The Nc
& Van ı
Dutch D   ⅃ɪ1ary

This comprehensive and contemporary two-way dictionary is ideal for Dutch language learners and users at all levels. Key features of the dictionary include:
- Over 33,000 Dutch entries
- The use of colloquial and idiomatic language
- Useful contextual information within glosses
- Phonetic transcription for all Dutch headwords, aiding pronunciation
- Gender markers for all Dutch nouns
- Appendix of Dutch irregular verbs
- A clear layout and format for easy referencing

This third edition has been systematically revised and updated throughout to provide:
- 2,000 new headwords and definitions, supported by 4,500 translations and a helpful pronunciation aid
- Expanded and updated information for a number of the previously existing headwords, including the addition of 2,200 new examples

The New Routledge & Van Dale Dutch Dictionary

Dutch–English/English–Dutch

Third Edition

Routledge
Taylor & Francis Group

LONDON AND NEW YORK

Utrecht - Antwerpen

Third English edition published 2021
by Routledge
2 Park Square, Milton Park, Abingdon, Oxon, OX14 4RN

and by Routledge
52 Vanderbilt Avenue, New York, NY 10017

Routledge is an imprint of the Taylor & Francis Group, an informa business

First published by Van Dale Lexicografie bv 2001 as *Ster Woordenboek Engels–Nederlands/
Nederlands–Engels,* Third edition, by R. Hempelman and N.E. Osselton
First English edition published by Routledge 2003
Second English edition published by Routledge 2014

British Library Cataloguing-in-Publication Data
A catalogue record for this book is available from the British Library

Library of Congress Cataloging-in-Publication Data
Names: Routledge (Firm)
Title: The new Routledge & Van Dale Dutch dictionary : Dutch-English/English-Dutch.
Other titles: New Routledge and Van Dale Dutch dictionary
Description: Third edition. | London ; New York : Routledge, 2020. |
Identifiers: LCCN 2020014978 | ISBN 9780367506575 (hardback) | ISBN 9780367506582
(paperback)
Subjects: LCSH: English language--Dictionaries--Dutch. | Dutch
language--Dictionaries--English.
Classification: LCC PF640 .N66 2020 | DDC 439.313/21--dc23
LC record available at https://lccn.loc.gov/2020014978

ISBN: 978-0-367-50657-5 (hbk)
ISBN: 978-0-367-50658-2 (pbk)

Typeset in Frutiger
by Pre Press Media Groep, Zeist, The Netherlands

MIX
Paper from
responsible sources
FSC
www.fsc.org
FSC™ C013985

Printed in the United Kingdom
by Henry Ling Limited

Contents

Foreword for the First Edition

This dictionary includes the past tense and past participle forms of Dutch irregular verbs.

In this dictionary all words appear in British spelling. To avoid confusion, American spellings have not been included. However, in many cases American spelling can easily be predicted on the basis of British spellings. For example, many words ending in *–our (humour)* and *–tre (centre)* are spelt *–or (humor)* and *–ter (center)* in American English. Also, unlike British spelling, American spelling does not always use double consonants, thus American English has "trave*l*er" and "jewe*l*er" rather than British "trave*ll*er" and "jewe*ll*er".

However, where British and American English differ lexically, there are entries for both: so for *apotheek* both chemist's, and [Am] drugstore are given.

The pronunciation of entries is represented by means of easy-to-understand symbols.

Detailed information about the layout of this dictionary is to be found in the Guide to the dictionary.

To make it easy to look up words, each entry appears at the beginning of a new line; in addition, all entries are printed in full.

Foreword for the Second Edition

For the second edition the dictionary has been systematically revised and updated throughout to offer two main improvements.

Firstly, there has been a substantial expansion of the headwords in the dictionary. In keeping with changes in the Dutch and English languages, the dictionary features 9,000 new headwords (an increase by 18% since the previous edition), supported by pronunciation aids. These new headwords are also accompanied by 9,000 new definitions, 18,000 translations and 3,000 new examples. A number of existing entries have also been revised and updated to reflect new developments in Dutch.

Secondly, the dictionary offers a substantially improved new layout design for clearer and easier referencing. Articles for Dutch nouns are presented at a glance, in the margin before the headwords, and conjugational information follows the Dutch verbs, after the headwords.

Foreword for the Third Edition

This third edition has been systematically revised and updated throughout to provide:

- 2,000 new headwords and definitions, supported by 4,500 translations and a helpful pronunciation aid
- Expanded and updated information for a number of the previously existing headwords, including the addition of 2,200 new examples, in particular phrases and expressions one can consider as fundamental for learners of Dutch: *dat gaat mijn begrip te boven, bekendheid krijgen, aan de bel trekken, er wordt gebeld, tot besluit, hem treft geen blaam, …*
- words only used in the Netherlands are now marked as Dutch.

List of Abbreviations

abbr	abbreviation	ind pron	indefinite pronoun
adj	adjective	inform	informal
adv	adverb	int	interjection
Am	American, in the USA	iron	ironical
approx	approximate	lit	literal
art	article	maths	mathematics
Austr	Australian, in Australia	m.b.t.	met betrekking tot
aux vb	auxiliary verb	med	medical
Belg	Belgian, in Belgium	mil	military
bldg	building	mus	music
bot	botany	n	noun
chem	chemistry	num	numeral
com	commerce	oft	often
comp	computer	pers	person
conj	conjunction	pers pron	personal pronoun
dem pron	demonstrative pronoun	pl	plural
depr	depreciatory	pol	politics
Dutch	Dutch, in the Netherlands	poss pron	possessive pronoun
econ	economics	prep	preposition
educ	education	pron	pronoun
eg	for example	ref pron	reflexive pronoun
elec	electricity	ref vb	reflexive verb
esp	especially	rel	religion
euph	euphemism	shipp	shipping
fig	figurative	s.o.	someone
fin	finance	socc	soccer
form	formal	sth.	something
geog	geography	techn	technics
graph	graphics	telecom	telecommunication
hist	historical	traf	traffic
hum	humorous	vb	verb
iem.	iemand	vulg	vulgar

Pronunciation Symbols

ɑ	as in French chat
a	as in after
ɛ	as in bed
e	as in late
ə	as in about
ɪ	as in bid
i	as in French ici
ɔ	as in lot
o	as in German Boot
ʏ	as in sun
y	as in French fumé
u	as in foot
b	as in back
c	as in cheek
d	as in door
f	as in far
ɣ	as in loch (but voiced)
χ	as in loch
g	as in goal
h	as in help
j	as in yet
k	as in car
l	as in like
m	as in mouse
n	as in nose
ŋ	as in wrong
ɲ	as in French campagne
p	as in paper
r	as in room
s	as in son
ʃ	as in fish
ʒ	as in pleasure
t	as in town
θ	as in thriller
v	as in verb
w	as in wax
z	as in zip
ø	as in German schön
ɛi	approx as in table, vein
œy	as in Latin neutrum
ɑu	as in mouth
oe:	as in nurse
ã	as in French chanson
ɛ̃	as in French vin
ɔ̃	as in French chanson
:	lengthening symbol, lenghtens the preceding vowel
ɑ:	as in barbecue
ɛ:	as in wear
i:	as in jeans
ɔ:	as in corner
u:	as in jury
ʏ:	as in service
y:	as in French pur

Guide to the Dictionary

The abbreviations and the pronunciation symbols used in this dictionary are explained in the *List of abbreviations* and the *Pronunciation symbols* on the preceding pages.

All entries appear in bold type	**aunt** tante
The vowel or vowels of stressed syllables of the English entries are underlined	**ab<u>o</u>lish** afschaffen, een eind maken aan **acr<u>o</u>ss-the-b<u>oa</u>rd** algemeen (geldend)
The pronunciation of the Dutch entries appears between slashes. The vowel or vowels of stressed syllables are underlined	**België** /b<u>ɛ</u>lɣijə/ Belgium
Dutch entries which are nouns, are preceded by the article **de** or **het** at the beginning of the line. If applicable, the plural form is given between brackets	de **satésaus** /sat<u>e</u>sɑus/ (pl: -sauzen) satay sauce het **satéstokje** /sat<u>e</u>stɔkjə/ (pl: -s) skewer
Dutch entries which are verbs, are followed by their conjugated forms (imperfect and past participle with the applicable auxiliary)	**creëren** /krej<u>e</u>rə(n)/ (creëerde, heeft gecreëerd) create **doorschuiven** /d<u>o</u>rsχœyvə(n)/ (schoof door, heeft/is doorgeschoven) pass on
Entries with identical spelling but different stress, pronunciation patterns or grammar are identified by a superscript numeral **1, 2** etc.	de **¹achteruit** /ɑχtər<u>œy</u>t/ reverse (gear): *een auto in zijn ~ zetten* put a car into reverse (gear) **²achteruit** /ɑχtər<u>œy</u>t/ (adv) back(wards) het **¹aas** /as/ bait: *levend ~* live bait; *van ~ voorzien* bait (the hook, trap) het/de **²aas** /as/ [cards] ace: *de ~ van harten, ruiten* the ace of hearts, diamonds
In the translations of English nouns the Dutch neuter nouns are marked with a superior h to mark the use of the Dutch article *het* In case the articles *het* and *de* are both allowed, the nouns are marked with +h	**accelerator** gaspedaal^h **ace 1** [cards] aas^{+h}, één; [fig] troef **2** [sport, esp tennis] ace **3** [inform] uitblinker: *an ~ at arithmetic* een hele piet in het rekenen
In entries which are abbreviations, the explanation is given first, printed in italics	**a.u.b.** /aub<u>e</u>/ (abbrev) *alstublieft* please
Commas are used to separate translations which are very close in meaning	de **aardbol** /<u>a</u>rdbɔl/ (pl: -len) earth, world, globe
Semicolons are used to separate translations which are less close in meaning. In many cases information about this small difference in meaning appears between brackets	**shutdown** sluiting; stopzetting [of business] **spotless** brandschoon, vlekkeloos; [fig also] onberispelijk
If an entry has significantly different translations, these are numbered **1, 2** etc.	**¹auxiliary** (n) **1** helper, hulpkracht, assistent **2** hulpmiddel^h **3** hulpwerkwoord^h
In some cases a translation requires clarification: eg restrictions as to the usage of a word, a field label, a brief explanation. This additional information appears between brackets	**acoustics 1** geluidsleer **2** akoestiek [in concert hall etc] **defuse** onschadelijk maken [also fig]; demonteren [explosives]: *~ a crisis* een crisis bezweren

In a number of cases the translation is followed by examples and expressions. These are in italics; the entry is represented by the symbol ~. To help you find your way through the examples, the most important word is printed in bold

For some entries no translations are given; they appear in one or more expressions

Expressions which do not clearly fit any of the given translations of an entry are dealt with at the end, after the || symbol

In case an expression has several meanings, these meanings are seperated by the letters **a)** and **b)**

Alternative forms appear between brackets and are introduced by *or*

Some entries are only used in fixed combinations with another word. In these cases the latter word is introduced by the sign +

Translations which are mainly used in American English are preceded by the abbreviation [Am]. This notation is also used in compounds and examples.

de **voorlichting** /vo̯rlɪ̯χtɪŋ/ (pl: -en) information: *de **afdeling** ~* public relations department; ***seksuele** ~* sex education; *goede ~ **geven*** give good advice

apegapen /a̯pəɣapə(n)/: *op ~ liggen* be at one's last gasp

de **balk** /bɑlk/ (pl: -en) beam || *het geld **over** de ~ gooien* spend money like water

de **groet** [...]: *de ~en!* **a)** [greeting] see you!; **b)** [forget it] not on your life!, no way!
de **aanplant** /a̯mplɑnt/ plantings, plants: *nieuwe* (or: *jonge*) ~ new (*or:* young) plantings

all-time van alle tijden: *an ~ **high*** (or: ***low***) een absoluut hoogtepunt (*or:* dieptepunt)

accessible (+ to) toegankelijk (voor), bereikbaar (voor); [fig] begrijpelijk (voor)

het **appartement** /ɑpɑrtəmɛnt/ (pl: -en) flat; [Am] apartment
de **etage** /etaʒə/ (pl: -s) floor, storey: *op de **eerste** ~* on the first floor; [Am] on the second floor

Dutch Irregular Verbs

Conjugated forms shown between brackets are regular.
Numbered forms represent the first, second and third person singular in the present tense.

infinitive	imperfect sing	imperfect pl	past participle
bakken	(bakte)		gebakken
bannen	(bande)		gebannen
barsten	(barstte)		gebarsten
bederven	bedierf	bedierven	bedorven
bedriegen	bedroog	bedrogen	bedrogen
beginnen	begon	begonnen	begonnen
begrijpen	begreep	begrepen	begrepen
belijden	beleed	beleden	beleden
bergen	borg		geborgen
bevelen	beval	bevalen	bevolen
bewegen	bewoog	bewogen	bewogen
bezwijken	bezweek	bezweken	bezweken
bidden	bad	baden	gebeden
bieden	bood	boden	geboden
bijten	beet	beten	gebeten
binden	bond		gebonden
blazen	blies	bliezen	geblazen
blijken	bleek	bleken	gebleken
blijven	bleef	bleven	gebleven
blinken	blonk		geblonken
braden	(braadde)		gebraden
breken	brak	braken	gebroken
brengen	bracht		gebracht
brouwen	(brouwde)		gebrouwen
buigen	boog	bogen	gebogen
delven	(delfde)/dolf	(delfden)/dolven	gedolven
denken	dacht		gedacht
dingen	dong		gedongen
doen	deed	deden	gedaan
1. doe 2. doet 3. doet			
dragen	droeg		gedragen
drijven	dreef	dreven	gedreven
dringen	drong		gedrongen
drinken	dronk		gedronken
druipen	droop	dropen	gedropen
duiken	dook	doken	gedoken
dunken	(dunkte)/docht		(gedunkt)/gedocht
dwingen	dwong		gedwongen
eten	at	aten	gegeten
fluiten	floot	floten	gefloten
gaan	ging		gegaan
1. ga 2. gaat 3. gaat			
gelden	gold		gegolden
genezen	genas	genazen	genezen
genieten	genoot	genoten	genoten
geven	gaf	gaven	gegeven
gieten	goot	goten	gegoten
glijden	gleed	gleden	gegleden
glimmen	glom	glommen	geglommen
graven	groef	groeven	gegraven
grijpen	greep	grepen	gegrepen
hangen	hing		gehangen
hebben	had	hadden	gehad
1. heb 2. hebt 3. heeft			
heffen	hief	hieven	geheven

infinitive	imperfect sing	imperfect pl	past participle
helpen	hielp		geholpen
heten	(heette)		geheten
hijsen	hees	hesen	gehesen
houden	hield		gehouden
houwen	hieuw		gehouwen
jagen	(jaagde)/joeg		(gejaagd)
kiezen	koos	kozen	gekozen
kijken	keek	keken	gekeken
klimmen	klom	klommen	geklommen
klinken	klonk		geklonken
kluiven	kloof	kloven	gekloven
knijpen	kneep	knepen	geknepen
komen	kwam	kwamen	gekomen
kopen	kocht		gekocht
krijgen	kreeg	kregen	gekregen
krimpen	kromp		gekrompen
kruipen	kroop	kropen	gekropen
kunnen	kon	konden	(gekund)
1. kan 2. kan/kunt 3. kan			
kwijten	kweet	kweten	gekweten
lachen	(lachte)		gelachen
laden	(laadde)		geladen
laten	liet		gelaten
lezen	las	lazen	gelezen
liegen	loog	logen	gelogen
liggen	lag	lagen	gelegen
lijden	leed	leden	geleden
lijken	leek	leken	geleken
lopen	liep		gelopen
malen	(maalde)		gemalen
melken	molk/(melkte)		gemolken
meten	mat/(meette)	maten/(meetten)	gemeten
mijden	meed	meden	gemeden
moeten	moest		gemoeten
mogen	mocht		gemogen
1. mag 2. mag 3. mag			
napluizen	ploos na	plozen na	nageplozen
nemen	nam	namen	genomen
ontginnen	ontgon	ontgonnen	ontgonnen
ontluiken	ontlook	ontloken	ontloken
ontspruiten	ontsproot	ontsproten	ontsproten
plegen			
- be in habit of	placht		-
- commit	(pleegde)		(gepleegd)
pluizen	(pluisde)		geplozen/(gepluisd)
prijzen			
- praise	prees	prezen	geprezen
- price	(prijsde)		(geprijsd)
raden	(raadde)		geraden
rieken	(riekte)/rook		geroken
rijden	reed	reden	gereden
rijgen	reeg	regen	geregen
rijten	reet	reten	gereten
rijzen	rees	rezen	gerezen
roepen	riep		geroepen
ruiken	rook	roken	geroken
scheiden	(scheidde)		gescheiden
schelden	schold		gescholden
schenden	schond		geschonden
schenken	schonk		geschonken

infinitive	imperfect sing	imperfect pl	past participle
scheppen			
- create	schiep		geschapen
- shovel	(schepte)		(geschept)
scheren			
- shave	schoor	schoren	geschoren
- skim	(scheerde)		(gescheerd)
schieten	schoot	schoten	geschoten
schijnen	scheen	schenen	geschenen
schijten	scheet	scheten	gescheten
schrijden	schreed	schreden	geschreden
schrijven	schreef	schreven	geschreven
schrikken			
- be scared	schrok	schrokken	geschrokken
- be quenched	(schrikte)		(geschrikt)
schuilen			
- hide	school	scholen	gescholen
- shelter	(schuilde)		(geschuild)
schuiven	schoof	schoven	geschoven
slaan	sloeg		geslagen
1. sla 2. slaat 3. slaat			
slapen	sliep		geslapen
slijpen	sleep	slepen	geslepen
slijten	sleet	sleten	gesleten
slinken	slonk		geslonken
sluipen	sloop	slopen	geslopen
sluiten	sloot	sloten	gesloten
smelten	smolt		gesmolten
smijten	smeet	smeten	gesmeten
snijden	sneed	sneden	gesneden
snuiten	snoot	snoten	gesnoten
snuiven	snoof	snoven	gesnoven
spannen	(spande)		gespannen
spijten	speet	speten	gespeten
spinnen	(spinde)/spon	(spinden)/sponnen	gesponnen
splijten	spleet	spleten	gespleten
spreken	sprak	spraken	gesproken
springen	sprong		gesprongen
spugen	(spuugde)		(gespuugd)/gespogen
spruiten	sproot	sproten	gesproten
spuiten	spoot	spoten	gespoten
staan	stond		gestaan
1. sta 2. staat 3. staat			
steken	stak	staken	gestoken
stelen	stal	stalen	gestolen
sterven	stierf	stierven	gestorven
stijgen	steeg	stegen	gestegen
stinken	stonk		gestonken
strijden	streed	streden	gestreden
strijken	streek	streken	gestreken
stuiven	stoof	stoven	gestoven
treden	trad	traden	getreden
treffen	trof	troffen	getroffen
trekken	trok	trokken	getrokken
vallen	viel		gevallen
vangen	ving		gevangen
varen	voer		gevaren
vechten	vocht		gevochten
verdwijnen	verdween	verdwenen	verdwenen
vergeten	vergat	vergaten	vergeten
verliezen	verloor	verloren	verloren

infinitive	imperfect sing	imperfect pl	past participle
verschuilen	verschool	verscholen	verscholen
verslinden	verslond		verslonden
verzinnen	verzon	verzonnen	verzonnen
vinden	vond		gevonden
vlechten	vlocht		gevlochten
vliegen	vloog	vlogen	gevlogen
vouwen	(vouwde)		gevouwen
vragen	vroeg		gevraagd
vreten	vrat	vraten	gevreten
vriezen	vroor	vroren	gevroren
waaien	(waaide)/woei		gewaaid
wassen			
- grow	wies		gewassen
- wash	(waste)		gewassen
wegen	woog	wogen	gewogen
werpen	wierp		geworpen
werven	wierf	wierven	geworven
weten	wist		geweten
weven	weefde		geweven
wezen	was	waren	(geweest)
wijken	week	weken	geweken
wijten	weet	weten	geweten
wijzen	wees	wezen	gewezen
willen	(wilde)/wou	(wilden)/wouden	(gewild)
1. wil 2. wilt 3. wil			
winden	wond		gewonden
winnen	won	wonnen	gewonnen
worden	werd		geworden
wreken	(wreekte)		gewroken
wrijven	wreef	wreven	gewreven
wringen	wrong		gewrongen
zeggen	zei/(zegde)	zeiden/(zegden)	(gezegd)
zenden	zond		gezonden
zien	zag	zagen	gezien
1. zie 2. ziet 3. ziet			
zijgen	zeeg	zegen	gezegen
zijn	was	waren	geweest
1. ben 2. bent 3. is			
zingen	zong		gezongen
zinken	zonk		gezonken
zinnen	zon/(zinde)	zonnen/(zinden)	gezonnen
zitten	zat	zaten	gezeten
zoeken	zocht		gezocht
zouten	(zoutte)		gezouten
zuigen	zoog	zogen	gezogen
zuipen	zoop	zopen	gezopen
zullen	zou	zouden	-
1. zal 2. zult 3. zal			
zwelgen	zwolg		gezwolgen
zwellen	zwol	zwollen	gezwollen
zwemmen	zwom	zwommen	gezwommen
zweren			
- swear	zwoer		gezworen
- fester	zwoor/(zweerde)	zworen/(zweerden)	gezworen
zwerven	zwierf	zwierven	gezworven
zwijgen	zweeg	zwegen	gezwegen

Dutch–English

a

het **06-nummer** /nɥlzɛsnʏmər/ (pl: -s) [Dutch] mobile (phone) number; [Am] cellphone number

de **3D-printer** /driedeprɪntər/ (pl: -s) 3D printer

de **a** /a/ (pl: a's) a, A: *van a tot z kennen* know from A to Z (*or:* from beginning to end); *wie a zegt, moet ook b zeggen* in for a penny, in for a pound

à /a/ (prep) **1** [roughly] (from …) to, [roughly] or: *2 à 3 maal* 2 or 3 times; *er waren zo'n 10 à 15 personen* there were some 10 to 15 people **2** at (the rate of): *5 meter à 6 euro, is 30 euro* 5 metres at 6 euros is 30 euros

het **A4'tje** /avɪrcə/ **1** A4 page **2** page: *een rapport van 10 ~s* a report of 10 pages

de **AA** /aa/ (pl) *Anonieme Alcoholisten* Alcoholics Anonymous

de **aai** /aj/ (pl: -en) stroke; caress; pet

aaibaar /ajbar/ (adj) cuddly, snuggly

aaien /ajə(n)/ (aaide, heeft geaaid) stroke; caress

de **aak** /ak/ (pl: aken) barge

de **aal** /al/ (pl: alen) eel

de **aalbes** /albɛs/ (pl: -sen) currant

de **aalmoes** /almus/ (pl: aalmoezen) alms

de **aalmoezenier** /almuzənjir/ (pl: -s) chaplain

de **aalscholver** /alsxɔlvər/ (pl: -s) cormorant

het **aambeeld** /ambelt/ (pl: -en) anvil

de **aambeien** /ambɛiə(n)/ (pl) piles

¹**aan** /an/ (adj) on: *een vrouw met een groene jurk ~* a woman in (*or:* wearing) a green dress; *de kachel is ~* the stove is on; *~/uit on/ off* ‖ *het is weer dik ~ tussen hen* it's on again between them; *daar is niets ~* **a)** there's nothing to it; **b)** it's dead easy; **c)** it's a waste of time

²**aan** /an/ (adv) (+ wat) about, around, away: *ik rotzooi maar wat ~* I'm just messing about ‖ *stel je niet zo ~!* stop carrying on like that!; *daar heeft zij niets ~* that's no use to her; *daar zijn we nog niet ~ toe* we haven't got that far yet; [fig] *zij weet niet waar zij ~ toe is* she doesn't know where she stands; *rustig ~!* calm down!, take it easy!; *van nu af ~* from now on; *van voren af ~* from the beginning; *van jongs af ~* from childhood; *jij kunt ervan op ~ dat …* you can count on it that …

³**aan** /an/ (prep) **1** on, at, by: *vruchten ~ de bomen* fruit on the trees; *~ een verslag werken* work on a report; *~ zee* (*or: de kust*) *wonen* live by the sea (*or:* on the coast) **2** by, with: *dag ~ dag* day by day; *doen ~* do, go in for; *twee ~ twee* two by two **3** to: *hij geeft les*

~ de universiteit he lectures at the university; *~ wal gaan* go ashore; *hoe kom je ~ dat spul?* how did you get hold of that stuff? **4** of, from: *sterven ~ een ziekte* die of a disease **5** of: *een tekort ~ kennis* a lack of knowledge **6** up to: *het is ~ mij ervoor te zorgen dat …* it is up to me to see that …; *dat ligt ~ haar* that's her fault ‖ *hij heeft het ~ zijn hart* he has got heart trouble; *hij is ~ het joggen* he's out jogging; *hij is ~ het strijken* he's (busy) ironing; *ze zijn ~ vakantie toe* they could do with (*or:* are badly in need of) a holiday

aanbakken /ambɑkə(n)/ (bakte aan, is aangebakken) burn, get burnt: *de aardappels zijn aangebakken* the potatoes are burnt

aanbellen /ambɛlə(n)/ (belde aan, heeft aangebeld) ring (at the door): *bij iem. ~* ring s.o.'s doorbell

aanbesteden /ambəstedə(n)/ (besteedde aan, heeft aanbesteed) put out to tender: *werk ~* put work out to tender, call for (*or:* invite) tenders for work

de **aanbesteding** /ambəstedɪŋ/ (pl: -en) tender; contract: *inschrijven op een ~* (submit a) tender for a contract; *een ~ houden* call for tenders

de **aanbetaling** /ambətalɪŋ/ (pl: -en) down payment; deposit: *een ~ doen van 200 euro* make a down payment of 200 euros

aanbevelen /ambəvelə(n)/ (beval aan, heeft aanbevolen) recommend: *dat kan ik je warm ~* I can recommend it warmly to you; *voor suggesties houden wij ons aanbevolen* we welcome any suggestions

aanbevelenswaardig /ambəvelə(n)swardəx/ (adj) recommendable, advisable

de **aanbeveling** /ambəvelɪŋ/ (pl: -en) recommendation: *het verdient ~ om …* it is advisable to …

aanbidden /ambɪdə(n)/ (aanbad, heeft aanbeden) **1** worship; venerate **2** [fig] worship; adore: *Jan aanbad zijn vrouw* Jan worshipped (*or:* adored) his wife

de **aanbidder** /ambɪdər/ (pl: -s) **1** worshipper **2** admirer: *een stille ~* a secret admirer

aanbieden /ambidə(n)/ (bood aan, heeft aangeboden) **1** offer, give: *iem. een geschenk ~* present a gift to s.o.; *hulp (or: diensten) ~* offer help (*or:* services); *zijn ontslag ~* tender one's resignation; *zijn verontschuldigingen ~* offer one's apologies **2** offer: *iets te koop* (or: *huur*) *~* put sth. up for sale (*or:* rent)

de **aanbieding** /ambidɪŋ/ (pl: -en) special offer, bargain: *goedkope* (or: *speciale*) *~* special offer, bargain; *koffie is in de ~* deze week coffee's on special offer this week, coffee's reduced this week

aanbinden /ambɪndə(n)/ (bond aan, heeft aangebonden) **1** fasten on **2** engage

aanblijven /amblɛivə(n)/ (bleef aan, is aangebleven) stay on: *zij blijft aan* **als** *minister* she is staying on as minister

de **aanblik** /<u>a</u>mblɪk/ **1** sight, glance: *bij de* **eerste** ~ at first sight (*or:* glance) **2** sight; [pers] appearance: *een* **troosteloze** ~ *opleveren* be a sorry sight, make a sorry spectacle

het **aanbod** /<u>a</u>mbɔt/ **1** offer: *iem. een* ~ **doen** make s.o. an offer; *zij* **nam** *het* ~ **aan** she accepted (*or:* took up) the offer; *zij* **sloeg** *het* ~ **af** she rejected the offer; *een* ~ *dat je niet kunt* **weigeren** an offer you can't refuse **2** supply: **vraag** *en* ~ supply and demand

aanboren /<u>a</u>mborə(n)/ (boorde aan, heeft aangeboord) tap, broach: *een nieuw vat* ~ tap (*or:* broach) a new barrel; [fig] *nieuwe* **belastingbronnen** ~ tap new sources of taxation

de **aanbouw** /<u>a</u>mbɑu/ **1** building; construction: *dit huis is* **in** ~ this house is under construction **2** extension, annexe: *een* ~ **aan** *een huis* an extension (*or:* annexe) to a house

aanbouwen /<u>a</u>mbɑuwə(n)/ (bouwde aan, heeft aangebouwd) build on, add: *een aangebouwde* **keuken** a built-on kitchen

aanbranden /<u>a</u>mbrɑndə(n)/ (brandde aan, is aangebrand) burn (on): *laat de* **aardappelen** *niet* ~ mind the potatoes don't boil dry (*or:* get burnt)

¹**aanbreken** /<u>a</u>mbrekə(n)/ (brak aan, is aangebroken) come, break; dawn; fall: *het* **moment** *was aangebroken om afscheid te nemen* the moment had come to say goodbye

²**aanbreken** /<u>a</u>mbrekə(n)/ (brak aan, heeft aangebroken) break into; break (into); open (up): *er staat nog een aangebroken* **fles** there's a bottle that's already been opened

aanbrengen /<u>a</u>mbrɛŋə(n)/ (bracht aan, heeft aangebracht) **1** put in, put on, install; introduce; apply: *verbeteringen* ~ make improvements; **make-up** ~ put on make-up **2** inform on; report: *een* **zaak** ~ report a matter

de **aandacht** /<u>a</u>ndɑχt/ attention, notice: *(persoonlijke)* ~ **besteden** *aan* give (*or:* pay) (personal) attention to; *aan de* ~ **ontsnappen** escape notice; *al zijn* ~ **richten** *op …* focus all one's attention on …; *iemands* ~ **trekken** attract s.o.'s attention, catch s.o.'s eye; *de* ~ **vestigen** *op* draw attention to; *onder de* ~ *komen* (*or:* brengen) **van** come (*or:* bring) to the attention of

aandachtig /<u>a</u>ndɑχtəχ/ (adj, adv) attentive, intent: ~ **luisteren** listen attentively (*or:* intently); *iets* ~ **bestuderen** examine sth. carefully (*or:* closely)

de **aandachtsboog** /<u>a</u>ndɑχ(t)sboχ/ attention span: *een* **korte** ~ *hebben* have a short attention span

het **aandachtspunt** /<u>a</u>ndɑχ(t)spʏnt/ (pl: -en) point of (special (*or:* particular)) interest: *een* ~ *van iets* **maken** draw special (*or:* particular)

attention to sth.

de **aandachtswijk** /<u>a</u>ndɑχ(t)swɛɪk/ (pl: -en) [Dutch] disadvantaged neighbourhood

de **aandachttrekker** /<u>a</u>ndɑχtrɛkər/ (pl: -s) attention-seeker

het **aandeel** /<u>a</u>ndel/ (pl: aandelen) **1** share, portion: ~ **hebben** *in een zaak* (*or:* de winst) have a share in a business (*or:* the profits) **2** contribution, part: *een* **actief** ~ *hebben in iets* take an active part in sth. **3** share (certificate); [Am] stock (certificate): ~ *op naam* nominative share, registered share

de **aandeelhouder** /<u>a</u>ndelhɑudər/ (pl: -s) shareholder

het **aandenken** /<u>a</u>ndɛŋkə(n)/ keepsake, memento: *iets bewaren* **als** ~ keep sth. as a keepsake

zich **aandienen** /<u>a</u>ndinə(n)/ (diende zich aan, heeft zich aangediend) present o.s. (as): *er diende zich een* **mogelijkheid** *aan om … an* opportunity to … presented itself

aandikken /<u>a</u>ndɪkə(n)/ (dikte aan, heeft aangedikt) embroider, pile (it) on

aandoen /<u>a</u>ndun/ (deed aan, heeft aangedaan) **1** put on **2** do to, cause: *iem. een* **proces** ~ take s.o. to court; *iem.* **verdriet, onrecht** ~ cause s.o. grief, do s.o. an injustice; *dat kun je niet* ~*!* you can't do that to her!; *wat doe je jezelf aan?* why put yourself through this? **3** call (in) at: *een* **haven** ~ call (in) at a port **4** turn on, switch on

de **aandoening** /<u>a</u>ndunɪŋ/ (pl: -en) disorder, complaint

aandoenlijk /<u>a</u>ndunlək/ (adj, adv) moving, touching

aandraaien /<u>a</u>ndrajə(n)/ (draaide aan, heeft aangedraaid) tighten, screw tighter

aandragen /<u>a</u>ndrayə(n)/ (droeg aan, heeft aangedragen) carry, bring (up/along/to)

de **aandrang** /<u>a</u>ndrɑŋ/ insistence, instigation: ~ **uitoefenen** *op* exert pressure on; ~ **hebben** need to go

aandrijven /<u>a</u>ndrɛivə(n)/ (dreef aan, heeft aangedreven) drive: *door een elektromotor aangedreven* driven by an electric motor

de **aandrijving** /<u>a</u>ndrɛivɪŋ/ (pl: -en) drive, power: **elektrische** ~ electric drive (*or:* power)

aandringen /<u>a</u>ndrɪŋə(n)/ (drong aan, heeft aangedrongen) **1** urge: *niet* **verder** ~ not press the point, not insist; *bij iem.* **op** *hulp* ~ urge s.o. to help **2** insist: *er* **sterk** *op* ~ *dat* strongly insist that; ~ **op** *iets* insist on sth.

aanduiden /<u>a</u>ndœydə(n)/ (duidde aan, heeft aangeduid) indicate: *niet* **nader** *aangeduid* unspecified; *iem.* ~ **als** *X* refer to s.o. as X

aandurven /<u>a</u>ndʏrvə(n)/ (durfde aan, heeft aangedurfd) dare to (do), feel up to: *een* **taak** ~ feel up to a task; *het* ~ *om* dare (*or:* presume) to

aanduwen /<u>a</u>ndywə(n)/ (duwde aan, heeft

aangeduwd) **1** push (on) **2** push home, press firm

aaneen /anen̯/ (adv): *jaren* ~ (for) years on end (*or:* at a time, stretch); *dicht* ~ close together; *kilometers* ~ kilometres at a stretch

aaneengesloten /anen̯ɣəslotə(n)/ (adj) unbroken, connected, continuous; [fig] united

de **aaneenschakeling** /anen̯sχakəlɪŋ/ (pl: -en) chain, succession, sequence: *een ~ van ongelukken* a series (*or:* sequence) of accidents

aanflitsen /anflɪtsə(n)/ (flitste aan, heeft aangeflitst) flash on

de **aanfluiting** /anflœytɪŋ/ (pl: -en) mockery

¹**aangaan** /anɣan/ (ging aan, is aangegaan) **1** go (towards), head (for/towards): *achter iem. (iets)* ~ **a)** chase s.o. (sth.) (up); **b)** [fig] go after s.o., go for sth. **2** go on; switch on; light

²**aangaan** /anɣan/ (ging aan, is aangegaan) **1** enter into; contract: *een lening* ~ contract a loan; *de strijd* ~ enter into combat (with), fight (with) **2** concern: *dat gaat hem niets aan* that's none of his business; *wat mij aangaat* as far as I'm concerned

aangaande /anɣandə/ (prep) as regards, regarding, with regard (*or:* respect) to, concerning

aangapen /anɣapə(n)/ (gaapte aan, heeft aangegaapt) gape (at), gawp at, gawk at: *sta me niet zo dom aan te gapen!* stop gaping at me like an idiot!

aangeboren /anɣəborə(n)/ (adj) innate, inborn; [med] congenital

aangedaan /anɣədan/ (adj) **1** moved, touched **2** affected

aangeharkt /anɣəhɑrkt/ (adj) [fig] manicured, immaculate: *het landschap ligt er ~ bij* the landscape looks well manicured

de **aangeklaagde** /anɣəklaɣdə/ (pl: -n) accused, defendant

aangelegd /anɣələχt/ (adj) -minded: *artistiek* ~ *zijn* have an artistic bent

de **aangelegenheid** /anɣələɣenhɛit/ (pl: -heden) affair, business, matter

aangenaam /anɣənam/ (adj, adv) pleasant; pleasing; congenial: *ze was ~ verrast* she was pleasantly surprised; *~ (met u kennis te maken)* pleased to meet you

aangenomen /anɣənomə(n)/ (adj): *~ werk* contract work; *een ~ kind* an adopted child

aangepast /anɣəpɑst/ (adj) (specially) adapted; adjusted: *een ~e versie* an adapted version; *een ~e ingang* an accessible entrance; *~e muziek* appropriately solemn music; *goed ~ zijn* be well-adapted (*or:* well-adjusted); *slecht ~ zijn* be poorly adapted (*or:* adjusted)

aangeschoten /anɣəsχotə(n)/ (adj) **1** under the influence, tipsy **2** unintentional: *~ hands* unintentional hands

aangeslagen /anɣəslaɣə(n)/ (adj) affected; shaken: *hij was ~ door het nieuws* he was shaken (or: deeply affected) by the news

aangetekend /anɣətekənt/ (adj) registered: *je moet die stukken ~ versturen* you must send those items by registered mail

aangetrouwd /anɣətraut/ (adj) related by marriage: *~e familie* in-laws

aangeven /anɣevə(n)/ (gaf aan, heeft aangegeven) **1** hand, pass **2** indicate, declare: *de trein vertrok op de aangegeven tijd* the train left on time; *tenzij anders aangegeven* except where otherwise specified, unless stated otherwise **3** report, notify; declare: *een diefstal* ~ report a theft (to the police); *een geboorte* (or: *huwelijk*) ~ register a birth (or: marriage); *hebt u nog iets aan te geven?* do you have anything (else) to declare?; *de dader heeft zichzelf aangegeven* the culprit turned himself in **4** indicate, mark: *de thermometer geeft 30 graden aan* the thermometer is registering 30 degrees; *de maat* ~ beat time **5** [socc] feed; [volleyball] set

de **aangever** /anɣevər/ (pl: -s) **1** informant; person submitting a declaration **2** [socc] feeder

aangewezen /anɣəwezə(n)/ (adj): *de ~ persoon* the obvious (*or:* right) person (for the job); *op iets ~ zijn* rely on sth.; *op zichzelf ~ zijn* be left to one's own devices; *zij zijn op elkaar ~* they depend (*or:* rely) on each other

het **aangezicht** /anɣəzɪχt/ (pl: -en) countenance, face

aangezien /anɣəzin/ (conj) since, as, seeing (that)

de **aangifte** /anɣɪftə/ (pl: -n) declaration; report; registration: *~ inkomstenbelasting* income tax return; *~ doen van een misdrijf* report a crime; *~ doen* make a declaration; *~ doen van geboorte* register a birth; *bij diefstal wordt altijd ~ gedaan* shoplifters will be prosecuted

het **aangifteformulier** /anɣɪftəformylir/ (pl: -en) tax form; declaration; registration form

aangrenzend /anɣrɛnzənt/ (adj) adjoining; adjacent; neighbouring

aangrijpen /anɣrɛipə(n)/ (greep aan, heeft aangegrepen) **1** grip; move; make a deep impression on: *dit boek heeft me zeer aangegrepen* this book has made a deep impression on me **2** seize (at/upon), grip: *een gelegenheid met beide handen ~* seize (at/upon) an opportunity with both hands

aangrijpend /anɣrɛipənt/ (adj, adv) moving, touching, poignant

aangroeien /anɣrujə(n)/ (groeide aan, is aangegroeid) **1** grow, increase **2** grow again: *doen ~* regenerate

aanhaken /anhakə(n)/ (haakte aan, heeft/is aangehaakt): *hij kon bij de kopgroep ~* he was able to join the leading group; *ik wilde graag* *even bij het zojuist gezegde* ~ I would like to come in here, could I just follow up on that? **aanhalen** /ɑnhalə(n)/ (haalde aan, heeft aangehaald) **1** caress, fondle **2** quote: *als voorbeeld* (or: *bewijs*) ~ quote as an example (or: as evidence) **3** pull in; haul in: *we moeten allemaal de buikriem* ~ we'll all have to tighten our belts || *de banden met China* ~ strengthen ties with China, seek closer relations with China

aanhalig /ɑnhaləx/ (adj, adv) affectionate: *hij kon zeer* ~ *doen* he could be very affectionate

de **aanhaling** /ɑnhalɪŋ/ (pl: -en) quotation; [inform] quote

het **aanhalingsteken** /ɑnhalɪŋstekə(n)/ (pl: -s) quotation mark; [inform] quote; inverted comma: *tussen* ~*s* in quotation marks, in inverted commas

de **aanhang** /ɑnhɑŋ/ following; supporters: *over een grote* ~ *beschikken* have a large following; *veel* ~ *vinden onder* find considerable support among, have a large following among

aanhangen /ɑnhɑŋə(n)/ (hing aan, heeft aangehangen) adhere to, be attached to, support: *een geloof* ~ adhere to a faith; *een partij* ~ support a party

de **aanhanger** /ɑnhɑŋər/ (pl: -s) **1** follower; supporter: *een vurig* (or: *trouw*) ~ *van* an ardent (or: a faithful) supporter of **2** trailer

aanhangig /ɑnhɑŋəx/ (adj) pending, before the courts: *een kwestie* ~ *maken bij de autoriteiten* take a matter up with the authorities

het **aanhangsel** /ɑnhɑŋsəl/ (pl: -s) appendix: *een* ~ *bij een polis* an appendix to a policy; *het wormvormig* ~ the vermiform appendix

de **aanhangwagen** /ɑnhɑŋwaɣə(n)/ (pl: -s) trailer

aanhankelijk /ɑnhɑŋkələk/ (adj, adv) affectionate, devoted

aanhebben /ɑnhɛbə(n)/ (had aan, heeft aangehad) have on, be wearing

aanhechten /ɑnhɛxtə(n)/ (hechtte aan, heeft aangehecht) attach; fasten on; affix

de **aanhechting** /ɑnhɛxtɪŋ/ (pl: -en) attachment

de **aanhef** /ɑnhɛf/ opening words; [letter] salutation

aanheffen /ɑnhɛfə(n)/ (hief aan, heeft aangeheven) start, begin; break into; raise

aanhollen /ɑnhɔlə(n)/: *komen* ~ come running (or: rushing) on/in

aanhoren /ɑnhorə(n)/ (hoorde aan, heeft aangehoord) listen to, hear: *iemands relaas geduldig* ~ listen patiently to s.o.'s story

¹**aanhouden** /ɑnhɑudə(n)/ (hield aan, heeft aangehouden) **1** keep on, go on, persist (in): *blijven* ~ persevere, insist; *je moet niet zo* ~ you shouldn't keep going on about it (like that) **2** go on, continue; hold, last, keep up **3** (+ op) keep [left or right]; make (for), head (for): *links* (or: *rechts*) ~ keep to the left (or: right); bear left (or: right)

²**aanhouden** /ɑnhɑudə(n)/ (hield aan, heeft aangehouden) **1** stop; arrest; hold: *een verdachte* ~ take a suspect into custody **2** hold on to, keep; continue; stick to **3** keep on **4** keep on, keep up; leave on; keep going || *als je het recept aanhoudt, kan er niets misgaan* if you stick to the recipe, nothing can go wrong

aanhoudend /ɑnhɑudənt/ (adj, adv) **1** continuous, persistent, constant, all the time: *een* ~*e droogte* a prolonged period of drought **2** continual, repeated, time and again, always

de **aanhouder** /ɑnhɑudər/ (pl: -s) sticker, go-getter: *de* ~ *wint* it's dogged that (or: as) does it; if at first you don't succeed, try, try, try again

de **aanhouding** /ɑnhɑudɪŋ/ (pl: -en) arrest

aanjagen /ɑnjaɣə(n)/ (jaagde aan/joeg aan, heeft aangejaagd) fill with: *iem. schrik* ~ frighten (or: terrify) s.o.

aankaarten /ɑnkartə(n)/ (kaartte aan, heeft aangekaart) raise: *een zaak* ~ *bij* raise a matter with

aankakken /ɑnkɑkə(n)/ [Dutch; inform]: *komen* ~ (or: *aangekakt*) come sauntering along (or: in), show (or: turn) up; *waar komen ze nou weer mee* ~? what have they come up with now?

aankijken /ɑnkɛikə(n)/ (keek aan, heeft aangekeken) look at: *elkaar veelbetekenend* ~ give each other a meaningful look; *het* ~ *niet waard* not worth looking at

de **aanklacht** /ɑnklɑxt/ (pl: -en) charge; indictment; complaint: *een* ~ *indienen tegen iem. (bij)* lodge a complaint against s.o. (with); *de* ~ *werd ingetrokken* the charge was dropped

aanklagen /ɑnklaɣə(n)/ (klaagde aan, heeft aangeklaagd) bring charges against, lodge a complaint against: *iem.* ~ *wegens diefstal* (or: *moord*) charge s.o. with theft (or: murder)

de **aanklager** /ɑnklaɣər/ (pl: -s) accuser; complainant; plaintiff; prosecutor: *openbare* ~ public prosecutor, Crown Prosecutor

aanklampen /ɑnklɑmpə(n)/ (klampte aan, heeft aangeklampt) stop; [fig] approach, apply to || ~ *bij de kopgroep* join the leaders

aankleden /ɑnkledə(n)/ (kleedde aan, heeft aangekleed) dress, get dressed; clothe; fit out: *je moet die jongen warm* ~ you must wrap the boy up well; *zich* ~ get dressed

de **aankleding** /ɑnkledɪŋ/ (pl: -en) furnishing; decor; furnishings; decor; set(ting)

aanklikken /ɑnklɪkə(n)/ (klikte aan, heeft aangeklikt) click (on)

aanklooien /ɑnklojə(n)/ (klooide aan, heeft aangeklooid): [inform] *maar wat* ~

mess around

aankloppen /ˈaŋklɔpə(n)/ (klopte aan, heeft aangeklopt) knock (at the door); [fig] come with a request; appeal (to): *tevergeefs bij iem. ~ om hulp* appeal to s.o. for help in vain

aanknopen /ˈaŋknopə(n)/ (knoopte aan, heeft aangeknoopt) **1** tie on **2** enter into: *betrekkingen ~ met* establish relations with; *onderhandelingen ~ met* enter into negotiations with; *een gesprek ~ met* begin (or: strike up) a conversation with

het **aanknopingspunt** /ˈaŋknopɪŋspʏnt/ (pl: -en) clue, lead; starting point

aankoeken /ˈaŋkukə(n)/ (koekte aan, is aangekoekt) cake, stick: *het eten was aangekoekt* the food had caked (or: stuck) on to the pan

¹**aankomen** /ˈaŋkomə(n)/ (kwam aan, is aangekomen) **1** arrive, reach; come in, pull in; [sport] finish: *de trein kan elk moment ~* the train is due at any moment; *daar komt iem. aan s.o. is coming; als derde ~* come in third **2** hit hard: *de klap is hard aangekomen* **a)** it was a heavy blow; **b)** [fig] it was a great blow to him **3** come (with): *en daar kom je nu pas mee aan?* and now you tell me!; *je hoeft met dat plan bij hem niet aan te komen* it's no use going to him with that plan **4** come (along), approach: *ik zag het ~* I could see it coming **5** touch, hit, come up (against): *niet (or: nergens) ~!* don't touch!, hands off! **6** put on weight

²**aankomen** /ˈaŋkomə(n)/ (kwam aan, is aangekomen) come (down) (to): *waar het op aankomt* what really matters; *als het op betalen aankomt* when it comes to paying; *we kunnen het er niet op aan laten komen* we cannot take the risk ‖ *als het erop aan komt* when it comes to the crunch

aankomend /ˈaŋkomənt/ (adj) prospective, future; budding; apprentice; trainee: *een ~ actrice* a starlet, an up-and-coming actress; *een ~ schrijver* a budding author

de **aankomst** /ˈaŋkɔmst/ arrival, coming (in); [sport] finish(ing); [aeroplane] landing: *in volgorde van ~* in (the) order of finishing; *bij ~* on arrival

de **aankomsttijd** /ˈaŋkɔmstɛit/ (pl: -en) time of arrival

aankondigen /ˈaŋkɔndəɣə(n)/ (kondigde aan, heeft aangekondigd) announce: *de volgende plaat ~* announce (or: introduce) the next record; *~ iets te zullen doen* announce that one will do sth.

de **aankondiging** /ˈaŋkɔndəɣɪŋ/ (pl: -en) announcement, notice; signal; foreboding; proclamation: *tot nadere ~* until further notice

de **aankoop** /ˈaŋkop/ (pl: aankopen) **1** buying: *bij ~ van drie flacons krijgt u een poster cadeau* (you get a) free poster with every three bottles **2** purchase(s): *grote aankopen doen* make large purchases

de **aankoopmakelaar** /ˈaŋkopmakəlar/ (pl: -s) purchasing agent, buyer's agent

aankopen /ˈaŋkopə(n)/ (kocht aan, heeft aangekocht) buy, purchase, acquire

aankrijgen /ˈaŋkrɛiɣə(n)/ (kreeg aan, heeft aangekregen) get going: *ik krijg de kachel niet aan* I can't get the stove to burn (or: light)

aankruisen /ˈaŋkrœysə(n)/ (kruiste aan, heeft aangekruist) tick: *~ wat van toepassing is* tick where appropriate

aankunnen /ˈaŋkʏnə(n)/ (kon aan, heeft aangekund) **1** be a match for, (be able to) hold one's own against: *het alleen ~* hold one's own **2** be equal (or: up) to, be able to manage (or: cope with): *zij kon het werk niet aan* she couldn't cope (with the work) ‖ *kan ik ervan op aan, dat je komt?* can I rely on your coming?

aanlanden /ˈanlɑndə(n)/ (landde aan, is aangeland) land (up), arrive at: *waar zijn we nu aangeland?* where have we got to now?

aanlandig /ˈanlɑndəx/ (adj) onshore: *de wind is ~* there is an onshore wind, the wind is blowing home

de **aanleg** /ˈanlɛx/ **1** construction, building; laying; digging; layout: *in ~* under construction; *~ van elektriciteit* installation of electricity **2** talent; aptitude: *~ tonen voor talen* show an aptitude for languages; *~ voor muziek* a talent for music; *daar moet je ~ voor hebben* it's a gift **3** tendency, predisposition, inclination: *~ voor griep hebben* be susceptible to flu ‖ [Belg] *rechtbank van eerste ~* [roughly] county court

¹**aanleggen** /ˈanlɛɣə(n)/ (legde aan, heeft aangelegd) [shipp] moor, tie up; touch (at); berth

²**aanleggen** /ˈanlɛɣə(n)/ (legde aan, heeft aangelegd) **1** construct, build; lay; dig; lay out; install; build up: *een spoorweg (or: weg) ~* construct a railway (or: road); *een nieuwe wijk ~* build a new estate; [Am] build a new development; *voorraden ~* build up stocks, stock up on provisions **2** aim

de **aanlegplaats** /ˈanlɛxplats/ (pl: -en) landing stage, landing place, mooring place; berth

de **aanleiding** /ˈanlɛidɪŋ/ (pl: -en) occasion, reason, cause: *er bestaat geen ~ om (or: tot)* there is no reason to (or: for); *iem. (geen) ~ geven* give s.o. (no) cause; *~ zijn (geven) tot* give rise to; *naar ~ van* as a result of

aanlengen /ˈanlɛŋə(n)/ (lengde aan, heeft aangelengd) dilute

aanleren /ˈanlerə(n)/ (leerde aan, heeft aangeleerd) **1** learn, acquire: *slechte manieren ~* acquire bad manners **2** teach: *een hond kunstjes ~* teach a dog tricks

aanleunen /ˈanlønə(n)/ (leunde aan, heeft aangeleund) lean (against/towards): ~ **tegen** bear (close) resemblance to || [Belg] ~ **bij** seek support (or: protection) from; zich iets **laten** ~ take (or: put up with, swallow) sth.

de **aanleunwoning** /ˈanlønwonɪŋ/ granny house, sheltered accommodation

aanlijnen /ˈanlɛinə(n)/ (lijnde aan, heeft aangelijnd) leash: aangelijnd **houden** keep on the leash (or: lead)

aanlokkelijk /anˈlɔkələk/ (adj) tempting, alluring, attractive

de **aanloop** /ˈanlop/ (pl: aanlopen) **1** run-up: een ~ **nemen** take a run-up; een sprong **met** (or: **zonder**) ~ a running (or: standing) jump; in de ~ **naar** de verkiezingen in the build-up to the elections **2** visitors, callers; customers: zij **hebben** altijd veel ~ they always have lots of visitors

de **aanloopkosten** /ˈanlopkɔstə(n)/ (pl) initial costs (or: expenses)

aanlopen /ˈanlopə(n)/ (liep aan, is aangelopen) **1** walk (towards), come (towards); drop in, drop by: **tegen** iets ~ **a)** walk into sth.; **b)** [fig] chance (or: stumble) on sth. **2** rub; drag **3** turn ... (in the face): **rood** ~ turn red in the face

de **aanmaak** /ˈamak/ manufacture, production

aanmaken /ˈamakə(n)/ (maakte aan, heeft aangemaakt) **1** mix; prepare: **sla** ~ dress a salad **2** light: een **vuur** (or: de **kachel**) ~ light a fire (or: the stove)

aanmanen /ˈamanə(n)/ (maande aan, heeft aangemaand) **1** urge: **tot** voorzichtigheid ~ urge caution **2** order: iem. **tot** betaling ~ demand payment from s.o.

de **aanmaning** /ˈamanɪŋ/ (pl: -en) **1** reminder: een **vriendelijke** ~ a gentle reminder **2** request for payment, notice to pay: ~ **tot** betaling **a)** reminder; **b)** final notice

zich **aanmatigen** /ˈamatəɣə(n)/ (matigde zich aan, heeft zich aangematigd): zich een **oordeel** ~ take it upon o.s. to pass judgement

aanmatigend /ˈamatəɣənt/ (adj, adv) presumptuous, arrogant, high-handed: op ~e **toon** spreken speak arrogantly (or: in a high-handed manner)

aanmelden /ˈamɛldə(n)/ (meldde aan, heeft aangemeld) **1** announce, report: uw komst is aangemeld **bij** de bewaking your arrival has been notified (or: announced) to security **2** register, sign up, put your name forward: heb jij je al aangemeld **voor** het toernooi? have you already signed up for the tournament?; meld je aan **met** je nieuwe gebruikersnaam sign up using your new user ID

de **aanmelding** /ˈamɛldɪŋ/ (pl: -en) entry; application; enlistment; enrolment: de ~ **is gesloten** applications will no longer be accepted

aanmeren /ˈamerə(n)/ (meerde aan, heeft aangemeerd) moor, tie up

aanmerkelijk /amˈɛrkələk/ (adj, adv) considerable; appreciable; marked, noticeable: een ~ **verschil** met vroeger a considerable change from the past; het gaat ~ **beter** things have improved noticeably

aanmerken /ˈamɛrkə(n)/ (merkte aan, heeft aangemerkt) comment, criticize: **op** zijn gedrag valt niets aan te merken his conduct is beyond reproach

de **aanmerking** /ˈamɛrkɪŋ/ (pl: -en) comment, criticism, remark: ~en **maken (hebben)** op find fault with, criticize || **in** ~ nemen consider; **in** ~ komen **voor** qualify for

aanmeten /ˈametə(n)/: zich een nieuw **kapsel** laten ~ change one's hairdo; [fig] zich een beleefde houding ~ assume a polite attitude, strike a polite pose

aanmodderen /ˈamɔdərə(n)/ (modderde aan, heeft aangemodderd): maar **wat** ~ mess around

aanmoedigen /ˈamudəɣə(n)/ (moedigde aan, heeft aangemoedigd) encourage; cheer on: iem. **tot** iets ~ encourage s.o. to do sth.

de **aanmoediging** /ˈamudəɣɪŋ/ (pl: -en) encouragement; cheers: **onder** ~ **van** het publiek while the spectators cheered him (or: her, them) on; hij had **weinig** ~ nodig he needed little encouragement

aanmonsteren /ˈamɔnstərə(n)/ (monsterde aan, heeft aangemonsterd) sign on

aannaaien /ˈanajə(n)/ (naaide aan, heeft aangenaaid): zich een oor laten **aannaaien** be taken for a ride

aannemelijk /anˈɡemələk/ (adj) **1** plausible: een ~e **verklaring** geven voor iets give a plausible explanation for sth. **2** acceptable, reasonable: tegen elk ~ **bod** any reasonable offer accepted; iets ~ **maken** make a reasonable case for sth.

aannemen /ˈanemə(n)/ (nam aan, heeft aangenomen) **1** take, accept; pick up, answer: kan ik een **boodschap** ~? can I take a message? **2** accept, take (on); pass; carry: een **aanbod** met beide handen ~ jump at an offer; een **opdracht** (or: **voorstel**) ~ accept a commission (or: proposal); de **uitdaging** ~ accept (or: take on) the challenge; **met** algemene stemmen ~ carry unanimously **3** accept, believe: **stilzwijgend** ~ tacitly accept; u kunt het **van** mij ~ you can take it from me; iets **voor** waar ~ accept (or: believe) sth. **4** assume, suppose: **algemeen** werd aangenomen dat ... it was generally assumed that ...; **als** vaststaand (vanzelfsprekend) ~ take for granted; aangenomen **dat** supposing (that), assuming (that) **5** undertake, contract for **6** engage, take on: iem. **op** proef ~ appoint s.o. for a trial period || vaste **vorm** ~ take (definite) shape, crystallize

de **aannemer** /ˈanemər/ (pl: -s) (building) contractor, builder

de **aanpak** /ampɑk/ approach: *de ~ van dit probleem* the way to deal with (*or:* tackle) this problem; *een zakelijke ~* a pragmatic approach

aanpakken /ampɑkə(n)/ (pakte aan, heeft aangepakt) **1** take, catch, get hold of **2** go (*or:* set) about (it); deal with; handle; tackle; seize; take: *vervuiling ~ bij de bron* reduce pollution at source; *een probleem ~* tackle a problem; *hoe zullen we dat ~?* how shall we set about it?; *een zaak goed* (or: *verkeerd*) *~* go the right (*or:* wrong) way about a matter; *hij weet van ~* he's a tremendous worker **3** deal with; attack; [law] proceed against: *iem. flink ~* take a firm line with s.o., be tough on s.o.

aanpappen /ampɑpə(n)/ (papte aan, heeft aangepapt) chum up (*or:* pal) up (with)

¹**aanpassen** /ampɑsə(n)/ (paste aan, heeft aangepast) **1** try on, fit on: *een nieuwe jas ~* try on a new coat **2** adapt (to), adjust (to), fit (to): *de lonen zullen opnieuw aangepast worden* wages will be readjusted

zich ²**aanpassen** /ampɑsə(n)/ (paste zich aan, heeft zich aangepast) adapt o.s. (to)

de **aanpassing** /ampɑsɪŋ/ (pl: -en) adaptation (to), adjustment (to)

het **aanpassingsvermogen** /ampɑsɪŋsfərmoɣə(n)/ adaptability (to); accommodation: *gebrek aan ~* lack of flexibility

het **aanplakbiljet** /amplɑgbɪljɛt/ (pl: -ten) poster, bill

het **aanplakbord** /amplɑgbɔrt/ (pl: -en) notice board; boarding; [Am] billboard

aanplakken /amplɑkə(n)/ (plakte aan, heeft aangeplakt) affix, paste (up); post (up): *verboden aan te plakken* no billposting

de **aanplant** /amplɑnt/ plantings, plants: *nieuwe* (or: *jonge*) *~* new (*or:* young) plantings

aanplanten /amplɑntə(n)/ (plantte aan, heeft aangeplant) plant (out), cultivate, grow; afforest

aanpoten /ampotə(n)/ (pootte aan, heeft aangepoot) hurry (up), slog away

aanpraten /amprɑtə(n)/ (praatte aan, heeft aangepraat) palm off on, talk into: *iem. iets ~* talk s.o. into (doing) sth., palm sth. off on s.o.

aanprijzen /amprɛizə(n)/ (prees aan, heeft aangeprezen) recommend, praise

het **aanraakscherm** /anraksxɛrm/ (pl: -en) [comp] touchscreen

aanraden /anradə(n)/ (raadde aan, heeft aangeraden) advise; recommend; suggest: *iem. dringend ~ iets te doen* advise s.o. urgently to do sth.; *dat is niet aan te raden* that is not advisable, to be recommended; *op ~ van* at/on the advice of

aanraken /anrakə(n)/ (raakte aan, heeft aangeraakt) touch: *verboden aan te raken*

(please) do not touch; *met geen vinger ~* not lay a finger on

de **aanraking** /anrakɪŋ/ (pl: -en) touch || *hij is nog nooit met de politie in ~ geweest* he has never been in trouble with the police (*or:* the law)

aanranden /anrandə(n)/ (randde aan, heeft aangerand) assault

de **aanrander** /anrandər/ (pl: -s) assailant

de **aanranding** /anrandɪŋ/ (pl: -en) (criminal, indecent) assault

het/de **aanrecht** /anrɛxt/ (pl: -en) kitchen (sink) unit

het **aanrechtblad** /anrɛxtblɑt/ (pl: -en) worktop, working top

aanreiken /anrɛikə(n)/ (reikte aan, heeft aangereikt) pass, hand; reach: *informatie ~* supply information; *iem. oplossingen ~* steer (*or:* direct) s.o. towards a solution strategy

aanrekenen /anrekənə(n)/ (rekende aan, heeft aangerekend) blame (for)

aanrennen /anrɛnə(n)/: *komen ~* come running (*or:* rushing) on/in

aanrichten /anrɪxtə(n)/ (richtte aan, heeft aangericht) cause, bring about: *een bloedbad ~* (onder) bring about a massacre (among); *grote verwoestingen ~* (bij) create (*or:* wreak) havoc (on)

aanrijden /anrɛidə(n)/ (reed aan, heeft aangereden) collide (with), crash (into), run into: *hij heeft een hond aangereden* he hit a dog; *tegen een muur ~* run (*or:* crash) into a wall

de **aanrijding** /anrɛidɪŋ/ (pl: -en) collision, crash: *een ~ hebben* be involved in a collision (*or:* crash)

aanroepen /anrupə(n)/ (riep aan, heeft aangeroepen) call on/upon; invoke

aanroeren /anrurə(n)/ (roerde aan, heeft aangeroerd) **1** touch: *het eten was nauwelijks aangeroerd* the food had hardly been touched **2** touch upon

aanrommelen /anromələ(n)/ (rommelde aan, heeft aangerommeld) mess around

aanrukken /anrʏkə(n)/: [hum] *nog een fles laten ~* have another bottle (up); *versterkingen laten ~* move up (*or:* call in) reinforcements

de **aanschaf** /ansxɑf/ purchase, buy, acquisition

aanschaffen /ansxɑfə(n)/ (schafte aan, heeft aangeschaft) purchase, acquire

aanscherpen /ansxɛrpə(n)/ (scherpte aan, heeft aangescherpt) **1** sharpen **2** [fig] accentuate, highlight

aanschieten /ansxitə(n)/ (schoot aan, heeft aangeschoten) **1** hit: *een aangeschoten hert* a wounded deer **2** buttonhole, accost: *een voorbijganger ~* buttonhole a passer-by

aanschouwelijk /ansxɑuwələk/ (adj) clear: *iets ~ maken* illustrate sth.; demonstrate sth.

aanschouwen /ansχ<u>au</u>wə(n)/ (aanschouwde, heeft aanschouwd) behold, see: *het levenslicht ~* (first) see the light; *met eigen ogen ~* behold (*or:* see) with one's own eyes
aanschuiven /ansχœyvə(n)/ (schoof aan, heeft aangeschoven) draw up, pull up: *~ bij een overleg* join (in on) the meeting; *schuif gezellig aan!* why don't you join us?
¹aanslaan /anslan/ (sloeg aan, is aangeslagen) **1** start **2** catch on, be successful: *dat plan is bij hen goed aangeslagen* that plan has caught on (well) with them **3** [med] have an effect, take effect: *de behandeling slaat nog niet aan* the treatment hasn't taken effect yet
²aanslaan /anslan/ (sloeg aan, heeft aangeslagen) **1** touch, strike, hit: *een toets ~ strike* a key; *een snaar ~* touch a string **2** estimate; assess; tax: *iem. hoog ~* think highly of s.o.
de **aanslag** /anslaχ/ (pl: -en) **1** [mus] touch: *een lichte* (or: *zware*) *~* a light (*or:* heavy) touch **2** ready: *met het geweer in de ~* with one's rifle at the ready **3** attempt, attack, assault: *een ~ op iemands leven plegen* make an attempt on s.o.'s life **4** deposit; moisture: *een vieze ~ op het plafond* a filthy (smoke) deposit on the ceiling **5** assessment: *een ~ van € 1000,- ontvangen* get assessed € 1000.00 ‖ [fig] *een ~ doen op iemands portemonnee* make inroads upon s.o.'s budget, hurt s.o.'s pocketbook
het **aanslagbiljet** /anslaχbɪljɛt/ (pl: -ten) assessment (notice); (income) tax return (*or:* form)
aanslepen /anslepə(n)/: *die kwestie blijft maar ~* that matter keeps dragging on; *dit product is niet aan te slepen* the demand for this product is through the roof
aanslibben /anslɪbə(n)/ (slibde aan, is aangeslibd) form a deposit: *aangeslibd land* alluvium, alluvial land
aansluipen /anslœypə(n)/: *komen ~* come sneaking along/up
¹aansluiten /anslœytə(n)/ (sloot aan, heeft aangesloten) connect, join, link: *een camera ~ op de computer* connect a camera to the computer
²aansluiten /anslœytə(n)/ (sloot zich aan, heeft zich aangesloten) fit: *deze treinen sluiten op elkaar aan* these trains connect, these are connecting trains; *achteraan ~ alstublieft* join the back of the queue please, go the end of the line please; *~ bij de wensen van de klant* meet the requirements of the customer
zich **³aansluiten** /anslœytə(n)/ (sloot zich aan, heeft zich aangesloten) join (in), become a member of: *zich bij de vorige spreker ~* agree with the preceding speaker; *zich bij een partij ~* join a party; *daar sluit ik me graag bij aan* I would like to second that
de **aansluiting** /anslœytɪŋ/ (pl: -en) **1** joining, association (with): *~ vinden bij iem.* (*iets*) join

in with s.o. (sth.); [fig] *~ zoeken bij* seek contact with **2** [traf] connection: *de ~ missen* miss the connection **3** connection: *~ op het gasnet* connection to the gas mains
aansmeren /ansmerə(n)/ (smeerde aan, heeft aangesmeerd) palm off (on): *iem. een veel te dure auto ~* cajole s.o. into buying far too expensive a car
aansnijden /ansnɛidə(n)/ (sneed aan, heeft aangesneden) **1** cut (into) **2** [fig] broach, bring up
aanspannen /anspanə(n)/ (spande aan, heeft aangespannen) institute: *een proces (tegen iem.) ~* institute (legal) proceedings (against s.o.)
aanspelen /anspelə(n)/ (speelde aan, heeft aangespeeld) [sport] pass, feed, play to
aanspoelen /anspulə(n)/ (spoelde aan, is aangespoeld) wash ashore, be washed ashore: *er is een fles met een briefje erin aangespoeld* a bottle containing a letter has been washed ashore
aansporen /ansporə(n)/ (spoorde aan, heeft aangespoord) urge (on); spur (on): *iem. ~ tot grotere inspanning* incite s.o. to greater efforts
de **aansporing** /ansporɪŋ/ (pl: -en): *op ~ van* at the instance of
de **aanspraak** /ansprak/ (pl: aanspraken) **1** claim: *~ maken op iets* lay claim to sth.; *geen ~ kunnen doen gelden (op iets)* not be able to lay any claim (to sth.) **2** contacts: *weinig ~ hebben* have few contacts
aansprakelijk /ansprakələk/ (adj) responsible (for); [law] liable (for): *zich voor iets ~ stellen* take responsibility for sth.; *iem. ~ stellen voor iets* hold s.o. responsible for sth.
de **aansprakelijkheid** /ansprakələkhɛit/ liability (for), responsibility: [Dutch] *wettelijke ~,* [Belg] *burgerlijke ~* (legal) liability, liability in law; *~ tegenover derden* third-party liability
de **aansprakelijkheidsverzekering** /ansprakələkhɛrtsfərzekərɪŋ/ (pl: -en) liability insurance, third party insurance
aanspreekbaar /ansprekbar/ (adj) approachable; get-at-able
aanspreken /ansprekə(n)/ (sprak aan, heeft aangesproken) **1** draw on, break into: *zijn kapitaal ~* break into one's capital **2** speak to, talk to, address: *iem. (op straat) ~* approach s.o. (in the street); *ik voel mij niet aangesproken* it doesn't concern me; *iem. met mevrouw* (*or:* meneer) *~* address s.o. as madam (*or:* sir); *iem. ~ op zijn verantwoordelijkheid* remind s.o. of their responsibilities; *iem. over zijn gedrag ~* talk to s.o. about his conduct **3** appeal to: *het boek sprak me niet erg aan* the book had little appeal for me
aanstaan /anstan/ (stond aan, heeft aangestaan) **1** please: *zijn gezicht staat mij niet*

aan I do not like the look of him **2** be running; be (turned) on

de **¹aanstaande** /anstạndə/ (pl: -n) fiancé; fiancée

²aanstaande /anstạndə/ (adj) **1** next; this: ~ *vrijdag* this Friday **2** (forth)coming; approaching: *een* ~ *moeder* an expectant mother, a mother-to-be

de **aanstalten** /anstạltə(n)/ (pl): ~ *maken om te vertrekken* get ready to leave; *geen* ~ *maken (om)* show no sign (*or:* intention) (of)

aanstampen /ạnstampə(n)/ (stampte aan, heeft aangestampt) tamp (down)

aanstaren /ạnstarə(n)/ (staarde aan, heeft aangestaard) stare at, gaze at: *iem.* **met** *open mond* ~ stare open-mouthed at s.o., gape at s.o.; *iem. vol bewondering* ~ gaze at s.o. admiringly

aanstekelijk /anstẹkələk/ (adj, adv) infectious, contagious, catching

aansteken /ạnstekə(n)/ (stak aan, heeft aangestoken) **1** light; kindle; turn on, switch on: *die* **brand** *is aangestoken* that fire was started deliberately; *een* **kaars** ~ light a candle **2** infect, contaminate: [fig] *ze steken* **elkaar** *aan* they are a bad (*or:* good) influence on one another

de **aansteker** /ạnstekər/ (pl: -s) (cigarette) lighter

¹aanstellen /ạnstɛlə(n)/ (stelde aan, heeft aangesteld) appoint: *iem.* **vast** ~ appoint s.o. permanently

zich **²aanstellen** /ạnstɛlə(n)/ (stelde zich aan, heeft zich aangesteld) show off, put on airs, act: *zich* **belachelijk** ~ make a fool of o.s.; *stel je* **niet** *aan!* be your age!, stop behaving like a child!

de **aansteller** /ạnstɛlər/ (pl: -s) poseur; [someone behaving childishly] baby

aanstellerig /anstẹlərəx/ (adj) affected, theatrical

de **aanstellerij** /anstɛlərɛi̯/ (pl: -en) affectation, pose, showing off || *is het nu uit* **met** *die* ~? are you quite finished?

de **aanstelling** /ạnstɛlɪŋ/ (pl: -en) appointment: *een* **vaste** (or: **tijdelijke**) ~ *hebben* have a permanent (*or:* temporary) appointment

aansterken /ạnstɛrkə(n)/ (sterkte aan, is aangesterkt) get stronger, recuperate, regain one's strength

aanstichten /ạnstɪxtə(n)/ (stichtte aan, heeft aangesticht) instigate

de **aanstichter** /ạnstɪxtər/ (pl: -s) instigator, originator: *de* ~ **van** *alle kwaad* the source of all evil

aanstippen /ạnstɪpə(n)/ (stipte aan, heeft aangestipt) **1** mention briefly, touch on **2** [med] dab

aanstoken /ạnstokə(n)/ (stak aan, heeft aangestoken) stir up, incite

aanstonds /ạnstɔn(t)s/ (adv): *zo* ~ presently, in a little while

de **aanstoot** /ạnstot/ offence: ~ *geven* give offence; ~ *nemen aan* take offence at

aanstootgevend /anstotxẹvənt/ (adj, adv) offensive, objectionable; [stronger] scandalous; [stronger] shocking: ~*e* **passages** *in een boek* offensive passages in a book

aanstormen /ạnstɔrmə(n)/: *komen* ~ come rushing up/along

aanstormend /ạnstɔrmənt/ (adj): ~ *talent* raging talent, up-and-coming talent

¹aanstoten /ạnstotə(n)/ (stootte aan, is aangestoten) knock (against), bump (into): *hij stootte* **tegen** *de tafel aan* he bumped into the table

²aanstoten /ạnstotə(n)/ (stootte aan, heeft aangestoten) nudge: *zijn* **buurman** ~ nudge one's neighbour

aanstrepen /ạnstrepə(n)/ (streepte aan, heeft aangestreept) mark, check (off), tick (off): *een* **plaats** *in een boek* ~ mark a place in a book

aansturen /ạnstyrə(n)/ (stuurde aan, heeft aangestuurd) (+ op) aim for, aim at, steer towards; drive at: *ik zou niet weten waar hij* **op** *aanstuurt* I don't know what he is driving at

het **aantal** /ạntal/ (pl: -len) number: *een* ~ *jaren lang* for a number of years; *een* ~ *gasten kwam te laat* a number of guests were late; *een* **flink** ~ *boeken* quite a few books; *het* **totale** ~ *werkende kinderen* the total number of working children

aantasten /ạntastə(n)/ (tastte aan, heeft aangetast) **1** affect; harm, attack: *dit zuur tast* **metalen** *aan* this acid corrodes metals; *die roddels tasten onze goede* **naam** *aan* those rumours damage (*or:* harm) our reputation **2** attack: *door een* **ziekte** *aangetast worden* be stricken with a disease

aantekenen /ạntekənə(n)/ (tekende aan, heeft aangetekend) **1** take (*or:* make) a note of, note down, write down, record; register: *brieven laten* ~ have letters registered **2** comment, note, remark: *daarbij tekende hij aan, dat ...* he further observed that ... || *hoger* **beroep** ~ enter (*or:* lodge) an appeal

de **aantekening** /ạntekənɪŋ/ (pl: -en) note: ~*en maken* take notes

de **aantijging** /ạntɛi̯ɣɪŋ/ (pl: -en) allegation, imputation, accusation: [Belg] *lasterlijke* ~ false allegation

de **aantocht** /ạntɔxt/: *in* ~ *zijn* be on the way

aantonen /ạntonə(n)/ (toonde aan, heeft aangetoond) demonstrate, prove, show: *er werd* **ruimschoots** *aangetoond dat ...* ample evidence was given to show that ...

aantoonbaar /antọmbar/ (adj) demonstrable: *dat is* ~ **onjuist** that is patently incorrect

aantreden /ạntredə(n)/ (trad aan, is aangetreden): *de manschappen laten* ~ fall the men in; *sinds het* ~ *van het* **kabinet** since the government took office

aantreffen /ɑntrɛfə(n)/ (trof aan, heeft aangetroffen) **1** meet, encounter, find: *iem. in bed* ~ find s.o. in bed; *iem. niet thuis* ~ find s.o. out **2** find, come across

aantrekkelijk /ɑntrɛkələk/ (adj) attractive; inviting: *ik vind ze erg* ~ I find them very attractive

¹**aantrekken** /ɑntrɛkə(n)/ (trok aan, heeft aangetrokken) **1** attract, draw: *de aarde wordt door de zon aangetrokken* the earth gravitates towards the sun **2** tighten: *een knoop* ~ tighten a knot **3** draw, attract: *zich aangetrokken voelen door* (or: *tot*) *iem. (iets)* feel attracted to s.o. (sth.); *dat trekt mij wel aan* that appeals to me **4** attract; draw: *nieuwe medewerkers* ~ take on (or: recruit) new staff **5** put on: *andere kleren* ~ change one's clothes; *ik heb niets om aan te trekken* I have nothing to wear

zich ²**aantrekken** /ɑntrɛkə(n)/ (trok zich aan, heeft zich aangetrokken) be concerned about, take seriously: *zich iemands lot* ~ be concerned about s.o.('s fate); *trek het je niet aan* don't let that worry you; *zich alles persoonlijk* ~ take everything personally

de **aantrekking** /ɑntrɛkɪŋ/ **1** attraction; gravitation **2** [fig] attraction, appeal

de **aantrekkingskracht** /ɑntrɛkɪŋskrɑxt/ **1** attraction, appeal: *een grote* ~ *bezitten voor iem.* hold (a) great attraction for s.o.; ~ *uitoefenen op iem.* attract s.o. **2** (force of) attraction; gravitational force

de **aan-uitknop** /ɑnœytknɔp/ (pl: -pen) on/off button

aanvaardbaar /ɑnvardbar/ (adj) acceptable: ~ *voor* acceptable to

aanvaarden /ɑnvardə(n)/ (aanvaardde, heeft aanvaard) **1** accept, agree to; take: *ik aanvaard uw aanbod* I accept your offer; *de consequenties* ~ take (or: accept) the consequences; *een voorstel* ~ accept a proposal **2** accept, assume: *de verantwoordelijkheid* ~ assume the responsibility

de **aanval** /ɑnvɑl/ (pl: -len) **1** attack, assault, offensive: *een* ~ *ondernemen* (or: *afslaan*) launch (or: beat off) an attack; *tot de* ~ *overgaan* take the offensive; *in de* ~ *gaan* go on the offensive; *de* ~ *is de beste verdediging* attack is the best form of defence **2** [med] attack, fit: *een* ~ *van koorts* an attack of fever; *een* ~ *van woede* an attack of anger

aanvallen /ɑnvɑlə(n)/ (viel aan, heeft aangevallen) attack, assail, assault: *de vijand in de rug* ~ attack (or: take) the enemy from the rear

aanvallend /ɑnvɑlənt/ (adj, adv) offensive, aggressive

de **aanvaller** /ɑnvɑlər/ (pl: -s) **1** assailant, attacker **2** [sport] attacker; [socc] forward; striker

de **aanvang** /ɑnvɑŋ/ beginning; commencement: *bij* ~ at the start, at the onset; *een* ~ *nemen* commence, open

aanvangen /ɑnvɑŋə(n)/ (ving aan, heeft aangevangen) begin, start, commence

aanvankelijk /ɑnvɑŋkələk/ (adv) initially, at first, in (or: at) the beginning

aanvaren /ɑnvarə(n)/ (voer aan, heeft aangevaren) run into, collide with: *een ander schip* ~ collide with another ship

de **aanvaring** /ɑnvarɪŋ/ (pl: -en) collision, crash: *in* ~ *komen met* collide with

aanvechtbaar /ɑnvɛxtbar/ (adj) contestable, disputable: *een* ~ *standpunt* a debatable point of view

aanvechten /ɑnvɛxtə(n)/ (vocht aan, heeft aangevochten) dispute: *een beslissing* ~ challenge a decision

de **aanvechting** /ɑnvɛxtɪŋ/ (pl: -en) [fig] temptation, impulse

aanvegen /ɑnveɣə(n)/ (veegde aan, heeft aangeveegd) sweep, sweep out

aanverwant /ɑnvərwɑnt/ (adj) related, allied: *de geneeskunde en* ~*e vakken* medicine and related professions

aanvinken /ɑnvɪŋkə(n)/ (vinkte aan, heeft aangevinkt) check (or: tick) off

¹**aanvliegen** /ɑnvliɣə(n)/ (vloog aan, heeft/is aangevlogen) fly (towards): *tegen iets* ~ fly (towards) against sth.; crash into sth.

²**aanvliegen** /ɑnvliɣə(n)/ (vloog aan, heeft aangevlogen) fly at, attack: *de hond vloog de postbode aan* the dog flew at the postman

de **aanvliegroute** /ɑnvlixrutə/ (pl: -s) approach route

aanvoegend /ɑnvuɣənt/ (adj): *de* ~*e wijs* the subjunctive mood

aanvoelen /ɑnvulə(n)/ (voelde aan, heeft aangevoeld) feel, sense: *iem.* ~ understand s.o.; [stronger] empathize with s.o.; *een stemming* ~ sense an atmosphere; *elkaar goed* ~ speak the same language || *het voelt koud aan* it feels cold

de **aanvoer** /ɑnvur/ supply, delivery: *de* ~ *van levensmiddelen* food supplies

de **aanvoerder** /ɑnvurdər/ (pl: -s) leader, captain

de **aanvoerdersband** /ɑnvurdərzbɑnt/ captain's arm band

aanvoeren /ɑnvurə(n)/ (voerde aan, heeft aangevoerd) **1** lead, command, captain: *een leger* ~ command an army **2** supply; import: *hulpgoederen werden per vliegtuig aangevoerd* relief supplies were flown in **3** bring forward, advance; produce; argue: *iets als verontschuldiging* ~ put forward sth. in one's defence, by way of an excuse

de **aanvoering** /ɑnvurɪŋ/ command, leadership, captaincy: *onder* ~ *van* under the command (or: leadership) of

de **aanvraag** /ɑnvrax/ (pl: aanvragen) **1** application, request; inquiry: *een ~ indienen* submit an application; *op ~ te vertonen* to be shown on demand; *~ voor een uitkering* application for social welfare payment **2** request, demand, order: *wij konden niet aan alle aanvragen voldoen* we couldn't meet the demand; *op ~ verkrijgbaar* available on request

aanvragen /ˈanvraɣə(n)/ (vroeg aan, heeft aangevraagd) **1** apply for, request: *ontslag ~* apply for permission to make redundant; *een vergunning ~* apply for a licence **2** request, order: *vraag een gratis folder aan* send for free brochure; *informatie ~ over treinen in Engeland* inquire about trains in England

de **aanvrager** /ˈanvraɣər/ (pl: -s) applicant

aanvreten /ˈanvretə(n)/ (vrat aan, heeft aangevreten) eat away (at), eat into: *door roest aangevreten* corroded by rust; *door gifgas aangevreten longen* lungs attacked by toxic gas

aanvullen /ˈanvʏlə(n)/ (vulde aan, heeft aangevuld) complete, finish, fill (up): *de voorraad ~* replenish stocks; *zij vullen elkaar goed aan* they complement each other well

aanvullend /ˈanvʏlənt/ (adj) supplementary, additional: *een ~e cursus* a follow-up course; *een ~ pensioen* a supplementary pension

de **aanvulling** /ˈanvʏlɪŋ/ (pl: -en) supplement, addition

aanvuren /ˈanvyrə(n)/ (vuurde aan, heeft aangevuurd) fire; rouse; incite: *de troepen ~* rouse the troops

aanwaaien /ˈanwajə(n)/ (waaide/woei aan, is aangewaaid) come naturally to: *alles waait hem zomaar aan* everything just falls into his lap

aanwakkeren /ˈanwɔkərə(n)/ (wakkerde aan, heeft aangewakkerd) **1** stir up: *het vuur ~* fan the fire **2** stimulate, stir up: *de kooplust ~* stimulate buying

de **aanwas** /ˈanwɔs/ (pl: -sen) growth, accretion

aanwenden /ˈanwɛndə(n)/ (wendde aan, heeft aangewend) apply, use: *zijn gezag ~* use one's authority; *zijn invloed ~* exert one's influence

zich **aanwennen** /ˈanwɛnə(n)/ (wende zich aan, heeft zich aangewend) get into the habit of: *zich slechte gewoonten ~* fall into (or: acquire) bad habits

aanwerven /ˈanwɛrvə(n)/ (wierf aan, heeft aangeworven) [Belg] recruit

aanwezig /anwˈeɣəx/ (adj) present: *Trudie is vandaag niet ~* Trudie is not in (or: here) today; *~ zijn bij* be present at; *niet ~* absent

de **aanwezige** /anwˈeɣəɣə/ (pl: -n) person present: *alle ~n keurden het plan goed* all (those) present approved the plan; *geachte ~n* ladies and gentlemen; *onder de ~n bevonden zich …* those present included

de **aanwezigheid** /anwˈeɣəxhɛit/ presence;

attendance: *uw ~ is niet noodzakelijk* your presence is not necessary (*or:* required); *in ~ van* in the presence of

aanwijsbaar /anwˈɛizbar/ (adj) demonstrable, provable, apparent

de **aanwijsstok** /ˈanwɛistɔk/ (pl: -ken) pointer

aanwijzen /ˈanwɛizə(n)/ (wees aan, heeft aangewezen) **1** point to, point out, indicate, show: *de dader ~* point out (*or:* to) the culprit; *een fout ~* point out a mistake; *gasten hun plaats ~* show guests to their seats **2** designate, assign, allocate: *een acteur ~ voor een rol* cast an actor for a part; *een erfgenaam ~* designate an heir **3** indicate, point to, show: *de klok wijst de tijd aan* the clock shows the time

aanwijzend /ˈanwɛizənt/ (adj): *~ voornaamwoord* demonstrative pronoun

de **aanwijzing** /ˈanwɛizɪŋ/ (pl: -en) **1** indication, sign, clue: *er bestaat geen enkele ~ dat …* there is no indication whatever that … **2** instruction, direction: *hij gaf nauwkeurige ~en* he gave precise instructions; *de ~en opvolgen* follow the directions; *~en voor het gebruik* directions for use

de **aanwinst** /ˈanwɪnst/ (pl: -en) **1** acquisition, addition: *een mooie ~ voor het museum* a beautiful acquisition for the museum **2** gain, improvement, asset: *hij is een echte ~ voor ons bedrijf* he is a great asset to our company

[1]**aanwrijven** /ˈanvrɛivə(n)/ (wreef aan, heeft aangewreven) rub against; graze against (*or:* past)

[2]**aanwrijven** /ˈanvrɛivə(n)/ (wreef aan, heeft aangewreven) impute, blame: *iem. iets ~* impute sth. to s.o.

aanzeggen /ˈanzɛɣə(n)/ (zegde aan/zei aan, heeft aangezegd) give notice, notify, announce: [fig] *iem. de wacht ~* issue a (serious) warning to s.o., give s.o. a talking to

de **aanzet** /ˈanzɛt/ (pl: -ten) start, initiative: *de (eerste) ~ geven tot iets* initiate sth., give the initial impetus to sth.

aanzetten /ˈanzɛtə(n)/ (zette aan, heeft aangezet) **1** put on, sew on, stitch on **2** start up, turn on: *de radio ~* turn on the radio **3** spur on, urge, incite, instigate: *iem. tot diefstal ~* incite s.o. to steal ‖ *ergens laat komen ~* turn up late somewhere; *met iets komen ~* turn up with sth.; come up with sth.

het **aanzicht** /ˈanzɪxt/ (pl: -en) aspect, look, view: *nu krijgt de zaak een ander ~* that puts a different light on the matter

het [1]**aanzien** /ˈanzin/ **1** looking (at), watching: *dat is het ~ waard* that is worth watching (*or:* looking at); *ten ~ van* with regard (*or:* respect) to **2** look, aspect, appearance: *iets een ander ~ geven* put a different complexion on sth. **3** standing, regard: *een man van ~* a man of distinction; *hij is sterk in ~ gestegen* his prestige has risen sharply

²**aanzien** /<u>a</u>nzin/ (zag aan, heeft aangezien) **1** look at, watch, see: *die film is niet om aan te zien* it's an awful film; *ik kon het niet langer ~* I couldn't bear to watch it any longer; *ik wil het nog even ~* I want to wait a bit, I want to await further developments **2** consider, regard: *waar zie je mij voor aan?* what do you take me for?; *iem. voor een ander ~* (mis)take s.o. for s.o. else ‖ *ik zie haar er best voor aan* I think she's quite capable of it; *naar het zich laat ~* to/by/from all appearances

aanzienlijk /anz<u>i</u>nlək/ (adj, adv) considerable, substantial: *~e schade* serious damage; *een ~e verbetering* a substantial improvement

het **aanzoek** /<u>a</u>nzuk/ (pl: -en) proposal: *de knappe prins deed het meisje een ~* the handsome prince proposed to the girl

aanzuigen /<u>a</u>nzœyγə(n)/ (zoog aan, heeft aangezogen) suck in ‖ *een ~de werking hebben* draw in more and more people

aanzuiveren /<u>a</u>nzœyvərə(n)/ (zuiverde aan, heeft aangezuiverd) pay off (*or:* up), settle: *een tekort ~* make up (*or:* good) a deficit

aanzwellen /<u>a</u>nzwɛlə(n)/ (zwol aan, is aangezwollen) swell (up, out), rise

de **aap** /ap/ (pl: apen) monkey; ape ‖ *~jes kijken* gawk at people; *voor ~ staan* be made a fool of

de **aar** /ar/ (pl: aren) ear

de **aard** /art/ **1** nature, disposition, character: *zijn ware ~ tonen* show one's true character **2** nature, sort, kind: *iets van dien ~* sth. of the sort, that sort, that nature; *schilderijen van allerlei ~* various kinds (*or:* all kinds) of paintings

de **aardappel** /<u>a</u>rdapəl/ (pl: -s, -en) potato: *gekookte* (or: *gebakken*) *~s* boiled (*or:* fried) potatoes

het **aardappelmeel** /<u>a</u>rdapəlmel/ potato flour

het **aardappelmesje** /<u>a</u>rdapəlmɛʃə/ (pl: -s) potato peeler

de **aardappelpuree** /<u>a</u>rdapəlpyre/ mashed potato(es)

de **aardas** /<u>a</u>rtas/ (pl: -sen) axis of the earth

de **aardbei** /<u>a</u>rdbɛi/ (pl: -en) strawberry

de **aardbeving** /<u>a</u>rdbevɪŋ/ (pl: -en) earthquake

de **aardbodem** /<u>a</u>rdbodəm/ surface (*or:* face) of the earth: *honderden huizen werden van de ~ weggevaagd* hundreds of houses were wiped off the face of the earth; [fig] *van de ~ verdwijnen* disappear off the face of the earth

de **aardbol** /<u>a</u>rdbɔl/ (pl: -len) earth, world, globe

de **aarde** /<u>a</u>rdə/ **1** earth, world: *in een baan om de ~* in orbit round the earth; *op ~* on earth, under the sun **2** ground; earth [electricity] **3** earth, soil: *dat zal bij haar niet in goede ~ vallen* she is not going to like that; *het plan viel in goede ~* the plan was well received; *ter ~ bestellen* commit to the earth, inhume, inter

het ¹**aardedonker** /ardəd<u>ɔ</u>ŋkər/ pitch-darkness: *in het ~* in pitch-darkness

²**aardedonker** /ardəd<u>ɔ</u>ŋkər/ (adj) pitch-dark

¹**aarden** /<u>a</u>rdə(n)/ (adj) earthen, clay

²**aarden** /<u>a</u>rdə(n)/ (aardde, heeft geaard) thrive: *zij kan hier niet ~* she can't settle in here, she can't find her niche; *ik aard hier best* I fit in here, I feel at home here; *dit diertje aardt hier goed* this animal thrives here

³**aarden** /<u>a</u>rdə(n)/ (aardde, heeft geaard) [electricity] earth; [Am] ground

het ¹**aardewerk** /<u>a</u>rdəwɛrk/ earthenware, pottery

²**aardewerk** /<u>a</u>rdəwɛrk/ (adj): *een ~ schotel* an earthenware dish

het **aardgas** /<u>a</u>rtχas/ natural gas

¹**aardig** /<u>a</u>rdəχ/ (adj) **1** nice, friendly: [iron] *wat doe je ~!* charming!, how charming you are!; *dat is ~ van je!* how nice of you! **2** nice, pretty: *het is een ~e meid* she's a nice girl; *een ~ tuintje* a nice (*or:* pretty) garden **3** fair, nice: *een ~ inkomen* a nice income

²**aardig** /<u>a</u>rdəχ/ (adv) nicely, pretty, fairly: *dat komt ~ in de richting* that's more like it; *~ wat mensen* quite a few people; *hij is ~ op weg om … te worden* he is well on his way to becoming …

de **aardigheid** /<u>a</u>rdəχhɛit/ (pl: -heden) small present: *ik heb een ~je meegebracht* I have brought a little sth.; *voor de ~* for the fun of it

de **aardkorst** /<u>a</u>rtkɔrst/ earth's crust

de **aardlekschakelaar** /<u>a</u>rtlɛksχakəlar/ (pl: -s) earth leakage circuit breaker

de **aardolie** /<u>a</u>rtoli/ petroleum

de **aardrijkskunde** /<u>a</u>rdrɛikskʏndə/ geography

aardrijkskundig /ardrɛikskʏndəχ/ (adj) geographic(al)

aards /arts/ (adj) earthly, worldly: *~e machten* earthly powers; *een ~ paradijs* paradise on earth; *~e genoegens* worldly pleasures

de **aardscheerder** /<u>a</u>rtsχerdər/ (pl: -s) near-earth asteroid *(NEA)*

de **aardschok** /<u>a</u>rtsχɔk/ (pl: -ken) earthquake; [fig] upheaval, shock

de **aardverschuiving** /<u>a</u>rtfərsχœyvɪŋ/ (pl: -en) landslide; [fig also] upheaval

de **aardworm** /<u>a</u>rtwɔrm/ (pl: -en) (earth)worm

de **aars** /ars/ (pl: aarzen) arse

het **aartsbisdom** /<u>a</u>rtsbɪzdɔm/ (pl: -men) archbishopric

de **aartsbisschop** /<u>a</u>rtsbɪsχɔp/ (pl: -pen) archbishop

de **aartsengel** /<u>a</u>rtsɛŋəl/ (pl: -en) archangel

de **aartshertog** /<u>a</u>rtshɛrtɔχ/ (pl: -en) archduke

de **aartsvader** /<u>a</u>rtsfadər/ (pl: -s, -en) patriarch

de **aartsvijand** /<u>a</u>rtsfɛiɑnt/ (pl: -en) arch-enemy

aarzelen /a̱rzələ(n)/ (aarzelde, heeft geaarzeld) hesitate: ~ *iets te doen* hesitate about doing sth.; *ik aarzel nog* I am still in doubt

de **aarzeling** /a̱rzəlɪŋ/ (pl: -en) hesitancy; hesitation; shilly-shallying; doubt: *na enige ~* after some hesitation

het **¹aas** /as/ bait: **levend** ~ live bait; *van ~ voorzien* bait (the hook, trap)

het/de **²aas** /as/ [cards] ace: *de ~ van harten, ruiten* the ace of hearts, diamonds

de **aasgier** /a̱sxir/ (pl: -en) vulture

het **abattoir** /abɑtwa̱r/ (pl: -s) abattoir, slaughterhouse

het **abc** /abese̱/ (pl: -'s) ABC: *het ~ van de kunst* the ABC of art

het **abces** /ɑpsɛs/ (pl: -sen) abscess

het **abc'tje** /abese̱cə/ (pl: -s) child's play: *het is een ~* it's child's play, it's a piece of cake

de **abdij** /ɑbdɛi̱/ (pl: -en) abbey

abject /ɑpjɛ̱kt/ (adj) despicable, abject

het **ABN** /abe̱n/ *Algemeen Beschaafd Nederlands* standard Dutch

abnormaal /ɑpnɔrma̱l/ (adj, adv) abnormal; deviant; aberrant; deformed: *een ~ groot hoofd* an abnormally large head

de **abonnee** /abone̱/ (pl: -s) subscriber (to)

het **abonneenummer** /abone̱nʏmər/ (pl: -s) subscriber('s) number

de **abonneetelevisie** /abone̱teləvizi/ pay television (or: cable), subscription television

het **abonnement** /abonəmɛ̱nt/ (pl: -en) **1** subscription (to); taking (or: buying) a season ticket: *een ~ nemen op ...* subscribe to ...; *een ~ opzeggen* (or: *vernieuwen*) cancel (or: renew) a subscription **2** season ticket

zich **abonneren** /abone̱rə(n)/ (abonneerde zich, heeft zich geabonneerd) subscribe (to), take out a subscription (to)

de **Aboriginal** /ɛbɔrɪ̱dʒənəl/ (pl: -s) Aboriginal

aborteren /abɔrte̱rə(n)/ (aborteerde, heeft geaborteerd) abort (a pregnancy), perform an abortion (on): *zij liet zich ~* she had an abortion

de **abortus** /abɔ̱rtʏs/ (pl: -sen) abortion

het **abracadabra** /abrakada̱bra/ abracadabra: [fig] *dat is ~ voor hem* that is all mumbo-jumbo (or: Chinese, double Dutch) to him
  Abraham /a̱braham/ || *hij heeft ~ gezien* he won't see fifty again; *hij weet waar ~ de mosterd haalt* he has been around

de **abri** /abri̱/ (pl: -'s) bus shelter

de **abrikoos** /abriko̱s/ apricot
  abrupt /aprʏ̱pt/ (adj, adv) abrupt, sudden: ~ *halt houden* stop abruptly (or: suddenly)
  abseilen /ɑ̱bzɑjlən/ (seilde ab, heeft abgeseild) abseil
  absent /ɑpsɛ̱nt/ (adj) absent

de **absentie** /ɑpsɛ̱nsi/ (pl: -s) absence

de **absolutie** /ɑpsoly̱(t)si/ [rel] absolution: ~ *geven* absolve
  absoluut /ɑpsoly̱t/ (adj, adv) absolute, perfect: ~ *gehoor* perfect pitch; *dat is ~ onmogelijk* that's absolutely impossible; ~ *niet* definitely (or: absolutely) not; *ik heb ~ geen tijd* I simply have no time; *weet je het zeker? ~!* are you sure? absolutely!; *op het absolute hoogtepunt van haar carrière* at the absolute peak (or: very height) of her career
  absorberen /ɑpsɔrbe̱rə(n)/ (absorbeerde, heeft geabsorbeerd) absorb: ~*d middel* absorbent, absorbing agent

de **absorptie** /ɑpsɔrpsi̱/ (pl: -s) absorption
  abstract /ɑpstrɑ̱kt/ (adj, adv) abstract: ~*e denkbeelden* abstract (or: theoretical) ideas; ~ *schilderen* paint abstractly

de **abstractie** /ɑpstrɑ̱ksi/ (pl: -s) abstraction: *onder ~ van* abstracting (from)
  abstraheren /ɑpstrahe̱rə(n)/ (abstraheerde, heeft geabstraheerd) abstract (from)
  absurd /ɑpsʏ̱rt/ (adj, adv) absurd, ridiculous, ludicrous: ~ *toneel* theatre of the absurd

de **absurditeit** /ɑpsʏrditɛ̱rt/ (pl: -en) absurdity; incongruity

de **abt** /ɑpt/ (pl: -en) abbot

het **¹abuis** /aby̱s/ mistake: *per ~* by mistake
  ²abuis /aby̱s/ (adj) mistaken: *u bent ~* you are mistaken
  abusievelijk /abysi̱vələk/ (adv) mistakenly, erroneously

de **acacia** /aka̱sia/ locust (tree), (false) acacia

de **academicus** /ɑkade̱mikʏs/ (pl: academici) university (or: college) graduate; academic

de **academie** /akade̱mi/ (pl: -s) university, college: *pedagogische ~* college of education; [Dutch] *sociale ~* college of social studies
  academisch /ɑkade̱mis/ (adj, adv) academic, university: *een ~e graad* a university degree; ~ *ziekenhuis* university (or: teaching) hospital; ~ *kwartiertje* [roughly] break between lectures; *een ~e vraag* an academic question

de **acceleratie** /ɑksɛlera̱(t)si/ acceleration
  accelereren /ɑksəlɛre̱rə(n)/ (accelereerde, heeft/is geaccelereerd) accelerate

het **accent** /ɑksɛ̱nt/ (pl: -en) accent; stress: *een sterk* (or: *licht*) *noordelijk ~* a strong (or: slight) northern accent; *het ~ hebben op de eerste lettergreep* have the accent on the first syllable; *het ~ leggen op* stress
  accentueren /ɑksɛntywe̱rə(n)/ (accentueerde, heeft geaccentueerd) stress, emphasize, accentuate
  acceptabel /ɑksɛpta̱bəl/ (adj, adv) acceptable
  accepteren /ɑksɛpte̱rə(n)/ (accepteerde, heeft geaccepteerd) accept, take: *een wissel ~* accept a bill (of exchange); *zijn gedrag kan ik niet ~* I can't accept (or: condone) his behaviour

de **acceptgiro** /ɑksɛptxi̱ro/ (pl: -'s) giro form (or: slip), payment slip

het **accessoire** /ɑsɛswa̱rə/ (pl: -s) accessory

de **accijns** /aksɛins/ (pl: accijnzen) excise (duty, tax): *accijnzen* **heffen** *(op)* charge excise (on)
de **acclamatie** /aklama(t)si/ (pl: -s) [Dutch]: *bij ~ aannemen* carry (or: pass) by acclamation; *bij ~ verkiezen* elect by acclamation
acclimatiseren /aklimatizɛrə(n)/ (acclimatiseerde, is geacclimatiseerd) acclimatize, become acclimatized
de **accolade** /akolɑdə/ (pl: -s) brace, bracket
de **accommodatie** /akɔmodɑ(t)si/ (pl: -s) accommodation; facilities: *er is ~ voor tien passagiers* there are facilities for ten passengers
het/de **accordeon** /akɔrdejɔn/ (pl: -s) accordion
de **account** /əkɑunt/ (pl: -s) **1** account: *een ~ aanmaken* make a new account **2** client meeting, client contact: *een ~ beheren* manage an account
de **accountant** /akɑuntənt/ (pl: -s) accountant; auditor
de **accountmanager** /əkɑuntmɛnədʒər/ (pl: -s) account manager
accrediteren /akreditɛrə(n)/ (accrediteerde, heeft geaccrediteerd) acknowledge, recognize
de **accu** /ɑky/ (pl: -'s) battery: *de ~ is leeg* the battery is dead; *de ~ opladen* charge (up) the battery; [fig] *recharge one's batteries*
accuraat /akyrɑt/ (adj, adv) accurate, precise, meticulous: *~ werken* work accurately
de **accuratesse** /akyratɛsə/ accuracy, precision, meticulousness
de **ace** /es/ (pl: -s) [tennis] ace
het/de **aceton** /asetɔn/ acetone
ach /ɑχ/ (int) oh, ah: *~ wat, ik doe het gewoon!* oh who cares, I'll just do it!; *~, je kunt niet alles hebben!* oh well, you can't have everything!
de **achilleshiel** /aχɪləshil/ (pl: -en) weakness, flaw, failing; [person also] Achilles heel; [plan also] (soft) underbelly
de **achillespees** /aχɪləspes/ (pl: -pezen) Achilles tendon
de **¹acht** /ɑχt/ (pl: -en) attention, consideration: *~ slaan op* a) pay attention to; b) take notice of; *de regels in ~ nemen* comply with (or: observe) the rules; *voorzichtigheid in ~ nemen* take due care
²acht /ɑχt/ (num) eight: *nog ~ dagen* another eight days, eight more days; *iets in ~-en breken* break sth. into eight pieces; *zij kwamen met hun ~en* eight of them came; *zij zijn met hun ~en* there are eight of them
de **achtbaan** /ɑχtban/ (pl: -banen) roller coaster: [fig] *een emotionele ~* an emotional roller coaster
achteloos /ɑχtəlos/ (adj, adv) careless; negligent, casual; inconsiderate
achten /ɑχtə(n)/ (achtte, heeft geacht) **1** esteem, respect **2** consider, think
¹achter /ɑχtər/ (adv) **1** behind, at the rear (or: back): *~ in de tuin* at the bottom of the

garden **2** slow, behind(hand): *jouw horloge loopt ~* your watch is slow ‖ *ik ben ~ met mijn werk* I am behind(hand) with my work; [sport] *~ staan* be behind (or: trailing); [sport] *vier punten ~ staan* be four points down
²achter /ɑχtər/ (prep) **1** behind, at the back (or: rear) of: *~ het huis* behind (or: at the back of) the house; *~ haar ouders' rug om* behind her parents' back; *zet een kruisje ~ je naam* put a tick against your name; *~ zijn computer* at his computer; *~ de tralies* behind bars; *pas op, ~ je!* mind your back **2** after: *~ elkaar* one after the other, in succession, in a row ‖ *~ iets komen* find out about sth.; get to the bottom of sth.; *~ iem. staan* stand behind s.o.; *~ iets staan* approve of sth., back sth.; *er zit (steekt) meer ~* there is more to it
achteraan /ɑχtəran/ (adv) at the back, at (or: in) the rear: *wij wandelden ~* we were walking at the back; *~ in de zaal* at the back of the hall
achteraangaan /ɑχtərɑŋɡan/ go after: *ik zou er maar eens ~* you'd better look into that, I'd do sth. about it if I were you
achteraankomen /ɑχtərɑŋkomə(n)/ (kwam achteraan, is achteraangekomen) come last: *wij komen wel achteraan* we'll follow on after
achteraanlopen /ɑχtəranlopə(n)/ (liep achteraan, heeft achteraangelopen) walk on behind
achteraf /ɑχtərɑf/ (adv) **1** at the back, in (or: at) the rear; [remote] out of the way: *~ wonen* live way out in the sticks, live in the middle of nowhere **2** afterwards, later (on), now, as it is: *~ bekeken zou ik zeggen dat ...* looking back I would say that ...; *~ is het makkelijk praten* it is easy to be wise after the event; *~ ben ik blij dat ...* now I'm glad that ...
de **achterbak** /ɑχtərbak/ (pl: -ken) boot
achterbaks /ɑχtərbɑks/ (adj, adv) underhand, sneaky
de **achterban** /ɑχtərban/ (pl: -nen) supporters, backing, grassroots (support)
de **achterband** /ɑχtərbant/ (pl: -en) back (or: rear) tyre
de **achterbank** /ɑχtərbaŋk/ (pl: -en) back seat
achterblijven /ɑχtərblɛivə(n)/ (bleef achter, is achtergebleven) **1** stay behind, remain (behind) **2** be (or: get) left (behind) **3** be left: *zij bleef achter met drie kinderen* she was left with three children ‖ *toen iedereen trakteerde, wou hij niet ~* when everyone else paid their round, he felt he had to follow suit
de **achterblijvende** /ɑχtərblɛivəndə/ (pl: -n) surviving relative
de **achterblijver** /ɑχtərblɛivər/ (pl: -s) **1** stay-behind **2** slow learner **3** surviving relative
de **achterbuurt** /ɑχtərbyrt/ (pl: -en) slum

de **achterdeur** /ɑχtərdør/ (pl: -en) back door; rear door [car]

de **achterdocht** /ɑχtərdɔχt/ suspicion (of, about): *hij begon ~ te **krijgen*** he began to get suspicious

achterdochtig /ɑχtərdɔχtəχ/ (adj, adv) suspicious

achtereen /ɑχtərɛn/ (adv) in succession: *hij won het kampioenschap **driemaal** ~* he won the championship three times in succession (or: in a row); *weken ~* (for) weeks on end, week after week

achtereenvolgend /ɑχtərenvɔlɣənt/ (adj) successive, consecutive

achtereenvolgens /ɑχtərenvɔlɣəns/ (adv) successively

het **achtereind** /ɑχtərɛint/ (pl: -en) rear end; hindquarters

achteren /ɑχtərə(n)/ (adv) (the) back: *verder naar ~* further back(wards); *van ~* from behind; *van ~ naar voren* back to front; backwards

achtergebleven /ɑχtərχəblevə(n)/ (adj) backward, underdeveloped: *~ gebieden* backward (or: underdeveloped) areas

de **achtergrond** /ɑχtərɣront/ (pl: -en) background: *de ~en van een conflict* the background to (or: of) a dispute || *zich op de ~ houden* keep in the background

de **achtergrondinformatie** /ɑχtərɣrontɪnforma(t)si/ background (information)

de **achtergrondmuziek** /ɑχtərɣrontmyzik/ background music; muzak

achterhaald /ɑχtərhalt/ (adj) out of date, irrelevant

achterhalen /ɑχtərhalə(n)/ (achterhaalde, heeft achterhaald) **1** overtake; catch up with: *de politie heeft de **dief** kunnen ~* the police were able to run down the thief **2** retrieve: *die gegevens zijn niet meer te ~* those data can no longer be accessed (or: retrieved) || *die gegevens zijn allang achterhaald* that information is totally out of date

de **achterhoede** /ɑχtərhudə/ (pl: -s) [sport] defence

het **achterhoedegevecht** /ɑχtərhudəɣəvɛχt/ (pl: -en) rearguard action

het **achterhoofd** /ɑχtərhoft/ (pl: -en) back of the head: *iets in zijn ~ houden* keep sth. at the back of one's mind; *hij is niet op zijn ~ gevallen* he was not born yesterday, there are no flies on him

achterhouden /ɑχtərhɑudə(n)/ (hield achter, heeft achtergehouden) **1** keep back, withhold **2** hold back

achterin /ɑχtərɪn/ (adv) in the back (or: rear); at the back (or: rear)

de **achterkamertjespolitiek** /ɑχtərkamərcəspolitik/ backroom (or: closed-door) politics

de **achterkant** /ɑχtərkɑnt/ (pl: -en) back, rear

(side), reverse (side): *op de ~ van het **papier*** on the back of the paper

de **achterklap** /ɑχtərklɑp/ backbiting, gossip, slander

de **achterkleindochter** /ɑχtərklɛindɔχtər/ (pl: -s) great-granddaughter

het **achterkleinkind** /ɑχtərklɛiŋkɪnt/ (pl: -eren) great-grandchild

de **achterkleinzoon** /ɑχtərklɛinzon/ (pl: -zonen, -s) great-grandson

de **achterklep** /ɑχtərklɛp/ (pl: -pen) lid of the boot [car]; hatchback, liftback

het **achterland** /ɑχtərlɑnt/ (pl: -en) hinterland

achterlaten /ɑχtərlatə(n)/ (liet achter, heeft achtergelaten) leave (behind): *een **bericht** (or: **boodschap**) ~* leave (behind) a note (or: message)

het **achterlicht** /ɑχtərlɪχt/ (pl: -en) back (or: rear) light; rear lamp

achterliggen /ɑχtərlɪɣə(n)/ (lag achter, heeft achtergelegen) lie behind; lag (behind): *drie **ronden** ~* be three laps behind, be trailing by three laps

het **achterlijf** /ɑχtərlɛif/ (pl: -lijven) **1** rump; abdomen **2** back

¹**achterlijk** /ɑχtərlək/ (adj) backward, (mentally) retarded: *hij is **niet** ~* he's no fool

²**achterlijk** /ɑχtərlək/ (adv) like a moron, like an idiot: *doe **niet** zo ~* don't be such a moron

achterlopen /ɑχtərlopə(n)/ (liep achter, heeft achtergelopen) **1** be slow, lose time; be behind, lag behind **2** be behind the times

achterna /ɑχtərna/ (adv) **1** after, behind **2** afterwards, after the event

de **achternaam** /ɑχtərnam/ (pl: -namen) surname, last name, family name

achternagaan /ɑχtərnaɣan/ (ging achterna, is achternagegaan) go after, follow (behind)

achternalopen /ɑχtərnalopə(n)/ (liep achterna, heeft/is achternagelopen) follow

achternazitten /ɑχtərnazɪtə(n)/ (zat achterna, heeft achternagezeten) chase: *de **politie** zit ons achterna* the police are after us (or: on our heels, on our tail)

de **achterneef** /ɑχtərnef/ (pl: -neven) second cousin; great-nephew

de **achternicht** /ɑχtərnɪχt/ (pl: -en) second cousin; great-niece

achterom /ɑχtərɔm/ (adv) round the back: *een **blik** ~* a backward glance

achterop /ɑχtərɔp/ (adv) **1** at (or: on) the back: *spring maar ~!* jump on behind me! **2** behind

achteropraken /ɑχtərɔprakə(n)/ (raakte achterop, is achteropgeraakt) get (or: fall) behind; drop behind

achterover /ɑχtərovər/ (adv) back(wards): *hij **viel** ~ op de stenen* he fell back(wards) onto the stones

achteroverdrukken /ɑχtərovərdrykə(n)/

(drukte achterover, heeft achteroverge-
drukt) pinch

de **achterpoot** /ɑxtərpot/ (pl: -poten) hind leg

de **achterruit** /ɑxtərœyt/ (pl: -en) rear window, back window

de **achterruitverwarming** /ɑxtərœytfər-
wɑrmɪŋ/ (rear window) demister

de **achterspeler** /ɑxtərspelər/ (pl: -s) back

achterst /ɑxtərst/ (adj) back, rear, hind-
(most): *de ~e rijen* the back rows

achterstaan /ɑxtərstan/ (stond achter,
heeft achtergestaan) be behind (*or:* down):
bij de rust stonden we met 3-1 achter at half-
time we were down 3 to 1

achterstallig /ɑxtərstɑlɛx/ (adj) back, overdue, in arrears: *~e huur* rent arrears, back
rent; *~ onderhoud* overdue maintenance

de **achterstand** /ɑxtərstɑnt/ arrears: [sport]
een grote ~ hebben be well down (*or:* behind); *de ~ inlopen* make up arrears, catch
up; *een ~ oplopen* fall behind; *de ploeg probeerde de ~ weg te werken* the team tried to
draw level

de **achterstandswijk** /ɑxtərstɑn(t)swɛik/ (pl:
-en) disadvantaged (*or:* underprivileged)
neighbourhood

het ¹**achterste** /ɑxtərstə/ (pl: -n) **1** back (part):
niet het ~ van zijn tong laten zien keep one's
cards close to one's chest, not commit o.s.
2 backside, rear (end): *op zijn ~ vallen* fall on
one's bottom

het/de ²**achterste** /ɑxtərstə/ (pl: -n) back one, hindmost one, rear(most) one

achterstellen /ɑxtərstɛlə(n)/ (stelde achter,
heeft achtergesteld) slight, neglect: *hij voelde zich achtergesteld* he felt discriminated
against

de **achtersteven** /ɑxtərstevə(n)/ (pl: -s) stern

achterstevoren /ɑxtərstəvorə(n)/ (adv)
back to front

de **achtertuin** /ɑxtərtœyn/ **1** back garden;
[Am] backyard **2** backyard

de ¹**achteruit** /ɑxtərœyt/ reverse (gear): *een
auto in zijn ~ zetten* put a car into reverse
(gear)

²**achteruit** /ɑxtərœyt/ (adv) back(wards)

achteruitgaan /ɑxtərœytxan/ (ging achteruit, is achteruitgegaan) **1** go back(wards);
go astern [ship]; reverse [car]; back [car]: *ga
eens wat achteruit!* stand back a little! **2** [fig]
decline, get worse, grow worse; fail: *zijn
prestaties gaan achteruit* his performance is
on the decline; *haar gezondheid gaat snel achteruit* her health is failing rapidly; *ik ben er per
maand honderd euro op achteruitgegaan* I am a
hundred euros worse off per month

de ¹**achteruitgang** /ɑxtərœytxɑŋ/ back exit,
rear exit, back door

de ²**achteruitgang** /ɑxtərœytxɑŋ/ decline: *de
huidige economische ~* the present economic
decline

de **achteruitkijkspiegel** /ɑxtərœytkɛik-
spiɣəl/ (pl: -s) rear-view mirror

achteruitlopen /ɑxtərœytlopə(n)/ (liep
achteruit, heeft/is achteruitgelopen) **1** walk
backwards: *de barometer loopt achteruit* the
barometer is falling **2** [fig] decline

achteruitrijden /ɑxtərœytrɛidə(n)/ (reed
achteruit, heeft/is achteruitgereden) reverse
(into), back (into)

achteruitwijken /ɑxtərœytwɛikə(n)/
(week achteruit, is achteruitgeweken) back
away, step back, fall back

achtervolgen /ɑxtərvɔlɣə(n)/ (achtervolg-
de, heeft achtervolgd) **1** follow: *die gedachte achtervolgt mij* that thought haunts (*or:*
obsesses) me **2** pursue; persecute

de **achtervolger** /ɑxtərvɔlɣər/ (pl: -s) pursuer

de **achtervolging** /ɑxtərvɔlɣɪŋ/ (pl: -en) pursuit; chase; persecution: *de ~ inzetten* pursue, set off in pursuit (of)

de **achtervolgingswaanzin** /ɑxtərvɔlɣɪŋs-
wanzɪn/ persecution complex (*or:* mania),
paranoia

¹**achterwaarts** /ɑxtərwarts/ (adj) backward,
rearward: *een ~e beweging* a backward
movement

²**achterwaarts** /ɑxtərwarts/ (adv) back-
(wards): *een stap ~* a step back(wards)

de **achterwand** /ɑxtərwɑnt/ (pl: -en) back
wall, rear wall

achterwege /ɑxtərweɣə/ (adv): *een antwoord bleef ~* an answer was not forthcoming; *~ laten* omit; leave undone

het **achterwerk** /ɑxtərwɛrk/ (pl: -en) backside,
rear (end)

het **achterwiel** /ɑxtərwil/ (pl: -en) back wheel,
rear wheel

de **achterzak** /ɑxtərzɑk/ (pl: -ken) back pocket

de **achterzijde** /ɑxtərzɛidə/ (pl: -n) back, rear

de **achting** /ɑxtɪŋ/ regard, esteem: *~ voor iem.
hebben* have respect for s.o.; *in (iemands) ~
dalen* come down in s.o.'s estimation; *in (iemands) ~ stijgen* go up in s.o.'s estimation

achtste /ɑxtstə/ (adj) eighth: *een ~ liter* one
eighth of a litre

achttien /ɑxtin/ (num) eighteen

achttiende /ɑxtində/ (num) eighteenth

achttiende-eeuws /ɑxtindeɛws/ (adj)
eighteenth-century

achturig /ɑxtyrəx/ (adj) eight-hour: *de ~e
werkdag* the eight-hour (working) day

de **acne** /ɑkne/ acne

de **acquisitie** /ɑkwizi(t)si/ (pl: -s) acquisition

de **acrobaat** /ɑkrobat/ (pl: acrobaten) acrobat

de **acrobatiek** /ɑkrobatik/ acrobatics

acrobatisch /ɑkrobatis/ (adj, adv) acrobatic

het **acryl** /ɑkril/ acrylic (fibre)

acteren /ɑkterə(n)/ (acteerde, heeft geac-
teerd) **1** act, perform **2** act: *~ op de bevindin-
gen* act on the findings

de **acteur** /ɑktør/ (pl: -s) actor, performer

de **actie** /ɑksi/ (pl: -s) **1** action, activity: *er zit geen ~ in dat toneelstuk* there's no action in that play; *in ~ komen* go into action **2** (protest) campaign: *~ voeren* [just once] hold a demonstration; *~ voeren tegen* campaign against

het **actiecomité** /ɑksikomite/ (pl: -s) action committee

actief /ɑktif/ (adj, adv) active [finance]; busy; energetic: *in actieve dienst* **a)** on active duty; **b)** [mil] on active service; *een actieve handelsbalans* a favourable balance of trade; *iets ~ en passief steunen* support sth. (both) directly and indirectly ‖ *actieve handel* export (trade)

de **actiegroep** /ɑksiɣrup/ (pl: -en) action group; [roughly] pressure group

het **actiepunt** /ɑksipʏnt/ point of action

de **actieradius** /ɑksiradijʏs/ radius of action, range

de **actievoerder** /ɑksivurdər/ (pl: -s) campaigner, activist

actievoeren /ɑksivurə(n)/ (voerde actie, heeft actiegevoerd): *~ tegen* agitate (*or:* campaign) against, carry on a campaign against

de **activa** /ɑktiva/ (pl) assets: *~ en passiva* assets and liabilities; *vaste ~* fixed assets; *vlottende ~* current assets

de **activatiecode** /ɑktiva(t)sikodə/ (pl: -s) activation code

activeren /ɑktivɛrə(n)/ (activeerde, heeft geactiveerd) activate

de **activist** /ɑktivɪst/ (pl: -en) activist, crusader

de **activiteit** /ɑktivitɛit/ (pl: -en) activity: *~en ontplooien* undertake activities; *buitenschoolse ~en* extramural activities, extracurricular activities

de **actrice** /ɑktrisə/ (pl: -s) actor, actress

actualiseren /ɑktywalizɛrə(n)/ (actualiseerde, heeft geactualiseerd) update

de **actualiteit** /ɑktywalitɛit/ (pl: -en) topical matter (*or:* subject); current event; news; current affairs

het **actualiteitenprogramma** /ɑktywalitɛrtə(n)proɣrama/ (pl: -'s) current affairs programme

actueel /ɑktywel/ (adj) current, topical: *een ~ onderwerp* a topical subject; current affairs

de **acupunctuur** /akypʏŋktyr/ acupuncture

[1]**acuut** /akyt/ (adj) acute, critical: *~ gevaar* acute danger

[2]**acuut** /akyt/ (adv) immediately, right away, at once

A.D. *anno Domini* AD

de **adamsappel** /adɑmsɑpəl/ (pl: -s) Adam's apple

het **adamskostuum** /adɑmskɔstym/ [hum]: *in ~* in one's birthday suit

de **adapter** /adɑptər/ (pl: -s) adapter

de **adder** /ɑdər/ (pl: -s) viper, adder: [fig] *er schuilt een ~(tje) onder het gras* there's a snake in the grass, there's a catch in it somewhere

additioneel /ɑdi(t)ʃonel/ (adj) additional, accessory

de **adel** /adəl/ nobility, peerage: *hij is van ~* he is a peer, he belongs to the nobility

de **adelaar** /adəlar/ (pl: -s) eagle

adellijk /adələk/ (adj) noble: *van ~e afkomst* of noble birth; *~ bloed* noble blood

de **adelstand** /adəlstɑnt/ nobility: *iem. in* (or: *tot) de ~ verheffen* ennoble s.o., raise s.o. to the peerage

de **adem** /adəm/ breath: *de laatste ~ uitblazen* breathe one's last; *slechte ~* bad breath, halitosis; *zijn ~ inhouden* [also fig] hold one's breath; *naar ~ happen* gasp for breath; *buiten ~ zijn* be out of breath; *in één ~* in the same breath; *weer op ~ komen* catch one's breath

adembenemend /adəmbənemənt/ (adj, adv) breathtaking: *een ~ schouwspel* a breathtaking scene

ademen /adəmə(n)/ (ademde, heeft geademd) breathe, inhale: *vrij ~* [also fig] breathe freely; *de lucht die we hier ~ is verpest* the air we are breathing here is poisoned

ademhalen /adəmhalə(n)/ (haalde adem, heeft ademgehaald) breathe: *weer adem kunnen halen* be able to breathe again; *haal eens diep adem* take a deep breath

de **ademhaling** /adəmhalɪŋ/ (pl: -en) breathing, respiration: *kunstmatige ~* artificial respiration; *een onrustige ~* irregular breathing

ademloos /adəmlos/ (adj, adv) breathless: *een ademloze stilte* a breathless hush

de **ademnood** /adəmnot/: *in ~ verkeren* be gasping for breath, find it difficult to breathe

de **adempauze** /adəmpauzə/ (pl: -s) breathing space, breather

de **ademtest** /adəmtɛst/ (pl: -s) breath test: *iem. de ~ afnemen* breathalyse s.o.

de **adept** /adɛpt/ (pl: -en) follower, adherent, disciple

adequaat /adəkwat/ (adj, adv) appropriate, effective; adequate: *~ reageren* react appropriately (*or:* effectively)

de **ader** /adər/ (pl: -s, -en) vein, blood vessel; artery: *een gesprongen ~* a burst blood vessel

de **aderlating** /adərlatɪŋ/ (pl: -en) bleeding; [fig] drain (on resources): *dat was een behoorlijke ~* it made a big hole in the budget

de **aderverkalking** /adərvərkɑlkɪŋ/ arteriosclerosis, hardening of the arteries

de **adh** *aanbevolen dagelijkse hoeveelheid* RDI (*recommended daily intake*)

ADHD /adehade/ *attention deficit hyperactivity disorder* ADHD

de **adhesie** /ɑthezi/ adherence

a.d.h.v. *aan de hand van* using, by means of

het **¹adjectief** /ɑtjɛktif/ (pl: adjectieven) adjective

²adjectief /ɑtjɛktif/ (adj) adjectival, adjective

de **adjudant** /ɑtjydɑnt/ (pl: -en) **1** adjutant, aide(-de-camp) **2** [Dutch] [roughly] warrant officer

de **adjunct-directeur** /ɑtjʏŋdirɛktør/ (pl: -en) deputy director (or: manager); [educ] deputy headmaster

de **administrateur** /ɑtministratør/ (pl: -en, -s) administrator: de ~ van een **universiteit** the administrative director of a university

de **administratie** /ɑtministra(t)si/ (pl: -s) **1** administration; management; accounts: de ~ **voeren** do the administrative work; keep the accounts **2** administrative department; [bldg] administrative building (or: offices): hij zit **op** de ~ he's in the administrative (or: clerical) department

administratief /ɑtministratif/ (adj, adv) administrative; clerical: ~ **personeel** administrative (or: clerical) staff; [Belg] ~ **centrum** administrative centre

de **administratiekosten** /ɑtministra(t)sikɔstə(n)/ (pl) administrative costs, service charge(s)

administreren /ɑtministrerə(n)/ (administreerde, heeft geadministreerd) administer; manage, run; keep accounts: een ~d **lichaam** an administrative body

de **admiraal** /ɑtmiral/ (pl: -s) admiral

de **adolescent** /ɑdolɛsɛnt/ (pl: -en) adolescent; youngster

de **adonis** /ɑdonɪs/ (pl: -sen) Adonis; Greek god

adopteren /ɑdoptərə(n)/ (adopteerde, heeft geadopteerd) adopt

de **adoptie** /ɑdɔpsi/ (pl: -s) adoption

het **adoptiekind** /ɑdɔpsikɪnt/ (pl: -eren) adopted child

de **adoptieouder** /ɑdɔpsiɑudər/ (pl: -s) adoptive parent

de **adrenaline** /ɑdrenalinə/ adrenaline

het **adres** /ɑdrɛs/ (pl: -sen) address, (place of) residence: hij verhuisde zonder een ~ **achter** te laten he moved without leaving a forwarding address; [fig] je bent aan het **juiste** ~ you've come to the right place; **per** ~ care of; [abbr] c/o; een **vertrouwd** ~ voor al uw reparaties a trusted source for all your repairs

de **adresbalk** /ɑdrɛzbɑlk/ (pl: -en) [comp] address bar, location bar

adresseren /ɑdrɛsərə(n)/ (adresseerde, heeft geadresseerd) address: een **brief** vergeten te ~ forget to address a letter

de **adreswijziging** /ɑdrɛswɛizəɣɪŋ/ (pl: -en) change of address

Adriatisch /ɑdrijatis/ (adj) Adriatic: ~e **Zee** Adriatic Sea

ADSL /ɑdeɛsɛl/ asymmetric digital subscriber line ADSL

de **advent** /ɑtfɛnt/ Advent

de **adverteerder** /ɑtfərterdər/ (pl: -s) advertiser

de **advertentie** /ɑtfərtɛnsi/ (pl: -s) advertisement, ad(vert): een ~ **plaatsen** put an advertisement in the paper(s)

adverteren /ɑtfərtɛrə(n)/ (adverteerde, heeft geadverteerd) advertise; announce: er wordt veel geadverteerd **voor** nieuwe computerspelletjes new computer games are being heavily advertised

het **advies** /ɑtfis/ (pl: adviezen) advice: ~ **geven** give advice; iemands ~ **opvolgen** follow s.o.'s advice; iem. **om** ~ vragen ask s.o.'s advice; een ~ a piece of advice; a recommendation; het ~ van deskundigen **inwinnen** obtain expert advice, get the opinion of experts

het **adviesbureau** /ɑtfizbyro/ (pl: -s) consultancy

de **adviesprijs** /ɑtfisprɛis/ (pl: -prijzen) recommended selling (or: retail) price

de **adviesraad** /ɑtfisrat/ (pl: -raden) advisory body

adviseren /ɑtfizerə(n)/ (adviseerde, heeft geadviseerd) **1** recommend, advise (s.o.): hij adviseerde mij de auto te laten repareren he advised me to have the car mended **2** advise, counsel: ik kan je in deze lastige kwestie niet ~ I can't offer you advice in this complicated matter

de **adviseur** /ɑtfizør/ (pl: -s) adviser, advisor, counsellor; consultant: **juridisch** ~ legal advisor, lawyer; solicitor

de **advocaat** /ɑtfokat/ (pl: advocaten) lawyer; barrister; solicitor: een ~ **nemen** engage a lawyer ‖ [fig] ~ van de **duivel** the devil's advocate

het **advocatenkantoor** /ɑtfokatə(n)kɑntor/ (pl: -kantoren) lawyer's office

de **advocatuur** /ɑtfokatyr/ Bar; legal profession: de **sociale** ~ [roughly] legal aid lawyers

de **aerobics** /ɛːrɔbɪks/ aerobics

aerodynamisch /ɛːrodinamis/ (adj) aerodynamic

het **¹af** /ɑf/: teruggaan **naar** af go back to square one

²af /ɑf/ (adj) **1** finished, done, completed; polished; well-finished: het werk **is** af the work is done (or: finished) **2** [game] out: zij **is** af she's out

³af /ɑf/ (adv) **1** off, away: mensen liepen af en **aan** people came and went; af en **toe** (every) now and then; klaar? af! ready, steady, go!; get set! go! **2** (+ van) from: van die dag af from that day (on, onwards); van kind af (aan) woon ik in deze straat since I was a child I have been living in this street; van de grond af from ground level **3** away, off: [fig] dat **kan** er bij ons niet af we can't afford that; de verf is **er** af the paint has come off; **ver** af a long way off; hij woont een eindje **van** de weg af he lives a little way away from the road; van *iem. af zijn* be rid of s.o.; *u bent nog niet van me af* you haven't seen (*or:* heard) the last of me; I haven't finished with you yet **4** down: *de trap af* down the stairs **5** to; towards; up to: *ze komen op ons af* they are coming towards us || *goed* (or: *beter, slecht*) *af zijn* have come off well (or: better, badly); *ik weet er niets van af* I don't know anything about it; *van voren af aan beginnen* start from scratch; start all over again

de **afasie** /afazi/ aphasia

afbakenen /ɑvbakənə(n)/ (bakende af, heeft afgebakend) mark out; stake out; define; demarcate; mark off

afbakken /ɑvbɑkə(n)/ (bakte af, heeft afgebakken) finish off in the oven: *broodjes om zelf af te bakken* par(t)-baked rolls

afbeelden /ɑvbɛldə(n)/ (beeldde af, heeft afgebeeld) depict, portray, picture

de **afbeelding** /ɑvbɛldɪŋ/ (pl: -en) picture, image; illustration; figure

afbekken /ɑvbɛkə(n)/ (bekte af, heeft afgebekt): [inform] *iem. ~* snap (*or:* snarl) at s.o.; jump down s.o.'s throat

afbellen /ɑvbɛlə(n)/ (belde af, heeft afgebeld) **1** cancel (by telephone) **2** ring round: *hij belde de halve stad af om een taxi* he rang round half the city for a taxi

afbestellen /ɑvbəstɛlə(n)/ (bestelde af, heeft afbesteld) cancel

afbetalen /ɑvbətalə(n)/ (betaalde af, heeft afbetaald) pay off; pay for [goods]: *het huis is helemaal afbetaald* the house is completely paid for

de **afbetaling** /ɑvbətalɪŋ/ (pl: -en) hire purchase, payment by instalment (*or:* in instalments): *op ~* on hire purchase

afbeulen /ɑvbølə(n)/ (beulde af, heeft afgebeuld) drive into the ground, work to death: *zich ~* slave; work one's guts out; knacker o.s.

afbieden /ɑvbidə(n)/ (bood af, heeft afgeboden) [Belg] bring (*or:* knock, beat) down

afbijten /ɑvbɛitə(n)/ (beet af, heeft afgebeten) **1** bite off **2** strip, remove

afbinden /ɑvbɪndə(n)/ (bond af, heeft afgebonden) **1** tie off **2** untie, undo: *de schaatsen ~* untie (*or:* undo) one's skates

afbladderen /ɑvblɑdərə(n)/ (bladderde af, is afgebladderd) **1** flake (off), peel (off): *de verf bladdert af* the paint is flaking (*or:* peeling) off **2** [fig] tarnish: *zijn imago is behoorlijk afgebladderd* his image is really tarnished, his image has been seriously dented

afblazen /ɑvblazə(n)/ (blies af, heeft afgeblazen) blow off (*or:* away): *stof van de tafel ~* blow the dust off the table || *de scheidsrechter had (de wedstrijd) al afgeblazen* the referee had already blown the final whistle

afblijven /ɑvblɛivə(n)/ (bleef af, is afgebleven) keep off, leave alone, let alone, keep

(*or:* stay) away (from): *blijf van de koekjes af* leave the biscuits alone

afboeken /ɑvbukə(n)/ (boekte af, heeft afgeboekt) **1** transfer **2** write off

afborstelen /ɑvbɔrstələ(n)/ (borstelde af, heeft afgeborsteld) brush (down): *zijn kleren ~* give one's clothes a brush

afbouwen /ɑvbɑuwə(n)/ (bouwde af, heeft afgebouwd) **1** cut back (on), down (on), phase out: *we zijn de therapie aan het ~* we're phasing out the therapy **2** complete, finish

de **afbraak** /ɑvbrak/ demolition

afbranden /ɑvbrɑndə(n)/ (brandde af, heeft/is afgebrand) burn down

afbreekbaar /ɑvbreɡbar/ (adj) decomposable, degradable; biodegradable: *biologisch afbreekbare wasmiddelen* biodegradable detergents

¹**afbreken** /ɑvbrekə(n)/ (brak af, is afgebroken) break off (*or:* away); snap (off): *de punt brak (van de stok) af* the end broke off (the stick)

²**afbreken** /ɑvbrekə(n)/ (brak af, heeft afgebroken) **1** break off, interrupt; cut short: *onderhandelingen ~* break off negotiations; *de wedstrijd werd afgebroken* the game was stopped **2** pull down, demolish; break down, tear down; break up; dismantle: *de boel ~* smash the place up **3** decompose, degrade || *afvalstoffen worden in het lichaam afgebroken* waste-products are broken down in the body

afbrengen /ɑvbrɛŋə(n)/ (bracht af, heeft afgebracht) put off: *ze zijn er niet van af te brengen* they can't be put off (*or:* deterred) || *het er goed ~* do well; *het er slecht ~* come off badly; *het er levend ~* escape with one's life; *het er heelhuids ~* come out of it unscathed

de **afbreuk** /ɑvbrøk/: *~ doen aan* harm, injure, damage

afbrokkelen /ɑvbrɔkələ(n)/ (brokkelde af, is afgebrokkeld) crumble (off, away), fragment: *het plafond brokkelt af* the ceiling is crumbling

afbuigen /ɑvbœyɣə(n)/ (boog af, is afgebogen) turn off, bear off, branch off: *hier buigt de weg naar rechts af* here the road bears (to the) right

het **afdak** /ɑvdɑk/ (pl: -en) lean-to

afdalen /ɑvdalə(n)/ (daalde af, is afgedaald) go down, come down, descend: *een berg ~* go (or: come) down a mountain

de **afdaling** /ɑvdalɪŋ/ (pl: -en) **1** descent **2** [skiing] downhill

afdanken /ɑvdɑŋkə(n)/ (dankte af, heeft afgedankt) **1** discard; cast off; (send for) scrap **2** dismiss; disband: *personeel ~* pay off staff

het **afdankertje** /ɑvdɑŋkərcə/ (pl: -s) cast-off, hand-me-down

afdekken /ɑvdɛkə(n)/ (dekte af, heeft afgedekt) cover (over, up)

de **afdeling** /ɑvdeːlɪŋə/ (pl: -en) department, division; section; ward: *de ~ Utrecht van onze vereniging* the Utrecht branch of our society; *Kees werkt op de ~ financiën* Kees works in the finance department

de **afdelingschef** /ɑvdeːlɪŋʃɛf/ (pl: -s) department(al) manager, head of department; floor manager

afdingen /ɑvdɪŋə(n)/ (dong af, heeft afgedongen) bargain (*or:* haggle) (with s.o.)

afdoen /ɑvdun/ (deed af, heeft afgedaan) **1** take off, remove: *zijn hoed ~* take off one's hat **2** take off: *iets van de prijs ~* knock a bit off the price, come down a bit (in price) ‖ [fig] *dat doet niets af aan het feit dat …* that doesn't alter the fact that …; *iets ~ als een incident* downplay sth., dismiss sth. as an incident

afdoend /ɑvdunt/ (adj, adv) sufficient, adequate; effective: *een ~ middel* an effective method

afdraaien /ɑvdraːjə(n)/ (draaide af, heeft afgedraaid) twist off: *de dop van een vulpen ~* unscrew the cap of a fountain pen ‖ *hier moet u rechts ~* you turn right (*or:* turn off to the right) here

afdragen /ɑvdraːɣə(n)/ (droeg af, heeft afgedragen) **1** make over, transfer, hand over, turn over **2** wear out: *afgedragen schoenen* worn-out shoes

afdrijven /ɑvdrɛivə(n)/ (dreef af, is afgedreven) drift off; [shipp] go adrift ‖ *de bui drijft af* the shower is blowing over

afdrogen /ɑvdroːɣə(n)/ (droogde af, heeft afgedroogd) dry (up); wipe dry: *zijn handen ~* dry one's hands (on a towel); *zich ~* dry o.s. (off)

de **afdronk** /ɑvdrɔŋk/ aftertaste

afdruipen /ɑvdrœypə(n)/ (droop af, is afgedropen) slink off (*or:* away), clear off

de **afdruk** /ɑvdrʏk/ (pl: -ken) print; imprint; mould; cast: *de wielen lieten een ~ achter* the wheels left an impression

afdrukken /ɑvdrʏkə(n)/ (drukte af, heeft afgedrukt) print (off); copy; run off

het **afdrukvoorbeeld** /ɑvdrʏkforbeːlt/ (pl: -en) print preview

afdwalen /ɑvdwaːlə(n)/ (dwaalde af, is afgedwaald) stray (off) (from), go astray; [fig also] wander (off): *zijn gedachten dwaalden af naar haar* his thoughts wandered off to her; *van zijn onderwerp ~* stray from one's subject

afdwingen /ɑvdwɪŋə(n)/ (dwong af, heeft afgedwongen) exact (from); extort (from)

de **affaire** /ɑfɛːrə/ (pl: -s) affair

het/de **affiche** /ɑfiʃə/ (pl: -s) poster; (play)bill

afgaan /ɑfxaːn/ (ging af, is afgegaan) **1** go down, descend: *de trap ~* go down the stairs **2** (+ op) [fig] rely on, depend on: *~de op wat hij zegt* judging by what he says; *op zijn gevoel*

~ play it by ear **3** come off; be deducted: *daar gaat 10 % van af* 10 % is taken off that **4** go off: *een geweer doen ~* fire a rifle **5** lose face, flop, fail ‖ *van school ~* leave school

de **afgang** /ɑfxɑŋ/ (pl: -en) (embarrassing) failure, flop

afgedraaid /ɑfxədrajt/ (adj) worn-out, completely exhausted

afgeladen /ɑfxəladə(n)/ (adj) (jam-)packed, crammed

afgelasten /ɑfxəlɑstə(n)/ (gelastte af, heeft afgelast) cancel; call off; [sport] postpone

afgeleefd /ɑfxəleeft/ (adj) used up, worn-out, spent

afgelegen /ɑfxəleɣə(n)/ (adj, adv) remote, far(-away), far-off: *een ~ dorp* a remote (*or:* an out-of-the-way) village

afgeleid /ɑfxəlɛit/ (adj) diverted, distracted: *hij is gauw ~* he is easily distracted

afgelopen /ɑfxəlopə(n)/ (adj) last, past: *de ~ maanden hadden wij geen woning* for the last few months we haven't had anywhere to live; *de ~ tijd* recently; *de ~ weken* the past weeks, the last few weeks ‖ *~!* stop it!, that's enough!

afgemeten /ɑfxəmetə(n)/ (adj, adv) **1** measured (off, out): *met ~ passen* with measured steps **2** formal, stiff

afgepeigerd /ɑfxəpɛiɣərt/ (adj) knackered, exhausted

afgericht /ɑfxərɪxt/ (adj) (well-)trained

afgerond /ɑfxərɔnt/ (adj) **1** (well-)rounded: *het vormt een ~ geheel* it forms a complete whole **2** round

afgesproken /ɑfxəsprokə(n)/ (adj) agreed, settled ‖ *dat is dan ~* it's a deal!

afgestompt /ɑfxəstɔmt/ (adj) dull(ed), deadened

de **afgestudeerde** /ɑfxəstyderdə/ (pl: -n) graduate

afgetrapt /ɑfxətrɑpt/ (adj) worn out

de **afgevaardigde** /ɑfxəvardəɣdə/ (pl: -n) delegate, representative; member (of parliament): *de geachte ~* the honourable member

¹**afgeven** /ɑfxevə(n)/ (gaf af, heeft afgegeven) **1** run **2** (+ op) run down: *op iem. ~* talk bad about s.o., be disparaging about s.o.

²**afgeven** /ɑfxevə(n)/ (gaf af, heeft afgegeven) **1** hand in; deliver; leave; hand over; give up: *hij weigerde zijn geld af te geven* he refused to part with his money; *een pakje bij iem. ~* leave a parcel with s.o. **2** give off: *de kachel geeft veel warmte af* the stove gives off a lot of heat **3** announce, expect: *een duidelijk signaal ~* send a clear message

afgewerkt /ɑfxəwɛrkt/ (adj) used (up), spent: *~e olie* used oil

afgewogen /ɑfxəwoɣə(n)/ (adj) balanced

afgezaagd /ɑfxəzaxt/ (adj) [fig] stale; hackneyed

de **afgezant** /ɑfxəzɑnt/ (pl: -en) envoy, ambassador

afgezien /ɑfχəzin/: ~ *van* besides, apart from; ~ *van* de kosten (or: *moeite*) apart from the cost (*or:* trouble)

afgezonderd /ɑfχəzɔndərt/ (adj, adv) isolated, cut off; segregated; remote

de **Afghaan** /ɑfχan/ (pl: Afghanen) Afghan

Afghaans /ɑfχans/ (adj) Afghan

Afghanistan /ɑfχanistɑn/ Afghanistan

afgieten /ɑfχitə(n)/ (goot af, heeft afgegoten) pour off; strain; drain: *aardappels* ~ drain potatoes; *groente* ~ strain vegetables

het **afgietsel** /ɑfχitsəl/ (pl: -s) cast, mould

de **afgifte** /ɑfχɪftə/ delivery; issue [tickets etc]

de **afgod** /ɑfχɔt/ (pl: -en) idol

afgooien /ɑfχojə(n)/ (gooide af, heeft afgegooid) throw down; fling down: *pas op dat je het* ***er*** *niet afgooit* take care that you don't knock it off

afgraven /ɑfχravə(n)/ (groef af, heeft afgegraven) dig up, dig off; level

afgrendelen /ɑfχrɛndələ(n)/ (grendelde af, heeft afgegrendeld) [fig] seal off, close off; [literally] bolt up

afgrijselijk /ɑfχrɛisələk/ (adj, adv) 1 horrible, horrid, atrocious: *een ~e* ***moord*** a gruesome murder 2 hideous, ghastly

het **afgrijzen** /ɑfχrɛizə(n)/ horror, dread: *met ~ vervullen* horrify

de **afgrond** /ɑfχrɔnt/ (pl: -en) abyss, chasm

de **afgunst** /ɑfχʏnst/ envy, jealousy

afgunstig /ɑfχʏnstəχ/ (adj) envious

de **afhaalmaaltijd** /ɑfhalmaltɛit/ takeaway (meal); [Am] take-out (meal/dinner)

het **afhaalrestaurant** /ɑfhalrɛstɔrɑnt/ (pl: -s) takeaway (restaurant); [Am] take-out (restaurant)

afhaken /ɑfhakə(n)/ (haakte af, heeft/is afgehaakt) pull out, drop out

afhakken /ɑfhɑkə(n)/ (hakte af, heeft afgehakt) chop off, cut off

afhalen /ɑfhalə(n)/ (haalde af, heeft afgehaald) 1 collect, call for 2 collect, meet: *ik* ***kom*** *je over een uur* ~ I'll pick you up in an hour; *iem. van de trein* ~ meet s.o. at the station || *bedden* ~ strip the beds

de **afhaler** /ɑfhalər/ (pl: -s) person collecting someone

afhandelen /ɑfhɑndələ(n)/ (handelde af, heeft afgehandeld) settle, conclude, deal with, dispose of: *de spreker handelde eerst de* ***bezwaren*** *af* the speaker first dealt with the objections

de **afhandeling** /ɑfhɑndəlɪŋ/ settlement, transaction

afhandig /ɑfhɑndəχ/ (adj): *iem. iets ~* ***maken*** *ken* trick s.o. out of sth.

afhangen /ɑfhɑŋə(n)/ (hing af, heeft afgehangen) depend (on): *hij danste alsof zijn leven* ***ervan*** *afhing* he danced for dear life (*or:* as though his life depended on it); *het hangt*

van het weer af it depends on the weather

afhankelijk /ɑfhɑŋkələk/ (adj) dependent (on), depending (on): *ik* ***ben*** *van niemand ~* I am quite independent; *de beslissing* ***is*** *~ van het weer* the decision is dependent on (*or:* depends on) the weather

de **afhankelijkheid** /ɑfhɑŋkələkhɛit/ dependence

afhelpen /ɑfhɛlpə(n)/ (hielp af, heeft afgeholpen) rid (of); cure (of): *iem.* ***van*** *zijn geld ~* relieve s.o. of his money

afhouden /ɑfhaudə(n)/ (hield af, heeft afgehouden) 1 keep off, keep out: *zij kon haar* ***ogen*** *niet van de taart ~* she couldn't keep her eyes off the cake; *iem.* ***van*** *zijn werk ~* keep s.o. from his work 2 keep back: *een* ***deel*** *van het loon ~* withhold a part of the wages

afhuren /ɑfhyrə(n)/ (huurde af, heeft afgehuurd) hire, rent

afijn /ɑfɛin/ (int) so, well

afkalven /ɑfkɑlvə(n)/ (kalfde af, is afgekalfd) cave in; [fig] be eroded

afkammen /ɑfkɑmə(n)/ (kamde af, heeft afgekamd) run down, tear (to pieces); [book also] slash (to shreds); slate

afkappen /ɑfkɑpə(n)/ (kapte af, heeft afgekapt) 1 chop off 2 cut (s.o.) short: *een* ***gesprek*** *~* break off (*or:* cut short) a conversation

de **afkeer** /ɑfker/ aversion (to), dislike (of): *een ~* ***hebben*** *(or:* ***tonen****)* have (*or:* display) an aversion (to)

afkeren /ɑfkerə(n)/ (keerde af, heeft afgekeerd) turn away (*or:* aside), avert: *het* ***hoofd*** *~* turn one's head away; *zich ~ van iem. (iets)* turn away from s.o. (sth.)

afkerig /ɑfkerəχ/ (adj) averse (to): *~ zijn van iets* be abhorrent of sth., abhor sth.; *niet ~ zijn van iets* not be ill-disposed toward sth.

afketsen /ɑfkɛtsə(n)/ (ketste af, is afgeketst) 1 bounce off, glance off 2 [fig] fall through, fail: *het* ***plan*** *is afgeketst op geldgebrek* the plan fell through because of a lack of money; *iets laten ~* reject sth.; defeat sth.; frustrate sth.

afkeuren /ɑfkørə(n)/ (keurde af, heeft afgekeurd) 1 reject, turn down, declare unfit: *hij is* ***voor*** *70 % afgekeurd* he has a 70 % disability 2 disapprove of, condemn || *een* ***doelpunt*** *~* disallow a goal

de **afkeuring** /ɑfkørɪŋ/ (pl: -en) disapproval, condemnation: *zijn ~* ***uitspreken*** *over* express one's disapproval of

het **afkickcentrum** /ɑfkɪksɛntrʏm/ (pl: -centra) rehab centre, drug rehabilitation centre

afkicken /ɑfkɪkə(n)/ (kickte af, heeft/is afgekickt) kick the habit; dry out: *hij is afgekickt* he has kicked the habit

de **afkickverschijnselen** /ɑfkɪkfərsχɛinsələ(n)/ (pl) withdrawal symptoms

afkijken /ɑfkɛikə(n)/ (keek af, heeft afgekeken) **1** copy, crib **2** see out, see to the end: *we hebben de **film** niet afgekeken* we didn't see the film out || *bij* (or: *van*) *zijn buurman ~ copy* (or: crib) from one's neighbour

afkleden /ɑfkledə(n)/ (kleedde af, heeft afgekleed) be slimming

afkloppen /ɑfklɔpə(n)/ (klopte af, heeft afgeklopt) knock on wood, touch wood: *even ~! touch wood!*

afkluiven /ɑfklœyvə(n)/ (kloof af, heeft afgekloven) gnaw off/on: *een **botje** ~* pick a bone

afknappen /ɑfknɑpə(n)/ (knapte af, is afgeknapt) break down, have a breakdown: *~ op iem. (iets)* get fed up with s.o. (sth.)

afknippen /ɑfknɪpə(n)/ (knipte af, heeft afgeknipt) cut (off); trim

afkoelen /ɑfkulə(n)/ (koelde af, is afgekoeld) cool (off, down); chill; refrigerate: *iets **laten** ~* leave sth. to cool

de **afkoeling** /ɑfkulɪŋ/ cooling (off (or: down))

afkoersen /ɑfkursə(n)/ (koerste af, heeft/is afgekoerst) (+ op) head straight for

afkomen /ɑfkomə(n)/ (kwam af, is afgekomen) **1** (+ op) come up to (or: towards): *(dreigend) **op** iem. ~* approach s.o. (menacingly); *zij zag de auto recht **op** zich ~* she saw the car heading straight for her (or: coming straight at her); *[fig] de dingen **op** zich laten ~* wait and see, let things take their course **2** get rid of; be done (or: finished) with; get off (or: away); get out of: *er **gemakkelijk** ~* get off easily (or: lightly)

de **afkomst** /ɑfkɔmst/ descent, origin; birth; [word] derivation: *Jean is van **Franse** ~* Jean is French by birth

afkomstig /ɑfkɔmstəx/ (adj) **1** from, coming (from), originating (from): *~ **uit** Spanje* of Spanish origin **2** originating (from), derived (from): *dat woord is ~ **uit** het Turks* that word is derived (or: borrowed) from Turkish

afkondigen /ɑfkɔndəɣə(n)/ (kondigde af, heeft afgekondigd) proclaim, give notice of

de **afkondiging** /ɑfkɔndəɣɪŋ/ (pl: -en) proclamation; declaration

de **afkoopsom** /ɑfkopsɔm/ (pl: -men) redemption money, compensation

afkopen /ɑfkopə(n)/ (kocht af, heeft afgekocht) buy (from), purchase (from), buy off; redeem; ransom: *een **hypotheek** ~* redeem a mortgage; *een **polis** ~* surrender a policy

afkoppelen /ɑfkɔpələ(n)/ (koppelde af, heeft afgekoppeld) uncouple; disconnect

afkorten /ɑfkortə(n)/ (kortte af, heeft afgekort) shorten; abbreviate

de **afkorting** /ɑfkortɪŋ/ (pl: -en) abbreviation, shortening

afkrabben /ɑfkrɑbə(n)/ (krabde af, heeft afgekrabd) scratch off, scrape off (or: from)

afkraken /ɑfkrakə(n)/ (kraakte af, heeft afgekraakt) run down: *de criticus kraakte haar boek **volledig** af* the reviewer ran her book into the ground

afkrijgen /ɑfkrɛiɣə(n)/ (kreeg af, heeft afgekregen) **1** get off, get out: *hij kreeg de **vlek** er niet af* he couldn't get the stain out **2** get done (or: finished): *het **werk** op tijd ~* get the work done (or: finished) in time

afkunnen /ɑfkʏnə(n)/ be able to get through, be able to cope with: *ik kan **het** zonder jou wel af* I can get along (very well) without you

de **aflaat** /ɑflat/ (pl: aflaten) [rel] indulgence

aflandig /ɑflɑndəx/ (adj) offshore

afleggen /ɑflɛɣə(n)/ (legde af, heeft afgelegd) **1** take off; lay down **2** make; take: *een **bezoek** ~* pay a visit; *een **examen** ~* take an exam(ination); sit (for) an examination; *een **getuigenis** ~* give evidence; testify **3** cover: *500 **mijl** per dag ~* cover 500 miles a day || *het (moeten) ~ **tegen** iem./iets op het gebied van* lose out to s.o./sth. on

afleiden /ɑflɛidə(n)/ (leidde af, heeft afgeleid) **1** lead (or: guide) away (from); divert (from) [road etc]; conduct [lightning]: *de **stroom** ~* divert the stream; *de **bliksem** ~* conduct lightning **2** divert, distract: *ik leidde **hem** af van zijn werk* I kept him from doing his work **3** trace back (to); derive (from): *'spraak' is afgeleid **van** 'spreken'* 'spraak' is derived from 'spreken'

de **afleiding** /ɑflɛidɪŋ/ (pl: -en) distraction, diversion: *ik **heb** echt ~ nodig* I really need sth. to take my mind off it (or: things); *voor ~ **zorgen*** take s.o.'s mind off things

de **afleidingsmanoeuvre** /ɑflɛidɪŋsmanœːvrə/ (pl: -s) diversion; [fig] red herring

afleren /ɑflerə(n)/ (leerde af, heeft afgeleerd) **1** unlearn, get out of (a habit): *ik heb het **stotteren** afgeleerd* I have overcome my stammer **2** cure of, break of: *ik zal je dat **liegen** wel ~* I'll teach you to tell lies || *nog eentje om het af te leren* one for the road

afleveren /ɑfleverə(n)/ (leverde af, heeft afgeleverd) **1** deliver: *de **bestelling** is op tijd afgeleverd* the order was delivered on time **2** [Belg] award, grant

de **aflevering** /ɑfleverɪŋ/ (pl: -en) **1** delivery: *bij ~ **betalen*** cash on delivery **2** episode

aflezen /ɑflezə(n)/ (las af, heeft afgelezen) **1** read out (the whole of) **2** read (off) || *[fig] de **woede** van iemands gezicht ~* tell the anger from, see the anger on s.o.'s face

aflikken /ɑflɪkə(n)/ (likte af, heeft afgelikt) lick: *zijn **vingers** (or: een **lepel**) ~* lick one's fingers (or: a spoon)

de **afloop** /ɑflop/ (pl: aflopen) **1** end, close: *na ~ **van de voorstelling*** after the performance **2** result, outcome: *ongeluk met dodelijke ~* fatal accident

aflopen /ɑflopə(n)/ (liep af, is afgelopen) **1** (come to an) end, finish; expire: *de **cursus** is* *afgelopen* the course is finished; *dit jaar loopt het huurcontract af* the lease expires this year; *het verhaal liep goed af* the story had a happy ending; *slecht* ~ turn out badly **2** run (*or:* go, walk) down

aflopend /ɑflopɛnt/ (adj): *het is een ~e zaak* we're fighting a losing battle

aflossen /ɑflɔsə(n)/ (loste af, heeft afgelost) **1** relieve: *laten we elkaar* ~ let's take turns **2** pay off: *een bedrag op een lening* ~ pay off an part of a loan

de **aflossing** /ɑflɔsɪŋ/ (pl: -en) **1** changing, change: *de* ~ *van de wacht* the changing of the guard **2** (re)payment **3** (re)payment (period), instalment: *een maandelijkse* (or: *jaarlijkse*) ~ a monthly (or: an annual) payment

afluisteren /ɑflœystərə(n)/ (luisterde af, heeft afgeluisterd) eavesdrop (on), listen in to (*or:* in on), monitor; (wire-)tap: *iem.* ~ eavesdrop on s.o.; monitor s.o.; *een telefoongesprek* ~ listen in to a phone call

afmaken /ɑfmakə(n)/ (maakte af, heeft afgemaakt) **1** finish, complete: *een werkje* ~ finish (*or:* complete) a bit of work **2** kill: *ze hebben de hond moeten laten* ~ they had to have the dog put down ‖ *hij maakte er zich met een grap van af* he brushed it aside with a joke; *zich er wat al te gemakkelijk van* ~ shrug sth. off too lightly

afmatten /ɑfmɑtə(n)/ (matte af, heeft afgemat) exhaust, wear out, tire out

afmelden /ɑfmɛldə(n)/ (meldde af, heeft afgemeld) cancel: *zich* ~ check (*or:* sign) (o.s.) out

afmeten /ɑfmetə(n)/ (mat af/meette af, heeft afgemeten) measure, judge: *de kwaliteit van een opleiding* ~ *aan het aantal geslaagden* judge the quality of a course from (*or:* by) the number of passes

de **afmeting** /ɑfmetɪŋ/ (pl: -en) dimension, proportion, size: *de ~en van de kamer* the dimensions (*or:* size) of the room

de **afname** /ɑfnamə/ **1** purchase: *bij* ~ *van 25 exemplaren* for quantities of 25, if 25 copies are ordered (*or:* bought) **2** sale **3** decline, decrease: *de* ~ *van de werkloosheid* the reduction in unemployment

afneembaar /ɑfnembar/ (adj) detachable, removable

¹**afnemen** /ɑfnemə(n)/ (nam af, is afgenomen) decrease, decline: *onze belangstelling nam af* our interest faded; *in gewicht* ~ lose weight

²**afnemen** /ɑfnemə(n)/ (nam af, heeft afgenomen) **1** take off (*or:* away), remove (from): *zijn hoed* ~ take off one's hat; raise one's hat; *het kleed van de tafel* ~ take (*or:* remove) the cloth from the table **2** remove: *iem. bloed* ~ take blood (*or:* a blood sample) **3** clean: *de tafel met een natte doek* ~ wipe the table with a damp cloth **4** deprive: *iem. zijn rijbewijs* ~

take away s.o.'s driving licence **5** hold, administer: *iem. de biecht* ~ hear s.o.'s confession; *iem. een eed* ~ administer an oath to s.o.; swear s.o. in; *iem. een examen* ~ examine s.o. **6** buy, purchase

de **afnemer** /ɑfnemər/ (pl: -s) buyer, customer: *Duitsland is onze grootste* ~ *van snijbloemen* Germany is our largest customer for cut flowers

afpakken /ɑfpɑkə(n)/ (pakte af, heeft afgepakt) take (away), snatch (away): *iem. een mes* ~ take away a knife from s.o.

afpassen /ɑfpɑsə(n)/ (paste af, heeft afgepast) measure (out): *een afgepaste portie* a measured (*or:* an adjusted) portion

afpersen /ɑfpɛrsə(n)/ (perste af, heeft afgeperst) extort (*or:* wring), force: *iem. geld* ~ extort money from s.o.

de **afperser** /ɑfpɛrsər/ (pl: -s) blackmailer

de **afpersing** /ɑfpɛrsɪŋ/ (pl: -en) extortion; blackmail

afpijnigen /ɑfpɛɪnəɣə(n)/ (pijnigde af, heeft afgepijnigd): *zijn hersens* ~ *(over)* rack (*or:* beat) one's brains (about)

afpikken /ɑfpɪkə(n)/ (pikte af, heeft afgepikt) [inform] pinch (from)

afpingelen /ɑfpɪŋələ(n)/ (pingelde af, heeft afgepingeld) haggle: *proberen af te pingelen* try to beat down the price

afplakken /ɑfplɑkə(n)/ (plakte af, heeft afgeplakt) tape up, cover with tape

afplukken /ɑfplʏkə(n)/ (plukte af, heeft afgeplukt) pick, pluck: *de veren van een kip* ~ pluck a chicken

afpoeieren /ɑfpujərə(n)/ (poeierde af, heeft afgepoeierd) brush off, put off

afprijzen /ɑfprɛizə(n)/ (prijsde af, heeft afgeprijsd) reduce, mark down: *alles is afgeprijsd* everything is reduced (in price)

afraden /ɑfradə(n)/ (raadde af, heeft afgeraden) advise against: *(iem.) iets* ~ dissuade (*or:* discourage) s.o. from (doing) sth.

afraffelen /ɑfrɑfələ(n)/ (raffelde af, heeft afgeraffeld) rush (through): *zijn huiswerk* ~ rush (through) one's homework

de **aframmeling** /ɑframəlɪŋ/ (pl: -en) beating, hiding

afranselen /ɑfrɑnsələ(n)/ (ranselde af, heeft afgeranseld) beat (up); flog; cane

de **afrastering** /ɑfrɑstərɪŋ/ (pl: -en) fencing, fence; railings

afreageren /ɑfrejaɣerə(n)/ (reageerde af, heeft afgereageerd) work off (*or:* vent) one's emotions, let off steam: *iets op iem.* ~ take sth. out on s.o.

afrekenen /ɑfrekənə(n)/ (rekende af, heeft afgerekend) settle (up), settle (*or:* pay) one's bill, settle one's account(s): *ober, mag ik ~!* waiter, the bill please! ‖ *met zijn vijanden* ~ deal with (*or:* polish off) one's enemies; *met iem., iets afgerekend hebben* be finished with (*or:* have done) with s.o., sth.; *iem.* ~ *op zijn resultaten* judge s.o. on his results

de **afrekening** /ɑfrekənɪŋ/ (pl: -en) **1** payment: ~ *geschiedt op 1 mei* payment is due on May 1st **2** punishment; hit, killing, murder: *een ~ in het criminele circuit* a revenge killing (*or:* murder) linked to organized crime **3** receipt; statement

afremmen /ɑfrɛmə(n)/ (remde af, heeft afgeremd) **1** slow down, brake, put the brake(s) on: *hij kon niet meer* ~ it was too late for him to brake; *voor een bocht* ~ slow down to take a curve **2** [fig] curb, check: *iem. in zijn enthousiasme* ~ curb s.o.'s enthusiasm

africhten /ɑfrɪxtə(n)/ (richtte af, heeft afgericht) train: *valken* ~ *voor de jacht* train falcons for hunting

¹**afrijden** /ɑfrɛidə(n)/ (reed af, heeft afgereden) drive down; ride down [on horseback]: *een heuvel* ~ ride (*or:* drive) down a hill

²**afrijden** /ɑfrɛidə(n)/ (reed af, heeft afgereden) drive to the end of; ride to the end of: *de hele stad* ~ ride (*or:* drive) all over town

Afrika /afrika/ Africa

de **Afrikaan** /afrikan/ (pl: Afrikanen) African

Afrikaans /afrikans/ (adj, adv) **1** African **2** South African

Afrikaans-Amerikaans /afrikansamerikans/ (adj) African American

het **afrikaantje** /afrikancə/ (pl: -s) [bot] African marigold

de **Afrikaner** /afrikanər/ Afrikaner, Boer

de **afrit** /ɑfrɪt/ (pl: -ten) exit: *op- en ~ten* slip roads; *bij de volgende* ~ at the next exit

de **afritsbroek** /ɑfrɪ(t)sbruk/ zip-off trousers

de **afroep** /ɑfrup/: *op* ~ *beschikbaar* available on demand; on call

afroepen /ɑfrupə(n)/ (riep af, heeft afgeroepen) call out; call off

het **afrokapsel** /afrokɑpsəl/ (pl: -s) Afro

afrollen /ɑfrolə(n)/ (rolde af, heeft afgerold) **1** unwind; unroll **2** roll down

afromen /ɑfromə(n)/ (roomde af, heeft afgeroomd) **1** skim **2** [fig] cream off

afronden /ɑfrondə(n)/ (rondde af, heeft afgerond) **1** wind up, round off: *wilt u (uw betoog)* ~? would you like to wind up (what you have to say)?; *een afgerond geheel vormen* form a complete whole **2** round off: *naar boven* (or: *beneden*) ~ round up (*or:* down); *een bedrag op hele euro* ~ round off an amount to the nearest euro

de **afronding** /ɑfrondɪŋ/ (pl: -en) winding up, rounding off, completion, conclusion: *als* ~ *van je studie moet je een werkstuk maken* to complete your study, you have to do a project

afruimen /ɑfrœymə(n)/ (ruimde af, heeft afgeruimd) clear (away), clear the table

afschaffen /ɑfsxɑfə(n)/ (schafte af, heeft afgeschaft) abolish, do away with: *de dood-*

straf ~ abolish capital punishment

de **afschaffing** /ɑfsxɑfɪŋ/ abolition: *de* ~ *van de slavernij* the abolition of slavery

het **afscheid** /ɑfsxɛit/ parting, leaving, farewell, departure: *van iem.* ~ *nemen* take leave of s.o.; *officieel* ~ *nemen (van)* take formal leave (of); *bij zijn* ~ *kreeg hij een gouden horloge* when he left he received a gold watch

afscheiden /ɑfsxɛidə(n)/ (scheidde af, heeft afgescheiden) **1** divide (off), partition off: *een ruimte met een gordijn* ~ curtain off an area **2** discharge; secrete: *sommige bomen scheiden hars af* some trees secrete (*or:* produce) resin

de **afscheiding** /ɑfsxɛidɪŋ/ (pl: -en) **1** separation; secession; schism; demarcation **2** partition; dividing line: *een ~ aanbrengen* put up a partition **3** discharge, secretion

afschepen /ɑfsxepə(n)/ (scheepte af, heeft afgescheept) (+ met) palm (sth.) off on (s.o.), fob (s.o.) off with (sth.): *zij laat zich niet zo gemakkelijk* ~ she is not so easily put off; *zich niet laten* ~ *(met een smoesje)* not be fobbed off (with an excuse)

afscheren /ɑfsxerə(n)/ (schoor af, heeft afgeschoren) shave (off); shear (off)

afschermen /ɑfsxɛrmə(n)/ (schermde af, heeft afgeschermd) screen; protect (from)

afscheuren /ɑfsxørə(n)/ (scheurde af, heeft afgescheurd) tear off

afschieten /ɑfsxitə(n)/ (schoot af, heeft afgeschoten) **1** fire (off); discharge: *een geweer* ~ fire a gun **2** shoot: *wild* ~ shoot game

afschilderen /ɑfsxɪldərə(n)/ (schilderde af, heeft afgeschilderd) **1** paint **2** portray, depict: *iem.* ~ *als* portray s.o. as, make s.o. out to be

afschilferen /ɑfsxɪlfərə(n)/ (schilferde af, heeft/is afgeschilferd) flake off; peel off

afschminken /ɑfʃmɪŋkə(n)/ (schminkte af, heeft afgeschminkt) remove make-up

afschrapen /ɑfsxrapə(n)/ (schraapte af, heeft afgeschraapt) scrape off

het **afschrift** /ɑfsxrɪft/ (pl: -en) copy: *een* ~ *van een (lopende) rekening* a current account statement

afschrijven /ɑfsxrɛivə(n)/ (schreef af, heeft afgeschreven) **1** debit: *geld van een rekening* ~ withdraw money from an account **2** write off: *die auto kun je wel* ~ you might as well write that car off; *we hadden haar al afgeschreven* we had already written her off **3** write down; write off (as depreciation)

de **afschrijving** /ɑfsxrɛivɪŋ/ (pl: -en) **1** debit **2** [fixed assets] depreciation; write-off; [intangible assets] amortization: *voor* ~ *op de machines* for depreciation of the machines

afschrikken /ɑfsxrɪkə(n)/ (schrikte af, heeft afgeschrikt) deter, put off; frighten off, scare off: *zo'n benadering schrikt de mensen af* an approach like that scares (*or:* puts) people off; *hij liet* zich door niets ~ he was not to be put off (*or:* deterred)

het **afschrikkingsmiddel** deterrent

afschrikwekkend /ɑfsχrɪkwɛ̠kənt/ (adj, adv) frightening, off-putting: *een ~ voorbeeld* a warning, a deterrent

afschudden /ɑfsχʏdə(n)/ (schudde af, heeft afgeschud) shake off; cast off: *een tegenstander van zich* ~ shake off an opponent

afschuimen /ɑfsχœymə(n)/ (schuimde af, heeft afgeschuimd) scour, comb: *de stad* ~ scour (*or:* comb) the city

afschuiven /ɑfsχœyvə(n)/ (schoof af, heeft afgeschoven) pass (on to s.o.): *de verantwoordelijkheid op een ander* ~ pass the buck; *zijn verantwoordelijkheid van zich* ~ shirk one's responsibility

afschuren /ɑfsχyrə(n)/ (schuurde af, heeft afgeschuurd) rub down; sand down

de **afschuw** /ɑfsχyw/ horror, disgust: *een ~ hebben van iets* loathe (*or:* detest) sth.; *van ~ vervuld* horrified, appalled

afschuwelijk /ɑfsχywələk/ (adj, adv) **1** horrible **2** shocking, awful, appalling: *ik heb een ~e dag gehad* I've had an awful day; *die rok staat je* ~ that dress looks awful on you

¹**afslaan** /ɑfslan/ (sloeg af, is afgeslagen) **1** turn (off); branch off: *links afslaan* turn (to the) left **2** cut out, stall ‖ *van zich* ~ hit out

²**afslaan** /ɑfslan/ (sloeg af, heeft afgeslagen) turn down; refuse; decline: *nou, een kopje koffie sla ik niet af* I won't say no to a cup of coffee

afslachten /ɑfslɑχtə(n)/ (slachtte af, heeft afgeslacht) slaughter, massacre

de **afslag** /ɑfslɑχ/ (pl: -en) **1** turn(ing); exit: *een ~ missen* miss the exit; [fig] miss an opportunity, let one's chance slip; *de verkeerde ~ nemen* take the wrong exit; [fig] take the wrong path in life; *neem de volgende ~ rechts* take the next right turn **2** Dutch auction: *bij ~ veilen* sell by Dutch auction; *~ van vis* fish auction

afslanken /ɑfslɑŋkə(n)/ (slankte af, is afgeslankt) slim (down), trim down: *het bedrijf moet aanzienlijk ~* the company has to slim down considerably

¹**afslijten** /ɑfslɛitə(n)/ (sleet af, is afgesleten) wear out, wear off

²**afslijten** /ɑfslɛitə(n)/ (sleet af, heeft afgesleten) wear (off, down)

afsloven /ɑfslovə(n)/ (sloofde zich af, heeft zich afgesloofd) wear out: *zich voor iem.* ~ wear o.s. out (*or:* kill o.s.) for s.o.

de **afsluitdijk** /ɑfslœydɛik/ (pl: -en) dam, causeway: *de Afsluitdijk* the IJsselmeer Dam

afsluiten /ɑfslœytə(n)/ (sloot af, heeft afgesloten) **1** close (off, up): *een weg ~ voor verkeer* close a road to traffic **2** lock (up); close: *heb je de voordeur goed afgesloten?*

have you locked the front door? **3** cut off, shut off, turn off, disconnect; exit: *de stroom ~* cut off the electricity **4** conclude; enter into; negotiate: *een levensverzekering ~* take out a life insurance policy **5** close, conclude: *een jaar ~* close a year ‖ *ik heb dat afgesloten* I've put that behind me

de **afsluiting** /ɑfslœytɪŋ/ (pl: -en) **1** closing off, closing up **2** locking (up, away) **3** shut-off, cut-off, disconnection **4** conclusion **5** closing; close; balancing **6** seclusion, isolation

afsnauwen /ɑfsnɑuwə(n)/ (snauwde af, heeft afgesnauwd) snap (*or:* snarl) at: *iem. ~* snap s.o.'s head off

afsnijden /ɑfsnɛidə(n)/ (sneed af, heeft afgesneden) cut off ‖ *de bocht ~* cut the corner; *een stuk* ~ take a short cut

afsnoepen /ɑfsnupə(n)/ (snoepte af, heeft afgesnoept) steal

de **afspeellijst** /ɑfspelɛɪst/ (pl: -en) playlist

¹**afspelen** /ɑfspelə(n)/ (speelde af, heeft afgespeeld) play

zich ²**afspelen** /ɑfspelə(n)/ (speelde zich af, heeft zich afgespeeld) happen, take place, occur

afspiegelen /ɑfspiɣələ(n)/ (spiegelde af, heeft afgespiegeld) depict, portray: *hij wordt afgespiegeld als een misdadiger* he is represented as a criminal

de **afspiegeling** /ɑfspiɣəlɪŋ/ (pl: -en) reflection, mirror image

¹**afsplitsen** /ɑfsplɪtsə(n)/ (splitste af, heeft afgesplitst) split off, separate

zich ²**afsplitsen** /ɑfsplɪtsə(n)/ (splitste zich af, heeft zich afgesplitst) split off

afspoelen /ɑfspulə(n)/ (spoelde af, heeft afgespoeld) rinse (down, off), wash (down, off): *het stof van zijn handen ~* rinse the dust off one's hands

de **afspraak** /ɑfsprak/ (pl: afspraken) appointment; engagement; agreement: *een ~ maken* (or: *hebben*) *bij de tandarts* make (*or:* have) an appointment with the dentist; *een ~ nakomen, zich aan een ~ houden* a) keep an appointment; b) stick to an agreement

het **afspraakje** /ɑfsprakjə/ (pl: -s) date

¹**afspreken** /ɑfsprekə(n)/ (sprak af, heeft afgesproken) make an appointment

²**afspreken** /ɑfsprekə(n)/ (sprak af, heeft afgesproken) agree (on), arrange: *een plan ~* agree on a plan; *dat is dus afgesproken* that's a deal, that's settled then; *~ iets te zullen doen* agree to do sth.; *zoals afgesproken* as agreed

afspringen /ɑfsprɪŋə(n)/ (sprong af, is afgesprongen) **1** jump down/off **2** fall through; break down

afstaan /ɑfstan/ (stond af, heeft afgestaan) give up; hand over: *zijn plaats ~* [eg to a younger colleague] step down

de **afstammeling** /ɑfstɑməlɪŋ/ (pl: -en) descendant

afstammen /ɑfstɑmə(n)/ (stamde af, is afgestamd) descend (from)

de **afstamming** /ɑfstɑmɪŋ/ descent: *van Italiaanse* ~ of Italian extraction

de **afstand** /ɑfstɑnt/ (pl: -en) **1** distance (to, from): *een* ~ *afleggen* cover a distance; ~ *houden* (or: *bewaren*) keep one's distance; [fig also] keep aloof; ~ *nemen van een onderwerp* distance o.s. from a subject; *op een* ~ **a)** at a distance; **b)** [fig] distant, aloof; *iem. op een* ~ *houden* [fig also] keep s.o. at arm's length **2** renunciation: ~ *doen van* renounce, disclaim; give up; ~ *doen van zijn bezit* part with one's possessions

afstandelijk /ɑfstɑndələk/ (adj, adv) distant, aloof

de **afstandsbediening** /ɑfstɑntsbədinɪŋ/ remote control (unit)

het **afstandsonderwijs** /ɑfstɑntsɔndərwɛis/ distance learning

het **afstapje** /ɑfstɑpjə/ (pl: -s) step: *denk om het* ~ mind the step

afstappen /ɑfstɑpə(n)/ (stapte af, is afgestapt) step down, come down, come off, dismount; get off (one's bike)

¹**afsteken** /ɑfsteːkə(n)/ (stak af, heeft afgestoken) stand out: *de kerktoren stak (donker) af tegen de hemel* the church tower stood out against the sky

²**afsteken** /ɑfsteːkə(n)/ (stak af, heeft afgestoken) **1** let off: *vuurwerk* ~ let off fireworks **2** deliver: *een speech* ~ hold forth, make a speech

het **afstel** /ɑfstɛl/ cancellation

afstellen /ɑfstɛlə(n)/ (stelde af, heeft afgesteld) adjust (to), set; tune (up)

afstemmen /ɑfstɛmə(n)/ (stemde af, heeft afgestemd) **1** tune (to); tune in (to): *een radio op een zender* ~ tune a radio in to a station **2** tune (to), coordinate, gear (to): *iets met iem.* ~ coordinate with s.o. on sth.; *alle werkzaamheden zijn op elkaar afgestemd* all activities are geared to one another

afstempelen /ɑfstɛmpələ(n)/ (stempelde af, heeft afgestempeld) stamp, cancel, postmark: *een paspoort* (or: *kaartje*) ~ stamp a passport (or: ticket)

afsterven /ɑfstɛrvə(n)/ (stierf af, is afgestorven) die (off); die back

afstevenen /ɑfsteːvənə(n)/ (stevende af, is afgestevend) (+ op) make for, head for (or: towards)

afstoffen /ɑfstɔfə(n)/ (stofte af, heeft afgestoft) dust (off)

¹**afstompen** /ɑfstɔmpə(n)/ (stompte af, is afgestompt) become blunt(ed) (or: numb)

²**afstompen** /ɑfstɔmpə(n)/ (stompte af, heeft afgestompt) blunt, dull, numb

afstotelijk /ɑfstoːtələk/ (adj) repulsive, repellent; off-putting

afstoten /ɑfstoːtə(n)/ (stootte af, heeft afgestoten) **1** dispose of; reject; hive off: *arbeidsplaatsen* ~ cut jobs **2** repel: *zo'n onvriendelijke behandeling stoot af* such unfriendly treatment is off-putting

afstraffen /ɑfstrɑfə(n)/ (strafte af, heeft afgestraft) punish

afstrijken /ɑfstrɛikə(n)/ (streek af, heeft afgestreken) **1** strike, light **2** wipe off, level (off): *een afgestreken eetlepel* a level tablespoonful

afstropen /ɑfstroːpə(n)/ (stroopte af, heeft afgestroopt) **1** strip (off): *een haas de huid* ~ skin a hare **2** pillage, ransack: *enkele benden stroopten het platteland af* a few bands pillaged the countryside

de **afstudeerscriptie** /ɑfstyderskrɪpsi/ (pl: -s) (Master's) thesis

afstuderen /ɑfstyderə(n)/ (studeerde af, heeft/is afgestudeerd) graduate (from), complete (or: finish) one's studies (at)

afstuiten /ɑfstœytə(n)/ (stuitte af, is afgestuit) rebound; be frustrated: *de bal stuit af tegen de paal* the ball rebounds off the post; *het voorstel stuitte af op haar koppigheid* the proposal fell through owing to her obstinacy

afsturen /ɑfstyrə(n)/ (stuurde af op, heeft afgestuurd op) (+ op) send (towards): *de hond op iem.* ~ set the dog on s.o.

aftakelen /ɑftakələ(n)/ (takelde af, is afgetakeld) go (or: run) to seed, go downhill: *hij begint al flink af te takelen* he really is starting to go downhill; [mentally] he is really starting to lose his faculties

de **aftakeling** /ɑftakəlɪŋ/ (pl: -en) deterioration, decline

de **aftakking** /ɑftɑkɪŋ/ (pl: -en) branch, fork

aftands /ɑftɑnts/ (adj) broken down, worn out: *een ~e piano* a worn-out (or: dilapidated) piano

aftappen /ɑftɑpə(n)/ (tapte af, heeft afgetapt) **1** draw off, drain: *als het hard vriest, moet je de waterleiding* ~ when it freezes hard you have to drain the pipes **2** tap: *stroom* ~ tap electricity; *de benzine* ~ siphon (off) the petrol; *een telefoonlijn* ~ tap a telephone line

aftasten /ɑftɑstə(n)/ (tastte af, heeft afgetast) **1** feel, sense: *een oppervlak* ~ explore a surface with one's hands **2** [fig] feel out, sound out

¹**aftekenen** /ɑfteːkənə(n)/ (tekende af, heeft afgetekend) **1** outline, mark off: *de plattegrond van een plein* ~ map out a (town) square **2** register, record: *ik heb mijn gewerkte uren laten* ~ I've had my working hours registered

zich ²**aftekenen** /ɑfteːkənə(n)/ (tekende zich af, heeft zich afgetekend) stand out, become visible: *zich* ~ *tegen* stand out against

aftellen /ɑftɛlə(n)/ (telde af, heeft afgeteld)

count (out, off): *de **dagen** ~ count the days*

de **afterparty** /ɑːftərpɑːrti/ after party

de **aftershave** /ɑftərʃɛf/ (pl: -s) aftershave

de **aftersun** /ɑːftərsʏn/ after sun

aftikken /ɑftɪkə(n)/ (tikte af, heeft afgetikt) **1** tag (out) **2** [inform] cough up, fork out: [auction] *afgetikt worden voor ... go for ...*

de **aftiteling** /ɑftitəlɪŋ/ (pl: -en) credit titles, credits

de **aftocht** /ɑftɔχt/ (pl: -en) retreat: *de ~ **blazen** beat a retreat*

de **aftrap** /ɑftrɑp/ (pl: -pen) kick-off: *de ~ **doen** kick off*

aftrappen /ɑftrɑpə(n)/ (trapte af, heeft afgetrapt) kick off

aftreden /ɑftredə(n)/ (trad af, is afgetreden) resign (one's post)

de **aftrek** /ɑftrɛk/ **1** deduction: *~ van **voorarrest** reduction in sentence for time already served; **na** ~ van onkosten less expenses* **2** deduction; allowance || ***gretig** ~ vinden sell like hot cakes; **geen** ~ vinden not sell*

aftrekbaar /ɑftrɛɡbaːr/ (adj) deductible; tax-deductible

aftrekken /ɑftrɛkə(n)/ (trok af, heeft afgetrokken) **1** subtract: *als je acht **van** veertien aftrekt houd je zes over if you take eight from fourteen you have six left* **2** deduct **3** masturbate, jerk off: *zich ~ masturbate*

de **aftrekpost** /ɑftrɛkpɔst/ (pl: -en) deduction, tax-deductible item (or: expense)

het **aftreksel** /ɑftrɛksəl/ (pl: -s) extract, infusion: [fig] *een **slap** ~ van het origineel a poor substitute for (or: rendering of) the original*

de **aftreksom** /ɑftrɛksɔm/ (pl: -men) subtraction (sum)

aftroeven /ɑftruvə(n)/ (troefde af, heeft afgetroefd) score (points) off

aftroggelen /ɑftrɔɣələ(n)/ (troggelde af, heeft afgetroggeld) wheedle out of: *iem. iets **weten** af te troggelen succeed in wheedling sth. out of s.o.*

aftuigen /ɑftœyɣə(n)/ (tuigde af, heeft afgetuigd) beat up, mug

afvaardigen /ɑfardəɣə(n)/ (vaardigde af, heeft afgevaardigd) send (or: appoint) as delegate: *hij was **naar** de leerlingenraad afgevaardigd he had been appointed as delegate to the students' council*

de **afvaardiging** /ɑfardəɣɪŋ/ (pl: -en) delegation

de **afvaart** /ɑfart/ (pl: -en) sailing, departure

het **afval** /ɑfɑl/ waste (matter); refuse; rubbish: ***radioactief** ~ radioactive waste*

de **afvalbak** /ɑfɑlbɑk/ litter bin (or: basket); dustbin; rubbish bin

afvallen /ɑfɑlə(n)/ (viel af, is afgevallen) **1** fall off (or: down): *de **bladeren** vallen af the leaves are falling* **2** drop out: *dat **alternatief** viel af that option was dropped (or: was no longer available)* **3** lose weight: *ik ben drie*

kilo afgevallen I've lost three kilos || ***iem.** ~ let s.o. down, desert (or: abandon) s.o.*

afvallig /ɑfɑləχ/ (adj) unfaithful, disloyal; lapsed

het **afvalproduct** /ɑfɑlprɔdʏkt/ (pl: -en) by-product, waste product

de **afvalrace** /ɑfɑlres/ (pl: -s) elimination race

de **afvalscheiding** /ɑfɑlsχɛidɪŋ/ separation of waste (products)

de **afvalstof** /ɑfɑlstɔf/ (pl: -fen) waste product; waste (matter): ***schadelijke** ~fen harmful (or: noxious) waste*

de **afvalverwerking** /ɑfɑlvərwɛrkɪŋ/ (pl: -en) processing of waste, waste disposal (or: treatment)

het **afvalwater** /ɑfɑlwatər/ waste water

de **afvalwedstrijd** /ɑfɑlwɛtstrɛit/ (pl: -en) heat, knock-out (or: elimination) competition

afvegen /ɑfeɣə(n)/ (veegde af, heeft afgeveegd) wipe (off), brush away, wipe away: *de **tafel** ~ wipe (off) the table*

afvinken /ɑfɪŋkə(n)/ (vinkte af, heeft afgevinkt) check (or: tick) off

afvloeien /ɑfluJə(n)/ (vloeide af, is afgevloeid) be made redundant, be laid off; be given early retirement

de **afvloeiing** /ɑflujɪŋ/ (pl: -en) release, gradual dismissal (or: discharge)

de **afvloeiingsregeling** /ɑflujɪŋsreɣəlɪŋ/ (pl: -en) redundancy pay (or: scheme)

de **afvoer** /ɑfur/ **1** transport, conveyance: *de ~ van **goederen** transport (or: removal) of goods* **2** drain(pipe), outlet; exhaust (pipe): *de ~ is **verstopt** the drain is blocked*

de **afvoerbuis** /ɑfurbœys/ (pl: -buizen) discharge (or: outlet) pipe; soil (or: waste) pipe; exhaust (pipe)

afvoeren /ɑfurə(n)/ (voerde af, heeft afgevoerd) **1** transport; drain away, drain off; lead away **2** carry off (or: down), lead down

de **afvoerstop** /ɑfurstɔp/ (pl: -pen) plug

zich **afvragen** /ɑfraɣə(n)/ (vroeg zich af, heeft zich afgevraagd) wonder, ask o.s.; (be in) doubt (as to): *ik vraag mij af, **wie** ... I wonder who ...; ik vraag mij af **of** dat juist is I wonder if (or: whether) that is correct*

afvuren /ɑfyrə(n)/ (vuurde af, heeft afgevuurd) fire, let off, discharge; launch

afwachten /ɑfwɑχtə(n)/ (wachtte af, heeft afgewacht) wait (for), await; anticipate: *zijn **beurt** ~ wait (for) one's turn; we **moeten** maar ~ we'll have to wait and see*

de **afwachting** /ɑfwɑχtɪŋ/ expectation; anticipation: *in ~ van uw antwoord we look forward to receiving your reply*

de **afwas** /ɑfwɑs/ **1** dishes, washing-up **2** doing (or: washing) the dishes, washing-up: *hij is **aan** de ~ he is washing up (or: doing) the dishes*

afwasbaar /ɑfwɑzbaːr/ (adj) washable

de **afwasborstel** /ɑfwɑzbɔrstəl/ (pl: -s) washing-up brush

de **afwasmachine** /ɑfwɑsmɑʃinə/ (pl: -s) dishwasher, washing-up machine

het **afwasmiddel** /ɑfwɑsmɪdəl/ washing-up liquid; [Am] dishwashing liquid

¹**afwassen** /ɑfwɑsə(n)/ (waste af, heeft afgewassen) do (or: wash) the dishes

²**afwassen** /ɑfwɑsə(n)/ (waste af, heeft afgewassen) **1** wash (up) **2** wash off (or: away): *bloed van zijn handen* ~ wash blood from his hands

de **afwatering** /ɑfwatərɪŋ/ (pl: -en) **1** drainage **2** drainage, drains

de **afweer** /ɑfwer/ defence

het **afweergeschut** /ɑfwerɣəsxʏt/ anti-aircraft guns

de **afweerreactie** /ɑfwerejɑksi/ (pl: -s) [med] immune response

het **afweersysteem** /ɑfwersistem/ (pl: -systemen) defence system; immune system

afwegen /ɑfweɣə(n)/ (woog af, heeft afgewogen) **1** weigh **2** weigh (up), consider: *de voor- en nadelen (tegen elkaar)* ~ weigh the pros and cons (against each other)

de **afweging** /ɑfweɣɪŋ/ (pl: -en) assessment; determination: *een* ~ *maken* consider the pros and cons, make a comparative assessment

afwenden /ɑfwɛndə(n)/ (wendde af, heeft afgewend) **1** turn away (or: aside); avert: *het hoofd* (or: *de ogen*) ~ turn one's head (or: eyes) away, look away; *de ogen niet* ~ *van iem. (iets)* not take one's eyes off s.o. (sth.) **2** avert, ward off, stave off; parry

afwennen /ɑfwɛnə(n)/ (wende af, heeft afgewend) cure of, break of: *iem. het nagelbijten proberen af te wennen* try to get s.o. out of the habit of biting his nails

afwentelen /ɑfwɛntələ(n)/ (wentelde af, heeft afgewenteld) shift (on to), transfer (to)

afweren /ɑfwerə(n)/ (weerde af, heeft afgeweerd) keep off (or: away), hold off; [fig] fend off, ward off: *nieuwsgierigen* ~ keep bystanders at a distance; *een aanval* (or: *aanvaller*) ~ repel an attack (or: attacker)

afwerken /ɑfwɛrkə(n)/ (werkte af, heeft afgewerkt) **1** finish (off): *een opstel* (or: *roman*) ~ add the finishing touches to an essay (or: a novel) **2** finish (off), complete: *een programma* ~ complete a programme

de **afwerking** /ɑfwɛrkɪŋ/ (pl: -en) finish(ing), finishing touch

afwerpen /ɑfwɛrpə(n)/ (wierp af, heeft afgeworpen) throw off

afweten /ɑfwetə(n)/: *het laten* ~ fail, refuse to work; not show up

afwezig /ɑfwezəx/ (adj) **1** absent; away, gone: *Jansen is op het ogenblik* ~ Jansen is away at the moment **2** absent-minded, preoccupied

de **afwezigheid** /ɑfwezəxɦɛit/ **1** absence: *tijdens Pauls* ~ during Paul's absence; *in (bij)* ~ *van* in the absence of **2** absent-mindedness: *in een moment van* ~ in a forgetful moment, in a momentary fit of absent-mindedness

afwijken /ɑfwɛikə(n)/ (week af, is afgeweken) **1** deviate (from); depart (from); diverge (from): *doen* ~ divert, turn (away); [fig] *van het rechte pad* ~ deviate from the straight and narrow **2** differ, deviate, vary; disagree (with)

afwijkend /ɑfwɛikənt/ (adj) different: ~ *gedrag* abnormal behaviour; *~e mening* different opinion

de **afwijking** /ɑfwɛikɪŋ/ (pl: -en) **1** defect, abnormality, aberration: *een geestelijke* ~ a mental abnormality; *een lichamelijke* ~ a physical defect **2** difference, deviation: *dit horloge vertoont een* ~ *van één seconde* this watch is accurate to within one second

afwijzen /ɑfwɛizə(n)/ (wees af, heeft afgewezen) **1** not admit, turn away: *de sollicitant werd afgewezen* the applicant was rejected **2** refuse, decline, reject; repudiate: *~d staan tegenover* be opposed to; *een verzoek* ~ refuse (or: turn down) a request; *een voorstel* ~ decline a proposal

de **afwijzing** /ɑfwɛizɪŋ/ (pl: -en) refusal, rejection; repudiation

afwikkelen /ɑfwɪkələ(n)/ (wikkelde af, heeft afgewikkeld) complete, settle: *een contract* (or: *kwestie*) ~ settle a contract (or: question)

afwimpelen /ɑfwɪmpələ(n)/ (wimpelde af, heeft afgewimpeld) not follow up, pass over; find an excuse (not to accept), get out of

afwinden /ɑfwɪndə(n)/ (wond af, heeft afgewonden) unwind

afwisselen /ɑfwɪsələ(n)/ (wisselde af, heeft afgewisseld) **1** alternate with, take turns; relieve: *elkaar* ~ take turns **2** vary: *zijn werk* ~ *met ontspanning* alternate one's work with relaxation

¹**afwisselend** /ɑfwɪsələnt/ (adj) **1** alternate **2** varied

²**afwisselend** /ɑfwɪsələnt/ (adv) alternately, in turn

de **afwisseling** /ɑfwɪsəlɪŋ/ (pl: -en) variety, variation, change: *een welkome* ~ *vormen* make a welcome change; *voor de* ~ for a change

afzakken /ɑfsɑkə(n)/ (zakte af, is afgezakt) **1** come down: *zich laten* ~ fall behind; go with (or: be taken by) the current **2** fall back

het **afzakkertje** /ɑfsɑkərcə/ (pl: -s) [inform] one for the road; nightcap

afzeggen /ɑfsɛɣə(n)/ (zei af/zegde af, heeft afgezegd) cancel, call off: *de staking werd afgezegd* the strike was called off

afzeiken /ɑfsɛikə(n)/ (zeikte af, heeft afgezeikt/gezeken) [inform] put down; [vulg] shit

akelig

all over: *zich niet **laten** ~ not let o.s. be put down*, not let people shit all over one

de **afzender** /ɑfsɛndər/ (pl: -s) sender; shipper [goods]: ~ … [on letter] from …

de **afzet** /ɑfsɛt/ **1** sale, market **2** sales

het **afzetgebied** /ɑfsɛtxəbit/ (pl: -en) outlet, opening, market

afzetten /ɑfsɛtə(n)/ (zette af, heeft afgezet) **1** switch off, turn off; disconnect **2** cut off, amputate **3** cheat, swindle; overcharge: *een klant **voor** tien euro* ~ cheat a customer out of ten euros **4** enclose, fence off, fence in; block off, close off: *een **bouwterrein** ~* fence off a building site **5** push off: [fig] *zich ~ tegen (iets, iem.)* react against (sth., s.o.); *zich ~ voor een sprong* take off **6** dismiss, remove: *een **koning** ~* depose a king **7** drop, set down, put down: *een vriend **thuis** ~* drop a friend at his home ‖ *dat moet je **van** je af (kunnen) zetten* (you should be able to) get that out of your mind

de **afzetter** /ɑfsɛtər/ (pl: -s) cheat, swindler

de **afzetterij** /ɑfsɛtərɛi/ swindle, cheat; rip-off

de **afzetting** /ɑfsɛtɪŋ/ (pl: -en) enclosure, fence; cordon

afzichtelijk /ɑfsɪxtələk/ (adj, adv) ghastly, hideous

afzien /ɑfsin/ (zag af, heeft afgezien) **1** (+ van) abandon, give up; renounce: *naderhand zagen ze toch **van** samenwerking af* afterwards they decided not to cooperate **2** have a hard time (of it), sweat it out: *dat **wordt** ~* we'd better roll up our sleeves

afzienbaar /ɑfsimbar/ (adj): *binnen afzienbare **tijd*** in the near future, within the foreseeable (or: not too distant) future

afzijdig /ɑfsɛidəx/ (adj) aloof: *zich ~ **houden** van*, *~ **blijven** van* keep aloof from

zich **afzonderen** /ɑfsɔndərə(n)/ (zonderde zich af, heeft zich afgezonderd) separate (or: seclude) o.s. (from), retire (from), withdraw (from): *zich **van** de wereld ~* withdraw from the world

de **afzondering** /ɑfsɔndərɪŋ/ (pl: -en) separation, isolation, seclusion: *in **strikte** ~* in strict isolation

afzonderlijk /ɑfsɔndərlək/ (adj) separate, individual, single: *in elk ~ **geval*** in each individual case; *~ **overeengekomen*** agreed separately

de **afzuigkap** /ɑfsœyxkap/ (pl: -pen) (cooker) hood

¹**afzwakken** /ɑfswɑkə(n)/ (zwakte af, is afgezwakt) subside, decrease

²**afzwakken** /ɑfswɑkə(n)/ (zwakte af, heeft afgezwakt) weaken, tone (or: play) down: *de scherpe **toon** ~* soften the sharp tone (of), tone down the sharpness (of)

afzwemmen /ɑfswɛmə(n)/ (zwom af, heeft afgezwommen) take a swimming test

afzweren /ɑfswerə(n)/ (zwoer af, heeft af-

gezworen) renounce, forswear: *de **drank** ~* **a)** give up drink(ing); **b)** swear off drink(ing); *zijn **geloof** (or: **beginselen**) ~* renounce one's faith (or: principles)

de **agenda** /aɣɛnda/ (pl: -'s) **1** [notebook] diary; [Am] calendar: *elektronische ~* organizer **2** agenda: *op de ~ staan* be on the agenda; *geheime (or: **verborgen**) ~* hidden agenda; *de ~'s **trekken*** settle on a date

agenderen /aɣɛndərə(n)/ (agendeerde, heeft geagendeerd) put on the agenda

de **agent** /aɣɛnt/ (pl: -en) **1** policeman, constable: *een **stille** ~*, *een ~ in burger* a plain-clothes policeman.**2** agent ‖ *een **geheim** ~* a secret agent

het **agentschap** /aɣɛntsxɑp/ (pl: -pen) branch (office)

ageren /aɣerə(n)/ (ageerde, heeft geageerd) agitate (or: manoeuvre) (against), (carry on a) campaign (against)

de **agf** fruit and vegetable sector

de **agglomeratie** /aɣlomera(t)si/ (pl: -s) conurbation

de **aggregatietoestand** /aɣreɣa(t)situstɑnt/ (pl: -en) physical state

de **agrariër** /aɣrarijər/ (pl: -s) farmer

agrarisch /aɣraris/ (adj) agrarian, agricultural, farming: *~e **school** school of agriculture

de **agressie** /aɣrɛsi/ (pl: -s) aggression: *een **daad** van ~* an act of aggression; *~ **opwekken*** provoke aggression

agressief /aɣrɛsif/ (adj, adv) aggressive: *een agressieve **politiek** voeren* pursue an aggressive policy

de **agressor** /aɣrɛsɔr/ (pl: -s) aggressor, attacker

¹**ah** /a/ (int) ah, oh

het/de ²**ah** /a/ (pl: -s): *oehs en ahs* oohs and aahs

aha /aha/ (int) aha

de **ahorn** /ahɔrn/ (pl: -en, -s) maple

a.h.w. *als het ware* as it were

ai /ɑj/ (int) ouch; ow; ah; oh ‖ *ai!, dat was maar net mis* oops! that was a close shave

de **aids** /ets/ Aids

de **aidspatiënt** /etspaʃɛnt/ (pl: -en) AIDS patient

de **aio** /ajo/ (pl: -'s) [Dutch] *assistent in opleiding* PhD student, research trainee

de **aios** /ajos/ (pl: -sen) [Dutch] *arts in opleiding tot specialist* trainee medical specialist

het **air** /ɛːr/ (pl: -s) air, look: *met het ~ van* with an air of

de **airbag** /ɛːrbɛːk/ (pl: -s) air bag

de **airconditioning** /ɛːrkɔndɪʃənɪŋ/ air-conditioning

de **ajuin** /ajœyn/ (pl: -en) [Belg] onion

akelig /akələx/ (adj) **1** unpleasant, nasty, dismal; dreary; bleak; ghastly: *een ~ **gezicht** (or: **beeld**)* a nasty sight (or: picture); *een ~ **verhaal** a ghastly story; *~ **weer*** nasty weath-

akkefietje

er **2** ill, sick: *ik word er ~ van* it turns my stomach

het **akkefietje** /ɑkəfi̯cə/ (pl: -s) **1** chore **2** (little) job **3** trifle ‖ *een ~ hebben met iem.* have a slight disagreement/misunderstanding with s.o., have a spat with s.o.

de **akker** /ɑkər/ (pl: -s) field

de **akkerbouw** /ɑkərbɑu/ (arable) farming, agriculture

de **akkerbouwer** /ɑkərbɑuwər/ (pl: -s) (crop) farmer, cultivator

het **akkerland** /ɑkərlɑnt/ arable land, plough land

het **akkoord** /ɑkort/ (pl: -en) **1** agreement, arrangement, settlement; bargain: *een ~ aangaan* (or: *sluiten*) come to an arrangement; *tot een ~ komen* reach an agreement **2** [mus] chord ‖ *~ gaan (met)* agree (to), be agreeable (to); *niet ~ gaan (met)* disagree (with)

de **akoestiek** /ɑkusti̯k/ acoustics

akoestisch /ɑkustis/ (adj) acoustic, sonic

de **akte** /ɑktə/ (pl: -n, -s) **1** deed; contract: *~ van geboorte* (or: *overlijden, huwelijk*) birth (or: death, marriage) certificate; *een ~ opmaken* draw up a deed; *~ opmaken van* make a record of **2** certificate; diploma; licence **3** [theatre, film] act ‖ *waarvan ~* duly noted, acknowledged

de **aktetas** /ɑktətɑs/ (pl: -sen) briefcase

¹**al** /ɑl/ (ind pron) **1** all, whole: *al de moeite* all our (or: their) trouble; *het was één en al geweld op tv gisteren* there was nothing but violence on TV yesterday **2** all (of) ‖ *al met al* all in all

²**al** /ɑl/ (adv) **1** yet; already: *al een hele tijd* for a long time now; *al enige tijd, al vanaf juli* for some time past (or: now), (ever) since July; *dat dacht ik al* I thought so; *is zij er nu al?* is she here already?; *is John here yet?*; *ik heb het altijd al geweten* I've known it all along; *daar heb je het al* there you are **2** all: *dat alleen al* that alone; *al te snel* (or: *spoedig*) far too fast (or: soon); *ze weten het maar al te goed* they know only too well; *hij had het toch al moeilijk* he had enough problems as it was ‖ *het is al laat* (or: *duur*) genoeg it is late (or: expensive) enough as it is; *dat lijkt er al meer op, dat is al beter* that's more like it

³**al** /ɑl/ (num) all (of); every; each: *al zijn gedachten* his every thought; *al de kinderen* all (of) the children

⁴**al** /ɑl/ (conj) though, although, even though, even if: *al ben ik arm, ik ben gelukkig* I may be poor, but I'm happy; *al zeg ik het zelf* even though I say so myself; *ook al is het erg* bad as it is (or: may be); *ik deed het niet, al kreeg ik een miljoen* I wouldn't do it for a million pounds

het **alarm** /ɑlɑrm/ alarm: *groot ~* full (or: red) alert; *loos (vals) ~* false alarm; *een stil ~* a si-

lent alarm; *~ slaan* (or: *geven*) give (or: sound) the alarm

de **alarmbelprocedure** /ɑlɑrmbɛlprosedyrə/ [Belg] constitutionally mandated procedure in Belgium to prevent discrimination against minorities

de **alarmcentrale** /ɑlɑrmsɛntralə/ (pl: -s) emergency centre, (general) emergency number

alarmeren /ɑlɑrme̯rə(n)/ (alarmeerde, heeft gealarmeerd) **1** alert, call out: *de brandweer ~* call (out) the fire brigade **2** alarm: *~de berichten* disturbing reports

het **alarmnummer** /ɑlɑrmnʏmər/ (pl: -s) emergency number

het **alarmpistool** /ɑlɑrmpistol/ (pl: -pistolen) alarm gun

de ¹**Albanees** /ɑlbane̯s/ (pl: Albanezen) [person] Albanian

het ²**Albanees** /ɑlbane̯s/ [language] Albanian

³**Albanees** /ɑlbane̯s/ (adj) Albanian

Albanië /ɑlbani̯jə/ Albania

het **albast** /ɑlbɑst/ (pl: -en) alabaster

de **albatros** /ɑlbatros/ (pl: -sen) albatross

de **albino** /ɑlbi̯no/ (pl: -'s) albino

het **album** /ɑlbʏm/ (pl: -s) album

de **alchemie** /ɑlχemi̯/ alchemy

de **alcohol** /ɑlkohol/ alcohol: *pure ~* pure alcohol; *verslaafd aan ~* addicted to alcohol

alcoholhoudend /ɑlkoholhɑudənt/ (adj) alcoholic: *~e dranken* alcoholic beverages, spirits

alcoholisch /ɑlkoholi̯s/ (adj) alcoholic: *~e dranken* alcoholic drinks; *een niet ~ drankje* a non-alcoholic drink

het **alcoholisme** /ɑlkoholi̯smə/ alcoholism

de **alcoholist** /ɑlkoholi̯st/ (pl: -en) alcoholic

het **alcoholpercentage** /ɑlkoholpɛrsɛntaʒə/ (pl: -s) alcohol by volume (ABV)

alcoholvrij /ɑlkoholvrɛi̯/ (adj) non-alcoholic, soft: *~e dranken* non-alcoholic beverages, soft drinks

aldaar /ɑldar/ (adv) there, at (or: of) that place

aldoor /ɑldor/ (adv) all along, all the time: *zij dacht ~ dat ...* she kept thinking that ...

aldus /ɑldʏs/ (adv) thus, so: *~ geschiedde* and so (or: thus) it happened; *~ de minister* according to (or: said) the minister

alert /ɑlɛrt/ (adj) alert: *~ zijn op spelfouten* be on the alert (or: lookout) for spelling mistakes

de **alfa** /ɑlfa/ (pl: -'s) [educ] [roughly] languages, humanities, arts ‖ *zij is een echte ~* all her talents are on the arts side

het **alfabet** /ɑlfabɛt/ (pl: -ten) alphabet: *alle letters van het ~* all the letters in the alphabet; *de boeken staan op ~* the books are arranged in alphabetical order

alfabetisch /ɑlfabe̯tis/ (adj, adv) alphabetical: *in ~e volgorde* in alphabetical order

alfabetiseren /ɑlfabɛtizerə(n)/ (alfabetiseerde, heeft gealfabetiseerd) alphabetize

alfanumeriek /ɑlfanymerik/ (adj) alphanumeric(al)

de **alg** /ɑlx/ (pl: -en) alga

· de **algebra** /ɑlɣebra/ algebra

algebraïsch /ɑlɣəbrɑis/ (adj, adv) algebraic(al)

algeheel /ɑlɣəhel/ (adj) complete, total: *met algehele **steun*** with (everyone's) full support; *met mijn algehele **instemming*** with my wholehearted consent; *tot algehele **tevredenheid*** to everyone's satisfaction

algemeen /ɑlɣəmen/ (adj, adv) **1** public, general, universal, common: *voor ~ **gebruik*** for general use; *algemene **middelen*** public funds; *algemene **ontwikkeling*** general knowledge; *een algemene **regel*** a general rule; *in algemene **zin*** in a general sense; *het is ~ **bekend*** it is common knowledge; *~ **beschouwd worden** als* be generally known as **2** general(ized), broad: *in algemene **bewoordingen*** in general terms || *in het ~ hebt u gelijk* on the whole, you're right; *zij zijn **in** het ~ betrouwbaar* for the most part they are reliable; *in (over) het ~* in general

de **algemeenheid** /ɑlɣəmenhɛit/ (pl: -heden) generality; indefiniteness || [Belg] *met ~ van stemmen* unanimously

Algerije /ɑlɣərɛiə/ Algeria

de **Algerijn** /ɑlɣərɛin/ (pl: -en) Algerian

Algerijns /ɑlɣərɛins/ (adj) Algerian

alhoewel /ɑlhuwɛl/ (conj) although

alias /alijɑs/ (adv) alias, also (*or:* otherwise) known as

het/de **alibi** /alibi/ (pl: -'s) alibi; excuse: *iem. een ~ **bezorgen (geven)*** cover up for s.o.

de **alien** /elijən/ alien

de **alimentatie** /alimɛnta(t)si/ maintenance (allowance, money); alimony

de **alinea** /alineja/ (pl: -'s) paragraph: *een nieuwe ~ **beginnen*** start a new paragraph

alla /ɑla/ (int) that's one thing

Allah /ɑla/ Allah

allang /ɑlɑŋ/ (adv) for a long time, a long time ago: *ik ben ~ **blij** dat je er bent* I'm pleased that you're here at all

¹**alle** /ɑlə/ (ind pron) all, every, each: *uit ~ **macht** iets proberen* try one's utmost; *hij had ~ **reden** om* he had every reason to; *boven ~ **twijfel*** beyond all doubt; *voor ~ **zekerheid*** to make quite (*or:* doubly) sure

²**alle** /ɑlə/ (num) all, every, each; everyone; everybody: *van ~ **kanten*** from all sides, from every side; *in ~ **opzichten*** in all respects; *zij gingen **met** hun ~n naar het zwembad they* went all together to the swimming pool; *geen **van** ~n wist het* not one of them knew

allebei /ɑləbɛi/ (num) both; either: *~ de **kinderen** waren bang* both (of the) children were afraid; *het was ~ **juist** geweest* either would

have been correct

alledaags /ɑledaxs/ (adj) daily, everyday: *de ~e **beslommeringen*** day-to-day worries; *de kleine, ~e **dingen** van het leven* the little everyday things of life; *dat is niet **iets** ~* that's not an everyday occurrence

¹**alleen** /alen/ (adj, adv) **1** alone, by o.s., on one's own: *hij **is** graag ~* he likes to be alone (*or:* by himself); *het ~ **klaarspelen*** manage it alone (*or:* on one's own); *helemaal ~* all (*or:* completely) alone; *een kamer voor **hem** ~* a room (all) to himself **2** only, alone: *~ in het weekeinde geopend* only open at weekends

²**alleen** /alen/ (adv) only, merely, just: *de gedachte ~ **al*** the mere (*or:* very) thought; *ik wilde u ~ **maar** even spreken* I just wanted to talk to you; *~ **maar** aan zichzelf denken* only think of o.s.; *niet ~ … maar ook* not only … but also

de **alleenheerschappij** /alenhersxɑpɛi/ absolute power; [fig] monopoly: *de ~ **voeren** (over)* reign supreme (over)

de **alleenheerser** /alenhersər/ (pl: -s) absolute sovereign, autocrat

alleen-lezen /alenlezə(n)/ (adj) [comp] read-only

het **alleenrecht** /alenrɛxt/ (pl: -en) exclusive right(s)

alleenstaand /alenstant/ (adj) single: *een ~e **ouder*** a single parent

de **alleenstaande** /alenstandə/ (pl: -n) single: *voor ~n* for singles; *een dansavond **voor** ~n* a singles' dance

de **alleenverdiener** /alenvərdinər/ (pl: -s) sole wage-earner

het **allegaartje** /aleɣarcə/ (pl: -s) mishmash, hotchpotch, jumble

de **allegorie** /aleɣorj/ (pl: -ën) allegory

allegorisch /aleɣoris/ (adj, adv) allegorical

¹**allemaal** /ɡləmal/ (adv) all, only: *hij zag ~ **sterretjes*** all he saw was little stars

²**allemaal** /ɡləmal/ (num) all; everybody; everyone; everything: *beste van ~* best of all; *~ **onzin*** all nonsense; *ik houd van **jullie** ~* I love you all; *zoals **wij** ~* like all of us; *~ **samen (tegelijk)*** all together; *tot ziens ~* goodbye everybody

allemachtig /aləmɔxtəx/ (adv) amazingly: *een ~ **groot** huis* an amazingly big house

alleman /ɡləmɑn/ (ind pron) everybody: *Jan en ~* one and all, all and sundry; *met **Jan** en ~ naar bed gaan* sleep around

allengs /alɛŋs/ (adv) gradually, little by little

allerbest /alərbɛst/ (adj, adv) very best: *zijn ~e **vrienden*** his very best friends; *ik wens je **het** ~e* I wish you all the best

allereerst /alərerst/ (adj, adv) first of all, very first: *vanaf het ~e **begin*** from the very beginning

het **allergeen** /alɛrɣen/ (pl: allergenen) allergen

de **allergie** /alɛryi/ (pl: -ën) allergy

allergisch /alɛryis/ (adj) allergic (to)

allerhande /alərhɑndə/ (adj) all sorts (of), all kinds (of)

Allerheiligen /alərhɛiləyə(n)/ All Saints' (Day)

allerhoogst /alərhoxst/ (adj) highest of all; very highest; supreme; paramount; maximum; top: *van het ~e belang* of supreme (*or:* paramount) importance; *het is de ~e tijd* it's high time

allerijl /alərɛil/: *in ~* with all speed, in great haste

allerlaatst /alərlatst/ (adj, adv) last of all, very last, very latest: *de ~e bus* the (very) last bus; *de ~e mode* the very latest style; *op het ~* at the very last moment; *tot op het ~* right up to the (very) end

allerlei /alərlɛi/ (adj) all sorts (*or:* kinds) of: *~ speelgoed* all sorts of toys

allerliefst /alərlifst/ (adj, adv) **1** (very) dearest (*or:* sweetest): *een ~ kind* a very dear (*or:* sweet) child **2** more than anything: *hij wil het ~ acteur worden* he wants to be an actor to be an actor more than anything

allerminst /alərmɪnst/ (adj) **1** least (of all): *ik heb er niet het ~e op aan te merken* I don't have the slightest objection **2** (very) least, (very) slightest: *op zijn ~* at the very least

Allerzielen /alərzilə(n)/ All Souls' (Day)

alles /ɡləs/ (ind pron) everything, all, anything: *hij heeft (van) ~ geprobeerd* he has tried everything; *is dat ~?* will that be all?; *dat is ~* that's it (*or:* everything); *ik weet er ~ van* I know all about it; *(het is) ~ of niets* it's all or nothing; *~ op ~ zetten* go all out; *van ~ (en nog wat)* all sorts of things; *~ bij elkaar viel het mee* all in all (*or:* all things considered) it was better than expected; *~ op zijn tijd* all in due course, all in good time; *dat slaat ~* that takes the cake

allesbehalve /aləzbəhɑlvə/ (adv) anything but: *het was ~ een succes* it was anything but a success; *~ vriendelijk* anything but friendly

de **alleseter** /ɡlesetər/ (pl: -s) omnivore

het **alles-in-éénpakket** /aləsɪnɛmpɑkɛt/ (pl: -ten) all-in-one package

allesomvattend /aləsomvɑtənt/ (adj) all-embracing, comprehensive, universal

allesoverheersend /aləsoverhɛrsənt/ (adj) overpowering: *een ~e smaak van knoflook* an overpowering taste of garlic

de **allesreiniger** /ɡləsrɛinəyər/ (pl: -s) all-purpose cleaner

alleszins /aləsɪns/ (adv) in every way, completely, in all respects, fully: *dat is ~ redelijk* that is perfectly reasonable

de **alliantie** /alijɑnsi/ (pl: -s) alliance

allicht /alɪxt/ (adv) most probably (*or:* likely), of course: *ja ~* yes, of course

de **alligator** /aliyɑtor/ (pl: -s) alligator

all-in /ɔːlɪn/ (adj, adv) all-in(clusive): *dat is € 1000 ~* that is € 1000 everything included

de **all-invakantie** /ɔːlɪnvakɑn(t)si/ (pl: -s) package holiday, all-inclusive holiday

de **¹allochtoon** /aloxton/ (pl: allochtonen) immigrant, foreigner

²allochtoon /aloxton/ (adj) foreign

allrisk /ɔːlrɪsk/ (adj, adv) [Dutch] comprehensive: *~ verzekerd zijn* have a comprehensive insurance policy

de **allriskverzekering** /ɔːlrɪskfərzekərɪŋ/ [Dutch] comprehensive insurance policy

allround /ɔːlrɑunt/ (adj) all-round

de **allure** /alyrə/ (pl: -s) air, style: *~ hebben* have style; *iem. van ~* a striking personality; *een gebouw met ~* an imposing building

de **allusie** /alyzi/ (pl: -s) allusion: [Belg] *~(s) maken op* hint at, allude to

almaar /ɡlmar/ (adv) constantly, continuously, all the time: *kinderen die ~ om snoep vragen* children who are always asking for sweets

de **almacht** /ɡlmɑxt/ omnipotence

almachtig /almɑxtəx/ (adj) almighty, all-powerful: *de Almachtige* the Almighty

de **almanak** /ɡlmanɑk/ (pl: -ken) almanac

de **alo** /alo/ *academie voor lichamelijke opvoeding* college of physical education

alom /alom/ (adv) everywhere, on all sides: *~ gevreesd* (*or:* **bekend**) generally feared (*or:* known)

de **alp** /alp/ (pl: -en) alp

alpineskiën /alpinəskijə(n)/ alpine (*or:* downhill) skiing

het **alpinisme** /alpinɪsmə/ alpinism, mountaineering

de **alpinist** /alpinɪst/ (pl: -en) alpinist, mountaineer

de **alpino** /alpino/ (pl: -'s) (Basque) beret

als /ɑls/ (conj) **1** like, as: *zich ~ een dame gedragen* behave like a lady; *hetzelfde ~ ik* the same as me, just like me; *hij is even groot ~ jij* he is as tall as you; *de brief luidt ~ volgt* the letter reads as follows; *zowel in de stad ~ op het land* both in the city and in the country **2** as, as if: *~ bij toverslag veranderde alles* as if by magic everything changed; *~ ware het je eigen kind* as if it were your own child **3** for, as: *poppen ~ geschenk* dolls for presents; *ik heb die man nog ~ jongen gekend* I knew that man when he was still a boy; *~ vrienden uit elkaar gaan* part as friends **4** when: *telkens ~ wij elkaar tegenkomen keert hij zich af* whenever we meet, he turns away **5** if, as long as: *~ zij er niet geweest was …* if she had not been there …; *maar wat ~ het regent, ~ het nu eens regent?* but what if it rains?; *~ het mogelijk is* if possible; *~ ze al komen* if they come at all

ALS /aːɛls/ *amyotrofe laterale sclerose* ALS *(amyotrophic lateral sclerosis);* Lou Gehrig's disease

alsjeblieft /alʃəbli̯ft/ (adv) **1** please: *10 euro,* ~ 10 euros, please; *een ogenblikje* ~ one moment, please; ~ *niet!* no, thank you!, please, don't! **2** here you are, there you go **3** yes please: *wil je koffie?* ~ would you like some coffee? yes please **4** ~ *zeg! mag het wat stiller?* oh come on! can you turn it down?; ~! *dat is pas een groot stuk chocola!* goodness! now that's what I call a big piece of chocolate!

alsmaar /ɑlsmar/ (adv) constantly, all the time: ~ *praten* talk constantly

alsmede /ɑlsme̯də/ (conj) as well as, and also

alsnog /ɑlsnɔχ/ (adv) still, yet: *je kunt je werkstuk* ~ *inleveren* you may still submit your paper; *je kunt* ~ *van studie veranderen* you can still change your course; *het vliegtuig mocht toen* ~ *vertrekken* the plane was then (finally) allowed to depart

alsof /ɑlsɔf/ (conj) as if: *je doet maar* ~ you're just pretending; *hij keek* ~ *hij mij niet begreep* he looked as if he didn't understand me

alsook /ɑlsok/ (conj) as well as

¹**alstublieft** /ɑlstybli̯ft/ (adv) please: *een ogenblikje* ~ just a minute, please; *wees* ~ *rustig* please be quiet

²**alstublieft** /ɑlstybli̯ft/ (int) please; here you are: ~, *dat is dan € 6,50* here you are, that will be € 6.50; *wilt u koffie?* ~! would you like some coffee? yes please!

de ¹**alt** /ɑlt/ [mus] [singer] alto

de ²**alt** /ɑlt/ [mus] [voice] alto

het **altaar** /ɑltar/ (pl: altaren) altar

het ¹**alternatief** /ɑltɛrnati̯f/ (pl: alternatieven) alternative: *er is geen enkel* ~ there is no alternative; *als* ~ as an alternative

²**alternatief** /ɑltɛrnati̯f/ (adj) alternative: *alternatieve geneeswijze* alternative treatment

althans /ɑltɑns/ (adv) at least

altijd /ɑltɛit/ (adv) always, forever: *ik heb het* ~ *wel gedacht* I've thought so all along; I've always thought so; *je kunt niet* ~ *winnen* you can't win them all; ~ *weer* again and again; *wat je ook doet, je verliest* ~ no matter what you do, you always lose; *bijna* ~ nearly always; *wonen ze nog* ~ *in Almere?* are they still living in Almere?; *voor eens en* ~ once and for all; *hetzelfde als* ~ the same as always, the usual; *ze ging* ~ *op woensdag winkelen* she always went shopping on Wednesdays

altijddurend /ɑltɛidyrənt/ (adj) everlasting

de **altsaxofoon** /ɑltsɑksofon/ (pl: -s, altsaxofonen) alto saxophone

de **altviolist** /ɑltfijolɪst/ violist

de **altviool** /ɑltfijol/ viola

de **aluin** /ɑlœyn/ (pl: -en) alum

het ¹**aluminium** /ɑlymi̯nijym/ aluminium; [Am] aluminum

²**aluminium** /ɑlymi̯nijym/ (adj) aluminium; [Am] aluminum

het/de **aluminiumfolie** /ɑlymi̯nijymfoli/ aluminium (*or:* tin, kitchen) foil

alvast /ɑlvɑst/ (adv) meanwhile, in the meantime: *begin maar* ~, *ik kom zo* just start, I'll be there in a moment; *jullie hadden* ~ *kunnen beginnen zonder mij* you could have started without me; *zijn naam kun je* ~ *doorstrepen* you can cross his name off now

de **alvleesklier** /ɑlvlesklir/ (pl: -en) pancreas

alvorens /ɑlvorə(n)s/ (adv) before: ~ *te vertrekken, graag het licht uitdoen* before you leave, please switch the light off

alweer /ɑlwe̯r/ (adv) **1** again, once more: *ben je er* ~? *je was er net ook al!* it's you again? you were just here! **2** already: *het is* ~ *laat* it's already late; *ben je er nu* ~? *ik dacht het langer zou duren!* you're back already! I thought it would take longer ‖ *hoe heet zij ook* ~? what was her name again?; *hoe zat het ook* ~? **a)** how does this work again?; **b)** remind me what that was all about?

alwetend /ɑlwe̯tənt/ (adj) omniscient, all-knowing

de **alzheimer** /ɑltshɛimər/ Alzheimer's (disease)

amai /ɑmɑi̯/ (int) oh boy

het **amalgaam** /ɑmɑlɣam/ (pl: amalgamen) amalgam

de **amandel** /ɑmɑndəl/ (pl: -en) **1** almond **2** tonsil: *zijn ~en laten knippen* have one's tonsils (taken) out

het **amandelschaafsel** /ɑmɑndəlsχafsəl/ flaked almonds

de **amanuensis** /ɑmanywɛnsɪs/ (pl: -sen, amanuenses) laboratory assistant

de **amateur** /ɑmatør/ (pl: -s) amateur

amateuristisch /ɑmatørɪstis/ (adj, adv) amateur(ish): ~*e sportbeoefening* amateur sports; *dat is zeer* ~ *gedaan* that was done very amateurishly

de **amazone** /ɑmazo̯ːnə/ (pl: -s) horsewoman

de **Amazone** /ɑmazo̯ːnə/ Amazon

het **ambacht** /ɑmbɑχt/ (pl: -en) trade, (handi)craft: *het* ~ *uitoefenen van* … practise the trade of … ‖ *het is met hem twaalf ~en, dertien ongelukken* he is a jack-of-all-trades (and master of none)

ambachtelijk /ɑmbɑχtələk/ (adj) according to traditional methods: *op ~e wijze bereid* prepared according to traditional methods

de **ambachtsman** /ɑmbɑχ(t)smɑn/ (pl: ambachtslieden) artisan, craftsman

de **ambassade** /ɑmbɑsa̯də/ (pl: -s) embassy

de **ambassadeur** /ɑmbɑsadø̯r/ (pl: -s) ambassador

de **amber** /ɑmbər/ amber

het **amber alert** /ɛmbərəlʏːrt/ (pl: -s): *er is een* ~ *uitgegaan* [UK] a Child Rescue Alert has been issued; [Am] an Amber Alert has been issued

de **ambiance** /ɑmbijā̯sə/ ambiance

ambiëren /ɑmbije̯rə(n)/ (ambieerde, heeft

geambieerd) aspire to: *een **baan** ~* aspire to a job

de **ambitie** /ɑmbi(t)si/ (pl: -s) ambition: *een man van grote ~* a man with great ambitions

ambitieus /ɑmbi(t)jøs/ (adj) ambitious: *ambitieuze plannen* ambitious plans

ambivalent /ɑmbivalɛnt/ (adj) ambivalent

het **ambt** /ɑmt/ (pl: -en) office: *een ~ uitoefenen* carry out one's duties; *iem. uit een ~ ontzetten* discharge s.o. from office

ambtelijk /ɑmtələk/ (adj, adv) official: *~e stukken* official documents

ambteloos /ɑmtəlos/ (adj) private: *een ~ burger* a private citizen

de **ambtenaar** /ɑmtənar/ (pl: ambtenaren) official, civil servant, public servant: *~ van de burgerlijke **stand*** registrar; [Am] county clerk; *burgerlijk ~* civil (*or:* public) servant

het **ambtenarenapparaat** /ɑmtənarə(n)ɑparat/ civil service

de **ambtenarij** /ɑmtənarɛi/ bureaucracy, red tape

de **ambtgenoot** /ɑmtxənot/ (pl: -genoten) colleague

de **ambtsaanvaarding** /ɑm(t)sanvardɪŋ/ accession to office, acceptance (*or:* assumption) of duties

de **ambtsdrager** /ɑm(t)sdraɣər/ (pl: -s) office holder

het **ambtsgeheim** /ɑm(t)sxəhɛim/ (pl: -en) professional secrecy (*or:* confidentiality); official secrecy

ambtshalve /ɑm(t)shɑlvə/ (adv) by virtue of one's office; in one's official capacity, officially

het **ambtsmisdrijf** /ɑm(t)smɪzdrɛif/ (pl: -misdrijven) malfeasance, misconduct

de **ambtstermijn** /ɑmtstɛrmɛin/ (pl: -en) term of office: *zijn ~ loopt af* his term of office is drawing to a close, his term of office is nearing its end

ambtswege /ɑm(t)sweɣə/: *van ~* officially, ex officio, by virtue of one's office

de **ambtswoning** /ɑm(t)swonɪŋ/ (pl: -en) official residence

de **ambulance** /ɑmbylɑsə/ (pl: -s) ambulance

de **ambulancebroeder** /ɑmbylɑsəbrudər/ (pl: -s) paramedic

ambulant /ɑmbylɑnt/ (adj) ambulatory, ambulant: *~e **zorg*** ambulatory care

het **amen** /amə(n)/ amen ‖ [fig] *ja en ~ op iets zeggen* bow to sth.; [Belg] *~ en uit* that's enough!, stop it!

het **amendement** /amɛndəmɛnt/ (pl: -en) amendment

amenderen /amɛndɛrə(n)/ (amendeerde, heeft geamendeerd) amend

Amerika /amerika/ America

de **Amerikaan** /amerikan/ (pl: Amerikanen) American: *tot ~ naturaliseren* naturalize as an American

Amerikaans /amerikans/ (adj) American: *de ~e **burgeroorlog*** the American Civil War; *het ~e **congres*** Congress; *~e **whiskey*** bourbon, rye, corn whiskey

de **Amerikaanse** /amerikansə/ American (woman)

het/de **amfetamine** /ɑmfetaminə/ (pl: -n) amphetamine

de **amfibie** /ɑmfibi/ (pl: -ën) amphibian

het **amfibievoertuig** /ɑmfibivurtœyx/ (pl: -en) amphibious vehicle, amphibian

het **amfitheater** /ɑmfitejatər/ (pl: -s) amphitheatre

amicaal /amikal/ (adj, adv) amicable, friendly: *~ **omgaan** met iem.* be on friendly terms with s.o.

het **aminozuur** /aminozyr/ (pl: -zuren) amino acid

de **ammonia** /amonija/ ammonia (water)

de **ammoniak** /amonijɑk/ ammonia

de **amnestie** /ɑmnɛsti/ (pl: -ën) amnesty: *~ **verlenen** (aan)* grant an amnesty (to)

de **amoebe** /amøbə/ (pl: -n) amoeba

amok /amɔk/: *~ **maken*** run amok

amoreel /amorɛl/ (adj, adv) amoral

amorf /amɔrf/ (adj) amorphous

ampel /ɑmpəl/ (adj, adv) ample: *na ~e **overweging*** after careful (*or:* full) consideration

amper /ɑmpər/ (adv) scarcely, barely, hardly: *hij kon ~ **schrijven*** he could barely write

de **ampère** /ɑmpɛːrə/ (pl: -s) ampere

de **ampul** /ɑmpyl/ (pl: -len) ampoule

de **amputatie** /ɑmpyta(t)si/ (pl: -s) amputation

amputeren /ɑmpytɛrə(n)/ (amputeerde, heeft geamputeerd) amputate

de **amulet** /amylɛt/ (pl: -ten) amulet

amusant /amyzɑnt/ (adj) amusing: *een ~ **verhaal*** an amusing story; *iets ~ **vinden*** find sth. amusing (*or:* entertaining)

het **amusement** /amyzəmɛnt/ (pl: -en) amusement, entertainment

de **amusementshal** /amyzəmɛn(t)shɑl/ (pl: -len) amusement arcade

zich **amuseren** /amyzɛrə(n)/ (amuseerde zich, heeft zich geamuseerd) amuse o.s., entertain o.s., enjoy o.s.: *zich **kostelijk** (uitstekend) ~* thoroughly enjoy o.s.

amuzikaal /amyzikal/ (adj) unmusical

de **amv** (pl: -'s) [Dutch] *alleenstaande minderjarige vreemdeling* unaccompanied minor immigrant

anaal /anal/ (adj, adv) anal

anabool /anabol/ (adj) anabolic: *anabole steroïden* anabolic steroids

het **anachronisme** /anaxronɪsmə/ (pl: -n) anachronism

het **anagram** /anaɣrɑm/ (pl: -men) anagram: *een ~ **vormen** van* make an anagram of

de **analfabeet** /analfabet/ (pl: analfabeten) illiterate

het **analfabetisme** /analfabetɪsmə/ illiteracy

de **analist** /analɪst/ (pl: -en) (chemical) analyst, lab(oratory) technician

de **analogie** /analoɣi/ (pl: -ën) analogy: *naar ~ van* by analogy with

analoog /analox/ (adj, adv) analogue

de **analyse** /analizə/ (pl: -s) analysis: *een kritische ~ van een roman* a critical analysis of a novel

analyseren /analizerə(n)/ (analyseerde, heeft geanalyseerd) analyse: *grondig ~* **a)** analyse thoroughly; **b)** [fig] dissect

analytisch /analitis/ (adj, adv) analytical: *~ denken* think analytically

de **ananas** /ananas/ (pl: -sen) pineapple

de **anarchie** /anarxi/ anarchy

het **anarchisme** /anarxɪsmə/ anarchism

de **anarchist** /anarxɪst/ (pl: -en) anarchist

anarchistisch /anarxɪstis/ (adj) **1** anarchist(ic) **2** anarchic

de **anatomie** /anatomi/ anatomy

anatomisch /anatomis/ (adj) anatomical

de **anchor** /ɛŋkər/ (pl: -s) anchorman, anchorwoman

de **ancien** /ãsjɛ̃/ (pl: -s) [Belg] veteran, ex-serviceman

de **anciënniteit** /ɑnsɛnitɛrt/ seniority, length of service

Andalusië /ɑndalysijə/ Andalusia

[1]**ander** /ɑndər/ (adj) **1** other, another: *aan de ~e kant* on the other hand; *een ~e keer misschien!* maybe some other time!; *(de) een of ~e voorbijganger* some passer-by; *met ~e woorden* in other words; *om de één of ~e reden* for some reason, for one reason or another **2** different: *ik voel me nu een ~ mens* I feel a different man (*or:* woman) now; *dat is een heel ~e zaak* that's quite a different matter, that's a different matter altogether

[2]**ander** /ɑndər/ (ind pron) **1** another; others: *de een of ~* somebody, s.o.; *sommigen wel, ~en niet* some do (*or:* are); some don't (*or:* aren't); *de ene of de ~e* (choose) one thing or the other **2** another matter (*or:* thing); other matters (*or:* things): *als geen ~* more than anybody else; *je hebt het een en ~ nodig om te ...* you need a few things in order to ...; *onder ~e* among other things, including; *of het één, of het ~!* you can't have it both ways

[3]**ander** /ɑndər/ (num) next, other: *om de ~e dag* every other day, on alternative days

anderhalf /ɑndərhɑlf/ (num) one and a half: *~ maal zoveel* half as much (*or:* many) again; *~ maal zo hoog* one and a half times as high; *~ uur* an hour and a half

[1]**anders** /ɑndərs/ (adj) different (from): *niemand ~* nobody else; *wilt u nog iets ~?* do you want anything else?; *over iets ~ beginnen (te praten)* change the subject; *er zit niets ~ op dan ...* there is nothing for it but to ...; *het is (nu eenmaal) niet ~* that's how it is (and there's nothing can be done about it)

[2]**anders** /ɑndərs/ (adv) **1** normally, differently: *het ~ aanpakken* handle it differently; *~ gezegd, ... in other words ...; in jouw geval liggen de zaken ~* in your case things are different; *(zo is het) en niet ~* that's the way it is (*or:* how things are) **2** otherwise: *net als ~* just as usual; *niet meer zo vaak als ~* less often than usual **3** otherwise, else: *wat kon ik ~ (doen) (dan ...)?* what else could I do (but ...); *~ niets?* will that be all? **4** else; otherwise: *waarom zou hij ~ zo koppig zijn?* why else should he be so stubborn? || *ergens ~* somewhere else

andersdenkend /ɑndərzdɛŋkənt/ (adj) dissentient, dissident

andersom /ɑndərsɔm/ (adv) the other way round

de **anderstalige** /ɑndərstaləɣə/ non-native speaker

anderszins /ɑndərsɪns/ (adv) [form] otherwise: *en/of ~* and/or otherwise

anderzijds /ɑndərzɛits/ (adv) on the other hand

de **andijvie** /ɑndɛivi/ endive

Andorra /ɑndɔra/ Andorra

de [1]**Andorrees** /ɑndores/ (pl: Andorrezen) Andorran

[2]**Andorrees** /ɑndores/ (adj) Andorran

het **andreaskruis** /ɑndrejaskrœys/ (pl: -en) cross of St Andrew

de **anekdote** /anɛgdotə/ (pl: -s) anecdote

de **anemoon** /anəmon/ (pl: anemonen) anemone

de **anesthesie** /anɛstezi/ anaesthesia: *lokale ~* local anaesthesia; *algehele ~* general anaesthesia

de **anesthesist** /anɛstezɪst/ (pl: -en) anaesthetist

de **angel** /aŋəl/ (pl: -s) sting

Angelsaksisch /aŋəlsɑksis/ (adj) **1** English(-speaking) **2** Anglo-Saxon

de **angina** /aŋɣina/ tonsillitis

de **anglicaan** /aŋxlikan/ (pl: anglicanen) Anglican

anglicaans /aŋxlikans/ (adj) Anglican: *de ~e kerk* the Church of England

de **anglist** /aŋxlɪst/ (pl: -en) specialist (*or:* student) of English (language and literature)

Angola /aŋxola/ Angola

de **Angolees** /aŋɣoles/ (pl: Angolezen) Angolan

de **angst** /aŋst/ (pl: -en) fear (of); dread, terror (of); anxiety: *~ aanjagen* frighten; [stronger] terrify; *~ hebben voor* be afraid (*or:* scared) of; *uit ~ voor straf* for fear of punishment; *verlamd van ~* numb with fear

angstaanjagend /aŋstanjaɣənt/ (adj, adv) terrifying, frightening

de **angstcultuur** /aŋstkʏltyr/ culture of fear

de **angsthaas** /aŋsthas/ (pl: -hazen) scaredy-cat

angstig /ɑnstəx/ (adj) **1** anxious; afraid: *een ~e schreeuw* an anxious cry; *dat maakte mij ~* that frightened me, that made me afraid **2** fearful, anxious, terrifying: *~e gedachten* anxious thoughts; *het waren ~e tijden* those were anxious times

angstvallig /ɑnstfɑləx/ (adj, adv) **1** scrupulous, meticulous: *zij vermeed ~ alle vreemde woorden* she scrupulously (*or:* carefully) avoided all foreign words **2** anxious, nervous

angstwekkend /ɑnstwɛkənt/ (adj, adv) frightening, terrifying

het **angstzweet** /ɑnstswet/ cold sweat

de **anijs** /anɛis/ aniseed

de **animatie** /anima(t)si/ (pl: -s) animation: [Belg] *kinderanimatie* children's activities (during an event)

het/de **animo** /animo/ zest (for), enthusiasm (for): *er is weinig ~ voor ...* there is little enthusiasm for ...

de **anjer** /ɑnər/ (pl: -s) carnation

het **anker** /ɑnkər/ (pl: -s) anchor: *het ~ lichten* raise (the) anchor; [also fig] get under way; *voor ~ liggen* be anchored, lie at anchor

de **ankerketting** /ɑnkərkɛtɪn/ (pl: -en) chain

de **ankerplaats** /ɑnkərplats/ (pl: -en) anchorage, berth

annex /anɛks/ (conj) cum; and; slash

de **annexatie** /anɛksa(t)si/ (pl: -s) annexation; incorporation [esp municipalities]

annexeren /anɛksɛrə(n)/ (annexeerde, heeft geannexeerd) annex; incorporate [esp municipalities]

anno /ɑno/ (prep) in the year: *~ 1981* in the year 1981; *~ nu* nowadays

de **annonce** /anõsə/ (pl: -s) advertisement, announcement

annonceren /anõnsɛrə(n)/ (annonceerde, heeft geannonceerd) **1** announce **2** bid; call

annuleren /anylɛrə(n)/ (annuleerde, heeft geannuleerd) cancel: *een bestelling ~* cancel an order

de **annulering** /anylɛrɪn/ (pl: -en) cancellation: *~ van een reservering* cancellation of a reservation

de **annuleringsverzekering** /anylɛrɪnsfərzekərɪn/ (pl: -en) cancellation insurance

de **anode** /anodə/ (pl: -n, -s) anode

anoniem /anonim/ (adj) anonymous, nameless, incognito

de **anonimiteit** /anonimitɛit/ anonymity

de **anorak** /anorak/ (pl: -s) anorak

de **anorexia** /anorɛksija/ anorexia

de **anorexiapatiënt** /anorɛksijapaʃɛnt/ (pl: -en) someone suffering from anorexia, anorexic: *hij was toen ~* he suffered from anorexia then, he was an anorexic then

de **ansichtkaart** /ɑnzɪxtkart/ (pl: -en) [Dutch] (picture) postcard

de **ansjovis** /anʃovɪs/ (pl: -sen) anchovy

Antarctica /ɑntɑrktika/ Antarctica

het **antecedent** /antəsədɛnt/ (pl: -en) antecedent: *iemands ~en natrekken* look into s.o.'s past record

de **antenne** /antɛnə/ (pl: -s) aerial; antenna

het **antibioticum** /antibijotikʏm/ (pl: antibiotica) antibiotic: *ik neem antibiotica* I'm taking antibiotics

anticiperen /antisipɛrə(n)/ (anticipeerde, heeft geanticipeerd) anticipate

de **anticlimax** /ɑntiklimɑks/ (pl: -en) anticlimax

de **anticonceptie** /antikɔnsɛpsi/ contraception, birth control

het **anticonceptiemiddel** /antikɔnsɛpsimɪdəl/ (pl: -en) contraceptive

de **anticonceptiepil** /antikɔnsɛpsipɪl/ (pl: -len) contraceptive pill

het **¹antiek** /antik/ antiques

²antiek /antik/ (adj) antique, ancient: *~e meubels* antique furniture

de **antiglobalist** /antiɣlobalɪst/ antiglobalist

de **antiheld** /ɑntihɛlt/ (pl: -en) antihero

antikraak /ɑntikrak/ (adv) anti-squat: *~ wonen* live somewhere as an anti-squatter

het **antilichaam** /ɑntilɪxam/ (pl: -lichamen) antibody

de **Antillen** /antɪlə(n)/ (pl) (the) Antilles: *de Nederlandse ~* the Netherlands Antilles

de **Antilliaan** /antɪl(i)jan/ (pl: Antillianen) Antillean

Antilliaans /antɪlijans/ (adj) Antillean

de **antilope** /antilopə/ (pl: -n) antelope

de **antipathie** /antipati/ (pl: -ën) antipathy (towards)

de **antiquair** /antikɛːr/ (pl: -s) antique dealer

het **antiquariaat** /antikwarijat/ (pl: antiquariaten) antiquarian (*or:* second-hand) bookshop

de **antireclame** /ɑntirəklamə/ [roughly] bad (*or:* negative) publicity

de **antiroosshampoo** /antiroʃampo/ (pl: -s) anti-dandruff shampoo

de **antisemiet** /antisemit/ (pl: -en) anti-Semite

antisemitisch /antisemitis/ (adj) anti-Semitic

het **antisemitisme** /antisemitɪsmə/ anti-Semitism

antiseptisch /antisɛptis/ (adj) antiseptic

de **antistof** /ɑntistɔf/ (pl: -fen) antibody

de **antithese** /antitezə/ (pl: -n, -s) antithesis

het/de **antivries** /antivris/ antifreeze

het/de **antraciet** /antrasit/ anthracite (coal)

de **antropologie** /antropoloɣi/ anthropology: *culturele ~* cultural anthropology, ethnology

de **antropoloog** /antropolox/ (pl: -logen) anthropologist

de **antroposofie** /antroposofi/ anthroposophy

Antwerpen /ɑntwɛrpə(n)/ Antwerp

het **antwoord** /ɑntwort/ (pl: -en) answer, reply: *een afwijzend (ontkennend) ~* a negative answer; *een bevestigend ~* an affirmative answer; *een positief* ~ a favourable answer; *het ~ schuldig (moeten) blijven* give no reply, remain silent; ~ *geven op* reply to, answer; *een ~ geven* give an answer; *in ~ op uw brief (schrijven)* in reply to your letter; *dat is geen ~ op mijn vraag* that doesn't answer my question

het **antwoordapparaat** /ɑntwortɑparat/ (pl: -apparaten) answering machine, answerphone

antwoorden /ɑntwordə(n)/ (antwoordde, heeft geantwoord) answer, reply, respond: *bevestigend (positief)* ~ answer in the affirmative; *ik antwoord niet op* zulke vragen I don't answer such questions

het **antwoordnummer** /ɑntwortnʏmər/ (pl: -s) [roughly] Freepost

de **anus** /anʏs/ anus

de **ANWB** /aɛnwebe/ *Algemene Nederlandse Wielrijdersbond* [roughly] Dutch AA, Royal Dutch Touring Club; [Am] Dutch AAA

het **aoc** (pl: -'s) [Dutch] *agrarisch opleidingscentrum* agricultural school; agricultural college

de **aorta** /aɔrta/ (pl: -'s) aorta

de **AOW** /aowe/ [Dutch] **1** *Algemene Ouderdomswet* general retirement pensions act **2** (old-age retirement) pension

de **AOW'er** /aowejər/ (pl: -s) [Dutch] OAP (old-age pensioner), senior citizen

apart /apɑrt/ (adj, adv) **1** separate, apart: *elk geval ~ behandelen* deal with each case individually; *iem. ~ nemen (spreken)* take s.o. aside; *onderdelen ~ verkopen* sell parts separately **2** special, exclusive: *zij vormen een klasse* ~ they are in a class of their own **3** different, unusual: *hij ziet er wat ~ uit* he looks a bit unusual

de **apartheid** /apɑrthɛit/ apartheid

apathisch /apatis/ (adj, adv) apathetic, impassive, indifferent

apegapen /apəɣapə(n)/: *op ~ liggen* be at one's last gasp

de **apenkop** /apə(n)kɔp/ (pl: -pen) monkey, brat

de **Apennijnen** /apɛnɛinə(n)/ (pl) Apennines

de **apennoot** /apənot/ peanut, monkey nut

het **apenstaartje** /apə(n)starcə/ (pl: -s) at sign

het **aperitief** /aperitif/ (pl: aperitieven) aperitif

apestoned /apəstɔnt/ (adj) [inform] stoned out of one's mind

de **apk-keuring** /apekakørɪŋ/ (pl: -en) [Dutch] motor vehicle test, MOT test

de **Apocalyps** /apokalɪps/ Apocalypse

de **apostel** /apɔstəl/ (pl: -en) apostle

de **apostrof** /apostrɔf/ (pl: -s) apostrophe

de **apotheek** /apotek/ (pl: apotheken) chemist's; [Am] drugstore

de **apotheker** /apotekər/ (pl: -s) pharmacist, dispenser

de **apothekersassistent** /apotekərsasistɛnt/ (pl: -en) pharmacist's assistant

de **app** /ɛp/ (pl: -s) app: *een ~ sturen* send an app

het **apparaat** /apɑrat/ (pl: apparaten) machine, appliance, device: *huishoudelijke apparaten* household appliances ‖ *het ambtelijk* ~ the administrative system, the Civil Service

de **apparatuur** /apɑratyr/ apparatus, equipment, machinery; hardware

het **appartement** /apɑrtəmɛnt/ (pl: -en) flat; [Am] apartment: *een driekamerappartement* a 2-bedroom flat

het **appartementsgebouw** /apɑrtəmɛntsxəbau/ (pl: -en) [Belg] block of flats

het **appbericht** /ɛbərɪxt/ (pl: -en) app: *een ~ sturen* send an app

de **¹appel** /ɑpəl/ (pl: -s) apple: *een ~tje voor de dorst* a nest egg; [inform] *een rotte* ~ a rotten apple

het **²appel** /apɛl/ (pl: -s) **1** call: ~ *houden* call the roll **2** appeal: *in ~ gaan* appeal ‖ *een ~ voor hands* an appeal for hands

de **appelboom** /ɑpəlbom/ (pl: -bomen) apple tree

de **appelflap** /ɑpəlflɑp/ (pl: -pen) apple turnover

de **appelflauwte** /ɑpəlflautə/ (pl: -s): *een ~ krijgen* go off in a swoon, swoon, sham a faint

het **appelgebak** /ɑpəlɣəbak/ [roughly] apple tart

de **appelkruimeltaart** /ɑpəlkrœym..ltart/ (pl: -en) apple crumble

appelleren /apɛlerə(n)/ (appelleerde, heeft geappelleerd) appeal: ~ *aan* appeal to; ~ *voor hands* appeal for hands

de **appelmoes** /ɑpəlmus/ apple-sauce

het **appelsap** /ɑpəlsap/ apple juice

de **appelsien** /apəlsin/ (pl: -en) [Belg] orange

de **appelstroop** /ɑpəlstrop/ apple spread

de **appeltaart** /ɑpəltart/ (pl: -en) apple pie

appen /ɛpə(n)/ (appte, heeft geappt) whatsapp, app

het/de **appendix** /apɛndɪks/ (pl: appendices) appendix

appetijtelijk /apətɛitələk/ (adj, adv) appetizing

het **appje** /ɛpjə/ (pl: -s) app: *een ~ sturen* send an app

applaudisseren /aplaudiserə(n)/ (applaudisseerde, heeft geapplaudisseerd) applaud, clap: ~ *voor iem.* applaud s.o.

het **applaus** /aplaus/ applause, clapping: *de motie werd met ~ begroet* the motion was received with applause; *een ~je voor Marleen!* let's give a big hand to Marleen!

appreciëren /apreʃerə(n)/ (apprecieerde, heeft geapprecieerd) appreciate

het/de **après-ski** /aprɛski/ après-ski

après-skiën /aprɛskijə(n)/ (après-skiede, heeft geaprès-skied) indulge in amusements after skiing

de **april** /aprɪl/ (pl: -s) April: **één ~** April Fools' Day

de **aprilgrap** /aprɪlɣrɑp/ (pl: -pen) April Fool's joke

het/de **¹à propos** /apropo/: *van zijn ~ raken* (or: *zijn*) lose the thread of one's argument

²à propos /apropo/ (int) apropos, by the way, incidentally

het **aquaduct** /akwadʏkt/ (pl: -en) aqueduct

aquajoggen /akwadʒɔɡə(n)/ (aquajogde, heeft/is geaquajogd) aquajog

de **aquaplaning** /akwaplenɪŋ/ aquaplaning; skidding

de **aquarel** /akwarɛl/ (pl: -len) water colour, aquarelle

het **aquarium** /akwarijʏm/ (pl: -s, aquaria) aquarium

de **¹ar** /ɑr/ (pl: arren) sleigh

²ar /ɑr/ (adj): *in arren moede iets doen* do sth. out of desperation

Arabië /arabijə/ Arabia

de **Arabier** /arabir/ (pl: -en) **1** Saudi (Arabian) **2** Arab

het **¹Arabisch** /arabis/ Arabic: *in het ~* in Arabic

²Arabisch /arabis/ (adj) Arabic; Arabian; Arab: *de ~e literatuur* Arabic literature

de **arbeid** /ɑrbɛit/ labour, work: *de Dag van de Arbeid* Labour Day; [Dutch] *de Partij van de Arbeid* the Labour Party; *ongeschoolde ~* unskilled labour (or: work); *~ verrichten* labour, work

de **arbeider** /ɑrbɛidər/ (pl: -s) worker, workman: *landarbeiders* agricultural labourers; *geschoolde ~s* skilled workers; *ongeschoolde ~s* unskilled workers

de **arbeidersklasse** /ɑrbɛidərsklɑsə/ working class(es)

de **arbeiderspartij** /ɑrbɛidərspɑrtɛi/ (pl: -en) Labour Party, Socialist Party

de **arbeidsbemiddeling** /ɑrbɛitsbəmɪdəlɪŋ/ employment-finding

het **arbeidsbureau** /ɑrbɛitsbyro/ (pl: -s) employment office, jobcentre: *zich inschrijven bij het ~* sign on at the employment office

het **arbeidsconflict** /ɑrbɛitskɔnflɪkt/ (pl: -en) labour dispute (or: conflict)

het **arbeidscontract** /ɑrbɛitskɔntrɑkt/ (pl: -en) employment contract

de **arbeidsinspectie** /ɑrbɛitsɪnspɛksi/ (pl: -s) labour inspectorate: *een ambtenaar van de ~* a labour inspector

arbeidsintensief /ɑrbɛitsɪntɛnzif/ (adj) labour-intensive

de **arbeidsmarkt** /ɑrbɛitsmɑrkt/ (pl: -en) labour market, job market: *de situatie op de ~* the employment situation

arbeidsongeschikt /ɑrbɛitsɔnɣəsxɪkt/ (adj) disabled, unable to work: *gedeeltelijk ~ verklaard worden* be declared partially disabled

de **arbeidsongeschiktheid** /ɑrbɛitsɔnɣə-sxɪkthɛit/ disability, inability to work: *volledige, gedeeltelijke ~* full, partial disability

de **arbeidsovereenkomst** /ɑrbɛitsovərəŋkɔmst/ (pl: -en) employment contract: *een collectieve ~* a collective agreement; *een individuele ~* an individual employment contract

de **arbeidsplaats** /ɑrbɛitsplats/ (pl: -en) job: *nieuwe ~en scheppen* create new jobs; *er gaan 20 ~en verloren* 20 jobs will be lost

de **arbeidstijdverkorting** /ɑrbɛitstɛitfərkortɪŋ/ reduction of working hours, shorter working week

de **arbeidsvoorwaarden** /ɑrbɛitsforwardə(n)/ (pl) terms (or: conditions) of employment: *secundaire ~* fringe benefits

arbeidzaam /ɑrbɛitsam/ (adj) industrious, hard-working, laborious: *na een ~ leven* after a useful life (or: a life of hard work)

de **arbiter** /ɑrbitər/ (pl: -s) [sport] referee; umpire

de **arbitrage** /ɑrbitraʒə/ **1** [sport] refereeing **2** [law] arbitration **3** [com] arbitrage

arbitrair /ɑrbitrɛːr/ (adj, adv) arbitrary: *~ te werk gaan* act arbitrarily

de **Arbowet** /ɑrbowɛt/ [Dutch] (Dutch) occupational health and safety act, Factories Act; [Am] [roughly] Labor Law

arceren /ɑrserə(n)/ (arceerde, heeft gearceerd) shade: *het gearceerde gedeelte* the shaded area

archaïsch /ɑrxais/ (adj) archaic; antiquated

het **archeologie** /ɑrxejoloɣi/ archaeology

archeologisch /ɑrxejoloɣis/ (adj, adv) archaeological: *~e opgravingen* archaeological excavation(s)

de **archeoloog** /ɑrxejolox/ (pl: -logen) archaeologist

het **archief** /ɑrxif/ (pl: archieven) archives; record office; registry (office); files: *iets in het ~ opbergen* file sth. (away)

de **archiefkast** /ɑrxifkɑst/ (pl: -en) filing cabinet

de **archipel** /ɑrxipɛl/ (pl: -s) archipelago

de **architect** /ɑrʃitɛkt/ (pl: -en) architect

architectonisch /ɑrʃitɛktonis/ (adj, adv) architectonic

de **architectuur** /ɑrʃitɛktyr/ architecture, building (style): *voorbeelden van moderne ~* examples of modern architecture

de **archivaris** /ɑrxivarɪs/ (pl: -sen) archivist, keeper of the archives (or: records); registrar

Arctisch /ɑrktis/ (adj) Arctic

de **Ardennen** /ɑrdɛnə(n)/ (pl) (the) Ardennes

de **are** /arə/ (pl: -n) are: *één ~ is honderd vierkante meter* one are is a hundred square metres

de **arena** /arenɑ/ (pl: -'s) arena

de **arend** /arənt/ (pl: -en) eagle

argeloos /ɑrɣəlos/ (adj, adv) unsuspecting, innocent

de **Argentijn** /ɑrɣəntɛin/ (pl: -en) Argentine,

Argentinian
Argentijns /arɣəntɛɪns/ (adj) Argentine,
Argentinian
Argentinië /arɣəntinijə/ Argentina
arglistig /arχlɪstəχ/ (adj, adv) crafty, cun-
ning

het **argument** /arɣymɛnt/ (pl: -en) argument:
*een **steekhoudend** ~* a watertight argument;
*~en **aanvoeren** voor iets* make out a case for
sth.; *~en **voor** en **tegen*** pros and cons; *dat is
geen ~* that's no reason

de **argumentatie** /arɣymɛnta(t)si/ (pl: -s) **1** argumentation, reasoning, line of reasoning
2 argument
argumenteren /arɣymɛntərə(n)/ (argumenteerde, heeft geargumenteerd) argue: *~
voor (or: **tegen**)* argue (*or:* make out a case)
for (*or:* against)

de **argusogen** /arɣysoɣə(n)/ (pl): *iets **met** ~ bekijken* look at sth. with Argus' eyes

de **argwaan** /arχwan/ suspicion: *~ **koesteren***
suspect (sth.); *~ **krijgen*** grow suspicious; *~
wekken* arouse (*or:* excite) suspicion
argwanend /arχwanənt/ (adj, adv) suspicious: *een ~e **blik*** a suspicious look

de **aria** /arija/ (pl: -'s) aria

de **aristocraat** /arɪstokrat/ (pl: aristocraten)
aristocrat

de **aristocratie** /arɪstokra(t)si/ (pl: -ën) aristocracy
aristocratisch /arɪstokratis/ (adj, adv) aristocratic

de **ark** /ark/ (pl: -en) **1** houseboat **2** Ark: *de ~
van **Noach*** Noah's Ark

de **¹arm** /arm/ (pl: -en) **1** arm: *een **gebroken** ~* a
broken (*or:* fractured) arm; *met **open** ~en
ontvangen* receive (*or:* welcome) with open
arms; *hij **sloeg** zijn ~en om haar heen* he threw
his arms around her; *zij liepen ~ **in** ~* they
walked arm in arm; *een advocaat **in** de ~ nemen* consult a solicitor **2** arm, sleeve
²arm /arm/ (adj) **1** poor: *de ~e **landen*** the
poor countries; *de ~en en de rijken* the rich
and the poor **2** poor (in), lacking **3** poor,
wretched: *het ~e **schaap*** the poor thing (*or:*
soul)

de **armatuur** /armatyr/ (pl: armaturen) fitting,
bracket

de **armband** /armbant/ (pl: -en) bracelet

het **¹Armeens** /armens/ Armenian
²Armeens /armens/ (adj) Armenian
Armenië /armenijə/ Armenia

de **Armeniër** /armenijər/ (pl: -s) Armenian
armetierig /armətirəχ/ (adj, adv) miserable, paltry
armlastig /armlɑstəχ/ (adj) poverty-strick-
en, needy

de **armleuning** /armlønɪŋ/ (pl: -en) arm(rest)

de **armoede** /armudə/ poverty; [stronger] des-
titution: *geestelijke ~* intellectual (*or:* spiri-

tual) poverty; *~ **lijden*** be poverty-stricken, be
in need; *schrijnende* (or: *bittere*) *~* abject (*or:*
grinding) poverty
armoedig /armudəχ/ (adj, adv) poor; shabby: *~ **gekleed*** shabbily dressed; *dat staat zo ~*
that looks so shabby

de **armoedzaaier** /armutsajər/ (pl: -s) [Dutch]
down-and-out(er); [Am] bum
armpjedrukken /armpjədrʏkə(n)/ arm-
wrestling

het **armsgat** /armsχat/ (pl: -en) armhole

de **armslag** /armslaχ/ (pl: -en) elbow room
armzalig /armzaləχ/ (adj, adv) poor, paltry,
miserable: *een ~ **pensioentje*** a meagre pension

het **aroma** /aroma/ aroma, flavour
aromatisch /aromatis/ (adj) aromatic

het **arrangement** /arãʒəmɛnt/ (pl: -en) arrangement; format; order: *een ~ **voor** orkest* piano an arrangement for piano
arrangeren /arãʒerə(n)/ (arrangeerde,
heeft gearrangeerd) **1** arrange; set out **2** arrange, organize, get up **3** arrange, score:
***voor** orkest ~* orchestrate, score

de **arrenslee** /arə(n)sle/ (pl: -ën) horse sleigh

het **arrest** /arɛst/ (pl: -en) **1** arrest, detention;
custody: *u staat **onder** ~* you are under arrest
2 [Dutch] judgement

de **arrestant** /arɛstɑnt/ (pl: -en) arrested man
(*or:* woman); detainee; prisoner

de **arrestatie** /arɛsta(t)si/ (pl: -s) arrest: *een ~
verrichten* make an arrest

het **arrestatiebevel** /arɛsta(t)sibəvɛl/ (pl: -en)
arrest warrant
arresteren /arɛstərə(n)/ (arresteerde, heeft
gearresteerd) arrest; detain: *iem. **laten** ~*
have s.o. arrested; place s.o. in charge
arriveren /ariverə(n)/ (arriveerde, is gearri-
veerd) arrive
arrogant /aroɣɑnt/ (adj, adv) arrogant; superior: *een ~e **houding** hebben* have a
haughty manner

de **arrogantie** /aroɣɑn(t)si/ arrogance, pre-
sumptuousness, superiority: *de ~ **van** de
macht* the arrogance of rank (*or:* power)

het **arrondissement** /arɔndisəmɛnt/ (pl: -en)
district

de **arrondissementsrechtbank** /arɔndisə-
mɛntsrɛχtbɑŋk/ (pl: -en) [Dutch] district court

het **arsenaal** /arsenal/ (pl: arsenalen) arsenal

het **arsenicum** /arsenikʏm/ arsenic
articuleren /artikylerə(n)/ (articuleerde,
heeft gearticuleerd) articulate, enunciate:
goed (or: *duidelijk*) *~* articulate well (*or:* dis-
tinctly); *slecht ~* articulate badly (*or:* poorly)

de **artiest** /artist/ (pl: -en) artist, entertainer;
performer

het **artikel** /artikəl/ (pl: -en) **1** article, paper;
story: *een redactioneel ~* an editorial; *de
krant wijdde er een **speciaal** ~ aan* the newspaper ran a feature on it **2** article, item:

huishoudelijke ~en household goods (*or:* items) **3** [law] article, section, clause: *~ 80 van de Grondwet* section 80 of the constitution

de **artillerie** /ɑrtɪləri/ (pl: -ën) artillery: *lichte* (or: *zware*) ~ light (*or:* heavy) artillery

¹**artisanaal** /ɑrtizanal/ (adj) [Belg] craft-

²**artisanaal** /ɑrtizanal/ (adv) [Belg] by craftsmen, by traditional methods

de **artisjok** /ɑrtiʃɔk/ (pl: -ken) artichoke

artistiek /ɑrtɪstik/ (adj, adv) artistic: *de ~ leider* the artistic director

de **artrose** /ɑrtrozə/ arthrosis, articular degeneration

de **arts** /ɑrts/ (pl: -en) doctor, physician: *zijn ~ raadplegen* consult one's doctor

de **artsenbezoeker** /ɑrtsə(n)bəzukər/ (pl: -s) medical representative; [Am esp] drug salesman (*or:* saleswoman)

Aruba /arubа/ Aruba

de **Arubaan** /aruban/ (pl: Arubanen) Aruban

Arubaans /arubans/ (adj) Aruban

de **as** /ɑs/ (pl: assen) **1** ashes; ash: *gloeiende as* (glowing) embers; *een stad in de as leggen* reduce a city to ashes **2** axle; shaft **3** [geometry] axis: *om zijn as draaien* revolve on its axis **4** [mus] A-flat

a.s. *aanstaande* next: *~ maandag* next Monday

de **asbak** /ɑzbɑk/ (pl: -ken) ashtray

het **asbest** /ɑzbɛst/ asbestos

asblond /ɑzblɔnt/ (adj) ash blond

de **asceet** /ɑset/ (pl: asceten) ascetic

ascetisch /ɑsetis/ (adj, adv) ascetic

aselect /aselɛkt/ (adj, adv) random, indiscriminate: *een ~e steekproef* a random sample (*or:* sampling)

het **asfalt** /ɑsfɑlt/ (pl: -en) asphalt

asfalteren /ɑsfɑltərə(n)/ (asfalteerde, heeft geasfalteerd) asphalt

het **asiel** /azil/ (pl: -en) **1** asylum, sanctuary: *politiek ~ vragen* (or: *krijgen*) seek (*or:* obtain) political asylum **2** animal home (*or:* shelter); pound

de **asielzoeker** /azilzukər/ (pl: -s) asylum seeker

het **asielzoekerscentrum** /azilzukərsɛntrʏm/ (pl: -centra) asylum seekers' centre, refugee centre

asjemenou /ɑʃəmənɑu/ (int) oh dear!, my goodness!

de ¹**aso** /aso/ (pl: -'s) [Dutch; inform] antisocial (person); [inform] plonker, idiot: *wat een ~! * what an idiot!, what a selfish plonker!

het ²**aso** /aɛso/ [Belg] general secondary education

³**aso** /aso/ (adj) [Dutch; inform] antisocial

¹**asociaal** /asoʃal/ (adj) antisocial, unsociable; asocial, selfish: *~ gedrag* antisocial behaviour; *zich ~ gedragen* behave antisocially; *een ~ grote auto* an obscenely large car

de ²**asociaal** /asoʃal/ (pl: asocialen) [inform] plonker, idiot

het **aspect** /ɑspɛkt/ (pl: -en) aspect: *we moeten alle ~en van de zaak bestuderen* we must consider every aspect of the matter

de **asperge** /ɑspɛrʒə/ (pl: -s) asparagus

de **asperger** /ɑspɛrɣər/ Asperger's syndrome

de **aspirant** /ɑspirɑnt/ (pl: -en) **1** trainee, student **2** junior: *hij speelt nog bij de ~en* he is still (playing) in the junior league

aspirant- prospective: *aspirant-student* prospective student

de **aspirant-koper** /ɑspirɑntkopər/ (pl: -s) prospective buyer

de **aspiratie** /ɑspira(t)si/ (pl: -s): *hij heeft ~s om voorzitter te worden* it is his ambition to be chairman, he aspires to be chairman

de **aspirine** /ɑspirinə/ aspirin

de **assemblage** /ɑsɛmblaʒə/ (pl: -s) assembly, assembling

assembleren /ɑsɛmblerə(n)/ (assembleerde, heeft geassembleerd) assemble

het **assenstelsel** /ɑsə(n)stɛlsəl/ (pl: -s) co-ordinate system

Assepoester /ɑsəpustər/ Cinderella

assertief /ɑsɛrtif/ (adj) assertive: *~ gedrag* assertive behaviour

de **assertiviteit** /ɑsɛrtivitɛit/ assertiveness

het **assessment** /ɑsɛsmənt/ (pl: -s) assessment

de **assessor** /ɑsɛsɔr/ (pl: -s) assessor

de **assisen** /ɑsizə(n)/: [Belg] *hof van ~* [British] [roughly] Crown Court; [Am] [roughly] District Court

het **assisenproces** /ɑsizə(n)prosɛs/ (pl: -sen) [Belg; law] [roughly] Crown Court proceedings

de **assist** /ɑsɪst/ assist

de **assistent** /ɑsistɛnt/ (pl: -en) assistant, aid, helper: [Belg] *sociaal ~* social worker

de **assistentie** /ɑsistɛnsi/ assistance, aid, help: *~ verlenen* give assistance; *de politie verzocht om ~* the police asked for assistance

assisteren /ɑsisterə(n)/ (assisteerde, heeft geassisteerd) assist, help, aid

de **associatie** /ɑsoʃa(t)si/ (pl: -s) association

associëren /ɑsoʃerə(n)/ (associeerde, heeft geassocieerd) (+ met) associate (with) || *zich ~ met* associate with

het **assortiment** /ɑsɔrtimɛnt/ (pl: -en) assortment, selection: *een ruim* (or: *beperkt*) *~ hebben* have a broad (*or:* limited) assortment

de **assurantie** /ɑsyrɑnsi/ (pl: assurantiën) insurance

de **aster** /ɑstər/ (pl: -s) aster

de **asterisk** /ɑstərɪsk/ (pl: -en) asterisk

het/de **astma** /ɑsma/ asthma: *~ hebben* suffer from (*or:* have) asthma

astmatisch /ɑsmatis/ (adj) asthmatic

de **astrologie** /ɑstroloɣi/ astrology

de **astroloog** /ɑstrolox/ (pl: -logen) astrologer

de **astronaut** /ɑstronɑut/ (pl: -en) astronaut

de **astronomie** /ɑstronomi/ astronomy

plonker, idiot

astronomisch /ɑstronomis/ (adj) **1** astronomical: ~e **kijker** astronomical telescope **2** astronomic(al): ~e **bedragen** astronomic amounts

de **astronoom** /ɑstronom/ (pl: -nomen) astronomer

Aswoensdag /ɑswunzdɑx/ Ash Wednesday

asymmetrisch /ɑsimetris/ (adj, adv) asymmetric(al)

het **at** /ɛt/ at; at-sign

de **atalanta** /ɑtɑlɑnta/ (pl: -'s) [zoology] red admiral

de **ATB** /ɑtebe/ (pl: -'s) ATB *(all-terrain bike)*

atechnisch /ɑtɛxnis/ (adj) untechnical

het **atelier** /ɑtəlje/ (pl: -s) studio; workshop: *werken **op** een ~* work in a studio

Atheens /ɑtens/ (adj) Athenian

het **atheïsme** /ɑtejɪsmə/ atheism

de **atheïst** /ɑtejɪst/ (pl: -en) atheist

Athene /ɑtenə/ Athens

het **atheneum** /ɑtənejvm/ (pl: -s) [Dutch] [roughly] grammar school; [Am] high school: *op het ~ zitten* [roughly] be at grammar school

Atlantisch /ɑtlɑntis/ (adj) Atlantic: *de ~e Oceaan* the Atlantic (Ocean)

de **atlas** /ɑtlɑs/ (pl: -sen) atlas

de **atleet** /ɑtlet/ (pl: atleten) athlete

de **atletiek** /ɑtletik/ athletics

atletisch /ɑtletis/ (adj) athletic

de **atmosfeer** /ɑtmosfer/ (pl: atmosferen) atmosphere; environment: *de hogere* (or: *lagere*) ~ the upper (or: lower) atmosphere

atmosferisch /ɑtmosferis/ (adj) atmospheric: ~e **druk** atmospheric pressure; ~e **storing** static interference, atmospheric disturbance

het **atol** /ɑtol/ (pl: -len) atoll

het **atoom** /ɑtom/ (pl: atomen) atom

de **atoombom** /ɑtombom/ (pl: -men) atom bomb, A-bomb

de **atoomenergie** /ɑtomenɛrʒi/ nuclear (or: atomic) energy (or: power)

het **atoomtijdperk** /ɑtomtɛitpɛrk/ nuclear (or: atomic) age

het **atoomwapen** /ɑtomwapə(n)/ (pl: -s) nuclear (or: atomic) weapon

het **atrium** /ɑtrijvm/ (pl: -s, atria) atrium

de **attaché** /ɑtɑʃe/ (pl: -s) [Belg] ministerial adviser

het/de **attachment** /ətɛtʃmənt/ (pl: -s) [comp] attachment

de **attaque** /ɑtɑk/ (pl: -s) **1** attack **2** stroke: *een ~ krijgen* suffer (or: have) a stroke

het **at-teken** /ɛtekə(n)/ at-sign

attenderen /ɑtɛndərə(n)/ (attendeerde, heeft geattendeerd) point out, draw attention to: *ik attendeer u erop dat ...* I draw your attention to (the fact that) ...

attent /ɑtɛnt/ (adj, adv) **1** attentive: *iem. ~*

maken op iets draw s.o.'s attention to sth. **2** considerate, thoughtful: *hij was altijd heel ~ voor* hen he was always very considerate towards them

de **attentie** /ɑtɛnsi/ (pl: -s) attention, mark of attention; present: *ik heb een kleine ~ meegebracht* I've brought a small present; *ter ~ van* for the attention of

het **attest** /ɑtɛst/ (pl: -en) certificate

de **attractie** /ɑtrɑksi/ (pl: -s) attraction: *zij is de grootste ~ vanavond* she is the main attraction this evening

attractief /ɑtrɑktif/ (adj, adv) attractive, catching

het **attractiepark** /ɑtrɑksipɑrk/ (pl: -en) amusement park

het **attribuut** /ɑtribyt/ (pl: attributen) attribute, characteristic

de **atv** /ɑteve/ *arbeidstijdverkorting* reduction of working hours

au /ɑu/ (int) ow, ouch

a.u.b. /aybe/ *alstublieft* please

de **aubade** /obɑdə/ (pl: -s) aubade: *een ~ brengen* perform an aubade, sing an aubade (to s.o.)

de **aubergine** /obɛrʒinə/ (pl: -s) aubergine, eggplant

de **audiëntie** /ɑud(i)jɛnsi/ (pl: -s) audience: ~ **geven** (or: **verlenen**) grant an audience (to s.o.); *op ~ gaan bij* have an audience with

het **audioboek** /ɑudijobuk/ (pl: -en) audio book

audiovisueel /ɑudijovizywel/ (adj) audiovisual

de **audit** /ɔːdɪt/ audit

de **auditie** /ɑudi(t)si/ (pl: -s) audition, try-out; screen test: *een ~ doen* (do an) audition

auditief /ɑuditif/ (adj, adv) auditive

de ¹**auditor** /ɑuditor/ (pl: -s) auditor

de ²**auditor** /ɑuditor/ (pl: -en) (student) listener

het **auditorium** /ɑuditorijvm/ (pl: auditoria, -s) auditorium

de **augurk** /ɑuɣvrk/ (pl: -en) gherkin

de **augustus** /ɑuɣvstvs/ August

de **aula** /ɑula/ (pl: -'s) great hall, auditorium

de **au pair** /opɛːr/ (pl: -s) au pair

de **aura** /ɑura/ (pl: -'s) aura, charisma: *de ~ van een groot kunstenaar* the aura (or: charisma) of a great artist; *iemands ~ lezen* read s.o.'s aura

het/de **aureool** /ɑurejol/ (pl: aureolen) **1** aureole, aureola, halo **2** [fig] aura: *een ~ van roem* an aura of fame

de **auspiciën** /ɑuspisijə(n)/ (pl) auspices, aegis: *onder ~ van* under the auspices (or: aegis) of, sponsored by

de **ausputzer** /ɑusputsər/ (pl: -s) [sport] sweeper

Australië /ɑustralijə/ Australia

de **Australiër** /ɑustralijər/ (pl: -s) Australian

Australisch /ɑustralis/ (adj) Australian

de **auteur** /autør/ (pl: -s) author, writer

het **auteursrecht** /autørsrɛxt/ (pl: -en) copyright: *overtreding van het* ~ infringement of copyright

de **authenticatie** /autɛntika(t)si/ (pl: -s) authentication

de **authenticiteit** /autɛntisitɛit/ authenticity

authentiek /autɛntik/ (adj) authentic; legitimate; genuine: *een ~e tekst* an authentic text; *een ~ kunstwerk* an original (*or*: authentic) work of art

de **autist** /autɪst/ (pl: -en) autistic person

autistisch /autɪstis/ (adj) autistic

de **auto** /auto/ (pl: -'s) car: *in een ~ rijden* drive, go by car; *het is een uur rijden met de ~* it's an hour's drive by car; *een elektrische ~* an electric car; *een zuinige ~* a fuel-efficient car

de **autoband** /autoband/ (pl: -en) (car) tyre

de **autobiografie** /autobijoɣrafi/ (pl: -ën) autobiography

de **autobom** /autobɔm/ (pl: -men) car bomb

de **autobotsing** /autobotsɪŋ/ (pl: -en) car crash

de **autobus** /autobʏs/ (pl: -sen) bus

de [1]**autochtoon** /autoxton/ (pl: autochtonen) autochthon, indigene, native

[2]**autochtoon** /autoxton/ (adj) autochthonous, indigenous, native

de **autocontrole** /autokontro:lə/ (pl: -s) [Belg] MOT (test) [UK]; (state) motor vehicle inspection [USA]

de **autocoureur** /autokurør/ (pl: -s) racing(-car) driver

de **autocratie** /autokra(t)si/ (pl: -ën) autocracy, dictatorship, autarchy

de **autocue** /autokju/ (pl: -s) autocue; [Am] teleprompter

de **autodidact** /autodidakt/ (pl: -en) autodidact, self-taught person

de **autodiefstal** /autodifstal/ (pl: -len) car theft

het **autogas** /autoɣas/ (pl: -sen) LPG [liquefied petroleum gas]

de **autogordel** /autoɣordəl/ (pl: -s) seat belt, safety belt: *het dragen van ~s is verplicht* the wearing of seat belts is compulsory

de **autohandelaar** /autohandəlar/ (pl: -s, -handelaren) car dealer

de **autokaart** /autokart/ (pl: -en) road map; road atlas

het **autokerkhof** /autokɛrkhɔf/ (pl: -hoven) junkyard, (used) car dump

de **autokeuring** /autokørɪŋ/ (pl: -en) MOT (test); (state) motor vehicle inspection: *verplichte, periodieke* ~ (compulsory, periodical) MOT (test), yearly (motor vehicle) inspection

de **autokraak** /autokrak/ (pl: -kraken) car break-in

autoluw /autolyw/ (adj) low-traffic: *de binnenstad ~ maken* limit (*or*: reduce) traffic in the city centre, make the city centre a low-

traffic area (*or*: zone)

de **automaat** /automat/ (pl: automaten) **1** automaton, robot **2** slot machine, vending machine; ticket machine: *munten in een ~ gooien* feed coins into a slot machine

de **automatenhal** /automatə(n)hal/ (pl: -len) [roughly] amusement arcade

de **automatiek** /automatik/ (pl: -en) automat

automatisch /automatis/ (adj, adv) automatic: *machtiging voor ~e afschrijving* standing order; *een ~e piloot* an automatic pilot, an autopilot; *iets ~ doen* do sth. automatically; ~ *sluitende deuren* self-closing doors

automatiseren /automatizerə(n)/ (automatiseerde, heeft geautomatiseerd) automate, automatize; computerize: *een administratie* ~ computerize an accounting department

de **automatisering** /automatizerɪŋ/ automation, computerization

het **automatisme** /automatɪsmə/ (pl: -n) automatism

de **automobiel** /automobil/ (pl: -en) (motor) car

de **automobilist** /automobilɪst/ (pl: -en) motorist, driver

de **automonteur** /automontør/ (pl: -s) car mechanic

de **autonomie** /autonomi/ autonomy, self-government

autonoom /autonom/ (adj, adv) autonomous

het **auto-ongeluk** /autoɔŋɣəlʏk/ (pl: -ken) car crash, (road) accident: *bij het* ~ *zijn drie mensen gewond geraakt* three people were injured in the car crash

de **autopapieren** /autopapirə(n)/ (pl) car (registration) papers

de **autopech** /autopɛx/ breakdown, car trouble

de **autoped** /autopɛt/ (pl: -s) scooter

de **autopsie** /autopsi/ (pl: -s, -ën) autopsy: ~ *verrichten op* perform an autopsy on

de **autopyromaan** /otopiroman, autopiroman/ (pl: -pyromanen) car arsonist

de **autorace** /autores/ (pl: -s) car race

de **autoradio** /autoradijo/ (pl: -'s) car radio

autorijden /autorɛidə(n)/ (reed auto, heeft autogereden) drive (a car)

de **autorijschool** /autorɛisxol/ (pl: -scholen) driving school

de **autorisatie** /autoriza(t)si/ (pl: -s) authorization, sanction, authority: *de* ~ *van de regering verkrijgen om* be authorized by the government to

autoritair /autoritɛ:r/ (adj, adv) authoritarian

de **autoriteit** /autoritɛit/ (pl: -en) authority: *de plaatselijke ~en* the local government; *een ~ op het gebied van slakken* an authority on snails de **autoruit** /<u>au</u>torœyt/ (pl: -en) car window; windscreen

de **autosnelweg** /<u>au</u>tosnɛlwɛɣ/ (pl: -en) motorway

het **autostoeltje** /<u>o</u>tostulcə, <u>au</u>tostulcə/ (pl: -s) child safety seat

de **autostop** /<u>au</u>tostɔp/: [Belg] ~ *doen* hitchhike

de **autostrade** /<u>au</u>tostradə/ [Belg] motorway

het **autoverkeer** /<u>au</u>tovərker/ car traffic

de **autowasstraat** /<u>au</u>towɑstrat/ automatic car wash

de **autoweg** /<u>au</u>towɛɣ/ (pl: -en) motorway

het **autowrak** /<u>au</u>tovrak/ (pl: -ken) wreck

de **avance** /av<u>ɑ̃</u>sə/ (pl: -s) advance, approach: *~s doen* make advances (*or:* approaches) (to)

de **avenue** /avən<u>y</u>/ (pl: -s) avenue

¹**averechts** /<u>a</u>vərɛxts/ (adj) **1** misplaced, wrong: *een ~e* **uitwerking** *hebben* have a contrary effect, be counter-productive **2** unsound, contrary, wrong

²**averechts** /<u>a</u>vərɛxts/ (adv) **1** back-to-front, inside out, upside down **2** (all) wrong: *het* **valt** *~* **uit** it goes all wrong

de **averij** /avər<u>ɛi</u>/ (pl: -en) damage; average: *zware ~* **oplopen** sustain heavy damage

de **aversie** /av<u>ɛ</u>rsi/ aversion: *een ~ krijgen* **tegen** take an aversion to

de **avg** *aardappelen, vlees, groente* [roughly] meat and two veg

de **AVG** /aveɣ<u>e</u>/ *Algemene Verordening Gegevensbescherming* GDPR *(General Data Protection Regulation)*

de **avocado** /avok<u>a</u>do/ (pl: -'s) avocado

de **avond** /<u>a</u>vɔnt/ (pl: -en) evening, night: *in de* **loop** *van de ~* during the evening; *de* **hele** *~* all evening, the whole evening; *het is zijn* **vrije** *~* it is his night off; *een ~je* **tv** *kijken* (or: *lezen*) spend the evening watching TV (*or:* reading); *een ~je* **uit** a night out, an evening out; *tegen de ~* towards the evening; *de ~* **voor** *de grote wedstrijd* the eve of the big match; *'s ~s* at night, in the evening

het **avondblad** /<u>a</u>vɔndblɑt/ (pl: -en) evening paper

de **avondcursus** /<u>a</u>vɔntkʏrzʏs/ (pl: -sen) evening classes

de **avonddienst** /<u>a</u>vɔndinst/ (pl: -en) evening shift; evening duty: *~* **hebben** be on the evening shift (*or:* duty)

het **avondeten** /<u>a</u>vɔntetə(n)/ dinner, supper, evening meal: *het ~* **klaarmaken** prepare dinner (*or:* supper)

de **avondjurk** /<u>a</u>vɔntjʏrk/ (pl: -en) evening gown (*or:* frock)

de **avondkleding** /<u>a</u>vɔntkledɪŋ/ evening dress (*or:* wear)

de **avondklok** /<u>a</u>vɔntklɔk/ (pl: -ken) curfew

het **Avondland** /<u>a</u>vɔntlɑnt/ Occident

het **avondmaal** /<u>a</u>vɔntmal/ dinner, supper: *het* **Laatste** *Avondmaal* the Last Supper; *het ~* *vieren* celebrate (Holy) Communion

de **avondmens** /<u>a</u>vɔntmɛns/ (pl: -en) night person; night owl

de **avondploeg** /<u>a</u>vɔntpluɣ/ (pl: -en) evening shift, late shift

het **avondrood** /<u>a</u>vɔntrot/ sunset (glow), evening glow, sunset sky

de **avondschool** /<u>a</u>vɔntsxol/ (pl: -scholen) night school; evening classes: *op een ~ zitten* go to night school

de **avondspits** /<u>a</u>vɔntspɪts/ (pl: -en) evening rush-hour

de **avonturier** /avɔntyr<u>i</u>r/ (pl: -s) adventurer, adventuress

het **avontuur** /avɔnt<u>y</u>r/ (pl: avonturen) **1** adventure: *een* **vreemd** *~ beleven* have a strange adventure; *op ~ (uit)gaan* set off on adventures; go solo **2** venture: *niet van avonturen* **houden** not like risky ventures **3** luck, chance: *het* **rad** *van ~* the wheel of fortune

avontuurlijk /avɔnt<u>y</u>rlək/ (adj, adv) **1** adventurous: *~ ingesteld zijn* have an adventurous spirit **2** full of adventure, exciting, adventurous: *een ~e* **vakantie** an exciting holiday

het **avontuurtje** /avɔnt<u>y</u>rcə/ (pl: -s) affair: *een ~* **hebben** *met …* have an affair with …

het **axioma** /ɑks(i)j<u>o</u>ma/ (pl: -'s) axiom

de **ayatollah** /ajɑt<u>ɔ</u>la/ (pl: -s) ayatollah

het **AZ** /az<u>ɛt</u>/ (pl: AZ's) [Belg] *Algemeen/Academisch Ziekenhuis* University Hospital, General Hospital

de **azalea** /az<u>a</u>leja/ (pl: -'s) azalea

het **azc** (pl: -'s) *asielzoekerscentrum* asylum seekers' centre, refugee centre

azen /<u>a</u>zə(n)/ (aasde, heeft geaasd) have one's eye (on)

de **Azerbeidzjaan** /ɑzɛrbɛidʒ<u>a</u>n/ (pl: Azerbeidzjanen) Azerbaijani

Azerbeidzjaans /ɑzɛrbɛidʒ<u>a</u>ns/ (adj) Azerbaijani

het **Azerbeidzjan** /ɑzɛrbɛidʒ<u>ɑ</u>n/ Azerbaijan

de **Azeri** /az<u>e</u>ri/ (pl: -'s) Azeri

de **Aziaat** /azij<u>a</u>t/ (pl: Aziaten) Asian

Aziatisch /azij<u>a</u>tis/ (adj) Asian

Azië /<u>a</u>zijə/ Asia

de **azijn** /az<u>ɛi</u>n/ (pl: -en) vinegar

het **azijnzuur** /az<u>ɛi</u>nzyr/ acetic acid

de **Azoren** /az<u>o</u>rə(n)/ (pl) Azores

de **Azteken** /ɑst<u>e</u>kə(n)/ (pl) Aztecs

het **azuur** /az<u>y</u>r/ azure

b

de **b** /be/ (pl: b's) b; B ‖ *wie a zegt, moet ook b zeggen* in for a penny, in for a pound

de **¹BA** *bachelor of arts* BA *(Bachelor of Arts)*

de **²BA** [Belg] *Burgerlijke Aansprakelijkheid* civil liability, (legal) liability, liability in law

de **baai** /baj/ (pl: -en) bay; [small] cove; inlet

de **baal** /bal/ (pl: balen) bag, sack; bale: *een ~ katoen* a bale of cotton

de **baaldag** /baldɑx/ (pl: -en) off-day

de **baan** /ban/ (pl: banen) **1** job: *een vaste ~ hebben* have a permanent job; [euph] *tussen twee banen zitten* be between jobs **2** path; lane: *iets op de lange ~ schuiven* shelve sth. **3** [sport] track; court; rink; speed-skating track; course: *starten in ~ drie* start in lane three **4** orbit: *een ~ om de aarde maken* orbit the earth

baanbrekend /banbrekənt/ (adj) pioneering, groundbreaking, pathbreaking: *~ werk verrichten* do pioneering work, break new ground

het **baanvak** /banvɑk/ (pl: -ken) **1** section (of track) **2** [Belg] (traffic) lane

de **baar** /bar/ **1** litter, stretcher **2** ingot, bar: *een ~ goud* a gold bar (*or:* ingot)

de **baard** /bart/ (pl: -en) beard: *hij krijgt de ~ in de keel* his voice is breaking; *zijn ~ laten staan* grow a beard

de **baarmoeder** /barmudər/ (pl: -s) womb

de **baars** /bars/ (pl: baarzen) perch, bass

de **baas** /bas/ (pl: bazen) **1** boss: *de situatie de ~ zijn* be in control of the situation; *je hebt altijd ~ boven ~* there's always s.o. bigger,better, …, there's always a bigger fish **2** boss, owner: *eigen ~ zijn* be one's own boss (*or:* master)

de **baat** /bat/ (pl: baten) **1** benefit, advantage: *~ hebben bij* benefit from, obtain relief from **2** profit(s), benefit ‖ *de gelegenheid te ~ nemen* take (*or:* seize) the opportunity

de **babbel** /bɑbəl/ (pl: -s) chat: *hij heeft een vlotte ~* he's a smooth talker

babbelen /bɑbələ(n)/ (babbelde, heeft gebabbeld) chatter, chat

de **babe** /beb/ babe

de **baby** /bebi/ (pl: -'s) baby: *een te vroeg geboren ~* a premature baby

het **babybedje** /bebibɛcə/ (baby's) cot

de **babyboom** /bebibu:m/ baby boom

de **babyboomer** /bebibu:mər/ baby boomer

de **babyface** /bebifes/ baby face

de **babyfoon** /bebifon/ (pl: -s) baby alarm

de **babysit** /bebisɪt/ (pl: -s) babysitter

babysitten /bebisɪtə(n)/ (babysitte, heeft gebabysit) babysit

de **babyverzorgingsruimte** /bebivərzɔrxɪŋsrœymtə/ (pl: -n, -s) baby care room

het **babyvet** /bebivɛt/ baby fat

de **bachelor** /bɛtʃələr/ (pl: -s) **1** bachelor's degree: *~ zijn* hold (*or:* have) a bachelor's degree; *zijn ~ hebben* hold (*or:* have) a bachelor's degree; *zijn ~ halen* get one's bachelor's degree **2** bachelor's degree course (*or:* program): *zijn ~ doen* do one's bachelor's, study for one's bachelor's degree

de **bacheloropleiding** /bɛtʃələrɔplɛidɪŋ/ (pl: -en) bachelor's degree course (*or:* program)

de **bacil** /bɑsɪl/ (pl: -len) bacillus, bacterium, germ; bug

de **back** /bɛk/ (pl: -s) back

de **backhand** /bɛkhɛnt/ [tennis] backhand(er), backhand stroke

de **backpacker** /bɛkpɛkər/ (pl: -s) backpacker

de **backslash** /bɛkslɛʃ/ (pl: -es) backslash

de **backspace** /bɛkspes/ backspace (key)

de **back-up** /bɛkʏp/ (pl: -s) backup: *een ~ maken van* make a backup of

het **bacon** /bekən/ bacon

de **bacterie** /bɑkteri/ (pl: bacteriën) bacterium, microbe: *bacteriën* bacteria

bacteriologisch /bɑkterijoloɣis/ (adj) bacteriological, bacterial, microbial

het **bad** /bɑt/ (pl: -en) **1** bath: *een ~ nemen* have a bath **2** pool

de **badeend** /bɑtent/ (pl: -en) rubber duck

¹baden /badə(n)/ (baadde, heeft gebaad) **1** bath; [Am] bathe; (go for a) swim, bathe; take a dip **2** roll (in), wallow (in), swim (in)

²baden /badə(n)/ (baadde, heeft gebaad) bath

de **badgast** /bɑtxɑst/ (pl: -en) seaside visitor, bather

het/de **badge** /bɛdʒ/ (pl: -s) (name) badge, (name) tag; insignia

de **badhanddoek** /bɑthɑnduk/ (pl: -en) bath towel

de **badjas** /bɑtjɑs/ (pl: -sen) (bath)robe, bath(ing) wrap

de **badkamer** /bɑtkamər/ (pl: -s) bathroom

de **badkleding** /bɑtkledɪŋ/ swimwear, bathing wear (*or:* gear)

de **badkuip** /bɑtkœyp/ (pl: -en) bathtub, bath

het **badlaken** /bɑtlakə(n)/ (pl: -s) bath towel (*or:* sheet)

de **badmeester** /bɑtmestər/ (pl: -s) bath superintendent (*or:* attendant), lifeguard

het **badminton** /bɛtmɪntɔn/ badminton

badmintonnen /bɛtmɪntɔnə(n)/ (badmintonde, heeft gebadmintond) play badminton

de **badmuts** /bɑtmʏts/ (pl: -en) bathing (*or:* swimming) cap

het **badpak** /bɑtpɑk/ (pl: -ken) swimsuit, bathing suit

de **badplaats** /bɑtplats/ (pl: -en) seaside resort

de **badstof** /bɑtstɔf/ (pl: -fen) towelling, terry (cloth) (or: towelling)

het **badwater** /bɑtwatər/ bath water

de **bagage** /baɣaʒə/ (pl: -s) **1** luggage **2** intellectual baggage, stock-in-trade

de **bagagedrager** /baɣaʒədraɣər/ (pl: -s) (rear) carrier

de **bagagekluis** /baɣaʒəklœys/ (pl: -kluizen) (luggage) locker

de **bagageruimte** /baɣaʒərœymtə/ (pl: -n, -s) boot; [Am] trunk

het/de **bagatel** /baɣatɛl/ (pl: -len) bagatelle, trifle

bagatelliseren /baɣatɛlizerə(n)/ (bagatelliseerde, heeft gebagatelliseerd) trivialize, play down

de **bagger** /bɑɣər/ (pl: -s) **1** mud; dredgings **2** rubbish, junk

baggeren /bɑɣərə(n)/ (baggerde, heeft gebaggerd) dredge

bah /bɑ/ (int) ugh!, yuck!

de **Bahama's** /bahamas/ (pl) the Bahamas

de **bahco** /bɑko/ (pl: -'s) adjustable spanner

Bahrein /bɑxrɛɪn/ Bahrain, Bahrein

de **Bahreiner** /bɑxrɛɪnər/ (pl: -s) Bahraini

Bahreins /bɑxrɛɪns/ (adj) Bahraini

de **bajes** /bajəs/ [Dutch; inform] can, cooler, jug, stir

de **bajesklant** /bajəsklɑnt/ (pl: -en) [inform] jailbird, lag, con

de **bajonet** /bajɔnɛt/ (pl: -ten) bayonet

de **bak** /bɑk/ (pl: -ken) **1** (storage) bin; cistern; tank; tray; trough; dish; bowl; tray: ~*ken met* **geld** *verdienen* earn loads of money **2** joke **3** can, jug, clink: *de* ~ *in draaien* go down, be put inside, be put locked up **4** cup (of coffee) || *(vol) aan de* ~ *moeten* (have to) pull out all the stops

het **bakbeest** /bɑgbest/ (pl: -en) whopper, monster

het **bakblik** /bɑgblɪk/ (pl: -ken) baking tin, cake tin

het **bakboord** /bɑgbort/ port

de **bakboordzijde** /bɑgbortsɛɪdə/: *aan* ~ on the port side

het **bakeliet**® /bakəlit/ bakelite

het **baken** /bakə(n)/ (pl: -s) [shipp] beacon

de **bakermat** /bakərmɑt/ (pl: -ten) cradle, origin

de **bakfiets** /bɑkfits/ (pl: -en) **1** carrier tricycle **2** delivery bicycle, carrier cycle

de **bakkebaard** /bɑkəbart/ (pl: -en) (side) whiskers; sideboards; muttonchop; muttonchop whisker

bakkeleien /bakəlɛɪjə(n)/ (bakkeleide, heeft gebakkeleid) [inform] squabble, wrangle

bakken /bɑkə(n)/ (bakte, heeft gebakken) **1** bake: *vers gebakken* **brood** freshly-baked bread **2** fry; deep-fry: *friet* ~ deep-fry chips

de **bakker** /bɑkər/ (pl: -s) **1** baker **2** bakery,

baker's shop: *een* **warme** ~ a fresh bakery || *(dat is)* **voor** *de* ~ that's settled (or: fixed)

de **bakkerij** /bakərɛi/ (pl: -en) bakery, baker's shop

het **bakkie** /bɑki/ (pl: -s) [Dutch; inform] **1** rig **2** cup: *zullen we een* ~ *doen?* shall we have a cup of coffee?

het **bakmeel** /bɑkmel/ self-raising flour

de **bakpan** /bɑkpɑn/ (pl: -nen) frying pan

het **bakpapier** /bɑkpapir/ greaseproof paper

de **bakplaat** /bɑkplat/ (pl: bakplaten) baking sheet (or: tray)

het **bakpoeder** /bɑkpudər/ baking powder

de **baksoda** /bɑksoda/ baking soda

de **baksteen** /bɑksten/ (pl: bakstenen) brick: *zinken* **als** *een* ~ sink (or: swim) like a stone; [fig] *iem. laten vallen* **als** *een* ~ drop s.o. like a hot potato, let s.o. down hard

de **bakvorm** /bɑkfɔrm/ (pl: -en) baking tin, cake tin

de **bakwedstrijd** /bɑkwɛtstrɛit/ (pl: -en) bake-off

het **bakzeil** /bɑksɛɪl/: ~ *halen* back down, climb down (from)

de ¹**bal** /bɑl/ (pl: -len) **1** [sport] ball: *iem. de* ~ *toespelen* pass (the ball to s.o.); [fig] *een* ~*letje over iets* **opgooien** put out feelers about sth.; *een* ~ *gehakt* a meatball; [Belg; fig] *de* ~ **misslaan** be wide of the mark; *een* ~*letje* **slaan** hit a ball; [fig] *toen is het* ~*letje gaan* **rollen** then the ball got rolling; *het kan me* **geen** ~ *schelen* I don't give a damn, I couldn't care less; *ik snap er* **geen** ~ *van* I don't get it (at all); *wie* **kaatst** *moet de* ~ *verwachten* those who play at bowls must look out for rubbers; [roughly] *do as you would be done by* **2** ball, nut **3** snob

het ²**bal** /bɑl/ (pl: -s) ball: *gekostumeerd* ~ fancy-dress ball

balanceren /balɑnserə(n)/ (balanceerde, heeft gebalanceerd) balance: ~ *op de rand van de dood* hover between life and death

de **balans** /balɑns/ (pl: -en) **1** balance, equilibrium: *uit zijn* ~ *zijn* be out of balance **2** (pair of) scales; balance **3** balance sheet, audit (report): *de* ~ **opmaken** a) draw up the balance sheet; b) [fig] take stock (of sth.)

de **balanspost** /balɑnspɔst/ (pl: -en) entry in the balance sheet

baldadig /baldadəx/ (adj, adv) rowdy, boisterous

het/de **baldakijn** /baldakɛin/ (pl: -en) canopy, baldachin

de **balein** /balɛin/ (pl: -en) whalebone, rib

de ¹**balen** /balə(n)/ (pl): *de* ~ *hebben* van iets have had (more than) enough of sth., be fed up with sth.

²**balen** /balə(n)/ (baalde, heeft gebaald) be fed up (with), be sick (and tired) (of)

de **balg** /bɑlx/ (pl: -en) bellows

de **balie** /bali/ (pl: -s) **1** counter; desk: *aan de* ~

kunt u alle informatie krijgen you can obtain all the information you need at the desk **2** bar

de **baliemedewerker** /bɑlimedəwɛrkər/ (pl: -s) desk clerk, receptionist

de **balk** /bɑlk/ (pl: -en) beam ‖ *het geld over de ~ gooien* spend money like water

de **Balkan** /bɑlkɑn/ (the) Balkans

balken /bɑlkə(n)/ (balkte, heeft gebalkt) bray

het **balkon** /bɑlkɔn/ (pl: -s) **1** balcony **2** [theatre] balcony, (dress) circle, gallery **3** platform

de **ballad** /bɛlət/ (pl: -s) ballad

de **ballade** /bɑlɑdə/ (pl: -n, -s) ballad

de **ballast** /bɑlɑst/ **1** ballast **2** lumber, dead weight; [of people] dead wood

¹**ballen** /bɑlə(n)/ (balde, heeft gebald) **1** play (with a) ball **2** [Dutch; vulg] fuck, ball

²**ballen** /bɑlə(n)/ (balde, heeft gebald) clench: *de vuist(en) ~* clench one's fist(s)

de **ballenbak** /bɑlə(n)bɑk/ (pl: -ken) ball pit

de **ballenjongen** /bɑlə(n)jɔŋə(n)/ (pl: -s) ball boy

ballerig /bɑlərəx/ (adj) arrogant, loud-mouthed, snooty

de **ballerina** /bɑlərinɑ/ ballerina

het **ballet** /bɑlɛt/ (pl: -ten) ballet: *op ~ zitten* take ballet lessons

de **balletdanser** /bɑlɛtdɑnsər/ (pl: -s) (ballet) dancer

de **balletdanseres** /bɑlɛtdɑnsərɛs/ (pl: -sen) ballet dancer

het **balletje-balletje** /bɑləcəbɑləcə/ shell game

de **balling** /bɑlɪŋ/ (pl: -en) exile

de **ballingschap** /bɑlɪŋsxɑp/ exile, banishment: *in ~ gaan* go into exile

de **ballon** /bɑlɔn/ (pl: -nen) balloon: *een ~ opblazen* blow up a balloon

de **ballpoint** /bɔlpɔjnt/ (pl: -s) ballpoint

balorig /bɑlorəx/ (adj) contrary, refractory, recalcitrant

de **balpen** /bɑlpɛn/ (pl: -nen) ballpoint (pen)

de **balsamicoazijn** /bɑlsɑmikoazɛɪn/ balsamic vinegar

de **balsem** /bɑlsəm/ (pl: -s) balm, balsam, ointment, salve

balsemen /bɑlsəmə(n)/ (balsemde, heeft gebalsemd) embalm, mummify

balsterk /bɑlstɛrk/ (adj) good with the ball: *een ~e spits* a handy striker

Baltisch /bɑltis/ (adj) Baltic: *~e Zee* Baltic (Sea), the Baltic

de **balts** /bɑlts/ display, courtship

de **balustrade** /bɑlystrɑdə/ (pl: -s) balustrade, railing; banister(s)

de **balzaal** /bɑlzal/ (pl: balzalen) ballroom

de **balzak** /bɑlzɑk/ (pl: -ken) scrotum, bag

de **bamastructuur** /bɑmastrʏktyr/ two-cycle university system

het/de ¹**bamboe** /bɑmbu/ bamboo

²**bamboe** /bɑmbu/ (adj) bamboo

de **bami** /bɑmi/ chow mein: *~ goreng* chow mein, fried noodles

het **bammetje** /bɑməcə/ (pl: -s) sandwich

de **ban** /bɑn/ (pl: -nen) **1** excommunication, ban: *in de ~ doen* (put under the) ban, outlaw **2** spell, fascination: *in de ~ van iets raken* fall under the spell of sth.

banaal /bɑnal/ (adj, adv) banal, trite

de **banaan** /bɑnan/ (pl: bananen) banana

de **banaliteit** /bɑnalitɛit/ (pl: -en) platitude, cliché

de **bananenschil** /bɑnanə(n)sxɪl/ (pl: -len) banana peel (*or*: skin): *uitglijden over een ~* slip on a banana skin

bancair /bɑŋkɛːr/ (adj) bank(ing), in (*or*: of, through) the bank(s): *~ geldverkeer* monetary exchange via the banks

de ¹**band** /bɑnt/ (pl: -en) **1** tape: *een ~ afspelen* play a tape back; *iets op de ~ opnemen* tape sth. **2** band, ribbon, tape; [martial arts] belt: *zwarte ~* black belt **3** tyre: *een lekke ~* a flat tyre, a puncture **4** conveyor (belt): *de lopende ~* the conveyor belt **5** tie, bond, link: *~en met China aanhalen* strengthen ties with China, seek closer relations with China; *~en van vriendschap* ties of friendship **6** (wave)band, wave **7** cushion, bank ‖ *aan de lopende ~ doelpunten scoren* pile on scores; *uit de ~ springen* get out of hand; *iets aan ~en leggen* check, curb, restrain sth.

de ²**band** /bɛnt/ (pl: -en) band, orchestra; group; combo

het ³**band** /bɑnt/ (pl: -en) tape; ribbon; string; band

de **bandage** /bɑndaʒə/ (pl: -s) bandage

bandeloos /bɑndəlos/ (adj) lawless; undisciplined; wild

de **bandenlichter** /bɑndə(n)lɪxtər/ (pl: -s) tyre lever

de **bandenpech** /bɑndə(n)pɛx/ tyre trouble; flat (tyre); puncture

de **bandiet** /bɑndit/ (pl: -en) **1** bandit; brigand **2** hooligan

het **bandje** /bɑncə/ (pl: -s) **1** band, strip, ribbon, string **2** tape **3** tape recording **4** strap

de **bandleider** /bɛntlɛidər/ (pl: -s) bandleader

de **bandopname** /bɑntopnamə/ (pl: -n, -s) tape recording

de **bandrecorder** /bɑntrikɔːrdər/ (pl: -s) tape recorder

banen /banə(n)/ (baande, heeft gebaand): *zich een weg ~* work (*or*: edge) one's way through; *gebaande wegen* beaten track(s)

bang /bɑŋ/ (adj) **1** afraid (of), frightened (of), scared (of); terrified (of): *~ in het donker* afraid of the dark; *~ maken* scare, frighten **2** frightening, anxious, scary **3** timid, fearful **4** afraid, anxious: *ik ben ~ dat het niet lukt* I'm afraid it won't work; *wees daar maar niet ~ voor* don't worry about it

bangelijk /bɑŋələk/ (adj) timid, fearful,

chicken-hearted: ~ *zijn* be a nervous type, be easily frightened

de **bangerd** /bɑŋərt/ (pl: -s) [Dutch] coward, chicken

Bangladesh /bɑŋlɑdɛʃ/ Bangladesh

de **banier** /banir/ (pl: -en) banner

de **banjo** /bɑnjo/ (pl: -'s) banjo

de **bank** /bɑŋk/ (pl: -en) **1** bench; couch; settee, sofa; seat **2** bank: *geld op* de ~ *hebben* have money in the bank **3** desk **4** pew **5** bank, shoal ‖ *door* de ~ *(genomen)* on average

het **bankafschrift** /bɑŋkɑfsχrɪft/ bank statement

het **bankbiljet** /bɑŋkbɪljɛt/ (pl: -ten) (bank)-note; paper currency

de **bankemployé** /bɑŋkɑmplwaje/ (pl: -s) bank employee

het **banket** /bɑŋkɛt/ (pl: -ten) **1** banquet, feast **2** [roughly] (almond) pastry

de **banketbakker** /bɑŋkɛdbɑkər/ (pl: -s) confectioner, pastry-cook

de **banketbakkerij** /bɑŋkɛdbɑkərɛi/ (pl: -en) confectionery, patisserie, confectioner's (shop)

de **banketletter** /bɑŋkɛtlɛtər/ (pl: -s) (almond) pastry letter

het **bankgeheim** /bɑŋkχəhɛɪm/ bank(ing) secrecy

de **bankhanger** /bɑŋkhɑŋər/ (pl: -s) couch potato

de **bankier** /bɑŋkir/ (pl: -s) banker

het **bankje** /bɑŋkjə/ (pl: -s) bench; stool, footrest

de **bankkaart** /bɑŋkart/ (pl: -en) [Belg] bank(er's) card

de **bankkluis** /bɑŋklœys/ (pl: -kluizen) bank vault (*or:* strongroom); [for client] safe-deposit box

de **bankoverval** /bɑŋkovərvɑl/ (pl: -len) bank hold-up, bank robbery

de **bankpas** /bɑŋkpɑs/ (pl: -sen) [Dutch] bank(er's) card

de **bankrekening** /bɑŋkrekənɪŋ/ (pl: -en) bank account: *een ~ openen bij een bank* open an account with a bank

het **¹bankroet** /bɑŋkrut/ (pl: -en) bankruptcy

²bankroet /bɑŋkrut/ (adj) bankrupt, broke; bust: ~ *gaan* go bankrupt; (go) bust

de **bankroof** /bɑŋkrof/ bank robbery

de **bankschroef** /bɑŋksχruf/ (pl: -schroeven) vice

het **bankstel** /bɑŋkstɛl/ (pl: -len) lounge suite

de **bankwerker** /bɑŋkwɛrkər/ (pl: -s) (bench) fitter, benchman

de **banneling** /bɑnəlɪŋ/ (pl: -en) exile

¹bannen /bɑnə(n)/ (bande, heeft gebannen) exile (from), expel (from); [esp fig] banish: *ban de bom* ban the bomb; *iets uit zijn geheugen* ~ efface sth. from one's memory

²bannen /bɛnə(n)/ (bande, heeft geband) [media] ban (from), block access (to)

de **banner** /bɛnər/ (pl: -s) banner

het **bantamgewicht** /bɑntɑmɣəwɪχt/ bantam-(weight)

de **bapao** /bɑpɑu/ Chinese steamed bread

de **¹bar** /bɑr/ (pl: -s) bar: *aan* de ~ *zitten* sit at the bar; *wie staat er achter de ~?* who's behind the bar?; *hakkenbar* heel bar

²bar /bɑr/ (adj) **1** barren **2** severe: ~ *weer* severe weather **3** rough, gross: *jij maakt het wat al te* ~ you are carrying things too far ‖ ~ *en boos* really dreadful

³bar /bɑr/ (adv) extremely, awfully

de **barak** /bɑrɑk/ (pl: -ken) shed, hut; barracks

de **barbaar** /bɑrbar/ (pl: barbaren) barbarian

barbaars /bɑrbars/ (adj, adv) barbarian, barbarous; barbaric; savage

de **Barbadaan** /bɑrbadan/ (pl: Barbadanen) Barbadian

Barbados /bɑrbedɔs/ Barbados

de **barbecue** /bɑːrbəkju/ (pl: -s) barbecue (party)

barbecueën /bɑːrbəkjuwə(n)/ (barbecue-de, heeft gebarbecued) barbecue

de **barbediende** /bɑrbədində/ (pl: -n, -s) barman, barwoman

de **barcode** /bɑrkodə/ (pl: -s) bar code

de **bareel** /bɑrel/ (pl: barelen) [Belg] barrier

het **barema** /bɑrema/ (pl: -'s) [Belg] wage scale, salary scale

baren /bɑrə(n)/ (baarde, heeft gebaard) bear, give birth to

de **barensnood** /bɑrə(n)snot/ labour: *in ~ verkeren* be in labour; [also hum] be in travail, labour

de **baret** /bɑrɛt/ (pl: -ten) beret, (academic) cap

het **¹Bargoens** /bɑrɣuns/ **1** (thieves') slang, argot **2** jargon

²Bargoens /bɑrɣuns/ (adj) slangy

de **bariton** /bɑriton/ (pl: -s) baritone (singer)

de **barjuffrouw** /bɑrjvfrɑu/ (pl: -en) barmaid

de **barkeeper** /bɑrkipər/ (pl: -s) barman

de **barkruk** /bɑrkrvk/ (pl: -ken) bar stool

barmhartig /bɑrmhɑrtəχ/ (adj, adv) merciful, charitable: *de ~e Samaritaan* the Good Samaritan

de **barmhartigheid** /bɑrmhɑrtəχhɛit/ mercy, clemency; charity

de **bar mitswa** /bɑrmɪtswa/ (pl: -'s) bar mitzvah

het/de **¹barok** /bɑrɔk/ baroque

²barok /bɑrɔk/ (adj) baroque

de **barometer** /bɑrometər/ (pl: -s) barometer: *de ~ staat op mooi weer* (or: *storm*) **a)** the barometer is set fair (*or:* is pointing to storm); **b)** [fig] things are looking good (*or:* bad)

de **baron** /bɑrɔn/ (pl: -nen) baron: *meneer de* ~ his (*or:* your) Lordship

de **barones** /bɑrɔnɛs/ (pl: -sen) baroness

de **barrage** /bɑraʒə/ (pl: -s) [sport] decider, play-off

de **barricade** /bɑrikadə/ (pl: -n) **1** barricade: *voor iets op de* ~ *gaan staan* [fig] fight on the

barricades for sth.; ~n **opwerpen** raise (or: throw up) barricades **2** [fig] barrier
barricaderen /barikad̲e̲rə(n)/ (barricadeerde, heeft gebarricadeerd) barricade; bar

de **barrière** /barij̲ɛːrə/ (pl: -s) barrier: een onoverkomelijke ~ an insurmountable barrier
bars /bars/ (adj, adv) stern, grim; forbidding; harsh

de **barst** /barst/ (pl: -en) crack; chap: er komen ~en in it is cracking ‖ ik geloof er **geen** ~ van I'm not buying that, I don't believe a single word of it
barsten /b̲a̲rstə(n)/ (barstte, is gebarsten) **1** crack, split; burst [also fig]; chapped **2** burst, explode ‖ het barst hier van de cafés the place is full of pubs; [inform] iem. **laten** ~ leave s.o. in the lurch; [inform] zich **te** ~ eten eat till one bursts; [fig] barst! damn!, go to hell!

de **bas** /bas/ (pl: -sen) **1** bass (singer, player); basso **2** double bass, (contra)bass: ~ **spelen** play the bass **3** bass (guitar)
basaal /baza̲l/ (adj) basal, fundamental, basic

het **basalt** /baz̲a̲lt/ basalt

de **¹base** /b̲a̲zə/ (pl: -n) base

de **²base** /bes/ free-base cocaine

het **baseball** /b̲e̲zbɔːl/ baseball
baseballen /b̲e̲zbɔlə(n)/ (baseballde, heeft gebaseballd) play baseball
¹baseren /baze̲rə(n)/ (baseerde, heeft gebaseerd) base (on), found (on)

zich **²baseren** /baze̲rə(n)/ (baseerde zich, heeft zich gebaseerd) base o.s. on, go on: we hadden niets om ons **op** te ~ we had nothing to go on

de **basgitaar** /b̲a̲sχitar/ (pl: basgitaren) bass (guitar)

het **basilicum** /baz̲i̲likʏm/ basil

de **basiliek** /bazil̲i̲k/ (pl: -en) basilica

de **basis** /b̲a̲zɪs/ (pl: bases) **1** basis, foundation: de ~ **leggen** voor iets lay the foundation of sth. **2** base, basis

de **basisbeurs** /b̲a̲zɪzbørs/ (pl: -beurzen) [Dutch] basic grant
basisch /b̲a̲zis/ (adj, adv) alkaline, basic: ~ **reageren** give (or: show) an alkaline reaction; ~e **zouten** basic salts

de **basiscursus** /b̲a̲zɪskʏrzʏs/ (pl: -sen) basic course, elementary course

het **basisinkomen** /b̲a̲zɪsɪŋkomə(n)/ (pl: -s) **1** guaranteed minimum income **2** basic income

het **basiskamp** /b̲a̲zɪskamp/ (pl: -en) base camp

het **basisonderwijs** /b̲a̲zɪsɔndərwɛis/ primary education

de **basisopstelling** /b̲a̲zɪsɔpstɛlɪŋ/ (pl: -en) (the team's) starting line-up

de **basisoptie** /b̲a̲zɪsɔpsi/ (pl: -s) [Belg] orientation subjects

de **basisschool** /b̲a̲zɪsχol/ (pl: -scholen) primary school

de **basisverzekering** /b̲a̲zɪsfərzekərɪŋ/ (pl: -en) basic (health) insurance (or: policy)

de **basisvorming** /b̲a̲zɪsfɔrmɪŋ/ [Dutch] basic (secondary school) curriculum

de **Bask** /bask/ (pl: -en) Basque
Baskenland /b̲a̲skə(n)lɑnt/ the Basque Country

de **¹basketbal** /b̲a̲ːskədbɑl/ (pl: -len) basketball

het **²basketbal** /b̲a̲ːskədbɑl/ basketball
basketballen /b̲a̲ːskədbɑlə(n)/ (basketbalde, heeft gebasketbald) play basketball

het **Baskisch** /b̲a̲skis/ Basque

het **bassin** /bas̲ɛ̲/ (pl: -s) **1** (swimming) pool **2** basin

de **bassist** /bas̲ɪ̲st/ (pl: -en) bass player

de **bassleutel** /b̲a̲ssløtəl/ (pl: -s) bass clef, F clef

de **bast** /bast/ (pl: -en) **1** bark; husk **2** [inform] skin, hide
basta /b̲a̲sta/ (int) stop!, enough!: en daarmee ~! and there's an end to it!

de **bastaard** /b̲a̲start/ (pl: -s) **1** bastard **2** mongrel, cross-breed **3** hybrid, cross(-breed)

de **basterdsuiker** /b̲a̲stərtsœykər/ soft brown sugar

het **bastion** /bastijɔn/ (pl: -s) bastion

het **bat** /bɛt/ (pl: -s) bat

het **bataljon** /bataljɔn/ (pl: -s) battalion

de **Batavier** /batav̲i̲r/ (pl: -en) Batavian

de **batch** /bɛtʃ/ (pl: -es) batch

de **bate** /b̲a̲tə/: ten ~ van for the benefit of
baten /b̲a̲tə(n)/ (baatte, heeft gebaat) avail: wij zouden **erbij** gebaat zijn it would be very helpful to us; baat het **niet,** dan schaadt het niet no harm in trying
batig /b̲a̲təχ/ (adj): ~ **saldo** surplus, credit balance
batikken /b̲a̲tɪkə(n)/ (batikte, heeft gebatikt) batik: gebatikte **stoffen** batiks

het **batje** /b̲ɛ̲cə/ bat

de **batterij** /batər̲ɛ̲i/ (pl: -en) battery: lege ~ dead battery; de ~ is **leeg a)** the battery is dead; **b)** [fig] he/she has run out of steam; de ~ **opladen a)** charge (up) the battery; **b)** [fig] charge one's batteries

de **batterijauto** /batərɛi̲a̲uto/ (pl: -'s) electric car

de **batterijlader** /batərɛi̲l̲adər/ battery charger

het **bauxiet** /bɔuks̲i̲t/ bauxite

de **baviaan** /bavij̲a̲n/ (pl: bavianen) baboon

de **baxter** /b̲ɛ̲kstər/ (pl: -s) [Belg; med] drip

de **bazaar** /baz̲a̲r/ (pl: -s) bazaar; (fancy)fair
bazelen /b̲a̲zələ(n)/ (bazelde, heeft gebazeld) drivel (on), waffle
bazig /b̲a̲zəχ/ (adj, adv) overbearing, domineering, bossy

de **bazin** /baz̲ɪ̲n/ (pl: -nen) **1** mistress **2** lady of the house

de **bb** [Dutch] basisberoepsgerichte leerweg

pre-vocational secondary education

het **beachvolleybal** /biːtʃfɔlibɑl/ beach volleyball

beademen /bəademə(n)/ (beademde,
heeft beademd) **1** breathe air into **2** apply
artificial respiration to

de **beademing** /bəademɪŋ/ (pl: -en) **1** breathing of air into **2** artificial respiration: *aan de ~
liggen* be on a ventilator

de **beambte** /bəɑmtə/ (pl: -n, -s) functionary,
(junior) official

beamen /bəamə(n)/ (beaamde, heeft be-
aamd) endorse; agree (with): *een bewering ~*
endorse a claim

de **beamer** /biːmər/ data projector

beangstigen /bəɑŋstəɣə(n)/ (beangstigde,
heeft beangstigd) alarm; frighten

¹**beantwoorden** /bəɑntwɔrdə(n)/ (beant-
woordde, heeft beantwoord) answer, meet,
comply with: *aan al de vereisten ~* meet all the
requirements; *niet ~ aan de verwachtingen* fall
short of expectations

²**beantwoorden** /bəɑntwɔrdə(n)/ (beant-
woordde, heeft beantwoord) answer; reply
to

beargumenteren /bəɑryymɛntərə(n)/ (be-
argumenteerde, heeft beargumenteerd)
substantiate: *zijn standpunt kunnen ~* be able
to substantiate one's point of view

de **beat** /biːt/ (pl: -s) beat

de **beatbox** /biːdbɔks/ (pl: -en) beatbox

de **beauty** /bjuːti/ (pl: -'s) beauty: *een ~ van een
doelpunt* a lovely (*or:* beautiful) goal, a beauty

de **beautycase** /bjuːtikes/ (pl: -s) vanity case

bebloed /bəblut/ (adj) bloody, blood-
stained: *zijn gezicht was geheel ~* his face was
completely covered in blood

beboeten /bəbutə(n)/ (beboette, heeft beboet) fine: *beboet worden* be fined, incur a
fine; *iem. ~ met 100 euro* fine s.o. 100 euros

bebossen /bəbɔsə(n)/ (beboste, heeft bebost) (af)forest: *bebost terrein* woodland

bebouwd /bəbɑut/ (adj) built-on: *de ~e
kom* the built-up area

bebouwen /bəbɑuwə(n)/ (bebouwde,
heeft bebouwd) **1** build on **2** cultivate, farm:
de grond ~ cultivate the land

de **bebouwing** /bəbɑuwɪŋ/ (pl: -en) buildings:
[Belg] *halfopen ~* semidetached house

becijferen /bəsɛifərə(n)/ (becijferde, heeft
becijferd) calculate; compute; estimate: *de
schade valt niet te ~* it is impossible to calculate the damage

becommentariëren /bəkɔmɛntarijərə(n)/
(becommentarieerde, heeft becommentari-
eerd) comment (on)

beconcurreren /bəkɔŋkyrərə(n)/ (becon-
curreerde, heeft beconcurreerd) compete
with: *de banken ~ elkaar scherp* there is fierce
competition among the banks

het **bed** /bɛt/ (pl: -den) bed: *het ~ (moeten) houden* be confined to bed; *haar ~je is gespreid*
she has got it made; *het ~ opmaken* make
the bed; *naar ~ gaan* go to bed; *naar ~ gaan
met iem.* go to bed with s.o.; *hij gaat ermee
naar ~ en staat er weer mee op* he can't stop
thinking about it; *dat is ver van mijn ~* that
does not concern me; *een ~ rozen* a bed of
roses

bedaard /bədart/ (adj, adv) **1** composed,
collected **2** calm, quiet: *~ optreden* act calmly

bedacht /bədɑxt/ (adj) prepared (for): *op
zoveel verzet waren ze niet ~ geweest* they had
not bargained for so much resistance

bedachtzaam /bədɑxtsam/ (adj, adv) cautious, circumspect; deliberate: *heel ~ te werk
gaan* set about sth. with great caution

de **bedankbrief** /bədɑŋgbrif/ (pl: -brieven)
letter of thanks

¹**bedanken** /bədɑŋkə(n)/ (bedankte, heeft
bedankt) decline, refuse

²**bedanken** /bədɑŋkə(n)/ (bedankte, heeft
bedankt) thank: *iem. voor iets ~* thank s.o. for
sth.; *je wordt bedankt!* thanks a million!,
thank you very much!

het **bedankje** /bədɑŋkjə/ (pl: -s) thank-you; letter of thanks; word of thanks: *er kon nauwelijks een ~ af!* (and) small thanks I got (for it)!

bedankt /bədɑŋkt/ (int) thanks: *reuze ~*
thanks a lot

bedaren /bədarə(n)/ (bedaarde, heeft bedaard) quiet down, calm down: *iem. tot ~
brengen* calm (*or:* quieten) s.o. down

de **bed-bad-broodvoorziening** /bɛdbɑd-
brotforzinɪŋ/ [Dutch] basic food and shelter

het **beddengoed** /bɛdə(n)ɣut/ (bed)clothes,
bedding

de **beddensprei** /bɛdə(n)sprɛi/ (pl: -en) bedspread

de **bedding** /bɛdɪŋ/ (pl: -en) bed, channel

bedeesd /bədest/ (adj) shy, diffident, timid

bedekken /bədɛkə(n)/ (bedekte, heeft bedekt) cover; cover up; cover over: *geheel ~
met iets* cover in sth.

de **bedekking** /bədɛkɪŋ/ (pl: -en) cover(ing)

bedekt /bədɛkt/ (adj) **1** covered; overcast
2 covert: *in ~e termen* in guarded terms

de **bedelaar** /bedəlar/ (pl: -s) beggar

de **bedelarij** /bedəlarɛi/ begging

de **bedelarmband** /bedəlarmbɑnt/ (pl: -en)
charm bracelet

de **bedelbrief** /bedəlbrif/ (pl: -brieven) beg-
ging-letter

bedelen /bedələ(n)/ (bedelde, heeft gebe-
deld) beg (for)

de **bedelstaf** /bedəlstɑf/: *aan de ~ raken* be reduced to beggary, be left a pauper

het **bedeltje** /bedəltʃə/ (pl: -s) charm

bedelven /bədɛlvə(n)/ (bedolf, heeft bedolven) bury; [fig also] swamp: *zij werden*

door het **puin** bedolven they were buried under the rubble

bedenkelijk /bədɛŋkələk/ (adj, adv) **1** worrying; dubious; questionable; serious: *een ~ geval* a worrying (*or:* serious) case **2** doubtful, dubious: *een ~ gezicht* a doubtful (*or:* serious) face

¹**bedenken** /bədɛŋkə(n)/ (bedacht, heeft bedacht) **1** think (about), consider: *als je bedenkt, dat ...* considering (*or:* bearing in mind) (that) ... **2** think of, think up, invent, devise

zich ²**bedenken** /bədɛŋkə(n)/ (bedacht zich, heeft zich bedacht) **1** think (about), consider: *zij zal zich wel tweemaal ~ voordat ...* she'll think twice before ...; *zonder zich te ~* without a moment's thought **2** change one's mind, have second thoughts: *ze heeft zich bedacht* she changed her mind

de **bedenking** /bədɛŋkɪŋ/ (pl: -en) objection: *~en hebben tegen iets* have objections to sth.

het **bedenksel** /bədɛŋksəl/ (pl: -s) fabrication

de **bedenktijd** /bədɛŋktɛit/ time for reflection: *hij kreeg drie dagen ~* he was given three days to think (the matter over) (*or:* to consider (the matter))

het **bederf** /bədɛrf/ decay, rot

bederfelijk /bədɛrfələk/ (adj) perishable: *~e goederen* perishables

¹**bederven** /bədɛrvə(n)/ (bedierf, is bedorven) decay, rot

²**bederven** /bədɛrvə(n)/ (bedierf, heeft bedorven) spoil: *die jurk is totaal bedorven* that dress is completely ruined; *iemands plezier ~* spoil s.o.'s fun

de **bedevaart** /bedəvart/ (pl: -en) pilgrimage: *een ~ doen* make (*or:* go) on a pilgrimage

de **bedevaartganger** /bedəvartxɑŋər/ (pl: -s) pilgrim

het **bedevaartsoord** /bedəvartsort/ (pl: -en) place of pilgrimage

de **bediende** /bədində/ (pl: -n, -s) **1** employee; clerk; assistant; attendant: *jongste ~* **a)** office junior; **b)** dogsbody **2** servant: *eerste ~* butler **3** [Belg] official

¹**bedienen** /bədinə(n)/ (bediende, heeft bediend) **1** serve: *iem. op zijn wenken ~* wait on s.o. hand and foot; *aan tafel ~* wait at (the) table **2** operate

zich ²**bedienen** /bədinə(n)/ (bediende zich, heeft zich bediend) use, make use of

de **bediening** /bədinɪŋ/ (pl: -en) **1** service: *al onze prijzen zijn inclusief ~* all prices include service (charges) **2** operation: *de ~ van een apparaat* the operation of a machine

het **bedieningspaneel** /bədinɪŋspanel/ (pl: -panelen) control panel; dash(board); [comp] console

het **beding** /bədɪŋ/ (pl: -en) condition, stipulation: *onder geen ~* under no circumstances

bedingen /bədɪŋə(n)/ (bedong, heeft be-

dongen) stipulate (for, that); insist on; require; agree (on)

bedisselen /bədɪsələ(n)/ (bedisselde, heeft bedisseld) fix (up), arrange

het **bedlampje** /bɛtlɑmpjə/ (pl: -s) bedside lamp, bedhead light

bedlegerig /bɛtleɣərəx/ (adj) ill in bed; bedridden

de **bedoeïen** /beduwin/ (pl: -en) Bedouin

bedoelen /bədulə(n)/ (bedoelde, heeft bedoeld) mean, intend: *wat bedoel je?* what do you mean?; *het was goed bedoeld* it was meant well (*or:* well meant); *~ met* mean by

de **bedoeling** /bədulɪŋ/ (pl: -en) **1** intention, aim, purpose, object: *dat was niet de ~* that was not intended (*or:* the intention); *met de ~ om te ...* with a view to (...ing); *hij zei dat zonder kwade ~en* he meant no harm by saying that **2** meaning; drift

de **bedoening** /bədunɪŋ/ (pl: -en) to-do, job, fuss: *het was een hele ~* it was quite a business

bedolven /bədɔlvə(n)/ (adj) **1** covered (with) **2** snowed under (with), swamped (with): *~ onder het werk* snowed under with work, up to one's ears in work

bedompt /bədɔmt/ (adj) stuffy; close; airless; stale: *een ~e atmosfeer* a stuffy atmosphere

bedonderen /bədɔndərə(n)/ (bedonderde, heeft bedonderd) [inform] cheat (on), trick, do (in the eye): *de kluit ~* take everybody for a ride

bedorven /bədɔrvə(n)/ (adj) bad, off; [fig] spoilt: *de melk is ~* the milk has gone off

bedotten /bədɔtə(n)/ (bedotte, heeft bedot) fool, take in

de **bedpartner** /bɛtpɑrtnər/ (pl: -s) bed partner

bedplassen /bɛtplɑsə(n)/ bed-wetting

de **bedrading** /bədradɪŋ/ (pl: -en) wiring, circuit

het **bedrag** /bədrɑx/ (pl: -en) amount, sum: *openstaand ~* unpaid amount; *een groot ~* a large amount (*or:* sum); *een klein ~* a small amount (*or:* sum); *een ~ ineens* a lump sum; *een rond ~* a round sum

bedragen /bədraɣə(n)/ (bedroeg, heeft bedragen) amount to; number; come to be

bedreigen /bədrɛiɣə(n)/ (bedreigde, heeft bedreigd) threaten: *bedreigde (dier- of planten)soorten* endangered species

de **bedreiging** /bədrɛiɣɪŋ/ (pl: -en) threat: *onder ~ van een vuurwapen* at gunpoint

bedreven /bədrevə(n)/ (adj) adept (at, in); skilled (in); skilful (in); (well-)versed (in): *niet ~ zijn in iets* lack experience in sth.

bedriegen /bədriɣə(n)/ (bedroog, heeft bedrogen) deceive, cheat; swindle: *als mijn ogen me niet ~* if my eyes do not deceive me; *hij bedriegt zijn vrouw* he cheats on his wife

bedwelmen

de **bedrieger** /bədriɣər/ (pl: -s) cheat, fraud, impostor; swindler

bedrieglijk /bədrixlək/ (adj, adv) deceptive, false; deceitful; fraudulent: *dit licht is ~* this light is deceptive

het **bedrijf** /bədrɛif/ (pl: bedrijven) **1** business, company, enterprise, firm; [large] concern; farm: *gemengd ~* mixed farm; *openbare bedrijven* public services **2** act **3** operation; (working) order: *buiten ~ zijn* be out of order

de **bedrijfsadministratie** /bədrɛifsɑtministra(t)si/ business administration; business accountancy, industrial accountancy

de **bedrijfsarts** /bədrɛifsɑrts/ (pl: -en) company doctor, company medical officer

de **bedrijfscultuur** /bədrɛifskʏltyr/ (pl: -culturen) corporate culture

de **bedrijfseconomie** /bədrɛifsekonomi/ business economics, industrial economics

bedrijfsgevoelig /bədrɛifsxəvuləx/ (adj) sensitive, confidential

de **bedrijfshulpverlener** /bədrɛifshʏlpfərlenər/ (pl: -s) [Dutch] health & safety officer

het **bedrijfskapitaal** /bədrɛifskapital/ (pl: -kapitalen) working capital

bedrijfsklaar /bədrɛifsklar/ (adj) in working order, in running order: *~ maken* put into working (*or:* running) order

de **bedrijfskunde** /bədrɛifskʏndə/ business administration, management

de **bedrijfsleider** /bədrɛifslɛidər/ (pl: -s) manager

de **bedrijfsleiding** /bədrɛifslɛidɪŋ/ (pl: -en) management, board (of directors)

het **bedrijfsleven** /bədrɛifslevə(n)/ business, trade and industry: *het particuliere ~* private enterprise

het **bedrijfsonderdeel** /bədrɛifsɔndərdel/ (pl: -onderdelen) department, business unit

het **bedrijfsongeval** /bədrɛifsɔŋɣəvɑl/ (pl: -len) industrial accident; [fig] unfortunate accident

het **bedrijfsresultaat** /bədrɛifsrezʏltat/ trading results, company results

de **bedrijfsrevisor** /bədrɛifsrevizɔr/ (pl: -s, -en) [Belg] auditor

de **bedrijfsruimte** /bədrɛifsrœymtə/ (pl: -n, -s) working (*or:* business) accommodation, work(ing) space

de **bedrijfssluiting** /bədrɛifslœytɪŋ/ (pl: -en) shutdown, close-down

de **bedrijfstak** /bədrɛifstɑk/ (pl: -ken) sector, industry, trade (*or:* business) (sector)

de **bedrijfsvereniging** /bədrɛifsfərenəɣɪŋ/ (pl: -en) [Dutch] industrial insurance board

de **bedrijfsvoering** /bədrɛifsfurɪŋ/ management

bedrijfszeker /bədrɛifsekər/ (adj) reliable

bedrijven /bədrɛivə(n)/ (bedreef, heeft bedreven) commit, perpetrate

bedrijvend /bədrɛivənt/ (adj): *de ~e vorm van een werkwoord* the active voice of a verb

het **bedrijvenpark** /bədrɛivə(n)pɑrk/ (pl: -en) business park; industrial estate; [Am] industrial park

het **bedrijventerrein** /bədrɛivə(n)tɛrɛin/ (pl: -en) business park; industrial estate; [Am] industrial park

bedrijvig /bədrɛivəx/ (adj) active, busy; industrious; bustling: *een ~ type* an industrious type

de **bedrijvigheid** /bədrɛivəxhɛit/ activity, busyness, industriousness: *economische ~* economic activity; *koortsachtige ~* feverish activity

zich **bedrinken** /bədrɪŋkə(n)/ (bedronk zich, heeft zich bedronken) get drunk

bedroefd /bədruft/ (adj) sad (about), dejected; upset (about), distressed (about)

de **bedroefdheid** /bədrufthɛit/ sadness, sorrow, dejection, distress

bedroeven /bədruvə(n)/ (bedroefde, heeft bedroefd) [form] sadden, grieve

¹**bedroevend** /bədruvənt/ (adj) **1** sad(dening), depressing **2** pathetic: *~e resultaten* pitiful results

²**bedroevend** /bədruvənt/ (adv) pathetically, miserably: *zijn werk is ~ slecht* his work is lamentable

het **bedrog** /bədrɔx/ **1** deceit, deception; fraud; swindle: *~ plegen* cheat, swindle, deceive, commit fraud **2** deception, delusion: *optisch ~* optical illusion

bedruipen /bədrœypə(n)/ (bedroop, heeft bedropen): *zichzelf (kunnen) ~* be able to pay one's way (*or:* support) o.s.

bedrukken /bədrʏkə(n)/ (bedrukte, heeft bedrukt) print, inscribe

bedrukt /bədrʏkt/ (adj) dejected, depressed

de **bedtijd** /bɛtɛit/ bedtime

beducht /bədʏxt/ (adj) anxious (for): *~ zijn voor zijn reputatie* be concerned (*or:* anxious) for one's reputation

beduiden /bədœydə(n)/ (beduidde, heeft beduid) signal, motion, indicate: *de agent beduidde mij te stoppen* the policeman signalled (to) me to stop

beduidend /bədœydənt/ (adj, adv) significant, considerable: *~ minder* considerably less

beduimeld /bədœyməlt/ (adj) well-thumbed: *een ~ boek* a well-thumbed book

beduusd /bədyst/ (adj) taken aback, flabbergasted

beduvelen /bədyvələ(n)/ (beduvelde, heeft beduveld) [inform] cheat (on), trick, do (in the eye); [fin also] swindle

het **bedwang** /bədwɑŋ/ control, restraint: *iem. in ~ houden* keep s.o. in check

bedwelmen /bədwɛlmə(n)/ (bedwelmde, heeft bedwelmd) stun, stupefy; intoxicate

bedwingen /bədwɪŋə(n)/ (bedwong, heeft bedwongen) suppress, subdue; restrain: *zijn tranen* ~ hold back one's tears; *zich niet langer kunnen* ~ lose control (of (*or:* over) o.s.)

beëdigd /bəedəχt/ (adj) sworn; chartered: ~ *getuige* sworn witness

beëdigen /bəedəɣə(n)/ (beëdigde, heeft beëdigd) swear (in), administer an oath to: *een getuige* ~ swear (in) a witness

de **beëdiging** /bəedəχɪŋ/ (pl: -en) **1** swearing, confirmation on oath **2** swearing (in), administration of the oath

beëindigen /bəeɪndəɣə(n)/ (beëindigde, heeft beëindigd) **1** end, finish; complete: *een vriendschap* ~ break off a friendship **2** end, close; discontinue; terminate

de **beek** /bek/ (pl: beken) brook, stream

het **beeld** /belt/ (pl: -en) **1** statue, sculpture **2** picture, image; view; illustration: *in* ~ *zijn* be on (the screen); *in* ~ *brengen* show (a picture, pictures of); [fig] *hij komt in* ~ *als lijsttrekker* he is being mentioned as party leader; *zich een* ~ *van iets vormen* form a picture (*or:* an image) of sth., visualize sth. **3** picture, description

beeldbepalend /beldbəpalənt/ (adj) iconic: ~e *gebouwen* iconic buildings

de **beeldbuis** /beldbœys/ (pl: -buizen) **1** cathode ray tube **2** screen; box: *elke avond voor de* ~ *zitten* sit in front of the box every evening

beeldend /beldənt/ (adj, adv) plastic, expressive: ~e *kunst* visual arts

de **beeldenstorm** /beldə(n)storm/ (pl: -en) **1** [fig] image breaking **2** iconoclasm

beeldhouwen /belthɑuwə(n)/ (beeldhouwde, heeft gebeeldhouwd) sculpture, sculpt; carve

de **beeldhouwer** /belthɑuwər/ (pl: -s) sculptor, sculptress; woodcarver

de **beeldhouwkunst** /belthɑukynst/ sculpture

het **beeldhouwwerk** /belthɑuwɛrk/ (pl: -en) sculpture; carving

beeldig /beldəχ/ (adj, adv) gorgeous, adorable: *die jas staat je* ~ that coat looks gorgeous on you

het **beeldmerk** /beltmɛrk/ (pl: -en) logo(type)

het/de **beeldpunt** /beltpynt/ (pl: -en) pixel

het **beeldscherm** /beltsχɛrm/ (pl: -en) (TV, television) screen; [comp] display

de **beeldschermbril** /beltsχɛrmbrɪl/ (pl: -len) computer glasses

beeldschoon /beltsχon/ (adj) gorgeous, ravishingly (*or:* stunningly) beautiful

de **beeldspraak** /beltsprak/ (pl: -spraken) metaphor, imagery, metaphorical language, figurative language

de **beeldvorming** /beltformɪŋ/ formation of an image: *bijdragen tot een bepaalde* ~ help to create (*or:* establish) a certain image

de **beeltenis** /bɛltənɪs/ (pl: -sen) likeness; effigy, image

het **been** /ben/ (pl: benen) **1** leg; [in expressions often] foot: [fig] *op zijn achterste benen gaan staan* rise up in arms; *met beide benen op de grond staan* [fig] have one's feet firmly on the ground; *op eigen benen staan* stand on one's own (two) feet; *de benen nemen* run for it; *op de* ~ *blijven* remain on one's feet, keep going; *ik kan niet meer op mijn benen staan* I'll drop dead (from exhaustion); *hij is met het verkeerde* ~ *uit bed gestapt* he got out of bed on the wrong side **2** leg **3** bone **4** bones **5** [maths] side, leg: *de benen van een driehoek* the sides of a triangle

de **beenbeschermer** /bembəsχɛrmər/ (pl: -s) leg-guard, pad

de **beenbreuk** /bembrøk/ (pl: -en) fracture of the leg: *gecompliceerde* ~ compound fracture (of the leg)

de **beenham** /bɛnhɑm/ ham off the bone

de **beenhouwer** /bɛnhɑuwər/ (pl: -s) [Belg] butcher

de **beenhouwerij** /bɛnhɑuwərɛi/ (pl: -en) [Belg] butcher's shop

het **beenmerg** /bemɛrχ/ bone marrow

de **beenruimte** /bɛnrœymtə/ legroom

de **beer** /ber/ (pl: beren) **1** bear **2** boar ‖ [astronomy] *de Grote Beer* the Big Dipper; [astronomy] *de Kleine Beer* the Little Dipper

de **beerput** /berpyt/ (pl: -ten) cesspool; cesspit: [fig] *de* ~ *opentrekken* blow (*or:* take) the lid off

het **beest** /best/ (pl: -en) **1** beast; animal: [fig] *het ~je bij zijn naam noemen* call a spade a spade **2** animal; beast; cattle **3** creepy-crawly ‖ [fig] *de* ~ *uithangen* behave like an animal; paint the town red

[1] **beestachtig** /bestɑχtəχ/ (adj) bestial; brutal; savage

[2] **beestachtig** /bestɑχtəχ/ (adv) terribly, dreadfully

de **beet** /bet/ (pl: beten) bite

beetgaar /betχar/ (adj) al dente

[1] **beethebben** /bethɛbə(n)/ (had beet, heeft beetgehad) [fishing] have a bite

[2] **beethebben** /bethɛbə(n)/ (had beet, heeft beetgehad) **1** have (got) (a) hold of **2** take in, cheat, fool; make a fool of

het [1] **beetje** /bɛcə/ (pl: -s) (little) bit, little: *een* ~ *Frans kennen* know a little French, have a smattering of French; *een* ~ *melk graag* a little milk (*or:* a drop of milk), please; *bij stukjes en bij* ~s bit by bit, little by little; *alle* ~s *helpen* every little helps; *een* ~ *technicus verhelpt dat zo* anyone who calls himself a technician could fix that in a jiffy; *een* ~ *kantoor heeft een koffieautomaat* any self-respecting office has got a coffee machine

[2] **beetje** /bɛcə/ (adv) (a) (little) bit, (a) little, rather: *dat is een* ~ *weinig* that's not very

much; *een ~ vervelend zijn* **a)** be a bit of a nuisance, be rather annoying; **b)** be rather boring, be a bit of a bore; *een ~ opschieten* get a move on

beetnemen /bḙtnemə(n)/ (nam beet, heeft beetgenomen) take in, make a fool of, fool: *je bent beetgenomen!* you've been had!

beetpakken /bḙtpɑkə(n)/ (pakte beet, heeft beetgepakt) lay hold of, get one's (*or:* lay) hands on

befaamd /bəfaːmt/ (adj) famous, renowned

begaafd /bəɣaːft/ (adj) **1** gifted, talented **2** gifted (with), endowed (with)

de **begaafdheid** /bəɣaːfthɛit/ **1** talent, ability; intelligence; genius **2** talent (for), gift (for)

¹**begaan** /bəɣaːn/: *iem.* **laten** *~* let s.o. do as he/she likes (*or:* pleases)

²**begaan** /bəɣaːn/ (beging, heeft begaan) commit; [mistakes also] make

begaanbaar /bəɣaːmbaːr/ (adj) passable, practicable

begeerlijk /bəɣeːrlək/ (adj, adv) desirable; eligible

de **begeerte** /bəɣeːrtə/ (pl: -n) desire (for), wish (for), craving (for)

begeleiden /bəɣəlɛidə(n)/ (begeleidde, heeft begeleid) **1** accompany, escort **2** guide, counsel, support; supervise; coach **3** accompany [mus also]; go with

begeleidend /bəɣəlɛidənt/ (adj) accompanying, attendant: *~e* **muziek** incidental music

de **begeleider** /bəɣəlɛidər/ (pl: -s) **1** companion; escort **2** guide, counsellor; supervisor, coach **3** [mus] accompanist

de **begeleiding** /bəɣəlɛidɪŋ/ (pl: -en) **1** accompaniment, accompanying; escort(ing) **2** guidance, counselling, support; supervision; coaching: *de ~ na de operatie was erg* **goed** the follow-up care after the operation was very good; *onder ~ van* under the guidance of **3** [mus] accompaniment

begeren /bəɣeːrə(n)/ (begeerde, heeft begeerd) desire, crave, long for: *alles wat zijn* **hartje** *maar kon ~* all one could possibly wish for

begerenswaardig /bəɣeːrənswaːrdəχ/ (adj) desirable; eligible; enviable

begerig /bəɣeːrəχ/ (adj, adv) desirous (of), longing (for), eager (for); hungry (for): *~e* **blikken** hungry looks

¹**begeven** /bəɣeːvə(n)/ (begaf, heeft begeven) **1** break down, fail; collapse; give way: *de* **auto** *kan het elk moment ~* the car is liable to break down any minute **2** forsake, leave; fail: *zijn* **stem** *begaf het* his voice broke

zich ²**begeven** /bəɣeːvə(n)/ (begaf zich, heeft zich begeven) proceed; embark (on, upon); adjourn (to): *zich op weg ~ (naar)* set out (for)

begieten /bəɣiːtə(n)/ (begoot, heeft begoten) water, wet

begiftigd /bəɣɪftəχt/ (adj): *~ met grote mu-*

zikaliteit endowed (*or:* gifted) with great musical talent

het **begin** /bəɣɪn/ beginning, start; opening: *~* **mei** early in May, (at) the beginning of May; *een* **veelbelovend** *~* a promising start; *dit* **is** *nog maar het ~* this is only the beginning; *een ~ maken met iets* begin (*or:* start) sth.; *(weer) helemaal* **bij** *het ~ (moeten) beginnen* (have to) start from scratch; *in het ~* at the beginning; at first, initially; *een boek van ~ tot eind lezen* read a book from cover to cover; *een* **goed** *~ is het halve werk* well begun is half done; the first blow is half the battle

de **beginletter** /bəɣɪnlɛtər/ (pl: -s) initial letter, first letter; initial

de **beginneling** /bəɣɪnəlɪŋ/ (pl: -en) beginner, novice

¹**beginnen** /bəɣɪnə(n)/ (begon, is begonnen) **1** begin, start (to do sth., doing sth.); commence; set about (doing): [inform] *begin* **maar!** go ahead!; fire away!; *laten we ~* let's get started; *het begint er op te* **lijken** that's more like it; *weer van voren af aan* **moeten** *~* go back to square one; *hij begon* **met** *te zeggen …* he began by saying …; *het begint donker te worden* it is getting dark; *je weet niet waar je* **aan** *begint* you don't know what you are letting yourself in for **2** (+ over) bring up, raise: *over politiek ~* bring up politics; *over iets anders ~* change the subject ǁ *daar kunnen we niet* **aan** *~* that's out of the question; *om te ~ …* for a start …; *voor zichzelf ~* start one's own business

²**beginnen** /bəɣɪnə(n)/ (begon, is begonnen) begin, start; open: *een* **gesprek** *~* begin (*or:* start) a conversation; *een* **zaak** *~* start a business

de **beginner** /bəɣɪnər/ (pl: -s) beginner: *cursus voor ~s* beginners' course

het **beginpunt** /bəɣɪmpʏnt/ (pl: -en) starting point, point of departure

het **beginsalaris** /bəɣɪnsalarɪs/ starting (*or:* initial) salary

het **beginsel** /bəɣɪnsəl/ (pl: -en) principle, rudiment: *in ~* in principle

de **beginselverklaring** /bəɣɪnsəlvərklarɪŋ/ (pl: -en) statement (*or:* declaration) of principles; manifesto

de **beglazing** /bəɣlazɪŋ/ (pl: -en) glazing

begluren /bəɣlyrə(n)/ (begluurde, heeft begluurd) peep at, spy on

de **begonia** /bəɣonija/ (pl: -'s) begonia

de **begraafplaats** /bəɣraːfplats/ (pl: -en) cemetery, graveyard, burial ground

de **begrafenis** /bəɣrafənɪs/ (pl: -sen) **1** funeral **2** burial

de **begrafenisondernemer** /bəɣrafənɪsɔndərnemər/ (pl: -s) undertaker, funeral director

de **begrafenisonderneming** /bəɣrafənɪsɔndərnemɪŋ/ (pl: -en) undertaker's (business), funeral parlour; [Am] funeral home

de **begrafenisstoet** /bəɣrafənɪstut/ (pl: -en) funeral procession

begraven /bəɣravə(n)/ (begroef, heeft begraven) bury: *dood en ~ zijn* be dead and gone

begrensd /bəɣrɛnst/ (adj) limited, finite, restricted

begrenzen /bəɣrɛnzə(n)/ (begrensde, heeft begrensd) 1 border: *door de zee begrensd* bordered by the sea 2 [fig] define 3 limit, restrict

¹**begrijpelijk** /bəɣrɛipələk/ (adj) 1 understandable, comprehensible, intelligible 2 natural, obvious: *dat is nogal ~* that is hardly surprising; *het is heel ~ dat hij bang is* it's only natural that he should be frightened

²**begrijpelijk** /bəɣrɛipələk/ (adv) clearly

begrijpen /bəɣrɛipə(n)/ (begreep, heeft begrepen) 1 understand, comprehend, grasp: *hij begreep de **hint*** he took the hint, he got the message; *dat **kan** ik ~* I (can) understand that; *o, ik begrijp **het*** oh, I see; *laten we dat **goed** ~* let's get that clear; *begrijp je me **nog?*** are you still with me?; *dat laat je voortaan, begrepen!* I'll have no more of that, is that clear? (*or:* do you hear?); *als je begrijpt wat ik bedoel* if you see what I mean 2 understand, gather: *begrijp me **goed*** don't get me wrong; *iem. (iets) **verkeerd** ~* misunderstand s.o. (sth.)

het **begrip** /bəɣrɪp/ (pl: -pen) 1 understanding, comprehension, conception: *vlug van ~* quick-witted 2 concept, idea, notion 3 understanding, sympathy: *~ voor iets kunnen **opbrengen*** appreciate; *ze was **vol** ~* she was very understanding; *dat gaat mijn ~ te **boven*** that is beyond me

begroeid /bəɣruit/ (adj) grown over (with), overgrown (with); wooded

begroeten /bəɣrutə(n)/ (begroette, heeft begroet) greet; hail; salute: *elkaar ~* exchange greetings; *het voorstel werd **met** applaus begroet* the proposal was greeted with applause

de **begroeting** /bəɣrutɪŋ/ (pl: -en) greeting, salutation

begroten /bəɣrotə(n)/ (begrootte, heeft begroot) estimate (at), cost (at): *de **kosten** van het gehele project worden begroot op 12 miljoen* the whole project is costed at 12 million

de **begroting** /bəɣrotɪŋ/ (pl: -en) estimate, budget: *een ~ **maken*** make an estimate

het **begrotingsoverschot** /bəɣrotɪŋsoʋərsχɔt/ (pl: -ten) budget surplus

het **begrotingstekort** /bəɣrotɪŋstəkɔrt/ (pl: -en) budget deficit

de **begunstigde** /bəɣʏnstəɣdə/ (pl: -n) beneficiary; payee

begunstigen /bəɣʏnstəɣə(n)/ (begunstig-

de, heeft begunstigd) favour

de **beha** /beha/ (pl: -'s) bra

behaaglijk /bəhaxlək/ (adj, adv) 1 pleasant, comfortable: *een ~ **gevoel*** a comfortable feeling 2 comfortable, relaxed 3 cosy, snug

behaagziek /bəhaxsik/ (adj, adv) coquettish

behaard /bəhart/ (adj) hairy: *de **huid** is daar ~* the skin is covered with hair there; *zwaar ~* very hairy

het ¹**behagen** /bəhaɣə(n)/ pleasure, delight: *~ **scheppen** in* take (a) pleasure (*or:* delight) in

²**behagen** /bəhaɣə(n)/ (behaagde, heeft behaagd) please: *het heeft Hare **Majesteit** behaagd om ...* Her Majesty has been graciously pleased to ...

³**behagen** /bəhaɣə(n)/ please

behalen /bəhalə(n)/ (behaalde, heeft behaald) gain, obtain, achieve, score, win: *een hoog **cijfer** ~* get (*or:* obtain) a high mark; *de **overwinning** ~* be victorious, carry the day

behalve /bəhalvə/ (prep) 1 except (for), but (for), with the exception of, excepting: *~ **mij** heeft hij geen enkele vriend* except for me he hasn't got a single friend 2 besides, in addition to

behandelen /bəhandələ(n)/ (behandelde, heeft behandeld) 1 handle, deal with, treat; attend to: *dergelijke **aangelegenheden** behandelt de rector zelf* the director attends to such matters himself; *eerlijk behandeld worden* be treated fairly; *de dieren werden **goed** behandeld* the animals were well looked after; *iem. **oneerlijk** ~* do s.o. (a) wrong; *iem. **voorzichtig** ~* go easy on s.o. 2 treat (of), discuss, deal with: *een **onderwerp** ~* discuss a subject 3 treat; nurse

de **behandeling** /bəhandəlɪŋ/ (pl: -en) 1 treatment, use, handling; operation; handling; management: *een wetsontwerp **in** ~ nemen* discuss a bill; *in ~ nemen* deal with 2 treatment, discussion 3 [med] treatment, attention: *zich **onder** ~ stellen* go to a doctor

de **behandelkamer** /bəhandəlkamər/ (pl: -s) surgery

het **behang** /bəhaŋ/ wallpaper

¹**behangen** /bəhaŋə(n)/ (behing, heeft behangen) (wall)paper (a room), hang (wallpaper)

²**behangen** /bəhaŋə(n)/ (behing, heeft behangen) (+ met) hang (with), drape (with)

de **behanger** /bəhaŋər/ (pl: -s) paperhanger

behapbaar /bəhabar/ (adj) manageable

behappen /bəhapə(n)/: *dat **kan** ik niet in m'n eentje ~* I can't handle that all at once on my own

behartenswaardig /bəhartə(n)swardəχ/ (adj) worthy of consideration

behartigen /bəhartəɣə(n)/ (behartigde, heeft behartigd) look after, promote de **behartiging** /bəhɑrtəɣɪŋ/ promotion (of), protection (of)

het **beheer** /bəhe̯r/ **1** management; control; supervision: *de penningmeester heeft het ~ over de kas* the treasurer is in charge of the funds **2** administration, management, rule: *dat eiland staat onder Engels ~* that island is under British administration

de **beheerder** /bəhe̯rdər/ (pl: -s) **1** manager **2** administrator, trustee **3** [comp] administrator

beheersbaar /bəhe̯rzbar/ (adj) manageable, controllable: *de inflatie ~ maken* bring inflation under control

beheersen /bəhe̯rsə(n)/ (beheerste, heeft beheerst) control, govern, rule; dominate: *die gedachte beheerst zijn leven* that thought dominates his life || *een vreemde taal ~* have a thorough command of a foreign language

de **beheersing** /bəhe̯rsɪŋ/ control; command: *de ~ over zichzelf verliezen* lose one's self-control

beheerst /bəhe̯rst/ (adj, adv) controlled, composed

beheksen /bəhɛksə(n)/ (behekste, heeft behekst) **1** bewitch, bedevil **2** [fig] bewitch, cast (or: put) a spell (or: charm) on

zich **behelpen** /bəhɛlpə(n)/ (behielp zich, heeft zich beholpen) manage, make do: *hij weet zich te ~* he manages, he can make do; *het is erg ~ zonder stroom* it's really roughing it without electricity

behelzen /bəhɛlzə(n)/ (behelsde, heeft behelsd) contain, include, comprehend: *we weten niet wat het plan behelst* we don't know what the plan amounts to; *het voorstel behelst het volgende* the proposal (or: suggestion) is this

behendig /bəhɛndəx/ (adj, adv) dexterous; adroit; skilful; clever; smart: *een ~e jongen* an agile boy; *~ klom ze achterop* she climbed nimbly up on the back

de **behendigheid** /bəhɛndəxhɛit/ dexterity, agility, skill

behept /bəhɛpt/ (adj) cursed (with), -ridden: *met vooroordelen ~* prejudice-ridden

beheren /bəhe̯rə(n)/ (beheerde, heeft beheerd) **1** manage; administer: *de financiën ~* control the finances **2** manage, run

behoeden /bəhu̯də(n)/ (behoedde, heeft behoed) **1** guard (from), keep (from), preserve (from): *iem. voor gevaar ~* keep s.o. from danger **2** guard, watch over

behoedzaam /bəhu̯tsam/ (adj, adv) cautious, wary

de **behoefte** /bəhu̯ftə/ (pl: -n) need (of, for); demand (for): *in eigen ~ (kunnen) voorzien* be self-sufficient; *~ hebben aan rust* have a need for quiet || *zijn ~ doen* relieve o.s.

behoeftig /bəhu̯ftəx/ (adj) needy, destitute; distressed: *de armen en de ~en* the poor

and the needy (or: destitute); *in ~ omstandigheden verkeren* find o.s. in needy (or: reduced) circumstances

het **behoeve** /bəhu̯və/: *ten ~ van* for the benefit of

behoeven /bəhu̯və(n)/ (behoefde, heeft behoefd) need, be in need of; require: *hulp ~* be in need of aid (or: support); *dit behoeft enige toelichting* this requires some explanation

¹**behoorlijk** /bəho̯rlək/ (adj) **1** decent, appropriate, proper, fitting: *producten van ~e kwaliteit* good quality products **2** adequate, sufficient **3** decent, respectable, presentable **4** considerable, substantial: *dat is een ~ eind lopen* that's quite a distance to walk

²**behoorlijk** /bəho̯rlək/ (adv) **1** decently, properly: *gedraag je ~* behave yourself **2** adequately, enough **3** pretty, quite: *~ wat* a fair amount (of) **4** decently, well (enough): *je kunt hier heel ~ eten* you can get a very decent meal here

behoren /bəho̯rə(n)/ (behoorde, heeft behoord) **1** belong (to); be owned by; be part of: *dat behoort nu tot het verleden* that's past history **2** require, need, be necessary, be needed: *naar ~* as it should be **3** should, ought (to): *jongeren ~ op te staan voor ouderen* young people should stand up for older people **4** belong (to), go together (or: with): *een tafel met de daarbij ~de stoelen* a table and the chairs to go with it; *dat behoort tot de mogelijkheden* that's an option; *hij behoort tot de betere leerlingen* he is one of the better pupils

het **behoud** /bəho̯ut/ **1** preservation, maintenance; conservation **2** preservation, conservation, care

behouden /bəho̯udə(n)/ (behield, heeft behouden) **1** preserve, keep; conserve; retain: *zijn zetel ~* retain one's seat **2** maintain, keep: *zijn vorm ~* keep fit || *ik wens u een ~ vaart* I wish you a safe journey

behoudend /bəho̯udənt/ (adj, adv) conservative: *hij behoort tot de ~e vleugel van de partij* he belongs to the conservative section of the party; *~ spelen* play a defensive game

behoudens /bəho̯udə(n)s/ (prep) **1** subject to: *~ goedkeuring door de gemeenteraad* subject to the council's approval **2** except (for): *~ enkele wijzigingen werd het plan goedgekeurd* except for (or: with) a few alterations, the plan was approved

de **behuizing** /bəhœyzɪŋ/ (pl: -en) **1** housing, accommodation; house; dwelling: *passende ~ zoeken* look for suitable accommodation **2** casing, housing

het **behulp** /bəhʏlp/: *met ~ van iets* with the help (or: aid) of sth.

behulpzaam /bəhʏlpsam/ (adj) helpful: *zij is altijd ~* she's always ready to help de **beiaard** /bɛiart/ (pl: -s) carillon

beide /bɛidə/ (num) both, either (one); two: *het is in ons ~r belang* it's in the interest of both of us; *een opvallend verschil tussen hun ~ dochters* a striking difference between their two daughters; *in ~ gevallen* in either case, in both cases; *ze zijn ~n getrouwd* they are both married, both (of them) are married; *wij ~n* both of us, the two of us; *ze weten het geen van ~n* neither of them knows

het **¹beige** /bɛːʒə/ beige

²beige /bɛːʒə/ (adj) beige

de **beignet** /bɛːɲe/ (pl: -s) fritter

zich **beijveren** /bɛivərə(n)/ (beijverde zich, heeft zich beijverd) apply o.s. (to)

beïnvloeden /bɛɪnvludə(n)/ (beïnvloedde, heeft beïnvloed) influence, affect: *zich door iets laten ~* be influenced by sth.

de **beïnvloeding** /bɛɪnvludɪŋ/: *~ van de jury* influencing the jury

Beiroet /bɛirut/ Beirut

de **beitel** /bɛitəl/ (pl: -s) chisel

beitelen /bɛitələ(n)/ (beitelde, heeft gebeiteld) 1 chisel 2 carve

het/de **beits** /bɛits/ (pl: -en) stain

beitsen /bɛitsə(n)/ (beitste, heeft gebeitst) stain

bejaard /bəjart/ (adj) elderly, aged, old

de **bejaarde** /bəjardə/ (pl: -n) elderly (or: old) person, senior citizen

het **bejaardentehuis** /bəjardə(n)təhœys/ (pl: -tehuizen) old people's home, home for the elderly

de **bejaardenverzorger** /bəjardə(n)vərzorɣər/ (pl: -s) geriatric helper

de **bejaardenzorg** /bəjardə(n)zorɣ/ care of the elderly (or: old)

bejegenen /bəjeɣənə(n)/ (bejegende, heeft bejegend) treat: *iem. onheus ~* snub (or: rebuff) s.o.

de **bek** /bɛk/ (pl: -ken) 1 bill; beak 2 snout, muzzle 3 mouth, trap, gob: *een grote ~ hebben* be loud-mouthed; *hou je grote ~* shut up!; *op zijn ~ gaan* come a cropper, fall flat on one's face 4 mug: *(gekke) ~ken trekken* make (silly) faces

bekaaid /bəkajt/ (adj): *er ~ afkomen* come off badly, get the worst of it, get a raw deal

bekaf /bɛkɑf/ (adj) all-in, knackered, dead tired

bekakt /bəkɑkt/ (adj, adv) affected, snooty

de **bekeerling** /bəkerlɪŋ/ (pl: -en) convert

bekend /bəkɛnt/ (adj) 1 known: *dit was mij ~* I knew (of) this; *het is algemeen ~* it's common knowledge; *voor zover mij ~* as far as I know; *voor zover ~* as far as is known 2 well-known, noted (for), known (for); notorious (for): *~ van radio en tv* of radio and TV fame 3 familiar: *u komt me ~ voor* haven't we met (somewhere) (before)?

de **bekende** /bəkɛndə/ (pl: -n) acquaintance

de **bekendheid** /bəkɛnthɛit/ 1 familiarity (with), acquaintance (with), experience (of) 2 reputation, name, fame: *~ krijgen* become (well-)known

bekendmaken /bəkɛntmakə(n)/ (maakte bekend, heeft bekendgemaakt) 1 announce 2 publish, make public (or: known): *de verkiezingsuitslag ~* declare the results of the election 3 familiarize (with), acquaint

de **bekendmaking** /bəkɛntmakɪŋ/ (pl: -en) 1 announcement 2 publication; notice; declaration

bekendstaan /bəkɛntstan/ (stond bekend, heeft bekendgestaan) be known (as), be known (or: reputed) (to be): *goed, slecht ~* have a good, bad reputation; *~ om* be noted (or: known) for

bekennen /bəkɛnə(n)/ (bekende, heeft bekend) 1 [law] confess; plead guilty (to) 2 confess, admit, acknowledge: *schuld ~* admit one's guilt; *je kunt beter eerlijk ~* you'd better come clean 3 see, detect: *hij was nergens te ~* there was no sign (or: trace) of him (anywhere)

de **bekentenis** /bəkɛntənɪs/ (pl: -sen) confession, admission, acknowledgement; plea of guilty: *een volledige ~ afleggen* make a full confession

de **beker** /bɛkər/ (pl: -s) beaker, cup; mug: *de ~ winnen* win the cup

bekeren /bəkerə(n)/ (bekeerde, heeft bekeerd) convert; reform

de **bekerfinale** /bɛkərfinalə/ (pl: -s) cup final

de **bekering** /bəkerɪŋ/ (pl: -en) conversion

de **bekerwedstrijd** /bɛkərwɛtstrɛit/ (pl: -en) cup-tie

bekeuren /bəkørə(n)/ (bekeurde, heeft bekeurd) fine (on the spot): *bekeurd worden voor te hard rijden* be fined for speeding

de **bekeuring** /bəkørɪŋ/ (pl: -en) (on-the-spot) fine, ticket

bekijken /bəkɛikə(n)/ (bekeek, heeft bekeken) 1 look at, examine: *iets vluchtig ~* glance at sth.; *van dichtbij ~* take a close(r) look at 2 look at, consider 3 see, look at, consider, view: *hoe je het ook bekijkt* whichever way you look at it ‖ *je bekijkt het maar!* please yourself!; *goed bekeken!* well done!; good thinking!

het **bekijks** /bəkɛiks/: *veel ~ hebben* attract a great deal of (or: a lot of) attention

het **¹bekken** /bɛkə(n)/ (pl: -s) 1 basin 2 [biology] pelvis 3 [mus] cymbal

²bekken /bɛkə(n)/ (bekte, heeft gebekt) snap (at) ‖ *dat bekt goed* that sounds right; *dat bekt niet lekker* that's hard to pronounce; that doesn't sound very elegant

de **bekkenbodem** /bɛkə(n)bodəm/ (pl: -s) pelvic floor

de **beklaagde** /bəklaɣdə/ (pl: -n) accused, defendant; prisoner (at the bar) de **beklaagdenbank** /bəkla̯ɣdə(n)bɑŋk/ (pl: -en) dock

bekladden /bəklɑ̯də(n)/ (bekladde, heeft beklad) blot; daub; plaster

het **beklag** /bəkla̯ɣ/ complaint

¹**beklagen** /bəkla̯ɣə(n)/ (beklaagde, heeft beklaagd) pity

zich ²**beklagen** /bəkla̯ɣə(n)/ (beklaagde zich, heeft zich beklaagd) complain (to s.o.), make a complaint (to s.o.): *zich ~ over de slechte service* complain (or: make a complaint) about the (poor) service

beklagenswaardig /bəkla̯ɣə(n)swa̯rdəχ/ (adj) pitiable, pitiful, piteous, lamentable, deplorable: *hij is ~* he is (much) to be pitied

bekleden /bəkle̯də(n)/ (bekleedde, heeft bekleed) 1 cover; coat; line: *een kamer ~* carpet a room 2 hold, occupy: *een hoge positie ~* hold a high position

de **bekleding** /bəkle̯dɪŋ/ (pl: -en) covering, coating, lining

beklemd /bəklɛmt/ (adj) jammed, wedged, stuck, trapped

beklemmen /bəklɛmə(n)/ (beklemde, heeft beklemd) 1 jam 2 oppress

beklemtonen /bəklɛmtonə(n)/ (beklemtoonde, heeft beklemtoond) stress, accent(uate); emphasize

beklijven /bəklɛi̯və(n)/ (beklijfde, heeft/is beklijfd) sink in, take root; leave a lasting impression

beklimmen /bəklɪmə(n)/ (beklom, heeft beklommen) climb, ascend, scale

beklinken /bəklɪŋkə(n)/ (beklonk, heeft/is beklonken) settle, clinch: *de zaak is beklonken* the matter's settled; the deal's sewn up

bekneld /bəknɛlt/ (adj) trapped: *door een botsing ~ raken in een auto* be trapped in a car after a collision

beknibbelen /bəknɪbələ(n)/ (beknibbelde, heeft beknibbeld) 1 cut back (on); skimp (on), stint (on) 2 [Belg] meddle with, interfere with

beknopt /bəknɔpt/ (adj, adv) brief(ly-worded), concise, succinct ‖ *een ~e uitgave* an abridged edition

beknotten /bəknɔtə(n)/ (beknotte, heeft beknot) curtail, cut short, restrict: *iemands vrijheid ~* curtail (or: restrict) s.o.'s freedom

bekocht /bəkɔχt/ (adj) cheated; taken in, taken for a ride: *zich ~ voelen* feel cheated (or: taken in)

bekoelen /bəkulə(n)/ (bekoelde, is bekoeld) 1 cool (off, down) 2 [fig] cool (off), dampen

bekogelen /bəko̯ɣələ(n)/ (bekogelde, heeft bekogeld) pelt, bombard

bekokstoven /bəkɔkstovə(n)/ (bekokstoofde, heeft bekokstoofd) cook up: *wat ben je nu weer aan 't ~?* what are you cooking up now?

bekomen /bəko̯mə(n)/ (bekwam, is bekomen) 1 agree with; suit; disagree with: *dat zal je slecht ~* you'll be sorry (for that) 2 recover, get over; come round, come to: *van de (eerste) schrik ~* get over the (initial) shock

zich **bekommeren** /bəkɔmərə(n)/ (bekommerde zich, heeft zich bekommerd) worry (about), bother (about), concern (or: trouble) o.s. (with, about)

de **bekomst** /bəkɔmst/: *zijn ~ van iets hebben* have had one's fill of sth.; be fed up with (or: sick and tired of) sth.

bekonkelen /bəkɔŋkələ(n)/ (bekonkelde, heeft bekonkeld) cook up; wheel and deal

bekoorlijk /bəko̯rlək/ (adj, adv) charming, lovely

bekopen /bəko̯pə(n)/ (bekocht, heeft bekocht) pay for

bekoren /bəko̯rə(n)/ (bekoorde, heeft bekoord) charm, seduce: *dat kan mij niet ~* it doesn't appeal to me; I don't think much of it

de **bekoring** /bəko̯rɪŋ/ (pl: -en) charm(s), appeal

bekorten /bəkɔrtə(n)/ (bekortte, heeft bekort) cut short, shorten, curtail: *zijn reis met een week ~* cut one's journey short by a week, cut a week off one's journey

bekostigen /bəkɔstəɣə(n)/ (bekostigde, heeft bekostigd) bear the cost of, pay for, fund: *ik kan dat niet ~* I can't afford that

bekrachtigen /bəkrɑχtəɣə(n)/ (bekrachtigde, heeft bekrachtigd) ratify, confirm; pass; assent to: *bekrachtigd worden* be passed

de **bekrachtiging** /bəkrɑχtəχɪŋ/ (pl: -en) 1 ratification, confirmation 2 upholding ‖ *stuurbekrachtiging* power steering

bekritiseren /bəkritize̯rə(n)/ (bekritiseerde, heeft bekritiseerd) criticize, find fault with

bekrompen /bəkrɔmpə(n)/ (adj, adv) narrow(-minded), petty, blinkered; [stronger] bigoted

bekronen /bəkro̯nə(n)/ (bekroonde, heeft bekroond) award a prize to: *een bekroond ontwerp* a prizewinning design, an award-winning design

de **bekroning** /bəkro̯nɪŋ/ (pl: -en) award

bekruipen /bəkrœy̯pə(n)/ (bekroop, heeft bekropen) come over, steal over: *het spijt me, maar nu bekruipt me toch het gevoel dat …* I'm sorry, but I've got a sneaking feeling that …

de **bekvechten** /bɛkfɛχtə(n)/ (bekvechtte, heeft gebekvecht) argue, bicker

bekwaam /bəkwa̯m/ (adj) competent, capable, able

de **bekwaamheid** /bəkwa̯mhɛit/ competence, (cap)ability, capacity, skill

zich **bekwamen** /bəkwa̯mə(n)/ (bekwaamde zich, heeft zich bekwaamd) qualify, train (o.s.), study, teach: *zich in iets ~* train for sth.

de **bel** /bɛl/ (pl: -len) **1** bell; chime; gong (bell): *de ~ gaat* there's s.o. at the door; *op de ~ drukken* press the bell; [fig] *aan de ~ trekken* raise the alarm (over sth.) **2** bubble: *~len blazen* blow bubbles

belabberd /bəlɑbərt/ (adj, adv) [inform] rotten, lousy, rough: *de bediening is ~* service is atrocious; *ik voel me nogal ~* I feel pretty rough (*or:* lousy)

belachelijk /bəlɑxələk/ (adj, adv) ridiculous, absurd, laughable, ludicrous: *doe niet zo ~* stop making such a fool of yourself; *zich ~ maken* make a fool of oneself; *op een ~ vroeg tijdstip* at some ungodly hour

¹**beladen** /bəlɑdə(n)/ (adj) emotionally charged

²**beladen** /bəlɑdə(n)/ (beladde, heeft beladen) load; burden

belagen /bəlɑɣə(n)/ (belaagde, heeft belaagd) **1** beset; [stronger] besiege **2** menace, endanger

belanden /bəlɑndə(n)/ (belandde, is beland) land (up), end up, finish, find o.s.: *~ bij* end up at, finish at; *waardoor hij in de gevangenis belandde* which landed him in prison

het **belang** /bəlɑŋ/ (pl: -en) **1** interest, concern; good: *het algemeen ~* the public interest; *~ bij iets hebben* have an interest in sth.; *in het ~ van uw gezondheid* for the sake of your health; *het is van het grootste ~ ...* it is imperative to ... **2** interest (in): *~ stellen in* be interested in, take an interest in **3** importance, significance: *veel ~ hechten aan iets* set great store by sth.

belangeloos /bəlɑŋəlos/ (adj, adv) unselfish, selfless: *belangeloze hulp* disinterested help

de **belangengroep** /bəlɑŋə(n)ɣrup/ (pl: -en) interest group, lobby, pressure group

de **belangenvereniging** /bəlɑŋə(n)vərenəɣɪŋ/ (pl: -en) interest group, pressure group, lobby

de **belangenverstrengeling** /bəlɑŋə(n)vərstrɛŋəlɪŋ/ conflict of interest

belanghebbend /bəlɑŋhɛbənt/ (adj) interested, concerned

de **belanghebbende** /bəlɑŋhɛbəndə/ (pl: -n) interested party, party concerned

belangrijk /bəlɑŋrɛik/ (adj) **1** important: *de ~ste gebeurtenissen* the main (*or:* major) events; *zijn gezin ~er vinden dan zijn carrière* put one's family before one's career; *en wat nog ~er is ...* and, more important(ly), ...; [iron] *lekker ~* hip, who cares **2** considerable, substantial, major: *in ~e mate* considerably, substantially

¹**belangstellend** /bəlɑŋstɛlənt/ (adj) interested: *ze waren heel ~* they were very attentive

²**belangstellend** /bəlɑŋstɛlənt/ (adv) interestedly, with interest

de **belangstellende** /bəlɑŋstɛləndə/ person interested, interested party

de **belangstelling** /bəlɑŋstɛlɪŋ/ interest (in): *in het middelpunt van de ~ staan* be the focus of attention; *een man met een brede ~* a man of wide interests; *zijn ~ voor iets verliezen* lose interest in sth.; *daar heb ik geen ~ voor* I'm not interested (in that)

belangwekkend /bəlɑŋwɛkənt/ (adj) interesting; of interest; conspicuous, prominent: *een ~e figuur* a conspicuous (*or:* prominent) person

belast /bəlɑst/ (adj) (+ met) responsible (for), in charge (of) ‖ [med] *erfelijk ~ zijn* have a hereditary defect

belastbaar /bəlɑstbar/ (adj) taxable: *~ inkomen* taxable income

belasten /bəlɑstə(n)/ (belastte, heeft belast) **1** load: *iets te zwaar ~* overload sth. **2** (place a) load (on) **3** make responsible (for), put in charge (of): *iem. te zwaar ~* overtax, overburden s.o.; *iem. met een taak ~* make s.o. responsible for of a task, put s.o. in charge of a task; *hij is belast met de taak om ...* he is charged with the duty of ..., he's responsible for ... **4** tax

belastend /bəlɑstənt/ (adj) aggravating; [law] incriminating; damning; damaging

belasteren /bəlɑstərə(n)/ (belasterde, heeft belasterd) slander; [written] libel

de **belasting** /bəlɑstɪŋ/ (pl: -en) **1** load, stress: *~ van het milieu met chemische producten* burdening of the environment with chemicals **2** burden, pressure: *de studie is een te grote ~ voor haar* studying is too much for her **3** tax, taxation; rate(s): *~ heffen* levy taxes; *~ ontduiken* evade tax

de **belastingaangifte** /bəlɑstɪŋaŋɪftə/ (pl: -n) tax return

de **belastingaanslag** /bəlɑstɪŋanslɑx/ (pl: -en) tax assessment

de **belastingaftrek** /bəlɑstɪŋaftrɛk/ tax deduction

de **belastingbetaler** /bəlɑstɪŋbətalər/ (pl: -s) taxpayer

de **belastingconstructie** /bəlɑstɪŋkɔnstryksi/ (pl: -s) tax avoidance scheme

de **belastingdienst** /bəlɑstɪŋdinst/ (pl: -en) tax department, Inland Revenue; [Am] IRS; Internal Revenue Service

de **belastingfraude** /bəlɑstɪŋfraudə/ tax fraud

de **belastingheffing** /bəlɑstɪŋhɛfɪŋ/ (pl: -en) taxation, levying of taxes

de **belastinginspecteur** /bəlɑstɪŋɪnspɛktør/ (pl: -s) tax inspector, inspector of taxes

de **belastingnomade** /bəlɑstɪŋnomadə/ (pl: -n) tax nomad

de **belastingontduiking** /bəlɑstɪŋɔndœykɪŋ/ (pl: -en) tax evasion, tax dodging

het **belastingparadijs** /bəlɑstɪŋparadɛis/ (pl:

-paradijzen) tax haven

de **belastingplichtige** /bəlɑstɪŋplɪxtəɣə/ (pl: -n) taxpayer

het **belastingstelsel** /bəlɑstɪŋstɛlsəl/ (pl: -s) tax system, system of taxation

het **belastingtarief** /bəlɑstɪŋtarif/ (pl: -tarieven) revenue tariff, tax rate

belastingvrij /bəlɑstɪŋvrɛi/ (adj) tax-free, duty-free; duty-paid; untaxed

belazeren /bəlazərə(n)/ (belazerde, heeft belazerd) [inform] cheat, make a fool of

de **belbundel** /bɛlbʏndəl/ (pl: -s) calling plan

beledigen /bəledəɣə(n)/ (beledigde, heeft beledigd) offend; [stronger] insult: *zich beledigd* **voelen** *door* be (*or:* feel) offended by

beledigend /bəledəɣənt/ (adj, adv) offensive (to), insulting (to), abusive

de **belediging** /bəledəɣɪŋ/ (pl: -en) insult, affront: *een* **grove** (or: **zware**) *~ a* gross insult

beleefd /bəleft/ (adj, adv) polite, courteous; well-mannered; civil: *dat is* **niet** *~* that's bad manners, that's not polite

de **beleefdheid** /bəleftheit/ (pl: -heden) politeness, courtesy

het **beleg** /bəlɛx/ **1** siege: *de* **staat** *van ~ afkondigen* declare martial law **2** (sandwich) filling

belegen /bəleɣə(n)/ (adj) mature(d); ripe; [fig] stale: *jong (licht) ~ kaas* semi-mature(d) cheese

belegeren /bəleɣərə(n)/ (belegerde, heeft belegerd) besiege, lay siege to

de **belegering** /bəleɣərɪŋ/ (pl: -en) siege

¹beleggen /bəlɛɣə(n)/ (belegde, heeft belegd) invest: *in effecten ~* invest in stocks and shares

²beleggen /bəlɛɣə(n)/ (belegde, heeft belegd) **1** convene, call: *een* **vergadering** *~* call a meeting **2** cover, fill; put meat (*or:* cheese) on [slice of bread]: *belegde* **broodjes** (ham, cheese etc.) rolls

de **belegger** /bəlɛɣər/ (pl: -s) investor

de **belegging** /bəlɛɣɪŋ/ (pl: -en) investment

het **beleggingsfonds** /bəlɛɣɪŋsfon(t)s/ (pl: -en) **1** investment trust (*or:* fund) **2** [roughly] gilt-edged (*or:* government) securities

het **beleid** /bəlɛit/ **1** policy: *het ~ van deze* **regering** the policies of this government; *ver-* **keerd** (or: **slecht**) *~* mismanagement **2** tact, discretion: *met ~ te werk gaan* handle things tactfully

belemmeren /bəlɛmərə(n)/ (belemmerde, heeft belemmerd) hinder, hamper; [stronger] impede; interfere with; [stronger] obstruct; block: *iem. het* **uitzicht** *~* obstruct (*or:* block) s.o.'s view; *de* **rechtsgang** *~* obstruct the course of justice

de **belemmering** /bəlɛmərɪŋ/ (pl: -en) hindrance, impediment, interference, obstruction: *een ~* **vormen** *voor* stand in the way of

belendend /bəlɛndənt/ (adj) adjoining, adjacent, neighbouring

belenen /bəlenə(n)/ (beleende, heeft beleend) pawn; borrow money on, raise a loan on

beleren /bələrə(n)/ lecture

het **beletsel** /bəlɛtsəl/ (pl: -s) obstacle, impediment

beletten /bəlɛtə(n)/ (belette, heeft belet) prevent (from), obstruct

beleven /bələvə(n)/ (beleefde, heeft beleefd) go through, experience: *de spannend-ste* **avonturen** *~* have the most exciting adventures; *plezier ~ aan* enjoy

de **belevenis** /bələvənɪs/ (pl: -sen) experience, adventure

belezen /bələzə(n)/ (adj) well-read, widely-read: *een ~* **man** a man of wide reading

de **Belg** /bɛlx/ (pl: -en) Belgian

België /bɛlɣijə/ Belgium

Belgisch /bɛlɣis/ (adj) Belgian

Belgrado /bɛlɣrado/ Belgrade

belichamen /bəlɪxamə(n)/ (belichaamde, heeft belichaamd) embody

de **belichaming** /bəlɪxamɪŋ/ (pl: -en) embodiment

belichten /bəlɪxtə(n)/ (belichtte, heeft belicht) **1** illuminate, light (up) **2** discuss, shed (*or:* throw) light on: *een* **probleem** *van verschillende kanten ~* discuss different aspects of a problem **3** expose

de **belichting** /bəlɪxtɪŋ/ lighting

het **¹believen** /bəlivə(n)/: *suiker toevoegen* **naar** *~* add sugar to taste

²believen /bəlivə(n)/ (beliefde, heeft beliefd) want, desire

belijden /bəlɛidə(n)/ (beleed, heeft beleden) profess, avow

de **belijdenis** /bəlɛidənɪs/ (pl: -sen) confession (of faith); confirmation

de **Belizaan** /bəlizan/ (pl: Belizanen) Belizian

Belizaans /bəlizans/ (adj) Belizian

Belize /bəlizə/ Belize

de **belkaart** /bɛlkart/ phone card

¹bellen /bɛlə(n)/ (belde, heeft gebeld) ring (the bell): *de* **fietser** *belde* the cyclist rang his bell; *er* **wordt** *gebeld* there's a ring at the door

²bellen /bɛlə(n)/ (belde, heeft gebeld) ring (up), call: *kan ik even ~?* may I use the (tele)-phone?

bellenblazen /bɛlə(n)blazə(n)/ blow bubbles

het **belletje** /bɛləcə/ (pl: -s) buzz, call, ring

de **belminuut** /bɛlminyt/ (pl: -minuten) (time) unit

de **belofte** /bəlɔftə/ (pl: -n) promise; pledge: *iem. een ~* **doen** make s.o. a promise; *zijn ~* **(ver)breken** break one's promise; *zijn ~* **houden** keep (*or:* live up) to one's promise (to s.o.), be as good as one's word; *~ maakt* **schuld** promise is debt

belonen /bəlonə(n)/ (beloonde, heeft beloond) pay, reward, repay

de **beloning** /bəlonɪŋ/ (pl: -en) reward; pay-(ment): *als ~ (van, voor)* in reward (for)

het **beloningscentrum** /bəlonɪŋsɛntrʏm/ re-ward (*or:* pleasure) centre

het **beloop** /bəlop/ (pl: belopen) course, way: *iets op zijn ~ laten* let sth. take (*or:* run) its course; let things slide

belopen /bəlopə(n)/ (beliep, heeft belopen) **1** walk: *die afstand is in één dag niet te ~* it's not a distance you can walk in one day **2** amount (*or:* come) to, total; run (in)to

beloven /bəlovə(n)/ (beloofde, heeft be-loofd) promise; vow; pledge: *dat belooft niet veel goeds* that does not augur well; *het be-looft een mooie dag te worden* it looks as if it'll be a lovely day; *dat belooft wat!* that's promising!; that spells trouble!

het **belspel** /bɛlspɛl/ (pl: -len) phone-in pro-gramme, phone-in contest

het **beltegoed** /bɛltəɣut/ (pl: -en) (calling) cred-it: *zijn ~ opvragen* check his calling credit; *zijn ~ opwaarderen* top up his calling credit

de **beltoon** /bɛlton/ (pl: beltonen) ringtone

beluisteren /bəlœystərə(n)/ (beluisterde, heeft beluisterd) **1** listen to; listen in to: *het programma is iedere zondag te ~* the pro-gramme is broadcast every Sunday **2** hear, overhear

belust /bəlʏst/ (adj) (+ op) bent (on); out (for)

de **belwaarde** /bɛlwardə/ (pl: -n) [Belg] credit (on prepaid phonecard)

bemachtigen /bəmɑxtəɣə(n)/ (bemachtig-de, heeft bemachtigd) **1** get hold of, get (*or:* lay) one's hands on: *een zitplaats ~* secure a seat **2** seize, capture, take (possession of); acquire

bemalen /bəmalə(n)/ (bemaalde, heeft be-maald/bemalen) drain

bemannen /bəmɑnə(n)/ (bemande, heeft bemand) man, staff; crew: *een bemand ruim-tevaartuig* a manned spacecraft

de **bemanning** /bəmɑnɪŋ/ (pl: -en) crew; ship's company; complement; garrison

het **bemanningslid** /bəmɑnɪŋslɪt/ (pl: -leden) crewman, member of the crew, hand

bemerken /bəmɛrkə(n)/ (bemerkte, heeft bemerkt) notice, note

bemesten /bəmɛstə(n)/ (bemestte, heeft bemest) manure; fertilize

bemeubelen /bəmøbələ(n)/ (bemeubelde, heeft bemeubeld) [Belg] furnish

de **bemiddelaar** /bəmɪdəlar/ (pl: -s) interme-diary; mediator; go-between

bemiddelbaar /bəmɪdəlbar/ (adj) employ-able

bemiddeld /bəmɪdəlt/ (adj) affluent, well-to-do

bemiddelen /bəmɪdələ(n)/ (bemiddelde, heeft bemiddeld) mediate: *~d optreden (in)*

act as a mediator (*or:* an arbitrator) (in)

de **bemiddeling** /bəmɪdəlɪŋ/ mediation

bemind /bəmɪnt/ (adj) dear (to), loved (by), much-loved: *door zijn charme maakte hij zich bij iedereen ~* his charm endeared him to eve-ryone

de **beminde** /bəmɪndə/ (pl: -n) beloved, sweetheart

beminnelijk /bəmɪnələk/ (adj) amiable

beminnen /bəmɪnə(n)/ (beminde, heeft bemind) love, hold dear

bemoedigen /bəmudəɣə(n)/ (bemoedig-de, heeft bemoedigd) encourage, hearten

de **bemoeial** /bəmujal/ (pl: -len) busybody

zich **bemoeien** /bəmujə(n)/ (bemoeide zich, heeft zich bemoeid) (+ met) meddle (in), in-terfere (in): *bemoei je niet overal mee!* mind your own business!; *daar bemoei ik me niet mee* I don't want to get mixed up in that

de **bemoeienis** /bəmujənɪs/ (pl: -sen) **1** con-cern: *geen ~ hebben met* not be concerned with, have nothing to do with **2** interference

bemoeilijken /bəmujləkə(n)/ (bemoeilijk-te, heeft bemoeilijkt) hamper, hinder; im-pede; aggravate; complicate

bemoeiziek /bəmujzik/ (adj) interfering, meddling: *~ zijn* be a meddler (*or:* busy-body); be a nos(e)y parker

de **bemoeizucht** /bəmujzʏxt/ meddlesome-ness, interference

benadelen /bənadelə(n)/ (benadeelde, heeft benadeeld) harm, put at a disadvan-tage, handicap; [law] prejudice: *iem. in zijn rechten ~* infringe s.o.'s rights

benaderbaar /bənadərbar/ (adj) ap-proachable

benaderen /bənadərə(n)/ (benaderde, heeft benaderd) **1** approach; [fig also] ap-proximate to; come close to: *moeilijk te ~* unapproachable **2** approach, get in touch with: *iem. ~ over een kwestie* approach s.o. on a matter **3** calculate (roughly), estimate (roughly)

de **benadering** /bənadərɪŋ/ (pl: -en) **1** ap-proach; [fig also] approximation (to) **2** (rough) calculation, (rough) estimate, ap-proximation ‖ *bij ~* approximately, roughly

benadrukken /bənadrʏkə(n)/ (benadruk-te, heeft benadrukt) emphasize, stress, un-derline

de **benaming** /bənamɪŋ/ (pl: -en) name, desig-nation

benard /bənɑrt/ (adj) awkward, perilous, distressing

benauwd /bənɑut/ (adj) **1** short of breath **2** close, muggy; stuffy: *een ~ gevoel op de borst* a tight feeling in one's chest; *~ warm* close, muggy, oppressive **3** anxious, afraid: *het ~ krijgen* feel anxious **4** upsetting **5** nar-row, cramped

de **benauwdheid** /bənɑuthɛit/ **1** tightness of

the chest **2** closeness, stuffiness **3** fear, anxiety

benauwen /bənɑuwə(n)/ (benauwde, heeft benauwd) weigh down on

de **bende** /bɛndə/ (pl: -s) **1** mess, shambles **2** mass; swarm; crowd **3** gang, pack

¹**beneden** /bənedə(n)/ (adv) down, below; downstairs; at the bottom: (via de trap) **naar** ~ gaan go down(stairs); de vijfde regel **van** ~ the fifth line up; the fifth line from the bottom

²**beneden** /bənedə(n)/ (prep) under, below, beneath: kinderen ~ de zes **jaar** children under six (years of age)

de **benedenverdieping** /bənedə(n)vərdipɪŋ/ (pl: -en) ground floor; lower floor

benedenwinds /bənedə(n)wɪnts/ (adj) leeward

de **benefietwedstrijd** /bənefitwɛtstrɛɪt/ (pl: -en) benefit (match)

de **Benelux** /benəlyks/ Benelux, the Benelux countries

benemen /bənemə(n)/ (benam, heeft benomen) take away (from)

benen /benə(n)/ (adj) bone

benepen /bənepə(n)/ (adj) **1** small-minded, petty **2** anxious, timid

benevelen /bənevələ(n)/ (benevelde, heeft beneveld) cloud, (be)fog: **lichtelijk** beneveld tipsy, woozy

Bengaals /bɛŋɑls/ (adj) Bengal; Bengali

de **Bengalees** /bɛŋɑles/ (pl: Bengalezen) Bangladeshi, Bengali

de **bengel** /bɛŋəl/ (pl: -s) (little) rascal, scamp, (little) terror

bengelen /bɛŋələ(n)/ (bengelde, heeft gebengeld) dangle, swing (to and fro)

benieuwd /bəniwt/ (adj) curious: ik **ben** ~ wat hij zal zeggen I wonder what he'll say; ze was **erg** ~ (te horen) wat hij ervan vond she was dying to hear what he thought of it

benieuwen /bəniwə(n)/: het zal mij ~ **of** hij komt I wonder if he'll come

benijden /bənɛɪdə(n)/ (benijdde, heeft benijd) envy, be envious (of), be jealous (of): al onze vrienden ~ ons **om** ons huis our house is the envy of all our friends

benijdenswaardig /bənɛɪdənswardəx/ (adj, adv) enviable

Benin /benɪn/ Benin

de **Beniner** /benɪnər/ (pl: -s) Beninese

benodigd /bənodəxt/ (adj) required, necessary, wanted

de **benodigdheden** /bənodəxthedə(n)/ requirements, necessities

benoemen /bənumə(n)/ (benoemde, heeft benoemd) appoint, assign (to), nominate: iem. **tot** burgemeester ~ appoint s.o. mayor

de **benoeming** /bənumɪŋ/ (pl: -en) appointment, nomination

het **benul** /bənyl/ notion, inkling, idea: hij **heeft** er geen (flauw) ~ van he hasn't got the fog-

giest idea

benutten /bənytə(n)/ (benutte, heeft benut) utilize, make use of: zijn **kansen** ~ make the most of one's opportunities; een **strafschop** ~ score from a penalty

B en W /beɛnwe/ (pl) [Dutch] Burgemeester en Wethouders Mayor and Aldermen

de **benzine** /bɛnzinə/ petrol; [Am] gas(oline): gewone **(normale)** ~ two star petrol; loodvrije ~ unleaded petrol

de **benzinemotor** /bɛnzinəmotər/ (pl: -en) petrol engine

de **benzinepomp** /bɛnzinəpomp/ (pl: -en) **1** petrol station, filling station **2** fuel pump

het **benzinestation** /bɛnzinəsta(t)ʃon/ (pl: -s) petrol station, filling station

de **benzinetank** /bɛnzinətɛŋk/ (pl: -s) petrol tank; [Am] gas(oline) tank

de **beoefenaar** /bəufənar/ (pl: -s) student; practitioner

beoefenen /bəufənə(n)/ (beoefende, heeft beoefend) practise, pursue, follow, study; go in for: **sport** ~ go in for sports

beogen /bəoɣə(n)/ (beoogde, heeft beoogd) have in mind, aim at, intend: het beoogde **resultaat** the intended (or: desired) result, the result aimed at

de **beoordelaar** /bəordelar/ (pl: -s) judge, assessor; reviewer

beoordelen /bəordelə(n)/ (beoordeelde, heeft beoordeeld) judge, assess: een **boek** ~ criticize a book; dat kan ik **zelf** wel ~! I can judge for myself (, thank you very much)!; dat is **moeilijk** te ~ that's hard to say; iem. **verkeerd** ~ misjudge s.o.

de **beoordeling** /bəordelɪŋ/ judgement, assessment, evaluation; [educ] mark; review

¹**bepaald** /bəpalt/ (adj) **1** particular, specific: heb je een ~ **iem.** in gedachten? are you thinking of anyone in particular? **2** specific, fixed, set, specified; given: **vooraf** ~ predetermined **3** certain, particular: om ~e **redenen** for certain reasons

²**bepaald** /bəpalt/ (adv) definitely: **niet** ~ slim not particularly clever

bepakken /bəpɑkə(n)/: bepakt en **bezakt** [roughly] with bag and baggage, [roughly] packed up and ready to go, [roughly] all ready to go

de **bepakking** /bəpɑkɪŋ/ (pl: -en) pack; (marching) kit

bepalen /bəpalə(n)/ (bepaalde, heeft bepaald) **1** prescribe, lay down, determine, stipulate: zijn **keus** ~ make one's choice; **vooraf** ~ predetermine; de prijs werd bepaald **op** € 100,- the price was set at 100 euros **2** determine, ascertain: u mag de **dag** zélf ~ (you can) name the day; het **tempo** ~ set the pace

de **bepaling** /bəpalɪŋ/ (pl: -en) **1** definition **2** provision, stipulation, regulation: een

wettelijke ~ a legal provision (*or:* stipulation)
3 condition **4** determination

¹**beperken** /bəpɛrkə(n)/ (beperkte, heeft beperkt) **1** limit, restrict **2** (+ tot) restrict (to), limit (to), confine (to), keep (to): *de uitgaven* ~ keep expenditure down; *tot het minimum* ~ keep (down) to a minimum

zich ²**beperken** /bəpɛrkə(n)/ (beperkte zich, heeft zich beperkt) restrict (o.s. to), confine (o.s. to)

de **beperking** /bəpɛrkɪŋ/ (pl: -en) **1** limitation, restriction: *zijn ~en kennen* know one's limitations; *~en opleggen aan* impose limits (*or:* limitations) on; [euph] *iem. met een* ~ s.o. with a disability (*or:* an impairment) **2** reduction, cutback: *een ~ van de uitgaven* a reduction of expenditure, a cut

beperkt /bəpɛrkt/ (adj, adv) limited, restricted, confined; reduced: ~ *blijven tot* be restricted to; *een ~e keuze* a limited choice; *verstandelijk* ~ mentally challenged (*or:* disabled)

beplanten /bəplɑntə(n)/ (beplantte, heeft beplant) plant (with); sow (with)

de **beplanting** /bəplɑntɪŋ/ (pl: -en) planting, plants, crop(s)

bepleiten /bəplɛitə(n)/ (bepleitte, heeft bepleit) argue, plead, advocate: *iemands zaak* ~ *(bij iem.)* plead s.o.'s case (with s.o.)

beppen /bɛpə(n)/ (bepte, heeft gebept) yack, chat

bepraten /bəpratə(n)/ (bepraatte, heeft bepraat) talk over/about, discuss: *wij zullen die zaak nader* ~ we will talk the matter over

beproefd /bəpruft/ (adj): *een ~e methode* a tried and tested (*or:* well-tried, approved) method

beproeven /bəpruvə(n)/ (beproefde, heeft beproefd) (put to the) test, try: *zijn geluk* ~ try one's luck

de **beproeving** /bəpruvɪŋ/ (pl: -en) **1** testing **2** ordeal, trial

het **beraad** /bərat/ consideration, deliberation; consultation: *na rijp* ~ after careful consideration

beraadslagen /bəratslaɣə(n)/ (beraadslaagde, heeft beraadslaagd) deliberate (upon), consider: *met iem. over iets* ~ consult with s.o. about sth.

de **beraadslaging** /bəratslaɣɪŋ/ (pl: -en) deliberation, consideration, consultation

zich **beraden** /bəradə(n)/ (beraadde zich, heeft zich beraden) consider, think over: *zich ~ over (op)* deliberate about

beramen /bəramə(n)/ (beraamde, heeft beraamd) **1** devise, plan: *een aanslag* ~ plot an attack **2** estimate, calculate

de **beraming** /bəramɪŋ/ (pl: -en) **1** planning, design **2** estimate, calculation, budget

de **Berber** /bɛrbər/ (pl: -s) Berber

het **berde** /bɛrdə/: *iets te* ~ *brengen* bring up a

matter, raise a point

berechten /bərɛɣtə(n)/ (berechtte, heeft berecht) try

de **berechting** /bərɛɣtɪŋ/ (pl: -en) trial; judgement; adjudication

bereden /bərɛdə(n)/ (adj) mounted

beredeneren /bərədənɛrə(n)/ (beredeneerde, heeft beredeneerd) argue, reason (out)

bereid /bərɛit/ (adj) **1** prepared **2** ready, willing, disposed: *tot alles* ~ *zijn* be prepared to do anything

bereiden /bərɛidə(n)/ (bereidde, heeft bereid) prepare, get ready; cook; make, fix: *een maaltijd* ~ prepare a meal; *iem. een hartelijke (warme) ontvangst* ~ give s.o. a warm welcome

de **bereidheid** /bərɛithɛit/ readiness, preparedness, willingness

de **bereiding** /bərɛidɪŋ/ (pl: -en) preparation, making, manufacture, production

de **bereidingswijze** /bərɛidɪŋswɛizə/ (pl: -n) method of preparation, process of manufacture, procedure

bereidwillig /bərɛitwɪləɣ/ (adj, adv) obliging, willing; helpful: ~ *iets doen* do sth. willingly

het **bereik** /bərɛik/ reach; range: *buiten (het)* ~ *van kinderen bewaren* keep away from children; *ik heb geen* ~ I'm not getting a signal; *het* ~ *van een elektrische auto* an electric car's range

bereikbaar /bərɛigbar/ (adj) accessible, attainable, within reach: *bent u telefonisch ~?* can you be reached by phone?

bereiken /bərɛikə(n)/ (bereikte, heeft bereikt) **1** reach, arrive in, arrive at, get to **2** reach, achieve, attain, gain: *zijn doel* ~ attain one's goal **3** reach, contact; get through (to)

berekend /bərɛkənt/ (adj) meant for, designed for; equal to, suited to: *hij is niet ~ voor zijn taak* he is not up to his job

berekenen /bərɛkənə(n)/ (berekende, heeft berekend) **1** calculate, compute, determine, figure out; add up **2** charge: *iem. te veel* (or: *weinig*) ~ overcharge (*or:* undercharge) s.o.

berekenend /bərɛkənənt/ (adj) calculating, scheming

de **berekening** /bərɛkənɪŋ/ (pl: -en) **1** calculation, computation: *naar (volgens) een ruwe* ~ at a rough estimate **2** calculation, evaluation, assessment: *een huwelijk uit* ~ a marriage of convenience

de **berg** /bɛrɣ/ (pl: -en) mountain; hill: *~en verzetten* move mountains; *ik zie er als een* ~ *tegenop* I'm not looking forward to it one little bit; [fig] *iem. gouden ~en beloven* promise s.o. the moon

bergachtig /bɛrɣɑɣtəɣ/ (adj) mountainous,

hilly
bergafwaarts /bɛrˣɐfwarts/ (adv) down-hill
bergbeklimmen /bɛrˠbəklɪmə(n)/ mountaineering, (rock)climbing
de **bergbeklimmer** /bɛrˠbəklɪmər/ (pl: -s) mountaineer, (mountain-)climber
bergen /bɛrˠə(n)/ (borg, heeft geborgen) **1** store, put away: *mappen in een la* ~ put files away in a drawer **2** [shipp] salvage **3** rescue, save; shelter; recover || *berg je* **maar!** watch out (for yourself)!
de **berggeit** /bɛrˣɛit/ (pl: -en) chamois, mountain goat
de **berghelling** /bɛrˣhɛlɪŋ/ (pl: -en) mountain slope, mountainside
het **berghok** /bɛrˣhɔk/ (pl: -ken) shed; storeroom; boxroom
de **berghut** /bɛrˣhʏt/ (pl: -ten) mountain hut, climbers' hut, mountain refuge
de **berging** /bɛrˠɪŋ/ (pl: -en) **1** [shipp] salvage, recovery **2** storeroom, boxroom; shed
de **bergkam** /bɛrˣkam/ (pl: -men) (mountain) ridge
de **bergketen** /bɛrˣketə(n)/ (pl: -s) mountain range (*or:* chain)
het **bergmeubel** /bɛrˣmøbəl/ (pl: -s) storage cabinet
bergop /bɛrˣɔp/ (adv) uphill
de **bergpas** /bɛrˣpɑs/ (pl: -sen) (mountain) pass, col
de **bergplaats** /bɛrˣplats/ (pl: -en) storage (space); storeroom; shed
de **bergschoen** /bɛrˣsˣun/ (pl: -en) mountaineering (*or:* climbing) boot
de **bergsport** /bɛrˣspɔrt/ mountaineering, (mountain) climbing; alpinism
de **bergtop** /bɛrˣtɔp/ (pl: -pen) summit, mountain top, peak; pinnacle
de **bergwand** /bɛrˣwɑnt/ (pl: -en) mountain side, face of a mountain, mountain wall
het **bericht** /bərɪˣt/ (pl: -en) message, notice, communication; report; news: *volgens de* **laatste** ~en according to the latest reports; *tot* **nader** ~ until further notice; *u krijgt* **schriftelijk** ~ you will receive written notice (*or:* notification); ~ **krijgen** *over* receive information about; ~ **achterlaten** *dat* leave a message that
berichten /bərɪˣtə(n)/ (berichtte, heeft bericht) report, send word, inform, advise
de **berichtgeving** /bərɪˣtˣevɪŋ/ reporting, (news) coverage, report(s)
berijden /bərɛidə(n)/ (bereed, heeft bereden) **1** ride **2** ride (on), drive (on)
de **berijder** /bərɛidər/ rider
berispen /bərɪspə(n)/ (berispte, heeft berispt) reprimand, admonish
de **berisping** /bərɪspɪŋ/ (pl: -en) reprimand, reproof
de **berk** /bɛrk/ (pl: -en) birch

Berlijn /bɛrlɛin/ Berlin
de **berm** /bɛrm/ (pl: -en) verge, roadside, shoulder
de **bermbom** /bɛrmbɔm/ (pl: -men) IED *(improvised explosive device)*; roadside bomb
de **bermuda** /bɛrmydɑ/ (pl: -'s) Bermuda shorts, Bermudas
de **Bermuda's** /bɛrmydɑs/ (pl) the Bermudas, Bermuda
beroemd /bərumt/ (adj) famous, renowned, celebrated, famed: ~ *om* famous for
de **beroemdheid** /bərumthɛit/ (pl: -heden) **1** fame, renown **2** celebrity
zich **beroemen** /bərumə(n)/ (beroemde zich, heeft zich beroemd) boast (about), take pride (in), pride o.s. (on)
het **beroep** /bərup/ (pl: -en) **1** occupation, profession, vocation; trade; business: *in de uit-* **oefening** *van zijn* ~ in the exercise of one's profession; *wat ben jij* **van** ~? what do you do for a living? **2** appeal: *raad van* ~ **a)** Court of Appeal; **b)** [Am] Court of Appeals; *in (hoger)* ~ *gaan* appeal (to a higher court), take one's case to a higher court || *een* ~ *doen op iem. (iets)* (make an) appeal to s.o. (sth.)
zich **beroepen** /bərupə(n)/ (beriep zich, heeft zich beroepen) (+ op) call (upon), appeal (to), refer (to)
beroeps /bərups/ (adj) professional: ~ *worden* turn professional
de **beroepsbevolking** /bərupsbəvɔlkɪŋ/ employed population, working population, labour force
de **beroepsdeformatie** /bərupsdeforma(t)si/ (pl: -s) occupational (*or:* job-related) disability
het **beroepsgeheim** /bərupsˣəhɛim/ (pl: -en) duty of professional confidentiality: *het* ~ *schenden* breach one's duty of professional confidentiality
beroepshalve /bərupshɑlvə/ (adv) professionally, in one's professional capacity
de **beroepskeuze** /bərupskøzə/ choice of (a) career (*or:* of profession): *begeleiding* **bij** *de* ~ careers counselling
de **beroepskeuzeadviseur** /bərupskøzəɑtfizør/ (pl: -s) counsellor, careers master
de **beroepsmilitair** /bərupsmilitɛːr/ (pl: -en) regular (soldier)
het **beroepsonderwijs** /bərupsɔndərwɛis/ vocational training, professional training
de **beroepsopleiding** /bərupsɔplɛidɪŋ/ (pl: -en) professional (*or:* vocational, occupational) training
de **beroepsschool** /bərupsˣol/ (pl: -scholen) [Belg] technical school
de **beroepsvaart** /bərupsfart/ commercial shipping
de **beroepsvoetballer** /bərupsfudbɑlər/ (pl: -s) professional football player

de **beroepsziekte** /bərupsiktə/ (pl: -n, -s) occupational disease (or: illness)
beroerd /bərurt/ (adj, adv) **1** miserable, wretched, rotten: *ik word er ~ van* it makes me sick; *hij ziet er ~ uit* he looks terrible **2** lazy: *hij is nooit te ~ om mij te helpen* he is always willing to help me
beroeren /bərurə(n)/ (beroerde, heeft beroerd) **1** touch **2** trouble, agitate
de **beroering** /bərurɪŋ/ (pl: -en) trouble, agitation, unrest, commotion
de **beroerte** /bərurtə/ (pl: -s) stroke
berokkenen /bərɔkənə(n)/ (berokkende, heeft berokkend) cause: *iem. schade ~* cause s.o. harm
berooid /bərojt/ (adj) destitute
het **berouw** /bərɑu/ remorse: *~ hebben over* regret; *~ tonen* show remorse (or: contrition)
berouwen /bərɑuwə(n)/ (berouwde, heeft berouwd) regret, rue, feel sorry for
beroven /bərovə(n)/ (beroofde, heeft beroofd) **1** rob: *iem. ~ van iets* rob s.o. of sth. **2** deprive of, strip: *iem. van zijn vrijheid ~* deprive s.o. of his freedom; *zich van het leven ~* take one's own life
de **beroving** /bərovɪŋ/ (pl: -en) robbery
berucht /bəryxt/ (adj) notorious (for), infamous
berusten /bərystə(n)/ (berustte, heeft berust) **1** (+ op) rest on, be based on, be founded on: *dit moet op een misverstand ~* this must be due to a misunderstanding **2** resign o.s. to **3** rest with, be deposited with: *de wetgevende macht berust bij het parlement* legislative power rests with parliament
de **berusting** /bərystɪŋ/ resignation, acceptance, acquiescence
de **bes** /bɛs/ **1** berry: *blauwe ~sen* blueberries; *rode ~sen* redcurrants **2** [mus] B-flat
beschaafd /bəsxaft/ (adj) cultured, civilized, refined, well-bred
beschaamd /bəsxamt/ (adj, adv) ashamed, shamefaced
beschadigd /bəsxadəxt/ (adj) damaged
beschadigen /bəsxadəɣə(n)/ (beschadigde, heeft beschadigd) damage: *door brand beschadigde goederen* fire-damaged goods
de **beschadiging** /bəsxadəɣɪŋ/ (pl: -en) damage
beschamen /bəsxamə(n)/ (beschaamde, heeft beschaamd) **1** (put to) shame **2** disappoint, betray: *iemands vertrouwen ~* betray s.o.'s confidence
beschamend /bəsxamənt/ (adj) shameful, humiliating, ignominious: *een ~e vertoning* a humiliating spectacle
de **beschaving** /bəsxavɪŋ/ (pl: -en) **1** civilization **2** culture, refinement, polish
bescheiden /bəsxɛidə(n)/ (adj, adv) **1** modest, unassuming: *zich ~ terugtrekken* withdraw discreetly; *naar mijn ~ mening* in my

humble opinion **2** modest, unpretentious: *een ~ optrekje* a modest little place
de **bescheidenheid** /bəsxɛidə(n)hɛit/ modesty, unpretentiousness: *valse ~* false modesty
de **beschermeling** /bəsxɛrməlɪŋ/ (pl: -en) ward, protégé
beschermen /bəsxɛrmə(n)/ (beschermde, heeft beschermd) protect, shield, preserve, (safe)guard, shelter: *een beschermd leventje* a sheltered life; *~ tegen de zon* screen from the sun
de **beschermengel** /bəsxɛrmɛŋəl/ (pl: -en) guardian angel
de **beschermer** /bəsxɛrmər/ (pl: -s) defender, guardian, protector
de **beschermheer** /bəsxɛrmher/ (pl: -heren) patron
de **beschermheilige** /bəsxɛrmhɛiləɣə/ (pl: -n) patron saint, patron, patroness
de **bescherming** /bəsxɛrmɪŋ/ (pl: -en) protection, (safe)guarding, shelter, cover: *~ bieden aan* offer protection to; *iem. in ~ nemen* take s.o. under one's protection; [fig] take s.o. under one's wing
de **beschermingsmiddelen** /bəsxɛrmɪŋsmɪdələ(n)/ (pl) protective equipment (or: gear)
de **beschermlaag** /bəsxɛrmlax/ protective layer (or: coating)
beschieten /bəsxitə(n)/ (beschoot, heeft beschoten) fire on, fire at, shell, bombard, pelt
beschikbaar /bəsxɪgbar/ (adj) available, at one's disposal, free
de **beschikbaarheid** /bəsxɪgbarhɛit/ availability
beschikken /bəsxɪkə(n)/ (beschikte, heeft beschikt) (+ over) dispose of, have (control of), have at one's disposal: *over genoeg tijd ~* have enough time at one's disposal; *over iemands lot ~* determine s.o.'s fate
de **beschikking** /bəsxɪkɪŋ/ (pl: -en) disposition, disposal: *ik sta tot uw ~* I am at your disposal; *ter ~ stellen* provide, supply, make available
beschilderen /bəsxɪldərə(n)/ (beschilderde, heeft beschilderd) paint
de **beschildering** /bəsxɪldərɪŋ/ (pl: -en) painting
beschimmeld /bəsxɪməlt/ (adj) mouldy: *~e papieren* musty papers
beschimmelen /bəsxɪmələ(n)/ (beschimmelde, is beschimmeld) become mouldy
beschimpen /bəsxɪmpə(n)/ (beschimpte, heeft beschimpt) taunt, jeer at, call names
beschonken /bəsxɔŋkə(n)/ (adj) drunk; intoxicated: *in ~ toestand* under the influence (of alcohol)
beschouwen /bəsxɑuwə(n)/ (beschouwde, heeft beschouwd) **1** consider, contemplate **2** consider, regard as, look upon as: *iets als*

zijn plicht ~ consider sth. (as, to be) one's duty

de **beschouwing** /bəsχɑuwɪŋ/ (pl: -en) consideration, view: *iets buiten* ~ *laten* leave sth. out of account, ignore sth.

beschrijven /bəsχrɛivə(n)/ (beschreef, heeft beschreven) **1** write (on) **2** describe, portray: *dat is met geen pen te* ~ it defies description **3** describe, trace: *een baan om de aarde* ~ trace a path around the earth

de **beschrijving** /bəsχrɛivɪŋ/ (pl: -en) description; depiction; sketch: *dat gaat alle* ~ *te boven* that defies description

beschroomd /bəsχromt/ (adj) timid, diffident, bashful

de **beschuit** /bəsχœyt/ (pl: -en) Dutch rusk, biscuit rusk, zwieback

de **beschuldigde** /bəsχʏldəɣdə/ (pl: -n) accused, defendant

beschuldigen /bəsχʏldəɣə(n)/ (beschuldigde, heeft beschuldigd) accuse (of), charge (s.o. with sth.), blame (s.o. for sth.): *ik beschuldig niemand, maar …* I won't point a finger, but …

beschuldigend /bəsχʏldəɣənt/ (adj) accusatory, denunciatory

de **beschuldiging** /bəsχʏldəɣɪŋ/ (pl: -en) accusation, imputation; charge; indictment: *iem. in staat van* ~ *stellen (wegens)* indict s.o. (for); *onder (op)* ~ *van diefstal (gearresteerd)* (arrested) on a charge of theft

beschut /bəsχʏt/ (adj) sheltered, protected || [Belg] ~*te werkplaats* sheltered workshop

beschutten /bəsχʏtə(n)/ (beschutte, heeft beschut) (+ tegen) shelter (from), protect (from, against); shield (from)

de **beschutting** /bəsχʏtɪŋ/ (pl: -en) shelter, protection: *(geen)* ~ *bieden* offer (no) protection; ~ *tegen de regen* protection from the rain

het **besef** /bəsɛf/ understanding, idea; sense: *tot het* ~ *komen dat* come to realize that

beseffen /bəsɛfə(n)/ (besefte, heeft beseft) realize, be aware (of); grasp; be conscious (of): *voor ik het besefte, had ik ja gezegd* before I knew it, I had said yes

¹**beslaan** /bəslan/ (besloeg, is beslagen) mist up (*or:* over), steam up (*or:* over): *toen ik binnenkwam, besloeg mijn bril* when I entered, my glasses steamed up

²**beslaan** /bəslan/ (besloeg, heeft beslagen) **1** take up, cover; run to: *deze kast beslaat de halve kamer* this cupboard takes up half the room **2** shoe

het **beslag** /bəslɑχ/ (pl: -en) **1** batter **2** fitting(s); ironwork; metalwork; shoe **3** possession: *iemands tijd in* ~ *nemen* take up s.o.'s time; *deze tafel neemt te veel ruimte in* ~ this table takes up too much space **4** attachment: *smokkelwaar in* ~ *nemen* confiscate contraband || ~ *leggen op iets* take possession of sth., lay (one's) hands on sth.

de **beslaglegging** /bəslɑχlɛɣɪŋ/ (pl: -en) [law] attachment, seizure, distress (on)

beslechten /bəslɛχtə(n)/ (beslechtte, heeft beslecht) settle: *het pleit is beslecht* the dispute has been settled

de **beslisboom** /bəslɪzbom/ (pl: -bomen) decision tree

beslissen /bəslɪsə(n)/ (besliste, heeft beslist) decide, resolve: *dit doelpunt zou de wedstrijd* ~ this goal was to decide the match

beslissend /bəslɪsənt/ (adj) decisive, conclusive; final; crucial: *in een* ~ *stadium zijn* have come to a head, be at a critical stage

de **beslissing** /bəslɪsɪŋ/ (pl: -en) decision; ruling

de **beslissingswedstrijd** /bəslɪsɪŋswɛtstrɛit/ (pl: -en) decider, play-off: *een* ~ *spelen* play off

¹**beslist** /bəslɪst/ (adj) **1** definite **2** decided

²**beslist** /bəslɪst/ (adv) certainly, definitely

de **beslommering** /bəslɔmərɪŋ/ (pl: -en) worry: *de dagelijkse* ~*en* the day-to-day worries

besloten /bəslotə(n)/ (adj) closed, private: *een* ~ *vergadering* a meeting behind closed doors; *in* ~ *kring* in a closed (*or:* private) circle, private(ly)

besluipen /bəslœypə(n)/ (besloop, heeft beslopen) steal up on, creep up on; stalk: *de vrees besloop hen* (the) fear crept over them

het **besluit** /bəslœyt/ (pl: -en) **1** decision, resolution, resolve: *een* ~ *nemen* take a decision; *mijn* ~ *staat vast* I'm quite determined **2** conclusion: *tot* ~, *wil ik opmerken …* winding up (*or:* in conclusion) I wish to remark … **3** order, decree

besluiteloos /bəslœytəlos/ (adj) indecisive, irresolute

besluiten /bəslœytə(n)/ (besloot, heeft besloten) **1** conclude, close, end **2** decide, resolve

besluitvaardig /bəslœytfɑrdəχ/ (adj) decisive, resolute

besmeren /bəsmerə(n)/ (besmeerde, heeft besmeerd) butter; daub [with paint]

besmet /bəsmɛt/ (adj) **1** infected, contaminated **2** tainted, contaminated, polluted

besmettelijk /bəsmɛtələk/ (adj) **1** infectious, contagious, catching: *een* ~*e ziekte* an infectious disease **2** (be) easily soiled

besmetten /bəsmɛtə(n)/ (besmette, heeft besmet) **1** infect (with), contaminate (with): *met griep besmet worden (door iem.)* catch the flu (from s.o.) **2** taint, soil

de **besmetting** /bəsmɛtɪŋ/ (pl: -en) infection; contagion; disease: *radioactieve* ~ radioactive contamination

besmeuren /bəsmørə(n)/ (besmeurde, heeft besmeurd) stain, soil: *met bloed besmeurde handen* blood-stained hands

besneden /bəsnedə(n)/ (adj) circumcised

besnijden /bəsnɛidə(n)/ (besneed, heeft

besneden) circumcise

de **besnijdenis** /bəsnɛ̯idənɪs/ circumcision

¹**besnoeien** /bəsnu̯jə(n)/ (besnoeide, heeft besnoeid) cut down (on): *op de uitgaven* ~ cut down (on) expenses

²**besnoeien** /bəsnu̯jə(n)/ (besnoeide, heeft besnoeid) prune; lop; trim

bespannen /bəspɑnə(n)/ (bespande, heeft bespannen) **1** stretch; string **2** harness (a horse to a cart): *een rijtuig met paarden* ~ put horses to a carriage

besparen /bəspɑrə(n)/ (bespaarde, heeft bespaard) **1** save **2** spare, save: *de rest zal ik je maar* ~ I'll spare you the rest; *die moeite had u zich wel kunnen* ~ you could have spared yourself the trouble

de **besparing** /bəspɑrɪŋ/ (pl: -en) **1** saving, economy **2** saving(s), economies: *een* ~ *op* a saving on

bespelen /bəspelə(n)/ (bespeelde, heeft bespeeld) **1** [sport] play on, play in [field] **2** [mus] play (on) **3** manipulate; play on: *een gehoor* ~ play to an audience

bespeuren /bəspørə(n)/ (bespeurde, heeft bespeurd) sense, notice, perceive, find

bespieden /bəspidə(n)/ (bespiedde, heeft bespied) spy (on), watch

bespioneren /bəspijonerə(n)/ (bespioneerde, heeft bespioneerd) spy on

bespoedigen /bəspudəyə(n)/ (bespoedigde, heeft bespoedigd) accelerate, speed up

bespottelijk /bəspɔtələk/ (adj, adv) ridiculous, absurd: *een* ~ *figuur slaan* (make o.s.) look ridiculous

bespotten /bəspɔtə(n)/ (bespotte, heeft bespot) ridicule, mock, deride, scoff at

bespreekbaar /bəspregbar/ (adj) debatable, discussible

het **bespreekgeval** /bəsprekxəvɑl/ (pl: -len) review case, discussion case

bespreken /bəsprekə(n)/ (besprak, heeft besproken) **1** discuss, talk about; consider: *een probleem* ~ go into a problem **2** discuss, comment on, examine; review **3** book, reserve: *kaartjes (plaatsen)* ~ make reservations

de **bespreking** /bəsprekɪŋ/ (pl: -en) **1** discussion, talk **2** meeting, conference, talks **3** review **4** booking, reservation

besprenkelen /bəsprɛŋkələ(n)/ (besprenkelde, heeft besprenkeld) sprinkle

bespringen /bəsprɪŋə(n)/ (besprong, heeft besprongen) pounce on, jump

besproeien /bəspru̯jə(n)/ (besproeide, heeft besproeid) **1** sprinkle **2** irrigate; spray; water

bespuiten /bəspœy̯tə(n)/ (bespoot, heeft bespoten) spray

het **bessensap** /bɛsə(n)sɑp/ (red)currant juice; blackcurrant juice

¹**best** /bɛst/ (adj) **1** best, better, optimum: *het* ~*e van het* ~*e* the best there is; *met de* ~*e bedoelingen* with the best of intentions; ~*e maatjes zijn met* be very thick with; *Peter ziet er niet al te* ~ *uit* Peter is looking the worse for wear; *hij kan koken als de* ~*e* he can cook with the best of them; *op een na de* ~*e* the second best; *het* ~*e ermee!* good luck!; best wishes! **2** well, all right: *(het is) mij* ~ I don't mind **3** dear, good: *Beste Jan* Dear Jan || *de eerste, de* ~*e* anyone, anything, any; *hij overnacht niet in het eerste het* ~*e hotel* he doesn't stay at just any (old) hotel

²**best** /bɛst/ (adv) **1** best: *jij kent hem het* ~*e* you know him best **2** sure: *je weet het* ~ you know perfectly well; *het zal* ~ *lukken* it'll work out (all right) **3** really: *hij heeft het er* ~ *moeilijk mee* it's really very difficult for him **4** possibly, well: *dat zou* ~ *kunnen* that's quite possible; *ze zou* ~ *willen ...* she wouldn't mind ... || *zijn* ~ *doen* do one's best; *hij is op zijn* ~ he is at his best; *ze is op haar* ~ *(gekleed)* she looks her best

het ¹**bestaan** /bəstan/ **1** existence: *die firma viert vandaag haar vijftigjarig* ~ that firm is celebrating its fiftieth anniversary today **2** living, livelihood

²**bestaan** /bəstan/ (bestond, heeft bestaan) **1** exist, be (in existence): *laat daar geen misverstand over* ~ let there be no mistake about it; *onze liefde zal altijd blijven* ~ our love will live on forever; *ophouden te* ~ cease to exist **2** (+ uit) consist (of); be made up (of): *dit werk bestaat uit drie delen* this work consists of three parts **3** be possible: *hoe bestaat het!* can you believe it!

bestaand /bəstant/ (adj) existing, existent, current

het **bestaansminimum** /bəstansminimʏm/ (pl: -minima) subsistence level

het **bestaansrecht** /bəstansrɛxt/ right to exist: *geen* ~ *hebben* have no right to exist; *zijn* ~ *ontlenen aan* be justified by

het ¹**bestand** /bəstɑnt/ (pl: -en) **1** truce; cease-fire **2** file

²**bestand** /bəstɑnt/ (adj): ~ *zijn tegen* withstand, resist; be immune to; *tegen hitte* ~ heat-resistant

het **bestanddeel** /bəstɑndel/ (pl: -delen) constituent, element; component (part); ingredient

besteden /bəstedə(n)/ (besteedde, heeft besteed) **1** spend, devote (to), give (to), employ for: *geen aandacht* ~ *aan* pay no attention to; *zorg* ~ *aan (werk)* take care over (work); *zoiets is niet aan haar besteed* such things are lost (or: wasted) on her **2** spend (on): *ik besteed elke dag een uur aan mijn huiswerk* every day I spend one hour on my homework

de **besteding** /bəstedɪŋ/ (pl: -en) spending: ~*en doen* spend money, invest

de **bestedingslimiet** /bəstedɪŋslimit/ (pl: -en) spending limit, credit limit

besteedbaar /bəstedbar/ (adj) disposable

het **bestek** /bəstɛk/ (pl: -ken) **1** cutlery: *(een) zilveren* ~ a set of silver cutlery **2** specifications || *iets in kort* ~ *uiteenzetten* explain sth. in brief

het **bestel** /bəstɛl/ (established) order

de **bestelauto** /bəstɛlauto/ (pl: -'s) delivery van; [Am] (panel) truck

bestelen /bəstelə(n)/ (bestal, heeft bestolen) rob

bestellen /bəstɛlə(n)/ (bestelde, heeft besteld) **1** order, place an order (for); send for: *een taxi* ~ call a taxi; *iets* ~ *bij* order sth. from **2** deliver **3** book, reserve

de **besteller** /bəstɛlər/ (pl: -s) **1** delivery man; postman **2** customer

de **bestelling** /bəstɛlɪŋ/ (pl: -en) **1** delivery **2** order: *een* ~ *doen bij, voor* place an order with, for **3** order, goods ordered: *~en afleveren* deliver goods ordered

de **bestemmeling** /bəstɛmǝlɪŋ/ (pl: -en) [Belg] addressee

bestemmen /bəstɛmǝ(n)/ (bestemde, heeft bestemd) mean, intend; design: *dit boek is voor John bestemd* this book was meant for John

de **bestemming** /bəstɛmɪŋ/ (pl: -en) **1** intention, purpose; allocation **2** destination; *plaats van* ~ destination; *hij is met onbekende ~ vertrokken* he has gone without leaving a forwarding address **3** destiny

het **bestemmingsplan** /bəstɛmɪŋsplɑn/ (pl: -nen) [Dutch] zoning plan (or: scheme)

bestempelen /bəstɛmpǝlǝ(n)/ (bestempelde, heeft bestempeld): *iets* ~ *als* designate sth. as, label (or: call) sth.

bestendig /bəstɛndǝx/ (adj, adv) **1** durable; lasting, enduring **2** stable, steady: ~ *weer* settled weather **3** -proof, -resistant: *hittebestendig* heat-resistant

bestendigen /bəstɛndǝɣǝ(n)/ (bestendigde, heeft bestendigd) continue: *als de economische groei wordt bestendigd* if economic growth continues

besterven /bəstɛrvǝ(n)/ (bestierf, is bestorven) [roughly] hang, [roughly] age || *het* ~ *van schrik* die of fright

bestijgen /bəstɛiɣǝ(n)/ (besteeg, heeft bestegen) **1** mount; ascend **2** climb, ascend

de **bestijging** /bəstɛiɣɪn/ (pl: -en) **1** mounting; ascent; accession (to) **2** climbing, ascent

bestoken /bəstokǝ(n)/ (bestookte, heeft bestookt) harass, press, shell; bomb(ard): *iem. met vragen* ~ bombard s.o. with questions

bestormen /bəstɔrmǝ(n)/ (bestormde, heeft bestormd) storm

de **bestorming** /bəstɔrmɪŋ/ (pl: -en) storming, assault

bestraffen /bəstrɑfǝ(n)/ (bestrafte, heeft

bestraft) punish

de **bestraffing** /bəstrɑfɪŋ/ (pl: -en) punishing, chastisement

bestralen /bəstralǝ(n)/ (bestraalde, heeft bestraald) give radiation treatment (or: radiotherapy)

de **bestraling** /bəstralɪŋ/ (pl: -en) irradiation; radiotherapy; radiation treatment

bestraten /bəstratǝ(n)/ (bestraatte, heeft bestraat) pave; surface; cobble

de **bestrating** /bəstratɪŋ/ (pl: -en) pavement, paving, surface, cobbles

bestrijden /bəstrɛidǝ(n)/ (bestreed, heeft bestreden) **1** dispute, challenge, contest; oppose; resist **2** combat, fight, counteract; control: *het alcoholisme* ~ combat alcoholism

het **bestrijdingsmiddel** /bəstrɛidɪŋsmɪdǝl/ (pl: -en) pesticide; herbicide; weed killer

bestrijken /bəstrɛikǝ(n)/ (bestreek, heeft bestreken) **1** cover: *deze krant bestrijkt de hele regio* this newspaper covers the entire area **2** spread; coat

bestrooien /bəstrojǝ(n)/ (bestrooide, heeft bestrooid) sprinkle (with); cover (with), spread (with); powder (with), dust (with): *gladde wegen met zand* ~ sand icy roads

de **bestseller** /bɛ(st)sɛlǝr/ (pl: -s) bestseller

bestuderen /bəstyderǝ(n)/ (bestudeerde, heeft bestudeerd) **1** study, pore over **2** study, investigate, explore

bestuiven /bəstœyvǝ(n)/ (bestoof, heeft bestoven) pollinate; dust; powder

besturen /bəstyrǝ(n)/ (bestuurde, heeft bestuurd) **1** drive, steer, navigate: *een schip* ~ steer a ship **2** control, operate **3** govern, administrate, manage, run

de **besturing** /bəstyrɪŋ/ (pl: -en) control(s), steering, drive

het **besturingssysteem** /bəstyrɪŋsistem/ (pl: -systemen) operating system

het **bestuur** /bəstyr/ (pl: besturen) **1** government; rule; administration; management: *de raad van* ~ *van deze school* the Board of Directors of this school; *onbehoorlijk* ~ misgovernment; bad (or: poor) governance **2** administration, government; management **3** government; council; corporation: *iem. in het* ~ *kiezen* elect s.o. to the board

bestuurbaar /bəstyrbar/ (adj) controllable, manageable; navigable: *gemakkelijk* ~ *zijn* be easy to steer (or: control); *niet meer* ~ *zijn* be out of control

de **bestuurder** /bəstyrdǝr/ (pl: -s) **1** driver; pilot; operator **2** administrator, manager: *de ~s van een instelling* the governors (or: managers) of an institution **3** director, manager

bestuurlijk /bəstyrlǝk/ (adj) administrative, governmental, managerial

het **bestuursakkoord** /bəstyrsakort/ (pl: -en) [Dutch] administrative agreement

het **bestuurslid** /bəstyrslɪt/ (pl: -leden) member of the board; committee member

de **bestwil** /bɛstwɪl/: *ik zeg het voor je (eigen)* ~ I'm saying this for your own good

de **bèta** /bɛːta/ science (side, subjects)

de **betaalapp** /bətalɛp/ (pl: -s) (mobile) payment app

de **betaalautomaat** /bətalɑutomat/ (pl: -automaten) point-of-sale terminal, point-of-pay(ment) terminal; ticket machine

betaalbaar /bətalbar/ (adj) affordable, reasonably priced

de **betaalcheque** /bətalʃɛk/ (pl: -s) (bank-)-guaranteed cheque

betaald /bətalt/ (adj) paid (for), hired, professional: ~ **voetbal** professional soccer ‖ *iem. iets ~ zetten* get even with s.o., get back at (*or:* on) s.o.

de **betaalkaart** /bətalkart/ (pl: -en) **1** [dated] (guaranteed) giro cheque **2** debit card **3** credit card

het **betaalmiddel** /bətalmɪdəl/ (pl: -en) tender, currency, circulating medium

de **betaalmuur** /bətalmyr/ (pl: -muren) paywall

de **betaalpas** /bətalpɑs/ (pl: -sen) debit card, bank card; smart card

de **betaal-tv** /bətalteve/ pay TV

de **bètablokker** /bɛːtablɔkər/ (pl: -s) betablocker

betalen /bətalə(n)/ (betaalde, heeft betaald) pay; pay for: *de kosten* ~ bear the cost; *(nog) te* ~ balance due; *contant* ~ pay (in) cash; *die huizen zijn niet te* ~ the price of these houses is prohibitive; *met cheques* ~ pay by cheque; *dit werk betaalt slecht* this work pays badly

betalend /bətalənt/ (adj) paying: *~e bezoekers* paying visitors/guests

de **betaler** /bətalər/ (pl: -s) payer

de **betaling** /bətalɪŋ/ (pl: -en) payment; reward; remuneration; settlement: ~ *in termijnen* payment in instalments

de **betalingsachterstand** /bətalɪŋsɑxtərstɑnt/ arrears (of payment): *een ~ hebben* be in arrears (of payment), be behind (on payment)

de **betalingsbalans** /bətalɪŋzbalɑns/ (pl: -en) balance of payments

het **betalingsbewijs** /bətalɪŋzbəwɛis/ (pl: -bewijzen) receipt

de **betalingsregeling** /bətalɪŋsreɣəlɪŋ/ (pl: -en) debt repayment scheme: *een ~ treffen* set up a debt repayment scheme

de **betalingstermijn** /bətalɪŋstɛrmɛin/ (pl: -en) instalment

betamelijk /bətaməl[ək]/ (adj, adv) decent, fit(ting), seemly, proper

betasten /bətɑstə(n)/ (betastte, heeft betast) feel, finger

betegelen /bəteɣələ(n)/ (betegelde, heeft betegeld) tile

betekenen /bətekənə(n)/ (betekende, heeft betekend) **1** mean, stand for, signify: *wat heeft dit te ~?* what's the meaning of this?; *wat betekent NN?* what does N.N. stand for? **2** mean, count, matter: *mijn auto betekent alles voor mij* my car means everything to me; *niet veel (weinig)* ~ be of little importance; *die baan betekent veel voor haar* that job means a lot to her **3** mean, entail: *dat betekent nog niet dat ...* that does not mean that ...

de **betekenis** /bətekənɪs/ (pl: -sen) **1** meaning, sense **2** significance, importance: *van doorslaggevende* ~ of decisive importance

beter /betər/ (adj, adv) **1** better: *het is ~ dat je nu vertrekt* you'd better leave now; *ze is ~ in wiskunde dan haar broer* she's better at maths than her brother; *dat is al ~* that's more like it; ~ *maken* improve; ~ *worden* improve; *wel wat ~s te doen hebben* have better things to do; ~ *laat dan nooit* better late than never; *hij is weer helemaal* ~ he has completely recovered; ~ *maken, weer ~ maken* cure; ~ *worden, weer ~ worden* recover, get well again; *het ~ doen (dan een ander)* do better than s.o. else; *je had ~ kunnen helpen* you would have done better to help; *de leerling kon ~* the student could do better; *John tennist ~ dan ik* John is a better tennis-player than me; [iron] *het ~ weten* know best; *ze weten niet ~ of ...* for all they know ...; *des te ~ (voor ons)* so much the better (for us); *hoe eerder hoe ~* the sooner the better; *de volgende keer ~* better luck next time **2** better (class of), superior: *uit ~e kringen* upper-class

de **beterschap** /betərsxɑp/ recovery (of health): ~*!* get well soon!

beteugelen /bətøɣələ(n)/ (beteugelde, heeft beteugeld) curb, check, suppress, control

beteuterd /bətøtərt/ (adj) taken aback, dismayed: ~ *kijken* look dismayed

de **betichte** /bətɪxtə/ (pl: -n) [Belg; law] accused, defendant

betichten /bətɪxtə(n)/ (betichtte, heeft beticht) accuse (of): *hij werd ervan beticht dat hij ... * he was alleged to have ...

betijen /bətɛiə(n)/: *laat hem maar* ~ let him be, leave him alone

betimmeren /bətɪmərə(n)/ (betimmerde, heeft betimmerd) board, panel

betitelen /bətitələ(n)/ (betitelde, heeft betiteld) call, label: *iets als onzin* ~ call (*or:* label) sth. nonsense

de **betoelaging** /bətulaɣɪŋ/ [Belg] subsidy

betogen /bətoɣə(n)/ (betoogde, heeft betoogd) demonstrate, march

de **betoger** /bətoɣər/ (pl: -s) demonstrator, marcher

de **betoging** /bətoɣɪŋ/ (pl: -en) demonstration, march

het **beton** /bətǫn/ concrete: *gewapend* ~ reinforced concrete; ~ *storten* pour concrete

betonen /bətǫnə(n)/ (betoonde, heeft betoond) show, display; extend

de **betonmolen** /bətǫmolə(n)/ (pl: -s) concrete mixer

betonnen /bətǫnə(n)/ (adj) concrete

het **betonrot** /bətǫnrɔt/ concrete cancer

het **betoog** /bətǫx/ (pl: betogen) argument; plea

betoveren /bətǫvərə(n)/ (betoverde, heeft betoverd) **1** put (*or:* cast) a spell on, bewitch: *betoverd door haar ogen* bewitched by her eyes **2** enchant

de **betovering** /bətǫvərɪŋ/ (pl: -en) **1** spell, bewitchment **2** enchantment, charm

betraand /bətrant/ (adj) tearfilled; bleary

betrachten /bətrɑxtə(n)/ (betrachtte, heeft betracht) practise, exercise; observe; show

de **betrachting** /bətrɑxtɪŋ/ (pl: -en) [Belg] aim, intention

betrappen /bətrɑpə(n)/ (betrapte, heeft betrapt) catch, surprise: *op heterdaad betrapt* caught redhanded

betreden /bətredə(n)/ (betrad, heeft betreden) **1** enter: *het is verboden dit* **terrein** *te* ~ no entry, keep out (*or:* off) **2** tread: *nieuwe* **paden** ~ break new (*or:* fresh) ground

betreffen /bətrɛfə(n)/ (betrof, heeft betroffen) **1** concern, regard: *waar het* **politiek** *betreft* when it comes to politics; *wat mij betreft is het in orde* as far as I'm concerned it's all right; *wat betreft je broer* with regard to your brother **2** concern, relate to

betreffende /bətrɛfəndə/ (prep) concerning, regarding

[1]**betrekkelijk** /bətrɛkələk/ (adj) relative: *dat is* ~ that depends (on how you look at it); *alles is* ~ everything is relative

[2]**betrekkelijk** /bətrɛkələk/ (adv) relatively, comparatively

de **betrekkelijkheid** /bətrɛkələkhɛit/ relativity

[1]**betrekken** /bətrɛkə(n)/ (betrok, is betrokken) **1** become overcast (*or:* cloudy), cloud over **2** cloud over; darken

[2]**betrekken** /bətrɛkə(n)/ (betrok, heeft betrokken) involve, concern: *betrokken zijn* **bij** be involved (*or:* implicated, mixed up) in; *zij deden alles zonder de anderen* **erin** *te* ~ they did everything without consulting the others || *iets* **op** *zichzelf* ~ take sth. personally

de **betrekking** /bətrɛkɪŋ/ (pl: -en) **1** post, job, position; office: *iem.* **aan** *een* ~ *helpen* engage s.o., help s.o. find a job **2** relation(ship): *nauwe* ~*en met iem.* **onderhouden** maintain close ties (*or:* connections) with s.o. **3** relation, connection: *met* ~ *tot* with regard to, with respect to; ~ *hebben* **op** relate (*or:* refer) to, concern

betreuren /bətrø̞rə(n)/ (betreurde, heeft

betreurd) **1** regret, be sorry for: *een* **vergissing** ~ regret a mistake **2** mourn (for, over), be sorry for

betreurenswaardig /bətrø̞rənswardəx/ (adj) regrettable, sad

betrokken /bətrɔkə(n)/ (adj) **1** concerned; involved: *de bij de ruzie* ~ **docent** the teacher involved in the argument; *de* ~ **persoon** the person in question **2** [face] gloomy; [air] overcast, cloudy **3** committed, engaged: *hij voelt zich* ~ **bij** *het milieu* he is committed to the environment

de **betrokkenheid** /bətrɔkənhɛit/ involvement, commitment, concern

betrouwbaar /bətrǫubar/ (adj) reliable, trustworthy, dependable: *uit betrouwbare* **bron** on good authority

de **betrouwbaarheid** /bətrǫubarhɛit/ reliability, dependability; trustworthiness

betuigen /bətœyɣə(n)/ (betuigde, heeft betuigd) express: *iem. zijn* **deelneming** (*or:* **medeleven**) ~ express one's condolences (*or:* sympathy) to s.o.

betwijfelen /bətwɛifələ(n)/ (betwijfelde, heeft betwijfeld) doubt, (call in) question: *het valt te* ~ *of …* it is doubtful whether …

betwisten /bətwɪstə(n)/ (betwistte, heeft betwist) dispute, contest, challenge

beu /bø/ (adj): *iets* ~ *zijn* be sick of sth.

de **beugel** /bøɣəl/ (pl: -s) brace: *een* ~ *dragen* wear braces, wear a brace || *dat kan niet* **door** *de* ~ that cannot pass (muster), that won't do

het **beugelslot** /bøɣəlslɔt/ U-lock

de **beuk** /bøk/ (pl: -en) beech

[1]**beuken** /bøkə(n)/ (adj) beech

[2]**beuken** /bøkə(n)/ (beukte, heeft gebeukt) batter, pound; lash: *op* (*or:* *tegen*) *iets* ~ hammer on sth., batter (away) at sth.

het **beukennootje** /bøkənocə/ (pl: -s) beechnut

de **beul** /bøl/ (pl: -en) **1** executioner; hangman **2** [fig] tyrant, brute

beunen /bønə(n)/ (beunde, heeft gebeund) [Dutch] moonlight

de **beunhaas** /bønhas/ (pl: -hazen) [Dutch] moonlighter

beunhazen /bønhazə(n)/ (beunhaasde, heeft gebeunhaasd) [Dutch] **1** bungle, botch **2** moonlight

de [1]**beurs** /børs/ (pl: beurzen) **1** scholarship, grant: *een* ~ *hebben, van een* ~ *studeren* have a grant; *een* ~ *krijgen* get a grant **2** exchange, market; [bldg] Stock Exchange: *naar de* ~ *gaan* float a company (on the stock market) **3** fair, show, exhibition: *antiekbeurs* antique(s) fair **4** purse

[2]**beurs** /børs/ (adj) overripe, mushy

de **beursindex** /børsɪndɛks/ (pl: -en) stock market price index

de **beurskoers** /børskurs/ share price, (exchange) rate

de **beursnotering** /bɘrsnoterɪŋ/ (pl: -en) quotation, share price; foreign exchange rate

de **beursstudent** /bɘrstydɛnt/ (pl: -en) student on a grant, scholar

de **beurswaarde** /bɘrswardə/ quoted value, stock exchange value

de **beurt** /bɘrt/ (pl: -en) turn: *een goede ~ maken* make a good impression; *een grote ~* [car] a big service; *de kamer een grondige ~ geven* give the room a good cleaning; *hij is aan de ~* it's his turn, he's next; *om de ~ iets doen* take turns doing sth.; *om de ~* in turn; *op je ~ wachten* wait your turn; *hij op zijn ~ ...* he in his turn ...

beurtelings /bɘrtəlɪŋs/ (adv) alternately, by turns, in turn: *het ~ warm en koud krijgen* go hot and cold (all over)

de **beurtrol** /bɘrtrɔl/ (pl: -len) [Belg] *see toerbeurt*

bevaarbaar /bəvarbar/ (adj) navigable

bevallen /bəvɑlə(n)/ (beviel, is bevallen) **1** give birth (to): *zij is van een dochter ~* she gave birth to a daughter **2** please, suit; give satisfaction: *hoe bevalt het je op school?* how do you like school?

bevallig /bəvɑləx/ (adj, adv) graceful, charming

de **bevalling** /bəvɑlɪŋ/ (pl: -en) delivery, childbirth

het **bevallingsverlof** /bəvɑlɪŋsfərlɔf/ (pl: -verloven) [Belg] maternity leave

bevangen /bəvɑŋə(n)/ (beving, heeft bevangen) seize, overcome: *hij werd door angst ~* he was panic-stricken

bevaren /bəvarə(n)/ (bevoer, heeft bevaren) navigate; sail

bevattelijk /bəvɑtələk/ (adj, adv) intelligible, comprehensible; *see vatbaar*

bevatten /bəvɑtə(n)/ (bevatte, heeft bevat) **1** contain, hold **2** comprehend, understand: *niet te ~* incomprehensible

het **bevattingsvermogen** /bəvɑtɪŋsfərmoɣə(n)/ comprehension: *zijn ~ te boven gaan* be beyond one's comprehension

bevechten /bəvɛxtə(n)/ (bevocht, heeft bevochten) **1** gain: *een zwaar bevochten positie* a hard-won (*or:* dearly won) position **2** fight (against)

beveiligen /bəvɛiləɣə(n)/ (beveiligde, heeft beveiligd) protect, secure; [fig also] safeguard

de **beveiliging** /bəvɛiləɣɪŋ/ (pl: -en) **1** protection, security; [fig also] safeguard(s) **2** safety (*or:* protective, security) device

de **beveiligingsdienst** /bəvɛiləɣɪŋzdinst/ (pl: -en) (private) security service

het **bevel** /bəvɛl/ (pl: -en) order, command; warrant: *~ geven tot* give the order to; *het ~ voeren over een leger* be in command of an army

bevelen /bəvelə(n)/ (beval, heeft bevolen) order, command

de **bevelhebber** /bəvɛlhɛbər/ (pl: -s) commander, commanding officer

beven /bevə(n)/ (beefde, heeft gebeefd) **1** shake, tremble, shiver: *~ van kou* shiver with cold **2** tremble, quake

de **bever** /bevər/ (pl: -s) beaver

bevestigen /bəvɛstəɣə(n)/ (bevestigde, heeft bevestigd) **1** fix, fasten, attach **2** confirm, affirm: *de uitzondering bevestigt de regel* the exception proves the rule

bevestigend /bəvɛstəɣənt/ (adj, adv) affirmative

de **bevestiging** /bəvɛstəɣɪŋ/ (pl: -en) **1** fixing, fastening, attachment **2** confirmation **3** affirmation, confirmation

het **bevind** /bəvɪnt/: *naar ~ van zaken handelen* act according to circumstances, use one's judgment

¹**bevinden** /bəvɪndə(n)/ (bevond, heeft bevonden) find: *gezien en goed bevonden* seen and approved; *schuldig ~ (aan een misdaad)* find guilty (of a crime)

zich ²**bevinden** /bəvɪndə(n)/ (bevond zich, heeft zich bevonden) be, find o.s.: *zich in gevaar ~* be in danger

de **bevinding** /bəvɪndɪŋ/ (pl: -en) finding, result; experience; conclusion

de **beving** /bevɪŋ/ (pl: -en) trembling; shiver

bevlekken /bəvlɛkə(n)/ (bevlekte, heeft bevlekt) soil, stain, spot: *met bloed bevlekt* bloodstained

de **bevlieging** /bəvliɣɪŋ/ (pl: -en) whim, impulse

bevloeien /bəvlujə(n)/ (bevloeide, heeft bevloeid) irrigate, water

bevlogen /bəvloɣə(n)/ (adj) animated, inspired, enthusiastic

bevochtigen /bəvɔxtəɣə(n)/ (bevochtigde, heeft bevochtigd) moisten, wet; humidify

de **bevochtiger** /bəvɔxtəɣər/ (pl: -s) humidifier

bevoegd /bəvuxt/ (adj) competent, qualified, authorized: *de ~e overheden (autoriteiten)* the proper authorities; *~e personen* authorized persons; *~ zijn* be qualified

de **bevoegdheid** /bəvuxtheit/ (pl: -heden) competence, qualification, authority; jurisdiction: *de bevoegdheden van de burgemeester* the powers of the mayor; *de ~ hebben om* have the power to; *zonder ~* unauthorized

bevoelen /bəvulə(n)/ (bevoelde, heeft bevoeld) feel, finger

bevolken /bəvɔlkə(n)/ (bevolkte, heeft bevolkt) populate, people

de **bevolking** /bəvɔlkɪŋ/ (pl: -en) population, inhabitants: *de inheemse ~* the native population

de **bevolkingsdichtheid** /bəvɔlkɪŋzdɪxtheit/ population density

de **bevolkingsgroep** /bəvɔlkɪŋsxrup/ (pl: -en)

community, section of the population

het **bevolkingsonderzoek** /bəvɔlkɪŋsɔndər-zuk/ (pl: -en) screening

het **bevolkingsregister** /bəvɔlkɪŋsrəyɪstər/ (pl: -s) register (of births, deaths and marriages)

bevolkt /bəvɔlkt/ (adj) populated: *een dicht-* (or: *dunbevolkte*) *streek* a densely (or: sparsely) populated region

bevoogden /bəvoydə(n)/ (bevoogdde, heeft bevoogd) patronize (s.o.)

bevoordelen /bəvordələ(n)/ (bevoordeelde, heeft bevoordeeld) benefit, favour: *familieleden* ~ *boven anderen* favour relatives above others

bevooroordeeld /bəvorordelt/ (adj) prejudiced, bias(s)ed: ~ *zijn tegen* (or: *voor*) be prejudiced against (or: in favour of)

bevoorraden /bəvoradə(n)/ (bevoorraadde, heeft bevoorraad) provision, supply, stock up

bevoorrechten /bəvorɛxtə(n)/ (bevoorrechtte, heeft bevoorrecht) privilege, favour: *een bevoorrechte positie innemen* occupy a privileged position

bevorderen /bəvɔrdərə(n)/ (bevorderde, heeft bevorderd) 1 promote, further, advance; boost; aid; encourage; stimulate; lead to; be conducive to: *dat bevordert de bloedsomloop* that stimulates one's blood circulation; *de verkoop van iets* ~ boost the sale of sth., push sth. 2 promote: *bevorderd worden* go up (to the next class); *een leerling naar een hogere klas* ~ move a pupil up to a higher class; *hij werd tot kapitein bevorderd* he was promoted to (the rank of) captain

de **bevordering** /bəvɔrdərɪŋ/ (pl: -en) 1 promotion, advancement; encouragement: *ter* ~ *van* for the promotion (or: advancement) of 2 promotion: *voor ~ in aanmerking komen* be eligible for promotion

bevorderlijk /bəvɔrdərlək/ (adj) beneficial (to), conducive (to), good (for): ~ *zijn voor* a) promote, further, advance; b) boost, aid; c) lead to, be conducive to

bevredigen /bəvredəyə(n)/ (bevredigde, heeft bevredigd) satisfy; gratify: *zijn nieuwsgierigheid* ~ gratify one's curiosity; *moeilijk te* ~ hard to please || *zichzelf* ~ masturbate

bevredigend /bəvredəyənt/ (adj) satisfactory, satisfying; gratifying: *een* ~e *oplossing* a satisfactory solution

de **bevrediging** /bəvredəyɪŋ/ (pl: -en) satisfaction, fulfilment; gratification: ~ *in iets vinden* find satisfaction in sth.

bevreemden /bəvremdə(n)/ (bevreemdde, heeft bevreemd) surprise: *dat bevreemdt mij* I'm surprised at it

bevreesd /bəvrest/ (adj) afraid, fearful

bevriend /bəvrint/ (adj) friendly (with): *een ~e mogendheid* a friendly nation (or: power); *goed ~ zijn (met iem.)* be close friends (with s.o.)

bevriezen /bəvrizə(n)/ (bevroor, heeft/is bevroren) 1 freeze (up, over), become (or: be frozen) (up, over): *het water is bevroren* the water is frozen; *alle leidingen zijn bevroren* all the pipes are (or: have) frozen (up); *de ruiten zijn bevroren* the windows are (or: have) frosted over; *ik ben half bevroren* I'm frozen to the bone, I'm freezing cold 2 freeze 3 freeze, block: *bevroren tegoed* frozen assets

de **bevriezing** /bəvrizɪŋ/ 1 freezing (over), frost, frostbite 2 freeze

bevrijden /bəvrɛidə(n)/ (bevrijdde, heeft bevrijd) free (from), liberate; release; set free; rescue; emancipate: *een land* ~ free (or: liberate) a country; *iem. uit zijn benarde positie* ~ rescue s.o. from a desperate position

de **bevrijding** /bəvrɛidɪŋ/ 1 liberation; release; rescue; emancipation: ~ *uit slavernij* emancipation from slavery 2 [fig] relief: *een gevoel van* ~ a feeling of relief

Bevrijdingsdag /bəvrɛidɪŋzdɑx/ Liberation Day

bevruchten /bəvrʏxtə(n)/ (bevruchtte, heeft bevrucht) fertilize; impregnate; inseminate

de **bevruchting** /bəvrʏxtɪŋ/ (pl: -en) fertilization, impregnation, insemination: *kunstmatige* ~ artificial insemination; ~ *buiten de baarmoeder* in vitro fertilization

bevuilen /bəvœylə(n)/ (bevuilde, heeft bevuild) soil, dirty, foul: *het eigen nest* ~ foul one's own nest

de **bewaarder** /bəwardər/ (pl: -s) 1 keeper, guardian; jailer; warder: *ordebewaarder* keeper of the peace 2 keeper

het **bewaarmiddel** /bəwarmɪdəl/ (pl: -en) [Belg; culinary] preservative

bewaken /bəwakə(n)/ (bewaakte, heeft bewaakt) guard, watch (over); monitor; [fig] watch; [fig] mind: *het budget* ~ watch the budget; *een gevangene* ~ guard a prisoner; *een terrein* ~ guard (over) an area; *zwaar* (or: *licht*) *bewaakte gevangenis* maximum (or: minimum) security prison

de **bewaker** /bəwakər/ (pl: -s) 1 guard 2 security guard

de **bewaking** /bəwakɪŋ/ guard(ing), watch(ing), surveillance, control: *onder strenge ~ staan* be kept under strict surveillance

de **bewakingscamera** /bəwakɪŋskaməra/ security camera

bewandelen /bəwɑndələ(n)/ (bewandelde, heeft bewandeld) 1 walk (on, over) 2 [fig] take (or: follow, steer) a … course: *de middenweg* ~ steer a middle course; *de officiële weg* ~ take the official line

bewapenen /bəwapənə(n)/ (bewapende, heeft bewapend) arm: *zich* ~ arm; *zwaar be-*

wapend heavily armed

de **bewapening** /bəwa̱pənɪŋ/ armament, arms

bewaren /bəwa̱rə(n)/ (bewaarde, heeft bewaard) **1** keep, save **2** keep, store; stock (up): *appels* ~ store apples; *een onderwerp tot de volgende keer* ~ leave a topic for the next time; ~ *voor later* save for a rainy day; *een geheim* ~ keep (*or:* guard) a secret **3** keep, maintain: *zijn kalmte* ~ keep calm; *zijn evenwicht* ~ keep (*or:* maintain) one's balance **4** preserve (from), save (from), guard (from, against) **5** [comp] store, save

de **bewaring** /bəwa̱rɪŋ/ **1** keeping, care; storage; custody: *in* ~ *geven (aan, bij)* deposit (at, with); entrust (to), leave (with) **2** custody, detention: *huis van* ~ house of detention

beweegbaar /bəwe̱ɣbar/ (adj) movable: *beweegbare delen* moving parts

beweeglijk /bəwe̱ɣlək/ (adj) agile, lively, active: *een zeer* ~ *kind* a very active child

de **beweegreden** /bəwe̱ɣredə(n)/ (pl: -en) motive; grounds: *de ~en van zijn gedrag* the motives underlying his behaviour

bewegen /bəwe̱ɣə(n)/ (bewoog, heeft bewogen) **1** move, stir: *op en neer* (*or: heen en weer*) ~ move up and down (*or:* to and fro); *zich* ~ move, stir; *ik kan me nauwelijks* ~ I can hardly move; *geen blad bewoog* not a leaf stirred; *~de delen* moving parts; *niet* ~! don't move! **2** exercise, be active: *we moeten meer* ~ we need to exercise more, we need to be more active physically

de **beweging** /bəwe̱ɣɪŋ/ (pl: -en) **1** movement, move, motion; gesture: *in* ~ *brengen*, *in* ~ *zetten* set in motion; start; *in* ~ *blijven* keep moving; *in* ~ *zijn* be moving, be in motion; *er is geen* ~ *in te krijgen* it won't budge (*or:* move); *een verkeerde* ~ *maken* make a wrong move **2** exercise: *aan* ~ *doen* exercise **3** movement: *de vredesbeweging* the peace movement

bewegingloos /bəwe̱ɣɪŋlos/ (adj) motionless, immobile

de **bewegingsmelder** /bəwe̱ɣɪŋsmɛldər/ (pl: -s) motion sensor

de **bewegingsvrijheid** /bəwe̱ɣɪŋsfrɛihɛit/ freedom of movement

bewegwijzeren /bəwɛ̱ɣxwɛizərə(n)/ (bewegwijzerde, heeft bewegwijzerd) signpost

beweren /bəwe̱rə(n)/ (beweerde, heeft beweerd) claim; contend; allege: *durven te* ~ *dat* dare to claim that; *dat zou ik niet willen* ~ I wouldn't (go as far as to) say that; *zij beweerde onschuldig te zijn* she claimed to be innocent; *dat is precies wat wij* ~ that's the very point we're making; *hij beweert dat hij niets gehoord heeft* he maintains that he did not hear anything

de **bewering** /bəwe̱rɪŋ/ (pl: -en) assertion, statement; allegation; claim; contention: *bij*

zijn ~ *blijven* stick to one's claim; *kun je deze* ~ *hard maken?* can you substantiate this claim?

bewerkelijk /bəwɛ̱rkələk/ (adj) laborious

bewerken /bəwɛ̱rkə(n)/ (bewerkte, heeft bewerkt) treat; work; process; edit; rewrite; revise; adapt: *de grond* ~ till the land (*or:* soil); *een studieboek voor het Nederlandse taalgebied* ~ adapt a textbook for the Dutch user; *geheel opnieuw bewerkt door* completely revised by; ~ *tot een film* adapt for the screen; *bewerkt voedsel* processed food

de **bewerker** /bəwɛ̱rkər/ (pl: -s) redactor; editor; orchestrator

de **bewerking** /bəwɛ̱rkɪŋ/ (pl: -en) **1** treatment; cultivation; process(ing); manufacturing; editing: *de derde druk van dit schoolboek is in* ~ the third edition of this textbook is in preparation **2** adaptation; version; arrangement; revision: *de Nederlandse* ~ *van dit boek* the Dutch version of this book; ~ *voor toneel* (*or: de film*) adaptation for stage (*or:* the screen) **3** manipulation, influencing **4** processing

bewerkstelligen /bəwɛrkstɛ̱ləɣə(n)/ (bewerkstelligde, heeft bewerkstelligd) bring about, effect, realize: *een ontmoeting* (*or: verzoening*) ~ bring about a meeting (*or:* reconciliation)

het **bewijs** /bəwɛ̱is/ (pl: bewijzen) **1** proof, evidence: [Belg] ~ *van goed gedrag en zeden* [roughly] certificate of good character; *het* ~ *leveren (dat, van)* produce evidence (that, of); *als* ~ *aanvoeren* quote (in evidence) **2** proof, evidence, sign: *als* ~ *van erkentelijkheid* as a token of gratitude; *het levende* ~ *zijn van* be the living proof of **3** proof, certificate: *betalingsbewijs* proof of payment, receipt; ~ *van goed gedrag* certificate of good conduct

de **bewijslast** /bəwɛ̱islɑst/ (pl: -en) burden of proof

het **bewijsmateriaal** /bəwɛ̱ismaterijal/ evidence, proof

bewijzen /bəwɛ̱izə(n)/ (bewees, heeft bewezen) **1** prove, establish, demonstrate: *dit bewijst dat* this proves that **2** render, show, prove: *de laatste eer* ~ *aan iem.* render the last honours to s.o., pay s.o. one's last respects ‖ *zichzelf moeten* ~ have to prove o.s.

het **bewind** /bəwɪ̱nt/ **1** government, regime, rule: *aan het* ~ *komen* come to power; *het* ~ *voeren over* govern, rule (over); manage, administer **2** administration, government

de **bewindsman** /bəwɪ̱n(t)smɑn/ (pl: -lieden, -personen) member of government (*or:* cabinet); minister, secretary

de **bewindsvrouw** /bəwɪ̱n(t)sfrɑu/ *see bewindsman*

de **bewindvoerder** /bəwɪ̱ntfurdər/ (pl: -s) administrator, director

bewogen /bəwo̱ɣə(n)/ (adj) **1** moved: *tot tranen toe* ~ moved to tears **2** stirring, event-

bezinksel

ful

de **bewolking** /bəwɔlkɪŋ/ (pl: -en) cloud(s):
laaghangende ~ low cloud(s)

bewolkt /bəwɔlkt/ (adj) cloudy, overcast

de **bewonderaar** /bəwɔndərar/ (pl: -s) admirer; [inform] fan

bewonderen /bəwɔndərə(n)/ (bewonderde, heeft bewonderd) admire, look up to

bewonderenswaardig /bəwɔndərənswardəχ/ (adj, adv) admirable, wonderful

de **bewondering** /bəwɔndərɪŋ/ admiration, wonder

bewonen /bəwonə(n)/ (bewoonde, heeft bewoond) inhabit, occupy; live in

de **bewoner** /bəwonər/ (pl: -s) inhabitant; occupant; resident

de **bewoning** /bəwonɪŋ/ occupation, residence

bewoonbaar /bəwombar/ (adj) (in)habitable; liveable

de **bewoordingen** /bəwordɪŋə(n)/ (pl) terms: *in krachtige* ~ strongly worded; warmly expressed

¹**bewust** /bəwʏst/ (adj) **1** concerned, involved: *op die ~e dag* on the day in question **2** aware, conscious: *ik ben me niet ~ van enige tekortkomingen* I am not aware of any shortcomings

²**bewust** /bəwʏst/ (adv) consciously, knowingly

bewusteloos /bəwʏstəlos/ (adj) unconscious, senseless: ~ *raken* pass out

de **bewusteloosheid** /bəwʏstəloshɛit/ unconsciousness

de **bewustwording** /bəwʏstwordɪŋ/ awakening (to), realization

het **bewustzijn** /bəwʏstsɛin/ consciousness; awareness: *zijn* ~ *verliezen* lose consciousness; *buiten* ~ *zijn* be unconscious; *weer tot* ~ *komen* regain (*or:* recover) consciousness

bezaaien /bəzajə(n)/ (bezaaide, heeft bezaaid) strew, stud: *bezaaid met* strewn with; studded with; littered with; dotted with

bezadigd /bəzadəχt/ (adj) sober, levelheaded, dispassionate

bezegelen /bəzeɣələ(n)/ (bezegelde, heeft bezegeld) seal

de **bezem** /bezəm/ (pl: -s) broom

de **bezemsteel** /bezəmstel/ (pl: -stelen) broomstick, broomhandle

¹**bezeren** /bəzerə(n)/ (bezeerde, heeft bezeerd) hurt, bruise

zich ²**bezeren** /bəzerə(n)/ (bezeerde zich, heeft zich bezeerd) hurt o.s., get hurt; [stronger] injure o.s.

bezet /bəzɛt/ (adj) **1** occupied; taken: ~ *gebied* occupied territory; *geheel* ~ full (up) **2** taken up, occupied **3** engaged, occupied, busy || *de lijn is* ~ the line is engaged, busy

bezeten /bəzetə(n)/ (adj) **1** possessed (by) **2** obsessed (by): ~ *van stripverhalen* mad

about comic strips **3** [fig] obsessed (by): ~ *zijn van, door* have an obsession about

de **bezetene** /bəzetənə/ (pl: -n) possessed person: *als een* ~ frenetically, madly; *als een* ~ *tekeergaan* go berserk

bezetten /bəzɛtə(n)/ (bezette, heeft bezet) occupy, take, fill: *een belangrijke plaats* ~ *in* occupy an important place in; feature in

de **bezetter** /bəzɛtər/ (pl: -s) occupier(s), occupying force(s)

de **bezetting** /bəzɛtɪŋ/ (pl: -en) **1** occupation; sit-in; filling; filling up **2** [theatre] cast

bezichtigen /bəzɪχtəɣə(n)/ (bezichtigde, heeft bezichtigd) (pay a) visit (to); see; tour; inspect: *een huis* ~ view a house

de **bezichtiging** /bəzɪχtəɣɪŋ/ (pl: -en) visit, view, inspection, tour

bezield /bəzilt/ (adj) **1** alive, living **2** animated, inspired

bezielen /bəzilə(n)/ (bezielde, heeft bezield) inspire, animate: *wat bezielt je!* what has got into you!

de **bezieling** /bəzilɪŋ/ inspiration, animation

bezien /bəzin/ (bezag, heeft bezien) see, consider, look on

de **bezienswaardigheid** /bəzinswardəχhɛit/ (pl: -heden) place of interest, sight

bezig /bezəχ/ (adj) **1** busy (with sth., doing sth.), working (on), preoccupied (with), engaged (in): *goed* ~ *zijn* go about things in the right way, do a good job, be on a roll; *de wedstrijd is al* ~ the match has already started; *als je er toch mee* ~ *bent* while you are at it (*or:* about it); *vreselijk lang met iets* ~ *zijn* be an awful long time over sth. **2** in process, underway: *de wegwerkzaamheden zijn al een jaar* ~ the roadworks have been going on for a year || *waar ben je eigenlijk mee* ~*!* what do you think you're up to?; *hij is weer* ~ he's at it again

bezigen /bezəɣə(n)/ (bezigde, heeft gebezigd) [form] employ, use: *verstandige taal* ~ talk sense

de **bezigheid** /bezəχhɛit/ (pl: -heden) activity, occupation, work

de **bezigheidstherapie** /bezəχhɛitsterapi/ occupational therapy

¹**bezighouden** /bezəχhɑudə(n)/ (hield bezig, heeft beziggehouden) **1** occupy, keep busy: *het houdt ons allemaal bezig* we are all concerned about it **2** employ; engage

zich ²**bezighouden** /bezəχhɑudə(n)/ (hield zich bezig, heeft zich beziggehouden) occupy (*or:* busy) o.s. (with), engage (o.s.) (in): *ik heb geen tijd om me daarmee bezig te houden* I have no time to attend to (*or:* bother with) that

bezinken /bəzɪŋkə(n)/ (bezonk, is bezonken) **1** settle (down), sink (to the bottom) **2** clarify, settle (out)

het **bezinksel** /bəzɪŋksəl/ (pl: -s) sediment, deposit, residue

zich **bezinnen** /bəzɪnə(n)/ (bezon zich, heeft zich bezonnen) **1** contemplate, reflect (on): *bezint eer ge begint* look before you leap **2** change one's mind

de **bezinning** /bəzɪnɪn/ reflection, contemplation

het **bezit** /bəzɪt/ possession, property: *in ~ houden* keep in one's possession

bezittelijk /bəzɪtələk/ (adj) [linguistics] possessive: *~ voornaamwoord* possessive pronoun

bezitten /bəzɪtə(n)/ (bezat, heeft bezeten) possess, own, have

de **bezitter** /bəzɪtər/ (pl: -s) owner; holder; possessor

de **bezitting** /bəzɪtɪn/ (pl: -en) property, possession, belongings; estate: *persoonlijke ~en* personal belongings; *waardevolle ~en* valuables

bezocht /bəzɔxt/ (adj) visited, attended, frequented: *een druk ~e receptie* a busy reception

bezoedelen /bəzudələ(n)/ (bezoedelde, heeft bezoedeld) defile, besmirch, sully

het **bezoek** /bəzuk/ (pl: -en) **1** visit; call: *op ~ gaan bij iem.* pay s.o. a visit **2** visitor(s), guest(s), caller(s)

het **bezoekadres** /bəzukadrɛs/ (pl: -sen) office address

bezoeken /bəzukə(n)/ (bezocht, heeft bezocht) visit, pay a visit to: *een school ~* attend a school; *een website ~* visit a website

de **bezoeker** /bəzukər/ (pl: -s) visitor, guest: *een site met een miljoen ~s per week* a site with a million visitors a week

het **bezoekerscentrum** /bəzukərsɛntrym/ (pl: -centra) visitors centre

de **bezoekregeling** /bəzukreɣəlɪn/ (pl: -en) visiting arrangements

het **bezoekuur** /bəzukyr/ (pl: -uren) visiting hour(s) (*or:* time)

de **bezoldiging** /bəzɔldəɣɪn/ (pl: -en) pay, salary

zich **bezondigen** /bəzɔndəɣə(n)/ (bezondigde zich, heeft zich bezondigd) be guilty of

bezopen /bəzopə(n)/ (adj) [inform] **1** sloshed, plastered **2** absurd

het **bezorgadres** /bəzɔrxadrɛs/ (pl: -sen) delivery address

bezorgd /bəzɔrxt/ (adj, adv) **1** concerned (for, about): *de ~e moeder* the caring mother **2** worried (about): *wees maar niet ~* don't worry

de **bezorgdheid** /bəzɔrxtɦɛit/ concern (for, about), worry

bezorgen /bəzɔrɣə(n)/ (bezorgde, heeft bezorgd) **1** get, provide: *iem. een baan ~* get s.o. a job; *dat bezorgt ons heel wat extra werk* that lands us with a lot of extra work **2** give, cause: *iem. een hoop last ~* put s.o. to great

inconvenience **3** deliver: *de post ~* deliver the post

de **bezorger** /bəzɔrɣər/ (pl: -s) delivery man (*or:* woman)

de **bezorging** /bəzɔrɣɪn/ (pl: -en) delivery

bezuinigen /bəzœynəɣə(n)/ (bezuinigde, heeft bezuinigd) economize, save

de **bezuiniging** /bəzœynəɣɪn/ (pl: -en) **1** economy, cut(back) **2** saving(s)

de **bezuinigingsmaatregel** /bəzœynəɣɪnsmatreɣəl/ (pl: -en) economy measure; expenditure (*or:* spending) cut

bezuren /bəzyrə(n)/: *dat zal je ~* you'll regret (*or:* pay for, suffer for) that

het **bezwaar** /bəzwar/ (pl: bezwaren) **1** drawback **2** objection; scruple: *~ maken tegen iets* object to sth.; *zonder enig ~* without any objection

bezwaard /bəzwart/ (adj) troubled

bezwaarlijk /bəzwarlək/ (adj) troublesome

het **bezwaarschrift** /bəzwarsxrɪft/ (pl: -en) protest, petition

bezweet /bəzwet/ (adj) sweaty, sweating

bezweren /bəzwerə(n)/ (bezwoer, heeft bezworen) **1** implore **2** avert

bezwijken /bəzwɛikə(n)/ (bezweek, is bezweken) **1** give (way, out): *onder een last ~* [also fig] collapse under a load **2** succumb, yield: *voor de verleiding ~* yield to (*or:* give in) to the temptation **3** go under: *aan een ziekte ~* succumb to a disease

de **Bhutaan** /butan/ (pl: Bhutanen) Bhutanese

Bhutaans /butans/ (adj) Bhutan(ese)

Bhutan /butan/ Bhutan

de **bhv'er** /beɦavejər/ (pl: -s) [Dutch] health & safety officer

bibberen /bɪbərə(n)/ (bibberde, heeft gebibberd) shiver (with)

de **bibliografie** /biblijoɣrafi/ (pl: -ën) bibliography

de **bibliothecaris** /biblijotekarəs/ (pl: -sen) librarian

de **bibliotheek** /biblijotek/ (pl: bibliotheken) library

de **biceps** /bisɛps/ (pl: -en) biceps

de ¹**bicultureel** /bikyltyrel/ (pl: biculturelen) bicultural

²**bicultureel** /bikyltyrel/ (adj) bicultural

bidden /bɪdə(n)/ (bad, heeft gebeden) **1** pray, say one's prayers: *tot God ~ om* pray to God for **2** implore

de **biecht** /bixt/ (pl: -en) confession: *iem. de ~ afnemen* hear s.o.'s confession

biechten /bixtə(n)/ (biechtte, heeft gebiecht) confess, go to confession

de **biechtstoel** /bixtstul/ (pl: -en) [rel] confessional (box)

bieden /bidə(n)/ (bood, heeft geboden) **1** offer; present **2** [cards] bid: *het is jouw beurt om te ~* it's your (turn to) bid now **3** (make an) offer, (make a) bid: *ik bied er* *twintig* **euro** *voor* I'll give you twenty euros for it

de **bieder** /bi̯dər/ (pl: -s) bidder

de **biefstuk** /bi̯fstʏk/ (pl: -ken) steak: ~ *van de* **haas** fillet steak

de **biels** /bils/ (pl: bielzen) (railway) sleeper; [Am] railroad tie

het **bier** /bir/ (pl: -en) beer: *donker* ~ stout, dark ale; [Belg] *klein* ~ small beer; *licht* ~ **a)** light ale; **b)** lager; ~ *van het vat* draught beer

het **bierblikje** /bi̯rblɪkjə/ (pl: -s) beer can

de **bierbrouwerij** /birbrɑuwərɛ̯i̯/ (pl: -en) brewery

de **bierbuik** /bi̯rbœyk/ (pl: -en) **1** beer belly, beer gut **2** beer guzzler

het **bierglas** /bi̯rɣlɑs/ (pl: -glazen) beer glass

de **bierkeet** /bi̯rket/ (pl: -keten) beer barn, beer joint

het **bierviltje** /bi̯rvɪltɕə/ (pl: -s) beer mat, coaster

de **bies** /bis/ (pl: biezen) **1** piping, border, edging **2** rush ‖ *zijn biezen* **pakken** make o.s. scarce

het **bieslook** /bi̯slok/ chives

de **biet** /bit/ (pl: -en) beet

bietsen /bi̯tsə(n)/ (bietste, heeft gebietst) [inform] scrounge, cadge

biezen /bi̯zə(n)/ (adj) rush: *een* ~ *zitting* a rush(-bottomed) seat; *see* bies

de **big** /bɪx/ (pl: -gen) piglet; piggy

de **bigbangtheorie** /bɪgbɛ̱ŋtejori/ Big Bang theory

biggelen /bɪ̯ɣələ(n)/ (biggelde, heeft/is gebiggeld) trickle

de ¹**bij** /bɛi̯/ (pl: -en) (honey) bee

²**bij** /bɛi̯/ (adj) **1** up-to-date: *de leerling* **is** *weer* (or: *nog niet*) ~ *met wiskunde* the pupil has now caught up on (or: is still behind in) mathematics **2** up-to-date: *(goed)* ~ *zijn* be (thoroughly) on top of things

³**bij** /bɛi̯/ (prep) **1** near (to), close (by, to): ~ *iem. gaan zitten* sit next to s.o. **2** at, to: ~ *een* **kruispunt** *komen* come to an intersection **3** to, with: *alles blijft* ~ *het* **oude** everything stays the same; *we zullen het* **er** *maar* ~ *laten* let's leave it at that **4** while, during: ~ *zijn dood* at his death **5** at: *zij was* ~ *haar tante* she was at her aunt's; *er niet* ~ *zijn met zijn gedachten* have only half one's mind on it **6** for, with: ~ *een* **baas** *werken* work for a boss; ~ *de* **marine** in the navy; ~ *ons* at our house; back home; in our country (or: family) **7** with, along: *zij had haar dochter* ~ *zich* she had her daughter with her; *ik heb geen geld* ~ *me* I have no money on me **8** with, to: *inlichtingen* ~ *de balie inwinnen* request information at the desk; ~ *zichzelf* (denken, zeggen) (think, say) to o.s. **9** by: *iem.* ~ *naam kennen* know s.o. by name **10** by, at: ~ *het* **lezen** *van de krant* (when) reading the newspaper; ~ *het* **ontbijt** at breakfast **11** in case of, if **12** for, in the eyes of: *zij kan* ~ *de* **buren** *geen goed doen*

she can do no good as far as the neighbours are concerned ‖ *de kamer is 6* ~ *5* the room is 6 by 5; *je bent er* ~ the game is up; gotcha!; [iron] *dat kon* **er** *ook nog wel* ~ things weren't bad enough, that's just what we were waiting for

het **bijbaantje** /bɛ̯i̯bancə/ (pl: -s) job on the side, second (or: secondary) job: *een* ~ **hebben** moonlight

de **bijbedoeling** /bɛ̯i̯bədulɪŋ/ ulterior motive (or: design)

bijbehorend /bɛi̯bəhorənt/ (adj) accompanying, matching

de **Bijbel** /bɛi̯bəl/ (pl: -s) Bible

Bijbels /bɛi̯bəls/ (adj) biblical

het **Bijbelvers** /bɛ̯i̯bəlvɛrs/ (pl: -verzen) Bible verse

bijbenen /bɛi̯benə(n)/ keep up (with)

bijbetalen /bɛi̯bətalə(n)/ (betaalde bij, heeft bijbetaald) pay extra, pay an additional (or: extra) charge

bijblijven /bɛi̯blɛi̯və(n)/ (bleef bij, is bijgebleven) **1** keep pace, keep up **2** stick in one's memory: *dat zal* **mij** *altijd* ~ I shall never forget it

bijboeken /bɛ̯i̯bukə(n)/ (boekte bij, heeft bijgeboekt) post; enter, write up: *een bedrag* ~ transfer an amount, credit an amount to s.o.'s account; *een* **weekje** ~ book an extra week, add a week (to one's stay)

bijbrengen /bɛi̯brɛŋə(n)/ (bracht bij, heeft bijgebracht) impart (to), convey (to), instil (into): *iem. bepaalde* **kennis** ~ convey (certain) knowledge to s.o.

bijdehand /bɛi̯dəhɑnt/ (adj) bright, sharp

de **bijdrage** /bɛ̯i̯draɣə/ (pl: -n) contribution, offering

bijdragen /bɛ̯i̯draɣə(n)/ (droeg bij, heeft bijgedragen) contribute, add: *zijn* **steentje** ~ do one's bit

bijeen /bɛi̯en/ (adv) together

bijeenbrengen /bɛ̯i̯embrɛŋə(n)/ (bracht bijeen, heeft bijeengebracht) bring together, get together, raise

bijeenkomen /bɛ̯i̯eŋkomə(n)/ (kwam bijeen, is bijeengekomen) meet, assemble

de **bijeenkomst** /bɛi̯eŋkɔmst/ (pl: -en) meeting, gathering

bijeenroepen /bɛ̯i̯enrupə(n)/ (riep bijeen, heeft bijeengeroepen) call together, convene

het ¹**bijeenzijn** /bɛɪ̯enzɛin/ gathering

²**bijeenzijn** /bɛɪ̯enzɛin/ (was bijeen, is bijeengeweest) be together (or: gathered): *de* **commissie** *is bijeengeweest* the commission has met

de **bijenhouder** /bɛ̯i̯ə(n)hɑudər/ (pl: -s) beekeeper

de **bijenkoningin** /bɛ̯i̯ə(n)konɪŋɪn/ (pl: -nen) queen bee

de **bijenkorf** /bɛ̯i̯ə(n)kɔrf/ (pl: -korven) (bee)-

hive

de **bijenteelt** /bɛiə(n)telt/ apiculture

het **bijenvolk** /bɛiə(n)vɔlk/ (pl: -en) (swarm of, hive of) bees

het/de **bijenwas** /bɛiə(n)wɑs/ beeswax

¹**bijgaand** /bɛɪɣant/ (adj) enclosed: *de ~e stukken* the enclosures

²**bijgaand** /bɛɪɣant/ (adv) enclosed: ~ *treft u aan ...* please find enclosed ...

het **bijgebouw** /bɛiɣəbɑu/ (pl: -en) annex, outbuilding

de **bijgedachte** /bɛiɣədɑχtə/ (pl: -n) **1** association **2** ulterior motive (*or:* design)

het **bijgeloof** /bɛiɣəlof/ superstition

bijgelovig /bɛiɣəloʋəχ/ (adj, adv) superstitious

de **bijgelovigheid** /bɛiɣəloʋəχhɛit/ superstition, superstitiousness

bijgenaamd /bɛiɣənamt/ (adj) called; nicknamed

bijhouden /bɛihɑudə(n)/ (hield bij, heeft bijgehouden) **1** hold out (*or:* up) (to): *houd je bord bij* hold out your plate **2** keep up (with), keep pace (with): *het onderwijs niet kunnen ~* be unable to keep up at school **3** keep up to date: *de stand ~* keep count (*or:* the score)

het **bijhuis** /bɛihœys/ (pl: bijhuizen) [Belg] branch

het **bijkantoor** /bɛikɑntor/ (pl: bijkantoren) branch (office)

de **bijkeuken** /bɛikøkə(n)/ (pl: -s) utility room

bijklussen /bɛiklʏsə(n)/ (kluste bij, heeft bijgeklust) have a sideline

bijkomen /bɛikomə(n)/ (kwam bij, is bijgekomen) **1** come to (*or:* round) **2** (re)gain (one's) breath, recover (o.s.): *niet meer ~ (van het lachen)* be overcome (with laughter)

bijkomend /bɛikomənt/ (adj) additional, incidental; subordinate

bijkomstig /bɛikɔmstəχ/ (adj) accidental, incidental; inessential; secondary; subordinate

de **bijkomstigheid** /bɛikɔmstəχhɛit/ (pl: -heden) incidental circumstance

de **bijl** /bɛil/ (pl: -en) axe ‖ *het ~tje erbij neerleggen* knock off, call it a day; call it quits

de **bijlage** /bɛilaɣə/ (pl: -n) **1** enclosure, appendix; supplement **2** [comp] attachment

bij lange /bɛilɑŋə/ (adv) ~ *na niet* not anything like (as nice, good, ...), not nearly (so nice, good, ...); not by a long shot (*or:* chalk)!; *dat is ~ na niet genoeg* that's not nearly enough; *het is ~ na niet af* it's nowhere near finished

bijleggen /bɛilɛɣə(n)/ (legde bij, heeft bijgelegd) **1** contribute, pay; make up **2** settle: *het ~* make up

de **bijles** /bɛilɛs/ (pl: -sen) coaching; [Am also] tutoring

bijlichten /bɛilɪχtə(n)/ (lichtte bij, heeft bijgelicht) light: *iem. ~* give (a) light to s.o.

de **bijna** /bɛina/ (adv) almost, nearly; close on; near: ~ *nooit* (*or:* *geen*) almost never (*or:* none), hardly ever (*or:* any)

de **bijnaam** /bɛinam/ (pl: bijnamen) nickname

de **bijna-doodervaring** /bɛinadotɛrvarɪŋ/ (pl: -en) near-death experience

het **bijou** /biʒu/ (pl: -s) jewel

bijpassen /bɛipɑsə(n)/ (paste bij, heeft bijgepast) pay; make up (the difference): *je zult moeten ~* you will have to pay (*or:* make up) the difference

bijpassend /bɛipɑsənt/ (adj) matching; to match

bijpraten /bɛipratə(n)/ (praatte bij, heeft bijgepraat) catch up: *iem. ~* bring s.o. up to date

het **bijproduct** /bɛiprodʏkt/ (pl: -en) by-product, spin-off

de **bijrijder** /bɛirɛidər/ (pl: -s) substitute-driver, driver's mate

de **bijrol** /bɛirɔl/ (pl: -len) supporting role (*or:* part) [also fig]

bijschaven /bɛisχavə(n)/ (schaafde bij, heeft bijgeschaafd) **1** plane (down) **2** [fig] polish (up): *een opstel ~* polish up an essay

bijscholen /bɛisχolə(n)/ (schoolde bij, heeft bijgeschoold) give further training

de **bijscholing** /bɛisχolɪŋ/ (extra) training

het **bijschrift** /bɛisχrɪft/ (pl: -en) **1** caption, legend **2** note

bijschrijven /bɛisχrɛivə(n)/ (schreef bij, heeft bijgeschreven) enter, include

de **bijschrijving** /bɛisχrɛivɪŋ/ (pl: -en) **1** entering (in the books) **2** amount entered, item entered

de **bijsluiter** /bɛislœytər/ (pl: -s) information leaflet, instruction leaflet

de **bijsmaak** /bɛismak/ (pl: bijsmaken) taste: *deze soep heeft een ~je* this soup has a funny taste to it, this soup doesn't taste right

bijspijkeren /bɛispɛikərə(n)/ (spijkerde bij, heeft bijgespijkerd) brush up: *een zwakke leerling ~* bring a weak pupil up to standard

bijspringen /bɛisprɪŋə(n)/ (sprong bij, heeft/is bijgesprongen) support, help out

¹**bijstaan** /bɛistan/ (stond bij, heeft bijgestaan) dimly recollect: *er staat me iets bij van een vergadering waar hij heen zou gaan* I seem to remember that he was to go to a meeting

²**bijstaan** /bɛistan/ (stond bij, heeft bijgestaan) assist, aid

de **bijstand** /bɛistɑnt/ **1** assistance, aid: ~ *verlenen* render assistance **2** [Dutch] social security; [Am] welfare: *hij leeft van de ~* he's on social security, he's on welfare **3** [Dutch] Social Security

de **bijstandsmoeder** /bɛistɑntsmudər/ (pl: -s) mother on social security; [Am] mother on welfare

de **bijstandsouder** /bɛistɑn(t)saudər/ (pl: -s) parent on social security; [Am] parent on welfare

de **bijstandsuitkering** /bɛistɑntsœytkerɪŋ/ (pl: -en) social security (payment)

de **bijstandswet** /bɛistɑntswɛt/ social security act

bijstellen /bɛistɛlə(n)/ (stelde bij, heeft bijgesteld) (re-)adjust: *de* **verwachtingen** *naar beneden* ~ lower (one's) expectations

de **bijstelling** /bɛistɛlɪŋ/ (pl: -en) (re-)adjustment

bijster /bɛistər/ (adv) unduly, (none) too: *de tuin is niet* ~ *groot* the garden is none too large ‖ *het spoor* ~ *zijn* have lost one's way

bijsturen /bɛistyrə(n)/ (stuurde bij, heeft bijgestuurd) **1** steer (away from, clear of, towards) **2** [fig] steer away from (or: clear of); adjust

de **bijt** /bɛit/ (pl: -en) hole (in the ice)

bijtanken /bɛitɛŋkə(n)/ (tankte bij, heeft bijgetankt) **1** refuel **2** [fig] replenish one's reserves, recharge one's battery

de **bijtelling** /bɛrtɛlɪŋ/ (pl: -en): [Dutch] *fiscale* ~ addition to taxable income

bijten /bɛitə(n)/ (beet, heeft gebeten) **1** bite: *van zich af* ~ give as good as one gets, stick up for o.s. **2** sting, smart

bijtend /bɛitənt/ (adj, adv) biting; corrosive

bijtijds /bɛitɛits/ (adv) **1** early **2** early, (well) in advance

bijtreden /bɛrtredə(n)/ (trad bij, is bijgetreden) [Belg] agree (with)

bijtrekken /bɛitrɛkə(n)/ (trok bij, is bijgetrokken) **1** straighten (out), improve **2** come (a)round

bijv. *bijvoorbeeld* e.g.

het **bijvak** /bɛivɑk/ (pl: -ken) subsidiary (subject)

de **bijval** /bɛivɑl/ approval; support

bijvallen /bɛrvɑlə(n)/ (viel bij, is bijgevallen) agree (with); support, back up: *iem.* ~ go along with s.o., agree with s.o.

de **bijvangst** /bɛivɑŋst/ (pl: -en) **1** [fishing] by-catch **2** [fig] incidental discovery

bijverdienen /bɛivərdinə(n)/ (verdiende bij, heeft bijverdiend) have an additional income: *een paar pond* ~ earn a few pounds extra (or: on the side)

de **bijverdienste** /bɛivərdinstə/ (pl: -n) extra earnings, extra income, additional income

het **bijverschijnsel** /bɛivərsχɛinsəl/ (pl: -en) side effect

bijvoegen /bɛivuɣə(n)/ (voegde bij, heeft bijgevoegd) add; enclose; attach

bijvoeglijk /bɛivuχlək/ (adj): ~ *naamwoord* adjective

het **bijvoegsel** /bɛivuχsəl/ (pl: -s) supplement, addition

bijvoorbeeld /bɛivɔrbelt/ (adv) for example, for instance, e.g.

bijvullen /bɛivʏlə(n)/ (vulde bij, heeft bijgevuld) top up (with); fill up (with)

bijwerken /bɛiwɛrkə(n)/ (werkte bij, heeft

bijgewerkt) improve, catch up (on); bring up to date; update

de **bijwerking** /bɛiwɛrkɪŋ/ (pl: -en) side effect

bijwonen /bɛiwonə(n)/ (woonde bij, heeft bijgewoond) attend, be present at

het **bijwoord** /bɛiwort/ (pl: -en) adverb

de **bijzaak** /bɛizak/ (pl: bijzaken) side issue, (minor) detail

bijzetten /bɛizɛtə(n)/ (zette bij, heeft bijgezet) **1** add **2** inter, bury

bijziend /bɛizint/ (adj) short-sighted

de **bijziendheid** /bɛizinthɛit/ short-sightedness

het **bijzijn** /bɛizɛin/: *in (het)* ~ *van* in the presence of

de **bijzin** /bɛizɪn/ (pl: -nen) (subordinate) clause: *betrekkelijke* ~ relative clause

¹**bijzonder** /bizɔndər/ (adj) **1** particular: *in het* ~ in particular, especially **2** special, unique **3** strange, peculiar **4** private

²**bijzonder** /bizɔndər/ (adv) **1** very (much) **2** particularly, in particular, especially

de **bijzonderheid** /bizɔndərhɛit/ (pl: -heden) detail, particular

biken /bɑjkə(n)/ (bikete, heeft gebiket) go mountain biking

de **bikini** /bikini/ (pl: -'s) bikini

bikkelhard /bɪkəlhɑrt/ (adj) **1** rock-hard **2** very hard

bikken /bɪkə(n)/ (bikte, heeft gebikt) chip (away)

de **bikramyoga** /bɪkrɑmjoɣə/ Bikram yoga

de **bil** /bɪl/ (pl: -len) buttock: *dikke* (or: *blote*) ~*len* a fat (or: bare) bottom

de/het **bila** /bila/ (pl: -'s) tête-à-tête, face-to-face (or: one-to-one) meeting

bilateraal /bilateral/ (adj) bilateral

biljard /bɪljɑrt/ (num) thousand billion(s); [Am] quadrillion

het **biljart** /bɪljɑrt/ (pl: -s) billiards, billiard table

de **biljartbal** /bɪljɑrdbɑl/ (pl: -len) billiard ball: *zo kaal als een* ~ as bald as a coot

biljarten /bɪljɑrtə(n)/ (biljartte, heeft gebiljart) play billiards

de **biljarter** /bɪljɑrtər/ billiards player

de **biljartkeu** /bɪljɑrtkø/ (pl: -s, -en) billiard cue

het **biljet** /bɪljɛt/ (pl: -ten) **1** ticket; bill; poster **2** note; [Am] bill

het **biljoen** /bɪljun/ (pl: -en) trillion

het/de **billboard** /bɪlbɔːrd/ (pl: -s) billboard

de **billenkoek** /bɪlə(n)kuk/: ~ *krijgen* get a smacking, get a spanking

billijk /bɪlək/ (adj, adv) fair, reasonable; moderate

billijken /bɪləkə(n)/ (billijkte, heeft gebillijkt) approve of: *dat kan ik* ~ I approve of that; *dat valt te* ~ that is quite reasonable

de **billijkheid** /bɪləkhɛit/ fairness, reasonableness

binair /binɛːr/ (adj) binary

¹**binden** /bɪndə(n)/ (bond, heeft gebonden)

1 tie (up), knot, bind, fasten; strap **2** tie (up) **3** bind: *door voorschriften gebonden zijn* be bound by regulations **4** bind **5** thicken

zich ²**binden** /bɪ̱ndə(n)/ (bond zich, heeft zich gebonden) commit o.s. (to), bind (*or:* pledge) o.s. (to)

bindend /bɪ̱ndənt/ (adj) binding: *een ~ referendum* a binding referendum

de **binding** /bɪ̱ndɪ̱ŋ/ (pl: -en) bond, tie

het **bindmiddel** /bɪ̱ntmɪdəl/ (pl: -en) binding agent, binder

het **bindweefsel** /bɪ̱ntwefsəl/ connective (*or:* interstitial) tissue

bingewatchen /bɪ̱ntʃwɔtʃə(n)/ binge viewing, binge watching

het **bingo** /bɪ̱ŋɡo/ bingo

de **bink** /bɪ̱ŋk/ (pl: -en) hunk: *de ~ uithangen* show off, play the tough guy

¹**binnen** /bɪ̱nə(n)/ (adv) inside, in; indoors: *hij is ~* he has got it made; *daar ~* inside, in there; *naar ~ gaan* go in, go inside, enter; *het wil me niet te ~ schieten* I can't bring it to mind; *van ~* (on the) inside; *'~!'* come in!

²**binnen** /bɪ̱nə(n)/ (prep) inside, within: *het ligt ~ mijn bereik* [also fig] it is within my reach

de **binnenbaan** /bɪ̱nə(n)ban/ (pl: -banen) [sport] **1** inside lane **2** indoor track; indoor court

het **binnenbad** /bɪ̱nə(n)bat/ (pl: -en) indoor (swimming) pool

de **binnenband** /bɪ̱nə(n)bant/ (pl: -en) (inner) tube

de **binnenbocht** /bɪ̱nə(n)bɔχt/ (pl: -en) inside bend

binnenboord /bɪnə(n)bo̱rt/ (adv) inboard || *zijn benen ~ houden* keep one's legs in(side)

binnenbrengen /bɪ̱nə(n)brɛŋə(n)/ (bracht binnen, heeft binnengebracht) bring in, take in, carry in

binnendoor /bɪnə(n)do̱r/ (adv): *~ gaan* take the direct route

binnendringen /bɪ̱nə(n)drɪŋə(n)/ (drong binnen, is binnengedrongen) penetrate (into), enter; break in(to); force one's way in(to)

binnendruppelen /bɪ̱nə(n)drʏpələ(n)/ (druppelde binnen, is binnengedruppeld) [also fig] trickle in(to)

binnengaan /bɪ̱nə(n)ɣan/ (ging binnen, is binnengegaan) enter, go in(to), walk in(to)

binnenhalen /bɪ̱nə(n)halə(n)/ (haalde binnen, heeft binnengehaald) fetch in, bring in; land

de **binnenhaven** /bɪ̱nə(n)havə(n)/ (pl: -s) inland harbour (*or:* port); inner harbour

binnenhengelen /bɪ̱nə(n)hɛŋələ(n)/ (hengelde binnen, heeft binnengehengeld) land, wangle, bring in: *nieuwe klanten ~* bring in new customers; *subsidies ~* wangle subsidies

het **Binnenhof** /bɪ̱nə(n)hɔf/ the Dutch Parlia-

ment

binnenhouden /bɪ̱nə(n)haudə(n)/ (hield binnen, heeft binnengehouden) keep in(doors)

de **binnenhuisarchitect** /bɪ̱nə(n)hœysarʃitɛkt/ (pl: -en) interior designer (and decorator)

binnenin /bɪnə(n)ɪ̱n/ (adv) inside

de **binnenkant** /bɪ̱nə(n)kant/ (pl: -en) inside, interior

binnenkomen /bɪ̱nə(n)komə(n)/ (kwam binnen, is binnengekomen) come in(to), walk in(to), enter; arrive || *hard ~ (bij iem.)* hit (s.o.) hard, hit home

de **binnenkomst** /bɪ̱nə(n)kɔmst/ entry, entrance; arrival

binnenkort /bɪnə(n)kɔ̱rt/ (adv) soon, shortly, before (very) long

binnenkrijgen /bɪ̱nə(n)krɛiɣə(n)/ (kreeg binnen, heeft binnengekregen) **1** get down, swallow **2** get, obtain

het **binnenland** /bɪ̱nə(n)lant/ (pl: -en) **1** interior, inland **2** home

binnenlands /bɪ̱nə(n)lants/ (adj) home, internal, domestic

binnenlaten /bɪ̱nə(n)latə(n)/ (liet binnen, heeft binnengelaten) let in(to), admit (to); show in(to), usher in(to)

binnenlopen /bɪ̱nə(n)lopə(n)/ (liep binnen, is binnengelopen) go in(to), walk in(to)

de **binnenmarkt** /bɪ̱nəmarkt/ internal market

de **binnenmuur** /bɪ̱nə(n)myr/ (pl: -muren) interior wall, inside wall

de **binnenplaats** /bɪ̱nə(n)plats/ (pl: -en) (inner) court(yard); yard

het **binnenpretje** /bɪ̱nə(n)prɛcə/ (pl: -s) secret amusement

de **binnenschipper** /bɪ̱nə(n)sχɪpər/ (pl: -s) skipper of a barge

binnenshuis /bɪnənshœ̱ys/ (adv) indoors, inside, within doors

binnensmonds /bɪnənsmɔ̱nts/ (adv) inarticulately, indistinctly

de **binnensport** /bɪ̱nə(n)spɔrt/ (pl: -en) indoor sport

de **binnenstad** /bɪ̱nə(n)stat/ (pl: -steden) town centre; city centre; inner city

het **binnenste** /bɪ̱nə(n)stə/ inside, in(ner)most part, inner part

binnenstebuiten /bɪnənstəbœ̱ytə(n)/ (adv) inside out, wrong side out

binnenstormen /bɪ̱nə(n)stɔrmə(n)/ (stormde binnen, is binnengestormd): *zij kwam de kamer ~* she came storming (*or:* dashing, rushing) into the room

binnenstromen /bɪ̱nə(n)stromə(n)/ (stroomde binnen, is binnengestroomd) [also fig] pour in(to), flow in(to); rush in(to), surge in(to)

binnentrekken /bɪ̱nə(n)trɛkə(n)/ (trok binnen, is binnengetrokken) march in(to), enter

de **binnenvaart** /bɪnə(n)vart/ inland shipping

binnenvallen /bɪnə(n)vɑlə(n)/ (viel binnen, is binnengevallen) burst in(to), barge in(to); invade: *bij iem.* **komen** ~ descend on s.o.

de **binnenvetter** /bɪnə(n)vɛtər/ (pl: -s) introvert

het **binnenwater** /bɪnə(n)watər/ (pl: -en) **1** inland waterway, canal, river **2** polder water

de **binnenweg** /bɪnə(n)wɛx/ (pl: -en) byroad; short cut

de **binnenzak** /bɪnə(n)zɑk/ (pl: -ken) inside pocket

de **binnenzee** /bɪnə(n)ze/ (pl: -ën) inland sea

het **bint** /bɪnt/ (pl: -en) beam; joist

de **biobak** /bijobɑk/ (pl: -ken) organic waste bin

de **bioboer** /bijobur/ biological farmer, organic farmer

de **biobrandstof** /bijobrɑntstɔf/ (pl: -fen) biofuel

de **biochemicus** /bijoxemikʏs/ (pl: biochemici) biochemist

de **biochemie** /bijoxemi/ biochemistry

biodynamisch /bijodinamis/ (adj) biodynamic

de **bio-energie** /bijoenɛrɣi/ bioenergy

de **biograaf** /bijoɣraf/ (pl: biografen) biographer

de **biografie** /bijoɣrafi/ (pl: -ën) biography

biografisch /bijoɣrafis/ (adj) biographic(al)

de **bio-industrie** /bijoɪndʏstri/ (pl: -ën) factory farming; agribusiness

de **biologie** /bijoloɣi/ biology

biologisch /bijoloɣis/ (adj, adv) biological, organic: ~ *afbreekbaar* biodegradable; ~*e* *groenten* organic vegetables; *haar* ~*e* *vader* her natural (*or:* biological) father

de **bioloog** /bijolox/ (pl: biologen) biologist

de **biomassa** /bijomɑsɑ/ biomass

het **biopt** /bijɔpt/ (pl: -en) biopsy specimen

het **bioritme** /bijorɪtmə/ (pl: -s) biorhythm

de **bioscoop** /bijoskop/ (pl: bioscopen) cinema; [Am] movie theater

bipolair /bipolɛːr/ (adj) bipolar: *een* ~*e* *stoornis hebben* have a bipolar disorder, be bipolar

de **bips** /bɪps/ (pl: -en) [child language] bottom, backside, buttocks

Birma /bɪrmɑ/ Burma

de **Birmaan** /bɪrman/ (pl: Birmanen) Burmese

Birmaans /bɪrmans/ (adj) Burmese

bis /bis/ (adv) (once) again, encore

het **biscuitje** /bɪskwicə/ biscuit; [Am] cookie

het **bisdom** /bɪzdɔm/ (pl: -men) diocese, bishopric

biseksueel /bisɛksywel/ (adj) bisexual

de **bisschop** /bɪsxɔp/ (pl: -pen) bishop

bisschoppelijk /bɪsxɔpələk/ (adj) episcopal

bissen /bɪsə(n)/ (biste, heeft gebist) [Belg; educ] repeat (the year)

de **bisser** /bisər/ (pl: -s) [Belg; educ] pupil who repeats a class

de **bistro** /bistro/ (pl: -'s) bistro

de **¹bit** /bɪt/ bit

het **²bit** /bɪt/ bit

de **bitch** /bɪtʃ/ (pl: bitches) bitch

de **bitcoin** /bɪtkɔjn/ (pl: -s) bitcoin

bits /bɪts/ (adj, adv) snappish, short(-tempered)

het/de **¹bitter** /bɪtər/ (gin and) bitters

²bitter /bɪtər/ (adj) **1** bitter **2** bitter, sour || ~ *weinig* precious little, next to nothing

de **bitterbal** /bɪtərbɑl/ (pl: -len) type of croquette served as an appetizer

de **bitterheid** /bɪtərhɛit/ bitterness

het **bitterkoekje** /bɪtərkukjə/ (pl: -s) (bitter) macaroon

het **bivak** /bivɑk/ (pl: -ken) bivouac: *zijn* ~ *opslaan* [fig] pitch one's tent

bivakkeren /bivɑkərə(n)/ (bivakkeerde, heeft gebivakkeerd) **1** bivouac **2** lodge, stay

bizar /bizɑr/ (adj, adv) bizarre

de **bizon** /bizɔn/ (pl: -s) bison

het **blaadje** /blacə/ (pl: -s) **1** leaf(let); sheet (of paper), piece (of paper); paper; tray **2** [bot] leaflet; petal || *bij iem. in een* **goed** ~ *staan* be in s.o.'s good books

de **blaam** /blam/: *hem treft* **geen** ~ he is not to blame; *iem. van* **alle** ~ *zuiveren* exonerate s.o.

de **blaar** /blar/ (pl: blaren) blister

de **blaas** /blas/ (pl: blazen) bladder, cyst

de **blaasbalg** /blazbɑlx/ (pl: -en) (pair of) bellows

het **blaasinstrument** /blasɪnstrymɛnt/ (pl: -en) wind instrument

de **blaaskaak** /blaskak/ (pl: -kaken) bighead, stuffed shirt, windbag

de **blaasontsteking** /blasɔntstekɪŋ/ (pl: -en) bladder infection, cystitis

het **blaasorkest** /blasɔrkɛst/ (pl: -en) wind orchestra; brass band

het **blaaspijpje** /blaspɛipjə/ (pl: -s) breathalyser

de **blaastest** /blastɛst/ (pl: -en) breathalyser (*or:* breath) test

de **blabla** /blablɑ/ **1** blah(-blah) **2** fuss

het **blad** /blɑt/ (pl: -en, -eren) **1** [bot] leaf; petal **2** tray **3** sheet, leaf; page **4** (news)paper; magazine **5** sheet; top; blade

de **bladblazer** /blɑdblazər/ leaf blower

bladderen /blɑdərə(n)/ (bladderde, heeft/is gebladderd) blister; bubble; flake; peel

het **bladerdeeg** /bladərdex/ puff pastry (*or:* paste)

bladeren /bladərə(n)/ (bladerde, heeft gebladerd) thumb, leaf

het **bladgoud** /blɑtxɑut/ gold leaf

het **bladgroen** /blɑtxrun/ chlorophyll

de **bladgroente** /blɑtxruntə/ (pl: -n, -s) green vegetables

de **bladluis** /blɑtlœys/ (pl: -luizen) greenfly, blackfly, aphis

de **bladmuziek** /blɑtmyzik/ sheet music
de **bladpeterselie** /blɑtpetərseli/ flat-leaf parsley
bladstil /blɑtstɪl/ (adj) dead calm: *het was ~* not a leaf stirred, it was dead calm
de **bladvulling** /blɑtfʏlɪŋ/ (pl: -en) in-fill, fill-up (article)
de **bladwijzer** /blɑtwɛizər/ (pl: -s) bookmark(er)
de **bladzijde** /blɑtsɛidə/ (pl: -n) page: *ik sloeg het boek open op ~ 58* I opened the book at page 58
blaffen /blɑfə(n)/ (blafte, heeft geblaft) bark
blaken /blakə(n)/ (blaakte, heeft geblaakt) burn (with), glow (with)
blakeren /blakərə(n)/ (blakerde, heeft geblakerd) scorch, burn: *door de zon geblakerd* sun-baked
de **blamage** /blamaʒə/ (pl: -s) disgrace
blancheren /blɑ̃ʃerə(n)/ (blancheerde, heeft geblancheerd) blanch
blanco /blɑŋko/ (adj, adv) blank: *~ stemmen* abstain (from voting)
blank /blɑŋk/ (adj) **1** white: *~ hout* natural wood **2** flooded: *de kelder staat ~* the cellar is flooded
de **blanke** /blɑŋkə/ (pl: -n) white (man, woman): *de ~n* the whites
blasé /blazɛ/ (adj) blasé
de **blasfemie** /blɑsfemi/ (pl: -ën) blasphemy
blaten /blatə(n)/ (blaatte, heeft geblaat) bleat
blauw /blɑu/ (adj) **1** blue: *in het ~ gekleed* dressed in blue **2** black, dark: *een ~e plek* a bruise; *iem. bont en ~ slaan* beat s.o. black and blue
de **blauwalg** /blɑuɑlx/ (pl: -en) blue algae
de **blauwbaard** /blɑubart/ (pl: -en) bluebeard
de **blauwdruk** /blɑudrʏk/ (pl: -ken) blueprint
de **blauwhelm** /blɑuhɛlm/ (pl: -en) blue helmet
het **blauwtje** /blɑucə/ (pl: -s): *een ~ lopen* be turned down, be rejected
de **blauwtong** /blɑutɔŋ/ bluetongue (disease)
¹**blazen** /blazə(n)/ (blies, heeft geblazen) **1** blow: *op de trompet, de fluit, het fluitje, de hoorn ~* sound the trumpet, play the flute, blow the whistle, play the horn **2** breathe into a breathalyser || *katten ~ als ze kwaad zijn* cats hiss when they are angry
²**blazen** /blazə(n)/ (blies, heeft geblazen) blow || *het is oppassen geblazen* we (*or:* you) need to watch out
de **blazer** /blazər/ (pl: -s) player of a wind instrument
het **blazoen** /blazun/ (pl: -en) blazon
bleek /blek/ (adj) **1** pale; wan: *~ zien* look pale (*or:* wan) **2** pale, white
de **bleekheid** /blekhɛit/ paleness; pallor
het **bleekmiddel** /blekmɪdəl/ bleach, bleaching agent
de **bleekselderij** /bleksɛldərɛi/ celery
het **bleekwater** /blekwatər/ bleach, bleaching agent
bleken /blekə(n)/ (bleekte, heeft gebleekt) bleach
blèren /blɛːrə(n)/ (blèrde, heeft geblèrd) **1** squall, howl **2** bleat
de **bles** /blɛs/ (pl: -sen) blaze, star
blesseren /blɛserə(n)/ (blesseerde, heeft geblesseerd) injure, hurt; wound
de **blessure** /blɛsyrə/ (pl: -s) injury
de **blessuretijd** /blɛsyrətɛit/ injury time
blèten /blɛːtə(n)/ (blètte, heeft geblèt) [Belg] bawl, blub
bleu /blø/ (adj) timid
blieven /blivə(n)/ (bliefde, heeft gebliefd) **1** [Dutch] like **2** please
blij /blɛi/ (adj) **1** glad, happy, pleased, cheerful, merry: *daar ben ik ~ om* I'm pleased about it; *~ zijn voor iem.* be glad for s.o.'s sake **2** happy, joyful, joyous
de **blijdschap** /blɛitsxɑp/ joy, gladness, cheer(fulness), happiness
blijf /blɛif/: [Belg] *geen ~ met iets weten* be at a loss, not know what to do about sth.
het **blijf-van-mijn-lijfhuis** /blɛifɑmənlɛifhœys/ [Dutch] women's refuge centre, shelter (for battered women)
de **blijheid** /blɛihɛit/ gladness, joy, happiness
het **blijk** /blɛik/ (pl: -en) mark, token: *~ geven van belangstelling* show one's interest
¹**blijkbaar** /blɛigbar/ (adj) evident, obvious, clear
²**blijkbaar** /blɛigbar/ (adv) apparently, evidently
blijken /blɛikə(n)/ (bleek, is gebleken) prove, turn out: *doen ~ van* show, express; *hij liet er niets van ~* he gave no sign of it; *dat moet nog ~* that remains to be seen
blijkens /blɛikə(n)s/ (prep) according to, as appears from, as is evident from
blijmoedig /blɛimudəx/ (adj, adv) cheerful, merry, gay
het **blijspel** /blɛispɛl/ (pl: -en) comedy
blijven /blɛivə(n)/ (bleef, is gebleven) **1** remain: *het blijft altijd gevaarlijk* it will always be dangerous; *rustig ~* keep quiet; *deze appel blijft lang goed* this apple keeps well; *jong ~* stay young **2** remain (doing), stay (on) (doing), continue (doing), keep (doing): *~ logeren* stay the night (in the house); *blijft u even aan de lijn?* hold the line, please; *blijf bij de reling vandaan* keep clear of the railings; *je moet op het voetpad ~* you have to keep to the footpath **3** be, keep: *~ staan* a) stand still, stop; b) remain standing; *waar zijn we gebleven?* where were we?; *waar is mijn portemonnee gebleven?* where has my purse got to? **4** perish, be left (*or:* remain) behind: *ergens in ~ (van het lachen)* a) choke; b) [fig] die

(laughing)

blijvend /blɛivənt/ (adj) lasting; enduring, permanent; durable

de ¹**blik** /blɪk/ **1** look; glance: *een ~ op iem. werpen* take a look at s.o., look s.o. over **2** look (in one's eyes), expression **3** view, outlook ‖ *een geoefende* (or: *scherpe*) *~ a* trained (*or:* sharp) eye

het ²**blik** /blɪk/ **1** tin(plate): *in ~* tinned **2** tin; [Am] can **3** dustpan

de **blikgroente** /blɪkxruntə/ (pl: -n, -s) tinned vegetables

¹**blikken** /blɪkə(n)/ (adj) tin: *~ doosjes* tin boxes (*or:* canisters)

²**blikken** /blɪkə(n)/ (blikte, heeft geblikt): *zonder ~ of blozen* without batting an eyelid

de **blikopener** /blɪkopənər/ (pl: -s) tin-opener

de **blikschade** /blɪksxadə/ bodywork damage: *een aanrijding met alleen ~* a collision with minor damage; [Am also] a fender bender

de **bliksem** /blɪksəm/ (pl: -s) lightning: *als door de ~ getroffen* thunderstruck; *de ~ slaat in* lightning strikes ‖ *er als de gesmeerde ~ vandoor gaan* take off like greased lightning

de **bliksemafleider** /blɪksəmaflɛidər/ (pl: -s) lightning conductor

het **bliksembezoek** /blɪksəmbəzuk/ (pl: -en) flying visit, lightning visit

de **bliksemcarrière** /blɪksəmkɑrijɛːrə/ (pl: -s) lightning career: *een ~ maken* rise rapidly

bliksemen /blɪksəmə(n)/ (bliksemde, heeft gebliksemd) flash, blaze

de **bliksemflits** /blɪksəmflɪts/ (pl: -en) (flash of) lightning

de **blikseminslag** /blɪksəmɪnslɑx/ (pl: -en) stroke (*or:* bolt) of lightning, thunderbolt

bliksemsnel /blɪksəmsnɛl/ (adj, adv) lightning, at (*or:* with) lightning speed, quick as lightning, like greased lightning

de **bliksemstart** /blɪksəmstɑrt/ lightning start

de **bliksemstraal** /blɪksəmstral/ (pl: -stralen) thunderbolt

de **blikvanger** /blɪkfɑŋər/ (pl: -s) eye-catcher

het **blikveld** /blɪkfɛlt/ field of vision; [fig] horizon, perspective

de ¹**blind** /blɪnt/ (pl: -en) (window) shutter, blind

²**blind** /blɪnt/ (adj) blind: *~ typen* touch-type; *zij is aan één oog ~* she is blind in one eye; *~ proeven* do a blind tasting

de **blind date** /blɑjndɛt/ blind date

de **blinddoek** /blɪnduk/ (pl: -en) blindfold

blinddoeken /blɪndukə(n)/ (blinddoekte, heeft geblinddoekt) blindfold

de **blinde** /blɪndə/ (pl: -n) blind person, blind man, blind woman: *de ~n* the blind

de **blindedarm** /blɪndədɑrm/ (pl: -en) appendix

de **blindedarmontsteking** /blɪndədɑrmɔntstekɪŋ/ (pl: -en) appendicitis

blindelings /blɪndəlɪŋs/ (adv) blindly: *~ volgen* follow blindly

de **blindengeleidehond** /blɪndə(n)ɣəlɛidəhɔnt/ (pl: -en) guide dog (for the blind)

blinderen /blɪndɛrə(n)/ (blindeerde, heeft geblindeerd) armour

de **blindganger** /blɪntxɑŋər/ (pl: -s) dud, unexploded bomb (*or:* shell)

de **blindheid** /blɪnthɛit/ blindness

zich **blindstaren** /blɪntstarə(n)/ (staarde zich blind, heeft zich blindgestaard): *zich ~ op* concentrate too much on; *je moet je niet ~ op details* don't let yourself be put off (*or:* obsessed) by details

het/de **blingbling** /blɪŋblɪŋ/ bling-bling

de **blini** /blini/ (pl: -'s) blini

blinken /blɪŋkə(n)/ (blonk, heeft geblonken) shine, glisten, glitter: *alles blinkt* er everything is spotless (*or:* spick and span)

blits /blɪts/ (adj) trendy, hip

blocken /blɔkə(n)/ (blockte, heeft geblockt) block

de **blocnote** /blɔknot/ (pl: -s) (writing) pad

het **bloed** /blut/ blood: *mijn eigen vlees en ~* my own flesh and blood; *~ vergieten* shed (*or:* spill) blood; *geen ~ kunnen zien* not be able to stand the sight of blood ‖ *in koelen ~e* in cold blood; *kwaad ~ zetten* breed (*or:* create) bad blood; *iem. het ~ onder de nagels vandaan halen* get under s.o.'s skin, exasperate s.o.

de **bloedarmoede** /blutarmudə/ anaemia

de **bloedbaan** /bludban/ (pl: -banen) bloodstream

het **bloedbad** /bludbɑt/ (pl: -en) bloodbath, massacre: *een ~ aanrichten onder de inwoners* massacre the inhabitants

de **bloedbank** /bludbɑŋk/ (pl: -en) blood bank

de **bloedcel** /blutsɛl/ (pl: -len) blood cell (*or:* corpuscle)

de **bloeddonor** /bludonɔr/ (pl: -en, -s) blood donor

bloeddoorlopen /bludorlopə(n)/ (adj) bloodshot: *met ~ ogen* with bloodshot eyes

bloeddorstig /bludɔrstəx/ (adj, adv) bloodthirsty

de **bloeddruk** /bludrʏk/ blood pressure: *de ~ meten* take s.o.'s blood pressure

bloedeigen /blutɛiɣə(n)/ (adj) (very) own: *mijn ~ kind* my own child

bloedeloos /bludəlos/ (adj) lifeless

bloeden /budə(n)/ (bloedde, heeft gebloed) bleed

bloederig /budərəx/ (adj) bloody, gory

de **bloedgroep** /blutxrup/ (pl: -en) blood group (*or:* type)

bloedheet /bluthet/ (adj) sweltering (hot), boiling (hot)

bloedhekel /bluthekəl/: *een ~ hebben aan iets* absolutely hate sth.

de **bloedhond** /bluthɔnt/ (pl: -en) bloodhound

bloedig /budəx/ (adj) bloody, gory

de **bloeding** /budɪŋ/ (pl: -en) bleeding; haemorrhage

het **bloedlichaampje** /blʊtlɪχampjə/ (pl: -s) blood corpuscle (or: cell)

bloedlink /blutlɪŋk/ (adj, adv) [inform] **1** bloody dangerous **2** hopping mad, furious: *hij werd ~ toen hij ervan hoorde* he went into a rage when he heard about it

de **bloedneus** /blʊtnøs/ (pl: -neuzen) bloody nose

het **bloedonderzoek** /blʊtɔndərzuk/ (pl: -en) blood test(s)

het **bloedplaatje** /blʊtplacə/ (pl: -s) (blood) platelet, thrombocyte

het **bloedplasma** /blʊtplɑsma/ (blood) plasma

de **bloedproef** /blʊtpruf/ (pl: -proeven) blood test

de **bloedprop** /blʊtprɔp/ (pl: -pen) blood clot, thrombus

bloedrood /blʊtrot/ (adj, adv) blood-red

bloedserieus /blutserijøs/ (adj) dead (or: utterly) serious

de **bloedsomloop** /blʊtsɔmlop/ (blood) circulation

bloedstollend /blutstɔlənt/ (adj) blood-curdling

de **bloedsuiker** /blʊtsœykər/ (pl: -s) blood sugar

de **bloedsuikerspiegel** /blʊtsœykərspiɣəl/ blood sugar level

de **bloedtransfusie** /blʊtrɑnsfyzi/ (pl: -s) (blood) transfusion

de **bloeduitstorting** /blʊtœytstɔrtɪŋ/ (pl: -en) extravasation (of blood)

het **bloedvat** /blʊtfɑt/ (pl: -en) blood vessel

de **bloedverdunner** /blʊtfərdʏnər/ (pl: -s) blood diluent

bloedvergieten /blʊtfərɣitə(n)/ bloodshed: *een revolutie zonder ~* a bloodless revolution

de **bloedvergiftiging** /blʊtfərɣɪftəɣɪŋ/ (pl: -en) blood poisoning

het **bloedverlies** /blʊtfərlis/ loss of blood

de **bloedverwant** /blʊtfərwɑnt/ (pl: -en) (blood) relation, relative, kinsman, kinswoman: *naaste ~en* close relatives, next of kin

de **bloedworst** /blʊtwɔrst/ (pl: -en) black pudding

de **bloedwraak** /blʊtvrak/ blood feud, vendetta

de **bloedzuiger** /blʊtsœyɣər/ (pl: -s) leech, bloodsucker

de **bloei** /bluj/ bloom, flower(ing); blossoming: *iem. in de ~ van zijn leven* s.o. in the prime of (his) life; *tot ~ komen* thrive, blossom

bloeien /blujə(n)/ (bloeide, heeft gebloeid) **1** bloom, flower; blossom **2** [fig] prosper, flourish

de **bloeiperiode** /blujperijodə/ (pl: -n, -s) **1** [bot] flowering time (or: season) **2** [fig] prime

de **bloem** /blum/ (pl: -en) **1** flower, bloom, blossom **2** flour

de **bloembak** /blʊmbɑk/ (pl: -ken) planter, flower box; window box

het **bloembed** /blʊmbɛt/ (pl: -den) flowerbed

de **bloembol** /blʊmbɔl/ (pl: -len) bulb

het/de **bloemencorso** /blumə(n)kɔrso/ (pl: -'s) flower parade

de **bloemenhandelaar** /blumə(n)hɑndəlar/ (pl: -s, -handelaren) florist

het **bloemenstalletje** /blumə(n)stɑləcə/ (pl: -s) flower stand, flower stall

de **bloemenvaas** /blumə(n)vas/ (pl: -vazen) (flower) vase

de **bloemenwinkel** /blumə(n)wɪŋkəl/ (pl: -s) florist's (shop), flower shop

het **bloemetje** /bluməcə/ (pl: -s) **1** (little) flower **2** flowers, nosegay || *de ~s buiten zetten* paint the town red

de **bloemist** /blumɪst/ (pl: -en) florist

de **bloemkool** /blumkol/ (pl: -kolen) cauliflower

het **bloemkoolroosje** /blumkolrojə/ (pl: -s) cauliflower floret

de **bloemkroon** /blumkron/ (pl: -kronen) corolla

de **bloemkwekerij** /blumkwekərɛi/ (pl: -en) **1** nursery, florist's (business) **2** floriculture, flower-growing industry

de **bloemlezing** /blumlezɪŋ/ (pl: -en) anthology

de **bloempot** /blumpɔt/ (pl: -ten) flowerpot

bloemrijk /blumrɛik/ (adj) flowery [also fig]

het **bloemschikken** /blumsχɪkə(n)/ (art of) flower arrangement

het **bloemstuk** /blumstʏk/ (pl: -ken) flower arrangement

de **bloemsuiker** /blumsœykər/ [Belg] icing sugar

de **bloes** /blus/ (pl: bloezen) blouse; shirt

de **bloesem** /blusəm/ (pl: -s) blossom, bloom, flower

het/de **blog** /blɔχ/ blog

de **blogger** /blɔɣər/ blogger

het **blok** /blɔk/ (pl: -ken) block, chunk; log: *een doos met ~ken* a box of building blocks; *als een ~ in slaap vallen* go out like a light || *iem. voor het ~ zetten* put a person on the spot; *een ~je omlopen* walk around the block

de **blokfluit** /blɔkflœyt/ (pl: -en) recorder

de **blokhut** /blɔkhʏt/ (pl: -ten) log cabin

het **blokje** /blɔkjə/ (pl: -s) cube, square

de **blokjescode** /blɔkjəskodə/ (pl: -s) QR code

de **blokkade** /blɔkadə/ (pl: -s) blockade

¹**blokken** /blɔkə(n)/ (blokte, heeft geblokt) cram, swot: *~ voor een tentamen* cram for an examination

²**blokken** /blɔkə(n)/ (blokte, heeft geblokt) **1** block: *zijn agenda ~* set aside time in one's schedule **2** block

de **blokkendoos** /blɔkə(n)dos/ (pl: -dozen) box of building blocks

bodybuilder

blokkeren /blɔkɛrə(n)/ (blokkeerde, heeft geblokkeerd) **1** blockade, block **2** freeze: *een **creditcard** ~* put a stop on a card, stop (*or:* cancel) a card **3** block, jam, lock **4** [sport] block, obstruct

de **blokletter** /blɔklɛtər/ (pl: -s) block letter, printing

blokletteren /blɔklɛtərə(n)/ (blokletterde, heeft geblokletterd) [Belg] headline, splash (news on the front page)

het **blokuur** /blɔkyr/ (pl: blokuren) [roughly] double period (*or:* lesson)

blond /blɔnt/ (adj) **1** blond, fair **2** golden

blonderen /blɔndərə(n)/ (blondeerde, heeft geblondeerd) bleach, peroxid(e)

de **blondine** /blɔndinə/ (pl: -s) blonde

het **¹bloot** /blot/ nudity

²bloot /blot/ (adj) bare, naked, nude: *op blote **voeten** lopen* go barefoot(ed); *uit het blote **hoofd** spreken* speak off the cuff, speak extempore; *met het blote **oog** iets waarnemen* observe sth. with the naked eye; *onder de blote **hemel*** in the open (air); *een jurk met blote **rug*** a barebacked dress

zich **blootgeven** /blotxevə(n)/ (gaf zich bloot, heeft zich blootgegeven) **1** expose o.s. **2** give o.s. away: *zich **niet** ~* not commit o.s., be non-committal

het **blootje** /blocə/: *in zijn ~* in the nude

blootleggen /blotlɛɣə(n)/ (legde bloot, heeft blootgelegd) lay open (*or:* bare), expose; [fig also] reveal

blootshoofds /blotshofts/ (adv) bareheaded

blootstaan /blotstan/ (stond bloot, heeft blootgestaan) be exposed (to); be subject (to), be open (to)

blootstellen /blotstɛlə(n)/ (stelde bloot, heeft blootgesteld) expose (to): *zich **aan** gevaar ~* expose o.s. to danger

blootsvoets /blotsfuts/ (adv) barefoot(ed): *~ **lopen*** go (*or:* walk) barefoot(ed)

de **blos** /blɔs/ (pl: -sen) **1** bloom: *een **gezonde** ~* a rosy complexion **2** flush; blush

de **blouse** /bluzə/ (pl: -s) blouse

blowen /blowə(n)/ (blowde, heeft geblowd) smoke dope

blozen /blozə(n)/ (bloosde, heeft gebloosd) **1** bloom (with) **2** flush (with); blush (with)

de **blubber** /blʏbər/ mud

de **blues** /blu:s/ blues

de **bluf** /blʏf/ **1** bluff(ing) **2** boast(ing), brag(ging), big talk

bluffen /blʏfə(n)/ (blufte, heeft gebluft) bluff; boast; brag, talk big

de **bluffer** /blʏfər/ (pl: -s) bluffer, boaster, braggart

het **blufpoker** /blʏfpokər/: *hij speelde een **partijtje** ~* he tried to brazen it out (*or:* bluff his way out)

de **blunder** /blʏndər/ (pl: -s) blunder: *een ~ **be**-*

gaan make a blunder

blunderen /blʏndərə(n)/ (blunderde, heeft geblunderd) blunder, make a blunder: *de keeper blunderde **vreselijk*** the keeper made a terrible blunder

de **blu-rayspeler** /blurespelər/ (pl: -s) Blu-ray player

blurren /blʏːrə(n)/ (blurde, heeft geblurd) blur

het **blusapparaat** /blʏsɑparat/ (pl: -apparaten) fire extinguisher

de **blusdeken** /blʏzdekə(n)/ (pl: -s) fire blanket

blussen /blʏsə(n)/ (bluste, heeft geblust) extinguish; put out

het **blusvliegtuig** /blʏsflixtœyx/ (pl: -en) fire-fighting plane

blut /blʏt/ (adj) broke, skint: *volkomen ~* stony-broke, flat broke

blz. *bladzijde* p.; pp.

de **BN'er** /beɛnər/ [Dutch] *bekende Nederlander* celebrity, famous Dutch person

bnp *bruto nationaal product* GNP

het **bo** /beo/ [Belg] *bijzonder onderwijs* special needs education

de **boa** /bowa/ (pl: -'s) boa

het **board** /bo:rd/ (pl: -s) hardboard, (fibre)-board

de **¹bob** /bɔp/ bobsleigh, bobsled

de **²bob**® /bɔp/ designated driver

de **bobbel** /bɔbəl/ (pl: -s) bump, lump

het **bobkapsel** /bɔpkɑpsəl/ (pl: -s) bob (cut)

de **bobo** /bobo/ bigwig, big shot

de **bobslee** /bɔpsle/ (pl: -ën) bob(sleigh)

bobsleeën /bɔpslejən/ bobsleigh

de **bochel** /bɔxəl/ (pl: -s) hump; hunchback

de **bocht** /bɔxt/ bend, curve: *zich in **allerlei** ~en wringen* try to wriggle one's way out of sth.; *uit de ~ vliegen* run off the road ‖ *dat is te kort **door** de ~* that's jumping to conclusions

bochtig /bɔxtəx/ (adj) winding

het **bod** /bɔt/ offer, bid: *een ~ **doen*** (*or:* **uitbrengen**) make a bid (*or:* an offer); *niet **aan** ~ komen* [fig] not get a chance

de **bode** /bodə/ (pl: -n, -s) messenger, postman

de **bodem** /bodəm/ (pl: -s) **1** bottom; base: *een dubbele ~* a hidden meaning; *op de ~ van de zee* at the bottom of the sea **2** ground, soil **3** territory, soil: *producten van **eigen** ~* home-grown products ‖ *een ~ **leggen** voor een avondje stappen* line your stomach before going out drinking; [fig] *iets **tot** de ~ uitzoeken* examine sth. down to the last detail

de **bodemgesteldheid** /bodəmɣəstɛlthɛɪt/ condition (*or:* composition) of the soil

bodemloos /bodəmlos/ (adj) bottomless

de **bodemprijs** /bodəmprɛɪs/ (pl: -prijzen) minimum price

de **bodemverontreiniging** /bodəmvərɔntrɛɪnəɣɪŋ/ (pl: -en) soil pollution

de **bodybuilder** /bɔdibʏldər/ (pl: -s) body-builder, muscleman het/de **bodybuilding** /bɔ̯dibɪldɪŋ/ body building

de **bodylotion** /bɔ̯dilo(t)ʃɔn/ (pl: -s) body lotion

de **bodypainting** /bɔ̯dipɛntɪŋ/ body painting

de **bodywarmer** /bɔ̯diwɔrmər/ (pl: -s) body warmer

boe /bu/ (int) boo; moo: ~ *roepen* boo, jeer ‖ *zonder* ~ *of bah te zeggen* without saying (*or:* uttering) a word, without opening one's mouth

Boedapest /bu̯dapɛst/ Budapest

Boeddha /bu̯da/ Buddha

het **boeddhisme** /budɪ̯smə/ Buddhism

de **boeddhist** /budɪ̯st/ (pl: -en) Buddhist

boeddhistisch /budɪ̯stis/ (adj) Buddhist

de **boedel** /bu̯dəl/ (pl: -s) property, household effects

de **boef** /buf/ (pl: boeven) scoundrel, rascal

de **boeg** /buχ/ (pl: -en) bow(s), prow: *het over een andere ~ gooien* change (one's) tack; change the subject

het **boegbeeld** /bu̯ybelt/ (pl: -en) figurehead

het **boegeroep** /bu̯yərup/ booing, hooting: *de premier moest onder ~ het podium verlaten* the prime minister was booed off the stage

de **boei** /buj/ (pl: -en) **1** buoy: *een kop* (or: *een kleur) als een ~* (a face) as red as a beetroot **2** chain, handcuff: *iem. in de ~en slaan* clap (*or:* put) s.o. in irons, (hand)cuff s.o.

¹boeien /bu̯jə(n)/ (boeide, heeft geboeid) **1** chain, (hand)cuff **2** fascinate, captivate: *het stuk kon ons niet (blijven) ~* the play failed to hold our attention

²boeien /bu̯jə(n)/ (int) **1** who cares! **2** boring!

boeiend /bu̯jənt/ (adj, adv) fascinating, gripping, captivating

het **boek** /buk/ (pl: -en) book: *altijd met zijn neus in de ~en zitten* always have one's nose in a book, always be at one's books; *een dik ~* a thick (*or:* fat) book; *een ~ over* a book on

Boekarest /bu̯karɛst/ Bucharest

de **boekbespreking** /bu̯ɡbəsprekɪŋ/ (pl: -en) book review

het **boekbinden** /bu̯ɡbɪndə(n)/ (book)binding

de **boekbinder** /bu̯ɡbɪndər/ (pl: -s) (book)-binder

de **boekbinderij** /buɡbɪndərɛ̯i/ (pl: -en) bindery, (book)binder's

het **boekdeel** /bu̯ɡdel/ (pl: -delen) volume

de **boekdrukkerij** /buɡdrʏkərɛ̯i/ (pl: -en) **1** printing house (*or:* office), print shop **2** printer's

de **boekdrukkunst** /bu̯ɡdrʏkʏnst/ (art of) printing, typography

boeken /bu̯kə(n)/ (boekte, heeft geboekt) book, post, enter (up)

de **boekenbeurs** /bu̯kə(n)børs/ (pl: -beurzen) book fair

de **boekenbon** /bu̯kə(n)bɔn/ (pl: -nen) book token

het **boekenfonds** /bu̯kə(n)fɔn(t)s/ (pl: -en) (educational) book fund

de **boekenkast** /bu̯kə(n)kɑst/ (pl: -en) bookcase

de **boekenlegger** /bu̯kə(n)lɛɣər/ (pl: -s) bookmark(er)

de **boekenlijst** /bu̯kə(n)lɛist/ (pl: -en) (required) reading list, booklist

de **boekenplank** /bu̯kə(n)plɑŋk/ (pl: -en) bookshelf

het **boekenrek** /bu̯kə(n)rɛk/ (pl: -ken) bookshelves

de **boekensteun** /bu̯kə(n)støn/ (pl: -en) bookend

de **boekentaal** /bu̯kə(n)tal/ **1** literary language **2** bookish language

de **Boekenweek**® /bu̯kə(n)wek/ (pl: -weken) book week

de **boekenwurm** /bu̯kə(n)wʏrm/ (pl: -en) bookworm

het **boeket** /bukɛt/ (pl: -ten) bouquet: *een ~je* a posy, a nosegay

de **boekhandel** /bu̯khɑndəl/ (pl: -s) bookshop

de **boekhandelaar** /bu̯khɑndəlar/ (pl: -s, -handelaren) bookseller

het **¹boekhouden** /bu̯khau̯də(n)/ bookkeeping, accounting

²boekhouden /bu̯khau̯də(n)/ keep the books, do the accounting, do (*or:* keep) the accounts

de **boekhouder** /bu̯khau̯dər/ (pl: -s) accountant, bookkeeper

de **boekhouding** /bu̯khau̯dɪŋ/ (pl: -en) **1** accounting, bookkeeping **2** accounting department (*or:* section), accounts department

boekhoudkundig /bukhau̯tkʏ̯ndəχ/ (adj, adv) accounting, bookkeeping

de **boeking** /bu̯kɪŋ/ (pl: -en) **1** booking, reservation **2** [socc] booking, caution **3** entry

het **boekjaar** /bu̯kjar/ (pl: -jaren) fiscal year, financial year

het **boekje** /bu̯kjə/ (pl: -s) (small, little) book, booklet ‖ *buiten zijn ~ gaan* exceed one's authority; *volgens het ~* according to the book

boekstaven /bu̯kstavə(n)/ (boekstaafde, heeft geboekstaafd) **1** (put on) record **2** substantiate

de **boekwaarde** /bu̯kwardə/ book value, balance sheet value

de **boekweit** /bu̯kwɛit/ buckwheat

het **boekwerk** /bu̯kwɛrk/ (pl: -en) book, work

de **boekwinkel** /bu̯kwɪŋkəl/ (pl: -s) bookshop

de **boel** /bul/ **1** things, matters; mess: *de hele ~ bij elkaar schreeuwen* scream one's head off, scream blue murder; *de ~ aan kant maken* straighten (*or:* tidy) things up; *hij kan zijn ~tje wel pakken* he can (*or:* might) as well pack it in (now) **2** affair, business, matter, situation: *er een dolle ~ van maken* make quite a party of it; *dit is foute ~* this is bad; *een mooie ~* a fine mess; *het is er een saaie* (or: *dooie*) *~* it's a dead-and-alive place **3** a lot, heaps, lots, loads

de **boeman** /bu̱mɑn/ (pl: -nen) bogeyman

de **boemel** /bu̱məl/ (pl: -s): *aan de ~ gaan* go (out) on the razzle

de **boemeltrein** /bu̱məltrɛin/ (pl: -en) slow train, stopping train

de **boemerang** /bu̱mərɑŋ/ (pl: -s) boomerang

de **boender** /bu̱ndər/ (pl: -s) scrubbing brush; [Am] scrub-brush

boenen /bu̱nə(n)/ (boende, heeft geboend) **1** polish **2** scrub

het/de **boenwas** /bu̱nwɑs/ beeswax, wax polish

de **boer** /bur/ (pl: -en) **1** farmer, peasant; [Am] rancher **2** boor, (country) bumpkin **3** burp, belch **4** jack

de **boerderij** /burdərɛi̯/ (pl: -en) farm

boeren /bu̱rə(n)/ (boerde, heeft geboerd) **1** farm, run a farm **2** burp, belch || *hij heeft goed* (or: *slecht*) *geboerd dit jaar* he has done well (or: badly) this year

het **boerenbedrog** /bu̱rə(n)bədrɔx/ [inform] fraud, humbug, bunk: *dat is je reinste ~* that is clearly humbug (or: total bunk)

de **boerenknecht** /bu̱rə(n)knɛxt/ (pl: -en) (farm)hand

de **boerenkool** /bu̱rə(n)ko̱l/ (pl: -kolen) kale

het **boerenverstand** /bu̱rə(n)vərstɑnt/: [inform] *daar kan ik niet bij met mijn ~* that's beyond me

de **boerin** /buri̱n/ (pl: -nen) **1** farmer's wife **2** woman farmer

de **boerka** /bu̱rka/ burqa, burk(h)a

boers /burs/ (adj, adv) rustic, rural, peasant: *een ~ accent* a rural accent

de **boete** /bu̱tə/ (pl: -s) **1** fine: *een ~ krijgen van € 100* be fined 100 euros; *iem. een ~ opleggen* fine s.o. **2** [rel] penance: *~ doen* do penance (for sins) **3** penalty: *schuld en ~* crime and punishment

het **boetekleed** /bu̱təklet/: *het ~ aantrekken* put on the hair shirt

boeten /bu̱tə(n)/ (boette, heeft geboet) pay ((the penalty, price) for); [rel] atone (for); [rel] do penance (for): *zwaar voor iets ~* pay a heavy penalty for sth.

de **boetiek** /buti̱k/ (pl: -s) boutique

de **boetseerklei** /butse̱rklɛi̯/ modelling clay

boetseren /butse̱rə(n)/ (boetseerde, heeft geboetseerd) model

boetvaardig /butfa̱rdəx/ (adj, adv) penitent

de **boeventronie** /bu̱və(n)troni/ (pl: -s) [inform] villain's face

de **boezem** /bu̱zəm/ (pl: -s) **1** bosom, breast: *een zware (flinke) ~ hebben* be full-bosomed **2** bosom, heart || *de hand in eigen ~ steken* acknowledge blame

de **boezemvriend** /bu̱zəmvrint/ (pl: -en) bosom friend

de **bof** /bɔf/ (pl: -fen) **1** (good) luck: *wat een ~,*

dat ik hem nog thuis tref I'm lucky (*or:* what luck) to find him still at home **2** mumps: *de ~ hebben* have mumps

boffen /bɔ̱fə(n)/ (bofte, heeft geboft) be lucky

de **bofkont** /bɔ̱fkɔnt/ (pl: -en) lucky dog

bogen /bo̱ɣə(n)/ (boogde, heeft geboogd): *kunnen ~ op* boast, pride o.s. ((up)on)

Bohemen /bohe̱mə(n)/ Bohemia

de **boiler** /bɔ̱i̯lər/ (pl: -s) water heater, boiler

de **bok** /bɔk/ (pl: -ken) **1** (male) goat, billy goat; buck; stag **2** vault

de **bokaal** /boka̱l/ (pl: bokalen) **1** goblet **2** beaker

bokken /bɔ̱kə(n)/ (bokte, heeft gebokt) sulk

de **bokkensprong** /bɔ̱kə(n)sprɔŋ/ (pl: -en) caper || *(rare) ~en maken* behave unpredictably (*or:* in a ridiculous way)

de **bokking** /bɔ̱kɪŋ/ (pl: -en) smoked herring

de **boksbal** /bɔ̱ksbɑl/ (pl: -len) punchball

de **boksbeugel** /bɔ̱ksbøɣəl/ (pl: -s) knuckleduster

boksen /bɔ̱ksə(n)/ (bokste, heeft gebokst) box

de **bokser** /bɔ̱ksər/ (pl: -s) boxer

de **bokshandschoen** /bɔ̱kshɑntsxun/ (pl: -en) boxing glove

bokspringen /bɔ̱ksprɪŋə(n)/ **1** (play) leapfrog **2** (squat) vaulting; vaulting exercise

de **bokswedstrijd** /bɔ̱kswɛtstrɛit̯/ (pl: -en) boxing match, (prize)fight

de ¹**bol** /bɔl/ (pl: -len) **1** ball; bulb: [fig] *ik heb geen glazen ~* I don't have a crystal ball **2** [maths] sphere || *uit zijn ~ gaan* go crazy, go out of one's mind

²**bol** /bɔl/ (adj, adv) round: *een ~le lens* a convex lens

de **bolcamera** /bɔ̱lkaməra/ (pl: -'s) dome camera

de **boleet** /bole̱t/ (pl: boleten) boletus

de **bolero** /bole̱ro/ bolero

de **bolhoed** /bɔ̱lhut/ (pl: -en) bowler (hat)

de **bolide** /boli̱də/ racing car

Bolivia /boli̱vija/ Bolivia

de **Boliviaan** /bolivija̱n/ (pl: Bolivianen) Boliviaan

Boliviaans /bolivija̱ns/ (adj) Bolivian

de **bolleboos** /bɔ̱ləbos/ (pl: bollebozen) highflyer

de **bollenkweker** /bɔ̱lə(n)kwekər/ (pl: -s) bulb grower

de **bollenteelt** /bɔ̱lə(n)telt/ bulb-growing (industry)

het **bollenveld** /bɔ̱lə(n)vɛlt/ (pl: -en) bulb field

het **bolletje** /bɔ̱ləcə/ (pl: -s) **1** (little) ball; globule **2** (soft) roll **3** [in document] bullet || *een ~ ijs* a scoop of ice cream

de **bolletjesslikker** /bɔ̱ləcəslɪkər/ (pl: -s) body packer, mule

de **bolsjewiek** /bɔlʃəwi̱k/ (pl: -en) Bolshevik

het **bolsjewisme** /bɔlʃəwɪsmə/ Bolshevism

de **bolster** /bɔlstər/ (pl: -s) shell: *ruwe ~, blanke pit* a rough diamond

bolvormig /bɔlvɔrməx/ (adj) spherical

de **bolwassing** /bɔlwasɪŋ/ (pl: -en) [Belg] dressing down

het **bolwerk** /bɔlwɛrk/ (pl: -en) bulwark; [fig also] stronghold; bastion

bolwerken /bɔlwɛrkə(n)/ manage, pull off; stick it out; hold one's own: *het (kunnen) ~* manage (it), pull it off; stick it out

de **bom** /bɔm/ (pl: -men) bomb: *het bericht sloeg in als een ~* the news came like a bombshell

de **bomaanslag** /bɔmanslax/ (pl: -en) bomb attack; bombing; bomb outrage

het **bomalarm** /bɔmalarm/ bomb alert; air-raid warning; bomb scare

het **bombardement** /bɔmbardəmɛnt/ (pl: -en) bombardment

bombarderen /bɔmbardɛrə(n)/ (bombardeerde, heeft gebombardeerd) **1** bomb **2** bombard; shell **3** [fig] bombard, shower

de **bombrief** /bɔmbrif/ (pl: bombrieven) letter bomb, mail bomb

de **bomgordel** /bɔmɣɔrdəl/ (pl: -s) explosive belt (*or:* vest), suicide belt (*or:* vest)

de **bommelding** /bɔmɛldɪŋ/ (pl: -en) bomb alert

bommen /bɔmə(n)/ (bomde, heeft gebomd): [inform] *(het) kan mij niet ~!* I couldn't care less (about it)!

de **bommenwerper** /bɔmə(n)wɛrpər/ (pl: -s) bomber

het **bommetje** /bɔmɛcə/ (pl: -s) cannonball: *een ~ doen* do a cannonball

de **bommoeder** /bɔmudər/ (pl: -s) [roughly] bachelor mother

bomvol /bɔmvɔl/ (adj) chock-full, cram-full, packed

de **bon** /bɔn/ (pl: -nen) **1** bill, receipt; cash-register slip: *iem. op de ~ slingeren* book s.o.; give s.o. a ticket **2** voucher, coupon; token; credit slip **3** ticket

bonafide /bonafidə/ (adj, adv) bona fide, in good faith

de **bonbon** /bɔmbɔn/ (pl: -s) [Dutch] chocolate, bonbon

de **bond** /bɔnt/ (pl: -en) **1** (con)federation, confederacy, alliance, union **2** union

de **bondgenoot** /bɔntxənot/ (pl: -genoten) ally; confederate

het **bondgenootschap** /bɔntxənotsxap/ (pl: -pen) alliance; confederacy, (con)federation

bondig /bɔndəx/ (adj, adv) concise, terse; pithy: *kort en ~* to the point, concise

het **bondsbestuur** /bɔn(t)sbəstyr/ society (*or:* association) executive; union executive

de **bondscoach** /bɔntskotʃ/ (pl: -es) national coach

de **Bondsdag** /bɔn(t)sdax/ Bundestag, (the Lower House of) the German Parliament

het **bondselftal** /bɔn(t)sɛlftal/ (pl: -len) national team

de **bondskanselier** /bɔntskansəlir/ (pl: -s) Federal Chancellor

de **Bondsrepubliek** /bɔntsrepyblik/: *~ Duitsland* Federal Republic (of Germany)

de **bonenstaak** /bonə(n)stak/ (pl: -staken) beanpole

het **boni** /boni/ profit, gains

de **bonje** /bɔnə/ [Dutch] rumpus, row

de **bonk** /bɔŋk/ (pl: -en) **1** lump: [Dutch] *één ~ zenuwen* a bundle of nerves **2** shooter

bonken /bɔŋkə(n)/ (bonkte, heeft/is gebonkt) **1** crash (against, into), bump (against, into) **2** bang, pound

bonkig /bɔŋkəx/ (adj): *een ~e stijl* a rough style

de **bonnefooi** /bonəfoj/ [Dutch]: *op de ~ ergens heen gaan* go somewhere on the off chance

de **bons** /bɔns/ (pl: bonzen) **1** thud, thump **2** (big) boss ‖ *iem. de ~ geven* give s.o. the push

de **bonsai** /bɔnsaj/ (pl: -s) bonsai

het ¹**bont** /bɔnt/ (pl: -en) fur: *met ~ gevoerd* fur-lined

²**bont** /bɔnt/ (adj, adv) **1** multicoloured; variegated: *~e kleuren* bright colours; *iem. ~ en blauw slaan* beat s.o. black and blue **2** colourful: *een ~ gezelschap* a) a colourful group of people; b) [depr] a motley crew ‖ *het te ~ maken* go too far

het **bontgoed** /bɔntxut/ (cotton) prints

de **bonthandel** /bɔnthandəl/ fur trade

de **bonthandelaar** /bɔnthandəlar/ (pl: -s, -handelaren) furrier

de **bontjas** /bɔntjas/ (pl: -sen) fur coat

de **bontmuts** /bɔntmyts/ (pl: -en) fur cap, fur hat

de **bonus** /bonys/ (pl: -sen) bonus, premium: *in de ~* on special offer (for loyalty card holders)

bonzen /bɔnzə(n)/ (bonsde, heeft gebonsd) **1** bang, hammer **2** bump (against, into), crash (against, into): *tegen iem. aan ~* bump into s.o., crash against (*or:* into) s.o. **3** pound

de **boodschap** /botsxap/ (pl: -pen) **1** purchase: *die kun je wel om een ~ sturen* [fig] you can leave things to him (*or:* her); *~pen doen* go (out) shopping, do the (*or:* one's) shopping **2** message: *een ~ voor iem. achterlaten* leave a message for s.o.; *een ~ krijgen* get a message **3** errand; mission

het **boodschappenlijstje** /botsxapə(n)lɛiʃə/ (pl: -s) shopping list

de **boodschappentas** /botsxapə(n)tas/ (pl: -sen) shopping bag

de **boodschapper** /botsxapər/ (pl: -s) messenger, courier

de **boog** /box/ (pl: bogen) **1** bow: *met pijl en ~* with bow and arrow **2** arch; span **3** arc; curve: *met een (grote) ~ om iets heenlopen* go out of one's way to avoid sth.

de **boogbal** /boɣbɑl/ (pl: -len) lob

de **boogscheut** /boxsxøt/ (pl: -en) [Belg] stone's throw: *op* een ~ *van* a stone's throw from

boogschieten /boxsxitə(n)/ archery

de **boogschutter** /boxsxʏtər/ (pl: -s) archer

de **Boogschutter** /boxsxʏtər/ (pl: -s) Sagittarius

de **bookmaker** /bukmekər/ bookmaker

de **bookmark** /bukmɑ:rk/ bookmark

de **boom** /bom/ (pl: bomen) 1 tree: *ze zien door de bomen het bos niet meer* they can't see the wood for the trees 2 bar, barrier, gate

de **boomgaard** /bomɣart/ (pl: -en) orchard

de **boomgrens** /bomɣrɛns/ tree line

boomklimmen /bomklɪmə(n)/ tree climbing

de **boomkwekerij** /bomkwekərɛi/ (pl: -en) tree nursery

de **boomschors** /bomsxɔrs/ (pl: -en) (tree) bark

de **boomstam** /bomstɑm/ (pl: -men) (tree) trunk

de **boomstronk** /bomstrɔŋk/ (pl: -en) tree stump

de **boon** /bon/ (pl: bonen) bean: *witte bonen* haricot beans; *honger maakt rauwe bonen zoet* hunger is the best sauce

het **boontje** /bonce/ (pl: -s): ~ *komt om zijn loontje* serves him right; *een heilig* ~ a goody-goody (or: prig)

de **boor** /bor/ (pl: boren) 1 brace 2 bit 3 drill

het/de **boord** /bort/ (pl: -en) 1 band, trim 2 collar 3 board: *van* ~ *gaan* disembark || [Belg] *iets goed* (or: *slecht*) *aan* ~ *leggen* set about it in the right (or: wrong) way

de **boordcomputer** /bortkɔmpjutər/ (pl: -s) (on)board computer

boordevol /bordəvɔl/ (adj) full (or: filled) to overflowing: ~ *nieuwe ideeën* bursting with new ideas; ~ *mensen* packed (or: crammed) with people

de **boordwerktuigkundige** /bortwɛrktœyxkʏndəɣə/ (pl: -n) flight engineer

het **booreiland** /borɛilɑnt/ (pl: -en) drilling rig (or: platform), oilrig

de **boormachine** /bormaʃinə/ (pl: -s) (electric) drill

het **boorplatform** /borplɑtfɔrm/ (pl: -s) drilling rig (or: platform); oil rig

de **boortoren** /bortorə(n)/ (pl: -s) derrick, drilling rig

boos /bos/ (adj, adv) 1 angry, cross, hostile: ~ *kijken (naar iem.)* scowl (at s.o.); ~ *worden op* iem. get angry at s.o. 2 evil, bad, malicious, wicked; vicious: *de (grote) boze wolf* the big bad wolf 3 evil, foul, vile: *de boze geesten* evil spirits

boosaardig /bosardəx/ (adj, adv) 1 malignant 2 malicious, vicious

de **boosdoener** /bozdunər/ (pl: -s) wrongdoer:

de ~ was een doorgebrande zekering the culprit was a blown fuse, a blown fuse was to blame

de **boosheid** /boshɛit/ anger; fury

de **boot** /bot/ (pl: boten) boat, vessel; [large] steamer; [large] ship; ferry: *de ~ missen* [also fig] miss the boat; *de ~ afhouden* [fig] refuse to commit o.s., keep one's distance

het **boothuis** /bothœys/ (pl: -huizen) boathouse

de **bootreis** /botrɛis/ (pl: -reizen) voyage, cruise

de **bootsman** /botsmɑn/ (pl: bootslui, bootslieden) boatswain

de **boottocht** /botɔxt/ (pl: -en) boat trip (or: excursion)

de **bootvluchteling** /botflʏxtəlɪŋ/ (pl: -en) boat person (or: refugee); boat people

het **bord** /bort/ (pl: -en) 1 plate: *alle probleemgevallen komen op zijn ~je terecht* he ends up with all the difficult cases on his plate; *van een* ~ *eten* eat off a plate 2 sign, notice: *de hele route is met ~en aangegeven* it is signposted all the way 3 board; (black)board; notice board || *een* ~ *voor zijn kop hebben* be thick-skinned

de **bordeaux** /bordo/ (pl: -s) bordeaux; claret

het **bordeel** /bordel/ (pl: bordelen) brothel, whorehouse

de **bordenwasser** /bordə(n)wɑsər/ (pl: -s) dishwasher

de **bordenwisser** /bordə(n)wɪsər/ (pl: -s) board eraser, board duster

de **border** /bo:rdər/ (pl: -s) border

de **borderliner** /bo:rdərlɑjnər/ borderliner

het **bordes** /bordɛs/ (pl: -sen) [roughly] steps

het **bordkrijt** /bortkrɛit/ chalk

borduren /bordyrə(n)/ (borduurde, heeft geborduurd) embroider

het **borduurwerk** /bordyrwɛrk/ (pl: -en) embroidery

boren /borə(n)/ (boorde, heeft geboord) bore, drill

de **borg** /bɔrx/ (pl: -en) 1 surety; bail: *zich ~ stellen voor een gevangene* stand bail for a prisoner 2 security; deposit

de **borgsom** /bɔrxsɔm/ (pl: -men) deposit, security (money)

de **borgtocht** /bɔrxtɔxt/ (pl: -en) bail, recognizance

de **boring** /borɪŋ/ (pl: -en) boring, drilling

de **borrel** /bɔrəl/ (pl: -s) [Dutch] drink || *iem. voor* een ~ *uitnodigen* ask s.o. round (or: invite s.o.) for a drink

borrelen /bɔrələ(n)/ (borrelde, heeft geborreld) 1 bubble; gurgle 2 have a drink

het **borrelhapje** /bɔrəlhɑpjə/ (pl: -s) snack, appetizer

het **borrelnootje**® /bɔrəlnocə/ (pl: -s) nut (to go with cocktails)

de **borrelpraat** /bɔrəlprat/ [Dutch] twaddle,

chitchat

de **borsjtsj** /borʃtʃ/ borscht

de **borst** /bɔrst/ **1** chest: *uit volle ~ zingen* sing lustily; *zich op de ~ slaan* (or: *kloppen*) congratulate o.s.; *dat stuit mij tegen de ~* that goes against the grain with me, that sticks in my gizzard; *maak je ~ maar nat!* prepare yourself for the worst! **2** breast: *een kind de ~ geven* breastfeed a child

het **borstbeeld** /bɔrstbelt/ (pl: -en) bust

het **borstbeen** /bɔrstben/ (pl: -benen) breastbone; sternum

de **borstcrawl** /bɔrstkrɔːl/ (front) crawl

de **borstel** /bɔrstəl/ (pl: -s) **1** brush **2** [Belg] broom ‖ [Belg] *ergens met de grove ~ door gaan* tackle sth. in a rough-and-ready way

borstelen /bɔrstələ(n)/ (borstelde, heeft geborsteld) brush

borstelig /bɔrstələχ/ (adj) bristly, bushy

de **borstkanker** /bɔrstkaŋkər/ breast cancer

de **borstkas** /bɔrstkas/ (pl: -sen) chest

de **borstslag** /bɔr(st)slaχ/ (pl: -en) breaststroke; (front) crawl

borstsparend /bor(st)sparənt/ (adj): *~e operatie* breast-conserving surgery

de **borstvergroting** /bɔrstfərγrotɪŋ/ (pl: -en) breast augmentation; [inform] boob job

de **borstvin** /bɔrs(t)fɪn/ (pl: -nen) pectoral fin

de **borstvoeding** /bɔrstfudɪŋ/ (pl: -en) breastfeeding

de **borstwering** /bɔrstwerɪŋ/ (pl: -en) parapet

de **borstwijdte** /bɔrstwɛitə/ (pl: -s) (width of the) chest; bust (measurement)

de **borstzak** /bɔrstsak/ (pl: -ken) breast pocket

de **¹bos** /bɔs/ bundle; bunch: *een flinke ~ haar* a fine head of hair

het **²bos** /bɔs/ wood(s), forest

het **bosbeheer** /bɔzbəher/ forestry

de **bosbes** /bɔzbɛs/ (pl: -sen) bilberry; [Am] blueberry

de **bosbouw** /bɔzbau/ forestry

de **bosbrand** /bɔzbrant/ (pl: -en) forest fire

het **bosje** /bɔʃə/ (pl: -s) **1** bundle, tuft; wisp **2** grove, coppice **3** bush, shrub

de **Bosjesman** /bɔʃəsman/ (pl: -nen) Bushman

de **bosklas** /bɔsklas/ (pl: -sen) [Belg] nature class (in the woods)

de **bosneger** /bɔsneγər/ (pl: -s) maroon

Bosnië en Herzegovina /bosnijəenhɛrtsegovina/ Bosnia and Herzegovina

de **Bosniër** /bɔsnijər/ (pl: -s) Bosnian

Bosnisch /bɔsnis/ (adj) Bosnian

het **bospad** /bɔspat/ (pl: -en) woodland path, forest path (or: trail)

de **Bosporus** /bɔsporʏs/ Bosp(h)orus

bosrijk /bɔsrɛik/ (adj) woody

de **bosui** /bɔsœy/ (pl: bosuien) spring onion; [Am] green onion

de **bosvrucht** /bɔsfrʏχt/ forest fruit, fruit of the forest

de **boswachter** /bɔswaχtər/ (pl: -s) forester;

[Am] (forest) ranger; gamekeeper

de **¹bot** /bɔt/ flounder ‖ [fig] *~ vangen* draw a blank, come away empty-handed

het **²bot** /bɔt/ bone: *tot op het ~ verkleumd zijn* chilled to the bone

³bot /bɔt/ (adj) **1** blunt, dull **2** blunt, curt: *een ~te opmerking* a blunt (or: curt) remark

de **botanicus** /botanikʏs/ (pl: botanici) botanist

botanisch /botanis/ (adj) botanic(al)

de **botbreuk** /bɔdbrøk/ (pl: -en) break, broken bone

de **boter** /botər/ (pl: -s) butter: *~ bij de vis* cash on the nail ‖ *hij heeft ~ op zijn hoofd* listen who's talking; *met zijn neus in de ~ vallen* find one's bread buttered on both sides, be in luck

de **boterbloem** /botərblum/ (pl: -en) buttercup

het **boterbriefje** /botərbrifjə/ (pl: -s) marriage lines, marriage certificate

boteren /botərə(n)/ (boterde, heeft geboterd): *het wil tussen hen niet ~* they can't get on

de **boterham** /botərham/ (pl: -men) **1** slice (or: piece) of bread: [fig] *iets op zijn ~ krijgen* get sth. on one's plate; *een ~ met ham* a ham sandwich **2** living, livelihood: *zijn ~ verdienen met ...* earn one's living by ...

de **boterhamworst** /botərhamwɔrst/ [roughly] luncheon meat

het **boter-kaas-en-eieren** /botərkasɛnɛijərə(n)/ [Dutch] noughts and crosses; [Am] tic-tac-toe

de **boterkoek** /botərkuk/ (pl: -en) **1** [Dutch] butter biscuit **2** [Belg] brioche

de **botervloot** /botərvlot/ (pl: -vloten) butter dish

boterzacht /botərzɑχt/ (adj) (as) soft as butter

de **botheid** /bɔthɛit/ **1** bluntness, dullness **2** bluntness, gruffness

de **botkanker** /bɔtkaŋkər/ bone cancer

de **botontkalking** /bɔtontkalkɪŋ/ osteoporosis

het **botsautootje** /bɔtsautocə/ (pl: -s) dodgem (car), bumper car

botsen /bɔtsə(n)/ (botste, heeft/is gebotst) **1** collide (with), bump into (or: against); crash into (or: against): *twee wagens botsten tegen elkaar* two cars collided **2** [fig] clash (with)

de **botsing** /bɔtsɪŋ/ (pl: -en) collision; crash: *met elkaar in ~ komen* collide with one another, run into one another

de **Botswaan** /botswan/ (pl: Botswanen) Botswanan

Botswaans /botswans/ (adj) Botswanan

Botswana /botswana/ Botswana

bottelen /bɔtələ(n)/ (bottelde, heeft gebotteld) bottle

botten /bɔtə(n)/ (botte, is gebot) bud (out), put out buds

de **botter** /bɔtər/ (pl: -s) smack, fishing boat

de **bottleneck** /bɔtəlnɛk/ (pl: -s) bottleneck

de **bottomline** /bɔtəmlɑjn/ bottom line

het **botulisme** /botylɪsmə/ botulism

botvieren /bɔtfirə(n)/ (vierde bot, heeft botgevierd): *zijn frustraties* ~ give (full) vent to one's frustrations; let o.s. go; *dat moet je niet op haar* ~ you mustn't take it out on her

botweg /bɔtwɛx/ (adv) bluntly, flatly; point-blank

boud /baut/ (adj, adv) bold, impudent: *een* ~*e* (or: *boute*) *bewering* an impudent (or: a bold) assertion

de **bougie** /buʒi/ (pl: -s) sparking plug

de **bouillon** /bujɔn/ (pl: -s) broth

het **bouillonblokje** /bujɔmblɔkjə/ (pl: -s) beef cube

de **boulevard** /buləvar/ (pl: -s) 1 boulevard, avenue 2 promenade

de **boulevardblad** /buləvarblɑt/ (pl: -en) [roughly] tabloid

de **boulimia nervosa** /bulimijanɛrvoza/ bulimia nervosa; [Am] bulimarexia

het **bouquet** /bukɛ/ bouquet

de **bourgogne** /burgɔɲə/ (pl: -s) burgundy

de **Bourgondiër** /burɣɔndijər/ (pl: -s) Burgundian

bourgondisch /burxɔndis/ (adj, adv) exuberant

de **bout** /baut/ (pl: -en) 1 (screw) bolt, pin 2 leg, quarter; drumstick

de **bouvier** /buvje/ (pl: -s) Bouvier des Flandres

de **bouw** /bau/ 1 building, construction 2 building industry (or: trade) 3 structure, construction; build

het **bouwbedrijf** /baubədrɛif/ (pl: -bedrijven) construction firm, builders

1bouwen /bauwə(n)/ (bouwde, heeft gebouwd) (+ op) rely on

2bouwen /bauwə(n)/ (bouwde, heeft gebouwd) build, construct; erect; put up

de **bouwer** /bauwər/ (pl: -s) builder; (building) contractor; shipbuilder

de **bouwgrond** /bauɣrɔnt/ (pl: -en) building land

de **bouwhelm** /bauhɛlm/ (pl: -en) safety helmet, hard hat

het **bouwjaar** /baujar/ (pl: -jaren) year of construction (or: manufacture): *te koop: auto van het* ~ *1981* for sale: 1981 car

de **bouwkunde** /baukyndə/ architecture

bouwkundig /baukyndəx/ (adj, adv) architectural, constructional, structural: ~ *ingenieur* structural engineer

de **bouwkundige** /baukyndəɣə/ (pl: -n) architect, structural engineer

de **bouwkunst** /baukynst/ building, construction, architecture

het **bouwland** /baulɑnt/ farmland: *stuk* ~ field

het **bouwmateriaal** /baumaterijal/ (pl: -materialen) building material

het **bouwpakket** /baupɑkɛt/ (pl: -ten) (do-it-yourself) kit

de **bouwplaats** /bauplats/ (pl: -plaatsen) building (or: construction) site

de **bouwpromotor** /baupromotər/ (pl: -en, -s) [Belg] (property) developer

de **bouwput** /baupʏt/ (pl: -ten) (building) excavation

bouwrijp /baurɛip/ (adj) ready for building: *een terrein* ~ *maken* prepare a site (for building)

de **bouwsteen** /bausten/ (pl: -stenen) 1 brick 2 building block

de **bouwstijl** /baustɛil/ (pl: -en) architecture

de **bouwstof** /baustɔf/ (pl: -fen) building material; [fig] material(s)

de **bouwtekening** /bautekənɪŋ/ (pl: -en) floor plan, drawing(s)

het **bouwterrein** /bautɛrɛin/ (pl: -en) 1 building land 2 building site, construction site

de **1bouwvak** /bauvɑk/ [Dutch] construction industry holiday

het **2bouwvak** /bauvɑk/ building (or: construction) industry

de **bouwvakker** /bauvɑkər/ (pl: -s) construction worker

het **bouwvakkersdecolleté** /bauvɑkərzdekɔlətə/ (pl: -s) builder's bum, plumber's crack

de **bouwval** /bauvɑl/ (pl: -len) ruin

bouwvallig /bauvɑləx/ (adj) crumbling, dilapidated, rickety

de **bouwvergunning** /bauvərɣʏnɪŋ/ (pl: -en) building (or: construction) permit

de **bouwwerf** /bauwɛrf/ (pl: -werven) [Belg] building (or: construction) site

het **bouwwerk** /bauwɛrk/ (pl: -en) building, structure, construction

1boven /bovə(n)/ (adv) 1 above, up; upstairs: *(naar)* ~ *brengen* take (or: carry) up; bring back; *woon je* ~ *of beneden?* do you live upstairs or down(stairs)?; *naar* ~ *afronden* round up 2 on top: *dat gaat mijn verstand (begrip) te* ~ that is beyond me; that's over my head; *de vierde regel van* ~ the fourth line from the top 3 above 4 (+ aan) on top, at the top: ~ *aan de lijst staan* be at the top (or: head) of the list || *te* ~ *komen* get over, overcome, recover from

2boven /bovə(n)/ (prep) 1 above; over: *hij woont* ~ *een bakker* he lives over a baker's shop; ~ *water komen* a) surface, come up for air; b) [fig] turn up; *de flat* ~ *ons* the flat overhead 2 above, beyond: *dat gaat* ~ *mijn verstand* that is beyond me 3 above, over: *hij stelt zijn carrière* ~ *zijn gezin* he puts his career before his family; *er gaat niets* ~ *Belgische friet* there's nothing like Belgian chips; *veiligheid* ~ *alles* safety first 4 over, above, beyond: *kinderen* ~ *de drie jaar* children over three; ~ *alle* *twijfel* beyond (all) doubt

bovenaan /bovə(n)a̱n/ (adv) at the top: ~ *staan* be (at the) top

bovenal /bovə(n)a̱l/ (adv) above all

de **bovenarm** /bo̱və(n)arm/ (pl: -en) upper arm

het **bovenbeen** /bo̱və(n)ben/ (pl: -benen) upper leg, thigh

de **bovenbouw** /bo̱və(n)bau/ **1** [educ] last 2 or 3 classes (of secondary school) **2** superstructure

de **bovenbuur** /bo̱və(n)byr/ (pl: -buren) upstairs neighbour

bovendien /bovəndi̱n/ (adv) moreover, in addition, furthermore, besides: ~, *hij is niet meerderjarig* besides, he's a minor

bovendrijven /bo̱və(n)drɛivə(n)/ float: *komen* ~ float (or: rise) to the surface, surface

bovengemiddeld /bovə(n)ɣəmɪ̱dəlt/ (adj) higher (or: more) than average: *~e temperaturen* higher than average temperatures; ~ *geïnteresseerd zijn in …* showing an unusual interest in …

bovengenoemd /bovə(n)ɣənu̱mt/ (adj) above(-mentioned), mentioned above, stated above; [law] (afore)said

de **bovengrens** /bo̱və(n)ɣrɛns/ (pl: -grenzen) upper limit

bovengronds /bovə(n)ɣrɔ̱nts/ (adj, adv) aboveground, surface, overhead

bovenhands /bovə(n)ha̱n(t)s/ (adj, adv) overarm: ~ *serveren* serve overarm

bovenin /bovə(n)ɪ̱n/ (adv) at the top, on top

de **bovenkaak** /bo̱və(n)kak/ (pl: -kaken) upper jaw

de **bovenkant** /bo̱və(n)kant/ (pl: -en) top

de **bovenkleding** /bo̱və(n)kledɪŋ/ outer clothes, outerwear

bovenkomen /bo̱və(n)komə(n)/ (kwam boven, is bovengekomen) **1** come up, come to the surface, break (the) surface, surface **2** come up(stairs)

de **bovenlaag** /bo̱və(n)laχ/ (pl: -lagen) upper layer, surface layer; top coat

de **bovenleiding** /bo̱və(n)lɛidɪŋ/ (pl: -en) overhead (contact) wire

het **bovenlijf** /bo̱və(n)lɛif/ (pl: -lijven) upper part of the body: *met ontbloot* ~ stripped to the waist

de **bovenlip** /bo̱və(n)lɪp/ (pl: -pen) upper lip

bovenmatig /bovəma̱təχ/ (adj, adv) extreme, excessive

bovenmenselijk /bovə(n)mɛ̱nsələk/ (adj, adv) superhuman

bovennatuurlijk /bovənaty̱rlək/ (adj, adv) supernatural

bovenop /bovə(n)ɔ̱p/ (adv) **1** on top: *het er te dik ~ leggen* lay it on too thick; [fig] *ergens ~ springen* pounce on sth.; [fig] *ergens ~ zitten* to keep a close eye on sth. **2** on one's

feet: *de zieke kwam er snel weer* ~ the patient made a quick recovery

bovenst /bo̱vənst/ (adj) top, topmost, upper(most): *van de ~e plank* first class; *de ~e verdieping* [also fig] the top storey

bovenstaand /bo̱və(n)stant/ (adj) above, above-mentioned

de **boventoon** /bo̱və(n)ton/ (pl: -tonen) dominant tone: [fig] *de ~ voeren* [pers] play first fiddle, monopolize the conversation; [feeling] predominate

bovenuit /bovə(n)œy̱t/ (adv) above: *zijn stem klonk overal* ~ his voice could be heard above everything

de **bovenverdieping** /bo̱və(n)vərdipɪŋ/ (pl: -en) upper storey, upper floor; top floor (or: storey)

bovenvermeld /bovə(n)vərmɛ̱lt/ (adj) above(-mentioned)

bovenwinds /bovə(n)wɪ̱nts/ (adj, adv) windward

de **bovenwoning** /bo̱və(n)wonɪŋ/ (pl: -en) upstairs flat

de **bovenzijde** /bo̱və(n)zɛidə/ (pl: -n) see *bovenkant*

de **bowl** /bowl/ (pl: -s) punch

bowlen /bo̱wlə(n)/ (bowlde, heeft gebowld) bowl

de **bowlingbaan** /bo̱lɪŋban/ (pl: -banen) bowling alley

de **box** /bɔks/ (pl: -en) **1** (loud)speaker **2** (loose) box, stall **3** storeroom **4** box **5** (play)pen

de **boxer** /bɔ̱ksər/ (pl: -s) boxer

de **boxershort** /bɔ̱ksərʃɔːrt/ (pl: -s) boxer shorts

de **boycot** /bɔ̱jkɔt/ (pl: -s) boycott

boycotten /bɔjkɔ̱tə(n)/ (boycotte, heeft geboycot) boycott; freeze out

boze /bo̱zə/: *het is uit den* ~ it is fundamentally wrong, it is absolutely forbidden

de **braadpan** /bra̱tpɑn/ (pl: -nen) casserole

de **braadworst** /bra̱twɔrst/ (pl: -en) **1** (frying) sausage **2** German sausage

braaf /braf/ (adj, adv) **1** good, honest; [oft iron] respectable; decent **2** well-behaved, obedient: [fig] *het ~ste jongetje van de klas* best in the class; best performing country

de **braafheid** /bra̱fhɛit/ goodness, decency, honesty; [sometimes iron] respectability; obedience

braak /brak/ (adj) **1** waste; fallow: ~ *laten liggen* leave (or: lay) fallow **2** [fig] fallow, undeveloped, unexplored

braakliggend /bra̱klɪɣənt/ (adj) fallow

het **braakmiddel** /bra̱kmɪdəl/ emetic, vomitive

de **braakneigingen** /bra̱knɛiɣɪŋə(n)/ (pl) queasiness, nausea: [fig] *daar krijg ik ~ van* it nauseates me

het **braaksel** /bra̱ksəl/ vomit

de **braam** /bram/ (pl: bramen) blackberry, bramble

brabbelen /bra̱bələ(n)/ (brabbelde, heeft

gebrabbeld) babble, jabber, gibber

braden /br<u>a</u>də(n)/ (braadde, heeft gebraden) roast; fry; pot-roast; grill

de **braderie** /bradəri/ (pl: -ën) fair

het **braille** /br<u>a</u>jə/ braille: *in* ~ in braille, brailled

brainstormen /br<u>ɛ</u>nstɔrmə(n)/ (brainstormde, heeft gebrainstormd) do some brainstorming: ~ *over* brainstorm on

brak /brɑk/ (adj) saltish, brinish

braken /br<u>a</u>kə(n)/ (braakte, heeft gebraakt) vomit, be sick, throw up, regurgitate

brallen /br<u>a</u>lə(n)/ (bralde, heeft gebrald) brag, boast

de **brancard** /brɑŋk<u>a</u>r/ (pl: -s) stretcher

de **branche** /br<u>ɑ̃</u>ʃ/ (pl: -s) branch, department; line (of business); (branch of) trade

de **brand** /brɑnt/ (pl: -en) fire, blaze: *er is gevaar voor* ~ there is a fire hazard; ~ *stichten* commit arson; *in* ~ *staan* be on fire; *in* ~ *vliegen* catch fire, burst into flames; ignite; *iets in* ~ *steken* set sth. on fire, set fire to sth. ‖ *iem. uit de* ~ *helpen* help s.o. out

het **brandalarm** /br<u>ɑ</u>ntalɑrm/ fire alarm (*or:* call)

brandbaar /br<u>ɑ</u>ndbar/ (adj) combustible; (in)flammable

de **brandblusinstallatie** /br<u>ɑ</u>ndblʏsɪnstala(t)si/ (pl: -s) sprinkler system

de **brandblusser** /br<u>ɑ</u>ndblʏsər/ (pl: -s) (fire) extinguisher

de **brandbom** /br<u>ɑ</u>ndbɔm/ (pl: -men) firebomb

de **brandbrief** /br<u>ɑ</u>ndbrif/ (pl: -brieven) appeal letter, letter of appeal

¹**branden** /br<u>ɑ</u>ndə(n)/ (brandde, heeft gebrand) burn, be on fire; blaze: *de lamp brandt* the lamp is on ‖ *ze was het huis niet uit te* ~ there was no way of getting her out of the house

²**branden** /br<u>ɑ</u>ndə(n)/ (brandde, heeft gebrand) burn; scald; roast: *zich de vingers* ~ [fig] burn one's fingers

de **brander** /br<u>ɑ</u>ndər/ (pl: -s) burner

branderig /br<u>ɑ</u>ndərəx/ (adj) irritant, caustic

de **brandewijn** /br<u>ɑ</u>ndəwɛin/ (pl: -en) brandy

de **brandgang** /br<u>ɑ</u>ntxɑŋ/ (pl: -en) fire lane, firebreak

het **brandgevaar** /br<u>ɑ</u>ntxəvar/ fire hazard, fire risk

brandgevaarlijk /br<u>ɑ</u>ntxəvarlək/ (adj) flammable

het **brandglas** /br<u>ɑ</u>ntxlɑs/ (pl: -glazen) burning-glass

de **brandhaard** /br<u>ɑ</u>nthart/ (pl: -en) seat of a fire; [fig] hotbed

het **brandhout** /br<u>ɑ</u>nthɑut/ (pl: -en) firewood: [fig] ~ *maken van iets* shoot sth. down in flames

de **branding** /br<u>ɑ</u>ndɪŋ/ (pl: -en) surf; breakers

de **brandkast** /br<u>ɑ</u>ntkɑst/ (pl: -en) safe

de **brandkraan** /br<u>ɑ</u>ntkran/ (pl: -kranen) (fire) hydrant, fireplug

de **brandladder** /br<u>ɑ</u>ntlɑdər/ (pl: -s) fire ladder; escape ladder

de **brandlucht** /br<u>ɑ</u>ntlʏxt/ smell of burning

de **brandmelder** /br<u>ɑ</u>ntmɛldər/ (pl: -s) fire alarm (system)

het **brandmerk** /br<u>ɑ</u>ntmɛrk/ (pl: -en) brand

brandmerken /br<u>ɑ</u>ntmɛrkə(n)/ (brandmerkte, heeft gebrandmerkt) brand

de **brandnetel** /br<u>ɑ</u>ntnetəl/ (pl: -s) nettle

het **brandpunt** /br<u>ɑ</u>ntpʏnt/ (pl: -en) **1** focus [also maths] **2** [fig] centre

het **brandraam** /br<u>ɑ</u>ntram/ (pl: -ramen) [Belg] stained-glass window

brandschoon /br<u>ɑ</u>ntsxon/ (adj) spotless

de **brandslang** /br<u>ɑ</u>ntslɑŋ/ (pl: -en) fire hose

de **brandspiritus** /br<u>ɑ</u>ntspiritʏs/ methylated spirit(s)

de **brandspuit** /br<u>ɑ</u>ntspœyt/ (pl: -en) fire engine: *drijvende* ~ fireboat

de **brandstapel** /br<u>ɑ</u>ntstapəl/ (pl: -s) stake

brandstichten /br<u>ɑ</u>ntstɪxtə(n)/ (stichtte brand, heeft brandgesticht) commit arson

de **brandstichter** /br<u>ɑ</u>ntstɪxtər/ (pl: -s) arsonist

de **brandstichting** /br<u>ɑ</u>ntstɪxtɪŋ/ (pl: -en) arson

de **brandstof** /br<u>ɑ</u>ntstɔf/ (pl: -fen) fuel

het **brandstoflabel** /br<u>ɑ</u>ntstɔflebəl/ (pl: -s) fuel economy label

de **brandtrap** /br<u>ɑ</u>ntrɑp/ (pl: -pen) fire escape

de **brandweer** /br<u>ɑ</u>ntwer/ fire brigade

de **brandweerauto** /br<u>ɑ</u>ntwerauto/ (pl: -'s) fire engine

de **brandweerkazerne** /br<u>ɑ</u>ntwerkazɛrnə/ (pl: -s) fire station

de **brandweerman** /br<u>ɑ</u>ntwermɑn/ (pl: -lieden) fireman

brandwerend /br<u>ɑ</u>ntwerənt/ (adj) fire-resistant

de **brandwond** /br<u>ɑ</u>ntwɔnt/ (pl: -en) burn

brassen /br<u>ɑ</u>sə(n)/ (braste, heeft gebrast) binge, guzzle

de **brasserie** /brasəri/ (pl: -ën) brasserie

bravo /br<u>a</u>vo/ (int) bravo!; hear! hear!

de **bravoure** /brav<u>u</u>r/ bravura: *met veel* ~ dashing

de **Braziliaan** /brazilij<u>a</u>n/ (pl: Brazilianen) Brazilian

Braziliaans /brazilij<u>a</u>ns/ (adj) Brazilian

Brazilië /braz<u>i</u>lijə/ Brazil

het **break-evenpoint** /breki̠vəmpɔjnt/ (pl: -s) break-even point

¹**breed** /bret/ (adj) wide, broad: *de kamer is 6 m lang en 5 m* ~ the room is 6 metres (long) by 5 metres (wide); *niet breder dan twee meter* not more than two metres wide (*or:* in width)

²**breed** /bret/ (adv) widely; loosely: *een* ~ *omgeslagen kraag* a wide (*or:* loose) collar

de **breedband** /br<u>e</u>dbɑnt/ [comp] broadband

het **breedbandinternet** /br<u>e</u>dbɑntɪntərnɛt/

broadband (Internet access)

het **breedbeeld** /brɛdbelt/ wide screen

de **breedbeeld-tv** /brɛdbelteve/ (pl: -'s) widescreen TV

breedgebouwd /bretχəbɑut/ (adj) broad(ly-built), square-built

breedgedragen /bretχədraɣə(n)/ (adj) widely supported: *een ~ plan* a widely supported plan

breedsprakig /bretsprakəχ/ (adj, adv) long-winded

de **breedte** /bretə/ (pl: -s) **1** width, breadth: *in de ~* breadthways **2** [geog] latitude

de **breedtegraad** /bretəɣrat/ (pl: -graden) parallel, degree of latitude

breeduit /bretœyt/ (adv) **1** spread (out): *~ gaan zitten* sprawl (on) **2** out loud

breedvoerig /bretfurəχ/ (adj, adv) circumstantial; detailed

breekbaar /brɛɡbar/ (adj) fragile; brittle

het **breekijzer** /brɛkɛizər/ (pl: -s) crowbar

het **breekpunt** /brɛkpʏnt/ (pl: -en) breaking point

de **breezer** /briːzər/ breezer

breien /brɛiə(n)/ (breide, heeft gebreid) knit

het **brein** /brɛin/ brain; [fig also] brains: *het ~ zijn achter een project* be the brain(s) behind a project, mastermind a project

de **breinaald** /brɛinalt/ (pl: -en) knitting needle

het **breiwerk** /brɛiwɛrk/ (pl: -en) knitting

¹**breken** /brekə(n)/ (brak, is gebroken) **1** break; fracture **2** break down: *toen hij dat hoorde, brak hij* when he heard that, he broke down **3** break: *met iem. ~* break off (relations) with s.o.; break up with s.o.; *met een gewoonte ~* break a habit

²**breken** /brekə(n)/ (brak, heeft gebroken) **1** break; [light] refract **2** break: *zijn belofte breken* break one's promise ‖ *een record ~* break a record; *de betovering* (or: *het verzet*) *~* break the spell (or: resistance)

de **brem** /brɛm/ broom

brengen /brɛŋə(n)/ (bracht, heeft gebracht) **1** bring; take: *mensen (weer) bij elkaar ~* bring (or: get) people together (again); *naar huis ~* take home; *een kind naar bed ~* put a child to bed **2** bring, take, give: *zijn mening naar voren ~* put forward, come out with one's opinion; *iets naar voren ~* bring sth. up; *een zaak voor het gerecht ~* take a matter to court **3** bring, send, put: *iem. tot een daad ~* drive s.o. to (sth.); *iem. aan het twijfelen ~* raise doubt(s) in s.o.'s mind ‖ *het ver ~* go far

de **bres** /brɛs/ (pl: -sen) breach; hole: *voor iem. in de ~ springen* step into the breach for s.o.

Bretagne /brətɒɲə/ Brittany

de **bretel** /brətɛl/ (pl: -s) braces; [Am] suspenders

de **breuk** /brøk/ (pl: -en) **1** break(ing), breakage **2** crack, split, fault **3** [med] fracture, hernia **4** rift, breach **5** [maths] fraction: *decimale (tiendelige) ~* decimal fraction; *samengestelde ~* complex (or: compound) fraction

de **breuklijn** /brøklɛin/ (pl: -en) (line of a) break; line of fracture [also med]; [geology] fault line

het **brevet** /brəvɛt/ (pl: -ten) certificate; [aviation] licence

de **brexit** /brɛksɪt/ Brexit: *een harde ~* a hard Brexit, a no-deal scenario; *een zachte ~* a soft Brexit

bridgen /brɪdʒə(n)/ (bridgede/bridgete, heeft gebridged/gebridget) play bridge

de **brief** /brif/ (pl: brieven) letter: *aangetekende ~* registered letter; *in antwoord op uw ~ van de 25e* in reply to your letter of the 25th

briefen /briːfə(n)/ (briefte, heeft gebrieft) brief

het **briefgeheim** /brifχəhɛim/ confidentiality of the mail(s)

het **briefhoofd** /brifhoft/ (pl: -en) letterhead, letter-heading

de **briefing** /briːfɪŋ/ (pl: -s) briefing

het **briefje** /brifjə/ (pl: -s) note: *dat geef ik je op een ~* you can take it from me

de **briefkaart** /brifkart/ (pl: -en) postcard

de **briefopener** /brifopənər/ (pl: -s) paperknife, letter-opener

het **briefpapier** /brifpapir/ writing paper, stationery

de **briefwisseling** /brifwɪsəlɪŋ/ (pl: -en) correspondence: *een ~ voeren (met)* correspond (with)

de **bries** /bris/ breeze

briesen /brisə(n)/ (brieste, heeft gebriest) roar; snort

de **brievenbus** /brivə(n)bʏs/ (pl: -sen) **1** postbox, letter box **2** letter box; [Am] mailbox

de **brigade** /briɣadə/ (pl: -s) **1** brigade **2** squad, team

de **brigadier** /briɣadir/ (pl: -s) **1** [Dutch] police sergeant **2** (school) crossing guard

de **brij** /brɛi/ **1** pulp **2** porridge ‖ *om de hete ~ heen draaien* beat about the bush

de **brik** /brɪk/ (pl: -ken): [Belg] *melk in ~* milk in cartons

de **bril** /brɪl/ (pl: -len) **1** (pair of) glasses; (pair of) goggles: *alles door een donkere* (or: *roze*) *~ zien* take a gloomy (or: rosy) view of everything **2** (toilet) seat

de **brildrager** /brɪldraɣər/ (pl: -s): *hij, zij is ~* he, she wears glasses

de ¹**briljant** /brɪljɑnt/ (pl: -en) (cut) diamond

²**briljant** /brɪljɑnt/ (adj, adv) brilliant

de **brille** /brɪljə/ brilliance

de **brillenkoker** /brɪlə(n)kokər/ (pl: -s) glasses case

het/de **brilmontuur** /brɪlmɔntyr/ (pl: -monturen) glasses frame de **brilslang** /brɪlslɑŋ/ (pl: -en) (spectacled) cobra

de **Brit** /brɪt/ (pl: -ten) Briton; Brit

de **brits** /brɪts/ (pl: -en) plank bed, wooden bed

Brits /brɪts/ (adj) British

de **broccoli** /brɔkoli/ broccoli

het **broccoliroosje** /brɔkoliroʃə/ (pl: -s) broccoli floret

de **broche** /brɔʃ/ (pl: -s) brooch

de **brochure** /broʃyrə/ (pl: -s) pamphlet

het **broddelwerk** /brɔdəlwɛrk/ botch-job, botch-up

brodeloos /brɔdəlos/ (adj) without means of support: *iem. ~ maken* leave s.o. without means of support

broeden /brudə(n)/ (broedde, heeft gebroed) brood ‖ *hij zit op iets te ~* he is working on sth.

de **broeder** /brudər/ (pl: -s) **1** brother **2** [Roman Catholicism] brother, friar **3** (male) nurse

broederlijk /brudərlək/ (adj, adv) fraternal; like brothers

de **broedermoord** /brudərmort/ (pl: -en) fratricide

de **broederschap** /brudərsχɑp/ (pl: -pen) brotherhood, fraternity

de **broedmachine** /brutmaʃinə/ (pl: -s) incubator, brooder

de **broedplaats** /brutplats/ (pl: -en) breeding ground

broeien /brujə(n)/ (broeide, heeft gebroeid) **1** heat, get heated, get hot **2** be sultry ‖ *er broeit iets* there is sth. brewing

broeierig /brujərəχ/ (adj, adv) **1** sultry, sweltering, muggy **2** sultry, sensual

de **broeihaard** /brujhart/ (pl: -en) hotbed: *een ~ van bacteriën* a breeding-ground for bacteria; *een ~ van verzet* a hotbed of resistance

de **broeikas** /brujkɑs/ (pl: -sen) hothouse, greenhouse

het **broeikaseffect** /brujkɑsɛfɛkt/ greenhouse effect

het **broeikasgas** /brujkɑsχɑs/ (pl: -sen) greenhouse gas

het **broeinest** /brujnɛst/ (pl: -en) [fig] hotbed

de **broek** /bruk/ (pl: -en) (pair of) trousers; shorts ‖ *het in zijn ~ doen* wet one's pants; *een proces aan zijn ~ krijgen* get taken to court; *iem. achter de ~ zitten* keep s.o. up to the mark, see that s.o. gets on with his work

het **broekje** /brukjə/ (pl: -s) briefs; panties; knickers

het **broekpak** /brukpɑk/ (pl: -ken) trouser suit

de **broekriem** /brukrim/ (pl: -en) belt: [also fig] *de ~ aanhalen* tighten one's belt

de **broekrok** /brukrɔk/ (pl: -ken) culottes, pantskirt

de **broekspijp** /brukspɛip/ (pl: -en) (trouser-)leg

de **broekzak** /brukzɑk/ (pl: -ken) trouser(s) pocket: *iets kennen als zijn ~* know sth. inside out (*or:* like the back of one's hand)

de **broekzakbellen** /brukzɑɡbɛlə(n)/ pocketdial

de **broer** /brur/ (pl: -s) brother

het **broertje** /brurcə/ (pl: -s) little brother ‖ *een ~ dood aan iets hebben* hate sth., detest sth.

het/de **brok** /brɔk/ (pl: -ken) piece, fragment, chunk: *~ken maken* a) smash things up; b) [fig] mess things up; *hij had een ~ in zijn keel* he had a lump in his throat

het **brokaat** /brokat/ brocade

brokkelen /brɔkələ(n)/ (brokkelde, heeft/is gebrokkeld) crumble

het **brokstuk** /brɔkstʏk/ (pl: -ken) (broken) fragment, piece; debris

de **brom** /brɔm/ buzz

de **bromfiets** /brɔmfits/ (pl: -en) moped

de **bromfietser** /brɔmfitsər/ (pl: -s) moped rider (*or:* driver)

brommen /brɔmə(n)/ (bromde, heeft/is gebromd) **1** hum; growl **2** mutter **3** ride a moped

de **brommer** /brɔmər/ (pl: -s) moped

de **brommobiel** /brɔmobil/ (pl: -en) [Dutch] motorized quadricycle, low-speed vehicle; motorized tricycle

de **bromscooter** /brɔmskutər/ (pl: -s) (motor) scooter

de **bromvlieg** /brɔmvliχ/ (pl: -en) bluebottle, blowfly

de **bron** /brɔn/ (pl: -nen) **1** well, spring: *hete ~* hot springs **2** source; spring, cause: *~nen van bestaan* means of existence; *een ~ van ergernis* an annoyance, a nuisance ‖ *hij heeft het uit betrouwbare ~* he has it from a reliable source; *een rijke (onuitputtelijke) ~ van informatie* a mine of information

de **bronchitis** /brɔnχitəs/ bronchitis

het **brons** /brɔns/ (pl: bronzen) bronze

de **bronstijd** /brɔnstɛit/ Bronze Age

de **bronvermelding** /brɔnvərmɛldɪŋ/ (pl: -en) acknowledgement of (one's) sources: *iets zonder ~ overnemen* copy sth. without acknowledgement (*or:* crediting the source)

het **bronwater** /brɔnwatər/ (pl: -en) spring water; [in bottle] mineral water

bronzen /brɔnzə(n)/ (adj) bronze: *een ~ medaille* a bronze (medal)

het **brood** /brot/ (pl: broden) **1** bread: *daar is geen droog ~ mee te verdienen* you won't (*or:* wouldn't) make a penny out of it; [fig] *~ op de plank hebben* be able to make ends meet **2** loaf (of bread): *een snee ~* a slice of bread; *twee broden* two loaves (of bread) **3** living

het **broodbeleg** /brodbəlɛχ/ sandwich filling

het **brooddeeg** /brodeχ/ (bread) dough

het **broodje** /brocə/ (pl: -s) (bread) roll, bun: *~ aap* monkey's sandwich ‖ *als warme ~s over de toonbank gaan* go (*or:* sell) like hot cakes

de **broodjeszaak** /brocəzak/ (pl: -zaken)

sandwich bar

de **broodkruimel** /brotkrœyməl/ (pl: -s) breadcrumb

de **broodmaaltijd** /brotmaltɛit/ (pl: -en) cold meal (or: lunch)

broodmager /brotmayər/ (adj) skinny, bony

broodnodig /brotnodəy/ (adj) much-needed, badly needed, highly necessary

het/de **broodrooster** /brotrostər/ (pl: -s) toaster

de **broodtrommel** /brotroməl/ (pl: -s)
1 breadbin **2** lunch box

de **broodwinner** /brotwɪnər/ (pl: -s) bread-winner

de **broodwinning** /brotwɪnɪŋ/ (pl: -en) livelihood

broos /bros/ (adj, adv) fragile, delicate, frail

bros /brɔs/ (adj) brittle, crisp(y)

brossen /brɔsə(n)/ (broste, heeft gebrost) [Belg] play truant, skip classes

brouwen /brɑuwə(n)/ (brouwde, heeft gebrouwen) brew; mix; concoct

de **brouwer** /brɑuwər/ (pl: -s) brewer

de **brouwerij** /brɑuwərɛi/ (pl: -en) brewery

het **brouwsel** /brɑusəl/ (pl: -s) brew, concoction

de **brownie** /brɑuni/ brownie

browsen /brɑuzə(n)/ (browsede/browsete, heeft gebrowsed/gebrowset) browse

de **browser** /brɑuzər/ browser

de **brug** /brʏx/ (pl: -gen) **1** bridge **2** bridge-(work) **3** [sport] parallel bars **4** [shipp] bridge ‖ *hij moet* **over** *de ~ komen* he has to deliver the goods (or: pay up)

Brugge /brʏɣə/ Bruges

het **bruggenhoofd** /brʏɣə(n)hoft/ (pl: -en) abutment; bridgehead

het **bruggetje** /brʏɣəcə/ (pl: -s) link

de **brugklas** /brʏxklɑs/ (pl: -sen) first class (or: form) (at secondary school)

de **brugklasser** /brʏxklɑsər/ (pl: -s) first-form-er

de **brugleuning** /brʏxlønɪŋ/ (pl: -en) bridge railing; parapet

het **brugpensioen** /brʏxpɛnʃun/ (pl: -en) [Belg] early retirement

de **brugwachter** /brʏxwɑxtər/ (pl: -s) bridge-keeper

de **brui** /brœy/: *er de ~ aan* **geven** chuck it (in)

de **bruid** /brœyt/ (pl: -en) bride

de **bruidegom** /brœydəyom/ (pl: -s) (bride)-groom

het **bruidsboeket** /brœytsbukɛt/ (pl: -ten) bri-dal bouquet

de **bruidsjapon** /brœytsjapon/ (pl: -nen) bridal gown, wedding dress

het **bruidsmeisje** /brœytsmɛiʃə/ bridesmaid

de **bruidsnacht** /brœytsnɑxt/ (pl: -en) wed-ding night

het **bruidspaar** /brœytspar/ (pl: -paren) bride and (bride)groom, bridal couple

de **bruidsschat** /brœytsxɑt/ (pl: -ten) dowry

de **bruidssuite** /brœytswitə/ (pl: -s) bridal suite

de **bruidstaart** /brœytstart/ (pl: -en) wedding cake

bruikbaar /brœygbar/ (adj) usable; useful; serviceable; employable

de **bruikleen** /brœyklen/ loan: *iets aan iem.* *in ~ geven* lend sth. to s.o.

de **bruiloft** /brœyloft/ (pl: -en) wedding

bruin /brœyn/ (adj, adv) brown ‖ *wat* **bak** *je ze weer ~* you're really going to town on it

het **bruinbrood** /brœymbrot/ (pl: -broden) brown bread

bruinen /brœynə(n)/ (bruinde, heeft/is ge-bruind) brown; tan; bronze: *de zon heeft zijn* **vel** *gebruind* the sun has tanned his skin

de **bruinkool** /brœyŋkol/ brown coal, lignite

de **bruinvis** /brœynvɪs/ (pl: -sen) porpoise

bruisen /brœysə(n)/ (bruiste, heeft ge-bruist) foam, effervesce: *~ van geestdrift* (or: *energie*) bubble with enthusiasm (or: energy)

bruisend /brœysənt/ (adj) exuberant

het/de **bruistablet** /brœystablɛt/ (pl: -ten) effer-vescent tablet

het **bruiswater** /brœyswatər/ [Belg] sparkling water, soda water

brullen /brʏlə(n)/ (brulde, heeft gebruld) roar, bawl, howl: *~ van het lachen* roar (or: howl) with laughter

de **brunch** /brʏnʃ/ (pl: -es) brunch

brunchen /brʏnʃə(n)/ (brunchte, heeft ge-bruncht) have brunch

Brunei /brunɛi/ Brunei

de **Bruneier** /brunɛijər/ (pl: -s) Bruneian

Bruneis /brunɛis/ (adj) Bruneian

de **brunette** /brynɛtə/ (pl: -s) brunette

Brussel /brʏsəl/ Brussels

Brussels /brʏsəls/ (adj) Brussels

brutaal /brytal/ (adj, adv) **1** insolent; cheeky; impudent: *zij was* **zo** *~ om ... she had the cheek (or: nerve) to ...* **2** bold, forward

de **brutaliteit** /brytalitɛit/ (pl: -en) cheek, im-pudence

bruto /bryto/ (adv) gross: *het concert heeft ~* *€ 1100 opgebracht* the concert raised 1100 euros gross

het **brutogewicht** /brytoyəwɪxt/ (pl: -en) gross weight

het **brutoloon** /brytolon/ (pl: -lonen) gross in-come

het **brutosalaris** /brytosalarɪs/ gross salary

de **brutowinst** /brytowɪnst/ (pl: -en) gross profit

bruusk /brysk/ (adj, adv) brusque, abrupt, curt: *een ~* **antwoord** an abrupt (or: curt) an-swer; *een ~* **optreden** a brusque manner

bruut /bryt/ (adj, adv) **1** brute; brutal **2** [in-form] sick, dope, cool, awesome: *een ~ feest* a wicked party; *dat is* **gewoon** *~* that's just sick, man

BSE /beɛze/ bovine spongiform encephalop-

athy BSE, mad cow disease

het **bsn** /beːsɛn/ (pl: -'s) [Dutch] *burgerservice-nummer* Citizen Service Number (CSN)

het **bso** /beːsoː/ [Belg] *beroepssecundair onderwijs* secondary vocational education

de **btw** /betewe/ *belasting op de toegevoegde waarde* VAT, value added tax: *ex* ~ excluding (*or:* plus VAT)

de **bubbel** /bʏbəl/ (pl: -s) bubble: *water met ~s* sparkling (*or:* soda) water; [fig] *in een ~ leven* live in a bubble

het **bubbelbad** /bʏbəlbɑt/ (pl: -en) whirlpool, jacuzzi

de **bubbels** /bʏbəls/ (pl) bubbly

de **bucketlist** /bʏkɪtlɪst/ (pl: -s) bucket list

het **budget** /bʏdʒɛt/ (pl: -ten) budget: *dat past niet in mijn* ~ that doesn't suit my budget

de **budgetbewaking** /bʏdʒɛdbəwakɪŋ/ budgetary control

de **budgetmaatschappij** /bʏdʒɛtmatsχɑpɛi/ (pl: -en) budget airline, low-cost carrier

budgettair /bʏdʒɛtɛːr/ (adj) budgetary

budgetteren /bʏdʒɛtɛrə(n)/ (budgetteerde, heeft gebudgetteerd) budget

de **buffel** /bʏfəl/ (pl: -s) buffalo

buffelen /bʏfələ(n)/ (buffelde, heeft gebuffeld) [inform] **1** wolf (down) **2** beaver away

de **buffer** /bʏfər/ (pl: -s) buffer

de **bufferstaat** /bʏfərstat/ (pl: -staten) buffer state

de **buffervoorraad** /bʏfərvorat/ (pl: -voorraden) buffer stock

de **bufferzone** /bʏfɛrzoːnə/ (pl: -s) buffer zone

het **buffet** /bʏfɛt/ (pl: -ten) sideboard; buffet: *koud* ~ cold buffet

de **bug** /bʏk/ (pl: -s) bug

de **bugel** /bʏɣəl/ (pl: -s) flugelhorn

de **bugfix** /bʏkfɪks/ (pl: -es) bug fix

de **buggy** /bʏgi/ (pl: -'s) buggy

de **bühne** /byːnə/ boards, stage

de **bui** /bœy/ (pl: -en) **1** shower; (short) storm: *hier en daar een* ~ scattered showers; *schuilen voor een* ~ take shelter from a storm; *winterse ~en* snow and hail showers; *de ~ zien hangen* [fig] see the storm coming **2** mood: *in een driftige* ~ in a fit of temper

de **buidel** /bœydəl/ (pl: -s) **1** purse: *diep in de ~ moeten tasten* have to reach deep (down) into one's pockets **2** pouch

het **buideldier** /bœydəldir/ (pl: -en) marsupial

de **buienradar** /bœyə(n)radɑr/ (pl: -s) precipitation radar

¹**buigen** /bœyɣə(n)/ (boog, heeft/is gebogen) **1** bow: *voor iem.* ~ bow to s.o. **2** (+ voor) bow (to), bend (before) **3** bend (over)

²**buigen** /bœyɣə(n)/ (boog, heeft gebogen) bend: *het hoofd* ~ [fig] bow (to), submit (to); *de weg buigt naar links* the road curves (*or:* bends) to the left; *zich over de balustrade* ~ lean over the railing

de **buiging** /bœyɣɪŋ/ (pl: -en) **1** bend, curve **2** bow; curtsy: *een* ~ *maken* bow, curtsy

buigzaam /bœyχsam/ (adj) **1** flexible, supple **2** [fig] flexible, adaptable, compliant

buiig /bœyəχ/ (adj) showery, gusty

de **buik** /bœyk/ (pl: -en) belly, stomach; abdomen: *een ~je krijgen* get a paunch; [fig] *er de ~ van vol hebben* be fed up (with it), be sick and tired of it; [fig] *schrijf het maar op je* ~ not on your life, forget it

buikdansen /bœyɡdɑnsə(n)/ (do a) belly dance

de **buikdanseres** /bœyɡdɑnsərɛs/ (pl: -sen) belly dancer

de **buikholte** /bœykhɔltə/ (pl: -n, -s) abdomen

de **buikkramp** /bœykrɑmp/ (pl: -en) stomach (*or:* abdominal) cramp

de **buiklanding** /bœyklɑndɪŋ/ (pl: -en) pancake landing, belly landing

de **buikloop** /bœyklop/ diarrhoea; the runs

de **buikpijn** /bœykpɛin/ (pl: -en) stomach ache, bellyache

de **buikriem** /bœykrim/ (pl: -en) belt: *de ~ aanhalen* tighten one's belt

de **buikspier** /bœykspir/ (pl: -en) stomach muscle, abdominal muscle

buikspreken /bœyksprekə(n)/ ventriloquize, throw one's voice

de **buikspreker** /bœyksprekər/ (pl: -s) ventriloquist

de **buikvliesontsteking** /bœykflisontstekɪŋ/ (pl: -en) peritonitis

de **buil** /bœyl/ (pl: -en) bump

de **buis** /bœys/ (pl: buizen) **1** tube, pipe; valve **2** box, TV **3** [Belg; inform] fail (mark)

de **buit** /bœyt/ **1** booty, spoils, loot **2** catch: *met een flinke* ~ *thuiskomen* come home with a big catch

buitelen /bœytələ(n)/ (buitelde, heeft/is gebuiteld) tumble, somersault

de **buiteling** /bœytəlɪŋ/ (pl: -en) tumble: *een lelijke* ~ *maken* take a nasty spill (*or:* tumble)

¹**buiten** /bœytə(n)/ (adv) outside, out, outdoors: *een dagje* ~ a day in the country; *daar wil ik* ~ *blijven* I want to stay out of that; *naar* ~ *gaan* **a)** go outside (*or:* outdoors); **b)** go into the country (*or:* out of town); *naar* ~ *brengen* take out; lead (*or:* show) out [pers]; *een gedicht van* ~ *leren* (or: *kennen*) learn (*or:* know) a poem by heart || *zich te* ~ *gaan (aan)* overindulge (o.s.) (in); *hou je er* ~*!* stay (*or:* keep) out of it!

²**buiten** /bœytə(n)/ (prep) **1** outside, beyond: ~ *het bereik van* out of reach of; *hij was* ~ *zichzelf van woede* he was beside himself with anger **2** out of: *iets* ~ *beschouwing laten* leave sth. out of consideration **3** without: *het is* ~ *mijn medeweten gebeurd* it happened without my knowledge

buitenaards /bœytəˀ(n)a͟rts/ (adj) extraterrestrial

buitenaf /bœytənɑf/ (adv) outside, external, from (or: on) the outside: *hulp van* ~ outside help; *zonder druk van* ~ without external pressure

de **buitenbaan** /bœytə(n)ban/ (pl: -banen) [sport] outside lane

buitenbaarmoederlijk /bœytə(n)barmudərlək/ (adj) ectopic: ~*e zwangerschap* ectopic pregnancy

het **buitenbad** /bœytə(n)bɑt/ (pl: -en) open-air (or: outdoor) pool

de **buitenband** /bœytə(n)bɑnt/ (pl: -en) tyre

het **buitenbeentje** /bœytə(n)bencə/ (pl: -s) odd man out, outsider

de **buitenbocht** /bœytə(n)bɔχt/ (pl: -en) outside curve (or: bend)

de **buitenboordmotor** /bœytə(n)bɔrtmotər/ (pl: -en) outboard motor

de **buitendeur** /bœytə(n)dør/ (pl: -en) front door, outside door

buitenechtelijk /bœytə(n)ɛχtələk/ (adj) extramarital: ~ *kind* illegitimate child

[1]**buitengewoon** /bœytə(n)γəwon/ (adj) special, extra; exceptional, unusual

[2]**buitengewoon** /bœytə(n)γəwon/ (adv) extremely, exceptionally

het **buitenhuis** /bœytə(n)hœys/ (pl: -huizen) country house

buitenissig /bœytənɪsəχ/ (adj) unusual, strange, eccentric

het **buitenkansje** /bœytə(n)kɑnʃə/ (pl: -s) stroke of luck

de **buitenkant** /bœytə(n)kɑnt/ (pl: -en) outside, exterior: *op de* ~ *afgaan* judge by appearances

het **buitenland** /bœytə(n)lɑnt/ foreign country (or: countries): *van* (or: *uit*) *het* ~ *terugkeren* return (or: come back) from abroad

de **buitenlander** /bœytə(n)lɑndər/ (pl: -s) foreigner, alien

buitenlands /bœytə(n)lɑnts/ (adj) foreign, international: *een* ~*e reis* a trip abroad

de **buitenlucht** /bœytə(n)lvχt/ open (air); country air

buitenom /bœytə(n)ɔm/ (adv) around; round the house, town, …

buitenparlementair /bœytə(n)pɑrləmɛntɛːr/ (adj, adv) extraparliamentary

buitenschools /bœytə(n)sχols/ (adj, adv) extracurricular, extramural: ~*e opvang* out-of-school care; after-school care

buitenshuis /bœytənshœys/ (adv) outside, out(side) of the house, outdoors: ~ *eten* eat out

buitensluiten /bœytə(n)slœytə(n)/ (sloot buiten, heeft buitengesloten) shut out; lock out

het **buitenspel** /bœytə(n)spɛl/ offside || [fig] *hij werd* ~ *gezet* he was sidelined

de **buitenspiegel** /bœytə(n)spiγəl/ (pl: -s) outside (or: wing) mirror

buitensporig /bœytənspɔrəχ/ (adj, adv) extravagant, excessive, exorbitant, inordinate

de **buitensport** /bœytə(n)spɔrt/ (pl: -en) outdoor sports

buitenst /bœytə(n)st/ (adj) out(er)most, exterior, outer

de **buitenstaander** /bœytə(n)standər/ (pl: -s) outsider

het **buitenverblijf** /bœytə(n)vərblɛɪf/ (pl: -verblijven) country house, country place

de **buitenwacht** /bœytə(n)wɑχt/ outside world, public; outsiders

de **buitenwereld** /bœytə(n)werəlt/ public (at large), outside world: *de boze* ~ the big, bad world (outside)

de **buitenwijk** /bœytə(n)wɛik/ (pl: -en) suburb; outskirts

de **buitenwipper** /bœytə(n)wɪpər/ (pl: -s) [Belg] bouncer

de **buitenzijde** /bœytə(n)zɛidə/ (pl: -n) outside, exterior; [esp fig] surface

buitmaken /bœytmakə(n)/ (maakte buit, heeft buitgemaakt) seize; capture [ship]

buizen /bœyzə(n)/ (buisde, heeft/is gebuisd) [Belg; inform] fail

de **buizerd** /bœyzərt/ (pl: -s) buzzard

[1]**bukken** /bʏkə(n)/ (bukte, heeft gebukt) stoop; duck: *hij gaat gebukt onder veel zorgen* he is weighed down by many worries

zich [2]**bukken** /bʏkə(n)/ (bukte zich, heeft zich gebukt) stoop, bend down

de **buks** /bʏks/ (pl: -en) (short) rifle

de **bul** /bʏl/ degree certificate

bulderen /bʏldərə(n)/ (bulderde, heeft gebulderd) roar, bellow

de **buldog** /bʏldɔχ/ (pl: -gen) bulldog

de **Bulgaar** /bʏlγar/ (pl: Bulgaren) Bulgarian

Bulgaars /bʏlγars/ (adj) Bulgarian

Bulgarije /bʏlγarɛiə/ Bulgaria

de **bulkartikelen** /bʏlkɑrtikələ(n)/ (pl) bulk, bulk(ed) goods

bulken /bʏlkə(n)/ (bulkte, heeft gebulkt): *hij bulkt van het geld* he is rolling in money

de **bulldozer** /bʏldozər/ (pl: -s) bulldozer

de **bullebak** /bʏləbɑk/ (pl: -ken) bully, ogre

het **bulletin** /bʏlətɛ̃/ (pl: -s) bulletin, report

de **bult** /bʏlt/ (pl: -en) **1** lump; bump **2** hunch, hump: *met een* ~ hunchbacked, humpbacked

de **bumper** /bʏmpər/ (pl: -s) bumper

de **bumperklever** /bʏmpərklevər/ tailgater

de **bundel** /bʏndəl/ (pl: -s) **1** bundle; sheaf **2** collection, volume **3** [telecom] (calling) plan, package: *buiten je* ~ *bellen* make out-of-plan calls

bundelen /bʏndələ(n)/ (bundelde, heeft gebundeld) bundle, cluster; combine: *krachten* ~ join forces

de **bungalow** /bʏŋgalow/ (pl: -s) bungalow; (summer) cottage; chalet

het **bungalowpark** /bʏŋgalowpɑrk/ (pl: -en)

holiday park

de **bungalowtent** /bʏŋɡalowtɛnt/ (pl: -en) family (frame) tent

bungeejumpen /bʏndʒidʒʏmpə(n)/ bungee jump

bungelen /bʏŋələ(n)/ (bungelde, heeft gebungeld) dangle, hang

de **bunker** /bʏŋkər/ (pl: -s) bunker, bomb shelter, air-raid shelter

bunkeren /bʏŋkərə(n)/ (bunkerde, heeft gebunkerd) **1** refuel **2** stoke up, stuff o.s.

de **bunzing** /bʏnzɪŋ/ (pl: -s, -en) polecat

de **burcht** /bʏrχt/ (pl: -en) castle, fortress, citadel, stronghold

het **bureau** /byro/ (pl: -s) **1** (writing) desk, bureau **2** office, bureau, department, (police) station; agency

het **bureaublad** /byroblɑt/ (pl: -en) desktop

de **bureaucraat** /byrokrat/ (pl: bureaucraten) bureaucrat

de **bureaucratie** /byrokra(t)si/ (pl: -ën) bureaucracy, officialdom

bureaucratisch /byrokratis/ (adj, adv) bureaucratic: *~e rompslomp* red tape

de **bureaula** /byrola/ (pl: -'s, -den) (desk) drawer

de **bureaulamp** /byrolɑmp/ (pl: -en) desk lamp

de **bureaustoel** /byrostul/ office chair, desk chair

het **bureel** /byrel/ (pl: burelen) [Belg] office

het **burengerucht** /byrə(n)ɣərʏχt/ [roughly] disturbance

de **burgemeester** /bʏrɣəmestər/ (pl: -s) mayor; [Scotland] provost: [Dutch] *~ en wethouders* mayor and aldermen; municipal executive; *see* schepen

de **burger** /bʏrɣər/ (pl: -s) **1** citizen **2** civilian: *militairen en ~s* soldiers and civilians ‖ *een agent in ~* a plain-clothes policeman

de **burgerbevolking** /bʏrɣərbəvɔlkɪŋ/ civilian population

de **burgerij** /bʏrɣərɛi/ (pl: -en) citizens; (petty) bourgeoisie, middle class

burgerlijk /bʏrɣərlək/ (adj, adv) **1** middleclass, bourgeois **2** [depr] bourgeois, conventional, middle-class; philistine; smug **3** civil, civic: *~e staat* marital status; *(bureau van de) ~e stand* Registry of Births, Deaths and Marriages; Registry Office **4** civil(ian)

de **burgerluchtvaart** /bʏrɣərlʏχtfart/ civil aviation

het **Burgernet** /bʏrɣərnɛt/ [Dutch] [roughly] Neighbourhood Watch; [Am] [roughly] Citizens Patrol

de **burgeroorlog** /bʏrɣərorlɔχ/ (pl: -en) civil war

de **burgerplicht** /bʏrɣərplɪχt/ civic duty

het **burgerrecht** /bʏrɣərɛχt/ (pl: -en) civil rights

het **burgerschap** /bʏrɣərsχɑp/ **1** citizenship **2** [Dutch] Citizenship

het **burgerservicenummer** /bʏrɣərsy:rvɪsnʏmər/ [Dutch] Citizen Service Number

de **burgervader** /bʏrɣərvadər/ (pl: -s) mayor

de ¹**burgerwacht** /bʏrɣərwɑχt/ (pl: -en) neighbourhood watch volunteer

de ²**burgerwacht** /bʏrɣərwɑχt/ (pl: -en) neighbourhood watch group

de **burgerzaken** /bʏrɣərzakə(n)/ (pl) civil affairs department

Burkina Faso /burkinafɑso/ Burkina Faso

de ¹**Burkinees** /burkines/ Burkinabe

²**Burkinees** /burkines/ (adj) Burkinabe

de **burn-out** /bʏːrnɑut/ burn-out

de **bursitis** /bʏrsitɪs/ bursitis

de ¹**Burundees** /burundes/ (pl: Burundezen) Burundian

²**Burundees** /burundes/ (adj) Burundian

Burundi /burundi/ Burundi

de **bus** /bʏs/ (pl: -sen) **1** bus; coach: *met de ~ gaan* go by bus; *~je* minibus; van **2** tin; [large] drum **3** box: *u krijgt de folders morgen in de ~* you will get the brochures in the post tomorrow ‖ *als winnaar uit de ~ komen* (turn out to) be the winner

de **busbaan** /bʏzban/ (pl: -banen) bus lane

de **buschauffeur** /bʏsʃofør/ bus driver, coach driver

de **busdienst** /bʏzdinst/ (pl: -en) bus service, coach service

de **bushalte** /bʏshɑltə/ (pl: -n, -s) bus stop, coach stop

het **bushokje** /bʏshɔkjə/ (pl: -s) bus shelter

het **busje** /bʏʃə/ (pl: -s) minibus; van

het **buskruit** /bʏskrœyt/ gunpowder

de **buslichting** /bʏslɪχtɪŋ/ (pl: -en) collection

de **buslijn** /bʏslɛin/ (pl: -en) bus route; coach route

het **busstation** /bʏsta(t)ʃɔn/ (pl: -s) bus station; coach station

de **buste** /bʏstə/ (pl: -s, -n) bust, bosom

de **bustehouder** /bʏstəhɑudər/ (pl: -s) brassiere

de **bustocht** /bʏstɔχt/ (pl: -en) coach trip; bus trip

het **butaan** /bytan/ butane

het **butagas** /bytaɣɔs/ butane (gas)

de **butler** /bʏtlər/ (pl: -s) butler

de **button** /bʏtən/ (pl: -s) badge

de **buur** /byr/ (pl: buren) neighbour: *de buren* the (next-door) neighbours

het **buurland** /byrlɑnt/ (pl: -en) neighbouring country

de **buurman** /byrmɑn/ (pl: buurlieden) (nextdoor) neighbour, man next door

de **buurt** /byrt/ (pl: -en) neighbourhood, area, district: *rosse ~* red-light district ‖ *de hele ~ bij elkaar schreeuwen* shout the place down; *in* (or: *uit*) *de ~ wonen* live nearby (or: a distance away); *je kunt maar beter bij hem uit de ~ blijven* you'd better give him a wide berth

de **buurtbewoner** /byrdbəwonər/ (pl: -s) local resident

het **buurtcentrum** /byrtsɛntrʏm/ (pl: -centra) community centre

buurten /byrtə(n)/ (buurtte, heeft gebuurt) visit the neighbours: *jullie moeten eens **komen*** ~ you must come round (*or:* over) some time

het **buurthuis** /byrthœys/ (pl: -huizen) community centre

de **buurtschap** /byrtsχap/ (pl: -pen) hamlet

de **buurtsuper** /byrtsypər/ (pl: -s) corner shop, local grocery store

de **buurtwacht** /byrtwɑχt/ (pl: -wachten) neighbourhood watch

de **buurtzorg** /byrtsɔrχ/ community healthcare service

de **buurvrouw** /byrvrɑu/ (pl: -en) neighbour, woman next door

de **buxus** /byksʏs/ (pl: -sen) box (tree)

de **buzzer** /byzər/ buzzer, pager

de **bv** /beve/ (pl: bv's) [Dutch] *besloten vennootschap* Ltd; [Am] Inc

bv. *bijvoorbeeld* e.g.

de **BV** *bekende Vlaming* celebrity, famous Flemish person

de **bvba** /bevebea/ [Belg] *besloten vennootschap met beperkte aansprakelijkheid* private company with limited liability

de **B-weg** /bɛwɛχ/ (pl: -en) B-road, secondary (*or:* minor) road

de **bypass** /bɑjpɑːs/ (pl: -es) bypass; (traffic) bypass

de **byte** /bɑjt/ (pl: -s) byte

Byzantijns /bizɑntɛins/ (adj) Byzantine

c

de **c** /se/ (pl: c's) c; C
   ca. *circa* approx.; ca.
het **cabaret** /kabarɛ(t)/ (pl: -s) cabaret
de **cabaretier** /kabarɛce/ (pl: -s) cabaret performer, cabaret artist(e)
de **cabine** /kabinə/ (pl: -s) **1** cabin **2** booth
de **cabriolet** /kabrijolɛt/ (pl: -s) convertible, drophead coupé
de **cacao** /kakou̯/ cocoa, (drinking) chocolate
het **cachegeheugen** /kɛʃǝhøɣǝ(n)/ (pl: -s) cache memory
het **cachet** /kaʃɛ/ (pl: -ten) cachet, (touch of) prestige: ~ *geven* aan iets lend style to sth.
de **cactus** /kɑktʏs/ (pl: -sen) cactus
het **CAD** /seadɛ/ (pl: -'s) *Computer Assisted Design* CAD
de **cadans** /kadɑns/ (pl: -en) cadence, rhythm
de ¹**caddie®** /kɛdi/ (pl: -s) caddie, (shopping) trolley; [Am] pushcart
de ²**caddie** /kɛdi/ (pl: -s) **1** (golf-)trolley; [Am] caddie (cart) **2** caddie, caddy
het **cadeau** /kado/ (pl: -s) present, gift: *iem. iets* ~ *geven* give a person sth. as a present; [iron] *dat krijg* je van me ~! you can keep it!; iets **niet** ~ *geven* not give sth. away
de **cadeaubon** /kadobɔn/ (pl: -nen) gift voucher
het **cadeaupapier** /kadopapir/ wrapping paper
de **cadet** /kadɛt/ (pl: -ten, -s) [Belg] junior member of sports club
het **cadmium** /kɑtmijʏm/ cadmium
het **café** /kafe/ (pl: -s) café, pub, bar
de **caféhouder** /kafɛhɑudǝr/ (pl: -s) café proprietor (or: owner)
de **cafeïne** /kafejinǝ/ caffeine
   cafeïnevrij /kafejinǝvrɛi/ (adj) decaffeinated
het **café-restaurant** /kafɛrɛstorɑnt/ (pl: -s) restaurant; café
de **cafetaria** /kafɛtarija/ (pl: -'s) cafeteria, snack bar
het **cahier** /kaje/ (pl: -s) exercise book
de **caissière** /kɑʃɛ:rǝ/ (pl: -s) [Dutch] cashier, check-out assistant
de **caisson** /kɛsɔ̃/ (pl: -s) caisson
de **caissonziekte** /kɛsɔ̃ziktǝ/ caisson disease, decompression sickness
de **cake** /kek/ (pl: -s) (madeira) cake
de **calamiteit** /kalamitɛit/ (pl: -en) calamity, disaster
het **calcium** /kɑlsijʏm/ calcium
de **calculatie** /kɑlkyla(t)si/ (pl: -s) calculation,

computation
de **calculator** /kɑlkylatɔr/ (pl: -s) calculator
   calculeren /kɑlkylerǝ(n)/ (calculeerde, heeft gecalculeerd) calculate, compute: [fig] *de ~de burger* the canny consumer, the citizen-consumer
de **caleidoscoop** /kalɛidoskop/ (pl: -scopen) kaleidoscope
   Californië /kalifɔrnijǝ/ California
het **callcenter** /kɔ:lsɛntǝr/ (pl: -s) call centre
de **calorie** /kalori/ (pl: -ën) calorie
   caloriearm /kaloriɑrm/ (adj) low-calorie, low in calories
   calorierijk /kalorirɛik/ (adj) high-calorie, rich in calories
het **calvinisme** /kɑlvinɪsmǝ/ Calvinism
de **calvinist** /kɑlvinɪst/ (pl: -en) Calvinist
   calvinistisch /kɑlvinɪstis/ (adj, adv) calvinistic(al)
   Cambodja /kɑmbɔca/ Cambodia
de **Cambodjaan** /kɑmbocɑn/ (pl: Cambodjanen) Cambodian
   Cambodjaans /kɑmbocɑns/ (adj) Cambodian
de **camcorder** /kɛmkɔ:rdǝr/ (pl: -s) camcorder
de **camembert** /kamambɛ:r/ Camembert (cheese)
de **camera** /kamǝra/ (pl: -'s) camera: *verborgen* ~ hidden camera; candid camera
de **camerabewaking** /kamǝrabǝwakɪŋ/ closed circuit tv, CCTV: *dit winkelgebied kent* ~ this shop area is protected by CCTV
de **camerabril** /kamǝrabrɪl/ (pl: -len) camera glasses
de **cameraman** /kamǝramɑn/ (pl: -nen) cameraman
de **cameraploeg** /kamǝrapluχ/ (pl: -en) camera crew (or: team)
het **cameratoezicht** /kamǝratuzɪχt/ closed circuit tv, CCTV
de **camouflage** /kamuflaʒǝ/ (pl: -s) camouflage; [fig] cover; front
   camoufleren /kamuflerǝ(n)/ (camoufleerde, heeft gecamoufleerd) camouflage, cover up, disguise
de **campagne** /kɑmpɑɲǝ/ (pl: -s) campaign, drive: ~ *voeren* (voor, tegen) campaign (for, against)
de **camper** /kɛmpǝr/ (pl: -s) camper
de **camping** /kɛmpɪŋ/ (pl: -s) camping site
de **campus** /kɛmpʏs/ (pl: -sen) campus
   Canada /kanada/ Canada
de **Canadees** /kanades/ (pl: Canadezen) Canadian
de **canapé** /kanape/ (pl: -s) sofa, settee, couch
de **Canarische Eilanden** /kanarisǝɛilɑndǝ(n)/ (pl) (the) Canaries, (the) Canary Islands
   cancelen /kɛnsǝlǝ(n)/ (cancelde, heeft gecanceld) cancel, annul
de **cannabis** /kɑnabɪs/ cannabis, hemp, marijuana

de **canon** /kₐnɔn/ (pl: -s) round, canon: *in ~ zin-gen* sing in a round (*or:* in canon) ‖ *de histo-rische ~ van Nederland* [roughly] the historical canon of the Netherlands

CANS /kɑns/ complaints of the arm, neck and/or shoulder

de **cantate** /kɑntₐtə/ (pl: -s, -n) cantata

de **cantharel** /kɑntɑrɛl/ (pl: -len) chanterelle

het **canvas** /kₐnvɑs/ canvas, tarpaulin

de **canyon** /kɛnən/ (pl: -s) canyon, gorge

de **cao** /seaₒ/ (pl: -'s) *collectieve arbeidsover-eenkomst* collective wage agreement

de **cao-onderhandelingen** /seaₒɔndər-hɑndəlɪŋə(n)/ (pl) collective bargaining

capabel /kɑpₐbəl/ (adj) capable, able; com-petent; qualified: *voor die functie leek hij ui-terst ~* he seemed very well qualified for the job; *ik acht hem ~ om die klus uit te voeren* I reckon he can cope with that job

de **capaciteit** /kɑpɑsitɛit/ (pl: -en) **1** capacity, power: *een motor met kleine ~* a low-powered engine **2** ability, capability: *Ans is een vrouw van grote ~en* Ans is a woman of great ability

de **cape** /kep/ (pl: -s) cape

de **capitulatie** /kɑpitylₐ(t)si/ (pl: -s) capitula-tion, surrender

capituleren /kɑpitylₑrə(n)/ (capituleerde, heeft gecapituleerd) capitulate, surrender

de **cappuccino** /kɑputʃino/ (pl: -'s) cappuccino

de **capriool** /kɑprijol/ (pl: capriolen) prank, ca-per

de **capslock** /kₑpslɔk/ (pl: -s) Caps Lock

de **capsule** /kɑpsylə/ (pl: -s) capsule

de **capuchon** /kɑpyʃɔn/ (pl: -s) hood

de **carambole** /kɑrɑmbol/ (pl: -s) cannon

de **caravan** /kₑrəvɛn/ (pl: -s) caravan; [Am] trailer (home)

de **carburator** /kɑrbyrₐtɔr/ (pl: -en) carburet-tor

het **cardiogram** /kɑrdijoɣrₐm/ (pl: -men) cardi-ogram

de **cardiologie** /kɑrdijoloɣi/ cardiology

de **cardioloog** /kɑrdijolₒx/ (pl: -logen) cardiol-ogist

Caribisch /kɑribis/ (adj) Caribbean: *het ~ gebied* the Caribbean

de **cariës** /kₐrijɛs/ caries, tooth decay, dental decay

het/de **carillon** /kɑrɪljɔn/ (pl: -s) [Dutch] carillon, chimes: *het spelen van het ~* the ringing of the bells

het **carnaval** /kₐrnɑvɑl/ (pl: -s) carnival (time)

de **carnavalsvakantie** /kₐrnɑvɑlsfakɑn(t)si/ carnival holiday, Shrovetide holiday

de **carnivoor** /kɑrnivₒr/ (pl: carnivoren) carni-vore

carpoolen /kₒːrpulə(n)/ (carpoolde, heeft/is gecarpoold) [Am] carpool

de **carport** /kₒːrpɔːrt/ (pl: -s) carport

de **carrière** /kɑrijɛːrə/ (pl: -s) career: *~ maken* make a career for oneself

de **carrièrejager** /kɑrijɛːrəjaɣər/ (pl: -s) career-ist; career woman

de **carrosserie** /kɑrɔsəri/ (pl: -ën) body, body-work

het/de **carrousel** /kɑrusɛl/ (pl: -s) merry-go-round; [Am] carousel

de **cartografie** /kɑrtoɣrafi/ cartography, map-making

de **cartoon** /kɑrtuːn/ (pl: -s) cartoon

de **cartoonist** /kɑrtunɪst/ (pl: -en) cartoonist

het **casco** /kₐsko/ (pl: -'s) body, vessel; hull

de **casestudy** /kₑstvdi/ (pl: -'s) case study

de **¹cash** /kɛʃ/ cash

²cash /kɛʃ/ (adv) cash

de **cashewnoot** /kₑʃunot/ (pl: -noten) cashew (nut)

het **casino** /kazino/ (pl: -'s) casino

de **cassatie** /kɑsₐ(t)si/ (pl: -s) annulment: *hof van ~* court of appeal

de **casselerrib** /kɑsələrɪp/ (pl: -s) cured side of pork

de **cassette** /kɑsɛtə/ (pl: -s) **1** box, casket; cof-fer; slip case; money box **2** cassette

het **cassettebandje** /kɑsɛtəbɑncə/ (pl: -s) cas-sette (tape)

de **cassettedeck** /kɑsɛtədɛk/ (pl: -s) cassette deck, tape deck

de **cassetterecorder** /kɑsɛtəriko:rdər/ (pl: -s) cassette (*or:* tape) recorder

de **cassis** /kₐsɪs/ cassis, black currant drink

de **castagnetten** /kɑstɑŋɛtə(n)/ (pl) castanets

castreren /kɑstrₑrə(n)/ (castreerde, heeft gecastreerd) castrate, neuter; doctor

de **catacomben** /katakₒmbə(n)/ (pl) cata-combs

Catalaans /katalₐns/ (adj) Catalan, Catalo-nian

catalogiseren /kataloɣizₑrə(n)/ (catalogi-seerde, heeft gecatalogiseerd) catalogue, record

de **catalogus** /katₐloɣvs/ (pl: catalogi) cata-logue

Catalonië /katalₒnijə/ Catalonia

de **catamaran** /katamₐrɑn/ (pl: -s) catamaran

catastrofaal /katastrofₐl/ (adj, adv) cata-strophic, disastrous

de **catastrofe** /katastrₒːfə/ (pl: -s, -n) catastro-phe, disaster

de **catechese** /katəxₑzə/ catechesis

de **catechisatie** /katəxizₐ(t)si/ (pl: -s) cate-chism, confirmation classes

de **catechismus** /katəxɪsmʏs/ (pl: -sen) cate-chism

de **categorie** /katəɣori/ (pl: -ën) category, clas-sification; bracket: *in drie ~ën indelen* distin-guish into three categories

categorisch /katəɣoris/ (adj, adv) categori-cal: *iets ~ weigeren* refuse sth. categorically

categoriseren /katəɣorizₑrə(n)/ (categori-seerde, heeft gecategoriseerd) categorize, class

cateren /kₑtərə(n)/ (caterde, heeft gecaterd) cater (for)

de **catering** /kɛtərɪŋ/ catering: *de ~ verzorgen* do the catering

de **catharsis** /katɑrsɪs/ (pl: -sen) catharsis

de **catwalk** /kɛtwɔ:k/ (pl: -s) catwalk

causaal /kauzal/ (adj) causal, causative: *~ verband* causal connection

de **cavalerie** /kavɑləri/ (pl: -s) cavalry, tanks

de **cavia** /kavija/ (pl: -'s) guinea pig, cavia

de **cayennepeper** /kajɛnəpepər/ cayenne (pepper), red pepper

cc /sese/ **1** *kubieke centimeter* cc **2** *kopie conform* [roughly] certified copy

cc'en /sesejə(n)/ (cc'de, heeft ge-cc'd) cc: *iem. ~* copy s.o. in, cc s.o.

de **cd** /sede/ (pl: cd's) compact disc CD

de **cd-box** /sedɛbɔks/ (pl: -en) CD box

de **cd-r** /sedeːr/ (pl: -'s) compact disc - recordable CD-R

het **cd-rek** /sedɛrɛk/ (pl: -ken) CD rack

de **cd-rom** /sedərɔm/ CD-ROM

de **cd-speler** /sedɛspelər/ (pl: -s) CD player

de **ceder** /sedər/ (pl: -s) cedar

de **cedille** /sedijə/ (pl: -s) cedilla

de **ceintuur** /sɛntyːr/ (pl: ceinturen) belt, waistband

de **cel** /sɛl/ (pl: -len) cell, (call) box; booth: *hij heeft een jaar ~ gekregen* he has been given a year; *in een ~ opsluiten* lock up in a cell || *een terroristische ~* a terrorist cell

de **celdeling** /sɛldelɪŋ/ (pl: -en) fission, cell division

het **celibaat** /selibat/ celibacy

de **celkern** /sɛlkɛrn/ (pl: -en) (cell) nucleus

de **cellist** /sɛlɪst/ (pl: -en) cellist

het **cello** /sɛlo/ (pl: -'s) (violon)cello

het **cellofaan** /sɛlofan/ cellophane: *in ~ verpakt* wrapped in cellophane

cellulair /sɛlylɛːr/ (adj) cellular

de **cellulitis** /sɛlylitɪs/ cellulite; cellulitis

het ¹**celluloid** /sɛlylɔjt/ celluloid

²**celluloid** /sɛlylɔjt/ (adj) celluloid

de **cellulose** /sɛlylozə/ cellulose

Celsius /sɛlsijʏs/ Celsius, centigrade

de **celstraf** /sɛlstrɑf/ (pl: -fen) solitary confinement: *iem. ~ geven* place s.o. in solitary confinement

de **celtherapie** /sɛlterapi/ cell therapy

de **celwand** /sɛlwɑnt/ cell wall

het/de **cement** /səmɛnt/ cement

censureren /sɛnzyrerə(n)/ (censureerde, heeft gecensureerd) censor; [fig] black out

de **censuur** /sɛnzyːr/ censorship

de **cent** /sɛnt/ (pl: -en) **1** cent: *iem. tot op de laatste ~ betalen* pay s.o. to the full; *zonder een ~ zitten* be penniless **2** [inform] penny, farthing: *ik vertrouw hem voor geen ~* I don't trust him an inch **3** money, cash: *het kost een paar ~en, maar dan heb je ook wat* it's not cheap, but it's so worth it (*or:* but it's worth every penny)

de **centiliter** /sɛntilitər/ (pl: -s) centilitre

de **centime** /sɛntim/ (pl: -s) centime

de **centimeter** /sɛntimetər/ (pl: -s) **1** centimetre: *een kubieke ~* a cubic centimetre; *een vierkante ~* a square centimetre **2** [Dutch] tape-measure

centraal /sɛntral/ (adj, adv) central: [fig] *een centrale figuur* a central (*or:* key) figure; *een ~ gelegen punt* a centrally situated point; *~ staan* be (the) central (point), be at the centre (stage)

de **Centraal-Afrikaan** /sɛntralafrikan/ (pl: Centraal-Afrikanen) Central African

Centraal-Afrikaans /sɛntralafrikans/ (adj) Central African

de **Centraal-Afrikaanse Republiek** /sɛntralafrikansərepyblik/ Central African Republic

de **centrale** /sɛntralə/ (pl: -s) **1** power station, powerhouse **2** (telephone) exchange; switchboard

de **centralisatie** /sɛntraliza(t)si/ (pl: -s) centralization

centraliseren /sɛntralizerə(n)/ (centraliseerde, heeft gecentraliseerd) centralize

centreren /sɛntrerə(n)/ (centreerde, heeft gecentreerd) centre

de **centrifuge** /sɛntrifyːʒə/ (pl: -s) centrifuge; spin-dryer

centrifugeren /sɛntrifyɣerə(n)/ (centrifugeerde, heeft gecentrifugeerd) centrifuge; spin-dry

centristisch /sɛntrɪstis/ (adj) centrist

het **centrum** /sɛntrʏm/ (pl: centra) centre: *in het ~ van de belangstelling staan* be the centre of attention; [pol] *links* (or: *rechts*) *van het ~* left (*or:* right) of centre; *in het ~ van de macht* at the seat of power

de **centrumspits** /sɛntrʏmspɪts/ (pl: -en) centre forward

de **ceremonie** /serəmoni/ (pl: -s, ceremoniën) ceremony

ceremonieel /serəmon(i)jel/ (adj, adv) ceremonial, formal: *een ceremoniële ontvangst* a formal reception

de **ceremoniemeester** /serəmonimestər/ (pl: -s) Master of Ceremonies; best man

het **certificaat** /sɛrtifikat/ (pl: certificaten) certificate

Ceylon /sɛilɔn/ Ceylon; Sri Lanka

de **cfk** /seɛfka/ (pl: -'s) chloorfluorkoolwaterstof CFC

de **chador** /tʃador/ (pl: -s) chador, chuddar

het ¹**chagrijn** /ʃaɣrɛin/ chagrin, annoyance

het/de ²**chagrijn** /ʃaɣrɛin/ (pl: -en) grouch, grumbler, sourpuss

chagrijnig /ʃaɣrɛinəx/ (adj, adv) miserable, grouchy: *doe niet zo ~* stop being such a misery; *~ zijn* sulk

het/de **chalet** /ʃalɛ/ (pl: -s) chalet, Swiss cottage

de **champagne** /ʃampɑɲə/ (pl: -s) champagne

de **champagnekurk** /ʃampɑɲəkyrk/ (pl: -en) champagne cork: *de ~en laten* **knallen** pop the corks

de **champignon** /ʃampijɔn/ (pl: -s) mushroom

het/de **chanson** /ʃɑ̃sɔ̃/ (pl: -s) song, chanson

de **chansonnier** /ʃɑ̃sɔ̃nje/ (pl: -s) (cabaret) singer

de **chantage** /ʃɑntaʒə/ (pl: -s) blackmail

chanteren /ʃɑnterə/ (chanteerde, heeft gechanteerd) blackmail

de **chaoot** /xaot/ (pl: chaoten) **1** scatterbrain **2** anarchist

de **chaos** /xaos/ chaos, disorder, havoc: *er* **heerst** *~ in het land* the country is in chaos

chaotisch /xaotis/ (adj, adv) chaotic

de **chaperon** /ʃaperɔn/ (pl: -s) chaperon(e)

de **charcuterie** /ʃarkytəri/ [Belg] cold cooked meats

de **charge** /ʃɑrʒə/ (pl: -s) charge [also sport]: *een ~* **uitvoeren** *(met de wapenstok)* make a (baton) charge

chargeren /ʃɑrʒerə/ (chargeerde, heeft gechargeerd) overdo, exaggerate (it)

het **charisma** /xarɪsma/ (pl: -'s) charisma

charitatief /xaritatif/ (adj) charitable: *charitatieve* **instelling** charity, charitable institution

de **charlatan** /ʃarlatɑn/ (pl: -s) charlatan, quack

charmant /ʃɑrmɑnt/ (adj) charming, engaging; winning; delightful, attractive: *een ~e* **jongeman** a charming young man

de **charme** /ʃɑrmə/ (pl: -s) charm: *zijn ~s in de* **strijd** *gooien* use one's charm, bring one's charm to bear

charmeren /ʃɑrmerə/ (charmeerde, heeft gecharmeerd) charm: *hij* **weet** *iedereen* **te** *~* he's a real charmer

de **charmeur** /ʃɑrmør/ (pl: -s) charmer; Prince Charming, ladies' man

het **charter** /tʃɑːrtər/ (pl: -s) **1** charter flight, charter(ed) plane **2** charter

charteren /ʃɑrterə/ (charterde, heeft gecharterd) charter, enlist, commission

het **chartervliegtuig** /tʃɑːrtərvlixtœyx/ (pl: -en) charter(ed) aircraft

de **chartervlucht** /tʃɑːrtərvlyxt/ (pl: -en) charter flight

het **chassis** /ʃasi/ chassis

de **chat** /tʃɛt/ (pl: -s) chat

de **chatbox** /tʃɛdbɔks/ chatbox

de **chatgroep** /tʃɛtyrup/ (pl: -en) chat group

de **chatroom** /tʃɛtruːm/ chat room

chatten /tʃɛtə(n)/ (chatte, heeft gechat) [comp] chat

de **chatter** /tʃɛtər/ (pl: -s) chatter

chaufferen /ʃoferə(n)/ (chauffeerde, heeft gechauffeerd) drive

de **chauffeur** /ʃofør/ (pl: -s) driver, chauffeur

het **chauvinisme** /ʃovinɪsmə/ chauvinism

de **chauvinist** /ʃovinɪst/ (pl: -en) chauvinist

chauvinistisch /ʃovinɪstis/ (adj, adv) chauvinist(ic)

check /tʃɛk/ (int) check

checken /tʃɛkə(n)/ (checkte, heeft gecheckt) check (up, out), verify

de **check-up** /tʃɛkʏp/ (pl: -s) check-up

de **cheeta** /tʃita/ (pl: -'s) cheetah

de **chef** /ʃɛf/ (pl: -s) leader; boss; head; chief; superior (officer); manager; stationmaster: *~ van een* **afdeling** head (*or:* manager) of a department; *~ d'équipe* team manager; *~ de mission* head of the delegation

de **chef de clinique** /ʃɛvdəklinik/ (pl: chefs de clinique) [roughly] senior consultant, [roughly] head of department

de **chef d'équipe** /ʃɛvdekip/ (pl: chefs d'équipe) team manager

de **chef-kok** /ʃɛfkɔk/ (pl: -s) chef

de **chef-staf** /ʃɛfstɑf/ (pl: -s, chefs van staven) Chief of Staff

de **chemicaliën** /xemikalijə(n)/ (pl) chemicals, chemical products

de **chemicus** /xemikʏs/ (pl: chemici) chemist

de **chemie** /xemi/ chemistry

chemisch /xemis/ (adj, adv) chemical: *kleren ~* **reinigen** dry-clean clothes; *~* **toilet** chemical lavatory; *~e* **wapens** chemical weapons

de **chemobak** /xemobɑk/ (pl: -ken) chemical waste bin

de **chemokuur** /xemokyr/ (pl: -kuren) course of chemotherapy

de **chemotherapie** /xemoterapi/ chemotherapy

de **cheque** /ʃɛk/ (pl: -s) cheque: *een* **blanco** *~ a* blank cheque; [fig also] carte blanche; *een* **ongedekte** *~ a* dud cheque; *een ~* **innen** cash a cheque

het **chequeboek** /tʃɛgbuk/ (pl: -en) chequebook

het **chiazaad** /tʃijazat/ chia seeds

de **¹chic** /ʃik/ chic, stylishness, elegance

²chic /ʃik/ (adj, adv) **1** chic, stylish, smart: *er ~* **uitzien** look (very) smart **2** elegant, distinguished; fashionable

chicaneren /ʃikanerə(n)/ (chicaneerde, heeft gechicaneerd) quibble (over)

de **Chileen** /ʃilen/ (pl: Chilenen) Chilean

Chileens /ʃilens/ (adj) Chilean

Chili /ʃili/ Chile

de **chili con carne** /ʃilikɔŋkɑrnə/ chilli con carne

de **chilipeper** /ʃilipepər/ **1** chilli pepper **2** chilli (powder)

chill /tʃɪl/ (adj) cool

chillen /tʃɪlə(n)/ (childe, heeft gechild) chill

de **chimpansee** /ʃɪmpɑnse/ (pl: -s) chimpanzee; chimp

China /ʃina/ China

de **chinees** /ʃines/ (pl: chinezen) Chinese restaurant; Chinese takeaway

de **¹Chinees** /ʃines/ (pl: Chinezen) **1** Chinese, Chinaman **2** Chinese restaurant; Chinese takeaway

het ²**Chinees** /ʃineːs/ [language] Chinese

³**Chinees** /ʃineːs/ (adj) Chinese: *Chinese wijk* (or: *buurt*) Chinatown

de **Chinese** /ʃineːsə/ Chinese (woman)

de **chip** /tʃɪp/ (pl: -s) **1** chip, integrated circuit **2** chip, microprocessor

de **chipkaart** /tʃɪpkɑrt/ (pl: -en) smart card, intelligent card

de **chippas** /tʃɪpɑs/ [Dutch] chip card

chippen /tʃɪpə(n)/ (chipte, is gechipt) [Dutch] pay by chip card

de **chips** /ʃɪps/ (pl) (potato) crisps; [Am] (potato) chips

de **Chiro** /xiro/ [Belg] Christian youth movement

de **chirurg** /ʃirʏrx/ (pl: -en) surgeon

de **chirurgie** /ʃirʏrɣi/ surgery

chirurgisch /ʃirʏrɣis/ (adj, adv) surgical: *een ~e ingreep* a surgical operation, surgery

de **chlamydia** /xlamiːdija/ chlamydia

het/de **chloor** /xloːr/ **1** chlorine **2** bleach

de **chloroform** /xlorofɔrm/ chloroform

het **chocolaatje** /ʃokolaːcə/ (pl: -s) chocolate

de **chocolade** /ʃokoladə/ **1** chocolate; choc: *pure ~* plain chocolate **2** (drinking) chocolate, cocoa

de **chocoladeletter** /ʃokoladəlɛtər/ (pl: -s) chocolate letter ‖ *een kop in ~s* an enormous headline, a banner headline

de **chocolademelk** /ʃokoladəmɛlk/ (drinking) chocolate, cocoa

de **chocoladepasta** /ʃokoladəpɑsta/ (pl: -'s) chocolate spread

de **cholera** /xoləra/ cholera

de **cholesterol** /xolɛstərɔl/ cholesterol: *een hoog ~ hebben* have high cholesterol

choqueren /ʃokeːrə(n)/ (choqueerde, heeft gechoqueerd) shock, give offence: *gechoqueerd zijn (door)* be shocked (at, by)

de **choreograaf** /xorejoɣraːf/ (pl: -grafen) choreographer

de **choreografie** /xorejoɣrafi/ choreography

¹**christelijk** /krɪstələk/ (adj) Christian: *een ~e school* a protestant school

²**christelijk** /krɪstələk/ (adv) decently

de **christen** /krɪstə(n)/ (pl: -en) Christian

de **christendemocraat** /krɪstə(n)demokraːt/ (pl: -democraten) Christian Democrat

het **christendom** /krɪstə(n)dɔm/ Christianity

Christus /krɪstʏs/ Christ ‖ *na ~* AD, after Christ; *voor ~* BC, before Christ

het **chromosoom** /xromozoːm/ (pl: chromosomen) chromosome

chronisch /xroːnis/ (adj, adv) chronic, lingering; recurrent: *een ~ zieke* a chronically sick patient

de **chronologie** /xronoloxi/ chronology

chronologisch /xronoloɣis/ (adj, adv) chronological

de **chronometer** /xroːnometər/ (pl: -s) stop-

watch, chronograph

het **chroom** /xrom/ chrome

de **chrysant** /xrizɑnt/ (pl: -en) chrysanthemum

de **ciabatta** /tʃabɑta/ (pl: -'s) ciabatta (bread)

de **cider** /siːdər/ cider

het **cijfer** /sɛifər/ (pl: -s) **1** figure, numeral, digit, cipher: *Romeinse ~s* Roman numerals; *twee ~s achter de komma* two decimal places; *getallen die in de vijf ~s lopen* five-figure numbers **2** mark, grade: *het hoogste ~* the highest mark

de **cijfercode** /sɛifərkodə/ (pl: -s) numeric code

cijferen /sɛifərə(n)/ (cijferde, heeft gecijferd) do (or: make) calculations

de **cijferlijst** /sɛifərlɛist/ (pl: -en) list of marks, (school) report

de **cilinder** /silɪndər/ (pl: -s) cylinder

de **cilinderinhoud** /silɪndərɪnhɑut/ cylinder capacity

de **cilinderkop** /silɪndərkɔp/ (pl: -pen) cylinder head

cilindrisch /silɪndris/ (adj) cylindrical

de **cineast** /sinejɑst/ (pl: -en) film maker (or: director)

de **cipier** /sipiːr/ (pl: -s) warder, jailer

de **cipres** /siprɛs/ (pl: -sen) cypress

circa /sɪrka/ (adv) approximately, about; circa

het **circuit** /sɪrkwiː/ (pl: -s) **1** [sport] circuit, (race)track **2** scene: *het zwarte ~* the black economy

circulair /sɪrkylɛːr/ (adj, adv) circular

de **circulaire** /sɪrkylɛːrə/ (pl: -s) circular (letter)

de **circulatie** /sɪrkyla(t)si/ (pl: -s) circulation: *geld in ~ brengen* put money into circulation

circuleren /sɪrkyleːrə(n)/ (circuleerde, heeft gecirculeerd) circulate, distribute: *geruchten laten ~* put about (or: circulate) rumours

het/de **circumflex** /sɪrkumflɛks/ (pl: -en) circumflex (accent)

het **circus** /sɪrkʏs/ (pl: -sen) circus

de **circustent** /sɪrkʏstɛnt/ (pl: -en) circus tent, big top, canvas

de **cirkel** /sɪrkəl/ (pl: -s) circle: *halve ~* semicircle; *een vicieuze ~* a vicious circle

cirkelen /sɪrkələ(n)/ (cirkelde, heeft/is gecirkeld) circle, orbit

de **cirkelomtrek** /sɪrkələmtrɛk/ (pl: -ken) perimeter

de **cirkelzaag** /sɪrkəlzax/ (pl: -zagen) circular saw

de **cisgender** /sɪdʒɛndər/ (pl: -s) cisgender

het **citaat** /sitaːt/ (pl: citaten) quotation, quote; citation: *einde ~* unquote, close quotes

de **citer** /siːtər/ (pl: -s) zither

citeren /siteːrə(n)/ (citeerde, heeft geciteerd) quote, cite

de **Cito-toets** /siːtotuts/ (pl: -en) [Dutch] secondary education aptitude test; [roughly] 11 plus test

de **citroen** /sitrun/ (pl: -en) lemon

het **citroengras** /sitrunɣrɑs/ lemongrass
het **citroensap** /sitrunsɑp/ (fresh) lemon juice
de **citrusvrucht** /sitrʏsfrʏxt/ (pl: -en) citrus fruit
de **city** /siti/ (pl: -'s) city centre
de **citytrip** /sititrɪp/ (pl: -s) city break
civiel /sivil/ (adj, adv) civil; civilian: ~ *ingenieur* civil engineer; *een politieman* in ~ plainclothes officer
civielrechtelijk /sivilrɛxtələk/ (adj, adv) civil: *iem.* ~ *vervolgen* bring a civil suit (*or*: action) against s.o.
de **civilisatie** /siviliza(t)si/ (pl: -s) civilization
civiliseren /sivilizɛrə(n)/ (civiliseerde, heeft geciviliseerd) civilize
de **ckv** /sekavé/ [Dutch] *culturele en kunstzinnige vorming* [roughly] culture and art classes
de **claim** /klem/ (pl: -s) claim: *een* ~ *indienen (bij)* lodge a claim (with)
claimen /klɛmə(n)/ (claimde, heeft geclaimd) (lay) claim (to), file (*or*: lodge) a claim: *een bedrag* ~ *bij de verzekering* claim on one's insurance
de **clamshell** /klɛmʃɛl/ (pl: -s) clamshell
de **clan** /klɛn/ (pl: -s) clan, clique, coterie
clandestien /klɑndɛstin/ (adj, adv) clandestine, illicit: *de* ~e *pers* underground press; ~ *gestookte whisky* bootleg whiskey, moonshine
de **clark** /klɑːrk/ (pl: -s) [Belg] fork-lift truck
de **classeur** /klɑsør/ (pl: -s) [Belg] file
het **classicisme** /klɑsisɪsmə/ classicism, classicalism
de **classicus** /klɑsikʏs/ (pl: classici) classicist
de **classificatie** /klɑsifika(t)si/ (pl: -s) classification, ranking, rating
classificeren /klɑsifisɛrə(n)/ (classificeerde, heeft geclassificeerd) classify, class, rank
de **claustrofobie** /klɑustrofobi/ claustrophobia
de **clausule** /klɑuzylə/ (pl: -s) clause, proviso, stipulation: *een* ~ *opnemen in* build a clause into
de **claxon** /klɑksɔn/ (pl: -s) (motor) horn: *op de* ~ *drukken* sound one's horn
claxonneren /klɑksɔnɛrə(n)/ (claxonneerde, heeft geclaxonneerd) sound one's horn, hoot
clean /kliːn/ (adj, adv) **1** clean, clinical **2** clean, off (drugs)
clement /klemɛnt/ (adj, adv) lenient
de **clementie** /klemɛn(t)si/ leniency: ~ *betrachten* be lenient, show mercy
de **clerus** /klerʏs/ clergy
het **cliché** /kliʃé/ (pl: -s) **1** cliché **2** plate, block
clichématig /kliʃematəx/ (adj, adv) cliché'd, commonplace, trite
de **cliënt** /klijɛnt/ (pl: -en) **1** client **2** customer, patron
de **clientèle** /klijɛntɛːlə/ clientele, custom(ers)
de **cliffhanger** /klɪfhɛŋər/ (pl: -s) cliffhanger

de **clignoteur** /kliɲotør/ (pl: -s) (direction) indicator, blinker
de **climax** /klimɑks/ (pl: -en) climax: *naar een* ~ *toewerken* build (up) to a climax
de **clinch** /klɪnʃ/: *in de* ~ *liggen met iem.* be at loggerheads with s.o.
de **clinicus** /klinikʏs/ (pl: clinici) clinician
de **clip** /klɪp/ (pl: -s) **1** paper clip; [large] bulldog clip **2** clip, pin **3** (video)clip
de **clitoris** /klitɔrɪs/ (pl: clitores) clitoris
close /klos/ (adj) close
het **closet** /klozɛt/ (pl: -s) lavatory, toilet
het **closetpapier** /klozɛtpɑpir/ toilet paper
de **close-up** /klosʏp/ (pl: -s) close-up
de **clou** /klu/ point, essence; punch line: *de* ~ *van iets niet snappen* miss the point (of sth.)
de **cloud** /klɑut/ [comp] cloud: *bestanden opslaan in de* ~ save files in the cloud
de **clown** /klɑun/ (pl: -s) clown, buffoon: *de* ~ *uithangen* clown around
clownesk /klɑunɛsk/ (adj, adv) clownish: *een* ~ *gebaar* a comic(al) gesture
de **club** /klʏp/ (pl: -s) **1** club [also golf]; society, association **2** crowd, group, gang
het **clubhuis** /klʏphœys/ (pl: -huizen) **1** club(house); pavilion **2** community centre; youth centre
de **clubkas** /klʏpkɑs/ (pl: -sen) club funds
de **cluster** /klʏstər/ (pl: -s) cluster
de **clusterbom** /klʏstərbɔm/ (pl: -men) cluster bomb
cm centimeter cm
de **co** /ko/ (pl: co's) *compagnon* partner
CO₂ /seotwé/ CO2, CO_2 *(carbon dioxide)*
CO₂-neutraal /seotwenøtrɑl/ (adj) carbonneutral
de **CO₂-voetafdruk** /seotwevutɑvdrʏk/ carbon footprint
de **coach** /kotʃ/ (pl: -es) coach, trainer; supervisor; tutor
coachen /kotʃə(n)/ (coachte, heeft gecoacht) coach, train; tutor
de **coalitie** /kowali(t)si/ (pl: -s) coalition
de **coalitiepartner** /kowali(t)sipɑrtnər/ (pl: -s) coalition partner
de **coassistent** /koɑsistɛnt/ (pl: -en) (assistant) houseman; [Am] intern(e)
de **cobra** /kobra/ (pl: -'s) cobra
de **cocaïne** /kokaɪnə/ cocaine: ~ *snuiven* snort (*or*: sniff) cocaine
de **cockpit** /kɔkpɪt/ (pl: -s) cockpit; flight deck
de **cocktail** /kɔktel/ (pl: -s) cocktail
de **cocktailbar** /kɔktelbɑːr/ cocktail lounge
de **cocktailparty** /kɔktelpɑːrti/ (pl: -'s) cocktail party
de **cocktailprikker** /kɔktelprɪkər/ (pl: -s) cocktail stick; [Am] cocktail pick
de **cocon** /kokɔn/ (pl: -s) cocoon; pod
de **code** /kodə/ (pl: -s) code, cipher: *een* ~ *ontcijferen* crack a code; [Dutch] ~ *rood* severe weather warning

coderen /kod_e_rə(n)/ (codeerde, heeft geco-
deerd) (en)code, encipher
het **codicil** /kodi_sil_/ (pl: -len) codicil
de **coëfficiënt** /koefi_ʃεnt_/ (pl: -en) coefficient
de **co-existentie** /koεksɪstɛn(t)si/ coexistence:
vreedzame ~ peaceful coexistence
de **coffeepad** /k_ɔ_fipεt/ (pl: -s) coffee pad
de **coffeeshop** /k_ɔ_fiʃɔp/ (pl: -s) coffee shop
de **cognac** /k_ɔ_ɲ_ɑ_k/ (pl: -s) cognac
cognitief /k_ɔ_ynitif/ (adj, adv) cognitive
coherent /koher_εnt_/ (adj, adv) coherent;
consistent
de **cohesie** /koh_e_zi/ cohesion
de **coïtus** /ko_i_tʏs/ coitus, coition, sexual intercourse
de **coke** /kok/ coke; snow
de **cokes** /koks/ coke
de **col** /kɔl/ (pl: -s) **1** roll-neck, polo neck **2** col,
(mountain) pass
de **cola** /k_o_la/ (pl: -'s) coke
de **cola-tic** /k_o_latɪk/ rum (*or:* gin) and coke
het/de **colbert** /kɔlbɛ:r/ (pl: -s) jacket
de **collaborateur** /kɔlaborat_ø_r/ (pl: -s) collaborator, quisling
de **collaboratie** /kɔlabor_a_(t)si/ collaboration
collaboreren /kɔlabor_e_rə(n)/ (collaboreer-
de, heeft gecollaboreerd) collaborate; work
together
de **collage** /kɔla_ʒə_/ (pl: -s) collage, montage,
paste-up
de **collectant** /kɔlεkt_ɑ_nt/ (pl: -en) collector;
sidesman
de **collect call** /kɔlεktk_ɔ:_l/ reverse charge call;
[Am] collect call
de **collecte** /kɔl_ε_ktə/ (pl: -s) collection; whip-
round
collecteren /kɔlεkt_e_rə(n)/ (collecteerde,
heeft gecollecteerd) collect, make a collection; [in church] take the collection
de **collectie** /kɔl_ε_ksi/ (pl: -s) **1** collection, show:
een fraaie ~ *schilderijen* a fine collection of
paintings **2** collection, accumulation
het **¹collectief** /kɔlεkt_i_f/ (pl: collectieven) collective
²collectief /kɔlεkt_i_f/ (adj, adv) collective,
corporate, joint, communal: *collectieve **arbeidsovereenkomst*** collective wage agreement; *collectieve **uitgaven*** public expenditure
het **collector's item** /kɔlɛktərsɑjtəm/ (pl: -s)
collector's item, collectible
de **collega** /kɔl_e_ɣa/ (pl: -'s, collegae) colleague,
associate; workmate
het **college** /kɔle_ʒə_/ (pl: -s) **1** college; (university) class; (formal) lecture: *de ~s zijn weer **begonnen*** term has started again; ~ **geven**
(over) lecture (on), give lectures (on); ~ **lopen**
attend lectures **2** board: [Dutch] ~ *van **bestuur* a)** Board of Governors; [Am] Board of
Regents; **b)** Board of Directors; [Dutch] *het ~
van **burgemeester** en **wethouders*** the (City,
Town) Council

het **collegegeld** /kɔle_ʒə_yɛlt/ tuition fee
de **collegezaal** /kɔle_ʒə_zal/ (pl: -zalen) lecture-
room; lecture-hall; lecture-theatre
collegiaal /kɔleɣ(i)j_a_l/ (adj, adv) fraternal,
brotherly, comradely: *zich* ~ ***opstellen*** be loyal to one's colleagues
de **collie** /k_ɔ_li/ (pl: -s) collie
het/de **collier** /kɔl_je_/ (pl: -s) necklace
het/de **colofon** /kolof_ɔ_n/ (pl: -s) colophon
Colombia /kol_ɔ_mbija/ Colombia
de **Colombiaan** /kolombij_a_n/ (pl: Colombia-
nen) Colombian
Colombiaans /kolombij_a_ns/ (adj) Colombian
de **colonne** /kol_ɔ_nə/ (pl: -s) column
colporteren /kɔlport_e_rə(n)/ (colporteerde,
heeft gecolporteerd) sell door-to-door,
hawk
de **coltrui** /k_ɔ_ltrœy/ (pl: -en) roll-neck (pullover, sweater); [Am] turtleneck (pullover,
sweater)
de **column** /k_ɔ_lʏm/ (pl: -s) column
de **columnist** /kɔlʏmnɪst/ (pl: -en) columnist
het **coma** /k_o_ma/ (pl: -'s) coma: *in* ~ *raken* lapse
into a coma
de **comapatiënt** /k_o_mapaʃɛnt/ (pl: -en) coma-
tose patient, patient in a coma
comazuipen /k_o_mazœypə(n)/ binge drink,
drink oneself into a coma
de **combi** /k_ɔ_mbi/ (pl: -'s) estate car, station
wagon
de **combiketel** /k_ɔ_mbiketəl/ (pl: -s) combination boiler
de **combinatie** /kɔmbin_a_(t)si/ (pl: -s) combination
de **combinatietang** /kɔmbin_a_(t)sitɑŋ/ (pl:
-en) combination pliers, electrician's pliers
de **combine** /kɔmb_ɑ_jn/ (pl: -s) combine (harvester)
¹combineren /kɔmbin_e_rə(n)/ (combineerde,
heeft gecombineerd) go (together), match:
*deze **kleuren*** ~ *niet* these colours don't go
(together) (*or:* don't match), these colours
clash
²combineren /kɔmbin_e_rə(n)/ (combineerde,
heeft gecombineerd) **1** combine (with): *twee
banen* ~ combine two jobs **2** associate (with),
link (with)
de **comeback** /kɔmb_ε_k/ (pl: -s) comeback: *een*
~ ***maken*** make (*or:* stage) a comeback
het **comfort** /kɔmf_ɔ:_r/ comfort; convenience: *dit
huis is voorzien van het **modernste*** ~ this house
is fully equipped with the latest conveniences
comfortabel /kɔmfort_a_bəl/ (adj, adv) comfortable
de **coming-out** /kɔmɪŋ_ɑ_ut/ coming out
het **comité** /komit_e_/ (pl: -s) committee: *uitvoerend* ~ executive committee
de **commandant** /komɑndɑnt/ (pl: -en)
1 commander, commandant **2** chief (fire)

officer, (fire) chief
commanderen /kɔmɑndɣrə(n)/ (commandeerde, heeft gecommandeerd) **1** command, be in command (of) **2** give orders; [depr] boss about, order about
het **commando** /kɔmɑndo/ (pl: -'s) **1** command: *het ~ voeren (over)* be in command (of) **2** (word of) command, order; [comp] command: *iets op ~ doen* do sth. to order; *huilen op ~* cry at will **3** [mil] commando
de **commandopost** /kɔmɑndopɔst/ (pl: -en) command post
het **commentaar** /kɔmɛntar/ (pl: commentaren) **1** comment(s), remark(s), observation(s); commentary (on): *~ op iets geven* (or: *leveren*) comment (or: make comments) on sth.; *geen ~* no comment **2** (unfavourable) comment, criticism: *een hoop ~ krijgen* receive a lot of unfavourable comment || *rechtstreeks ~* (running) commentary
de **commentaarstem** /kɔmɛntarstɛm/ (pl: -men) voice-over
de **commentator** /kɔmɛntatɔr/ (pl: -en) commentator
commenten /kɔmɛntə(n)/ (commentte, heeft gecomment) comment, leave a comment
de **commercie** /kɔmɛrsi/ commerce, trade
commercieel /kɔmɛrfel/ (adj, adv) commercial: *op niet-commerciële basis* on a non-profit(-making) basis
het **commissariaat** /kɔmɪsarijat/ (pl: commissariaten) **1** commissionership: *een ~ bekleden bij een bedrijf* sit on the board of a company **2** commissioner's office
de **commissaris** /kɔmɪsarɪs/ (pl: -sen) **1** commissioner, governor: [Dutch] *~ van de Koning* (or: *Koningin*) (Royal) Commissioner, governor; *~ van politie* Chief Constable, Chief of Police, police commissioner; *raad van ~sen* supervisory board **2** official, officer
de **commissie** /kɔmɪsi/ (pl: -s) **1** committee, board, commission: *de Europese Commissie* the European Commission; *een ~ instellen* appoint (or: set up) a committee **2** [com] commission
de **commissiebasis** /kɔmɪsibazɪs/: *werken op ~* work on a commission basis
zich **committeren** /kɔmitɣrə(n)/ (committeerde zich, heeft zich gecommitteerd) commit o.s.
de **commode** /kɔmodə/ (pl: -s) chest of drawers
de **commotie** /kɔmo(t)si/ (pl: -s) commotion; fuss: *~ veroorzaken* cause a commotion, make a fuss
communautair /kɔmynotɛːr/ (adj) **1** communal; Community: *~e wetgeving* Community legislation **2** [Belg] community, communal: *de ~e kwestie* the community question; *~e relaties* relations between the linguistic communities

de **commune** /kɔmynə/ (pl: -s) commune
de **communicant** /kɔmynikɑnt/ (pl: -en) **1** s.o. making his (or: her) first Communion **2** communicant
de **communicatie** /kɔmynika(t)si/ (pl: -s) communication
communicatief /kɔmynikatif/ (adj, adv) communicative
het **communicatiemiddel** /kɔmynika(t)simɪdəl/ (pl: -en) means of communication
de **communicatiestoornis** /kɔmynika(t)sistɔrnɪs/ (pl: -sen) breakdown in communication(s)
communiceren /kɔmynisɣrə(n)/ (communiceerde, heeft gecommuniceerd) communicate (with): *~de vaten* communicating vessels
de **communie** /kɔmyni/ (pl: -s) (Holy) Communion: *eerste* (or: *plechtige*) *~* first (or: solemn) Communion
het **communiqué** /kɔmynike/ (pl: -s) communiqué, statement: *een ~ uitgeven* issue a communiqué, put out a statement
het **communisme** /kɔmynɪsmə/ Communism
de **communist** /kɔmynɪst/ (pl: -en) Communist
communistisch /kɔmynɪstis/ (adj, adv) communist: *de ~e partij* the communist party
compact /kɔmpɑkt/ (adj, adv) compact
de **compact disc** /kɔmpɑkdɪsk/ (pl: -s) compact disc
de **compagnie** /kɔmpɑɲi/ (pl: -s) company; partnership: *de Oost-Indische Compagnie* the Dutch East India Company
de **compagnon** /kɔmpɑɲɔn/ (pl: -s) **1** partner, (business) associate: *de ~ van iem. worden* go into partnership with s.o. **2** pal, buddy, chum
het **compartiment** /kɔmpɑrtimɛnt/ (pl: -en) compartment
de **compassie** /kɔmpɑsi/ compassion
compatibel /kɔmpatibəl/ (adj) compatible
de **compensatie** /kɔmpɛnza(t)si/ (pl: -s) compensation: *als ~ voor, ter ~ van* by way of compensation for
compenseren /kɔmpɛnsɣrə(n)/ (compenseerde, heeft gecompenseerd) compensate for, counterbalance, make good: *dit compenseert de nadelen* this outweighs the disadvantages; *een tekort ~* make good a deficiency (or: deficit)
competent /kɔmpətɛnt/ (adj) **1** competent, able, capable: *hij is (niet) ~ op dat gebied* he is (not) competent in that field **2** competent, qualified, authorized: *dit hof is in deze kwestie niet ~* this court is not competent to settle this matter
de **competentie** /kɔmpətɛnsi/ (pl: -s) competence; capacity
competentiegericht /kɔmpətɛn(t)siɣərɪxt/ (adj) competency-based, skill-based: *~ leren* competency-based teaching (or: learning)
de **competitie** /kɔmpəti(t)si/ (pl: -s) league

de **compilatie** /kɔmpilа̱(t)si/ (pl: -s) compilation

compleet /kɔmple̱t/ (adj, adv) **1** complete: *deze jaargang is niet ~* this volume is incomplete **2** complete, total, utter: *complete onzin* utter (or: sheer) nonsense; *ik was ~ vergeten de oven aan te zetten* I'd clean (or: completely) forgotten to switch the oven on

het **complement** /kɔmpləme̱nt/ (pl: -en) complement

complementair /kɔmplemɛntɛ̱:r/ (adj) complementary

completeren /kɔmplete̱rə(n)/ (completeerde, heeft gecompleteerd) complete, make up

het **¹complex** /kɔmplɛ̱ks/ (pl: -en) complex, aggregate: *een heel ~ van regels* a whole complex of rules

²complex /kɔmplɛ̱ks/ (adj) complex, complicated, intricate: *een ~ probleem* a complex problem; *een ~ verschijnsel* a complex phenomenon

de **complicatie** /kɔmplikа̱(t)si/ (pl: -s) complication: *bij dit soort operaties treden zelden ~s op* with this type of surgery complications hardly ever arise

compliceren /kɔmplise̱rə(n)/ (compliceerde, heeft gecompliceerd) complicate: *een gecompliceerde breuk* a compound fracture; *een ~de factor* a complicating factor

het **compliment** /kɔmplime̱nt/ (pl: -en) **1** compliment: *iem. een ~ maken over iets* pay s.o. a compliment on sth., compliment s.o. on sth. **2** regard; respect: *de ~en van vader en of u even wilt komen* father sends his regards and would you mind calling around

complimenteren /kɔmplimɛnte̱rə(n)/ (complimenteerde, heeft gecomplimenteerd) compliment: *iem. ~ met iets* compliment s.o. on sth.

complimenteus /kɔmplimɛnto̱s/ (adj, adv) complimentary

het **complot** /kɔmplɔ̱t/ (pl: -ten) **1** plot: *een ~ smeden* hatch a plot, conspire **2** conspiracy

de **component** /kɔmpone̱nt/ (pl: -en) component

componeren /kɔmpone̱rə(n)/ (componeerde, heeft gecomponeerd) compose

de **componist** /kɔmponı̱st/ (pl: -en) composer

het/de **composiet** /kɔmpozi̱t/ composite

de **compositie** /kɔmpozi̱(t)si/ (pl: -s) composition

de **compositiefoto** /kɔmpozi̱(t)sifoto/ (pl: -'s) [Dutch] photofit

het/de **compost** /kɔmpɔ̱st/ compost

composteren /kɔmposte̱rə(n)/ (composteerde, heeft gecomposteerd) compost

de **compote** /kɔmpo̱:t/ (pl: -s) stewed fruit

de **compressie** /kɔmprɛ̱si/ (pl: -s) compression

de **compressor** /kɔmprɛ̱sɔr/ (pl: -en) compressor

comprimeren /kɔmprime̱rə(n)/ (comprimeerde, heeft gecomprimeerd) compress, condense

het **compromis** /kɔmpromi̱/ (pl: -sen) compromise: *een ~ aangaan* (or: *sluiten*) come to (or: reach) a compromise

compromitteren /kɔmpromite̱rə(n)/ (compromitteerde, heeft gecompromitteerd) compromise

compromitterend /kɔmpromite̱rənt/ (adj) compromising, incriminating: *~e verklaringen* (or: *papieren*) incriminating statements (or: documents)

de **computer** /kɔmpju̱tər/ (pl: -s) computer: *achter de ~ zitten* sit at (or: in front of) the computer; *gegevens invoeren in een ~* feed data into a computer

het **computerbestand** /kɔmpju̱tərbəstɑnt/ (pl: -en) computer file

de **computerbril** /kɔmpju̱tərbrɪl/ (pl: -len) computer glasses

computeren /kɔmpju̱tərə(n)/ (computerde, heeft gecomputerd) be at (or: work on, play on) the computer

de **computerfanaat** /kɔmpju̱tərfanat/ computer fanatic (or: freak)

computergestuurd /kɔmpju̱tərɣəstyrt/ (adj) computer-controlled

de **computerkraker** /kɔmpju̱tərkrakər/ (pl: -s) hacker

het **computernetwerk** /kɔmpju̱tərnɛtwɛrk/ (pl: -en) computer network

het **computerprogramma** /kɔmpju̱tərproɣrama/ (pl: -'s) computer program

het **computerspelletje** /kɔmpju̱tərspɛləcə/ (pl: -s) computer game

het **computervirus** /kɔmpju̱tərvirʏs/ computer virus

het **concentraat** /kɔnsɛntra̱t/ (pl: concentraten) concentrate, extract

de **concentratie** /kɔnsɛntra̱(t)si/ (pl: -s) concentration: *~ van het gezag* concentration of authority; *zijn ~ verliezen* lose one's concentration

de **concentratieboog** /kɔnsɛntra̱(t)sibox/ attention span: *een korte ~ hebben* have a short attention span

het **concentratiekamp** /kɔnsɛntra̱(t)sikɑmp/ (pl: -en) concentration camp

de **concentratieschool** /kɔnsɛntra̱(t)sisχol/ (pl: -scholen) [Belg] school for ethnic minority children

¹concentreren /kɔnsɛntre̱rə(n)/ (concentreerde, heeft geconcentreerd) concentrate, centre; mass; strengthen: *een geconcentreerde oplossing* a concentrated solution

zich **²concentreren** /kɔnsɛntre̱rə(n)/ (concentreerde zich, heeft zich geconcentreerd) concentrate (on): *zijn hoop concentreerde zich op de zomervakantie* his hopes were pinned on the summer holidays

concentrisch /kɔnsɛntris/ (adj, adv) concentric

het **concept** /kɔnsɛpt/ (pl: -en) **1** (rough, first) draft, outline: *een ~ maken van* draft **2** concept

de **conceptie** /kɔnsɛpsi/ (pl: -s) conception

de **conceptnota** /kɔnsɛptnota/ (pl: -'s) draft proposal

de **conceptovereenkomst** /kɔnsɛptovərenkɔmst/ (pl: -en) draft agreement

het **concern** /kɔnsy:rn/ (pl: -s) group

het **concert** /kɔnsɛrt/ (pl: -en) **1** concert; recital: *naar een ~ gaan* go to a concert **2** concerto

concerteren /kɔnsɛrterə(n)/ (concerteerde, heeft geconcerteerd) perform (*or:* give) a concert

het **concertgebouw** /kɔnsɛrtxəbɑu/ (pl: -en) concert hall

de **concertmeester** /kɔnsɛrtmestər/ (pl: -s) (orchestra) leader

de **concertzaal** /kɔnsɛrtsal/ (pl: -zalen) concert hall, auditorium

de **concessie** /kɔnsɛsi/ (pl: -s) concession; franchise; licence ‖ *~s doen* aan iem. make concessions to s.o.

de **conciërge** /kɔnʃɛ:rʒə/ (pl: -s) caretaker, janitor, porter

het **concilie** /kɔnsili/ (pl: -s, conciliën) [rel] council

het **conclaaf** /kɔnklaf/ (pl: conclaven) conclave: *met iem. in ~ gaan* discuss sth. with s.o.

concluderen /kɔnklyderə(n)/ (concludeerde, heeft geconcludeerd) conclude, deduce: *wat kunnen we daaruit ~?* what can we conclude from that?

de **conclusie** /kɔnklyzi/ (pl: -s) conclusion, deduction; findings: *de ~ trekken* draw the conclusion

het/de **concours** /kɔnkur/ (pl: -en) competition, contest

concreet /kɔnkret/ (adj, adv) **1** concrete, material, real, actual, tangible: *een ~ begrip* a concrete term; *een ~ geval* van a specific case of **2** definite: *concrete toezeggingen* definite promises; *het overleg heeft niets ~s opgeleverd* the discussion did not result in anything concrete

concretiseren /kɔnkretizerə(n)/ (concretiseerde, heeft geconcretiseerd) concretize; make concrete

de **concurrent** /kɔnkyrɛnt/ (pl: -en) competitor; rival

de **concurrentie** /kɔnkyrɛnsi/ competition, contest, rivalry

de **concurrentiepositie** /kɔnkyrɛnsipozi(t)si/ (pl: -s) competitive position, competitiveness

de **concurrentievervalsing** /kɔnkyrɛn(t)sivərvalsɪŋ/ distortion of competition, unfair competition

concurreren /kɔnkyrerə(n)/ (concurreerde, heeft geconcurreerd) compete

concurrerend /kɔŋkyrɛrənt/ (adj, adv) competitive [price]; competing; rival; conflicting

het **condens** /kɔndɛns/ condensation

de **condensatie** /kɔndɛnsa(t)si/ condensation

condenseren /kɔndɛnzerə(n)/ (condenseerde, heeft/is gecondenseerd) condense; boil down; evaporate

het **condenswater** /kɔndɛnswatər/ (water from) condensation

de **conditie** /kɔndi(t)si/ (pl: -s) **1** condition, proviso; terms: *een ~ stellen* make a condition; *onder (op) ~ dat* on (the) condition that **2** condition, state; form; shape: *de speler is in goede ~* the player is in good shape (*or:* is fit); *je hebt geen ~* you're (badly) out of condition

de **conditietraining** /kɔndi(t)sitrenɪŋ/ fitness training: *aan ~ doen* work out

conditioneel /kɔndi(t)ʃonel/ (adj, adv) conditional

de **condoleance** /kɔndolejɑ̃sə/ (pl: -s) condolences, sympathy

condoleren /kɔndolerə(n)/ (condoleerde, heeft gecondoleerd) offer one's condolences (to s.o.)

het **condoom** /kɔndom/ (pl: -s) condom; rubber

de **condor** /kɔndor/ (pl: -s) (Andean) condor

de **conducteur** /kɔndʏktør/ (pl: -s) conductor, ticket collector

confabuleren /kɔnfabylerə(n)/ (confabuleerde, heeft geconfabuleerd) confabulate

de **confectie** /kɔnfɛksi/ ready-to-wear clothes, ready-made clothes

de **confederatie** /kɔnfedəra(t)si/ (pl: -s) confederation, confederacy

de **conference** /kɔnferɑ̃sə/ **1** (solo) act, (comic) monologue **2** talk

de **conferencier** /kɔnferɑ̃ʃe/ (pl: -s) entertainer

de **conferentie** /kɔnferɛnsi/ (pl: -s) conference, meeting

de **confessie** /kɔnfɛsi/ (pl: -s) confession, admission

confessioneel /kɔnfɛʃonel/ (adj) confessional; denominational

de **confetti** /kɔnfɛti/ confetti

confidentieel /kɔnfidɛnʃel/ (adj, adv) confidential

de **configuratie** /kɔnfiɣyra(t)si/ (pl: -s) configuration

confisqueren /kɔnfɪskerə(n)/ (confisqueerde, heeft geconfisqueerd) confiscate

de **confituren** /kɔnfityrə(n)/ (pl) conserves

de **confituur** /kɔnfityr/ [Belg] jam

het **conflict** /kɔnflɪkt/ (pl: -en) conflict, clash: *in ~ komen met* come into conflict with

conform /kɔnfɔrm/ (adj, adv) in accordance with

zich **conformeren** /kɔnformerə(n)/ (conformeerde zich, heeft zich geconformeerd) conform (to), comply (with): *zich ~ aan de* *publieke opinie* bow to public opinion

de **conformist** /kɔnfɔrmɪst/ (pl: -en) conformist

de **confrontatie** /kɔnfrɔnta(t)si/ (pl: -s) confrontation

confronteren /kɔnfrɔnterə(n)/ (confronteerde, heeft geconfronteerd) confront (with): *met de werkelijkheid geconfronteerd worden* be faced (*or*: confronted) with reality

confuus /kɔnfys/ (adj) confused

het **conglomeraat** /kɔŋɣlomerat/ (pl: conglomeraten) conglomerate

Congo /kɔŋɣo/ Congo

de ¹**Congolees** /kɔŋɣoles/ (pl: Congolezen) Congolese

²**Congolees** /kɔŋɣoles/ (adj) Congolese

de **congregatie** /kɔŋɣreya(t)si/ (pl: -s) [rel] congregation

het **congres** /kɔŋɣrɛs/ (pl: -sen) conference; congress

het **congresgebouw** /kɔŋɣrɛsɣəbɑu/ conference hall

congruent /kɔŋɣrywɛnt/ (adj) congruent

de **conifeer** /konifer/ (pl: coniferen) conifer

conjunctureel /kɔnjʏŋktyrel/ (adj, adv) cyclical: *problemen van conjuncturele **aard*** cyclical problems, problems caused by fluctuations in the market

de **conjunctuur** /kɔnjʏŋktyr/ (pl: conjuncturen) economic situation, market conditions, trade cycle

de **connectie** /kɔnɛksi/ (pl: -s) connection, link ‖ *goede ~s hebben* be well connected

de **conrector** /kɔnrɛktɔr/ (pl: -s) [roughly] deputy headmaster

consciëntieus /kɔnʃɛnʃøs/ (adj, adv) conscientious, scrupulous, painstaking

de **consecratie** /kɔnsekra(t)si/ (pl: -s) consecration

de **consensus** /kɔnsɛnzʏs/ consensus

consequent /kɔnsəkwɛnt/ (adj, adv) **1** logical: *~ **handelen*** act logically, be consistent **2** consistent (with)

de **consequentie** /kɔnsəkwɛnsi/ (pl: -s) implication, consequence: *de ~s **trekken*** draw the obvious conclusion

de **conservatie** /kɔnsɛrva(t)si/ conservation, preservation

de ¹**conservatief** /kɔnsɛrvatif/ (pl: conservatieven) conservative; Tory

²**conservatief** /kɔnsɛrvatif/ (adj, adv) conservative; [pol] Conservative: *de conservatieve **partij*** the Conservative (*or*: Tory) Party

de **conservator** /kɔnsɛrvatɔr/ (pl: -s, -en) curator; keeper; custodian

het **conservatorium** /kɔnsɛrvatorijʏm/ (pl: conservatoria) academy of music, conservatory

de **conserven** /kɔnsɛrvə(n)/ (pl) canned food(s), tinned food(s), preserved food(s)

het **conservenblik** /kɔnsɛrvə(n)blɪk/ (pl: -ken)

can, tin (can)

conserveren /kɔnsɛrverə(n)/ (conserveerde, heeft geconserveerd) preserve, conserve; can; tin: *goed geconserveerd zijn* be well preserved

de **conservering** /kɔnzɛrverɪŋ/ **1** preservation; conservation **2** preserving; canning

het **conserveringsmiddel** /kɔnsɛrverɪŋsmɪdəl/ (pl: -en) preservative

de **consideratie** /kɔnsidəra(t)si/ (pl: -s) consideration: *geen enkele ~ hebben* be completely inconsiderate

de **consignatie** /kɔnsɪna(t)si/ (pl: -s) consignment

consolideren /kɔnsolidərə(n)/ (consolideerde, heeft geconsolideerd) **1** consolidate, strengthen **2** consolidate, fund

de **consorten** /kɔnsɔrtə(n)/ (pl) confederates, associates, buddies: *Hans **en** ~* Hans and his pals

het **consortium** /kɔnsɔr(t)sijʏm/ (pl: -s) consortium, syndicate

constant /kɔnstɑnt/ (adj, adv) constant, steady, continuous; staunch; loyal: *een ~e **grootheid** (or: **waarde**) a constant quantity (or: value); hij houdt me ~ voor de gek* he is forever pulling my leg (*or*: making a fool of me)

de **constante** /kɔnstɑntə/ (pl: -n) constant

constateren /kɔnstaterə(n)/ (constateerde, heeft geconstateerd) establish; ascertain; record; detect; observe: *ik constateer slechts het **feit** dat* I'm merely stating the fact that, all I'm saying is that

de **constatering** /kɔnstaterɪŋ/ (pl: -en) observation; establishment

de **consternatie** /kɔnstɛrna(t)si/ (pl: -s) consternation, alarm: *dat **gaf** heel wat ~* it caused quite a stir

de **constipatie** /kɔnstipa(t)si/ constipation: *last hebben van ~* be constipated

de **constitutie** /kɔnstity(t)si/ (pl: -s) **1** constitution, physique: *een **slechte** ~ hebben* have a weak constitution **2** constitution

constitutioneel /kɔnstity(t)ʃonel/ (adj, adv) constitutional: *constitutionele **monarchie*** constitutional monarchy

de **constructeur** /kɔnstrʏktør/ (pl: -s) designer

de **constructie** /kɔnstrʏksi/ (pl: -s) construction, building, erection, structure

constructief /kɔnstrʏktif/ (adj, adv) **1** constructive, useful: *~ te werk gaan* go about sth. in a constructive way **2** constructional, structural

de **constructiefout** /kɔnstrʏksifɑut/ (pl: -en) structural (*or*: construction) defect (*or*: fault)

construeren /kɔnstrywerə(n)/ (construeerde, heeft geconstrueerd) construct; build; erect; design

de **consul** /kɔnsʏl/ (pl: -s) consul

het **consulaat** /kɔnsylat/ (pl: consulaten) consulate

het **consulaat-generaal** /kɔnsylatχenərɑl/ (pl: consulaten-generaal) consulate general

de **consulent** /kɔnsylɛnt/ (pl: -en) consultant, adviser

het **consult** /kɔnsylt/ (pl: -en) consultation; visit

de **consultant** /kɔnsyltənt/ consultant

het **consultatiebureau** /kɔnsylta(t)sibyro/ (pl: -s) clinic, health centre: ~ *voor* zuigelingen infant welfare centre, child health centre; well-baby clinic

consulteren /kɔnsyltərə(n)/ (consulteerde, heeft geconsulteerd) **1** consult **2** confer, discuss

de **consument** /kɔnsymɛnt/ (pl: -en) consumer

de **consumentenbond** /kɔnsymɛntə(n)bɔnt/ (pl: -en) consumers' organization

consumeren /kɔnsymerə(n)/ (consumeerde, heeft geconsumeerd) **1** consume, eat, drink **2** deplete, exhaust

de **consumptie** /kɔnsympsi/ (pl: -s) **1** consumption: *(on)geschikt voor* ~ (un)fit for (human) consumption **2** food, drink(s), refreshment(s)

de **consumptiebon** /kɔnzymsibɔn/ (pl: -nen) food voucher

consumptief /kɔnsymptif/ (adj) consumptive: ~ *krediet* consumer credit

de **consumptiegoederen** /kɔnsympsiɣudərə(n)/ (pl) consumer goods: *duurzame* ~ consumer durables

het **contact** /kɔntɑkt/ (pl: -en) **1** contact, connection, touch: *telefonisch* ~ *opnemen* get in touch by phone; ~ *opnemen met iem. (over iets)* contact s.o., get in touch with s.o. (about sth.); *in* ~ *blijven met* keep in touch with **2** contact, terms: *een goed* ~ *met iem. hebben* have a good relationship with s.o. **3** contact (man); connection: *~en hebben in bepaalde kringen* have connections in certain circles **4** contact, switch; ignition: *het sleuteltje in het* ~ *steken* put the key in(to) the ignition

de **contactadvertentie** /kɔntɑktɑtfərtɛnsi/ (pl: -s) personal ad(vert), advert in the personal column

contactarm /kɔntɑktɑrm/ (adj) socially inhibited; socially isolated

de **contactdoos** /kɔntɑɡdos/ (pl: -dozen) socket; appliance inlet

contacten /kɔntɑktə(n)/ (contactte, heeft gecontact) [Dutch] get in touch: *we moeten even* ~ *over …* we'll have to get in touch about …

de **contactlens** /kɔntɑktlɛns/ (pl: -lenzen) contact lens; contacts

de **contactlijm** /kɔntɑktlɛim/ contact adhesive

contactloos /kɔntɑktlos/ (adj) contactless: ~ *betalen* make contactless payments, wave-and-pay

de **contactpersoon** /kɔntɑktpɛrson/ (pl: -personen) contact (person)

de **contactsleutel** /kɔntɑktsløtəl/ (pl: -s) ignition key

contactueel /kɔntɑktywel/ (adj, adv) contactual

het **contactverbod** /kɔntɑktfərbɔt/ restraining order

de **container** /kɔntɛnər/ (pl: -s) **1** container **2** (rubbish) skip

het **containerpark** /kɔntɛnərpɑrk/ (pl: -en) [Belg] recycling centre, amenity centre

de **contaminatie** /kɔntɑmina(t)si/ (pl: -s) contamination

contant /kɔntɑnt/ (adj, adv) cash, ready: *tegen ~e betaling* on cash payment; cash down; ~ *geld* ready money

de **contanten** /kɔntɑntə(n)/ (pl) cash, ready money, cash in hand

het **content** /kɔntɛnt/ (adj) content (with), satisfied (with)

de **context** /kɔntɛkst/ (pl: -en) context, framework, background: *je moet dat in de juiste* ~ *zien* you must put that into its proper context

het **continent** /kɔntinɛnt/ (pl: -en) continent

continentaal /kɔntinɛntɑl/ (adj) continental

het **contingent** /kɔntɪŋɡɛnt/ (pl: -en) **1** contingent **2** quota, share, proportion; allocation; allotment

¹**continu** /kɔntiny/ (adj) continuous; unbroken

²**continu** /kɔntiny/ (adv) continuously: *hij loopt ~ te klagen* he is always complaining

het **continubedrijf** /kɔntinybədrɛif/ (pl: -bedrijven) continuous working plant

continueren /kɔntinywerə(n)/ (continueerde, heeft gecontinueerd) **1** continue (with), carry on (with) **2** continue, retain

de **continuïteit** /kɔntinywitɛit/ **1** continuity **2** continuation

het **conto** /kɔnto/ (pl: -'s) account: [fig] *iets op iemands ~ schrijven* hold s.o. accountable for sth.; [fig] *iets op zijn ~ schrijven* achieve

de **contour** /kɔntur/ (pl: -en) contour

contra /kɔntra/ (prep) contra, against; [law] versus: *alle argumenten pro en ~ bekijken* consider all the arguments for and against

de **contrabas** /kɔntrabɑs/ (pl: -sen) (double) bass

de **contraceptie** /kɔntrasɛpsi/ contraception

het **contract** /kɔntrɑkt/ (pl: -en) contract, agreement: *zijn ~ loopt af* his contract is running out; *een ~ opzeggen* (or: *verbreken*) terminate (or: break) a contract; *een ~ (af)sluiten* enter into (or: make) a contract; *een ~ (onder)tekenen* sign a contract; *volgens ~* according to contract

de **contractbreuk** /kɔntrɑktbrøk/ breach of contract: ~ *plegen* commit a breach of contract

contracteren /kɔntrɑkterə(n)/ (contracteerde, heeft gecontracteerd) **1** engage;

sign (up, on) **2** contract: *~de **partijen*** contracting parties

de **¹contractueel** /kɔntrɑktywel/ (pl: contractuelen) [Belg] contractual worker

²contractueel /kɔntrɑktywel/ (adj, adv) contractual: *iets ~ **vastleggen** lay sth. down (or: stipulate sth.)* in a contract

de **contradictie** /kɔntrɑdɪksi/ (pl: -s) contradiction

de **contramine** /kɔntrɑminə/: *in de ~ zijn* be perverse, be contrary

contraproductief /kɔntrɑprodʏktif/ (adj) counterproductive

de **contraspionage** /kɔntrɑspijonaʒə/ (pl: -s) counter-espionage

het **contrast** /kɔntrɑst/ (pl: -en) contrast: *een schril ~* a harsh contrast; *een (sterk) ~ **vormen** met* form a sharp contrast with (or: to)

contrasteren /kɔntrɑsterə(n)/ (contrasteerde, heeft gecontrasteerd) contrast (with), be in contrast (with/to)

contrastief /kɔntrɑstif/ (adj, adv) contrastive

de **contreien** /kɔntrɛiə(n)/ (pl) parts, regions

de **contributie** /kɔntribʏ(t)si/ (pl: -s) subscription; contribution

de **controle** /kɔntroːlə/ (pl: -s) **1** check (on), checking, control; supervision (of, over); [med] check-up; monitoring: *~ van de **bagage*** baggage check; *de ~ van de **boekhouding*** the audit of accounts, the examination of the books; *de ~ **over** het stuur verliezen* lose control of the steering-wheel **2** control (point), checkpoint; (ticket) gate: *zijn kaartje **aan** de ~ afgeven* hand in one's ticket at the gate

controleerbaar /kɔntrolerbaːr/ (adj) verifiable

de **controlepost** /kɔntroːləpɔst/ (pl: -en) control (point), checkpoint

controleren /kɔntrolerə(n)/ (controleerde, heeft gecontroleerd) **1** supervise, superintend; monitor: *~d **geneesheer*** [roughly] medical officer **2** check (up, on), inspect, examine; verify: *de **boeken** ~* audit the books (or: accounts); *kaartjes ~* inspect tickets; *iets extra (dubbel) ~* double-check sth.

de **controleur** /kɔntrolør/ (pl: -s) inspector, controller, checker; ticket inspector (or: collector); auditor

de **controller** /kɔntroːlər/ controller

de **controltoets** /kɔntroːltuts/ (pl: -en) Control (key)

de **controverse** /kɔntrovɛrsə/ (pl: -n, -s) controversy

controversieel /kɔntrovɛrsjel/ (adj) controversial; contentious, much debated

het **convenant** /kɔnvənɑnt/ (pl: -en) covenant

het **convent** /kɔnvɛnt/ (pl: -en) monastery; convent

de **conventie** /kɔnvɛnsi/ (pl: -s) convention: *in strijd met de ~ zijn* go against the accepted norm

conventioneel /kɔnvɛnʃonel/ (adj, adv) conventional

de **conversatie** /kɔnvɛrsa(t)si/ (pl: -s) conversation, talk

converseren /kɔnvɛrserə(n)/ (converseerde, heeft geconverseerd) converse (with), engage in conversation (with)

de **conversie** /kɔnvɛrsi/ (pl: -s) conversion

converteren /kɔnvɛrterə(n)/ (converteerde, heeft geconverteerd) convert (into, to)

cool /kuːl/ (adj) cool

de **coolingdown** /kuːlɪŋdɑun/ cooling down

de **coöperatie** /koːopəra(t)si/ (pl: -s) **1** cooperation, collaboration **2** cooperative (society)

coöperatief /koːopəratif/ (adj, adv) cooperative

de **coördinaat** /koːɔrdinaːt/ (pl: coördinaten) co-ordinate

de **coördinatie** /koːɔrdina(t)si/ (pl: -s) coordination

de **coördinator** /koːɔrdinaːtɔr/ (pl: -en) coordinator

coördineren /koːɔrdinerə(n)/ (coördineerde, heeft gecoördineerd) coordinate, arrange, organize: *werkzaamheden ~* supervise work

COPD /seopedeː/ *chronic obstructive pulmonary disease* COPD

copieus /kopijøs/ (adj, adv) copious, abundant: *een ~ diner* a lavish dinner

de **copiloot** /kopilot/ (pl: copiloten) co-pilot

de **coproductie** /koprodʏksi/ (pl: -s) joint production, co-production

copuleren /kopylerə(n)/ (copuleerde, heeft gecopuleerd) copulate; mate

copy-pasten /kɔpipɛstə(n)/ (copy-pastte, heeft gecopy-past) copy-paste, cut and paste

het **copyright** /kɔpirɑjt/ (pl: -s) copyright

corduroy /kɔrdyrɔj/ (adj) cord(uroy); corded

het **cornedbeef** /kɔrnɛdbif/ corned beef, bully (beef)

de **corner** /kɔːrnər/ (pl: -s) corner

de **corporatie** /kɔrpora(t)si/ (pl: -s) corporation, corporate body

het **corps** /kɔːr/ (pl: corpora) [Dutch] corps

de **corpsstudent** /kɔːrstydɛnt/ (pl: -en) [Dutch] member of a student association

corpulent /kɔrpylɛnt/ (adj) corpulent

correct /kɔrɛkt/ (adj, adv) **1** correct; right; exact: *~ antwoorden* get the answer(s) right, answer correctly **2** correct, right, proper: *~e houding* proper conduct (or: behaviour); *~e kleding* suitable dress

de **correctheid** /kɔrɛktheit/ **1** correctness, precision **2** correctness, propriety

de **correctie** /kɔrɛksi/ (pl: -s) correction; adjustment; revision; marking: *~s aanbrengen* make corrections; adjust, make adjustments

correctioneel /kɔrɛkʃonel/ (adj) [Belg] criminal: *correctionele rechtbank* [roughly]

Crown Court

de **corrector** /kɔrɛktɔr/ (pl: -s, -en) proofreader, corrector, reviser

de **correlatie** /kɔrela(t)si/ (pl: -s) correlation

de **correspondent** /kɔrɛspɔndɛnt/ (pl: -en) correspondent: *van onze ~ in Parijs* from our Paris correspondent

de **correspondentie** /kɔrɛspɔndɛnsi/ (pl: -s) correspondence: *een drukke ~ voeren* carry on a lively correspondence

het **correspondentieadres** /kɔrɛspɔndɛn(t)siadrɛs/ (pl: -sen) postal (*or:* mailing) address

corresponderen /kɔrɛspɔnderə(n)/ (correspondeerde, heeft gecorrespondeerd) **1** correspond (with), write (to) **2** correspond (to, with), match (with), agree (with)

de **corridor** /kɔridɔːr/ corridor

corrigeren /kɔriɣerə(n)/ (corrigeerde, heeft gecorrigeerd) **1** correct; adjust **2** correct; mark

de **corrosie** /kɔrozi/ (pl: -s) corrosion

corrumperen /kɔrʏmperə(n)/ (corrumpeerde, heeft gecorrumpeerd) corrupt, pervert: *macht corrumpeert* power corrupts

corrupt /kɔrʏpt/ (adj, adv) corrupt, dishonest

de **corruptie** /kɔrʏpsi/ (pl: -s) corruption

het/de **corsage** /kɔrsaʒə/ (pl: -s) corsage

Corsica /kɔrsika/ Corsica

het **corso** /kɔrso/ (pl: -'s) pageant, parade, procession

de **corvee** /kɔrve/ (pl: -s) (household) chores: *~ hebben* do the chores

de **coryfee** /kɔrife/ (pl: -ën) star, lion, celebrity

het **coschap** /kɔsχɑp/ (pl: -pen) clerkship; (assistant) housemanship; [Am] intern(e)ship

de **cosinus** /kosinʏs/ cosine

de **cosmetica** /kɔsmetika/ (pl) cosmetics

cosmetisch /kɔsmetis/ (adj) cosmetic

Costa Rica /kɔstarika/ Costa Rica

de **Costa Ricaan** /kɔstarikan/ (pl: Costa Ricanen) Costa Rican

Costa Ricaans /kɔstarikans/ (adj) Costa Rican

de **couchette** /kuʃɛt(ə)/ (pl: -s) couchette, berth

de **coulance** /kulɑ̃sə/ considerateness

coulant /kulɑnt/ (adj, adv) accommodating, obliging, reasonable

de **coulisse** /kulisə/ (pl: -n) (side) wing

de **counter** /kɑuntər/ (pl: -s) counter-attack, countermove: *op de ~ spelen* rely on the counter-attack

counteren /kɑuntərə(n)/ (counterde, heeft gecounterd) [sport] counter(-attack)

de **countrymuziek** /kɑuntrimyzik/ country music

de **coup** /kup/ (pl: -s) coup (d'état): *een ~ plegen* stage a coup

de **coupe** /kup/ (pl: -s) **1** cut; style **2** coupe: *~ royale* [roughly] sundae

de **coupé** /kupe/ (pl: -s) **1** compartment **2** coupé

couperen /kuperə(n)/ (coupeerde, heeft gecoupeerd) cut: *een hond ~ dock* a dog's tail

de **coupe soleil** /kupsolɛi/ (pl: coupes soleils) highlights

het **couplet** /kuplɛt/ (pl: -ten) stanza, verse; couplet

de **coupon** /kupɔn/ (pl: -s) **1** remnant **2** coupon

de **coupure** /kupyrə/ (pl: -s) **1** cut, deletion **2** [finance] denomination

courant /kurɑnt/ (adj) current

de **coureur** /kurør/ (pl: -s) (racing) cyclist; racing motorcyclist; racing car driver

de **courgette** /kurʒɛt(ə)/ (pl: -s) courgette; [Am] zucchini

de **courtage** /kurtaʒə/ (pl: -s) brokerage, (broker's) commission

de **couscous** /kuskus/ couscous

de **couture** /kutyrə/ couture, dressmaking

de **couturier** /kutyrje/ (pl: -s) couturier, (fashion) designer

het **couvert** /kuvɛːr/ (pl: -s) **1** cover, envelope **2** cover; cutlery

de **couveuse** /kuvøzə/ (pl: -s) incubator

het **couveusekind** /kuvøzəkɪnt/ (pl: -eren) premature baby

het/de **cover** /kɑvər/ (pl: -s) **1** cover **2** cover (version), remake

de **cowboy** /kɑubɔj/ (pl: -s) cowboy

de **coyote** /kojotə/ (pl: -s) coyote

c.q. /seky/ *casu quo* and, or

de **crack** /krɛk/ (pl: -s) **1** crack player, ace; [Am] hotshot **2** crack

de **cracker** /krɛkər/ (pl: -s) cracker

de **crash** /krɛʃ/ (pl: -es) crash

het **crashdieet** /krɛʃdijet/ (pl: -diëten) crash diet

crashen /krɛʃə(n)/ (crashte, heeft/is gecrasht) **1** crash: *het toestel crashte bij de landing* the plane crashed on landing **2** crash, go bankrupt **3** [comp] crash

de **crawl** /krɔːl/ crawl

crawlen /krɔːlə(n)/ (crawlde, heeft/is gecrawld) do the crawl

de **creatie** /kreja(t)si/ (pl: -s) creation: *de nieuwste ~s van Dior* Dior's latest creations

creatief /krejatif/ (adj, adv) creative, original, imaginative: *~ bezig zijn* do creative work; *~ boekhouden* indulge in creative accounting

de **creativiteit** /krejativitɛit/ creativity, creativeness: [fig] *haar oplossingen getuigen van ~* her solutions show creative talent

de **crèche** /krɛʃ/ (pl: -s) crèche, day-care centre, day nursery

het **credit** /kredɪt/ credit: *debet en ~* debit and credit; *iets op iemands ~ schrijven* [also fig] put sth. to s.o.'s credit, credit s.o. with sth.

de **creditcard** /krɛdɪtkɑːrt/ (pl: -s) credit card

crediteren /kredɪterə(n)/ (crediteerde, heeft gecrediteerd) credit de **crediteur** /kreditør/ (pl: -en) creditor; accounts payable

de **creditnota** /krḛdɪtnota/ (pl: -'s) credit note (or: slip)

het **credo** /krḛdo/ (pl: -'s) **1** credo, creed **2** Credo, Creed

creëren /krejḛrə(n)/ (creëerde, heeft gecreëerd) create

de **crematie** /kremɑ(t)si/ (pl: -s) cremation

het **crematorium** /krematṓrijʏm/ (pl: crematoria) crematorium

de **crème** /krɛːm/ (pl: -s) **1** cream: ~ *op zijn gezicht smeren* rub cream on one's face **2** crème ‖ *een* ~ *japon* a cream(-coloured) dress

cremeren /krəmḛrə(n)/ (cremeerde, heeft gecremeerd) cremate

de **creool** /krejṓl/ (pl: creolen) Creole

het **¹creools** /krejṓls/ creole

²creools /krejṓls/ (adj) creole

het **crêpepapier** /krɛ̄ːpapir/ crêpe paper

creperen /krepḛrə(n)/ (crepeerde, is gecrepeerd) **1** die: *ze lieten haar gewoon* ~ they let her die like a dog **2** suffer: ~ *van de pijn* be racked with pain

het **cricket** /krɪkət/ cricket

cricketen /krɪkətə(n)/ (crickette, heeft gecricket) play cricket

de **crime** /krim/ disaster: *het is een* ~ it is a disaster

de **criminaliteit** /kriminalitɛ̄it/ (pl: -en) criminality: *de kleine* ~ petty crime

de **¹crimineel** /kriminḛl/ (pl: criminelen) criminal

²crimineel /kriminḛl/ (adj) criminal: *het criminele circuit* the (criminal) underworld, (the world of) organized crime

³crimineel /kriminḛl/ (adv) [inform] horribly, terribly: *het is* ~ *koud* it's wickedly cold

de **criminologie** /kriminoloɣi/ criminology

de **crisis** /krḭzɪs/ (pl: crises) crisis: *de* ~ *van de jaren dertig* the depression of the 1930s; *een* ~ *doormaken* go through a crisis; *een* ~ *doorstaan* weather a crisis

de **crisismanager** /krḭzɪsmɛnədʒər/ (pl: -s) crisis manager

het **criterium** /kritḛrijʏm/ (pl: criteria) **1** criterion: *aan de criteria voldoen* meet the criteria; *een* ~ *vaststellen* lay down a criterion **2** [cycling] criterium

de **criticaster** /kritikɑstər/ (pl: -s) criticaster

de **criticus** /krḭtikʏs/ (pl: critici) critic, reviewer: *door de critici toegejuicht worden* receive critical acclaim

de **croissant** /krwɑsɑ̄/ (pl: -s) croissant

de **croque-monsieur** /krɔkməsjø̄/ (pl: -s) [Belg] toasted ham and cheese sandwich

de **cross** /krɔs/ (pl: -es) cross

crossen /krɔ̄sə(n)/ (croste, heeft/is gecrost) **1** take part in a cross-country (event); do cross-country; do autocross (or: rallycross)

[car] **2** tear about: *hij crost heel wat af op die fiets* he is always tearing about on that bike of his

de **crossfiets** /krɔ̄sfits/ (pl: -en) cyclo-cross bike; BMX bike

de **crossmotor** /krɔ̄smotər/ cross-country motorcycle

de **croupier** /krupjē/ (pl: -s) croupier

de **¹cru** /kry/ (pl: -'s) vintage

²cru /kry/ (adj, adv) **1** crude, rude; rough: *dat klinkt misschien* ~, *maar …* that sounds a bit harsh, but … **2** blunt; cruel

cruciaal /krysi̠jāl/ (adj) crucial

het **crucifix** /krysifɪks/ (pl: -en) crucifix

de **cruise** /kruːs/ (pl: -s) cruise

de **cruisecontrol** /kruːskəntrol/ cruise control

cryptisch /krɪptis/ (adj, adv) cryptic(al), obscure

het **cryptogram** /krɪptoɣrɑ̄m/ (pl: -men) cryptogram

Cuba /kȳba/ Cuba

de **Cubaan** /kybān/ (pl: Cubanen) Cuban

Cubaans /kybāns/ (adj) Cuban

culinair /kylinɛ̄ːr/ (adj) culinary

culmineren /kʏlminḛrə(n)/ (culmineerde, heeft geculmineerd) culminate (in)

cultiveren /kʏltivḛrə(n)/ (cultiveerde, heeft gecultiveerd) **1** cultivate; till **2** cultivate, improve: *gecultiveerde kringen* cultured (or: sophisticated) circles

cultureel /kʏltyrḛl/ (adj, adv) cultural: ~ *werk* cultural activities, social and creative activities

de **cultus** /kȳltʏs/ (pl: culten) cult

de **cultuur** /kʏltȳr/ (pl: culturen) **1** culture, cultivation: *een stuk grond in* ~ *brengen* bring land into cultivation **2** culture, civilization: *de oosterse* ~ eastern civilization

de **cultuurbarbaar** /kʏltȳrbɑrbar/ (pl: -barbaren) [offensive] Philistine

de **cultuurdrager** /kʏltȳrdraɣər/ (pl: -s) vehicle of culture; purveyor of culture

de **cultuurgeschiedenis** /kʏltȳrɣəsxidənɪs/ history of civilization; cultural history

cultuurhistorisch /kʏltyrhɪstoris/ (adj) connected with the history of civilization; historico-cultural, cultural-historical

cum laude /kumlɑudə/ (adv) with distinction

de **cumulatie** /kymylɑ(t)si/ (pl: -s) (ac)cumulation: ~ *van ambten* plurality

cumulatief /kymylatif/ (adj) cumulative

¹cumuleren /kymylḛrə(n)/ (cumuleerde, heeft gecumuleerd) [Belg] have several jobs

²cumuleren /kymylḛrə(n)/ (cumuleerde, heeft gecumuleerd) (ac)cumulate: *verschillende functies* ~ pluralize

de **cup** /kʏp/ (pl: -s) cup

Cupido /kȳpido/ Cupid, Eros

de **cupmaat** /kȳpmat/ (pl: -maten) cup size

Curaçao /kyrasɑ̄u/ Curaçao

de **curatele** /kyrat̲e̲lə/ legal restraint; wardship; receivership: *onder ~ staan* a) be under legal restraint; **b)** be made a ward of court; **c)** be in receivership

de **curator** /kyra̲tor/ (pl: -s, -en) curator ‖ *de firma staat onder het **beheer** van een ~* the firm is in receivership

curieus /kyrij̲ø̲s/ (adj, adv) curious, strange: *ik **vind** het maar ~* I find it rather strange

de **curiositeit** /kyrijozit̲ɛi̲t/ (pl: -en) curiosity, oddity, strangeness: *... en **andere** ~en ...* and other curiosities (*or:* curiosa)

het **curriculum** /kyri̲kylʏm/ (pl: curricula) curriculum: *~ vitae* curriculum vitae; [Am] résumé

cursief /kyrs̲i̲f/ (adj, adv) italic, italicized, cursive: *~ **drukken** print in italics

de **cursist** /kyrs̲ɪ̲st/ (pl: -en) student

de **cursor** /k̲y̲rsor/ (pl: -s) cursor

de **cursus** /k̲y̲rzʏs/ (pl: -sen) course (of study, lectures): *zich opgeven voor een ~ **Frans** sign up for a French course; *een **schriftelijke** ~* a correspondence course; *een ~ **volgen** (bij iem.)* take a course (with s.o.); *een ~ voor **beginners*** a beginners' course; *een ~ voor **gevorderden*** an advanced course

het **cursusboek** /k̲y̲rzʏzbuk/ (pl: -en) textbook; coursebook

de **curve** /k̲y̲rvə/ (pl: -n) curve

de **custard** /k̲y̲stɑrt/ custard (powder)

de **cut** /kʏt/ (pl: -s) [film] cut(ting)

de **cutter** /k̲y̲tər/ (pl: -s) **1** slicer **2** Stanley (*or:* carpet) knife

de **¹cv** /sev̲e̲/ (pl: cv's) **1** *commanditaire vennootschap* Limited Partnership, Special Partnership **2** *coöperatieve vereniging* co-op

de **²cv** /sev̲e̲/ *centrale verwarming* central heating

het **³cv** /sev̲e̲/ *curriculum vitae* cv; [Am] résumé

CVA /seve̲a̲/ *cerebrovasculair accident* CVA, cerebrovascular accident

de **cv-ketel** /sev̲e̲ketəl/ (pl: -s) central-heating boiler

CVS /seve̲ɛ̲s/ *chronischevermoeidheidssyndroom* Chronic Fatigue Syndrome, CFS

het **CWI** /sewe̲i̲/ [Dutch] *Centrum voor Werk en Inkomen* [roughly] Job Centre

het **cyanide** /sijan̲i̲də/ (pl: -n) cyanide

de **cyberaanval** /s̲ɑ̲jbəranval/ (pl: -len) cyber attack

de **cybernetica** /sibɛrn̲e̲tika/ cybernetics

cyberpesten /s̲ɑ̲jbərpɛstə(n)/ cyber-bully

de **cyberspace** /s̲ɑ̲jbərspes/ [comp] cyberspace

de **cyclaam** /sikl̲a̲m/ (pl: cyclamen) cyclamen

de **cyclecross** /s̲ɑ̲jkəlkrɔs/ (pl: -es) cyclo-cross

cyclisch /s̲i̲klis/ (adj, adv) cyclic(al): *~e **verbindingen** cyclic compounds

de **cycloon** /sikl̲o̲n/ (pl: cyclonen) cyclone, hurricane

de **cycloop** /sikl̲o̲p/ (pl: cyclopen) Cyclops

de **cyclus** /s̲i̲klʏs/ (pl: cycli) cycle

de **cynicus** /s̲i̲nikʏs/ (pl: cynici) cynic

cynisch /s̲i̲nis/ (adj, adv) cynical

het **cynisme** /sin̲i̲smə/ cynicism

de **Cyprioot** /siprij̲o̲t/ (pl: Cyprioten) Cypriot

Cyprus /s̲i̲prʏs/ Cyprus

cyrillisch /sir̲i̲lis/ (adj) Cyrillic

de **cyste** /k̲i̲stə/ (pl: -n) cyst

d

de **d** /de/ (pl: d's) d; D

de **daad** /dat/ (pl: daden) act(ion), deed, activity: *een goede ~ verrichten* do a good deed; *de ~ bij het woord voegen* suit the action to the word

de **daadkracht** /dɑtkrɑχt/ decisiveness, energy, vigour

daadwerkelijk /dɑtwɛrkələk/ (adj, adv) actual, active, practical

¹**daags** /daχs/ (adj) daily, everyday

²**daags** /daχs/ (adv) a day, per day, daily: *tweemaal ~* twice a day

¹**daar** /dar/ (adv) **1** (over) there: *hier en ~* here and there; *zie je dat huis ~* (do you) see that house (over there)?; *tot ~* up to there **2** (just, over, right) there: *wie is ~?* who is it? (*or:* there?)

²**daar** /dar/ (conj) as, because, since

daaraan /daran/ (adv) on (to) it (*or:* them): *wat heb je ~* what good is that

daarachter /darɑχtər/ (adv) **1** behind (it, that, them, there): [fig] *wat zou ~ zitten?* I wonder what's behind it **2** beyond (it, that, them, there)

daarbij /darbɛi/ (adv) **1** with it (*or:* that); with these (*or:* those): *~ blijft het* that's how it is, we'll keep it like that **2** besides, moreover, furthermore: *~ komt, dat …* what's more …

daarbinnen /darbɪnə(n)/ (adv) in there, inside, in it (*or:* that); in these (*or:* those): *~ is het warm* it's warm in there

daarboven /darbovə(n)/ (adv) up there, above it

daardoor /dardor/ (adv) **1** through it (*or:* that); through these (*or:* those) **2** therefore; so, consequently; by this (*or:* that) means: *zij weigerde, en ~ gaf zij te kennen … she refused, and by doing so made it clear …; ~ werd hij ziek* that is (*or:* was) what made him ill, because of this (*or:* that) he became ill

daarenboven /darə(n)bovə(n)/ (adv) besides, moreover, in addition, furthermore: *hij was knap en ~ rijk* he was handsome and rich besides

daarentegen /darəntexə(n)/ (adv) on the other hand: *hij is zeer radicaal, zijn broer ~ conservatief* he is a strong radical, his brother, on the other hand, is conservative

daargelaten /darχəlatə(n)/ (adv): *uitzonderingen ~* apart from (*or:* except for) exceptions

daarheen /darhen/ (adv) (to) there: *wij wil-len ~* we want to go (over) there

daarin /darɪn/ (adv) **1** in there (*or:* it, those) **2** in that: *hij is ~ handig* he is good at it

daarlangs /darlɑŋs/ (adv) by (*or:* past, along) that: *we kunnen beter ~ gaan* we had better go that way

daarmee /darme/ (adv) with, by that (*or:* it, those): *~ kun je het vastzetten* you can fasten it with that (*or:* those); *en ~ uit!* and that's that! (*or:* all there is to it!)

daarna /darna/ (adv) after(wards), next, then: *de dag ~* the day after (that); *snel* (*or:* *kort*) *~* soon (*or:* shortly) after (that); *eerst … en ~ …* first … and then …

daarnaar /darnar/ (adv) **1** at (*or:* to, for) that **2** accordingly, according to that: *~ moet je handelen* you must act accordingly

daarnaartoe /darnartu/ (adv) (to) there: *wij willen ~* we want to go there

daarnaast /darnast/ (adv) **1** beside it, next to it **2** besides, in addition (to this): *~ is hij nog brutaal ook* what's more he is cheeky (too)

daarnet /darnɛt/ (adv) just now, only a little while ago, only a minute ago

daarom /darɔm/ (adv) **1** around it **2** therefore, so, because of this (*or:* that), for that reason: *hij wil het niet hebben, ~ doe ik het juist* he doesn't like it, and that's exactly why I do it; *waarom niet? ~ niet!* why not? because (I say so)!; that's why!

daaromheen /darɔmhɛn/ (adv) around it (*or:* them): *een tuin met een hek ~* a garden with a fence around it

daaromtrent /darɔmtrɛnt/ (adv) **1** about that: *ik kan u ~ geen inlichtingen geven* I can't give you any information about that **2** thereabout, or so: *€ 100 of ~* a hundred euros or thereabout (*or:* so); *rond vier uur of ~* around four o'clock

daaronder /darɔndər/ (adv) under(neath) it

daarop /darɔp/ (adv) **1** (up)on that, on top of that (*or:* those): *de tafel en het kleed ~* the table and the cloth on top of it **2** on that, to that: *uw antwoord* (*or:* *reactie*) *~* your reply (*or:* reaction) (to that) **3** thereupon: *de dag ~* the next (*or:* following) day, the day after (that); *kort ~* shortly afterwards, soon after (that)

daaropvolgend /darɔpfɔlɣənt/ (adj, adv) next, following: *hij kwam in juli en vertrok in juni ~* he arrived in July and left the following June

daarover /darovər/ (adv) **1** on top of it, on (*or:* over, above) that: *~ lag een zeil* there was a tarpaulin on top of (*or:* over, across) it **2** about that: *genoeg ~* enough said, enough of that

daartegen /dartexə(n)/ (adv) **1** against it, next to it **2** against it (*or:* them): *eventuele bezwaren ~* any objections to it

daartegenaan /dɑrteɣə(n)ɑn/ (adv) (right) up against it (*or:* them), (right) onto it (*or:* them): *onze schuur is ~ gebouwd* our shed is built up against (*or:* onto) it

daartegenover /dɑrteɣə(n)ovər/ (adv) **1** opposite (*or:* facing) it/them: *de kerk met de pastorie* ~ the church with the vicarage opposite it (*or:* facing it) **2** on the other hand, (but) then again …: ~ *staat dat dit systeem duurder is* (but) on the other hand this system costs more

daartoe /dɑrtu/ (adv) **1** for that, to that **2** for that (purpose), to that end: ~ *gemachtigd zijn* be authorized to do it

daartussen /dɑrtʏsə(n)/ (adv) **1** between them, among them: *die twee ramen en de ruimte* ~ those two windows and the space between (them) **2** between them: *wat is het verschil* ~? what's the difference (between them)?

daaruit /dɑrœyt/ (adv) **1** out of that (*or:* those): *het water spuit* ~ the water spurts out of it **2** from that: ~ *kun je afleiden dat …* from this it can be deduced that …

daarvan /dɑrvɑn/ (adv) **1** from it (*or:* that, there) **2** of it (*or:* that), thereof **3** of it (*or:* that): ~ *wordt plastic gemaakt* plastic is made of that, that is used for making plastic ‖ *niets* ~ nothing of the sort

daarvandaan /dɑrvɑndɑn/ (adv) **1** (away) from there, away (from it) **2** hence, therefore

daarvoor /dɑrvor/ (adv) **1** in front of it, before that (*or:* those) **2** before (that): *de week* ~ the week before (that), the previous week **3** for that (purpose): ~ *heb ik geen tijd* I've no time for that **4** for it (*or:* them): ~ *(in de plaats) heb ik een boek gekregen* I got a book instead **5** that's why: ~ *ben ik ook gekomen* that's what I've come for; *daar zijn het kinderen voor* that's children for you

de **dadel** /dɑdəl/ date

dadelijk /dɑdələk/ (adv) **1** immediately, at once, right away **2** directly, presently: *ik kom (zo)* ~ *bij u* I'll be right with you

de **dadelpalm** /dɑdəlpɑlm/ (pl: -en) date palm

de **dadendrang** /dɑdə(n)drɑŋ/ dynamism, thirst for action

de **dader** /dɑdər/ (pl: -s) perpetrator, offender: *de vermoedelijke* ~ the suspect

het **daderprofiel** /dɑdərprofil/ (pl: -en) offender profile: *een ~ opstellen* compile an offender profile

de **¹dag** /dɑχ/ (pl: -en) **1** day, daybreak, daytime: ~ *en nacht bereikbaar* available day and night; *bij klaarlichte* ~ in broad daylight; *het is kort* ~ time is running out (fast), there is not much time (left); *het is morgen vroeg* ~ we must get up early (*or:* an early start) tomorrow; *iem. de* ~ *van zijn leven bezorgen* give s.o. the time of his life; *lange ~en maken* work long hours; *er*

gaat geen ~ voorbij of ik denk aan jou not a day passes but I think of you; *het is vandaag mijn ~ niet* it just isn't my day (today); *wat is het voor ~?* what day (of the week) is it?; *morgen komt er weer een ~* tomorrow is another day; ~ *in,* ~ *uit* day in day out; ~ *na* ~ day by day, day after day; *het wordt met de ~ slechter* it gets worse by the day; *om de drie ~en* every three days; *24 uur per* ~ 24 hours a day; *van* ~ *tot* ~ daily, from day to day; *van de ene* ~ *op de andere* from one day to the next; *over veertien ~en* in two weeks' time; in a fortnight **2** daylight: *voor de* ~ *komen* come to light, surface, appear; *met iets voor de* ~ *komen* **a)** come up with sth.; **b)** come forward, present o.s.; *voor de* ~ *ermee!* **a)** out with it!; **b)** show me!; *goed voor de* ~ *komen* make a good impression **3** day(s), time: *ouden van ~en* the elderly **4** hello; hi (there); bye(-bye); goodbye

²dag /dɑχ/ (int) hello, hi; bye(-bye); goodbye: *dáág!* bye(-bye)!, bye then; *ja, dáág!* forget it!

de **dagbehandeling** /dɑɣbəhɑndəlɪŋ/ (pl: -en) outpatients' treatment

het **dagblad** /dɑɣblɑt/ (pl: -en) (daily) newspaper, (daily) paper

het **dagboek** /dɑɣbuk/ (pl: -en) diary, journal: *een ~ (bij)houden* keep a diary

het **dagdeel** /dɑɣdel/ (pl: -delen) part of the day; shift; morning; afternoon; evening; night

dagdromen /dɑɣdromə(n)/ (dagdroomde, heeft gedagdroomd) daydream

¹dagelijks /dɑɣələks/ (adj) **1** daily: *zijn ~e bezigheden* his daily routine; *voor ~ gebruik* for everyday use **2** everyday, ordinary: ~ *bestuur* executive (committee); *in het ~ leven* in everyday life; *dat is ~ werk voor hem* that's routine for him

²dagelijks /dɑɣələks/ (adv) daily, each day, every day: *dat komt ~ voor* it happens every day

dagen /dɑɣə(n)/ (daagde, heeft gedaagd) **1** summon(s); subpoena: *iem. voor het gerecht ~* summon(s) s.o. **2** dawn: *het begon mij te ~* it began to dawn on me

dagenlang /dɑɣə(n)lɑŋ/ (adj) lasting (for) days

het **dag-en-nachtritme** /dɑχɛnɑχtrɪtmə/ day-night cycle: *een verstoord ~ hebben* have a disrupted circadian rhythm

de **dageraad** /dɑɣərat/ dawn, daybreak, break of day

het **dagje** /dɑχjə/ (pl: -s) day: *een ~ ouder worden* be getting on (a bit); *een ~ uit* a day out

de **dagjesmensen** /dɑχjəsmɛnsə(n)/ (pl) (day) trippers

de **dagkaart** /dɑχkart/ (pl: -en) day-ticket

het **daglicht** /dɑχlɪχt/ daylight, light of day: *bij iem. in een kwaad ~ staan* be in s.o.'s bad books; *iem. in een kwaad ~ stellen* put s.o. in the wrong (with)

het **dagmenu** /d<u>a</u>xmənY/ daily menu

de **dagopvang** /d<u>a</u>xɔpfɑŋ/ day nursery, day-care centre

het **dagretour** /d<u>a</u>xrətur/ (pl: -s) day return, day (return) ticket

de **dagschotel** /d<u>a</u>xsxotəl/ (pl: -s) plat du jour, dish of the day; today's special

de **dagtaak** /d<u>a</u>xtak/ (pl: dagtaken) **1** daily work **2** day's work: *daar heb ik een ~ aan* that is a full day's work (*or:* a full-time job)

de **dagtekening** /d<u>a</u>xtekənɪŋ/ date

de **dagtocht** /d<u>a</u>xtɔxt/ (pl: -en) day trip

dagvaarden /d<u>a</u>xfardə(n)/ (dagvaardde, heeft gedagvaard) summon: *gedagvaard worden* be summoned (to appear in court)

de **dagvaarding** /d<u>a</u>xfardɪŋ/ (pl: -en) (writ of) summons, writ; subpoena

het **dagverblijf** /d<u>a</u>xfərblɛif/ (pl: dagverblijven) **1** day room: *een ~ voor kinderen* a day-care centre, a day nursery, a crèche **2** outdoor enclosure, outside cage, outside pen

dagvers /d<u>a</u>xfɛrs/ (adj) fresh daily, fresh each day

de **dahlia** /d<u>a</u>lija/ (pl: -'s) dahlia

het **dak** /dɑk/ (pl: -en) roof: *auto met open ~* convertible; soft-top; *een ~ boven het hoofd hebben* have a roof over one's head; [fig] *iets van de ~en schreeuwen* shout sth. from the rooftops; [fig] *het ~ gaat eraf* it's going to be one big party; [fig] *uit zijn ~ gaan* a) go crazy, freak out; b) blow one's top

de **dakbedekking** /d<u>a</u>gbədɛkɪŋ/ (pl: -en) roofing material

de **dakdekker** /d<u>a</u>gdɛkər/ (pl: -s) roofer

de **dakgoot** /d<u>a</u>gxot/ (pl: dakgoten) gutter

het **dakje** /d<u>a</u>kjə/ (pl: -s) **1** rooflet **2** circumflex (accent) ‖ *het ging van een leien ~* it was plain (*or:* smooth) sailing all the way

de **dakkapel** /d<u>a</u>kapɛl/ (pl: -len) dormer (window)

dakloos /d<u>a</u>klos/ (adj) homeless, (left) without a roof over one's head

de **dakloze** /d<u>a</u>klozə/ homeless person; street people

de **daklozenkrant** /d<u>a</u>kloze(n)krɑnt/ [roughly] Big Issue

de **dakpan** /d<u>a</u>kpɑn/ (pl: -nen) (roof(ing)) tile

het **dakraam** /d<u>a</u>kram/ (pl: dakramen) skylight, attic window, garret window

het **dakterras** /d<u>a</u>ktɛrɑs/ (pl: -sen) terrace, roof garden

het **dal** /dɑl/ (pl: -en) valley, dale ‖ *hij is door een diep ~ gegaan* he has had a very hard (*or:* rough) time

dalen /d<u>a</u>lə(n)/ (daalde, is gedaald) **1** descend, go down, come down, drop, fall: *het vliegtuig daalt* the (aero)plane is descending; *de temperatuur daalde tot beneden het vriespunt* the temperature fell below zero **2** fall, go down, come down, drop; decline; de-

crease: *de prijzen zijn een paar* **euro** *gedaald* prices are down by a couple of euros

de **daling** /d<u>a</u>lɪŋ/ (pl: -en) **1** descent, fall(ing), drop: *~ van de zeespiegel* drop in the sea level **2** slope, incline, descent, drop; [small] dip **3** decrease, drop, slump: *de ~ van het* **geboortecijfer** the fall in the birth rate

de **daluren** /d<u>a</u>lyrə(n)/ (pl) off-peak hours

de **dam** /dɑm/ **1** dam: *een ~ leggen* build a dam **2** [draughts] king, crowned man: *een ~ halen* crown a man

het **damast** /dam<u>a</u>st/ (pl: -en) damask

het **dambord** /d<u>a</u>mbɔrt/ (pl: -en) draughtboard

de **dame** /d<u>a</u>mə/ (pl: -s) **1** lady: *~s en heren* ladies and gentlemen **2** [chess, cards] queen: *een ~ halen* queen a pawn

het **damesblad** /d<u>a</u>məzblɑt/ (pl: -en) women's magazine

de **damesfiets** /d<u>a</u>məsfits/ (pl: -en) women's (*or:* lady's) bike

de **dameskapper** /d<u>a</u>məskɑpər/ (pl: -s) ladies' hairdresser

de **damesmode** /d<u>a</u>məsmodə/ (pl: -s) **1** ladies' fashion **2** ladies' clothing

het **damhert** /d<u>a</u>mhɛrt/ (pl: -en) fallow deer

dammen /d<u>a</u>mə(n)/ (damde, heeft gedamd) play draughts; [Am] play checkers

de **dammer** /d<u>a</u>mər/ (pl: -s) draughts player; [Am] checkers player

de **damp** /dɑmp/ (pl: -en) **1** steam; vapour; mist **2** smoke; fume: *schadelijke ~en* noxious fumes

dampen /d<u>a</u>mpə(n)/ (dampte, heeft gedampt) **1** steam **2** smoke **3** vape

dampend /d<u>a</u>mpənt/ (adj) steamy

de **dampkap** /d<u>a</u>mpkɑp/ (pl: -pen) [Belg] cooker hood, extractor hood

de **dampkring** /d<u>a</u>mpkrɪŋ/ (pl: -en) (earth's) atmosphere

de **damschijf** /d<u>a</u>msxɛif/ (pl: damschijven) draught(sman)

het **damspel** /d<u>a</u>mspɛl/ (pl: -len) **1** draughts **2** set of draughts

de **damwand** /d<u>a</u>mwɑnt/ (pl: -en) sheet piling

¹dan /dɑn/ (adv) **1** then: *morgen zijn we vrij, ~ gaan we uit* we have a day off tomorrow, so we're going out; *nu eens dit, ~ weer dat* first one thing, then another; *tot ~* till then; see you then; *hij zei dat hij ~ en ~ zou komen* he said he'd come at such and such a time; *en je broer ~?* and what about your brother then?; *wat ~ nog?* so what!; *ook goed, ~ niet* all right, we won't then; *al ~ niet groen* green or otherwise, whether green or not; *en ~ zeggen ze nog dat ...* and still they say that ...; *hij heeft niet gewerkt; hij is ~ ook gezakt* he didn't work, so not surprisingly he failed **2** then; besides: *eerst werken, ~ spelen* business before pleasure; *zelfs ~ gaat het niet* even so it won't work; *en ~?* and then what?

²dan /dɑn/ (conj) **1** than: *hij is groter ~ ik* he is bigger than me **2** but, except: *hij heeft nie-mand ~ zijn moeder* he has no one but (*or:* except) his mother

de **dance** /dɛːns/ dance

het **dancefestival** /dɛːnsfɛstival/ (pl: -s) EDM festival

de **dancing** /dɛnsɪŋ/ (pl: -s) dance hall, disco-theque

danig /danəx/ (adv) soundly, thoroughly, well: *~ in de knoei zitten* be in a terrible mess

de **dank** /dɑŋk/ thanks, gratitude: *iets niet in ~ afnemen* take sth. in bad part; *geen ~* you're welcome; *met ~ aan ...* thanks to ...; *stank voor ~ krijgen* get little thanks for one's pains; *bij voorbaat ~* thank you in advance; *tegen wil en ~* unwilling, willy-nilly

dankbaar /dɑŋgbar/ (adj, adv) **1** grateful, thankful: *ik zou u zeer ~ zijn als ...* I should be most grateful to you (*or:* obliged) if ... **2** rewarding, grateful: *een dankbare taak* a rewarding task

de **dankbaarheid** /dɑŋgbarhɛit/ gratitude, thankfulness: *uit ~ voor* in appreciation of

de **dankbetuiging** /dɑŋgbətœyɣɪŋ/ (pl: -en) expression of gratitude (*or:* thanks)

¹**danken** /dɑŋkə(n)/ (dankte, heeft gedankt) decline (with thanks)

²**danken** /dɑŋkə(n)/ (dankte, heeft gedankt) **1** thank: *ja graag, dank je* yes, please, thank you; *niets te ~* not at all, you're welcome **2** owe, be indebted: *dit heb ik aan jou te ~* I owe this to you; I have you to thank for this

het **dankwoord** /dɑŋkwort/ (pl: -en) word(s) of thanks

dankzeggen /dɑŋksɛɣə(n)/ (zegde dank/zei dank, heeft dankgezegd) thank, express (one's) thanks (*or:* gratitude) to

dankzij /dɑŋksɛi/ (prep) thanks to

de **dans** /dɑns/ (pl: -en) dance, dancing: *iem. ten ~ vragen* ask s.o. to dance (*or:* for a dance) ‖ *de ~ ontspringen* get off scot-free

dansen /dɑnsə(n)/ (danste, heeft/is gedanst) dance: *uit ~ gaan* go (out) dancing; *~ op muziek* (or: *een plaat*) dance to music (*or:* a record)

de **danser** /dɑnsər/ (pl: -s) dancer

de **danseres** /dɑnsərɛs/ (pl: -sen) dancer

de **dansles** /dɑnslɛs/ (pl: -sen) dancing class (*or:* lesson); dancing classes

het **dansorkest** /dɑnsɔrkɛst/ (pl: -en) dance band

de **danspas** /dɑnspɑs/ (pl: -sen) (dance) step

de **dansschool** /dɑnsxol/ (pl: -scholen) dancing school

de **dansvloer** /dɑnsflur/ (pl: -en) dance floor

de **danszaal** /dɑnsal/ (pl: -zalen) dance hall; ballroom

dapper /dɑpər/ (adj, adv) **1** brave, coura-geous: *zich ~ verdedigen* put up a brave fight **2** plucky, tough: *klein maar ~* small but tough

de **dapperheid** /dɑpərhɛit/ bravery, courage

de **dar** /dɑr/ (pl: -ren) drone

de **darm** /dɑrm/ (pl: -en) intestine, bowel: *dikke ~* the large intestine; *dunne ~* small intes-tine; *twaalfvingerige ~* duodenum

de **darmflora** /dɑrmflora/ intestinal flora

dartel /dɑrtəl/ (adj, adv) playful, frisky, frol-icsome

dartelen /dɑrtələ(n)/ (dartelde, heeft/is ge-darteld) romp, frolic, gambol

darten /dɑːrtə(n)/ (dartte, heeft gedart) play darts

de **darter** /dɑːrtər/ (pl: -s) darts player

het **darts** /dɑːrts/ darts

het **dartsbord** /dɑːrtsbɔrt/ dartboard

de **das** /dɑs/ **1** badger **2** tie: *dat deed hem de ~ om* that did for him, that finished him **3** [Dutch] scarf

het **dashboard** /dɛʒbɔːrt/ (pl: -s) dashboard

het **dashboardkastje** /dɛʒbɔːrtkɑʃə/ (pl: -s) glove compartment

de **dashcam** /dɛʃkɛm/ (pl: -s) dashboard (*or:* dash) camera

¹**dat** /dɑt/ (dem pron) that: *ben ik ~?* is that me?; *~ is het hem nu juist* that's just it, that's the problem; *ziezo, ~ was ~* right, that's that (then), so much for that; *~ lijkt er meer op* that's more like it; *mijn boek en ~ van jou* my book and yours; *~ mens* that (dreadful) woman

²**dat** /dɑt/ (pron) **1** that, which; [of pers] that; who, whom: *het bericht ~ mij gebracht werd ...* the message that (*or:* which) was brought me ...; *het jongetje ~ ik een appel heb gegeven* the little boy (that, who) I gave an apple to **2** which; [of pers] who; [of pers] whom: *het huis, ~ onlangs opgeknapt was, werd verkocht* the house, which had recently been done up, was sold

³**dat** /dɑt/ (conj) **1** that [usually not translat-ed]: *in plaats (van) ~ je me het vertelt ...* instead of telling me, you ...; *de reden ~ hij niet komt is ...* the reason (why) he is not coming is ...; *ik denk ~ hij komt* I think (that) he'll come; *zonder ~ ik het wist* without me knowing; *het regende ~ het goot* it was pouring (down) **2** that, because: *hij is kwaad ~ hij niet mee mag* he is angry that (*or:* because) he can't come **3** so that: *doe het zo, ~ hij het niet merkt* do it in such a way that he won't notice **4** as far as: *is hier ook een bioscoop? niet ~ ik weet* is there a cinema here? not that I know **5** that: *~ mij nu juist zoiets moest overkomen!* that such a thing should happen to me now!

de **data** /data/ (pl) **1** data **2** dates

de **databank** /databɑŋk/ (pl: -en) data bank

het **databeheer** /databeher/ [comp] data man-agement

de **datacompressie** /datakɔmprɛsi/ data compression

de **datakabel** /datakabəl/ (pl: -s) data cable

de **datalimiet** /datalimit/ data limit

de **dataroaming** /dⱥtaromɪŋ/ data roaming

de **date** /detʃ/ (pl: -s) date: *een ~ hebben met iem.* have a date with s.o.

daten /dⱥtə(n)/ (datete, heeft gedatet) date

¹**dateren** /datⱥrə(n)/ (dateerde) date (from), go back (to): *het huis dateert al uit de veertiende eeuw* the house goes all the way back to the fourteenth century; *de brief dateert van 6 juli* the letter is dated 6th July

²**dateren** /datⱥrə(n)/ (dateerde, heeft gedateerd) date

datgene /dⱥtxenə/ (dem pron) what, that which: *~ wat je zegt, is waar* what you say is true

dato /dⱥto/ (adv) date, dated: *drie weken na ~* three weeks later

de **datum** /dⱥtʏm/ (pl: data) date, time: *zonder ~* undated; *er staat geen ~ op* there is no date on it; *over ~* past its date, past its sell-by date

de **datumprikker** /dⱥtʏmprɪkər/ (pl: -s) (digital) meeting planner

de **dauw** /dɑu/ dew ‖ [Belg] *van de hemelse ~ leven* live the life of Riley

dauwtrappen /dⱥutrⱥpə(n)/ [roughly] taking a walk at dawn

daveren /dⱥvⱥrə(n)/ (daverde, heeft gedaverd) thunder, shake, roar; resound: *de vrachtwagen daverde voorbij* the truck thundered (or: roared) past

daverend /dⱥvⱥrənt/ (adj, adv) resounding, thunderous: *een ~ applaus* thunderous applause; *een ~ succes* a resounding success

de **davidster** /dⱥvɪtstⱥr/ (pl: -ren) Star of David

d.d. *de dato* dd

de /də/ (art) the: *eens in de week* once a week; *ze kosten twintig euro de kilo* they are twenty euros a kilo; *dat is dé man voor dat karwei* he is (just) the man for the job

de **deadline** /dɛtlɑjn/ (pl: -s) deadline

dealen /diːlə(n)/ (dealde, heeft gedeald) deal (in), push: *hij dealt in heroïne* he deals in (or: pushes) heroin ‖ *met iets kunnen ~* be able to deal (or: cope, put up) with sth.

de **dealer** /diːlər/ (pl: -s) dealer; pusher

het/de **debacle** /debⱥkəl/ (pl: -s) disaster; failure; downfall

het **debat** /dəbⱥt/ (pl: -ten) debate; argument

debatteren /debⱥtⱥrə(n)/ (debatteerde, heeft gedebatteerd) debate; argue

het **debet** /debɛt/ debit(s), debtor side, debit side: *~ en credit* debit(s) and credit(s)

de **debetkaart** /debɛtkart/ (pl: -en) debit card

de ¹**debiel** /dəbiːl/ (pl: -en) [offensive] moron, imbecile, cretin

²**debiel** /dəbiːl/ (adj, adv) [offensive] feeble-minded: *doe niet zo ~* don't be such an idiot

debiteren /debitⱥrə(n)/ (debiteerde, heeft gedebiteerd) debit, charge

de **debiteur** /debitⱥr/ (pl: -en) debtor, debt receivable, account(s) receivable

de **debriefing** /dibriːfɪŋ/ (pl: -s) debriefing

de **debutant** /debytⱥnt/ (pl: -en) novice; newcomer

debuteren /debytⱥrə(n)/ (debuteerde, heeft gedebuteerd) make a (or: one's) debut

het **debuut** /debyt/ (pl: debuten) debut: *zijn ~ maken* make one's debut (or: first appearance)

de **decaan** /dekⱥn/ (pl: decanen) **1** dean **2** student counsellor

decadent /dekadɛnt/ (adj) decadent

de **decadentie** /dekadɛn(t)si/ decadence, degeneration

de **decafé** /dekⱥfe/ decaf(f), decaffeinated coffee

de **decameter** /dekⱥmetər/ decametre

de **december** /desɛmbər/ December

het **decennium** /desⱥnijʏm/ (pl: decennia) decade

de **decentralisatie** /desɛntraliza(t)si/ decentralization; deconcentration; localization

decentraliseren /desɛntralizⱥrə(n)/ (decentraliseerde, heeft gedecentraliseerd) decentralize; deconcentrate; localize

de **deceptie** /desɛpsi/ (pl: -s) disappointment; disillusionment

de **decharge** /deʃɑrʒ/: *iem. ~ verlenen* release (or: relieve) s.o. (from/of); *getuige à ~* witness for the defence

de **decibel** /desibɛl/ (pl: -s) decibel

de **deciliter** /desilitər/ (pl: -s) decilitre

de ¹**decimaal** /desimⱥl/ (pl: decimalen) decimal (place): *tot op zes decimalen uitrekenen* calculate to six decimal places

²**decimaal** /desimⱥl/ (adj) decimal: *decimale breuk* decimal fraction, decimal

decimeren /desimⱥrə(n)/ (decimeerde, heeft gedecimeerd) decimate

de **decimeter** /desimetər/ (pl: -s) decimetre

de **declamatie** /deklamⱥ(t)si/ (pl: -s) declamation; recitation

declameren /deklamⱥrə(n)/ (declameerde, heeft gedeclameerd) declaim, recite

de **declaratie** /deklarⱥ(t)si/ (pl: -s) expenses claim; account; claim (form): *zijn ~ indienen* put in one's claim

declareren /deklarⱥrə(n)/ (declareerde, heeft gedeclareerd) declare: *een bedrag* (or: *driehonderd euro*) *~* charge an amount (or: three hundred euros); *heeft u nog iets te ~?* have you anything to declare?

de **decoder** /dikⱥdər/ decoder

decoderen /dekⱥdⱥrə(n)/ (decodeerde, heeft gedecodeerd) decode

het **decolleté** /dekⱥlⱥte/ (pl: -s) low neckline, cleavage

het **decor** /dekoːr/ (pl: -s) **1** decor, scenery, setting(s); [film] set: *~ en kostuums* scenery and costumes **2** [fig] background

de **decoratie** /dekorⱥ(t)si/ (pl: -s) decoration, adornment

decoratief /dekⱥratif/ (adj, adv) decorative,

ornamental
decoreren /dekɔrɐrə(n)/ (decoreerde, heeft gedecoreerd) decorate
het **decorum** /dekɔrʏm/ decorum, propriety: *het ~ bewaren* maintain decorum (*or:* the proprieties)
de **decoupeerzaag** /dekupɐrzaχ/ (pl: -zagen) jigsaw
het **decreet** /dəkret/ (pl: decreten) decree
het **deeg** /deχ/ (pl: degen) dough; pastry
de **deegrol** /deχrɔl/ (pl: -len) rolling pin
de **deegwaren** /deχwarə(n)/ (pl) pasta
de **deejay** /diːdʒe/ (pl: -s) deejay
het **deel** /del/ **1** part, piece: *één ~ bloem op één ~ suiker* one part (of) flour to one part (of) sugar; *voor een groot ~* to a great extent; *voor het grootste ~* for the most part; *~ uitmaken van* be part of, belong to **2** share: *zijn ~ van de winst* his share of the profits **3** volume ‖ *het viel hem ten ~* it fell to him (*or:* to his lot)
deelbaar /delbar/ (adj) divisible: *tien is ~ door twee* ten is divisible by two
de **deeleconomie** /delekonomi/ sharing economy
de **deelgenoot** /delɣənot/ (pl: -genoten) partner (in), sharer (in): *iem. ~ maken van een geheim* confide a secret to s.o.
de **deelname** /delnamə/ participation: *~ aan een wedstrijd* taking part in a contest (*or:* competition, race); *bij voldoende ~* if there are enough entries
deelnemen /delnemə(n)/ (nam deel, heeft deelgenomen) participate (in), take part (in); attend; enter; compete (in); join (in): *aan een wedstrijd ~* take part in a contest; *~ aan een examen* take an exam
de **deelnemer** /delnemər/ (pl: -s) participant; conferee; competitor; entrant; contestant: *een beperkt aantal ~s* a limited number of participants
de **deelneming** /delnemɪŋ/ **1** participation, attendance, entry **2** sympathy; condolence(s): *zijn ~ betuigen* extend one's sympathy; *met oprechte ~* with deepest sympathy
de **deelregering** /delrəɣerɪŋ/ (pl: -en) [Belg] regional government (*or:* administration)
de **deelrepubliek** /delrepyblik/ (pl: -en) autonomous republic
deels /dels/ (adv) partly, part
de **deelstaat** /delstat/ (pl: -staten) (federal) state
het **deelteken** /deltekə(n)/ (pl: -s) division sign
de **deeltijd** /deltɛit/ part-time, half-time
de **deeltijdbaan** /deltɛidban/ (pl: -banen) part-time job
het **deeltijdwerk** /deltɛitwɛrk/ part-time work, half-time work
het **deeltje** /delcə/ (pl: -s) particle
het **deelwoord** /delwort/ (pl: -en) participle: *het onvoltooid ~* the present participle; *het voltooid ~* the past participle

de **Deen** /den/ (pl: Denen) Dane
het **¹Deens** /dens/ Danish
²Deens /dens/ (adj) Danish
deerniswekkend /dernɪswɛkənt/ (adj) pitiful, pitiable, pathetic: *in ~e toestand* in a pitiful (*or:* sorry) state
de-escaleren /deɛskalɐrə(n)/ de-escalate
het **¹defect** /dəfɛkt/ (pl: -en) fault, defect; flaw: *we hebben het ~ aan de machine kunnen verhelpen* we've managed to sort out the trouble with the machine
²defect /dəfɛkt/ (adj) faulty, defective; out of order; damaged: *~ out of order*
de **defensie** /defɛnsi/ defence: *de minister van ~* the Minister of Defence
het **defensief** /defɛnsif/ defensive: *in het ~ zijn* be on the defensive
de **defibrillator** /defibrilatɔr/ (pl: -en, -s) defibrillator
het **defilé** /defileɣ/ (pl: -s) parade
definiëren /defin(i)jerə(n)/ (definieerde, heeft gedefinieerd) define: *iets nader ~* define sth. more closely, be more specific about sth.
de **definitie** /definitsi/ (pl: -s) definition: *per ~* by definition
definitief /definitif/ (adj, adv) definitive, final: *de definitieve versie* the definitive version
de **deflatie** /defla(t)si/ (pl: -s) deflation
deftig /dɛftəχ/ (adj, adv) distinguished, fashionable, stately: *een ~e buurt* a fashionable quarter
¹degelijk /deɣələk/ (adj) **1** reliable, respectable, solid, sound: *een ~ persoon* a respectable person **2** sound, reliable, solid: *een ~ fabricaat* a reliable product
²degelijk /deɣələk/ (adv) thoroughly, soundly, very much ‖ *wel ~* really, actually, positively; *ik meen het wel ~* I am quite serious
de **degen** /deɣə(n)/ (pl: -s) sword; foil
degene /dəɣenə/ (dem pron) he, she; those: *~ die ...* he who, she who
de **degeneratie** /deɣenəra(t)si/ (pl: -s) degeneration
de **degradatie** /deɣrada(t)si/ (pl: -s) demotion; [esp sport] relegation
de **degradatiewedstrijd** /deɣrada(t)siwɛtstrɛit/ (pl: -en) relegation match
¹degraderen /deɣradɐrə(n)/ (degradeerde, is gedegradeerd) be relegated (to), be downgraded (to)
²degraderen /deɣradɐrə(n)/ (degradeerde, heeft gedegradeerd) degrade, downgrade (to); demote (to); [esp sport] relegate (to)
deinen /dɛinə(n)/ (deinde, heeft gedeind) **1** heave: *de zee deinde sterk* the sea surged wildly **2** bob, roll
de **deining** /dɛinɪŋ/ (pl: -en) **1** swell, roll **2** rocking motion **3** commotion: *~ veroorzaken* cause a stir
het **dek** /dɛk/ (pl: -ken) **1** cover(ing); horse-cloth

2 [shipp] deck: *alle hens aan ~* all hands on deck

het **dekbed** /dɛgbɛt/ (pl: -den) continental quilt, duvet

het/de **dekbedovertrek** /dɛgbɛtovərtrɛk/ (pl: -ken) eiderdown cover

de **deken** /dekə(n)/ **1** blanket: *onder de ~s kruipen* pull the blankets over one's head **2** dean

de **dekhengst** /dɛkhɛnst/ (pl: -en) stud(-horse), (breeding) stallion

dekken /dɛkə(n)/ (dekte, heeft gedekt) **1** cover; coat: *de tafel ~* set the table **2** agree (with), correspond (with, to) **3** cover (for), protect: *iem. in de rug ~* support s.o., stand up for s.o.; *zich ~* cover (or: protect) o.s. **4** cover, meet: *deze cheque is niet gedekt* this cheque is not covered; *de verzekering dekt de schade* the insurance covers the damage **5** cover; service

de **dekking** /dɛkɪŋ/ **1** [mil] cover, shelter: *~ zoeken* seek (or: take) cover (from) **2** service **3** [fin] cover **4** cover: *ter ~ van de (on)kosten* to cover (or: meet, make up) the expenses **5** coverage **6** [socc] marking; cover; guard [boxing etc]

de **deklaag** /dɛklax/ (pl: -lagen) **1** finishing coat **2** covering layer

de **dekmantel** /dɛkmɑntəl/ (pl: -s) cover, cloak; blind; front: *iem. (iets) als ~ gebruiken* use s.o. (sth.) as a front

het/de **dekmatras** /dɛkmatrɑs/ (pl: -sen) mattress topper

het/de **deksel** /dɛksəl/ (pl: -s) lid; top; cover: *het ~ op zijn neus krijgen* get the door slammed in one's face

het **dekzeil** /dɛksɛil/ (pl: -en) tarpaulin, canvas

de **delegatie** /deleɣa(t)si/ (pl: -s) delegation

delegeren /deleɣerə(n)/ (delegeerde, heeft gedelegeerd) delegate

delen /delə(n)/ (deelde, heeft gedeeld) **1** divide, split **2** share, divide: *je moet kiezen of ~* take it or leave it; *eerlijk ~* share and share alike; *samen ~* go halves; *het verschil ~* split the difference; [media] *een bericht ~* share a message (or: post) **3** divide; [educ] do division: *honderd ~ door tien* divide one hundred by ten ‖ *een mening ~* share an opinion; *iem. in zijn vreugde laten ~* share one's joy with s.o.

de **deler** /delər/ (pl: -s) divisor

deleten /diliːtə(n)/ (deletete, heeft gedeletet) [comp] delete

de **delfstof** /dɛlfstɔf/ (pl: -fen) mineral

delibereren /delibererə(n)/ (delibereerde, heeft gedelibereerd) deliberate (over/(up)on); debate: *na lang ~ werden zij het eens* they agreed after much debate

delicaat /delikat/ (adj) delicate

de **delicatesse** /delikatɛsə/ (pl: -n) delicacy

het **delict** /delɪkt/ (pl: -en) offence; indictable offence: *plaats ~* scene of the crime

de **deling** /delɪŋ/ (pl: -en) division

de **delinquent** /delɪŋkwɛnt/ (pl: -en) delinquent, offender

het **delirium** /delirijʏm/ (pl: deliria) delirium

de **delta** /dɛlta/ (pl: -'s) **1** delta **2** delta wing

deltavliegen /dɛltavliɣə(n)/ hang-gliding

delven /dɛlvə(n)/ (delfde/dolf, heeft gedolven) **1** dig **2** extract: *goud* (or: *grondstoffen*) *~ mine* gold (or: raw materials)

de **demagogie** /demaɣoɣi/ demagogy

de **demagoog** /demaɣox/ (pl: demagogen) demagogue

demarreren /demarerə(n)/ (demarreerde, heeft/is gedemarreerd) break away, take a flyer

dement /demɛnt/ (adj) demented

dementeren /demɛntərə(n)/ (dementeerde, is gedementeerd) grow demented, get demented

de **dementie** /demɛnsi/ dementia

demilitariseren /demilitarizerə(n)/ (demilitariseerde, heeft gedemilitariseerd) demilitarize

demissionair /demɪʃonɛːr/ (adj) [Dutch] outgoing: *het kabinet is ~* the cabinet has resigned (or: tendered) its resignation

de **demo** /demo/ (pl: -'s) **1** demo (tape) **2** demo

de **demobilisatie** /demobiliza(t)si/ demobilization

de **democraat** /demokrat/ (pl: democraten) democrat

de **democratie** /demokra(t)si/ (pl: -ën) democracy, self-government

democratisch /demokratis/ (adj, adv) democratic

democratiseren /demokratizerə(n)/ (democratiseerde, heeft/is gedemocratiseerd) democratize

de **demografie** /demoɣrafi/ demography

de **demon** /demɔn/ (pl: -en) demon, devil, evil spirit

demoniseren /demonizerə(n)/ (demoniseerde, heeft gedemoniseerd) demonize

de **demonstrant** /demɔnstrɑnt/ (pl: -en) demonstrator, protester

de **demonstratie** /demɔnstra(t)si/ (pl: -s) **1** demonstration, display, show(ing), exhibition **2** demonstration, (protest) march: *een ~ tegen kernwapens* a demonstration against nuclear arms

demonstratief /demɔnstratif/ (adj, adv) ostentatious, demonstrative, showy: *zij liet op demonstratieve wijze haar ongenoegen blijken* she pointedly showed her displeasure

¹**demonstreren** /demɔnstrerə(n)/ (demonstreerde, heeft gedemonstreerd) demonstrate, march, protest: *~ tegen* (or: *voor*) *iets* demonstrate against (or: in support of) sth.

²**demonstreren** /demɔnstrerə(n)/ (demonstreerde, heeft gedemonstreerd) demonstrate, display, show, exhibit

de **demontage** /demɔntaːʒə/ (pl: -s) dismantling, disassembling, taking apart; removal; defusing

demonteren /demɔnt‿erə(n)/ (demonteerde, heeft gedemonteerd) **1** disassemble, dismantle, take apart; remove; knock down **2** deactivate; defuse; disarm

demoraliseren /demoralizɛrə(n)/ (demoraliseerde, heeft gedemoraliseerd) demoralize

demotiveren /demotivɛrə(n)/ (demotiveerde, heeft gedemotiveerd) remove (or: reduce) (s.o.'s) motivation, discourage, dishearten

dempen /dɛmpə(n)/ (dempte, heeft gedempt) **1** fill (up, in), close (up), stop (up) **2** subdue; tone down; muffle; deaden; dim; shade [light]: *gedempt licht* subdued (or: dimmed, soft) light

de **demper** /dɛmpər/ (pl: -s) silencer; [Am] muffler

de **den** /dɛn/ (pl: -nen) pine (tree), fir

denderen /dɛndərə(n)/ (denderde, heeft/is gedenderd) rumble, thunder; hurtle; roar

denderend /dɛndərənt/ (adj, adv): *ik vind dat boek niet* ~ I don't think that book is so marvellous, I'm not exactly wild about that book

Denemarken /denəmɑrkə(n)/ Denmark

denigrerend /deniɣrɛrənt/ (adj, adv) disparaging, belittling

het **denim** /dɛnɪm/ denim

denkbaar /dɛŋgbaːr/ (adj) conceivable, imaginable, possible

het **denkbeeld** /dɛŋgbeːlt/ (pl: -en) **1** concept, idea, thought, notion: *zich een* ~ *vormen van* form some idea of; *een verkeerd* ~ *hebben van* have a wrong conception (or: idea) of **2** opinion, idea, view: *hij houdt er verouderde ~en op na* he has some antiquated ideas

denkbeeldig /dɛŋgbeːldəx/ (adj) **1** notional, theoretical, hypothetical **2** imaginary, illusory, unreal; fictitious: *het gevaar is niet ~ dat* ... there's a (very) real danger that ...

¹**denken** /dɛŋkə(n)/ (dacht, heeft gedacht) **1** think, consider, reflect, ponder: *het doet ~ aan* it reminds one of ...; *dit doet sterk aan omkoperij ~* this savours strongly of bribery; *waar zit je aan te ~?* what's on your mind?; *ik moet er niet aan ~* I can't bear to think about it; *ik denk er net zo over* I feel just the same about it; *ik zal eraan ~* I'll bear it in mind; *nu ik eraan denk* (now I) come to think of it; *aan iets ~* think (or: be thinking) of sth.; *ik probeer er niet aan te ~* I try to put it out of my mind; *iem. aan het ~ zetten* set s.o. thinking; *ik dacht bij mezelf* I thought (or: said) to myself; *denk om je hoofd* mind your head; *er verschillend* (or: *anders*) *over ~* take a different view (of the matter); *zij denkt er nu anders over* she feels differently about it (now); *dat had ik niet*

van hem gedacht I should never have thought it of him **2** think of (or: about), intend (to), plan (to): *ik denk erover met roken te stoppen* I'm thinking of giving up smoking ‖ *geen ~ aan!* it's out of the question!

²**denken** /dɛŋkə(n)/ (dacht, heeft gedacht) **1** think, be of the opinion, consider: *ik weet niet wat ik ervan moet ~* I don't know what to think; *wat dacht je van een ijsje?* what would you say to an ice cream?; *dat dacht je maar, dat had je maar gedacht* that's what you think!; *ik dacht van wel* (or: *van niet*) I thought it was (or: wasn't); *wie denk je wel dat je bent?* (just) who do you think you are? **2** think, suppose, expect, imagine: *wie had dat kunnen ~* who would have thought it?; *u moet niet ~ (dat)* ... you mustn't suppose (or: think) (that) ...; *dat dacht ik al* I thought so; *dacht ik het niet!* just as I thought! **3** think, understand, imagine, appreciate, consider: *de beste arts die je je maar kunt ~* the best (possible) doctor; *denk eens (aan)* imagine!, just think of it! **4** think of (or: about), intend, be going (to), plan: *wat denk je nu te doen?* what do you intend to do now?

de **denker** /dɛŋkər/ (pl: -s) thinker

de **denkfout** /dɛŋkfaut/ (pl: -en) logical error, error of reasoning

de **denkpiste** /dɛŋkpistə/ (pl: -s, -n) [Belg] cast of mind

de **denksport** /dɛŋkspɔrt/ (pl: -en) puzzle solving, problem solving

de **denktank** /dɛŋktɛŋk/ (pl: -s) think tank

de **denkwijze** /dɛŋkwɛizə/ (pl: -n) way of thinking, mode of thought

de **dennenappel** /dɛnə(n)ɑpəl/ (pl: -s) pine cone; fir cone

de **dennenboom** /dɛnə(n)bom/ (pl: -bomen) pine (tree), fir

de **dennenprocessierups** /dɛnə(n)prosɛsirʏps/ (pl: -en) pine processionary caterpillar

de **deodorant** /dejodorɑnt/ (pl: -s, -en) deodorant

depanneren /depɑnɛrə(n)/ (depanneerde, heeft gedepanneerd) [Belg] **1** [car] repair, put back on the road **2** [s.o.] help out

het **departement** /depɑrtəmɛnt/ (pl: -en) department, ministry

depenaliseren /depenalizɛrə(n)/ (depenaliseerde, heeft gedepenaliseerd) [Belg] decriminalize

de **dependance** /depɛndɑ̃s/ (pl: -s) annex(e)

deplorabel /deploraːbəl/ (adj) deplorable, lamentable

deponeren /deponɛrə(n)/ (deponeerde, heeft gedeponeerd) **1** deposit, place, put (down): *documenten bij de notaris* ~ deposit documents with the notary's **2** file; lodge

deporteren /depɔrtɛrə(n)/ (deporteerde, heeft gedeporteerd) deport; transport: *een gedeporteerde* a deportee (or: transportee) het **deposito** /depozito/ (pl: -'s) deposit

het/de **depot** /depo/ (pl: -s) **1** deposit(ing), committing to safe keeping **2** (goods on) deposit, deposited goods (or: documents) **3** depot, store

deppen /dɛpə(n)/ (depte, heeft gedept) dab; pat (dry)

de **depressie** /deprɛsi/ (pl: -s) depression

depressief /deprɛsif/ (adj) depressed, depressive, low, dejected

depri /depri/ (adj) down, depressed: *zich ~ voelen* feel down (or: depressed)

deprimeren /deprimɛrə(n)/ (deprimeerde, heeft gedeprimeerd) depress, deject; oppress; dishearten

de **deputatie** /depyta(t)si/ (pl: -s) deputation, delegation: [Belg] *bestendige ~* provincial council, executive

der /dɛr/ (art) of (the)

de **derby** /dyrbi/ (pl: derbies) local derby

de ¹**derde** /dɛrdə/ (pl: -n) **1** third party: *in aanwezigheid van ~n* in the presence of a third party **2** third form: *in de ~ zitten* be in the third form

het ²**derde** /dɛrdə/ (pl: -n) third: *twee ~ van de kiezers* two thirds of the voters; *ten ~* thirdly, in the third place

³**derde** /dɛrdə/ (num) third: *de ~ mei* the third of May

derdegraads /dɛrdəɣrats/ (adj) third-rate

derderangs /dɛrdərɑŋs/ (adj) third-rate, third-class

de **derde wereld** /dɛrdəwɛrəlt/ Third World

het **derdewereldland** /dɛrdəwɛrəltlɑnt/ Third World country, developing country

dereguleren /dereɣylɛrə(n)/ (dereguleerde, heeft gedereguleerd) deregulate

deren /dɛrə(n)/ (deerde, heeft gedeerd) hurt, harm, injure

dergelijk /dɛrɣələk/ (dem pron) similar, (the) like, such(like): *en ~e* and the like; *wijn, bier en ~e dranken* wine, beer and drinks of that sort; *iets ~s heb ik nog nooit meegemaakt* I have never experienced anything like it

derhalve /dɛrhɑlvə/ (adv) therefore, so

het **derivaat** /derivat/ (pl: derivaten) derivative

dermate /dɛrmatə/ (adv) so (much), to such an extent, such (that)

de **dermatologie** /dɛrmatoloɣi/ dermatology

de **dermatoloog** /dɛrmatolox/ (pl: -logen) dermatologist

dertien /dɛrtin/ (num) thirteen; [in dates] thirteenth: *~ is een ongeluksgetal* thirteen is an unlucky number; *zo gaan er ~ in een dozijn* they are two a penny

dertiende /dɛrtində/ (num) thirteenth

dertig /dɛrtəx/ (num) thirty; [in dates] thirtieth: *zij is rond de ~* she is thirtyish

dertigste /dɛrtəxstə/ (num) thirtieth

derven /dɛrvə(n)/ (derfde, heeft gederfd) lose, miss

¹**des** /dɛs/ (adv) wherefore, on that (or: which) count ‖ *~ te beter* all the better; *hoe meer mensen er komen, ~ te beter ik me voel* the more people come, the better I feel

²**des** /dɛs/ (art) of (the), (the) …'s: *de heer ~ huizes* the master of the house

desalniettemin /dɛsɑlnitəmɪn/ (adv) nevertheless, nonetheless

desastreus /dezɑstrøs/ (adj, adv) disastrous: *de wedstrijd verliep ~* the match turned into a disaster

desbetreffend /dɛzbətrɛfənt/ (adj) relevant; appropriate; respective: *de ~e afdelingen* the departments concerned (or: in question)

deselecteren /deselɛktərə(n)/ (deselecteerde, heeft gedeselecteerd) deselect

deserteren /dezɛrtərə(n)/ (deserteerde, is gedeserteerd) desert: *uit het leger ~* desert (the army)

de **deserteur** /dezɛrtør/ (pl: -s) deserter

de **desertie** /dezɛr(t)si/ (pl: -s) desertion

desgevraagd /dɛsɣəvraxt/ (adv) if required (or: requested): *~ deelde zij mee* on being asked, she declared

desgewenst /dɛsɣəwɛnst/ (adv) if required (or: desired): *~ wordt het boek u toegestuurd* the book will be sent to you on request

het **design** /dizɑjn/ design; designer: *designjeans* designer jeans

de **desillusie** /dɛsɪlyzi/ (pl: -s) disillusion; disillusionment

desinfecteren /dɛsɪnfɛktərə(n)/ (desinfecteerde, heeft gedesinfecteerd) disinfect

de **desintegratie** /dɛsɪntəɣra(t)si/ disintegration, decomposition

de **desinteresse** /dɛsɪntərɛsə/ lack of interest

deskundig /dɛskyndəx/ (adj, adv) expert (in, at), professional: *een zaak ~ beoordelen* judge a matter expertly; *zij is zeer ~ op het gebied van* she's an authority on

de **deskundige** /dɛskyndəɣə/ (pl: -n) expert (in, at), authority (on), specialist (in)

de **deskundigheid** /dɛskyndəxɦɛit/ expertise, professionalism: *zijn grote ~ op dit gebied* his great expertise in this field

desnoods /dɛsnots/ (adv) if need be, if necessary; in an emergency; at a pinch: *~ gaan we wat eerder weg* we can leave a little earlier if necessary; *werk ~ wat langer door* work a little longer if you have to

desolaat /dezolat/ (adj) desolate

desondanks /dɛsondɑŋks/ (adv) in spite of this, in spite of (all) that, all the same, for all that: *~ protesteerde hij niet* in spite of all that he did not protest

de **desoriëntatie** /dɛsorijɛnta(t)si/ disorientation

desperaat /dɛsperat/ (adj, adv) desperate

de **despoot** /dɛspot/ (pl: despoten) despot, autocrat, tyrant het **dessert** /dɛsɛːr/ (pl: -en) dessert, pudding: *wat wil je als ~?* what would you like for dessert?

het **dessin** /dɛsɛ̃/ (pl: -s) design, pattern

destabiliseren /destabilizerə(n)/ (destabiliseerde, heeft/is gedestabiliseerd) destabilize

destijds /dɛstɛits/ (adv) at the (*or*: that) time, then, in those days: *~ waren er nog geen computers* there were no computers (yet) in those days

de **destructie** /dɛstrʏksi/ (pl: -s) destruction

destructief /dɛstrʏktif/ (adj, adv) destructive

detacheren /detɑʃerə(n)/ (detacheerde, heeft gedetacheerd) **1** second, send on secondment **2** attach (to), second, post (to)

het **detail** /detɑj/ (pl: -s) detail, particular; specifics: *in ~s treden* go into detail(s)

de **detailhandel** /detɑjhɑndəl/ retail trade

de **detaillist** /detɑjɪst/ (pl: -en) retailer

detecteren /detɛktɛrə(n)/ (detecteerde, heeft gedetecteerd) detect, discover

de **detectiepoort** /detɛksipoort/ (pl: -en) security gate, metal detector

de **detective** /ditɛktɪf/ (pl: -s) **1** detective: *particulier ~* private detective (*or*: investigator) **2** detective novel, whodunit

de **detector** /detɛktɔr/ (pl: -s, -en) detector

de **detentie** /detɛnsi/ (pl: -s) detention, arrest, custody

determineren /detɛrminɛrə(n)/ (determineerde, heeft gedetermineerd) **1** determine, establish **2** [biology] identify

detineren /detinɛrə(n)/ (detineerde, heeft gedetineerd) detain: *in Scheveningen gedetineerd zijn* be on remand in Scheveningen (prison)

detoneren /detonɛrə(n)/ (detoneerde, heeft/is gedetoneerd) **1** be out of tune [also fig]: *het gebouw detoneert met de omgeving* the building is out of tune with (*or*: clashes with) its surroundings **2** detonate, explode

het **deuce** /djus/ deuce

de **deugd** /døxt/ (pl: -en) **1** virtuousness, morality **2** virtue, merit

deugdelijk /døxdələk/ (adj) sound, good, reliable

deugdzaam /døxtsam/ (adj, adv) virtuous, good, upright, honest

de **deugdzaamheid** /døxtsamhɛit/ virtuousness, uprightness, honesty

deugen /døɣə(n)/ (deugde, heeft gedeugd) **1** be no good; be good for nothing: *die jongen heeft nooit willen ~* that boy has always been a bad lot **2** be wrong (*or*: unsuitable, unfit): *die man deugt niet voor zijn werk* that man's no good at his job

de **deugniet** /døxnit/ (pl: -en) rascal, scamp, scallywag

de **deuk** /døk/ (pl: -en) **1** dent **2** [fig] blow,

shock: *zijn zelfvertrouwen heeft een flinke ~ gekregen* his self-confidence took a terrible knock **3** fit: *we lagen in een ~* we were in stitches

deuken /døkə(n)/ (deukte, heeft gedeukt) dent; [fig] damage

de **deun** /døn/ (pl: -en) tune

de **deur** /dør/ (pl: -en) door: *voor een gesloten ~ komen* find no one in; *de ~ voor iemands neus dichtdoen (dichtgooien)* shut (*or*: slam) the door in s.o.'s face; *zij komt de ~ niet meer uit* she never goes out any more; *iem. de ~ uitzetten* turn s.o. out of the house; *aan de ~ kloppen* knock at (*or*: on) the door; *vroeger kwam de bakker bij ons aan de ~* the baker used to call at the house; *buiten de ~ eten* eat out; *met de ~en gooien* slam doors; *met de ~ in huis vallen* come straight to the point

de **deurbel** /dørbɛl/ (pl: -len) doorbell

de **deurdranger** /dørdrɑŋər/ (pl: -s) doorspring

de **deurknop** /dørknɔp/ (pl: -pen) doorknob

de **deurmat** /dørmɑt/ (pl: -ten) doormat

de **deuropening** /døropənɪŋ/ (pl: -en) doorway

de **deurpost** /dørpɔst/ (pl: -en) doorpost

de **deurwaarder** /dørwardər/ (pl: -s) process-server, bailiff; usher

de **devaluatie** /devalywa(t)si/ (pl: -s) devaluation

devalueren /devalywɛrə(n)/ (devalueerde, heeft gedevalueerd) devalue: *de yen is 10 % gedevalueerd* the yen has been devalued by 10 %

het **devies** /dəvis/ (pl: deviezen) motto, device

de **deviezen** /dəvizə(n)/ (foreign) exchange

de **¹devoot** /devot/ (pl: devoten) devotee

²devoot /devot/ (adj, adv) devout

de **devotie** /devo(t)si/ (pl: -s) devotion

deze /dezə/ (dem pron) this; these; this one; these (ones): *wil je ~ (hier)?* do you want this one? (*or*: these ones?); *een ~r dagen* one of these days ‖ *bij ~n meld ik u* I herewith inform you

dezelfde /dezɛlvdə/ (dem pron) the same: *van ~ datum* of the same date; *wil je weer ~?* (would you like the) same again?; *op precies ~ dag* on the very same day

dhr. *de heer* Mr

de **dia** /dija/ (pl: -'s) slide, transparency

de **diabetes** /dijabetəs/ diabetes: *~ hebben* have diabetes, be a diabetic

de **diabeticus** /dijabetikʏs/ (pl: diabetici) diabetic

het/de **diadeem** /dijadem/ (pl: diademen) diadem

het **diafragma** /dijafrɑɣma/ (pl: -'s) diaphragm, stop

de **diagnose** /dijɑɣnozə/ (pl: -n, -s) diagnosis

diagnosticeren /dijɑɣnɔstisɛrə(n)/ (diagnosticeerde, heeft gediagnosticeerd) diagnose

de **¹diagonaal** /dijayonal/ diagonal
²diagonaal /dijayonal/ (adj) diagonal
het **diagram** /dijayrŏm/ (pl: -men) diagram, graph, chart
de **diaken** /dijakə(n)/ (pl: -s, -en) deacon
het **dialect** /dijalɛkt/ (pl: -en) dialect
de **dialoog** /dijalox/ (pl: dialogen) dialogue
het **dialoogvenster** /dijaloxfɛnstər/ (pl: -s) dialog box
de **dialyse** /dijalizə/ (pl: -n) dialysis, (haemo)-dialysis
het/de **diamant** /dijamŏnt/ (pl: -en) diamond: ~ *slijpen* polish (or: cut) a diamond
diamanten /dijamŏntə(n)/ (adj) diamond: *een ~ broche* a diamond brooch
de **diameter** /dijametər/ (pl: -s) diameter
diametraal /dijametral/ (adj, adv) diame-tral: [fig] *dat staat er ~ tegenover* that is dia-metrically opposed to it
de **diaprojector** /dijaprojɛktər/ (pl: -s) slide projector
de **diarree** /dijarē/ diarrhoea
de **diaspora** /dijŏspora/ Diaspora
¹dicht /dɪxt/ (adj) **1** closed, shut; drawn; off: *mondje ~* mum's the word; *de afvoer zit ~* the drain is blocked (up) **2** tight **3** close-lipped, tight-lipped, close-(mouthed) **4** close, thick, dense, compact: *een gebied met een ~e be-volking* a densely populated area; *~e mist* thick (or: dense) fog
²dicht /dɪxt/ (adv) close (to), near: *ze zaten ~ opeengepakt* they sat tightly packed to-gether; *hij woont ~ in de buurt* he lives near here
dichtbegroeid /dɪxtbəyrujt/ (adj) thick, dense, thickly wooded
dichtbevolkt /dɪxtbəvolkt/ (adj) densely populated
dichtbij /dɪxtbɛi/ (adv) close by, near by, nearby: *van ~* from close up
dichtbinden /dɪxtbɪndə(n)/ (bond dicht, heeft dichtgebonden) tie up
de **dichtbundel** /dɪxtbʏndəl/ (pl: -s) collection of poems, book of poetry
dichtdoen /dɪxtdun/ (deed dicht, heeft dichtgedaan) close, shut; draw: *geen oog ~* not sleep a wink
dichtdraaien /dɪxtdrajə(n)/ (draaide dicht, heeft dichtgedraaid) turn off; close
dichten /dɪxtə(n)/ (dichtte, heeft gedicht) **1** write poetry, compose verses **2** stop (up), fill (up); seal: *een gat ~* stop a gap; mend a hole
de **dichter** /dɪxtər/ (pl: -s) poet: [Dutch] *~ des vaderlands* [roughly] poet laureate
dichterbij /dɪxtərbɛi/ (adv) nearer, closer
dichterlijk /dɪxtərlək/ (adj, adv) poetic(al): *~e vrijheid* poetic licence
dichtgaan /dɪxtxan/ (ging dicht, is dichtge-gaan) close; shut; heal: *de deur gaat niet dicht* the door won't shut; *op zaterdag gaan de*

winkels vroeg dicht the shops close early on Saturdays
dichtgooien /dɪxtxojə(n)/ (gooide dicht, heeft dichtgegooid) **1** slam (to, shut); bang **2** fill up, fill in
dichtgroeien /dɪxtxrujə(n)/ (groeide dicht, is dichtgegroeid) **1** close; heal (up); grow thick **2** get fat, gain weight
de **dichtheid** /dɪxthɛit/ density; thickness, compactness
dichtklappen /dɪxtklɑpə(n)/ (klapte dicht, heeft/is dichtgeklapt) snap shut, snap to; slam (shut) || *hij klapte volkomen dicht* he clammed up completely
dichtknijpen /dɪxtkneipə(n)/ (kneep dicht, heeft dichtgeknepen) squeeze: *de handen ~* clench one's fingers
dichtknopen /dɪxtknopə(n)/ (knoopte dicht, heeft dichtgeknoopt) button (up), fas-ten
de **dichtkunst** /dɪxtkʏnst/ (art of) poetry
dichtmaken /dɪxtmakə(n)/ (maakte dicht, heeft dichtgemaakt) close, fasten
dichtplakken /dɪxtplɑkə(n)/ (plakte dicht, heeft dichtgeplakt) seal (up); stick down; close; stop
¹dichtslaan /dɪxtslan/ (sloeg dicht, is dicht-geslagen) slam shut, bang shut
²dichtslaan /dɪxtslan/ (sloeg dicht, heeft dichtgeslagen) bang (shut), slam (shut); snap shut: *de deur voor iemands neus ~* slam the door in s.o.'s face
dichtslibben /dɪxtslɪbə(n)/ (slibde dicht, is dichtgeslibd) **1** silt up, become silted up **2** become (or: get) blocked
dichtspijkeren /dɪxtspɛikərə(n)/ (spijkerde dicht, heeft dichtgespijkerd) nail up (or: down), board up
dichtstbijzijnd /dɪxtstbɛizɛint/ (adj) near-est
dichtstoppen /dɪxtstopə(n)/ (stopte dicht, heeft dichtgestopt) stop (up); fill (up); plug (up)
dichttimmeren /dɪxtɪmərə(n)/ (timmerde dicht, heeft dichtgetimmerd) **1** board up **2** [fig]: *een akkoord ~* make a watertight agreement
dichttrekken /dɪxtrɛkə(n)/ (trok dicht, heeft dichtgetrokken) close; draw: *de deur achter zich ~* pull the door to behind one
de **dichtvorm** /dɪxtform/: *in ~* in poetic form, in verse
dichtvouwen /dɪxtfɑuwə(n)/ (vouwde dicht, heeft dichtgevouwen) fold up
dichtvriezen /dɪxtfrizə(n)/ (vroor dicht, is dichtgevroren) freeze (over, up); be frozen (up); be frozen over
dichtzitten /dɪxtsɪtə(n)/ (zat dicht, heeft dichtgezeten) be closed, be blocked (or: locked): *mijn neus zit dicht* my nose is blocked up

het **dictaat** /dɪkt̪a̠t/ (pl: dictaten) **1** (lecture) notes **2** dictation

de **dictator** /dɪkt̪a̠tɔr/ (pl: -s) dictator

dictatoriaal /dɪkt̪atorija̠l/ (adj, adv) dictatorial

de **dictatuur** /dɪkt̪atŷr/ (pl: dictaturen) dictatorship

het **dictee** /dɪkte̠/ (pl: -s) dictation

dicteren /dɪkte̠rə(n)/ (dicteerde, heeft gedicteerd) dictate

de **didacticus** /didɑ̠ktikʏs/ (pl: didactici) didactician

de **didactiek** /didɑktik̠/ didactics

didactisch /didɑ̠ktis/ (adj, adv) didactic

¹die /di/ (dem pron) **1** that; those; that one; those (ones): *heb je ~ nieuwe **film** van Spielberg al gezien?* have you seen this new film by Spielberg?; *~ **grote** of ~ **kleine?*** the big one or the small one?; *niet **deze** maar ~ (daar)* not this one, that one; *mevrouw ~ **en** ~* Mrs so and so, Mrs such and such **2** that; those; that one; those (ones): *mijn **boeken** en ~ van mijn zus* my books and my sister's (*or:* those of my sister); *~ **tijd** is voorbij* those times are over; *~ **van** mij, jou, hem, haar, ons, jullie, hen* mine, yours, his, hers, ours, yours, theirs; *ze draagt altijd **van** ~ korte rokjes* she always wears (those) short skirts; *ken je ~ **van** ~ Belg ~ ...* do you know the one about the Belgian who ...?; *~ is goed* that's a good one; *o, ~!* oh, him! (*or:* her!); *waar is je auto?* ~ *staat in de garage* where's your car? it's in the garage; *~ zit!* bullseye!, touché!

²die /di/ (pron) that; [pers also] who; whom; which: *de **kleren** ~ u besteld heeft* the clothes (that, which) you ordered; *de **man** ~ daar loopt, is mijn vader* the man (that is, who is) walking over there is my father; *de **mensen** ~ ik spreek, zijn heel vriendelijk* the people (who, that) I talk to are very nice; *dezelfde ~ ik heb* the same one (as) I've got; *zijn **vrouw,** ~ arts is, rijdt in een grote Volvo* his wife, who's a doctor, drives a big Volvo

het **dieet** /dije̠t/ (pl: diëten) diet: *op ~ zijn* be on a diet; *een ~ **volgen*** be on a diet

de **dief** /dif/ (pl: dieven) thief, robber; burglar: *houd de ~!* stop thief!

de **diefstal** /di̠fstɑl/ (pl: -len) theft; robbery; burglary

diegene /diɣe̠nə/ (pron) he, she: *~n **die*** those who

dienaangaande /dinaŋɣa̠ndə/ (adv) as to that, with respect (*or:* reference) to that

de **dienaar** /di̠nar/ (pl: dienaren) servant

het **dienblad** /di̠mblɑt/ (pl: -en) (dinner-)tray, (serving) tray

¹dienen /di̠nə(n)/ (diende, heeft gediend) **1** serve: *dat dient nergens **toe*** that is (of) no use **2** serve as, serve for, be used as (*or:* for): *vensters ~ om licht en lucht toe te laten* windows serve the purpose of letting in light

and air **3** need, should, ought to: *u dient onmiddellijk te **vertrekken*** you are to leave immediately **4** [law] come up: *wanneer dient die **zaak** voor de rechtbank?* when does this case come up in court?

²dienen /di̠nə(n)/ (diende, heeft gediend) **1** serve, attend (to), minister **2** serve, help: *dat dient het algemeen **belang*** it is in the public interest ‖ *iem. **van** advies ~* give s.o. advice; *hij was **er** niet **van** gediend* none of that with him, he didn't want that

dienovereenkomstig /dinovəreŋkɔ̠mstəχ/ (adv) accordingly

diens /dins/ (dem pron) his

de **dienst** /dinst/ (pl: -en) **1** service: *zich **in** ~ stellen van* place o.s. in the service of; *ik ben een maand geleden als verkoper **in** ~ getreden bij deze firma* a month ago I joined this company as a salesman; *in ~ **nemen*** take on, engage; *in ~ **zijn*** do one's military service **2** duty: *ik **heb** morgen geen ~* I am off duty tomorrow **3** service, department: *de ~ **open-bare werken*** the public works department **4** service, office: *iem. een goede ~ **bewijzen*** do s.o. a good turn; *je kunt me een ~ **bewijzen*** you can do me a favour **5** place, position: *in **vaste** (or: **tijdelijke**) ~ zijn* hold a permanent (*or:* temporary) appointment; *iem. **in** ~ hebben* employ s.o.; *in ~ zijn bij iem.* be in s.o.'s service ‖ *de ~ **uitmaken*** run the show, call the shots; *tot uw ~* you're welcome; *iem. **van** ~ zijn met* be of service to s.o. with

de **dienstapotheek** /di̠nstapotek/ (pl: -apotheken) pharmacy on duty, out of hours pharmacy

de **dienstauto** /di̠nstɑuto/ (pl: -'s) official car; company car

dienstbaar /di̠nstbar/ (adj) helpful: *zich ~ **opstellen*** be of service

de **dienstbode** /di̠nstbodə/ (pl: -n, -s) servant (girl), maid(servant)

dienstdoen /di̠nsdun/ (deed dienst, heeft dienstgedaan) serve (as/for), be used (as/for)

dienstdoend /di̠nzdunt/ (adj) on duty; in charge; acting

het **dienstencentrum** /di̠nstə(n)sɛntrʏm/ (pl: -centra) social service centre

de **dienstencheque** /di̠nstə(n)ʃɛk/ (pl: -s) [Belg] service voucher

de **dienstensector** /di̠nstə(n)sɛktɔr/ services sector, service industries

het **dienstjaar** /di̠nstjar/ (pl: -jaren) year of service; seniority

de **dienstlift** /di̠nstlɪft/ (pl: -en) service lift

de **dienstmededeling** /di̠nstmedədelɪŋ/ (pl: -en) staff announcement

het **dienstmeisje** /di̠nstmɛiʃə/ maid(servant), housemaid

de **dienstorder** /di̠nstɔrdər/ (pl: -s) (official) order, instructions

het **dienstpistool** /di̠nstpistol/ (pl: -pistolen)

diesel

duty weapon

de **dienstplicht** /dịnstplɪχt/ (compulsory) military service, conscription: *vervangende* ~ alternative national service; community service

dienstplichtig /dinstplɪχtəχ/ (adj) eligible for military service: *de ~e leeftijd bereiken* become of military age; *niet* ~ exempt from military service

de **dienstplichtige** /dịnstplɪχtəχə/ conscript

de **dienstregeling** /dịnstreχəlɪŋ/ (pl: -en) timetable: *een vlucht met vaste* ~ a scheduled flight

de **diensttijd** /dịnstɛit/ (period, length of) service, term of office: *buiten* (or: *onder*) ~ when off (or: on) duty

het **dienstverband** /dịnstfərbɑnt/ employment: *in los* (or: *vast*) ~ *werken* be employed on a temporary (or: permanent) basis

de **dienstverlening** /dịnstfərlenɪŋ/ service(s)

de **dienstweigeraar** /dịnstwɛiχərɑr/ (pl: -s) conscientious objector

dientengevolge /dintɛnχəvɔ̣lχə/ (adv) consequently, as a consequence

¹**diep** /dip/ (adj) deep; [fig also] profound; total, impenetrable: *twee meter* ~ two metres deep; *~er maken* deepen; *in het ~e gegooid worden* be thrown in at the deep end; *een ~e duisternis* utter darkness; *in* ~ *gepeins verzonken* (sunk) deep in thought; *alles was in ~e rust* everything was utterly peaceful; *een ~e slaap* a deep sleep; *in zijn hart* deep (down) in one's heart; *uit het ~ste van zijn hart* from the bottom of one's heart ‖ *een ~e stem* a deep voice; ~ *blauw* deep blue

²**diep** /dip/ (adv) deep(ly), low: ~ *zinken (vallen)* sink low; ~ *ongelukkig zijn* be deeply unhappy; *hij is* ~ *verontwaardigd* he is deeply (or: mortally) indignant; ~ *ademhalen* breathe deeply; take a deep breath; ~ *nadenken* think hard; *de haat zit* ~ the hatred runs deep

diepgaand /dịpχɑnt/ (adj, adv) profound, searching, in-depth: *~e discussie* in-depth (or: deep) discussion

de **diepgang** /dịpχɑŋ/ **1** draught **2** depth, profundity

de **dieplink** /dịplɪŋk/ (pl: -s) deep link

dieplinken /dịplɪŋkə(n)/ deep-link

de **diepte** /dịptə/ (pl: -n, -s) **1** depth, depth(s), profundity **2** trough, hollow

het **diepte-interview** /dịptəɪntərvju:/ (pl: -s) in-depth interview

het **dieptepunt** /dịptəpʏnt/ (pl: -en) **1** (absolute) low **2** all-time low, rock bottom: *een* ~ *in een relatie* a low point in a relationship

de **diepvries** /dịpfris/ deep-freeze, freezer

de **diepvrieskist** /dịpfriskɪst/ (pl: -en) (chest-type) freezer, deep-freeze

de **diepvriesmaaltijd** /dịpfrismɑltɛit/ (pl: -en) freezer meal; [Am] TV dinner

de **diepvriezen** /dịpfrizə(n)/ (vroor diep, heeft diepgevroren) (deep-)freeze

de **diepvriezer** /dịpfrizər/ (pl: -s) deepfreeze, freezer

diepzeeduiken /dipsẹdœykə(n)/ deep-sea diving

diepzinnig /dipsɪnəχ/ (adj, adv) **1** profound, discerning **2** profound, pensive: *een ~e blik* a thoughtful (or: pensive) look

de **diepzinnigheid** /dipsɪnəχhɛit/ profundity, profoundness, depth

het **dier** /dir/ (pl: -en) animal, creature; beast

dierbaar /dịrbar/ (adj) dear, much-loved, beloved: *mijn dierbaren* my loved ones

de **dierenambulance** /dịrə(n)ɑmbylɑ̃sə/ (pl: -s) animal ambulance

de **dierenarts** /dịrə(n)ɑrts/ (pl: -en) veterinary surgeon, vet

het **dierenasiel** /dịrə(n)azil/ (pl: -en) animal home (or: shelter)

de **dierenbescherming** /dịrə(n)bəsχɛrmɪŋ/ animal protection, prevention of cruelty to animals

de **dierenbeul** /dịrə(n)bøl/ (pl: -en) s.o. who is cruel to animals

de **dierendag** /dịrə(n)dɑχ/ [roughly] animal day, pets' day

het **dierenleed** /dịrə(n)let/ animal suffering

de **dierenmishandeling** /dịrə(n)mɪshɑndəlɪŋ/ cruelty to animals, maltreatment of animals

het **dierenpension** /dịrə(n)pɛnʃɔn/ (pl: -s) (boarding) kennel(s)

de **dierenrechten** /dịrə(n)rɛχtə(n)/ (pl) animal rights

de **dierenriem** /dịrə(n)rim/ zodiac

het **dierenrijk** /dịrə(n)rɛik/ animal kingdom (or: world)

de **dierentemmer** /dịrə(n)tɛmər/ (pl: -s) animal trainer; lion-tamer

de **dierentuin** /dịrə(n)tœyn/ (pl: -en) zoo, animal park

de **dierenvriend** /dịrə(n)vrint/ (pl: -en) animal (or: pet) lover

het **dierenwelzijn** /dịrə(n)wɛlzɛin/ animal welfare

de **dierenwinkel** /dịrə(n)wɪŋkəl/ (pl: -s) pet shop

de **diergeneeskunde** /dịrχəneskʏndə/ veterinary medicine

dierlijk /dịrlək/ (adj) animal; [depr] bestial; brute; brutish: *de ~e aard (natuur)* animal nature

de **dierproef** /dịrpruf/ (pl: -proeven) animal experiment (or: test)

de **diersoort** /dịrsort/ (pl: -en) animal species: *bedreigde ~en* endangered species (of animals)

diervriendelijk /dirvrịndələk/ (adj) animal-friendly

de **diesel** /dịzəl/ (pl: -s, -s) diesel (oil, fuel), derv:

op ~ rijden take diesel

de **dieselmotor** /dizəlmotər/ (pl: -en) diesel engine

de **dieselolie** /dizəloli/ diesel oil (*or:* fuel)

de **diëtist** /dijetɪst/ (pl: -en) dietitian

de **dievegge** /divɛɣə/ (pl: -s) thief; shoplifter

de **dievenklauw** /divə(n)klɑu/ (pl: -en) security lock

het **dievenpoortje** /divə(n)porcə/ (pl: -s) security label detector, anti-shoplifting alarm

diezelfde /dizɛlvdə/ (dem pron) the same, this same, that same: *ik heb hem nog ~ dag gezien* I saw him that very (*or:* same) day

de **differentiaal** /dɪfərɛnʃal/ (pl: differentialen) differential

de **differentiaalrekening** /dɪfərɛn(t)ʃalrekənɪŋ/ differential calculus

de **differentiatie** /dɪfərɛn(t)ʃa(t)si/ (pl: -s) differentiation

het **differentieel** /dɪfərɛn(t)ʃel/ differential (gear)

differentiëren /dɪfərɛnʃerə(n)/ (differentieerde, heeft gedifferentieerd) differentiate (between), distinguish (between)

de **diffusie** /dɪfyzi/ diffusion, mixture

diffuus /dɪfys/ (adj) diffuse; scattered

de **difterie** /dɪftəri/ diphtheria

de **diggelen** /dɪɣələ(n)/ (pl): *aan ~ slaan* smash to smithereens

de **digibeet** /diɣibet/ (pl: digibeten) computer illiterate

het **digibord** /diɣibort/ (pl: -en) interactive whiteboard

de **digicode** /diɣikodə/ (pl: -s) digicode, digital code

digitaal /diɣital/ (adj, adv) digital

digitaliseren /diɣitalizerə(n)/ (digitaliseerde, heeft gedigitaliseerd) digit(al)ize

de **dij** /dɛi/ (pl: -en) thigh; ham

het **dijbeen** /dɛiben/ (pl: dijbenen) thigh bone

de **dijk** /dɛik/ (pl: -en) bank, embankment; [in the Netherlands] dike: *een ~ (aan)leggen* throw up a bank (*or:* an embankment) || *iem. aan de ~ zetten* sack s.o., lay s.o. off

de **dijkdoorbraak** /dɛɪgdorbrak/ (pl: -braken) bursting of a dike, giving way of a dike

¹**dik** /dɪk/ (adj) **1** thick: *10 cm ~* 10 cm thick; *de ~ke darm* the large intestine; *een ~ke honderd euro* a good hundred euros; *ze stonden tien rijen ~* they stood ten (rows) deep; *~ worden* thicken, set, congeal **2** thick, fat, bulky: *een ~ke buik* a paunch **3** fat, stout, corpulent: *een ~ke man* a fat man **4** swollen: *~ke vingers* plump fingers **5** thick, close, great: *~ke vrienden zijn* be great (*or:* close) friends || *~ doen* swank, swagger, boast

²**dik** /dɪk/ (adv) **1** thick, ample, good: *~ tevreden (zijn)* (be) well-satisfied; *~ onder het stof* thick with dust; *het er ~ bovenop leggen* lay it on thick; *dat zit er ~ in* that's quite on the cards **2** thick, heavy, dense || *door ~ en*

dun gaan go through thick and thin

de **dikdoenerij** /dɪgdunərɛi/ bragging, boasting

dikhuidig /dɪkhœydəɣ/ (adj) pachyderm(at)ous, thick-skinned

de **dikkerd** /dɪkərt/ (pl: -s) fatty, piggy: *dat is een gezellige ~* he/she is round (*or:* fat) and cuddly

de **dikkop** /dɪkɔp/ (pl: -pen) tadpole

de **dikmaker** /dɪkmakər/ (pl: -s) fattening food/drink

de **dikte** /dɪktə/ (pl: -s) **1** fatness, thickness **2** thickness; gauge: *een ~ van vier voet* four feet thick **3** thickness, density

dikwijls /dɪkwəls/ (adv) often, frequently

de **dikzak** /dɪksɑk/ (pl: -ken) fatty, fatso

het **dilemma** /dilɛma/ (pl: -'s) dilemma

de **dilettant** /dilɛtɑnt/ (pl: -en) dilettante, amateur

de **dille** /dɪlə/ (pl: -n) dill

de **dimensie** /dimɛnsi/ (pl: -s) **1** dimension, measurement, meaning **2** dimension, perspective

het **dimlicht** /dɪmlɪxt/ (pl: -en) dipped headlights

¹**dimmen** /dɪmə(n)/ (dimde, heeft gedimd) cool it: *effe ~, da's niet leuk meer* cool it, it's not funny any more

²**dimmen** /dɪmə(n)/ (dimde, heeft gedimd) dip (the headlights), shade

de **dimmer** /dɪmər/ (pl: -s) dimmer(-switch)

de **dimsum** /dɪmsʊm/ (pl: -) dimsum

het **diner** /dine/ (pl: -s) dinner: *aan het ~* at dinner

dineren /dinerə(n)/ (dineerde, heeft gedineerd) dine, have dinner

het **ding** /dɪŋ/ (pl: -en) **1** thing, object; gadget: *en (al) dat soort ~en* and (all) that sort of thing **2** thing, matter, affair: *doe geen gekke ~en* don't do anything foolish; *de ~en bij hun naam noemen* call a spade a spade || *dat is echt een ~* it's a really big thing; [inform] *een lekker ~* a nice (*or:* sweet) little thing; [inform] *dat is niet mijn ~* that's not my thing, that's not my cup of tea; *dat is best een ~etje aan het worden* that is becoming quite an issue

dingen /dɪŋə(n)/ (dong, heeft gedongen) compete (for), strive (after/for)

de **dinges** /dɪŋəs/ [inform] thingummy, what's-his-name, what's-her-name

de **dinosaurus** /dinosɑurʏs/ (pl: -sen) dinosaur

de **dinsdag** /dɪnzdɑx/ (pl: -en) Tuesday: [Belg] *vette ~* Shrove Tuesday

dinsdags /dɪnzdɑxs/ (adj) Tuesday

de **diode** /dijodə/ (pl: -n, -s) diode

het **dioxine** /dijoksinə/ dioxin

de **dip** /dɪp/ (pl: -s) dip: *in een ~ zitten* be going through a bad patch

het **diploma** /diploma/ (pl: -'s) diploma, certificate: *een ~ behalen* qualify, graduate

de **diplomaat** /diplomat/ (pl: diplomaten) di-

plomat
het **diplomatenkoffertje** /diplomatə(n)-
kofərcə/ (pl: -s) attaché case
de **diplomatie** /diploma(t)si/ **1** diplomacy
2 diplomatic corps, diplomats: *hij gaat in de ~*
he is going to enter the diplomatic service
diplomatiek /diplomatik/ (adj, adv) **1** diplomatic: *langs ~e weg* by diplomacy **2** diplomatic, tactful
diplomeren /diplomerə(n)/ (diplomeerde,
heeft gediplomeerd) certificate: *niet gediplo-*
meerd unqualified, untrained
dippen /dɪpə(n)/ (dipte, heeft gedipt) **1** dip
2 dip, insert
de **dipsaus** /dɪpsɑus/ (pl: -sauzen) dip
¹**direct** /dirɛkt/ (adj) **1** direct, immediate,
straight: *zijn ~e chef* his immediate superior;
de ~e oorzaak the immediate cause; *~e uit-*
zending live broadcast **2** prompt, immediate: *~e levering* prompt delivery
²**direct** /dirɛkt/ (adv) **1** direct(ly), at once:
kom ~ come at once (*or:* straightaway); *per ~*
straightaway; [Am] right now **2** presently,
directly: *ik ben ~ klaar* I'll be ready in a minute ‖ *niet ~ vriendelijk* not exactly kind
de **directeur** /dirɛktør/ (pl: -en, -s) manager;
(managing) director; principal; headmaster;
superintendent; governor
de **directeur-grootaandeelhouder** /dirɛk-
tørɣrotɑndelhɑudər/ (pl: directeuren-groot-
aandeelhouders) director and majority
shareholder
de **directie** /dirɛksi/ (pl: -s) management
het **directielid** /dirɛksilɪt/ (pl: -leden) member of the board
(of directors)
de **directiesecretaresse** /dirɛksisɪkrətarɛsə/
(pl: -s) executive secretary
de **directory** /dɑjrɛktəri/ (pl: -'s) [comp] directory
de **directrice** /dirɛktrisə/ (pl: -s) *see directeur*
de **dirigeerstok** /diriɣerstok/ (pl: -ken) baton
de **dirigent** /diriɣɛnt/ (pl: -en) conductor;
choirmaster
dirigeren /diriɣerə(n)/ (dirigeerde, heeft
gedirigeerd) conduct; control
de **dis** /dɪs/ (pl: -sen) [form] table
de **discipel** /disipəl/ (pl: -en) disciple, follower
disciplinair /disiplinɛːr/ (adj, adv) disciplinary: *een ~e maatregel* a disciplinary measure
de **discipline** /disiplinə/ discipline
disciplineren /disiplinerə(n)/ (disciplineer-
de, heeft gedisciplineerd) discipline, train: *hij*
werkt zeer gedisciplineerd aan zijn nieuwe ro-
man he applies himself to his new novel with
strict self-discipline
de **discman** /dɪskmɛːn/ (pl: -s) discman
de **disco** /dɪsko/ (pl: -'s) disco
het **disconto** /dɪskɔnto/ (pl: -'s) discount
de **discotheek** /dɪskotek/ (pl: discotheken)
1 record library (*or:* collection) **2** record li-

brary **3** discotheque
discreet /dɪskret/ (adj, adv) **1** discreet, delicate, tactful **2** discreet, unobtrusive: *een ~*
tikje op de kamerdeur a discreet tap on the
door **3** delicate, secret
de **discrepantie** /dɪskrepɑnsi/ discrepancy
de **discretie** /dɪskreti/ **1** discretion, tact **2** discretion, secrecy
de **discriminatie** /dɪskriminа(t)si/ discrimination
discrimineren /dɪskriminerə(n)/ (discrimi-
neerde, heeft gediscrimineerd) discriminate
(against); [with direct object] segregate
de **discus** /dɪskʏs/ (pl: -sen) discus, disc
de **discussie** /dɪskʏsi/ (pl: -s) discussion, debate: *(het) onderwerp van ~ (zijn)* (be) under
discussion; *een hevige (verhitte) ~* a heated
discussion; *ter ~ staan* be under discussion, be
open to discussion; *iets ter ~ stellen* a) bring
sth. up for discussion; b) call sth. into question
discussiëren /dɪskʏʃerə(n)/ (discussieerde,
heeft gediscussieerd) discuss, debate, argue
discuswerpen /dɪskʏswɛrpə(n)/ discus
throwing
discutabel /dɪskytabəl/ (adj) debatable,
dubious, disputable
de **disk** /dɪsk/ (pl: -s) disk
de **diskdrive** /dɪsgdrɑjf/ (pl: -s) disk drive
de **diskette** /dɪskɛtə/ (pl: -s) diskette, floppy
(disk)
de **diskjockey** /dɪskdʒoki/ (pl: -s) disc jockey
het **diskrediet** /dɪskrədit/ discredit: *in ~ raken*
fall into discredit
diskwalificeren /dɪskwalifiserə(n)/ (dis-
kwalificeerde, heeft gediskwalificeerd) disqualify
de **dispensatie** /dɪspɛnsa(t)si/ (pl: -s) dispensa-
tion, exemption: *~ verlenen (van)* grant dis-
pensation (*or:* exemption) (from)
de **display** /dɪsplɛj/ (pl: -s) display
het **dispuut** /dɪspyt/ (pl: disputen) debating society
de **disruptie** /dɪsrʏpsi/ (pl: -s) disruption
disruptief /dɪsrʏptif/ (adj) disruptive: *dis-*
ruptieve innovaties disruptive innovations
dissen /dɪsə(n)/ (diste, heeft gedist) insult,
diss
de **dissertatie** /dɪsɛrta(t)si/ (pl: -s) (doctoral)
dissertation, (doctoral) thesis
de ¹**dissident** /dɪsidɛnt/ (pl: -en) dissident
²**dissident** /dɪsidɛnt/ (adj) dissident
de **dissonant** /dɪsonɑnt/ (pl: -en) dissonance,
discord: [fig] *er was geen ~ te horen* not a
note of discord was heard
zich **distantiëren** /dɪstɑnʃerə(n)/ (distantieerde
zich, heeft zich gedistantieerd) distance, dissociate
de **distel** /dɪstəl/ (pl: -s) thistle
de **distillatie** /dɪstila(t)si/ (pl: -s) distillation
distilleren /dɪstilerə(n)/ (distilleerde, heeft

gedistilleerd) **1** distil **2** deduce, infer: *iets uit iemands woorden* ~ deduce sth. from what s.o. says

distribueren /dɪstribywe̯rə(n)/ (distribueerde, heeft gedistribueerd) distribute, dispense, hand out

de **distributieketen** /dɪstriby̱(t)sike̯tə(n)/ (pl: -s) distribution chain

het **district** /dɪstrɪ̱kt/ (pl: -en) district, county

dit /dɪt/ (dem pron) this; these: *in* ~ *geval* in this case; *wat zijn* ~*?* what are these?

ditmaal /dɪ̱tmal/ (adv) this time, for once

de **diva** /di̱va/ (pl: -'s) diva

het **divagedrag** /di̱vayədraχ/ diva behaviour

Divali /diva̱li/ Diwali

de **divan** /di̱vɑn/ (pl: -s) divan, couch

divers /di̱vɛrs/ (adj) **1** diverse, various: *een* ~*e samenleving* a diverse society **2** various, several: ~*e keren* several times

de **diversen** /di̱vɛrsə(n)/ (pl) sundries, miscellaneous

de **diversiteit** /divɛrsite̱it/ diversity, variety

het **dividend** /dividɛ̱nt/ (pl: -en) dividend

de **divisie** /divi̱zi/ (pl: -s) division; league; class

dizzy /dɪ̱zi/ (adj) dizzy: *ik word* ~ *van die stortvloed aan informatie* there's such a torrent of information it makes me dizzy

de **dj** /di̱:dʒe/ (pl: dj's) *diskjockey* DJ

de **djellaba** /dʒɛla̱ba/ (pl: -'s) djellaba

de **djembé** /dʒɛ̱mbe/ djembe

Djibouti /djibu̱ti/ Djibouti

de **Djiboutiaan** /djibucɑ̱n/ (pl: Djiboutianen) Djiboutian

Djiboutiaans /djibucɑ̱ns/ (adj) Djiboutian

dm *decimeter* dm

d.m.v. *door middel van* by means of

het **DNA** /deɛ̱na/ DNA: *ondernemen zit in zijn* ~ business is in his genes, he's a born entrepreneur

het **DNA-onderzoek** /deɛna̱ondərzuk/ DNA-test

de **DNA-spray** /deɛ̱naspre/ (pl: -s) DNA spray

de **do** /do/ (pl: do's) do(h)

dobbelen /dɔ̱bələ(n)/ (dobbelde, heeft gedobbeld) dice, play (at) dice

het **dobbelspel** /dɔ̱bəlspɛl/ (pl: -len) dicing, game of dice

de **dobbelsteen** /dɔ̱bəlsten/ (pl: -stenen) **1** dice: *met dobbelstenen gooien* throw the dice **2** dice, cube

de **dobber** /dɔ̱bər/ (pl: -s) float ‖ *hij had er een zware* ~ *aan* he found it a tough job

dobberen /dɔ̱bərə(n)/ (dobberde, heeft gedobberd) float, bob: *op het water* ~ bob up and down on the water

de **dobermannpincher** /do̱bərmɑnpɪnʃər/ (pl: -s) Doberman(n) (pinscher)

de **docent** /dosɛ̱nt/ (pl: -en) teacher, instructor: ~ *aan de universiteit* university lecturer

de **docentenkamer** /dosɛ̱ntə(n)kamər/ (pl: -s) staffroom

de **doceren** /dose̱rə(n)/ (doceerde, heeft gedoceerd) teach; lecture

doch /dɔχ/ (conj) yet, but: *hij had haar gewaarschuwd,* ~ *zij wilde niet luisteren* he had warned her, yet (*or:* but, still) she wouldn't listen

de **dochter** /dɔ̱χtər/ (pl: -s) daughter, (little) girl

de **dochtermaatschappij** /dɔ̱χtərmatsχɑpɛi/ (pl: -en) subsidiary (company)

de **doctor** /dɔ̱ktor/ (pl: -en, -s) doctor

het **¹doctoraal** /dɔktora̱l/ [Dutch] Master's (degree (*or:* exam)); [roughly] MA, MSc: *zijn* ~ *doen* do one's MA/MSc/Master's

²doctoraal /dɔktora̱l/ (adj) [Dutch] [roughly] Master's, (post)graduate

het **doctoraat** /dɔktora̱t/ (pl: doctoraten) doctorate

de **doctorandus** /dɔktorɑ̱ndʏs/ (pl: -sen, doctorandi) [Dutch] (title of) university graduate

de **doctrine** /dɔktri̱nə/ (pl: -s) doctrine, dogma

het **document** /dokymɛ̱nt/ (pl: -en) document, paper

documentair /dokymɛntɛ̱ːr/ (adj) documentary

de **documentaire** /dokymɛntɛ̱rə/ (pl: -s) documentary

de **documentatie** /dokymɛnta̱(t)si/ documentation

documenteren /dokymɛnte̱rə(n)/ (documenteerde, heeft gedocumenteerd) document, support with evidence

de **dode** /do̱də/ (pl: -n) dead person, the deceased

de **dodehoekspiegel** /dodəhu̱kspiɣəl/ (pl: -s) blind spot mirror

dodelijk /do̱dələk/ (adj, adv) **1** deadly, mortal, lethal, fatal: *een* ~ *ongeluk, een ongeval met* ~*e afloop* a fatal accident; *een* ~*e dosis* a lethal dose; *een* ~ *gif* a deadly poison; *een* ~ *slachtoffer* a fatality, a casualty **2** dead(ly), mortal: ~ *geschrokken* frightened to death; ~ *vermoeid* dead beat, dead tired

doden /do̱də(n)/ (doodde, heeft gedood) kill, murder, slay: *de tijd* ~ kill time

de **dodencel** /do̱də(n)sɛl/ (pl: -len) death cell (*or:* row)

de **dodenherdenking** /do̱də(n)hɛrdɛŋkɪŋ/ (pl: -en) commemoration of the dead

het **dodental** /do̱də(n)tɑl/ (pl: -len) number of deaths (*or:* casualties), death toll

de **doedelzak** /du̱dəlzɑk/ (pl: -ken) bagpipes: *op een* ~ *spelen* play the bagpipes

de **doe-het-zelfzaak** /duətsɛ̱lfsak/ (pl: -zaken) do-it-yourself shop, DIY shop

de **doe-het-zelver** /duətsɛ̱lvər/ (pl: -s) do-it-yourselfer, DIY

doei /duj/ (int) [Dutch; inform] bye(-bye), cheerio, cheers: *dikke* ~ bye, catch ya later, see ya

het/de **doek** /duk/ **1** cloth, fabric **2** screen: *het witte*

~ the silver screen **3** canvas, painting **4** curtain; backcloth: *het ~ gaat op* the curtain rises || *iets uit de ~en doen* disclose sth.

het **doekje** /dʊkjə/ (pl: -s) (piece of) cloth; tissue

het **doel** /dul/ (pl: -en) **1** target, purpose, object(ive), aim, goal; destination: *zijn ~ bereiken* achieve one's aim; *ten ~ hebben* aim at, be intended to; *goede ~en* charity, charities; *iets schenken aan een goed ~* make a charitable donation **2** goal; net: *in eigen ~ schieten* score an own goal || *het ~ heiligt de middelen (niet)* the end justifies (*or:* does not justify) the means

doelbewust /dulbəwʏst/ (adj, adv) determined, resolute

het **doeleinde** /dulɛində/ (pl: -n) **1** purpose, aim, design **2** end, aim, purpose, destination: *voor eigen* (*or: privé*) *~n* for one's own (*or:* private) ends

doelen /dulə(n)/ (doelde, heeft gedoeld) aim (at), refer (to), mean: *waar ik op doel is dit* what I mean (*or:* am referring to, am driving at) is this

het **doelgebied** /dulɣəbit/ (pl: -en) goal area

doelgericht /dulɣərɪxt/ (adj, adv) purposeful, purposive

de **doelgroep** /dulɣrup/ (pl: -en) target group (*or:* audience)

de **doellijn** /dulɛɪn/ (pl: -en) goal line: *de bal van de ~ halen* kick the ball from the line, (make a) save on the line

doelloos /dulos/ (adj, adv) aimless, idle; pointless

de **doelman** /dulmɑn/ (pl: -nen) goalkeeper

doelmatig /dulmatəx/ (adj, adv) suitable, appropriate, functional, effective

de **doelmatigheid** /dulmatəxhɛit/ suitability, expediency, effectiveness

de **doelpaal** /dulpal/ (pl: -palen) (goal)post

het **doelpunt** /dulpʏnt/ (pl: -en) goal, score: *een ~ afkeuren* disallow a goal; *een ~ maken* kick (*or:* score) a goal; *met twee ~en verschil verliezen* lose by two goals

het **doelsaldo** /dulsɑldo/ (pl: -'s, -saldi) goal difference

de **doelstelling** /dulstɛlɪŋ/ (pl: -en) aim, object(ive)

de **doeltrap** /dultrɑp/ (pl: -pen) goal kick

doeltreffend /dultrɛfənt/ (adj, adv) effective, efficient

de **doelverdediger** /dulvərdedəɣər/ (pl: -s) (goal)keeper; [Am] (goal)tender; goalie

het **doelwit** /dulwɪt/ (pl: -ten) target, aim, object: *een dankbaar ~ vormen* make an easy victim (*or:* target)

de **doem** /dum/ doom

de **Doema** /duma/ duma

doemdenken /dumdɛŋkə(n)/ doom-mongering, defeatism

doemen /dumə(n)/ doom, destine

het **doemscenario** /dumsənarijo/ worst-case scenario

¹**doen** /dun/ (deed, heeft gedaan) **1** do, act, behave: *gewichtig ~* act important; *~ alsof* pretend; *je doet maar* go ahead, suit yourself **2** do, be: *ik doe er twee uur over* it takes me two hours; *aan sport ~* do sport(s), take part in sport(s) || *dat is geen manier van ~* that's no way to behave

²**doen** /dun/ (deed, heeft gedaan) **1** do, make, take: *een oproep ~* make an appeal; *uitspraak ~* pass judgement; *doe mij maar een witte wijn* for me a white wine, I'll have a white wine; *wat kom jij ~?* what do you want?; *helemaal niets ~* do nothing at all; *wat doet hij (voor de kost)?* what does he do (for a living)? **2** put: *iets in zijn zak ~* put sth. in one's pocket **3** make, do: *dat doet me plezier* I'm glad about that; *iem. verdriet* (*or: pijn*) *~* hurt s.o., cause s.o. grief (*or:* pain) **4** (+ het) work: *de remmen ~ het niet* the brakes don't work || *dat doet er niet toe* that's beside the point; *anders krijg je met mij te ~* or else you'll have me to deal with; *het ~ en laten* all one's actions, one's every movement; *we weten wat ons te ~ staat* we know what (we have, are) to do; *niets aan te ~* can't be helped; [inform] *niets* (or: *niks*) *meer aan ~* it's just right as it is

het **doetje** /ducə/ (pl: -s) softy, milksop, wet

de **doevakantie** /duvakan(t)si/ (pl: -s) action holiday; [Am] action vacation

dof /dof/ (adj, adv) **1** dim, dull; mat(t); tarnished: *~fe tinten* dull (*or:* muted) hues (*or:* tints)? **2** dull, muffled: *een ~fe knal (dreun)* a muffled boom

de **doffer** /dofər/ (pl: -s) cock-pigeon

de **dofheid** /dofhɛit/ dullness, dimness

de **dog** /dox/ (pl: -gen) mastiff

het **dogma** /doɣma/ (pl: -'s) dogma

dogmatisch /doxmatis/ (adj, adv) dogmatic(al)

het **dok** /dok/ (pl: -ken) dock(yard)

de **doka** /doka/ (pl: -'s) darkroom

dokken /dokə(n)/ (dokte, heeft gedokt) [inform] fork out, cough up

de **dokter** /doktər/ (pl: -s, doktoren) doctor; GP: *een ~ roepen* (or: *laten komen*) send for (*or:* call in) a doctor || *~tje spelen* play doctors and nurses

dokteren /doktərə(n)/ (dokterde, heeft gedokterd) **1** practise **2** tinker (with (*or:* at)): *aan iets ~* tinker with sth.

het **doktersadvies** /doktərsatfis/ (pl: -adviezen) doctor's advice, medical advice

de **doktersassistente** /doktərsasistɛntə/ (medical) receptionist

het **doktersattest** /doktərsatɛst/ (pl: -en) medical (*or:* doctor's) certificate

de **doktersbehandeling** /doktərzbəhandəlɪŋ/: *onder ~ zijn* be under medical treatment

het **doktersvoorschrift** /dɔktərsforsχrɪft/ medical instructions, doctor's orders

dol /dɔl/ (adj) **1** mad, crazy: *het is om ~ van te worden* it is enough to drive you crazy; *~ op iets (iem.) zijn* be crazy about sth. (s.o.) **2** mad, wild, crazy: *door het ~le heen zijn* be beside o.s. with excitement (*or:* joy) **3** foolish, silly, daft: *~le pret hebben* have great fun **4** worn, slipping, stripped: *die schroef is ~* the screw is stripped (*or:* slipping) **5** crazy, whirling (round in circles): *het kompas is ~* the compass has gone crazy **6** mad, rabid

dolblij /dɔlblɛi/ (adj) overjoyed (about): *~ zijn met iets* be over the moon about sth.

doldwaas /dɔldwas/ (adj) nutty, potty, absolutely crazy: *doldwaze verwikkelingen* hilarious twists and turns, a crazy mix-up

dolen /dolə(n)/ (doolde, heeft/is gedoold) wander (about), roam

de **dolfijn** /dɔlfɛin/ (pl: -en) dolphin

het **dolfinarium** /dɔlfinarijʏm/ (pl: -s, dolfinaria) dolphinarium

dolgraag /dɔlɣraχ/ (adv) with the greatest of pleasure: *ga je mee? ~ are you coming?* I'd love to

de **dolk** /dɔlk/ (pl: -en) dagger

de **dolksteek** /dɔlkstek/ (pl: -steken) daggerthrust, stab

de **dollar** /dɔlar/ (pl: -s) dollar

het **dollarteken** /dɔlartekə(n)/ (pl: -s) dollar sign || *~s in de ogen hebben* see a lot of dollar signs in front of s.o.'s eyes; [British] have a pound sign for a brain

de **dolleman** /dɔləman/ (pl: -nen) madman, lunatic

dollen /dɔlə(n)/ (dolde, heeft gedold) lark about, horse around

de **¹dom** /dɔm/ (pl: -men) cathedral

²dom /dɔm/ (adj, adv) **1** stupid, simple, dumb: *zo ~ als het achtereind van een varken* as thick as two (short) planks **2** silly, daft: *sta niet zo ~ te grijnzen!* wipe that silly grin off your face! **3** sheer, pure: *~ geluk* sheer luck, a fluke **4** ignorant: *zich van de ~me houden* play ignorant, play (the) innocent

de **dombo** /dɔmbo/ (pl: -'s) [Dutch; inform] dumbo

het **domein** /dɔmɛin/ (pl: -en) domain, territory

de **domeinnaam** /dɔmɛinam/ domain name

de **domheid** /dɔmhɛit/ (pl: -heden) stupidity, idiocy

het **domicilie** /domisili/ domicile: *~ kiezen ten kantore van* elect domicile at the office of

dominant /dominɑnt/ (adj) dominant, overriding

de **dominee** /domine/ (pl: -s) minister

domineren /dominerə(n)/ (domineerde, heeft gedomineerd) dominate

Dominica /dominika/ Dominica

de **Dominicaan** /dominikan/ (pl: Dominicanen) Dominican

Dominicaans /dominikans/ (adj) Dominican || *de ~e Republiek* the Dominican Republic

de **Dominicaanse Republiek** /dominikansərepyblik/ Dominican Republic

het **domino** /domino/ (pl: -'s) dominoes

het **domino-effect** /dominoɛfɛkt/ (pl: -en) knock-on effect; [pol] domino effect

het **dominospel** /dominospɛl/ **1** dominoes **2** set of dominoes

de **dominosteen** /dominosten/ (pl: -stenen) domino

dommelen /dɔmələ(n)/ (dommelde, heeft gedommeld) doze, drowse

de **domoor** /dɔmor/ (pl: domoren) idiot, fool, blockhead, dunce

dompelen /dɔmpələ(n)/ (dompelde, heeft gedompeld) plunge, dip, immerse

de **domper** /dɔmpər/ (pl: -s): *dit onverwachte bericht zette een ~ op de feestvreugde* this unexpected news put a damper on the party

de **dompteur** /dɔmtør/ (pl: -s) animal trainer (*or:* tamer)

domweg /dɔmwɛχ/ (adv) (quite) simply, without a moment's thought, just

de **donateur** /donatør/ (pl: -s) donor; contributor; supporter

de **donatie** /dona(t)si/ (pl: -s) donation, gift

de **Donau** /donau/ Danube

de **donder** /dɔndər/ (pl: -s) **1** thunder **2** [inform] carcass; [pers] devil: *op zijn ~ krijgen* get a roasting **3** [inform] hell, damn(ation) || *daar kun je ~ op zeggen* you can bet your boots on that, you can bank on that

de **donderbui** /dɔndərbœy/ (pl: -en) thunderstorm, thunder-shower

de **donderdag** /dɔndərdɑχ/ (pl: -en) Thursday: *Witte Donderdag* Maundy Thursday

donderdags /dɔndərdɑχs/ (adj) Thursday

¹donderen /dɔndərə(n)/ (donderde, heeft/is gedonderd) **1** thunder away, bluster **2** tumble (down): *hij is van de trap gedonderd* he tumbled down the stairs

²donderen /dɔndərə(n)/ (donderde, heeft gedonderd) thunder

donderjagen /dɔndərjaɣə(n)/ (donderjaagde, heeft gedonderjaagd) [inform] be a nuisance, be a pain (in the neck)

de **donderslag** /dɔndərslɑχ/ (pl: -en) **1** thunderclap, thunderbolt, roll (*or:* crack) of thunder **2** [fig] thunderbolt, bombshell: *als een ~ bij heldere hemel* like a bolt from the blue

doneren /donerə(n)/ (doneerde, heeft gedoneerd) donate

het **¹donker** /dɔnkər/ dark(ness), gloom

²donker /dɔnkər/ (adj) **1** dark, gloomy: *het wordt ~* it's getting dark **2** dark, dismal, gloomy: *een ~e toekomst* a gloomy future **3** dark, dusky **4** low(-pitched) **5** darkskinned

³donker /dɔnkər/ (adv) dismally, gloomily: *de*

toekomst ~ *inzien* take a gloomy view of the future

donkerblauw /dɔŋkərblɑu̯/ (adj) dark (*or:* deep) blue

de **donor** /dónɔr/ (pl: -en, -s) donor

het **donorcodicil** /dónɔrkodisil/ (pl: -len) donor card

het **donororgaan** /dónɔrɔryan/ donor organ

het **dons** /dɔns/ down, fuzz

de **donut** /dónʏt/ (pl: -s) doughnut

donzen /dɔ́nzə(n)/ (adj) down(-filled): *een ~ dekbed* a down(-filled) quilt (*or:* duvet)

de **¹dood** /dot/ death, end: *aan de ~ ontsnappen* escape death; *dat wordt zijn ~* that will be the death of him; *iem. ter ~ veroordelen* condemn (*or:* sentence) s.o. to death; *de een zijn ~ is de ander zijn brood* one man's death is another man's breath ‖ *(zo bang) als de ~ voor iets zijn* be scared to death of sth.

²dood /dot/ (adj) **1** dead, killed: *hij was op slag ~* he died (*or:* was killed) instantly **2** dead, extinct: *een dooie boel* a dead place; *op een ~ spoor zitten* be at a dead end; *een dode vulkaan* an extinct volcano ‖ *op zijn dooie gemak* at one's leisure; *een dode hoek* a blind angle

doodbloeden /dódbludə(n)/ (bloedde dood, is doodgebloed) **1** bleed to death **2** [fig] run down, peter out

de **dooddoener** /dódunər/ (pl: -s) unanswerable remark, bromide

doodeenvoudig /dotɛnvɑu̯dəx/ (adj, adv) perfectly simple, quite simple

doodeng /dotɛ́ŋ/ (adj, adv) really scary; dead scary: *ik vind het allemaal ~* it really gives me the creeps

zich **doodergeren** /dótɛryərə(n)/ (ergerde zich dood, heeft zich doodgeërgerd) be (*or:* get) exasperated (with); be extremely annoyed

doodernstig /dótɛrnstəx/ (adj) deadly serious, solemn

doodgaan /dótxan/ (ging dood, is doodgegaan) die: *van de honger ~* starve to death

doodgeboren /dótxəborə(n)/ (adj) stillborn

doodgemoedereerd /dotxəmudərért/ (adj, adv) quite (*or:* perfectly) calm; dead calm (*or:* cool), (as) cool as a cucumber

doodgewoon /dótxəwon/ (adj, adv) perfectly common (ordinary): *iets ~s* sth. quite ordinary

doodgooien /dótxojə(n)/ (gooide dood, heeft doodgegooid) bombard, swamp

de **doodgraver** /dótxravər/ (pl: -s) gravedigger, sexton

doodkalm /dotkɑlm/ (adj, adv) quite (*or:* perfectly) calm

de **doodkist** /dótkɪst/ (pl: -en) coffin

de **doodklap** /dótklɑp/ (pl: -pen) **1** death blow, final blow, coup de grâce **2** almighty blow

zich **doodlachen** /dótlɑxə(n)/ (lachte zich dood, heeft zich doodgelachen) kill o.s. (laughing), split one's sides: *het is om je dood te lachen* it's a scream

doodleuk /dótløk/ (adv) coolly, blandly

doodlopen /dótlopə(n)/ (liep dood, is doodgelopen) **1** come to an end (*or:* a dead end), peter out: *~d steegje* blind alley; *een ~de straat* a dead end **2** lead nowhere, lead to nothing

doodmaken /dótmakə(n)/ (maakte dood, heeft doodgemaakt) kill

doodmoe /dótmu/ (adj) dead tired, dead on one's feet, worn out

doodongerust /dotɔŋɣərʏst/ (adj) worried to death, worried sick

doodop /dotɔ́p/ (adj) worn out, washed-out

doodrijden /dótrɛidə(n)/ (reed dood, heeft doodgereden) run over and kill

doods /dots/ (adj) **1** deathly, deathlike: *een ~e stilte* a deathly silence **2** dead, dead-and-alive

de **doodsangst** /dótsɑŋst/ (pl: -en) agony, mortal fear

doodsbang /dótsbɑŋ/ (adj, adv) (+ voor) terrified (of), scared to death: *iem. ~ maken* terrify s.o.

de **doodsbedreiging** /dótsbədrɛiɣɪŋ/ (pl: -en) death threat

doodsbleek /dotsblék/ (adj) deathly pale, as white as a sheet: *er ~ uitzien* look as white as a sheet

zich **doodschamen** /dótsxamə(n)/ (schaamde zich dood, heeft zich doodgeschaamd) be terribly embarrassed

doodschieten /dótsxitə(n)/ (schoot dood, heeft doodgeschoten) shoot (dead), shoot and kill: *zichzelf ~* shoot o.s.

het **doodseskader** /dótsɛskadər/ (pl: -s) death squad

het **doodshoofd** /dótshoft/ (pl: -en) skull

de **doodskist** /dótskɪst/ (pl: -en) coffin

¹doodslaan /dótslan/ (sloeg dood, is doodgeslagen) fizzle out: *het bier slaat dood* the beer's gone flat

²doodslaan /dótslan/ (sloeg dood, heeft doodgeslagen) beat to death; strike dead: *een vlieg ~* swat a fly

de **doodslag** /dótslɑx/ (pl: -en) manslaughter

de **doodsnood** /dótsnot/ death agony; [fig] death throes, fight to survive: *in ~ verkeren* be in one's death agony, be fighting to survive

de **doodsoorzaak** /dótsorzak/ (pl: -oorzaken) cause of death

de **doodsstrijd** /dótstrɛit/ death agony

de **doodsteek** /dótstek/ coup de grâce, death blow, final blow: *dat betekende de ~ voor het vredesproces* that dealt a death blow to the peace process

doodsteken /dótstekə(n)/ (stak dood,

heeft doodgestoken) stab to death, stab and kill

doodstil /dotstɪl/ (adj) deathly quiet (or: still); quite still; dead silent: *het werd opeens ~ toen hij binnenkwam* there was a sudden hush when he came in

de **doodstraf** /dotstraf/ (pl: -fen) death penalty: *hier staat de ~ op* this is punishable by death

de **doodsverachting** /dotsfəraχtɪŋ/ contempt (or: disregard) for death

doodvallen /dotfalə(n)/ (viel dood, is doodgevallen) **1** drop (or: fall) dead: *ik mag ~ als het niet waar is* if that isn't so I'll eat my hat; *val dood!* drop dead!, go to hell! **2** [of conversation] flag, peter out

het **doodvonnis** /dotfɔnɪs/ (pl: -sen) death sentence

doodziek /dotsik/ (adj) **1** critically ill, terminally ill **2** sick and tired: *ik word ~ van die kat* I'm (getting) sick and tired of that cat

de **¹doodzonde** /dotsɔndə/ **1** mortal sin **2** mortal sin, deadly sin

²doodzonde /dotsɔndə/ (adj) a terrible pity; a terrible waste

doodzwijgen /dotswɛɪɣə(n)/ (zweeg dood, heeft doodgezwegen) hush up, smother, keep quiet

doof /dof/ (adj, adv) **1** deaf: *~ blijven voor* turn a deaf ear to; *~ aan één oor* deaf in one ear; *zo ~ als een kwartel* as deaf as a (door)-post, stone-deaf **2** numb: *dove vingers* numb fingers

de **doofheid** /dofhɛit/ deafness

de **doofpot** /dofpɔt/ (pl: -ten) extinguisher, cover-up: *die hele zaak is in de ~ (gestopt)* that whole business has been hushed up

doofstom /dofstɔm/ (adj) deaf-and-dumb, deaf mute

de **doofstomme** /dofstɔmə/ (pl: -n) deaf mute

de **dooi** /doj/ thaw

dooien /dojə(n)/ (dooide, heeft gedooid) thaw: *het begon te ~* the thaw set in

de **dooier** /dojər/ (pl: -s) (egg) yolk

de **doolhof** /dolhɔf/ (pl: -hoven) maze, labyrinth

de **doop** /dop/ (pl: dopen) **1** christening, baptism **2** [fig] inauguration, christening: *de ~ van een schip* the naming of a ship **3** [Belg] initiation (of new students)

het/de **doopceel** /dopsel/ (pl: doopcelen): *iemands ~ lichten* bring out s.o.'s past

de **doopnaam** /dopnam/ (pl: -namen) Christian name, baptismal name, given name

het **doopsel** /dopsəl/ (pl: -s) baptism, christening

de **doopsuiker** /dopsœykər/ [Belg] sugared almonds

het **doopvont** /dopfɔnt/ (pl: -en) font

¹door /dor/ (adv) through: *de hele dag ~* all day long, throughout the day; *het kan ermee*

~ it's passable; *de tunnel gaat onder de rivier ~* the tunnel passes under the river ‖ *tussen de buien ~* between showers; *ik ben ~ en ~ nat* I'm wet through (and through); *~ en ~ slecht* rotten to the core

²door /dor/ (prep) **1** through: *~ heel Europa* throughout Europe; *~ rood (oranje) rijden* jump the lights **2** through, into: *zout ~ het eten doen* mix salt into the food; *alles lag ~ elkaar* everything was in a mess **3** by (means of): *~ ijverig te werken, kun je je doel bereiken* you can reach your goal by working hard; *~ haar heb ik hem leren kennen* it was thanks to her that I met him **4** because of, owing to, by, with: *~ het slechte weer* because of (or: owing to) the bad weather; *~ ziekte verhinderd* prevented by illness from coming (or: attending, going); *dat komt ~ jou* that's (all) because of you **5** by: *zij werden ~ de menigte toegejuicht* they were cheered by the crowd; *~ wie is het geschreven?* who was it written by? ‖ *~ de jaren heen* over the years; *~ de week* through the week

doorbakken /dorbɑkə(n)/ (adj) well-done

doorbelasten /dorbəlɑstə(n)/ (belastte door, heeft doorbelast) pass on (or: through): *de kosten worden doorbelast aan de werkgever* the costs will be passed on (or: through) to the employer

doorberekenen /dorbərekənə(n)/ (berekende door, heeft doorberekend) pass on, on-charge

doorbetalen /dorbətalə(n)/ (betaalde door, heeft doorbetaald) keep paying, continue paying

doorbijten /dorbɛitə(n)/ (beet door, heeft doorgebeten) **1** bite (hard): *de hond beet niet door* the dog didn't bite hard **2** keep biting, continue biting (or: to bite); [fig] keep trying; [fig] keep at it: *even ~!* just grin and bear it!

doorbladeren /dorbladərə(n)/ (bladerde door, heeft doorgebladerd) leaf through, glance through; thumb through

doorboren /dorborə(n)/ (doorboorde, heeft doorboord) drill (through), bore (a hole in); tunnel; pierce; stab

de **doorbraak** /dorbrak/ (pl: -braken) **1** bursting, collapse **2** breakthrough; [sport] break: *~ van een politieke partij* the breakthrough of a political party

doorbranden /dorbrɑndə(n)/ (brandde door, heeft/is doorgebrand) **1** burn through, burn properly **2** burn out: *een doorgebrande lamp* a blown (light) bulb

¹doorbreken /dorbrekə(n)/ (doorbrak, heeft doorbroken) break (through), burst (through); breach: *de sleur ~* get out of the rut

²doorbreken /dorbrekə(n)/ (brak door, is doorgebroken) **1** break (apart, in two), break up, burst, perforate: *het gezwel brak*

door the swelling ruptured **2** break through, come through: *de **tandjes** zullen snel ~ the* teeth will come through fast **3** break through, make it

³**doorbreken** /dọrbrekə(n)/ (brak door, heeft doorgebroken) break (in two); snap (in two): *ze brak zijn wandelstok door (in tweeën)* she broke her walking stick in two

doorbrengen /dọrbrɛŋə(n)/ (bracht door, heeft doorgebracht) spend: *ergens de **nacht** ~* spend the night (*or:* stay overnight) somewhere

doorbuigen /dọrbœyɣə(n)/ (boog door, is doorgebogen) **1** bend, sag: *de **vloer** boog sterk door* the floor sagged badly **2** bend further (over), bow deeper

doordacht /dọrdɑχt/ (adj) well-thought-out, well-considered

doordat /dọrdɑt/ (conj) because (of the fact that), owing to, as a result of, on account of (the fact that), in that: *~ er gebrek aan geld was* through lack of money

doordenken /dọrdɛŋkə(n)/ (dacht door, heeft doorgedacht) reflect, think, consider: *als je **even** doordenkt* (or: *door had gedacht*) if you think (*or:* had thought) for a moment

doordeweeks /dordəweːks/ (adj) weekday, workaday: *op een ~e **dag*** on a weekday

doordraaien /dọrdrajə(n)/ (draaide door, heeft/is doorgedraaid) **1** keep turning, continue turning (*or:* to turn); [fig] go on; [fig] keep moving: *de motor **laten** ~* keep the engine running (*or:* on) **2** slip, not bite, have stripped, be stripped

doordrammen /dọrdrɑmə(n)/ (dramde door, heeft doorgedramd) nag, go on: *~ **over** iets* keep harping on (about) sth.

de **doordrammer** /dọrdrɑmər/ (pl: -s) nagger, pest

doordraven /dọrdravə(n)/ (draafde door, heeft/is doorgedraafd) rattle on

doordrenken /dọrdrɛŋkə(n)/ (doordrenkte, heeft doordrenkt) soak (through), saturate, drench

¹**doordrijven** /dọrdrɛivə(n)/ (dreef door, heeft doorgedreven) nag: *je **moet** niet zo ~* stop nagging!

²**doordrijven** /dọrdrɛivə(n)/ (dreef door, heeft doorgedreven) push through, force through, enforce, impose: *iets te **ver** ~* carry things too far

¹**doordringen** /dọrdrɪŋə(n)/ (doordrong, heeft doordrongen) persuade, convince: *doordrongen **zijn** van de noodzaak …* be convinced of the necessity of …

²**doordringen** /dọrdrɪŋə(n)/ (drong door, is doorgedrongen) penetrate, get through, occur: *~ **in** penetrate; permeate; filter through; het drong niet **tot** me door dat hij mij wilde spreken* it didn't occur to me that he wanted to see me; *niet **tot** iem. kunnen ~* not be able

to get through to s.o.

doordringend /dordrɪŋənt/ (adj) piercing; penetrating; pungent: *iem. ~ **aankijken*** give s.o. a piercing look

doordrukken /dọrdrʏkə(n)/ (drukte door, heeft doorgedrukt) push through, force through: *zijn eigen **mening** ~* impose one's own view

dooreen /dorẹn/ (adv) jumbled up, higgledy-piggledy

dooreten /dọretə(n)/ (at door, heeft doorgegeten) carry on eating, keep (on) eating: *eet eens **even** door!* eat up now!

¹**doorgaan** /dọrɣan/ (ging door, is doorgegaan) **1** go on, walk on, continue: *deze trein gaat door **naar** Amsterdam* this train goes on to Amsterdam **2** continue (doing, with), go (*or:* carry) on (doing, with), persist (in, with), proceed (with): *hij **bleef** er maar over ~* he just kept on about it; *dat gaat in één moeite door* we can do that as well while we're about it **3** continue, go on, last **4** go through, pass through, pass **5** take place, be held: *het **feest** gaat door* the party is on; *niet ~* be off **6** pass for, pass o.s. off as; be considered (as): *zij gaat **voor** erg intelligent door* she is said to be very intelligent

²**doorgaan** /dọrɣan/ (ging door, is doorgegaan) go through, pass through

doorgaand /dọrɣant/ (adj) through: *~ **verkeer*** through traffic

doorgaans /dọrɣans/ (adv) generally, usually

de **doorgang** /dọrɣaŋ/ (pl: -en) **1** occurrence: *(geen) ~ **hebben** (not) take place **2** passage(-way), way through, gangway; aisle

het **doorgeefluik** /dọrɣeflœyk/ (pl: -en) (serving-)hatch; [fig] intermediary, middleman

doorgestoken /dọrɣəstokə(n)/ (adj): *dat is ~ **kaart** it's been arranged behind our backs, it's fixed, it's a put-up job

doorgeven /dọrɣevə(n)/ (gaf door, heeft doorgegeven) **1** pass (on, round), hand on (*or:* round): *geef de **fles** eens door* pass the bottle round (*or:* on) **2** pass (on): *een boodschap **aan** iem. ~* pass a message on to s.o. **3** pass on, hand on, hand over **4** pass on, let (s.o.) know about: *dat zal ik **moeten** ~ aan je baas* I will have to tell your boss about this

doorgewinterd /dọrɣəwɪntərt/ (adj) seasoned, experienced

doorgronden /dorɣrọndə(n)/ (doorgrondde, heeft doorgrond) fathom, penetrate

doorhakken /dọrhɑkə(n)/ (hakte door, heeft doorgehakt) chop in half (*or:* two), split: [fig] *de knoop **doorhakken** cut the (Gordian) knot, take the plunge

doorhalen /dọrhalə(n)/ (haalde door, heeft doorgehaald) cross out, delete: *~ wat niet van toepassing is* delete where not applicable

doorhebben /dọrhɛbə(n)/ (had door, heeft

doorgehad) see (through), be on to: *hij had het dadelijk door* **dat** *... he saw at once that ...*
doorheen /dorhe̱n/ (adv) through: *zich* **er** *~ slaan* get through (it) somehow or other
doorkijken /do̱rkɛikə(n)/ (keek door, heeft doorgekeken) look through
doorklikken /do̱rklɪkə(n)/ (klikte door, heeft doorgeklikt) click (on the link)
doorklinken /do̱rklɪŋkə(n)/ (klonk door, heeft doorgeklonken) be heard: *de berusting die* **uit** *zijn woorden doorklinkt* the resignation that can be heard in his words
doorkneed /dorkne̱t/ (adj) experienced
doorknippen /do̱rknɪpə(n)/ (knipte door, heeft doorgeknipt) cut through, cut in half (or: in two)
doorkomen /do̱rkomə(n)/ (kwam door, is doorgekomen) **1** come through (or: past, by), pass (through, by): *de* **stoet** *moet hier ~* the procession must come past here **2** get through (to the end): *de* **dag** *~* make it through the day; *er is geen ~ aan* **a)** [book, work etc] there is no way I'm going to get this finished; **b)** [crowd, traffic] I don't stand a hope of getting through **3** come through, get through: *de* **zon** *komt door* the sun is breaking through
doorkruisen /dorkrœ̱ysə(n)/ (doorkruiste, heeft doorkruist) **1** traverse, roam; scour: *hij heeft heel* **Frankrijk** *doorkruist* he has travelled all over France **2** thwart: *dat voorstel doorkruist mijn* **plannen** that proposal has thwarted my plans
doorlaten /do̱rlatə(n)/ (liet door, heeft doorgelaten) let through (or: pass), allow through (or: to pass): *geen* **geluid** *~* be soundproof
doorleefd /dorle̱ft/ (adj) wrinkled, aged
doorleren /do̱rlerə(n)/ (leerde door, heeft doorgeleerd) keep (on) studying, continue with one's studies, stay on at school
doorleven /dorle̱və(n)/ (doorleefde, heeft doorleefd) live through, spend
¹**doorlezen** /do̱rlezə(n)/ (las door, heeft doorgelezen) read on, keep (on) reading
²**doorlezen** /do̱rlezə(n)/ (las door, heeft doorgelezen) read (to the end (or: through)): *ik heb dat* **boek** *slechts vluchtig doorgelezen* I have only glanced (or: skimmed) through that book
doorlichten /do̱rlɪxtə(n)/ (lichtte door, heeft doorgelicht) investigate, examine carefully; screen [pers]
doorliggen /do̱rlɪɣə(n)/ (lag door, heeft/is doorgelegen) have bedsores, get bedsores: *zijn* **rug** *is doorgelegen* he has (got) bedsores on his back
doorlinken /do̱rlɪŋkə(n)/ (linkte door, heeft doorgelinkt) redirect (to)
¹**doorlopen** /dorlo̱pə(n)/ (doorliep, heeft/is doorlopen) **1** walk through, go through,

pass through **2** go through, pass through; complete: *alle* **stadia** *~* pass through (or: complete) every stage **3** run through, glance through
²**doorlopen** /do̱rlopə(n)/ (liep door, heeft/is doorgelopen) **1** walk (or: go, pass) through: *hij liep* **tussen** *de struiken door* he walked (or: went) through the bushes **2** keep (on) walking (or: going/moving); continue walking (or: going/moving); continue to walk (or: to go/move); walk on (or: go/move on): *~ a.u.b.!* move along now, please! **3** run: *het* **blauw** *is doorgelopen* the blue has run **4** run on, carry on through, continue; be consecutive: *de eetkamer loopt door* **in** *de keuken* the dining room runs through into the kitchen **5** hurry up
doorlopend /dorlo̱pənt/ (adj, adv) continuous, continuing; continual; consecutive: *~* **krediet** revolving (or: continuous) credit; *hij is ~* **dronken** he is constantly drunk
doormaken /do̱rmakə(n)/ (maakte door, heeft doorgemaakt) go through, pass through, live through, experience, undergo: *een moeilijke* **tijd** *~* have a hard time (of it)
doormidden /dormɪ̱də(n)/ (adv) in two, in half
de **doorn** /dorn/ (pl: -en) thorn: *dat is mij een ~* **in** *het oog* that is a thorn in my flesh
doornat /dorna̱t/ (adj) wet through, soaked (through)
doornemen /do̱rnemə(n)/ (nam door, heeft doorgenomen) **1** go through (or: over): *een artikel* **vluchtig** *~* skim through an article **2** go over: *iets* **met** *elkaar ~* go over sth. together
Doornroosje /dornro̱ʃə/ Sleeping Beauty
doorprikken /do̱rprɪkə(n)/ (prikte door, heeft doorgeprikt) burst, prick, puncture
de **doorreis** /do̱rɛis/ stopover, stopoff: *hij is* **op** *~ (naar Rome)* he is passing through (or: stopping over) (on his way to Rome)
doorrijden /do̱rɛidə(n)/ (reed door, heeft/is doorgereden) **1** keep on (or: continue) driving/riding: *rijdt deze bus door* **naar** *het station?* does this bus go on to the station? **2** drive on, ride on, proceed, continue: *~* **na** *een aanrijding* fail to stop after an accident **3** drive faster, ride faster, increase speed: *als we* **wat** *~, zijn we er in een uur* if we step on it, we will be there in an hour
de **doorrijhoogte** /do̱rɛihoxtə/ (pl: -n) clearance, headway
doorschemeren /do̱rsxemərə(n)/ (schemerde door, heeft/is doorgeschemerd) be hinted at, be implied: *hij* **liet** *~ dat hij trouwplannen had* he hinted that he was planning to marry
doorscheuren /do̱rsxørə(n)/ (scheurde door, heeft/is doorgescheurd) tear up; tear in half

doorschieten /dɔrsχitə(n)/ (schoot door, is doorgeschoten) shoot through (*or:* past)

doorschijnend /dorsχεinənt/ (adj, adv) translucent; see-through; transparent

doorschuiven /dɔrsχœyvə(n)/ (schoof door, heeft/is doorgeschoven) pass on

doorslaan /dorslan/ (sloeg door, heeft/is doorgeslagen) **1** tip, dip: *de balans doen* ~ tip the scales **2** blow, melt; fuse; break down: *de stop is doorgeslagen* the fuse has blown **3** talk

doorslaand /dorslant/ (adj) conclusive, decisive: *een* ~ *succes* a resounding success

de **doorslag** /dorslɑχ/ (pl: -en) **1** turn (*or:* tip) (of the scale): *dat gaf bij mij de* ~ that decided me; *dat geeft de* ~ that settles it **2** carbon (copy), duplicate

doorslaggevend /dorslɑχεvənt/ (adj) decisive: *van* ~ *belang* of overriding importance

doorslikken /dorslɪkə(n)/ (slikte door, heeft doorgeslikt) swallow

doorsmeren /dorsmerə(n)/ (smeerde door, heeft doorgesmeerd) lubricate: *de auto laten* ~ have the car lubricated

de **doorsnede** /dorsnedə/ (pl: -n) **1** section, cross-section, profile: *een* ~ *van een bol maken* make a cross-section of a sphere **2** diameter: *die bal heeft een* ~ *van 5 cm* this ball has a diameter of 5 cm

doorsnee /dorsne/ (adj) average, mean: *de* ~ *burger* the man in (*or:* on) the street; *in* ~ on average, in the main

¹**doorsnijden** /dorsnɛidə(n)/ (sneed door, heeft doorgesneden) cut, sever; cut in(to) two; bisect: *hij heeft alle banden met zijn familie doorgesneden* he has severed (*or:* cut) all ties with his family

²**doorsnijden** /dorsnɛidə(n)/ (doorsneed, heeft doorsneden) cut (through)

doorspekken /dorspεkə(n)/ (doorspekte, heeft doorspekt) interlard (with), intersperse (with), punctuate (with)

¹**doorspelen** /dorspelə(n)/ (speelde door, heeft doorgespeeld) play on, continue to play: *het orkest speelde door alsof er niets gebeurd was* the orchestra played on as if nothing had happened

²**doorspelen** /dorspelə(n)/ (speelde door, heeft doorgespeeld) pass on, leak: *informatie aan een krant* ~ pass on information to a newspaper; *de bal* ~ *naar …* pass (the ball) to …

doorspoelen /dorspulə(n)/ (spoelde door, heeft doorgespoeld) **1** wash down (*or:* out, through): *je eten* ~ *met wijn* wash down your food with wine **2** flush out; flush **3** wind on

doorspreken /dorsprekə(n)/ (sprak door, heeft doorgesproken) discuss, go into (in depth)

doorstaan /dorstan/ (doorstond, heeft doorstaan) endure, bear, (with)stand, come

through: *een proef* ~ come through a test

de **doorstart** /dorstɑrt/ (pl: -s) **1** aborted landing **2** [economics] new start; bankruptcy restructuring

¹**doorstarten** /dorstɑrtə(n)/ (startte door, heeft/is doorgestart) **1** abort a landing **2** start up again

²**doorstarten** /dorstɑrtə(n)/ (startte door, heeft/is doorgestart) start up again

doorstoten /dorstotə(n)/ (stootte door, heeft/is doorgestoten) **1** keep on (*or:* continue) pushing **2** advance, push on (*or:* through); break through, burst through: ~ *tot de kern van de zaak* get to the heart of the matter

doorstrepen /dorstrepə(n)/ (streepte door, heeft doorgestreept) cross out, delete, strike out (*or:* through)

doorstromen /dorstromə(n)/ (stroomde door, is doorgestroomd) **1** move up, move on **2** flow (through)

de **doorstroming** /dorstromɪŋ/ **1** moving up, moving on **2** flow, circulation: *een vlottere* ~ *van het verkeer* a freer flow of traffic

doorstuderen /dorstyderə(n)/ (studeerde door, heeft doorgestudeerd) continue (with) one's studies

doorsturen /dorstyrə(n)/ (stuurde door, heeft doorgestuurd) send on; forward; send away: *een brief* ~ forward a letter; *een e-mail* ~ forward an email; *een patiënt naar een specialist* ~ refer a patient to a specialist

doortastend /dortɑstənt/ (adj, adv) vigorous, bold

de **doortocht** /dortɔχt/ (pl: -en) **1** crossing, passage through, way through **2** passage, thoroughfare: *de* ~ *versperren* block the way through

doortrapt /dortrɑpt/ (adj, adv) **1** cunning, crafty **2** base, villainous

¹**doortrekken** /dortrεkə(n)/ (trok door, heeft/is doorgetrokken) travel through, pass through, journey through, roam

²**doortrekken** /dortrεkə(n)/ (trok door, heeft doorgetrokken) **1** extend, continue: *een lijn* ~ follow the same line (*or:* course); *een vergelijking* ~ carry a comparison (further) **2** flush

doorverbinden /dorvərbɪndə(n)/ (verbond door, heeft doorverbonden) connect; put through (to)

doorvertellen /dorvərtεlə(n)/ (vertelde door, heeft doorverteld) pass on: *aan niemand* ~, *hoor!* don't tell anyone else!

doorverwijzen /dorvərwεizə(n)/ (verwees door, heeft doorverwezen) refer

de **doorvoer** /dorvur/ (pl: -en) transit

de **doorvoerhaven** /dorvurhavə(n)/ (pl: -s) transit port

doorwaadbaar /dorwadbar/ (adj) fordable, wad(e)able: *doorwaadbare plaats* ford

doorweekt /dorwe̲kt/ (adj) wet through, soaked, drenched

¹**doorwerken** /do̲rwɛrkə(n)/ (werkte door, heeft doorgewerkt) **1** go (*or:* keep) on working, continue to work, work on; work overtime: *er werd dag en nacht doorgewerkt* they worked night and day **2** make headway, get on (with the job): *je kunt hier nooit ~* you can never get on with your work here **3** affect sth., make itself felt: *zijn houding werkt door op anderen* his attitude has its effect on others

²**doorwerken** /do̲rwɛrkə(n)/ (werkte door, heeft doorgewerkt) work (one's way) through, get through, go through: *een heleboel stukken door moeten werken* have to plough through a mass of documents

¹**doorzagen** /do̲rzaɣə(n)/ (zaagde door, heeft doorgezaagd) keep (*or:* go, moan) on (about sth.)

²**doorzagen** /do̲rzaɣə(n)/ (zaagde door, heeft doorgezaagd) saw (sth.) through, saw in two || *iem. over iets blijven ~* force sth. down s.o.'s throat; question s.o. closely, grill s.o.

doorzakken /do̲rzakə(n)/ (zakte door, is doorgezakt) **1** sag, give (way) **2** go on drinking (*or:* boozing), make a night of it

¹**doorzetten** /do̲rzɛtə(n)/ (zette door, heeft doorgezet) **1** become stronger, become more intense: *de weeën zetten door* the contractions are increasing (in intensity) **2** persevere: *nog even ~!* don't give up now!; *van ~ weten* not give up easily

²**doorzetten** /do̲rzɛtə(n)/ (zette door, heeft doorgezet) **1** press (*or:* go) ahead with **2** go through with: *iets tot het einde toe ~* see sth. through

de **doorzetter** /do̲rzɛtər/ (pl: -s) go-getter, stayer

het **doorzettingsvermogen** /do̲rzɛtɪŋsfərmoɣə(n)/ perseverance, drive

doorzeven /dorze̲və(n)/ (doorzeefde, heeft doorzeefd) riddle: *met kogels doorzeefd* bullet-riddled

doorzichtig /dorzɪxtəɣ/ (adj) **1** transparent; see-through: *gewoon glas is ~, matglas doorschijnend* plain glass is transparent, frosted glass is translucent **2** [fig] transparent, thin, obvious

de **doorzichtigheid** /dorzɪxtəɣhɛit/ transparency

doorzien /dorzi̲n/ (doorzag, heeft doorzien) see through; be on to [pers]: *hij doorzag haar bedoelingen* he saw what she was up to

doorzoeken /dorzu̲kə(n)/ (doorzocht, heeft doorzocht) search through, go through; ransack: *zijn zakken ~* turn one's pockets (inside) out

de **doos** /dos/ (pl: dozen) box; case: *een ~ bonbons* a box of chocolates; *de ~ van Pandora* Pandora's box; [aviation] *de zwarte ~* the black box

de **dop** /dɔp/ (pl: -pen) **1** shell; pod; husk **2** cap; top **3** [Belg; inform] dole, unemployment benefit || *een advocaat in de ~* a budding lawyer; *kijk uit je ~pen!* watch where you're going!

de **dopamine** /dopami̲nə/ dopamine

de ¹**dope** /dop/ dope: *helemaal onder de ~ zitten* be stoned, be doped up to the eyeballs

²**dope** /dop/ (adj) [inform] (really) dope, awesome

dopen /do̲pə(n)/ (doopte, heeft gedoopt) **1** sop, dunk (in): *zijn pen in de inkt ~* dip one's pen in the ink **2** [rel] baptize, christen: *iem. tot christen ~* baptize s.o. **3** [Belg] initiate, rag

de **doper** /do̲pər/ (pl: -s) baptizer: *Johannes de Doper* John the Baptist

de **doperwt** /do̲pɛrt/ (pl: -en) green pea

de **doping** /do̲pɪŋ/ drug(s)

de **dopingcontrole** /do̲pɪŋkontro:lə/ (pl: -s) dope test

het **dopje** /do̲pjə/ (pl: -s) cap, top

¹**doppen** /do̲pə(n)/ (dopte, heeft gedopt) [Belg] be on benefit, be on the dole

²**doppen** /do̲pə(n)/ (dopte, heeft gedopt) (un)shell; pod; hull; peel; (un)husk; hull

dor /dor/ (adj) **1** barren, arid **2** withered

het **dorp** /dɔrp/ (pl: -en) village; [Am] town: *het hele ~ weet het* it's all over town

de **dorpel** /do̲rpəl/ (pl: -s) threshold, doorstep

de **dorpeling** /do̲rpəlɪŋ/ (pl: -en) villager; village people

de **dorpsbewoner** /do̲rpsbəwonər/ (pl: -s) villager

het **dorpshuis** /do̲rpshœys/ (pl: -huizen) community centre

dorsen /do̲rsə(n)/ (dorste, heeft gedorsen) thresh

de **dorst** /dɔrst/ thirst: *~ hebben* be thirsty; *zijn ~ lessen* quench one's thirst; *ik verga van de ~* I'm dying of thirst

dorstig /do̲rstəɣ/ (adj) thirsty, parched

doseren /doze̲rə(n)/ (doseerde, heeft gedoseerd) dose

de **dosering** /doze̲rɪŋ/ (pl: -en) quantity; dose; dosage

de **dosis** /do̲zɪs/ (pl: doses) dose, measure: *een flinke ~ gezond verstand* a good measure of common sense

het **dossier** /doʃe̲/ (pl: -s) file, documents, records: *een ~ bijhouden van iets (iem.)* keep a file on sth. (s.o.)

de **dot** /dɔt/ (pl: -ten) tuft || *een flinke ~ slagroom* a dollop of cream; *een ~ van een kans* a golden opportunity

de **douane** /duwa̲nə/ (pl: -n, -s) customs

de **douanebeambte** /duwa̲nəbəɑmtə/ (pl: -n) customs officer

de **douanerechten** /duwa̲nərɛxtə(n)/ (pl) customs duties

de **double** /dɒbəl/ (pl: -s) double
doubleren /dublerə(n)/ (doubleerde, heeft gedoubleerd) [Dutch] repeat (a class)
de **douche** /duʃ/ (pl: -s) shower: [fig] *een koude* ~ a rude awakening
de **douchecel** /duʃsɛl/ (pl: -len) shower (cubicle)
de **douchekop** /duʃkɔp/ (pl: -pen) shower head
douchen /duʃə(n)/ (douchte, heeft gedoucht) shower, take (*or:* have) a shower
het **douchetoilet** /duʃtwalɛt/ (pl: -ten) toilet bidet
douwen /dɒuwə(n)/ (douwde, heeft gedouwd) shove, push; crowd
de **dove** /dovə/ (pl: -n) deaf person
de **dovemansoren** /dovəmɑnsorə(n)/ (pl): *dat is niet aan* ~ *gezegd* that did not fall on deaf ears; *voor* ~ *spreken* not find any hearing
¹**doven** /dovə(n)/ (doofde, is gedoofd) die down, go out: [fig] *het vuur is gedoofd* the fire is gone/has gone out
²**doven** /dovə(n)/ (doofde, heeft gedoofd) extinguish, put out; turn out, turn off [light]
de **dovenetel** /dovənetəl/ (pl: -s) dead nettle
down /dɑun/ (adj) down, down-hearted ‖ ~ *gaan* fail, go down
de **download** /dɑunlot/ (pl: -s) download
downloaden /dɑunlodə(n)/ (downloadde, heeft gedownload) download
het **downsyndroom** /dɑunsɪndrom/ Down's syndrome
het **dozijn** /dozɛin/ (pl): *een* ~ *eieren* one dozen eggs
de **draad** /drat/ (pl: draden) **1** thread; fibre: *tot op de* ~ *versleten* worn threadbare; *de* ~ *weer opnemen* pick up the thread; *de* ~ *kwijt zijn* flounder **2** fibre; string
het **draadje** /dracə/ (pl: -s) **1** thread, strand, fibre: *aan een zijden* ~ *hangen* hang by a thread; *er zit een* ~ *los bij hem* he has a screw loose **2** wire, piece of wiring **3** [on Internet forum] thread
draadloos /dratlos/ (adj, adv) wireless: ~ *internet* wireless Internet; *draadloze telefoon* cellular (tele)phone
draagbaar /draybar/ (adj) portable, transportable
de **draagbalk** /draybɑlk/ (pl: -en) breastsummer, girder
de **draagkracht** /draxkrɑxt/ capacity, strength: *financiële* ~ financial strength (*or:* capacity, means)
draaglijk /draxlək/ (adj, adv) bearable, endurable
de **draagmoeder** /draxmudər/ (pl: -s) surrogate mother
de **draagstoel** /draxstul/ (pl: -en) sedan (chair)
de **draagtas** /draxtɑs/ (pl: -sen) carrier bag; [Am] bag
het **draagvermogen** /draxfərmoɣə(n)/ bearing (*or:* supporting) power; lift

het **draagvlak** /draxflɑk/ (pl: -ken) [literally] bearing surface, basis; support: *het maatschappelijk* ~ *van een wetsontwerp* the public support for a bill
de **draagwijdte** /draxwɛitə/ range; [fig also] scope, bearing
de **draai** /drai/ (pl: -en) **1** turn, twist, bend: *een* ~ *van 180° maken* make an about-turn **2** turn, twist; screw: *iem. een* ~ *om de oren geven* box s.o.'s ears ‖ *hij kon zijn* ~ *niet vinden* he couldn't settle down
draaibaar /draibar/ (adj) revolving, rotating, swinging: *een draaibare (bureau)stoel* a swivel chair
de **draaibank** /draibɑŋk/ (pl: -en) (turning) lathe
het **draaiboek** /draibuk/ (pl: -en) script, screenplay, scenario
de **draaicirkel** /draisɪrkəl/ (pl: -s) turning circle
de **draaideur** /draidør/ (pl: -en) revolving door
¹**draaien** /draiə(n)/ (draaide, heeft/is gedraaid) **1** turn (around), revolve, rotate; orbit; pivot: *in het rond* ~ turn round, spin round; *daar draait het om* that's what it's all about **2** turn, swerve: *de wind draait* the wind is changing **3** work, run, do: *met winst* (*or:* *verlies*) ~ work at a profit (*or:* loss) ‖ *aan de knoppen* ~ turn the knobs; *die film draait nog steeds* that film is still on; *er omheen* ~ evade the question; *zich eronderuit* ~ wriggle out of it
²**draaien** /draiə(n)/ (draaide, heeft gedraaid) **1** turn (around); twirl; spin: *het gas hoger* (*or:* *lager*) ~ turn the gas up (*or:* down); *een deur op slot* ~ lock a door **2** turn (around), swerve **3** dial **4** play: *een film* ~ show a film **5** DJ: *wie draait er vanavond?* who's DJ'ing tonight? ‖ *een nachtdienst* ~ work a night shift; *de zaak ~de houden* keep things going
draaierig /draiərəx/ (adj) dizzy
het **draaihek** /draihɛk/ turnstile, swing gate
de **draaikolk** /draikɔlk/ (pl: -en) whirlpool
de **draaimolen** /draimolə(n)/ (pl: -s) merry-go-round
het **draaiorgel** /draiɔrɣəl/ (pl: -s) barrel organ; hand organ: *de orgelman speelde zijn* ~ the organgrinder was grinding his barrel organ
de **draaischijf** /draisxɛif/ (pl: -schijven) **1** potter's wheel **2** turntable **3** dial **4** [fig] hub
de **draaistoel** /draistul/ (pl: -en) swivel chair, revolving chair
de **draaitafel** /draitafəl/ (pl: -s) turntable
de **draak** /drak/ (pl: draken) dragon
het/de **drab** /drɑp/ **1** dregs, sediment **2** ooze
het/de **drachme** /drɑxmə/ (pl: -n) drachma
de **dracht** /drɑxt/ (pl: -en) **1** gestation; pregnancy **2** costume, dress
drachtig /drɑxtəx/ (adj) with young, bearing: ~ *zijn* be with young
draconisch /drakonis/ (adj, adv) draconian
de **draf** /draf/ trot: *in volle* ~ at full trot; *op een*

~je lopen run along, trot

¹dragen /drayə(n)/ (droeg, heeft gedragen) rest on, be supported: *een ~de balk* a supporting beam

²dragen /drayə(n)/ (droeg, heeft gedragen) **1** support, bear, carry; [fig also] sustain: *iets bij zich ~* have sth. on one **2** wear, have on: *die schoenen kun je niet bij die jurk ~* those shoes don't go with that dress **3** take, have: *de gevolgen ~* bear (or: take) the consequences **4** bear, endure: *de spanning was niet langer te ~* the tension had become unbearable

de **drager** /drayər/ (pl: -s) **1** bearer; carrier **2** medium; data carrier

de **dragon** /drayɔn/ tarragon

de **drain** /dren/ (pl: -s) drain

draineren /drɛnerə(n)/ (draineerde, heeft gedraineerd) drain

dralen /dralə(n)/ (draalde, heeft gedraald) linger, hesitate

het **drama** /drama/ (pl: -'s) **1** tragedy, drama: *de Griekse ~'s* the Greek tragedies; *een ~ opvoeren* perform a tragedy **2** tragedy, catastrophe || *een ~ van iets maken* make a drama of sth.

dramatisch /dramatis/ (adj, adv) **1** dramatic: *~e effecten* theatrical effects **2** tragic; theatrical: *doe niet zo ~* don't make such a drama of it

dramatiseren /dramatizerə(n)/ (dramatiseerde, heeft gedramatiseerd) **1** dramatize, make a drama of **2** dramatize; adapt for the stage

drammen /dramə(n)/ (dramde, heeft gedramd) nag, go on

drammerig /dramərəx/ (adj, adv) nagging, insistent, tiresome

de **drang** /draŋ/ **1** urge, instinct: *de ~ tot zelfbehoud* the survival instinct **2** pressure, force: *met zachte ~* with gentle insistence

het **dranghek** /draŋhɛk/ (pl: -ken) barrier

de **drank** /draŋk/ (pl: -en) drink; beverage: *alcoholhoudende ~en* alcoholic beverages; *aan de ~ zijn* drink, be an alcoholic

het **drankje** /draŋkjə/ (pl: -s) drink: *een ~ klaarmaken* mix a drink

het **drankmisbruik** /draŋkmɪzbrœyk/ alcohol abuse

het **drankorgel** /draŋkɔrɣəl/ (pl: -s) drunk(ard), hard drinker

de **drankvergunning** /draŋkfərɣʏnɪŋ/ (pl: -en) liquor licence

draperen /draperə(n)/ (drapeerde, heeft gedrapeerd) drape

drassig /drasəx/ (adj) boggy, swampy

drastisch /drɑstis/ (adj, adv) drastic: *de prijzen* (or: *belastingen*) *~ verlagen* slash prices (or: taxes)

de **draufgänger** /droufgɛnər/ (pl: -s) go-getter

draven /dravə(n)/ (draafde, heeft/is ge-

draafd) **1** trot **2** hurry about

de **dreef** /dref/ (pl: dreven) **1** (+ op) in form, in one's stride: *niet op ~ zijn* be off form; *hij is aardig* (or: *geweldig*) *op ~* he's in good (or: splendid) form **2** avenue, lane

de **dreggen** /drɛɣə(n)/ (dregde, heeft gedregd) drag

de **dreigbrief** /drɛɣybrif/ (pl: -brieven) threatening letter

het **dreigement** /drɛiɣəmɛnt/ (pl: -en) threat

¹dreigen /drɛiɣə(n)/ (dreigde, heeft gedreigd) **1** threaten, menace: *~ met straf* threaten punishment **2** threaten, be in danger: *de vergadering dreigt uit te lopen* the meeting threatens to go on longer than expected

²dreigen /drɛiɣə(n)/ (dreigde, heeft gedreigd) threaten

dreigend /drɛiɣənt/ (adj) **1** threatening, ominous, menacing: *iem. ~ aankijken* scowl at s.o. **2** imminent, threatening

de **dreiging** /drɛiɣɪŋ/ (pl: -en) threat, menace

de **dreigmail** /drɛixmel/ (pl: -s) threatening (e)mail

de **dreigtweet** /drɛixtwiːt/ (pl: -s) threatening tweet

de **drek** /drɛk/ dung, muck; manure

de **drempel** /drɛmpəl/ (pl: -s) **1** threshold, doorstep **2** threshold, barrier

de **drenkeling** /drɛŋkəlɪŋ/ (pl: -en) drowning person; drowned body (or: person)

drenken /drɛŋkə(n)/ (drenkte, heeft gedrenkt) drench, soak, saturate

drentelen /drɛntələ(n)/ (drentelde, heeft/is gedrenteld) saunter, stroll

de **dresscode** /drɛskodə/ dress code

dresseren /drɛserə(n)/ (dresseerde, heeft gedresseerd) train

de **dresseur** /drɛsør/ (pl: -s) (animal) trainer

het/de **dressoir** /drɛswar/ (pl: -s) sideboard, buffet

de **dressuur** /drɛsyr/ training, drilling; dressage; schooling

de **dreumes** /drøməs/ (pl: -en) toddler, tot

de **dreun** /drøn/ (pl: -en) **1** boom, rumble; drone: *er klonk een doffe ~* there was a dull boom (or: rumble) **2** drone, monotone **3** blow, thump: *iem. een ~ verkopen (geven)* sock s.o. one

dreunen /drønə(n)/ (dreunde, heeft gedreund) **1** hum, drone, rumble: *het hele huis dreunt ervan* the whole house is rocking with it **2** boom, crash, thunder, roar: *hij sloeg de deur ~d dicht* he slammed the door shut

dribbelen /drɪbələ(n)/ (dribbelde, heeft/is gedribbeld) dribble

drie /dri/ (num) three; [in dates] third: *een auto in z'n ~ zetten* put a car into third gear; *met ~ tegelijk* in threes; *zij waren met hun ~ën* there were three of them; *het is tegen* (or: *bij*) *~ën* it's almost three o'clock; *met 3-0 verliezen* lose by three goals to nil

dringend

driedaags /dridaxs/ (adj) three-day
driedelig /dridel̥əx/ (adj) tripartite; three-piece
driedimensionaal /dridimɛnʃonal/ (adj) three-dimensional
driedubbel /dridybəl/ (adj, adv) **1** threefold, triple **2** treble, triple
de **Drie-eenheid** /driɛnhɛɪt/ the (Blessed (or: Holy)) Trinity
het **driegangendiner** /driɣɑŋə(n)dine/ (pl: -s) three-course dinner
de **driehoek** /drihuk/ (pl: -en) **1** triangle **2** [Dutch] the mayor, public prosecutor and chief of police
driehoekig /drihukəx/ (adj, adv) triangular, three-cornered
de **driehoeksverhouding** /drihuksfərhaudɪŋ/ (pl: -en) triangular (or: three-cornered) relationship
driehonderd /drihɔndərt/ (num) three hundred
driehoog /drihox/ (adv) three floors up; [Am] four floors up: *driehoog-achter* a garret (room)
driejarig /drijarəx/ (adj) **1** three-year-old: *op ~e leeftijd* at the age of three **2** three-year
de **driekleur** /driklør/ tricolour
Driekoningen /drikɔnɪŋə(n)/ (feast of (the)) Epiphany, Twelfth Night
driekwart /drikwɑrt/ (adj, adv) three-quarter: *(voor) ~ leeg* three parts empty; *(voor) ~ vol* three-quarters full
de **driekwartsmaat** /drikwɑrtsmat/ three-four (time)
drieledig /driledəx/ (adj) three-part: *een ~ doel* a threefold purpose
de **drieling** /drilɪŋ/ (pl: -en) (set of) triplets: *de geboorte van een ~* the birth of triplets
het **drieluik** /drilœyk/ (pl: -en) triptych
driemaal /drimal/ (adv) three times: *~ zo veel (groot) geworden* increased threefold; *~ is scheepsrecht* third time lucky
driemaandelijks /drimandələks/ (adj, adv) quarterly, three-monthly: *een ~ tijdschrift* a quarterly
de **driemaster** /drimɑstər/ (pl: -s) three-master
de **driesprong** /drisprɔŋ/ (pl: -en) three-forked road
driest /drist/ (adj, adv) reckless, foolhardy
het **driesterrenrestaurant** /dristɛrə(n)rɛstorɑnt/ (pl: -s) three-star restaurant
het **drietal** /dritɑl/ (pl: -len) threesome, trio, triad
de **drietand** /dritɑnt/ (pl: -en) **1** trident: *de ~ van Neptunus* Neptune's trident **2** three-pronged, three-tined fork
de **drietrapsraket** /dritrɑpsrakɛt/ (pl: -ten) three-stage rocket
het **drievoud** /drivɑut/ (pl: -en) **1** treble, triplicate: *een formulier in ~ ondertekenen* sign a

form in triplicate **2** multiple of three
drievoudig /drivɑudəx/ (adj) treble, triple: *we moesten het ~e (bedrag) betalen* we had to pay three times as much
de **driewieler** /driwilər/ (pl: -s) tricycle; [car] three-wheel car
de **drift** /drɪft/ (pl: -en) **1** (fit of) anger, (hot) temper, rage: *in ~ ontsteken* fly into a rage **2** passion, urge **3** drift
de **driftbui** /drɪftbœy/ (pl: -en) fit (or: outburst) of anger
¹**driftig** /drɪftəx/ (adj) **1** angry, heated: *je moet je niet zo ~ maken* you must not lose your temper **2** short-tempered
²**driftig** /drɪftəx/ (adv) **1** angry, hot-headed: *~ spreken* speak in anger **2** vehement, heated: *hij stond ~ te gebaren* he was making vehement gestures; *zij maakte ~ aantekeningen* she was busily taking notes
de **driftkop** /drɪftkɔp/ (pl: -pen) hothead
het **drijfgas** /drɛɪfxɑs/ (pl: -sen) propellant
het **drijfijs** /drɛɪfɛɪs/ drift ice
de **drijfjacht** /drɛɪfjɑxt/ (pl: -en) drive, battue
drijfnat /drɛɪfnɑt/ (adj) soaking wet, sopping wet, drenched, soaked
de **drijfveer** /drɛɪfer/ (pl: -veren) motive, mainspring
het **drijfzand** /drɛɪfsɑnt/ quicksand(s)
¹**drijven** /drɛɪvə(n)/ (dreef, heeft/is gedreven) **1** float, drift: *het pakje bleef ~* the package remained afloat **2** float, drift, glide **3** be soaked: *~ van het zweet* be dripping with sweat
²**drijven** /drɛɪvə(n)/ (dreef, heeft gedreven) **1** drive, push, move: *de menigte uit elkaar ~* break up the crowd **2** drive, push, compel: *iem. tot het uiterste ~* push s.o. to the extreme **3** run, conduct, manage: *handel ~ met een land* trade with a country; *de spot met iem. ~* make fun of s.o. **4** drive; propel; operate: *door stoom gedreven schepen* steam-driven (or: steam-propelled) ships
drijvend /drɛɪvənt/ (adj) floating, drifting
de **drijver** /drɛɪvər/ (pl: -s) **1** driver; drover; beater **2** float: *~s van een watervliegtuig* floats of a seaplane
de **drilboor** /drɪlbor/ (pl: -boren) drill
drillen /drɪlə(n)/ (drilde, heeft gedrild) drill
¹**dringen** /drɪŋə(n)/ (drong, is gedrongen) **1** push, shove, penetrate: *hij drong door de menigte heen* he pushed (or: elbowed, forced) his way through the crowd; *naar voren ~* push forward **2** push, press: *het zal wel ~ worden om een goede plaats* we'll probably have to fight for a good seat **3** press, urge, compel: *de tijd dringt* time is short
²**dringen** /drɪŋə(n)/ (drong, heeft gedrongen) push, force
¹**dringend** /drɪŋənt/ (adj) **1** urgent; pressing; acute; dire **2** urgent; earnest; insistent, pressing: *op ~ verzoek van* at the urgent re-

quest of

²dringend /drɪŋənt/ (adv) urgently, acutely, direly: *ik moet u ~ spreken* I must speak to you immediately

drinkbaar /drɪŋbar/ (adj) drinkable; potable

de **drinkbeker** /drɪŋbekər/ (pl: -s) drinking cup, goblet

drinken /drɪŋkə(n)/ (dronk, heeft gedronken) **1** drink; sip: *wat wil je ~?, wat drink jij?* what are you having?, what'll it be?; *ik drink op ons succes* here's to our success! **2** soak (up) **3** drink: *te veel ~* drink (to excess)

de **drinker** /drɪŋkər/ (pl: -s) drinker

de **drinkplaats** /drɪŋkplats/ (pl: -en) watering place

het **drinkwater** /drɪŋkwatər/ drinking water, potable water

de **drinkyoghurt** /drɪŋkjoɣʏrt/ (pl: -s) drinking yoghurt

de **drive-inbioscoop** /drajvɪmbijoskop/ (pl: -bioscopen) drive-in-cinema

droef /druf/ (adj, adv) sad, sorrowful

de **droefenis** /drufənɪs/ [form] sadness, sorrow, grief: *in diepe ~* in deep distress

droefgeestig /drufxestəx/ (adj) melancholy, mournful; doleful

de **droefheid** /drufhɛit/ sorrow, sadness, grief

de **droesem** /drusəm/ (pl: -s) dregs, lees

¹droevig /druvəx/ (adj) **1** sad, sorrowful, miserable **2** sad, melancholy: *een ~e blik* a sad (*or:* melancholy) look **3** depressing, saddening: *een ~ lied* a sad (*or:* melancholy) song **4** depressing, miserable

²droevig /druvəx/ (adv) **1** sadly, dolefully, sorrowfully **2** depressingly, pathetically: *het is ~ gesteld met hem* he's in a distressing situation

¹drogen /droɣə(n)/ (droogde, heeft/is gedroogd) dry: *de was te ~ hangen* hang out the laundry to dry

²drogen /droɣə(n)/ (droogde, heeft gedroogd) dry, air; wipe: *iets laten ~* leave sth. to dry

de **droger** /droɣər/ (pl: -s) drier

drogeren /droɣərə(n)/ (drogeerde, heeft gedrogeerd) dope

de **drogist** /droɣɪst/ (pl: -en) **1** chemist **2** chemist's

de **drogisterij** /droɣɪstərɛi/ (pl: -en) chemist's

de **drogreden** /droxredə(n)/ (pl: -en) fallacy, sophism

de **drol** /drɔl/ (pl: -len) turd || [inform] *dat kost geen ~* it's dirt cheap, it costs next to nothing

de **drom** /drɔm/ (pl: -men) crowd, horde, throng

de **dromedaris** /dromədarəs/ (pl: -sen) dromedary, (Arabian) camel

¹dromen /dromə(n)/ (droomde, heeft gedroomd) **1** dream **2** (day)dream, muse

²dromen /dromə(n)/ (droomde, heeft ge-

droomd) dream, imagine

de **dromer** /dromər/ (pl: -s) dreamer, stargazer, rainbow chaser

¹dromerig /dromərəx/ (adj) **1** dreamy, faraway **2** dreamy, dreamlike, illusory: *een ~e sfeer* a dreamlike feeling

²dromerig /dromərəx/ (adv) dreamily: *~ uit zijn ogen kijken* gaze dreamily

de **drone** /dron/ (pl: -s) drone

de **dronepiloot** /drompilot/ (pl: -piloten) drone pilot

de **dronk** /drɔŋk/ (pl: -en) **1** toast **2** drinking

de **dronkaard** /drɔŋkart/ (pl: -s) drunk(ard)

dronken /drɔŋkə(n)/ (adj) drunken, drunk: *de wijn maakt hem ~* the wine is making him drunk; *iem. ~ voeren* ply s.o. with liquor

de **dronkenlap** /drɔŋkə(n)lap/ drunk

de **dronkenman** /drɔŋkəman/ drunk

de **dronkenschap** /drɔŋkənsxap/ drunkenness, intoxication, inebriety: *in kennelijke staat van ~ (verkeren)* (be) under the influence of drink

droog /droɣ/ (adj) dry; arid; dried out: *hij zit hoog en ~* he is sitting high and dry

de **droogbloem** /droɣblum/ (pl: -en) dried flower

de **droogdoek** /droɣduk/ (pl: -en) tea towel

de **droogkap** /droxkap/ (pl: -pen) (hair)dryer (hood)

droogkoken /droxkokə(n)/ (kookte droog, is drooggekookt) boil dry

de **droogkuis** /droxkœys/ [Belg] dry-cleaning

droogleggen /droxlɛɣə(n)/ (legde droog, heeft drooggelegd) reclaim; [esp in the Netherlands] impolder

het **droogrek** /droxrɛk/ (pl: -ken) drying rack

droogscheren /droxsxerə(n)/ (schoor droog, heeft drooggeschoren) dry-shave

de **droogte** /droxtə/ (pl: -n) dryness; aridity; drought

de **droogtrommel** /droxtrɔməl/ (pl: -s) dryer, drying machine, tumble(r) dryer

het **droogvoer** /droxfur/ dry feed; dry food, cat/dog biscuits

droogzwemmen /droxswɛmə(n)/ (zwom droog, heeft drooggezwommen) **1** practise swimming on (dry) land **2** [fig] do a dry run

de **droom** /drom/ (pl: dromen) dream, fantasy: *het meisje van zijn dromen* the girl of his dreams; *een natte ~* a wet dream || *iem. uit de ~ helpen* disillusion (*or:* disenchant) s.o.

het **droombeeld** /drombelt/ (pl: -en) picture from a dream; fantasy, illusion

de **droomprins** /dromprɪns/ (pl: -en) Prince Charming

de **droomwereld** /dromwerəlt/ dream-world, fantasy world, fool's paradise

het/de **drop** /drɔp/ liquorice: *Engelse ~* liquorice all-sorts

het **dropdownmenu** /drɔbdouməny/ (pl: -'s) drop-down menu

droppen /drɔpə(n)/ (dropte, heeft gedropt) drop off

de **dropping** /drɔpɪŋ/ (pl: -s) drop

de **drug** /drʏɡ/ (pl: -s) drug, narcotic: ~s *gebruiken* take (*or:* use) drugs, be on drugs; *handelen* in ~s, ~s *verkopen* deal in (*or:* sell) drugs

de **drugsdealer** /drʏksdi:lər/ (pl: -s) (drug) dealer, pusher

het **drugsgebruik** /drʏksχəbrœyk/ use of drugs, drug abuse

de **drugsgebruiker** /drʏ:ɡsχəbrœykər/ (pl: -s) drug user

de **drugshandel** /drʏkshɑndəl/ dealing (in drugs), drug trade

de **drugsrunner** /drʏ:ɡsrʏnər/ drug trafficker

de **drugsstaat** /drʏkstat/ (pl: -staten) narco-state

de **drugsverslaafde** /drʏksfərslavdə/ (pl: -n) drug addict, junkie

de **druïde** /drywidə/ (pl: -n) druid

de **druif** /drœyf/ grape: *een tros druiven* a bunch of grapes

druilerig /drœylərəχ/ (adj) drizzly

de **druiloor** /drœylor/ (pl: -oren) mope(r)

druipen /drœypə(n)/ (droop, heeft gedropen) drip, trickle

de **druiper** /drœypər/ (pl: -s) **1** the clap, gonorrhoea **2** run, drip

druipnat /drœypnɑt/ (adj) soaking wet, soaked through

de **druipneus** /drœypnøs/ (pl: -neuzen) runny nose: *ik heb een* ~ my nose is running

het/de **druipsteen** /drœypsten/ stalactite; [hanging] stalagmite [standing]

de **druivenoogst** /drœyvə(n)oχst/ (pl: -en) grape harvest, vintage

het **druivensap** /drœyvə(n)sɑp/ grape-juice

de **druivensuiker** /drœyvə(n)sœykər/ grape sugar, dextrose

de **druiventros** /drœyvə(n)trɔs/ (pl: -sen) bunch of grapes

de ¹**druk** /drʏk/ (pl: -ken) **1** pressure: ~ *uitoefenen (op)* exert pressure (on) **2** strain, stress: *de tegenstander onder* ~ *zetten* put one's opponent under pressure; [sport] ~ *zetten* press **3** edition: *een herziene* ~ a revised edition

²**druk** /drʏk/ (adj) **1** busy, demanding, active, lively: *een ~ke baan* a demanding job; *een ~ leven hebben* lead a busy life **2** active, lively, boisterous: *~ke kinderen* boisterous children; *zich ~ maken over iets* worry about sth.

³**druk** /drʏk/ (adv) **1** busily: ~ *bezet* busy; ~ *bezig zijn (met iets)* be very busy (with, doing sth.) **2** busily, noisily, excitedly

drukbezet /drʏɡbəzɛt/ (adj) busy

de **drukfout** /drʏkfɑut/ (pl: -en) misprint, printing error, erratum

¹**drukken** /drʏkə(n)/ (drukte, heeft gedrukt) press, push

²**drukken** /drʏkə(n)/ (drukte, heeft gedrukt) **1** push, press: *iem. de hand* ~ shake hands with s.o. **2** force: *iem. tegen zich aan* ~ hold s.o. close (to o.s.) **3** push down: *de prijzen* (*or: kosten*) ~ keep down prices (*or:* costs) **4** print: *10.000 exemplaren van een boek* ~ print (*or:* run off) 10,000 copies of a book **5** stamp, impress

drukkend /drʏkənt/ (adj) **1** oppressive, heavy, burdensome **2** sultry; close

de **drukker** /drʏkər/ (pl: -s) printer

de **drukkerij** /drʏkərɛi/ (pl: -en) printer, printing office (*or:* business), printer's

de **drukkingsgroep** /drʏkɪŋsχrup/ (pl: -en) [Belg] pressure group

de **drukknoop** /drʏknop/ (pl: -knopen) press stud, press fastener, popper

de **drukknop** /drʏknɔp/ (pl: -pen) push-button

de **drukletter** /drʏklɛtər/ (pl: -s) **1** (block, printed) letter **2** type, letter

de **drukpers** /drʏkpɛrs/ (pl: -en) printing press

de **drukproef** /drʏkpruf/ (pl: -proeven) proof, galley (proof), printer's proof

de **drukte** /drʏktə/ **1** busyness, pressure (of work): *door de* ~ *heb ik de bestelling vergeten* it was so busy (*or:* hectic) I forgot the order **2** bustle, commotion, stir: *de* ~ *voor Kerstmis* the Christmas rush **3** fuss, ado: *veel* ~ *over iets maken* make a big fuss about sth.

de **druktemaker** /drʏktəmakər/ (pl: -s) noisy (*or:* rowdy) person, show-off

de **druktoets** /drʏktuts/ (pl: -en) (push-)button

het **drukwerk** /drʏkwɛrk/ (pl: -en) printed matter (*or:* papers)

de **drum** /drʏm/ (pl: -s) drum

de **drumband** /drʏmbɛnt/ (pl: -s) drum band

drummen /drʏmə(n)/ (drumde, heeft gedrumd) **1** drum, play the drum(s) **2** [Belg] push and shove

de **drummer** /drʏmər/ (pl: -s) drummer

het **drumstel** /drʏmstɛl/ (pl: -len) drum set, (set of) drums

de **druppel** /drʏpəl/ (pl: -s) drop(let); bead: *alles tot de laatste* ~ *opdrinken* drain to the (very) last drop; *zij lijken op elkaar als twee ~s water* they are as like as two peas in a pod; [fig] *dat is de* ~ *die de emmer doet overlopen* that's the straw that breaks the camel's back

druppelen /drʏpələ(n)/ (druppelde, heeft gedruppeld) drip, trickle, ooze: *iets in het oog* ~ put drops in one's eye

de **druppellader** /drʏpəladər/ (pl: -s) trickle charger

de **druppelstop** /drʏpəlstɔp/ (pl: -pen) drip stop (mechanism)

het **dualisme** /dywalɪsmə/ dualism

¹**dubbel** /dʏbəl/ (adj) **1** double, duplicate, dual: *een ~e bodem* a double (*or:* hidden) meaning **2** double (the size), twice (as big) || *een* ~ *leven leiden* lead a double life

²**dubbel** /dʏbəl/ (adv) **1** double, twice: *ik heb dat boek* ~ I have two copies of that book; ~

liggen be doubled up **2** doubly, twice: *dat is ~ erg* that's twice as bad; *hij verdient het ~ en dwars* he deserves every bit of it

de **dubbeldekker** /dɣbəldɛkər/ (pl: -s) double-deck(er) (bus)

de **dubbelepunt** /dʏbələpʏnt/ (pl: -en) colon

de **dubbelganger** /dɣbəlɣaŋər/ (pl: -s) double, lookalike, doppelgänger

het **dubbelglas** /dʏbəlɣlas/ double glazing

dubbelklikken /dɣbəlklɪkə(n)/ (dubbelklikte, heeft gedubbelklikt) double-click

het **dubbelleven** /dʏbəlevə(n)/: *een ~ leiden* lead a double life

dubbelop /dʏbəlɔp/ (adv) double

dubbelparkeren /dɣbəlparkerə(n)/ double-park

de **dubbelrol** /dʏbəlrɔl/ (pl: -len) double role, twin roles

het **dubbelspel** /dʏbəlspɛl/ (pl: -en) [sport] doubles

de **dubbelspion** /dʏbəlspijɔn/ (pl: -nen) double agent

het **dubbeltje** /dʏbəlcə/ (pl: -s) [Dutch] ten-cent piece: *zo plat als een ~* (as) flat as a pancake; [fig] *het is een ~ op zijn kant* it's a toss-up, it's touch and go

dubbelvouwen /dʏbəlvauwə(n)/ (vouwde dubbel, heeft dubbelgevouwen) fold in two, bend double (or: in two)

dubbelzijdig /dʏbəlzɛɪdəɣ/ (adj) double(-sided), two-sided: *~ kopiëren* make double-sided copies

dubbelzinnig /dʏbəlzɪnəɣ/ (adj) **1** ambiguous: *een ~ antwoord* an ambiguous (or: evasive) answer **2** suggestive, with a double meaning

de **dubbelzinnigheid** /dʏbəlzɪnəɣhɛit/ (pl: -heden) **1** ambiguity **2** ambiguous remark; suggestive remark

dubben /dʏbə(n)/ (dubde, heeft gedubd) brood, ponder: *~ over iets* brood about sth.

dubieus /dybijøs/ (adj) **1** dubious, doubtful **2** dubious, questionable

duchten /dʏxtə(n)/ (duchtte, heeft geducht) fear

de **ducttape** /dʏktep/ (pl: -s) duct tape

het **duel** /dywɛl/ (pl: -s) duel, fight, single combat

duelleren /dywɛlerə(n)/ (duelleerde, heeft geduelleerd) duel, fight

het **duet** /dywɛt/ (pl: -ten) duet, duo

duf /dʏf/ (adj, adv) **1** musty, stuffy, mouldy: *het rook daar ~* it smelled musty **2** [fig] stuffy, stale

duidelijk /dœydələk/ (adj, adv) **1** clear, clear-cut, plain: *zich in ~e bewoordingen (taal) uitdrukken* speak plainly; *ik heb hem ~ gemaakt dat …* I made it clear to him that …; *om ~ te zijn, om het maar eens ~ te zeggen* to put it (quite) plainly **2** clear, distinct, plain: *een ~e voorkeur hebben voor iets* have a dis-

tinct preference for sth.; *~ zichtbaar* (or: *te merken*) *zijn* be clearly visible (or: noticeable)

de **duidelijkheid** /dœydələkhɛit/ clearness, clarity, obviousness

duiden /dœydə(n)/ (duidde, heeft geduid) **1** point (to, at) **2** point (to), indicate: *verschijnselen die op tuberculose ~* symptoms that indicate tuberculosis

de **duif** /dœyf/ (pl: duiven) pigeon, dove: *onder iemands duiven schieten* poach on s.o.'s territory

duigen /dœyɣə(n)/: *in ~ vallen* fall to pieces, collapse

de **duik** /dœyk/ (pl: -en) dive, diving, plunge: *een ~ nemen* take a dip

de **duikboot** /dœyɣbot/ (pl: -boten) submarine; sub; U-boat

de **duikbril** /dœyɣbrɪl/ (pl: -len) diving goggles

duikelen /dœykələ(n)/ (duikelde, is geduikeld) **1** (turn a) somersault, go (or: turn) head over heels, tumble **2** (take a) tumble, fall head over heels **3** drop, dive; plunge (downward)

de **duikeling** /dœykəlɪŋ/ (pl: -en) **1** somersault, roll **2** fall, tumble

duiken /dœykə(n)/ (dook, heeft/is gedoken) **1** dive, plunge, duck, go under; submerge: [sport] *naar een bal ~* dive for (or: after) a ball **2** duck (down, behind): *in een onderwerp ~* go (deeply) into a subject

de **duiker** /dœykər/ (pl: -s) diver

het **duikerpak** /dœykərpak/ (pl: -ken) wetsuit, diving suit

de **duikplank** /dœykplaŋk/ (pl: -en) diving board

de **duiksport** /dœyksport/ diving

de **duikvlucht** /dœykflʏxt/ (pl: -en) (nose) dive

de **duim** /dœym/ (pl: -en) **1** thumb: *de ~ opsteken* give the thumbs up; *onder de ~ houden* keep under one's thumb **2** inch || [Belg] *de ~en leggen* surrender; throw in the sponge; *iets uit zijn ~ zuigen* dream sth. up

het **duimbreed** /dœymbret/ inch: *geen ~ toegeven* not budge an inch

duimen /dœymə(n)/ (duimde, heeft geduimd) **1** keep one's fingers crossed **2** suck one's thumb

duimendik /dœymə(n)dɪk/ (adv) an inch deep (or: thick): *het stof ligt er ~ op* the dust is an inch thick on top of it; [fig] *het ligt er ~ (boven)op* it's as plain as the nose on your face, it sticks out a mile

het **duimpje** /dœympjə/ (pl: -s): *Klein Duimpje* Tom Thumb; *iets op zijn ~ kennen* know sth. like the back of one's hand; know sth. (off) by heart

de **duimschroef** /dœymsxruf/ (pl: -schroeven) thumbscrew: *(iem.) de duimschroeven aandraaien* tighten the screws (on s.o.); turn on the heat on (s.o.)

de **duimstok** /dœymstɔk/ (pl: -ken) folding

ruler

duimzuigen /dœymzœyɣə(n)/ thumb sucking

het/de **duin** /dœyn/ (pl: -en) (sand) dune, sand hill

Duinkerken /dœynkɛrkə(n)/ Dunkirk

de **duinpan** /dœympɑn/ (pl: -nen) dip (in the dunes)

het ¹**duister** /dœystər/ dark, darkness: *in het ~ tasten* be in the dark

²**duister** /dœystər/ (adj, adv) **1** dark; gloomy; [fig] dim; black **2** shady, dubious

de **duisternis** /dœystərnɪs/ (pl: -sen) darkness, dark

de **duit** /dœyt/ (pl: -en): *ook een ~ in het zakje doen* put in a word

Duits /dœyts/ (adj) German ‖ *~e herdershond* Alsatian

de **Duitse** /dœytsə/ German woman, German girl: *zij is een ~* she is German

de **Duitser** /dœytsər/ (pl: -s) German

Duitsland /dœytslɑnt/ Germany

Duitstalig /dœytstaləx/ (adj) **1** German-speaking **2** German

de **duivel** /dœyvəl/ (pl: -s) **1** [rel] devil **2** demon

duivels /dœyvəls/ (adj, adv) **1** diabolic(al), devilish, demonic: *een ~ plan* a diabolical plan **2** livid, (raving) mad, furious

de **duivelskunstenaar** /dœyvəlskynstənar/ (pl: -s) wizard

de **duivenmelker** /dœyvə(n)mɛlkər/ (pl: -s) pigeon fancier; pigeon flyer

de **duiventil** /dœyvə(n)tɪl/ (pl: -len) dovecote, pigeon house

duizelen /dœyzələ(n)/ (duizelde, heeft geduizeld) become dizzy, reel: *het duizelt mij* my head is spinning (*or:* swimming)

duizelig /dœyzələx/ (adj) dizzy (with), giddy (with): *de drukte maakte hem ~* the crowds made his head spin

de **duizeligheid** /dœyzələxhɛit/ dizziness

de **duizeling** /dœyzəlɪŋ/ (pl: -en) dizziness, dizzy spell; vertigo: *soms last hebben van ~en* suffer from dizzy spells

duizelingwekkend /dœyzəlɪŋwɛkənt/ (adj, adv) dizzy, giddy; staggering

duizend /dœyzənt/ (num) (a, one) thousand: *~ pond* (*or:* *dollar*) a thousand pounds (*or:* dollars); *dat werk heeft (vele) ~en gekost* that work cost thousands; *~ tegen één* a thousand to one; *hij is er één uit ~en* he is one in a thousand

duizend-en-een /dœyzəntɛnen/ (num) a thousand and one: *~ mogelijkheden* thousands of possibilities

de **duizendpoot** /dœyzəntpot/ (pl: -poten) **1** centipede **2** jack of all trades

duizendste /dœyzəntstə/ (num) thousandth

het **duizendtal** /dœyzəntɑl/ (pl: -len) **1** thousand **2** thousands

de **dukaat** /dykat/ (pl: dukaten) ducat

dulden /dʏldə(n)/ (duldde, heeft geduld) **1** endure, bear, put up with: *geen tegenspraak ~* not bear being contradicted **2** tolerate, permit, allow: *de leraar duldt geen tegenspraak* the teacher won't put up with any contradiction

dumpen /dʏmpə(n)/ (dumpte, heeft gedumpt) dump

de **dumpprijs** /dʏmprɛɪs/ (pl: -prijzen) bulk-purchase price; clearance (*or:* knockdown) price

¹**dun** /dʏn/ (adj) **1** thin; slender; fine: *~ne darm* small intestine **2** sparse, light, fine, scant **3** thin, light, runny

²**dun** /dʏn/ (adv) thinly, sparsely, lightly; meanly

dunbevolkt /dʏmbəvɔlkt/ (adj) thinly populated, sparsely populated

de **dunk** /dʏŋk/ **1** opinion **2** [basketball] dunk (shot)

dunken /dʏŋkə(n)/ (docht/dunkte, heeft gedocht/gedunkt): *mij dunkt, dat ...* it seems to me that ..., I think that ...

de **dunne** /dʏnə/: *aan de ~ zijn* have the trots (*or:* runs)

dunnetjes /dʏnəcəs/ (adv) thin(ly) ‖ *iets nog eens ~ overdoen* go ahead and do it all over again

het **duo** /dywo/ (pl: -'s) duo, pair

de **dupe** /dypə/ victim, dupe: *wie zal daar de ~ van zijn?* who will be the one to suffer for it? (*or:* pay for it?)

duperen /dypərə(n)/ (dupeerde, heeft gedupeerd) let down, fail

de **duplex** /dyplɛks/ (pl: -en) [Belg] [roughly] duplex (appartment)

het **duplicaat** /dyplikat/ (pl: duplicaten) duplicate (copy), transcript, facsimile

duplo /dyplo/: *in ~* in duplicate

duren /dyrə(n)/ (duurde, heeft geduurd) last, take, go on: *het duurt nog een jaar* it will take another year; *het duurde uren* (*or:* *eeuwen, een eeuwigheid*) it lasted hours (*or:* ages, an eternity); *het duurt nog wel even (voor het zover is)* it will be a while yet (before that happens); *de tentoonstelling duurt nog tot oktober* the exhibition runs until October; *zolang als het duurt* as long as it lasts

de **durf** /dyrf/ daring, nerve, guts

de **durfal** /dyrfɑl/ (pl: -len) daredevil

durven /dyrvə(n)/ (durfde, heeft gedurfd) dare, venture (to, upon): *hoe durf je!* how dare you!; *als het erop aan kwam durfde hij niet* he got cold feet when it came to the crunch

dus /dʏs/ (conj) so, therefore, then: *ik kan ~ op je rekenen?* I can count on you then?

dusdanig /dʏzdanəx/ (adv) so, in such a way (*or:* manner); to such an extent: *hij werd ~ toegetakeld dat hij naar het ziekenhuis moest* he was beaten up so badly that he had to go hospital

de **duster** /dʏstər/ (pl: -s) [Dutch] housecoat; [Am] duster

dusver /dʏsfɛr/ (adv): *tot* ~ so far, up to now; *tot* ~ *is alles in orde* so far so good

het **dutje** /dʏcə/ nap, snooze, forty winks: *een ~ doen* have a nap (*or:* snooze)

de ¹**duur** /dyr/ duration, length; life; term: *van korte* ~ short-lived; *op de lange* ~ in the long run; finally; *op den* ~ in the long run

²**duur** /dyr/ (adj) expensive, dear, costly: *die auto is* ~ *(in het gebruik)* that car is expensive to run; *hoe* ~ *is die fiets?* how much is that bicycle?; *dat is te* ~ *voor mij* I can't afford it

³**duur** /dyr/ (adv) expensively, dearly: *iets* ~ *betalen* pay a high price for sth.; pay dearly for sth.; [fig] ~ *te staan komen* cost (s.o.) dearly

de **duurloop** /dyrlop/ (pl: -lopen) endurance race

¹**duurzaam** /dyrzam/ (adj) **1** durable; hard-wearing; (long-)lasting; enduring; sustainable; permanent: *duurzame energie* renewable energy; *duurzame landbouw* sustainable agriculture; *duurzame verbruiksgoederen* durable consumer goods **2** permanent, (long-)lasting: *voor* ~ *gebruik* for permanent use

²**duurzaam** /dyrzam/ (adv) permanently, durably: ~ *gescheiden* permanently separated

de **duurzaamheid** /dyrzamhɛit/ durability, endurance; (useful, service) life

de **duw** /dyw/ (pl: -en) push, shove; nudge; poke; jab; dig: *hij gaf me een* ~ *(met de elleboog)* he nudged me; *de zaak een ~tje geven* help the matter along; *iem. een ~tje (omhoog, in de rug) geven* give s.o. a boost

de **duwboot** /dywbot/ (pl: duwboten) pusher tug

¹**duwen** /dywə(n)/ (duwde, heeft geduwd) press, push, jostle: *een ~de en dringende massa* a jostling crowd

²**duwen** /dywə(n)/ (duwde, heeft geduwd) **1** push; shove; wheel: *een kinderwagen* ~ wheel (*or:* push) a pram **2** push, thrust, shove; nudge: *iem. opzij* ~ push (*or:* elbow) s.o. aside

de **duwvaart** /dywvart/ push-towing, pushing

de **dvd** /devede/ DVD

de **dvd-brander** /devedɛbrandər/ (pl: -s) DVD burner

de **dvd-recorder** /devedɛriko:rdər/ DVD recorder

de **dvd-speler** /devedɛspelər/ DVD player

het **dwaalspoor** /dwalspor/ (pl: -sporen) wrong track, false scent: *iem. op een* ~ *brengen* mislead (*or:* misguide) s.o.

de ¹**dwaas** /dwas/ (pl: dwazen) fool, idiot, ass, dope, dummy, nincompoop

²**dwaas** /dwas/ (adj) foolish, silly, stupid: *een ~ idee* a crazy idea

³**dwaas** /dwas/ (adv) foolishly, stupidly, crazily

de **dwaasheid** /dwashɛit/ (pl: -heden) foolishness, folly, stupidity

dwalen /dwalə(n)/ (dwaalde, heeft gedwaald) **1** stray, wander **2** wander, roam: *wij dwaalden twee uur in het bos* we wandered through the forest for two hours **3** stray, travel

de **dwaling** /dwalɪŋ/ (pl: -en) error, mistake: *een rechterlijke* ~ a miscarriage of justice

de **dwang** /dwaŋ/ compulsion, coercion; force; obligation; pressure: *onder* ~ under duress, involuntarily; *met zachte* ~ by persuasion

de **dwangarbeid** /dwaŋarbɛit/ hard labour, forced labour

de **dwangarbeider** /dwaŋarbɛidər/ (pl: -s) convict

het **dwangbevel** /dwaŋbəvɛl/ (pl: -en) [law] injunction, enforcement order: *iem. een* ~ *betekenen* serve a writ on s.o., slap an injunction on s.o.

het **dwangbuis** /dwaŋbœys/ (pl: -buizen) straitjacket

de **dwangsom** /dwaŋsɔm/ (pl: -men) penalty (*or:* damages) (imposed on a daily basis in case of non-compliance)

dwarrelen /dwarələ(n)/ (dwarrelde, heeft/is gedwarreld) whirl; twirl; swirl; flutter

dwars /dwars/ (adj, adv) transverse, diagonal, crosswise: ~ *tegen iets ingaan* go right against sth.; *ergens* ~ *doorheen gaan* go right through (*or:* across) sth.; ~ *door het veld* straight across the field; ~ *door iem. heen kijken* look straight through s.o.

de **dwarsbalk** /dwarzbalk/ (pl: -en) transverse beam, crossbeam

dwarsbomen /dwarzbomə(n)/ (dwarsboomde, heeft gedwarsboomd) thwart; frustrate

de **dwarsdoorsnede** /dwarzdorsnedə/ (pl: -n) cross-section

de **dwarsfluit** /dwarsflœyt/ (pl: -en) flute

de **dwarslaesie** /dwarslezi/ spinal cord lesion; paraplegia

dwarsliggen /dwarslɪɣə(n)/ (lag dwars, heeft dwarsgelegen) be obstructive, be contrary, be a troublemaker

de **dwarsligger** /dwarslɪɣər/ (pl: -s) **1** obstructionist, troublemaker **2** sleeper; [Am] railroad tie

de **dwarsstraat** /dwarstrat/ (pl: -straten) side street: [fig] *ik noem maar een* ~ just to give an example

het **dwarsverband** /dwarsfərbant/ (pl: -en) (unexpected) connection; interconnections

dwarszitten /dwarsɪtə(n)/ (zat dwars, heeft dwarsgezeten) cross, thwart, hamper: *iem.* ~ frustrate s.o.('s plans); *wat zit je dwars?* what's worrying (*or:* bugging) you?

de **dweil** /dwɛil/ (pl: -en) (floor-)cloth, rag; mop
dweilen /dwɛ̱ilə(n)/ (dweilde, heeft ge-
dweild) mop (down); mop (up): *dat is ~ met
de kraan open* it's like swimming against the
tide

het **dweilorkest** /dwɛ̱ilɔrkɛst/ (pl: -en) Carnival
band, Oompah band
dwepen /dwe̱pə(n)/ (dweepte, heeft ge-
dweept) be enthusiastic: *~ met* be enthusiastic about

de **dwerg** /dwɛrχ/ (pl: -en) **1** gnome, dwarf, elf:
Sneeuwwitje en de zeven ~en Snow White
and the Seven Dwarfs **2** dwarf, midget

de **dwergstaat** /dwɛ̱rχstat/ (pl: -staten) micro-
state, ministate
dwingen /dwɪ̱ŋə(n)/ (dwong, heeft gedwongen) force, compel, oblige, coerce,
make (s.o. do sth.): *hij was wel gedwongen
(om) te antwoorden* he was obliged to answer; *iem. ~ een overhaast besluit te nemen*
rush s.o. into making a hasty decision; *niets
dwingt je daartoe* you are not obliged to do it;
iem. ~ tot gehoorzaamheid force s.o. to obey

¹**dwingend** /dwɪ̱ŋənt/ (adj) compelling,
compulsory: *~e redenen* compelling reasons
²**dwingend** /dwɪ̱ŋənt/ (adv) authoritatively:
iem. iets ~ voorschrijven make sth. compulsory for s.o.
d.w.z. *dat wil zeggen* i.e.

de **dynamica** /dina̱mika/ dynamics

de **dynamiek** /dinami̱k/ dynamics, vitality, dynamism

het **dynamiet** /dinami̱t/ dynamite
dynamisch /dina̱mis/ (adj) dynamic, energetic, forceful

de **dynamo** /dina̱mo/ (pl: -'s) dynamo, generator

de **dynastie** /dinɑsti̱/ dynasty

de **dysenterie** /dɪsɛntəri̱/ dysentery
dyslectisch /dɪslɛktis/ (adj) dyslexic

de **dyslexie** /dɪslɛksi̱/ dyslexia

e

de **e** /e/ (pl: e's) e, E: *E groot* (or: *klein*) E major (*or:* minor)
e.a. *en andere(n)* et al.
de **eau de cologne** /odəkɔlɔɲə/ (pl: eaux de cologne) cologne, eau de Cologne
de **eb** /ɛp/ **1** ebb(-tide), outgoing tide: *het is eb* the tide is out **2** low tide: *bij* eb at low tide
het **ebbenhout** /ɛbə(n)hʌut/ ebony
het **echie** /ɛxi/: [inform] *om* (or: *voor*) *het ~* for real; [inform] *spelen om het ~* play for real
de **echo** /ɛxo/ (pl: -'s) echo, reverberation; blip: *de ~ weerkaatste zijn stem* his voice was echoed
echoën /ɛxowə(n)/ (echode, heeft geëchood) echo, reverberate, resound, ring
de **echoscopie** /ɛxoskopi/ (pl: -ën) ultrasound scan
¹**echt** /ɛxt/ (adj) **1** real, genuine; authentic; true; actual: *een ~e vriend* a true (*or:* real) friend **2** real, regular, true (blue, born): *het is een ~ schandaal* it's an absolute scandal **3** legitimate
²**echt** /ɛxt/ (adv) **1** really, truly, genuinely, honestly: *dat is ~ Hollands* that's typically Dutch; *dat is ~ iets voor hem* that's him all over; *ik heb het ~ niet gedaan* I honestly didn't do it **2** real, genuine(ly)
de **echtbreuk** /ɛxtbrøk/ (pl: -en) adultery
echtelijk /ɛxtələk/ (adj) conjugal, marital: *een ~e ruzie* a domestic quarrel
echter /ɛxtər/ (adv) however, nevertheless, yet, but: *dat is ~ niet gebeurd* however, that did not happen
de **echtgenoot** /ɛxtxənot/ (pl: -genoten) husband: *de aanstaande echtgenoten* the husband and wife to be
de **echtgenote** /ɛxtxənotə/ (pl: -n, -s) wife
de **echtheid** /ɛxtheit/ authenticity, genuineness
het **echtpaar** /ɛxtpar/ (pl: -paren) married couple: *het ~ Keizers* Mr and Mrs Keizers
de **echtscheiding** /ɛxtsxeidɪŋ/ (pl: -en) divorce
de **eclips** /eklɪps/ (pl: -en) eclipse
het **ecoduct** /ekodʏkt/ (pl: -en) wildlife viaduct
de **ecologie** /ekoloɣi/ ecology
ecologisch /ekoloɣis/ (adj, adv) ecological; biological
de **econometrie** /ekonometri/ econometry
de **economie** /ekonomi/ (pl: -ën) **1** economy **2** economy, frugality, thrift **3** economics, political economy
economisch /ekonɔmis/ (adj, adv) **1** economical, frugal, thrifty **2** economic: *de ~e as-*

pecten van het uitgeversbedrijf the economics of publishing
de **econoom** /ekonom/ (pl: economen) economist
het **ecosysteem** /ekosistem/ eco system
de **ecu** /eky/ (pl: -'s) ecu
Ecuador /ekwadɔr/ Ecuador
de **Ecuadoraan** /ekwadoran/ (pl: Ecuadoranen) Ecuadorian
Ecuadoraans /ekwadorans/ (adj) Ecuadorian
het **eczeem** /ɛksem/ (pl: eczemen) eczema
e.d. *en dergelijke* and the like
de **edammer** /edɑmər/ Edam (cheese)
edel /edəl/ (adj, adv) **1** noble, aristocratic: *van ~e geboorte* high-born **2** noble, magnanimous ‖ *~e delen* privates; family jewels
edelachtbaar /edəlɑxtbar/ (adj): *Edelachtbare* Your Honour
het **edelgas** /edəlɣɑs/ (pl: -sen) inert gas
het **edelhert** /edəlhɛrt/ (pl: -en) red deer
de **edelman** /edəlmɑn/ (pl: edellieden) noble, nobleman, peer
het **edelmetaal** /edəlmetal/ (pl: -metalen) precious metal
edelmoedig /edəlmudəx/ (adj, adv) noble, generous, magnanimous
de **edelsmid** /edəlsmɪt/ (pl: -smeden) worker in precious metals
de **edelsteen** /edəlsten/ (pl: -stenen) precious stone, gem(stone)
de **editie** /edi(t)si/ (pl: -s) edition; issue; version
de **educatie** /edyka(t)si/ (pl: -s) education
educatief /edykatif/ (adj, adv) educational
de **eed** /et/ (pl: eden) oath, vow: *een ~ afleggen* take (*or:* swear) an oath, swear; *iets onder ede verklaren* declare sth. on oath
het **eeg** /eeɣ/ (pl: -'s) *elektro-encefalogram* EEG
de **EEG** /eeɣe/ *Europese Economische Gemeenschap* EEC
de **eekhoorn** /ekhorn/ (pl: -s) squirrel
het **eekhoorntjesbrood** /ekhorncəzbrot/ cep, boletus
het **eelt** /elt/ hard skin; callus: *~ op zijn ziel hebben* be hardened
¹**een** /ən/ (art) **1** a; an: *op ~ (goeie) dag* one (fine) day; *neem ~ Oprah Winfrey* take s.o. like an Oprah Winfrey **2** a, some: *over ~ dag of wat* in a few days **3** a, some: *wat ~ mooie bloemen!* what beautiful flowers!; *wat ~ idee!* what an idea!
²**een** /en/ (num) one: *het ~ en ander* this and that; *van het ~ komt het ander* one thing leads to another; *op één dag* in one day; on the same day; *~ en dezelfde* one and the same; *de weg is ~ en al modder* the road is nothing but mud; *op ~ na de laatste* the last but one; *op ~ na de beste* the second best; *~ voor ~* one by one; one at a time ‖ *~ april* April Fools' Day; *hij gaf hem er ~ op de neus* he gave him one on the nose; *geef me er nog ~* give

me another (one), give me one more; *zich ~ voelen met de natuur* be at one with nature

de **eenakter** /ẹnɑktər/ (pl: -s) one-act play

eencellig /ensẹləx/ (adj) unicellular, single-celled

de **eend** /ent/ (pl: -en) **1** duck; duckling; drake: *zich een **vreemde** ~ in de bijt voelen* feel the odd man out **2** (Citroën) 2 CV, deux-chevaux

eendaags /endạxs/ (adj) **1** (once) daily **2** one-day

de **eendagsvlieg** /ẹndɑxsflix/ (pl: -en) **1** may-fly **2** nine days' wonder

het **eendenkroos** /ẹndə(n)kros/ duckweed

de **eendracht** /ẹndrɑxt/ harmony, concord

eendrachtig /endrạxtəx/ (adj, adv) united: *~ samenwerken* work together in unison, work harmoniously together

eenduidig /endọydəx/ (adj, adv) unequivocal, unambiguous

eeneiig /enẹiəx/ (adj) monovular, monozygotic: *een ~e tweeling* identical twins

de **eengezinswoning** /eŋɣəzɪnswonɪŋ/ (pl: -en) (small) family dwelling

de **eenheid** /ẹnhɛit/ (pl: -heden) **1** unity, oneness; uniformity: *de ~ **herstellen** (or: **verbreken**)* restore (or: destroy) unity **2** unit: *eenheden en **tientallen*** units and tens **3** unit, entity: [Dutch] *de **mobiele** ~* riot police; *een (hechte, gesloten) ~ **vormen*** form a (tight, closed) group

de **eenheidsprijs** /ẹnhɛitsprɛis/ (pl: -prijzen) **1** unit price, price per unit **2** uniform price

de **eenheidsworst** /ẹnhɛrtsworst/ (pl: -en) sameness

de **eenhoorn** /ẹnhorn/ (pl: -s) unicorn

eenjarig /ẹnjarəx/ (adj) **1** one-year(-old), yearling **2** one-year('s): *een ~e **plant*** an annual

het **eenkamerappartement** /eŋkạmərɑpartəmɛnt/ (pl: -en) single-room (or: one-room) apartment, studio apartment

de **eenkamerflat** /eŋkạmərflɛt/ (pl: -s) single-room flat; [Am] single-room apartment

eenkennig /eŋkẹnəx/ (adj) shy

de **eenling** /ẹnlɪŋ/ (pl: -en) (solitary) individual, lone wolf, loner

eenmaal /ẹmal/ (adv) **1** once, one time: *~, andermaal, verkocht* going, going, gone! **2** once; one day; some day: *als het ~ zover komt* if it ever comes to it **3** just, simply: *dat is nu ~ zo* that's just the way it is; *ik ben nu ~ zo* that's the way I am

eenmalig /ẹmaləx/ (adj) once-only, one-off: *een ~ **optreden (concert)*** a single performance

de **eenmanszaak** /ẹmɑnsak/ (pl: -zaken) one-man business

eenmotorig /emotọrəx/ (adj) single-engine(d)

een-op-een /enɔpẹn/ (adv) one-on-one: [sport] *~ **verdedigen*** defend one-on-one; *de*

*kinderen **worden** ~ **begeleid*** the children are individually supervised, the children receive one-to-one attention; *dat kun je niet zomaar ~ **overnemen*** it isn't a perfect parallel

het **eenoudergezin** /enọudərɣəzɪn/ (pl: -nen) single-parent family

eenparig /empạrəx/ (adj, adv) uniform: *~ versneld* uniformly accelerated

het **eenpersoonsbed** /empɛrsọnzbɛt/ (pl: -den) single bed

de **eenpersoonskamer** /empɛrsọnskamər/ (pl: -s) single room; single

de **eenpitter** /ẹmpɪtər/ (pl: -s) **1** self-employed person **2** loner

het **eenrichtingsverkeer** /enrɪxtɪŋsfərker/ one-way traffic: ***straat** met ~* one-way street

¹**eens** /ens/ (adj) agreed, in agreement: *het over de prijs ~ **worden*** agree on a (or: about the) price; *het niet ~ zijn **met** iem.* disagree with s.o.

²**eens** /ens/ (adv) **1** once: *voor ~ en altijd* once and for all; *~ in de week (or: drie maanden)* once a week (or: every three months) **2** some day, one day; sometime; once: ***kom** ~ langs* drop in (or: by) sometime; *er was ~* once upon a time there was **3** just: ***denk** ~ even (goed) na* just think (carefully); *niet ~ tijd hebben om* not even have the time to; *nog ~* once more, (once) again; *nu ~, dan weer* off and on, on and off

eensgezind /ensxẹzɪnt/ (adj, adv) unanimous, united; concerted: *~ **voor** (or: **tegen**) iets zijn* be unanimously for (or: against) sth.

de **eensgezindheid** /ensxẹzɪnthɛit/ unanimity, consensus, harmony, accord

eensklaps /ẹnsklɑps/ (adv) suddenly, all of a sudden

eensluidend /enslœ̣ydənt/ (adj) identical (in content), uniform (with): *tot een ~ **oordeel** komen* come to a uniform (or: unanimous) opinion (or: judgment)

eenstemmig /enstẹməx/ (adj, adv) **1** unanimous, by common assent (or: consent) **2** in unison, for one voice

eentje /ẹncə/ (ind pron) one: *neem er nog ~* have another (one, glass); *op (or: in) z'n ~ (by) o.s.*; (on) one's own

eentonig /entọnəx/ (adj, adv) monotonous, monotone; drab; dull: *een ~ **leven (bestaan)** leiden* lead a humdrum (or: dull) existence; *~ werk* tedious (or: monotonous) work; drudgery

de **eentonigheid** /entọnəxhɛit/ monotony, monotonousness, tedium

een-twee-drie /entwedrị/ (adv) just like that: *niet ~* not just like that

het **een-tweetje** /entwẹcə/ (pl: -s) **1** one-two; wall pass **2** joint pact, joint deal; stitch-up: *een ~ **met** iem. opzetten* prearrange a deal with s.o.; *een ~ **met** de minister* a joint deal with the minister

de **eenvoud** /ẹnvɑut/ **1** simplicity, simpleness; plainness **2** simplicity, straightforwardness, naivety, innocence: *hij zei dat in zijn* ~ he said that in his naivety (*or:* innocence)

¹**eenvoudig** /envọudəχ/ (adj) **1** simple, uncomplicated; plain; easy: *dat is het ~ste* that's the easiest way; *zo* ~ *ligt dat niet* it's not that simple **2** simple, unpretentious, ordinary **3** simple, plain, ordinary; low(ly); humble; modest, unpresuming, simple-hearted

²**eenvoudig** /envọudəχ/ (adv) **1** simply, plainly: *(al) te* ~ *voorstellen* (over)simplify **2** simply, just

eenvoudigweg /envọudəχwɛχ/ (adv) simply, just

de **eenwording** /ẹnwɔrdɪŋ/ (pl: -en) unification, integration: *de politieke* ~ *van Europa* the political unification (*or:* integration) of Europe

eenzaam /ẹnzam/ (adj, adv) **1** solitary, isolated, lonely, lone(some): *een* ~ *leven leiden* live a solitary life **2** solitary, isolated, lonely, secluded

de **eenzaamheid** /ẹnzamhɛit/ solitude, solitariness, loneliness; isolation; retirement, seclusion

de **eenzaat** /ẹnzat/ (pl: eenzaten) [Belg] loner, lone wolf

eenzelvig /enzɛlvəχ/ (adj, adv) self-contained, introverted

eenzijdig /enzẹidəχ/ (adj, adv) **1** one-sided, unilateral, limited: *hij is erg* ~ he is very one-sided **2** one-sided, biased, partial

de **eer** /er/ **1** honour, respect: *de ~ redden* save one's face; *aan u de* ~ *(om te beginnen)* you have the honour (of starting); *naar* ~ *en geweten antwoorden* answer to the best of one's knowledge; *op mijn (woord van)* ~ I give you my word (of honour); *de ~ aan zichzelf houden* take the honourable way out **2** honour(s), credit: *iem. de laatste ~ bewijzen* pay s.o. one's last respects; *het zal me een (grote, bijzondere) ~ zijn* I will be (greatly) honoured; *ter ere van* in honour of (s.o., sth.)

eerbaar /ẹrbar/ (adj, adv) honourable

het **eerbetoon** /ẹrbətoːn/ (mark of) honour: *met veel ~ ontvangen* receive with full honours

de **eerbied** /ẹrbit/ respect, esteem, regard; reverence; veneration; worship: *iem. ~ verschuldigd zijn* owe s.o. respect

eerbiedig /erbịdəχ/ (adj, adv) respectful

eerbiedigen /erbịdəγə(n)/ (eerbiedigde, heeft geëerbiedigd) respect, regard; observe: *de mening van anderen ~* respect the opinions of others

eerbiedwaardig /erbitwạrdəχ/ (adj) respectable

eerdaags /ẹrdaχs/ (adv) one of these days

¹**eerder** /ẹrdər/ (adj) earlier

²**eerder** /ẹrdər/ (adv) **1** before (now), sooner, earlier: *ik heb u al eens ~ gezien* I have seen you (somewhere) before; *hoe ~ hoe beter (liever)* the sooner the better **2** rather, sooner, more (likely): *ik zou ~ denken dat* I am more inclined to think that

het **eergevoel** /ẹryəvul/ (sense, feeling of) honour, pride

eergisteren /erɣịstərə(n)/ (adv) the day before yesterday

het **eerherstel** /ẹrhɛrstɛl/ rehabilitation

¹**eerlijk** /ẹrlək/ (adj) **1** honest, fair, sincere: ~ *is* ~ fair is fair **2** honest, true, genuine: *een ~e zaak* a square deal **3** fair, square, honest: ~ *spel* fair play

²**eerlijk** /ẹrlək/ (adv) **1** sincerely; honestly; frankly: ~ *gezegd* to be honest **2** honestly, really and truly: *ik heb het niet gedaan*, ~ *(waar)!* honestly, I didn't do it! **3** fairly, squarely: ~ *delen!* fair shares!

de **eerlijkheid** /ẹrləkhɛit/ honesty, fairness, sincerity

eerst /erst/ (adv) **1** first: *hij zag de brand het* ~ he was the first to see the fire; *(het) ~ aan de beurt zijn* be first (*or:* next); *voor het ~* for the first time, first **2** first(ly), at first: ~ *was hij verlegen, later niet meer* at first he was shy, but not later

eerste /ẹrstə/ (num) first; chief; prime; senior; earliest: *als ~ bezochten we het museum* we started by visiting the museum; *hij kwam als ~ binnen* he was the first to enter; *de ~ vier dagen* (for) the next four days; *hij is niet de ~ de beste* he is not just anybody; *informatie uit de ~ hand* first-hand information; *ten ~* first(ly), in the first place; *van de ~ tot de laatste* down to the last one, every man jack (of them); *één keer moet de ~ zijn* there's a first time for everything

eerstegraads /ẹrstəɣrats/ (adj, adv) first-degree

de **eerstehulppost** /ẹrstəhʏlpɔst/ (pl: -en) first-aid post (*or:* station)

eerstejaars /ẹrstəjars/ (adj) first-year

het **Eerste Kamerlid** /ẹrstəkạmərlɪt/ (pl: -leden) [Dutch] Member of the Upper Chamber (*or:* Upper House) (of the Dutch Parliament)

eersteklas /ẹrstəklɑs/ (adj, adv) first-rate, first-class

de **eersteklasser** /ẹrstəklɑsər/ (pl: -s) first-former

de **eerstelijnszorg** /ẹrstəlɛinsɔrχ/ primary health care

eersterangs /ẹrstərɑns/ (adj) first-rate, top-class

eerstkomend /erstkọmənt/ (adj) next: *~e woensdag* next Wednesday

eerstvolgend /erstfọlɣənt/ (adj) next: *de ~e trein* the next train due

¹**eervol** /ẹrvɔl/ (adj) **1** honourable, glorious, creditable: *de ~le verliezers* the worthy losers; *een ~le vermelding* an honourable men-

tion **2** with honour, without loss of face

²eervol /ervol/ (adv) honourably, worthily, gloriously, creditably

de **eerwraak** /ervrak/ honour killing

eerzaam /erzam/ (adj, adv) respectable, virtuous, decent, honest

de **eerzucht** /erzʏχt/ ambition

eerzuchtig /erzʏχtəχ/ (adj, adv) ambitious, aspiring

eetbaar /edbar/ (adj) edible, fit for (human) consumption, fit to eat; eatable; palatable

het **eetcafé** /etkafe/ (pl: -s) pub serving meals; beanery

de **eetgelegenheid** /etχəleɣə(n)hɛɪt/ (pl: -gelegenheden) place to eat, eating-house

het **eetgerei** /etχərɛi/ cutlery, tableware

de **eetgewoonte** /etχəwontə/ (pl: -n, -s) eating habit; diet

de **eethoek** /ethuk/ (pl: -en) **1** dinette **2** dining table and chairs

het **eethuis** /ethœys/ (pl: eethuizen) eating house, (small) restaurant

de **eetkamer** /etkamər/ dining room

de **eetlepel** /etlepəl/ (pl: -s) soup spoon; dessertspoon; tablespoon(ful)

het **eetlust** /etlʏst/ appetite

het **eetservies** /etsɛrvis/ (pl: -serviezen) dinner service, dinner set, tableware

het **eetstokje** /etstɔkjə/ (pl: -s) chopstick

de **eetstoornis** /etstornɪs/ eating disorder

de **eetwaar** /etwar/ (pl: eetwaren) foodstuff(s), eatables, food

de **eetzaal** /etsal/ (pl: eetzalen) dining room (or: hall); canteen

de **eeuw** /ew/ (pl: -en) **1** century: *in de loop der ~en* through the centuries (or: ages); *in het Londen van de achttiende ~* in eighteenth-century London **2** ages, (donkey's) years: *het is ~en geleden dat ik van haar iets gehoord heb* I haven't heard from her for ages; *dat heeft een ~ geduurd* that took ages **3** age, era, epoch: [Dutch] *de gouden ~* the golden age

eeuwenlang /ewə(n)lɑŋ/ (adv) for centuries (or: ages)

eeuwenoud /ewə(n)ɑut/ (adj) age-old, centuries-old

¹eeuwig /ewəχ/ (adj) **1** eternal, everlasting, perennial, perpetual, never-ending: *~e sneeuw* perpetual snow **2** lifelong, undying: *~e vriendschap* undying (or: lifelong) friendship **3** endless, incessant, interminable, never-ending: *een ~e optimist* an incorrigible optimist

²eeuwig /ewəχ/ (adv) **1** forever, eternally, perpetually **2** forever, incessantly, endlessly, interminably, eternally

eeuwigdurend /ewəɣdyrənt/ (adj) perpetual, everlasting

de **eeuwigheid** /ewəχhɛit/ ages, eternity: *ik heb je in geen ~ gezien* I haven't seen you for ages

de **eeuwwisseling** /ewɪsəlɪŋ/ (pl: -en) turn of the century

het **effect** /ɛfɛkt/ (pl: -en) **1** effect, result, outcome, consequence: *een averechts ~ hebben* have a contrary effect, be counter-productive; *~ hebben* have an effect, be effective **2** spin; side: *een bal ~ geven* put spin on a ball **3** [com] stock, share, security

het **effectbejag** /ɛfɛktbəjɑχ/ aiming at effect, straining after effect: *uit ~* for (the sake of) effect

de **effectenbeurs** /ɛfɛktə(n)børs/ (pl: -beurzen) stock exchange

de **effectenmarkt** /ɛfɛktəmɑrkt/ stock market

effectief /ɛfɛktif/ (adj, adv) **1** real, actual, effective, active **2** effective, efficacious **3** [Belg; law] non-suspended

effen /ɛfə(n)/ (adj, adv) **1** even, level, smooth **2** plain, uniform, unpatterned: *~ rood* solid red

effenen /ɛfənən/ (effende, heeft geëffend) level, smooth: *de weg ~ voor iem.* pave the way for s.o.

de **efficiency** /ɛfɪʃənsi/ efficiency

efficiënt /ɛfiʃɛnt/ (adj, adv) efficient, businesslike

de **efficiëntie** /ɛfiʃɛn(t)si/ efficiency

de **eg** /ɛχ/ (pl: eggen) harrow

de **EG** /eɣe/ *Europese Gemeenschap* EC

egaal /eɣal/ (adj, adv) even, level, smooth; uniform; solid

egaliseren /eɣalizərə(n)/ (egaliseerde, heeft geëgaliseerd) level, equalize, smooth

Egeïsch /eɣeis/ (adj) Aegean

de **egel** /eɣəl/ (pl: -s) hedgehog

eggen /ɛɣə(n)/ (egde, heeft geëgd) harrow

het **ego** /eɣo/ ego

¹egocentrisch /eɣosɛntris/ (adj) egocentric, self-centred

²egocentrisch /eɣosɛntris/ (adv) in an egocentric (or: a self-centred) way

het **egoïsme** /eɣowɪsmə/ egoism, selfishness

de **egoïst** /eɣowɪst/ (pl: -en) egoist

egoïstisch /eɣowɪstis/ (adj, adv) egoistic(al), selfish

de **egotripper** /eɣotrɪpər/ (pl: -s) egomaniac

Egypte /eɣɪptə/ Egypt

de **Egyptenaar** /eɣɪptənar/ (pl: Egyptenaren) Egyptian

Egyptisch /eɣɪptis/ (adj) Egyptian

eh /ə/ (int) er

de **EHBO** /ehabeo/ *Eerste Hulp Bij Ongelukken* first aid; first-aid post (or: station); accident and emergency ward (or: department)

de **EHBO'er** /ehabeoər/ (pl: -s) first-aider

de **EHBO-post** /ehabeopost/ (pl: -en) first-aid post (or: station)

het **ei** /ɛi/ (pl: eieren) **1** egg: *een hard(gekookt) ei* a hard-boiled egg; *dat is het hele eieren eten* that's all there is to it; *een ei leggen* lay an egg; *een ei uitbroeden* hatch an egg; *voor* een appel en een ei for a song, for next to nothing; eieren **kiezen** voor zijn geld make the best of a bad job **2** ovum, egg ‖ [Belg] ei zo na very nearly

de **eicel** /ɛisɛl/ (pl: -len) egg cell, ovum, female germ cell

de **eierdooier** /ɛiərdojər/ (pl: -s) egg yolk

de **eierdop** /ɛiərdɔp/ (pl: -pen) eggshell

het **eierdopje** /ɛiərdɔpjə/ (pl: eierdopjes) egg-cup

de **eierschaal** /ɛiərsχal/ (pl: -schalen) eggshell

de **eierstok** /ɛiərstɔk/ (pl: -ken) ovary

de **eierwekker** /ɛiərwɛkər/ (pl: -s) egg-timer

de **Eiffeltoren** /ɛifəltorə(n)/ Eiffel Tower

het **eigeel** /ɛiɣel/ egg yolk

eigen /ɛiɣə(n)/ (adj) **1** own; private; personal: voor ~ **gebruik** for one's (own) private use; mensen met een ~ **huis** people who own their own house; wij hebben ieder een ~ **(slaap)kamer** we have separate (bed)rooms; ~ **weg** private road; op zijn geheel ~ **wijze** in his very own way; bemoei je met je ~ **zaken** mind your own business **2** typical, characteristic, individual: bier met een geheel ~ **smaak** beer with a distinctive taste **3** own, native, domestic

de **eigenaar** /ɛiɣənar/ (pl: eigenaren) owner, possessor; holder: de **rechtmatige** ~ the rightful owner; deze auto is drie keer **van** ~ veranderd this car changed hands three times

¹eigenaardig /ɛiɣənardəχ/ (adj) **1** peculiar, personal, idiosyncratic: een ~ **geval** a peculiar case **2** peculiar, strange, odd, curious: hij was een ~e **jongen** he was a strange boy

²eigenaardig /ɛiɣənardəχ/ (adv) peculiarly, oddly

het **eigenbelang** /ɛiɣə(n)bəlɑŋ/ self-interest: **uit** ~ handelen act out of self-interest

de **eigendom** /ɛiɣəndɔm/ (pl: -men) **1** ownership, title: **in** ~ hebben own (sth.) **2** property, possession; belongings: dat boek is **mijn** ~ that book belongs to me

de **eigendunk** /ɛiɣə(n)dʏŋk/ (self-)conceit, self-importance, arrogance

eigengemaakt /ɛiɣə(n)ɣəmakt/ (adj) home-made

eigengereid /ɛiɣə(n)ɣərɛit/ (adj) headstrong, self-willed

eigenhandig /ɛiɣə(n)hɑndəχ/ (adj, adv) (made, done) with one's own hand(s), (do sth.) o.s., personally

¹eigenlijk /ɛiɣə(n)lək/ (adj) real, actual, true, proper: de ~e **betekenis** van een woord the true meaning of a word

²eigenlijk /ɛiɣə(n)lək/ (adv) really, in fact, exactly, actually: u heeft ~ **gelijk** you are right, really; wat **is** een pacemaker ~? what exactly is a pacemaker?; ~ **mag** ik je dat niet vertellen actually, I'm not supposed to tell you

eigenmachtig /ɛiɣəmɑχtəχ/ (adj, adv) self-willed, self-opinionated: ~ **handelen** act on one's own authority

de **eigennaam** /ɛiɣənam/ (pl: -namen) proper name

de **eigenschap** /ɛiɣənsχɑp/ (pl: -pen) quality; property; [comp] attribute: **goede** ~pen qualities (or: strong points, strengths)

eigentijds /ɛiɣə(n)tɛits/ (adj) contemporary, modern

de **eigenwaarde** /ɛiɣə(n)wardə/ self-respect, self-esteem: **gevoel** van ~ sense of dignity, self-respect

eigenwijs /ɛiɣə(n)wɛis/ (adj, adv) cocky, conceited, pigheaded: **doe** niet zo ~ don't think you know it all

eigenzinnig /ɛiɣə(n)zɪnəχ/ (adj, adv) self-willed; stubborn; obstinate; unamenable; wayward

de **eik** /ɛik/ (pl: -en) oak (tree)

de **eikel** /ɛikəl/ (pl: -s) **1** acorn **2** glans (penis) **3** [inform] jerk, dick, asshole

het **¹eiken** /ɛikə(n)/ oak

²eiken /ɛikə(n)/ (adj) oak

de **eikenboom** /ɛikə(n)bom/ (pl: -bomen) oak (tree)

de **eikenprocessierups** /ɛikə(n)prosɛsirʏps/ (pl: -en) oak processionary caterpillar

het **eiland** /ɛilɑnt/ (pl: -en) island: op het ~ **Man** on (or: in) the Isle of Man; een **kunstmatig** ~ an artificial island, a man-made island

de **eilandbewoner** /ɛilɑndbəwonər/ (pl: -s) islander, island dweller

de **eilandengroep** /ɛilɑndə(n)ɣrup/ (pl: -en) archipelago, group of islands

de **eileider** /ɛilɛidər/ (pl: -s) Fallopian tube

het **eind** /ɛint/ (pl: -en) **1** way; distance; piece: het is een **heel** ~ it's a long way; het is nog een **heel** ~ it's still a long way; daar **kom** ik een heel ~ mee that will go a long way; [fig] aan het **kortste** ~ trekken get the worst of it, come off worst; [fig] aan het **langste** ~ trekken come off best, get the best of it **2** end, extremity; ending: ~ **mei** at the end of May; het **andere** ~ van de stad the other end of the town ‖ het bij het **rechte** ~ hebben be right

de **eindbaas** /ɛindbas/ (pl: -bazen) [inform] top dog

de **eindbestemming** /ɛindbəstɛmɪŋ/ (pl: -en) final destination; terminal

het **eindbod** /ɛindbɔt/ final offer

het **eindcijfer** /ɛintsɛifər/ (pl: -s) final figure, grand total; final mark

het **einddiploma** /ɛindiploma/ (pl: -'s) diploma, certificate; certificate of qualification

het **einde** /ɛində/ (pl: -n) **1** end: er komt geen ~ aan there's no end to it **2** end; ending: **aan** zijn ~ **komen** meet one's end; aan het ~ van de middag in the late afternoon; laten we er nu maar een ~ aan **maken** let's finish off now; een verhaal met een **open** ~ an story with an open ending; **ten** ~ lopen come to an end; expire; **ten** ~ raad zijn be at one's wits' end; van het begin **tot** het ~ from beginning to end; [fig] *dat is niet het ~ van de **wereld*** that's not the end of the world; *eind goed, al goed* all's well that ends well

de **eindejaarspremie** /ɛɪndəjaːrspremi/ (pl: -s) [Belg] end-of-year bonus

de **eindejaarsuitkering** /ɛɪndəjaːrsœytkerɪŋ/ (pl: -en) [Dutch] year-end bonus

eindelijk /ɛɪndələk/ (adv) finally, at last, in the end

eindeloos /ɛɪndəlos/ (adj, adv) **1** endless, infinite, interminable **2** endless, perpetual, interminable, unending: *ik moest ~ **lang** wachten* I had to wait for ages

de **einder** /ɛɪndər/ horizon

het **eindexamen** /ɛɪntɛksamə(n)/ (pl: -s) final exam: *voor zijn ~ slagen* (or: *zakken*) pass (or: fail) one's final exams

de **eindexamenkandidaat** /ɛɪntɛksamə(n)-kandidaːt/ (pl: -kandidaten) examinee, A-level candidate

het **eindexamenvak** /ɛɪntɛksamə(n)vak/ (pl: -ken) final examination subject, school certificate subject

eindig /ɛɪndəx/ (adj) **1** finite: *~e **getallen*** (or: *reeksen*) finite numbers (*or:* progressions) **2** limited

¹**eindigen** /ɛɪndəɣə(n)/ (eindigde, is geëindigd) **1** end, finish, come to an end, stop: *~ **waar** je begonnen bent* end up where one started (from) **2** end, finish, come to an end, terminate; run out; expire: *dit woord eindigt **op** een klinker* this word ends in a vowel ‖ *zij eindigde **als** eerste* she finished first

²**eindigen** /ɛɪndəɣə(n)/ (eindigde, heeft geëindigd) finish (off), end, bring to a close, terminate

het **eindje** /ɛɪncə/ (pl: -s) **1** piece, bit: *een ~ **touw*** a length of rope; a piece of string **2** short distance: *een ~ **verder*** a bit further **3** (loose) end: *de ~s met moeite aan elkaar **kunnen knopen*** be hardly able to make (both) ends meet

de **eindmeet** /ɛɪntmet/ (pl: -meten) [Belg] finishing line

het **eindoordeel** /ɛɪntoːrdel/ (pl: -oordelen) final judgement; final conclusion(s)

het **eindproduct** /ɛɪntproдʏkt/ (pl: -en) final product, end-product, final result, end-result

het **eindpunt** /ɛɪntpʏnt/ (pl: -en) end; terminus

het **eindrapport** /ɛɪntraːport/ (pl: -en) **1** (school) leaving report **2** final report

de **eindredacteur** /ɛɪntredaktør/ (pl: -en, -s) [roughly] editor-in-chief

het **eindresultaat** /ɛɪntrezʏltaːt/ (pl: -resultaten) final result, end result; conclusion; final total

de **eindscriptie** /ɛɪntskrɪpsi/ (pl: -s) final paper, thesis, dissertation

het **eindsignaal** /ɛɪntsɪɣnaːl/ (pl: -signalen) final whistle

de **eindsprint** /ɛɪntsprɪnt/ (pl: -s) final sprint

het **eindstadium** /ɛɪntstaːdijʏm/ (pl: -stadia) final stage; terminal stage

de **eindstand** /ɛɪntstɑnt/ (pl: -en) final score

het **eindstation** /ɛɪntstaː(t)ʃɔn/ (pl: -s) terminal (station)

de **eindstreep** /ɛɪntstrep/ (pl: -strepen) finish(ing line): *de ~ niet **halen*** [fig] not make it

de **eindstrijd** /ɛɪntstrɛit/ final(s), final contest

de **eindterm** /ɛɪntɛrm/ final attainment level

de **eindzege** /ɛɪntseɣə/ (pl: -s) first place

de **einzelgänger** /ɑjntsəlɡɛnər, ɛɪntsəlɡɛnər/ (pl: -s) loner, lone wolf

de **eis** /ɛis/ (pl: -en) **1** requirement, demand, claim: *hoge ~en stellen aan iem.* make great demands of s.o.; *iemands ~en **inwilligen*** comply with s.o.'s demands; *aan de ~en **voldoen*** meet the requirements, be up to standard **2** demand, terms: *akkoord gaan met iemands ~en* agree to s.o.'s demands **3** [law] claim, suit; sentence demanded

eisen /ɛisə(n)/ (eiste, heeft geëist) **1** demand, require, claim: *iets **van** iem. ~* demand sth. from s.o. **2** [law] demand, sue for: *schadevergoeding ~* claim damages

de **eiser** /ɛisər/ (pl: -s) **1** requirer, claimer **2** [law] plaintiff; prosecutor; claimant

het **eitje** /ɛicə/ (pl: -s, eiertjes) (small) egg; ovum: [fig] *dat **is** een ~* it's a piece of cake; [fig] *een zacht(gekookt) ~* a soft-boiled egg

eivormig /ɛivɔrməx/ (adj) egg-shaped, oval

het **eiwit** /ɛiwɪt/ (pl: -ten) **1** egg white, white of an egg **2** protein, albumin

de **ejaculatie** /ejakyla(t)si/ (pl: -s) ejaculation

het/de **EK** /eka/ *Europees kampioenschap* European Championship

de **ekster** /ɛkstər/ (pl: -s) magpie

het **eksteroog** /ɛkstərox/ (pl: -ogen) corn

het **elan** /elã/ élan, panache, zest

de **eland** /elant/ (pl: -en) elk, moose

de **elasticiteit** /elastisitɛit/ elasticity

het **elastiek** /elastik/ (pl: -en) **1** rubber, elastic **2** rubber band, elastic band

het **elastiekje** /elastikjə/ (pl: -s) rubber band

elastisch /elɑstis/ (adj) elastic

elders /ɛldərs/ (adv) elsewhere

het **eldorado** /ɛldoraːdo/ eldorado

electoraal /elɛktoraːl/ (adj) electoral

het **electoraat** /elɛktoraːt/ (pl: electoraten) electorate

elegant /eleɣɑnt/ (adj, adv) elegant; refined

de **elegantie** /eleɣɑnsi/ elegance

het/de **elektra** /elɛktra/ electricity

de **elektricien** /elɛktriʃɛ̃/ (pl: -s) electrician

de **elektriciteit** /elɛktrisitɛit/ electricity: *de ~ **is** nog niet **aangesloten*** we aren't connected to the mains yet

de **elektriciteitscentrale** /elɛktrisitɛitsɛntraːlə/ power station

elektrificeren /elɛktrifisɛrə(n)/ (elektrificeerde, heeft geëlektrificeerd) electrify

elektrisch /elɛktris/ (adj, adv) electric(al): *een ~e **centrale*** a power station; *een ~e **deken*** an electric blanket; *~ **koken*** cook with electricity

het **elektrocardiogram** /elɛktrokɑrdijoɣrɑm/ (pl: -men) electrocardiogram

elektrocuteren /elɛktrokytərə(n)/ (elektrocuteerde, heeft geëlektrocuteerd) electrocute

de **elektrocutie** /elɛktroky(t)si/ (pl: -s) electrocution

de **elektrode** /elɛktrodə/ (pl: -n, -s) electrode

de **elektrolyse** /elɛktroli:zə/ electrolysis

de **elektromagneet** /elɛktromɑɣnet/ (pl: -magneten) electromagnet

de **elektromotor** /elɛktromotər/ (pl: -en, -s) electric motor

het **elektron** /elɛktrɔn/ (pl: -en) electron

de **elektronica** /elɛktronika/ electronics

elektronisch /elɛktronis/ (adj, adv) electronic: ~e **post** electronic mail; e-mail

de **elektroshock** /elɛktroʃɔk/ (pl: -s) electroshock

de **elektrotechniek** /elɛktrotɛxnik/ electrotechnology

elektrotechnisch /elɛktrotɛxnis/ (adj) electrical: ~ **ingenieur** electrical engineer

het **element** /eləmɛnt/ (pl: -en) element, component

elementair /eləmɛntɛ:r/ (adj) elementary; fundamental, basic

de ¹**elf** /ɛlf/ (pl: -en, elven) elf, pixie, fairy

²**elf** /ɛlf/ (num) eleven; [in dates] eleventh: *het is bij elven* it's close on eleven

elfde /ɛlvdə/ (num) eleventh

elfendertigst /ɛlfəndɛrtəxst/ (num): *op zijn ~* at a snail's pace; in a roundabout way

het **elfje** /ɛlfjə/ fairy

de **Elfstedentocht** /ɛlfstedə(n)tɔxt/ (pl: -en) 11-city race; skating marathon in Friesland

het **elftal** /ɛlftɑl/ (pl: -len) team: *het nationale ~* the national team; *het tweede ~* the reserves

de **eliminatie** /elimina(t)si/ (pl: -s) elimination, removal

elimineren /eliminerə(n)/ (elimineerde, heeft geëlimineerd) eliminate, remove

elitair /elitɛ:r/ (adj) elitist

de **elite** /elitə/ elite

het **elitekorps** /elitəkɔrps/ elite troop

het **elixer** /elɪksər/ (pl: -s) elixir

elk /ɛlk/ (ind pron) **1** each (one); every one: *van ~ vier (stuks)* four of each **2** everyone, everybody: *~e tweede* every other one **3** each; every; any: *ze kunnen ~e dag komen* they can come any day; *ze komen ~e dag* they come every day; *~e keer dat hij komt* every time he comes

elkaar /ɛlkɑr/ (pron) each other, one another: *in ~s gezelschap* in each other's company; *uren achter ~* for hours on end; *vier keer achter ~* four times in a row; *alles bij ~* in the end; *bij ~ komen* meet, come together; *meer dan alle anderen bij ~* more than all the others put together; *wij blijven bij ~* we stick (or: keep)

together; *door ~ raken* get mixed up (or: confused); *in ~ zakken* collapse; *zij werden het met ~ eens* they came to an agreement; *naast ~ zitten* (or: *liggen*) sit (or: lie) side by side; *op ~ liggen* lie one on top of the other; *die auto valt bijna (van ellende) uit ~* that car is dropping to bits; *(personen of zaken) (goed) uit ~ kunnen houden* be able to tell (people, things) apart; *uit ~ gaan* **a)** break up; **b)** split up, break up; *zij zijn familie van ~* they are related; *iets niet voor ~ kunnen krijgen* not manage (to do) sth.

de **elleboog** /ɛləboх/ (pl: ellebogen) **1** elbow **2** forearm: *ze moesten zich met de ellebogen een weg uit de winkel banen* they had to elbow their way out of the shop

de **ellende** /ɛlɛndə/ **1** misery **2** trouble, bother: *dat geeft alleen maar (een hoop) ~* that will only cause (a lot of) trouble

de **ellendeling** /ɛlɛndəlɪŋ/ (pl: -en) wretch, pain in the neck

¹**ellendig** /ɛlɛndəɣ/ (adj) **1** awful, dreadful, miserable: *ik voelde me ~* I felt rotten **2** wretched, miserable **3** awful, dreadful: *ik kan die ~e sommen niet maken* I can't do those awful sums

²**ellendig** /ɛlɛndəɣ/ (adv) awfully, miserably

de **ellepijp** /ɛləpɛɪp/ (pl: -en) ulna

de **ellips** /ɛlɪps/ (pl: -en) ellipse, oval

de **els** /ɛls/ (pl: elzen) alder

El Salvador /ɛlsɑlvɑdor/ El Salvador

de **Elzas** /ɛlzɑs/ Alsace

het **elzenhout** /ɛlzə(n)hɑut/ alder-wood

het **email** /emɑj/ enamel

de **e-mail** /imel/ e-mail: *een ~ versturen* send an email, email

het **e-mailadres** /imeladrɛs/ e-mail address

e-mailen /imelə(n)/ (e-mailde, heeft ge-e-maild) e-mail

de **emancipatie** /emɑnsipa(t)si/ (pl: -s) emancipation, liberation

emanciperen /emɑnsiperə(n)/ (emancipeerde, heeft geëmancipeerd) emancipate

de **emballage** /ɑmbɑlaʒə/ packing, packaging

het **embargo** /ɛmbɑrɣo/ (pl: -'s) (trade) embargo ‖ *een ~ opheffen* lift an embargo

het **embleem** /ɛmblem/ (pl: emblemen) emblem

de **embolie** /ɛmboli/ embolism

het **embryo** /ɛmbrijo/ (pl: -'s) embryo

embryonaal /ɛmbrijonɑl/ (adj) embryonic, embryonal: *in embryonale toestand* in embryo (or: germ), in the embryo stage

het **emeritaat** /emeritat/ superannuation, [roughly] retirement: *met ~ gaan* [roughly] retire

emeritus /emeritvs/ (adj) emeritus, retired: *een ~ hoogleraar* an emeritus professor, a professor emeritus

de **emigrant** /emiɣrɑnt/ (pl: -en) emigrant

de **emigratie** /emiɣra(t)si/ (pl: -s) emigration

emigreren /emiɣrẹrə(n)/ (emigreerde, is geëmigreerd) emigrate

eminent /eminɛnt/ (adj) eminent, distinguished

de **emir** /emir/ (pl: -s) emir

het **emiraat** /emirat/ (pl: emiraten) emirate

de **emissie** /emɪsi/ (pl: -s) emission, issue

het **emissierecht** /emɪsirɛxt/ (pl: -en) emissions rights

de **emmer** /ɛmər/ (pl: -s) bucket, pail: *met* **hele** *~s tegelijk* by the bucketful

de **emoe** /emu/ (pl: -s) emu

het **emoticon** /emotikɔn/ (pl: -s) emoticon

de **emotie** /emo(t)si/ (pl: -s) emotion, feeling; excitement: *~s* **losmaken** release emotions; *de ~s* **liepen** *hoog* **op** emotions (*or:* feelings) were running high; *zij liet haar ~s de vrije loop* she let herself go

de **emotie-tv** /emo(t)siteve/ emotion tv

¹**emotioneel** /emo(t)ʃonel/ (adj) emotional, sensitive: *een emotionele* **benadering** *vermijden* avoid an emotional approach; *~* **worden** get emotional

²**emotioneel** /emo(t)ʃonel/ (adv) emotionally

het **emplacement** /ãplasəmɛnt/ (pl: -en) yard

de **employé** /ãmplwajẹ/ (pl: -s) employee

de **EMU** /eemy/ *Economische en Monetaire Unie* EMU, Economic and Monetary Union

en /ɛn/ (conj) **1** and; plus: *twee is vier two and two is four; two plus two is four* **2** and: *én* **boete** *én* **gevangenisstraf** *krijgen* get both a fine and a prison sentence **3** and, but, so: *en* **waarom** *doe je het niet?* so why don't you do it?; *en* **toch** *and still;* **nou** *en?* so what?, and …? || *vind je het fijn? (nou) en* **of!** do you like it? I certainly do!, I'll say!

de **enclave** /ãklavə/ (pl: -s) enclave

de **encycliek** /ɛnsiklịk/ (pl: -en) encyclical

de **encyclopedie** /ãsiklopedị/ (pl: -ën) encyclopaedia

de **endeldarm** /ɛndɛldɑrm/ (pl: -en) rectum

endogeen /ɛndoɣẹn/ (adj) endogenous

ene /enə/ (ind pron) a, an, one: *woont hier ~* **Bertels?** does a Mr (*or:* Ms) Bertels live here?

enenmale /enənmalə/ (adv): *dat is* **ten** *~ onmogelijk* that is absolutely (*or:* entirely, completely) impossible

de **energie** /enɛrɣị/ (pl: -ën) energy, power: *duurzame ~* renewable energy; *schone ~* clean energy; *overlopen van ~* be bursting with energy

het **energiebedrijf** /enɛrɣibədrɛif/ (pl: -bedrijven) electricity company, power company

de **energiebesparing** /enɛrɣibəsparɪŋ/ energy saving

energiebewust /enɛrɣibəwʏst/ (adj) energy-conscious

de **energiebron** /enɛrɣibrɔn/ (pl: -nen) source of energy (*or:* power)

de **energiedrank** /enɛrɣidrɑŋk/ (pl: -en) energy drink

energiek /enɛrɣik/ (adj, adv) energetic, dynamic

energieneutraal /enɛrɣinøtral/ (adj) energy-neutral, zero-energy

de **energietransitie** /enɛrɣitranzi(t)si/ energy transition

de **energievoorziening** /enɛrɣivorzinɪŋ/ power supply

enerverend /enɛrvẹrənt/ (adj) exciting, nerve-racking

enerzijds /enərzɛits/ (adv) on the one hand: *~ …,* **anderzijds** *…* on the one hand …, on the other (hand) …

eng /ɛŋ/ (adj, adv) **1** scary, creepy: *een ~* **beest** a nasty (*or:* creepy, scary) animal; a creepy-crawly **2** narrow

het **engagement** /ɑŋɡaʒəmɛnt/ (pl: -en) commitment, involvement

de **engel** /ɛŋəl/ (pl: -en) angel

Engeland /ɛŋəlɑnt/ England

de **engelbewaarder** /ɛŋəlbəwardər/ (pl: -s) guardian angel

het **engelengeduld** /ɛŋələ(n)ɣədʏlt/ patience of a saint

Engels /ɛŋəls/ (adj) English || *iets van het Nederlands* **in** *het ~* **vertalen** translate sth. from Dutch into English

de **Engelse** /ɛŋəlsə/ Englishwoman: *zij* **is** *een ~* she is English

de **Engelsman** /ɛŋəlsmɑn/ (pl: Engelsen) Englishman

Engelstalig /ɛŋəlstaləχ/ (adj) **1** English-language, English **2** English-speaking

de **engerd** /ɛŋərt/ (pl: -s) creep, ghoul

de **engte** /ɛŋtə/ (pl: -n, -s) narrow(s)

¹**enig** /enəχ/ (adj) only, sole: *~* **erfgenaam** sole heir; *dit was de ~e* **keer** *dat …* this was the only time that …; *hij is* **de** *~e die het kan* he is the only one who can do it; **het** *~e wat ik kon zien was* all I could see was

²**enig** /enəχ/ (adj, adv) wonderful, marvellous, lovely

³**enig** /enəχ/ (ind pron) **1** some: *~e moeite doen* go to some trouble; *zonder ~e* **twijfel** without any doubt **2** any, a single: *zonder ~ incident* without a single incident **3** some, a few: *er kwamen ~e* **bezoekers** a few visitors came

enigerlei /enəɣərlɛi/ (adj) any: *in ~* **mate** to any extent; *in ~* **vorm** in any form, in some form or other

enigermate /enəɣərmatə/ (adv) somewhat, a bit, a little, to some extent

enigszins /enəχsɪns/ (adv) **1** somewhat, rather: *hij was ~* **verlegen** he was rather (*or:* somewhat) shy **2** at all, in any way: *indien (ook maar) ~* **mogelijk** if at all possible; *zodra ik maar ~* **kan** as soon as I possibly can

de ¹**enkel** /ɛŋkəl/ (pl: -s) ankle: *een* **verstuikte** *~* a sprained ankle

²**enkel** /ɛŋkəl/ (adj) single: *een kaartje ~e reis* a single (ticket)

³**enkel** /ɛŋkəl/ (adv) 1 singly 2 only, just: *hij doet het ~ voor zijn plezier* he only does it for fun; *ik doe het ~ en alleen om jou* I'm doing it simply and solely for you

⁴**enkel** /ɛŋkəl/ (num) 1 sole, solitary, single: *in één ~e klap* at one blow; *er is geen ~ gevaar* there is not the slightest danger; *geen ~e kans hebben* have no chance at all; *op geen ~e manier* (in) no way 2 a few: *in slechts ~e gevallen* in only a few cases 3 a few: *in ~e dagen* in a few days

de **enkelband** /ɛŋkəlbɑnt/ (pl: -en) 1 ankle ligament: *zijn ~en scheuren* tear one's ankle ligaments 2 anklet 3 electronic tag, ankle tag

de **enkeling** /ɛŋkəlɪŋ/ (pl: -en) individual: *slechts een ~ weet hiervan* only one or two people know about this

de **enkelsok** /ɛŋkəlsɔk/ (pl: -ken) ankle sock; [Am] anklet

het **enkelspel** /ɛŋkəlspɛl/ (pl: -en) singles

het **enkeltje** /ɛŋkəlcə/ (pl: -s) single (ticket)

het **enkelvoud** /ɛŋkəlvɑut/ (pl: -en) singular

enkelzijdig /ɛŋkəlzɛidəx/ (adj, adv) one-sided, unilateral: *~ kopiëren* make single-sided copies

enorm /enɔrm/ (adj, adv) 1 enormous, huge: *een ~ succes* an enormous success 2 tremendous: *~ groot* gigantic, immense

de **enquête** /ɑŋkɛːtə/ (pl: -s) 1 poll, survey: *een ~ houden naar* conduct (*or:* do, make) a survey of 2 inquiry, investigation

het **enquêteformulier** /ɑŋkɛːtəfɔrmylir/ (pl: -en) questionnaire

ensceneren /ɑːsənərə(n)/ (ensceneerde, heeft geënsceneerd) stage, put on

het **ensemble** /ɑːsɑ̃blə/ (pl: -s) ensemble, company, troupe

de **ent** /ɛnt/ (pl: -en) graft

enten /ɛntə(n)/ (entte, heeft geënt) graft

de **enter** /ɛntər/ [comp] enter

enteren /ɛntərə(n)/ (enterde, heeft geënterd) board

de **entertoets** /ɛntərtuts/ (pl: -en) enter (key)

het **enthousiasme** /ɑntuːʒɑsmə/ enthusiasm

enthousiast /ɑntuːʒɑst/ (adj, adv) enthusiastic

de **entourage** /ɑnturaːʒə/ (pl: -s) entourage

de **entrecote** /ɑntrəkɔt/ (pl: -s) entrecôte

de **entree** /ɑ̃treː/ (pl: -s) 1 entrance, entrance hall 2 entry, entrance, admission: *vrij ~* admission free; free entrance 3 admission: *~ heffen* charge for admission

de **entreeprijs** /ɑ̃trɛprɛis/ (pl: -prijzen) admission (price)

de **enveloppe** /ɛnvəlɔp/ (pl: -n) envelope

enz. enzovoort etc.

enzovoorts /ɛnzovorts/ et cetera, and so on, etc.

het **enzym** /ɛnzim/ (pl: -en) enzyme

het **epicentrum** /episɛntrʏm/ epicentre

de **epidemie** /epidemiː/ (pl: -ën) epidemic

de **epilepsie** /epilɛpsiː/ epilepsy

epileptisch /epilɛptis/ (adj) epileptic

epileren /epilɛrə(n)/ (epileerde, heeft geëpileerd) depilate

de **epiloog** /epilɔx/ (pl: epilogen) epilogue

episch /epis/ (adj, adv) epic(al), heroic

de **episode** /epizɔdə/ (pl: -n, -s) episode

het/de **epistel** /epɪstəl/ (pl: -s) epistle

de **epo** /epo/ EPO

het **epos** /epos/ (pl: epen) epic (poem), epos

de **equator** /ekwator/ equator

Equatoriaal-Guinea /ekwatorijalɣineja/ Equatorial Guinea

de **Equatoriaal-Guineeër** /ekwatorijalɣinejər/ (pl: -s) Equatorial Guinean

Equatoriaal-Guinees /ekwatorijalɣines/ (adj) Equatorial Guinean

de **equipe** /ekip/ (pl: -s) team

het ¹**equivalent** /ek(w)ivalɛnt/ (pl: -en) equivalent: *een ~ vinden voor* find an equivalent for

²**equivalent** /ek(w)ivalɛnt/ (adj) equivalent (to)

¹**er** /ɛr/ (pron) of them [often not translated]: *ik heb er nog* (or: *nóg*) *twee* I have got two left (*or:* more); *ik heb er geen (meer)* I haven't got any (left); *hij kocht er acht* he bought eight (of them); *er zijn er die ...* there are those who ...

²**er** /ɛr/ (adv) 1 there: *ik zal er even langsgaan* I'll just call in (*or:* look in, drop in); *dat boek is er niet* that book isn't there; *wie waren er?* who was (*or:* were) there?; *we zijn er* here we are, we've arrived 2 there [often not translated]: *er gebeuren rare dingen* strange things (can) happen; *heeft er iem. gebeld?* did anybody call?; *wat is er?* what is it?, what's the matter?; *is er iets?* is anything wrong? (*or:* the matter?); *er is* (or: *zijn*) *... there is (or: are) ...; *er wordt gezegd dat ...* it is said that ...; *er was eens een koning* once upon a time there was a king ‖ *het er slecht afbrengen* make a bad job of it; *er slecht afkomen* come off badly; *ik zit er niet mee* it doesn't worry me

eraan /ɛrɑn/ (adv) on (it), attached (to it): *kijk eens naar het kaartje dat ~ zit* have a look at the card that's on it (*or:* attached to it) ‖ *de hele boel ging ~* the whole lot was destroyed; *wat kan ik ~ doen?* what can I do about it?; *ik kom ~* I'm on my way

erachter /ɛrɑxtər/ (adv) behind (it): *het hek en de tuin ~* the hedge and the garden behind (it)

eraf /ɛrɑf/ (adv) off (it): *het knopje is ~* the button has come off; *de lol is ~* the fun has gone out of it

erbarmelijk /ɛrbɑrmələk/ (adj, adv) abominable, pitiful, pathetic

erbij /ɛrbɛi̯/ (adv) **1** there, included at (or: with) it **2** at it, to it: *ik blijf ~ dat ...* I still believe (or: maintain) that ...; *zout ~ doen* add salt; *hoe kom je ~!* the very idea!, what can you be thinking of!; *het ~ laten* leave it at that (or: there) ‖ *je bent ~* your game (or: number) is up

erboven /ɛrbo̯və(n)/ (adv) above, over (it)

erbovenop /ɛrbo̯və(n)ɔp/ (adv) on (the) top, on top of it (or: them) ‖ *nu is hij ~* **a)** he has got over it now; **b)** he has pulled through; **c)** [finance] he is on his feet again

erdoor /ɛrdo̯r/ (adv) **1** through it: *die saaie zondagen, hoe zijn we ~ gekomen?* those boring Sundays, however did we get through them? **2** by (or: because) of it: *hij raakte zijn baan ~ kwijt* it cost him his job ‖ *ik ben ~* I've passed; *ik wil ~* I'd like to get past (or: through)

erdoorheen /ɛrdorhe̯n/ (adv) through, through it: *ik ben ~* I'm through (it); *je moet er even doorheen* you just have to work your way through it, you have to give it time; *~ zitten* be completely drained, be completely burnt-out

de **e-reader** /iːriːdər/ (pl: -s) e-book reader, e-reader

de **ereburger** /e̯rəbʏrɣər/ (pl: -s) freeman; honorary citizen

de **erecode** /e̯rəko̯də/ (pl: -n, -s) code of honour

de **erectie** /erɛksi/ (pl: -s) erection

de **eredienst** /e̯rədinst/ (pl: -en) worship, service

de **eredivisie** /e̯rədivizi/ [Dutch] premier league

het **eredoctoraat** /e̯rədɔktorat/ (pl: eredoctoraten) honorary doctorate

de **eregast** /e̯rəɣɑst/ (pl: -en) guest of honour

de **erekwestie** /e̯rəkwɛsti/ (pl: -s) matter of honour

het **erelid** /e̯rəlɪt/ (pl: ereleden) honorary member

het **ereloon** /e̯rəlon/ (pl: erelonen) [Belg] fee

het **eremetaal** /e̯rəmetal/ medal of honour

eren /e̯rə(n)/ (eerde, heeft geëerd) honour

de **ereplaats** /e̯rəplats/ (pl: -en) place of honour: *een ~ innemen* have an honoured place

het **erepodium** /e̯rəpodijʏm/ (pl: erepodia) rostrum, podium

de **eretitel** /e̯rətitəl/ (pl: -s) honorary title, title of honour

de **eretribune** /e̯rətribynə/ (pl: -s) seats of honour, grandstand

het **erewoord** /e̯rəwort/ word of honour

het **erf** /ɛrf/ (pl: erven) **1** property **2** (farm)yard, estate; grounds: *huis en ~ property*

het **erfdeel** /ɛrvdel/ (pl: erfdelen) inheritance, portion

erfelijk /ɛrfələk/ (adj, adv) hereditary

de **erfelijkheid** /ɛrfələkhɛit/ heredity

de **erfelijkheidsleer** /ɛrfələkhɛitsler/ genetics

de **erfenis** /ɛrfənɪs/ (pl: -sen) **1** inheritance; [esp fig] heritage: *een ~ krijgen* be left an inheritance (or: a legacy) **2** legacy, inheritance; estate

de **erfgenaam** /ɛrfɣənam/ (pl: erfgenamen) heir: *iem. tot ~ benoemen* appoint s.o. (one's) heir

het **erfgoed** /ɛrfɣut/ (pl: -eren) inheritance: *cultureel ~* cultural heritage

de **erfpacht** /ɛrfpɑχt/ (pl: -en) [roughly] long lease

het **erfstuk** /ɛrfstʏk/ (pl: -ken) (family) heirloom

de **erfzonde** /ɛrfsɔndə/ original sin

¹**erg** /ɛrχ/: *geen ~ in iets hebben* not be aware (or: be unaware) of sth.

²**erg** /ɛrχ/ (adj) bad: *in het ~ste geval* if the worst comes to the worst; *van de ~ste soort* of the (very) worst kind; *vind je het ~ als ik er niet ben?* do you mind if I'm not there?; *wat ~!* how awful!; *het is (zo) al ~ genoeg* it's bad enough as it is

³**erg** /ɛrχ/ (adv) very: *het spijt me ~* I'm very sorry; *hij ziet er ~ slecht uit* he looks awful (or: dreadful, terrible)

ergens /ɛrɣəns/ (adv) **1** somewhere, anywhere: *~ anders* somewhere else **2** somewhere: *ik heb dat ~ gelezen* I've read that somewhere **3** somehow: *ik kan hem ~ toch wel waarderen* (I have to admit that) he has his good points **4** sth.: *hij zocht ~ naar* he was looking for sth. (or other)

¹**ergeren** /ɛrɣərə(n)/ (ergerde, heeft geërgerd) annoy, irritate

zich ²**ergeren** /ɛrɣərə(n)/ (ergerde zich, heeft zich geërgerd) feel (or: get) annoyed (at); be shocked; take offence

ergerlijk /ɛrɣərlək/ (adj, adv) annoying, aggravating

de **ergernis** /ɛrɣərnɪs/ (pl: -sen) annoyance, irritation: *tot (grote) ~ van de aanwezigen* to the (great) annoyance of those present

ergonomisch /ɛrɣonomis/ (adj, adv) ergonomic; [Am] biotechnological

de **ergotherapeut** /ɛrɣoterapœyt/ (pl: -en) occupational therapist

de **ergotherapie** /ɛrɣoterapi/ (pl: -ën) occupational therapy

erheen /ɛrhe̯n/ (adv) there

erin /ɛrɪn/ (adv) in(to) it, (in) there: *~ lopen* [fig] walk right into it; fall for it

Eritrea /eritrei̯a/ Eritrea

de **Eritreeër** /eritrei̯ər/ (pl: -s) Eritrean

Eritrees /eritre̯s/ (adj) Eritrean

erkend /ɛrkɛnt/ (adj) **1** recognized, acknowledged **2** recognized; authorized; certified: *een internationaal ~ diploma* an internationally recognized certificate

erkennen /ɛrke̯nə(n)/ (erkende, heeft erkend) recognize, acknowledge; admit: *zijn ongelijk ~* admit to being (in the) wrong; *iets* *niet* ~ disown sth.; *een natuurlijk* **kind** ~ acknowledge a natural child; *een document* **als** *echt* ~ recognize a document as genuine

de **erkenning** /ɛrkɛnɪŋ/ (pl: -en) recognition, acknowledgement

erkentelijk /ɛrkɛntələk/ (adj) thankful, grateful

de **erkentelijkheid** /ɛrkɛntələkhɛɪt/ appreciation, recognition: *iem. zijn* ~ *voor iets* **betuigen** show one's appreciation of sth. to s.o.; *uit* ~ *voor* in recognition of, in gratitude for

de **erker** /ɛrkər/ (pl: -s) bay (window)

erlangs /ɛrlɑŋs/ (adv) past (it), alongside (it): *wil je deze brief even op de bus doen als je* ~ **komt?** could you pop this letter in the (post)box when you're passing?

de **erlenmeyer** /ɛrlə(n)mɛijər/ (pl: -s) Erlenmeyer flask

ermee /ɛrme/ (adv) with it: *hij bemoeide zich* ~ he concerned himself with it; he interfered with it; *wat* **doen** *we* ~? what shall we do about (or: with) it?

erna /ɛrna/ (adv) afterwards, after (it), later: *de* **morgen** ~ the morning after

ernaar /ɛrnar/ (adv) to (or: towards, at) it: ~ **kijken** look at it

ernaartoe /ərnartu, ɛrnartu/ (adv) there: *ga je* ~? are you going there?; *op de* **weg** ~ on the way (there)

ernaast /ɛrnast/ (adv) **1** beside it, next to it: *de fabriek en de* **directeurswoning** ~ the factory and the manager's house next to it **2** off the mark: ~ **zitten** be wide of the mark, be wrong

de **ernst** /ɛrnst/ **1** seriousness, earnest(ness): *in alle* ~ in all seriousness; *het is* **bittere** ~ it is dead serious; a serious matter **2** seriousness, gravity: *de* ~ *van de* **toestand** *inzien* recognize the seriousness of the situation

¹**ernstig** /ɛrnstəx/ (adj) **1** serious, grave: *de situatie* **wordt** ~ the situation is becoming serious **2** serious, earnest, sincere: *dat is mijn* ~*e* **overtuiging** that is my sincere conviction **3** serious, severe, grave: ~*e* **gevolgen** *hebben* have grave (or: serious) consequences

²**ernstig** /ɛrnstəx/ (adv) **1** seriously, gravely: *iem.* ~ **toespreken** have a serious talk with s.o.; ~ **ziek** seriously ill **2** seriously, earnestly, sincerely: *het* ~ **menen** be serious

e-roken /eroke(n)/ vape

erom /ɛrɔm/ (adv) **1** around it, round (about) it: *een tuin met een* **schutting** ~ a garden enclosed by a fence **2** for it: *als hij* ~ **vraagt** if he asks for it || *denk je* ~? you won't forget, will you?; *het gaat* ~ *dat ...* the thing is that ...; *hij* **doet** *het* ~ he is doing it on purpose

eromheen /ɛrɔmhen/ (adv) around it, round (about) it

eronder /ɛrɔndər/ (adv) under it, underneath (it), below it: *hij zat op een bank en zijn*

hond **lag** ~ he sat on a bench and his dog lay underneath (or: under) it **2** as a result of it, because of it, under it: *hij* **lijdt** ~ he suffers from it || *(iem.)* ~ **krijgen** beat, defeat (s.o.)

eronderdoor /ɛrɔndərdor/ (adv) underneath it: ~ **gaan a)** go to pieces; **b)** go bust

erop /ɛrɔp/ (adv) **1** on it, on them: ~ *of er-*onder all or nothing **2** up it, up them, on(to) it: ~ **slaan** hit it, bang on it; hit out **3** up it, up them then: ~ **klimmen** climb up it; mount it **4** to it: *het* **vervolg** ~ the sequel to it || *de* **dag** ~ the following day; ~ **staan** insist on it; *het* **zit** ~ that's it (then)

eropaan /ɛrɔpan/ (adv) to(wards) it || *als het* ~ **komt** when it comes to the crunch

eropaf /ɛrɔpɑf/ (adv) to (it): ~ **gaan** go towards it

eropuit /ɛrɔpœʏt/ (adv): *een dagje* ~ **gaan** go off (or: away) for the day; *hij* **is** ~ *mij dwars te zitten* he is out to frustrate me

de **erosie** /erozi/ (pl: -s) erosion

de **erotica** /erotika/ (pl) erotica

de **erotiek** /erotik/ eroticism

erotisch /erotis/ (adj, adv) erotic

erotiseren /erotizere(n)/ (erotiseerde, heeft geërotiseerd) eroticize: *macht eroti-seert* power is an aphrodisiac

erover /ɛrovər/ (adv) **1** over it, across it: *het kleed dat* ~ **ligt** the cloth which covers it **2** over it: *hij* **gaat** ~ he is in charge of it **3** about it, of it: *hoe* **denk** *je* ~? what do you think about it?

eroverheen /ɛrovərhen/ (adv) over it, across it: **strooi** *de kaas* ~ sprinkle the cheese over it; *het heeft lang geduurd eer ze* ~ **waren** it took them a long time to get over it

ertegen /ɛrteyə(n)/ (adv) **1** against it, at it: *hij gooide de* **bal** ~ he threw the ball at it **2** against (it): *ik* **ben** ~ I am against it; ~ **vechten** fight (against) it, oppose it || ~ **kunnen** feel up to it; be able to put up with it

ertegenover /ɛrteyə(n)ovər/ (adv) **1** opposite (to) it: *het* **huis** ~ the house opposite **2** against it; towards it: ~ **staat** *dat ...* on the other hand ... || *hoe* **sta** *je* ~? where do you stand on that?

ertoe /ɛrtu/ (adv) **1** to: *de* **moed** ~ *hebben* have the courage for it (or: to do it); *iem.* ~ **brengen** *om iets te doen* persuade s.o. to do sth.; ~ **komen** get round to it; *hoe* **kwam** *je* ~? what made you do it? **2** to (it): *de vogels die* ~ **behoren** the birds which belong to it || *wat* **doet** *dat* ~? what does it matter?; what has that got to do with it?

het **erts** /ɛrts/ (pl: -en) ore

ertussen /ɛrtʏsə(n)/ (adv) **1** (in) between (it): *het lukte me niet* ~ *te* **komen** I couldn't get a word in (edgeways) **2** in the middle, among other things

ertussenuit /ɛrtʏsə(n)œʏt/ (adv) **1** out (of it) **2** out, loose: *een dagje* ~ **gaan** slip off for the day; ~ *knijpen* slip off (*or:* away, out) (unnoticed), slope off

eruit /ɛrœyt/ (adv) **1** out: ~ *!* (get) out! **2** out, gone: ~ *liggen* be out of favour; [sport] be eliminated

eruitzien /ɛrœytzin/ (zag eruit, heeft eruit-gezien) **1** look **2** look like, look as if: *hij is niet zo dom* **als** *hij eruitziet* he's not as stupid as he looks **3** look a mess

de **eruptie** /erʏpsi/ (pl: -s) eruption

ervan /ɛrvɑn/ (adv) from it, of it: *dat is het aantrekkelijke* ~ that's what is so attractive about it; *ik ben* ~ *overtuigd* I am convinced of it; *ik schrok* ~ it gave me a fright

ervandaan /ɛrvɑndan/ (adv) **1** away (from there): *ik kom* ~ I have just come from there **2** from there: *hij woont dertig kilometer* ~ he lives twenty miles from there

ervandoor /ɛrvɑndor/ (adv) off: *met het geld* ~ *gaan* make off with the cash; *zij ging* ~ *met een zeeman* she ran off with a sailor

ervanlangs /ɛrvɑnlɑns/: *iem.* ~ *geven* let s.o. have it; ~ *krijgen* (really) get (*or:* catch) it

¹**ervaren** /ɛrvarə(n)/ (adj) experienced (in); skilled (in)

²**ervaren** /ɛrvarə(n)/ (ervoer/ervaarde, heeft ervaren) experience; discover

de **ervarenheid** /ɛrvarənhɛɪt/ skill, experience, practice

de **ervaring** /ɛrvarɪŋ/ (pl: -en) experience: *veel* ~ *hebben* be highly experienced; ~ *hebben met iets* know about sth., be familiar with sth.; *de nodige* ~ *opdoen* (*or:* *missen*) gain (*or:* lack) the necessary experience

erven /ɛrvə(n)/ (erfde, heeft geërfd) inherit: *iets (van iem.)* ~ inherit sth. (from s.o.)

ervoor /ɛrvor/ (adv) **1** in front (of it) **2** before (it): *dat was* ~, *niet erna* that was before, not after(wards) **3** for it: *dat dient* ~ *om ...* that is for ..., that serves to ...; *hij moet* ~ *boeten* he will pay for it (*or:* this); ~ *zorgen dat ...* see to it that ... **4** for it, in favour (of it): *ik ben* ~ I am in favour of it **5** for it, instead (of it): ~ *doorgaan* pass for (sth. else); *wat krijg ik* ~*?* what will I get for it? ‖ *er alleen voor staan* be on one's own; *zoals de zaken* ~ *staan* as things stand

de **erwt** /ɛrt/ (pl: -en) pea

de **erwtensoep** /ɛrtə(n)sup/ pea soup

de **es** /ɛs/ ash

de **escalatie** /ɛskala(t)si/ (pl: -s) escalation

¹**escaleren** /ɛskalerə(n)/ (escaleerde, is geëscaleerd) escalate; rocket; shoot up

²**escaleren** /ɛskalerə(n)/ (escaleerde, heeft geëscaleerd) (cause to) escalate; force up

de **escapade** /ɛskapadə/ (pl: -s) escapade

de **escapetoets** /ɛskeptuts/ (pl: -en) [comp] escape (key)

het **escorte** /ɛskɔrtə/ (pl: -s) escort

de **esculaap** /ɛskylap/ (pl: esculapen) staff of Aesculapius

de **esdoorn** /ɛzdorn/ (pl: -s) maple; sycamore

de **e-sigaret** /esiɣarɛt/ (pl: -ten) e-cigarette

het **eskader** /ɛskadər/ (pl: -s) squadron

de **Eskimo** /ɛskimo/ (pl: -'s) Eskimo

de **esp** /ɛsp/ (pl: -en) aspen

het **Esperanto** /ɛsperɑnto/ Esperanto

de **espresso** /ɛsprɛso/ (pl: -'s) espresso

de **espressobar** /ɛsprɛsobɑːr/ café, coffee bar

het **essay** /ɛse/ (pl: -s) essay

de **essentie** /ɛsɛnsi/ essence

essentieel /ɛsɛnʃel/ (adj, adv) essential: *een* ~ *verschil* a fundamental difference

de **Est** /ɛst/ (pl: -en) Estonian

het **establishment** /ɛstɛblɪʃmənt/ establishment

de **estafette** /ɛstafɛtə/ (pl: -s) relay (race)

het **estafettestokje** /ɛstafɛtəstɔkjə/ (pl: -s) baton

de **e-step** /iːstɛp/ e-scooter

esthetisch /ɛstetis/ (adj, adv) aesthetic

Estland /ɛstlɑnt/ Estonia

de **Estlander** /ɛstlɑndər/ (pl: -s) Estonian

Estlands /ɛstlɑn(t)s/ (adj) Estonian

de **etage** /etaʒə/ (pl: -s) floor, storey: *op de eerste* ~ on the first floor; [Am] on the second floor

de **etalage** /etalaʒə/ (pl: -s) shop window, display window: ~*s (gaan)* *kijken* (go) window-shopping

de **etalagepop** /etalaʒəpɔp/ (pl: -pen) (shop-window) dummy, mannequin

etaleren /etalerə(n)/ (etaleerde, heeft geëtaleerd) display

de **etaleur** /etalør/ (pl: -s) window dresser

de **etappe** /etɑpə/ (pl: -s) **1** stage; lap **2** [sport] stage, leg

etc. *et cetera* etc.

het ¹**eten** /etə(n)/ **1** food: *hij houdt van lekker* ~ he is fond of good food **2** meal; dinner: *warm* ~ hot meal, dinner; *het* ~ *is klaar* dinner is ready; *ik ben niet thuis* *met* *het* ~ I won't be home for dinner

²**eten** /etə(n)/ (at, heeft gegeten) eat, dine: *blijf je* ~*?* will you stay for dinner?; *wij zitten net te* ~ we've just sat down to dinner; *uit* ~ *gaan* go out for a meal

³**eten** /etə(n)/ (at, heeft gegeten) eat: *het is niet te* ~ it's inedible; it tastes awful; *wat* ~ *we vandaag?* what's for dinner today?; *je kunt hier lekker* ~ the food is good here; *eet smakelijk* enjoy your meal

de **etensbak** /etə(n)zbɑk/ trough; food bowl

de **etensresten** /etənsrɛstə(n)/ (pl) leftovers

de **etenstijd** /etənstɛit/ dinnertime, time for dinner: *onder* ~ at dinnertime

de **etenswaren** /etənswarə(n)/ (pl) foodstuff(s), eatables, food

het **etentje** /etəntɕə/ (pl: -s) dinner, meal

de **eter** /etər/ (pl: -s) eater

de **ether** /etər/ **1** ether **2** air: *in de* ~ *zijn* be on the air

de **ethiek** /etik/ ethics
Ethiopië /etijopijə/ Ethiopia
de **Ethiopiër** /etijopijər/ (pl: -s) Ethiopian
Ethiopisch /etijopis/ (adj) Ethiopian
ethisch /etis/ (adj, adv) ethical, moral
het **etiket** /etikɛt/ (pl: -ten) label; ticket; tag; sticker
de **etiquette** /etikɛtə/ etiquette, good manners
het **etmaal** /ɛtmal/ (pl: etmalen) twenty-four hours
etnisch /ɛtnis/ (adj, adv) ethnic: *~e **minderheden*** ethnic minorities; *~ **profileren*** racial profiling; *~e **zuivering*** ethnic cleansing
de **ets** /ɛts/ (pl: -en) etching
etsen /ɛtsə(n)/ (etste, heeft geëtst) etch
ettelijke /ɛtələkə/ (num) dozens of, masses of
de **etter** /ɛtər/ pus
etteren /ɛtərə(n)/ (etterde, heeft geëtterd) fester
de **etude** /etydə/ (pl: -s) étude
het **etui** /etwi/ (pl: -s) case
de **etymologie** /etimoloɣi/ (pl: -ën) etymology
etymologisch /etimoloɣis/ (adj, adv) etymological
de **EU** /ey/ *Europese Unie* EU
de **eucalyptus** /œykalɪptys/ (pl: -sen) eucalyptus (tree)
de **eucharistie** /œyxarɪsti/ Eucharist, celebration of the Eucharist; (the) Mass; (Holy) Communion
het **eufemisme** /œyfemɪsmə/ (pl: -n) euphemism
de **euforie** /œyfori/ euphoria
euforisch /œyforis/ (adj) euphoric
de **Eufraat** /øfrat/ Euphrates
de **eunuch** /œynyx/ (pl: -en) eunuch
de **euregio** /øreɣijo/ (pl: -'s) Euregio
eureka /œyreka/ (int) eureka
de **euro** /øro/ euro: *dat kost drie ~* that's three euros
de **eurocent** /ørosɛnt/ (pl: -en) (euro) cent
de **eurocheque** /øroʃɛk/ (pl: -s) Eurocheque
de **Eurocommissaris** /ørokɔmɪsarɪs/ (pl: -sen) Member of the European Commission
de **Eurocommissie** /ørokɔmɪsi/ (pl: -s) European Commission
het **euroland** /ørolɑnt/ (pl: -en) euro country
de **euromunt** /øromʏnt/ (pl: -en) **1** euro **2** euro coin
Europa /øropa/ Europe
het **Europarlement** /øroparləmɛnt/ European Parliament
de **Europarlementariër** /øroparləmɛntarijər/ (pl: -s) member of the European Parliament; Euro-MP
de **Europeaan** /øropejan/ (pl: Europeanen) European
Europees /øropes/ (adj, adv) European
eurosceptisch /ørosɛptis/ (adj) Eurosceptic

het **euroteken** /øroteka(n)/ (pl: -s) euro symbol
het **Eurovisiesongfestival** /ørovizisɔnfɛstival/ (pl: -s) Eurovision Song Contest
de **eurozone** /ørozɔːnə/ eurozone
euthanaseren /œytanazɛrə(n)/ (euthanaseerde, heeft geëuthanaseerd) euthanize
de **euthanasie** /œytanazi/ euthanasia
het **euvel** /øvəl/ (pl: -s) fault, defect: *aan hetzelfde ~ mank gaan* suffer from the same flaw (*or:* fault); *een ~ **verhelpen*** remedy a fault (*or:* defect)
Eva /eva/ Eve
de **evacuatie** /evakywa(t)si/ (pl: -s) evacuation
de **evacué** /evakywe/ (pl: -s) evacuee
[1] **evacueren** /evakywɛrə(n)/ (evacueerde, is geëvacueerd) be evacuated
[2] **evacueren** /evakywɛrə(n)/ (evacueerde, heeft geëvacueerd) evacuate
de **evaluatie** /evalywa(t)si/ (pl: -s) **1** evaluation, assessment **2** evaluation
evalueren /evalywɛrə(n)/ (evalueerde, heeft geëvalueerd) evaluate, assess
het **evangelie** /evɑnɣeli/ (pl: evangeliën) **1** gospel **2** Gospel: *het ~ van **Marcus*** the Gospel according to St Mark
evangelisch /evɑnɣelis/ (adj, adv) evangelical
de **evangelist** /evɑnɣelɪst/ (pl: -en) evangelist
[1] **even** /evə(n)/ (adj) even ‖ *om het ~ wie* whoever, no matter who
[2] **even** /evə(n)/ (adv) **1** (just) as: *ze zijn ~ **groot*** they're equally big; *in ~ **grote** aantallen* in equal numbers; *hij is ~ **oud** als ik* he is (just) as old as I am **2** just: *zij is altijd ~ **opgewekt*** she's always nice and cheerful **3** just, just a moment (*or:* while): *het duurt nog wel ~* it'll take a bit (*or:* while) longer; *mag ik u ~ **storen?*** may I disturb you just for a moment?; *heel ~* just for a second (*or:* minute); *~ **later** shortly* afterwards; *nu ~ **niet!*** not (right) now!; *eens ~ **zien** let me see* **4** (only) just, barely **5** just (a bit): *nog ~ **doorzetten** go on for just a bit* longer ‖ *als het maar éven **kan*** if it is at all possible
de **evenaar** /evənar/ (pl: -s) equator
evenals /evə(n)ɑls/ (conj) (just) like; (just) as: *hun zaak ging failliet, ~ **die** van veel andere kleine ondernemers* their business went bankrupt, just like many other small businesses
evenaren /evənarə(n)/ (evenaarde, heeft geëvenaard) equal, (be a) match (for)
het **evenbeeld** /evə(n)belt/ (pl: -en) image: *zij is het ~ van haar moeder* she is the spitting image of her mother; she is a carbon copy of her mother
eveneens /evə(n)ens/ (adv) also, too, as well
het **evenement** /evənəmɛnt/ (pl: -en) event
evengoed /evə(n)ɣut/ (adv) **1** just as: *jij bent ~ **schuldig** als je broer* you are just as guilty as your brother **2** just as well: *je kunt dat ~ zo*

doen you can just as well do it like this **3** all the same, just the same: *ik weet van niets, maar word er ~ wel op aangekeken* I know nothing about it, but I am suspected all the same

evenmin /evə(n)mɪn/ (adv) (just) as little as, no(t any) more than; neither; nor: *~ als zijn moeder hield hij van vis* he didn't like fish any more than his mother did; *ik kom niet en mijn broer ~* I am not coming and neither is my brother; *de economie krimpt niet, maar groeit ~* the economy is not shrinking, but neither is it growing

evenredig /evə(n)redəχ/ (adj, adv) proportional (to); commensurate (with): *het loon is ~ aan de inspanning* the pay is in proportion to the effort; [maths] *omgekeerd ~ met* inversely proportional to

eventjes /evə(n)cəs/ (adv) **1** (only) just: *~ aanraken* (only) just touch **2** (for) (just) a little while: *hij is ~ hier geweest* he was here for (just) a little while **3** only, merely: *het kostte maar ~ € 1200* it only cost 1200 euros, it cost a mere 1200 euros

¹eventueel /evə(n)tywel/ (adj) any (possible), such … as, potential: *eventuele klachten indienen bij …* (any) complaints should be lodged with …; *eventuele klanten* prospective (or: potential) customers

²eventueel /evə(n)tywel/ (adv) possibly, if necessary; alternatively: *alles of ~ de helft* all of it, or alternatively half; *wij zouden ~ bereid zijn om …* we might be prepared to …

evenveel /evə(n)vel/ (num) (just) as much; just as; equally: *iedereen heeft er ~ recht op* everyone is equally entitled to it; *ieder krijgt ~* everyone gets the same amount

evenwel /evə(n)wel/ (adv) however, nevertheless, nonetheless, yet

het **evenwicht** /evə(n)wɪχt/ balance: *wankel ~* unsteady balance; *zijn ~ bewaren* (or: *verliezen*) keep (or: lose) one's balance; *het juiste ~ vinden* achieve the right balance; *de twee partijen houden elkaar in ~* the two parties balance each other out; *in ~ zijn* be well-balanced, be in equilibrium; *zijn ~ kwijt zijn* have lost one's balance

¹evenwichtig /evə(n)wɪχtəχ/ (adj) (well-)balanced, steady, stable; [fig] level-headed

²evenwichtig /evə(n)wɪχtəχ/ (adv) evenly, equally, uniformly

de **evenwichtsbalk** /evə(n)wɪχtsbalk/ (pl: -en) (balance) beam

het **evenwichtsorgaan** /evə(n)wɪχ(t)sorɣan/ (pl: -organen) organ of balance

evenwijdig /evə(n)wɛidəχ/ (adj, adv) parallel (to, with)

evenzeer /evə(n)zer/ (adv) **1** (just) as much (as) **2** likewise, also

evenzo /evə(n)zo/ (adv) likewise

het **everzwijn** /evərzwɛin/ (pl: -en) wild boar

evident /evidɛnt/ (adj, adv) obvious, (self-)evident; clearly

evolueren /evolywerə(n)/ (evolueerde, heeft/is geëvolueerd) evolve

de **evolutie** /evoly(t)si/ (pl: -s) evolution

de **evolutieleer** /evoly(t)siler/ theory of evolution, evolutionism

de **ex** /ɛks/ (pl: exen) ex

¹exact /ɛksɑkt/ (adj) exact, precise: *~e wetenschappen* (exact) sciences

²exact /ɛksɑkt/ (adv) accurately, precisely

ex aequo /ɛksekwo/ (adv) joint: *Short en Anand eindigden ~ op de tweede plaats* Short and Anand finished joint second

het **examen** /ɛksamə(n)/ (pl: -s) exam(ination): *mondeling* (or: *schriftelijk*) *~* oral (or: written) exam; *een ~ afleggen, ~ doen* take (or: sit) an exam; *zakken voor een ~* fail an exam

de **examenkandidaat** /ɛksamə(n)kɑndidat/ (pl: -kandidaten) examinee, examination candidate

het **examenvak** /ɛksamə(n)vɑk/ (pl: -ken) examination subject

de **examenvrees** /ɛksamə(n)vres/ fear of exam(ination)s; (pre-)exam nerves

de **examinator** /ɛksaminator/ (pl: -en) examiner

examineren /ɛksaminerə(n)/ (examineerde, heeft geëxamineerd) examine

excellent /ɛksɛlɛnt/ (adj, adv) excellent, splendid

de **excellentie** /ɛksɛlɛnsi/ (pl: -s) Excellency

excentriek /ɛksɛntrik/ (adj, adv) eccentric

exceptioneel /ɛksɛpʃonel/ (adj) exceptional

het **exces** /ɛksɛs/ (pl: -sen) excess; extravagance

excessief /ɛksɛsif/ (adj) excessive; extravagant

¹exclusief /ɛksklyzif/ (adj) exclusive

²exclusief /ɛksklyzif/ (adv) excluding, excl.: *~ btw* excluding VAT, plus VAT

excommuniceren /ɛkskɔmyniserə(n)/ (excommuniceerde, heeft geëxcommuniceerd) excommunicate

de **excursie** /ɛkskyrsi/ (pl: -s) **1** excursion **2** (study) visit; field trip

excuseren /ɛkskyzerə(n)/ (excuseerde, heeft geëxcuseerd) excuse, pardon: *Jack vraagt of we hem willen ~, hij voelt zich niet lekker* Jack asks to be excused, he is not feeling well; *wilt u mij even ~* please excuse me for a moment; *zich ~ voor* offer one's excuses (or: apologies) for

het **excuus** /ɛkskys/ (pl: excuses) **1** apology: *zijn excuses aanbieden* apologize **2** excuse: *een slap ~* a poor excuse

executeren /ɛksekyterə(n)/ (executeerde, heeft geëxecuteerd) execute

de **executie** /ɛkseky(t)si/ (pl: -s) execution: *uitstel van ~* stay of execution

de **executieveiling** /ɛkseky(t)sivɛilɪŋ/ (pl: -en)

forced sale, sale under execution

het **exemplaar** /ɛksɛmplaːr/ (pl: exemplaren) **1** specimen, sample **2** copy

exemplarisch /ɛksɛmplaːris/ (adj, adv) exemplary, illustrative

de **exercitie** /ɛksɛrsi(t)si/ (pl: -s) exercise, drill

het **exhibitionisme** /ɛksibi(t)ʃonɪsmə/ exhibitionism

de **exhibitionist** /ɛksibiʃonɪst/ (pl: -en) exhibitionist

existentieel /ɛksɪstɛn(t)ʃel/ (adj) existential

exit /ɛksɪt/ exit: *zijn ~ uit de politiek* his exit from politics; *~ John* exit John, farewell (to) John, that's the end of John

de **exitpoll** /ɛksɪtpɔl/ exit poll

de **exodus** /ɛksodʏs/ (pl: -sen) exodus

exogeen /ɛksoɣen/ (adj) exogenous

exorbitant /ɛksɔrbitɑnt/ (adj, adv) exorbitant, excessive, extravagant

het **exorcisme** /ɛksɔrsɪsmə/ exorcism

het **exoskelet** /ɛksoskəlɛt/ (pl: -ten) (robotic) exoskeleton

exotisch /ɛksotis/ (adj) exotic

de **expansie** /ɛkspɑnsi/ (pl: -s) expansion

het **expansievat** /ɛkspɑnsivɑt/ (pl: -en) expansion tank

de **expat** /ɛkspɛt/ expat

de **expediteur** /ɛkspediˈtøːr/ (pl: -en) shipping agent, forwarding agent; shipper; carrier

de **expeditie** /ɛkspedi(t)si/ (pl: -s) **1** shipping department, forwarding department **2** expedition: *op ~ gaan (naar)* go on an expedition (to) **3** dispatch, shipping, forwarding: *voor een snelle ~ van de goederen zorgen* ensure that the goods are forwarded rapidly

het **experiment** /ɛksperimɛnt/ (pl: -en) experiment: *een wetenschappelijk ~ uitvoeren (op)* perform a scientific experiment (on)

experimenteel /ɛksperimɛntel/ (adj, adv) experimental

experimenteren /ɛksperimɛntərə(n)/ (experimenteerde, heeft geëxperimenteerd) experiment

de **expert** /ɛkspɛːr/ (pl: -s) expert

de **expertise** /ɛkspɛrtiːzə/ (pl: -s, -n) (expert's) assessment

expliciet /ɛksplisit/ (adj, adv) explicit

exploderen /ɛksplodərə(n)/ (explodeerde, is geëxplodeerd) explode

de **exploitant** /ɛksplwɑtɑnt/ proprietor, owner, licensee

de **exploitatie** /ɛksplwɑtaː(t)si/ (pl: -s) exploitation; development

exploiteren /ɛksplwɑterə(n)/ (exploiteerde, heeft geëxploiteerd) exploit; develop: *een stuk grond ~* develop a plot of land

de **explosie** /ɛksplozi/ (pl: -s) explosion

het **1explosief** /ɛksplozif/ (pl: explosieven) explosive

2explosief /ɛksplozif/ (adj, adv) explosive: *explosieve stoffen* explosives

de **explosievengordel** /ɛksplozivə(n)ɣɔrdəl/ (pl: -s) explosive belt (*or:* vest)

de **exponent** /ɛkspoˈnɛnt/ (pl: -en) exponent

exponentieel /ɛksponɛn(t)ʃel/ (adj, adv) exponential

de **export** /ɛkspɔrt/ export

exporteren /ɛkspɔrterə(n)/ (exporteerde, heeft geëxporteerd) export

de **exporteur** /ɛkspɔrtøːr/ (pl: -s) exporter

exposeren /ɛkspozerə(n)/ (exposeerde, heeft geëxposeerd) exhibit, display, show

de **expositie** /ɛkspozi(t)si/ (pl: -s) exhibition, show

expres /ɛksprɛs/ (adv) on purpose, deliberately

de **expressie** /ɛksprɛsi/ (pl: -s) expression

het **expressionisme** /ɛksprɛʃonɪsmə/ expressionism

de **expresweg** /ɛksprɛswɛx/ (pl: -en) [Belg] [roughly] major arterial road

de **extase** /ɛkstaːzə/ ecstasy, rapture

1extatisch /ɛkstaːtis/ (adj, adv) ecstatic

2extatisch /ɛkstaːtis/ (adv) ecstatically; in ecstasy

de **extensie** /ɛkstɛnsi/ (pl: -s) (file) extension

extensief /ɛkstɛnsif/ (adj) extensive

het **1exterieur** /ɛkster(i)øːr/ (pl: -en) exterior

2exterieur /ɛkster(i)øːr/ (adj) exterior, external, outside

extern /ɛkstɛrn/ (adj) **1** non-resident; living-out **2** external, outside

1extra /ɛkstra/ (adj) extra, additional: *er zijn geen ~ kosten aan verbonden* there are no extras (involved); *iets ~'s* sth. extra

2extra /ɛkstra/ (adv) **1** extra: *hij kreeg 20 euro ~* he got 20 euros extra **2** specially: *de leerlingen hadden ~ hun best gedaan* the pupils had made a special effort

het **extraatje** /ɛkstraːcə/ (pl: -s) bonus

het **extract** /ɛkstrɑkt/ (pl: -en) extract; excerpt, abstract

extrapoleren /ɛkstrapolerə(n)/ (extrapoleerde, heeft geëxtrapoleerd) extrapolate

de **extra's** /ɛkstras/ (pl) **1** bonuses; perquisites; perks **2** extras

extravagant /ɛkstravaɣɑnt/ (adj, adv) extravagant, outrageous

extravert /ɛkstravɛrt/ (adj) extrovert(ed), outgoing

1extreem /ɛkstrem/ (adj) extreme

2extreem /ɛkstrem/ (adv) **1** extremely **2** ultra-, far: *extreemlinks* extreme left-wing

het **1extreemrechts** /ɛkstremrɛx(t)s/ (the) extreme (*or:* far) right

2extreemrechts /ɛkstremrɛx(t)s/ (adj) extreme right, ultra-right

het **extremisme** /ɛkstremɪsmə/ extremism

de **extremist** /ɛkstremɪst/ (pl: -en) extremist

de **ezel** /ezəl/ (pl: -s) **1** donkey: *zo koppig als een ~* be as stubborn as a mule; *een ~ stoot zich in 't gemeen geen tweemaal aan dezelfde steen* once bitten, twice shy **2** easel

het **ezelsbruggetje** /ẹzəlzbrʏɣəcə/ memory
aid, mnemonic

het **ezelsoor** /ẹzəlsor/ (pl: -oren) dog-ear

f

de **f** /ɛf/ (pl: f's) f, F

de **fa** /fa/ (pl: fa's) [mus] fa(h)

de **faalangst** /falɑŋst/ fear of failure

de **faam** /fam/ fame, renown

de **fabel** /fabəl/ (pl: -s) fable, fairy-tale

fabelachtig /fabəlɑxtəx/ (adj, adv) fantastic, incredible

het **fabricaat** /fabrikat/ (pl: fabricaten) manufacture, make: *Nederlands* ~ made in the Netherlands

de **fabricage** /fabrikaʒə/ manufacture, production

fabriceren /fabrisɛrə(n)/ (fabriceerde, heeft gefabriceerd) **1** manufacture, produce **2** make, construct

de **fabriek** /fabrik/ (pl: -en) factory

de **fabrieksarbeider** /fabriksɑrbɛɪdər/ (pl: -s) factory worker

de **fabriekshal** /fabrikshɑl/ (pl: -len) **1** factory (building) **2** workshop

het **fabrieksterrein** /fabrikstɛrɛɪn/ factory site

de **fabrikant** /fabrikɑnt/ (pl: -en) manufacturer, producer; factory owner

de **façade** /fasadə/ (pl: -s) façade, front

facebooken /fɛzbukə(n)/ (facebookte, heeft gefacebookt) go (*or:* be) on Facebook

de **facelift** /feslɪft/ (pl: -s) face-lift: *het bedrijf heeft een* ~ *ondergaan* the company has had a face-lift

faceliften /feslɪftə(n)/ (faceliftte, heeft gefacelift) give a facelift (to)

het **facet** /fasɛt/ (pl: -ten) aspect, facet

de **faciliteit** /fasilitɛɪt/ (pl: -en) facility, convenience, amenity

de **faciliteitengemeente** /fasilitɛɪtə(n)ɣəmentə/ (pl: -n, -s) [Belg] municipality with (linguistic) facilities

factchecken /fɛktʃɛkə(n)/ (factcheckte, heeft gefactcheckt) do a fact check, check the facts

de **factor** /fɑktɔr/ (pl: -en) factor: [maths] *een getal in* ~*en ontbinden* resolve a number into factors; *de beslissende* ~ the determining (*or:* determinant) factor; *een zonnebrandcrème met* ~ *30* a factor 30 sun cream (*or:* sunscreen)

factureren /fɑktyrerə(n)/ (factureerde, heeft gefactureerd) invoice, bill

de **factuur** /fɑktyr/ (pl: facturen) invoice, bill

facultatief /fɑkʏltatif/ (adj) optional, elective

de **faculteit** /fɑkʏltɛɪt/ (pl: -en) faculty

de **fagot** /faɣɔt/ (pl: -ten) bassoon

Fahrenheit /farənhɑjt/ Fahrenheit

failliet /fajit/ (adj, adv) bankrupt: ~ *gaan* go bankrupt

het **faillissement** /fajisəmɛnt/ (pl: -en) bankruptcy

fair /fɛːr/ (adj, adv) fair: *iem.* ~ *behandelen* treat s.o. fairly; *dat is niet* ~ that's not playing the game

de **fair trade** /fɛːrtreːt/ fair trade

de **¹fake** /fek/ (pl: -s) fake

²fake /fek/ (adj) fake: *dat hele verhaal is* ~ the whole story's a fake, the whole story's a sham

de **fakir** /fakir/ (pl: -s) fakir

de **fakkel** /fɑkəl/ (pl: -s) torch

de **fakkeldrager** /fɑkəldraɣər/ (pl: -s) torchbearer

de **falafel** /falɑfɛl/ falafel

falen /falə(n)/ (faalde, heeft gefaald) fail; make an error (of judgment), make a mistake

de **faling** /falɪŋ/ [Belg] bankruptcy

de **fall-out** /fɔlɑut/ fall-out

de **fallus** /fɑlʏs/ (pl: -sen) phallus

de **falsetstem** /fɑlsɛtstɛm/ falsetto

fameus /famøs/ (adj, adv) famous, celebrated

familiaal /familijal/ (adj) familial: [Belg] *familiale verzekering* family insurance

familiair /familijɛːr/ (adj, adv) familiar: *al te* ~ *met* iem. omgaan treat s.o. with too much familiarity, take liberties with s.o.

de **familie** /famili/ (pl: -s) **1** family: [fig] *het is één grote* ~ they are one great big happy family; [Belg] *een politieke* ~ a political family; *bij de* ~ *Jansen* at the Jansens **2** family, relatives, (blood) relations: *wij zijn verre* ~ *(van elkaar)* we are distant relatives; *het zit in de* ~ it runs in the family

het **familiedrama** /familidrama/ (pl: -'s) family tragedy, family murder-suicide

het **familielid** /famililɪt/ (pl: -leden) member of the family; relative; relation: *zijn naaste familieleden* his next of kin

de **familienaam** /familinam/ (pl: -namen) family name, surname; [esp Am] last name

het **familiewapen** /familiwapə(n)/ (pl: -s) family (coat of) arms

familieziek /familizik/ (adj) overfond of one's relations

de **fan** /fɛn/ (pl: -s) fan

de **fanaat** /fanat/ (pl: fanaten) fanatic

de **fanaticus** /fanatikʏs/ (pl: fanatici) *see fanaat*

fanatiek /fanatik/ (adj, adv) fanatical, crazy: *een* ~ *schaker* a chess fanatic

de **fanatiekeling** /fanatikəlɪŋ/ (pl: -en) [iron] fanatic

het **fanatisme** /fanatɪsmə/ fanaticism; zealotry

de **fanclub** /fɛnklʏp/ (pl: -s) fan club

fancy /fɛnsi/ (adj) cool, chic, stylish: ~ *kle-*

feilbaar

ding stylish clothes

de **fancy fair** /fɛnsifɛːr/ (pl: -s) bazaar, jumble sale

de **fanfare** /fɑnfɑ̯rə/ (pl: -s) brass band

de **fanmail** /fɛnmel/ fan mail

¹**fantaseren** /fɑntazḛrə(n)/ (fantaseerde, heeft gefantaseerd) fantasize (about), dream (about)

²**fantaseren** /fɑntazḛrə(n)/ (fantaseerde, heeft gefantaseerd) dream up, make up, imagine, invent

de **fantasie** /fɑntazi̯/ (pl: -ën) imagination

de **fantast** /fɑntɑst/ (pl: -en) dreamer, visionary, storyteller; liar

¹**fantastisch** /fɑntɑstis/ (adj) **1** fantastic, fanciful: *~e verhalen* fanciful (*or:* wild) stories **2** fantastic, marvellous

²**fantastisch** /fɑntɑstis/ (adv) fantastically, terrifically

de **fantasy** /fɛntəzi/ fantasy

het **fantoom** /fɑntom/ (pl: fantomen) phantom

de **fantoompijn** /fɑntompɛɪn/ phantom limb pain

de **farao** /fɑ̯rao/ (pl: -'s) pharaoh

de **farce** /fɑrs/ (pl: -n, -s) farce

de **farde** /fɑrdə/ [Belg] **1** file **2** carton (of cigarettes)

de **farizeeën** /fɑrizḛ̯ə(n)/ (pl) Pharisees

farmaceutisch /fɑrmasœytis/ (adj) pharmaceutic(al)

de **fascinatie** /fɑsina(t)si/ (pl: -s) fascination

fascineren /fɑsinḛrə(n)/ (fascineerde, heeft gefascineerd) fascinate, captivate

fascinerend /fɑsinḛrənt/ (adj) fascinating

het **fascisme** /fɑʃɪsmə/ fascism

de **fascist** /fɑʃɪst/ (pl: -en) fascist

fascistisch /fɑʃɪstis/ (adj, adv) fascist

de **fase** /fɑ̯zə/ (pl: -s, -n) phase: [Dutch] *eerste ~* undergraduate course of studies; [Dutch] *tweede ~* postgraduate course of studies

faseren /fɑzḛrə(n)/ (faseerde, heeft gefaseerd) phase

het **fastfood** /fɑ̯ːstfuːt/ fast food

de **fat** /fɑt/ (pl: -ten) dandy, fop

fataal /fɑtal/ (adj, adv) fatal; terminal; lethal; mortal: *dat zou ~ zijn voor mijn reputatie* that would ruin my reputation

fatalistisch /fɑtalɪstis/ (adj, adv) fatalistic

de **fata morgana** /fɑtɑmɔryɑ̯na/ (pl: -'s) fata morgana, mirage

het **fatsoen** /fɑtsṵn/ decorum, decency, propriety: *geen enkel ~ hebben* lack all basic sense of propriety (*or:* decency); *zijn ~ houden* behave (o.s.)

fatsoeneren /fɑtsunḛrə(n)/ (fatsoeneerde, heeft gefatsoeneerd) **1** (re-)model, shape: *zijn haar ~* do (*or:* fix) one's hair **2** lick into shape, civilize

fatsoenlijk /fɑtsṵnlək/ (adj, adv) **1** decent; respectable: *op een ~e manier aan de kost komen* make an honest living **2** decent; respectable; fair

fatsoenshalve /fɑtsunshɑ̯lvə/ (adv) for decency's sake, for the sake of decency

de **fatwa** /fɑtwa/ fatwa(h)

de **fauna** /fṵna/ fauna

de **fauteuil** /fotœy/ (pl: -s) armchair, easy chair

de ¹**favoriet** /favorɪt/ (pl: -en) favourite

²**favoriet** /favorɪt/ (adj) favourite; [pers] favoured

de **fax** /fɑks/ (pl: -en) fax

faxen /fɑ̯ksə(n)/ (faxte, heeft gefaxt) fax

de **fazant** /fazɔnt/ (pl: -en) pheasant

het **fbo** /ɛfbeo/ [Dutch] basic secondary education

de **februari** /febrywa̯ri/ February

de **fecaliën** /fekali̯ə(n)/ (pl) faeces

federaal /fedərɑ̯l/ (adj) federal

federaliseren /fedəralizḛrə(n)/ (federaliseerde, heeft gefederaliseerd) federalize, (con)federate

het **federalisme** /fedəralɪsmə/ federalism

de **federatie** /fedəra̯(t)si/ (pl: -s) federation, confederation

de **fee** /fe/ (pl: -ën) fairy

de **feedback** /fiːdbɛk/ feedback: *iem. ~ geven* give s.o. feedback

feeëriek /fejərɪk/ (adj) enchanting, magic(al), fairylike

de **feeks** /feks/ (pl: -en) shrew, vixen

de **feeling** /fiːlɪŋ/ feel(ing), knack: *~ hebben voor iets* have a feel(ing) for sth.

het **feest** /fest/ (pl: -en) **1** party: *een ~ geven* give (*or:* have) a party; *een ~je bouwen* throw a party **2** feast, treat: *dat ~ gaat niet door* you can put that (idea) right out of your head

de **feestartikelen** /fḛstɑrtikələ(n)/ (pl) party goods (*or:* gadgets)

de **feestavond** /fḛstavɔnt/ (pl: -en) gala night; social evening

de **feestdag** /fḛstdɑx/ (pl: -en) holiday: *op zonen ~en* on Sundays and public holidays; *prettige ~en* **a)** Merry Christmas; **b)** Happy Easter

feestelijk /fḛstələk/ (adj, adv) festive: *een ~e jurk* a party dress

de **feestelijkheden** /fḛstələkhedə(n)/ (pl) festivities, celebrations

feesten /fḛstə(n)/ (feestte, heeft gefeest) celebrate, make merry

de **feestganger** /fḛstxɑŋər/ (pl: -s) party-goer, guest

het **feestmaal** /fḛstmal/ (pl: -malen) feast, banquet

de **feestneus** /fḛstnøs/ (pl: -neuzen) **1** false nose **2** party-goer

het **feestvarken** /fḛstfɑrkə(n)/ (pl: -s) birthday boy (*or:* girl), guest of honour

feestvieren /fḛstfirə(n)/ (vierde feest, heeft feestgevierd) celebrate

feilbaar /fɛɪlbar/ (adj) fallible, liable to error

feilloos /fɛ̱ilos/ (adj, adv) infallible; unerring; faultless; flawless: ~ de weg terug **vinden** find one's way back unerringly

het **feit** /fɛit/ (pl: -en) fact; circumstance; event: het **is** (or: **blijft**) een ~ dat ... the fact is (or: remains) that ...; de ~en **spreken** voor zichzelf the facts speak for themselves; **in** ~e in fact, actually

[1]**feitelijk** /fɛ̱itələk/ (adj) actual: de ~e **macht** the de facto (or: real, actual) power

[2]**feitelijk** /fɛ̱itələk/ (adv) actually, practically

de **feitenkennis** /fɛ̱itə(n)kɛnɪs/ knowledge of (the) facts, factual knowledge

feitenvrij /fɛitə(n)vrɛi̱/ (adj) fact-free: ~e **politiek** fact-free politics

fel /fɛl/ (adj, adv) **1** fierce; bitter; sharp; bright; vivid; blazing [light]; glaring [light]: een **felroze** jurk a brilliant pink dress; een ~le **pijn** a sharp pain **2** fierce, sharp; keen; violent; bitter: een ~le **brand** a blazing (or: raging) fire **3** fierce; fiery; vehement; spirited [pers]; scathing; biting: ~ **tegen** iets zijn be dead set against sth.

de **felicitatie** /felisita(t)si/ (pl: -s) congratulation(s)

feliciteren /felisite̱rə(n)/ (feliciteerde, heeft gefeliciteerd) congratulate on: iem. ~ **met** iets congratulate s.o. on sth.; gefeliciteerd en nog vele jaren happy birthday and many happy returns (of the day)

felrood /fɛlro̱t/ (adj) bright red

het **feminisme** /feminɪ̱smə/ feminism, Women's Liberation

de **feminist** /feminɪ̱st/ (pl: -en) feminist

feministisch /feminɪ̱stis/ (adj, adv) feminist

het **fenomeen** /fenome̱n/ (pl: fenomenen) phenomenon

fenomenaal /fenomena̱l/ (adj, adv) phenomenal

feodaal /fejoda̱l/ (adj, adv) feudal

het **feodalisme** /fejodalɪ̱smə/ feudalism, feudal system

ferm /fɛrm/ (adj, adv) firm; resolute

fermenteren /fɛrmɛnte̱rə(n)/ (fermenteerde, heeft gefermenteerd) ferment

de **fermette** /fɛrmɛ̱tə/ (pl: -s) [Belg] restored farmhouse (as second home)

fervent /fɛrvɛ̱nt/ (adj, adv) fervent, ardent

het **festijn** /fɛstɛi̱n/ (pl: -en) feast, fête

het **festival** /fɛ̱stival/ (pl: -s) festival

de **festiviteit** /fɛstivitɛi̱t/ (pl: -en) festivity, celebration

de **fetisj** /fe̱tiʃ/ (pl: -en) fetish

de **fetisjist** /fetiʃɪ̱st/ (pl: -en) fetishist

het/de **feuilleton** /fœyətɔ̱n/ (pl: -s) serial (story)

de **fez** /fɛs/ (pl: -zen) fez

het **fiasco** /fija̱sko/ (pl: -'s) fiasco, disaster

het **fiat** /fi̱jɑt/ fiat, authorization: zijn ~ **geven** authorize; give the green light

fiatteren /fijɑte̱rə(n)/ (fiatteerde, heeft gefiatteerd) authorize; attach (or: give) one's

fiat to

het/de **fiche** /fi̱ʃə/ (pl: -s) **1** counter, token, chip **2** index card, filing card

de **fictie** /fɪ̱ksi/ (pl: -s) fiction

fictief /fɪkti̱f/ (adj, adv) fictitious, imaginary: een ~ **bedrag** an imaginary sum

de **fiducie** /fidy̱si/ faith: ik **heb** er geen ~ in I've no faith in it

fier /fir/ (adj, adv) proud

de **fierheid** /fi̱rhɛit/ pride, high spirits

de **fiets** /fits/ (pl: -en) bike, bicycle: we gaan **op** (or: **met**) de ~ we're going by bike; **op** zijn ~ stappen get on one's bike (or: bicycle); een **elektrische** ~ an electric bicycle, an e-bike || **op** die ~! like that, in that way

de **fietsband** /fi̱tsbɑnt/ (pl: -en) bike (or: bicycle, cycle) tyre

de **fietsbel** /fi̱tsbɛl/ bike (or: bicycle) bell

de **fietsdrager** /fi̱tsdraɣər/ (pl: -s) bike (or: bicycle) carrier/rack

fietsen /fi̱tsə(n)/ (fietste, heeft/is gefietst) ride (a bike, bicycle), cycle, bike: het is een **uur** ~ it takes an hour (to get there) by bike

de **fietsenmaker** /fi̱tsə(n)makər/ (pl: -s) **1** bicycle repairer (or: mender) **2** bicycle repair shop

het **fietsenrek** /fi̱tsə(n)rɛk/ (pl: -ken) **1** bike (or: bicycle, cycle) stand **2** [roughly] gappy teeth

de **fietsenstalling** /fi̱tsə(n)stɑlɪŋ/ bicycle shed, bicycle stands, bicycle park

de **fietser** /fi̱tsər/ (pl: -s) (bi)cyclist

het **fietsknooppunt** /fi̱tsknopʏnt/ (pl: -en) cycling junction

de **fietsmand** /fi̱tsmɑnt/ (pl: -en) bike (or: bicycle) basket

het **fietspad** /fi̱tspɑt/ (pl: -en) bicycle track (or: path)

de **fietspomp** /fi̱tspɔmp/ (pl: -en) bicycle pump

het **fietssleuteltje** /fi̱tsløtəlcə/ (pl: -s) bike (or: bicycle) key

de **fietsstraat** /fi̱tstrat/ (pl: -straten) [roughly] quietway

de **fietstas** /fi̱tstɑs/ (pl: -sen) saddlebag

de **fietstocht** /fi̱tstɔxt/ (pl: -en) bicycle ride (or: trip, tour), cycling trip (or: tour): een ~je gaan **maken** go for a bicycle ride

fiftyfifty /fɪftifɪ̱fti/ (adv) fifty-fifty: ~ **doen** split (sth.) fifty-fifty (with s.o.), go halves (with s.o.)

de **figurant** /fiɣurɑ̱nt/ (pl: -en) extra, walk-on

figureren /fiɣure̱rə(n)/ (figureerde, heeft gefigureerd) **1** act, perform **2** be an extra

het/de **figuur** /fiɣy̱r/ (pl: figuren) figure; character; individual: een **goed** ~ a good figure; geen gek ~ **slaan** naast not come off badly compared with; wat is hij voor een ~? what sort of person is he?

figuurlijk /fiɣy̱rlək/ (adj, adv) figurative, metaphorical: ~ **gesproken** metaphorically speaking

de **figuurzaag** /fiɣy̱rzaɣ/ (pl: -zagen) fretsaw;

jigsaw

figuurzagen /fiɣʏrzaɣə(n)/ do fretwork; jigsaw

Fiji /fidʒi/ Fiji

de **Fiji-eilanden** /fidʒiɛilɑndə(n)/ (pl) Fiji Islands

de **Fijiër** /fidʒijər/ (pl: -s) Fijian

Fijisch /fidʒis/ (adj) Fijian

¹**fijn** /fɛin/ (adj) **1** fine: ~e *sneeuw* fine snow; ~e *instrumenten* delicate instruments **2** delicate **3** nice, lovely, fine, great, grand: *nog een ~e dag* have a nice day!; *een ~e tijd* a good time **4** subtle, fine: *een ~e neus* a fine (*or:* subtle) nose ‖ *ik weet er het ~e niet van I* don't know the finer (*or:* specific) details

²**fijn** /fɛin/ (adv) nice: *ons huis is ~ groot* our house is nice and big

³**fijn** /fɛin/ (int) that's nice, lovely: *we gaan op vakantie, ~!* we're going on holiday, great!

fijnbesnaard /fɛimbəsnart/ (adj) highly-strung, delicate(ly balanced), sensitive

fijngevoelig /fɛiɲɣəvuləx/ (adj, adv) **1** sensitive **2** tactful

fijnmaken /fɛimakə(n)/ (maakte fijn, heeft fijngemaakt) crush (fine); pulverize

fijnmalen /fɛimalə(n)/ (maalde fijn, heeft fijngemalen) grind (up/down), crush

fijnmazig /fɛimazəx/ (adj) fine(-meshed): *een ~e structuur* a finely-woven structure

de **fijnproever** /fɛimpruvər/ (pl: -s) connoisseur; gourmet

fijnsnijden /fɛinsnɛidə(n)/ (sneed fijn, heeft fijngesneden) cut fine(ly), slice thinly

fijnstampen /fɛinstɑmpə(n)/ (stampte fijn, heeft fijngestampt) crush, pound, pulverize; mash

het **fijnstof** /fɛinstɔf/ particulate matter *(PM)*; particulates

fijntjes /fɛintʃəs/ (adv) cleverly, subtly: *~ opmerken* make a knowing (*or:* subtle) remark

de **fik** /fɪk/ (pl: -ken) [inform] fire: *in de ~ steken* set fire to

¹**fikken** /fɪkə(n)/ (fikte, heeft gefikt) [inform] burn

de ²**fikken** /fɪkə(n)/ (pl) paws: *blijf af met je ~* keep your paws off

Fikkie /fɪki/ [Dutch] doggy ‖ *geef mijn portie maar aan ~* (you can) count me out

fiks /fɪks/ (adj) sturdy, firm

fiksen /fɪksə(n)/ (fikste, heeft gefikst) [inform] fix (up), manage

de **filantroop** /filɑntrop/ (pl: filantropen) philanthropist

de **filatelist** /filatəlɪst/ (pl: -en) philatelist

de ¹**file** /filə/ (pl: -s) [traf] queue; line; row; tailback; traffic jam: *in een ~ staan* (or: *raken*) be in (or: get into) a traffic jam

de ²**file** /fɑjl/ (pl: -s) [comp] file

fileren /filerə(n)/ (fileerde, heeft gefileerd) **1** fillet **2** pick holes in, tear to shreds

het/de **filet** /file/ (pl: -s) fillet

de **filevorming** /filəvɔrmɪŋ/ buildup (of traffic): *er is ~ over 3 km* traffic is backed up for 3 km

filharmonisch /filhɑrmonis/ (adj) philharmonic

het **filiaal** /filijal/ (pl: filialen) branch; chain store

de **filiaalhouder** /filijalhaudər/ (pl: -s) branch manager

de **Filipijn** /filipɛin/ (pl: -en) Filipino

de **Filipijnen** /filipɛinə(n)/ (pl) (the) Philippines

Filipijns /filipɛins/ (adj) Philippine, Filipino

de **film** /fɪlm/ (pl: -s) film; [Am] movie: *een stomme ~* a silent film (*or:* picture); *welke ~ draait er in die bioscoop?* what's on at that cinema?; *wij gaan naar de ~* we're going to the cinema (*or:* the movie)

de **filmacademie** /fɪlmakademi/ (pl: -s) film academy (*or:* school)

de **filmacteur** /fɪlmɑktør/ (pl: -s) film actor

de **filmcamera** /fɪlmkamərə/ (pl: -'s) (cine-)camera; (film)camera; motion-picture camera

filmen /fɪlmə(n)/ (filmde, heeft gefilmd) film, make (a film), shoot (a film)

de **filmer** /fɪlmər/ (pl: -s) film-maker

het **filmhuis** /fɪlmhœys/ (pl: -huizen) art cinema, cinema club

de **filmkeuring** /fɪlmkørɪŋ/ (pl: -en) film censorship; film censorship board; board of film censors

de **filmmuziek** /fɪlmyzik/ soundtrack

de **filmopname** /fɪlmɔpnamə/ (pl: -n, -s) shot, sequence, take: *een ~ maken van* make (*or:* shoot) a film of

de **filmproducent** /fɪlmprodysɛnt/ (pl: -en) film producer

de **filmregisseur** /fɪlmreɣisør/ (pl: -s) film director

de **filmrol** /fɪlmrɔl/ (pl: -len) **1** role (*or:* part) in a film **2** reel of film

de **filmster** /fɪlmstɛr/ (pl: -ren) (film) star, movie star

filosoferen /filozoferə(n)/ (filosofeerde, heeft gefilosofeerd) philosophize

de **filosofie** /filozofi/ (pl: -ën) philosophy: *de ~ van Plato* Plato's philosophy

filosofisch /filozofis/ (adj, adv) philosophic(al)

de **filosoof** /filozof/ (pl: filosofen) philosopher

het/de **filter** /fɪltər/ (pl: -s) filter

¹**filteren** /fɪltərə(n)/ (filterde, is gefilterd) filter through (*or:* into); percolate (through)

²**filteren** /fɪltərə(n)/ (filterde, heeft gefilterd) filter; percolate

de **filtersigaret** /fɪltərsiɣarɛt/ (pl: -ten) filter (tip), filter-tipped cigarette

het **filterzakje** /fɪltərzɑkjə/ (pl: -s) (coffee) filter

de **Fin** /fɪn/ (pl: -nen) Finn, Finnish woman

finaal /final/ (adj, adv) **1** final **2** complete, total: *ik ben het ~ vergeten* I clean forgot (it)

de **finale** /finalə/ (pl: -s) [mus] finale; [sport] fi-
nal(s)

de **finalist** /finalɪst/ (pl: -en) finalist

financieel /finɑnʃel/ (adj, adv) financial

financieel-economisch /finɑnʃel-
ekonɔmis/ (adj) financial and economic

de **financiën** /finɑnsijə(n)/ (pl) finance, finances, funds

de **financier** /finɑnsir/ (pl: -s) financier

financieren /finɑnsirə(n)/ (financierde,
heeft gefinancierd) finance, fund; back

de **financiering** /finɑnsirɪŋ/ financing

het **financieringstekort** /finɑnsirɪŋstəkɔrt/
(pl: -en) financing deficit, [roughly] budget
deficit

het **fineer** /finer/ veneer

fineren /finerə(n)/ (fineerde, heeft gefi-
neerd) veneer, finish, overlay, face

de **finesse** /finɛsə/ (pl: -s) nicety, subtlety: *de ~s
van iets* the ins and outs of sth.

fingeren /fɪŋɣerə(n)/ (fingeerde, heeft gefingeerd) 1 feign, sham; stage: *een gefingeerde overval* a staged robbery 2 invent,
make up, dream up: *een gefingeerde naam* a
fictitious name; an assumed name

de **finish** /fɪnɪʃ/ finish, finishing line

finishen /fɪnɪʃə(n)/ (finishte, heeft/is gefi-
nisht) finish: *als tweede ~* finish second, come
(in) second

Finland /fɪnlɑnt/ Finland

het ¹**Fins** /fɪns/ Finnish

²**Fins** /fɪns/ (adj) Finnish

de **firewall** /fɑjərwɔːl/ firewall

de **firma** /fɪrma/ (pl: -'s) firm, partnership, company: *de ~ Smith & Jones* the firm of Smith
and Jones

het **firmament** /fɪrmamɛnt/ [form] firmament,
heaven(s)

de **fis** /fis/ (pl: -sen) [mus] F sharp

fiscaal /fɪskal/ (adj, adv) tax(-), fiscal: *~ aftrekbaar* tax-deductible; *~ nummer* tax identification number; [USA] social security number

de **fiscus** /fɪskʏs/ 1 the Inland Revenue, the
Treasury; [inform] the taxman 2 treasury;
[UK] (HM) Inland Revenue; [Am] IRS

fit /fɪt/ (adj) fit; fresh: *niet ~ zijn* be out of
condition; be under the weather

de **fitness** /fɪtnəs/ fitness training; keep-fit exercises: *aan ~ doen* do fitness training; work
out

het **fitnesscentrum** /fɪtnəsɛntrʏm/ (pl: -cen-
tra) fitness club, health club

fitnessen /fɪtnəsə(n)/ (fitneste, heeft gefit-
nest) work out, exercise

de **fitting** /fɪtɪŋ/ (pl: -s, -en) socket; screw(cap);
fitting

het **fixeer** /fɪkser/ fixer, fixative

fixen /fɪksə(n)/ (fixte, heeft gefixt) [sport]
fix; *see fiksen*

fixeren /fɪkserə(n)/ (fixeerde, heeft ge-

fixeerd) fix

de **fjord** /fjɔrt/ (pl: -en) fjord, fiord

de **flacon** /flakɔn/ (pl: -s) bottle, flask; flagon

fladderen /flɑdərə(n)/ (fladderde, heeft/is
gefladderd) 1 flap about; flutter 2 flutter;
flap; stream

flagrant /flaɣrɑnt/ (adj) flagrant, blatant,
glaring: *dat is een ~e leugen* that is a blatant
(*or:* bald, barefaced) lie; *in ~e tegenspraak
met* in flat contradiction to (*or:* with)

flakkeren /flɑkərə(n)/ (flakkerde, heeft ge-
flakkerd) flicker

flamberen /flɑmberə(n)/ (flambeerde,
heeft geflambeerd) flambé

flamboyant /flɑmbwɑjɑnt/ (adj) flamboyant

de **flamenco** /flamɛnko/ (pl: -'s) flamenco

de **flamingo** /flamɪŋo/ (pl: -'s) flamingo

het **flanel** /flanɛl/ (pl: -len) flannel; flannelette

flaneren /flanerə(n)/ (flaneerde, heeft/is
geflaneerd) stroll, parade

de **flank** /flɑŋk/ (pl: -en) flank, side

flankeren /flɑŋkerə(n)/ (flankeerde, heeft
geflankeerd) flank

flansen /flɑnsə(n)/ (flanste, heeft geflanst)
(+ in elkaar) knock together, put together

de **flap** /flɑp/ (pl: -pen) 1 flap 2 turnover
3 [Dutch] (bank) note 4 flysheet

de **flapdrol** /flɑbdrɔl/ (pl: -len) [inform] wally

het **flapoor** /flɑpor/ protruding ear, sticking-
out ear

flappen /flɑpə(n)/ (flapte, heeft geflapt)
fling down, bang down, plonk down || *eruit
~* blab(ber), blurt out

de **flapuit** /flɑpœyt/ (pl: -s) blab, blabber

de **flard** /flɑrt/ (pl: -en) 1 shred, tatter: *aan ~en
scheuren* tear to shreds 2 fragment; scrap:
enkele ~en van het gesprek a few fragments
(*or:* snatches) of the conversation

de **flashback** /flɛʃbɛk/ (pl: -s) flashback

de **flat** /flɛt/ (pl: -s) 1 block of flats; block of
apartments 2 flat; [Am] apartment: *op een ~*
in a flat

de **flater** /flatər/ (pl: -s) blunder, howler

het **flatgebouw** /flɛtxəbɑu/ (pl: -en) *see flat*

het/de **flatscreen** /flɛtskriːn/ flat screen

flatteren /flɑterə(n)/ (flatteerde, heeft geflatteerd) flatter: *een geflatteerd portret* a
flattering portrait; *een geflatteerde voorstelling van iets geven* paint (*or:* present) a rosy
picture of sth.

flatteus /flɑtøs/ (adj) 1 becoming, flattering 2 flattering

flauw /flɑu/ (adj, adv) 1 bland, tasteless;
washy; watery 2 faint, feeble, weak; dim: *ik
heb geen ~ idee* I haven't the faintest idea
3 feeble: *een ~e grap* a feeble (*or:* corny, silly) joke 4 silly; chicken(-hearted); unsport-
ing; faint-hearted: *ik wil niet ~ doen, maar ...* I
don't want to spoil the party but ..., I hate to
be a downer but ... 5 gentle, slight

de **flauwekul** /fl<u>ou</u>wəkʏl/ [inform] rubbish, nonsense

de **flauwte** /fl<u>ou</u>tə/ (pl: -s) faint, fainting fit: *van een ~ bijkomen* come round (*or:* to)

flauwtjes /fl<u>ou</u>cəs/ (adj, adv) faint; [light] dim; bland; dull; silly: *~ glimlachen* smile weakly

flauwvallen /fl<u>ou</u>vɑlə(n)/ (viel flauw, is flauwgevallen) faint, pass out: *~ van de pijn* faint with pain

de **¹fleece** /fliːs/ (pl: -s) fleece

het/de **²fleece** /fliːs/ fleece

het **flensje** /flɛɲʃə/ (pl: -s) crêpe, thin pancake

de **fles** /flɛs/ (pl: -sen) bottle; jar: *de baby krijgt de ~* the baby is bottle-fed; *op de ~ gaan* crash, go bust

de **flesopener** /flɛsopənər/ (pl: -s) bottle-opener

¹flessen /flɛsə(n)/ (fleste, is geflest) [Belg] fail

²flessen /flɛsə(n)/ (fleste, heeft geflest) **1** swindle, con, cheat, rip off **2** fool, pull s.o.'s leg

de **flessentrekkerij** /flɛsə(n)trɛkərɛɪ/ (pl: -en) swindle, con(fidence trick), fraud

flets /flɛts/ (adj, adv) **1** pale, wan: *er ~ uitzien* look pale (*or:* washed-out) **2** pale, dull: *~e kleuren* pale (*or:* faded, dull) colours

fleurig /fl<u>ø</u>rəx/ (adj, adv) colourful, cheerful

flexibel /flɛksibəl/ (adj) flexible, pliable; [fig also] supple; [fig also] elastic: *~e werktijden* flexible hours; flexitime

de **flexibiliteit** /flɛksibilit<u>ɛi</u>t/ flexibility; [fig also] elasticity

de **flexitariër** /flɛksit<u>a</u>rijər/ (pl: -s) flexitarian, semivegetarian

de **flexplek** /flɛksplɛk/ (pl: -ken) hot desk

de **flexwerker** /flɛkswɛrkər/ (pl: -s) **1** temporary employee **2** flexiworker

de **flik** /flɪk/ (pl: -ken) **1** [Belg; inform] cop **2** [Dutch] chocolate drop

flikflooien /flɪkflojə(n)/ (flikflooide, heeft geflikflooid) pet, cuddle: *met iem. ~* get off (*or:* neck, snog) with s.o.

flikken /flɪkə(n)/ (flikte, heeft geflikt) bring off, pull off; get away with: *dat moet je me niet meer ~* don't you dare try that one on me again

de **flikker** /flɪkər/ (pl: -s) queen, poofter; [Am] faggot, fag ‖ *het kan hem geen ~ schelen* he doesn't give a damn; *hij heeft geen ~ uitgevoerd* he hasn't done a bloody thing; *iem. op zijn ~ geven* give s.o. a good hiding; give s.o. a proper dressing-down

¹flikkeren /flɪkərə(n)/ (flikkerde, heeft geflikkerd) **1** flicker; blink: *het ~de licht van een kaars* the flickering light of a candle **2** glitter, sparkle: *de zon flikkert op het water* the sun shimmers on the water

²flikkeren /flɪkərə(n)/ (flikkerde, is geflikkerd) [inform] fall, tumble: *van de trap ~*

nosedive (*or:* tumble) down the stairs

¹flink /flɪŋk/ (adj) **1** robust, stout, sturdy **2** considerable, substantial: *een ~e dosis* a stiff dose; *een ~e wandeling* a good (long) walk **3** firm; plucky: *een ~e meid* a big girl; *zich ~ houden* put on a brave front (*or:* face)

²flink /flɪŋk/ (adv) considerably, thoroughly, soundly: *~ wat mensen* quite a number of people, quite a few people; *iem. er ~ van langs geven* give s.o. what for

flinterdun /flɪntərd<u>y</u>n/ (adj) wafer-thin, paper-thin: [fig] *~ bewijs* flimsy evidence

de **flip-over** /flɪp<u>o</u>vər/ (pl: -s) flipchart

flipperen /flɪpərə(n)/ (flipperde, heeft geflipperd) play pinball

de **flipperkast** /flɪpərkɑst/ (pl: -en) pinball machine

de **flirt** /flʏːrt/ (pl: -s, -en) flirtation

flirten /fl<u>ʏː</u>rtə(n)/ (flirtte, heeft geflirt) flirt

de **flits** /flɪts/ (pl: -en) **1** [photography] flash(bulb), flash(light) **2** flash, streak **3** flash; split second **4** clip, flash: *~en van een voetbalwedstrijd* highlights of a football match

¹flitsen /flɪtsə(n)/ (flitste, heeft/is geflitst) flash: *er flitste een bliksemstraal in de lucht* (a bolt of) lightning flashed through the sky

²flitsen /flɪtsə(n)/ (flitste, heeft geflitst) flash: *geflitst worden* get flashed

flitsend /flɪtsənt/ (adj) **1** stylish, snappy, snazzy **2** brilliant

het **flitslicht** /flɪtslɪxt/ flash(light)

de **flitspaal** /flɪtspal/ speed camera, camera speed trap

de **flodder** /fl<u>ɔ</u>dər/ (pl: -s): *losse ~s* dummy (*or:* blank) cartridges, blanks

flodderig /fl<u>ɔ</u>dərəx/ (adj, adv) **1** baggy, floppy **2** sloppy, shoddy, messy

flonkeren /fl<u>ɔ</u>ŋkərə(n)/ (flonkerde, heeft geflonkerd) twinkle; sparkle; glitter: *~de ogen* sparkling eyes

de **flonkering** /fl<u>ɔ</u>ŋkərɪŋ/ (pl: -en) sparkle; sparkling; twinkling

de **flop** /flɔp/ (pl: -s) flop

floppen /fl<u>ɔ</u>pə(n)/ (flopte, is geflopt) flop

de **floppydisk** /fl<u>ɔ</u>pidɪsk/ (pl: -s) floppy disk, diskette

de **floppydrive** /fl<u>ɔ</u>pidrɑjf/ (pl: -s) disk drive

de **flora** /fl<u>o</u>ra/ flora

floreren /flor<u>e</u>rə(n)/ (floreerde, heeft gefloreerd) flourish, bloom, thrive

het/de **floret** /flor<u>ɛ</u>t/ (pl: -ten) foil

de **florijn** /flor<u>ɛi</u>n/ (pl: -en) florin, guilder

florissant /florisɑnt/ (adj) flourishing, blooming, thriving; well; healthy: *dat ziet er niet zo ~ uit* that doesn't look so good

flossen /fl<u>ɔ</u>sə(n)/ (floste, heeft geflost) floss one's teeth

de **fluctuatie** /flʏktyw<u>a</u>(t)si/ (pl: -s) fluctuation; swing

fluctueren /flʏktyw<u>e</u>rə(n)/ (fluctueerde, heeft gefluctueerd) fluctuate

fluisteren /flœystərə(n)/ (fluisterde, heeft gefluisterd) whisper

de **fluit** /flœyt/ (pl: -en) **1** flute; fife **2** whistle

het **fluitconcert** /flœytkɔnsɛrt/ (pl: -en) **1** flute concerto, concerto for flute; flute recital (or: concert) **2** catcalls, hissing: *op een ~ onthaald worden* be catcalled

¹**fluiten** /flœytə(n)/ (floot, heeft gefloten) **1** whistle, blow a whistle: *de scheidsrechter floot voor buitenspel* the referee blew (or: whistled) for off-side **2** play the flute **3** whistle; sing; [ship] pipe; hiss || *daar kun je naar ~* you can whistle for it

²**fluiten** /flœytə(n)/ (floot, heeft gefloten) **1** whistle; play; sing **2** referee, act as referee in

de **fluitist** /flœytɪst/ (pl: -en) flautist, flute(-player)

het **fluitje** /flœycə/ (pl: -s) whistle || *een ~ van een cent* a doddle; a piece of cake

de **fluitketel** /flœytketəl/ (pl: -s) whistling kettle

het **fluitsignaal** /flœytsɪnal/ whistle(-signal)

de **fluittoon** /flœyton/ (pl: -tonen) whistle, whistling; whine; b(l)eep

het **fluor** /flywɔr/ fluorine

het **fluweel** /flywel/ (pl: fluwelen) velvet

fluwelen /flywelə(n)/ (adj) velvet, velvety

flyeren /flɑjərə(n)/ (flyerde, heeft geflyerd) distribute (or: hand out) flyers

de **fly-over** /flɑjovər/ (pl: -s) overpass, flyover

fnuikend /fnœykənt/ (adj) fatal, destructive: *~ voor* fatal to

de **fobie** /fobi/ (pl: -ën) phobia: *een ~ voor katten* a phobia about cats

het/de **focus** /fokʏs/ (pl: -sen) **1** focal point, focus **2** [fig] focus: *de ~ leggen op …* focus completely on …, zoom in on …

focussen /fokʏsə(n)/ (focuste, heeft gefocust) focus, focalize: *~ op een probleem* focus on a problem

de **FOD** [Belg] *Federale Overheidsdienst* Federal Government Service

het **foedraal** /fudral/ (pl: foedralen) case, cover, sheath

foefelen /fufələ(n)/ (foefelde, heeft gefoefeld) [Belg] cheat, fiddle

het **foefje** /fufjə/ (pl: -s) trick

foei /fuj/ (int) naughty naughty!

foeilelijk /fujlelək/ (adj) hideous, ugly as sin (or: hell)

de **foelie** /fuli/ mace

foeteren /futərə(n)/ (foeterde, heeft gefoeterd) grumble, grouse

foetsie /futsi/ (adv) [inform] gone, vanished (into thin air): *ineens was mijn portemonnee ~* suddenly my purse was gone (or: had vanished)

het/de **foetus** /føtʏs/ (pl: -sen) fetus

de **foetushouding** /føtʏshɑudɪŋ/ fetal position

de **föhn** /føn/ (pl: -s) **1** [meteorology] föhn **2** blow-dryer

föhnen /fønə(n)/ (föhnde, heeft geföhnd) blow-dry

de ¹**fok** /fɔk/ (pl: -ken) foresail

de ²**fok** /fɔk/ breeding || [inform] *wat de ~?* WTF *(what the fuck)*

³**fok** /fɔk/ (int) blast!

¹**fokken** /fɔkə(n)/ (fokte, heeft gefokt) **1** breed; rear; raise: *schapen ~* breed sheep **2** [inform] take the piss (out of s.o.); wind s.o. up

²**fokken** /fɔkə(n)/ (fokte, heeft gefokt) be a pain in the neck (or: ass): *lopen te ~* being a pain in the neck; *met iem. ~* wind s.o. up

de **fokker** /fɔkər/ (pl: -s) breeder; stockbreeder; cattle-raiser; fancier

de **fokkerij** /fɔkərɛi/ (pl: -en) **1** (cattle-)breeding, cattle-raising; (live)stock farming **2** breeding farm, stock farm; breeding kennel(s); stud farm

fokking /fɔkɪŋ/ (adj) [inform] [vulg] bloody, effing: *een ~ hekel hebben aan iets* really hate sth., hate sth. with a vengeance

de **fokstier** /fɔkstir/ (pl: -en) (breeding) bull

de **folder** /fɔldər/ (pl: -s) leaflet, brochure, folder

het/de **folie** /foli/ (pl: -s) (tin)foil

de **folk** /fɔk/ folk (music)

de **folklore** /fɔklorə/ folklore

folkloristisch /fɔklorɪstis/ (adj) folklor-(ist)ic

de **folkmuziek** /fɔkmyzik/ folk music

de **folteraar** /fɔltərar/ (pl: -s) torturer

folteren /fɔltərə(n)/ (folterde, heeft gefolterd) torture; [fig also] rack; [fig also] torment

de **foltering** /fɔltərɪŋ/ (pl: -en) torture, torment

de **fondant** /fɔndɑnt/ [Dutch] fondant

het **fonds** /fɔnts/ (pl: -en) **1** fund, capital, resources, funds **2** fund, trust

de **fondue** /fɔndy/ (pl: -s) fondue

fonduen /fɔndywə(n)/ (fondude, heeft gefonduud) eat fondue, have fondue

de **fonetiek** /fonetik/ phonetics

fonetisch /fonetis/ (adj, adv) phonetic

fonkelen /fɔŋkələ(n)/ (fonkelde, heeft gefonkeld) **1** sparkle, glitter; twinkle **2** sparkle, effervesce

fonkelnieuw /fɔŋkəlniw/ (adj) brand-new

de **fontein** /fɔntɛin/ (pl: -en) fountain

de **foodtruck** /fu:trʏk/ (pl: -s) food truck

de **fooi** /foj/ (pl: -en) **1** tip, gratuity **2** [fig] pittance; starvation wages

de **foor** /for/ (pl: foren) [Belg] fair

foppen /fɔpə(n)/ (fopte, heeft gefopt) fool, hoax, trick

de **fopspeen** /fɔpspen/ (pl: fopspenen) dummy (teat), soother; [Am] pacifier

¹**forceren** /fɔrserə(n)/ (forceerde, heeft ge-

forceerd) **1** force; enforce: *de zaak* ~ force the issue, rush things **2** force, strain, overtax, overwork: *zijn stem* ~ (over)strain one's voice

zich ²**forceren** /fɔrs=rə(n)/ (forceerde zich, heeft zich geforceerd) force o.s., overtax o.s., overwork o.s.

de **forel** /forɛl/ (pl: -len) trout

de **forens** /forɛns/ (pl: forenzen) commuter

forensisch /forɛnzis/ (adj) [law] forensic: *~e geneeskunde* forensic medicine

het **forfait** /forfɛ/ (pl: -s): [Belg; sport] ~ *geven* fail to turn up

het **formaat** /format/ (pl: formaten) size; format; [fig] stature; [fig] class: *een document in A4-~* a document in A4 format; [fig] *een prestatie van* ~ a feat

formaliseren /formalizɛrə(n)/ (formaliseerde, heeft geformaliseerd) formalize, standardize

formalistisch /formalɪstis/ (adj, adv) formalist(ic), legalistic

de **formaliteit** /formalitɛit/ (pl: -en) formality, matter of routine: *de nodige ~en* **vervullen** go through the necessary formalities

het/de **format** /fɔrmɑt/ format

de **formateur** /formatør/ (pl: -s) person charged with forming a new government

de **formatie** /forma(t)si/ (pl: -s) **1** formation **2** band, group

formatteren /formatɛrə(n)/ (formatteerde, heeft geformatteerd) format

formeel /formɛl/ (adj, adv) formal; official: *~ heeft u gelijk* technically speaking you are right

formeren /formɛrə(n)/ (formeerde, heeft geformeerd) **1** form, create **2** form, create, make **3** form, shape

het ¹**formica** /fɔrmika/ formica

²**formica** /fɔrmika/ (adj) formica

formidabel /formidabəl/ (adj, adv) formidable, tremendous

de **formule** /formylə/ (pl: -s) formula: *de ~ van* **water** *is H₂O* the formula for water is H_2O

de **formule 1** /formylɛən/ formula 1

de **formule 1-coureur** /formylɛənkurør/ formula 1 driver

formuleren /formylɛrə(n)/ (formuleerde, heeft geformuleerd) formulate, phrase: *iets* **anders** ~ rephrase sth.

de **formulering** /formylɛrɪŋ/ (pl: -en) formulation, phrasing, wording: *de* **juiste** ~ *is als volgt* the correct wording is as follows

het **formulier** /formylir/ (pl: -en) form: *een ~* **invullen** fill in a form; [Am] fill out a form

het **fornuis** /fɔrnœys/ (pl: fornuizen) **1** cooker **2** furnace

fors /fɔrs/ (adj, adv) **1** sturdy; robust; loud; vigorous; forceful; massive [bldg]; heavy: *een ~ kerel* a big fellow **2** substantial, considerable: *een ~ bedrag* a substantial sum

forsgebouwd /fɔrsχəbɑut/ (adj) sturdily

(*or:* strongly, solidly) built

het **fort** /fɔrt/ (pl: -en) fort(ress)

het **fortuin** /fɔrtœyn/ (pl: -en) **1** (good) fortune, (good) luck: *zijn ~* **zoeken** seek one's fortune **2** fortune

fortuinlijk /fɔrtœynlək/ (adj, adv) fortunate, lucky: *erg ~ zijn* be very lucky, have very good luck

het **forum** /fɔrym/ (pl: -s) **1** forum, panel discussion **2** panel

forumen /fɔrymə(n)/ (forumde, heeft geforumd) participate in internet forums

het **fosfaat** /fɔsfat/ (pl: fosfaten) phosphate

het/de **fosfor** /fɔsfor/ phosphorus

fossiel /fɔsil/ (adj) fossil, fossilized

de **foto** /fɔto/ (pl: -'s) photograph, picture, photo: *een ~ nemen van iem.* take a photo (*or:* picture) of s.o.; *wil je niet* **op** *de ~?* don't you want to be in the picture?

het **fotoalbum** /fɔtoɑlbʏm/ (pl: -s) photo album

de **fotocamera** /fɔtokamɛra/ (pl: -'s) camera

de **fotofinish** /fɔtofɪnɪʃ/ photo finish

fotogeniek /fɔtoʒənik/ (adj) photogenic

de **fotograaf** /fotoɣraf/ (pl: -grafen) photographer

fotograferen /fotoɣrafɛrə(n)/ (fotografeerde, heeft gefotografeerd) photograph, take a photograph (of)

de **fotografie** /fotoɣrafi/ (pl: -ën) photography

fotografisch /fotoɣrafis/ (adj) photographic(al): *een ~ geheugen* a photographic memory

de **fotokopie** /fotokopi/ (pl: -ën) photocopy, xerox: *een ~ maken van iets* photocopy sth.

fotokopiëren /fotokopijɛrə(n)/ (fotokopieerde, heeft gefotokopieerd) photocopy, xerox

het **fotomodel** /fɔtomodɛl/ (pl: -len) model, photographer's model, cover girl

de **fotoreportage** /fɔtoreportaʒə/ (pl: -s) photo-reportage

fotoshoppen /fɔtoʃɔpə(n)/ (fotoshopte, heeft gefotoshopt) photo shop

het **fototoestel** /fɔtotustɛl/ (pl: -len) camera

fouilleren /fujɛrə(n)/ (fouilleerde, heeft gefouilleerd) search; frisk

de **fouillering** /fujɛrɪŋ/ (body) search

de ¹**fout** /fɑut/ (pl: -en) **1** fault, flaw, defect: *zijn ~ is dat …* the trouble with him is that …; *niemand is* **zonder** *~en* nobody's perfect **2** mistake, error; foul; fault: *zijn ~* **goedmaken** make good one's mistake; *in de ~ gaan* a) make a mistake; b) slip up; *menselijke ~* human error; *~ op* **stapelen** make one mistake after another

²**fout** /fɑut/ (adj, adv) **1** wrong; incorrect; erroneous: *de boel ging ~* everything went wrong; *een ~ antwoord* a wrong answer **2** inappropriate, tasteless, questionable: *~e*

grappen maken tell inappropriate jokes; *~e*
kleren uncool clothing; *een ~e opmerking* an
inappropriate remark, a tasteless remark
3 questionable, dubious: *wat een ~e man* he
is a bad person, he's no good
foutief /fɑutif/ (adj, adv) wrong, incorrect
foutloos /fɑutlos/ (adj, adv) faultless, perfect
de **foutmarge** /fɑutmɑrʒə/ (pl: -s) margin of
error
de **foutmelding** /fɑutmɛldɪŋ/ (pl: -en) [comp]
error message
foutparkeren /fɑutpɑrkərə(n)/ park illegally
de **foyer** /fwɑjɛ/ (pl: -s) foyer
fraai /fraj/ (adj, adv) **1** pretty; fine **2** fine,
splendid
de **fractie** /frɑksi/ (pl: -s) fraction: *in een ~ van
een seconde* in a fraction of a second
de **fractieleider** /frɑksilɛidər/ (pl: -s) [roughly]
leader of the (*or:* a) parliamentary party;
[Am] [roughly] floor leader
de **fractuur** /frɑktyr/ (pl: fracturen) fracture
fragiel /fraʒil/ (adj) fragile
het **fragment** /fraymɛnt/ (pl: -en) fragment,
section
fragmentarisch /frɑxmɛntaris/ (adj) frag-
mentary
de **framboos** /frɑmbos/ raspberry
het **frame** /frem/ (pl: -s) frame
framen /fremə(n)/ (framede, heeft ge-
framed) frame: *iem. als onbetrouwbaar ~*
make s.o. look unreliable
de **Française** /frɑsɛːzə/ (pl: -s) Frenchwoman
de **franchise** /frɑnʃizə/ franchise
franco /frɑnko/ (adv) prepaid; postage paid;
[goods] carriage paid
de **franje** /frɑnjə/ (pl: -s) **1** fringe, fringing
2 [fig] frill, trimmings: *zonder (overbodige) ~*
stripped of all its frills
de **frank** /frɑnk/ (pl: -en) franc ‖ [Belg] *zijn ~ valt*
the penny has dropped
frankeren /frɑnkerə(n)/ (frankeerde, heeft
gefrankeerd) stamp; frank; [Am] meter; prepay: *onvoldoende gefrankeerd* under-
stamped; postage due
Frankrijk /frɑnkrɛik/ France
het **¹Frans** /frɑns/ French: *in het ~* in French
²Frans /frɑns/ (adj) French: *de ~en* the French;
twee ~en two French people; two French-
men
de **Fransman** /frɑnsmɑn/ (pl: Fransen) Frenchman
frappant /frɑpɑnt/ (adj, adv) striking, remarkable
de **frase** /frazə/ (pl: -n) phrase
de **frater** /fratər/ (pl: -s) friar, brother
de **fratsen** /frɑtsə(n)/ (pl) whims, fads, caprices
de **fraude** /frɑudə/ (pl: -s) fraud; embezzlement: *~ plegen* commit fraud; commit a
fraud

frauderen /frɑudɛrə(n)/ (fraudeerde, heeft
gefraudeerd) commit fraud
de **fraudeur** /frɑudør/ (pl: -s) fraud, cheat
frauduleus /frɑudyløs/ (adj, adv) fraudulent; crooked
de **freak** /friːk/ (pl: -s) **1** freak, nut, fanatic,
buff: *een filmfreak* a film buff **2** freak,
weirdo
freelance /frilɑs/ (adj, adv) freelance
de **freelancer** /frilɑsər/ (pl: -s) freelance(r)
de **frees** /fres/ (pl: frezen) fraise
de **freeware** /friːwɛːr/ freeware
het **fregat** /freyɑt/ (pl: -ten) frigate
frêle /frɛːlə/ (adj, adv) frail, delicate
frequent /frekwɛnt/ (adj, adv) frequent
de **frequentie** /frekwɛnsi/ (pl: -s) frequency: *de
~ van zijn hartslag* his pulse (rate)
het **fresco** /fresko/ (pl: -'s) fresco
de **fresia** /frezija/ (pl: -'s) freesia
de **¹fret** /frɛt/ (pl: -ten) fret
het **²fret** /frɛt/ (pl: -ten) ferret
freudiaans /frɔjdijans/ (adj) Freudian: *een
~e vergissing (verspreking)* a Freudian slip
de **freule** /frøːlə/ (pl: -s) [roughly] gentlewom-
an, lady: *~ Jane A.* [roughly] the Honourable
Jane A.
frezen /frezə(n)/ (freesde, heeft gefreesd)
mill
de **fricandeau** /frikɑndo/ (pl: -s) fricandeau
de **frictie** /frɪksi/ (pl: -s) friction
friemelen /frimələ(n)/ (friemelde, heeft
gefriemeld) fiddle: *~ aan (met)* fiddle with
de **Fries** /fris/ Frisian
Friesland /frislɑnt/ Friesland
de **friet** /frit/ (pl: -en) chips; [Am] French fries:
~je oorlog chips with mayonnaise and peanut sauce; *~je zonder* just chips (no sauce)
het **frietkot** /fritkɔt/ (pl: -en) [Belg] [roughly]
fish and chips stand; [Am] [roughly] hot dog
stand
de **frigo** /friyo/ (pl: -'s) [Belg] fridge
de **frigobox** /friyoboks/ (pl: -en) [Belg] cool box
de **frik** /frɪk/ (pl: -ken) schoolmaster, schoolmistress
de **frikandel** /frikɑndɛl/ (pl: -len) minced-meat
hot dog
het **¹fris** /frɪs/ soft drink; pop: *een glaasje ~* a soft
drink, a glass of pop
²fris /frɪs/ (adj) **1** fresh; fit; lively: *met ~se
moed* with renewed vigour **2** fresh, airy,
breezy: *het ruikt hier niet ~* it's stuffy (in) here
3 clean **4** cool(ish), chilly
het **frisbee** /frɪzbi/ (pl: -s) frisbee
frisbeeën /frɪzbijə(n)/ (frisbeede, heeft ge-
frisbeed) frisbee
de **frisdrank** /frɪzdrɑnk/ (pl: -en) soft drink;
pop
frisjes /frɪʃəs/ (adj) chilly, nippy
de **friteuse** /fritøzə/ (pl: -s) deep fryer, chip pan
frituren /frityrə(n)/ (frituurde, heeft gefri-
tuurd) deep-fry

de **frituur** /fritʏr/ chip shop

de **frituurpan** /frityrpɑn/ (pl: -nen) deep frying pan; deep fryer; chip pan

het **frituurvet** /frityrvɛt/ (pl: -ten) frying fat

frivool /frivol/ (adj, adv) frivolous

¹**frommelen** /frɔmələ(n)/ (frommelde, heeft gefrommeld) fiddle, fumble: *aan* het tafelkleed ~ fiddle with the tablecloth

²**frommelen** /frɔmələ(n)/ (frommelde, heeft gefrommeld) **1** crumple (up), rumple, crease: *iets in* elkaar ~ crumple sth. up **2** stuff away

de **frons** /frɔns/ (pl: -en) **1** wrinkle **2** frown; scowl

fronsen /frɔnsə(n)/ (fronste, heeft gefronst) frown; scowl: *de wenkbrauwen* ~ frown; knit one's brow(s)

het **front** /frɔnt/ (pl: -en) front; façade; forefront: [fig] *een gesloten* ~ *vormen* form a united front; *het vijandelijke* ~ the enemy front

frontaal /frɔntal/ (adj, adv) frontal; head-on

het **fruit** /frœyt/ fruit ‖ *Turks* ~ Turkish delight

de **fruitautomaat** /frœytɑutomat/ (pl: -automaten) fruit machine; [Am] slot machine; one-armed bandit

fruiten /frœytə(n)/ (fruitte, heeft gefruit) fry, sauté

het **fruithapje** /frœythɑpjə/ (pl: -s) fruit purée

fruitig /frœytəx/ (adj) fruity ‖ *fris* en ~ bright-eyed and bushy-tailed, full of beans

de **fruitsalade** /frœytsaladə/ (pl: -s) fruit salad

het **fruitsap** /frœytsɑp/ (pl: -pen) [Belg] fruit juice

de **fruitteler** /frœytelər/ fruit grower, fruit farmer

frunniken /frʏnəkə(n)/ (frunnikte, heeft gefrunnikt) fiddle

de **frustraat** /frʏstrat/ frustrated person

de **frustratie** /frʏstra(t)si/ (pl: -s) frustration

frustreren /frʏstrerə(n)/ (frustreerde, heeft gefrustreerd) **1** frustrate **2** thwart

de **f-sleutel** /ɛfsløtəl/ [Dutch] F clef

de **fte** /ɛftee/ *fulltime-equivalent* fte, full-time equivalent

de **fuchsia** /fʏksija/ (pl: -'s) fuchsia

¹**fucking** /fʏkɪŋ/ (adj) [vulg] [inform] bloody: ~ *teringzooi* the whole bloody business

²**fucking** /fʏkɪŋ/ (adv) [vulg] [inform] bloody: ~ *vervelend* bloody annoying

de **fuga** /fʏɣa/ (pl: -'s) fugue

de **fuif** /fœyf/ (pl: fuiven) party; bash: *een* ~ *geven (houden)* give (or: have) a party

het **fuifnummer** /fœyfnʏmər/ (pl: -s) partygoer, merrymaker: *hij is een echt* ~ he's a party-going type

de **fuik** /fœyk/ (pl: -en) fyke (net); [fig] snare, trap: [fig] *in de* ~ *lopen* walk (or: fall) into a trap

full colour /fulkɔlər/ (adj) full colour

fulltime /fultɑjm/ (adj, adv) full-time

de **fulltimer** /fultɑjmər/ (pl: -s) full-timer

de **functie** /fʏŋksi/ (pl: -s) post, position, duties: *een hoge* ~ *bekleden* hold an important position; *in* ~ *treden* take up office ‖ [maths] *x is een* ~ *van* y x is a function of y

de **functiebeschrijving** /fʏŋksibəsχrɛivɪŋ/ (pl: -en) job description, job specification

de **functie-eis** /fʏŋksiɛis/ (pl: -en) job requirement

de **functionaris** /fʏŋkʃonarɪs/ (pl: -sen) official

functioneel /fʏŋkʃonel/ (adj) functional

functioneren /fʏŋkʃonerə(n)/ (functioneerde, heeft gefunctioneerd) **1** act, function, serve **2** work, function, perform: *niet* (or: *goed*) ~*d* out of order, in working order

het **functioneringsgesprek** /fʏŋkʃonerɪŋsχəsprɛk/ (pl: -ken) performance interview

het **fundament** /fʏndamɛnt/ (pl: -en) foundation; [fig also] fundamental(s): *de* ~*en leggen (voor)* lay the foundations (for)

het **fundamentalisme** /fʏndamɛntalɪsmə/ fundamentalism

de **fundamentalist** /fʏndamɛntalɪst/ (pl: -en) fundamentalist

fundamenteel /fʏndamɛntel/ (adj, adv) fundamental, basic

funderen /fʏnderə(n)/ (fundeerde, heeft gefundeerd) **1** found, build **2** [fig also] base, ground

de **fundering** /fʏnderɪŋ/ (pl: -en) foundation(s); [fig also] basis; groundwork: *de* ~ *leggen* lay the foundation(s)

funest /fynɛst/ (adj) disastrous, fatal: *de droogte is* ~ *voor de tuin* (the) drought is disastrous for the garden

fungeren /fʏŋɣerə(n)/ (fungeerde, heeft gefungeerd) **1** act as, function as **2** be the present ... (or: acting ..., officiating ...)

de **furie** /fyri/ (pl: -s, furiën) fury, shrew: *tekeergaan als een* ~ go raving mad

furieus /fyrijøs/ (adj, adv) furious, enraged

de **furore** /fyrorə/ furore: ~ *maken* be all the rage, be the thing

fuseren /fyzerə(n)/ (fuseerde, is gefuseerd) merge (with), incorporate

de **fusie** /fyzi/ (pl: -s) merger: *een* ~ *aangaan* merge

fusilleren /fyzijerə(n)/ (fusilleerde, heeft gefusilleerd) execute by firing squad

het **fust** /fʏst/ (pl: -en) cask, barrel: *een* ~ *aanslaan* broach a cask

de **fut** /fʏt/ go, energy, zip: *de* ~ *is eruit bij hem* there's no go in him anymore; *geen* ~ *hebben om iets te doen* not have the energy (or: strength) to do sth.

futiel /fytil/ (adj) futile

de **futiliteit** /fytilitɛit/ (pl: -en) trifle, futility

het **futsal** /fʏtsɑl/ futsal, indoor soccer

futuristisch /fytyrɪstis/ (adj, adv) futuristic)

de **fuut** /fyt/ (pl: futen) great crested grebe

de **fysica** /fizika/ physics
de **fysicus** /fizikʏs/ (pl: fysici) physicist
  fysiek /fizik/ (adj, adv) physical
de **fysiologie** /fizijoloɣi/ physiology
de **fysiotherapeut** /fizijoterapœyt/ (pl: -en)
  [Dutch] physiotherapist
de **fysiotherapie** /fizijoterapi/ **1** [Dutch]
  physiotherapy **2** [Belg] rehabilitation
  fysisch /fizis/ (adj, adv) physical

g

de **g** /ɣe/ (pl: g's) g, G

gaaf /ɣaf/ (adj) **1** whole, intact; sound: *een ~ gebit* a perfect set of teeth **2** great, super: *hij speelde een gave partij* he played a great game

de **gaai** /ɣaj/ jay: *Vlaamse ~* jay

¹**gaan** /ɣan/ (ging, is gegaan) **1** go, move: *hé, waar ga jij naartoe?* where are you going?; where do you think you're going?; *het gaat niet zo best* (or: *slecht*) met de patiënt the patient isn't doing so well (or: so badly) **2** go, leave; be off: *hoe laat gaat de trein?* what time does the train go?; *ik moet nu ~* I must go now, I must be going (or: off) now; *ik ga ervandoor* I'm going (or: off); *ga nu maar* off you go now **3** go, be going to: *aan het werk ~* set to work; *~ kijken* go and (have a) look; *~ liggen* lie down; *~ staan* stand up; *ze ~ trouwen* they're getting married; *hoe is het gegaan?* how was it?, how did it (or: things) go? **5** (+ over) run, be in charge (of): *daar ga ik niet over* that's not my responsibility **6** (+ over) be (about): *waar gaat die film over?* what's that film about? ‖ *zich laten ~* let o.s. go; *dat gaat er bij hem niet in* he won't accept (or: believe) that, that's a no-go for him; *dat gaat gewoon niet* it just won't work; [fig] *dat gaat mij te ver* I think that is going too far; *eraan ~* have had it; [pers also] be (in) for it; *daar ~ we weer* (t)here we go again; *we hebben nog twee uur te ~* we've got two hours to go; *aan de kant ~* move aside; *zijn gezin gaat bij hem boven alles* his family comes first (with him)

²**gaan** /ɣan/ (ging, is gegaan) **1** be, go, happen: *het is toch nog gauw gegaan* things went pretty fast (after all) **2** (+ om) be (about): *daar gaat het juist om* that's the whole point; *het gaat erom of ...* the point is whether ...; *het gaat om het principe* it's the principle that matters; *het gaat om je baan* your job is at stake ‖ *het ga je goed* all the best; *hoe gaat het (met u)?* how are you?, how are things with you?; *hoe gaat het op het werk?* how is your work (going)?, how are things (going) at work?; *ik ga voor de entrecote* I'll go for the steak, I'll have the steak; *het gaat* it's all right; it's OK; *dat zal niet ~* that just won't work; I'm afraid that's not on

³**gaan** /ɣan/ (aux vb) be going to: *het gaat gebeuren* it's going to happen; *dat gaat niet lukken* that's not going to happen; *dat gaat niet werken* that won't work

gaande /ɣandə/ (adj) **1** going, running: *een gesprek ~ houden* keep a conversation going **2** going on, up: *~ zijn* be going on, be in progress

gaandeweg /ɣandəwɛɣ/ (adv) gradually

gaans /ɣans/ walk: *nog geen tien minuten ~ van* within ten minutes walk from/of; *een uur ~* an hour's walk

de **gaap** /ɣap/ (pl: gapen) yawn

gaar /ɣar/ (adj) **1** done; cooked: *de aardappels zijn ~* the potatoes are cooked (or: done); *het vlees is goed* (or: *precies*) ~ the meat is well done (or: done to a turn); *iets ~ koken* cook sth. **2** done, tired (out): *ik ben helemaal ~ van die reis* that journey really did for me **3** [inform] dumb, lame: *een ~ filmpje* a dumb (or: lame) movie

de **gaarheid** /ɣarhɛɪt/ readiness (to eat, serve, ...)

de **gaarkeuken** /ɣarkøkə(n)/ (pl: -s) soup kitchen

gaarne /ɣarnə/ (adv) gladly, with pleasure

het **gaas** /ɣas/ (pl: gazen) **1** gauze; net(ting): *fijn* (or: *grof*) ~ fine-meshed (or: large-meshed) gauze **2** wire mesh; (wire) netting; (wire) gauze: *het ~ van een hor* the wire gauze of a screen

het **gaatje** /ɣacə/ (pl: -s) (little, small) hole; puncture: *~s in de oren laten prikken* have one's ears pierced; *ik had geen ~s* I had no cavities ‖ *ik zal eens kijken of ik voor u nog een ~ kan vinden* I'll see if I can fit (or: squeeze) you in

de **gabber** /ɣɑbər/ (pl: -s) [inform] mate, pal, chum, buddy

Gabon /ɣabɔn/ Gabon

de ¹**Gabonees** /ɣabones/ (pl: Gabonezen) Gabonese

²**Gabonees** /ɣabones/ (adj) Gabonese

gadeslaan /ɣadəslan/ (sloeg gade, heeft gadegeslagen) **1** observe, watch **2** follow, watch (closely)

de **gading** /ɣadɪŋ/: *hij kon niets van zijn ~ vinden* he couldn't find anything to suit him (or: to his liking, he wanted); *was er iets van je ~ bij?* was there anything you fancied there?

de **gaffel** /ɣɔfəl/ (pl: -s) (two-pronged) fork

de **gage** /ɣaʒə/ (pl: -s) pay; fee; salary

het **gajes** /ɣajəs/ [Dutch; inform] rabble, riff-raff

de **gal** /ɣɔl/ (pl: -len) bile; gall

het **gala** /ɣala/ gala

de **gala-avond** /ɣalaavɔnt/ (pl: -en) gala night

het **galadiner** /ɣaladine/ (pl: -s) state banquet, gala dinner

galant /ɣalɔnt/ (adj, adv) chivalrous, gallant: *~e manieren* elegant manners

de **galavoorstelling** /ɣalavorstɛlɪŋ/ (pl: -en)

gala performance

de **galblaas** /ɣɑlblas/ (pl: galblazen) gall bladder: *een operatie aan de* ~ a gall bladder operation

de **galei** /ɣalɛi/ (pl: -en) galley

de **galeislaaf** /ɣalɛislaf/ (pl: -slaven) galley slave

de **galerie** /ɣaləri/ (pl: -s) (art) gallery

de **galeriehouder** /ɣalərihaudər/ (pl: -s) gallery owner; manager of a gallery

de **galerij** /ɣalərɛi/ (pl: -en) gallery; walkway; (shopping) arcade

de **galg** /ɣalɣ/ (pl: -en) gallows: *aan de* ~ *ophangen* hang on the gallows; ~*je spelen* play hangman; *hij groeit voor* ~ *en rad op* he'll come to no good

de **galgenhumor** /ɣalɣə(n)hymɔr/ gallows humour

het **galgenmaal** /ɣalɣəmal/ (pl: -malen) last meal: *het* ~ *nuttigen* eat one's last meal

Galilea /ɣalilɛja/ Galilee

het **galjoen** /ɣaljun/ (pl: -en) galleon

de **galm** /ɣalm/ (pl: -en) sound; peal(ing) || *de luide* ~ *van zijn stem* his booming voice

¹**galmen** /ɣalmə(n)/ (galmde, heeft gegalmd) resound, boom; peal: *de klokken* ~ the bells peal

²**galmen** /ɣalmə(n)/ (galmde, heeft gegalmd) bellow

de **galop** /ɣalɔp/ (pl: -s) gallop: *in* ~ at a gallop; *in* ~ *overgaan* break into a gallop

galopperen /ɣaloperə(n)/ (galoppeerde, heeft/is gegaloppeerd) gallop: *een paard laten* ~ gallop a horse

de **galsteen** /ɣalsten/ (pl: -stenen) gallstone, bilestone

Gambia /ɣɑmbija/ (The) Gambia

de **Gambiaan** /ɣɑmbijan/ (pl: Gambianen) Gambian

Gambiaans /ɣɑmbijans/ (adj) Gambian

de **game** /gem/ (pl: -s) game

de **gamepad** /gempɛt/ (pl: -s) game pad

het/de **gamma** /ɣɑma/ (pl: -'s) [mus] scale, gamut

gammel /ɣɑməl/ (adj) **1** rickety, wobbly, ramshackle: *een* ~*e constructie* a ramshackle construction **2** shaky, faint: *ik ben een beetje* ~ I don't feel up to much

de **gang** /ɣaŋ/ (pl: -en) **1** passage(way), corridor, hall(way) **2** passage(way), tunnel: *een ondergrondse* ~ an underground passage(way) **3** walk, gait: *herkenbaar aan zijn moeizame* ~ recognizable by his laboured gait **4** movement; speed: *er* ~ *achter zetten* speed it up; *de les was al aan de* ~ the lesson had already started (*or:* got going); *een motor aan de* ~ *krijgen* get an engine going; *goed op* ~ *komen* [also fig] get into one's stride; *iem. op* ~ *helpen* help s.o. to get going, give s.o. a start **5** course, run: *de* ~ *van zaken is als volgt* the procedure is as follows; *de dagelijkse* ~ *van zaken* the daily routine; *verantwoordelijk zijn*

voor de goede ~ *van zaken* be responsible for the smooth running of things; *het feest is in volle* ~ the party is in full swing; *alles gaat weer zijn gewone* ~ everything's back to normal **6** course: *het diner bestond uit vijf* ~*en* it was a five-course dinner || *ga je* ~ *maar* **a)** (just, do) go ahead; **b)** (just, do) carry on; **c)** after you; *zijn eigen* ~ *gaan* go one's own way

gangbaar /ɣɑŋbar/ (adj) **1** current, contemporary, common: *een gangbare uitdrukking* a common expression **2** popular: *een gangbare maat* a common size

de **Ganges** /ɣɑŋəs/ the (River) Ganges

het **gangetje** /ɣɑŋəcə/ (pl: -s) **1** pace, rate **2** alley(way); passage(way); narrow corridor (*or:* passage) || *alles gaat z'n* ~ things are going all right

de **gangmaker** /ɣɑŋmakər/ (pl: -s) [Dutch] (the) life and soul of the party

het **gangpad** /ɣɑŋpɑt/ (pl: -en) aisle

het **gangreen** /ɣɑŋɣren/ gangrene: ~ *krijgen* get gangrene; [part of the body] become gangrenous

de **gangster** /gɛŋstər/ (pl: -s) gangster

de ¹**gans** /ɣɑns/ (pl: ganzen) goose: *de sprookjes van Moeder de Gans* the (fairy) tales of Mother Goose

²**gans** (adj): *van* ~*er harte* with all one's heart

het **ganzenbord** /ɣɑnzə(n)bɔrt/ (pl: -en) (game of) goose

de **ganzenlever** /ɣɑnzə(n)levər/ (pl: -s) goose liver, foie gras

de **ganzenpas** /ɣɑnzə(n)pɑs/ (pl: -sen) goose step

gapen /ɣapə(n)/ (gaapte, heeft gegaapt) **1** yawn: ~ *van verveling* yawn with boredom **2** gape, gawk (at) **3** yawn, gape: *een* ~*de afgrond* [also fig] a yawning abyss

gappen /ɣɑpə(n)/ (gapte, heeft gegapt) pinch, swipe

de **garage** /ɣaraʒə/ (pl: -s) garage: *de auto moet naar de* ~ the car has to go to the garage

de **garagedeur** /ɣaraʒədør/ garage door

de **garagehouder** /ɣaraʒəhaudər/ (pl: -s) garage owner; garage manager

de **garagist** /ɣaraʒɪst/ (pl: -en) [Belg] **1** garage owner **2** motor mechanic

garanderen /ɣarɑndərə(n)/ (garandeerde, heeft gegarandeerd) guarantee, warrant: *gegarandeerd echt goud* guaranteed solid gold; *ik kan niet* ~ *dat je slaagt* I cannot guarantee that you will succeed; *dat garandeer ik je* I guarantee you that

de **garant** /ɣarɑnt/ (pl: -en) guarantor; guarantee underwriter; [law] surety: ~ *staan voor de schulden van zijn vrouw* stand surety for one's wife's debts; *zijn aanwezigheid staat* ~ *voor een gezellige avond* his presence ensures an enjoyable evening

de **garantie** /ɣarɑnsi/ (pl: -s) guarantee, warranty: *dat valt niet **onder** de ~* that is not covered by the guarantee; *drie jaar ~ **op** iets krijgen* get a three-year guarantee on sth.

het **garantiebewijs** /ɣarɑnsibəwɛis/ guarantee (card), warranty, certificate of guarantee

de **garde** /ɣɑrdə/ (pl: -n) 1 guard: *de **nationale** ~* the national guard 2 whisk, beater

de **garderobe** /ɣɑrdərˌoːbə/ (pl: -s) 1 wardrobe: *een **uitgebreide** ~ bezitten* possess an extensive wardrobe 2 cloakroom; [Am] checkroom

het **gareel** /ɣarˌeːl/ (pl: garelen): *iem. (weer) **in** het ~ brengen* bring s.o. to heel, make s.o. toe the line; *in het ~ lopen* toe the line

het **garen** /ɣaːrə(n)/ (pl: -s) thread, yarn: *een klosje ~* a reel of thread

de **garnaal** /ɣɑrnaːl/ (pl: garnalen) shrimp; prawn

de **garnalencocktail** /ɣɑrnaːlə(n)kɔktel/ (pl: -s) shrimp cocktail, prawn cocktail

garneren /ɣɑrnˌeːrə(n)/ (garneerde, heeft gegarneerd) garnish

de **garnering** /ɣɑrnˌeːrɪŋ/ (pl: -en) garnishing

het **garnituur** /ɣɑrnitˌyr/ (pl: garnituren) 1 garnishing, trim, trimming(s) 2 accessories; set, ensemble

het **garnizoen** /ɣɑrnizˌun/ (pl: -en) garrison

het **gas** /ɣɑs/ (pl: -sen) gas: *~, **water** en elektra* gas, water and electricity; *vloeibaar ~* liquid gas; *het ~ **aansteken** (or: **uitdraaien**)* light (or: turn off) the gas; *op ~ **koken*** cook with (or: by) gas; *~ **geven*** step on the gas; *vol ~ de bocht door* (round the bend) at full speed; *de auto rijdt **op** ~* the car runs on LPG

de **gasbel** /ɣɑzbɛl/ (pl: -len) 1 gas bubble (or: pocket) 2 gasfield, gas deposit

de **gasbeving** /ɣɑzbevɪŋ/ (pl: -en) earthquake caused by gas drilling

de **GAS-boete** /ɣɑzbuːtə/ (pl: -s) [Belg] municipal administrative fine

de **gasbrander** /ɣɑzbrɑndər/ (pl: -s) gas burner

de **gasfitter** /ɣɑsfɪtər/ (pl: -s) gas fitter; plumber

de **gasfles** /ɣɑsflɛs/ (pl: -sen) gas cylinder

het **gasfornuis** /ɣɑsfɔrnœys/ (pl: gasfornuizen) gas cooker

de **gaskachel** /ɣɑskɑχəl/ (pl: -s) gas heater

de **gaskamer** /ɣɑskamər/ (pl: -s) gas chamber, gas oven

de **gaskraan** /ɣɑskran/ (pl: gaskranen) gas tap: *de ~ **opendraaien** (or: **dichtdraaien**)* turn on (or: off) the gas (tap)

de **gasleiding** /ɣɑslɛidɪŋ/ (pl: -en) gas pipe(s); service pipe; gas main(s)

het **gaslek** /ɣɑslɛk/ (pl: -ken) gas leak(age)

de **gaslucht** /ɣɑslʏχt/ smell of gas

het **gasmasker** /ɣɑsmɑskər/ (pl: -s) gas mask

de **gasmeter** /ɣɑsmetər/ (pl: -s) gas meter

het/de **gaspedaal** /ɣɑspədal/ (pl: gaspedalen) accelerator (pedal): *het ~ **indrukken** (or: **intrappen**)* step on (or: press down) the accel-

erator

de **gaspit** /ɣɑspɪt/ (pl: -ten) gas ring, gas burner

het **gasstel** /ɣɑstɛl/ (pl: -len) gas ring (or: burner)

de **gast** /ɣɑst/ (pl: -en) 1 guest, visitor: *~en **ontvangen*** entertain (guests); *bij iem. **te** ~ zijn* be s.o.'s guest 2 customer: *vaste ~en* a) regular guests; b) regular customers 3 [inform] bloke, chap; [Am] guy, bro, dude: *hé ~, hoe is het?* hey dude/bro, how you doing?

de **gastarbeider** /ɣɑstɑrbɛidər/ (pl: -s) immigrant worker

het **gastcollege** /ɣɑstkɔleʒə/ (pl: -s) guest lecture

de **gastdocent** /ɣɑzdosɛnt/ (pl: -en) visiting lecturer

het **gastenboek** /ɣɑstə(n)buk/ (pl: -en) visitors' book, guest book

het **gastgezin** /ɣɑstχəzɪn/ (pl: -nen) host family

de **gastheer** /ɣɑsther/ (pl: -heren) host: *als ~ optreden* act as host

het **gastland** /ɣɑstlɑnt/ (pl: -en) host country

het **gastoptreden** /ɣɑstoptredə(n)/ (pl: -s) guest appearance (or: performance)

de **gastrol** /ɣɑstrɔl/ (pl: -len) guest appearance

de **gastronomie** /ɣɑstronomj/ gastronomy

gastronomisch /ɣɑstronˌomis/ (adj, adv) gastronomic

de **gastspreker** /ɣɑstsprekər/ (pl: -s) guest speaker

gastvrij /ɣɑstfrɛi/ (adj, adv) hospitable, welcoming: *iem. ~ **onthalen*** entertain s.o. well; *iem. ~ **ontvangen*** welcome s.o. (warmly)

de **gastvrijheid** /ɣɑstfrɛihɛit/ hospitality: *bij iem. ~ **genieten*** enjoy s.o.'s hospitality

de **gastvrouw** /ɣɑstfrau/ (pl: -en) hostess

gasvormig /ɣɑsfɔrməχ/ (adj) gaseous

het **gat** /ɣɑt/ (pl: -en) 1 hole, gap: *een ~ **dichten*** stop (or: fill) a hole; *een ~ **maken** in* make a hole in (sth.); [fig] *ergens ~en in schieten* shoot holes in sth.; *zwart ~* black hole 2 opening: [fig] *een ~ **in** de markt ontdekken* discover a gap (or: hole) in the market 3 hole, cavity: *een ~ **in** je kies* a hole (or: cavity) in your tooth 4 hole, dump 5 cut, gash: *zij viel een ~ **in** haar hoofd* she fell and cut her head || *hij heeft een ~ **in** zijn hand* he spends money like water; *iets **in** de ~en hebben* realize sth., be aware of sth.; *iem. (iets) **in** de ~en houden* keep an eye on s.o. (sth.); *niets **in** de ~en hebben* be quite unaware of anything; *in de ~en lopen* attract (too much) attention

de **gate** /get/ (pl: -s) gate

¹**gauw** /ɣau/ (adj, adv) quick, fast; hasty: *ga zitten en ~ een **beetje*** sit down and hurry up about it! (or: and make it snappy!); *dat heb je ~ **gedaan**, dat is* ~ that was quick (work); *ik zou maar ~ een jurk **aantrekken*** (if I were you) I'd just slip into a dress

²**gauw** /ɣau/ (adv) 1 soon, before long: *hij had er **al** ~ genoeg van* he had soon had

enough (of it); *hij zal nu wel ~ **hier** zijn* he won't be long now; *dat zou ik zo ~ niet weten* I couldn't say offhand **2** easily: *ik ben niet ~ **bang**, maar …* I'm not easily scared, but …; *dat **kost** al ~ € 100* that can easily cost 100 euros || *zo ~ ik iets weet, zal ik je bellen* as soon as I hear anything I'll ring you

de **gauwigheid** /ɣɑuwəxhɛɪt/ hurriedness, hurry

de **gave** /ɣavə/ (pl: -n) **1** gift, donation, endowment **2** gift, talent

de **gayscene** /ɡeːsiːn/ gay scene

de **Gazastrook** /ɣazastrok/ Gaza Strip

de **gazelle** /ɣazɛlə/ (pl: -n) gazelle

de **gazet** /ɣazɛt/ (pl: -ten) [Belg] newspaper

het **gazon** /ɣazɔn/ (pl: -s) lawn

ge /ɣə/ (pers pron) **1** thou **2** [Belg] you: *wat zegt ge?* what did you say?

geaard /ɣəart/ (adj) **1** earthed; [Am] grounded: *een ~ **stopcontact*** an earthed socket **2** natured, inclined, tempered

de **geaardheid** /ɣəarthɛit/ disposition, nature, inclination: *seksuele ~* sexual orientation

geabonneerd /ɣəabɔnɛrt/ (adj): *~ **zijn** (op)* have a subscription (to)

geacht /ɣəɑxt/ (adj) respected, esteemed: *Geachte **Heer*** (or: ***Mevrouw***) Dear Sir (or: Madam); *~e **luisteraars*** Ladies and Gentlemen

de **geadresseerde** /ɣəadrɛsɛrdə/ (pl: -n) addressee; consignee

geaffecteerd /ɣəɑfɛktɛrt/ (adj, adv) affected, mannered: *~ **spreken*** talk posh; *~ **Engels** spreken* mince one's English

geagiteerd /ɣəaɣitɛrt/ (adj, adv) excited, agitated: *~ **zijn*** be in a flutter

de **geallieerden** /ɣəaliˌjɛrdə(n)/ (pl) Allies

geamuseerd /ɣəamyzɛrt/ (adj, adv) amused: *~ **naar iets kijken*** watch sth. in amusement

geanimeerd /ɣəanimɛrt/ (adj) animated, lively, warm: *een ~ **gesprek*** an animated (or: a lively) conversation

gearmd /ɣəɑrmt/ (adj, adv) arm in arm

geavanceerd /ɣəavɑnsɛrt/ (adj) advanced, latest: *~e **technieken*** advanced techniques

het **gebaar** /ɣəbar/ (pl: gebaren) **1** gesture, sign(al): *expressie in **woord** en ~* expression in word and gesture; *door een ~ beduidde zij hem bij haar te komen* she motioned him to come over; *met gebaren iets duidelijk maken* signal sth. (by means of gestures) **2** gesture, move: *een **vriendelijk** ~ aan zijn adres* a gesture of friendliness towards him

het **gebak** /ɣəbɑk/ pastry, confectionery, cake(s): *~ van **bladerdeeg*** puff (pastry); *vers ~* fresh pastry (or: confectionery); *koffie **met** ~* coffee and cake(s)

het **gebakje** /ɣəbɑkjə/ (pl: -s) (fancy) cake, pastry: *op ~s **trakteren*** treat (s.o.) to cake(s)

gebakken /ɣəbɑkə(n)/ (adj) baked; fried: *~*

aardappelen (or: *vis*) fried potatoes (or: fish)

gebaren /ɣəbarə(n)/ (gebaarde, heeft gebaard) gesture, gesticulate; signal; motion: *met armen en benen ~* gesticulate wildly

de **gebarentaal** /ɣəbarə(n)tal/ sign language

de **gebarentolk** /ɣəbarə(n)tɔlk/ sign (language) interpreter

het **gebed** /ɣəbɛt/ (pl: -en) prayer, devotions; grace: *mijn ~en **werden verhoord*** my prayers were answered; *het ~ **vóór** de maaltijd* (saying) grace

het **gebedel** /ɣəbedəl/ begging

de **gebedsgenezer** /ɣəbɛtsxənezər/ (pl: -s) faith healer

het **gebedskleedje** /ɣəbɛtsklecə/ prayer mat

het **gebeente** /ɣəbentə/ (pl: -n) bones: *wee je ~!* woe betide you!, don't you dare!

gebeiteld /ɣəbɛitəlt/ (adj): *hij **zit** ~* he's sitting pretty, he's got it made

het **gebergte** /ɣəbɛrxtə/ (pl: -n, -s) **1** mountains **2** mountain range, chain of mountains

het **gebeurde** /ɣəbørdə/ incident, event: *hij wist zich niets **van** het ~ te herinneren* he couldn't remember anything of what had happened

het **¹gebeuren** /ɣəbørə(n)/ (pl: -s) event, incident, happening: *een **eenmalig** ~* a unique event

²gebeuren /ɣəbørə(n)/ (gebeurde, is gebeurd) **1** happen, occur, take place: *er is een **ongeluk** gebeurd* there's been an accident; *voor ze (goed) wist wat **er** gebeurde* (the) next thing she knew; *er gebeurt hier nooit **iets*** nothing ever happens here; *alsof er **niets** gebeurd was* as if nothing had happened; *wat is er **met** jou gebeurd?* what's happened to you?; *voor als er iets gebeurt* just in case; *er **moet** nog heel wat ~, voor het zover is* we have a long way to go yet; *het is **zó** gebeurd* it'll only take a second (or: minute); *er moet nog het een en ander **aan** ~* it needs a bit more doing to it; *dat gebeurt wel meer* these things do happen **2** happen, occur: *dat **kan** de beste ~* it could happen to anyone; *er kan **niets** (mee) ~* nothing's can happen (to it)

de **gebeurtenis** /ɣəbørtənɪs/ (pl: -sen) **1** event, occurrence, incident: *dat is een **belangrijke** ~* that's a major event; *een **onvoorziene** ~* an unforeseen occurrence (or: incident) **2** event: *een **eenmalige** ~* a unique occasion

het **gebied** /ɣəbit/ (pl: -en) **1** territory, domain **2** area, district, region: *onderontwikkelde* (or: *achtergebleven*) *~en* underdeveloped (or: depressed) areas/regions **3** field, department: *op **ecologisch** ~* in the field of ecology; *vragen op **financieel** ~* financial problems; *wij verkopen alles **op** het ~ van …* we sell everything (which has) to do with … **4** territory, land

gebieden /ɣəbidə(n)/ (gebood, heeft geboden) **1** order, dictate: *iem. ~ **te zwijgen*** im-

pose silence on s.o., bind s.o. to secrecy
2 compel, necessitate: *de grootste voorzichtigheid is geboden* the situation calls for the
utmost caution, great caution is required
gebiedend /ɣəbidənt/ (adj, adv) imperative, vital, compulsive ‖ *op ~e toon* with a
voice of command, in a peremptory tone; *~e
wijs* imperative mood, imperative

het **gebiedsdeel** /ɣəbitsdel/ (pl: -delen) territory: *de overzeese gebiedsdelen* the overseas
territories

het **gebit** /ɣəbɪt/ (pl: -ten) **1** (set of) teeth: *een
goed ~ hebben* have a good set of teeth; *een
regelmatig* (or: *onregelmatig, sterk*) *~* regular (or: irregular, strong) teeth **2** (set of)
dentures, (set of) false teeth

de **gebitscorrectie** /ɣəbɪtskɔrɛksi/ (pl: -s) or-
thodontic (or: teeth) straightening

de **gebitsverzorging** /ɣəbɪtsfərzɔrɣɪŋ/ dental
care

het **gebladerte** /ɣəbladərtə/ foliage

het **geblaf** /ɣəblɑf/ barking, baying

geblesseerd /ɣəblɛsert/ (adj) injured

de **geblesseerde** /ɣəblɛserdə/ (pl: -n) [sport]
injured player

geblindeerd /ɣəblɪndert/ (adj) shuttered;
blacked out; armoured

gebloemd /ɣəblumt/ (adj) floral (pat-
terned), flowered: *~ behang* floral (pat-
terned) wallpaper

geblokkeerd /ɣəblɔkert/ (adj) **1** blockad-
ed; ice-bound **2** blocked **3** blocked, frozen:
een ~e rekening a frozen account ‖ *de wielen
raakten ~* the wheels locked

geblokt /ɣəblɔkt/ (adj) chequered

gebocheld /ɣəbɔxəlt/ (adj) hunchbacked,
humpbacked

het **gebod** /ɣəbɔt/ (pl: -en) order, command:
~en en verboden do's and don'ts; *een ~ uitvaardigen* issue an order (or: injunction); *de
tien ~en* the Ten Commandments

¹**geboeid** /ɣəbujt/ (adj) handcuffed

²**geboeid** /ɣəbujt/ (adj) captivated, fasci-
nated: *~ toekijken* watch with great interest

gebogen /ɣəboɣə(n)/ (adj) bent, curved:
met ~ hoofd with bowed head, with head
bowed

gebonden /ɣəbɔndə(n)/ (adj) **1** bound, tied
(up), committed: *niet contractueel ~* not
bound by contract; *aan huis ~* housebound;
niet aan regels ~ not bound by rules **2** bound:
een ~ boek a hardback ‖ *~ aspergesoep*
cream of asparagus (soup)

de **geboorte** /ɣəbortə/ (pl: -n, -s) birth; delivery: *bij de ~ woog het kind ...* the child
weighed ... at birth

de **geboorteakte** /ɣəbortəɑktə/ (pl: -n, -s)
birth certificate, certificate of birth

de **geboortebeperking** /ɣəbortəbəpɛrkɪŋ/
(pl: -en) **1** birth control, family planning
2 contraception, family-planning methods

het **geboortecijfer** /ɣəbortəsɛifər/ (pl: -s) birth
rate

de **geboortedag** /ɣəbortədɑx/ (pl: -en)
1 birthday: *de honderdste* (or: *tweehon-
derdste*) *~* the centenary (or: bicentenary) of
s.o.'s birth **2** day of birth

de **geboortedatum** /ɣəbortədatʏm/ date of
birth, birth date

de **geboortegolf** /ɣəbortəɣɔlf/ (pl: -golven)
baby boom

het **geboortejaar** /ɣəbortəjar/ (pl: -jaren) year
of birth

het **geboortekaartje** /ɣəbortəkarcə/ (pl: -s)
birth announcement card

het **geboorteland** /ɣəbortəlɑnt/ (pl: -en) native country, country of origin

het **geboorteoverschot** /ɣəbortəovərsxɔt/
(pl: -ten) excess (of) births (over deaths)

de **geboorteplaats** /ɣəbortəplats/ (pl: -en)
place of birth, birthplace

de **geboorteregeling** /ɣəbortəreɣəlɪŋ/ birth
control

het **geboorteregister** /ɣəbortərəɣɪstər/ (pl: -s)
register of births

geboren /ɣəborə(n)/ (adj) born: *een ~ leraar*
a born teacher; *mevrouw Jansen, ~ Smit* Mrs
Jansen née Smit; *~ en getogen in Amsterdam*
born and bred in Amsterdam; *waar* (or: *wanneer*) *bent u ~?* where (or: when) were you
born?; *een te vroeg ~ kind* a premature baby

de **geborgenheid** /ɣəbɔrɣənhɛit/ security,
safety

het **gebouw** /ɣəbou/ (pl: -en) building, structure, construction: *een groot* (or: *ruim*) *~* a
large (or: spacious) building; *een houten
~(tje)* a wooden structure

gebouwd /ɣəbout/ (adj) built, constructed:
hij is fors (stevig) ~ he is well-built; *mooi ~ zijn*
have a fine figure, be well-proportioned

het **gebouwencomplex**
/ɣəbouwə(n)kɔmplɛks/ (pl: -en) block (or:
group) of buildings

het **gebral** /ɣəbrɑl/ bragging, bluster, tub-
thumping

gebrand /ɣəbrɑnt/ (adj) roasted, burnt: *~e
amandelen* burnt (or: roasted) almonds ‖
erop ~ zijn te be keen on, be eager for

het **gebrek** /ɣəbrɛk/ (pl: -en) **1** lack, shortage,
deficiency: *groot ~ hebben aan* be greatly
lacking in; [stronger] be in desperate need
of; *~ aan personeel hebben* be short-handed,
be understaffed; *bij ~ aan beter* for want of
anything (or: sth.) better **2** want, need: *~ lijden* be in want (or: need), go short **3** ailment, infirmity: *de ~en van de ouderdom* the
ailments of old age **4** shortcoming, weakness: *alle mensen hebben hun ~en* we all have
our faults, no one is perfect **5** flaw, fault,
defect: *een ~ verhelpen* correct a fault; *(ernstige) ~en vertonen* be (seriously) defective,
show serious flaws ‖ *zonder ~en* flawless,

faultless, perfect; *in ~e blijven* a) fail (to do sth.); b) (be in) default

¹gebrekkig /ɣəbrɛkəx/ (adj, adv) **1** infirm, ailing; lame: *een ~ mens* an ailing person **2** faulty, defective; inadequate; poor: *~e huisvesting* poor housing; *een ~e kennis van het Engels* poor (knowledge of) English

²gebrekkig /ɣəbrɛkəx/ (adv) poorly, inadequately: *een taal ~ spreken* speak a language poorly

de **gebroeders** /ɣəbrudərs/ (pl) brothers: *de ~ Jansen, handelaren in wijnen* Jansen Brothers (*or:* Bros.), wine merchants

gebroken /ɣəbrokə(n)/ (adj) **1** broken; fractured: *~ lijn* broken line; *een ~ rib* a broken (*or:* fractured) rib **2** broken: *zich ~ voelen* be a broken man (*or:* woman) **3** broken: *hij sprak haar in ~ Frans aan* he addressed her in broken French

het **gebruik** /ɣəbrœyk/ (pl: -en) **1** use, application; consumption; be on; take; taking: *het ~ van sterkedrank* (the) consumption of spirits; *voor algemeen ~* for general use; *voor eigen ~* for personal use; *alleen voor uitwendig ~* for external use (*or:* application) only; *(geen) ~ van iets maken* (not) make use of sth.; *van de gelegenheid ~ maken* take (*or:* seize) the opportunity; *iets in ~ nemen* put sth. into use **2** custom, habit: *de ~en van een land* the customs of a country

gebruikelijk /ɣəbrœykələk/ (adj) usual, customary; common: *de ~e naam van een plant* the common name of a plant; *op de ~e wijze* in the usual way

¹gebruiken /ɣəbrœykə(n)/ (gebruikte, heeft gebruikt) be on drugs, take drugs

²gebruiken /ɣəbrœykə(n)/ (gebruikte, heeft gebruikt) use, apply; take: *de auto gebruikt veel brandstof* the car uses (*or:* consumes) a lot of fuel; *slaapmiddelen ~* take sleeping pills (*or:* tablets); *zijn verstand ~* use one's common sense; *dat kan ik net goed ~* I could just use that; *dat kan ik goed ~* that comes in handy; *ik zou best wat extra geld kunnen ~* I could do with some extra money; *zich gebruikt voelen* feel used; *zijn tijd goed ~* make good use of one's time, put one's time to good use

de **gebruiker** /ɣəbrœykər/ (pl: -s) **1** user; consumer: *de ~s van een computer* computer users **2** drug user; drug addict

de **gebruikersnaam** /ɣəbrœykərsnam/ (pl: -namen) username

gebruikersvriendelijk /ɣəbrœykərsfrɪndələk/ (adj, adv) user-friendly, easy to use; convenient

gebruikmaken /ɣəbrœykmakə(n)/ (maakte gebruik, heeft gebruikgemaakt) (+ van) use, make use of: *van de gelegenheid ~* take (*or:* seize) the opportunity; *~ van een mogelijkheid* use a possibility

de **gebruikmaking** /ɣəbrœykmakɪn/ use: *met ~ van* (by) using, with the benefit of

de **gebruiksaanwijzing** /ɣəbrœyksanwɛizɪn/ (pl: -en) directions (for use); instructions (for use)

gebruiksklaar /ɣəbrœyksklar/ (adj) ready for use

gebruiksvriendelijk /ɣəbrœyksfrɪndələk/ (adj, adv) user-friendly, easy to use; convenient

de **gebruikswaarde** /ɣəbrœykswardə/ practical value, utility value

gebruind /ɣəbrœynt/ (adj) tanned, sunburnt

het **gebrul** /ɣəbrʏl/ roar(ing), howling

gebukt /ɣəbʏkt/ (adj): *~ gaan onder zorgen* be weighed down (*or:* be burdened) with worries

gecharmeerd /ɣəʃɑrmert/ (adj): *niet erg ~ zijn van iets* be none too happy with sth., be not exactly thrilled with sth.; *van iem. (iets) ~ zijn* be taken with s.o. (sth.)

geciviliseerd /ɣəsivilizert/ (adj) civilized

gecompliceerd /ɣəkɔmplisert/ (adj) complicated, involved: *een ~e breuk* a compound fracture; *een ~ geval* a complicated case

geconcentreerd /ɣəkɔnsɛntrert/ (adj, adv) **1** concentrated **2** concentrated, intent; with concentration: *~ werken* work with (great) concentration

geconserveerd /ɣəkɔnsɛrvert/ (adj) preserved; canned: *goed ~ zijn* be well-preserved

de **gedaagde** /ɣədaɣdə/ (pl: -n) defendant; respondent

gedaan /ɣədan/ (adj) **1** done, finished, over: *dan is het ~ met de rust* then there won't be any peace and quiet **2** done, finished, over (with): *ik kan alles van hem ~ krijgen* he'll do anything for me; *iets ~ krijgen* get sth. done; *van iem. iets ~ krijgen* get sth. out of s.o.

de **gedaante** /ɣədantə/ (pl: -n, -s) form, figure, shape; [fig esp] guise: *een andere ~ aannemen* take on another form, change (its) shape; *in menselijke ~* in human form (*or:* shape); *zijn ware ~ tonen* show (o.s. in) one's true colours

de **gedaanteverwisseling** /ɣədantəvərwɪsəlɪn/ (pl: -en) transformation, metamorphosis: *een ~ ondergaan* be(come) transformed

de **gedachte** /ɣədɑxtə/ (pl: -n) **1** thought: *iemands ~n ergens van afleiden* take s.o.'s mind off sth.; *(diep) in ~ zijn* be deep in thought; *iets in ~n doen* do sth. absent-mindedly, do sth. with one's mind elsewhere; *iets in ~n houden* keep one's mind on sth.; bear sth. in mind; *er niet bij zijn met ~n* have one's mind on sth. else **2** thought, idea: *de achterliggende ~ is dat ...* the underlying idea (*or:* thought) is that ...; *zijn ~n bij iets houden* keep one's mind on sth.; *de ~ niet kunnen verdragen dat ...* not be able to bear the thought (*or:* bear to think) that ...; *de ~ al-*

leen al ... the very thought (*or*: idea) ...; *(iem.)* *op de* ~ *brengen* give (s.o.) the idea; *van* ~*n wisselen over* exchange ideas on, discuss **3** opinion, view: *iem. tot andere* ~*n brengen* make s.o. change his mind **4** idea: *van* ~*n veranderen* change one's mind

de **gedachtegang** /ɣədɑxtəɣɑŋ/ (pl: -en) train of thought; (line of) reasoning

het **gedachtegoed** /ɣədɑxtəɣut/ range of thought (*or*: ideas)

gedachtelezen /ɣədɑxtəlezə(n)/ mind-reading, thought-reading

gedachteloos /ɣədɑxtəlos/ (adj, adv) unthinking, thoughtless

de **gedachtenis** /ɣədɑxtənɪs/ memory: *ter* ~ *van iem.* in memory of s.o.

de **gedachtesprong** /ɣədɑxtəsprɔŋ/ (pl: -en) mental leap (*or*: jump): *een* ~ *maken* make a mental leap (*or*: jump), jump from one idea to another

de **gedachtewisseling** /ɣədɑxtəwɪsəlɪŋ/ (pl: -en) exchange of ideas (*or*: opinions): *een* ~ *houden over* exchange ideas on, compose notes on

gedag /ɣədɑx/ (int): ~ *zeggen* say hello (*or*: goodbye)

de **gedagvaarde** /ɣədɑxfardə/ (pl: -n) person summon(s)ed

gedateerd /ɣədatert/ (adj) (out)dated, archaic

gedecideerd /ɣədesidert/ (adj, adv) decisive, resolute

het **gedeelte** /ɣədeltə/ (pl: -n, -s) part, section; instalment: *het bovenste* (*or*: *onderste*) ~ the top (*or*: bottom) part; *het grootste* ~ *van het jaar* most of the year; *voor een* ~ partly

¹**gedeeltelijk** /ɣədeltələk/ (adj) partial: *een* ~*e vergoeding voor geleden schade* partial compensation for damage sustained

²**gedeeltelijk** /ɣədeltələk/ (adv) partly, partially: *dat is slechts* ~ *waar* that is only partly (*or*: partially) true

gedegen /ɣədeɣə(n)/ (adj) thorough: *een* ~ *studie* a thorough study

gedeisd /ɣədeist/ (adj, adv) quiet, calm: *zich* ~ *houden* lie low

gedekt /ɣədɛkt/ (adj) **1** covered **2** [fin] covered: *een* ~*e cheque* a covered cheque

de **gedelegeerde** /ɣədeleɣerdə/ (pl: -n) delegate, representative: *een* ~ *bij de VN* a delegate to the UN

gedemotiveerd /ɣədemotivert/ (adj) demoralized, dispirited: ~ *raken* lose one's motivation

gedempt /ɣədɛmpt/ (adj) subdued, faint; muffled; hushed: *op* ~*e toon* in a low (*or*: subdued) voice

gedenken /ɣədɛŋkə(n)/ (gedacht, heeft gedacht) commemorate; remember: *iem. in zijn testament* ~ remember s.o. in one's will

de **gedenksteen** /ɣədɛŋksten/ (pl: -stenen) memorial stone

het **gedenkteken** /ɣədɛŋktekə(n)/ (pl: -en, -s) memorial: *een* ~ *voor* a memorial to

gedenkwaardig /ɣədɛnkwardəx/ (adj) memorable: *een* ~*e gebeurtenis* a memorable event

gedeprimeerd /ɣədeprimert/ (adj) depressed

gedeputeerd /ɣədepytert/ (adj): *Gedeputeerde Staten* [roughly] the provincial executive

de **gedeputeerde** /ɣədepyterdə/ (pl: -n) **1** delegate, representative **2** member of parliament **3** [Dutch] [roughly] member of the provincial executive

gedesillusioneerd /ɣədɛsɪlyʃonert/ (adj) disillusioned

gedesoriënteerd /ɣədɛsorijəntert/ (adj) disorient(at)ed

¹**gedetailleerd** /ɣədetɑjert/ (adj) detailed: *een* ~ *verslag* a detailed report

²**gedetailleerd** /ɣədetɑjert/ (adv) in detail

de **gedetineerde** /ɣədetinerdə/ (pl: -n) prisoner, inmate

het **gedicht** /ɣədɪxt/ (pl: -en) poem: *een* ~ *maken* (or: *voordragen*) write (*or*: recite) a poem

de **gedichtenbundel** /ɣədɪxtə(n)byndəl/ (pl: -s) volume of poetry (*or*: verse), collection of poems

gedienstig /ɣədinstəx/ (adj, adv) obliging, helpful

gedijen /ɣədɛiə(n)/ (gedijde, heeft gedijd) thrive, prosper, do well

het **geding** /ɣədɪŋ/ (pl: -en) (law)suit, (legal) action, (legal) proceedings: *in kort* ~ *behandelen* discuss in summary proceedings; *een* ~ *aanspannen (beginnen) tegen* institute proceedings against

gediplomeerd /ɣədiplomert/ (adj) qualified, certified; registered

het **gedistilleerd** /ɣədɪstilert/ spirits; [esp Am] liquor: *handel in* ~ *en wijnen* trade in wines and spirits

gedistingeerd /ɣədɪstɪŋɣert/ (adj, adv) distinguished: *een* ~ *voorkomen* a distinguished appearance

gedocumenteerd /ɣədokymɛntert/ (adj) documented: *een goed* ~ *rapport* a well-documented report

het **gedoe** /ɣədu/ business, stuff, carry on: *zenuwachtig* ~ fuss

gedogen /ɣədoɣə(n)/ (gedoogde, heeft gedoogd) tolerate, put up with

het **gedonder** /ɣədɔndər/ **1** thunder(ing), rumble: *het* ~ *weerklonk door het gebergte* the thunder rolled through the mountains **2** trouble, hassle: *daar kun je een hoop* ~ *mee krijgen* that can land you in a good deal of trouble

gedoodverfd /ɣədotfɛrft/ (adj): *een* ~*e*

winnaar a hot favourite, a dead certainty; *de ~e winnaar zijn* be tipped to win

het **gedrag** /ɣədrɒx/ behaviour, conduct: *een bewijs van goed ~* evidence of good behaviour; certificate of good character; *wegens slecht ~* for bad behaviour (or: misconduct); *iemands ~ goedkeuren* (or: **afkeuren**) approve of (or: disapprove of) s.o.'s behaviour

zich **gedragen** /ɣədraɣə(n)/ (gedroeg zich, heeft zich gedragen) behave; behave o.s.: *hij beloofde zich voortaan **beter** te zullen ~* he promised to behave better in future; *zich goed* (or: *slecht*) *~* behave well (or: badly); *zich niet (slecht) ~* misbehave (o.s.); *gedraag je!* behave (yourself)!

de **gedragslijn** /ɣədrɒxslɛin/ (pl: -en) course (of action), line of conduct: *een ~ volgen* persue a course of action

het **gedragspatroon** /ɣədrɒxspatron/ (pl: -patronen) pattern of behaviour

de **gedragsregel** /ɣədrɒxsreɣəl/ (pl: -s) rule of conduct (or: behaviour)

de **gedragswetenschappen** /ɣədrɒxswetənsxapə(n)/ (pl) behavioural sciences

het **gedrang** /ɣədrɒn/ jostling, pushing: *in het ~ komen* a) end up (or: find o.s.) in a crush; b) get into a tight corner

gedreven /ɣədreːvə(n)/ (adj) passionate; fanatic(al): *een ~ kunstenaar* s.o. who lives for his art

gedrieën /ɣədrijə(n)/ (num) (the) three (of): *zij zaten ~ op de bank* the three of them sat on the bench

het **gedrocht** /ɣədrɒxt/ (pl: -en) monster, freak

gedrongen /ɣədrɒŋə(n)/ (adj): *een ~ gestalte* a stocky (or: thickset, squat) figure

gedroomd /ɣədromt/ (adj) ideal: *de ~e kandidaat* the ideal (or: dream) candidate

gedrukt /ɣədrʏkt/ (adj) **1** printed **2** [com] depressed, dull: *de markt was ~* the market was depressed

geducht /ɣədʏxt/ (adj, adv) formidable, fearsome: *een ~e tegenstander* a formidable opponent

het **geduld** /ɣədʏlt/ patience: *zijn ~ bewaren* remain patient; *~ hebben met iem.* be patient with s.o.; *zijn ~ verliezen* lose (one's) patience; *even ~ a.u.b.* one moment, please; *veel van iemands ~ vergen, iemands ~ op de proef stellen* try s.o.'s patience

geduldig /ɣədʏldəx/ (adj, adv) patient: *~ afwachten* wait patiently

gedupeerd /ɣədypeːrt/ (adj) duped

de **gedupeerde** /ɣədypeːrdə/ victim, dupe

gedurende /ɣədyrəndə/ (prep) during, for, over; in the course of: *~ de hele dag* all through the day; *~ het hele jaar* throughout the year; *~ vier maanden* for (a period of) four months; *~ het onderzoek* during the enquiry; *~ de laatste (afgelopen) drie weken* over the past three weeks

gedurfd /ɣədʏrft/ (adj) daring; provocative: *een zeer ~ optreden* a highly provocative performance

gedwee /ɣədweː/ (adj) meek, submissive

gedwongen /ɣədwɒŋə(n)/ (adj, adv) (en)forced, compulsory, involuntary: *~ ontslag* compulsory redundancy; *een ~ verkoop* a forced sale; *~ ontslag nemen* be forced to resign

geel /ɣeːl/ (adj) yellow || (*in de Ronde van Frankrijk*) *in het ~ rijden* be wearing the yellow jersey (in the Tour de France); *de scheidsrechter toonde hem het ~* the referee showed him the yellow card

de **geelzucht** /ɣeːlzʏxt/ jaundice

geëmancipeerd /ɣeːemɒnsipeːrt/ (adj) liberated, emancipated

geëmotioneerd /ɣeːemoː(t)ʃoneːrt/ (adj, adv) emotional, touched, moved

¹**geen** /ɣeːn/ (num) none; not a, not any; no: *hij heeft ~ auto* he doesn't have a car, he hasn't got a car; *hij heeft ~ geld* he doesn't have any money, he has no money; *er zijn bijna ~ koekjes meer* we're nearly out of cookies; *bijna ~* almost none, hardly any; *~ van die jongens* (or: *beiden*) none of those lads, neither (of them)

²**geen** /ɣeːn/ (art) **1** not a, no: *nog ~ tien minuten later* not ten minutes later; *nog ~ twee jaar geleden* less than two years ago; *~ enkele reden hebben om te* have no reason whatsoever to **2** not a(ny), no: *hij kent ~ Engels* he doesn't know (any) English; *~ één* not (a single) one

geeneens /ɣeːneːns/ (adv) [inform] not even, not so much as

geëngageerd /ɣeːɑŋɡaʒeːrt/ (adj) committed

geenszins /ɣeːnsɪns/ (adv) by no means, not at all

geërgerd /ɣeːɛrɣərt/ (adj) upset, irritated

de **geest** /ɣeːst/ (pl: -en) **1** mind, consciousness: *iets voor de ~ halen* call sth. to mind **2** soul: *zijn auto gaf de ~* his car gave up the ghost **3** spirit, character: *jong van ~ zijn* be young at heart **4** ghost, spirit: *de Heilige Geest* the Holy Ghost (or: Holy Spirit); *een boze (kwade) ~* an evil spirit, a demon; *in ~en geloven* believe in ghosts **5** spirit, vein, intention

geestdodend /ɣeːstdoːdənt/ (adj) stultifying; monotonous; dull

de **geestdrift** /ɣeːstdrɪft/ enthusiasm, passion; zeal

geestdriftig /ɣeːstdrɪftəx/ (adj) enthusiastic

geestelijk /ɣeːstələk/ (adj, adv) **1** mental, intellectual; psychological; spiritual: *~e aftakeling* mental deterioration; *een ~ gehandicapte* a mentally handicapped person; *~e inspanning* mental effort; *~ gestoord* mentally disturbed (or: deranged) **2** spiritual: *~e bijstand verlenen aan iem.* a) give (spiritual)

geheel

counselling to s.o.; **b)** [rel] minister to s.o.
3 clerical

de **geestelijke** /ɣestələkə/ (pl: -n) clergyman;
[Protestantism] minister; [esp Roman Cathol-
icism] priest

de **geestelijkheid** /ɣestələkhɛit/ **1** clergy
2 spirituality

de **geestesgesteldheid** /ɣestəsχəstɛlthɛit/
state (or: frame) of mind

het **geesteskind** /ɣestəskɪnt/ (pl: -eren) brain-
child

de **geestestoestand** /ɣestəstustant/ state of
mind, mental state

de **geesteswetenschappen** /ɣestəswetən-
sχapə(n)/ (pl) humanities, arts

geestesziek /ɣestəsik/ (adj) mentally ill

geestig /ɣestəχ/ (adj, adv) witty, humorous,
funny

de **geestigheid** /ɣestəχhɛit/ (pl: -heden) witticism, quip

geestrijk /ɣestrɛik/ (adj): ~ **vocht** hard liquor, strong drink

geestverruimend /ɣestfərœymənt/ (adj)
mind-expanding; hallucinogenic

de **geestverschijning** /ɣestfərsχɪnɪŋ/ (pl:
-en) apparition, phantom, spectre, ghost

de **geestverwant** /ɣestfərwant/ (pl: -en) kindred spirit; [pol] sympathizer

de **geeuw** /ɣew/ (pl: -en) yawn

geeuwen /ɣewə(n)/ (geeuwde, heeft ge-
geeuwd) yawn: ~ **van** slaap yawn with sleepiness

de **geeuwhonger** /ɣewhɔŋər/ ravenous hunger

gefaseerd /ɣəfazert/ (adj) phased, in
phases

gefeliciteerd /ɣəfelisitert/ (int) congratulations: ~ **met** je verjaardag happy birthday!

gefingeerd /ɣəfɪŋɣert/ (adj) fictitious,
fake(d); feigned

geflatteerd /ɣəflatert/ (adj) flattering

het **geflirt** /ɣəflɪːrt/ flirtation, flirting

het **gefluister** /ɣəflœystər/ whisper(ing)(s),
murmur

het **gefluit** /ɣəflœyt/ whistling; warbling; singing

geforceerd /ɣəfɔrsert/ (adj, adv) forced,
contrived, artificial

gefortuneerd /ɣəfɔrtynert/ (adj) moneyed,
monied, wealthy: een ~ **man** a man of means

gefrustreerd /ɣəfrʏstrert/ (adj) frustrated

gefundeerd /ɣəfʏndert/ (adj) (well-)found-
ed, (well-)grounded

de **gegadigde** /ɣəɣadəɣdə/ (pl: -n) applicant;
candidate; prospective buyer; interested
party: een ~ **voor** iets **vinden** find a (potential)
buyer for sth.

¹gegarandeerd /ɣəɣarandert/ (adj, adv)
guaranteed

²gegarandeerd /ɣəɣarandert/ (adv) [fig]
definitely: dat **gaat** ~ **mis** that's bound (or:

sure) to go wrong

gegeneerd /ɣəʒənert/ (adj) embarrassed,
uncomfortable: zich ~ **voelen** feel embarrassed (or: uncomfortable)

het **¹gegeven** /ɣəɣevə(n)/ (pl: -s) data, datum,
fact, information; data; entry, item: nadere
~s further information; **persoonlijke** ~s personal details; ~s **opslaan** (or: **invoeren, op-**
vragen) store (or: input, retrieve) data
2 theme, subject

²gegeven /ɣəɣevə(n)/ (adj) given, certain: op
een ~ **moment** begin je je af te vragen … there
comes a time when you begin to wonder …

het **gegevensbestand** /ɣəɣevə(n)zbəstant/
(pl: -en) database, data file

de **gegevensverwerking** /ɣəɣevənsfər-
wɛrkɪŋ/ data processing

het **gegiechel** /ɣəɣixəl/ giggle(s), giggling;
snigger(ing): **onderdrukt** ~ stifled giggling

de **gegijzelde** /ɣəɣizəldə/ (pl: -n) hostage

het **gegil** /ɣəɣɪl/ screaming, screams

gegoed /ɣəɣut/ (adj) well-to-do, well-off,
moneyed, monied: de ~e **burgerij** the upper
middle class

het **gegoochel** /ɣəɣoχəl/ juggling

gegoten /ɣəɣotə(n)/ (adj): die jurk zit als ~
that dress fits you like a glove

het **gegrinnik** /ɣəχrɪnək/ snigger, grinning

gegrond /ɣəɣrɔnt/ (adj) (well-)founded,
valid, legitimate

gehaaid /ɣəhajt/ (adj, adv) smart, sharp

gehaast /ɣəhast/ (adj, adv) hurried, hasty,
in a hurry

gehaat /ɣəhat/ (adj) hated, hateful: zich (bij
iem.) ~ **maken** incur s.o.'s hatred

het **gehakt** /ɣəhakt/ minced meat, mince

de **gehaktbal** /ɣəhaktbal/ (pl: -len) meatball

de **gehaktmolen** /ɣəhaktmolə(n)/ (pl: -s)
mincer

het **gehalte** /ɣəhaltə/ (pl: -s) content, percentage, proportion: een **hoog** (or: **laag**) ~ **aan** a
high (or: low) content of

gehandicapt /ɣəhɛndikɛpt/ (adj) handicapped; disabled; challenged: **verstandelijk**
~ mentally disabled (or: handicapped, challenged)

de **gehandicapte** /ɣəhɛndikɛptə/ (pl: -n)
handicapped person; mentally handicapped
person: de (lichamelijk) ~n the (physically)
handicapped, the disabled

het **gehannes** /ɣəhɑnəs/ [Dutch] fumbling

gehard /ɣəhɑrt/ (adj) **1** tough, hardened,
seasoned: ~ **tegen** hardened against **2** tempered

het **geharrewar** /ɣəhɑrəwar/ squabble(s), bick-
ering(s), squabbling

gehavend /ɣəhavənt/ (adj) battered, tattered

gehecht /ɣəhɛχt/ (adj) attached (to);
[stronger] devoted (to)

het **¹geheel** /ɣəhel/ **1** whole, entity, unit(y)

2 whole, entirety: *in zijn ~* in its entirety ‖
over het ~ genomen on the whole

²**geheel** /ɣəheˌl/ (adv) entirely, fully, completely, totally: *~ en al* entirely, fully; *ik voel mij een ~ ander mens* I feel a different person altogether; revised

de **geheelonthouder** /ɣəheˌlɔnthaudər/ (pl: -s) teetotaller

geheid /ɣəhɛɪt/ (adj, adv): *die strafschop gaat er ~ in* he can't miss that penalty, that penalty's a (dead) cert; *dat wordt ~ een succes* it's bound to be a success

het ¹**geheim** /ɣəhɛim/ (pl: -en) secret: *een ~ toevertrouwen* (or: *bewaren*) confide (or: keep) a secret; *een ~ verraden* give away a secret, let the cat out of the bag; *in het ~* secretly

²**geheim** /ɣəhɛim/ (adj) 1 secret, hidden, concealed, clandestine; undercover: *dat moet ~ blijven* this must remain private (or: a secret); *een ~e bijeenkomst* a secret meeting 2 secret, classified, confidential, private: *uiterst ~e documenten* top-secret documents ‖ *een ~ telefoonnummer* an unlisted telephone number

geheimhouden /ɣəhɛimhaudə(n)/ (hield geheim, heeft geheimgehouden) keep (a) secret, keep under cover, keep dark

de **geheimhouding** /ɣəhɛimhaudɪŋ/ secrecy, confidentiality, privacy

het **geheimschrift** /ɣəhɛimsχrɪft/ (pl: -en) (secret) code, cipher

de **geheimtaal** /ɣəhɛimtal/ (pl: -talen) secret (or: private) language

¹**geheimzinnig** /ɣəhɛimzɪnəχ/ (adj) mysterious, unexplained, cryptic

²**geheimzinnig** /ɣəhɛimzɪnəχ/ (adv) mysteriously, secretly: *erg ~ doen (over iets)* be very secretive (about sth.)

de **geheimzinnigheid** /ɣəhɛimzɪnəχhɛit/ 1 secrecy, stealth 2 mysteriousness, mystery

het **gehemelte** /ɣəheˌməltə/ (pl: -s) palate, roof of the mouth

het **geheugen** /ɣəhøɣə(n)/ (pl: -s) 1 memory; mind: *dat ligt nog vers in mijn ~* it's still fresh in my memory (or: mind); *iemands ~ opfrissen* refresh s.o.'s memory; *mijn ~ laat me in de steek* my memory is letting me down 2 memory, storage

de **geheugenkaart** /ɣəhøɣə(n)kart/ (pl: -en) memory card

het **geheugensteuntje** /ɣəhøɣə(n)støncə/ (pl: -s) reminder, prompt

de **geheugenstick** /ɣəhøɣə(n)stɪk/ memory stick

het **geheugenverlies** /ɣəhøɣə(n)vərlis/ amnesia, loss of memory: *tijdelijk ~* a blackout

het **gehoor** /ɣəhoˌr/ (sense of) hearing, ear(s): *bij geen ~* if there's no reply; *geen muzikaal ~ hebben* have no ear for music

het **gehoorapparaat** /ɣəhoˌraparat/ (pl: -apparaten) hearing aid

het **gehoorbeentje** /ɣəhoˌrbencə/ auditory ossicle

de **gehoorbeschermer** /ɣəhoˌrbəsχɛrmər/ (pl: -s) (pair of) ear defenders, (pair of) ear muffs

de **gehoorgang** /ɣəhoˌrɣaŋ/ (pl: -en) auditory duct (or: passage)

gehoorgestoord /ɣəhoˌrɣəstort/ (adj) hearing-impaired, hard of hearing, deaf

het **gehoororgaan** /ɣəhoˌrɔrɣan/ (pl: -organen) ear, auditory organ, organ of hearing

de **gehoorsafstand** /ɣəhoˌrsafstant/ earshot, hearing

het **gehoorverlies** /ɣəhoˌrvərlis/ hearing loss

gehoorzaam /ɣəhoˌrzam/ (adj, adv) obedient

de **gehoorzaamheid** /ɣəhoˌrzamhɛrt/ obedience

gehoorzamen /ɣəhoˌrzamə(n)/ (gehoorzaamde, heeft gehoorzaamd) obey; comply (with)

gehorig /ɣəhoˌrəχ/ (adj) noisy, thin-walled

gehouden /ɣəhaudə(n)/ (adj) obliged (to), liable (to): *~ zijn tot* be obliged (or: liable) to

het **gehucht** /ɣəhʏχt/ (pl: -en) hamlet, settlement

het **gehuil** /ɣəhœyl/ crying: *het ~ van de wind* the howling (or: moaning) of the wind

gehuisvest /ɣəhœysfɛst/ (adj) housed, lodged

gehuwd /ɣəhʏwt/ (adj) married

de **geigerteller** /ɡɑjɡərtɛlər/ (pl: -s) Geiger counter

geijkt /ɣɛɪkt/ (adj) 1 calibrated 2 standard: *hij komt altijd met het ~e antwoord* he always comes up with the standard reply

geil /ɣɛil/ (adj, adv) [inform] horny, randy: *~ worden* get horny, get turned on

geilen /ɣɛilə(n)/ (geilde, heeft gegeild) [inform] be hot for; [Am] have the hots (for)

geïmproviseerd /ɣəɪmprovizert/ (adj) improvised, ad lib

de **gein** /ɣɛin/ [Dutch; inform] fun, merriment: *~ trappen* make merry; *voor de ~* (just) for fun, (just) for the hell of it

geinig /ɣɛinəχ/ (adj, adv) [inform] funny, cute

geïnteresseerd /ɣəɪntərɛsert/ (adj, adv) interested

de **geïnterneerde** /ɣəɪntɛrnerdə/ (pl: -n) detainee, inmate

de **geïnterviewde** /ɣəɪntərvjudə/ (pl: -n) interviewee

het **geintje** /ɣɛincə/ (pl: -s) joke, prank, (wise)-crack: *~s uithalen* play jokes

de **geiser** /ɣɛizər/ (pl: -s) geyser

de **geisha** /ɣɛiʃa/ (pl: -'s) geisha

geïsoleerd /ɣəizolert/ (adj) isolated

de **geit** /ɣɛit/ (pl: -en) goat

de **geitenkaas** /ɣɛitə(n)kas/ goat's cheese

het **geitenpad** /ɣɛitə(n)pat/ goat path; [fig] makeshift way

gejaagd /ɣəjaːxt/ (adj, adv) hurried, agitated

het **gejammer** /ɣəjɑmər/ moaning, lamentation(s)

het **gejank** /ɣəjɑŋk/ whining, whine; whimper

het **gejoel** /ɣəjuːl/ shouting, cheering, cheers; jeering

het **gejuich** /ɣəjœyx/ cheer(ing)

de ¹**gek** /ɣɛk/ (pl: -ken) **1** lunatic; loony; nut(case): *rijden als een ~* drive like a maniac **2** fool, idiot: *iem. voor de ~ houden* pull s.o.'s leg, make a fool of s.o.; *zichzelf voor de ~ houden* fool o.s.; *voor ~ lopen* look absurd (*or:* ridiculous); *iem. voor ~ zetten* make a fool of s.o.

²**gek** /ɣɛk/ (adj) **1** mad, crazy (with), insane: *je lijkt wel ~* you must be mad; *het is om je ~ te lachen* it's hilarious, it's surreal; *zich niet ~ laten maken* remain calm and collected, be unflappable **2** mad; silly; stupid; foolish: *dat is geen ~ idee* that's not a bad idea; *je zou wel ~ zijn als je het niet deed* you'd be crazy (*or:* mad) not to (do it) **3** crazy, ridiculous; bad: *op de ~ste plaatsen* in the oddest (*or:* most unlikely) places; *~ genoeg* oddly (*or:* strangely) enough; *niet ~, hè?* not bad, eh? **4** fond (of), keen (on), mad (about), crazy (about): *hij is ~ op die meid* he's crazy about that girl

³**gek** /ɣɛk/ (adv) silly; badly: *doe niet zo ~* don't act (*or:* be) so silly

gekant /ɣəkɑnt/ (adj): *tegen iets ~ zijn* be set against sth., be opposed to sth.

gekarteld /ɣəkɑrtəlt/ (adj) [bot] crenated, serrated

de **gekheid** /ɣɛkhɛit/ joking, banter: *alle ~ op een stokje* (all) joking apart

het **gekibbel** /ɣəkɪbəl/ squabbling, bickering(s), squabble(s)

de **gekkekoeienziekte** /ɣɛkəkujə(n)ziktə/ mad cow disease; [scientific] BSE

het **gekkenhuis** /ɣɛkə(n)hœys/ (pl: -huizen) [inform] madhouse, nuthouse: *wat is dat hier voor een ~?* what kind of a madhouse is this?

het **gekkenwerk** /ɣɛkə(n)wɛrk/ [inform] a mug's game, madness

de **gekkigheid** /ɣɛkəxhɛit/ (pl: -heden) folly, foolishness, madness

het **geklaag** /ɣəklaːx/ complaining, moaning

gekleed /ɣəkleːt/ (adj) dressed: *hij is slecht (slordig) ~* he is badly dressed

het **geklets** /ɣəklɛts/ chatter, waffle: *~ in de ruimte* hot air

gekleurd /ɣəklørt/ (adj) coloured; [fig also] colourful: *iets door een ~e bril zien* have a coloured view of sth.

het **geklungel** /ɣəklʏŋəl/ [inform] fiddling (about), bungling

gekmakend /ɣɛkmaːkənt/ (adj) maddening, nerve-wracking

geknipt /ɣəknɪpt/ (adj): *ergens voor ~ zijn* be cut out for sth.

het **geknoei** /ɣəknuj/ **1** messing, splashing about **2** mess(-up): *dat ~ kun je niet inleveren* you can't hand that mess in **3** fraud: *~ bij de verkiezingen* rigging (*or:* fraudulent practices) in the elections; *met de boekhouding* juggling with the accounts

gekoeld /ɣəkult/ (adj) cooled, frozen

gekostumeerd /ɣəkɔstymeːrt/ (adj): *een ~ bal* a fancy dress ball, a costume ball

het **gekrakeel** /ɣəkrakeːl/ squabbling(s), wrangling

gekreukeld /ɣəkrøkəlt/ (adj) wrinkled, wrinkly, (c)rumpled, creased

het **gekreun** /ɣəkrøn/ groan(s), moan(s), groaning, moaning

het **gekrijs** /ɣəkrɛis/ scream(ing); screech(ing)

het **gekrioel** /ɣəkrijul/ swarming

gekruid /ɣəkrœyt/ (adj) spiced, spicy, seasoned

gekruist /ɣəkrœyst/ (adj) crossed; crossbred

gekscherend /ɣɛksxerənt/ (adj, adv) joking, bantering

de **gekte** /ɣɛktə/ **1** lunacy, insanity **2** [fig] mania, madness, craze: *de ~ op de huizenmarkt* housing market madness (*or:* mania)

gekuist /ɣəkœyst/ (adj) expurgated, edited, cut

gekunsteld /ɣəkʏnstəlt/ (adj, adv) artificial, affected

gekwalificeerd /ɣəkwalifiseːrt/ (adj) qualified, skilled

het **gekwebbel** /ɣəkwɛbəl/ chatter

gekweld /ɣəkwɛlt/ (adj) tormented, anguished

gekwetst /ɣəkwɛtst/ (adj) **1** hurt, wounded, injured **2** hurt, offended: *zich ~ voelen* take offence

het/de **gel** /dʒɛl/ (pl: -s) gel, jelly

gelaagd /ɣəlaːxt/ (adj) layered: *een ~e maatschappij* a stratified society

gelaarsd /ɣəlaːrst/ (adj) booted: *de Gelaarsde Kat* Puss in Boots

het **gelaat** /ɣəlaːt/ (pl: gelaten) countenance, face

de **gelaatskleur** /ɣəlaːtsklør/ complexion

de **gelaatsscan** /ɣəlaːtskɛn/ facial scan

de **gelaatstrekken** /ɣəlaːtstrɛkə(n)/ (pl) features: *scherpe ~* sharp (*or:* chiselled) features

de **gelaatsuitdrukking** /ɣəlaːtsœydrʏkɪŋ/ (pl: -en) (facial) expression

het **gelach** /ɣəlɑx/ laughter: *in luid ~ uitbarsten* burst out laughing

geladen /ɣəlaːdə(n)/ (adj) loaded, charged

het **gelag** /ɣəlɑx/ (pl: -en): *het ~ betalen* foot the bill; *een hard ~* a bad break, a raw deal

gelasten /ɣəlɑstə(n)/ (gelastte, heeft gelast) order, direct, instruct, charge: *iem. ~ het pand te ontruimen* order s.o. to vacate the premises

gelaten /ɣəlātə(n)/ (adj) resigned, uncomplaining

de **gelatine** /ʒelatinə/ gelatine; gel; jelly

het **geld** /ɣɛlt/ (pl: -en) **1** money, currency, cash: *elektronisch ~* electronic money, e-money; *met gepast ~ betalen* pay the exact amount; *vals ~* counterfeit money; *zwart ~* undisclosed income; *bulken van* (or: *zwemmen in*) *het ~* be loaded, be rolling in money (or: in it); *het ~ groeit mij niet op de rug* I'm not made of money; *iem. ~ uit de zak **kloppen*** wheedle money out of s.o.; *waar **voor** zijn ~ krijgen* get value for money; *je ~ of je **leven*** your money or your life! **2** money, cash, funds, resources: *iem. ~ **afpersen*** extort money from s.o.; *contant ~* cash; *zonder ~ zitten* be broke **3** money, amount, sum, price, rate: *kinderen betalen half ~* children half-price; *voor geen ~ ter wereld* not for love or money

de **geldautomaat** /ɣɛltautomat/ (pl: -automaten) cash dispenser, cashpoint

de **geldboete** /ɣɛldbutə/ (pl: -s) fine

geldelijk /ɣɛldələk/ (adj, adv) financial

gelden /ɣɛldə(n)/ (gold, heeft gegolden) **1** count **2** apply, obtain, go for: *hetzelfde geldt **voor** jou* that goes for you too

geldend /ɣɛldənt/ (adj) valid, applicable, current: *een algemeen ~e regel* a universal rule

het **geldgebrek** /ɣɛltxəbrɛk/ lack of money, shortage (or: want) of money

geldig /ɣɛldəɣ/ (adj) valid, legitimate; current

de **geldigheid** /ɣɛldəxɦɛit/ validity, legitimacy, currency

de **geldingsdrang** /ɣɛldɪŋzdraŋ/ assertiveness

de **geldinzameling** /ɣɛltɪnzaməlɪŋ/ (pl: -en) fund-raising

de **geldmarkt** /ɣɛltmɑrkt/ (pl: -en) **1** money-market **2** stock exchange

de **geldmiddelen** /ɣɛltmɪdələ(n)/ (pl) funds, (financial) resources, (financial) means

de **geldnood** /ɣɛltnot/ financial trouble, financial problems

de **geldontwaarding** /ɣɛltɔntwardɪŋ/ inflation

de **geldschieter** /ɣɛltsxitər/ (pl: -s) money-lender; sponsor

de **geldsom** /ɣɛltsɔm/ (pl: -men) sum of money

het **geldstuk** /ɣɛltstʏk/ (pl: -ken) coin

geldverslindend /ɣɛltfərslɪndənt/ (adj, adv) costly, expensive

de **geldverspilling** /ɣɛltfərspɪlɪŋ/ (pl: -en) waste of money, extravagance

de **geldwolf** /ɣɛltwɔlf/ (pl: -wolven) money-grubber

de **geldzorgen** /ɣɛltsɔrɣə(n)/ (pl) financial worries (or: problems), money troubles

geleden /ɣələdə(n)/ (adj) ago, back, before, previously, earlier: *kort ~* recently, lately, not long ago; *het is een hele tijd ~, dat …* it has

been a long time since …; *ik had het een **week** ~ nog gezegd* I had said so a week before; *het is donderdag drie **weken** ~ gebeurd* it happened three weeks ago this (or: last Thursday)

de **geleding** /ɣələdɪŋ/ (pl: -en) section, part

geleed /ɣəlet/ (adj) jointed, articulate(d): *een ~ dier* a segmental animal

geleerd /ɣəlert/ (adj) learned, scholarly; erudite; academic

de **geleerde** /ɣəlerdə/ (pl: -n) scholar, man of learning; scientist: *daarover zijn de ~n het nog niet eens* the experts are not yet agreed on the matter

gelegen /ɣəleɣə(n)/ (adj) **1** situated, lying: *op het zuiden ~* facing south **2** convenient, opportune: *kom ik ~?* are you busy?, am I disturbing you?

de **gelegenheid** /ɣəleɣənɦɛit/ (pl: -heden) **1** place, site **2** opportunity, chance, facilities: *een **gunstige** ~ afwachten* wait for the right moment; *die streek **biedt** volop ~ voor fietstochten* that area offers ample facilities for cycling; *als de ~ zich **voordoet*** when the opportunity presents itself; *bij ~* sometime; *in de ~ zijn om …* be able to, have the opportunity to …; *ik maak **van** de ~ gebruik om …* I take this opportunity to … **3** eating place; [roughly] restaurant; eating house: *openbare gelegenheden* public places **4** occasion: *een feestelijke ~* a festive occasion; *ter ~ **van*** on the occasion of

de **gelegenheidskleding** /ɣəleɣənɦɛitskledɪŋ/ formal dress, full dress

de **gelei** /ʒəlɛi/ (pl: -en) jelly, preserve

geleid /ɣəlɛit/ (adj) guided: *~e **projectielen*** guided missiles; *~e economie* planned economy

het **geleide** /ɣəlɛidə/ escort: *onder militair ~* under military escort; *ten ~* introduction

de **geleidehond** /ɣəlɛidəhɔnt/ (pl: -en) guide-dog

geleidelijk /ɣəlɛidələk/ (adj, adv) gradual, by degrees, by (or: in) (gradual) stages

geleiden /ɣəlɛidə(n)/ (geleidde, heeft geleid) **1** guide, conduct, accompany, lead **2** conduct, transmit: *koper geleidt goed* copper is a good conductor

de **geleider** /ɣəlɛidər/ (pl: -s) conductor

het **gelid** /ɣəlɪt/ (pl: gelederen) [mil] rank, file, order: *in het ~ **staan*** stand in line; *in de **voorste** gelederen* in the front ranks, in the forefront

geliefd /ɣəlift/ (adj) **1** beloved, dear, well-liked **2** favourite, cherished, pet: *zijn ~ **onderwerp*** his favourite subject **3** favourite, popular: *hij is niet erg ~ **bij** de leerlingen* he is not very popular with the pupils

de **geliefde** /ɣəlivdə/ (pl: -n) sweetheart; lover

gelieven /ɣəlivə(n)/ (geliefde, heeft geliefd): *gelieve geen fietsen **te plaatsen*** please do not park bicycles here

het **¹gelijk** /ɣəlɛik/ right: *iem. ~ geven* agree with s.o.; *(groot, volkomen) ~ hebben* be (perfectly) right

²gelijk /ɣəlɛik/ (adj) **1** equal, the same: *twee mensen een ~e behandeling geven* treat two people (in) the same (way); [sport] *~ spel* a draw; *tweemaal twee is ~ aan vier* two times two is four **2** equal, equivalent: *veertig ~* deuce, forty all **3** right

³gelijk /ɣəlɛik/ (adv) **1** likewise, alike, in the same way (*or:* manner), similarly: *zij zijn ~ gekleed* they are dressed alike (*or:* the same) **2** equally **3** level **4** simultaneously, at the same time: *de twee treinen kwamen ~ aan* the two trains came in simultaneously (*or:* at the same time) **5** [Dutch] at once, straightaway, immediately; in a minute: *ik kom ~ bij u* I'll be with you in a moment; I'll be right with you

gelijkaardig /ɣəlɛikɑrdəɣ/ (adj) [Belg] similar

gelijkbenig /ɣəlɛiɣbenəɣ/ (adj) isosceles

de **gelijke** /ɣəlɛikə/ (pl: -n) equal, peer

gelijkelijk /ɣəlɛikələk/ (adv) equally, evenly

gelijken /ɣəlɛikə(n)/ (geleek, heeft geleken) [form] resemble

de **gelijkenis** /ɣəlɛikənɪs/ (pl: -sen) resemblance, similarity, likeness: *~ vertonen met* bear (a) resemblance to

de **gelijkheid** /ɣəlɛikhɛit/ equality

gelijklopen /ɣəlɛiklopə(n)/ (liep gelijk, heeft gelijkgelopen) be right, keep (good) time

¹gelijkmaken /ɣəlɛikmakə(n)/ (maakte gelijk, heeft gelijkgemaakt) [sport] equalize, draw level, tie (*or:* level) the score

²gelijkmaken /ɣəlɛikmakə(n)/ (maakte gelijk, heeft gelijkgemaakt) **1** level, make even, smooth (out), even (out) **2** equate, make even (*or:* equal), even up, level up, bring into line (with)

de **gelijkmaker** /ɣəlɛikmakər/ (pl: -s) equalizer, a game-tying goal

gelijkmatig /ɣəlɛikmatəɣ/ (adj, adv) even, equal, constant; smooth: *een ~e druk* (a) steady pressure; *~ verdelen* distribute evenly

gelijknamig /ɣəlɛiknaməɣ/ (adj) of the same name

gelijkschakelen /ɣəlɛiksχakələ(n)/ (schakelde gelijk, heeft gelijkgeschakeld) regard (*or:* treat) as equal(s)

gelijksoortig /ɣəlɛiksortəɣ/ (adj) similar, alike, analogous

het **gelijkspel** /ɣəlɛikspɛl/ (pl: gelijke spelen) draw, tie(d game)

gelijkspelen /ɣəlɛikspelə(n)/ (speelde gelijk, heeft gelijkgespeeld) draw, tie; halve: *A. speelde gelijk tegen F.* A. drew with F.

gelijkstaan /ɣəlɛikstan/ (stond gelijk, heeft gelijkgestaan) **1** be equal (to); be tantamount (to) **2** be level (with); be all square

(with): *op punten ~* be level(-pegging)

gelijkstellen /ɣəlɛikstɛlə(n)/ (stelde gelijk, heeft gelijkgesteld) equate (with); put on a par (*or:* level) (with); give equal rights (to): *voor de wet ~* make equal before the law

de **gelijkstroom** /ɣəlɛikstrom/ direct current, DC

gelijktijdig /ɣəlɛiktɛidəɣ/ (adj, adv) simultaneous, at the same time: *~ vertrekken* leave at the same time

de **gelijktijdigheid** /χəlɛiktɛidəɣhɛit/ simultaneity

gelijktrekken /ɣəlɛiktrɛkə(n)/ (trok gelijk, heeft gelijkgetrokken) level (up), equalize

gelijkvloers /ɣəlɛikflurs/ (adj, adv) on the ground floor, ground-floor; [Am also] first-floor

gelijkvormig /ɣəlɛikfɔrməɣ/ (adj) identical: *~e driehoeken* similar triangles

gelijkwaardig /ɣəlɛikwardəɣ/ (adj) equal (to, in), equivalent (to), of the same value (*or:* quality) (as), equally matched, evenly matched

de **gelijkwaardigheid** /χəlɛikwardəɣhɛit/ equivalence, equality, parity

gelijkzetten /ɣəlɛiksɛtə(n)/ (zette gelijk, heeft gelijkgezet) set (by): *laten we onze horloges (met elkaar) ~* let's synchronize (our) watches

gelijkzijdig /ɣəlɛiksɛidəɣ/ (adj) equilateral

gelikt /ɣəlɪkt/ (adj) **1** licked, highly finished; slick **2** slick, flashy: *een ~e website* a slick website

gelinieerd /ɣəlinijɛrt/ (adj) lined; ruled

de **gelofte** /ɣəlɔftə/ (pl: -n, -s) vow, oath, pledge

het **geloof** /ɣəlof/ (pl: geloven) **1** faith, belief, trust; conviction: *een vurig ~ in God* ardent faith in God; *~ in de mensheid hebben* have faith in humanity; *van zijn ~ vallen* lose one's faith; lose one's moral compass **2** faith, religion, creed, (religious) belief: *zijn ~ belijden* profess one's faith

de **geloofsbelijdenis** /ɣəlofsbəlɛidənɪs/ (pl: -sen) profession of faith: *zijn ~ afleggen* (solemnly) profess one's faith

de **geloofsovertuiging** /ɣəlofsovərtœyɣɪŋ/ (pl: -en) religious conviction

geloofwaardig /ɣəlofwardəɣ/ (adj, adv) credible; reliable; plausible, convincing

¹geloven /ɣəlovə(n)/ (geloofde, heeft geloofd) **1** (+ in) believe (in), have faith (in): *~ in God* believe in God **2** (+ aan) believe (in) || *ik geloof van wel* I think so; *je zult eraan moeten ~* you'll just have to, you'd better face (up to) it

²geloven /ɣəlovə(n)/ (geloofde, heeft geloofd) **1** believe, credit: *je kunt me ~ of niet* believe it or not; *niet te ~!* incredible!; *iem. op zijn woord ~* take s.o. at his word **2** think, believe: *hij is het er, geloof ik, niet mee eens* I don't think he agrees

gelovig /ɣəl̪o̯vəχ/ (adj, adv) religious; pious; faithful: *een ~ christen* a faithful Christian

de **gelovige** /ɣəl̪o̯vəɣə/ (pl: -n) believer

het **geluid** /ɣəlœyt/ (pl: -en) **1** sound; noise: *sneller dan het ~* faster than sound; supersonic; *het ~ van krekels* the sound of crickets; *verdachte ~en* suspicious noises **2** tone, timbre, sound: *er zit een mooi ~ in die viool* that violin has a beautiful tone **3** [fig] note, voice, noise: *er klinken ~en om de btw te verhogen* there are motions to raise VAT

geluiddempend /ɣəlœydɛmpənt/ (adj) soundproof(ing), muffling

de **geluiddemper** /ɣəlœydɛmpər/ (pl: -s) silencer; mute

geluiddicht /ɣəlœydɪχt/ (adj) soundproof

geluidloos /ɣəlœytlos/ (adj, adv) silent

de **geluidsbarrière** /ɣəlœytsbarijɛːrə/ (pl: -s) [Dutch] sound barrier: *de ~ doorbreken* break the sound barrier

het **geluidseffect** /ɣəlœytsɛfɛkt/ (pl: -en) sound effect

de **geluidshinder** /ɣəlœytshɪndər/ noise nuisance

de **geluidsinstallatie** /ɣəlœytsɪnstɑla(t)si/ (pl: -s) sound (reproducing) equipment, stereo; public-address system

de **geluidsisolatie** /ɣəlœytsizola(t)si/ sound insulation, soundproofing

de **geluidsman** /ɣəlœytsmɑn/ sound recordist

de **geluidsmuur** /ɣəlœytsmyr/ (pl: -muren) [Belg] **1** sound barrier **2** noise barrier

de **geluidsoverlast** /ɣəlœytsovərlɑst/ noise nuisance

het **geluidsscherm** /ɣəlœytsχɛrm/ (pl: -en) noise-reducing wall

het **geluidssignaal** /ɣəlœytsɪɲal/ (pl: -signalen) sound (or: acoustic) signal

de **geluidssterkte** /ɣəlœytstɛrktə/ (pl: -s) sound intensity; volume

de **geluidstechnicus** /ɣəlœytstɛχnikʏs/ (pl: -technici) sound engineer (or: technician)

de **geluidswal** /ɣəlœytswɑl/ (pl: -len) noise barrier

de **geluidsweergave** /ɣəlœytsweˑrɣavə/ (pl: -n) sound reproduction

het **geluk** /ɣəlʏk/ **1** (good) luck, (good) fortune: *dat brengt ~* that will bring (good) luck; *iem. ~ toewensen* wish s.o. luck (or: happiness); *veel ~!* good luck!; *dat is meer ~ dan wijsheid* that is more (by) good luck than good judgement **2** happiness, good fortune; [stronger] joy: *hij kon zijn ~ niet op* he was beside himself with joy **3** lucky thing, piece (or: bit) of luck; lucky break: *wat een ~ dat je thuis was* a lucky thing you were (at) home; *hij mag van ~ spreken dat …* he can count yourself lucky that …, he can thank your (lucky) stars that …

¹**gelukkig** /ɣəlʏkəχ/ (adj) **1** lucky, fortunate:

de ~e eigenaar the lucky owner **2** happy, lucky: *een ~e keuze* a happy choice **3** fortunate; happy; successful; prosperous: *~ kerstfeest* happy (or: merry) Christmas ‖ *een ~ paar* a happy couple

²**gelukkig** /ɣəlʏkəχ/ (adv) **1** well, happily: *zijn woorden ~ kiezen* choose one's words well **2** luckily, fortunately: *~ was het nog niet te laat* luckily (or: fortunately) it wasn't too late

de **gelukkige** /ɣəlʏkəɣə/ (pl: -n) happy man (or: woman); lucky one; winner: *tot de ~n behoren* be one of the lucky ones

het **geluksgetal** /ɣəlʏksχətɑl/ (pl: -len) lucky number

het **gelukskoekje** /ɣəlʏkskukjə/ (pl: -s) fortune cookie

het **geluksspel** /ɣəlʏkspɛl/ (pl: -en) game of chance

het **gelukstelegram** /ɣəlʏksteləɣrɑm/ (pl: -men) telegram of congratulation

de **geluksvogel** /ɣəlʏksfoɣəl/ (pl: -s) lucky devil, lucky dog

de **gelukwens** /ɣəlʏkwɛns/ (pl: -en) congratulation; birthday wish: *mijn ~en!* congratulations!

gelukwensen /ɣəlʏkwɛnsə(n)/ (wenste geluk, heeft gelukgewenst) (+ met) congratulate (on), offer one's congratulations (on): *iem. met zijn verjaardag ~* wish s.o. many happy returns (of the day)

gelukzalig /ɣəlʏksaləχ/ (adj) blissful, blessed, beatific: *een ~e glimlach* a beatific smile

de **gelukzoeker** /ɣəlʏksukər/ (pl: -s) **1** fortunehunter, adventurer **2** [depr] fortune seeker

het **gelul** /ɣəlʏl/ [inform] (bull)shit

gemaakt /ɣəmakt/ (adj, adv) **1** pretended, sham: *een ~e glimlach* an artificial (or: a forced) smile **2** affected

de ¹**gemaal** /ɣəmal/ consort

het ²**gemaal** /ɣəmal/ **1** pumping-engine **2** fuss, bother

de **gemachtigde** /ɣəmɔχtəɣdə/ (pl: -n) deputy, authorized representative; endorsee; [law] proxy

het **gemak** /ɣəmɑk/ (pl: -ken) **1** ease, leisure: *zijn ~ nemen* take things easy **2** quiet, calm: *zich niet op zijn ~ voelen* feel ill at ease, feel awkward; *iem. op zijn ~ stellen* put (or: set) s.o. at his ease **3** ease, facility: *met ~ winnen* win easily; win hands down, have a walkover; *voor het ~* for convenience's sake

¹**gemakkelijk** /ɣəmɑkələk/ (adj, adv) **1** easy; easygoing: *de ~ste weg kiezen* take the line of least resistance; *~ in de omgang* easy to get on with **2** comfortable; convenient

²**gemakkelijk** /ɣəmɑkələk/ (adv) **1** easily: *dat is ~er gezegd dan gedaan* that's easier said than done **2** comfortably

gemakshalve /ɣəmɑkshɑlvə/ (adv) for convenience('s sake), for the sake of convenience

de **gemakzucht** /ɣəmɑksʏχt/ laziness: *uit (pure) ~ from (or: out) of (pure) laziness*
gemakzuchtig /ɣəmɑksʏχtəχ/ (adj) lazy, easygoing

de **gemalin** /ɣəmalɪn/ (pl: -nen) consort
gemankeerd /ɣəmɑŋkert/ (adj) failed, broken down: *een ~ dichter* a failed (or: would-be) poet
gemarineerd /ɣəmarinert/ (adj) marinaded, pickled, soused
gemaskerd /ɣəmɑskərt/ (adj) masked
gematigd /ɣəmatəχt/ (adj, adv) moderate; measured

de **gember** /ɣɛmbər/ ginger

¹**gemeen** /ɣəmen/ (adj) **1** nasty; vicious; malicious; low; vile; shabby: *een gemene hond* a vicious dog; *een gemene streek* a dirty trick; *dat was ~ van je* that was a mean (or: rotten) thing to do **2** common, joint: *veel met iem. ~ hebben* have a lot in common with s.o.; *de (grootste) gemene deler* a) [maths] the highest common factor; b) [fig] the (common) denominator

²**gemeen** /ɣəmen/ (adv) **1** nastily; viciously, maliciously: *iem. ~ behandelen* treat s.o. badly **2** awfully: *het is ~ koud* it's awfully cold
gemeend /ɣəment/ (adj) sincere

het **gemeengoed** /ɣəmenɣut/ common (or: public) property: *die denkbeelden zijn ~ geworden* those ideas have become generally accepted

de **gemeenplaats** /ɣəmemplats/ (pl: -en) commonplace, cliché

de **gemeenschap** /ɣəmensχɑp/ (pl: -pen) **1** community: *in ~ van goederen trouwen* have community of property **2** [Belg] federal region **3** intercourse
gemeenschappelijk /ɣəmensχɑpələk/ (adj) **1** common, communal: *een ~e bankrekening* a joint bank account; *een ~e keuken* a communal kitchen **2** joint, common; concerted; united ‖ *onze ~e kennissen* our mutual acquaintances

het **gemeenschapsgeld** /ɣəmensχɑpsχɛlt/ (pl: -en) public funds (or: money)

het **gemeenschapsonderwijs** /ɣəmensχɑps-ondərwɛis/ [Belg] education controlled by regional authorities

de **gemeenschapsraad** /ɣəmensχɑpsrat/ (pl: -raden) [Belg] community council

de **gemeenschapszin** /ɣəmensχɑpsɪn/ community (or: public) spirit

de **gemeente** /ɣəmentə/ (pl: -n, -s) **1** local authority (or: council); metropolitan city (or: town, parish) council: *bij de ~ werken* work for the local council **2** district, borough, city, town, parish: *de ~ Eindhoven* the city of Eindhoven
gemeente- [also] municipal

de **gemeenteadministratie** /ɣəmentəɑtmi-nistra(t)si/ local government

de **gemeenteambtenaar** /ɣəmentəɑmtənar/ (pl: -ambtenaren) local government official

het **gemeentebedrijf** /ɣəmentəbədrɛif/ (pl: -bedrijven): *de gemeentebedrijven* public works

de **gemeentebelasting** /ɣəmentəbəlɑstɪŋ/ (pl: -en) council tax

het **gemeentebestuur** /ɣəmentəbəstyr/ (pl: -besturen) district council, local authority (or: authorities)

het **gemeentehuis** /ɣəmentəhœys/ (pl: -huizen) local government offices; town hall, city hall
gemeentelijk /ɣəmentələk/ (adj) local authority, council, community, municipal: *het ~ vervoerbedrijf* the municipal (or: corporation, city) transport company

de **gemeentepolitie** /ɣəmentəpoli(t)si/ municipal police; [Am] city police

de **gemeenteraad** /ɣəmentərat/ (pl: -raden) council, town (or: city, parish) council: *in de ~ zitten* be on the council

het **gemeenteraadslid** /ɣəmentəratslɪt/ (pl: -raadsleden) local councillor, member of the (local) council

de **gemeenteraadsverkiezing** /ɣəmen-təratsfərkizɪŋ/ (pl: -en) local election(s)

de **gemeentereiniging** /ɣəmentərɛinəɣɪŋ/ environmental (or: public) health department

de **gemeentesecretaris** /ɣəmentəsɪkrətarɪs/ (pl: -sen) [roughly] Town Clerk

de **gemeenteverordening** /ɣəmentəverɔr-dənɪŋ/ (pl: -en) by(e)law; [Am] city ordinance

de **gemeentewerken** /ɣəmentəwɛrkə(n)/ (pl) public works (department)
gemêleerd /ɣəmɛːlert/ (adj) mixed, blended: *een ~ gezelschap* a mixed bunch of people

het **gemenebest** /ɣəmenəbɛst/ (pl: -en) commonwealth: *het Gemenebest van Onafhankelijke Staten* the Commonwealth of Independent States; *het Britse Gemenebest* the (British) Commonwealth (of Nations)
gemengd /ɣəmɛŋt/ (adj, adv) mixed; blended; miscellaneous
gemeubileerd /ɣəməbilert/ (adj) furnished

¹**gemiddeld** /ɣəmɪdəlt/ (adj) **1** average: *iem. van ~e grootte* s.o. of average (or: medium) height **2** average, mean: *de ~e hoeveelheid regen per jaar* the average (or: mean) annual rainfall

²**gemiddeld** /ɣəmɪdəlt/ (adv) on average, an average (of)

het **gemiddelde** /ɣəmɪdəldə/ average, mean: *boven* (or: *onder*) *het ~* above (or: below) (the) average

het **gemis** /ɣəmɪs/ **1** lack, want, absence, deficiency **2** loss: *zijn dood wordt als een groot ~ gevoeld* his death is felt as a great loss

het **gemodder** /ɣəmɔdər/ muddling, bungling,

messing

het **gemoed** /ɣəmut̪/ (pl: -eren) mind, heart: *de ~eren raakten* **verhit** feelings started running high; *de ~eren* **sussen** pour oil on troubled waters; *op iemands ~ werken* pluck (at) s.o.'s heart strings

gemoedelijk /ɣəmud̪ələk/ (adj, adv) agreeable, pleasant; amiable; easygoing

de **gemoedsrust** /ɣəmut̪srʏst/ peace (*or:* tranquillity) of mind, inner peace (*or:* calm)

de **gemoedstoestand** /ɣəmut̪stustɑnt̪/ state of mind, frame of mind

gemoeid /ɣəmujt̪/ (adj): *alsof haar leven* **er mee** ~ *was* as if her life depended on it (*or:* were at stake); *er is een hele dag mee* ~ it will take a whole day

het **gemompel** /ɣəmɔmpəl/ murmur, murmuring: *er ging een verontwaardigd ~* **op** *onder het publiek* an indignant murmur (*or:* a murmur of indignation) rose from the audience

het **gemopper** /ɣəmɔpər/ grumbling, grousing, complaints

gemotiveerd /ɣəmotivert̪/ (adj) **1** reasoned, well-founded **2** motivated

gemotoriseerd /ɣəmotorizert̪/ (adj) motorized

de **gems** /ɣɛms/ (pl: gemzen) chamois

gemunt /ɣəmʏnt̪/ (adj) coined ‖ *het op iem. ~ hebben* have it in for s.o.

het **gen** /ɣɛn/ (pl: -en) gene: [fig] *het zit* **in** *zijn ~en* it's in his genes, it's part of his genetic make-up

genaamd /ɣənamt̪/ (adj) **1** named, called **2** (also) known as, alias, going by the name of

de **genade** /ɣənad̪ə/ **1** mercy, grace; quarter: *geen ~* **hebben met** have no mercy on **2** mercy, pardon, forgiveness ‖ *goeie ~!* my goodness!

genadeloos /ɣənad̪əlos/ (adj, adv) merciless, ruthless

de **genadeslag** /ɣənad̪əslɑx/ (pl: -en) death blow

genadig /ɣənad̪əx/ (adj, adv) merciful: *een ~e straf* a light punishment; *er ~ (van)* **afkomen** get off (*or:* be let off) lightly

gênant /ʒənɑnt̪/ (adj) embarrassing

de **gendarme** /ʒɑndɑrm(ə)/ (pl: -s, -n) [Belg] member of national police force

de **gender** /dʒɛndər, ɣɛndər/ gender

de **genderidentiteit** /dʒɛndəridɛntitɛrt̪/ gender identity

genderneutraal /ɣɛndərnøtral/ (adj) gender-neutral

gene /ɣenə/ (dem pron) that, the other: *deze* of ~ somebody (or other)

de **gêne** /ʒɛːnə/ embarrassment, discomfiture: *zonder enige ~* without embarrassment, unashamedly, without (any) inhibition

de **genealogie** /ɣenejaloɣi/ (pl: -ën) genealogy

de **geneesheer** /ɣənesher/ (pl: -heren) physi-cian, doctor

geneeskrachtig /ɣəneskrɑxtəx/ (adj) therapeutic, healing: *~e* **bronnen** medicinal springs

de **geneeskunde** /ɣəneskʏnd̪ə/ medicine, medical science: *een student* **in** *de ~* a medical student

geneeskundig /ɣəneskʏnd̪əx/ (adj, adv) medical, medicinal, therapeutic

het **geneesmiddel** /ɣənesmɪd̪əl/ (pl: -en) medicine, drug, remedy: *rust is een* **uitstekend** *~* rest is an excellent cure

de **geneeswijze** /ɣəneswɛizə/ (pl: -n) (form of) treatment, therapy

genegen /ɣəneɣə(n)/ (adj) willing, prepared: *hij* **is** *niet ~ toestemming te geven* he is not prepared to give permission

de **genegenheid** /ɣəneɣənhɛit̪/ affection, fondness, attachment

geneigd /ɣənɛixt̪/ (adj) **1** inclined, apt, prone: *~ tot luiheid* inclined to be lazy (*or:* to laziness) **2** inclined, disposed: *ik* **ben** *~ je te geloven* I am inclined to believe you

de ¹**generaal** /ɣenəral/ (pl: -s) general

²**generaal** /ɣenəral/ (adj) general: *de generale repetitie* (the) (full) dress-rehearsal

de **generalisatie** /ɣenəraliza(t̪)si/ (pl: -s) generalization, sweeping statement

generaliseren /ɣenəralizerə(n)/ (generaliseerde, heeft gegeneraliseerd) generalize

de **generatie** /ɣenəra(t̪)si/ (pl: -s) generation

de **generatiekloof** /ɣenəra(t̪)siklof/ (pl: -kloven) generation gap: *de ~* **overbruggen** bridge the generation gap

de **generator** /ɣenərat̪or/ (pl: -en) generator, dynamo

zich **generen** /ʒənərə(n)/ (geneerde zich, heeft zich gegeneerd) be embarrassed, feel shy (*or:* awkward)

genereren /ɣenərerə(n)/ (genereerde, heeft gegenereerd) generate

genereus /ɣenərøs/ (adj, adv) generous

de **generiek** /ɣenərik/ [Belg] credits, credit titles

Genesis /ɣenəzɪs/ Genesis

de **genetica** /ɣənetika/ genetics

genetisch /ɣənetis/ (adj, adv) genetic: *~e manipulatie* genetic engineering, gene splicing

de **geneugte** /ɣənøxtə/ (pl: -n) pleasure, delight(s)

Genève /ʒənɛːvə/ Geneva

¹**genezen** /ɣənezə(n)/ (genas, is genezen) recover, get well again: *van een ziekte ~* recover from an illness; [fig] *daar was hij snel* **van** *~* he soon got over that, that was short-lived

²**genezen** /ɣənezə(n)/ (genas, heeft genezen) cure; heal

de **genezing** /ɣənezɪŋ/ (pl: -en) cure; recovery; healing

geniaal /ɣənijal/ (adj, adv) brilliant: *een ge-*

niale **vondst (zet)** a stroke of genius

de **genialiteit** /ɣenijalɪtɛɪt/ ingenuity, brilliance, brilliancy

de **¹genie** /ʒəni/ (pl: -ën) [mil] military engineering

het **²genie** /ʒəni/ (pl: -ën) genius: *een **groot** ~* an absolute genius

het **geniep** /ɣənip/: *in het ~* on the sly, on the quiet; sneakily

geniepig /ɣənipəɣ/ (adj, adv) sly; sneaky: *op een ~e **manier*** on the sly

¹genieten /ɣənitə(n)/ (genoot, heeft genoten) enjoy o.s., have a good time, have fun: *van het leven ~* enjoy life; *ik heb genoten!* I really enjoyed myself!

²genieten /ɣənitə(n)/ (genoot, heeft genoten) enjoy, have the advantage of: *een goede opleiding genoten hebben* have received a good training (*or:* education) ‖ *hij **is** vandaag niet te ~* he's unbearable today, he's in a bad mood today

de **genieter** /ɣənitər/ (pl: -s) **1** sensualist: *hij is een **echte** ~* he really knows how to enjoy life **2** recipient, beneficiary

de **genietroepen** /ʒənitrupə(n)/ (pl) (Military (*or:* Royal)) Engineers

de **genitaliën** /ɣenitalijə(n)/ (pl) genitals

de **genocide** /ɣenosidə/ genocide

de **genodigde** /ɣənodəɣdə/ (pl: -n) (invited) guest, invitee

¹genoeg /ɣənuɣ/ (adv) enough, sufficiently: *ben ik **duidelijk** ~ geweest* have I made myself clear; *jammer ~* regrettably, unfortunately; *je kunt niet **voorzichtig** ~ zijn* one can't be too careful; *vreemd ~* strangely enough, strange to say

²genoeg /ɣənuɣ/ (num) enough, plenty, sufficient; adequate: *er is **eten** ~* there is plenty of food; *ik **heb** ~ aan een gekookt ei* a boiled egg will do for me; *ik **weet** ~* I've heard enough; *er is ~ **voor** allemaal* there is enough to go round; *er zijn al **slachtoffers** ~* there are too many victims (as it is); *er schoon ~ van hebben* have had it up to here, be heartily sick of it; *zo is het wel ~* that will do ‖ *alsof dat nog niet ~ was ...* as if that wasn't enough ..., and to top it all ...

de **genoegdoening** /ɣənuɣdunɪŋ/ redress, restitution, satisfaction: *~ van iem. **eisen** voor iets* claim redress from s.o. for sth.

het **genoegen** /ɣənuɣə(n)/ (pl: -s) **1** satisfaction, gratification: *~ **nemen** met iets* put up with sth. **2** pleasure, satisfaction: *iem. een ~ **doen*** do s.o. a favour, oblige s.o.; *met ~* with pleasure; *het was mij een **waar** ~* it was a real pleasure

genoeglijk /ɣənuɣlək/ (adj, adv) enjoyable, pleasant: *zij **zaten** ~ bij elkaar* they were sitting happily together

genoegzaam /ɣənuɣsam/ (adj, adv) sufficient, satisfactory: *dat is toch ~ **bekend*** that is

(surely) sufficiently well known (*or:* well enough known)

genoemd /ɣənumt/ (adj) (above-)mentioned, said

het **genootschap** /ɣənotsxɑp/ (pl: -pen) society, association, fellowship

het **genot** /ɣənot/ (pl: genietingen) enjoyment, pleasure, delight, benefit, advantage: *onder het ~ van een glas wijn* over a glass of wine

het **genotmiddel** /ɣənotmɪdəl/ (pl: -en) stimulant; [pl] luxury foods

het **genre** /ʒãrə/ (pl: -s) genre

Gent /ɣɛnt/ Ghent

de **gentechnologie** /ɣɛntɛxnoloɣi/ genetic engineering

de **gentherapie** /ɣɛnterapi/ gene therapy

gentrificeren /ɣɛntrifisɛrə(n)/ be (*or:* become) gentrified

genuanceerd /ɣənywɑnsɛrt/ (adj, adv) subtle

het **genus** /ɣenʏs/ (pl: genera) **1** genus **2** gender

de **geodriehoek** /ɣejodrihuk/ (pl: -en) combination of a protractor and a setsquare

geoefend /ɣəufənt/ (adj) experienced, trained: *een ~ **pianist*** an accomplished pianist

de **geografie** /ɣejoɣrafi/ geography

geografisch /ɣejoɣrafis/ (adj) geographic(al)

geolied /ɣəolit/ (adj) oiled; lubricated

de **geologie** /ɣejoloɣi/ geology

geologisch /ɣejoloɣis/ (adj) geological: *een ~ **tijdperk*** a geological age

de **geoloog** /ɣejolox/ (pl: geologen) geologist

de **geometrie** /ɣejometri/ geometry

geometrisch /ɣejometris/ (adj) geometric(al)

geoorloofd /ɣəorloft/ (adj) permitted, permissible: *een ~ **middel** lawful means, a lawful method

georganiseerd /ɣəorɣanizɛrt/ (adj) organized: *een ~e **reis*** a package tour

Georgië /ɣejɔrɣijə/ Georgia

de **Georgiër** /ɣejɔrɣijər/ (pl: -s) Georgian

het **¹Georgisch** /ɣejɔrɣis/ Georgian

²Georgisch /ɣejɔrɣis/ (adj) Georgian

georiënteerd /ɣəorijɛntɛrt/ (adj) oriented, orientated

gepaard /ɣəpart/ (adj) coupled (with), accompanied (by), attendant (on), attached (to): *de risico's die daarmee ~ **gaan*** the risks involved

gepakt /ɣəpɑkt/ (adj): *~ en **gezakt*** ready for off, all ready to go

gepantserd /ɣəpɑntsərt/ (adj) armoured, in armour: *een ~e auto* an armour-plated car

geparfumeerd /ɣəpɑrfymɛrt/ (adj) perfumed, scented

gepast /ɣəpɑst/ (adj, adv) **1** (be)fitting, becoming, proper: *dat is **niet** ~* that is not done

2 exact: *met ~ geld betalen* pay the exact amount

gepatenteerd /ɣəpatɛntɛrt/ (adj) patent(ed) ‖ [fig] *een ~ leugenaar* a patent (*or:* an arrant) liar

het **gepeins** /ɣəpɛɪns/ musing(s), meditation(s), pondering

gepensioneerd /ɣəpɛnʃonɛrt/ (adj) retired, pensioned-off, superannuated

de **gepensioneerde** /ɣəpɛnʃonɛrdə/ (pl: -n) (old age) pensioner; [Am] retiree

gepeperd /ɣəpepərt/ (adj) peppery, peppered; [fig also] spicy: *zijn rekeningen zijn nogal ~* his bills are a bit steep

het **gepeupel** /ɣəpøpəl/ mob, rabble

het **gepiep** /ɣəpip/ **1** squeak(ing) **2** peep(ing); chirp, cheep(ing); squeak(ing); squeal(ing); screech(ing) **3** wheeze, wheezing

gepikeerd /ɣəpikert/ (adj) piqued, nettled: *gauw ~ zijn* be touchy

geplaatst /ɣəplatst/ (adj) qualified, qualifying

het **geploeter** /ɣəplutər/ drudgery, slaving; plodding

gepokt /ɣəpɔkt/ (adj): *~ en gemazeld zijn* be tried and tested

het **gepraat** /ɣəprat/ talk, gossip, chat, (tittle-)tattle: *hun huwelijk leidde tot veel ~* their marriage caused a lot of talk

geprefabriceerd /ɣəprefabrisert/ (adj) prefabricated, prefab

geprikkeld /ɣəprɪkəlt/ (adj) irritated, irritable: *gauw ~ zijn* be huffish (*or:* huffy)

geprononceerd /ɣəpronɔnsert/ (adj, adv) pronounced

geraakt /ɣərakt/ (adj) **1** offended, hurt **2** moved, touched

het **geraamte** /ɣəramtə/ (pl: -n, -s) **1** skeleton: [fig] *een wandelend* (*or: levend*) *~* a walking (*or:* living) skeleton **2** [fig] frame(work)

het **geraas** /ɣəras/ din, roar(ing), noise

geradbraakt /ɣərɑdbrakt/ (adj) shattered, exhausted; [Am] bushed ‖ *~ Frans* broken French

geraden /ɣəradə(n)/ (adj, adv) advisable, expedient ‖ *dat is je ~ ook!* you'd better!

geraffineerd /ɣərɑfinɛrt/ (adj, adv) **1** refined **2** refined, subtle: *een ~ plan* an ingenious plan **3** crafty, clever

geraken /ɣərakə(n)/ (geraakte, is geraakt) [Belg] *see ¹raken*

de **gerammel** /ɣərɑmməl/ rattle, rattling, clank-(ing) jingling, clatter(ing)

de **geranium** /ɣəranijʏm/ (pl: -s) geranium

de **gerant** /ʒerɑ̃/ (pl: -en, -s) manager

geraspt /ɣərɑspt/ (adj) grated

het **¹gerecht** /ɣərɛxt/ (pl: -en) dish; course: *als volgende ~ hebben we …* the next course is …

het **²gerecht** /ɣərɛxt/ (pl: -en) court (of justice), court of law, law court, tribunal: *voor het ~*

gedaagd worden be summoned (to appear in court); *voor het ~ verschijnen* appear in court

¹gerechtelijk /ɣərɛxtələk/ (adj) **1** judicial, legal, court: [Belg] *~e politie* criminal investigation department; *~e stappen ondernemen* take legal action (*or:* proceedings) **2** forensic, legal: *~e geneeskunde* forensic medicine

²gerechtelijk /ɣərɛxtələk/ (adv) legally, judicially: *iem. ~ vervolgen* take (*or:* institute) (legal) proceedings against s.o.; prosecute s.o.

gerechtigd /ɣərɛxtəxt/ (adj) authorized; qualified; entitled: *hij is ~ dat te doen* he is authorized to do that

de **gerechtigheid** /ɣərɛxtəxhɛit/ justice

het **gerechtshof** /ɣərɛxtshɔf/ (pl: -hoven) court (of justice)

gerechtvaardigd /ɣərɛxtfardəxt/ (adj, adv) justified, warranted: *~e eisen* just (*or:* legitimate) claims

gereed /ɣəret/ (adj) (all) ready; finished

de **gereedheid** /ɣərethɛit/ readiness: *alles in ~ brengen* (*maken*) get everything ready (*or:* in readiness)

gereedmaken /ɣəretmakə(n)/ (maakte gereed, heeft gereedgemaakt) make ready, get ready, prepare

het **gereedschap** /ɣəretsxɑp/ (pl: -pen) tools, equipment, apparatus; utensils: *een stuk ~* a tool, a piece of equipment

de **gereedschapskist** /ɣəretsxɑpskɪst/ (pl: -en) toolbox

gereedstaan /ɣəretstan/ (stond gereed, heeft gereedgestaan) be ready, stand ready, be waiting; [pers also] stand by

gereformeerd /ɣəreformert/ (adj) (Dutch) Reformed

geregeld /ɣəreɣəlt/ (adj) **1** regular, steady: *hij komt ~ te laat* he is often (*or:* nearly always) late **2** orderly, well-ordered: *een ~ leven gaan leiden* settle down, start keeping regular hours

het **gerei** /ɣərɛi/ gear, things; tackle; kit: *keukengerei* kitchen utensils; *scheergerei* shaving things (*or:* kit); *schrijfgerei* writing materials

geremd /ɣərɛmt/ (adj, adv) inhibited

gerenommeerd /ɣərenomert/ (adj) renowned, illustrious; well-established: *een ~ hotel* a reputable hotel

gereserveerd /ɣərezɛrvert/ (adj, adv) **1** reserved, distant: *een ~e houding aannemen* keep one's distance **2** reserved, booked

gerespecteerd /ɣərɛspɛktert/ (adj) respected

geribbeld /ɣərɪbəlt/ (adj) *see geribd*

geribd /ɣərɪpt/ (adj) ribbed; corded; corrugated: *~ katoen* corduroy

gericht /ɣərɪxt/ (adj, adv) directed (at, towards), aimed (at, towards); [fig] specific: *~e vragen* carefully chosen (*or:* selected) questions

het **gerief** /ɣərif/ [Belg] accessories: *schoolgerief* school needs

gerieflijk /ɣərif…lək/ (adj, adv) comfortable

gerimpeld /ɣərɪmpəlt/ (adj) wrinkled, wrinkly; shrivelled: *een ~ voorhoofd* a furrowed brow

gering /ɣərɪŋ/ (adj) **1** small, little: *een ~e kans* a slim (*or:* remote) chance; *in ~e mate* to a small extent (*or:* degree) **2** petty, slight, minor: *een ~ bedrag* a petty (*or:* trifling) sum; *da's niet ~* that's quite sth.

geringschattend /ɣərɪŋsxɑtənt/ (adj, adv) disparaging: *iem. ~ behandelen* slight s.o., be disparaging towards s.o.

het **geritsel** /ɣərɪtsəl/ rustling, rustle

het ¹**Germaans** /ɣɛrmans/ Germanic

²**Germaans** /ɣɛrmans/ (adj) Germanic, Teutonic

de **Germanen** /ɣɛrmanə(n)/ (pl) Germans, Teutons

het **gerochel** /ɣərɔxəl/ hawk(ing)

het **geroddel** /ɣərɔdəl/ gossip(ing), tittle-tattle

het **geroep** /ɣərup/ calling, shouting, crying, call(s), shout(s), cries, cry: *hij hoorde hun ~ niet* he did not hear them calling

geroepen /ɣərupə(n)/ (adj) called: *je komt als ~* you're just the person we need

het **geroezemoes** /ɣəruzəmus/ buzz(ing), hum: *met al dat ~ kan ik jullie niet verstaan* I can't make out what you're saying with all the din

het **gerommel** /ɣərɔməl/ **1** rumbling, rumble: *~ in de buik* rumbling in one's stomach **2** rummaging (about, around) **3** messing, fiddling about

geronnen /ɣərɔnə(n)/ (adj) clotted

gerookt /ɣərokt/ (adj) smoked

geroutineerd /ɣərutinert/ (adj, adv) experienced, practised

de **gerst** /ɣɛrst/ barley

het **gerucht** /ɣərʏxt/ (pl: -en) rumour: *het ~ gaat dat ...* there is a rumour that ...; *dat zijn maar ~en* it is only hearsay

geruchtmakend /ɣərʏxtmakənt/ (adj) controversial, sensational

geruim /ɣərœym/ (adj) considerable

geruisloos /ɣərœyslos/ (adj, adv) noiseless, silent; [fig] quietly

geruit /ɣərœyt/ (adj) check(ed)

¹**gerust** /ɣərʏst/ (adj) easy, at ease: *een ~ geweten* (or: *gemoed*) an easy (*or:* a clear) conscience, an easy mind; *met een ~ hart de toekomst tegemoet zien* face the future with confidence; *ik ben er niet ~ op* I am not happy (*or:* easy) about it

²**gerust** /ɣərʏst/ (adv) safely, with confidence, without any fear (*or:* problem): *ga ~ je gang* (do) go ahead!, feel free to ...; *vraag ~ om hulp* don't hesitate to ask for help

geruststellen /ɣərʏstɛlə(n)/ (stelde gerust,

heeft gerustgesteld) reassure, put (*or:* set) (s.o.'s) mind at rest

geruststellend /ɣərʏstɛlənt/ (adj) reassuring

de **geruststelling** /ɣərʏstɛlɪŋ/ (pl: -en) reassurance, comfort; relief

het **geruzie** /ɣəruzi/ arguing, quarrelling, bickering

het **geschater** /ɣəsxatər/ peals (*or:* roars) of laughter

gescheiden /ɣəsxɛidə(n)/ (adj) **1** separated, apart: *twee zaken strikt ~ houden* keep two things strictly separate; *~ leven (van)* live apart (from) **2** divorced: *~ gezin* broken home

het **geschenk** /ɣəsxɛŋk/ (pl: -en) present, gift

geschieden /ɣəsxidə(n)/ (geschiedde, is geschied) occur, take place, happen

de **geschiedenis** /ɣəsxidənɪs/ (pl: -sen) **1** history: *de ~ herhaalt zich* history repeats itself **2** tale, story: *dat is een andere ~* that's another story **3** [comp] history: *zijn ~ wissen* erase (*or:* delete) one's (Internet) history

geschiedkundig /ɣəsxitkʏndəx/ (adj, adv) historical

de **geschiedvervalsing** /ɣəsxitfərvɑlsɪŋ/ (pl: -en) falsification (*or:* rewriting) of history

geschift /ɣəsxɪft/ (adj) **1** crazy, nuts **2** curdled

geschikt /ɣəsxɪkt/ (adj, adv) suitable, fit, appropriate: *is twee uur een ~e tijd?* will two o'clock be convenient?; *~ zijn voor het doel* serve the purpose; *dat boek is niet ~ voor kinderen* that book is not suitable for children

het **geschil** /ɣəsxɪl/ (pl: -len) dispute, disagreement, quarrel: *een ~ bijleggen* settle a dispute (with s.o.)

geschoold /ɣəsxolt/ (adj) trained, skilled

het **geschreeuw** /ɣəsxrew/ shouting, yelling, shouts: *hou op met dat ~* stop yelling || *veel ~ maar weinig wol* much cry and little wool; much ado about nothing

het **geschrift** /ɣəsxrɪft/ (pl: -en) writing: *de heilige ~en* the Scriptures; *in woord en ~* orally and in written form; *valsheid in ~e plegen* commit forgery

het **geschut** /ɣəsxʏt/ artillery

de **gesel** /ɣesəl/ (pl: -s, -en) **1** whip **2** [fig] scourge

geselen /ɣesələ(n)/ (geselde, heeft gegeseld) whip, flog

gesetteld /ɣəsɛtəlt/ (adj) settled: *~ zijn* be settled

het **gesis** /xəsɪs/ hiss(ing); fizz(le); sizzle

gesitueerd /ɣəsitywert/ (adj) situated: *de beter ~e klassen* the better-off classes

het **gesjoemel** /ɣəʃuməl/ dirty tricks, trickery

geslaagd /ɣəslaxt/ (adj) successful

het **geslacht** /ɣəslɔxt/ (pl: -en) **1** family, line, house: *uit een nobel* (or: *vorstelijk*) *~ stammen* be of noble (*or:* royal) descent **2** sex **3** generation

geslachtelijk /ɣəslɑxtələk/ (adj) sexual: ~e **voortplanting** sexual reproduction

de **geslachtsdaad** /ɣəslɑxtsdat/ sex(ual) act; [med] coitus

de **geslachtsdelen** /ɣəslɑxtsdelə(n)/ (pl) genitals, sex organs, genital organs; private parts

de **geslachtsdrift** /ɣəslɑx(t)sdrɪft/ sex(ual) drive, sexual urge, libido

de **geslachtsgemeenschap** /ɣəslɑxtsxəmensxɑp/ sexual intercourse (or: relations), sex

geslachtsneutraal /ɣəslɑx(t)snøtral/ (adj) gender-neutral

het **geslachtsorgaan** /ɣəslɑx(t)sɔrɣan/ (pl: -organen) sex(ual) organ, genital organ; [pl also] genitals

de **geslachtsverandering** /ɣəslɑx(t)sfərɑndərɪŋ/ (pl: -en) sex change

het **geslachtsverkeer** /ɣəslɑx(t)sfərker/ sexual intercourse (or: relations)

de **geslachtsziekte** /ɣəslɑxtsiktə/ (pl: -n, -s) venereal disease, VD

geslepen /ɣəslepə(n)/ (adj, adv) sly, cunning, sharp

gesloten /ɣəslotə(n)/ (adj) **1** closed, shut; drawn: achter ~ **deuren** behind closed doors, in private; in camera; een ~ **geldkist** (or: **enveloppe, goederenwagon**) a sealed chest (or: envelope, goods wagon); een **hoog** ~ bloes a high-necked blouse **2** close(-mouthed), tight-lipped: dat **kind** is nogal ~ that child doesn't say much (for himself, herself); een ~ **circuit** a closed circuit

gesmeerd /ɣəsmert/ (adj, adv) **1** greased, buttered **2** smoothly: ervoor zorgen dat het ~ **gaat** make sure everything goes smoothly

gesmoord /ɣəsmort/ (adj) **1** stifled, smothered **2** braised

het **gesnauw** /ɣəsnɑu̯/ snarling, snapping

het **gesnik** /ɣəsnɪk/ sobbing, sobs

het **gesnurk** /ɣəsnʏrk/ snore, snoring

het **gesoebat** /ɣəsubɑt/ imploring (for)

gesorteerd /ɣəsɔrtert/ (adj) sorted: op kleur ~ sorted according to colour; ~e **koekjes** assorted biscuits

de **gesp** /ɣɛsp/ (pl: -en) buckle, clasp

gespannen /ɣəspɑnə(n)/ (adj, adv) **1** tense(d), taut; bent **2** tense, strained; [pers also] nervous; on edge: te hoog ~ **verwachtingen** exaggerated expectations; ~ **luisteren** listen intently; **tot** het uiterste ~ at full strain

gespecialiseerd /ɣəspeʃalizert/ (adj) specialized; specializing

gespeend /ɣəspent/ (adj): ~ **van** devoid of, utterly lacking (in)

gespen /ɣɛspə(n)/ (gespte, heeft gegespt) buckle; strap

gespierd /ɣəspirt/ (adj) muscular; brawny; beefy

gespikkeld /ɣəspɪkəlt/ (adj) spotted, speck-

led; dotted

gespitst /ɣəspɪtst/ (adj) keen: ~ zijn **op** iets be keen on sth. (or: to do sth.) ‖ met ~e **oren** with one's ears pricked up, all ears

gespleten /ɣəspletə(n)/ (adj) split; cleft; cloven

het **gesprek** /ɣəsprɛk/ (pl: -ken) **1** talk, conversation; call: het ~ met iem. **aangaan** discuss sth. with s.o., broach a subject with s.o.; het ~ op iets anders **brengen** change the subject; een ~ **voeren** hold a conversation; het ~ van de **dag** zijn be the talk of the town; (het nummer is) **in** ~ (the number's) engaged; een ~ onder vier ogen a private discussion **2** discussion, consultation: **inleidende** ~ken introductory talks

de **gesprekskosten** /ɣəsprɛkskɔstə(n)/ (pl) call charge(s)

de **gesprekspartner** /ɣəsprɛkspɑrtnər/ (pl: -s) person one is (or: was)… speaking to; discussion (or: conversation) partner

de **gespreksstof** /ɣəsprɛkstɔf/ topic(s) of conversation, subject(s) for discussion

het **gespuis** /ɣəspœy̯s/ riff-raff, rabble, scum

gestaag /ɣəstax/ (adj, adv) steady: gestage **arbeid** steady work; het aantal **nam** ~ **toe** the number rose steadily; het werk **vordert** ~ the work is progressing steadily

de **gestalte** /ɣəstɑltə/ (pl: -n, -s) **1** figure; build: **fors** van ~ heavily-built; een **slanke** ~ a slim figure **2** shape, form ‖ ~ **geven** (aan) give shape (to); ~ **krijgen** take shape

gestampt /ɣəstɑmt/ (adj) crushed; mashed: ~e **muisjes** aniseed (sugar) crumble

het/de **gestand** /ɣəstɑnt/: zijn belofte ~ **doen** be as good as one's word, keep one's promise

gestationeerd /ɣəsta(t)ʃonert/ (adj) stationed, based

de **geste** /ʒɛstə/ (pl: -s) gesture: een ~ **doen** make a gesture

het **gesteente** /ɣəstentə/ (pl: -n, -s) rock, stone

het **gesteggel** /ɣəstɛɣəl/ bickering, squabbling

het **gestel** /ɣəstɛl/ (pl: -len) **1** constitution **2** system: het **zenuwgestel** the nervous system

gesteld /ɣəstɛlt/ (adj) **1** keen (on), fond (of): zij zijn **erop** ~ (dat) they would like it (if), they are set on (…-ing); erg **op** comfort ~ zijn like one's comfort **2** appointed: binnen de ~e **tijd** within the time specified

de **gesteldheid** /ɣəstɛltheit/ state, condition; constitution

gestemd /ɣəstɛmt/ (adj) disposed: hij is **goed** ~ he's in a good mood; **gunstig** ~ favourably disposed (towards)

gesteriliseerd /ɣəsterilizert/ (adj) sterilized

het **gesticht** /ɣəstɪxt/ (pl: -en) mental home (or: institution)

gesticuleren /ɣɛstikylerə(n)/ (gesticuleerde, heeft gegesticuleerd) gesticulate

gestippeld /ɣəstɪpəlt/ (adj) **1** dotted: een

~e **lijn** a dotted line **2** spotted, speckled; dotted

gestoffeerd /ɣəstɔfe̞rt/ (adj) **1** upholstered **2** (fitted) with curtains and carpets

gestoord /ɣəsto̞rt/ (adj) disturbed: [fig] *ergens ~ van worden* be sick to one's back teeth of sth.; *prettig ~* slightly eccentric

het **gestotter** /ɣəsto̞tər/ stammer(ing), stutter(ing)

gestreept /ɣəstre̞pt/ (adj) striped

gestrekt /ɣəstrɛkt/ (adj) (out)stretched

gestrest /ɣəstrɛst/ (adj) stressed

gestroomlijnd /ɣəstro̞mlɛɪnt/ (adj) streamlined, aerodynamic: *een ~e organisatie* a streamlined organization

het **gesuis** /ɣəsœys/ sough(ing), murmur(ing); ringing

het **gesukkel** /ɣəsʏkəl/ **1** ailing **2** difficulties

het **getal** /ɣətɑl/ (pl: -len) number, figure: *een rond ~* a round number (or: figure); *een ~ van drie cijfers* a three-digit (or: three-figure) number

getalenteerd /ɣətalɛnte̞rt/ (adj) talented

het **getalm** /ɣətɑlm/ lingering

getalsmatig /ɣətɑlsmatəχ/ (adj) numerical

getand /ɣətɑnt/ (adj) [bot] dentate, denticulate

getapt /ɣətɑpt/ (adj) popular (with)

het **geteisem** /ɣəte̞ɪsəm/ riff-raff, scum

getekend /ɣəte̞kənt/ (adj) **1** marked, branded: *een fraai ~e kat* a cat with beautiful markings; *voor het leven ~ zijn* be marked for life **2** lined

het **getier** /ɣəti̞r/ howl(ing), roar(ing): *gevloek en ~* cursing and swearing

het **getij** /ɣəte̞ɪ/ (pl: -en) tide

het **getik** /ɣətɪk/ tick(ing); tapping

getikt /ɣətɪkt/ (adj) **1** crazy, cracked, nuts: *hij is compleet ~* he's completely off his rocker **2** typed

getint /ɣətɪnt/ (adj) tinted, dark

getiteld /ɣətite̞lt/ (adj) entitled

het **getob** /ɣətɔp/ worry(ing), brooding

het **getoeter** /ɣətu̞tər/ hoot(ing), honk(ing), beep(ing)

het **getouwtrek** /ɣətɑutrɛk/ tug-of-war

getralied /ɣətralit/ (adj) latticed, grated; barred

getrapt /ɣətrɑpt/ (adj) multi-stage; indirect

getraumatiseerd /ɣətrɑumatize̞rt/ (adj) traumatized

het **getreiter** /ɣətrɛɪtər/ vexation, nagging, teasing

getroebleerd /ɣətruble̞rt/ (adj): *~e verhoudingen* troubled (or: difficult) relations

getroffen /ɣətrɔfə(n)/ (adj) **1** hit, struck **2** stricken, afflicted: *de ~ ouders* the stricken parents; the bereaved parents

zich **getroosten** /ɣətro̞stə(n)/ (getroostte zich, heeft zich getroost) undergo, suffer: *zich de moeite ~ om iets te doen* take (the) trouble

(or: put o.s. out) to do sth.

getrouw /ɣətrɑu/ (adj) faithful, true: *een ~e vertaling* (or: *weergave*) a faithful translation (or: representation)

getrouwd /ɣətrɑut/ (adj) married; wed(ded): *hij is ~ met zijn werk* he is married to his work; [fig] *zo zijn we niet ~* that wasn't what we agreed on (at all)

het **getto** /ɣɛto/ (pl: -'s) ghetto

de **gettoblaster** /ɣɛtoblɑːstər/ (pl: -s) ghetto blaster

de **getuige** /ɣətœyɣə/ (pl: -n) witness

de **getuige-deskundige** /ɣətœyɣədɛskʏndəɣə/ (pl: -n) expert witness

¹**getuigen** /ɣətœyɣə(n)/ (getuigde, heeft getuigd) **1** give evidence (or: testimony), testify (to) **2** speak: *alles getuigt voor* (or: *tegen*) *haar* everything speaks in her favour (or: against her) **3** be evidence (or: a sign) (of), show, indicate: *die daad getuigt van moed* that act shows courage

²**getuigen** /ɣətœyɣə(n)/ (getuigde, heeft getuigd) testify (to), bear witness (to)

het/de **getuigenis** /ɣətœyɣənɪs/ (pl: -sen) **1** evidence **2** testimony, evidence, statement

het **getuigenverhoor** /ɣətœyɣə(n)vərho̞r/ (pl: -verhoren) hearing (or: examination) of witnesses

de **getuigenverklaring** /ɣətœyɣə(n)vərklarɪŋ/ (pl: -en) testimony, deposition

het **getuigschrift** /ɣətœyχsχrɪft/ (pl: -en) certificate; report; reference

de **geul** /ɣøl/ (pl: -en) **1** channel **2** trench, ditch, gully

de **geur** /ɣør/ (pl: -en) smell; perfume; scent; aroma: *een onaangename ~ verspreiden (afgeven)* give off an unpleasant smell ‖ *iets in ~en en kleuren vertellen* tell all the (gory) details of sth.

geuren /ɣørə(n)/ (geurde, heeft gegeurd) **1** smell **2** show off, flaunt

geurig /ɣørəχ/ (adj) fragrant, sweet-smelling

de **geus** /ɣøs/ (pl: geuzen) [historical] Beggar

het **gevaar** /ɣəvar/ (pl: gevaren) danger, risk: *hij is een ~ op de weg* he's a menace on the roads; *~ bespeuren* (or: *ruiken*) sense (or: scent) danger; *het ~ bestaat dat het bedrijf failliet gaat* there is a distinct possibility that the company will go bankrupt; *~ lopen* be in danger, run a risk; *~ voor brand* fire hazard; *het is niet zonder ~* it is not without its dangers; *het ~ bestaat dat* there is a risk that ‖ *iem. (iets) in ~ brengen* endanger s.o. (sth.)

gevaarlijk /ɣəvarlək/ (adj) dangerous; hazardous; risky: *zich op ~ terrein begeven* tread on thin ice

het **gevaarte** /ɣəvartə/ (pl: -n, -s) monster, colossus

het **geval** /ɣəvɑl/ (pl: -len) **1** case, affair: *een lastig ~* an awkward case **2** circumstances, position: *in* **uw** ~ *zou ik het nooit doen* in your position I'd never do that **3** case, circumstances: *in het* **uiterste** ~ at worst, if the worst comes to the worst; *in* ~ *van oorlog* (or: *brand, ziekte*) in the event of war (or: *fire, illness*); *in negen van de tien* ~*len* nine times out of ten; *in enkele* ~*len* in some cases; *voor het* ~ *dat* (just) in case **4** chance, luck: *wat* **wil** *nou het* ~*?* guess what

gevallen /ɣəvɑlə(n)/ (adj) fallen: *de* ~*en* the dead

gevangen /ɣəvɑŋə(n)/ (adj) caught, captive; imprisoned

de **gevangenbewaarder** /ɣəvɑŋə(n)bəwardər/ (pl: -s) warder, jailer

de **gevangene** /ɣəvɑŋənə/ (pl: -n) prisoner, inmate; convict; captive

gevangenhouden /ɣəvɑŋə(n)hɑudə(n)/ (hield gevangen, heeft gevangengehouden) imprison, detain, keep in confinement (or: prison)

de **gevangenis** /ɣəvɑŋənɪs/ (pl: -sen) prison, jail: *hij heeft tien jaar* **in** *de* ~ *gezeten* he has served ten years in prison (or: jail)

de **gevangenisstraf** /ɣəvɑŋənɪstrɑf/ (pl: -fen) imprisonment, prison sentence, jail sentence, prison term: *tot één* **jaar** ~ *veroordeeld worden* be sentenced to one year's imprisonment; *levenslange* ~ life imprisonment

gevangennemen /ɣəvɑŋəneme(n)/ (nam gevangen, heeft gevangengenomen) arrest; capture; take prisoner (or: captive)

de **gevangenschap** /ɣəvɑŋə(n)sxɑp/ captivity, imprisonment

de **gevarendriehoek** /ɣəvarə(n)drihuk/ (pl: -en) warning triangle, emergency triangle; [Am] [roughly] flares

gevarieerd /ɣəvarijert/ (adj) varied

gevat /ɣəvɑt/ (adj, adv) quick(-witted), sharp; quick, ready: *een* ~ **antwoord** a ready (or: quick) retort

het **gevecht** /ɣəvɛxt/ (pl: -en) **1** [mil] fight(ing), combat: *een* ~ *van man* **tegen** *man* hand-to-hand combat **2** fight, struggle: *een* ~ *op leven en dood* a life-or-death struggle

het **gevechtsvliegtuig** /ɣəvɛx(t)sflixtœyx/ (pl: -en) fighter (plane (or: aircraft))

geveinsd /ɣəvɛinst/ (adj) pretended, feigned

de **gevel** /ɣevəl/ (pl: -s) façade, (house)front; outside wall, outer wall

de **geveltoerist** /ɣevəlturɪst/ (pl: -en) **1** cat burglar **2** urban climber; spiderman protester

¹**geven** /ɣevə(n)/ (gaf, heeft gegeven) **1** be fond of: *niets (geen cent)* **om** *iem.* ~ not care a thing about s.o. **2** matter: *dat geeft* **niks** it doesn't matter a bit (or: at all)

²**geven** /ɣevə(n)/ (gaf, heeft gegeven) give; donate; hand: *geschiedenis* ~ teach history; *geef mij maar een* **glaasje wijn** I'll have a glass

of wine; *kunt u me de* **secretaresse** *even* ~*?* can I please speak to the secretary?; *kun je me het* **zout** ~*?* could you give (or: pass, hand) me the salt?; [cards] *wie* **moet** *er* ~*?* whose deal is it?; *geef op!* (come on,) hand it over!

de **gever** /ɣevər/ (pl: -s) giver, donor: *een* **gulle** ~ a generous giver

gevestigd /ɣəvɛstəxt/ (adj) old-established, long-standing: *de* ~*e* **orde** the established order

gevierd /ɣəvirt/ (adj) celebrated

gevleid /ɣəvlɛit/ (adj) flattered: *zich* ~ *voelen* feel flattered

gevlekt /ɣəvlɛkt/ (adj) spotted, specked; stained; mottled

gevleugeld /ɣəvløɣəlt/ (adj) winged

het **gevlij** /ɣəvlɛi/: *bij iem.* **in** *het* ~ *proberen te komen* butter s.o. up

gevlogen /ɣəvloɣə(n)/ (adj) flown, gone

gevoeglijk /ɣəvuxlək/ (adv) properly, suitably: *dat* **kun** *je* ~ *vergeten* you can simply rule that out

het **gevoel** /ɣəvul/ (pl: -ens) **1** touch, feel(ing): *op het* ~ *af* by feel (or: touch) **2** feeling, sensation: *een* **brandend** ~ *in de maag* a burning sensation in one's stomach; *ik vind het wel een* **lekker** ~ I like the feeling; *ik* **heb** *geen* ~ *meer in mijn vinger* my finger's gone numb, I've got no feeling left in my finger **3** feeling, sense: *het* ~ **hebben** *dat ...* have a feeling that ..., feel that ... **4** feeling(s), emotion(s): *op zijn* ~ *afgaan* play it by ear; *zijn* ~*ens* **tonen** show one's feelings **5** sense (of), feeling (for): *geen* ~ *voor humor hebben* have no sense of humour ‖ ~*ens van spijt* feelings of regret

het **gevoelen** /ɣəvulə(n)/ (pl: -s) **1** feeling, emotion: *zijn* ~*s* **tonen** show one's feelings **2** feeling, sentiment: ~*s van spijt* feelings of regret **3** feeling, opinion

gevoelig /ɣəvuləx/ (adj) **1** sensitive (to); sore; tender; allergic (to) **2** sensitive (to), susceptible (to); touchy: *een* ~ **mens** a sensitive person **3** sore: *een* ~*e* **klap** a painful (or: nasty) blow **4** sensitive, delicate: *die vraag* **ligt** ~ that's a sensitive issue

de **gevoeligheid** /ɣəvuləxhɛit/ (pl: -heden) sensitivity (to), susceptibility (to)

gevoelloos /ɣəvulos/ (adj) **1** numb **2** insensitive (to), unfeeling: *een* ~ **mens** an unfeeling person

de **gevoelloosheid** /ɣəvulosheit/ numbness; insensitivity; callousness

het **gevoelsleven** /ɣəvulslevə(n)/ emotional (or: inner) life

gevoelsmatig /ɣəvulsmatəx/ (adj, adv) instinctive

de **gevoelsmens** /ɣəvulsmɛns/ (pl: -en) man (or: woman) of feeling; emotional person

de **gevoelstemperatuur** /ɣəvulstɛmpəratyr/ windchill factor

de **gevoelswaarde** /ɣəvulswardə/ **1** sentimental (*or:* emotional) value **2** connotation

het **gevogelte** /ɣəvoɣəltə/ poultry, fowl: *wild en ~* game and fowl

het **gevolg** /ɣəvɔlx/ (pl: -en) consequence; result; effect; outcome; success: *met goed ~ examen doen* pass an exam; *~ geven* (or: *gevend*) *aan een opdracht* carry out (*or:* according to) instructions; *(geen) nadelige ~en hebben* have (no) adverse effects; *met alle ~en van dien* with all its consequences; *tot ~ hebben* result in

de **gevolgtrekking** /ɣəvɔlxtrɛkɪŋ/ (pl: -en) conclusion, deduction

gevolmachtigd /ɣəvɔlmɑxtəxt/ (adj) authorized, having (full) power of attorney

gevorderd /ɣəvɔrdərt/ (adj) advanced

gevormd /xəvɔrmt/ (adj) **1** -formed, (-)shaped: *een stel fraai ~e benen* a pair of shapely legs; *een goed ~e neus* a regular nose **2** fully formed: *een ~ karakter* a fully developed character

gevraagd /xəvraxt/ (adj) in demand: *een ~ boek* a book that is much (*or:* greatly) in demand

gevreesd /ɣəvrest/ (adj) dreaded

gevuld /ɣəvʏlt/ (adj) **1** full, plump: *een ~ figuur* a full figure **2** stuffed, filled: *een ~e kies* a filled tooth; *~e tomaten* stuffed tomatoes

het **gewaad** /ɣəwat/ (pl: gewaden) garment, attire, robe, gown

gewaagd /ɣəwaxt/ (adj) **1** hazardous, risky: *een ~e sprong* a daring leap **2** daring, suggestive

gewaarworden /ɣəwarwɔrdə(n)/ (werd gewaar, is gewaargeworden) perceive, observe, notice

de **gewaarwording** /ɣəwarwɔrdɪŋ/ (pl: -en) perception; sensation

het **gewag** /ɣəwɑx/: *~ maken van* mention, report

gewapend /ɣəwapənt/ (adj) armed; reinforced: *~ beton* reinforced concrete

gewapenderhand /ɣəwapəndərhɑnt/ (adv) by force of arms: *~ tussenbeide komen* intervene militarily

het **gewas** /ɣəwɑs/ (pl: -sen) plant

gewatteerd /ɣəwatert/ (adj) quilted: *een ~e deken* a quilt; a duvet

het **gewauwel** /ɣəwɑuwəl/ claptrap, drivel

het **geweer** /ɣəwer/ (pl: geweren) rifle, gun: *een ~ aanleggen* aim a rifle (*or:* gun)

het **geweervuur** /ɣəwervyr/ gunfire

het **gewei** /ɣəwɛi/ (pl: -en) antlers

het **geweld** /ɣəwɛlt/ violence, force; strength: *~ gebruiken* use violence; *grof ~* brute force (*or:* strength); *huiselijk ~* domestic violence; *verbaal ~* verbal violence (*or:* assault); *de waarheid ~ aandoen* stretch the truth || *hij wilde met alle ~ naar huis* he wanted to go home at all costs

de **gewelddaad** /ɣəwɛldat/ (pl: -daden) (act of) violence, outrage

gewelddadig /ɣəwɛldadəx/ (adj, adv) violent, forcible

geweldig /ɣəwɛldəx/ (adj, adv) **1** tremendous, enormous: *een ~ bedrag* a huge sum; *een ~e eetlust* an enormous appetite; *zich ~ inspannen* go to great lengths **2** terrific, fantastic, wonderful: *je hebt me ~ geholpen* you've been a great help; *hij is ~* he's a great guy; *die jurk staat haar ~* that dress looks smashing on her; *hij zingt ~* he sings wonderfully; *~!* great!, terrific! **3** tremendous, terrible

geweldloos /ɣəwɛltlos/ (adj, adv) nonviolent: *~ verzet* nonviolent (*or:* peaceful) resistance

het **gewelf** /ɣəwɛlf/ (pl: gewelven) **1** vault(ing), arch **2** vault

gewelfd /ɣəwɛlft/ (adj) vaulted, arched

gewend /ɣəwɛnt/ (adj) used (to), accustomed (to); in the habit (of); inured (to): *~ raken aan zijn nieuwe huis* settle down in one's new house; *dat zijn we niet van hem ~* that's not like him at all, that's quite unlike him!

gewenst /ɣəwɛnst/ (adj) desired, wished for

gewerveld /ɣəwɛrvəlt/ (adj) vertebrate

het **gewest** /ɣəwɛst/ (pl: -en) **1** district, region **2** province, county; [Belg] region: *overzeese ~en* overseas territories

gewestelijk /ɣəwɛstələk/ (adj, adv) regional, provincial

het **geweten** /ɣəwetə(n)/ conscience: *een slecht ~ hebben* have a bad (*or:* guilty) conscience; *veel op zijn ~ hebben* have a lot to answer for

gewetenloos /ɣəwetənlos/ (adj, adv) unscrupulous, unprincipled

het **gewetensbezwaar** /ɣəwetə(n)zbəzwar/ (pl: -bezwaren) scruple, conscientious objection

de **gewetensnood** /ɣəwetə(n)snot/ moral dilemma

gewetensvol /ɣəwetənsfɔl/ (adj, adv) conscientious, scrupulous; painstaking

de **gewetensvraag** /ɣəwetə(n)sfrax/ (pl: -vragen): *dat is een ~* now you're asking me one, that's quite a question

gewettigd /ɣəwɛtəxt/ (adj) **1** legitimate, justified; well-founded **2** legitimated

gewezen /ɣəwezə(n)/ (adj) former, ex-

het **gewicht** /ɣəwɪxt/ (pl: -en) weight; importance: *maten en ~en* weights and measures; *zaken van het grootste ~* matters of the utmost importance; *soortelijk ~* specific gravity; *op zijn ~ letten* watch one's weight; *beneden het ~* underweight

gewichtheffen /ɣəwɪxthɛfə(n)/ weightlifting

¹**gewichtig** /ɣəwɪxtəx/ (adj) weighty, important; grave: *~e gebeurtenissen* important events; *hij zette een ~ gezicht* he put on a

grave face

²**gewichtig** /ɣəwɪxtəx/ (adv) (self-)impor-
tantly, pompously: ~ *doen* be important
(about sth.)

de **gewichtsklasse** /ɣəwɪxtsklɑsə/ (pl: -n)
weight

gewiekst /ɣəwikst/ (adj) sharp, shrewd, fly

gewijd /ɣəwɛit/ (adj) **1** consecrated, holy: ~
water holy water **2** ordained

gewild /ɣəwɪlt/ (adj) sought-after, popular;
in demand

¹**gewillig** /ɣəwɪləx/ (adj) **1** willing; docile;
obedient: *zich ~ tonen* show (one's) willingness **2** willing, ready: *een ~ oor lenen aan iem.*
lend a ready ear to s.o.

²**gewillig** /ɣəwɪləx/ (adv) willingly, readily,
voluntarily: *hij ging ~ mee* he came along
willingly

het **gewin** /ɣəwɪn/ gain, profit

het **gewoel** /ɣəwul/ **1** tossing (and turning);
struggling **2** bustle

gewond /ɣəwɒnt/ (adj) injured; wounded;
hurt: ~ *aan het been* injured (*or:* wounded) in
the leg

de **gewonde** /ɣəwɒndə/ injured person,
wounded person, casualty

gewonnen /ɣəwɒnə(n)/ (adj): *zich ~ geven*
admit defeat

¹**gewoon** /ɣəwon/ (adj) **1** usual, regular,
customary, ordinary: *in zijn gewone doen zijn*
be o.s.; *zijn gewone gang gaan* go about one's
business, carry on as usual **2** common: *dat is
~ that's natural* **3** ordinary, common(place),
plain: *het gewone leven* everyday life; *de gewone man* the common man; *de ~ste zaak ter
wereld* (sth.) perfectly normal

²**gewoon** /ɣəwon/ (adv) **1** normally: *doe
maar ~* (do) act normal(ly), behave yourself
2 normally, ordinarily, usually **3** simply, just:
zij praatte er heel ~ over she was very casual
about it

gewoonlijk /ɣəwonlək/ (adv) usually, normally: *zoals ~ kwam ze te laat* as usual, she
was late

de **gewoonte** /ɣəwontə/ (pl: -n, -s) **1** custom,
practice **2** habit, custom: *de macht der ~* the
force of habit; *tegen zijn ~* contrary to his
usual practice; *hij heeft de ~ om* he has a habit
(*or:* way) of; *uit ~* from (*or:* out of, by) habit

het **gewoontedier** /ɣəwontədir/ (pl: -en) creature of habit

gewoontegetrouw /ɣəwontəɣətrɑu/
(adv) as usual, according to custom

gewoonweg /ɣəwonwɛx/ (adv) simply, just

het **gewricht** /ɣəvrɪxt/ (pl: -en) joint, articulation

de **gewrichtsontsteking** /ɣəvrɪx(t)sɔntste-
kɪŋ/ rheumatoid arthritis

het **gewriemel** /ɣəvriməl/ fiddling (with)

gezaagd /ɣəzaxt/ (adj) [bot] serrate

het **gezag** /ɣəzɑx/ **1** authority, power; [mil]

command; rule; dominion: *ouderlijk ~* parental authority; *het ~ voeren over* command,
be in command of **2** authority, authorities:
het bevoegd ~ the competent authorities
3 authority, weight: *op eigen ~* on one's own
authority; *op ~ van* on the authority of

gezaghebbend /ɣəzɑxhɛbənt/ (adj, adv)
authoritative, influential: *iets vernemen uit ~e
bron* have sth. on good authority

de **gezagsdrager** /ɣəzɑxdrayər/ (pl: gezags-
dragers) person in charge (*or:* authority)

de **gezagvoerder** /ɣəzɑxfurdər/ (pl: -s) captain; skipper

¹**gezamenlijk** /ɣəzamə(n)lək/ (adj) collective, combined, united, joint: *met ~e krachten* with united forces

²**gezamenlijk** /ɣəzamə(n)lək/ (adv) together

het **gezang** /ɣəzɑŋ/ (pl: -en) song, singing

het **gezanik** /ɣəzanək/ **1** nagging, moaning
2 trouble: *dat geeft een hoop ~* that causes a
lot of trouble

de **gezant** /ɣəzɑnt/ (pl: -en) envoy, ambassador, representative, delegate

het **gezantschap** /ɣəzɑntsxɑp/ (pl: -pen) mission

gezapig /ɣəzapəx/ (adj) lethargic, indolent,
complacent

het **gezegde** /ɣəzɛɣdə/ (pl: -n, -s) **1** saying,
proverb **2** [linguistics] predicate: *naamwoordelijk ~* nominal predicate

gezegend /ɣəzeɣənt/ (adj, adv) blessed;
fortunately; luckily

de **gezel** /ɣəzɛl/ (pl: -len) companion; mate

gezellig /ɣəzɛləx/ (adj, adv) **1** enjoyable,
pleasant; sociable; companionable: *het zijn
~e mensen* they are good company (*or:* very
sociable) **2** pleasant, comfortable; cosy: *een ~
hoekje* a snug (*or:* cosy) corner

de **gezelligheid** /ɣəzɛləxhɛit/ **1** sociability: *hij
houdt van ~* he is fond of company **2** cosi-
ness, snugness

het **gezelschap** /ɣəzɛlsxɑp/ (pl: -pen) **1** company, companionship: *iem. ~ houden* keep s.o.
company; *in ~ van* in the company of **2** company, society **3** company, party: *zich bij het ~
voegen* join the party

het **gezelschapsspel** /ɣəzɛlsxɑpspɛl/ (pl: -en)
party game

gezet /ɣəzɛt/ (adj) **1** set, regular **2** stout,
thickset

het **gezeur** /ɣəzør/ moaning, nagging; fuss(ing):
hou nu eens op met dat eeuwige ~! for goodness' sake stop that perpetual moaning!

het **gezicht** /ɣəzɪxt/ (pl: -en) **1** sight: *liefde op
het eerste ~* love at first sight; *dat is geen ~!*
you look a fright, that is hideous; *een vreselijk ~* a gruesome sight **2** face: *iem. in zijn ~
uitlachen* laugh in s.o.'s face; *iem. van ~ kennen* know s.o. by sight **3** face, expression,
look(s): *ik zag aan zijn ~ dat* I could tell by the

look on his face that; [fig] *dat geeft scheve ~en* that will make people jealous (*or:* envious); *een ~ zetten alsof* look as if **4** view, sight: *aan het ~ onttrekken* conceal

het **gezichtsbedrog** /ɣəzɪxtsbədrɔx/ optical illusion

het **gezichtspunt** /ɣəzɪxtspʏnt/ (pl: -en) point of view, angle || *een heel nieuw ~* an entirely fresh perspective (*or:* viewpoint, angle)

de **gezichtssluier** /ɣəzɪx(t)slœyjər/ (face) veil

het **gezichtsveld** /ɣəzɪxtsfɛlt/ (pl: -en) field (*or:* range) of vision, sight

het **gezichtsverlies** /ɣəzɪxtsfərlis/ loss of face: *~ lijden* lose face, suffer a loss of face

het **gezichtsvermogen** /ɣəzɪxtsfərmoɣə(n)/ (eye)sight

gezien /ɣəzin/ (adj) **1** esteemed, respected, popular **2** seen (by me), endorsed || *het voor ~ houden* pack it in

het **gezin** /ɣəzɪn/ (pl: -nen) family: *een samengesteld ~* a patchwork family

gezind /ɣəzɪnt/ (adj) (pre)disposed (to), inclined (to): *iem. vijandig ~ zijn* be hostile toward s.o.

de **gezindheid** /ɣəzɪnthɛit/ (pl: gezindheden) inclination, disposition: *vijandige ~* hostility (towards)

de **gezindte** /ɣəzɪntə/ (pl: -n, -s) denomination

de **gezinsbijslag** /ɣəzɪnzbɛislɔx/ [Belg] child benefit (*or:* allowance)

het **gezinsdrama** /ɣəzɪnzdrama/ (pl: -'s) family tragedy, family murder-suicide

de **gezinshereniging** /ɣəzɪnshɛrenəɣɪŋ/ (pl: -en) reunification (*or:* reuniting) of the family

het **gezinshoofd** /ɣəzɪnshoft/ (pl: -en) head of the family

de **gezinshulp** /ɣəzɪnshʏlp/ (pl: -en) home help

het **gezinsleven** /ɣəzɪnslevə(n)/ family life

het **gezinslid** /ɣəzɪnslɪt/ (pl: -leden) member of the family, family member

de **gezinsuitbreiding** /ɣəzɪnsœydbrɛidɪŋ/ (pl: -en) addition to the family

de **gezinsverpakking** /ɣəzɪnsfərpɑkɪŋ/ (pl: -en) family(-size(d)) pack(age), king-size(d) pack(age), jumbo pack(age)

de **gezinsverzorgster** /ɣəzɪnsfərzɔrxstər/ (pl: -s) home help

de **gezinszorg** /ɣəzɪnsɔrx/ (pl: -en) home help

gezocht /ɣəzɔxt/ (adj) strained, contrived, forced; far-fetched

¹**gezond** /ɣəzɔnt/ (adj) **1** able-bodied, fit: *~ en wel* safe and sound **2** robust: *~e wangen* rosy cheeks

²**gezond** /ɣəzɔnt/ (adj, adv) **1** healthy, sound; well [after vb]: *zo ~ als een vis* as fit as a fiddle **2** sound, good: *~ verstand* common sense

de **gezondheid** /ɣəzɔnthɛit/ health: *naar iemands ~ vragen* inquire after s.o.('s health);

op uw ~! here's to you!, here's to your health!, cheers!; *zijn ~ gaat achteruit* his health is failing || *~!* (God) bless you!

de **gezondheidsdienst** /ɣəzɔnthɛitsdinst/ (pl: -en) (public) health service

de **gezondheidsredenen** /ɣəzɔnthɛitsredənə(n)/ (pl): *om ~* for health reasons, for reasons of health

de **gezondheidstoestand** /ɣəzɔnthɛitstustɑnt/ health, state of health

de **gezondheidszorg** /ɣəzɔnthɛitsɔrx/ **1** health care, medical care **2** health service(s)

gezouten /ɣəzɑutə(n)/ (adj) salt(ed), salty

de **gezusters** /ɣəzʏstərs/ (pl) sisters

het **gezwam** /ɣəzwɑm/ drivel, piffle: *~ in de ruimte* hot air

het **gezwel** /ɣəzwɛl/ (pl: -len) swelling; growth; tumour: *een goedaardig* (or: *kwaadaardig*) *~* a benign (*or:* malignant) tumour

het **gezwets** /ɣəzwɛts/ drivel, rubbish

gezwollen /ɣəzwɔlə(n)/ (adj) swollen

gezworen /ɣəzwɔrə(n)/ (adj) sworn

het **gft-afval** /ɣeɛftɑfɑl/ [roughly] organic waste

de **gft-bak** /ɣeɛftɑbɑk/ (pl: -ken) organic waste bin

Ghana /ɣana/ Ghana

de ¹**Ghanees** /ɣanes/ (pl: Ghanezen) Ghanaian

²**Ghanees** /ɣanes/ (adj) Ghanaian

de **ghostwriter** /ɡostrɑjtər/ (pl: -s) ghostwriter

de **gids** /ɣɪts/ (pl: -en) **1** guide; mentor: *iemands ~ zijn* be s.o.'s guide (*or:* mentor) **2** guide(book); handbook; manual **3** (Girl) Guide; [Am] Girl Scout **4** (telephone) directory, telephone book: *de gouden gids®* the yellow pages

giechelen /ɣixələ(n)/ (giechelde, heeft gegiecheld) giggle, titter

de **giek** /ɣik/ (pl: -en) **1** [shipp] boom **2** jib

de ¹**gier** /ɣir/ (pl: -en) vulture

de ²**gier** /ɣir/ (pl: -en) [Dutch] liquid manure, slurry

gieren /ɣirə(n)/ (gierde, heeft gegierd) shriek, scream, screech

gierig /ɣirəx/ (adj) miserly, stingy

de **gierigaard** /ɣirəxart/ (pl: -s) miser, skinflint

de **gierigheid** /ɣirəxhɛit/ miserliness, stinginess

de **gierst** /ɣirst/ millet

gieten /ɣitə(n)/ (goot, heeft gegoten) **1** pour: *het regent dat het giet* it's pouring (down (*or:* with rain)) **2** cast; found; mould: *die kleren zitten (hem) als gegoten* his clothes fit (him) like a glove **3** water

de **gieter** /ɣitər/ (pl: -s) watering can

de **gieterij** /ɣitərɛi/ (pl: -en) foundry

het **gietijzer** /ɣitɛizər/ cast iron

het **gif** /ɣɪf/ (pl: -fen) poison; venom; toxin

de **gifbeker** /ɣɪvbekər/ (pl: -s) poisoned cup

de **gifbelt** /ɣɪvbɛlt/ (pl: -en) (illegal) dump for

toxic waste

het **gifgas** /ɣɪfχɑs/ (pl: -sen) poison(ous) gas

gifgroen /ɣɪfχrun/ (adj) bilious (or: fluorescent) green

de **gifslang** /ɣɪfslɑŋ/ (pl: -en) poisonous (or: venomous) snake

de **gift** /ɣɪft/ (pl: -en) gift; donation; contribution

de **giftand** /ɣɪftɑnt/ (pl: -en) poison fang, venom tooth

giftig /ɣɪftəχ/ (adj) **1** poisonous; venomous **2** venomous, vicious: toen hij dat hoorde, werd hij ~ when he heard that he was furious

gifvrij /ɣɪfrɛi/ (adj) non-toxic, non-poisonous

de **gifwolk** /ɣɪfwɔlk/ (pl: -en) toxic cloud

giga /ɣiɣɑ/ (adv) mega, huge

de **gigabyte** /ɣiɣabɑjt/ (pl: -s) gigabyte

de **gigant** /ɣiɣɑnt/ (pl: -en) giant

gigantisch /ɣiɣɑntis/ (adj, adv) gigantic, huge

de **gigolo** /dʒiɣolo/ (pl: -'s) gigolo

gij /ɣɛi/ (pers pron) thou

de **gijzelaar** /ɣɛizəlɑr/ (pl: -s) hostage

gijzelen /ɣɛizələ(n)/ (gijzelde, heeft gegijzeld) take hostage; kidnap; hijack

de **gijzeling** /ɣɛizəlɪŋ/ (pl: -en) taking of hostages; kidnapping; hijack(ing): iem. in ~ houden hold s.o. hostage

de **gijzelnemer** /ɣɛizəlnemər/ (pl: -s) hostage taker

de **gijzelsoftware** /ɣɛizəlsɔftwɛːr/ ransomware

de **gil** /ɣɪl/ (pl: -len) scream, yell; screech; squeal; shriek: als je me nodig hebt, **geef** dan even een ~ if you need me just give (me) a shout

het/de **gilde** /ɣɪldə/ (pl: -n) guild

het **gilet** /ʒilɛt/ (pl: -s) gilet

gillen /ɣɪlə(n)/ (gilde, heeft gegild) **1** scream; screech; squeal; shriek: het is **om** te ~ it's a (perfect) scream; ~ **als** een mager speenvarken squeal like a (stuck) pig **2** [train, siren, machine] scream; [brakes] screech

de **giller** /ɣɪlər/ (pl: -s) [inform]: het is een ~! what a scream (or: howl, gas)!

ginds /ɣɪns/ (adj, adv) over there; up there, down there

ginnegappen /ɣɪnəɣɑpə(n)/ (ginnegapte, heeft geginnegapt) giggle, snigger: wat **zitten** jullie weer te ~? (just) what are you sniggering about/at?, what's so funny?

de **gin-tonic** /dʒɪntɔnɪk/ gin and tonic

het **gips** /ɣɪps/ **1** plaster (of Paris): zijn been zit **in** het ~ his leg is in plaster; ~ **aanmaken** mix plaster **2** plaster cast

de **gipsafdruk** /ɣɪpsɑvdrʏk/ (pl: -ken) plaster cast

gipsen /ɣɪpsə(n)/ (adj) plaster

het **gipsverband** /ɣɪpsfərbɑnt/ (pl: -en) (plaster) cast

giraal /ɣiral/ (adj) giro

de **giraffe** /ʒirɑf/ (pl: -n, -s) giraffe

gireren /ɣirərə(n)/ (gireerde, heeft gegireerd) pay (or: transfer) by giro

de **giro** /ɣiro/ [Dutch] **1** giro **2** giro account **3** transfer by bank (or: giro), bank transfer, giro transfer

het **gironummer** /ɣironʏmər/ (pl: -s) [Dutch] Girobank (account) number

de **giropas** /ɣiropɑs/ (pl: -sen) [Dutch] (giro cheque) guarantee card

de **girorekening** /ɣirorekənɪŋ/ (pl: -en) [Netherlands; dated] Girobank/giro account; Check account

gissen /ɣɪsə(n)/ (giste, heeft gegist) guess (at), estimate

de **gissing** /ɣɪsɪŋ/ (pl: -en) guess; guesswork; speculation: dit **zijn** allemaal (maar) ~en this is just (or: mere) guesswork

de **gist** /ɣɪst/ yeast

gisten /ɣɪstə(n)/ (gistte, heeft gegist) ferment

gisteravond /ɣɪstərɑvɔnt/ (adv) last night, yesterday evening

gisteren /ɣɪstərə(n)/ (adv) yesterday: de krant **van** ~ yesterday's paper; ~ **over** een week yesterday week, a week from yesterday; [fig] hij is niet **van** ~ he wasn't born yesterday, he's nobody's fool

gistermiddag /ɣɪstərmɪdɑχ/ (adv) yesterday afternoon

gisternacht /ɣɪstərnɑχt/ (adv) last night

gisterochtend /ɣɪstərɔχtənt/ (adv) yesterday morning

de **gisting** /ɣɪstɪŋ/ (pl: -en) fermentation, ferment; effervescence

de **gitaar** /ɣitar/ (pl: gitaren) guitar

de **gitarist** /ɣitarɪst/ (pl: -en) guitarist, guitar player

gitzwart /ɣɪtswɑrt/ (adj) jet-black

de **G-kracht** /ɣekrɑχt/ (pl: -en) G-force

het **glaasje** /χlaʃə/ (pl: -s) **1** (small) glass; slide **2** drop, drink: te diep in het ~ **gekeken hebben** have had one too many

¹**glad** /χlɑt/ (adj) **1** slippery; icy: het is ~ op de wegen the roads are slippery **2** [fig] slippery, slick: hij heeft een ~**de tong** he has a glib tongue **3** shiny; glossy; polished **4** smooth, even: ~**de banden** bald tyres; een ~**de kin** a clean-shaven chin (or: face)

²**glad** /χlɑt/ (adv) smoothly

gladgeschoren /χlɑtχəsχorə(n)/ (adj) clean-shaven

de **gladheid** /χlɑtheit/ slipperiness; iciness: ~ op de **wegen** icy patches on the roads

de **gladiator** /χladijɑtɔr/ (pl: -en) gladiator

de **gladiool** /χladijol/ (pl: gladiolen) gladiolus

de **gladjanus** /χlɑtjanʏs/ (pl: -sen) smooth operator (or: customer); smoothie

gladmaken /χlɑtmakə(n)/ (maakte glad, heeft gladgemaakt) smooth(en), even; polish

gladstrijken /ɣlɑtstrɛikə(n)/ (streek glad, heeft gladgestreken) smooth (out, down); iron out: *moeilijkheden* ~ iron out difficulties; *zijn* **veren** ~ preen one's feathers

de **glans** /ɣlɑns/ (pl: -en, glanzen) **1** glow **2** gleam, lustre; gloss; sheen: *P. geeft uw meubelen een* **fraaie** ~ *P.* gives your furniture a beautiful shine

het **glansmiddel** /ɣlɑnsmɪdəl/ polish

glansrijk /ɣlɑnsrɛik/ (adj, adv) splendid, brilliant; glorious

de **glansrol** /ɣlɑnsrɔl/ (pl: -len) star part, star role

het **glansspoelmiddel** /ɣlɑnspulmɪdəl/ dishwasher rinse aid

de **glansverf** /ɣlɑnsfɛrf/ gloss (paint)

¹**glanzen** /ɣlɑnzə(n)/ (glansde, heeft geglansd) **1** gleam, shine: ~*d* **papier** glossy (*or:* high-gloss) paper **2** shine, glow; twinkle: ~*d* **haar** glossy (*or:* sleek) hair

²**glanzen** /ɣlɑnzə(n)/ (glansde, heeft geglansd) polish; glaze; gloss

het **glas** /ɣlɑs/ (pl: glazen) glass; (window-)pane: *een* ~ **bier** a (glass of) beer; **dubbel** ~ double glazing; **geslepen** ~ cut glass; *laten we het* ~ **heffen** *op* ... let's drink to ...; ~ *in lood* leaded glass; stained glass

de **glasbak** /ɣlɑzbɑk/ (pl: -ken) bottle bank

glasblazen /ɣlɑzblazə(n)/ glassblowing

de **glascontainer** /ɣlɑskɔntənər/ (pl: -s) bottle bank

glashard /ɣlɑshɑrt/ (adj, adv) unfeeling: *hij ontkende* ~ he flatly denied

glashelder /ɣlɑshɛldər/ (adj, adv) crystal-clear; as clear as a bell

het **glas-in-loodraam** /ɣlɑsɪnlotram/ (pl: -ramen) leaded window; stained-glass window

de **glasplaat** /ɣlɑsplat/ (pl: -platen) sheet of glass; glass plate; glass top

de **glastuinbouw** /ɣlɑstœymbɑu/ greenhouse farming

de **glasverzekering** /ɣlɑsfərzekərɪŋ/ glass insurance

de **glasvezel** /ɣlɑsfezəl/ (pl: -s) **1** glass fibre, fibreglass **2** optical fibre, fibre optics

het **glaswerk** /ɣlɑswɛrk/ glass(ware)

de **glaswol** /ɣlɑswɔl/ glass wool

glazen /ɣlazə(n)/ (adj) glass

de **glazenwasser** /ɣlazə(n)wɑsər/ (pl: -s) window cleaner

glazig /ɣlazəχ/ (adj) **1** glassy **2** waxy

glazuren /ɣlazyrə(n)/ (glazuurde, heeft geglazuurd) glaze; enamel

het **glazuur** /ɣlazyr/ **1** glaze, glazing; enamel **2** icing

de **gletsjer** /ɣlɛtʃər/ (pl: -s) glacier

de **gleuf** /ɣløf/ (pl: gleuven) **1** groove; slot; slit **2** trench, ditch; fissure

glibberen /ɣlɪbərə(n)/ (glibberde, heeft geglibberd) slither, slip, slide

glibberig /ɣlɪbərəχ/ (adj) slippery, slithery;

slimy; greasy: [fig] *zich op* ~ **terrein** *bevinden* have got onto a tricky subject

de **glijbaan** /ɣlɛiban/ (pl: -banen) slide, chute

glijden /ɣlɛidə(n)/ (gleed, heeft/is gegleden) **1** slide, glide **2** slip, slide: *het boek was uit haar handen gegleden* the book had slipped from her hands

glijdend /ɣlɛidənt/ (adj) sliding, flexible: *een ~e* **belastingschaal** a sliding tax scale

de **glijvlucht** /ɣlɛivlʏχt/ (pl: -en) gliding flight; glide(-down)

de **glimlach** /ɣlɪmlɑχ/ smile; grin: *een stralende* ~ a radiant smile

glimlachen /ɣlɪmlɑχə(n)/ (glimlachte, heeft geglimlacht) smile; grin: **blijven** ~ keep (on) smiling

glimmen /ɣlɪmə(n)/ (glom, heeft geglommen) **1** glow, shine **2** shine, gleam: *de tafel glimt* **als** *een spiegel* the table is shining like a mirror **3** shine, glitter: *haar ogen glommen* **van** *blijdschap* her eyes shone with pleasure

de **glimp** /ɣlɪmp/ (pl: -en) glimpse: [fig] *een* ~ *van iem.* **opvangen (zien)** catch a glimpse of s.o.

glinsteren /ɣlɪnstərə(n)/ (glinsterde, heeft geglinsterd) **1** glitter, sparkle; glisten **2** shine, gleam, sparkle

glippen /ɣlɪpə(n)/ (glipte, is geglipt) **1** slide: *naar buiten* ~ sneak (*or:* steal) out **2** slip, drop: *hij liet het glas* **uit** *de handen* ~ he let the glass slip from his hands

de **glitter** /ɣlɪtər/ (pl: -s) glitter: *een bloes* **met** ~ a sequined blouse ‖ ~ *en* **glamour** glitter and glamour, tinsel

globaal /ɣlobal/ (adj, adv) rough, broad

de **globalisering** /ɣlobalizerɪŋ/ globalization

de **globe** /ɣlobə/ (pl: -s) globe

de **globetrotter** /ɣlobətrɔtər/ (pl: -s) globetrotter

de **gloed** /ɣlut/ **1** glow; blaze: *in* ~ *zetten* (*or:* *staan*) set (*or:* be) aglow **2** glow; glare; blush

gloednieuw /ɣlutniw/ (adj) brand new

gloedvol /ɣlutfɔl/ (adj, adv) glowing, fervent, impassioned: *een ~* **betoog** a glowing speech, an impassioned speech

gloeien /ɣlujə(n)/ (gloeide, heeft gegloeid) **1** glow, shine, burn **2** smoulder, glow **3** be red-hot (*or:* white-hot), glow

gloeiend /ɣlujənt/ (adj, adv) **1** glowing, red-hot, white-hot **2** red-hot; boiling hot: *gloeiend heet* burning hot, red-hot **3** glowing, fervent ‖ *je bent* **er** ~ **bij** you're in for it now, (I) caught you red-handed; *een ~e* **hekel** *aan iem. hebben* hate s.o.'s guts

de **gloeilamp** /ɣlujlamp/ (pl: -en) (light) bulb

glooien /ɣlojə(n)/ (glooide, heeft geglooid) slope, slant

glooiend /ɣlojənt/ (adj) sloping, slanted; rolling

de **glooiing** /ɣlojɪŋ/ (pl: -en) slope, slant

gloren /ɣlorə(n)/ (gloorde, heeft gegloord)

gleam, glimmer: *de ochtend begon* te ~ day was breaking (*or:* dawning); *er gloorde iets van hoop* there was a glimmer of hope

de **glorie** /ɣlo̱ri/ (pl: gloriën, -s) glory; [rel] gloria: *in volle* ~ in full glory (*or:* splendour)

glorierijk /ɣlo̱rirɛɪk/ (adj, adv) glorious

de **glorietijd** /ɣlo̱ritɛit/ (pl: -en) heyday, golden age: *in zijn* ~ in his heyday

glorieus /ɣlorijø̱s/ (adj, adv) glorious

de **gloss** /ɡlɔs/ gloss

de **glossy** /ɡlɔ̱si/ glossy

de **glucose** /ɣlyko̱zə/ glucose, grape-sugar

de **gluiperd** /ɣlœy̱pərt/ (pl: -s) [Dutch] shifty character, sneak

gluiperig /ɣlœy̱pərəɣ/ (adj, adv) shifty, sneaky

glunderen /ɣly̱ndərə(n)/ (glunderde, heeft geglunderd) smile happily

gluren /ɣly̱rə(n)/ (gluurde, heeft gegluurd) peep, peek

het **gluten** /ɣly̱tə(n)/ gluten

glutenvrij /ɣlytə(n)vrɛɪ̱/ (adj) gluten-free

de **gluurder** /ɣly̱rdər/ (pl: -s) peeping Tom

de **glycerine** /ɣlisəri̱nə/ glycerine

het **gmo** /ɣeɛmo̱/ (pl: -'s) GMO *(genetically modified organism)*

gniffelen /ɣnɪ̱fələ(n)/ (gniffelde, heeft gegniffeld) snigger, chuckle

de **gnoe** /ɣnu̱/ (pl: -s) gnu

de **go** /ɡo/ (pl: go's) go-ahead: *een go krijgen* get the go-ahead

de **goal** /ɡol/ (pl: -s) goal: *een* ~ *maken* score a goal

de **god** /ɣɔt/ (pl: -en) god; idol: [fig] *aan de ~en overgeleverd zijn* be left to one's fate

God /ɣɔt/ God: *in* ~ *geloven* believe in God; *leven als* ~ *in Frankrijk* be in the clover, have a place in the sun

goddank /ɣɔ̱dɑŋk/ (int) thank God (*or:* goodness)

goddelijk /ɣɔ̱dələk/ (adj, adv) divine: *wat een* ~ *weer!* such glorious weather!

goddeloos /ɣɔ̱delos/ (adj) **1** irreligious, godless **2** wicked

de **godheid** /ɣɔ̱thɛit/ (pl: -heden) deity, god(head)

de **godin** /ɣodɪ̱n/ (pl: -nen) goddess

godlasterend /ɣɔtlɑ̱stərənt/ (adj) blasphemous

de **godsdienst** /ɣɔ̱tsdinst/ (pl: -en) religion

godsdienstig /ɣɔtsdi̱nstəɣ/ (adj, adv) religious, devout

het **godsdienstonderwijs** /ɣɔtsdinstɔndərwɛis/ religious education (*or:* instruction)

de **godsdienstvrijheid** /ɣɔtsdinstfrɛɪhɛit/ freedom of religion

het **godshuis** /ɣɔ̱tshœys/ (pl: -huizen) house of God, place of worship, church

de **godslastering** /ɣɔ̱tslɑstərɪŋ/ (pl: -en) **1** blasphemy **2** profanity

godsnaam /ɣɔ̱tsnam/: *in* ~ for heaven's sake

godswil /ɣɔ̱tswɪl/: *om* ~ for heaven's sake!; *hoe is het om* ~ *mogelijk* how on earth is it possible?

het **¹goed** /ɣut/ (pl: -eren) **1** goods, ware(s) **2** goods, property; estate: *onroerend* ~ real estate **3** clothes: *schoon* ~ *aantrekken* put on clean clothes **4** material, fabric, cloth: *wit* (*or:* *bont*) ~ white (*or:* coloured) wash; whites, coloureds

²goed /ɣut/ (adj) **1** good; kind; nice: *ik ben wel* ~ *maar niet gek* I'm not as stupid as you think; *ik voel me heel* ~ I feel fine (*or:* great); *zou u zo* ~ *willen zijn ...* would (*or:* could) you please ..., would you be so kind as to ..., do (*or:* would) you mind ... **2** well, fine: *daar word ik niet* ~ *van* [also fig] that makes me (feel) sick || ~ *en kwaad* good and evil, right and wrong

³goed /ɣut/ (adj, adv) **1** good; well; right, correct: *alle berekeningen zijn* ~ all the calculations are correct; *hij bedoelt (meent) het* ~ he means well; *begrijp me* ~ don't get me wrong; *als je* ~ *kijkt* if you look closely; *dat zit wel* ~ that's all right, don't worry about it; *net* ~*!* serves you right!; *het is ook nooit* ~ *bij hem* nothing's ever good enough for him; *precies* ~ just (*or:* exactly) right **2** well: *hij was* ~ *nijdig* he was really annoyed; *het betaalt* ~ it pays well; *toen ik* ~ *en wel in bed lag* when I finally (*or:* at last) got into bed; ~ *bij zijn* be clever || *we hebben het nog nooit zo* ~ *gehad* we've never had it so good; *(heel)* ~ *Engels spreken* speak English (very) well, speak (very) good English; *die jas staat je* ~ that coat suits you (*or:* looks good on you); *de melk is niet* ~ *meer* the milk has gone off; *dat komt* ~ *uit* that's (very) convenient; *komt* ~*!* no worries!; *hij maakt het* ~ he is doing well (*or:* all right); [fig] *hij staat er* ~ *voor* his prospects are good; *de rest hou je nog te* ~ I'll owe you the rest; *dat hebben we nog te* ~ that's still in store for us; ~ *zo!* good!, that's right!; well done!, that's the way!; *ook* ~ very well, all right; *de opbrengst komt ten* ~*e van het Rode Kruis* the proceeds go to the Red Cross; *zij is* ~ *in wiskunde* she is good at mathematics; *dat is te veel van het* ~*e* that is too much of a good thing; *het is maar* ~ *dat ...* it's a good thing that ...; ~ *dat je 't zegt* that reminds me; *dat was maar* ~ *ook* it was just as well

goedaardig /ɣu̱tardəɣ/ (adj) **1** good-natured, kind-hearted **2** [med] benign

goedbedoeld /ɣudbədu̱lt/ (adj) well-intended

goedbetaald /ɣudbəta̱lt/ (adj) well-paid: *een* ~*e baan* a well-paid job

goeddoen /ɣu̱dun/ (deed goed, heeft goedgedaan) do good, help

het **goeddunken** /ɣu̱dʏŋkə(n)/: *naar eigen* ~ *handelen* act on one's own discretion, act as one sees fit

goedemiddag /ɣudəmɪdɑx/ (int) good afternoon

goedemorgen /ɣudəmɔrɣə(n)/ (int) good morning

goedenacht /ɣudənɑxt/ (int) good night

goedenavond /ɣudə(n)avɔnt/ (int) good evening; good night

goedendag /ɣudə(n)dɑx/ (int) **1** good day, hello **2** goodbye, good day **3** hello!, well now!

de **goederen** /ɣudərə(n)/ (pl) **1** goods; [economics] commodities; merchandise: ~ ~ laden (or: lossen) load (or: unload) goods **2** goods, property

de **goederenlift** /ɣudərə(n)lɪft/ (pl: -en) goods lift; [Am] service elevator

de **goederentrein** /ɣudərə(n)trɛin/ (pl: -en) goods train; [Am] freight train

de **goederenwagen** /ɣudərə(n)waɣə(n)/ (pl: -s) goods carriage; [Am] freight car

goedgeefs /ɣutxefs/ (adj) generous, liberal

goedgehumeurd /ɣutxəhymørt/ (adj) good-humoured, good-natured

goedgelovig /ɣutxəlovəx/ (adj) credulous, gullible

goedgemutst /ɣutxəmʏtst/ (adj) good-humoured, good-natured

goedgezind /ɣutxəzɪnt/ (adj): iem. ~ zijn be well-disposed towards s.o.

goedhartig /ɣuthɑrtəx/ (adj, adv) kind(ly), friendly

de **goedheid** /ɣuthɛit/ **1** goodness: hij is de ~ zelf he is goodness personified **2** benevolence, indulgence

¹goedhouden /ɣuthɑudə(n)/ (hield goed, heeft goedgehouden) keep, preserve: melk kun je niet zo lang ~ you can't keep milk very long

zich **²goedhouden** /ɣuthɑudə(n)/ (hield zich goed, heeft zich goedgehouden) control o.s.; keep a straight face; keep a stiff upper lip: hij kon zich niet ~ he couldn't help laughing (or: crying, …)

goedig /ɣudəx/ (adj, adv) gentle; meek

het **goedje** /ɣucə/ stuff

goedkeuren /ɣutkørə(n)/ (keurde goed, heeft goedgekeurd) **1** approve (of); pass: [med] goedgekeurd worden pass one's medical **2** approve; adopt

goedkeurend /ɣutkørənt/ (adj, adv) approving, favourable: ~ knikken (or: glimlachen) nod (or: smile) (one's) approval

de **goedkeuring** /ɣutkørɪŋ/ (pl: -en) approval, consent

¹goedkoop /ɣutkop/ (adj) **1** cheap, inexpensive: ~ tarief cheap rate; off-peak tariff **2** [fig] cheap

²goedkoop /ɣutkop/ (adv) cheaply, at a low price: er ~ afkomen get off cheap(ly)

goedlachs /ɣutlɑxs/ (adj) cheery: zij is ~

she's quick to laugh

goedmaken /ɣutmakə(n)/ (maakte goed, heeft goedgemaakt) **1** make up (or: amends) for: iets weer ~ bij iem. make amends to s.o. for sth. **2** make up for, compensate (for) **3** cover, make good

goedmoedig /ɣutmudəx/ (adj, adv) good-natured, good-humoured

goedpraten /ɣutpratə(n)/ (praatte goed, heeft goedgepraat) explain away, justify; gloss over

goedschiks /ɣutsxɪks/ (adv) willingly: ~ of kwaadschiks willing(ly) or unwilling(ly)

het **¹goedvinden** /ɣutfɪndə(n)/ permission, consent; agreement

²goedvinden /ɣutfɪndə(n)/ (vond goed, heeft goedgevonden) approve (of), consent (to): als jij het goedvindt if you agree

de **goedzak** /ɣutsɑk/ (pl: -ken) softy: 't is een echte ~ he's soft as butter

de **goegemeente** /ɣuɣəmɛntə/ the ordinary man in the street

goeiemorgen /ɣujəmɔrɣə(n)/ (int) **1** good morning **2** come again?, you're kidding

de **goeroe** /ɣuru/ (pl: -s) guru

de **goesting** /ɣustɪŋ/ [Belg] liking, fancy, appetite

de **gok** /ɣɔk/ gamble: zullen we een ~je wagen? shall we have a go (at it)?

de **gokautomaat** /ɣɔkɑutomat/ (pl: -automaten) gambling (or: gaming) machine

de **gokhal** /ɣɔkhɑl/ (pl: -len) gambling arcade, slot club

gokken /ɣɔkə(n)/ (gokte, heeft gegokt) gamble, (place a) bet (on): ~ op een paard (place a) bet on a horse

de **gokker** /ɣɔkər/ (pl: -s) gambler

het **gokpaleis** /ɣɔkpalɛis/ casino

het **gokspel** /ɣɔkspɛl/ (pl: -en) game of chance, gambling (game)

gokverslaafd /ɣɔkfərslaft/ (adj) addicted to gambling

de **gokverslaafde** /ɣɔkfərslavdə/ (pl: -n) gambling addict

de **gokverslaving** /ɣɔkfərslavɪŋ/ gambling addiction

de **¹golf** /ɣɔlf/ (pl: golven) **1** wave: korte (or: lange) ~ short (or: long) wave **2** gulf, bay **3** stream, flood **4** [fig] wave; surge: een ~ van geweld a wave of violence

het **²golf** /ɡɔlf/ (pl: golven) golf

de **golfbaan** /ɣɔlvban/ (pl: -banen) golf course (or: links)

de **golfbreker** /ɣɔlvbrekər/ (pl: -s) breakwater, mole

golfen /ɡɔlfə(n)/ (golfde/golfte, heeft gegolfd/gegolft) play golf

de **golflengte** /ɣɔlflɛŋtə/ (pl: -n, -s) wavelength: (niet) op dezelfde ~ zitten [also fig] (not) be on the same wavelength

de **golfslag** /ɣɔlfslɑx/ surge, swell: sterke ~

heavy sea

de **golfstok** /gɔlfstɔk/ (pl: -ken) golf club

de **Golfstroom** /ɣɔlfstrom/ Gulf Stream

golven /ɣɔlvə(n)/ (golfde, heeft gegolfd) **1** undulate, wave; heave; surge: *de wind deed het **water** ~* the wind ruffled the surface of the water **2** gush, flow

golvend /ɣɔlvənt/ (adj) undulating, wavy || *een ~ **terrein*** rolling terrain

het **gom** /ɣɔm/ rubber; [esp Am] eraser

de **gondel** /ɣɔndəl/ (pl: -s) gondola

de **gong** /ɣɔŋ/ (pl: -s) gong

de **goniometrie** /ɣonijometri/ goniometry

de **gonorroe** /ɣonorø/ gonorrhoea

gonzen /ɣɔnzə(n)/ (gonsde, heeft gegonsd) buzz, hum

de **goochelaar** /ɣoxəlar/ (pl: -s) conjurer, magician

goochelen /ɣoxələ(n)/ (goochelde, heeft gegoocheld) **1** conjure, do (conjuring, magic) tricks: *~ **met** kaarten* do (*or:* perform) card tricks **2** juggle (with): *~ **met** cijfers* juggle with figures

de **goochelkunst** /ɣoxəlkʏnst/ conjuring

de **goocheltruc** /ɣoxəltryk/ (pl: -s) conjuring trick, magic trick

goochem /ɣoxəm/ (adj) [Dutch] smart, crafty

de **goodwill** /ɡutwɪl/ goodwill

googelen® /ɡuɡələ(n)/ (googelde, heeft gegoogeld) google

de **gooi** /ɣoj/ (pl: -en) throw, toss: [fig] *een ~ doen **naar** het presidentschap* make a bid for the Presidency

gooien /ɣoje(n)/ (gooide, heeft gegooid) throw, toss; fling (at), hurl (at): *geld **ertegenaan** ~* spend a lot of money on (sth.); *iem. er**uit** ~* throw s.o. out; *met de deur ~* slam the door

het **gooi-en-smijtwerk** /ɣojɛnsmɛıtwɛrk/ knockabout, slapstick

goor /ɣor/ (adj, adv) **1** filthy, foul **2** bad, nasty: *~ **smaken** (or: **ruiken**)* taste (*or:* smell) revolting

de **goot** /ɣot/ (pl: goten) **1** wastepipe, drain(pipe); gutter **2** gutter, drain: [fig] *in de ~ terechtkomen* end up in the gutter

de **gootsteen** /ɣotsten/ (pl: -stenen) (kitchen) sink: *iets **door** de ~ spoelen* pour sth. down the sink

de **gordel** /ɣɔrdəl/ (pl: -s) belt

de **gordelroos** /ɣɔrdəlros/ shingles

het/de **gordijn** /ɣordɛın/ (pl: -en) curtain

de **gordijnrail** /ɣordɛınrel/ (pl: -s) curtain rail (*or:* track)

gorgelen /ɣɔrɣələ(n)/ (gorgelde, heeft gegorgeld) gargle

de **gorilla** /ɣorɪla/ (pl: -'s) gorilla

de **gort** /ɣɔrt/ pearl barley, groats || *iets **aan** ~ slaan* smash sth. to smithereens

gortig /ɣɔrtəx/ (adj): *dat wordt (me) te ~* it's

too much (for me), it's more than I can take

het **GOS** /ɣos/ Gemenebest van Onafhankelijke Staten CIS (Commonwealth of Independent States)

gothic /ɡoːθɪk/ (adj) gothic

de **gotiek** /ɣotik/ Gothic

gotisch /ɣotis/ (adj) Gothic

het **goud** /ɣaut/ gold: *zulke kennis is ~ **waard*** such knowledge is invaluable; ***voor** geen ~ not for all the tea in China; ik zou me daar **voor** geen ~ vertonen* I wouldn't be seen dead there; *het is niet alles ~ wat er blinkt* all that glitters is not gold

goudbruin /ɣaudbrœyn/ (adj) golden brown, auburn

goudeerlijk /ɣauterlək/ (adj) honest through and through

gouden /ɣaudə(n)/ (adj) **1** gold; [esp fig] golden: *een ~ **ring** a* gold ring **2** golden

de **goudkoorts** /ɣautkorts/ gold fever, gold rush

de **goudmijn** /ɣautmɛın/ (pl: -en) gold mine: *een ~ **ontdekken*** [fig] strike oil

de **goudsmid** /ɣautsmɪt/ (pl: -smeden) goldsmith

het **goudstuk** /ɣautstʏk/ (pl: -ken) gold coin

de **goudvis** /ɣautfɪs/ (pl: -sen) goldfish

de **goulash** /ɡulaʃ/ goulash

de **gourmet** /ɡurmɛ/ (pl: -s) **1** gourmet, epicure **2** fondue Bourguignonne

gourmetten /ɡurmɛtə(n)/ (gourmette, heeft gegourmet) [roughly] have a fondue Bourguignonne

de **gouvernante** /ɣuvərnɑntə/ (pl: -s) governess; nanny

het **gouvernement** /ɣuvɛrnəmɛnt/ (pl: -en) [Belg] provincial government (*or:* administration)

de **gouverneur** /ɣuvərnør/ (pl: -s) **1** governor **2** [Belg] provincial governor

de **gozer** /ɣozər/ (pl: -s) [inform] guy, fellow: *een **leuke** ~ a* nice guy (*or:* fellow)

het **gps** /ɣepeɛs/ global positioning system gps

de **graad** /ɣrat/ (pl: graden) degree; [mil] rank: *een **academische** ~ a* university degree; *de vader is eigenwijs, maar de zoon is nog een -je **erger*** the father is conceited, but the son is even worse; *18° Celsius* 18 degrees Celsius; *een draai van **180** graden maken* make a 180-degree turn; *tien graden onder nul* ten degrees below zero

de **graadmeter** /ɣratmetər/ (pl: -s) graduator, gauge, measure

de **graaf** /ɣraf/ (pl: graven) count, earl

de **graafmachine** /ɣrafmaʃinə/ (pl: -s) excavator

het **graafschap** /ɣrafsxɑp/ (pl: -pen) county

graag /ɣrax/ (adv) **1** gladly, with pleasure: *~ **gedaan** you're* welcome; *ik wil je ~ **helpen** I'd* be glad to help (you); ***hoe** ~ ik het ook zou doen* much as I would like to do it; *~ **of niet***

take it or leave it; *(heel)* ~*!* (okay) thank you very much!, yes please! **2** willingly, readily: *zij praat niet ~ over die tijd* she dislikes talking about that time; *dat wil ~ geloven* I can quite believe that, I'm not surprised

de **graai** /ɣraj/ (pl: -en) grab: *een ~ in de kassa doen* put one's hand in the till

graaien /ɣrajə(n)/ (graaide, heeft gegraaid) grabble, rummage: *~de politici* money-grubbing politicians

de **graaier** /ɣrajər/ (pl: -s) money-grubber

de **graal** /ɣral/ the (Holy) Grail

het **graan** /ɣran/ (pl: granen) grain, corn ‖ *een ~tje meepikken* get one's share, get in on the act

de **graanschuur** /ɣransxyr/ (pl: -schuren) granary

de **graat** /ɣrat/ (pl: graten) **1** (fish) bone **2** bones ‖ *niet zuiver op de ~* unreliable; [Belg] *ergens geen graten in zien* see nothing wrong with

grabbel /ɣrɔbəl/: *zijn goede naam te ~ gooien* throw away one's reputation

grabbelen /ɣrɔbələ(n)/ (grabbelde, heeft gegrabbeld) rummage (about, around), grope (about, around): *de kinderen ~ naar de pepernoten* the children are scrambling for the ginger nuts

de **grabbelton** /ɣrɔbəltɔn/ (pl: -nen) lucky dip; [Am] grab bag

de **gracht** /ɣraxt/ (pl: -en) canal; moat: *aan een ~ wonen* live on a canal

gracieus /ɣraføs/ (adj, adv) graceful, elegant

de **gradatie** /ɣrada(t)si/ (pl: -s) degree, level: *in verschillende ~s van moeilijkheid* with different steps (*or:* levels) of difficulty

de **gradenboog** /xradə(n)box/ (pl: -bogen) protractor

gradueel /ɣradywel/ (adj, adv) of degree, in degree, gradual

het **graf** /ɣraf/ (pl: graven) grave, tomb: *zijn eigen ~ graven* dig one's own grave ‖ *zwijgen als het ~* be quiet (*or:* silent) as the grave

de **graffiti** /ɣrɛfɪti/ graffiti

de **grafiek** /ɣrafik/ (pl: -en) graph, diagram

het **grafiet** /ɣrafit/ graphite

grafisch /ɣrafis/ (adj, adv) graphic

de **grafkelder** /ɣrafkɛldər/ (pl: -s) tomb; vault, crypt

de **grafrede** /ɣrafredə/ funeral oration

de **grafschennis** /ɣrafsxɛnɪs/ desecration of graves

het **grafschrift** /ɣrafsxrɪft/ (pl: -en) epitaph

de **grafsteen** /ɣrafsten/ (pl: -stenen) gravestone, tombstone

de **grafstem** /ɣrafstɛm/ (pl: -men) sepulchral voice

het/de **gram** /ɣram/ (pl: -men) gram: *vijf ~ zout* five grams of salt

de **grammatica** /ɣramatika/ grammar

grammaticaal /ɣramatikal/ (adj, adv) grammatical

de **grammofoon** /ɣramofon/ (pl: -s) gramophone

de **grammofoonplaat** /ɣramofomplat/ (pl: -platen) (gramophone) record

de **granaat** /ɣranat/ grenade; shell

de **granaatappel** /ɣranatapəl/ (pl: -en, -s) pomegranate

de **granaatscherf** /ɣranatsxɛrf/ (pl: -scherven) piece of shrapnel, shell fragment; shrapnel

het **grand café** /ɡrãkafe/ grand café

grandioos /ɣrandijos/ (adj, adv) monumental, mighty

het **graniet** /ɣranit/ granite

granieten /ɣranitə(n)/ (adj) granite

de **grap** /ɣrap/ (pl: -pen) joke, gag: *een flauwe ~* a feeble (*or:* poor) joke; *~pen vertellen* tell (*or:* crack) jokes; *een ~ met iem. uithalen* play a joke on s.o.; *ze kan wel tegen een ~* she can take a joke; *voor de ~* for fun ‖ *dat wordt een dure ~* that will be an expensive business

de **grapefruit** /ɡrepfrut/ (pl: -s) grapefruit

de **grapjas** /ɣrapjas/ (pl: -sen) *see grappenmaker*

het **grapje** /ɣrapjə/ (pl: -s) (little) joke: *het was maar een ~* I was only joking (*or:* kidding); *~?!* you must be joking!; *iets met een ~ afdoen* shrug sth. off with a joke; *kun je niet tegen een ~?* can't you take a joke?

de **grappenmaker** /ɣrapə(n)makər/ (pl: -s) joker, wag

grappig /ɣrapəx/ (adj, adv) **1** funny, amusing: *zij probeerden ~ te zijn* they were trying to be funny **2** funny, comical, amusing; humorous: *het was een ~ gezicht* it was a funny (*or:* comical) sight; *een ~e opmerking* a humorous remark; *wat is daar nou zo ~ aan?* what's so funny about that? **3** attractive; [Am] cute

het **gras** /ɣras/ (pl: -sen) grass: *het ~ maaien* mow the lawn; [fig] *iem. het ~ voor de voeten wegmaaien* cut the ground from under s.o.'s feet; [fig] *ze hebben er geen ~ over laten groeien* they did not let the grass grow under their feet

grasduinen /ɣrazdœynə(n)/ (grasduinde, heeft gegrasduind) browse (through)

het **grasland** /ɣraslɑnt/ grassland, meadow; pasture

de **grasmaaier** /ɣrasmajər/ (pl: -s) (lawn)mower

de **grasmat** /ɣrasmɑt/ (pl: -ten) grass, turf; field, pitch: *de ~ lag er prachtig bij* the grass looked fantastic

de **grasspriet** /ɣrasprit/ (pl: -en) blade of grass

het **grasveld** /ɣrasfɛlt/ (pl: -en) field (of grass)

de **graszode** /ɣrasodə/ (pl: -n) turf, sod

de **gratie** /ɣra(t)si/ **1** grace **2** favour: *bij iem. uit de ~ raken* fall out of favour with s.o. **3** mercy **4** pardon: *~ krijgen* be pardoned

de **gratificatie** /ɣratifika(t)si/ (pl: -s) gratuity, bonus

gratineren /ɣratinerə(n)/ (gratineerde, heeft gegratineerd) cover with breadcrumbs (or: cheese): *gegratineerde schotel* dish au gratin

gratis /ɣratɪs/ (adj, adv) free (of charge): ~ *en voor niks* gratis, absolutely free

grauw /ɣrɑu/ (adj) grey, ashen

het **gravel** /ɣrɛvəl/ gravel

de **gravelbaan** /ɣrɛvəlban/ (pl: -banen) clay court

graven /ɣravə(n)/ (groef, heeft gegraven) **1** dig; excavate; delve; mine: *een put* ~ sink a well; *een tunnel* ~ dig a tunnel, tunnel **2** dig; burrow

graveren /ɣraverə(n)/ (graveerde, heeft gegraveerd) engrave

de **graveur** /ɣravør/ (pl: -s) engraver

de **gravin** /ɣravɪn/ (pl: -nen) countess

de **gravure** /ɣravyrə/ (pl: -s) engraving, print

grazen /ɣrazə(n)/ (graasde, heeft gegraasd) graze, (be at) pasture: *het vee laten* ~ let the cattle out to graze || *te* ~ *genomen worden* be had, be taken in; *iem. te* ~ *nemen* take s.o. for a ride, take s.o. in

de **greep** /ɣrep/ (pl: grepen) **1** grasp, grip, grab: ~ *krijgen op iets* get a grip on sth.; *vast in zijn* ~ *hebben* have firmly in one's grasp **2** random selection (or: choice): *doe maar een* ~ take your pick

het **greintje** /ɣrɛincə/ (pl: -s) (not) a bit (of): *geen* ~ *hoop* not a ray of hope; *geen* ~ *gezond verstand* not a grain of common sense

de **grendel** /ɣrɛndəl/ (pl: -s) bolt: *achter slot en* ~ *zitten* be under lock and key

grendelen /ɣrɛndələ(n)/ (grendelde, heeft gegrendeld) bolt

grenen /ɣrenə(n)/ (adj) pine(wood), deal

het **grenenhout** /ɣrenə(n)hɑut/ pine(wood)

de **grens** /ɣrɛns/ (pl: grenzen) border; boundary; limit; bounds: *aan de Duitse* ~ at the German border; *we moeten ergens een* ~ *trekken* we have to draw the line somewhere; *binnen redelijke grenzen* within reason; [fig] *een* ~ *overschrijden* pass a limit; [fig] *grenzen verleggen* push back frontiers

de **grenscontrole** /ɣrɛnskɔntrɔːlə/ (pl: -s) border (or: customs) check

het **grensgebied** /ɣrɛnsɣəbit/ (pl: -en) **1** border region **2** [fig] borderline, grey area; fringe (area)

het **grensgeval** /ɣrɛnsɣəvɑl/ (pl: -len) borderline case

de **grenslijn** /ɣrɛnslɛin/ (pl: -en) boundary line; [fig] dividing line

de **grensovergang** /ɣrɛnsovərɣɑŋ/ (pl: -en) border crossing(-point)

grensoverschrijdend /ɣrɛnsovərsχrɛidənt/ (adj) **1** cross-border, international **2** [fig] unacceptable: ~ *gedrag* unacceptable behaviour

de **grensrechter** /ɣrɛnsrɛχtər/ (pl: -s) linesman [socc]; line judge

de **grensstreek** /ɣrɛnstrek/ (pl: -streken) border region

grensverleggend /ɣrɛnsfərlɛɣənt/ (adj) pushing back frontiers, opening up new horizons, revealing

grenzeloos /ɣrɛnzəlos/ (adj, adv) infinite, boundless

grenzen /ɣrɛnzə(n)/ (grensde, heeft gegrensd) **1** border (on); be adjacent to: *hun tuinen* ~ *aan elkaar* their gardens border on one another **2** [fig] border (on), verge (on); approach: *dat grenst aan het ongelofelijke* that verges on the incredible

de **greppel** /ɣrɛpəl/ (pl: -s) channel; trench; ditch

gretig /ɣretəχ/ (adj, adv) **1** eager; greedy: ~ *aftrek vinden* sell like hot cakes **2** ambitious: *een ~e voetballer* an ambitious football player

de **grief** /ɣrif/ (pl: grieven) objection, grievance, complaint

de **Griek** /ɣrik/ (pl: -en) Greek

Griekenland /ɣrikə(n)lɑnt/ Greece

Grieks /ɣriks/ (adj) Greek

grienen /ɣrinə(n)/ (griende, heeft gegriend) snivel, blub(ber)

de **griep** /ɣrip/ (the) flu; (a) cold: ~ *oplopen* catch the flu

grieperig /ɣripərəχ/ (adj) ill with flu: *ik ben wat* ~ I've got a touch of flu

de **griepprik** /ɣriprɪk/ (pl: -ken) influenza vaccination

het **griesmeel** /ɣrismel/ semolina

de **griet** /ɣrit/ bird, chick, doll

grieven /ɣrivə(n)/ (griefde, heeft gegriefd) hurt, offend

grievend /ɣrivənt/ (adj, adv) hurtful, offensive, cutting: *een ~e opmerking* a cutting remark

de **griezel** /ɣrizəl/ (pl: -s) ogre, terror; [pers] creep; [pers] weirdo

griezelen /ɣrizələ(n)/ (griezelde, heeft gegriezeld) shudder, shiver, get the creeps

de **griezelfilm** /ɣrizəlfɪlm/ (pl: -s) horror film

griezelig /ɣrizələχ/ (adj, adv) gruesome, creepy

het **griezelverhaal** /ɣrizəlvərhal/ (pl: -verhalen) horror story

grif /ɣrɪf/ (adj, adv) ready; adept; rapid; prompt: *ik geef* ~ *toe dat ...* I readily admit to ... (-ing); ~ *van de hand gaan* sell like hot cakes

de **griffie** /ɣrɪfi/ (pl: -s) registry; clerk of the court's office

de **griffier** /ɣrɪfir/ (pl: -s) [roughly] registrar, clerk

de **grijns** /ɣrɛins/ grin, smirk; sneer

grijnzen /ɣrɛinzə(n)/ (grijnsde, heeft gegrijnsd) **1** smirk, sneer **2** grin: *sta niet zo dom* *te* ~! wipe that silly grin off your face!

¹grijpen /ɣrɛipə(n)/ (greep, heeft gegrepen) grab; reach (for): *dat is te **hoog** gegrepen* that is aiming too high; *naar de fles* ~ reach for (*or:* turn to) the bottle; *het **vuur** grijpt om zich heen* the fire is spreading

²grijpen /ɣrɛipə(n)/ (greep, heeft gegrepen) grab (hold of), seize, grasp; snatch: *de **dief** werd gegrepen* the thief was nabbed; *hij greep zijn **kans*** he grabbed (*or:* seized) his chance; [fig] *door iets gegrepen zijn* be affected (*or:* moved) by sth.; *voor het* ~ *liggen* be there for the taking

de **grijper** /ɣrɛɪpər/ (pl: -s) bucket, claw, grab

het **¹grijs** /ɣrɛis/ grey

²grijs /ɣrɛis/ (adj) grey: *een grijze **dag*** an overcast day; *in een* ~ *verleden* in the dim and distant past; *hij **wordt** al aardig* ~ he is getting quite grey

de **grijsaard** /ɣrɛisart/ (pl: -s) old man

de **gril** /ɣrɪl/ (pl: -len) whim, fancy

de **grill** /ɣrɪl/ (pl: -s) grill

grillen /ɣrɪlə(n)/ (grilde, heeft gegrild) grill

grillig /ɣrɪləɣ/ (adj, adv) whimsical, fanciful, capricious: ~ *weer* changeable weather

de **grilligheid** /ɣrɪləɣhɛit/ (pl: -heden) capriciousness, whimsicality, fickleness

de **grimas** /ɣrimɑs/ (pl: -sen) grimace

de **grime** /ɣrim/ (pl: -s) make-up, greasepaint

grimeren /ɣrimerə(n)/ (grimeerde, heeft gegrimeerd) make up

de **grimeur** /ɣrimør/ (pl: -s) make-up artist

grimmig /ɣrɪməɣ/ (adj, adv) **1** furious, irate **2** fierce, forbidding: *een ~e **kou*** a severe cold

het **grind** /ɣrɪnt/ gravel; shingle

grinniken /ɣrɪnəkə(n)/ (grinnikte, heeft gegrinnikt) chuckle; snigger: *zit niet zo dom te* ~! stop that silly sniggering!

de **grip** /ɣrɪp/ grip; traction: ~ *hebben op* [also fig] have a grip on

grissen /ɣrɪsə(n)/ (griste, heeft gegrist) snatch, grab

de **grizzlybeer** /ɣrɪzliber/ (pl: -beren) grizzly (bear)

de **groef** /ɣruf/ (pl: groeven) groove, furrow; slot

de **groei** /ɣruj/ **1** growth, development: *een broek die **op** de ~ gemaakt is* trousers which allow for growth **2** growth, increase; expansion: *economische* ~ economic growth

de **groeiachterstand** /ɣrujɑχtərstɑnt/ growth delay (*or:* failure)

de **groeibriljant** /ɣrujbrɪljɑnt/ (pl: -en) **1** trade-up diamond **2** rising star

groeien /ɣrujə(n)/ (groeide, is gegroeid) grow, develop: *hij groeit **als** kool* a) he is shooting up; b) he's coming on well; *zijn baard **laten** ~* grow a beard; [fig] *er groeit iets moois tussen hen* love is in the air; *het geld groeit mij niet **op** de rug* I am not made of money

het **groeihormoon** /ɣrujhɔrmon/ (pl: -hormonen) growth hormone

de **groeikern** /ɣrujkɛrn/ (pl: -en) centre of urban growth

de **groeipijn** /ɣrujpɛin/ (pl: -en) growing pains

de **groeistuip** /ɣrujstœyp/ (pl: -en) growing pain; [fig also] teething troubles, initial problems

groeizaam /ɣrujzam/ (adj, adv) favourable (to growth): ~ *weer* growing weather

het **¹groen** /ɣrun/ **1** green: *ze was **in** het ~ (gekleed)* she was (dressed) in green **2** green space

²groen /ɣrun/ (adj, adv) **1** green: *deze **aardbeien** zijn nog* ~ these strawberries are still green; *het verkeerslicht sprong **op** ~* the traffic lights changed to green **2** green: ~ *beleggen* make a green investment

de **groenbak** /ɣrunbɑk/ (pl: -ken) organic waste bin

Groenland /ɣrunlɑnt/ Greenland

de **Groenlander** /ɣrunlɑndər/ (pl: -s) Greenlander

Groenlands /ɣrunlɑn(t)s/ (adj) Greenland(ic)

de **groenstrook** /ɣrunstrok/ (pl: -stroken) **1** green belt, green space (*or:* area) **2** grass strip, centre strip

de **groente** /ɣruntə/ (pl: -n, -s) vegetable: *vlees en twee verschillende **soorten** ~* meat and two vegetables

de **groenteboer** /ɣruntəbur/ (pl: -en) greengrocer, greengrocer's (shop)

de **groentesoep** /ɣruntəsup/ vegetable soup

de **groentetuin** /ɣruntətœyn/ (pl: -en) vegetable garden, kitchen garden

de **groentewinkel** /ɣruntəwɪŋkəl/ (pl: -s) greengrocer's (shop), greengrocery

het **groentje** /ɣruncə/ (pl: -s) greenhorn; new boy, new girl; fresher; freshman

de **groentjes** /ɣruncəs/ (pl) [Belg; inform] vegetables

de **groep** /ɣrup/ (pl: -en) group; party: *een grote* ~ *van de **bevolking*** a large section of the population; *leeftijdsgroep* age group (*or:* bracket); *in* ~*jes van vijf of zes* in groups of five or six; *we gingen in **een** ~ rond de gids staan* we formed a group round the guide

¹groeperen /ɣruperə(n)/ (groepeerde, heeft gegroepeerd) group: *anders (opnieuw)* ~ regroup

zich **²groeperen** /ɣruperə(n)/ (groepeerde zich, heeft zich gegroepeerd) **1** cluster (round), gather (round); huddle (round) **2** group (together), form a group

de **groepering** /ɣruperɪŋ/ (pl: -en) grouping, faction

de **groepsdruk** /ɣrupsdrʏk/ peer pressure

het **groepshoofd** /ɣrupshoft/ (pl: -en) **1** [sport] (top) seed **2** group leader

de **groepsleider** /ɣrupslɛidər/ (pl: -s) group

leader

de **groepspraktijk** /ɣrupsprɑktɛɪk/ group practice

de **groepsreis** /ɣrupsrɛis/ (pl: -reizen) group travel

het **groepsverband** /ɣrupsfərbɑnt/: *in* ~ in a group (or: team); *werken in* ~ work as a team

de **groepsverkrachting** /ɣrupsfərkrɑχtɪŋ/ (pl: -en) gang rape

de **groet** /ɣrut/ (pl: -en) greeting; [mil] salute: *doe hem de ~en van mij* give him my best wishes; tell him I said hello; *je moet de ~en van haar hebben*. O, *doe haar de ~en terug* she sends (you) her regards (or: love). Oh, the same to her; *een korte ~ tot afscheid* a parting word; *met vriendelijke ~* with kind(est) regards, best wishes; *de ~en!* a) [greeting] see you!; b) [forget it] not on your life!, no way!

groeten /ɣrutə(n)/ (groette, heeft gegroet) greet, say hello: *wees gegroet Maria* Hail Mary

de **groeve** /ɣruvə/ (pl: -n) quarry

groezelig /ɣruzələχ/ (adj) grubby, grimy, dirty

grof /ɣrof/ (adj, adv) **1** coarse, hefty **2** coarse, rough, crude: *grove gelaatstrekken* coarse features; *iets ~ schetsen* a) make a (rough) sketch of sth.; b) [fig also] sketch sth. in broad outlines **3** gross; rude: *een grove fout* a glaring error; *je hoeft niet meteen ~ te worden* there's no need to be rude

grofgebouwd /ɣrɔfχəbaut/ (adj) heavily-built

de **grofheid** /ɣrɔfhɛit/ (pl: -heden) coarseness; rudeness; roughness; grossness

grofvuil /ɣrɔfœyl/ (adv) (collection of) bulky refuse: *iets bij het ~ zetten* put sth. out as trash; [fig] bin sth., dump sth.

grofweg /ɣrɔfwɛχ/ (adv) roughly, about, in the region of

de **grog** /ɣrɔk/ (pl: -s) grog, (hot) toddy

groggy /ɣrɔgi/ (adj) groggy, dazed; punch-drunk

de **grol** /ɣrɔl/ (pl: -len) joke, gag

¹**grommen** /ɣrɔmə(n)/ (gromde, heeft gegromd) growl, snarl: *de hond begon tegen mij te ~* the dog began to growl at me

²**grommen** /ɣrɔmə(n)/ (gromde, heeft gegromd) grumble, mutter: *hij gromde iets onduidelijks* he muttered sth. indistinct

de **grond** /ɣrɔnt/ (pl: -en) **1** ground, land: *er zit een flink stuk ~ bij het huis* the house has considerable grounds; *een stuk ~* a plot of land; *braakliggende ~* waste land; *iem. tegen de ~ slaan* knock s.o. flat; *zij heeft haar bedrijf van de ~ af opgebouwd* she built up her firm from scratch **2** ground, earth: *schrale* (or: *onvruchtbare*) *~* barren (or: poor) soil; *iem. nog verder de ~ in trappen* kick s.o. when he is down **3** ground; floor: *de begane ~* the ground floor; [Am] the first floor; *ik had wel door de ~ kunnen gaan* I wanted the ground to open up and swallow me **4** bottom: *aan de ~ zitten* be on the rocks **5** ground, foundation, basis: *op ~ van zijn huidskleur* because of (or: on account of) his colour; *op ~ van artikel 461* by virtue of section 461 **6** bottom; essence: *dat komt uit de ~ van zijn hart* that comes from the bottom of his heart ‖ *zichzelf te ~e richten* dig one's own grave, cut one's own throat

het **grondbeginsel** /ɣrɔndbəɣɪnsəl/ (pl: -en) (basic, fundamental) principle; fundamentals; basics

het **grondbezit** /ɣrɔndbəzɪt/ **1** landownership, ownership of land **2** landed property, (landed, real) estate

de **grondbezitter** /ɣrɔndbəzɪtər/ (pl: -s) landowner

het **grondgebied** /ɣrɔntχəbit/ (pl: -en) [also fig] territory; soil

de **grondgedachte** /ɣrɔntχədɑχtə/ basic idea, underlying idea, fundamental idea

grondig /ɣrɔndəχ/ (adj, adv) thorough; radical: *een ~e hekel aan iets hebben* loathe sth., dislike sth. intensely; *iets ~ bespreken* talk sth. out (or: through); *iets ~ onderzoeken* examine sth. thoroughly

de **grondigheid** /ɣrɔndəχhɛit/ thoroughness; soundness; validity

de **grondlaag** /ɣrɔntlaχ/ (pl: -lagen) undercoat

de **grondlegger** /ɣrɔntlɛɣər/ (pl: -s) founder, (founding) father

de **grondlegging** /ɣrɔntlɛɣɪŋ/ foundation, establishment, founding

het **grondpersoneel** /ɣrɔntpɛrsonel/ ground crew

de **grondprijs** /ɣrɔntprɛis/ (pl: -prijzen) the price of land

het **grondrecht** /ɣrɔntrɛχt/ (pl: -en) basic right; civil rights

de **grondregel** /ɣrɔntreɣəl/ (pl: -s) basic rule, fundamental rule, cardinal rule

de **grondslag** /ɣrɔntslɑχ/ (pl: -en) [fig] basis, foundation(s): *de ~ leggen van iets* lay the foundation for sth.; *ten ~ liggen aan* a) be at the bottom of; b) underlie

de **grondsoort** /ɣrɔntsort/ (pl: -en) (type, kind of) soil

de **grondstewardess** /ɣrɔntscuwɑrdɛs/ (pl: -en) ground hostess; [Am] ground stewardess

de **grondstof** /ɣrɔntstɔf/ (pl: -fen) raw material; raw produce

de **grondverf** /ɣrɔntfɛrf/ primer

de **grondvest** /ɣrɔntfɛst/ (pl: -en) foundation **grondvesten** /ɣrɔntfɛstə(n)/ (grondvestte, heeft gegrondvest) **1** lay the foundations of **2** [fig] found, base: *gegrondvest op* based on

het **grondvlak** /ɣrɔntflɑk/ (pl: -ken) base

het **grondwater** /ɣrɔntwɑtər/ groundwater

het **grondwerk** /ɣrɔntwɛrk/ (pl: -en) groundwork

de **grondwet** /ɣrɔntwɛt/ (pl: -ten) constitution: *in strijd met de ~* unconstitutional

grondwettelijk /ɣrɔntwɛtələk/ (adj) constitutional

het **grondzeil** /ɣrɔntsɛɪl/ (pl: -en) groundsheet

groot /ɣrot/ (adj) **1** big, large: *een tamelijk grote kamer* quite a big (*or:* large) room; *de kans is ~ dat …* there's a good chance that …; *met grote moeite* with great difficulty; *op één na de ~ste* the next to largest **2** big, tall: *wat ben jij ~ geworden!* how you've grown!; *de ~ste van de twee* the bigger of the two **3** big; grown-up: *zij heeft al grote kinderen* she has (already) got grown-up children; *daar ben je te ~ voor* you're too big for that (sort of thing) **4** in size: *het stuk land is twee hectare ~* the piece of land is two hectares in area; *twee keer zo ~ als deze kamer* twice as big as this room **5** great, large: *een ~ gezin* a large family; *de grote massa* the masses; *een steeds groter aantal* an increasing (*or:* a growing) number; *in het ~ inkopen* (*or: verkopen*) buy (*or:* sell) in bulk || *Karel de Grote* Charlemagne; *Alexander de Grote* Alexander the Great; *je hebt ~ gelijk!* you are quite (*or:* perfectly) right!

het **grootboek** /ɣrodbuk/ (pl: -en) ledger

grootbrengen /ɣrodbrɛŋə(n)/ (bracht groot, heeft grootgebracht) bring up, raise: *een kind met de fles ~* bottle-feed a child

Groot-Brittannië /ɣrodbrɪtɑn(i)jə/ Great Britain

het **grootgrondbezit** /ɣrotxrɔndbəzɪt/ large(-scale) landownership

de **grootgrondbezitter** /ɣrotxrɔndbəzɪtər/ (pl: -s) large landowner

de **groothandel** /ɣrothɑndəl/ (pl: -s) wholesaler's, wholesale business

de **grootheid** /ɣrothɛit/ quantity

de **grootheidswaan** /ɣrothɛitswan/ megalomania

de **groothertog** /ɣrothɛrtɔx/ (pl: -en) grand duke

het **groothertogdom** /ɣrothɛrtɔɣdɔm/ (pl: -men) grand duchy

de **groothoeklens** /ɣrothuklɛns/ (pl: -lenzen) wide-angle lens

zich **groothouden** /ɣrothɑudə(n)/ (hield zich groot, heeft zich grootgehouden) **1** bear up (well, bravely) **2** keep up appearances, keep a stiff upper lip

de **grootmacht** /ɣrotmɑxt/ (pl: -en) superpower

de **grootmeester** /ɣrotmestər/ (pl: -s) **1** grandmaster **2** (great, past) master

de **grootmoeder** /ɣrotmudər/ (pl: -s) grandmother

grootmoedig /ɣrotmudəx/ (adj, adv) magnanimous, generous: *dat was erg ~ van hem* that was very noble of him

de **grootouders** /ɣrotɑudərs/ (pl) grandparents

groots /ɣrots/ (adj, adv) **1** grand, magnificent, majestic **2** spectacular, large-scale; ambitious: *~e plannen hebben* have ambitious plans; *het ~ aanpakken* a) go about it on a grand scale; b) [inform] think big

grootschalig /ɣrotsxaləx/ (adj, adv) large-scale, ambitious

grootscheeps /ɣrotsxeps/ (adj, adv) large-scale, great, massive; full-scale

de **grootspraak** /ɣrotsprak/ **1** boast(ing): *waar blijf je nu met al je ~!* where's all your boasting now? **2** hyperbole, overstatement

de **grootte** /ɣrotə/ (pl: -n, -s) size: *onder de normale ~* undersize(d); *een model op ware ~* a life-size model; *ter ~ van* the size of

de **grootvader** /ɣrotfadər/ (pl: -s) grandfather

de **grootverbruiker** /ɣrotfərbrœykər/ (pl: -s) large-scale consumer, bulk consumer

het **gros** /ɣros/ (pl: -sen) **1** majority, larger part: *het ~ van de mensen* the majority of the people, the people at large **2** gross

de **grossier** /ɣrosir/ (pl: -s) wholesaler

de **grot** /ɣrot/ (pl: -ten) cave

grotendeels /ɣrotəndels/ (adv) largely

grotesk /ɣrotɛsk/ (adj, adv) grotesque

het **gruis** /ɣrœys/ grit

het **grut** /ɣryt/ toddlers, small fry, young fry

de **grutto** /ɣryto/ (pl: -'s) (black, bar-tailed) godwit

de **gruwel** /ɣrywəl/ (pl: -en) horror

de **gruweldaad** /ɣrywəldat/ (pl: -daden) atrocity: *gruweldaden bedrijven* commit atrocities

gruwelijk /ɣrywələk/ (adj, adv) **1** horrible, gruesome: *een ~e misdaad* a horrible crime; an atrocity **2** terrible, enormous: *een ~e hekel aan iem. hebben* hate s.o.'s guts; *zich ~ vervelen* be bored stiff (*or:* to death) **3** [inform] wicked, awesome

gruwen /ɣrywə(n)/ (gruwde, heeft gegruwd) be horrified (by): *ik gruw bij de gedachte aan al die ellende* I'm horrified by the thought of all this misery

de **gruzelementen** /ɣryzələmɛntə(n)/ (pl): *iets aan ~ slaan* knock sth. to pieces (*or:* matchwood), shatter sth.; *aan ~ liggen* have fallen to pieces (*or:* smithereens)

de **g-sleutel** /ɣesløtəl/ (pl: -s) [Dutch] G clef, Treble clef

de **gsm**® /ɣeɛsɛm/ (pl: -'s) GSM

het **gsm'etje**® /ɣeɛsɛmøcə/ (pl: -s) mobile (phone); [Am] cellphone

het **gsm-nummer**® /ɣeɛsɛmnʏmər/ (pl: -s) mobile (phone) number; [Am] cellphone number

Guatemala /ɣuwatəmala/ Guatemala

de **Guatemalteek** /ɣwatəmɑltek/ (pl: Guatemalteken) Guatemalan

Guatemalteeks /ɣwatəmɑlteks/ (adj) Guatemalan

de **guerrilla** /gərɪlja/ (pl: -'s) guer(r)illa (warfare)

de **guerrillaoorlog** /gerɪljaorlɔχ/ (pl: -en) guer(r)illa war(fare)

de **guerrillastrijder** /gərɪljastrɛɪdər/ (pl: -s) guer(r)illa (fighter)

de **guillotine** /gijotɪnə/ (pl: -s) guillotine

Guinee /χinə/ Guinea

Guinee-Bissau /χinebisɑu/ Guinea-Bissau

de **Guinee-Bissauer** /χinebisɑuwər/ (pl: -s) inhabitant (or: native) of Guinea Bissau

Guinee-Bissaus /χinebisɑus/ (adj) of/from Guinea Bissau

de **Guineeër** /χinəjər/ (pl: -s) Guinean

Guinees /χinəs/ (adj) Guinean

de **guirlande** /girlɑ̄də/ (pl: -s) festoon, garland

guitig /χœytəχ/ (adj, adv) roguish, mischievous

¹gul /χʏl/ (adj) **1** generous: *met ~le hand (geven)* (give) generously; *~ zijn* **met** *iets* be liberal with sth. **2** cordial: *een ~le lach* a hearty laugh

²gul /χʏl/ (adv) cordially

de **gulden** /χʏldə(n)/ (pl: -s) (Dutch) guilder, florin; [abbr] Dfl; NLG

de **gulheid** /χʏlhɛit/ **1** generosity **2** cordiality

de **gulp** /χʏlp/ (pl: -en) fly (front); zip: *je ~ staat open* your fly is open

gulpen /χʏlpə(n)/ (gulpte, is gegulpt) gush: *het bloed gulpte uit de wond* blood gushed from the wound

gulzig /χʏlzəχ/ (adj, adv) greedy: *met ~e blikken* with greedy eyes

het/de **gum** /χʏm/ rubber; [Am] eraser

het/de **gummi** /χʏmi/ rubber

de **gummiknuppel** /χʏmiknʏpəl/ (pl: -s) baton; [Am] club

de **gummistok** /χʏmistɔk/ (pl: -ken) baton

gunnen /χʏnə(n)/ (gunde, heeft gegund) **1** grant: *iem. een blik op iets ~* let s.o. have a look at sth.; *hij gunde zich de tijd niet om te eten* he did not allow himself time to eat **2** not begrudge: *het is je van harte gegund* you're very welcome to it

de **gunst** /χʏnst/ (pl: -en) favour: *iem. een ~ bewijzen* do s.o. a favour

gunstig /χʏnstəχ/ (adj, adv) **1** favourable, kind: *~ staan tegenover* sympathize with **2** favourable, advantageous: *een ~e gelegenheid* a good (or: favourable) opportunity; *in het ~ste geval* at best; *met ~e uitslag* with a favourable (or: satisfactory) result; *~e voortekenen* favourable (or: hopeful) signs; *~ voor* ... favourable (or: good) for ... **3** favourable, agreeable: *~ bekendstaan* have a good reputation

het **gunsttarief** /χʏnstarif/ (pl: -tarieven) [Belg] concessionary rate

gutsen /χʏtsə(n)/ (gutste, heeft gegutst) gush, pour

guur /χyr/ (adj, adv) bleak; rough; wild; cutting

de **Guyaan** /χijan/ (pl: Guyanen) Guyanese

Guyaans /χijans/ (adj) Guyanese

Guyana /χijana/ Guyana

de **¹gym** /χɪm/ gym

het **²gym** /χɪm/ [roughly] grammar school; [Am] high school; [Dutch] gymnasium

gymmen /χɪmə(n)/ (gymde, heeft gegymd) **1** do gym(nastics) **2** have gym

de **gymnasiast** /χɪmnaʒɑst/ (pl: -en) [Dutch] [roughly] grammar-school student; [Am] [roughly] high-school student; [Dutch etc.] gymnasium student

het **gymnasium** /χɪmnazijʏm/ (pl: -s, gymnasia) [roughly] grammar school; [Am] high school; [Dutch] gymnasium

de **gymnast** /χɪmnɑst/ (pl: -en) gymnast

de **gymnastiek** /χɪmnɑstik/ gymnastics: *op ~ zijn* be at gymnastics

de **gynaecologie** /χinekoloχi/ gynaecology

de **gynaecoloog** /χinekoloχ/ (pl: -logen) gynaecologist

de **gyros** /χirɔs/ gyros

h

de **h** /ha/ (pl: h's) h, H, aitch

ha /ha/ (int) ah!: *ha! ben je daar?* ah! so there you are; *ha! dat dacht je maar!* aha! that's what you thought || *haha, die is goed!* ha, ha that's (a) good (one)!

de **haag** /haχ/ (pl: hagen) hedge(row)

de **haai** /haj/ (pl: -en) shark: *naar de ~en gaan* go down the drain

de **haaientanden** /haja(n)tɑndə(n)/ **1** shark's teeth **2** triangular road marking (at junction)

de **haaienvinnensoep** /haja(n)vɪnə(n)sup/ shark-fin soup

de **haak** /hak/ (pl: haken) hook: *er zitten veel haken en ogen aan* it's a tricky business || *dat is niet in de ~* that's not quite right; *de hoorn van de ~ nemen* take the receiver off the hook

het **haakje** /hakjə/ (pl: -s) bracket, parenthesis: *~ openen* (or: *sluiten*) open (or: close) (the) brackets; *tussen (twee) ~s* **a)** in brackets; **b)** [fig] incidentally, by the way

de **haaknaald** /haknalt/ (pl: -en) crochet hook (or: needle)

haaks /haks/ (adj, adv) square(d) || *hou je ~* (keep your) chin up

het **haakwerk** /hakwɛrk/ (pl: -en) crochet (work), crocheting

de **haal** /hal/ (pl: halen) **1** tug, pull: *met een flinke ~ trok hij het schip aan de wal* with a good tug he pulled the boat ashore **2** stroke || *aan de ~ gaan met* run off with

haalbaar /halbar/ (adj) attainable, feasible

de **haalbaarheid** /halbarhɛit/ feasibility

de **haan** /han/ (pl: hanen) cock: *daar kraait geen ~ naar* no one will know a thing; *de ~ spannen (overhalen)* cock the gun

het **haantje** /hancə/ (pl: -s) young cock; chicken

de **haantje-de-voorste** /hancədəvorstə/ ringleader: *~ zijn* be (the) cock-of-the-walk

het ¹**haar** /har/ hair: *met lang ~, met kort ~* long-haired, short-haired; *z'n ~ laten knippen* have a haircut; *z'n ~ verven* dye one's hair

het/de ²**haar** /har/ hair: *iets met de haren erbij slepen* drag sth. in; *geen ~ op m'n hoofd die eraan denkt* I would not dream of it; *elkaar in de haren vliegen* fly at each other; *het scheelde maar een ~ of ik had hem geraakt* I only just missed hitting him; *op een ~ na* very nearly

³**haar** /har/ (pers pron) her; it: *vrienden van ~* friends of hers; *hij gaf het ~* he gave it to her; *die van ~ is wit* hers is white

⁴**haar** /har/ (poss pron) her; its: *Els ~ schoenen* Elsie's shoes

de **haarborstel** /harborstəl/ (pl: -s) hairbrush

het **haarbreed** /harbret/: *hij week geen ~* he did not give an inch

de **haard** /hart/ (pl: -en) **1** stove: *eigen ~ is goud waard* there's no place like home **2** hearth: *huis en ~* hearth and home; *een open ~* a fireplace; *bij de ~* by (or: at) the fireside

de **haardos** /hardos/ (pl: -sen) (head of) hair: *een dichte* (or: *volle*) *~* a thick head of hair

de **haardracht** /hardrɑχt/ (pl: -en) hair style

de **haardroger** /hardroɣər/ (pl: -s) hairdryer

het **haardvuur** /hartfyr/ (pl: -vuren) open fire, fire on the hearth

haarfijn /harfɛin/ (adv): *iets ~ uitleggen* explain sth. in great detail, explain the ins and outs of sth.

de **haargrens** /harɣrɛns/ hairline

de **haargroei** /harɣruj/ hair growth

de **haarkloverij** /harklovərɛi/ **1** hairsplitting **2** quibbling

het/de **haarlak** /harlɑk/ (pl: -ken) hair spray

de **haarlok** /harlɔk/ (pl: -ken) lock (of hair)

haarscherp /harsχɛrp/ (adj, adv) very sharp; exact

het **haarscheurtje** /harsχørcə/ (pl: -s) haircrack

de **haarspeld** /harspɛlt/ (pl: -en) **1** hairslide; [Am] hair clasp **2** hairpin

de **haarspeldbocht** /harspɛldbɔχt/ hairpin bend

de **haarspoeling** /harspulɪŋ/ hair colouring

de **haarspray** /harsprɛ/ (pl: -s) hair spray

het **haarstukje** /harstʏkjə/ (pl: -s) hairpiece

de **haaruitval** /harœytfɑl/ hair loss

het **haarvat** /harvɑt/ (pl: -en) capillary

de **haarversteviger** /harvərstevəɣər/ (pl: -s) hair conditioner

de **haarwortel** /harwortəl/ (pl: -s) **1** hair-root: *kleuren tot in de ~s* blush to the roots of one's hair **2** [bot] root-hair

de **haas** /has/ (pl: hazen) **1** hare **2** fillet: *een biefstuk van de ~* fillet steak **3** [sport] pacemaker || *het ~je zijn* be for it; *mijn naam is ~* I'm saying nothing, I know nothing about it

het **haasje-over** /hajəovər/: *~ springen* (play) leapfrog

de ¹**haast** /hast/ hurry, haste: *in grote ~* in a great hurry, in haste; *er is ~ bij* the matter is urgent, the matter cannot wait; *~ hebben* be in a hurry; *~ maken* make haste, hurry up; *waarom zo'n ~?* what's the rush?

²**haast** /hast/ (adv) almost, nearly; hardly: *je zou ~ denken dat ...* you would almost think that ...; *hij was ~ gevallen* he nearly fell; *hij zei ~ niets toen hij wegging* he said hardly anything when he left; *~ niet* hardly; *~ nooit* scarcely ever

zich **haasten** /hastə(n)/ (haastte zich, heeft zich gehaast) hurry; hurry up: *we hoeven ons niet te ~* there's no need to hurry; *haast je maar niet!* don't hurry!, take your time!

haastig /hastəχ/ (adj, adv) hasty, rash: *niet*

zo ~! (take it) easy!

het **haastwerk** /ha̱stwɛrk/ **1** hasty (*or:* rushed) work **2** urgent (*or:* pressing) work

de **haat** /hat/ hatred, hate: *blinde* ~ blind hate; *~ zaaien* stir up (*or:* sow) hatred

haatdragend /hadra̱ɣənt/ (adj) resentful, rancorous, spiteful

de **haat-liefdeverhouding** /hatli̱vdəvərhaudɪŋ/ love-hate relationship

de **habbekrats** /ha̱bəkrɑts/ [inform]: *voor een ~* for a song

het **habijt** /habɛi̱t/ (pl: -en) habit

de **habitat** /ha̱bitɑt/ (pl: -s) habitat

het/de **hachee** /haʃe̱/ [Dutch] stew, hash

hachelijk /hɑ̱xələk/ (adj) precarious

het **hachje** /hɑ̱xjə/ (pl: -s) skin: *zijn ~ redden* save one's skin; *alleen aan zijn eigen ~ denken* only think of one's own safety

hacken /hɛ̱kə(n)/ (hackte, heeft gehackt) hack: *zijn computer is gehackt* his computer has been hacked; *een netwerk ~* hack into a network

de **hacker** /hɛ̱kər/ hacker

de **hadj** /hɑdʒ/ hadj

de **hadji** /hɑ̱dʒi/ hadji

de **hagedis** /ha̱ɣədɪs/ (pl: -sen) lizard

de **hagel** /ha̱ɣəl/ (pl: -s) **1** hail **2** (lead, ball) shot

de **hagelbui** /ha̱ɣəlbœy/ (pl: -en) hailstorm

hagelen /ha̱ɣələ(n)/ (hagelde, heeft gehageld) hail: *het hagelt* it hails, it is hailing

de **hagelslag** /ha̱ɣəlslɑx/ chocolate strands

de **hagelsteen** /ha̱ɣəlsten/ (pl: -stenen) hailstone

hagelwit /ha̱ɣəlwɪt/ (adj) (as) white as snow: *~te tanden* pearly-white teeth

haha /haha̱, haha/ *see* ha

de **haiku** /ha̱jku/ (pl: -'s) haiku

de **hairextension** /hɛːrɛkstɛnʃən/ (hair) extension

Haïti /ha̱iti/ Haiti

de **Haïtiaan** /haitija̱n/ (pl: Haïtianen) Haitian

Haïtiaans /haitija̱ns/ (adj) Haitian

de **hak** /hɑk/ **1** heel: *schoenen met hoge* (*or: lage*) *~ken* high-heeled (*or:* flat-heeled) shoes; *met de ~ken over de sloot slagen* pass by the skin of one's teeth **2** heel: [fig] *de ~ken in het zand zetten* dig one's heels in **3** cut ‖ *van de ~ op de tak springen* skip from one subject to another; *iem. een ~ zetten* play s.o. a nasty trick, do s.o. a bad turn

de **hakbijl** /hɑ̱gbɛɪl/ (pl: -en) hatchet, chopper

het **hakblok** /hɑ̱gblɔk/ (pl: -ken) chopping block, butcher's block

¹**haken** /ha̱kə(n)/ (haakte, heeft gehaakt) catch: *hij bleef met zijn jas aan een spijker ~* he caught his coat on a nail

²**haken** /ha̱kə(n)/ (haakte, heeft gehaakt) crochet

het **hakenkruis** /ha̱kə(n)krœys/ (pl: -kruizen) swastika

hakkelen /hɑ̱kələ(n)/ (hakkelde, heeft ge-

hakkeld) stammer (out), stumble (over one's words)

¹**hakken** /hɑ̱kə(n)/ (hakte, heeft gehakt) hack (at) ‖ *dat hakt erin* **a)** that costs a packet, that's a nasty blow to our budget; **b)** that's a big blow

²**hakken** /hɑ̱kə(n)/ (hakte, heeft gehakt) **1** chop (up): *in stukjes ~* cut (*or:* chop) (up) **2** cut (off, away) **3** cut (out)

het **hakmes** /hɑ̱kmɛs/ (pl: -sen) **1** chopper, machete **2** chopping knife

de **hal** /hɑl/ (pl: -len) (entrance) hall: *in de ~ van het hotel* in the hotel lobby (*or:* lounge, foyer)

halal /halɑ̱l/ (adj) halal

halen /ha̱lə(n)/ (haalde, heeft gehaald) **1** pull; drag: *ervan alles bij ~* drag in everything (but the kitchen sink); *ik kan er mijn kosten niet uit ~* it doesn't cover my expenses; *eruit ~ wat erin zit* get the most out of sth.; *overhoop ~* turn upside down; *waar haal ik het geld vandaan?* where shall I find the money?; *zijn zakdoek uit zijn zak ~* pull out one's handkerchief; *iem. uit zijn concentratie ~* break s.o.'s concentration; *geld van de bank ~* (with)draw money from the bank **2** fetch, get: *de post ~* collect the mail; *ik zal het gaan ~* I'll go and get it; *ik zal je morgen komen ~* I'll come for you tomorrow; *iem. van de trein ~* meet s.o. at the station; *twee ~ een betalen* two for the price of one **3** fetch, go for: *de dokter ~* go for the doctor; *iem. (iets) laten ~* send for s.o. (sth.) **4** get; take; pass: *goede cijfers ~* get good marks **5** reach; catch; get; make; compare; pull through: *hij heeft de finish niet gehaald* he did not make it to the finish; *daar haalt niets het bij* nothing can touch (*or:* beat) it; [Belg] *Anderlecht haalde het met 2-1 van Standard* Anderlecht beat Standard 2 to 1 ‖ *je haalt twee zaken door elkaar* you are mixing up two things

het ¹**half** /hɑlf/ (pl: halven) half: *twee halven maken een heel* two halves make a whole

²**half** /hɑlf/ (adj) **1** half: *voor ~ geld* (at) half price; *vier en een halve mijl* four and a half miles; *de halve stad spreekt ervan* half the town is talking about it **2** halfway up/down (*or:* along, through): *ik ga ~ april* I'm going in mid-April; *er is een bus telkens om vier minuten vóór ~* there is a bus every four minutes to the half-hour; *het is ~ elf* **a)** it is half past ten; **b)** it is half ten

³**half** /hɑlf/ (adv) half, halfway: *een glas ~ vol schenken* pour half a glass; *met het raam ~ dicht* with the window halfway down (*or:* open)

halfacht /hɑlfɑ̱xt/ (adv) half past seven, seven-thirty

halfbakken /hɑlvbɑ̱kə(n)/ (adj, adv) half-baked: *hij deed alles maar ~* he did everything in a half-baked way (*or:* by halves)

hand

halfbewolkt /hɑlvbəwɔlkt/ (adj) rather cloudy, with some clouds

de **halfbloed** /hɑlvblut/ (pl: -en) half-breed, half-blood

de **halfbroer** /hɑlvbrur/ (pl: -s) half-brother

het **halfdonker** /hɑlvdɔŋkər/ semidarkness, half-dark(ness)

halfdood /hɑlvdot/ (adj) half-dead

de **halfedelsteen** /hɑlfedəlsten/ (pl: -stenen) semiprecious stone

het **halffabricaat** /hɑlfabrikat/ (pl: -fabricaten) semimanufacture

halfgaar /hɑlfxar/ (adj) **1** half-done **2** half-witted

de **halfgeleider** /hɑlfxələɛidər/ (pl: -s) semiconductor

de **halfgod** /hɑlfxɔt/ (pl: -en) demigod

halfhartig /hɑlfhɑrtəx/ (adj, adv) half-hearted

het **halfjaar** /hɑlfjar/ (pl: -jaren) six months, half a year

halfjaarlijks /hɑlfjarləks/ (adj, adv) half-yearly, biannual: *te betalen in ~e* **termijnen** payable in biannual instalments, payable every six months

het **halfpension** /hɑlfpɛnʃɔn/ half board

het **halfrond** /hɑlfrɔnt/ (pl: -en) hemisphere

halfslachtig /hɑlfslɑxtəx/ (adj, adv) half-hearted, half: *~e* **maatregelen** half(way) measures

halfstok /hɑlfstɔk/ (adv) at half-mast: *vlaggen ~* **hangen** fly flags at half-mast

het **halfuur** /hɑlfyr/ half (an) hour: *om het ~* every half hour, half-hourly

halfvol /hɑlfɔl/ (adj) **1** half-full: *bij hem is het* **glas** *altijd ~* for him the glass is always half-full **2** low-fat, half-fat

de **halfwaardetijd** /hɑlfwardɛit/ half-life

halfweg /hɑlfwɛx/ (prep) halfway

halfzacht /hɑlfsɑxt/ (adj) **1** soft-boiled **2** soft-headed, soft (in the head)

de **halfzuster** /hɑlfsystər/ (pl: -s) half-sister

halleluja /hɑlelyja/ (int) alleluia, halleluja(h)

hallo /hɑlo/ (int) hello, hallo, hullo

de **hallucinatie** /hɑlysina(t)si/ (pl: -s) hallucination

hallucineren /hɑlysinerə(n)/ (hallucineerde, heeft gehallucineerd) hallucinate, hear things, see things

de **halm** /hɑlm/ (pl: -en) stalk; blade

de **halo** /hɑlo/ (pl: -'s) halo; [around moon] corona

het **halogeen** /hɑloxen/ (pl: halogenen) halogen

de **halogeenlamp** /hɑloxenlɑmp/ (pl: -en) halogen lamp

de **hals** /hɑls/ (pl: halzen) **1** neck: *de ~ van een* **gitaar** the neck of a guitar; *iem. om de ~ val-len* throw one's arms round s.o.'s neck; *een japon met laag* **uitgesneden** *~* a low-necked

dress **2** throat **3** nape ‖ *hij heeft het zichzelf op de ~* **gehaald** he has brought it on himself

de **halsband** /hɑlzbɑnt/ (pl: -en) **1** collar **2** necklace

halsbrekend /hɑlzbrekənt/ (adj) daredevil

de **halsdoek** /hɑlzduk/ (pl: -en) scarf

de **halsketting** /hɑlskɛtɪŋ/ (pl: -en) **1** necklace **2** collar

de **halsmisdaad** /hɑlsmɪzdat/ (pl: -misdaden) capital crime (*or:* offence)

halsoverkop /hɑlsoverkɔp/ (adv) in a hurry (*or:* rush); headlong; head over heels: *~* **ver-liefd** *worden* fall head over heels in love; *~ naar het ziekenhuis* **gebracht** *worden* be rushed to hospital; *~ de trap af* **komen** come tumbling downstairs

halsreikend /hɑlsrɛikənt/ (adv) eagerly: *~ naar iets* **uitzien** look forward eagerly to sth.

de **halsslagader** /hɑlslɑxadər/ (pl: -s, -en) carotid (artery)

halsstarrig /hɑlstɑrəx/ (adj) obstinate, stubborn

het/de **halster** /hɑlstər/ (pl: -s) halter

het **¹halt** /hɑlt/ stop: *iem. een ~* **toeroepen** stop s.o.; *~* **houden** halt

²halt /hɑlt/ (int) halt!, stop!, wait!

de **halte** /hɑltə/ (pl: -s) stop

de **halter** /hɑltər/ (pl: -s) dumb-bell; bar bell

de **halvarine** /hɑlvarinə/ (pl: -s) low-fat margarine

de **halvemaan** /hɑlvəman/ (pl: -manen) **1** half-moon **2** crescent

halveren /hɑlverə(n)/ (halveerde, heeft gehalveerd) **1** divide into halves **2** halve

halverwege /hɑlverweɣə/ (adv) halfway, halfway through ‖ *~* **blijven steken** *in een boek* get stuck halfway through a book

de **ham** /hɑm/ (pl: -men) ham: *een* **broodje** *~* a ham roll

de **hamam** /hɑmɑm/ hammam

de **hamburger** /hɑmbyrɣər/ (pl: -s) hamburger, beefburger: *~ met* **kaas** cheeseburger

de **hamer** /hɑmər/ (pl: -s) hammer: [fig] *onder de ~ brengen* bring under the hammer

hameren /hɑmərə(n)/ (hamerde, heeft gehamerd) hammer: *er bij iem.* **op** *blijven ~* keep on at s.o. about sth.

het **hamerpunt** /hɑmərpʏnt/ (pl: -en) formality

de **hamster** /hɑmstər/ (pl: -s) hamster

de **hamsteraar** /hɑmstərar/ (pl: -s) hoarder

hamsteren /hɑmstərə(n)/ (hamsterde, heeft gehamsterd) hoard (up)

de **hamstring** /hɛmstrɪŋ/ (pl: -s) hamstring

de **hamvraag** /hɑmvrax/ (pl: -vragen) key question

de **hand** /hɑnt/ (pl: -en) hand: *er is iets* **aan** *de ~* there's sth. the matter (*or:* up); *wat is er er* **aan** *de ~?* what's going on?; *niks* **aan** *de ~!* there's nothing wrong; not to worry; *blote ~en* bare hands; *in* **goede** (*or:* **verkeerde**) *~en vallen* fall into the right (*or:* wrong) hands;

*iem. de **helpende** ~ bieden* lend s.o. a (helping) hand; *de laatste ~ aan iets leggen* put the finishing touches to sth.; *niet met lege ~en komen* not come empty-handed; *de ~en vol hebben aan iem. (iets)* have one's hands full with s.o. (sth.); *dat kost ~en vol geld* that costs lots of money; *iem. de ~ drukken* (or: *geven, schudden*) shake hands with s.o., give s.o. one's hand; *iemands ~ lezen* read s.o.'s palm; *de ~ ophouden* [fig] hold out one's hand for a tip; beg; *zijn ~en uit de mouwen steken* [fig] roll up one's sleeves, get down to it; *hij kan zijn ~en niet thuishouden* he can't keep his hands to himself; *zijn ~ uitsteken* indicate; *~en omhoog!* (*of ik schiet*) hands up! (or I'll shoot); *~en thuis!* hands off!; *wat geld achter de ~ houden* keep some money for a rainy day; *in de ~en klappen* clap one's hands; [fig] *iets in de ~ hebben* have sth. under control; *de macht in ~en hebben* have power, be in control; *in ~en vallen van de politie* fall into the hands of the police; *met de ~ gemaakt* handmade; *iets omhanden hebben* have sth. to do; *iem. onder ~en nemen* take s.o. in hand (or: to task); *iem. op zijn ~ hebben* have s.o. on one's side; *uit de ~ lopen* get out of hand; *iem. werk uit ~en nemen* take work off s.o.'s hands; *iets van de ~ doen* sell sth., part with sth., dispose of sth.; *dat ligt voor de ~* that speaks for itself, is self-evident; *aan de winnende ~ zijn* be winning

de **handbagage** /hɑndbaɣaʒə/ (pl: -s) hand-luggage

het **handbal** /hɑndbɑl/ handball

handballen /hɑndbɑlə(n)/ (handbalde, heeft gehandbald) play handball

het **handbereik** /hɑndbərɛik/ reach: *onder* (or: *binnen*) ~ within reach

de **handboei** /hɑndbuj/ (pl: -en) handcuffs

het **handboek** /hɑndbuk/ (pl: -en) **1** handbook **2** reference book

het **handbreed** /hɑndbret/ hand('s-)breadth: *geen ~ wijken* not budge, give an inch

de **handdoek** /hɑnduk/ (pl: -en) towel

de **handdruk** /hɑndrʏk/ (pl: -ken) handshake

de **handel** /hɑndəl/ **1** trade, business: *~ drijven* trade (with), do business (with); *binnenlandse ~* domestic trade; *zwarte ~* black market; *~ in verdovende middelen* drug trafficking **2** merchandise, goods **3** business; shop

de **handelaar** /hɑndəlar/ (pl: -s, handelaren) trader; merchant; dealer; [depr] trafficker

handelbaar /hɑndəlbar/ (adj) manageable, docile

¹**handelen** /hɑndələ(n)/ (handelde, heeft gehandeld) **1** trade, do business, transact business; [depr] traffic: *hij handelt in drugs* he traffics in drugs **2** act: *~d optreden* take action; *ik zal naar eer en geweten ~* I shall act in all conscience **3** (+ *over*) treat (of), deal (with)

²**handelen** /hɛndələ(n)/ (handelde, heeft gehandeld) handle, deal with: *een situatie kunnen ~* be able to handle a situation

de **handeling** /hɑndəlɪŋ/ (pl: -en) **1** act, deed **2** action, plot: *de plaats van ~* the scene (of the action)

handelingsbekwaam /hɑndəlɪŋzbəkwam/ (adj) [law] having capacity (or: competence) to act

het **handelsakkoord** /hɑndəlsakort/ (pl: -en) trade agreement

het **handelsartikel** /hɑndəlsɑrtikəl/ (pl: -en) commodity; goods; merchandise

de **handelsbalans** /hɑndəlzbalɑns/ (pl: -en) balance of trade, trade balance

de **handelsbetrekkingen** /hɑndəlzbətrɛkɪŋ/ (pl) trade relations, commercial relations

de **handelskamer** /hɑndəlskamər/ (pl: -s) **1** producers' cooperative **2** [Dutch] Commercial Court

de **handelskennis** /hɑndəlskɛnɪs/ knowledge of commerce (or: business); business studies

het **handelsmerk** /hɑndəlsmɛrk/ (pl: -en) trademark; brand name

de **handelsmissie** /hɑndəlsmɪsi/ (pl: -s) trade mission (or: delegation)

de **handelsonderneming** /hɑndəlsondərnemɪŋ/ (pl: -en) commercial enterprise, business enterprise

de **handelsovereenkomst** /hɑndəlsoverenkomst/ (pl: -en) trade agreement (or: pact)

de **handelspartner** /hɑndəlspɑrtnər/ (pl: -s) business partner, trading partner

het **handelsrecht** /hɑndəlsrɛxt/ commercial law

de **handelsrechtbank** /hɑndəlsrɛxtbɑŋk/ (pl: -en) [Belg] commercial court

het **handelsregister** /hɑndəlsrəɣɪstər/ (pl: -s) company (or: commercial, trade) register

de **handelsreiziger** /hɑndəlsrɛizəɣər/ (pl: -s) sales representative

het **handelstekort** /hɑndəlstəkort/ (pl: -en) trade deficit

het **handelsverdrag** /hɑndəlsfərdrɑx/ (pl: -en) commercial treaty

het **handelsverkeer** /hɑndəlsfərker/ (pl:) trade, business

de **handelswaar** /hɑndəlswar/ (pl: -waren) commodity, article; merchandise; goods

de **handenarbeid** /hɑndə(n)ɑrbɛit/ hand(i)-craft, industrial art, manual training

de **handendroger** /hɑndə(n)droɣər/ (pl: -s) hand dryer

de **hand-en-spandiensten** /hɑntɛnspɑndinstə(n)/ (pl): *~ verrichten* lend a helping hand; aid and abet

handenwringend /hɑndə(n)vrɪŋənt/ (adj) [fig] beside o.s. with despair

het **handgebaar** /hɑntχəbar/ (pl: -gebaren) gesture

het **handgemeen** /hɑntχəmen/ (hand-to-hand) fight

de **handgranaat** /hɑntχranat/ (pl: -granaten) (hand) grenade

de **handgreep** /hɑntχrep/ handle; grip

¹**handhaven** /hɑnthavə(n)/ (handhaafde, heeft gehandhaafd) **1** maintain; keep up; uphold; enforce: *de* **orde** ~ maintain (*or:* keep, preserve) order **2** maintain, stand by: *zijn* **bezwaren** ~ stand by one's objections

zich ²**handhaven** /hɑnthavə(n)/ (handhaafde zich, heeft zich gehandhaafd) hold one's own

de **handhaving** /hɑnthavɪŋ/ maintenance; upholding; enforcement

de **handicap** /hɛndikɛp/ (pl: -s) handicap: *speciale voorzieningen voor mensen* **met** *een* ~ special facilities for the disabled

handig /hɑndəχ/ (adj, adv) **1** skilful; dexterous; handy: *een* ~ **formaat** a handy size; ~ **in (met)** *iets zijn* be good (*or:* handy) at sth. **2** clever: *hij* **legde** *het* ~ **aan** he set about it cleverly

de **handigheid** /hɑndəχhɛit/ (pl: -heden) **1** skill **2** knack

het **handje** /hɑncə/ (pl: -s) hand(shake) ‖ *een* ~ **helpen** give (*or:* lend) a (helping) hand; *ergens een* ~ *van* **hebben** have a tendency to do sth.; ~ *contantje* **betalen** pay cash (down)

de **handkar** /hɑntkɑr/ (pl: -ren) handcart

de **handkus** /hɑntkʏs/ (pl: -sen) kiss on the hand: *iem. een* ~ **geven** kiss s.o.'s hand

de **handlanger** /hɑntlɑŋər/ (pl: -s) accomplice

de **handleiding** /hɑntlɛidɪŋ/ (pl: -en) manual, handbook; directions (*or:* instructions) (for use)

handlezen /hɑntlezə(n)/ palmistry, palmreading

handmatig /hɑntmatəχ/ (adj) manual

de **handomdraai** /hɑntomdraːj/: *in een* ~ *in* (less than) no time

de **handoplegging** /hɑntopleɣɪŋ/ (pl: -en) laying on of hands; faith healing

de **hand-out** /hɛndɑut/ (pl: -s) hand-out

de **handpalm** /hɑntpɑlm/ (pl: -en) palm (of the hand)

de **handreiking** /hɑntrɛikɪŋ/ (pl: -en) help(ing hand), assistance

de **handrem** /hɑntrɛm/ (pl: -men) handbrake

het **hands** /hɛnts/ hands, handling (the ball), handball: *aangeschoten* ~ unintentional hands

de **handschoen** /hɑntsχun/ (pl: -en) glove: *een* **paar** ~*en* a pair of gloves; *iem. met* **fluwelen** ~*en aanpakken* handle s.o. with kid gloves

het **handschoenenkastje** /hɑntsχunə(n)kɑʃə/ (pl: -s) glove compartment

het **handschrift** /hɑntsχrɪft/ (pl: -en) **1** handwriting **2** manuscript

handsfree /hɛn(t)sfriː/ (adj) handsfree: ~ **bellen** call in handsfree mode, make a handsfree call

de **handstand** /hɑntstɑnt/ (pl: -en) handstand

de **handtas** /hɑntɑs/ (pl: -sen) (hand)bag

handtastelijk /hɑntɑstələk/ (adj) free, (over)familiar: ~ **worden** paw s.o.

de **handtekening** /hɑntekənɪŋ/ (pl: -en) signature; autograph

de **handtekeningenactie** /hɑntekənɪŋə(n)- ɑksi/ (pl: -s) petition

de **handvaardigheid** /hɑntfɑrdəχhɛit/ (handi)craft(s)

het **handvat** /hɑntfɑt/ (pl: -ten) handle; hilt; butt: *het* ~ *van een* **koffer** the handle of a suitcase

het **handvest** /hɑntfɛst/ (pl: -en) charter

de **handvol** /hɑntfol/ handful

handwarm /hɑntwɑrm/ (adj) lukewarm

het **handwerk** /hɑntwɛrk/ (pl: -en) **1** handiwork: *dit tapijt* **is** ~ this carpet is handmade **2** needlework; embroidery; crochet(ing) **3** manual work; trade

de **handwerksman** /hɑntwɛrksmɑn/ (pl: handwerkslieden, handwerkslui) craftsman, artisan

handzaam /hɑntsam/ (adj) handy

de **hanenkam** /hanə(n)kɑm/ (pl: -men) **1** (cocks)comb **2** Mohawk haircut

de **hanenpoot** /hanə(n)pot/ (pl: -poten) **1** cock's foot **2** [illegible handwriting] scrawl

de **hang** /hɑŋ/: *de* ~ *naar* **vrijheid** the longing for freedom; *zij heeft een sterke* ~ *naar* **luxe** she has a strong craving for luxury

de **hangar** /hɑŋɡar/ (pl: -s) hangar

de **hangbrug** /hɑŋbrʏχ/ (pl: -gen) suspension bridge

de **hangbuik** /hɑŋbœyk/ (pl: -en) pot-belly

het **hangbuikzwijn** /hɑŋbœykswɛin/ potbellied pig

¹**hangen** /hɑŋə(n)/ (hing, heeft gehangen) **1** hang: *de zeilen* ~ **slap** the sails are slack, the sails are hanging (loose); *het schilderij hangt* **scheef** the painting is (hanging) crooked; *aan het plafond* ~ hang (*or:* swing, be suspended) from the ceiling; *de hond liet zijn* **staart** ~ the dog hung its tail **2** sag: *het koord hangt* **slap** the rope is sagging (*or:* slack) **3** lean (over), hang (over); loll; slouch; hang around: *hij hing* **op** *zijn stoel* he lay sprawled in a chair, he lolled in his chair **4** stick (to), cling (to); be (*or:* get) stuck (in): [fig] **blijven** ~ linger (*or:* stay, hang) (on); get hung up (*or:* stuck); [fig] *ze* ~ *erg* **aan** *elkaar* they are devoted to (*or:* wrapped up in) each other ‖ *de wolken* ~ **laag** the clouds are (hanging) low; *de bloemen zijn gaan* ~ the flowers are wilting

²**hangen** /hɑŋə(n)/ (hing, heeft gehangen) **1** hang (up): *de was* **buiten** ~ hang out the washing (to dry); *zijn jas* **aan** *de kapstok* ~ hang (up) one's coat on the peg **2** hang

hangend /hɑŋənt/ (adj) hanging; drooping

het **hang-en-sluitwerk** /hɑŋənslœytwɛrk/

fastenings, hinges and locks

de **hanger** /hɑŋər/ (pl: -s) **1** (clothes) hanger, coat-hanger **2** pendant, pendent; pendant earring, drop earring

hangerig /hɑŋərəx/ (adj) listless

het **hangijzer** /hɑŋɛizər/ (pl: -s) pot-hook: *een heet ~* a controversial issue, hot potato

de **hangjongere** /hɑŋjɔŋərə/ (pl: -n) loitering teen; mallrat

de **hangkast** /hɑŋkɑst/ (pl: -en) wardrobe

de **hanglamp** /hɑŋlɑmp/ (pl: -en) hanging lamp

de **hangmap** /hɑŋmɑp/ (pl: -pen) suspension file

de **hangmat** /hɑŋmɑt/ (pl: -ten) hammock

de **hangplant** /hɑŋplɑnt/ (pl: -en) hanging plant

de **hangplek** /hɑŋplɛk/ hangout

het **hangslot** /hɑŋslɔt/ (pl: -en) padlock

hannesen /hɑnəsə(n)/ (hanneste, heeft gehannest) [Dutch; inform] mess about (*or:* around): *wat zit je toch te ~* you are making a mess of it

de **hansworst** /hɑnswɔrst/ (pl: -en) buffoon, clown

hanteerbaar /hɑntɛrbar/ (adj) manageable

hanteren /hɑntɛrə(n)/ (hanteerde, heeft gehanteerd) **1** handle, operate, employ; wield: *de botte bijl ~* take heavy-handed, crude measures; *moeilijk te ~* unwieldy, difficult (*or:* awkward) to handle, unmanageable **2** manage, manoeuvre

de **Hanzestad** /hɑnzəstɑt/ Hanseatic town

de **hap** /hɑp/ (pl: -pen) **1** bite; peck: *in één ~ was het op* it was gone in one (*or:* in a single) bite; *een snelle ~* a quick bite **2** bite, mouthful: *een ~ nemen* take a bite (*or:* mouthful)

haperen /hapərə(n)/ (haperde, heeft gehaperd) **1** stick, get stuck: *de conversatie haperde* the conversation flagged **2** have sth. wrong (*or:* the matter) with o.s.

het **hapje** /hɑpjə/ (pl: -s) **1** bite, mouthful: *wil je ook een ~ mee-eten?* would you like to join us (for a bite, meal)?; *ergens een ~ gaan eten* go somewhere for a bite to eat **2** snack, bite to eat, hors d'oeuvre, appetizer: *voor (lekkere) ~s zorgen* serve refreshments ‖ [med] *een ~ weefsel* a tissue sample

hapklaar /hɑpklar/ (adj) ready-to-eat

happen /hɑpə(n)/ (hapte, heeft gehapt) **1** bite (at), snap (at): *naar lucht ~* gasp for air **2** bite (into), take a bite (out of)

de **happening** /hɛpənɪŋ/ (pl: -s) happening

happig /hɑpəx/ (adj) (+ op) keen (on), eager (for)

het **happy end** /hɛpiɛnt/ happy ending

het **harakiri** /harakiri/ hara-kiri

haram /harɑm/ (adj) haram

¹**hard** /hɑrt/ (adj) **1** hard; firm; solid: *~e bewijzen* firm proof, hard evidence; *~ worden*

harden, become hard; set **2** stiff, rigid: *~e schijf* hard disk **3** hard; loud: *~e muziek* loud music; *~e wind* strong (*or:* stiff) wind **4** hard; harsh: *een ~e politiek* a tough policy; *een ~ vonnis* a severe sentence **5** harsh; garish: *~e trekken* harsh features

²**hard** /hɑrt/ (adv) **1** hard: *~ lachen* laugh heartily; *een band ~ oppompen* pump a tyre up hard; *hij ging er nogal ~ tegenaan* he went at it rather hard; *zijn rust ~ nodig hebben* be badly in need of a rest; *dit onderdeel is ~ aan vervanging toe* this part is in urgent need of replacement **2** loudly: *niet zo ~ praten!* keep your voice down!; *de tv ~er zetten* turn up the TV **3** fast, quickly: *~ achteruitgaan* deteriorate rapidly (*or:* fast); *te ~ rijden* drive (*or:* ride) too fast, speed **4** hard, harshly: *iem. ~ aanpakken* be hard on s.o.

het **hardboard** /hɑːrdbɔːrd/ hardboard

de **hardcopy** /hɑːrtkɔpi/ (pl: -'s) hard copy

de **hardcore** /hɑːrtkɔːr/ hardcore

de **harddisk** /hɑrdɪsk/ (pl: -s) hard disk

de **harddiskrecorder** /hɑːrdɪskrikɔːrdər/ hard disk recorder

¹**harden** /hɑrdə(n)/ (hardde, is gehard) harden, become hard; dry; set

²**harden** /hɑrdə(n)/ (hardde, heeft gehard) **1** harden, temper **2** toughen (up): *hij is gehard door weer en wind* he has been hardened (*or:* seasoned) by wind and weather **3** bear, stand; take; stick: *deze hitte is niet te ~* this heat is unbearable

hardgekookt /hɑrtxəkɔkt/ (adj) hard-boiled

hardhandig /hɑrthɑndəx/ (adj, adv) hard-handed, rough; heavy-handed: *~ optreden* take hard-handed (*or:* harsh, drastic) action, use strong-arm tactics

de **hardheid** /hɑrthɛit/ hardness; toughness; harshness

hardhorend /hɑrthɔrənt/ (adj) hard of hearing: *~ zijn* be hard of hearing

het **hardhout** /hɑrthɑut/ hardwood: *tropisch ~* tropical hardwood

hardleers /hɑrtlɛrs/ (adj) **1** dense, slow, thick(-skulled) **2** headstrong, stubborn

de **hardliner** /hɑːrdlɑjnər/ (pl: -s) hard liner

hardlopen /hɑrtlopə(n)/ (liep hard, heeft hardgelopen) run, race, run a race

de **hardloper** /hɑrtlopər/ (pl: -s) runner

hardmaken /hɑrtmakə(n)/ (maakte hard, heeft gehard) prove: *kun je dat ook ~?* have you got any proof for that?, can you prove that (with figures)?

hardnekkig /hɑrtnɛkəx/ (adj, adv) stubborn, obstinate; persistent: *een ~ gerucht* a persistent rumour

de **hardnekkigheid** /hɑrtnɛkəxhɛit/ obstinacy, stubbornness

hardop /hɑrtɔp/ (adv) aloud, out loud: *~ denken* (*or:* *lachen*) think/laugh aloud (*or:*

out loud); *iets ~ zeggen* say sth. out loud

hardrijden /hɑrtrɛidə(n)/ (reed hard, heeft hardgereden) [sport] race; speed-skate

de **hardrijder** /hɑrtrɛidər/ (pl: -s) racer; speedskater; racing cyclist

hardvochtig /hɑrtfɔxtəχ/ (adj, adv) hard(-hearted); unfeeling

de **hardware** /hɑːrdwɛːr/ hardware

de **harem** /hɑrəm/ (pl: -s) harem

harentwil /hɑrəntwɪl/: *om ~* for her sake

harig /hɑrəχ/ (adj) hairy; furry

de **haring** /hɑrɪŋ/ (pl: -en) **1** herring; kipper: *een school ~en* a shoal of herring; *nieuwe* (or: *zure*) ~ new (or: pickled) herring; *als ~en in een ton* (packed) like sardines **2** tent peg, tent stake

de **hark** /hɑrk/ (pl: -en) rake

harken /hɑrkə(n)/ (harkte, heeft geharkt) rake (up, together)

de **harlekijn** /hɑrləkɛin/ (pl: -s) **1** harlequin **2** jumping jack **3** clown

de **harmonica** /hɑrmonika/ (pl: -'s) **1** accordion **2** harmonica, mouth-organ

de **harmonicawand** /hɑrmonikawɑnt/ (pl: -en) folding partition

de **harmonie** /hɑrmoni/ (pl: -ën, -s) **1** harmony, concord, agreement: *in* (or: *niet in) ~ zijn met* be in (or: out of) harmony with **2** (brass)band

harmonieus /hɑrmonijøs/ (adj, adv) harmonious, melodious

harmonisch /hɑrmonis/ (adj, adv) **1** harmonic: *een ~ geheel* vormen blend (in), go well (together) **2** harmonious

harmoniseren /hɑrmonizerə(n)/ (harmoniseerde, heeft geharmoniseerd) harmonize: *de belastingen* in Europa ~ harmonize taxes within Europe

het **harnas** /hɑrnɑs/ (pl: -sen) (suit of) armour: *in het ~ sterven* die in harness; *iem. tegen zich in het ~ jagen* put s.o.'s back up

de **harp** /hɑrp/ (pl: -en) harp

de **harpist** /hɑrpɪst/ (pl: -en) harpist, harp player

de **harpoen** /hɑrpun/ (pl: -en) harpoon

harpoeneren /hɑrpunerə(n)/ (harpoeneerde, heeft geharpoeneerd) harpoon

de **harpsluiting** /hɑrpslœytɪŋ/ (pl: -en) shackle

het/de **hars** /hɑrs/ (pl: -en) resin; rosin

de **harses** /hɑrsəs/ (pl) [Dutch; inform] nut, conk, skull: *hou je ~!* shut your trap!

het **hart** /hɑrt/ (pl: -en) **1** heart: *uit de grond van zijn ~* from the bottom of one's heart; *in ~ en nieren* through and through, to the core; *met ~ en ziel* with all one's heart; *met een gerust* ~ with an easy mind; *een zwak ~ hebben* have a weak heart; *iemands ~ breken* break s.o.'s heart; *het ~ op de juiste plaats hebben* have one's heart in the right place; *ik hield mijn ~ vast* my heart missed a beat; *je kunt je ~ ophalen* you can enjoy it to your heart's

content; *zijn ~ uitstorten* pour out (or: unburden, open) one's heart (to s.o.); *(diep) in zijn ~ hield hij nog steeds van haar* in his heart (of hearts) he still loved her; *waar het ~ van vol is, loopt de mond van over* what the heart thinks, the tongue speaks **2** heart, nerve: *heb het ~ eens!* don't you dare!, just you try it!; *iem. een ~ onder de riem steken* hearten s.o., buck s.o. up; *het ~ zonk hem in de schoenen* he lost heart **3** heart, centre || *iets niet over zijn ~ kunnen verkrijgen* not find it in one's heart to do sth.; *van ~e gefeliciteerd* my warmest congratulations; *het ging niet van ~e* it didn't come from the heart; he/she had to be pushed

de **hartaanval** /hɑrtanval/ (pl: -len) heart attack

de **hartchirurgie** /hɑrtʃirʏrɣi/ cardiac (or: heart) surgery

[1]**hartelijk** /hɑrtələk/ (adj) **1** hearty, warm: ~ *dank voor ...* many thanks for ...; *~e groeten aan je vrouw* kind regards to your wife **2** warm-hearted, open-hearted, cordial: ~ *tegen iem. zijn* be friendly towards s.o.

[2]**hartelijk** /hɑrtələk/ (adv) heartily, warmly: ~ *bedankt voor ...* thank you very much for ...; ~ *gefeliciteerd* sincere congratulations

de **hartelijkheid** /hɑrtələkhɛit/ **1** cordiality, warm-heartedness **2** cordiality, hospitality

de **harten** /hɑrtə(n)/ (pl: -) hearts: *hartenboer* jack (or: knave) of hearts

de **hartenlust** /hɑrtə(n)lʏst/: *naar ~* to one's heart's content

de **hart- en vaatziekten** /hɑrtɛnvatsiktə(n)/ (pl) cardiovascular diseases

de **hartenwens** /hɑrtə(n)wɛns/ (pl: -en) heart's desire, fondest wish

het **hartfalen** /hɑrtfalə(n)/ heart failure

hartgrondig /hɑrtχrɔndəχ/ (adj) whole-hearted, hearty

hartig /hɑrtəχ/ (adj, adv) **1** tasty; well-seasoned; hearty **2** salt(y)

het **hartinfarct** /hɑrtɪnfɑrkt/ (pl: -en) coronary (thrombosis)

het **hartje** /hɑrcə/ (pl: -s) **1** (little) heart: *hij heeft een grote mond, maar een klein ~* he's not all what he makes out to be **2** heart, centre: *~ winter* the dead of winter; *~ zomer* the height of summer

de **hartkamer** /hɑrtkamər/ (pl: -s) ventricle (of the heart)

de **hartklacht** /hɑrtklɑχt/ (pl: -en) heart complaint (or: condition)

de **hartklep** /hɑrtklɛp/ (pl: -pen) heart valve, valve (of the heart)

de **hartklopping** /hɑrtklɔpɪŋ/ (pl: -en) palpitation (of the heart)

de **hartkwaal** /hɑrtkwal/ (pl: -kwalen) heart condition

de **hartpatiënt** /hɑrtpaʃɛnt/ (pl: -en) cardiac patient

de **hartritmestoornis** /hɑrtrɪtməstornɪs/ (pl: -sen) cardiac arrhythmia

de **hartslag** /hɑrtslɑх/ (pl: -en) heartbeat, pulse; heart rate

hartstikke /hɑrtstɪkə/ (adv) awfully, terribly; completely: ~ **gek** stark staring mad; crazy; ~ **goed** fantastic, terrific, smashing; ~ **bedankt!** thanks awfully (*or:* ever so much)

de **hartstilstand** /hɑrtstɪlstɑnt/ (pl: -en) cardiac arrest

de **hartstocht** /hɑrtstoхt/ (pl: -en) passion; emotion [esp pl]

¹**hartstochtelijk** /hɑrtstoхtələk/ (adj) 1 passionate, emotional; excitable 2 passionate, ardent, fervent: *hij is een ~ skiër* he is an ardent skier

²**hartstochtelijk** /hɑrtstoхtələk/ (adv) passionately, ardently

de **hartstreek** /hɑrtstrek/ heart (*or:* cardiac) region

de **hartverlamming** /hɑrtfərlɑmɪŋ/ heart failure

hartverscheurend /hɑrtfərsхørənt/ (adj, adv) heartbreaking, heart-rending

hartverwarmend /hɑrtfərwɑrmənt/ (adj, adv) heart-warming

de **hashtag** /hɛʃtɛk/ (pl: -s) hashtag

de **hasj** /hɑʃ/ hash

de **haspel** /hɑspəl/ (pl: -s) reel; spool

hatelijk /hɑtələk/ (adj, adv) nasty, spiteful; snide

de **hatelijkheid** /hɑtələkhɛit/ (pl: -heden) nasty remark, snide remark, gibe, (nasty) crack

de **hatemail** /hɛtmel/ hatemail

haten /hɑtə(n)/ (haatte, heeft gehaat) hate

hatsjie /hɑtʃi/ (int) atishoo

de **hattrick** /hɛtrɪk/ (pl: -s) [sport] hat trick: *een zuivere ~ scoren* score a pure hat trick

hautain /hotɛ̃/ (adj, adv) haughty, arrogant

de **have** /hɑvə/: *levende ~* livestock; *~ en goed verliezen* lose everything

haveloos /hɑvəlos/ (adj) 1 shabby, scruffy; delapidated: *wat ziet hij er ~ uit* how scruffy he looks 2 shabby, beggarly; down-and-out

de **haven** /hɑvə(n)/ (pl: -s) harbour; port; [fig] (safe) haven: [fig] *een veilige ~ vinden* find refuge; *een ~ binnenlopen (aandoen)* put into a port

de **havenarbeider** /hɑvə(n)ɑrbɛidər/ (pl: -s) dockworker

het **havenhoofd** /hɑvə(n)hoft/ (pl: -en) mole, jetty

de **havenmeester** /hɑvəmestər/ (pl: -s) harbour master; [Am] port warden

de **havenstad** /hɑvə(n)stɑt/ (pl: -steden) port; seaport (town)

de **haver** /hɑvər/ oat; oats

de **haverklap** /hɑvərklɑp/: *om de ~* a) every other minute, continually; b) at the drop of a hat

de **havermout** /hɑvərmɑut/ 1 rolled oats, oat-

meal 2 (oatmeal) porridge

de **havik** /hɑvɪk/ (pl: -en) 1 goshawk 2 [pol] hawk

de **haviksneus** /hɑvɪksnøs/ (pl: -neuzen) hooked nose

de **havo** /hɑvo/ (pl: -'s) [Dutch] *hoger algemeen voortgezet onderwijs* school for higher general secondary education

het **hawaïhemd** /hɑwɔjhɛmt/ (pl: -en) Hawaiian shirt

de **hazelaar** /hɑzəlɑr/ (pl: -s) hazel

de **hazelnoot** /hɑzəlnot/ 1 hazel 2 hazelnut

de **hazenlip** /hɑzə(n)lɪp/ (pl: -pen) harelip

het **hazenpad** /hɑzə(n)pɑt/ (pl: -en): *het ~ kiezen* take to one's heels

de **hazenpeper** /hɑzə(n)pepər/ [roughly] jugged hare

het **hazenslaapje** /hɑzə(n)slapjə/ power nap

de **hazewind** /hɑzəwɪnt/ (pl: -en) greyhound

het/de **hbo** /habeo/ [Dutch] *hoger beroepsonderwijs* (school for) higher vocational education

hé /he/ (int) hey!, hello; oh (really)?

hè /hɛ/ (int) oh (dear); ah: *hè, dat doet zeer!* oh (*or:* ouch), that hurts!; *hè, blij dat ik zit! phew, glad I can take the weight off my feet!* || *lekker weertje, hè?* nice day, isn't it?

headbangen /hɛːdbɛŋə(n)/ (headbangde, heeft geheadbangd) headbanging

de **header** /hɛdər/ (pl: -s) [comp] header

de **headhunter** /hɛːthʏntər/ (pl: -s) headhunter

de **headset** /hɛːtsɛt/ headset

het/de **heao** /heao/ (pl: -'s) [Dutch] *hoger economisch en administratief onderwijs* school (institute) for business administration and economics

heavy /hɛvi/ (adj) [inform] heavy

het **hebbeding** /hɛbədɪŋ/ (pl: -en) thingummy, gadget

de **hebbelijkheid** /hɛbələkhɛrt/ (pl: -heden) habit: *de ~ hebben om* have the (nasty (*or:* annoying)) habit of …

¹**hebben** /hɛbə(n)/ (had, heeft gehad) 1 have (got), own: *iets bij zich ~* be carrying sth., have sth. with (*or:* on) one; *geduld ~* be patient; *iets moeten ~* need sth. 2 have: *die pantoffels heb ik van mijn vrouw* I got those slippers from my wife; *van wie heb je dat?* who told (*or:* gave) you that? 3 (+ aan) be of use (to): *je weet niet wat je aan hem hebt* you never know where you are with him || *verdriet ~* be sad; *wat heb je?* what's the matter (*or:* wrong) with you?; *wat heb je toch* what's come over you?; *het koud* (or: *warm*) *~* be cold (*or:* hot); *hij heeft iets tegen mij* he has a grudge against me; *ik heb nooit Spaans gehad* I've never learned Spanish; *niets ~ met voetbal* not be into football; *ik moet er niets van ~* I want nothing to do with it; *dat heb je ervan* that's what you get; *daar heb je het al* I told you so; *zo wil ik het ~* that's how I want

it; *iets gedaan* **willen** ~ want (to see) sth.
done; *ik weet niet waar je het* **over** hebt I don't
know what you're talking about; *daar heb ik
het straks nog* **over** I'll come (back) to that
later on (*or:* in a moment); *nu we het daar
toch* **over** ~ now that you mention it …; *hoe
ecologisch* **wil** *je het* ~? just how eco-friendly
do you want it to be?

²**hebben** /hɛbə(n)/ (aux vb, had) have: *had ik
dat maar* **geweten** if (only) I had known
(that); *had dat maar* **gezegd** if only you'd told
me (that); *ik heb met Marco B. op school* **gezeten** I was at school with Marco B.

hebberig /hɛbərəx/ (adj) greedy

hebbes /hɛbəs/ (int) got you; gotcha!; got it

het ¹**Hebreeuws** /hebrews/ Hebrew

²**Hebreeuws** /hebrews/ (adj) Hebrew

de **Hebriden** /hebridə(n)/ (pl) Hebrides

de **hebzucht** /hɛpsʏxt/ greed: **uit** ~ out of
greed

hebzuchtig /hɛpsʏxtəx/ (adj) greedy, avaricious

hecht /hɛxt/ (adj, adv) solid; [fig] strong;
tight; tightly-knit; close(ly)-knit: *een* ~e
vriendschap a close friendship

¹**hechten** /hɛxtə(n)/ (hechtte, heeft gehecht)
1 adhere, stick **2** be attached (to), devoted
(to), adhere (to): *ik hecht niet* **aan** *deze dure
auto* I'm not very attached to this expensive
car

²**hechten** /hɛxtə(n)/ (hechtte, heeft gehecht)
1 stitch, suture: *een* **wond** ~ sew up, stitch a
wound **2** attach, fasten, (af)fix: *een* **prijskaartje** *aan iets* ~ put a price tag on sth. **3** attach: **waarde** (*or:* **belang**) *aan iets* ~ attach
value (*or:* importance) to sth.

zich ³**hechten** /hɛxtə(n)/ (hechtte zich, heeft zich
gehecht) (+ aan) become attached to, cling
to: *hij hecht zich gemakkelijk* **aan** *mensen* he
gets attached to people easily

de **hechtenis** /hɛxtənɪs/ **1** custody, detention:
voorlopige ~ preventive custody, detention
on remand **2** [Dutch] imprisonment, prison

de **hechting** /hɛxtɪŋ/ (pl: -en) stitches, su-
ture(s): *de* ~en **verwijderen** take out the
stitches

de **hechtpleister** /hɛxtplɛɪstər/ (pl: -s) adhesive plaster

de **hectare** /hɛktarə/ (pl: -n) hectare

hectisch /hɛktis/ (adj, adv) hectic

het **hectogram** /hɛktoɣrɑm/ hectogram

de **hectoliter** /hɛktolitər/ hectolitre

de **hectometer** /hɛktometər/ hectometre

het ¹**heden** /hedə(n)/ present (day)

²**heden** /hedə(n)/ (adv) [form] today, now-
(adays), at present: **tot op** ~ up to (*or:* till/un-
til) now; **vanaf** ~, *met ingang van* ~ as from
today

hedendaags /hedə(n)daxs/ (adj) contemporary, present-day: *woordenboeken voor* ~
taalgebruik dictionaries of current usage

het **hedonisme** /hedonɪsmə/ (pl: -n) hedonism

¹**heel** /hel/ (adj) **1** intact: *het ei was nog* ~ the
egg was unbroken **2** whole, entire, all: ~ **Engeland** all England; *een* ~ **jaar** a whole year
3 quite a, quite some: *het is een* ~ **eind** *(weg)*
it's a good way (off); *een hele* **tijd** quite some
time

²**heel** /hel/ (adv) **1** very (much), really: *dat is* ~
gewoon that's quite normal; *een* ~ **klein**
beetje a tiny bit; *dat kostte* ~ **wat** *moeite* that
took a great deal of effort; *je weet het* ~
goed! you know perfectly well!; ~ **vaak** very
often (*or:* frequently) **2** completely, entirely,
wholly: *dat is iets* ~ **anders** that's a different
matter altogether

het **heelal** /helɑl/ universe

heelhuids /helhœyts/ (adv) unharmed, unscathed, whole: ~ **terugkomen** return safe
and sound; *er* ~ **afkomen** escape unharmed

de **heelmeester** /helmestər/ (pl: -s) surgeon:
zachte ~*s maken stinkende wonden* [roughly]
desperate diseases need desperate remedies

het **heemraadschap** /hemratsxɑp/ **1** polder
(*or:* dike) board **2** polder (district)

heen /hen/ (adv) **1** gone, away: ~ *en* **weer**
lopen walk/pace up and down (*or:* back and
forth) **2** on the way there, out ‖ *je kunt* **daar**
niet ~ you cannot go there; **langs** *elkaar* ~
praten talk at cross purposes; *je kunt niet* **om**
hem ~ you can't ignore him

het ¹**heengaan** /henɣan/ **1** passing away **2** departure

²**heengaan** /henɣan/ (ging heen, is heengegaan) **1** depart, leave **2** pass away

het **heenkomen** /henkomə(n)/: *een goed* ~
zoeken seek safety in flight

de **heenreis** /henrɛis/ way there, outward
journey, journey out

de **heenwedstrijd** /henwɛtstrɛɪt/ (pl: -en)
[Belg] first game (*or:* match)

de **heenweg** /henwɛx/ way there, way out

de **heer** /her/ (pl: heren) **1** man **2** Mr; Sir; gentlemen: **dames** *en heren!* ladies and gentlemen! **3** gentleman: *een* **echte** ~ a real gentleman **4** Lord: *als de Heer het* **wil** God (*or:* the
Lord) willing **5** lord, master: *mijn* **oude** ~ my
old man **6** [cards] king

heerlijk /herlək/ (adj, adv) **1** delicious, gorgeous **2** delightful, lovely, wonderful, splendid: *het is een* ~ **gevoel** it feels great

de **heerschappij** /hersxɑpɛi/ dominion, mastery, rule

heersen /hersə(n)/ (heerste, heeft geheerst)
1 rule (over); reign **2** dominate **3** be, be
prevalent: *er heerst griep* there's a lot of flu
about

heersend /hersənt/ (adj) ruling, prevailing:
de ~*e* **klassen** the ruling class(es); *de* ~*e* **mode**
the current fashion

de **heerser** /hersər/ (pl: -s) ruler

heerszuchtig /hersʏxtəx/ (adj) imperious,

domineering

hees /hes/ (adj) hoarse: *een hese **keel** a sore
throat

de **heesheid** /heshɛit/ hoarseness; huskiness

de **heester** /hestər/ (pl: -s) shrub

heet /het/ (adj) **1** hot: *een hete **adem** a fiery
breath; *in het ~st van de strijd* in the thick (or:
heat) of the battle; *~ van de **naald** up-to-the-
minute, latest **2** [fig] hot; heated; fiery
3 hot, spicy: *hete **kost** spicy food **4** [inform]
hot, horny

heetgebakerd /hetχəba̱kərt/ (adj) hot-
tempered, quick-tempered

de **heethoofd** /hethoft/ (pl: -en) hot-head,
hot-heated person

de **hefboom** /hɛvbom/ (pl: hefbomen) lever

de **hefbrug** /hɛvbrɣ/ (pl: -gen) **1** (vertical) lift
bridge **2** (hydraulic) lift

heffen /hɛfə(n)/ (hief, heeft geheven) **1** lift,
raise: *het glas ~* raise one's glass (to), drink
(to) **2** levy, impose: *belasting ~* levy taxes (on
s.o.)

de **heffing** /hɛfɪŋ/ (pl: -en) levy, charge

het **heft** /hɛft/ (pl: -en) handle; haft; hilt: *het ~ in
handen **hebben** be in control, command

heftig /hɛftəχ/ (adj, adv) violent; fierce; furious; intense; severe; heated: *~ **protesteren**
protest vigorously

de **heftruck** /hɛftryk/ (pl: -s) fork-lift truck

de **heg** /hɛχ/ (pl: -gen) hedge

de **heggenschaar** /hɛɣə(n)sχar/ (pl: -scharen)
garden shears, hedge trimmer

de **hei** /hɛi/ (pl: -en) **1** heath(land) **2** [bot]
heather

de **heibel** /hɛibəl/ row, racket

de **heide** /hɛidə/ heath

de **heidedag** /hɛidədɑχ/ policy day

de **heiden** /hɛidə(n)/ (pl: -en) heathen, pagan

heidens /hɛidəns/ (adj, adv) **1** heathen, pagan **2** atrocious, abominable; infernal; rotten

heien /hɛiə(n)/ (heide, heeft geheid) drive
(piles)

heiig /hɛiəχ/ (adj) [Dutch] hazy

het **heil** /hɛil/ good: *ik zie er **geen** ~ in* I do not see
the point of it ‖ *het **Leger** des Heils* the Salvation Army

de **Heiland** /hɛilɑnt/ Saviour

de **heilbot** /hɛilbot/ (pl: -ten) halibut

heilig /hɛiləχ/ (adj) holy, sacred: *~e **koe** sacred cow; *de Heilige **Schrift** (Holy) Scripture,
Holy Writ; *de Heilige **Stoel** the Holy See; *hem
is niets ~* nothing is sacred to him; *die prijs is
voor mij **niet** ~* that price is negotiable, as far
as I'm concerned; *iem. ~ **verklaren** canonize
s.o.

het **heiligdom** /hɛiləχdom/ (pl: -men) sanctuary

de **heilige** /hɛiləɣə/ (pl: -n) saint

heiligen /hɛiləɣə(n)/: *het **doel** heiligt de middelen* the end justifies the means

het **heiligenbeeld** /hɛiləɣə(n)belt/ (pl: -en)

image of a saint, holy figure

de **heiligschennis** /hɛiləχsχɛnɪs/ sacrilege,
desecration

heilloos /hɛilos/ (adj, adv) fatal, disastrous

heilzaam /hɛilzam/ (adj) **1** curative, healing; wholesome; healthful **2** salutary, beneficial: *een heilzame **werking** (or: **invloed**) hebben* have a beneficial effect (or: influence)

heimelijk /hɛiməlǝk/ (adj, adv) secret; clandestine; surreptitious; sneaking

het **heimwee** /hɛimwe/ homesickness: *ik kreeg
~ (naar)* I became homesick (for)

Hein /hɛin/: *Magere ~* the Grim Reaper

heinde /hɛində/ (adv): *van ~ en **verre** from
far and near (or: wide)

de **heipaal** /hɛipal/ (pl: heipalen) pile

het **hek** /hɛk/ (pl: -ken) **1** fence; barrier: [fig] *het
~ is van de dam* things are getting out of hand
2 gate; wicket(-gate)

de **hekel** /hɛkəl/ hackle ‖ *een ~ aan iem. (iets)
hebben* hate s.o. (sth.)

hekelen /hɛkələ(n)/ (hekelde, heeft gehe-
keld) criticize, denounce

het **hekje** /hɛkjə/ (pl: -s) **1** small gate (or: door)
2 [comp, telecom] hash; [Am] number sign

de **hekkensluiter** /hɛkə(n)slœytər/ (pl: -s) last
comer: *hij (or: is) de ~ op de ranglijst* he is last
on the list, he is at the bottom of the list

de **heks** /hɛks/ (pl: -en) **1** witch **2** shrew **3** hag

de **heksenjacht** /hɛksə(n)jɑχt/ (pl: -en) witch-
hunt

de **heksenketel** /hɛksə(n)ketəl/ (pl: -s) bedlam, pandemonium

de **heksenkring** /hɛksə(n)krɪŋ/ (pl: -en) fairy
ring

de **heksentoer** /hɛksə(n)tur/ (pl: -en) tough
job, complicated job

de **hekserij** /hɛksərɛi/ (pl: -en) sorcery, witchcraft

het **hekwerk** /hɛkwɛrk/ (pl: -en) fencing; railings

de **¹hel** /hɛl/ hell

²hel /hɛl/ (adj, adv) vivid, bright

helaas /helas/ (adv) unfortunately: *~ **kunnen** wij u niet helpen* I'm afraid (or: sorry) we
can't help you

de **held** /hɛlt/ (pl: -en) hero ‖ *hij is geen ~ in rekenen* he is not much at figures

de **heldendaad** /hɛldə(n)dat/ (pl: -daden) heroic deed (or: feat), act of heroism; exploit

het **heldendicht** /hɛldə(n)dɪχt/ (pl: -en) heroic
poem, epic poem, epic

de **heldendood** /hɛldə(n)dot/ heroic death: *de
~ **sterven** die a hero, die a hero's death

de **heldenmoed** /hɛldəmut/ heroism: *met ~
heroically, with heroism

de **heldenrol** /hɛldə(n)rol/ hero's part (or: role)

helder /hɛldər/ (adj, adv) **1** clear: *een ~e **lach**
a ringing laugh **2** clear, bright: *~ **wit** (or:
groen) brilliant white, bright green **3** clear,
lucid ‖ *zo ~ **als** kristal* (or: glas) as clear as crys-

tal, crystal-clear

de **helderheid** /hɛldərhɛit/ **1** clearness, clarity **2** brightness, vividness **3** brightness **4** clarity, lucidity

helderziend /hɛldərzint/ (adj) clairvoyant

de **helderziende** /hɛldərzində/ (pl: -n) clairvoyant: ik **ben** toch geen ~ I'm not a mind-reader

de **helderziendheid** /hɛldərzinthɛit/ clairvoyance, second sight

heldhaftig /hɛlthɑftəχ/ (adj, adv) heroic, valiant

de **heldin** /hɛldɪn/ (pl: -nen) heroine

de **heleboel** /helǝbul/ (quite) a lot, a whole lot: **een** ~ mensen zouden het niet met je eens zijn an awful lot of people wouldn't agree with you

helemaal /helǝmal/ (adv) **1** completely, entirely: ik heb het ~ **alleen** gedaan I did it all by myself; ~ **nat** zijn be wet through; **ben** je nu ~ gek geworden? are you completely out of your mind?; ~ **niets** nothing at all; het kan mij ~ **niets** schelen I couldn't care less; ~ **niet** absolutely not; **niet** ~ juist not quite correct; ~ **in** het begin right at the beginning (or: start) **2** right; all the way: ~ **bovenaan** right at the top; ~ in het noorden way up in the north

¹**helen** /helǝ(n)/ (heelde, is geheeld) heal: de **wond** heelt langzaam the wound is healing slowly

²**helen** /helǝ(n)/ (heelde, heeft geheeld) **1** [law] receive **2** [med] heal: de tijd heelt alle **wonden** time cures all things; time is the great healer

de **heler** /helǝr/ (pl: -s) receiver; [fig] fence

de **helft** /hɛlft/ (pl: -en) half: ieder de ~ **betalen** pay half each, go halves, go Dutch; **meer** dan de ~ more than half; de ~ **minder** half as much (or: many); de ~ **van** tien is vijf half of ten is five; de **tweede** ~ van een wedstrijd the second half of a match

de **helikopter** /helikɔptǝr/ (pl: -s) helicopter; chopper

de **heling** /helɪŋ/ receiving

het **helium** /helijʏm/ helium

hellen /hɛlǝ(n)/ (helde, heeft geheld) slope, lean (over), slant: de **muur** helt naar links the wall is leaning

het **hellenisme** /hɛlenɪsmǝ/ Hellenism

de **helleveeg** /hɛləveχ/ (pl: -vegen) shrew, hellcat

de **helling** /hɛlɪŋ/ (pl: -en) **1** slope, incline; ramp **2** inclination

de **hell's angel** /hɛlsɛndʒǝl/ Hells Angel

de **helm** /hɛlm/ (pl: -en) helmet; hard hat

het **helmgras** /hɛlmɣrɑs/ marram (grass)

help /hɛlp/ (int): **lieve** ~ oh, Lord/dear!, good heavens!, dear me!

de **helpdesk** /hɛlbdɛsk/ (pl: -s) help desk

helpen /hɛlpǝ(n)/ (hielp, heeft geholpen) **1** help, aid: kun je mij **aan** honderd euro ~? can

you let me have a hundred euros?; help! help! **2** attend to: welke **specialist** heeft u geholpen? which specialist did you see? (or: have?); u **wordt** morgen geholpen you are having your operation tomorrow **3** help, assist: iem. een **handje** ~ give (or: lend) s.o. a hand; ik help het je **hopen** I'll keep my fingers crossed for you; help **me** eraan denken, wil je? remind me, will you? **4** help (out): iem. **aan** een baan ~ get s.o. fixed up with a job **5** help, serve: wordt u **al** geholpen? are you being served? ‖ **kan** ik 't ~ dat hij zich zo gedraagt? is it my fault if he behaves like that?; **wat** helpt het? what good would it do?, what is the use?; dat helpt **tegen** hoofdpijn that's good for a headache

de **helper** /hɛlpǝr/ (pl: -s) helper, assistant

hels /hɛls/ (adj, adv) infernal: een ~ **karwei** a (or: the) devil of a job

hem /hɛm/ (pers pron) him; it: dit boek is van ~ this book is his; vrienden **van** ~ friends of his ‖ dat is het ~ **nu** juist that's just it (or: the point)

het **hemd** /hɛmt/ (pl: -en) **1** vest; [Am] undershirt: iem. het ~ van zijn lijf **vragen** want to know everything (from s.o.); pester s.o. (with questions); [fig] iem. **in** zijn ~ zetten make s.o. look a fool **2** shirt

de **hemdsmouw** /hɛm(t)smɑu/ (pl: -en) shirt-sleeve: **in** ~en in one's shirt-sleeves

de **hemel** /hemǝl/ (pl: -en) sky, heaven(s): hij heeft er ~ en **aarde** om bewogen he moved heaven and earth for it; een **heldere** (or: **blauwe, bewolkte**) ~ a clear (or: blue, cloudy) sky; Onze Vader die **in** de ~en zijt Our Father who (or: which) art in heaven; hij was in de **zevende** ~ he was in seventh heaven

het **hemellichaam** /hemǝlɪχam/ (pl: -lichamen) heavenly body, celestial body

hemels /hemǝls/ (adj, adv) sublime, divine

hemelsblauw /hemǝlzblɑu/ (adj) sky-blue

hemelsbreed /hemǝlzbret/ (adj, adv) **1** vast, enormous **2** as the crow flies, in a straight line

hemeltergend /hemǝltɛrɣǝnt/ (adj, adv) outrageous

Hemelvaartsdag /hemǝlvartsdɑχ/ (pl: -en) Ascension Day

de **hemofilie** /hemofili/ haemophilia

de ¹**hen** /hɛn/ (pl: -nen) hen

²**hen** /hɛn/ (pers pron) them: ik heb ~ nog niet **ontmoet** I haven't met them yet; dit boek is **van** ~ this book is theirs; vrienden **van** ~ friends of theirs

het/de **hendel** /hɛndǝl/ (pl: -s) handle, lever

de **hengel** /hɛŋǝl/ (pl: -s) fishing rod

de **hengelaar** /hɛŋǝlar/ (pl: -s) angler

hengelen /hɛŋǝlǝ(n)/ (hengelde, heeft gehengeld) angle, fish

het **hengsel** /hɛŋsǝl/ (pl: -s) **1** handle **2** hinge

de **hengst** /hɛŋst/ (pl: -en) stallion; stud (horse)

de **hennep** /hɛnəp/ hemp; cannabis

de **hennepkwekerij** /hɛnəpkwekərɛi/ (pl: -en) grow house, cannabis farm

de **hens** /hɛns/ (pl): *alle ~ aan dek!* all hands on deck!

de **hepatitis** /hepatitɪs/ hepatitis

her /hɛr/ (adv) hither, here: *~ en der* here and there; *~ en der verspreid liggen* lie scattered all over the place

de **heraldiek** /hɛraldik/ heraldry

het **herbarium** /hɛrbarijʏm/ (pl: -s, herbaria) herbarium

herbebossen /hɛrbəbɔsə(n)/ (herbeboste, heeft herbebost) reafforest; [esp Am] reforest

herbeleven /hɛrbəlevə(n)/ (herbeleefde, heeft herbeleefd) relive

herbenoemen /hɛrbənumə(n)/ (herbenoemde, heeft herbenoemd) reappoint

de **herberg** /hɛrbɛrχ/ (pl: -en) inn, tavern

herbergen /hɛrbɛrɣə(n)/ (herbergde, heeft geherbergd) accommodate, house; harbour: *de zaal kan 2000 mensen ~* the hall seats 2000 people

de **herbergier** /hɛrbɛrɣir/ (pl: -s) innkeeper, publican, victualler

herbewapenen /hɛrbəwapənə(n)/ (herbewapende, heeft herbewapend) rearm, remilitarize

de **herbivoor** /hɛrbivor/ (pl: herbivoren) herbivore

herboren /hɛrborə(n)/ (adj) reborn, born again

de **herbouw** /hɛrbɑu/ rebuilding, reconstruction

herbouwen /hɛrbɑuwə(n)/ (herbouwde, heeft herbouwd) rebuild, reconstruct

herdenken /hɛrdɛŋkə(n)/ (herdacht, heeft herdacht) commemorate

de **herdenking** /hɛrdɛŋkɪŋ/ (pl: -en) commemoration

de **herder** /hɛrdər/ (pl: -s) **1** cowherd; shepherd **2** pastor

de **herdershond** /hɛrdərshɔnt/ (pl: -en) sheepdog; Alsatian; [Am] German shepherd (dog)

de **herdruk** /hɛrdrʏk/ (pl: -ken) (new) edition; reprint

herdrukken /hɛrdrʏkə(n)/ (herdrukte, heeft herdrukt) reprint

de **heremiet** /herəmit/ (pl: -en) hermit

het **herenakkoord** /herə(n)ɑkort/ (pl: -en) gentleman's agreement

het **herendubbel** /herə(n)dʏbəl/ men's doubles

het **herenenkelspel** /herə(n)ɛŋkəlspɛl/ men's singles

de **herenfiets** /herə(n)fits/ (pl: -en) men's bike (*or*: bicycle)

het **herenhuis** /herə(n)hœys/ (pl: -huizen) mansion, (imposing) town house, (desirable) residence

herenigen /hɛrenəɣə(n)/ (herenigde, heeft herenigd) reunite; reunify

de **hereniging** /hɛrenəɣɪŋ/ (pl: -en) reunification, reunion

de **herenkapper** /herə(n)kɑpər/ (pl: -s) men's hairdresser's

de **herenkleding** /herə(n)kledɪŋ/ menswear, men's clothes (*or*: clothing)

het **herexamen** /hɛrɛksamə(n)/ (pl: -s) re-examination, resit

de **herfst** /hɛrfst/ autumn; [Am] fall: *in de ~ in* (the) autumn, in the fall

de **herfstkleur** /hɛrfstklør/ (pl: -en) autumn(al) colour; [Am] fall colour

de **herfstvakantie** /hɛrfstfakɑnsi/ (pl: -s) autumn half-term (holiday); [Am] fall break, mid-term break

het **hergebruik** /hɛrɣəbrœyk/ **1** reuse **2** recycling

hergebruiken /hɛrɣəbrœykə(n)/ (hergebruikte, heeft hergebruikt) reuse; recycle

hergroeperen /hɛrɣrupərə(n)/ (hergroepeerde, heeft gehergroepeerd) regroup, reform

herhaald /hɛrhalt/ (adj) repeated: *~e pogingen doen* make repeated attempts

herhaaldelijk /hɛrhaldələk/ (adv) repeatedly: *dat komt ~ voor* that happens time and again

¹**herhalen** /hɛrhalə(n)/ (herhaalde, heeft herhaald) repeat, redo; revise; [Am] review: *iets in het kort ~* summarize sth.

zich ²**herhalen** /hɛrhalə(n)/ (herhaalde zich, heeft zich herhaald) repeat o.s.; recur

de **herhaling** /hɛrhalɪŋ/ (pl: -en) **1** recurrence, repetition; replay; repeat; rerun: *voor ~ vatbaar zijn* bear repetition (*or*: repeating); *dat is niet voor ~ vatbaar* I wouldn't do that again, once is (more than) enough **2** repetition; revision; [Am] review: *in ~en vervallen* repeat o.s.

de **herhalingscursus** /hɛrhalɪŋskʏrzʏs/ refresher course

het **herhalingsrecept** /hɛrhalɪŋsrəsɛpt/ (pl: -en) repeat prescription

het **herhalingsteken** /hɛrhalɪŋstekə(n)/ (pl: -s) [mus] repeat (mark)

herindelen /hɛrɪndelə(n)/ (herindeelde, heeft geherindeeld) regroup

de **herindeling** /hɛrɪndelɪŋ/ (pl: -en) redivision, regrouping

¹**herinneren** /hɛrɪnərə(n)/ (herinnerde, heeft herinnerd) remind, recall: *die geur herinnerde mij aan mijn jeugd* that smell reminded me of my youth; *herinner mij eraan dat ...* remind me that ... (*or*: to ...)

zich ²**herinneren** /hɛrɪnərə(n)/ (herinnerde zich, heeft zich herinnerd) remember, recall: *kun je je die ler nog ~?* do you remember that Irishman?; *als ik (het) me goed herinner* if I remember correctly (*or*: rightly); *zich iets vaag ~*

have a vague recollection of sth.; *voor zover ik mij herinner* as far as I can remember

de **herinnering** /hɛrɪnərɪŋ/ (pl: -en) **1** recollection, remembrance: *iets in ~ brengen* recall sth.; *in ~ roepen* (*or:* call) to mind **2** memory: *iets in zijn ~ voor zich zien* see sth. before one **3** memory, reminiscence: *ter ~ aan* in memory of **4** souvenir, reminder || *een tweede ~ van de bibliotheek* a second reminder from the library

herintreden /hɛrɪntredə(n)/ (trad herin, is heringetreden) return to work || *een ~de vrouw* a (woman) returner

herinvoeren /hɛrɪnvurə(n)/ reintroduce, bring back: *de dienstplicht ~ reintroduce* military service

de **herkansing** /hɛrkɑnsɪŋ/ (pl: -en) repêchage; extra heat

herkauwen /hɛrkɑuwə(n)/ (herkauwde, heeft herkauwd) ruminate

de **herkauwer** /hɛrkɑuwər/ (pl: -s) ruminant

herkenbaar /hɛrkɛmbar/ (adj) recognizable: *een herkenbare situatie* a familiar situation

herkennen /hɛrkɛnə(n)/ (herkende, heeft herkend) recognize, identify, spot: *ik herkende hem aan zijn manier van lopen* I recognized him by his walk; *iem. ~ als de dader* identify s.o. as the culprit

de **herkenning** /hɛrkɛnɪŋ/ (pl: -en) recognition, identification

de **herkenningsmelodie** /hɛrkɛnɪŋsmelodi/ (pl: -ën) signature tune, theme song

het **herkenningsteken** /hɛrkɛnɪŋstekə(n)/ (pl: -s) distinguishing (*or:* identifying) mark

de **herkeuring** /hɛrkørɪŋ/ (pl: -en) re-examination, reinspection

herkiesbaar /hɛrkizbar/ (adj) eligible for re-election

herkiezen /hɛrkizə(n)/ (herkoos, heeft herkozen) re-elect

de **herkomst** /hɛrkɔmst/ (pl: -en) origin, source: *het land van ~* the country of origin

herleidbaar /hɛrlɛidbar/ (adj) reducible (to): *die breuk is niet ~* that fraction is irreducible

herleiden /hɛrlɛidə(n)/ (herleidde, heeft herleid) reduce (to), convert (into): *een breuk ~ reduce* (to) a fraction

herleven /hɛrlevə(n)/ (herleefde, is herleefd) revive: *~d fascisme* resurgent fascism

herlezen /hɛrlezə(n)/ (herlas, heeft herlezen) reread

de **hermafrodiet** /hɛrmafrodit/ (pl: -en) hermaphrodite

de **¹hermelijn** /hɛrməlɛin/ (pl: -en) [animal] ermine

het **²hermelijn** /hɛrməlɛin/ [fur] ermine

hermetisch /hɛrmetis/ (adj, adv) hermetic: *~ gesloten* hermetically sealed

hernemen /hɛrnemə(n)/ (hernam, heeft

hernomen) resume, regain

de **hernia** /hɛrnija/ (pl: -'s) slipped disc

hernieuwen /hɛrniwə(n)/ (hernieuwde, heeft hernieuwd) renew: *een hernieuwde belangstelling voor rock-'n-roll* a renewed interest in rock 'n' roll; *met hernieuwde kracht* with renewed strength

de **heroïne** /herowinə/ heroin

heroïsch /herowis/ (adj, adv) heroic

herontdekken /hɛrɔndɛkə(n)/ (herontdekte, heeft herontdekt) rediscover

heropenen /hɛropənə(n)/ (heropende, heeft heropend) reopen

de **heropvoeding** /hɛrɔpfudɪŋ/ re-education

heroriënteren /hɛrorijɛnterə(n)/ (heroriënteerde, heeft geheroriënteerd) reorient(ate)

heroveren /hɛrovərə(n)/ (heroverde, heeft heroverd) recapture; recover; retake; regain: *hij wilde zijn oude plaats ~* he wanted to regain his old seat (*or:* place)

de **herovering** /hɛrovərɪŋ/ recapture

heroverwegen /hɛrovərweɣə(n)/ (heroverwoog, heeft heroverwogen) reconsider, rethink

de **herpes** /hɛrpɛs/ herpes

de **herrie** /hɛri/ **1** noise, din, racket: *maak niet zo'n ~* don't make such a racket **2** bustle; commotion; turmoil; fuss: *~ schoppen* make trouble

de **herriemaker** /hɛrimakər/ (pl: -s) noisy person

de **herrieschopper** /hɛrisχɔpər/ (pl: -s) troublemaker

herrijzen /hɛrɛizə(n)/ (herrees, is herrezen) rise again: *hij is als uit de dood herrezen* it is as if he has come back from the dead

de **herrijzenis** /hɛrɛizənɪs/ resurrection

herroepen /hɛrupə(n)/ (herriep, heeft herroepen) revoke; repeal; retract; reverse

herscheppen /hɛrsχɛpə(n)/ (herschiep, heeft herschapen) transform, convert

herscholen /hɛrsχolə(n)/ (herschoolde, heeft herschoold) retrain

herschrijven /hɛrsχrɛivə(n)/ (herschreef, heeft herschreven) rewrite

de **hersenbloeding** /hɛrsə(n)bludɪŋ/ (pl: -en) cerebral haemorrhage

de **hersenen** /hɛrsənə(n)/ (pl) brain

de **hersenhelft** /hɛrsə(n)hɛlft/ (pl: -en) (cerebral) hemisphere, half of the brain

het **herseninfarct** /hɛrsə(n)ɪnfɑrkt/ (pl: -en) cerebral infarction

het **hersenletsel** /hɛrsə(n)lɛtsəl/ brain damage

de **hersens** /hɛrsəns/ (pl) **1** brain(s): *een goed stel ~ hebben* have a good head on one's shoulders; *hoe haal je het in je ~!* have you gone off your rocker? **2** skull: *iem. de ~ inslaan* beat s.o.'s brains out

de **hersenschim** /hɛrsə(n)sχɪm/ (pl: -men) chim(a)era: *~men najagen* run after (*or:*

chase) a shadow

de **hersenschudding** /hɛrsə(n)sχʏdɪŋ/ (pl: -en) concussion

de **hersenspoeling** /hɛrsə(n)spulɪŋ/ (pl: -en) brainwashing

de **hersenvliesontsteking** /hɛrsə(n)vlisɔntstekɪŋ/ (pl: -en) meningitis

herstarten /hɛrstɑrtə(n)/ (herstartte, heeft herstart) start again, restart; reboot

het **herstel** /hɛrstɛl/ **1** repair, mending; rectification; correction **2** recovery; convalescence; recuperation: *het ~ van de economie* the recovery of the economy; *voor ~ van zijn gezondheid* to recuperate, to convalesce **3** restoration

herstelbaar /hɛrstɛlbar/ (adj) reparable

¹**herstellen** /hɛrstɛlə(n)/ (herstelde, is hersteld) recover, recuperate: *snel* (or: *goed*) *~ van een ziekte* recover quickly (or: well) from an illness

²**herstellen** /hɛrstɛlə(n)/ (herstelde, heeft hersteld) **1** repair, mend; restore **2** restore; re-establish: *de rust ~* restore quiet; *een gebruik in ere ~* re-establish a custom **3** right; repair; rectify; correct: *een onrecht ~* right a wrong; *de heer Blaak, herstel: Braak* Mr Blaak, correction: Braak

de **herstelwerkzaamheden** /hɛrstɛlwɛrksamhedə(n)/ (pl) repairs

herstructureren /hɛrstrʏktyrerə(n)/ (herstructureerde, heeft geherstructureerd) restructure, remodel, reorganize

de **herstructurering** /hɛrstrʏktyrerɪŋ/ restructuring, reorganization

het **hert** /hɛrt/ (pl: -en) deer; red deer

de **hertenkamp** /hɛrtə(n)kɑmp/ (pl: -en) deer park, deer forest

de **hertog** /hɛrtɔχ/ (pl: -en) duke

het **hertogdom** /hɛrtɔχdɔm/ (pl: -men) duchy, dukedom

de **hertogin** /hɛrtoɣɪn/ (pl: -nen) duchess

hertrouwen /hɛrtrɑuwə(n)/ (hertrouwde, is hertrouwd) remarry, marry again

hervatten /hɛrvɑtə(n)/ (hervatte, heeft hervat) resume, continue, restart: *onderhandelingen ~* resume (or: reopen) negotiations; *het spel ~* resume (or: continue) the game; *het werk ~* return to work, go back to work

de **herverdeling** /hɛrvərdelɪŋ/ (pl: -en) redistribution, reorganization, reshuffle

de **herverkaveling** /hɛrvərkavəlɪŋ/ reallocation (of land)

herverzekeren /hɛrvərzekərə(n)/ (herverzekerde, heeft herverzekerd) reinsure

hervormd /hɛrvɔrmt/ (adj) **1** reformed **2** [rel] Reformed; Protestant [as opposed to Catholicism]: *de ~e kerk* the Reformed Church

hervormen /hɛrvɔrmə(n)/ (hervormde, heeft hervormd) reform

de **hervormer** /hɛrvɔrmər/ (pl: -s) reformer

de **hervorming** /hɛrvɔrmɪŋ/ (pl: -en) **1** reformation **2** reform

herwaarderen /hɛrwardərə(n)/ (herwaardeerde, heeft geherwaardeerd) revalue; [fig] reassess

de **herwaardering** /hɛrwardərɪŋ/ revaluation, reassessment

herwinnen /hɛrwɪnə(n)/ (herwon, heeft herwonnen) recover, regain

herzien /hɛrzin/ (herzag, heeft herzien) revise: *een nieuwe, ~e uitgave* a new, revised edition || *een beslissing ~* reconsider a decision

de **herziening** /hɛrzinɪŋ/ (pl: -en) revision, review: *een ~ van de grondwet* an amendment to the constitution

de **hes** /hɛs/ (pl: -sen) smock, blouse

het **hesje** /hɛʃə/ (pl: -s) vest; [sport] training bib (or: vest): *een reflecterend ~* a safety vest

de **hesp** /hɛsp/ (pl: -en) [Belg] ham

¹**het** /ət/ (pron) it: *ik denk* (or: *hoop*) *~* I think (or: hope) so; *wie is ~? ben jij ~?* who is it? is that you? yes, it is me; *zij waren ~ die ...* it were they who ...; *als jij ~ zegt* if you say so; *~ kind heeft honger; geef ~ een boterham* the child is hungry; give him (or: her) a sandwich; *de machine doet ~* the machine works; *hoe gaat ~? ~ gaat* how are you? I'm all right (or: O.K.); *wat geeft ~? wat zou ~?* what does it matter? who cares?; *~ regent* it is raining

²**het** /ət/ (art) the: *in ~ zwart gekleed* dressed in black; *Nederland is ~ land van de tulpen* Holland is the country for tulips; *die vind ik ~ leukst* that's the one I like best; *zij was er ~ eerst* she was there first

¹**heten** /hetə(n)/ (heette, heeft geheten) be called (or: named): *een jongen, David geheten* a boy by the name of David; *het boek heet ...* the book is called ...; *hoe heet dat?, hoe heet dat in het Arabisch?* what is that called?, what is that in Arabic? (or: the Arabic for that?)

²**heten** /hetə(n)/ (heette, heeft geheten) bid: *ik heet u welkom* I bid you welcome

de **heterdaad** /hetərdat/: *iem. op ~ betrappen* catch s.o. in the act, catch s.o. red-handed

de ¹**hetero** /hetəro/ (pl: -'s) hetero

²**hetero** /hetəro/ (adj) hetero, straight

heterogeen /hetəroɣen/ (adj) heterogeneous

de ¹**heteroseksueel** /hetərosɛksywel/ (pl: -seksuelen) heterosexual

²**heteroseksueel** /hetərosɛksywel/ (adj) heterosexual

hetgeen /ətχen/ (pron) **1** that which, what: *ik blijf bij ~ ik gezegd heb* I stand by what I said **2** which: *hij kon niet komen, ~ hij betreurde* he could not come, which he regretted

de **hetze** /hɛtsə/ (pl: -s) witch hunt: *een ~ voeren tegen* conduct a witch hunt (or: smear campaign) against

hetzelfde /ətsɛlvdə/ (dem pron) the same: *wie zou niet ~ doen?* who wouldn't (do the same)?; *het is (blijft) mij ~* it's all the same to me; *(van) ~* (the) same to you

hetzij /ətsɛi/ (conj) either, whether: *~ warm of koud* either hot or cold

heuglijk /høxlək/ (adj) happy, glad, joyful

heulen /højlə(n)/ (heulde, heeft geheuld) collaborate, be in league with

de **heup** /høp/ (pl: -en) hip

het **heupgewricht** /høpxəvrɪxt/ (pl: -en) hip joint

heupwiegen /høpwiɣə(n)/ (heupwiegde, heeft geheupwiegd) sway (*or:* wiggle) one's hips, waggle

heus /høs/ (adj, adv) real, true: *een ~e diamant* a real (*or:* genuine) diamond; *hij doet het ~ wel* he is sure to do it; [hum] *maar niet ~!* but not really!, just kidding!

de **heuvel** /høvəl/ (pl: -s) hill; [small] hillock; mound

heuvelachtig /høvəlɑxtəx/ (adj) hilly

de **heuvelrug** /høvəlrʏx/ (pl: -gen) **1** ridge **2** range (of hills)

¹**hevig** /heːvəx/ (adj) **1** violent, intense: *~e angst* acute terror; *een ~e brand* a raging fire; *een ~e koorts* a raging fever; *~e pijnen* severe pains **2** violent, vehement, fierce: *onder ~ protest* under strong (*or:* vehement) protest; *~e uitvallen* violent outbursts

²**hevig** /heːvəx/ (adv) violently, fiercely, intensely: *hij was ~ verontwaardigd* he was highly indignant; *~ bloeden* bleed profusely; *zij snikte ~* she cried her eyes out

de **hevigheid** /heːvəxhɛit/ violence, vehemence, intensity, fierceness, acuteness

de **hiel** /hil/ (pl: -en) heel: *iem. op de ~en zitten* be (close) on s.o.'s heels; [fig] *de ~en lichten* take to one's heels

de **hielenlikker** /hilə(n)lɪkər/ (pl: -s) bootlick(er)

hier /hir/ (adv) **1** here: *dit meisje ~* this girl; *ik ben ~ nieuw* I'm new here; *wie hebben we ~!* look who's here!; *~ is het gebeurd* this is where it happened; *~ is de krant* here's the newspaper; *~ staat dat ...* it says here that ...; *~ of daar* vinden wij wel wat we'll find sth. somewhere or other; *het zit me tot ~* I've had it up to here **2** this: *~ moet je het mee doen* you'll have to make do with this

hieraan /hiraːn/ (adv) to this, at/on (*or:* by, from) this: *~ valt niet te twijfelen* there is no doubt about this

hierachter /hirɑxtər/ (adv) behind this; after this: *~ ligt een grote tuin* there is a large garden at the back

de **hiërarchie** /hijərɑrxi/ (pl: -ën) hierarchy

hiërarchisch /hijərɑrxis/ (adj, adv) hierarchic(al)

hierbeneden /hirbəneːdə(n)/ (adv) down here

hierbij /hirbɛi/ (adv) at this, with this; herewith; hereby: *~ bericht ik u, dat ...* I hereby inform you that ...; *~ komt nog dat hij ...* in addition (to this), he ...

hierbinnen /hirbɪnə(n)/ (adv) in here, inside

hierboven /hirboːvə(n)/ (adv) up here; above: *~ woont een drummer* a drummer lives upstairs

hierbuiten /hirbœytə(n)/ (adv) outside

hierdoor /hirdoːr/ (adv) **1** through here, through this, by doing so: *~ wil hij ervoor zorgen dat ...* by doing so he wants to ensure that ... **2** because of this: *~ werd ik opgehouden* this held me up

hierheen /hirheːn/ (adv) (over) here, this way: *op de weg ~* on the way here; *hij kwam helemaal ~ om ...* he came all this way ...

hierin /hirɪn/ (adv) in here, within, in this

hierlangs /hirlɑŋs/ (adv) past here, along here, by here

hiermee /hirmeː/ (adv) with this, by this: *in verband ~* in this connection

hierna /hirnaː/ (adv) **1** after this **2** below

hiernaartoe /hirnaːrtuː/ (adv) (over) here: *ze komen ~* they are coming here

hiernaast /hirnaːst/ (adv) next door; alongside: *de illustratie op de bladzijde ~* the illustration on the facing page; *~ hebben ze twee auto's* the next-door neighbours have two cars

het **hiernamaals** /hirnaːmaːls/ hereafter, next world, (great) beyond

de **hiëroglief** /hijəroɣlif/ (pl: -en) hieroglyph; hieroglyphics

hierom /hirɔm/ (adv) **1** (a)round this: *dat ringetje moet ~* that ring belongs around this **2** because of this, for this reason: *~ blijf ik thuis* this is why I'm staying at home

hieromheen /hirɔmheːn/ (adv) (a)round this: *~ loopt een gracht* there is a canal surrounding this

hieronder /hirɔndər/ (adv) **1** under here, underneath, below: *zoals ~ aangegeven* as stated below **2** among these: *~ zijn veel personen van naam* among them there are many people of note ‖ *~ versta ik ...* by this I understand ...

hierop /hirɔp/ (adv) **1** (up)on this: *het komt ~ neer* it comes down to this **2** after this, then

hierover /hiroːvər/ (adv) **1** over this **2** about this, regarding this, on this

hiertegen /hirteːɣə(n)/ (adv) against this

hiertegenover /hirteːɣə(n)oːvər/ (adv) opposite; across the street; over the way

hiertoe /hirtuː/ (adv) **1** (up to) here: *tot ~* so far, up to now **2** to this, for this: *wat heeft u ~ gebracht?* what brought you to do this?

hieruit /hirœyt/ (adv) **1** out of here: *van ~ vertrekken* depart from here **2** from this: *~*

volgt, dat ... it follows (from this) that ...
hiervan /hi̯rvɑn/ (adv) of this
hiervandaan /hirvɑndan̲/ (adv) from here, away
hiervoor /hi̯rvor/ (adv) **1** in front (of this); before this **2** of this: *~ hoeft u niet bang te zijn* you needn't be afraid of this **3** for this purpose, to this end **4** (in exchange, return) for this
de **hifi-installatie** /hɑjfɔ̲jɪnstɑla(t)si/ (pl: -s) hifi (set)
het **higgsdeeltje** /hɪksdelcə/ (pl: -s) Higgs particle (*or:* boson)
de **high five** /hɑjfɑj̲f/ high five
het/de **highlight** /hɑ̲jlɑjt/ (pl: -s) highlight: *de ~s van de rondreis* the highlights of the trip
hightech /hɑjtɛ̲k/ (adj) high-tech, hi-tech
hihi /hihi̲/ (int) ha, ha!
hij /hɛi/ (pers pron) he; it: *iedereen is trots op het werk dat ~ zelf **doet*** everyone is proud of the work they do themselves; *~ **is** het* it's him; *~ **daar*** him over there
hijgen /hɛi̯ɣə(n)/ (hijgde, heeft gehijgd) pant, gasp
de **hijger** /hɛi̯ɣər/ (pl: -s) heavy breather: *ik **had** weer een ~ vandaag* I had another obscene phone-call today
¹**hijgerig** /hɛi̯ɣ̲ərəχ/ (adj) **1** panting, wheezing **2** sensation-hungry, sensationalist: *de ~e **pers*** the sensation-hungry press
²**hijgerig** /hɛi̯ɣ̲ərəχ/ (adv) in gasps
de **hijs** /hɛis/ (pl: -en) whack
hijsen /hɛi̯sə(n)/ (hees, heeft gehesen) **1** hoist, lift: *de **vlag** (in top) ~* hoist (*or:* run up) the flag **2** haul, heave
de **hijskraan** /hɛi̯skran/ (pl: -kranen) crane
de **hik** /hɪk/ (pl: -ken) hiccup
hikken /hɪ̲kə(n)/ (hikte, heeft gehikt) hiccup
|| *tegen iets aan ~* shrink from sth.
de **hilariteit** /hilariˈtɛi̲t/ hilarity, mirth
de **Himalaya** /himalaja̲/ (the) Himalayas
de **hinde** /hɪ̲ndə/ (pl: -n) hind, doe
de **hinder** /hɪ̲ndər/ nuisance, bother; hindrance; obstacle: *het verkeer **ondervindt** veel ~ van de sneeuw* traffic is severely disrupted by the snow
hinderen /hɪ̲ndərə(n)/ (hinderde, heeft gehinderd) impede, hamper, obstruct: *zijn lange jas hinderde hem **bij** het lopen* his long coat got in his way as he walked
de **hinderlaag** /hɪ̲ndərlaχ/ (pl: -lagen) ambush; [fig also] trap: *de vijand in een ~ lokken* lure the enemy into an ambush
¹**hinderlijk** /hɪ̲ndərlək/ (adj) **1** annoying, irritating **2** objectionable, disturbing **3** unpleasant, disagreeable: *ik vind de **warmte** niet ~* the heat does not bother me
²**hinderlijk** /hɪ̲ndərlək/ (adv) annoyingly, blatantly
de **hindernis** /hɪ̲ndərnɪs/ (pl: -sen) obstacle, barrier; [fig also] hindrance; [fig also] imped-

iment
de **hindernisloop** /hɪ̲ndərnɪslop/ (pl: -lopen) steeplechase
de **hinderpaal** /hɪ̲ndərpal/ (pl: -palen) obstacle, impediment
de **Hinderwet** /hɪ̲ndərwɛt/ [Dutch] [roughly] Nuisance Act
de **hindoe** /hɪ̲ndu/ Hindu
het **hindoeïsme** /hɪnduwɪ̲smə/ Hinduism
de **Hindoestaan** /hɪndustan̲/ (pl: Hindoestanen) Hindu(stani)
hinkelen /hɪ̲ŋkələ(n)/ (hinkelde, heeft/is gehinkeld) hop; play hopscotch
hinken /hɪ̲ŋkə(n)/ (hinkte, heeft/is gehinkt) **1** limp, have a limp, walk with a limp, hobble (along) **2** hop
de **hink-stap-sprong** /hɪŋkstɑpspron̲/ triple jump, hop, step and jump
hinniken /hɪ̲nəkə(n)/ (hinnikte, heeft gehinnikt) neigh; whinny
de **hint** /hɪnt/ (pl: -s) hint, tip(-off): *(iem.) een ~ geven* drop (s.o.) a hint
hip /hɪp/ (adj) hip, trendy
de **hiphop** /hɪ̲phɔp/ hip hop
de **hippie** /hɪ̲pi/ (pl: -s) hippie
de **historicus** /hɪstoˈrikʏs/ (pl: historici) historian
de **historie** /hɪstoˈri/ (pl: historiën) **1** history **2** story, anecdote **3** affair, business
historisch /hɪstoˈris/ (adj) **1** historic: *wij beleven een ~ **moment*** we are witnessing a historic moment **2** historical; period: *een ~e **roman*** a historical novel **3** historical, true: *dat **is** ~* that's a historical fact (*or:* a true story)
de **hit** /hɪt/ (pl: -s) hit (record)
de **Hitlergroet** /hi̲tlərɣrut/ Hitler (*or:* Nazi) salute: *de ~ **brengen*** make the Hitler salute
de **hitlijst** /hɪ̲tlɛist/ (pl: -en) chart(s), hit parade
hitsig /hɪ̲tsəχ/ (adj, adv) **1** hot-blooded **2** [inform] hot; randy; horny
de **hitte** /hɪ̲tə/ heat
hittebestendig /hɪtəbəstɛ̲ndəχ/ (adj) heat-resistant, heatproof
de **hittegolf** /hɪ̲təɣɔlf/ (pl: -golven) heatwave
het **hiv** /hɑive̲/ *human immunodeficiency virus* HIV
de **hiv-remmer** /ɛ̲tsrɛmər/ (pl: hiv-remmers) antiretroviral
hm /həm/ (int) (a)hem
ho /ho/ (int) **1** stop: *zeg maar 'ho'* say when **2** come on!, that's not fair!
de **hoax** /hoks/ (pl: -es, -en) hoax
de **hobbel** /hɔ̲bəl/ (pl: -s) bump
hobbelen /hɔ̲bələ(n)/ (hobbelde, heeft/is gehobbeld) bump, jolt, lurch
hobbelig /hɔ̲bələχ/ (adj) bumpy, irregular
het **hobbelpaard** /hɔ̲bəlpart/ (pl: -en) rocking horse
de **hobby** /hɔ̲bi/ (pl: -'s) hobby: [fig] *een uit de **hand** gelopen ~* a hobby that turned into a passion; [depr] *linkse ~'s* (expensive) left-

wing hobbies

de **hobo** /hobo̱/ (pl: -'s) oboe

de **hoboïst** /hobowɪ̱st/ (pl: -en) oboist

het **hobu** /ho̱by/ [Belg] *hoger onderwijs buiten de universiteit* non-university higher education

het **hockey** /hɔ̱ki/ hockey; [Am] field hockey
hockeyen /hɔ̱kijə(n)/ (hockeyde, heeft gehockeyd) play hockey

de **hockeystick** /hɔ̱kistɪk/ (pl: -s) hockey stick

het/de **hocus pocus** /hokʏspo̱kʏs/ hocus-pocus; mumbo-jumbo

hoe /hu/ (adv) **1** how: *je kunt wel nagaan ~ blij zij was* you can imagine how happy she was; *~ dan?* but how?, I don't get it; *~ eerder ~ beter* the sooner the better; *het gaat ~ langer ~ beter* it is getting better all the time; *~ leuk is dat!* what fun!; *~ ouder ze wordt, ~ minder ze ziet* the older she gets, the less she sees; *~ fietst zij naar school?* which way does she cycle to school?; *~ moet het nu verder?* where do we go from here?; *~ dan ook* **a)** anyway, anyhow; **b)** no matter how; **c)** by hook or by crook; **d)** no matter what; *~ vreemd het ook lijkt* strange as it may seem; *~ duur het ook is, ik wil het hebben* no matter how expensive it is, I want it; *~ kom je erbij?* how can you think such a thing?; *hoezo?, ~ dat zo?* how (or: what) do you mean?, why do you ask?; *~ vind je mijn kamer?* what do you think of my room? **2** what: *~ noemen jullie de baby?* what are you going to call the baby?

de **hoed** /hut/ (pl: -en) hat: *een hoge ~* a top hat

de **hoedanigheid** /hudanəxhɛɪt/ (pl: -heden) capacity: *in de ~ van* in one's capacity as

de **hoede** /hu̱də/ **1** care, protection; custody; charge; (safe) keeping: *iem. onder zijn ~ nemen* take charge of s.o., take a person under one's care (or: protection) **2** guard: *op zijn ~ zijn (voor)* be on one's guard (against)

¹**hoeden** /hu̱də(n)/ (hoedde, heeft gehoed) tend, keep watch over, look after

zich ²**hoeden** /hu̱də(n)/ (hoedde zich, heeft zich gehoed) (+ voor) guard (against), beware (of), be on one's guard (against)

de **hoedenplank** /hu̱də(n)plɑŋk/ (pl: -en) shelf; [car] rear (or: parcel, back) shelf

het **hoedje** /hu̱cə/ (pl: -s) (little) hat: *onder één ~ spelen met* be in league with; *zich een ~ schrikken* be frightened to out of one's wits

de **hoef** /huf/ (pl: hoeven) hoof

het **hoefijzer** /hu̱fɛɪzər/ (pl: -s) (horse)shoe

de **hoefsmid** /hu̱fsmɪt/ (pl: -smeden) farrier, blacksmith

hoegenaamd /hu̱ɣənamt/ (adv) at all, absolutely, completely

de **hoek** /huk/ (pl: -en) **1** corner: *in de ~ staan* (or: *zetten*) stand (or: put) in the corner; *de ~ omslaan* turn the corner; *(vlak) om de ~ (van de straat)* (just) around the corner **2** [maths] angle: [fig] *iets vanuit een andere ~ bekijken* look at sth. from a different angle; *in een rechte ~* at right angles; *een scherpe* (or: *een stompe*) *~* an acute (or: obtuse) angle; *die lijnen snijden elkaar onder een ~ van 45°* those lines meet at an angle of 45° **3** quarter, point of the compass: *dode ~* blind spot

het **hoekhuis** /hu̱khœys/ (pl: -huizen) corner house; end house
hoekig /hu̱kəχ/ (adj, adv) angular; craggy; rugged; jagged

het **hoekje** /hu̱kjə/ (pl: -s) corner; nook ‖ *het ~ omgaan* kick the bucket

het **hoekpunt** /hu̱kpʏnt/ (pl: -en) vertex, angular point

de **hoekschop** /hu̱ksχɔp/ (pl: -pen) corner (kick)

de **hoeksteen** /hu̱ksten/ (pl: -stenen) cornerstone; [fig] keystone; linchpin; pillar

de **hoektand** /hu̱ktɑnt/ (pl: -en) canine tooth, eye-tooth; fang
hoelang /hulɑ̱ŋ/ (adv) how long

het **hoen** /hun/ (pl: -ders) hen, chicken; poultry; (domestic) fowl

de **hoepel** /hu̱pəl/ (pl: -s) hoop
hoepla /hu̱pla/ (int) whoops; oops(-a-daisy); ups-a-daisy; here we go

de **hoer** /hur/ (pl: -en) [inform] whore
hoera /hura̱/ (int) hooray, hurray, hurrah

de **hoes** /hus/ (pl: hoezen) cover(ing), case

de **hoest** /hust/ cough

de **hoestbui** /hu̱stbœy/ (pl: -en) fit of coughing, coughing fit
hoesten /hu̱stə(n)/ (hoestte, heeft gehoest) cough

de **hoestsiroop** /hu̱(st)sirop/ cough syrup

de **hoeve** /hu̱və/ (pl: -n) farm(stead); farmhouse; homestead
hoeveel /huve̱l/ (num) how much, how many: *~ appelen zijn er?* how many apples are there?; *~ geld heb je bij je?* how much money do you have on you?; *~ is vier plus vier?* what do four and four make?; how much is four plus four?; *met hoevelen waren jullie?* how many of you were there?; how many were you?

de **hoeveelheid** /huve̱lhɛɪt/ (pl: -heden) amount, quantity; volume; dose
hoeveelste /huve̱lstə/ (num): *de ~ juli ben je jarig?* when in July is your birthday?; *voor de ~ keer vraag ik het je nu?* how many times have I asked you?; *de ~ is het vandaag?* what day of the month is it today?; *het ~ deel van een liter is 10 cm³?* what fraction of a litre is 10cc?

¹**hoeven** /hu̱və(n)/ (hoefde, heeft gehoefd) matter, be necessary: *het had niet gehoeven* you didn't have to do that, you shouldn't have done that; *het mag wel, maar het hoeft niet* you can but you don't have to

²**hoeven** /hu̱və(n)/ (hoefde, heeft gehoefd) need (to), have to: *dat had je niet ~ (te) doen* you shouldn't have (done that); *daar hoef je*

*niet bang voor te **zijn*** you needn't worry about that

hoever /huvɛr/ (adv) how far: *in ~re* to what extent

hoewel /huwɛl/ (conj) **1** (al)though, even though: *~ het pas maart is, zijn de bomen al groen* even though it's only March the trees are already in leaf **2** (al)though, however

hoezeer /huzer/ (adv) how much: *ik kan je niet zeggen ~ het mij spijt* I can't tell you how sorry I am

hoezo /huzo/ (int) what (*or:* how) do you mean?, in what way? (*or:* respect?): *~ crisis?* crisis? what crisis?

het **hof** /hɔf/ **1** [law] court **2** court, royal household

de **hofdame** /hɔvdamə/ (pl: -s) lady-in-waiting; maid of honour

hoffelijk /hɔfələk/ (adj, adv) courteous, polite

de **hofhouding** /hɔfhaudɪŋ/ (pl: -en) (royal) household, court

de **hofleverancier** /hɔfleverɑnsir/ (pl: -s) purveyor to the Royal Household, purveyor to His (Her) Majesty the King (Queen), Royal Warrant Holder

de **hofnar** /hɔfnɑr/ (pl: -ren) court jester, fool

het **hogedrukgebied** /hoɣədrykxəbit/ (pl: -en) anticyclone

de **hogedrukspuit** /hoɣədrykspœyt/ (pl: -en) high-pressure paint spray, high-pressure spraying pistol

de **hogepriester** /hoɣəpristər/ (pl: -s) high priest

de **hogerhand** /hoɣərhɑnt/: *op bevel van ~* by order of the authorities

het **Hogerhuis** /hoɣərhœys/ House of Lords, Upper House

hogerop /hoɣərɔp/ (adv) higher up: *hij wil ~* he wants to get on

de **hogeschool** /hoɣəsxol/ (pl: -scholen) [Dutch] college (of advanced, higher education), polytechnic, academy: *Economische ~* School of Economics; *Technische ~* College (*or:* Institute) of Technology; Polytechnic (College)

de **hogesnelheidstrein** /hoɣəsnɛlhɛitstrɛin/ (pl: -en) high-speed train

hoi /hɔj/ (int) hi, hello; hurray; whoopee

het **hok** /hɔk/ (pl: -ken) **1** shed; storeroom **2** pen; (dog) kennel; (pig)sty; dovecote; hen house, hen-coop

het **hokje** /hɔkjə/ (pl: -s) **1** cabin; (sentry) box; cubicle; booth **2** compartment; pigeon-hole; square; box: *het ~ aankruisen (invullen)* put a tick in the box

hokken /hɔkə(n)/ (hokte, heeft gehokt) shack up (with)

het **¹hol** /hɔl/ (pl: -en) **1** cave, cavern, grotto: *een donker ~* a dark, gloomy hole **2** hole; lair; den; burrow: *zich in het ~ van de leeuw wagen*

beard (*or:* brave) the lion in his den **3** hole; haunt ‖ *een op ~ geslagen paard* a runaway (horse)

²hol /hɔl/ (adj, adv) **1** hollow; female; sunken; gaunt: *een ~ geslepen brillenglas* a concave lens; *het ~le van de hand* (*or:* *voet*) the hollow of the hand, the arch of the foot **2** hollow; empty: *~ klinken* a) sound hollow; b) sound empty **3** hollow, cavernous ‖ *in het ~st van de nacht* at dead of night

de **holbewoner** /hɔlbəwonər/ (pl: -s) cave-dweller

de **holding** /hoːldɪŋ/ (pl: -s) holding

de **hold-up** /holdyp/ (pl: -s) [Belg] robbery, hold-up

de **holebi** /holebi/ (pl: -'s) [Belg] *homo, lesbienne of biseksueel* LGB (lesbian, gay, bisexual): *~'s en transgenders* LGBT (lesbian, gay, bisexual, transgender)

Holland /hɔlɑnt/ the Netherlands, Holland

de **Hollander** /hɔlɑndər/ (pl: -s) **1** Dutchman **2** inhabitant of North or South Holland

Hollands /hɔlɑnts/ (adj) **1** from (the province of) North or South Holland **2** Dutch, Netherlands: *~e nieuwe* Dutch (*or:* salted) herring

de **Hollandse** /hɔlɑntsə/ Dutchwoman

hollen /hɔlə(n)/ (holde, heeft/is gehold) **1** bolt, run away **2** run, race: *het is met hem ~ of stilstaan* it's always all or nothing with him

de **holocaust** /holokɔːst/ (pl: -en) holocaust

het **hologram** /holoɣrɑm/ (pl: -men) hologram

de **holster** /hɔlstər/ (pl: -s) holster

de **holte** /hɔltə/ (pl: -s, -n) **1** cavity, hollow, hole; niche **2** hollow; socket; pit; crook **3** draught, depth

de **hom** /hɔm/ (pl: -men) milt: [fig] *~ of kuit willen hebben* want to know, one way or the other

de **homeopathie** /homejopati/ homoeopathy

homeopathisch /homejopatis/ (adj, adv) homoeopathic

de **homepage** /hɔmpetʃ/ (pl: -s) [comp] home page

de **hometrainer** /hɔmtrenər/ (pl: -s) home trainer

de **hommage** /ɔmaʒə/ (pl: -s) homage

de **hommel** /hɔməl/ (pl: -s) bumblebee

de **homo** /homo/ (pl: -'s) **1** gay; fairy; queen **2** [offensive] poof; [Am] pussy, sissy

de **¹homofiel** /homofil/ (pl: -en) homosexual

²homofiel /homofil/ (adj) homosexual

homogeen /homoɣen/ (adj) homogeneous, uniform

het **homohuwelijk** /homohywələk/ (pl: -en) same-sex marriage, gay marriage; (gay) blessing

de **homoscene** /homosiːn/ gay scene

de **homoseksualiteit** /homosɛksywalitɛit/ homosexuality; lesbianism

de **¹homoseksueel** /homosɛksyw<u>e</u>l/ (pl: -sek-
suelen) homosexual
²homoseksueel /homosɛksyw<u>e</u>l/ (adj) homosexual
de **homp** /homp/ (pl: -en) chunk, hunk, lump
de **hond** /hont/ (pl: -en) **1** dog; hound: *pas op
voor de ~* beware of the dog; *de ~ uitlaten*
take the dog (out) for a walk; let the dog
out; *~en aan de lijn!* dogs must be kept on the
lead (leash)!; *geen ~* not a soul, nobody; *je
moet geen slapende ~en wakker maken* let
sleeping dogs lie; *blaffende ~en bijten niet*
[roughly] his bark is worse than his bite; [fig]
de ~ in de pot vinden come too late for dinner
2 dog, cur: *ondankbare ~!* ungrateful swine!
het **hondenasiel** /h<u>o</u>ndə(n)azil/ (pl: -en) dogs'
home
de **hondenbaan** /h<u>o</u>ndə(n)ban/ (pl: -banen)
lousy (*or:* rotten, awful) job
het **hondengevecht** /h<u>o</u>ndə(n)ɣəvɛχt/ (pl: -en)
dogfight
het **hondenhok** /h<u>o</u>ndə(n)hok/ (pl: -ken) (dog)
kennel
het **hondenras** /h<u>o</u>ndə(n)rɑs/ (pl: -sen) breed of
dog
de **hondenuitlaatservice** /h<u>o</u>ndə(n)œyt-
latsɪ:rvɪs/ (pl: -s) dog-walking service
het **hondenweer** /h<u>o</u>ndə(n)wer/ foul weather,
filthy weather
het **¹honderd** /h<u>o</u>ndərt/ (pl: -en) hundred, hun-
dred(s): *~en jaren* (or: *keren*) hundreds of
years (*or:* times); *zij sneuvelden bij ~en* they
died in their hundreds || *alles loopt in het ~*
everything is going haywire
²honderd /h<u>o</u>ndərt/ (num) hundred: *een
bankbiljet van ~ euro* a hundred-euro (bank)-
note; *dat heb ik nu al (minstens) ~ keer gezegd*
(if I've said it once) I've said it a hundred
times; *ik voel me niet helemaal ~ procent* I'm
feeling a bit under the weather; *~ procent
zeker zijn (van)* be absolutely positive; *er zijn er
over de ~* there are more than a hundred
honderdduizend /hondərdœyzənt/ (num)
a (*or:* one) hundred thousand: *(enige) ~en
(mensen)* hundreds of thousands (of people)
honderdduizendste /hondərdœyzəntstə/
(num) (one) hundred thousandth
honderd-en-een /hondərtɛnən/ (num) a
hundred and one; [fig also] a ton (of)
het **honderdje** /h<u>o</u>ndərcə/ (pl: -s) hundred-
guilder note
honderdste /h<u>o</u>ndərstə/ (num) hundredth:
ik probeer het nu al voor de ~ maal I've tried it
a hundred times
het **hondje** /h<u>o</u>ncə/ (pl: -s) doggy, little dog;
bowwow
honds /honts/ (adj, adv) despicable, shameful, scandalous
de **hondsdolheid** /hontsd<u>o</u>lhɛit/ rabies
Honduras /hond<u>u</u>rɑs/ Honduras
de **¹Hondurees** /hondur<u>e</u>s/ (pl: Hondurezen)

Honduran
²Hondurees /hondur<u>e</u>s/ (adj) Honduran
honen /h<u>o</u>nə(n)/ (hoonde, heeft gehoond)
jeer
de **Hongaar** /hoŋ<u>ɣ</u>ar/ (pl: Hongaren) Hungarian
het **¹Hongaars** /hoŋɣars/ Hungarian
²Hongaars /hoŋɣars/ (adj) Hungarian
Hongarije /hoŋɣar<u>ɛi</u>ə/ Hungary
de **honger** /h<u>o</u>ŋər/ appetite, hunger: *ik heb
toch een ~!* I'm starving; *~ hebben* be (*or:*
feel) hungry; *van ~ sterven* die of hunger,
starve to death
de **hongerdood** /h<u>o</u>ŋərdot/ death by starvation: *de ~ sterven* starve to death, die of
starvation
hongeren /h<u>o</u>ŋərə(n)/ (hongerde, heeft ge-
hongerd) starve, hunger: *~ naar* hanker after; hunger (*or:* be hungry) for
hongerig /h<u>o</u>ŋərəχ/ (adj, adv) hungry; famished; peckish
de **hongerklop** /h<u>o</u>ŋərklop/ [cycling] bonk,
hunger pang: *de ~ krijgen* bonk, hit the bonk
het **hongerloon** /h<u>o</u>ŋərlon/ (pl: -lonen) pittance, subsistence wages, starvation wages
de **hongersnood** /h<u>o</u>ŋərsnot/ (pl: -noden)
famine, starvation; dearth
de **hongerstaking** /h<u>o</u>ŋərstakɪŋ/ (pl: -en) hunger strike
de **honing** /h<u>o</u>nɪŋ/ honey
de **honingraat** /h<u>o</u>nɪŋrat/ (pl: -raten) honey-
comb
het **honk** /hoŋk/ (pl: -en) base
het **¹honkbal** /h<u>o</u>ŋgbɑl/ baseball
de **²honkbal** /h<u>o</u>ŋgbɑl/ (pl: -len) baseball
de **honkbalknuppel** /h<u>o</u>ŋgbɑlknʏpəl/ (pl: -s)
(baseball) bat
honkballen /h<u>o</u>ŋgbɑlə(n)/ (honkbalde,
heeft gehonkbald) play baseball
de **honneurs** /hon<u>ø</u>rs/ (pl): *de ~ waarnemen* do
the honours
honorair /honor<u>ɛ</u>:r/ (adj): *~ consul* honorary consul
het **honorarium** /honor<u>a</u>rijʏm/ (pl: honoraria,
-s) fee, salary; royalty; honorarium
honoreren /honor<u>e</u>rə(n)/ (honoreerde,
heeft gehonoreerd) **1** pay, remunerate; fee
2 honour, give due recognition; recognize
het **hoofd** /hoft/ (pl: -en) **1** head: *met gebogen
~* with head bowed; *een ~ groter* (or: *kleiner*)
zijn dan be a head taller (*or:* shorter) than;
een hard ~ in iets hebben have grave doubts
about sth.; *het ~ laten hangen* hang one's
head, be downcast; [fig] *iem. het ~ op hol
brengen* turn s.o.'s head; [fig] *het ~ boven water houden* keep one's head above water,
keep afloat; *het werk is hem boven het ~ gegroeid* he can't cope with his work any more;
het succes is hem naar het ~ gestegen success
has gone to his head; *iets over het ~ zien*
overlook sth. **2** head, mind, brain(s): *mijn ~*

staat er niet naar I'm not in the mood for it; *zijn ~ erbij houden* stay focused; *hij heeft veel aan zijn ~* he has a lot of things on his mind; *iets uit het ~ kennen* learn sth. by heart (*or:* rote); *uit het ~ zingen* sing from memory; *iem. het ~ op hol brengen* turn s.o.'s head; *per ~ van de bevolking* per head of (the) population **3** head; top **4** head, front, vanguard **5** head, chief, leader; principal; headmaster; headmistress **6** main, chief: *hoofdbureau* head office ‖ *uit ~e van zijn functie* in his capacity as …

de **hoofdagent** /h<u>o</u>ftaɣɛnt/ (pl: -en) [Dutch] senior police officer

het **hoofdartikel** /h<u>o</u>ftɑrtikəl/ (pl: -en) editorial, leading article, leader

de **hoofdbrekens** /h<u>o</u>fdbrekə(n)s/ (pl): *dat zal mij heel wat ~ kosten* I shall have to rack my brains over that, that's going to take a lot of thought

de **hoofdcommissaris** /h<u>o</u>ftkɔmɪsɑrɪs/ (pl: -sen) [Dutch] (chief) superintendent (of police), commissioner

het **hoofddeksel** /h<u>o</u>vdɛksəl/ (pl: -s) headgear; headwear

de **hoofddoek** /h<u>o</u>vduk/ (pl: -en) (head)scarf

het **hoofdeind** /h<u>o</u>ftɛint/ head

hoofdelijk /h<u>o</u>vdələk/ (adj, adv): *~e stemming* poll, voting by call; *~ aansprakelijk zijn* be severally liable (*or:* responsible)

het **hoofdgebouw** /h<u>o</u>ftɣəbɑu/ (pl: -en) main (*or:* central) building

het **hoofdgerecht** /h<u>o</u>ftɣərɛɣt/ (pl: -en) main course

het/de **hoofdhaar** /h<u>o</u>fthɑr/ hair (of the head)

de **hoofdhuid** /h<u>o</u>fthœyt/ scalp

de **hoofding** /h<u>o</u>vdɪŋ/ (pl: -en) [Belg] letterhead

de **hoofdinspecteur** /h<u>o</u>ftɪnspɛktør/ (pl: -s) [Dutch] chief inspector; chief medical officer; inspector general

het **hoofdkantoor** /h<u>o</u>ftkɑntor/ (pl: -kantoren) head office, headquarters

het **hoofdkussen** /h<u>o</u>ftkʏsə(n)/ (pl: -s) pillow

het **hoofdkwartier** /h<u>o</u>ftkwɑrtir/ (pl: -en) headquarters

de **hoofdletter** /h<u>o</u>ftlɛtər/ (pl: -s) capital (letter)

de **hoofdlijn** /h<u>o</u>ftlɛin/ (pl: -en) outline

de **hoofdluis** /h<u>o</u>ftlœys/ (pl: -luizen) head louse

de **hoofdmaaltijd** /h<u>o</u>ftmaltɛit/ main meal

de **hoofdmoot** /h<u>o</u>ftmot/ (pl: -moten) principal part

de **hoofdpersoon** /h<u>o</u>ftpɛrson/ (pl: -personen) principal person, leading figure; main character

de **hoofdpijn** /h<u>o</u>ftpɛin/ (pl: -en) headache: *barstende ~* splitting headache

het **hoofdpijndossier** /h<u>o</u>ftpɛindɔʃe/ (pl: -s) headache

het **hoofdpodium** /h<u>o</u>ftpodijʏm/ main stage

de **hoofdprijs** /h<u>o</u>ftprɛis/ (pl: -prijzen) first prize

de **hoofdredacteur** /h<u>o</u>ftredɑktør/ (pl: -en) editor(-in-chief)

het **hoofdrekenen** /h<u>o</u>ftrekənə(n)/ mental arithmetic

de **hoofdrol** /h<u>o</u>ftrɔl/ (pl: -len) leading part: *de ~ spelen* play the leading part, be the leading man (*or:* lady)

de **hoofdrolspeler** /h<u>o</u>ftrɔlspelər/ (pl: -s) leading man, star; [fig] main figure

de **hoofdschakelaar** /h<u>o</u>ftsχakəlar/ (pl: -s) main switch

hoofdschuddend /h<u>o</u>ftsχʏdənt/ (adv) shaking one's head

de **hoofdstad** /h<u>o</u>ftstɑt/ (pl: -steden) capital (city); provincial capital

hoofdstedelijk /hoftst<u>e</u>dələk/ (adj) metropolitan

de **hoofdsteun** /h<u>o</u>ftstøn/ (pl: -en) headrest

de **hoofdstraat** /h<u>o</u>ftstrat/ (pl: -straten) high street, main street

het **hoofdstuk** /h<u>o</u>ftstʏk/ (pl: -ken) chapter

het **hoofdtelwoord** /h<u>o</u>ftɛlwort/ (pl: -en) cardinal number

het **hoofdvak** /h<u>o</u>ftfɑk/ (pl: -ken) main subject

de **hoofdverpleegkundige** /hoftfərpleɣkʏndəɣə/ charge nurse

de **hoofdvogel** /h<u>o</u>ftfoɣəl/ (pl: -s) [Belg] main prize ‖ *de ~ afschieten* make (*or:* commit) a serious blunder

de **hoofdweg** /h<u>o</u>ftwɛɣ/ (pl: -en) main road

de **hoofdwond** /h<u>o</u>ftwɔnt/ (pl: -en) head wound (*or:* injury)

de **hoofdzaak** /h<u>o</u>ftsak/ (pl: -zaken) main point (*or:* thing); essentials: *~ is, dat we slagen* what matters is that we succeed

hoofdzakelijk /hofts<u>a</u>kələk/ (adv) mainly

de **hoofdzin** /h<u>o</u>ftsɪn/ (pl: -nen) main sentence (*or:* clause)

de **hoofdzonde** /h<u>o</u>ftsɔndə/ (pl: -n) cardinal sin

de **hoofdzuster** /h<u>o</u>ftsʏstər/ (pl: -s) charge nurse

hoofs /hofs/ (adj, adv): *de ~e liefde* courtly love

hoog /hoχ/ (adj, adv) high, tall: *een hoge ambtenaar* a senior official; *een hoge bal* a high ball; *een hoge C* a high C, a top C; *naar een hogere klas overgaan* move up (*or:* be moved up) to a higher class; *een ~ stemmetje* (or: *geluid*) a high-pitched voice (*or:* sound); *de ~ste verdieping* the top floor; *een stapel van drie voet ~* a three-foot high pile; *het water staat ~* the water is high; *~ in de lucht* high up in the air; *hij woont drie ~* he lives on the third floor; [Am] he lives on the second floor; *de ruzie liep ~ op* the quarrel became heated; *de verwarming staat ~* the heating is on high; *de temperatuur mag niet hoger zijn dan 60°* the temperature must not go above (*or:* exceed) 60°; *het zit hem* ~ it rankles him

hoogachten /ho̯χɑχtə(n)/ (achtte hoog, heeft hooggeacht) esteem highly, respect highly: ~*d* yours faithfully

hoogbegaafd /ho̯ybəya̯ft/ (adj) highly gifted (*or:* talented): *scholen voor* ~*e kinderen* schools for highly-gifted children

de **hoogbouw** /ho̯ybɑu/ high-rise building (*or:* flats)

de **hoogconjunctuur** /ho̯χkɔnyŋktyr/ (period of) boom

de **hoogdag** /ho̯yɑχ/ (pl: -en) [Belg] feast day

hoogdravend /ho̯ydra̯vənt/ (adj) high-flown, bombastic

het **hooggebergte** /ho̯χəbɛrχtə/ (pl: -n, -s) high mountains

hooggeëerd /ho̯χəe̯rt/ (adj) highly honoured: ~ *publiek!* Ladies and Gentlemen!

hooggeplaatst /ho̯χəpla̯tst/ (adj) high-placed, highly placed

het **hooggerechtshof** /ho̯χərɛχ(t)shɔf/ (pl: -hoven) Supreme Court

hooghartig /ho̯χhɑrtəχ/ (adj, adv) haughty

de **hoogheid** /ho̯χhɛit/ (pl: -heden) highness

hooghouden /ho̯χhaudə(n)/ (hield hoog, heeft hooggehouden) honour; keep up: *de eer* ~ keep one's honour

de **hoogleraar** /ho̯χle̯rar/ (pl: -leraren) professor

hooglopend /ho̯χlo̯pənt/ (adj) violent

de **hoogmis** /ho̯χmɪs/ (pl: -sen) high mass

de **hoogmoed** /ho̯χmut/ pride: ~ *komt voor de val* pride goes before a fall

de **hoogmoedswaanzin** /ho̯χmutswanzɪn/ megalomania

hoognodig /ho̯χno̯dəχ/ (adj, adv) highly necessary, much needed, urgently needed: *er moet* ~ *iets gebeuren* sth. needs to be done urgently

hoogoplopend /ho̯χo̯plopənt/ (adj): *een ~e ruzie* a screaming row

de **hoogoven** /ho̯χovə(n)/ (pl: -s) blast furnace

het **hoogseizoen** /ho̯χsɛizun/ (pl: -en) high season: *buiten het* ~ out of season

de **hoogspanning** /ho̯χspɑnɪŋ/ high tension (*or:* voltage): [fig] *onder* ~ *staan* be under stress, be subjected to great stress

hoogspringen /ho̯χsprɪŋə(n)/ high-jump, high-jumping

het ¹**hoogst** /ho̯χst/ **1** top, highest **2** utmost: *je krijgt op zijn* ~ *wat strafwerk* at the very worst you'll be given some lines

²**hoogst** /ho̯χst/ (adv) highly, extremely: ~ *(on)waarschijnlijk* highly (un)likely

hoogstaand /ho̯χstant/ (adj) high-minded; edifying: *het was geen* ~ *schouwspel* it was a rather unedifying spectacle

het **hoogstandje** /ho̯χstɑncə/ (pl: -s) tour de force

hoogsteigen /ho̯χstɛiɣə(n)/ (adj): *de Konin-gin in* ~ *persoon* the Queen, no less; no less a person than the Queen

hoogstens /ho̯χstəns/ (adv) **1** at the most, at (the very) most, up to, no(t) more than: ~ *twaalf* twelve at the (very) most **2** at worst: ~ *kan hij u de deur wijzen* the worst he can do is show you the door **3** at best

hoogstnodig /ho̯χstnodəχ/ (adj) absolutely necessary, strictly necessary: *alleen het* ~*e kopen* buy only the bare necessities

hoogstpersoonlijk /ho̯χs(t)pɛrsonlək/ (adv) in person, personally

hoogstwaarschijnlijk /ho̯χstwarsχɛinlək/ (adj, adv) most likely (*or:* probable), in all probability

de **hoogte** /ho̯χtə/ (pl: -n, -s) **1** height: *de* ~ *ingaan* go up, rise; ascend; *hij deed erg uit de* ~ he was being very superior; *lengte, breedte en* ~ length, breadth and height **2** height; level: *de* ~ *van de waterspiegel* the water level; *tot op zekere* ~ *hebt u gelijk* up to a point you're right **3** level, latitude; elevation, altitude: *er staat een file ter* ~ *van Woerden* there is a traffic jam near Woerden ‖ *zich van iets op de* ~ *stellen* acquaint o.s. with sth.; *op de* ~ *blijven* keep o.s. informed; keep in touch; *ik kan geen* ~ *van hem krijgen* I don't understand him; I can't figure him out

de **hoogtelijn** /ho̯χtəlɛin/ (pl: -en) altitude

het **hoogtepunt** /ho̯χtəpʏnt/ (pl: -en) height, peak, highlight: *naar een* ~ *voeren, een* ~ *doen bereiken* bring to a climax

de **hoogtevrees** /ho̯χtəvres/ fear of heights

de **hoogteziekte** /ho̯χtəziktə/ altitude sickness

de **hoogtezon** /ho̯χtəzɔn/ (pl: -nen) sun lamp

het **hoogtij** /ho̯χtɛi/: ~ *vieren* be (*or:* run) rampant; *de corruptie viert* ~ corruption is rampant (*or:* rife)

hooguit /ho̯χœyt/ (adv) at the most, at (the very) most, no(t) more than

het **hoogverraad** /ho̯χfərat/ high treason

de **hoogvlakte** /ho̯χflɑktə/ (pl: -n, -s) plateau

de **hoogvlieger** /ho̯χfliyər/ (pl: -s) [fig] high-flyer; whizz kid: *het is geen* ~ he's no genius

hoogwaardig /ho̯χwardəχ/ (adj) high-quality

de **hoogwaardigheidsbekleder** /ho̯χwardəχhɛitsbəkledər/ (pl: -s) dignitary

het **hoogwater** /ho̯χwatər/ high water, high tide: *bij (met)* ~ at high tide

de **hoogwerker** /ho̯χwɛrkər/ (pl: -s) tower waggon

het **hooi** /hoj/ hay: *te veel* ~ *op zijn vork nemen* bite off more than one can chew

de **hooiberg** /hojbɛrχ/ (pl: -en) haystack

hooien /hojə(n)/ (hooide, heeft gehooid) make hay

de **hooikoorts** /hojkorts/ hay fever

de **hooimijt** /hojmɛit/ (pl: -en) haystack

de **hooivork** /hojvɔrk/ (pl: -en) pitchfork

de **hooiwagen** /hojwayə(n)/ (pl: -s) **1** haycart, hay-wagon **2** daddy-long-legs

de **hooligan** /hulɪɡən/ (pl: -s) hooligan

het **hoongelach** /honɣəlɑχ/ jeering, jeers

de **¹hoop** /hop/ (pl: hopen) **1** heap, pile: *op een ~ leggen* pile up, stack up; *je kunt niet alles* (or: *iedereen*) *op één ~ gooien* you can't lump everything (or: everyone) together **2** great deal, good deal, lot: *een hele ~* a good many; *ik heb nog een ~ te doen* I've still got a lot (or: lots) to do **3** business ‖ *te ~ lopen tegen iets* rise up in arms against sth., protest against sth.

de **²hoop** /hop/ (pl: hopen) hope: *goede ~ hebben* have high hopes; *valse ~ wekken* raise false hopes; *zolang er leven is, is er ~* while there's life there's hope; *weer (nieuwe) ~ krijgen* regain hope; *op ~ van zegen* ... and hoping for the best; with one's fingers crossed; *de ~ opgeven* (or: *verliezen*) *dat* ... give up (or: lose) hope that ...

hoopgevend /hopχevənt/ (adj) hopeful

hoopvol /hopfol/ (adj) hopeful; promising: *de toekomst zag er niet erg ~ uit* the future did not look very promising

hoorbaar /horbar/ (adj, adv) audible

het **hoorcollege** /horkɔleʒə/ (pl: -s) (formal) lecture

de **hoorn** /horn/ (pl: -s) **1** horn: *de stier nam hem op zijn ~s* the bull tossed him (on his horns) **2** receiver: *de ~ erop gooien* slam down the receiver; *de ~ van de haak nemen* lift the receiver **3** horn **4** conch

de **hoornist** /hornɪst/ (pl: -en) horn player

het **hoornvlies** /hornvlis/ (pl: -vliezen) cornea

het **hoorspel** /horspɛl/ (pl: -en) radio play

de **hoorzitting** /horzɪtɪŋ/ (pl: -en) hearing

de **hop** /hop/ (pl: -pen) hop(plant), hops

hopelijk /hopələk/ (adv) I hope, let's hope, hopefully: *~ komt hij morgen* I hope (or: let's hope) he is coming tomorrow

hopeloos /hopəlos/ (adj, adv) hopeless, desperate: *hij is ~ verliefd op* he's hopelessly (or: desperately) in love with

¹hopen /hopə(n)/ (hoopte, heeft gehoopt) hope (for): *~ op betere tijden* hope for better times

²hopen /hopə(n)/ (hoopte, heeft gehoopt) **1** hope (for): *dat is niet te ~* I hope (or: let's hope) not; *ik hoop van wel* (or: *van niet*) I hope so (or: hope not); *ik hoop dat het goed met u gaat* I hope you are well; *tegen beter weten in (blijven) ~* hope against hope; *blijven ~* keep (on) hoping **2** pile (up): *op elkaar gehoopt* heaped

de **hopman** /hopmɑn/ (pl: -nen) Scoutmaster

de **hor** /hor/ (pl: -ren) screen

de **horde** /hordə/ (pl: -s) **1** horde: *~n mensen* hordes of people **2** [sport] hurdle: *een ~ nemen* take (or: clear) a hurdle

de **hordeloop** /hordəlop/ hurdle race

de **horeca** /horəka/ (hotel and) catering (industry)

de **horecagelegenheid** /horekaɣəleɣə(n)hɛit/ (pl: -gelegenheden) catering facility; bars and restaurants

¹horen /horə(n)/ (hoorde, heeft gehoord) **1** hear: *hij hoort slecht* he is hard of hearing **2** belong: *wij ~ hier niet* we don't belong here; *de kopjes ~ hier* the cups go here **3** be done, should be **4** belong (to) ‖ *dat hoor je te weten* you should (or: ought to) know that; *dat hoort niet* it is not done; *dat hoort zo* that's how it should be

²horen /horə(n)/ (hoorde, heeft gehoord) **1** hear: *we hoorden de baby huilen* we heard the baby crying; *nu kun je het me vertellen, hij kan ons niet meer ~* you can tell me now, he is out of earshot; *ik heb het alleen van ~ zeggen* I only have it on hearsay; *ik hoor het hem nog zeggen* I can still hear him saying it; *hij deed alsof hij het niet hoorde* he pretended not to hear (it); *ik kon aan zijn stem ~ dat hij zenuwachtig was* I could tell by his voice that he was nervous **2** listen to **3** hear, be told, get to know: *Johan kreeg te ~ dat het zo niet langer kon* Johan was told that it can't go on like that; *wij kregen heel wat te ~* we were given a hard time of it; *laat eens iets van je ~* keep in touch; *zij wil geen nee ~* she won't take no for an answer; *hij vertelde het aan iedereen die het maar ~ wilde* he told it to anyone who would listen; *toevallig ~* overhear; *hij wilde er niets meer over ~* he didn't want to hear any more about it; *daar heb ik nooit van gehoord* I've never heard of it; *daarna hebben we niets meer van hem gehoord* that was the last we heard from him; *u hoort nog van ons* you'll be hearing from us; *nou hoor je het ook eens van een ander* so I'm not the only one who says so; *ik hoor het nog wel* let me know (about it) **4** listen (to): *moet je ~!* just listen!, listen to this!; *moet je ~ wie het zegt!* look who is talking!; *hoor eens* listen, I say

de **horizon** /horizon/ (pl: -nen) horizon: *zijn ~ verbreden* broaden (or: extend) one's horizon(s)

horizontaal /horizontal/ (adj) horizontal; [crossword puzzle] across

het **horloge** /horloʒə/ (pl: -s) watch

het **horlogebandje** /horloʒəbɑncə/ (pl: -s) watchband, watch strap

het **hormoon** /hormon/ (pl: hormonen) hormone

de **hormoonhuishouding** /hormonhœyshaudɪŋ/ hormone (or: hormonal) regulation

de **horoscoop** /horoskop/ (pl: horoscopen) horoscope: *een ~ trekken (opmaken)* cast a horoscope

de **horrorfilm** /hororfɪlm/ (pl: -s) horror film

het **horrorverhaal** /hororverhal/ (pl: -verhalen) horror story: *horrorverhalen over oplichting via* *internet* horror stories about online fraud

de **hort** /hɔrt/ (pl: -en) jerk: *met ~en en stoten spreken* speak haltingly ‖ *de ~ op zijn* be on a spree, be on the loose

de **hortensia** /hɔrtɛnsija/ (pl: -'s) hydrangea

de **horzel** /hɔrzəl/ (pl: -s) hornet

de **hospes** /hɔspɛs/ (pl: -sen) [Dutch] landlord; host

het/de **hospice** /hɔspis(ə)/ (pl: -s) hospice

de **hospita** /hɔspita/ (pl: -'s) [Dutch] landlady

het **hospitaal** /hɔspital/ (pl: hospitalen) hospital

hospitaliseren /hɔspitalizɛrə(n)/ (hospitaliseerde, heeft/is gehospitaliseerd) [Belg] hospitalize

de **hospitant** /hɔspitɑnt/ (pl: -en) student teacher

hospiteren /hɔspitɛrə(n)/ (hospiteerde, heeft gehospiteerd) **1** do one's teaching practice **2** be interviewed for a room in a student residence

hossen /hɔsə(n)/ (hoste, heeft/is gehost) dance (*or:* leap) about (arm in arm)

de **host** /host/ [comp] host

de **hostess** /hɔstəs/ (pl: -es) hostess

de **hostie** /hɔsti/ (pl: -s) host

de **hosting** /hostɪŋ/ [comp] hosting

de **hotdog** /hɔdɔg/ (pl: -s) hotdog

het **hotel** /hotɛl/ (pl: -s) hotel

de **hotelhouder** /hotɛlhɑudər/ (pl: -s) hotelkeeper

de **hotelschool** /hotɛlsxol/ (pl: -scholen) hotel and catering school: *hogere ~* hotel management school

de **hotspot** /hɔtspɔt/ hot spot

houdbaar /hɑudbar/ (adj) **1** not perishable: *beperkt houdbaar* perishable; *ten minste ~ tot* best before **2** tenable

de **houdbaarheid** /hɑudbarhɛit/ shelf life, storage life [of foods etc]

de **houdbaarheidsdatum** /hɑudbarhɛitsdatʏm/ use-by date, best-before date

¹**houden** /hɑudə(n)/ (hield, heeft gehouden) **1** (+ van) love: *wij ~ van elkaar* we love each other **2** (+ van) like, care for: *je moet ervan ~* it's an acquired taste; *niet van dansen ~* not like dancing; *hij houdt wel van een grapje* he can stand a joke; *ik hou meer van bier dan van wijn* I prefer beer to wine **3** hold; stick: *het ijs houdt nog niet* the ice isn't yet strong enough to hold your weight

²**houden** /hɑudə(n)/ (hield, heeft gehouden) **1** keep: *je mag het ~* you can keep (*or:* have) it; *kippen* (or: *duiven*) *~* keep hens (*or:* pigeons); *de blik op iets gericht ~* keep looking at sth.; *laten we het gezellig ~* let's keep it (*or:* the conversation) pleasant; *ik zal het kort ~* I'll keep it short; *iem. aan de praat ~* keep s.o. talking; *hij kon er zijn gedachten niet bij ~* he couldn't keep his mind on it; *iets tegen het licht ~* hold sth. up to the light; *ik kon hun na-*

men niet uit elkaar ~ I kept getting their names mixed up; *contact met iem. ~* keep in touch with s.o.; *orde ~* keep order **2** hold: [sport] *die had hij gemakkelijk kunnen ~* he could have easily stopped that one; *de balk hield het niet* the beam didn't hold; the beam gave way **3** hold; organize; give: *een lezing ~* give (*or:* deliver) a lecture **4** (+ voor) take to be, consider to be (*or:* as): *iets voor gezien ~* leave it at that, call it a day **5** take, stand: *het was er niet om te ~ van de hitte* the heat was unbearable; *ik hou het niet meer* I can't take it any more (*or:* longer) ‖ *rechts ~* keep (to the) right; *William houdt nooit zijn woord* (or: *beloften*) William never keeps his word (*or:* promises); *we ~ het op de 15e* let's make it the 15th, then

zich ³**houden** /hɑudə(n)/ (hield zich, heeft zich gehouden) **1** (+ aan) keep to; adhere to; abide by; comply with; observe **2** keep: *hij kon zich niet goed ~* he couldn't help laughing (*or:* crying)

de **houder** /hɑudər/ (pl: -s) **1** holder; bearer: *de ~ van het wereldrecord* the holder of the world record **2** [law] keeper; holder **3** keeper, manager; proprietor **4** holder, container

de **houdgreep** /hɑutxrep/ (pl: -grepen) hold

de **houding** /hɑudɪŋ/ (pl: -en) **1** position, pose: *in een andere ~ gaan liggen (zitten)* assume a different position **2** pose, air: *zich geen ~ weten te geven* feel awkward **3** attitude, manner

de **house** /haus/ house (music)

de **houseparty** /hauspɑːrti/ (pl: -'s) house party

de **housewarming** /hauswɔːrmɪŋ/ (pl: -s) housewarming (party)

het **hout** /hɑut/ wood: *~ sprokkelen* gather wood (*or:* sticks) ‖ [fig] *hij is uit het goede ~ gesneden* he is made of the right stuff; [Belg] *niet meer weten van welk ~ pijlen te maken* not know which way to turn, be at a complete loss

de **houtblazers** /hɑudblazərs/ (pl) woodwinds

houten /hɑutə(n)/ (adj) wooden

houterig /hɑutərəx/ (adj, adv) wooden: *zich ~ bewegen* move woodenly

de **houthakker** /hɑuthɑkər/ (pl: -s) lumberjack

de **houthandel** /hɑuthɑndəl/ (pl: -s) **1** timber trade **2** timber yard

het **houtje** /hɑucə/ (pl: -s) bit of wood ‖ *iets op eigen ~ doen* do sth. on one's own (initiative); *op een ~ bijten* have difficulty in keeping body and soul together

de **houtlijm** /hɑutlɛim/ wood glue

de **houtskool** /hɑutskol/ charcoal

de **houtsnede** /hɑutsnedə/ (pl: -n, -s) woodcut

het **houtsnijwerk** /hɑutsnɛiwɛrk/ (pl: -en) woodcarving

het **houtvuur** /hɑutfyr/ wood (*or:* log) fire

de **houtworm** /hɑutwɔrm/ (pl: -en) wood-

worm
de **houtzagerij** /hɑutsɑɣərɛi/ (pl: -en) sawmill
het **houvast** /hɑuvɑst/ hold, grip: *niet veel* (or: *geen enkel*) ~ *geven* provide little (or: no) hold; *iem.* ~ *bieden* [also fig] give s.o. sth. to hold on to
de **houw** /hɑu/ gash: *iem. een* ~ *geven* gash s.o.
de **houwdegen** /hɑudeɣə(n)/ (pl: -s) **1** backsword **2** [fig] old war-horse
het **houweel** /hɑuwel/ (pl: houwelen) pickaxe
houwen /hɑuwə(n)/ (hieuw, heeft gehouwen) **1** chop, hack; carve; hew: *uit marmer gehouwen* carved out of marble **2** chop down
de **hovenier** /hovənir/ (pl: -s) horticulturist, gardener
hozen /hozə(n)/ (hoosde, heeft gehoosd) bail (out) || *het hoost* it is pouring down (or: with rain)
de **hsl** /hɑɛsɛl/ (pl: -'s) hogesnelheidslijn high-speed rail link
het **hso** /hɑɛso/ [Belg] *hoger secundair onderwijs* senior general secondary education
de **hst** /hɑɛste/ *hogesnelheidstrein* high-speed train, HST
de **hts** /hɑteɛs/ (pl: -'en) [Dutch] *hogere technische school* Technical College
de **hufter** /hʏftər/ (pl: -s) [inform] shithead, asshole, jerk, moron
hufterproof /hʏftərpruːf/ (adj) vandal proof
de **hugenoot** /hyɣənot/ (pl: hugenoten) Huguenot
huggen /hʏɣə(n)/ (hugde, heeft gehugd) hug
de **huichelaar** /hœyxəlar/ (pl: -s) hypocrite
de **huichelarij** /hœyxəlɑrɛi/ (pl: -en) hypocrisy
¹**huichelen** /hœyxələ(n)/ (huichelde, heeft gehuicheld) play the hypocrite, be hypocritical
²**huichelen** /hœyxələ(n)/ (huichelde, heeft gehuicheld) feign, sham
de **huid** /hœyt/ (pl: -en) **1** skin: *hij heeft een dikke* ~ he is thick-skinned; *zijn* ~ *duur verkopen* fight to the bitter end; *iem. de* ~ *vol schelden* call s.o. everything under the sun; *iem. op zijn* ~ *zitten* keep on at s.o. **2** hide; skin
de **huidarts** /hœytɑrts/ (pl: -en) dermatologist
huidig /hœydəx/ (adj) present, current
de **huidkanker** /hœytkɑŋkər/ skin cancer
de **huidskleur** /hœytsklør/ (skin) colour
de **huiduitslag** /hœytœytslɑx/ rash
de **huidziekte** /hœytsiktə/ (pl: -n, -s) skin disease
de **huifkar** /hœyfkɑr/ (pl: -ren) covered wagon
de **huig** /hœyx/ (pl: -en) uvula
de **huilbaby** /hœylbebi/ (pl: -'s) whiny baby
de **huilbui** /hœylbœy/ (pl: -en) crying fit
de **huilebalk** /hœyləbɑlk/ (pl: -en) cry-baby
huilen /hœylə(n)/ (huilde, heeft gehuild) **1** cry; whine; snivel: *ze kon wel* ~ she could

have cried; *half lachend, half* ~*d* between laughing and crying; ~ *om iets* cry about sth.; ~ *van blijdschap* (or: *pijn*) cry with joy (or: pain) **2** howl
het **huis** /hœys/ (pl: huizen) **1** house, home: ~ *van bewaring* remand centre; ~ *en haard* hearth and home; *halfvrijstaand* ~ semi-detached; [Am] duplex; *open* ~ *houden* have an open day; [Am] have an open house; *het ouderlijk* ~ *verlaten, uit* ~ *gaan* leave home; *dicht bij* ~ near home; *heel wat in* ~ *hebben* [fig] have a lot going for one; *nu de kinderen het* ~ *uit zijn* now that the children have all left; *een* ~ *van drie verdiepingen* a three-storeyed house; *ik kom van* ~ I have come from home; *dan zijn we nog verder van* ~ then we will be even worse off; [Dutch] *vanuit* ~ *werken* work from home; *(op kosten) van het* ~ on the house; *het is niet om over naar* ~ *te schrijven* it is nothing to write home about; *van* ~ *uit* originally, by birth **2** House: *het Koninklijk* ~ the Royal Family || [Belg] *daar komt niets van in* ~ **a)** that's not on; **b)** it won't work, nothing will come of it
het **huis-aan-huisblad** /hœysanhœyzblɑt/ (pl: -en) free local paper
het **huisarrest** /hœysɑrɛst/ house arrest: ~ *hebben* be under house arrest; be kept in
de **huisarts** /hœysɑrts/ (pl: -en) family doctor
de **huisartsenpost** /hœysɑrtsə(n)post/ (pl: -en) [roughly] doctor's surgery
de **huisbaas** /hœyzbas/ (pl: -bazen) landlord
het **huisbezoek** /hœyzbəzuk/ (pl: -en) house call
de **huisdeur** /hœyzdør/ (pl: -en) front door
het **huisdier** /hœyzdir/ (pl: -en) pet
huiselijk /hœysələk/ (adj) **1** domestic, home; family: *in de* ~*e kring* in the family circle **2** homelike, homey: *een* ~ *type* a home-loving type
de **huisgenoot** /hœysxənot/ (pl: -genoten) housemate; member of the family
het **huisgezin** /hœysxəzɪn/ (pl: -nen) family
huishoudelijk /hœyshɑudələk/ (adj) domestic, household
het ¹**huishouden** /hœyshɑudə(n)/ (pl: -s) **1** housekeeping: *het* ~ *doen* run the house, do the housekeeping **2** household: *woningen voor een- en tweepersoonshuishoudens* houses for single people and couples
²**huishouden** /hœyshɑudə(n)/ (hield huis, heeft huisgehouden) carry on, cause damage (or: havoc)
de **huishoudfolie** /hœyshɑutfoli/ cling film
het **huishoudgeld** /hœyshɑutxɛlt/ housekeeping (money)
de **huishouding** /hœyshɑudɪŋ/ (pl: -en) housekeeping: *een gemeenschappelijke* ~ *voeren* have a joint household
de **huishoudster** /hœyshɑutstər/ (pl: -s) housekeeper

het **huisje** /hœyʃə/ (pl: -s) bungalow, cottage, small house, little house
huisje-boompje-beestje /hœyʃəbompjəbeʃə/ (adj) suburban bliss
de **huisjesmelker** /hœyʃəsmɛlkər/ (pl: -s) rackrenter; [Am] slumlord
de **huiskamer** /hœyskamər/ (pl: -s) living room
de **huisman** /hœysmɑn/ (pl: -nen) househusband
de **huismeester** /hœysmestər/ (pl: -s) caretaker, warden
het **huismiddel** /hœysmɪdəl/ (pl: -en) home remedy
de **huismoeder** /hœysmudər/ (pl: -s) housewife
de **huismus** /hœysmʏs/ (pl: -sen) **1** house sparrow **2** stay-at-home
het **huisnummer** /hœysnʏmər/ (pl: -s) house number
het **huispak** /hœyspɑk/ (pl: -ken) onesie, jumpsuit
de **huisraad** /hœysrat/ household effects
de **huisregels** /hœysreɣəls/ (pl) house rules
de **huisschilder** /hœysxɪldər/ (pl: -s) house painter
de **huissleutel** /hœysløtəl/ (pl: -s) latchkey, front-door key
de **huisstijl** /hœystɛɪl/ (pl: -en) house style
de **huisstofmijt** /hœystɔfmɛɪt/ (pl: -en) house dust mite
de **huisvader** /hœysfadər/ (pl: -s) family man, father (of the family)
huisvesten /hœysfɛstə(n)/ (huisvestte, heeft gehuisvest) house, accommodate
de **huisvesting** /hœysfɛstɪŋ/ **1** housing **2** accommodation: *ergens ~ **vinden*** find accommodation somewhere
de **huisvredebreuk** /hœysfredəbrøk/ [law] unlawful entry, trespass (in s.o.'s house)
de **huisvriend** /hœysfrint/ (pl: -en) family friend, friend of the family
de **huisvrouw** /hœysfrɑu/ (pl: -en) housewife
het **huisvuil** /hœysfœyl/ household refuse
huiswaarts /hœyswarts/ (adv) homeward(s)
het **huiswerk** /hœyswɛrk/ homework: *~ **maken*** do one's homework; *~ **opgeven*** assign homework
het **huiswerkinstituut** /hœyswɛrkɪnstityt/ (pl: -instituten) homework coaching institute, homework club
de **huiswijn** /hœyswɛɪn/ (pl: -en) house wine
de **huiszoeking** /hœysukɪŋ/ (pl: -en) (house) search
het **huiszoekingsbevel** /hœysukɪŋzbəvɛl/ (pl: -en) search warrant
huiveren /hœyvərə(n)/ (huiverde, heeft gehuiverd) **1** shiver; shudder; tremble: *~ van de kou* shiver with cold; *luister en huiver* wait for it, listen to this **2** recoil (from), shrink (from)
huiverig /hœyvərəx/ (adj) hesitant, wary

de **huivering** /hœyvərɪŋ/ (pl: -en) shiver, shudder
huiveringwekkend /hœyvərɪŋwɛkənt/ (adj, adv) horrible, terrifying
het **huize** /hœyzə/: *je moet van **goeden** ~ komen om hem te verslaan* you'd have to be very good to beat him
het **huizenblok** /hœyzə(n)blɔk/ (pl: -ken) row of houses
huizenhoog /hœyzə(n)hox/ (adj, adv) towering: *huizenhoge **golven*** mountainous waves; *~ **favoriet** zijn* be the hot favourite
de **huizenjacht** /hœyzə(n)jɑxt/: *op ~ gaan* go house-hunting
de **huizenmarkt** /hœyzəmɑrkt/ housing market
de **hulde** /hʏldə/ homage, tribute
het **huldeblijk** /hʏldəblɛɪk/ tribute
huldigen /hʏldəɣə(n)/ (huldigde, heeft gehuldigd) honour, pay tribute (to): *de mening **huldigen** dat …* be of the opinion that …, take the view that …
de **huldiging** /hʏldəɣɪŋ/ (pl: -en) homage, tribute
¹**hullen** /hʏlə(n)/ (hulde, heeft gehuld) wrap up in; [fig also] veil (in), cloak (in)
zich ²**hullen** /hʏlə(n)/ (hulde zich, heeft zich gehuld) wrap o.s. (up); [fig also] veil (or: cloak, shroud) o.s. (in)
de **hulp** /hʏlp/ (pl: -en) **1** help, assistance: *om ~ roepen* call (out) for help; *iem. **te** ~ komen* come to s.o.'s aid; *eerste ~ (bij ongelukken)* first aid; *~ **verlenen*** render assistance, assist **2** helper, assistant: *~ **in** de huishouding* home help
hulpbehoevend /hʏlpbəhuvənt/ (adj) in need of help; invalid; infirm; needy
de **hulpbron** /hʏlpbrɔn/ (pl: -nen) resource
de **hulpdienst** /hʏlbdinst/ (pl: -en) auxiliary service(s); emergency service(s): *telefonische ~* helpline
hulpeloos /hʏlpəlos/ (adj, adv) helpless
het **hulpgeroep** /hʏlpxərup/ a cry (or: call) for help
het **hulpmiddel** /hʏlpmɪdəl/ (pl: -en) aid, help, means
de **hulppost** /hʏlpɔst/ (pl: -en) aid station; first-aid post
het **hulpstuk** /hʏlpstʏk/ (pl: -ken) accessory, attachment
de **hulptroepen** /hʏlptrupə(n)/ (pl) auxiliary troops (or: forces); reinforcements
hulpvaardig /hʏlpfardəx/ (adj) helpful
de **hulpverlener** /hʏlpfərlenər/ (pl: -s) social worker
de **hulpverlening** /hʏlpfərlenɪŋ/ assistance, aid; relief
het **hulpwerkwoord** /hʏlpwɛrkwort/ (pl: -en) auxiliary
de **huls** /hʏls/ (pl: hulzen) **1** case, cover, container **2** cartridge case, shell

de **hulst** /hʏlst/ holly
humaan /hymạn/ (adj, adv) humane
de **humaniora** /hymanijọra/ [Belg] [roughly] grammar school education
het **humanisme** /hymanɪsmə/ humanism
de **humanist** /hymanɪst/ (pl: -en) humanist
humanitair /hymanitɛːr/ (adj, adv) humanitarian
het **humeur** /hymọr/ (pl: -en) humour, temper, mood: *in een* **goed** ~ *zijn* be in a good humour (*or:* temper, mood)
humeurig /hymọrəx/ (adj, adv) moody
de **hummel** /hʏməl/ (pl: -s) toddler, (tiny) tot
de **hummus** /hʏmus/ hummus
de **humor** /hymɔr/ humour: *gevoel* **voor** ~ sense of humour
de **humorist** /hymorɪst/ (pl: -en) humorist; comic
humoristisch /hymorɪstis/ (adj, adv) humorous: *een ~e* **opmerking** a humorous remark
de **humus** /hymʏs/ humus
¹**hun** /hʏn/ (pers pron) them: *ik zal het ~* **geven** I'll give it to them; *heb je ~ al* **geroepen?** have you already called them?
²**hun** /hʏn/ (poss pron) their: *~* **kinderen** their children
het **hunebed** /hynəbɛt/ (pl: -den) megalith(ic tomb, monument, grave)
hunkeren /hʏŋkərə(n)/ (hunkerde, heeft gehunkerd) long for, yearn for
hup /hʏp/ (int) **1** come on, go (to it): *~* **Henk** *~!* come on Henk! **2** hup, oops-a-daisy: *een, twee, … ~!* one, two, … up you go!
huppeldepup /hʏpəldəpʏp/ what's-his-name, what's-her-name
huppelen /hʏpələ(n)/ (huppelde, heeft/is gehuppeld) hop, skip, frolic
huren /hyrə(n)/ (huurde, heeft gehuurd) **1** rent; charter: *een* **huis** ~ rent a house; *ka-mers* ~ live in rooms **2** hire, take on: *een* **kok** ~ hire (*or:* take on) a cook
hurken /hʏrkə(n)/ (hurkte, is gehurkt) squat: *zij* **zaten** *gehurkt op de grond* they were squatting on the ground ‖ *op zijn ~ (gaan) zitten* squat (on one's haunches)
het **hurktoilet** /hʏrktwalɛt/ (pl: -ten) squat toilet
de **hut** /hʏt/ (pl: -ten) **1** hut: *een* **lemen** ~ a mud hut **2** cabin
hutjemutje /hʏcəmʏcə/ (adv): *we zaten er ~* we sat closely (*or:* tightly) packed together, we were like sardines in a can
de **hutkoffer** /hʏtkɔfər/ (pl: -s) cabin trunk
hutselen /hʏtsələ(n)/ (hutselde, heeft gehutseld) mix (up), shake (up): *dominostenen door elkaar ~* shuffle dominoes
de **hutspot** /hʏtspɔt/ [Dutch] hot(ch)-pot(ch)
de **huur** /hyr/ (pl: huren) rent; lease: *achterstal-lige* ~ rent in arrears, back rent; *kale* ~ basic rent; *iem. de ~* **opzeggen** give s.o. notice (to

leave, quit); *dit huis is* **te** ~ this house is to let; [Am] this house is for rent; *hij* **betaalt** *€ 800,-* ~ *voor dit huis* he pays 800 euros rent for this house
de **huurachterstand** /hyraxtərstant/ arrears of rent
de **huurauto** /hyrauto/ (pl: -'s) rented car, hire(d) car
het **huurcontract** /hyrkɔntrakt/ (pl: -en) rental agreement; lease: *een ~* **aangaan** sign a lease; *een ~* **opzeggen** terminate a lease
de **huurder** /hyrdər/ (pl: -s) renter; tenant; hirer: *de* **huidige** *~s* the sitting tenants
het **huurhuis** /hyrhœys/ (pl: -huizen) rented house
de **huurkoop** /hyrkop/ instalment buying, hire purchase (system)
de **huurling** /hyrlɪŋ/ (pl: -en) hireling; mercenary
de **huurmoord** /hyrmort/ (pl: -en) assassination; hit
de **huurmoordenaar** /hyrmordənar/ (pl: -s) (hired) assassin
de **huurovereenkomst** /hyrovəreŋkɔmst/ (pl: -en) *see* huurcontract
de **huurprijs** /hyrprɛis/ (pl: -prijzen) rent; rental (price)
de **huurschuld** /hyrsxʏlt/ (pl: -en) rent arrears, arrears of rent: *de ~* **bedraagt** *€ 5000,-* the rent arrears amount to € 5000
de **huurtoeslag** /hyrtuslɔx/ (pl: -en) [Dutch] rent subsidy, housing benefit
de **huurverhoging** /hyrvərhoɣɪŋ/ rent increase
de **huurwoning** /hyrwonɪŋ/ (pl: -en) rented house (*or:* flat)
huwbaar /hywbar/ (adj) marriageable: *de huwbare* **leeftijd** *bereiken* reach marriageable age
het **huwelijk** /hywələk/ (pl: -en) **1** marriage, wedding: *in het ~* **treden** *met* get married to; *gemengd ~* mixed marriage; *een* **wettig** *~* a lawful marriage; *een ~* **inzegenen** perform a marriage service; *een ~* **sluiten (aangaan)** *met* get married to; *een kind,* **buiten** *~ geboren* a child born out of wedlock; *zijn ~* **met** his marriage to; *een meisje* **ten** *~ vragen* propose to a girl; *een ~* **uit** *liefde* a love match; *een* **burgerlijk** *~* a civil wedding; *een* **kerkelijk** *~* a church wedding; *een ~* **voltrekken** perform a marriage service, celebrate a marriage **2** matrimony: *na 25 jaar ~* after 25 years of matrimony
huwelijks /hywələks/ (adj) marital, married: *~e* **voorwaarden** marriage settlement (*or:* articles)
het **huwelijksaanzoek** /hywələksanzuk/ (pl: -en) proposal (of marriage): *een ~* **doen** propose (to s.o.); *een ~* **krijgen** receive a proposal (of marriage)
de **huwelijksakte** /hywələksɑktə/ (pl: -n, -s)

marriage certificate

het **huwelijksgeschenk** /ɦʏwələksxɛsxɛŋk/ (pl: -en) wedding present (or: gift)

de **huwelijksnacht** /ɦʏwələksnɑxt/ (pl: -en) wedding night: *de eerste* ~ the wedding night

de **huwelijksplechtigheid** /ɦʏwələksplɛxtəxɦɛit/ (pl: -heden) wedding, marriage ceremony, wedding ceremony

de **huwelijksreis** /ɦʏwələksrɛis/ (pl: -reizen) honeymoon (trip): *zij zijn* **op** ~ they are on (their) honeymoon (trip)

huwen /ɦʏwə(n)/ (huwde, heeft/is gehuwd) marry

de **huzaar** /ɦyzaːr/ (pl: huzaren) hussar

de **huzarensalade** /ɦyzaːrə(n)salaːdə/ (pl: -s) [roughly] Russian salad

de **hyacint** /hijasɪnt/ (pl: -en) hyacinth

de **hybride** /hibriːdə/ (pl: -n) **1** hybrid, cross **2** hybrid, hybrid car, hybrid bike

de **hybrideauto** /hibriːdəauto/ (pl: -'s) hybrid car

hydraulisch /hidrɑulis/ (adj, adv) hydraulic: ~*e* **pers** (or: *remmen*) hydraulic press (or: brakes)

de **hyena** /hijeːna/ (pl: -'s) hy(a)ena

de **hygiëne** /hiɣi)jeːnə/ hygiene: *persoonlijke* (or: *intieme*) ~ personal hygiene

[1]**hygiënisch** /hiɣ(i)jeːnis/ (adj) hygienic, sanitary: ~*e* **omstandigheden** sanitary conditions; ~*e* **voorschriften** hygienic (or: sanitary) regulations

[2]**hygiënisch** /hiɣ(i)jeːnis/ (adv) hygienically: ~ **verpakt** hygienically packed (or: wrapped)

de **hymne** /hɪmnə/ (pl: -n) hymn

de **hype** /hɑjp/ (pl: -s) hype, fad, craze

hypen /hɑjpə(n)/ (hypete, heeft gehypet) hype

de [1]**hyper** /hiːpər/ (pl: -s) [med] hyperglycemia, hyper: *hij had vanochtend een* ~ he became hyperglycemic this morning, he had a hyper this morning

[2]**hyper** /hiːpər/ (adj) [inform] hyper: *ik was* **helemaal** ~ I was totally hyper

hyper- /hiːpər-/ hyper-, ultra-, super-

hyperactief /hipərɑktiːf/ (adj) hyperactive

de **hyperbool** /hipərboːl/ (pl: hyperbolen) **1** [maths] hyperbola **2** [exaggeration] hyperbole

hypercorrect /hipərkɔrɛkt/ (adj) hypercorrect

de **hyperlink** /hɑjpərlɪŋk/ hyperlink

de **hypermarkt** /hiːpərmɑrkt/ (pl: -en) hypermarket

hypermodern /hipərmodɛrn/ (adj, adv) ultramodern; super-fashionable: *een* ~ *interieur* an ultramodern interior

de **hyperventilatie** /hiːpərvɛntila(t)si/ hyperventilation

hyperventileren /hiːpərvɛntileːrə/ (hyperventileerde, heeft gehyperventileerd) hy-

perventilate

de **hypnose** /hipnoːzə/ hypnosis: *iem.* **onder** ~ *brengen* put s.o. under hypnosis

hypnotisch /hipnoːtis/ (adj, adv) hypnotic: ~*e* **blik** hypnotic gaze

hypnotiseren /hipnotizeːrə(n)/ (hypnotiseerde, heeft gehypnotiseerd) hypnotize

de **hypnotiseur** /hipnotizøːr/ (pl: -s) hypnotist, hypnotherapist

de **hypo** /hiːpo/ (pl: -'s) [med] hypoglycemia, hypo: *hij had vanochtend een* ~ he became hypoglycemic this morning, he had a hypo this morning

de **hypochonder** /hipoxɔndər/ (pl: -s) hypochondriac

de [1]**hypocriet** /hipokriːt/ (pl: -en) hypocrite

[2]**hypocriet** /hipokriːt/ (adj) hypocritical, insincere

de **hypocrisie** /hipokriziː/ hypocrisy

de **hypotenusa** /hipotenyːza/ (pl: -'s) hypotenuse

hypothecair /hipoteːkɛːr/ (adj) mortgage: ~*e* **lening** mortgage (loan)

de **hypotheek** /hipoteːk/ (pl: hypotheken) mortgage: *een* ~ **aflossen** pay off a mortgage; *een* ~ **afsluiten** take out a mortgage; *een* ~ **nemen** *op een huis* take out a mortgage on a house

de **hypotheekrente** /hipoteːkrɛntə/ mortgage (interest)

de **hypothese** /hipoteːzə/ (pl: -n, -s) hypothesis *een* ~ **opstellen** formulate a hypothesis

hypothetisch /hipoteːtis/ (adj, adv) hypothetical

de **hysterie** /hɪsteriː/ hysteria

hysterisch /hɪsteːris/ (adj, adv) hysterical: ~ **gekrijs** hysterical screams; *doe niet zo* ~! don't be so (or: get) hysterical!

i

i /i/ (pl: i's) i, I: *de puntjes* **op** *de i zetten* dot one's i's and cross one's t's

Iberisch /ibɛris/ (adj) Iberian: *het ~ Schiereiland* the Iberian Peninsula

de **ibis** /ibɪs/ (pl: -sen) ibis

de **icetea** /ɑjsti:/ ice tea

iconisch /ikonis/ (adj) iconic

de **icoon** /ikon/ (pl: iconen) icon: *zij is een ~ van de jaren tachtig* she's an eighties icon

de **ICT** /isete/ *informatie- en communicatietechnologie* ICT, information and communication technology

de **ICT'er** ICT specialist

het ¹**ideaal** /idejal/ (pl: idealen) **1** ideal: *zich iem. tot ~ stellen* take s.o. as a model **2** ideal, ambition: *het ~ van zijn jeugd was arts te worden* the ambition of his youth was to become a doctor; *een ~ nastreven* pursue an ideal (*or*: ambition), follow a dream

²**ideaal** /idejal/ (adj, adv) ideal, perfect

idealiseren /idejalizerə(n)/ (idealiseerde, heeft geïdealiseerd) idealize, glamorize

het **idealisme** /idejalɪsmə/ idealism

de **idealist** /idejalɪst/ (pl: -en) idealist

idealistisch /idejalɪstis/ (adj) idealistic

idealiter /idejalitɛr/ (adv) ideally, theoretically, in theory

het/de **idee** /ide/ (pl: -ën) **1** idea: *ik heb een ~* I've got an idea; *op een ~ komen* think of sth., hit upon an idea; *zich een ~ vormen van iets* form an idea of sth. **2** idea, notion, concept(ion): *het gaat om het ~* **a)** the idea was good; **b)** just to give an idea; *ik heb geen (flauw) ~* I haven't the faintest (*or*: foggiest) idea **3** idea, view

ideëel /idejel/ (adj) idealistic

de **ideeënbus** /idejə(n)bʏs/ (pl: -sen) suggestion box

het/de **idee-fixe** /idefɪks/ (pl: -n) obsession

idem /idɛm/ (adv) ditto, idem

identiek /idɛntik/ (adj) identical (with, to): *~ aan* identical to; *beide versies zijn ~* the two versions are identical

de **identificatie** /idɛntifika(t)si/ (pl: -s) identification

de **identificatieplicht** /idɛntifika(t)siplɪxt/ obligation to carry identification

identificeren /idɛntifiserə(n)/ (identificeerde, heeft geïdentificeerd) identify

de **identiteit** /idɛntitɛit/ identity

het **identiteitsbewijs** /idɛntitɛitsbəwɛis/ (pl: -bewijzen) identity card, ID card

de **identiteitsfraude** /idɛntitɛitsfraudə/ identity theft

de **identiteitskaart** /idɛntitɛrtskart/ (pl: -en) identity card; ID (card)

de **ideologie** /idejoloɣi/ (pl: -ën) ideology

ideologisch /idejoloɣis/ (adj, adv) ideological

het **idioom** /idijom/ (pl: idiomen) idiom

de ¹**idioot** /idijot/ (pl: idioten) idiot; fool: *een volslagen ~* an absolute fool

²**idioot** /idijot/ (adj, adv) ridiculous, idiotic; foolish: *doe niet zo ~* don't be such a fool (*or*: an idiot); *~ hoge prijzen* ridiculously high prices

idolaat /idolat/ (adj, adv): *~ van* infatuated with, mad about

het **idool** /idol/ (pl: idolen) idol

de **idylle** /idɪlə/ (pl: -n, -s) idyl(l)

idyllisch /idɪlis/ (adj, adv) idyllic

ieder /idər/ (ind pron) **1** every; each; any: *het kan ~e dag afgelopen zijn* it may be over any day (now); *werkelijk ~e dag* every single day; *ze komt ~e dag* she comes every day **2** everyone, everybody; each (one), anyone, anybody: *tot ~s verbazing* to everyone's surprise; *~ van ons* each of us, every one of us; *~ voor zich* every man for himself

iedereen /idəren/ (ind pron) everyone, everybody, all; anybody; anyone: *jij bent niet ~* you're not just anybody

iel /il/ (adj, adv) thin, puny

iemand /imɑnt/ (ind pron) someone, somebody; anyone; anybody: *is daar ~?* is anybody there?; *hij is niet zomaar ~* he's not just anybody; *hij wilde niet dat ~ het wist* he didn't want anyone to know; *zij maakte de indruk van ~ die* she gave the impression of being s.o. (*or*: a woman) who

de **iep** /ip/ (pl: -en) elm

de **Ier** /ir/ (pl: -en) Irishman: *tien ~en* ten Irishmen

Ierland /irlɑnt/ Ireland, Republic of Ireland

het ¹**Iers** /irs/ Irish

²**Iers** /irs/ (adj) Irish

¹**iets** /its/ (ind pron) **1** anything **2** something; anything: *~ lekkers* (or: *moois*) something tasty (*or*: beautiful); *beter ~ dan niets* something is better than nothing; *~ dergelijks* something like that **3** something, a little, a bit: *een mysterieus ~* something mysterious, a mysterious something; *hij heeft ~ wat ik niet begrijp* there is something about him which I don't understand

²**iets** /its/ (adv) a bit, a little, slightly: *als zij er ~ om gaf* if she cared at all; *het is ~ te zuur* it's a bit too sour; *we moeten ~ vroeger weggaan* we must leave a bit (*or*: slightly) earlier

ietwat /itwɑt/ (adv) somewhat, slightly

de **iftar** /ɪftɑr/ (pl: -s) iftar

de **iglo** /iɣlo/ (pl: -'s) igloo

de **i-grec** /iɣrɛk/ (pl: -s) y

ijdel /ɛidəl/ (adj, adv) vain, conceited: *~e*

hoop wishful thinking

de **ijdelheid** /ɛ̲idəlhɛit/ (pl: -heden) vanity, conceit

de **ijdeltuit** /ɛ̲idəltœyt/ (pl: -en) vain person

ijken /ɛ̲ikə(n)/ (ijkte, heeft geijkt) calibrate

het **ijkpunt** /ɛ̲ikpʏnt/ (pl: -en) benchmark (figure)

ijl /ɛil/ (adj) rarefied: *~e lucht* thin (*or:* rarefied) air

ijlen /ɛ̲ilə(n)/ (ijlde, heeft geijld) be delirious, ramble; rave

ijlings /ɛ̲ɪlɪŋs/ (adv) with all speed, in great haste

het **ijs** /ɛis/ **1** ice: *zich op glad ~ bevinden (begeven)* skate on thin ice; *het ~ breken* break the ice; *hij gaat niet over één nacht ~* he doesn't take any chances; *de haven was door ~ gesloten* the port was icebound **2** ice cream

de **ijsafzetting** /ɛ̲ɪsɑfsɛtɪŋ/ icing up; ice accretion

de **ijsbaan** /ɛ̲izban/ (pl: ijsbanen) skating rink, ice(-skating) rink

de **ijsbeer** /ɛ̲izber/ (pl: ijsberen) polar bear

ijsberen /ɛ̲izberə(n)/ (ijsbeerde, heeft geijsbeerd) pace up and down

de **ijsberg** /ɛ̲izbɛrχ/ (pl: -en) iceberg

de **ijsbergsla** /ɛ̲izbɛrχsla/ iceberg lettuce

de **ijsbloemen** /ɛ̲ɪzblumə(n)/ (pl) frostwork

het **ijsblokje** /ɛ̲izblɔkjə/ (pl: -s) ice cube

de **ijsbreker** /ɛ̲ɪzbrekər/ (pl: -s) icebreaker

de **ijscoman** /ɛ̲iskoman/ (pl: -nen) [Dutch] ice-cream man

ijselijk /ɛ̲isələk/ (adj, adv) hideous, dreadful

de **ijsemmer** /ɛ̲ɪsɛmər/ (pl: -s) ice bucket

het **ijshockey** /ɛ̲ishɔki/ ice hockey; [Am] hockey

ijshockeyen /ɛ̲ɪshɔkijə(n)/ (ijshockeyde, heeft geijshockeyd) play ice hockey; [Am] play hockey

het **ijsje** /ɛ̲iʃə/ (pl: -s) ice (cream)

de **ijskar** /ɛ̲iskar/ ice-cream cart

de **ijskast** /ɛ̲iskɑst/ (pl: -en) fridge, refrigerator: *iets in de ~ zetten* a) put sth. in the fridge; b) [fig] shelve sth., put sth. on ice

de **ijskoffie** /ɛ̲iskɔfi/ iced coffee, ice coffee

ijskoud /ɛiskɑut/ (adj, adv) **1** ice-cold, icy(-cold) **2** [fig] icy, (as) cold as ice: *een ~e ontvangst* an icy welcome; *een ~e wind* an icy wind

de **ijskrabber** /ɛ̲ɪskrɑbər/ (pl: -s) ice scraper

IJsland /ɛ̲islɑnt/ Iceland

de **IJslander** /ɛ̲ɪslɑndər/ (pl: -s) Icelander

IJslands /ɛ̲islɑnts/ (adj) Icelandic

de **ijslolly** /ɛ̲islɔli/ (pl: -'s) ice lolly; [Am] popsicle

de **ijsmuts** /ɛ̲ismʏts/ (pl: -en) [Dutch] [roughly] woolly hat

de **ijspegel** /ɛ̲ispeɣəl/ (pl: -s) icicle

de **ijssalon** /ɛ̲isalɔn/ (pl: -s) ice-cream parlour

de **ijsschots** /ɛ̲isχɔts/ (pl: -en) (ice) floe

de **ijstaart** /ɛ̲istart/ (pl: -en) ice-cream cake

de **ijsthee** /ɛ̲iste/ ice(d) tea

de **ijstijd** /ɛ̲istɛit/ (pl: -en) ice age, glacial period

(*or:* epoch)

de **ijsvogel** /ɛ̲isfoɣəl/ (pl: -s) kingfisher

ijsvrij /ɛisfrɛ̲i/ (adj) clear of ice || *~ hebben* have a day off to go skating

de **ijver** /ɛ̲ivər/ diligence

de **ijveraar** /ɛ̲ivərar/ (pl: -s) advocate, zealot

ijveren /ɛ̲ɪvərə(n)/ (ijverde, heeft geijverd) devote o.s. (to), work (for)

ijverig /ɛ̲ivərəχ/ (adj, adv) diligent: *een ~ scholier* an industrious (*or:* a diligent) pupil; *~ werken aan …* apply oneself to …

de **ijzel** /ɛ̲izəl/ black ice

ijzelen /ɛ̲izələ(n)/ (ijzelde, heeft geijzeld) freeze over: *het ijzelt* it is freezing over

het **ijzer** /ɛ̲izər/ (pl: -s) iron: *~ smeden* (*or: gieten*) forge (*or:* cast) iron; *je moet het ~ smeden als het heet is* strike while the iron is hot

het/de **ijzerdraad** /ɛ̲izərdrat/ (iron) wire

ijzeren /ɛ̲izərə(n)/ (adj) iron: *een ~ gezondheid* an iron constitution

het **ijzererts** /ɛ̲izərɛrts/ (pl: -en) iron ore

de **ijzerhandel** /ɛ̲izərhɑndəl/ (pl: -s) **1** hardware store, ironmonger's shop **2** hardware trade, ironmongery

ijzerhoudend /ɛizərhɑudənt/ (adj) ferriferous; ferrous

ijzersterk /ɛ̲izərstɛrk/ (adj) iron, cast-iron: *hij kwam met ~e argumenten* he produced very strong arguments; *een ~ geheugen* an excellent (*or:* infallible) memory

de **ijzertijd** /ɛ̲izərtɛit/ Iron Age

de **ijzerwaren** /ɛ̲izərwarə(n)/ (pl) hardware, ironmongery

de **ijzerzaag** /ɛ̲izərzaχ/ (pl: -zagen) metal saw

ijzig /ɛ̲izəχ/ (adj, adv) icy, freezing: *~e kalmte* steely composure

ijzingwekkend /ɛizɪŋwɛ̲kənt/ (adj, adv) horrifying, gruesome

ik /ɪk/ (pers pron) I: *ik ben het* it's me; *als ik er niet geweest was …* if it hadn't been for me …; *ze is beter dan ik* she's better than I am

de **ik-figuur** /ɪ̲kfiɣyr/ (pl: ik-figuren) first-person narrator

ikzelf /ɪksɛ̲lf/ (I) myself

illegaal /ileɣa̲l/ (adj, adv) **1** illegal **2** underground: *~ werk* underground work

de **illegaliteit** /ɪleɣalitɛ̲ɪt/ (pl: -en) **1** illegality **2** resistance (movement)

de **illusie** /ɪlyzi/ (pl: -s) illusion, (pipe)dream; delusion: *maakt u zich (daarover) geen ~s* you need have no illusions about that; *een ~ verstoren* shatter an illusion; *een ~ wekken* create an illusion

de **illusionist** /ɪlyzi(j)onɪ̲st/ (pl: -en) conjurer

illuster /ɪly̲stər/ (adj) illustrious, distinguished

de **illustratie** /ɪlystra̲(t)si/ (pl: -s) illustration

illustratief /ɪlystrati̲f/ (adj) illustrative: *~ in dit verband is …* a case in point is …

de **illustrator** /ɪlystra̲tor/ (pl: -s, -en) illustrator

illustreren /ɪlystre̲rə(n)/ (illustreerde, heeft

geïllustreerd) illustrate; exemplify

het/de **image** /ɪmɪtʃ/ image

imaginair /imaʒinɛːr/ (adj, adv) imaginary: *een ~ getal* an imaginary number

het/de **imago** /imayo/ (pl: -'s) image

de **imam** /imɑm/ (pl: -s) imam

de **imbeciel** /ɪmbesil/ (pl: -en) imbecile

het **IMF** /iɛmɛf/ *Internationaal Monetair Fonds* IMF

de **imitatie** /imita(t)si/ (pl: -s) imitation, copy, copying; impersonation: *een slechte ~* a poor (*or:* bad) imitation

de **imitator** /imitɑtor/ (pl: -s, -en) imitator, impersonator

imiteren /imiterə(n)/ (imiteerde, heeft geïmiteerd) imitate, copy; impersonate

de **imker** /ɪmkər/ (pl: -s) bee-keeper

de **imkerij** /ɪmkərɛi/ **1** beekeeping, apiculture **2** beekeeping business, apiary

immens /ɪmɛns/ (adj, adv) immense

immer /ɪmər/ (adv) ever, always

immers /ɪmərs/ (adv) **1** after all: *hij komt ~ morgen* after all, he is coming tomorrow; he is coming tomorrow, isn't he? **2** for, since

de **immigrant** /imiyrɑnt/ (pl: -en) immigrant

de **immigratie** /imiyra(t)si/ (pl: -s) immigration

immigreren /imiyrerə(n)/ (immigreerde, is geïmmigreerd) immigrate

de **immobiliën** /ɪmobilijə(n)/ (pl) [Belg] property, real estate

immoreel /imorɛl/ (adj, adv) immoral

de **immuniteit** /imynitɛit/ (pl: -en) immunity

de **immunotherapie** /imynoterapi/ (pl: -ën) immunotherapy

immuun /imyn/ (adj) immune: *~ voor kritiek* immune to criticism

het **immuunsysteem** /imynsistem/ immune system

het/de **i-mode** /ɑimod/ i-mode

de **impact** /ɪmpɛkt/ impact, effect

de **impasse** /ɪmpɑsə/ (pl: -s, -n) impasse, deadlock

het/de **imperiaal** /ɪmperijal/ (pl: -s) roof-rack

het **imperialisme** /ɪmperijalɪsmə/ imperialism

de **imperialist** /ɪmperijalɪst/ (pl: -en) imperialist

imperialistisch /ɪmperijalɪstis/ (adj, adv) imperialist(ic)

het **imperium** /ɪmperijʏm/ (pl: -s, imperia) empire

impertinent /ɪmpɛrtinɛnt/ (adj, adv) impertinent

het **implantaat** /ɪmplɑntat/ (pl: implantaten) implant

implanteren /ɪmplɑnterə(n)/ (implanteerde, heeft geïmplanteerd) implant

implementeren /ɪmplemɛnterə(n)/ (implementeerde, heeft geïmplementeerd) implement

de **implicatie** /ɪmplika(t)si/ (pl: -s) implication

impliceren /ɪmpliserə(n)/ (impliceerde, heeft geïmpliceerd) imply

impliciet /ɪmplisit/ (adj, adv) implicit

imploderen /ɪmploderə(n)/ (implodeerde, is geïmplodeerd) implode

de **implosie** /ɪmplozi/ (pl: -s) implosion

imponeren /ɪmponerə(n)/ (imponeerde, heeft geïmponeerd) impress, overawe: *laat je niet ~ door die deftige woorden* don't be overawed by those posh words

impopulair /ɪmpopylɛːr/ (adj) unpopular: *~e maatregelen nemen* take unpopular measures

de **import** /ɪmpɔrt/ **1** import(ation) **2** import(s)

importeren /ɪmpɔrterə(n)/ (importeerde, heeft geïmporteerd) import

de **importeur** /ɪmpɔrtør/ (pl: -s) importer

imposant /ɪmpozɑnt/ (adj) impressive, imposing

impotent /ɪmpotɛnt/ (adj) impotent

impregneren /ɪmprɛɣnerə(n)/ (impregneerde, heeft geïmpregneerd) impregnate

het **impresariaat** /ɪmprɛsarijat/ [roughly] managership; agency

de **impresario** /ɪmprɛsarijo/ (pl: -'s) impresario

de **impressie** /ɪmprɛsi/ (pl: -s) impression

het **impressionisme** /ɪmprɛʃonɪsmə/ impressionism

improductief /ɪmprodʏktif/ (adj) unproductive

de **improvisatie** /ɪmproviza(t)si/ (pl: -s) improvisation

improviseren /ɪmprovizerə(n)/ (improviseerde, heeft geïmproviseerd) improvise

de **impuls** /ɪmpʏls/ (pl: -en) **1** impulse, impetus **2** impulse, urge: *hij handelde in een ~* he acted on (an) impulse

impulsief /ɪmpʏlsif/ (adj, adv) impulsive, impetuous

¹**in** /ɪn/ (adj) in: *de bal was in* the ball was in

²**in** /ɪn/ (adv) **1** in, into, inside: *dat wil er bij mij niet in* I find that hard to believe; *dag in dag uit* day in (and) day out **2** in, inside: *tussen twee huizen in* (in) between two houses || *tegen alle verwachtingen in* contrary to all expectations

³**in** /ɪn/ (prep) **1** in, at: *een vertegenwoordiger in het bestuur* a representative on the board; *puistjes in het gezicht* pimples on one's face; *in heel het land* throughout (*or:* all over) the country; *hij is nog nooit in Londen geweest* he has never been to London; *hij zat niet in dat vliegtuig* he wasn't on that plane; *in slaap* asleep **2** into: *in de hoogte kijken* look up; *in het Japans vertalen* translate into Japanese **3** in, at; during: *in het begin* at the beginning; *een keer in de week* once a week **4** in: *er gaan 100 cm in een meter* there are 100 centimetres to a metre; *twee meter in omtrek* two metres in circumference; *in een rustig tempo* at an easy pace; *in tweeën snijden* cut

in two || *professor in de* **natuurkunde** professor of physics; *zij is goed in* **wiskunde** she's good at mathematics; *uitbarsten in gelach* burst into laughter

inacceptabel /ɪnɑksɛptɑbəl/ (adj, adv) unacceptable

de **inachtneming** /ɪnɑxtnemɪŋ/ regard, consideration, observation: *met ~ van* having regard to, considering, taking into account; *met ~ van de voorschriften* in compliance with the regulations

inademen /ɪnadəmə(n)/ (ademde in, heeft ingeademd) inhale, breathe in

de **inauguratie** /ɪnɑuɣyra(t)si/ (pl: -s) inauguration

inaugureel /ɪnɑuɣyrel/ (adj) inaugural

inaugureren /ɪnɑuɣyrerə(n)/ (inaugureerde, heeft geïnaugureerd) inaugurate

inbedden /ɪmbɛdə(n)/ (bedde in, heeft ingebed) bed, embed

zich **inbeelden** /ɪmbeldə(n)/ (beeldde zich in, heeft zich ingebeeld) imagine: *dat beeld je je maar in* that's just your imagination

de **inbeelding** /ɪmbeldɪŋ/ (pl: -en) imagination

inbegrepen /ɪmbəɣrepə(n)/ (adj) included, including: *dat is* **bij** *de prijs ~* it's included in the price

het **inbegrip** /ɪmbəɣrɪp/: *met ~ van* including

inbellen /ɪmbɛlə(n)/ (belde in, heeft ingebeld) [comp] dial up

de **inbewaringstelling** /ɪmbəwarɪŋstɛlɪŋ/ (pl: -en) [Dutch] **1** arrest, taking into custody **2** sectioning

inbinden /ɪmbɪndə(n)/ (bond in, heeft ingebonden) bind

inblazen /ɪmblazə(n)/ (blies in, heeft ingeblazen) blow into; [fig] breathe into: *iets nieuw* **leven** *~* breathe new life into sth.

inblikken /ɪmblɪkə(n)/ (blikte in, heeft ingeblikt) can, tin

de **inboedel** /ɪmbudəl/ (pl: -s) moveables, furniture, furnishings: *een ~* **verzekeren** [roughly] insure the contents of one's house against fire and theft

de **inboedelverzekering** /ɪmbudəlvərzekərɪŋ/ (pl: -en) [roughly] fire and theft insurance

inboeten /ɪmbutə(n)/ (boette in, heeft ingeboet) lose

inboezemen /ɪmbuzəmə(n)/ (boezemde in, heeft ingeboezemd) inspire

de **inboorling** /ɪmborlɪŋ/ (pl: -en) native

de **inborst** /ɪmbɔrst/ disposition, character

inbouwen /ɪmbɑuwə(n)/ (bouwde in, heeft ingebouwd) build in

de **inbouwkeuken** /ɪmbɑukøkə(n)/ (pl: -s) built-in kitchen

de **inbox** /ɪmbɔks/ in box

de **inbraak** /ɪmbrak/ (pl: inbraken) breaking in, burglary: *~* **plegen** *in* break into, burgle

het **inbraakalarm** /ɪmbrakalɑrm/ burglar (*or:* intrusion) alarm

inbreken /ɪmbrekə(n)/ (brak in, heeft ingebroken) **1** break in(to) (a house), burgle (a house): *~ in een* **computersysteem** break into a computer system; *er is alweer* **bij** *ons ingebroken* our house has been broken into (*or:* burgled) again **2** [fig] butt in, interrupt: *mag ik even ~?* may I interrupt (for a moment)?; sorry to interrupt, but …

de **inbreker** /ɪmbrekər/ (pl: -s) burglar; [in computer] hacker

de **inbreng** /ɪmbrɛŋ/ (pl: -en) contribution

inbrengen /ɪmbrɛŋə(n)/ (bracht in, heeft ingebracht) **1** bring in(to); insert; inject **2** contribute **3** bring (forward): *daar valt niets* **tegen** *in te brengen* there is nothing to be said against this

de **inbreuk** /ɪmbrøk/ (pl: -en) infringement, violation

inburgeren /ɪmbyrɣərə(n)/ (burgerde in, is ingeburgerd) naturalize, settle down, settle in

de **inburgeringscursus** /ɪmbyrɣərɪŋskʏrsʏs/ (pl: -sen) citizenship course

de **inbussleutel** /ɪmbʏsløtəl/ (pl: -s) Allen key

de **Inca** /ɪŋka/ Inca

incalculeren /ɪŋkɑlkylerə(n)/ (calculeerde in, heeft ingecalculeerd) calculate in

de **incarnatie** /ɪŋkɑrna(t)si/ (pl: -s) incarnation

incasseren /ɪŋkɑserə(n)/ (incasseerde, heeft geïncasseerd) **1** collect; cash (in) **2** accept, take

het **incasseringsvermogen** /ɪŋkɑserɪŋsfərmoɣə(n)/ stamina, resilience: *hij* **heeft** *een groot ~* he can take a lot

het **incasso** /ɪŋkɑso/ collection: *automatische ~* direct debit

de **incest** /ɪnsɛst/ incest

incestueus /ɪnsɛstywøs/ (adj) incestuous

inchecken /ɪntʃekə(n)/ (checkte in, heeft ingecheckt) [airport] check in; [Dutch; public transport] touch in; [hotel] register: *zijn* **bagage** *~* check one's luggage

het **incident** /ɪnsidɛnt/ (pl: -en) incident

incidenteel /ɪnsidɛntel/ (adj, adv) incidental, occasional: *dit verschijnsel* **doet** *zich ~* **voor** this phenomenon occurs occasionally

inclusief /ɪŋklyzif/ (adv) including; [abbr: incl.] inclusive (of): *45 euro ~ (bedieningsgeld)* 45 euros, including service

incognito /ɪŋkɔɣnito/ (adv) incognito

incompetent /ɪŋkɔmpətɛnt/ (adj) incompetent, unqualified

incompleet /ɪŋkɔmplet/ (adj) incomplete

in concreto /ɪŋkɔŋkreto/ in the concrete, in this particular case

inconsequent /ɪŋkɔnsəkwɛnt/ (adj, adv) inconsistent

incontinent /ɪŋkɔntinɛnt/ (adj) incontinent

de **incontinentie** /ɪŋkɔntinɛn(t)si/ incontinence

incorrect /ɪnkɔrɛkt/ (adj, adv) incorrect
incourant /ɪnkurɑnt/ (adj) unsaleable, unmarketable: *~e maten* off-sizes
de **Incrowd** /ɪŋkraud/ (pl: -s) in-crowd
de **incubatietijd** /ɪŋkyba(t)sitɛit/ (pl: -en) incubation period
indammen /ɪndɑmə(n)/ (damde in, heeft ingedamd) dam (up): *een conflict ~* keep a conflict under control
zich **indekken** /ɪndɛkə(n)/ (dekte zich in, heeft zich ingedekt) cover o.s. (against)
indelen /ɪndelə(n)/ (deelde in, heeft ingedeeld) **1** divide, order, class(ify): *zijn dag ~* plan one's day **2** group, class(ify)
de **indeling** /ɪndelɪŋ/ (pl: -en) division, arrangement, classification; lay-out: *de ~ van een gebied in districten* the division of a region into districts
zich **indenken** /ɪndɛŋkə(n)/ (dacht zich in, heeft zich ingedacht) imagine: *zich in iemands situatie ~* put o.s. in s.o.'s place (*or:* shoes)
inderdaad /ɪndərdat/ (adv) indeed; really; sure enough: *ik heb dat ~ gezegd, maar ...* I did say that, but ...; *het lijkt er ~ op dat het helpt* it really does seem to help; *dat is ~ het geval* that is indeed the case; *~, dat dacht ik nu ook!* exactly, that's what I thought, too!
indertijd /ɪndərtɛit/ (adv) at the time
¹**indeuken** /ɪndøkə(n)/ (deukte in, is ingedeukt) be dented
²**indeuken** /ɪndøkə(n)/ (deukte in, heeft ingedeukt) dent
de **index** /ɪndɛks/ (pl: -en) index
het **indexcijfer** /ɪndɛksɛifər/ (pl: -s) index (number)
indexeren /ɪndɛkserə(n)/ (indexeerde, heeft geïndexeerd) index
India /ɪndija/ India
de **indiaan** /ɪndijan/ (pl: indianen) (American) Indian
indiaans /ɪndijans/ (adj) Indian
Indiaas /ɪndijas/ (adj) Indian
het **indianenverhaal** /ɪndijanə(n)vərhal/ (pl: -verhalen) tall story
de **indicatie** /ɪndika(t)si/ (pl: -s) indication
Indië /ɪndijə/ the Dutch East Indies; India
indien /ɪndin/ (conj) if, in case; supposing
indienen /ɪndinə(n)/ (diende in, heeft ingediend) submit: *een wetsontwerp ~* introduce a bill
de **indiensttreding** /ɪndinstredɪŋ/ taking up one's duties, commencement of employment
de **Indiër** /ɪndijər/ (pl: -s) Indian
de **indigestie** /ɪndiɣɛsti/ indigestion
indikken /ɪndɪkə(n)/ (dikte in, heeft/is ingedikt) thicken
indirect /ɪndirɛkt/ (adj, adv) indirect; roundabout: *op ~e manier* in an indirect way, in a roundabout way; *~e vrije trap* indirect free kick

Indisch /ɪndis/ (adj) (East) Indian
indiscreet /ɪndɪskret/ (adj, adv) indiscreet: *zonder ~ te zijn* without being indiscreet
het/de **individu** /ɪndividy/ (pl: -en) individual; person
het **individualisme** /ɪndividywalɪsmə/ individualism
de **individualist** /ɪndividywalɪst/ (pl: -en) individualist
¹**individueel** /ɪndividywel/ (adj) individual, particular
²**individueel** /ɪndividywel/ (adv) individually, singly
de **indoctrinatie** /ɪndɔktrina(t)si/ (pl: -s) indoctrination
indommelen /ɪndɔmələ(n)/ (dommelde in, is ingedommeld) doze off
Indonesië /ɪndonezijə/ Indonesia
de **Indonesiër** /ɪndonezijər/ (pl: -s) Indonesian
Indonesisch /ɪndonezis/ (adj) Indonesian
indoor- indoor
¹**indraaien** /ɪndrajə(n)/ (draaide in, is ingedraaid) turn in(to): *de auto draaide de straat in* the car turned into the street
²**indraaien** /ɪndrajə(n)/ (draaide in, heeft ingedraaid) screw in(to): *een schroef ~* drive (*or:* screw) in a screw
indringen /ɪndrɪŋə(n)/ (drong in, is ingedrongen) penetrate (into), intrude (into); soak (into)
indringend /ɪndrɪŋənt/ (adj) penetrating: *een ~e blik* a penetrating gaze, a piercing look
de **indringer** /ɪndrɪŋər/ (pl: -s) intruder, trespasser
indrinken /ɪndrɪŋkə(n)/ (dronk in, heeft ingedronken) **1** drink in: *zich moed ~* take Dutch courage **2** have pre-drink drinks; preload
indruisen /ɪndrœysə(n)/ (druiste in, heeft/is ingedruist) go against, conflict with
de **indruk** /ɪndrʏk/ (pl: -ken) **1** impression; air; idea: *diepe (grote) ~ maken* make a deep impression; *ik kon niet aan de ~ ontkomen dat* I could not escape the impression that; *dat geeft* (*or:* *wekt*) *de ~ ...* that gives (*or:* creates) the impression that ...; *ik kreeg de ~ dat* I got the impression that; *weinig ~ maken op iem.* make little impression on s.o. **2** impression, (im)print: *op de sneeuw waren ~ken van vogelpootjes zichtbaar* in the snow the prints (*or:* imprints) of birds' feet were visible
indrukken /ɪndrʏkə(n)/ (drukte in, heeft ingedrukt) push in, press
indrukwekkend /ɪndrʏkwɛkənt/ (adj, adv) impressive
induiken /ɪndœykə(n)/ (dook in, heeft/is ingedoken) **1** dive in(to): *zijn bed* (*or:* *de koffer*) *~* turn in, hit the sack **2** plunge in(to): *ergens dieper ~* delve deeper into sth.
industrialiseren /ɪndʏstrijalizerə(n)/ (in-

dustrialiseerde, heeft geïndustrialiseerd) industrialize

de **industrie** /ɪndystri/ (pl: -ën) (manufacturing) industry

industrieel /ɪndystrijel/ (adj) industrial

het **industriegebied** /ɪndystrijəbit/ (pl: -en) industrial area; industrial estate (or: park); trading estate

het **industrieland** /ɪndystrilɑnt/ (pl: -en) industrialized nation (or: country)

het **industrieterrein** /ɪndystritɛrɛin/ (pl: -en) industrial zone (or: estate, park)

indutten /ɪndʏtə(n)/ (dutte in, is ingedut) doze off, nod off

induwen /ɪndywə(n)/ (duwde in, heeft ingeduwd) push in(to)

ineengedoken /ɪneŋɣədokə(n)/ (adj) crouched, hunched (up)

ineenkrimpen /ɪneŋkrɪmpə(n)/ (kromp ineen, is ineengekrompen) curl up, double up; [fig] flinch

ineens /ɪnens/ (adv) **1** (all) at once: bij betaling ~ krijg je korting you get a discount for cash payment **2** all at once, all of a sudden, suddenly: zomaar ~ just like that

ineenstorten /ɪnɛnstɔrtə(n)/ (stortte ineen, is ineengestort) collapse

de **ineenstorting** /ɪnɛnstɔrtɪŋ/ collapse

ineffectief /ɪnɛfɛktif/ (adj, adv) ineffective, inefficient

inefficiënt /ɪnɛfiʃɛnt/ (adj, adv) inefficient

inenten /ɪnɛntə(n)/ (entte in, heeft ingeënt) vaccinate, inoculate

de **inenting** /ɪnɛntɪŋ/ (pl: -en) vaccination, inoculation

het **inentingsbewijs** /ɪnɛntɪŋzbəwɛis/ (pl: -bewijzen) vaccination certificate

de **infanterie** /ɪnfɑntəri/ infantry

infantiel /ɪnfɑntil/ (adj, adv) infantile: doe niet zo ~ don't be such a baby

het **infarct** /ɪnfɑrkt/ (pl: -en) infarct(ion); heart attack

infecteren /ɪnfɛktɛrə(n)/ (infecteerde, heeft geïnfecteerd) infect

de **infectie** /ɪnfɛksi/ (pl: -s) infection

inferieur /ɪnferijør/ (adj) inferior, low-grade

het **inferno** /ɪnfɛrno/ (pl: -'s) inferno

de **infiltrant** /ɪnfɪltrɑnt/ (pl: -en) infiltrator

de **infiltratie** /ɪnfɪltra(t)si/ (pl: -s) infiltration

infiltreren /ɪnfɪltrɛrə(n)/ (infiltreerde, is geïnfiltreerd) infiltrate: ~ in een beweging infiltrate (into) a movement

de **inflatie** /ɪnfla(t)si/ (pl: -s) inflation: [fig] het woord 'fascisme' is aan ~ **onderhevig** the meaning of the word 'fascism' is widening

inflatoir /ɪnflatwar/ (adj) inflationary

de **influenza** /ɪnflywɛnza/ influenza

influisteren /ɪnflœystərə(n)/ (fluisterde in, heeft ingefluisterd) whisper (in s.o.'s ear)

de **info** /ɪnfo/ (pl: -'s) [inform] info

de **informant** /ɪnfɔrmɑnt/ (pl: -en) informant

de **informateur** /ɪnfɔrmatør/ (pl: -s) politician who investigates whether a proposed cabinet formation will succeed

de **informatica** /ɪnfɔrmatika/ computer science, informatics

de **informaticus** /ɪnfɔrmatikʏs/ (pl: informatici) information scientist, computer scientist

de **informatie** /ɪnfɔrma(t)si/ (pl: -s) **1** information; data **2** information; intelligence: om nadere ~ verzoeken request further information; ~ **inwinnen** (bij ...) make inquiries (of ...), obtain information (from ...); ter ~ for your information

de **informatiedrager** /ɪnfɔrma(t)sidrayər/ (pl: -s) data carrier

informatief /ɪnfɔrmatif/ (adj) informative

de **informatietechnologie** /ɪnfɔrma(t)sitɛxnoloɣi/ information technology (IT)

de **informatieverwerking** /ɪnfɔrma(t)siverwɛrkɪŋ/ data processing (or: handling)

de **informatisering** /ɪnfɔrmatizerɪŋ/ (pl: -en) computerization

informeel /ɪnfɔrmel/ (adj, adv) informal, unofficial; casual

¹**informeren** /ɪnfɔrmɛrə(n)/ (informeerde, heeft geïnformeerd) inquire, enquire, ask: ik heb **ernaar** geïnformeerd I have made inquiries about it; ~ **bij** iem. ask s.o.; naar de aanvangstijden ~ inquire about opening times

²**informeren** /ɪnfɔrmɛrə(n)/ (informeerde, heeft geïnformeerd) inform

de **infostress** /ɪnfostrɛs/ info-stress

infrarood /ɪnfrarot/ (adj) infra-red

de **infrastructuur** /ɪnfrastrʏktyr/ (pl: -structuren) infrastructure

het **infuus** /ɪnfys/ (pl: infusen) drip: aan het ~ liggen a) be on a drip; b) [fig] need an injection

de **infuuszak** /ɪnfysɑk/ (pl: -ken) IV bag, infusion bag

ingaan /ɪŋɣan/ (ging in, is ingegaan) **1** go in(to): een deur ~ go through a door **2** go in(to), come in(to), enter: een weg ~ turn into a road **3** examine, go into: uitgebreid ~ op consider at length **4** agree with, agree to, comply with: op een aanbod ~ accept an offer **5** take effect: de regeling gaat 1 juli in the regulation is effective as from (or: of) July 1st || ~ **tegen** run counter to

de **ingang** /ɪŋɣaŋ/ (pl: -en) **1** entrance, entry, doorway; acceptance: de nieuwe ideeën vonden gemakkelijk ~ bij het publiek the new ideas found a ready reception with the public **2** commencement: met ~ van 1 april as from (or: of) April 1st; met onmiddellijke ~ to take effect at once, starting immediately

ingebed /ɪŋɣəbɛt/ (adj) embedded

ingebeeld /ɪŋɣəbelt/ (adj) imaginary

ingebonden /ɪŋɣəbɔndə(n)/ (adj) bound

ingebouwd /ɪŋɣəbaut/ (adj) built-in

de **ingebruikneming** /ɪŋəbrœyknemɪŋ/ introduction; occupation

ingeburgerd /ɪŋəbʏrɣərt/ (adj) **1** naturalized **2** established: ~ **raken** take hold

ingehouden /ɪŋəhɑudə(n)/ (adj) **1** restrained **2** subdued; bated

ingelegd /ɪŋəlɛχt/ (adj) inlaid

ingemaakt /ɪŋəmakt/ (adj) preserved, bottled

ingenaaid /ɪŋənajt/ (adj) stitched

de **ingenieur** /ɪnʒeɲør/ (pl: -s) engineer

ingenieus /ɪŋenijøs/ (adj, adv) ingenious

ingenomen /ɪŋənomə(n)/ (adj) (+ met) pleased (with), satisfied (with)

ingesloten /ɪŋɣəslotə(n)/ (adj, adv) **1** enclosed **2** surrounded

ingespannen /ɪŋɣəspɑnə(n)/ (adj, adv) **1** intensive, intense: ~ **luisteren** listen intently **2** strenuous: *na drie dagen van* ~ **arbeid** after three strenuous days

de **ingesprektoon** /ɪŋɣəsprɛkton/ engaged signal; [Am] busy signal

ingetogen /ɪŋətoɣə(n)/ (adj, adv) modest

ingeval /ɪŋɣəvɑl/ (conj) in case, in the event of

ingevallen /ɪŋɣəvɑlə(n)/ (adj) hollow; sunken

ingeven /ɪŋɣevə(n)/ (gaf in, heeft ingegeven) inspire: *doe wat uw hart **u** ingeeft* follow the dictates of your heart

de **ingeving** /ɪŋɣevɪŋ/ (pl: -en) inspiration, intuition: *een ~ **krijgen*** have a flash of inspiration, have a brainwave

ingevolge /ɪŋɣəvɔlɣə/ (prep) [form] in accordance with; under, by virtue of

ingevroren /ɪŋɣəvrorə(n)/ (adj) icebound; frozen

de **ingewanden** /ɪŋɣəwɑndə(n)/ (pl) intestines

de **ingewijde** /ɪŋɣəwɛidə/ (pl: -n) initiate; [fig also] insider; adept

ingewikkeld /ɪŋɣəwɪkəlt/ (adj, adv) complicated

ingeworteld /ɪŋɣəwɔrtəlt/ (adj) deep-rooted

de **ingezetene** /ɪŋɣəzetənə/ (pl: -n) resident, inhabitant

ingezonden /ɪŋɣəzɔndə(n)/ (adj) sent in: ~ **brieven** letters to the editor

de **ingooi** /ɪŋoj/ (pl: -en) throw-in

[1]**ingooien** /ɪŋojə(n)/ (gooide in, heeft ingegooid) [sport] throw in

[2]**ingooien** /ɪŋojə(n)/ (gooide in, heeft ingegooid) **1** throw in(to) **2** smash

ingraven /ɪŋrɑvə(n)/ (groef in, heeft ingegraven) bury: *zich (in de grond)* ~ dig (o.s.) in; burrow

het **ingrediënt** /ɪŋredijɛnt/ (pl: -en) ingredient

de **ingreep** /ɪŋrep/ (pl: ingrepen) intervention

ingrijpen /ɪŋrɛipə(n)/ (greep in, heeft ingegrepen) **1** interfere **2** intervene

ingrijpend /ɪŋrɛipənt/ (adj, adv) radical

ingroeien /ɪŋrujə(n)/ (groeide in, is ingegroeid) grow in(to): *een ingegroeide **nagel*** an ingrown nail

de **inhaalmanoeuvre** /ɪnhalmanœ:vrə/ (pl: -s) overtaking manoeuvre

de **inhaalrace** /ɪnhalres/ (pl: -s) race to recover lost ground, race to catch up

de **inhaalstrook** /ɪnhalstrok/ (pl: -stroken) fast lane

het **inhaalverbod** /ɪnhalvərbɔt/ overtaking prohibition; [Am] passing restriction

de **inhaalwedstrijd** /ɪnhalwɛtstrɛit/ (pl: -en) rearranged fixture, postponed match

inhaken /ɪnhakə(n)/ (haakte in, heeft/is ingehaakt) (+ op) take up

inhakken /ɪnhɑkə(n)/ (hakte in, heeft ingehakt) (+ op) pitch into

[1]**inhalen** /ɪnhalə(n)/ (haalde in, heeft ingehaald) [traf] overtake, pass

[2]**inhalen** /ɪnhalə(n)/ (haalde in, heeft ingehaald) **1** draw in, take in; haul in **2** catch up with; outrun **3** make up (for); recover: *de verloren **tijd*** ~ make up for lost time **4** bring in

inhaleren /ɪnhalɣrə(n)/ (inhaleerde, heeft geïnhaleerd) inhale; [only with direct object] draw in

inhalig /ɪnhaləχ/ (adj) greedy

de **inham** /ɪnhɑm/ (pl: -men) bay, cove, creek

inheems /ɪnhems/ (adj) native: *~e **planten*** indigenous plants

de **inhoud** /ɪnhɑut/ (pl: -en) **1** content, capacity **2** content **3** contents **4** import

[1]**inhouden** /ɪnhɑudə(n)/ (hield in, heeft ingehouden) **1** restrain, hold (in, back): *de **adem*** ~ hold one's breath **2** deduct: *een zeker **percentage** van het loon* ~ withhold a certain percentage of the wages **3** contain, hold **4** involve, mean: *wat houdt dit in voor onze klanten?* what does this mean for our customers? **5** hold in

zich [2]**inhouden** /ɪnhɑudə(n)/ (hield zich in, heeft zich ingehouden) control o.s.: *zich ~ om niet in lachen uit te barsten* keep a straight face

de **inhouding** /ɪnhɑudɪŋ/ (pl: -en) deduction; amount withheld

de **inhoudsmaat** /ɪnhɑutsmat/ (pl: -maten) measure of capacity (or: volume)

de **inhoudsopgave** /ɪnhɑutsɔpχavə/ (pl: -n) (table of) contents

inhuldigen /ɪnhʏldəɣə(n)/ (huldigde in, heeft ingehuldigd) inaugurate, install

de **inhuldiging** /ɪnhʏldəɣɪŋ/ (pl: -en) inauguration

inhuren /ɪnhʏrə(n)/ (huurde in, heeft ingehuurd) engage

de **initiaal** /ini(t)ʃal/ (pl: initialen) initial

het **initiatief** /ini(t)ʃatif/ (pl: initiatieven) initiative; enterprise: *op **eigen** ~* on one's own initiative

de **initiatiefnemer** /ini(t)ʃatifnemər/ (pl: -s)

initiator
de **initiator** /ini(t)ʃatɔr/ (pl: -s, -en) initiator
initiëren /ini(t)ɣerə(n)/ (initieerde, heeft geïnitieerd) initiate (into)
injecteren /ɪnjɛktɣerə(n)/ (injecteerde, heeft geïnjecteerd) inject
de **injectie** /ɪnjɛksi/ (pl: -s) injection
de **injectienaald** /ɪnjɛksinalt/ (pl: -en) (hypodermic) needle
inkapselen /ɪŋkɑpsələ(n)/ (kapselde in, heeft ingekapseld) encase
de **inkeer** /ɪŋker/ repentance: *tot ~ komen* think better of it
inkepen /ɪŋkepə(n)/ (keepte in, heeft ingekeept) notch; groove
de **inkeping** /ɪŋkepɪŋ/ (pl: -en) notch
de **inkijk** /ɪŋkɛɪk/ looking (in), view (of the inside); cleavage
inkijken /ɪŋkɛikə(n)/ (keek in, heeft ingekeken) take a look at
de **inkjet** /ɪŋkjɛt/ inkjet
inklappen /ɪŋklɑpə(n)/ (klapte in, heeft ingeklapt) fold in, fold up
inklaren /ɪŋklɑrə(n)/ (klaarde in, heeft ingeklaard) clear (inwards)
inkleden /ɪŋkledə(n)/ (kleedde in, heeft ingekleed) frame, express: *hoe zal ik mijn **verzoek** ~?* how shall I put my request?
inkleuren /ɪŋklørə(n)/ (kleurde in, heeft ingekleurd) colour
de **inklimmer** /ɪŋklɪmər/ (pl: -s) **1** cat burglar **2** illegal migrant trying to board a truck heading for Britain
inklinken /ɪŋklɪŋkə(n)/ (klonk in, is ingeklonken) settle
de **inkom** /ɪŋkɔm/ [Belg] admission, entrance fee
het ¹**inkomen** /ɪŋkomə(n)/ (pl: -s) income; revenue
²**inkomen** /ɪŋkomə(n)/ (kwam in, is ingekomen) enter, come in(to): *ingekomen **stukken*** (or: *brieven*) incoming correspondence (or: letters) ‖ *daar **kan** ik ~* (can) appreciate that, I quite understand that; *daar **komt** niets **van** in* that's out of the question, no way!
het **inkomgeld** /ɪŋkomɣɛlt/ (pl: -en) [Belg] admission (charge), entrance fee
de **inkomsten** /ɪŋkɔmstə(n)/ (pl) income; earnings; revenue(s)
de **inkomstenbelasting** /ɪŋkɔmstə(n)bəlɑstɪŋ/ (pl: -en) [Dutch] income tax
de **inkoop** /ɪŋkop/ (pl: inkopen) purchase, purchasing, buying: *inkopen **doen*** go shopping
de **inkoopprijs** /ɪŋkoprɛis/ (pl: -prijzen) cost price
inkopen /ɪŋkopə(n)/ (kocht in, heeft ingekocht) buy, purchase
de **inkoper** /ɪŋkopər/ (pl: -s) buyer, purchasing agent
inkoppen /ɪŋkɔpə(n)/ (kopte in, heeft ingekopt) head (the ball) in(to the goal)

het **inkoppertje** /ɪŋkɔpərcə/ easy score
inkorten /ɪŋkɔrtə(n)/ (kortte in, heeft ingekort) shorten, cut down
inkrimpen /ɪŋkrɪmpə(n)/ (kromp in, heeft ingekrompen) reduce, cut (down)
de **inkrimping** /ɪŋkrɪmpɪŋ/ (pl: -en) reduction; cut(s)
de **inkt** /ɪŋkt/ (pl: -en) ink: *met ~ schrijven* write in ink
de **inktvis** /ɪŋktfɪs/ (pl: -sen) octopus; squid
de **inktvlek** /ɪŋktflɛk/ (pl: -ken) ink blot
inladen /ɪnladə(n)/ (laadde in, heeft ingeladen) load
de **inlander** /ɪnlɑndər/ (pl: -s) native
inlands /ɪnlɑnts/ (adj) native; internal; domestic, home-grown
inlassen /ɪnlɑsə(n)/ (laste in, heeft ingelast) insert: *een pauze **inlassen*** take a break
zich **inlaten** /ɪnlatə(n)/ (liet zich in, heeft zich ingelaten) meddle (with, in), concern o.s. (with): *zich ~ **met** dergelijke mensen* associate with such people
de **inleg** /ɪnlɛɣ/ **1** deposit(ing); deposit **2** stake
inleggen /ɪnlɛɣə(n)/ (legde in, heeft ingelegd) **1** deposit; stake; invest **2** put, throw in (or: down) **3** preserve
het **inlegkruisje** /ɪnlɛɣkrœyʃə/ (pl: -s) panty shield
het **inlegvel** /ɪnlɛɣfɛl/ (pl: -len) insert
inleiden /ɪnlɛidə(n)/ (leidde in, heeft ingeleid) introduce
inleidend /ɪnlɛidənt/ (adj) introductory; opening
de **inleider** /ɪnlɛidər/ (pl: -s) (opening) speaker
de **inleiding** /ɪnlɛidɪŋ/ (pl: -en) **1** introductory remarks, opening remarks, preamble **2** introduction, preface, foreword
zich **inleven** /ɪnlevə(n)/ (leefde zich in, heeft zich ingeleefd) put (or: imagine) o.s. (in), empathize (with)
inleveren /ɪnlevərə(n)/ (leverde in, heeft ingeleverd) hand in, turn in
inlezen /ɪnlezə(n)/ (las in, heeft ingelezen): *zich ~* read up (on), study the literature; *gegevens ~* read in data
inlichten /ɪnlɪxtə(n)/ (lichtte in, heeft ingelicht) inform
de **inlichting** /ɪnlɪxtɪŋ/ (pl: -en) **1** (piece of) information: *~en inwinnen* make inquiries, ask for information **2** information (office); inquiries; intelligence (service)
de **inlichtingendienst** /ɪnlɪxtɪŋə(n)dinst/ (pl: -en) **1** information office, inquiries office **2** intelligence (service), secret service
inlijsten /ɪnlɛistə(n)/ (lijstte in, heeft ingelijst) frame
inlijven /ɪnlɛivə(n)/ (lijfde in, heeft ingelijfd) incorporate (in/with); annex
de **inlineskate** /ɪnlɑjnsket/ (pl: -s) in-line skate
inlineskaten /ɪnlɑjnsketə(n)/ inline skate
de **inloggegevens** /ɪnlɔɣəɣevə(n)s/ (pl) login

(*or:* user) credentials, login data
inloggen /ɪnlɔɣə(n)/ (logde in, heeft ingelogd) log on, log in (on)

het **inlogscherm** /ɪnlɔxsxɛrm/ (pl: -en) login screen

¹**inlopen** /ɪnlopə(n)/ (liep in, is ingelopen) **1** walk into, step into; [bldg] enter; turn into **2** catch up: *op iem. ~* catch up on s.o.

²**inlopen** /ɪnlopə(n)/ (liep in, heeft ingelopen) **1** wear in **2** make up ‖ *zich ~* warm up

inlossen /ɪnlɔsə(n)/ (loste in, heeft ingelost) redeem

inluiden /ɪnlœydə(n)/ (luidde in, heeft ingeluid) herald

¹**inmaken** /ɪmakə(n)/ (maakte in, heeft ingemaakt) preserve; conserve

²**inmaken** /ɪmakə(n)/ (maakte in, heeft ingemaakt) [fig] slaughter

zich **inmengen** /ɪmɛŋə(n)/ (mengde zich in, heeft zich ingemengd) interfere (in, with)

de **inmenging** /ɪmɛŋɪŋ/ (pl: -en) interference (in, with)

inmiddels /ɪmɪdəls/ (adv) meanwhile, in the meantime: *dat is ~ bevestigd* this has since (*or:* now) been confirmed

in natura /ɪnatyra/ (adj) in kind

innemen /ɪnemə(n)/ (nam in, heeft ingenomen) **1** take: *een standpunt ~* take a stand **2** take (up); occupy: *zijn plaats ~* take one's seat **3** capture

innemend /ɪnemənt/ (adj, adv) captivating, engaging, winning

innen /ɪnə(n)/ (inde, heeft geïnd) collect; cash

het ¹**innerlijk** /ɪnərlək/ (pl: -en) inner self, inner nature

²**innerlijk** /ɪnərlək/ (adj, adv) inner

¹**innig** /ɪnəx/ (adj) **1** profound, deep(est) **2** ardent, fervent **3** close, deep, intimate

²**innig** /ɪnəx/ (adv) (most) deeply

de **inning** /ɪnɪŋ/ (pl: -en) **1** collection; cashing **2** innings; inning

de **innovatie** /ɪnova(t)si/ (pl: -s) innovation

innovatief /ɪnovatif/ (adj, adv) innovative

¹**inpakken** /ɪmpakə(n)/ (pakte in, heeft ingepakt) pack in: *~ en wegwezen* pack up and go

²**inpakken** /ɪmpakə(n)/ (pakte in, heeft ingepakt) **1** pack (up) **2** wrap (up) ‖ *zich laten ~* come off worst; be taken to the cleaners, be taken in

inpalmen /ɪmpalmə(n)/ (palmde in, heeft ingepalmd) charm, win over

inparkeren /ɪmparkerə(n)/ parallel park

inpassen /ɪmpasə(n)/ (paste in, heeft ingepast) fit in

inpeperen /ɪmpepərə(n)/ (peperde in, heeft ingepeperd) [fig] get even with (s.o.) (for)

inperken /ɪmpɛrkə(n)/ (perkte in, heeft ingeperkt) restrict, curtail

in petto /ɪmpɛto/ (adv) in reserve, in store

inpikken /ɪmpɪkə(n)/ (pikte in, heeft ingepikt) **1** grab, snap up; pinch **2** [Belg] take up

inplakken /ɪmplakə(n)/ (plakte in, heeft ingeplakt) stick (*or:* glue, paste) in

inpluggen /ɪmplʏɣə(n)/ (plugde in, heeft ingeplugd) plug in

inpolderen /ɪmpɔldərə(n)/ (polderde in, heeft ingepolderd) drain, impolder

de **inpoldering** /ɪmpɔldərɪŋ/ (pl: -en) (land) reclamation, impoldering

inpompen /ɪmpɔmpə(n)/ pump in(to)

inpraten /ɪmpratə(n)/ (praatte in, heeft ingepraat) talk (s.o.) into (sth.): *op iem. ~* work on s.o.

inprenten /ɪmprɛntə(n)/ (prentte in, heeft ingeprent) impress (on), instil (in(to)); imprint

de **input** /ɪmput/ (pl: -s) input

de **inquisitie** /ɪŋkwizi(t)si/ inquisition

inregenen /ɪnreɣənə(n)/ (regende in, heeft ingeregend) rain in: *het regent hier in* the rain's coming in (*or:* through)

het **inreisverbod** /ɪnrɛisfərbɔt/ (re-)entry ban; [Am] travel ban

inrekenen /ɪnrekənə(n)/ (rekende in, heeft ingerekend) pull in; round up

het ¹**inrichten** /ɪnrɪxtə(n)/ [Belg] organize: *de ~de macht* the (school) administration (*or:* management)

²**inrichten** /ɪnrɪxtə(n)/ (richtte in, heeft ingericht) equip; furnish: *een compleet ingerichte keuken* a fully-equipped kitchen

de **inrichter** /ɪnrɪxtər/ [Belg] organizer

de **inrichting** /ɪnrɪxtɪŋ/ (pl: -en) **1** design; layout **2** institution

¹**inrijden** /ɪnrɛidə(n)/ (reed in, is ingereden) ride in(to); [car] drive in(to)

²**inrijden** /ɪnrɛidə(n)/ (reed in, heeft ingereden) run in; break in

de **inrit** /ɪnrɪt/ (pl: -ten) drive(way)

inroepen /ɪnrupə(n)/ (riep in, heeft ingeroepen) call in, call upon: *iemands hulp ~* call in s.o.'s help

inroosteren /ɪnrostərə(n)/ (roosterde in, heeft ingeroosterd) schedule

de **inruil** /ɪnrœyl/ exchange, trade-in, part exchange: *€ 2000,- bij ~ van* uw oude auto 2,000 euros in part exchange for your old car

inruilen /ɪnrœylə(n)/ (ruilde in, heeft ingeruild) **1** exchange **2** trade in, part-exchange

de **inruilwaarde** /ɪnrœylwardə/ (pl: -n) trade-in (*or:* part-exchange) value

inruimen /ɪnrœymə(n)/ (ruimde in, heeft ingeruimd) clear (out)

inrukken /ɪnrʏkə(n)/ (rukte in, is ingerukt) dismiss, withdraw: *ingerukt mars!* dismiss!

inschakelen /ɪnsxakələ(n)/ (schakelde in, heeft ingeschakeld) **1** switch on; connect **2** call in, bring in, involve

inschalen /ɪnsxalə(n)/ (schaalde in, heeft

ingeschaald) rank; grade, classify; [salary] put on a/the scale

inschatten /ˈɪnsxatə(n)/ (schatte in, heeft ingeschat) estimate, assess

inschenken /ˈɪnsxɛŋkə(n)/ (schonk in, heeft ingeschonken) pour (out)

inschepen /ˈɪnsxepə(n)/ (scheepte in, heeft ingescheept) embark

inscheuren /ˈɪnsxørə(n)/ (scheurde in, is ingescheurd) tear

¹**inschieten** /ˈɪnsxitə(n)/ (schoot in, is inge- schoten) **1** fall through: *mijn lunch zal er wel bij* ~ then I can say goodbye to my lunch **2** shoot in(to): *een zijstraat* ~ shoot into a side street **3** score

²**inschieten** /ˈɪnsxitə(n)/ (schoot in, heeft in- geschoten) **1** lose **2** shoot into the net

inschikkelijk /ˈɪnsxɪkələk/ (adj, adv) accom- modating: *niet erg* ~ rather uncompromising

inschikken /ˈɪnsxɪkə(n)/ (schikte in, heeft/is ingeschikt) move up: *als iedereen even wat in- schikt* if everyone can just move up a bit

het **inschrijfgeld** /ˈɪnsxrɛifxɛlt/ (pl: -en) regis- tration fee; entry fee; enrolment fee

¹**inschrijven** /ˈɪnsxrɛivə(n)/ (schreef in, heeft ingeschreven) bid, submit a bid

²**inschrijven** /ˈɪnsxrɛivə(n)/ (schreef in, heeft ingeschreven) register; enter; enrol; sign up: *zich (laten)* ~ sign up, register (o.s.); *zich als student* ~ enrol as a student

de **inschrijving** /ˈɪnsxrɛivɪŋ/ (pl: -en) **1** regis- tration; entry; enrolment **2** [com] subscrip- tion; bid: *een* ~ *openen* call for bids (*or:* ten- ders)

het **inschrijvingsformulier** /ˈɪnsxrɛivɪŋsfor- mylir/ (pl: -en) application form; enrolment form

inschuiven /ˈɪnsxœyvə(n)/ (schoof in, heeft ingeschoven) push in, slide in

de **inscriptie** /ɪnskrɪpsi/ (pl: -s) inscription; leg- end

het **insect** /ɪnsɛkt/ (pl: -en) insect

de **insectenbeet** /ɪnsɛktə(n)bet/ (pl: -beten) insect bite

het **insecticide** /ɪnsɛktisidə/ (pl: -n, -s) insecti- cide

inseinen /ˈɪnsɛinə(n)/ (seinde in, heeft inge- seind) tip off

de **inseminatie** /ɪnseminˈa(t)si/ insemination: *kunstmatige* ~ artificial insemination

de **insert** /ɪnsyːrt/ (pl: -s) [comp] Insert (key)

insgelijks /ɪnsxəlɛiks/ (adv) likewise; (and) the same to you

de **insider** /ˈɪnsɔjdər/ (pl: -s) insider

het **insigne** /ɪnsˈinə/ (pl: -s) badge

de **insinuatie** /ɪnsinywa(t)si/ (pl: -s) insinuation

insinueren /ɪnsinywerə(n)/ (insinueerde, heeft geïnsinueerd) insinuate

insjallah /ɪnʃˈɑla/ (int) inshallah

¹**inslaan** /ˈɪnslan/ (sloeg in, is ingeslagen) **1** take; turn into: [fig] *een verkeerde weg* ~

take the wrong path (*or:* turning), go the wrong way; [fig] *nieuwe wegen* ~ break new ground, blaze a (new) trail **2** strike, hit ‖ *het nieuws sloeg in als een bom* the news came as a bombshell

²**inslaan** /ˈɪnslan/ (sloeg in, heeft ingeslagen) **1** smash (in), beat (in) **2** stock (up on, with)

de **inslag** /ˈɪnslɑx/ (pl: -en) **1** impact **2** streak [pers]; slant; bias

inslapen /ˈɪnslapə(n)/ (sliep in, is ingeslapen) **1** fall asleep, drop off (*or:* go) to sleep **2** pass away, pass on

inslikken /ˈɪnslɪkə(n)/ (slikte in, heeft inge- slikt) swallow

de **insluiper** /ˈɪnslœypər/ (pl: -s) sneak-thief, in- truder

insluiten /ˈɪnslœytə(n)/ (sloot in, heeft inge- gesloten) **1** enclose; surround: *een ant- woordformulier* ~ enclose an answer form **2** shut in, lock in

¹**insmeren** /ˈɪnsmerə(n)/ (smeerde in, heeft ingesmeerd) rub (with); put … on

zich ²**insmeren** /ˈɪnsmerə(n)/ (smeerde zich in, heeft zich ingesmeerd) put oil on: *zich* ~ *met bodylotion* rub o.s. with body lotion

insneeuwen /ˈɪnsnewə(n)/ (sneeuwde in, is ingesneeuwd) snow in

insnijden /ˈɪnsnɛidə(n)/ (sneed in, heeft in- gesneden) cut into; [med] lance: *een wond* ~ make an incision in a wound

inspannen /ˈɪnspanə(n)/ (spande in, heeft ingespannen) use; exert: *zich* ~ *voor iets* take a lot of trouble about sth.; *zich moeten* ~ *om wakker te blijven* have to struggle to stay awake

inspannend /ˈɪnspɑnənt/ (adj) strenuous, laborious; exacting

de **inspanning** /ˈɪnspɑnɪŋ/ (pl: -en) effort, ex- ertion; strain: *met een laatste* ~ *van zijn krach- ten* with a final effort, with one last effort

inspecteren /ɪnspɛkterə(n)/ (inspecteerde, heeft geïnspecteerd) inspect, examine, sur- vey

de **inspecteur** /ɪnspɛktør/ (pl: -s) inspector, ex- aminer

de **inspectie** /ɪnspɛksi/ (pl: -s) **1** inspection, ex- amination, survey **2** inspectorate

¹**inspelen** /ˈɪnspelə(n)/ (speelde in, heeft in- gespeeld) **1** anticipate **2** go along with; cap- italize on; take advantage of; feel for

²**inspelen** /ˈɪnspelə(n)/ (speelde in, heeft in- gespeeld) [sport] practise, warm up

de **inspiratie** /ɪnspira(t)si/ (pl: -s) inspiration

inspireren /ɪnspirerə(n)/ (inspireerde, heeft geïnspireerd) inspire: *geïnspireerd wor- den door iets (iem.)* be inspired by sth. (s.o.)

inspirerend /ɪnspirerənt/ (adj, adv) inspir- ing

de **inspraak** /ˈɪnsprak/ participation, involve- ment; say (in sth.)

inspreken /ˈɪnsprekə(n)/ (sprak in, heeft ingesproken) record: *u kunt nu uw **boodschap** ~* you may leave (*or:* record) your message now ‖ *iem. **moed** ~* put heart into s.o.

inspringen /ˈɪnsprɪŋə(n)/ (sprong in, is ingesprongen) **1** stand in: *voor een collega ~* stand in for a colleague **2** jump on(to), leap on(to), seize (up)on ‖ *deze **regel** moet een beetje ~* this line needs to be indented slightly

inspuiten /ˈɪnspœytə(n)/ (spoot in, heeft ingespoten) inject; fix

instaan /ˈɪnstan/ (stond in, heeft ingestaan) answer, be answerable (*or:* responsible); guarantee; vouch: *voor iem. ~* vouch for s.o.

instabiel /ɪnstaˈbil/ (adj) unstable

de **instabiliteit** /ɪnstabiliˈtɛit/ instability

de **installateur** /ɪnstalaˈtør/ (pl: -s) fitter, installer; electrician

de **installatie** /ɪnstaˈla(t)si/ (pl: -s) **1** installation **2** installation, plant, equipment, machinery; fittings: *een nieuwe **stereo-installatie*** a new hifi-set **3** installation, inauguration

installeren /ɪnstaˈlerə(n)/ (installeerde, heeft geïnstalleerd) install; inaugurate: *iem. als lid ~* initiate s.o. as a member

de **instandhouding** /ɪnstʌntˈhɑudɪŋ/ maintenance, preservation

de **instantie** /ɪnˈstɑnsi/ (pl: -s) **1** body, authority: *de **officiële** ~s* the government agencies, the official bodies **2** [law] instance ‖ *in eerste ~ dachten we dat het waar was* initially we thought it was true

instappen /ˈɪnstɑpə(n)/ (stapte in, is ingestapt) get in; get on; board

insteken /ˈɪnstekə(n)/ (stak in, heeft ingestoken) put in: *de **stekker** ~* plug in, put in the plug

instellen /ˈɪnstɛlə(n)/ (stelde in, heeft ingesteld) **1** establish, create **2** set up, start **3** adjust; focus; tune: *een **camera** (scherp) ~* focus a camera; *zakelijk ingesteld zijn* have a businesslike attitude (*or:* mentality)

de **instelling** /ˈɪnstɛlɪŋ/ (pl: -en) **1** institute, institution **2** setting; tuning: [comp] *instellingen* settings **3** attitude, mentality: *een **negatieve** ~* a negative attitude

instemmen /ˈɪnstɛmə(n)/ (stemde in, heeft ingestemd) agree (with, to)

de **instemming** /ˈɪnstɛmɪŋ/ approval

het **instinct** /ɪnˈstɪŋkt/ (pl: -en) instinct

instinctief /ɪnstɪŋkˈtif/ (adj, adv) instinctive

instinctmatig /ɪnˈstɪŋktmatəx/ (adj, adv) instinctive: *~ **handelen*** act on one's instinct(s)

de **instinker** /ˈɪnstɪŋkər/ tricky question

institutioneel /ɪnstity(t)ʃoˈnel/ (adj) institutional

het **instituut** /ɪnstiˈtyt/ (pl: instituten) institution, institute

instoppen /ˈɪnstɔpə(n)/ (stopte in, heeft ingestopt) **1** put in **2** tuck in: *iem. **lekker** ~* tuck

s.o. in nice and warm

instorten /ˈɪnstɔrtə(n)/ (stortte in, is ingestort) **1** collapse; fall down; cave in: *de zaak staat **op** ~* the business is at the point of collapse **2** collapse, break down

de **instorting** /ˈɪnstɔrtɪŋ/ (pl: -en) collapse [bldg]; breakdown; caving, cave-in

de **instroom** /ˈɪnstrom/ (pl: instromen) influx, inflow: *de ~ van eerstejaars **studenten*** the intake of first-year students

de **instructeur** /ɪnstrʏkˈtør/ (pl: -s) instructor

de **instructie** /ɪnˈstrʏksi/ (pl: -s) instruction; order; directive

instructief /ɪnstrʏkˈtif/ (adj, adv) instructive, informative

instrueren /ɪnstryˈwerə(n)/ (instrueerde, heeft geïnstrueerd) instruct

het **instrument** /ɪnstryˈmɛnt/ (pl: -en) **1** instrument: *~en **aflezen*** read instruments (*or:* dials) **2** tool **3** (musical) instrument: *een ~ **bespelen*** play an instrument

instrumentaal /ɪnstrymɛnˈtal/ (adj) instrumental

instuderen /ˈɪnstyderə(n)/ (studeerde in, heeft ingestudeerd) practise, learn: *een **muziekstuk** ~* practise a piece of music

de **instuif** /ˈɪnstœyf/ (pl: instuiven) **1** (informal) party **2** youth centre

insturen /ˈɪnstyrə(n)/ (stuurde in, heeft ingestuurd) **1** send in, submit **2** steer into; sail into [ship]

de **insuline** /ɪnsyˈlinə/ insulin

intact /ɪnˈtɑkt/ (adj) intact

de **intake** /ˈɪntek/ (pl: -s) register

het **intakegesprek** /ˈɪntekxəsprɛk/ (pl: -ken) interview on admission

de **inteelt** /ˈɪntelt/ inbreeding

integendeel /ɪnteˈɣə(n)del/ (adv) on the contrary: *ik lui? ~!* me lazy? quite the contrary!

integer /ɪnˈteɣər/ (adj, adv) upright, honest

de **¹integraal** /ɪnteˈɣral/ (pl: integralen) [maths] integral

²integraal /ɪnteˈɣral/ (adj, adv) integral, complete

de **integraalhelm** /ɪnteˈɣralhɛlm/ (pl: -en) regulation (crash-)helmet

de **integratie** /ɪnteˈɣra(t)si/ integration

integreren /ɪnteˈɣrerə(n)/ (integreerde, heeft/is geïntegreerd) integrate: *~ in de samenleving* integrate into society

de **integriteit** /ɪnteɣriˈtɛit/ integrity

¹intekenen /ˈɪntekənə(n)/ (tekende in, heeft ingetekend) subscribe, sign up

²intekenen /ˈɪntekənə(n)/ (tekende in, heeft ingetekend) register, enter

de **intekenlijst** /ˈɪnteke(n)lɛist/ (pl: -en) subscription list

het **intellect** /ɪntɛˈlɛkt/ intellect

intellectueel /ɪntɛlɛktyˈwel/ (adj, adv) intellectual

intelligent /ɪntɛliɣɛnt/ (adj, adv) intelligent, bright

de **intelligentie** /ɪntɛliɣɛnsi/ intelligence

het **intelligentiequotiënt** /ɪntɛliɣɛnsikoʃɛnt/ (pl: -en) intelligence quotient, IQ

de **intelligentietest** /ɪntɛliɣɛnsitɛst/ (pl: -s) intelligence test

de **intelligentsia** /ɪntɛliɣɛn(t)sija/ intelligentsia

intens /ɪntɛns/ (adj, adv) intense: ~ *gelukkig* blissfully happy; ~ *genieten* enjoy immensely

intensief /ɪntɛnzif/ (adj, adv) intensive

de **intensiteit** /ɪntɛnzitɛit/ intensity, intenseness

de **intensive care** /ɪntɛnsɪfkɛːr/ intensive care: *op* de ~ *liggen* be in intensive care

intensiveren /ɪntɛnzivərə(n)/ (intensiveerde, heeft geïntensiveerd) intensify

de **intentie** /ɪntɛnsi/ (pl: -s) intention, purpose: *de* ~ *hebben* om intend to

de **interactie** /ɪntərɑksi/ (pl: -s) interaction

interactief /ɪntərɑktif/ (adj, adv) interactive

de **intercedent** /ɪntərsedɛnt/ intermediary

de **intercity** /ɪntərsɪti/ (pl: -'s) intercity (train): *de* ~ *nemen* go by intercity (train)

de **intercom** /ɪntərkɔm/ (pl: -s) intercom: *iets over* de ~ *omroepen* announce sth. over (*or:* on) the intercom

de **intercommunale** /ɪntərkɔmynalə/ (pl: -s) [Belg] [roughly] intermunicipal (utility) company (with state and/or private participation)

intercontinentaal /ɪntərkɔntinɛntal/ (adj, adv) intercontinental

interdisciplinair /ɪntərdisiplinɛːr/ (adj, adv) interdisciplinary

interen /ɪntərə(n)/ (teerde in, heeft/is ingeteerd) eat into (one's capital)

interessant /ɪntərɛsɑnt/ (adj, adv) **1** interesting: ~ *willen zijn (doen)* show off **2** advantageous, profitable

het/de **interesse** /ɪntərɛsə/ (pl: -s) interest: *een brede* ~ *hebben* have wide interests

¹**interesseren** /ɪntərɛsɛrə(n)/ (interesseerde, heeft geïnteresseerd) interest: *wie het gedaan heeft interesseert me niet* I am not interested in who did it

zich ²**interesseren** /ɪntərɛsɛrə(n)/ (interesseerde zich, heeft zich geïnteresseerd) be interested

de **interest** /ɪntərɛst/ (pl: -en) interest: *samengestelde* ~ compound interest; *tegen* 9 % ~ at the rate of 9 %

de **interface** /ɪntərfes/ (pl: -s) interface

het **interieur** /ɪntər(i)jør/ (pl: -s) interior, inside

het **interim** /ɪntərɪm/ (pl: -s) **1** interim: *de directeur ad* ~ the acting manager **2** [Belg] temporary replacement (*or:* job)

het **interimbureau** /ɪntərɪmbyro/ (pl: -s) [Belg] employment agency

de **interland** /ɪntərlɑnt/ (pl: -s) international (match); test match

interlokaal /ɪntərlokal/ (adj, adv) trunk

intermenselijk /ɪntərmɛnsələk/ (adj) interpersonal: ~*e verhoudingen* human relations

het **intermezzo** /ɪntərmɛdzo/ (pl: -'s) intermezzo; [fig] interlude

intern /ɪntɛrn/ (adj, adv) **1** resident: ~*e patiënten* in-patients **2** internal, domestic: *uitsluitend voor* ~ *gebruik* confidential

het **internaat** /ɪntərnat/ (pl: internaten) boarding school

internationaal /ɪntərnɑ(t)ʃonal/ (adj, adv) international

de **international** /ɪntərnɛʃənəl/ (pl: -s) [sport] international

internationaliseren /ɪntərnɑ(t)ʃonalizɛrə(n)/ (internationaliseerde, heeft geïnternationaliseerd) internationalize

interneren /ɪntɛrnɛrə(n)/ (interneerde, heeft geïnterneerd) intern

het **internet** /ɪntərnɛt/ Internet

het **internetadres** /ɪntərnɛtadrɛs/ (pl: -sen) Internet address

internetbankieren /ɪntərnɛtbɑŋkirə(n)/ (internetbankierde, heeft geïnternetbankierd) e-banking, Internet banking

internetbellen /ɪntərnɛtbɛlə(n)/ (internetbelde, heeft geïnternetbeld) voip

het **internetcafé** /ɪntərnɛtkafe/ (pl: -s) Internet café, cybercafé

internetdaten /ɪntərnɛdetə(n)/ (internetdatete, heeft geïnternetdatet) date online, online dating

de **internetprovider** /ɪntərnɛtprovɑjdər/ (pl: -s) Internet (service) provider

de **internettelevisie** Internet television

internetten /ɪntərnɛtə(n)/ (internette, heeft geïnternet) surf the Net

de **internetter** /ɪntərnɛtər/ (pl: -s) netter, nettie, nethead

de **internetveiling** /ɪntərnɛtfɛilɪŋ/ internet auction

de **internetverbinding** /ɪntərnɛtfɛrbɪndɪŋ/ (pl: -en) Internet connection

internetwinkelen /ɪntərnɛtwɪŋkələ(n)/ shop online, online shopping

de **internist** /ɪntərnɪst/ (pl: -en) internist

de **interpellatie** /ɪntərpɛla(t)si/ (pl: -s) interpellation

interpelleren /ɪntərpɛlɛrə(n)/ (interpelleerde, heeft geïnterpelleerd) interpellate: *de minister* ~ *over* interpellate the minister about

de **interpretatie** /ɪntərpreta(t)si/ (pl: -s) interpretation, reading: *foute (verkeerde)* ~ misinterpretation

interpreteren /ɪntərpretɛrə(n)/ (interpreteerde, heeft geïnterpreteerd) interpret

de **interpunctie** /ɪntərpʏŋksi/ punctuation

interrumperen /ɪntərʏmpɛrə(n)/ (interrumpeerde, heeft geïnterrumpeerd) interrupt

de **interruptie** /ɪntərʏpsi/ (pl: -s) interruption

het **interval** /ɪntərvɑl/ (pl: -len) interval

de **interventie** /ɪntərvɛnsi/ (pl: -s) intervention

het **interview** /ɪntərvju/ (pl: -s) **1** interview **2** job interview

interviewen /ɪntərvjuwə(n)/ (interviewde, heeft geïnterviewd) interview

intiem /ɪntim/ (adj, adv) **1** intimate **2** cosy: *een ~ gesprek* a cosy chat

de **intifada** /ɪntifɑda/ (pl: -'s) intifada

intikken /ɪntɪkə(n)/ (tikte in, heeft ingetikt) **1** smash, break **2** type in ‖ *de bal* ~ flick the ball in (*or:* home)

de **intimidatie** /ɪntimida(t)si/ (pl: -s) intimidation, bullying: *seksuele intimidatie* sexual harassment

intimideren /ɪntimidɛrə(n)/ (intimideerde, heeft geïntimideerd) intimidate

de **intimiteit** /ɪntimitɛit/ (pl: -en) **1** intimacy, familiarity **2** liberty: *ongewenste ~en* sexual harassment

de **intocht** /ɪntɔxt/ (pl: -en) entry: *zijn ~ houden in* make one's entry into

intoetsen /ɪntutsə(n)/ (toetste in, heeft ingetoetst) key in, enter

intolerant /ɪntolerɑnt/ (adj) intolerant

de **intolerantie** /ɪntolerɑn(t)si/ intolerance

intomen /ɪntomə(n)/ (toomde in, heeft ingetoomd) curb, restrain, check

de **intonatie** /ɪntona(t)si/ (pl: -s) intonation

het **intranet** /ɪntranɛt/ intranet

intrappen /ɪntrɑpə(n)/ (trapte in, heeft ingetrapt) kick in (*or:* down)

intraveneus /ɪntravenøs/ (adj, adv) intravenous

de **intrede** /ɪntredə/ entry: *zijn ~ doen* set in

intreden /ɪntredə(n)/ (trad in, is ingetreden) **1** enter a convent (*or:* monastery) **2** set in, occur, take effect

de **intrek** /ɪntrɛk/ residence: *bij iem. zijn ~ nemen* move in with s.o.

¹**intrekken** /ɪntrɛkə(n)/ (trok in, is ingetrokken) **1** move in (with): *bij zijn vriendin ~* move in with one's girlfriend **2** be absorbed, soak in: *de verf moet nog ~* the paint must soak in first

²**intrekken** /ɪntrɛkə(n)/ (trok in, heeft ingetrokken) **1** draw in, draw up, retract **2** withdraw; cancel; abolish; drop; repeal: *een verlof ~* cancel leave

de **intrekking** /ɪntrɛkɪŋ/ (pl: -en) withdrawal; abolition; cancellation; repeal

de **intrigant** /ɪntriɣɑnt/ (pl: -en) intriguer, schemer

de **intrige** /ɪntriʒə/ (pl: -s) intrigue, plot

intrigeren /ɪntriɣerə(n)/ (intrigeerde, heeft geïntrigeerd) intrigue, fascinate

intrigerend /ɪntriɣerənt/ (adj) intriguing, fascinating

het/de **intro** /ɪntro/ (pl: -'s) intro

de **introducé** /ɪntrodysɛ/ (pl: -s) guest, friend

introduceren /ɪntrodysɛrə(n)/ (introduceerde, heeft geïntroduceerd) **1** introduce; initiate **2** introduce, phase in

de **introductie** /ɪntrodʏksi/ (pl: -s) **1** introduction, presentation **2** launch(ing)

de **introductieweek** /ɪntrodʏksiwek/ orientation week

introvert /ɪntrovɛrt/ (adj) introverted

de **intuïtie** /ɪntywi(t)si/ (pl: -s) intuition, instinct: *op zijn ~ afgaan* act on one's intuition

intuïtief /ɪntywitif/ (adj, adv) intuitive, instinctive: ~ *aanvoelen* know intuitively

intussen /ɪntʏsə(n)/ (adv) meanwhile, in the meantime

intypen /ɪntipə(n)/ (typte in, heeft ingetypt) type in, enter

de **inval** /ɪnvɑl/ (pl: -len) **1** raid, invasion: *een ~ doen in* raid [bldg]; invade **2** (bright) idea

de **invalide** /ɪnvalidə/ (adj) invalid, handicapped

de **invalidenwagen** /ɪnvalidə(n)waɣə(n)/ (pl: -s) car for disabled; motorized quadricycle

invallen /ɪnvɑlə(n)/ (viel in, is ingevallen) **1** raid, invade **2** set in; fall; close in **3** stand in (for), (act as a) substitute (for) **4** fall down, come down, collapse: *ingevallen wangen* hollow (*or:* sunken) cheeks

de **invaller** /ɪnvɑlər/ (pl: -s) substitute; replacement

de **invalshoek** /ɪnvɑlshuk/ (pl: -en) **1** angle of incidence **2** approach, point of view

de **invalsweg** /ɪnvɑlswɛx/ (pl: -en) approach road

de **invasie** /ɪnvazi/ (pl: -s) invasion

de **inventaris** /ɪnvɛntarɪs/ (pl: -sen) **1** inventory, list (of contents) **2** stock (in trade), inventory; fittings; furniture

de **inventarisatie** /ɪnvɛntariza(t)si/ (pl: -s) stocktaking, making (*or:* drawing up) an inventory

inventariseren /ɪnvɛntarizɛrə(n)/ (inventariseerde, heeft geïnventariseerd) **1** (make an) inventory, take stock (of), draw up a statement of assets and liabilities **2** list

inventief /ɪnvɛntif/ (adj) inventive, ingenious

de **inventiviteit** /ɪnvɛntivitɛit/ inventiveness, ingenuity

de **investeerder** /ɪnvɛstɛrdər/ (pl: -s) investor

investeren /ɪnvɛstɛrə(n)/ (investeerde, heeft geïnvesteerd) invest

de **investering** /ɪnvɛstɛrɪŋ/ (pl: -en) investment

de **investeringskosten** /ɪnvɛstɛrɪŋskɔstə(n)/ (pl) investment; invested capital

de **investeringsmaatschappij** /ɪnvɛstɛrɪŋsmatsχɑpɛi/ (pl: -en) investment company

invetten /ɪnvɛtə(n)/ (vette in, heeft ingevet) grease

de **invitatie** /ɪnvitaː(t)si/ (pl: -s) invitation

de **in-vitrofertilisatie** /ɪnviːtrofɛrtiliza(t)si/ in vitro fertilization

invliegen /ɪnvliɣə(n)/ (vloog in, heeft ingevlogen): *er ~* be had, be fooled

de **invloed** /ɪnvluːt/ (pl: -en) influence: *~ uitoefenen op iem.* influence s.o., exert/exercise (an) influence on s.o.; *zijn ~ gebruiken* exert (*or:* use) one's influence; *rijden onder ~* drive under the influence, drink and drive

invloedrijk /ɪnvluːtrɛik/ (adj) influential

¹**invoegen** /ɪnvuɣə(n)/ (voegde in, heeft ingevoegd) join the (stream of) traffic, merge

²**invoegen** /ɪnvuɣə(n)/ (voegde in, heeft ingevoegd) insert (into)

de **invoegstrook** /ɪnvuxstroːk/ (pl: -stroken) acceleration lane

de **invoer** /ɪnvuːr/ (pl: -en) **1** import; [goods] imports **2** input

invoeren /ɪnvurə(n)/ (voerde in, heeft ingevoerd) **1** import **2** introduce **3** enter, input (to); read in(to)

de **invoerrechten** /ɪnvurɛxtə(n)/ (pl) import duty

het **invoerverbod** /ɪnvurvərbɔt/ import ban

invreten /ɪnvretə(n)/ (vrat in, heeft ingevreten) corrode

invriezen /ɪnvrizə(n)/ (vroor in, heeft ingevroren) freeze

de **invrijheidstelling** /ɪnvrɛihɛitstɛlɪŋ/ (pl: -en) release, discharge: *vervroegde ~* early release

het **invulformulier** /ɪnvʏlfɔrmylir/ (pl: -en) form (for completion)

invullen /ɪnvʏlə(n)/ (vulde in, heeft ingevuld) fill in: [fig] *iets voor iem. ~* decide sth. for s.o., tell s.o. what to do (and think)

de **invulling** /ɪnvʏlɪŋ/ (pl: -en) interpretation

inweken /ɪnwekə(n)/ (weekte in, heeft/is ingeweekt) soak

inwendig /ɪnwɛndəx/ (adj, adv) internal, inner; inside: *voor ~ gebruik* for internal use

¹**inwerken** /ɪnwɛrkə(n)/ (werkte in, heeft ingewerkt) (+ op) act on, affect: *op elkaar ~* interact

²**inwerken** /ɪnwɛrkə(n)/ (werkte in, heeft ingewerkt) show the ropes, break in

de **inwerking** /ɪnwɛrkɪŋ/ (pl: -en) action, effect

de **inwerkingtreding** /ɪnwɛrkɪŋtredɪŋ/ coming into force, taking effect

de **inwerktijd** /ɪnwɛrktɛit/ (pl: -en) training period

inwerpen /ɪnwɛrpə(n)/ (wierp in, heeft ingeworpen) throw in; insert

inwijden /ɪnwɛidə(n)/ (wijdde in, heeft ingewijd) **1** inaugurate, dedicate; consecrate **2** initiate

de **inwijding** /ɪnwɛidɪŋ/ (pl: -en) **1** inauguration, dedication; consecration **2** initiation

de **inwijkeling** /ɪnwɛikəlɪŋ/ (pl: -en) [Belg] immigrant

het **inwijken** /ɪnwɛikə(n)/ [Belg] immigrate

inwikkelen /ɪnwɪkələ(n)/ (wikkelde in, heeft ingewikkeld) wrap (up)

inwilligen /ɪnwɪləɣə(n)/ (willigde in, heeft ingewilligd) grant, comply with, agree to: *zijn eisen ~* comply with (*or:* agree to) his demands

inwinnen /ɪnwɪnə(n)/ (won in, heeft ingewonnen) obtain, gather

inwisselbaar /ɪnwɪsəlbar/ (adj) exchangeable; convertible; redeemable

inwisselen /ɪnwɪsələ(n)/ (wisselde in, heeft ingewisseld) exchange; convert; cash; change; redeem

inwonen /ɪnwonə(n)/ (woonde in, heeft ingewoond) live; live in: *Gerard woont nog bij zijn ouders in* Gerard still lives with his parents

inwonend /ɪnwonənt/ (adj) resident, living in: *~e kinderen* children living at home

de **inwoner** /ɪnwonər/ (pl: -s) inhabitant, resident

de **inwoning** /ɪnwonɪŋ/ living together: *kost en ~* board and lodging, room and board

de **inworp** /ɪnwɔrp/ (pl: -en) throwing in; insertion

inwrijven /ɪnvrɛivə(n)/ (wreef in, heeft ingewreven) rub in(to): *dat zal ik hem eens ~* I'll rub his nose in it

inzaaien /ɪnzajə(n)/ (zaaide in, heeft ingezaaid) sow, seed

de **inzage** /ɪnzaɣə/ inspection: *een exemplaar ter ~* an inspection copy

inzake /ɪnzaːkə/ (prep) concerning, with regard to, in respect of, as far as … is concerned

inzakken /ɪnzakə(n)/ (zakte in, is ingezakt) **1** collapse; give way **2** [com] collapse, slump

inzamelen /ɪnzaməl(n)/ (zamelde in, heeft ingezameld) collect; raise

de **inzameling** /ɪnzaməlɪŋ/ (pl: -en) collection

inzegenen /ɪnzeɣənə(n)/ (zegende in, heeft ingezegend) solemnize

de **inzegening** /ɪnzeɣənɪŋ/ (pl: -en) solemnization

inzenden /ɪnzɛndə(n)/ (zond in, heeft ingezonden) send in, submit; contribute

de **inzending** /ɪnzɛndɪŋ/ (pl: -en) **1** submission; contribution **2** entry, contribution; exhibit

inzepen /ɪnzepə(n)/ (zeepte in, heeft ingezeept) soap; lather

de **inzet** /ɪnzɛt/ (pl: -ten) **1** effort: *de spelers vochten met enorme ~* the players gave it all they'd got **2** stake, bet: *de ~ verhogen* raise one's bet (*or:* the stakes)

inzetbaar /ɪnzɛdbar/ (adj) usable; available

¹**inzetten** /ɪnzɛtə(n)/ (zette in, heeft ingezet) set in

²**inzetten** /ɪnzɛtə(n)/ (zette in, heeft ingezet) **1** stake, bet: *hoog ~* a) play for high stakes; b) [fig] set the bar high **2** start; strike up

³**inzetten** /ɪnzɛtə(n)/ (zette in, heeft ingezet) **1** put in; set **2** start, launch: *de aanval* ~ go onto the attack; *de achtervolging* ~ set off in pursuit **3** bring into action

zich ⁴**inzetten** /ɪnzɛtə(n)/ (zette zich in, heeft zich ingezet) do one's best: *zich voor een zaak* ~ devote o.s. to a cause

het **inzicht** /ɪnzɪxt/ (pl: -en) **1** insight, understanding: *een beter* ~ *krijgen in* gain an insight into **2** view, opinion

inzichtelijk /ɪnzɪxtələk/ (adj): *een kwestie* ~ *maken* clarify an issue

¹**inzien** /ɪnzin/: *mijns* ~*s* in my view (*or:* opinion), to my mind; *bij nader* ~ on (further) consideration, on second thoughts

²**inzien** /ɪnzin/ (zag in, heeft ingezien) **1** have a look at: *stukken* ~ examine documents; *een boek vluchtig* ~ leaf through a book **2** see, recognize: *de noodzaak gaan* ~ *van* come to recognize the necessity of **3** take a … view of, consider: *ik zie het somber in* I'm pessimistic about it

de **inzinking** /ɪnzɪŋkɪŋ/ (pl: -en) breakdown: *ik had een kleine* ~ it was one of my off moments

inzitten /ɪnzɪtə(n)/ (zat in, heeft ingezeten) sit in: [fig] *dat zit er niet in* there's no chance of that || *ergens over* ~ be worried about sth.

de **inzittende** /ɪnzɪtəndə/ (pl: -n) occupant, passenger

inzoomen /ɪnzumə(n)/ (zoomde in, heeft ingezoomd) zoom in (on): ~ *op* *een onderwerp* zoom in on a subject

het **ion** /ijɔn/ (pl: -en) ion

het **IP-adres** /ipeadrɛs/ (pl: -sen) IP address

i.p.v. *in plaats van* instead of

het **IQ** /iky/ (pl: IQ's) *intelligentiequotiënt* IQ

Iraaks /iraks/ (adj) Iraqi

Iraans /irans/ (adj) Iranian

Irak /irɑk/ Iraq

de **Irakees** /irakes/ (pl: Irakezen) Iraqi

Iran /iran/ Iran

de **Iraniër** /iranijər/ (pl: -s) Iranian

de **iris** /iris/ (pl: -sen) iris

de **irisscan** /irɪskɛn/ (pl: -s) iris scan

de **ironie** /ironi/ irony

ironisch /ironis/ (adj, adv) ironic(al)

irrationeel /ɪra(t)ʃonel/ (adj, adv) irrational

irreëel /ɪrejel/ (adj) unreal, imaginary

irrelevant /ɪreləvɑnt/ (adj) irrelevant: *dat is* ~ that's beside the point

de **irrigatie** /ɪriɣa(t)si/ (pl: -s) irrigation

irrigeren /ɪriɣerə(n)/ (irrigeerde, heeft geïrrigeerd) irrigate

irritant /iritɑnt/ (adj, adv) irritating, annoying

de **irritatie** /irita(t)si/ (pl: -s) irritation

irriteren /iriterə(n)/ (irriteerde, heeft geïrriteerd) irritate, annoy: *het irriteert mij* it is getting on my nerves

de/het **IS** /ɪɛs/ *Islamitische Staat* IS (*Islamic State*);

ISIS (*Islamic State of Iraq and Syria*)

de **ischias** /ɪsxijɑs/ sciatica

de **islam** /ɪslɑm/ Islam

de **islamiet** /ɪslamit/ (pl: -en) Islamite

het **islamisme** /ɪslamɪsmə/ Islamism

islamitisch /ɪslamitis/ (adj) Islamic

de **isolatie** /izola(t)si/ (pl: -s) **1** insulation **2** isolation

de **isoleercel** /izolɛrsɛl/ (pl: -len) isolation cell; padded cell

het **isolement** /izoləmɛnt/ isolation

¹**isoleren** /izolerə(n)/ (isoleerde, heeft geïsoleerd) [elec] insulate (from, against)

²**isoleren** /izolerə(n)/ (isoleerde, heeft geïsoleerd) isolate; quarantine; cut off

Israël /ɪsrael/ Israel

de **Israëli** /ɪsraeli/ (pl: -'s) Israeli

de **Israëliër** /ɪsraelijər/ (pl: -s) Israeli

Israëlisch /ɪsraelis/ (adj) Israeli

het/de **issue** /ɪʃu/ (pl: -s) issue: *een hot* ~ a burning issue

de **IT** /ite/ *informatietechnologie* IT, information technology

de **italiaan** /itɑljan/ (pl: italianen) Italian restaurant

de **Italiaan** /itɑljan/ (pl: Italianen) Italian

het ¹**Italiaans** /itɑljans/ Italian

²**Italiaans** /itɑljans/ (adj) Italian

Italië /italijə/ Italy

het **item** /ɑjtəm/ (pl: -s) item, topic: *een hot* ~ a burning issue

de **IT'er** /itejər/ IT specialist

i.t.t. *in tegenstelling tot* in contrast with, as opposed to

de **ivf** /ivɛf/ *in-vitrofertilisatie* IVF

i.v.m. *in verband met* in connection with

het **ivoor** /ivor/ (pl: ivoren) ivory

Ivoorkust /ivorkyst/ Ivory Coast

ivoren /ivorə(n)/ (adj) ivory

de **Ivoriaan** /ivorijan/ (pl: Ivorianen) Ivory Coaster

het **Ivriet** /ivrit/ (modern) Hebrew

j

de **j** /je/ (pl: j's) j, J

ja /ja/ (int) **1** yes; yeah; all right, OK: *ja knik-*
ken nod (agreement); *en **zo** ja* and if so
2 really, indeed: *o ja?* oh yes?; (oh) really? ‖ *o*
ja, nu ik je toch spreek … oh, yes, by the way …

de **jaap** /jap/ (pl: japen) cut, gash, slash

het **jaar** /jar/ (pl: jaren) year: *een **half** ~* half a
year; *het hele ~ **door*** throughout the year; *~*
in**, ~ **uit year after year; *in de laatste paar ~, de*
laatste jaren in the last few years, in recent
years; *om de twee ~* every other year; *over vijf*
~ five years from now; *per ~* yearly, a year;
*een kind **van** zes ~* a six-year-old (child); *vorige*
*week dinsdag is ze **twaalf** ~ geworden* she was
twelve last Tuesday; *de jaren **tachtig, negen-***
tig the eighties, nineties; *de jaren **tien*** [21st
century] the twenty-tens; *de jaren **nul*** [21st
century] the noughties; *uit het ~ **nul*** from the
year dot

de **jaarbeurs** /jarbørs/ (pl: -beurzen) **1** (annual) fair, trade fair **2** exhibition centre

het **jaarboek** /jarbuk/ (pl: -en) yearbook, annual

de **jaarcijfers** /jarsɛifərs/ (pl) annual returns

de **jaargang** /jarɣɑŋ/ (pl: -en) volume, year (of
publication)

de **jaargenoot** /jarɣənot/ (pl: -genoten) classmate

het **jaargetijde** /jarɣətɛidə/ (pl: -n) season

de **jaarkaart** /jarkart/ (pl: -en) annual season
ticket

jaarlijks /jarləks/ (adj, adv) annual, yearly:
*dit feest **wordt** ~ **gevierd*** this celebration
takes place every year

de **jaarmarkt** /jarmɑrkt/ (pl: -en) (annual) fair

de **jaarring** /jarɪŋ/ (pl: -en) annual ring, growth
(*or:* tree) ring

het **jaartal** /jartɑl/ (pl: -len) year, date

de **jaartelling** /jartɛlɪŋ/ (pl: -en) era: *de **chris-***
***telijke** ~* the Christian era

de **jaarvergadering** /jarvərɣadərɪŋ/ (pl: -en)
annual meeting

het **jaarverslag** /jarvərsfɑɣ/ (pl: -en) annual report: *financieel ~* annual financial report;
sociaal ~ social balance sheet

de **jaarwisseling** /jarwɪsəlɪŋ/ (pl: -en) turn of
the year: *goede (prettige) ~!* Happy New
Year!

het **JAC** /jɑk/ *Jongerenadviescentrum* young
people's advisory centre

de ¹**jacht** /jɑxt/ (pl: -en) **1** hunting; shooting: *op*
~ gaan **a)** go (out) hunting; **b)** go (out) shooting; **c)** go hunting, prowl **2** hunt; shoot

3 hunt, chase: *~ **maken** op oorlogsmisdadigers*
hunt down war criminals

het ²**jacht** /jɑxt/ (pl: -en) yacht

jachten /jɑxtə(n)/ (jachtte, heeft/is gejacht)
hurry, rush

het **jachtgebied** /jɑxtxəbit/ (pl: -en) hunt(ing
ground); shoot(ing); shooting ground

het **jachtgeweer** /jɑ(xt)xəwer/ (pl: -geweren)
shotgun

de **jachthaven** /jɑxthavə(n)/ (pl: -s) yacht basin; marina

de **jachthond** /jɑxthɔnt/ (pl: -en) hound

jachtig /jɑxtəx/ (adj, adv) hurried, hectic

de **jachtluipaard** /jɑxtlœypart/ (pl: -en) cheetah

de **jachtopziener** /jɑxtɔpsinər/ (pl: -s) game-
warden

het **jachtseizoen** /jɑxtsɛizun/ (pl: -en) hunting
season, shooting season

de **jachtvergunning** /jɑxtfərɣʏnɪŋ/ (pl: -en)
hunting licence

het **jack** /jɛk/ (pl: -s) jacket, coat

de **jackpot** /dʒɛkpɔt/ (pl: -s) jackpot

het/de **jacquet** /ʒɑkɛt/ (pl: -ten) morning coat

de **jacuzzi**® /dʒakuzi/ (pl: -'s) jacuzzi

het/de **jade** /jadə/ jade

jagen /jaɣə(n)/ (jaagde/joeg, heeft gejaagd)
1 hunt, hunt for; shoot: *op patrijs ~* hunt partridge **2** drive; put; race; rush: *prijzen **om-***
***hoog** (or: **omlaag**) ~* drive prices up (*or:*
down)

de **jager** /jaɣər/ (pl: -s) hunter

de **jaguar** /dʒɛɡuwɑr/ (pl: -s) jaguar

Jahweh /jawɛ/ Yahweh

jaja /jaja/ (int) **1** [iron] whatever, oh yeah?:
~, het zal wel yeah, whatever **2** yes!: *~! het is*
gelukt! yes! we did it!

de **jakhals** /jɑkhɑls/ (pl: jakhalzen) jackal

jakkeren /jɑkərə(n)/ (jakkerde, heeft/is ge-
jakkerd) ride hard, rush along

jakkes /jɑkəs/ (int) [inform] ugh!, bah!,
pooh!

de **jaknikker** /jɑknɪkər/ (pl: -s) **1** yes-man
2 pumpjack; nodding donkey

Jakob /jakɔp/ James, Jacob: *de ware ~* Mr
Right

de **jakobsschelp** /jakɔpsxɛlp/ (pl: -en) scallop

jaloers /jalurs/ (adj, adv) jealous (of), envious (of)

de **jaloezie** /ʒaluzi/ (pl: -ën) **1** envy; jealousy
2 (Venetian) blind

de **jam** /ʒɛm/ (pl: -s) jam

Jamaica /jamɑjka/ Jamaica

de **Jamaicaan** /jamɑjkan/ (pl: Jamaicanen) Jamaican

Jamaicaans /dʒamɑjkans/ (adj) Jamaican

jammen /dʒɛmə(n)/ (jamde, heeft gejamd)
gig, jam

jammer /jɑmər/ (adj) a pity, a shame, too
bad, bad luck: *een typisch **geval** van ~* it's a
shame, but what can you do?; *het **is** ~ dat …*

a) it's a pity (*or:* shame) that ...; **b)** too bad that ...; *het is erg ~ voor hem* it's very hard on him; *wat ~!* what a pity! (*or:* shame!); *~, hij is net weg* (a) pity (*or:* bad luck), he has just left

jammeren /j<u>a</u>mərə(n)/ (jammerde, heeft gejammerd) moan

jammerlijk /j<u>a</u>mərlək/ (adj, adv) pitiful, miserable: *~ mislukken* fail miserably

de **jampot** /z<u>ɛ</u>mpɔt/ (pl: -ten) jam jar

Jan /jɑn/ John: *~ en alleman* every Tom, Dick and Harry; *~ Klaassen en Katrijn* Punch and Judy; *~ met de pet* the (ordinary) man in the street; *~ Rap en zijn maat* ragtag and bobtail

de **janboel** /j<u>a</u>mbul/ shambles, mess

janboerenfluitjes /jɑmburə(n)fl<u>œy</u>cəs/: *op zijn ~* anyhow, any old how

de **janet** /zɑn<u>ɛ</u>t/ (pl: -ten) [Belg] homo, poof(ter), pansy

janken /j<u>a</u>ŋkə(n)/ (jankte, heeft gejankt) whine, howl; [inform] blubber

de **januari** /jɑnyw<u>a</u>ri/ January

de **jap** /jɑp/ (pl: -pen) Jap

Japan /jap<u>ɑ</u>n/ Japan

de **Japanner** /jap<u>ɑ</u>nər/ (pl: -s) Japanese

het ¹**Japans** /jap<u>ɑ</u>ns/ Japanese

²**Japans** /jap<u>ɑ</u>ns/ (adj) Japanese

de **japon** /jap<u>ɔ</u>n/ (pl: -nen) dress; gown

¹**jarenlang** /j<u>a</u>rə(n)lɑŋ/ (adj) many years': *een ~e vriendschap* a friendship of many years' (standing)

²**jarenlang** /j<u>a</u>rə(n)lɑŋ/ (adv) for years and years

het **jargon** /jɑry<u>ɔ</u>n/ (pl: -s) jargon: *ambtelijk ~* officialese

jarig /j<u>a</u>rəx/ (adj): *de ~e Job* (*or: Jet*) the birthday boy (*or:* girl); *ik ben vandaag ~* it's my birthday today; *dan ben je nog niet ~* it won't be the happiest day of your life

de **jarige** /j<u>a</u>rəyə/ (pl: -n) person celebrating his (*or:* her) birthday, birthday boy (*or:* girl)

de **jarretelle** /zɑrət<u>ɛ</u>l/ (pl: -s) suspender; [Am] garter

de **jas** /jɑs/ (pl: -sen) **1** coat **2** jacket ‖ *in een nieuw ~je steken* give (*or:* get) a facelift

het **jasje** /j<u>a</u>ʃə/ (pl: -s) **1** (short, little) coat **2** jacket

de **jasmijn** /jɑsm<u>ɛi</u>n/ (pl: -en) jasmine

jasses /j<u>a</u>səs/ (int) [Dutch; inform] ugh!

de **jat** /jɑt/ (pl: -ten) [inform] paw

jatten /j<u>a</u>tə(n)/ (jatte, heeft gejat) [inform] pinch, nick

Java /j<u>a</u>va/ Java

de **Javaan** /jav<u>a</u>n/ (pl: Javanen) Javan(ese)

jawel /jaw<u>ɛ</u>l/ (int) (oh) yes; certainly: *~ meneer* certainly sir

het **jawoord** /j<u>a</u>wort/ consent; [roughly] 'I will'

jazeker /jaz<u>e</u>kər/ (int) yes, certainly, indeed

de **jazz** /dʒɛːz/ jazz

het **jazzballet** /dʒ<u>ɛː</u>sbɑlɛt/ jazz ballet

de **jazzband** /dʒ<u>ɛː</u>sbɛnt/ (pl: -s) jazz band

¹**je** /jə/ (pers pron) you: *jullie zouden je moeten schamen* you ought to be ashamed of yourselves

²**je** /jə/ (poss pron) your: *één van je vrienden* a friend of yours

³**je** /jə/ (ind pron) you: *zoiets doe je niet* you don't do things like that

jee /je/ (int) (oh) Lord!, dear me!

de **jeep** /dʒip/ (pl: -s) jeep

jegens /j<u>e</u>yəns/ (prep) towards: *diep wantrouwen koesteren ~ iem.* have a deep distrust of s.o.

Jehova /jəh<u>o</u>va/ Jehovah: *~'s getuigen* Jehovah's Witnesses

Jemen /j<u>e</u>mə(n)/ (the) Yemen

de **Jemeniet** /jemən<u>i</u>t/ (pl: -en) Yemeni

Jemenitisch /jemən<u>i</u>tis/ (adj) Yemenite

de **jenaplanschool** /j<u>e</u>naplɑnsxol/ (pl: -scholen) [roughly] Summerhill school

de **jenever** /jən<u>e</u>vər/ (pl: -s) Dutch gin, jenever

de **jeneverbes** /jən<u>e</u>vərbɛs/ (pl: -sen) juniper berry

jengelen /j<u>ɛ</u>ŋələ(n)/ (jengelde, heeft gejengeld) **1** whine, moan **2** drone: *~ op een gitaar* twang (away) on a guitar

jennen /j<u>ɛ</u>nə(n)/ (jende, heeft gejend) badger, pester

de **jerrycan** /dʒ<u>ɛ</u>rikɛn/ (pl: -s) jerrycan

Jeruzalem /jer<u>y</u>zalɛm/ Jerusalem

de **jet** /dʒɛt/ (pl: -s) jet (aircraft)

de **jetlag** /dʒ<u>ɛ</u>tlɛːk/ (pl: -s) jet lag

de **jetset** /dʒ<u>ɛ</u>tsɛt/ jet set

de **jetski®** /dʒ<u>ɛ</u>tski/ (pl: -'s) jet-ski

het **jeu de boules** /ʒødəb<u>u</u>l/ boule

de **jeugd** /jøxt/ **1** youth **2** young people: *de ~ van tegenwoordig* young people nowadays

de **jeugdbende** /j<u>ø</u>xtbɛndə/ gang of youths

de **jeugdherberg** /j<u>ø</u>xthɛrbɛrx/ (pl: -en) youth hostel

de **jeugdherinnering** /j<u>ø</u>xthɛrɪnərɪŋ/ (pl: -en) reminiscence of childhood, childhood memory

jeugdig /j<u>ø</u>ydəx/ (adj) youthful, young(ish): *een programma voor ~e kijkers* a programme for younger viewers

het **jeugdjournaal** /j<u>ø</u>xtʃurnal/ (pl: -s) news broadcast for young people

de **jeugdliefde** /j<u>ø</u>xtlivdə/ (pl: -s) youthful love, adolescent love, calf-love; [pers] old flame: *zij is een van zijn ~s* she's one of his old loves

de **jeugdpuistjes** /j<u>ø</u>xtpœyʃəs/ (pl) acne, spots, pimples

de **jeugdrechter** /j<u>ø</u>xtrɛxtər/ (pl: -s) [Belg] juvenile court magistrate

de **jeugdvriend** /j<u>ø</u>xtfrint/ (pl: -en) old (girl) friend

de **jeugdwerkloosheid** /j<u>ø</u>xtwɛrklosheit/ youth unemployment

de **jeugdzonde** /j<u>ø</u>xtsɔndə/ (pl: -n) sin of one's youth

de **jeuk** /jøk/ itch(ing): *ik heb overal ~* I'm itching

all over; [fig] *ergens ~ van krijgen* get hot under the collar about sth., get worked up about sth.

jeuken /jøkə(n)/ (jeukte, heeft gejeukt) itch: *mijn handen ~ om hem een pak slaag te geven* I'm (just) itching to give him a good thrashing; [inform] *het zal me ~* it's all the same to me

jeukerig /jøkərəχ/ (adj) itchy

de **je-weet-wel** /jəwetwɛl/ [of pers] what's-his-name; you know …

jezelf /jəzɛlf/ (ref pron) yourself: *kijk naar ~* look at yourself

de **jezidi** /jezidi/ (pl: -'s) Yezidi

de **jezuïet** /jezywit/ (pl: -en) Jesuit

Jezus /jezʏs/ Jesus

de **jicht** /jɪχt/ gout

het ¹**Jiddisch** /jɪdis/ Yiddish

²**Jiddisch** /jɪdis/ (adj) Yiddish

de **jihad** /dʒihat/ jihad, jehad

de **jihadstrijder** /dʒihatstrɛɪdər/ (pl: -s) jihadist, jihadi

jij /jɛi/ (pers pron) you: *zeg, ~ daar!* hey, you!; *~ hier?* goodness, are you here?

de **jij-bak** /jɛɪbɑk/ (pl: -ken) comeback

jijen /jɛɪjə(n)/: *~ en jouen* be on familiar (*or*: christian-name) terms (with s.o.)

de **jingle** /dʒɪŋəl/ (pl: -s) jingle

jippie /jɪpi/ (int) yippee

het **jiujitsu** /jiujɪtsu/ ju-jitsu

jl. *jongstleden* ult; inst

de **job** /dʒɔp/ (pl: -s) job

Job /jɔp/ Job: *zo arm als ~* as poor as a church mouse

de **jobdienst** /dʒɔbdinst/ (pl: -en) [Belg] (student) employment agency

de **jobstijding** /jɔpstɛidɪŋ/ (pl: -en) bad tidings; bad news

de **jobstudent** /dʒɔpstydɛnt/ (pl: -en) [Belg] student with part-time job

het **joch** /jɔχ/ lad

het **jochie** /jɔχi/ (pl: -s) (little) lad

de **jockey** /dʒɔki/ (pl: -s) jockey

jodelen /jodələ(n)/ (jodelde, heeft gejodeld) yodel

het **jodendom** /jodəndɔm/ Judaism

het **Jodendom** /jodəndɔm/ Jews, Jewry

de **Jodenvervolging** /jodə(n)vərvɔlɣɪŋ/ persecution of the Jews

de **jodin** /jodɪn/ (pl: -nen) Jewess

de **Jodin** /jodɪn/ (pl: -nen) Jewess

het **jodium** /jodijʏm/ iodine

de **Joegoslaaf** /juɣoslaf/ (pl: Joegoslaven) Yugoslav(ian)

Joegoslavië /juɣoslavijə/ Yugoslavia

Joegoslavisch /juɣoslavis/ (adj) Yugoslav(ian)

de **joekel** /jukəl/ (pl: -s) whopper: *wat een ~ van een huis!* what a whacking great house!

joelen /julə(n)/ (joelde, heeft gejoeld) whoop, roar: *een ~de menigte* a roaring crowd

joggen /dʒɔɡə(n)/ (jogde, heeft/is gejogd) jog

de **jogger** /dʒɔɡər/ (pl: -s) jogger

de **jogging** /dʒɔɡɪŋ/ **1** jogging **2** [Belg] track suit

het **joggingpak** /dʒɔɡɪŋpɑk/ (pl: -ken) tracksuit

joh /jɔ/ (int) [inform] you: *hé ~, kijk een beetje uit* hey (you), watch out; *kop op, ~* (come on) cheer up, (old boy, girl)

Johannes /johɑnəs/ John: *~ de Doper* John the Baptist

de **joint** /dʒɔjnt/ (pl: -s) joint, stick

de **joint venture** /dʒɔjntvɛncər/ (pl: -s) joint venture

de **jojo** /jojo/ (pl: -'s) yo-yo

de **joker** /jokər/ (pl: -s) joker: *er voor Jan Joker bij zitten* sit there like a spare part; *iem. voor ~ zetten* make s.o. look a fool, make a fool of s.o.

de **jokkebrok** /jɔkəbrɔk/ (pl: -ken) (little) fibber

jokken /jɔkə(n)/ (jokte, heeft gejokt) fib, tell a fib

jolig /joləχ/ (adj, adv) jolly

het ¹**jong** /jɔŋ/ (pl: -en) **1** young (one); pup(py) **2** kid, child

²**jong** /jɔŋ/ (adj) **1** young: *op ~e leeftijd* at an early age; *~ en oud* young and old **2** recent, late: *de ~ste berichten* the latest news **3** young, new, immature: *~e kaas* unmatured (*or*: green) cheese

de **jongedame** /jɔŋədamə/ (pl: -s) young lady

de **jongeheer** /jɔŋəhɛr/ (pl: -heren) young gentleman

de **jongelui** /jɔŋəlœy/ (pl) youngsters, young people

de **jongeman** /jɔŋəmɑn/ (pl: -nen) young man

de ¹**jongen** /jɔŋə(n)/ (pl: -s) **1** boy, youth, lad: *is het een ~ of een meisje?* is it a boy or a girl? **2** boy, lad, guy: *onze ~s hebben zich dapper geweerd* our boys put up a brave defence **3** kids; lads; chaps; folks; guys: *gaan jullie mee, ~s?* are you coming, you lot?

²**jongen** /jɔŋə(n)/ (jongde, heeft gejongd) give birth, drop (their) young, bear young; litter: *onze kat heeft vandaag gejongd* our cat has had kittens today

jongensachtig /jɔŋənsɑχtəχ/ (adj, adv) boyish: *zich ~ gedragen* behave like a boy

de **jongensdroom** /jɔŋə(n)zdrom/ (pl: -dromen) boyish dream; childhood dream

de **jongere** /jɔŋərə/ (pl: -n) young person, youngster

het **jongerencentrum** /jɔŋərə(n)sɛntrʏm/ (pl: -centra) [roughly] youth centre

het **jongerenwerk** /jɔŋərə(n)wɛrk/ youth work

jongleren /jɔŋlerə(n)/ (jongleerde, heeft gejongleerd) juggle

de **jongleur** /jɔŋlør/ (pl: -s) juggler, acrobat

jongstleden /jɔŋstledə(n)/ (adj) last: *de 14e*

~ the 14th of this month

de **jonkheer** /jɔŋkher/ (pl: -heren) esquire

het **jonkie** /jɔŋki/ (pl: -s) [Dutch; inform] young one

de **jonkvrouw** /jɔŋkfrɑu/ (pl: -en) [roughly] Lady

de **jood** /jot/ (pl: joden) Jew

de **Jood** /jot/ (pl: Joden) Jew

joods /jots/ (adj, adv) Jewish, Judaic

Joods /jots/ (adj, adv) Jewish, Judaic

joods-christelijk /jotskrɪstələk/ (adj) Judaeo-Christian

Joost /jost/: ~ *mag het weten* God knows, search me, hanged if I know

de **Jordaan** /jɔrdan/ (the river) Jordan

Jordaans /jɔrdans/ (adj) Jordanian

Jordanië /jɔrdanijə/ Jordan

de **Jordaniër** /jɔrdanijər/ (pl: -s) Jordanian

de **jota** /jota/ (pl: -'s) iota

jou /jɑu/ (pers pron) you: ~ *moet ik* **hebben** you're just the person I need; *is dit boek van* ~? is this book yours?

de **joule** /ʒul/ (pl: -s) joule

het **journaal** /ʒurnal/ (pl: journalen) news, newscast: *het* ~ *van 8 uur* the 8 o'clock news

de **journalist** /ʒurnalɪst/ (pl: -en) journalist

de **journalistiek** /ʒurnalɪstik/ journalism

jouw /jɑu/ (poss pron) your: *is dat* ~ **werk?** is that your work?; *dat potlood is* **het** ~*e* that pencil is yours

joviaal /jovijal/ (adj, adv) jovial

het/de **joyriding** /dʒɔjrɑjdɪŋ/ joyriding

de **joystick** /dʒɔjstɪk/ (pl: -s) joystick

jr. *junior* Jr.

jubelen /jybələ(n)/ (jubelde, heeft gejubeld) shout with joy, be jubilant

de **jubelstemming** /jybəlstɛmɪŋ/ jubilant mood

de **jubilaris** /jybilarɪs/ (pl: -sen) [roughly] person celebrating his (or: her) jubilee

jubileren /jybilerə(n)/ (jubileerde, heeft gejubileerd) celebrate one's jubilee (or: anniversary)

het **jubileum** /jybilejvm/ (pl: jubilea) anniversary; jubilee: *gouden* ~ golden jubilee, 50th anniversary

het **judo** /jydo/ judo

de **judoka** /jydoka/ (pl: -'s) judoka, judoist

de **juf** /jʏf/ (pl: -s, -fen) teacher; [form of address] Miss

het **juffershondje** /jʏfərshɔncə/ (pl: -s) lapdog: *beven als een* ~ shake like a jelly (or: leaf)

de **juffrouw** /jʏfrɑu/ (pl: -en) madam

juichen /jœyxə(n)/ (juichte, heeft gejuicht) shout with joy, be jubilant: *de* **menigte** *juichte toen het doelpunt werd gemaakt* the crowd cheered when the goal was scored

de **juichkreet** /jœyxkret/ (pl: -kreten) shout of joy (or: jubilation)

¹**juist** /jœyst/ (adj, adv) **1** right, correct: *de* ~*e* **tijd** the right (or: correct) time; *is dit de* ~*e*

spelling? is this the right spelling? **2** right, proper: *precies op het* ~*e* **moment** just at the right moment

²**juist** /jœyst/ (adv) **1** just, exactly, of all times (or: places, people); no, on the contrary: *ze bedoelde* ~ *het* **tegendeel** she meant just the opposite; ~, **ja** right; *gelukkig? ik ben* ~ **diepbedroefd!** happy? no (or: on the contrary), I'm terribly sad!; **daarom** ~ that's exactly why; ~ **op** *dat moment kwam zij binnen* just at that very moment (or: right at that moment) she came in **2** just

de **juistheid** /jœystheit/ correctness, accuracy; truth; appropriateness

het **juk** /jʏk/ (pl: -ken) yoke

het **jukbeen** /jʏgben/ (pl: -deren) cheekbone

de **jukebox** /dʒugbɔks/ (pl: -en) jukebox

de **juli** /jyli/ July

¹**jullie** /jʏli/ (pers pron) you: ~ **hebben** *gelijk* you're right

²**jullie** /jʏli/ (poss pron) your: *is die auto van* ~? is that car yours?

de **jumbojet** /dʒʏmbodʒɛt/ (pl: -s) jumbo jet

jumpen /dʒʏmpə(n)/ (jumpte, heeft gejumpt) jump

de **jungle** /dʒʏŋɡəl/ (pl: -s) jungle

de **juni** /jyni/ June

de **junior** /jynijɔr/ (pl: -en) junior

de **junk** /dʒʏŋk/ (pl: -s) **1** junkie, junk **2** junkie, addict: *een* **koffiejunkie** a coffee enthusiast, a coffee addict; *een* **politieke** ~*ie* a politics enthusiast (or: freak)

het **junkfood** /dʒʏŋkfuːt/ junk food

de **junta** /xʏnta/ (pl: -'s) junta

jureren /ʒyrɛrə(n)/ (jureerde, heeft gejureerd) adjudicate

de **jurering** /ʒyrɛrɪŋ/ (pl: -en) adjudication

juridisch /jyridis/ (adj, adv) legal, law

de **jurisdictie** /jyrɪzdɪksi/ (pl: -s) jurisdiction; competence

de **jurisprudentie** /jyrɪsprydɛnsi/ jurisprudence

de **jurist** /jyrɪst/ (pl: -en) jurist, lawyer

de **jurk** /jʏrk/ (pl: -en) dress: *een* **blote** ~ a revealing dress

de **jury** /ʒyri/ (pl: -'s) jury

het **jurylid** /ʒyrilɪt/ (pl: -leden) **1** member of the jury **2** (panel of) judges

de **juryrechtspraak** /ʒyrirɛxtsprak/ trial by jury

de **jus** /ʒy/ gravy

de **jus d'orange** /ʒydorɑ̃ʃ/ [Dutch] orange juice

de **juskom** /ʒykɔm/ (pl: -men) gravy boat

de **justitie** /jʏsti(t)si/ **1** justice: *minister van* ~ Minister of Justice; *officier van* ~ public prosecutor **2** judiciary; the law; the police: *met* ~ *in aanraking komen* come into conflict with the law

justitieel /jʏsti(t)ʃel/ (adj) judicial: *een* ~ **onderzoek** a judicial inquiry (or: investigation)

het **justitiepaleis** /jʏsti(t)sipalɛis/ (pl: -palei-
zen) [Belg] Palace of Justice

de ¹**jute** /jʏtə/ jute

²**jute** /jʏtə/ (adj) jute

juten /jʏtə(n)/ (adj) jute, burlap

Jutland /jʏtlɑnt/ Jutland

jutten /jʏtə(n)/ (jutte, heeft gejut) search
beaches

de **jutter** /jʏtər/ (pl: -s) beachcomber

het **juweel** /jywel/ (pl: juwelen) **1** jewel, gem
2 jewellery

het **juwelenkistje** /jywelə(n)kɪʃə/ (pl: -s) jewel
case

de **juwelier** /jywəlir/ (pl: -s) jeweller

k

de **¹k** /ka/ (pl: k's) k: *Kunst met een **grote** K* Art with a capital A

²k 1 *kilo* K **2** [euph] *kanker* the big C ‖ [inform] *dat is **zwaar** k* that sucks

K /ka/ 1024 bytes, kilobyte K: *een bestand van 2506 K* a 2506K file

de **kaaiman** /kɑjmɑn/ (pl: -nen) cayman

de **kaak** /kak/ (pl: kaken) jaw

het **kaakbeen** /kɑgben/ (pl: -deren, -benen) jawbone

de **kaakchirurg** /kakʃirʏrx/ (pl: -en) oral surgeon, dental surgeon

het **kaakje** /kakjə/ (pl: -s) biscuit

de **kaakslag** /kakslɑx/ (pl: -en) slap in the face; punch in the face: *iem. een ~ **geven*** slap (*or:* punch) s.o. in the face

kaal /kal/ (adj) **1** bald: *zo ~ **als** een biljartbal zijn* be (as) bald as a coot **2** (thread)bare: *de kale **huur*** the basic rent; *een kale **plek*** a (thread)bare spot **3** bare: *de bomen **worden** ~* the trees are losing their leaves

de **kaalkop** /kalkɔp/ (pl: -pen) [inform] baldy

kaalplukken /kalplʏkə(n)/ (plukte kaal, heeft kaalgeplukt) [inform] **1** squeeze dry, bleed white **2** seize the criminal assets of

kaalscheren /kalsxerə(n)/ (schoor kaal, heeft kaalgeschoren) shave

de **kaalslag** /kalslɑx/ deforestation

de **kaap** /kap/ (pl: kapen) cape: *~ de Goede Hoop* Cape of Good Hope

Kaapstad /kapstɑt/ Cape Town

Kaapverdië /kapfɛrdijə/ Cape Verde (Islands)

de **Kaapverdiër** /kapfɛrdijər/ (pl: -s) Cape Verdean

Kaapverdisch /kapfɛrdis/ (adj) Cape Verdean

de **Kaapverdische Eilanden** /kapfɛrdisəɛilɑndə(n)/ (pl) Cape Verde Islands

de **kaars** /kars/ (pl: -en) candle

het **kaarslicht** /karslɪxt/ candlelight

kaarsrecht /karsrɛxt/ (adj, adv) dead straight; bolt upright

het **kaarsvet** /karsfɛt/ candle-grease

de **kaart** /kart/ (pl: -en) **1** card: *de gele* (*or:* **rode***) ~ krijgen* be shown the yellow (*or:* red) card **2** menu **3** cards, hand: *een spel ~en* a pack of cards **4** ticket **5** map; chart: *in ~ brengen* **a)** map; **b)** [sea] chart; **c)** [fig] map out, record ‖ *dat is geen **haalbare** ~* it's not a viable proposition; *open ~ spelen* put all one's cards on the table; *van de ~ zijn* be upset

kaarten /kartə(n)/ (kaartte, heeft gekaart) play cards

de **kaartenbak** /kartə(n)bɑk/ (pl: -ken) cardindex box (*or:* drawer)

het **kaartenhuis** /kartə(n)hœys/ (pl: -huizen) house of cards: *instorten **als** een ~* collapse like a house of cards

de **kaarting** /kartɪŋ/ (pl: -en) [Belg] drive, bridge drive, whist drive

het **kaartje** /karcə/ (pl: -s) **1** (business) card **2** ticket

kaartlezen /kartlezə(n)/ read maps

het **kaartspel** /kartspɛl/ card playing, card game; cards: *geld verliezen **bij** het ~* lose money at cards

het **kaartsysteem** /kartsistem/ (pl: -systemen) card index

de **kaartverkoop** /kartfɛrkop/ ticket sales

de **kaas** /kas/ (pl: kazen) cheese: *belegen ~* matured cheese; *jonge ~* unmatured (*or:* green) cheese; *oude ~* fully mature cheese ‖ *hij heeft er geen ~ van **gegeten*** he's not much good at it, he doesn't know the first thing about it; *zich de ~ niet van het brood **laten eten*** be able to stand up for oneself

de **kaasboer** /kazbur/ (pl: -en) cheesemonger

de **kaasfondue** /kasfɔndy/ (pl: -s) cheese fondue

de **kaasschaaf** /kasxaf/ (pl: -schaven) cheese slicer

de **kaasstolp** /kastɔlp/ (pl: -en) **1** cheese cover **2** ivory tower

kaatsen /katsə(n)/ (kaatste, heeft gekaatst) bounce

het **kabaal** /kabal/ racket, din: *~ **maken*** make a racket

kabbelen /kɑbələ(n)/ (kabbelde, heeft gekabbeld) lap; [also fig] ripple; babble, murmur

de **kabel** /kabəl/ (pl: -s) **1** cable **2** wire; cable

de **kabelbaan** /kabəlban/ (pl: -banen) funicular (railway), cable-lift

de **kabelexploitant** /kabələksplwatɑnt/ (pl: -en) operator of a cable TV system

de **kabeljauw** /kabəljɑu/ (pl: -en) cod(fish)

het **kabelnet** /kabəlnɛt/ (pl: -ten) cable television network: *aangesloten zijn **op** het ~* receive cable television

het **kabelslot** /kabəlslɔt/ (pl: -en) cable lock

de **kabeltelevisie** /kabələtələvizi/ cable television

het **kabinet** /kabinɛt/ (pl: -ten) cabinet, government: *het ~ **is gevallen*** the government has fallen; *het ~-Rutte* the Rutte cabinet (*or:* government)

de **kabinetschef** /kabinɛtʃɛf/ (pl: -s) [roughly] principal private secretary

de **kabinetscrisis** /kabinɛtskrizɪs/ (pl: -crises) fall of the government

de **kabinetsformatie** /kabinɛtsfɔrma(t)si/ (pl: -s) formation of a (new) government (*or:*

cabinet)

de **kabouter** /kabɑutər/ (pl: -s) **1** gnome, pixie; little people: *dat hebben de ~tjes gedaan* it must have been the fairies (*or*: the little people) **2** Brownie

de **kachel** /kɑxəl/ (pl: -s) stove; heater; fire; fire

het **kadaster** /kadɑstər/ **1** [roughly] land register **2** [roughly] land registry

het **kadaver** /kadavər/ (pl: -s) (dead) body; corpse

de **kade** /kadə/ (pl: -n) quay, wharf: *het schip ligt aan de ~* the ship lies by the quay(side)

het **kader** /kadər/ (pl: -s) **1** frame(work): *in het ~ van* within the framework (*or*: scope) of, as part of **2** executives

het **kadetje** /kadɛtɕə/ (pl: -s) (bread) roll

het **kaf** /kɑf/ chaff

de **kaffer** /kɑfər/ (pl: -s) boor, lout

de **Kaffer** /kɑfər/ (pl: -s) Kaffir

het/de **kaft** /kɑft/ (pl: -en) **1** cover **2** jacket

de **kaftan** /kɑftɑn/ (pl: -s) kaftan

kaften /kɑftə(n)/ (kaftte, heeft gekaft) cover

het **kaftpapier** /kɑftpapir/ wrapping paper, brown paper

de **kajak** /kajɑk/ (pl: -s) kayak

de **kajotter** /kajɔtər/ (pl: -s) [Belg] member of KAJ

de **kajuit** /kajœyt/ (pl: -en) saloon

de **kak** /kɑk/ **1** [inform] shit, crap **2** la-di-da people, snooty people, snobs ‖ *kale (kouwe) ~* swank, la-di-da behaviour

kakelbont /kakəlbɔnt/ (adj) gaudy

kakelen /kakələ(n)/ (kakelde, heeft gekakeld) cackle; [fig also] chatter

kakelvers /kakəlvɛrs/ (adj) farm-fresh

de **kaketoe** /kakətu/ (pl: -s) cockatoo

het **kaki** /kaki/ khaki

kakken /kɑkə(n)/ (kakte, heeft gekakt) [inform] crap, shit

de **kakkerlak** /kɑkərlɑk/ (pl: -ken) cockroach

de **kalebas** /kaləbɑs/ (pl: -sen) gourd, calabash

de **kalender** /kalɛndər/ (pl: -s) calendar

het **kalenderjaar** /kalɛndərjar/ (pl: -jaren) calendar year

het **kalf** /kɑlf/ (pl: kalveren) calf: *de put dempen als het ~ verdronken is* lock the stable door after the horse has bolted

het **kalfsleer** /kɑlfsler/ calf, calfskin

het **kalfsmedaillon** /kɑlfsmedajɔn/ (pl: -s) medallion of veal

de **kalfsoester** /kɑlfsustər/ (pl: -s) veal escalope

het **kalfsvlees** /kɑlfsfles/ veal

het **kaliber** /kalibər/ (pl: -s) calibre, bore

de **kalief** /kalif/ (pl: -en) caliph

het **kalifaat** /kalifat/ (pl: kalifaten) caliphate

het **kalium** /kalijʏm/ potassium, potash

de **kalk** /kɑlk/ **1** lime; (quick)lime; slaked lime **2** (lime) mortar **3** plaster; whitewash

de **kalkaanslag** /kɑlkanslɑx/ scale, fur

kalken /kɑlkə(n)/ (kalkte, heeft gekalkt) **1** scribble **2** chalk

de **kalknagel** /kɑlknaɣəl/ fungal nail

de **kalkoen** /kɑlkun/ (pl: -en) turkey

het/de **kalksteen** /kɑlksten/ (pl: -stenen) limestone

kalligraferen /kaliɣrafere(n)/ (kalligrafeerde, heeft gekalligrafeerd) write in calligraphy (*or*: fine handwriting)

de **kalligrafie** /kaliɣrafi/ (pl: -ën) calligraphy, penmanship

kalm /kɑlm/ (adj, adv) **1** calm, cool, composed **2** peaceful, quiet: *~ aan!* take it easy!, easy does it!

kalmeren /kɑlmere(n)/ (kalmeerde, heeft gekalmeerd) calm down, soothe, tranquillize: *een ~d effect* a calming (*or*: soothing, tranquillizing) effect

het **kalmeringsmiddel** /kɑlmerɪŋsmɪdəl/ sedative, tranquillizer

kalmpjes /kɑlmpjəs/ (adv) calmly

de **kalmte** /kɑlmtə/ **1** calm(ness), composure: *zijn ~ bewaren* keep one's head/composure (*or*: self-control, cool) **2** calm(ness), tranquillity, quietness

kalven /kɑlvə(n)/ (kalfde, heeft gekalfd) calve

de **kalverliefde** /kɑlvərlivdə/ (pl: -s) calf love

de **kam** /kɑm/ (pl: -men) comb: [fig] *alles over één ~ scheren* lump everything together, generalize

de **kameel** /kamel/ (pl: kamelen) camel

het/de **kameleon** /kamelejɔn/ (pl: -s) chameleon

de **kamer** /kamər/ (pl: -s) **1** room, chamber **2** room, apartment: *~s verhuren* take in lodgers; *~ met ontbijt* Bed and Breakfast, B & B; *Renske woont op ~s* Renske is (*or*: lives) in lodgings; *op ~s gaan wonen* move into lodgings **3** chamber, house: [Belg] *Kamer van Volksvertegenwoordigers* Lower House (of Parliament); [Dutch] *de Eerste Kamer* a) the Upper Chamber (*or*: Upper House); b) the (House of) Lords, the Upper House; c) [Am] the Senate; [Dutch] *de Tweede Kamer* a) the Lower Chamber (*or*: Lower House); b) the (House of) Commons; c) [Am] the House (of Representatives) **4** chamber, board: *de Kamer van Koophandel* the Chamber of Commerce

de **kameraad** /kamərat/ (pl: kameraden) comrade, companion, mate, pal, buddy

de **kameraadschap** /kaməratsxɑp/ companionship, (good-)fellowship, camaraderie

kameraadschappelijk /kaməratsxɑpələk/ (adj, adv) companionable, friendly: *~ met iem. omgaan* fraternize with s.o.

de **kamerbewoner** /kamərbəwonər/ (pl: -s) lodger

kamerbreed /kamərbret/ (adj) wall-to-wall

het **Kamerdebat** /kamərdebɑt/ (pl: -ten) parliamentary debate; congressional debate

de **kamergenoot** /kamərɣənot/ (pl: -genoten)

room-mate

de **kamerjas** /kɑmərjɑs/ (pl: -sen) dressing gown

het **Kamerlid** /kɑmərlɪt/ (pl: -leden) Member of Parliament, MP

het **kamermeisje** /kɑmərmɛiʃə/ (pl: -s) chambermaid

de **kamermuziek** /kɑmərmyzik/ chamber music

Kameroen /kɑmərun/ Cameroon

de **Kameroener** /kɑmərunər/ (pl: -s) Cameroonian

Kameroens /kɑməruns/ (adj) Cameroonian

het **kamerorkest** /kɑmərɔrkɛst/ (pl: -en) chamber orchestra

de **kamerplant** /kɑmərplɑnt/ (pl: -en) house plant, indoor plant

de **kamertemperatuur** /kɑmərtɛmpəratyr/ room temperature

de **Kamerverkiezing** /kɑmərvərkizɪŋ/ (pl: -en) parliamentary elections; [Am] congressional elections

de **Kamerzetel** /kɑmərzetəl/ (pl: -s) seat

de **kamfer** /kɑmfər/ camphor

het **kamgaren** /kɑmɣarə(n)/ worsted (yarn)

de **kamikaze** /kamikazə/ (pl: -s) kamikaze, suicide pilot

de **kamikazepiloot** /kamikazəpilot/ (pl: -piloten) kamikaze pilot

de **kamille** /kamɪlə/ camomile

kammen /kɑmə(n)/ (kamde, heeft gekamd) comb

het **kamp** /kɑmp/ (pl: -en) camp

de **kampeerboerderij** /kɑmperburdərɛi/ (pl: -en) farm campsite

de **kampeerder** /kɑmperdər/ (pl: -s) camper

het **kampeerterrein** /kɑmpertɛrɛin/ (pl: -en) camp(ing) site; caravan park (or: site)

de **kampeerwagen** /kɑmperwaɣə(n)/ (pl: -s) 1 caravan 2 camper

het **kampement** /kɑmpəmɛnt/ (pl: -en) camp, encampment

kampen /kɑmpə(n)/ (kampte, heeft gekampt) contend (with), struggle (with), wrestle (with): met tegenslag **te** ~ hebben have to cope with setbacks

de **kamper** /kɑmpər/ mobile home resident

kamperen /kɑmperə(n)/ (kampeerde, heeft/is gekampeerd) camp (out), encamp, pitch (one's) tents, bivouac: **vrij** (or: bij de boer) ~ camp wild (or: on a farm)

de **kamperfoelie** /kɑmpərfuli/ (pl: -s) honeysuckle

de **kampioen** /kɑmpijun/ (pl: -en) champion, titleholder

het **kampioenschap** /kɑmpijunsxɑp/ (pl: -pen) championship, contest, competition, tournament

het **kampvuur** /kɑmpfyr/ (pl: -vuren) campfire

de **kan** /kɑn/ (pl: -nen) jug: de zaak is in ~nen en **kruiken** it's in the bag

het **kanaal** /kanal/ (pl: kanalen) 1 canal, channel: Het Kanaal the (English) Channel 2 canal, duct

de **Kanaaleilanden** /kanalɛilɑndə(n)/ (pl) Channel Islands (or: Isles)

de **Kanaaltunnel** /kanaltynəl/ Channel Tunnel, Chunnel

kanaliseren /kanalizerə(n)/ (kanaliseerde, heeft gekanaliseerd) [fig] channel

de **kanarie** /kanari/ (pl: -s) canary (bird)

kanariegeel /kanariɣel/ (adj) canary yellow

de **kandelaar** /kɑndəlar/ (pl: -s) candlestick, candleholder

de **kandidaat** /kɑndidat/ (pl: kandidaten) 1 candidate; applicant: zich ~ **stellen** (voor) run (for) 2 candidate, examinee

de **kandidatuur** /kɑndidatyr/ (pl: kandidaturen) candidature, nomination

kandideren /kɑndiderə(n)/ (kandideerde, heeft gekandideerd) nominate, put forward: **zich** ~ put o.s. up (for); [esp Am] run (for)

de **kandij** /kɑndɛi/ candy

het/de **kaneel** /kanel/ cinnamon

de **kangoeroe** /kɑŋɣəru/ (pl: -s) kangaroo

de **kangoeroewoning** /kɑŋɣəruwonɪŋ/ (pl: -en) house with a granny flat

de **kanjer** /kɑɲər/ (pl: -s) 1 wizard, humdinger, whizz kid; [sport] star (player) 2 whopper, colossus: een ~ **van** een vis (or: appel) a whopping fish (or: apple)

de **kanker** /kɑŋkər/ cancer; carcinoma: aan ~ **doodgaan** die of cancer

de **kankeraar** /kɑŋkərar/ (pl: -s) grouser

de **kankerbestrijding** /kɑŋkərbəstrɛidɪŋ/ fight against cancer, cancer control; (anti-)-cancer campaign

kankeren /kɑŋkərə(n)/ (kankerde, heeft gekankerd) grouse, grumble, gripe: ~ **op** de maatschappij grouse about society

het **kankergezwel** /kɑŋkərɣəzwɛl/ (pl: -len) cancerous tumour

de **kankerpatiënt** /kɑŋkərpaʃɛnt/ (pl: -en) cancer patient

kankerverwekkend /kɑŋkərvərwɛkənt/ (adj) carcinogenic

de **kannibaal** /kanibal/ (pl: kannibalen) cannibal, man-eater

het **kannibalisme** /kanibalɪsmə/ cannibalism

de **kano** /kano/ (pl: -'s) canoe

het **kanon** /kanɔn/ (pl: -nen) 1 gun, cannon 2 big shot, big name

het **kanonschot** /kanɔnsxɔt/ (pl: -en) gunshot, cannonshot

de **kanonskogel** /kanɔnskoɣəl/ (pl: -s) cannonball

de **kanovaarder** /kanovardər/ (pl: -s) canoeist

de **kans** /kɑns/ (pl: -en) 1 chance, possibility, opportunity; liability; risk: vijftig **procent** ~ equal chances, even odds; (een) **grote** ~ dat ... a good chance that ...; hij **heeft** een goede (or: veel) ~ te winnen he stands (or: has) a good chance of winning; *de ~en* **keren** the tide (*or:* his luck) is turning; *geen ~* **maken** *op* stand no chance of (sth., doing sth.); *ik zie er wel ~* **toe** I think I can manage it; *~ zien te ontkomen* manage to escape; *de ~ is honderd tegen één* (*or:* chances) are a hundred to one **2** opportunity, chance, break: *zijn ~* **afwachten** await one's chances; *zijn ~en* **grijpen** seize the opportunity; *een* **gemiste** *~* a lost (*or:* missed) opportunity; *iem. een* **tweede** *~ geven* give s.o. a second chance; *zijn ~ schoon* **zien** see one's chance, see one's way clear (to); *geen schijn van ~* not a chance in the world

KANS complaints of the arm, neck and/or shoulder

kansarm /kɑnsɑrm/ (adj) underprivileged, deprived

de **kansberekening** /kɑnzbərekənɪŋ/ (pl: -en) theory of probability; calculation of probability

de **kansel** /kɑnsəl/ (pl: -s) pulpit

de **kanselier** /kɑnsəliːr/ (pl: -s) chancellor

de **kanshebber** /kɑnshɛbər/ (pl: -s) likely candidate (*or:* winner): *de grootste ~* the favourite; *~ zijn* **voor** … be in line for

kansloos /kɑnsloːs/ (adj, adv) prospectless: *hij was ~* **tegen** *hem* he didn't stand a chance against him

kansrijk /kɑnsrɛik/ (adj) likely [candidate]; strong

het **kansspel** /kɑnspɛl/ (pl: -en) game of chance

de **kant** /kɑnt/ (pl: -en) **1** edge, side; margin: *aan de ~!* out of the way!; *aan de ~ gaan staan* stand (*or:* step) aside; *zijn auto aan de ~ zetten* pull up (*or:* over) **2** lace **3** bank, edge: *op de ~ klimmen* climb ashore **4** side, face, surface; [fig] aspect; [fig] facet; [fig] angle; [fig] view: *zich van zijn* **goede** *~ laten zien* show one's good side; *iemands* **sterke** (or: **zwakke**) *~en* s.o.'s strong (*or:* weak) points; *deze ~ boven* this side up **5** side, end, edge: *iets op zijn ~ zetten* put sth. on its side; *de* **scherpe** *~en van iets afnemen* tone sth. down (a bit); *scherpe ~* (cutting) edge **6** way, direction: *zij kan nog* **alle** *~en op* she has kept her options open; *deze ~ op, alstublieft* this way, please; *van alle ~en op* all sides; *geen ~ meer op kunnen* have nowhere (left) to go **7** side, part(y): *familie van* **vaders** (or: **moeders**) *~* relatives on one's father's (*or:* mother's) side; *ik sta van jouw ~* I'm on your side ‖ *iets* **over** *~ laten gaan* take sth. (lying down), stand for sth.; *iem. van ~ maken* do s.o. in

de **kanteel** /kɑnteːl/ (pl: kantelen) merlon

¹**kantelen** /kɑntələ(n)/ (kantelde, is gekanteld) topple over, turn over: [fig] *door dat doelpunt kantelde de* **wedstrijd** this goal changed the game, this goal swung the game (in …'s favour)

²**kantelen** /kɑntələ(n)/ (kantelde, heeft ge-

kanteld) tilt, tip (over, to one side), turn over: *niet ~!* this side up!

het **kantelraam** /kɑntəlram/ (pl: -ramen) swing (*or:* cantilever) window

kanten /kɑntə(n)/ (adj) (of) lace, lacy

kant-en-klaar /kɑntɛŋklaːr/ (adj) ready-to-use, ready for use, ready-made; instant; ready-to-wear; off the peg: *geen kant-en-klare* **oplossing** *hebben* have no cut-and-dried solution

de **kant-en-klaarmaaltijd** /kɑntɛŋklaːrmaltɛit/ ready meal

de **kantine** /kɑntinə/ (pl: -s) canteen; [Am] cafeteria

het **kantje** /kɑncə/ (pl: -s) **1** edge, verge: *dat was op het ~ af, het was ~* **boord** that was a near thing (*or:* close shave) **2** page, side: *een opstel van drie ~s* a three-page essay ‖ *er de ~s* **aflopen** cut corners

de **kantlijn** /kɑntlɛin/ (pl: -en) margin

het **kanton** /kɑntɔn/ (pl: -s) canton, district

het **kantongerecht** /kɑntɔŋɣərɛxt/ (pl: -en) [Netherlands] cantonal court; [England] [roughly] magistrates' court; [Am] [roughly] municipal (*or:* police, Justice) of the Peace court

de **kantonrechter** /kɑntɔnrɛxtər/ (pl: -s) [Dutch] cantonal judge, magistrate, JP; [Am] Justice of the Peace

het **kantoor** /kɑntoːr/ (pl: kantoren) office: *na ~ een borrel pakken* have a drink after office hours; *naar ~ gaan* go to the office; *hij is* **op** *zijn ~* he is in his office; *overdag ben ik op (mijn) ~* I am at the office in the daytime; *op ~ werken* work in an office

de **kantoorbaan** /kɑntoːrban/ (pl: -banen) office job, clerical job

de **kantoorboekhandel** /kɑntoːrbukhandəl/ (pl: -s) (office) stationer's (shop)

het **kantoorgebouw** /kɑntoːrɣəbau/ (pl: -en) office block (*or:* building)

het **kantoorpersoneel** /kɑntoːrpɛrsoneːl/ office staff (*or:* employees, workers)

de **kantoortijd** /kɑntoːrtɛit/ office (*or:* business) hours: *onder ~* during office (*or:* business) hours

de **kanttekening** /kɑntekənɪŋ/ (pl: -en) (short, marginal) comment

de **kap** /kɑp/ (pl: -pen) **1** hood **2** cap **3** hood; bonnet; [Am] hood: *het ~je van het* **brood** the end slice, the crust; *twee (huizen)* **onder** *één ~* two semi-detached houses; a semi-detached house ‖ [Belg] *op iemands ~ zitten* pester s.o.

de **kapel** /kɑpɛl/ (pl: -len) **1** chapel **2** dormer (window) **3** band

de **kapelaan** /kɑpəlaːn/ (pl: -s) curate, assistant priest

kapen /kaːpə(n)/ (kaapte, heeft gekaapt) hijack

de **kaper** /kaːpər/ (pl: -s) hijacker: *er zijn ~s* **op** *de kust* we've got plenty of competitors (*or:* rivals)

de **kaping** /kɑpɪŋ/ (pl: -en) hijack(ing)

het **kapitaal** /kapitɑl/ **1** fortune: een ~ aan boeken a (small) fortune in books **2** capital

de **kapitaalgoederen** /kapitɑlɣudərə(n)/ (pl) capital goods, investment goods

kapitaalkrachtig /kapitɑlkrɑxtəɣ/ (adj) wealthy, substantial

de **kapitaalmarkt** /kapitɑlmɑrkt/ capital market

de **kapitaalrekening** /kapitɑlrekənɪŋ/ (pl: -en) capital account

de **kapitaalvernietiging** /kapitɑlvərnitəɣɪŋ/ (pl: -en) **1** destruction of capital **2** waste of talent

het **kapitalisme** /kapitalɪsmə/ capitalism

de **kapitalist** /kapitalɪst/ (pl: -en) capitalist

kapitalistisch /kapitalɪstis/ (adj) capitalist(ic)

de **kapitein** /kapitɛin/ (pl: -s) captain; skipper

het **kapittel** /kapɪtəl/ (pl: -s, -en) chapter

het **kapje** /kɑpjə/ (pl: -s) **1** cap; (face)mask **2** heel

de **kaplaars** /kɑplars/ (pl: kaplaarzen) top boot, jackboot

het **kapmes** /kɑpmɛs/ (pl: -sen) chopping-knife; cleaver; machete

de **kapok** /kapɔk/ kapok

kapot /kapɔt/ (adj) **1** broken, in bits: die jas is ~ that coat is torn **2** broken; broken down [car]: de **koffieautomaat** is ~ the coffee machine is out of order **3** dead beat, worn out: zich ~ **werken** work one's fingers to the bone; hij is niet ~ te krijgen he's a tough one (or: cookie) **4** devastated, cut up, brokenhearted: ergens ~ **van** zijn be devastated by sth.

kapotgaan /kapɔtxan/ (ging kapot, is kapotgegaan) **1** break, fall apart; break down **2** wear down, get knackered: in de laatste beklimming ging ik **helemaal** kapot the last climb finished me off; hij gaat **eraan** kapot it's wearing him down, it's killing him

het **kapotje** /kapɔcə/ (pl: -s) rubber, French letter

kapotmaken /kapɔtmakə(n)/ (maakte kapot, heeft kapotgemaakt) break (up), destroy, wreck, ruin

kapotvallen /kapɔtfɑlə(n)/ (viel kapot, is kapotgevallen) fall to pieces, fall and break, smash

¹**kappen** /kɑpə(n)/ (kapte, heeft gekapt) chop, cut || ik kap **er mee** I'm knocking off

²**kappen** /kɑpə(n)/ (kapte, heeft gekapt) **1** cut down, chop down, fell **2** do one's (or: s.o.'s) hair: zich **laten** ~ have one's hair done **3** cut, hew

de **kapper** /kɑpər/ (pl: -s) hairdresser, hairstylist; barber

de **kappertjes** /kɑpərcəs/ (pl) capers

het/de **kapsalon** /kɑpsalɔn/ (pl: -s) hairdresser's;

barber's shop

kapseizen /kɑpsɛizə(n)/ (kapseisde, is gekapseisd) capsize, keel over

het **kapsel** /kɑpsəl/ (pl: -s) **1** hairstyle, haircut **2** hairdo

de **kapsones** /kapsɔnəs/ (pl): ~ **hebben** be full of o.s.

de **kapstok** /kɑpstɔk/ (pl: -ken) hallstand; hatstand; hat rack; coat hooks

de **kaptafel** /kɑptafəl/ (pl: -s) dressing table

de **kapucijner** /kapyscɛinər/ (pl: -s) [roughly] marrowfat (pea)

de **kar** /kɑr/ (pl: -ren) **1** cart, barrow: [fig] de ~ **trekken** do the dirty work **2** car

het **karaat** /karat/ (pl: -s, karaten) carat

de **karabijn** /karabɛin/ (pl: -en) carbine

de **karaf** /karɑf/ (pl: -fen) carafe, decanter

het **karakter** /karɑktər/ (pl: -s) **1** character, nature: iem. met een **sterk** ~ s.o. with (great) strength of character **2** character, personality, spirit: ~ **tonen** show character (or: spirit); zonder ~ without character, spineless **3** character, symbol

de **karaktereigenschap** /karɑktərɛiɣə(n)sxɑp/ (pl: -pen) character trait

karakteriseren /karɑkterizerə(n)/ (karakteriseerde, heeft gekarakteriseerd) characterize

karakteristiek /karɑkterɪstik/ (adj) characteristic (of), typical (of)

karakterloos /karɑktərlos/ (adj) characterless, insipid

de **karaktertrek** /karɑktərtrɛk/ (pl: -ken) characteristic, feature, trait

de **karamel** /karamɛl/ (pl: -s) caramel, toffee

het **karaoke** /karaɔkə/ karaoke

het **karate** /karatə/ karate

de **karatetrap** /karatətrɑp/ (pl: -pen) karate kick

de **karavaan** /karavan/ (pl: karavanen) caravan, train

de **karbonade** /kɑrbonadə/ (pl: -s) [Dutch] chop, cutlet

de **kardinaal** /kɑrdinɑl/ (pl: kardinalen) cardinal

Karel /karəl/ Charles: ~ de **Grote** Charlemagne

de **kariboe** /karibu/ (pl: -s) caribou

karig /karəx/ (adj) **1** sparing, mean, frugal **2** meagre, scant(y), frugal: een ~ **maal** a frugal meal

de **karikatuur** /karikatyr/ (pl: karikaturen) caricature

het/de **karkas** /kɑrkɑs/ (pl: -sen) carcass

het **karma** /kɑrma/ karma

de **karnemelk** /kɑrnəmɛlk/ buttermilk

karnen /kɑrnə(n)/ (karnde, heeft gekarnd) churn

de **karper** /kɑrpər/ (pl: -s) carp

het **karpet** /kɑrpɛt/ (pl: -ten) rug

karren /kɑrə(n)/ (karde, heeft/is gekard)

ride; bike

het **karrenspoor** /kɑrə(n)spor/ (pl: -sporen) cart track

de **karrenvracht** /kɑrə(n)vrɑxt/ (pl: -en) cartload

het **karretje** /kɑrəcə/ (pl: -s) (little) cart, car; trap; trolley; soapbox

het **kartel** /kɑrtɛl/ **1** cartel, trust **2** cartel

kartelen /kɑrtələ(n)/ (kartelde, heeft gekarteld) serrate, notch; mill

het **kartelmes** /kɑrtəlmɛs/ (pl: -sen) serrated knife

de **kartelrand** /kɑrtəlrɑnt/ (pl: -en) milled edge

karten /kɑːrtə(n)/ (kartte, heeft/is gekart) (go-)kart

het **karting** /kɑːrtɪŋ/ karting

het **karton** /kɑrtɔn/ (pl: -s) **1** cardboard **2** carton, cardboard box

kartonnen /kɑrtɔnə(n)/ (adj) cardboard: een ~ **bekertje** a paper cup

de **karwats** /kɑrwɑts/ (pl: -en) (riding) crop, (riding) whip

het/de **karwei** /kɑrwɛi/ (pl: -en) **1** job, work: een heidens ~ a hell of a job **2** odd job, chore **3** job, task, chore

de **karwij** /kɑrwɛi/ caraway (seed)

de **kas** /kɑs/ (pl: -sen) **1** greenhouse, hothouse **2** cashdesk, cashier's office **3** cash, fund(s): de kleine ~ petty cash; de ~ **beheren** (or: houden) manage (or: keep) the cash; krap (slecht) bij ~ zitten be short of cash (or: money) **4** socket

het **kasboek** /kɑzbuk/ (pl: -en) cash book, account(s) book

de **kasbon** /kɑzbɔn/ (pl: -nen) [Belg] (type of) savings certificate

de **kasgroente** /kɑsxruntə/ (pl: -n, -s) greenhouse vegetables

het **kasjmier** /kɑʃmir/ cashmere

de **Kaspische Zee** /kɑspisəze/ Caspian Sea

de **kasplant** /kɑsplɑnt/ (pl: -en) hothouse plant

de ¹**kassa** /kɑsa/ (pl: -'s) **1** cash register, till **2** cash desk; checkout; box office, booking office: bij de ~ at the till, at checkout

²**kassa** /kɑsa/ (int) ker-ching!, bingo!, jackpot!

de **kassabon** /kɑsabɔn/ (pl: -nen) receipt, sales slip, docket

het **kassaldo** /kɑsaldo/ (pl: -'s) cash balance

de **kassamedewerker** /kɑsamedəwɛrkər/ (pl: -s) cashier, checker, check-out assistant

de **kassei** /kɑsɛi/ (pl: -en) cobble(stone), paving stone, sett

de **kassier** /kɑsir/ (pl: -s) cashier; teller

het **kassucces** /kɑsyksɛs/ (pl: -sen) box-office success, box-office hit

de **kast** /kɑst/ (pl: -en) **1** cupboard; wardrobe; chest of drawers; cabinet: iem. **op** de ~ jagen (krijgen) get a rise out of s.o.; alles **uit** de ~ halen pull out all the stops **2** barracks; barn: een

~ **van** een huis a barn of a house ‖ **uit** de ~ komen come out (of the closet)

de **kastanje** /kɑstɑnə/ (Spanish, sweet) chestnut: gepofte ~s roast chestnuts

de **kastanjeboom** /kɑstɑnəbom/ (pl: -bomen) chestnut (tree)

het ¹**kastanjebruin** /kɑstɑnəbrœyn/ chestnut, auburn

²**kastanjebruin** /kɑstɑnəbrœyn/ (adj) chestnut, auburn

de **kaste** /kɑstə/ (pl: -n) caste

het **kasteel** /kɑstel/ (pl: kastelen) castle

de **kastelein** /kɑstəlɛin/ (pl: -s) innkeeper, publican, landlord

het **kastenstelsel** /kɑstəstɛlsəl/ caste system

het **kasticket** /kɑstikɛt/ (pl: -s) [Belg] receipt

kastijden /kɑstɛidə(n)/ (kastijdde, heeft gekastijd) chastise, castigate, punish

het **kastje** /kɑʃə/ (pl: -s) **1** cupboard, locker: van het ~ naar de muur gestuurd worden be sent (or: driven) from pillar to post **2** box

de **kat** /kɑt/ (pl: -ten) **1** cat: [fig] de ~ op het spek binden set the fox to watch the geese; leven als ~ en **hond** be like cat and dog; de **Gelaarsde** Kat Puss in Boots; [fig] de ~ uit de boom **kijken** wait to see which way the wind blows; **maak** dat de ~ **wijs** pull the other one, tell it to the marines **2** snarl: iem. een ~ **geven** snarl (or: snap) at s.o.

katachtig /kɑtɑxtəx/ (adj) catlike

de **katalysator** /kɑtalizator/ (pl: -s, -en) (catalytic) converter [of car]

de **katapult** /kɑtapylt/ (pl: -en) catapult

de **kater** /kɑtər/ (pl: -s) **1** tomcat **2** hangover **3** disillusionment

het/de **katern** /kɑtɛrn/ (pl: -en) quire, gathering

de **katheder** /kɑtedər/ (pl: -s) lectern

de **kathedraal** /kɑtedral/ (pl: kathedralen) cathedral

de **katheter** /kɑtetər/ (pl: -s) catheter: een ~ **inbrengen** bij catheterize

de **kathode** /kɑtodə/ (pl: -n, -s) cathode

het **katholicisme** /kɑtolisɪsmə/ (Roman) Catholicism

katholiek /kɑtolik/ (adj) (Roman) Catholic

het **katje** /kɑcə/ (pl: -s) **1** kitten **2** [bot] catkin

het/de **katoen** /kɑtun/ cotton

katoenen /kɑtunə(n)/ (adj) cotton

de **katoenplantage** /kɑtumplɑntaʒə/ cotton plantation

de **katrol** /kɑtrɔl/ (pl: -len) **1** (fishing) reel **2** pulley

het **kattebelletje** /kɑtəbɛləcə/ (pl: -s) (scribbled) note, memo

katten /kɑtə(n)/ (katte, heeft gekat) snap (at), snarl (at)

de **kattenbak** /kɑtə(n)bɑk/ (pl: -ken) **1** cat('s) box **2** [Dutch] dicky seat; [Am] rumble seat

de **kattenbakkorrels** /kɑtə(n)bɑkɔrəls/ (pl) cat litter

de **kattenbrokken** /kɑtə(n)brɔkə(n)/ (pl) dry

cat food, cat biscuits

de **kattenkop** /kɑtə(n)kɔp/ (pl: -pen) **1** cat's head **2** cat, bitch

het **kattenkwaad** /kɑtə(n)kwat/ mischief: ~ *uithalen* get into mischief

het **kattenluik** /kɑtə(n)lœyk/ cat flap

de **kattenpis** /kɑtə(n)pɪs/: *dat is geen* ~ no kidding; that's not to be sneezed at

het **kattenvoer** /kɑtə(n)vur/ cat food

katterig /kɑtərəx/ (adj) under the weather; hung over; disappointed, disillusioned

kattig /kɑtəx/ (adj, adv) catty

de **katzwijm** /kɑtswɛɪm/: *in* ~ *vallen* faint

de **kauw** /kɑu/ (pl: -en) jackdaw

kauwen /kɑuwə(n)/ (kauwde, heeft gekauwd) chew: [fig] *op iets* ~ chew sth. over

het/de **kauwgom** /kɑuɣɔm/ chewing gum

de **kavel** /kavəl/ (pl: -s) lot, parcel; share

de **kaviaar** /kavijar/ caviar

de **Kazach** /kazɑx/ Kazakh

het ¹**Kazachs** /kazɑxs/ Kazakh

²**Kazachs** /kazɑxs/ (adj) Kazakh

Kazachstan /kazɑkstɑn/ Kazakhstan

de **kazerne** /kazɛrnə/ (pl: -s) barrack(s) [mil]; station

het **kazuifel** /kazœyfəl/ (pl: -s) chasuble

de **kb** [Dutch; educ] *kaderberoepsgerichte leerweg* middle-management vocational training

KB /kilobɑjt(s)/ *kilobyte* K, KB

de **kebab** /kebɑb/ kebab

de **keel** /kel/ (pl: kelen) throat: *het hangt me (mijlenver) de ~ uit* I'm fed up with it; *een ~ opzetten* start yelling; *zijn ~ schrapen* clear one's throat; [fig] *dat grijpt je naar de ~* it grabs you by the throat, it's gut-wrenching

het **keelgat** /kelɣɑt/ (pl: -en) gullet: *in het verkeerde ~ schieten* **a)** go down the wrong way; **b)** [fig] not go down very well (with s.o.)

de **keelholte** /kelhɔltə/ pharynx

de **keelontsteking** /kelɔntstekɪŋ/ (pl: -en) throat infection, laryngitis

de **keelpijn** /kelpɛɪn/ sore throat

keepen /kipə(n)/ (keepte, heeft gekeept) be in goal, keep goal

de **keeper** /kipər/ (pl: -s) (goal)keeper; goalie

de **keer** /ker/ (pl: keren) time: *een doodenkele ~* once in a blue moon; *een enkele ~* once or twice; *geen enkele ~* not once; *een andere ~* another time; *nou vooruit, voor deze ~ dan!* all right then, but just this once!; *nog een ~(tje)* (once) again, once more; *(op) een ~* one day; *één enkele ~, slechts één ~* only once; *negen van de tien ~* nine times out of ten; *dat heb ik nu al tien* (or: *honderd*) *~ gehoord* I've already heard that dozens of times (or: a hundred times); *twee ~* twice; *twee ~ twee is vier* twice two is four; *~ op ~* time after time, time and again; *binnen de kortste keren* in no time (at all)

de **keerkring** /kerkrɪŋ/ (pl: -en) tropic

het **keerpunt** /kerpʏnt/ (pl: -en) turning point

de **keerzijde** /kerzɛidə/ (pl: -n) other side; reverse

de **keet** /ket/ (pl: keten) **1** hut, shed **2** racket: ~ *trappen* (or: *schoppen*) horse about (around)

keffen /kɛfə(n)/ (kefte, heeft gekeft) yap

het **keffertje** /kɛfərcə/ (pl: -s) yapper

de **kegel** /keɣəl/ (pl: -s) **1** cone **2** ninepin; skittle

de **kegelbaan** /keɣəlban/ (pl: -banen) skittle alley

kegelen /keɣələ(n)/ (kegelde, heeft gekegeld) play skittles (or: ninepins)

de **kei** /kɛi/ (pl: -en) **1** boulder **2** cobble(stone); set(t) ‖ *Eric is een ~ in wiskunde* Eric is brilliant at maths

keihard /kɛihɑrt/ (adj, adv) **1** rock-hard, hard; as hard as rock [after vb] **2** hard, tough ‖ ~ *schreeuwen* shout at the top of one's voice; *de radio stond ~ aan* the radio was on full blast (or: was blaring away)

keilen /kɛilə(n)/ (keilde, heeft gekeild) throw, chuck, fling: *iem. de deur uit* ~ throw (or: chuck) s.o. out (of the door)

de **keizer** /kɛizər/ (pl: -s) emperor

de **keizerin** /kɛizərɪn/ (pl: -nen) empress

keizerlijk /kɛizərlək/ (adj, adv) imperial

het **keizerrijk** /kɛizərɛik/ (pl: -en) empire

de **keizersnede** /kɛizərsnedə/ (pl: -n) Caesarean (section)

de **kelder** /kɛldər/ (pl: -s) cellar, basement

kelderen /kɛldərə(n)/ (kelderde, is gekelderd) plummet, tumble

het **kelderluik** /kɛldərlœyk/ (pl: -en) trapdoor (to a cellar)

kelen /kelə(n)/ (keelde, heeft gekeeld) **1** cut (s.o.'s) throat **2** strangle, throttle

de **kelk** /kɛlk/ (pl: -en) **1** goblet **2** calyx

de **kelner** /kɛlnər/ (pl: -s) waiter

de **Kelten** /kɛltə(n)/ (pl) Celts

het ¹**Keltisch** /kɛltis/ Celtic

²**Keltisch** /kɛltis/ (adj) Celtic

de **kemphaan** /kɛmphan/ (pl: -hanen) **1** ruff **2** fighting cock: *vechten als kemphanen* fight like fighting cocks

de **kenau** /kenɑu/ (pl: -s) battle-axe, virago

kenbaar /kɛmbar/ (adj) known

het **kengetal** /kɛnɣətɑl/ (pl: -len) dialling code; [Am] area code; prefix

Kenia /kenija/ Kenya

de **Keniaan** /kenijan/ (pl: Kenianen) Kenyan

Keniaans /kenijans/ (adj) Kenyan

het **kenmerk** /kɛnmɛrk/ (pl: -en) (identifying) mark; hallmark [also fig]; reference [abbr: ref]

kenmerken /kɛnmɛrkə(n)/ (kenmerkte, heeft gekenmerkt) characterize, mark, typify

kenmerkend /kɛnmɛrkənt/ (adj, adv) (+ voor) characteristic (of), typical (of); specific (to): *~e eigenschappen* distinctive characteristics

de **kennel** /kɛnəl/ (pl: -s) kennel

¹**kennelijk** /kɛ̱nələk/ (adj) evident, apparent; clear; obvious; unmistakable

²**kennelijk** /kɛ̱nələk/ (adv) evidently, clearly, obviously: *het is ~ zonder opzet gedaan* it was obviously done unintentionally

kennen /kɛ̱nə(n)/ (kende, heeft gekend) know, be acquainted with: *iem. leren ~* get to know s.o.; *elkaar (beter) leren ~* get (better) acquainted; *ken je deze al?* have you heard this one?; *ik ken haar al jaren* I've known her for years; *sinds ik jou ken …* since I met you …; *iem. van naam ~* know s.o. by name; *iem. door en door ~* know s.o. inside out; *iets van buiten ~, iets uit zijn hoofd ~* know sth. by heart; *ons kent ons* we know what to expect, we know each others ways; [fig] *laat je niet ~!* give 'em hell!

de **kenner** /kɛ̱nər/ (pl: -s) **1** connoisseur **2** authority (on), expert (on)

de **kennersblik** /kɛ̱nərzblɪk/ (pl: -ken) expert('s) eye

de **kennis** /kɛ̱nɪs/ (pl: -sen) **1** knowledge (of); acquaintance (with): *met ~ van zaken* knowledgeably; *~ is macht* knowledge is power **2** consciousness: *zij is weer bij ~ gekomen* she has regained consciousness, she has come round **3** knowledge, information; learning; know-how: *een grondige ~ van het Latijn hebben* have a thorough knowledge of Latin **4** acquaintance: *hij heeft veel vrienden en ~sen* he has a lot of friends and acquaintances

de **kennisgeving** /kɛ̱nɪsxevɪŋ/ (pl: -en) notification, notice: *iets voor ~ aannemen* take note of sth.

de **kennismaatschappij** /kɛ̱nɪsmatsxɑpɛɪ/ knowledge (*or:* information) society

kennismaken /kɛ̱nɪsmakə(n)/ (maakte kennis, heeft kennisgemaakt) get acquainted (with), meet, get to know, be introduced: *aangenaam kennis te maken!* pleased to meet you

de **kennismaking** /kɛ̱nɪsmakɪŋ/ (pl: -en) **1** acquaintance **2** introduction (to)

kennisnemen /kɛ̱nɪsnemə(n)/ (nam kennis van, heeft heeft kennisgenomen van) take note (of)

de **kennisneming** /kɛ̱nɪsnemɪŋ/ examination, inspection: *na ~ van de stukken* after examination of the documents; *ter ~* for your information

de **kennissenkring** /kɛ̱nɪssə(n)krɪŋ/ (pl: -en) (circle of) acquaintances

kenschetsen /kɛ̱nsxɛtsə(n)/ (kenschetste, heeft gekenschetst) characterize

het **kenteken** /kɛ̱ntekə(n)/ (pl: -s) registration number; [Am] license number

het **kentekenbewijs** /kɛ̱ntekə(n)bəwɛis/ (pl: -bewijzen) [roughly] vehicle registration document; logbook

de **kentekenplaat** /kɛ̱ntekə(n)plat/ (pl: -pla-ten) number plate; [Am] license plate

kenteren /kɛ̱ntərə(n)/ (kenterde, heeft gekenterd) turn

de **kentering** /kɛ̱ntərɪŋ/ (pl: -en) turn: *~ in de publieke opinie* turn (*or:* change) of public opinion

de **keper** /ke̱pər/: *op de ~ beschouwd* on closer inspection; when all is said and done

het **keppeltje** /kɛ̱pəlcə/ (pl: -s) yarmulka

de **keramiek** /kerami̱k/ ceramics; pottery

keramisch /kera̱mis/ (adj) ceramic, pottery: *een ~e kookplaat* a ceramic hob; [Am] a ceramic stove top

de **kerel** /ke̱rəl/ (pl: -s) **1** (big) fellow, (big) guy, (big) chap (*or:* bloke) **2** he-man: *kom naar buiten als je een ~ bent* come outside if you're man enough

¹**keren** /ke̱rə(n)/ (keerde, is gekeerd) turn (round); shift: *~ verboden* no U-turns

²**keren** /ke̱rə(n)/ (keerde, heeft gekeerd) **1** turn **2** turn (towards) **3** turn (back); stem: *het water ~* stem the (flow of) water

zich ³**keren** /ke̱rə(n)/ (keerde zich, heeft zich gekeerd) **1** turn (round): *zich ergens niet kunnen wenden of ~* not have room to move **2** turn ‖ *in zichzelf gekeerd zijn* be introverted, keep to o.s.

de **kerf** /kɛrf/ (pl: kerven) notch, nick; groove

de **kerfstok** /kɛ̱rfstɔk/ (pl: -ken): *heel wat op zijn ~ hebben* have a lot to answer for

de **kerk** /kɛrk/ (pl: -en) church: *naar de ~ gaan* **a)** go to church; **b)** be a churchgoer

de **kerkbank** /kɛ̱rgbɑŋk/ pew

de **kerkdienst** /kɛ̱rgdinst/ (pl: -en) (divine) service, church; mass

kerkelijk /kɛ̱rkələk/ (adj) church, ecclesiastical

de **kerkenraad** /kɛ̱rkə(n)rat/ (pl: -raden) **1** church council meeting **2** (parochial) church council

de **kerker** /kɛ̱rkər/ (pl: -s) dungeon, prison, jail

de **kerkganger** /kɛ̱rkxɑŋər/ (pl: -s) churchgoer

het **kerkgebouw** /kɛ̱rkxəbɑu/ (pl: -en) church (building)

het **kerkgenootschap** /kɛ̱rkxənotsxɑp/ (pl: -pen) (religious) denomination, (religious) community

het **kerkhof** /kɛ̱rkhɔf/ (pl: -hoven) churchyard, graveyard

de **kerkklok** /kɛ̱rklɔk/ (pl: -ken) **1** church bell **2** church clock

het **kerkkoor** /kɛ̱rkor/ (pl: -koren) **1** choir **2** church choir

de **kerkmuziek** /kɛ̱rkmyzik/ church music, religious music

het **kerkplein** /kɛ̱rkplɛin/ (pl: -en) [roughly] village square

de **kerktoren** /kɛ̱rktorə(n)/ (pl: -s) church tower; steeple; spire

de **kerkuil** /kɛ̱rkœyl/ (pl: -en) barn owl

kermen /kɛ̱rmə(n)/ (kermde, heeft gekermd) moan; whine; wail

de **kermis** /kɛrməs/ (pl: -sen) fair

de **kermisexploitant** /kɛrmɪsɛksplwɑtɑnt/ (pl: -en) showman

de **kern** /kɛrn/ (pl: -en) **1** core; heart; pith **2** [fig] core, heart, essence: *tot de ~ van een zaak doordringen* get (down) to the (very) heart of the matter; *de ~ van het probleem* the fundamental issue **3** central

kernachtig /kɛrnɑxtəx/ (adj, adv) pithy, concise, terse

het **kernafval** /kɛrnɑfɑl/ nuclear waste

de **kernbom** /kɛrmbɔm/ (pl: -men) nuclear bomb

de **kerncentrale** /kɛrnsɛntrɑlə/ (pl: -s) nuclear (*or:* atomic) power station, nuclear plant, atomic plant

het **kerndoel** /kɛrndul/ (pl: -en) primary objective, chief aim

de **kernenergie** /kɛrnenɛrʒi/ nuclear energy

de **kernfusie** /kɛrnfyzi/ nuclear fusion

de **kernfysica** /kɛrnfizikɑ/ nuclear physics

de **kernfysicus** /kɛrnfizikʏs/ (pl: -fysici) nuclear physicist, atomic physicist

kerngezond /kɛrnɣəzɔnt/ (adj) perfectly healthy, in perfect health; as fit as a fiddle

de **kernmacht** /kɛrnmɑxt/ (pl: -en) nuclear power

de **kernoorlog** /kɛrnorlɔx/ (pl: -en) nuclear war

de **kernproef** /kɛrmpruf/ (pl: -proeven) nuclear test, atomic test

de **kernreactie** /kɛrnrejɑksi/ (pl: -s) nuclear reaction

de **kernreactor** /kɛrnrejɑktɔr/ (pl: -s, -en) (nuclear, atomic) reactor

de **kerntaak** /kɛrntak/ (pl: -taken) core task

het **kernwapen** /kɛrnwapə(n)/ (pl: -s) nuclear weapon, atomic weapon

de **kerosine** /kerozinə/ kerosene

de **kerrie** /kɛri/ curry

de **kers** /kɛrs/ cherry: [fig] *de ~ op de taart* the icing on the cake

de **kersenbonbon** /kɛrsə(n)bɔmbɔn/ (pl: -s) cherry liqueur chocolate

de **kerst** /kɛrst/ Christmas: *een witte ~* a white Christmas

de **kerstavond** /kɛrstavɔnt/ (pl: -en) evening of Christmas Eve

de **kerstboom** /kɛrstbom/ (pl: -bomen) Christmas tree: *een cadeautje voor onder de ~* a Christmas gift, a gift from Santa; *de ~ opzetten* decorate the Christmas tree

de **kerstdag** /kɛrzdɑx/ (pl: -en) Christmas Day: *prettige ~en!* Merry (*or:* Happy) Christmas!; *eerste ~* Christmas Day; *tweede ~* Boxing Day

kerstenen /kɛrstənə(n)/ (kerstende, heeft gekerstend) christianize

het **kerstfeest** /kɛrstfest/ (pl: -en) (feast, festival of) Christmas: *zalig (gelukkig) ~!* Merry Christmas!

de **kerstkaart** /kɛrstkart/ Christmas card

de **kerstkrans** /kɛrstkrɑns/ (pl: -en) (almond) pastry ring

het **kerstlied** /kɛrstlit/ (pl: -eren) (Christmas) carol

de **Kerstman** /kɛrstmɑn/ (pl: -nen) Santa (Claus), Father Christmas

Kerstmis /kɛrstmɪs/ Christmas

de **kerstnacht** /kɛrstnɑxt/ (pl: -en) Christmas night

de **kerstomaat** /kɛrstomat/ (pl: -tomaten) cherry tomato

het **kerstpakket** /kɛrstpɑkɛt/ (pl: -ten) Christmas hamper (*or:* box)

de **kerststal** /kɛrstɑl/ (pl: -len) crib

de **Kerstster** /kɛr(st)stɛr/ Star of Bethlehem

de **kerststol** /kɛr(st)stɔl/ (pl: -len) (Christmas) stollen

de **kerstvakantie** /kɛrstfakan(t)si/ (pl: -s) Christmas holiday(s); [Am] Christmas vacation

kersvers /kɛrsfɛrs/ (adj) fresh, new: *~ uit de winkel* fresh (*or:* straight) from the shop

de **kervel** /kɛrvəl/ chervil

¹**kerven** /kɛrvə(n)/ (kerfde, is gekerfd) gouge (out), cut

²**kerven** /kɛrvə(n)/ (kerfde, heeft gekerfd) **1** notch, nick, cut; score **2** carve (out), cut (out): *zij kerfden hun naam in de boom* they carved their names in the tree

de **ketchup** /kɛtʃʏp/ ketchup

de **ketel** /ketəl/ (pl: -s) **1** kettle; cauldron **2** boiler

het/de **ketelsteen** /ketəlsten/ (boiler) scale

de **keten** /ketə(n)/ (pl: -s) **1** chains **2** chain **3** chain, series

ketenen /ketənə(n)/ (ketende, heeft geketend) **1** chain (up) **2** chain **3** [fig] curb

de **ketjap** /kɛtjɑp/ soy sauce

ketsen /kɛtsə(n)/ (ketste, heeft/is geketst) **1** glance off, ricochet (off) **2** misfire, fail to go off: *het geweer ketste* the gun misfired

de **ketter** /kɛtər/ (pl: -s) heretic ‖ *roken als een ~* smoke like a chimney

de **ketterij** /kɛtərɛi/ (pl: -en) heresy

ketters /kɛtərs/ (adj, adv) heretical

de **ketting** /kɛtɪŋ/ (pl: -en) chain: *aan de ~ leggen* chain up

de **kettingbotsing** /kɛtɪŋbotsɪŋ/ (pl: -en) multiple collision (*or:* crash), pile-up

de **kettingbrief** /kɛtɪŋbrif/ (pl: -brieven) chain letter

de **kettingkast** /kɛtɪŋkɑst/ (pl: -en) chain guard

de **kettingreactie** /kɛtɪŋrejɑksi/ (pl: -s) chain reaction

de **kettingroker** /kɛtɪŋrokər/ (pl: -s) chain smoker

het **kettingslot** /kɛtɪŋslɔt/ chain lock

de **kettingzaag** /kɛtɪŋzax/ (pl: -zagen) chainsaw

de **keu** /køˌ/ (pl: -s) (billiard) cue

de **keuken** /kø̞kə(n)/ (pl: -s) **1** kitchen **2** (art of) cooking, cuisine: *de Franse* ~ French cooking (*or:* cuisine)

de **keukendoek** /kø̞kə(n)duk/ (pl: -en) kitchen towel

de **keukenhulp** /kø̞kə(n)hʏlp/ (pl: -en) food processor

de **keukenkast** /kø̞kə(n)kɑst/ (pl: -en) kitchen cabinet (*or:* cupboard)

het **keukenkruid** /kø̞kə(n)krœyt/ kitchen herb

de **keukenmachine** /kø̞kə(n)maʃinə/ (pl: -s) food processor

de **keukenrol** /kø̞kə(n)rɔl/ (pl: -len) kitchen roll

het **keukenschort** /kø̞kə(n)sxɔrt/ apron

Keulen /kø̞lə(n)/ Cologne ‖ *het in* ~ *horen donderen* be (utterly) staggered

de **keur** /kør/ (pl: -en) **1** hallmark **2** choice (selection)

keuren /kø̞rə(n)/ (keurde, heeft gekeurd) test; inspect; sample; taste; examine: *films* ~ classify films; *iem. geen blik waardig* ~ not deign to look at s.o.

¹**keurig** /kø̞rəx/ (adj) **1** neat, tidy: *er* ~ *uitzien* look neat (and tidy), look smart **2** smart, nice: *een* ~ *handschrift* a neat hand **3** fine, choice: *een* ~ *rapport* (*or:* *opstel*) an excellent report (*or:* essay)

²**keurig** /kø̞rəx/ (adv) nicely; neatly ‖ ~ *netjes gekleed* properly dressed

de **keuring** /kø̞rɪŋ/ (pl: -en) **1** test; inspection; examination: *een medische* ~ a medical (examination) **2** testing; inspection; sampling; tasting; examination

de **keuringsarts** /kø̞rɪŋsɑrts/ medical examiner

de **keuringsdienst** /kø̞rɪŋzdinst/ (pl: -en) inspection service: *Keuringsdienst van Waren* commodity inspection department

het **keurkorps** /kørkɔrps/ (pl: -en) crack troops

de **keurmeester** /kørmestər/ (pl: -s) inspector; [gold and silver] assay-master

het **keurmerk** /kørmɛrk/ (pl: -en) hallmark; quality mark

het **keurslijf** /kørslɛif/ (pl: -lijven) straitjacket: [fig] *in een* ~ *zitten* have one's hands tied

de **keus** /køs/ (pl: keuzen) **1** choice, selection **2** choice, option, alternative: *er is volop* ~ there's a lot to choose from; *aan u de* ~ the choice is yours **3** choice, assortment: *een grote* ~ a large choice (*or:* assortment), a wide range

de **keutel** /kø̞təl/ (pl: -s) droppings; pellet

keuvelen /kø̞vələ(n)/ (keuvelde, heeft gekeuveld) (have a) chat, talk

de **keuze** /kø̞zə/ (pl: -n) *see* keus

het **keuzemenu** /kø̞zəməny/ (pl: -'s) **1** set menu, fixed price menu **2** menu

het **keuzepakket** /kø̞zəpɑkɛt/ (pl: -ten) options; choice of subjects (*or:* courses)

het **keuzevak** /kø̞zəvɑk/ (pl: -ken) option, optional subject (*or:* course)

de **keuzevrijheid** /kø̞zəvrɛihɛit/ freedom of choice

de **kever** /ke̞vər/ (pl: -s) **1** beetle **2** Beetle

het **keyboard** /kiːbɔːrd/ (pl: -s) keyboard

de **keycard** /kiːkɑːrt/ keycard

de **keycord** /kikɔːrt/ keycord

kg *kilogram* kg

de **ki** /kai/ **1** *kunstmatige inseminatie* AI (artificial insemination) **2** *kunstmatige intelligentie* AI (artificial intelligence)

kibbelen /kɪbələ(n)/ (kibbelde, heeft gekibbeld) bicker, squabble

de **kibbeling** /kɪbəlɪŋ/ cod parings

de **kibboets** /kɪbuts/ (pl: -en, kibboetsim) kibbutz

de **kick** /kɪk/ (pl: -s) kick

kickboksen /kɪɡbɔksə(n)/ kickboxing

kicken /kɪkə(n)/ (kickte, heeft gekickt) get a kick (out of); [Am] get off (on), dig: *dat is* ~! that's cool!

kidnappen /kɪtnɛpə(n)/ (kidnapte, heeft gekidnapt) kidnap

de **kidnapper** /kɪtnɛpər/ (pl: -s) kidnapper

de **kids** /kɪts/ (pl) [inform] kids

kiekeboe /kikəbu/ (int) peekaboo!

het **kiekje** /kikjə/ (pl: -s) snap(shot)

de **kiel** /kil/ (pl: -en) **1** smock **2** [shipp] keel

kielekiele /kiləkilə/: *het was* ~ it was touch and go, it was a close shave

kielhalen /kilhalə(n)/ (kielhaalde, heeft gekielhaald) keelhaul

het **kielzog** /kilzɔx/ wake, wash: *in iemands* ~ *varen* follow in s.o.'s wake (*or:* track(s))

de **kiem** /kim/ (pl: -en) germ, seed

kiemen /kimə(n)/ (kiemde, heeft/is gekiemd) germinate

kien /kin/ (adj, adv) sharp, keen

de **kiepauto** /kipauto/ (pl: -'s) tip up truck

¹**kiepen** /kipə(n)/ (kiepte, is gekiept) topple, tumble: *het glas is van de tafel gekiept* the glass toppled off the table

²**kiepen** /kipə(n)/ (kiepte, heeft gekiept) tip over, topple (over)

¹**kieperen** /kipərə(n)/ (kieperde, is gekieperd) tumble, topple

²**kieperen** /kipərə(n)/ (kieperde, heeft gekieperd) [inform] dump

de **kier** /kir/ (pl: -en) chink, slit; crack: *door een* ~ *van de schutting* through a crack in the fence; *de deur staat op een* ~ the door is ajar

kierewiet /kirəwit/ (adj) [inform] mad, bananas: *het is om* ~ *van te worden!* it's enough to drive me mad (*or:* bananas)

de **kies** /kis/ (pl: kiezen) molar, back tooth: *een rotte* ~ a bad (*or:* decayed) molar; [fig] a rotten apple (in the barrel); [fig] *iets voor zijn kiezen krijgen* be forced to swallow sth.

de **kiesbrief** /kizbrif/ (pl: -brieven) [Belg] polling card het **kiesdistrict** /ki̱zdɪstrɪkt/ (pl: -en) electoral district, constituency

de **kiesdrempel** /ki̱zdrɛmpəl/ (pl: -s) electoral threshold

kieskeurig /kiskøːrəx/ (adj) choosy, fussy

de **kieskring** /ki̱skrɪŋ/ (pl: -en) electoral district, constituency; ward

de **kiespijn** /ki̱spɛin/ toothache: *ik kan hem missen als ~* I need him like I need a hole in the head

het **kiesrecht** /ki̱srɛxt/ (pl: -en) suffrage, right to vote, (the) vote

het **kiesstelsel** /ki̱stɛlsəl/ (pl: -s) electoral (or: voting) system

de **kiestoon** /ki̱ston/ dialling tone

kietelen /ki̱tələ(n)/ (kietelde, heeft gekieteld) tickle

de **kieuw** /kiw/ (pl: -en) gill

de **kieviet** /ki̱vit/ (pl: -en) lapwing, peewit, plover

het **kiezel** /ki̱zəl/ (pl: -s) gravel; shingle

de **kiezelsteen** /ki̱zəlsten/ (pl: -stenen) pebble

¹**kiezen** /ki̱zə(n)/ (koos, heeft gekozen)
1 choose, decide: *zorgvuldig ~* pick and choose; *~ tussen* choose between; *je kunt uit drie kandidaten ~* you can choose from three candidates **2** vote: *voor een vrouwelijke kandidaat ~* vote for a woman candidate

²**kiezen** /ki̱zə(n)/ (koos, heeft gekozen)
1 choose, select, pick (out): *partij ~* take sides **2** vote (for); elect **3** choose, elect || *een nummer ~* dial a number

de **kiezer** /ki̱zər/ (pl: -s) voter, constituent; electorate

de **kift** /kɪft/ [Dutch; inform]: *dat is de ~* sour grapes!

de **kijf** /kɛif/: *dat staat buiten ~* that is beyond dispute (or: question(ing))

de **kijk** /kɛik/ view, outlook; insight: *~ op iets hebben* have a good eye for sth.; [fig] *iem. te ~ zetten* expose s.o.; [inform] *tot ~!* see you (later)!

het **kijkcijfer** /kɛiksɛifər/ (pl: -s) rating

de **kijkdichtheid** /kɛiɡdɪxtɦɛit/ ratings

¹**kijken** /kɛikə(n)/ (keek, heeft gekeken)
1 look, see: *ga eens ~ wie er is* go and see who's there; *daar sta ik van te ~* well I'll be blowed; *kijk eens wie we daar hebben* look who's here!; *goed ~* watch closely; [fig] *naar iets ~* have a look at (or: see) about sth.; *zij ~ niet op geld (een paar euro)* money is no object with them; *uit het raam ~* look out (of) the window; *even de andere kant op ~* look the other way **2** look, search: *we zullen ~ of dat verhaal klopt* we shall see whether that story checks out **3** look, appear || *laat eens ~, wat hebben we nodig* let's see, what do we need

²**kijken** /kɛikə(n)/ (keek, heeft gekeken) look at, watch: *kijk haar eens (lachen)* look at her (laughing)

de **kijker** /kɛikər/ (pl: -s) **1** spectator, onlooker; viewer **2** binoculars; opera-glass(es)

de **kijkfile** /kɛikfilə/ (pl: -s) traffic jam caused by rubbernecking

het **kijkje** /kɛikjə/ (pl: -s) (quick) look, glance: *de politie zal een ~ nemen* the police will have a look

de **kijkoperatie** /kɛikopəra(t)si/ (pl: -s) keyhole operation (or: surgery); exploratory operation (or: surgery)

de **kijkwoning** /kɛikwonɪŋ/ (pl: -en) [Belg] show house

kijven /kɛivə(n)/ (kijfde, heeft gekijfd) quarrel, wrangle, rail (at)

de **kik** /kɪk/ sound || *zonder een ~ te geven* without a sound (or: murmur)

kikken /kɪkə(n)/ (kikte, heeft gekikt) open one's mouth, give a sound (or: peep)

de **kikker** /kɪkər/ (pl: -s) frog

het **kikkerbad** /kɪkərbat/ paddling pool, wading pool

het **kikkerbilletje** /kɪkərbɪləcə/ (pl: -s) frog's leg

het **kikkerdril** /kɪkərdrɪl/ frogspawn, frogs' eggs

de **kikkererwt** /kɪkərɛrt/ (pl: -en) chickpea

het **kikkerland** /kɪkərlant/ chilly country

het **kikkervisje** /kɪkərvɪʃə/ (pl: -s) tadpole

de **kikvors** /kɪkfɔrs/ (pl: -en) frog

de **kikvorsman** /kɪkfɔrsman/ (pl: -nen) frogman

kil /kɪl/ (adj, adv) chilly, cold

de **killer** /kɪlər/ (pl: -s) killer

het/de **kilo** /ki̱lo/ (pl: -'s) kilo

de **kilocalorie** /ki̱lokalori/ (pl: -ën) kilocalorie

het/de **kilogram** /ki̱loɣram/ (pl: -men) kilogram(me)

de **kilometer** /ki̱lometər/ (pl: -s) kilometre: *op een ~ afstand* at a distance of one kilometre; *90 ~ per uur rijden* drive at 90 kilometres an hour; *vierkante ~* square kilometre

de **kilometerteller** /ki̱lometərtɛlər/ (pl: -s) milometer; [Am] odometer

de **kilometervergoeding** /ki̱lometərvərɣudɪŋ/ mileage (allowance)

de **kilowatt** /ki̱lowat/ (pl: -s) kilowatt

het **kilowattuur** /ki̱lowatyr/ kilowatt-hour

de **kilt** /kɪlt/ (pl: -s) kilt

de **kilte** /kɪltə/ chilliness

de **kim** /kɪm/ (pl: -men) horizon

de **kimono** /kimo̱no/ (pl: -'s) kimono

de **kin** /kɪn/ (pl: -nen) chin || [Belg] *op zijn ~ kloppen* get nothing to eat

het **kind** /kɪnt/ (pl: -eren) child, baby: *een ~ hebben van* have a child by; *een ~ krijgen* have a baby; *~eren opvoeden* bring up children; *een ~ van zes jaar* a child of six, a six-year-old (child); [fig] *een ~ kan de was doen* that's child's play, it's as simple as ABC; *van ~ af aan, van ~s af* since (or: from) childhood, since I/he/… was a child

de **kindbruid** /kɪndbrœyt/ (pl: -en) child bride

kinderachtig /kɪndərɑχtəχ/ (adj, adv) **1** childlike; child(ren)'s **2** [depr] childish, infantile: *doe niet zo* ~ grow up!, don't be such a baby!

de **kinderarbeid** /kɪndərɑrbɛit/ child labour

de **kinderarts** /kɪndərɑrts/ (pl: -en) paediatrician

de **kinderbescherming** /kɪndərbəsχɛrmɪŋ/ child welfare: *Raad voor de Kinderbescherming* child welfare council

de **kinderbijslag** /kɪndərbɛislɑχ/ family allowance, child benefit

het **kinderboek** /kɪndərbuk/ (pl: -en) children's book

de **kinderboerderij** /kɪndərburdɛrɛi/ (pl: -en) children's farm

het **kinderdagverblijf** /kɪndərdɑχfərblɛif/ (pl: -verblijven) crèche, day-care centre

de **kinderhand** /kɪndərhɑnt/ (pl: -en) child(ren)'s hand

de **kinderjaren** /kɪndərjɑrə(n)/ (pl) childhood (years): *sinds mijn* ~ since I was a child

de **kinderkamer** /kɪndərkɑmər/ (pl: -s) nursery

kinderlijk /kɪndərlək/ (adj, adv) childlike; childish

kinderloos /kɪndərlos/ (adj) childless

het **kindermeisje** /kɪndərmɛiʃə/ (pl: -s) nurse-(maid), nanny

het **kindermenu** /kɪndərməny/ (pl: -'s) children's menu

de **kindermishandeling** /kɪndərmɪshɑndəlɪŋ/ child abuse

de **kinderoppas** /kɪndərɔpɑs/ (pl: -sen) babysitter, childminder

de **kinderopvang** /kɪndərɔpfɑŋ/ (day) nursery, day-care centre, crèche

de **kinderporno** /kɪndərpɔrno/ child pornography

de **kinderrechter** /kɪndərɛχtər/ (pl: -s) [Dutch] [roughly] magistrate of (*or:* in) a juvenile court

kinderrijk /kɪndərɛik/ (adj) (blessed) with many children: *een* ~ *gezin* a large family

het **kinderslot** /kɪndərslɔt/ (pl: -en) childproof lock

het **kinderspel** /kɪndərspɛl/ (pl: -en) **1** children's games; [fig] child's play **2** children's game

de **kindersterfte** /kɪndərstɛrftə/ child mortality

de **kinderstoel** /kɪndərstul/ (pl: -en) high chair

het **kindertehuis** /kɪndərtəhœys/ (pl: -tehuizen) children's home

de **kindertelefoon**® /kɪndərteləfon/ (pl: -s) children's helpline, childline

de **kindertijd** /kɪndərtɛit/ childhood (days)

de **kinderverlamming** /kɪndərvərlɑmɪŋ/ polio

de **kinderwagen** /kɪndərwɑɣə(n)/ (pl: -s) baby buggy, pram

de **kinderziekte** /kɪndərziktə/ (pl: -n, -s) childhood disease; [fig] teething troubles; growing pains: *de* ~*n (nog niet) te boven zijn* still have teething troubles

het **kinderzitje** /kɪndərzɪcə/ (pl: -s) baby seat, child's seat

het **kindhuwelijk** /kɪnthywələk/ (pl: -en) child marriage

kinds /kɪnts/ (adj) senile, in one's second childhood || *van* ~ *af aan* from childhood (on), since childhood

kindsbeen /kɪn(t)sben/: *van* ~ *(af)* from childhood (on), since childhood

de **kindsoldaat** /kɪntsɔldat/ child soldier

de **kinesist** /kinezɪst/ (pl: -en) [Belg] physiotherapist

de **kinesitherapie** /kinezɪterɑpi/ [Belg] physiotherapy

de **kinine** /kinḭnə/ quinine

de **kink** /kɪŋk/ (pl: -en): *er zit een* ~ *in de kabel* there's a hitch (somewhere)

de **kinkhoest** /kɪŋkhust/ whooping cough

kinky /kɪŋki/ (adj, adv) kinky

de **kiosk** /kijɔsk/ (pl: -en) kiosk; newspaper stand, book stand

de **kip** /kɪp/ (pl: -pen) **1** chicken, hen: *er was geen* ~ *te zien* (or: *te bekennen*) there wasn't a soul to be seen **2** chicken, poultry

het **kip-eiprobleem** /kɪpɛiproblem/ chicken-and-egg problem

het/de **kipfilet** /kɪpfile/ (pl: -s) chicken breast(s)

kiplekker /kɪplɛkər/ (adj) as fit as a fiddle

de **kippenborst** /kɪpə(n)bɔrst/ (pl: -en) chicken breast

het **kippenboutje** /kɪpə(n)bɑucə/ (pl: -s) chicken leg

het **kippengaas** /kɪpə(n)ɣas/ chicken wire

het **kippenhok** /kɪpə(n)hɔk/ (pl: -ken) **1** chicken coop **2** [fig] pandemonium, chicken coop

de **kippenren** /kɪpə(n)rɛn/ (pl: -nen) chicken run

de **kippensoep** /kɪpə(n)sup/ chicken soup

het **kippenvel** /kɪpə(n)vɛl/ goosebumps

kippig /kɪpəχ/ (adj) short-sighted, near-sighted

de **Kirgies** /kɪrɣis/ (pl: Kirgiezen) Kyrgyz

Kirgizië /kɪrɣḭzijə/ Kirghizistan

het ¹**Kirgizisch** /kɪrɣḭzis/ Kyrgyz

²**Kirgizisch** /kɪrɣḭzis/ (adj) Kyrgyz

kirren /kɪrə(n)/ (kirde, heeft gekird) coo, gurgle

de **kirsch** /kɪrʃ/ kirsch

de **kissebissen** /kɪsəbɪsə(n)/ (kissebiste, heeft gekissebist) squabble, bicker

de **kist** /kɪst/ (pl: -en) **1** chest **2** coffin **3** box; case; crate

kisten /kɪstə(n)/ (kistte, heeft gekist): [inform] *laat je niet* ~ don't let them walk all over you

het/de **kit** /kɪt/ cement, glue, sealant

kitesurfen /kɑjtsʏrfə(n)/ (kitesurfte/kitesurfde, heeft gekitesurft/gekitesurfd) kite

surf
kits /kɪts/ (adj): *alles ~?* how's things?, everything O.K.? (*or:* all right?)
de **kitsch** /kitʃ/ kitsch
de **kittelaar** /kɪtəlar/ (pl: -s) clitoris
kitten /kɪtə(n)/ (kitte, heeft gekit) seal (tight)
kittig /kɪtəχ/ (adj, adv) spirited
de **kiwi** /kiwi/ (pl: -'s) kiwi
klaaglijk /klaχlək/ (adj, adv) plaintive
de **Klaagmuur** /klaχmyr/ Wailing Wall
de **klaagzang** /klaχsɑŋ/ (pl: -en) lament(ation): *een ~ aanheffen* raise one's voice in complaint
klaar /klar/ (adj, adv) **1** clear **2** pure **3** ready: *de boot is ~ voor vertrek* the boat is ready to sail; *~ voor de strijd* ready for action; *~ terwijl u wacht* ready while you wait; *~? af!* ready, get set, go! **4** finished, done: *ik ben zo ~* I won't be a minute (*or:* second); *~ is Kees* (and) that's that!; *ergens ~ mee zijn* a) have finished sth.; b) [fig] have had (more than) enough of sth., have had it with sth.; *we zijn ~ met eten* (or: *opruimen*) we've finished eating (*or:* clearing up)
klaarblijkelijk /klarblɛɪkələk/ (adv) evidently, obviously
klaarkomen /klarkomə(n)/ (kwam klaar, is klaargekomen) **1** (be) finish(ed), complete; settle things **2** come
klaarleggen /klarlɛɣə(n)/ (legde klaar, heeft klaargelegd) put ready; lay out
klaarlicht /klarlɪχt/ (adj): *op ~e dag* in broad daylight
klaarliggen /klarlɪɣə(n)/ (lag klaar, heeft klaargelegen) be ready: *iets hebben ~* have sth. ready
klaarmaken /klarmakə(n)/ (maakte klaar, heeft klaargemaakt) **1** get ready, prepare **2** make; get ready; prepare; cook: *het ontbijt ~* get breakfast ready
de **klaar-over** /klarovər/ member of the school crossing patrol, lollipop boy (*or:* girl)
klaarspelen /klarspelə(n)/ (speelde klaar, heeft klaargespeeld) manage (to do), pull off
klaarstaan /klarstan/ (stond klaar, heeft klaargestaan) be ready, be waiting; stand by: *zij moet altijd voor hem ~* he expects her to be at his beck and call
klaarstomen /klarstomə(n)/ (stoomde klaar, heeft klaargestoomd) cram: *iem. voor een examen ~* cram s.o. for an exam
klaarwakker /klarwɑkər/ (adj) wide awake; [fig] (on the) alert
klaarzetten /klarzɛtə(n)/ (zette klaar, heeft klaargezet) put ready, put out, set out
Klaas /klas/ Nick, Nicholas: *~ Vaak* the sandman, Wee Willie Winkie
de **klacht** /klɑχt/ (pl: -en) **1** complaint; symptom: *wat zijn de ~en van de patiënt?* what are

the patient's symptoms?; *zijn ~en uiten* air one's grievances; *~en behandelen* deal with complaints **2** lament, complaint
de **klachtenbrief** /klɑχtə(n)brif/ (pl: -brieven) letter of complaint
de **klachtenlijn** /klɑχtə(n)lɛɪn/ (pl: -en) complaints service
het **klad** /klɑt/ (pl: -den) (rough) draft: *een brief in ~ schrijven* draft a letter, write a letter out in rough (*or:* draft) || *de ~ komt erin* business is falling off
het **kladblaadje** /klɑdblacə/ (pl: -s) (piece of) scrap paper
het **kladblok** /klɑdblɔk/ (pl: -ken) scribbling-pad
¹**kladden** /klɑdə(n)/ (kladde, heeft geklad) make a mess
de ²**kladden** /klɑdə(n)/ (pl): [inform] *iem. bij de ~ grijpen* catch (*or:* grab, seize) hold of s.o.; [inform] *het publiek bij de ~ hebben* seize (*or:* grab) the audience's attention
kladderen /klɑdərə(n)/ (kladderde, heeft gekladderd) make blots (*or:* smudges)
het **kladje** /klɑcə/ (rough) draft; (piece of) scrap paper
het **kladpapier** /klɑtpapir/ (pl: -en) scrap paper
de **kladversie** /klɑtfɛrzi/ (pl: -s) rough version (*or:* copy)
klagen /klaɣə(n)/ (klaagde, heeft geklaagd) complain
de **klager** /klaɣər/ (pl: -s) complainer
klakkeloos /klɑkələos/ (adj, adv) unthinking; indiscriminate; groundless: *iets ~ aannemen* accept sth. unthinkingly (*or:* uncritically)
klakken /klɑkə(n)/ (klakte, heeft geklakt) click, clack
klam /klɑm/ (adj, adv) clammy, damp
de **klamboe** /klɑmbu/ (pl: -s) mosquito net
de **klandizie** /klɑndizi/ clientele, customers
de **klank** /klɑŋk/ (pl: -en) sound
het **klankbord** /klɑŋbɔrt/ (pl: -en) sounding board: [fig] *een ~ vormen* be, act as a sounding board (for)
de **klant** /klɑnt/ (pl: -en) customer, client; [in catering industry] guest: *een vaste ~* a regular (customer); a patron; a habitué; *de ~ is koning* the customer is always right
de **klantenbinding** /klɑntə(n)bɪndɪŋ/ customer relations
de **klantenkaart** /klɑntə(n)kart/ loyalty card
de **klantenkring** /klɑntə(n)krɪŋ/ (pl: -en) customers, clientele
de **klantenservice** /klɑntə(n)sʏrvɪs/ after-sales service; [Am] customer service; service department
klantvriendelijk /klɑntfrɪndələk/ (adj) customer-friendly
de **klap** /klɑp/ (pl: -pen) **1** bang, crash; crack: *met een ~ dichtslaan* slam (shut) **2** slap, smack; [fig] blow: *iem. een ~ geven* hit s.o.;

iem. een ~ *om de oren geven* box s.o.'s ears ‖ *als* ~ *op de vuurpijl* to crown (*or:* top, cap) it all, the crowning touch

de **klapband** /klɑbɑnt/ (pl: -en) blow-out, flat

de **klapdeur** /klɑbdør/ (pl: -en) swing-door, self-closing door

de **klaplong** /klɑplɔŋ/ (pl: -en) pneumothorax

de **klaploper** /klɑplopər/ (pl: -s) sponger, scrounger

¹**klappen** /klɑpə(n)/ (klapte, heeft geklapt) clap; flap; slam: *in de handen* ~ clap (one's hands)

²**klappen** /klɑpə(n)/ (klapte, is geklapt) burst: *de voorband is geklapt* the front tyre has burst; *in elkaar* ~ collapse ‖ *uit de school* ~, [Belg] *uit de biecht* ~ tell tales

de **klapper** /klɑpər/ (pl: -s) **1** folder, file **2** smash, hit

klapperen /klɑpərə(n)/ (klapperde, heeft geklapperd) bang, rattle; chatter

klappertanden /klɑpərtɑndə(n)/ (klappertandde, heeft geklappertand) [roughly] shiver

de **klaproos** /klɑpros/ (pl: -rozen) poppy

de **klapschaats** /klɑpsχats/ (pl: -en) clap skate

de **klapstoel** /klɑpstul/ (pl: -en) folding chair; tip-up seat, theatre seat

het **klapstuk** /klɑpstʏk/ (pl: -ken) **1** rib of beef **2** highlight

de **klaptafel** /klɑptafəl/ (pl: -s) folding table

de **klapzoen** /klɑpsun/ (pl: -en) smacking kiss, smack(er)

de **klare** /klarə/ jenever, Dutch gin

klaren /klarə(n)/ (klaarde, heeft geklaard) **1** clarify **2** settle, manage: *kan hij dat klusje alleen* ~? can he manage that job alone?

de **klarinet** /klarinɛt/ (pl: -ten) clarinet

de **klas** /klɑs/ (pl: -sen) **1** classroom: *de* ~ *uit gestuurd worden* be sent out of the (class)room; *voor de* ~ *staan* be a teacher **2** class **3** form; [Am] grade: *in de vierde* ~ *zitten* be in the fourth form **4** class, grade; [sport] league; [sport] division

de **klasgenoot** /klɑsχənot/ (pl: -genoten) classmate

het **klaslokaal** /klɑslokal/ (pl: -lokalen) classroom

de **klasse** /klɑsə/ (pl: -n) class, league: *dat is grote* ~! that's first-rate!

het **klassement** /klɑsəmɛnt/ (pl: -en) list of rankings (*or:* ratings); [sport] league table: *hij staat bovenaan (in) het* ~ he is (at the) top of the league (table)

het **klassenboek** /klɑsə(n)buk/ (pl: -en) class register, form register; [Am] roll book

de **klassenjustitie** /klɑsəjʏsti(t)si/ class justice

de **klassenleraar** /klɑsə(n)lerar/ (pl: -leraren) form teacher, class teacher; [Am] homeroom teacher

de **klassenstrijd** /klɑsəstrɛit/ class struggle

de **klassenvertegenwoordiger** /klɑsə(n)vərteɣə(n)wordəɣər/ (pl: -s) class representative (*or:* spokesman)

¹**klasseren** /klɑserə(n)/ (klasseerde, heeft geklasseerd) **1** classify **2** [Belg] list

zich ²**klasseren** /klɑserə(n)/ (klasseerde zich, heeft zich geklasseerd) qualify, rank: *zich* ~ *voor de finale* qualify for the final(s)

de **klassering** /klɑserɪŋ/ (pl: -en) classification

klassiek /klɑsik/ (adj) classic(al), traditional: *de* ~*e oudheid* classical antiquity; *een* ~ *voorbeeld* a classic example

de **klassieker** /klɑsikər/ (pl: -s) classic

klassikaal /klɑsikal/ (adj, adv) class, group: *iets* ~ *behandelen* deal with sth. in class

de **klastitularis** /klɑstitylarɪs/ (pl: -sen) [Belg] class teacher

klateren /klatərə(n)/ (klaterde, heeft geklaterd) splash; gurgle

het **klatergoud** /klatərɣaut/ tinsel, gilt

klauteren /klɑutərə(n)/ (klauterde, heeft/is geklauterd) clamber, scramble

de **klauw** /klɑu/ (pl: -en) claw; clutch(es); talon ‖ *dat kost ~en met geld* that costs loads of money; *uit de ~en lopen* get out of hand (*or:* control)

het/de **klavecimbel** /klavəsɪmbəl/ (pl: -s) harpsichord, (clavi)cembalo

de **klaver** /klavər/ (pl: -s) clover

het **klaverblad** /klavərblɑt/ (pl: -en) cloverleaf

de **klaveren** /klavərə(n)/ clubs

klaverjassen /klavərjɑsə(n)/ (klaverjaste, heeft geklaverjast) play (Klaber)jass

het **klavertjevier** /klavərcəvir/ (pl: -en) four-leaf clover

het **klavier** /klavir/ (pl: -en) keyboard

de **kledder** /klɛdər/ (pl: -s) blob, dollop

kledderen /klɛdərə(n)/ (kledderde, heeft gekledderd) slop

kleddernat /klɛdərnɑt/ (adj) soaking (wet); soaked

kleden /kledə(n)/ (kleedde, heeft gekleed) dress, clothe

de **klederdracht** /kledərdrɑχt/ (pl: -en) (traditional, national) costume (*or:* dress)

de **kledij** /kledɛi/ attire

de **kleding** /kledɪŋ/ clothing, clothes, garments

het **kledingstuk** /kledɪŋstʏk/ (pl: -ken) garment, article of clothing

het **kleed** /klet/ (pl: kleden) **1** carpet; rug; (table)cloth **2** [Belg] dress

het **kleedgeld** /kletχɛlt/ dress (*or:* clothing) allowance

het **kleedhokje** /klethɔkjə/ (pl: -s) changing cubicle

de **kleedkamer** /kletkamər/ (pl: -s) dressing room; [sport] changing room

de **kleefrijst** /klefrɛist/ sticky rice

de **kleefstof** /klefstɔf/ (pl: -fen) adhesive

de **kleerborstel** /klerbɔrstəl/ (pl: -s) clothes brush

de **kleerhanger** /klerhɑŋər/ (pl: -s) coat-hanger, clothes hanger

de **kleerkast** /kl<u>e</u>rkɑst/ (pl: -en) wardrobe

de **kleermaker** /kl<u>e</u>rmakər/ (pl: -s) tailor

de **kleermakerszit** /kl<u>e</u>rmakərzɪt/: *in ~ zitten* sit cross-legged

de **kleerscheuren** /kl<u>e</u>rsχørə(n)/ (pl): *er zonder ~ afkomen* escape unscathed (*or:* unhurt); get off scot-free

klef /klɛf/ (adj) **1** sticky, clammy **2** sticky; gooey; doughy **3** clinging

de **klei** /klɛi/ clay

de **kleiduif** /kl<u>ɛi</u>dœyf/ (pl: -duiven) clay pigeon

kleien /kl<u>ɛi</u>ə(n)/ (kleide, heeft gekleid) work with clay

klein /klɛin/ (adj) **1** small, little: *een ~ beetje* a little bit; *een ~ eindje* a short distance; a little way; *~ maar fijn* good things come in small packages **2** little, young: *van ~s af aan* from childhood (on), since childhood **3** small, minor: *hebt u het niet ~er?* have you got nothing smaller?

kleinbehuisd /klɛɪmbəhœyst/ (adj): *~ zijn* live in a small house

kleinburgerlijk /klɛimb<u>y</u>rɣərlək/ (adj) lower middle class, petty bourgeois; narrow-minded

de **kleindochter** /kl<u>ɛi</u>ndɔχtər/ (pl: -s) grand-daughter

Klein Duimpje /klɛind<u>œy</u>mpjə/ Tom Thumb

kleineren /klɛin<u>e</u>rə(n)/ (kleineerde, heeft gekleineerd) belittle, disparage

kleingeestig /klɛin<u>ɣ</u>estəχ/ (adj) narrow-minded, petty

het **kleingeld** /kl<u>ɛi</u>nɣɛlt/ (small) change

de **kleinigheid** /kl<u>ɛi</u>nəχhɛit/ (pl: -heden) **1** little thing: *ik heb een ~je meegebracht* I have brought you a little sth. **2** trivial matter, unimportant matter, trifle

het **kleinkind** /kl<u>ɛi</u>nkɪnt/ (pl: -eren) grandchild

kleinkrijgen /kl<u>ɛi</u>nkrɛɪɣə(n)/ (kreeg klein, heeft kleingekregen) subdue, bring (s.o.) to his knees

de **kleinkunst** /kl<u>ɛi</u>nkʏnst/ cabaret

kleinmaken /kl<u>ɛi</u>makə(n)/ (maakte klein, heeft kleingemaakt) cut small, cut up

het **kleinood** /kl<u>ɛi</u>not/ (pl: kleinoden, kleinodiën) jewel, gem, bijou

kleinschalig /klɛinsχ<u>a</u>ləχ/ (adj) small-scale

het **kleintje** /kl<u>ɛi</u>ncə/ (pl: -s) **1** small one, short one; shorty **2** little one; baby

kleinzerig /klɛinz<u>e</u>rəχ/ (adj): *hij is altijd ~* he always makes a fuss about a little bit of pain

kleinzielig /klɛinz<u>i</u>ləχ/ (adj) petty, narrow-minded

de **kleinzoon** /kl<u>ɛi</u>nzon/ (pl: -s, -zonen) grandson

de **¹klem** /klɛm/ (pl: -men) **1** grip **2** emphasis, stress: *met ~ beweren dat …* insist on the fact that … **3** trap **4** clip

²klem /klɛm/ (adj) jammed, stuck ‖ *zich ~ zui-*

pen get smashed

¹klemmen /kl<u>ɛ</u>mə(n)/ (klemde, heeft geklemd) stick, jam: *de deur klemt* the door sticks

²klemmen /kl<u>ɛ</u>mə(n)/ (klemde, heeft geklemd) clasp, press

klemrijden /kl<u>ɛ</u>mrɛidə(n)/ (reed klem, heeft klemgereden): *een auto ~ force a car to stop*

de **klemtoon** /kl<u>ɛ</u>mton/ (pl: -tonen) stress, accent; [fig] emphasis: *de ~ ligt op de eerste lettergreep* the stress (*or:* accent) is on the first syllable

klemvast /klɛmv<u>ɑ</u>st/ (adj) jammed, stuck: *de bal ~ hebben* have the ball safely in his hands

de **klep** /klɛp/ (pl: -pen) **1** lid; valve; key **2** flap; ramp **3** flap; fly **4** visor

de **klepel** /kl<u>e</u>pəl/ (pl: -s) clapper

kleppen /kl<u>ɛ</u>pə(n)/ (klepte, heeft geklept) **1** clack **2** peal, toll

klepperen /kl<u>ɛ</u>pərə(n)/ (klepperde, heeft geklepperd) clatter, rattle

de **kleptomaan** /klɛptom<u>a</u>n/ (pl: -manen) kleptomaniac

de **kleren** /kl<u>e</u>rə(n)/ (pl) clothes: *andere* (*or:* *schone*) *~ aantrekken* change (into sth. else, into clean clothes); *zijn ~ uittrekken* undress

de **klerezooi** /kl<u>e</u>rəzoj/ bloody mess

klerikaal /klerik<u>a</u>l/ (adj) clerical

de **klerk** /klɛrk/ (pl: -en) clerk

de **klets** /klɛts/ **1** rubbish, twaddle **2** splash

kletsen /kl<u>ɛ</u>tsə(n)/ (kletste, heeft gekletst) **1** chatter, chat **2** gossip: *laat ze maar ~* let them talk **3** talk nonsense (*or:* rubbish), babble

de **kletskoek** /kl<u>ɛ</u>tskuk/ [inform] nonsense, twaddle

de **kletskous** /kl<u>ɛ</u>tskɑus/ (pl: -en) [inform] chatterbox, garrulous chap

de **kletsmajoor** /kl<u>ɛ</u>tsmajor/ (pl: -s) [inform] twaddler, gossipmonger

kletsnat /klɛtsn<u>ɑ</u>t/ (adj) soaking (wet)

kletteren /kl<u>ɛ</u>tərə(n)/ (kletterde, heeft gekletterd) clash; clang; patter; rattle: *de borden kletterden op de grond* the plates crashed to the floor

kleumen /kl<u>ø</u>mə(n)/ (kleumde, heeft gekleumd) be half frozen

de **kleur** /klør/ (pl: -en) **1** colour: *wat voor ~ ogen heeft ze?* what colour are her eyes?; *primaire ~en* primary colours; *mensen van ~* people of colour **2** complexion: *een ~ krijgen* flush, blush **3** [cards] suit: *~ bekennen* a) follow suit; b) [fig] show one's colours

de **kleurdoos** /kl<u>ø</u>rdos/ (pl: -dozen) paintbox

kleurecht /klørɛ<u>χ</u>t/ (adj) colour fast

kleuren /kl<u>ø</u>rə(n)/ (kleurde, heeft gekleurd) colour, paint; dye; tint: *binnen de lijnen ~* a) colour in (neatly); b) [fig] stick to the rules

kleurenblind /kl<u>ø</u>rə(n)blɪnt/ (adj) colour-blind

de **kleurenfoto** /klørə(n)foto/ (pl: -'s) colour photo(graph), colour picture

de **kleurenpiet** /klørə(n)pit/ (pl: -en) Colour Pete, Sint Nicholas' attendant

het **kleurenspectrum** /klørə(n)spɛktrʏm/ (pl: -spectra) colour spectrum

de **kleurentelevisie** /klørə(n)teləvizi/ (pl: -s) colour television

kleurig /klørəχ/ (adj, adv) colourful

de **kleurling** /klørlɪŋ/ (pl: -en) coloured person

kleurloos /klørlos/ (adj) **1** colourless; pale **2** colourless, dull

het **kleurpotlood** /klørpɔtlot/ (pl: -potloden) colour pencil, (coloured) crayon

kleurrijk /klørɛik/ (adj) colourful

de **kleurspoeling** /klørspulɪŋ/ (pl: -en) colour rinse

de **kleurstof** /klørstɔf/ (pl: -fen) **1** colour; dye; colouring (matter): *(chemische) ~fen **toevoegen** add colouring matters* **2** pigment

het **kleurtje** /klørcə/ (pl: -s) colour; flush; blush

de **kleuter** /kløtər/ (pl: -s) pre-schooler (in a nursery class); [Am] kindergartner

het **kleuterbad** /kløtərbɑt/ (pl: -en) paddling pool, wading pool

de **kleuterleidster** /kløtərlɛitstər/ (pl: -s) nursery school teacher; [Am] kindergarten teacher

het **kleuteronderwijs** /kløtərɔndərwɛis/ pre-school education, nursery education

de **kleuterschool** /kløtərsχol/ (pl: -scholen) nursery school; [Am] kindergarten

kleven /klevə(n)/ (kleefde, heeft gekleefd) **1** stick (to), cling (to): *zijn overhemd kleefde **aan** zijn rug* his shirt stuck (or: clung) to his back; [fig] *dat blijft **aan** hem ~* it's given him a bad name **2** be sticky: *mijn **handen** ~* my hands are sticky

kleverig /klevərəχ/ (adj) sticky

kliederen /klidərə(n)/ (kliederde, heeft gekliederd) make a mess, mess about (or: around)

de **kliek** /klik/ (pl: -en) clique

het **kliekje** /klikjə/ (pl: -s) leftover(s)

de **klier** /klir/ **1** gland **2** pain in the neck

klieren /klirə(n)/ (klierde, heeft geklierd) [inform] be a pest, be a pain in the neck; [Am] be a pain in the ass

klieven /klivə(n)/ (kliefde, heeft gekliefd) cleave

de **klif** /klɪf/ (pl: -fen) cliff

de **klik** /klɪk/ (pl: -ken) click

klikken /klɪkə(n)/ (klikte, heeft geklikt) **1** click **2** tell (on s.o.), snitch (on), blab: *je mag niet ~* don't tell tales **3** click, hit it off: *het klikte meteen **tussen** hen* they hit it off immediately

de **klikspaan** /klɪkspan/ (pl: -spanen) tell-tale

de **klim** /klɪm/ climb

het **klimaat** /klimat/ (pl: klimaten) climate

de **klimaatbeheersing** /klimadbəhersɪŋ/ air conditioning

klimaatneutraal /klimatnøtral/ (adj) carbon-neutral: *~ **produceren** produce in a carbon neutral way*

de **klimaatverandering** /klimatfərɑndərɪŋ/ (pl: -en) climatic change

klimmen /klɪmə(n)/ (klom, heeft/is geklommen) climb (up, down), clamber (about): *in een boom ~* climb (up) a tree; *met het ~ der jaren* with advancing years

de **klimmer** /klɪmər/ (pl: -s) climber

de **klimmuur** /klɪmyr/ climbing wall

het/de **klimop** /klɪmɔp/ ivy

de **klimplant** /klɪmplɑnt/ (pl: -en) climber, climbing plant, creeper

het **klimrek** /klɪmrɛk/ (pl: -ken) **1** climbing frame **2** wall bars

de **klimwand** /klɪmwɑnt/ climbing wall

de **kling** /klɪŋ/ (pl: -en): *iem. **over** de ~ jagen* put s.o. to the sword

klingelen /klɪŋələ(n)/ (klingelde, heeft geklingeld) tinkle, jingle

de **kliniek** /klinik/ (pl: -en) clinic

klinisch /klinis/ (adj, adv) clinical

de **klink** /klɪŋk/ (pl: -en) **1** (door)handle **2** latch

klinken /klɪŋkə(n)/ (klonk, heeft geklonken) sound, resound; clink; ring: *die naam klinkt me **bekend** (in de oren)* that name sounds familiar to me; *dat klinkt **goed*** that sounds great

de **klinker** /klɪŋkər/ (pl: -s) **1** vowel **2** clinker

klinkklaar /klɪŋklar/ (adj): *klinkklare **onzin*** plain (or: utter) nonsense

de **klinknagel** /klɪŋknaɣəl/ (pl: -s) rivet

de **klip** /klɪp/ (pl: -pen) rock; cliff: *hun huwelijk is **op** de ~pen gelopen* their marriage has gone on the rocks

klip-en-klaar /klɪpɛnklar/ (adv) crystal-clear: *iets ~ **formuleren** say sth. in plain language (or: words)*

de **klipper** /klɪpər/ (pl: -s) clipper

het **klissen** /klɪsə(n)/ [Belg] arrest, run in: *een **inbreker** ~ arrest a burglar*

de **klit** /klɪt/ (pl: -ten) tangle

klitten /klɪtə(n)/ (klitte, heeft geklit) **1** stick: *aan elkaar ~* hang (or: stick) together **2** become entangled, get entangled

het **klittenband** /klɪtə(n)bɑnt/ (pl: -en) Velcro

de **klodder** /klɔdər/ (pl: -s) daub; clot; blob: *een ~ **mayonaise** a dollop of mayonnaise*

klodderen /klɔdərə(n)/ (klodderde, heeft geklodderd) **1** mess (about, around) **2** daub

de ¹**kloek** /kluk/ (pl: -en) broody hen

²**kloek** /kluk/ (adj) stout, sturdy, robust

de **klojo** /klojo/ (pl: -'s) [inform] jerk

de **klok** /klɔk/ (pl: -ken) **1** clock: *hij kan nog geen ~ kijken* he can't tell (the) time yet; *dat klinkt als een ~* that's perfect; *de ~ **loopt voor** (or: **achter, gelijk**)* the clock is fast (or: slow, on time); *met de ~ mee* clockwise; *tegen de ~ in* anticlockwise; [Am] counter-clockwise; [fig] *iets aan de grote ~ hangen* make a fuss about sth., tell everyone about sth.; [fig] *daar kun je de ~ op gelijkzetten* you can set your watch by it; *de ~ terugzetten* turn the clock back **2** bell

het **klokgelui** /klɔkχəlœy/ (bell-)ringing, chiming; bell tolling

het **klokhuis** /klɔkhœys/ (pl: -huizen) core

klokken /klɔkə(n)/ (klokte, heeft geklokt) [sport] time, clock

de **klokkenluider** /klɔkə(n)lœydər/ **1** bellringer **2** [fig] whistle-blower

het **klokkenspel** /klɔkə(n)spɛl/ (pl: -len) **1** carillon, chimes **2** glockenspiel

de **klokkentoren** /klɔkə(n)torə(n)/ (pl: -s) bell tower, belfry

klokkijken /klɔkɛɪkə(n)/ tell (the) time

de **klokslag** /klɔkslɑχ/ (pl: -en): *~ vier uur* on (*or:* at) the stroke of four

klokvast /klɔkfɑst/ (adj) [Belg] punctual: *~e treinen* punctual trains

de **klomp** /klɔmp/ (pl: -en) **1** clog; [Am] wooden shoe: [fig] *nu breekt mijn ~!* that's the limit!; [fig] *dat kun je op je ~en aanvoelen* that stands (*or:* sticks) out a mile **2** clod, lump

de **klompvoet** /klɔmpfut/ (pl: -en) club-foot

klonen /klonə(n)/ (kloonde, heeft gekloond) clone

de **klont** /klɔnt/ (pl: -en) **1** lump, dab: *de saus zit vol ~en* the sauce is full of lumps (*or:* is lumpy) **2** clot

klonteren /klɔntərə(n)/ (klonterde, heeft geklonterd) become lumpy, get lumpy; clot; curdle

klonterig /klɔntərəχ/ (adj) lumpy

het **klontje** /klɔncə/ (pl: -s) **1** lump, dab **2** sugar lump (*or:* cube) ‖ *zo klaar als een ~* as plain as the nose on your face

de **kloof** /klof/ (pl: kloven) **1** split **2** crevice, chasm, cleft **3** [fig] gap, gulf

klooien /klojə(n)/ (klooide, heeft geklooid) bungle, mess up

de **kloon** /klon/ (pl: klonen) clone

het **klooster** /klostər/ (pl: -s) monastery, convent; nunnery; cloister

de **kloosterling** /klostərlɪŋ/ (pl: -en) religious, monk, nun

de **kloot** /klot/ (pl: kloten) [inform] ball ‖ *naar de kloten zijn* be screwed up

de **klootzak** /klotsɑk/ (pl: -ken) [offensive; inform] bastard, son-of-a-bitch

de **klop** /klɔp/ (pl: -pen) **1** knock **2** lick(ing): *~ krijgen* get a lick, get licked

de **klopboor** /klɔbor/ (pl: -boren) hammer drill

de **klopgeest** /klɔpχest/ (pl: -en) poltergeist

de **klopjacht** /klɔpjɑχt/ (pl: -en) round-up; drive

¹**kloppen** /klɔpə(n)/ (klopte, heeft geklopt) **1** knock (at, on); tap: *er wordt geklopt* there's a knock at the door **2** beat, throb: *met ~d*

hart with one's heart racing (*or:* pounding) **3** agree: *dat klopt* that's right

²**kloppen** /klɔpə(n)/ (klopte, heeft geklopt) knock; tap; beat: *eieren ~ beat (*or:* whisk) eggs; *iem. op de schouder ~* pat s.o. on the back

de **klopper** /klɔpər/ knocker

de **klos** /klɔs/ (pl: -sen) bobbin, reel ‖ *de ~ zijn* be the fall guy

klossen /klɔsə(n)/ (kloste, heeft/is geklost) clump, stump

klote /klotə/ (adj, adv) [vulg]: *een klotedag* a bloody awful day; *zich ~ voelen* feel shitty (*or:* crappy); *kloteweer* bloody awful weather, rotten weather; *een klotewijf* a bitch; *klotezooi* bloody mess; *dat is zwaar ~* that's really bloody awful

klotsen /klɔtsə(n)/ (klotste, heeft/is geklotst) slosh, splash

kloven /klovə(n)/ (kloofde, heeft gekloofd) split, cleave; cut

de **klucht** /klʏχt/ (pl: -en) farce

de **kluif** /klœyf/ (pl: kluiven) knuckle(bone); [fig] big job, tough job

de **kluis** /klœys/ (pl: kluizen) safe, safe-deposit box

kluisteren /klœystərə(n)/ (kluisterde, heeft gekluisterd): *aan het ziekbed gekluisterd zijn* be bedridden, be confined to one's sickbed; *aan de televisie gekluisterd zitten* be glued to the television

de **kluit** /klœyt/ (pl: -en) **1** lump, clod: *zich niet met een ~je in het riet laten sturen* not let o.s. be fobbed off (*or:* be given the brush-off) **2** ball of earth (*or:* soil)

kluiven /klœyvə(n)/ (kloof, heeft gekloven) gnaw

de **kluizenaar** /klœyzənar/ (pl: -s) hermit, recluse

klunen /klynə(n)/ (kluunde, heeft/is gekluund) walk (on skates)

de **klungel** /klʏŋəl/ (pl: -s) clumsy oaf

klungelen /klʏŋələ(n)/ (klungelde, heeft geklungeld) bungle, botch (up)

klungelig /klʏŋələχ/ (adj, adv) clumsy, bungling

de **kluns** /klʏns/ (pl: klunzen) dimwit, oaf, bungler

de **klus** /klʏs/ (pl: -sen) **1** big job, tough job **2** small job, chore: *~jes opknappen* do odd jobs

de **klusjesman** /klʏʃəsmɑn/ (pl: -nen) handyman, odd-job man

klussen /klʏsə(n)/ (kluste, heeft geklust) **1** do odd jobs **2** moonlight

de **kluts** /klʏts/: *de ~ kwijt zijn (raken)* be lost (*or:* confused); *be shaken* (*or:* rattled)

klutsen /klʏtsə(n)/ (klutste, heeft geklutst) beat (up)

de **kluunschaats** /klynsχats/ (pl: -en) ice-skate with detachable blade

het **kluwen** /klywə(n)/ (pl: -s) ball
het **klysma** /klɪsma/ (pl: -'s) enema
　　 km *kilometer* km
het **KMI** /kaɛmi/ [Belg] *Koninklijk Meteorologisch Instituut* (Belgian) Royal Meteorological Institute
de **kmo** /kaɛmo/ *kleine of middelgrote onderneming* [Belg] SMB, small and medium-sized businesses
　　 km/u *kilometer per uur* km/h, mph
het **knaagdier** /knaɣdir/ (pl: -en) rodent
de **knaagtand** /knaxtɑnt/ (pl: -en) (rodent) incisor
de **knaap** /knap/ (pl: knapen) boy, lad
　　 knabbelen /knɡbələ(n)/ (knabbelde, heeft geknabbeld) nibble (on), munch (on)
het **knabbeltje** /knɡbəlcə/ (pl: -s) nibble(s), snack
het **knäckebröd** /knɛkəbrøt/ crispbread, knäckebröd
　　 knagen /knaɣə(n)/ (knaagde, heeft geknaagd) gnaw, eat: *een ~d geweten* pangs of conscience; [fig] *het blijft ~* it keeps gnawing at me, it keeps nagging away at me
de **knak** /knɑk/ (pl: -ken) crack, snap
　　 knakken /knɑkə(n)/ (knakte, heeft/is geknakt) snap, break; crack
de **knakker** /knɑkər/ (pl: -s) [inform] character, customer
de **knakworst** /knɑkwɔrst/ (pl: -en) [roughly] frankfurter
de **knal** /knɑl/ (pl: -len) bang, pop
　　 knallen /knɑlə(n)/ (knalde, heeft geknald) 1 bang; crack; pop 2 [sport] go all-out
de **knalpot** /knɑlpɔt/ (pl: -ten) silencer; [Am] muffler
　　 ¹knap /knɑp/ (adj, adv) 1 good-looking; handsome; pretty 2 clever, bright: *een ~pe kop* a brain, a whizz kid 3 smart, capable, clever; handy: *een ~ stuk werk* a clever piece of work
　　 ²knap /knɑp/ (adv) cleverly, well
　　 ¹knappen /knɑpə(n)/ (knapte, heeft geknapt) crackle; crack
　　 ²knappen /knɑpə(n)/ (knapte, is geknapt) crack; snap
de **knapperd** /knɑpərt/ (pl: -s) brain, whiz(z) kid
　　 knapperen /knɑpərə(n)/ (knapperde, heeft geknapperd) crackle; crack
　　 knapperig /knɑpərəɣ/ (adj) crisp; crunchy; brittle; crusty
de **knapzak** /knɑpsɑk/ (pl: -ken) knapsack
　　 knarsen /knɑrsə(n)/ (knarste, heeft geknarst) crunch: *de deur knarst in haar scharnieren* the door creaks (or: squeaks) on its hinges
　　 knarsetanden /knɑrsətɑndə(n)/ (knarsetandde, heeft geknarsetand) grind one's teeth
de **knauw** /knɑu/ (pl: -en) 1 bite 2 [fig] blow

　　 knauwen /knɑuwə(n)/ (knauwde, heeft geknauwd) gnaw (at), chew; crunch (on)
de **knecht** /knɛxt/ (pl: -en) servant; farmhand
　　 kneden /knedə(n)/ (kneedde, heeft gekneed) knead, mould
　　 kneedbaar /knedbar/ (adj) 1 kneadable, workable 2 [fig] pliable: *iem. ~ maken* make s.o. putty in one's hands
de **kneep** /knep/ (pl: knepen) 1 pinch (mark) 2 [fig] knack: *de ~jes van het vak kennen* know the tricks of the trade
de **¹knel** /knɛl/ (pl: -len) 1 catch 2 fix, jam
　　 ²knel /knɛl/ (adj) stuck, caught: *~ komen te zitten* get stuck (or: caught)
　　 ¹knellen /knɛlə(n)/ (knelde, heeft gekneld) squeeze; pinch
　　 ²knellen /knɛlə(n)/ (knelde, heeft gekneld) squeeze, press
het **knelpunt** /knɛlpʏnt/ (pl: -en) bottleneck
　　 knetteren /knɛtərə(n)/ (knetterde, heeft geknetterd) crackle; sputter
　　 knettergek /knɛtərɣɛk/ (adj) nuts, (stark staring) mad; [Am] (raving) mad
de **kneus** /knøs/ (pl: kneuzen) 1 old crock (or: wreck) [esp cars] 2 [educ] drop-out
　　 kneuterig /knøtərəɣ/ (adj, adv) snug, cosy
　　 kneuzen /knøzə(n)/ (kneusde, heeft gekneusd) bruise
de **kneuzing** /knøzɪŋ/ (pl: -en) bruise, bruising
de **knevel** /knevəl/ (pl: -s) moustache
　　 knevelen /knevələ(n)/ (knevelde, heeft gekneveld) tie down, tie up; gag
　　 knibbelen /knɪbələ(n)/ (knibbelde, heeft geknibbeld) haggle, bargain
de **knie** /kni/ (pl: -ën) knee: *iets onder de ~ krijgen* master sth., get the hang (or: knack) of sth.; *door de ~ën gaan* give in
de **knieband** /knibɑnt/ (pl: -en) 1 knee protector (or: supporter) 2 hamstring
de **kniebeschermer** /knibəsχɛrmər/ (pl: -s) knee-pad
de **kniebroek** /knibruk/ (pl: -en) knee breeches
de **kniebuiging** /knibœyɣɪŋ/ (pl: -en) 1 kneeling 2 knee bend
het **kniegewricht** /kniɣəvrɪxt/ (pl: -en) knee joint
de **knieholte** /kniholtə/ (pl: -s, -n) hollow (or: back) of the knee
　　 knielen /knilə(n)/ (knielde, heeft/is geknield) kneel
de **knieschijf** /knisχɛif/ (pl: -schijven) kneecap
de **kniesoor** /knisor/ (pl: kniesoren) moper, moaner: *een ~ die daarop let* details, details, but that is a (mere) detail
de **knieval** /knival/ (pl: -len) genuflection: *een ~ doen voor iem.* fall to one's knees before s.o.
　　 kniezen /knizə(n)/ (kniesde, heeft gekniesd) grumble (about), moan (about), mope
　　 knijpen /knɛipə(n)/ (kneep, heeft gekne-

pen) **1** pinch **2** press, squeeze ‖ [inform] *'m ~ have the wind up*; [inform] *ertussenuit ~ slip off* (*or:* away/out) (unnoticed)

de **knijper** /kn£ipər/ (pl: -s) (clothes) peg, clip

de **knijpfles** /kn£ipflɛs/ (pl: -sen) squeeze-bottle

de **knijpkat** /kn£ipkɑt/ (pl: -ten) dynamo torch

de **knik** /knɪk/ (pl: -ken) **1** crack; kink **2** twist, kink **3** nod

knikkebollen /knɪkəbolə(n)/ (knikkebolde, heeft geknikkebold) nod

¹**knikken** /knɪkə(n)/ (knikte, is geknikt) **1** crack, snap **2** bend, buckle

²**knikken** /knɪkə(n)/ (knikte, heeft) nod

³**knikken** /knɪkə(n)/ (knikte, heeft geknikt) bend, twist

de **knikker** /knɪkər/ (pl: -s) marble

¹**knikkeren** /knɪkərə(n)/ (knikkerde, heeft geknikkerd) play marbles: [fig] *ik heb nog met hem geknikkerd* [roughly] I knew him when he was in short pants

²**knikkeren** /knɪkərə(n)/ (knikkerde, heeft geknikkerd) [inform] kick out, chuck out: *iem. eruit ~* chuck s.o. out

de **knip** /knɪp/ (pl: -pen) **1** snap; (spring) catch; clasp **2** catch

het **knipmes** /knɪpmɛs/ (pl: -sen) clasp-knife: *buigen als een ~* bow and scrape, grovel

knipogen /knɪpoɣə(n)/ (knipoogde, heeft geknipoogd) wink

de **knipoog** /knɪpoːx/ (pl: -ogen) wink: *hij gaf mij een ~* he winked at me; [fig] *met een ~ naar ...* with a nod towards ...; *een vette ~* an unsubtle wink; *een bericht met een ~* a message with a wink

¹**knippen** /knɪpə(n)/ (knipte, heeft geknipt) cut, snip

²**knippen** /knɪpə(n)/ (knipte, heeft geknipt) **1** cut (off, out): *de heg ~* clip (*or:* trim) the hedge; *zijn nagels ~* cut (*or:* clip) one's nails **2** [comp] cut: *~ en plakken* cut and paste

knipperen /knɪpərə(n)/ (knipperde, heeft geknipperd) **1** blink **2** flash **3** flash on and off

het **knipperlicht** /knɪpərlɪxt/ (pl: -en) indicator; flashing light

het **knipsel** /knɪpsəl/ (pl: -s) cutting

het **KNMI** /kaɛnɛmiˑ/ *Koninklijk Nederlands Meteorologisch Instituut* Royal Dutch Meteorological Institute

de **kno-arts** /kaɛnoɑrts/ (pl: -en) [Dutch] ENT specialist

de **knobbel** /knɔbəl/ (pl: -s) **1** knob; knot; bump **2** [fig] gift, talent: *een wiskundeknobbel hebben* have a gift for mathematics

de ¹**knock-out** /nɔkaut/ (pl: -s) knock-out

²**knock-out** /nɔkaut/ (adj) knock-out

de **knoei** /knuj/ (pl: -s) *lelijk in de ~ zitten* be in a terrible mess (*or:* fix)

de **knoeiboel** /knujbul/ mess

knoeien /knujə(n)/ (knoeide, heeft geknoeid) **1** make a mess, spill **2** make a mess (of) **3** tinker (with), monkey about (with) **4** cheat, tamper (with), swindle: *met de boeken ~* cook the books

de **knoeier** /knujər/ (pl: -s) **1** messy person **2** bungler **3** cheat

de **knoest** /knust/ (pl: -en) knot

de **knoet** /knut/ (pl: -en) cat-o'-nine-tails: [fig] *onder de ~ zitten* be oppressed

het/de **knoflook** /knɔflok/ garlic

knokig /knɔkəx/ (adj) bony

de **knokkel** /knɔkəl/ (pl: -s) knuckle

knokken /knɔkə(n)/ (knokte, heeft geknokt) **1** fight **2** [fig] fight hard

de **knokpartij** /knɔkpɑrtɛi/ (pl: -en) fight, scuffle

de **knokploeg** /knɔkpluːx/ (pl: -en) (bunch, gang of) thugs; henchmen

de **knol** /knɔl/ (pl: -len) **1** tuber **2** turnip

het **knolgewas** /knɔlɣəwɑs/ (pl: -sen) tuberous plant

de **knolraap** /knɔlrap/ (pl: -rapen) swede, kohlrabi

de **knolselderij** /knɔlsɛldərɛi/ celeriac

de **knoop** /knop/ (pl: knopen) **1** button **2** knot: *een ~ leggen* (*or:* *maken*) tie (*or:* make) a knot; *(met zichzelf) in de ~ zitten* be at odds with oneself ‖ *het schip voer negen knopen* the ship was doing nine knots; [fig] *de ~ doorhakken* cut the (Gordian) knot, take the plunge

het **knooppunt** /knopʏnt/ (pl: -en) intersection; interchange

het **knoopsgat** /knopsxɑt/ (pl: -en) buttonhole

de **knop** /knɔp/ (pl: -pen) **1** button, switch: *met een druk op de ~* presto, with a press of the button; [fig] *de ~ omzetten* switch over, turn the corner **2** button, handle: *de ~ van een deur* the handle of a door **3** bud: *de roos is nog in de ~* the rose bush is in bud (*or:* is not fully out yet) **4** button ‖ *naar de ~pen gaan* **a)** [eg relation] go on the rocks; **b)** [things] go on the blink

knopen /knopə(n)/ (knoopte, heeft geknoopt) knot, make a knot, tie: *twee touwen aan elkaar ~* tie two ropes together

knorren /knɔrə(n)/ (knorde, heeft geknord) grunt

knorrig /knɔrəx/ (adj, adv) grumbling: *in een zeer ~e bui zijn* have the grumps, be grouchy

de **knot** /knɔt/ (pl: -ten) knot, ball; tuft

de ¹**knots** /knɔts/ (pl: -en) **1** club **2** whopper

²**knots** /knɔts/ (adj, adv) [inform] crazy, loony

knotten /knɔtə(n)/ (knotte, heeft geknot) top, head

de **knotwilg** /knɔtwɪlx/ (pl: -en) pollard willow

de **knowhow** /nohɑu/ know-how

knudde /knʏdə/ (adj) [inform] no good at all, rubbishy

de **knuffel** /knʏfəl/ (pl: -s) **1** cuddle, hug **2** soft

toy, cuddly toy
het **knuffeldier** /knʏfəldir/ (pl: -en) soft toy,
cuddly toy, teddy (bear)
knuffelen /knʏfələ(n)/ (knuffelde, heeft
geknuffeld) cuddle
de **knuist** /knœyst/ (pl: -en) fist
de **knul** /knʏl/ (pl: -len) fellow, guy, chap, bloke
knullig /knʏləx/ (adj, adv) awkward: *dat is ~
gedaan* that has been done clumsily
de **knuppel** /knʏpəl/ (pl: -s) **1** club; truncheon
2 stick; joystick
knus /knʏs/ (adj, adv) cosy, homey
de **knutselaar** /knʏtsəlar/ (pl: -s) handyman,
do-it-yourselfer
knutselen /knʏtsələ(n)/ (knutselde, heeft
geknutseld) knock together, knock up
het **knutselwerk** /knʏtsəlwɛrk/ **1** odd jobs,
tinkering **2** handiwork, handicraft(s)
de **koala** /kowala/ (pl: -'s) koala (bear)
het **kobalt** /kobɑlt/ cobalt
de **koe** /ku/ (pl: koeien) **1** cow: [fig] *een waarheid als een ~* a truism; [fig] *over ~tjes en kalf-
jes praten* talk about one thing and another;
[Dutch; fig] *oude koeien uit de sloot halen*
open old wounds (*or*: sores); [fig] *de ~ bij de
hoorns **vatten*** take the bull by the horns
2 giant
de **koehandel** /kuhɑndəl/ [depr] horse trading
de **koeienletters** /kujə(n)lɛtərs/ (pl) giant letters
koeiig /kujəx/ (adj) bovine: *~e **ogen** cow
eyes*
koeioneren /kujonerə(n)/ (koeioneerde,
heeft gekoeioneerd) bully
de **koek** /kuk/ (pl: -en) **1** cake: *dat is andere ~!*
that is another (*or*: a different) kettle of fish;
*een gevulde **koek*** [roughly] an almond paste
cake; *dat gaat erin als (gesneden) ~* it is a huge
success; it's selling like hot cakes **2** biscuit;
[Am] cooky, cookie: *een ~je van eigen deeg
krijgen* get a taste of one's own medicine
de **koekenpan** /kukə(n)pɑn/ (pl: -nen) frying
pan
de **koekoek** /kukuk/ (pl: -en) cuckoo
de **koekoeksklok** /kukuksklɔk/ (pl: -ken) cuckoo clock
de **koektrommel** /kuktrɔməl/ (pl: -s) biscuit
tin; [Am] cooky tin
koel /kul/ (adj) **1** cool; chilly **2** cool, calm
koelbloedig /kulbludəx/ (adj, adv) cold-
blooded, calm, cool
de **koelbox** /kulbɔks/ (pl: -en) cool box, cooler
de **koelcel** /kulsɛl/ (pl: -len) cold store
koelen /kulə(n)/ (koelde, heeft gekoeld)
cool (down, off); chill
de **koeler** /kulər/ (pl: -s) cooler; ice bucket
het **koelhuis** /kulhœys/ (pl: -huizen) cold store
de **koeling** /kulɪŋ/ **1** cold store **2** cooling; re-
frigeration
de **koelkast** /kulkɑst/ (pl: -en) fridge, refrigerator: *iets in de ~ zetten* put sth. in the fridge

de **koeltas** /kultɑs/ (pl: -sen) thermos bag
de **koelte** /kultə/ cool(ness)
koeltjes /kulcəs/ (adj) (a bit) chilly || *~ rea-
geren* respond coolly
de **koeltoren** /kultorə(n)/ cooling tower
de **koelvloeistof** /kulvlujstɔf/ (pl: -fen) cool-
ant
het **koelwater** /kulwatər/ cooling-water
koen /kun/ (adj, adv) [form] bold
de **koepel** /kupəl/ (pl: -s) dome
de **koepelorganisatie** /kupəlɔrɣaniza(t)si/
umbrella organisation
de **koepeltent** /kupəltɛnt/ dome tent
de **Koerd** /kurt/ (pl: -en) Kurd
Koerdisch /kurdis/ (adj) Kurdish
Koerdistan /kurdistɑn/ Kurdistan
koeren /kurə(n)/ (koerde, heeft gekoerd)
coo
de **koerier** /kurir/ (pl: -s) courier
de **koers** /kurs/ **1** course: *van ~ **veranderen***
change course (*or*: tack); *~ **zetten** naar* head
for **2** route **3** price; (exchange) rate
de **koersdaling** /kurzdalɪŋ/ (pl: -en) fall in
prices; depreciation
koersen /kursə(n)/ (koerste, heeft/is ge-
koerst) (+ op) set course for
de **koersschommeling** /kursxɔməlɪŋ/ (pl:
-en) price fluctuation (*or*: variation), market
fluctuation
de **koerswijziging** /kurswɛizəɣɪŋ/ (pl: -en)
change in course (*or*: direction)
de **koerswinst** /kurswɪnst/ (pl: -en) stock market profit, gain(s) (made by stock fluctuations)
koest /kust/ (adj): *zich ~ **houden*** keep quiet,
keep a low profile
koesteren /kustərə(n)/ (koesterde, heeft
gekoesterd) cherish, foster: *hoop ~* nurse
hopes
het **koeterwaals** /kutərwals/ gibberish
de **koets** /kuts/ (pl: -en) coach, carriage
de **koetsier** /kutsir/ (pl: -s) coachman
de **koevoet** /kuvut/ (pl: -en) crowbar
Koeweit /kuwɛit/ Kuwait
de **Koeweiter** /kuwɛitər/ (pl: -s) Kuwaiti
Koeweits /kuwɛits/ (adj) Kuwaiti
de **koffer** /kɔfər/ (pl: -s) (suit)case, (hand)bag;
trunk
de **kofferbak** /kɔfərbɑk/ (pl: -ken) boot; [Am]
trunk
de **koffie** /kɔfi/ coffee: *~ **drinken*** have coffee; *~
verkeerd* café au lait; *~ **zonder** melk* black
coffee; [fig] *dat is geen **zuivere** ~* there's sth.
fishy about it, it looks suspicious
de **koffieboon** /kɔfibon/ (pl: -bonen) coffee
bean
het **koffiedik** /kɔfidɪk/ coffee grounds: *het is zo
helder **als** ~* it is as clear as mud; *ik kan geen ~
kijken* I can't read tea-leaves, I am not a crystal-gazer
de **koffiekan** /kɔfikɑn/ (pl: -nen) coffeepot

het **koffiekopje** /kɔfikɔpjə/ (pl: -s) coffee cup

de **koffiemelk** /kɔfimɛlk/ evaporated milk

de **koffiepad** /kɔfipɛt/ (pl: -s) coffee pad

de **koffiepot** /kɔfipɔt/ (pl: -ten) coffeepot

de **koffieshop** /kɔfiʃɔp/ (pl: -s) **1** coffee shop **2** cannabis coffee shop

de **koffietafel** /kɔfitafəl/ (pl: -s) (light) lunch

de **koffietent** /kɔfitɛnt/ (pl: -en) coffee shop, coffee house

de **koffietijd** /kɔfitɛɪt/ coffee time; lunch time

het **koffiezetapparaat** /kɔfizɛtɑparɑt/ (pl: -apparaten) coffee-maker

koffiezetten /kɔfizɛtə(n)/ (zette koffie, heeft koffiegezet) make coffee, put coffee on

de **kogel** /koɣəl/ (pl: -s) **1** bullet; ball: *de ~ krijgen* be shot; *een verdwaalde ~* a stray bullet **2** shot ‖ *de ~ is door de kerk* the die is cast

de **kogelbiefstuk** /koɣəlbifstʏk/ (pl: -ken) round steak

het **kogelgewricht** /koɣəlɣəvrɪxt/ (pl: -en) ball(-and-socket) joint

de **kogellager** /koɣəlaɣər/ (pl: -s) ball-bearing

kogelslingeren /koɣəlslɪŋərə(n)/ hammer (throw)

kogelstoten /koɣəlstotə(n)/ shot-put(ting)

kogelvrij /koɣəlvrɛi/ (adj) bulletproof

de **koikarper** /kɔjkɑrpər/ koi (carp)

de **kok** /kɔk/ (pl: -s) cook: *de chef-~* the chef

koken /kokə(n)/ (kookte, heeft gekookt) **1** boil: *water kookt bij 100 °C* water boils at 100 °C **2** cook, do the cooking ‖ *~ van woede* boil (or: seethe) with rage

kokendheet /kokənthet/ (adj) piping (or: boiling, scalding) hot

de **koker** /kokər/ (pl: -s) **1** case **2** cylinder **3** shaft; chute

koket /kokɛt/ (adj) **1** coquettish **2** smart, stylish

kokhalzen /kɔkhɑlzə(n)/ (kokhalsde, heeft gekokhalsd) retch, heave

kokkerellen /kɔkərɛlə(n)/ (kokkerelde, heeft gekokkereld) cook

het **kokos** /kokɔs/ **1** coconut **2** coconut fibre

de **kokosmat** /kokɔsmɑt/ (pl: -ten) coconut matting

de **kokosnoot** /kokɔsnot/ coconut

de **kokospalm** /kokɔspɑlm/ (pl: -en) coconut palm

het **kokoswater** /kokɔswɑtər/ coconut water

de **koksmuts** /kɔksmʏts/ (pl: -en) chef's hat

de **kolder** /kɔldər/ nonsense, rubbish

de **kolen** /kolə(n)/ (pl) coal: *op hete ~ zitten* be on tenterhooks

de **kolencentrale** /kolə(n)sɛntralə/ (pl: -s) coal-fired power station

de **kolenmijn** /kolə(n)mɛin/ (pl: -en) coal mine

de **kolere** /kolɛrə/: [vulg] *krijg de ~!* get stuffed!, drop dead!

de **kolf** /kɔlf/ (pl: kolven) **1** butt **2** flask; retort **3** cob ‖ *dat is een ~je naar haar hand* that is

just up her street

de **kolibrie** /kolibri/ (pl: -s) hummingbird

het/de **koliek** /kolik/ (pl: -en) colic

de **kolk** /kɔlk/ (pl: -en) eddy, whirlpool

kolken /kɔlkə(n)/ (kolkte, heeft gekolkt) swirl, eddy

de **kolom** /kolɔm/ (pl: -men) column

de **kolonel** /kolonɛl/ (pl: -s) colonel

koloniaal /kolonijal/ (adj) colonial

het **kolonialisme** /kolonijalɪsmə/ colonialism

de **kolonie** /koloni/ (pl: -s, koloniën) colony

de **kolonisatie** /koloniza(t)si/ colonization

koloniseren /kolonizɛrə(n)/ (koloniseerde, heeft gekoloniseerd) colonize

de **kolonist** /kolonɪst/ (pl: -en) colonist, settler

de **kolos** /kolɔs/ (pl: -sen) colossus

kolossaal /kolɔsal/ (adj, adv) colossal, immense

kolven /kɔlvə(n)/ (kolfde, heeft gekolfd) express milk

de **¹kom** /kɔm/ (pl: -men) **1** bowl; washbasin **2** basin, bowl **3** socket: *haar arm is uit de ~ geschoten* her arm is dislocated ‖ *de bebouwde ~* the built-up area; [Am] the city limits

²kom /kɔm/ (int) come on!: *~ nou, dat maak je me niet wijs* come on (now) (or: look), don't give me that; *~, ik stap maar weer eens op* right, I'm off now!; *~ op!* come on!

de **komaf** /kɔmɑf/ origin, birth: *van goede ~* upper-crust, high-born ‖ [Belg] *~ maken met iets* give short shrift to sth.

de **kombuis** /kɔmbœys/ (pl: kombuizen) galley

de **komediant** /komedijɑnt/ (pl: -en) comedy actor, comedian

de **komedie** /komedi/ (pl: -s) comedy; [fig also] (play-)acting

de **komeet** /komet/ (pl: kometen) comet

komen /komə(n)/ (kwam, is gekomen) **1** come, get: *er komt regen* it is going to rain; *er kwam bloed uit zijn mond* there was blood coming out of his mouth; *ergens bij kunnen ~* be able to get at sth.; *de politie laten ~* send for (or: call) the police; *ik kom eraan!* (or: *al!*) (I'm) coming!, I'm on my way!; *kom eens langs!* come round some time!; *ergens achter ~* find out sth., get to know sth.; *hoe kom je erbij!* what(ever) gave you that idea?; *ergens overheen ~* get over sth.; [fig] *we kwamen er niet uit* we couldn't work it out; *hoe kom je van hier naar het museum?* how do you get to the museum from here?; *hij komt uit Engeland* he's from England; *wie het eerst komt, het eerst maalt* first come, first served **2** come ((a)round, over), call: *er ~ mensen vanavond* there are (or: we've got) people coming this evening **3** (+ aan) touch: *kom nergens aan!* don't touch (anything)! **4** come (about), happen: *hoe komt het?* how come?, how did that happen?; *daar komt niets van in* that's out of the question; *dat komt ervan als je niet luistert* that's what you get (or: what happens) if you don't listen **5** (+ aan) come (by), get (hold of): *aan geld zien te ~* get hold of some money; *daar kom ik straks nog op* I'll come round to that in a moment || *daar komt nog bij dat …* what's more …, besides …; *kom nou!* don't be silly!, come off it!

komend /kˈomənt/ (adj) coming, to come; next: *~e week* next week

de **komiek** /komˈik/ (pl: -en) comedian, comic

de **komijn** /komˈɛin/ cumin

komisch /kˈomis/ (adj, adv) comic(al), funny

de **komkommer** /komkˈomər/ (pl: -s) cucumber

de **komkommertijd** /komkˈomərtɛit/ silly season

de **komma** /kˈoma/ (pl: -'s) **1** comma **2** (decimal) point: *tot op vijf cijfers na de ~ uitrekenen* calculate to five decimal places; *nul ~ drie (0,3)* nought point three (0.3); [Am] zero point three (0.3)

de **kommer** /kˈomər/ sorrow: *~ en kwel* sorrow and misery

het **kompas** /kompˈas/ (pl: -sen) compass

de **kompasnaald** /kompˈasnalt/ (pl: -en) compass needle

het **kompres** /komprˈɛs/ (pl: -sen) compress

de **komst** /komst/ coming, arrival: *er is storm op ~* there is a storm brewing

het **konijn** /konˈɛin/ (pl: -en) rabbit; bunny

het **konijnenhok** /konˈɛinə(n)hok/ (pl: -ken) rabbit hutch

het **konijnenhol** /konˈɛinə(n)hol/ (pl: -en) rabbit hole (*or*: burrow)

de **koning** /kˈonɪŋ/ (pl: -en) king

de **koningin** /konɪŋˈɪn/ (pl: -nen) queen

Koninginnedag /konɪŋˈɪnədɑx/ [Dutch] Queen's Birthday

Koningsdag /kˈonɪŋzdɑx/ King's Day

koningsgezind /kˈonɪŋsxəzɪnt/ (adj) royalist(ic), monarchist

het **koningshuis** /kˈonɪŋshœys/ (pl: -huizen) royal family (*or*: house)

de **koningsnacht** /kˈonɪŋsnɑxt/ (pl: -en) [Dutch] King's night, Dutch King's Day Eve

de **koningsspelen** /kˈonɪŋspelə(n)/ (pl) [Dutch] King's Games, National Primary Schools Sports Day

koninklijk /kˈonɪŋklək/ (adj) royal; regal: *het Koninklijk Huis* the Royal Family

het **koninkrijk** /kˈonɪŋkrɛik/ (pl: -en) kingdom

de **koninkrijksrelaties** /kˈonɪŋkrɛiksrela(t)sis/ (pl): [Dutch] *ministerie van Binnenlandse Zaken en Koninkrijksrelaties* Ministry of the Interior and Kingdom Relations

het **koninkrijksstatuut** /kˈonɪŋkrɛiksstatyt/ Charter for the Kingdom of the Netherlands

konkelen /kˈoŋkələ(n)/ (konkelde, heeft gekonkeld) scheme, intrigue

de **kont** /kont/ (pl: -en) [inform] bottom, behind, bum: *je kunt hier je ~ niet keren* you couldn't swing a cat here; *in zijn blote ~* stark naked; in one's birthday suit

het **konvooi** /konvˈoi/ (pl: -en) convoy

de **kooi** /koj/ (pl: -en) **1** cage **2** pen; coop; fold; sty **3** berth, bunk

de **kook** /kok/ boil: *aan de ~ brengen* bring to the boil; *volkomen van de ~ raken* go to pieces, get very upset

het **kookboek** /kˈogbuk/ (pl: -en) cookery book

de **kookgelegenheid** /kˈokxəleyə(n)hɛit/ cooking facilities

de **kookkunst** /kˈokkynst/ cookery, (the art of) cooking, culinary art

de **kookplaat** /kˈokplat/ (pl: -platen) hotplate, hob

het **kookpunt** /kˈokpynt/ (pl: -en) boiling point: *het ~ bereiken* [also fig] reach boiling point

de **kookwekker** /kˈokwɛkər/ (pl: -s) kitchen timer

de **kool** /kol/ (pl: kolen) **1** cabbage: *Chinese ~* napa cabbage, pe tsai **2** coal

het **kooldioxide** /kˈoldijoksidə/ carbon dioxide

het **koolhydraat** /kˈolhidrat/ (pl: -hydraten) carbohydrate: [dietary] *koolhydraten* carbs

de **koolmees** /kˈolmes/ (pl: -mezen) great tit

het **koolmonoxide** /kˈolmonoksidə/ carbon monoxide

de **koolraap** /kˈolrap/ (pl: -rapen) kohlrabi, turnip cabbage

de **koolrabi** /kolrˈabi/ kohlrabi

de **koolstof** /kˈolstof/ carbon

de **koolvis** /kˈolvɪs/ (pl: -sen) pollack

de **koolwaterstof** /kolwˈatərstof/ (pl: -fen) hydrocarbon

het **koolwitje** /kˈolwɪcə/ (pl: -s) cabbage white (butterfly)

het **koolzaad** /kˈolzat/ (rape)seed, colza

het **koolzuur** /kˈolzyr/ carbon dioxide

koolzuurhoudend /kolzyrhˈaudənt/ (adj) carbonated

de **koon** /kon/ (pl: konen) cheek

de **koop** /kop/ (pl: kopen) buy, sale, purchase: *~ en verkoop* buying and selling; *de ~ gaat door* the deal (*or*: sale) is going through; [fig] *iets op de ~ toe nemen* (be prepared to) put up with sth.; *te ~ (zijn, staan)* (be) for sale; *te ~ of te huur* to buy or let; *te ~ gevraagd* wanted; [fig] *met iets te ~ lopen* parade (*or*: flaunt) sth.

de **koopakte** /kˈopɑktə/ (pl: -n, -s) deed of sale (*or*: purchase)

de **koopavond** /kˈopavont/ (pl: -en) late-night shopping, late opening

het **koopcontract** /kˈopkontrɑkt/ (pl: -en) contract (*or*: bill) of sale; purchase deed, title deed; deed of purchase

koopgraag /kˈopxrax/ (adj) acquisitive, eager to spend money

de **koophandel** /kˈophɑndəl/ commerce, trade: *Kamer van Koophandel* Chamber of Commerce

het **koophuis** /kˈophœys/ owner-occupied house

het **koopje** /kˈopjə/ (pl: -s) bargain, good buy

(*or:* deal)

de **koopjesjager** /kopjəsjaɣər/ (pl: -s) bargain hunter, snapper-up

de **koopkracht** /kopkraxt/ buying power

de **koopman** /kopman/ (pl: kooplieden) merchant, businessman

de **koopsom** /kopsɔm/ (pl: -men) purchase price

de **koopvaardij** /kopfardɛi/ merchant navy

de **koopwaar** /kopwar/ (pl: -waren) merchandise, wares

koopziek /kopsik/ (adj) shopaholic, addicted to buying

de **koopzondag** /kopsɔndax/ shopping Sunday

het **koor** /kor/ (pl: koren) choir, chorus: *een gemengd ~* a mixed (voice) choir ‖ *in ~* with one voice, in unison

het/de **koord** /kort/ (pl: -en) cord, (thick) string, (light) rope

koorddansen /kordansə(n)/ walk a tightrope

de **koorddanser** /kordansər/ (pl: -s) tightrope walker, high wire walker

de **koorknaap** /korknap/ (pl: -knapen) choirboy: [fig] *hij is geen ~* he's no choirboy (*or:* angel)

de **koorts** /korts/ fever: *~ hebben* have a fever; *bij iem. de ~ opnemen* take s.o.'s temperature

koortsachtig /kortsaxtəx/ (adj, adv) feverish: *~e bedrijvigheid* frenzied activity

koortsig /kortsəx/ (adj) feverish

de **koortslip** /kortslɪp/ (pl: -pen) cold sore

de **koortsthermometer** /kortstɛrmometər/ (pl: -s) clinical thermometer

de **koortsuitslag** /kortsœytslax/ cold sore

koortsvrij /kortsfrɛi/ (adj) free of fever, without fever

de **koorzang** /korzaŋ/ choral singing

koosjer /koʃər/ (adj) kosher: [fig] *dat zaakje is niet ~* that business doesn't look too kosher

de **koosnaam** /kosnam/ pet name, term of endearment

het **kootje** /kocə/ (pl: -s) phalanx

de **kop** /kɔp/ (pl: -pen) **1** head: *er zit ~ noch staart aan* you can't make head or tail of it; *~ dicht!* shut up!; *een mooie ~ met haar* a beautiful head of hair; *een rooie ~ krijgen* go red, flush; *iem. op zijn ~ geven* give s.o. what for; *dat zal je de ~ niet kosten* it's not going to kill you **2** head, brain: *zijn ~ erbij houden* stay focused; *dat is een knappe ~* he is a clever (*or:* smart) fellow **3** head, top: *de ~ van Overijssel* the north of Overijssel; *de ~ van een spijker* (*or:* *hamer*) the head of a nail (*or:* hammer); *op ~ liggen* be in the lead; *over de ~ slaan* overturn, somersault; *over de ~ gaan* go broke, fold **4** cup, mug: *een ~ koffie* a cup of coffee **5** headline, heading ‖ *~ of munt* heads or tails; *iets de ~ indrukken* suppress (*or:* crush, clamp down on) sth.; *het is vijf uur*

op de ~ af it is exactly five o'clock; *iets op de ~ tikken* pick sth. up, get hold of sth.; *de ~ opsteken* surface, crop up

de **kopbal** /kɔbal/ (pl: -len) header

kopen /kopə(n)/ (kocht, heeft gekocht) **1** buy, purchase: *wat koop ik ervoor?* what good will it do me? **2** buy (off)

de **kop-en-schotel** /kopɛnsxotəl/ (pl: -s) cup and saucer

de **¹koper** /kopər/ (pl: -s) buyer

het **²koper** /kopər/ (pl: -s) **1** copper **2** brass **3** brass (section)

het/de **koperdraad** /kopərdrat/ copper (*or:* brass) wire

koperen /kopərə(n)/ (adj) brass, copper

het **koperwerk** /kopərwɛrk/ copper work, brass work, brassware

de **kopgroep** /kɔpxrup/ (pl: -en) leading group; break(away)

de **kopie** /kopi/ (pl: -ën) **1** copy, duplicate **2** (photo)copy

het **kopieerapparaat** /kopijeraparat/ (pl: -apparaten) photocopier

kopiëren /kopijerə(n)/ (kopieerde, heeft gekopieerd) **1** copy, make a copy (of); transcribe **2** (photo)copy, xerox

de **kopij** /kopɛi/ (pl: -en) copy, manuscript

het **kopje** /kɔpjə/ (pl: -s) (small, little) cup ‖ *~ duikelen* turn somersaults; *de poes gaf haar steeds ~s* the cat kept nuzzling (up) against her; *iem. een ~ kleiner maken* do s.o. in, bump s.o. off

kopjeduikelen /kɔpjədœykələ(n)/ (duikelde kopje, heeft kopjegeduikeld) (turn, do a) somersault

kopje-onder /kopjəɔndər/ (adv): *hij ging ~* he got a ducking

de **koplamp** /kɔplamp/ (pl: -en) headlight

de **koploper** /kɔplopər/ (pl: -s) leader, front runner; trendsetter

de **¹koppel** /kɔpəl/ (sword) belt

het **²koppel** /kɔpəl/ **1** couple, pair; group; bunch; set **2** couple: *een aardig ~* a nice couple

de **koppelaar** /kɔpəlar/ (pl: -s) matchmaker, marriage broker

de **koppelbaas** /kɔpəlbas/ (pl: -bazen) (illegal) labour subcontractor

koppelen /kɔpələ(n)/ (koppelde, heeft gekoppeld) **1** couple (with, to) **2** link, relate: *twee mensen proberen te ~* try to pair two people off

de **koppeling** /kɔpəlɪŋ/ (pl: -en) clutch (pedal): *de ~ intrappen* let out the clutch

het **koppelteken** /kɔpəltekə(n)/ (pl: -s) hyphen

het **koppelwerkwoord** /kɔpəlwɛrkwort/ (pl: -en) copula

koppen /kɔpə(n)/ (kopte, heeft gekopt) head

koppensnellen /kɔpə(n)snɛlə(n)/ headhunt

kosten

koppig /kɔpəx/ (adj, adv) **1** stubborn, head-strong: *(zo) ~ als een ezel* (as) stubborn as a mule **2** heady

de **koppigaard** /kɔpəxart/ (pl: -s) [Belg] stub-born person, obstinate person

de **koppigheid** /kɔpəxhɛit/ stubbornness

de **koprol** /kɔprɔl/ (pl: -len) somersault

kopschuw /kɔpsxyw/ (adj) shy, withdrawn: *iem. ~ maken* scare (or: frighten) s.o. off

de **kop-staartbotsing** /kɔpstardbɔtsɪŋ/ (pl: -en) rear-end collision

de **kopstem** /kɔpstɛm/ (pl: -men) falsetto

de **kopstoot** /kɔpstot/ (pl: kopstoten) butt (of the head): *iem. een ~ geven* headbutt s.o.

het **kopstuk** /kɔpstʏk/ (pl: -ken) head man, boss

de **koptelefoon** /kɔptələfon/ (pl: -s) head-phone(s), earphone(s), headset

de **kopzorg** /kɔpsɔrx/ (pl: -en) worry, headache

het **koraal** /koral/ (pl: koralen) coral

het **koraaleiland** /koralɛilɑnt/ (pl: -en) coral is-land

het **koraalrif** /koralrɪf/ (pl: -fen) coral reef

de **Koran** /koran/ Koran

kordaat /kordat/ (adj, adv) firm, plucky, bold

het **kordon** /kordɔn/ (pl: -s) cordon

Korea /koreja/ Korea

de **Koreaan** /korejan/ (pl: Koreanen) Korean

het **¹Koreaans** /korejans/ Korean

²Koreaans /korejans/ (adj) Korean

het **koren** /korə(n)/ (pl: -s) corn; [Am] wheat; grain

de **korenbloem** /korə(n)blum/ (pl: -en) corn-flower

de **korenschuur** /korə(n)sxyr/ (pl: -schuren) granary

de **korenwolf** /korə(n)wɔlf/ (pl: -wolven) Eu-ropean hamster

de **korf** /kɔrf/ (pl: korven) basket; hive

het **korfbal** /kɔrvbal/ korfball

korfballen /kɔrvbalə(n)/ (korfbalde, heeft gekorfbald) play korfball

het **korhoen** /kɔrhun/ (pl: -ders) black grouse

de **koriander** /korijɑndər/ coriander (seed)

de **kornuit** /kɔrnœyt/ (pl: -en) mate; [Am] bud-dy

de **korporaal** /kɔrporal/ (pl: -s) corporal

het **korps** /kɔrps/ (pl: -en) corps, body; staff; force

de **korpschef** /kɔrpʃɛf/ (pl: -s) [Dutch] superin-tendant

de **korrel** /kɔrəl/ (pl: -s) granule, grain: *iets met een ~(tje) zout nemen* take sth. with a pinch of salt

korrelig /kɔrələx/ (adj) granular

het **korset** /kɔrsɛt/ (pl: -ten) corset

de **korst** /kɔrst/ (pl: -en) crust; scab; rind

het **korstmos** /kɔrstmɔs/ (pl: -sen) lichen

kort /kɔrt/ (adj, adv) short; brief: *alles ~ en klein slaan* smash everything to pieces; *een ~ overzicht* a brief (or: short) summary; *~*

daarvoor shortly before; *iets ~ uiteenzetten* explain sth. briefly; *tot voor ~* until recently; *in het ~* in short, briefly

kortaangebonden /kɔrtaŋəbɔndə(n)/ (adj) short-spoken; crusty

kortademig /kɔrtadəməx/ (adj) short of breath; [also fig] short-winded

kortaf /kɔrtɑf/ (adj, adv) curt, abrupt

korten /kɔrtə(n)/ (kortte, heeft gekort) cut (back): *~ op de uitkeringen* cut back on social security

het **kortetermijngeheugen** /kɔrtətɛrmɛinyə-høyə(n)/ short-term memory

de **korting** /kɔrtɪŋ/ (pl: -en) discount, conces-sion; cut: *~ geven op de prijs* give a discount off the price

de **kortingscode** /kɔrtɪŋskodə/ (pl: -s) dis-count code

de **kortingskaart** /kɔrtɪŋskart/ (pl: -en) con-cession (or: reduced-fare) card/pass; discount card

kortom /kɔrtɔm/ (adv) in short, to put it briefly (or: shortly)

kortsluiten /kɔrtslœytə(n)/ (sloot kort, heeft kortgesloten) short-circuit: [fig] *de za-ken ~* align (or: fine-tune) matters

de **kortsluiting** /kɔrtslœytɪŋ/ (pl: -en) short circuit, short

kortstondig /kɔrtstɔndəx/ (adj) short-lived, brief

kortweg /kɔrtwɛx/ (adv) briefly, shortly

kortwieken /kɔrtwikə(n)/ (kortwiekte, heeft kortgewiekt) clip the wings of

kortzichtig /kɔrtsɪxtəx/ (adj, adv) short-sighted

kosmisch /kɔsmis/ (adj) cosmic

de **kosmonaut** /kɔsmonɑut/ (pl: -en) cosmo-naut

de **kosmos** /kɔsmɔs/ cosmos

de **kost** /kɔst/ (pl: -en) **1** see ¹*kosten* **2** living: *wat doe jij voor de ~?* what do you do for a living?; *de ~ verdienen* make a living (as a ..., by ...-ing) **3** board(ing), keep: *~ en inwoning* board and lodging **4** fare, food: *dagelijkse ~* ordinary food

kostbaar /kɔstbar/ (adj) **1** expensive **2** val-uable; [stronger] precious

de **kostbaarheden** /kɔstbarhedə(n)/ (pl) valu-ables

kostelijk /kɔstələk/ (adj, adv) precious; ex-quisite; delicious; excellent

¹kosteloos /kɔstəlos/ (adj) free

²kosteloos /kɔstəlos/ (adv) free of charge

de **¹kosten** /kɔstə(n)/ (pl) cost, expense; outlay; charge: *de ~ dekken* cover the costs; *~ van le-vensonderhoud* cost of living; *op haar eigen ~* at her own expense; *op ~ van* at the ex-pense of; *~ noch moeite sparen* spare no trouble or expense

²kosten /kɔstə(n)/ (kostte, heeft gekost) cost, be, take: *hoeveel kost het?* what does it cost?, how much is it?; *het heeft ons **maanden** gekost om dit te regelen* it took us months to organize this; *het ongeluk kostte (aan) drie kinderen het **leven*** three children died (*or:* lost their lives) in the accident; *dit karwei zal heel wat **tijd** ~* this job will take (up) a great deal of time

de **kosten-batenanalyse** /kɔstə(n)bɑtə(n)analiːzə/ (pl: -s) cost-benefit analysis

kostenbesparend /kɔstə(n)bəspɑrənt/ (adj) money-saving, cost-cutting

kostendekkend /kɔstə(n)dɛkənt/ (adj) cost-effective, self-supporting

de **kostenstijging** /kɔstə(n)stɛiɣɪŋ/ increase in costs

de **koster** /kɔstər/ (pl: -s) verger

de **kostganger** /kɔstχɑŋər/ (pl: -s) boarder, lodger

het **kostgeld** /kɔstχɛlt/ (pl: -en) board (and lodging)

het **kostje** /kɔʃə/ (pl: -s): *zijn ~ **is gekocht*** he has it made

de **kostprijs** /kɔstprɛis/ cost price

de **kostschool** /kɔstsχol/ (pl: -scholen) boarding school; public school: *op een ~ zitten* attend a boarding school

het **kostuum** /kɔstym/ (pl: -s) **1** suit **2** costume, dress

de **kostwinner** /kɔstwɪnər/ (pl: -s) breadwinner

het **kot** /kɔt/ (pl: -ten) **1** hovel **2** [Belg] student apartment (*or:* room): *op ~ zitten* be in digs

de **kotbaas** /kɔdbas/ (pl: kotbazen) [Belg] landlord

de **kotelet** /kotəlɛt/ (pl: -ten) chop, cutlet

de **koter** /kotər/ (pl: -s) [inform] youngster, kid

de **kotmadam** /kɔtmadɑm/ (pl: -men, -s) [Belg] landlady

kotsbeu /kɔtsbø/ (adj): [Belg; inform] *iets ~ zijn* be sick and tired of sth.

kotsen /kɔtsə(n)/ (kotste, heeft gekotst) [inform] puke: *de boel **onder** ~* be sick all over the place

kotsmisselijk /kɔtsmɪsələk/ (adj) [inform] sick as a dog (*or:* cat): [fig] *ik **word** er ~ van* I'm sick to death of it, it makes me sick

de **kotter** /kotər/ (pl: -s) cutter

de **kou** /kɑu/ cold(ness), chill: *~ **lijden*** suffer from the cold, freeze

koud /kɑut/ (adj) cold; chilly: *het **laat** mij ~* it leaves me cold; *het ~ **hebben*** be (*or:* feel) cold

koudbloedig /kɑudbludəχ/ (adj) cold-blooded

het **koudvuur** /kɑutfyr/ gangrene

de **koudwatervrees** /kɑutwɑtərvres/ cold feet

het **koufront** /kɑufrɔnt/ (pl: -en) cold front

de **koukleum** /kɑukløm/ (pl: -en) shivery type

de **kous** /kɑus/ (pl: -en) stocking; sock

kouvatten /kɑuvɑtə(n)/ (vatte kou, heeft kougevat) catch cold

kouwelijk /kɑuwələk/ (adj, adv) chilly, sensitive to cold

de **Kozak** /kozɑk/ (pl: -ken) Cossack

de **¹kozijn** /kozɛin/ [Belg] cousin

het **²kozijn** /kozɛin/ (window, door) frame

de **kraag** /kraχ/ (pl: kragen) **1** collar: *iem. **bij (in)** zijn ~ grijpen* grab s.o. by the collar; collar s.o. **2** head

de **kraai** /kraj/ (pl: -en) crow

kraaien /krajə(n)/ (kraaide, heeft gekraaid) crow

het **kraaiennest** /krajənɛst/ (pl: -en) crow's-nest

de **kraaienpootjes** /krajə(n)poces/ (pl) crow's-feet

de **kraak** /krak/ (pl: kraken) break-in

het **kraakbeen** /krakben/ (pl: -deren) cartilage

het **kraakpand** /krakpɑnt/ (pl: -en) squat

de **kraakstem** /krakstɛm/ grating (*or:* rasping) voice

de **kraal** /kral/ (pl: kralen) bead

de **kraam** /kram/ (pl: kramen) stall, booth

de **kraamafdeling** /kramɑvdelɪŋ/ (pl: -en) maternity ward

het **kraambed** /krambɛt/ childbed: *een lang ~* a long period of lying-in

de **kraamhulp** /kramhylp/ (pl: -en) maternity assistant

de **kraamkamer** /kramkamər/ (pl: -s) delivery room; [before delivery] labour room

de **kraamkliniek** /kramklinik/ (pl: -en) maternity clinic

de **kraamverzorgster** /kramvərzɔrχstər/ (pl: -s) maternity nurse

het **kraamvisite** /kramvizitə/ (pl: -s): *op ~ komen* come to see the new mother and her baby

de **kraamvrouw** /kramvrɑu/ (pl: -en) woman in childbed; mother of newly-born baby

de **kraamzorg** /kramzɔrχ/ maternity care

de **kraan** /kran/ (pl: kranen) **1** tap; [Am] faucet; (stop)cock; valve **2** crane

de **kraandrijver** /krandrɛivər/ (pl: -s) crane driver (*or:* operator)

de **kraanvogel** /kranvoɣəl/ (pl: -s) (common) crane

de **kraanwagen** /kranwaɣə(n)/ (pl: -s) breakdown lorry (*or:* truck); [Am] tow truck

het **kraanwater** /kranwatər/ tap water

de **krab** /krɑp/ (pl: -ben) crab

de **krabbel** /krɑbəl/ (pl: -s) **1** scratch (mark) **2** scrawl

¹krabbelen /krɑbələ(n)/ (krabbelde, heeft gekrabbeld) scratch || *(weer) **overeind** ~* scramble to one's feet

²krabbelen /krɑbələ(n)/ (krabbelde, heeft gekrabbeld) scrawl

het **krabbeltje** /krɑbəlcə/ (pl: -s) scrawl

¹krabben /krɑbə(n)/ (krabde, heeft gekrabd) scratch: *zijn **hoofd** ~* scratch one's head

²krabben /ˈkrɑbə(n)/ (krabde, heeft gekrabd) scratch out, scratch off

de **krach** /krɑχ/ (pl: -s) [Dutch] crash

de **kracht** /krɑχt/ (pl: -en) strength, power; force: *drijvende ~ achter* moving force (or: spirit) behind; *op eigen ~* on one's own, by o.s.; *op volle* (or: *halve*) *~ (werken)* operate at full (or: half) speed/power; *met zijn laatste ~en* with a final effort; *het vergt veel van mijn ~en* it's a great drain on my energy; *van ~ zijn* be valid (or: effective); *zijn ~en meten met iem.* measure one's strength with s.o., pit one's strength against s.o.; *zijn woorden ~ bijzetten* reinforce his words, suit the action to the word; *~ putten uit* draw strength from; *op ~en komen* regain one's strength, recuperate

de **krachtbron** /ˈkrɑχtbrɔn/ (pl: -nen) source of energy (or: power); power station

de **krachtcentrale** /ˈkrɑχtsɛntralə/ (pl: -s) power station

krachtdadig /krɑχˈdadəχ/ (adj, adv) energetic, vigorous

krachteloos /ˈkrɑχtəlos/ (adj) weak; limp; powerless

krachtens /ˈkrɑχtəns/ (prep) by virtue of, under

krachtig /ˈkrɑχtəχ/ (adj, adv) **1** strong, powerful: *een ~e motor* a powerful engine; *matige tot ~e wind* moderate to strong winds **2** powerful, forceful: *kort maar ~* **a)** brief and to the point; **b)** [fig] short but (or: and) sweet; *~ optreden* take vigorous action, take strong measures **3** potent

de **krachtmeting** /ˈkrɑχtmetɪŋ/ (pl: -en) contest, trial of strength

de **krachtpatser** /ˈkrɑχtpatsər/ (pl: -s) muscleman, bruiser

de **krachtsinspanning** /ˈkrɑχtsɪnspanɪŋ/ (pl: -en) effort

de **krachtsport** /ˈkrɑχtspɔrt/ (pl: -en) strength sport

de **krachtterm** /ˈkrɑχtɛrm/ (pl: -en) swearword: *hij gebruikte nogal veel ~en* he used a lot of swearwords (or: strong language)

de **krachttraining** /ˈkrɑχtrenɪŋ/ (pl: -en) weight training

de **krak** /krɑk/ (pl: -ken) crack, snap

krakelen /ˈkrakələ(n)/ (krakeelde, heeft gekrakeeld) quarrel, row

de **krakeling** /ˈkrakəlɪŋ/ (pl: -en) type of biscuit; [Am] type of cookie: *zoute ~en* pretzels

¹kraken /ˈkrakə(n)/ (kraakte, heeft gekraakt) crack; creak; crunch: *een ~de stem* a grating voice

²kraken /ˈkrakə(n)/ (kraakte, heeft gekraakt) **1** crack **2** break into [bldg]; crack; hack **3** pan, slate || *het pand is gekraakt* the building has been broken into by squatters

de **kraker** /ˈkrakər/ (pl: -s) **1** squatter **2** [comp] hacker **3** smash (hit)

krakkemikkig /ˈkrɑkəmɪkəχ/ (adj, adv) [inform] rickety

de **kram** /krɑm/ (pl: -men) clamp; cramp (iron); clasp || [Belg] *uit zijn ~men schieten* blow one's top

de **kramiek** /kraˈmik/ (pl: -en) [Belg] currant loaf

de **kramp** /krɑmp/ (pl: -en) cramp: [fig] *in een ~ schieten* tense up

krampachtig /krɑmˈpɑχtəχ/ (adj, adv) **1** forced: *met een vertrokken gezicht* grimacing **2** frenetic: *zich ~ aan iem. (iets) vasthouden* cling to s.o. (sth.) for dear life **3** convulsive

kranig /ˈkranəχ/ (adj) plucky, brave

krankjorum /krɑŋkˈjorʏm/ (adj, adv) [inform] bonkers, nuts

krankzinnig /krɑŋkˈsɪnəχ/ (adj) **1** mentally ill, insane, mad: *~ worden* go insane, go out of one's mind **2** crazy, mad || *~ duur* extremely expensive

de **krankzinnige** /krɑŋkˈsɪnəɣə/ (pl: -n) madman, madwoman

de **krans** /krɑns/ (pl: -en) **1** wreath **2** ring: *een ~ om de zon* (or: *de maan*) a corona round the sun (or: moon)

de **kransslagader** /ˈkrɑnslɑχadər/ (pl: -s) coronary artery

de **krant** /krɑnt/ (pl: -en) (news)paper: *een digitale ~* a digital newspaper; *een papieren ~* a print newspaper

het **krantenartikel** /ˈkrɑntə(n)ɑrtikəl/ (pl: -en) newspaper article

het **krantenbericht** /ˈkrɑntə(n)bərɪχt/ (pl: -en) newspaper report

de **krantenbezorger** /ˈkrɑntə(n)bəzɔrɣər/ (pl: -s) (news)paper boy (or: girl)

de **krantenkiosk** /ˈkrɑntə(n)kijɔsk/ (pl: -en) newspaper kiosk (or: stand)

het **krantenknipsel** /ˈkrɑntə(n)knɪpsəl/ (pl: -en) newspaper cutting, press cutting

de **krantenkop** /ˈkrɑntə(n)kɔp/ (pl: -pen) (newspaper) headline

de **krantenwijk** /ˈkrɑntə(n)wɛik/ (pl: -en) (news)paper round; [Am] (news)paper route: *een ~ hebben* have a (news)paper round

krap /krɑp/ (adj, adv) **1** tight; narrow **2** tight, scarce: *een ~pe markt* a small market; *~ (bij kas) zitten* be short of money (or: cash) || *met een ~pe meerderheid* with a bare majority

de **¹kras** /krɑs/ (pl: -sen) scratch

²kras /krɑs/ (adj, adv) **1** strong, vigorous; hale and hearty **2** strong, drastic: *dat is een nogal ~se opmerking* that is a rather crass remark

het **kraslot** /ˈkrɑslɔt/ (pl: -en) scratch card

¹krassen /ˈkrɑsə(n)/ (kraste, heeft gekrast) **1** scrape: *zijn ring kraste over het glas* his ring scraped across the glass **2** rasp; scrape; croak; hoot; screech

²krassen /ˈkrɑsə(n)/ (kraste, heeft gekrast)

scratch; carve

het krat /krɑt/ (pl: -ten) crate: *een ~ bier* a crate of beer

de krater /krɑtər/ (pl: -s) crater: *een ~ slaan* leave a crater

het krediet /krədit/ (pl: -en) **1** credit: *veel ~ hebben* enjoy great trust **2** credit, respect

de kredietbank /krədidbɑŋk/ (pl: -en) [roughly] finance company

de kredietcrisis /krəditkrizɪs/ (pl: -crises) credit crunch, credit crisis

de kredietinstelling /krəditɪnstɛlɪŋ/ (pl: -en) credit institution (*or:* company)

kredietwaardig /krəditwardəx/ (adj) creditworthy

de kreeft /kreft/ (pl: -en) lobster

de Kreeft /kreft/ (pl: -en) [astrology] Cancer

de Kreeftskeerkring /kreftskerkrɪŋ/ tropic of Cancer

de kreek /krek/ (pl: kreken) **1** creek, cove **2** stream

de kreet /kret/ (pl: kreten) **1** cry **2** slogan, catchword

de krekel /krekəl/ (pl: -s) cricket

het kreng /krɛŋ/ (pl: -en) **1** beast, bastard; bitch **2** wretched thing **3** carrion

krenken /krɛŋkə(n)/ (krenkte, heeft gekrenkt) offend, hurt

de krent /krɛnt/ currant: *de ~en uit de pap* the best bits; *op zijn ~ zitten* laze, idle

de krentenbol /krɛntə(n)bɔl/ (pl: -len) currant bun

het krentenbrood /krɛntə(n)brot/ (pl: -broden) currant loaf

krenterig /krɛntərəx/ (adj, adv) stingy

Kreta /kretɑ/ Crete

de kreukel /krøkəl/ (pl: -s) crease

¹kreukelen /krøkələ(n)/ (kreukelde, is gekreukeld) get creased (*or:* rumpled)

²kreukelen /krøkələ(n)/ (kreukelde, heeft gekreukeld) crease: *het zat in gekreukeld papier* it was wrapped in crumpled paper

kreukelig /krøkələx/ (adj) crumpled, creased

de kreukelzone /krøkəlzɔːnə/ (pl: -s) crumple zone

¹kreuken /krøkə(n)/ (kreukte, is gekreukt) get creased (*or:* rumpled)

²kreuken /krøkə(n)/ (kreukte, heeft gekreukt) crease, crumple

kreukvrij /krøkfrɛi/ (adj) crease-resistant

kreunen /krønə(n)/ (kreunde, heeft gekreund) groan, moan

kreupel /krøpəl/ (adj, adv) **1** lame **2** poor, clumsy

het kreupelhout /krøpəlhɑut/ undergrowth

de krib /krɪp/ (pl: -ben) manger, crib

kribbig /krɪbəx/ (adj, adv) grumpy, catty

de kriebel /kribəl/ (pl: -s) itch, tickle: *ik krijg daar de ~s van* it gets on my nerves

kriebelen /kribələ(n)/ (kriebelde, heeft ge-

kriebeld) tickle; itch: *dat kriebelt!* that's tickly!; *deze trui kriebelt* this jumper itches; [fig] *het begint weer te ~* I'm getting that itch again

de kriebelhoest /kribəlhust/ tickling cough

kriebelig /kribələx/ (adj) crabbed || *~ van iets worden* get irritated by sth.

de kriek /krik/ (pl: -en) **1** black cherry **2** [Belg] cherry beer || *zich een ~ lachen* laugh one's head off

krieken /krikə(n)/: *met (bij) het ~ van de dag* at (the crack of) dawn

de krielkip /krilkɪp/ (pl: -pen) bantam hen

het krieltje /krilcə/ (pl: -s) (small) new potato

krijgen /krɛiyə(n)/ (kreeg, heeft gekregen) get; receive; catch: *aandacht ~* receive attention; *je krijgt de groeten van … …* sends (you) his regards; *zij kreeg er hoofdpijn van* it gave her a headache; *slaap* (or: *trek*) *~* feel sleepy (or: hungry); *iets af ~* get sth. done (*or:* finished); *dat goed is niet meer te ~* you can't get hold of that stuff any more; *iem. te pakken ~* get (hold of) s.o.; *ik krijg nog geld van je* you (still) owe me some money; *iets voor elkaar ~* manage sth.

de krijger /krɛiyər/ (pl: -s) warrior

het krijgertje /krɛiyərcə/: *~ spelen* play tag (*or:* tig)

de krijgsgevangene /krɛixsxəvɑŋənə/ (pl: -n) prisoner of war

krijgshaftig /krɛixshɑftəx/ (adj, adv) warlike

de krijgsheer /krɛixsher/ warlord

het Krijgshof /krɛixshɔf/ [Belg] military high court

de krijgslist /krɛixslɪst/ (pl: -en) stratagem, ruse

de krijgsmacht /krɛixsmɑxt/ (pl: -en) armed forces, army

de krijgsraad /krɛixsrat/ (pl: -raden) court-martial

krijsen /krɛisə(n)/ (krijste, heeft gekrijst) **1** shriek, screech **2** scream

het krijt /krɛit/ chalk; crayon || *bij iem. in het ~ staan* owe s.o. sth.

krijten /krɛitə(n)/ (krijtte, heeft gekrijt) chalk

het krijtje /krɛicə/ (pl: -s) piece of chalk

de krijtrots /krɛitrɔts/ (pl: -en) chalk cliff

krijtwit /krɛitwɪt/ (adj) (as) white as chalk

de krik /krɪk/ (pl: -s) jack

de Krim /krɪm/: *de ~* (the) Crimea

de krimp /krɪmp/ shrinkage: *~ van de bevolking* demographic shrinkage; *economische ~* economic shrinkage (*or:* contraction) || *geen ~ geven* not flinch

krimpen /krɪmpə(n)/ (kromp, is gekrompen) shrink, contract

de krimpfolie /krɪmpfoli/ clingfilm, shrink-wrapping

krimpvrij /krɪmpfrɛi/ (adj) shrink-proof,

shrink-resistant

de **kring** /krɪŋ/ (pl: -en) circle, ring; circuit: *in besloten* ~ in a closed (*or:* private) circle, private(ly); *in politieke* ~*en* in political circles; *de huiselijke* ~ the family (*or:* domestic) circle; ~*en onder de ogen hebben* have bags under one's eyes; ~*en maken op een tafelblad* make rings on a table top; *in een* ~ *zitten* sit in a ring (*or:* circle)

kringelen /krɪŋələ(n)/ (kringelde, heeft gekringeld) spiral

de **kringloop** /krɪŋlop/ cycle; circulation

het **kringlooppapier** /krɪŋlopapir/ recycled paper

de **kringloopwinkel** /krɪŋlopwɪŋkəl/ (pl: -s) shop specialized in recycled goods

de **kringspier** /krɪŋspir/ (pl: -en) orbicularis, sphincter(-muscle)

krioelen /krijulə(n)/ (krioelde, heeft gekrioeld) swarm, teem

kriskras /krɪskrɑs/ (adv) criss-cross

het **kristal** /krɪstɑl/ (pl: -len) crystal

kristalhelder /krɪstɑlhɛldər/ (adj) crystal-clear; lucid

kristallen /krɪstɑlə(n)/ (adj) crystal

de **kristalsuiker** /krɪstɑlsœykər/ granulated sugar

de **¹kritiek** /kritik/ (pl: -en) **1** criticism: *opbouwende* (*or: afbrekende*) ~ constructive (*or:* destructive) criticism **2** (critical) review: *goede* (*or: slechte*) ~*en krijgen* get good (*or:* bad) reviews

²kritiek /kritik/ (adj) critical; crucial: *de toestand van de patiënt was* ~ the patient's condition was critical

kritiekloos /kritiklos/ (adj, adv) uncritical: *iets* ~ *aanvaarden* accept sth. without question

kritisch /kritis/ (adj, adv) **1** critical **2** fault-finding: *een* ~ *iem.* a fault-finder

kritiseren /kritizerə(n)/ (kritiseerde, heeft gekritiseerd) criticize; review

de **Kroaat** /krowat/ (pl: Kroaten) Croat, Croatian

Kroatië /krowa(t)sijə/ Croatia

het **¹Kroatisch** /krowatis/ Croatian

²Kroatisch /krowatis/ (adj) Croatian

de **kroeg** /krux/ (pl: -en) pub: *altijd in de* ~ *zitten* always be in the pub

de **kroegbaas** /kruɣbas/ (pl: -bazen) publican

de **kroegentocht** /kruɣə(n)tɔxt/ (pl: -en) pub-crawl; [Am] bar-hopping

de **kroegloper** /kruxlopər/ (pl: -s) pub-crawler

de **kroepoek** /krupuk/ prawn crackers, shrimp crackers

de **kroes** /krus/ (pl: kroezen) mug

het **kroeshaar** /krushar/ (pl: -haren) frizzy hair, curly hair

kroezen /kruzə(n)/ (kroesde, heeft gekroesd) frizzle, curl (up)

krokant /krokɑnt/ (adj) crisp(y), crunchy

de **kroket** /krokɛt/ croquette

de **krokodil** /krokodɪl/ (pl: -len) crocodile

de **krokodillentranen** /krokodɪlə(n)tranə(n)/ (pl): ~ *huilen* shed crocodile tears

de **krokus** /krokʏs/ (pl: -sen) crocus

de **krokusvakantie** /krokʏsfakɑnsi/ [roughly] spring half-term; [Am] [roughly] semester break

krols /krɔls/ (adj) on heat

krom /krɔm/ (adj, adv) **1** bent, crooked; curved: ~*me benen* bow-legs **2** clumsy: ~ *Nederlands* bad Dutch

krombuigen /krɔmbœyɣə(n)/ (boog krom, heeft/is kromgebogen) bend

kromgroeien /krɔmɣrujə(n)/ (groeide krom, is kromgegroeid) grow crooked

kromliggen /krɔmlɪɣə(n)/ (lag krom, heeft kromgelegen) scrimp and save

de **kromme** /krɔmə/ (pl: -n) **1** curve **2** graph

¹krommen /krɔmə(n)/ (kromde, is gekromd) bend

²krommen /krɔmə(n)/ (kromde, heeft gekromd) bend

de **krommenaas** /krɔmənas/: [Belg] *zich van* ~ *gebaren* act dumb, pretend not to hear

de **kromming** /krɔmɪŋ/ (pl: -en) bend(ing), curving; curvature

kromtrekken /krɔmtrɛkə(n)/ (trok krom, is kromgetrokken) warp; buckle

kronen /kronə(n)/ (kroonde, heeft gekroond) crown

de **kroniek** /kronik/ (pl: -en) chronicle

de **kroning** /kronɪŋ/ (pl: -en) crowning; coronation

de **kronkel** /krɔŋkəl/ (pl: -s) twist(ing); kink

kronkelen /krɔŋkələ(n)/ (kronkelde, heeft/is gekronkeld) twist, wind; wriggle: ~ *van pijn* writhe in agony

kronkelig /krɔŋkələɣ/ (adj) twisting, winding

de **kronkelweg** /krɔŋkəlwɛx/ (pl: -en) twisting road, winding road, crooked path

de **kroon** /kron/ (pl: kronen) **1** crown; [of flower] corolla **2** Crown: *een benoeming door de* ~ a Crown appointment ‖ *dat is de* ~ *op zijn werk* that is the crowning glory of his work; *dat spant de* ~ that takes the cake

de **kroongetuige** /kronɣətœyɣə/ (pl: -n) crown witness

het **kroonjaar** /kronjar/ (pl: -jaren) jubilee year

het **kroonjuweel** /kronjywel/ [literally and fig] crown jewel

de **kroonkurk** /kronkʏrk/ (pl: -en) crown cap

de **kroonlijst** /kronlɛist/ (pl: -en) cornice

de **kroonluchter** /kronlʏxtər/ (pl: -s) chandelier

de **kroonprins** /kromprɪns/ (pl: -en) crown prince; [fig] heir-apparent

de **kroonprinses** /kromprɪnsɛs/ (pl: -sen) crown princess

het **kroonsteentje** /kronstencə/ (pl: -s) connector

het **kroos** /kros/ duckweed

het **kroost** /krost/ offspring

de **krop** /krɔp/ (pl: -pen) **1** head: *een ~ sla* a head of lettuce **2** crop, gizzard

het **krot** /krɔt/ (pl: -ten) slum (dwelling), hovel

de **krottenwijk** /krɔ̯tə(n)wɛik/ (pl: -en) slum(s)

het **kruid** /krœyt/ (pl: -en) **1** herb: [fig] *daar is geen ~ tegen gewassen* there is no cure for that; *geneeskrachtige ~en* medicinal herbs **2** herb, spice

kruiden /krœydə(n)/ (kruidde, heeft gekruid) season, flavour; [fig also] spice (up)

de **kruidenboter** /krœydə(n)botər/ herb butter

de **kruidenier** /krœydənir/ (pl: -s) grocer

het **kruidenrekje** /krœydə(n)rɛkjə/ (pl: -s) spice rack

de **kruidenthee** /krœydə(n)te/ herb(al) tea

kruidig /krœydəx/ (adj) spicy

het **kruidje-roer-mij-niet** /krœycərurmənit/ (pl: kruidjes-roer-mij-niet) **1** [bot] touch-me-not **2** [fig] thin-skinned (*or:* touchy) person

de **kruidkoek** /krœytkuk/ [roughly] spiced gingerbread

de **kruidnagel** /krœytnaɣəl/ (pl: -s, -en) clove

¹**kruien** /krœyə(n)/ (kruide, heeft gekruid) break up, drift

²**kruien** /krœyə(n)/ (kruide, heeft gekruid) wheel

de **kruier** /krœyər/ (pl: -s) porter

de **kruik** /krœyk/ (pl: -en) **1** jar, pitcher, crock **2** hot-water bottle

het **kruim** /krœym/ (pl: -en) **1** crumb **2** [Belg] the pick of the bunch, the very best

de **kruimel** /krœyməl/ (pl: -s) crumb

het **kruimeldeeg** /krœyməldex/ crumbly pastry; [Am] crumb crust

de ¹**kruimeldief** /krœyməldif/ (pl: -dieven) petty thief

de ²**kruimeldief**® /krœyməldif/ (pl: -dieven) crumb-sweeper, dustbuster

kruimelen /krœymələ(n)/ (kruimelde, heeft gekruimeld) crumble

de **kruimeltaart** /krœyməltart/ (pl: -en) fruit crumble

het **kruimelwerk** /krœyməlwɛrk/ **1** odd jobs **2** pottering (about)

kruimig /krœyməx/ (adj) mealy, floury

de **kruin** /krœyn/ (pl: -en) crown

kruipen /krœypə(n)/ (kroop, heeft/is gekropen) **1** creep, crawl **2** crawl (along); drag: *de uren kropen voorbij* time dragged (on)

kruiperig /krœypərəx/ (adj, adv) cringing, slimy, servile

het **kruis** /krœys/ (pl: kruizen) **1** cross **2** crotch, seat **3** crotch, groin **4** head: *~ of munt?* heads or tails? ‖ [Belg; fig] *een ~ over iets maken* put an end to sth.; *een ~ slaan* cross o.s.

de **kruisband** /krœyzbɑnt/ (pl: -en) cruciate ligament

het **kruisbeeld** /krœyzbelt/ (pl: -en) crucifix

de **kruisbes** /krœyzbɛs/ (pl: -sen) gooseberry

de **kruisbestuiving** /krœyzbəstœyvɪŋ/ (pl: -en) cross-pollination [also fig]

de **kruisboog** /krœyzbox/ (pl: -bogen) **1** ogive **2** crossbow

kruiselings /krœysəlɪŋs/ (adj, adv) crosswise, crossways

kruisen /krœysə(n)/ (kruiste, heeft gekruist) cross, intersect: *onze brieven hebben elkaar gekruist* our letters crossed (each other)

de **kruiser** /krœysər/ (pl: -s) **1** cruiser **2** cabin cruiser

kruisigen /krœysəɣə(n)/ (kruisigde, heeft gekruisigd) crucify

de **kruisiging** /krœysəɣɪŋ/ (pl: -en) crucifixion

de **kruising** /krœysɪŋ/ (pl: -en) **1** crossing, junction, intersection; crossroads **2** crossing, hybridization; cross-fertilization **3** cross, hybrid; cross-breed

het **kruisje** /krœyʃə/ (pl: -s) **1** cross; mark **2** sign of the cross **3** [comp] close icon, close

de **kruiskopschroevendraaier** /krœyskopsxruvə(n)drajər/ (pl: -s) Phillips screwdriver

het **kruispunt** /krœyspʏnt/ (pl: -en) crossing, junction, intersection; crossroad(s): [fig] *op een ~ staan* stand at the crossroads

de **kruisraket** /krœysrakɛt/ (pl: -ten) cruise missile

de **kruisridder** /krœysrɪdər/ (pl: -s) crusader

de **kruissnelheid** /krœysnɛlhɛit/ cruising speed

de **kruisspin** /krœyspɪn/ (pl: -nen) diadem spider

de **kruissteek** /krœystek/ (pl: -steken) cross-stitch

het **kruisteken** /krœystekə(n)/ (pl: -s) (sign of the) cross

de **kruistocht** /krœystɔxt/ (pl: -en) crusade

de **kruisvaarder** /krœysfardər/ (pl: -s) crusader

het **kruisverhoor** /krœysfərhor/ (pl: -verhoren) cross-examination: *iem. aan een ~ onderwerpen* cross-examine s.o.

de **kruiswoordpuzzel** /krœyswortpʏzəl/ (pl: -s) crossword (puzzle)

het **kruit** /krœyt/ (gun)powder

de **kruitdamp** /krœydɑmp/ (pl: -en) gunsmoke: [fig] *toen de ~ was opgetrokken* when the smoke (of battle) had cleared

het **kruitvat** /krœytfat/ (pl: -en) powder keg

de **kruiwagen** /krœywaɣə(n)/ (pl: -s) **1** (wheel)barrow **2** [fig] connections: *~s gebruiken* pull strings

de **kruk** /krʏk/ **1** stool **2** crutch **3** (door) handle

de **krukas** /krʏkɑs/ (pl: -sen) crankshaft

de **krul** /krʏl/ (pl: -len) **1** curl; ringlet **2** [socc] looping shot, curling ball

krullen /krʏlə(n)/ (krulde, heeft gekruld) **1** curl **2** [socc] curl: *hij krulde de bal over de muur* he curled the ball over the wall

de **krullenbol** /krȳlə(n)bɔl/ (pl: -len) curly (head)

de **krulspeld** /krȳlspɛlt/ (pl: -en) curler, roller

de **krultang** /krȳltɑŋ/ (pl: -en) curling iron

het **kso** /kɑɛsō/ [Belg] secondary fine arts education

kubiek /kybı̄k/ (adj) cubic: *kubieke meter* cubic metre

de **kubus** /kybʏs/ (pl: -sen) cube

kuchen /kʏχə(n)/ (kuchte, heeft gekucht) cough

de **kudde** /kȳdə/ (pl: -s) herd; flock

het **kuddedier** /kȳdədir/ (pl: -en) **1** herd animal **2** one of the herd (*or:* mob)

kuieren /kœ̄yərə(n)/ (kuierde, heeft/is gekuierd) stroll, go for a walk

de **kuif** /kœyf/ (pl: kuiven) **1** forelock; quiff **2** (head of) hair **3** crest, tuft

het **kuiken** /kœ̄ykə(n)/ (pl: -s) chick(en)

de **kuil** /kœyl/ (pl: -en) pit, hole; hollow; pothole

het **kuiltje** /kœ̄ylcə/ (pl: -s) dimple; cleft

de **kuip** /kœyp/ (pl: -en) tub; barrel

het **kuipje** /kœ̄ypjə/ (pl: -s) tub

de **¹kuis** /kœys/ (pl: kuizen) [Belg] (house)cleaning: *grote* ~ spring-cleaning

²kuis /kœys/ (adj, adv) chaste, pure

kuisen /kœ̄ysə(n)/ (kuiste, heeft gekuist) [Belg] clean

de **kuisheid** /kœ̄yshɛit/ chastity, purity

de **kuisheidsgordel** /kœ̄yshɛitsχɔrdəl/ (pl: -s) chastity belt

de **kuisvrouw** /kœ̄ysfrɑu/ (pl: -en) [Belg] cleaning lady (*or:* woman)

de **kuit** /kœyt/ (pl: -en) **1** [anatomy] calf **2** spawn

het **kuitbeen** /kœ̄ydben/ (pl: -benen) fibula

kukeleku /kykələkȳ/ (int) cock-a-doodle-doo

kukelen /kȳkələ(n)/ (kukelde, is gekukeld) [Dutch] go flying, tumble

de **kul** /kʏl/ (pl: -len) [inform] rubbish

de **kummel** /kȳməl/ cum(m)in; caraway (seed)

de **kumquat** /kumkwɑt/ (pl: -s) cumquat

de **kunde** /kȳndə/ knowledge, learning

kundig /kȳndəχ/ (adj, adv) able, capable, skilful: *iets ~ repareren* repair sth. skilfully

de **kunne** /kȳnə/ sex: *van beiderlei* ~ of both sexes

¹kunnen /kȳnə(n)/ (kon, heeft gekund) may, might, could, it is possible that ...: *het kan een vergissing zijn* it may be a mistake

²kunnen /kȳnə(n)/ (kon, heeft gekund) be acceptable: *zo kan het niet langer* it (*or:* things) can't go on like this; *die trui kán gewoon niet* that sweater's just impossible

³kunnen /kȳnə(n)/ (kon, heeft gekund) can, could, be able to; be possible: *een handige man kan alles* a handy man can do anything; *dat kon er nog wel bij* to add insult to injury ..., to make matters worse ...; *buiten iets ~*

do without sth.; *het deksel kan er niet af* the lid won't come off; *hij kan niet meer* he can't go on; *morgen kan ik niet* tomorrow's impossible for me; *hij liep wat hij kon* he ran as fast as he could; *hij kan goed zingen* he's a good singer || *moet ~* yes, why not?, fine by me

⁴kunnen /kȳnə(n)/ (aux vb, kon, heeft gekund) can, be allowed to; may; could; be allowed to, might: *zoiets kun je niet doen* you can't do that sort of thing; *de gevangene kon ontsnappen* the prisoner was able to (*or:* managed to) escape; *je had het me wel ~ vertellen* you might (*or:* could) have told me

de **kunst** /kʏnst/ (pl: -en) **1** art: *een handelaar in* ~ an art dealer **2** art, skill: *zwarte* ~ black magic; *dat is uit de* ~ that's amazing! **3** trick

de **kunstacademie** /kȳnstakademi/ (pl: -s) art academy

het **kunstbeen** /kȳnstben/ (pl: -benen) artificial leg

de **kunstbloem** /kȳnstblum/ (pl: -en) artificial flower

de **kunstcriticus** /kȳnstkritikʏs/ (pl: -critici) art critic

de **kunstenaar** /kȳnstənar/ (pl: -s) artist

het **kunst- en vliegwerk** /kȳnstɛnvliχwɛrk/: *met* ~ by pulling out all the stops

de **kunstgalerij** /kȳns(t)χɑlərɛi/ (pl: -en) (art) gallery

het **kunstgebit** /kȳnstχəbɪt/ (pl: -ten) (set of) false teeth, (set of) dentures; (dental) plate

de **kunstgeschiedenis** /kȳnstχəsχidənɪs/ history of art; [subject] art history

het **kunstgras** /kȳnstχrɑs/ artificial grass (*or:* turf)

de **kunstgreep** /kȳnstχrep/ (pl: -grepen) trick, manoeuvre

de **kunsthandelaar** /kȳnsthɑndəlar/ (pl: -s, -handelaren) art dealer

het/de **kunsthars** /kȳnsthɑrs/ synthetic resin; phenolic resin

de **kunstheup** /kȳnsthøp/ (pl: -en) artificial hip

kunstig /kȳnstəχ/ (adj, adv) ingenious, skilful

het **kunstijs** /kȳnstɛis/ artificial ice, man-made ice; (ice) rink

de **kunstijsbaan** /kȳnstɛizban/ (pl: -banen) ice rink, skating rink

het **kunstje** /kȳnʃə/ (pl: -s) **1** knack, trick: *dat is een koud* ~ that's child's play, there's nothing to it **2** trick: *geen* ~s! none of your tricks!

het **kunstleer** /kȳnstler/ imitation leather

het **kunstlicht** /kȳnstlɪχt/ artificial light

de **kunstliefhebber** /kȳnstlifhɛbər/ art lover

de **kunstmaan** /kȳnstman/ (pl: -manen) satellite

kunstmatig /kȳnstmɑtəχ/ (adj, adv) artificial; synthetic; man-made; imitation

de **kunstmest** /kȳnstmɛst/ fertilizer

kunstrijden /kȳnstrɛidə(n)/ figure-skate

het **kunstschaatsen** /kȳn(st)sχatsə(n)/ figure-skating

de **kunstschat** /kʏn(st)sχɑt/ (pl: -ten) art treasure

de **kunstschilder** /kʏnstsχɪldər/ (pl: -s) artist, painter

de **kunststof** /kʏnstɔf/ (pl: -fen) synthetic (material, fibre), plastic: *van* ~ synthetic, plastic

het **kunststuk** /kʏnstʏk/ (pl: -ken) work of art; feat; stunt: *een journalistiek ~je* a masterpiece of journalism; *dat is een ~ dat ik je niet na zou doen* that's a feat I couldn't match

de **kunstverzameling** /kʏnstfərzaməlɪŋ/ (pl: -en) art collection

de **kunstvezel** /kʏnstfezəl/ (pl: -s) man-made fibre, synthetic fibre

het **kunstvoorwerp** /kʏnstforwɛrp/ (pl: -en) work of art; artefact

de **kunstvorm** /kʏnstfɔrm/ (pl: -en) art form, medium (of art)

het **kunstwerk** /kʏnstwɛrk/ (pl: -en) work of art, masterpiece: *dat is een klein ~je* it's a little gem (*or:* masterpiece)

kunstzinnig /kʏnstsɪnəχ/ (adj) artistic(ally-minded): *~e vorming* art(istic) training (*or:* education)

de **kür** /kyr/ (pl: -en) **1** performance (to music) **2** freestyle dressage to music

de ¹**kuren** /kyrə(n)/ (pl) quirks; moods: *hij heeft altijd van die vreemde* ~ he's quirky (*or:* moody); *vol* ~ **a)** moody; **b)** awkward

²**kuren** /kyrə(n)/ (kuurde, heeft gekuurd) take a cure

de ¹**kurk** /kʏrk/ cork: *doe de* ~ *goed op de fles* cork the bottle properly

het/de ²**kurk** /kʏrk/ cork: *wij hebben* ~ *in de gang* we've got cork flooring in the hall

kurkdroog /kʏrgdroχ/ (adj) (as) dry as a bone, bone-dry

de **kurkentrekker** /kʏrkə(n)trɛkər/ (pl: -s) corkscrew

de **kurkuma** /kʏrkuma/ turmeric

de **kus** /kʏs/ (pl: -sen) kiss: *geef me eens een* ~ give me a kiss; how about a kiss?; *een ~ krijgen van iem.* get a kiss from (*or:* be kissed by) s.o.; *iem. een ~ toewerpen* blow s.o. a kiss; *~jes!* (lots of) love (and kisses)

het **kushandje** /kʏshɑncə/ (pl: -s) a blown kiss: *~s geven* blow kisses (to s.o.)

het ¹**kussen** /kʏsə(n)/ (pl: -s) cushion; pillow; pad: *de ~s (op)schudden* plump up the pillows

²**kussen** /kʏsə(n)/ (kuste, heeft gekust) kiss: *iem. gedag (vaarwel)* ~ kiss s.o. goodbye; *elkaar* ~ kiss (each other)

het/de **kussensloop** /kʏsə(n)slop/ (pl: -slopen) pillowcase, pillowslip

de **kust** /kʏst/ (pl: -en) **1** coast, (sea)shore: *de* ~ *is veilig* the coast is clear; *een huisje aan de* ~ a cottage by the sea; *onder (voor) de* ~ off the coast, offshore; *inshore*; *vijftig kilometer uit de* ~ fifty kilometres offshore (*or:* off the coast) **2** seaside

het **kustgebied** /kʏstχəbit/ (pl: -en) coastal area (*or:* region)

de **kustlijn** /kʏstlɛin/ (pl: -en) coastline, shoreline

de **kustplaats** /kʏstplats/ (pl: -en) seaside town, coastal town

de **kuststreek** /kʏ(st)strek/ coastal region

de **kuststrook** /kʏ(st)strok/ coastal strip

de **kustvaarder** /kʏstfardər/ (pl: -s) coaster

de **kustwacht** /kʏstwɑχt/ coast guard (service)

de ¹**kut** /kʏt/ (pl: -ten) [vulg] cunt

²**kut** /kʏt/ (adj): [inform] *het ~te is, dat ...* the shitty thing is that ...

³**kut** /kʏt/ (int) [vulg] fuck!, fucking hell!

kutten /kʏtə(n)/ (kutte, heeft gekut) [inform] **1** be a pain in the neck: *hij loopt weer te* ~ he's being a pain in the neck again **2** struggle, mess: *ik ben al tien minuten met dit slot aan het* ~ I've been struggling (*or:* messing) with this lock for the last ten minutes

de **kuub** /kyp/ cubic metre: *te koop voor een tientje de* ~ on sale for ten euros a cubic metre

de **kuur** /kyr/ (pl: kuren) cure, course of treatment

het **kuuroord** /kyrort/ (pl: -en) health resort; spa

het ¹**kwaad** /kwat/ (pl: kwaden) **1** wrong, harm: *een noodzakelijk* ~ a necessary evil; *van* ~ *tot erger vervallen* go from bad to worse **2** harm, damage: *meer ~ dan goed doen* do more harm than good; *dat kan geen* ~ it can't do any harm

²**kwaad** /kwat/ (adj) bad; vicious: ~ *bloed zetten* breed (*or:* create) bad blood; *hij is de ~ste niet* he's not a bad guy

³**kwaad** /kwat/ (adj, adv) **1** bad, wrong: *het te* ~ *krijgen* be overcome (by); break down **2** bad; evil: *ze bedoelde er niets ~s mee* she meant no harm (*or:* offence) **3** angry: *zich ~ maken,* ~ *worden* get angry; *iem.* ~ *maken* make s.o. angry; ~ *zijn op iem.* be angry at (*or:* with) s.o.; ~ *zijn om iets* be angry at (*or:* about) sth.

kwaadaardig /kwatardəχ/ (adj, adv) **1** malicious; vicious **2** pernicious; malignant

kwaaddenkend /kwadɛnkənt/ (adj) suspicious

de **kwaadheid** /kwathɛit/ anger: *rood worden van* ~ turn red with anger (*or:* fury)

kwaadschiks /kwatsχɪks/ (adv) unwillingly

kwaadspreken /kwatsprekə(n)/ (sprak kwaad, heeft kwaadgesproken) speak ill (*or:* badly): ~ *van (iem.)* speak ill (*or:* badly) of (s.o.); slander (s.o.)

kwaadwillig /kwatwɪləχ/ (adj) malevolent

de **kwaal** /kwal/ (pl: kwalen) **1** complaint, disease, illness: *een hartkwaal* a heart condition **2** trouble, problem

de **kwab** /kwɑp/ (pl: -ben) (roll of) fat (*or:* flab), jowl het **kwadraat** /kwɑdra̱t/ (pl: kwadraten) square: *drie ~* three squared

kwadratisch /kwɑdra̱tis/ (adj) quadratic

de **kwajongen** /kwajɔ̱ŋə(n)/ (pl: -s) **1** mischievous boy, naughty boy, brat **2** rascal

kwajongensachtig /kwajɔ̱ŋənsɑxtəx/ (adj, adv) boyish, mischievous

de **kwajongensstreek** /kwajɔ̱ŋə(n)strek/ (pl: -streken) (boyish) prank, practical joke: *een ~ uithalen* play a practical joke

de **kwak** /kwɑk/ (pl: -ken) **1** dab; blob; dollop: *een ~ eten* a dollop of food **2** thud, thump, smack

kwaken /kwa̱kə(n)/ (kwaakte, heeft gekwaakt) quack; croak

de **kwakkel** /kwɑ̱kəl/ (pl: -s) [Belg] canard, unfounded rumour (*or:* story)

kwakkelen /kwɑ̱kələ(n)/ (kwakkelde, heeft gekwakkeld) drag on; linger; be fitful

het **kwakkelweer** /kwɑ̱kəlwer/ unsteady weather, changeable weather

¹kwakken /kwɑ̱kə(n)/ (kwakte, is gekwakt) bump, crash, fall with a thud: *hij kwakte tegen de grond* he landed with a thud on the floor

²kwakken /kwɑ̱kə(n)/ (kwakte, heeft gekwakt) dump, chuck; dab: *zij kwakte haar tas op het bureau* she smacked her bag down on the desk

de **kwakzalver** /kwɑ̱ksɑlvər/ (pl: -s) quack (doctor)

de **kwakzalverij** /kwɑksɑlvəri̱/ quackery

de **kwal** /kwɑl/ (pl: -len) **1** jellyfish **2** jerk

de **kwalificatie** /kwalifika̱(t)si/ (pl: -s) qualification(s)

de **kwalificatiewedstrijd** /kwalifika̱(t)siwɛtstrɛit/ (pl: -en) qualifying match

¹kwalificeren /kwalifise̱rə(n)/ (kwalificeerde, heeft gekwalificeerd) **1** call, describe as **2** qualify

zich **²kwalificeren** /kwalifise̱rə(n)/ (kwalificeerde zich, heeft zich gekwalificeerd) qualify (for)

kwalijk /kwa̱lək/ (adj, adv) evil, vile, nasty; vilely; nastily, badly: *de ~e gevolgen van het roken* the bad (*or:* detrimental) effects of smoking; *dat is een ~e zaak* that is a nasty business ‖ *neem me niet ~, dat ik te laat ben* excuse my being late, excuse me for being late; *neem(t) (u) mij niet ~* I beg your pardon; *iem. iets ~ nemen* blame s.o. for sth.; *je kunt hem dat toch niet ~ nemen* you can hardly blame him

kwalitatief /kwalitati̱f/ (adj, adv) qualitative: *een ~ verschil* a difference in quality

de **kwaliteit** /kwalite̱it/ (pl: -en) **1** quality: *~ leveren* deliver a quality product; *hout van slechte ~* low-quality wood; *van slechte ~* (of) poor quality **2** characteristic

de **kwaliteitsgarantie** /kwalitɛ̱itsxarɑn(t)si/ guarantee, warranty of quality

kwantificeren /kwɑntifise̱rə(n)/ (kwantificeerde, heeft gekwantificeerd) quantify

de **kwantiteit** /kwɑntitɛ̱it/ (pl: -en) quantity, amount

het **kwantum** /kwɑ̱ntʏm/ (pl: -s) quantum

de **kwantumkorting** /kwɑ̱ntʏmkɔrtɪŋ/ quantity rebate

de **kwantumtheorie** /kwɑ̱ntʏmtejori/ quantum theory

de **kwark** /kwɑrk/ fromage frais, curd cheese

de **kwarktaart** /kwɑ̱rktart/ (pl: -en) [roughly] cheesecake

het **kwart** /kwɑrt/ (pl: -en) quarter: *voor een ~ leeg* a quarter empty; *het is ~ voor* (*or:* over) *elf* it is a quarter to (*or:* past) eleven; *het is ten forty-five* (*or:* eleven fifteen)

het **kwartaal** /kwɑrta̱l/ (pl: kwartalen) quarter, trimester; [educ] term: *(eenmaal) per ~* quarterly

de **kwartaalcijfers** /kwɑrta̱lsɛifərs/ (pl) quarterly balance

de **kwartel** /kwɑ̱rtəl/ (pl: -s) quail: *zo doof als een ~* as deaf as a post

het **kwartet** /kwɑrtɛ̱t/ (pl: -ten) quartet: *een ~ voor strijkers* a string quartet

het **kwartetspel** /kwɑrtɛ̱tspɛl/ (pl: -en) happy families; [Am] old maid

kwartetten /kwɑrtɛ̱tə(n)/ (kwartette, heeft gekwartet) play happy families; [Am] play old maid

de **kwartfinale** /kwɑ̱rtfinalə/ (pl: -s) quarter-finals: *de ~ halen* make the quarter-finals

de **kwartfinalist** /kwɑ̱rtfinalɪst/ quarter-finalist

het **kwartier** /kwɑrti̱r/ (pl: -en) quarter (of an hour): *het duurde een ~* **a)** it took a quarter of an hour; **b)** it lasted a quarter of an hour; *om het ~* every quarter (of an hour) of an hour; *drie ~* three-quarters of an hour

het **kwartje** /kwɑ̱rcə/ (pl: -s) [Dutch] 25-cent piece; [Am] quarter: *het kost twee ~s* it costs fifty cents; *het ~ is gevallen* the penny has dropped, it's finally clicked

de **kwartnoot** /kwɑrtnot/ (pl: -noten) crotchet; [Am] quarter note

het **kwarts** /kwɑrts/ quartz

de **kwartslag** /kwɑ̱rtslɑx/ (pl: -en) quarter (of a) turn

de **kwast** /kwɑst/ (pl: -en) **1** brush **2** tassel; [small] tuft: *met ~en (versierd)* tasselled **3** (lemon) squash, lemonade

de **kwatong** /kwa̱tɔŋ/ (pl: -en) [Belg] scandalmonger: *~en beweren …* it is rumoured that …

het **kwatrijn** /kwatrɛ̱in/ (pl: -en) quatrain

de **kwebbel** /kwɛ̱bəl/ chatterbox ‖ *houd je ~ dicht* shut your trap

kwebbelen /kwɛ̱bələ(n)/ (kwebbelde, heeft gekwebbeld) chatter

de **kweek** /kwek/ **1** cultivation; culture; growing **2** culture, growth: *eigen ~* homegrown

(players)

de **kweekplaats** /kwe̯kplats/ (pl: -en) **1** nursery; [fig also] breeding ground **2** [fig] hotbed

de **kweekvijver** /kwe̯kfɛivər/ (pl: -s) fishbreeding pond; [fig] breeding ground

de **kweepeer** /kwe̯per/ (pl: -peren) quince

kweken /kwe̯kə(n)/ (kweekte, heeft gekweekt) **1** grow, cultivate: *gekweekte planten* cultivated plants; *zelf gekweekte tomaten* home-grown tomatoes **2** raise, breed: *oesters* ~ breed oysters **3** [fig] breed, foster: *goodwill* ~ foster goodwill

de **kweker** /kwe̯kər/ (pl: -s) grower; (market) gardener; nurseryman

de **kwekerij** /kwekərɛi/ (pl: -en) nursery; market garden

kwekken /kwe̯kə(n)/ (kwekte, heeft gekwekt) chatter, jabber

de **kwelgeest** /kwe̯lɣest/ (pl: -en) tormentor, teaser, pest

kwellen /kwe̯lə(n)/ (kwelde, heeft gekweld) **1** hurt; [stronger] torment; torture **2** torment: *gekweld worden door geldgebrek* be troubled by lack of money; *een ~de pijn* an excruciating pain **3** trouble, worry: *die gedachte bleef hem* ~ the thought kept troubling him; *gekweld door wroeging* (or: *een obsessie*) haunted by remorse (or: by an obsession)

de **kwelling** /kwe̯lɪŋ/ (pl: -en) **1** torture, torment **2** torment, agony: *een brief schrijven is een ware ~ voor hem* writing a letter is sheer torment for him

het **kwelwater** /kwe̯lwatər/ seepage (water)

de **kwestie** /kwe̯sti/ (pl: -s) question, matter; issue: *een netelige ~* a delicate question (or: matter); *een slepende ~* a matter that drags on; *de persoon* (or: *de zaak*) *in ~* the person (or: matter) in question; *een ~ van smaak* a question (or: matter) of taste; *een ~ van vertrouwen* a matter of confidence

kwetsbaar /kwe̯tsbar/ (adj) vulnerable: *dit is zijn kwetsbare plek* (or: *zijde*) this is his vulnerable spot (or: side)

de **kwetsbaarheid** /kwe̯tsbarhɛit/ vulnerability

kwetsen /kwe̯tsə(n)/ (kwetste, heeft gekwetst) injure, wound, hurt, bruise: *iemands gevoelens* ~ hurt s.o.'s feelings; *gekwetste trots* wounded pride

de **kwetsuur** /kwe̯tsyr/ (pl: kwetsuren) injury

kwetteren /kwe̯tərə(n)/ (kwetterde, heeft gekwetterd) twitter

de **kwibus** /kwi̯bʏs/ (pl: -sen) joker: *een rare ~* a weird chap (or: customer)

kwiek /kwik/ (adj, adv) alert, spry

het/de **kwijl** /kwɛil/ slobber

kwijlen /kwɛi̯lə(n)/ (kwijlde, heeft gekwijld) slobber: *om van te ~* mouth-watering

kwijnen /kwɛi̯nə(n)/ (kwijnde, heeft ge-

kwijnd): *een ~d bestaan leiden* linger on

kwijt /kwɛit/ (adj) **1** lost: *ik ben mijn sleutels* ~ I have lost my keys; *zijn verstand ~ zijn* have lost one's mind **2** rid (of): *ik ben mijn kiespijn* ~ my toothache is gone (or: over); *hij is al die zorgen* ~ he is rid of all those troubles; *die zijn we gelukkig* ~ we are well rid of him, good riddance to him **3** deprived (of): *ik ben zijn naam* ~ I've forgotten his name; [fig] *nu ben ik het* ~ it has slipped my memory; *de weg ~ zijn* be lost, have lost one's way || *ik kan mijn auto nergens* ~ I can't park my car anywhere

zich **kwijten** /kwɛi̯tə(n)/ (kweet zich, heeft zich gekweten): *zich van zijn taak* ~ acquit o.s. of one's task

kwijtraken /kwɛi̯trakə(n)/ (raakte kwijt, is kwijtgeraakt) **1** lose: *zijn evenwicht* ~ [also fig] lose one's balance (or: composure); *de weg* ~ lose one's way **2** dispose of, sell: *die zul je makkelijk* ~ you will easily dispose (or: get rid) of those

kwijtschelden /kwɛi̯tsxɛldə(n)/ (schold kwijt, heeft kwijtgescholden) forgive, let off: *hij heeft mij de rest kwijtgescholden* he has let me off the rest; *van zijn straf is (hem) 2 jaar kwijtgescholden* he had 2 years of his punishment remitted; *iem. een straf* ~ let s.o. off a punishment

het **kwik** /kwɪk/ mercury: *het ~ stijgt* (or: *daalt*) the thermometer is rising (or: falling)

de **kwikstaart** /kwɪkstart/ (pl: -en) wagtail

het **kwikzilver** /kwɪksɪlvər/ mercury

de **kwinkslag** /kwɪŋkslɑx/ (pl: -en) witticism

het **kwintet** /kwɪntɛt/ (pl: -ten) quintet

kwispelen /kwɪspələ(n)/ (kwispelde, heeft gekwispeld) wag: *met de staart* ~ wag one's tail

kwistig /kwɪstəx/ (adj, adv) lavish

de **kwitantie** /kwitɑnsi/ (pl: -s) receipt || *een ~ innen* collect payment

I

de **l** /ɛl/ (pl: l's) l, L
de **¹la** /la/ (pl: la's) [mus] la
de **²la** /la/ (pl: la's) drawer; till: *de la uittrekken* (or: *dichtschuiven*) open (*or:* shut) a drawer
de **laadbak** /ladbɑk/ (pl: -ken) (loading) platform
de **laadpaal** /latpal/ (pl: -palen) charging point; EV charging station
het **laadpunt** /latpʏnt/ (pl: -en) **1** charging station, charging point **2** smart card charging machine
het **laadruim** /latrœym/ (pl: -en) cargo hold; cargo compartment, freight compartment
het **laadvermogen** /latfərmoɣə(n)/ carrying capacity
de **¹laag** /laɣ/ (pl: lagen) **1** layer; coating; film; sheet; coat **2** stratum: *in brede lagen van de bevolking* in large sections of the population || *de volle ~ krijgen* get the full blast (of s.o.'s disapproval)
²laag /laɣ/ (adj, adv) **1** low: *een ~ bedrag* a small amount; *het gas ~ draaien* turn the gas down; *de barometer stond ~* the barometer was low **2** low, mean
laag-bij-de-gronds /laɣbɛidəɣrɔnts/ (adj, adv) commonplace: *~e opmerkingen* crude remarks
de **laagbouw** /laɣbɑu/ low-rise building
laagdrempelig /laɣdrɛmpələɣ/ (adj) **1** approachable, get-at-able, (easily) accessible **2** accessible
laaggeletterd /laɣɣəlɛtərt/ (adj) functionally illiterate
de **laaggeletterdheid** /laɣɣəlɛtərthɛit/ functional illiteracy
laaggeschoold /laɣɣəsxolt/ (adj) semiskilled: *~ werk* unskilled work
laaghartig /laɣhɑrtəɣ/ (adj, adv) mean, low
het **laagseizoen** /laxsɛizun/ (pl: -en) low season, off season
laagstaand /laɣstant/ (adj) low-lying: *~e zon* low sun
de **laagte** /laɣtə/ (pl: -n, -s) depression; hollow
de **laagvlakte** /laɣflɑktə/ (pl: -n, -s) lowland plain, lowland(s)
laagvliegen /laɣfliɣə(n)/ fly low, hedgehop
het **laagwater** /laɣwatər/ low tide
laaien /lajə(n)/ (laaide, heeft gelaaid) blaze
laaiend /lajənt/ (adj, adv) **1** wild: *~ enthousiast zijn over iets* be wildly enthusiastic about sth. **2** furious
laakbaar /lagbar/ (adj, adv) reprehensible

de **laan** /lan/ (pl: lanen) avenue: *iem. de ~ uitsturen* sack s.o., fire s.o.; send s.o. packing
de **laars** /lars/ (pl: laarzen) boot
laat /lat/ (adj, adv) late: *van de vroege morgen tot de late avond* from early in the morning till late at night; *een wat late reactie* a rather belated reaction; *is het nog ~ geworden gisteravond?* did the people stay late last night?; *het ~ maken* keep late hours, make a (late) night of it; *~ opblijven* stay up late; *gisteravond ~* late last night; *hoe ~ is het?* what's the time?, what time is it?; *'s avonds ~* late at night; *te ~ komen (op school, op kantoor, op je werk)* be late (for school, at the office, for work); *een dag te ~* a day late (*or:* overdue); *~ in de middag* (or: *het voorjaar*) in the late afternoon (*or:* spring); *beter ~ dan nooit* better late than never; [fig] *is het weer zo ~?* here we go again!
de **laatbloeier** /ladblujər/ (pl: -s) late-bloomer
laatdunkend /ladʏŋkənt/ (adj, adv) conceited, condescending: *zich ~ uitlaten over iem.* be condescending about s.o.
de **laatkomer** /latkomər/ (pl: -s) latecomer
¹laatst /latst/ (adj) **1** last: *dat zou het ~e zijn wat ik zou doen* that is the last thing I would do **2** latest, last: *in de ~e jaren* in the last few years, in recent years; *de ~e tijd* recently, lately **3** final, last: *voor de ~e keer optreden* make one's last (*or:* final) appearance **4** latter: *in de ~e helft van juli* in the latter (*or:* second) half of July; *ik heb voorkeur voor de ~e* I prefer the latter
²laatst /latst/ (adv) **1** recently, lately: *ik ben ~ nog bij hem geweest* I visited him recently **2** last: *morgen op zijn ~* tomorrow at the latest; *op het ~ waren ze allemaal dronken* they all ended up drunk; *voor het ~* for the last time; *toen zag hij haar voor het ~* that was the last time he saw her
de **laatstgenoemde** /latstɣənumdə/ last (named, mentioned); latter
laattijdig /latɛidəɣ/ (adj, adv) [Belg] tardy, tardily
het **lab** /lɑp/ (pl: -s) lab
het/de **label** /lebəl/ (pl: -s) label; sticker; address tag
labelen /lebələ(n)/ (labelde, heeft gelabeld) label
het **labeur** /labør/ [Belg] labour, chore
labeuren /labørə(n)/ [Belg] slave away, toil
labiel /labil/ (adj) unstable
het **labo** /labo/ (pl: -'s) [Belg] lab
de **laborant** /laborɑnt/ (pl: -en) laboratory assistant (*or:* technician)
het **laboratorium** /laboratorijʏm/ (pl: laboratoria) lab(oratory)
de **labradoedel** /labradudəl/ (pl: -s) labradoodle
de **labrador** /labrador/ Labrador
het **labyrint** /labirɪnt/ (pl: -en) labyrinth
de **lach** /lɑx/ laugh, (burst of) laughter: *de slap-*

pe ~ *hebben* have the giggles; *in* de ~ *schieten* burst out laughing; [Am also] crack up

de **lachbui** /lɑχbœy/ (pl: -en) fit of laughter
lachen /lɑχə(n)/ (lachte, heeft gelachen) **1** laugh; smile: *iem.* **aan** *het* ~ *maken* make s.o. laugh; *hij kon zijn* ~ *niet* **inhouden** he couldn't help laughing; *laat me niet* ~ don't make me laugh; *er* **is (valt)** *niets te* ~ this is no laughing matter; *om* (or: *over*) *iets* ~ laugh about (or: at); *tegen iem.* ~ laugh at s.o.; *wie het laatst lacht, lacht het best* he who laughs last laughs longest **2** (+ om) laugh at: *daar kun je nu wel* **om** ~, *maar ...* it's all very well to laugh, but ...
lachend /lɑχənt/ (adj) laughing, smiling

de **lacher** /lɑχər/ (pl: -s) laugher
lacherig /lɑχərəχ/ (adj) giggly

het **lachertje** /lɑχərcə/ (pl: -s) laugh, joke

de **lachfilm** /lɑχfɪlm/ (pl: -s) comedy

het **lachgas** /lɑχɑs/ laughing gas

het **lachsalvo** /lɑχsɑlvo/ (pl: -'s) burst of laughter

de **lachspiegel** /lɑχspiɣəl/ (pl: -s) carnival mirror

de **lachspier** /lɑχspir/ (pl: -en): *op* de ~*en werken* get s.o. laughing
lachwekkend /lɑχwɛkənt/ (adj) laughable; ridiculous
laconiek /lakonik/ (adj, adv) laconic

de **lacune** /lakynə/ (pl: -s) gap

de **ladder** /lɑdər/ (pl: -s) ladder, scale || *een* ~ *in je kous* a run (or: ladder) in your stocking

de **ladderwagen** /lɑdərwaɣə(n)/ (pl: -s) ladder truck
ladderzat /lɑdərzɑt/ (adj) smashed, blind drunk

de **lade** /lɑdə/ (pl: -n, -s) drawer; till

de **ladekast** /lɑdəkɑst/ (pl: -en) chest (of drawers); filing cabinet
laden /lɑdə(n)/ (laadde, heeft geladen) **1** load: ~ *en lossen* loading (and unloading); *koffers* **uit** *de auto* ~ unload the bags from the car **2** charge: *een geladen* **atmosfeer** a charged atmosphere

de **lader** /lɑdər/ (pl: -s) charger

de **lading** /lɑdɪŋ/ (pl: -en) **1** cargo; [ship] load: *te zware* ~ overload **2** charge

de **ladyshave** /lɛdiʃef/ (pl: -s) ladyshave, women's shaver
laf /lɑf/ (adj, adv) cowardly

de **lafaard** /lɑfart/ (pl: -s) coward
lafhartig /lɑfhɑrtəχ/ (adj, adv) see *laf*

de **lafheid** /lɑfhɛit/ (pl: -heden) cowardice

het **lagedrukgebied** /laɣədrykχəbit/ (pl: -en) low-pressure area

het **lagelonenland** /laɣəlonə(n)lɑnt/ low-wage country

het **lager** /laɣər/ (pl: -s) bearing

het **Lagerhuis** /laɣərhœys/ Lower House; [Great Britain and Canada] House of Commons

de **lagerwal** /laχərwɑl/ lee shore: *aan* ~ *raken*

come down in the world, go to seed

de **lagune** /laɣynə/ (pl: -s) lagoon

het/de **lak** /lɑk/ (pl: -ken) lacquer, varnish; polish: *de* ~ *is beschadigd* the paintwork is damaged || *daar* **heb** *ik* ~ *aan* I couldn't care less

de **lakei** /lakɛi/ (pl: -en) lackey

het **laken** /lɑkə(n)/ (pl: -s) **1** sheet; tablecloth: [fig] *de* ~*s* **uitdelen** rule the roost, run the show **2** cloth, worsted: *het* ~ *van een* **biljart** the cloth of a billiard table || [Dutch] *van hetzelfde* ~ *een* **pak** *krijgen*, [Belg] *van hetzelfde* ~ *een* **broek** *krijgen* have a taste of one's own medicine
lakken /lɑkə(n)/ (lakte, heeft gelakt) **1** lacquer, varnish; polish **2** paint, enamel

de **lakmoesproef** /lɑkmuspruf/ (pl: -proeven) [also fig] litmus test
laks /lɑks/ (adj, adv) lax

het **lakwerk** /lɑkwɛrk/ paint(work)
lallen /lɑlə(n)/ (lalde, heeft gelald) slur one's words

het **¹lam** /lɑm/ (pl: lammeren) lamb
²lam /lɑm/ (adj, adv) **1** paralysed; [fig also] out of action **2** numb

de **lama** /lɑma/ (pl: -'s) llama

de **lambrisering** /lambrizerɪŋ/ (pl: -en) wainscot(t)ing, panelling

de **lamel** /lamɛl/ (pl: -len) plate, (laminated) layer; strip

de **lamheid** /lɑmhɛit/: *met* ~ *geslagen zijn* be struck dumb

het **laminaat** /laminat/ (pl: laminaten) laminate
lamleggen /lɑmlɛɣə(n)/ (legde lam, heeft lamgelegd) paralyse: *het* **verkeer** ~ bring the traffic to a standstill
lamlendig /lɑmlɛndəχ/ (adj, adv) shiftless

de **lamp** /lɑmp/ (pl: -en) lamp, light; bulb: *er gaat een* ~*je bij mij* **branden** that rings a bell; *tegen de* ~ *lopen* get caught

de **lampion** /lampijɔn/ (pl: -s, -nen) Chinese lantern

het **lamsvlees** /lɑmsfles/ lamb

de **lamswol** /lɑmswɔl/ lambswool

de **lanceerbasis** /lɑnserbazɪs/ (pl: -bases) launch site, launch pad

het **lanceerplatform** /lɑnserplɑtfɔrm/ (pl: -s) launching site
lanceren /lɑnserə(n)/ (lanceerde, heeft gelanceerd) launch; blast, lift off: *een* **bericht** (or: *een* **gerucht**) ~ spread a report (or: a rumour)

de **lancering** /lɑnserɪŋ/ (pl: -en) launch(ing); blast-off, lift-off

het **lancet** /lɑnsɛt/ (pl: -ten) lancet

het **land** /lɑnt/ (pl: -en) **1** land: *aan* ~ *gaan* go ashore; *te* ~ *en ter zee* on land and sea; ~ *in zicht!* land ho! **2** country: ~ *van* **herkomst** country of origin; *in ons* ~ in this country; *het* **beloofde** ~ the Promised Land; *de* **Lage** *Landen* the Low Countries; *veilige* ~*en* safe countries || *er is met hem geen* ~ *te* **bezeilen** you won't get anywhere with him, you're wasting your time with him

de **landarbeider** /lɑntɑrbɛidər/ (pl: -s) farm worker, agricultural worker

de **landbouw** /lɑndbɑu/ farming; ~ en veeteelt a) arable farming and stockbreeding; b) arable and dairy farming

het **landbouwbedrijf** /lɑndbɑubədrɛif/ (pl: -bedrijven) farm

het **landbouwbeleid** /lɑndbɑubəlɛit/ agricultural policy

de **landbouwer** /lɑndbɑuwər/ (pl: -s) farmer

de **landbouwgrond** /lɑndbɑuɣront/ (pl: -en) agricultural land, farming land, farmland

landbouwkundig /lɑndbɑukʏndəɣ/ (adj) agricultural

de **landbouwmachine** /lɑndbɑumɑʃinə/ (pl: -s) agricultural machine, farming machine

de **landbouwuniversiteit** /lɑndbɑuwynivɛrzitɛit/ (pl: -universiteiten) [Dutch] agricultural university; [as a name] University of Agriculture

de **landeigenaar** /lɑntɛiɣənɑr/ (pl: -s, -eigenaren) landowner

landelijk /lɑndələk/ (adj, adv) **1** national **2** rural, country

landen /lɑndə(n)/ (landde, is geland) land: ~ op Zaventem land at Zaventem

de **landengte** /lɑntɛŋtə/ (pl: -n, -s) isthmus, neck of land

de **landenwedstrijd** /lɑndə(n)wɛtstrɛit/ (pl: -en) international match (or: contest)

landerig /lɑndərəɣ/ (adj) down in the dumps, listless

de **landerijen** /lɑndərɛiə(n)/ (pl) (farm)land(s)

de **landgenoot** /lɑntɣənot/ (pl: -genoten) (fellow) countryman

het **landgoed** /lɑntɣut/ (pl: -eren) country estate

het **landhuis** /lɑnthœys/ (pl: -huizen) country house

de **landing** /lɑndɪŋ/ (pl: -en) landing: een zachte ~ a smooth landing

de **landingsbaan** /lɑndɪŋzban/ (pl: -banen) runway

het **landingsgestel** /lɑndɪŋsxəstɛl/ (pl: -len) landing gear, undercart

de **landingstroepen** /lɑndɪŋstrupə(n)/ (pl) landing force(s)

het **landingsvaartuig** /lɑndɪŋsfartœyx/ (pl: -en) landing craft

landinwaarts /lɑntɪnwarts/ (adv) inland

de **landkaart** /lɑntkart/ (pl: -en) map

het **landklimaat** /lɑntklimat/ continental climate

de **landloper** /lɑntlopər/ (pl: -s) tramp, vagrant

de **landmacht** /lɑntmɑxt/ army, land forces

het **landmark** /lɛntmɑːrk/ landmark

de **landmeter** /lɑntmetər/ (pl: -s) (land) surveyor

de **landmijn** /lɑntmɛin/ (pl: -en) landmine

het **landnummer** /lɑntnʏmər/ (pl: -s) international (dialling) code

de **landrot** /lɑntrɔt/ (pl: -ten) landlubber

het **landsbelang** /lɑn(t)sbəlɑŋ/ (pl: -en) national interest: iets doen in het ~ do sth. in the national interest

het **landschap** /lɑntsxɑp/ (pl: -pen) landscape

de **landsgrens** /lɑn(t)sxrɛns/ (pl: -grenzen) border

de **landskampioen** /lɑn(t)skɑmpijun/ (pl: -en) national champion

de **landstreek** /lɑntstrek/ (pl: -streken) region, district

de **landsverdediging** /lɑntsfərdedəɣɪŋ/ [Belg] defence

de **landtong** /lɑntɔŋ/ (pl: -en) spit of land, headland

het **landverraad** /lɑntfərat/ (high) treason

de **landverrader** /lɑntfəradər/ (pl: -s) traitor (to one's country)

de **landweg** /lɑntwɛx/ (pl: -en) country road lane; (country) track

de **landwijn** /lɑntwɛin/ (pl: -en) local wine

de **landwind** /lɑntwɪnt/ land wind

de **landwinning** /lɑntwɪnɪŋ/ (pl: -en) land reclamation

¹**lang** /lɑŋ/ (adj) long; tall: de kamer is zes meter ~ the room is six metres long; een ~e vent a tall guy

²**lang** /lɑŋ/ (adv) **1** long, (for) a long time: ik blijf geen dag ~er I won't stay another day, I won't stay a day longer; ~ duren take a long time, last long (or: a long time); ~ geleden long ago; ze leefden ~ en gelukkig they lived happily ever after; ~ zal hij leven! for he's a jolly good fellow!; ~ meegaan last (a long time); ~ opblijven stay up late; ze kan niet ~er wachten she can't wait any longer (or: more); dat kan zo niet ~er things can't go on like this **2** far (from), (not) nearly: dat smaakt ~ niet slecht it doesn't taste at all bad; hij is nog ~ niet zover he hasn't got nearly as far as that; wij zijn er nog ~ niet we've (still got) a long way to go; bij ~e na niet far from it ‖ we hebben het er ~ en breed over gehad we've talked about it at great length

langdradig /lɑŋdradəɣ/ (adj, adv) long-winded

langdurig /lɑŋdyrəɣ/ (adj, adv) long(-lasting), lengthy; long-standing, long-established

de **langeafstandsraket** /lɑŋəɣfstɑn(t)srakɛt/ (pl: -ten) long-range missile

de **langeafstandsvlucht** /lɑŋəɣfstɑn(t)sflʏxt/ (pl: -en) long-distance flight

het **langetermijngeheugen** /lɑŋətɛrmɛinɣəhøɣə(n)/ long-term memory

langgerekt /lɑŋɣərɛkt/ (adj) long-drawn-out, elongated

langlaufen /lɑŋlɑufə(n)/ (langlaufte, heeft is gelanglauft) ski cross-country

langlopend /lɑŋlopənt/ (adj) long-term

de **langoustine** /lɑŋgustinə/ (pl: -s) langoustine

¹**langs** /lɑŋs/ (adv) **1** along: *in een boot de kust ~ varen* sail along the coast, skirt the coast **2** round, in, by: *ik kom nog weleens ~* I'll drop in (*or:* round, by) sometime **3** past: *hij kwam net ~* he just came past || *ervan ~ krijgen* catch it

²**langs** /lɑŋs/ (prep) **1** along: *~ de rivier wandelen* go for a walk along the river **2** via, by (way, means of): *~ de regenpijp naar omlaag* down the drainpipe; *hier* (or: *daar*) *~ this* (*or:* that) way **3** past: *~ elkaar heen praten* talk at cross purposes **4** in at: *wil jij even ~ de bakker rijden?* could you just drop in at the bakery?

langsgaan /lɑŋsxan/ (ging langs, is langsgegaan) **1** pass (by) **2** call in (at)

langskomen /lɑŋskomə(n)/ (kwam langs, is langsgekomen) **1** come past, come by, pass by **2** come round (*or:* over), drop by, drop in

de **langslaper** /lɑŋslapər/ (pl: -s) late riser

de **langspeelplaat** /lɑŋspelplat/ (pl: -platen) long-playing record, LP

langsrijden /lɑŋsrɛidə(n)/ (reed langs, is langsgereden) ride past; drive past

de **langstlevende** /lɑŋstlevəndə/ (pl: -n) survivor

langszij /lɑŋsɛi/ (adv) alongside: *~ komen* **a)** [ship] come alongside; **b)** [sport] equalize

languit /lɑŋœyt/ (adv) (at) full-length, stretched out

langverwacht /lɑŋvərwɑxt/ (adj) long-awaited

langwerpig /lɑŋwɛrpəx/ (adj, adv) elongated, long

langzaam /lɑŋzam/ (adj, adv) **1** slow: *een langzame dood sterven* die a slow (*or:* lingering) death; *~ aan!* slow down!, (take it) easy!; *het ~ aan doen* take things eas(il)y; *~ maar zeker* slowly but surely **2** gradual, bit by bit, little by little: *~ werd hij wat beter* he gradually got a bit better

langzaamaan /lɑŋzaman/ (adv) gradually: *het ~ doen* go slow

de **langzaamaanactie** /lɑŋzamanaksi/ (pl: -s) go-slow

langzamerhand /lɑŋzamərhɑnt/ (adv) gradually, bit by bit, little by little: *ik krijg er ~ genoeg van* I'm beginning to get tired of it

lankmoedig /lɑŋkmudəx/ (adj, adv) long-suffering

de **lans** /lɑns/ (pl: -en) lance

de **lantaarn** /lɑntarn/ (pl: -s) **1** street lamp, street light **2** lantern; torch; [Am] flashlight

de **lantaarnpaal** /lɑntarmpal/ (pl: -palen) lamp post

lanterfanten /lɑntərfɑntə(n)/ (lanterfantte, heeft gelanterfant) lounge (about), loaf (about); sit about (*or:* around)

Laos /laos/ Laos: *Democratische volksrepubliek ~* People's Democratic Republic of Laos

de **Laotiaan** /lao(t)ʃan/ (pl: Laotianen) Laotian
Laotiaans /lao(t)ʃans/ (adj) Laotian

de **lap** /lɑp/ (pl: -pen) piece, length; rag: *een lap grond* a piece of land; *dat werkt op hem als een rode ~ op een stier* that's like a red rag to him

de **Lap** /lɑp/ (pl: -pen) Lapp

het **lapje** /lɑpjə/ (pl: -s): *iem. voor het ~ houden* have s.o. on, pull s.o.'s leg

de **lapjeskat** /lɑpjəskɑt/ (pl: -ten) tabby-and-white cat; [Am] calico cat
Lapland /lɑplɑnt/ Lapland

de **Laplander** /lɑplɑndər/ (pl: -s) Lapp, Laplander
Laplands /lɑplɑn(t)s/ (adj) Lapp(ish)

het **lapmiddel** /lɑpmɪdəl/ makeshift (measure), stopgap
lappen /lɑpə(n)/ (lapte, heeft gelapt) patch, mend; cobble || *ramen ~* cobble the windows; *dat zou jij mij niet moeten ~* don't try that (one) on me; *iem. erbij ~* blow the whistle on s.o.

de **lappendeken** /lɑpə(n)dekə(n)/ (pl: -s) patchwork quilt

de **lappenmand** /lɑpəmɑnt/ (pl: -en): *in de ~ zijn* be laid up, be on the sick list

de **laptop** /lɛptɔp/ laptop (computer)
larderen /lɑrderə(n)/ (lardeerde, heeft gelardeerd) lard; [fig] (inter)lard

de **larie** /lari/ rubbish

de **lariekoek** /larikuk/ (stuff and) nonsense, rubbish

de ¹**lariks** /larɪks/ (pl: -en) [tree] larch

het ²**lariks** /larɪks/ [wood] larch

de **larve** /lɑrvə/ (pl: -n) larva

de **las** /lɑs/ (pl: -sen) weld; joint; [film] splice

de **lasagne** /lazɑnə/ lasagna

het **lasapparaat** /lɑsaparat/ (pl: lasapparaten) welding apparatus, welder; [film] splicer

de **lasbril** /lɑzbrɪl/ (pl: -len) welding goggles

de **laser** /lezər/ (pl: -s) laser

de **laserprinter** /lezərprɪntər/ (pl: -s) laser printer

de **lasershow** /lezərʃo/ laser show

de **laserstraal** /lezərstral/ (pl: -stralen) laser beam

het **laserwapen** /lezərwapə(n)/ laser weapon

de **lasnaad** /lɑsnat/ (pl: -naden) weld

¹**lassen** /lɑsə(n)/ (laste, heeft gelast) weld; join; [film] splice

²**lassen** /lɑsə(n)/ (laste, heeft gelast) put in; [also fig] insert

de **lasser** /lɑsər/ (pl: -s) welder

de **lasso** /lɑso/ (pl: -'s) lasso

de **last** /lɑst/ (pl: -en) **1** load; burden: *hij bezweek haast onder de ~* he nearly collapsed under the burden **2** cost(s), expense(s): *sociale ~en* National Insurance contributions; [Am] social security premiums **3** trouble; inconvenience: *iem. tot ~ zijn* bother s.o.; *wij hebben veel ~ van onze buren* our neighbours are a great nuisance to us **4** charge: *iem. iets ten* ~*e leggen* charge s.o. with sth.

het **lastdier** /lɑstdir/ (pl: -en) beast of burden

de **lastenverlichting** /lɑstə(n)vərlɪχtɪŋ/ (pl: -en) reduction in the tax burden

de **lastenverzwaring** /lɑstə(n)vərzwarɪŋ/ (pl: -en) increase in the tax burden

de **laster** /lɑstər/ slander; libel

de **lastercampagne** /lɑstərkampɑɲə/ (pl: -s) smear campaign

lasteren /lɑstərə(n)/ (lasterde, heeft gelasterd) slander; libel

de **lastgeving** /lɑstχevɪŋ/ (pl: -en) order, instruction(s)

lastig /lɑstəχ/ (adj, adv) difficult: *een ~ vraagstuk* a tricky problem; *een ~ kind* a troublesome (*or:* difficult) child

lastigvallen /lɑstəχfɑlə(n)/ (viel lastig, heeft lastiggevallen) bother, trouble; harass

de ¹**last minute** /lɑːstmɪnɪt/ (pl: -s) last-minute holiday (*or:* break)

²**last minute** /lɑːstmɪnɪt/ (adj) last-minute

de **lastpost** /lɑstpɔst/ (pl: -en) nuisance, pest

de **lat** /lɑt/ (pl: -ten) slat: *zo mager als een ~* (as) thin as a rake; *de bal kwam tegen de ~* the ball hit the crossbar; [fig] *de ~ te hoog leggen* set the bar too high; [Belg; fig] *de ~ gelijk leggen* give everyone the same odds

¹**laten** /lɑtə(n)/ (liet, heeft gelaten) **1** omit, keep from: *laat dat!* stop that!; *hij kan het niet ~* he can't help (doing) it; *laat maar!* never mind! **2** leave, let: *waar heb ik dat potlood gelaten?* where did I leave (*or:* put) that pencil?; *daar zullen we het bij ~!* let's leave it at that! **3** put: *waar moet ik het boek ~?* where shall I put (*or:* leave) the book? **4** let (be): *iem. ~ halen* **a)** send for s.o.; **b)** have s.o. fetched **5** show (into), let (into): *hij werd in de kamer gelaten* he was shown into the room **6** let, allow: *laat de kinderen maar* just let the kids be

²**laten** /lɑtə(n)/ (aux vb, liet, heeft gelaten) let: ~ *we niet vergeten, dat …* don't let us forget that …

latent /latɛnt/ (adj, adv) latent

¹**later** /lɑtər/ (adj) later, subsequent; future: *op ~e leeftijd* at an advanced age, late in life

²**later** /lɑtər/ (adv) later (on), afterwards; presently: *enige tijd ~* after some time (*or:* a while), a little later (on); *even ~* soon after, presently; *niet ~ dan twee uur* no later than two o'clock; *~ op de dag* later that (same) day, later in the day

lateraal /lateral/ (adj) lateral

het **Latijn** /latɛin/ Latin

Latijns-Amerika /latɛinsamerika/ Latin America

Latijns-Amerikaans /latɛinsamerikans/ (adj) Latin-American

de **latrelatie** /lɑtrela(t)si/: *ze hebben een ~* they are living apart together

de **laurier** /lɑurir/ (pl: -en) **1** laurel **2** bay [culinary]

lauw /lɑu/ (adj, adv) lukewarm

de **lauweren** /lɑuwərə(n)/ (pl) laurels: *op zijn ~ rusten* rest on one's laurels

lauwwarm /lɑuwɑrm/ (adj) lukewarm

de **lava** /lava/ (pl: -'s) lava

de **lavabo** /lavabo/ (pl: -'s) [Belg] washbasin

laveloos /lavəlos/ (adj) [inform] sloshed, loaded

laven /lavə(n)/ (laafde, heeft gelaafd): *zich ~ aan* refresh o.s. at

de **lavendel** /lavɛndəl/ lavender

laveren /lavərə(n)/ (laveerde, heeft/is gelaveerd) tack; [fig] steer a middle course

het **lawaai** /lawaj/ noise, din; [stronger] racket

lawaaierig /lawajərəχ/ (adj, adv) noisy

de **lawaaimaker** /lawajmakər/ (pl: -s) noise-maker

de **lawine** /lawinə/ (pl: -s) avalanche; [fig also] barrage

het **lawinegevaar** /lawinəχəvar/ danger of avalanches

het **laxeermiddel** /lɑksermɪdəl/ laxative

laxeren /lɑkserə(n)/ (laxeerde, heeft gelaxeerd) purge: *dat werkt ~d* that is a laxative

het **lazarus** /lazərʏs/: *zich het ~ schrikken* get the shock of one's life

de **lazer** /lazər/ body: *iem. op zijn ~ geven* beat the crap out of s.o.; bawl (*or:* chew) s.o. out

lazeren /lazərə(n)/ [vulg] tumble: *hij lazerde van de trap af* he fell arse over elbow down the stairs

het **lcd-scherm** /ɛlsedɛsχɛrm/ LCD display, LCD screen

de **leaseauto** /liːsɑuto/ (pl: -'s) leased car

leasen /liːsə(n)/ (leasede/leasete, heeft geleased/geleaset) lease

de **lector** /lɛktɔr/ (pl: -en, -s) **1** lecturer **2** [Belg] lector

de **lectuur** /lɛktyr/ reading (matter)

de **ledematen** /ledəmatə(n)/ (pl) limbs

het **ledental** /ledə(n)tal/ (pl: -len) membership (figure)

lederen /ledərə(n)/ (adj) leather

de **lederwaren** /ledərwarə(n)/ (pl) leather goods (*or:* articles)

het **ledikant** /ledikɑnt/ (pl: -en) bed(stead)

de **ledlamp** /lɛtlɑmp/ (pl: -en) LED lamp, LED light

het **leed** /let/ sorrow, grief

het **leedvermaak** /letfərmak/ malicious pleasure

het **leedwezen** /letwezə(n)/ [form]: *tot mijn ~ …* I regret to say …

leefbaar /levbar/ (adj) liveable, bearable; endurable: *een huis ~ maken* make a house inhabitable

de **leefgemeenschap** /lefχəmensχɑp/ (pl: -pen) commune; community

het **leefklimaat** /lefklimat/ social climate

het **leefloon** /lẹflon/ (pl: -lonen) social security; welfare

het **leefmilieu** /lẹfmɪljø/ (pl: -s) environment

de **leeftijd** /lẹftɛit/ (pl: -en) age: *Gerard is op een moeilijke* ~ Gerard is at an awkward age; *hij bereikte de* ~ *van 65 jaar* he lived to be 65; *op vijftienjarige* ~ at the age of (*or*: aged) fifteen; *een man op* ~ an elderly man; *Eric ziet er jong uit voor zijn* ~ Eric looks young for his age; [Belg] *de derde* ~ the elderly; [Am] senior citizens

de **leeftijdgenoot** /lẹftɛitχənot/ (pl: -genoten) contemporary, peer

de **leeftijdsdiscriminatie** /lẹftɛrtzdɪskrimina(t)si/ age discrimination

de **leeftijdsgrens** /lẹftɛitsχrɛns/ (pl: -grenzen) age limit

de **leefwijze** /lẹfwɛizə/ (pl: -n) lifestyle, way of life, manner of living

leeg /leχ/ (adj) 1 empty; vacant; flat; blank: *een lege accu* a flat battery; *met lege handen vertrekken* [fig] leave empty-handed 2 idle, empty 3 [fig] empty, hollow

leegeten /lẹχetə(n)/ (at leeg, heeft leeggegeten) finish, empty: *zijn bord* ~ finish (*or*: empty) one's plate; [fig] *die partij wordt helemaal leeggegeten* the party is losing more and more supporters (to)

het **leeggoed** /lẹχut/ [Belg] empties

leeghalen /lẹχhalə(n)/ (haalde leeg, heeft leeggehaald) empty; clear out [bldg]; turn out; ransack

het **leeghoofd** /lẹχhoft/ (pl: -en) nitwit, empty-headed person

leeglopen /lẹχlopə(n)/ (liep leeg, is leeggelopen) (become) empty; become deflated; go flat; run down

leegmaken /lẹχmakə(n)/ (maakte leeg, heeft leeggemaakt) empty; finish; clear: *zijn zakken* ~ turn out one's pockets

leegstaan /lẹχstan/ (stond leeg, heeft leeggestaan) be empty (*or*: vacant)

de **leegstand** /lẹχstant/ vacancy

de **leegte** /lẹχtə/ (pl: -s, -n) emptiness: *hij liet een grote* ~ *achter* he left a great void (behind him)

de **leek** /lek/ (pl: leken) layman

het/de **leem** /lem/ loam

de **leemte** /lẹmtə/ (pl: -n, -s) gap, blank

het **leen** /len/ (pl: lenen) loan: *iets van iem. te* ~ *hebben* have sth. on loan from s.o.

de **leenheer** /lẹnher/ (pl: -heren) liege (lord)

de **leenman** /lẹman/ (pl: -nen) vassal

het **leenstelsel** /lẹnstɛlsəl/ (pl: -s) 1 feudal system 2 student loan system

leep /lep/ (adj, adv) cunning, canny

de ¹**leer** /ler/ apprenticeship: *in de* ~ *zijn (bij)* serve one's apprenticeship (with)

het ²**leer** /ler/ leather

het **leerboek** /lẹrbuk/ (pl: -en) textbook

de **leergang** /lẹrχaŋ/ (pl: -en) (educational) method, methodology

het **leergeld** /lẹrχɛlt/ (pl: -en) apprenticeship fee: [fig] ~ *betalen* pay one's dues, learn one's lesson

leergierig /lẹrχirəχ/ (adj, adv) inquisitive, eager to learn

het **leerjaar** /lẹrjar/ (pl: -jaren) (school) year: *beroepsvoorbereidend* ~ vocational training year

de **leerkracht** /lẹrkraχt/ (pl: -en) teacher, instructor

de **leerling** /lẹrlɪŋ/ (pl: -en) 1 student, pupil: *de beste* ~ *van de klas* a) top of his (*or*: her) class; b) the best (in) 2 apprentice, trainee: *leerling-verpleegster* trainee nurse

leerlooien /lẹrlojə(n)/ tan

de **leerlooierij** /lerlojərɛi/ (pl: -en) 1 tanning 2 tannery

de **leermeester** /lẹrmestər/ (pl: -s) master

de **leermethode** /lẹrmetodə/ teaching method, training method

het **leermiddelen** /lẹrmɪdələ(n)/ educational aids

het **leerplan** /lẹrplan/ (pl: -nen) syllabus, curriculum

de **leerplicht** /lẹrplɪχt/ compulsory education

leerplichtig /lerplɪχtəχ/ (adj) of school age

leerrijk /lẹrik/ (adj) instructive, informative

de **leerschool** /lẹrsχol/ (pl: -scholen) school: *dat was een goede* ~ *voor hem* that was good training (*or*: experience) for him

de **leerstoel** /lẹrstul/ (pl: -en) chair

de **leerstof** /lẹrstof/ subject matter, (subject) material

het **leertje** /lẹrcə/ (pl: -s) washer

het **leervak** /lẹrvak/ (pl: -ken) subject

de **leerweg** /lẹrwɛχ/ [Dutch] (learning) track, study option: *de basisberoepsgerichte* ~ the basic vocational track; *de gemengde* ~ the combined track; *de kaderberoepsgerichte* ~ the advanced vocational track; *de theoretische* ~ the theoretical track

het **leer-werktraject** /lerwɛrktrajɛkt/ (pl: -en) work study programme

leerzaam /lẹrzam/ (adj, adv) instructive, informative: *een leerzame ervaring* a valuable experience

leesbaar /lẹzbar/ (adj, adv) 1 legible 2 readable

de **leesbevestiging** /lẹzbəvɛstəɣɪŋ/ (pl: -en) read receipt: *om een* ~ *vragen* ask for a read receipt

leesblind /lẹzblɪnt/ (adj) dyslexic

de **leesblindheid** /lẹzblɪntɛit/ dyslexia

het **leesboek** /lẹzbuk/ (pl: -en) reader

de **leesbril** /lẹzbrɪl/ reading glasses

de **leeslamp** /lẹslamp/ (pl: -en) reading lamp

de **leesmoeder** /lẹsmudər/ (pl: -s) (parent) volunteer reading teacher

de **leest** /lest/ (pl: -en) last

het **leesteken** /lẹstekə(n)/ (pl: -s) punctuation

mark
de **leesvaardigheid** /lesf**ɑ**rdəxhɛit/ reading proficiency (or: skill)
het **leesvoer** /l**e**sfur/ something to read
de **leeswijzer** /l**e**swɛizər/ (pl: -s) **1** (book)-mark(er) **2** reader's guide
de **leeszaal** /l**e**sal/ (pl: -zalen) reading room; public library
de **leeuw** /lew/ (pl: -en) lion: *zo sterk als een* ~ as strong as an ox
de **Leeuw** /lew/ (pl: -en) [astrology] Leo
het **leeuwendeel** /l**e**wə(n)del/ lion's share
de **leeuwentemmer** /l**e**wə(n)tɛmər/ (pl: -s) li-on-tamer
de **leeuwerik** /l**e**wərɪk/ (pl: -en) lark
de **leeuwin** /lewɪn/ (pl: -nen) lioness
het/de **lef** /lɛf/ guts, nerve: ~ *hebben* have nerve (or: guts); *heb het* ~ *niet om dat te doen* don't you dare do that
de **lefgozer** /lɛfxozər/ (pl: -s) [inform] hotshot; show-off
de **leg** /lɛx/: *van de* ~ *zijn* have stopped laying; [fig] *tweede* ~ offspring from a second marriage or relationship
legaal /ley**a**l/ (adj, adv) legal
het **legaat** /ley**a**t/ (pl: legaten) legacy
legaliseren /leyaliz**e**rə(n)/ (legaliseerde, heeft gelegaliseerd) legalize
de **legbatterij** /lɛxbɑtərɛi/ (pl: -en) battery (cage)
legen /l**e**yə(n)/ (leegde, heeft geleegd) empty
de **legenda** /ləy**ɛ**nda/ (pl: -'s) legend
legendarisch /leyɛnd**a**ris/ (adj) legendary
de **legende** /ləy**ɛ**ndə/ (pl: -n, -s) legend
het **leger** /l**e**yər/ (pl: -s) **1** army; armed forces: *een* ~ *op de been brengen* raise an army; *in het* ~ *gaan* join the army **2** lair
de **legerbasis** /l**e**yərbazɪs/ (pl: -bases) army base
legeren /l**e**yərə(n)/ (legerde, heeft gelegerd) **1** encamp **2** quarter; billet
legergroen /l**e**yərɣrun/ (adj) olive drab (or: green)
de **legering** /l**e**yərɪŋ/ alloy
de **legermacht** /l**e**yərmɑxt/ (pl: -en) armed forces; army
de **leges** /l**e**yɛs/ (pl) (legal) dues, fees
leggen /l**ɛ**yə(n)/ (legde, heeft gelegd) **1** lay (down); floor: *een kind op bed* ~ put a child to bed **2** lay **3** put: *op volgorde* ~ put in order
de **legger** /l**ɛ**yər/ (pl: -s) [gymnastics] bar: *gelijke* ~*s* parallel bars; *ongelijke* ~*s* asymmetric bars; [Am] uneven bars
de **legging** /l**ɛ**ɡɪŋ/ (pl: -s) leggings
legio /l**e**yijo/ (adj) countless: *hij maakte* ~ *fouten* the errors he made were legion
het **legioen** /leyij**u**n/ (pl: -en) **1** legion **2** supporters
de **legionella** /leyijonɛla/ **1** Legionella pneumophila **2** legionnaires' disease

de **legislatuur** /leyɪslat**y**r/ (pl: legislaturen) **1** (exercise of) legislative power **2** [Belg] term
legitiem /leyit**i**m/ (adj, adv) legitimate
de **legitimatie** /leyitim**a**(t)si/ (pl: -s) identification, proof of identity, ID: *geen geldige* ~ *bij zich hebben* be unable to prove one's identity
het **legitimatiebewijs** /leyitim**a**(t)sibəwɛis/ (pl: -bewijzen) identity papers (or: card); ID
de **legitimatieplicht** /leyitim**a**(t)siplɪxt/ compulsory identification
[1]**legitimeren** /leyitim**e**rə(n)/ (legitimeerde, heeft gelegitimeerd) legitimize, justify: *dat legitimeert nog niet het gebruik van geweld* that doesn't justify the use of violence
zich [2]**legitimeren** /leyitim**e**rə(n)/ (legitimeerde zich, heeft zich gelegitimeerd) identify o.s., prove one's identity
de **legkast** /l**ɛ**xkɑst/ (pl: -en) cupboard (with shelves)
de **legkip** /l**ɛ**xkɪp/ (pl: -pen) laying hen
de **legpuzzel** /l**ɛ**xpyzəl/ (pl: -s) jigsaw (puzzle)
de **leguaan** /leyw**a**n/ (pl: leguanen) iguana
de **lei** /lɛi/ slate: (weer) *met een schone* ~ *beginnen* start again with a clean slate
de **leiband** /l**ɛ**ibɑnt/ (pl: -en) leash: [fig] *hij loopt aan de* ~ *van* ... he's spoonfed by ...
leiden /l**ɛ**idə(n)/ (leidde, heeft geleid) **1** lead, bring, guide: *iem.* ~ *naar* lead (or: steer) s.o. towards; *de nieuwe bezuinigingen zullen ertoe* ~ *dat* ... as a result of the new cutbacks, ...; *de weg leidde ons door het dorpje* the road took (or: led) us through the village; *zij leidde hem door de gangen* she led (or: guided) him through the corridors; *tot niets* ~ lead nowhere **2** manage; conduct; direct: *zich laten* ~ *door* be guided (or: ruled) by **3** [sport] (be in the) lead || *een druk leven* ~ lead a busy life
de **leider** /l**ɛ**idər/ (pl: -s) leader; [com] director; manager; guide
het **leiderschap** /l**ɛ**idərsxɑp/ leadership
de **leiding** /l**ɛ**idɪŋ/ (pl: -en) **1** guidance, direction: *onder zijn bekwame* ~ under his (cap)able leadership; ~ *geven* (aan) direct; lead; manage, run; govern; preside over, chair; *wie heeft er hier de* ~? who's in charge here? **2** direction; management; managers; (board of) directors; leadership: *de* ~ *heeft hier gefaald* the management is at fault here **3** pipe; wire; cable: *elektrische* ~ electric wire (or: cable) **4** lead: *Ajax heeft de* ~ *met 2 tegen 1* Ajax leads 2-1
leidinggeven /l**ɛ**idɪŋyevə(n)/ (+ aan) [work] direct; [team] lead; [business] manage, run; [country, association] govern; [meeting] preside over/chair: *gewend om leiding te geven* used/accustomed to taking control/to managing people; *leiding kunnen geven* have leadership qualities; *ik geef (aan) zestig mensen leiding* I manage a staff of six-

ty, I have sixty people under me

leidinggevend /lɛidɪŋɣevənt/ (adj) executive, managerial: *een ~e **functie** hebben* be in management, have a managerial role

de **leidinggevende** /lɛidɪŋɣevəndə/ (pl: -n) manager, supervisor: *iemands **direct** ~ s.o.'s immediate supervisor*, s.o.'s manager

het **leidingwater** /lɛidɪŋwatər/ tap water

de **leidraad** /lɛidrat/ (pl: leidraden) guide(line)

het **leidsel** /lɛitsəl/ (pl: -s) rein

de **leidsman** /lɛitsman/ (pl: -nen, leidslieden) guide, leader

leien /lɛiə(n)/ (adj) slate

het/de **leisteen** /lɛisten/ slate

het **¹lek** /lɛk/ (pl: -ken) leak(age), puncture; flat: *een ~ **dichten*** stop a leak

²lek /lɛk/ (adj) leaky, punctured; flat: *een ~ke **band** krijgen* get a puncture

de **lekkage** /lɛkaʒə/ (pl: -s) leak(age)

¹lekken /lɛkə(n)/ (lekte, heeft gelekt) **1** leak, be leaking; take in water; drip **2** leak: *informatie ~ **naar** de pers* leak information to the press

²lekken /lɛkə(n)/ (lekte, is gelekt) leak, seep

¹lekker /lɛkər/ (adj) **1** nice, good, tasty; delicious: *ze weet wel wat ~ **is*** she knows a good thing when she sees it; *is het ~? ja, het **heeft** me ~ **gesmaakt*** do you like it? yes, I enjoyed it **2** nice, sweet **3** well, fine: *ik **ben** niet ~* I'm not feeling too well **4** nice, pleasant **5** nice; comfortable; lovely: *~ **rustig*** nice and quiet; *~ **weer*** lovely weather

²lekker /lɛkər/ (adv) **1** well, deliciously: *~ (kunnen) **koken*** be a good cook **2** nicely, fine: [inform] *gaat ie ~?* are you managing?; *slaap ~, **droom** maar ~* sleep tight, sweet dreams; *het ~ **vinden** om* like to || *~ **puh*** hard cheese, yah boo sucks to you

de **lekkerbek** /lɛkərbɛk/ (pl: -ken) gourmet, foodie

het **lekkerbekje** /lɛkərbɛkjə/ (pl: -s) [Dutch] fried fillet of haddock

de **lekkernij** /lɛkərnɛi/ (pl: -en) delicacy; sweet

het **lekkers** /lɛkərs/ sweet(s); snack: *zin hebben in iets ~* fancy sth. sweet (*or:* a snack)

de **lel** /lɛl/ clout

de **lelie** /leli/ (pl: -s) (madonna) lily

het **lelietje-van-dalen** /lelicəvandalə(n)/ (pl: lelietjes-van-dalen) lily of the valley

¹lelijk /lelək/ (adj) **1** ugly: *het was een ~ **gezicht*** it looked awful **2** bad, nasty: *een ~ **hoestje*** a bad cough

²lelijk /lelək/ (adv) badly, nastily: *zich ~ **vergissen** in iem. (iets)* be badly mistaken about s.o. (sth.)

de **lelijkerd** /leləkərt/ (pl: -s) **1** ugly man; hag, witch **2** rascal, ugly customer

lemen /lemə(n)/ (adj) loam

het **lemmet** /lɛmət/ (pl: -en) blade

de **lemming** /lɛmɪŋ/ (pl: -s, -en) lemming: [fig] *als ~en* like lemmings (off a cliff)

de **lende** /lɛndə/ (pl: -nen) **1** lumbar region, small of the back **2** loin, haunch

de **lendenbiefstuk** /lɛndəbifstʏk/ (pl: -ken) sirloin

de **lendendoek** /lɛndə(n)duk/ (pl: -en) loincloth

lenen /lenə(n)/ (leende, heeft geleend) **1** lend (to); [Am] loan: *ik heb hem **geld** geleend* I have lent him some money **2** borrow (of, from): *mag ik je **fiets** vandaag ~?* can I borrow your bike today?

de **lener** /lenər/ (pl: -s) **1** lender **2** borrower

lengen /lɛŋə(n)/: *de dagen ~* the days are growing longer (*or:* drawing) out

de **lengte** /lɛŋtə/ (pl: -n, -s) **1** length: *een plank in de ~ **doorzagen*** saw a board lengthways (*or:* lengthwise) **2** length, height: *hij lag in zijn **volle** ~ op de grond* he lay full-length on the ground || *over een ~ **van** 60 meter* for a distance of 60 metres; *tot in ~ van dagen* for many years to come

de **lengteas** /lɛŋtəas/ (pl: -sen) longitudinal axis

de **lengtecirkel** /lɛŋtəsɪrkəl/ (pl: -s) meridian

de **lengtemaat** /lɛŋtəmat/ (pl: -maten) linear (*or:* longitudinal) measurement

de **lengterichting** /lɛŋtərɪxtɪŋ/ longitudinal direction, linear direction

lenig /lenəx/ (adj, adv) lithe

de **lenigheid** /lenəxhɛit/ litheness

de **lening** /lenɪŋ/ (pl: -en) loan: *iem. een ~ **verstrekken*** grant s.o. a loan

de **lens** /lɛns/ (pl: lenzen) lens; [contact lenses also] contacts

de **lente** /lɛntə/ (pl: -s) spring: *in de ~* in (the) spring, in springtime; *één zwaluw **maakt** nog geen ~* one swallow doesn't make a summer

lenteachtig /lɛntəɑxtəx/ (adj, adv) springlike

het **lente-uitje** /lɛntəœycə/ (pl: -s) spring onion; [Am] green onion

de **lepel** /lepəl/ (pl: -s) **1** spoon; ladle; teaspoon: *een baby **met** een ~ voeren* spoonfeed a baby **2** spoonful

de **lepelaar** /lepəlar/ (pl: -s) spoonbill

lepelen /lepələ(n)/ (lepelde, heeft gelepeld): *iets **naar** binnen ~* spoon sth. up

de **lepra** /lepra/ leprosy

de **leraar** /lerar/ (pl: leraren) teacher: *hij is ~ **Engels*** he's an English teacher

de **lerarenopleiding** /lerarə(n)oplɛidɪŋ/ (pl: -en) secondary teacher training (course): *de **tweedefaselerarenopleiding*** post-graduate teacher training (course)

de **lerares** /lerarɛs/ (pl: -sen) see leraar

¹leren /lerə(n)/ (adj) leather

²leren /lerə(n)/ (leerde, heeft geleerd) **1** learn ((how) to do): *een **vak** ~* learn a trade; *iem. ~ **kennen*** get to know s.o.; *op dat gebied **kun** je nog heel wat van hem ~* he can still teach you a thing or two; *hij wil ~ **schaatsen***

he wants to learn (how) to skate; *iets al doen-de* ~ pick sth. up as you go along; *iets van buiten* ~ learn sth. by heart **2** teach: *de ervaring leert … experience teaches …* **3** study, learn: *haar kinderen kunnen goed* (or: *niet*) ~ her children are good (or: no good) at school

³**leren** /lᴇrə(n)/ (leerde, heeft geleerd) **1** teach (s.o. (how) to do sth.): *iem. ~ lezen en schrijven* teach s.o. to read and write **2** pick up, learn: *hij leert het al aardig* he is beginning to get the hang of it

de **lering** /lᴇrɪŋ/ (pl: -en): ~ *uit iets trekken* learn (a lesson) from sth.

de **les** /lᴇs/ (pl: -sen) **1** lesson, class: *ik heb ~ van 9 tot 12* I have lessons (or: classes) from 9 to 12; *een ~ laten uitvallen* drop a class; ~ *in tekenen* drawing (or: art) classes **2** [fig] lecture, lesson: *bij de* ~ *blijven* be alert; *dat is een goede* ~ *voor hem geweest* that's been a good lesson to him; *iem. de* ~ *lezen,* [Belg] *iem. de* ~ *spellen* give s.o. a talking-to; *een wijze* ~ a wise lesson

de **lesauto** /lᴇsɑuto/ (pl: -'s) learner car; [Am] driver education car

de **lesbienne** /lᴇzb(i)jɛnə/ (pl: -s) lesbian

lesbisch /lᴇzbis/ (adj) lesbian

het **lesgeld** /lᴇsxɛlt/ tuition fee(s)

lesgeven /lᴇsxevə(n)/ (gaf les, heeft lesgegeven) teach

het **leslokaal** /lᴇslokal/ (pl: leslokalen) classroom

de **Lesothaan** /ləsotan/ (pl: Lesothanen) Mosotho

Lesothaans /ləsotans/ (adj) Lesotho

Lesotho /ləsoto/ Lesotho

het **lesrooster** /lᴇsrostər/ (pl: -s) school timetable; [Am] school schedule

lessen /lᴇsə(n)/ (leste, heeft gelest) quench

de **lessenaar** /lᴇsənar/ (pl: -s) (reading, writing) desk, lectern

lest /lᴇst/ (adj, adv): *ten langen ~e* at (long) last, finally

het **lesuur** /lᴇsyr/ (pl: lesuren) lesson, period

de **Let** /lᴇt/ (pl: -ten) Latvian

de **lethargie** /letɑrɣi/ lethargy

Letland /lᴇtlɑnt/ Latvia

de **Letlander** /lᴇtlɑndər/ (pl: -s) *see Let*

Letlands /lᴇtlɑn(t)s/ (adj) *see ²Lets*

het ¹**Lets** /lᴇts/ Latvian

²**Lets** /lᴇts/ (adj) Latvian

het **letsel** /lᴇtsəl/ injury

letten /lᴇtə(n)/ (lette, heeft gelet) **1** pay attention (to): *daar heb ik niet op gelet* I didn't notice; *op zijn gezondheid* ~ watch one's health; *let op mijn woorden* mark my words; *let maar niet op haar* don't pay any attention to her; *let wel* mind you, note **2** take care of: *goed op iem.* ~ take good care of s.o.; *er wordt ook op de uitspraak gelet* pronunciation is also taken into consideration (or: account) ‖ *wat let je?* what's keeping (or: stopping) you?

de **letter** /lᴇtər/ (pl: -s) letter; [pl, notice] lettering: *met grote ~s* in capitals

de **letteren** /lᴇtərə(n)/ (pl) language and literature, arts: ~ *studeren* be an arts student

de **lettergreep** /lᴇtərɣrep/ (pl: -grepen) syllable

de **letterkunde** /lᴇtərkʏndə/ literature

letterkundig /lᴇtərkʏndəɣ/ (adj, adv) literary

letterlijk /lᴇtərlək/ (adj, adv) literal: *iets al te ~ opvatten* take sth. too literally

het **letterteken** /lᴇtərtekə(n)/ (pl: -s) character

het **lettertype** /lᴇtərtipə/ (pl: -s) typeface, font

de **leugen** /løɣə(n)/ (pl: -s) lie: *een ~tje om bestwil* a white lie

de **leugenaar** /løɣənar/ (pl: -s) liar

leugenachtig /løɣənɑxtəɣ/ (adj) lying

de **leugendetector** /løɣə(n)detɛktɔr/ (pl: -s) lie detector

leuk /løk/ (adj, adv) **1** funny, amusing: *hij denkt zeker dat hij ~ is* he seems to think he is funny; *ik zie niet in wat daar voor ~s aan is* I don't see the funny side of it **2** pretty, nice: *een ~ bedrag* quite a handsome sum; *echt een ~e vent (knul)* a really nice guy; *dat staat je ~* that suits you **3** nice, pleasant: *ik vind het ~ werk* I enjoy the work; *iets ~ vinden* enjoy (or: like) sth.; *laten we iets ~s gaan doen* let's do sth. nice; ~ *dat je gebeld hebt* it was nice of you to call

de **leukemie** /løykəmi/ leukaemia

de **leukerd** /løkərt/ (pl: -s) funny man (or: guy)

het/de **leukoplast**® /løkoplɑst/ sticking plaster

leunen /lønə(n)/ (leunde, heeft geleund) lean (on, against): *achterover* ~ lean back, recline

de **leuning** /lønɪŋ/ (pl: -en) **1** (hand)rail **2** back, arm (rest) **3** rail(ing), guard rail

de **leunstoel** /lønstul/ (pl: -en) armchair

leuren /lørə(n)/ (leurde, heeft geleurd) peddle

de **leus** /løs/ (pl: leuzen) slogan, motto

de **leut** /løt/ fun: *voor de* ~ for fun

leuteren /løtərə(n)/ (leuterde, heeft geleuterd) drivel

Leuven /løvə(n)/ Leuven, Louvain

leve /levə/ long live: ~ *de koning!* long live the King!; *lang* ~ *de lol* let the good times roll

het ¹**leven** /levə(n)/ (pl: -s) **1** life, existence: *de aanslag heeft aan twee mensen het* ~ *gekost* the attack cost the lives of two people; *om het* ~ *komen* lose one's life, be killed; *iem. om het* ~ *brengen* kill s.o., take s.o.'s life; *het* ~ *schenken aan* give birth to; *zijn* ~ *wagen* risk one's life; *een voltooid* ~ a completed life; *nog in* ~ *zijn* be still alive; *hoe staat het* ~*?* how is life?; *zijn* ~ *niet (meer) zeker zijn* be not safe here (any more) **2** life, reality: *een organisatie in het* ~ *roepen* set up an organization **3** life, lifetime: *zijn hele verdere* ~ for the rest of his life; *hun* ~ *lang hebben ze hard gewerkt* they

worked hard all their lives; *voor het* ~ for life
4 life, living: *het* ~ *wordt steeds* **duurder** the
cost of living is going up all the time; *zijn* ~
beteren mend one's ways **5** life, liveliness: *er
kwam* ~ *in de brouwerij* things were beginning to liven up

²**leven** /l̲e̲və(n)/ (leefde, heeft geleefd) **1** live,
be alive: *blijven* ~ stay alive; *en zij leefden nog
lang en gelukkig* and they lived happily ever
after; ~ *en laten* **leven** live and let live; *leef je
nog?* are you still alive?; *stil gaan* ~ retire;
naar iets toe ~ look forward to sth. **2** [fig] live
(on) **3** live (on, by); live off: *zij moet ervan* ~
she has to live on it
levend /l̲e̲vənt/ (adj) living; live; alive: *het er*
~ *vanaf brengen* escape with one's life
levendig /l̲e̲vəndəx/ (adj, adv) **1** lively
2 lively, vivacious: ~ *van aard* **zijn** have a vivacious nature **3** vivid, clear: *ik kan mij die dag
nog* ~ *herinneren* I remember that day clearly **4** vivid, spirited: *over een* ~*e* **fantasie** *beschikken* have a vivid imagination
levenloos /l̲e̲və(n)los/ (adj) lifeless, dead:
iem. ~ *aantreffen* find s.o. dead
levensbedreigend /l̲e̲vənzbədr̲e̲i̲yənt/
(adj) life-threatening
de **levensbehoefte** /l̲e̲vənzbəhuftə/ (pl: -n)
1 necessity of life **2** necessities (of life)
het **levensbelang** /l̲e̲vənzbəlɑŋ/ (pl: -en) vital
importance
de **levensbeschouwing** /l̲e̲və(n)zbəsxɑuwɪŋ/
(pl: -en) philosophy of life
de **levensbeschrijving** /l̲e̲vənzbəsxr̲e̲i̲vɪŋ/ (pl:
-en) biography, curriculum vitae
de **levensduur** /l̲e̲vənzdyr/ [fig] **1** lifespan: *de
gemiddelde* ~ *van de Nederlander* the life expectancy of the Dutch **2** life
¹**levensecht** /levəns̲ɛ̲xt/ (adj) lifelike
²**levensecht** /levəns̲ɛ̲xt/ (adv) in a lifelike
way (*or:* manner)
de **levenservaring** /l̲e̲vənsɛrvarɪŋ/ (pl: -en)
experience of life
de **levensfase** /l̲e̲və(n)sfazə/ (pl: -s) stage of
life
de **levensgenieter** /l̲e̲və(n)sxenitər/ (pl: -s)
[roughly] bon vivant, pleasure-lover
het **levensgevaar** /l̲e̲vənsxəvar/ danger of life,
peril to life: *buiten* ~ *zijn* be out of danger
levensgevaarlijk /l̲e̲vənsxəv̲a̲rlək/ (adj,
adv) perilous
de **levensgezel** /l̲e̲vənsxəzɛl/ (pl: -len) life
partner (*or:* companion)
levensgroot /levənsxr̲o̲t/ (adj) **1** life-size(d)
2 huge, enormous
de **levenskunstenaar** /l̲e̲və(n)skʏnstənar/ (pl:
-s) master in the art of living
¹**levenslang** /levənsl̲ɑ̲ŋ/ (adj) lifelong: ~*e
herinneringen* lasting memories || *hij* **kreeg** ~
he was sentenced to life (imprisonment)
²**levenslang** /levənsl̲ɑ̲ŋ/ (adv) all one's life
het **levenslied** /l̲e̲və(n)slit/ (pl: -liederen)

[roughly] sentimental song
de **levensloop** /l̲e̲vənslop/ **1** course of life
2 curriculum vitae
de **levenslust** /l̲e̲və(n)slʏst/ joy of living
levenslustig /levənsl̲ʏ̲stəx/ (adj) high-spirited
de **levensmiddelen** /l̲e̲vənsmɪdələ(n)/ (pl)
food(s)
de **levensomstandigheden** /l̲e̲vənsomstandəxhedə(n)/ (pl) living conditions, circumstances (*or:* conditions) of life
het **levensonderhoud** /l̲e̲vənsondərhaut/ support, means of sustaining life: *de* **kosten** *van*
~ *stijgen* (or: *dalen*) living costs are rising (*or:*
falling)
de **levensovertuiging** /l̲e̲və(n)sovərtœyɣɪŋ/
philosophy of life
de **levenspartner** /l̲e̲vənspartnər/ (pl: -s) life
partner, life companion
de **levensstandaard** /l̲e̲vənstandart/ standard of living
de **levensstijl** /l̲e̲vənstɛil/ (pl: -en) lifestyle,
style of living
het **levensteken** /l̲e̲və(n)stekə(n)/ (pl: -s, -en)
sign of life
levensvatbaar /levə(n)sf̲ɑ̲dbar/ (adj) viable; feasible
de **levensverwachting** /l̲e̲vənsfərwaxtɪŋ/
1 expectation of (*or:* from) life **2** life expectancy
de **levensverzekering** /l̲e̲vənsfərzekərɪŋ/ (pl:
-en) life insurance (policy)
de **levensvreugde** /l̲e̲və(n)sfrøydə/ joy of living
de **levenswandel** /l̲e̲vənswandəl/ conduct (in
life), life
het **levenswerk** /l̲e̲vənswɛrk/ life's work, lifework
de **levenswijsheid** /l̲e̲və(n)sw̲ɛ̲i̲shɛit/ wisdom
de **levenswijze** /l̲e̲vənsw̲ɛizə/ way of life
de **lever** /l̲e̲vər/ (pl: -s) liver: [Belg] *het ligt* **op** *zijn*
~ it rankles him || *iets* **op** *zijn* ~ *hebben* have
sth. on one's mind
de **leverancier** /levəransir/ (pl: -s) supplier
de **leverantie** /levərɑnsi/ (pl: -s) delivery, supply(ing)
leverbaar /l̲e̲vərbar/ (adj) available, ready
for delivery: *niet meer* ~ out of stock
leveren /l̲e̲vərə(n)/ (leverde, heeft geleverd) **1** supply, deliver **2** furnish, provide:
iem. stof ~ *voor een verhaal* provide s.o. with
material for a story **3** fix, do, bring off: *ik
weet niet hoe hij* **het** *hem geleverd heeft* I don't
know how he pulled it off
de **levering** /l̲e̲vərɪŋ/ (pl: -en) **1** delivery: ~ *op
krediet* sell on credit **2** [law] transfer (of
ownership): *akte van* ~ deed of transfer,
deed of conveyance
de **leveringstermijn** /l̲e̲vərɪŋstɛrmɛin/ delivery period (*or:* time)
de **leverpastei** /l̲e̲vərpastɛi/ (pl: -en) liver paté

de **levertijd** /le̱vərtɛit/ (pl: -en) delivery time

de **leverworst** /le̱vərwɔrst/ (pl: -en) liver sausage

lezen /le̱zə(n)/ (las, heeft gelezen) **1** read: *je handschrift is* **niet** *te ~* your (hand)writing is illegible; *veel ~* **over** *een schrijver* (or: *een bepaald onderwerp)* read up on a writer (or: on a particular subject); *ik lees hier dat ... it* says here that ... **2** read (out, aloud) ‖ *de angst stond op zijn gezicht te ~* anxiety was written all over his face

de **lezer** /le̱zər/ (pl: -s) reader: *het* **aantal** *~s van deze krant neemt nog steeds toe* the readership of this newspaper is still increasing

de **lezing** /le̱zɪŋ/ (pl: -en) **1** reading: *bij* **opper-vlakkige** (or: *nauwkeurige) ~* on a cursory (or: a careful reading) **2** lecture

de **lhbt'er** /ɛlhabete̱jər/ (pl: -s) lesbienne, homo, biseksueel, transgender LGBT *(lesbian, gay, bisexual, transgendered)*

de **liaan** /lija̱n/ (pl: lianen) liana, liane

de **Libanees** /libane̱s/ (pl: Libanezen) Lebanese

Libanon /li̱banɔn/ (the) Lebanon

de **libel** /libɛ̱l/ (pl: -len) dragonfly

de ¹**liberaal** /libera̱l/ (pl: liberalen) Liberal; Conservative

²**liberaal** /libera̱l/ (adj, adv) **1** liberal; [in the Netherlands also] conservative **2** liberal, broad-minded

liberaliseren /liberalize̱rə(n)/ (liberaliseerde, heeft geliberaliseerd) liberalize

het **liberalisme** /liberalɪ̱smə/ liberalism

Liberia /libe̱rija/ Liberia

de **Liberiaan** /liberija̱n/ (pl: Liberianen) Liberian

Liberiaans /liberija̱ns/ (adj) Liberian

de **libero** /li̱bəro/ (pl: -'s) [sport] sweeper

de **libido** /li̱bido/ libido, sex drive

Libië /li̱bijə/ Libya

de **Libiër** /li̱bijər/ (pl: -s) Libyan

Libisch /li̱bis/ (adj) Libyan

de ¹**licentiaat** /lisɛnsja̱t/ [Belg] licentiate

het ²**licentiaat** /lisɛnsja̱t/ licentiate, licence

de **licentie** /lisɛ̱nsi/ (pl: -s) **1** licence **2** permit

het **lichaam** /lɪ̱χam/ (pl: lichamen) **1** body: *over zijn hele ~ beven* shake all over **2** trunk

de **lichaamsbeweging** /lɪ̱χamzbəweɣɪŋ/ (pl: -en) (physical) exercise; gymnastics

de **lichaamsbouw** /lɪ̱χamzbɑu/ build, figure

het **lichaamsdeel** /lɪ̱χamzdel/ (pl: -delen) part of the body; limb

de **lichaamstaal** /lɪ̱χamstal/ body language

de **lichaamsverzorging** /lɪ̱χamsfərzɔrχɪŋ/ personal hygiene

lichamelijk /lɪ̱χamələk/ (adj, adv) physical

het ¹**licht** /lɪχt/ (pl: -en) light: *tussen ~ en* **donker** in the twilight; *waar zit de* **knop** *van het ~?* where's the light switch?; *groot ~* full beam; *dat werpt een* **nieuw** *~ op de zaak* that puts things in a different light; *het ~* **aandoen** (or: *uitdoen)* put the light on (or: off); *toen ging*

er een ~je (bij me) **op** then it dawned on me; *het ~* **staat** *op rood* the light is red; **aan** *het ~ komen* come to light; *het ~* **zien** see the light

²**licht** /lɪχt/ (adj) **1** light, delicate: *zij* **voelde** *zich ~ in het hoofd* she felt light in the head; *een kilo* **te** *~* a kilogram underweight **2** light, bright: *het* **wordt** *al ~* it is getting light **3** light; pale **4** light, easy **5** light, slight: *een ~e* **afwijking** *hebben* be a bit odd; *een ~e* **blessure** a minor injury

³**licht** /lɪχt/ (adv) **1** lightly; light: *~* **slapen** sleep light **2** slightly **3** easily: *~* **verteerbaar** (easily) digestible, light **4** highly: *~* **ontvlam-bare** *stoffen* highly (in)flammable materials

de **lichtbak** /lɪ̱χtbak/ (pl: -ken) **1** light box **2** illuminated sign

lichtbewolkt /lɪχtbəwɔ̱lkt/ (adj) rather cloudy, with some clouds

lichtblauw /lɪχtbla̱u/ (adj) light (or: pale) blue

de **lichtbron** /lɪ̱χtbrɔn/ (pl: -nen) light source, source of light

de **lichtbundel** /lɪ̱χtbʏndəl/ (pl: -s) beam of light

lichtelijk /lɪ̱χtələk/ (adv) slightly

lichten /lɪ̱χtə(n)/ (lichtte, heeft gelicht) **1** lift, raise **2** remove: *iem. van zijn bed ~* arrest s.o. in his bed

lichtend /lɪ̱χtənt/ (adj) shining: *een ~* **voor-beeld** a shining example

lichterlaaie /lɪχtərla̱jə/: *het gebouw stond in ~* the building was in flames (or: ablaze)

lichtgelovig /lɪχtɣəlo̱vəχ/ (adj) gullible

lichtgeraakt /lɪ̱(χt)χəra̱kt/ (adj) touchy: *~ zijn* be quick to take offence

lichtgevend /lɪ̱(χt)χe̱vənt/ (adj) luminous

lichtgevoelig /lɪ(χt)χəvu̱ləχ/ (adj) (light) sensitive

het **lichtgewicht** /lɪ̱(χt)χəwɪχt/ (pl: -en) lightweight

lichtgewond /lɪ(χt)χəwɔ̱nt/ (adj) slightly injured (or: wounded)

de **lichting** /lɪ̱χtɪŋ/ (pl: -en) **1** levy, draft **2** collection

het **lichtjaar** /lɪ̱χtjar/ (pl: -jaren) light year

het **lichtjesfeest** /lɪ̱χjəsfest/ Diwali, Festival of Lights

de **lichtkogel** /lɪ̱χtkoɣəl/ (pl: -s) (signal) flare

de **lichtkrans** /lɪ̱χtkrɑns/ (pl: -en) halo; aureole

de **lichtkrant** /lɪ̱χtkrɑnt/ (pl: -en) illuminated news trailer

de **lichtmast** /lɪ̱χtmɑst/ (pl: -en) lamp-post, lamp standard

het **lichtnet** /lɪ̱χtnɛt/ (pl: -ten) (electric) mains, lighting system: *een apparaat* **op** *het ~ aanslui-ten* connect an appliance to the mains; *op het ~ werken* run off the mains

de **lichtpen** /lɪ̱χtpɛn/ (pl: -nen) light pen(cil)

het **lichtpunt** /lɪ̱χtpʏnt/ (pl: -en) **1** point (or: spot) of light **2** [fig] ray of hope

de **lichtreclame** /lɪ̱χtrəklamə/ illuminated advertising, neon signs (or: advertising)

de **lichtschakelaar** /lɪxtsχakəlar/ (pl: -s) light switch

de **lichtshow** /lɪxtʃoː/ (pl: -s) light show

het **lichtsignaal** /lɪxtsɪnal/ (pl: -signalen) light signal, flash: *een ~ geven* flash

de **lichtsterkte** /lɪxtstɛrktə/ brightness; luminous intensity

de **lichtstraal** /lɪxtstral/ (pl: -stralen) ray of light; beam (or: shaft) of light

lichtvaardig /lɪxtfardəχ/ (adj, adv) rash

de **lichtval** /lɪxtfɑl/ light

lichtvoetig /lɪxtfutəχ/ (adj, adv) light-footed

lichtzinnig /lɪxtsɪnəχ/ (adj, adv) **1** frivolous: *~ omspringen met* trifle with **2** light, loose: *~ leven* live a loose life

de **lichtzinnigheid** /lɪxtsɪnəχhɛit/ frivolity

het **lid** /lɪt/ (pl: leden) **1** member: *het aantal leden bedraagt … the membership is …; ~ van de gemeenteraad* (town) councillor; *~ van de Kamer* Member of Parliament, M.P.; *deze omroep heeft 500.000 leden* this broadcasting company has a membership of 500,000; *~ worden van* join, become a member of; *~ zijn van de bibliotheek* belong to the library; *~ zijn van* be a member of; be (or: serve) on; *zich als ~ opgeven* apply for membership **2** part, member; limb: *recht van lijf en leden* straightlimbed; *het (mannelijk) ~* the (male) member

het **lidgeld** /lɪtχɛlt/ [Belg] subscription

de **lidkaart** /lɪtkart/ (pl: -en) [Belg] membership card

het **lidmaatschap** /lɪtmatsχɑp/ (pl: -pen) membership: *bewijs van ~* membership card; *iem. van het ~ van een vereniging uitsluiten* exclude s.o. from membership of a club; *het ~ kost € 25,-* the membership fee is 25 euros; *zijn ~ opzeggen* resign one's membership

de **lidmaatschapskaart** /lɪtmatsχɑpskart/ (pl: -en) membership card

de **lidstaat** /lɪtstat/ (pl: lidstaten) member state

het **lidwoord** /lɪtwort/ (pl: -en) article: *bepaald en onbepaald ~* definite and indefinite article

Liechtenstein /lixtənstɛin/ Liechtenstein

de **Liechtensteiner** /lixtənstɛinər/ (pl: -s) Liechtensteiner

Liechtensteins /lixtənstɛins/ (adj) Liechtenstein

het **lied** /lit/ (pl: -eren) song: *het hoogste ~ zingen* be wild with joy

de **lieden** /lidə(n)/ (pl) folk, people: *dat kun je verwachten bij zulke ~* that's what you can expect from people like that

liederlijk /lidərlək/ (adj, adv) debauched

het **liedje** /licə/ (pl: -s) song: *het is altijd hetzelfde ~* it's the same old story

het **¹lief** /lif/ **1** girlfriend, boyfriend, beloved **2** joy: *~ en leed met iem. delen* share life's joys

and sorrows with s.o.

²lief /lif/ (adj) **1** dear, beloved: *(maar) mijn lieve kind* (but) my dear; [in letters] *Lieve Maria* Dear Maria; *zijn ~ste wens* his dearest (or: fondest) wish **2** nice, sweet: *een ~ karakter* a sweet nature, a kind heart; *zij zijn erg ~ voor elkaar* they are very devoted to each other; *dat was ~ van haar om jou mee te nemen* it was nice of her to take you along **3** dear, sweet: *er ~ uitzien* look sweet (or: lovely) **4** dear, treasured: *iets voor ~ nemen* put up with sth.; make do with sth.; *tegenslagen voor ~ nemen* take the rough with the smooth

³lief /lif/ (adv) sweetly, nicely: *iem. ~ aankijken* give s.o. an affectionate look ‖ *ik ga net zo ~ niet* I'd (just) as soon not go

liefdadig /livdadəχ/ (adj) charitable: *een ~ doel* a good cause; *het is voor een ~ doel* it is for charity; *~e instellingen* charitable institutions

de **liefdadigheid** /livdadəχhɛit/ charity, benevolence, beneficence: *~ bedrijven* do charitable work

de **liefdadigheidsinstelling** /livdadəχhɛitsɪnstɛlɪŋ/ (pl: -en) charity, charitable institution

de **liefde** /livdə/ (pl: -s, -n) love: *haar grote ~* her great love; *kinderlijke ~* childish love (or: affection); filial love (or: affection); *een ongelukkige ~ achter de rug hebben* have suffered a disappointment in love; *vrije ~* free love; *de ware ~* true love; *iemands ~ beantwoorden* return s.o.'s love (or: affection); *de ~ bedrijven* make love; *geluk hebben in de ~* be fortunate (or: successful) in love; *~ op het eerste gezicht* love at first sight; *hij deed het uit ~* he did it for love; *trouwen uit ~* marry for love; *de ~ voor het vaderland* (the) love of one's country; *~ voor de kunst* love of art; *~ is blind* love is blind

liefdeloos /livdəlos/ (adj, adv) loveless

de **liefdesbrief** /livdəzbrif/ (pl: -brieven) love letter

het **liefdesleven** /livdəslevə(n)/ (pl: -s) love life

het **liefdesnest** /livdəsnɛst/ (pl: -en) love nest

het **liefdesverdriet** /livdəsfərdrit/ pangs of love: *~ hebben* be disappointed in love

liefdevol /livdəvol/ (adj, adv) loving: *~le verzorging* tender loving care; *iem. ~ aankijken* give s.o. a loving look

het **liefdewerk** /livdəwɛrk/ (pl: -en) charity, charitable work: *het is ~ oud papier* it's for love only

liefhebben /lifhɛbə(n)/ (had lief, heeft liefgehad) love

de **liefhebber** /lifhɛbər/ (pl: -s) lover: *een ~ van chocola* a chocolate lover; *een ~ van opera* an opera lover (or: buff); *zijn er nog ~s?* (are there) any takers?; *daar zullen wel ~s voor zijn* there are sure to be customers for that

de **liefhebberij** /lifhɛbərɛi/ (pl: -en) hobby,

pastime: *een **dure** ~* [fig] an expensive hobby; *tuinieren is zijn **grootste** ~* gardening is his favourite pastime

het **liefje** /lifjə/ (pl: -s) sweetheart

liefkozen /lifkozə(n)/ (liefkoosde, heeft geliefkoosd) caress, fondle, cuddle

de **liefkozing** /lifkozɪŋ/ (pl: -en) caress

liefst /lifst/ (adv) **1** dearest, sweetest: *zij **zag** er van allen het ~ **uit*** she looked the sweetest (*or:* prettiest) of them all **2** rather, preferably: *men neme een banaan, ~ een **rijpe** …* take a banana, preferably a ripe one …; *wat zou je het ~ **doen?*** what would you rather do?, what would you really like to do?; *in welke auto **rijd** je het ~?* which car do you prefer to drive?

de **liefste** /lifstə/ (pl: -n) sweetheart, darling: **mijn** ~ my dear(est) (*or:* love)

liegen /liɣə(n)/ (loog, heeft gelogen) lie, tell a lie: *hij **staat** gewoon te ~!* he's a downright liar!; ***tegen** iem. ~* lie to s.o.; *hij liegt **alsof** het gedrukt staat, hij liegt dat hij barst* he is telling barefaced lies; *dat is allemaal gelogen* that's a pack of lies

de **lier** /lir/ (pl: -en) lyre

de **lies** /lis/ (pl: liezen) groin

de **liesbreuk** /lizbrøk/ (pl: -en) inguinal hernia

de **lieslaars** /lislars/ (pl: -laarzen) wader

het **lieveheersbeestje** /livəhɛrzbeɕə/ (pl: -s) ladybird; [Am] ladybug

de **lieveling** /livəlɪŋ/ (pl: -en) **1** darling, sweetheart: *zij is de ~ van de **familie*** she's the darling of the family **2** favourite, darling: *de ~ van het **publiek*** the darling (*or:* favourite) of the public

liever /livər/ (adv) rather: *ik **drink** ~ koffie dan thee* I prefer coffee to tea; *ik zou ~ **gaan** (dan blijven)* I'd rather go than stay; *ik weet het, of ~ **gezegd**, ik denk het* I know, at least, I think so; *als je ~ **hebt** dat ik wegga, hoef je het maar te zeggen* if you'd sooner (*or:* rather) I'd leave, just say so; *ik **zie** hem ~ gaan dan komen* I'm glad to see the back of him; *hoe meer, **hoe** ~ the* more the better; *hij ~ **dan** ik* rather him than me

de **lieverd** /livərt/ (pl: -s) darling: [iron] *het **is** me een ~je* he's (*or:* she's) a nice one

de **lift** /lɪft/ (pl: -en) **1** lift; [Am] elevator: *de ~ **nemen*** take the lift **2** lift, ride: *iem. een ~ **geven*** give s.o. a lift (*or:* ride); *een ~ **krijgen*** get (*or:* hitch) a lift; *een ~ **vragen*** thumb (*or:* hitch) a lift ‖ *in de ~ **zitten*** be on the way up, be on the rise

liften /lɪftə(n)/ (liftte, heeft/is gelift) hitch-(hike)

de **lifter** /lɪftər/ (pl: -s) hitchhiker

de **liftkoker** /lɪftkokər/ (pl: -s) lift shaft; [Am] elevator shaft

de **liga** /liɣa/ (pl: -'s) league

het **ligbad** /lɪɣbɑt/ (pl: -en) bath; [Am] (bath)tub

de **ligdag** /lɪɣdɑx/ (pl: -en) lay day

de **ligfiets** /lɪxfits/ (pl: -en) recumbent bike

liggen /lɪɣə(n)/ (lag, heeft gelegen) **1** lie; be laid up: *er lag een halve meter **sneeuw*** there was half a metre of snow; *lekker tegen iem. aan **gaan*** ~ snuggle up to s.o.; *lig je **lekker? (goed?)*** are you comfortable?; *ik **blijf** morgen ~ tot half tien* I'm going to stay in bed till 9.30 tomorrow; ***gaan** ~* lie down; *hij ligt **in** bed* he is (lying) in bed; *op* sterven ~ lie (*or:* be) dying **2** (+ aan) depend (on); be caused by; be due to: *dat ligt **eraan*** it depends; *ik denk dat het **aan** je versterker ligt* I think that it's your amplifier that's causing the trouble; ***aan** mij zal het niet* ~ it won't be my fault; *is het nou zo koud of ligt het **aan** mij?* is it really so cold, or is it just me?; *het ligt **aan** die rotfiets van me* it's that bloody bike of mine; *als het **aan** mij ligt niet* not if I can help it; *waar zou dat **aan** ~?* what could be the cause of that?; *het lag misschien ook een beetje **aan** mij* I may have had sth. to do with it; *het kan **aan** mij ~, maar …* it may be just me, but …; *als het **aan** mij ligt* if it is up to me **3** die down: *de wind **ging** ~* the wind died down **4** suit: *ze ~ **elkaar** niet zo erg* they don't get on (with each other) **5** (+ te): *hij ligt te **slapen*** he's asleep; *zij lagen de hele dag te **zonnen*** they spent the whole day lying in the sun ‖ *die zaak ligt nogal **gevoelig*** the matter is a bit delicate; *dat werk is voor ons **blijven** ~* that work has been left for us; *ik **heb** (nog) een paar flessen wijn ~* I have a few bottles of wine (left); [Belg] *iem. ~ **hebben*** take s.o. in; *ik heb dat boek **laten** ~* I left that book (behind); *dit bed ligt **lekker*** (*or:* hard) this bed is comfortable (*or:* hard); *de zaken ~ nu heel **anders*** things have changed a lot (since then); *het plan, zoals het **er** nu ligt, is onaanvaardbaar* as it stands, the plan is unacceptable; *uw bestelling ligt **klaar*** your order is ready (for dispatch, collection); ***zo** ~ de zaken nu eenmaal* I'm afraid that's the way things are; *Antwerpen ligt **aan** de Schelde* Antwerp lies on the Scheldt; *de schuld ligt **bij** mij* the fault is mine; ***onder** het gemiddelde* ~ be below average; *de bal ligt **op** de grond* the ball is on the ground; *op het zuiden* ~ face (the) south; *ze ~ **voor** het grijpen* they're all over the place

liggend /lɪɣənt/ (adj) lying, horizontal: *een ~e **houding*** a lying (*or:* recumbent) posture

de **ligging** /lɪɣɪŋ/ (pl: -en) position, situation, location: *de ~ van de **heuvels*** the lie of the hills; *de **schilderachtige** ~ van dat kasteel* the picturesque location of the castle

light /lajt/ (adj) lite, diet: *cola ~* diet coke

de **lightrail** /lajtrel/ light rail

de **ligplaats** /lɪxplats/ (pl: -en) berth, mooring (place)

de **ligstoel** /lɪxstul/ (pl: -en) reclining chair (*or:* seat); deckchair

de **liguster** /liɣystər/ (pl: -s) privet

lijdelijk /lɛɪdələk/ (adj, adv) resigned ‖ ~ **toezien** look on passively

het **¹lijden** /lɛɪdə(n)/ suffering; pain; agony; grief; misery: *nu is hij uit zijn ~ verlost* a) he is now released from his suffering; b) [fig] that's put him out of his misery; *een dier uit zijn ~ verlossen* put an animal out of its misery

²lijden /lɛɪdə(n)/ (leed, heeft geleden) suffer: *zij leed het ergst van al* she was (the) hardest hit of all; *aan een kwaal ~* suffer from a complaint; *zijn gezondheid leed er onder* his health suffered (from it)

³lijden /lɛɪdə(n)/ (leed, heeft geleden) suffer, undergo: *hevige pijn ~* suffer (or: be in) terrible pain; *een groot verlies ~* suffer (or: sustain) a great loss; *honger ~* starve ‖ *het leed is geleden* the suffering is over, what's done is done

lijdend /lɛɪdənt/ (adj) suffering: *de lijdende vorm* the passive voice

de **lijdensweg** /lɛɪdə(n)swɛχ/ (pl: -en): *haar afstuderen werd een ~* she went through hell getting her degree

lijdzaam /lɛɪtsam/ (adj, adv) patient; passive: *~ toezien* stand by and watch

het **lijf** /lɛif/ (pl: lijven) body: *in levenden lijve* a) in person; b) alive and well; *een strak ~* a fit body; *bijna geen kleren aan zijn ~ hebben* have hardly a shirt to one's back; *iets aan den lijve ondervinden* experience (sth.) personally; *iem. te ~ gaan* go for (or: attack) s.o.; *iem. (toevallig) tegen het ~ lopen* run into s.o., stumble upon s.o.; *ik kon hem niet van het ~ houden* I couldn't keep him off me; *gezond van ~ en leden* able-bodied ‖ *dat heeft niets om het ~* there's nothing to it, that's nothing, it's a piece of cake

de **lijfarts** /lɛɪfɑrts/ (pl: -en) personal physician

de **lijfeigene** /lɛɪfɛɪɣənə/ (pl: -n) serf

lijfelijk /lɛɪfələk/ (adj, adv) physical: *zij was ~ aanwezig* she was there in person

de **lijfrente** /lɛɪfrɛntə/ (pl: -n, -s) annuity

de **lijfrentepolis** /lɛɪfrɛntəpolɪs/ (pl: -sen) annuity insurance policy

de **lijfspreuk** /lɛɪfsprøk/ (pl: -en) motto

de **lijfstraf** /lɛɪfstrɑf/ (pl: -fen) corporal punishment

de **lijfwacht** /lɛɪfwɑχt/ bodyguard

het **lijk** /lɛik/ (pl: -en) 1 corpse, (dead) body: *over mijn ~!* over my dead body!; *over ~en gaan* let nothing (or: no one) stand in one's way 2 [fig] carcass: *een levend ~* a walking corpse

lijkbleek /lɛiɡblek/ (adj) deathly pale, ashen

lijken /lɛikə(n)/ (leek, heeft geleken) 1 be like, look (a)like, resemble: *je lijkt je vader wel* you act (or: sound, are) just like your father; *het lijkt wel wijn* it's almost like wine; *zij lijkt op haar moeder* she looks like her mother; *ze ~ helemaal niet op elkaar* they're not a bit alike; *dat lijkt nergens op (naar)* it is absolutely hopeless (or: useless) 2 seem, appear, look:

hij lijkt jonger dan hij is he looks younger than he is; *dat lijkt me vreemd* it seems odd to me; *het lijkt maar zo* it only seems that way 3 suit, fit: *dat lijkt me wel wat* I like the sound (or: look) of that; *het lijkt me niets* I don't think much of it

de **lijkenpikker** /lɛɪkə(n)pɪkər/ (pl: -s) vulture

de **lijkkist** /lɛɪkɪst/ (pl: -en) coffin

de **lijkschouwer** /lɛiksχɑuwər/ (pl: -s) autopsist, medical examiner; [law] coroner

de **lijkschouwing** /lɛiksχɑuwɪŋ/ (pl: -en) autopsy

de **lijkwagen** /lɛɪkwaɣə(n)/ (pl: -s) hearse

de **lijm** /lɛim/ (pl: -en) glue

lijmen /lɛɪmə(n)/ (lijmde, heeft gelijmd) 1 glue (together); [also fig] patch up; [also fig] mend: [fig] *de brokken ~* pick up the pieces; *de scherven aan elkaar ~* glue (or: stick) the pieces together 2 talk round, win over: *zich niet laten ~* refuse to be roped in

de **lijmpoging** /lɛɪmpoɣɪŋ/ attempt to patch up

de **lijmsnuiver** /lɛɪmsnœyvər/ (pl: -s) glue sniffer

de **lijn** /lɛin/ (pl: -en) 1 line, rope; leash; lead: *~en trekken* (or: *krassen*) op draw (or: scratch) lines on; *een hond aan de ~ houden* keep a dog on the leash 2 line, crease: *de scherpe ~en om de neus* the deep lines around the nose 3 (out)line, contour: *iets in grote ~en aangeven* sketch sth. in broad outlines; *in grote ~en* broadly speaking, on the whole; *aan de ~ doen* slim, be on a diet 4 line, rank: *op dezelfde* (or: *op één*) *~ zitten* be on the same wavelength 5 line, route: *de ~ Haarlem-Amsterdam* the Haarlem-Amsterdam line; *die ~ bestaat niet meer* that service (or: route) no longer exists; *blijft u even aan de ~ a.u.b.* hold the line, please; *ik heb je moeder aan de ~* your mother is on the phone 6 [fig] line, course, trend: *de grote ~en uit het oog verliezen* lose o.s. in details ‖ *iem. aan het ~tje houden* keep s.o. dangling

de **lijndienst** /lɛindinst/ (pl: -en) regular service, scheduled service, line: *een ~ onderhouden op* run a regular service on

lijnen /lɛinə(n)/ (lijnde, heeft gelijnd) slim, diet

de **lijnkaart** /lɛinkart/ [Belg] smart card for payment on public transport

de **lijnolie** /lɛinoli/ linseed oil

¹lijnrecht /lɛinrɛχt/ (adj) (dead) straight

²lijnrecht /lɛinrɛχt/ (adv) 1 straight, right: *~ naar beneden* straight down 2 directly, flatly: *~ staan tegenover* be diametrically (or: flatly) opposed to

de **lijnrechter** /lɛinrɛχtər/ (pl: -s) linesman

het **lijnstuk** /lɛinstʏk/ (pl: -ken) line segment

het **lijntoestel** /lɛintustɛl/ (pl: -len) airliner, scheduled plane

de **lijnvlucht** /lɛinvlʏχt/ (pl: -en) scheduled

flight

het **lijnzaad** /lɛɪnzat/ linseed

lijp /lɛip/ (adj, adv) [Dutch; inform] silly, daft: *doe niet zo ~!* don't be silly! (*or:* daft!)

de **lijst** /lɛist/ (pl: -en) **1** list, record, inventory, register: *~en bijhouden van de uitgaven* keep records of the costs; *zijn naam staat bovenaan de ~* he is (at the) top of the list; *iem. (iets) op een ~ zetten* put s.o. (sth.) on a list **2** frame: *een vergulde ~* a gilt frame

de **lijstaanvoerder** /lɛistanvurdər/ (pl: -s) (league) leader

de **lijster** /lɛistər/ (pl: -s) thrush

de **lijsterbes** /lɛistərbɛs/ rowan (tree), mountain ash

de **lijsttrekker** /lɛistrɛkər/ (pl: -s) [roughly] party leader (during election campaign)

lijvig /lɛivəx/ (adj) corpulent, hefty

lijzig /lɛizəx/ (adj, adv) drawling: *een ~e stem* a sing-song voice

de **lijzijde** /lɛɪzɛɪdə/ lee (side)

de **lik** /lɪk/ (pl: -ken) **1** lick: *ik kreeg een ~ van de hond* the dog licked me **2** lick, dab: *een ~je verf* a lick of paint **3** clink, cage ǁ *~ op stuk geven* (or: *krijgen*) give (or: get) tit for tat

de **likdoorn** /lɪgdorn/ (pl: -s) corn

de **like** /lɑjk/ (pl: -s) [media] like

liken /lɑjkə(n)/ (likete, heeft geliket) like

de **likeur** /likør/ (pl: -en) liqueur

likkebaarden /lɪkəbardə(n)/ (likkebaardde, heeft gelikkebaard) lick one's lips

likken /lɪkə(n)/ (likte, heeft gelikt) lick

likmevestje /lɪkməvɛʃə/: *een organisatie van ~* crummy (*or:* lousy) organization

het **lik-op-stukbeleid** /lɪkɔpstʏgbəlɛit/ tit-for-tat policy (*or:* strategy)

lila /lila/ (adj) lilac; lavender

de **lilliputter** /lilipʏtər/ (pl: -s) midget, dwarf

Limburg /lɪmbʏrx/ Limburg

de **Limburger** /lɪmbʏrɣər/ (pl: -s) Limburger

Limburgs /lɪmbʏrxs/ (adj) Limburg

de **limerick** /lɪmərɪk/ (pl: -s) limerick

het **limiet** /limit/ (pl: -en) limit

limiteren /limiterə(n)/ (limiteerde, heeft gelimiteerd) limit, confine

de **¹limo** /limo/ (pl: -'s) *limousine* limo

de **²limo®** /limo/ (pl: -'s) [inform] *limonade* lemonade, soft drink

de **limoen** /limun/ (pl: -en) lime

de **limonade** /limonadə/ (pl: -s) lemonade: *priklimonade, ~ gazeuse* fizzy (*or:* aerated, sparkling) lemonade

de **limonadesiroop** /limonadəsirop/ lemon syrup

de **limousine** /limuzinə/ (pl: -s) limousine, limo

de **linde** /lɪndə/ (pl: -n) lime (tree), linden

lineair /linejɛːr/ (adj) linear ǁ *~e hypotheek* level repayment mortgage

linea recta /linejarɛkta/ (adv) straight: *~ gaan naar* go straight to

linedansen /lɑjndansə(n)/ (linedanste,

heeft gelinedanst) line dance

de **lingerie** /lɛ̃ʒəri/ lingerie, women's underwear, ladies' underwear

de **linguïst** /lɪŋɣwɪst/ (pl: -en) linguist

het/de **liniaal** /linijal/ (pl: linialen) ruler

de **linie** /lini/ (pl: -s) line, rank: *door de vijandelijke ~ (heen)breken* break through the enemy lines ǁ *over de hele ~* on all points, across the board

de **¹link** /lɪŋk/ (pl: -s) link; [comp] (hyper)link: *een ~ leggen tussen twee gebeurtenissen* link two events

²link /lɪŋk/ (adj) **1** risky, dicey: *~e jongens* a nasty bunch **2** sly, cunning **3** mad: *~ worden* get furious

linken /lɪŋkə(n)/ (linkte, heeft gelinkt) (hyper)link

linker /lɪŋkər/ (adj) left, left-hand; nearside: *~ rijbaan* left lane; *het ~ voorwiel* the nearside wheel

de **linkerarm** /lɪŋkərɑrm/ left arm

het **linkerbeen** /lɪŋkərben/ (pl: -benen) left leg: *hij is met zijn ~ uit bed gestapt* he got out of bed on the wrong side

de **linkerhand** /lɪŋkərhɑnt/ (pl: -en) left hand: *twee ~en hebben* be all fingers and thumbs

de **linkerkant** /lɪŋkərkɑnt/ (pl: -en) left(-hand) side, left

de **linkervleugel** /lɪŋkərvløɣəl/ (pl: -s) **1** left wing: *de ~ van een gebouw* (or: *een voetbalelftal*) the left wing of a building (*or:* football team) **2** left (wing), Left

de **linkerzijde** /lɪŋkərzɛɪdə/ (pl: -n) left(-hand) side, left, nearside: *zij zat aan mijn ~* she was sitting on my left

links /lɪŋks/ (adj, adv) **1** left, to (*or:* on) the left: *de tweede straat ~* the second street on the left; *~ en rechts* [also fig] right and left, on all sides; *~ houden* keep (to the) left; *iem. ~ laten liggen* ignore s.o., pass s.o. over, give s.o. the cold shoulder; *iets ~ laten liggen* ignore sth., pass sth. over; *~ van iem. zitten* sit to (or: on) s.o.'s left **2** left, left-handed, anticlockwise: *~ afslaan* turn (to the) left; *~ de bocht om rijden* take the left-hand bend (*or:* turn) **3** left-handed; left-footed: *~ schrijven* write with one's left hand **4** left-wing, leftist, socialist

de **linksachter** /lɪŋksɑxtər/ (pl: -s) left back

linksaf /lɪŋksɑf/ (adv) (to the) left, leftwards: *bij de brug moet u ~ (gaan)* turn left at the bridge

de **linksback** /lɪŋksbɛk/ (pl: -s) left back

de **linksbuiten** /lɪŋksbœytə(n)/ (pl: -s) outside left, left-wing(er)

linkshandig /lɪŋkshɑndəx/ (adj) left-handed

linksom /lɪŋksɔm/ (adv) left: *~ draaien* turn (to the) left ǁ *~ of rechtsom* one way or the other

linnen /lɪnə(n)/ (adj) linen, flax: *~ onder-*

goed linen underwear, linen

het **linnengoed** /lɪnə(n)ɣut/ linen

de **linnenkast** /lɪnə(n)kɑst/ (pl: -en) linen cupboard

het/de **¹linoleum** /linolejym/ linoleum

²linoleum /linolejym/ (adj) linoleum

het **linolzuur** /linolzyr/ (pl: -zuren) linoleic acid

het **lint** /lɪnt/ (pl: -en) ribbon, tape; (bias) binding; band: *het ~ van een schrijfmachine* a (typewriter) ribbon; *door het ~ gaan* blow one's top, fly off the handle

het **lintje** /lɪncə/ (pl: -s) decoration: *een ~ krijgen* be decorated, get a medal

de **lintmeter** /lɪntmetər/ (pl: -s) [Belg] tape measure

de **lintworm** /lɪntwɔrm/ (pl: -en) tapeworm

de **linze** /lɪnzə/ (pl: -n) lentil

de **lip** /lɪp/ (pl: -pen) lip: *dikke ~pen* thick (*or:* full) lips; *gesprongen ~pen* chapped (*or:* cracked) lips; *zijn ~pen ergens bij aflikken* lick (*or:* smack) one's lips; *aan iemands ~pen hangen* hang on s.o.'s lips (*or:* every word); [fig] *iem. op de ~ zitten* sit very close to s.o., be sticky

de **lipgloss** /lɪpɡlɔs/ lipgloss

het **lipje** /lɪpjə/ tab; lip

liplezen /lɪplezə(n)/ lip-read

de **liposuctie** /liposʏksi/ (pl: -s) liposuction

de **lippenbalsem** /lɪpə(n)bɑlsəm/ (pl: -s) lip balm

de **lippenstift** /lɪpə(n)stɪft/ (pl: -en) lipstick

de **liquidatie** /likwida(t)si/ (pl: -s) **1** liquidation, elimination **2** liquidation, winding-up, break-up, dissolution; settlement

liquide /likidə/ (adj) liquid, fluid: *~ middelen* liquid (*or:* fluid) assets

liquideren /likwidərə(n)/ (liquideerde, heeft geliquideerd) **1** [com] wind up, liquidate **2** eliminate, dispose of

de **lire** /lirə/ (pl: -s) lira

de **lis** /lɪs/ (pl: -sen) [bot] flag, iris

de **lisdodde** /lɪzdɔdə/ (pl: -n) reed mace

lispelen /lɪspələ(n)/ (lispelde, heeft gelispeld) lisp, speak with a lisp

Lissabon /lɪsabɔn/ Lisbon

de **list** /lɪst/ (pl: -en) trick, ruse, stratagem; cunning; craft, deception: *~ en bedrog* double-crossing, double-dealing; *een ~ verzinnen* invent a ruse, think of a solution

listig /lɪstəɣ/ (adj, adv) cunning, crafty, wily

de **litanie** /litani/ (pl: -ën) litany

de **liter** /litər/ (pl: -s) litre: *twee ~ melk* two litres of milk

literair /litərɛːr/ (adj, adv) literary: *~ tijdschrift* literary journal

de **literatuur** /litəratyr/ literature

de **literatuurlijst** /litəratyrlɛist/ (pl: -en) reading list, bibliography

de **literfles** /litərflɛs/ (pl: -sen) litre bottle

de **litho** /lito/ (pl: -'s) litho

Litouwen /litɑuwə(n)/ Lithuania

de **Litouwer** /litɑuwər/ (pl: -s) Lithuanian

het **¹Litouws** /litɑus/ Lithuanian

²Litouws /litɑus/ (adj) Lithuanian

het **lits-jumeaux** /liʒymo/ (pl: -) twin beds

het **litteken** /lɪtekə(n)/ (pl: -s) scar, mark: *met ~s op zijn gezicht* with a scarred face

de **liturgie** /litʏrɣi/ (pl: -ën) liturgy, rite

liturgisch /litʏrɣis/ (adj) liturgical

live /lɑjf/ (adj) live

het **liveoptreden** /lɑjfɔptredə(n)/ (pl: -s) live performance

de **liveshow** /lɑjfʃo/ (pl: -s) live show

livestreamen /lɑjfstri:mə(n)/ live-stream

de **living** /lɪvɪŋ/ (pl: -s) living room

de **livrei** /livrɛi/ (pl: -en) livery

de **lob** /lɔp/ (pl: -ben, -s) **1** seed leaf **2** [sport] lob

lobben /lɔbə(n)/ (lobde, heeft gelobd) lob

de **lobbes** /lɔbəs/ (pl: -en) **1** big, good-natured dog **2** kind soul, good-natured fellow, big softy

de **lobby** /lɔbi/ (pl: -'s) **1** lobby **2** [in hotel] lobby; lounge, foyer, hall

lobbyen /lɔbijə(n)/ (lobbyde, heeft gelobbyd) lobby

de **locatie** /loka(t)si/ (pl: -s) location

de **locoburgemeester** /lokobʏrɣəmestər/ (pl: -s) deputy mayor, acting mayor

de **locomotief** /lokomotif/ (pl: locomotieven) engine, locomotive

loden /lodə(n)/ (adj) **1** lead, leaden: *~ pijp* lead pipe **2** [fig] leaden, heavy

het/de **loeder** /ludər/ (pl: -s) [inform] brute, bastard

de **loef** /luf/: [fig] *iem. de ~ afsteken* steal a march on s.o.

de **loefzijde** /lufsɛidə/ windward (side)

de **loei** /luj/ [inform] thump; bash; sizzler; cracker: *een ~ verkopen (uitdelen)* hit (*or:* lash) out (at s.o.)

loeien /lujə(n)/ (loeide, heeft geloeid) **1** moo; low; bellow **2** howl; whine; roar; blare; hoot; wail: *de motor laten ~* race the engine; *met ~de sirenes* with blaring sirens

loeihard /lujhɑrt/ (adj, adv) [inform] **1** amazingly fast **2** blaring, deafening

de **loempia** /lumpija/ (pl: -'s) spring roll, egg roll

loensen /lunzə(n)/ (loenste, heeft geloenst) squint, be cross-eyed

de **loep** /lup/ (pl: -en) magnifying glass, lens: *iets onder de ~ nemen* scrutinize sth., take a close look at sth.

loepzuiver /lupsœyvər/ (adj, adv) flawless, perfect: *een ~e diamant* a flawless diamond; *een ~e pass* a flawless (*or:* perfect) pass

de **loer** /lur/ **1** lurking: *op de ~ liggen* [also fig] lie in wait (for), lurk, be on the lookout (for) **2** trick: *iem. een ~ draaien* play a nasty (*or:* dirty) trick on s.o.

loeren /lurə(n)/ (loerde, heeft geloerd) leer (at); peer at; spy on: *het gevaar loert overal* there is danger lurking everywhere; *op iem. (iets)* ~ lie in wait for s.o. (sth.)

de **¹lof** /lɔf/ **1** praise, commendation: ~ *oogsten* win praise; *iem.* ~ *toezwaaien* give (high) praise to s.o., pay tribute to s.o.; *niets dan* ~ *voor …* full marks to …, hats off to …; *vol* ~ *zijn over* speak highly of, be full of praise for **2** honour, credit

het **²lof** /lɔf/ chicory

loffelijk /lɔ̞fələk/ (adj, adv) praiseworthy

het **loflied** /lɔ̞flit/ (pl: -liederen) hymn, song of praise: *een* ~ *op de natuur* an ode to nature

de **loftrompet** /lɔ̞frɔmpɛt/: *de* ~ *over iem.* **steken** trumpet forth (*or:* sing) s.o.'s praises

de **loftuiting** /lɔ̞ftœytɪŋ/ (pl: -en) (words of) praise, eulogy

de **lofzang** /lɔ̞fsɑŋ/ (pl: -en) ode

de **¹log** [comp] computer log

²log /lɔχ/ (adj, adv) unwieldy, cumbersome, ponderous, clumsy, heavy; sluggish; lumbering: *een* ~ *gevaarte* a cumbersome (*or:* an unwieldy) monster; *een ~ge* **olifant** a ponderous elephant; *met ~ge* **tred** *lopen* lumber (along), move with heavy gait

de **logaritme** /loɣarɪtmə/ (pl: -n) logarithm

het **logbestand** /lɔɣbəstɑnt/ (pl: -en) log file

het **logboek** /lɔɣbuk/ (pl: -en) log(book), journal: *in het* ~ *opschrijven* log

de **loge** /lo:ʒə/ (pl: -s) box, loge

de **logé** /loʒe/ (pl: -s) guest, visitor: *we krijgen een* ~ we are having a visitor (*or:* s.o. to stay)

het **logeerbed** /loʒerbɛt/ (pl: -den) spare bed

de **logeerkamer** /loʒerkamər/ (pl: -s) guest room, spare (bed)room, visitor's room

de **logeerpartij** /loʒerpartɛi/ (pl: -en) stay; [Am] slumber party, pyjama party

logen /loɣə(n)/ (loogde, heeft geloogd) soak in (*or:* treat with) lye

logenstraffen /loɣə(n)strɑfə(n)/ (logenstrafte, heeft gelogenstraft) belie

logeren /loʒerə(n)/ (logeerde, heeft/is gelogeerd) stay, put up; board; lodge: *blijven* ~ stay the night, stay over; *ik logeer bij een vriend* I'm staying at a friend's (home) (*or:* with a friend); *kan ik bij jou* ~? could you put me up (for the night)?; *in een hotel* ~ stay at a hotel; *iem.* **te** ~ *krijgen* have s.o. staying

de **logica** /loɣika/ logic: *er zit geen* ~ *in wat je zegt* there is no logic in what you're saying

het **logies** /loʒis/ accommodation, lodging(s): ~ *met ontbijt* bed and breakfast

de **login** /lɔχɪn/ (pl: -s) login

de **logingegevens** /lɔχɪnɣəɣevə(n)s/ (pl) login details

de **loginnaam** /lɔχɪnam/ log-in name

logisch /loɣis/ (adj, adv) logical, rational: *een ~e* **tegenstrijdigheid** a logical paradox; ~ *denken* think logically (*or:* rationally); *dat is nogal* ~ that's only logical, that figures

de **logistiek** /loɣɪstik/ logistics

het **logo** /loɣo/ (pl: -'s) logo

de **logopedie** /loɣopedi/ speech therapy

de **logopedist** /loɣopedɪst/ (pl: -en) speech therapist

de **loipe** /lɔjpə/ (pl: -s, -n) (ski) run

de **lok** /lɔk/ (pl: -ken) **1** lock, strand of hair; tress; curl; ringlet **2** locks, hair; tresses

het **¹lokaal** /lokal/ (pl: lokalen) (class)room

²lokaal /lokal/ (adj) local; topical: *om 10 uur lokale* **tijd** at 10 o'clock local time; *lokale* **verdoving** local anaesthesia

het **lokaas** /lɔkas/ (pl: lokazen) bait

lokaliseren /lokalizerə(n)/ (lokaliseerde, heeft gelokaliseerd) locate

het **loket** /lokɛt/ (pl: -ten) (office) window; booking office, ticket office; box-office (window); counter

de **lokettist** /lokɛtɪst/ (pl: -en) booking-clerk, ticket-clerk; box-office clerk; counter clerk

lokken /lɔkə(n)/ (lokte, heeft gelokt) **1** entice, lure: *in de val* ~ lure into a trap **2** tempt, entice, attract

het **lokkertje** /lɔkərcə/ (pl: -s) bait, carrot; loss leader; special offer

de **lokroep** /lɔkrup/ (pl: -en) call (note)

de **lol** /lɔl/ [inform] laugh, fun, lark: *zeg,* **doe** *me een* ~ *(en hou op)* do me a favour (and knock it off, will you); ~ *hebben* have fun, have a great time; *zijn* ~ *wel* **op** *kunnen* be in for a hell of a time; *voor de* ~ for a laugh, for fun (*or:* a lark); *ik doe dit niet* **voor** *de* ~ I'm not doing this for the good of my health; *de* ~ *was er gauw* **af** the fun was soon over

de **lolbroek** /lɔlbruk/ (pl: -en) [inform] clown, joker

het **lolletje** /lɔləcə/ (pl: -s) [inform]: *dat* **is** *geen* ~ it's not exactly a laugh a minute

lollig /lɔləχ/ (adj, adv) [inform] jolly, funny

de **lolly** /lɔli/ (pl: -'s) lollipop, lolly

de **lommerd** /lɔmərt/ (pl: -en) pawnshop

lommerrijk /lɔmərɛik/ (adj) shady

de **¹lomp** /lɔmp/ (pl: -en) rag; tatter

²lomp /lɔmp/ (adj, adv) **1** ponderous, unwieldy: *~e* **schoenen** clumsy shoes; *zich* ~ **bewegen** move clumsily, he got in an ungainly manner **2** clumsy, awkward, ungainly **3** rude, unmannerly, uncivil: *iem.* ~ **behandelen** treat s.o. rudely, be uncivil to s.o.

de **lomschool** /lɔmsχol/ (pl: -scholen) [Dutch] remedial school

Londen /lɔndə(n)/ London

Londens /lɔndə(n)s/ (adj) London

lonen /lonə(n)/ (loonde, heeft geloond) be worth: *dat loont de* **moeite** *niet* it is not worth one's while

lonend /lonənt/ (adj) paying, rewarding; profitable; remunerative: *dat is* **niet** ~ that doesn't pay

de **long** /lɔŋ/ (pl: -en) lung

de **longarts** /lɔŋarts/ (pl: -en) lung specialist

de **longdrink** /lɔŋdrɪŋk/ (pl: -s) long drink

het **longemfyseem** /lɔŋɛmfizem/ (pl: -emfysemen) (pulmonary) emphysema

de **longkanker** /lɔŋkɑŋkər/ lung cancer

de **longlist** /lɔŋlɪst/ longlist

de **longontsteking** /lɔŋɔntstekɪŋ/ (pl: -en) pneumonia

lonken /lɔŋkə(n)/ (lonkte, heeft gelonkt) make eyes at

de **lont** /lɔnt/ (pl: -en) fuse; touchpaper: [fig] *een kort ~je hebben* have a short fuse

loochenen /loxənə(n)/ (loochende, heeft geloochend) deny

het **lood** /lot/ **1** lead: *met ~ in de schoenen* with a heavy heart **2** lead, shot, ammunition ‖ *dat is ~* (or: *om*) *oud ijzer* it's six of one and half a dozen of the other; *uit het ~ (geslagen) zijn* be thrown off one's balance

de **loodgieter** /lotxitər/ (pl: -s) plumber

het **loodje** /loce/ (pl: -s) (lead) seal ‖ *de laatste ~s wegen het zwaarst* the last mile is the longest one; *het ~ leggen* **a)** come off badly, get the short end of the stick; **b)** kick the bucket

de **loodlijn** /lotlɛin/ (pl: -en) perpendicular (line), normal (line)

loodrecht /lotrɛxt/ (adj, adv) perpendicular (to), plumb; sheer: *~ op iets staan* be at right angles to sth.

de **¹loods** /lots/ pilot

de **²loods** /lots/ shed; hangar

loodsen /lotsə(n)/ (loodste, heeft geloodst) pilot, steer, conduct; shepherd

loodvrij /lotfrɛi/ (adj) lead-free, unleaded

loodzwaar /lotswar/ (adj, adv) heavy

het **loof** /lof/ foliage, leaves; green

de **loofboom** /lovbom/ (pl: -bomen) deciduous tree

het **Loofhuttenfeest** /lofhytə(n)fest/ Feast of Tabernacles

het/de **loog** /lox/ (pl: logen) caustic (solution), lye

looien /loɪjə(n)/ (looide, heeft gelooid) tan

het **looizuur** /loɪzyr/ tannic acid, tannin

de **¹look** /luk/ (pl: -s) look

het/de **²look** /lok/ allium

loom /lom/ (adj, adv) **1** heavy, leaden; slow; sluggish: *zich ~ bewegen* move heavily (or: sluggishly) **2** languid, listless

het **loon** /lon/ (pl: lonen) **1** pay, wage(s): *een hoog ~ verdienen* earn high wages **2** deserts, reward: *hij gaf hem zijn verdiende ~* he gave him his just deserts

de **loonadministratie** /lonatmɪnistra(t)si/ (pl: -s) wages administration (or: records)

de **loonbelasting** /lombəlastɪŋ/ (pl: -en) [Dutch] income tax

de **loondienst** /londinst/ (pl: -en) paid employment, salaried employment

de **loonlijst** /lonlɛist/ (pl: -en) payroll

de **loonmatiging** /lomatəɣɪŋ/ wage restraint

het **loonstrookje** /lonstrokjə/ (pl: -s) payslip

de **loonsverhoging** /lonsfərhoɣɪŋ/ (pl: -en) wage increase, pay increase, increase in wages (or: pay), rise; [Am] raise

de **loop** /lop/ (pl: lopen) **1** course, development: *de ~ van de Rijn* the course of the Rhine; *zijn gedachten de vrije ~ laten* give one's thoughts (or: imagination) free rein; *in de ~ der jaren* through the years **2** barrel **3** run, flight

de **loopafstand** /lopɑfstɔnt/ walking distance: *op ~* within walking distance

de **loopbaan** /lobɑn/ (pl: -banen) career

de **loopbaanbegeleiding** /lobambəɣəlɛidɪŋ/ career counseling

de **loopbrug** /lobrʏx/ footbridge

de **loopgraaf** /lopxraf/ (pl: -graven) trench

de **loopgravenoorlog** /lopxravə(n)orlɔx/ (pl: -en) trench war(fare) [also fig]

het **loopje** /lopjə/ (pl: -s) [mus] run, roulade ‖ *een ~ met iem. nemen* pull s.o.'s leg, make fun of s.o.

de **loopjongen** /lopjɔŋə(n)/ (pl: -s) errand boy, messenger boy

de **looplamp** /loplɑmp/ (pl: -en) portable inspection lamp

de **loopneus** /lopnøs/ (pl: -neuzen) runny nose, running nose

de **looppas** /lopɑs/ jog, run: *in ~* at a jog, at the double

de **loopplank** /loplɑŋk/ (pl: -en) gangplank, gangway

het **looprek** /loprɛk/ (pl: -ken) walking frame, walker

loops /lops/ (adj) on heat, in heat, in season

de **looptijd** /loptɛit/ (pl: -en) term, (period of) currency, duration

het **loopvlak** /lopflɑk/ tread

loos /los/ (adj) false, empty: *~ alarm* false alarm ‖ *er is iets ~* something's up (or: going on)

de **loot** /lot/ (pl: loten) shoot, cutting

het **lootje** /loce/ (pl: -s) lottery ticket, raffle ticket, lot: *~s trekken* draw lots

¹lopen /lopə(n)/ (liep, heeft/is gelopen) **1** walk, go: *iem. in de weg ~* get in s.o.'s way; *de trap op ~* run (or: go, walk) up the stairs; *op handen en voeten ~* walk on one's hands and feet, walk on all fours; *de straat uit ~* walk down the street **2** run: *het op een ~ zetten* take to one's heels **3** run, go: *het is anders gelopen* it worked out (or: turned out) otherwise ‖ *dit horloge loopt uitstekend* this watch keeps excellent time; *de kraan loopt niet meer* the tap's stopped running; *een motor die loopt op benzine* an engine that runs on petrol; *alles loopt gesmeerd* everything's running smoothly; *iets laten ~* **a)** let sth. go; **b)** let sth. slide (or: slip); *niet over zich heen laten ~* not let oneself get walked over

²lopen /lopə(n)/ (liep, heeft gelopen) go to, attend: *college ~* attend lectures

lopend /lopənt/ (adj) **1** running, moving: *~e band* conveyor belt; assembly line; [fig] *aan de ~e band* continually, ceaselessly **2** current, running: *het ~e jaar* the current year **3** running; streaming; runny

de **loper** /lopər/ (pl: -s) **1** walker; courier; messenger **2** carpet (strip); runner **3** bishop **4** pass-key, master key, skeleton key, picklock

het/de **lor** /lor/ (pl: -ren) rag

los /los/ (adj, adv) **1** loose, free; undone; detachable; movable: *er is een schroef ~* a screw has come loose; *~!* let go! **2** loose, separate, odd, single: *thee wordt bijna niet meer ~ verkocht* tea is hardly sold loose any more **3** slack, loose ‖ *met ~se handen rijden* ride with no hands; *ze leven er maar op ~* they live from one day to the next; *~ van* apart from, besides; *dat is niet ~ te zien van* this cannot be detached from

losbandig /lozbɑndəχ/ (adj, adv) lawless; loose; fast, dissipated

losbarsten /lozbɑrstə(n)/ (barstte los, is losgebarsten) break out, burst out, flare up, erupt; blow up

de **losbol** /lozbɔl/ (pl: -len) fast liver, rake

losbranden /lozbrɑndə(n)/ (brandde los, is losgebrand) fire (*or:* blaze) away: *brand maar los!* fire away!

¹**losbreken** /lozbrekə(n)/ (brak los, is losgebroken) **1** break out (*or:* free), escape: *de hond is losgebroken* the dog has torn itself free **2** burst out, blow up: *een hevig onweer brak los* a heavy thunderstorm broke

²**losbreken** /lozbrekə(n)/ (brak los, heeft losgebroken) break off, tear off (*or:* loose), separate

losdraaien /lozdrajə(n)/ (draaide los, heeft losgedraaid) **1** unscrew, untwist **2** take off, twist off, loosen

de **loser** /luːzər/ loser

losgaan /losxan/ (ging los, is losgegaan) **1** come loose, work loose, become untied (*or:* unstuck, detached) **2** let oneself go, let one's hair down ‖ *hij ging helemaal los na dat mailtje* he freaked out completely after that email; *Twitter ging los* Twitter exploded

het **losgeld** /losxɛlt/ (pl: -en) ransom (money)

losjes /loʃəs/ (adv) **1** loosely: *zij droeg haar sjaal ~ om haar nek* she wore her scarf draped loosely around her neck **2** airily, casually: *~ op iets gebaseerd zijn* be loosely based on sth.

loskloppen /losklopə(n)/ (klopte los, heeft losgeklopt) beat, knock loose (*or:* off)

losknopen /losknopə(n)/ (knoopte los, heeft losgeknoopt) undo, untie

loskomen /loskomə(n)/ (kwam los, is losgekomen) **1** come loose, come off, break loose (*or:* free), come apart: *hij kan niet ~ van zijn verleden* he cannot forget his past **2** come out, unbend, relax

loskoppelen /loskopələ(n)/ (koppelde los, heeft losgekoppeld) detach, uncouple, disconnect, separate

loskrijgen /loskrɛiɣə(n)/ (kreeg los, heeft losgekregen) **1** get loose; get undone; get free (*or:* released): *een knoop ~* get a knot untied **2** secure, extract, (manage to) obtain; raise

¹**loslaten** /loslatə(n)/ (liet los, heeft losgelaten) come off, peel off, come loose (*or:* unstuck, untied), give way

²**loslaten** /loslatə(n)/ (liet los, heeft losgelaten) **1** release, set free, let off, let go, discharge; unleash: *laat me los!* let go of me!, let me go!; [fig] *een formule ~ op de gegevens* apply a formula to the data **2** reveal, speak; release; leak: *geen woord ~ over iets* keep mum (*or:* close) about sth. **3** let go, relinquish

losliggend /loslɪɣənt/ (adj) loose

loslippig /loslɪpəχ/ (adj) loose-lipped, loose-tongued

loslopen /loslopə(n)/ (liep los, heeft losgelopen) walk about (freely), run free; be at large; stray ‖ *het zal wel ~* it will be all right, it'll sort itself out

loslopend /loslopənt/ (adj) stray, unattached

losmaken /losmakə(n)/ (maakte los, heeft losgemaakt) **1** release, set free; untie: *de hond ~* unleash the dog; *een knoop ~* untie a knot, undo a button **2** loosen (up); rake **3** stir up: *die tv-film heeft een hoop losgemaakt* that TV film has created quite a stir

de **losprijs** /losprɛis/ (pl: -prijzen) ransom (money)

losraken /losrakə(n)/ (raakte los, is losgeraakt) come loose (*or:* off, away), dislodge, become detached

losrukken /losrʏkə(n)/ (rukte los, heeft losgerukt) tear loose, rip off, wrench, yank away (*or:* off)

de **löss** /lʏs/ loess

losscheuren /losχørə(n)/ (scheurde los, heeft losgescheurd) tear loose, rip off (*or:* away)

losschroeven /losχruvə(n)/ (schroefde los, heeft losgeschroefd) unscrew, loosen; screw off; disconnect

lossen /losə(n)/ (loste, heeft gelost) **1** unload, discharge **2** discharge; shoot; fire: *een schot op (het) doel ~* shoot at goal

losslaan /loslan/ (sloeg los, is losgeslagen) **1** break away **2** [fig] go astray: *die jongen is helemaal losgeslagen* that boy has gone completely astray

losstaan /lostan/ (stond los, heeft losgestaan): *~ van* be unrelated to

losstaand /lostant/ (adj) detached; isolated; free-standing; disconnected

lostrekken /lostrɛkə(n)/ (trok los, heeft losgetrokken) pull loose, loosen, draw loose

los-vast /losfɑst/ (adj) half-fastened; [fig] casual

¹losweken /lɔswekə(n)/ (weekte los, is losgeweekt) become unstuck

²losweken /lɔswekə(n)/ (weekte los, heeft losgeweekt) soak off; steam off (*or:* open)

loszitten /lɔsɪtə(n)/ (zat los, heeft losgezeten) be loose; be slack: *die knoop zit los* that button is coming off

het **lot** /lɔt/ (pl: -en) **1** lottery ticket; raffle ticket **2** lot, share: [fig] *zij is een ~ uit de loterij* she is one in a thousand **3** fortune, chance **4** lot, fate, destiny: *iem. aan zijn ~ overlaten* leave s.o. to fend for himself, leave s.o. to his fate; *berusten in zijn ~* resign o.s. to one's fate

loten /lotə(n)/ (lootte, heeft geloot) draw lots

de **loterij** /lotərɛi/ (pl: -en) lottery

de **lotgenoot** /lɔtxənot/ (pl: lotgenoten) companion (in misfortune, adversity), fellow-sufferer

de **loting** /lotɪŋ/ (pl: -en) drawing lots

de **lotion** /loʃɔn/ (pl: -s) lotion, wash

de **lotto** /lɔto/ (pl: -'s) lottery

de **lotus** /lotʏs/ (pl: -sen) lotus

louche /luʃ(ə)/ (adj) shady, suspicious(-looking)

de **lounge** /laundʒ/ (pl: -s) lounge

¹louter /lautər/ (adj) sheer, pure; mere; bare: *uit ~ medelijden* purely out of compassion; *door ~ toeval* by pure coincidence

²louter /lautər/ (adv) purely, merely, only: *het heeft ~ theoretische waarde* it has only theoretical value

loven /lovə(n)/ (loofde, heeft geloofd) **1** praise, commend, laud **2** [rel] praise, bless, glorify: *looft de Heer* praise the Lord

lovend /lovənt/ (adj, adv) laudatory, approving; full of praise

de **loverboy** /lovərbɔi/ (pl: -s) lover boy

het **lovertje** /lovərcə/ (pl: -s) spangle, sequin

de **lowbudgetfilm** /lobʏdʒɛtfɪlm/ (pl: -s) low-budget film, film made on a shoestring

loyaal /lojal/ (adj, adv) loyal, faithful, steadfast

de **loyaliteit** /lwajalitɛit/ loyalty

¹lozen /lozə(n)/ (loosde, heeft geloosd) drain, empty: *~ in (op) de zee* discharge into the sea

²lozen /lozə(n)/ (loosde, heeft geloosd) get rid of, send off, dump

de **lozing** /lozɪŋ/ (pl: -en) drainage, discharge, dumping

de **lp** /ɛlpe/ (pl: lp's) LP

het **lpg** /ɛlpeɣe/ *liquefied petroleum gas* LPG, LP gas

het **lso** /ɛlɛso/ [Belg] *lager secundair onderwijs* junior secondary general education

de **lucht** /lʏxt/ (pl: -en) **1** air: *~ krijgen* a) breathe; b) [fig] get room to breathe; *ik krijg geen ~* I can't breathe **2** air: *in de ~ vliegen* blow up, explode; *de ~ ingaan* a) [aeroplane] take to the air; b) [radio] go on the air; [fig]

die bewering is uit de ~ gegrepen that statement is totally unfounded; [fig] *uit de ~ komen vallen* appear out of thin air; [Belg] be dumbfounded; [fig] *de ~ klaren* clear the air; [fig] *dat komt niet uit de ~ vallen* it was to be expected, it is not unexpected **3** smell, scent, odour **4** sky: *de ~ betrekt* the sky is becoming overcast ‖ *gebakken ~* hot air

de **luchtaanval** /lʏxtanvɑl/ (pl: -len) air raid

de **luchtafweer** /lʏxtɑfwer/ anti-aircraft guns

het **luchtafweergeschut** /lʏxtɑfwerɣəsxʏt/ anti-aircraft guns

het **luchtalarm** /lʏxtalɑrm/ (pl: -en) air-raid warning (*or:* siren), (air-raid) alert

de **luchtballon** /lʏxtbɑlɔn/ (pl: -nen) (hot-air) balloon

het **luchtbed** /lʏxtbɛt/ (pl: -den) air-bed, Lilo, inflatable bed

de **luchtbel** /lʏxtbɛl/ (pl: -len) air bubble (*or:* bell)

de **luchtbevochtiger** /lʏxtbəvɔxtəɣər/ (pl: -s) humidifier

de **luchtbrug** /lʏxtbrʏx/ (pl: -gen) **1** overhead bridge **2** airlift

luchtdicht /lʏxdɪxt/ (adj, adv) airtight, hermetic

de **luchtdruk** /lʏxdrʏk/ (atmospheric) pressure, air pressure

het **luchtdrukpistool** /lʏxdrʏkpistol/ (pl: -pistolen) air pistol

luchten /lʏxtə(n)/ (luchtte, heeft gelucht) air, ventilate: *zijn hart ~ bij iem.* pour out one's feelings to s.o.; *iem. niet kunnen ~ of zien* hate the sight of s.o.

de **luchter** /lʏxtər/ (pl: -s) candelabrum, chandelier

het/de **luchtfilter** /lʏxtfɪltər/ (pl: -s) air filter (*or:* cleaner)

de **luchtfoto** /lʏxtfoto/ (pl: -'s) aerial photo(graph), aerial view

luchtgekoeld /lʏ(x)txəkult/ (adj) air-cooled

het **luchtgevecht** /lʏ(x)txəvɛxt/ (pl: -en) dogfight

luchthartig /lʏxthɑrtəx/ (adj, adv) light-hearted, carefree

de **luchthaven** /lʏxthavə(n)/ (pl: -s) airport

de **luchthavenbelasting** /lʏxthavə(n)bəlɑstɪŋ/ airport tax

luchtig /lʏxtəx/ (adj) **1** light, airy **2** light, cool, thin **3** airy, light-hearted: *iets op ~e toon meedelen* announce sth. casually **4** airy, vivacious, light ‖ *~ gekleed* lightly dressed

het **luchtje** /lʏxjə/ (pl: -s) smell, scent, odour: *er zit een ~ aan* [fig] there is sth. fishy about it ‖ *een ~ scheppen* take a breath of fresh air, get a bit of fresh air

het **luchtkasteel** /lʏxtkɑstel/ (pl: -kastelen) castle in the air, daydream: *luchtkastelen bouwen* build castles in the air

de **luchtkoker** /lʏxtkokər/ (pl: -s) air (*or:* ventilating) shaft het **luchtkussen** /lʏχtkʏsə(n)/ (pl: -s) air cushion (or: pillow)

de **luchtlaag** /lʏχtlaχ/ (pl: -lagen) layer of air

de **luchtlandingstroepen** /lʏχtlɑndɪŋstrupə(n)/ (pl) airborne troops

luchtledig /lʏχtlɛdəχ/ (adj) exhausted (or: void) of air

het **luchtledige** /lʏχtlɛdəɣə/: in het ~ praten talk hot air

de **luchtmacht** /lʏχtmɑχt/ (pl: -en) air force

de **luchtmachtbasis** /lʏχtmɑχtbazɪs/ (pl: -bases) air(-force) base

luchtmobiel /lʏχtmobil/ (adj) airborne

de **luchtpijp** /lʏχtpɛip/ (pl: -en) windpipe, trachea

de **luchtpost** /lʏχtpɔst/ airmail

het **luchtruim** /lʏχtrœym/ atmosphere, airspace, air

het **luchtschip** /lʏχtsχɪp/ (pl: -schepen) airship, dirigible

de **luchtspiegeling** /lʏχtspiɣəlɪŋ/ (pl: -en) mirage

de **luchtsprong** /lʏχtsprɔŋ/ (pl: -en) jump in the air, caper

de **luchtstreek** /lʏχtstrek/ (pl: -streken) zone, region

de **luchtstroom** /lʏχtstrom/ (pl: -stromen) air current, flow of air

de **luchtvaart** /lʏχtfart/ aviation, flying

de **luchtvaartmaatschappij** /lʏχtfartmatsχɑpɛi/ (pl: -en) airline (company): de Koninklijke Luchtvaartmaatschappij Royal Dutch Airlines, KLM

de **luchtverfrisser** /lʏχtfərfrɪsər/ (pl: -s) air freshener

het **luchtverkeer** /lʏχtfərker/ air traffic

de **luchtverkeersleider** /lʏχtfərkerslɛidər/ (pl: -s) air traffic controller

de **luchtverversing** /lʏχtfərvɛrsɪŋ/ ventilation

de **luchtvervuiling** /lʏχtfərvœylɪŋ/ air pollution

de **luchtvochtigheid** /lʏχtfɔχtəχhɛit/ humidity

de **luchtweerstand** /lʏχtwerstɑnt/ drag, air resistance

de **luchtwegen** /lʏχtweɣə(n)/ (pl) bronchial tubes

de **luchtzak** /lʏχtsɑk/ (pl: -ken) air pocket, air hole

luchtziek /lʏχtsik/ (adj) airsick

de **luchtziekte** /lʏχtsiktə/ airsickness

de **lucifer** /lysifɛr/ (pl: -s) match

het **lucifersdoosje** /lysifɛrzdoʃə/ (pl: -s) matchbox

het **lucifershoutje** /lysifɛrshɑucə/ (pl: -s) matchstick

lucky /lʏki/ (adj) lucky

lucratief /lykratif/ (adj, adv) lucrative, profitable

ludiek /lydik/ (adj, adv) playful: ~e protestacties happenings

luguber /lyɣybər/ (adj, adv) lugubrious, sinister

de [1]**lui** /lœy/ (pl) people, folk: zijn **ouwe** ~ his old folks (or: parents)

[2]**lui** /lœy/ (adj, adv) lazy, idle, indolent; slow; heavy: een ~e **stoel** an easy chair; liever ~ **dan** moe zijn be bone idle

de **luiaard** /lœyart/ (pl: -s) 1 lazybones 2 sloth

luid /lœyt/ (adj, adv) loud: ~ en **duidelijk** loud and clear; met ~e **stem** in a loud voice

[1]**luiden** /lœydə(n)/ (luidde, heeft geluid) 1 sound, ring; toll: de **klok** luidt the bell is ringing (or: tolling) 2 read, run: het **vonnis** luidt … the verdict is …; de brief luidt als **volgt** the letter reads as follows

[2]**luiden** /lœydə(n)/ (luidde, heeft geluid) ring, sound

luidkeels /lœytkels/ (adv) loudly, at the top of one's voice: ~ **lachen** laugh at the top of one's voice

luidop /lœytɔp/ (adv) [Belg] aloud, out loud

luidruchtig /lœytrʏχtəχ/ (adj, adv) noisy, boisterous

de **luidspreker** /lœytsprekər/ (pl: -s) (loud)speaker

de **luier** /lœyər/ (pl: -s) nappy; [Am] diaper: een baby een **schone** ~ omdoen change a baby's nappy (or: diaper)

luieren /lœyərə(n)/ (luierde, heeft geluierd) be idle (or: lazy), laze

de **luifel** /lœyfəl/ (pl: -s) awning

de **luiheid** /lœyhɛit/ laziness, idleness

het **luik** /lœyk/ (pl: -en) hatch; trapdoor; shutter

Luik /lœyk/ Liège

de **luilak** /lœylɑk/ (pl: -ken) lazybones, sluggard

Luilekkerland /lœylɛkərlɑnt/ (land of) Cockaigne, land of plenty

de **luim** /lœym/ (pl: -en) humour, mood, temper

de **luipaard** /lœypart/ (pl: -en) leopard

de **luis** /lœys/ (pl: luizen) louse; aphid ‖ een ~ in de **pels** a thorn in the side (of)

de **luister** /lœystər/ lustre, splendour: een gebeurtenis ~ **bijzetten** add lustre to an event

de **luisteraar** /lœystərar/ (pl: -s) listener

het **luisterboek** /lœystərbuk/ (pl: -en) audio book

luisteren /lœystərə(n)/ (luisterde, heeft geluisterd) 1 listen: goed **kunnen** ~ be a good listener; luister eens listen …, say … 2 eavesdrop, listen (in) 3 listen, respond: naar hem wordt toch niet geluisterd nobody pays any attention to (or: listens to) him anyway ‖ dat luistert **nauw** that requires precision, it's very precise work

luisterrijk /lœystərɛik/ (adj, adv) splendid, glorious, magnificent

de **luistertoets** /lœystərtuts/ (pl: -en) listening comprehension test

de **luistervaardigheid** /lœystərvardəχhɛit/

listening (skill)

de **luistervink** /lœystərvɪŋk/ (pl: -en) eaves-dropper

de **luit** /lœyt/ (pl: -en) lute

de **luitenant** /lœytənɑnt/ (pl: -s) lieutenant

de **luiwammes** /lœywɑməs/ (pl: -en) [inform] lazybones

luizen /lœyzə(n)/ (luisde, heeft geluisd): *iem. erin ~* take s.o. in, trick s.o. into sth.; trip s.o. up

de **luizenbaan** /lœyzə(n)ban/ (pl: -banen) soft job, cushy job

het **luizenleven** /lœyzə(n)levə(n)/ (pl: -s) cushy life: *een ~ leiden* have an easy (*or:* a cushy) life

lukken /lʏkə(n)/ (lukte, is gelukt) succeed, be successful, work, manage: *gaat ~!* we can do it!, we'll get there!; this is going to work!; *die foto is goed gelukt* that photo has come out well; *het is niet gelukt* it didn't work, it didn't go through, it was no go; *het lukte hem te ontsnappen* he managed to escape

lukraak /lʏkrak/ (adj, adv) haphazard, random, wild, hit-or-miss

de **lul** /lʏl/ (pl: -len) [inform] **1** prick, cock **2** prick, drip: *voor ~ staan* stand there like an idiot

lullen /lʏlə(n)/ (lulde, heeft geluld) [inform] (talk) bullshit, drivel: *je lult!* you're talking bullshit

lullig /lʏləx/ (adj, adv) [inform] shitty, (bloody) stupid, pathetic: *doe niet zo ~* don't be such a jerk (*or:* tit)

lumineus /lyminøs/ (adj) brilliant, bright

de **lummel** /lʏməl/ (pl: -s) [inform] clodhopper, gawk

lummelen /lʏmələ(n)/ (lummelde, heeft gelummeld) [inform] hang around, fool around

de **lunch** /lʏnʃ/ (pl: -es) lunch(eon)

het **lunchconcert** /lʏnʃkɔnsɛrt/ (pl: -en) lunch concert

lunchen /lʏnʃə(n)/ (lunchte, heeft geluncht) lunch, have (*or:* eat, take) lunch

het **lunchpakket** /lʏnʃpɑkɛt/ (pl: -ten) packed lunch

de **lunchpauze** /lʏnʃpauzə/ (pl: -s) lunch break

de **lunchroom** /lʏnʃruːm/ (pl: -s) tearoom; [Am] [roughly] coffee shop

de **luren** /lyrə(n)/ (pl): *iem. in de ~ leggen* take s.o. in, take s.o. for a ride

lurken /lʏrkə(n)/ (lurkte, heeft gelurkt) suck noisily

de **lurven** /lʏrvə(n)/ (pl): [inform] *iem. bij zijn ~ pakken* get s.o., grab s.o.

de **lus** /lʏs/ (pl: -sen) loop; noose

de **lust** /lʏst/ (pl: -en) **1** desire, interest: *tijd en ~ ontbreken me om ...* I have neither the time nor the energy to (*or:* for) ... **2** lust, passion, desire **3** delight, joy: *~en en lasten* joys and burdens; *zwemmen is zijn ~ en zijn leven*

swimming is all the world to him, swimming is his ruling passion; *een ~ voor het oog* a sight for sore eyes

lusteloos /lʏstəlos/ (adj, adv) listless, languid, apathetic

lusten /lʏstə(n)/ (lustte, heeft gelust) like, enjoy, be fond of, have a taste for: *ik zou wel een pilsje ~* I could do with a beer; [fig] *hij zal ervan ~* he's going to pay for this; [fig] *ik lust hem rauw* let me get my hands on him

lustig /lʏstəx/ (adj, adv) cheerful, gay, merry

de **lustmoord** /lʏstmort/ (pl: -en) sex murder (*or:* killing)

het **lustobject** /lʏstɔpjɛkt/ (pl: -en) sex object

het **lustrum** /lʏstrʏm/ (pl: lustra) lustrum

luthers /lytərs/ (adj) Lutheran

luttel /lʏtəl/ (adj) little, mere; few; inconsiderable

luwen /lywə(n)/ (luwde, is geluwd) subside, die down

de **luwte** /lywtə/ (pl: -n) lee, shelter

de **luxaflex®** /lʏksaflɛks/ Venetian blinds

de **¹luxe** /lʏksə/ luxury: *het zou geen (overbodige) ~ zijn* it would certainly be no luxury, it's really necessary

²luxe /lʏksə/ (adj) luxury, fancy, de luxe: *een ~ tent* a posh (*or:* fancy) place

het **luxeartikel** /lʏksəartikəl/ (pl: -en) luxury article; [pl] luxury goods

Luxemburg /lʏksəmbʏrx/ Luxembourg

de **Luxemburger** /lʏksəmbʏryər/ (pl: -s) Luxembourger

Luxemburgs /lʏksəmbʏrxs/ (adj) (of/from) Luxembourg

het **luxeprobleem** /lʏksəproblem/ (pl: -problemen) luxury problem: *een ~ hebben* be spoilt for choice

luxueus /lyksywøs/ (adj, adv) luxurious, opulent, plush

het **lyceum** /lisejʏm/ (pl: lycea) [Dutch] [roughly] grammarschool; [Am] high school

Lyme /lajm/ [med]: *de ziekte van ~* Lyme Disease, Lyme borreliosis

de **lymfe** /lɪmfə/ lymph

de **lymfeklier** /lɪmfəklir/ (pl: lymfeklieren) lymph node (*or:* gland)

lynchen /lɪnʃə(n)/ (lynchte, heeft gelyncht) lynch

de **lynx** /lɪŋks/ (pl: -en) lynx

de **lyriek** /lirik/ lyric(al) (poetry)

lyrisch /liris/ (adj, adv) lyric(al)

m

de **m** /ɛm/ (pl: m's) m, M

de **ma** /ma/ (pl: ma's) mum; [Am] mom: *pa en
ma* Mum (*or:* Mom) and Dad

de **MA** (pl: MA's) *master of arts* MA *(Master of
Arts)*

de **maag** /maχ/ (pl: magen) stomach: *mijn ~
draaide zich om* it made my stomach turn, it
turned my stomach; *ergens mee in zijn ~ zitten*
be worried about sth., be troubled by sth.;
iem. iets in de ~ splitsen unload sth. onto s.o.

de **maagband** /maχbɑnt/ (pl: -en) gastric
band, lap band

de **maagd** /maχt/ (pl: -en) virgin

de **Maagd** /maχt/ (pl: -en) [astrology] Virgo

de **maag-, darm- en leverarts** /maχdɑrmɛn-
leverɑrts/ (pl: -en) [Dutch] gastroenterologist

het **maag-darmkanaal** /maχdɑrmkanal/ (pl:
-kanalen) gastrointestinal tract

maagdelijk /maχdələk/ (adj, adv) virginal:
~ wit virgin white

de **maagdelijkheid** /maχdələkhɛit/ virginity

het **maagdenvlies** /maχdə(n)vlis/ (pl: -vliezen)
hymen

de **maagklacht** /maχklɑχt/ (pl: -en) stomach
disorder

de **maagkramp** /maχkrɑmp/ (pl: -en) stomach
cramps

de **maagpijn** /maχpɛin/ (pl: -en) stomach ache

het **maagsap** /maχsɑp/ gastric juice

de **maagsonde** /maχsɔndə/ (pl: -s) stomach
(*or:* gastric) tube

het **maagzuur** /maχsyr/ heartburn

de **maagzweer** /maχswer/ (pl: -zweren) ulcer

maaien /majə(n)/ (maaide, heeft gemaaid)
mow, cut: *het gras ~* a) cut (*or:* mow) the
grass; b) mow the lawn

de **maaier** /majər/ (pl: -s) mower

de **maaimachine** /majmaʃinə/ (pl: -s) (lawn)-
mower

de **maak** /mak/: *er zijn plannen in de ~ om ...*
plans are being made to ...

het **¹maal** /mal/ meal: *een feestelijk ~* a festive
meal

het/de **²maal** /mal/ **1** time: *een paar ~* once or twice,
several times; *anderhalf ~ zoveel* half as much
(*or:* many) (again) **2** times: *lengte ~ breedte
~ hoogte* length times width times height;
tweemaal drie is zes two times three is six

de **maalstroom** /malstrom/ (pl: -stromen)
whirlpool; [fig] vortex

het **maalteken** /maltekə(n)/ (pl: -s) multiplication sign

de **maaltijd** /maltɛit/ (pl: -en) meal, dinner

de **maaltijdbox** /maltɛidbɔks/ (pl: -en) food
box

de **maaltijdcheque** /maltɛrtʃɛk/ (pl: -s) [Belg]
luncheon voucher

het **maaltijdpakket** /maltɛitpɑkɛt/ (pl: -ten)
meal kit

de **maan** /man/ (pl: manen) moon

de **maand** /mant/ (pl: -en) month: *de ~ januari*
the month of January; *een ~ vakantie* a
month's holiday; *drie ~en lang* for three
months; *binnen een ~* within a month; *een
baby van vier ~en* a four-month-old baby

het **maandabonnement** /mantabɔnəmɛnt/
(pl: -en) monthly subscription; monthly season ticket

de **maandag** /mandɑχ/ (pl: -en) Monday: *ik
train altijd op ~* I always train on Mondays; *ik
doe het ~ wel* I will do it on Monday; *'s ~s on*
Mondays, every Monday

¹maandags /mandɑχs/ (adj) Monday

²maandags /mandɑχs/ (adv) on Mondays

het **maandblad** /mantblɑt/ (pl: -en) monthly
(magazine)

maandelijks /mandələks/ (adj, adv)
monthly, once a month, every month: *in ~e
termijnen* in monthly instalments

maandenlang /mandə(n)lɑŋ/ (adj, adv) for
months, months long

de **maandkaart** /mantkart/ (pl: -en) monthly
(season) ticket

het **maandsalaris** /mantsalarɪs/ monthly salary

het **maandverband** /mantfərbɑnt/ (pl: -en)
sanitary towel; [Am] sanitary napkin

de **maanfase** /manfazə/ phase (of the moon)

de **maanlanding** /manlɑndɪŋ/ (pl: -en) moon
landing

het **maanlandschap** /manlɑntsχɑp/ (pl: -pen)
moonscape, lunarscape

het **maanlicht** /manlɪχt/ moonlight

het **maanmannetje** /manmɑnəcə/ man in the
moon

de **maansverduistering** /mansfərdœystərɪŋ/
(pl: -en) eclipse of the moon, lunar eclipse

het **maanzaad** /manzat/ poppy seed

¹maar /mar/ (adv) **1** but, only, just: *zeg het ~:
koffie of thee?* which will it be: coffee or tea?;
kom ~ binnen come on in; *dat komt ~ al te
vaak voor* that happens only (*or:* all) too often; *het is ~ goed dat je gebeld hebt* it's a good
thing you rang; *als ik ook ~ een minuut te lang
wegblijf* if I stay away even a minute too long;
doe het nu ~ just do it; *let ~ niet op hem* don't
pay any attention to him; *ik zou ~ uitkijken*
you'd better be careful **2** only, as long as: *als
het ~ klaar komt* as long as (*or:* so long as) it is
finished **3** (if) only: *ik hoop ~ dat hij het vindt* I
only hope he finds it || *wat je ~ wil* whatever
you want; *ik vind het ~ niks* I'm none too
happy about it; *zoveel als je ~ wilt* as much
(*or:* many) as you like

²maar /mar/ (conj) but: *klein, ~ dapper* small

but tough || *ja* ~, *als dat nu niet zo is* yes, but what if that isn't true?; *nee* ~*!* really!

de **maarschalk** /m*a*rsχɑlk/ (pl: -en) Field Marshal; [Am] General of the Army

de **maart** /mart/ March

de **maas** /mas/ (pl: mazen) mesh: *door de mazen (van het net) glippen* slip through the net

de **Maas** /mas/ Meuse

de **¹maat** /mat/ **1** size, measure; measurements: *in hoge mate* to a great degree, to a large extent; *in toenemende mate* increasingly, more and more; *welke* ~ *hebt u?* what size do you take? **2** measure: *maten en gewichten* weights and measures **3** moderation **4** [mus] time; beat: *(geen)* ~ *kunnen houden* be (un)able to keep time **5** [mus] bar, measure: *de eerste maten van het volkslied* the first few bars of the national anthem || *de* ~ *is vol* that's the limit

de **²maat** /mat/ **1** pal, mate **2** (team)mate; [cards] partner

de **maatbeker** /m*a*dbekər/ (pl: -s) measuring cup

maatgevend /matχevənt/ (adj) normative; indicative: *dat is toch niet* ~*?* that is not a criterion, is it?

het **maatgevoel** /m*a*tχəvul/ sense of rhythm

het **maatglas** /m*a*tχlɑs/ measuring glass, measuring cup; graduated cylinder

maathouden /m*a*thɑudə(n)/ (hield maat, heeft maatgehouden) [mus] keep time

het **maatje** /m*a*cə/ (pl: -s) chum, pal: *goede* ~*s zijn met iem.* be the best of friends with s.o.; *goede* ~*s worden met iem.* chum up with s.o.

de **maatjesharing** /m*a*cəshariŋ/ (pl: -en) [roughly] young herring

het **maatkostuum** /m*a*tkostym/ (pl: -s) custom-made suit, tailored suit

de **maatpak** /m*a*tpɑk/ (pl: -ken) custom-made suit, tailor-made suit

de **maatregel** /m*a*trəɣəl/ (pl: -en) measure: ~*en nemen* (or: *treffen*) take steps

de **maatschap** /m*a*tsχɑp/ (pl: -pen) partnership

maatschappelijk /matsχɑpələk/ (adj, adv) **1** social: *hij zit in het* ~ *werk* he's a social worker **2** joint: *het* ~ *kapitaal* nominal capital

de **maatschappij** /matsχɑpɛi/ (pl: -en) **1** society, association **2** company

de **maatschappijleer** /matsχɑpɛiler/ social studies

de **maatstaf** /m*a*tstɑf/ (pl: -staven) criterion, standard(s)

het **maatwerk** /m*a*twɛrk/ custom-made clothes (or: shoes)

macaber /mak*a*bər/ (adj, adv) macabre

de **macaroni** /makar*o*ni/ macaroni

Macedonië /masəd*o*nijə/ Macedonia

de **Macedoniër** /masəd*o*nijər/ (pl: -s) Macedonian

het **¹Macedonisch** /masəd*o*nis/ Macedonian

²Macedonisch /masəd*o*nis/ (adj) Macedonian

de **machete** /mɑ(t)ʃ*e*tə/ (pl: -s) machete

¹machinaal /maʃin*a*l/ (adj) mechanized, machine

²machinaal /maʃin*a*l/ (adv) mechanically, by machine

de **machine** /maʃ*i*nə/ (pl: -s) machine; machinery

de **machinebankwerker** /maʃinəbɑŋkwɛrkər/ (pl: -s) lathe operator

het **machinegeweer** /maʃinəɣəwer/ (pl: -geweren) machine-gun

de **machinekamer** /maʃinəkɑmər/ (pl: -s) engine room

de **machinist** /maʃin*i*st/ (pl: -en) **1** [railways] engine driver; [Am] engineer **2** [shipp] engineer

de **¹macho** /m*ɑ*tʃo/ (pl: -'s) macho

²macho /m*ɑ*tʃo/ (adj) macho

de **macht** /mɑχt/ (pl: -en) **1** power, force: *(naar) de* ~ *grijpen* (attempt to) seize power; *aan de* ~ *zijn* be in power; *iem. in zijn* ~ *hebben* have s.o. in one's power; *de* ~ *over het stuur verliezen* lose control of the wheel **2** authority: *rechterlijke* ~ the judicial branch, the judiciary; *de uitvoerende* (or: *wetgevende*) ~ the executive (or: legislative) branch **3** power, force: *dat gaat boven mijn* ~ that is beyond my power; *met (uit) alle* ~ with all one's strength || [maths] *een getal tot de vierde* ~ *verheffen* raise a number to the fourth power; [maths] *drie tot de derde* ~ three cubed

machteloos /m*ɑ*χtəlos/ (adj, adv) powerless: *machteloze woede* impotent (or: helpless) anger

de **machteloosheid** /m*ɑ*χtəlosɛit/ powerlessness

de **machthebber** /m*ɑ*χthɛbər/ (pl: -s) ruler, leader

machtig /m*ɑ*χtəχ/ (adj) **1** powerful, mighty: *haar gevoelens werden haar te* ~ she was overcome by her emotions **2** rich, heavy **3** competent (in)

machtigen /m*ɑ*χtəɣə(n)/ (machtigde, heeft gemachtigd) authorize

de **machtiging** /m*ɑ*χtəɣiŋ/ (pl: -en) authorization

het **machtsblok** /m*ɑ*χ(t)sblɔk/ (pl: -ken) power block

de **machtshonger** /m*ɑ*χ(t)shɔŋər/ lust for power

het **machtsmiddel** /m*ɑ*χ(t)smɪdəl/ (pl: -en) means of (exercising) power, weapon

het **machtsmisbruik** /m*ɑ*χ(t)smɪzbrœyk/ abuse of power

de **machtsovername** /m*ɑ*χ(t)sovərnamə/ (pl: -s) assumption of power; take-over

de **machtspolitiek** /m*ɑ*χ(t)spolitik/ power politics

de **machtspositie** /mɑx(t)spozi(t)si/ (pl: -s) position of power

de **machtsstrijd** /mɑxtstrɛit/ (pl: -en) struggle for power, power struggle

het **machtsvacuüm** /mɑx(t)sfakywʏm/ power vacuum

machtsverheffen /mɑx(t)sfərhɛfə(n)/ raise to the power

het **machtsvertoon** /mɑxtsfərton/ display of power, show of strength

het **macramé** /makramɛ/ macramé

macro /mɑkro/ (adv) macro

macrobiotisch /makrobijotis/ (adj) macrobiotic

Madagaskar /madayɑskar/ Madagascar

de **madam** /madɑm/ (pl: -men) lady: *de ~ spelen (uithangen)* act the lady

de **made** /madə/ (pl: -n) maggot, grub

het **madeliefje** /madəlifjə/ (pl: -s) daisy

de **madonna** /madɔna/ (pl: -'s) Madonna

Madrileens /madrilens/ (adj) of/from Madrid; Madrid

maf /mɑf/ (adj, adv) [inform] crazy, nuts: *doe niet zo ~* don't be so daft, stop goofing around

maffen /mɑfə(n)/ (mafte, heeft gemaft) [inform] sleep, snooze, kip

de **maffia** /mɑfija/ mafia

de **maffioso** /mafijozo/ (pl: maffiosi) mafioso

de **mafkees** /mɑfkes/ (pl: mafkezen) [inform] goof(ball), nut

het **magazijn** /mayazɛin/ (pl: -en) **1** warehouse; stockroom; supply room **2** magazine

de **magazijnbediende** /maxazɛimbədində/ (pl: -n, -s) warehouseman; supply clerk

het **magazine** /mɛgəzin/ (pl: -s) **1** magazine **2** current affairs programme

mager /mayər/ (adj, adv) **1** thin; skinny **2** lean: *~e riblappen* lean beef (ribs) **3** feeble

de **magie** /mayi/ magic

magisch /mayis/ (adj) magic(al)

magistraal /mayistral/ (adj) magisterial; [fig also] masterly

de **magistraat** /mayistrat/ (pl: magistraten) magistrate

het **magma** /mɑyma/ magma

de **magnaat** /maynat/ (pl: magnaten) magnate, tycoon

de **magneet** /maynet/ (pl: magneten) magnet

de **magneetkaart** /mɑxnetkart/ swipe card

de **magneetzweeftrein** /mɑxnetzweftrɛin/ magnetic levitation train, maglev train

het **magnesium** /maynezijʏm/ magnesium

magnetisch /maynetis/ (adj) magnetic

de **magnetiseur** /maxnetizør/ (pl: -s) magnetizer

het **magnetisme** /maynetɪsmə/ magnetism

de **magnetron** /maynetrɔn/ (pl: -s) microwave: *iets in de ~ opwarmen* microwave sth.; [inform] nuke sth.

de **magnetronmaaltijd** /maxnetromaltɛit/ (pl: -en) microwave meal

magnifiek /mɑɲifik/ (adj, adv) magnificent

de **magnolia** /maynolija/ (pl: -'s) magnolia

de **maharadja** /maharɑtja/ (pl: -'s) maharaja(h)

het **¹mahonie** /mahoni/ mahogany

²mahonie /mahoni/ (adj) mahogany

de **mail** /mel/ (pl: -s) (e-)mail

het **mailadres** /meladrɛs/ mail address

de **mailbox** /melbɔks/ mail box

mailen /melə(n)/ (mailde, heeft gemaild) **1** e-mail **2** do a mailshot

de **mailing** /melɪŋ/ (pl: -s) mailing

de **mailinglijst** /melɪŋlɛist/ (pl: -en) mailing list

de **mailinglist** /melɪŋlɪst/ (pl: -s) mailing list

de **maillot** /majo/ (pl: -s) tights

het **mailtje** /melcə/ e-mail

de **mailwisseling** /melwɪsəlɪŋ/ (pl: -en) emails; correspondence

de **mainport** /menpɔːrt/ (pl: -s) transport hub

de **mais** /majs/ maize; [Am] corn: *gepofte ~* popcorn

de **maiskolf** /mɑjskɔlf/ (pl: -kolven) corn-cob

de **maiskorrel** /mɑjskɔrəl/ (pl: -s) kernel of maize; [Am] kernel of corn

de **maîtresse** /mɛːtrɛsə/ (pl: -s) mistress

de **maizena** /majzɛna/ cornflour; [Am] cornstarch

de **majesteit** /majəstɛit/ (pl: -en) Majesty

majestueus /majɛstywøs/ (adj, adv) majestic(al)

de **majeur** /mazør/ major: *in ~ spelen* play in a major key

de **majoor** /major/ (pl: -s) major

de **majoraan** /majoran/ (sweet) marjoram

de **majorette** /majorɛtə/ (pl: -s) (drum) majorette

mak /mɑk/ (adj, adv) **1** tame(d) **2** [fig] meek, gentle

de **makelaar** /makəlar/ (pl: -s) **1** estate agent; [Am] real estate agent **2** broker, agent: *~ in assurantiën* insurance broker

de **makelaardij** /makəlardɛi/ brokerage, agency; estate agency

de **makelij** /makəlɛi/ make, produce: *van eigen ~* home-grown, home-produced

maken /makə(n)/ (maakte, heeft gemaakt) **1** repair, fix: *zijn auto kan niet meer gemaakt worden* his car is beyond repair; *zijn auto laten ~* have one's car repaired (*or:* fixed) **2** make, produce; manufacture: *fouten ~* make mistakes; *cider wordt van appels gemaakt* cider is made from apples **3** cause || *je hebt daar niets te ~* you have no business there; *dat heeft er niets mee te ~* that's got nothing to do with it; *ze wil niets meer met hem te ~ hebben* she doesn't want anything more to do with him; *het (helemaal) ~* make it (to the top); *anders krijg je met mij te ~* or you'll have to deal with me; *hij zal het niet lang meer ~* he is not long for this world; *je hebt het **ernaar** gemaakt* you('ve) asked for it; *ik weet het **goed** gemaakt* I'll tell you what, I'll make you an offer; *hoe maakt u het?* how do you do?; *hoe maakt je broer het?* how is your brother?; *maak **dat** je wegkomt!* get out of here!

de **maker** /makər/ (pl: -s) maker, producer; artist

de **make-up** /mekʏp/ make-up

[1]**makkelijk** /makələk/ (adj) easy, simple: [inform] *dat is ~ **zat*** it's simple enough

[2]**makkelijk** /makələk/ (adv) easily, readily: *jij hebt ~ **praten*** it's easy (enough) for you to talk

de **makker** /makər/ (pl: -s) pal, mate

het **makkie** /maki/ (pl: -s) piece of cake; cushy job, easy job

de **makreel** /makrel/ (pl: makrelen) mackerel

de [1]**mal** /mal/ (pl: -len) mould, template ‖ *iem. **voor** de ~ houden* make fun of s.o., pull s.o.'s leg

[2]**mal** /mal/ (adj, adv) silly, foolish: *nee, ~le meid (jongen)* no, silly!; *ben je ~?* are you kidding?, of course not!

malafide /malafidə/ (adj) fraudulent, crooked

de **Malagassiër** /malaɣasijər/ (pl: -s) Malagasy
Malagassisch /malaɣasis/ (adj) Malagasy

de **malaise** /malɛːzə/ **1** malaise **2** depression, slump

de **malaria** /malarija/ malaria
Malawi /malawi/ Malawi

de **Malawiër** /malawijər/ (pl: -s) Malawian
Malawisch /malawis/ (adj) Malawian

de **Malediven** /maledivə(n)/ (pl) Maldive Islands, Maldives
Maleis /malɛis/ (adj) Malay; [Am] Malayan
Maleisië /malɛisijə/ Malaysia

de **Maleisiër** /malɛisijər/ (pl: -s) Malaysian
Maleisisch /malɛizis/ (adj) Malaysian

[1]**malen** /malə(n)/ (maalde, heeft gemaald) turn, grind

[2]**malen** /malə(n)/ (maalde, heeft gemalen) grind; crush

het **mali** /mali/ [Belg] deficit, shortfall
Mali /mali/ Mali

de **maliënkolder** /malijənkɔldər/ (pl: -s) coat of mail

de [1]**Malinees** /malines/ (pl: Malinezen) Malian

[2]**Malinees** /malines/ (adj) Malian

de **maling** /malɪŋ/ grind ‖ *daar heb ik ~ **aan*** I don't care two hoots (or: give a hoot); *~ **aan** iets (iem.) hebben* not care (or: not give a rap) about sth. (s.o.); *iem. **in** de ~ nemen* pull s.o.'s leg, fool s.o.

de **mallemoer** /maləmur/: *dat gaat je **geen** ~ aan* that's none of your damn (or: bloody) business; *naar zijn ~* ruined, finished

de **malloot** /malot/ (pl: malloten) idiot, fool
mals /mals/ (adj, adv) tender

het/de **malt** /malt/ [Dutch] low alcohol beer, non-alcoholic beer

Malta /malta/ Malta
Maltees /maltes/ (adj) Maltese
Maltezer /maltezər/ (adj) Maltese

de **malus** /malʏs/ (pl: -sen) (financial) penalty

de **malversatie** /malvɛrsa(t)si/ (pl: -s) malversation; embezzlement

de **mama** /mama/ (pl: -'s) mam(m)a

de **mammoet** /mamut/ (pl: -en, -s) mammoth

de **mammoettanker** /mamutɛŋkər/ (pl: -s) mammoth tanker, supertanker

de [1]**man** /man/ (pl: -nen) **1** man: *op de ~ spelen* **a)** go for the man (or: player); **b)** [fig] get personal; *een ~ **uit** duizenden* a man in a million; *een ~ **van** weinig woorden* a man of few words; *hij is een ~ **van** zijn woord* he is as good as his word **2** man, human: *de **gewone (kleine)** ~* the man in the street, the common man; *vijf ~ **sterk*** five strong; *met hoeveel ~ zijn we?* how many are we?, how many of us are there? **3** husband ‖ *met **man** en macht* with might and main

[2]**man** /man/ (int): [inform] *wat doe je nou, ~?* WTF!

het **management** /mɛnədʒmənt/ management

het **managementteam** /mɛnədʒmənti:m/ (pl: -s) management team
managen /mɛnədʒə(n)/ (managede, heeft gemanaged) manage

de **manager** /mɛnədʒər/ (pl: -s) manager

de **manche** /mãʃ(ə)/ (pl: -s) **1** heat **2** game

de **manchet** /manʃɛt/ (pl: -ten) cuff

de **manchetknoop** /manʃɛtknop/ (pl: -knopen) cuff link

het **manco** /maŋko/ (pl: -'s) **1** defect, shortcoming **2** shortage

de **mand** /mant/ (pl: -en) basket ‖ *bij een verhoor **door** de ~ vallen* have to own up (or: come clean); *door de ~ vallen als coach* fail as a coach, be a failure as a coach

het **mandaat** /mandat/ (pl: mandaten) mandate: [Belg] *een **dubbel** ~* a double mandate

de **mandarijn** /mandarɛin/ (pl: -en) mandarin; [small] tangerine

het **Mandarijn** /mandarɛin/ Mandarin

de **mandataris** /mandatarɪs/ (pl: -sen) **1** mandatary **2** [Belg] representative

de **mandekking** /mandɛkɪŋ/ man-to-man marking; [Am] man-on-man coverage

de **mandoline** /mandolinə/ (pl: -s) mandolin

de **mandril** /mandrɪl/ (pl: -s) mandrill

de **manege** /manɛʒə/ (pl: -s) riding school, manège

de [1]**manen** /manə(n)/ (pl) mane

[2]**manen** /manə(n)/ (maande, heeft gemaand) **1** remind; [stronger] demand: *iem. **om** geld ~* demand payment from s.o. **2** urge ‖ *iem. **tot** kalmte ~* calm s.o. down

de **maneschijn** /manəsxɛin/ moonlight

het **mangaan** /maŋɣan/ manganese

het **mangat** /mɑŋɣɑt/ (pl: -en) manhole

de **mangel** /mɑŋəl/ (pl: -s): [fig] *door de* ~ *gehaald worden* be put through the wringer; be crucified

de **mango** /mɑŋɡo/ (pl: -'s) mango

de **mangrove** /mɑŋɣroːvə/ (pl: -n, -s) mangrove

manhaftig /mɑnhɑftəχ/ (adj, adv) manful, manly: *zich ~ gedragen* act manfully (*or:* bravely)

de **maniak** /manijɑk/ (pl: -ken) maniac; freak; buff; fan

maniakaal /manijakaːl/ (adj, adv) maniacal

de **manicure** /manikyːrə/ (pl: -n) manicurist

de **manie** /mani/ (pl: -s) mania

de **manier** /maniːr/ (pl: -en) **1** way, manner: *daar is hij ook niet op een eerlijke ~ aangekomen* he didn't get that by fair means; *hun ~ van leven* their way of life; *op een fatsoenlijke ~* in a decent manner, decently; *op de een of andere ~* somehow or other; *op de gebruikelijke ~* (in) the usual way; *dat is geen ~ (van doen)* that is no way to behave **2** manners: *wat zijn dat voor ~en!* what kind of behaviour is that!

het **manifest** /manifɛst/ (pl: -en) manifesto

de **manifestatie** /manifɛsta(t)si/ (pl: -s) demonstration; happening; event

zich **manifesteren** /manifɛsteːrə(n)/ (manifesteerde zich, heeft zich gemanifesteerd) manifest o.s.

de **manipulatie** /manipyla(t)si/ (pl: -s) manipulation: *genetische ~* genetic engineering

manipuleren /manipyleːrə(n)/ (manipuleerde, heeft gemanipuleerd) manipulate

manisch-depressief /manizdeprɛsif/ (adj) manic-depressive

het **manjaar** /mɑnjaːr/ (pl: manjaren) man-year

mank /mɑŋk/ (adj, adv) lame: *~ lopen* (walk with a) limp; *deze vergelijking gaat ~* this comparison falls short

het **mankement** /mɑŋkəmɛnt/ (pl: -en) defect; bug

¹**mankeren** /mɑŋkeːrə(n)/ (mankeerde, heeft gemankeerd) be wrong, be the matter: *wat mankeert je toch?* what's wrong (*or:* the matter) with you?; *er mankeert nogal wat aan* there's a fair amount wrong with it

²**mankeren** /mɑŋkeːrə(n)/ (mankeerde, heeft gemankeerd) have sth. the matter: *ik mankeer niets* I'm all right, there's nothing wrong with me

de **mankracht** /mɑŋkrɑχt/ manpower

het **manna** /mɑna/ manna: *als ~ uit de hemel neerdalen* fall like manna from heaven, be manna from heaven

mannelijk /mɑnələk/ (adj, adv) male, masculine: *een ~e stem* a masculine voice

het **mannenkoor** /mɑnə(n)koːr/ (pl: -koren) male choir, men's chorus

de **mannenstem** /mɑnə(n)stɛm/ male voice, man's voice

de **mannequin** /mɑnəkɛ̃/ (pl: -s) model

het **mannetje** /mɑnəcə/ **1** little fellow, little guy **2** man: *daar heeft hij zijn ~s voor* he leaves that to his underlings **3** male || *zijn ~ staan* hold one's (own) ground, stick up for o.s.

de **mannetjesputter** /mɑnəcəspʏtər/ (pl: -s) strapper, he-man, she man

de **manoeuvre** /manœːvrə/ (pl: -s) manoeuvre

manoeuvreren /manuvreːrə(n)/ (manoeuvreerde, heeft gemanoeuvreerd) manoeuvre: *iem. in een onaangename positie ~* manoeuvre s.o. into an awkward position

de **manometer** /manomeːtər/ (pl: -s) manometer, pressure gauge

mans /mɑns/ (adj): *zij is er ~ genoeg voor* she can handle it

de **manschappen** /mɑnsχɑpə(n)/ men

manshoog /mɑnshoχ/ (adj) man-size(d), of a man's height

de **mantel** /mɑntəl/ (pl: -s) **1** coat; [also fig] cloak: [fig] *iets met de ~ der liefde bedekken* cover sth. with the cloak of charity **2** [technology] casing, housing

de **mantelorganisatie** /mɑntəlorɣaniza(t)si/ (pl: -s) umbrella organization

het **mantelpak** /mɑntəlpɑk/ (pl: -ken) suit

de **mantelzorg** /mɑntəlzɔrχ/ volunteer aid

de/het **mantra** /mɑntra/ (pl: -'s) mantra

de **manufacturen** /manyfɑktyːrə(n)/ (pl) drapery

het **manuscript** /manyskrɪpt/ (pl: -en) manuscript; typescript

het **manusje-van-alles** /manyʃəvɑnɑləs/ (pl: manusjes-van-alles) jack-of-all-trades; (general) dogsbody

het **manuur** /mɑnyr/ (pl: manuren) man-hour

het **manwijf** /mɑnwɛif/ (pl: -wijven) mannish woman, battle-axe

de **map** /mɑp/ (pl: -pen) **1** file folder **2** file **3** [comp] folder

de **maquette** /makɛtə/ (pl: -s) (scale-)model

de **maraboe** /maraˈbu/ (pl: -s) marabou

de **marathon** /maraton/ (pl: -s) marathon: *halve ~* half-marathon

de **marathonloop** /maratonlop/ (pl: -lopen) marathon race

marchanderen /mɑrʃɑndeːrə(n)/ (marchandeerde, heeft gemarchandeerd) bargain

marcheren /mɑrʃeːrə(n)/ (marcheerde, heeft/is gemarcheerd) march

de **marconist** /mɑrkonɪst/ (pl: -en) radio operator

de **marechaussee** /mareʃoseː/ (pl: -s) [Dutch] military police, MP

de **maretak** /maːrətak/ (pl: -ken) mistletoe

de **margarine** /mɑrɣarinə/ (pl: -s) margarine

de **marge** /mɑrːʒə/ (pl: -s) **1** margin: *gerommel in de ~* fiddling about **2** band

marginaal /mɑrɣinaːl/ (adj) marginal

de **margriet** /mɑrɣrit/ (pl: -en) marguerite, (ox-eye) daisy

Maria-Hemelvaart /marijahe̱məlvart/ Assumption (of the Virgin Mary)

de **marihuana** /marijuwa̱na/ marijuana, marihuana

de **marine** /mari̱nə/ navy

de **marinebasis** /mari̱nəbazɪs/ (pl: -bases) naval base

marineren /marine̱rə(n)/ (marineerde, heeft gemarineerd) marinate, marinade

de **marinier** /marini̱r/ (pl: -s) marine: [Dutch] het *Korps Mariniers* the Marine Corps; the Marines

de **marionet** /marijone̱t/ puppet

maritiem /mariti̱m/ (adj) maritime

de **marjolein** /marjole̱in/ marjoram

de **mark** /mɑrk/ (pl: -en) mark

markant /mɑrkɑnt/ (adj) striking

de **markeerstift** /mɑrke̱rstɪft/ (pl: -en) marker, marking pen

markeren /mɑrke̱rə(n)/ (markeerde, heeft gemarkeerd) mark

de **marketing** /mɑ̱ːrkətɪŋ/ marketing

de **markies** /mɑrki̱s/ (pl: markiezen) marquis

de **markiezin** /mɑrkizɪ̱n/ (pl: -nen) marquise

de **markt** /mɑrkt/ (pl: -en) market: *een dalende* (or: *stijgende*) ~ a bear (or: bull) market; *naar de* ~ *gaan* go to market; *van alle* ~*en thuis zijn* be able to turn one's hand to anything; *zichzelf uit de* ~ *prijzen* price o.s. out of the market || [Belg] *het niet onder de* ~ *hebben* be having a hard time

het **marktaandeel** /mɑ̱rktandel/ (pl: -aandelen) market share, share of the market

de **marktdag** /mɑ̱rgdɑx/ (pl: -en) market day

de **markteconomie** /mɑ̱rktekonomi/ (pl: -ën) market economy

de **markthal** /mɑ̱rkthɑl/ (pl: -len) market hall, covered market

de **marktkoopman** /mɑ̱rktkopmɑn/ (pl: -nen, marktkooplui) market vendor, stallholder

de **marktkraam** /mɑ̱rktkram/ (pl: -kramen) market stall (or: booth)

de **marktleider** /mɑ̱rktlɛidər/ (pl: -s) market leader

het **marktonderzoek** /mɑ̱rktondərzuk/ market research

de **marktwaarde** /mɑ̱rktwardə/ market value

de **marktwerking** /mɑ̱rktwɛrkɪŋ/ free-market system, free competition

de **marmelade** /mɑrməla̱də/ (pl: -s) marmalade

het **marmer** /mɑ̱rmər/ (pl: -s) marble

marmeren /mɑ̱rmərə(n)/ (adj) marble

de **marmot** /mɑrmɔ̱t/ (pl: -ten) **1** marmot **2** guinea pig

de **Marokkaan** /mɑroka̱n/ (pl: Marokkanen) Moroccan

Marokkaans /mɑroka̱ns/ (adj) Moroccan

Marokko /mɑrɔ̱ko/ Morocco

de **mars** /mɑrs/ (pl: -en) march || *hij heeft niet veel in zijn* ~ **a)** he hasn't got much about him;

b) he is pretty ignorant; **c)** he isn't very bright; **d)** he's not up to much; *hij heeft heel wat in zijn* ~ **a)** he has a lot to offer; **b)** he is pretty knowledgeable; **c)** he's a clever chap; *voorwaarts* ~*!* forward march!; *ingerukt* ~*!* dismiss!

Mars /mɑrs/ Mars

het/de **marsepein** /mɑrsəpɛi̱n/ marzipan

de **marskramer** /mɑ̱rskramər/ (pl: -s) hawker, pedlar

het **marsmannetje** /mɑ̱rsmɑnəcə/ (pl: -s) Martian

de **martelaar** /mɑ̱rtəlar/ (pl: martelaren) martyr

het **martelaarschap** /mɑ̱rtəlarsxɑp/ martyrdom

de **marteldood** /mɑ̱rtəldot/ death through torture

martelen /mɑ̱rtələ(n)/ (martelde, heeft gemarteld) torture

de **martelgang** /mɑ̱rtəlɣɑŋ/ (pl: -en) [also fig] calvary

de **marteling** /mɑ̱rtəlɪŋ/ (pl: -en) torture

de **¹marter** /mɑ̱rtər/ (pl: -s) [animal] marten

het **²marter** /mɑ̱rtər/ [fur] marten

de **Martinikaan** /mɑrtinika̱n/ (pl: Martinikanen) inhabitant (or: native) of Martinique

Martinikaans /mɑrtinika̱ns/ (adj) of/from Martinique

Martinique /mɑrtini̱k/ Martinique

het **marxisme** /mɑrksɪ̱smə/ Marxism

de **marxist** /mɑrksɪ̱st/ (pl: -en) Marxist

de **mascara** /mɑska̱ra/ mascara

de **mascotte** /mɑskɔ̱tə/ (pl: -s) mascot

het **masker** /mɑ̱skər/ (pl: -s) mask

de **maskerade** /mɑskəra̱də/ (pl: -s) **1** masked procession **2** masquerade

maskeren /mɑske̱rə(n)/ (maskeerde, heeft gemaskeerd) mask, hide: *hij maskeerde zijn slechte bedoelingen* he masked his evil intentions

het **masochisme** /mɑsoxɪ̱smə/ masochism

de **masochist** /mɑsoxɪ̱st/ (pl: -en) masochist

de **massa** /mɑ̱sa/ (pl: -'s) **1** mass, heaps: *hij heeft een* ~ *vrienden* he has heaps (or: loads) of friends; ~*'s mensen* masses (or: swarms) of people **2** mass, crowd; [pol] masses: *met de* ~ *meedoen* go with (or: follow) the crowd

massaal /mɑsa̱l/ (adj, adv) massive: ~ *verzet* massive resistance; *de aanhangers van de president gingen de straat op* the president's supporters took to the streets; *massale vissterfte* massive fish mortality

de **massabijeenkomst** /mɑ̱sabɛiɛnkomst/ (pl: -en) mass meeting

de **massage** /mɑsa̱ʒə/ massage

het **massagraf** /mɑ̱saɣraf/ (pl: -graven) mass grave

de **massamedia** /mɑ̱samedija/ (pl) mass media

de **massamoord** /mɑ̱samort/ (pl: -en) mass murder

de **massaproductie** /mɑsaprodɣksi/ mass production
de **massasprint** /mɑsasprɪnt/ (pl: -s) [cycling] bunch sprint
het **massavernietigingswapen** /mɑsavərnitəyɪŋswapə(n)/ weapon of mass destruction
masseren /maserə(n)/ (masseerde, heeft gemasseerd) massage, do a massage on
de **masseur** /masør/ (pl: -s) masseur
massief /masif/ (adj) solid, massive, heavy: *een ring van ~ zilver* a ring of solid silver
de **mast** /mɑst/ (pl: -en) **1** mast: *de ~ strijken* lower the mast **2** pylon
de **master** /mɑːstər/ **1** master's degree: *~ zijn* hold (*or:* have) a master's degree; *zijn ~ hebben* hold (*or:* have) a master's degree; *zijn ~ halen* get one's master's degree **2** master's degree course (*or:* program): *zijn ~ doen* do one's master's, study for one's master's degree
de **masteropleiding** /mɑːstəroplɛɪdɪŋ/ (pl: -en) master's (course): *ze volgt een ~ Engelse letterkunde* she's doing a (*or:* her) master's in English Literature
het **masterplan** /mɑːstərplɑn/ (pl: -nen) master plan
de **masterscriptie** /mɑːstərskrɪpsi/ (pl: -s) master's degree thesis (*or:* dissertation)
masturberen /mɑstʏrberə(n)/ (masturbeerde, heeft gemasturbeerd) masturbate
de **¹mat** /mɑt/ (pl: -ten) mat: *~ten kloppen* beat (*or:* shake) mats
²mat /mɑt/ (adj) checkmate: *~ staan* be checkmated; *iem. ~ zetten* checkmate s.o.
³mat /mɑt/ (adj, adv) **1** mat(t); dull; dim [light]; pearl **2** mat(t); frosted
de **matador** /matadɔr/ (pl: -s) matador
de **match** /mɛtʃ/ (pl: -es) match: *er was geen ~ tussen hen* they didn't click, they were not well-matched; *de politie vond geen ~* the police found no match; *op zoek zijn naar een goede ~* be looking for a compatible match, be looking for a soulmate
het **matchpoint** /mɛtʃpojnt/ (pl: -s) match point: *op ~ staan* be at match point
het **matchpunt** /mɛtʃpʏnt/ (pl: -en) match point: *op ~ staan* be at match point
de **mate** /matə/ (pl: -n) measure, extent, degree: *in dezelfde ~* equally, to the same extent; *in mindere ~* to a lesser degree; *in grote* (*or: hoge*) *~* to a great (*or:* large) extent, largely; *met ~* in moderation, moderately
mateloos /matəlos/ (adj, adv) immoderate, excessive: *~ rijk* immensely rich
de **matennaaier** /matənajər/ rat
het **materiaal** /mater(i)jal/ (pl: materialen) material(s)
de **materialist** /materijalɪst/ (pl: -en) materialist
materialistisch /mater(i)jalɪstis/ (adj, adv) materialistic
de **materie** /materi/ (pl: -s) matter; (subject) matter
het **¹materieel** /materijel/ material(s), equipment: *rollend ~* rolling stock
²materieel /materijel/ (adj) material: *materiële schade* property (*or:* material) damage
de **materniteit** /matɛrnitɛit/ [Belg] maternity ward
het **matglas** /mɑtxlɑs/ frosted glass
de **mathematicus** /matematikɣs/ mathematician
mathematisch /matematis/ (adj, adv) mathematical
matig /matəx/ (adj, adv) **1** moderate **2** moderate, mediocre
matigen /matəyə(n)/ (matigde, heeft gematigd) moderate, restrain: *matig uw snelheid* reduce your speed
de **matiging** /matəyɪŋ/ moderation
de **matinee** /matine/ (pl: -s) matinee
matineus /matinøs/ (adj) early
het **matje** /mɑcə/ (pl: -s) mat: *op het ~ moeten komen* **a)** be put on the spot; **b)** be (put) on the carpet
de **matrak** /matrɑk/ (pl: -ken) [Belg] truncheon, baton
het/de **matras** /matrɑs/ (pl: -sen) mattress
de **matrijs** /matrɛis/ (pl: matrijzen) mould, matrix
de **matrix** /matrɪks/ (pl: matrices) matrix
de **matroos** /matros/ (pl: matrozen) sailor
de **matse** /mɑtsə/ (pl: -s) matzo
matsen /mɑtsə(n)/ (matste, heeft gematst) [Dutch; inform] do a favour; wangle
de **mattenklopper** /mɑtə(n)klɔpər/ (pl: -s) carpet-beater
de **mattie** /mɑti/ (pl: -s) [Dutch; inform] [Am] homie; [British] mate
Mauritaans /mɑuritɑns/ (adj) Mauritanian
Mauritanië /mɑuritanijə/ Mauretania
de **Mauritaniër** /mɑuritanijər/ (pl: -s) Mauritanian
de **Mauritiaan** /mɑuri(t)ʃan/ (pl: Mauritianen) Mauritian
Mauritiaans /mɑuri(t)ʃans/ (adj) Mauritian
Mauritius /mɑuritsijɣs/ (island of) Mauritius
het **mausoleum** /mɑuzolejɣm/ (pl: -s, mausolea) mausoleum
mauwen /mɑuwə(n)/ (mauwde, heeft gemauwd) **1** miaow, mew **2** whine
de **mavo** /mavo/ (pl: -'s) [Dutch] school for lower general secondary education
m.a.w. *met andere woorden* in other words
het **maxi** /mɑksi/ maxi
¹maximaal /mɑksimal/ (adj) maximum, maximal
²maximaal /mɑksimal/ (adv) at (the) most: *dit werk duurt ~ een week* this work takes a week at most
het **maximum** /mɑksimɣm/ (pl: maxima) maxi-

mum

de **maximumsnelheid** /mɑksimʏmsnɛlheit/ (pl: -heden) speed limit; maximum speed

de **maximumtemperatuur** /mɑksimʏmtɛmpərɑtyr/ maximum temperature

de **mayonaise** /majɔnɛːzə/ mayonnaise: *patat met* ~ chips with mayonnaise; [Am] French fries with mayonnaise

de **mazelen** /maːzələ(n)/ (pl) measles

de **mazout** /mazʏt/ [Belg] (heating) oil

de **mazzel** /mɑzəl/ [inform] (good) luck: *de ~!* see you!; ~ *hebben* have (good) luck

mazzelen /mɑzələ(n)/ (mazzelde, heeft gemazzeld) [inform] have (good) luck

het **mbo** /ɛmbeo/ [Dutch] *middelbaar beroepsonderwijs* intermediate vocational education

m.b.v. *met behulp van* by means of

de **mdl-arts** /ɛmdeɛlɑrts/ (pl: -en) [Dutch] *maag-, darm- en leverarts* gastroenterologist

me /mə/ (pers pron) me

de **ME** /ɛmeː/ (pl: ME's) [Dutch] *mobiele eenheid* anti-riot squad

de **meander** /mejɑndər/ (pl: -s) meander

het **meao** /meao/ (pl: -'s) [Dutch] *middelbaar economisch en administratief onderwijs* intermediate business education

de **mecanicien** /mekaniʃɛ/ (pl: -s) mechanic

de **meccano** /mɛkano/ (pl: -'s) meccano (set)

de **mechanica** /meχanika/ mechanics

het/de **mechaniek** /meχaniːk/ (pl: -en) mechanism

de **mechanisatie** /meχanizaː(t)si/ mechanization

mechanisch /meχanis/ (adj, adv) mechanical: ~ *speelgoed* clockwork toys

mechaniseren /meχanizeːrə(n)/ (mechaniseerde, heeft gemechaniseerd) mechanize

het **mechanisme** /meχanɪsmə/ (pl: -n) mechanism; [fig also] machinery

de **medaille** /medɑjə/ (pl: -s) medal

het **medaillon** /medɑjɔn/ (pl: -s) medallion; locket

mede /meːdə/ (adv) [form] also: ~ *hierdoor* as a consequence of this and other factors; ~ *namens* also on behalf of; ~ *wegens* partly due to

de **medeburger** /meːdəbʏrɣər/ (pl: -s) fellow citizen

mededeelzaam /medədeːlzam/ (adj) communicative

de **mededeling** /meːdədeːlɪŋ/ (pl: -en) announcement, statement

het **mededelingenbord** /meːdədeːlɪŋə(n)bɔrt/ (pl: -en) notice board

de **mededinger** /meːdədɪŋər/ (pl: -s) rival; competitor

het **mededogen** /meːdədoɣə(n)/ compassion

de **mede-eigenaar** /meːdəɛiɣənar/ (pl: -s, mede-eigenaren) joint owner

de **medeklinker** /meːdəklɪŋkər/ (pl: -s) consonant

de **medeleerling** /meːdəleːrlɪŋ/ (pl: -en) fellow pupil

het **medeleven** /meːdəleːvə(n)/ sympathy: *oprecht* ~ sincere sympathy; *mijn* ~ *gaat uit naar* my sympathy lies with; *zijn* ~ *tonen* express one's sympathy

het **medelijden** /meːdəlɛidə(n)/ pity, compassion: *heb* ~ *(met)* have mercy (upon); ~ *met zichzelf hebben* feel sorry for o.s.

de **medemens** /meːdəmɛns/ (pl: -en) fellow man

medeplichtig /medəplɪχtəχ/ (adj) accessory

de **medeplichtige** /medəplɪχtəɣə/ (pl: -n) accessory (to), accomplice; partner

de **medereiziger** /meːdərɛizəɣər/ (pl: -s) fellow traveller (*or:* passenger)

medeschuldig /medəsχʏldəχ/ (adj) implicated (in), also guilty, also to blame

de **medestander** /meːdəstɑndər/ (pl: -s) supporter

medeverantwoordelijk /meːdəvərɑntwordələk/ (adj) jointly responsible (for), co-responsible (for)

de **medewerker** /meːdəwɛrkər/ (pl: -s) 1 fellow worker, co-worker; collaborator; contributor, correspondent: *onze juridisch (or: economisch)* ~ our legal (*or:* economics) correspondent 2 employee, staff member

de **medewerking** /meːdəwɛrkɪŋ/ cooperation, assistance: *met ~ van* assisted by, with the cooperation of; *de politie riep de ~ in van het publiek* the police made an appeal to the public for cooperation

het **medeweten** /meːdəweːtə(n)/ (fore)knowledge: *dit is buiten mijn ~ gebeurd* this occurred unknown to me (*or:* without my knowledge)

de **medezeggenschap** /medəzɛɣə(n)sχɑp/ say; participation

de **media** /meːdija/ (pl) media: *de sociale* ~ the social media

mediageniek /medijaʒənik/ (adj) mediagenic

de **mediaspeler** /meːdijaspeler/ (pl: -s) 1 media player 2 (portable) media player

de **mediastilte** /meːdijastɪltə/ media silence

de **mediatheek** /meːdijatɛk/ (pl: mediatheken) multimedia centre (*or:* library)

de **mediator** /miːdijətər/ mediator

mediawijs /medijawɛis/ (adj) media-savvy

het **medicament** /medikamɛnt/ (pl: -en) medicament, medicine

de **medicijn** /medisɛin/ (pl: -en) medicine: *een student (in de) ~en* a medical student

het **medicijnkastje** /medisɛinkɑʃə/ (pl: -s) medicine chest (*or:* cabinet)

de **medicus** /meːdikʏs/ (pl: medici) doctor, medical practitioner

medio /meːdijo/ (adv) in the middle of: ~ *september* in mid-September

medisch /mɛdis/ (adj, adv) medical: *op ~ advies* on the advice of one's doctor

de **meditatie** /medita(t)si/ (pl: -s) meditation

mediteren /mediterə(n)/ (mediteerde, heeft gemediteerd) meditate

mediterraan /meditɛran/ (adj) Mediterranean

het ¹**medium** /medijʏm/ (pl: media) medium

²**medium** /medijʏm/ (adj) medium(-sized)

mee /me/ (adv) with, along: *waarom ga je niet ~?* why don't you come along? ‖ *met de klok ~* clockwise; *kan ik ook ~?* can I come too?; *hij heeft zijn uiterlijk ~* he has his looks going for him; *dat kan nog jaren ~* that will last for years; *het kan er ~ door* it's all right, it'll do; *ergens te vroeg* (or: *te laat*) *~ komen* be too early (or: late) with sth.

meebrengen /mebrɛŋə(n)/ (bracht mee, heeft meegebracht) **1** bring (along) (with one): *wat zal ik voor je ~?* what shall I bring you? **2** involve: *de moeilijkheden die dit met zich heeft meegebracht* the difficulties which resulted from this

¹**meedelen** /medelə(n)/ (deelde mee, heeft meegedeeld) share (in), participate (in): *alle erfgenamen delen mee* all heirs are entitled to a share

²**meedelen** /medelə(n)/ (deelde mee, heeft meegedeeld) inform (of), let … know; notify, announce; report: *ik zal het haar voorzichtig ~* I shall break it to her gently; *hierbij deel ik u mee, dat …* I am writing to inform you that …

meedingen /medɪŋə(n)/ (dong mee, heeft meegedongen) compete

meedoen /medun/ (deed mee, heeft meegedaan) join (in), take part (in): *mag ik ~?* can I join in (or: you)?; *~ aan een wedstrijd* compete in a game; *~ aan een project* (or: *staking*) take part in a project (or: strike); *oké, ik doe mee* okay, count me in

meedogenloos /medoɣə(n)los/ (adj, adv) merciless

mee-eten /meetə(n)/ (at mee, heeft meegegeten) eat with (s.o.)

de **mee-eter** /meetər/ (pl: -s) blackhead, whitehead

meegaan /meɣan/ (ging mee, is meegegaan) **1** go along (or: with), accompany, come along (or: with): *is er nog iem. die meegaat?* is anyone else coming (or: going)? **2** [fig] go (along) with, agree (with): *met de mode ~* keep up with (the) fashion **3** last: *dit toestel gaat jaren mee* this machine will last for years

meegaand /meɣant/ (adj) compliant, pliable

¹**meegeven** /meɣevə(n)/ (gaf mee, heeft meegegeven) give (way), yield: *de planken geven niet mee* there is no give in the boards

²**meegeven** /meɣevə(n)/ (gaf mee, heeft meegegeven) give: *iem. een boodschap ~* send a message with s.o.

meehelpen /mehɛlpə(n)/ (hielp mee, heeft meegeholpen) help (in, with), assist (with)

¹**meekomen** /mekomə(n)/ (kwam mee, is meegekomen) **1** come (also), come along **2** keep up (with)

²**meekomen** /mekomə(n)/ (kwam mee, is meegekomen) **1** come (along, with, also): *ik heb er geen bezwaar tegen als hij meekomt* I don't object to his coming (along) **2** keep up (with)

meekrijgen /mekrɛiɣə(n)/ (kreeg mee, heeft meegekregen) **1** get, receive: *kan ik het geld direct ~?* can I have the money immediately? **2** win over, get on one's side **3** get, receive, hear: *heb je het nieuws over X nog meegekregen?* have you heard the news on X yet?

het **meel** /mel/ flour

de **meeldraad** /meldrat/ (pl: -draden) stamen

meeleven /melevə(n)/ (leefde mee, heeft meegeleefd) sympathize

meelijwekkend /melɛiwɛkənt/ (adj) pitiful

meelopen /melopə(n)/ (liep mee, is meegelopen) walk along (with), accompany

de **meeloper** /melopər/ (pl: -s) hanger-on

meeluisteren /melœystərə(n)/ (luisterde mee, heeft meegeluisterd) listen (in)

meemaken /memakə(n)/ (maakte mee, heeft meegemaakt) experience; go through; live; see; take part (in): *had hij dit nog maar mee mogen maken* if he had only lived to see this; *ze heeft heel wat meegemaakt* she has seen (or: been through) a lot

meenemen /menemə(n)/ (nam mee, heeft meegenomen) **1** take along (or: with): [in restaurant] *~ graag* to take away please; *een koffie om mee te nemen* a coffee to go; *neem een tas mee* take a bag with you **2** enthuse, unite: *zijn achterban ~* rally one's supporters ‖ *dat is meegenomen* that's a (welcome) bonus, that's (always) sth.

meepraten /meprate(n)/ (praatte mee, heeft meegepraat) take part (or: join) in a conversation: *daar kan ik over ~* I know sth. about that, you don't have to tell me

het ¹**meer** /mer/ (pl: meren) lake

²**meer** /mer/ (num) **1** more: *~ dood dan levend* more dead than alive; *des te ~* all the more (so); *min of ~* more or less; *steeds ~* more and more; *hij heeft ~ boeken dan ik* he has got more books than I (have) **2** more, further: *wie waren er nog ~?* who else was there?; *wat kan ik nog ~ doen?* what else can I do? **3** any more, no more, (any) longer: *zij is geen kind ~* she is no longer a child; *hij had geen appels ~* he had no more apples, he was out of apples **4** more (often): *we moeten dit ~ doen* we must do this more often ‖ *onder ~* among other things; among others; *zonder ~*

a) naturally, of course; b) right away

de **ME'er** /ɛmejər/ [Dutch] riot policeman

meerdaags /merdaxs/ (adj) of (or: for) more than one day: ~e **weerprognose** weather forecast for the coming days

de ¹**meerdere** /merdərə/ (pl: -n) superior; superior officer

²**meerdere** /merdərə/ (num) several, a number of

de **meerderheid** /merdərhɛit/ majority: in de ~ zijn a) be in the majority; b) [pol] hold a/the majority

meerderjarig /merdərjarəx/ (adj) of age: ~ worden come of age

de **meerderjarige** /merdərjarəyə/ (pl: -n) adult

de **meerderjarigheid** /merdərjarəxhɛit/ adulthood, legal age

meerderlei /merdərlɛi/ (pron) multiple

meerekenen /merekənə(n)/ (rekende mee, heeft meegerekend) count (in)

meerijden /merɛidə(n)/ (reed mee, heeft/is meegereden) come (or: ride) (along) with: ik vroeg of ik mee **mocht** rijden I asked for a lift

meerjarig /merjarəx/ (adj) of more than one year; long-term

de **meerkeuzetoets** /merkøzətuts/ (pl: -en) multiple-choice test

de **meerkeuzevraag** /merkøzəvrax/ (pl: -vragen) multiple-choice question

de **meerkoet** /merkut/ coot

meermaals /mermals/ (adv) several times, more than once

meeroken /merokə(n)/ (rookte mee, heeft meegerookt) be subjected to passive smoking

het **meeroudergezin** /meroudərɣəzin/ (pl: -nen) multi-parent family

het **meerouderschap** /meroudərsxap/ multiple parenting

de **meerpaal** /merpal/ (pl: -palen) mooring post

meerstemmig /merstɛmǝx/ (adj, adv) many-voiced

het **meervoud** /mervaut/ (pl: -en) plural: in het ~ (in the) plural

¹**meervoudig** /mervoudǝx/ (adj) plural

²**meervoudig** /mervoudǝx/ (adv) poly-, multi-: ~ onverzadigde vetzuren polyunsaturated fatty acids

de **meerwaarde** /merwardə/ surplus (or: excess) value

het **meerwerk** /merwɛrk/ additional (or: extra) work

meerzijdig /merzɛidǝx/ (adj) multilateral

de **mees** /mes/ (pl: mezen) tit

meesjouwen /mesjauwə(n)/ (sjouwde mee, heeft meegesjouwd) lug; [Am] tote

meeslepen /meslepə(n)/ (sleepte mee, heeft meegesleept) **1** drag (along) **2** carry (with, away): zich laten ~ get carried away

meeslepend /meslepənt/ (adj, adv) compelling, moving

meesleuren /meslørə(n)/ (sleurde mee, heeft meegesleurd) sweep away (or: along)

meesmuilen /mesmœylə(n)/ (meesmuilde, heeft gemeesmuild) smirk

meespelen /mespelə(n)/ (speelde mee, heeft meegespeeld) take part (or: join) in a game; play (along with); be a cast member

¹**meest** /mest/ (adj) **1** most, the majority of: op zijn ~ at (the) most **2** most, greatest

²**meest** /mest/ (adv) most, best: de ~ gelezen krant the most widely read newspaper

meestal /mestal/ (adv) mostly, usually

de **meester** /mestər/ (pl: -s) **1** master: ~ in de rechten [roughly] Master of Laws; pas tegen de ochtend kon het sein **'brand** ~' worden gegeven it took all night for the fire brigade to get the fire under control **2** teacher, (school)master

het **meesterbrein** /mestərbrɛin/ (pl: -en) mastermind

de **meesteres** /mestarɛs/ (pl: -sen) mistress

de **meesterhand** /mestərhant/ master-hand, touch of the master

de **meesterknecht** /mestərknɛxt/ (pl: -en) [cycling] lieutenant

meesterlijk /mestərlǝk/ (adj, adv) masterly

het **meesterschap** /mestərsxap/ mastery, skill

het **meesterstuk** /mestərstvk/ (pl: -ken) masterpiece

het **meesterwerk** /mestərwɛrk/ (pl: -en) masterpiece, masterwork

de **meet** /met/ (pl: meten): van ~ af aan from the beginning

meetbaar /medbar/ (adj) measurable

¹**meetellen** /metɛlə(n)/ (telde mee, heeft meegeteld) count: dat telt **niet** mee that doesn't count

²**meetellen** /metɛlə(n)/ (telde mee, heeft meegeteld) count also, count in, include

de **meeting** /mi:tɪŋ/ (pl: -s) meeting

het **meetinstrument** /metɪnstrymɛnt/ (pl: -en) measuring instrument

de **meetkunde** /metkyndə/ geometry

de **meetlat** /metlat/ (pl: -ten) measuring rod: [fig] iem. langs de ~ **leggen** judge s.o.

het **meetlint** /metlɪnt/ (pl: -en) tape-measure

meetronen /metronə(n)/ (troonde mee, heeft meegetroond) coax along

de **meeuw** /mew/ (pl: -en) (sea)gull

meevallen /mevalə(n)/ (viel mee, is meegevallen) turn out (or: prove, be) better than expected: dat zal wel ~ it won't be so bad

de **meevaller** /mevalər/ (pl: -s) piece (or: bit) of luck: een **financiële** ~ a windfall

meevoelen /mevulə(n)/ (voelde mee, heeft meegevoeld) sympathize (with)

meevoeren /mevurə(n)/ (voerde mee, heeft meegevoerd) carry (along)

meewarig /mewarəx/ (adj, adv) pitying:

met een ~*e **blik** keek ze hem aan* she looked at him pityingly

meewerken /mɐ̯wɛrkə(n)/ (werkte mee, heeft meegewerkt) **1** cooperate, work together: *we werkten allemaal een **beetje** mee* we all pulled together, we all did our little bit **2** assist: *allen werkten mee **om** het concert te laten slagen* everyone assisted in making the concert a success ‖ ~*d **voorwerp*** indirect object

meezingen /mɐ̯zɪŋə(n)/ (zong mee, heeft meegezongen) sing along (with)

meezitten /mɐ̯zɪtə(n)/ (zat mee, heeft meegezeten) be favourable: *het zat hem **niet** mee* luck was against him; *als alles meezit* if all goes well, if everything runs smoothly

de **megabioscoop** /mɐ̯ɣabijoskop/ multiplex

de **megabyte** /mɐ̯ɣabɑjt/ megabyte

de **megafoon** /mɐ̯ɣafon/ (pl: -s, megafonen) megaphone

de **megahertz** /mɐ̯ɣahɛrts/ megahertz

megalomaan /mɐ̯ɣaloman/ (adj) megalomaniac(al)

de **mei** /mɛi/ May

de **meid** /mɛit/ (pl: -en) girl, (young) woman: *je bent al een **hele** ~* you're quite a woman (*or:* girl)

de **meidengroep** /mɛidə(n)ɣrup/ (pl: -en) female band

de **meidoorn** /mɛidorn/ (pl: -s) hawthorn

de **meikever** /mɛikevər/ (pl: -s) May-bug, cockchafer

de **meineed** /mɛinet/ (pl: meineden) perjury

het **meisje** /mɛiʃə/ (pl: -s) **1** girl, daughter **2** girl, young woman (*or:* lady) **3** girlfriend **4** girl, maid

meisjesachtig /mɛiʃəsɑxtəx/ (adj, adv) girlish, girl-like

de **meisjesnaam** /mɛiʃəsnam/ (pl: -namen) maiden name

mej. *Mejuffrouw* Miss

de **mejuffrouw** /məjʏfrɑu/ (pl: -en) Miss; Ms

mekaar /məkar/ (ref pron) [inform] each other, one another ‖ *komt **voor** ~* OK, I'll see to it

het **mekka** /mɛka/ (pl: -'s) Mecca

mekkeren /mɛkərə(n)/ (mekkerde, heeft gemekkerd) **1** bleat **2** keep on (at s.o. about sth.), nag

melaats /melats/ (adj) leprous

de **melaatsheid** /melatsheit/ leprosy

de **melancholie** /melɑŋxoli/ melancholy

melancholiek /melɑŋxolik/ (adj, adv) melancholy

de **melange** /melɑ̃ʒə/ (pl: -s) blend, mélange

[1]**melden** /mɛldə(n)/ (meldde, heeft gemeld) report, inform (of); announce: *u moet zich ~ **bij** de receptie* please report to reception; *ze heeft **zich** ziek gemeld* she has reported (herself) sick; she called in sick; *niets **te** ~ hebben* [fig] have nothing to report

zich [2]**melden** /mɛldə(n)/ (meldde zich, heeft zich gemeld) report, check in

de **melding** /mɛldɪŋ/ (pl: -en) mention(ing), report(ing)

de **meldkamer** /mɛltkamər/ (pl: -s) centre; emergency room

melig /meləx/ (adj, adv) corny

de **melk** /mɛlk/ milk: *halfvolle ~* low-fat milk; *koffie **met** ~* coffee with milk; [British] white coffee; *koffie **zonder** ~* black coffee

de **melkboer** /mɛlgbur/ (pl: -en) milkman

de **melkbus** /mɛlgbʏs/ (pl: -sen) milk churn

melken /mɛlkə(n)/ (molk/melkte, heeft gemolken) milk

de **melkfles** /mɛlkflɛs/ (pl: -sen) milk bottle

het **melkgebit** /mɛlkxəbɪt/ (pl: -ten) milk teeth

de **melkkoe** /mɛlku/ **1** dairy cow **2** [fig] milch cow

het/de **melkpoeder** /mɛlkpudər/ powdered milk, dehydrated milk

de **melktand** /mɛlktɑnt/ (pl: -en) milk tooth

het **melkvee** /mɛlkfe/ dairy cattle

de **melkveehouder** /mɛlkfehɑudər/ (pl: -s) dairy farmer

de **Melkweg** /mɛlkwɛx/ (pl: -en) Milky Way

de **melodie** /melodi/ (pl: -ën) melody, tune

melodieus /melod(i)jøs/ (adj, adv) melodious

het **melodrama** /melodrama/ (pl: -'s) melodrama

melodramatisch /melodramatis/ (adj, adv) melodramatic(al)

de **meloen** /məlun/ (pl: -en) melon

het/de **membraan** /mɛmbran/ (pl: membranen) membrane

het/de **memo** /memo/ (pl: -'s) memo

de **memoires** /memwarəs/ (pl) memoirs

memorabel /memorabəl/ (adj) memorable

het **memorandum** /memorɑndʏm/ (pl: -s, memoranda) memorandum, note

memoreren /memorerə(n)/ (memoreerde, heeft gememoreerd) mention, remind

de **memorie** /memori/ (pl: -s) **1** memory: *kort van ~ zijn* have a short memory **2** memorandum: *~ van **toelichting*** explanatory memorandum

men /mɛn/ (ind pron) **1** one; people; they: *~ zegt* it is said, people (*or:* they) say; *~ zegt dat hij ziek is* he is said to be ill **2** one; you: *~ kan hen niet **laten omkomen*** they cannot be allowed to die; *~ **zou zeggen** dat …* by the look of it … **3** one; they: *~ **had** dat kunnen voorzien* that could have been foreseen; *~ **hoopt** dat …* it is hoped that …

de **meneer** /məner/ (pl: meneren) gentleman; [before surname] Mr

menen /menə(n)/ (meende, heeft gemeend) **1** mean: *dat meen je niet!* you can't be serious!; *ik meen **het!*** I mean it! **2** intend, mean: *het **goed** met iem. ~* mean well towards s.o. **3** think: *ik meende dat …* I thought

...

menens /mɛnəns/ (adj): *het is* ~ it's serious

de **mengeling** /mɛŋəlɪŋ/ (pl: -en) mixture

het **mengelmoes** /mɛŋəlmus/ mishmash, jumble

¹**mengen** /mɛŋə(n)/ (mengde, heeft gemengd) **1** mix, blend: *door elkaar* ~ mix together **2** mix, bring in: *mijn naam wordt er ook in gemengd* my name was also brought in (*or:* dragged in)

zich ²**mengen** /mɛŋə(n)/ (mengde zich, heeft zich gemengd) get (o.s.) involved (in), get (o.s.) mixed up (in): *zich in de discussie* ~ join in the discussion

de **mengkleur** /mɛŋklør/ mixed (*or:* blended) colour

de **mengkraan** /mɛŋkran/ (pl: -kranen) mixer tap

het **mengpaneel** /mɛŋpanel/ (pl: -panelen) mixing console, mixer

het **mengsel** /mɛŋsəl/ (pl: -s) mixture, blend

de **menie** /meni/ red lead

meniën /menijə(n)/ (meniede, heeft gemenied) red-lead

menig /menəx/ (num) many; many a: *in* ~ *opzicht* in many respects

menigeen /menəxen/ (ind pron) many (people)

menigmaal /menəxmal/ (adv) many times, many a time

de **menigte** /menəxtə/ (pl: -n, -s) crowd

de **mening** /menɪŋ/ (pl: -en) opinion, view: *afwijkende* ~ dissenting view (*or:* opinion); *zijn* ~ *geven* give one's opinion (*or:* view); *naar mijn* ~ in my opinion (*or:* view), I think, I feel; *van* ~ *veranderen* change one's opinion (*or:* view); *de ~en hierover zijn* **verdeeld** opinions are divided on this (problem/issue); *voor zijn* ~ *durven uitkomen* stand up for one's opinion

de **meningsuiting** /menɪŋsœytɪŋ/ (expression of) opinion, speech: *vrijheid van* ~ freedom of speech

het **meningsverschil** /menɪŋsfərsxɪl/ (pl: -len) difference of opinion

de **meniscus** /menɪskʏs/ meniscus, kneecap

mennen /mɛnə(n)/ (mende, heeft gemend) drive

de **menopauze** /menopauzə/ menopause

de ¹**mens** /mɛns/ **1** human (being), man; man(kind): *ik ben ook maar een* ~ I'm only human; *dat* **doet** *een* ~ *goed* that does you good; *geen* ~ not a soul **2** people: *de gewone ~en* ordinary people; *beste ~en* (hello,) everybody!; [inform] people! **3** person: *een onmogelijk* ~ *zijn* be impossible (to deal with)

het ²**mens** /mɛns/ thing, creature: *het is een braaf (best)* ~ she's a good (old) soul

de **mensa** /mɛnza/ (pl: -'s) refectory; (student) cafeteria

de **mensaap** /mɛnsap/ (pl: -apen) anthropoid (ape), man ape

het **mensbeeld** /mɛnzbelt/ (pl: -en) portrayal of man(kind)

menselijk /mɛnsələk/ (adj) **1** human: *vergissen is* ~ to err is human **2** humane: *niet* ~ inhumane, inhuman

de **menselijkheid** /mɛnsələkhɛit/ humanity: *misdaden tegen de* ~ crimes against humanity

de **menseneter** /mɛnsə(n)etər/ (pl: -s) cannibal

de **mensengedaante** /mɛnsə(n)ɣədantə/ human form

de **mensenhandel** /mɛnsə(n)handəl/ human trafficking

de **mensenhater** /mɛnsə(n)hatər/ (pl: -s) misanthrope

de **mensenheugenis** /mɛnsə(n)høɣənɪs/ human memory: *sinds* ~ from (*or:* since) time immemorial

de **mensenkennis** /mɛnsə(n)kɛnɪs/ insight into (human) character (*or:* human nature)

het **mensenleven** /mɛnsə(n)levə(n)/ (pl: -s) (human) life

de **mensenmassa** /mɛnsəmɑsa/ (pl: -'s) crowd

de **mensenrechten** /mɛnsə(n)rɛxtə(n)/ (pl) human rights

mensenschuw /mɛnsə(n)sxʏw/ (adj) shy, afraid of people

de **mensensmokkel** /mɛnsə(n)smɔkəl/ people smuggling

de **mensenvriend** /mɛnsə(n)vrint/ philanthropist

het **mens-erger-je-niet** /mɛnsɛrɣərjənit/ ludo; [Am] sorry

de **mensheid** /mɛnshɛit/ human nature, humanity

menslievend /mɛnslivənt/ (adj, adv) charitable, humanitarian; philanthropic

mensonterend /mɛnsɔntərənt/ (adj) degrading, disgraceful

mensonwaardig /mɛnsɔnwardəx/ (adj) degrading

de **menstruatie** /mɛnstrywa(t)si/ menstruation, period

de **menstruatiepijn** /mɛnstrywa(t)sipɛin/ (pl: -en) menstrual pain

menstrueren /mɛnstrywerə(n)/ (menstrueerde, heeft gemenstrueerd) menstruate

menswaardig /mɛnswardəx/ (adj) decent, dignified

de **menswetenschappen** /mɛnswetə(n)sxɑpə(n)/ (pl) life sciences; social sciences

mentaal /mɛntal/ (adj, adv) mental

de **mental coach** /mɛntəlkotʃ/ mental coach

de **mentaliteit** /mɛntalitɛit/ mentality

de **menthol** /mɛntɔl/ menthol

de **mentor** /mɛntɔr/ (pl: -en) **1** tutor; [Am] student adviser **2** mentor

het **menu** /məny/ (pl: -'s) menu

de **menubalk** /mənybalk/ (pl: -en) menu bar, button bar

het/de **menuet** /menywɛt/ (pl: -ten) minuet

de **menukaart** /mənykart/ (pl: -en) menu

de **mep** /mɛp/ (pl: -pen) smack || *de volle* ~ the full whack

meppen /mɛpə(n)/ (mepte, heeft gemept) smack

merci /mɛrsi/ (int) thanks

Mercurius /mɛrkyrijʏs/ Mercury

de **merel** /mɛrəl/ (pl: -s) blackbird

meren /mɛrə(n)/ (meerde, heeft gemeerd) moor

het **merendeel** /mɛrə(n)del/ greater part; majority

merendeels /mɛrə(n)dels/ (adv) **1** for the most part **2** mostly

het **merg** /mɛrx/ (bone) marrow: *die kreet ging door ~ en been* it was a harrowing (*or:* heart-rending) cry

de **mergel** /mɛrɣəl/ marl

de **meridiaan** /meridijan/ (pl: meridianen) meridian

het **merk** /mɛrk/ (pl: -en) **1** brand (name), trademark; make **2** mark; hallmark

het **merkartikel** /mɛrkɑrtikəl/ proprietary brand

merkbaar /mɛrgbar/ (adj, adv) noticeable

merken /mɛrkə(n)/ (merkte, heeft gemerkt) **1** notice, see: *dat is (duidelijk) te* ~ it shows; *hij liet niets* ~ he gave nothing away; *je zult het wel* ~ you'll find out; *ik merkte het aan zijn gezicht* I could tell (*or:* see) by the look on his face **2** mark; brand

de **merkkleding** /mɛrkledɪŋ/ designer wear (*or:* clothes)

merkwaardig /mɛrkwardəx/ (adj, adv) peculiar: *het ~e van de zaak is …* the curious (*or:* odd) thing (about it) is …

de **merrie** /mɛri/ (pl: -s) mare

het **mes** /mɛs/ (pl: -sen) knife; blade: *het ~ snijdt aan twee kanten* it is doubly advantageous

mesjogge /məʃɔɣə/ (adj) [Dutch; inform] crazy, nutty

het **mespunt** /mɛspʏnt/ (pl: -en): *een ~je zout* toe a pinch of salt

de **mess** /mɛs/ (pl: -es) mess (hall), messroom

messcherp /mɛsxɛrp/ (adj) razor-sharp

de **Messias** /mɛsijɑs/ Messiah

het **messing** /mɛsɪŋ/ brass

de **messteek** /mɛstek/ (pl: messteken) stab (of a knife)

de **mest** /mɛst/ **1** manure **2** fertilizer

mesten /mɛstə(n)/ (mestte, heeft gemest) fertilize; fatten

de **mesthoop** /mɛsthop/ (pl: -hopen) dunghill

het **mestkalf** /mɛstkɑlf/ (pl: -kalveren) fatting calf

de **mestvaalt** /mɛstfalt/ (pl: -en) dunghill

het **mestvee** /mɛstfe/ beef cattle, store cattle, fatstock

de **mestvork** /mɛstfɔrk/ dung fork

met /mɛt/ (prep) **1** (along) with, of: *~ Janssen* [on the telephone] Janssen speaking (*or:*

here); ~ *wie spreek ik?* [on the telephone] who am I speaking to?; *spreken* ~ *iem.* speak to s.o.; ~ *(zijn) hoevelen zijn zij?* how many of them are there? **2** with, and; including: ~ *rente* with interest; ~ *vijf* plus (*or:* and) five; *tot en* ~ *hoofdstuk drie* up to and including chapter three **3** (mixed) with, and **4** with, by, through, in: ~ *de trein van acht uur* by the eight o'clock train **5** with, by, at: *ik kom* ~ *Kerstmis* I'm coming at Christmas || *een zak* ~ *geld* a bag of money

de **¹metaal** /metal/ metal industry; steel industry

het **²metaal** /metal/ metal: *zware metalen* heavy metals

metaalachtig /metalɑxtəx/ (adj, adv) metallic: *het klinkt* ~ it sounds metallic

de **metaalbewerking** /metalbəwɛrkɪŋ/ metalworking

de **metaaldetector** /metaldetɛktor/ (pl: -s, -en) metal detector

de **metaalindustrie** /metalɪndʏstri/ (pl: -ën) metallurgical industry

de **metaalmoeheid** /metalmuhɛit/ metal fatigue

de **metafoor** /metafor/ (pl: metaforen) metaphor: *om een* ~ *te gebruiken* metaphorically speaking

metafysisch /metafizis/ (adj, adv) metaphysical

metalen /metalə(n)/ (adj) **1** metal, metallic **2** metallic

metallic /metɛlɪk/ (adj) metallic

de **metamorfose** /metamɔrfozə/ (pl: -n, -s) metamorphosis

meteen /məten/ (adv) **1** immediately, at once, right (*or:* straight) away: *ze kwam* ~ *toen ze het hoorde* she came as soon as she heard it; *dat zeg ik u zo* ~ I'll tell you in (just) a minute; *ze was* ~ *dood* she was killed instantly; *nu* ~ (right) now, this (very) minute **2** at the same time, too: *koop er ook* ~ *eentje voor mij* buy one for me (too) while you're about it || *zo* ~ *verklapt hij het nog* next thing, he'll be giving it all away; *zo* ~ *val je nog* if you don't watch out, you'll fall (over/down)

meten /metə(n)/ (mat/meette, heeft gemeten) measure; meter

de **meteoor** /metejor/ (pl: meteoren) meteor

de **meteoriet** /metejorit/ (pl: -en) meteorite

de **meteorologie** /metejoroloɣi/ meteorology

meteorologisch /metejoroloɣis/ (adj) meteorological

de **meteoroloog** /metejorolox/ (pl: -logen) meteorologist

de **¹meter** /metər/ **1** metre: *méters boeken* yards of books; *vierkante* (or: *kubieke*) ~ square (*or:* cubic) metre; *~s maken* [fig] put in the miles, get a lot done **2** meter, gauge: *de ~ opnemen* read the meter **3** indicator, (meter) needle || *voor geen* ~ not at all, no way de **²meter** /mɛtər/ godmother

de **meterkast** /mɛtərkɑst/ (pl: -en) meter cupboard

de **metgezel** /mɛtχəzɛl/ (pl: -len) companion

het **methaan** /metɑn/ methane

het **methadon** /metadɔn/ methadone

de **methode** /metodə/ (pl: -n, -s) method, system

de **methodiek** /metodik/ (pl: -en) methodology

de **meting** /mɛtɪŋ/ (pl: -en) measuring, measurement

metriek /metrik/ (adj) metric

de **metro** /mɛtro/ (pl: -'s) underground (railway); [Am] subway; tube; metro

de **metronoom** /metronom/ (pl: -nomen) metronome

de **metropool** /metropol/ (pl: -polen) metropolis

het **metrostation** /mɛtrosta(t)ʃɔn/ (pl: -s) undergroundstation; [Am] subway station; tube station; metro station

het **metrum** /mɛtrʏm/ (pl: -s, metra) metre

de **metselaar** /mɛtsəlɑr/ (pl: -s) bricklayer

metselen /mɛtsələ(n)/ (metselde, heeft gemetseld) build (in brick, with bricks); lay bricks

de **metten** /mɛtə(n)/ (pl): *korte ~ maken (met)* make short (*or:* quick) work (of)

metterdaad /mɛtərdat/ (adv) indeed, in fact

het **meubel** /møbəl/ (pl: -s, -en) piece of furniture; furniture

de **meubelboulevard** /møbəlbuləvɑr/ (pl: -s) furniture heaven (*or:* strip)

de **meubelmaker** /møbəlmakər/ (pl: -s) furniture maker

de **meubelzaak** /møbəlzak/ (pl: -zaken) furniture business (*or:* shop)

het **meubilair** /møbilɛːr/ furniture, furnishings

meubileren /møbilɛrə(n)/ (meubileerde, heeft gemeubileerd) furnish

de **meug** /møχ/: *iets tegen heug en ~ opeten* force down sth.; *ieder zijn ~* to each his own, there's no accounting for taste

de **meute** /møtə/ (pl: -s) gang, crowd

de **mevrouw** /məvrɑu/ (pl: -en) **1** madam, ma'am, miss **2** Mrs; Ms

de **Mexicaan** /mɛksikan/ (pl: Mexicanen) Mexican

Mexicaans /mɛksikans/ (adj) Mexican

Mexico /mɛksiko/ Mexico

mezelf /məzɛlf/ (ref pron) myself, me: *ik vermaak ~ wel* I'll look after myself

de **mezzosopraan** /mɛtsosopran/ (pl: -sopranen) mezzo-soprano

m.i. *mijns inziens* in my opinion

miauw /mijɑu/ (int) miaow, mew

miauwen /mijɑuwə(n)/ (miauwde, heeft gemiauwd) miaow, mew

de **micro** /mikro/ (pl: -'s) [Belg] mike

de **microbe** /mikrobə/ (pl: -n) microbe

de **microfilm** /mikrofɪlm/ (pl: -s) microfilm

de **microfoon** /mikrofɔn/ (pl: -s) microphone; mike

de **microgolf** /mikroɣɔlf/ (pl: -golven) [Belg] microwave

het **microkrediet** /mikrokrədit/ (pl: -en) microcredit

het **micro-organisme** /mikroorɣanɪsmə/ (pl: -n) micro-organism

de **microprocessor** /mikroprosɛsɔr/ (pl: -s) microprocessor

de **microscoop** /mikroskop/ (pl: microscopen) microscope

microscopisch /mikroskopis/ (adj, adv) microscopic: *~ klein* microscopic

de **middag** /mɪdɑχ/ (pl: -en) **1** afternoon: *'s ~s* in the afternoon; *om 5 uur 's ~s* at 5 o'clock in the afternoon, at 5 p.m. **2** noon: *tussen de ~* at lunchtime

het **middagdutje** /mɪdɑɣdʏcə/ (pl: -s) afternoon nap

het **middageten** /mɪdɑχetə(n)/ lunch(eon)

de **middagpauze** /mɪdɑχpɑuzə/ (pl: -s) lunch hour, lunchtime, lunch-hour break

de **middagtemperatuur** /mɪdɑχtɛmpəratyr/ afternoon temperature

het **middaguur** /mɪdɑχyr/ noon

het **middel** /mɪdəl/ (pl: -en) **1** waist **2** means: *het is een ~, geen doel* it's a means to an end; *door ~ van* by means of **3** remedy: *een ~tje tegen hoofdpijn* a headache remedy; *het ~ is soms erger dan de kwaal* the remedy may be worse than the disease

middelbaar /mɪdəlbar/ (adj) middle; [educ] secondary

de **middeleeuwen** /mɪdələwə(n)/ (pl) Middle Ages

middeleeuws /mɪdəlɛws/ (adj) medieval: *~e geschriften* medieval documents; *~e opvattingen* medieval ideas

het **middelgebergte** /mɪdəlɣəbɛrχtə/ (pl: -n, -s) low mountain range

middelgroot /mɪdəlɣrot/ (adj) medium-size(d)

middellands /mɪdəlɑn(t)s/ (adj) Mediterranean: *de Middellandse Zee* the Mediterranean (Sea)

middellang /mɪdəlɑŋ/ (adj) **1** medium (length (*or:* range)) **2** medium length (*or:* term): *op ~e termijn* in the medium term

de **middellijn** /mɪdəlɛin/ (pl: -en) diameter

de **middelmaat** /mɪdəlmat/ average

middelmatig /mɪdəlmatəχ/ (adj, adv) average, mediocre: *ik vind het maar ~* I think it's pretty middling

de **middelmatigheid** /mɪdəlmatəχhɛit/ mediocrity

het **middelpunt** /mɪdəlpʏnt/ (pl: -en) centre, middle

middelpuntvliedend /mɪdəlpʏntflidənt/

(adj) centrifugal

middels /mɪdəls/ (prep) by means of

middelst /mɪdəlst/ (adj) middle(most)

de **middelvinger** /mɪdəlvɪŋər/ (pl: -s) middle finger

het **¹midden** /mɪdə(n)/ (pl: -s) **1** middle, centre: *dat laat ik in het ~* I won't go into that; *de waarheid ligt in het ~* the truth lies (somewhere) in between **2** middle, midst: *te ~ van* in the midst of, among

²midden /mɪdə(n)/ (adv) in the middle of: *~ in de zomer* in the middle of (the) summer; *hij is ~ (in de) veertig* he is in his middle forties (*or:* mid-forties); *~ op de dag* in the middle of the day

Midden-Amerika /mɪdə(n)amerika/ Central America

de **middenberm** /mɪdə(n)bɛrm/ (pl: -en) central reservation

middendoor /mɪdə(n)dor/ (adv) in two

Midden-Europa /mɪdə(n)øropa/ Central Europe

Midden-Europees /mɪdə(n)øropes/ (adj) Central-European

de **middengolf** /mɪdə(n)ɣolf/ medium wave

middenin /mɪdə(n)ɪn/ (adv) in the middle (*or:* centre)

de **middenjury** /mɪdə(n)ʒyri/ [Belg] central examination committee

het **middenkader** /mɪdə(n)kadər/ middle management

de **middenklasse** /mɪdə(n)klɑsə/ medium range (*or:* size)

de **middenklassenauto** /mɪdə(n)klɑsə(n)auto/ (pl: -'s) car in the medium-price range, average-priced car

de **middenmoot** /mɪdə(n)mot/ middle bracket (*or:* group): *die sportclub hoort thuis in de ~* that's just an average club

de **middenmoter** /mɪdəmotər/ (pl: -s) [roughly] average joe; [Am] average guy

het **middenoor** /mɪdə(n)or/ (pl: -oren) middle ear

het **Midden-Oosten** /mɪdə(n)ostə(n)/ Middle East

het **middenpad** /mɪdə(n)pɑt/ (centre) aisle; gangway

het **middenrif** /mɪdə(n)rɪf/ midriff, diaphragm

het **middenschip** /mɪdə(n)sxɪp/ nave

de **middenstand** /mɪdə(n)stɑnt/ (the) self-employed, tradespeople

de **middenstander** /mɪdə(n)stɑndər/ (pl: -s) tradesman, shopkeeper

het **middenstandsdiploma** /mɪdə(n)stɑntsdiploma/ (pl: -'s) [Dutch] [roughly] retailer's certificate (*or:* diploma)

de **middenstip** /mɪdə(n)stɪp/ (pl: -pen) centre spot

het **middenveld** /mɪdə(n)vɛlt/ midfield

de **middenvelder** /mɪdə(n)vɛldər/ (pl: -s) midfielder, midfield player

de **middenweg** /mɪdə(n)wɛx/ (pl: -en) [fig] middle course, medium: *de gulden ~* the golden mean, the happy medium

de **middernacht** /mɪdərnɑxt/ midnight

middernachtelijk /mɪdərnɑxtələk/ (adj) midnight

het **midgetgolf** /mɪdʒətɣolf/ miniature golf, midget golf

de **midlifecrisis** /mɪtlɑjfkrɑjsəs/ (pl: -crises) midlife crisis

de **midvoor** /mɪtfor/ centre forward

de **midweek** /mɪtwek/ (pl: -weken) midweek

de **midwinter** /mɪtwɪntər/ (pl: -s) midwinter

de **mie** /mi/ (Chinese) noodles

de **miep** /mip/ (pl: -en) bird; [Am] broad

de **mier** /mir/ (pl: -en) ant

de **miereneter** /mirə(n)etər/ (pl: -s) ant-eater

de **mierenhoop** /mirə(n)hop/ (pl: -hopen) ant-hill

de **mierenneuker** /mirənøkər/ (pl: -s) [inform] nitpicker

het **mierikswortel** /mirɪkswortəl/ horseradish

het **mietje** /micə/ (pl: -s) [offensive; inform] **1** gay, pansy **2** softy, wet; chicken

miezeren /mizərə(n)/ (miezerde, heeft gemiezerd) drizzle

miezerig /mizərəx/ (adj) **1** drizzly **2** tiny, puny

de **migraine** /migrɛːnə/ migraine

de **migrant** /miɣrɑnt/ (pl: -en) migrant

de **migratie** /miɣra(t)si/ (pl: -s) migration

de **migratieachtergrond** /miɣra(t)siɑxtərɣront/ migrant background

migreren /miɣrerə(n)/ (migreerde, is gemigreerd) migrate

de **mihoen** /mihun/ (thin) Chinese noodles

mij /mɛi/ (pers pron) **1** me: *hij had het (aan) ~ gegeven* he had given it to me; *dat is van ~* that's mine; *een vriend van ~* a friend of mine; *dat is ~ te duur* that's too expensive for me **2** myself: *ik schaam ~ zeer* I am deeply ashamed

mijden /mɛɪdə(n)/ (meed, heeft gemeden) avoid

de **mijl** /mɛil/ (pl: -en) mile

mijlenver /mɛilə(n)vɛr/ (adj, adv) miles (away); for miles

de **mijlpaal** /mɛilpal/ (pl: mijlpalen) milestone: *een ~ bereiken* reach a milestone

mijmeren /mɛimərə(n)/ (mijmerde, heeft gemijmerd) muse (on), (day)dream (about)

de **¹mijn** /mɛin/ (pl: -en) mine: *op een ~ lopen* strike (*or:* hit) a mine

²mijn /mɛin/ (poss pron) my ‖ *daar moet ik het ~e van weten* I must get to the bottom of this

de **mijnbouw** /mɛɪmbau/ mining (industry)

de **mijnenlegger** /mɛɪnə(n)lɛɣər/ minelayer; minecraft

de **mijnenveger** /mɛɪnə(n)veɣər/ (pl: -s) minesweeper

het **mijnenveld** /mɛɪnə(n)vɛlt/ (pl: -en) mine-

field
mijnerzijds /mɛɪnərzɛɪts/ (adv) [form] on (or: for) my part

de **mijnheer** /mənər/ (pl: mijnheren) **1** sir: ~ *de voorzitter* Mr chairman; ~ *Jansen* Mr Jansen **2** gentleman

de **mijnschacht** /mɛɪnsxɑxt/ (pl: -en) mine shaft

de **mijnwerker** /mɛɪnwɛrkər/ (pl: -s) miner

de **mijt** /mɛɪt/ (pl: -en) mite

de **mijter** /mɛɪtər/ (pl: -s) mitre

mijzelf /mɛɪzɛlf/ (ref pron) myself

mikken /mɪkə(n)/ (mikte, heeft gemikt) (take) aim: ~ *op iets* (take) aim at sth.

de **mikmak** /mɪkmɑk/ [inform] caboodle: *de hele* ~ the lot, the whole caboodle

het **mikpunt** /mɪkpʏnt/ (pl: -en) butt, target

Milaan /milan/ Milan

mild /mɪlt/ (adj, adv) mild; soft; gentle

de **milicien** /miliɕɛ̃/ (pl: -s) [Belg; historical] conscript

het **milieu** /miljø/ (pl: -s) **1** milieu: *iem. uit een ander* ~ s.o. from a different social background (or: milieu); *het criminele* ~ criminal circles; *uit een voortreffelijk* ~ *komen* be of excellent stock, have impeccable lineage **2** environment: *de vervuiling van het* ~ environmental pollution

het **milieubeheer** /miljøbəheːr/ conservation (of nature), environmental protection

de **milieubescherming** /miljøbəsxɛrmɪŋ/ conservation, environmental protection

de **milieubeweging** /miljøbəweːxɪŋ/ (pl: -en) ecology movement, environmental movement

milieubewust /miljøbəwʏst/ (adj) environment-minded, environmentally conscious

de **milieueffectrapportage** /miljøɛfɛktrapoːrtaʒə/ (pl: -s) environmental impact statement

de **milieuheffing** /miljøhɛfɪŋ/ (pl: -en) environmental tax (or: fee)

de **milieuramp** /miljørɑmp/ (pl: -en) environmental disaster

de **milieuvervuiling** /miljøvərvœylɪŋ/ environmental pollution

milieuvriendelijk /miljøvrɪndələk/ (adj, adv) ecologically sound, environmentally friendly (or: safe)

de **milieuwetgeving** /miljøwɛtxevɪŋ/ environmental legislation

de **milieuzone** /miljøzoːnə/ (pl: -s) low emission zone

de **¹militair** /militɛːr/ (pl: -en) soldier, serviceman

²militair /militɛːr/ (adj, adv) military: *in ~e dienst* gaan do one's military service, join the Army

de **militant** /militɑnt/ (pl: -en) [Belg] activist

militaristisch /militarɪstis/ (adj, adv) militarist(ic)

de **militie** /mili(t)si/ [Belg; historical] compulsory military service

miljard /mɪljɑrt/ (num) billion, (a, one) thousand million: *de schade loopt in de ~en euro's* the damage runs into billions of euros

de **miljardair** /mɪljɑrdɛːr/ (pl: -s) multimillionaire

miljardste /mɪljɑrtstə/ (num) billionth

het **miljoen** /mɪljun/ (pl: -en) million

de **miljoenennota** /mɪljunənota/ (pl: -'s) [Dutch] budget

de **miljoenenschade** /mɪljunə(n)sxadə/ damage amounting to millions

de **miljoenenstad** /mɪljunə(n)stɑt/ city with over a million inhabitants

de **miljoenste** /mɪljunstə/ millionth

de **miljonair** /mɪljonɛːr/ (pl: -s) millionaire

de **milkshake** /mɪlkʃek/ (pl: -s) milk shake

het **mille** /mil/ (one) thousand

het **millennium** /milɛnijʏm/ (pl: millennia) millennium

de **millibar** /milibar/ (pl: -en, -s) millibar

het **milligram** /miliɣrɑm/ (pl: -men) milligram

de **milliliter** /mililitər/ (pl: -s) millilitre

de **millimeter** /milimetər/ (pl: -s) millimetre

millimeteren /milimetərə(n)/ (millimeterde, heeft gemillimeterd) crop

de **milt** /mɪlt/ (pl: -en) spleen

het **miltvuur** /mɪltfyr/ anthrax

de **mime** /mim/ mime

de **mimespeler** /mimspelər/ (pl: -s) mime artist

de **mimiek** /mimik/ facial expression

de **mimosa** /mimoza/ (pl: -'s) mimosa

de **¹min** /mɪn/ (pl: -nen) minus; minus (sign) ‖ *zij heeft op haar rapport een zeven* ~ she has a seven minus on her report; *de thermometer staat op* ~ *10°* the thermometer is at minus 10°; *tien* ~ *drie* is zeven ten minus three equals seven; ~ *of meer* more or less

²min /mɪn/ (adj) **1** poor: *arbeiders waren haar te* ~ workmen were beneath her **2** little, few: *zo* ~ *mogelijk fouten maken* make as few mistakes as possible

minachten /mɪnɑxtə(n)/ (minachtte, heeft geminacht) disdain, hold in contempt

minachtend /mɪnɑxtənt/ (adj, adv) disdainful, contemptuous: ~ *behandelen* treat with contempt

de **minachting** /mɪnɑxtɪŋ/ contempt, disdain: *uit* ~ *voor* in contempt of

de **minaret** /minarɛt/ (pl: -ten) minaret

de **minarine** /minarinə/ [Belg] low-fat margarine

minder /mɪndər/ (adj) **1** less, fewer; smaller: *hij heeft niet veel geld, maar nog* ~ *verstand* he has little money and even less intelligence; *dat was* ~ *geslaagd* that was less successful; *hoe* ~ *erover gezegd wordt, hoe beter* the less said about it the better; *vijf minuten meer of* ~ give or take five minutes; *groepen van negen en* ~ groups of nine and under **2** worse: *mijn* *ogen* **worden** ~ my eyes are not what they used to be

minderbedeeld /mɪndərbədɛlt/ (adj) less fortunate

de **mindere** /mɪndərə/ (pl: -n) inferior

minderen /mɪndərə(n)/ (minderde, heeft geminderd) decrease: *vaart* ~ slow down; ~ *met (roken)* cut down on (smoking)

de **minderheid** /mɪndərhɛit/ (pl: -heden) minority

de **mindering** /mɪndərɪŋ/ (pl: -en) decrease: *iets in* ~ *brengen (op)* deduct sth. (from)

minderjarig /mɪndərjarəx/ (adj) minor; underage: ~ *zijn* be a minor

de **minderjarigheid** /mɪndərjarəxhɛit/ minority

minderwaardig /mɪndərwardəx/ (adj) inferior (to)

de **minderwaardigheid** /mɪndərwardəxhɛit/ inferiority

het **minderwaardigheidscomplex** /mɪndərwardəxhɛrtskɔmplɛks/ (pl: -en) inferiority complex

mineraal /minəral/ (adj) mineral ‖ *rijk aan mineralen* rich in minerals

het **mineraalwater** /minəralwatər/ mineral water

de **mineur** /minør/ minor: *in* ~ *zijn* be depressed

het **mini** /mini/ mini

de **miniatuur** /minijatyr/ (pl: miniaturen) miniature

de **minibar** /minibɑ:r/ minibar

de ¹**miniem** /minim/ (pl: -en) [Belg] junior member (10, 11 years) of sports club

²**miniem** /minim/ (adj, adv) small, slight, negligible

de **minima** /minima/ (pl) minimum wage earners

minimaal /minimal/ (adj, adv) **1** minimal, minimum: ~ *presteren* perform very poorly **2** at least

minimaliseren /minimalizərə(n)/ (minimaliseerde, heeft geminimaliseerd) minimize

minimalistisch /minimalɪstis/ (adj) minimalist

het **minimum** /minimʏm/ (pl: minima) minimum

de **minimumleeftijd** /minimʏmleftɛit/ (pl: -en) minimum age

het **minimumloon** /minimʏmlon/ (pl: -lonen) minimum wage

de **minimumtemperatuur** /minimʏmtɛmpəratyr/ minimum temperature

de **minirok** /minirɔk/ (pl: -ken) miniskirt

de **minister** /minɪstər/ (pl: -s) minister, secretary of state; [Am] secretary: ~ *van Binnenlandse Zaken* Minister of the Interior; Home Secretary; [Am] Secretary of the Interior; ~ *van Buitenlandse Zaken* Minister for Foreign Affairs; Secretary of State for Foreign and Commonwealth Affairs; Foreign Secretary; [Am] Secretary of State; ~ *van Defensie* Minister of Defence; Secretary of State for Defence; [Am] Secretary of Defense; Defense Secretary; ~ *van Economische Zaken* Minister for Economic Affairs; Secretary of State for Trade and Industry; [Am] [roughly] Secretary for Commerce; ~ *van Financiën* Minister of Finance; Chancellor of the Exchequer; [Am] Secretary of the Treasury; [Dutch] ~ *van Justitie en Veiligheid* Minister of Justice; [roughly] Lord (High) Chancellor; [Am] [roughly] Attorney General; ~ *van Landbouw en Visserij* Minister of Agriculture and Fisheries; ~ *van Onderwijs en Wetenschappen* Minister of Education and Science; [Am] Secretary of Education; ~ *van Ontwikkelingssamenwerking* Minister for Overseas Development; ~ *van Sociale Zaken en Werkgelegenheid* Minister for Social Services and Employment; [Am] [roughly] Secretary of Labor; ~ *van Verkeer en Waterstaat* Minister of Transport and Public Works; [Am] Secretary of Transportation; ~ *van Volkshuisvesting, Ruimtelijke Ordening en Milieubeheer* Minister for Housing, Regional Development and the Environment; [Am] [roughly] Secretary for Housing and Urban Development; ~ *van Volksgezondheid, Welzijn en Sport* Minister of Health, Welfare and Sport; [Am] [roughly] Secretary of Health and Human Services; *eerste* ~ prime minister, premier

het **ministerie** /minɪstəri/ (pl: -s) ministry, department: ~ *van Buitenlandse Zaken* Ministry of Foreign Affairs; Foreign (and Commonwealth) Office; [Am] State Department; ~ *van Defensie* Ministry of Defence; [Am] Department of Defense; (the) Pentagon; ~ *van Financiën* Ministry of Finance; Treasury; [Am] Treasury Department ‖ *het Openbaar Ministerie* the Public Prosecutor

ministerieel /minɪstərijel/ (adj) ministerial: *de ministeriële verantwoordelijkheid* ministerial responsibility

de **minister-president** /minɪstərprezidɛnt/ (pl: -en) prime minister, premier

de **ministerraad** /minɪstərat/ (pl: -raden) **1** council of ministers **2** cabinet (meeting)

de **ministerspost** /minɪstərspɔst/ ministerial post

de **minnaar** /mɪnar/ (pl: -s) lover, mistress

de **minne** /mɪnə/: *iets in der* ~ *schikken* settle sth. amicably (*or:* by mutual agreement); settle sth. out of court

minnetjes /mɪnəcəs/ (adj, adv) poor

het **minpunt** /mɪmpʏnt/ (pl: -en) minus (point)

minst /mɪnst/ (adj, adv) **1** slightest, lowest: *niet de (het)* ~*e …* not a shadow of …, not the slightest … **2** least: *op z'n* ~ at (the very) least; *niet in het* ~ not at all; *bij het* ~*e of geringste* at the least little thing; *ten* ~*e* at least

3 least; fewest: *zij verdient het ~e* **geld** she earns the least money; *de ~e* **fouten** the fewest mistakes

minstens /mɪnstəns/ (adv) at least: *ik moet ~ vijf* euro hebben I need five euros at least

de **minstreel** /mɪnstrel/ (pl: minstrelen) minstrel

het **minteken** /mɪntekə(n)/ (pl: -s) minus (sign)

minus /minʏs/ (prep) minus

minuscuul /minʏskyl/ (adj, adv) tiny, minuscule, minute

de **minutenwijzer** /minytə(n)wɛizər/ (pl: -s) minute hand

minutieus /miny(t)ʃøs/ (adj, adv) meticulous: *iets ~* **beschrijven** describe sth. in meticulous (or: minute) detail

de **minuut** /minyt/ (pl: minuten) **1** minute: *het is tien minuten* **lopen** it's a ten-minute walk **2** second, minute: *de situatie verslechterde* **met** *de ~* the situation was getting worse by the minute; *op de ~ af* to the (very) minute

het **mirakel** /mirakəl/ (pl: -s, -en) miracle, wonder

de **mirre** /mɪrə/ myrrh

de **¹mis** /mɪs/ (pl: -sen) Mass: *naar de ~ gaan* go to Mass

²mis /mɪs/ (adj, adv) **1** out, off target: *~ poes!* tough (luck)!; *was het ~ of* **raak?** was it a hit or a miss? **2** wrong: *het* **liep** *~* it went wrong; *daar is niks ~ mee* there's nothing wrong with that

het **misbaar** /mɪzbar/ uproar, hullabaloo

het **misbaksel** /mɪzbɑksəl/ (pl: -s) bastard, louse

het **misbruik** /mɪzbrœyk/ (pl: -en) abuse, misuse; excess: *~ van iem.* **maken** take advantage of s.o., use s.o., exploit s.o.; *seksueel ~* sexual abuse

misbruiken /mɪzbrœykə(n)/ (misbruikte, heeft misbruikt) **1** abuse, misuse; impose upon **2** violate

de **misdaad** /mɪzdat/ (pl: misdaden) crime

de **misdaadbestrijding** /mɪzdadbəstrɛidɪŋ/ crime prevention, fight against crime

misdadig /mɪzdadəχ/ (adj, adv) criminal

de **misdadiger** /mɪzdadəγər/ (pl: -s) criminal

de **misdadigheid** /mɪzdadəχhɛit/ crime, criminality

de **misdienaar** /mɪzdinar/ (pl: -s) acolyte; altar boy

misdoen /mɪzdun/ (misdeed, heeft misdaan) do wrong

zich **misdragen** /mɪzdraγə(n)/ (misdroeg zich, heeft zich misdragen) misbehave; be (a) naughty (boy, girl)

het **misdrijf** /mɪzdrɛif/ (pl: misdrijven) criminal offence, criminal act, crime; [law] felony

de **misdruk** /mɪzdrʏk/ (pl: -ken) bad copy

miserabel /mizerabəl/ (adj, adv) miserable, wretched

de **misère** /mizɛːrə/ (pl: -s) misery

misgaan /mɪsχan/ (ging mis, is misgegaan) go wrong: *dit* **plan** *moet haast wel ~* this plan is almost sure to fail

misgrijpen /mɪsχrɛipə(n)/ (greep mis, heeft misgegrepen) **1** miss one's hold **2** find that sth. is sold out || *~* **bij** *een sollicitatie* fail to get hired

misgunnen /mɪsχʏnə(n)/ (misgunde, heeft misgund) (be)grudge, resent

mishandelen /mɪshɑndələ(n)/ (mishandelde, heeft mishandeld) ill-treat, maltreat; batter: *dieren ~* be cruel to (or: maltreat) animals

de **mishandeling** /mɪshɑndəlɪŋ/ (pl: -en) ill-treatment, maltreatment; [law] battery

miskennen /mɪskɛnə(n)/ (miskende, heeft miskend) misunderstand: *een miskend* **genie** (or: **talent**) a misunderstood genius (or: talent)

de **miskenning** /mɪskɛnɪŋ/ denial

de **miskleun** /mɪskløn/ (pl: -en) blunder, boob

de **miskoop** /mɪskop/ (pl: miskopen) bad bargain, bad buy

de **miskraam** /mɪskram/ (pl: miskramen) miscarriage

misleiden /mɪslɛidə(n)/ (misleidde, heeft misleid) mislead, deceive: *iem. ~* deceive s.o., lead s.o. up the garden path; *een ~de* **advertentie** a misleading advertisement

de **misleiding** /mɪslɛidɪŋ/ (pl: -en) deception

¹mislopen /mɪslopə(n)/ (liep mis, is misgelopen) go wrong, miscarry: *het* **plan** *liep mis* the plan miscarried (or: was a failure)

²mislopen /mɪslopə(n)/ (liep mis, heeft misgelopen) miss (out on): [hum] *hij is zijn* **carrière** *misgelopen* he missed his vocation, he's in the wrong business

de **mislukkeling** /mɪslʏkəlɪŋ/ (pl: -en) failure

mislukken /mɪslʏkə(n)/ (mislukte, is mislukt) fail, be unsuccessful, go wrong; fall through; break down: *een mislukte* **advocaat** (or: **schrijver**) a failed lawyer (or: writer); *een mislukte* **poging** an unsuccessful attempt

de **mislukking** /mɪslʏkɪŋ/ (pl: -en) failure

mismaakt /mɪsmakt/ (adj) deformed

de **mismaaktheid** /mɪsmakthɛit/ deformity

mismoedig /mɪsmudəχ/ (adj) dejected, dispirited, discouraged

misnoegd /mɪsnuχt/ (adj) displeased (with/at)

het **misnoegen** /mɪsnuγə(n)/ displeasure

de **mispel** /mɪspəl/ (pl: -s, -en) medlar

mispeuteren /mɪspøtərə(n)/ (mispeuterde, heeft mispeuterd) [Belg] do sth. wrong, be up to

misplaatst /mɪsplatst/ (adj) out of place, misplaced; uncalled-for

misprijzen /mɪsprɛizə(n)/ (misprees, heeft misprezen) disapprove of: *een ~de* **blik** a look of disapproval, a disapproving look

het **mispunt** /mɪspʏnt/ (pl: -en) pain (in the

neck), bastard, louse

zich **misrekenen** /mɪsre̱kənə(n)/ (misrekende zich, heeft zich misrekend) miscalculate

het **missaal** /mɪsa̱l/ (pl: missalen) missal

misschien /mɪsxi̱n/ (adv) perhaps, maybe: *bent u ~ mevrouw Hendriks?* are you Mrs Hendriks by any chance?; *heeft u ~ een paperclip voor me?* do you happen to have (*or:* could you possibly let me have) a paper clip?; *het is ~ beter als …* it may be better (*or:* perhaps it's better) if …; *~ vertrek ik morgen, ~ ook niet* maybe I'll leave tomorrow, maybe not; *zoals je ~ weet* as you may know; *wilt u ~ een kopje koffie?* would you care for some coffee?

misselijk /mɪ̱sələk/ (adj, adv) **1** sick (in the stomach): *om ~ van te worden* sickening, nauseating, disgusting **2** nasty; disgusting; revolting: *een ~e grap* a sick joke ‖ *das is niet ~* that's quite sth.

de **misselijkheid** /mɪ̱sələkhɛit/ (feeling of) sickness, nausea

¹**missen** /mɪ̱sə(n)/ (miste, heeft gemist) **1** [Dutch] be missing: *er ~ een paar bladzijden uit dat boek* there are a few pages missing from that book **2** miss: *~ voor open doel* miss an easy shot ‖ *dat kan niet ~* that can't fail (*or:* go wrong), that's bound to work (*or:* happen)

²**missen** /mɪ̱sə(n)/ (miste, heeft gemist) miss, go without; spare; afford; lack; lose: *de trein ~* miss the train; [fig] *zijn doel ~* miss the mark; *iem. ontzettend ~* miss s.o. badly; *ik kan mijn bril niet ~* I can't get along without my glasses; *kun je je fiets een paar uurtjes ~?* can you spare your bike for a couple of hours?; *ze kunnen elkaar niet ~* they can't get along without one another; *ik zou het voor geen geld willen ~* I wouldn't part with it (*or:* do without it) for all the world

de **misser** /mɪ̱sər/ (pl: -s) **1** failure, mistake, flop **2** miss; bad shot, poor shot; misthrow; bad throw; miscue

de **missie** /mɪ̱si/ (pl: -s) mission; missionary work

de **missionaris** /mɪʃona̱rɪs/ (pl: -sen) missionary

misslaan /mɪ̱slan/ (sloeg mis, heeft misgeslagen) miss

misstaan /mɪsta̱n/ (misstond, heeft misstaan) not suit ‖ *een verontschuldiging zou niet ~* an apology would not be out of place

de **misstand** /mɪ̱stɑnt/ (pl: -en) abuse, wrong

de **misstap** /mɪ̱stɑp/ (pl: -pen) **1** false step, wrong step **2** slip: *een ~ begaan* make a slip; slip up

de **missverkiezing** /mɪ̱sfərkizɪŋ/ (pl: -en) beauty contest

de **mist** /mɪst/ fog; mist: *dichte ~* (a) thick fog; *de ~ ingaan* a) go wrong (*or:* fail) completely; b) fall flat; c) go wrong, be all at sea ‖ *~ creë-*

ren use smoke and mirrors

de **mistbank** /mɪ̱stbɑŋk/ (pl: -en) fog bank

misten /mɪ̱stə(n)/ (mistte, heeft gemist) be foggy, be misty

het **mistgordijn** /mɪ̱stxɔrdɛin/ curtain of fog

de **misthoorn** /mɪ̱sthɔrn/ (pl: -s) foghorn

mistig /mɪ̱stəx/ (adj) foggy; misty

de **mistlamp** /mɪ̱stlɑmp/ (pl: -en) fog lamp

de **mistletoe** /mɪ̱səlto/ mistletoe

mistroostig /mɪstro̱stəx/ (adj) **1** dispirited, dejected **2** dismal, miserable

de **misvatting** /mɪ̱sfɑtɪŋ/ (pl: -en) misconception, fallacy: *een populaire ~* a popular misconception, a popular fallacy

het **misverstand** /mɪ̱sfərstɑnt/ (pl: -en) misunderstanding: *een ~ uit de weg ruimen* clear up a misunderstanding

misvormd /mɪsfɔ̱rmt/ (adj) deformed, disfigured; [fig] distorted

de **misvorming** /mɪsfɔ̱rmɪŋ/ (pl: -en) **1** deformation; [fig] distortion **2** deformity; [fig] distortion

de **mitella** /mitɛ̱la/ (pl: -'s) sling

de **mitrailleur** /mitrajø̱r/ (pl: -s) machine-gun

mits /mɪts/ (conj) if, provided that: *~ goed bewaard, kan het jaren meegaan* (if) stored well, it can last for years

de **mix** /mɪks/ (pl: -en, -es) mix

de **mixdrank** /mɪ̱ksdrɑŋk/ mix

mixen /mɪ̱ksə(n)/ (mixte, heeft gemixt) mix

de **mixer** /mɪ̱ksər/ (pl: -s) mixer; liquidizer; blender

het **mkb** /ɛmkabe̱/ [Dutch] *midden- en kleinbedrijf* small and medium-sized businesses

MKZ /ɛmkazɛ̱t/ *mond-en-klauwzeer* foot and mouth (disease)

ml *milliliter* ml

de **mlk-school** /ɛmɛlka̱sxol/ school for children with learning problems

mm *millimeter* mm

de **mms** *multimedia message service* MMS message

m.m.v. *met medewerking van* with the co-operation of

mobiel /mobi̱l/ (adj) mobile: *~ nummer* mobile (phone) number; [Am] cellphone number; *~e telefoon* mobile (phone); [Am] cellphone

het **mobieltje** /mobi̱lcə/ (pl: -s) mobile (phone); [Am] cellphone

het/de **mobilhome** /mo̱bəlhom/ [Belg] camper (van)

de **mobilisatie** /mobiliza̱(t)si/ (pl: -s) mobilization

mobiliseren /mobilize̱rə(n)/ (mobiliseerde, heeft gemobiliseerd) mobilize

de **mobiliteit** /mobilitɛ̱it/ (pl: -en) mobility

de **mobilofoon** /mobilofo̱n/ (pl: -s) radio-telephone

de **mocassin** /mɔkasɛ̱/ (pl: -s) moccasin

modaal /moda̱l/ (adj) average

de **modaliteit** /modalitɛɪt/ **1** modality **2** term
de **modder** /mɔdər/ mud; sludge
het **modderbad** /mɔdərbɑt/ (pl: -en) mudbath
modderen /mɔdərə(n)/ (modderde, heeft gemodderd) muddle (along, through)
het/de **modderfiguur** /mɔdərfiɣyr/: *een ~ slaan* cut a sorry figure, look like a fool
modderig /mɔdərəx/ (adj) muddy
de **modderpoel** /mɔdərpul/ (pl: -en) quagmire; [fig] mire
de **modderschuit** /mɔdərsxœyt/ (pl: -en): *dat staat als een vlag op een ~* it looks totally out of place
moddervet /mɔdərvɛt/ (adj) gross(ly fat)
de **mode** /mɔdə/ (pl: -s) fashion: *zich naar de laatste ~ kleden* dress after the latest fashion; *(in de) ~ zijn* be fashionable
modebewust /mɔdəbəwʏst/ (adj, adv) fashion-conscious
het **modeblad** /mɔdəblɑt/ (pl: -en) fashion magazine
de **modegek** /mɔdəɣɛk/ fashion plate
de **modegril** /mɔdəɣrɪl/ (pl: -len) fashion fad
het **model** /mɔdɛl/ (pl: -len) **1** model, type, style: *~ staan voor* serve as a model (*or:* pattern) for; *als ~ nemen voor iets* model sth. (*or:* o.s.) on **2** model, design: *het ~ van een overhemd* the style of a shirt **3** model, style: *goed in ~ blijven* stay in shape
de **modelbouw** /mɔdɛlbɑu/ model making, modelling (to scale)
het **modellenbureau** /mɔdɛlə(n)byro/ (pl: -s) modelling agency
modelleren /mɔdɛlɛrə(n)/ (modelleerde, heeft gemodelleerd) model: *~ naar* fashion after, model on
de **modelwoning** /mɔdɛlwonɪŋ/ (pl: -en) show house
het/de **modem** /mɔdəm/ (pl: -s) modem
de **modeontwerper** /mɔdəontwɛrpər/ (pl: -s) fashion designer
modern /mɔdɛrn/ (adj, adv) modern: *het huis is ~ ingericht* the house has a modern interior; *de ~ste technieken* most modern (*or:* state-of-the-art) technology
moderniseren /mɔdɛrnizərə(n)/ (moderniseerde, heeft gemoderniseerd) modernize
de **modernisering** /mɔdɛrnizərɪŋ/ (pl: -en) modernization
modernistisch /mɔdɛrnɪstis/ (adj, adv) modernist(ic), ultra-modern
de **modeshow** /mɔdəʃow/ (pl: -s) fashion show
het **modewoord** /mɔdəwort/ (pl: -en) vogue word
de **modezaak** /mɔdəzak/ (pl: -zaken) clothes shop, clothes store; fashion store
modieus /modijøs/ (adj, adv) fashionable: *een modieuze dame* a lady of fashion
modificeren /modifisərə(n)/ (modificeerde, heeft gemodificeerd) modify
de **modulatie** /modyla(t)si/ modulation

de **module** /modylə/ (pl: -s) module
de **modus** /mɔdʏs/ (pl: modi) mode
de **¹moe** /mu/ mum(my); [Am] mom ǁ *nou ~!* well I say!
²moe /mu/ (adj) **1** tired: *~ van het wandelen* tired with walking **2** tired (of), weary (of): *zij is het warme weer ~* she is (sick and) tired of the hot weather
de **moed** /mut/ **1** courage, nerve: *al zijn ~ bijeenrapen (verzamelen)* muster up (*or:* summon up, pluck up) one's courage **2** courage, heart: *de ~ erin houden* keep one's spirits up; *met frisse ~ beginnen* begin with fresh courage; come up smiling; *de ~ opgeven* lose heart; *~ putten uit* take heart from; *de ~ zonk hem in de schoenen* his heart sank into his boots
moedeloos /mudəlos/ (adj, adv) despondent, dejected
de **moedeloosheid** /mudəlosheit/ despondency, dejection
de **moeder** /mudər/ (pl: -s) mother: *een alleenstaande ~* a single mother; *hij is niet bepaald ~s mooiste* he's no oil-painting; *bij ~s pappot (blijven) zitten* be (*or:* remain) tied to one's mother's apron strings; *vadertje en ~tje spelen* play house
het **moederbedrijf** /mudərbədrɛɪf/ (pl: -bedrijven) parent company
Moederdag /mudərdɑx/ Mother's Day
het **moederhuis** /mudərhœys/ (pl: -huizen) [Belg] maternity home
de **moederkoek** /mudərkuk/ (pl: -en) placenta
het **moederland** /mudərlɑnt/ motherland
moederlijk /mudərlək/ (adj, adv) **1** motherly **2** maternal
de **moedermaatschappij** /mudərmatsxɑpɛɪ/ (pl: -en) parent company
de **moedermelk** /mudərmɛlk/ mother's milk
het **moederschap** /mudərsxɑp/ motherhood
de **moederskant** /mudərskɑnt/ mother's side, maternal side: *grootvader van ~* maternal grandfather
het **moederskindje** /mudərskɪncə/ (pl: -s) **1** mother's child **2** mummy's boy (*or:* girl)
de **moedertaal** /mudərtal/ (pl: -talen) mother tongue: *iem. met Engels als ~* a native speaker of English
de **moedervlek** /mudərvlɛk/ (pl: -ken) birthmark, mole
de **moederziel** /mudərzil/: *~ alleen* all alone
moedig /mudəx/ (adj, adv) brave; plucky
moedwillig /mutwɪləx/ (adj, adv) wilful, malicious
de **moeflon** /muflɔn/ (pl: -s) mouf(f)lon
de **moeheid** /muheit/ tiredness, weariness
moeilijk /mujlək/ (adj, adv) **1** difficult: *~ opvoedbare kinderen* problem children; *doe niet zo ~* don't make such a fuss; *het ~ hebben* have a rough time, have a (hard (*or:* bad)) time of it **2** hard, difficult: *het is ~ te geloven*

it's hard to believe; *hij **maakte** het ons ~* he gave us a hard (*or:* difficult) time **3** hardly: *daar kan ik ~ iets over **zeggen*** it's hard for me to say ‖ *zij is een ~ **persoon*** she is hard to please

de **moeilijkheid** /mujləkhɛit/ (pl: -heden) difficulty, trouble, problem: *om moeilijkheden **vragen*** be asking for trouble; *in moeilijkheden verkeren* be in trouble; *daar **zit (ligt)** de ~* there's the catch

de **moeite** /mujtə/ **1** effort, trouble: *vergeefse ~* wasted effort; *bespaar je de ~* (you can) save yourself the trouble (*or:* bother); *~ **doen*** take pains (*or:* trouble); *u hoeft geen extra ~ te **doen*** you need not bother, don't put yourself out; [Belg] *eraan zijn **voor** de ~* have done it all for nothing; *het **is** de ~ niet (waard)* it's not worth it (*or:* the effort, the bother); *het is de ~ **waard** om het te proberen* it's worth a try (*or:* trying); *het was zeer de ~ **waard*** it was most rewarding; *dank u wel **voor** de ~!* thank you very much!, sorry to have troubled you!; *dat is me te **veel** ~!* that's too much trouble **2** trouble, difficulty; bother: *ik **heb** ~ met zijn gedrag* I find his behaviour hard to take (*or:* accept)

moeiteloos /mujtəlos/ (adj, adv) effortless, easy: *leer ~ Engels!* learn English without tears!

moeizaam /mujzam/ (adj) laborious ‖ *zich ~ een weg **banen** (door)* make one's way with difficulty (through)

de **moer** /mur/ **1** nut **2** mother **3** doe; queen (bee); vixen ‖ *daar schiet je **geen** ~ mee op* that doesn't get you anywhere; *dat gaat je **geen** ~ aan* that's none of your damn (*or:* bloody) business

het **moeras** /murɑs/ (pl: -sen) swamp, marsh

het **moerasgebied** /murɑsxəbit/ marshland

moerassig /murɑsəx/ (adj) swampy

de **moersleutel** /mursløtəl/ (pl: -s) spanner; [Am] wrench

het **moes** /mus/ purée

de **moesson** /musɔn/ (pl: -s) monsoon

de **moestuin** /mustœyn/ (pl: -en) kitchen garden, vegetable garden

¹moeten /mutə(n)/ (moest, heeft gemoeten) like: *ik moet die **man** niet* I don't like that man

²moeten /mutə(n)/ (aux vb, moest, heeft gemoeten) **1** must, have to, should, ought to: *ik moest wel **lachen*** I couldn't help laughing; *ik moet **zeggen**, dat …* I must say (*or:* have to say) that …; *het heeft zo ~ **zijn*** it had to be (like that); *als het moet* if I (*or:* we) must **2** want, need: *ik moet er niet aan **denken** wat het kost* I hate to think (of) what it costs; *~ jullie niet **eten**?* don't you want to eat?; *dat moet ik nog **zien*** I'll have to see; *dat moet dan **maar*** all right then, there's no getting round it; *het huis moet **nodig** eens geschilderd worden* the house badly needs a coat of paint; *wat*

moet dat? what's all this about?; *wat moet je?* what do you want? **3** should, ought to: *dat moet **gezegd (worden)*** it has to be said; *moet je eens **horen*** listen (to this); *de trein moet om vier uur **vertrekken*** the train is due to leave at four o'clock; *je moest eens **weten** …* if only you knew …; *dat moet jij (zelf) **weten*** it's up to you; *moet je nu al **weg**?* are you off already?; *ze moet er nodig eens uit* she needs a day out **4** must; be supposed to, said to: *zij moet vroeger een mooi meisje **geweest zijn*** she must have been a pretty girl once **5** [Belg] need (to), have (to): *u moet niet komen* you needn't come

de **moezelwijn** /muzəlwɛin/ (pl: -en) Moselle (wine)

de **¹mof** /mɔf/ (pl: -fen) [offensive] kraut

de **²mof** /mɔf/ (pl: -fen) (coupling) sleeve, bush, socket

¹mogelijk /moɣələk/ (adj) possible, likely, potential: *hoe **is** het ~ dat je je daarin vergist hebt?* how could you possibly have been mistaken about this?; *het **is** ~ dat hij wat later komt* he may come a little later; *het is **heel goed** ~ dat hij het niet gezien heeft* he may very well not have seen it; *het is **ons** niet ~ …* it's impossible for us to, we cannot possibly …; *al **het** ~e doen* do everything possible; *zo ~* if possible; *zoveel ~* as far/often/much as possible

²mogelijk /moɣələk/ (adv) possibly, perhaps

mogelijkerwijs /moɣələkərwɛis/ (adv) possibly, perhaps, conceivably

de **mogelijkheid** /moɣələkhɛit/ (pl: -heden) **1** possibility; chance; eventuality: *geen ~* not possibly; *zij **onderschat** haar mogelijkheden* she underestimates herself; *dat **behoort** tot de mogelijkheden* that's an option **2** possibilities, prospects: *nieuwe mogelijkheden **voor** de export* new openings (*or:* prospects) for export

¹mogen /moɣə(n)/ (mocht, heeft gemogen) like: *ik mag hem **wel*** I quite (*or:* rather) like him

²mogen /moɣə(n)/ (aux vb, mocht, heeft gemogen) **1** can, be allowed to, may, must, should, ought to: *mag ik een **kilo** peren van u?* (can I have) a kilo of pears, please?; *mag ik uw **naam** even?* could (*or:* may) I have your name, please?; *er mag hier niet **gerookt worden*** you're not allowed to smoke here; *je mag **gaan spelen**, maar je mag je niet vuilmaken* you can go out and play, but you're not to get dirty; *als ik **vragen** mag* if you don't mind my asking; *mag ik **even**?* do you mind?, may I?; *mag ik er even **langs**?* excuse me (please) **2** should, ought to: *je **had** me weleens ~ **waarschuwen*** you might (*or:* could) have warned me; *hij mag blij **zijn** dat …* he ought to (*or:* should) be happy that …; *ik mag niet **mopperen*** I mustn't complain

3 may, might || *het mocht niet **baten*** it didn't help, it was to no avail; *dat ik dit nog mag **meemaken!*** that I should live to see this!; *dat mocht je **willen*** wouldn't you just like that; you'd like that, wouldn't you?; *het heeft niet zo ~ **zijn*** it was not to be; *zo mag ik het **horen*** (or: *zien*) that's what I like to hear (or: see)

de **mogendheid** /mo̯yənthɛit/ (pl: -heden) power

het ¹**mohair** /mohɛːr/ mohair

²**mohair** /mohɛːr/ (adj) mohair

Mohammed /mohɑmɛt/ Mohammed

de **mohammedaan** /mohɑməda̱n/ (pl: mohammedanen) Mohammedan

mohammedaans /mohɑməda̱ns/ (adj) Mohammedan

de **Mohikanen** /mohika̱nə(n)/ (pl) Mohicans

de **mok** /mɔk/ (pl: -ken) mug

de **moker** /mo̱kər/ (pl: -s) sledgehammer

de **mokerslag** /mo̱kərslɑx/ (pl: -en) sledgehammer blow [also fig]: *dat nieuws kwam aan **als** een ~* that news came as a terrible blow

de **mokka** /mo̱ka/ mocha (coffee)

het/de **mokkel** /mo̱kəl/ [inform] chick, cracker

mokken /mo̱kə(n)/ (mokte, heeft gemokt) grouse, sulk

de ¹**mol** /mɔl/ [mus] **1** flat **2** minor

de ²**mol** /mɔl/ mole

Moldavië /mɔlda̱vijə/ Moldavia

de **Moldaviër** /mɔlda̱vijər/ (pl: -s) Moldavian

Moldavisch /mɔlda̱vis/ (adj) Moldovan

moleculair /molekylɛːr/ (adj) molecular

het/de **molecule** /moleky̱l(ə)/ (pl: -n) molecule

de **molen** /mo̱lə(n)/ (pl: -s) **1** (wind)mill **2** [angling] reel || *het zit in de ~* it is in the pipeline

de **molenaar** /mo̱lənar/ (pl: -s) miller

de **molensteen** /mo̱lə(n)sten/ (pl: -stenen) millstone

de **molenwiek** /mo̱lə(n)wik/ (pl: -en) sail arm, wing

molesteren /molɛstḛrə(n)/ (molesteerde, heeft gemolesteerd) molest

mollen /mɔ̱lə(n)/ (molde, heeft gemold) wreck, bust (up)

mollig /mɔ̱ləx/ (adj) plump; chubby

het/de **molm** /mɔlm/ mouldered wood

de **molotovcocktail** /mo̱lotɔfkɔktel/ (pl: -s) Molotov cocktail

de **molshoop** /mɔ̱lshop/ (pl: -hopen) molehill

het **molton** /mɔ̱lton/ flannel

de **Molukken** /moly̱kə(n)/ (pl) Moluccas, Molucca Islands

de **Molukker** /moly̱kər/ (pl: -s) Moluccan

Moluks /moly̱ks/ (adj) Molucca(n)

het/de **mom** /mɔm/: *onder het ~ van de weg te vragen* on (or: under) the pretext of asking the way

het **moment** /momɛnt/ (pl: -en) moment, minute: *één ~, ik kom zó* one moment please, I'm coming; hang on a minute, I'm coming; *op een **bepaald** ~* at a certain moment; *hij kan*

elk ~ binnenkomen he could come in any moment (or: minute) (now); *op **enig** ~* at any moment; *geen ~ aarzelen* not hesitate for a second (or: moment); *op dit ~ kan ik u niet helpen* I can't help you just now (or: at the moment); *daar heb ik **geen** ~ aan gedacht* it never occurred to me

momenteel /momɛnte̱l/ (adv) at present, at the moment, currently

de **momentopname** /momɛntɔpnamə/ (pl: -n, -s) random indication (or: picture)

mompelen /mɔ̱mpələ(n)/ (mompelde, heeft gemompeld) mumble, mutter

Monaco /mo̱nako/ Monaco

de **monarch** /monɑ̱rx/ (pl: -en) monarch

de **monarchie** /monɑrxi̱/ (pl: -ën) monarchy

de **monarchist** /monɑrxɪ̱st/ (pl: -en) monarchist; royalist

de **mond** /mɔnt/ (pl: -en) mouth; muzzle: *een grote ~ hebben* **a)** be loud-mouthed; **b)** be cheeky, give s.o. lip; **c)** talk big; *iem. een **grote** ~ geven* talk back at (or: to) s.o., give s.o. lip; *hij kan zijn **grote** ~ niet houden* he can't keep his big mouth shut; *dat is een **hele** ~ vol* that's quite a mouthful; *zijn ~ **houden*** keep quiet; shut up; *iem. **naar** de ~ praten* play up to s.o.; *zijn ~ **opendoen*** **a)** open one's mouth; **b)** speak up; *iem. de ~ **snoeren*** silence s.o.; *zijn ~ **voorbijpraten*** spill the beans; *met de ~ vol tanden staan* be at a loss for words, be tongue-tied

mondain /mɔndɛ̱/ (adj) fashionable: *een ~e **badplaats*** a sophisticated resort, a luxury resort

monddood /mɔndo̱t/ (adj): *~ **maken*** silence

mondeling /mɔ̱ndəlɪŋ/ (adj, adv) oral; verbal; by word of mouth: *een ~ **examen*** an oral (exam(ination)); *een ~e **toezegging*** (or: *afspraak*) a verbal agreement (or: arrangement)

het **mond-en-klauwzeer** /mɔntɛŋkla̱uzer/ foot-and-mouth disease

de **mondharmonica** /mɔ̱nthɑrmonika/ (pl: -'s) harmonica

de **mondhoek** /mɔ̱nthuk/ (pl: -en) corner of the mouth

mondiaal /mɔndija̱l/ (adj, adv) worldwide, global

de **mondialisering** /mɔndijalizɛ̱rɪŋ/ globalization

mondig /mɔ̱ndəx/ (adj) of age; mature, independent

de **monding** /mɔ̱ndɪŋ/ (pl: -en) mouth; estuary

het **mondje** /mɔ̱ncə/ (pl: -s) mouthful; taste: *een ~ **Turks** spreken* have a smattering of Turkish; *(denk erom,) ~ **dicht*** mum's the word; *hij is niet **op** zijn ~ gevallen* **a)** he has a ready tongue; **b)** he gives as good as he gets

mondjesmaat /mɔ̱ncəsmat/ (adv) scantily, sparsely

het **mondkapje** /mɔntkɑpjə/ surgical mask

de **mond-op-mondbeademing** /mɔntɔp-mɔndbəademɪŋ/ mouth-to-mouth (resuscitation, respiration), rescue breathing

het **mondstuk** /mɔntstʏk/ (pl: -ken) **1** mouthpiece; nozzle **2** filter

de **mond-tot-mondreclame** /mɔntɔtmɔntrəklamə/ advertisement by word of mouth, word-of-mouth advertising

de **mondvol** /mɔntfɔl/ mouthful

de **mondvoorraad** /mɔntforat/ provisions, supplies

de **Monegask** /moneɣɑsk/ (pl: -en) Monegasque

Monegaskisch /moneɣɑskis/ (adj) Monegasque

monetair /monetɛːr/ (adj, adv) monetary: *het Internationaal Monetair **Fonds*** the International Monetary Fund

de **moneybelt** /mɔnibɛlt/ money belt

Mongolië /mɔŋɣolijə/ Mongolia

mongoloïde /mɔŋɣolowidə/ (adj) mongoloid

Mongoloïde /mɔŋɣolowidə/ (adj) Mongoloid

de **mongool** /mɔŋɣol/ (pl: mongolen) **1** [dated] s.o. with Down's syndrome **2** [offensive] moron, idiot

de **Mongool** /mɔŋɣol/ (pl: Mongolen) Mongol(ian)

het **1Mongools** /mɔŋɣols/ Mongolian

2Mongools /mɔŋɣols/ (adj) Mongolian: *de ~e volksrepubliek* the Mongolian People's Republic

de **monitor** /mɔnitɔr/ (pl: -s) **1** monitor **2** [Belg] youth leader **3** [Belg] tutor

monitoren /mɔnitorə(n)/ (monitorde, heeft gemonitord) monitor

de **monnik** /mɔnək/ (pl: -en) monk

het **monnikenwerk** /mɔnəkə(n)wɛrk/ drudgery, donkey work

mono /mono/ (adv) mono

de **monocle** /monɔklə/ (pl: -s) monocle

de **monocultuur** /monokʏltyr/ (pl: -culturen) monoculture

monogaam /monoɣam/ (adj) monogamous

de **monogamie** /monoɣami/ monogamy

de **monografie** /monoɣafi/ (pl: -ën) monograph

het **monogram** /monoɣrɑm/ (pl: -men) monogram

de **monoloog** /monolox/ (pl: -logen) monologue

monomaan /monoman/ (adj) monomaniac(al)

het **monopolie** /monopoli/ (pl: -s) monopoly

de **monopoliepositie** /monopolipozi(t)si/ monopoly position

de **monopolist** /monopolɪst/ (pl: -en) monopolist

monotoon /monoton/ (adj, adv) monotonous, in a monotone

de **monseigneur** /monsɛŋør/ (pl: -s) Monsignor

het **monster** /mɔnstər/ (pl: -s) **1** monster **2** sample, specimen **3** monster, giant

monsteren /mɔnstərə(n)/ (monsterde, heeft gemonsterd) **1** examine, inspect **2** review, inspect

monsterlijk /mɔnstərlək/ (adj, adv) monstrous, hideous

de **monsterzege** /mɔnstərzeɣə/ (pl: -s) mammoth victory

de **montage** /montaʒə/ **1** assembly, mounting **2** [film] editing

de **montagefoto** /montaʒəfoto/ (pl: -'s) **1** photomontage **2** [Dutch] Photofit (picture)

de **Montenegrijn** /montəneɣrɛɪn/ (pl: -en) Montenegran

het **Montenegrijns** /montəneɣrɛɪns/ Montenegrin

Montenegro /montəneɣro/ Montenegro

monter /mɔntər/ (adj, adv) lively, cheerful, vivacious

monteren /montərə(n)/ (monteerde, heeft gemonteerd) **1** assemble; install **2** mount, fix **3** edit; cut [film]; assemble **4** fix; mount

de **montessorischool** /montɛsorisxol/ (pl: -scholen) Montessori school

de **monteur** /montør/ (pl: -s) mechanic; serviceman; repairman

het/de **montuur** /montyr/ (pl: monturen) frame: *een bril zonder ~* rimless glasses

het **monument** /monymɛnt/ (pl: -en) monument: *een ~ ter herinnering aan de doden* a memorial to the dead

monumentaal /monymɛntal/ (adj, adv) monumental

de **monumentenlijst** /monymɛntə(n)lɛist/ (pl: -en) [roughly] list of national monuments and historic buildings

1mooi /moj/ (adj) **1** beautiful: *iets ~ vinden* think sth. is nice **2** good-looking, handsome; pretty, beautiful **3** lovely, beautiful: *zij ziet er ~ uit* she looks lovely; *deze fiets is er niet ~er op worden* this bicycle isn't what it used to be **4** smart: *zich ~ maken* dress up **5** good; excellent: *~e cijfers halen* get good marks; [Am] get good grades **6** good, fine; nice, handsome: *het kon niet ~er* it couldn't have been better; *te ~ om waar te zijn* too good to be true **7** good, nice: *een ~ verhaal* a nice (or: good) story; *het is ~ (geweest)* zo! that's enough now!, all right, that'll do!

2mooi /moj/ (adv) well, nicely: *jij hebt ~ praten* it's all very well for you to talk; *dat is ~ meegenomen* that is so much to the good; *~ zo!* good!, well done!

het **moois** /mojs/ fine thing(s), sth. beautiful: [iron] *dat is ook wat ~!* a nice state of affairs!

moonen /mu̱:nə(n)/ (moonde, heeft gemoond) moon

de **moord** /mort/ (pl: -en) murder; assassination; [law] homicide: *een ~ plegen* commit murder, take a life; *~ en brand schreeuwen* scream blue murder

de **moordaanslag** /mo̱rtanslɑx/ (pl: -en) attempted murder

moorddadig /morda̱dəx/ (adj) murderous

moorden /mo̱rdə(n)/ (moordde, heeft gemoord) kill, murder

de **moordenaar** /mo̱rdənar/ (pl: -s) murderer, killer

moordend /mo̱rdənt/ (adj) murderous, deadly; fatal: *~e concurrentie* cut-throat competition

de **moordkuil** /mo̱rtkœyl/: *van zijn hart geen ~ maken* make no disguise of one's feelings

de **moordpartij** /mo̱rtpɑrtɛı/ (wholesale) massacre, slaughter

de **moordzaak** /mo̱rtsak/ (pl: -zaken) murder case

de **moorkop** /mo̱rkɔp/ (pl: -pen) [Dutch] chocolate éclair

de **moot** /mot/ (pl: moten) piece: *een ~ zalm* a salmon steak

de **mop** /mɔp/ (pl: -pen) joke: *een schuine ~* a dirty joke

de **mopperaar** /mo̱pərar/ (pl: -s) grumbler

mopperen /mo̱pərə(n)/ (mopperde, heeft gemopperd) grumble, grouch: *ik mag niet ~* I mustn't complain

de **moraal** /mora̱l/ morality, moral(s)

moraliseren /moralize̱rə(n)/ (moraliseerde, heeft gemoraliseerd) moralize

moralistisch /moralı̱stis/ (adj, adv) moralistic

het **moratorium** /morato̱rijʏm/ (pl: -s, moratoria) moratorium; ban

morbide /morbi̱də/ (adj) morbid

mordicus /mo̱rdikʏs/ (adv): *ergens ~ tegen zijn* be dead against sth.

het ¹**moreel** /more̱l/ morale: *het ~ hoog houden* keep up morale

²**moreel** /more̱l/ (adj, adv) moral

de **mores** /mo̱rəs/ (pl) mores ‖ *iem. ~ leren* teach s.o. a lesson

de **morfine** /morfi̱nə/ morphine

morfologisch /morfolo̱ɣis/ (adj, adv) morphologic(al)

de ¹**morgen** /mo̱rɣə(n)/ (pl: -s) morning: *de hele ~* all morning; *'s ~s* in the morning; *(goede) ~!* (good) morning!; *om 8 uur 's ~s* at 8 a.m.

²**morgen** /mo̱rɣə(n)/ (adv) tomorrow: *vandaag of ~* one of these days; *~ over een week* a week tomorrow; *tot ~!* see you tomorrow!, till tomorrow!; *de krant van ~* tomorrow's (news)paper

morgenavond /morɣə(n)a̱vɔnt/ (adv) tomorrow evening

morgenmiddag /morɣə(n)mı̱dɑx/ (adv) tomorrow afternoon

morgenochtend /morɣə(n)ɔ̱xtənt/ (adv) tomorrow morning

het **morgenrood** /mo̱rɣə(n)rot/ aurora, red morning sky

morgenvroeg /morɣə(n)vrʏx/ (adv) tomorrow morning

het **mormel** /mo̱rməl/ (pl: -s) mutt: *een verwend ~* a spoilt brat

de **mormoon** /mormo̱n/ (pl: mormonen) Mormon; Latter-day Saint

de **morning-afterpil** /mornıŋa̱:ftərpıl/ (pl: -len) morning-after pill

morrelen /mo̱rələ(n)/ (morrelde, heeft gemorreld) fiddle

morren /mo̱rə(n)/ (morde, heeft gemord) grumble: *zonder ~* ungrudgingly, uncomplainingly

morsdood /mo̱rzdot/ (adj) (as) dead as a doornail

het **morse** /mo̱rsə/ Morse (code)

morsen /mo̱rsə(n)/ (morste, heeft gemorst) (make a) mess (on, of), spill: *het kind zit te ~ met zijn eten* the child is messing around with his food

het **morseteken** /mo̱rsətekə(n)/ (pl: -s) Morse sign

morsig /mo̱rsəx/ (adj, adv) dirty, messy

de **mortel** /mo̱rtəl/ mortar

het/de **mortier** /morti̱r/ (pl: -en) mortar

de **mortiergranaat** /morti̱rɣranat/ mortar bomb

het **mortuarium** /mortywa̱rijʏm/ (pl: mortuaria) **1** mortuary **2** funeral parlour; [Am] funeral home

het **mos** /mɔs/ (pl: -sen) moss

de **moskee** /moske̱/ (pl: -ën) mosque

Moskou /mo̱skɑu/ Moscow

de **moslim** /mo̱slım/ (pl: -s) Muslim, Moslem

de **moslima** /mo̱slıma/ Muslimah

de **mossel** /mo̱səl/ (pl: -en) mussel

de **mosterd** /mo̱stərt/ mustard: *hij weet waar Abraham de ~ haalt* he knows what's what; *als ~ na de maaltijd komen* come (too) late in the day

het **mosterdgas** /mo̱stərtxɑs/ mustard gas

de **mot** /mɔt/ (pl: -ten) moth

het **motel** /mote̱l/ (pl: -s) motel

de **motie** /mo̱(t)si/ (pl: -s) motion

het **motief** /moti̱f/ (pl: motieven) **1** motive **2** motif, design

de **motivatie** /motiva̱(t)si/ motivation

motiveren /motive̱rə(n)/ (motiveerde, heeft gemotiveerd) **1** explain, account for; defend; justify **2** motivate

de **motor** /mo̱tər/ (pl: -en) **1** engine; motor: *de ~ starten* (or: *afzetten*) start (or: turn off) the engine **2** motorcycle **3** driving force

de **motoragent** /mo̱tərɑɣɛnt/ (pl: -en) motorcycle policeman

het **motorblok** /mo̱tərblɔk/ (pl: -ken) engine

block

de **motorboot** /mo̱tərbot/ (pl: -boten) motor-boat

de **motorcoureur** /mo̱tərkurør/ (pl: -s) motorcycle racer; rider

de **motorcross** /mo̱tərkrɔs/ (pl: -es) motocross

de **motorfiets** /mo̱tərfits/ (pl: -en) motorcycle, motorbike, bike: ~ *met zijspan* sidecar motorcycle

de **motoriek** /motori̱k/ (loco)motor system, locomotion

motorisch /moto̱ris/ (adj, adv) motor: *een ~ gehandicapte* a disabled person; *hij is ~ gestoord* he has a motor disability

het **motorjacht** /mo̱tərjɑxt/ (pl: -en) motor yacht

de **motorkap** /mo̱tərkɑp/ (pl: -pen) bonnet; [Am] hood

de **motorolie** /mo̱toroli/ (engine) oil

de **motorpech** /mo̱tərpɛx/ engine trouble

de **motorrace** /mo̱tores/ (pl: -s) motorcycle race

de **motorrijder** /mo̱tərɛidər/ (pl: -s) motorcyclist

de **motorrijtuigenbelasting** /mo̱tərɛitœyɣə(n)bəlɑstɪŋ/ [Dutch] [roughly] road tax

de **motorsport** /mo̱tərsport/ motorcycle racing

het **motorvoertuig** /mo̱tərvurtœyx/ (pl: -en) motor vehicle; [Am] automobile

de **motregen** /mo̱treɣə(n)/ (pl: -s) drizzle

motregenen /mo̱treɣənə(n)/ (motregende, heeft gemotregend) drizzle

mottig /mo̱təx/ (adj) moth-eaten, scruffy

het **motto** /mo̱to/ (pl: -'s) motto; slogan

de **mountainbike** /mau̯ntənbɑjk/ (pl: -s) mountain bike

de **mousse** /mus/ (pl: -s) mousse

mousseren /musɛ̱rə(n)/ (mousseerde, heeft gemousseerd) sparkle, fizz

het/de **mout** /mɑut/ malt

de **mouw** /mɑu/ (pl: -en) sleeve: *de ~en opstropen* roll up one's sleeves; *ergens een ~ aan weten te passen* find a way (a)round sth.; *iem. iets op de ~ spelden* tell s.o. tales, take s.o. for a ride

mouwloos /mau̯los/ (adj) sleeveless

het **mozaïek** /mozai̯k/ (pl: -en) mosaic

de **Mozambikaan** /mozɑmbikaːn/ (pl: Mozambikanen) Mozambican

Mozambikaans /mozɑmbikaːns/ (adj) Mozambican

Mozambique /mozɑmbi̱k/ Mozambique

Mozes /mo̱zəs/ Moses

de **mp3** MP3

de **mp3-speler** /ɛmpedri̱spelər/ MP3 player

de **MRI-scan** /ɛmɛriskɛn/ MRI scan

MS /ɛmɛs/ *multiple sclerose* MS

het **mt** *managementteam* management team

de **mts** /ɛmtɛɣs/ (pl: -'en) [Dutch] *middelbare technische school* intermediate technical school

de **muesli** /my̱sli/ muesli

de **muezzin** /muwɣ̱dzɪn/ muezzin

muf /mʏf/ (adj) musty, stale; stuffy

de **mug** /mʏx/ (pl: -gen) mosquito; [small] gnat: *van een ~ een olifant maken* make a mountain out of a molehill

de **muggenbeet** /mʏɣə(n)bet/ (pl: -beten) mosquito bite

de **muggenbult** /mʏɣə(n)bʏlt/ mosquito bite

de **muggenolie** /mʏɣə(n)oli/ insect repellent

muggenziften /mʏɣə(n)zɪftə(n)/ (muggenziftte, heeft gemuggenzift) niggle, split hairs, nit-pick

de **muggenzifter** /mʏɣə(n)zɪftər/ (pl: -s) niggler, hairsplitter, nit-picker

de **muil** /mœyl/ mouth, muzzle

het **muildier** /mœyldir/ (pl: -en) mule

de **muilezel** /mœylezəl/ (pl: -s) hinny

de **muilkorf** /mœylkorf/ (pl: -korven) muzzle

muilkorven /mœylkorvə(n)/ (muilkorfde, heeft gemuilkorfd) muzzle

de **muis** /mœys/ (pl: muizen) mouse; [hand] ball: *de ~ van de hand* the ball of the thumb/hand; *een optische ~* an optical mouse

de **muisarm** /mœysɑrm/ (pl: -en) mouse arm

de **muiscursor** /mœyskʏrsɔr/ (pl: -s) mouse cursor

muisgrijs /mœysxrɛis/ (adj) dun(-coloured)

de **muisklik** /mœysklɪk/ mouse click

het **muismatje** /mœysmat/ mouse mat, mousepad

muisstil /mœystɪl/ (adj) (as) still (*or:* quiet) as a mouse

de **muiten** /mœytə(n)/ (muitte, heeft gemuit) mutiny

de **muiterij** /mœytərɛi̱/ (pl: -en) mutiny: *er brak ~ uit* a mutiny broke out

de **muizenissen** /mœyzənɪsə(n)/ (pl) worries

de **muizenval** /mœyzə(n)vɑl/ (pl: -len) mousetrap

mul /mʏl/ (adj) loose, sandy

de **mulat** /mylɑt/ (pl: -ten) mulatto

multicultureel /mʏltikʏltyreḻ/ (adj) multicultural

multifunctioneel /mʏltifʏŋkʃoneḻ/ (adj) multifunctional

de **multimedia** /mʏltimedi̱ja/ (pl) multimedia

de **multimiljonair** /mʏltimɪljonɛːr/ (pl: -s) multimillionaire

de **multinational** /mʏltinɛʃənəl/ (pl: -s) multinational

multiple /mʏltipəl/ (adj) multiple

de **multiplechoicetest** /mʏltɪpəltʃ[o̱jstɛst/ (pl: -s) multiple choice test

het **multiplex** /mʏltiplɛks/ multi-ply (board)

multiresistent /mʏltirezistɛnt/ (adj) multiresistant: *~e bacteriën* multiresistant bacteria

de **multitasking** /mʏltitaːskɪŋ/ multitasking, task-juggling de **multivitamine** /mʏltivitaminə/ multivitamin

het **mum** /mʏm/: *in een ~ (van tijd)* in a jiffy (*or:* trice)

de **mummie** /mʏmi/ (pl: -s) mummy

München /mʏnʃə(n)/ Munich

de **munitie** /myni(t)si/ (am)munition, ammo

de **munt** /mʏnt/ (pl: -en) **1** coin: *iem. met gelijke ~ terugbetalen* give s.o. a taste of their own medicine **2** token

de **munteenheid** /mʏntenhɛit/ (pl: -heden) monetary unit

munten /mʏntə(n)/ (muntte, heeft gemunt) **1** mint, coin **2** coin ‖ [fig] *het op iem. gemunt hebben* have it in for s.o., be down on s.o.; *zij hebben het op mijn leven gemunt* they're after my life

het **muntgeld** /mʏntxɛlt/ coin, coinage

het **muntstelsel** /mʏntstɛlsəl/ monetary system

het **muntstuk** /mʏntstʏk/ (pl: -ken) coin

de **muntthee** /mʏnte/ (fresh) mint tea

murmelen /mʏrmələ(n)/ (murmelde, heeft gemurmeld) mumble, murmur

murw /mʏrf/ (adj) tender, soft

de **mus** /mʏs/ (pl: -sen) sparrow

het **museum** /mʏzejʏm/ (pl: musea) museum; (art) gallery

de **museumjaarkaart** /mʏzejʏmjaɾkart/ (pl: -en) annual museum pass

de **musical** /mjuzəkəl/ (pl: -s) musical

musiceren /mʏziserə(n)/ (musiceerde, heeft gemusiceerd) make music

de **musicoloog** /mʏzikolox/ (pl: -logen) musicologist

de **musicus** /mʏzikʏs/ (pl: musici) musician

de **muskaatdruif** /mʏskadrœyf/ (pl: -druiven) muscadine

de **muskaatwijn** /mʏskatwɛin/ muscatel

de **musketier** /mʏskətiɾ/ (pl: -s) musketeer

de **muskiet** /mʏskit/ (pl: -en) mosquito

het **muskietengaas** /mʏskitə(n)ɣas/ mosquito net(ting)

de **muskusrat** /mʏskʏsrɑt/ (pl: -ten) muskrat

de **must** /mʏst/ must

de **mutant** /mʏtɑnt/ (pl: -en) mutant

de **mutatie** /mʏta(t)si/ (pl: -s) **1** mutation; transaction **2** mutation; turnover

muteren /mʏterə(n)/ (muteerde, heeft gemuteerd) mutate

de **muts** /mʏts/ (pl: -en) hat, cap

de **mutualiteit** /mʏtywalitɛit/ [Belg] health insurance scheme

de **muur** /mʏr/ (pl: muren) wall: *een blinde ~ a* blank wall; *de muren komen op mij af* the walls are closing in on me; [sport] *een ~tje vormen (opstellen)* make a wall; *uit de ~ eten, iets uit de ~ trekken* [roughly] eat from a vending machine

het **muurbloempje** /mʏrblumpjə/ wallflower

de **muurkrant** /mʏrkrɑnt/ (pl: -en) wall poster

de **muurschildering** /mʏrsχildərɪŋ/ (pl: -en)

mural

muurvast /mʏrvɑst/ (adj, adv) firm, solid; unyielding; unbending: *de besprekingen zitten ~* the talks have reached total deadlock

de **muurverf** /mʏrvɛrf/ masonry paint

de **muzak** /mʏzɑk/ muzak

de **muze** /mʏzə/ (pl: -n) **1** muse **2** (the) Muses: *zich aan de ~n wijden* devote o.s. to the arts

de **muziek** /mʏzik/ music: *op de maat van de ~ dansen* dance in time to the music; *klassieke ~* classical music; *lichte ~* light music; *oude ~* early music; *~ maken* make music; *op ~ dansen* dance to music; *dat klinkt mij als ~ in de oren* it's music to my ears

het **muziekinstrument** /mʏzikɪnstrymɛnt/ (pl: -en) musical instrument

het **muziekje** /mʏzikjə/ (pl: -s) bit (*or:* piece) of music: *een ~ opzetten* play a bit of music

de **muziekkapel** /mʏzikapɛl/ (pl: -len) band

de **muziekles** /mʏzikles/ music lesson

het **muziekmobieltje** /mʏzikmobilcə/ (pl: -s) music cellphone (*or:* mobile phone)

de **muzieknoot** /mʏziknot/ (pl: -noten) (musical) note

het **muziekpapier** /mʏzikpapir/ music paper

de **muziekschool** /mʏziksχol/ (pl: -scholen) school of music

de **muzieksleutel** /mʏziksløtəl/ (pl: -s) clef

de **muziekstandaard** /mʏzikstɑndart/ (pl: -en, -s) music stand

het **muziekstuk** /mʏzikstʏk/ (pl: -ken) piece of music, composition

de **muziekuitvoering** /mʏzikœytfurɪŋ/ (pl: -en) musical performance

muzikaal /mʏzikal/ (adj, adv) musical: *~ gevoel* feel for music

de **muzikant** /mʏzikɑnt/ (pl: -en) musician

mw. *mevrouw of mejuffrouw* Ms

Myanmar /mijɑnmɑr/ Myanmar

de [1]**Myanmarees** /mijɑnmares/ (pl: Myanmarezen) inhabitant (*or:* native) of Myanmar

[2]**Myanmarees** /mijɑnmares/ (adj) Myanmar

het **mysterie** /mɪsteri/ (pl: -s) mystery

mysterieus /mɪster(i)jøs/ (adj, adv) mysterious

mystiek /mɪstik/ (adj) **1** mystic, mysterious **2** mystical: *een ~e ervaring* a mystical experience

de **mythe** /mitə/ (pl: -n) myth; [pers] legend

mythisch /mitis/ (adj) mythic(al)

de **mythologie** /mitoloɣi/ (pl: -ën) mythology

mythologisch /mitoloɣis/ (adj) mythological

n

de **n** /ɛn/ (pl: n's) n, N: *x tot de **macht** n* x to the nth power
na /na/ (prep) after: *de ene **blunder** na de andere maken* make one blunder after the other (*or*: another); *na u!* after you! ‖ *wat eten we na?* what's for dessert?; *op een paar uitzonderingen na* with a few exceptions; *de op één na grootste* (or: *sterkste*) the second biggest (*or*: strongest); *het op drie na grootste bedrijf* the fourth largest company

de **naad** /nat/ (pl: naden) seam; joint ‖ *zich **uit** de ~ werken* work o.s. to death

het **naadje** /naːcə/: *het ~ van de kous willen weten* want to know all the ins and outs
naadloos /natlos/ (adj) seamless

de **naaf** /naf/ (pl: naven) hub

het **naaiatelier** /najatəljeː/ (pl: -s) tailor's (shop): *illegale ~s* sweatshops

de **naaidoos** /najdos/ (pl: -dozen) sewing box
naaien /najə(n)/ (naaide, heeft genaaid) **1** sew: *een **knoop** aan een jas ~* sew a button on(to) a coat **2** [inform] screw

het **naaigaren** /najɣarə(n)/ (pl: -s) sewing thread (*or*: cotton): *een **klosje** ~* a reel of thread (*or*: cotton)

de **naaimachine** /najmaʃinə/ (pl: -s) sewing machine

de **naaister** /najstər/ (pl: -s) seamstress
naakt /nakt/ (adj, adv) **1** naked, nude: *~ **slapen*** sleep in the nude **2** bare

de **naaktloper** /naktlopər/ (pl: -s) nudist

de **naaktslak** /naktslɑk/ slug

het **naaktstrand** /naktstrɑnt/ (pl: -en) nude beach

de **naald** /nalt/ (pl: -en) needle: *het **oog** van een ~* the eye of a needle

de **naaldboom** /naldbom/ (pl: -bomen) conifer

het **naaldbos** /naldbɔs/ (pl: -sen) coniferous forest

de **naaldhak** /nalthɑk/ (pl: -ken) stiletto(heel); [Am] spike heel

het **naaldhout** /nalthaut/ softwood, coniferous wood

de **naam** /nam/ (pl: namen) name; reputation: *een **goede** (or: **slechte**) ~ hebben* have a good (*or*: bad) reputation; *zijn ~ **eer** aandoen* live up to one's reputation (*or*: name); [Dutch] *dat mag geen ~ **hebben*** that's not worth mentioning; *~ **maken*** make a name for o.s. (with, as); *de dingen **bij** de ~ noemen* call a spade a spade; *een cheque uitschrijven **op** ~ van* make out a cheque to; *ten name van, op*

*~ **van** in the name of; wat was uw ~ ook weer?* what did you say your name was?

het **naambordje** /nambɔrcə/ (pl: -s) nameplate

de **naamdag** /namdɑx/ (pl: -dagen) [Roman Catholicism] name day

de **naamgenoot** /namɣənot/ (pl: -genoten) namesake

het **naamkaartje** /namkarcə/ (pl: -s) calling-card, business card
naamloos /namlos/ (adj, adv) anonymous, unnamed

het **naamplaatje** /namplacə/ nameplate

de **naamval** /namvɑl/ (pl: -len) case

het **naamwoord** /namwort/ (pl: -en) noun: *een bijvoeglijk ~* an adjective; *een **zelfstandig** ~* a noun
naamwoordelijk /namwordələk/ (adj) nominal

na-apen /naapə(n)/ (aapte na, heeft nageaapt) ape, mimic

de **na-aper** /naapər/ (pl: -s) mimic, copycat

[1] **naar** /nar/ (adj, adv) nasty, horrible

[2] **naar** /nar/ (prep) **1** to, for: *~ **huis** gaan* go home; *~ de **weg** vragen* ask the way; *op **zoek** ~* in search of; *~ iem. **vragen*** ask for (*or*: after) s.o. **2** (according) to: *ruiken* (or: *smaken*) *~* smell (*or*: taste) of
naargeestig /narɣestəx/ (adj, adv) gloomy, dismal

[1] **naargelang** /narɣəlɑŋ/ (prep) according to, depending on: *al ~ de **leeftijd*** depending on (one's) age

[2] **naargelang** /narɣəlɑŋ/ (conj) as: *~ je ouder wordt …* as you get older
naarmate /narmatə/ (conj) as: *~ je meer **verdient**, ga je ook meer belasting betalen* the more you earn, the more tax you pay
naartoe /nartu/ (adv): *waar moet dit ~?* where will this lead us?

[1] **naast** /nast/ (adj) **1** near(est), closest; immediate: *de ~e **bloedverwanten*** the next of kin **2** out, off (target): *hij **schoot** ~* he shot wide

[2] **naast** /nast/ (prep) **1** next to, beside; wide of: *~ iem. **gaan zitten*** sit down next to (*or*: beside) s.o. **2** alongside, next to: *~ **elkaar*** side by side, next to one another **3** after, next to

de **naaste** /nastə/ (pl: -n) neighbour

de **naastenliefde** /nastə(n)livdə/ charity

de **nabehandeling** /nabəhɑndəlɪŋ/ after-care

de **nabeschouwing** /nabəsxɑuwɪŋ/ (pl: -en) summing-up; recap, review
nabespreken /nabəsprekə(n)/ (besprak na, heeft nabesproken) discuss afterwards

de **nabestaande** /nabəstandə/ (pl: -n) (surviving) relative; next of kin
nabestellen /nabəstɛlə(n)/ (bestelde na, heeft nabesteld) reorder, have copies made of

[1] **nabij** /nabɛi/ (adj) close, near: *de ~e **omgeving*** the immediate surroundings

²**nabij** /nabɛi̯/ (prep) near (to), close to: *om en ~ de duizend euro* roughly (*or:* around, about) a thousand euros

nabijgelegen /nabɛi̯ɣəleɣə(n)/ (adj) nearby

de **nabijheid** /nabɛi̯hɛit/ neighbourhood, vicinity

nablijven /nablɛivə(n)/ (bleef na, is nagebleven) stay behind

nablussen /nablʏsə(n)/ damp down

nabootsen /nabotsə(n)/ (bootste na, heeft nagebootst) imitate, copy; mimic

de **nabootsing** /nabotsɪŋ/ (pl: -en) imitation, copying; copy

naburig /nabyrəx/ (adj) neighbouring, nearby

de **nacht** /naxt/ (pl: -en) night: *de afgelopen ~* last night; *de komende ~* tonight; *het werd ~* night (*or:* darkness) fell; *tot laat in de ~* deep into the night; *'s ~s* at night; *om drie uur 's ~s* at three o'clock in the morning, at three a.m.; *zo lelijk als de ~* (as) ugly as sin; *bij ~ en ontij* at ungodly hours

nachtblind /naxtblɪnt/ (adj) night-blind

nachtbraken /naxtbrakə(n)/ (nachtbraakte, heeft genachtbraakt) **1** stay out till the early hours **2** work into the early hours

de **nachtbraker** /naxtbrakər/ (pl: -s) **1** night-reveller **2** night owl

de **nachtclub** /naxtklʏp/ (pl: -s) nightclub

de **nachtdienst** /naxdinst/ (pl: -en) night shift

het **nachtdier** /naxdir/ (pl: -en) nocturnal animal

de **nachtegaal** /naxtəɣal/ (pl: nachtegalen) nightingale

nachtelijk /naxtələk/ (adj, adv) **1** night **2** nocturnal, of night **3** night(time)

het **nachthemd** /naxthɛmt/ (pl: -en) nightgown

de **nachtjapon** /naxtjapɔn/ (pl: -nen) nightgown, nightdress, nightie

de **nachtkaars** /naxtkars/ (pl: -en): *uitgaan als een ~* peter out (like a damp squib)

het **nachtkastje** /naxtkaʃə/ (pl: -s) night table, bedside table

het **nachtleven** /naxtlevə(n)/ nightlife

de **nachtmerrie** /naxtmɛri/ (pl: -s) nightmare

de **nachtmis** /naxtmɪs/ (pl: -sen) midnight mass

de **nachtploeg** /naxtpluх/ (pl: -en) night shift

de **nachtrust** /naxtrʏst/ night's rest

het **nachtslot** /naxtslɔt/ (pl: -en) double lock: *de deur op het ~ doen* double-lock the door

de **nachttrein** /naxtrɛin/ (pl: -en) night train

het **nachtverblijf** /naxtfərblɛif/ (pl: -verblijven) night's lodging; night-quarters

de **nachtvlucht** /naxtflʏxt/ (pl: -en) night flight

de **nachtvoorstelling** /naxtforstɛlɪŋ/ (pl: -en) late-night performance

de **nachtvorst** /naxtfɔrst/ night frost; ground frost

de **nachtwake** /naxtwakə/ (pl: -n) vigil, night watch

de **nachtwaker** /naxtwakər/ (pl: -s) night watchman

het **nachtwerk** /naxtwɛrk/ nightwork

de **nachtzoen** /naxtsun/ (pl: -en) good-night kiss: *iem. een ~ geven* kiss s.o. good night

de **nachtzuster** /naxtsʏstər/ (pl: -s) night nurse

de **nacompetitie** /nakɔmpəti(t)si/ (pl: -s) [socc] play-offs

de **nadagen** /nadaɣə(n)/ (pl): *in de ~ van zijn carrière* in the twilight (*or:* the latter days) of one's career, towards the end of one's career

de **nadarafsluiting** /nadɑrɑfslœytɪŋ/ (pl: -en) [Belg] crush barrier

nadat /nadɑt/ (conj) after: *het moet gebeurd zijn ~ ze vertrokken waren* it must have happened after they left

het **nadeel** /nadel/ (pl: nadelen) disadvantage; damage; drawback: *zo zijn voor- en nadelen hebben* have its pros and cons; *al het bewijsmateriaal spreekt in hun ~* all the evidence is against them; *ten nadele van* to the detriment of

nadelig /nadeləх/ (adj, adv) adverse, harmful

nadenken /nadɛŋkə(n)/ (dacht na, heeft nagedacht) **1** think: *even ~* let me think; *ik heb er niet bij nagedacht* I did it without thinking; *ik moet er eens over ~* I'll think about it **2** think, reflect (on, upon), consider: *zonder erbij na te denken* without (even, so much as) thinking; *stof tot ~* food for thought

nadenkend /nadɛŋkənt/ (adj, adv) thoughtful

nader /nadər/ (adj, adv) **1** closer, nearer: *partijen ~ tot elkaar proberen te brengen* try to bring parties closer together **2** closer; further; more detailed (*or:* specific): *bij ~e kennismaking* on further (*or:* closer) acquaintance

naderbij /nadərbɛi̯/ (adv) closer, nearer

naderen /nadərə(n)/ (naderde, heeft genaderd) approach

naderhand /nadərhɑnt/ (adv) afterwards

nadien /nadin/ (adv) after(wards), later

nadoen /nadun/ (deed na, heeft nagedaan) **1** copy **2** imitate, copy; mimic: *de scholier deed zijn leraar na* the schoolboy mimicked his teacher

de **nadruk** /nadrʏk/ (pl: -ken) emphasis, stress

nadrukkelijk /nadrʏkələk/ (adj, adv) emphatic, express

nagaan /naɣan/ (ging na, is nagegaan) **1** check (up): *we zullen die zaak zorgvuldig ~* we will look carefully into the matter **2** work out (for o.s.), examine: *voor zover we kunnen ~* as far as we can gather (*or:* ascertain) **3** imagine: *kun je ~!* just imagine!

de **nageboorte** /naɣəbortə/ (pl: -n) afterbirth

de **nagedachtenis** /naɣədɑxtənɪs/ memory: *ter ~ aan mijn moeder* in memory of my mother

de **nagel** /naɣəl/ (pl: -s) nail; claw: *op zijn ~s bijten* bite one's nails

nagelbijten /naɣəlbɛitə(n)/ bite one's nails

het/de **nagellak** /naɣəlɑk/ (pl: -ken) nail polish (or: varnish)

de **nagelriem** /naɣəlrim/ (pl: -en) cuticle

nagenoeg /naɣənux/ (adv) almost, nearly

het **nagerecht** /naɣərɛxt/ (pl: -en) dessert (course)

het **nageslacht** /naɣəslɑxt/ (pl: -en) offspring, descendants

nahouden /nahɑudə(n)/ keep (in) (after hours), detain (after hours)

naïef /naif/ (adj, adv) naive

de **na-ijver** /naɛivər/ envy, jealousy

de **naïviteit** /naivitɛit/ naïveté

het **najaar** /najar/ autumn

de **najaarsmode** /najarsmodə/ autumn fashion(s)

najagen /najaɣə(n)/ (jaagde na/joeg na, heeft nagejaagd) 1 chase 2 go for (or: after), pursue: *een doel* ~ pursue a goal

nakaarten /nakartə(n)/ (kaartte na, heeft nagekaart) have a chat afterwards

het **nakie** /naki/ [inform]: *in zijn ~ staan* stand naked (to the world)

nakijken /nakɛikə(n)/ (keek na, heeft nagekeken) 1 watch, follow (with one's eyes): *zij keek de wegrijdende auto na* she watched the car drive off 2 check, have (or: take) a look at: *zich laten ~* have a check-up 3 correct: *veel proefwerken ~* mark a lot of papers; [Am] grade a lot of papers || *hij had het ~* he could whistle for it

de **nakomeling** /nakoməlɪŋ/ (pl: -en) descendant; offspring

¹**nakomen** /nakomə(n)/ (kwam na, is nagekomen) come later, arrive later, come after(wards)

²**nakomen** /nakomə(n)/ (kwam na, is nagekomen) observe; perform; fulfil: *een belofte* ~ keep a promise

het **nakomertje** /nakomərcə/ (pl: -s) afterthought

nalaten /nalatə(n)/ (liet na, heeft nagelaten) 1 leave (behind); bequeath (to) 2 refrain from (-ing): *hij kan het niet ~ een grapje te maken* he cannot resist making a joke

de **nalatenschap** /nalatənsxɑp/ (pl: -pen) estate, inheritance

nalatig /nalatəx/ (adj, adv) negligent

de **nalatigheid** /nalatəxhɛit/ negligence

naleven /naleɣə(n)/ (leefde na, heeft nageleefd) observe; comply with

de **naleving** /naleɣɪŋ/ observance, compliance (with)

nalezen /nalezə(n)/ (las na, heeft nagelezen) read again

nalopen /nalopə(n)/ (liep na, heeft nagelopen) 1 walk after, run after 2 check

de **namaak** /namak/ imitation, copy; fake; counterfeit

namaken /namakə(n)/ (maakte na, heeft nagemaakt) 1 imitate, copy 2 fake, counterfeit

name /namə/: *met* ~ especially, particularly; *ze heeft je niet met ~ genoemd* she didn't mention your name (specifically)

namelijk /namələk/ (adv) 1 namely 2 you see, as it happens, it so happens (that): *ik had ~ beloofd dat …* it so happens I had promised that …

namens /naməns/ (prep) on behalf of

nameten /nametə(n)/ (mat na/meette na, heeft nagemeten) check (or: verify) (the measurements of)

Namibië /namibijə/ Namibia

de **Namibiër** /namibijər/ (pl: -s) Namibian

Namibisch /namibis/ (adj) Namibian

de **namiddag** /namidɑx/ (pl: -en) afternoon

de **nanny** /nɛni/ (pl: -'s) nanny

naoorlogs /naorlɔxs/ (adj) postwar

het **napalm** /napɑlm/ napalm

Napels /napəls/ Naples

napluizen /naplœyzə(n)/ (ploos na, heeft nageplozen) examine closely, scrutinize, unravel

het ¹**nappa** /nɑpa/ nap(p)a (leather), sheepskin

²**nappa** /nɑpa/ (adj) nap(p)a (leather), sheepskin

napraten /napratə(n)/ (praatte na, heeft nagepraat) echo, parrot

de **nar** /nɑr/ (pl: -ren) fool, idiot

de **narcis** /nɑrsɪs/ (pl: -sen) [white] narcissus; [yellow] daffodil

de **narcose** /nɑrkozə/ narcosis; anaesthetic: *volledige* ~ general anaesthetic; *bijkomen van de* ~ come out of the anaesthetic

narekenen /narekənə(n)/ (rekende na, heeft nagerekend) go over (or: through) (again), check

de **narigheid** /narəxhɛit/ trouble

naroepen /narupə(n)/ (riep na, heeft nageroepen) 1 call after 2 jeer at

narrig /nɑrəx/ (adj, adv) peevish: *~ reageren* react peevishly

nasaal /nazal/ (adj, adv) nasal

de **naschok** /nasxɔk/ (pl: -ken) aftershock

de **nascholing** /nasxolɪŋ/ (pl: -en) refresher course, continuing education

de **nascholingscursus** /nasxolɪŋskyrzys/ continuing-education course; refresher course

het **naschrift** /nasxrɪft/ (pl: -en) postscript

het **naseizoen** /nasɛizun/ (pl: -en) late season

de **nasi** /nɑsi/ rice: *~ goreng* fried rice

de **nask** /nɑsk/ *natuur- en scheikunde* physics and chemistry

naslaan /naslan/ (sloeg na, heeft nageslagen): *het woordenboek erop* ~ consult a dictionary

het **naslagwerk** /nɑslɑχwɛrk/ (pl: -en) reference book (or: work)

de **nasleep** /nɑslep/ aftermath, (after)effects, consequences

de **nasmaak** /nɑsmak/ (pl: nasmaken) aftertaste

naspelen /nɑspelə(n)/ (speelde na, heeft nagespeeld) [mus] repeat (by ear); play (sth.) after (s.o.); represent; play (out), act (out)

nassen /nɑsə(n)/ (naste, heeft genast) [Dutch; inform]: *dat is niet te ~* it's inedible, it's not fit for a dog

nastaren /nɑstarə(n)/ (staarde na, heeft nagestaard) stare (or: gaze) after

nastreven /nɑstrevə(n)/ (streefde na, heeft nagestreefd) aim for, aim at, strive for (or: after): *geluk ~* seek happiness

nasynchroniseren /nɑsɪnχronizerə(n)/ (synchroniseerde na, heeft nagesynchroniseerd) dub

het **¹nat** /nɑt/ liquid; juice

²nat /nɑt/ (adj, adv) **1** wet; moist; damp: *~ worden* get wet; *door en door ~* drenched (or: soaked) (to the skin) **2** wet; rainy

natafelen /nɑtafələ(n)/ (tafelde na, heeft nagetafeld) linger at the table

natekenen /nɑtekənə(n)/ (tekende na, heeft nagetekend) draw

natellen /nɑtɛlə(n)/ (telde na, heeft nageteld) count again, check

de **natie** /nɑ(t)si/ (pl: -s) nation, country

nationaal /nɑ(t)ʃonal/ (adj, adv) national

het **nationaalsocialisme** /nɑ(t)ʃonalsoʃalɪsmə/ National Socialism; Nazism

de **nationaalsocialist** /nɑ(t)ʃonalsoʃalɪst/ (pl: -en) National Socialist, Nazi

de **nationalisatie** /nɑ(t)ʃonaliza(t)si/ (pl: -s) nationalization

nationaliseren /nɑ(t)ʃonalizerə(n)/ (nationaliseerde na, heeft genationaliseerd) nationalize

het **nationalisme** /nɑ(t)ʃonalɪsmə/ nationalism

de **nationalist** /nɑ(t)ʃonalɪst/ (pl: -en) nationalist

nationalistisch /nɑ(t)ʃonalɪstis/ (adj, adv) nationalist(ic)

de **nationaliteit** /nɑ(t)ʃonalitɛit/ (pl: -en) nationality: *hij is van Britse ~* he has the British nationality

natmaken /nɑtmakə(n)/ (maakte nat, heeft natgemaakt) wet; moisten

natrappen /nɑtrɑpə(n)/ (trapte na, heeft nagetrapt) kick s.o. when he is down

natrekken /nɑtrɛkə(n)/ (trok na, heeft nagetrokken) check (out); investigate

het **natrium** /nɑtrijʏm/ sodium

natscheren /nɑtsχerə(n)/ (schoor nat, heeft natgeschoren) wet-shave

het **nattevingerwerk** /nɑtəvɪnərwɛrk/ guesswork

de **nattigheid** /nɑtəχhɛit/ damp: *~ voelen* smell a rat, be uneasy (about sth.)

de **natura** /nɑtyra/: *in ~* in kind

de **naturalisatie** /nɑtyraliza(t)si/ (pl: -s) naturalization

naturaliseren /nɑtyralizerə(n)/ (naturaliseerde, heeft genaturaliseerd) naturalize: *zich laten ~* be naturalized

naturel /nɑtyrɛl/ (adj) **1** natural: *~ leer* natural leather; *~ linnen* unbleached linen **2** [sport] natural **3** [fig] genuine-looking, natural: *een ~ acteur* a natural actor

het **naturisme** /nɑtyrɪsmə/ naturism, nudism

de **naturist** /nɑtyrɪst/ (pl: -en) naturist

de **natuur** /nɑtyr/ **1** nature; country(side); scenery: *wandelen in de vrije ~* (take a) walk (out) in the country(side); *terug naar de ~* back to nature **2** nature, character: *twee tegengestelde naturen* two opposite natures (or: characters); *dat is zijn tweede ~* that's become second nature (to him); *van nature* by nature

het **natuurbeheer** /nɑtyrbəher/ (nature) conservation

de **natuurbescherming** /nɑtyrbəsχɛrmɪn/ (nature) conservation, protection of nature

de **natuurbrand** /nɑtyrbrɑnt/ (pl: -en) wildfire

het **natuurgebied** /nɑtyrɣəbit/ (pl: -en) scenic area; nature reserve; wildlife area

de **natuurgenezer** /nɑtyrɣənezər/ (pl: -s) healer

natuurgetrouw /nɑtyrɣətrɑu/ (adj, adv) true to nature (or: life)

de **natuurkunde** /nɑtyrkʏndə/ physics

natuurkundig /nɑtyrkʏndəχ/ (adj) physical, physics

de **natuurkundige** /nɑtyrkʏndəɣə/ (pl: -n) physicist

de **natuurliefhebber** /nɑtyrlifhɛbər/ (pl: -s) nature lover, lover of nature

natuurlijk /nɑtyrlək/ (adj, adv) natural; true to nature (or: life): *maar ~!* why, of course! (or: naturally!)

het **natuurmonument** /nɑtyrmonymɛnt/ (pl: -en) nature reserve

het **natuurproduct** /nɑtyrprodʏkt/ (pl: -en) natural product

het **natuurreservaat** /nɑtyrezɛrvat/ (pl: -reservaten) nature reserve

het **natuurschoon** /nɑtyrsχon/ natural (or: scenic) beauty

het **natuurtalent** /nɑtyrtalɛnt/ (pl: -en) gift; natural talent, born talent; [pers] gifted (or: naturally talented) person

het **natuurverschijnsel** /nɑtyrvərsχɛinsəl/ (pl: -en, -s) natural phenomenon

de **natuurvoeding** /nɑtyrvudɪn/ (pl: -en) organic food, natural food, wholefood

de **natuurwetenschap** /nɑtyrwetənsχɑp/ (pl: -pen) (natural) science

het **¹nauw** /nɑu/ (tight) spot (or: corner): *iem. in*

het ~ drijven drive s.o. into a corner, put s.o. in a (tight) spot

²**nauw** /nɑu/ (adj, adv) **1** narrow **2** close: *een ~e samenhang* a close connection **3** precise, particular: *wat geld betreft kijkt hij niet zo ~* he's not so fussy (*or:* strict) when it comes to money **4** narrow, close-fitting; tight

nauwelijks /nɑuwələks/ (adv) hardly, scarcely, barely || *ik was ~ thuis, of ...* I'd only just got home when ...

nauwgezet /nɑuɣəzɛt/ (adj, adv) painstaking, conscientious, scrupulous; punctual

nauwkeurig /nɑukørəx/ (adj, adv) accurate, precise; careful; close: *tot op de millimeter ~* accurate to (within) a millimetre

de **nauwkeurigheid** /nɑukørəxhɛit/ accuracy, precision, exactness: *met de grootste ~* with clockwork precision

nauwlettend /nɑulɛtənt/ (adj, adv) close; conscientious; careful: *~ toezien op* keep a close watch on

n.a.v. *naar aanleiding van* in connection with, with reference to

de **navel** /navəl/ (pl: -s) navel

de **navelsinaasappel** /navəlsinɑsɑpəl/ (pl: -s) navel orange

navelstaren /navəlstarə(n)/ indulgence in navel-gazing

de **navelstreng** /navəlstrɛŋ/ (pl: -en) umbilical cord, navel string

het **naveltruitje** /navəltrœycə/ (pl: -s) crop top

navenant /navənɑnt/ (adj, adv): *de prijzen zijn ~ hoog* the prices are correspondingly (*or:* proportionately) high; *de prijs is laag en de kwaliteit is ~* the price is low and so is the quality

navertellen /navərtɛlə(n)/ (vertelde na, heeft naverteld) repeat, retell: *hij zal het niet ~ he won't live to tell the tale*

de **navigatie** /naviɣa(t)si/ navigation

navigeren /naviɣerə(n)/ (navigeerde, heeft genavigeerd) navigate

de **NAVO** /navo/ *Noord-Atlantische Verdragsorganisatie* NATO

navolgen /navɔlɣə(n)/ (volgde na, heeft nagevolgd) follow, imitate: *iemands voorbeeld ~* follow s.o.'s example

de **navolger** /navɔlɣər/ (pl: -s) follower, imitator, copier

de **navolging** /navɔlɣɪŋ/ (pl: -en) imitation, following

de **navraag** /navrax/ inquiry: *~ doen bij* inquire with

navragen /navraɣə(n)/ (vraagde na/vroeg na, heeft nagevraagd) inquire (about, into)

navrant /navrɑnt/ (adj, adv) distressing: *een ~ geval* a sad case

navulbaar /navʏlbar/ (adj) refillable

de **navulverpakking** /navʏlvərpɑkɪŋ/ (pl: -en) refillable packaging

de **naweeën** /nawejə(n)/ (pl) **1** afterpains, aftereffects **2** aftereffects; aftermath

de **nawerking** /nawɛrkɪŋ/ (pl: -en) aftereffect(s)

nawijzen /nawɛizə(n)/ (wees na, heeft nagewezen) point at (*or:* after): *iem. met de vinger ~* point the finger at s.o.

het **nawoord** /nawort/ (pl: -en) afterword, epilogue

de **nazaat** /nazat/ (pl: nazaten) descendant, offspring

nazeggen /nazɛɣə(n)/ (zegde na/zei na, heeft nagezegd) repeat: *zeg mij na* repeat after me

nazenden /nazɛndə(n)/ (zond na, heeft nagezonden) send on (*or:* after), forward

de **nazi** /natsi/ (pl: -'s) Nazi

nazien /nazin/ (zag na, heeft nagezien) look over (*or:* through), check

de **nazit** /nazɪt/ (pl: -ten) [Dutch] informal gathering after a meeting, performance, ...

de **nazomer** /nazomər/ (pl: -s) late summer

de **nazorg** /nazɔrx/ **1** aftercare **2** maintenance

NB /ɛnbe/ *nota bene* NB

n.Chr. *na Christus* AD (Anno Domini)

de **neanderthaler** /nejɔndərtalər/ (pl: -s) Neanderthal (man)

de **necropolis** /nekropolɪs/ (pl: -sen) necropolis

de **nectar** /nɛktɑr/ nectar

de **nectarine** /nɛktarinə/ (pl: -s) nectarine

nederig /nedərəx/ (adj, adv) humble, modest

de **nederlaag** /nedərlax/ (pl: -lagen) defeat; setback: *een ~ lijden* suffer a defeat, be defeated

Nederland /nedərlɑnt/ the Netherlands, Holland

de **Nederlander** /nedərlɑndər/ (pl: -s) Dutchman: *de ~s* the Dutch

het **Nederlanderschap** /nedərlɑndərsxɑp/ Dutch nationality: *het ~ verliezen* lose one's Dutch nationality

het **Nederlands** /nedərlɑnts/ Dutch: *het Algemeen Beschaafd ~* Standard Dutch

Nederlandstalig /nedərlɑntstaləx/ (adj) Dutch-speaking: *een ~ lied* a song in Dutch

de **nederzetting** /nedərzɛtɪŋ/ (pl: -en) settlement, post

nee /ne/ (int) **1** no: *geen ~ kunnen zeggen* not be able to say no; *daar zeg ik geen ~ tegen* I wouldn't say no (to that); *~ toch* you can't mean it; really?; surely not; *~ heb je, ja kun je krijgen* you never know until you ask **2** really, you're joking (*or:* kidding)

de **neef** /nef/ (pl: neven) **1** nephew **2** cousin: *zij zijn ~ en nicht* they are cousins

de **nee-jasticker** /nejastɪkər/ (pl: -s) 'no junk mail' sticker

de **nee-neesticker** /nenestɪkər/ (pl: -s) 'no circulars' sticker

neer /ner/ (adv) down

neerbuigend /nerbœyɣənt/ (adj) condescending, patronizing

neerdalen /nerdalə(n)/ (daalde neer, is
neergedaald) come down, go down, descend

neergaan /nerɣan/ (ging neer, is neerge-
gaan): *de straat* (*or:* trap) *op-* en ~ go up and
down the street (*or:* stairs)

neergooien /nerɣojə(n)/ (gooide neer,
heeft neergegooid) throw down, toss down:
het bijltje er bij ~ throw in the towel

neerhalen /nerhalə(n)/ (haalde neer, heeft
neergehaald) **1** take down, pull down, lower
2 pull (*or:* take, knock) down, raze **3** take
down, bring down

neerkijken /nerkɛikə(n)/ (keek neer, heeft
neergekeken) look down (on), look down
one's nose (at)

neerkomen /nerkomə(n)/ (kwam neer, is
neergekomen) **1** come down, descend, fall,
land: *waar is het* **vliegtuig** *neergekomen?*
where did the aeroplane land? **2** fall (on): *alles komt* **op** *mij neer* it all falls on my shoulders
3 come (*or:* boil) down (to), amount (to): *dat
komt* **op** *hetzelfde neer* it comes (*or:* boils
down) to the same thing

de **neerlandicus** /nerlɑndikʏs/ (pl: neerlandi-
ci) Dutch specialist, student of (*or:* authority
on) Dutch

neerleggen /nerlɛɣə(n)/ (legde neer, heeft
neergelegd) **1** put (down), lay (down), set
(down): *een bevel* **naast** *zich* ~ disregard (*or:*
ignore) a command **2** put aside, lay down:
zijn **ambt** ~ resign (from) one's office

neerploffen /nerplɔfə(n)/ (plofte neer, is
neergeploft) flop down, plump down

neersabelen /nersabələ(n)/ (sabelde neer,
heeft neergesabeld) **1** put to the sword, cut
down (with a sword) **2** [fig] tear apart, tear
to pieces; torpedo

neerschieten /nersxitə(n)/ (schoot neer,
heeft neergeschoten) **1** shoot (down)
2 bring down, down

¹neerslaan /nerslan/ (sloeg neer, is neergeslagen) fall down; drop down: *een wolk van
stof sloeg neer* **op** *het plein* a cloud of dust settled on the square

²neerslaan /nerslan/ (sloeg neer, heeft
neergeslagen) **1** turn down; let down; lower:
de **ogen** ~ lower one's eyes **2** strike down,
knock down; [sport] floor || *een* **opstand** ~
put down (*or:* crush) an insurrection (*or:* a
rebellion)

neerslachtig /nerslɑxtəx/ (adj, adv) dejected, depressed

de **neerslag** /nerslɑx/ (pl: -en) precipitation;
rain; rainfall; layer; fall: **kans** *op* ~ chance of
rain; *winterse* ~ snow and hail showers

neersteken /nerstekə(n)/ (stak neer, heeft
neergestoken) stab (to death)

neerstorten /nerstɔrtə(n)/ (stortte neer, is
neergestort) crash down, thunder down;

crash: ~*d* **puin** falling rubble

neerstrijken /nerstrɛikə(n)/ (streek neer, is
neergestreken) **1** alight, settle (on), perch
(on) **2** descend (on); settle (on): *op een terras-
je* ~ descend on a terrace

neertellen /nertɛlə(n)/ (telde neer, heeft
neergeteld) pay (out), fork out

neervallen /nervalə(n)/ (viel neer, is neer-
gevallen) **1** fall down, drop down: *werken tot
je* **erbij** *neervalt* work till you drop **2** drop
(down), flop (down)

neerwaarts /nerwarts/ (adj, adv) down-
ward(s), down

neerzetten /nerzɛtə(n)/ (zette neer, heeft
neergezet) put down, lay down, place; set
down; erect: *een goede* **tijd** ~ record a good
time

de **neet** /net/ (pl: neten) nit

het **¹negatief** /neɣatif/ (pl: negatieven) negative
(plate, film)

²negatief /neɣatif/ (adj, adv) **1** negative;
[esp maths, science] minus: *een* ~ **getal** a
negative (*or:* minus) (number) **2** negative,
critical

negen /neɣə(n)/ (num) nine: ~ *op (van)* de
tien keer nine times out of ten

negende /neɣəndə/ (num) ninth

negentien /neɣə(n)tin/ (num) nineteen

negentiende /neɣə(n)tində/ (num) nineteenth

negentiende-eeuws /neɣə(n)tindeews/
(adj) nineteenth-century

negentig /neɣəntəx/ (num) ninety: *hij was
in de* ~ he was in his nineties

de **neger** /neɣər/ (pl: -s) (African, American)
black (person); [offensive] Negro

negeren /nəɣerə(n)/ (negeerde, heeft genegeerd) ignore, take no notice of; [pers
also] give the cold shoulder; disregard; brush
aside: *iem.* **volkomen** ~ cut s.o. dead

neigen /nɛiɣə(n)/ (neigde, heeft geneigd)
incline (to, towards), be inclined (to, towards), tend (to, towards)

de **neiging** /nɛiɣɪŋ/ (pl: -en) inclination, tendency

de **nek** /nɛk/ (pl: -ken) nape (*or:* back) of the
neck: *je* ~ **breken** over de rommel trip over the
rubbish; *zijn* ~ **uitsteken** stick one's neck out;
tot aan zijn ~ *in de schulden zitten* be up to
one's ears in debt; *iem. in zijn* ~ **hijgen** be close
on s.o.'s heels; *uit zijn* ~ **praten** talk out of the
back of one's neck; [Dutch] *over zijn* ~ *gaan*
heave, puke

de **nek-aan-nekrace** /nɛkɑnɡkres/ (pl: -s)
neck-and-neck race

de **nekhernia** /nɛkhɛrnija/ (pl: -'s) herniated
cervical disc

nekken /nɛkə(n)/ (nekte, heeft genekt)
break (*or:* wring) s.o.'s neck

de **nekklem** /nɛklɛm/ (pl: -men) chokehold,
stranglehold

de **nekkramp** /nɛkramp/ spotted fever

het **nekvel** /nɛkfɛl/ scruff of the neck: *iem.* (or: *een hond*) *in zijn ~ pakken* take s.o. (or: a dog) by the scruff of the neck

nemen /nemə(n)/ (nam, heeft genomen) **1** take: *maatregelen ~* take steps (or: measures); *de moeite ~ om* take the trouble to; *ontslag ~* resign; *een kortere weg ~* take a short cut; *iem. iets kwalijk ~* take sth. ill of s.o.; *iem. (niet) serieus ~* (not) take s.o. seriously; *strikt genomen* strictly (speaking); *iem. (even) apart ~* take s.o. aside; *voor zijn rekening ~* deal with, account for **2** have: *wat neem jij?* what are you having?; *neem nog een koekje* (do) have another biscuit **3** take, get, have, take out: *een dag vrij ~* have (or: take) a day off **4** take, use: *de bus ~* catch (or: take) the bus, go by bus **5** take; seize; capture

het **neofascisme** /nejofaʃɪsmə/ neo-Fascism

het **neon** /nejon/ neon

de **neonazi** /nejonatsi/ (pl: -'s) neo-Nazi

de **neonreclame** /nejonrəklamə/ (pl: -s) neon sign(s)

de **nep** /nɛp/ sham, fake, swindle; rip-off: *het is allemaal ~* it's bogus (or: fake, a sham)

Nepal /nepal/ Nepal

de **Nepalees** /nepales/ (pl: Nepalezen) Nepalese, Nepali

het **nepnieuws** /nɛpniws/ fake news

neppen /nɛpə(n)/ (nepte, heeft genept) [Dutch; inform] humbug, bamboozle, cheat: *ze hebben me aardig genept met dit horloge* I've really been ripped off with this watch

de **nepper** /nɛpər/ [Dutch; inform] fake

Neptunus /nɛptynʏs/ Neptune

de **nerd** /nʏːrd/ (pl: -s) nerd

nerderig /nʏːrdərəx/ (adj) nerdy

de **nerf** /nɛrf/ (pl: nerven) grain(ing), texture; vein; rib

nergens /nɛrɣəns/ (adv) **1** nowhere: *met onbeleefdheid kom je ~ naartoe* being rude will get you nowhere; *ik kon ~ naartoe* I had nowhere to go **2** nothing: *~ aan komen!* don't touch!; *dit gaat helemaal ~ over* this is rubbish, this is a lot of nonsense; *ik weet ~ van* I know nothing about it

de **nering** /nerɪŋ/ (pl: -en): *de tering naar de ~ zetten* cut one's coat according to one's cloth

de **¹nerts** /nɛrts/ (pl: -en) [animal] mink

het **²nerts** /nɛrts/ [fur] mink

nerveus /nɛrvøs/ (adj, adv) nervous, tense, high(ly)-strung

de **nervositeit** /nɛrvozitɛɪt/ nervousness

het **nest** /nɛst/ (pl: -en) **1** nest; eyrie; den; hole **2** litter, nest; brood **3** jam, spot, fix: *zich in de ~en werken* get into trouble, be in a mess (or: jam)

nestelen /nɛstələ(n)/ (nestelde, heeft genesteld) nest

het **¹net** /nɛt/ (pl: -ten) **1** net: *achter het ~ vissen* miss out, miss the boat **2** network, system; net; mains; grid: *een ~ van telefoonverbindingen* a network of telephone connections

²net /nɛt/ (adj) **1** neat, tidy; trim: *iets in het ~ schrijven* copy out sth. **2** respectable, decent: *een ~te buurt* a respectable (or: genteel) neighbourhood

³net /nɛt/ (adv) just, exactly: *~ goed* serves you/him (or: her, them) right; *het gaat maar ~* it's a tight fit; *zij ging ~ vertrekken* she was about to leave; *~ iets voor hem* **a)** just the thing for him; **b)** just like him, him all over; *~ wat ik dacht* just as I thought; *dat is ~ wat ik nodig heb* that's exactly what I need; *ze is ~ zo goed als hij* she's every bit as good as he is; *zo is het maar ~* right you are!, just as you say!; *we hadden ~ zo goed niets kunnen doen* we might just as well have done nothing; *we kwamen ~ te laat* we came just too late; *~ echt* just like the real thing; *wij zijn ~ thuis* we've (only) just come home

de **netbal** /nɛdbal/ (pl: -len) netball

netelig /netələx/ (adj) thorny, knotty, tricky

de **netelroos** /netəlros/ nettle rash

de **netheid** /nɛtheit/ neatness, tidiness; cleanliness; smartness

netjes /nɛɡəs/ (adj, adv) **1** neat, tidy, clean **2** neat, smart: *~ gekleed* all dressed up **3** decent, respectable, proper: *gedraag je ~* behave yourself

het **netnummer** /nɛtnʏmər/ (pl: -s) dialling code; [Am] area code

de **netspanning** /nɛtspanɪŋ/ mains voltage

de **nettiquette** /nɛtikɛtə/ netiquette

netto /nɛto/ (adj, adv) net, nett, clear, real: *het ~ maandsalaris* the take-home pay; *de opbrengst bedraagt ~ € 2000,-* the net(t) profit is € 2,000

de **nettowinst** /nɛtowɪnst/ net profit

het **netvlies** /nɛtflis/ (pl: netvliezen) retina: [fig] *dat staat op zijn ~ gebrand* it's etched in his memory

het **netwerk** /nɛtwɛrk/ network, criss-cross pattern; [fig also] system: *een ~ van intriges* a web of intrigue

netwerken /nɛtwɛrkə(n)/ (netwerkte, heeft genetwerkt) network

neukbaar /nøgbar/ (adj) [vulg] fuckable

neuken /nøkə(n)/ (neukte, heeft geneukt) [inform] screw, fuck

neuraal /nøyral/ (adj) neural

neuriën /nørijə(n)/ (neuriede, heeft geneuried) hum

de **neurochirurgie** /nøroʃirʏrɣi/ neurosurgery

de **neurologie** /nøroloɣi/ neurology, neuroscience

de **neuroloog** /nørolox/ (pl: -logen) neurologist

de **neuroot** /nørot/ (pl: neuroten) neurotic, psycho, nutcase

de **neurose** /nørozə/ (pl: -n, -s) neurosis

neurotisch /nørotis/ (adj) neurotic

de **neus** /nøs/ (pl: neuzen) **1** nose, scent; [fig also] flair: *iem. iets door de ~ boren* do (*or:* diddle) s.o. out of sth.; *een fijne ~ voor iets hebben* have a good nose for sth., have an eye for sth.; *een frisse ~ halen* get a breath of fresh air; *doen alsof zijn ~ bloedt* play (*or:* act) dumb; [Belg] *van zijn ~ maken* show off, make a fuss; *zijn ~ ophalen* sniff; [fig] *de ~ voor iem. (iets) ophalen* turn up one's nose at s.o. (sth.); look down one's nose at s.o. (sth.); *zijn ~ snuiten* blow one's nose; *zijn ~ in andermans zaken steken* stick one's nose into other people's affairs; *iem. met zijn ~ op de feiten drukken* make s.o. face the facts; *niet verder kijken dan zijn ~ lang is* be unable to see further than (the end of) one's nose; *dat ga ik jou niet aan je ~ hangen* that's none of your business; [fig] *tussen ~ en lippen door* as you go along **2** nose; nozzle; (toe)cap; toe || *dat examen is een wassen ~* that exam is just a mere formality

de **neusdruppels** /nøzdrʏpəls/ (pl) nose drops

het **neusgat** /nøsχɑt/ (pl: -en) nostril

de **neushoorn** /nøshorn/ (pl: -s) rhinoceros, rhino

het **neusje** /nøʃə/: *het ~ van de zalm* the pick of the bunch, the crème de la crème

de **neuslengte** /nøslɛŋtə/ (pl: -n, -s) nose, hair('s breadth)

neuspeuteren /nøspøtərə(n)/ pick one's nose

de **neusvleugel** /nøsfløɣəl/ (pl: -s) nostril

het **neuswiel** /nøswil/ (pl: -en) nosewheel

de **neut** /nøt/ (pl: -en) drop, snort(er)

neutraal /nøtral/ (adj) neutral, impartial

neutraliseren /nøtralizerə(n)/ (neutraliseerde, heeft geneutraliseerd) neutralize, counteract

de **neutraliteit** /nøtralitɛit/ neutrality: *de ~ schenden* violate neutrality

de **neutronenbom** /nøytronə(n)bɔm/ (pl: -men) neutron bomb

neuzen /nøzə(n)/ (neusde, heeft geneusd) browse, nose around (*or:* about)

de **nevel** /nevəl/ (pl: -en) mist; [light] haze; spray

nevelig /nevələχ/ (adj) misty, hazy

de **nevenactiviteit** /nevə(n)ɑktivitɛit/ sideline

het **neveneffect** /nevə(n)ɛfɛkt/ (pl: -en) side effect

de **nevenfunctie** /nevə(n)fʏŋksi/ (pl: -s) additional job

de **neveninkomsten** /nevə(n)ɪŋkɔmstə(n)/ (pl) additional income

de **newfoundlander** /nufaundlɛndər/ (pl: -s) Newfoundland (dog)

de **ngo** /ɛŋɣeo/ (pl: -'s) NGO

Nicaragua /nikaraɡuwa/ Nicaragua

de **Nicaraguaan** /nikaraɡwan/ (pl: Nicaraguanen) Nicaraguan

Nicaraguaans /nikaraɡwans/ (adj) Nicara-guan

de **nicht** /nɪχt/ **1** niece **2** cousin **3** fairy, queen, poofter; [Am] faggot

nichterig /nɪχtərəχ/ (adj, adv) fairy, poofy

de **nicotine** /nikotinə/ nicotine

niemand /nimɑnt/ (ind pron) no one, nobody: *voor ~ onderdoen* be second to none; *~ anders dan* none other than

het **niemandsland** /nimɑntslɑnt/ no-man's-land

de **nier** /nir/ (pl: -en) kidney; [fig] *in hart en ~en* through and through, to the core

de **niersteen** /nirsten/ (pl: -stenen) kidney stone

de **niesbui** /nizbœy/ (pl: -en) attack (*or:* fit) of sneezing

¹**niet** /nit/ (ind pron) nothing, nought: *dat is ~ meer dan een suggestie* that's nothing more than a suggestion

²**niet** /nit/ (adv) not: *~ geslaagd* (or: *gereed*) unsuccessful (*or:* unprepared); *ik hoop van ~* I hope not; *hoe vaak heb ik ~ gedacht ...* how often have I thought ...; *geloof jij dat verhaal ~?* ik ook *~* don't you believe this story? neither (*or:* nor) do I; *~ alleen ..., maar ook ...* not only ... but also ...; *het betaalt goed, daar ~ van* it's well-paid, that's not the point, but; *helemaal ~* not at all; no way; *denk dat maar ~* don't you believe it!; *ik neem aan van ~* I don't suppose so, I suppose not; *ze is ~ al te slim* she is none too bright

nieten /nitə(n)/ (niette, heeft geniet) staple

nietes /nitəs/ (int) [inform] it isn't: *het is jouw schuld! ~! welles!* it's your fault! - oh no it isn't! - oh yes it is!

nietig /nitəχ/ (adj) **1** invalid, null (and void): *~ verklaren* declare invalid (*or:* null (and void)) **2** puny

het **nietje** /nicə/ (pl: -s) staple

de **nietmachine** /nitmaʃinə/ (pl: -s) stapler

niet-roken /nitrokə(n)/ (adv) non-smoking

niets /nits/ (ind pron) **1** not at all: *dat bevalt mij ~* I don't like that at all **2** nothing, not anything: *weet je ~ beters?* don't you know (of) anything better?; *zij moet ~ van hem hebben* she will have nothing to do with him; *~ nieuws* nothing new; *verder ~?* is that all?; *ik geloof er ~ van* I don't believe a word of it; *voor ~* **a)** for nothing, gratis, free (of charge); **b)** for nothing; *niet voor ~* not for nothing, for good reason; *dat is ~ voor mij* that's not my cup of tea; *dit is ~ dan opschepperij* that's just (*or:* mere) boasting || *in het ~ verdwijnen* disappear into thin air

de **nietsnut** /nitsnʏt/ (pl: -ten) good-for-nothing

nietsontziend /nitsɔntsint/ (adj) unscrupulous, uncompromising

nietsvermoedend /nitsfərmudənt/ (adj, adv) unsuspecting

nietszeggend /nitsɛɣənt/ (adj) meaningless; empty: *een ~e* **opmerking** a triviality, a purposeless remark

niettegenstaande /ni̯teɣənstandə/ (prep) notwithstanding, despite, in spite of: ~ *het feit dat* ... notwithstanding (*or:* despite, in spite of) the fact that ...

niettemin /nitəmɪn/ (adv) nevertheless, nonetheless, even so, still: ~ *is het waar dat* ... it is nevertheless true that ...

nietwaar /nitwar/ (int) is(n't) it?, do(n't) you?, have(n't) we?: *jij kent zijn pa, ~?* you know his dad, don't you?; *dat is mogelijk, ~?* it's possible, isn't it?

nieuw /niw/ (adj) **1** new, recent: *het ~ste op het gebied van* the latest thing in **2** new; un-worn; unused: *zo goed als* ~ as good as new **3** fresh; young: *~e haring* early-season her-ring(s) **4** new, fresh; original; novel: *een ~ begin maken* make a fresh start; *ik ben hier ~* I'm new here **5** new; modern

de **nieuwbouw** /ni̯wbau/ **1** construction of new buildings **2** new(ly built) houses

de **nieuwbouwwijk** /ni̯wbauwɛik/ (pl: -en) new housing estate (*or:* development)

de **nieuweling** /ni̯wəlɪŋ/ (pl: -en) **1** novice, be-ginner **2** new boy (*or:* girl, pupil)

de **nieuwemaan** /ni̯wəman/ new moon

Nieuw-Guinea /niwɣine̯ja/ New Guinea

het **nieuwjaar** /niwjar/: *gelukkig ~!* Happy New Year!

Nieuwjaar /niwjar/ New Year, New Year's Day

de **nieuwjaarsdag** /niwjarzdɔx/ (pl: -en) New Year's Day

de **nieuwjaarswens** /niwjarswɛns/ (pl: -en) New Year's greeting(s)

de **nieuwkomer** /ni̯wkomər/ (pl: -s) newcom-er; new boy (*or:* girl, pupil): *een ~ in de top veertig* a newcomer to the top twenty

het **nieuws** /niws/ news; piece of news: *buiten-lands* (or: *binnenlands*) ~ foreign (*or:* do-mestic) news; *ik heb goed ~* I have (some) good news; *volop in het ~ komen* hit the headlines; *dat is oud ~* that's stale news; that's ancient history; *het ~ van acht uur* the eight o'clock news; *is er nog ~?* any news?, what's new?

het **nieuwsbericht** /ni̯wzbərɪxt/ (pl: -en) news report; news bulletin; news flash

de **nieuwsbrief** /ni̯wzbrif/ (pl: -brieven) news-letter

de **nieuwsdienst** /ni̯wzdinst/ (pl: -en) news service, press service

nieuwsgierig /niwsxiˈrəx/ (adj, adv) curious (about), inquisitive, nosy

de **nieuwsgierigheid** /niwsxiˈrəxhɛit/ curiosi-ty, inquisitiveness: *branden van* ~ be dying from curiosity

de **nieuwsgroep** /ni̯wsxrup/ (pl: -en) news-group

de **nieuwslezer** /ni̯wslezər/ (pl: -s) newsreader

het **nieuwsoverzicht** /ni̯wsovərzɪxt/ (pl: -en) news summary: *kort* ~ rundown on the news

de **nieuwswaarde** /ni̯wswardə/ news value

de **nieuwszender** /ni̯wsɛndər/ (pl: -s) news network

het **nieuwtje** /ni̯wcə/ (pl: -s) piece (*or:* item, bit) of news

Nieuw-Zeeland /niwze̯lant/ New Zealand

de **Nieuw-Zeelander** /niwze̯landər/ (pl: -s) New Zealander

Nieuw-Zeelands /niwze̯lan(t)s/ (adj) New Zealand; of, from New Zealand

niezen /nizə(n)/ (niesde, heeft geniesd) sneeze

de **¹Niger** /niˈɣər/ Niger

²Niger /niˈɣər/ Niger

de **¹Nigerees** /niˈɣeres/ (pl: Nigerezen) Nigerien

²Nigerees /niˈɣeres/ (adj) Nigerien

Nigeria /niˈɣerija/ Nigeria

de **Nigeriaan** /niˈɣerijan/ (pl: Nigerianen) Nige-rian

Nigeriaans /niˈɣerijans/ (adj) Nigerian

nihil /nihɪl/ (adj) nil, zero

de **nijd** /nɛit/ envy, jealousy: *groen en geel wor-den van* ~ *over iets* be green with envy at sth.; *haat en* ~ hatred and malice

nijdig /nɛidəx/ (adj, adv) angry, annoyed, cross

de **Nijl** /nɛil/ Nile

het **nijlpaard** /nɛilpart/ (pl: -en) hippopotamus; hippo

nijpend /nɛipənt/ (adj) pinching, biting: *het ~ tekort aan* the acute shortage of

de **nijptang** /nɛiptɑŋ/ (pl: -en) (pair of) pincers

nijver /nɛivər/ (adj, adv) industrious, hard-working

de **nijverheid** /nɛivərhɛit/ industry

de **nikab** /nikɑp/ (pl: -s) niqab, face veil

het **nikkel** /nɪkəl/ nickel

nikkelen /nɪkələ(n)/ (adj) **1** nickel **2** nickel-plated

niks /nɪks/ (ind pron) [inform] nothing; [Am] zilch: *dat wordt* ~ that won't work; *nou, ik vind het maar ~!* well I don't think much of it; *dat kost drie keer* ~ that costs next to nothing, that's dirt cheap; *dat is niet* ~ that's quite something

niksen /nɪksə(n)/ [inform] sit around, loaf about, laze about, do nothing

de **niksnut** /nɪksnʏt/ (pl: -ten) [inform] good-for-nothing, layabout

de **nimf** /nɪmf/ (pl: -en) nymph

nimmer /nɪmər/ (adv) never

nippen /nɪpə(n)/ (nipte, heeft genipt) sip (at), take a sip

het **nippertje** /nɪpərcə/: *op het* ~ at the very last moment (*or:* second), in the nick of time; *dat was op het* ~ that was a close (*or:* near) thing; *de student haalde op het* ~ *zijn examen* the stu-dent only passed by the skin of his teeth

het **nirwana** /nɪrvana/ nirvana

de **nis** /nɪs/ (pl: -sen) niche, alcove

het **nitraat** /nitra̱t/ (pl: nitraten) nitrate

het **nitriet** /nitri̱t/ (pl: -en) nitrite

het **niveau** /nivo̱/ (pl: -s) level, standard: *rugby op hoog* ~ top-class rugby; *het* ~ *daalt* the tone (of the conversation) is dropping; *onder zijn* ~ *werken* work below one's capability

nivelleren /nivɛle̱rə(n)/ (nivelleerde, heeft genivelleerd) level (out)

de **nivellering** /nivɛle̱rɪŋ/ (pl: -en) levelling (out), evening out

de **nko-arts** /ɛŋkao̱ɑrts/ (pl: -en) [Belg] ENT specialist

nl. *namelijk* viz.

Noach /no̱wɑx/ Noah: *de ark van* ~ Noah's ark

nobel /no̱bəl/ (adj, adv) noble(-minded), generous

de **Nobelprijs** /nobɛ̱lprɛis/ (pl: -prijzen) Nobel prize: *de* ~ *voor de vrede* the Nobel Peace prize

noch /nɔx/ (conj) neither, nor: ~ *de een* ~ *de ander* neither the one nor the other

nochtans /nɔxtɑ̱ns/ (adv) [form] nevertheless, nonetheless

de **no-claimkorting** /nokle̱mkɔrtɪŋ/ no claim(s) bonus

nodeloos /no̱dəlos/ (adj, adv) unnecessary: *zich* ~ *ongerust maken* worry over nothing

¹**nodig** /no̱dəx/ (adj, adv) **1** necessary, needful: *zij hadden* al *hun tijd* ~ they had no time to waste (*or:* spare); *iets* ~ *hebben* need (*or:* require) sth.; *er is moed voor* ~ *om* it takes courage to; *dat is hard (dringend)* ~ that is badly needed, that is vital; *zo (waar)* ~ if need be, if necessary **2** usual, customary

²**nodig** /no̱dəx/ (adv) necessarily, needfully, urgently ‖ *dat moet jij* ~ *zeggen* look who's talking

de **noedels** /nu̱dəls/ (pl) noodles

noemen /nu̱mə(n)/ (noemde, heeft genoemd) **1** call, name: *noem jij dit een gezellige avond?* is this your idea of a pleasant evening?; *dat noem ik nog eens moed* that's what I call courage!; *iem. bij zijn voornaam* ~ call s.o. by his first name; *een kind naar zijn vader* ~ name a child after his father **2** mention, cite; name: *om maar eens iets te* ~ to name (but) a few

noemenswaardig /numənswa̱rdəx/ (adj, adv) appreciable, considerable, noticeable, worthy of mention: *niet* ~ inappreciable; nothing to speak of

de **noemer** /nu̱mər/ (pl: -s) denominator: [fig] *onder één* ~ *brengen* lump (*or:* heap) together

nog /nɔx/ (adv) **1** still, so far: *niemand heeft dit* ~ *geprobeerd* no one has tried this (as) yet; *zelfs nu* ~ even now; *tot* ~ *toe* so far, up to now **2** still **3** even, still: ~ *groter* even larger, larger still **4** from now (on), more: ~ *drie nachtjes slapen* three (more) nights

5 again, (once) more: ~ *één woord en ik schiet* one more word and I'll shoot; *neem er* ~ *eentje!* have another (one)! ‖ *ik zag hem vorige week* ~ I saw him only last week; *verder* ~ *iets?* anything else?; *ze zijn er* ~ *maar net* they've only just arrived; ~ *geen maand geleden* less than a month ago

de **noga** /no̱ɣa/ nougat

nogal /nɔɣɑ̱l/ (adv) rather, fairly, quite, pretty: *ik vind het* ~ *duur* I think it is rather (*or:* quite) expensive; *er waren er* ~ *wat* there were quite a few (of them)

nogmaals /nɔ̱xmals/ (adv) again, once again (*or:* more): ~ *bedankt* thanks again

de **no-goarea** /nogoɛ̱:rijə/ no-go area

de **nok** /nɔk/ (pl: -ken) ridge, crest, peak

de **nomade** /noma̱də/ (pl: -n) nomad

nominaal /nomina̱l/ (adj) nominal

de **nominatie** /nomina̱(t)si/ (pl: -s) nomination (list)

nomineren /nomine̱rə(n)/ (nomineerde, heeft genomineerd) nominate

de **non** /nɔn/ (pl: -nen) nun, sister

het **non-actief** /nɔnɑkti̱f/: *(tijdelijk) op* ~ *staan* be suspended

non-binair /nɔmbinɛ̱:r/ (adj) non-binary

de **nonchalance** /nɔnʃɑlɑ̱̃sə/ nonchalance, casualness

nonchalant /nɔnʃɑlɑ̱nt/ (adj, adv) nonchalant, casual

de **nonnenschool** /nɔ̱nə(n)sxol/ (pl: -scholen) convent (school)

non-profit /nɔmprɔ̱fɪt/ (adj) nonprofit

de **nonsens** /nɔ̱nsɛns/ nonsense, rubbish

non-stop /nɔnstɔ̱p/ (adj) nonstop

de **nood** /not/ (pl: noden) distress; extremity; (time(s) of) emergency: *geen* ~*!* don't worry!; *uiterste* ~ dire need; *in geval van* ~ in an emergency, in case of need; *mensen in* ~ people in distress (*or:* trouble); *in* ~ *verkeren* be in distress (*or:* trouble); *in* ~ *leer je je vrienden kennen* a friend in need is a friend indeed; ~ *breekt wet* necessity knows no law; *van de* ~ *een deugd maken* make a virtue of necessity ‖ [Belg] ~ *hebben aan* need

de **noodgang** /no̱tχɑŋ/ breakneck speed: *met een* ~ at breakneck speed

het **noodgebouw** /no̱tχəbɑu/ temporary building, makeshift building

noodgedwongen /notχədwɔ̱ŋə(n)/ (adv) out of (*or:* from) (sheer) necessity: *wij moeten* ~ *andere maatregelen treffen* we are forced to take other measures

het **noodgeval** /no̱tχəval/ (pl: -len) (case of) emergency

de **noodhulp** /no̱thʏlp/ (pl: -en) **1** temporary help, worker **2** emergency relief, emergency aid

de **noodklok** /no̱tklɔk/ (pl: -ken) alarm (bell)

de **noodkreet** /no̱tkret/ (pl: -kreten) cry of distress, call for help

de **noodlanding** /nɔtlɑndɪŋ/ (pl: -en) forced landing, emergency landing, belly landing, crash landing

noodlijdend /notlɛɪdənt/ (adj) destitute, indigent, needy

het **noodlot** /nɔtlɔt/ fate

noodlottig /notlɔtəx/ (adj, adv) fatal (to), disastrous (to), ill-fated: *een ~e reis* an ill-fated journey

de **noodmaatregel** /nɔtmatreɣəl/ emergency measure

de **noodoplossing** /nɔtɔplɔsɪŋ/ (pl: -en) temporary solution

de **noodrem** /nɔtrɛm/ (pl: -men) emergency brake, safety brake: *aan de ~ trekken* a) pull the communication cord; b) [fig] take emergency measures

de **noodsituatie** /nɔtsitywa(t)si/ (pl: -s) emergency (situation), difficult position, precarious position

de **noodsprong** /nɔtsprɔŋ/ (pl: -en) desperate move (*or:* measure)

de **noodstop** /nɔtstɔp/ (pl: -pen) emergency stop

de **noodtoestand** /nɔtustɑnt/ (pl: -en) emergency (situation), crisis

de **nooduitgang** /nɔtœytxɑŋ/ (pl: -en) emergency exit; fire-escape

de **noodvaart** /nɔtfart/ breakneck speed: *met een ~* at breakneck speed

het **noodverband** /nɔtfərbɑnt/ first-aid (*or:* emergency, temporary) dressing

de ¹**noodweer** /nɔtwer/ self-defence

het ²**noodweer** /nɔtwer/ heavy weather, storm, filthy weather

de **noodzaak** /nɔtsak/ necessity, need: *ik zie de ~ daarvan niet in* I don't see the need for this

noodzakelijk /nɔtsakələk/ (adj) necessary, imperative, essential, vital: *het hoogst ~e* the bare necessities

noodzakelijkerwijs /notsakələkərwɛis/ (adv) necessarily, inevitably, of necessity

noodzaken /nɔtsakə(n)/ (noodzaakte, heeft genoodzaakt) force, oblige, compel

nooit /nojt/ (adv) **1** never: *bijna ~* hardly ever, almost never; *~ van mijn leven* never in my life; *~ van gehoord!* never heard of it (*or:* him) **2** never, certainly not, definitely not, no way: *je moet het ~ doen* you must never do that; *~ ofte nimmer* absolutely not, never ever; *dat ~!* never!

de **Noor** /nor/ (pl: Noren) Norwegian

noord /nort/ (adj, adv) north(erly), northern

Noord-Afrika /nortɑfrika/ North Africa

Noord-Amerika /nortamerika/ North America

Noord-Amerikaans /nortamerikans/ (adj) North American

Noord-Atlantisch /nortɑtlɑntis/ (adj) North Atlantic

Noord-Brabant /nordbrɑbɑnt/ North Brabant

noordelijk /nɔrdələk/ (adj, adv) north-(erly), northern, northerly, northward: *de wind is ~* the wind is northerly; *een ~e koers kiezen* steer a northerly course; *het ~ halfrond* the northern hemisphere

het **noorden** /nɔrdə(n)/ north; North: *ten ~ van* (to the) north of; *in het hoge Noorden* in the extreme North

de **noordenwind** /nɔrdə(n)wɪnt/ (pl: -en) north(erly) wind

de **noorderbreedte** /nɔrdərbretə/ north latitude: *Madrid ligt op 40 graden ~* Madrid lies in 40° north latitude

de **noorderkeerkring** /nɔrdərkerkrɪŋ/ Tropic of Cancer

het **noorderlicht** /nɔrdərlɪxt/ aurora borealis, northern lights

de **noorderling** /nɔrdərlɪŋ/ (pl: -en) northerner

de **noorderzon** /nɔrdərzɔn/: *met de ~ vertrekken* do a moonlight flit; abscond; skeddadle

Noord-Holland /nortɦɔlɑnt/ North Holland

de **Noord-Ier** /nortir/ (pl: -en) inhabitant (*or:* native) of Northern Ireland

Noord-Ierland /nortirlɑnt/ Northern Ireland

Noord-Iers /nortirs/ (adj) (of) Northern Ireland

de **Noordkaap** /nortkap/ North Cape, Arctic Cape

Noord-Korea /nortkoreja/ North Korea

de **Noord-Koreaan** /nortkorejan/ (pl: Noord-Koreanen) North Korean

Noord-Koreaans /nortkorejans/ (adj) North Korean

de **noordkust** /nɔrtkʏst/ north(ern) coast

Noord-Macedonië /nortmɑsədonijə/ North Macedonia

de **Noord-Macedoniër** /nortmɑsədonijər/ (pl: -s) North Macedonian

Noord-Macedonisch /nortmɑsədonis/ (adj) North Macedonian

noordoost /nortost/ (adj) northeast(erly)

het **noordoosten** /nortostə(n)/ north-east

de **noordpool** /nɔrtpol/ North Pole

de **Noordpool** /nɔrtpol/ Arctic

de **noordpoolcirkel** /nɔrtpolsɪrkəl/ Arctic Circle

het **noordpoolgebied** /nɔrtpolɣəbit/ Arctic (region)

noordwaarts /nɔrtwarts/ (adj, adv) northward(s), northward

noordwest /nortwɛst/ (adj) northwest(erly)

het **noordwesten** /nortwɛstə(n)/ north-west

de **Noordzee** /nɔrtse/ North Sea

de **Noorman** /norman/ (pl: -nen) Norseman, Viking

het ¹**Noors** /nors/ Norwegian

²**Noors** /nors/ (adj) Norwegian

Noorwegen /nọrweyə(n)/ Norway

de **noot** /not/ (pl: noten) **1** nut: *een **harde** ~ (om te kraken)* a tough (or: hard) nut (to crack) **2** [mus] note: *hele* (or: *halve*) *noten spelen* play semibreves (or: minims); *een **kwart** ~ a* crotchet; *een **valse** ~* a wrong note **3** (foot)-note: *ergens een **kritische** ~ bij plaatsen* comment (critically) on sth.

de **nootmuskaat** /notmʏska̱t/ nutmeg

de **nop** /nɔp/ (pl: -pen) nix: *voor ~* for nothing, for free

nopen /nọpə(n)/ (noopte, heeft genoopt) impel, compel

de **nopjes** /nɔpjəs/ (pl): *in zijn ~ zijn* be (as) pleased as Punch, be delighted

noppes /nɔpəs/ (ind pron): *je kunt er **voor** ~ naar binnen* you can go there for nothing (or: for free); *heb ik nou alles voor ~ gedaan?* has it all been an utter waste of time?

de **nor** /nɔr/ (pl: -ren) [inform] clink, nick

het **nordic walking** /nɔrdɪkwọ:kɪŋ/ Nordic Walking

de **noren** /nọrə(n)/ (pl) racing skates

de **norm** /nɔrm/ (pl: -en) standard, norm: *~en en **waarden*** norms and values, standards

¹**normaal** /nɔrma̱l/ (adj, adv) normal, standard, usual: *een normale **auto*** a standard car; *temperaturen **boven** ~* higher than normal temperatures; *doe eens ~!* behave yourself!, grow up!; *~ **gesproken*** generally speaking, in the normal course of events; *~ ben ik al thuis om deze tijd* I am normally (or: usually) home by this time

het ²**normaal** /nɔrma̱l/: *het nieuwe ~* the new normal

de **normaalschool** /nɔrma̱lsxol/ (pl: -scholen) [Belg] training college for primary school teachers

normaliseren /nɔrmalize̱rə(n)/ (normaliseerde, heeft genormaliseerd) normalize

normaliter /nɔrmalitər/ (adv) normally, usually, as a rule

Normandië /nɔrma̱ndijə/ Normandy

de **Normandiër** /nɔrma̱ndijər/ (pl: -s) Norman

Normandisch /nɔrma̱ndis/ (adj) Norman

het **normbesef** /nɔrmbəsɛf/ sense of standards (or: values)

het **normen-en-waardenpatroon** /nɔrmə(n)ɛnwa̱rdə(n)patron/ (pl: -patronen) value system, values

de **normering** /nɔrme̱rɪŋ/ (pl: -en) standard

normoverschrijdend /nɔrmovərsxre̱ɪdənt/ (adj) deviant: *~ **gedrag*** deviant (or: anti-social) behaviour

de **normvervaging** /nɔrmvərva̱yɪŋ/ (pl: -en) blurring of (moral) standards

nors /nɔrs/ (adj, adv) surly, gruff, grumpy

de **nostalgie** /nɔstalyi̱/ nostalgia

nostalgisch /nɔsta̱lyis/ (adj, adv) nostalgic

de **nota** /nọta/ (pl: -'s) **1** account, bill **2** memorandum

de **notabele** /nota̱bələ/ (pl: -n) dignitary, leading citizen

nota bene /notabe̱nə/ nota bene, please note ‖ *ze heeft ~ alwéér een andere auto* she's got yet another new car, would you believe

het **notariaat** /notar(i)ja̱t/ (pl: notariaten) **1** office of notary (public) **2** notary's practice

notarieel /notar(i)je̱l/ (adj, adv) notarial: *een notariële **akte*** a notarial act (or: deed)

de **notaris** /nota̱rɪs/ (pl: -sen) notary (public)

het **notariskantoor** /nota̱rɪskantor/ (pl: -kantoren) notary('s) office

de **notatie** /nota̱(t)si/ notation; notation system

het/de **notebook** /nọdbuk/ (pl: -s) notebook (computer)

de **notenbalk** /nọtə(n)balk/ (pl: -en) staff, stave

de **notenboom** /nọtə(n)bom/ (pl: -bomen) walnut (tree)

de **notendop** /nọtə(n)dɔp/ (pl: -pen) nutshell: [fig] *in een ~* in a nutshell

het **notenhout** /nọtə(n)haut/ walnut

de **notenkraker** /nọtə(n)krakər/ (pl: -s) (pair of) nutcrackers

het **notenschrift** /nọtə(n)sxrɪft/ (pl: -en) (musical) notation; staff notation

¹**noteren** /note̱rə(n)/ (noteerde, heeft genoteerd) list; quote

²**noteren** /note̱rə(n)/ (noteerde, heeft genoteerd) **1** note (down), make a note of, record, register; book: *een **telefoonnummer** ~* jot down (or: make a note) of a telephone number **2** quote: *aan de beurs genoteerd zijn* be listed on the (stock) market

de **notering** /note̱rɪŋ/ (pl: -en) quotation; quoted price; rate

de **notie** /nọ(t)si/ (pl: -s) **1** notion, idea: *geen flauwe ~* not the faintest notion **2** notion: *de ~ 'samenleving'* the notion of society

de **notitie** /noti̱(t)si/ (pl: -s) note; memo(randum): *~s **maken*** take notes

het **notitieblok** /noti̱(t)siblɔk/ (pl: -ken) notepad, memo pad; scribbling pad

het **notitieboekje** /noti̱(t)sibukjə/ (pl: -s) notebook, memorandum book

notoir /notwa̱r/ (adj) notorious

de **notulen** /nọtylə(n)/ (pl) minutes

notuleren /notyle̱rə(n)/ (notuleerde, heeft genotuleerd) take (the) minutes

de **notulist** /notyli̱st/ minutes secretary

¹**nou** /nau/ (adv) [Dutch; inform] now: *wat moeten we ~ doen?* what do we (have to) do now?

²**nou** /nau/ (int) [inform] **1** now, well: *kom je ~?* well, are you coming? **2** well, really: *meen je dat ~?* do you really mean it?; *hoe kan dat ~?* how on earth can that be? (or: have happened?); *~ dan!* exactly, couldn't agree more!; *~, en of!* you bet! **3** again: *wanneer ga je ~ ook weer weg?* when were you leaving

again? **4** oh (very) well, never mind: ~ *ja, zo erg is 't niet* never mind, it's not all that bad; *dat is ~ niet bepaald eenvoudig* well, that's not so easy **5** oh, now, … on earth, … ever: *waar bleef je ~?* where on earth have you been? || ~ *en?* so what?; ~, *dat was het dan* well (*or:* so), that was that
Nova Zembla /novazɛmbla/ Novaya Zemlya

de **novelle** /novɛlə/ (pl: -n) short story, novella

de **november** /novɛmbər/ November

de **NSB'er** /ɛnɛzbejər/ (pl: -s) [Dutch] **1** NSB member **2** [offensive] traitor
nu /ny/ (adv) **1** now, at the moment: *nu en dan* now and then, at times, occasionally; *ik kan nu niet* I can't (right, just) now; *nu nog niet* not yet; *tot nu (toe)* up to now, so far; *van nu af aan* from now on **2** now(adays), these days || *het hier en het nu* the here and now

de **nuance** /nywāsə/ (pl: -s) nuance
nuanceren /nywansɛrə(n)/ (nuanceerde, heeft genuanceerd) nuance; differentiate; qualify
nuchter /nʏxtər/ (adj) **1** fasting; newborn: *voor de operatie moet je ~ zijn* you must have an empty stomach before surgery **2** sober: ~ *worden* sober up **3** sober, plain: *de ~e waarheid* the plain (*or:* simple) truth **4** sober(-minded), sensible, level-headed
nucleair /nyklejɛːr/ (adj, adv) nuclear

de **nudist** /nydɪst/ (pl: -en) nudist, naturist
nuffig /nʏfəx/ (adj) [Dutch] prim, prissy

de **nuk** /nʏk/ (pl: -ken) mood, quirk
nukkig /nʏkəx/ (adj) quirky, moody, sullen

de **nul** /nʏl/ (pl: -len) nought; zero; 0: *tien graden onder ~* ten (degrees) below zero; *PSV heeft met 2-0 verloren* PSV lost two-nil || *nul op het rekest krijgen* meet with a refusal; be turned down

de **nulmeridiaan** /nʏlmeridijan/ (pl: -meridianen) prime meridian

het **nulpunt** /nʏlpʏnt/ zero (point): *het absolute ~* absolute zero

het **nulzesnummer** /nʏlzɛsnʏmər/ (pl: -s) mobile (phone) number; [Am] cellphone number
numeriek /nymerik/ (adj) numerical, numeric

het **nummer** /nʏmər/ (pl: -s) **1** number, figure: ~ *één van de klas zijn* be top of one's class **2** number: *mobiel ~* mobile (phone) number; [Am] cellphone number; *vast ~* landline number **3** number, issue: *een ~ van een tijdschrift* a number (*or:* issue) of a periodical; *een oud ~* a back issue (*or:* number) **4** number; track: *een ~ draaien* play a track **5** act, routine, number: *een ~ brengen* do a routine (*or:* an act); [fig] *dat etentje is een verplicht ~* the dinner is compulsory || *iem. op zijn ~ zetten* put s.o. in his (*or:* her) place

het **nummerbord** /nʏmərbɔrt/ (pl: -en) number plate; [Am] license plate
nummeren /nʏmərə(n)/ (nummerde, heeft genummerd) number

de **nummering** /nʏmərɪŋ/ (pl: -en) numeration

de **nummermelder** /nʏmərmɛldər/ caller ID

het **nummertje** /nʏmərcə/ (pl: -s) **1** number: *een ~ trekken* take a number **2** [inform] bang: *een ~ maken met iem.* bang s.o.

de **nummerweergave** /nʏmərwɛryavə/ caller ID
nurks /nʏrks/ (adj, adv) gruff

het **nut** /nʏt/ use(fulness); benefit; point; value; purpose: *het heeft geen enkel ~ om …* it is useless (*or:* pointless) to …; *ik zie er het ~ niet van in* I don't see the point of it

het **nutsbedrijf** /nʏtsbədrɛif/ (pl: -bedrijven): *openbare nutsbedrijven* public utilities
nutteloos /nʏtəlos/ (adj, adv) **1** useless: *een nutteloze vraag* a pointless question **2** fruitless

de **nutteloosheid** /nʏtəloshɛit/ uselessness, futility
nuttig /nʏtəx/ (adj, adv) **1** useful: *zich ~ maken* make o.s. useful **2** advantageous: *zijn tijd ~ besteden* make good use of one's time
nuttigen /nʏtəyə(n)/ (nuttigde, heeft genuttigd) consume, take, partake of

de **nv** /ɛnve/ (pl: nv's) *naamloze vennootschap* plc (public limited company); [Am] Inc (incorporated)
n.v.t. *niet van toepassing* n/a

het/de **nylon** /nɛilɔn/ nylon

de **nymfomane** /nɪmfomānə/ (pl: -n, -s) nymphomaniac

O

o /o/ (int) O, oh, ah ‖ *o zo verleidelijk* ever so tempting

o.a. *onder andere* among other things, for instance

de **oase** /owazə/ (pl: -s) oasis

de **obelisk** /obəlɪsk/ (pl: -en) obelisk

de **O-benen** /obenə(n)/ (pl) bandy legs, bow-legs: *met ~* bandy-legged, bow-legged

de **ober** /obər/ (pl: -s) waiter

de **obesitas** /obezitɑs/ obesity

het **object** /opjɛkt/ (pl: -en) object

objectief /opjɛktif/ (adj, adv) objective

de **objectiviteit** /opjɛktivitɛit/ objectiveness, objectivity, impartiality

obligaat /obliɣat/ (adj, adv) obligatory: *obligate toespraken* standard speeches

de **obligatie** /obliɣa(t)si/ (pl: -s) bond, debenture

obsceen /opsen/ (adj) obscene

obscuur /opskyr/ (adj) **1** obscure, dark **2** shady, obscure: *een ~ zaakje* a shady (*or:* doubtful) business

obsederen /opsederə(n)/ (obsedeerde, heeft geobsedeerd) obsess

de **observatie** /opsɛrva(t)si/ (pl: -s) observation

de **observatiepost** /opsɛrva(t)sipost/ (pl: -en) observation post

de **observator** /opsɛrvator/ (pl: -s, -en) observer

het **observatorium** /opsɛrvatorijʏm/ (pl: observatoria) observatory

observeren /opsɛrverə(n)/ (observeerde, heeft geobserveerd) observe, watch

de **obsessie** /opsɛsi/ (pl: -s) obsession, hang-up

het **obstakel** /opstakəl/ (pl: -s) obstacle, obstruction, impediment: *een belangrijk ~ vormen* constitute a major obstacle

obstinaat /opstinat/ (adj) obstinate, stubborn

de **obstipatie** /opstipa(t)si/ constipation

de **obstructie** /opstrʏksi/ (pl: -s) obstruction: *~ plegen* commit obstruction

de **occasie** /okazi/ (pl: -s) [Belg] bargain

de **occasion** /okeʒən/ (pl: -s) [Dutch] used car

occult /okʏlt/ (adj) occult

het **occultisme** /okʏltɪsmə/ occultism

de **oceaan** /osejan/ (pl: oceanen) ocean, sea: *de Stille (Grote) Oceaan* the Pacific (Ocean)

Oceanië /osejanijə/ Oceania

och /ox/ (int) oh, o, ah: *~ kom* oh, go on (with you)

de **ochtend** /oxtənt/ (pl: -en) morning; dawn; daybreak: *de hele ~* all morning; *om 7 uur 's*

~s at 7 o'clock in the morning, at 7 a.m.

het **ochtendblad** /oxtəndblɑt/ (pl: -en) morning (news)paper

het **ochtendgebed** /oxtəntχəbɛt/ (pl: -en) morning prayers

het **ochtendgloren** /oxtəntχlorə(n)/ [form] daybreak

het **ochtendhumeur** /oxtənthymør/ (pl: -en) (early) morning mood: *een ~ hebben* have got up on the wrong side of the bed

de **ochtendjas** /oxtəntjɑs/ (pl: -sen) dressing gown; housecoat

de **ochtendkrant** /oxtəntkrɑnt/ (pl: -en) morning (news)paper

de **ochtendmens** /oxtəntmɛns/ (pl: -en) early bird (*or:* riser)

de **ochtendschemering** /oxtəntsχemərɪŋ/ dawn

de **ochtendspits** /oxtəntspɪts/ morning rush hour

het/de **octaaf** /oktaf/ (pl: octaven) octave, eighth

het **octaan** /oktan/ octane

de **octopus** /oktopʏs/ (pl: -sen) octopus

het **octrooi** /oktroj/ (pl: -en) patent: *~ aanvragen* apply for a patent

de **ode** /odə/ (pl: -n, -s) ode: *een ~ brengen aan iem.* pay tribute to s.o.

oecumenisch /œykymenis/ (adj) ecumenical, interfaith

het **oedeem** /œydem/ (pl: oedemen) (o)edema

het **oedipuscomplex** /œydipʊskomplɛks/ (pl: -en) Oedipus complex

oef /uf/ (int) phew, whew, oof

het **oefenboek** /ufəmbuk/ (pl: -en) workbook, exercise book

¹**oefenen** /ufənə(n)/ (oefende, heeft geoefend) train, practise; rehearse; drill [mil]: *~ voor een voorstelling* rehearse for a performance

²**oefenen** /ufənə(n)/ (oefende, heeft geoefend) train, coach; [mil] drill: *geduld ~* exercise patience

de **oefening** /ufənɪŋ/ (pl: -en) exercise: *dat is een goede ~ voor je* it is good practice for you; *~ baart kunst* practice makes perfect

het **oefenterrein** /ufə(n)tɛrɛin/ (pl: -en) practice ground, training ground

de **oefenwedstrijd** /ufə(n)wɛtstrɛit/ (pl: -en) training (*or:* practice, warm-up) match; sparring match

de **oehoe** /uhu/ (pl: -s) eagle owl

oei /uj/ (int) oops; ouch

het ¹**Oekraïens** /ukrains/ Ukrainian

²**Oekraïens** /ukrains/ (adj) Ukrainian

Oekraïne /ukrainə/ Ukraine

de **Oekraïner** /ukrainər/ (pl: -s) Ukrainian

de **oen** /un/ (pl: -en) [inform] blockhead, dummy

oeps /ups/ (int) oops, whoops

de **Oeral** /ural/: *de ~* the Urals; the Ural Mountains

het **oerbos** /ˈurbɔs/ (pl: -sen) primeval forest

oergezellig /uryəzˈɣlex/ (adj, adv) [inform] very pleasant; delightful

het **oergraan** /ˈuryran/ (pl: -granen) ancient grain

de **oerknal** /ˈurknɑl/ Big Bang

de **oermens** /ˈurmɛns/ (pl: -en) primitive (or: prehistoric) man

oeroud /urˈɑut/ (adj) ancient, prehistoric, primeval

oersaai /ursˈaj/ (adj, adv) [inform] deadly dull

de **oertijd** /ˈurtɛit/ (pl: -en) prehistoric times

het **oerwoud** /ˈurwɑut/ (pl: -en) **1** primeval forest, virgin forest; jungle **2** [fig] jungle, chaos, hotchpotch

de **OESO** /ˈuzo/ OECD

de **oester** /ˈustər/ (pl: -s) oyster

de **oesterbank** /ˈustərbɑŋk/ (pl: -en) oyster bank

de **oesterzwam** /ˈustərzwɑm/ (pl: -men) oyster mushroom

het **oestrogeen** /œystroˈɣen/ (pl: oestrogenen) oestrogen

het **oeuvre** /ˈœːvrə/ oeuvre, works, body of work

de **oever** /ˈuvər/ (pl: -s) bank; shore: *de rivier is* **buiten** *haar ~s getreden* the river has burst its banks

oeverloos /ˈuvərlos/ (adj) endless, interminable: *~ gezwets* blather, claptrap

de **Oezbeek** /uzbˈek/ Uzbek

het **¹Oezbeeks** /uzbˈeks/ Uzbek

²Oezbeeks /uzbˈeks/ (adj) Uzbek

Oezbekistan /uzbˈekistɑn/ Uzbekistan

of /ɔf/ (conj) **1** (either ...) or: *je krijgt of het* **een** *of het ander* you get either the one or the other; *het is óf het* **een** *óf het ander* it is either or, you can't have it both ways; *Lisa zei weinig of* **niets** Lisa said little or nothing; **min** *of* **meer** more or less; **vroeg** *of* **laat** sooner or later, eventually **2** or: *de influenza of* **griep** influenza, or flu **3** (hardly ...) when, (no sooner ...) than: *ik weet* **niet** *beter of ...* for all I know ... **4** although, whether ... or (not), no matter (how, what, where): *of je het nu leuk vindt of niet* whether you like it or not **5** as if, as though: *hij* **doet** *of er niets gebeurd is* he is behaving (or: acts) as if nothing has happened; *het is* **net** *of het regent* it looks just as though it were raining **6** whether, if: *ik* **vraag** *me af of hij komen zal* I wonder whether (or: if) he'll come ǁ *ik weet niet,* **wie** *of het gedaan heeft* I don't know who did it; **wanneer** *of ze komt, ik weet 't niet* when she is coming I don't know; *een dag of* **tien** about ten days, ten days or so

het **offensief** /ɔfɛnsˈif/ (pl: offensieven) offensive: *in het ~ gaan* go on the offensive

het **offer** /ˈɔfər/ (pl: -s) offering, sacrifice, gift, donation: *een ~* **brengen** make a sacrifice;

zware ~s eisen take a heavy toll

de **offerande** /ɔfərandə/ (pl: -n, -s) offering, sacrifice; offertory

offeren /ˈɔfərə(n)/ (offerde, heeft geofferd) sacrifice, offer (up)

het **offerfeest** /ˈɔfərfest/ (pl: -en) ceremonial offering

het **Offerfeest** /ˈɔfərfest/ [Islam] Eid al-Adha, Celebration of Sacrifice

de **offerte** /ɔfˈɛrtə/ (pl: -s) offer; tender; quotation

de **official** /ɔfˈɪʃəl/ (pl: -s) official

officieel /ɔfiʃˈel/ (adj, adv) **1** official, formal: *iets ~* **meedelen** announce sth. officially **2** formal, ceremonial

de **officier** /ɔfisˈir/ (pl: -en) officer: [Dutch] **officier** *van justitie* public prosecutor

officieus /ɔfiʃˈøs/ (adj, adv) unofficial, semi-official

offline /ɔflˈɑjn/ (adj) offline

offpiste /ɔfpˈistə/ (adv) off-piste: *~ skiën* ski off-piste

offshore /ɔfˈɔːr/ (adj) offshore

de **offshoring** /ɔfʃɔːrɪŋ/ offshoring

ofschoon /ɔfsxˈon/ (conj) (al)though, even though: *~ hij rijk is, is hij niet gelukkig* although he is rich, he is not happy

ofte /ˈɔftə/ (conj): *nooit ~* **nimmer** not ever

oftewel /ɔftəwˈɛl/ (conj) *see ofwel*

ofwel /ɔfwˈɛl/ (conj) **1** either ... or **2** or, that is, i.e.: *de cobra ~* **brilslang** the cobra, or hooded snake

het **ogenblik** /ˈoɣə(n)blɪk/ (pl: -ken) **1** moment, instant, minute, second: *een ~* **rust** a moment's peace; *in een ~* in a moment; *juist* **op** *dat ~* just at that very moment (or: instant); *(heeft u) een ~je?* just a moment (or: minute); would you mind waiting a moment? **2** moment, time, minute

ogenblikkelijk /ˈoɣə(n)blɪkələk/ (adv) immediately, at once, this instant: *ga ~ de dokter* **halen** go and fetch the doctor immediately (or: at once)

ogenschijnlijk /ˈoɣə(n)sxɛɪnlək/ (adj, adv) apparent, ostensible; at first sight

ogenschouw /ˈoɣə(n)sxɑu/: *iets in ~ nemen* take stock of sth.

o.g.v. *op grond van* on the basis of

het/de **ohm** /om/ (pl: -s) ohm

de **ok** /ˈokɑ/ *operatiekamer* operating theatre

OK /okˈe/ (int) OK

de **okapi** /okˈapi/ (pl: -'s) okapi

oké /okˈej/ (int) OK, okay: *dat vind ik niet ~* that's not right, it's wrong

de **oker** /ˈokər/ (pl: -s) ochre

de **oksel** /ˈɔksəl/ (pl: -s) armpit

de **oktober** /ɔktˈobər/ (pl: -s) October

de **oldtimer** /ˈɔltɑjmər/ vintage car

de **oleander** /olejˈɑndər/ (pl: -s) oleander

de **olie** /ˈoli/ (pl: oliën) oil: *~ op het vuur* **gooien** add fuel to the fire

de **oliebol** /ˈolibɔl/ (pl: -len) **1** [roughly] dough-nut ball **2** [fig] idiot, fathead

de **olieboycot** /ˈolibɔjkɔt/ (pl: -s) oil boycott

de **oliebron** /ˈolibrɔn/ (pl: -nen) oil well

de **oliecrisis** /ˈolikrizɪs/ oil crisis

oliedom /olidɔm/ (adj, adv) (as) dumb as an ox

de **oliekachel** /ˈolikaχəl/ (pl: -s) oil heater

de **olielamp** /ˈolilamp/ (pl: -en) oil lamp

oliën /ˈolijə(n)/ (oliede, heeft geolied) oil, lu-bricate; grease

de **olieraffinaderij** /ˈolirɑfinadərɛi/ (pl: -en) oil refinery

het **oliesel** /ˈolisəl/ anointing, extreme unction, last rites: *het laatste (Heilig)* ~ *toedienen* ad-minister extreme unction (*or:* the last rites)

de **olietanker** /ˈolitɛŋkər/ (pl: -s) (oil) tanker

de **olieverf** /ˈolivɛrf/ oil colour(s), oil paint

de **olievlek** /ˈolivlɛk/ (pl: -ken) (oil-)slick: *zich als een ~ uitbreiden* spread unchecked

de **olievlekwerking** /ˈolivlɛkwɛrkɪŋ/ uncon-trollable expansion

de **olifant** /ˈolifɑnt/ (pl: -en) elephant: *als een ~ in een porseleinkast* like a bull in a china shop

de **olifantshuid** /ˈolifɑn(t)shœyt/ [fig] *een ~ hebben* have a thick skin, have a hide like a rhinoceros

de **oligarchie** /oliɣɑrˈχi/ (pl: -ën) oligarchy

de **olijf** /olɛif/ (pl: olijven) olive

de **Olijfberg** /olɛivbɛrχ/ Mount of Olives

de **olijfboom** /olɛivbom/ (pl: -bomen) olive (tree)

de **olijfolie** /olɛifoli/ olive oil

olijk /olək/ (adj, adv) [form] roguish, arch

de **olm** /olm/ (pl: -en) elm (tree)

o.l.v. *onder leiding van* conducted by

O.L.V. *Onze-Lieve-Vrouw* BVM; Our (Bless-ed) Lady

de **olympiade** /olɪmpijˈadə/ (pl: -s) Olympiad, Olympics, Olympic Games

olympisch /olɪmpis/ (adj) Olympic: *de Olympische Spelen* the Olympic Games, the Olympics; *het ~ vuur* the Olympic flame

¹**om** /ɔm/ (adj) **1** roundabout, circuitous: *een straatje (blokje) om* round the block **2** over, up, finished: *voor het jaar om is* before the year is out; *uw tijd is om* your time is up

²**om** /ɔm/ (adv) **1** (a)round, about; on: *doe je das om* put your scarf on; *toen zij de hoek om kwamen* when they came (a)round the cor-ner **2** about: *waar gaat het om?* what's it about?; what's the matter?

³**om** /ɔm/ (prep) **1** (a)round, about: *om de hoek* (just) round the corner **2** at: *ik zie je vanavond om acht uur* I'll see you tonight at eight (o'clock); *om een uur of negen* around nine (o'clock) **3** every: *om beurten* in turn; *om en om* in turns; *om de twee uur* every two hours **4** for (reasons of), on account of, be-cause of: *om deze reden* for this reason **5** to, in order to, so as to: *niet om te eten* not fit to eat, inedible

het **OM** /oɣm/ *Openbaar Ministerie* Public Prose-cutor

de **oma** /oma/ (pl: -'s) gran(ny), grandma, grandmother

de **omafiets** /omafits/ (pl: -en) [roughly] sit-up-and-beg type bicycle

Oman /omɑn/ Oman

de **Omaniet** /omanit/ (pl: -en) Omani

Omanitisch /omanitis/ (adj) Omani

omarmen /omɑrmə(n)/ (omarmde, heeft omarmd) embrace; hug: *een voorstel ~* ac-cept a proposal with open arms

ombinden /ɔmbɪndə(n)/ (ombond, heeft ombonden) tie on (*or:* round)

ombouwen /ɔmbɑuwə(n)/ (bouwde om, heeft omgebouwd) convert; reconstruct; re-build; alter

ombrengen /ɔmbrɛŋə(n)/ (bracht om, heeft omgebracht) kill, murder

de **ombudsman** /ɔmbʏtsmɑn/ (pl: -nen) om-budsman

ombuigen /ɔmbœyɣə(n)/ (boog om, heeft/ is omgebogen) **1** restructure, adjust, change (the direction of) **2** bend (round, down, back)

omcirkelen /ɔmsɪrkələ(n)/ (omcirkelde, heeft omcirkeld) (en)circle, ring; [fig also] surround: *de politie omcirkelde het gebouw* the police surrounded the building

omdat /ɔmdɑt/ (conj) because, as: *juist ~ ...* precisely because ...; *waarom ga je niet mee? ik er geen zin in heb* why don't you come along? because I don't feel like it

omdoen /ɔmdun/ (deed om, heeft omge-daan) put on: *zijn veiligheidsgordel ~* fasten one's seat belt

omdopen /ɔmdopə(n)/ (doopte om, heeft omgedoopt) rename

¹**omdraaien** /ɔmdrajə(n)/ (draaide om, is omgedraaid) **1** turn (round): *de brandweer-auto draaide de hoek om* the fire engine turned the corner **2** turn back (*or:* round)

²**omdraaien** /ɔmdrajə(n)/ (draaide om, heeft omgedraaid) **1** turn (round), turn over: *zich ~* roll over (on one's side) **2** reverse, swing round

omduwen /ɔmdywə(n)/ (duwde om, heeft omgeduwd) push over; knock over

de **omega** /omeɣa/ (pl: -'s) omega

de **omelet** /oməlɛt/ (pl: -ten) omelette

omfloerst /ɔmflurst/ (adj) shrouded: *met ~e stem* in a muffled voice

omgaan /ɔmɣan/ (ging om, is omgegaan) **1** go round; turn; round: *de hoek ~* turn the corner; *een blokje ~* go for (a) walk around the block **2** go about (with), associate (with); handle; manage: *zo ga je niet met mensen om* that's no way to treat people

omgaand /ɔmɣant/ (adj, adv): *per ~e ant-woorden* answer by return (of post, mail) de **omgang** /ɔmɣaŋ/ contact, association: *hij is gemakkelijk* (or: *lastig*) *in de ~* he is easy (or: difficult) to get on with

de **omgangsregeling** /ɔmɣaŋsreɣəlɪŋ/ (pl: -en) arrangement(s) concerning parental access

de **omgangstaal** /ɔmɣaŋstal/ everyday speech

de **omgangsvormen** /ɔmɣaŋsfɔrmə(n)/ (pl) manners, etiquette

¹**omgekeerd** /ɔmɣəkert/ (adj) **1** turned round; upside down; inside out; back to front: *~ evenredig* inversely proportional (to) **2** opposite, reverse

²**omgekeerd** /ɔmɣəkert/ (adv) the other way round: *het is precies ~* it's just the other way round

omgeven /ɔmɣevə(n)/ (omgaf, heeft omgeven) surround, encircle: *geheel door land ~* landlocked

de **omgeving** /ɔmɣevɪŋ/ neighbourhood, vicinity, surrounding area (or: districts)

omgooien /ɔmɣojə(n)/ (gooide om, heeft omgegooid) **1** knock over, upset **2** change round

de **omhaal** /ɔmhal/ (pl: omhalen) overhead kick ‖ *met veel ~ van woorden* in a roundabout way

omhakken /ɔmhakə(n)/ (hakte om, heeft omgehakt) chop down, cut down, fell

het **omhalen** /ɔmhalə(n)/ [Belg] collect, make a collection

de **omhaling** /ɔmhalɪŋ/ (pl: -en) [Belg] collection

omhanden /ɔmhandə(n)/ (adv): *niets ~ hebben* have nothing to do; be at a loose end

omhangen /ɔmhaŋə(n)/ (hing om, heeft omgehangen) hang over (or: round)

omheen /ɔmhen/ (adv) round (about), around: *ergens ~ draaien* talk round sth., beat about the bush; [fig] *ergens niet ~ kunnen* not be able to get round sth.

omheinen /ɔmhɛɪnə(n)/ (omheinde, heeft omheind) fence off (or: in)

de **omheining** /ɔmhɛɪnɪŋ/ (pl: -en) fence, enclosure

omhelzen /ɔmhɛlzə(n)/ (omhelsde, heeft omhelsd) embrace, hug: *iem. stevig ~ give s.o. a good hug*

de **omhelzing** /ɔmhɛlzɪŋ/ (pl: -en) embrace, hug

omhoog /ɔmhox/ (adv) **1** up (in the air) **2** up(wards); in(to) the air: *handen ~!* hands up!

omhooggaan /ɔmhoxan/ (ging omhoog, is omhooggegaan) go up(wards), rise: *de prijzen gaan omhoog* prices are going up (or: are rising)

omhooghouden /ɔmhoxhaudə(n)/ (hield omhoog, heeft omhooggehouden) hold up

omhoogkomen /ɔmhoxkomə(n)/ (kwam omhoog, is omhooggekomen) **1** come (or: get) up **2** [fig] get on (or: ahead)

omhoogzitten /ɔmhoxsɪtə(n)/ (zat omhoog, heeft omhooggezeten) [Dutch]: *met iets ~* be stuck over (or: on) sth.; be stuck with sth.

omhullen /ɔmhylə(n)/ (omhulde, heeft omhuld) envelop, wrap

het **omhulsel** /ɔmhylsəl/ (pl: -s) covering, casing, envelope, shell; husk; hull; pod

de **omissie** /ɔmɪsi/ (pl: -s) omission

de **omkadering** /ɔmkadərɪŋ/ (pl: -en) [Belg] staff-pupil ratio

omkeerbaar /ɔmkerbar/ (adj) reversible

¹**omkeren** /ɔmkerə(n)/ (keerde om, is omgekeerd) turn back, turn round

²**omkeren** /ɔmkerə(n)/ (keerde om, heeft omgekeerd) **1** turn (round); turn; invert: *zich ~* turn (a)round **2** switch (round), change (round); twist (round)

omkijken /ɔmkɛikə(n)/ (keek om, heeft omgekeken) **1** look round: *hij keek niet op of om* he didn't even look up **2** look after; worry about, bother about: *niet naar iem. ~* not worry (or: bother) about s.o.; leave s.o. to his own devices; *je hebt er geen ~ naar* it needs no looking after **3** [fig] look back: *~ naar het voorbije jaar* look back over the past year

omkleden /ɔmkledə(n)/ (kleedde om, heeft omgekleed) change, put other clothes on

omkomen /ɔmkomə(n)/ (kwam om, is omgekomen) **1** die; be killed: *~ van honger* starve to death **2** come round, turn: *hij zag haar juist de hoek ~* he saw her just (as she was) coming round (or: turning) the corner

omkoopbaar /ɔmkobar/ (adj) bribable, corruptible

omkopen /ɔmkopə(n)/ (kocht om, heeft omgekocht) bribe, buy (over), corrupt: *zich laten ~* accept a bribe

de **omkoperij** /ɔmkopərɛi/ bribery, corruption

omlaag /ɔmlax/ (adv) down, below: *naar ~* down(wards)

omlaaggaan /ɔmlaxan/ (ging omlaag, is omlaaggegaan) go down

omleggen /ɔmlɛɣə(n)/ (legde om, heeft omgelegd) **1** put round; [Am] put around; put on **2** kill

omleiden /ɔmlɛidə(n)/ (leidde om, heeft omgeleid) divert, re-route; train

de **omleiding** /ɔmlɛidɪŋ/ (pl: -en) [traf] (traffic) diversion, detour; relief route, alternative route

omliggend /ɔmlɪɣənt/ (adj) surrounding

omlijnen /ɔmlɛinə(n)/ (omlijnde, heeft omlijnd) outline

de **omlijsting** /ɔmlɛistɪŋ/ (pl: -en) frame; [fig] setting

de **omloop** /ɔmlop/ (pl: omlopen) circulation: *geld in ~ brengen* put money into circulation; *er zijn heel wat geruchten over haar in ~* there are plenty of rumours going round about her

de **omloopsnelheid** /ɔmlopsnɛlhɛɪt/ **1** rate of circulation **2** orbital velocity

¹**omlopen** /ɔmlopə(n)/ (liep om, is omgelopen) walk round, go round: *ik loop wel even om* I'll go round the back

²**omlopen** /ɔmlopə(n)/ (liep om, heeft omgelopen) (run into and) knock over

de **ommekeer** /ɔməker/ turn(about); about-turn; about-face, U-turn, revolution

het **ommetje** /ɔməcə/ (pl: -s) stroll, (little) walk

het **ommezien** /ɔməzin/: *in een ~ was hij terug* (or: *klaar*) he was back (or: finished) in a jiffy

de **ommezijde** /ɔməzɛidə/ (pl: -n) reverse (side), back, other side: *zie ~* see overleaf

de **ommezwaai** /ɔməzwaj/ (pl: -en) revolution; reversal, U-turn: *een politieke ~* a political U-turn

de **omnisport** /ɔmnispɔrt/ (pl: -en) [Belg] multifaceted sports program at youth sport camps

de **omnivoor** /ɔmnivọr/ (pl: omnivoren) omnivore

omploegen /ɔmpluɣə(n)/ (ploegde om, heeft omgeploegd) **1** plough (up) **2** plough in (or: under)

ompraten /ɔmpratə(n)/ (praatte om, heeft omgepraat) persuade, bring round, talk round; talk into; talk out of: *zich laten ~* give in, be brought around

de **omrastering** /ɔmrɑstərɪŋ/ (pl: -en) fencing, fence(s)

omrekenen /ɔmrekənə(n)/ (rekende om, heeft omgerekend) convert (to), turn (into)

¹**omrijden** /ɔmrɛidə(n)/ (reed om, heeft/is omgereden) make a detour, take a roundabout route, take the long way round

²**omrijden** /ɔmrɛidə(n)/ (reed om, heeft omgereden) knock down, run down

omringen /ɔmrɪŋə(n)/ (omringde, heeft omringd) surround, enclose

de **omroep** /ɔmrup/ (pl: -en) broadcasting corporation (or: company), (broadcasting) network

omroepen /ɔmrupə(n)/ (riep om, heeft omgeroepen) **1** broadcast, announce (over the radio, on TV) **2** call (over the PA, intercom): *iemands naam laten ~* have s.o. paged

de **omroeper** /ɔmrupər/ (pl: -s) announcer

de **omroepinstallatie** /ɔmrupɪnstɑla(t)si/ (pl: -s) sound system

omroeren /ɔmrurə(n)/ (roerde om, heeft omgeroerd) stir, churn

omruilen /ɔmrœylə(n)/ (ruilde om, heeft omgeruild) exchange, trade (in), change (over, round, places), swap

omschakelen /ɔmsxakələ(n)/ (schakelde om, heeft omgeschakeld) convert, change (or: switch) over (to)

de **omschakeling** /ɔmsxakəlɪŋ/ (pl: -en)

switch, shift, changeover

omscholen /ɔmsxolə(n)/ (schoolde om, heeft omgeschoold) retrain, re-educate: *waarom laat je je niet ~?* why don't you get retrained?

de **omscholing** /ɔmsxolɪŋ/ retraining, re-education

omschoppen /ɔmsxɔpə(n)/ (schopte om, heeft omgeschopt) kick over

omschrijven /ɔmsxrɛivə(n)/ (omschreef, heeft omschreven) **1** describe, determine **2** define, specify, state: *iemands bevoegdheden nader ~* define s.o.'s powers

de **omschrijving** /ɔmsxrɛivɪŋ/ (pl: -en) **1** description, paraphrase **2** definition, specification, characterization

omsingelen /ɔmsɪŋələ(n)/ (omsingelde, heeft omsingeld) surround, besiege

¹**omslaan** /ɔmslan/ (sloeg om, is omgeslagen) **1** turn; round: *de hoek omslaan* turn the corner **2** change; break; swing (round), veer (round): *het weer slaat om* the weather is breaking **3** overturn, topple, keel (over); capsize [ship]

²**omslaan** /ɔmslan/ (sloeg om, heeft omgeslagen) **1** fold over (or: back); turn down; turn back **2** turn (over) || *een jas ~* put a coat on

omslachtig /ɔmslɑxtəx/ (adj, adv) laborious; time-consuming; lengthy; wordy; long-winded; roundabout

het/de **omslag** /ɔmslɑx/ **1** cuff **2** cover; dust jacket

de **omslagdoek** /ɔmslɑxduk/ (pl: -en) shawl, wrap

het **omslagpunt** /ɔmslɑxpʏnt/ (pl: -en) turning point

omsluiten /ɔmslœytə(n)/ (omsloot, heeft omsloten) enclose, surround

omsmelten /ɔmsmɛltə(n)/ (smolt om, heeft omgesmolten) melt down, re-melt

omspitten /ɔmspɪtə(n)/ (spitte om, heeft omgespit) dig up, break up, turn over

omspoelen /ɔmspulə(n)/ (spoelde om, heeft omgespoeld) rinse (out), wash out, wash up

omspringen /ɔmsprɪŋə(n)/ (sprong om, heeft/is omgesprongen) deal (with): *slordig met andermans boeken ~* be careless with s.o. else's books

de **omstander** /ɔmstɑndər/ (pl: -s) bystander, onlooker, spectator: *de ~s* bystanders

omstandig /ɔmstɑndəx/ (adj, adv) elaborate: *iets ~ uitleggen* elaborate (or: amplify) on sth.

de **omstandigheid** /ɔmstɑndəxhɛit/ (pl: -heden) circumstance; situation; condition: *naar omstandigheden* considering (or: under) the circumstances; *in de gegeven omstandigheden* under (or: in) the circumstances; *wegens omstandigheden* for family reasons

omstoten /ɔmstotə(n)/ (stootte om, heeft

omgestoten) knock over

omstreden /ɔmstredə(n)/ (adj) controversial; debatable; contentious; contested; disputed: *een ~ boek* a controversial book

omstreeks /ɔmstreks/ (prep) (round) about, (a)round, towards, in the region (*or:* neighbourhood) of

de **omstreken** /ɔmstrekə(n)/ (pl) neighbourhood, district; environs; surroundings: *de stad Antwerpen en ~* the city of Antwerp and (its) environs

omtoveren /ɔmtovərə(n)/ (toverde om, heeft omgetoverd) transform

de **omtrek** /ɔmtrɛk/ (pl: -ken) **1** [maths] perimeter; circumference; periphery **2** contour(s), outline(s), silhouette; skyline **3** surroundings, vicinity, environs, surrounding district (*or:* area): *in de wijde ~* for miles around

omtrekken /ɔmtrɛkə(n)/ (omtrok, heeft omtrokken) pull down ‖ *een ~de beweging maken* **a)** make an enveloping (*or:* outflanking) movement; **b)** [fig] (try to) circumvent the issue

¹**omtrent** /ɔmtrɛnt/ (adv) about, approximately

²**omtrent** /ɔmtrɛnt/ (prep) **1** about, (a)round **2** concerning, with reference to, about

omturnen /ɔmtʏrnə(n)/ (turnde om, heeft omgeturnd) win over, bring round; [Am] bring around

omvallen /ɔmvalə(n)/ (viel om, is omgevallen) fall over (*or:* down); turn over (*or:* on its side): *~ van de slaap* be dead tired

de **omvang** /ɔmvaŋ/ **1** girth, circumference, bulk(iness) **2** dimensions, size, volume, magnitude, scope: *de volle ~ van de schade* the full extent of the damage

omvangrijk /ɔmvaŋrɛik/ (adj) sizeable; bulky; extensive

omvatten /ɔmvatə(n)/ (omvatte, heeft omvat) contain, comprise, include, cover

omver /ɔmvɛr/ (adv) over, down

omvergooien /ɔmvɛrɣojə(n)/ (gooide omver, heeft omvergegooid) knock over, bowl over, upset, overturn

omverlopen /ɔmvɛrlopə(n)/ (liep omver, heeft omvergelopen) knock, run down (*or:* over), bowl over: *omvergelopen worden* be knocked off one's feet

omverrijden /ɔmvɛrɛidə(n)/ (reed omver, heeft omvergereden) run, knock down (*or:* over)

omverwerpen /ɔmvɛrwɛrpə(n)/ (wierp omver, heeft omvergeworpen) **1** knock over (*or:* down), throw down **2** [fig] overthrow

omvliegen /ɔmvliɣə(n)/ (vloog om, is omgevlogen) **1** fly past, fly by, rush by: *een bocht ~* tear round a corner **2** fly round, tear round, race round: *de tijd vloog om* the time flew by

omvormen /ɔmvɔrmə(n)/ (vormde om,

heeft omgevormd) transform, convert (into)

omvouwen /ɔmvɑuwə(n)/ (vouwde om, heeft omgevouwen) fold down (*or:* over); turn down

omwaaien /ɔmwajə(n)/ (waaide/woei om, is omgewaaid) be (*or:* get) blown down, blow down; be blown off one's feet

de **omweg** /ɔmwɛx/ (pl: -en) detour, roundabout route, roundabout way: *langs een ~* indirectly; *een ~ maken* make a detour, take a roundabout route

de **omwenteling** /ɔmwɛntəlɪŋ/ (pl: -en) **1** rotation, revolution, turn; orbit **2** [pol] revolution, upheaval

omwille /ɔmwɪlə/ (adv): [form] *~ van* for (the sake of), because of

¹**omwisselen** /ɔmwɪsələ(n)/ (wisselde om, heeft omgewisseld) change places, swap places, change seats

²**omwisselen** /ɔmwɪsələ(n)/ (wisselde om, heeft omgewisseld) exchange (for), swap: *dollars ~ in euro* change dollars into euros

omzeilen /ɔmzɛilə(n)/ (omzeilde, heeft omzeild) skirt, get round; by-pass

de **omzendbrief** /ɔmzɛndbrif/ (pl: -brieven) [Belg] circular (letter)

de **omzet** /ɔmzɛt/ (pl: -ten) **1** turnover, volume of trade (*or:* business) **2** returns, sales, business

de **omzetbelasting** /ɔmzɛdbəlastɪŋ/ sales tax, turnover tax

omzetten /ɔmzɛtə(n)/ (zette om, heeft omgezet) **1** turn over, sell: *goederen ~* sell goods **2** convert (into), turn (into): *een terdoodveroordeling in levenslang ~* commute a sentence from death to life imprisonment

omzichtig /ɔmzɪxtəx/ (adj, adv) cautious, circumspect, prudent

omzien /ɔmzin/ (zag om, heeft omgezien) look (after)

omzwaaien /ɔmzwajə(n)/ (zwaaide om, is omgezwaaid) change subject(s)

de **omzwerving** /ɔmzwɛrvɪŋ/ (pl: -en) wandering, ramble: *nachtelijke ~en* nocturnal rambles

onaangedaan /ɔnaŋədan/ (adj) unmoved: *~ blijven* remain unmoved

onaangekondigd /ɔnaŋəkɔndəxt/ (adj) unannounced: *een ~ bezoek* a surprise visit

onaangenaam /ɔnaŋənam/ (adj, adv) unpleasant, disagreeable

onaangepast /ɔnaŋəpast/ (adj) maladjusted: *~ gedrag vertonen* show maladjusted behaviour

onaangetast /ɔnaŋətast/ (adj) unaffected; intact

onaannemelijk /ɔnaŋəmələk/ (adj) implausible, incredible, unbelievable

onaantastbaar /ɔnantɑstbar/ (adj) unassailable, impregnable

onaantrekkelijk /ɔnantrɛkələk/ (adj) unattractive, unprepossessing, unappealing

onaanvaardbaar /ɔnanvardbar/ (adj) unacceptable

onaardig /ɔnardəχ/ (adj, adv) unpleasant, unfriendly, unkind

onachtzaam /ɔnɔχtsam/ (adj, adv) inattentive, careless; negligent

onaf /ɔnɑf/ (adj) unfinished, incomplete

onafgebroken /ɔnɑfχəbrokə(n)/ (adj, adv) **1** continuous, sustained: *40 jaar ~ dienst* 40 years continuous service **2** unbroken, uninterrupted: *we hebben drie dagen ~ regen gehad* the rain hasn't let up for three days

onafhankelijk /ɔnɑfhɑŋkələk/ (adj, adv) independent (of)

de **onafhankelijkheid** /ɔnɑfhɑŋkələkhɛit/ independence

onafscheidelijk /ɔnɑfsχɛidələk/ (adj, adv) inseparable (from)

onafzienbaar /ɔnɑfsimbar/ (adj, adv) immense, vast

onbaatzuchtig /ɔmbatsyχtəχ/ (adj, adv) unselfish

onbarmhartig /ɔmbɑrmhɑrtəχ/ (adj, adv) merciless, unmerciful, ruthless

onbedaarlijk /ɔmbədarlək/ (adj, adv) uncontrollable

de **onbedachtzaamheid** /ɔmbədɔχ(t)samhɛit/ thoughtlessness, rashness

onbedekt /ɔmbədɛkt/ (adj, adv) uncovered, exposed

onbedoeld /ɔmbədult/ (adj, adv) unintentional, inadvertent: *iem. ~ kwetsen* hurt s.o. unintentionally

onbedorven /ɔmbədɔrvə(n)/ (adj) unspoilt, untainted

onbeduidend /ɔmbədœydənt/ (adj) insignificant, trivial, inconsequential

onbegaanbaar /ɔmbəɣambar/ (adj) impassable

onbegonnen /ɔmbəɣɔnə(n)/ (adj) hopeless, impossible

onbegrensd /ɔmbəɣrɛnst/ (adj) unlimited, boundless, infinite

onbegrijpelijk /ɔmbəɣrɛipələk/ (adj, adv) incomprehensible, unintelligible

het **onbegrip** /ɔmbəɣrɪp/ incomprehension, lack of understanding, ignorance

onbehaaglijk /ɔmbəhaχlək/ (adj) uncomfortable

het **onbehagen** /ɔmbəhaɣə(n)/ discomfort (about)

onbeheerd /ɔmbəhert/ (adj) abandoned, unattended, ownerless: *laat uw bagage niet ~ achter* do not leave your baggage unattended

onbeheerst /ɔmbəherst/ (adj, adv) uncontrolled, unrestrained

onbeholpen /ɔmbəhɔlpə(n)/ (adj, adv) awkward, clumsy, inept

onbehoorlijk /ɔmbəhorlək/ (adj, adv) un-

seemly; improper, indecent: *hij gedraagt zich ~* he behaves in an unseemly manner; *~e taal* indecent language; *het was nogal ~ van hem om ...* it was rather unbecoming of him to ...

onbehouwen /ɔmbəhɑuwə(n)/ (adj) coarse, crude

onbekend /ɔmbəkɛnt/ (adj) unknown, out-of-the-way, unfamiliar: *met ~e bestemming vertrekken* leave for an unknown destination

de **onbekende** /ɔmbəkɛndə/ (pl: -n) unknown (person), stranger

onbekommerd /ɔmbəkɔmərt/ (adj, adv) carefree, unconcerned

onbekwaam /ɔmbəkwam/ (adj) incompetent, incapable

onbelangrijk /ɔmbəlɑŋrɛik/ (adj, adv) unimportant, insignificant; inconsiderable: *iets ~s* sth. trivial

onbeleefd /ɔmbəleft/ (adj, adv) impolite, rude

de **onbeleefdheid** /ɔmbəlefthɛit/ impoliteness, rudeness, incivility, discourtesy; insult

onbelemmerd /ɔmbəlɛmərt/ (adj, adv) unobstructed

onbemand /ɔmbəmɑnt/ (adj) unmanned

de **onbenul** /ɔmbənyl/ (pl: -len) fool, idiot

onbenullig /ɔmbənyləχ/ (adj, adv) inane, stupid, fatuous

onbepaald /ɔmbəpalt/ (adj) **1** indefinite, unlimited **2** indefinite, indeterminate, undefined: *~ lidwoord* indefinite article

onbeperkt /ɔmbəpɛrkt/ (adj, adv) unlimited, unbounded

onbeproefd /ɔmbəpruft/ (adj) untried: *geen middel ~ laten* leave no stone unturned

onbereikbaar /ɔmbərɛigbar/ (adj) **1** inaccessible **2** unattainable, out of (*or:* beyond) reach: *een ~ ideaal* an unattainable ideal

onberekenbaar /ɔmbərekəmbar/ (adj, adv) unpredictable

onberispelijk /ɔmbərɪspələk/ (adj, adv) perfect; irreproachable

onbeschaafd /ɔmbəsχaft/ (adj, adv) **1** uncivilized **2** uneducated, unrefined

onbeschadigd /ɔmbəsχadəχt/ (adj) undamaged, intact

onbescheiden /ɔmbəsχɛidə(n)/ (adj, adv) **1** immodest, forward **2** indiscreet, indelicate **3** presumptuous, bold: *zo ~ zijn om ...* be so bold as to ...

onbeschoft /ɔmbəsχɔft/ (adj, adv) rude, illmannered, boorish

onbeschreven /ɔmbəsχrevə(n)/ (adj) blank

onbeschrijfelijk /ɔmbəsχrɛifələk/ (adj, adv) indescribable; beyond description (*or:* words) [after vb]; [depr] unspeakable: *het is ~* it defies (*or:* beggars) description

onbeslist /ɔmbəslɪst/ (adj) undecided, unresolved: *de wedstrijd eindigde ~* the match ended in a draw

onbespeelbaar /ɔmbəspelbar/ (adj) unplayable; not fit (*or:* unfit) for play

onbespoten /ɔmbəspoːtə(n)/ (adj) unsprayed

onbespreekbaar /ɔmbəspreːkbaːr/ (adj) taboo

onbesproken /ɔmbəsproːkə(n)/ (adj): *van ~ gedrag* of irreproachable (*or:* blameless) conduct

onbestaanbaar /ɔmbəstaːmbaːr/ (adj) impossible

onbestelbaar /ɔmbəstɛlbaːr/ (adj) undeliverable

onbestemd /ɔmbəstɛmt/ (adj) vague

onbestendig /ɔmbəstɛndəχ/ (adj) unsettled, variable: *het weer is ~* the weather is changeable (*or:* variable)

onbestuurbaar /ɔmbəstyːrbaːr/ (adj) **1** uncontrollable, out of control; unmanageable **2** ungovernable

onbesuisd /ɔmbəsœyst/ (adj, adv) rash

onbetaalbaar /ɔmbətaːlbaːr/ (adj) **1** prohibitive, impossibly dear **2** priceless, invaluable **3** priceless, hilarious

onbetaald /ɔmbətaːlt/ (adj) unpaid (for); outstanding; unsettled; undischarged

onbetekenend /ɔmbəteːkənənt/ (adj) insignificant

onbetrouwbaar /ɔmbətrɔubaːr/ (adj) unreliable; [pers also] untrustworthy; shady; shifty

onbetuigd /ɔmbətœyχt/ (adj): *zich niet ~ laten* keep one's end up

onbetwist /ɔmbətʋɪst/ (adj) undisputed: *de ~e kampioen* the unrivalled champion

onbevangen /ɔmbəvɑŋə(n)/ (adj, adv) open(-minded)

onbevestigd /ɔmbəvɛstəχt/ (adj) unconfirmed: *volgens ~e berichten …* there are unconfirmed reports that …

onbevlekt /ɔmbəvlɛkt/ (adj) immaculate

onbevoegd /ɔmbəvuχt/ (adj) unauthorized; unqualified

de **onbevoegde** /ɔmbəvuːɣdə/ (pl: -n) unauthorized person; unqualified person

onbevooroordeeld /ɔmbəvoːroːrdeːlt/ (adj, adv) unprejudiced, open-minded

onbevredigend /ɔmbəvreːdəɣənt/ (adj) unsatisfactory

onbewaakt /ɔmbəwaːkt/ (adj) unguarded, unattended

onbeweeglijk /ɔmbəweːɣlək/ (adj, adv) motionless

onbewerkt /ɔmbəwɛrkt/ (adj) unprocessed, raw

onbewezen /ɔmbəweːzə(n)/ (adj) unproved, unproven

onbewogen /ɔmbəwoːɣə(n)/ (adj, adv) **1** immobile **2** unmoved

onbewolkt /ɔmbəwɔlkt/ (adj) cloudless, clear

onbewoonbaar /ɔmbəwoːmbaːr/ (adj) uninhabitable

onbewoond /ɔmbəwoːnt/ (adj) uninhabited: *een ~ eiland* a desert island

onbewust /ɔmbəwʏst/ (adj, adv) unconscious (of): *iets ~ doen* do sth. unconsciously

onbezoldigd /ɔmbəzɔldəχt/ (adj) unpaid

onbezonnen /ɔmbəzɔnə(n)/ (adj, adv) unthinking, rash, thoughtless: *een ~ daad* a heedless action

onbezorgd /ɔmbəzɔrχt/ (adj, adv) carefree, unconcerned: *een ~e oude dag* a carefree old age

onbillijk /ɔmbɪlək/ (adj, adv) unfair, unreasonable

onbrandbaar /ɔmbrɑndbaːr/ (adj) incombustible, non-flammable

onbreekbaar /ɔmbreːkbaːr/ (adj) unbreakable, non-breakable

het **onbruik** /ɔmbrœyk/: *in ~ raken* fall (*or:* pass) into disuse, go out of date

onbruikbaar /ɔmbrœyɡbaːr/ (adj) unusable; useless

onbuigzaam /ɔmbœyχsam/ (adj) inflexible

de **oncoloog** /ɔŋkoloːχ/ (pl: -logen) oncologist

oncomfortabel /ɔnkɔmfɔrtaːbəl/ (adj) uncomfortable

oncontroleerbaar /ɔŋkɔntroleːrbaːr/ (adj) unverifiable

onconventioneel /ɔŋkɔnvɛn(t)ʃoneːl/ (adj, adv) unconventional

ondankbaar /ɔndɑŋkbaːr/ (adj, adv) ungrateful: *een ondankbare taak* a thankless (*or:* an unrewarding) task

de **ondankbaarheid** /ɔndɑŋkbaːrhɛit/ ingratitude

ondanks /ɔndɑŋks/ (prep) in spite of, contrary to: *~ haar inspanningen lukte het (haar) niet* for (*or:* despite) all her efforts, she didn't succeed

ondeelbaar /ɔndeːlbaːr/ (adj) indivisible: *een ~ getal* a prime number

ondefinieerbaar /ɔndefiniːjɛrbaːr/ (adj) indefinable

ondemocratisch /ɔndemokraːtis/ (adj) undemocratic

ondenkbaar /ɔndɛŋkbaːr/ (adj) inconceivable, unthinkable

¹**onder** /ɔndər/ (adv) below, at the bottom: *~ aan de bladzijde* at the foot (*or:* bottom) of the page ‖ *ten ~ gaan* go down

²**onder** /ɔndər/ (prep) **1** under, below, underneath: *hij zat ~ de prut* he was covered with mud; *de tunnel gaat ~ de rivier door* the tunnel goes (*or:* passes) under(neath) the river; *zes graden ~ nul* six degrees below zero **2** among(st): *er was ruzie ~ de supporters* there was a fight among the supporters; *~ andere* among other things; *~ ons gezegd (en gezwegen)* between you and me (and the doorpost) ‖ *~ toezicht van de politie* under police surveillance; *zij leed erg ~ het verlies* she

suffered greatly from the loss

onderaan /ondər<u>a</u>n/ (adv) at the bottom, below: ~ op de **bladzijde** at the bottom (or: foot) of the page; [fig] ~ **staan** come in last

de **onderaannemer** /<u>o</u>ndəranemər/ (pl: -s) subcontractor

onderaards /ondər<u>a</u>rts/ (adj) subterranean

onderaf /ondər<u>o</u>f/ (adv): hij heeft zich van ~ opgewerkt he has worked his way up from the bottom of the ladder

de **onderafdeling** /<u>o</u>ndəravdelɪŋ/ (pl: -en) subdepartment

de **onderarm** /<u>o</u>ndərarm/ (pl: -en) forearm

het **onderbeen** /<u>o</u>ndərben/ (pl: -benen) (lower) leg; shin; calf

onderbelicht /ondərbəlɪ<u>x</u>t/ (adj) 1 underexposed 2 [fig] neglected, give too little attention

onderbewust /ondərbəw<u>y</u>st/ (adj, adv) subconscious

het **onderbewuste** /ondərbəw<u>y</u>stə/ subconscious, unconscious

het **onderbewustzijn** /ondərbəw<u>y</u>(st)sɛɪn/ subconscious

de **onderbezetting** /<u>o</u>ndərbəzɛtɪŋ/ undermanning, being short-handed

de **onderbouw** /<u>o</u>ndərbou/ the lower classes of secondary school

onderbouwen /ondərb<u>ou</u>wə(n)/ (onderbouwde, heeft onderbouwd) build, found; [fig also] substantiate

onderbreken /ondərbr<u>e</u>kə(n)/ (onderbrak, heeft onderbroken) 1 interrupt, break 2 interrupt, cut short; break in (on)

de **onderbreking** /ondərbr<u>e</u>kɪŋ/ (pl: -en) 1 interruption: urenlang praten zonder ~ talk on (and on) for hours 2 break

onderbrengen /<u>o</u>ndərbrɛŋə(n)/ (bracht onder, heeft ondergebracht) 1 accommodate; lodge; house; put up: zijn kinderen **bij** iem. ~ lodge one's children with s.o. 2 class(ify) (with, under, in)

de **onderbroek** /<u>o</u>ndərbruk/ (pl: -en) underpants; panties

de **onderbuik** /<u>o</u>ndərbœyk/ (pl: -en) abdomen

het **onderbuikgevoel** /<u>o</u>ndərbœykɣəvul/ (instinctive) envy, hate, rancour

de **onderdaan** /<u>o</u>ndərdan/ (pl: onderdanen) subject

het **onderdak** /<u>o</u>ndərdak/ accommodation; shelter; lodging: iem. ~ **geven** accommodate (or: lodge) s.o., get s.o. a place; ~ **vinden** find accommodation

onderdanig /ondərd<u>a</u>nəx/ (adj) submissive, humble

het **onderdeel** /<u>o</u>ndərdel/ (pl: -delen) part, (sub)division; branch: het **volgend** ~ van ons programma the next item on our programme

de **onderdirecteur** /<u>o</u>ndərdirɛktør/ (pl: -en) assistant manager: ~ van een **school** deputy headmaster

onderdoen /<u>o</u>ndərdun/ (deed onder, heeft ondergedaan) be inferior (to): **voor** niemand ~ yield to no one, be second to none

onderdompelen /<u>o</u>ndərdompələ(n)/ (dompelde onder, heeft ondergedompeld) immerse, submerge

onderdoor /ondərd<u>o</u>r/ (adv) under

onderdrukken /ondərdr<u>y</u>kə(n)/ (onderdrukte, heeft onderdrukt) 1 oppress 2 suppress, repress: een **glimlach** ~ suppress a smile

de **onderdrukking** /ondərdr<u>y</u>kɪŋ/ (pl: -en) oppression

onderduiken /<u>o</u>ndərdœykə(n)/ (dook onder, is ondergedoken) 1 go into hiding, go underground 2 dive (in)

de **onderduiker** /<u>o</u>ndərdœykər/ (pl: -s) person in hiding

onderen /<u>o</u>ndərə(n)/ (adv) 1 (+ naar) down(wards); downstairs 2 (+ van) below, underneath 3 (+ van) from below; from downstairs: van ~ **af** beginnen start from scratch (or: the bottom)

[1] **ondergaan** /<u>o</u>ndərɣan/ (ging onder, is ondergegaan) go down; set: de ~de **zon** the setting sun

[2] **ondergaan** /ondərɣ<u>a</u>n/ (onderging, heeft ondergaan) undergo, go through

de **ondergang** /<u>o</u>ndərɣaŋ/ 1 ruin, (down)fall: dat **was** zijn ~ that was his undoing 2 setting

ondergeschikt /ondərɣəsx<u>ɪ</u>kt/ (adj) 1 subordinate 2 minor, secondary

de **ondergeschikte** /ondərɣəsx<u>ɪ</u>ktə/ (pl: -n) subordinate

ondergeschoven /<u>o</u>ndərɣəsxovə(n)/ (adj): [fig] een ~ **kindje** an issue that deserves more attention, a neglected issue

de **ondergetekende** /ondərɣətek<u>e</u>ndə/ (pl: -n) 1 undersigned: **ik,** ~ I, the undersigned 2 yours truly

het **ondergoed** /<u>o</u>ndərɣut/ underwear

de **ondergrens** /<u>o</u>ndərɣrɛns/ (pl: -grenzen) lower limit: een ~ **stellen** set a lower limit

de **ondergrond** /<u>o</u>ndərɣront/ (pl: -en) base; basis; foundation: witte sterren op een **blauwe** ~ white stars on a blue background

ondergronds /ondərɣr<u>o</u>nts/ (adj) underground

de **ondergrondse** /ondərɣr<u>o</u>ntsə/ (pl: -n, -s) 1 underground; [Am] subway 2 underground, resistance

onderhand /ondərh<u>a</u>nt/ (adv) meanwhile

de **onderhandelaar** /ondərh<u>a</u>ndəlar/ (pl: -s, -handelaren) negotiator

onderhandelen /ondərh<u>a</u>ndələ(n)/ (onderhandelde, heeft onderhandeld) negotiate; bargain

de **onderhandeling** /ondərh<u>a</u>ndəlɪŋ/ (pl: -en) 1 negotiation; bargaining 2 negotiation; talks

onderhands /ondərh<u>a</u>nts/ (adj, adv) 1 underhand(ed), backstairs, underhand: iets ~

regelen make hole-and-corner arrangements **2** private **3** [sport] underhand, underarm: ~ *serveren* serve underarm

onderhavig /ɔndərhavəχ/ (adj) present, in question, in hand: *in het ~e geval* in the present case

onderhevig /ɔndərhevəχ/ (adj) liable (to), subject (to)

het **onderhoud** /ɔndərhaut/ maintenance, upkeep

onderhouden /ɔndərhaudə(n)/ (onderhield, heeft onderhouden) **1** maintain, keep up; service: *het huis was slecht ~* the house was in bad repair; *betrekkingen ~ met* maintain (or: have) relations with; *een contact ~* keep in touch **2** maintain, support

onderhoudend /ɔndərhaudənt/ (adj, adv) entertaining, amusing

de **onderhoudsbeurt** /ɔndərhautsbørt/ (pl: -en) overhaul, service

de **onderhuur** /ɔndərhyr/ sublet: *iets in ~ hebben* have the subtenancy of sth.

de **onderhuurder** /ɔndərhyrdər/ (pl: -s) subtenant

¹**onderin** /ɔndərɪn/ (adv) below, at the bottom

²**onderin** /ɔndərɪn/ (prep) at the bottom of: *het ligt ~ die kast* it's at the bottom of that cupboard

de **onderjurk** /ɔndərjʏrk/ (pl: -en) slip

de **onderkaak** /ɔndərkak/ (pl: -kaken) lower jaw; mandible

de **onderkant** /ɔndərkant/ (pl: -en) underside, bottom

onderkennen /ɔndərkɛnə(n)/ (onderkende, heeft onderkend) recognize

de **onderkin** /ɔndərkɪn/ (pl: -nen) double chin

onderkoeld /ɔndərkult/ (adj) **1** hypothermic: *ernstig ~e slachtoffers* people suffering from hypothermia; *~ raken* (start to) suffer from hypothermia (or: exposure) **2** cool: *een ~e reactie* an unemotional reaction, a cold reaction

het **onderkomen** /ɔndərkomə(n)/ (pl: -s) somewhere to go (or: sleep, stay), accommodation; shelter

de **onderkruiper** /ɔndərkrœypər/ (pl: -s) **1** scab **2** squirt, shrimp

de **onderlaag** /ɔndərlaχ/ (pl: -lagen) lower layer; foundation; undercoat: [fig] *de ~ van de maatschappij* the dregs of society

onderlangs /ɔndərlɑŋs/ (adv) along the bottom (or: foot), underneath

onderlegd /ɔndərlɛχt/ (adj) (well-)grounded: *zij is goed ~* she's well educated

het **onderlichaam** /ɔndərlɪχam/ (pl: -lichamen) lower part of the body

het **onderlijf** /ɔndərlɛif/ (pl: -lijven) lower part of the body

onderling /ɔndərlɪŋ/ (adj, adv) mutual, among ourselves, among them(selves), to-

gether: *de partijen konden de kwestie ~ regelen* the parties were able to arrange the matter between (or: among) themselves

de **onderlip** /ɔndərlɪp/ (pl: -pen) lower lip: *de ~ laten hangen* [roughly] pout

onderlopen /ɔndərlopə(n)/ (liep onder, is ondergelopen) be flooded

ondermijnen /ɔndərmɛinə(n)/ (ondermijnde, heeft ondermijnd) undermine, subvert

¹**ondernemen** /ɔndərnemə(n)/ (ondernam, heeft ondernomen) undertake, take upon o.s.: *een poging ~ om* make an attempt to; *stappen ~ om* take steps to; *iets ~ tegen* do sth. about, take action against

²**ondernemen** /ɔndərnemə(n)/ (ondernam, heeft ondernomen) manage (or: run) a business: *~ zit hem in het bloed* he is a born businessman; *duurzaam ~* implement sustainable business practices, set up a sustainable business

ondernemend /ɔndərnemənt/ (adj) enterprising

de **ondernemer** /ɔndərnemər/ (pl: -s) entrepreneur, employer; operator; owner

het **ondernemerschap** /ɔndərnemərsχap/ [econ] entrepreneurship

de **onderneming** /ɔndərnemɪŋ/ (pl: -en) **1** undertaking, enterprise; venture: *het is een hele ~* it's quite an undertaking **2** company, business; [large] concern: *een ~ runnen* run a business

de **ondernemingsraad** /ɔndərnemɪŋsrat/ (pl: -raden) works council, employees council

de **onderofficier** /ɔndərɔfisir/ (pl: -en) NCO, non-commissioned officer

het **onderonsje** /ɔndərɔnʃə/ (pl: -s) private chat

onderontwikkeld /ɔndərɔntwɪkəlt/ (adj) underdeveloped, backward

onderop /ɔndərɔp/ (adv) at the bottom, below

het **onderpand** /ɔndərpant/ (pl: -en) pledge, security, collateral: *tegen ~ lenen* borrow on security

de **onderpastoor** /ɔndərpastor/ (pl: -s) [Belg; Roman Catholicism] curate, priest in charge

onderpresteren /ɔndərprɛstərə(n)/ underperform; [esp educ] underachieve

het **onderricht** /ɔndərɪχt/ instruction, tuition

onderrichten /ɔndərɪχtə(n)/ (onderrichtte, heeft onderricht) instruct, teach

onderschatten /ɔndərsχɑtə(n)/ (onderschatte, heeft onderschat) underestimate

het **onderscheid** /ɔndərsχɛit/ difference, distinction: *een ~ maken tussen ...* distinguish ... from ... (or: between) ...

¹**onderscheiden** /ɔndərsχɛidə(n)/ (onderscheidde, heeft onderscheiden) **1** distinguish, discern: *niet te ~ zijn van* be indistinguishable from **2** decorate: *~ worden met een medaille* be awarded a medal

zich ²**onderscheiden** /ɔndərsχɛidə(n)/ (onderscheidde zich, heeft zich onderscheiden) distinguish o.s. (for)

de **onderscheiding** /ɔndərsχɛidɪŋ/ (pl: -en) decoration, honour: [Belg] *met* ~ with distinction

onderscheppen /ɔndərsχɛpə(n)/ (onderschepte, heeft onderschept) intercept

het **onderschrift** /ɔndərsχrɪft/ (pl: -en) caption, legend

onderschrijven /ɔndərsχrɛivə(n)/ (onderschreef, heeft onderschreven) subscribe to, endorse

het **onderspit** /ɔndərspɪt/: *het* ~ *delven* get the worst (of it)

onderst /ɔndərst/ (adj) bottom(most), under(most)

onderstaand /ɔndərstant/ (adj) (mentioned) below

ondersteboven /ɔndərstəbovə(n)/ (adv) **1** upside down: *je houdt het* ~ you have it the wrong way up **2** upset: ~ *zijn van iets* be upset (*or:* cut up) about sth.

de **ondersteek** /ɔndərstek/ (pl: -steken) bedpan

het **onderstel** /ɔndərstɛl/ (pl: -len) chassis, undercarriage; landing gear

ondersteunen /ɔndərstønə(n)/ (ondersteunde, heeft ondersteund) **1** support; back (up) **2** [comp] support: *deze software ondersteunt de volgende bestandsformaten* this software supports the following file formats

de **ondersteuning** /ɔndərstønɪŋ/ **1** support **2** support, (public) assistance

onderstrepen /ɔndərstrepə(n)/ (onderstreepte, heeft onderstreept) underline

het **onderstuk** /ɔndərstʏk/ (pl: -ken) base, lower part

ondertekenen /ɔndərtekənə(n)/ (ondertekende, heeft ondertekend) sign

de **ondertekening** /ɔndərtekənɪŋ/ (pl: -en) **1** signing **2** signature

ondertitelen /ɔndərtitələ(n)/ (ondertitelde, heeft ondertiteld) subtitle

de **ondertiteling** /ɔndərtitəlɪŋ/ (pl: -en) subtitles

de **ondertoon** /ɔndərton/ (pl: -tonen) undertone; [fig also] undercurrent, overtone

ondertussen /ɔndərtʏsə(n)/ (adv) meanwhile, in the meantime

onderuit /ɔndərœyt/ (adv) **1** (out) from under: *je kunt er niet* ~ *haar ook te vragen* you can't avoid inviting her, too **2** down; flat; over **3** sprawled, sprawling

onderuitgaan /ɔndərœytχan/ (ging onderuit, is onderuitgegaan) topple over, be knocked off one's feet; trip; slip

onderuithalen /ɔndərœythalə(n)/ (haalde onderuit, heeft onderuitgehaald) **1** [sport] bring down, take down **2** trip up, floor: *hij werd volledig onderuitgehaald* they wiped the floor with him

ondervangen /ɔndərvɑŋə(n)/ (onderving, heeft ondervangen) overcome

onderverdelen /ɔndərvərdelə(n)/ (verdeelde onder, heeft onderverdeeld) (sub)divide; break down

de **onderverdeling** /ɔndərvərdelɪŋ/ (pl: -en) subdivision, breakdown

onderverhuren /ɔndərvərhyrə(n)/ (onderverhuurde, heeft onderverhuurd) sublet, sublease

onderverzekerd /ɔndərvərzekərt/ (adj) underinsured

ondervinden /ɔndərvɪndə(n)/ (ondervond, heeft ondervonden) experience: *medeleven* ~ meet with sympathy; *moeilijkheden* (or: *concurrentie*) ~ be faced with difficulties (*or:* competition)

de **ondervinding** /ɔndərvɪndɪŋ/ (pl: -en) experience

ondervoed /ɔndərvut/ (adj) undernourished

de **ondervoeding** /ɔndərvudɪŋ/ undernourishment; malnutrition

de **ondervraagde** /ɔndərvraɣdə/ (pl: -n) interviewee; person heard (*or:* questioned)

ondervragen /ɔndərvraɣə(n)/ (ondervroeg, heeft ondervraagd) **1** interrogate; question; examine; hear **2** interview

de **ondervraging** /ɔndərvraɣɪŋ/ (pl: -en) questioning, interrogation, examination, interview

onderwaarderen /ɔndərwardərə(n)/ (onderwaardeerde, heeft ondergewaardeerd) underestimate

onderweg /ɔndərwɛχ/ (adv) **1** on (*or:* along) the way; in transit; en route: *we zijn het* ~ *verloren* we lost it on the way **2** on one's (*or:* its, the) way

de **onderwereld** /ɔndərwerəlt/ underworld

het **onderwerp** /ɔndərwɛrp/ (pl: -en) subject (matter)

onderwerpen /ɔndərwɛrpə(n)/ (onderwierp, heeft onderworpen) subject

onderwijl /ɔndərwɛil/ (adv) meanwhile

het **onderwijs** /ɔndərwɛis/ education, teaching: *academisch* ~ university education; [Dutch] *bijzonder* ~ private education; [Belg] *buitengewoon* ~ special needs education; *hoger* ~ higher education; *lager* ~ primary education; *middelbaar (voortgezet)* ~ secondary education; [Dutch] *openbaar* ~ state education; *algemeen secundair* ~ general secondary education; [Dutch] *speciaal* ~ special needs education; [Belg] *technisch secundair* ~ secondary technical education; *voortgezet* ~ secondary education

de **onderwijsinspectie** /ɔndərwɛisɪnspɛksi/ (pl: -s) schools inspectorate

de **onderwijsinstelling** /ɔndərwɛisɪnstɛlɪŋ/ (pl: -en) educational institution

de **onderwijskunde** /ɔndərwɛiskʏndə/ didactics, theory of education

het **onderwijsprofiel** /ɔndərwɛisprofil/ educational profile

onderwijzen /ɔndərwɛizə(n)/ (onderwees, heeft onderwezen) teach, instruct: *iem.* **iets** ~ instruct s.o. in sth., teach s.o. sth.

de **onderwijzer** /ɔndərwɛizər/ (pl: -s) (school)teacher, schoolmaster, schoolmistress

de **onderzeeër** /ɔndərzejər/ (pl: -s) submarine

de **onderzetter** /ɔndərzɛtər/ (pl: -s) **1** mat, coaster **2** mat, stand

de **onderzijde** /ɔndərzɛidə/ (pl: -n) underside

het **onderzoek** /ɔndərzuk/ **1** investigation, examination, study, research: *bij nader* ~ on closer examination (*or:* inspection) **2** investigation; inquiry: *een* ~ *instellen naar* inquire into, examine, investigate **3** [med] examination, check-up

onderzoeken /ɔndərzukə(n)/ (onderzocht, heeft onderzocht) **1** examine, inspect, investigate; search; test (for): *de dokter onderzocht zijn ogen* the doctor examined his eyes **2** investigate, examine, inquire into: *mogelijkheden* ~ examine (*or:* investigate) possibilities **3** inquire into, investigate, examine ‖ *het bloed* ~ carry out a blood test

de **onderzoeker** /ɔndərzukər/ (pl: -s) researcher, research worker (*or:* scientist), investigator

de **onderzoeksrechter** /ɔndərzuksrɛxtər/ (pl: -s) [Belg] [roughly] examining magistrate

ondeskundig /ɔndɛskʏndəx/ (adj, adv) incompetent: ~ *gerepareerd* repaired amateurishly

de **ondeugd** /ɔndøxt/ vice

ondeugdelijk /ɔndøydələk/ (adj) inferior

ondeugend /ɔndøyənt/ (adj, adv) naughty, mischievous

ondiep /ɔndip/ (adj) shallow; superficial: *een* ~*e tuin* a short garden

het **ondiepe** /ɔndipə/ shallow end

het **ondier** /ɔndir/ (pl: -en) monster, beast

het **onding** /ɔndɪŋ/ (pl: -en) rotten thing, useless thing

ondoelmatig /ɔndulmatəx/ (adj, adv) inefficient

ondoenlijk /ɔndunlək/ (adj) unfeasible, impracticable

ondoordacht /ɔndordɔxt/ (adj, adv) inadequately considered, rash

ondoordringbaar /ɔndordrɪŋbar/ (adj) impenetrable; impermeable (to): *ondoordringbare duisternis* (or: *wildernis*) impenetrable darkness (*or:* wilderness)

ondoorgrondelijk /ɔndorɣrɔndələk/ (adj) unfathomable; inscrutable

ondoorzichtig /ɔndorzɪxtəx/ (adj) **1** nontransparent, opaque **2** [fig] obscure

ondraaglijk /ɔndraxlək/ (adj, adv) unbearable

ondrinkbaar /ɔndrɪŋbar/ (adj) undrinkable

ondubbelzinnig /ɔndʏbəlzɪnəx/ (adj, adv) unambiguous; unmistakable

onduidelijk /ɔndœydələk/ (adj, adv) indistinct; obscure; unclear: *de situatie is* ~ the situation is obscure (*or:* unclear); ~ *spreken* speak indistinctly

de **onduidelijkheid** /ɔndœydələkhɛit/ (pl: -heden) indistinctness, lack of clarity; [stronger] obscurity

onecht /ɔnɛxt/ (adj) **1** illegitimate **2** false **3** fake(d)

oneens /ɔnens/ (adj) in disagreement, at odds: *het met iem.* ~ *zijn* over iets disagree with s.o. about sth.

oneerbaar /ɔnerbar/ (adj, adv) indecent, improper

oneerbiedig /ɔnerbidəx/ (adj, adv) disrespectful

oneerlijk /ɔnerlək/ (adj, adv) dishonest, unfair

de **oneerlijkheid** /ɔnerləkhɛit/ (pl: -heden) dishonesty, unfairness

oneetbaar /ɔnedbar/ (adj) inedible; not fit to eat [after vb]: *dit oude brood is* ~ this stale bread is not fit to eat

oneffen /ɔnɛfə(n)/ (adj) uneven

oneigenlijk /ɔnɛiɣə(n)lək/ (adj, adv) improper: ~ *gebruik* improper use

oneindig /ɔnɛindəx/ (adj, adv) infinite, endless: ~ *groot* (or: *klein*) infinite(ly large), infinitesimal(ly)

de **oneindigheid** /ɔnɛindəxhɛit/ infinity

de **onenigheid** /ɔnenəxhɛit/ (pl: -heden) discord, disagreement

onervaren /ɔnɛrvarə(n)/ (adj, adv) inexperienced

de **onervarenheid** /ɔnɛrvarənhɛit/ inexperience, lack of experience (*or:* skill)

de **onesie** /wɔnzi/ (pl: -s) onesie

oneven /ɔnevə(n)/ (adj, adv) odd, uneven

onevenredig /ɔnevə(n)redəx/ (adj, adv) disproportionate

onevenwichtig /ɔnevə(n)wɪxtəx/ (adj) unbalanced, unstable

onfatsoenlijk /ɔnfɑtsunlək/ (adj, adv) illmannered, bad-mannered; offensive; improper; indecent

onfeilbaar /ɔnfɛilbar/ (adj, adv) infallible

onfortuinlijk /ɔnfɔrtœynlək/ (adj, adv) unfortunate, unlucky

onfris /ɔnfrɪs/ (adj, adv) **1** unsavoury; stale; musty; stuffy: *er* ~ *uitzien* not look fresh; [of pers] look unsavoury **2** unsavoury, shady: *een* ~*se affaire* an unsavoury (*or:* a shady) business

ongeacht /ɔnɣəɑxt/ (prep) irrespective of, regardless of

ongeboren /ɔnɣəborə(n)/ (adj) unborn

ongebreideld /ɔnɣəbrɛidəlt/ (adj, adv) unbridled, unrestrained

ongebruikelijk /ɔŋəbrœykələk/ (adj) unusual

ongebruikt /ɔŋəbrœykt/ (adj) unused; new

ongecompliceerd /ɔŋəkɔmplisert/ (adj, adv) uncomplicated

ongedaan /ɔŋədan/ (adj) undone: *dat kun je niet meer ~ maken* you can't go back on it now

ongedeerd /ɔŋədert/ (adj) unhurt, uninjured, unharmed

ongedekt /ɔŋədɛkt/ (adj, adv) uncovered

het **ongedierte** /ɔŋədirtə/ vermin

de **ongedocumenteerde** /ɔŋədokymɛnterdə/ (pl: -n) undocumented immigrant, illegal immigrant

het **ongeduld** /ɔŋədʏlt/ impatience

ongeduldig /ɔŋədʏldəχ/ (adj, adv) impatient

ongedurig /ɔŋədyrəχ/ (adj) restless, restive, fidgety

ongedwongen /ɔŋədwɔŋə(n)/ (adj, adv) relaxed, informal

ongeëvenaard /ɔŋəevənart/ (adj, adv) unequalled, unmatched

ongefrankeerd /ɔŋəfraŋkert/ (adj) unstamped

ongegeneerd /ɔŋəʒənert/ (adj, adv) unashamed, impertinent

ongegrond /ɔŋəγrɔnt/ (adj, adv) unfounded, groundless: *~e klachten* unfounded complaints

ongehinderd /ɔŋəhɪndərt/ (adj, adv) unhindered: *~ werken* work undisturbed

ongehoord /ɔŋəhort/ (adj, adv) outrageous: *~ laat* outrageously late

ongehoorzaam /ɔŋəhorzam/ (adj) disobedient

de **ongehoorzaamheid** /ɔŋəhorzamhɛit/ disobedience

ongehuwd /ɔŋəhywt/ (adj) single, unmarried

ongeïnteresseerd /ɔŋəɪntərɛsert/ (adj, adv) uninterested: *~ toekijken* watch with indifference

ongekend /ɔŋəkɛnt/ (adj, adv) unprecedented: *~ lage prijzen* unprecedentedly low prices; *dat is iets ~s voor hem* that is sth. quite new for him

ongekroond /ɔŋəkrɔnt/ (adj) uncrowned

ongekunsteld /ɔŋəkʏnstəlt/ (adj, adv) artless, unaffected

ongeldig /ɔŋɣɪldəχ/ (adj) invalid

ongelegen /ɔŋəleɣə(n)/ (adj, adv) inconvenient, awkward

ongeletterd /ɔŋəlɛtərt/ (adj) **1** unlettered **2** illiterate

het ¹**ongelijk** /ɔŋəlɛik/ wrong: *ik geef je geen ~* I don't blame you; *ongelijk hebben* be wrong

²**ongelijk** /ɔŋəlɛik/ (adj, adv) **1** unequal: *het is ~ verdeeld in de wereld* there's a lot of in-

justice in the world; *een ~e strijd* an unequal (*or:* a one-sided) fight **2** uneven

de **ongelijkheid** /ɔŋəlɛikhɛit/ **1** inequality; difference **2** unevenness

ongelijkmatig /ɔŋəlɛikmatəχ/ (adj, adv) uneven, unequal; irregular

ongelofelijk /ɔŋəlofələk/ (adj, adv) incredible, unbelievable

het **ongeloof** /ɔŋəlof/ disbelief

ongeloofwaardig /ɔŋəlofwardəχ/ (adj) incredible, implausible

ongelovig /ɔŋəloveχ/ (adj, adv) **1** disbelieving, incredulous **2** unbelieving

het **ongeluk** /ɔŋəlʏk/ (pl: -ken) accident: *een ~ krijgen* have an accident; *zich een ~ lachen* split one's sides (laughing), laugh one's head off; *per ~ iets verklappen* inadvertently let sth. slip; *een ~ zit in een klein hoekje* accidents will happen

het **ongelukje** /ɔŋəlʏkjə/ (pl: -s) mishap: *een ~ hebben* have a little accident

ongelukkig /ɔŋəlʏkəχ/ (adj, adv) **1** unhappy: *iem. diep ~ maken* make s.o. deeply unhappy **2** unlucky **3** unfortunate: *hij is ~ terechtgekomen* he landed awkwardly

de **ongeluksdag** /ɔŋəlʏksdaχ/ (pl: -en) unlucky day

het **ongeluksgetal** /ɔŋəlʏksχətal/ (pl: -len) unlucky number

de **ongeluksvogel** /ɔŋəlʏksfoɣəl/ (pl: -s) unlucky person

het **ongemak** /ɔŋəmak/ (pl: -ken) inconvenience, discomfort

ongemakkelijk /ɔŋəmɑkələk/ (adj, adv) uncomfortable

ongemanierd /ɔŋəmanirt/ (adj, adv) illmannered

ongemerkt /ɔŋəmɛrkt/ (adj, adv) unnoticed: *~ (weten te) ontsnappen* (manage to) escape without being noticed

ongemoeid /ɔŋəmujt/ (adj) undisturbed: *iem. ~ laten* leave s.o. alone

ongemotiveerd /ɔŋəmotivert/ (adj, adv) unmotivated, without motivation

ongenaakbaar /ɔŋənagbar/ (adj) **1** unapproachable **2** indomitable

de **ongenade** /ɔŋənadə/ **1** disgrace, disfavour: *in ~ vallen* fall into disfavour **2** displeasure

ongenadig /ɔŋənadəχ/ (adj, adv) merciless(ly): *het is ~ koud* it is bitterly cold; *hij kreeg een ~ pak voor zijn broek* he got a merciless thrashing

ongeneeslijk /ɔŋəneslək/ (adj, adv) incurable: *~ ziek* incurably ill

ongenietbaar /ɔŋənidbar/ (adj) disagreeable

het **ongenoegen** /ɔŋənuɣə(n)/ (pl: -s) displeasure, dissatisfaction

ongenood /ɔŋənot/ (adj) uninvited; unwanted: *ongenode gasten* uninvited (*or:* unwelcome) guests; [inform] gatecrashers

ongenuanceerd /ɔŋənywɑnsɛrt/ (adj, adv) over-simplified: ~ *denken* think simplistically; *een ~e uitlating* a blunt remark

ongeoorloofd /ɔŋəoɔrloft/ (adj) illegal, illicit, improper

ongepast /ɔŋəpɑst/ (adj, adv) improper; inappropriate: ~ *gedrag* inappropriate behaviour

de **ongerechtigheid** /ɔŋərɛxtəxhɛit/ (pl: -heden) **1** injustice **2** flaw

het **ongerede** /ɔŋəredə/: *in het ~ raken* break down; get lost; get mixed up

ongeregeld /ɔŋərəɣəlt/ (adj, adv) **1** disorderly, disorganized **2** irregular: *op ~e tijden* at odd times ‖ *een zootje ~* a mixed bag; a motley crew

de **ongeregeldheden** /ɔŋərəɣəlthedə(n)/ (pl) disturbances, disorders

ongerept /ɔŋərɛpt/ (adj) untouched, unspoilt

het **ongerief** /ɔŋərif/ inconvenience

ongerijmd /ɔŋərɛɪmt/ (adj, adv) absurd: *een bewijs uit het ~e* an indirect demonstration (*or*: proof)

ongerust /ɔŋərʏst/ (adj, adv) worried, anxious (for): *ik begin ~ te worden* I'm beginning to get worried

de **ongerustheid** /ɔŋərʏsthɛit/ concern, worry

ongeschikt /ɔŋəsxɪkt/ (adj, adv) unsuitable

ongeschonden /ɔŋəsxɔndə(n)/ (adj) intact, undamaged

ongeschoold /ɔŋəsxolt/ (adj) unskilled, untrained

ongeslagen /ɔŋəslaɣə(n)/ (adj) unbeaten

ongesteld /ɔŋəstɛlt/ (adj): *zij is ~* she is having her period

ongestoord /ɔŋəstort/ (adj, adv) **1** undisturbed **2** clear: *~e ontvangst* clear reception

ongestraft /ɔŋəstrɑft/ (adj, adv) unpunished: *iets ~ doen* get away with sth.

ongetrouwd /ɔŋətrɑut/ (adj) unmarried, single: *~e oom* bachelor uncle; *~e tante* maiden aunt

ongetwijfeld /ɔŋətwɛɪfəlt/ (adv) no doubt, without a doubt, undoubtedly

ongevaarlijk /ɔŋəvarlək/ (adj) harmless, safe

het **ongeval** /ɔŋəvɑl/ (pl: -len) accident

de **ongevallenverzekering** /ɔŋəvɑlə(n)vərzekərɪŋ/ (pl: -en) accident insurance

ongeveer /ɔŋəver/ (adv) about, roughly, around: *dat is het ~* that's about it

ongevoelig /ɔŋəvuləx/ (adj, adv) insensitive (to), insensible (to)

de **ongevoeligheid** /ɔŋəvuləxhɛit/ insensitivity

ongevraagd /ɔŋəvraxt/ (adj) unasked(-for), uninvited

ongewapend /ɔŋəwapənt/ (adj) unarmed

ongewenst /ɔŋəwɛnst/ (adj) unwanted, undesired; undesirable

ongewerveld /ɔŋəwɛrvəlt/ (adj) invertebrate: *~e dieren* invertebrates

ongewijzigd /ɔŋəwɛɪzəxt/ (adj) unaltered, unchanged

ongewild /ɔŋəwɪlt/ (adj, adv) **1** unintentional, unintended **2** unwanted

ongewis /ɔŋəwɪs/ (adj) uncertain

ongewoon /ɔŋəwon/ (adj, adv) unusual

ongezellig /ɔŋəzɛləx/ (adj, adv) **1** unsociable **2** cheerless, comfortless **3** unenjoyable, dreary, no fun

ongezien /ɔŋəzin/ (adj, adv) **1** unseen, unnoticed: *hij verliet ~ de kamer* he left the room unnoticed **2** (sight) unseen: *hij kocht het huis ~* he bought the house (sight) unseen **3** unprecedented

ongezoet /ɔŋəzut/ (adj) unsweetened

ongezond /ɔŋəzɔnt/ (adj, adv) **1** unhealthy **2** unsound, unhealthy

ongezouten /ɔŋəzɑutə(n)/ (adj) **1** unsalted, saltless **2** unvarnished; strong, outspoken

ongrijpbaar /ɔŋɣrɛibar/ (adj) elusive

ongunstig /ɔŋɣʏnstəx/ (adj, adv) unfavourable: *in het ~ste geval* at (the) worst; *op een ~ moment* at an awkward moment

onguur /ɔnɣyr/ (adj) **1** unsavoury **2** rough

onhaalbaar /ɔnhalbar/ (adj) unfeasible

onhandelbaar /ɔnhɑndəlbar/ (adj) unmanageable, unruly, intractable

onhandig /ɔnhɑndəx/ (adj, adv) clumsy, awkward: *zij is erg ~* she's all fingers and thumbs

de **onhandigheid** /ɔnhɑndəxhɛit/ (pl: -heden) clumsiness, awkwardness

onhebbelijk /ɔnhɛbələk/ (adj, adv) unmannerly: *de ~e gewoonte hebben om … have* the objectionable habit of …

het **onheil** /ɔnhɛil/ (pl: -en) calamity, disaster; doom

onheilspellend /ɔnhɛilspɛlənt/ (adj, adv) ominous

de **onheilsprofeet** /ɔnhɛilsprofet/ (pl: -profeten) prophet of doom

onherbergzaam /ɔnhɛrbɛrxsam/ (adj, adv) inhospitable

onherkenbaar /ɔnhɛrkɛmbar/ (adj, adv) unrecognizable

onherroepelijk /ɔnhɛrupələk/ (adj, adv) irrevocable

onherstelbaar /ɔnhɛrstɛlbar/ (adj, adv) irreparable: *~ beschadigd* damaged beyond repair

onheus /ɔnhøs/ (adj, adv) impolite

on hold /ɔnhoːlt/ (adv): *een project ~ zetten* put a project on hold

onhoorbaar /ɔnhorbar/ (adj, adv) inaudible

onhoudbaar /ɔnhɑudbar/ (adj) **1** unbearable, intolerable **2** unstoppable

onhygiënisch /ɔnhiɣ(i)jenis/ (adj, adv) unhygienic, insanitary

onjuist /ɔnjœyst/ (adj, adv) **1** inaccurate, false **2** incorrect, mistaken

onkerkelijk /ɔnkɛrkələk/ (adj) nondenominational; nonchurchgoing

onkies /ɔnkis/ (adj, adv) indelicate

onklaar /ɔnklar/ (adj): *iets ~ maken* put sth. out of order, inactivate sth.

de **onkosten** /ɔnkɔstə(n)/ (pl) **1** expense(s), expenditure: *~ vergoed* (all) expenses covered **2** extra expense(s)

de **onkostenvergoeding** /ɔnkɔstə(n)vərɣudɪŋ/ (pl: -en) payment (*or:* reimbursement) of expenses; mileage allowance

onkreukbaar /ɔnkrøgbar/ (adj) upright, unimpeachable

het **onkruid** /ɔnkrœyt/ weed(s): *~ vergaat niet* ill weeds grow apace

onkuis /ɔnkœys/ (adj, adv) **1** improper, indecent **2** unchaste, impure

de **onkunde** /ɔnkyndə/ ignorance

onkwetsbaar /ɔnkwɛtsbar/ (adj, adv) invulnerable

onlangs /ɔnlɑŋs/ (adv) recently, lately: *ik heb hem ~ nog gezien* I saw him just the other day

onleesbaar /ɔnlezbar/ (adj, adv) **1** illegible **2** unreadable

online /ɔnlɑjn/ (adj) online: *altijd ~ zijn* always be online

onlogisch /ɔnloɣis/ (adj, adv) illogical

de **onlusten** /ɔnlʏstə(n)/ (pl) riots, disturbances

de **onmacht** /ɔmɑxt/ impotence, powerlessness

onmatig /ɔmatəɣ/ (adj, adv) intemperate, immoderate, excessive

de **onmens** /ɔmɛns/ (pl: -en) brute, beast

onmenselijk /ɔmɛnsələk/ (adj, adv) inhuman

onmerkbaar /ɔmɛrgbar/ (adj, adv) unnoticeable, imperceptible

onmetelijk /ɔmetələk/ (adj) immense, immeasurable

onmiddellijk /ɔmɪdələk/ (adj, adv) immediate, immediately, directly, at once, straightaway: *ik kom ~ naar Utrecht* I'm coming to Utrecht straightaway (*or:* at once, immediately)

de **onmin** /ɔmɪn/: *met iem. in ~ leven* be at odds with s.o.

onmisbaar /ɔmɪzbar/ (adj, adv) indispensable, essential

onmiskenbaar /ɔmɪskɛmbar/ (adj, adv) unmistakable, indisputable: *hij lijkt ~ op zijn vader* he looks decidedly like his father

onmogelijk /ɔmoɣələk/ (adj, adv) impossible: *een ~ verhaal* a preposterous story; *ik kan ~ langer blijven* I can't possibly stay any longer; *iem. het leven ~ maken* pester the life out of s.o.; *zich ~ maken* make oneself impossible

onmondig /ɔmɔndəɣ/ (adj) incapable (of self-government)

onnadenkend /ɔnadɛnkənt/ (adj, adv) unthinking: *~ handelen* act without thinking

onnatuurlijk /ɔnatyrlək/ (adj, adv) unnatural

onnauwkeurig /ɔnɑukørəɣ/ (adj, adv) inaccurate

de **onnauwkeurigheid** /ɔnɑukørəɣhɛit/ inaccuracy

onnavolgbaar /ɔnavɔlɣbar/ (adj, adv) inimitable

onnodig /ɔnodəɣ/ (adj, adv) unnecessary, needless, superfluous: *~ te zeggen dat ...* needless to say ...

onnozel /ɔnozəl/ (adj, adv) foolish, silly: *met een ~e grijns* with a sheepish grin

de **onnozelaar** /ɔnozəlar/ (pl: -s) [Belg; depr] Simple Simon, birdbrain

onofficieel /ɔnofiɕel/ (adj, adv) unofficial

onomstotelijk /ɔnɔmstotələk/ (adj) indisputable, conclusive

onomwonden /ɔnɔmwɔndə(n)/ (adj, adv) frank, plain

ononderbroken /ɔnɔndərbrokə(n)/ (adj, adv) continuous, uninterrupted

onontbeerlijk /ɔnɔntberlək/ (adj) indispensable

onontkoombaar /ɔnɔntkombar/ (adj, adv) inescapable, inevitable: *dat leidt ~ tot verlies* that inevitably leads to loss(es)

onooglijk /ɔnoxlək/ (adj, adv) unsightly, ugly

onopgemerkt /ɔnɔpxəmɛrkt/ (adj, adv) unnoticed, unobserved

onophoudelijk /ɔnɔphɑudələk/ (adj, adv) continuous, ceaseless, incessant

onoplettend /ɔnɔplɛtənt/ (adj, adv) inattentive, inadvertent

onoplosbaar /ɔnɔplɔzbar/ (adj) **1** insoluble, indissoluble **2** unsolvable

onopvallend /ɔnɔpfɑlənt/ (adj, adv) inconspicuous, nondescript; unobtrusive; discreet: *~ te werk gaan* act discreetly

onopzettelijk /ɔnɔpsɛtələk/ (adj, adv) unintentional, inadvertent

onovergankelijk /ɔnovərɣɑŋkələk/ (adj, adv) [linguistics] intransitive

onoverkomelijk /ɔnovərkɔmələk/ (adj) insurmountable

onovertroffen /ɔnovərtrɔfə(n)/ (adj) unsurpassed, unrivalled

onoverwinnelijk /ɔnovərwɪnələk/ (adj) invincible

onoverzichtelijk /ɔnovərzɪxtələk/ (adj, adv) cluttered, poorly organized (*or:* arranged)

onpaar /ɔmpar/ (adj) unpaired, odd

onparlementair /ɔmpɑrləmɛntɛːr/ (adj)
unparliamentary

onpartijdig /ɔmpɑrtɛidəχ/ (adj, adv) impartial, unbiased

de **onpartijdigheid** /ɔmpɑrtɛidəχhɛit/ impartiality

onpasselijk /ɔmpɑsələk/ (adj) sick

onpeilbaar /ɔmpɛilbɑr/ (adj) **1** unfathomable **2** unlimited

onpersoonlijk /ɔmpərsonlək/ (adj, adv)
impersonal

onplezierig /ɔmpləzirəχ/ (adj, adv) unpleasant, nasty

onpraktisch /ɔmprɑktis/ (adj, adv) impractical

onprettig /ɔmprɛtəχ/ (adj, adv) unpleasant,
disagreeable, nasty

onproductief /ɔmprodyktif/ (adj, adv) unproductive

het **onraad** /ɔnrat/ trouble, danger: ~ *bespeu-*
ren smell a rat

onrealistisch /ɔnrejalɪstis/ (adj) unrealistic

het **onrecht** /ɔnrɛχt/ injustice, wrong: *iem.* ~
(aan)doen do s.o. wrong; *sociaal* ~ social injustice; *ten* ~*e* a) erroneously, mistakenly;
b) wrongfully, improperly

onrechtmatig /ɔnrɛχtmatəχ/ (adj, adv) unlawful, illegal; wrongful; unjust

onrechtvaardig /ɔnrɛχtfɑrdəχ/ (adj, adv)
unjust

de **onrechtvaardigheid** /ɔnrɛχtfɑrdəχhɛit/
(pl: -heden) injustice, wrong

onredelijk /ɔnredələk/ (adj, adv) unreasonable, unfounded

onregelmatig /ɔnreɣəlmatəχ/ (adj, adv) irregular

onreglementair /ɔnreɣləmɛntɛːr/ (adj) not
regulatory

onrein /ɔnrɛin/ (adj, adv) unclean

onrendabel /ɔnrɛndabəl/ (adj) uneconomic

onrijp /ɔnrɛip/ (adj) **1** unripe, unseasoned
2 immature

onroerend /ɔnrurənt/ (adj) immovable:
makelaar in ~ *goed* estate agent

de **onroerendezaakbelasting** /ɔnrurəndə-
zaɡbəlɑstɪŋ/ [Dutch] property tax(es)

de **onrust** /ɔnryst/ restlessness, agitation: ~
zaaien stir up trouble

onrustbarend /ɔnrystbarənt/ (adj, adv)
alarming

onrustig /ɔnrystəχ/ (adj, adv) restless, turbulent

de **onruststoker** /ɔnrystokər/ (pl: -s) troublemaker, agitator

het **¹ons** /ɔns/ (pl: -en, onzen) quarter of a pound,
four ounces: *een* ~ *ham* a quarter of ham

²ons /ɔns/ (pers pron) us: *het is* ~ *een genoe-*
gen (it's) our pleasure; *onder* ~ *gezegd* (just)
between ourselves; *dat is van* ~ that's ours,
that belongs to us

³ons /ɔns/ (poss pron) our: ~ *huis* our house;

uw boeken en die van ~ your books and ours

onsamenhangend /ɔnsamə(n)hɑŋənt/
(adj, adv) incoherent, disconnected

onschadelijk /ɔnsχadələk/ (adj, adv) harmless; innocent; non-noxious: *een bom* ~ *ma-*
ken defuse a bomb

onschatbaar /ɔnsχɑdbar/ (adj, adv) invaluable: *van onschatbare waarde zijn* be invaluable

onschendbaar /ɔnsχɛndbar/ (adj) immune

onscherp /ɔnsχɛrp/ (adj) out of focus,
blurred

de **onschuld** /ɔnsχʏlt/ innocence

onschuldig /ɔnsχʏldəχ/ (adj) **1** innocent,
guiltless **2** innocent, harmless

onsmakelijk /ɔnsmakələk/ (adj, adv) **1** distasteful, unpalatable **2** distasteful, disagreeable, unsavoury

onsportief /ɔnspɔrtif/ (adj, adv) unsport-
ing, unsportsmanlike: *hij heeft zich* ~ *gedra-*
gen he behaved unsportingly

onstabiel /ɔnstabil/ (adj, adv) unstable

onsterfelijk /ɔnstɛrfələk/ (adj, adv) immortal: *zich* ~ *belachelijk maken* make an absolute fool of oneself

de **onsterfelijkheid** /ɔnstɛrfələkhɛit/ immortality

onstuimig /ɔnstœyməχ/ (adj) **1** turbulent
2 passionate, tempestuous

onstuitbaar /ɔnstœydbar/ (adj, adv) unstoppable

onsympathiek /ɔnsɪmpatik/ (adj, adv) un-
congenial: *een* ~*e houding* an unengaging
manner

onszelf /ɔnsɛlf/ (ref pron) ourselves

ontaard /ɔntart/ (adj) degenerate

ontaarden /ɔntardə(n)/ (ontaardde, is ontaard) degenerate (into), deteriorate

ontactisch /ɔntɑktis/ (adj) impolitic

ontberen /ɔntberə(n)/ (ontbeerde, heeft
ontbeerd) lack: *iets moeten* ~ do (*or:* go)
without sth.

de **ontbering** /ɔntberɪŋ/ (pl: -en) hardship,
(de)privation

ontbieden /ɔntbidə(n)/ (ontbood, heeft
ontboden) summon, send for

het **ontbijt** /ɔntbɛit/ breakfast: *een kamer met* ~
bed and breakfast, B & B

ontbijten /ɔntbɛitə(n)/ (ontbeet, heeft
ontbeten) (have) breakfast

de **ontbijtkoek** /ɔntbɛitkuk/ (pl: -en) [Dutch]
[roughly] gingercake, gingerbread

ontbinden /ɔntbɪndə(n)/ (ontbond, heeft
ontbonden) dissolve; disband; annul

de **ontbinding** /ɔntbɪndɪŋ/ (pl: -en) **1** annulment **2** decomposition, decay; corruption
[also fig]: *tot* ~ *overgaan* decompose, decay;
in staat van ~ in a state of decomposition

ontbloot /ɔntblot/ (adj) bare, naked

ontbloten /ɔntblotə(n)/ (ontblootte, heeft
ontbloot) bare; expose

de **ontboezeming** /ɔndbu̱zəmɪŋ/ (pl: -en) outpouring

ontbossen /ɔndbɔ̱sə(n)/ (ontboste, heeft ontbost) deforest

ontbranden /ɔndbrɑ̱ndə(n)/ (ontbrandde, is ontbrand) ignite

ontbreken /ɔndbre̱kə(n)/ (ontbrak, heeft ontbroken) **1** be lacking (in): *waar het aan ontbreekt is ...* what's lacking is ...; *er ontbreekt nog veel aan* there's still much to be desired **2** be absent, be missing

ontcijferen /ɔntsɛi̱fərə(n)/ (ontcijferde, heeft ontcijferd) decipher

ontdaan /ɔnda̱n/ (adj) upset, disconcerted

ontdekken /ɔndɛ̱kə(n)/ (ontdekte, heeft ontdekt) discover: *iets bij toeval ~* hit upon (*or:* stumble on) sth.

de **ontdekker** /ɔndɛ̱kər/ (pl: -s) discoverer

de **ontdekking** /ɔndɛ̱kɪŋ/ (pl: -en) discovery, find: *een ~ doen* make a discovery

de **ontdekkingsreiziger** /ɔndɛ̱kɪŋsrɛizəɣər/ (pl: -s) explorer, discoverer

zich **ontdoen** /ɔndu̱n/ (ontdeed zich, heeft zich ontdaan) (+ van) dispose of, get rid of, remove

ontdooien /ɔndo̱jə(n)/ (ontdooide, is ontdooid) thaw, defrost; melt

ontduiken /ɔndœy̱kə(n)/ (ontdook, heeft ontdoken) evade, elude, dodge: *de belasting ~ evade* (paying one's) taxes

ontegenzeglijk /ɔnteɣənzɛ̱ɣlək/ (adj) undeniable, incontestable

onteigenen /ɔntɛi̱ɣənə(n)/ (onteigende, heeft onteigend) **1** expropriate **2** dispossess

ontelbaar /ɔntɛ̱lbaːr/ (adj, adv) countless, innumerable

ontembaar /ɔntɛ̱mbaːr/ (adj) untameable, indomitable

onterecht /ɔntərɛ̱xt/ (adj, adv) undeserved, unjust

onteren /ɔnte̱rə(n)/ (onteerde, heeft onteerd) dishonour, violate

onterven /ɔntɛ̱rvə(n)/ (onterfde, heeft onterfd) disinherit

ontevreden /ɔntəvre̱də(n)/ (adj, adv) dissatisfied (with): *je mag niet ~ zijn* (you) mustn't grumble

de **ontevredenheid** /ɔntəvre̱dənhɛit/ dissatisfaction (about, with)

zich **ontfermen** /ɔntfɛ̱rmə(n)/ (ontfermde zich, heeft zich ontfermd) (+ over) take pity on

ontfutselen /ɔntfʏ̱tsələ(n)/ (ontfutselde, heeft ontfutseld) filch, pilfer

ontgaan /ɔntxa̱n/ (ontging, is ontgaan) **1** escape, pass (by): *de overwinning kon ons niet meer ~* victory was ours **2** escape, miss, fail to notice: *het kon niemand ~ dat* no one could fail to notice that **3** escape, elude: *de logica daarvan ontgaat mij* the logic of it escapes me

ontgelden /ɔntxɛ̱ldə(n)/: *hij heeft het moe-*

ten ~ he got it in the neck, he had to pay for it

ontginnen /ɔntxɪ̱nə(n)/ (ontgon, heeft ontgonnen) reclaim; cultivate

de **ontginning** /ɔntxɪ̱nɪŋ/ exploitation, development; reclamation

ontglippen /ɔntxlɪ̱pə(n)/ (ontglipte, is ontglipt) slip, get away: *de bal ontglipte hem* the ball slipped out of his hands

de **ontgoocheling** /ɔntxo̱xəlɪŋ/ (pl: -en) disillusionment

ontgroeien /ɔntxru̱jə(n)/ (ontgroeide, is ontgroeid) outgrow: [fig] *de kinderschoenen* (*or: schoolbanken*) *ontgroeid zijn* have left one's childhood (*or:* schooldays) behind

de **ontgroening** /ɔntxru̱nɪŋ/ ragging; [Am] hazing

het **onthaal** /ɔntha̱l/ **1** welcome, reception **2** [Belg] reception

de **onthaalouder** /ɔntha̱laudər/ [Belg] temporary host to (foreign) children

onthaasten /ɔntha̱stə(n)/ (onthaastte, heeft onthaast) de-stress, relax, calm down

onthalen /ɔntha̱lə(n)/ (onthaalde, heeft onthaald) entertain: *iem. warm ~* give s.o. a warm welcome

onthand /ɔntha̱nt/ (adj) [Dutch] inconvenienced

ontharen /ɔntha̱rə(n)/ (onthaarde, heeft onthaard) depilate

onthecht /ɔnthɛ̱xt/ (adj) detached

ontheemd /ɔnthe̱mt/ (adj) homeless; [fig] uprooted

ontheffen /ɔnthɛ̱fə(n)/ (onthief, heeft ontheven) exempt, release

de **ontheffing** /ɔnthɛ̱fɪŋ/ (pl: -en) exemption; release: *~ hebben van* be released from

onthoofden /ɔntho̱vdə(n)/ (onthoofdde, heeft onthoofd) behead, decapitate

de **onthoofding** /ɔntho̱vdɪŋ/ (pl: -en) decapitation, beheading

¹onthouden /ɔntho̱udə(n)/ (onthield, heeft onthouden) remember: *goed gezichten kunnen ~* have a good memory for faces; *ik zal het je helpen ~* I'll remind you of it

zich **²onthouden** /ɔntho̱udə(n)/ (onthield zich, heeft zich onthouden) abstain (from), refrain (from)

de **onthouding** /ɔntho̱udɪŋ/ **1** abstention **2** continence, abstinence

onthullen /ɔnthʏ̱lə(n)/ (onthulde, heeft onthuld) **1** unveil **2** reveal, disclose, divulge

de **onthulling** /ɔnthʏ̱lɪŋ/ (pl: -en) **1** unveiling **2** revelation, disclosure: *opzienbarende ~en* startling disclosures

onthutst /ɔnthʏ̱tst/ (adj, adv) disconcerted, dismayed

¹ontkennen /ɔntkɛ̱nə(n)/ (ontkende, heeft ontkend) plead not guilty

²ontkennen /ɔntkɛ̱nə(n)/ (ontkende, heeft ontkend) deny, negate: *hij ontkende iets met*

de zaak te maken te hebben he denied any involvement in the matter

ontkennend /ɔntkɛnənt/ (adj, adv) negative

de **ontkenning** /ɔntkɛnɪŋ/ (pl: -en) denial, negation

de **ontkerkelijking** /ɔntkɛrkələkɪŋ/ secularization

ontketenen /ɔntketənə(n)/ (ontketende, heeft ontketend) let loose; unchain; unleash

ontkiemen /ɔntkimə(n)/ (ontkiemde, is ontkiemd) germinate; [fig also] bud

ontkleden /ɔntkledə(n)/ (ontkleedde, heeft ontkleed) undress: *zich* ~ undress

de **ontknoping** /ɔntknopɪŋ/ (pl: -en) ending, dénouement: *zijn* ~ *naderen* reach a climax

ontkomen /ɔntkomə(n)/ (ontkwam, is ontkomen) **1** escape, get away **2** evade, get round

ontkoppelen /ɔntkɔpələ(n)/ (ontkoppelde, heeft ontkoppeld) uncouple; [fig] disconnect, unlink

ontkrachten /ɔntkrɑxtə(n)/ (ontkrachtte, heeft ontkracht) enfeeble: *een bewijs* ~ take the edge off a piece of evidence

ontkurken /ɔntkʏrkə(n)/ (ontkurkte, heeft ontkurkt) uncork, unstop(per)

ontladen /ɔntladə(n)/ (ontlaadde, heeft ontladen) unload; discharge: [fig] *zich* ~ be released

de **ontlading** /ɔntladɪŋ/ (pl: -en) **1** release **2** discharge

¹**ontlasten** /ɔntlɑstə(n)/ (ontlastte, heeft ontlast) unburden, relieve: *we moeten hem wat* ~ we've got to take some of the weight off his shoulders

zich ²**ontlasten** /ɔntlɑstə(n)/ (ontlastte zich, heeft zich ontlast) empty (*or:* move, open) one's bowels

de **ontlasting** /ɔntlɑstɪŋ/ stools, (human) excrement; faeces

ontleden /ɔntledə(n)/ (ontleedde, heeft ontleed) **1** dissect, anatomize **2** analyse: *een zin* ~ analyse (*or:* parse) a sentence

de **ontleding** /ɔntledɪŋ/ (pl: -en) **1** dissection **2** analysis

ontlenen /ɔntlenə(n)/ (ontleende, heeft ontleend) derive (from), borrow (from), take (from): *aan deze verklaring kunnen geen rechten worden ontleend* no rights may be derived from this statement

ontlokken /ɔntlɔkə(n)/ (ontlokte, heeft ontlokt) elicit (from)

ontlopen /ɔntlopə(n)/ (ontliep, is ontlopen) differ from: *die twee* ~ *elkaar* niet veel they don't differ greatly

ontluiken /ɔntlœykə(n)/ (ontlook, is ontloken) burgeon, bud: *een ~de liefde* an awakening love; *een ~d talent* a burgeoning (*or:* budding) talent

ontmaagden /ɔntmaɣdə(n)/ (ontmaagd-

de, heeft ontmaagd) deflower

ontmantelen /ɔntmɑntələ(n)/ (ontmantelde, heeft ontmanteld) dismantle, strip

ontmaskeren /ɔntmɑskərə(n)/ (ontmaskerde, heeft ontmaskerd) unmask, expose

ontmoedigen /ɔntmudəɣə(n)/ (ontmoedigde, heeft ontmoedigd) discourage, demoralize; deter: *we zullen ons niet laten* ~ *door … we* won't let … get us down

ontmoeten /ɔntmutə(n)/ (ontmoette, heeft ontmoet) **1** meet, run into, bump into **2** meet, see

de **ontmoeting** /ɔntmutɪŋ/ (pl: -en) meeting, encounter: *een toevallige* ~ a chance meeting (*or:* encounter)

de **ontmoetingsplaats** /ɔntmutɪŋsplats/ (pl: -en) meeting place

ontnemen /ɔntnemə(n)/ (ontnam, heeft ontnomen) take away

de **ontnieter** /ɔntnitər/ staple extractor

de **ontnuchtering** /ɔntnʏxtərɪŋ/ disillusionment, disenchantment

ontoegankelijk /ɔntuɣɑŋkələk/ (adj) inaccessible, impervious (to)

ontoelaatbaar /ɔntuladbar/ (adj) inadmissible

ontoereikend /ɔnturɛikənt/ (adj, adv) inadequate

ontoerekeningsvatbaar /ɔnturekənɪŋsfɑdbar/ (adj) not responsible; [law] of unsound mind

ontoonbaar /ɔntombar/ (adj) unpresentable

ontploffen /ɔntplɔfə(n)/ (ontplofte, is ontploft) explode, blow up: *ik dacht dat hij zou* ~ I thought he'd explode

de **ontploffing** /ɔntplɔfɪŋ/ (pl: -en) explosion

ontplooien /ɔntplojə(n)/ (ontplooide, heeft ontplooid) develop

zich **ontpoppen** /ɔntpɔpə(n)/ (ontpopte zich, heeft zich ontpopt) reveal o.s. (as), turn out (to be)

ontrafelen /ɔntrafələ(n)/ (ontrafelde, heeft ontrafeld) unravel, disentangle

ontredderd /ɔntrɛdərt/ (adj) upset, broken down: *in ~e toestand* in a desperate situation

ontregeld /ɔntreɣəlt/ (adj) unsettled, disordered

ontregelen /ɔntreɣələ(n)/ (ontregelde, heeft ontregeld) disorder, disorganize, dislocate

ontroeren /ɔntrurə(n)/ (ontroerde, heeft ontroerd) move, touch

ontroerend /ɔntrurənt/ (adj) moving, touching; tear-jerking

de **ontroering** /ɔntrurɪŋ/ (pl: -en) emotion

ontroostbaar /ɔntrostbar/ (adj) inconsolable, broken-hearted

de ¹**ontrouw** /ɔntrɑu/ **1** disloyalty, unfaithfulness **2** unfaithfulness, infidelity

²**ontrouw** /ɔntrɑu/ (adj) **1** disloyal (to), un-

true (to) **2** unfaithful

ontruimen /ɔntrœymə(n)/ (ontruimde, heeft ontruimd) **1** clear, vacate **2** clear, evacuate: *de politie moest het **pand** ~* the police had to clear the building

de **ontruiming** /ɔntrœymɪŋ/ (pl: -en) **1** evacuation **2** eviction

ontschepen /ɔntsxepə(n)/ (ontscheepte, is ontscheept) disembark

ontschieten /ɔntsxitə(n)/ (ontschoot, is ontschoten) slip, elude

ontsieren /ɔntsirə(n)/ (ontsierde, heeft ontsierd) mar, blot

ontslaan /ɔntslan/ (ontsloeg, heeft ontslagen) **1** dismiss, discharge: *ontslagen **worden*** be dismissed; *iem. op staande voet ~* dismiss s.o. on the spot **2** relieve, discharge: *een patiënt ~ **uit** een ziekenhuis* discharge a patient from hospital

het **ontslag** /ɔntslɔx/ (pl: -en) **1** dismissal, discharge: *eervol ~* honourable discharge; *~ nemen* resign, hand in one's notice (*or:* resignation) **2** resignation, notice **3** exemption

de **ontslagbrief** /ɔntslɑxbrif/ (pl: -brieven) notice; (letter of) resignation

de **ontslagvergoeding** /ɔntslɑxfərɣudɪŋ/ severance pay

de **ontsluiting** /ɔntslœytɪŋ/ **1** opening up: *de ~ van een **gebied*** the opening up of an area **2** dilat(at)ion

ontsmetten /ɔntsmɛtə(n)/ (ontsmette, heeft ontsmet) disinfect

de **ontsmetting** /ɔntsmɛtɪŋ/ disinfection, decontamination

het **ontsmettingsmiddel** /ɔntsmɛtɪŋsmɪdəl/ disinfectant, antiseptic

ontsnappen /ɔntsnɑpə(n)/ (ontsnapte, is ontsnapt) **1** escape (from): *aan de dood ~* escape death **2** escape, get away, get out: *weten te ~* make one's getaway **3** escape, elude: *aan de aandacht ~* escape notice **4** pull (*or:* break) away (from)

de **ontsnapping** /ɔntsnɑpɪŋ/ (pl: -en) escape

¹ontspannen /ɔntspɑnə(n)/ (adj) relaxed, easy: *zich ~ **gedragen*** have an easy manner

²ontspannen /ɔntspɑnə(n)/ (ontspande, heeft ontspannen) **1** slacken, unbend **2** relax: *zich ~* relax

de **ontspanning** /ɔntspɑnɪŋ/ (pl: -en) relaxation, recreation

ontsporen /ɔntsporə(n)/ (ontspoorde, is ontspoord) **1** be derailed **2** [fig] go (*or:* run) off the rails

de **ontsporing** /ɔntsporɪŋ/ (pl: -en) derailment; [fig] lapse

ontspringen /ɔntsprɪŋə(n)/ (ontsprong, is ontsprongen) rise: *de rivier ontspringt in de bergen* the river rises in the mountains || [fig] *de **dans** ~* have a lucky escape

ontspruiten /ɔntsprœytə(n)/ (ontsproot, is ontsproten) originate (from)

het **¹ontstaan** /ɔntstan/ origin; creation; development, coming into existence

²ontstaan /ɔntstan/ (ontstond, is ontstaan) **1** come into being, arise: *door haar vertrek ontstaat een **vacature*** her departure has created a vacancy **2** originate, start

ontsteken /ɔntstekə(n)/ (ontstak, is ontstoken) be(come) inflamed

de **ontsteking** /ɔntstekɪŋ/ (pl: -en) **1** inflammation **2** ignition

ontsteld /ɔntstɛlt/ (adj, adv) dismayed

de **ontsteltenis** /ɔntstɛltənɪs/ **1** dismay, confusion **2** dismay; horror

ontstemd /ɔntstɛmt/ (adj) untuned, out of tune

de **ontstentenis** /ɔntstɛntənɪs/: *bij ~ van* in the absence of

ontstijgen /ɔntstɛɪɣə(n)/ (ontsteeg, is ontstegen) mount, rise (up)

ontstoken /ɔntstokə(n)/ (adj) inflamed

ontstoppen /ɔntstɔpə(n)/ (ontstopte, heeft ontstopt) **1** unblock, unclog **2** unstop(per), uncork

de **ontstopper** /ɔntstɔpər/ (pl: -s) plunger

zich **onttrekken** /ɔntrɛkə(n)/ (onttrok zich, heeft zich onttrokken) withdraw (from), back out of

onttronen /ɔntronə(n)/ (onttroonde, heeft onttroond) dethrone, depose

de **ontucht** /ɔntʏxt/ illicit sexual acts, sexual abuse

ontvallen /ɔntfɑlə(n)/ (ontviel, is ontvallen) **1** pass away: *zijn **vrouw** is hem vroeg ~* he lost his wife early **2** escape, (let) slip: *zich een **opmerking** laten ~* let slip a remark

ontvangen /ɔntfɑŋə(n)/ (ontving, heeft ontvangen) **1** receive; collect; draw: *in dank ~* received with thanks **2** receive; welcome: *iem. **hartelijk** (or: met open armen) ~* receive s.o. with open arms, make s.o. very welcome

de **ontvanger** /ɔntfɑŋər/ (pl: -s) **1** receiver, recipient **2** receiver

de **ontvangst** /ɔntfɑŋst/ (pl: -en) **1** receipt: *in ~ nemen* [eg flowers] receive; [money] collect; [goods] take delivery of; *na ~ van uw brief* on receipt of your letter; *tekenen **voor** ~* sign for receipt **2** collection **3** reception: *een **hartelijke** (or: **gunstige**) ~* a warm (*or:* favourable) reception

het **ontvangstbewijs** /ɔntfɑŋstbəwɛis/ (pl: -bewijzen) receipt

ontvankelijk /ɔntfɑŋkələɣ/ (adj) **1** susceptible (to): *~ **voor*** open to, receptive to **2** admissible, sustainable

ontvasten /ɔntfɑstə(n)/ (ontvastte, heeft ontvast) break the fast

ontvlambaar /ɔntflɑmbar/ (adj) inflammable

ontvlammen /ɔntflɑmə(n)/ (ontvlamde, is ontvlamd) inflame

ontvluchten /ɔntflʏxtə(n)/ (ontvluchtte, is

ontvlucht) **1** escape (from), run away from **2** flee

de **ontvoerder** /ɔntfu̯rdər/ (pl: -s) kidnapper

ontvoeren /ɔntfu̯rə(n)/ (ontvoerde, heeft ontvoerd) kidnap

de **ontvoering** /ɔntfu̯rɪŋ/ (pl: -en) kidnapping

ontvolgen /ɔntfɔ̯lɣə(n)/ (ontvolgde, heeft ontvolgd) unfollow

ontvouwen /ɔntfɑ̯uwə(n)/ (ontvouwde, heeft ontvouwd/ontvouwen) unfold

ontvreemden /ɔntfre̯mdə(n)/ (ontvreemd-de, heeft ontvreemd) steal

ontvrienden /ɔntfri̯ndə(n)/ (ontvriendde, heeft ontvriend) unfriend, defriend

ontwaken /ɔntwa̯kə(n)/ (ontwaakte, is ontwaakt) awake, (a)rouse

ontwapenen /ɔntwa̯pənə(n)/ (ontwapen-de, heeft ontwapend) disarm: *een ~de* **glim-lach** a disarming smile

de **ontwapening** /ɔntwa̯pənɪŋ/ disarmament

ontwaren /ɔntwa̯rə(n)/ (ontwaarde, heeft ontwaard) [form] descry

ontwarren /ɔntwa̯rə(n)/ (ontwarde, heeft ontward) disentangle

ontwennen /ɔntwɛ̯nə(n)/ (ontwende, is ontwend) get out of the habit

de **ontwenningskuur** /ɔntwɛ̯nɪŋskyr/ (pl: -kuren) detoxification

de **ontwenningsverschijnselen** /ɔnt-wɛ̯nɪŋsfərsxɛɪnsələ(n)/ (pl) withdrawal symptoms

het **ontwerp** /ɔntwɛ̯rp/ (pl: -en) draft; design

ontwerpen /ɔntwɛ̯rpə(n)/ (ontwierp, heeft ontworpen) **1** design; plan **2** devise, plan; formulate; draft; draw up

de **ontwerper** /ɔntwɛ̯rpər/ (pl: -s) designer, planner

ontwijken /ɔntwɛ̯ikə(n)/ (ontweek, heeft ontweken) avoid

ontwijkend /ɔntwɛ̯ikənt/ (adj, adv) evasive

de **ontwikkelaar** /ɔntwɪ̯kəlar/ (pl: -s) developer

ontwikkeld /ɔntwɪ̯kəlt/ (adj) **1** developed, mature **2** educated, informed; cultivated; cultured

¹**ontwikkelen** /ɔntwɪ̯kələ(n)/ (ontwikkelde, heeft ontwikkeld) **1** develop **2** educate: *zich ~* educate o.s. ‖ *foto's ~ en afdrukken* process a film

zich ²**ontwikkelen** /ɔntwɪ̯kələ(n)/ (ontwikkelde zich, heeft zich ontwikkeld) develop (into): *we zullen zien hoe de zaken zich ~* we'll see how things develop

de **ontwikkeling** /ɔntwɪ̯kəlɪŋ/ (pl: -en) **1** development, growth: *tot ~* **komen** develop **2** education: *algemene ~* general knowledge

de **ontwikkelingshulp** /ɔntwɪ̯kəlɪŋshylp/ foreign aid, development assistance

het **ontwikkelingsland** /ɔntwɪ̯kəlɪŋslɑnt/ (pl: -en) developing country

de **ontwikkelingsmaatschappij** /ɔnt-wɪ̯kəlɪŋsmatsxɑpɛɪ/ (pl: -en) development company

ontworstelen /ɔntwɔ̯rstələ(n)/ (ontwor-stelde, heeft ontworsteld): *zij ontworstelde* **zich** *aan zijn greep* she struggled out of his grasp

ontwortelen /ɔntwɔ̯rtələ(n)/ (ontwortel-de, heeft ontworteld) uproot

ontwrichten /ɔntwrɪ̯xtə(n)/ (ontwrichtte, heeft ontwricht) **1** disrupt **2** dislocate

het **ontzag** /ɔntsɑ̯x/ awe, respect

ontzaglijk /ɔntsɑ̯xlək/ (adj) tremendous, enormous: *~ veel* an awful lot, terribly much

¹**ontzeggen** /ɔntsɛ̯ɣə(n)/ (ontzegde/ontzei, heeft ontzegd) refuse, deny: *iem. de toegang* **ontzeggen** refuse s.o. admittance

zich ²**ontzeggen** /ɔntsɛ̯ɣə(n)/ (ontzegde zich/ontzei zich, heeft zich ontzegd) deny o.s.: *hij ontzegde zich veel om …* he made many sacrifices to …

de **ontzegging** /ɔntsɛ̯ɣɪŋ/ (pl: -en) denial, refusal: *~ van de* **rijbevoegdheid** disqualification from driving

ontzenuwen /ɔntse̯nywə(n)/ (ontzenuw-de, heeft ontzenuwd) refute, disprove

ontzet /ɔntsɛ̯t/ (adj) relief

ontzetten /ɔntsɛ̯tə(n)/ (ontzette, heeft ont-zet) **1** expel, remove **2** relieve; rescue **3** appal, horrify

¹**ontzettend** /ɔntsɛ̯tənt/ (adj) **1** appalling **2** terrific, immense, tremendous

²**ontzettend** /ɔntsɛ̯tənt/ (adv) awfully, tremendously: *het spijt me ~* I'm terribly (*or:* awfully) sorry; *~ veel bloemen* an awful lot of flowers

de **ontzetting** /ɔntsɛ̯tɪŋ/ (pl: -en) **1** deprivation; removal: *~ uit een recht* disfranchisement **2** relief; rescue **3** horror, dismay: *tot onze ~* to our dismay (*or:* horror)

ontzien /ɔntsi̯n/ (ontzag, heeft ontzien) spare: *iem. ~* spare s.o.

onuitgenodigd /ɔnœ̯ytxənodəxt/ (adj) uninvited; unwanted: *~ binnenvallen (op een feestje)* gatecrash (a party)

onuitputtelijk /ɔnœ̯ytpʏtələk/ (adj, adv) inexhaustible

onuitroeibaar /ɔnœ̯ytrujbar/ (adj) ineradicable; indestructible

onuitspreekbaar /ɔnœ̯ytspre̯gbar/ (adj) unpronounceable

onuitsprekelijk /ɔnœ̯ytspre̯kələk/ (adj, adv) unspeakable

onuitstaanbaar /ɔnœ̯ytsta̯mbar/ (adj, adv) unbearable, insufferable: *die kerel vind ik ~* I can't stand that guy

onvast /ɔnvɑ̯st/ (adj, adv) unsteady, unstable

onveilig /ɔnvɛ̯iləx/ (adj, adv) unsafe, dangerous

de **onveiligheid** /ɔnvɛ̯iləxhɛit/ danger(ous-

ness)
onveranderd /ɔnvərɑndərt/ (adj) unchanged, unaltered
¹**onveranderlijk** /ɔnvərɑndərlək/ (adj) unchanging, unvarying
²**onveranderlijk** /ɔnvərɑndərlək/ (adv) invariably
onverantwoord /ɔnvərɑntwort/ (adj, adv) irresponsible
onverantwoordelijk /ɔnvərɑntwordələk/ (adj, adv) irresponsible; unjustifiable
onverbeterlijk /ɔnvərbetərlək/ (adj) incorrigible
onverbiddelijk /ɔnvərbɪdələk/ (adj, adv) unrelenting, implacable
onverdeeld /ɔnvərdelt/ (adj) undivided
onverdiend /ɔnvərdint/ (adj, adv) undeserved
onverdraagzaam /ɔnvərdraxsam/ (adj) intolerant (towards)
de **onverdraagzaamheid** /ɔnvərdraxsamhɛit/ intolerance
onverenigbaar /ɔnvərenəybar/ (adj) incompatible (with)
onvergeeflijk /ɔnvəryeflək/ (adj, adv) unforgivable, inexcusable
onvergelijkbaar /ɔnvɛryəlɛigbar/ (adj, adv) incomparable
onvergetelijk /ɔnvəryetələk/ (adj, adv) unforgettable
onverhard /ɔnvərhɑrt/ (adj) unpaved
onverhoeds /ɔnvərhuts/ (adj, adv) unexpected
¹**onverholen** /ɔnvərholə(n)/ (adj) unconcealed
²**onverholen** /ɔnvərholə(n)/ (adv) openly
onverhoopt /ɔnvərhopt/ (adj) unhoped-for, unexpected; in the unlikely event
onverklaarbaar /ɔnvərklarbar/ (adj, adv) inexplicable, unaccountable: op onverklaarbare **wijze** unaccountably
onverkoopbaar /ɔnvərkobar/ (adj) unsaleable
onverkort /ɔnvərkɔrt/ (adj, adv) **1** unabridged **2** unimpaired: ~ van toepassing fully applicable
onverkwikkelijk /ɔnvərkwɪkələk/ (adj) nasty
de **onverlaat** /ɔnvərlat/ (pl: onverlaten) miscreant
onverlet /ɔnvərlɛt/ (adj) [Dutch]: dat laat ~ dat ... the fact remains that ...
onvermijdelijk /ɔnvərmɛidələk/ (adj, adv) inevitable: ~e fouten unavoidable mistakes
¹**onverminderd** /ɔnvərmɪndərt/ (adj, adv) undiminished: ~ van kracht blijven remain in full force
²**onverminderd** /ɔnvərmɪndərt/ (prep) without prejudice to
onvermoeibaar /ɔnvərmujbar/ (adj) indefatigable, tireless

het **onvermogen** /ɔnvərmoyə(n)/ impotence, powerlessness; inability
onvermurwbaar /ɔnvərmyrfbar/ (adj) unrelenting
onverricht /ɔnvərɪxt/ (adj): ~er zake terugkeren return without having achieved one's aim
¹**onverschillig** /ɔnvərsxɪləx/ (adj) indifferent (to): hij zat daar met een ~ gezicht he sat there looking completely indifferent (or: unconcerned)
²**onverschillig** /ɔnvərsxɪləx/ (adv) indifferently: iem. ~ behandelen treat s.o. with indifference
de **onverschilligheid** /ɔnvərsxɪləxhɛit/ indifference
onverschrokken /ɔnvərsxrɔkə(n)/ (adj, adv) fearless
onverslijtbaar /ɔnvərslɛidbar/ (adj) indestructible; durable [goods]
onverstaanbaar /ɔnvərstambar/ (adj, adv) unintelligible; inarticulate; inaudible
onverstandig /ɔnvərstɔndəx/ (adj, adv) foolish, unwise
onverstoorbaar /ɔnvərstorbar/ (adj, adv) imperturbable, unflappable
onverteerbaar /ɔnvərterbar/ (adj, adv) indigestible; [fig also] unacceptable
onvertogen /ɔnvərtoyə(n)/ (adj) indecent: er is geen ~ woord gevallen there was no bad feeling
onvervalst /ɔnvərvɑlst/ (adj) pure, unadulterated; broad
onvervangbaar /ɔnvərvɑnbar/ (adj) irreplaceable
onvervreemdbaar /ɔnvərvremdbar/ (adj, adv) inalienable
onvervuld /ɔnvərvʏlt/ (adj) unfulfilled
onverwacht /ɔnvərwɑxt/ (adj, adv) unexpected, surprise: dat soort dingen gebeurt altijd ~ that sort of thing always happens when you least expect it
onverwachts /ɔnvərwɑxts/ (adj, adv) unexpected, sudden, surprise
onverwarmd /ɔnvərwɑrmt/ (adj) unheated
onverwoestbaar /ɔnvərwustbar/ (adj) indestructible; tough; durable
onverzadigbaar /ɔnvərzadəybar/ (adj) insatiable
onverzadigd /ɔnvərzadəxt/ (adj) **1** insatiate(d) **2** unsaturated
onverzekerd /ɔnvərzekərt/ (adj) uninsured; uncovered
onverzettelijk /ɔnvərzɛtələk/ (adj, adv) unbending, intransigent
onverzoenlijk /ɔnvərzunlək/ (adj, adv) irreconcilable
onverzorgd /ɔnvərzɔrxt/ (adj) careless, untidy; uncared-for; untended: zij ziet er ~ uit she neglects her appearance
onvindbaar /ɔnvɪndbar/ (adj) untraceable;

not to be found

onvoldaan /ɔnvɔldan/ (adj) **1** unpaid **2** unsatisfied

de **¹onvoldoende** /ɔnvɔldundə/ (pl: -s) unsatisfactory mark; [Am] unsatisfactory grade; fail: *een ~ halen* fail (an exam, a test); *hij had twee ~s* he had two unsatisfactory marks

²onvoldoende /ɔnvɔldundə/ (adj, adv) insufficient, unsatisfactory: *een ~ hoeveelheid* an insufficient amount

onvolkomen /ɔnvɔlkomə(n)/ (adj) imperfect

onvolledig /ɔnvɔledəx/ (adj, adv) incomplete

onvolprezen /ɔnvɔlprezə(n)/ (adj) unsurpassed

onvoltooid /ɔnvɔltojt/ (adj) unfinished: *~ verleden tijd* simple past (tense), imperfect (tense)

onvolwassen /ɔnvɔlwɑsə(n)/ (adj) immature: *~ reageren* react in an adolescent way

¹onvoorbereid /ɔnvorbərɛit/ (adj) unprepared

²onvoorbereid /ɔnvorbərɛit/ (adv) unaware(s), by surprise

onvoordelig /ɔnvordeləx/ (adj, adv) unprofitable, uneconomic(al): *~ uit zijn* pay too high a price

onvoorspelbaar /ɔnvorspɛlbar/ (adj, adv) unpredictable

onvoorstelbaar /ɔnvorstɛlbar/ (adj) inconceivable, unimaginable, unthinkable; beyond belief: *het is ~!* it's unbelievable!, it's incredible!

onvoorwaardelijk /ɔnvorwardələk/ (adj, adv) unconditional, unquestioning: *~e straf* non-suspended sentence

onvoorzichtig /ɔnvorzɪxtəx/ (adj, adv) careless; [stronger] reckless: *je hebt zeer ~ gehandeld* you have acted most imprudently

de **onvoorzichtigheid** /ɔnvorzɪxtəxhɛit/ carelessness; [stronger] recklessness; lack of caution

¹onvoorzien /ɔnvorzin/ (adj) unforeseen: *~e uitgaven* incidental expenditure(s)

²onvoorzien /ɔnvorzin/ (adv) accidentally

de **onvrede** /ɔnvredə/ dissatisfaction (with)

onvriendelijk /ɔnvrindələk/ (adj, adv) unfriendly, hostile

onvrij /ɔnvrɛi/ (adj) unfree

onvrijwillig /ɔnvrɛiwɪləx/ (adj, adv) involuntary

onvruchtbaar /ɔnvrʏxtbar/ (adj) infertile, barren

de **onvruchtbaarheid** /ɔnvrʏx(t)barhɛit/ infertility

onwaar /ɔnwar/ (adj) untrue, false

onwaardig /ɔnwardəx/ (adj) unworthy (of)

onwaarschijnlijk /ɔnwarsxɛinlək/ (adj) unlikely, improbable: *het is hoogst ~ dat* it is most (or: highly) unlikely that

de **onwaarschijnlijkheid** /ɔnwarsxɛinlək-hɛit/ improbability, unlikelihood

het **onweer** /ɔnwer/ (pl: onweren) thunderstorm: *we krijgen ~* we're going to have a thunderstorm

onweerlegbaar /ɔnwerlɛxbar/ (adj, adv) irrefutable

de **onweersbui** /ɔnwerzbœy/ (pl: -en) thunder(y) shower

onweerstaanbaar /ɔnwerstambar/ (adj, adv) irresistible, compelling

onwel /ɔnwɛl/ (adj) unwell, ill, indisposed

onwelkom /ɔnwɛlkom/ (adj) unwelcome

onwennig /ɔnwɛnəx/ (adj) unaccustomed, ill at ease: *zij staat er nog wat ~ tegenover* she has not quite got used to the idea

onweren /ɔnwerə(n)/ (onweerde, heeft geonweerd) thunder: *het heeft geonweerd* there has been a thunderstorm

onwerkbaar /ɔnwɛrgbar/ (adj) unworkable: *een onwerkbare situatie* an impossible situation

onwerkelijk /ɔnwɛrkələk/ (adj) unreal

onwetend /ɔnwetənt/ (adj) **1** ignorant **2** unaware

de **onwetendheid** /ɔnwetənthɛit/ ignorance: *uit (or: door) ~* out of (or: through) ignorance

onwetenschappelijk /ɔnwetənsxɑpələk/ (adj, adv) unscientific, unscholarly

onwettig /ɔnwɛtəx/ (adj, adv) **1** illegal; illicit; unlawful **2** illegitimate

onwezenlijk /ɔnwezə(n)lək/ (adj) unreal

onwijs /ɔnwɛis/ (adv) [Dutch] awfully, fabulously, terrifically, ever so: *~ gaaf* brill; *~ hard werken* work like mad (or: crazy)

de **onwil** /ɔnwɪl/ unwillingness: *uit pure ~* out of sheer stubbornness; [Am] out of sheer bloody-mindedness

onwillekeurig /ɔnwɪləkørəx/ (adj) **1** involuntary **2** inadvertently, unconsciously || *~ lachte hij* he laughed in spite of himself

onwillig /ɔnwɪləx/ (adj, adv) unwilling

onwrikbaar /ɔnvrɪgbar/ (adj, adv) irrefutable

onzalig /ɔnzaləx/ (adj, adv) unlucky: *wie kwam er op die ~e gedachte?* whose silly idea was it?

onzedelijk /ɔnzedələk/ (adj, adv) indecent, obscene

de **onzedelijkheid** /ɔnzedələkhɛit/ immorality, indecency, immodesty

onzeker /ɔnzekər/ (adj, adv) **1** insecure, unsure **2** uncertain, unsure; precarious: *het aantal gewonden is nog ~* the number of injured is not yet known; *hij nam het zekere voor het ~e* he decided to play safe

de **onzekerheid** /ɔnzekərhɛit/ (pl: -heden) uncertainty, doubt: *in ~ laten* (or: *verkeren*) keep (or: be) in a state of suspense

onzelfstandig /ɔnzɛlfstɑndəx/ (adj) dependent (on others)

Onze-Lieve-Heer /ɔnzəlivəhɛr/ Our Lord, (the good) God

Onze-Lieve-Vrouw /ɔnzəlivəvrɑu/ Our Lady

het **onzevader** /ɔnzəvadər/ (pl: -s) Lord's Prayer: *het ~ bidden* say the Lord's Prayer

onzichtbaar /ɔnzɪxtbar/ (adj) invisible

onzijdig /ɔnzɛidəx/ (adj) neutral

de **onzin** /ɔnzɪn/ nonsense: *klinkklare ~* utter nonsense; *~ verkopen* talk nonsense

onzindelijk /ɔnzɪndələk/ (adj, adv) not toilet-trained

onzinnig /ɔnzɪnəx/ (adj, adv) absurd, senseless; nonsensical

onzorgvuldig /ɔnzɔrxfʏldəx/ (adj, adv) careless, negligent

¹**onzuiver** /ɔnzœyvər/ (adj) **1** impure **2** gross **3** inaccurate, imperfect

²**onzuiver** /ɔnzœyvər/ (adv) out of tune

het **oog** /ox/ (pl: ogen) **1** eye: *een blauw ~* a black eye; *dan kun je het met je eigen ogen zien* then you can see for yourself; *goede ogen hebben* have good eyesight; *geen ~ dichtdoen* not sleep a wink; *zijn ogen geloven* (or: *vertrouwen*) believe (or: trust) one's eyes; *hij had alleen ~ voor haar* he only had eyes for her; *aan één ~ blind* blind in one eye; *iem. iets onder vier ogen zeggen* say sth. to s.o. in private; *goed uit zijn ogen kijken* keep one's eyes open; *kun je niet uit je ogen kijken?* can't you look where you're going?; *zijn ogen de kost geven* take it all in; *~ om ~, tand om tand* an eye for an eye, a tooth for a tooth **2** look, glance, eye: *zij kon haar ogen niet van hem afhouden* she couldn't take (or: keep) her eyes off him; *(zo) op het ~* on the face of it; *iem. op het ~ hebben* have s.o. in mind, have one's eye on s.o.; *wat mij voor ogen staat* what I have in mind **3** view, eye: *zo ver het ~ reikt* as far as the eye can see; *in het ~ lopend* conspicuous, noticeable; *in het ~ houden* **a)** keep an eye on; **b)** [fig] keep in mind; *iets uit het ~ verliezen* lose sight of sth.; *uit het ~, uit het hart* out of sight, out of mind ‖ *in mijn ogen* in my opinion (or: view); *met het ~ op* with a view to; in view of; *hoge ogen gooien* have an excellent chance

de **oogappel** /oxapəl/ (pl: -s) apple of one's eye: *hij was zijn moeders ~* he was the apple of his mother's eye

de **oogarts** /oxarts/ (pl: -en) ophthalmologist, eye specialist

de **oogbol** /oxbɔl/ (pl: -len) eyeball

de **ooggetuige** /oxətœyɣə/ (pl: -n) eyewitness

het **ooggetuigenverslag** /oxətœyɣə(n)vərslax/ (pl: -en) eyewitness report

de **ooghoek** /oxhuk/ (pl: -en) corner of the eye

de **ooghoogte** /oxhoxtə/ eye level: *op ~* at eye level

het **oogje** /oxjə/ (pl: -s) **1** eye: *een ~ dichtknijpen*

(or: *dichtdoen*) close (or: shut) one's eyes (to) **2** glance, look, peep: *een ~ in het zeil houden* keep a lookout ‖ *een ~ hebben op* have one's eye on

de **oogklep** /oxklɛp/ (pl: -pen) blinker; [Am] blinder; [fig] *~pen voor hebben* be blind to, be blinkered

het **ooglid** /oxlɪt/ (pl: oogleden) (eye)lid

oogluikend /oxlœykənt/ (adj): *iets ~ toelaten (toestaan)* turn a blind eye to sth.

het **oogmerk** /oxmɛrk/ (pl: -en): *met het ~ om* with a view to, with the object (or: intention) of

de **oogopslag** /oxopslax/ glance, look, glimpse

het **oogpunt** /oxpʏnt/ (pl: -en) viewpoint, point of view

de **oogschaduw** /oxsxadyw/ eyeshadow

de **oogst** /oxst/ (pl: -en) **1** harvesting, reaping **2** harvest, crop: *de ~ binnenhalen* bring in the harvest

oogsten /oxstə(n)/ (oogstte, heeft geoogst) harvest; pick

oogstrelend /oxstrɛlənt/ (adj) delightful

de **oogsttijd** /oxstɛit/ (pl: -en) harvest(ing) time

oogverblindend /oxfərblɪndənt/ (adj) blinding, dazzling: *een ~e schoonheid* a raving beauty

de **oogwenk** /oxwɛŋk/ (pl: -en) moment, instant

de **oogwimper** /oxwɪmpər/ (pl: -s) (eye)lash

het **oogwit** /oxwɪt/ white of the eye

de **ooi** /oj/ (pl: -en) ewe

de **ooievaar** /ojəvar/ (pl: -s) stork

ooit /ojt/ (adv) ever, at any time: *Jan, die ~ een vriend van me was* John, who was once a friend of mine; *groter dan ~ tevoren* bigger than ever (before); *de beste prestatie ~* the best-ever performance

ook /ok/ (adv) **1** also, too: *zijn er ~ brieven?* are there any letters?; *morgen kan ~ nog* tomorrow will be all right too; *ik hou van tennis en hij ~* I like tennis and so does he; *ik ben er ~ nog* I'm here too; *hij kookte en heelgoed ~* he did the cooking and very well too; *hij heeft niet gewacht, en ik trouwens ~ niet* he didn't wait and neither did I; *zo vreselijk moeilijk is het nu ~ weer niet* it's not all that difficult (after all); *dat hebben we ~ weer gehad* so much for that, that's over and done with; *opa praatte ~ zo* grandpa used to talk like that (too); *dat is waar ~!* that's true, of course!; oh, I almost forgot! **2** even: *~ al is hij niet rijk* even though he's not rich **3** anyhow, anyway: *hoe jong ik ~ ben …* (as) young as I may be (or: am) …; *hoe het ~ zij, laten we nu maar gaan* anyway, let's go now; *wat je ~ doet* whatever you do; *wie (dan) ~* whoever; *hoe zeer zij zich ~ inspande* however she tried **4** again, too: *dat gezanik ~* all that fuss (too); *jij hebt ~ nooit tijd!* you never have any time!;

hoe heet hij ~ weer? what was his name again?

de **oom** /om/ (pl: -s) uncle

het **oor** /or/ (pl: oren) **1** ear: *met een half ~ mee-luisteren* listen with only an ear; *dat gaat het ene ~ in, het andere uit* it goes (at) in one ear and out (at) the other; *zijn oren (niet) geloven* (not) believe one's ears; *een en al ~ zijn* be all ears; [Belg] *op zijn beide* (or: *twee*) *oren slapen* have no worries, sleep the sleep of the just; *doof aan één ~* deaf in one ear; *gaatjes in de oren hebben* have pierced ears; *iets in de oren knopen* get sth. into one's head; *ik stond wel even met mijn oren te klapperen* I couldn't believe my ears (or: what I was hearing); *iem. met iets om de oren slaan* blow s.o. up over sth.; *dat is ons ter ore gekomen* that has come to our attention (or: ears), we have heard (that); *tot over de oren verliefd zijn* be head over heels in love; [fig] *het zit tussen je oren* it's all in your head **2** handle, ear ‖ *iem. een ~ aannaaien* fool s.o., take s.o. for a ride

de **oorarts** /orɑrts/ (pl: -en) otologist, ear specialist

de **oorbel** /orbɛl/ (pl: -len) earring

het **oord** /ort/ (pl: -en) region, place; resort

het **oordeel** /ordel/ (pl: oordelen) judgement; verdict; sentence

oordelen /ordelə(n)/ (oordeelde, heeft geoordeeld) **1** judge, pass judgement; sentence **2** judge, make up one's mind

het **oordopje** /ordɔpjə/ (pl: -s) **1** earplug **2** earphone, bud

de **oordruppels** /ordrʏpəls/ (pl) eardrops

de **oorkonde** /orkɔndə/ (pl: -n) document, charter, deed

de **oorlel** /orlɛl/ (pl: -len) lobe (of the ear)

de **oorlog** /orlɔx/ (pl: -en) war: *het is ~* there's a war on; *de ~ verklaren aan* declare war on; *~ voeren* wage war

de **oorlogsheld** /orlɔxshɛlt/ (pl: -en) war hero

de **oorlogsmisdadiger** /orlɔxsmɪzdadəyər/ (pl: -s) war criminal

het **oorlogspad** /orlɔxspɑt/: *op het ~ zijn* be on the warpath

het **oorlogsschip** /orlɔxsxɪp/ (pl: -schepen) warship

de **oorlogssterkte** /orlɔxstɛrktə/: *op ~* at fighting strength

de **oorlogsverklaring** /orlɔxsfərklarɪŋ/ (pl: -en) declaration of war

oorlogszuchtig /orlɔxsʏxtəx/ (adj, adv) warlike, war-minded

de **oorlogvoering** /orlɔxfurɪŋ/ conduct (or: waging) of the war, warfare

oormerken /ormɛrkə(n)/ (oormerkte, heeft geoormerkt) earmark

de **oorontsteking** /orɔntstekɪŋ/ (pl: -en) inflammation of the ear

de **oorpijn** /orpɛin/ (pl: -en) earache

de **oorring** /orɪŋ/ (pl: -en) earring

de **oorschelp** /orsxɛlp/ (pl: -en) auricle

het/de **oorsmeer** /orsmer/ ear wax

de **oorsprong** /orsprɔŋ/ (pl: -en) origin, source: *van ~* originally

¹**oorspronkelijk** /orsprɔŋkələk/ (adj) original, innovative: *een ~ kunstenaar* an original (or: innovative) artist

²**oorspronkelijk** /orsprɔŋkələk/ (adv) originally, initially

de **oorspronkelijkheid** /orsprɔŋkələkhɛit/ originality

het **oortje** /orcə/ earphone

oorverdovend /orvərdovənt/ (adj, adv) deafening

de **oorvijg** /orvɛix/ (pl: -en) box on the ear

de **oorworm** /orwɔrm/ earwig

de **oorwurm** /orwʏrm/ (pl: -en) **1** [zoology] earwig: *een gezicht als een ~ zetten* pull a long face **2** [mus] earworm

de **oorzaak** /orzak/ (pl: oorzaken) cause, origin: *~ en gevolg* cause and effect

oorzakelijk /orzakələk/ (adj): *~ verband* causal connection, causality

oost /ost/ (adj) east: *~ west, thuis best* east, west, home's best

het **Oostblok** /ostblɔk/ Eastern bloc

Oost-Duitsland /osdœytslɑnt/ East Germany; German Democratic Republic

oostelijk /ostələk/ (adj, adv) **1** eastern **2** [to the east] easterly; eastward; [from the east] easter(ly) [wind]: *een ~e wind* an easterly wind

het **oosten** /ostə(n)/ east: *ten ~ van* (to the) east of; *het ~ van Frankrijk* eastern France

Oostende /ostɛndə/ Ostend

Oostenrijk /ostə(n)rɛik/ Austria

de **Oostenrijker** /ostə(n)rɛikər/ (pl: -s) Austrian

Oostenrijks /ostə(n)rɛiks/ (adj) Austrian

de **oostenwind** /ostə(n)wɪnt/ (pl: -en) east wind, easterly

de **oosterburen** /ostərbyrə(n)/ (pl) neighbours to the east

de **oosterlengte** /ostərlɛŋtə/ eastern longitude

oosters /ostərs/ (adj) oriental

Oost-Europa /ostøropa/ Eastern Europe

Oost-Europees /ostøropes/ (adj) East European

Oost-Indisch /ostɪndis/ (adj, adv) East Indian ‖ *~ doof zijn* pretend not to hear

de **oostkust** /ostkʏst/ (pl: -en) east(ern) coast

oostwaarts /ostwarts/ (adv) eastward

de **Oostzee** /ostse/ Baltic (Sea)

het **ootje** /ocə/: *iem. in het ~ nemen* take s.o. for a ride, pull s.o.'s leg

ootmoedig /otmudəx/ (adj, adv) humble

¹**op** /ɔp/ (adj) used up, gone: *het geld* (or: *mijn geduld*) *is op* the money (or: my patience) has run out; *hij is op van de zenuwen* he is a nervous wreck

²op /ɔp/ (adv) up: *trap op en trap af* up and down the stairs; *de straat op en neer lopen* walk up and down the street; *zij had een nieuwe hoed op* she had a new hat on

³op /ɔp/ (prep) **1** in, on, at: *op een motor rijden* ride a motorcycle; *op de hoek wonen* live on the corner; *later op de dag* later in the day; *op negenjarige leeftijd* at the age of nine; *op maandag* (on) Monday; *op een maandag* on a Monday; *op vakantie* on holiday; *op zijn vroegst* at the earliest; *op haar eigen manier* in her own way; *op zijn minst* at (the very) least; *op zijn snelst* at the quickest **2** in, to: *op de eerste plaats* in the first place, first(ly); in first place; *de auto loopt 1 op 8* the car does 8 km to the litre; *één op de duizend* one in a thousand; *op één na de laatste* the last but one

de **opa** /ˈoːpaː/ (pl: -'s) grandpa, grandad

de **¹opaal** /oːˈpaːl/ (pl: opalen) [stone] opal

het **²opaal** /oːˈpaːl/ [mineral] opal

opbaren /ˈɔbaːrə(n)/ (baarde op, heeft opgebaard) place on a bier: *opgebaard liggen* lie in state

opbellen /ˈɔbɛlə(n)/ (belde op, heeft opgebeld) (tele)phone, call, ring (up): *ik zal je nog wel even ~* I'll give you a call (or: ring)

opbergen /ˈɔbɛrɣə(n)/ (borg op, heeft opgeborgen) put away, store; file (away)

opbeuren /ˈɔbøːrə(n)/ (beurde op, heeft opgebeurd) cheer up

opbiechten /ˈɔbixtə(n)/ (biechtte op, heeft opgebiecht) confess: *alles eerlijk ~* make a clean breast of it

opbieden /ˈɔbiːdə(n)/ (bood op, heeft opgeboden): *tegen iem. ~* bid against s.o.

opblaasbaar /ˈɔblaːzbaːr/ (adj) inflatable

de **opblaasboot** /ˈɔblaːzboːt/ (pl: -boten) inflatable boat

opblazen /ˈɔblaːzə(n)/ (blies op, heeft opgeblazen) blow up, inflate: *iets geweldig ~* blow sth. up out of all proportion

opblijven /ˈɔblɛivə(n)/ (bleef op, is opgebleven) stay up

opbloeien /ˈɔbluːjə(n)/ (bloeide op, is opgebloeid) **1** bloom **2** flourish, prosper

het **opbod** /ˈɔbɔt/: *iets bij ~ verkopen* sell sth. by auction

opboksen /ˈɔbɔksə(n)/ (bokste op, heeft opgebokst) compete

opborrelen /ˈɔbɔrələ(n)/ (borrelde op, is opgeborreld) bubble up

de **opbouw** /ˈɔbɑu/ **1** construction **2** structure

opbouwen /ˈɔbɑuwə(n)/ (bouwde op, heeft opgebouwd) build up, set up: *het weefsel is uit cellen opgebouwd* the tissue is made up (or: composed) of cells

opbouwend /ˈɔbɑuwənt/ (adj) constructive

opbranden /ˈɔbrɑndə(n)/ (brandde op, is opgebrand) be burned up (or: down)

opbreken /ˈɔbreːkə(n)/ (brak op, heeft op-

gebroken) **1** break up, take down (or: apart) **2** break up, tear up: *de straat ~ dig* (or: break) up the street

opbrengen /ˈɔbrɛŋə(n)/ (bracht op, heeft opgebracht) **1** bring in, yield: *dat kan ik niet ~* a) I can't afford that; **b)** [fig] I can't bring myself to that **2** work up: *begrip* (or: *belangstelling*) *~ voor* show understanding for (or: an interest in) **3** apply

de **opbrengst** /ˈɔbrɛŋst/ (pl: -en) yield, profit; revenue

opdagen /ˈɔbdaːɣə(n)/ (daagde op, is opgedaagd) turn up, show up

opdat /ɔbdɑt/ (conj) so that

opdienen /ˈɔbdiːnə(n)/ (diende op, heeft opgediend) serve (up), dish up

opdiepen /ˈɔbdiːpə(n)/ (diepte op, heeft opgediept) dig up

zich **opdirken** /ˈɔbdɪrkə(n)/ (dirkte zich op, heeft zich opgedirkt) [inform] doll (or: jazz) o.s. up

opdissen /ˈɔbdɪsə(n)/ (diste op, heeft opgedist) serve up, dish up

opdoeken /ˈɔbduːkə(n)/ (doekte op, heeft opgedoekt) shut down

opdoemen /ˈɔbduːmə(n)/ (doemde op, is opgedoemd) loom (up), appear

opdoen /ˈɔbdun/ (deed op, heeft opgedaan) **1** gain, get: *kennis ~* acquire knowledge; *inspiratie ~* gain inspiration **2** apply, put on: *doe je muts op* put your hat on

zich **opdoffen** /ˈɔbdɔfə(n)/ (dofte zich op, heeft zich opgedoft) doll o.s. up

de **opdoffer** /ˈɔbdɔfər/ (pl: -s) **1** punch **2** setback

de **opdonder** /ˈɔbdɔndər/ (pl: -s) punch

opdonderen /ˈɔbdɔndərə(n)/ (donderde op, is opgedonderd) get lost: *donder op!* get lost!

opdraaien /ˈɔbdraːjə(n)/ (draaide op, heeft/ is opgedraaid): *ik wil hier niet voor ~* I don't want to take any blame for this; *voor de kosten ~* foot the bill; *iem. voor iets laten ~* land (or: saddle) s.o. with sth.

de **opdracht** /ˈɔbdrɑxt/ (pl: -en) assignment, order: *we kregen ~ om ...* we were told to ..., given orders to ...

de **opdrachtgever** /ˈɔbdrɑxtxeːvər/ (pl: -s) client, customer

opdragen /ˈɔbdraːɣə(n)/ (droeg op, heeft opgedragen) charge, commission, assign

opdraven /ˈɔbdraːvə(n)/ (draafde op, is opgedraafd) show up, put in an appearance

opdreunen /ˈɔbdrøːnə(n)/ (dreunde op, heeft opgedreund) rattle off, reel off, drone

opdrijven /ˈɔbdrɛivə(n)/ (dreef op, heeft opgedreven) force up, drive up

¹opdringen /ˈɔbdrɪŋə(n)/ (drong op, is opgedrongen) push forward, press forward; press on, push on

²opdringen /ˈɔbdrɪŋə(n)/ (drong op, heeft opgedrongen) force on, press on; intrude on, impose on: *dat werd **ons** opgedrongen* that was forced on us

zich ³**opdringen** /ǫbdrɪŋə(n)/ (drong zich op, heeft zich opgedrongen) force o.s. on, impose o.s. (on), impose one's company (on): *ik **wil** me niet* ~ I don't want to intrude

opdringerig /ɔbdrɪŋərəx/ (adj, adv) obtrusive; pushy: *~ **reclameboodschappen*** aggressive advertising

opdrinken /ǫbdrɪŋkə(n)/ (dronk op, heeft opgedronken) drink (up)

opdrogen /ǫbdroɣə(n)/ (droogde op, is opgedroogd) dry (up); run dry

de **opdruk** /ǫbdrvk/ (pl: -ken) (im)print

opdrukken /ǫbdrvkə(n)/ (drukte op, heeft opgedrukt) **1** print on(to), impress on(to); stamp on(to) **2** push up, press up: *zich* ~ do press-ups

opduikelen /ǫbdœykələ(n)/ (duikelde op, heeft opgeduikeld) dig up

opduiken /ǫbdœykə(n)/ (dook op, is opgedoken) **1** surface, rise (*or:* come) to the surface **2** turn up

opduwen /ǫbdywə(n)/ (duwde op, heeft opgeduwd) push up, press up

opdweilen /ǫbdwɛilə(n)/ (dweilde op, heeft opgedweild) mop up

opeen /ɔpen/ (adv) together

opeens /ɔpens/ (adv) suddenly, all at once, all of a sudden

de **opeenstapeling** /ɔpenstapəlɪŋ/ (pl: -en) accumulation, build-up

opeenvolgend /ɔpenvɔlɣənt/ (adj) successive, consecutive

de **opeenvolging** /ɔpenvɔlɣɪŋ/ (pl: -en) succession

opeisen /ɔpɛisə(n)/ (eiste op, heeft opgeëist) claim, demand: *de **aandacht*** ~ demand (*or:* compel) attention; *een **aanslag*** ~ claim responsibility for an attack

open /ǫpə(n)/ (adj, adv) open; unlocked; vacant: *de **deur** staat* ~ the door is ajar (*or:* open); *met* ~ **ogen** with one's eyes open; *een* ~ **plek** *in het bos* a clearing in the woods; *tot hoe laat zijn de **winkels** ~?* what time do the shops close?; *~ en **bloot*** openly, for all (the world) to see

openbaar /ǫpə(n)bar/ (adj, adv) public, open: *de openbare **orde** verstoren* disturb the peace; *iets ~ **maken*** make sth. public, disclose (*or:* publish) sth. || *in het* ~ in public, publicly

de **openbaarheid** /ǫpə(n)barhɛit/ publicity

de **openbaarmaking** /ǫpə(n)barmakɪŋ/ publication, disclosure

¹**openbaren** /ɔpəmbarə(n)/ (openbaarde, heeft geopenbaard) reveal

zich ²**openbaren** /ɔpəmbarə(n)/ (openbaarde zich, heeft zich geopenbaard) manifest o.s.

de **openbaring** /ɔpə(n)barɪŋ/ (pl: -en) revelation

openbarsten /ǫpə(n)barstə(n)/ (barstte

open, is opengebarsten) burst open

openbreken /ǫpə(n)brekə(n)/ (brak open, heeft opengebroken) break (open), force open, prise open: *een **slot*** ~ force a lock

de **opendeurdag** /ɔpə(n)dǫrdax/ (pl: -en) [Belg] open day

¹**opendoen** /ǫpə(n)dun/ (deed open, heeft opengedaan) open the door; answer the door (*or:* bell, ring): *er werd **niet** opengedaan* there was no answer

²**opendoen** /ǫpə(n)dun/ (deed open, heeft opengedaan) open

opendraaien /ǫpə(n)drajə(n)/ (draaide open, heeft opengedraaid) open; turn on; unscrew

openduwen /ǫpə(n)dywə(n)/ (duwde open, heeft opengeduwd) push open

¹**openen** /ǫpənə(n)/ (opende, heeft geopend) open, begin: [cards] *met* schoppen ~ lead spades

²**openen** /ǫpənə(n)/ (opende, heeft geopend) **1** open; turn on; unscrew: *een **bestand*** ~ open a file, get into a file **2** open, start

de **opener** /ǫpənər/ (pl: -s) opener

opengaan /ǫpə(n)ɣan/ (ging open, is opengegaan) open

openhalen /ǫpə(n)halə(n)/ (haalde open, heeft opengehaald) tear: *ik heb mijn jas opengehaald **aan** een spijker* I tore my coat on a nail

openhartig /ɔpənhɑrtəx/ (adj, adv) frank, candid; straightforward: *een* ~ **gesprek** a heart-to-heart (talk)

de **openhartigheid** /ɔpə(n)hɑrtəxhɛit/ frankness, candour

de **openheid** /ǫpənhɛit/ openness, sincerity: *in alle* ~ in all candour

openhouden /ǫpə(n)haudə(n)/ (hield open, heeft opengehouden) keep open: *de **deur** voor iem.* ~ hold the door (open) for s.o.

de **opening** /ǫpənɪŋ/ (pl: -en) opening; gap: [Dutch] *van **zaken** geven over iets* disclose sth.

de **openingsplechtigheid** /ǫpənɪŋsplɛxtəxhɛit/ (pl: -heden) opening ceremony, inauguration

openlaten /ǫpə(n)latə(n)/ (liet open, heeft opengelaten) **1** leave open; leave on, leave running **2** leave blank; leave open

openlijk /ǫpə(n)lək/ (adj, adv) **1** open, overt: *~ voor iets **uitkomen*** openly admit sth. **2** public: *iets ~ **verkondigen*** declare sth. in public

de **openlucht** /ɔpə(n)lvxt/ open air: *in de* ~ slapen sleep in the open air

het **openluchtmuseum** /ɔpə(n)lvxtmyzejvm/ (pl: -musea) open-air museum, historical village

het **openluchttheater** /ɔpə(n)lvxtejatər/ (pl: -s) open-air theatre

openmaken /ọpə(n)makə(n)/ (maakte open, heeft opengemaakt) open (up)

openslaan /ọpə(n)slan/ (sloeg open, heeft opengeslagen) open

openslaand /ọpə(n)slant/ (adj): ~e **deuren** double doors

opensnijden /ọpə(n)snɛidə(n)/ (sneed open, heeft opengesneden) cut (open)

openstaan /ọpə(n)stan/ (stond open, heeft opengestaan) **1** be open; be unlocked: *mijn huis staat altijd voor jou open* my door will always be open to (or: for) you; *de kraan staat open* the tap is on (or: is running); ~ **voor** *kritiek* be open to criticism **2** [comp] be open, be opened

openstellen /ọpə(n)stɛlə(n)/ (stelde open, heeft opengesteld) open

opentrekken /ọpə(n)trɛkə(n)/ (trok open, heeft opengetrokken) pull open, open: *een fles* ~ open (or: uncork) a bottle

openvallen /ọpə(n)valə(n)/ (viel open, is opengevallen) fall open, drop open

openvouwen /ọpə(n)vauwə(n)/ (vouwde open, heeft opengevouwen) unfold, open (out)

openzetten /ọpə(n)zɛtə(n)/ (zette open, heeft opengezet) open; turn on

de **opera** /ọpera/ (pl: -'s) opera

de **operatie** /opera(t)si/ (pl: -s) operation, surgery: *een grote* (or: *kleine*) ~ **ondergaan** undergo major (or: minor) surgery

operatief /operatịf/ (adj, adv) surgical, operative

de **operatiekamer** /opera(t)sikamər/ (pl: -s) operating room

de **operatietafel** /opera(t)sitafəl/ (pl: -s) operating table

operationeel /opera(t)ʃonẹl/ (adj) operational; in running (or: working) order

opereren /opərẹrə(n)/ (opereerde, heeft geopereerd) **1** work; use **2** operate, perform surgery (or: an operation): *iem.* ~ operate on s.o.; *zij is geopereerd* **aan** *de longen* she has had an operation on the lungs

de **operette** /opərɛtə/ (pl: -s) light opera

opeten /ọpetə(n)/ (at op, heeft opgegeten) eat (up), finish

opfleuren /ọpflørə(n)/ (fleurde op, heeft/is opgefleurd) cheer up, brighten up

opflikkeren /ọpflɪkərə(n)/ (flikkerde op, is opgeflikkerd) **1** flare up, flicker **2** [vulg] bugger off, piss off: *flikker* **toch** *op!* bugger (or: piss) off!

opfokken /ọpfokə(n)/ (fokte op, heeft opgefokt) work up, whip up, stir up

de **opfriscursus** /ọpfrɪskʏrsʏs/ (pl: -sen) refresher course

opfrissen /ọpfrɪsə(n)/ (friste op, heeft/is opgefrist) freshen (up): *zijn* **Engels** ~ brush up (on) one's English; *zich* ~ freshen up; [Am] wash up

opgaan /ọpχan/ (ging op, is opgegaan) **1** go up; climb **2** come up, rise **3** go, be finished **4** hold good (or: true), apply: *dit gaat niet op* **voor** *arme mensen* this doesn't apply to (or: this is not true of) poor people || *als het die kant opgaat* **met** *de maatschappij dan … if that is the way society is going …*; **in** *vlammen* ~ go up in flames

opgaand /ọpχant/ (adj) rising

de **opgang** /ọpχaŋ/ (pl: -en): ~ **maken** catch on, take (on)

de **opgave** /ọpχavə/ (pl: -n) **1** statement, specification: *zonder* ~ *van redenen* without reason given **2** question: *schriftelijke* ~*n* written assignments **3** task, assignment

opgeblazen /ọpχəblazə(n)/ (adj) puffy, bloated, swollen

opgebrand /ọpχəbrant/ (adj) burnt-out, worn-out

opgefokt /ọpχəfokt/ (adj) worked up

opgeilen /ọpχɛilə(n)/ (geilde op, heeft opgegeild) [inform] turn on

opgelaten /ọpχəlatə(n)/ (adj) embarrassed: *zich* ~ *voelen* feel embarrassed

het **opgeld** /ọpχɛlt/ (pl: -en): ~ **doen** catch on, take (on)

opgelucht /ọpχəlʏχt/ (adj) relieved: ~ **ademhalen** heave a sigh of relief

opgeruimd /ọpχərœymt/ (adj) tidy, neat: ~ *staat netjes* good riddance (to bad rubbish)

opgescheept /ọpχəsχept/ (adj): *met iem. (iets)* ~ *zitten* be stuck with s.o. (sth.)

opgeschoten /ọpχəsχotə(n)/ (adj) lanky

opgetogen /ọpχətoɣə(n)/ (adj) delighted, overjoyed

opgeven /ọpχevə(n)/ (gaf op, heeft opgegeven) **1** give up, abandon: *de* **moed** ~ lose heart; *(het)* **niet** ~ not give in (or: up), hang on; *je moet* **nooit** *(niet te gauw)* ~ never say die **2** give, state: *zijn* **inkomsten** ~ *aan de belasting* declare one's income to the tax inspector; *als reden* ~ give (or: state) as one's reason **3** give, assign **4** enter: *zich* ~ *voor een cursus* enrol (or: sign up) for a course; *als vermist* ~ report (as) missing **5** give (up), surrender

opgewassen /ọpχəwasə(n)/ (adj) equal (to); up (to): *hij bleek niet* ~ **tegen** *die taak* the task proved beyond him (or: too much for him)

opgewekt /ọpχəwɛkt/ (adj, adv) cheerful, good-humoured: *hij is altijd heel* ~ he is always in good spirits (or: bright and breezy)

opgewonden /ọpχəwondə(n)/ (adj, adv) **1** excited **2** agitated, in a fluster

opgezet /ọpχəzɛt/ (adj) **1** swollen, bloated **2** [Belg] happy, content: ~ *zijn met iets* be pleased about sth.

de **opgieting** /ọpχitɪŋ/ (pl: -en) sauna infusion

opgooien /ọpχojə(n)/ (gooide op, heeft opgegooid) throw up, toss up

opgraven /ɔpχravə(n)/ (groef op, heeft opgegraven) dig up, unearth; excavate; exhume

de **opgraving** /ɔpχravɪŋ/ (pl: -en) **1** dig(ging); excavation; exhumation: ~*en vonden plaats in …* excavations were carried out in … **2** excavation, dig, (archaeological) site

opgroeien /ɔpχrujə(n)/ (groeide op, is opgegroeid) grow (up): *met iets opgegroeid zijn* have grown up with sth.

de **ophaalbrug** /ɔphalbrʏχ/ (pl: -gen) lift bridge, drawbridge

de **ophaaldienst** /ɔphaldinst/ (pl: -en) collecting service, collection service

ophalen /ɔphalə(n)/ (haalde op, heeft opgehaald) **1** raise, draw up, pull up; hoist **2** collect: *vuilnis* ~ collect refuse (*or:* rubbish); [Am] collect garbage; *kom je me vanavond* ~*?* are you coming round for me tonight? **3** bring up, bring back, recall: *herinneringen* ~ *aan de goede oude tijd* reminisce about the good old days **4** collect: *geld* ~ collect money **5** brush up (on), polish up: *rapportcijfers* ~ improve on one's (report) marks **6** download: *bestanden* ~ retrieve (*or:* download) files

ophanden /ɔphɑndə(n)/: ~ *zijn* be imminent, be close at hand, be approaching

¹**ophangen** /ɔphɑŋə(n)/ (hing op, heeft opgehangen) hang up, ring off

²**ophangen** /ɔphɑŋə(n)/ (hing op, heeft opgehangen) hang (up); post: *de was* ~ hang out the wash(ing) ‖ *zich* ~ hang o.s.

ophebben /ɔphɛbə(n)/ (had op, heeft opgehad) **1** wear, have on **2** have finished, have had

de **ophef** /ɔphɛf/ fuss, noise, song (and dance): ~ *maken over iets* kick up (*or:* make a fuss) about sth.; *zonder veel* ~ without much ado

opheffen /ɔphɛfə(n)/ (hief op, heeft opgeheven) **1** raise, lift: *met opgeheven hoofd* with (one's) head held high **2** cancel (out), neutralize: *het effect* ~ *van iets* counteract sth. **3** remove; discontinue: *de club werd na een paar maanden opgeheven* the club was disbanded after a couple of months

de **opheffingsuitverkoop** /ɔphɛfɪŋsœytfər-kop/ closing-down sale

ophefmakend /ɔphɛfma̱kənt/ (adj, adv) [Belg] sensational

ophelderen /ɔphɛldərə(n)/ (helderde op, heeft opgehelderd) clear up, clarify

de **opheldering** /ɔphɛldərɪŋ/ (pl: -en) explanation

ophemelen /ɔphemələ(n)/ (hemelde op, heeft opgehemeld) praise to the skies, extol

ophijsen /ɔpheisə(n)/ (hees op, heeft opgehesen) pull up, hoist (up); raise

ophitsen /ɔphɪtsə(n)/ (hitste op, heeft opgehitst) **1** egg on, goad: *een hond* ~ tease (*or:* bait) a dog; *iem.* ~ get s.o.'s hackles up

2 incite, stir up: *de mensen tegen elkaar* ~ set people at one another's throats

ophoepelen /ɔphupələ(n)/ (hoepelde op, is opgehoepeld) [inform] get lost: *hoepel op!* get lost!

ophogen /ɔphoɣə(n)/ (hoogde op, heeft opgehoogd) raise

ophokken /ɔphɔkə(n)/ (hokte op, heeft opgehokt): *pluimvee* ~ keep poultry indoors

zich **ophopen** /ɔphopə(n)/ (hoopte zich op, heeft zich opgehoopt) pile up, accumulate: *de sneeuw heeft zich opgehoopt* the snow has banked up

¹**ophouden** /ɔphaudə(n)/ (hield op, heeft/is opgehouden) stop; quit; (come to an) end: *de straat hield daar op* the street ended there; *dan houdt alles op* then there's nothing more to be said; *plotseling* ~ break off; *ze hield maar niet op met huilen* she (just) went on crying (and crying); ~ *met roken* give up (*or:* stop) smoking; *het is opgehouden met regenen* the rain has stopped; *even* ~ *met werken* have a short break in one's work; *hou op!* stop it!, cut it out!; *laten we erover* ~ let's leave it at that

²**ophouden** /ɔphaudə(n)/ (hield op, heeft opgehouden) **1** hold up, delay; [pers also] keep; [pers also] detain: *iem. niet langer* ~ not take up any more of s.o.'s time; *dat houdt de zaak alleen maar op* that just slows things down; *ik werd opgehouden* I was delayed (*or:* held up) **2** keep on **3** hold (up): *een plas* ~ hold one's water ‖ *de schijn* ~ keep up appearances, go through the motions

de **opinie** /opini/ (pl: -s) opinion, view

het **opinieblad** /opiniblɑt/ (pl: -en) [roughly] news magazine

de **opiniepeiling** /opinipɛilɪŋ/ (pl: -en) (opinion) poll: *(een)* ~*(en) houden (over)* canvass opinion (on)

het/de **opium** /opijʏm/ opium

opjagen /ɔpjaɣə(n)/ (jaagde op/joeg op, heeft opgejaagd) hurry, rush; hound

opjutten /ɔpjʏtə(n)/ (jutte op, heeft opgejut) [inform] needle, give (s.o.) the jitters

opkalefateren /ɔpkaləfatərə(n)/ (kalefaterde op, heeft opgekalefaterd) patch (up), doctor (up)

opkijken /ɔpkɛikə(n)/ (keek op, heeft opgekeken) **1** look up: ~ *tegen iem.* look up to s.o. **2** sit up, be surprised: *daar kijk ik van op* I'd never have thought it

opkikkeren /ɔpkɪkərə(n)/ (kikkerde op, is opgekikkerd): *daar zal je van* ~ it'll pick you up, it'll do you good

het **opklapbed** /ɔpklɑbɛt/ (pl: -den) foldaway bed

opklappen /ɔpklɑpə(n)/ (klapte op, heeft opgeklapt) fold up

opklaren /ɔpklarə(n)/ (klaarde op, is opgeklaard) brighten up, clear up: *de lucht klaart* *op* the sky's clearing up

opklimmen /ɔpklɪmə(n)/ (klom op, is opgeklommen) climb

opkloppen /ɔpklɔpə(n)/ (klopte op, heeft opgeklopt) **1** beat up: *slagroom* ~ whip cream **2** exaggerate

de **opknapbeurt** /ɔpknɑbørt/ (pl: -en) redecoration, facelift

¹**opknappen** /ɔpknɑpə(n)/ (knapte op, is opgeknapt) pick up, revive: *het weer is opgeknapt* the weather has brightened up; *hij zal er erg van* ~ it'll do him all the good in the world

²**opknappen** /ɔpknɑpə(n)/ (knapte op, heeft opgeknapt) **1** tidy up, do up, redecorate; restore: *het dak moet nodig eens opgeknapt worden* the roof needs repairing (*or:* fixing) **2** fix, carry out: *dat zal zij zelf wel* ~ she'll take care of it herself

zich ³**opknappen** /ɔpknɑpə(n)/ (knapte zich op, heeft zich opgeknapt) freshen (o.s.) up

opknopen /ɔpknopə(n)/ (knoopte op, heeft opgeknoopt) string up

opkomen /ɔpkomə(n)/ (kwam op, is opgekomen) **1** come up; rise; come in: [econ] ~*de landen* emerging countries; *spontaan* (*or: vanzelf*) ~ crop up **2** rise, ascend **3** occur; recur: *het komt niet bij hem op* it doesn't occur to him; *het eerste wat bij je opkomt* the first thing that comes into your mind **4** come on; set in; rise: *ik voel een verkoudheid* (*or: de koorts*) ~ I can feel a cold (*or:* the fever) coming on **5** [theatre] enter, come on (stage) **6** fight (for), stand up (for): *steeds voor elkaar* ~ stick together || *kom op, we gaan* come on, let's go; *kom maar op als je durft!* come on if you dare!

de **opkomst** /ɔpkomst/ **1** rise **2** attendance; turnout **3** entrance **4** rise, boom

opkopen /ɔpkopə(n)/ (kocht op, heeft opgekocht) buy up

opkrabbelen /ɔpkrɑbələ(n)/ (krabbelde op, is opgekrabbeld) struggle up (*or:* to) one's feet

opkrikken /ɔpkrɪkə(n)/ (krikte op, heeft opgekrikt) **1** jack up **2** hype up, pep up: *het moreel* ~ boost morale

opkroppen /ɔpkrɔpə(n)/ (kropte op, heeft opgekropt) bottle up, hold back

opkuisen /ɔpkœysə(n)/ (kuiste op, heeft opgekuist) [Belg] clean (up), tidy (up)

oplaadbaar /ɔplɑdbar/ (adj) rechargeable

de **oplaadkabel** /ɔplɑdkabəl/ (pl: -s) charging cable

het **oplaadpunt** /ɔplatpʏnt/ (pl: -en) charging point (*or:* station)

oplaaien /ɔplajə(n)/ (laaide op, is opgelaaid) flare (*or:* flame, blaze) up: *de strijd laait weer op* fighting has flared up again; *door de wind laaide het vuur weer op* the wind caused the fire to flare up again

opladen /ɔpladə(n)/ (laadde op, heeft opgeladen) charge

de **oplader** /ɔplader/ (pl: -s) charger: *mobiele* ~ powerbank

de **oplage** /ɔplaɣə/ (pl: -n) edition, issue; circulation: *een krant met een grote* ~ a newspaper with a wide circulation

oplappen /ɔplɑpə(n)/ (lapte op, heeft opgelapt) patch up

oplaten /ɔplatə(n)/ (liet op, heeft opgelaten) fly; release; launch

de **oplawaai** /ɔplawaj/ (pl: -en) wallop

oplazeren /ɔplazərə(n)/ (lazerde op, is opgelazerd) [Dutch; inform] bugger off, piss off, beat it

opleggen /ɔplɛɣə(n)/ (legde op, heeft opgelegd) enforce, impose: *wetten* ~ enforce (*or:* impose, lay down) laws; *iem. het zwijgen* ~ [also fig] silence s.o., put (*or:* reduce) s.o. to silence

de **oplegger** /ɔplɛɣər/ (pl: -s) semi-trailer, trailer: *truck met* ~ articulated lorry; [Am] articulated truck

opleiden /ɔplɛidə(n)/ (leidde op, heeft opgeleid) educate, instruct: *hij is tot advocaat opgeleid* he has been trained as a lawyer

de **opleiding** /ɔplɛidɪŋ/ (pl: -en) **1** education, training: *een* ~ *volgen (krijgen)* receive training, train; *zij volgt een* ~ *voor secretaresse* she is doing a secretarial course; *een wetenschappelijke* ~ an academic (*or:* a university) education **2** institute, (training) college; academy

het **opleidingscentrum** /ɔplɛidɪŋsɛntrʏm/ (pl: -centra) training centre

opletten /ɔplɛtə(n)/ (lette op, heeft opgelet) **1** watch, take care: *let op waar je loopt* look where you're going; *let maar eens op* mark my words; wait and see **2** pay attention: *opgelet!, let op!* attention please!, take care!

oplettend /ɔplɛtənt/ (adj, adv) **1** observant, observing: *zij sloeg hem* ~ *gade* she watched him carefully (*or:* closely) **2** attentive

de **oplettendheid** /ɔplɛtəntɦɛit/ attention, attentiveness

opleuken /ɔpløkə(n)/ (leukte op, heeft opgeleukt) liven up, brighten up

opleven /ɔplevə(n)/ (leefde op, is opgeleefd) revive

opleveren /ɔpleverə(n)/ (leverde op, heeft opgeleverd) **1** deliver; surrender: *tijdig* ~ deliver on time **2** yield: *wat levert dat baantje op?* what does (*or:* how much does) the job pay?; *voordeel* ~ yield profit; *het schrijven van boeken levert weinig op* writing (books) doesn't bring in much **3** produce: *het heeft me niets dan ellende opgeleverd* it brought me nothing but misery

de **oplevering** /ɔpleverɪŋ/ (pl: -en) delivery;

[bldg] completion

de **opleving** /ˈɔplevɪŋ/ revival; recovery; upturn, pick-up: *een **plotselinge** ~* an upsurge

oplezen /ˈɔpleze(n)/ (las op, heeft opgelezen) read (out), call (out, off)

oplichten /ˈɔplɪҳtə(n)/ (lichtte op, heeft opgelicht) swindle, cheat, con: *iem. ~ voor 2 ton* swindle (*or:* con) s.o. out of 200,000 euros

de **oplichter** /ˈɔplɪҳtər/ (pl: -s) swindler, crook, con(fidence) man (woman)

de **oplichterij** /ɔplɪҳtərɛɪ̯/ (pl: -en) swindle, con(-trick)

de **oplichting** /ˈɔplɪҳtɪŋ/ fraud, con(-trick)

oplikken /ˈɔplɪkə(n)/ (likte op, heeft opgelikt) lick up, lap up

de **oploop** /ˈɔplop/ **1** crowd **2** riot, tumult

¹**oplopen** /ˈɔplopə(n)/ (liep op, is opgelopen) **1** go up, run up, walk up: *de trap ~* run (*or:* go, walk) up the stairs **2** increase, mount, rise: *de spanning laten ~* build up the tension **3** bump into, run into

²**oplopen** /ˈɔplopə(n)/ (liep op, heeft opgelopen) catch, get: *een **verkoudheid** ~* catch a cold || *achterstand ~* get behind, fall behind

oplopend /ˈɔplopənt/ (adj) **1** rising, sloping (upwards) **2** increasing, mounting: *een hoog ~e ruzie* a flaming row

oplosbaar /ɔplɔzbar/ (adj) solvable

de **oploskoffie** /ˈɔploskɔfi/ instant coffee

het **oplosmiddel** /ˈɔplɔsmɪdəl/ solvent; thinner

¹**oplossen** /ˈɔplɔsə(n)/ (loste op, is opgelost) dissolve: *die **vlekken** lossen op als sneeuw voor de zon* those stains will vanish in no time

²**oplossen** /ˈɔplɔsə(n)/ (loste op, heeft opgelost) **1** solve **2** (re)solve: *dit zou het **probleem** moeten ~* this should settle (*or:* solve) the problem

de **oplossing** /ˈɔplɔsɪŋ/ (pl: -en) solution; answer

opluchten /ˈɔplʏҳtə(n)/ (luchtte op, heeft opgelucht) relieve: *dat lucht op!* what a relief!; *opgelucht ademhalen* draw a breath of relief

de **opluchting** /ˈɔplʏҳtɪŋ/ relief: *tot mijn grote ~* to my great relief, much to my relief

opluisteren /ˈɔplœystərə(n)/ (luisterde op, heeft opgeluisterd) grace, add lustre to

de **opmaak** /ˈɔpmak/ **1** layout, set-out, mock-up; format **2** embellishment; trimming

de **opmaat** /ˈɔpmat/ overture(s), prelude

opmaken /ˈɔpmakə(n)/ (maakte op, heeft opgemaakt) **1** finish (up), use up: *al zijn geld ~* spend all one's money **2** make up: *zich ~* make o.s. up **3** draw up: *de balans ~* weigh the pros and cons, take stock **4** lay out, make up **5** gather: *moet ik daaruit ~ dat ...* do I gather (*or:* conclude) from it that ... || *het bed ~* make (up) the bed; *zich ~ om te vertrekken* prepare to leave

de **opmars** /ˈɔpmars/ (pl: -en) [also fig] march, advance

opmerkelijk /ɔpmɛrkələk/ (adj, adv) remarkable, striking

opmerken /ˈɔpmɛrkə(n)/ (merkte op, heeft opgemerkt) **1** observe; note **2** note, notice **3** observe, remark: *mag ik misschien even iets ~?* may I make an observation?

de **opmerking** /ˈɔpmɛrkɪŋ/ (pl: -en) remark, observation, comment: *hou je brutale ~en voor je* keep your comments to yourself

opmerkzaam /ˈɔpmɛrksam/ (adj, adv) attentive, observant

opmeten /ˈɔpmetə(n)/ (mat op/meette op, heeft opgemeten) measure; survey

opnaaien /ˈɔpnajə(n)/ (naaide op, heeft opgenaaid) needle: *laat je toch niet zo ~* keep your hair (*or:* shirt) on

de **opname** /ˈɔpnamə/ (pl: -n, -s) **1** admission **2** shot; [film] shooting; take; recording **3** withdrawal

opnemen /ˈɔpnemə(n)/ (nam op, heeft opgenomen) **1** withdraw: *een snipperdag ~* take a day off **2** take: *iets (te) gemakkelijk ~* be (too) casual about sth. **3** record; [film] shoot: *een concert ~* record a concert **4** measure: *de gasmeter ~* read the (gas)meter; *de temperatuur ~* take the temperature; *de tijd ~ (van)* time a person **5** take down **6** admit, introduce, include: *laten ~ in een ziekenhuis* hospitalize; *in het ziekenhuis opgenomen worden* be admitted to hospital **7** admit, receive: *ze werd snel opgenomen in de groep* she was soon accepted as one of the group **8** answer: *er wordt niet opgenomen* there's no answer **9** absorb || *het tegen iem. ~* take s.o. on; *hij kan het tegen iedereen ~* he can hold his own against anyone; *het voor iem. ~* speak (*or:* stick) up for s.o.

opnieuw /ɔpni̯w/ (adv) **1** (once) again, once more: *telkens (steeds) ~* again and again; time and (time) again **2** (once) again, once more: *nu moet ik weer helemaal ~ beginnen* now I'm back to square one

opnoemen /ˈɔpnumə(n)/ (noemde op, heeft opgenoemd) name, call (out); enumerate: *te veel om op te noemen* too much (*or:* many) to mention

de **opoe** /ˈɔpu/ (pl: -s) [Dutch] gran(ny), gran(d)ma

opofferen /ˈɔpɔfərə(n)/ (offerde op, heeft opgeofferd) sacrifice

de **opoffering** /ˈɔpɔfərɪŋ/ (pl: -en) sacrifice; [fig] expense

het **oponthoud** /ˈɔpɔnthɑut/ stop(page), delay: *~ hebben* be delayed

oppakken /ˈɔpɑkə(n)/ (pakte op, heeft opgepakt) **1** run in, pick up, round up

de **oppas** /ˈɔpɑs/ (pl: -sen) babysitter, childminder

oppassen /ˈɔpɑsə(n)/ (paste op, heeft opgepast) **1** look out, be careful: *pas op voor zakkenrollers* beware of pickpockets **2** babysit

de **oppasser** /ɔpɑsər/ (pl: -s) keeper

oppeppen /ɔpɛpə(n)/ (pepte op, heeft opgepept) pep (up)

opperbest /ɔpərbɛst/ (adj, adv) splendid, excellent: *in een ~ humeur* in high spirits

het **opperbevel** /ɔpərbəvɛl/ supreme command, high command

de **opperbevelhebber** /ɔpərbəvɛlhɛbər/ (pl: -s) commander-in-chief, supreme commander

opperen /ɔpərə(n)/ (opperde, heeft geopperd) put forward, propose, suggest

het **opperhoofd** /ɔpərhoft/ (pl: -en) chief, chieftain

de **opperhuid** /ɔpərhœyt/ epidermis

oppermachtig /ɔpərmɑxtəx/ (adj, adv) supreme

opperst /ɔpərst/ (adj) supreme, complete

het **oppervlak** /ɔpərvlɑk/ (pl: -ken) **1** surface, face **2** (surface) area

oppervlakkig /ɔpərvlɑkəx/ (adj, adv) superficial, shallow: *(zo) ~ beschouwd* on the face of it; *iem. ~ kennen* have a nodding acquaintance with s.o., know s.o. slightly

de **oppervlakkigheid** /ɔpərvlɑkəxhɛit/ (pl: -heden) superficiality, shallowness

de **oppervlakte** /ɔpərvlɑktə/ (pl: -n, -s) **1** surface, face **2** surface (area)

het **oppervlaktewater** /ɔpərvlɑktəwatər/ (pl: -en) surface water

het **Opperwezen** /ɔpərwezə(n)/ Supreme Being

oppiepen /ɔpipə(n)/ (piepte op, heeft opgepiept) bleep

oppikken /ɔpɪkə(n)/ (pikte op, heeft opgepikt) pick up, collect: *ik pik je bij het station op* I will pick you up at the station

oppimpen /ɔpɪmpə(n)/ (pimpte op, heeft opgepimpt) pimp up, sex up

opplakken /ɔplɑkə(n)/ (plakte op, heeft opgeplakt) stick (on), glue (on), paste (on), affix

oppoetsen /ɔputsə(n)/ (poetste op, heeft opgepoetst) polish (up): *[fig] zijn Frans ~* brush up one's French

oppompen /ɔpɔmpə(n)/ (pompte op, heeft opgepompt) pump up; blow up [socc]; inflate

de **opponent** /ɔponɛnt/ (pl: -en) opponent

de **opportunist** /ɔportynɪst/ (pl: -en) opportunist

opportunistisch /ɔportynɪstis/ (adj, adv) opportunistic

de **oppositie** /ɔpozi(t)si/ (pl: -s) opposition

de **oppositieleider** /ɔpozi(t)silɛidər/ (pl: -s) opposition leader, leader of the opposition

oppotten /ɔpotə(n)/ (potte op, heeft opgepot) hoard (up)

oprakelen /ɔprakələ(n)/ (rakelde op, heeft opgerakeld) rake up, drag up

opraken /ɔprakə(n)/ (raakte op, is opgeraakt) run out (*or:* short, low), be low; run out

oprapen /ɔprapə(n)/ (raapte op, heeft opgeraapt) pick up, gather

oprecht /ɔprɛxt/ (adj, adv) sincere, heartfelt

de **oprechtheid** /ɔprɛxthɛit/ sincerity: *in alle ~* in all sincerity

oprichten /ɔprɪxtə(n)/ (richtte op, heeft opgericht) set up, establish; start; found: *een onderneming ~* establish (*or:* start) a company

de **oprichter** /ɔprɪxtər/ (pl: -s) founder

de **oprichting** /ɔprɪxtɪŋ/ (pl: -en) foundation; establishment; formation

oprijden /ɔprɛidə(n)/ (reed op, is opgereden) ride along; drive along: *een oprijlaan ~* turn into a drive; *tegen iets ~* crash into (*or:* collide with) sth.

de **oprijlaan** /ɔprɛilan/ (pl: -lanen) drive(way)

oprijzen /ɔprɛizə(n)/ (rees op, is opgerezen) rise, tower

de **oprit** /ɔprɪt/ (pl: -ten) **1** drive, access **2** approach road, slip road

de **oproep** /ɔprup/ **1** call, appeal: *een dringende oproep doen* make an urgent call (*or:* appeal) (to) **2** call: *een gemiste ~* a missed call

oproepen /ɔprupə(n)/ (riep op, heeft opgeroepen) **1** summon, call (up); page: *als getuige ~* call as a witness; *opgeroepen voor militaire dienst* conscripted (*or:* drafted) into military service **2** call up, evoke, conjure up; arouse

de **oproepkracht** /ɔprupkrɑxt/ (pl: -en) standby employee (*or:* worker)

het **oproer** /ɔprur/ (pl: -en) revolt; insurrection

de **oproerkraaier** /ɔprurkrajər/ (pl: -s) agitator, insurgent

de **oproerpolitie** /ɔprurpoli(t)si/ riot police

oprollen /ɔprolə(n)/ (rolde op, heeft opgerold) **1** roll up, curl up; coil up; wind **2** round up

de **oprotpremie** /ɔprotpremi/ (pl: -s) [inform] **1** severance pay **2** repatriation bonus

oprotten /ɔprotə(n)/ (rotte op, is opgerot) [vulg] piss off, sod off, bugger off

opruien /ɔprœyjə(n)/ (ruide op, heeft opgeruid) incite, agitate

opruimen /ɔprœymə(n)/ (ruimde op, heeft opgeruimd) clean (out), clear (out), tidy (up), clear (up): *de rommel ~* clear (*or:* tidy) away the mess; *opgeruimd staat netjes* a) that's things nice and tidy again; b) [iron] good riddance (to bad rubbish)

de **opruiming** /ɔprœymɪŋ/ (pl: -en) clearance; (clearance) sale; clear-out

de **opruimingsuitverkoop** /ɔprœymɪŋsœytfərkop/ (stock-)clearance sale

oprukken /ɔprʏkə(n)/ (rukte op, is opgerukt) advance

opschalen /ɔpsxalə(n)/ scale up: *de productie ~* scale up production; *de tropische storm* *werd opgeschaald **naar** een orkaan* the tropical storm was upgraded to a hurricane

opscharrelen /ɔpsχɑrələ(n)/ (scharrelde op, heeft opgescharreld) rake up, dig up

opschepen /ɔpsχepə(n)/ (scheepte op, heeft opgescheept) saddle with, palm off on: *iem. **met** iets* ~ saddle s.o. with sth., plant sth. on s.o.

de **opscheplepel** /ɔpsχɛplepəl/ (pl: -s) table-spoon, server

¹**opscheppen** /ɔpsχɛpə(n)/ (schepte op, heeft opgeschept) brag, boast: ~ **met** *(over) zijn nieuwe auto* show off one's new car

²**opscheppen** /ɔpsχɛpə(n)/ (schepte op, heeft opgeschept) dish up, serve out, spoon out; ladle out: *mag ik je nog eens ~?* may I give you (or: will you have) another helping?

de **opschepper** /ɔpsχɛpər/ (pl: -s) boaster, braggart

opschepperig /ɔpsχɛpərəχ/ (adj, adv) boastful

de **opschepperij** /ɔpsχɛpərɛi/ (pl: -en) bragging; exhibitionism; show

opschieten /ɔpsχitə(n)/ (schoot op, is opgeschoten) **1** hurry up, push on (or: ahead) **2** get on, make progress (or: headway): *daar schiet je niks mee op* that's not going to get you anywhere **3** get on (or: along): *ze kunnen goed **met** elkaar* ~ they get on very well (together)

opschorten /ɔpsχɔrtə(n)/ (schortte op, heeft opgeschort) adjourn; suspend; postpone, put on hold

het **opschrift** /ɔpsχrɪft/ (pl: -en) **1** legend; inscription; lettering **2** headline; heading; caption; direction

opschrijven /ɔpsχrɛivə(n)/ (schreef op, heeft opgeschreven) write/take/put (or: note, jot) down: *schrijf het maar voor mij op* charge it to (or: put it on) my account

opschrikken /ɔpsχrɪkə(n)/ (schrikte op, is opgeschrikt) start, startle, jump

opschudden /ɔpsχʏdə(n)/ (schudde op, heeft opgeschud) **1** shake up, fluff up, plump up: *de **kussens** ~* shake (or: plump, fluff) up the pillows **2** shake (up): *ze werd opgeschud **uit** haar dromen* she was shaken out of her dreams; *een ingeslapen **organisatie** ~* shake things up at a sleepy organization

de **opschudding** /ɔpsχʏdɪŋ/ (pl: -en) commotion, disturbance

opschuiven /ɔpsχœyvə(n)/ (schoof op, is opgeschoven) move up (or: over), shift up, shove up

opslaan /ɔpslan/ (sloeg op, heeft opgeslagen) **1** lay up, store **2** hit up; serve **3** lift, raise **4** save: *gegevens* ~ store data

de **opslag** /ɔpslɑχ/ (pl: -en) **1** rise; [Am] raise; surcharge: ~ **krijgen** get (or: receive) a rise **2** [sport] serve; service; ball **3** storage

de **opslagplaats** /ɔpslɑχplats/ (pl: -en) warehouse, (storage) depot; store; depository [goods]

de **opslagtank** /ɔpslɑχtɛŋk/ storage tank

opslokken /ɔpslɔkə(n)/ (slokte op, heeft opgeslokt) swallow up (or: down)

¹**opsluiten** /ɔpslœytə(n)/ (sloot op, heeft opgesloten) shut up, lock up; confine; put (or: place) under restraint; cage; pound: *opgesloten in zijn kamertje **zitten*** be cooped up in one's room

zich ²**opsluiten** /ɔpslœytə(n)/ (sloot zich op, heeft zich opgesloten) shut o.s. in, lock o.s. up

de **opsluiting** /ɔpslœytɪŋ/ confinement, imprisonment: *eenzame* ~ solitary confinement

de **opsmuk** /ɔpsmʏk/ finery, gaudery: *zonder* ~ unadorned, plain

opsnorren /ɔpsnɔrə(n)/ (snorde op, heeft opgesnord) [inform] ferret out, rake out

opsnuiven /ɔpsnœyvə(n)/ (snoof op, heeft opgesnoven) sniff (up), snuff; inhale; snort

opsodemieteren /ɔpsodəmitərə(n)/ (sodemieterde op, is opgesodemieterd) [Dutch; inform] piss off, bugger off: *sodemieter op!* go to hell!

het **opsolferen** /ɔpsɔlfərə(n)/ [Belg] palm off (on): *iem. iets* ~ palm sth. off on s.o.

opsommen /ɔpsɔmə(n)/ (somde op, heeft opgesomd) enumerate, recount

de **opsomming** /ɔpsɔmɪŋ/ (pl: -en) enumeration, list, run-down

opsouperen /ɔpsupərə(n)/ (soupeerde op, heeft opgesoupeerd) squander, spend

opsparen /ɔpsparə(n)/ (spaarde op, heeft opgespaard) save up; hoard (up)

opspelden /ɔpspɛldə(n)/ (speldde op, heeft opgespeld) pin up/on

opspelen /ɔpspelə(n)/ (speelde op, heeft opgespeeld) play up

opsplitsen /ɔpsplɪtsə(n)/ (splitste op, heeft opgesplitst) split up (into), break up (into)

opsporen /ɔpspɔrə(n)/ (spoorde op, heeft opgespoord) track, trace; detect; track down, hunt down

de **opsporing** /ɔpspɔrɪŋ/ (pl: -en) location, tracing

de **opsporingsdienst** /ɔpspɔrɪŋzdinst/ (pl: -en) investigation service (or: department)

de **opspraak** /ɔpsprak/ discredit: *in* ~ *komen* get o.s. talked about

opspringen /ɔpsprɪŋə(n)/ (sprong op, is opgesprongen) jump/leap (or: spring, start) up; spring (or: jump, start) to one's feet; bounce

opstaan /ɔpstan/ (stond op, is opgestaan) stand up, get up, get (or: rise) to one's feet, get on one's feet: *met **vallen** en* ~ with ups and downs; *hij staat altijd **vroeg** op* he's an early riser (or: bird), he is always up early

de **opstand** /ɔpstɑnt/ (pl: -en) (up)rising, revolt, rebellion, insurrection de **opstandeling** /ɔ̱pstɑndəlɪŋ/ (pl: -en) rebel, insurgent

opstandig /ɔpstɑ̱ndəχ/ (adj) rebellious, mutinous, insurgent

de **opstanding** /ɔ̱pstɑndɪŋ/ resurrection: *de ~ van Christus* the Resurrection of Christ

de **opstap** /ɔ̱pstɑp/ (pl: -pen) step: *struikel niet over het ~je* don't stumble over the step, mind the step

¹**opstapelen** /ɔ̱pstapələ(n)/ (stapelde op, heeft opgestapeld) pile up, heap up, stack (up); amass; accumulate

zich ²**opstapelen** /ɔ̱pstapələ(n)/ (stapelde zich op, heeft zich opgestapeld) pile up, accumulate, mount up

opstappen /ɔ̱pstɑpə(n)/ (stapte op, is opgestapt) go away, move on; be off; resign

¹**opsteken** /ɔ̱psteke(n)/ (stak op, is opgestoken) rise, get up: *de wind steekt op* the wind is getting up (*or:* rising)

²**opsteken** /ɔ̱psteke(n)/ (stak op, heeft opgestoken) **1** put up, hold up, raise: *een paraplu ~* put up an umbrella **2** learn; pick up: *zij hebben er niet veel van opgestoken* they have not taken much of it in **3** gather up, pin up

de **opsteker** /ɔ̱pstekər/ (pl: -s) windfall, piece of (good) luck

het **opstel** /ɔ̱pstɛl/ (pl: -len) (school) essay, composition: *een ~ maken over* write/do an essay (*or:* a paper) on

¹**opstellen** /ɔ̱pstɛlə(n)/ (stelde op, heeft opgesteld) **1** set up (*or:* erect); post, place (sth., s.o.); arrange; dispose, line up; deploy: [sport] *opgesteld staan* be lined up **2** draw up, formulate; draft: *een plan ~* draw up a plan

zich ²**opstellen** /ɔ̱pstɛlə(n)/ (stelde zich op, heeft zich opgesteld) **1** take up a position; form; line up, station o.s., post o.s. **2** take up a position (on), adopt an attitude (towards); pose (as): *zich keihard ~* take a hard line

de **opstelling** /ɔ̱pstɛlɪŋ/ (pl: -en) **1** placing, erection; deployment; position; arrangement **2** position, attitude **3** [sport] line-up

opstijgen /ɔ̱pstɛiɣə(n)/ (steeg op, is opgestegen) **1** ascend, rise; go up; take off; lift off **2** mount

opstoken /ɔ̱pstokə(n)/ (stookte op, heeft opgestookt) incite (to), put up (to sth.)

het **opstootje** /ɔ̱pstocə/ (pl: -s) disturbance, (street) row

de **opstopping** /ɔ̱pstɔpɪŋ/ (pl: -en) stoppage, blockage; traffic jam; congestion

opstrijken /ɔ̱pstrɛikə(n)/ (streek op, heeft opgestreken) pocket, rake in, scoop in, scoop up

opstropen /ɔ̱pstropə(n)/ (stroopte op, heeft opgestroopt) roll up, turn up

opstuiven /ɔ̱pstœyvə(n)/ (stoof op, is opgestoven) **1** fly up **2** dash up, tear up; flare out/up

opsturen /ɔ̱pstyrə(n)/ (stuurde op, heeft opgestuurd) send, post, mail

optekenen /ɔ̱ptekənə(n)/ (tekende op, heeft opgetekend) write, note, take down

optellen /ɔ̱ptɛlə(n)/ (telde op, heeft opgeteld) add (up), count up, total up: *twee getallen (bij elkaar) ~* add up two numbers

de **optelling** /ɔ̱ptɛlɪŋ/ (pl: -en) **1** addition **2** (addition) sum

opteren /ɔpte̱rə(n)/ (opteerde, heeft geopteerd): *~ voor* opt for, choose

de **opticien** /ɔptiʃɛ̱/ (pl: -s) optician

de **optie** /ɔ̱psi/ (pl: -s) **1** option; choice, alternative: *een ~ op een huis hebben* have an option on a house; *verliezen is geen ~* losing is not an option **2** [Belg] optional subject

de **optiebeurs** /ɔ̱psibørs/ (pl: -beurzen) options market

de **optiek** /ɔpti̱k/ point of view, angle

optillen /ɔ̱ptɪlə(n)/ (tilde op, heeft opgetild) lift (up), raise

¹**optimaal** /ɔptima̱l/ (adj) optimum

²**optimaal** /ɔptima̱l/ (adv) optimal

optimaliseren /ɔptimalize̱rə(n)/ (optimaliseerde, heeft geoptimaliseerd) optimize

het **optimisme** /ɔptimɪ̱smə/ optimism

de **optimist** /ɔptimɪ̱st/ (pl: -en) optimist

optimistisch /ɔptimɪ̱stis/ (adj, adv) optimistic: *de zaak ~ bekijken* look on the bright side

optioneel /ɔpʃone̱l/ (adj) optional

optisch /ɔ̱ptis/ (adj) optic(al), visual

de **optocht** /ɔ̱ptɔχt/ (pl: -en) procession, parade; march

optornen /ɔ̱ptɔrnə(n)/ (tornde op, is opgetornd) battle (with), struggle (against)

het ¹**optreden** /ɔ̱ptredə(n)/ (pl: -s) **1** action; way of acting; behaviour; attitude; manner; bearing; demeanour: *het ~ van de politie werd fel bekritiseerd* the conduct of the police was strongly criticized **2** appearance, performance; show; gig

²**optreden** /ɔ̱ptredə(n)/ (trad op, heeft opgetreden) **1** appear; perform: *in een film ~* appear in a film **2** act (as), serve (as) **3** act, take action: *streng ~* take firm action; *~ tegen iem.* take action against s.o.

het **optrekje** /ɔ̱ptrɛkjə/ (pl: -s) pied-à-terre

¹**optrekken** /ɔ̱ptrɛkə(n)/ (trok op, is opgetrokken) **1** accelerate **2** be busy (with); take care (of); hang around (with): *samen ~* hang around together **3** rise, lift

²**optrekken** /ɔ̱ptrɛkə(n)/ (trok op, heeft opgetrokken) pull up, haul up, raise; hoist (up): *met opgetrokken knieën* with one's knees pulled up; *een muur ~* put up a wall

optrommelen /ɔ̱ptrɔmələ(n)/ (trommelde op, heeft opgetrommeld) drum up

optuigen /ɔ̱ptœyɣə(n)/ (tuigde op, heeft opgetuigd) dress up, tart up

opvallen /ɔ̱pfɑlə(n)/ (viel op, is opgevallen)

strike, be conspicuous, attract attention (or: notice): ~ **door** *zijn kleding* attract attention because of (or: on account of) one's clothes; *wat het **meest** opvalt* ... what strikes one most ...

opvallend /ɔpfɑlənt/ (adj, adv) striking, conspicuous, marked: *het ~ste **kenmerk*** the most striking feature

de **opvang** /ɔpfɑŋ/ relief, emergency measures

opvangen /ɔpfɑŋə(n)/ (ving op, heeft opgevangen) **1** catch, receive **2** overhear, pick up, catch: *flarden van een gesprek* ~ overhear scraps of conversation **3** take care of; receive: *de **kinderen** ~ als ze uit school komen* take care of (or: look after) the children after school **4** catch, collect

het **opvanghuis** /ɔpfɑŋhœys/ (pl: -huizen) reception centre, relief centre

opvatten /ɔpfɑtə(n)/ (vatte op, heeft opgevat) take, interpret: *iets **verkeerd** (fout)* ~ misinterpret (or: misunderstand) sth.

de **opvatting** /ɔpfɑtɪŋ/ (pl: -en) view, notion, opinion

opvegen /ɔpfeɣə(n)/ (veegde op, heeft opgeveegd) sweep up

opvijzelen /ɔpfɛɪzələ(n)/ (vijzelde op, heeft opgevijzeld) boost

opvissen /ɔpfɪsə(n)/ (viste op, heeft opgevist) **1** dredge up **2** [fig] fish out/up, dig up

opvliegen /ɔpfliɣə(n)/ (vloog op, is opgevlogen) **1** fly up **2** jump to one's feet **3** flare out/up

opvliegend /ɔpfliɣənt/ (adj) short-tempered, quick-tempered

de **opvlieger** /ɔpfliɣər/ (pl: -s) flush

opvoeden /ɔpfudə(n)/ (voedde op, heeft opgevoed) bring up, raise: *goed* (or: *slecht*) *opgevoed* well-bred (or: ill-bred); well (or: badly) brought up

de **opvoeder** /ɔpfudər/ (pl: -s) educator, tutor, governess

de **opvoeding** /ɔpfudɪŋ/ (pl: -en) upbringing, education: *een **strenge** ~* a strict upbringing

opvoedkundig /ɔpfutkʏndəx/ (adj, adv) educational, educative, pedagogic(al)

opvoeren /ɔpfurə(n)/ (voerde op, heeft opgevoerd) **1** increase; step up; speed up; accelerate: *een **motor** ~* tune (up) an engine; *de **snelheid** ~* raise (or: step up) the pace; increase speed **2** perform, put on, present

de **opvoering** /ɔpfurɪŋ/ (pl: -en) **1** production, presentation **2** performance

opvolgen /ɔpfɔlɣə(n)/ (volgde op, heeft opgevolgd) **1** succeed **2** follow up, observe; comply with; obey: *iemands **advies** ~* follow (or: take) s.o.'s advice

de **opvolger** /ɔpfɔlɣər/ (pl: -s) successor (to)

opvouwbaar /ɔpfɑubar/ (adj) folding, fold-up, foldaway; collapsible

opvouwen /ɔpfɑuwə(n)/ (vouwde op, heeft opgevouwen) fold up; fold away

opvragen /ɔpfraɣə(n)/ (vraagde op/vroeg op, heeft opgevraagd) ask for, request; check: *informatie* ~ request information; *zijn **beltegoed** ~* check his calling credit

¹**opvreten** /ɔpfretə(n)/ (vrat op, heeft opgevreten) eat up, devour: [hum] *ik **kan** je wel ~* I could just eat you up

zich ²**opvreten** /ɔpfretə(n)/ (vrat zich op, heeft zich opgevreten) get worked up (about sth.), get more and more upset

opvrolijken /ɔpfroləkə(n)/ (vrolijkte op, heeft opgevrolijkt) cheer (s.o.) up, brighten (s.o., sth.) up

opvullen /ɔpfʏlə(n)/ (vulde op, heeft opgevuld) stuff, fill

opwaaien /ɔpwajə(n)/ (waaide op/woei op, is opgewaaid) (get) blow(n) up

opwaarderen /ɔpwardərə(n)/ (waardeerde op, heeft opgewaardeerd) revalue, upgrade, uprate: *zijn **beltegoed** ~* top up his phone (or: balance)

opwaarts /ɔpwarts/ (adj, adv) upward; upwards: *~e **druk*** upward pressure, upthrust; [of a liquid] buoyancy

opwachten /ɔpwɑxtə(n)/ (wachtte op, heeft opgewacht) lie in wait for

de **opwachting** /ɔpwɑxtɪŋ/: *zijn ~ **maken*** appear; *welke bands zullen hun ~ **maken** tijdens het festival?* which bands will be playing at the festival?; *zijn ~ bij iem. **maken*** pay one's respects to s.o.

¹**opwarmen** /ɔpwɑrmə(n)/ (warmde op, is opgewarmd) **1** warm up, heat up **2** [sport] warm up, loosen up, limber up

²**opwarmen** /ɔpwɑrmə(n)/ (warmde op, heeft opgewarmd) warm up, heat up, reheat

opwegen /ɔpweɣə(n)/ (woog op, heeft opgewogen) be equal (to); make up (for); compensate (for)

opwekken /ɔpwɛkə(n)/ (wekte op, heeft opgewekt) **1** arouse; excite; stir: *de **eetlust** (van iem.) ~* whet (s.o.'s) appetite **2** generate, create: *elektriciteit* ~ generate electricity

opwekkend /ɔpwɛkənt/ (adj, adv) **1** cheerful **2** tonic

opwellen /ɔpwɛlə(n)/ (welde op, is opgeweld) well up, rise

de **opwelling** /ɔpwɛlɪŋ/ (pl: -en) impulse: *in een ~ iets doen* do sth. on impulse

zich **opwerken** /ɔpwɛrkə(n)/ (werkte zich op, heeft zich opgewerkt) work one's way up, climb the ladder

opwerpen /ɔpwɛrpə(n)/ (wierp op, heeft opgeworpen) **1** throw up: *een **muntstuk** ~* toss a coin **2** raise **3** raise, erect: *barricades ~* raise (or: erect) barriers ‖ *zich ~ **als*** set o.s. up as

¹**opwinden** /ɔpwɪndə(n)/ (wond op, heeft opgewonden) **1** wind up **2** wind **3** excite, wind (or: key, tense) up

zich ²**opwinden** /ɔpwɪndə(n)/ (wond zich op,

heeft zich opgewonden) become incensed, get excited, fume: *zich ~ over iets* get worked up about sth.

opwindend /ɔpwɪndənt/ (adj) **1** exciting, thrilling: *het was heel ~* it was quite a thrill **2** sexy, suggestive

de **opwinding** /ɔpwɪndɪŋ/ (pl: -en) excitement; tension: *voor de nodige ~ zorgen* cause quite a stir

opzadelen /ɔpsadələ(n)/ (zadelde op, heeft opgezadeld) saddle: [fig] *iem. met iets ~* saddle s.o. with sth.

opzeggen /ɔpsɛɣə(n)/ (zegde op/zei op, heeft opgezegd) **1** cancel, terminate; resign; give notice: *zijn baan ~* resign from one's job; *een contract ~* terminate a contract; *de huur ~* cancel (*or:* terminate) a tenancy **2** read out; recite

de **opzegtermijn** /ɔpsɛɣtɛrmɛin/ (pl: -en) (period, term of) notice

de ¹**opzet** /ɔpsɛt/ **1** organization; scheme; idea; layout; design, plan; set-up **2** intention, aim

het ²**opzet** /ɔpsɛt/ intention, purpose: *met ~* on purpose; [Dutch] *het was geen boze ~*, [Belg] *het was geen kwaad ~* no harm was intended

de **opzetborstel** /ɔpsɛdbɔrstəl/ (pl: -s) (tooth)brush head

het **opzetje** /ɔpsɛcə/ (pl: -s) **1** rough draft, first attempt **2** setup

opzettelijk /ɔpsɛtələk/ (adj, adv) deliberate, intentional; on purpose: *hij deed het ~* he did it on purpose

¹**opzetten** /ɔpsɛtə(n)/ (zette op, is opgezet) blow up; arise; gather; rise, set in

²**opzetten** /ɔpsɛtə(n)/ (zette op, heeft opgezet) **1** put up, raise; stand (sth., s.o.) up: *een tent ~* pitch (*or:* put up) a tent; *zijn kraag ~* turn up (*or:* raise) one's collar **2** put on: *zijn hoed ~* put one's hat on; *theewater ~* put the kettle on (for tea) **3** set up, start (off): *een zaak ~* set up in business, set up shop **4** stuff

het **opzicht** /ɔpsɪxt/ (pl: -en) respect, aspect: *ten ~e van* a) compared with (*or:* to), in relation to; b) with respect (*or:* regard) to, as regards; *in geen enkel ~* in no way, not in any sense

de **opzichter** /ɔpsɪxtər/ (pl: -s) **1** supervisor; overseer; superintendent **2** inspector; (site) foreman

opzichtig /ɔpsɪxtəx/ (adj, adv) showy; blatant

het ¹**opzien** /ɔpsin/ stir, fuss; amazement: *veel ~ baren* cause quite a stir (*or:* fuss)

²**opzien** /ɔpsin/ (zag op, heeft opgezien) **1** look up: *daar zullen ze van ~* that'll make them sit up (and take notice) **2** (+ tegen) not be able to face, shrink from: *ergens als (tegen) een berg tegen ~* dread sth.

opzienbarend /ɔpsimbarənt/ (adj) sensational, spectacular, stunning

de **opziener** /ɔpsinər/ (pl: -s) supervisor, inspector

opzij /ɔpsɛi/ (adv) **1** aside, out of the way **2** at (*or:* on) one side

opzijgaan /ɔpsɛiɣan/ (ging opzij, is opzijgegaan) give way to, make way for, go to one side

opzijleggen /ɔpsɛileɣə(n)/ (legde opzij, heeft opzijgelegd): *geld ~* put money aside; *hij legde het boek opzij tot 's avonds* he put the book aside till the evening

opzijzetten /ɔpsɛizɛtə(n)/ (zette opzij, heeft opzijgezet) put (*or:* set) aside, table, discard, scrap

opzitten /ɔpsɪtə(n)/ (zat op, heeft opgezeten) sit up (and beg) ‖ *hij heeft er 20 jaar tropen ~* he's been in the tropics 20 years

opzoeken /ɔpsukə(n)/ (zocht op, heeft opgezocht) **1** look up, find: *een adres ~* look up an address **2** look up, call on: *je moet me eens komen ~* you must come and see me sometime

opzuigen /ɔpsœyɣə(n)/ (zoog op, heeft opgezogen) suck up; hoover up, vacuum up: *limonade door een rietje ~* drink lemonade through a straw

opzwellen /ɔpswɛlə(n)/ (zwol op, is opgezwollen) swell (up, out), bulge; billow; balloon

opzwepen /ɔpswepə(n)/ (zweepte op, heeft opgezweept) whip up

oraal /oral/ (adj, adv) oral

het **orakel** /orakəl/ (pl: -s) oracle

de **orang-oetan** /oraŋutan/ (pl: -s) orang-utan

het ¹**oranje** /oraɲə/ (pl: -s) [color] orange; [traffic lights] amber

²**oranje** /oraɲə/ (adj) orange; [traffic lights] amber

Oranje /oraɲə/ (pl: -s) **1** (the house of) Orange **2** the Dutch team

de **oratie** /ora(t)si/ (pl: -s) oration

het **oratorium** /oratorijʏm/ (pl: -s, oratoria) **1** oratorio **2** oratory

de **orchidee** /ɔrxide/ (pl: -ën) orchid

de **orde** /ɔrdə/ (pl: -n, -s) order; discipline: *verstoring van de openbare ~* disturbance of the peace; *dat komt (wel) in ~* it will turn out all right (*or:* OK); *in ~!* all right!, fine!, OK!; *voor de goede ~ wijs ik u erop dat …* for the record, I would like to remind you that …; *zijn leven op ~ hebben* have his life under control; *~ op zaken stellen* put (*or:* set) things right; *iem. tot de ~ roepen* call s.o. to order ‖ *iem. een ~ verlenen* invest s.o. with a decoration, decorate s.o.; *dat is van een heel andere ~* that is of an entirely different order; *aan de ~ van de dag zijn* be the order of the day

ordelijk /ɔrdələk/ (adj, adv) neat, tidy

ordeloos /ɔrdəlos/ (adj, adv) disorganized, disorderly

ordenen /ɔrdənə(n)/ (ordende, heeft geordend) arrange, sort (out) de **ordening** /ɔrdənɪŋ/ (pl: -en) **1** arrangement, organization **2** regulation, structuring

ordentelijk /ɔrdɛntələk/ (adj, adv) respectable, decent

de **order** /ɔrdər/ (pl: -s) order, instruction, command: *uitstellen tot nader ~* put off until further notice; *een ~ plaatsen voor twee vrachtauto's bij D.* order two lorries from D.

de **ordeverstoring** /ɔrdəvərstorɪŋ/ (pl: -en) disturbance, disturbance (*or:* breach) of the peace

ordinair /ɔrdinɛːr/ (adj, adv) **1** common, vulgar; coarse; crude **2** common, ordinary, normal

de **ordner** /ɔrtnər/ (pl: -s) (document) file

de **oregano** /oreɣano/ oregano

oreren /orerə(n)/ (oreerde, heeft georeerd) **1** deliver a speech **2** orate

het **orgaan** /ɔrɣan/ (pl: organen) organ

de **orgaandonatie** /ɔrɣandona(t)si/ (pl: -s) organ donation

de **orgaantransplantatie** /ɔrɣantrɑnsplɑnta(t)si/ organ transplant(ation)

de **organisatie** /ɔrɣaniza(t)si/ (pl: -s) **1** organization, arrangement **2** organization, society, association

de **organisatieadviseur** /ɔrɣaniza(t)siɑtfizør/ (pl: -s) organization consultant

de **organisator** /ɔrɣanizator/ (pl: -en) organizer

organisatorisch /ɔrɣanizatoris/ (adj, adv) organizational

organisch /ɔrɣanis/ (adj, adv) organic

organiseren /ɔrɣanizerə(n)/ (organiseerde, heeft georganiseerd) **1** organize, arrange **2** organize, fix up, stage

het **organisme** /ɔrɣanɪsmə/ (pl: -n) organism

de **organist** /ɔrɣanɪst/ (pl: -en) organist, organ player

het **orgasme** /ɔrɣɑsmə/ (pl: -n) orgasm, climax

het **orgel** /ɔrɣəl/ (pl: -s) (pipe) organ: *een ~ draaien* grind an organ

de **orgelman** /ɔrɣəlmɑn/ organ-grinder

de **orgie** /ɔrɣi/ (pl: -ën) orgy, revelry

de **Oriënt** /orijɛnt/ Orient

de **oriëntatie** /orijɛnta(t)si/ orientation, information: *zijn ~ kwijtraken* lose one's bearings

zich **oriënteren** /orijɛnterə(n)/ (oriënteerde zich, heeft zich georiënteerd) **1** orientate o.s. **2** look around

het **oriënteringsvermogen** /orijɛnterɪŋsfərmoɣə(n)/ sense of direction

de **originaliteit** /oriʒinalitɛit/ originality

de **origine** /oriʒinə/ origin: *zij zijn van Franse ~* they are of French origin (*or:* extraction)

het **¹origineel** /oriʒinel/ (pl: originelen) original

²origineel /oriʒinel/ (adj, adv) original

de **orka** /ɔrka/ (pl: -'s) orc(a)

de **orkaan** /ɔrkan/ (pl: orkanen) hurricane

de **orkaankracht** /ɔrkɑnkrɑxt/ hurricane force

het **orkest** /ɔrkɛst/ (pl: -en) orchestra

orkestreren /ɔrkɛstrerə(n)/ (orkestreerde, heeft georkestreerd) orchestrate

het **ornaat** /ɔrnat/: [hum] *in vol ~* in best bib and tucker, dressed (up) to the nines

het **ornament** /ɔrnamɛnt/ (pl: -en) ornament

de **orthodontist** /ɔrtodɔntɪst/ (pl: -en) orthodontist

orthodox /ɔrtodɔks/ (adj) orthodox

de **orthopedie** /ɔrtopedi/ orthop(a)edics

orthopedisch /ɔrtopedis/ (adj) orthop(a)edic

de **os** /ɔs/ (pl: ossen) bullock, ox: *slapen als een os* sleep like a log

de **OS** /oɛs/ (pl) *Olympische Spelen* Olympic Games

de **ossenhaas** /ɔsə(n)has/ (pl: -hazen) tenderloin

de **ossenstaartsoep** /ɔsə(n)startsup/ oxtail soup

de **otter** /ɔtər/ (pl: -s) otter

oubollig /aubɔləx/ (adj) corny, waggish

oud /aut/ (adj) **1** old: *zo'n veertig jaar ~* fortyish; *vijftien jaar ~* fifteen years old (*or:* of age), aged fifteen; *hij werd honderd jaar ~* he lived to (be) a hundred; *de ~ste zoon* **a)** the elder son; **b)** the oldest son; *haar ~ere zusje* her elder (*or:* big) sister; *hoe ~ ben je?* how old are you?; *toen zij zo ~ was als jij* when she was your age; *zij zijn even ~* they are the same age; *hij is vier jaar ~ dan ik* he is four years older than me; *kinderen van zes jaar en ~er* children from six upwards **2** old, aged: *de ~e dag* old age; *je bent nooit te ~ om te leren* you are never too old to learn **3** old, ancient; long-standing: *een ~e mop* a corny joke; *~ papier* waste paper; *~er in dienstjaren* senior **4** ancient; outdated; archaic: *~ nummer* back issue **5** ex-, former, old ‖ *jong en ~* young and old; *~ en nieuw vieren* see in the New Year; *alles bij het ~e laten* leave everything as it was; *hij is weer helemaal de ~e* he's back to normal again

oudbakken /audbɑkə(n)/ (adj) stale

de **oudedagsvoorziening** /audədɑxsforzinɪŋ/ (pl: -en) provision for old age

de **oudejaarsavond** /audəjarsavɔnt/ (pl: -en) New Year's Eve

de **ouder** /audər/ (pl: -s) parent: *mijn ~s* my parents; my folks

de **ouderavond** /audəravɔnt/ (pl: -en) parents' evening

de **ouderdom** /audərdɔm/ age, (old) age

de **ouderdomsdiabetes** /audərdɔmzdijabetəs/ type-2 diabetes, adult-onset diabetes

de **ouderdomskwaal** /audərdɔmskwal/ (pl: -kwalen) old person's complaint

de **ouderejaars** /audərəjars/ older student, senior student

ouderlijk /audərlək/ (adj) parental: *het ~ huis* the parental home

de **ouderling** /audərlɪŋ/ (pl: -en) church warden, elder

de **ouderraad** /ɑudərat/ (pl: -raden) parents' council

het **ouderschapsverlof** /ɑudərsχɑpsfərlɔf/ (pl: -verloven) maternity leave; parental leave

ouderwets /ɑudərwɛts/ (adj, adv) old-fashioned; outmoded

de **oudgediende** /ɑutχədjndə/ (pl: -n) old hand, veteran

de **oudheid** /ɑuthɛit/ antiquity, ancient times

de **oudheidkunde** /ɑuthɛitkʏndə/ arch(a)eology

het **oudjaar** /ɑutjar/ New Year's Eve

het **oudje** /ɑucə/ (pl: -s) old person, old chap, old fellow, old dear, old girl

de **oud-leerling** /ɑutlerlɪŋ/ (pl: -en) former pupil

de **oudoom** /ɑutom/ (pl: -s) great-uncle

oudsher /ɑutshɛr/ (adv): *van* ~ of old, from way back

de **oudste** /ɑutstə/ (pl: -n) **1** oldest, eldest: *wie is de* ~, *jij of je broer?* who is older, you or your brother? **2** (most) senior

de **oud-strijder** /ɑutstrɛidər/ (pl: -s) war veteran

de **oudtante** /ɑutɑntə/ (pl: -s) great-aunt

out /ɑut/ (adj): [inform] ~ *gaan* pass out

de **outbox** /ɑudbɔks/ outbox

de **outcast** /ɑutkɑːst/ outcast

de **outfit** /ɑutfɪt/ (pl: -s) outfit

de **outlet** /ɑutlɛt/ outlet

het/de **outplacement** /ɑutplɛsmənt/ outplacement

de **output** /ɑutpʏt/ (pl: -s) output: *als* ~ *leveren* output

de **outsider** /ɑutsɑjdər/ (pl: -s) outsider

de **outsourcing** /ɑutsɔːrsɪŋ/ outsourcing

de **ouverture** /uvɛrtyrə/ (pl: -s, -n) overture, prelude

de **ouwe** /ɑuwə/ (pl: -n) [inform] **1** chief, boss **2** old man || *een gouwe* ~ a golden oldie

de **ouwehoer** /ɑuwəhur/ [Dutch; inform] windbag

ouwehoeren /ɑuwəhurə(n)/ (ouwehoerde, heeft geouwehoerd) [Dutch; inform] go on

de **ouwel** /ɑuwəl/ wafer

ouwelijk /ɑuwələk/ (adj, adv) oldish, elderly

het **ov** /ovẹ/ *openbaar vervoer* public transport

het **¹ovaal** /oval/ (pl: ovalen) oval

²ovaal /oval/ (adj) oval

de **ovatie** /ova(t)si/ (pl: -s) ovation

de **ov-chipkaart** /ovetʃɪpkart/ (pl: -en) [Dutch] public transport pass

de **oven** /ovə(n)/ (pl: -s) oven

de **ovenfriet** /ovə(n)frit/ oven chips; [Am] oven-baked fries

de **ovenschaal** /ovə(n)sχal/ (pl: -schalen) baking dish, casserole

de **ovenschotel** /ovə(n)sχotəl/ (pl: -s) oven dish

ovenvast /ovə(n)vɑst/ (adj) oven-proof

de **ovenwant** /ovə(n)wɑnt/ oven glove; [Am] oven mitt

¹over /ovər/ (adj) over, finished: *de pijn is al* ~ the pain has gone

²over /ovər/ (adv) **1** across, over: *zij zijn* ~ *uit Ankara* they are over from Ankara; ~ *en weer* back and forth; from both sides **2** left, over: *als er genoeg tijd* ~ *is* if there is enough time left; *het is* ~ *van gisteren* that's left over from yesterday; *er is 10 euro* ~ there are 10 euros left

³over /ovər/ (prep) **1** over, above: ~ *een periode van … over a period of …* **2** across, over: *hij werkt* ~ *de grens* he works across (*or:* over) the border; ~ *de heuvels* over (*or:* beyond) the hills; ~ *straat lopen* walk around; ~ *de hele lengte* all along **3** about: *de winst* ~ *het vierde kwartaal* the profit over the fourth quarter **4** by way of, via: *zij communiceren* ~ *de mobilofoon* they communicate by mobile telephone; *zij reed* ~ *Nijmegen naar Zwolle* she drove to Zwolle via Nijmegen; *een brug* ~ *de rivier* a bridge over (*or:* across) the river **5** about: *verheugd* ~ delighted at (*or:* with) **6** over, across **7** after, in: *zaterdag* ~ *een week* a week on Saturday **8** over, past: *zij is twee maanden* ~ *tijd* she is two months overdue; *tot* ~ *zijn oren in de problemen zitten* be up to one's neck in trouble; *het is kwart* ~ *vijf* it is a quarter past five; *het is vijf* ~ *half zes* it is twenty-five to six

overal /ovərɑl/ (adv) **1** everywhere; anywhere: ~ *bekend* widely known; *van* ~ from everywhere, from all over the place **2** everything: *zij weet* ~ *van* she knows about everything

de **overall** /ovərɔːl/ (pl: -s) overalls

overbekend /ovərbəkɛnt/ (adj) very well-known

overbelast /ovərbəlɑst/ (adj) overloaded, overburdened

overbelasten /ovərbəlɑstə(n)/ (overbelastte, heeft overbelast) overload, overburden, overtax

de **overbelasting** /ovərbəlɑstɪŋ/ stress, strain

overbelichten /ovərbəlɪχtə(n)/ (belichtte over, heeft overbelicht) overexpose

de **overbevolking** /ovərbəvɔlkɪŋ/ overpopulation

overbevolkt /ovərbəvɔlkt/ (adj) overpopulated

overbezet /ovərbəzɛt/ (adj) overcrowded: *mijn agenda is al* ~ my programme is already overbooked

de **overblijf** /ovərblɛif/: *op de* ~ *zitten* stay at school during the lunch break; *deze school heeft geen* ~ at this school you cannot stay at school during the lunch break

het **overblijfsel** /ovərblɛifsəl/ (pl: -en) **1** relic; remnant; remains **2** remains; leftovers; rem-

nant
overblijven /ǫvərblɛivə(n)/ (bleef over, is overgebleven) **1** be left, remain: *van al mijn goede voornemens blijft zo **niets** over* all my good intentions are coming to nothing now **2** be left (over)
de **overblijver** /ǫvərblɛivər/ (pl: -s) school-luncher
overbluffen /ovərblʏfə(n)/ (overblufte, heeft overbluft) confound, dumbfound: *laat je door hem niet ~* don't let him come it over (*or:* with) you
overbodig /ovərbǫdəχ/ (adj, adv) superfluous, redundant; unnecessary: ~ *te zeggen* needless to say; *het is geen ~e **luxe*** it would be no luxury, it's really necessary
[1]**overboeken** /ǫvərbukə(n)/ (boekte over, heeft overgeboekt) transfer
[2]**overboeken** /ovərbukə(n)/ (overboekte, heeft overboekt) overbook
de **overboeking** /ǫvərbukɪŋ/ (pl: -en) transfer (into, to)
overboord /ovərbort/ (adv) overboard: *man ~!* man overboard!
overbrengen /ǫvərbrɛŋə(n)/ (bracht over, heeft overgebracht) **1** take (*or:* bring, carry) (across), move, transfer **2** convey, communicate: *boodschappen* (or: *iemands **groeten**) ~* convey messages (*or:* s.o.'s greetings) **3** pass (on)
overbruggen /ovərbrʏɣə(n)/ (overbrugde, heeft overbrugd) bridge; tide over
de **overbruggingsperiode** /ovərbrʏɣɪŋsperi-jodə/ (pl: -s) interim (period)
de **overcapaciteit** /ǫvərkapasitɛit/ overcapacity
de **overdaad** /ǫvərdat/ excess
overdadig /ovərdadəχ/ (adj, adv) excessive, profuse; extravagant; lavish; wasteful
overdag /ovərdɑχ/ (adv) by day, during the daytime
overdekken /ovərdɛkə(n)/ (overdekte, heeft overdekt) cover
overdekt /ovərdɛkt/ (adj) covered: *een ~ zwembad* an indoor swimming pool
overdenken /ovərdɛŋkə(n)/ (overdacht, heeft overdacht) consider, think over
overdoen /ǫvərdun/ (deed over, heeft overgedaan) do again: *een **examen** ~* resit an examination; [fig] *iets (nog eens) **dunnetjes** ~* give a repeat performance, have another try (*or:* go) (at sth.)
overdonderen /ovərdǫndərə(n)/ (overdonderde, heeft overdonderd) overwhelm, confound: *een ~d **succes*** an overwhelming success
de **overdosis** /ǫvərdozɪs/ (pl: -doses) overdose
de **overdracht** /ǫvərdrɑχt/ (pl: -en) transfer, handing over
overdrachtelijk /ovərdrɑχtələk/ (adj, adv) metaphorical

overdragen /ǫvərdraɣə(n)/ (droeg over, heeft overgedragen) hand over, assign; delegate
overdreven /ovərdrevə(n)/ (adj, adv) exaggerated: *dat **is** sterk ~* that is highly exaggerated; that is way out of proportion; *hij **doet** wel wat ~* he lays it on a bit thick
overdrijven /ovərdrɛivə(n)/ (overdreef, heeft overdreven) **1** overdo (it, sth.), go too far (with sth.): *je mustn't* overdo it (*or:* things) **2** exaggerate
de **overdrijving** /ovərdrɛivɪŋ/ (pl: -en) exaggeration; overstatement
de **overdruk** /ǫvərdrvk/ (pl: -ken) overpressure
overduidelijk /ovərdœydələk/ (adj, adv) patently obvious, evident
overdwars /ovərdwɑrs/ (adv) crosswise, transversely
overeen /ovərẹn/ (adv) **1** to the same thing **2** crossed ‖ [Belg] *de armen ~* arms crossed
[1]**overeenkomen** /ovərẹŋkomə(n)/ (kwam overeen, is overeengekomen) **1** correspond (to): ~ *met de beschrijving* fit the description **2** be similar (to): *geheel ~ **met*** fully correspond to (*or:* with)
[2]**overeenkomen** /ovərẹŋkomə(n)/ (kwam overeen, is overeengekomen) agree (on), arrange: *zoals* overeengekomen as agreed; *iets **met** iem. ~* arrange sth. with s.o.
de **overeenkomst** /ovərẹŋkɔmst/ (pl: -en) **1** similarity, resemblance: ~ *vertonen* **met** show similarity to, resemble **2** agreement: *een ~ **sluiten** met iem.* make (*or:* enter into) an agreement with s.o.
overeenkomstig /ovərẹŋkɔmstəχ/ (prep) in accordance with, according to: ~ *de **verwachtingen*** in line with expectations
overeenstemmen /ovərẹnstɛmə(n)/ (stemde overeen, heeft overeengestemd) *see* [1]*overeenkomen*
de **overeenstemming** /ovərẹnstɛmɪŋ/ **1** harmony, conformity, agreement: *niet **in** ~ met* out of line (*or:* keeping) with, inconsistent with **2** agreement: *tot ~ komen* come to terms, reach an agreement
overeind /ovərẹint/ (adv) **1** upright; on end: ~ *gaan staan* stand up (straight), get to one's feet **2** standing: ~ *blijven* keep upright; keep one's footing; [fig] *een stelling ~ houden* hold onto (*or:* stick to) a theory
overgaan /ǫvərɣan/ (ging over, is overgegaan) **1** move over (*or:* across), go over, cross (over): *de **brug** ~* go over the bridge, cross (over) the bridge **2** transfer, pass **3** move up: *van de vierde **naar** de vijfde klas ~* move up from the fourth to the fifth form **4** change, convert, turn: *de kleuren gingen **in** elkaar over* the colours shaded into one another **5** move on to; proceed to, turn to; change (over) (to); switch (over) (to): ~ *tot de aanschaf van* (or: *het gebruik van*) … start buying (*or:* using) …

6 pass (over, away); wear off; blow over: *de pijn zal wel ~* the pain will wear off **7** ring

de **overgang** /ˈoʊvərɣɑŋ/ (pl: -en) **1** transitional stage, link **2** transition, change(over) **3** change of life, menopause: *in de ~ zijn* be at the change of life

de **overgangsperiode** /ˈoʊvərɣɑŋsperijodə/ (pl: -n, -s) transition(al) period

overgankelijk /oʊvərˈɣɑŋkələk/ (adj) [linguistics] transitive

de **overgave** /ˈoʊvərɣavə/ **1** surrender, capitulation **2** dedication, devotion, abandon(ment): *zij doet haar werk met ~* she's a very dedicated worker

¹**overgeven** /ˈoʊvərɣevə(n)/ (gaf over, heeft overgegeven) be sick, vomit, throw up

zich ²**overgeven** /ˈoʊvərɣevə(n)/ (gaf zich over, heeft zich overgegeven) surrender

overgevoelig /oʊvərɣəˈvuləχ/ (adj, adv) hypersensitive, oversensitive

het **overgewicht** /ˈoʊvərɣəwɪχt/ **1** overweight, extra (weight) **2** excess baggage

¹**overgieten** /oʊvərˈɣitə(n)/ (overgoot, heeft overgoten) bathe [light]; cover

²**overgieten** /ˈoʊvərɣitə(n)/ (goot over, heeft overgegoten) pour (into)

de **overgooier** /ˈoʊvərɣojər/ (pl: -s) pinafore dress

het **overgordijn** /ˈoʊvərɣɔrdɛin/ (pl: -en) (long, heavy, lined) curtain

overgroot /oʊvərˈɣrot/ (adj) vast, huge: *met overgrote meerderheid* by an overwhelming majority

de **overgrootmoeder** /ˈoʊvərɣrotmudər/ (pl: -s) great-grandmother

de **overgrootvader** /ˈoʊvərɣrotfadər/ (pl: -s) great-grandfather

overhaast /oʊvərˈhast/ (adj, adv) rash, hurried, (over)hasty

overhaasten /oʊvərˈhastə(n)/ (overhaastte, heeft overhaast) rush, hurry

overhalen /ˈoʊvərhalə(n)/ (haalde over, heeft overgehaald) **1** persuade, talk (s.o.) into (sth.): *iem. tot iets ~* talk s.o. into doing sth. **2** pull (on): *de trekker ~* pull the trigger

de **overhand** /ˈoʊvərhɑnt/ upper hand, advantage: *de ~ hebben* have the upper hand, be on top

overhandigen /oʊvərˈhɑndəɣə(n)/ (overhandigde, heeft overhandigd) hand (over), present; *iem. iets ~* hand sth. over to s.o.

de **overheadkosten** /ˈoʊvərhɛːtkɔstə(n)/ (pl) overhead cost (or: expenses)

de **overheadprojector** /ˈoʊvərhɛːtprojɛktɔr/ (pl: -s) overhead projector

overhebben /ˈoʊvərhɛbə(n)/ (had over, heeft overgehad) **1** have (for), be prepared to give (for); not begrudge (s.o. sth.): *ik zou er alles voor ~* I would do (or: give) anything for it **2** have over, have left: *geen geld meer ~* have no more money left

overheen /oʊvərˈhen/ (adv) **1** over: *daar groeit hij wel ~* he will grow out of it **2** across, over: *er een doek* (or: *dweil*) *~ halen* run a cloth (or: mop) over it **3** past ‖ *ergens ~ lezen* miss (or: overlook) sth.; *zich ergens ~ zetten* get the better of sth., overcome sth., get over it

overheerlijk /oʊvərˈhɛrlək/ (adj, adv) absolutely delicious

overheersen /oʊvərˈhɛrsə(n)/ (overheerste, heeft overheerst) dominate, predominate

de **overheerser** /oʊvərˈhɛrsər/ (pl: -s) oppressor, dictator

de **overheersing** /oʊvərˈhɛrsɪŋ/ (pl: -en) rule, oppression

de **overheid** /ˈoʊvərhɛit/ (pl: -heden) **1** government **2** authority: *de plaatselijke ~* the local authorities

het **overheidsbedrijf** /ˈoʊvərhɛitsbədrɛif/ (pl: -bedrijven) public enterprise, state enterprise; a public utility company

de **overheidsdienst** /ˈoʊvərhɛitsdinst/ (pl: -en) government service, public service, the civil service

de **overheidsinstelling** /ˈoʊvərhɛitsɪnstɛlɪŋ/ (pl: -en) government institution (or: agency)

overheidswege /ˈoʊvərhɛitsweɣə/: *van ~* by the authorities, officially

overhellen /ˈoʊvərhɛlə(n)/ (helde over, heeft overgeheld) lean (over), tilt (over)

het **overhemd** /ˈoʊvərhɛmt/ (pl: -en) shirt

overhevelen /ˈoʊvərhevələ(n)/ (hevelde over, heeft overgeheveld) transfer

overhoophalen /oʊvərˈhophalə(n)/ (haalde overhoop, heeft overhoopgehaald) turn upside down

overhoopliggen /oʊvərˈhoplɪɣə(n)/ (lag overhoop, heeft overhoopgelegen) **1** be in a mess **2** be at loggerheads (with): *ze liggen altijd met elkaar overhoop* they're always at loggerheads (with one another)

overhoren /oʊvərˈhorə(n)/ (overhoorde, heeft overhoord) test

de **overhoring** /oʊvərˈhorɪŋ/ (pl: -en) test

overhouden /ˈoʊvərhɑudə(n)/ (hield over, heeft overgehouden) have left, still have: *dat houdt niet over* it's only (just) adequate, it's no better than it should be

overig /ˈoʊvərəχ/ (adj) remaining, other: *voor het ~e* for the rest, otherwise

overigens /ˈoʊvərəɣəns/ (adv) anyway, for that matter, though

overjarig /oʊvərˈjarəχ/ (adj) more than one year old

de **overjas** /ˈoʊvərjɑs/ (pl: -sen) overcoat

de **overkant** /ˈoʊvərkɑnt/ other side, opposite side: *zij woont aan de ~* she lives across the street

de **overkapping** /oʊvərˈkɑpɪŋ/ (pl: -en) covering, roof

overkijken /ˈoʊvərkɛikə(n)/ (keek over, heeft

overgekeken) look over: *zijn les ~* look through one's lesson

overkoepelend /ovərk**u**pələnt/ (adj, adv) coordinating

overkoken /**o**vərkokə(n)/ (kookte over, is overgekookt) boil over

¹**overkomen** /**o**vərkomə(n)/ (kwam over, is overgekomen) **1** come over: *oma is uit Marokko overgekomen* granny has come over from Morocco **2** come across, get across

²**overkomen** /ovərk**o**mə(n)/ (overkwam, is overkomen) happen to, come over: *dat kan de beste ~* that could happen to the best of us; *ik wist niet wat mij overkwam* I didn't know what was happening to me

¹**overladen** /ovərl**a**də(n)/ (adj) overloaded, overburdened

²**overladen** /ovərl**a**də(n)/ (overlaadde, heeft overladen) shower, heap on (*or:* upon): *hij werd ~ met werk* he was overloaded with work

³**overladen** /**o**vərladə(n)/ (laadde over, heeft overgeladen) transfer; trans-ship

overlangs /**o**vərlɑŋs/ (adj, adv) lengthwise; longitudinal: *iets ~ doorsnijden* cut sth. lengthwise

overlappen /ovərl**ɑ**pə(n)/ (overlapte, heeft overlapt) overlap

de **overlast** /**o**vərlɑst/ inconvenience, nuisance: *~ veroorzaken* cause trouble (*or:* annoyance)

overlaten /**o**vərlatə(n)/ (liet over, heeft overgelaten) **1** leave: *laat dat maar aan mij over!* just leave that to me! **2** leave (over): *veel* (*or: niets*) *te wensen ~* leave much (*or:* nothing) to be desired

overleden /ovərl**e**də(n)/ (adj) dead

de **overledene** /ovərl**e**dənə/ (pl: -n) deceased

het **overleg** /**o**vərlɛx/ **1** thought, consideration **2** consultation, deliberation: *~ voeren (over)* consult (on); *in (nauw) ~ met* in (close) consultation with; *in onderling ~* by mutual agreement

¹**overleggen** /ovərl**ɛ**xə(n)/ (overlegde, heeft overlegd) **1** consider: *hij overlegt wat hem te doen staat* he is considering what he has to do **2** consult, confer: *iets met iem. ~* consult (with) s.o. on sth.

²**overleggen** /**o**vərlɛxə(n)/ (legde over, heeft overgelegd) [Dutch] produce: *stukken ~* produce/submit (*or:* hand in) documents

overleven /ovərl**e**və(n)/ (overleefde, heeft overleefd) survive, outlive

de **overlevende** /ovərl**e**vəndə/ (pl: -n) survivor

overleveren /**o**vərlevərə(n)/ (leverde over, heeft overgeleverd) hand over, turn over, turn in

de **overlevering** /**o**vərlevərɪŋ/ (pl: -en) tradition: *via mondelinge ~* via oral tradition

overlezen /**o**vərlezə(n)/ (las over, heeft overgelezen) read over (*or:* through): *een ar-*

tikel vluchtig ~ skim through an article

overlijden /ovərl**ɛi**də(n)/ (overleed, is overleden) die

het **overlijdensbericht** /ovərl**ɛi**də(n)zbərɪxt/ (pl: -en) death announcement: *de ~en* the obituaries; the deaths

de **overloop** /**o**vərlop/ (pl: -lopen) landing

overlopen /**o**vərlopə(n)/ (liep over, is overgelopen) **1** walk over (*or:* across) **2** go over, defect: *~ naar de vijand* desert (*or:* defect) to the enemy **3** overflow || *~ van* enthousiasme be brimming (*or:* bubbling) (over) with enthusiasm

de **overloper** /**o**vərlopər/ (pl: -s) deserter, defector

de **overmaat** /**o**vərmat/ excess: *tot ~ van ramp* to make matters worse

de **overmacht** /**o**vərmɑxt/ **1** superior numbers (*or:* strength, forces): *tegenover een geweldige ~ staan* face fearful odds **2** circumstances beyond one's control, force majeure; Act of God

overmaken /**o**vərmakə(n)/ (maakte over, heeft overgemaakt) transfer, remit

overmannen /ovərm**ɑ**nə(n)/ (overmande, heeft overmand) overcome, overpower, overwhelm

overmatig /ovərm**a**təx/ (adj, adv) excessive

overmeesteren /ovərm**e**stərə(n)/ (overmeesterde, heeft overmeesterd) overpower, overcome

de **overmoed** /**o**vərmut/ overconfidence, recklessness

overmoedig /ovərm**u**dəx/ (adj, adv) overconfident, reckless

overmorgen /**o**vərmɔrɣə(n)/ (adv) the day after tomorrow

overnachten /ovərn**ɑ**xtə(n)/ (overnachtte, heeft overnacht) stay (*or:* spend) the night, stay (over)

de **overnachting** /ovərn**ɑ**xtɪŋ/ (pl: -en) **1** stay **2** night: *het aantal ~en* the number of nights (spent, slept)

de **overname** /**o**vərnamə/ takeover, purchase, taking-over

overnemen /**o**vərnemə(n)/ (nam over, heeft overgenomen) **1** receive **2** take (over): *de macht ~* assume power **3** adopt: *de gewoonten van een land ~* adopt the customs of a country **4** take over, buy

overpad /**o**vərpɑt/ *het recht van ~ hebben* have (a/the) right of way

de **overpeinzing** /ovərp**ɛi**nzɪŋ/ (pl: -en) reflection

overplaatsen /**o**vərplatsə(n)/ (plaatste over, heeft overgeplaatst) transfer

de **overplaatsing** /**o**vərplatsɪŋ/ (pl: -en) transfer, move

overplanten /**o**vərplɑntə(n)/ (plantte over, heeft overgeplant) **1** transplant **2** transplant, graft

de **overproductie** /overprodʏksi/ overproductie

overreden /overredə(n)/ (overreedde, heeft overreed) persuade

¹**overrijden** /overɛidə(n)/ (reed over, heeft overgereden) drive over; ride over

²**overrijden** /overɛidə(n)/ (overreed, heeft overreden) run over, knock down

overrijp /overɛip/ (adj) overripe

overrompelen /overɔmpələ(n)/ (overrompelde, heeft overrompeld) (take by) surprise, catch off guard, catch napping

overrulen /overulə(n)/ (overrulede, heeft overruled) overrule

overschaduwen /oversχadywə(n)/ (overschaduwde, heeft overschaduwd) overshadow, put in the shade

overschakelen /oversχakələ(n)/ (schakelde over, heeft/is overgeschakeld) **1** switch over **2** switch (or: change, go) over: *op de vierdaagse werkweek* ~ go over to a four-day week

de **overschakeling** /oversχakəlɪŋ/ switchover, changeover

overschatten /oversχɑtə(n)/ (overschatte, heeft overschat) overestimate, overrate

de **overschatting** /oversχɑtɪŋ/ (pl: -en) overestimation; overrating

overschieten /oversχitə(n)/ (schoot over, is overgeschoten) be left (over)

het **overschot** /oversχɔt/ (pl: -ten) remainder; remains; residue; remnant(s): *het stoffelijk* ~ the (mortal) remains, the body || [Belg] ~ *van* be absolutely right

overschreeuwen /oversχrewə(n)/ (overschreeuwde, heeft overschreeuwd) shout down: [fig] *zijn angst* ~ try to drown one's fear

overschrijden /oversχrɛidə(n)/ (overschreed, heeft overschreden) exceed, go beyond

¹**overschrijven** /oversχrɛivə(n)/ (overschreef, heeft overschreven) overwrite

²**overschrijven** /oversχrɛivə(n)/ (schreef over, heeft overgeschreven) **1** copy; [depr] crib: *iets in het net* ~ copy sth. out neatly **2** transfer; put in (s.o.'s) name

de **overschrijving** /oversχrɛivɪŋ/ (pl: -en) **1** putting in s.o. (else)'s name; [sport] transfer **2** remittance

¹**overslaan** /overslan/ (sloeg over, is overgeslagen) **1** jump (over); be infectious; be catching **2** break, crack: *met ~de stem* with a catch in one's voice

²**overslaan** /overslan/ (sloeg over, heeft overgeslagen) miss (out), skip, leave out, omit: *één beurt* ~ miss one turn; *een bladzijde* ~ skip a page; *een jaar* ~ skip a year

de **overslag** /overslɑχ/ (pl: -en) transfer, transshipment

overspannen /overspɑnə(n)/ (adj) **1** over-

strained, overtense(d) **2** overwrought: *hij is erg* ~ he is suffering from severe (over)strain

het **overspel** /overspɛl/ adultery

overspelen /overspelə(n)/ (speelde over, heeft overgespeeld) **1** replay: *de wedstrijd moest overgespeeld worden* the match had to be replayed **2** [sport] play on (to), pass the ball on to

overspelig /overspeləχ/ (adj) adulterous

overspoelen /overspulə(n)/ (overspoelde, heeft overspoeld) wash over; flood (across), inundate

het **overstaan** /overstan/: *ten* ~ *van* in the presence of, before

overstag /overstɑχ/ (adv): ~ *gaan* tack; [fig] change one's mind

de **overstap** /overstɑp/ (pl: -pen) changeover, switch-over

overstappen /overstɑpə(n)/ (stapte over, is overgestapt) **1** step over, cross **2** change, transfer: ~ *op de trein naar Groningen* change to the Groningen train

de **overste** /overstə/ (pl: -n) **1** lieutenant-colonel **2** (father, mother) superior, prior, prioress

de **oversteek** /overstek/ (pl: -steken) crossing

de **oversteekplaats** /overstekplats/ (pl: -en) crossing(-place); pedestrian crossing

oversteken /overstekə(n)/ (stak over, is overgestoken) cross (over), go across, come across

overstelpen /overstɛlpə(n)/ (overstelpte, heeft overstelpt) shower, swamp, inundate

overstemmen /overstɛmə(n)/ (overstemde, heeft overstemd) drown (out); shout down

¹**overstromen** /overstromə(n)/ (stroomde over, is overgestroomd) **1** flow over, flood **2** overflow

²**overstromen** /overstromə(n)/ (overstroomde, heeft overstroomd) **1** flood, inundate **2** flood, swamp: *de markt* ~ *met* flood the market with

de **overstroming** /overstromɪŋ/ (pl: -en) flood

overstuur /overstyr/ (adj, adv) upset; shaken: *mijn maag is* ~ my stomach is upset, I've got an upset stomach

de **overtocht** /overtɔχt/ (pl: -en) crossing; voyage

overtollig /overtɔləχ/ (adj, adv) **1** surplus, excess **2** superfluous, redundant

overtreden /overtredə(n)/ (overtrad, heeft overtreden) break, violate

de **overtreder** /overtredər/ (pl: -s) offender, wrongdoer

de **overtreding** /overtredɪŋ/ (pl: -en) offence, violation (or: breach) (of the rules); [sport] foul: *een zware* ~ a bad foul; *een* ~ *begaan tegenover een tegenspeler* foul an opponent; *een* ~ *op Janssen* a foul on (or: against) Janssen

overtreffen /ovərtrɛ́fə(n)/ (overtrof, heeft overtroffen) exceed, surpass, excel

het/de **overtrek** /óvərtrɛk/ (pl: -ken) cover, case

¹**overtrekken** /óvərtrɛkə(n)/ (trok over, is overgetrokken) pass (over)

²**overtrekken** /óvərtrɛkə(n)/ (trok over, heeft overgetrokken) trace: *met* inkt ~ trace in ink

³**overtrekken** /ovərtrɛ́kə(n)/ (overtrok, heeft overtrokken) cover; upholster

overtuigd /ovərtœ́yxt/ (adj) confirmed, convinced: *hij was ervan ~ te zullen slagen* he was confident (*or:* sure) that he would succeed; *ik ben er (vast, heilig) van ~ dat ...* I'm (absolutely) convinced that ...

overtuigen /ovərtœ́yɣə(n)/ (overtuigde, heeft overtuigd) convince, persuade

overtuigend /ovərtœ́yɣənt/ (adj, adv) convincing, cogent; persuasive; conclusive

de **overtuiging** /ovərtœ́yɣɪŋ/ (pl: -en) conviction, belief, persuasion: *godsdienstige ~* religious persuasion (*or:* beliefs); *vol (met) ~* with conviction

overtypen /óvərtipə(n)/ (typte over, heeft overgetypt) retype; type out

het **overuur** /óvəryr/ (pl: -uren) overtime hour; overtime: *overuren maken* work overtime

de **overval** /óvərval/ (pl: -len) surprise attack; raid; hold-up; stick-up

de **overvalknop** /óvərvalknɔp/ (pl: -pen) panic alarm button

overvallen /ovərvɑ́lə(n)/ (overviel, heeft overvallen) **1** raid; hold up; assault [pers]; surprise **2** surprise, take by surprise; overtake

de **overvaller** /óvərvɑlər/ (pl: -s) raider, attacker

¹**overvaren** /óvərvarə(n)/ (voer over, is overgevaren) cross (over), sail across

²**overvaren** /óvərvarə(n)/ (voer over, heeft overgevaren) ferry, take across, put across

oververhit /ovərvərhɪ́t/ (adj) overheated: *de gemoederen raakten ~* feelings ran high

oververhitten /óvərvərhɪtə(n)/ (oververhitte, heeft oververhit) overheat

oververmoeid /ovərvərmújt/ (adj) overtired, exhausted

de **oververtegenwoordiging** /óvərvərteɣə(n)wordəɣɪŋ/ overrepresentation

de **oververzekering** /óvərvərzekərɪŋ/ overinsurance

overvleugelen /ovərvlǿɣələ(n)/ (overvleugelde, heeft overvleugeld) outstrip, eclipse

de **overvloed** /óvərvlut/ abundance ‖ *in ~* in plenty, in abundance; *ten ~e ...* needless to say ...; *misschien ten ~e herinneren wij u eraan dat ...* we would like to remind you - perhaps unnecessarily - that ...

overvloedig /ovərvlúdəx/ (adj, adv) abundant, plentiful, copious

overvloeien /óvərvlujə(n)/ (vloeide over,

heeft/is overgevloeid) **1** overflow, run over **2** (+ van) overflow (with): *~ van enthousiasme* bubble (over) with enthusiasm **3** flow (over); fade: *kleuren in elkaar laten ~* run the colours into one another; *het ene beeld in het andere laten ~* fade one image into another

overvoeren /ovərvúrə(n)/ (overvoerde, heeft overvoerd) [Dutch] glut, overstock, oversupply, surfeit

overvol /óvərvɔl/ (adj) overfull; overcrowded; packed

overvragen /ovərvrátɣə(n)/ (overvraagde/overvroeg, heeft overvraagd) overcharge, ask too much

overwaaien /óvərwajə(n)/ (waaide over/woei over, is overgewaaid) blow over

de **overwaarde** /óvərwardə/ surplus value: *de ~ van een huis* home equity

overwaarderen /óvərwardərə(n)/ (waardeerde over, heeft overgewaardeerd) overvalue, overrate

de ¹**overweg** /óvərwɛx/ level crossing; [Am] railroad crossing: *een bewaakte ~* a guarded (*or:* manned) level crossing

²**overweg** /ovərwɛ́x/ (adv): *met een nieuwe machine ~ kunnen* know how to handle a new machine; *goed met elkaar ~ kunnen* get along well

overwegen /ovərwéɣə(n)/ (overwoog, heeft overwogen) consider, think over, think out: *de nadelen (risico's) ~* count the cost; *wij ~ een nieuwe auto te kopen* we are thinking of (*or:* considering) buying a new car

overwegend /óvərwéɣənt/ (adv) predominantly, mainly, for the most part

de **overweging** /ovərwéɣɪŋ/ (pl: -en) **1** consideration, thought: *in ~ nemen* consider **2** consideration, ground, reason: *uit financiële ~en* for financial reasons

overweldigen /ovərwɛ́ldəɣə(n)/ (overweldigde, heeft overweldigd) overwhelm, overcome

overweldigend /ovərwɛ́ldəɣənt/ (adj) overwhelming, overpowering: *een ~e meerderheid halen* win a landslide victory

het **overwerk** /óvərwɛrk/ overtime (work)

overwerken /óvərwɛrkə(n)/ (werkte over, heeft overgewerkt) work overtime

overwerkt /óvərwɛ́rkt/ (adj) overworked, overstrained

het **overwicht** /óvərwɪxt/ ascendancy, preponderance; authority

de **overwinnaar** /ovərwɪ́nar/ (pl: -s) victor, winner; conqueror

overwinnen /ovərwɪ́nə(n)/ (overwon, heeft overwonnen) **1** defeat, overcome **2** conquer, overcome **3** conquer, overcome, surmount: *moeilijkheden ~* overcome/surmount (*or:* get over) difficulties

de **overwinning** /ovərwɪ́nɪŋ/ (pl: -en) victory, conquest, triumph; win: *een ~ behalen* win a victory, be victorious, win, triumph; *een **verpletterende** ~* a sweeping victory

de **overwinteraar** /ovərwɪntərar/ (pl: -s) **1** hibernator **2** s.o. spending the winter in a warm country; [Am] snowbird

overwinteren /ovərwɪntərə(n)/ (overwinterde, heeft overwinterd) **1** (over)winter: *~ in Spanje* spend the winter in Spain **2** hibernate

de **overwintering** /ovərwɪntərɪŋ/ (pl: -en) (over)wintering, hibernation

overwoekeren /ovərwukərə(n)/ (overwoekerde, heeft overwoekerd) overgrow, overrun: *overwoekerd worden **door** onkruid* become overgrown with weeds

overzees /ovərzes/ (adj) oversea(s)

overzetten /ovərzɛtə(n)/ (zette over, heeft overgezet) take across (*or:* over); ferry (across, over): *iem. de **grens** ~* deport s.o.

het **overzicht** /ovərzɪxt/ (pl: -en) **1** survey, view: *~ **vanuit** de lucht* bird's-eye view; *ik heb **geen** enkel ~ meer* I have lost all track of the situation **2** survey, (over)view, summary; review

overzichtelijk /ovərzɪxtələk/ (adj, adv) well-organized; clearly set out

overzien /ovərzin/ (overzag, heeft overzien) survey; overlook; command (a view of); review: *de **gevolgen** zijn niet te ~* the consequences are incalculable

de **overzijde** /ovərzɛidə/ other side, opposite side: *aan de ~ van het gebouw* opposite the building

overzwemmen /ovərzwɛmə(n)/ (zwom over, heeft/is overgezwommen) swim (across): *het **Kanaal** ~* swim the Channel

de **ov-jaarkaart** /ovejarkart/ (pl: -en) [Dutch] annual season ticket, travel card

de **OVSE** /ovecse/ *Organisatie voor Veiligheid en Samenwerking in Europa* OSCE

de **ovulatie** /ovyla(t)si/ (pl: -s) ovulation

de **oxidatie** /ɔksida(t)si/ (pl: -s) oxidation

het **oxide** /ɔksidə/ (pl: -n, -s) oxide

oxideren /ɔksiderə(n)/ (oxideerde, is geoxideerd) oxidize

de **ozb** /ozɛdbe/ *onroerendezaakbelasting* property tax(es)

het/de **ozon** /ozɔn/ ozone

de **ozonlaag** /ozɔnlax/ ozone layer

p

de **p** /pe/ (pl: p's) p, P

de **pa** /pa/ (pl: pa's) dad(dy), pa: *haar pa en* **ma** her mum and dad(dy)

p/a /pea/ *per adres* c/o

het **paadje** /pacə/ (pl: -s) path; trail

paaien /pajə(n)/ (paaide, heeft gepaaid) placate, appease

de **paal** /pal/ (pl: palen) **1** post, stake, pole; pile **2** (goal)post: *hij schoot* **tegen (op)** *de* ~ he hit the (goal)post ‖ **voor** ~ *staan* look foolish (*or:* stupid)

paaldansen /paldansə(n)/ (paaldanste, heeft gepaaldanst) pole dancing

de **paalwoning** /palwonɪŋ/ (pl: -en) pile dwelling

het **paar** /par/ (pl: paren) **1** pair, couple: *twee* ~ *sokken* two pairs of socks **2** (a) few, (a) couple of: *in een* ~ **woorden** in a couple of (*or:* a few) words

het **paard** /part/ (pl: -en) **1** horse: *op het* **verkeerde** ~ *wedden* back the wrong horse; *je moet een gegeven* ~ *niet in de bek kijken* never look a gift horse in the mouth; *over het* ~ *getild zijn* be swollen-headed, be puffed up; *het* ~ *achter de wagen* **spannen** a) make things difficult for o.s.; b) put the cart before the horse **2** (vaulting) horse **3** knight

de **paardenbloem** /pardə(n)blum/ (pl: -en) dandelion

de **paardenkastanje** /pardə(n)kastɑɲə/ (pl: -s) horse chestnut

de **paardenkracht** /pardə(n)krɑxt/ (pl: -en) horsepower

het **paardenmiddel** /pardəmɪdəl/ (pl: -en) rough remedy

de **paardenrennen** /pardə(n)rɛnə(n)/ (pl) horse races

de **paardensport** /pardə(n)spɔrt/ equestrian sport(s); horse racing

de **paardensprong** /pardə(n)sprɔŋ/ (pl: -en) **1** jump **2** knight's move

de **paardenstaart** /pardə(n)start/ (pl: -en) **1** horsetail **2** ponytail

de **paardenstal** /pardə(n)stɑl/ (pl: -len) stable

de **paardenvijg** /pardə(n)vɛɪx/ (pl: -en) horse-droppings; horse-dung

paardrijden /partrɛɪdə(n)/ (reed paard, heeft paardgereden) ride (horseback): *zij zit op* ~ she is taking riding lessons

de **paardrijder** /partrɛɪdər/ (pl: -s) horseman, horsewoman; rider

het **paarlemoer** /parləmur/ mother-of-pearl

paars /pars/ (adj) purple

de **paartijd** /partɛit/ mating season; rut

het **paartje** /parcə/ (pl: -s) couple, pair: *een pas getrouwd* ~ a newly wed couple, newlyweds

paasbest /pazbɛst/ (adj): *op zijn* ~ *zijn* be all dressed up

de **paasdag** /pazdɑx/ (pl: -en) Easter Day: *eerste* ~ Easter Sunday

het **paasei** /pasɛi/ (pl: -eren) Easter egg

het **paasfeest** /pasfest/ (pl: -en) Easter

de **paashaas** /pashas/ (pl: -hazen) Easter bunny (*or:* rabbit)

de **paasvakantie** /pasfakɑnsi/ (pl: -s) Easter holidays

de **pabo** /pabo/ (pl: -'s) [Dutch] teacher training college (for primary education)

de **pacemaker** /pesmekər/ (pl: -s) pacemaker

de **pacht** /pɑxt/ (pl: -en) lease: *in* ~ *nemen* lease, take on lease

pachten /pɑxtə(n)/ (pachtte, heeft gepacht) lease, rent

de **pachter** /pɑxtər/ (pl: -s) leaseholder, lessee; tenant (farmer)

de **pachtsom** /pɑxtsɔm/ (pl: -men) rent, rental

het **pacifisme** /pɑsifɪsmə/ pacifism

de **pacifist** /pɑsifɪst/ (pl: -en) pacifist

pacifistisch /pɑsifɪstis/ (adj, adv) pacifist(ic)

het **pact** /pɑkt/ (pl: -en) pact, treaty

de ¹**pad** /pɑt/ (pl: -den) toad ‖ [Belg] *een* ~ *in iemands* **korf** *zetten* thwart s.o.; set off

het ²**pad** /pɑt/ (pl: -en) **1** path, walk; track; trail; gangway; aisle: [fig] *platgetreden* ~*en bewandelen* walk the beaten path (*or:* tracks) **2** path, way: *iem. op het* **slechte** ~ *brengen* lead s.o. astray; *hij is het* **slechte** ~ *opgegaan* he has taken to crime; *iemands* ~ *kruisen* cross s.o.'s path ‖ *op* ~ *gaan* set off; [inform] *van het* ~*je zijn* be off the rails, have lost one's marbles

de **paddenstoel** /pɑdəstul/ (pl: -en) [general] fungus; [poisonous] toadstool; [edible] mushroom

de **paddo** /pɑdo/ shroom, magic mushroom

de **padvinder** /pɑtfɪndər/ (pl: -s) (boy) scout, girl guide

de **padvinderij** /pɑtfɪndərɛi/ scouting

de **paella** /paɛlja/ paella

paf /pɑf/ (adj): *iem.* ~ *doen staan* make s.o. gasp, stagger s.o.; *ik sta* ~ I'm flabbergasted!, well, blow me down!

paffen /pɑfə(n)/ (pafte, heeft gepaft) [inform] puff

pafferig /pɑfərəx/ (adj) doughy; puffy

pag. *pagina* p.

de **page** /paʒə/ (pl: -s) page

de **pagina** /paɣina/ (pl: -'s) **1** page: ~ *2 en 3* pages 2 and 3 **2** web page

de **pagode** /paɣodə/ (pl: -n, -s) pagoda

paintballen /pɛndbɔlə(n)/ (paintballde, heeft gepaintballd) go paintballing

de **pais** /pɑjs/: *alles is weer* ~ *en* **vree** peace

reigns once more

het pak /pɑk/ (pl: -ken) **1** pack(age); packet; parcel; carton: *een ~ melk* a carton of milk; *een ~ sneeuw* a layer of snow **2** suit: *een nat ~ halen* get drenched, get a drenching **3** bale; batch; bundle; packet: *een ~ oud papier* a batch (*or:* bundle) of waste paper ‖ *bij de ~ken neerzitten* throw in the towel, give up; *dat is een ~ van mijn hart* that takes a load off my mind, that's a great relief; *een kind een ~ slaag geven* spank (*or:* wallop) a child, give a child a spanking; [Belg] *een ~ beter* much better; [Belg] *een ~ mensen* a ton of people

het pakhuis /pɑkhœys/ (pl: pakhuizen) warehouse, storehouse

het pakijs /pɑkɛɪs/ pack (ice)

de Pakistaan /pakistan/ (pl: Pakistani) Pakistani

Pakistaans /pakistans/ (adj) Pakistan(i), of Pakistan, from Pakistan

Pakistan /pakistɑn/ Pakistan

het pakje /pɑkjə/ (pl: -s) parcel, present

¹pakken /pɑkə(n)/ (pakte, heeft gepakt) hold; grip; bite; take

²pakken /pɑkə(n)/ (pakte, heeft gepakt) **1** get, take, fetch: *een pen ~* get a pen; *pak een stoel* grab a chair; *~ wat je pakken kan* take everything you can get, grab what you can **2** catch, grasp, grab; seize: *de daders zijn nooit gepakt* the offenders were never caught; *iem. op iets ~* get s.o. on sth.; *proberen iem. te ~ te krijgen* try to get hold of s.o.; *iets te ~ krijgen* lay one's hands on sth.; *iem. te ~ nemen* have a go at s.o.; *nou heb ik je te ~* got you!; *als ik hem te ~ krijg* if I catch him, if I lay hands on him; *hij heeft het behoorlijk te ~* he has it badly; *pak me dan, als je kan!* catch me if you can! **3** pack; wrap up: *zijn koffers ~* pack one's bags

pakkend /pɑkənt/ (adj) catching; catchy; fascinating, appealing; fetching; arresting; gripping; catching; attractive: *een ~e titel* a catchy (*or:* an arresting) title

de pakkerd /pɑkərt/ (pl: -s) hug and a kiss

het pakket /pɑkɛt/ (pl: -ten) **1** parcel **2** pack; kit; [fig] package

de pakketpost /pɑkɛtpɔst/ parcel post

pakkie-an /pɑkiɑn/ [Dutch]: *dat is niet mijn ~* that's not my department

de pakking /pɑkɪŋ/ (pl: -en) gasket, packing

het pakpapier /pɑkpapir/ packing paper, wrapping paper

de paksoi /pɑksɔj/ pak-choi cabbage

pakweg /pɑkwɛx/ (adv) roughly, approximately, about, around

de ¹pal /pɑl/ (pl: -len) catch

²pal /pɑl/ (adv) directly: *de wind staat ~ op het raam* the wind blows right on the window; *hij stond ~ voor mijn neus* he stood directly in front of me ‖ [fig] *~ staan voor iets* stand firm

for sth.

het paleis /palɛis/ (pl: paleizen) **1** palace; court **2** hall

de Palestijn /paləstɛin/ (pl: -en) Palestinian

Palestijns /paləstɛins/ (adj) Palestinian, Palestine

Palestina /paləstina/ Palestine

het palet /palɛt/ (pl: -ten) palette

de paling /palɪŋ/ (pl: -en) eel, eels: *gerookte ~* smoked eel(s)

de palissade /palisadə/ (pl: -n, -s) palisade, stockade

de pallet /pɛlət/ (pl: -s) pallet (board)

de palm /pɑlm/ (pl: -en) palm

de palmboom /pɑlmbom/ (pl: -bomen) palm

de palmolie /pɑlmoli/ palm oil

Palmpasen /pɑlmpasə(n)/ [Dutch] Palm Sunday

de palmtak /pɑlmtɑk/ (pl: -ken) palm

de palmtop /pɑlmtɔp/ palmtop

Palmzondag /pɑlmzɔndɑx/ Palm Sunday

het pamflet /pɑmflɛt/ (pl: -ten) pamphlet; broadsheet

pamperen /pɛmpərə(n)/ (pamperde, heeft gepamperd) pamper

het pampus /pɑmpʏs/: *voor ~ liggen* be dead to the world, be out cold

de pan /pɑn/ (pl: -nen) **1** pan: [fig] *dat swingt de ~ uit* that's really far out; [fig] *de ~ uit rijzen* soar, snowball, rocket **2** (pan)tile ‖ *in de ~ hakken* cut to ribbons (*or:* pieces), make mincemeat of

Panama /panama/ Panama

de Panamees /panames/ (pl: Panamezen) Panamanian

het/de pancreas /pɑŋkrejas/ pancreas

het pand /pɑnt/ **1** premises, property, building, house **2** pawn, pledge, security

de panda /pɑnda/ (pl: -'s) panda

de pandjesjas /pɑncəsjɑs/ (pl: -sen) tailcoat

het paneel /panel/ (pl: panelen) panel

het paneermeel /panermel/ breadcrumbs

het panel /pɛnəl/ (pl: -s) panel

paneren /panerə(n)/ (paneerde, heeft gepaneerd) bread(crumb)

de panfluit /pɑnflœyt/ (pl: -en) pan pipe(s)

pang /pɑŋ/ (int) pow, bang

de paniek /panik/ (pl: -en) panic, alarm; terror: *in ~ raken* panic; *er ontstond ~* panic broke out; *~ zaaien* spread panic (*or:* alarm); *geen ~!* don't panic

paniekerig /panikərəx/ (adj, adv) panicky, panic-stricken: *~ reageren* panic (in reaction to)

het paniekvoetbal /panikfudbɑl/ **1** panicky play **2** [fig] panic measure(s) (*or:* behaviour): *~ spelen* be panicking

de paniekzaaier /paniksajər/ (pl: -s) panic-monger, alarmist

panisch /panis/ (adj, adv) panic, frantic: *een ~e angst hebben voor iets* (*or:* om iets te doen) be terrified (of doing) sth.

panklaar /paŋklar/ (adj) **1** ready to cook **2** [fig] ready-made: *een panklare oplossing* an instant solution

de **panne** /pɑnə/ breakdown: ~ *hebben* have a breakdown, have engine trouble

de **pannenkoek** /pɑnə(n)kuk/ (pl: -en) **1** pancake **2** [inform] dumbo, pin-head: *hij is geen* ~ he's no dumbo; *hij is een* ~ *als trainer* he is useless as a trainer

de **pannenlap** /pɑnə(n)lɑp/ (pl: -pen) oven cloth; oven glove

de **pannenset** /pɑnə(n)sɛt/ (pl: -s) set of (pots and) pans

de **pannenspons** /pɑnə(n)spɔns/ (pl: -sponzen) scourer, scouring pad

het **panorama** /panorama/ (pl: -'s) panorama

de **pantalon** /pɑntalɔn/ (pl: -s) (pair of) trousers; (pair of) slacks: *twee* ~s two pair(s) of trousers

de **panter** /pɑntər/ (pl: -s) panther; leopard

de **pantoffel** /pɑntɔfəl/ (pl: -s) (carpet) slipper

de **pantoffelheld** /pɑntɔfəlhɛlt/ (pl: -en) faint-heart

de **pantomime** /pɑntomimə/ (pl: -s, -n) mime, dumbshow

het **pantser** /pɔntsər/ (pl: -s) **1** (plate) armour, armour-plating **2** (suit of) armour

de **pantserdivisie** /pɑn(t)sərdivizi/ (pl: -s) armoured division

pantseren /pɔntsərə(n)/ (pantserde, heeft gepantserd) armour(-plate)

de **pantserwagen** /pɑn(t)sərwaɣə(n)/ (pl: -s) armoured car

de **panty** /pɛnti/ (pl: -'s) (pair of) tights: *drie* ~'s three pairs of tights

de **pap** /pɑp/ (pl: -pen) porridge; pap: *ik lust er wel* ~ *van* this is meat and drink to me ‖ *geen* ~ *meer kunnen zeggen* **a)** be (dead)beat; **b)** be whacked (out), be fagged (out); **c)** be full up

de **papa** /papa/ (pl: -'s) papa, dad(dy)

de **papadag** /pɑpadɑx/ (pl: -en) daddy's stay-at-home day

de **papaja** /papaja/ (pl: -'s) papaya, pawpaw

de **paparazzo** /paparɔtso/ (pl: paparazzi) paparazzo

de **papaver** /papavər/ (pl: -s) poppy

de **papegaai** /papəɣaj/ (pl: -en) parrot

de **paper** /pepər/ (pl: -s) paper

de **paperassen** /papərɑsə(n)/ (pl) papers, paperwork; bumf

de **paperback** /pepərbɛk/ (pl: -s) paperback

de **paperclip** /pepərklɪp/ (pl: -s) paperclip

het **Papiamento** /papijamɛnto/ Papiamento

het **papier** /papir/ (pl: -en) **1** paper: *zijn gedachten op* ~ *zetten* put one's thoughts down on paper **2** paper; document ‖ *het loopt aardig in de* ~*en* it (soon) mounts up

de **papiercontainer** /papirkɔntenər/ (pl: -s) paper recycling bin

papieren /papirə(n)/ (adj) paper

het **papiergeld** /papirɣɛlt/ paper money: *€ 100,- in* ~ 100 euros in notes

het **papier-maché** /pɑpirmɑʃe/ papier-mâché

het **papiertje** /papircə/ (pl: -s) piece of paper; wrapper

de **papierversnipperaar** /papirvərsnɪpərar/ (pl: -s) (paper) shredder

het **papierwerk** /papirwɛrk/ paperwork

de **papierwinkel** /papirwɪŋkəl/ mass of paperwork

de **papil** /papɪl/ (pl: -len) papilla

het **papkind** /pɑpkɪnt/ (pl: -eren) sissy

de **paplepel** /pɑplepəl/ (pl: -s): *dat is hem met de* ~ *ingegeven* he learned it at his mother's knee

Papoea-Nieuw-Guinea /papuwaniwɣineja/ Papua New Guinea

de **pappa** /pɑpa/ (pl: -'s) papa, dad, daddy

de **pappenheimer** /pɑpə(n)hɛɪmər/ (pl: -s): *hij kent zijn* ~s he knows his people (*or:* customers)

papperig /pɑpərəx/ (adj) **1** mushy **2** puffy

de **pappie** /pɑpi/ (pl: -s) daddy

de **paprika** /paprika/ (pl: -'s) (sweet) pepper

het **paprikapoeder** /paprikapudər/ paprika

de **paps** /pɑps/ dad, daddy

de **papyrus** /papirys/ (pl: -sen) papyrus

de **papzak** /pɑpsɑk/ (pl: -ken) potbelly

de **paraaf** /paraf/ (pl: parafen) initials

paraat /parat/ (adj) ready, prepared: *parate kennis* ready knowledge; ~ *staan* be ready, be prepared; *dat heb ik even niet* ~ I'll need to look that up

de **parabel** /parabəl/ (pl: -s, -en) parable

de **parabool** /parabol/ (pl: parabolen) parabola

de **parachute** /paraʃyt/ (pl: -s) parachute

parachutespringen /paraʃytsprɪŋə(n)/ parachuting

de **parachutist** /paraʃytɪst/ (pl: -en) parachutist

de **parade** /paradə/ (pl: -s) parade

het **paradepaard** /paradəpart/ (pl: -en) showpiece

paraderen /paradərə(n)/ (paradeerde, heeft geparadeerd) parade

het **paradijs** /paradɛis/ (pl: paradijzen) paradise

paradijselijk /paradɛisələk/ (adj, adv) heavenly

de **paradox** /paradɔks/ (pl: -en) paradox

paradoxaal /paradɔksal/ (adj, adv) paradoxical

paraferen /parafərə(n)/ (parafeerde, heeft geparafeerd) initial

de **paraffine** /parafinə/ (pl: -n) paraffin wax

de **parafrase** /parafrazə/ (pl: -n, -s) paraphrase

de **paragnost** /paraɣnɔst/ (pl: -en) psychic

de **paragraaf** /paraɣraf/ (pl: -grafen) section

Paraguay /paraɣwɑj/ Paraguay

de **Paraguayaan** /paraɣwajan/ (pl: Paraguayanen) Paraguayan

Paraguayaans /paragwajans/ (adj) Paraguayan

de **¹parallel** /paralɛl/ (pl: -len) parallel: *deze ~ kan nog verder doorgetrokken worden* this parallel (*or:* analogy) can be carried further

²parallel /paralɛl/ (adj, adv) **1** parallel (to, with): *die wegen lopen ~ aan (met) elkaar* those roads run parallel to each other; *~ schakelen* shunt **2** parallel (to), analogous (to, with)

het **parallellogram** /paralɛloɣrɑm/ (pl: -men) parallelogram

de **parallelweg** /paralɛlwɛx/ (pl: -en) parallel road

paralympisch /paralɪmpis/ (adj): *de Paralympische Spelen* the Paralympic Games, the Paralympics

paramedisch /paramedis/ (adj) paramedical

de **parameter** /parametər/ (pl: -s) parameter

paramilitair /paramilitɛːr/ (adj) paramilitary

de **paranoia** /paranɔja/ paranoia

paranoïde /paranowidə/ (adj) paranoid

paranormaal /paranɔrmal/ (adj, adv) paranormal, psychic

de **paraplu** /paraply/ (pl: -'s) umbrella

de **parapsychologie** /parapsixoloɣi/ parapsychology, psychic research

de **parasiet** /parasit/ (pl: -en) **1** parasite **2** parasite, sponge(er)

parasiteren /parasiterə(n)/ (parasiteerde, heeft geparasiteerd) parasitize; [fig] sponge (on, off)

de **parasol** /parasɔl/ (pl: -s) sunshade, parasol

parastataal /parastatal/ (adj) [Belg] semigovernmental: *parastatale instelling* semigovernmental institution, [roughly] quango

de **paratroepen** /paratrupə(n)/ (pl) paratroopers

de **paratyfus** /paratifys/ paratyphoid (fever)

het **parcours** /parkur(s)/ (pl: -en) track

pardoes /pardus/ (adv) bang, slap, smack

het **¹pardon** /pardɔn/ pardon, mercy: *generaal ~* amnesty; *zonder ~* without mercy, mercilessly

²pardon /pardɔn/ (int) pardon (me), I beg your pardon, excuse me, (so) sorry: *stond ik op uw tenen? ~!* sorry, did I step on your toe?

de **parel** /parəl/ (pl: -s) pearl

parelen /parələ(n)/ (parelde, heeft gepareld) pearl: *het zweet parelde op haar voorhoofd* her forehead was beaded with sweat

het **parelhoen** /parəlhun/ (pl: -ders) guinea fowl; guinea hen

¹paren /parə(n)/ (paarde, heeft gepaard) mate (with)

²paren /parə(n)/ (paarde, heeft gepaard) [fig] combine (with), couple (with): *gepaard gaan met* go (hand in hand) with

pareren /parerə(n)/ (pareerde, heeft gepareerd) parry

het/de **parfum** /parfym/ (pl: -s) perfume, scent

parfumeren /parfymerə(n)/ (parfumeerde, heeft geparfumeerd) scent, perfume

de **paria** /parija/ (pl: -'s) pariah, outcast

Parijs /pariɛs/ Paris

de **paring** /parɪŋ/ (pl: -en) **1** mating **2** pairing

de **Parisienne** /parizɛnə/ Parisian

de **pariteit** /paritɛit/ parity

het **park** /pɑrk/ (pl: -en) **1** park **2** fleet; plant

de **parka** /pɑrka/ (pl: -'s) parka

de **parkeerautomaat** /pɑrkerautomat/ (pl: -automaten) (car-park) ticket machine (*or:* dispenser); [Am] (parking lot) ticket machine

de **parkeerbon** /pɑrkerbɔn/ (pl: -nen) parking ticket

de **parkeergarage** /pɑrkeryaraʒə/ (pl: -s) (underground) car park; [Am] (underground) parking garage

het **parkeergeld** /pɑrkerɣɛlt/ parking fee

de **parkeergelegenheid** /pɑrkerɣəleɣə(n)hɛit/ parking facilities

de **parkeermeter** /pɑrkermetər/ parking meter

de **parkeerplaats** /pɑrkerplats/ (pl: -en) parking place (*or:* space); car park; [Am] parking lot

de **parkeerschijf** /pɑrkersxɛif/ (pl: -schijven) (parking) disc

het **parkeerterrein** /pɑrkertɛrɛin/ (pl: -en) car park; [Am] parking lot

het **parkeerverbod** /pɑrkervərbɔt/ parking ban; [on notice] No Parking: *hier geldt een ~* this is a no-parking zone

parkeren /pɑrkerə(n)/ (parkeerde, heeft geparkeerd) park; pull in (*or:* over)

het **parket** /pɑrkɛt/ (pl: -ten) **1** parquet (floor) **2** public prosecutor ‖ *in een lastig ~ zitten* find o.s. in a difficult (*or:* an awkward) position

de **parketvloer** /pɑrkɛtflur/ (pl: -en) parquet (floor)

de **parkiet** /pɑrkit/ (pl: -en) parakeet

de **parking** /pɑːrkɪŋ/ (pl: -s) [Belg] car park; [Am] parking lot

de **parkinson** /pɑrkɪnsɔn/ Parkinson's disease

het **parlement** /pɑrləmɛnt/ (pl: -en) parliament: *in het ~* in parliament

parlementair /pɑrləmɛntɛːr/ (adj) parliamentary

de **parlementariër** /pɑrləmɛntarijər/ (pl: -s) member of (a) parliament, parliamentarian; representative

de **parlementsverkiezing** /pɑrləmɛn(t)sfərkizɪŋ/ (pl: -en) parliamentary election

parmantig /pɑrmɑntəx/ (adj, adv) jaunty, dapper

parochiaal /parɔxijal/ (adj) parochial

de **parochiaan** /parɔxijan/ (pl: parochianen) parishioner

de **parochie** /parɔxi/ (pl: -s) parish

de **parodie** /parodi/ (pl: -ën) parody (of, on); travesty (of)
parodiëren /parodijɛrə(n)/ (parodieerde, heeft geparodieerd) parody

het **parool** /parol/ (pl: parolen) watchword, slogan: *opletten is het ~* pay attention is the motto

het **part** /pɑrt/ share, portion || *voor mijn ~* for all I care, as far as I'm concerned; *iem. ~en spelen* play tricks on s.o.

het/de **parterre** /pɑrtɛ:rə/ (pl: -s) ground floor; [Am also] first floor

de **participatie** /pɑrtisipa(t)si/ (pl: -s) participation

de **participatiemaatschappij** /pɑrtisipa-(t)simatsχɑpɛi/ **1** holding company **2** participation society
participeren /pɑrtisipɛrə(n)/ (participeerde, heeft geparticipeerd) participate (in), take part (in)

de **¹particulier** /pɑrtikylir/ (pl: -en) private individual (*or:* person): *geen verkoop aan ~en* trade (sales) only
²particulier /pɑrtikylir/ (adj, adv) private: *het ~ initiatief* private enterprise

de **partij** /pɑrtɛi/ (pl: -en) **1** party, side: *de strijdende ~en* the warring parties; *~ kiezen* take sides **2** set, batch, lot; consignment; shipment: *bij* (or: *in*) *~en verkopen* sell in lots **3** [mus] part **4** game

het **partijbestuur** /pɑrtɛibəstyr/ (pl: -besturen) party executive (committee)

het **partijcongres** /pɑrtɛikɔŋɣrɛs/ (pl: -sen) party congress; party conference; party convention
partijdig /pɑrtɛidəχ/ (adj, adv) bias(s)ed, partial

de **partijleider** /pɑrtɛilɛidər/ (pl: -s) party leader

de **¹partijpolitiek** /pɑrtɛipolitik/ party politics
²partijpolitiek /pɑrtɛipolitik/ (adj) party political

de **partituur** /pɑrtityr/ (pl: partituren) score

de **partizaan** /pɑrtizan/ (pl: partizanen) partisan

de **partner** /pɑrtnər/ (pl: -s) **1** partner, companion **2** (co-)partner, associate

het **partnerregister** /pɑrtnərəɣɪstər/ [Dutch] register in which cohabitation contracts are officially recorded

het **partnerschap** /pɑrtnərsχɑp/ partnership: [Dutch] *een geregistreerd ~* a civil partnership
parttime /pɑ:rtɑjm/ (adj) part-time

de **parttimebaan** /pɑ:rtɑjmban/ part-time job

de **parttimer** /pɑ:rtɑjmər/ (pl: -s) part-timer

de **party** /pɑ:rti/ (pl: -'s) party

de **partydrug** /pɑ:rtidrʏɣ/ party drug

de **partytent** /pɑ:rtitɛnt/ (pl: -en) party tent

de **parvenu** /pɑrvəny/ (pl: -'s) parvenu

de **¹pas** /pɑs/ **1** step, pace; gait: *iem. de ~ afsnij-* den cut (*or:* head) s.o. off **2** pass **3** pass; passport || *het leger moest er aan te ~ komen* the army had to step in; *goed van ~ komen* come in handy (*or:* useful); *dat komt uitstekend van ~* that's just the thing; *altijd wel van ~ komen* always come in handy; *te ~ en te onpas* all the time, whether it is relevant or not

²pas /pɑs/ (adv) **1** (only) just, recently: *hij begint ~* he is just beginning, he has only just started; *~ geplukt* freshly picked; *een ~ getrouwd stel* a newly-wed couple; *~ geverfd* wet paint; *ik werk hier nog maar ~* I'm new here (*or:* to this job) **2** only, just: *hij is ~ vijftig (jaar)* he's only fifty **3** only, not until: *~ toen vertelde hij het mij* it was only then that he told me; *~ toen hij weg was, begreep ik ...* it was only after he had left that I understood ...; *~ geleden, ~ een paar dagen terug* only recently, only the other day **4** really: *dat is ~ een vent* he's (what I call) a real man; *dat is ~ hard werken!* now, that really is hard work!

Pascha /pɑsχɑ/ Pesach

Pasen /pasə(n)/ Easter: *vrolijk ~!* Happy Easter!

de **pasfoto** /pɑsfoto/ (pl: -'s) passport photo(graph)
pasgeboren /pɑsχəborə(n)/ (adj) newborn, newly born
pasgetrouwd /pɑsχətrɑut/ (adj) newly married

het **pashokje** /pɑshɔkjə/ (pl: -s) fitting room

het **pasje** /pɑʃə/ (pl: -s) **1** step **2** pass

de **paskamer** /pɑskamər/ (pl: -s) fitting room
pasklaar /pɑsklar/ (adj) (made) to measure; fitted; [fig] ready-made

het **paspoort** /pɑsport/ (pl: -en) passport

de **paspoortcontrole** /pɑsportkɔntrɔ:lə/ passport control

de **pass** /pɑ:s/ (pl: -es) [sport] pass: *een goede ~ geven* make a good pass

de **passaat** /pɑsat/ (pl: passaten) trade wind

de **passage** /pɑsaʒə/ (pl: -s) passage, extract: *een ~ uit een gedicht voorlezen* read an extract from a poem

de **passagier** /pɑsaʒir/ (pl: -s) passenger

het **passagiersschip** /pɑsaʒirsχɪp/ (pl: -schepen) passenger ship
passant /pɑsɑnt/: *en ~ in* passing; [chess] *en ~ slaan* take (a pawn) en passant

¹passen /pɑsə(n)/ (paste, heeft gepast) **1** fit: *het past precies* it fits like a glove; *deze sleutel past op de meeste sloten* this key fits most locks **2** (+ bij) fit, go (with), match: *deze hoed past er goed bij* this hat is a good match; *ze ~ goed* (or: *slecht*) *bij elkaar* they are well-matched (*or:* ill-matched) **3** (+ op) look after, take care of: *op de kinderen ~* look after the children; *pas op het afstapje* (or: *je hoofd*) watch/mind the step (*or:* your head); *op zijn woorden ~* mind what one says; mind one's language **4** [cards] pass

²**passen** /pɑsə(n)/ (paste, heeft gepast) **1** fit: ~ *en meten* try it in all different ways; *met wat ~ en meten komen we wel rond* with a bit of juggling we'll manage **2** pay with the exact money: *hebt u het niet gepast?* haven't you got the exact change? (*or:* money?) **3** try on

³**passen** /pɑsə(n)/ (passte, heeft gepasst) [socc] pass

passend /pɑsənt/ (adj, adv) **1** suitable (for), suited (to), appropriate: *niet bij elkaar ~e partners* incompatible partners; *niet bij elkaar ~e sokken* odd socks; *slecht bij elkaar ~* ill-matched **2** proper, becoming: *een ~ gebruik maken van* make proper use of

de **passer** /pɑsər/ (pl: -s) compass

de **passerdoos** /pɑsərdos/ (pl: -dozen) compass case

¹**passeren** /pɑserə(n)/ (passeerde, is gepasseerd) pass, overtake: *de auto passeerde (de fietser)* the car overtook (the cyclist); *een huis ~ pass (by) a house

²**passeren** /pɑserə(n)/ (passeerde, heeft/is gepasseerd) **1** pass through; cross: *de grens* (or: *een brug*) ~ cross the border (*or:* a bridge); *de vijftig gepasseerd zijn* have turned fifty **2** [sport] pass: *de doelman ~* go past the keeper **3** pass over: *zich gepasseerd voelen* feel passed over

de **passie** /pɑsi/ (pl: -s) passion (for); zeal (for), enthusiasm (for)

passief /pɑsif/ (adj, adv) passive

het **passiespel** /pɑsispɛl/ (pl: -en) passion play

de **passievrucht** /pɑsivrʏxt/ (pl: -en) passion fruit

de **passiva** /pɑsiva/ (pl) liabilities

het **password** /pɑ:swʏ:rt/ (pl: -s) password

de **pasta** /pɑsta/ (pl: -'s) **1** paste **2** pasta

de **pastei** /pɑstɛi/ (pl: -en) pasty, pie

het **pastel** /pɑstɛl/ (pl: -s) pastel

de **pasteltint** /pɑstɛltɪnt/ (pl: -en) pastel shade (*or:* tone)

pasteuriseren /pɑstørizerə(n)/ (pasteuriseerde, heeft gepasteuriseerd) pasteurize

de **pastille** /pɑstijə/ (pl: -s) pastille, lozenge

de **pastinaak** /pɑstinak/ (pl: pastinaken) parsnip

de **pastoor** /pɑstor/ (pl: -s) (parish) priest; padre: *Meneer Pastoor* Father

de **pastor** /pɑstɔr/ (pl: -s, pastores) pastor, minister; [Roman Catholicism] priest

pastoraal /pɑstoral/ (adj, adv) **1** pastoral: ~ *medewerker* church worker **2** pastoral, bucolic

het **pastoraat** /pɑstorat/ **1** pastoral care **2** priesthood

de **pastorie** /pɑstori/ (pl: -ën) parsonage; [Roman Catholicism] presbytery

de **pasvorm** /pɑsfɔrm/ (pl: -en) fit

pat /pɑt/ (adj) stalemate: *iem. ~ zetten* stalemate s.o.

de **patat** /pɑtɑt/ **1** [Dutch] chips, French fries: *een zakje ~* a bag of chips; *~ met* chips with mayonnaise **2** [Belg] potato

het **patatje** /pɑtɑcə/ (pl: -s) [Dutch] (portion of) chips

de **patatkraam** /pɑtɑtkram/ (pl: -kramen) [Dutch] [roughly] fish and chips stand; [Am] [roughly] hot dog stand

de **patch** /pɛtʃ/ patch

de **paté** /pɑte/ (pl: -s) pâté

het **patent** /pɑtɛnt/ (pl: -en) patent

patenteren /pɑtɛnterə(n)/ (patenteerde, heeft gepatenteerd) (grant a) patent ‖ *een gepatenteerde leugenaar* a patent liar

de **pater** /pɑtər/ (pl: -s) father

de ¹**paternoster** /pɑtərnɔstər/ (pl: -s) rosary

het ²**paternoster** /pɑtərnɔstər/ paternoster, Our Father

pathetisch /pɑtetis/ (adj, adv) pathetic

het **pathos** /pɑtos/ pathos; melodrama

het **patience** /pɑʃ̃ɑs/ patience; [Am] solitaire

de **patiënt** /pɑʃɛnt/ (pl: -en) patient: *zijn ~en bezoeken* do one's rounds

de **patio** /pɑ(t)s(i)jo/ (pl: -'s) patio

de **patisserie** /pɑtisəri/ (pl: -ën) **1** pastries **2** pastry shop

de **patriarch** /pɑtrijɑrx/ (pl: -en) patriarch

de **patrijs** /pɑtrɛis/ (pl: patrijzen) partridge

de **patrijspoort** /pɑtrɛisport/ (pl: -en) porthole

de **patriot** /pɑtrijɔt/ (pl: -ten) patriot

patriottisch /pɑtrijɔtis/ (adj) patriotic

het **patronaat** /pɑtronat/ (pl: patronaten) [Belg] employers

de **patrones** /pɑtronɛs/ (pl: -sen) **1** patron (saint) **2** patron(ess)

de ¹**patroon** /pɑtron/ **1** patron **2** boss

de ²**patroon** /pɑtron/ cartridge: *een losse ~* a blank

het ³**patroon** /pɑtron/ **1** pattern, design: *volgens een vast ~* according to an established pattern **2** pattern, style

de **patrouille** /pɑtrujə/ (pl: -s) patrol

patrouilleren /pɑtrujerə(n)/ (patrouilleerde, heeft gepatrouilleerd) patrol

pats /pɑts/ (int) wham, bang: *pats-boem* wham bam

de **patser** /pɑtsər/ (pl: -s) show-off

patserig /pɑtsərəx/ (adj, adv) flashy

de **patstelling** /pɑtstɛlɪŋ/ stalemate [also fig]

de **pauk** /pauk/ (pl: -en) kettledrum; timpani

de **paukenist** /paukənɪst/ (pl: -en) kettledrummer

de **paus** /paus/ (pl: -en) pope

pauselijk /pɑusələk/ (adj) papal, pontifical: ~ *gezag* papacy, papal authority

de **pauw** /pau/ (pl: -en) peacock; [female also] peahen

de **pauze** /pɑuzə/ (pl: -s) interval, break, intermission; [sport] (half-)time: *een kwartier ~ houden* take (*or:* have) a fifteen-minute break; *een ~ inlassen* introduce an extra break

pauzeren /pɑuzɛrə(n)/ (pauzeerde, heeft gepauzeerd) pause, take a break, have a rest

het **paviljoen** /pɑvɪljun/ (pl: -en, -s) pavilion

de **pavlovreactie** /pɑflofrejɑksi/ (pl: -s) Pavlovian response

het **pay-per-view** /pepərvju:/ pay-per-view

de **pc** /pese/ (pl: pc's) *personal computer* pc

de **pech** /pɛx/ **1** bad (*or:* hard, tough) luck: ~ *gehad* hard (*or:* tough) luck **2** breakdown || ~ *met* de auto car trouble

de **pechdienst** /pɛxdinst/ (pl: -en) [Belg] breakdown service

de **pechstrook** /pɛxstrok/ (pl: -stroken) [Belg] hard shoulder

de **pechvogel** /pɛxfoɣəl/ (pl: -s) unlucky person: *hij is een echte* ~ he's a walking disaster area

het/de **pedaal** /pədal/ (pl: pedalen) treadle; pedal

de **pedaalemmer** /pədalɛmər/ (pl: -s) pedal bin

de **pedagogiek** /pedaɣoɣik/ (theory of) education, educational theory (*or:* science); pedagogy

pedagogisch /pedaɣoɣis/ (adj, adv) pedagogic(al): ~*e academie* teacher(s') training college

de **pedagoog** /pedaɣox/ (pl: -gogen) education(al)ist

pedant /pədɑnt/ (adj, adv) pedantic

de **peddel** /pɛdəl/ (pl: -s) paddle

peddelen /pɛdələ(n)/ (peddelde, heeft/is gepeddeld) paddle

de **pedicure** /pedikyrə/ (pl: -s) chiropodist, pedicure

de ¹**pedofiel** /pedofil/ (pl: -en) paedophile

²**pedofiel** /pedofil/ (adj) paedophile

de **pee** /pe/ [Dutch; inform]: *(ergens) de* ~ *(over) in hebben* be annoyed about sth.

de **peen** /pen/ (pl: penen) carrot || ~*tjes zweten* be in a cold sweat

de **peer** /per/ (pl: peren) **1** pear **2** bulb

de **peerreview** /pirivju/ (pl: -s) peer review

de **pees** /pes/ (pl: pezen) tendon, sinew

de **peesontsteking** /pesontstekɪŋ/ (pl: -en) tendinitis

de **peetmoeder** /petmudər/ (pl: -s) godmother

de **peetoom** /petom/ (pl: -s) godfather

de **peettante** /petɑntə/ (pl: -s) godmother

de **peetvader** /petfadər/ (pl: -s) godfather

de **pegel** /peɣəl/ (pl: -s) icicle

de **peignoir** /pɛɲwar/ (pl: -s) dressing gown, housecoat

het **peil** /pɛil/ (pl: -en) **1** level, standard: *het* ~ *van de conversatie daalde* the level of conversation dropped **2** mark, level: *zijn conditie op* ~ *brengen* (or: *houden*) get o.s. into condition, keep fit (*or:* in shape) || *dat is beneden* ~ that is below the mark

de **peildatum** /pɛildatym/ (pl: -data) set day, reference date

de **peilen** /pɛilə(n)/ (peilde, heeft gepeild) **1** sound, fathom **2** [fig] gauge; sound (out): *ik zal Bernard even* ~, *kijken wat die ervan vindt* I'll sound Bernard out, see what he thinks

het **peilglas** /pɛilɣlɑs/ (pl: -glazen) gaugeglass

de **peiling** /pɛilɪŋ/ (pl: -en) **1** sounding **2** poll: *op kop gaan in de* ~*en* take the lead in the polls

het **peillood** /pɛilot/ (pl: -loden) plumb (*or:* lead) line

peilloos /pɛilos/ (adj) unfathomable

de **peilstok** /pɛilstɔk/ (pl: -ken) sounding rod; gauging-rod; dipstick

peinzen /pɛinzə(n)/ (peinsde, heeft gepeinsd) (+ over) think about, contemplate: *hij peinst er niet over* he won't even contemplate (*or:* consider) it; *hij peinst zich suf over een oplossing* he is racking his brains to find a solution

het/de **pek** /pɛk/ pitch

de **pekel** /pekəl/ salt, grit

het **pekelvlees** /pekəlvles/ salted meat

de **pekinees** /pekineːs/ (pl: pekinezen) pekinese

de **pelgrim** /pɛlɣrɪm/ (pl: -s) pilgrim

de **pelgrimstocht** /pɛlɣrɪmstɔxt/ (pl: -en) pilgrimage

de **pelikaan** /pelikan/ (pl: pelikanen) pelican

pellen /pɛlə(n)/ (pelde, heeft gepeld) peel, skin; blanch; husk; hull; shell

de **pellet** /pɛlət/ (pl: -s) (wood) pellet

het **peloton** /pelətɔn/ (pl: -s) **1** platoon **2** [sport] pack, (main)bunch

de **pels** /pɛls/ (pl: pelzen) fleece, fur

het **pelsdier** /pɛlzdir/ (pl: -en) furred animal, furbearing animal

de **pelsjager** /pɛlsjaɣər/ (pl: -s) trapper

de **pen** /pɛn/ (pl: -nen) **1** pen: [fig] *in de* ~ *klimmen* put pen to paper **2** pin; needle

de **penalty** /pɛnəlti/ (pl: -'s) [sport] penalty (kick, shot): *een* ~ *nemen* take a penalty

de **penaltystip** /pɛnəltistɪp/ penalty spot

de **penarie** /pənari/ [inform]: *in de* ~ *zitten* be in real trouble

het/de **pendant** /pɛndɑnt/ (pl: -en) counterpart

de **pendel** /pɛndəl/ (pl: -s) commuting

de **pendelaar** /pɛndəlar/ (pl: -s) commuter

de **pendeldienst** /pɛndəldinst/ (pl: -en) shuttle service

pendelen /pɛndələ(n)/ (pendelde, heeft gependeld) commute

het **pendelverkeer** /pɛndəlvərker/ commuter traffic

de **pendule** /pɛndylə/ (pl: -s) (mantel) clock (with pendulum)

penetrant /penətrɑnt/ (adj, adv) penetrating

de **penetratie** /penətra(t)si/ (pl: -s) penetration

penetreren /penətrerə(n)/ (penetreerde,

heeft gepenetreerd) penetrate
penibel /penibəl/ (adj) painful, awkward
de **penicilline** /penisiljnə/ penicillin
de **penis** /penɪs/ penis
penitentiair /peniten(t)ʃɛːr/ (adj) penitentiary: *een ~e inrichting* a penitentiary; a pen
de **penlight** /pɛnlɑjt/ **1** penlight **2** penlight battery
pennen /pɛnə(n)/ (pende, heeft gepend) **1** scribble, pen **2** [chess] pin
de **pennenstreek** /pɛnə(n)strek/ (pl: -streken) penstroke: *met één ~* with one stroke of the pen
de **pennenvrucht** /pɛnə(n)vrʏxt/ (pl: -en) product of one's pen
de **penning** /pɛnɪŋ/ (pl: -en) **1** token **2** [chess] pin
de **penningmeester** /pɛnɪŋmestər/ (pl: -s) treasurer
de **pens** /pɛns/ (pl: -en) paunch, belly, gut
het **penseel** /pɛnsel/ (pl: penselen) (paint)brush
het **pensioen** /pɛnʃun/ (pl: -en) **1** pension, retirement (pay); superannuation: *~ aanvragen* apply for a pension; *met ~ gaan* retire **2** retirement: *wat gaat u doen na uw ~?* what are you going to do when you retire?
het **pensioenfonds** /pɛnʃunfɔn(t)s/ (pl: -en) pension fund
het **pensioengat** /pɛnʃuŋɑt/ (pl: -en) pension gap
pensioengerechtigd /pɛnʃuŋɣərɛxtəxt/ (adj) pensionable: *de ~e leeftijd bereiken* reach retirement age
de **pensioenuitkering** /pɛnʃunœytkerɪŋ/ (pl: -en) pension, retirement pay
het **pension** /pɛnʃɔn/ (pl: -s) **1** guest house, boarding house **2** bed and board: *vol ~* full board; *in ~ zijn* be a lodger **3** kennel
het **pensionaat** /pɛnʃonɑt/ (pl: pensionaten) boarding school
de **pensionado** /pɛnʃonɑdo/ (pl: -'s) **1** (retired) bon vivant; [Am] gray panther **2** pensioner; [Am] retiree
de **pensionhouder** /pɛnʃɔnhɑudər/ (pl: -s) landlord
de **pensionhoudster** /pɛnʃɔnhɑutstər/ landlady
de **penvriend** /pɛnvrint/ (pl: -en) pen-friend; [Am] pen pal
de **peper** /pepər/ (pl: -s) pepper: *een snufje ~* a dash of pepper
peperduur /pepərdyr/ (adj) very expensive, pricey
de **peperkoek** /pepərkuk/ (pl: -en) [roughly] gingerbread, gingercake
de **peperkorrel** /pepərkɔrəl/ (pl: -s) peppercorn
de **pepermolen** /pepərmolə(n)/ (pl: -s) pepper mill
de **pepermunt** /pepərmʏnt/ (pl: -en) peppermints: *een rolletje ~* a tube of peppermints

de **pepernoot** /pepərnot/ (pl: -noten) [roughly] spiced ginger nut
het **pepmiddel** /pɛpmɪdəl/ (pl: -en) pep pill
de **pepperspray** /pɛpərspre/ (pl: -s) pepper spray
de **peptalk** /pɛptɔːk/ pep talk
per /pɛr/ (prep) **1** per, a, by: *iets ~ post verzenden* send sth. by post (*or:* mail); *het aantal inwoners ~ vierkante kilometer* the number of inhabitants per square kilometre; *iets ~ kilo* (*or: paar*) *verkopen* sell sth. by the kilo (*or:* in pairs); *ze kosten 3 euro ~ stuk* they cost 3 euros apiece (*or:* each); *~ uur betaald worden* be paid by the hour; *~ vliegtuig* by plane, by air **2** from, as of: *de nieuwe tarieven worden ~ 1 februari van kracht* the new rates will take effect on February 1
het **perceel** /pɛrsel/ (pl: percelen) **1** property **2** parcel, lot, section
het **percent** /pɛrsɛnt/ (pl: -en) per cent
het **percentage** /pɛrsɛntaːʒə/ (pl: -s) percentage
de **percussie** /pɛrkysi/ (pl: -s) percussion
de **perenboom** /perə(n)bom/ (pl: -bomen) pear (tree)
perfect /pɛrfɛkt/ (adj, adv) perfect: *hij gaf een ~e imitatie van die zangeres* he did a perfect imitation of that singer; *in ~ staat* **a)** in mint condition; **b)** in perfect condition; *alles is ~ in orde* everything is perfect
de **perfectie** /pɛrfɛksi/ (pl: -s) perfection
perfectioneren /pɛrfɛkʃonərə(n)/ (perfectioneerde, heeft geperfectioneerd) perfect, bring to perfection
de **perfectionist** /pɛrfɛkʃonɪst/ (pl: -en) perfectionist
perfectionistisch /pɛrfɛkʃonɪstis/ (adj) perfectionist
de **perforator** /pɛrforɑtor/ (pl: -s) perforator, punch
perforeren /pɛrforerə(n)/ (perforeerde, heeft geperforeerd) perforate: *een geperforeerde long* a perforated lung
de **pergola** /pɛrɣolɑ/ (pl: -'s) pergola
de **periferie** /periferi/ (pl: -ën) periphery
de **periode** /perijodə/ (pl: -s) period, time; phase; episode, chapter: *~n met zon* sunny periods; *verkozen voor een ~ van twee jaar* elected for a two-year term (of office)
het/de **¹periodiek** /perijodik/ (pl: -en) **1** periodical **2** increment
²periodiek /perijodik/ (adj, adv) periodic(al): *het ~ systeem* the periodic table
de **periscoop** /periskop/ (pl: periscopen) periscope
het **perk** /pɛrk/ (pl: -en) **1** bed; flower bed **2** bound, limit: *binnen de ~en houden* limit, contain; *dat gaat alle ~en te buiten* that's the very limit
het **perkament** /pɛrkamɛnt/ (pl: -en) parchment
de **¹permanent** /pɛrmanɛnt/ (pl: -s) permanent

(wave)

²**permanent** /pɛrmanɛnt/ (adj) **1** permanent, perpetual **2** permanent, enduring; lasting; standing

³**permanent** /pɛrmanɛnt/ (adv) permanently, perpetually, all the time

permanenten /pɛrmanɛntə(n)/ (permanentte, heeft gepermanent) give a permanent wave, perm

de **permissie** /pɛrmɪsi/ (pl: -s) permission, leave

permitteren /pɛrmitərə(n)/ (permitteerde zich, heeft zich gepermitteerd) permit, grant permission, allow: *ik kan me niet ~ dat te doen* I can't afford to do that

perplex /pɛrplɛks/ (adj) perplexed, baffled, flabbergasted

het **perron** /pɛrɔn/ (pl: -s) platform

de **pers** /pɛrs/ (pl: -en) **1** press: *de ~ te woord staan* talk to the press **2** (printing) press: *ter ~e gaan* go to press

de **Pers** /pɛrs/ (pl: Perzen) Persian

het **persagentschap** /pɛrsaɣɛntsχɑp/ (pl: -pen) press (*or*: news) agency

het **persbericht** /pɛrzbərɪχt/ (pl: -en) press report, newspaper report

het **persbureau** /pɛrsbyro/ (pl: -s) news agency, press agency, press bureau

de **persconferentie** /pɛrskɔnfɛrɛnsi/ (pl: -s) press conference, news conference

per se /pɛrse/ (adv) at any price, at all costs: *hij wilde haar ~ zien* he was set on seeing (*or*: determined to see) her

¹**persen** /pɛrsə(n)/ (perste, heeft geperst) press, compress: *je moet harder ~* you must press harder

²**persen** /pɛrsə(n)/ (perste, heeft geperst) **1** press; stamp (out) **2** press (out), squeeze (out) **3** press, squeeze, push: *zich door een nauwe doorgang ~* squeeze (o.s.) through a narrow gap

de **persfotograaf** /pɛrsfotoɣraf/ (pl: -grafen) press photographer, newspaper photographer

de **persiflage** /pɛrsiflaʒə/ (pl: -s) (+ op) parody (of)

de **perskaart** /pɛrskart/ (pl: -en) press card (*or*: pass)

het/de **personage** /pɛrsonaʒə/ (pl: -s) character, role

de **personalia** /pɛrsonalija/ (pl) personal particulars (*or*: details)

het **personeel** /pɛrsonel/ personnel, staff; employees; workforce; crew; (factory) hands: *tien man ~* a staff of ten; *wij hebben een groot tekort aan ~* we are badly understaffed (*or*: short-staffed); *onderwijzend ~* teaching staff

de **personeelschef** /pɛrsonelʃɛf/ (pl: -s) personnel manager, staff manager

de **personeelszaken** /pɛrsonelzakə(n)/ (pl)

1 personnel matters, staff matters **2** personnel department

de **personenauto** /pɛrsonə(n)ɑuto/ (pl: -'s) (private, passenger) car

de **personificatie** /pɛrsonifika(t)si/ (pl: -s) personification

de **persoon** /pɛrson/ (pl: personen) person, individual; people: *een tafel voor één ~* a table for one || *ze kwam in (hoogst)eigen ~* she came personally (*or*: in person)

¹**persoonlijk** /pɛrsonlək/ (adj) **1** personal, private: *om ~e redenen* for personal (*or*: private) reasons, for reasons of one's own; *een ~ onderhoud* a personal talk; *~ worden* get (*or*: become) personal **2** personal, individual

²**persoonlijk** /pɛrsonlək/ (adv) personally || *~ vind ik hem een kwal* personally, I think he's a pain

de **persoonlijkheid** /pɛrsonləkhɛit/ (pl: -heden) personality, character

de **persoonsbeschrijving** /pɛrsonzbəsχrɛivɪŋ/ (pl: -en) personal description

het **persoonsbewijs** /pɛrsonzbəwɛis/ (pl: -bewijzen) identity card

persoonsgebonden /pɛrsonsχəbɔndə(n)/ (adj) personal

de **persoonsvorm** /pɛrsonsfɔrm/ (pl: -en) finite verb

het **perspectief** /pɛrspɛktif/ (pl: perspectieven) **1** prospect, perspective **2** perspective, context: *iets in breder ~ zien* look at (*or*: see) sth. in a wider context || *in ~ tekenen* draw in perspective

de **perssinaasappel** /pɛrsinaːsɑpəl/ (pl: -s) juice orange

de **persvrijheid** /pɛrsfrɛihɛit/ freedom of the press

pertinent /pɛrtinɛnt/ (adj) definite(ly), emphatic(ally): *~ volhouden* maintain categorically

Peru /peru/ Peru

de **Peruaan** /peruwan/ (pl: Peruanen) Peruvian

Peruaans /peruwans/ (adj) Peruvian

pervers /pɛrvɛrs/ (adj, adv) perverted, degenerate; unnatural

Perzië /pɛrzijə/ Persia

de **perzik** /pɛrzɪk/ (pl: -en) peach: *wilde ~* flat peach; [Am] donut peach

Perzisch /pɛrzis/ (adj) Persian: *~ tapijt* Persian rug (*or*: carpet)

de **peseta** /peseta/ (pl: -'s) peseta

het **pessimisme** /pɛsimɪsmə/ pessimism

de **pessimist** /pɛsimɪst/ (pl: -en) pessimist

pessimistisch /pɛsimɪstis/ (adj, adv) pessimistic, gloomy

de **pest** /pɛst/ **1** (bubonic) plague, pestilence **2** miserable || [Dutch] *de ~ in hebben* be in a foul mood; *de ~ aan iets (iem.) hebben* loathe/detest sth. (s.o.)

pesten /pɛstə(n)/ (pestte, heeft gepest) pester, tease; [at school] bully: *hij zit mij altijd te ~*

he is always on at me

het **pesticide** /pɛstisi̱də/ (pl: -n, -s) pesticide

de **pestkop** /pɛ̱stkɔp/ (pl: -pen) [inform] pest, nuisance

de **pesto** /pɛ̱sto/ pesto

de **pet** /pɛt/ (pl: -ten) **1** cap: *met de ~ naar iets gooien* make a half-hearted attempt at sth., have a shot at sth.; *met de ~ rondgaan* pass the hat round **2** [fig] upstairs: *dat gaat **boven** mijn ~* that is beyond me; *ik kan er **met mijn** ~ niet bij* it beats me ǁ *geen **hoge** ~ op hebben van* not think much of, have a low opinion of

het **petekind** /pe̱təkɪnt/ (pl: -eren) godchild

de **peter** /pe̱tər/ (pl: -s) godfather

de **peterselie** /petərse̱li/ parsley

de **petfles** /pɛ̱tflɛs/ (pl: -sen) PET-bottle, (reusable) plastic bottle

de **petitie** /pəti̱(t)si/ (pl: -s) petition: *een ~ **indienen*** file a petition

de **petroleum** /petro̱lejʏm/ petroleum, mineral oil

petto /pɛ̱to/: *iets **in** ~ hebben* have sth. in reserve (*or:* in hand)

de **petunia** /pety̱nija/ (pl: -'s) petunia

de **peuk** /pøk/ (pl: -en) **1** butt, stub **2** fag

de **peul** /pøl/ (pl: -en) pod, capsule

de **peulenschil** /pø̱lə(n)sxɪl/ (pl: -len) [Dutch] trifle: *dat **is** maar een ~(letje) voor hem* **a)** that's peanuts (*or:* chicken feed) to him; **b)** he can do it standing on his head

de **peulvrucht** /pø̱lvrʏxt/ (pl: -en) dried legume

de **peuter** /pø̱tər/ (pl: -s) pre-schooler, toddler

peuteren /pø̱tərə(n)/ (peuterde, heeft gepeuterd) pick: *in zijn neus ~* pick one's nose

de **peuterleidster** /pø̱tərlɛitstər/ (pl: -s) nursery-school teacher

de **peuterspeelzaal** /pø̱tərspelzal/ (pl: -zalen) playgroup

de **peutertuin** /pø̱tərtœyn/ (pl: -en) day nursery, crèche

pezen /pe̱zə(n)/ (peesde, heeft gepeesd) [inform] slave

pezig /pe̱zəx/ (adj) sinewy, stringy

de **pfeiffer** /pfɔj̱fər/ glandular fever

het **pgb** /peɣebe̱/ (pl: -'s) [Dutch] *persoonsgebonden budget* personal budget

het **phishing** /fɪ̱ʃɪŋ/ phishing

de **pH-waarde** /pehawardə/ pH value

de **pi** /pi/ (pl: pi's) pi

de **pianist** /pijani̱st/ (pl: -en) pianist, piano player

de **piano** /pija̱no/ (pl: -'s) piano

het **pianoconcert** /pija̱nokɔnsɛrt/ (pl: -en) **1** piano recital: *een ~ **geven*** give a piano recital **2** piano concerto

de **pianoles** /pija̱nolɛs/ piano lesson

pianospelen /pija̱nospelə(n)/ play(ing) the piano

de **pianostemmer** /pija̱nostɛmər/ (pl: -s) piano tuner

de **pias** /pija̱s/ (pl: -sen) [Dutch] clown, buffoon

de **piccalilly** /pɪkalɪ̱li/ [Dutch] piccalilli

de **piccolo** /pi̱kolo/ (pl: -'s) **1** bell-boy **2** piccolo

de **picknick** /pɪ̱knɪk/ (pl: -s) picnic

picknicken /pɪ̱knɪkə(n)/ (picknickte, heeft gepicknickt) picnic

de **picknickmand** /pɪ̱knɪkmɑnt/ (pl: -en) picnic hamper (*or:* basket)

de **pick-up** /pɪ̱kʏp/ (pl: -s) record player

pico bello /pikobɛ̱lo/ (adj, adv) splendid, outstanding

het **pictogram** /pɪ̱ktoɣrɑm/ (pl: -men) pictogram

de **picture** /pɪ̱kçər/: *in de ~ komen* come to the fore; *hij is **in** de ~ als lijsttrekker* he is being mentioned as party leader

de **pief** /pif/ (pl: -en) [inform] type, sort: *zich een **hele** ~ voelen* think one is a big shot (*or:* cheese)

de **piek** /pik/ (pl: -en) **1** spike: *een ~ **haar*** a spike of hair **2** peak, summit **3** finial

pieken /pi̱kə(n)/ (piekte, heeft gepiekt) **1** be spiky, stand out: *~d **haar*** straggly hair **2** peak: *de olieprijs piekte **op** 122 euro* the price of oil peaked at 122 euros; *te **vroeg** ~* peak too early

de **piekeraar** /pi̱kərar/ (pl: -s) worrier, brooder

piekeren /pi̱kərə(n)/ (piekerde, heeft gepiekerd) worry, brood

piekfijn /pikfɛi̱n/ (adj, adv) posh, smart

het **piekuur** /pi̱kyr/ (pl: -uren) peak hour; rush hour

de **piemel** /pi̱məl/ (pl: -s) willie

pienter /pɪ̱ntər/ (adj) bright, sharp, shrewd

piep /pip/ (int) squeak; peep; cheep

piepen /pi̱pə(n)/ (piepte, heeft gepiept) squeak; peep; cheep; creak; pipe

de **pieper** /pi̱pər/ (pl: -s) **1** b(l)eeper **2** spud

piepjong /pipjɔ̱ŋ/ (adj): *niet (zo) ~ meer **zijn*** be no chicken

piepklein /pipklɛi̱n/ (adj) teeny(-weeny), teensy

het **piepschuim** /pi̱psxœym/ styrofoam, polystyrene foam

de **piepstem** /pi̱pstɛm/ (pl: -men) squeaky voice

de **pieptoon** /pi̱pton/ (pl: -tonen) bleep, beep

de **piepzak** /pi̱psɑk/ [inform]: *in de ~ zitten* have the wind up

de **pier** /pir/ (pl: -en) **1** worm, earthworm **2** pier

de **piercing** /pi̱rsɪŋ/ piercing

het **pierenbad** /pi̱rə(n)bɑt/ paddling pool

de **pies** /pis/ [inform] pee, wee

piesen /pi̱sə(n)/ (pieste, heeft gepiest) [inform] pee, wee

de **piet** /pit/ (pl: -en) geezer, feller: *hij vindt zichzelf een **hele** ~* he thinks he's really s.o.; *een **hoge** ~* a great card

Piet /pit/: *Jan, ~ en Klaas* Tom, Dick and Harry; *er voor ~ **Snot** bijzitten* sit there like a fool; *Zwarte ~* St Nicholas' helper

de **piëteit** /pijetɛɪt/ piety
pietepeuterig /pitəpøtərəx/ (adj, adv) [inform] **1** finical, finicky **2** microscopic(al)
het **pietje-precies** /picəprəsis/: *een ~ zijn* be a fusspot
pietluttig /pitlytəx/ (adj) meticulous, petty, niggling
het **pigment** /pɪymɛnt/ pigment
de **pigmentvlek** /pɪymɛntflɛk/ (pl: -ken) birthmark, mole
de **pij** /pɛɪ/ (pl: -en) (monk's) habit, frock
de **pijl** /pɛil/ (pl: -en) arrow: *nog meer ~en op zijn boog hebben* have more than one string to one's bow; *volg de ~en* follow the arrows (*or:* signs)
de **pijl-en-boog** /pɛɪlɛmbox/ (pl: pijl-en-bogen) bow and arrow
de **pijler** /pɛilər/ (pl: -s) pillar
pijlsnel /pɛilsnɛl/ (adj, adv) (as) swift as an arrow
het **pijltje** /pɛilcə/ (pl: -s) dart
de **pijltjestoets** /pɛɪlcəstuts/ (pl: -en) [comp] scroll arrow
de **pijn** /pɛin/ (pl: -en) pain; ache: *~ in de buik hebben* have (a) stomach ache, have a pain in one's stomach; *~ in de keel hebben* have a sore throat; *~ lijden* be in pain; *iem. ~ doen* hurt s.o., give s.o. pain || *met veel ~ en moeite iets gedaan krijgen* get sth. accomplished with a great deal of trouble (*or:* a great effort)
de **pijnappel** /pɛinapəl/ (pl: -s) pine cone
de **pijnbank** /pɛimbɑŋk/ (pl: -en) rack
de **pijnboom** /pɛimbom/ (pl: -bomen) pine (tree)
de **pijngrens** /pɛiŋɣrɛns/ pain threshold
pijnigen /pɛinəɣə(n)/ (pijnigde, heeft gepijnigd) **1** torture **2** torment: *zijn hersens ~ beat one's brains out*
¹**pijnlijk** /pɛinlək/ (adj) **1** painful, sore: *~ aanvoelen* hurt, be painful **2** painful, hurtful: *een ~e opmerking* an embarrassing remark **3** painful, awkward, embarrassing: *er viel een ~e stilte* there was an uncomfortable silence
²**pijnlijk** /pɛinlək/ (adv) painfully: *~ getroffen zijn* be pained
pijnloos /pɛinlos/ (adj) painless
de **pijnstiller** /pɛinstɪlər/ (pl: -s) painkiller
de **pijp** /pɛip/ (pl: -en) **1** pipe, tube **2** leg
pijpen /pɛɪpə(n)/ (pijpte, heeft gepijpt) [inform] blow; suck off: *gepijpt worden* be blown (*or:* sucked (off)) || [fig] *naar iemands ~ dansen* dance attendance (up)on s.o.
de **pijpenkrul** /pɛɪpə(n)krʏl/ (pl: -len) corkscrew curl
de **pijpensteel** /pɛɪpə(n)stel/ (pl: -stelen): *het regent pijpenstelen* it's raining cats and dogs
de **pijpleiding** /pɛiplɛidɪŋ/ (pl: -en) piping; pipeline
de **pik** /pɪk/ [inform] penis: *een stijve ~* a hard-on || *de ~ op iem. hebben* have it in for s.o.

pikant /pikɑnt/ (adj) piquant
pikdonker /pɪɡdɔŋkər/ (adj) pitch-dark, pitch-black
het **pikhouweel** /pɪkhɑuwel/ (pl: -houwelen) pickaxe
¹**pikken** /pɪkə(n)/ (pikte, heeft gepikt) peck
²**pikken** /pɪkə(n)/ (pikte, heeft gepikt) [inform] **1** lift, pinch: *zij heeft dat geld gepikt* she stole that money **2** take, put up with: *pik jij dat allemaal maar?* do you just put up with all that?; *we ~ het niet langer* we won't take it any longer
pikzwart /pɪkswɑrt/ (adj) pitch-black: *~ haar* raven-(black) hair
de **pil** /pɪl/ (pl: -len) **1** pill: *het is een bittere ~ voor hem* it is a bitter pill for him to swallow; *de ~ slikken* be on the pill **2** tome
de **pilaar** /pilɑr/ (pl: pilaren) pillar
de **piloot** /pilot/ (pl: piloten) pilot: *automatische ~* automatic pilot
de **pilot** /pɑjlət/ (pl: -s) pilot
het/de **pils** /pɪls/ beer, lager
pimpelen /pɪmpələ(n)/ (pimpelde, heeft gepimpeld) tipple, booze
de **pimpelmees** /pɪmpəlmes/ blue tit
pimpelpaars /pɪmpəlpɑrs/ (adj) (lurid) purple: *hij is ~ van de kou* he is blue with cold
pimpen /pɪmpə(n)/ (pimpte, heeft gepimpt) pimp
de **pin** /pɪn/ (pl: -nen) peg, pin
het **pinapparaat** /pɪnɑpɑrɑt/ (pl: -apparaten) PIN-code reader
de **pinautomaat** /pɪnɑutomɑt/ [roughly] EFTPOS, Electronic Fund Transfer at Point Of Sale: *kan ik de ~ gebruiken?* can I use my direct debit card?, can I use Chip and PIN?
het/de **pincet** /pɪnsɛt/ (pl: -ten) (pair of) tweezers
de **pincode** /pɪŋkodə/ (pl: -s) PIN code
de **pinda** /pɪndɑ/ (pl: -'s) peanut
de **pindakaas** /pɪndɑkas/ peanut butter
de **pindasaus** /pɪndɑsɑus/ (pl: -sauzen) peanut sauce
de **pineut** /pinøt/ dupe: *de ~ zijn* be the dupe
de **ping** /pɪŋ/ **1** [inform] cash, shekels **2** ping
de **pingelaar** /pɪŋəlɑr/ (pl: -s) **1** [socc] player who holds on to the ball **2** haggler
pingelen /pɪŋələ(n)/ (pingelde, heeft gepingeld) **1** haggle (over, about) **2** hold on to the ball
pingen /pɪŋə(n)/ (pingde, heeft gepingd) ping
het **pingpong** /pɪŋpɔŋ/ ping-pong
pingpongen /pɪŋpɔŋə(n)/ (pingpongde, heeft gepingpongd) play ping-pong
de **pinguïn** /pɪŋɡwɪn/ (pl: -s) penguin
de **pink** /pɪŋk/ (pl: -en) little finger || *bij de ~en zijn* be all there
de **pinksterbloem** /pɪŋkstərblum/ (pl: -en) cuckoo flower, lady's smock
de **pinksterdag** /pɪŋkstərdɑx/ (pl: -en): *eerste ~* Whit Sunday; [esp Am] Pentecost; *tweede*

~ Whit Monday
Pinksteren /pɪŋkstərə(n)/ Whitsun(tide);
[esp Am] Pentecost
de **pinkstergemeente** /pɪŋkstərɣəmentə/ (pl:
-n, -s) Pentecostal church
pinnen /pɪnə(n)/ (pinde, heeft gepind)
[Dutch] **1** withdraw cash from a cashpoint
2 pay with his (debit) card
pinnig /pɪnəɣ/ (adj, adv) tart; snappish
de **pinpas** /pɪmpɑs/ (pl: -sen) [Dutch] cash card;
switch card
de **pint** /pɪnt/ (pl: -en) pint
het **pintje** /pɪncə/ (pl: -s) [Belg] pint (of beer)
de **pioen** /pijun/ (pl: -en) peony
de **pion** /pijɔn/ (pl: -nen) **1** counter, piece
2 pawn **3** traffic cone: *oranje ~nen* orange
traffic cones
de **pionier** /pijonir/ (pl: -s) pioneer
het/de **pipet** /pipɛt/ (pl: -ten) pipette
pips /pɪps/ (adj) washed out, pale
de **piraat** /pirat/ (pl: piraten) pirate
de **piramide** /piramidə/ (pl: -n, -s) pyramid
het **piramidespel** /piramidəspɛl/ pyramid
scheme
de **piranha** /pirɑna/ (pl: -'s) piranha
de **piratenzender** /piratə(n)zɛndər/ (pl: -s) pirate (radio station)
de **piraterij** /piratərɛɪ/ piracy: *~ op internet* Internet piracy
de **pirouette** /piruwɛt(ə)/ (pl: -n, -s) pirouette
de **pis** /pɪs/ [inform] piss
de **pisang** /pisɑŋ/ banana || [Dutch] *de ~ zijn* be
left holding the baby
pisnijdig /pɪsnɛɪdəɣ/ (adj, adv) [inform]
pissed off
de **pispaal** /pɪspal/ (pl: -palen) [inform] target
de **pispot** /pɪspɔt/ (pl: -ten) piss-pot
de **pissebed** /pɪsəbɛt/ (pl: -den) woodlouse
pissen /pɪsə(n)/ (piste, heeft gepist) [in-
form] piss
pissig /pɪsəɣ/ (adj, adv) [inform] pissed off,
bloody annoyed
de **pistache** /pistɑʃ/ (pl: -s) pistachio (nut)
de **piste** /pistə/ (pl: -s) **1** ring **2** [cycling] track
3 [skiing] piste
de **pistolet** /pistolɛt/ (pl: -s) bread roll
het **pistool** /pistol/ (pl: pistolen) pistol, gun:
nietpistool staple gun
de ¹**pit** /pɪt/ (pl: -ten) **1** seed; pip; stone **2** wick
3 burner
het/de ²**pit** /pɪt/ spirit: *er zit ~ in die meid* she's a girl
with spirit
het **pitabroodje** /pitabrocə/ (pl: -s) pitta
(bread)
de **pitbullterriër** /pɪtbultɛrijər/ (pl: -s) pit bull
(terrier)
de **pits** /pɪts/ pit(s)
de **pitsstraat** /pɪtstrat/ (pl: -straten) pit lane
pitten /pɪtə(n)/ (pitte, heeft gepit) [inform]
turn in, kip: *gaan ~* hit the sack
pittig /pɪtəɣ/ (adj, adv) **1** lively, pithy; racy

2 [fig] stiff **3** spicy, hot, strong **4** tough
pittoresk /pitorɛsk/ (adj, adv) picturesque;
scenic
de **pixel** /pɪksəl/ pixel
de **pizza** /pidza/ (pl: -'s) pizza: *een stuk ~* a slice
of pizza
de **pizzabodem** /pidzabodəm/ (pl: -s) pizza
base
de **pizzakoerier** /pitsakurir/ (pl: -s) pizza deliv-
erer, pizza delivery boy
de **pizzeria** /pidzərija/ (pl: -'s) pizzeria
de **pk** /peka/ (pl: pk's) *paardenkracht* h.p.
de **PKN** *Protestantse Kerk in Nederland* Dutch
United Protestant Chruches
de **plaag** /plax/ (pl: plagen) plague
de **plaaggeest** /plaxest/ (pl: -en) tease(r)
de **plaat** /plat/ (pl: platen) **1** plate; sheet; slab
2 record **3** plate, print || [inform] *uit zijn ~
gaan* be over the moon; hit the roof
het **plaatje** /placə/ (pl: -s) **1** plate; sheet; slab;
identity disc **2** snapshot, photo **3** picture
de **plaats** /plats/ (pl: -en) **1** place, position: *de ~
van bestemming* the destination; *de juiste
man op de juiste ~* the right man in the right
place; *op uw ~en!* klaar, af on your marks, get
set, go; *in (op) de eerste ~* in the first place; *op
de eerste ~ komen* come first, take first place;
op de eerste ~ eindigen be (placed) first; *ter ~e
op* the spot; on the scene; [Belg] *ter ~e trappelen* be stuck **2** room, space: *deze tafel
neemt veel ~* in this table takes up a lot of
room (*or:* space) **3** town **4** place; seat: *neemt
u a.u.b. ~* please take your seats; *van ~ wisse-
len* change places || *in ~ van* instead of
de **plaatsbepaling** /platsbəpalɪŋ/ orientation
de **plaatsbespreking** /platsbəsprekɪŋ/ booking, reservation
het **plaatsbewijs** /platsbəwɛis/ (pl: -bewijzen)
ticket
¹**plaatselijk** /platsələk/ (adj) local: *tien uur ~e
tijd* ten o'clock local time; *een ~e verdoving* a
local anaesthetic
²**plaatselijk** /platsələk/ (adv) **1** locally, on
the spot: *iets ~ onderzoeken* investigate sth.
on the spot **2** in some places: *~ regen* local
showers
¹**plaatsen** /platsə(n)/ (plaatste, heeft geplaatst) **1** place, put: *de ladder tegen het
schuurtje ~* lean (*or:* put) the ladder against
the shed; *iets niet kunnen ~* [also fig] not be
able to place sth. **2** rank || *een advertentie ~*
put an advertisement in the paper; *een order
~* place an order
zich ²**plaatsen** /platsə(n)/ (plaatste zich, heeft
zich geplaatst) qualify (for)
het **plaatsgebrek** /platsxəbrɛk/ lack of space
plaatshebben /platshɛbə(n)/ (had plaats,
heeft plaatsgehad) take place
de **plaatsing** /platsɪŋ/ (pl: -en) **1** placement,
positioning **2** [sport] ranking; qualification
plaatsmaken /platsmakə(n)/ (maakte

plasticsoep

plaats, heeft plaatsgemaakt) make room (or: space) (for)

de **plaatsnaam** /platsnam/ (pl: -namen) place name

plaatsnemen /platsnemə(n)/ (nam plaats, heeft plaatsgenomen) take a seat

het **plaatstaal** /platstal/ sheet steel, steelplate

plaatsvervangend /platsfərvaŋənt/ (adj) substitute; temporary: ~e *schaamte* vicarious shame

de **plaatsvervanger** /platsfərvaŋər/ (pl: -s) substitute, replacement; deputy

plaatsvinden /platsfɪndə(n)/ (vond plaats, heeft plaatsgevonden) take place, happen

de **placebo** /plasebo/ (pl: -'s) placebo

de **placemat** /plɛsmɛt/ (pl: -s) place mat

de **placenta** /plasɛnta/ (pl: -'s) placenta

de **pladijs** /pladɛis/ (pl: pladijzen) [Belg] plaice

het **plafond** /plafɔn/ (pl: -s) ceiling: *het glazen ~* the glass ceiling

de **plag** /plɑx/ (pl: -gen) sod, turf

plagen /plaɣə(n)/ (plaagde, heeft geplaagd) tease: *iem. met iets* ~ tease s.o. about sth.

plagerig /plaɣərəx/ (adj, adv) teasing

de **plagerij** /plaɣərɛi/ (pl: -en) teasing

het **plagiaat** /plaɣijat/ (pl: plagiaten) plagiarism: ~ *plegen* plagiarize

de **plagiaatscanner** /plaɣijatskɛnər/ (pl: -s) plagiarism checker

de **plaid** /plet/ (pl: -s) travelling rug; [Am] plaid blanket

de **plak** /plɑk/ (pl: -ken) **1** slice: *iets in ~ken snijden* slice sth. **2** (dental) plaque || *onder de ~ zitten* be henpecked

het **plakband** /plɑgbɑnt/ adhesive tape

het **plakboek** /plɑgbuk/ (pl: -en) scrapbook

het **plakkaat** /plɑkat/ (pl: plakkaten) placard, poster

de **plakkaatverf** /plɑkatfɛrf/ poster paint

¹**plakken** /plɑkə(n)/ (plakte, heeft geplakt) stick; paste || *ergens blijven ~* stick (or: hang) around somewhere; outstay one's welcome

²**plakken** /plɑkə(n)/ (plakte, heeft geplakt) **1** stick (to, on), glue (to, on) **2** repair: *een band ~* repair a puncture

de **plakker** /plɑkər/ (pl: -s) billsticker

plakkerig /plɑkərəx/ (adj) sticky

het **plakplaatje** /plɑkplacə/ (pl: -s) transfer

het **plaksel** /plɑksəl/ (pl: -s) paste

de **plakstift** /plɑkstɪft/ (pl: -en) Pritt stick

het **plakwerk** /plɑkwɛrk/ sticking, glueing

plamuren /plamyrə(n)/ (plamuurde, heeft geplamuurd) fill

de **plamuur** /plamyr/ filler

het **plamuurmes** /plamyrmɛs/ (pl: -sen) filling-knife

het **plan** /plɑn/ (pl: -nen) **1** plan: *een ~ uitvoeren* carry out a plan; *een ~ maken (voor ...)* draw up a plan for sth., plan sth.; *het ~ opvatten (om)* plan (to), intend (to), propose (to); *een ~ smeden (tegen)* scheme (against), plot

(against); *zijn ~ trekken* [Belg] manage, cope; *wat ben je van ~?* what are you going to do?; *we waren net van ~ om ...* we were just about (or: going) to ... **2** plan, design

het **plan de campagne** /plɑndəkɑmpɑɲə/ plan (or: scheme) of action

de **planeconomie** /plɑnekonomi/ (pl: -ën) planned economy

de **planeet** /planet/ (pl: planeten) planet: *[hum] van welke ~ kom jij?* which planet are you living on?

het **planetarium** /planetarijʏm/ (pl: -s, planetaria) planetarium

de **plank** /plɑŋk/ (pl: -en) plank; board; shelf: *[Dutch] de ~ misslaan* be wide of the mark

de **plankenkoorts** /plɑŋkə(n)korts/ stage fright

het **plankgas** /plɑŋkxɑs/ [roughly] full throttle: ~ *geven* step on the gas

de **plankton** /plɑŋkton/ plankton

plankzeilen /plɑŋksɛilə(n)/ windsurfing, boardsailing

planmatig /plɑmatəx/ (adj, adv) systematic; according to plan

plannen /plɛnə(n)/ (plande, heeft gepland) plan

de **planning** /plɛnɪŋ/ plan, planning

de **planologie** /planoloɣi/ (town and country) planning

de **plant** /plɑnt/ (pl: -en) plant: *de ~en water geven* water the plants

plantaardig /plɑntardəx/ (adj) vegetable

de **plantage** /plɑntaʒə/ (pl: -s) plantation

planten /plɑntə(n)/ (plantte, heeft geplant) plant; plant out

de **plantenbak** /plɑntə(n)bɑk/ (pl: -ken) flower box

de **planteneter** /plɑntə(n)etər/ (pl: -s) herbivore

de **plantengroei** /plɑntə(n)ɣruj/ **1** plant growth **2** vegetation

de **plantenkas** /plɑntə(n)kɑs/ (pl: -sen) greenhouse

de **planter** /plɑntər/ (pl: -s) planter

de **plantkunde** /plɑntkʏndə/ botany

het **plantsoen** /plɑntsun/ (pl: -en) public garden(s), park

de **plaque** /plɑk/ (pl: -s) plaque

de **plas** /plɑs/ (pl: -sen) **1** puddle, pool **2** water, pee: *een ~je (moeten) doen* (have to) go (to the toilet, loo); (have to) do a wee(-wee) **3** pool, pond

het **plasma** /plɑsma/ (pl: -'s) plasma

¹**plassen** /plɑsə(n)/ (plaste, heeft geplast) **1** go (to the toilet, loo), (have a) pee: *ik moet nodig ~* I really have to go **2** splash

²**plassen** /plɑsə(n)/ (plaste, heeft geplast) pass: *bloed ~* pass blood (in one's urine)

het ¹**plastic** /plɛstɪk/ plastic

²**plastic** /plɛstɪk/ (adj) plastic

de **plasticsoep** /plɛstɪksup/ plastic soup

de **¹plastiek** /plɑstik/ (pl: -en) **1** plastic art(s) **2** model

het **²plastiek** /plɑstik/ [Belg] plastic

plastificeren /plɑstifisɛrə(n)/ (plastificeerde, heeft geplastificeerd) plasticize

plastisch /plɑstis/ (adj) plastic

plat /plɑt/ (adj, adv) **1** flat: *een ~te tv* a flatscreen TV **2** closed down, shut down: *de haven **gaat** morgen* ~ tomorrow the port will be shut down ‖ *de **zaal** ~ krijgen* **a)** carry the audience with one; **b)** bring the house down; ~ **praten** speak in dialect; ~ **uitgedrukt** to put it crudely (*or:* coarsely)

de **¹plataan** /platan/ (pl: platanen) [tree] plane (tree)

het **²plataan** /platan/ [wood] plane (tree)

platbranden /plɑdbrɑndə(n)/ (brandde plat, heeft platgebrand) burn to the ground

het **plateau** /plato/ (pl: -s) **1** dish, platter **2** plateau

de **plateauzool** /platozol/ (pl: -zolen) platform sole

de **platenspeler** /platə(n)spelər/ (pl: -s) record player

de **platenzaak** /platə(n)zak/ (pl: -zaken) record shop

het **platform** /plɑtfɔrm/ (pl: -s) platform

platgaan /plɑtxan/ (lag plat, heeft platgelegen) **1** be bowled over by (s.o.): *de zaal ging plat* the audience was rolling in the aisles **2** [comp] fail, go down **3** [business] be (completely) closed/shut down; be strikebound

het **¹platina** /platina/ platinum

²platina /platina/ (adj) platinum

platleggen /plɑtlɛɣə(n)/ (legde plat, heeft platgelegd) **1** lay flat **2** bring to a standstill

platliggen /plɑtlɪɣə(n)/ (lag plat, heeft platgelegen) be at a standstill

platlopen /plɑtlopə(n)/ (liep plat, heeft platgelopen) trample down

platonisch /platonis/ (adj, adv) platonic

platspuiten /plɑtspœytə(n)/ (spoot plat, heeft platgespoten) [inform] knock out with sedatives

de **plattegrond** /platəɣrɔnt/ (pl: -en) **1** (street) map **2** floor plan

de **plattekaas** /platəkas/ [Belg] cottage cheese, cream cheese

het **platteland** /platəlɑnt/ country(side)

de **plattelandsbevolking** /platəlɑn(t)sbəvɔlkɪŋ/ rural population

plattrappen /plɑtrɑpə(n)/ (trapte plat, heeft platgetrapt) trample down

plattreden /plɑtredə(n)/ (trad plat, heeft platgetreden) trample down: *platgetreden paden* well-trodden paths

de **platvis** /plɑtfɪs/ (pl: -sen) flatfish

platvloers /plɑtflurs/ (adj) coarse, crude

de **platvoet** /plɑtfut/ (pl: -en) flatfoot

platzak /plɑtsɑk/ (adj) (flat) broke

plausibel /plɑuzibəl/ (adj) plausible

plaveien /plavɛijə(n)/ (plaveide, heeft geplaveid) pave

het **plaveisel** /plavɛisəl/ (pl: -s) paving, pavement

de **plavuis** /plavœys/ (pl: plavuizen) (floor) tile; flag(stone)

het/de **playback** /plejbɛk/ (pl: -s) miming

playbacken /plejbɛkə(n)/ (playbackte, heeft geplaybackt) mime (to one's own, another person's voice)

de **playboy** /plejbɔj/ (pl: -s) playboy

het **plebs** /plɛps/ plebs

plechtig /plɛxtəx/ (adj, adv) solemn: ~ **beloven** *(te)* solemnly promise (to)

de **plechtigheid** /plɛxtəxhɛit/ (pl: -heden) ceremony

plechtstatig /plɛxtstatəx/ (adj, adv) solemn

het **plectrum** /plɛktrʏm/ (pl: -s, plectra) plectrum

de **plee** /ple/ (pl: -s) [inform] loo; [Am] john: *op de ~ zitten* be in the loo

het **pleeggezin** /pleɣəzɪn/ (pl: -nen) foster home

het **pleegkind** /pleɣkɪnt/ (pl: -eren) fosterchild: *(iem.) als ~ opnemen* take (s.o.) in as foster-child

de **pleegouders** /pleɣɑudərs/ (pl) foster-parents

plegen /pleɣə(n)/ (pleegde, heeft gepleegd) commit: *verzet* ~ offer resistance; *een telefoontje* ~ make a (phone) call

het **pleidooi** /plɛidɔj/ (pl: -en) **1** plea: *een ~ houden voor* make a plea for **2** counsel's speech (*or:* argument)

het **plein** /plɛin/ (pl: -en) square, plaza: *op (aan) het ~* in the square

de **pleinvrees** /plɛinvres/ agoraphobia

de **¹pleister** /plɛistər/ (sticking) plaster

het **²pleister** /plɛistər/ plaster

pleisteren /plɛistərə(n)/ (pleisterde, heeft gepleisterd) **1** plaster **2** put a plaster on

de **pleisterplaats** /plɛistərplats/ (pl: -en) stopping place

het **pleisterwerk** /plɛistərwɛrk/ plasterwork, plaster(ing)

het **pleit** /plɛit/ **1** (law)suit: *het ~ winnen* win one's suit **2** dispute: *het ~ beslechten* decide the argument

de **pleitbezorger** /plɛidbəzɔrɣər/ (pl: -s) [fig] advocate, champion, supporter

pleiten /plɛitə(n)/ (pleitte, heeft gepleit) plead: *dat pleit voor hem* that is to his credit

de **pleiter** /plɛitər/ (pl: -s) counsel

de **plek** /plɛk/ (pl: -ken) **1** spot: *een blauwe ~* a bruise; *iemands zwakke ~ raken* find s.o.'s weak spot **2** spot, place: *ter ~ke* on site, in situ

plenair /plenɛːr/ (adj) plenary

plengen /plɛŋə(n)/ (plengde, heeft geplengd): *tranen* ~ shed tears, weep de **plensbui** /plɛnzbœy/ (pl: -en) downpour

¹**plenzen** /plɛnzə(n)/ (plensde, heeft geplensd) pour

²**plenzen** /plɛnzə(n)/ (plensde, heeft geplensd) splash

het **pleonasme** /plejonɔsmə/ (pl: -n) pleonasm

pletten /plɛtə(n)/ (plette, heeft geplet) **1** crush **2** flatten; squash

pletter /plɛtər/: *te ~ slaan tegen de rotsen* be dashed against the rocks; *zich te ~ vervelen* be bored stiff (*or:* to death)

pleuren /plɵrə(n)/ (pleurde, heeft gepleurd) [inform] chuck: *hij pleurde zijn rommel in de kast* he chucked his junk in the closet || *pleur op!* piss off!

het/de **pleuris** /plɵrɪs/ [inform]: *de ~ breekt uit* the shit hits the fan; *ik schrok me de ~* I was frightened to death, I was scared out of my wits; *krijg de ~* go to hell

de **plevier** /pləvir/ (pl: -en) plover

het **plexiglas**® /plɛksiɣlɑs/ plexiglass

plezant /pləzɑnt/ (adj) [Belg] pleasant

het **plezier** /pləzir/ **1** pleasure, fun: *iem. een ~ doen* do s.o. a favour; *~ hebben* have fun, enjoy o.s.; *veel ~!* enjoy yourself! **2** pleasure, enjoyment: *met alle ~* with pleasure; *ik heb hier altijd met ~ gewerkt* I have always enjoyed working here

plezieren /pləzirə(n)/ (plezierde, heeft geplezierd): *als ik je ermee kan ~* if that's what makes you happy; *iem. met iets ~* oblige s.o. with sth.

plezierig /pləzirəχ/ (adj, adv) pleasant

het **plezierjacht** /pləzirjɑχt/ (pl: -en) pleasure yacht

de **plezierreis** /pləzirɛɪs/ (pl: -reizen) (pleasure) trip, outing

de **plicht** /plɪχt/ (pl: -en) duty: *het is niet meer dan je ~ (om …)* you are in duty bound (to …); *de ~ roept* duty calls; *zijn ~ doen* (or: *vervullen*) do one's duty, perform one's duty; *zijn ~ verzaken* neglect one's duty

plichtmatig /plɪχtmatəχ/ (adj, adv) dutiful: *een ~ bezoekje* a duty call

de **plichtpleging** /plɪχtpleɪ̯ɪŋ/ (pl: -en) ceremony: *met veel ~en* with considerable ceremony; *zonder ~en* unceremonious(ly), without ceremony

het **plichtsbesef** /plɪχtsbəsɛf/ sense of duty

plichtsgetrouw /plɪχtsχətrɑu̯/ (adj, adv) dutiful

het **plichtsverzuim** /plɪχ(t)sfərzœym/ neglect of duty

de **plint** /plɪnt/ (pl: -en) skirting board; [Am] baseboard

de **ploeg** /pluχ/ (pl: -en) **1** gang; shift: *in ~en werken* work (in) shifts **2** [sport] team; side **3** plough

ploegen /pluɣə(n)/ (ploegde, heeft/is geploegd) plough: *een akker* (or: *het land*) *~* plough a field (*or:* the land)

de **ploegendienst** /pluɣə(n)dinst/ (pl: -en) shift work: *in ~ werken* work (in) shifts

de **ploeggenoot** /pluɣənot/ (pl: -genoten) teammate

de **ploegleider** /pluɣlɛidər/ (pl: -s) [sport] team manager; captain

het **ploegverband** /pluɣfərbɑnt/: [sport] *in ~* as a team

de **ploert** /plurt/ (pl: -en) cad, scab

de **ploeteraar** /plutərar/ (pl: -s) plodder, slogger

ploeteren /plutərə(n)/ (ploeterde, heeft geploeterd) plod (away, along)

de **plof** /plɔf/ (pl: -fen) thud, bump, plop

ploffen /plɔfə(n)/ (plofte, is geploft) **1** thud, flop **2** pop, bang || *in een stoel ~* plump down (*or:* flop) into a chair

de **plofkraak** /plɔfkrak/ (pl: -kraken) safecracking with explosives

plomp /plɔmp/ (adj, adv) plump; squat; cumbersome

plompverloren /plɔmpfərlorə(n)/ (adv) bluntly

de **plons** /plɔns/ (pl: -en, plonzen) splash || *~! daar viel de steen in het water* splash! went the stone into the water

plonzen /plɔnzə(n)/ (plonsde, heeft/is geplonsd) splash

de **plooi** /ploj/ (pl: -en) pleat, fold || *zijn gezicht in de ~ houden* keep a straight face

plooibaar /plojbar/ (adj) pliable, flexible

plooien /plojə(n)/ (plooide, heeft geplooid) fold, pleat, crease

de **plooifiets** /plojfits/ (pl: -en) [Belg] folding (*or:* collapsible) bike

de **plooirok** /plojrɔk/ (pl: -ken) pleated skirt

de **plopkap** /plɔpkɑp/ (pl: -pen) microphone windscreen

de **plot** /plɔt/ (pl: -s) plot

¹**plotseling** /plɔtsəlɪŋ/ (adj) sudden, unexpected

²**plotseling** /plɔtsəlɪŋ/ (adv) suddenly, unexpectedly

het/de **pluche** /plyʃ(ə)/ plush || [pol] *op het ~ zitten* be in power

pluchen /plyʃə(n)/ (adj) plush, stuffed: *een ~ ezel* a stuffed donkey

de **plug** /plʏχ/ (pl: -gen) plug

pluggen /plʏɣə(n)/ (plugde, heeft geplugd) plug, promote: *een plan ~* plug a project

de **pluim** /plœym/ (pl: -en) **1** plume, feather **2** plume; [small] tuft: *een ~ van rook* a plume of smoke || *iem. een ~ geven* pat s.o. on the back

de **pluimage** /plœymaʒə/ (pl: -s) plumage

het **pluimvee** /plœymve/ poultry

de **pluis** /plœys/ bit of fluff || *het is daar niet ~* there's sth. fishy there

pluizen /plœyzə(n)/ (pluisde, heeft geplozen/gepluisd) give off fluff; pill

de **pluk** /plʏk/ (pl: -ken) **1** tuft, wisp **2** crop

plukken /plɣkə(n)/ (plukte, heeft geplukt)
1 pick: *pluk de **dag*** live for the moment
2 pluck

de **pluktuin** /plɣktœyn/ (pl: -en) pick-your-own garden (*or:* farm)

de **plumeau** /plymo̯/ (pl: -s) feather duster

de **plumpudding** /plɣmpʏdɪŋ/ (pl: -en, -s) plum pudding

de **plunderaar** /plɣndərar/ (pl: -s) plunderer, looter

plunderen /plɣndərə(n)/ (plunderde, heeft geplunderd) **1** plunder, loot **2** plunder, raid; rifle through: *de **koelkast** ~* raid the fridge

de **plundering** /plɣndərɪŋ/ (pl: -en) plundering, looting

de **plunje** /plɣɲə/ togs, duds

de **plunjezak** /plɣɲəzak/ (pl: -ken) kitbag

het/de **¹plus** /plʏs/ (pl: -sen) **1** plus (sign) **2** plus (pole)

²plus /plʏs/ (prep) plus: *twee ~ **drie** is vijf* two plus (*or:* and) three is five || **vijfenzestig ~** over-65

de **plusklas** /plʏsklɑs/ (pl: -sen) [Dutch] special class for gifted pupils

plusminus /plʏsmi̯nʏs/ (adv) approximately, about: *~ **duizend** euro* approximately (*or:* about) a thousand euros

het **pluspunt** /plʏspʏnt/ (pl: -en) plus, asset: *ervaring **is** bij sollicitaties een ~* experience is a plus (*or:* an asset) when applying for a job

het **plusteken** /plʏstekə(n)/ (pl: -s) plus (sign)

het **plutonium** /plyto̯nijʏm/ plutonium

pneumatisch /pnøma̯tis/ (adj, adv) pneumatic

de **po** /po̯/ (pl: po's) chamber pot, po

pochen /pɔxə(n)/ (pochte, heeft gepocht) boast, brag

pocheren /pɔʃe̯rə(n)/ (pocheerde, heeft gepocheerd) poach

de **pochet** /pɔʃɛt/ (pl: -ten) dress-pocket handkerchief, breast-pocket handkerchief

het **pocketboek** /pɔkədbuk/ (pl: -en) paperback

de **podcast** /pɔtkɑːst/ (pl: -s) podcast

het **podium** /po̯dijʏm/ (pl: podia) **1** stage: *op het ~ staan* **a)** [theatre] be on (the) stage; **b)** [sport] be on the podium **2** platform, podium: *een ~ **bieden** aan jonge kunstenaars* provide a platform for young artists

de **podiumplaats** /po̯dijʏmplats/ (pl: -en) [sport] podium place

de **poedel** /pu̯dəl/ (pl: -s) poodle

poedelnaakt /pu̯dəlnakt/ (adj) stark naked, in one's birthday suit

de **poedelprijs** /pu̯dəlprɛis/ (pl: -prijzen) [Dutch] booby prize

het **poeder** /pu̯dər/ (pl: -s) powder

de **poederblusser** /pu̯dərblʏsər/ (pl: -s) powder extinguisher

de **poederbrief** /pu̯dərbrif/ powder letter

de **poederdoos** /pu̯dərdos/ (pl: -dozen) compact

poederen /pu̯dərə(n)/ (poederde, heeft gepoederd) powder: *zich (het gezicht) ~* powder one's face (*or:* nose)

de **poedermelk** /pu̯dərmɛlk/ dried milk, powdered milk

de **poedersneeuw** /pu̯dərsnew/ powder snow

de **poedersuiker** /pu̯dərsœykər/ icing sugar

de **poedervorm** /pu̯dərvɔrm/: *in ~* in powder form

de **poef** /puf/ (pl: -en) hassock

het/de **poeha** /puha̯/ hoo-ha, fuss

de **poel** /pul/ (pl: -en) pool; puddle

de **poelier** /puli̯r/ (pl: -s) poulterer('s)

de **poema** /pu̯ma/ (pl: -'s) puma

het/de **poen** /pun/ dough, dosh

de **¹poep** /pup/ [inform] crap, shit; dog-do; bird-do

de **²poep** /pup/ (pl: -en) [Belg; inform] bum; [Am] fanny: *op zijn ~ krijgen* get (*or:* be) spanked

poepen /pu̯pə(n)/ (poepte, heeft gepoept) [inform] **1** (have a) crap: *in zijn broek ~* do it in one's pants **2** [Belg] bang, bonk

de **poes** /pus/ (pl: poezen) (pussy)cat: *een jong ~je* a kitten || *mis ~!* wrong!; *dat is niet **voor** de ~* that's no child's play, that's not to be sneezed at

het **poesiealbum** /pu̯sialbʏm/ (pl: -s) album (of verses)

poeslief /pusli̯f/ (adj, adv) suave, bland, smooth; honeyed; sugary; silky: *iets ~ **vragen*** purr a question, ask sth. in the silkiest tones

de **poespas** /pu̯spɑs/ hoo-ha, song and dance: *laat die ~ maar achterwege* stop making such a song and dance about it

de **poesta** /pu̯sta/ (pl: -'s) puszta

de **poet** /put/ [Dutch; inform] loot

poëtisch /powe̯tis/ (adj, adv) poetic

de **poets** /puts/ (pl: -en): *iem. een ~ **bakken*** play a trick (*or:* hoax) on s.o.; [Belg] *~ wederom* tit for tat

de **poetsdoek** /pu̯tsduk/ (pl: -en) cleaning cloth, cleaning rag

poetsen /pu̯tsə(n)/ (poetste, heeft gepoetst) clean; polish: *zijn **tanden** ~* brush one's teeth

de **poetsvrouw** /pu̯tsfrɑu/ (pl: -en) cleaning woman

de **poëzie** /powezi̯/ poetry

de **pof** /pɔf/: *op de ~* on tick, on credit

de **pofbroek** /pɔvbruk/ (pl: -en) knickerbockers

poffen /pɔfə(n)/ (pofte, heeft gepoft) roast; pop

het **poffertje** /pɔfərcə/ (pl: -s) kind of small pancake

pogen /po̯ɣə(n)/ (poogde, heeft gepoogd) [form] endeavour, attempt, seek

de **poging** /po̯ɣɪŋ/ (pl: -en) attempt, try; effort: *een ~ **wagen*** have a try at sth.; *~ **tot** moord* attempted murder; *een **vergeefse** ~* a vain (*or:* futile, useless) attempt

de **pogrom** /poɣrɔm/ (pl: -s) pogrom

de **pointe** /pwɛ:ntə/ (pl: -s) point: *hij **heeft** de ~ niet **begrepen*** he missed the point

pokdalig /pogdaləɣ/ (adj) pockmarked

poken /pokə(n)/ (pookte, heeft gepookt) poke

het **poker** /pokər/ poker

pokeren /pokərə(n)/ (pokerde, heeft gepokerd) play poker

de **pokken** /pokə(n)/ smallpox

het **pokkenweer** /pokə(n)wer/ [inform] filthy (*or:* lousy) weather

de **pol** /pɔl/ (pl: -len) clump

polair /polɛ:r/ (adj) polar

de **polarisatie** /polariza(t)si/ (pl: -s) polarization

polariseren /polarizerə(n)/ (polariseerde, heeft gepolariseerd) polarize

de **polder** /pɔldər/ (pl: -s) polder

het **poldermodel** /pɔldərmɔdɛl/ (pl: -len) polder model

de **polemiek** /polemik/ (pl: -en) polemic: *een ~ **voeren*** engage in a polemic (*or:* controversy)

Polen /polə(n)/ Poland

de **poli** /poli/ (pl: -'s) [Dutch] outpatients'

de **poliep** /polip/ (pl: -en) polyp

polijsten /polɛistə(n)/ (polijstte, heeft gepolijst) polish (up); sand(paper)

de **polikliniek** /poliklinik/ (pl: -en) outpatient clinic

poliklinisch /poliklinis/ (adj): *~e **patiënt*** outpatient; *~e **behandeling*** treatment in an outpatients' department

de **polio** /polijo/ polio

de **polis** /polɪs/ (pl: -sen) (insurance) policy

de **polishouder** /polɪshɑudər/ (pl: -s) policyholder

de **polisvoorwaarden** /polɪsforwardə(n)/ (pl) terms (*or:* conditions) of a policy

de **politicologie** /politikoloɣi/ political science

de **politicus** /politikʏs/ (pl: politici) politician

de **politie** /poli(t)si/ (pl: -s) police (force)

de **politieagent** /poli(t)siaɣɛnt/ (pl: -en) police officer, policeman

de **politieauto** /poli(t)siɑuto/ (pl: -'s) police car, patrol car

het **politiebericht** /poli(t)sibərɪχt/ (pl: -en) police message

de **politiebewaking** /poli(t)sibəwakɪŋ/ police protection

het **politiebureau** /poli(t)sibyro/ (pl: -s) police station

de **politiecommissaris** /poli(t)sikɔmɪsarɪs/ (pl: -sen) Chief of Police

de **politiehond** /poli(t)sihɔnt/ (pl: -en) police dog

de **¹politiek** /politik/ **1** politics: *in de ~ **zitten*** be in politics, be a politician **2** policy: *binnenlandse* (or: *buitenlandse*) ~ internal (*or:* for-

eign) policy

²politiek /politik/ (adj, adv) political

de **politiemacht** /poli(t)simɑχt/ body of police, police presence: *er was een **grote** ~ op de* been the police were present in force

de **politieman** /poli(t)siman/ (pl: -nen) policeman, police officer

de **politierechter** /poli(t)sirɛχtər/ (pl: -s) [Dutch] magistrate

de **politiestaat** /poli(t)sistat/ (pl: -staten) police state

het **politietoezicht** /poli(t)situzɪχt/ police supervision

de **politieverordening** /poli(t)siverɔrdənɪŋ/ (pl: -en) by-law; [Am] local ordinance

de **polka** /pɔlka/ (pl: -'s) polka

de **poll** /pɔl/ (pl: -s) poll

de **pollen** /pɔlə(n)/ pollen

de **pollepel** /pɔlepəl/ (pl: -s) wooden spoon

het **polo** /polo/ **1** polo **2** sports shirt

de **polonaise** /polonɛ:zə/ (pl: -s) **1** conga: *een ~ **houden*** do the conga **2** polonaise

het **poloshirt** /poloʃʏrt/ (pl: -s) sports shirt, tennis shirt

de **pols** /pɔls/ (pl: -en) **1** wrist **2** pulse: *iem. de ~ **voelen*** feel (or: take) s.o.'s pulse

het **polsbandje** /pɔlsbɑncə/ wrist band

polsen /pɔlsə(n)/ (polste, heeft gepolst): *iem. ~ **over** iets* sound s.o. out on (*or:* about) sth.

het **polsgewricht** /pɔlsχəvrɪχt/ wrist (joint)

het **polshorloge** /pɔlshɔrloʒə/ (pl: -s) wristwatch

de **polsslag** /pɔlslɑχ/ (pl: -en) pulse

de **polsstok** /pɔlstɔk/ (pl: -ken) (jumping) pole

de **polsstokhoogspringen** /pɔlstɔkhoχsprɪŋə(n)/ pole vaulting

de **polyester** /polijɛstər/ (pl: -s) polyester

de **polyether** /polietər/ polyether; foam rubber

de **¹polyfoon** /polifon/ polyphonic ringtone

²polyfoon /polifon/ (adj) polyphonic

de **polygamie** /poliɣami/ polygamy

Polynesisch /polinɛzis/ (adj) Polynesian

de **pomp** /pɔmp/ (pl: -en) pump

de **pompbediende** /pɔmbdində/ (pl: -n, -s) service (*or:* petrol) station attendant

de **pompelmoes** /pɔmpəlmus/ (pl: -moezen) grapefruit

pompen /pɔmpə(n)/ (pompte, heeft gepompt) pump

pompeus /pɔmpøs/ (adj, adv) pompous

de **pomphouder** /pɔmphɑudər/ (pl: -s) petrol station owner; [Am] gas station owner

de **pompoen** /pɔmpun/ (pl: -en) pumpkin

het **pompstation** /pɔmpsta(t)ʃɔn/ (pl: -s) filling station, service station

de **poncho** /pɔnʃo/ (pl: -'s) poncho

het **pond** /pɔnt/ (pl: -en) half a kilo(gram), 500 grams; [approx] pound; [currency] pound: *het **weegt** een ~* it weighs half a kilo ‖ *het* *volle* ~ *moeten betalen* have to pay the full price

poneren /pon̪ɣrə(n)/ (poneerde, heeft geponeerd) postulate, advance: *een stelling* ~ advance a thesis

ponsen /pɔnsə(n)/ (ponste, heeft geponst) punch

de **ponskaart** /pɔnskart/ (pl: -en) **1** punch(ed) card **2** embossed card

de **pont** /pont/ (pl: -en) ferry(boat)

pontificaal /pontifikaːl/ (adj, adv) pontifical

het/de **ponton** /pontɔn/ (pl: -s) pontoon

de **pontonbrug** /pontɔmbrʏɣ/ (pl: -gen) pontoon bridge

de **pony** /poni/ **1** pony **2** fringe

de **pooier** /pojər/ (pl: -s) pimp

de **pook** /pok/ (pl: poken) **1** poker **2** gear lever, (gear)stick

de **pool** /pol/ (pl: polen) pole

de **Pool** /pol/ (pl: Polen) Pole

het **poolbiljart** /poːlbɪljart/ pool

de **poolcirkel** /poːlsɪrkəl/ (pl: -s) polar circle

poolen /puːlə(n)/ (poolde, heeft gepoold) **1** carpool **2** play pool **3** pool (resources)

de **poolexpeditie** /poːlɛkspedi(t)si/ (pl: -s) polar expedition

het **poolgebied** /poːlɣəbit/ (pl: -en) polar region

het **poolijs** /poːlɛɪs/ polar ice

het **poollicht** /poːlɪxt/ polar lights; aurora polaris

het **¹Pools** /pols/ Polish
²Pools /pols/ (adj) Polish

de **poolshoogte** /poːlshoxtə/ latitude, altitude of the pole: ~ *nemen* **a)** [shipp] take one's bearings; **b)** [fig] size up the situation

de **Poolster** /poːlstɛr/ (the) Pole Star, Polaris

de **poon** /pon/ (pl: ponen) gurnard

de **poort** /port/ (pl: -en) gate, gateway: [fig] *aan de* ~ *rammelen* knock at the door; [educ] *selecteren aan de* ~ pre-select, select at entry **2** [comp] port: *seriële* ~ serial port

de **poos** /pos/ (pl: pozen) while, time: *een hele* ~ a good while, a long time

de **poot** /pot/ (pl: poten) **1** paw, leg: *de poten van een tafel* the legs of a table; [fig] *zijn* ~ *stijf houden* stand firm, stick to one's guns; *geen* ~ *hebben* om op te staan not have a leg to stand on **2** queer, gay (man) ‖ *op zijn achterste poten gaan staan* get (up) on one's hind legs; *de* ~ *van een bril* the arms of a pair of glasses; [fig] *alles kwam op zijn* ~*jes terecht* everything turned out all right; *op hoge poten* in high dudgeon; *iets op poten zetten* set up (*or:* start) sth.

het **pootgoed** /potxut/ seeds

pootjebaden /poːtjəbadə(n)/ paddle

de **pop** /pɔp/ (pl: -pen) **1** doll **2** puppet: *daar heb je de* ~*pen al aan het dansen* here we go, now we're in for it **3** dummy: *zij is net een aangeklede* ~ she looks like a dressed-up doll

het **popcorn** /pɔpkɔːrn/ popcorn

popelen /pɔpələ(n)/ (popelde, heeft gepopeld) quiver: *zitten te* ~ *om weg te mogen* be raring (*or:* itching) to go

het **popfestival** /pɔpfɛstival/ pop festival, rock festival

de **popgroep** /pɔpxrup/ (pl: -en) pop group, rock group, rock band

popiejopie /popijopi/ (adj) [Dutch] palsy-walsy: ~ *doen* get palsy-walsy, be all chummy

de **popmuziek** /pɔpmyzik/ rock music, pop music

het **poppenhuis** /pɔpə(n)hœys/ (pl: -huizen) doll's house

de **poppenkast** /pɔpə(n)kast/ (pl: -en) **1** puppet theatre **2** puppet show

de **poppenwagen** /pɔpə(n)waɣə(n)/ (pl: -s) doll's pram; [Am] baby carriage

popperig /pɔpərəx/ (adj) doll-like, pretty-pretty

het **poppodium** /pɔpodijʏm/ (pl: -podia) pop venue

de **popster** /pɔpstɛr/ (pl: -ren) pop star, rock star

populair /popylɛːr/ (adj, adv) popular

populairwetenschappelijk /popylɛːrwetə(n)sxɑpələk/ (adj, adv) popular-science

populariseren /popylarizɛrə(n)/ (populariseerde, heeft gepopulariseerd) popularize

de **populariteit** /popylaritɛit/ popularity

de **populatie** /popyla(t)si/ (pl: -s) population

de **populier** /popylir/ (pl: -en) poplar

het **populisme** /popylɪsmə/ populism

de **pop-up** /pɔpʏp/ pop-up

de **pop-upwinkel** /pɔpʏpwɪŋkəl/ (pl: -s) pop-up shop

de **por** /pɔr/ (pl: -ren) jab, prod, dig

poreus /porøs/ (adj) porous

de **porie** /pori/ (pl: poriën) pore

de **porno** /pɔrno/ porn(o)

de **pornografie** /pɔrnoɣrafi/ pornography

pornografisch /pɔrnoɣrafis/ (adj, adv) pornographic

porren /pɔrə(n)/ (porde, heeft gepord) **1** prod: *iem. in de zij* ~ poke s.o. in the ribs **2** [media] poke ‖ *hij is wel te* ~ *voor die baan* he won't take much persuading to take the job, he can be tempted to take the job

het **porselein** /pɔrsəlɛin/ china(ware), porcelain

porseleinen /pɔrsəlɛinə(n)/ (adj) china, porcelain

de **porseleinkast** /pɔrsəlɛinkast/ (pl: -en) china cabinet

de **¹port** /pɔrt/ (pl: -en) port (wine)

het/de **²port** /pɔrt/ (pl: -en) **1** postage **2** surcharge

het **portaal** /pɔrtaːl/ (pl: portalen) porch, hall; portal

portable /pɔːrtəbəl/ (adj) portable

de **portal** /pɔːrtəl/ (pl: -s) portal

de **portefeuille** /pɔrtəfœyə/ (pl: -s) wallet

de **portemonnee** /pɔrtəmɔnɛ/ (pl: -s) purse,

wallet: *een maatregel in zijn ~ voelen* be hit financially by a policy change

het/de **portfolio** /pɔrtfo̱lijo/ (pl: -'s) portfolio

de **portie** /pɔ̱rsi/ (pl: -s) **1** share, portion: *zijn ~ wel gehad hebben* have had one's fair share **2** portion; serving; helping: *een grote (flinke) ~ geduld* a good deal of patience

het/de **portiek** /pɔrti̱k/ (pl: -en) porch; doorway

de ¹**portier** /pɔrti̱r/ doorkeeper, gatekeeper

het ²**portier** /pɔrti̱r/ door

het/de **porto** /pɔ̱rto/ (pl: porti) postage

de **portofoon** /pɔrtofo̱n/ (pl: -s) walkie-talkie

de **portokosten** /pɔ̱rtokɔstə(n)/ (pl) postage charges (*or:* expenses)

de **Porto Ricaan** /portorika̱n/ (pl: Porto Ricanen) Puerto Rican

Porto Ricaans /portorika̱ns/ (adj) Puerto Rican

Porto Rico /portori̱ko/ Puerto Rico

het **portret** /pɔrtrɛ̱t/ (pl: -ten) portrait

de **portretschilder** /pɔrtrɛ̱tsxɪldər/ (pl: -s) portrait-painter

portretteren /pɔrtrɛte̱rə(n)/ (portretteerde, heeft geportretteerd) portray

Portugal /pɔ̱rtyɣɑl/ Portugal

Portugees /pɔrtyɣe̱s/ (adj) Portuguese

portvrij /pɔrtfrɛ̱i/ (adj) post-paid, postage free

de **pose** /po̱zə/ (pl: -s) pose, posture: *een ~ aannemen* assume a pose

poseren /poze̱rə(n)/ (poseerde, heeft geposeerd) pose, sit

de **positie** /pozi̱(t)si/ (pl: -s) **1** position, posture: *~ kiezen* (or: *innemen*) choose (*or:* take) up a position **2** position, attitude: *in een conflict ~ nemen* (or: *kiezen*) take (*or:* choose) sides in a conflict **3** position, situation **4** position, post **5** (social) position, status, (social) rank: *een hoge ~* a high position (*or:* rank) (in society)

positief /poziti̱f/ (adj, adv) **1** positive, affirmative **2** positive, favourable: *positieve kritiek* constructive criticism; *iets ~ benaderen* approach sth. positively

de **positiekleding** /pozi̱(t)sikledɪŋ/ maternity clothes

de **positieveling** /pozi̱tivəlɪŋ/ (pl: -en) person who always looks on the bright side, upbeat person

de **positieven** /pozi̱tivə(n)/ (pl): *weer bij zijn ~ komen* come to one's senses

de ¹**post** /pɔst/ (pl: -en) **1** post office, postal services **2** post, mail: *aangetekende ~* registered mail; *elektronische ~* electronic mail, e-mail **3** post; post office; letterbox **4** post, jamb **5** item; entry: *de ~ salarissen* the salary item **6** post, position: *een ~ bekleden* hold a post, occupy a position

de ²**post** (pl: -s) post

het **postadres** /pɔ̱stadrɛs/ (pl: -sen) address

het **postagentschap** /pɔ̱staɣɛntsxɑp/ (pl: -pen)

sub-post office

de **postbezorging** /pɔ̱stbəzɔrɣɪŋ/ (pl: -en) postal delivery, delivery of the post; [Am] mail delivery, delivery of the mail

de **postbode** /pɔ̱stbodə/ (pl: -s) postman; [Am] mailman

de **postbus** /pɔ̱stbʏs/ (pl: -sen) **1** postoffice box, PO Box **2** [email] mailbox

de **postcode** /pɔ̱stkodə/ (pl: -s) [Dutch] postal code; [Am] ZIP code

de ¹**postdoc** /pɔsdɔk/ (pl: -s) postdoc(toral); [Am also] postgraduate

²**postdoc** /pɔsdɔk/ (adj) postdoctoral; [Am also] postgraduate

de **postduif** /pɔ̱zdœyf/ (pl: -duiven) carrier pigeon, homing pigeon

de **postelein** /pɔstəlɛ̱in/ purslane

¹**posten** /pɔ̱stə(n)/ (postte, heeft gepost) stand guard

²**posten** /pɔ̱stə(n)/ (postte, heeft gepost) post; [Am] mail; send off

de **poster** /po̱stər/ (pl: -s) poster

posteren /poste̱rə(n)/ (posteerde, heeft geposteerd) post

poste restante /postərɛstɑ̱ntə/ (adv) poste restante; [Am] general delivery: *De heer H. de Vries, ~ Hoofdpostkantoor Brighton* Mr H. de Vries, c/o Main Post Office, Brighton

de **posterijen** /postərɛ̱iə(n)/ (pl) Post Office, Postal Services

de **posting** /po̱stɪŋ/ (pl: -s) post

de **postkamer** /pɔ̱stkamər/ (pl: -s) post room

het **postkantoor** /pɔ̱stkɑntor/ (pl: -kantoren) post office

de **postkoets** /pɔ̱stkuts/ (pl: -en) stagecoach

postmodern /pɔstmodɛ̱rn/ (adj) postmodern

postnataal /pɔstnata̱l/ (adj) postnatal

het **postnummer** /pɔ̱stnʏmər/ (pl: -s) [Belg] postcode, postal code

de **postorder** /pɔ̱stɔrdər/ (pl: -s) mail order

het **postorderbedrijf** /pɔ̱stɔrdərbədrɛif/ (pl: -bedrijven) mail-order firm (*or:* company), catalogue house

het **postpakket** /pɔ̱stpɑkɛt/ (pl: -ten) parcel, parcel-post package

het **postpapier** /pɔ̱stpapir/ writing paper, letter paper, notepaper: *~ en enveloppen* stationery

de **postrekening** /pɔ̱strekənɪŋ/ (pl: -en) giro bank account

het **poststempel** /pɔ̱stɛmpəl/ postmark

postuum /pɔsty̱m/ (adj, adv) posthumous

het **postuur** /pɔsty̱r/ (pl: posturen) figure, shape; build; stature

het **postvak** /pɔ̱stfɑk/ (pl: -ken) **1** pigeon-hole **2** [email] mailbox: *~ in* inbox; *~ uit* outbox

postvatten /pɔ̱stfɑtə(n)/ (vatte post, heeft postgevat) **1** take up one's station, post o.s. **2** take form

de **postwissel** /pɔ̱stwɪsəl/ (pl: -s) postal order,

money order

de **postzegel** /pɔstseɣəl/ (pl: -s) stamp: *voor een euro aan ~s bijplakken* stamp an excess amount of one euro; *voor drie euro aan ~s bijsluiten* enclose three euros in stamps

de **postzegelverzameling** /pɔ(st)seɣəlvərzaməlɪŋ/ (pl: -en) stamp collection

de **¹pot** /pɔt/ [inform] dyke, dike; gay

de **²pot** /pɔt/ **1** pot; jar: *een ~ jam* a jar of jam **2** pot, chamber pot: *hij kan (me) de ~ op* he can get stuffed **3** pot, saucepan: *eten wat de ~ schaft* eat whatever's going **4** kitty, pool ‖ *dat is één ~ nat* you can't really tell the difference; [of pers] they're birds of a feather

potdicht /pɔdɪxt/ (adj) tight, locked, sealed: *de deur is ~* the door is shut tight

poten /poːtə(n)/ (pootte, heeft gepoot) plant; set; put in

potent /potɛnt/ (adj) potent, virile

de **potentaat** /potɛntaːt/ (pl: potentaten) potentate

de **potentiaal** /potɛn(t)ʃaːl/ (pl: potentialen) potential

de **potentie** /potɛn(t)si/ (pl: -s) potence

het **¹potentieel** /potɛnʃeːl/ potential; capacity

²potentieel /potɛnʃeːl/ (adj, adv) **1** potential: *potentiële koper* prospective (*or:* would-be) buyer **2** latent, potential

de **potgrond** /pɔtxrɔnt/ potting compost (soil)

potig /poːtəx/ (adj) burly, sturdy, husky

het **potje** /pɔcə/ (pl: -s) **1** (little) pot; terrine: *zijn eigen ~ koken* [fig] fend for o.s. **2** game: *een ~ kaarten, biljarten* play a game of cards, billiards **3** fund ‖ *er een ~ van maken* mess (*or:* muck) things up

het **potjeslatijn** /pɔcəslatɛɪn/ gibberish; mumbo jumbo

het **potlood** /pɔtloːt/ (pl: potloden) pencil: *met ~ tekenen* draw in pencil

de **potloodslijper** /pɔtloːtslɛɪpər/ (pl: -s) pencil sharpener

de **potloodventer** /pɔtloːtfɛntər/ (pl: -s) flasher

de **potplant** /pɔtplɑnt/ (pl: -en) pot plant, potted plant

het/de **potpourri** /pɔtpori/ (pl: -'s) potpourri, medley

potsierlijk /pɔtsiːrlək/ (adj) clownish, ridiculous, grotesque

potten /pɔtə(n)/ (potte, heeft gepot) **1** hoard; stash (away) **2** pot

pottenbakken /pɔtə(n)bɑkə(n)/ pottery(-making), ceramics

de **pottenbakker** /pɔtə(n)bɑkər/ (pl: -s) potter

de **pottenbakkerij** /pɔtə(n)bɑkərɛɪ/ (pl: -en) pottery

de **pottenkijker** /pɔtə(n)kɛikər/ (pl: -s) Nosy Parker, snooper

potverteren /pɔtfərterə(n)/ squander

de **potvis** /pɔtfɪs/ (pl: -sen) sperm whale

de **poule** /pul/ (pl: -s) group

pover /poːvər/ (adj, adv) poor, meagre, miserable: *een ~ resultaat* a poor result

de **pr** /peːɛr/ public relations PR

Praag /praːx/ Prague

de **praal** /praːl/ splendour, pomp: *met pracht en ~* with pomp and circumstance

het **praalgraf** /praːlɣraf/ (pl: -graven) mausoleum

de **praat** /praːt/ talk: *met iem. aan de ~ raken* get talking to s.o. ‖ *een auto aan de ~ krijgen* get a car to start

de **praatgroep** /praːtxrup/ (pl: -en) discussion group

het **praatje** /praːcə/ (pl: -s) **1** chat, talk **2** talk, speech: *mooie ~s* fine words **3** airs: *~s krijgen* put on airs

de **praatjesmaker** /praːcəsmaːkər/ (pl: -s) **1** boaster, braggart **2** windbag, gasbag

de **praatpaal** /praːtpaːl/ (pl: -palen) emergency telephone

de **praatshow** /praːtʃo/ (pl: -s) chat show, talk show

de **praatstoel** /praːtstuːl/: *hij zit weer op zijn ~* he's on again

de **pracht** /prɑxt/ **1** magnificence, splendour **2** [fig] beauty, gem

prachtig /prɑxtəx/ (adj, adv) **1** splendid, magnificent **2** exquisite, gorgeous ‖ *~!* excellent!

de **prachtkerel** /prɑxtkerəl/ (pl: -s) a fine man; a great guy

het **practicum** /prɑktikʏm/ (pl: practica) practical, lab(oratory): *ik heb vanmiddag ~* I've got a practical this afternoon

de **pragmaticus** /prɑxmatikʏs/ (pl: pragmatici) pragmatist

pragmatisch /prɑxmatis/ (adj) pragmatic(al)

de **prairie** /prɛːri/ (pl: -s) prairie

de **prak** /prɑk/ mash, mush ‖ *een auto in de ~ rijden* smash (up) a car

prakken /prɑkə(n)/ (prakte, heeft geprakt) mash

prakkiseren /prɑkizerə(n)/ (prakkiseerde, heeft geprakkiseerd) [inform] **1** brood, worry: *zich suf ~* worry o.s. sick **2** muse, think

de **praktijk** /prɑktɛik/ (pl: -en) practice; experience: *echt een man van de ~* a doer (rather than a thinker); *een eigen ~ beginnen* start a practice of one's own; *in de ~* in (actual) practice; *iets in ~ brengen* put sth. into practice, apply (*or:* implement) sth.

de **praktijkervaring** /prɑktɛikɛrvarɪŋ/ practical experience

praktijkgericht /prɑktɛikxərɪxt/ (adj) practically-oriented

het **praktijkonderwijs** /prɑktɛikɔndərwɛis/ [Dutch] practical training

¹praktisch /prɑktis/ (adj, adv) **1** practical, handy, useful: *~e kennis* working knowledge **2** practical, realistic; businesslike

²**praktisch** /prɑktis/ (adv) practically, almost: *de was is ~ **droog*** the laundry's practically dry

praktiseren /prɑktizɘrɘ(n)/ (praktiseerde, heeft gepraktiseerd) practise

de **praline** /pralinɘ/ (pl: -s) chocolate (praline)

prangend /prɑŋɘnt/ (adj): *een ~e **vraag*** a burning question, a pressing issue

prat /prɑt/ (adj, adv) proud: *~ **gaan** op zijn intelligentie* boast (or: brag) about one's intelligence

praten /pratɘ(n)/ (praatte, heeft gepraat) talk, speak: *we ~ **er** niet meer **over*** let's forget it, let's leave it at that; *je hebt **gemakkelijk** ~* it's easy (or: it's all right) for you to talk; *daarover **valt** te ~* that's a matter for discussion; *iedereen praat **erover*** it's the talk of the town, everyone is talking about it; ***langs** iem. **heen** ~* talk across s.o.; *hij kan ~ **als** Brugman* he can talk the hind legs off a donkey

de **prater** /pratɘr/ (pl: -s) talker: *hij is geen **grote** ~* he isn't much of a talker

de **prauw** /prɑu/ (pl: -en) proa

het/de **pre** /pre/ (pl: -'s) preference: *een ~ **hebben*** have the preference; *kennis van het Frans **is** een ~* knowledge of French is an advantage (or: an asset, a plus)

precair /prekɛːr/ (adj, adv) precarious, delicate

het **precedent** /presɘdɛnt/ (pl: -en) precedent: *een ~ **scheppen*** establish (or: create) a precedent

¹**precies** /prɘsis/ (adj, adv) precise, exact, accurate, specific: *~ **een kilometer*** one kilometre exactly; *dat is ~ **hetzelfde*** that is precisely (or: exactly) the same (thing); *om ~ **te zijn*** to be precise; *~ **in** het midden* right in the middle; *~ **om** twaalf uur* at twelve (o'clock) sharp, on the stroke of twelve; *~ **op** tijd* right on time; *~ **drie** jaar geleden* exactly (or: precisely) three years ago

²**precies** /prɘsis/ (int) precisely, exactly

preciseren /presizerɘ(n)/ (preciseerde, heeft gepreciseerd) specify: *kunt u dat **nader** ~?* could you be more specific?

de **precisie** /presizi/ precision, accuracy

het **predicaat** /predikat/ **1** title **2** [linguistics] predicate

de **predikant** /predikɑnt/ (pl: -en) **1** minister, pastor; vicar, rector; parson [Anglican Church]; clergyman **2** [Roman Catholicism] preacher

prediken /predɪkɘ(n)/ (predikte, heeft gepredikt) preach

de **preek** /prek/ (pl: preken) **1** sermon, homily (on): *een ~ **houden*** deliver a sermon **2** sermon, lecture (on)

de **preekstoel** /prekstul/ (pl: -en) pulpit

prefabriceren /prefabriserɘ(n)/ (prefabriceerde, heeft geprefabriceerd) prefabricate

preferent /preferɛnt/ (adj) preferred, preferential

prefereren /prefererɘ(n)/ (prefereerde, heeft geprefereerd) prefer: *dit is te ~ **boven** dat* this is preferable to that

de **prehistorie** /prehɪstori/ prehistory

prehistorisch /prehɪstoris/ (adj) prehistoric

de **prei** /prɛi/ (pl: -en) leek

preken /prekɘ(n)/ (preekte, heeft gepreekt) **1** preach, deliver (or: preach) a sermon **2** preach, moralize

de **prelude** /prelydɘ/ (pl: -s) prelude

prematuur /prematyr/ (adj) premature

de **premie** /premi/ (pl: -s) **1** premium, bonus, gratuity **2** premium; (insurance) contribution: *de sociale ~s* social insurance (or: security) contributions

de **premier** /prɘmje/ (pl: -s) prime minister, premier

de **première** /prɘmjɛːrɘ/ (pl: -s) première; first night; opening performance

de **preminiem** /preminim/ (pl: -en) [Belg] junior member (6-10 years) of sports club

prenataal /prenatal/ (adj) antenatal; [Am] prenatal

de **prent** /prɛnt/ (pl: -en) print, illustration; cartoon

de **prentbriefkaart** /prɛndbrifkart/ (pl: -en) (picture) postcard

prenten /prɛntɘ(n)/: [fig] *zich iets **in** het geheugen ~* fix sth. in one's mind

het **prentenboek** /prɛntɘ(n)buk/ (pl: -en) picture book

prepaid /priːpet/ (adj) pay-as-you-go, prepay: *~ **beltegoed*** prepaid phone credit

het **preparaat** /preparat/ (pl: preparaten) preparation

prepareren /preparerɘ(n)/ (prepareerde, heeft geprepareerd) prepare

het **prepensioen** /prepɛnʃun/ (pl: -en) pre-pension scheme; [Am] pre-pension plan

de **presbyteriaan** /prɛzbiterijan/ (pl: -rianen) Presbyterian

de **preselectie** /presɘlɛksi/ [Belg] qualifying round

het ¹**present** /prezɛnt/ (pl: -en) present, gift

²**present** /prezɛnt/ (adj) present; in attendance: *ze **waren** allemaal ~* they were all present; *~! present!, here!

de **presentatie** /prezɛnta(t)si/ (pl: -s) presentation, introduction: *de ~ **is** in handen van Joris* the programme is presented by Joris

de **presentator** /prezɛntator/ (pl: -en) presenter; host, hostess, anchorman

het **presenteerblaadje** /prɘzɛntɘrblacɘ/ tray, platter: *de baan werd hem **op** een ~ aangeboden* the job was handed to him on a silver platter

presenteren /prezɛnterɘ(n)/ (presenteerde, heeft gepresenteerd) **1** present, introduce **2** present; offer **3** pass off (as) **4** present, host

de **presentie** /prezɛn(t)si/ presence

de **presentielijst** /prezɛnsilɛist/ (pl: -en) attendance list, (attendance) roll, (attendance) register

de **president** /prezidɛnt/ (pl: -en) President

de **president-directeur** /prezidɛndirɛktør/ (pl: -en) chairman (of the board)

presidentieel /prezidɛn(t)jel/ (adj) presidential

de **presidentsverkiezing** /prezidɛn(t)sfərkizɪŋ/ presidential election

pressen /prɛsə(n)/ (preste, heeft geprest) press, put pressure on

de **pressie** /prɛsi/ (pl: -s) pressure

de **prestatie** /prɛsta(t)si/ (pl: -s) performance, achievement, feat: *een* **hele** ~ quite an achievement; *een* ~ *leveren* achieve sth., perform well, do well

het **prestatieloon** /prɛsta(t)silon/ (pl: -lonen) merit pay

presteren /prɛstɛrə(n)/ (presteerde, heeft gepresteerd) achieve, perform: *hij heeft nooit veel gepresteerd* he has never done anything to speak of; *slecht* ~ perform well

het **prestige** /prɛstiːʒə/ prestige

prestigieus /prɛstiʒøs/ (adj) prestigious

de **pret** /prɛt/ **1** fun, hilarity: ~ *hebben* (or: *maken*) have fun, have a good time; *dat was dolle* ~ it was great (or: glorious) fun; *dat mag de* ~ *niet drukken* never mind **2** fun, enjoyment **3** fun, entertainment: *(het is) uit met de* ~! the party is over

pretenderen /pretɛndɛrə(n)/ (pretendeerde, heeft gepretendeerd) profess (to be), make out, pretend (to be)

de **pretentie** /pretɛn(t)si/ (pl: -s) pretension: *ik heb niet de* ~ ... I make no pretension(s) to ..., I don't pretend to ...

pretentieus /pretɛn(t)jøs/ (adj, adv) pretentious

het **pretje** /prɛcə/ (pl: -s) bit of fun: *dat is geen* ~ that's no picnic

de **pretogen** /prɛtoɣə(n)/ (pl) twinkling eyes

het **pretpark** /prɛtpɑrk/ (pl: -en) amusement park

prettig /prɛtəx/ (adj, adv) pleasant, nice: ~ *weekend!* have a pleasant (or: nice) weekend; *deze krant leest* ~ this paper is nice to read

preuts /prøts/ (adj, adv) prudish, prim (and proper)

de **preutsheid** /prøtshɛit/ prudishness, primness

prevaleren /prevalɛrə(n)/ (prevaleerde, heeft geprevaleerd) prevail

prevelen /prevələ(n)/ (prevelde, heeft gepreveld) mumble, murmur

de **preventie** /prevɛnsi/ (pl: -s) prevention

preventief /prevɛntif/ (adj, adv) preven(ta)tive, precautionary

de **pr-functionaris** /peːrfɣŋkʃonarɪs/ PR officer

het **prieel** /prijel/ (pl: priëlen) summerhouse, arbour

priegelen /priɣələ(n)/ (priegelde, heeft gepriegeld) [Dutch] do fine (or: delicate) (needle)work

het **priegelwerk** /priɣəlwɛrk/ [Dutch] close work, delicate work

de **priem** /prim/ (pl: -en) awl, bodkin

het **priemgetal** /primɣətɑl/ (pl: -len) prime (number)

de **priester** /pristər/ (pl: -s) priest

prijken /prɛikə(n)/ (prijkte, heeft geprijkt) be resplendent, adorn

de **prijs** /prɛis/ (pl: prijzen) **1** price; fare; charge: *voor een zacht ~je* at a bargain price; *tot elke* ~ at any price (or: cost), at all costs **2** price (tag): *het ~je hangt er nog aan* it has still got the price on **3** prize, award: *een ~ uitloven* put up a prize; *in de prijzen vallen* be among the winners **4** reward, prize || *iets op* ~ *stellen* appreciate sth.

prijsbewust /prɛizbəwʏst/ (adj) cost-conscious

de **prijsdaling** /prɛizdalɪŋ/ (pl: -en) fall (or: drop, decrease) in price

prijsgeven /prɛisɣevə(n)/ (gaf prijs, heeft prijsgegeven) give up, abandon, consign

het **prijskaartje** /prɛiskarcə/ (pl: -s) price tag

de **prijsklasse** /prɛisklɑsə/ (pl: -n) price range, price bracket

de **prijslijst** /prɛislɛist/ (pl: -en) price list

de **prijsopgave** /prɛisopχavə/ (pl: -n) estimate; quotation; tender

de **prijsuitreiking** /prɛisœytrɛikɪŋ/ (pl: -en) distribution of prizes; prize-giving (ceremony)

de **prijsvechter** /prɛisfɛχtər/ **1** discounter **2** prize fighter

de **prijsverhoging** /prɛisfərhoɣɪŋ/ price increase, rise

de **prijsverlaging** /prɛisfərlaɣɪŋ/ price reduction, price cut

de **prijsvraag** /prɛisfraχ/ (pl: -vragen) competition, (prize) contest

de **prijswinnaar** /prɛiswɪnar/ (pl: -s) prizewinner

¹**prijzen** /prɛizə(n)/ (prees, heeft geprezen) praise, commend: *een veelgeprezen boek* a highly-praised book || *zich gelukkig* ~ *met* call (or: consider) o.s. lucky that

²**prijzen** /prɛizə(n)/ (prijsde, heeft geprijsd) price; ticket; mark: *vele artikelen zijn tijdelijk lager geprijsd* many articles have been temporarily marked down

prijzig /prɛizəx/ (adj) expensive, pricey

de **prik** /prɪk/ (pl: -ken) **1** prick, prod **2** injection, shot **3** pop, fizz: *mineraalwater zonder* ~ still mineral water || *dat is vaste* ~ that happens all the time

de **prikactie** /prɪkɑksi/ (pl: -s) lightning strike

het **prikbord** /prɪgbɔrt/ (pl: -en) noticeboard;

[Am] bulletin board

het **prikje** /prɪkjə/ (pl: -s): *iets voor een ~ kopen* buy sth. dirt cheap (*or:* for next to nothing)

de **prikkel** /prɪkəl/ (pl: -s) incentive, stimulant, stimulus

prikkelbaar /prɪkəlbar/ (adj) touchy, irritable

het/de **prikkeldraad** /prɪkəldrat/ barbed wire

¹**prikkelen** /prɪkələ(n)/ (prikkelde, heeft geprikkeld) prickle, tingle; sting: *mijn been prikkelt* my leg is tingling

²**prikkelen** /prɪkələ(n)/ (prikkelde, heeft geprikkeld) irritate, vex

¹**prikken** /prɪkə(n)/ (prikte, heeft geprikt) sting, tingle: *de rook prikt in mijn ogen* the smoke is making my eyes smart

²**prikken** /prɪkə(n)/ (prikte, heeft geprikt) **1** prick; prod: *een ballon lek ~* pop a balloon **2** stick (to), affix (to): *een poster op de muur ~* pin a poster on the wall **3** inject

de **prikklok** /prɪklɔk/ (pl: -ken) time clock

de **priklimonade** /prɪklimonadə/ (pl: -s) pop

pril /prɪl/ (adj) early, fresh, young

¹**prima** /prima/ (adj, adv) excellent, great, terrific, fine: *een ~ vent* a nice chap; [Am] a great guy

²**prima** /prima/ (int) great

het **primaat** /primat/ primacy, pre-eminence

¹**primair** /primɛːr/ (adj) primary, basic

²**primair** /primɛːr/ (adj, adv) **1** primary, initial, first **2** primary, principal, essential, chief

primen /prɔjmə(n)/ (primede, heeft geprimed) prime, apply primer to

de **primeur** /primør/ (pl: -s) sth. new; scoop

primitief /primitif/ (adj, adv) **1** primitive, elemental **2** primitive, makeshift: *het ging er heel ~ toe* it was very rough and ready there

de **primula** /primyla/ (pl: -'s) primula, primrose

het **principe** /prɪnsipə/ (pl: -s) principle: *een man met hoogstaande ~s* a man of high principles; *in ~* in principle, basically; *uit ~* on principle, as a matter of principle

principieel /prɪnsipjel/ (adj, adv) **1** fundamental, essential, basic **2** on principle, of principle: *een ~ dienstweigeraar* a conscientious objector (to military service)

de **prins** /prɪns/ (pl: -en) prince: *de ~ op het witte paard* Prince Charming

prinselijk /prɪnsələk/ (adj) princely

de **prinses** /prɪnsɛs/ (pl: -sen) princess

Prinsjesdag /prɪnʃəzdɑx/ (pl: -en) [Dutch] [roughly] day of the Queen's (*or:* King's) speech

de **print** /prɪnt/ (pl: -s) **1** print-out **2** print

printen /prɪntə(n)/ (printte, heeft geprint) print

de **printer** /prɪntər/ (pl: -s) printer

printvriendelijk /prɪntfrɪndələk/ (adj) printer-friendly

de **prior** /prijor/ (pl: -s) prior

de **prioriteit** /prijoritɛit/ (pl: -en) priority: *~en*

stellen establish priorities; get one's priorities right

het **prisma** /prɪsma/ (pl: -'s) prism

het **privaatrecht** /privatrɛxt/ private law

de **privacy** /prɑjvəsi/ privacy, seclusion: *iemands ~ schenden* infringe (on) s.o.'s privacy, invade s.o.'s privacy

privatiseren /privatizerə(n)/ (privatiseerde, heeft geprivatiseerd) privatize, denationalize

privé /prive/ (adj, adv) private, confidential, personal: *ik zou je graag even ~ willen spreken* I'd like to talk to you privately (*or:* in private) for a minute; *dat moet strikt ~ blijven* that must remain strictly private

de **privédetective** /priveditɛktɪf/ (pl: -s) private detective

het **privédomein** /privedomɛɪn/ (pl: -en): *dat behoort tot het ~* that's a private matter

het **privéleven** /privelevə(n)/ private life

de **privéschool** /privesxol/ (pl: -scholen) private school

de **privésfeer** /privesfer/: *in de ~* personal, private

het **privilege** /priviles̬ə/ (pl: -s) privilege

de **pr-medewerker** /peɡrmedəwɛrkər/ (pl: -s) PR person, public relations officer

pro /pro/ (adj) pro(-) ‖ *het ~ en het contra horen* hear the pros and cons

probaat /probat/ (adj, adv) effective, efficacious: *een ~ middel* an efficacious remedy, a tried and tested remedy

het **probeersel** /probersəl/ (pl: -s) experiment, try-out

proberen /proberə(n)/ (probeerde, heeft geprobeerd) **1** try (out), test: *het met water en zeep ~* try soap and water **2** try, attempt: *dat hoef je niet eens te ~* you needn't bother (trying that)

het **probleem** /problem/ (pl: problemen) problem, difficulty, trouble: *in de problemen zitten* be in difficulties (*or:* trouble); *geen ~!* no problem!; *ergens geen ~ van maken* not make a problem of (*or:* about) sth., not make difficulties about sth.

het **probleemgeval** /problemɣəvɑl/ (pl: -len) problematical case

probleemloos /problemlos/ (adj, adv) uncomplicated, smooth, trouble-free: *alles verliep ~* things went very smoothly (*or:* without a hitch)

de **probleemstelling** /problemstɛlɪŋ/ (pl: -en) definition (*or:* formulation) of a problem

de **problematiek** /problematik/ problem(s), issue

problematisch /problematis/ (adj) problematic(al)

het **procedé** /prosede/ (pl: -s) process, technique

procederen /prosəderə(n)/ (procedeerde, heeft geprocedeerd) litigate, take legal action, proceed (against); prosecute: *gaan* ~ go to court

de **procedure** /prosədy̱rə/ (pl: -s) **1** procedure, method **2** (law)suit, action, legal proceedings (*or:* procedure): *een* ~ *tegen iem.* **aanspannen** start legal proceedings against s.o.

de **procedurefout** /prosədy̱rəfaut/ (pl: -en) procedural mistake, mistake in procedure

het **procent** /prosɛnt/ (pl: -en) per cent, percent: *honderd* ~ *zeker* dead certain (*or:* sure)

procentueel /prosɛntywe̱l/ (adj) in terms of percentage

het **proces** /prosɛs/ (pl: -sen) **1** (law)suit; trial; action, legal proceedings: *iem. een* ~ *aandoen* take s.o. to court; *zonder* **vorm** *van* ~ summarily, without trial **2** process

de **proceskosten** /prosɛskɔstə(n)/ (pl) (legal) costs

de **processie** /prosɛsi/ (pl: -s) procession

de **processierups** /prosɛsiryps/ (pl: -en) processionary caterpillar

de **processor** /prosɛsɔr/ (pl: -s, -en) processor

het **proces-verbaal** /prosɛsfərba̱l/ (pl: processen-verbaal) charge; summons; ticket: *een* ~ *aan zijn broek* **krijgen** be booked, get a ticket; ~ *opmaken tegen iem.* take s.o.'s name and address, book s.o.

de **proclamatie** /proklama̱(t)si/ (pl: -s) **1** proclamation **2** [Belg] public announcement of the results (of a competition, exams, ...)

proclameren /proklame̱rə(n)/ (proclameerde, heeft geproclameerd) proclaim

de **procuratiehouder** /prokyra̱(t)sihaudər/ (pl: -s) deputy manager

de **procureur** /prokyrø̱r/ (pl: -s) [law] [roughly] solicitor; [Am] [roughly] attorney: [Belg] ~ *des* **Konings** [roughly] public prosecutor

de **procureur-generaal** /prokyrørɣenəra̱l/ (pl: procureurs-generaal) Procurator-General; [roughly] Attorney General

pro Deo /prode̱jo/ (adv) free (of charge), for nothing

de **pro-Deoadvocaat** /prode̱joatfokat/ (pl: -advocaten) legal aid counsel; [Am] public defender

de **producent** /prodysɛnt/ (pl: -en) producer

de **producer** /prodju̱:sər/ (pl: -s) producer

produceren /prodyse̱rə(n)/ (produceerde, heeft geproduceerd) produce, make, manufacture; generate

het **product** /prody̱kt/ (pl: -en) product, production; commodity: *het bruto* **nationaal** ~ the gross national product; the GNP

de **productie** /prody̱ksi/ (pl: -s) **1** production: *uit de* ~ *nemen* stop producing (*or:* production) **2** production; output; yield; produce

productief /prodykti̱f/ (adj) **1** productive, fruitful **2** productive, prolific: *een* ~ *dagje* a good day's work

de **productiekosten** /prody̱ksikɔstə(n)/ (pl) cost(s) of production

de **productieleider** /prody̱ksile̱idər/ (pl: -s) production manager; producer

de **productiemaatschappij** /prody̱ksimatsχɑpɛi/ (pl: -en) film production company

het **productieproces** /prody̱ksiprosɛs/ (pl: -sen) production process, manufacture

de **productiviteit** /prodyktivitɛi̱t/ productivity, productive capacity

het **productschap** /prody̱ktsχɑp/ (pl: -pen) [Dutch] [roughly] Commodity Board

de **proef** /pruf/ (pl: proeven) **1** test, examination, trial: *op de* ~ *stellen* put to the test; *proeven* **nemen** carry out experiments **2** test, try, trial, probation: *iets een week* **op** ~ *krijgen* have sth. on a week's trial; *op* ~ on probation **3** proof || *de* ~ *op de som nemen* test sth., put it to the test, try (out) sth.

de **proefballon** /pru̱vbɑlɔn/ trial balloon: [fig] *een* ~*netje* **oplaten** float a trial balloon, put out a feeler

het **proefdier** /pru̱vdir/ (pl: -en) laboratory animal

proefdraaien /pru̱vdrajə(n)/ (draaide proef, heeft proefgedraaid) trial run, test run

het **proefkonijn** /pru̱fkonɛin/ (pl: -en) guinea pig

het **proeflokaal** /pru̱flokal/ (pl: -lokalen) public house

de **proefneming** /pru̱fnemɪŋ/ (pl: -en) test(ing)

proefondervindelijk /prufɔndərvɪndələk/ (adj, adv) experimental, by experiment (*or:* experience)

de **proefperiode** /pru̱fperijodə/ (pl: -n, -s) trial period; probationary period; probation

de **proefpersoon** /pru̱fpɛrsɔn/ (pl: -personen) (experimental, test) subject

het **proefproces** /pru̱fprosɛs/ (pl: -sen) test case

de **proefrit** /pru̱frɪt/ (pl: -ten) test drive; trial run: *een* ~ **maken** *met de auto* test-drive the car

het **proefschrift** /pru̱fsχrɪft/ (pl: -en) (doctoral, Ph D) thesis, dissertation

de **proeftijd** /pru̱ftɛit/ probation, probationary period, trial period: [law] *voorwaardelijk veroordeeld* **met** *een* ~ *van twee jaar* a suspended sentence with two years' probation

de **proeftuin** /pru̱ftœyn/ (pl: -en) experimental garden (*or:* field)

het **proefwerk** /pru̱fwɛrk/ (pl: -en) test (paper): *een* ~ *opgeven* set a test

proesten /pru̱stə(n)/ (proestte, heeft geproest) **1** sneeze **2** snort, splutter

de **proeve** /pru̱və/: *een* ~ *van* **bekwaamheid** proof of competence

proeven /pru̱və(n)/ (proefde, heeft geproefd) taste, try, sample, test: *van het eten* ~ try some of the food

de **proeverij** /pruvərɛi̱/ tasting

de **prof** /prɔf/ (pl: -s) **1** prof **2** pro

profaan /profan/ (adj) profane

de **profclub** /prɔfklʏp/ (pl: -s) professional club

de **profeet** /profet/ (pl: profeten) prophet, prophetess

professioneel /profɛʃonel/ (adj) professional || *iets ~ aanpakken* approach sth. in a professional way

de **professor** /profɛsɔr/ (pl: -en) professor: *~ in de taalwetenschap* a professor of linguistics; *een verstrooide ~* an absent-minded professor

de **profetie** /profe(t)si/ (pl: -ën) prophecy

profetisch /profetis/ (adj, adv) prophetic

proficiat /profisijat/ (int) congratulations: *~ met je verjaardag* happy birthday!

het **profiel** /profil/ (pl: -en) profile: [Internet] *een ~ aanmaken* make a personal profile

de **profielschets** /profilsxɛts/ (pl: -en) profile

het **profielwerkstuk** /profilwɛrkstʏk/ (pl: -ken) [Dutch] school project

de **profielzool** /profilzol/ (pl: -zolen) grip sole, sole with a tread

het **profijt** /profɛit/ (pl: -en) profit, benefit

profileren /profilerə(n)/ (profileerde, heeft geprofileerd) **1** characterize, make known **2** profile, mould

profiteren /profiterə(n)/ (profiteerde, heeft geprofiteerd) profit (from, by), take advantage (of), exploit: *zoveel mogelijk ~ van* make the most of

de **profiteur** /profitør/ (pl: -s) profiteer

pro forma /proforma/ (adv) for form's sake, for appearance's sake

de **pro-formazitting** /proformazitɪŋ/ (pl: -en) [Dutch] pre-trial hearing

het **profvoetbal** /prɔfudbal/ professional football

de **prognose** /proɣnozə/ (pl: -s) prognosis, forecast

het **programma** /proɣrama/ (pl: -'s) **1** programme: *het hele ~ afwerken* go (or: get) through the whole programme **2** [comp] program

het **programmaboekje** /proɣramabukjə/ programme

de **programmagids** /proɣramaɣɪts/ [roughly] listings; [Am] TV guide

de **programmamaker** /proɣramamakər/ (pl: -s) programme maker (or: writer), producer

de **programmatuur** /proɣramatyr/ software; programs

de **programmeertaal** /proɣramertal/ (pl: -talen) computer language

¹**programmeren** /proɣramerə(n)/ (programmeerde, heeft geprogrammeerd) [comp] program

²**programmeren** /proɣramerə(n)/ (programmeerde, heeft geprogrammeerd) programme, schedule: *de uitzending is geprogrammeerd voor woensdag* the programme is to be broadcast on Wednesday

de **programmeur** /proɣramør/ (pl: -s) programmer

de **progressie** /proɣrɛsi/ (pl: -s) **1** progress **2** progression

progressief /proɣrɛsif/ (adj, adv) progressive; liberal

het **project** /projɛkt/ (pl: -en) project

projecteren /projɛkterə(n)/ (projecteerde, heeft geprojecteerd) project

de **projectie** /projɛksi/ (pl: -s) projection

het **projectiel** /projɛktil/ (pl: -en) missile, projectile: [fig] *een ongeleid ~* a loose cannon

de **projectleider** /projɛktlɛidər/ (pl: -s) project manager

de **projectontwikkelaar** /projɛktɔntwɪkəlar/ (pl: -s) property developer; [Am] real estate developer

de **projector** /projɛktɔr/ (pl: -s) projector

de **proleet** /prolet/ (pl: proleten) [depr] plebeian

het **proletariaat** /proletarijat/ proletariat

de **proletariër** /proletarijər/ (pl: -s) proletarian

prolongeren /prolɔŋɣerə(n)/ (prolongeerde, heeft geprolongeerd) prolong, extend: *zijn titel ~* retain one's (championship) title

de **proloog** /prolox/ (pl: prologen) prologue

de **promenade** /promənadə/ (pl: -s) shopping precinct, shopping mall

het **promillage** /promilaʒə/ (pl: -s) blood alcohol level

het **promille** /promil/ (pl: -n) per thousand, per mil(le): *acht ~* 0.8 percent

prominent /prominɛnt/ (adj) prominent

promoten /promotə(n)/ (promootte, heeft gepromoot) promote

de **promotie** /promo(t)si/ (pl: -s) promotion: *~ maken* get promotion

de **promotor** /promotər/ (pl: -s) **1** [roughly] tutor (or: supervisor) (of a PhD student) **2** promoter

de **promovendus** /promovɛndʏs/ (pl: promovendi) **1** doctoral (or: PhD) student **2** promoted player (or: team)

promoveren /promoverə(n)/ (promoveerde, is gepromoveerd) **1** take one's doctoral degree (or: one's Ph D): *hij is gepromoveerd op een onderzoek naar ...* he obtained his doctorate with a thesis on ... **2** [sport] be promoted, go up

prompt /prɔmt/ (adj, adv) **1** prompt, speedy **2** punctual, prompt: *~ op tijd* right (or: dead) on time

pronken /prɔŋkə(n)/ (pronkte, heeft gepronkt) flaunt (o.s., sth.); prance; strut: *zij loopt graag te ~ met haar zoon* she likes to show off her son

de **prooi** /proj/ (pl: -en) **1** prey; quarry **2** prey, victim: *ten ~ vallen aan* become prey to

proost /prost/ (int) cheers

proosten /prostə(n)/ (proostte, heeft geproost) toast, raise one's glass de **prop** /prɔp/ (pl: -pen) ball: *een ~ watten* a wad of cotton wool ‖ *met iets op de ~pen komen* come up with sth.

de **propaganda** /propaɣɔnda/ propaganda

propageren /propaɣe̱rə(n)/ (propageerde, heeft gepropageerd) propagate

de **propedeuse** /propədœ̱yzə/ foundation course

propedeutisch /propədœ̱ytis/ (adj) preliminary, introductory

de **propeller** /propɛ̱lər/ (pl: -s) (screw) propeller, (air)screw

proper /pro̱pər/ (adj) neat, tidy; clean

de **proportie** /propɔ̱rsi/ (pl: -s) **1** proportion, relation: *iets in (de juiste) ~(s) zien* keep sth. in perspective **2** proportion, dimension

proportioneel /proporʃone̱l/ (adj, adv) proportional

proppen /prɔ̱pə(n)/ (propte, heeft gepropt) shove, stuff, cram, pack: *iedereen werd in één auto gepropt* everyone was squeezed (*or:* packed) into one car

propvol /prɔpfo̱l/ (adj) full to the brim (*or:* to bursting), chock-full, crammed; packed (tight): *een ~le bus* an overcrowded bus

het/de **prospectus** /prospɛ̱ktʏs/ (pl: -sen) prospectus

de **prostaat** /prosta̱t/ (pl: prostaten) prostate (gland)

de **prostaatkanker** /prosta̱tkɑŋkər/ cancer of the prostate

de **prostituee** /prostitywe̱/ (pl: -s) prostitute

de **prostitutie** /prostity̱(t)si/ prostitution

het **protectionisme** /protɛkʃonɪsmə/ protectionism

het/de **proteïne** /protei̱nə/ protein

het **protest** /protɛ̱st/ (pl: -en) protest: *uit ~ (tegen)* in protest (against); *~ aantekenen tegen* enter (*or:* lodge) a protest against, raise an objection against

de **protestant** /protɛstɑ̱nt/ (pl: -en) Protestant

protestants /protɛstɑ̱nts/ (adj, adv) Protestant; [non-Anglican] dissenting; Nonconformist

de **protestbeweging** /protɛ̱stbəweɣɪŋ/ (pl: -en) protest movement

protesteren /protɛste̱rə(n)/ (protesteerde, heeft geprotesteerd) protest

de **protestmars** /protɛ̱stmɑrs/ (pl: -en) protest march

de **prothese** /prote̱zə/ (pl: -n, -s) prothesis, prosthesis; dentures; false teeth

het **protocol** /protoko̱l/ (pl: -len) **1** protocol **2** record

protocollair /protokolɛ̱:r/ (adj) required by protocol, according to protocol

het **proton** /pro̱tɔn/ (pl: -en) proton

de **protonkaart** /pro̱tɔnkart/ (pl: -en) [Belg] rechargeable smart card

het **prototype** /pro̱totipə/ (pl: -n, -s) prototype

protserig /prɔ̱tsərəx/ (adj, adv) flash(y)

het/de **proviand** /provijɑ̱nt/ provisions: *~ inslaan* stock (up) provisions, victual

de **provider** /provɑ̱jdər/ provider

provinciaal /provɪnʃa̱l/ (adj, adv) provincial: *een provinciale weg* [roughly] a secondary road

de **provincie** /provɪ̱nsi/ (pl: -s) province, region: *de ~ Limburg* the Province of Limburg

de **provisie** /provi̱zi/ (pl: -s) [Dutch] commission; brokerage

provisorisch /provizo̱ris/ (adj, adv) provisional, temporary

provoceren /provose̱rə(n)/ (provoceerde, heeft geprovoceerd) provoke, incite

provocerend /provose̱rənt/ (adj, adv) provocative, provoking

het **proza** /pro̱za/ prose

prozaïsch /proza̱is/ (adj, adv) prosaic

de **pruik** /prœyk/ (pl: -en) wig, toupee

pruilen /prœ̱ylə(n)/ (pruilde, heeft gepruild) pout, sulk

de **pruim** /prœym/ **1** plum; prune **2** plug, wad

pruimen /prœ̱ymə(n)/ (pruimde, heeft gepruimd) chew tobacco

de **pruimenboom** /prœ̱ymə(n)bom/ (pl: -bomen) plum (tree)

Pruisen /prœ̱ysə(n)/ Prussia

Pruisisch /prœ̱ysis/ (adj, adv) Prussian

het **prul** /prʏl/ (pl: -len) **1** piece of waste paper **2** (piece of) trash, piece of rubbish (*or:* junk)

de **prullaria** /prʏla̱rija/ (pl) nicknacks, knickknacks

de **prullenbak** /prʏ̱lə(n)bɑk/ (pl: -ken) **1** bin, waste paper basket, wastebasket **2** [comp] recycle bin, trash can

de **prullenmand** /prʏ̱lə(n)mɑnt/ (pl: -en) wastepaperbasket; [esp Am] wastebasket: *dat gaat rechtstreeks de ~ in* that is going straight into the wastepaperbasket

de **prut** /prʏt/ **1** mud, ooze, sludge **2** mush **3** grounds

de **pruts** /prʏts/ (pl: -en) [Belg] trinket

prutsen /prʏ̱tsə(n)/ (prutste, heeft geprutst) mess about (*or:* around), potter (about), tinker (about): *je moet niet zelf aan je tv gaan zitten ~* you shouldn't mess about with your TV-set yourself

de **prutser** /prʏ̱tsər/ (pl: -s) botcher, bungler

het **prutswerk** /prʏ̱tswɛrk/ botch(-up)

pruttelen /prʏ̱tələ(n)/ (pruttelde, heeft geprutteld) simmer, perk; percolate

het **PS** /peɛs/ *postscriptum* PS

de **psalm** /psɑlm/ (pl: -en) psalm

het **psalmboek** /psɑ̱lmbuk/ (pl: -en) psalmbook, psalter

het **pseudoniem** /psœydoni̱m/ (pl: -en) pseudonym

de **psoriasis** /psorija̱zɪs/ psoriasis

pst /pst/ (int) ps(s)t: *~! kom eens hier!* ps(s)t! come here!

de **psyche** /psi̱xə/ psyche

psychedelisch /psɪxədɛlis/ (adj) psychedelic

de **psychiater** /psɪxijatər/ (pl: -s) psychiatrist: *je moet naar een ~* you should see a psychiatrist

de **psychiatrie** /psɪxijatri/ psychiatry

psychiatrisch /psɪxijatris/ (adj) psychiatric: *een ~e inrichting* a mental hospital

psychisch /psɪxis/ (adj, adv) psychological, mental: *~ gestoord* emotionally disturbed; *dat is ~, niet lichamelijk* that is psychological, not physical

de **psychoanalyse** /psɪxoanalizə/ (pl: -n, -s) psychoanalysis

de **psychologie** /psɪxoloɣi/ psychology

psychologisch /psɪxoloɣis/ (adj, adv) psychological

de **psycholoog** /psɪxolox/ (pl: -logen) psychologist

de **psychopaat** /psɪxopat/ (pl: -paten) psychopath

de **psychose** /psɪxozə/ (pl: -n, -s) psychosis

psychosomatisch /psɪxosomatis/ (adj, adv) psychosomatic

de **psychotherapeut** /psɪxoterapœyt/ (pl: -en) psychotherapist

de **psychotherapie** /psɪxoterapi/ psychotherapy, psychotherapeutics

psychotisch /psɪxotis/ (adj) psychotic

PTSS PTSD *(post-traumatic stress disorder)*

de **PTT** /petete/ [Dutch] *Post, Telegrafie, Telefonie* Post Office

de **puber** /pybər/ (pl: -s) adolescent

puberaal /pybəral/ (adj, adv) adolescent

puberen /pybərə(n)/ (puberde, heeft gepuberd) reach puberty

de **puberteit** /pybərtɛit/ puberty, adolescence: *in de ~ zijn* be going through one's adolescence

de **publicatie** /pyblika(t)si/ (pl: -s) publication

publiceren /pybliserə(n)/ (publiceerde, heeft gepubliceerd) publish

de **publiciteit** /pyblisitɛit/ publicity: *~ krijgen* attract attention, get publicity; *iets in de ~ brengen* bring sth. to public notice; *in de ~ treden met iets* make sth. public

de **public relations** /pʏblɪkrilefəns/ (pl) public relations

het ¹**publiek** /pyblik/ **1** public; [sport] crowd; audience; readership; clientele; visitors: *een breed ~ proberen te bereiken* try to cater for a broad public; *veel ~ trekken* attract (*or:* draw) a good crowd, be well attended; *het grote ~* the general public, the millions **2** (general) public: *toegankelijk voor (het) ~* open to the (general) public

²**publiek** /pyblik/ (adj, adv) public: *er was veel ~e belangstelling* it was well attended; *de ~e sector* the public sector

de **publieksprijs** /pybliksprɛis/ prize awarded by the public

de **publiekstrekker** /pyblikstrɛkər/ (pl: -s) crowd-puller; (good) box-office draw; box-office success, box-office hit

de **publiekswissel** /pyblɪkswɪsəl/ (pl: -s) [Dutch] last-minute substitution

de **pubquiz** /pʏpkwɪs/ (pl: -zen) pub quiz

de **pudding** /pydɪŋ/ (pl: -en, -s) pudding

de **puf** /pʏf/ (get up and) go, energy: *ergens de ~ niet meer voor hebben* not feel up to sth. any more

puffen /pʏfə(n)/ (pufte, heeft gepuft) **1** pant: *~ van de warmte* pant with the heat **2** puff (on an inhaler)

het **pufje** /pʏfjə/ (pl: -s) puff

de **pui** /pœy/ (pl: -en) (lower) front, (lower) façade; shopfront

puik /pœyk/ (adj, adv) **1** choice; top quality **2** great, first-rate

puilen /pœylə(n)/ bulge

het/de **puimsteen** /pœymsten/ pumice (stone)

het **puin** /pœyn/ rubble: *~ ruimen* a) clear up the rubble; b) [fig] pick up the pieces, sort sth. out; *in ~ liggen* lie (*or:* be) in ruins; be smashed (up, to bits)

de **puinhoop** /pœynhop/ (pl: -hopen) **1** heap of rubble (*or:* rubbish) **2** mess, shambles: *jij hebt er een ~ van gemaakt* you have made a mess of it

puinruimen /pœynrœymə(n)/ (ruimde puin, heeft puingeruimd) **1** clear up the debris **2** [fig] pick up the pieces

de **puist** /pœyst/ (pl: -en) pimple, spot: *~jes uitknijpen* squeeze spots

de **pukkel** /pʏkəl/ (pl: -s) pimple, spot

de **pul** /pʏl/ (pl: -len) tankard, mug

pulken /pʏlkə(n)/ (pulkte, heeft gepulkt) pick: *zit niet zo in je neus te ~* stop picking your nose

de **pullover** /pʏlovər/ (pl: -s) pullover, sweater

de **pulp** /pʏlp/ **1** pulp: *tot ~ geslagen* beaten to a pulp **2** pulp, junk (reading)

de **pulpfilm** /pʏlpfɪlm/ (pl: -s) trashy film

pulseren /pʏlserə(n)/ (pulseerde, heeft gepulseerd) pulsate

pulsvissen /pʏlsfɪsə(n)/ electric pulse fishing

de **pummel** /pʏməl/ (pl: -s) lout, boor

de **pump** /pʏmp/ (pl: -s) pump

de **punaise** /pynɛːzə/ (pl: -s) drawing pin; [Am] thumbtack

de **punctie** /pʏŋksi/ (pl: -s) [med] puncture: *lumbale ~* lumbar puncture

punctueel /pʏŋktywel/ (adj, adv) punctual

de **punk** /pʏŋk/ punk

de **punker** /pʏŋkər/ (pl: -s) punk

de ¹**punt** /pʏnt/ (pl: -en) **1** point, tip; corner; angle: *het ligt op het ~je van mijn tong* it's on the tip of my tongue; *ergens een ~ achter zetten* a) put a stop to sth.; b) call it a day; *een ~ aan een potlood slijpen* sharpen a pencil; *op het ~je van zijn stoel zitten* be (sitting) on the edge of his seat **2** wedge || [Belg] *op ~ stellen* arrange, fix up

het ²**punt** /pʏnt/ (pl: -en) **1** point, place: *het laagste ~ bereiken* reach rock-bottom **2** point, moment: *hij stond op het ~ om te vertrekken* he was (just) about to leave **3** point; item; count; matter; question; issue: *zijn ~ maken* make one's point; *dat is niet zijn sterkste ~* that is not his strength; *zijn zwakke ~* his weak point; *tot in de ~jes verzorgd* **a)** impeccably dressed; **b)** shipshape; *geen ~!* no problem!

het/de ³**punt** /pʏnt/ (pl: -en) **1** full stop; decimal (point): *~en en strepen* dots and dashes; *de dubbelepunt* the colon; *ik was gewoon kwaad, ~, uit!* I was just angry, full stop **2** point: *hoeveel ~en hebben jullie?* what's your score?; *op ~en winnen (verslaan)* win on points; *hij is twee ~en vooruitgegaan* he has gone up (by) two marks **3** mark

het **puntdak** /pʏndɑk/ (pl: -en) gable(d) roof, peaked roof

punten /pʏntə(n)/ (puntte, heeft gepunt) **1** sharpen, point **2** trim

de **puntendeling** /pʏntə(n)delɪŋ/ (pl: -en) draw

het **puntenklassement** /pʏntə(n)klɑsəmɛnt/ (pl: -en) points classification

de **puntenlijst** /pʏntə(n)lɛist/ (pl: -en) scorecard; scoresheet; report

de **puntenslijper** /pʏntə(n)slɛipər/ (pl: -s) (pencil) sharpener

de **puntentelling** /pʏntə(n)tɛlɪŋ/ (pl: -en) scoring

de **punter** /pʏntər/ (pl: -s) **1** punt **2** toe-kick, toe-shot

puntgaaf /pʏntxaf/ (adj, adv) perfect, flawless

het **punthoofd** /pʏnthoft/ (pl: -en): *ik krijg er een ~ van* it is driving me crazy (*or:* up the wall)

puntig /pʏntəx/ (adj, adv) pointed, sharp: *~e uitsteeksels* sharp points; *~e bladeren* pointed leaves

het **puntje** /pʏncə/ (pl: -s) **1** (small, little) point, tip, dot: *de ~s op de i zetten* dot the i's and cross the t's **2** [roughly] roll **3** dot; spot || *als ~ bij paaltje komt* when it comes to the crunch (*or:* point)

de **puntkomma** /pʏntkɔma/ (pl: -'s) semicolon

de **puntmuts** /pʏntmʏts/ (pl: -en) pointed cap, pointed hat

puntsgewijs /pʏntsxəwɛis/ (adj, adv) point by point, step by step

de **puntzak** /pʏntsɑk/ (pl: -ken) cornet, cone

de **pupil** /pypɪl/ **1** pupil, student **2** [sport] [roughly] junior

de **puppy** /pʏpi/ (pl: -'s) puppy

de **puppytraining** /pʏpitrenɪŋ/ (pl: -en) puppy training (course)

de **puree** /pyre/ puree; mashed potatoes || *in de ~ zitten* be in hot water (*or:* the soup)

pureren /pyrerə(n)/ (pureerde, heeft gepureerd) puree, mash

purgeren /pʏrɣerə(n)/ (purgeerde, heeft gepurgeerd) purge (of/from): *een ~d middel* a laxative

puriteins /pyritɛins/ (adj, adv) puritan(ic(al))

het ¹**purper** /pʏrpər/ purple

²**purper** /pʏrpər/ (adj) purple

de **purser** /pʏːrsər/ (pl: -s) purser

het/de **pus** /pʏs/ pus

het **pushbericht** /puʃbərɪxt/ (pl: -en) push message

pushen /puʃə(n)/ (pushte, heeft gepusht) push (on), urge (on), drive (on)

de **push-upbeha** /puʃybeha/ (pl: -'s) wonderbra, push-up bra

de **put** /pʏt/ (pl: -ten) **1** well: *dat is een bodemloze ~* it's a bottomless pit; *diep in de ~ zitten* be down, feel low; *iem. uit de ~ halen* cheer s.o. up **2** drain || *geld in een bodemloze ~ gooien* pour (*or:* throw) money down the drain

de **putsch** /putʃ/ (pl: -en) putsch

putten /pʏtə(n)/ (putte, heeft geput) draw (from, on)

puur /pyr/ (adj) **1** pure: *pure chocola* plain chocolate; *~ goud* solid gold; *een whisky ~ graag* a straight whisky, please **2** pure, absolute, sheer: *het was ~ toeval dat ik hem zag* it was pure chance that I saw him

de **puzzel** /pʏzəl/ (pl: -s) puzzle

puzzelen /pʏzələ(n)/ (puzzelde, heeft gepuzzeld) do puzzles, solve crossword, jigsaw puzzles

het **pvc** /pevese/ PVC

de **pygmee** /pɪɣme/ (pl: -ën) pygmy

de **pyjama** /pijama/ (pl: -'s) pyjamas: *twee ~'s* two pairs of pyjamas

de **pylon** /pilɔn/ (pl: -en) (traffic) cone

de **pyloon** /pilɔn/ (pl: pylonen) pylon

de **Pyreneeën** /pirənɛjə(n)/ (adj) Pyrenees

de **pyromaan** /piromaːn/ (pl: pyromanen) pyromaniac, firebug

de **pyrrusoverwinning** /pɪrʏsovərwɪnɪŋ/ (pl: -en) Pyrrhic victory

Pythagoras /pitaɣorɑs/ Pythagoras: *stelling van ~* Pythagorean theorem

de **python** /pitɔn/ (pl: -s) python

q

de **q** /ky/ (pl: q's) q

Qatar /kat<u>o</u>r/ Qatar

de **¹Qatarees** /katar<u>e</u>s/ (pl: Qatarezen) Qatari

  ²Qatarees /katar<u>e</u>s/ (adj) Qatari

de **Q-koorts** /k<u>y</u>korts/ Q fever

qua /kwa/ (prep) as regards, as far as … goes

de **quarantaine** /karɑntɛ:nə/ quarantine: *in ~ gehouden worden* be kept in quarantine

quartair /kwɑrtɛ:r/ (adj) quaternary: *de ~e sector* the government (*or:* public) sector

quasi /kw<u>a</u>si/ (adv) **1** quasi(-), pseudo-: *een quasi-intellectueel* a pseudo-intellectual **2** [Belg] almost, nearly: *het is ~ onmogelijk* it is scarcely (*or:* hardly) possible

het **quatre-mains** /kɑtrəmɛ̃/ (piano) duet, composition for four hands

de **quatsch** /kwɑtʃ/ nonsense, rubbish: *ach, ~!* nonsense!

de **querulant** /kwerylɑnt/ (pl: -en) quarrel-monger, troublemaker

de **quiche** /kiʃ/ (pl: -s) quiche

de **quilt** /kwɪlt/ (pl: -s) quilt

quilten /kwɪltə(n)/ (quiltte, heeft gequilt) quilt

de **quinoa** /k<u>i</u>nwa/ quinoa

quitte /kit/ (adj) quits, even: *~ spelen* break even; *~ staan met* be quits with

het **qui-vive** /kiviːvə/: *op* zijn *~ zijn* be on the qui vive (*or:* the alert)

de **quiz** /kwɪs/ quiz

de **quizleider** /kwɪslɛidər/ (pl: -s) quizmaster

het **quorum** /kw<u>o</u>rʏm/ (pl: -s) quorum

de **quota** /kw<u>o</u>ta/ quota, share

het **quotiënt** /koʃɛnt/ quotient

het **quotum** /kw<u>o</u>tʏm/ (pl: -s, quota) quota

r

de **r** /ɛr/ (pl: r's) r, R
de **¹ra** /ra/ (pl: ra's) [shipp] yard
²ra /ra/ (int): *ra, ra, wie is dat?* guess who?
de **raad** /rat/ (pl: raden) **1** advice: *iem. ~ geven* advise s.o.; *luister naar mijn ~* take my advice **2** council, board: *de ~ van bestuur* (or: *van commissarissen*) the board (of directors, of management); *de Raad van State* the Council of State || *met voorbedachten rade* intentionally, deliberately; *moord met voorbedachten rade* premeditated (or: wilful) murder; *hij weet overal ~ op* he's never at a loss; *geen ~ weten met iets* not know what to do with sth.; not know how to cope with sth.; *ten einde ~ zijn* be at one's wits' end
het **raadhuis** /rathœys/ (pl: -huizen) town hall, city hall
raadplegen /ratpleɣə(n)/ (raadpleegde, heeft geraadpleegd) consult, confer with
het **raadsbesluit** /ratsbəslœyt/ (pl: -en) decision (of the council)
het **raadsel** /ratsəl/ (pl: -s) **1** riddle: *een ~ opgeven* ask a riddle **2** mystery: *het is mij een ~ hoe dat zo gekomen is* it's a mystery to me how that could have happened; *voor een ~ staan* be mystified, puzzled, baffled
raadselachtig /ratsəlɑχtəχ/ (adj, adv) mysterious, puzzling
het **raadslid** /ratslɪt/ (pl: -leden) councillor
de **raadsman** /ratsmɑn/ (pl: raadslieden) legal adviser
de **raadzaal** /ratsal/ (pl: -zalen) council chamber
raadzaam /ratsam/ (adj) advisable, wise
de **raaf** /raf/ (pl: raven) raven
raak /rak/ (adj, adv) home: *~ schieten* hit the mark; *ieder schot was ~* every shot went home; [iron] *het is weer ~* they're at it again || *maar ~* at random; *maar ~ slaan* hit right and left; *klets maar ~* say what you like
de **raaklijn** /raklɛin/ (pl: -en) tangent (line)
het **raakpunt** /rakpʏnt/ (pl: -en) point of contact: *ze hebben geen enkel ~* they have absolutely nothing in common
het **raakvlak** /rakflɑk/ (pl: -ken) **1** tangent plane **2** interface, common ground: *de taalkunde heeft ~ken met andere disciplines* linguistics has much ground in common with other disciplines; *het ~ tussen* the interface between
het **raam** /ram/ (pl: ramen) window, casement: *het ~pje omlaag draaien* wind down the car window

het **raamkozijn** /ramkozɛin/ (pl: -en) window frame
de **raamvertelling** /ramvərtɛlɪŋ/ (pl: -en) frame story
het **raamwerk** /ramwɛrk/ (pl: -en) framework; outline: *het Europese ~* the shared institutions of the EU; *het ~ van haar scriptie is af* the outline of her thesis is finished
de **raap** /rap/ (pl: rapen) turnip || *recht voor zijn ~* straight from the shoulder
de **raapstelen** /rapstelə(n)/ (pl) turnip tops (or: greens)
¹raar /rar/ (adj) odd, funny, strange: *een rare* an odd fish, an oddball; *een rare snuiter* a strange guy, a weirdo
²raar /rar/ (adv) oddly, strangely: *daar zul je ~ van opkijken* you'll be surprised
raaskallen /raskɑlə(n)/ (raaskalde, heeft geraaskald) rave, talk gibberish, talk rot
de **raat** /rat/ (pl: raten) (honey)comb
de **rabarber** /rabɑrbər/ rhubarb
het **rabat** /rabɑt/ discount
de **rabbi** /rɑbi/ (pl: -'s) rabbi
de **rabbijn** /rɑbɛin/ (pl: -en) rabbi
rabiaat /rabijat/ (adj, adv) rabid
de **rabiës** /rabijəs/ rabies
de **race** /res/ (pl: -s) race: *nog in de ~ zijn* still be in the running; *een ~ tegen de klok* a race against time; *het is een gelopen ~* it's a foregone conclusion
de **raceauto** /resauto/ (pl: -'s) racing car
de **racebaan** /rezban/ (pl: -banen) (race)track
de **racefiets** /resfits/ (pl: -en) racing bicycle (or: bike)
racen /resə(n)/ (racete, heeft/is geracet) race
het **racisme** /rasɪsmə/ racism
de **racist** /rasɪst/ (pl: -en) racist
racistisch /rasɪstis/ (adj, adv) racist
het **racket** /rɛkət/ (pl: -s) racket
het **rad** /rɑt/ (pl: -eren) (cog)wheel: *het ~ van avontuur* the wheel of Fortune; *iem. een ~ voor (de) ogen draaien* pull the wool over s.o.'s eyes
de **radar** /radɑr/ (pl: -s) radar
radeloos /radəlos/ (adj) desperate
raden /radə(n)/ (raadde, heeft geraden) guess: *raad eens wie daar komt* guess who's coming; *goed geraden* you've guessed it; *mis (fout) ~* guess wrong; *naar iets ~* guess (at) sth.; *je raadt het toch niet* you'll never guess; *je mag driemaal ~ wie het gedaan heeft* you'll never guess who did it || *dat is je geraden* you'd better
het **radertje** /radərcə/ (pl: -s) cog(wheel): *een klein ~ in het geheel zijn* be just a cog in the machine
het **raderwerk** /radərwɛrk/ wheels, gear(s)
de **radiator** /radijator/ (pl: -en) radiator
radicaal /radikal/ (adj) radical, drastic: *een ~ geneesmiddel* a radical cure; *een radicale partij* a radical party

radicaliseren /radikalizerə(n)/ (radicaliseerde, is geradicaliseerd) radicalize

de **radijs** /radɛis/ (pl: radijzen) radish

de **radio** /radijo/ (pl: -'s) radio, radio set: *de ~ uitzetten* switch off (*or:* turn off) the radio; *naar de ~ luisteren* listen to the radio

radioactief /radijoaktif/ (adj) radioactive: *~ afval* radioactive waste

de **radioactiviteit** /radijoaktivitɛit/ radioactivity

radiografisch /radijoɣrafis/ (adj, adv) radiographic ‖ *~ bestuurd* radio-controlled

de **radiologie** /radijoloɣi/ radiology

de **radioloog** /radijolox/ (pl: -logen) radiologist

de **radio-omroep** /radijoomrup/ (pl: -en) broadcasting service

het **radioprogramma** /radijoproɣrama/ (pl: -'s) radio programme

het **radiostation** /radijosta(t)ʃɔn/ (pl: -s) radio (*or:* broadcasting) station

het **radiotoestel** /radijotustɛl/ (pl: -len) radio (set)

de **radio-uitzending** /radijoœytsɛndɪŋ/ (pl: -en) radio broadcast (*or:* transmission)

de **radiozender** /radijozɛndər/ (pl: -s) radio transmitter

het **radium** /radijʏm/ radium

de **radius** /radijʏs/ (pl: -sen, radii) radius

de **radslag** /ratslɑx/ (pl: -en) cartwheel: *~en maken* turn cartwheels

de **rafel** /rafəl/ (pl: -s) frayed end, loose end: *de ~s hangen erbij* it is falling apart

rafelen /rafələ(n)/ (rafelde, heeft gerafeld) fray: *een gerafeld vloerkleed* a frayed carpet

rafelig /rafələx/ (adj) frayed

de **raffinaderij** /rafinadərɛi/ (pl: -en) refinery

het **raffinement** /rafinəmɛnt/ refinement, subtlety

raffineren /rafinerə(n)/ (raffineerde, heeft geraffineerd) refine

het **rag** /rɑx/ cobweb(s)

de **rage** /raʒə/ (pl: -s) craze, rage: *het is een ~* it's all the rage; *de nieuwste ~* the latest craze

de **ragebol** /raɣəbɔl/ (pl: -len) ceiling mop

ragfijn /rɑxfɛin/ (adj) as light (*or:* fine, thin) as gossamer

de **ragout** /raɣu/ (pl: -s) ragout: *~ van rundvlees* beef ragout (*or:* stew)

de **rail** /reːl/ (pl: -s) **1** rail: [fig] *de boel weer op de ~s hebben* get things back track again **2** rail(way): *vervoer per ~* rail transport; *uit de ~s lopen* derail, be derailed, leave the tracks

de **raison** /rɛzɔ̃/ [Dutch] *à ~ van ...* on payment of ...; *~ d'être* raison d'être

rakelings /rakəlɪŋs/ (adv) closely, narrowly: *de steen ging ~ langs zijn hoofd* the stone narrowly missed his head

¹**raken** /rakə(n)/ (raakte, is geraakt) get, become: *betrokken ~ bij* become involved in; *gewend ~ aan* get used to; [sport] *uit vorm ~*

lose one's form; *aan de drank ~* turn to drink, start drinking (heavily); [inform] hit the bottle

²**raken** /rakə(n)/ (raakte, heeft geraakt) **1** hit **2** affect, hit: *dat raakt me totaal niet* that leaves me cold **3** touch: *de auto raakte heel even het paaltje* the car grazed the post

de **raket** /rakɛt/ (pl: -ten) missile, rocket: *een ~ lanceren* launch a missile (*or:* rocket)

de **raketbasis** /rakɛdbazɪs/ (pl: -bases) missile base, rocket base

het **raketschild** /rakɛtsxɪlt/ space shield, rocket shield

de **raketwetenschap** /rakɛtwetənsxɑp/: *dat is geen ~* that's not rocket science

de **rakker** /rɑkər/ (pl: -s) rascal

de **rally** /rɛli/ (pl: -'s) rally

de **ram** /rɑm/ (pl: -men) ram

de **Ram** /rɑm/ (pl: -men) [astrology] Aries

de **ramadan** /rɑmadɑn/ Ramadan

ramen /ramə(n)/ (raamde, heeft geraamd) estimate

de **raming** /ramɪŋ/ (pl: -en) estimate

de **ramkoers** /rɑmkurs/: *op ~ liggen* be on a collision course, be heading for a direct confrontation

de **ramkraak** /rɑmkrak/ (pl: -kraken) ram raid

de **rammel** /rɑməl/ (pl: -s) beating: *een pak ~* a beating

de **rammelaar** /rɑməlar/ (pl: -s) rattle

¹**rammelen** /rɑmələ(n)/ (rammelde, heeft gerammeld) **1** rattle: *aan de deur ~* rattle the door; *met z'n sleutels ~* clink one's keys **2** be ramshackle: *dit plan rammelt aan alle kanten* this plan is totally unsound ‖ *ik rammelde van de honger* my stomach was rumbling with hunger

²**rammelen** /rɑmələ(n)/ (rammelde, heeft gerammeld) shake: *een kind door elkaar ~* give a child a shaking

rammen /rɑmə(n)/ (ramde, heeft geramd) ram, bash in (*or:* down): *de deur ~* bash the door down; *de auto ramde een muur* the car ran into a wall

de **rammenas** /rɑmənɑs/ (pl: -sen) winter radish

de **ramp** /rɑmp/ (pl: -en) disaster: *een ~ voor het milieu* an environmental disaster; *ik zou het geen ~ vinden als hij niet kwam* I wouldn't shed any tears if he didn't come; *tot overmaat van ~* to make matters worse

het **rampenplan** /rɑmpə(n)plɑn/ (pl: -nen) contingency plan

het **rampgebied** /rɑmpxəbit/ (pl: -en) disaster area

de **rampspoed** /rɑmpsput/ (pl: -en) misfortune, adversity

rampzalig /rɑmpsaləx/ (adj, adv) disastrous

de **rancune** /rɑŋkynə/ (pl: -s) rancour: *~ koesteren jegens iem.* hold a grudge against s.o.; *sans ~* no hard feelings

rancuneus /rɑŋkynø̞s/ (adj, adv) vindictive

de **rand** /rɑnt/ (pl: -en) **1** edge, rim: *de ~ van een bord* (or: *schaal*) the rim of a plate (*or*: dish); *een opstaande ~* a raised edge; *een brief met een zwarte ~* a black-edged letter; *aan de ~ van de stad* on the outskirts of the town; *aan de ~ van de samenleving* on the fringes of society **2** border, edge: *een ~ langs het tafelkleed* a border on the tablecloth **3** frame, rim: *de ~ van een spiegel* the frame of a mirror; *een bril met gouden ~en* gold-rimmed glasses **4** edge, brink, (b)rim, verge: *aan de ~ van de afgrond* **a)** on the brink of the precipice; **b)** [fig] on the verge of disaster; *tot de ~ gevuld* filled to the brim **5** rand ‖ *zwarte ~en onder zijn nagels hebben* have dirt under one's fingernails

de **randaarde** /rɑntardə/ earth (connection)

de **randapparatuur** /rɑntɑparatyr/ peripheral equipment

de **randgemeente** /rɑntxəmentə/ (pl: -n, -s) suburb

de **randgroepjongere** /rɑntxrupjoŋərə/ (pl: -n) young drop-out

het **randje** /rɑncə/ (pl: -s) edge, border, rim; [fig] verge; [fig] brink ‖ *op het ~ (af)* on the borderline; *dat was op het ~* that was close (*or*: touch and go)

de **Randstad** /rɑntstɑt/: *de ~ the cities* (*or*: conurbation) of western Holland

het **randverschijnsel** /rɑntfərsχɛinsəl/ (pl: -en) marginal phenomenon

de **randvoorwaarde** /rɑntforwardə/ (pl: -n) precondition

de **rang** /rɑŋ/ (pl: -en) **1** rank, position: *een ~ hoger dan hij* one rank above him; *mensen van alle ~en en standen* people from all walks of life **2** circle: *we zaten op de tweede ~* we were in the upper circle

het **rangeerterrein** /rɑnʒɛrtɛrɛin/ (pl: -en) marshalling yard

rangeren /rɑnʒerə(n)/ (rangeerde, heeft gerangeerd) shunt: *een trein op een zijspoor ~* shunt a train into a siding

de **ranglijst** /rɑŋlɛist/ (pl: -en) (priority) list, list (of candidates); (league) table: *bovenaan de ~ staan* be at the top of the list

het **rangnummer** /rɑŋnʏmər/ (pl: -s) number

de **rangorde** /rɑŋordə/ (pl: -n, -s) order

rangschikken /rɑŋsχɪkə(n)/ (rangschikte, heeft gerangschikt) **1** classify, order, class **2** arrange: *alfabetisch ~* arrange in alphabetical order

de **rangschikking** /rɑŋsχɪkɪŋ/ **1** classification **2** arrangement, order

het **rangtelwoord** /rɑŋtɛlwort/ (pl: -en) ordinal (number)

de **ranja**® /rɑnja/ orange squash, orangeade

de **rank** /rɑŋk/ (pl: -en) tendril

de **ransel** /rɑnsəl/ (pl: -s) knapsack

ranselen /rɑnsələ(n)/ (ranselde, heeft geranseld) flog, thrash

de **ransomware** /rɛnsəmwɛːr/ ransomware

het **rantsoen** /rɑntsun/ (pl: -en) ration, allowance: *een ~ boter* a ration (*or*: an allowance) of butter

rantsoeneren /rɑn(t)sunerə(n)/ (rantsoeneerde, heeft gerantsoeneerd) ration

ranzig /rɑnzəχ/ (adj) rancid

rap /rɑp/ (adj, adv) quick, swift: *iets ~ doen* do sth. quickly

de **rapedrug** /repdrʏːɡ/ (pl: -s) date-rape drug

rapen /rapə(n)/ (raapte, heeft geraapt) pick up, collect: *kastanjes ~* pick up (*or*: collect) chestnuts; *een bij elkaar geraapt stelletje* (or: *zootje*) a motley crew

de **rapmuziek** /rɛpmyzik/ rap music

rappen /rɛpə(n)/ (rapte, heeft gerapt) rap

de **rapper** /rɛpər/ (pl: -s) rapper

het **rapport** /rɑpɔrt/ (pl: -en) report, despatch: *~ uitbrengen* (or: *opmaken*) *over* produce (*or*: make) a report on; *een onvoldoende op zijn ~ krijgen* get a fail mark in one's report

de **rapportage** /rɑpɔrtaʒə/ (pl: -s) report(ing)

het **rapportcijfer** /rɑpɔrtsɛifər/ (pl: -s) report mark

de **rapportenvergadering** /rɑpɔrtə(n)vərɣadərɪŋ/ meeting to discuss pupils' reports

rapporteren /rɑpɔrterə(n)/ (rapporteerde, heeft gerapporteerd) report; cover: *~ aan* report to

de **rapsodie** /rɑpsodi/ (pl: -ën) rhapsody

de **raptekst** /rɛptɛkst/ (pl: -en) rap lyrics

rara /rara/ (int): *~, wat is dat?* guess what this is; *~, wie ben ik?* guess who

de **rariteit** /raritɛit/ (pl: -en) curio(sity): *een handeltje in ~en* an antique shop

het **¹ras** /rɑs/ (pl: -sen) race; breed; variety: *van gemengd ~* of mixed race

²ras /rɑs/ (adj, adv) swift; rapid, quick: *met ~se schreden* swiftly, rapidly

de **rasartiest** /rɑsartist/ born artist

rasecht /rɑsɛχt/ (adj) (true) born

de **rashond** /rɑshont/ pedigree dog, pure-bred dog

de **rasp** /rɑsp/ (pl: -en) grater

het **raspaard** /rɑspart/ (pl: -en) thoroughbred

raspen /rɑspə(n)/ (raspte, heeft geraspt) grate: *kaas ~* grate cheese

de **rassendiscriminatie** /rɑsə(n)dɪskriminaː(t)si/ racial discrimination

de **rassenhaat** /rɑsə(n)hat/ racial hatred

de **rasta** /rɑsta/ Rasta(farian)

de **raster** /rɑstər/ fence, lattice

raszuiver /rɑsœyvər/ (adj) pure-blooded; pure-bred

de **rat** /rɑt/ (pl: -ten) rat: *hij zat als een ~ in de val* he was caught out

de **rataplan** /rɑtaplɑn/: *de hele ~* the whole caboodle (*or*: lot)

de **ratel** /ratəl/ (pl: -s) rattle

ratelen /ratələ(n)/ (ratelde, heeft gerateld)

rattle: *de* **wekker** *ratelt* the alarm clock is jangling

de **ratelslang** /rɑtəlslɑŋ/ (pl: -en) rattlesnake

ratificeren /ratifisɛrə(n)/ (ratificeerde, heeft geratificeerd) ratify

de **ratio** /ra(t)sijo/ **1** reason **2** ratio

rationeel /ra(t)ʃonel/ (adj, adv) rational

het/de **ratjetoe** /rɑcətu/ (pl: -s) hotchpotch, mishmash

rato /rato/: *naar ~* pro rata, in proportion

de **rats** /rɑts/ [Dutch]: [inform] *in de ~ zitten (over)* have the wind up (about)

het **rattengif** /rɑtə(n)ɣɪf/ rat poison

het **rattenkruit** /rɑtə(n)krœyt/ arsenic

¹rauw /rɑu/ (adj) **1** raw: *~e biefstuk* raw steak **2** sore: *een ~e plek* a raw spot **3** rough, tough ‖ *dat viel ~ op mijn dak* that was an unexpected blow; *ik lust hem ~* I let him do his worst

²rauw /rɑu/ (adv) rawly, sorely, roughly

de **rauwkost** /rɑukɔst/ vegetables eaten raw

rauwmelks /rɑumɛlks/ (adj) raw-milk, unpasteurised: *~e kaas* raw-milk cheese, unpasteurised cheese

de **ravage** /ravaʒə/ (pl: -s) **1** ravage(s), havoc: *die hevige storm heeft een ~ aangericht* that violent storm has wreaked havoc **2** debris

de **rave** /rev/ rave

het **ravijn** /ravɛin/ (pl: -en) ravine, gorge

de **ravioli** /ravijoli/ ravioli

ravotten /ravɔtə(n)/ (ravotte, heeft geravot) romp, horse around

het **rayon** /rɛjɔn/ (pl: -s) district; territory: *hij heeft Limburg als zijn ~* he works Limburg

de **rayonchef** /rɛjɔnʃɛf/ (pl: -s) area supervisor

razen /razə(n)/ (raasde, heeft/is geraasd) race, tear: *de auto's ~ over de snelweg* the cars are racing along the motorway

razend /razənt/ (adj, adv) **1** furious: *iem. ~ maken* infuriate s.o.; *als een ~e tekeergaan* rave like a madman **2** terrific: *hij heeft het ~ druk* he's up to his neck in work; *~ snel, in ~e vaart* at a terrific pace, at breakneck speed

razendsnel /razəntsnɛl/ (adj, adv) superfast, high-speed

de **razernij** /razərnɛi/ frenzy, rage: *in blinde ~* in a blind rage; *iem. tot ~ brengen* infuriate s.o.

de **razzia** /razija/ (pl: -'s) razzia

de **r&b** /arɛmbiː/ R&B, rhythm and blues

de **re** /re/ (pl: re's) re, D

de **reactie** /rejɑksi/ (pl: -s) reaction, response: *als ~ op* in reaction to; [media] *een ~ plaatsen* leave a comment; *snelle ~s* sharp reflexes; *een ~ vertonen* respond

de **reactiesnelheid** /rejɑksisnɛlhɛit/ speed of reaction

de **¹reactionair** /rejɑkʃonɛːr/ (pl: reactionairen) reactionary

²reactionair /rejɑkʃonɛːr/ (adj, adv) reactionary

de **reactor** /rejɑktɔr/ (pl: -s) reactor: *snelle ~* fast reactor

de **reader** /riːdər/ (pl: -s) reader

de **reageerbuis** /rejaɣɛrbœys/ (pl: -buizen) test tube: *bevruchting in een ~* test-tube (*or:* in vitro) fertilization

de **reageerbuisbaby** /rejaɣɛrbœyzbebi/ (pl: -'s) test-tube baby

reageren /rejaɣɛrə(n)/ (reageerde, heeft gereageerd) react (to); respond: *te sterk ~* overreact; *moet je eens kijken hoe hij daarop reageert* look how he reacts to that; *ze reageerde positief op de behandeling* she responded to the treatment

realiseerbaar /rejalizɛrbar/ (adj) realizable, feasible

¹realiseren /rejalizɛrə(n)/ (realiseerde, heeft gerealiseerd) realize: *dat is niet te ~* that is impracticable

zich **²realiseren** /rejalizɛrə(n)/ (realiseerde zich, heeft zich gerealiseerd) realize

het **realisme** /rejalɪsmə/ realism

de **realist** /rejalɪst/ (pl: -en) realist

realistisch /rejalɪstis/ (adj, adv) realistic: *~ beschrijven* (or: *schilderen*) describe (*or:* paint) realistically

de **realiteit** /rejalitɛit/ (pl: -en) reality: *we moeten de ~ onder ogen zien* we must face facts (*or:* reality)

de **realiteitszin** /rejalitɛitsɪn/ sense of reality

de **realitysoap** /rijɛlətisop/ reality soap

de **reallifesoap** /rilɑjfsop/ real-life soap

de **reanimatie** /reanima(t)si/ resuscitation, reanimation

reanimeren /reanimɛrə(n)/ (reanimeerde, heeft gereanimeerd) resuscitate, revive

de **rebel** /rəbɛl/ (pl: -len) rebel

rebelleren /rəbɛlɛrə(n)/ (rebelleerde, heeft gerebelleerd) rebel: *~ tegen ... * rebel against ...

de **rebellie** /rəbɛli/ rebellion

rebels /rəbɛls/ (adj, adv) rebellious

de **rebound** /ribaunt/ rebound

de **rebus** /rebys/ (pl: -sen) rebus

recalcitrant /rekɑlsitrɑnt/ (adj, adv) recalcitrant

recapituleren /rekɑpitylɛrə(n)/ (recapituleerde, heeft gerecapituleerd) recapitulate, summarize

de **recensent** /resɛnsɛnt/ (pl: -en) reviewer, critic

recenseren /resɛnsɛrə(n)/ (recenseerde, heeft gerecenseerd) review

de **recensie** /resɛnsi/ (pl: -s) review, notice: *lovende (juichende) ~s krijgen* get rave reviews

recent /resɛnt/ (adj) recent

het **recept** /resɛpt/ (pl: -en) **1** prescription: *alleen op ~ verkrijgbaar* available only on prescription **2** recipe

de **receptie** /resɛpsi/ (pl: -s) **1** reception: *staande ~* stand-up reception **2** reception (desk):

melden **bij** *de* ~ report to the reception (desk)

de **receptionist** /resɛpʃɔnɪst/ (pl: -en) receptionist

de **recessie** /rəsɛsi/ recession

de **recette** /rəsɛtə/ (pl: -s) receipts

de **recherche** /reʃɛrʒə/ (pl: -s) criminal investigation department

de **rechercheur** /reʃɛrʃør/ (pl: -s) detective

het **¹recht** /rɛxt/ (pl: -en) **1** justice, right: *iem.* ~ *doen* do s.o. justice; *iem. (iets) geen* ~ *doen* be unfair to s.o. (sth.); *het* ~ *handhaven* uphold the law; *het* ~ *aan zijn kant hebben* be in the right **2** law: *student (in de)* ~*en* law student; *burgerlijk* ~ civil law; *het* ~ *in eigen handen nemen* take the law into one's own hands; ~*en studeren* read (*or:* study) law; *volgens Engels* ~ under English law **3** right: ~ *van bestaan hebben* have a right to exist; *het* ~ *van de sterkste* the law of the jungle; *dat is mijn goed* ~ that is my right; *het volste* ~ *hebben om ...* have every right to ...; *niet het* ~ *hebben iets te doen* have no right to do sth.; *goed tot zijn* ~ *komen* show up well; *voor zijn* ~*(en) opkomen* defend one's right(s) **4** rights: *de* ~*en van de mens* human rights **5** right, claim: ~ *op een uitkering* entitlement to a benefit; ~ *hebben op iets* have the right to sth. **6** (copy)right(s): *alle* ~*en voorbehouden* all rights reserved ‖ *iets tot zijn* ~ *laten komen* do justice to sth., give sth. its due

²recht /rɛxt/ (adj, adv) **1** straight: *de auto kwam* ~ *op ons af* the car was coming straight at us; *iets* ~ *leggen* put sth. straight; ~ *op iem. (iets) afgaan* go straight for s.o. (sth.); *iem.* ~ *in de ogen kijken* look s.o. straight in the eye; ~ *voor zich uitkijken* look straight ahead; *hij woont* ~ *tegenover mij* he lives straight across from me; ~ *tegenover elkaar* face-to-face **2** straight (up), upright: ~ *zitten* (or: *staan*) sit (*or:* stand) up straight; ~ *overeind* straight up; bolt upright **3** right; direct; directly: *de* ~*e zijde van een voorwerp* the right side of an object **4** right; true: *op het* ~*e pad blijven* keep to the straight and narrow ‖ ~*e hoek* right angle

de **rechtbank** /rɛxtbɑŋk/ (pl: -en) **1** court (of law, justice), lawcourt: *voor de* ~ *moeten komen* have to appear in court (*or:* before the court) **2** court, law courts, magistrates' court; [Am] courthouse

de **rechtbanktekening** /rɛxtbɑŋktekənɪŋ/ (pl: -en) court drawing, courtroom sketch

rechtbreien /rɛx(t)brɛiə(n)/ (breide recht, heeft rechtgebreid) put right, rectify

rechtbuigen /rɛx(t)bœyɣə(n)/ (boog recht, heeft rechtgebogen) straighten (out), bend straight

rechtdoor /rɛxtdor/ (adv) straight on (*or:* ahead)

rechtdoorzee /rɛɣdorze/ (adj) straight, honest, sincere

de **¹rechter** /rɛxtər/ (pl: -s) judge, magistrate: *naar de* ~ *stappen* go to court; *voor de* ~ *moeten verschijnen* have to appear in court

²rechter /rɛxtər/ (adj) right; right(-hand): *de* ~ *deur* the door on the (*or:* your) right

de **rechterarm** /rɛxtərɑrm/ right arm

het **rechterbeen** /rɛxtərben/ right leg

de **rechter-commissaris** /rɛxtərkɔmɪsɑrɪs/ (pl: rechters-commissarissen) examining judge (*or:* magistrate)

de **rechterhand** /rɛxtərhɑnt/ (pl: -en) right hand: *de tweede straat aan uw* ~ the second street on your right

de **rechterkant** /rɛxtərkɑnt/ right(-hand) side: *aan de* ~ on the right(-hand) side

rechterlijk /rɛxtərlək/ (adj, adv) judicial, court: *de* ~*e macht* the judiciary

de **rechtervleugel** /rɛxtərvløɣəl/ (pl: -s) **1** right wing: *de* ~ *van een gebouw* (or: *een voetbalelftal*) the right wing of a building (*or:* football team) **2** right (wing), Right

de **rechtervoet** /rɛxtərvut/ right foot

de **rechterzijde** /rɛxtərzɛidə/ right(-hand) side: *pijn in de* ~ *hebben* have a pain in one's right side; *aan de* ~ on the right(-hand side)

rechtgeaard /rɛ(xt)xəart/ (adj) right-minded: *iedere* ~*e Fransman* every true Frenchman

de **rechthoek** /rɛxthuk/ (pl: -en) rectangle, oblong

rechthoekig /rɛxthukəx/ (adj, adv) **1** right-angled, at right angles: *een* ~*e driehoek* a right-angled triangle **2** rectangular, oblong: *een* ~*e kamer* a rectangular room

rechtmatig /rɛxtmatəx/ (adj, adv) rightful; lawful; legitimate: *de* ~*e eigenaars* the rightful (*or:* legitimate) owners

rechtop /rɛxtɔp/ (adv) upright, straight (up); on end: ~ *lopen* walk upright; ~ *zitten* sit up straight

rechts /rɛxts/ (adj, adv) **1** right(-hand): *de eerste deur* ~ the first door on (*or:* to) the right; ~ *afslaan* turn (off to the) right; ~ *houden* keep (to the) right; ~ *rijden* drive on the right; ~ *boven* (or: *beneden*) top (*or:* bottom) right; *hij zat* ~ *van mij* he sat on my right(-hand side) **2** right-handed: ~ *schrijven* write with one's right hand **3** [pol] right-wing

de **rechtsachter** /rɛxtsɑxtər/ (pl: -s) right back

rechtsaf /rɛxtsɑf/ (adv) (to the, one's) right: *bij de splitsing moet u* ~ you have to turn right at the junction

de **rechtsbescherming** /rɛxtsbəsxɛrmɪŋ/ legal protection

de **rechtsbijstand** /rɛxtsbɛistɑnt/ legal aid

de **rechtsbuiten** /rɛxtsbœytə(n)/ (pl: -s) right-winger, outside right

rechtschapen /rɛxtsxapə(n)/ (adj, adv) righteous, honest

het **rechtsgebied** /rɛx(t)sxəbit/ jurisdiction

rechtsgeldig /rɛxtsxɛldəx/ (adj) (legally)

valid, lawful

de **rechtsgeldigheid** /rɛxtsxɛldəxhɛit/ legality, legal force (or: validity)

de **rechtsgeleerde** /rɛx(t)sxəlerdə/ (pl: -n) lawyer

de **rechtsgelijkheid** /rɛxtsxəlɛikhɛit/ equality before the law, equality of rights (or: status)

het **rechtsgevoel** /rɛx(t)sxəvul/ sense of justice

rechtshandig /rɛxtshɑndəx/ (adj) right-handed

de **rechtshulp** /rɛxtshʏlp/ legal aid: [Dutch] *bureau voor ~* legal advice centre

rechtsom /rɛx(t)sɔm/ (adv) (to the) right

rechtsomkeert /rɛxtsɔmkert/ (adv): *~ maken* a) [mil] do an about-turn; b) [fig] make a U-turn

de **rechtsongelijkheid** /rɛxtsɔŋəlɛikhɛit/ inequality of status, legal inequality

de **rechtsorde** /rɛxtsɔrdə/ legal order, system of law(s)

de **rechtspersoon** /rɛxtspɛrsɔn/ (pl: -personen) legal body (or: entity, person)

de **rechtspositie** /rɛxtspozi(t)si/ legal position

de **rechtspraak** /rɛxtsprak/ **1** administration of justice (or: of the law) **2** jurisdiction: *de ~ in strafzaken* criminal jurisdiction

rechtspreken /rɛxtsprekə(n)/ (sprak recht, heeft rechtgesproken) administer justice: *de ~de macht* the judicature; the judiciary; *~ in een zaak* judge a case

de **rechtsstaat** /rɛxtstat/ (pl: -staten) constitutional state

rechtstreeks /rɛxtstreks/ (adj, adv) **1** direct, straight(forward): *een ~e verbinding* a direct connection; *~ naar huis gaan* go straight (or: right) home **2** direct, immediate: *een ~e uitzending* a direct broadcast; *hij wendde zich ~ tot de minister* he went straight to the minister

de **rechtsvervolging** /rɛxtsfərvɔlɣɪŋ/ (pl: -en) legal proceedings, prosecution: *een ~ tegen iem. instellen* institute legal proceedings against s.o.; *ontslaan van ~* acquit

de **rechtsvordering** /rɛx(t)sfɔrdərɪŋ/ (pl: -en) **1** (legal) action **2** legal procedure

de **rechtswinkel** /rɛxtswɪŋkəl/ (pl: -s) law centre (or: clinic)

de **rechtszaak** /rɛxtsak/ (pl: -zaken) lawsuit: *ergens een ~ van maken* take a matter to court

de **rechtszaal** /rɛxtsal/ (pl: -zalen) courtroom

de **rechtszitting** /rɛxtsɪtɪŋ/ (pl: -en) sitting (or: session) of the court

rechttoe /rɛxtu/ (adv): *~, rechtaan* straightforward; *het was allemaal ~ rechtaan* it was plain sailing all the way

rechttrekken /rɛxtrɛkə(n)/ (trok recht, heeft rechtgetrokken) set right, put right

rechtuit /rɛxtœyt/ (adv) straight on (or: ahead): *~ lopen* walk straight on

rechtvaardig /rɛxtfardəx/ (adj, adv) just, fair: *een ~ oordeel* a fair judgement; *iem. ~*

behandelen treat s.o. fairly

rechtvaardigen /rɛxtfardəɣə(n)/ (rechtvaardigde, heeft gerechtvaardigd) justify; warrant: *zich tegenover iem. ~* justify o.s. to s.o.

de **rechtvaardigheid** /rɛxtfardəxhɛit/ justice

de **rechtvaardiging** /rɛxtfardəɣɪŋ/ justification

rechtzetten /rɛxtsɛtə(n)/ (zette recht, heeft rechtgezet) **1** put right, set right, rectify **2** adjust **3** set up, put up, raise

rechtzinnig /rɛxtsɪnəx/ (adj, adv) [Dutch] orthodox; [Protestantism] Reformed

de **recidivist** /residivɪst/ (pl: -en) recidivist, repeated offender

het **recital** /risɡjtəl/ (pl: -s) recital

de **reclamatie** /reklama(t)si/ **1** reclamation **2** claim

de **reclame** /rəklamə/ (pl: -s) **1** advertising, publicity: *~ maken (voor iets)* advertise (sth.) **2** ad(vertisement), sign

de **reclameaanbieding** /rəklaməambidɪŋ/ (pl: -en) special offer

de **reclameboodschap** /rəklaməbotsxɑp/ (pl: -pen) commercial

het **reclamebureau** /rəklaməbyro/ advertising agency

de **reclamecampagne** /rəklaməkɑmpɑɲə/ (pl: -s) advertising campaign: *een ~ voeren* run (or: conduct) an advertising campaign

de **reclamefolder** /rəklaməfɔldər/ (pl: -s) advertising brochure (or: pamphlet)

reclameren /reklamɛrə(n)/ (reclameerde, heeft gereclameerd) complain, put in a claim

de **reclamespot** /rəklaməspɔt/ (pl: -s) commercial, (advertising) spot

de **reclamestunt** /rəklaməstʏnt/ (pl: -s) advertising stunt, publicity stunt

de **reclassering** /reklɑserɪŋ/ after-care and rehabilitation

de **reclasseringsambtenaar** /reklɑserɪŋsɑmtənar/ probation officer

de **reconstructie** /rekɔnstrʏksi/ (pl: -s) reconstruction

reconstrueren /rekɔnstrywɛrə(n)/ (reconstrueerde, heeft gereconstrueerd) reconstruct

de **reconversie** /rekɔnvɛrsi/ (pl: -s) [Belg] switch

het **record** /rəkoːr/ (pl: -s) record: *een ~ breken* (or: *vestigen*) break (or: establish) a record

de **recorder** /rikoːdər/ (pl: -s) recorder

de **recordhouder** /rəkoːrhɑudər/ (pl: -s) record-holder

de **recordpoging** /rəkoːrpoɣɪŋ/ (pl: -en) attempt on a record

de **recreant** /rekrejɑnt/ (pl: -en) **1** [roughly] holiday-maker; [Am] vacationer **2** recreational athlete: *professionele tennissers en ~en* professional and recreational tennis players

de **recreatie** /rekreja(t)si/ (pl: -s) recreation,

leisure
recreatief /rekrejatif/ (adj) recreational
recreëren /rekrejere(n)/ (recreëerde, heeft gerecreëerd) relax
rectaal /rɛktal/ (adj, adv) rectal
de **rectificatie** /rɛktifika(t)si/ (pl: -s) rectification
rectificeren /rɛktifisere(n)/ (rectificeerde, heeft gerectificeerd) rectify
de **rector** /rɛktɔr/ (pl: -en, -s) **1** headmaster; [esp Am] principal **2** rector
het **reçu** /rəsy/ (pl: -'s) receipt
recyclen /risɑjk(ə)lə(n)/ (recyclede, heeft gerecycled) [Dutch] recycle
recycleren /resiklere(n)/ (recycleerde, heeft gerecycleerd) [Belg] recycle
de **recycling** /risɑjklɪŋ/ [Dutch] recycling
de **redacteur** /redaktør/ (pl: -en, -s) editor
de **redactie** /redɑksi/ (pl: -s) editors, editorial staff
redactioneel /redɑkʃonel/ (adj) editorial: *een ~ artikel* an editorial
reddeloos /rɛdəlos/ (adv): *hij is ~ verloren* he is irretrievably lost, he is beyond redemption; *het bedrijf is ~ verloren* the company is beyond saving, the company cannot be salvaged
¹**redden** /rɛdə(n)/ (redde, heeft gered) **1** save, rescue; salvage: *de ~de hand toesteken* be the saving of a person; *we moeten zien te ~ wat er te ~ valt* we must make the best of a bad job; *gered zijn* be helped; *een ~de engel* a ministering angel **2** (+ het) manage: *de zieke zal het niet ~* the patient won't pull through ‖ *Jezus redt* Jesus saves
zich ²**redden** /rɛdə(n)/ (redde zich, heeft zich gered) manage, cope: *ik red me best!* I can manage all right!
de **redder** /rɛdər/ (pl: -s) rescuer, saviour
de **redding** /rɛdɪŋ/ (pl: -en) rescue, salvation
de **reddingsactie** /rɛdɪŋsɑksi/ (pl: -s) rescue operation
de **reddingsboot** /rɛdɪŋzbot/ (pl: -boten) lifeboat
de **reddingsbrigade** /rɛdɪŋzbriɣadə/ (pl: -s, -n) rescue party (or: team)
de **reddingsdeken** /rɛdɪŋzdekə(n)/ (pl: -s) emergency blanket; [Am] space blanket
de **reddingsoperatie** /rɛdɪŋsopəra(t)si/ (pl: -s) rescue operation
de **reddingspoging** /rɛdɪŋspoɣɪŋ/ (pl: -en) rescue attempt (or: bid, effort): *hun ~en mochten hem niet baten* their attempts (or: efforts) to rescue him were in vain
het **reddingswerk** /rɛdɪŋswɛrk/ rescue work (or: operations)
reddingszwemmen /rɛdɪŋswɛmə(n)/ lifesaving
de **rede** /redə/ (pl: -s) **1** reason, sense: *hij is niet voor ~ vatbaar* he won't listen to (or: see) reason **2** speech; address: *een ~ houden*

make a speech **3** reason, intelligence, intellect ‖ *iem. in de ~ vallen* interrupt s.o.; *directe, indirecte ~* direct, indirect speech
¹**redelijk** /redələk/ (adj) **1** rational, sensible **2** reasonable, fair: *binnen ~e grenzen* within (reasonable) limits; *een ~e prijs* a reasonable price; *een ~e kans maken* stand a reasonable chance
²**redelijk** /redələk/ (adv) **1** rationally: *~ denken* think rationally **2** reasonably, fairly: *ik ben ~ gezond* I am in reasonably good health
redelijkerwijs /redələkərwɛis/ (adv) in fairness: *~ kunt u niet meer verlangen* in all fairness you cannot expect more
de **redelijkheid** /redələkhɛit/: *dat kan in ~ niet van ons gevraagd worden* that cannot in reasonableness (or: fairness) be asked of us
redeloos /redəlos/ (adj, adv) **1** irrational **2** unreasonable
de **reden** /redə(n)/ (pl: -en) **1** reason, cause, occasion: *om persoonlijke ~en* for personal reasons; *ik heb er mijn ~voor* I have my reasons; *om die ~* for that reason; *geen ~ tot klagen hebben* have no cause (or: ground) for complaint; *een ~ te meer om ... * all the more reason why ... **2** reason, motive: *zonder opgaaf van ~en* without reason; *~ geven tot* give cause for
de **redenaar** /redənar/ (pl: -s) speaker, orator
redeneren /redənere(n)/ (redeneerde, heeft geredeneerd) reason, argue (about): *daartegen is (valt) niet te ~* there is no arguing with that
de **redenering** /redənerɪŋ/ (pl: -en) reasoning, argumentation: *een fout in de ~* a flaw in the reasoning; *een logische ~* a logical line of argument
de **reder** /redər/ (pl: -s) shipowner
de **rederij** /redərɛi/ (pl: -en) shipping company, shipowner(s)
redetwisten /redətwɪstə(n)/ (redetwistte, heeft geredetwist) argue
de **redevoering** /redəvurɪŋ/ (pl: -en) speech, address: *een ~ houden* make (or: deliver) a speech
redigeren /rediɣere(n)/ (redigeerde, heeft geredigeerd) edit
het **redmiddel** /rɛtmɪdəl/ (pl: -en) remedy: *een laatste ~* a last resort
reduceren /redysere(n)/ (reduceerde, heeft gereduceerd) reduce, decrease: *gereduceerd tarief* reduced rate
de **reductie** /redʏksi/ (pl: -s) reduction, decrease; cut; cutback: *~ geven* give a discount
het/de **ree** /re/ (pl: -ën) roe(deer)
de **reebok** /rebɔk/ (pl: -ken) roebuck
reeds /rets/ (adv) [form] already: *~ bij het begin* already from the (very) beginning; *~ lang* for a long time
reëel /rejel/ (adj, adv) **1** real, actual: *reële groei van het inkomen* growth of real income

2 realistic, reasonable: *je moet ~ blijven* you've got to stay realistic, let's be realistic (here); *een reële kijk op het leven hebben* have a realistic outlook on life

de **reeks** /reks/ (pl: -en) **1** series, row; string **2** series, succession, sequence: *een ~ ongelukken* a string (*or:* succession) of accidents

de **reep** /rep/ (pl: repen) **1** strip; thong; band; sliver: *de komkommer in ~jes snijden* slice the cucumber thinly **2** (chocolate) bar

de **reet** /ret/ (pl: reten) **1** crack, chink **2** [vulg] arse; [Am] ass; backside

het **referaat** /refərɑt/ (pl: referaten) lecture, paper: *een ~ houden over iets* read a paper on sth.

het **referendum** /refərɛndʏm/ (pl: -s, referenda) referendum: *een bindend ~* a binding referendum

de **referentie** /refərɛnsi/ (pl: -s) reference; [pers also] referee: *mag ik u als ~ opgeven?* may I use you as a reference?

het **referentiekader** /refərɛn(t)sikɑdər/ (pl: -s) frame of reference

refereren /refərerə(n)/ (refereerde, heeft gerefereerd) refer (to)

reflecteren /reflɛkterə(n)/ (reflecteerde, heeft gereflecteerd) reflect, mirror

de **reflectie** /reflɛksi/ (pl: -s) reflection

de **reflector** /reflɛktɔr/ (pl: -en) reflector; Catseye

de **reflex** /reflɛks/ (pl: -en) reflex: *een aangeboren ~* an innate reflex

de **reformwinkel** /refɔrmwɪŋkəl/ (pl: -s) [Dutch] health food shop, wholefood shop

het **refrein** /rəfrɛin/ (pl: -en) refrain, chorus: *iedereen zong het ~ mee* everybody joined in the chorus

de **refter** /rɛftər/ (pl: -s) refectory

de **regatta** /reɣɑta/ (pl: -'s) regatta

het **regeerakkoord** /rəɣerakort/ (pl: -en) coalition agreement

de **regeerperiode** /rəɣerperijodə/ period of office, period of government

de **regel** /reɣəl/ (pl: -s) **1** line: *een ~ overslaan* skip a line; leave a line blank; *tussen de ~s door lezen* read between the lines **2** rule: *het is ~ dat …* it is a (general) rule that …; *in de ~* as a rule, ordinarily **3** rule, regulation; law: *tegen alle ~s in* contrary to (*or:* against) all the rules

de **regelafstand** /reɣəlɑfstɑnt/ (pl: -en) line space, spacing: *op enkele ~* single-spaced; *de ~ instellen* set the line interval

regelbaar /reɣəlbar/ (adj) regulable; adjustable

regelen /reɣələ(n)/ (regelde, heeft geregeld) **1** regulate; arrange; fix (up); settle; control [traf]; adjust; order: *de geluidssterkte ~* adjust the volume; *de temperatuur ~* regulate (*or:* control) the temperature; *het verkeer ~* direct the traffic; *ik zal dat wel even*

~ I'll take care of that **2** regulate, lay down rules for

de **regelgeving** /reɣəlɣevɪŋ/ rules; instructions

de **regeling** /reɣəlɪŋ/ (pl: -en) **1** regulation, arrangement, settlement, ordering; control [traf]; adjustment: *de ~ van de geldzaken* the settling of money matters; *een ~ treffen* make an arrangement (*or:* a settlement) **2** arrangement, settlement; scheme

de **regelmaat** /reɣəlmat/ regularity: *met de ~ van de klok* as regular as clockwork

regelmatig /reɣəlmatəɣ/ (adj, adv) **1** regular, orderly: *een ~e ademhaling* regular (*or:* even) breathing; *een ~ leven leiden* lead a regular (*or:* an orderly) life **2** regular; frequent: *~ naar de kerk gaan* be a regular churchgoer; *dat komt ~ voor* that happens regularly

de **regelneef** /reɣəlnef/ (pl: -neven) [iron] busybody, organizer

regelrecht /reɣəlrɛxt/ (adj, adv) straight, direct; right: *de kinderen kwamen ~ naar huis* the children came straight home

de **regen** /reɣə(n)/ (pl: -s) **1** rain: *aanhoudende ~* persistent rain; *in de stromende ~* in the pouring rain; [fig] *van de ~ in de drup komen* jump out of the frying pan into the fire; *zure ~* acid rain **2** rain; shower

regenachtig /reɣənɑxtəɣ/ (adj) rainy, showery: *een ~e dag* a rainy day

de **regenboog** /reɣə(n)box/ (pl: -bogen) rainbow

de **regenboogtrui** /reɣə(n)boxtrœy/ (pl: -en) [sport] rainbow jersey

het **regenboogvlies** /reɣə(n)boxflis/ (pl: -vliezen) iris

de **regenbui** /reɣə(n)bœy/ (pl: -en) shower (of rain); downpour

de **regencape** /reɣə(n)kep/ (pl: -s) rain cape

de **regendruppel** /reɣə(n)drʏpəl/ (pl: -s, -en) raindrop

regenen /reɣənə(n)/ (regende, heeft geregend) rain; [light] shower; drizzle: *het heeft flink geregend* there was quite a downpour; *het regent dat het giet* it is pouring

de **regenjas** /reɣə(n)jɑs/ (pl: -sen) raincoat, mackintosh

de **regenkleding** /reɣə(n)kledɪŋ/ rainproof clothing, rainwear

de **regenmeter** /reɣə(n)metər/ (pl: -s) rain gauge

het **regenpak** /reɣə(n)pɑk/ (pl: -ken) waterproof suit

de **regenpijp** /reɣə(n)pɛip/ (pl: -en) drainpipe

de **regent** /rəɣɛnt/ (pl: -en) **1** regent **2** [Belg] teacher for lower classes in secondary school

de **regentijd** /reɣə(n)tɛit/ (pl: -en) rainy season, rains: *in de ~* during the rainy season

de **regenton** /reɣə(n)tɔn/ (pl: -nen) water butt

de **regenval** /reɣə(n)vɑl/ rain(fall); shower

de **regenvlaag** /reɣə(n)vlax/ (pl: -vlagen) scud,

rainy squall

het **regenwater** /reɣə(n)watər/ rainwater

de **regenworm** /reɣə(n)wɔrm/ (pl: -en) earthworm

het **regenwoud** /reɣə(n)waut/ (pl: -en) rainforest

regeren /rəɣerə(n)/ (regeerde, heeft geregeerd) rule (over); reign; govern, control: *de ~de partij* the party in power

de **regering** /rəɣerɪŋ/ (pl: -en) government: *de ~ is afgetreden* the government has resigned

het **regeringsbeleid** /rəɣerɪŋzbəlɛit/ government policy

het **regeringsbesluit** /rəɣerɪŋzbəslœyt/ (pl: -en) government decision

de **regeringsleider** /rəɣerɪŋslɛidər/ (pl: -s) leader of the government

de **regeringspartij** /rəɣerɪŋspɑrtɛi/ (pl: -en) party in office (*or:* power), government party

de **regeringsverklaring** /rəɣerɪŋsfərklarɪŋ/ (pl: -en) government policy statement

de **regie** /reʒi/ (pl: -s) direction, production || *de ~ kwijt zijn over iets* no longer be in charge of sth., lose one's hold over sth.; *de ~ voeren over iets* be in charge of sth.

het **regime** /reʒim/ (pl: -s) regime

het **regiment** /reʒimɛnt/ (pl: -en) regiment

de **regio** /reɣijo/ (pl: -'s) region, area: *in hogere ~nen* in higher spheres

het **regiokorps** /reɣijokɔrps/ (pl: -en) [Dutch] regional police force

regionaal /reɣ(i)jonal/ (adj, adv) regional

regisseren /reɣiserə(n)/ (regisseerde, heeft geregisseerd) direct, produce

de **regisseur** /reɣisør/ (pl: -s) director, producer

het **register** /rəɣɪstər/ (pl: -s) 1 register, record: *de ~s van de burgerlijke stand* the register of births, deaths and marriages; *een alfabetisch ~* an alphabetical register 2 index, table of contents

de **registeraccountant** /rəɣɪstərɑkauntənt/ (pl: -s) [Dutch] chartered accountant, certified public accountant

de **registratie** /reɣistra(t)si/ (pl: -s) registration

registreren /reɣistrerə(n)/ (registreerde, heeft geregistreerd) register, record

het **reglement** /reɣləmɛnt/ (pl: -en) regulation(s), rule(s); rule book; rules and regulations: *huishoudelijk ~* regulations

reglementair /reɣləmɛntɛːr/ (adj, adv) regulation, prescribed, official: *iets ~ vaststellen* prescribe sth.; *~ winnen* be declared the winner(s)

regressief /reɣrɛsif/ (adj, adv) regressive

reguleren /reɣylerə(n)/ (reguleerde, heeft gereguleerd) regulate, control, adjust

regulier /reɣylir/ (adj) regular, normal: [sport] *de ~e speeltijd* regular playing time

de **rehabilitatie** /rehabilita(t)si/ (pl: -s) rehabilitation, vindication

rehabiliteren /rehabiliterə(n)/ (rehabiliteerde, heeft gerehabiliteerd) rehabilitate, vindicate

de **rei** /rɛi/ (pl: -en) [Belg] town canal, city canal

de **reiger** /rɛiɣər/ (pl: -s) heron

reiken /rɛikə(n)/ (reikte, heeft gereikt) reach, extend: *zo ver het oog reikt* as far as the eye can see; *iem. de hand ~* hold out a hand to s.o.; [fig] reach out to s.o.

reikhalzend /rɛikhɑlzənt/ (adj) longingly, anxiously

de **reikwijdte** /rɛikwɛitə/ range, scope

reilen /rɛilə(n)/: *het ~ en zeilen van de politiek* the ins and outs of politics; *zoals het nu reilt en zeilt* as things are at the moment

rein /rɛin/ (adj, adv) clean || *~e dieren* clean animals

de **reïncarnatie** /rɛiŋkɑrna(t)si/ (pl: -s) reincarnation

het **reine** /rɛinə/: *in het ~ komen met zichzelf* sort oneself out, come to terms with one's conscience

reinigen /rɛinəɣə(n)/ (reinigde, heeft gereinigd) clean (up), wash; cleanse: *chemisch ~* dry-clean

de **reiniging** /rɛinəɣɪŋ/ cleaning, cleansing, washing, purification: *chemische ~* dry-cleaning

de **reinigingsdienst** /rɛinəɣɪŋzdinst/ (pl: -en) cleansing service (*or:* department)

het **reinigingsmiddel** /rɛinəɣɪŋsmɪdəl/ cleansing agent, clean(s)er; detergent

de **reis** /rɛis/ (pl: reizen) 1 trip, journey; voyage; passage; flight: *enkele ~* single (journey); [Am] one-way; *goede ~* have a good (*or:* pleasant) journey; *een ~ om de wereld maken* go round the world; *op ~ gaan* go on a journey 2 trip, tour: *een geheel verzorgde ~* a package tour (*or:* holiday)

het **reisbureau** /rɛizbyro/ (pl: -s) travel agency; travel agent's

de **reischeque** /rɛisʃɛk/ (pl: -s) traveller's cheque

het **reisgezelschap** /rɛisɣəzɛlsχɑp/ (pl: -pen) tour(ing) group (*or:* party); coach party

de **reisgids** /rɛisχɪts/ (pl: -en) 1 travel brochure (*or:* leaflet) 2 guidebook, (travel) guide 3 (travel) guide, courier

de **reiskosten** /rɛiskɔstə(n)/ (pl) travelling expenses: *reis- en verblijfkosten* travel and living expenses

de **reiskostenvergoeding** /rɛiskɔstə(n)vərɣudɪŋ/ (pl: -en) travelling allowance

de **reisleider** /rɛislɛidər/ (pl: -s) (travel, tour) guide, courier

de **reisorganisatie** /rɛisɔrɣaniza(t)si/ (pl: -s) travel organization (*or:* company), tour operator

de **reisorganisator** /rɛisɔrɣanizatɔr/ (pl: -en) tour operator

de **reisplanner** /rɛisplɛnər/ (pl: -s) journey

planner

de **reisverzekering** /rɛisfərzekərɪŋ/ (pl: -en) travel insurance

de **reiswieg** /rɛiswix/ (pl: -en) carrycot, portable crib

de **reisziekte** /rɛɪsiktə/ travel sickness

reizen /rɛizə(n)/ (reisde, heeft/is gereisd) travel, go on a trip (or: journey): *op en neer* ~ travel up and down; *per spoor* ~ travel by train

de **reiziger** /rɛizəɣər/ (pl: -s) **1** traveller, tourist; passenger: *~s naar Londen hier overstappen* passengers for London change here **2** travelling salesman

de **¹rek** /rɛk/ elasticity, give, flexibility: *de ~ is er uit* the party is over

het **²rek** /rɛk/ rack; shelves

rekbaar /rɛɡbar/ (adj) elastic: *een ~ begrip* an elastic concept, a broad notion

¹rekenen /rekənə(n)/ (rekende, heeft gerekend) **1** calculate, do sums (or: figures), reckon: *goed kunnen* ~ be good at figures; *in euro's* ~ calculate (or: think) in euros **2** consider, include, take into consideration (or: account): *daar had ik niet op gerekend* I hadn't counted on (or: expected) that; *daar mag je wel op* ~ you'd better allow for that **3** (+ op) rely, count on, trust: *kan ik op je* ~? can I count on you?; *reken maar niet op ons* count us out **4** (+ op) expect: *je kunt op 40 gasten* ~ you can expect 40 guests

²rekenen /rekənə(n)/ (rekende, heeft gerekend) **1** count: *alles bij elkaar gerekend* all told; in all **2** charge, ask: *hoeveel rekent u daarvoor?* how much do you charge for that? **3** count, number: *zich* ~ *tot* count o.s. as (or: among) **4** bear in mind, remember, allow for: *reken maar!* you bet!

de **rekenfout** /rekənfaut/ (pl: -en) miscalculation

het **Rekenhof** /rekənhɔf/ [Belg] (the) Treasury

de **rekening** /rekənɪŋ/ (pl: -en) **1** bill; [Am also] check; invoice: *een hoge ~* a stiff bill; *een ~ betalen* (or: *voldoen*) pay/settle an account (or: a bill); *ober, mag ik de ~?* waiter, may I have the bill please? **2** account: *iets in ~ brengen* charge for sth.; *een ~ openen (bij een bank)* open an account (at a bank); *op ~ van* at the expense of; *dat is voor mijn ~* I'll take care of that, leave that to me; *kosten voor zijn ~ nemen* pay the costs **3** (+ voor) expense: *voor eigen ~* at one's own expense ‖ *~ houden met iets* take sth. into account; *je moet een beetje ~ houden met je ouders* you should show some consideration for your parents

de **rekening-courant** /rekənɪŋkurɑnt/ (pl: rekeningen-courant) current account

de **rekeninghouder** /rekənɪŋhaudər/ (pl: -s) account holder

het **rekeningnummer** /rekənɪŋnʏmər/ account number

de **Rekenkamer** /rekə(n)kamər/ audit office, auditor's office

de **rekenkunde** /rekə(n)kʏndə/ arithmetic, maths

rekenkundig /rekə(n)kʏndəx/ (adj, adv) arithmetic(al)

de **rekenliniaal** /rekə(n)linijal/ (pl: -linialen) slide rule

de **rekenmachine** /rekə(n)maʃinə/ (pl: -s) calculator

de **rekenschap** /rekənsxɑp/ account, explanation: *ik ben u geen ~ verschuldigd* I don't owe you any explanation ‖ *zich ~ van iets geven* realise; give account of sth.

de **rekensom** /rekə(n)sɔm/ (pl: -men) **1** sum; number work **2** [fig] problem, question: *het is een eenvoudig ~metje* it's just a matter of adding two and two; *een eenvoudige ~ leert dat ...* it is easy to calculate that ...

het **rekenvoorbeeld** /rekənvorbelt/ (pl: -en) sample calculation

het **rekest** /rekɛst/ (pl: -en) petition

¹rekken /rɛkə(n)/ (rekte, heeft/is gerekt) stretch: *dat elastiek rekt niet goed meer* that elastic has lost its stretch

²rekken /rɛkə(n)/ (rekte, heeft gerekt) **1** stretch (out) **2** drag out, draw out; prolong: *het leven van een stervende* ~ prolong a dying person's life; [socc] *tijd* ~ use delaying tactics

rekruteren /rekrytərə(n)/ (rekruteerde, heeft gerekruteerd) recruit

de **rekruut** /rekryt/ (pl: rekruten) recruit

de **rekstok** /rɛkstɔk/ (pl: -ken) horizontal bar, high bar

het **rekwisiet** /rekwizit/ (pl: -en) (stage-)property, prop

de **rel** /rɛl/ (pl: -len) **1** disturbance, riot: *~letjes trappen* riot **2** [fig] storm, fuss, scandal: *een ~ in de media* a storm in the media; *een politieke ~* a political storm, political fuss; *een ~ schoppen* kick up (or: cause) a row

het **relaas** /rəlas/ (pl: relazen) account: *zijn ~ doen* tell one's story

het **relais** /rəlɛː/ relay

relateren /relatərə(n)/ (relateerde, heeft gerelateerd) relate

de **relatie** /rela(t)si/ (pl: -s) **1** relation(s), connection, relationship, contact: *~s onderhouden (met)* maintain relations (with); *in ~ staan tot* have relations with **2** affair, relationship: *een ~ hebben met iem.* have a relationship with s.o.

de **relatiebreuk** /rela(t)sibrøk/ break-up

het **relatiebureau** /rela(t)sibyro/ (pl: -s) dating agency

relatief /relatif/ (adj, adv) relative, comparative

het **relatiegeschenk** /rela(t)siɣəsxɛŋk/ (pl: -en) business gift

relationeel /rela(t)ʃonel/ (adj): *problemen in*

*de relationele **sfeer** domestic problems*
relativeren /relativɐrǝ(n)/ (relativeerde, heeft gerelativeerd) put into perspective
relaxed /rilɛkst/ (adj, adv) relaxed, cool, laid-back
relaxen /rilɛksǝ(n)/ (relaxte, heeft gerelaxt) relax
de **relaxfauteuil** /rilɛksfotœy/ (pl: -s) reclining armchair, recliner
relevant /relǝvɑnt/ (adj) relevant: *die **vraag** is niet* ~ that question is irrelevant
de **relevantie** /relǝvɑnsi/ relevance
het **reliëf** /reljɛf/ relief
de **religie** /reliɣi/ (pl: -s) religion
religieus /reliɣjøs/ (adj, adv) religious
de **relikwie** /relikwi/ relic
de **reling** /relɪŋ/ (pl: -en) rail
rellen /rɛlǝ(n)/ (relde, heeft gereld) start a riot: ~*de jongeren* rioting youths, young rioters
relschoppen /rɛlsχopǝ(n)/ start a riot: ~*de jongeren* young people causing trouble, rioting youths
de **relschopper** /rɛlsχopǝr/ (pl: -s) rioter, hooligan
de **rem** /rɛm/ (pl: -men) brake: *op de* ~ *gaan staan* slam (*or:* jam) on the brakes; *alle* ~*men losgooien* throw caution to the winds; [inform] let it all hang out, let one's hair down
de **rembekrachtiging** /rɛmbǝkrɑχtǝɣɪŋ/ power(-assisted) brakes
het **remblok** /rɛmblɔk/ (pl: -ken) brake block
het **rembours** /rɑmbuːrs/ (pl: -en) cash on delivery, COD: *onder* ~ *versturen* send (sth.) COD
het/de **remedie** /rǝmeːdi/ (pl: -s) remedy: *dat is de aangewezen* ~ that is the obvious remedy
de **remise** /rǝmiːzǝ/ (pl: -s) draw, tie, drawn game
het **remlicht** /rɛmlɪχt/ (pl: -en) brake light
remmen /rɛmǝ(n)/ (remde, heeft geremd) brake; [fig also] curb; check; inhibit: *geremd in zijn ontwikkeling* curbed in its development
de **remming** /rɛmɪŋ/ (pl: -en) check; [fig] inhibition
het/de **rempedaal** /rɛmpǝdal/ (pl: -pedalen) brake pedal
het **remspoor** /rɛmspoːr/ (pl: remsporen) skid mark
de **remweg** /rɛmwɛχ/ braking distance
de **ren** /rɛn/ run
de **renaissance** /renɛsɑ̃sǝ/ renaissance
de **renbaan** /rɛmban/ (pl: renbanen) (race)track, (race)course
rendabel /rɛndabǝl/ (adj) profitable, cost-effective
het **rendement** /rɛndǝmɛnt/ (pl: -en) **1** return, yield, output: *het* ~ *van obligaties* the return (*or:* yield) on bonds **2** efficiency, output, performance: *het* ~ *van een elektrische lamp* the efficiency (*or:* output) of an electric lamp
renderen /rɛndeːrǝ(n)/ (rendeerde, heeft

gerendeerd) pay (a profit): *niet* ~*d* not commercially viable
het **rendier** /rɛndir/ (pl: -en) reindeer
rennen /rɛnǝ(n)/ (rende, heeft/is gerend) run, race: *we zijn laat, we **moeten*** ~ we're late; we must dash (off) (*or:* must fly)
de **renner** /rɛnǝr/ (pl: -s) rider
de **renovatie** /renova(t)si/ (pl: -s) renovation, redevelopment
renoveren /renoveːrǝ(n)/ (renoveerde, heeft gerenoveerd) renovate; redevelop
het **renpaard** /rɛmpart/ (pl: -en) racehorse, thoroughbred
de **rentabiliteit** /rɛntabilitɛit/ productivity, cost-effectiveness, profitability
de **rente** /rɛntǝ/ (pl: -n, -s) interest: ~ *opbrengen* yield interest; ~ *op* ~ compound interest; *een lening **tegen** vijf procent* ~ a loan at five per cent interest
renteloos /rɛntǝlos/ (adj) **1** interest-free **2** non-productive
de **rentenier** /rɛntǝnir/ (pl: -s) person of independent (*or:* private) means
rentenieren /rɛntǝnirǝ(n)/ (rentenierde, heeft gerentenierd) **1** live off one's investments **2** lead a life of leisure
het **rentepercentage** /rɛntǝpɛrsɛntaʒǝ/ interest rate
de **rentestand** /rɛntǝstɑnt/ (pl: -en) interest rate
de **renteverhoging** /rɛntǝvǝrhoɣɪŋ/ rise in interest rates
de **renteverlaging** /rɛntǝvǝrlaɣɪŋ/ fall in interest rates
de **rentevoet** /rɛntǝvut/ interest rate, rate of interest
rentevrij /rɛntǝvrɛi/ (adj) interest-free, zero-interest
de **rentmeester** /rɛntmesstǝr/ (pl: -s) steward, manager
de **rentree** /rɑ̃tre/ (pl: -s) comeback, re-entry: *zijn* ~ *maken* make one's comeback
de **reorganisatie** /reɔrɣaniza(t)si/ (pl: -s) reorganization
reorganiseren /reɔrɣanizeːrǝ(n)/ (reorganiseerde, heeft gereorganiseerd) reorganize: *het **onderwijs*** ~ reorganize the educational system
de **rep** /rɛp/: *het hele land was in* ~ *en roer* the entire country was in (an) uproar
de **reparateur** /reparatøːr/ (pl: -s) repairer, repairman; service engineer
de **reparatie** /repara(t)si/ (pl: -s) repair: *mijn horloge is in (de)* ~ my watch is being repaired
repareren /repareːrǝ(n)/ (repareerde, heeft gerepareerd) repair, mend, fix: *dat **is** niet meer **te*** ~ it's beyond repair
repatriëren /repatrijeːrǝ(n)/ (repatrieerde, heeft gerepatrieerd) repatriate
het **repertoire** /repɛrtwaːr/ (pl: -s) repertoire, repertory: *het **klassieke*** ~ the classics; *zijn* ~

afwerken do one's repertoire

¹repeteren /repetere(n)/ (repeteerde, heeft gerepeteerd) **1** rehearse **2** repeat, circulate

²repeteren /repetere(n)/ (repeteerde, heeft gerepeteerd) rehearse; run through, go through

de **repetitie** /repeti(t)si/ (pl: -s) rehearsal; run-through; practice: *generale* ~ dress rehearsal; *final* (or: *last*) rehearsal

de **replica** /replika/ (pl: -'s) replica, copy

de **repliek** /replik/ (pl: -en) retort, response: *iem. van* ~ *dienen* put s.o. in his place

de **reportage** /reportaʒe/ (pl: -s) report, coverage; commentary: *de* ~ *van een voetbalwedstrijd* the coverage of a football match

de **reporter** /riporter/ (pl: -s) reporter

reppen /repe(n)/ (repte, heeft gerept) **1** mention **2** hurry, rush

de **represaille** /represajje/ (pl: -s) reprisal, retaliation: ~*s nemen* (tegen) retaliate (or: take reprisals) (against)

representatief /reprezentatif/ (adj) **1** representative (of), typical (of): *een representatieve groep van de bevolking* a cross-section of the population; *een representatieve steekproef* a representative sample **2** representative, presentable: *een representatieve functie* a representative position

representeren /reprezentere(n)/ (representeerde, heeft gerepresenteerd) represent

de **repressie** /represi/ (pl: -s) repression

repressief /represif/ (adj, adv) repressive

de **reprimande** /reprimande/ (pl: -s) reprimand; rebuke; talking-to

reproduceren /reprodysere(n)/ (reproduceerde, heeft gereproduceerd) reproduce, copy

de **reproductie** /reprodyksi/ (pl: -s) reproduction, copy

het **reptiel** /reptil/ (pl: -en) reptile

de **republiek** /republik/ (pl: -en) republic

de **republikein** /republikein/ (pl: -en) republican

republikeins /republikeins/ (adj, adv) republican

de **reputatie** /repyta(t)si/ (pl: -s) reputation, name; fame: *een goede* (or: *slechte*) ~ *hebben* have a good (or: bad) reputation; *iemands* ~ *schaden, slecht zijn voor iemands* ~ damage s.o.'s reputation

het **requiem** /rekwijɛm/ (pl: -s) requiem (mass)

de **research** /risy:rtʃ/ research

het **reservaat** /rezɛrvat/ (pl: reservaten) reserve, preserve: *indianenreservaat* Indian reservation; *natuurreservaat* nature reserve

de **reserve** /rezɛrve/ (pl: -s) **1** reserve(s): *zijn* ~*s aanspreken* draw on one's reserves **2** reserve, reservation: *zonder enige* ~ without reservations

de **reservebank** /rezɛrvebaŋk/ (pl: -en) reserve(s') bench, sub bench

het **reserveonderdeel** /rezɛrveonderdel/ (pl: -onderdelen) spare part

reserveren /rezɛrvere(n)/ (reserveerde, heeft gereserveerd) **1** reserve, put aside (or: away, by): *1000 euro* ~ *voor* set aside 1000 euros for; *een artikel voor iem.* ~ put aside an article for s.o. **2** book, reserve: *een tafel* ~ reserve (or: book) a table

de **reservering** /rezɛrverɪŋ/ (pl: -en) booking, reservation

de **reservesleutel** /rezɛrvesløtəl/ (pl: -s) spare key

het **reservewiel** /rezɛrvewil/ (pl: -en) spare wheel

het **reservoir** /rezɛrvwar/ (pl: -s) reservoir, tank

resetten /risɛte(n)/ (resette, heeft gereset) reset

resistent /rezistɛnt/ (adj) resistant (to): ~ *worden tegen antibiotica* become resistant (or: immune) to antibiotics

de **resolutie** /rezolytsi/ (pl: -s) resolution

resoluut /rezolyt/ (adj, adv) resolute, determined

resoneren /rezonere(n)/ (resoneerde, heeft geresoneerd) resonate

het **resort** /rizɔːrt/ (pl: -s) resort

resp. *respectievelijk* resp (respectively)

het **respect** /rɛspɛkt/ respect; regard; deference: ~ *afdwingen* command respect; *voor iets (iem.)* ~ *tonen* show respect for sth. (s.o.); *met alle* ~ with all (due) respect

respectabel /rɛspɛktabəl/ (adj, adv) respectable; considerable

respecteren /rɛspɛktere(n)/ (respecteerde, heeft gerespecteerd) respect, appreciate: *zichzelf* ~*d* self-respecting; *iemands opvattingen* ~ respect s.o.'s views

respectievelijk /rɛspɛktivələk/ (adj, adv) respective: *bedragen van* ~ *10, 20 en 30 euro* sums of 10, 20 and 30 euros respectively

respectloos /rɛspɛktlos/ (adj) disrespectful: *iem.* ~ *behandelen* treat s.o. disrespectfully

het **respijt** /rɛspɛit/ respite, grace, delay

het/de **respons** /rɛspɔns/ response, reaction

responsief /rɛsponsif/ (adj) responsive: ~ *ontwerp* responsive design

het **ressentiment** /rɛsɛntimɛnt/ (pl: -en) resentment

het **ressort** /rɛsɔrt/ (pl: -en) [Dutch] jurisdiction

ressorteren /rɛsɔrtere(n)/ (ressorteerde, heeft geressorteerd): ~ *onder* come under

de **rest** /rɛst/ (pl: -en) rest, remainder: *de* ~ *van het materiaal* the remainder of the material; *voor de* ~ *geen nieuws* otherwise no news

het **restant** /rɛstɑnt/ (pl: -en) remainder, remnant

het **restaurant** /rɛstorɑnt/ (pl: -s) restaurant

de **restauratie** /rɛstora(t)si/ (pl: -s) restoration

restaureren /rɛstorere(n)/ (restaureerde, heeft gerestaureerd) restore

resten /rɛste(n)/ (restte, heeft/is gerest) re-

main, be left: *hem* restte niets meer dan ...
there was nothing left for him but to ...; *nu
rest mij* nog te verklaren ... now it only remains for me to say ...
resteren /rɛstē̯rə(n)/ (resteerde, is geres-
teerd) be left, remain
restitueren /rɛstitywē̯rə(n)/ (restitueerde,
heeft gerestitueerd) refund, pay back

de **restitutie** /rɛstity(t)si/ (pl: -s) refund

het **restje** /rɛʃə/ (pl: -s): *ik heb nog een ~ van gisteren* I've got a few scraps (left over) from
yesterday

de **restrictie** /rɛstrɪksi/ (pl: -s) restriction

de **restwarmte** /rɛstwɑrmtə/ residual heat (*or:*
warmth)
restylen /ristɑ̯jlə(n)/ give sth./s.o. a makeover

het **resultaat** /rezyltā̯t/ (pl: resultaten) **1** result,
effect, outcome: *het plan had het beoogde ~*
the plan had the desired effect; *resultaten
behalen* achieve results; *met het ~ dat ...* with
the result that ...; *zonder ~* with no result
2 result; returns
resulteren /rezyltē̯rə(n)/ (resulteerde,
heeft geresulteerd) result: *het daaruit ~de
verlies* the loss resulting from it, the resulting
loss; *~ in* result in, lead up to; *dit heeft geresulteerd in zijn ontslag* this has resulted in his
dismissal; *wanneer het signaal sterk is dan zal
dat ~ in een goede ontvangst* if the signal is
strong, high quality reception will be the result; *wat resulteert is ...* the result (*or:* outcome, upshot) is ...

het **resumé** /rezymē̯/ (pl: -s) summary, abstract
resumeren /rezymē̯rə(n)/ (resumeerde,
heeft geresumeerd) **1** summarize **2** recapitulate

de **resusfactor** /rē̯zysfɑktɔr/ (pl: -en) Rhesus
factor
rete- /rē̯tə/ very

de **retoriek** /retorī̯k/ rhetoric: *holle ~* empty
rhetoric
retorisch /retorī̯s/ (adj, adv) rhetorical: *een
~e vraag* a rhetorical question

de **retort** /rətɔ̄rt/ (pl: -en) retort
retoucheren /retuʃē̯rə(n)/ (retoucheerde,
heeft geretoucheerd) retouch, touch up

het ¹**retour** /rətū̯r/ (pl: -s) return (ticket); [Am]
round-trip (ticket): *een ~ eerste klas Utrecht* a
first-class return (ticket) to Utrecht; *op zijn ~*
past his (*or:* its) best
²**retour** /rətū̯r/ (adv) back: *~ komen* come
back, be returned; *~ afzender* return to
sender; *drie euro ~* three euros change

het **retourbiljet** /rətū̯rbɪljɛt/ (pl: -ten) return
ticket; [Am] round-trip ticket

de **retourenveloppe** /rətū̯rɛnvəlɔp/ (pl: -n)
self-addressed envelope
retourneren /returnē̯rə(n)/ (retourneerde,
heeft geretourneerd) return
retourpinnen /rətū̯rpɪnə(n)/ (pinde retour,

heeft retourgepind) refund (a customer via a
PIN pad)

het **retourtje** /rətū̯rcə/ return; [Am] round-trip

de **retourvlucht** /rətū̯rvlʏxt/ (pl: -en) **1** return
flight **2** return flight; [Am] round-trip flight

het **retrospectief** /retrospɛktī̯f/ (pl: retrospec-
tieven) retrospective: *in ~* in retrospect

de **return** /rity̆ːrn/ (pl: -s) **1** return **2** return
match, return game **3** return: *een harde ~* a
hard return; *een zachte ~* a soft return

de **retweet** /rī̯twiːt/ (pl: -s) retweet
retweeten /ritwī̯ːtə(n)/ (retweette, heeft
geretweet) retweet

de **reu** /rø/ (pl: -en) male dog

de **reuk** /røk/ (pl: -en) **1** smell, odour: *een onaangename ~ verspreiden* give off an unpleasant smell **2** smell; scent: *op de ~ afgaan*
hunt by scent
reukloos /rø̆klos/ (adj, adv) odourless;
scentless

de **reukzin** /rø̆ksɪn/ (sense of) smell

het **reuma** /rø̆ma/ rheumatism
reumatisch /rømatī̯s/ (adj) rheumatic

de **reünie** /rejynī̯/ (pl: -s) reunion

de **reuring** /rø̆rɪŋ/ [Dutch] **1** buzz, hum **2** stir:
voor ~ zorgen cause a stir (*or:* an uproar),
rock the boat

de **reus** /røs/ (pl: reuzen) giant
reusachtig /røzɑ̆xtəx/ (adj) **1** gigantic,
huge **2** great, terrific
reuze /rø̆zə/ (adv) [inform] enormously: *~
veel* an awful lot; *~ bedankt* thanks awfully

de **reuzel** /rø̆zəl/ (pl: -s) lard

het **reuzenrad** /rø̆zə(n)rɑt/ (pl: -eren) Ferris
wheel

de **revalidatie** /revalidā̯(t)si/ rehabilitation

het **revalidatiecentrum** /revalidā̯(t)sisɛntrʏm/
(pl: -centra) rehabilitation centre
revalideren /revalidē̯rə(n)/ (revalideerde,
heeft/is gerevalideerd) recover, convalesce

de **revaluatie** /revalywā̯(t)si/ revaluation
revalueren /revalywē̯rə(n)/ (revalueerde,
heeft gerevalueerd) revalue

de **revanche** /revɑ̃̄ʃ/ revɛnge: *~ nemen (op iem.)*
take revenge (on s.o.)

zich **revancheren** /rəvɑ̃ʃē̯rə(n)/ (revancheerde
zich, heeft zich gerevancheerd) revenge
(o.s.), be revenged

de **revers** /rəvɛ̄ːr/ lapel
reviseren /revizē̯rə(n)/ (reviseerde, heeft
gereviseerd) overhaul

de **revisie** /revī̯zi/ (pl: -s) **1** revision; review
2 overhaul, going-over

de **revolte** /revɔ̆ltə/ (pl: -s) revolt, insurgence

de **revolutie** /revoly̆(t)si/ (pl: -s) revolution: *de
Amerikaanse Revolutie* the American War of
Independence
revolutionair /revoly(t)ʃonɛ̄ːr/ (adj, adv)
revolutionary: *een ~e ontdekking* a revolutionary discovery

de **revolver** /revɔ̆lvər/ (pl: -s) revolver

de **revue** /rəvy̆/ (pl: -s) **1** revue, show **2** review
Rhodos /rodɔs/ Rhodes

het/de **Riagg** /rijɑχ/ [Dutch] *Regionale Instelling voor Ambulante Geestelijke Gezondheidszorg* regional institute for mental welfare

riant /rijɑnt/ (adj, adv) ample, spacious: *een ~e villa* a spacious villa

de **rib** /rɪp/ (pl: -ben) rib: *een gebroken ~* a broken (*or:* fractured) rib; *een gekneusde ~* a bruised rib; *de zwevende ~ben* the floating ribs; *je kunt zijn ~ben tellen* he is a bag of bones || *dat is een ~ uit je lijf* that costs an arm and a leg

de **ribbel** /rɪbəl/ (pl: -s) rib, ridge; ripple

de **ribbelstrook** /rɪbəlstrok/ (pl: -stroken) tactile paving

de **ribbenkast** /rɪbə(n)kɑst/ (pl: -en) rib cage

de **ribbroek** /rɪbruk/ (pl: -en) cord(uroy) trousers

de **ribeye** /rɪpɑj/ ribeye

het **ribfluweel** /rɪpflywel/ cord(uroy)

de **ribkarbonade** /rɪpkɑrbonɑdə/ (pl: -s) [Dutch] rib chop

de **richel** /rɪχəl/ (pl: -s) ledge, ridge

¹**richten** /rɪχtə(n)/ (richtte, heeft gericht) **1** direct, aim, orient: *gericht op* aimed at, directed at, oriented towards; *zijn ogen op iets ~ focus one's eyes on sth.; *het geweer op iem. ~* aim a gun at s.o. **2** direct, address; extend: *een brief, aan mij gericht* a letter addressed to me; *een vraag ~ tot de voorzitter* direct a question to the chairman **3** align: *naar het oosten gericht* facing east

zich ²**richten** /rɪχtə(n)/ (richtte zich, heeft zich gericht) **1** (+ tot) address (o.s. to): *richt u met klachten tot ons bureau* address any complaints to our office **2** (+ naar) conform to: *zich ~ naar de omstandigheden* be guided by circumstances

de **richting** /rɪχtɪŋ/ (pl: -en) direction: *zij gingen ~ Amsterdam* they went in the direction of (*or:* they headed for) Amsterdam; *iem. een zetje in de goede ~ geven* give s.o. a push in the right direction; [traf] *~ aangeven* indicate direction, signal; *dat komt aardig in de ~* that's looks sth. like it; *van ~ veranderen* change direction; [fig] *~ geven aan iets get* sth. moving in the right direction

de **richtingaanwijzer** /rɪχtɪŋanwɛizər/ (pl: -s) (direction) indicator

de **richtingscoëfficiënt** /rɪχtɪŋskoɛfiʃɛnt/ (pl: -en) [maths] gradient, slope

het **richtingsgevoel** /rɪχtɪŋsɣəvul/ sense of direction

de **richtlijn** /rɪχtlɛin/ (pl: -en) guideline; directions: *iets volgens de ~en uitvoeren* do sth. in the prescribed way

de **richtmicrofoon** /rɪχtmikrofon/ (pl: -s) directional microphone

het **richtsnoer** /rɪχtsnur/ (pl: -en) guideline; directions

de **ridder** /rɪdər/ (pl: -s) knight: *iem. tot ~ slaan* dub s.o. a knight; knight s.o.

ridderen /rɪdərə(n)/ (ridderde, heeft geridderd) knight: *geridderd worden* be knighted, receive a knighthood

ridderlijk /rɪdərlək/ (adj) chivalrous || *hij kwam er ~ voor uit* he frankly (*or:* openly) admitted it

de **ridderorde** /rɪdərɔrdə/ (pl: -n, -s) knighthood, order

de **ridderzaal** /rɪdərzal/ (pl: -zalen) great hall: [Netherlands] *de Ridderzaal* (the) Knights' Hall

ridicuul /ridikyl/ (adj, adv) ridiculous

de **riedel** /rɪdəl/ (pl: -s) tune, jingle

de **riek** /rik/ (pl: -en) (three-pronged) fork

rieken /rikə(n)/ (rook/riekte, heeft geroken) smack (of), smell (of), reek (of): *die riekt naar verraad* this smacks of treason

de **riem** /rim/ (pl: -en) **1** belt **2** strap; belt; sling; leash **3** seat belts

het **riet** /rit/ reed; cane

rieten /ritə(n)/ (adj) reed; rush; cane; wicker(work): *~ stoel* cane (*or:* wicker) chair; *~ dak* thatched roof

het **rietje** /riĉə/ (pl: -s) **1** straw **2** reed

de **rietsuiker** /ritsœykər/ cane sugar

het **rif** /rɪf/ (pl: -fen) reef

rigoureus /riɣorøs/ (adj, adv) rigorous

de **rij** /rɛi/ (pl: -en) **1** row, line: *~en auto's* rows of cars; queues of cars; *een ~ bomen* a line of trees; *een ~ mensen* a) a row of people; b) a line (*or:* queue) of people; *in de eerste* (*or:* *voorste*) *~en* in the front seats (*or:* rows); *in de ~ staan* queue; [Am] stand in line; [fig] *de ~en sluiten* close (up) the ranks **2** row; string: *een ~ getallen* a) a column of figures; b) a row of figures; *ze niet allemaal op een ~tje hebben* have a screw loose

de **rijbaan** /rɛiban/ (pl: rijbanen) roadway; lane: *weg met gescheiden rijbanen* dual carriageway

het **rijbewijs** /rɛibəwɛis/ (pl: rijbewijzen) driving licence; [Am] driver's license: *z'n ~ halen* pass one's driving test; *groot ~* large goods vehicle licence; [Am] commercial driver's license

de **rijbroek** /rɛibruk/ (pl: -en) jodhpurs, riding breeches

rijden /rɛidə(n)/ (reed, heeft/is gereden) **1** drive; ride: *honderd kilometer per uur ~* drive (*or:* do) a hundred kilometres an hour; *het is twee uur ~* it's a two-hour drive; *hij werd bekeurd omdat hij te hard reed* he was fined for speeding; *door het rode licht ~* go through a red light; *in een auto ~* drive (in) a car; *op een (*or:* *te*) *paard ~* ride a horse (*or:* on horseback) **2** drive [car]; ride; move; run; do: *hoeveel heeft je auto al gereden?* how many miles (*or:* kilometres) has your car done?; *(te) dicht op elkaar ~* not keep one's distance; *de tractor* *rijdt op dieselolie* the tractor runs (*or:* operates) on diesel oil; *die auto rijdt lekker* that car is pleasant to drive **3** skate

rijdend /rɛidənt/ (adj) **1** mobile: *~e bibliotheek* mobile (*or:* travelling) library; [Am] bookmobile **2** moving

de **rijder** /rɛidər/ (pl: -s) rider; driver [car]; cyclist

het **rijdier** /rɛidir/ (pl: -en) riding animal, mount

rijendik /rɛijə(n)dɪk/ (adj) packed

het **rijexamen** /rɛiɛksamə(n)/ (pl: -s) driving test: *~ doen* take one's driving test

het **rijgedrag** /rɛiхədrɑх/ driving (behaviour), motoring performance

rijgen /rɛiуə(n)/ (reeg, heeft geregen) thread, string

de **rijglaars** /rɛiхlars/ (pl: -laarzen) lace-up boot

de **rijinstructeur** /rɛiɪnstrүktør/ (pl: -s) driving instructor

het **¹rijk** /rɛik/ (pl: -en) **1** realm; state; kingdom; empire: *het Britse Rijk* the British Empire; *het ~ der hemelen* the Kingdom of Heaven; *het Derde Rijk* the Third Reich; *iets naar het ~ der fabelen verwijzen* dismiss sth. as a myth **2** [Dutch] government, State: *door het Rijk gefinancierd* State-financed ‖ *het ~ alleen hebben* have the place (all) to o.s.

²rijk /rɛik/ (adj) **1** rich, wealthy: *stinkend ~ zijn* be filthy rich **2** rich; fertile; generous: *hij heeft een ~e verbeelding* he has a fertile imagination ‖ *ik ben je liever kwijt dan ~* I'd rather see the back of you

de **rijkaard** /rɛikart/ (pl: -s) rich person; moneybags

de **rijkdom** /rɛiɡdɔm/ (pl: -men) **1** wealth, affluence **2** resource: *natuurlijke ~men* natural resources

rijkelijk /rɛikələk/ (adj, adv) rich, copious, sumptuous, in abundance: *~ versierd* richly decorated; *een ~ maal* a sumptuous meal; *iem. ~ belonen* reward s.o. handsomely; *het bier vloeide ~* the beer flowed freely; *die maatregel kwam ~ laat* the measure came way too late

de **rijkelui** /rɛikəlœy/ (pl) [inform] rich people

het **rijkeluiskind** /rɛikəlœyskɪnt/ (pl: -eren) [inform] rich man's son, rich man's daughter

rijklaar /rɛiklar/ (adj): *een auto ~ maken* prepare a car for sale; *deze tweedehands fiets is ~* this second-hand bike is ready to go

de **rijksambtenaar** /rɛiksɑmtənar/ (pl: -ambtenaren) public servant

de **rijksbegroting** /rɛiksbəуrotɪŋ/ (pl: -en) [Dutch] (national) budget

de **rijksdaalder** /rɛiksdaldər/ (pl: -s) two-and-a-half guilder coin

de **rijksdienst** /rɛiksdinst/ (pl: -en) national agency

de **rijksinstelling** /rɛiksɪnstɛlɪŋ/ government institution (*or:* institute)

het **rijksmuseum** /rɛiksmyzejʏm/ (pl: -musea) national museum; national gallery

de **rijksoverheid** /rɛiksovərhɛit/ (pl: -heden) central government, national government

de **rijkspolitie** /rɛikspoli(t)si/ [Dutch] national police (force)

het **rijksregisternummer** /rɛiksrəуɪstərnʏmər/ [Belg] Citizen Service Number (CSN)

de **rijksuniversiteit** /rɛiksyniverzitɛit/ (pl: -en) state university

de **Rijksvoorlichtingsdienst** /rɛiksforlɪхtɪŋzdinst/ [Dutch] government information service

de **rijkswacht** /rɛikswɑхt/ [Belg] state police

de **rijkswachter** /rɛikswɑхtər/ (pl: -s) [Belg] state policeman

Rijkswaterstaat /rɛikswatərstat/ [Dutch] [roughly] Department (*or:* Ministry) of Waterways and Public Works

de **rijksweg** /rɛikswɛх/ (pl: -en) national trunk road; [Am] state highway

de **rijlaars** /rɛilars/ (pl: -laarzen) riding boot

de **rijles** /rɛilɛs/ (pl: -sen) driving lesson; riding lesson: *~ nemen* take driving (*or:* riding) lessons

het **rijm** /rɛim/ (pl: -en) rhyme; verse: *op ~* rhyming, in rhyme

de **rijmelarij** /rɛiməlarɛi/ (pl: -en) doggerel (verse)

rijmen /rɛimə(n)/ (rijmde, heeft gerijmd) **1** be in rhyme (*or:* verse), rhyme (with): *deze woorden ~ op elkaar* these words rhyme (with each other) **2** rhyme, versify ‖ *dat viel niet te ~ met ...* that could not be reconciled with ...

het **rijmpje** /rɛimpjə/ (pl: -s) rhyme, short verse

de **Rijn** /rɛin/ Rhine

de **rijnaak** /rɛinak/ (pl: rijnaken) Rhine barge

de **¹rijp** /rɛip/ (white) frost, hoarfrost

²rijp /rɛip/ (adj) **1** ripe: *~ maken (worden)* ripen, mature **2** mature: *op ~ere leeftijd* at a ripe age **3** (+ voor) ripe (for), ready (for): *~ voor de sloop* ready for the scrap heap **4** serious: *na ~ beraad* after careful consideration

het **rijpaard** /rɛipart/ (pl: -en) saddle horse

rijpen /rɛipə(n)/ (rijpte, heeft/is gerijpt) ripen; mature

de **rijpheid** /rɛiphɛit/ ripeness, maturity: *tot ~ komen* ripen, mature

de **rijschool** /rɛisхol/ (pl: rijscholen) driving school; riding school (*or:* academy)

het **rijshout** /rɛishaut/ osier, brush(wood)

de **rijst** /rɛist/ rice

de **rijstebrij** /rɛistəbrɛi/ rice pudding

de **rijstijl** /rɛistɛil/ (pl: -en) driving style

de **rijstkorrel** /rɛistkorəl/ (pl: -s) grain of rice

de **rijstrook** /rɛistrok/ (traffic) lane

de **rijsttafel** /rɛistafəl/ (pl: -s) (Indonesian) rice meal

de **rijstwafel** /rɛistwafəl/ (pl: -s) rice cake

de **rijtijd** /rɛitɛit/ (pl: -en) driving time; travel time het **rijtjeshuis** /rɛ̲icəshœys/ (pl: -huizen) [Dutch] terrace(d) house; [Am] row house

het **rijtuig** /rɛ̲itœyx/ (pl: -en) **1** carriage **2** carriage; [Am] car

de **rijvaardigheid** /rɛivɑ̲rdəxhɛit/ driving ability (or: proficiency)

het **rijverbod** /rɛ̲ɪvərbɔt/ (pl: -en) driving ban

de **rijweg** /rɛ̲iwɛx/ (pl: -en) road(way)

het **rijwiel** /rɛ̲iwil/ (pl: -en) (bi)cycle

het **rijwielpad** /rɛ̲iwilpɑt/ (pl: -en) cycle path, cycle track

de **rijwielstalling** /rɛ̲iwilstɑlɪŋ/ (pl: -en) (bi)cycle lock-up

rijzen /rɛ̲izə(n)/ (rees, is gerezen) rise: *laat het deeg ~* leave the dough to rise; *de prijzen ~ de pan uit* prices are soaring

rijzig /rɛ̲ɪzəx/ (adj, adv) tall: *~ van gestalte* tall in build (or: stature)

de **rikketik** /rɪ̲kətɪk/ (pl: -ken) ticker

de **riksja** /rɪ̲kʃa/ (pl: -'s) rickshaw

rillen /rɪ̲lə(n)/ (rilde, heeft gerild) shiver, shudder, tremble: *hij rilde van de kou* he shivered with cold

rillerig /rɪ̲lərəx/ (adj) shivery

de **rilling** /rɪ̲lɪŋ/ (pl: -en) shiver, shudder, tremble: *koude ~en hebben* have the shakes (or: shivers); *er liep een ~ over mijn rug* a shiver ran down my spine

de **rimboe** /rɪ̲mbu/ (pl: -s) jungle

de **rimpel** /rɪ̲mpəl/ (pl: -s) wrinkle: *een gezicht vol ~s* a wrinkled face

rimpelen /rɪ̲mpələ(n)/ (rimpelde, heeft/is gerimpeld) **1** wrinkle (up): *het voorhoofd ~* wrinkle one's forehead **2** crinkle (up)

rimpelig /rɪ̲mpələx/ (adj) wrinkled: *een ~e appel* a wizened apple

de **ring** /rɪŋ/ (pl: -en) ring

de **ringbaard** /rɪ̲ŋbart/ (pl: -en) goatee and moustache, ringbeard

de **ringband** /rɪ̲ŋbɑnt/ (pl: -en) ring-binder

ringeloren /rɪ̲ŋəlorə(n)/: *zich laten ~* let o.s. be bullied (or: browbeat)

ringen /rɪ̲ŋə(n)/ (ringde, heeft geringd) ring

de **ringmap** /rɪ̲ŋmɑp/ (pl: -pen) ring-binder

de **ringslang** /rɪ̲ŋslɑŋ/ (pl: -en) grass snake, ring(ed) snake

de **ringtone** /rɪ̲ŋton/ ring tone

de **ringvaart** /rɪ̲ŋvart/ (pl: -en) ring canal, belt canal

de **ringvinger** /rɪ̲ŋvɪŋər/ (pl: -s) ring finger

de **ringweg** /rɪ̲ŋwɛx/ (pl: -en) ring road

de **ringworm** /rɪ̲ŋwɔrm/ (pl: -en) ringworm

rinkelen /rɪ̲ŋkələ(n)/ (rinkelde, heeft gerinkeld) jingle, tinkle; ring; chink: *~de ruiten* rattling panes of glass; *de ~de tamboerijn* the jingling tambourine

de **rinoceros** /rinos̲erɔs/ (pl: -sen) rhinoceros, rhino

de **riolering** /rijol̲erɪŋ/ (pl: -en) sewerage, sewer system

het **riool** /rijo̲l/ (pl: riolen) sewer: *een open ~* an open sewer

de **riooljournalistiek** /rijol̲ʒurnalɪstik/ gutter journalism

de **rioolwaterzuivering** /rijo̲lwatərzœyvərɪŋ/ **1** sewage treatment **2** sewage works (or: plant)

het **risico** /ri̲ziko/ (pl: -'s) risk: *dat behoort tot de ~'s van het vak* that's an occupational hazard; *het ~ lopen (van)* run the risk (of); *te veel ~'s nemen* run too many risks; *op eigen ~* at one's own risk; *voor ~ van de eigenaar* at the owner's risk; *geen ~ willen nemen* not want to take any chances

risicodragend /rizikodra̲yənt/ (adj) risk-bearing

de **risicogroep** /ri̲zikoyrup/ (pl: -en) high-risk group

de **risicowedstrijd** /ri̲zikowɛtstrɛɪt/ high-risk match

riskant /rɪskɑ̲nt/ (adj) risky: *een ~e onderneming* a risky enterprise

riskeren /rɪske̲rə(n)/ (riskeerde, heeft geriskeerd) risk

de **rit** /rɪt/ (pl: -ten) **1** ride, run; drive: *een ~je maken* go for a ride **2** [cycling] stage, ride: *[fig] de zaak weer op ~ krijgen* get things back on track (or: the rails)

het **ritme** /rɪ̲tmə/ (pl: -s) rhythm: *uit zijn ~ raken* lose one's rhythm

ritmisch /rɪ̲tmis/ (adj, adv) rhythmic(al): *~ bewegen* move rhythmically

de **rits** /rɪts/ (pl: -en) **1** zipper, zip **2** bunch; string; batch; battery: *een ~ kinderen* a whole string of children

ritselen /rɪ̲tsələ(n)/ (ritselde, heeft geritseld) rustle: *ik hoor een muis ~ achter het behang* I can hear a mouse scuffling behind the wallpaper; *~ met* een papiertje rustle a paper

ritsen /rɪ̲tsə(n)/ (ritste, heeft geritst) zipper merge, merge alternately

de **ritssluiting** /rɪ̲tslœytɪŋ/ (pl: -en) zipper, zip: *kun je me even helpen met mijn ~?* can you help zip me up? (or: unzip me?)

het **¹ritueel** /rityw̲el/ (pl: rituelen) ritual
²ritueel /rityw̲el/ (adj) ritual

de **ritzege** /rɪ̲tseyə/ (pl: -s) stage victory: *een ~ behalen* win a stage

de **rivaal** /riva̲l/ (pl: rivalen) rival

de **rivaliteit** /rivalit̲eit/ rivalry

de **rivier** /rivi̲r/ (pl: -en) river: *een ~ oversteken* cross a river; *een huis aan de ~* a house on the river

de **Rivièra** /rivjɛ̲:ra/ Riviera

de **rivierarm** /rivi̲rɑrm/ (pl: -en) arm of a river

de **riviermond** /rivi̲rmɔnt/ (pl: -en) river mouth; estuary

de **rob** /rɔp/ (pl: -ben) seal

de **robbenjacht** /rɔ̲bə(n)jɑxt/ seal hunting

de **¹robijn** /robɛ̲in/ [gem] ruby

het **²robijn** /robɛ̲in/ [mineral] ruby

de **robot** /ro̲bɔt/ (pl: -s) robot: *hij lijkt wel een ~*

he is like a robot

de **robotfoto** /rǫbotfoto/ (pl: -'s) [Belg] photo-fit

de **robotstofzuiger** /rǫbotstofsœyɣər/ (pl: -s) robot vacuum cleaner

robuust /robyst/ (adj, adv) robust; solid: *een ~e gezondheid* robust health

de **rochel** /rǫχəl/ (pl: -s) **1** lump of spit **2** hawk

rochelen /rǫχələ(n)/ (rochelde, heeft gerocheld) hawk (up)

de **rock-'n-roll** /rokənrǫl/ rock 'n' roll

de **rockzanger** /rǫksaŋər/ (pl: -s) rock singer

het **rococo** /rokokǫ/ rococo

de **roddel** /rǫdəl/ (pl: -s) gossip: *de nieuwste ~s uit de showwereld* the latest gossip in show business; *~ en achterklap* gossip

de **roddelaar** /rǫdəlar/ (pl: -s) gossip

het **roddelblad** /rǫdəlblɑt/ (pl: -en) gossip magazine

roddelen /rǫdələ(n)/ (roddelde, heeft geroddeld) gossip (about)

de **roddelpers** /rǫdəlpɛrs/ gutter press, gossip papers

de **rodehond** /rodəhǫnt/ German measles, rubella

de **rodekool** /rodəkǫl/ (pl: -kolen) red cabbage

het **Rode Kruis** /rodəkrœys/ Red Cross

de **rodelbaan** /rǫdəlban/ (pl: -banen) toboggan run; luge run

rodelen /rǫdələ(n)/ (rodelde, heeft/is gerodeld) toboggan; luge run

de **rodeo** /rodejo/ (pl: -'s) rodeo

de **rododendron** /rododɛndron/ (pl: -s) rhododendron

de **roe** /ru/ (pl: -s) rod

de **roebel** /rubəl/ (pl: -s) rouble

de **roede** /rudə/ (pl: -n, -s) rod

het **roedel** /rudəl/ (pl: -s) herd; pack

de **roeibaan** /rujban/ (pl: -banen) rowing course

de **roeiboot** /rujbot/ (pl: -boten) rowing boat

roeien /rujə(n)/ (roeide, heeft/is geroeid) row: *met grote slagen ~* take big strokes

de **roeier** /rujər/ (pl: -s) rower, oarsman

de **roeispaan** /rujspan/ (pl: -spanen) oar; scull; paddle

de **roeiwedstrijd** /rujwɛtstrɛit/ (pl: -en) boat race, rowing race; regatta

roekeloos /rukəlos/ (adj, adv) reckless: *~ rijden* drive recklessly

de **roem** /rum/ glory, fame, renown: *op zijn ~ teren* rest on one's laurels

de **Roemeen** /rumęn/ (pl: Roemenen) Romanian

het **Roemeens** /rumęns/ Romanian

roemen /rumə(n)/ (roemde, heeft geroemd) praise, speak highly of

Roemenië /rumęnijə/ Romania

de **roemer** /rumər/ (pl: -s) rummer

roemloos /rumlos/ (adj) inglorious: *~ ten onder gaan* lose unceremoniously

roemrijk /rumrɛik/ (adj, adv) glorious: *een ~ verleden* a glorious past

roemrucht /rumryχt/ (adj) illustrious, renowned

de **roep** /rup/ call; cry; shout

¹**roepen** /rupə(n)/ (riep, heeft geroepen) call, cry, shout; clamour: *om hulp ~* call (*or:* cry) out for help; *een ~de in de woestijn* a voice (crying) in the wilderness

²**roepen** /rupə(n)/ (riep, heeft geroepen) **1** call, summon: *de ober ~* call the waiter; *iem. op het matje ~* carpet s.o.; *de plicht roept (mij)* duty calls; *ik zal je om zeven uur ~* I'll call you at seven; *je komt als geroepen* (you're) just the person we need; *daar voel ik mij niet toe geroepen* I don't quite feel like it **2** [depr] proclaim: *je roept dat nu wel, maar ...* you say that now, but ...; *van alles ~ over buitenlanders* say all kinds of (nasty) things about foreigners

de **roepia** /rupija/ (pl: -'s) rupiah

de **roeping** /rupɪŋ/ (pl: -en) vocation, mission, calling

de **roepnaam** /rupnam/ (pl: -namen) nickname

het **roer** /rur/ (pl: -en) **1** rudder **2** helm; tiller: *het ~ niet uit handen geven* remain at the helm; *het ~ omgooien* change course (*or:* tack)

roerbakken /rurbakə(n)/ (roerbakte, heeft geroerbakt/roergebakken) stir-fry

het **roerei** /rurɛi/ (pl: -eren) scrambled eggs

roeren /rurə(n)/ (roerde, heeft geroerd) stir, mix: *de soep ~* stir the soup; *door elkaar ~* mix together

roerend /rurənt/ (adj, adv) moving, touching ‖ *het ~ eens zijn* be of one (*or:* the same) mind

de **roerganger** /rurɣaŋər/ (pl: -s) helmsman, steersman: *de grote ~* the Great Helmsman

roerig /rurəχ/ (adj) lively, active, restless

roerloos /rurlos/ (adj, adv) motionless, immovable, immobile

het **roerstaafje** /rurstafjə/ coffee stirrer

de **roes** /rus/ (pl: roezen) **1** flush; high: *in een ~* in a whirl (of excitement) **2** fuddle, intoxication; high: *zijn ~ uitslapen* sleep it off

het/de **roest** /rust/ (pl: -en) rust: *een laag ~* a layer of rust ‖ *oud ~* scrap iron

roestbruin /rustbrœyn/ (adj) rust, rust-coloured

roesten /rustə(n)/ (roestte, heeft/is geroest) rust, get rusty

roestig /rustəχ/ (adj) rusty

roestvrij /rustfrɛi/ (adj) rustproof, rust-resistant: *~ staal* stainless steel

het **roet** /rut/ soot: *zo zwart als* ~ as black as soot; [fig] *~ in het eten gooien* throw a spanner into the works

het/de **roetfilter** /rutfɪltər/ (pl: -s) soot filter, particle filter

roetsjen /rutʃə(n)/ (roetsjte, heeft/is ge-

roetsjt) slide
roetzwart /rutswɑrt/ (adj) black, pitch-black

de **roffel** /rɔfəl/ (pl: -s) roll; ruffle
roffelen /rɔfələ(n)/ (roffelde, heeft geroffeld) roll: **met** *de vingers op de tafel* ~ drum (one's fingers) on the table

de **rog** /rɔχ/ (pl: -gen) ray

de **rogge** /rɔɣə/ rye: *brood* **van** ~ bread made from rye

het **roggebrood** /rɔɣəbrot/ (pl: -broden) rye bread, pumpernickel

de **rok** /rɔk/ (pl: -ken) **1** skirt; petticoat: *Schotse* ~ kilt; *een* **wijde** ~ a full skirt **2** tail coat, tails: *de heren waren* **in** ~ the men wore evening dress

de **rokade** /rokɑdə/ (pl: -s) castling: *de* **korte** (or: *lange*) ~ castling on the king's side (or: queen's side)
roken /rokə(n)/ (rookte, heeft gerookt) **1** smoke, puff (at): *stoppen* **met** ~ stop (or: give up) smoking; *verboden te* ~ no smoking; *minder gaan* ~ cut down on smoking; *de* **schoorsteen** *rookt* the chimney is smoking **2** smoke, cure

de **roker** /rokər/ (pl: -s) smoker
rokerig /rokərəχ/ (adj) smoky

de **rokkenjager** /rɔkə(n)jaɣər/ (pl: -s) womanizer

het **rokkostuum** /rɔkostym/ (pl: -s) dress suit

de **rol** /rɔl/ (pl: -len) **1** part, role: *zijn* ~ *instuderen* learn one's part; *een* ~ **spelen** a) play a part, play-act; b) play a part (in), enter in(to); *de* ~*len* **omkeren** reverse roles; *turn the tables*; **uit** *zijn* ~ *vallen* forget oneself **2** roll; cylinder; coil; scroll; reel; spool: *een* ~ **behang** a roll of wallpaper; *een* ~ **beschuit** a packet of rusks **3** roller; rolling pin

het/de **rolgordijn** /rɔlɣɔrdɛin/ (pl: -en) (roller) blind: *een* ~ **ophalen** (or: *laten zakken*) let up (or: down) a blind

de **rolkoffer** /rɔlkɔfər/ (pl: -s) wheeled suitcase

de **rollade** /rolɑdə/ (pl: -s) rolled meat

de **rollator** /rolɑtɔr/ Zimmer frame, rollator
rollebollen /rɔləbɔlə(n)/ (rollebolde, heeft gerollebold) **1** turn (or: go) head over heels **2** mess around, get it on **3** romp (around): [fig] ~*d over* **straat** *gaan* argue in public, disagree violently with each other

¹**rollen** /rɔlə(n)/ (rolde, heeft/is gerold) roll: *er gaan* **koppen** ~ heads will roll; *de zaak* **aan** *het* ~ *brengen* set the ball rolling

²**rollen** /rɔlə(n)/ (rolde, heeft gerold) **1** roll (up): *een* **sigaret** ~ roll a cigarette **2** wrap, roll (up): *zich* **in** *een deken* ~ wrap o.s. up in a blanket **3** lift: *zakken* ~ pick pockets

het **rollenpatroon** /rɔlə(n)patron/ (pl: -patronen) sex role

het **rollenspel** /rɔlə(n)spɛl/ role-playing

de **roller** /rɔlər/ (pl: -s) roller

het **rolletje** /rɔləcə/ (pl: -s) (small) roll; roller: *een*

~ **drop** a packet of liquorice; *alles liep* **op** ~*s* everything went like clockwork (*or:* went smoothly)

het **rolluik** /rɔllœyk/ (pl: -en) roll-down shutter

het **rolmodel** /rɔlmodɛl/ (pl: -len) role model

de **rolschaats** /rɔlsχats/ (pl: -en) roller skate
rolschaatsen /rɔlsχatsə(n)/ (rolschaatste, heeft/is gerolschaatst) roller skate

de **rolschaatser** /rɔlsχatsər/ (pl: -s) roller skater

de **rolstoel** /rɔlstul/ (pl: -en) wheelchair: *toegankelijk* **voor** ~*en* with access for wheelchairs

de **roltrap** /rɔltrɑp/ (pl: -pen) escalator, moving staircase

de **rolverdeling** /rɔlvərdelɪŋ/ (pl: -en) cast(ing); [fig] division of roles

de **Roma** /roma/ (pl) Roma (gypsies)
Romaans /romans/ (adj) **1** Latin: *de* ~*e* **volken** the Latin peoples **2** Romance, Latin

de **roman** /romɑn/ (pl: -s) novel

de **romance** /romɑ̃sə/ (pl: -s) romance

de **romanschrijver** /romɑnsχrɛivər/ (pl: -s) novelist, fiction writer

de **romanticus** /romɑntikʏs/ (pl: romantici) romantic

de **romantiek** /romɑntik/ romance: *een* **vleugje** ~ a touch of romance
romantisch /romɑntis/ (adj, adv) romantic
romantiseren /romɑntizerə(n)/ (romantiseerde, heeft geromantiseerd) romanticize
Rome /romə/ Rome: *het* **oude** ~ Ancient Rome; *zo oud als de weg naar* ~ as old as the hills

de **Romein** /romɛin/ (pl: -en) Roman
Romeins /romɛins/ (adj) Roman: *uit de* ~*e* **oudheid** from Ancient Rome; *het* ~ **recht** Roman law; *het* ~*e* **Rijk** the Roman Empire
romig /roməχ/ (adj) creamy

de **rommel** /rɔməl/ **1** mess, shambles: ~ **maken** make a mess **2** junk, rubbish, trash
rommelen /rɔmələ(n)/ (rommelde, heeft gerommeld) **1** rumble, roll: *de* **donder** *rommelt in de verte* the thunder is rumbling in the distance **2** rummage: *in zijn papieren* ~ shuffle one's papers
rommelig /rɔmələχ/ (adj, adv) messy, untidy

de **rommelmarkt** /rɔməlmɑrkt/ (pl: -en) flea market, jumble sale

de **romp** /rɔmp/ (pl: -en) **1** trunk; torso **2** shell; hull

de **romper** /rɔmpər/ (pl: -s) rompers

de **rompslomp** /rɔmpslɔmp/ fuss, bother: *ambtelijke* ~ red tape, bureaucracy; *papieren* ~ paperwork

¹**rond** /rɔnt/ (adj, adv) **1** round, circular **2** arranged, fixed (up): *de zaak* **is** ~ everything is arranged (*or:* fixed) **3** around, about ‖ *een mooi* ~ **bedrag** a nice round figure

²**rond** /rɔnt/ (prep) **1** round; [fig] surround-

ing: *in de berichtgeving ~ de affaire* in the reporting of the affair **2** around, about: *~ de middag* around midday; *~ de 2000 betogers* approximately (*or:* about, some) 2000 demonstrators

rondbazuinen /rɔndbazœynə(n)/ (bazuinde rond, heeft rondgebazuind) broadcast, trumpet (around)

rondbrengen /rɔndbrɛŋə(n)/ (bracht rond, heeft rondgebracht) bring round

de **ronddelen** /rɔndelə(n)/ (deelde rond, heeft rondgedeeld) hand round (*or:* around); deal: *wie moet de kaarten ~?* whose deal is it?, who's dealing?

ronddraaien /rɔndrajə(n)/ (draaide rond, heeft/is rondgedraaid) turn (round); spin (round): *~ in een cirkel, kringetje* go round in circles

ronddwalen /rɔndwalə(n)/ (dwaalde rond, heeft rondgedwaald) wander, wander around

de **ronde** /rɔndə/ (pl: -n) **1** rounds; beat: *de ~ doen* go on one's rounds **2** round(s): *de eerste ~ van onderhandelingen* the first round of talks; *de praatjes doen de ~* stories are going around **3** lap, circuit: *laatste ~* bell lap; *twee ~n voor* (or: *achter*) *liggen* be two laps ahead (*or:* behind) **4** tour; race: *de ~ van Frankrijk* the Tour de France

de **rondtafelconferentie** /rɔndətafəlkɔnfɛrɛn(t)si/ (pl: -s) round-table conference

rondgaan /rɔntxan/ (ging rond, is rondgegaan) **1** go round: *~ als een lopend vuurtje* spread like wildfire **2** go round, pass round: *laat de schaal nog maar eens ~* pass the plate round again

de **rondgang** /rɔntxaŋ/ (pl: -en) **1** circuit **2** tour

rondhangen /rɔnthaŋə(n)/ (hing rond, heeft rondgehangen) hang around (*or:* about)

de **ronding** /rɔndɪŋ/ (pl: -en) curve

het **rondje** /rɔncə/ (pl: -s) **1** round: *een ~ van de zaak* (a round of) drinks on the house; *hij gaf een ~* he stood a round (of drinks) **2** [sport] lap; circuit

rondkijken /rɔntkɛikə(n)/ (keek rond, heeft rondgekeken) look round: *goed ~ voor je iets koopt* shop around

rondkomen /rɔntkomə(n)/ (kwam rond, is rondgekomen) manage, get by; live: *hij kan er net mee ~* he can just manage (*or:* get by) on it

rondleiden /rɔntlɛidə(n)/ (leidde rond, heeft rondgeleid) **1** lead round **2** show round, take round: *mensen in een museum ~* show (*or:* take) people round a museum

de **rondleiding** /rɔntlɛidɪŋ/ (pl: -en) (guided, conducted) tour

rondlopen /rɔntlopə(n)/ (liep rond, heeft/is rondgelopen) go around, walk around: *je*

moet daar niet mee blijven ~ you shouldn't let that weigh (*or:* prey) on your mind

rondneuzen /rɔntnøzə(n)/ (neusde rond, heeft rondgeneusd) nose about, prowl

¹**rondom** /rɔntɔm/ (adv) all round, on all sides: *het plein met de huizen ~* the square with houses round it

²**rondom** /rɔntɔm/ (prep) (a)round

het **rondpunt** /rɔntpʏnt/ (pl: -en) [Belg] roundabout

de **rondreis** /rɔntrɛis/ (pl: -reizen) tour, circular tour: *op haar ~ door de Verenigde Staten* on her tour of America

rondreizen /rɔntrɛizə(n)/ (reisde rond, heeft/is rondgereisd) travel around (*or:* about): *de wereld ~* travel round the globe (*or:* world)

rondrennen /rɔntrɛnə(n)/ (rende rond, heeft rondgerend) run around, chase about

rondrijden /rɔntrɛidə(n)/ (reed rond, heeft/is rondgereden) go for a drive (*or:* run, ride)

de **rondrit** /rɔntrɪt/ (pl: -ten) tour

het **rondschrijven** /rɔntsχrɛivə(n)/ (pl: -s) circular (letter)

rondslingeren /rɔntslɪŋərə(n)/ (slingerde rond, heeft rondgeslingerd) lie about (*or:* around): *zijn boeken laten ~* leave his books lying around (*or:* about)

rondsturen /rɔntstyrə(n)/ (stuurde rond, heeft rondgestuurd) send round: *circulaires ~* distribute circulars

de **rondte** /rɔntə/ (pl: -n, -s) circle, round(ness): *in de ~ zitten* sit in a circle

rondtrekken /rɔntrɛkə(n)/ (trok rond, heeft/is rondgetrokken) travel (a)round: *~de seizoenarbeiders* migrant seasonal workers

ronduit /rɔntœyt/ (adv) plain, straight(forward), frank: *het is ~ belachelijk* absolutely (*or:* simply) ridiculous; *iem. ~ de waarheid zeggen* tell s.o. the plain truth

de **rondvaart** /rɔntfart/ (pl: -en) round trip, circular trip (*or:* tour); cruise: *een ~ door de grachten maken* make (*or:* go) for a tour of the canals

de **rondvaartboot** /rɔntfardbot/ (pl: -boten) boat for canal trips

rondvertellen /rɔntfərtɛlə(n)/ (vertelde rond, heeft rondverteld) put about, spread about: *hij heeft dat overal rondverteld* he spread (*or:* put) that about everywhere

rondvliegen /rɔntfliɣə(n)/ (vloog rond, heeft/is rondgevlogen) fly about (*or:* around): *geraakt worden door ~de kogels* be hit by flying bullets

de **rondvlucht** /rɔntflʏχt/ (pl: -en) round trip (by plane/helicopter): *een ~ boven de stad maken* go for a round trip over the town

de **rondvraag** /rɔntfraχ/ **1** (any) other business **2** a short survey

de **rondweg** /rɔntwɛχ/ (pl: -en) ring road, bypass, relief road: *een ~ aanleggen om L.* bypass L.

rondzwerven /rɔntswɛrvə(n)/ (zwierf rond, heeft rondgezworven) roam about, wander about: *op straat* ~ **a)** hang about the streets; **b)** roam the streets

ronken /rɔŋkə(n)/ (ronkte, heeft geronkt) **1** snore **2** throb ‖ *in* ~*de* **bewoordingen** in highfalutin terms

ronselen /rɔnsələ(n)/ (ronselde, heeft geronseld) recruit

de **röntgenfoto** /rʏntχə(n)foto/ (pl: -'s) X-ray, roentgenogram, roentgenograph: *een ~ laten maken* have an X-ray taken

het **röntgenonderzoek** /rʏntχənɔndərzuk/ X-ray

de **röntgenstralen** /rʏntχə(n)stralə(n)/ (pl) X-rays, roentgen rays

rood /rot/ (adj) red; ginger; ruddy; copper(y); ginger: *met een ~ hoofd van de inspanning* flushed with exertion; *iem. de rode kaart tonen* show s.o. the red card; *door ~ (licht) rijden* jump the lights; ~ *worden* go red (*or:* scarlet), flush, blush; *het licht sprong op* ~ the light changed to red; *over de rooie gaan* flip one's lid, lose one's cool ‖ ~ *staan* be in the red; *in het* ~ *(gekleed)* dressed in red

roodbont /rodbɔnt/ (adj) red and white; skewbald

het **roodborstje** /rodbɔrʃə/ (pl: -s) robin (redbreast)

roodbruin /rodbrœyn/ (adj) reddish brown, russet; sorrel: *het* ~ *van herfstbladeren* the russet (colour) of autumn leaves

roodgloeiend /rotχlujənt/ (adj) red-hot: *de telefoon staat* ~ the telephone hasn't stopped ringing

roodharig /rotharəχ/ (adj) red-haired, redheaded

de **roodhuid** /rodhœyt/ (pl: -en) redskin

Roodkapje /rotkɑpjə/ Little Red Riding Hood

de **roodvonk** /rotfɔŋk/ scarlet fever

het **rood-wit-blauw** /rotwɪtblɑu/ the Dutch flag

de **roof** /rof/ (pl: roven) **1** robbery: *op* ~ *uitgaan* commit robbery **2** preying, hunting

de **roofbouw** /rovbɑu/ exhaustion, overuse: ~ *plegen op zijn gezondheid* undermine one's health; ~ *plegen op zijn lichaam* wear o.s. out

het **roofdier** /rovdir/ (pl: -en) animal (*or:* beast) of prey, predator

de **roofmoord** /rofmort/ (pl: -en) robbery with murder

de **roofoverval** /rofovərvɑl/ (pl: -len) robbery, hold-up: *een ~ plegen op een juwelierszaak* rob a jeweller's

de **rooftocht** /roftɔχt/ (pl: -en) raid

de **roofvogel** /rofoɣəl/ (pl: -s) bird of prey

de **rooibosthee** /rojbɔste/ rooibos tea

rooien /rojə(n)/ (rooide, heeft gerooid) dig up; lift, raise; uproot: *een bos* ~ clear a wood

(*or:* forest)

de **rook** /rok/ smoke; fume(s): *je kunt er de* ~ *snijden* it's thick with smoke in here; *in* ~ *opgaan* go up in smoke; *onder de* ~ *van de stad wonen* live a stone's throw from the town; *waar* ~ *is, is vuur* there's no smoke without fire

de **rookbom** /roɡbɔm/ (pl: -men) smoke bomb

het **rookgordijn** /rokχɔrdɛin/ (pl: -en) smokescreen: *een ~ leggen* put up (*or:* lay) a smokescreen

het **rookkanaal** /rokanal/ (pl: -kanalen) flue

de **rooklucht** /roklʏχt/ smell of smoke

de **rookmelder** /rokmɛldər/ (pl: -s) smoke alarm, smoke detector

de **rookpaal** /rokpal/ [roughly] pillar indicating 'smoking zone' on a railway platform

de **rookpauze** /rokpɑuzə/ (pl: -s) cigarette break: *een ~ inlassen* take a break for a cigarette

de **rookschade** /roksχadə/ smoke damage

het **rooksignaal** /roksɪnal/ (pl: -signalen) smoke signal

het **rookverbod** /rokfərbɔt/ ban on smoking

het **rookvlees** /rokfles/ [roughly] smoke-dried beef (*or:* meat)

rookvrij /rokfrɛi/ (adj) no(n)-smoking: *een ~ gebouw* a non-smoking building, a smoke-free building

de **rookwolk** /rokwɔlk/ (pl: -en) cloud (*or:* pall) of smoke

de **rookworst** /rokwɔrst/ (pl: -en) [roughly] smoked sausage

de **room** /rom/ cream: *dikke ~* double cream; *zure ~* sour cream

de **roomboter** /rombotər/ butter

het **roomijs** /romɛis/ ice cream

de **roomkaas** /romkas/ (pl: -kazen) cream cheese

rooms /roms/ (adj) Roman Catholic

Rooms /roms/ (adj) Roman

de **roomsaus** /romsɑus/ (pl: -sauzen) cream sauce

het **rooms-katholicisme** /romskatolisɪsmə/ Roman Catholicism

rooms-katholiek /romskatolik/ (adj) Roman Catholic

de **roomsoes** /romsus/ (pl: -soezen) cream puff

de **roos** /ros/ (pl: rozen) **1** rose: [fig] *op rozen zitten* lie on a bed of roses; *slapen als een ~* sleep like a log **2** bull's-eye: *in de ~ schieten* score a bull's-eye; *(midden) in de ~ bang* in the middle **3** dandruff

rooskleurig /rosklørəχ/ (adj, adv) rosy, rose-coloured: *een ~e toekomst* a rosy (*or:* bright) future

het/de **rooster** /rostər/ (pl: -s) **1** grid, grating, grate; grille; gridiron: *het ~ van de kachel* the stove grate; [Belg] *iem. op het ~ leggen* grill s.o. **2** grid **3** schedule; timetable, roster: *een ~ opstellen (opmaken)* draw up a roster (*or:*

rota)
roosteren /rostərə(n)/ (roosterde, heeft geroosterd) **1** grill, roast, broil **2** toast **3** grill: *een verdachte ~* grill a suspect

het **ros** /rɔs/ (pl: -sen) steed

de **rosbief** /rɔzbif/ roast beef

de **rosé** /rozɐ/ rosé (wine)

rossig /rɔsəχ/ (adj) reddish, ruddy; sandy

rot /rɔt/ (adj) **1** rotten, bad; decayed; putrid: *door en door ~, zo ~ als een mispel* rotten to the core **2** rotten, lousy, wretched: *zich ~ lachen* split one's sides laughing; *zij schrok zich ~* she got the fright of her life, she was scared out of her wits; *zich ~ vervelen* be bored to tears

het/de **rotan** /rotɑn/ rattan

de **rotatie** /rota(t)si/ (pl: -s) rotation, revolution

het **rotding** /rɔdɪŋ/ [inform] damn thing, bloody thing

roteren /rotɛrə(n)/ (roteerde, heeft geroteerd) rotate: *een ~de beweging* a rotary motion

het **rotje** /rɔcə/ (pl: -s) (fire)cracker, squib, banger

het **rotjong** /rɔtjɔŋ/ [inform] brat, little pest

de **rotonde** /rotɔndə/ (pl: -s) roundabout

de **rotopmerking** /rɔtopmɛrkɪŋ/ (pl: -en) nasty remark

de **rotor** /rotɔr/ (pl: -s) rotor

de **rots** /rɔts/ (pl: -en) rock, cliff; crag: *als een ~ in de branding* as steady as a rock; *het schip liep op de ~en* the ship struck the rocks

rotsachtig /rɔtsɑχtəχ/ (adj) rocky, rugged

het **rotsblok** /rɔtsblɔk/ (pl: -ken) boulder

de **rotskust** /rɔtskʏst/ rocky coast

de **rotstreek** /rɔtstrek/ (pl: rotstreken) dirty trick, mean trick: *iem. een ~ leveren* play a dirty trick on s.o.

de **rotstuin** /rɔtstœyn/ (pl: -en) rock garden, rockery

rotsvast /rɔtsfɑst/ (adj, adv) rock-solid, rocklike: *een ~e overtuiging* a deep-rooted conviction

de **rotswand** /rɔtswɑnt/ (pl: -en) rock face, cliff face

rotten /rɔtə(n)/ (rotte, heeft/is gerot) rot, decay: *~d hout* rotting wood

rottig /rɔtəχ/ (adj, adv) [inform] rotten, nasty

de **rottigheid** /rɔtəχhɛit/ [inform] misery, wretchedness

de **rottweiler** /rɔtwɑjlər/ (pl: -s) Rottweiler

de **rotvent** /rɔtfɛnt/ (pl: -en) [inform] bastard, jerk

het **rotweer** /rɔtwer/ [inform] awful weather

de **rotzak** /rɔtsɑk/ (pl: -ken) [inform] bastard, jerk

de **rotzooi** /rɔtsoj/ [inform] **1** (piece of) junk, trash **2** mess, shambles

rotzooien /rɔtsojə(n)/ (rotzooide, heeft gerotzooid) [inform] **1** mess about: *~ met de*

boekhouding tamper with the accounts, cook the books **2** fool around

het/de **rouge** /ruːʒɐ/ rouge, blusher

de **roulatie** /rula(t)si/ circulation: *in ~ brengen* bring into circulation [film]

rouleren /rulɛrə(n)/ (rouleerde, heeft gerouleerd) **1** circulate, be in circulation **2** rotate, take turns; work in shifts

de **roulette** /rulɛtɐ/ (pl: -s) roulette (table)

de **route** /rutə/ (pl: -s) route, way; round

de **routekaart** /rutəkart/ (pl: -en) **1** key map **2** road-map

de **routeplanner** /rutəplɛnər/ (pl: -s) route planner

de **routine** /rutinə/ **1** practice, skill, knack **2** routine, grind: *de dagelijkse ~* the daily grind

de **routineklus** /rutinəklʏs/ routine job

routinematig /rutinəmatəχ/ (adj) routine

het **routineonderzoek** /rutinəondərzuk/ (pl: -en) routine check-up

routineus /rutinøs/ (adj) routine

de **rouw** /rɑu/ mourning; sorrow; grief: *in ~ dompelen* plunge into mourning; *in de ~ zijn* be in mourning; *een dag van nationale ~* a day of national mourning

de **rouwadvertentie** /rɑuɑtfərtɛn(t)si/ (pl: -s) death announcement

de **rouwband** /rɑubɑnt/ (pl: -en) mourning band, black armband

rouwen /rɑuwə(n)/ (rouwde, heeft gerouwd) mourn, grieve

rouwig /rɑuwəχ/ (adj) regretful, sorry: *ergens niet ~ om zijn* not regret sth.

de **rouwkaart** /rɑukart/ (pl: -en) mourning card; memorial service invitation

de **rouwkrans** /rɑukrɑns/ funeral wreath

de **rouwstoet** /rɑustut/ (pl: -en) funeral procession

roven /rovə(n)/ (roofde, heeft geroofd) steal, rob

de **rover** /rovər/ (pl: -s) robber

het **roversnest** /rovərsnɛst/ (pl: -en) den of thieves

royaal /rojal/ (adj, adv) **1** generous, open-handed: *een royale beloning* a handsome (*or:* generous) reward **2** spacious, ample: *een royale meerderheid* a comfortable majority

royeren /rwajɛrə(n)/ (royeerde, heeft geroyeerd) expel (from)

roze /rɔːzə/ (adj) pink, rose: [fig] *op een ~ wolk zitten* be on cloud nine

de **rozemarijn** /rozəmarɛin/ rosemary

de **rozenbottel** /rozə(n)bɔtəl/ (pl: -s) rose hip

de **rozengeur** /rozə(n)ɣør/ smell (*or:* scent) of roses: *het is er niet alleen ~ en maneschijn* it's not all sweetness and light there

de **rozenkrans** /rozə(n)krɑns/ (pl: -en) rosary: *de ~ bidden* say the rosary

de **rozenstruik** /rozə(n)strœyk/ (pl: -en) rose

bush
rozig /r<u>o</u>zəχ/ (adj) languid
de **rozijn** /roz<u>ɛi</u>n/ (pl: -en) raisin
RSI /ɛrɛsi/ RSI
het/de **rubber** /r<u>ʏ</u>bər/ rubber
de **rubberboot** /r<u>ʏ</u>bərbot/ (pl: -boten) (rubber) dinghy
rubberen /r<u>ʏ</u>bərə(n)/ (adj) rubber
de **rubberlaars** /r<u>ʏ</u>bərlars/ rubber boot, wellington
rubriceren /rybris<u>e</u>rə(n)/ (rubriceerde, heeft gerubriceerd) class, classify
de **rubriek** /rybr<u>i</u>k/ (pl: -en) **1** column, feature, section: *de **advertentierubriek(en)*** the advertising columns **2** section, group
de **ruchtbaarheid** /r<u>ʏ</u>χtbarhɛit/ publicity: ~ *aan iets **geven*** give publicity to sth.
rücksichtslos /r<u>ʏ</u>ksiχ(t)slos/ (adj, adv) unscrupulous, thoughtless
de **rucola** /r<u>y</u>kola/ (pl: -'s) rocket; [Am] arugula
rudimentair /rydimɛnt<u>ɛ:</u>r/ (adj, adv) rudimentary
de **rug** /rʏχ/ (pl: -gen) back: *achter de ~ van iem. kwaadspreken* talk about s.o. behind his back; *ik zal blij zijn als het **achter** de ~ is* I'll be glad to get it over and done with; *hij heeft een moeilijke tijd **achter** de ~* he had a difficult time; *een duwtje* (or: *steuntje*) *in de ~* a bit of encouragement (or: support), a helping hand, a leg up; *het schoot hem **in** de ~* he felt a stab of pain in his back; *met de ~ tegen de muur* with one's back to the wall; *het (geld) groeit mij niet **op** de ~* I am not made of money; *op zijn ~ liggen* **a)** be six feet under; **b)** be stagnant; *iem. de ~ **toekeren*** turn one's back on s.o.
het **rugby** /r<u>ʏ</u>gbi/ rugby
rugbyen /r<u>ʏ</u>gbijə(n)/ (rugbyde, heeft gerugbyd) play rugby (or: rugger)
de **rugdekking** /r<u>ʏ</u>γdɛkɪŋ/ backing: *iem. ~ **geven*** [sport] cover a team-mate; [fig] back s.o.
ruggelings /r<u>ʏ</u>γəlɪŋs/ (adv) **1** back to back **2** backward(s)
de **ruggengraat** /r<u>ʏ</u>γə(n)γrat/ (pl: -graten) backbone, spine
het **ruggenmerg** /r<u>ʏ</u>γə(n)mɛrχ/ spinal marrow (or: cord)
de **ruggensteun** /r<u>ʏ</u>γə(n)støn/ (pl: -en) **1** back support **2** backing, support: *iem. ~ **geven*** give s.o. backing
de **ruggespraak** /r<u>ʏ</u>γəsprak/ consultation: ~ *met iem. **houden*** consult s.o.
de **rugklachten** /r<u>ʏ</u>χklɑχtə(n)/ (pl) back trouble, backache
de **rugleuning** /r<u>ʏ</u>χlønɪŋ/ (pl: -en) back (of a chair)
het **rugnummer** /r<u>ʏ</u>χnʏmər/ (pl: -s) (player's) number
de **rugpijn** /r<u>ʏ</u>χpɛin/ pain in the back, backache
de **rugslag** /r<u>ʏ</u>χslɑχ/ backstroke, back-crawl
de **rugwind** /r<u>ʏ</u>χwɪnt/ (pl: -en) tail wind, following wind

de **rugzak** /r<u>ʏ</u>χsɑk/ (pl: -ken) rucksack, backpack
rugzwemmen /r<u>ʏ</u>χswɛmə(n)/ swim backstroke
de **rui** /rœy/ **1** moult(ing) **2** [Belg] covered canal, roofed-over canal
ruien /r<u>œy</u>ə(n)/ (ruide, heeft geruid) moult, shed one's feathers
de **ruif** /rœyf/ (pl: ruiven) rack
ruig /rœyχ/ (adj) **1** rough: *een ~ **feest** a rowdy party **2** shaggy, hairy
¹**ruiken** /r<u>œy</u>kə(n)/ (rook, heeft geroken) **1** smell: *aan iets ~* have a smell (or: sniff) at sth.; *honden **kunnen** goed ~* dogs have a good scent (or: sense of smell); *die bloemen ~ **lekker*** those flowers smell nice; *het ruikt hier **naar** parfum* the place smells of perfume **2** smell, stink, reek: *hij ruikt **uit** zijn mond* his breath smells
²**ruiken** /r<u>œy</u>kə(n)/ (rook, heeft geroken) [also fig] smell, scent: *hoe **kon** ik dat nu ~!* how could I possibly know!; *onraad ~* scent (or: sense) danger
de **ruiker** /r<u>œy</u>kər/ (pl: -s) posy, bouquet
de **ruil** /rœyl/ (pl: -en) exchange, swap
¹**ruilen** /r<u>œy</u>lə(n)/ (ruilde, heeft geruild) change: *ik zou niet **met** hem willen ~* I would not change places with him
²**ruilen** /r<u>œy</u>lə(n)/ (ruilde, heeft geruild) exchange, swap
de **ruilhandel** /r<u>œy</u>lhɑndəl/ barter (trade): ~ *drijven* barter
het **ruilmiddel** /r<u>œy</u>lmɪdəl/ (pl: -en) means (or: medium) of exchange
de **ruilverkaveling** /r<u>œy</u>lvərkavəlɪŋ/ (pl: -en) land consolidation
het ¹**ruim** /rœym/ (pl: -en) hold: *in ~e mate* in great measure, to a large extent
²**ruim** /rœym/ (adj, adv) **1** spacious, large; roomy: *een ~ **assortiment*** a large assortment; ~ *wonen* live spaciously **2** free: ~ *baan maken* make way; *in de ~ste **zin*** in the broadest sense **3** wide, roomy, loose: *die jas **zit** ~* that coat is loose-fitting **4** ample, liberal: *een ~e **meerderheid*** a big majority
³**ruim** /rœym/ (adv) (rather) more than, sth. over, well over: ~ *een **uur** well over an hour; *dat is ~ **voldoende*** that is amply sufficient
ruimdenkend /r<u>œy</u>mdɛnkənt/ (adj) broad(-minded)
ruimen /r<u>œy</u>mə(n)/ (ruimde, heeft geruimd) **1** clear out **2** clear away: *iem. **uit** de weg ~* get rid of (or: kill) s.o.
ruimhartig /r<u>œy</u>mhɑrtəχ/ (adj) generous, warm-hearted
ruimschoots /r<u>œy</u>msχots/ (adv) amply, plentifully: ~ *de tijd* (or: *gelegenheid*) *hebben* have ample time (or: opportunity); ~ *op tijd aankomen* arrive in ample time
de **ruimte** /r<u>œy</u>mtə/ (pl: -n, -s) room; space: *wegens **gebrek** aan ~* for lack of room (or:

space); *de begrippen ~ en tijd* the concepts of time and space; *te weinig ~ hebben* be cramped for space; *~ uitsparen* save space; *iem. de ~ geven* give s.o. elbow room

het **ruimtegebrek** /rœymtəɣəbrɛk/ lack (*or:* shortage) of space

het **ruimtelaboratorium** /rœymtəlaboratorijʏm/ (pl: -laboratoria) spacelab

ruimtelijk /rœymtələk/ (adj, adv) **1** spatial, spacial, space: *~e ordening* environmental (*or:* town and country) planning **2** three-dimensional: *~ inzicht hebben* have good spatial skills

het **ruimtepak** /rœymtəpɑk/ (pl: -ken) space suit

het **ruimteschip** /rœymtəsχɪp/ (pl: -schepen) spacecraft

het **ruimtestation** /rœymtəsta(t)ʃɔn/ (pl: -s) space station

de **ruimtevaarder** /rœymtəvardər/ (pl: -s) spaceman, astronaut

de **ruimtevaart** /rœymtəvart/ space travel

het **ruimtevaartuig** /rœymtəvartœyχ/ (pl: -en) spacecraft

het **ruimteveer** /rœymtəver/ (pl: -veren) (space) shuttle

de **ruin** /rœyn/ (pl: -en) gelding

de **ruïne** /rywinə/ (pl: -s) ruins, ruin; [pers] wreck

ruïneren /rywinɣrə(n)/ (ruïneerde, heeft geruïneerd) ruin

de **ruis** /rœys/ noise; murmur

ruisen /rœysə(n)/ (ruiste, heeft geruist) rustle; gurgle

de **ruit** /rœyt/ (pl: -en) **1** (window)pane, window **2** diamond; check

de [superscript]**1ruiten** /rœytə(n)/ diamonds: *ruitenvrouw* queen of diamonds; *ruitenboer* jack (*or:* knave) of diamonds; *~ is troef* diamonds are trumps

[superscript]**2ruiten** /rœytə(n)/ (adj) check(ed), chequered

de **ruitenkrabber** /rœytə(n)krɑbər/ (pl: -s) ice scraper

de **ruitensproeier** /rœytə(n)sprujər/ (pl: -s) screenwasher; [Am] windshield washer

de **ruitenwisser** /rœytə(n)wɪsər/ (pl: -s) windscreen wiper, wiper

de **ruiter** /rœytər/ (pl: -s) horseman, rider

de **ruiterij** /rœytərɛi/ cavalry, horse

ruiterlijk /rœytərlək/ (adj, adv) frank: *iets ~ toegeven* admit sth. frankly

het **ruiterpad** /rœytərpɑt/ (pl: -en) bridle path

de **ruitersport** /rœytərsport/ equestrian sport(s), riding

het **ruitjespapier** /rœycəspapir/ squared paper

de [superscript]**1ruk** /rʏk/ (pl: -ken) **1** jerk, tug **2** gust (of wind) **3** distance, way **4** time, spell: *in één ~ doorwerken* work on at one stretch; [inform] *dat kan me geen ~ schelen* I don't give a damn

[superscript]**2ruk** /rʏk/ (adj) [inform] the pits, crappy

[superscript]**1rukken** /rʏkə(n)/ (rukte, heeft gerukt) **1** tug

(at) **2** [vulg] wank; [Am] jerk (off)

[superscript]**2rukken** /rʏkə(n)/ (rukte, heeft gerukt) tear, wrench: *iem. de kleren van het lijf ~* tear the clothes from s.o.'s body

de **rukker** /rʏkər/ (pl: -s) [inform] wanker; [Am] jerk

de **rukwind** /rʏkwɪnt/ (pl: -en) squall, gust (of wind)

rul /rʏl/ (adj) loose, sandy

de **rum** /rʏm/ rum

de **rumboon** /rʏmbon/ (pl: rumbonen) [Dutch] rum bonbon

de **rum-cola** /rʏmkola/ rum and coke

het **rumoer** /rymur/ (pl: -en) noise; din; racket, row: *~ maken* make a noise

rumoerig /rymurəχ/ (adj) noisy

de **run** /rʏn/ (pl: -s) run: *er was een ~ op die bank* there was a run on that bank

het **rund** /rʏnt/ (pl: -eren) **1** cow; cattle; ox **2** cow; bull; cattle **3** idiot, fool: *een ~ van een vent* a prize idiot ‖ *bloeden als een ~* bleed like a pig

het **rundergehakt** /rʏndərɣəhɑkt/ minced beef, mince

de **runderlap** /rʏndərlɑp/ (pl: -pen) braising steak

de **runderrollade** /rʏndərɔladə/ collared beef, rolled beef

het **rundvee** /rʏntfe/ cattle: *twintig stuks ~* twenty head of cattle

het **rundvlees** /rʏntfles/ beef

de **rune** /rynə/ (pl: -n) rune

runnen /rʏnə(n)/ (runde, heeft gerund) run, manage: *hij runt het bedrijf in z'n eentje* he runs the company all by himself

de **running** /rʏnɪŋ/: *in de ~ zijn voor …* be in the running for …; *uit de ~ zijn* be out of the running

de **rups** /rʏps/ (pl: -en) caterpillar

de **rupsband** /rʏpsbɑnt/ (pl: -en) caterpillar (track)

het **rupsvoertuig** /rʏpsfurtœyχ/ (pl: -en) caterpillar

de **Rus** /rʏs/ (pl: -sen) Russian

Rusland /rʏslɑnt/ Russia

de **Russin** /rʏsɪn/ (pl: -nen) see *Rus*

Russisch /rʏsis/ (adj) Russian ‖ *een ~ ei* egg mayonnaise; *~ roulette* Russian roulette

de **rust** /rʏst/ **1** rest; relaxation **2** rest; lie-down **3** quiet: *gun hem wat ~* give him a break; *nooit* (*or:* *geen moment*) *~ hebben* never have a moment's peace; *wat ~ nemen* take a break; *laat me met ~!* leave me alone!; *tot ~ komen* settle (*or:* calm) (down) **4** (peace and) quiet; still(ness): *alles was in diepe ~* all was quiet **5** [sport] half-time, interval

de **rustdag** /rʏzdɑχ/ (pl: -en) rest day; day off; holiday

rusteloos /rʏstəlos/ (adj, adv) restless

rusten /rʏstə(n)/ (rustte, heeft gerust) **1** rest, relax, take (*or:* have) a rest: *even ~*

have (*or:* take) a break **2** rest, sleep: *hij **ligt te** ~* he is resting **3** rest, pause **4** weigh; be burdened (*or:* encumbered) with: *op hem rust een zware verdenking* he is under strong suspicion || *we moeten het verleden **laten** ~* we've got to let bygones be bygones

rustgevend /rʏstxevənt/ (adj) **1** comforting **2** restful, calming

het **rusthuis** /rʏsthœys/ (pl: -huizen) rest home

rustiek /rʏstik/ (adj) rural; pastoral

¹**rustig** /rʏstəx/ (adj, adv) **1** peaceful, quiet **2** calm, still: *het **water** is* ~ the water's calm **3** steady: *een ~e **ademhaling*** even breathing **4** calm: *~ **weer*** calm weather; *~ **antwoorden*** answer calmly; *zich ~ **houden*** keep calm; *hij **komt** ~ een uur te laat* he quite happily (*or:* cheerfully) comes an hour late; *ze **zat** ~ te lezen* she sat quietly reading; *het ~ aan doen* take it easy **5** quiet; smooth; uneventful: *daar **kan** ik ~ **studeren*** I can study there in peace; *het is hier **lekker** ~* it's nice and quiet here

²**rustig** /rʏstəx/ (adv) safely: *je **kunt** me ~ **bellen*** feel free to call me; *dat **mag** je ~ **weten*** I don't mind if you know that

de **rustplaats** /rʏstplats/ (pl: -en) resting place: *de **laatste** ~* the final resting place; *naar zijn **laatste** ~ brengen* lay to rest

het **rustpunt** /rʏstpʏnt/ (pl: -en) pause; period

de **ruststand** /rʏstɑnt/ (pl: -en) [sport] halftime score

de **rustverstoring** /rʏstfərstorɪŋ/ disturbance

ruw /ryw/ (adj, adv) **1** rough: *een ~e **plank*** a rough plank; *een ~e **schets*** a rough draft; *een ~ **spel*** a rough game; *iets ~ **afbreken*** break sth. off abruptly; *iem. ~ **behandelen*** treat s.o. roughly **2** raw, crude; rough-hewn: *~e **olie*** crude oil

ruwweg /rywɛx/ (adv) roughly: *~ **geschat*** at a rough estimate (*or:* guess)

de **ruzie** /ryzi/ (pl: -s) quarrel, argument: *slaande ~ hebben* have a blazing row; *een ~ **bijleggen*** patch up a quarrel; *~ **krijgen** met iem.* have an argument with s.o.; *~ **zoeken*** look for trouble (*or:* a fight); *~ hebben **met** iem.* (or: **om** iets) quarrel with s.o. (*or:* over sth.)

ruziën /ryzijə(n)/ (ruziede, heeft geruzied) quarrel

de **ruziezoeker** /ryzizukər/ (pl: -s) quarrelsome person

Rwanda /ruwɑnda/ Rwanda

de ¹**Rwandees** /ruwɑndes/ (pl: Rwandezen) Rwandan

²**Rwandees** /ruwɑndes/ (adj) Rwandan

S

de **s** /ɛs/ (pl: s'en) s, S
saai /saj/ (adj, adv) boring, dull
de **saamhorigheid** /samhoːrəxhɛɪt/ solidarity
de **sabbat** /sɑbɑt/ (pl: -ten) sabbath
het **sabbatical year** /səbɛtɪkəljir/ sabbatical
year
sabbelen /sɑbələ(n)/ (sabbelde, heeft ge-
sabbeld) suck: ~ *aan* een *lolly* suck a lollipop
de **sabel** /sɑbəl/ sabre
de **sabotage** /sabotaʒə/ sabotage
saboteren /sabotɛrə(n)/ (saboteerde, heeft
gesaboteerd) **1** commit sabotage (on) **2** sabotage, undermine
de **saboteur** /sabotør/ (pl: -s) saboteur
het **sacrament** /sɑkramɛnt/ (pl: -en) sacrament
de **sacristie** /sɑkrɪstiː/ (pl: -ën) sacristy
het **sadisme** /sadɪsmə/ sadism
de **sadist** /sadɪst/ (pl: -en) sadist
sadistisch /sadɪstis/ (adj, adv) sadistic
het **sadomasochisme** /sadomasoχɪsmə/ sado-
masochism
de **safari** /safaːri/ (pl: -'s) safari: *op* ~ *gaan* go on
safari
de **safe** /sef/ (pl: -s) safe, safe-deposit box
de **¹saffier** /sɑfir/ (pl: -en) [gem] sapphire
het **²saffier** /sɑfir/ [mineral] sapphire
de **saffraan** /sɑfran/ saffron
de **sage** /saɣə/ (pl: -n) legend
de **Sahara** /sahaːra/ Sahara
saillant /sɑjɑnt/ (adj, adv) salient
Saksisch /sɑksis/ (adj) Saxon
de **salade** /saladə/ (pl: -s) salad
de **salamander** /salamɑndər/ (pl: -s) salamander
de **salami** /salaːmi/ salami
de **salariëring** /salarijɛrɪŋ/ payment
het **salaris** /salaːrɪs/ (pl: -sen) salary, pay
de **salarisschaal** /salaːrɪsχal/ (pl: -schalen) salary scale
de **salarisverhoging** /salaːrɪsfərhoɣɪŋ/ (pl:
-en) (salary) increase, (pay) rise
het **saldo** /sɑldo/ (pl: -'s, saldi) balance: *een positief* ~ a credit balance; *een negatief* ~ a
deficit; *per* ~ on balance
het **saldotekort** /sɑldotəkɔrt/ (pl: -en) deficit;
overdraft
de **salie** /saːli/ sage
de **salmiak** /sɑlmijɑk/ [Dutch] salty liquorice
powder
de **salmonella** /sɑlmoːnɛla/ salmonella
het **salomonsoordeel** /saːlomɔnsordel/ (pl:
-oordelen) judgment of Solomon
het/de **salon** /salɔn/ (pl: -s) drawing room, salon

salonfähig /salɔnfɛjiχ/ (adj) socially acceptable
de **salontafel** /salɔntafəl/ (pl: -s) coffee table
het **salpeterzuur** /sɑlpeːtərzyr/ nitric acid
de **salto** /sɑlto/ (pl: -'s) somersault
salueren /salywɛrə(n)/ (salueerde, heeft
gesalueerd) salute
het **saluut** /salyt/ salute
het **saluutschot** /salyːtsχɔt/ (pl: -schoten) salute
het **salvo** /sɑlvo/ (pl: -'s) salvo, volley
de **Samaritaan** /samaritan/ (pl: Samaritanen)
Samaritan ‖ *de barmhartige* ~ the good Samaritan
de **samba** /sɑmba/ (pl: -'s) samba
de **sambal** /sɑmbɑl/ sambal
samen /saːmə(n)/ (adv) **1** together; in chorus: *zij hebben* ~ *een kamer* they share a room
2 with each other, with one another: *het* ~
goed kunnen vinden get on well (together);
zij zijn het ~ *eens* they agree (with each other)
3 in all, altogether: ~ *is dat 21 euro* that
makes 21 euros altogether (*or:* in all)
samenbrengen /saːmə(n)brɛŋə(n)/ (bracht
samen, heeft samengebracht) bring together
samendrukken /saːmə(n)drʏkə(n)/ (drukte
samen, heeft samengedrukt) compress
samengaan /saːmə(n)ɣan/ (ging samen, is
samengegaan) go together, go hand in
hand: *niet* ~ *met* not go (together) with
samengesteld /saːmə(n)ɣəstɛlt/ (adj) compound
de **samenhang** /saːmə(n)hɑŋ/ connection
samenhangen /saːmə(n)hɑŋə(n)/ (hing samen, heeft samengehangen) be connected,
be linked: *dat hangt samen met het klimaat*
that has to do with the climate
samenhangend /saːmə(n)hɑŋənt/ (adj,
adv) related, connected: *een hiermee* ~ *probleem* a related problem
samenknijpen /saːmə(n)knɛipə(n)/ (kneep
samen, heeft samengeknepen) squeeze together; screw up
samenkomen /saːmə(n)komə(n)/ (kwam
samen, is samengekomen) come together,
meet (together); converge (on)
de **samenkomst** /saːmə(n)kɔmst/ (pl: -en)
meeting
samenleven /saːmə(n)levə(n)/ (leefde samen, heeft samengeleefd) live together
de **samenleving** /saːmə(n)levɪŋ/ society: *de
huidige* ~ modern society
het **samenlevingscontract** /saːmə(n)-
levɪŋskɔntrɑkt/ (pl: -en) cohabitation agreement
de **samenloop** /saːmə(n)lop/ concurrence, conjunction: *een* ~ *van omstandigheden* a combination of circumstances
samenpersen /saːmə(n)pɛrsə(n)/ (perste samen, heeft samengeperst) compress, press
together

het **samenraapsel** /sa̱mə(n)rapsəl/ (pl: -s) pack; ragbag

samenscholen /sa̱mə(n)sxolə(n)/ (schoolde samen, heeft/is samengeschoold) assemble

de **samenscholing** /sa̱mə(n)sxolɪŋ/ (pl: -en) gathering, assembly

samensmelten /sa̱mə(n)smɛltə(n)/ (smolt samen, is samengesmolten) fuse (together)

samenspannen /sa̱mə(n)spanə(n)/ (spande samen, heeft/is samengespannen) conspire, plot (together)

het **samenspel** /sa̱mə(n)spɛl/ combined action (or: play); teamwork

de **samenspraak** /sa̱mə(n)sprak/: iets **in** ~ beslissen decide sth. in consultation

het **samenstel** /sa̱mə(n)stɛl/ composition, system

samenstellen /sa̱mə(n)stɛlə(n)/ (stelde samen, heeft samengesteld) **1** put together, make up, compose: samengesteld zijn **uit** be made up (or: composed) of **2** draw up, compose; compile

de **samensteller** /sa̱mə(n)stɛlər/ (pl: -s) compiler; composer

de **samenstelling** /sa̱mə(n)stɛlɪŋ/ (pl: -en) **1** composition, make-up **2** [linguistics] compound

samentrekken /sa̱mə(n)trɛkə(n)/ (trok samen, is samengetrokken) contract, shrink

samenvallen /sa̱mə(n)valə(n)/ (viel samen, is samengevallen) coincide (with); correspond: gedeeltelijk ~ overlap

samenvatten /sa̱mə(n)vatə(n)/ (vatte samen, heeft samengevat) summarize, sum up: kort samengevat (to put it) in a nutshell; iets in een paar woorden ~ sum sth. up in a few words

de **samenvatting** /sa̱mə(n)vatɪŋ/ (pl: -en) summary; highlights

samenvoegen /sa̱mə(n)vuɣə(n)/ (voegde samen, heeft samengevoegd) join (together)

samenwerken /sa̱mə(n)wɛrkə(n)/ (werkte samen, heeft samengewerkt) cooperate, work together: gaan ~ join forces (with); nauw ~ cooperate closely

de **samenwerking** /sa̱mə(n)wɛrkɪŋ/ cooperation, teamwork: in **nauwe** ~ met in close collaboration with

samenwonen /sa̱mə(n)wonə(n)/ (woonde samen, heeft samengewoond) **1** live together, cohabit **2** live (together) with, share a house (or: flat)

het **samenzijn** /sa̱mə(n)zɛɪn/ gathering

de **samenzweerder** /sa̱mə(n)zwerdər/ (pl: -s) conspirator

samenzweren /sa̱mə(n)zwerə(n)/ (zwoer samen, heeft samengezworen) conspire, plot: tegen iem. ~ conspire (or: plot) against s.o.

de **samenzwering** /sa̱mə(n)zwerɪŋ/ (pl: -en) conspiracy, plot

de **samoerai** /samuraɪ/ (pl: -) samurai

samsam /samsa̱m/ (adv) [Dutch; inform] fifty-fifty: ~ **doen** go halves (with s.o.)

het **sanatorium** /sanato̱rijʏm/ (pl: sanatoria) sanatorium

de **sanctie** /sa̱ŋksi/ (pl: -s) sanction: ~s **opleggen** aan impose sanctions against (or: on); ~s **verbinden** aan apply sanctions to

sanctioneren /saŋkʃone̱rə(n)/ (sanctioneerde, heeft gesanctioneerd) sanction

de **sandaal** /sanda̱l/ (pl: sandalen) sandal

de **sandwich** /sɛntwɪtʃ/ (pl: -es) **1** sandwich **2** [Belg] bridge roll

sandwichen /sɛntwɪtʃə(n)/ (sandwichte, heeft gesandwicht): gesandwicht worden **tussen** ... be sandwiched between ...; [fig] be squashed between ...

saneren /sane̱rə(n)/ (saneerde, heeft gesaneerd) **1** put in order, see to: zijn **gebit** laten ~ have one's teeth seen to **2** reorganize, redevelop: de **binnenstad** ~ redevelop the town centre

de **sanering** /sane̱rɪŋ/ **1** [roughly] course of dental treatment **2** reorganization; redevelopment; clean-up (operation)

het **¹sanitair** /sanitɛ̱ːr/ sanitary fittings, bathroom fixtures

²sanitair /sanitɛ̱ːr/ (adj) sanitary: ~e **artikelen** bathroom equipment; een ~e **stop** maken stop to go to the bathroom; ~e **voorzieningen** toilet facilities

San Marino /samari̱no/ San Marino

het **Sanskriet** /sa̱nskrit/ Sanskrit: dat **is** ~ voor hem that is Greek to him

de **santenkraam** /sa̱ntə(n)kram/: de **hele** ~ the whole lot (or: caboodle); [Am] the whole shebang (or: enchilada)

het **sap** /sap/ (pl: -pen) juice; sap; fluid: het ~ uit een citroen **knijpen** squeeze the juice from a lemon

de **sapcentrifuge** /sa̱psɛntrifyːʒə/ (pl: -s) juice extractor, juicer

het **sapje** /sa̱pjə/ (pl: -s) (fruit) juice

sappel /sa̱pəl/ [Dutch; inform]: zich te ~ **maken** over iets worry about sth.

sappelen /sa̱pələ(n)/ (sappelde, heeft gesappeld) [Dutch] slave (or: slog) (away), drudge

sappig /sa̱pəx/ (adj) juicy: ~ vlees juicy (or: succulent) meat

het **sarcasme** /sɑrkɑ̱smə/ (pl: -n) sarcasm

sarcastisch /sɑrkɑ̱stis/ (adj, adv) sarcastic: ~e **opmerkingen** snide remarks

de **sarcofaag** /sɑrkofa̱x/ (pl: -fagen) sarcophagus

de **sardine** /sɑrdi̱nə/ (pl: -s) sardine

Sardinië /sɑrdi̱nijə/ Sardinia

de **sarong** /sa̱rɔŋ/ (pl: -s) sarong

sarren /sa̱rə(n)/ (sarde, heeft gesard) bait, (deliberately) provoke, needle de **sas** /sɑs/: *hij is zeer in zijn ~ met* zijn nieuwe *auto* he's delighted (or: over the moon, very pleased) with his new car

de **satan** /sɑtɑn/ (pl: -s) devil, fiend

Satan /sɑtɑn/ Satan

satanisch /sɑtɑnis/ (adj, adv) satanic(al), diabolic: *een ~e blik* (or: *lach*) a fiendish look (or: laugh)

de **saté** /sɑte/ satay

de **satelliet** /sɑtəlit/ (pl: -en) satellite

de **satellietschotel** /sɑtəlitsχotəl/ satellite dish

de **satellietstaat** /sɑtəlitstɑt/ (pl: -staten) satellite (state)

de **satellietverbinding** /sɑtəlitfərbɪndɪŋ/ (pl: -en) satellite link(-up)

de **satésaus** /sɑtesɑus/ (pl: -sauzen) satay sauce

het **satéstokje** /sɑtestɔkjə/ (pl: -s) skewer

het **satijn** /sɑtɛin/ (pl: -en) satin

satijnen /sɑtɛinə(n)/ (adj) satin

de **satire** /sɑtirə/ (pl: -s) satire: *een ~ schrijven op* satirize, write a satire on

satirisch /sɑtiris/ (adj, adv) satiric(al)

Saturnus /sɑtʏrnʏs/ Saturn

de **saucijs** /sɔsɛis/ (pl: saucijzen) sausage

het **saucijzenbroodje** /sɔsɛizə(n)broцə/ (pl: -s) [Dutch] sausage roll

Saudi-Arabië /sɑudiɑrɑbijə/ Saudi Arabia

Saudi-Arabisch /sɑudiɑrɑbis/ (adj) Saudi (Arabian)

de **Saudiër** /sɑudijər/ (pl: -s) Saudi (Arabian)

Saudisch /sɑudis/ (adj) Saudi (Arabian)

de **sauna** /sɔunɑ/ (pl: -'s) sauna (bath)

de **saus** /sɑus/ (pl: sauzen) sauce; gravy; (salad) dressing: *zoetzuur ~* sweet and sour (sauce)

de **sauskom** /sɑuskɔm/ (pl: -men) sauce boat

de **sauslepel** /sɑuslepəl/ (pl: -s) sauce spoon (or: ladle)

sauteren /soterə(n)/ (sauteerde, heeft gesauteerd) sauté

¹**sauzen** /sɔuzə(n)/ (sausde, heeft gesausd) distemper, colour-wash

²**sauzen** /sɔuzə(n)/ (sausde, heeft gesausd): *het saust* it's pouring

de **savanne** /sɑvɑnə/ (pl: -n) savannah

saven /sevə(n)/ (savede, heeft gesaved) [comp] save

de **savooiekool** /sɑvojəkol/ (pl: -kolen) savoy (cabbage)

de **sax** /sɑks/ (pl: -en) sax(ophone)

de **saxofonist** /sɑksofonɪst/ (pl: -en) saxophonist, saxophone player

de **saxofoon** /sɑksofon/ (pl: -s) saxophone

de **S-bocht** /ɛzbɔχt/ (pl: -en) S-bend

het **scala** /skɑlɑ/ (pl: -'s) scale, range: *een breed ~ van artikelen* a wide range of items

de **scalp** /skɑlp/ (pl: -en) scalp

het **scalpel** /skɑlpɛl/ (pl: -s) scalpel

scalperen /skɑlperə(n)/ (scalpeerde, heeft gescalpeerd) scalp

de **scan** /skɛn/ (pl: -s) scan

scanderen /skɑndɛrə(n)/ (scandeerde, heeft gescandeerd) chant

Scandinavië /skɑndinɑvijə/ Scandinavia

de **Scandinaviër** /skɑndinɑvijər/ (pl: -s) Scandinavian

Scandinavisch /skɑndinɑvis/ (adj) Scandinavian

scannen /skɛnə(n)/ (scande, heeft gescand) scan

de **scanner** /skɛnər/ (pl: -s) scanner

het **scenario** /sənɑrijo/ (pl: -'s) scenario; screenplay [film]; script

de **scene** /si:n/ (pl: -s) scene

de **scène** /sɛːnə/ scene: *hij had de overval zelf in ~ gezet* he had faked the robbery himself

de **scepsis** /skɛpsɪs/ scepticism

de **scepter** /sɛptər/ (pl: -s) sceptre: *de ~ zwaaien* hold sway (over)

sceptisch /sɛptis/ (adj, adv) sceptical

de **schaaf** /sχɑf/ (pl: schaven) **1** plane **2** slicer

het **schaafsel** /sχɑfsəl/ (pl: -s) shavings: *van parmezaan* Parmesan shavings

de **schaafwond** /sχɑfwɔnt/ (pl: -en) graze, scrape

het ¹**schaak** /sχɑk/ chess: *een partij ~* a game of chess

²**schaak** /sχɑk/ (adj) in check: *~ staan* be in check; *iem. ~ zetten* put s.o. in check

het **schaakbord** /sχɑgbɔrt/ (pl: -en) chessboard

schaakmat /sχɑkmɑt/ (adj) checkmate: *~ staan* be checkmated; *iem. ~ zetten* checkmate s.o.

de **schaakpartij** /sχɑkpɑrtɛi/ (pl: -en) game of chess

het **schaakspel** /sχɑkspɛl/ (pl: -len) **1** chess **2** chess set

het **schaakstuk** /sχɑkstʏk/ (pl: -ken) piece, chessman

het **schaaktoernooi** /sχɑkturnoj/ (pl: -en) chess tournament

de **schaal** /sχɑl/ (pl: schalen) **1** scale: *er wordt op grote ~ misbruik van gemaakt* it is misused on a large scale; *op ~ tekenen* draw to scale; *~ 4:1* a scale of four to one **2** dish, plate: *een ~ met fruit* a bowl of fruit; [fig] *gewicht in de ~ leggen* carry much weight

het **schaaldier** /sχɑldir/ (pl: -en) crustacean

het **schaalmodel** /sχɑlmodɛl/ (pl: -len) scale model

de **schaalverdeling** /sχɑlvərdelɪŋ/ (pl: -en) graduation, scale division: *een ~ op iets aanbrengen* graduate sth.

de **schaalvergroting** /sχɑlvərɣrotɪŋ/ (pl: -en) increase (in scale), expansion

het **schaambeen** /sχɑmben/ (pl: -deren) pubis, pubic bone

het **schaamdeel** /sχɑmdel/ (pl: -delen) genital(s), private part(s): *de vrouwelijke* (or: *mannelijke*) *schaamdelen* the female (or: male) genitals

het **schaamhaar** /sχɑmhɑr/ (pl: -haren) pubic

hair

de **schaamlippen** /sxamlɪpə(n)/ (pl) labia: *de grote* (or: *de kleine*) ~ the labia majora (or: minora)

het **schaamrood** /sxamrot/: *iem. het ~ naar de kaken jagen* bring a blush (of shame) to s.o.'s cheeks; *met het ~ op de kaken moet ik bekennen dat …* I plead guilty to …, I'm deeply embarrassed to admit that …

de **schaamte** /sxamtə/ shame: *blozen* (or: *rood worden*) *van ~* blush (or: go red) with shame; *plaatsvervangende ~ voelen* be ashamed for s.o. (else)

schaamteloos /sxamtəlos/ (adj, adv) shameless

het **schaap** /sxap/ (pl: schapen) sheep: *een kudde schapen* a flock of sheep; *het zwarte ~ (van de familie) zijn* be the black sheep (of the family); *~jes tellen* count sheep

schaapachtig /sxapɑxtəx/ (adj, adv) silly: *iem. ~ aankijken* look stupidly at s.o.; *~ lachen* grin sheepishly

de **schaapherder** /sxaphɛrdər/ (pl: -s) shepherd

de **schaar** /sxar/ (pl: scharen) **1** (pair of) scissors: *de ~ in iets zetten* take the scissors (or: a pair of scissors) to sth.; *één ~* one pair of scissors; *twee scharen* two (pairs of) scissors **2** pincers; claws

¹**schaars** /sxars/ (adj) scarce: *mijn ~e vrije ogenblikken* my rare free moments; *~ zijn* be in short supply

²**schaars** /sxars/ (adv) sparingly, sparsely; scantily: *~ verlicht* dimly lit

de **schaarste** /sxarstə/ scarcity, shortage

de **schaats** /sxats/ (pl: -en) skate: *de ~en onderbinden* put on one's skates

de **schaatsbaan** /sxatsban/ (pl: -banen) (skating) rink

schaatsen /sxatsə(n)/ (schaatste, heeft/is geschaatst) skate

de **schaatser** /sxatsər/ (pl: -s) skater

schabouwelijk /sxabouwələk/ (adj) [Belg] wretched, dismal

de **schacht** /sxaxt/ (pl: -en) **1** shaft; shank; [bot] stem **2** [Belg] fresher, first-year student

de **schade** /sxadə/ (pl: -n) **1** loss(es): *de ~ inhalen* recoup one's losses; *~ lijden* suffer a loss **2** damage; [pers also] harm: *~ aanrichten* damage sth.; *~ aan iets toebrengen* (or: *berokkenen*) do (or: cause) damage to sth.; *zijn auto heeft heel wat ~ opgelopen* his car has suffered quite a lot of damage; *de ~ loopt in de miljoenen* the damage runs into millions || *door ~ en schande wijs worden* live and learn, learn the hard way

de **schadeclaim** /sxadəklem/ (pl: -s) insurance claim (for damage): *een ~ afhandelen* settle a claim

de **schade-expert** /sxadɛkspɛːr/ (pl: -s) loss adjuster; [Am] insurance adjuster

het **schadeformulier** /sxadəfɔrmylir/ (pl: -en) claim form

schadelijk /sxadələk/ (adj, adv) harmful, damaging: *~e dieren* pests, vermin; *~e gewoonten* pernicious habits

schadeloosstellen /sxadəlostɛlə(n)/ (stelde schadeloos, heeft schadeloosgesteld) compensate; repay; reimburse: *zich ergens voor ~* compensate (o.s.) for sth.

de **schadeloosstelling** /sxadəlostɛlɪŋ/ (pl: -en) compensation: *volledige ~ betalen* pay full damages

schaden /sxadə(n)/ (schaadde, heeft geschaad) damage, harm: *roken schaadt de gezondheid* smoking damages your health; *baat het niet, het schaadt ook niet* it can't do any harm and it may do some good

de **schadepost** /sxadəpɔst/ (pl: -en) loss, (financial) setback

de **schadevergoeding** /sxadəvərɣudɪŋ/ (pl: -en) compensation; damages: *volledige ~ betalen* pay full damages; *~ eisen voor* claim compensation (or: damages) for; *€ 1000,- ~ krijgen* receive 1000 euros in damages

de **schaduw** /sxadyw/ (pl: -en) shade, shadow: *in iemands ~ staan* be the outshone (or: overshadowed) by s.o.; *uit de ~ treden* come out of the shadows; *een ~ werpen over iets* cast a shadow over sth.

de **schaduweconomie** /sxadywekonomi/ shadow economy

schaduwen /sxadywə(n)/ (schaduwde, heeft geschaduwd) shadow, tail: *iem. laten ~* have s.o. shadowed (or: tailed)

het **schaduwkabinet** /sxadywkabinɛt/ (pl: -ten) shadow cabinet

de **schaduwzijde** /sxadywzɛidə/ (pl: -n) **1** shady side **2** drawback: *de ~ van een overigens nuttige maatregel* the drawback to an otherwise useful measure

schaffen /sxɑfə(n)/: *eten wat de pot schaft* eat whatever's going

schaften /sxɑftə(n)/ (schaftte, heeft geschaft) break (for lunch, dinner)

de **schakel** /sxakəl/ (pl: -s) link: *een belangrijke ~* a vital link; *de ontbrekende ~* the missing link

de **schakelaar** /sxakəlar/ (pl: -s) switch

de **schakelarmband** /sxakəlɑrmbɑnt/ (pl: -en) chain bracelet

schakelen /sxakələ(n)/ (schakelde, heeft geschakeld) **1** connect: *parallel* (or: *in serie*) *~* connect in parallel (or: in series) **2** change, change gear(s): *naar de tweede versnelling ~* change to second (gear)

de **schakeling** /sxakəlɪŋ/ (pl: -en) **1** connection, circuit **2** gear change: *automatische ~* automatic gear change

de **schakelkast** /sxakəlkɑst/ (pl: -en) switch box, switch cupboard

schaken /sxakə(n)/ (schaakte, heeft geschaakt) play chess: *een partijtje* ~ play a game of chess; *simultaan* ~ play simultaneous chess

de **schaker** /sχɑkər/ (pl: -s) chess player

de **schakering** /sχɑkerɪŋ/ (pl: -en) **1** diversity **2** pattern(ing)

het **schaliegas** /sχɑliɣɑs/ shale gas

schalks /sχɑlks/ (adj) mischievous, sly

schallen /sχɑlə(n)/ (schalde, heeft geschald) (re)sound; peal

schamel /sχɑməl/ (adj, adv) poor, shabby: *een* ~ *pensioentje* a meagre (*or:* miserable) pension

zich **schamen** /sχɑmə(n)/ (schaamde zich, heeft zich geschaamd) be ashamed (of), be embarrassed: *zich dood* (or: *rot*) ~ die with shame; *daar hoef je je niet voor te* ~ there's no need to be ashamed of that; *zich nergens voor* ~ not be ashamed of anything

schamper /sχɑmpər/ (adj) scornful, sarcastic, sneering

schamperen /sχɑmpərə(n)/ (schamperde, heeft geschamperd) sneer

het **schampschot** /sχɑmpsχɔt/ (pl: -schoten) grazing shot

het **schandaal** /sχɑndɑl/ (pl: schandalen) **1** scandal, outrage: *een publiek* (or: *een politiek*) ~ a public outrage, a political scandal **2** shame, disgrace: *een grof* ~ a crying shame

de **schandaalpers** /sχɑndɑlpɛrs/ gutter press

schandalig /sχɑndɑləχ/ (adj, adv) scandalous, outrageous, disgraceful: ~ *duur* outrageously expensive; *het is* ~ *zoals hij ons behandelt* it's disgraceful the way he treats us

de **schande** /sχɑndə/ disgrace, shame: *het is een* ~ it's a disgrace; ~ *van iets spreken* cry out against sth.

schandelijk /sχɑndələk/ (adj, adv) scandalous, outrageous: *een* ~ *boek* an infamous book

de **schandpaal** /sχɑntpal/ (pl: -palen): *iem. aan de* ~ *nagelen* pillory s.o.

de **schandvlek** /sχɑntflɛk/ (pl: -ken) **1** blot **2** disgrace

de **schans** /sχɑns/ (pl: -en) ski jump

schansspringen /sχɑnsprɪŋə(n)/ ski jump

het/de **schap** /sχɑp/ (pl: -pen) shelf: *de ~pen bijvullen* re-stock the shelves

de **schapenkaas** /sχɑpə(n)kas/ sheep's (*or:* ewe's) cheese

de **schapenscheerder** /sχɑpə(n)sχerdər/ (pl: -s) sheepshearer

de **schapenvacht** /sχɑpə(n)vɑχt/ (pl: -en) sheepskin, fleece

het **schapenvlees** /sχɑpə(n)vles/ mutton, lamb

de **schapenwol** /sχɑpə(n)wɔl/ sheep's wool

de **schapenwolkjes** /sχɑpə(n)wɔlkjəs/ (pl) fleecy clouds

schappelijk /sχɑpələk/ (adj, adv) reasonable, fair

de **schar** /sχɑr/ (pl: -ren) dab, sheepdog

¹**scharen** /sχɑrə(n)/ (schaarde, is geschaard) jackknife

²**scharen** /sχɑrə(n)/ (schaarde, heeft geschaard) range: *zich om het vuur* ~ gather round the fire; [fig] *zich achter iem.* ~ side with s.o.

het/de **scharminkel** /sχɑrmɪŋkəl/ (pl: -s) scrag(gy person): *een mager* ~ a bag of bones

het **scharnier** /sχɑrnir/ (pl: -en) hinge: *om een* ~ *draaien* hinge

scharnieren /sχɑrnirə(n)/ (scharnierde, heeft gescharnierd) hinge

de **scharrel** /sχɑrəl/ (pl: -s) [inform] **1** flirt **2** flirtation: *aan de* ~ *zijn* fool around

de **scharrelaar** /sχɑrəlar/ (pl: -s) odd-jobber

het **scharrelei** /sχɑrəlɛi/ (pl: -eren) free-range egg

scharrelen /sχɑrələ(n)/ (scharrelde, heeft gescharreld) **1** rummage (about): *hij scharrelt de hele dag in de tuin* he potters about in the garden all day (long) **2** scratch

de **scharrelkip** /sχɑrəlkɪp/ (pl: -pen) free-range chicken

de **schat** /sχɑt/ (pl: -ten) **1** treasure: *een verborgen* ~ a hidden treasure **2** treasure, riches: *~ten aan iets verdienen* make a fortune out of sth.; *een* ~ *aan gegevens* (or: *materiaal*) a wealth of data (*or:* material) **3** darling, dear, honey: *zijn het geen ~jes?* aren't they sweet?

de **schatbewaarder** /sχɑdbəwardər/ (pl: -s) [Belg] treasurer

schateren /sχɑtərə(n)/ (schaterde, heeft geschaterd) roar (with laughter): *de kinderen* ~ *van plezier* the children shouted with pleasure

de **schaterlach** /sχɑtərlɑχ/ loud laughter

de **schatgraver** /sχɑtχravər/ (pl: -s) treasure digger

de **schatkamer** /sχɑtkamər/ (pl: -s) treasury, treasure house

de **schatkist** /sχɑtkɪst/ (pl: -en) **1** treasure chest **2** treasury, (the) Exchequer

schatplichtig /sχɑtplɪχtəχ/ (adj) tributary: ~ *zijn aan iem.* be indebted to s.o.

schatrijk /sχɑtrɛik/ (adj) wealthy: *ze zijn schat- en* ~ they are fabulously wealthy

de **schattebout** /sχɑtəbɑut/ (pl: -en) dear, darling

schatten /sχɑtə(n)/ (schatte, heeft geschat) value; estimate; assess; appraise: *de afstand* ~ estimate the distance; *hoe oud schat je hem?* how old do you take him to be?; *de schade* ~ *op* assess the damage at

schattig /sχɑtəχ/ (adj, adv) sweet, lovely: *zij ziet er* ~ *uit* she looks lovely

de **schatting** /sχɑtɪŋ/ (pl: -en) estimate, assessment: *een voorzichtige* ~ a conservative estimate; *naar* ~ *drie miljoen* an estimated three million

schaven /sχɑvə(n)/ (schaafde, heeft geschaafd) **1** plane: *planken* ~ plane boards **2** graze, scrape **3** slice, shred: *komkommers* ~ slice cucumbers

het **schavot** /sxavɔt/ (pl: -ten) scaffold: *iem. op het ~ brengen* **a)** condemn s.o. to the scaffold; **b)** [fig] cause s.o.'s downfall

de **schavuit** /sxavœyt/ (pl: -en) rascal

de **schede** /sxedə/ (pl: -n, -s) **1** sheath **2** vagina

de **schedel** /sxedəl/ (pl: -s) skull

de **schedelbasisfractuur** /sxedəlbazısfraktyr/ (pl: -fracturen) fracture of the base of the skull

scheef /sxef/ (adj, adv) **1** crooked; oblique; leaning; slanting; sloping: *scheve hoeken* oblique angles; *een ~ gezicht trekken* pull a wry face; *een scheve neus hebben* have a crooked nose; *het schilderij hangt ~* the picture is crooked **2** wrong, distorted: *de zaak gaat (loopt) ~* things are going wrong

de **scheefgroei** /sxefxruj/ [fig] adverse development

scheel /sxel/ (adj, adv) cross-eyed

scheelzien /sxelzin/ (zag scheel, heeft scheelgezien) squint

de **scheen** /sxen/ (pl: schenen) shin: *iem. tegen de schenen schoppen* tread on s.o.'s toes

het **scheenbeen** /sxemben/ (pl: -deren, -benen) shinbone

de **scheenbeschermer** /sxembəsxɛrmər/ (pl: -s) shinguard

de **scheepsbouw** /sxepsbau/ shipbuilding (industry)

de **scheepsbouwer** /sxepsbauwər/ (pl: -s) shipbuilder

de **scheepshut** /sxepshʏt/ (pl: -ten) (ship's) cabin

de **scheepslading** /sxepsladıŋ/ (pl: -en) shipload, (ship's) cargo

de **scheepsramp** /sxepsramp/ (pl: -en) shipping disaster

het **scheepsrecht** /sxepsrɛxt/: *driemaal is ~* third time lucky

het **scheepsruim** /sxepsrœym/ (pl: -en) (ship's) hold

de **scheepswerf** /sxepswɛrf/ (pl: -werven) shipyard

de **scheepvaart** /sxepfart/ shipping (traffic), navigation

het **scheepvaartverkeer** /sxepfartfərker/ shipping (traffic)

het **scheerapparaat** /sxeraparat/ (pl: -apparaten) shaver

de **scheerkwast** /sxerkwast/ (pl: -en) shaving brush

de **scheerlijn** /sxerlɛın/ (pl: -en) **1** stretching wire **2** guy (rope)

het **scheermes** /sxɛrmɛs/ (pl: -sen) razor

het **scheermesje** /sxɛrmɛʃə/ (pl: -s) razor blade

de **scheerwol** /sxerwɔl/ (virgin) wool: *zuiver ~* pure new wool

de **scheerzeep** /sxerzep/ shaving soap

de **scheet** /sxet/ (pl: scheten) [inform] fart: *een ~ laten* fart

scheidbaar /sxɛidbar/ (adj, adv) separable

¹**scheiden** /sxɛidə(n)/ (scheidde, is gescheiden) **1** part (company), separate: *hier ~ onze wegen* here our ways part; ~ *van* part (or: separate) from; *als vrienden ~* part (as) friends **2** divorce; separate: *zij gaan ~* they are getting divorced

²**scheiden** /sxɛidə(n)/ (scheidde, heeft gescheiden) **1** separate, divide: *dooier en eiwit ~* separate the yolk from the (egg) white; *het hoofd van de romp ~* sever the head from the body; *twee vechtende jongens ~* separate two fighting boys; *huisvuil ~* sort the household waste **2** divorce; separate: *zich laten ~* get a divorce

de **scheiding** /sxɛidıŋ/ (pl: -en) **1** separation, detachment: *een ~ maken (veroorzaken) (in)* rupture, disrupt **2** divorce: *in ~ liggen* be getting a divorce; ~ *van tafel en bed* legal separation **3** parting

de **scheidingswand** /sxɛidıŋswant/ dividing wall

de **scheidslijn** /sxɛitslɛin/ (pl: -en) dividing line; [fig] borderline

de **scheidsmuur** /sxɛitsmyr/ (pl: -muren) partition; [fig] barrier

de **scheidsrechter** /sxɛitsrɛxtər/ (pl: -s) umpire; referee: *als ~ optreden bij een wedstrijd* umpire (or: referee) a match

de **scheikunde** /sxɛikʏndə/ chemistry

scheikundig /sxɛikʏndəx/ (adj, adv) chemical

schel /sxɛl/ (adj, adv) shrill: *een ~le stem* a shrill (or: piercing) voice

de **Schelde** /sxɛldə/ Scheldt

schelden /sxɛldə(n)/ (schold, heeft gescholden) curse, swear: *vloeken en ~* curse and swear; *op iem. ~* scold s.o., call s.o. names

de **scheldkanonnade** /sxɛltkanɔnadə/ (pl: -s) [Dutch] torrent of abuse

de **scheldnaam** /sxɛltnam/ (pl: -namen) term of abuse

het **scheldwoord** /sxɛltwort/ (pl: -en) term of abuse

schelen /sxelə(n)/ (scheelde, heeft gescheeld) **1** differ: *ze ~ twee maanden* they are two months apart **2** concern, matter: *het kan mij niets* (or: *geen bal*) ~ I don't give a hoot (or: care two hoots); *het kan me niet ~* I don't care; *I don't mind; kan mij wat ~!* why should I care! ‖ *het scheelde geen haar* it was a close shave; *dat scheelt (me) weer een ritje* that saves (me) another trip; *wat scheelt je?* what's the matter with you?; *het scheelde weinig, of hij was verdronken* he narrowly escaped being drowned

de **schelm** /sxɛlm/ (pl: -en) crook

de **schelp** /sxɛlp/ (pl: -en) **1** shell **2** auricle

de **schelpdieren** /sxɛlbdirə(n)/ (pl) shellfish

de **schelvis** /sxɛlvɪs/ (pl: -sen) haddock

het **schema** /sxema/ (pl: -'s) **1** diagram, plan **2** plan, outline **3** schedule: *we liggen weer op* ~ we're back on schedule; *achter* (or: *voor*) *op het* ~ behind (or: ahead of) schedule

schematisch /sxematis/ (adj, adv) schematic, diagrammatic: *iets* ~ *voorstellen (aangeven)* represent sth. in diagram form

de **schemer** /sxemər/ twilight: *de* ~ *valt* evening is falling

het **schemerdonker** /sxemərdɔŋkər/ twilight, half-light; dusk

schemeren /sxemərə(n)/ (schemerde, heeft geschemerd) grow dark; become light: *het begint te* ~ it is getting dark (or: light); twilight is setting in

schemerig /sxemərəx/ (adj, adv) dusky

de **schemering** /sxemərɪŋ/ twilight, dusk, dawn

de **schemerlamp** /sxemərlɑmp/ (pl: -en) floor lamp, standard lamp

de **schemertoestand** /sxemərtustɑnt/ twilight state

schenden /sxɛndə(n)/ (schond, heeft geschonden) **1** damage **2** break, violate: *een verdrag* (or: *mensenrechten*) ~ violate a treaty (or: human rights)

de **schending** /sxɛndɪŋ/ (pl: -en) violation; breach

de **schenkel** /sxɛŋkəl/ (pl: -s) shank

schenken /sxɛŋkə(n)/ (schonk, heeft geschonken) **1** pour (out) **2** give: *zijn hart* ~ *aan* give one's heart to ‖ *geen aandacht* ~ *aan iem.* take no notice (or: account) of s.o., pay no attention to s.o.

de **schenking** /sxɛŋkɪŋ/ (pl: -en) gift, donation: *een* ~ *doen* make a gift (or: donation)

de **schennis** /sxɛnɪs/ (pl: -sen) violation: ~ *plegen* commit indecent exposure

de **schep** /sxɛp/ **1** scoop; shovel **2** (table)-spoon(ful), scoop(ful): *drie ~pen ijs* three scoops of ice cream

de **schepen** /sxepə(n)/ (pl: -en) [Belg] alderman

het **schepencollege** /sxepə(n)kɔleʒə/ (pl: -s) [Belg] bench of (Mayor and) Aldermen

het **schepijs** /sxɛpɛis/ (easy-scoop) ice cream

het **schepje** /sxɛpjə/ (pl: -s) **1** (small) spoon **2** spoon(ful): *een* ~ *suiker* a spoonful of sugar ‖ *er een* ~ *(boven)op doen* a) add a little extra; b) heighten (the effect)

het **schepnet** /sxɛpnɛt/ (pl: -ten) dip (or: landing) net

¹**scheppen** /sxɛpə(n)/ (schepte, heeft geschept) scoop, shovel: *een emmer water* ~ draw a bucket of water; *leeg* ~ empty; *vol* ~ fill; *zand op een kruiwagen* ~ shovel sand into a wheelbarrow

²**scheppen** /sxɛpə(n)/ (schiep, heeft geschapen) create: *God schiep de hemel en de aarde* God created heaven and earth

de **schepper** /sxɛpər/ (pl: -s) creator

de **schepping** /sxɛpɪŋ/ (pl: -en) creation

het **scheppingsverhaal** /sxɛpɪŋsfərhal/ story of the Creation

het **schepsel** /sxɛpsəl/ (pl: -en, -s) creature

¹**scheren** /sxerə(n)/ (schoor, heeft geschoren) shave; shear: *zich* ~ shave; *geschoren schapen* shorn sheep

²**scheren** /sxerə(n)/ (scheerde, heeft/is gescheerd): *scheer je weg!* get away!, buzz off!

de **scherf** /sxɛrf/ (pl: scherven) fragment; splinter: *in scherven (uiteen)vallen* fall to pieces; *scherven brengen geluk* [roughly] no good crying over spilt milk

de **schering** /sxerɪŋ/ (pl: -en): *dat is* ~ *en inslag* that is the order of the day

het **scherm** /sxɛrm/ (pl: -en) **1** screen, shade **2** curtain: *de man achter de ~en* the man behind the scenes **3** screen, display

de **schermafdruk** /sxɛrmɑvdrʏk/ (pl: -ken) screenshot, print screen

schermen /sxɛrmə(n)/ (schermde, heeft geschermd) fence

de **schermutseling** /sxɛrmʏtsəlɪŋ/ (pl: -en) skirmish, clash

het ¹**scherp** /sxɛrp/ **1** edge: *op het* ~ *van de snede balanceren* be on a knife-edge **2** ball: *met* ~ *schieten* fire (with) live ammunition; *op* ~ *staan* be on edge

²**scherp** /sxɛrp/ (adj) **1** sharp, pointed; [maths] acute: *een* ~ *kin* a pointed chin **2** sharp, pungent, hot; spicy; cutting; biting: *~e mosterd* (or: *kerrie*) hot mustard (or: curry) **3** strict, severe: ~ *toezicht* close control **4** sharp, harsh: *~e kritiek* sharp criticism **5** sharp, clear-cut: *een* ~ *contrast vormen* be in sharp contrast with; ~ *stellen* focus **6** live; armed

scherpen /sxɛrpə(n)/ (scherpte, heeft gescherpt) sharpen

scherpomlijnd /sxɛrpɔmlɛint/ (adj) clear-cut, well-defined

de **scherpschutter** /sxɛrpsxʏtər/ (pl: -s) sharpshooter; sniper

de **scherpslijper** /sxɛrpslɛipər/ (pl: -s) quibbler

de **scherpte** /sxɛrptə/ (pl: -n, -s) sharpness, keenness: *de* ~ *van het beeld* the sharpness of the picture; *de* ~ *van een foto* the focus of a picture; [fig] ~ *missen* lack focus, not be on the ball

scherpzinnig /sxɛrpsɪnəx/ (adj, adv) **1** acute, discerning, sharp(-witted): *een ~e geest* a subtle mind **2** shrewd, clever: ~ *antwoorden* give a shrewd answer

de **scherts** /sxɛrts/ joke, jest

schertsen /sxɛrtsə(n)/ (schertste, heeft geschertst) joke, jest

de **schertsfiguur** /sxɛrtsfiɣyr/ (pl: -figuren) joke, nonentity

de **schertsvertoning** /sxɛrtsfərtonɪŋ/ (pl: -en) joke

de **schets** /sxɛts/ (pl: -en) sketch: *een eerste* ~ a

first draft; *een ruwe* (or: *korte*) ~ *van mijn leven* a rough (or: brief) outline of my life

het **schetsboek** /sxɛtsbuk/ (pl: -en) sketchbook
schetsen /sxɛtsə(n)/ (schetste, heeft geschetst) sketch: *een beeld ~ van* paint a picture of; *ruw (in grote lijnen) ~* give a rough sketch (of)

schetteren /sxɛtərə(n)/ (schetterde, heeft geschetterd) blare

de **scheur** /sxør/ (pl: -en) **1** crack, crevice; split: *een ~ in een muur* a crack in a wall **2** tear: *hij heeft een ~ in mijn nieuwe boek gemaakt* he has torn my new book || *zijn ~ opentrekken* open one's big mouth

de **scheurbuik** /sxørbœyk/ scurvy: *aan ~ lijdend* scorbutic

¹**scheuren** /sxørə(n)/ (scheurde, is gescheurd) tear (apart); crack; split: *pas op, het papier zal ~* be careful, the paper will tear; *de auto scheurde door de bocht* the car came screeching round the corner

²**scheuren** /sxørə(n)/ (scheurde, heeft gescheurd) tear: *zijn kleren ~* tear one's clothes

de **scheuring** /sxørɪŋ/ (pl: -en) rift, split; schism

de **scheurkalender** /sxørkalɛndər/ (pl: -s) block-calendar

de **scheut** /sxøt/ (pl: -en) **1** shoot, sprout **2** twinge, stab (of pain) **3** dash; shot: *een ~ melk* a dash of milk

scheutig /sxøtəx/ (adj) generous: *hij is ~ met de wijn* he pours the wine generously; *niet ~ zijn met informatie* be stingy with information || [Belg] *~ op iets zijn* be keen on sth.

schichtig /sxɪxtəx/ (adj, adv) nervous, timid; skittish

schielijk /sxilək/ (adv) quickly, rapidly

het **schiereiland** /sxirɛilɑnt/ (pl: -en) peninsula

de **schietbaan** /sxidban/ (pl: -banen) shooting range

¹**schieten** /sxitə(n)/ (schoot, heeft geschoten) **1** shoot; fire: *op iem. ~* shoot (or: take a shot) at s.o.; [fig] *niet geschoten is altijd mis* you can always try **2** (+ laten) let go, release; drop [pers]; forget [pers]: *laat hem ~* forget (about) him

²**schieten** /sxitə(n)/ (schoot, is geschoten) shoot, dash: *de prijzen ~ omhoog* prices are soaring; *het kind was plotseling de weg over geschoten* the child had suddenly dashed (out) across the road || *de tranen schoten haar in de ogen* tears rushed to her eyes; *weer te binnen ~* come back (to mind); *iem. te hulp ~* rush to s.o.'s aid (or: assistance)

³**schieten** /sxitə(n)/ (schoot, heeft geschoten) shoot: *hij kon haar wel ~* he could (cheerfully) have murdered her; *zich een kogel door het hoofd ~* blow out one's brains; *naast ~* miss; *in het doel ~* net (the ball)

het **schietgebed** /sxitxəbɛt/ (pl: -en) short prayer, quick prayer: *een ~je doen* say a quick prayer

de **schietpartij** /sxitpɑrtɛi/ (pl: -en) shoot-out, shooting

het **schietschijf** /sxitsxɛif/ (pl: -schijven) target

de **schietstoel** /sxitstul/ (pl: -en) ejector seat, ejection seat

de **schiettent** /sxitɛnt/ (pl: -en) rifle gallery, shooting gallery

¹**schiften** /sxɪftə(n)/ (schiftte, is geschift) curdle, turn

²**schiften** /sxɪftə(n)/ (schiftte, heeft geschift) sort (out), sift (through)

de **schifting** /sxɪftɪŋ/ (pl: -en) **1** sifting: *Jan is bij de eerste ~ afgevallen* Jan was weeded out in the first round **2** curdling

de **schijf** /sxɛif/ (pl: schijven) **1** disc **2** disc, plate; (potter's) wheel **3** slice: *een ~je citroen* a slice of lemon **4** disk

de **schijfrem** /sxɛifrɛm/ (pl: -men) disc brake

de **schijn** /sxɛin/ **1** appearance, semblance: *op de uiterlijke ~ afgaan* judge by (outward) appearances; *~ bedriegt* appearances are deceptive; *de ~ ophouden tegenover de familie* keep up appearances in front of the family **2** show, appearances: *schone ~* glamour, cosmetics, gloss **3** shadow, gleam: *geen ~ van kans hebben* not have the ghost of a chance

schijnbaar /sxɛimbar/ (adj, adv) seeming, apparent: *~ oprecht* seemingly sincere

de **schijnbeweging** /sxɛimbəwexɪŋ/ (pl: -en) feint, dummy (movement, pass): *een ~ maken* (make a) feint

de ¹**schijndood** /sxɛindot/ apparent death, suspended animation

²**schijndood** /sxɛindot/ (adj) apparently dead, in a state of suspended animation

schijnen /sxɛinə(n)/ (scheen, heeft geschenen) **1** shine: *de zon schijnt* the sun is shining; *met een zaklantaarn in iemands gezicht ~* flash a torch in s.o.'s face **2** seem, appear: *het schijnt zo* it looks like it; *hij schijnt erg rijk te zijn* apparently he is very rich

schijnheilig /sxɛinhɛiləx/ (adj, adv) hypocritical, sanctimonious: *met een ~ gezicht* sanctimoniously

het **schijnhuwelijk** /sxɛinhywələk/ (pl: -en) marriage of convenience

het **schijnsel** /sxɛinsəl/ (pl: -s) shine, light

het **schijntje** /sxɛincə/ (pl: -s): *ik kocht het voor een ~* I bought it for a song

de **schijnvertoning** /sxɛinvərtonɪŋ/ (pl: -en) diversion

de **schijnwerper** /sxɛinwɛrpər/ (pl: -s) floodlight; spotlight: *iem. in de ~s zetten* spotlight s.o.; [fig] *in de ~s staan* be in the limelight, be the centre of attention

het/de **schijt** /sxɛit/ [inform] shit, crap

schijten /sxɛitə(n)/ (scheet, heeft gescheten) [inform] shit, crap

de **schijterd** /sxɛitərt/ (pl: -s) [Dutch; inform] funk, scaredy-cat

schijterig /sxɛitərəx/ (adj, adv) [inform]

chicken-hearted

de **schijterij** /sχɛitərɛi̯/ [inform] shits; trots; runs: *aan de ~ zijn* have the shits (*or:* trots, runs)

de **schik** /sχɪk/ contentment, fun: *~ hebben in zijn werk* enjoy one's work

schikken /sχɪkə(n)/ (schikte, heeft geschikt) arrange, order: *de boeken in volgorde ~* put the books in order; *zich naar iem. ~* go along with s.o.

de **schikking** /sχɪkɪŋ/ (pl: -en) arrangement, ordering || *een ~ treffen (met)* reach an understanding (with)

de **schil** /sχɪl/ (pl: -len) skin; rind; peel

het **schild** /sχɪlt/ (pl: -en) **1** shield; shell: *een menselijk ~* a human shield **2** sign

de **schilder** /sχɪldər/ (pl: -s) **1** (house-)painter; (house-)decorator **2** painter

schilderachtig /sχɪldəraχtəχ/ (adj, adv) picturesque; scenic

schilderen /sχɪldərə(n)/ (schilderde, heeft geschilderd) paint, decorate: *zijn huis laten ~* have one's house painted

het **schilderij** /sχɪldərɛi̯/ (pl: -en) painting, picture: *een ~ in olieverf* an oil painting

de **schildering** /sχɪldərɪŋ/ (pl: -en) painting, picture: *~en op een wand* murals

de **schilderkunst** /sχɪldərkʏnst/ (art of) painting

het **schildersbedrijf** /sχɪldərzbədrɛif/ (pl: -bedrijven) painter and decorator's business

de **schildersezel** /sχɪldərsezəl/ (pl: -s) (painter's) easel

het **schilderstuk** /sχɪldərstʏk/ (pl: -ken) painting, picture

het **schilderwerk** /sχɪldərwɛrk/ **1** painting: *het ~ op de wand* the mural (painting) **2** paintwork: *het ~ aanbesteden* give out the paintwork by contract

de **schildklier** /sχɪltklir/ (pl: -en) thyroid gland

de **schildknaap** /sχɪltknap/ (pl: -knapen) shield-bearer, squire

de **schildpad** /sχɪltpɑt/ (pl: -den) tortoise; turtle

de **schildwacht** /sχɪltwɑχt/ (pl: -en) sentry, guard: *~en aflossen* change the guard

de **schilfer** /sχɪlfər/ (pl: -s) scale; flake; chip; sliver

schilferen /sχɪlfərə(n)/ (schilferde, heeft/is geschilferd) flake (off), peel (off)

schillen /sχɪlə(n)/ (schilde, heeft geschild) peel: *aardappels ~* peel potatoes

de **schim** /sχɪm/ (pl: -men) shadow: *~men in het donker* shadows in the dark

de **schimmel** /sχɪməl/ (pl: -s) **1** mould, mildew: *de ~ van kaas afhalen* scrape the mould off cheese; *er zit ~ op die muur* there is mildew on the wall **2** [bot] fungus **3** grey **4** fungal infection

schimmelen /sχɪmələ(n)/ (schimmelde, is geschimmeld) mould, become mouldy (*or:* mildewed)

schimmelig /sχɪmələχ/ (adj) mouldy

de **schimmelinfectie** /sχɪmməlɪnfɛksi/ (pl: -s) fungal infection

het **schimmenspel** /sχɪmə(n)spɛl/ shadow theatre, shadow play

schimmig /sχɪmməχ/ (adj) **1** shadowy **2** [fig] vague, sketchy: *een ~ verhaal* a strange tale

schimpen /sχɪmpə(n)/ (schimpte, heeft geschimpt) scoff, jeer, sneer

het **schip** /sχɪp/ (pl: schepen) ship; vessel; barge; boat: *per ~* by ship (*or:* boat); [fig] *zijn schepen achter zich verbranden* burn one's boats; [fig] *het zinkende ~ verlaten* leave the sinking ship; [fig] *schoon ~ maken* make a clean sweep, clean things up

de **schipbreuk** /sχɪbrøk/ (pl: -en) shipwreck, wreck: *~ lijden* **a)** founder, be wrecked; **b)** be shipwrecked

de **schipbreukeling** /sχɪbrøkəlɪŋ/ (pl: -en) shipwrecked person

de **schipper** /sχɪpər/ (pl: -s) master (of a ship), captain, skipper

schipperen /sχɪpərə(n)/ (schipperde, heeft geschipperd) give and take: *je moet een beetje weten te ~* you've got to give and take (a bit)

de **schipperstrui** /sχɪpərstrœy̯/ (pl: -en) seaman's pullover

het **schisma** /sχɪsma/ (pl: -'s, -ta) schism

schitteren /sχɪtərə(n)/ (schitterde, heeft geschitterd) **1** glitter, shine, twinkle: *zijn ogen schitterden van plezier* his eyes twinkled with amusement **2** shine (in, at), excel (in, at): *~ in gezelschap* be a social success; *~ door afwezigheid* be conspicuous by one's absence

schitterend /sχɪtərənt/ (adj, adv) **1** brilliant, sparkling: *het weer was ~* the weather was gorgeous **2** splendid, magnificent: *een ~ doelpunt* a marvellous goal

de **schittering** /sχɪtərɪŋ/ (pl: -en) brilliance, radiance

schizofreen /sχidzofren/ (adj) schizophrenic

de **schizofrenie** /sχidzofreni/ schizophrenia

de **schlager** /ʃlaɡər/ (pl: -s) (schmalzy) pop(ular) song

de **schlemiel** /ʃləmil/ (pl: -en) [Dutch; inform] wally

de **schmink** /ʃmɪŋk/ **1** greasepaint, make-up **2** make-up, make-up room: *hij zit nog in de ~* he is still in make-up

schminken /ʃmɪŋkə(n)/ (schminkte, heeft geschminkt) make (s.o.) up: *zich ~* make (o.s.) up

de **schnabbel** /ʃnɑbəl/ (pl: -s) (bit of a) job on the side: *daar heb ik een leuke ~ aan* it brings in a bit extra for me

de **schnitzel** /ʃnɪtsəl/ (pl: -s) (veal, pork) cutlet, schnitzel

het **schoeisel** /sχujsəl/ footwear

de **schoen** /sχun/ (pl: -en) shoe: *twee **paar** ~en* two pairs of shoes; *hoge ~en* boots; [Belg] *in nauwe ~tjes zitten* be in dire straits; *zijn ~en aantrekken* put on one's shoes; *zijn ~en uittrekken* take off one's shoes; [fig] *de stoute ~en aantrekken* take the plunge; *ik zou niet graag in zijn ~en willen staan* I wouldn't like to be in his shoes; *iem. iets in de ~en schuiven* pin sth. on (to) s.o., lay sth. at s.o.'s door

de **schoenenzaak** /sχunə(n)zak/ (pl: -zaken) shoe shop

de **schoener** /sχunər/ (pl: -s) schooner

de **schoenlepel** /sχunlepəl/ (pl: -s) shoehorn

de **schoenmaat** /sχumat/ (pl: -maten) shoe size

de **schoenmaker** /sχumakər/ (pl: -s) cobbler, shoemaker: *die schoenen moeten **naar** de ~* those shoes need repairing

het/de **schoensmeer** /sχunsmer/ shoe polish, shoe cream

de **schoenveter** /sχunvetər/ (pl: -s) shoelace: *zijn ~s **strikken** (or: **vastmaken**)* lace up (or: tie) one's shoes

de **schoenzool** /sχunzol/ (pl: -zolen) sole

de **schoep** /sχup/ (pl: -en) blade

de **schoffel** /sχɔfəl/ (pl: -s) hoe

schoffelen /sχɔfələ(n)/ (schoffelde, heeft geschoffeld) **1** weed **2** [Dutch] do community service

schofferen /sχɔfɛrə(n)/ (schoffeerde, heeft geschofferd) treat with contempt

het **schoffie** /sχɔfi/ (pl: -s) [Dutch] rascal

de **schoft** /sχɔft/ **1** bastard **2** shoulder; withers

schofterig /sχɔftərəχ/ (adj, adv) rascally

de **schok** /sχɔk/ (pl: -en) **1** shock: *dat nieuws zal een ~ **geven*** that news will come as quite a shock; *de ~ te boven komen* get over the shock **2** jolt: *een ~ **krijgen*** receive a shock; *de ~ken van een **aardbeving*** earthquake tremors; *de ~ was zo **hevig** dat …* the (force of the) impact was so great that …

het **schokbeton** /sχɔgbeton/ vibrated concrete

de **schokbreker** /sχɔgbrekər/ (pl: -s) shock absorber

de **schokdemper** /sχɔgdɛmpər/ (pl: -s) shock absorber

het **schokeffect** /sχɔkɛfɛkt/ (pl: -en) shock, impact: *voor een ~ **zorgen*** create a shock

¹**schokken** /sχɔkə(n)/ (schokte, heeft geschokt) shake, jolt

²**schokken** /sχɔkə(n)/ (schokte, heeft geschokt) shock: *die **beelden** shocking scenes

de ¹**schol** /sχɔl/ (pl: -len) plaice

²**schol** /sχɔl/ (int) [Belg] cheers!

de **scholekster** /sχɔlɛkstər/ (pl: -s) oystercatcher

scholen /sχolə(n)/ (schoolde, heeft geschoold) school, train

de **scholengemeenschap** /sχolə(n)ɣemensχɔp/ (pl: -pen) [roughly] comprehensive school

de **scholier** /sχolir/ (pl: -en) **1** pupil; [Am] student **2** [Belg] junior member (14, 15 years) of sports club

de **scholing** /sχolɪŋ/ training, schooling: *een man **met** weinig ~* a man of little schooling (or: education)

de **schommel** /sχɔməl/ (pl: -s) swing

schommelen /sχɔmələ(n)/ (schommelde, heeft/is geschommeld) **1** swing; rock; roll **2** swing, rock: *ze zijn **aan** het ~* they are playing on the swings **3** fluctuate

de **schommeling** /sχɔməlɪŋ/ (pl: -en) fluctuation, swing

de **schommelstoel** /sχɔməlstul/ (pl: -en) rocking chair

de **schoof** /sχof/ (pl: schoven) sheaf

schooien /sχojə(n)/ (schooide, heeft geschooid) beg: *die hond schooit **bij** iedereen om een stukje vlees* that dog begs a piece of meat from everybody

de **schooier** /sχojər/ (pl: -s) tramp, vagrant; [Am] bum

de **school** /sχol/ (pl: scholen) **1** school: *een **bijzondere** ~* a denominational school; *de **lagere** ~* primary school; *de **middelbare** ~* secondary school; [Am] high school; *een **neutrale** ~* a non-denominational school; *een **openbare** ~* a state school; [Am] a public school; *vrije ~* Rudolf Steiner School; *een **witte, zwarte** ~* a predominantly white, black school; *naar ~ gaan* go to school; *de kinderen zijn **naar** de ~* the children are at school; *op de middelbare ~ zitten* go to (or: attend) secondary school; *uit ~ komen* come home from school; *als de kinderen **van** ~ zijn* when the children have finished school; *zij werd **van** ~ gestuurd* she was expelled from school; *een ~ **voor** voortgezet onderwijs* a secondary school **2** school: *een ~ **haringen*** a school of herring ǁ *uit de ~ **klappen*** tell tales

de **schoolagenda** /sχolaɣɛnda/ (pl: -'s) school diary

de **schoolarts** /sχolɑrts/ (pl: -en) school doctor

de **schoolbank** /sχolbɑŋk/ (pl: -en) school desk: *ik heb met hem **in** de ~en gezeten* we went to school together, we were schoolmates

de **schoolbel** /sχolbɛl/ (pl: -len) school bell

het **schoolbestuur** /sχolbəstyr/ (pl: -besturen) board of governors

schoolblijven /sχolblɛivə(n)/ (bleef school, is schoolgebleven) stay in (after school), be kept in (after school)

het **schoolboek** /sχolbuk/ (pl: -en) school book, textbook

het **schoolbord** /sχolbort/ (pl: -en) blackboard

de **schoolbus** /sχolbʏs/ (pl: -sen) school bus

de **schooldag** /sχoldɑχ/ (pl: -en) school day: *de **eerste** ~* the first day of school

het **schoolexamen** /sχolɛksamə(n)/ (pl: -s) [Dutch] exam(ination) het **schoolfeest** /sxolfest/ (pl: -en) school party

schoolgaand /sxolɣant/ (adj) schoolgoing: ~e *kinderen* children of school age

het **schoolgebouw** /sxolɣəbɑu/ (pl: -en) school (building)

het **schoolgeld** /sxolɣɛlt/ (pl: -en) tuition, fee(s)

het **schoolhoofd** /sxolhoft/ (pl: -en) principal, headmaster, headmistress

het **schooljaar** /sxoljar/ (pl: -jaren) school year: *het eerste* ~ *over moeten doen* have to repeat the first year

de **schooljeugd** /sxoljøxt/ school-age children, school-agers

de **schooljongen** /sxoljɔŋə(n)/ (pl: -s) schoolboy

de **schooljuffrouw** /sxoljʏfrɑu/ (pl: -en) (school)teacher

de **schoolkeuze** /sxolkøzə/ choice of school

de **schoolklas** /sxolklɑs/ (pl: -sen) class, form

de **schoolkrant** /sxolkrɑnt/ (pl: -en) school (news)paper

het **schoollokaal** /sxolokal/ (pl: -lokalen) schoolroom

de **schoolmeester** /sxolmestər/ (pl: -s) **1** schoolteacher **2** pedant, prig: *de* ~ *spelen (uithangen)* be a pedant

het **schoolmeisje** /sxolmɛiʃə/ (pl: -s) schoolgirl

de **schoolopleiding** /sxolopleidɪŋ/ (pl: -en) education: *een goede* ~ *genoten hebben* have had the advantage of a good education

het **schoolplein** /sxolplɛin/ (pl: -en) (school) playground: *de kinderen spelen op het* ~ the children were playing in the playground

de **schoolreis** /sxolrɛis/ (pl: -reizen) school trip

de **schoolreünie** /sxolrejyni/ school reunion

schools /sxols/ (adj, adv) **1** school, schoolish **2** scholastic

het **schoolschrift** /sxolsxrɪft/ (pl: -en) school notebook

de **schoolslag** /sxolslɑx/ breaststroke

de **schooltas** /sxoltɑs/ (pl: -sen) schoolbag; satchel

de **schooltelevisie** /sxolteləvizi/ educational television

de **schooltijd** /sxoltɛit/ (pl: -en) school time (*or:* hours): *de* ~en *variëren soms van school tot school* school hours can vary from school to school; *buiten* (or: *na*) ~ outside (*or:* after) school; *gedurende de* ~, *onder* ~ during school (time)

het **schoolvak** /sxolvɑk/ (pl: -ken) school subject

de **schoolvakantie** /sxolvakɑnsi/ (pl: -s) school holidays

de **schoolverlater** /sxolvərlatər/ (pl: -s) school leaver; [Am] recent graduate; drop-out

het **schoolverzuim** /sxolvərzœym/ school absenteeism

het **schoolvoorbeeld** /sxolvorbelt/ (pl: -en) classic example: *dit is een van* hoe het niet *moet* this is a classic example of how it shouldn't be done

de **schoolvriend** /sxolvrint/ (pl: -en) school friend

schoolziek /sxolzik/ (adj) shamming, malingering

schoolzwemmen /sxolzwɛmə(n)/ swimming (in school)

het **¹schoon** /sxon/ beauty: *het vrouwelijk* ~ female beauty

²schoon /sxon/ (adj) **1** clean; neat: [fig] *schone handen houden* stay squeaky clean, keep one's nose clean; ~ *water* clean (*or:* fresh) water **2** beautiful, fine: *de schone kunsten* the fine arts **3** clear; after tax: *50 pond* ~ *per week verdienen* make 50 pounds a week net (*or:* after tax) **4** [Belg] fine, pretty ‖ *tachtig kilo* ~ *aan de haak* eighty kilo's net (weight); eighty kilo's without clothes; *zijn kans* ~ *zien* see one's chance (*or:* opportunity)

de **schoonbroer** /sxombrur/ (pl: -s) brother-in-law

de **schoondochter** /sxondɔxtər/ (pl: -s) daughter-in-law

de **schoonfamilie** /sxonfamili/ (pl: -s) in-laws

de **schoonheid** /sxonhɛit/ (pl: -heden) beauty

het **schoonheidsfoutje** /sxonhɛitsfɑucə/ little slip, flaw

het/de **schoonheidssalon** /sxonhɛitsalɔn/ (pl: -s) beauty salon (*or:* parlour)

de **schoonheidsspecialiste** /sxonhɛitspeʃalɪstə/ (pl: -s) beautician; cosmetician

het **schoonheidsvlekje** /sxonhɛitsflɛkjə/ (pl: -s) beauty spot

de **schoonheidswedstrijd** /sxonhɛitswɛtstrɛit/ (pl: -en) beauty contest

schoonhouden /sxonhɑudə(n)/ (hield schoon, heeft schoongehouden) clean: *een kantoor* ~ clean an office

de **schoonmaak** /sxomak/ (house) cleaning, clean-up: *de grote* ~ the spring-cleaning; *grote* ~ *houden* spring-clean; make a clean sweep

de **schoonmaakartikelen** /sxomakɑrtikələ(n)/ (pl) cleaning products, cleanser(s)

schoonmaken /sxomakə(n)/ (maakte schoon, heeft schoongemaakt) clean

de **schoonmaker** /sxomakər/ (pl: -s) cleaner

de **schoonmoeder** /sxomudər/ (pl: -s) mother-in-law

de **schoonouders** /sxonɑudərs/ (pl) in-laws

het **schoonschrift** /sxonsxrɪft/ (pl: -en) calligraphy

schoonspoelen /sxonspulə(n)/ (spoelde schoon, heeft schoongespoeld) rinse (out)

schoonspringen /sxonsprɪŋə(n)/ platform diving

de **schoonvader** /sxonvadər/ (pl: -s) father-in-law

de **schoonzoon** /sxonzon/ (pl: -s, -zonen) son-in-law

de **schoonzus** /sxonzʏs/ (pl: -sen) sister-in-law

schoonzwemmen /sxonzwɛmə(n)/ synchronized swimming

de **schoorsteen** /sxorsten/ (pl: -stenen) chimney: *de ~ trekt niet goed* the chimney doesn't draw well; *de ~ vegen* sweep the chimney

de **schoorsteenmantel** /sxorstemantəl/ (pl: -s) mantelpiece

de **schoorsteenpiet** /sxorstempit/ (pl: -en) St Nicholas' helper with soot on his/her face

de **schoorsteenveger** /sxorstenveyər/ (pl: -s) chimney sweep

schoorvoetend /sxorvutənt/ (adj) reluctantly

de **schoot** /sxot/ (pl: schoten) lap: *bij iem. op ~ kruipen* clamber onto s.o.'s lap; [fig] *het wordt hem zomaar in de ~ geworpen* it simply falls into his lap

het **schoothondje** /sxothɔncə/ (pl: -s) lapdog

de **schop** /sxɔp/ **1** kick: *een vrije ~* a free kick; *iem. een ~ onder zijn kont geven* kick s.o. on (*or:* up) the behind **2** shovel; spade: *het centrum gaat op de ~* the city centre will be (completely) rebuilt (*or:* redeveloped); *het rechtssysteem moet op de ~* the legal system needs to be overhauled

de **¹schoppen** /sxɔpə(n)/ (pl: -) spades: *~ is troef* spades are trump; *één ~* one spade

²schoppen /sxɔpə(n)/ (schopte, heeft geschopt) kick: *tegen een bal ~* kick a ball || *het ver ~* go far (in the world)

het/de **schoppenaas** /sxɔpə(n)as/ ace of spades

schor /sxɔr/ (adj, adv) hoarse, husky

het **schorem** /sxorəm/ riff-raff, scum

de **schorpioen** /sxɔrpijun/ (pl: -en) scorpion

de **Schorpioen** /sxɔrpijun/ (pl: -en) [astrology] Scorpio

de **schors** /sxɔrs/ (pl: -en) bark

schorsen /sxɔrsə(n)/ (schorste, heeft geschorst) **1** adjourn **2** suspend: *een speler voor drie wedstrijden ~* suspend a player for three games; *als lid ~* suspend s.o. from membership

de **schorseneer** /sxɔrsəner/ (pl: schorseneren) scorzonera

de **schorsing** /sxɔrsɪŋ/ (pl: -en) suspension: *door zijn gedrag een ~ oplopen* be suspended for bad conduct

het/de **schort** /sxɔrt/ (pl: -en) apron: *een ~ voordoen* put on an apron

schorten /sxɔrtə(n)/ (schortte, heeft geschort): *het schort aan ...* the trouble is ...; *wat schort eraan?* what's wrong?, what's the matter?

het **schot** /sxɔt/ (pl: -en) **1** shot: *een ~ in de roos* a bull's-eye; *een ~ op goal* a shot at goal **2** range: *buiten ~ blijven, zich buiten ~ houden* keep out of range; *iem. (iets) onder ~ hebben* have s.o. (sth.) within range; *onder ~ houden* keep covered; *onder ~ nemen* cover **3** movement: *er komt (zit) ~ in de zaak* things are beginning to get going (*or:* to move)

4 partition

de **Schot** /sxɔt/ (pl: -ten) Scot

de **schotel** /sxotəl/ (pl: -s) **1** dish; [small] saucer: *een vuurvaste ~* an ovenproof dish **2** dish: *een warme ~* a hot dish || *een vliegende ~* a flying saucer

de **schotelantenne** /sxotəlantɛnə/ (satellite) dish, dish aerial, saucer aerial

Schotland /sxɔtlant/ Scotland

de **schots** /sxɔts/ (pl: -en) (ice) floe || *~ en scheef* higgledy-piggledy, topsy-turvy

Schots /sxɔts/ (adj) Scottish, Scots; Scotch: *~e whisky* Scotch (whisky)

de **schotwond** /sxɔtwɔnt/ (pl: -en) bullet wound, gunshot wound

de **schouder** /sxaudər/ (pl: -s) shoulder: *de ~s ophalen* shrug one's shoulders; *iem. op zijn ~ kloppen* pat s.o. on the back; *over iemands ~ meekijken* a) look over s.o.'s shoulder; b) keep a close eye on s.o.; [fig] *een last van iemands ~s nemen* take a weight off s.o.'s shoulders; [fig] *zijn ~s onder iets zetten* buckle down to sth.

de **schouderband** /sxaudərbant/ (pl: -en) shoulder strap: *zonder ~jes* strapless

het **schouderblad** /sxaudərblat/ (pl: -en) shoulder blade (*or:* bone)

het **schouderklopje** /sxaudərklɔpjə/ (pl: -s) pat on the back: *iem. een schouderklopje geven* give s.o. a pat on the shoulder

de **schoudertas** /sxaudərtas/ (pl: -sen) shoulder bag

de **schoudervulling** /sxaudərvʏlɪŋ/ (pl: -en) shoulder pad

de **schouw** /sxau/ (pl: -en) mantel(piece)

de **schouwarts** /sxauarts/ (pl: -en) [Dutch] forensic expert

de **schouwburg** /sxaubʏrx/ (pl: -en) theatre: *naar de ~ gaan* go to the theatre

het **schouwspel** /sxauspɛl/ (pl: -en) spectacle; sight; show: *een aangrijpend ~* a touching sight

schraal /sxral/ (adj, adv) **1** lean: *een schrale opkomst bij de verkiezingen* a poor turnout at the elections **2** poor; arid **3** bleak; cutting **4** dry: *schrale handen* chapped hands

schragen /sxrayə(n)/ (schraagde, heeft geschraagd) **1** prop (up) **2** [fig] support, buoy (up)

de **schram** /sxram/ (pl: -men) scratch, scrape: *geen ~metje hebben* not have a scratch; *vol ~men zitten* be all scratched

schrander /sxrandər/ (adj, adv) clever, sharp

schranzen /sxranzə(n)/ (schransde, heeft geschransd) gormandize, stuff o.s.

schrap /sxrap/ (adv) braced: *zich ~ zetten* brace o.s.; dig (one's heels) in

schrapen /sxrapə(n)/ (schraapte, heeft geschraapt) **1** clear: *de keel ~* clear one's throat **2** scrape: *geld bij elkaar ~* scrape money together

schrappen /sxrɑpə(n)/ (schrapte, heeft ge-schrapt) **1** scrape; scale **2** strike off, strike out, delete: *iem. als lid ~ drop s.o. from membership*

de **schrede** /sxredə/ (pl: -n) pace, step: [fig] *op zijn ~n terugkeren* retrace one's (foot)steps

de **schreef** /sxref/ (pl: schreven): *over de ~ gaan* overstep the mark

de **schreeuw** /sxrew/ (pl: -en) shout, cry: *een ~ geven* (let out a) yell, give a cry

¹**schreeuwen** /sxrewə(n)/ (schreeuwde, heeft geschreeuwd) **1** scream, cry (out), yell (out) **2** cry out (for): *deze problemen ~ om een snelle oplossing* these problems are crying out for a quick solution **3** scream, shout: *hij schreeuwt tegen iedereen* he shouts at everyone **4** cry; screech; squeal

²**schreeuwen** /sxrewə(n)/ (schreeuwde, heeft geschreeuwd) shout (out), yell (out): *een bevel ~* shout (or: yell) (out) an order

¹**schreeuwend** /sxrewənt/ (adj) glaring, screaming, in-your-face: *~e kleuren* loud (or: garish) colours; *er is een ~ tekort aan technische specialisten* there's a dire shortage of technical experts

²**schreeuwend** /sxrewənt/ (adv) terribly, impossibly, outrageously

de **schreeuwlelijk** /sxrewlelək/ (pl: -en) **1** loudmouth, bigmouth **2** squaller, screamer

schreien /sxrɛiə(n)/ (schreide, heeft geschreid) weep, cry (out) ‖ *bittere (or: hete) tranen ~* weep bitter (or: hot) tears

schriel /sxril/ (adj) thin, meagre

het **schrift** /sxrɪft/ (pl: -en) **1** writing: *iets op ~ stellen* put sth. in writing; *ik heb het op ~* I have it in writing **2** (hand)writing: *duidelijk leesbaar ~* legible handwriting **3** exercise book, notebook

de **Schrift** /sxrɪft/ Scripture(s): *de Heilige ~* (Holy) Scripture, the Scriptures

schriftelijk /sxrɪftələk/ (adj, adv) written, in writing: *een ~e cursus* a correspondence course; *~ bevestigen* confirm in writing; *iets ~ vastleggen* put sth. in writing ‖ *voor het ~ zakken* fail one's written exams

schrijden /sxrɛidə(n)/ (schreed, heeft/is geschreden) stride, stalk

de **schrijfbenodigdheden** /sxrɛivbənodəxthedə(n)/ (pl) stationery, writing materials

het **schrijfblok** /sxrɛivblɔk/ (pl: -ken) writing pad, (note)pad

de **schrijffout** /sxrɛifɑut/ (pl: -en) writing error, slip of the pen

het **schrijfgerei** /sxrɛifxərɛi/ stationery

de **schrijfmachine** /sxrɛifmaʃinə/ (pl: -s) typewriter

het **schrijfpapier** /sxrɛifpɑpir/ writing paper

de **schrijfster** /sxrɛifstər/ (pl: -s) writer

de **schrijftaal** /sxrɛiftal/ written language

de **schrijfvaardigheid** /sxrɛifardəxhɛit/ writing skill

schrijlings /sxrɛilɪŋs/ (adj, adv) straddling, astride: *~ op een paard zitten* sit astride a horse

schrijnen /sxrɛinə(n)/ (schrijnde, heeft geschrijnd) **1** chafe **2** smart

het ¹**schrijven** /sxrɛivə(n)/ (pl: schrijvens) letter

²**schrijven** /sxrɛivə(n)/ (schreef, heeft geschreven) write: *een vriend ~* write to a friend; *voluit ~* write (out) in full; *op een advertentie ~* answer an advertisement; *op het moment waarop ik dit schrijf* at the time of writing

de **schrijver** /sxrɛivər/ (pl: -s) writer, author

de **schrik** /sxrɪk/ (pl: -ken) **1** terror, shock, fright: *iem. ~ aanjagen* give s.o. a fright; *van de ~ bekomen* get over the shock; *met de ~ vrijkomen* have a lucky escape; *tot mijn ~* to my alarm (or: horror); *tot hun grote ~* to their horror **2** fright, fear **3** terror: *hij is de ~ van de buurt* he is the terror of the neighbourhood

schrikaanjagend /sxrɪkaɲaxənt/ (adj) terrifying, frightening

schrikbarend /sxrɪgbarənt/ (adj, adv) alarming, shocking: *~ hoge prijzen* staggering prices

het **schrikbeeld** /sxrɪgbelt/ (pl: -en) phantom, spectre, bogey: *het ~ van de werkloosheid* the spectre of unemployment

het **schrikbewind** /sxrɪgbəwɪnt/ (pl: -en) reign of terror: [fig] *een ~ voeren* terrorize the place, conduct a reign of terror

de **schrikdraad** /sxrɪgdrat/ (pl: -draden) electric fence

de **schrikkeldag** /sxrɪkəldɑx/ (pl: -en) leap day

het **schrikkeljaar** /sxrɪkəljar/ (pl: -jaren) leap year

de **schrikkelmaand** /sxrɪkəlmant/ (pl: -en) February

schrikken /sxrɪkə(n)/ (schrok, is geschrokken) be shocked (or: scared, frightened): *ik schrik me kapot (dood)* I'm scared stiff (or: to death); *wakker ~* wake with a start; *iem. laten ~* frighten s.o.; *hij schrok ervan* it frightened him; *van iets ~* be frightened by sth.; *iem. aan het ~ maken* give s.o. a fright

schril /sxril/ (adj, adv) **1** shrill; squeaky: *een ~le stem* a shrill voice **2** sharp; glaring: *~ afsteken bij iets* be in sharp contrast to sth., contrast sharply with sth.

schrobben /sxrɔbə(n)/ (schrobde, heeft geschrobd) scrub

de **schroef** /sxruf/ (pl: schroeven) **1** screw: *alles staat weer op losse schroeven* everything's unsettled (or: up in the air) again; [fig] *de schroeven aandraaien* put the screws on; *een ~ vastdraaien* (or: losdraaien) tighten (or: loosen) a screw; *er zit een ~je bij hem los* he has a screw loose **2** screw propeller

het **schroefdeksel** /sxruvdɛksəl/ (pl: -s) screw

cap, screw-on lid

de **schroefdop** /sxruvdɔp/ (pl: -pen) screw cap, screw top: *de ~ van een **fles** losdraaien* screw the top off a bottle; *wijn **met** ~* screw-cap wine

de **schroefdraad** /sxruvdrat/ (pl: -draden) (screw) thread

schroeien /sxrujə(n)/ (schroeide, heeft geschroeid) **1** singe; sear: *zijn **kleren** ~* singe one's clothes **2** scorch: *de zon schroeide het **gras*** the sun scorched the grass

schroeven /sxruvə(n)/ (schroefde, heeft geschroefd) screw: *iets **in** elkaar ~* screw sth. together; *iets **uit** elkaar ~* unscrew sth.

de **schroevendraaier** /sxruvə(n)drajər/ (pl: -s) screwdriver

schrokken /sxrɔkə(n)/ (schrokte, heeft geschrokt) cram down, gobble: *zit niet zo **te** ~* don't bolt your food like that

schromelijk /sxromələk/ (adj, adv) gross: *~ **overdreven*** grossly exaggerated

schromen /sxromə(n)/ (schroomde, heeft geschroomd) hesitate

schrompelen /sxrɔmpələ(n)/ (schrompelde, is geschrompeld) shrivel

de **schroom** /sxrom/ hesitation, diffidence

de **¹schroot** /sxrot/ lath: *een muur **met** ~jes betimmeren* lath a wall

het **²schroot** /sxrot/ **1** scrap (iron, metal) **2** lumps

de **schroothoop** /sxrothop/ (pl: -hopen) scrap heap: *deze auto is rijp **voor** de ~* this car is fit for the scrap heap

de **schub** /sxʏp/ (pl: -ben) scale

schuchter /sxʏxtər/ (adj, adv) shy, timid: *een ~e **poging*** a timid attempt

schudden /sxʏdə(n)/ (schudde, heeft geschud) shake; shuffle: *~ **voor gebruik*** shake before use; *elkaar **de hand** ~* shake hands; *nee ~ (met het hoofd)* shake one's head; *iem. **door** elkaar ~* shake s.o. up; *iem. **van** zich af ~* shake s.o. off || *dat **kun** je wel ~!* forget it!, nothing doing!

de **schuier** /sxœyər/ (pl: -s) [Dutch] brush

de **schuif** /sxœyf/ (pl: schuiven) bolt: *de ~ **op** de deur doen* bolt the door

de **schuifbalk** /sxœyvbalk/ [comp] scroll bar

het **schuifdak** /sxœyvdak/ (pl: -en) sunroof

de **schuifdeur** /sxœyvdør/ (pl: -en) sliding door

schuifelen /sxœyfələ(n)/ (schuifelde, heeft geschuifeld) shuffle: *met de voeten ~* shuffle one's feet

het **schuifje** /sxœyfjə/ (pl: -s) (small) bolt

de **schuifladder** /sxœyfladər/ (pl: -s) extension ladder

de **schuifpui** /sxœyfpœy/ (pl: -en) sliding patio doors, sliding French window; [Am] sliding French door

het **schuifraam** /sxœyfram/ (pl: -ramen) sash window; sliding window

de **schuiftrombone** /sxœyftrombɔːnə/ (pl: -s)

slide trombone

de **schuiftrompet** /sxœyftrɔmpɛt/ (pl: -ten) trombone

de **schuifwand** /sxœyfwɑnt/ (pl: -en) sliding wall

schuilen /sxœylə(n)/ (schuilde, heeft gescholen/geschuild) **1** hide: *daarin schuilt een groot **gevaar*** that carries a great risk (with it) **2** shelter (from)

schuilgaan /sxœylɣan/ (ging schuil, is schuilgegaan) be hidden: *de zon ging schuil **achter** donkere wolken* the sun was hidden (or: went) behind dark clouds

zich **schuilhouden** /sxœylhɑudə(n)/ (hield zich schuil, heeft zich schuilgehouden) be in hiding, hide o.s. away

de **schuilkelder** /sxœylkɛldər/ (pl: -s) air-raid shelter

de **schuilnaam** /sxœylnam/ (pl: -namen) pseudonym, pen-name

de **schuilplaats** /sxœylplats/ (pl: -en) **1** hiding place, (place of) shelter; hideout: *iem. een ~ **verlenen*** give shelter to s.o. **2** shelter: *een ~ **zoeken*** take shelter

het **schuim** /sxœym/ foam; froth; lather

het **schuimbad** /sxœymbɑt/ (pl: -en) bubble bath

schuimbekken /sxœymbɛkə(n)/ (schuimbekte, heeft geschuimbekt) foam: *~ **van** woede* foam with rage

het **schuimblusapparaat** /sxœymblʏsɑparat/ (pl: -apparaten) foam extinguisher

schuimen /sxœymə(n)/ (schuimde, heeft geschuimd) foam, froth; lather: *die **zeep** schuimt niet* that soap does not lather

de **schuimkraag** /sxœymkraɣ/ (pl: -kragen) head

het **schuimpje** /sxœympjə/ (pl: -s) meringue

het **¹schuimplastic** /sxœymplɛstɪk/ foam plastic

²schuimplastic /sxœymplɛstɪk/ (adj) foam plastic

de **¹schuimrubber** /sxœymrʏbər/ foam rubber

²schuimrubber /sxœymrʏbər/ (adj) foam rubber

de **schuimspaan** /sxœymspan/ (pl: -spanen) skimmer

de **schuimwijn** /sxœymwɛin/ (pl: -en) sparkling wine

schuin /sxœyn/ (adj, adv) **1** slanting, sloping: *~e **rand*** bevelled edge; *een ~e **streep*** a slash; *een stuk hout ~ **afzagen*** saw a piece of wood slantwise; *iets ~ **houden*** slant sth.; *~ **oversteken*** cross diagonally; *~ **schrijven*** write in italics; *hier ~ **tegenover*** diagonally across from here **2** smutty, dirty || *met een ~ **oog** kijken naar* look at … with envious eyes, cast envious looks at

schuingedrukt /sxœynɣədrʏkt/ (adj) (printed) in italics

de **schuinsmarcheerder** /sxœynsmɑrʃerdər/ (pl: -s) debauchee de **schuit** /sχœyt/ (pl: -en) barge, boat

het **schuitje** /sχœycə/ (pl: -s) boat: *in hetzelfde ~ zitten* be in the same boat

¹**schuiven** /sχœyvə(n)/ (schoof, heeft/is geschoven) **1** slide: *de lading ging ~ the cargo shifted*; *in elkaar ~* slide into one another, telescope **2** move (*or:* bring) one's chair: *dichterbij ~* bring one's chair closer || *laat hem maar ~* let him get on with it; *met data ~* rearrange dates

²**schuiven** /sχœyvə(n)/ (schoof, heeft geschoven) push, shove: *een stoel bij de tafel ~* pull up a chair; *iets (iem.) terzijde ~* brush sth. (s.o.) aside; *iets voor zich uit ~* put sth. off, postpone sth.

de **schuiver** /sχœyvər/ (pl: -s) skid, lurch: *een ~ maken* skid, lurch

de **schuld** /sχʏlt/ (pl: -en) **1** debt: *zijn ~en afbetalen* pay off (*or:* settle) one's debts; *~en hebben* have debts, be in debt; *zich in de ~en steken* incur debts, get into debt **2** guilt, blame: *iem. de ~ van iets geven* blame s.o. for sth.; *het is mijn eigen ~* it is my own fault; *eigen ~ dikke bult* it's your own fault; *schuld bekennen* confess; *de ~ krijgen* get the blame

de **schuldbekentenis** /sχʏldbəkɛntənɪs/ (pl: -sen) **1** bond; IOU **2** admission (*or:* confession) of guilt: *een volledige ~ afleggen* make a full confession

schuldbewust /sχʏldbəwʏst/ (adj) conscious of guilt, contrite

de **schuldeiser** /sχʏltɛisər/ (pl: -s) creditor

de **schuldenaar** /sχʏldənar/ (pl: -s, schuldenaren) debtor

het **schuldgevoel** /sχʏltχəvul/ (pl: -ens) feeling of guilt, guilty conscience

schuldig /sχʏldəχ/ (adj) **1** owing: *hoeveel ben ik u ~?* how much do I owe you? **2** guilty: *zich ~ voelen* feel guilty; *de rechter heeft hem ~ verklaard* the judge has declared him guilty

de **schuldige** /sχʏldəɣə/ (pl: -n) culprit, guilty party; offender

de **schuldsanering** /sχʏltsanerɪŋ/ (pl: -en) debt restructuring

de **schuldvraag** /sχʏltfraχ/ (pl: -vragen) the question of guilt

de **schulp** /sχʏlp/ (pl: -en) shell: *in zijn ~ kruipen* withdraw (*or:* retire) into one's shell

schunnig /sχʏnəχ/ (adj) shabby; filthy

schuren /sχyrə(n)/ (schuurde, heeft/is geschuurd) **1** grate, scour **2** sand(paper) || *dat schuurt* there is friction

de **schurft** /sχʏrft/ scabies; mange: *de ~ aan iem. hebben* hate s.o.'s guts

de **schurk** /sχʏrk/ (pl: -en) scoundrel, villain

de **schurkenstaat** /sχʏrkə(n)stat/ (pl: -staten) rogue state

de **schurkenstreek** /sχʏrkə(n)strek/ (pl: -streken) piece of villainy

het **schut** /sχʏt/ (pl: -ten) shelter, cover || *iem.*

voor ~ zetten make s.o. look a fool; *voor ~ staan* look a fool (*or:* an idiot)

het **schutblad** /sχʏdblɑt/ (pl: -en) **1** endpaper, end leaf **2** [bot] bract

de **schutkleur** /sχʏtklør/ (pl: -en) camouflage

de **schutsluis** /sχʏtslœys/ (pl: -sluizen) lock

de **schutspatroon** /sχʏtspatron/ (pl: -patronen) patron (saint)

schutten /sχʏtə(n)/ (schutte, heeft geschut) lock

de **schutter** /sχʏtər/ (pl: -s) **1** rifleman, marksman; gunman **2** [socc] striker || *hij is een goede ~* he is a crack shot

schutteren /sχʏtərə(n)/ (schutterde, heeft geschutterd) **1** fumble **2** falter, stammer

de **schutting** /sχʏtɪŋ/ (pl: -en) fence: *een ~ om een bouwterrein zetten* fence off a construction site

de **schuttingtaal** /sχʏtɪŋtal/ foul language, obscene language: *~ uitslaan* use foul (*or:* obscene) language

het **schuttingwoord** /sχʏtɪŋwort/ (pl: -en) four-letter word, obscenity

de **schuur** /sχyr/ (pl: schuren) shed; barn: *de oogst in de ~ brengen* bring in the harvest

de **schuurmachine** /sχyrmaʃinə/ (pl: -s) sander, sanding machine

het **schuurmiddel** /sχyrmɪdəl/ abrasive

het **schuurpapier** /sχyrpapir/ sandpaper

het/de **schuurpoeder** /sχyrpudər/ scouring powder

de **schuurspons** /sχyrspons/ (pl: -sponzen) scourer

schuw /sχyw/ (adj, adv) shy, timid

schuwen /sχywə(n)/ (schuwde, heeft geschuwd) shun, shrink from

de **schwalbe** /ʃwɑlbə/ (pl: -s) deliberate dive to draw a penalty

de **schwung** /ʃwʊŋ/ verve, dash

de **sciencefiction** /sɑjənsfɪkʃən/ science fiction, sci-fi

de **sclerose** /sklerozə/ (pl: -n, -s) sclerosis: *multiple ~* multiple sclerosis

de **scooter** /skutər/ (pl: -s) (motor) scooter

de **scootmobiel** /skutmobil/ miniscooter, mobility scooter

de **score** /skorə/ (pl: -s) score: *een gelijke ~* a draw (*or:* tie); *een ~ behalen van ...* make a score of ...

het **scorebord** /skorəbort/ (pl: -en) scoreboard

scoren /skorə(n)/ (scoorde, heeft gescoord) **1** score: *een doelpunt ~* score (a goal) **2** [inform] do it (with s.o.)

de **scout** /skɑut/ (pl: -s) **1** Scout **2** talent-scout

de **scouting** /skɑutɪŋ/ Scouting

scrabbelen® /skrɛbələ(n)/ (scrabbelde, heeft gescrabbeld) play Scrabble

screenen /skriːnə(n)/ (screende, heeft gescreend) screen; vet: *een sollicitant ~* screen an applicant; *iem. ~ op borstkanker* screen s.o. for breast cancer de **screensaver** /skri:nsevər/ screensaver

het/de **screenshot** /skri:nʃɔt/ (pl: -s) screenshot, print screen

het **script** /skrɪpt/ (pl: -s) script

de **scriptie** /skrɪpsi/ (pl: -s) thesis, term paper: *een ~ schrijven over* write a thesis about (*or:* on)

scrollen /skrɔlə(n)/ (scrolde, heeft gescrold) scroll

het **scrotum** /skrɔtʏm/ (pl: -s) scrotum

de **scrupule** /skrypylə/ (pl: -s) scruple, qualm

scrupuleus /skrypylø:s/ (adj, adv) scrupulous

de **sculptuur** /skʏlpty:r/ (pl: sculpturen) sculpture

het **se** (pl: se's) *schoolexamen* exam, test

de **seance** /sejɑ̃:sə/ (pl: -s) seance

sec /sɛk/ *seconde* sec

de **seconde** /səkɔndə/ (pl: -n) **1** second: *in een onderdeel van een ~* in a split second **2** second, moment: *hij houdt geen ~ zijn mond* he never stops talking

de **secondelijm** /səkɔndəlɛim/ superglue

de **secondewijzer** /səkɔndəwɛizər/ (pl: -s) second hand

het **secreet** /səkre:t/ (pl: secreten) (dirty) swine, sod; bitch

de **secretaire** /sɪkrətɛ:r(ə)/ (pl: -s) writing desk

de **secretaresse** /sɪkrətɑrɛsə/ (pl: -s) secretary

het **secretariaat** /sɪkrətarijat/ (pl: secretariaten) secretariat; secretary's office

de **secretaris** /sɪkrətɑrɪs/ (pl: -sen) secretary; clerk

de **secretaris-generaal** /sɪkrətɑrɪsxenərɑl/ (pl: secretarissen-generaal) secretary-general

de **sectie** /sɛksi/ (pl: -s) **1** autopsy; post-mortem (examination); dissection: *~ verrichten* carry out a post-mortem (*or:* an autopsy) **2** section; department: *de ~ betaald voetbal* the Football League; *de ~ Frans* the French department

de **sector** /sɛktɔr/ (pl: -en) sector: *de agrarische ~* the agricultural sector; *de zachte ~* the social sector

de **secularisatie** /sekylariza(t)si/ secularization

seculier /sekyli:r/ (adj) secular

secundair /sekʏndɛ:r/ (adj, adv) secondary, minor: *van ~ belang* of minor importance

secuur /səky:r/ (adj, adv) precise, meticulous

sedert /se:dərt/ (prep) since; for: *~ enige tijd* for some time

seffens /sɛfə(n)s/ (adv) [Belg] at once, straightaway

het **segment** /sɛɣmɛnt/ (pl: -en) segment: *de ~en van een tunnel* the sections of a tunnel; *producten uit het hoogste ~* products from the upper segment (*or:* from the top shelf), top-of-the-range products

de **SEH** [UK] A & E (*Accident and Emergency*); [Am] ER (*Emergency Room*)

het **sein** /sɛin/ (pl: -en) **1** signal, sign: *het ~ op veilig zetten* set the sign at clear **2** tip, hint: *geef me even een ~tje als je hulp nodig hebt* just let me know if you need any help

seinen /sɛinə(n)/ (seinde, heeft geseind) **1** signal; flash **2** telegraph; radio

de **seinwachter** /sɛinwɑxtər/ (pl: -s) signalman

seismisch /sɛismis/ (adj) seismic

de **seismograaf** /sɛismoɣra:f/ (pl: -grafen) seismograph

het **seizoen** /sɛizun/ (pl: -en) season: *weer dat past bij het ~* seasonable weather; *buiten het ~* in the off-season, out of season; off-season

de **seizoenarbeid** /sɛizunɑrbɛit/ seasonal work (*or:* employment)

de **seizoenarbeider** /sɛizunɑrbɛidər/ (pl: -s) seasonal worker

de **seizoenkaart** /sɛizunkart/ (pl: -en) season ticket

de **seizoenopruiming** /sɛizunɔprœymɪŋ/ end-of-season sale

de **seizoenwerkloosheid** /sɛizunwɛrkloshɛit/ seasonal unemployment

de **seks** /sɛks/ sex: *~ hebben* have sex; *onveilige ~* unprotected sex

de **sekse** /sɛksə/ (pl: -n) sex: *iem. van de andere ~* s.o. of the opposite sex

de **seksfilm** /sɛksfɪlm/ (pl: -s) sex film; skin-flick

de **seksist** /sɛksɪst/ (pl: -en) sexist; male chauvinist

seksistisch /sɛksɪstis/ (adj, adv) sexist, like a sexist: *een ~e opmerking* a sexist remark

het **seksleven** /sɛkslevə(n)/ sex life

de **seksshop** /sɛkʃɔp/ (pl: -s) sex shop, porn shop

het **sekssymbool** /sɛkssɪmbol/ (pl: -symbolen) sex symbol

de **seksualiteit** /sɛksywalitɛit/ sexuality

seksueel /sɛksywel/ (adj, adv) sexual: *seksuele voorlichting* sex education; *~ overdraagbare aandoeningen* sexually transmitted disease(s)

de **seksuoloog** /sɛksywolox/ (pl: -logen) sexologist

de **sekte** /sɛktə/ (pl: -n, -s) sect

de **selderij** /sɛldərɛi/ celery

select /səlɛkt/ (adj) select: *een ~ gezelschap* a select group

selecteren /selɛktərə(n)/ (selecteerde, heeft geselecteerd) select, pick (out): *hij werd niet geselecteerd voor die wedstrijd* he was not picked (*or:* selected) for that match

de **selectie** /səlɛksi/ (pl: -s) selection: [sport] *de ~ bekendmaken* announce the selection, name the squad

selectief /səlɛktif/ (adj, adv) selective

de **selectieprocedure** /səlɛksiprosedyrə/ (pl: -s) selection procedure

de **selectiewedstrijd** /səlɛksiwɛtstrɛit/ (pl: -en) selection match; preliminary match

de **selfie** /sɛlfi/ (pl: -s) selfie

de **selfiestick** /sɛlfistɪk/ (pl: -s) selfie stick
de **semafoon** /semafo̱n/ (pl: -s) [roughly] radio(tele)phone
het **semester** /semɛstər/ (pl: -s) six months, semester, term (of six months)
de **semieten** /semi̱tə(n)/ (pl) Semites
het **seminarie** /semina̱ri/ (pl: -s) seminary: *op het ~ zitten* be at a seminary
het **semioverheidsbedrijf** /se̱miovərhɛitsbədrɛif/ (pl: -bedrijven) semi state-controlled company
de **senaat** /sena̱t/ (pl: senaten) senate
de **senator** /sena̱tor/ (pl: -en) senator: *tot ~ gekozen worden* be elected (as) senator
Senegal /se̱neɣɑl/ Senegal
de [1]**Senegalees** /seneɣale̱s/ (pl: Senegalezen) Senegalese
[2]**Senegalees** /seneɣale̱s/ (adj) Senegalese
seniel /seni̱l/ (adj) senile
de **seniliteit** /senilitɛi̱t/ senility
de **senior** /se̱nijor/ (pl: -en) senior
de **seniorenpas** /senijo̱rə(n)pɑs/ (pl: -sen) pensioner's ticket (*or:* pass), senior citizen's pass (*or:* reduction card)
de **sensatie** /sɛnsa̱(t)si/ (pl: -s) sensation, feeling; thrill; stir: *op ~ belust zijn* be looking for sensation
sensatiebelust /sɛnsa̱(t)sibəlʏst/ (adj) sensationalist
de **sensatiepers** /sɛnsa̱(t)sipɛrs/ gutter press
de **sensatiezucht** /sɛnsa̱(t)sizʏxt/ sensationalism
sensationeel /sɛnsa(t)ʃone̱l/ (adj, adv) sensational; spectacular
sensibel /sɛnsi̱bəl/ (adj) sensitive (to)
sensitief /sɛnsiti̱f/ (adj) sensitive
de **sensor** /sɛ̱nsor/ (pl: -s, -en) sensor
sensueel /sɛnsywe̱l/ (adj, adv) sensual
het **sentiment** /sɛntimɛ̱nt/ (pl: -en) sentiment: *vals ~* cheap sentiment
sentimenteel /sɛntimɛnte̱l/ (adj, adv) sentimental: *een sentimentele film* a sentimental film; a tear-jerker
de **SEO** (pl: -'s) SEO (*search engine optimization*)
separaat /separa̱t/ (adj) separate
de **separatist** /separati̱st/ (pl: -en) separatist
seponeren /sepone̱rə(n)/ (seponeerde, heeft geseponeerd) dismiss, drop
de **september** /sɛptɛ̱mbər/ September
septisch /sɛ̱ptis/ (adj) septic: *~e put* septic tank
sereen /sere̱n/ (adj, adv) serene
de **serenade** /serena̱də/ (pl: -s) serenade: *iem. een ~ brengen* serenade s.o.
de **sergeant** /sɛrʒa̱nt/ (pl: -s) sergeant
de **sergeant-majoor** /sɛrʒɑntmajo̱r/ (pl: -s) [Dutch] sergeant major
de **serie** /se̱ri/ (pl: -s) series; serial: *een Amerikaanse ~ op de tv* an American serial on TV
de **seriemoordenaar** /se̱rimordənar/ (pl: -s) serial killer
het **serienummer** /se̱rinʏmər/ (pl: -s) serial number
de **serieproductie** /se̱riprodʏksi/ serial production, series production
serieus /serijø̱s/ (adj, adv) serious; straight: *een serieuze zaak* no laughing matter; *~?* seriously?, really?
de **sering** /se̱rɪŋ/ (pl: -en) lilac: *een boeket ~en* a bouquet of lilac
seropositief /seropoziti̱f/ (adj) HIV-positive
het **serpent** /sɛrpɛ̱nt/ (pl: -en) **1** serpent **2** shrew, bitch
de **serpentine** /sɛrpɛnti̱nə/ (pl: -s) streamer
de **serre** /sɛ̱rə/ (pl: -s) **1** sunroom **2** conservatory
het **serum** /se̱rʏm/ (pl: sera) serum
de **serveerster** /sɛrve̱rstər/ waitress
de **server** /sʏ̱rvər/ (pl: -s) server
serveren /sɛrve̱rə(n)/ (serveerde, heeft geserveerd) serve: *koel ~* serve chilled; *onderhands* (*or:* *bovenhands*) *~* serve underarm (*or:* overarm)
het **servet** /sɛrvɛ̱t/ (pl: -ten) napkin
de **service** /sʏ̱rvɪs/ **1** service: *dat is nog eens ~!* that is what I call service! **2** service charge: *~ inbegrepen* service charges included
de **servicebeurt** /sʏ̱rvɪsbørt/ (pl: -en) service: *met je auto naar de garage gaan voor een ~* take the car to be serviced
de **serviceflat** /sʏ̱rvɪsflɛt/ (pl: -s) service flat
de **servicekosten** /sʏ̱rvɪskostə(n)/ (pl) service charge(s)
Servië /sɛ̱rvijə/ Serbia
de **Serviër** /sɛ̱rvijər/ (pl: -s) Serb(ian)
het **servies** /sɛrvi̱s/ (pl: serviezen) service: *theeservies* tea service (*or:* set); *30-delig ~* 30-piece service
het **serviesgoed** /sɛrvi̱sxut/ (pl: -eren) crockery
het [1]**Servisch** /sɛ̱rvis/ Serbian
[2]**Servisch** /sɛ̱rvis/ (adj) Serbian
het **sesamzaad** /se̱zɑmzat/ (pl: -zaden) sesame seed(s)
de **sessie** /sɛ̱si/ (pl: -s) session, sitting; jam session
de **set** /sɛt/ (pl: -s) set
het **setpoint** /sɛ̱tpojnt/ (pl: -s) set point
de **setter** /sɛ̱tər/ (pl: -s) setter: *Ierse ~* Irish setter
het/de **sexappeal** /sɛksəpi:l/ sex appeal
de **sextant** /sɛksta̱nt/ (pl: -en) sextant
het **sextet** /sɛkstɛ̱t/ (pl: -ten) sextet(te)
sexy /sɛ̱ksi/ (adj) sexy
de **Seychellen** /seʃɛ̱lə(n)/ (pl) the Seychelles
de **sfeer** /sfer/ (pl: sferen) **1** atmosphere **2** atmosphere; character; ambience: *een huis met een heel eigen ~* a house with a distinctive character **3** sphere: *in hogere sferen zijn* have one's head in the clouds
sfeervol /sfe̱rvol/ (adj) attractive

de **sfinx** /sfɪŋks/ (pl: -en) sphinx

de **shag** /ʃɛk/ hand-rolling tobacco: ~ *roken* roll one's own

de **shampoo** /ʃɑmpo/ (pl: -s) shampoo

het **shantykoor** /ʃɛntikor/ (pl: -koren) shanty choir

de **sharia** /ʃarija/ sharia(h)

de **sheet** /ʃi:t/ (pl: -s) sheet

de **sheriff** /ʃɛrɪf/ (pl: -s) sheriff

de **sherry** /ʃɛri/ (pl: -'s) sherry

de **shetlander** /ʃɛtlɑndər/ (pl: -s) Shetland (pony)

shinen /ʃɑjnə(n)/ [inform] shine

het **shirt** /ʃy:rt/ (pl: -s) shirt; blouse

de **shirtreclame** /ʃy:rtrəklamə/ (pl: -s) shirt advertising

de **¹shit** /ʃɪt/ **1** shit: *een* **hoop** ~ *over zich heen krijgen* get a ton of shit **2** shit || [inform] *vette* ~ totally phat; [inform] *heftige* ~ heavy stuff

²shit /ʃɪt/ (int) [inform] [vulg] shit!

de **shitstorm** /ʃɪtstɔrm/ (verbal) abuse: *een* ~ *over zich heen krijgen* be subjected to a barrage of (internet) abuse

de **shoarma** /ʃwɑrma/ doner kebab: *een* **broodje** ~ a doner kebab

de **shock** /ʃɔk/ (pl: -s) shock: *in* **een** ~ *verkeren* be in shock

shockeren /ʃɔkerə(n)/ (shockeerde, heeft geshockeerd) *see* choqueren

de **shocktherapie** /ʃɔkterapi/ shock treatment (*or:* therapy)

de **shocktoestand** /ʃɔktustɑnt/ (pl: -en) state of shock: *hij is* **in** ~ he is in (a state of) shock

shoppen /ʃɔpə(n)/ (shopte, heeft geshopt) shop; shop around

de **short** /ʃɔ:rt/ shorts

de **shortlist** /ʃɔ:rtlɪst/ (pl: -s) shortlist

het **shorttrack** /ʃɔ:rtrɛk/ short-track speed skating

de **shot** /ʃɔt/ (pl: -s) **1** shot: *een* ~ *nemen* take a shot; shoot up **2** shot: *een* ~ *wodka* a shot of vodka

het **shotje** /ʃɔcə/ (pl: -s) [inform] shot, shooter: *we bestelden drie ~s wodka* we ordered three vodka shooters

de **shovel** /ʃɔvəl/ (pl: -s) [Dutch] shovel

de **show** /ʃow/ (pl: -s) show, display

de **showbusiness** /ʃobɪznɪs/ show business

showen /ʃowə(n)/ (showde, heeft geshowd) show, display

het **showproces** /ʃoprosɛs/ (pl: -sen) show trial

de **showroom** /ʃoru:m/ (pl: -s) show room

de **shredder** /ʃrɛdər/ (pl: -s) shredder

de **shuttle** /ʃʏtəl/ (pl: -s) shuttle

de **si** /si/ (pl: si's) [mus] ti, si

de **siamees** /sijamɛs/ (pl: siamezen) Siamese (cat)

Siamees /sijamɛs/ (adj) Siamese: *een Siamese tweeling* Siamese twins

Siberië /siberijə/ Siberia

Siberisch /siberis/ (adj, adv) Siberian

de **Siciliaan** /sisilijan/ (pl: Sicilianen) Sicilian

Sicilië /sisilijə/ Sicily

sidderen /sɪdərə(n)/ (sidderde, heeft gesidderd) tremble, shiver: *ik sidderde* **bij** *de gedachte alleen al* the very thought of it made me shudder

de **siddering** /sɪdərɪŋ/ (pl: -en) shudder, shiver: *er* **ging** *een* ~ *door de menigte* a shudder (*or:* shiver) went through the crowd

de **sier** /sir/ show: *dat is alleen maar* **voor** *de* ~ it's only for show || *goede* ~ *maken (met iets)* try to cut a dash (with sth.), show off (sth.)

het **sieraad** /sirat/ (pl: sieraden) jewel; jewellery

sieren /sirə(n)/ (sierde, heeft gesierd) adorn: *dat siert* **hem** it is to his credit

sierlijk /sirlək/ (adj, adv) elegant, graceful

de **sierlijkheid** /sirləkhɛit/ elegance, grace(fulness)

de **sierplant** /sirplɑnt/ (pl: -en) ornamental plant

Sierra Leone /sɛralejonə/ Sierra Leone

de **Sierra Leoner** /sɛralejonər/ (pl: -s) Sierra Leonean

Sierra Leoons /sɛralejons/ (adj) Sierra Leonian

de **sierstrip** /sirstrɪp/ (pl: -s) trim

de **siësta** /sijɛsta/ (pl: -'s) siesta: ~ *houden* have a siesta

de **sigaar** /siɣar/ (pl: sigaren) cigar: *een* ~ **opsteken** light a cigar || *de* ~ *zijn* have had it; get the blame

het **sigarenbandje** /siɣarə(n)bɑncə/ (pl: -s) cigar band

de **sigarenwinkel** /siɣarə(n)wɪŋkəl/ cigar shop, tobacconist's

de **sigaret** /siɣarɛt/ (pl: -ten) cigarette: *een* **elektronische** ~ an electronic cigarette; *een* **pakje** ~*ten* a packet of cigarettes; [Am] a pack of cigarettes; *een* ~ **opsteken** (*or:* **uitmaken**) light (*or:* put out) a cigarette

de **sigarettenautomaat** /siɣarɛtə(n)automat/ (pl: -automaten) cigarette (vending) machine

het **signaal** /sɪnal/ (pl: signalen) signal, sign: *het* ~ **voor** *de aftocht geven* sound the retreat; *een* *duidelijk* ~ **afgeven** send a clear message

het **signalement** /sɪnaləmɛnt/ (pl: -en) description: *hij beantwoordt niet* **aan** *het* ~ he doesn't fit the description

signaleren /sɪnalerə(n)/ (signaleerde, heeft gesignaleerd) **1** see, spot: *hij was* **in** *een nachtclub gesignaleerd* he had been seen in a nightclub **2** point out: *problemen* (*or:* **misstanden**) ~ point out problems (*or:* evils)

de **signalisatie** /sɪnaliza(t)si/ [Belg] traffic signs, road signs

de **signatuur** /sɪnatyr/ (pl: signaturen) **1** signature **2** nature, character

signeren /sɪnerə(n)/ (signeerde, heeft gesigneerd) sign, autograph: *een door de auteur gesigneerd* **exemplaar** a signed (an autographed) copy

significant /sɪɣnifikɒnt/ (adj, adv) significant

sijpelen /sɛipələ(n)/ (sijpelde, heeft/is gesijpeld) trickle, ooze, seep

de **sik** /sɪk/ (pl: -ken) goatee

de **sikh** /sɪk/ (pl: -s) Sikh

de **sikkel** /sɪkəl/ (pl: -s) sickle

sikkeneurig /sɪkənørəx/ (adj, adv) [Dutch] peevish, grouchy

de **sikkepit** /sɪkəpɪt/ whit, bit

het/de **silhouet** /siluwɛt/ (pl: -ten) silhouette

het **silicium** /silisijʏm/ silicon

het/de **siliconenkit** /silikɔnə(n)kɪt/ silicone paste, fibre-glass paste

de **silo** /silo/ (pl: -'s) silo

de **simkaart** /sɪmkart/ (pl: -en) SIM card

simpel /sɪmpəl/ (adj, adv) simple: ~e *kost* simple (or: modest) fare; *zo ~ ligt dat!* it's as simple as that!

de **simulant** /simylɒnt/ (pl: -en) simulator

simuleren /simylerə(n)/ (simuleerde, heeft gesimuleerd) simulate, sham

simultaan /simyltan/ (adj, adv) simultaneous: [sport] ~ *spelen* give a simultaneous display

de **simultaanpartij** /simyltampartɛi/ (pl: -en) simultaneous game

simultaanschaken /simyltansxakə(n)/ play simultaneous chess

de **sinaasappel** /sinasapəl/ (pl: -en, -s) orange

de **sinaasappelkist** /sinasapəlkɪst/ orange crate, orange box

het **sinaasappelsap** /sinasapəlsɑp/ orange juice

de **sinas** /sinɑs/ [Dutch] orangeade, orange soda

¹**sinds** /sɪnts/ (prep) since; for: *ik ben hier al ~ jaren* niet meer geweest I haven't been here for years; *ik heb hem ~ maandag niet meer gezien* I haven't seen him since Monday; *~ kort* recently; for a short time now

²**sinds** /sɪnts/ (conj) since; ever since: *~ ik Jan ken* since I met (or: have known) Jan

sindsdien /sɪn(t)sdin/ (adv) since: *~ is er van hen niets meer vernomen* they have not been heard of (ever) since; *~ werkt hij niet meer* he hasn't worked since (then)

Singapore /sɪŋapur/ Singapore

de ¹**Singaporees** /sɪŋapores/ (pl: Singaporezen) Singaporean

²**Singaporees** /sɪŋapores/ (adj) Singaporean

de **singel** /sɪŋəl/ (pl: -s) **1** canal **2** webbing

de **singer-songwriter** /sɪŋərsɒŋrɑjtər/ singersong writer

de **single** /sɪŋɡəl/ (pl: -s) single

de **singlet** /sɪŋɡlɛt/ (pl: -s) singlet; [Am] undershirt

sinister /sinɪstər/ (adj, adv) sinister: *~e plannen* sinister designs

de **sint** /sɪnt/ (pl: -en) **1** saint **2** St Nicholas

de **sint-bernardshond** /sɪndbɛrnɑrtshɔnt/ (pl: -en) St Bernard (dog)

de **sintel** /sɪntəl/ (pl: -s) cinder: *gloeiende ~s* glowing embers

de **sintelbaan** /sɪntəlban/ (pl: -banen) cinder track

Sinterklaas /sɪntərklas/ see Sint-Nicolaas

de **sinterklaasavond** /sɪntərklasavɔnt/ (pl: -en) St Nicholas' Eve

het **sinterklaasgedicht** /sɪntərklasxədɪxt/ (pl: -en) St Nicholas' poem

de **sint-juttemis** /sɪntjʏtəmɪs/: *wachten tot ~* wait till the cows come home

Sint-Nicolaas /sɪntnikolas/ **1** St Nicholas **2** feast of St Nicholas

de **sinus** /sinʏs/ (pl: -sen) sine (of angle)

sip /sɪp/ (adj) glum, crestfallen: *~ kijken* look glum

sire /sirə/ your Majesty, Sire

de **sirene** /sirenə/ (pl: -s) siren: *met loeiende ~* with wailing sirens

de **siroop** /sirɔp/ (pl: siropen) syrup: *vruchten op lichte* (or: *zware*) *~ fruit* in light (or: heavy) syrup

de **sisklank** /sɪsklɑŋk/ (pl: -en) sibilant

de **sissen** /sɪsə(n)/ (siste, heeft gesist) **1** hiss: *een ~d geluid* maken make a hissing noise **2** sizzle: *het spek siste in de pan* the bacon was sizzling in the pan

de **sisser** /sɪsər/ (pl: -s): *met een ~ aflopen* blow over; fizzle out

de **sisyfusarbeid** /sizifʏsɑrbɛit/ Sisyphean task

de ¹**site** /sɑjt/ site, website: *mobiele ~* mobile website

de ²**site** /sitə/ [Belg] (archaeological) site/dig

de **situatie** /sitywa(t)si/ (pl: -s) situation, position: *een moeilijke ~* a difficult situation; *in de huidige ~* as things stand, in the present situation

situeren /sitywerə(n)/ (situeerde, heeft gesitueerd) place, locate, set: *waar is de handeling van het verhaal gesitueerd?* where is the story set?, where does the action of the story take place?

de **sjaak** /ʃak/: [inform] *de ~ zijn* be the sucker, be muggins

de **sjaal** /ʃal/ (pl: -s) scarf: *een ~ omslaan* put on a scarf

de **sjabloon** /ʃablɔn/ (pl: sjablonen) **1** stencil (plate); template; [fig] stereotype **2** [comp] template

de **sjacheraar** /ʃɑxərar/ (pl: -s) haggler, horsetrader

de **sjah** /ʃa/ (pl: -s) shah

de **sjalot** /ʃalɔt/ (pl: -ten) shallot

de **sjans** /ʃɑns/: *~ hebben* make a hit (with s.o.)

sjansen /ʃɑnsə(n)/ (sjanste, heeft gesjanst) [Dutch; inform] flirt, make eyes at s.o.: *~ met de buurman* flirt with the neighbour de **sjasliek** /ʃɑslik/ shashlik

de **sjeik** /ʃɛik/ (pl: -s) sheik(h)

het **sjekkie** /ʃɛki/ (pl: -s) [Dutch; inform] (hand-rolled) cigarette, roll-up: *een ~ draaien* roll a cigarette

de **sjerp** /ʃɛrp/ (pl: -en) sash

¹sjezen /ʃeːzə(n)/ (sjeesde, heeft/is gesjeesd) race, rocket

²sjezen /ʃeːzə(n)/ (sjeesde, is gesjeesd) [Dutch] drop out

de **sjiiet** /ʃiit/ (pl: -en) Shiite

de **sjoege** /ʃuɣə/ [Dutch]: [inform] *hij gaf geen ~* he didn't react

de **sjoelbak** /ʃulbɑk/ (pl: -ken) shovelboard

sjoelen /ʃulə(n)/ (sjoelde, heeft gesjoeld) play at shovelboard

sjoemelen /ʃumələ(n)/ (sjoemelde, heeft gesjoemeld) [inform] cheat

de **sjoemelsoftware** /ʃuməlsɔftwɛːr/ defeat device

sjofel /ʃofəl/ (adj, adv) shabby

sjokken /ʃɔkə(n)/ (sjokte, heeft/is gesjokt) trudge

de **sjonnie** /ʃɔni/ (pl: -s) [Dutch] greaser

sjorren /ʃɔrə(n)/ (sjorde, heeft gesjord) lug, heave

sjotten /ʃɔtə(n)/ (sjotte, heeft gesjot) [Belg] **1** play soccer **2** shoot, kick

sjouwen /ʃɑuwə(n)/ (sjouwde, heeft/is gesjouwd) lug, drag: *lopen ~* trudge; traipse

de **sjouwer** /ʃɑuwər/ (pl: -s) porter; docker

het **¹skai** /skɑj/ imitation leather

²skai /skɑj/ (adj) imitation leather

het **skateboard** /skɛdbɔːrd/ (pl: -s) skateboard

skaten /skɛtə(n)/ (skatete, heeft/is geskatet) skateboard

de **skeeler** /skilər/ (pl: -s) skeeler

skeeleren /skilərə(n)/ (skeelerde, heeft/is geskeelerd) rollerblade

het **skelet** /skəlɛt/ (pl: -ten) skeleton; frame

de **skelter** /skɛltər/ (pl: -s) (go-)kart

skelteren /skɛltərə(n)/ (skelterde, heeft/is geskelterd) go-kart: *het ~* go-karting

de **sketch** /skɛtʃ/ (pl: -es) sketch

de **ski** /ski/ (pl: -'s) ski

het **skicentrum** /skisɛntrʏm/ (pl: skicentra) ski resort

skiën /skijə(n)/ (skiede, heeft/is geskied) ski: *gaan ~* go skiing

de **skiër** /skijər/ (pl: -s) skier

de **skiff** /skɪf/ (pl: -s) skiff

het **skigebied** /skiɣəbit/ (pl: -en) skiing area (*or:* centre)

de **skihal** /skihɑl/ (pl: -len) ski centre

de **skileraar** /skilerar/ (pl: skileraren) ski instructor

de **skilift** /skilɪft/ (pl: -en) ski lift

skimmen /skɪmə(n)/ (skimde, heeft geskimd) skim

skinny /skɪni/ (adj) **1** skinny **2** skinny; tight-fitting

de **skipiste** /skipistə/ (pl: -s, -n) ski run

de **skischans** /skisxɑns/ (pl: -en) ski jump

de **skischoen** /skisxun/ (pl: -en) ski boot

skispringen /skisprɪŋə(n)/ ski-jumping

de **skistok** /skistɔk/ (pl: -ken) ski stick; [Am] ski pole

skypen /skɑjpə(n)/ (skypete, heeft geskypet) skype: *zullen we zo even ~?* shall we Skype?

de **sla** /sla/ lettuce; salad: *een krop ~* a head of lettuce; *de ~ aanmaken* dress the salad

de **slaaf** /slaf/ (pl: slaven) slave: *tot ~ gemaakte* enslaved (person)

slaafgemaakt /slafxəmakt/ (adj) enslaved

slaafs /slafs/ (adj, adv) slavish, servile: *~e gehoorzaamheid* servile obedience

de **slaag** /slax/: [also fig] *iem. een pak ~ geven* give s.o. a beating

slaags /slaxs/ (adv): *~ raken met iem.* come to blows (*or:* grips) with s.o.

slaan /slan/ (sloeg, heeft geslagen) **1** hit, strike; slap; beat: *de klok slaat ieder kwartier* the clock strikes the quarters; *zich ergens doorheen ~* pull through; *zijn hart ging sneller ~* his heart beat faster; *een paal in de grond ~* drive a stake into the ground; *met de vleugels ~* flap one's wings; *met de deur ~* slam the door; *iem. in elkaar ~* beat s.o. up; *hij is er niet (bij) weg te ~* wild horses couldn't drag him away **2** take, capture **3** (+ op) refer to: *waar slaat dat nu weer op?* what do you mean by that?; *dat slaat op mij* that is meant for (*or:* aimed at) me; *dat slaat nergens op* that makes no sense at all || *over de kop ~* overturn; *een mantel om iem. heen ~* wrap a coat round s.o.; *de armen om de hals van iem. ~* fling one's arms around s.o.'s neck; *de benen over elkaar ~* cross one's legs

de **slaap** /slap/ **1** sleep: *in ~ vallen* fall asleep **2** sleepiness: *~ hebben* be (*or:* feel) sleepy; *~ krijgen* get sleepy **3** temple

de **slaapbank** /slabɑŋk/ (pl: -en) sofa bed

slaapdronken /slabdrɔŋkə(n)/ (adj) half asleep, drowsy

het **slaapgebrek** /slapxəbrɛk/ lack of sleep

de **slaapgelegenheid** /slapxələxənhɛit/ (pl: -heden) sleeping accommodation, place to sleep

de **slaapkamer** /slapkamər/ (pl: -s) bedroom

de **slaapkop** /slapkɔp/ (pl: -pen) **1** sleepyhead **2** dope

het **slaapliedje** /slaplicə/ (pl: -s) lullaby

het **slaapmiddel** /slapmɪdəl/ (pl: -en) sleeping pill

de **slaapmuts** /slapmʏts/ (pl: -en) nightcap

het **slaapmutsje** /slapmʏtʃə/ (pl: -s) nightcap

de **slaappil** /slapɪl/ (pl: -len) sleeping pill

de **slaapplaats** /slaplats/ (pl: -en) place to sleep, bed

de **slaapstad** /slapstɑt/ (pl: -steden) dormitory suburb; dormitory town

de **slaapstand** /slapstant/ [comp] sleep mode
de **slaapster** /slapstər/ (pl: -s): *de Schone Slaap-ster* Sleeping Beauty
de **slaaptrein** /slaptrɛin/ (pl: -en) sleeper, overnight train
slaapverwekkend /slapfərwɛkənt/ (adj) sleep-inducing; [fig] soporific: *een ~ boek* a tedious book
de **slaapwandelaar** /slapwandəlar/ (pl: -s) sleepwalker
slaapwandelen /slapwandələ(n)/ (slaap-wandelde, heeft geslaapwandeld) walk in one's sleep: *het ~* sleepwalking
de **slaapzaal** /slapsal/ (pl: -zalen) dormitory, dorm
de **slaapzak** /slapsak/ (pl: -ken) sleeping bag
het **slaatje** /slacə/ (pl: -s) salad || *hij wil overal een ~ uit slaan* he tries to cash in on everything
de **slab** /slap/ (pl: -ben) bib: *een kind een ~ voordoen* put a child's bib on
de **slabak** /slabak/ (pl: -ken) salad bowl
slabakken /slabakə(n)/ (slabakte, heeft ge-slabakt) [Belg] hang fire, do badly: *de ~de economie* the stagnating economy
de **slacht** /slaxt/ slaughter(ing)
het **slachtafval** /slaxtafal/ offal
de **slachtbank** /slaxtbaŋk/ (pl: -en): *naar de ~ geleid worden* be led to the slaughter
slachten /slaxtə(n)/ (slachtte, heeft ge-slacht) slaughter, butcher: *geslachte koeien* slaughtered cows
het **slachthuis** /slaxthœys/ (pl: -huizen) slaugh-terhouse
de **slachting** /slaxtɪŋ/ (pl: -en) slaughter(ing); massacre
het **slachtoffer** /slaxtɔfər/ (pl: -s) victim; casual-ty: *~ worden van* fall victim (*or:* prey) to
de **slachtofferhulp** /slaxtɔfərhʏlp/ help (*or:* aid) to victims
de **slachtpartij** /slaxtpartɛi/ (pl: -en) slaughter, massacre
het **slachtvee** /slaxtfe/ stock (*or:* cattle) for slaughter(ing), beef cattle
de **¹slag** /slax/ **1** blow; punch; lash: *iem. een (zware) ~ toebrengen* deal s.o. a heavy blow **2** stroke; drive: *een ~ in de lucht* a shot in the dark **3** [mil] battle: *in de ~ bij Nieuwpoort* at the Battle of Nieuwpoort; [Belg] *zich uit de ~ trekken* get out of a difficult situation **4** bang, bump **5** wave: *hij heeft een mooie ~ in zijn haar* he has a nice wave in his hair **6** stroke; beat: *(totaal) van ~ zijn* be (com-pletely) thrown out **7** knack: *de ~ van iets te pakken krijgen* get the knack (*or:* hang) of sth. **8** [cards] trick: *iem. een ~ voor zijn* be one up on s.o. **9** take, capture **10** stroke: *vrije ~* freestyle || *aan de ~ gaan* get to work; *een ~ naar iets slaan* have a shot (*or:* stab) at sth.; *een goede ~ slaan* make a good deal; *een ~ om de arm houden* refuse to commit oneself; *hij was op ~ dood* he was killed instantly;

zonder ~ of stoot [fig] without striking a blow, without any resistance
het **²slag** /slax/ sort, kind: *dat is niet voor ons ~ mensen* that's not for the likes of us; *iem. van jouw ~* s.o. like you
de **slagader** /slaxadər/ (pl: -s) artery: *grote ~* aorta
de **slagboom** /slaxbom/ (pl: -bomen) barrier
slagen /slaɣə(n)/ (slaagde, is geslaagd) **1** (+ in, met) succeed (in); be successful (in): *ben je erin geslaagd?* did you pull it off, did you manage? **2** succeed in (-ing), manage (to): *ik slaagde er niet in de top te bereiken* I failed to make it to the top **3** (+ voor) pass; qualify (as, for): *hij is voor zijn Frans geslaagd* he has passed (his) French **4** be successful: *de ope-ratie is geslaagd* the operation was successful; *de tekening is goed geslaagd* the drawing has turned out well
de **slager** /slaɣər/ (pl: -s) butcher
de **slagerij** /slaɣərɛi/ (pl: -en) butcher's (shop)
het **slaghout** /slaxhaut/ (pl: -en) bat
het **slaginstrument** /slaxɪnstrymɛnt/ (pl: -en) percussion instrument
de **slagpen** /slaxpɛn/ (pl: -nen) **1** flight feather **2** firing pin
de **slagregen** /slaxreɣə(n)/ (pl: -s) driving (*or:* torrential) rain
de **slagroom** /slaxrom/ whipped cream: *aard-beien met ~* strawberries and whipped cream
het **slagschip** /slaxsxɪp/ (pl: -schepen) battle-ship
de **slagtand** /slaxtant/ (pl: -en) **1** tusk **2** fang
slagvaardig /slaxfardəx/ (adj) decisive
het **slagveld** /slaxfɛlt/ (pl: -en) battlefield
het **slagwerk** /slaxwɛrk/ (pl: -en) percussion (section); rhythm section
de **slagwerker** /slaxwɛrkər/ (pl: -s) percussion-ist; drummer
de **slagzij** /slaxsɛi/ list [ship]; bank: *dat schip maakt zware ~* that ship is listing heavily
de **slagzin** /slaxsɪn/ (pl: -nen) slogan, catch-phrase
de **slak** /slak/ (pl: -ken) **1** snail; slug: *op alle ~ken zout leggen* find fault with everything, split hairs **2** slag, dross
slaken /slakə(n)/ (slaakte, heeft geslaakt) give, utter: *een kreet ~* give a cry, shriek; *een zucht ~* give (*or:* heave) a sigh
de **slakkengang** /slakə(n)ɣaŋ/ snail's pace
het **slakkenhuis** /slakə(n)hœys/ (pl: -huizen) **1** snail's shell **2** [med] cochlea
de **slalom** /slalɔm/ (pl: -s) slalom
slalommen /slalɔmə(n)/ (slalomde, heeft/is geslalomd) slalom
de **slamix** /slamɪks/ (pl: -en) salad dressing
de **slang** /slaŋ/ (pl: -en) **1** snake: *giftige ~en* poisonous snakes **2** hose
de **slangenbeet** /slaŋə(n)bet/ (pl: -beten) snakebite
het **slangengif** /slaŋə(n)ɣɪf/ snake poison

de **slangenmens** /slɑ̃nəmɛns/ (pl: -en) contortionist

slank /slɑŋk/ (adj) slender; slim

de **slaolie** /slɑoli/ salad oil

slap /slɑp/ (adj) **1** slack: [fig] *een ~pe tijd* a slack season; *het touw hangt ~* the rope is slack; *~pe koffie* weak coffee **2** soft, limp **3** weak, flabby: *~pe spieren* flabby muscles; *we lagen ~ van het lachen* we were in stitches **4** empty, feeble: *een ~ excuus* a lame (*or:* feeble) excuse; *~ geklets* empty talk, slip-slop

slapeloos /slɑpəlos/ (adj, adv) sleepless

de **slapeloosheid** /slɑpəloshɛit/ insomnia, sleeplessness: *aan ~ lijden* suffer from insomnia

slapen /slɑpə(n)/ (sliep, heeft geslapen) **1** sleep: *gaan ~* go to bed; go to sleep; *hij kon er niet van ~* it kept him awake; *slaap lekker* sleep well; *bij iem. blijven ~* spend the night at s.o.'s house (*or:* place); spend the night with s.o.; *ik wil er een nachtje over ~* I'd like to sleep on it; *hij slaapt als een os* (*or:* roos) he sleeps like a log; [fig] *hij heeft zitten ~* he took his eye off the ball **2** sleep (with) ‖ *mijn been slaapt* I've got pins and needles in my leg

slapend /slɑpənt/ (adj) sleeping: *~e rijk worden* make money without any effort

slaperig /slɑpərəx/ (adj, adv) sleepy; drowsy

de **slapjanus** /slɑpjɑnʏs/ (pl: -sen) [inform] wimp, weed

de **slappeling** /slɑpəlɪŋ/ (pl: -en) weakling, softie

de **slapte** /slɑptə/ slackness

de **slasaus** /slɑsɑus/ (pl: -sauzen) salad dressing

de **slash** /slɛʃ/ (pl: -es) slash

de **slavenarbeid** /slɑvə(n)ɑrbɛit/ slave labour

de **slavenhandel** /slɑvə(n)hɑndəl/ slave trade

de **slavernij** /slɑvərnɛi/ slavery: *afschaffing van de ~* abolition of slavery

de **slavin** /slɑvɪn/ (pl: -nen) (female) slave

slecht /slɛxt/ (adj, adv) **1** bad; poor: *een ~ gebit* bad teeth; *~ betaald* badly (*or:* low) paid; *~ nieuws* bad news; *~ er worden* worsen, deteriorate; *~ ter been zijn* have difficulty (in) walking **2** bad, unfavourable: *hij heeft het ~ getroffen* he has been unlucky; *het er ~ afbrengen* come off badly, be badly off **3** bad, ill: *het gaat ~ met me* I'm in a bad way, I'm not doing well; *het loopt nog eens ~ met je af* you will come to no good **4** bad, wrong: *zich op het ~e pad begeven* go astray

slechtbetaald /slɛxtbətɑlt/ (adj) badly-paid, poorly-paid

de **slechterik** /slɛxtərɪk/ (pl: -en) baddie, bad guy, villain

slechtgehumeurd /slɛxtxəhymørt/ (adj) bad-tempered

slechtgemanierd /slɛ(xt)xəmanirt/ (adj) bad-mannered, ill-mannered

slechthorend /slɛxthorənt/ (adj) hard of hearing

slechts /slɛxts/ (adv) only, merely, just: *in ~ enkele gevallen* in only (*or:* just) a few cases

slechtziend /slɛxtsint/ (adj) visually handicapped: *~ zijn* have bad eyesight

de **sledehond** /slɛdəhont/ (pl: -en) husky

de **slee** /sle/ (pl: -ën) sledge; [Am] sled

sleeën /slejə(n)/ (sleede, heeft/is gesleed) sledge; [Am] sled; sleigh

de **sleep** /slep/ (pl: slepen) **1** train **2** train: *een ~ kinderen* an army of kids **3** tow: *iem. op ~ nemen* give s.o. a tow, take s.o. in tow

de **sleepboot** /slebot/ (pl: -boten) tug(boat)

de **sleepkabel** /slepkabəl/ (pl: -s) tow rope

het **sleepnet** /slepnɛt/ (pl: -ten) trawl (net), dragnet

het **sleeptouw** /sleptɑu/ (pl: -en) tow rope: *iem. op ~ nemen* take s.o. in tow

de **sleepwagen** /slepwaɣə(n)/ (pl: -s) breakdown truck, breakdown van; [Am] tow truck

sleets /slets/ (adj) [Dutch] worn

slenteren /slɛntərə(n)/ (slenterde, heeft/is geslenterd) stroll, amble: *op straat ~* loaf about the streets

slepen /slepə(n)/ (sleepte, heeft gesleept) **1** drag, haul: *iem. door een examen ~* pull s.o. through an exam; *iem. voor de rechter ~* take s.o. to court **2** tow **3** [comp] drag and drop

slepend /slepənt/ (adj) **1** dragging: *een ~e gang hebben* drag (*or:* shuffle) one's feet **2** lingering, long-drawn-out

de **slet** /slɛt/ (pl: -ten) slut

de **sleuf** /sløf/ (pl: sleuven) **1** slot; slit: *de ~ van een spaarpot* the slot in a piggybank **2** groove; trench

de **sleur** /slør/ rut, grind: *de alledaagse ~* the daily grind

sleuren /slørə(n)/ (sleurde, heeft gesleurd) drag, haul

de **sleutel** /sløtəl/ (pl: -s) **1** key **2** [fig] key, clue **3** spanner; [Am] wrench: *een Engelse ~* a monkey wrench **4** [mus] clef

het **sleutelbedrijf** /sløtəlbədrɛif/ (pl: -bedrijven) **1** key business (*or:* company) **2** rental agency

het **sleutelbeen** /sløtəlben/ (pl: -deren) collarbone, clavicle

de **sleutelbos** /sløtəlbɔs/ (pl: -sen) bunch of keys

sleutelen /sløtələ(n)/ (sleutelde, heeft gesleuteld) **1** work (on), repair **2** [fig] fiddle (with), tinker (with): *er moet nog wel wat aan de tekst gesleuteld worden* the text needs a certain amount of touching up

de **sleutelfiguur** /sløtəlfiɣyr/ (pl: -figuren) key figure

het **sleutelgat** /sløtəlɣat/ (pl: -en) keyhole: *aan het ~ luisteren* listen (*or:* eavesdrop) at the keyhole; *door het ~ kijken* peep through the keyhole

de **sleutelhanger** /sløtəlhɑŋər/ (pl: -s) keyring

de **sleutelpositie** /sløtəlpozi(t)si/ (pl: -s) key

position

de **sleutelring** /sløtəlrɪŋ/ (pl: -en) keyring

het **slib** /slɪp/ silt; sludge

de **sliding** /slɑjdɪŋ/ (pl: -s) sliding tackle

de **sliert** /slirt/ (pl: -en) **1** string, thread; wisp: ~en **rook** wisps of smoke **2** pack, bunch: een **hele** ~ a whole bunch

het **slijk** /slɛik/ mud, mire: iem. (or: iemands naam) **door** het ~ sleuren drag s.o. (or: s.o.'s name) through the mud/mire

het/de **slijm** /slɛim/ (pl: -en) **1** mucus; phlegm **2** [bot] slime **3** [toy product] slime

de **slijmbal** /slɛimbɑl/ (pl: -len) [inform] toady, bootlicker

de **slijmbeurs** /slɛimbørs/ (pl: -beurzen) bursa

de **slijmbeursontsteking** /slɛimbørsɔntstekɪŋ/ (pl: -en) bursitis

slijmen /slɛimə(n)/ (slijmde, heeft geslijmd) butter up, soft-soap: ~ **tegen** iem. butter s.o. up

slijmerig /slɛimərəχ/ (adj, adv) slimy

het **slijmvlies** /slɛimvlis/ (pl: -vliezen) mucous membrane

slijpen /slɛipə(n)/ (sleep, heeft geslepen) **1** sharpen **2** grind, polish; cut: **diamant** ~ cut diamonds **3** cut

de **slijpsteen** /slɛipsten/ (pl: -stenen) grindstone

de **slijtage** /slɛitaʒə/ wear (and tear): **tekenen** van ~ vertonen show signs of wear; **aan** ~ onderhevig zijn be subject to wear

slijten /slɛitə(n)/ (sleet, heeft/is gesleten) **1** wear (out): die jas is **kaal** gesleten that coat is worn bare **2** wear away, wear off; waste (away) **3** spend, pass: zijn **leven** in eenzaamheid ~ spend one's days in solitude

de **slijter** /slɛitər/ (pl: -s) wine merchant; [Am] liquor dealer ‖ ik **ga** naar de ~ I'm going to the wine shop

de **slijterij** /slɛitərɛi/ (pl: -en) wine shop; [Am] liquor store

slijtvast /slɛitfɑst/ (adj) hard-wearing, wear-resistant

slikken /slɪkə(n)/ (slikte, heeft geslikt) **1** swallow; gulp (down) **2** swallow, put up with: je **hebt** het maar te ~ you just have to put up with it

slim /slɪm/ (adj, adv) clever, smart: ~me **oogjes** shrewd eyes; een ~me **zet** a clever move; iem. te ~ af zijn be too clever for s.o.

de **slimheid** /slɪmhɛit/ cleverness

de **slimmigheid** /slɪməχhɛit/ dodge, trick: hij wist zich **door** een ~je eruit te redden he weaseled his way out of it

de **slinger** /slɪŋər/ (pl: -s) **1** festoon, streamer; garland **2** swing, sway **3** pendulum

de **slingerbeweging** /slɪŋərbəweɣɪŋ/ (pl: -en) **1** swing **2** swerve

[1]**slingeren** /slɪŋərə(n)/ (slingerde, heeft/is geslingerd) **1** swing, sway: ~ **op** zijn benen sway on one's legs **2** sway, lurch; yaw [ship]

3 lie about (or: around): **laat** je boeken niet altijd op mijn bureau ~! don't always leave your books lying around on my desk! **4** wind

[2]**slingeren** /slɪŋərə(n)/ (slingerde, heeft geslingerd) **1** sling, fling: bij de botsing werd de bestuurder **uit** de auto geslingerd in the crash the driver was flung out of the car **2** swing, sway

zich [3]**slingeren** /slɪŋərə(n)/ (slingerde zich, heeft zich geslingerd) wind; wind (o.s.)

de **slingerplant** /slɪŋərplɑnt/ (pl: -en) creeper, runner

slinken /slɪŋkə(n)/ (slonk, is geslonken) shrink: de **voorraad** slinkt the supply is dwindling

slinks /slɪŋks/ (adj, adv) cunning, devious: op ~e **wijze** by devious means

de **slip** /slɪp/ skid: **in** een ~ raken go into a skid

het **slipgevaar** /slɪpχəvar/ risk of skidding

het **slipje** /slɪpjə/ (pl: -s) (pair of) briefs (or: panties), (pair of) knickers

slippen /slɪpə(n)/ (slipte, is geslipt) slip; skid

de **slipper** /slɪpər/ (pl: -s) mule; slipper

het **slippertje** /slɪpərcə/ (pl: -s): een ~ **maken** have a bit on the side

de **sliptong** /slɪptɔŋ/ (pl: -en) slip, sole

slissen /slɪsə(n)/ (sliste, heeft geslist) lisp

slobberen /slɔbərə(n)/ (slobberde, heeft geslobberd) **1** bag, sag: zijn jasje slobbert **om** zijn lijf his baggy coat hangs around his body **2** slobber, slurp

de **slobbertrui** /slɔbərtrœy/ (pl: -en) baggy sweater

de **sloddervos** /slɔdərvɔs/ (pl: -sen) slob

de **sloeber** /sluber/ (pl: -s): een **arme** ~ a poor wretch (or: devil)

de **sloep** /slup/ (pl: -en) cutter: de ~ **strijken** lower the boat

de **sloerie** /sluri/ (pl: -s) slut

de **slof** /slɔf/ (pl: -fen) **1** slipper, mule: zij kan het **op** haar ~fen af she can do it with her eyes shut (or: with one hand tied behind her back); **uit** zijn ~ schieten hit the roof **2** carton **3** oval-shaped fruit pie; turnover

sloffen /slɔfə(n)/ (slofte, heeft/is gesloft) shuffle: **loop** niet zo te ~! don't shuffle (or: drag) your feet!

de **slogan** /slogən/ (pl: -s) slogan

de **slok** /slɔk/ (pl: -ken) **1** drink; sip [small]: **grote** ~ken nemen gulp **2** swallow, gulp ‖ een ~ **op** hebben have had one too many

de **slokdarm** /slɔgdɑrm/ (pl: -en) gullet

de **slokop** /slɔkɔp/ (pl: -pen) glutton

de **slons** /slɔns/ (pl: slonzen) slattern, sloven, slut

slonzig /slɔnzəχ/ (adj, adv) slovenly, sloppy

de **sloof** /slof/ (pl: sloven) (household) drudge

sloom /slom/ (adj, adv) listless, slow: **doe** niet zo ~ come on, I haven't got all day

de [1]**sloop** /slop/ (pl: slopen) **1** demolition **2** demolition firm; scrapyard: rijp **voor** de ~

on its last legs, fit for the scrap heap

het/de **²sloop** /slop/ (pl: slopen) pillowcase: *lakens en slopen* bedlinen

de **sloopauto** /sl̥opɑuto/ (pl: -'s) scrap car, wreck

de **sloophamer** /sl̥ophamər/ (pl: -s) jackhammer

het **slooppand** /sl̥opɑnt/ (pl: -en) building due for demolition

de **sloot** /slot/ (pl: sloten) **1** ditch, channel **2** buckets, gallons: [fig] *dat kost sloten met geld* it costs heaps of money; *een ~ water* a large amount of water

slootjespringen /sl̥ocəsprɪŋə(n)/ leap (over) ditches

het **slootwater** /sl̥otwatər/ ditchwater; [fig] dishwater

het **slop** /slɔp/ (pl: -pen) alley(way); blind alley: *in het ~ raken* come to a dead end

slopen /sl̥opə(n)/ (sloopte, heeft gesloopt) **1** demolish **2** break up; scrap **3** undermine: *~d werk* exhausting (*or:* back-breaking) work; *een ~de ziekte* a wasting disease

de **sloper** /sl̥opər/ (pl: -s) demolition contractor

de **sloperij** /slopərɛi/ (pl: -en) demolition firm (*or:* contractors); scrapyard

de **sloppenwijk** /sl̥ɔpə(n)wɛik/ (pl: -en) slums, slum area

slordig /sl̥ɔrdəx/ (adj, adv) careless; untidy; sloppy: *wat zit je haar ~* how untidy your hair is; *~ schrijven* scribble ‖ *dat kost een ~e miljoen* that costs a cool million

de **slordigheid** /sl̥ɔrdəxhɛit/ (pl: -heden) carelessness, sloppiness

het **slot** /slɔt/ (pl: -en) **1** lock; fastening: *iem. achter ~ en grendel zetten* put s.o. behind bars; *achter ~ en grendel* under lock and key; *een deur op ~ doen* lock a door; *alles op ~ doen* lock up; *op ~ zitten* **a)** be locked; **b)** [fig] be deadlocked **2** end, conclusion: *ten ~te* finally, eventually, at last; *~ volgt* to be concluded **3** castle ‖ *per ~ van rekening* after all, on balance; all things considered

het **slotakkoord** /sl̥ɔtakort/ (pl: -en) **1** final chord **2** final agreement: *het ~ van de conferentie* the summit's final agreement

de **slotenmaker** /sl̥otə(n)makər/ (pl: -s) locksmith

de **slotfase** /sl̥ɔtfazə/ (pl: -s, -n) final stage

de **slotgracht** /sl̥ɔtxrɑxt/ (pl: -en) (castle) moat

de **slotkoers** /sl̥ɔtkurs/ (pl: -en) closing price(s)

de **slotscène** /sl̥ɔtsɛ:nə/ final scene

de **slotsom** /sl̥ɔtsɔm/ conclusion

het **slotwoord** /sl̥ɔtwort/ closing word(s)

de **Sloveen** /slovḛn/ (pl: Slovenen) Slovene, Slovenian

het **¹Sloveens** /slovḛns/ Slovene

²Sloveens /slovḛns/ (adj) Slovenian

sloven /sl̥ovə(n)/ (sloofde, heeft gesloofd) drudge

Slovenië /slovḛnijə/ Slovenia

de **Slowaak** /slowak/ (pl: Slowaken) Slovak

het **¹Slowaaks** /slowaks/ Slovak

²Slowaaks /slowaks/ (adj) Slovak(ian)

Slowakije /slowakɛiə/ Slovakia

de **slow motion** /slomoʃən/ (pl: -s) slow motion

de **sluier** /sl̥œyər/ (pl: -s) veil

sluik /sl̥œyk/ (adj) straight, lank

de **sluikreclame** /sl̥œykrəklamə/ (pl: -s) product placement

sluikstorten /sl̥œykstɔrtə(n)/ [Belg] dump (illegally)

sluimeren /sl̥œymərə(n)/ (sluimerde, heeft gesluimerd) slumber

sluipen /sl̥œypə(n)/ (sloop, is geslopen) **1** steal, sneak; stalk: *naar boven ~* steal (*or:* sneak) upstairs **2** creep

de **sluipmoord** /sl̥œypmort/ (pl: -en) assassination

de **sluipmoordenaar** /sl̥œypmordənar/ (pl: -s) assassin ‖ *overgewicht is een ~* overweight is an unseen killer

de **sluiproute** /sl̥œyprutə/ (pl: -s) short cut

de **sluipschutter** /sl̥œypsχʏtər/ (pl: -s) sniper

het **sluipverkeer** /sl̥œypfərker/ cut-through traffic

de **sluipweg** /sl̥œypwɛx/ (pl: -en) secret route

de **sluis** /sl̥œys/ (pl: sluizen) lock; sluice: *door een ~ varen* pass through a lock

de **sluiswachter** /sl̥œyswɑχtər/ (pl: -s) lockkeeper

¹sluiten /sl̥œytə(n)/ (sloot, heeft gesloten) balance: *de begroting ~d maken* balance the budget ‖ *over en ~* over and out

²sluiten /sl̥œytə(n)/ (sloot, heeft gesloten) **1** shut, close; close down: *de grenzen ~* close the frontiers; *het raam ~* shut (*or:* close) the window; *de winkel (zaak) ~* **a)** close (the shop) down; **b)** [fig] shut up shop; *dinsdagmiddag zijn alle winkels gesloten* it is early closing day on Tuesday **2** conclude, enter into: *een verbond ~ (met)* enter into an alliance (with); *vrede ~* make peace; make up (with s.o.) **3** close, conclude

de **sluiting** /sl̥œytɪŋ/ (pl: -en) **1** shutting (off); closure; conclusion: *~ van de rekening* balancing of the account **2** fastening, fastener; lock; clasp: *de ~ van deze jurk zit op de rug* this dress does up at the back

de **sluitingsdatum** /sl̥œytɪŋzdatʏm/ (pl: -data) closing date

de **sluitingstijd** /sl̥œytɪŋstɛit/ (pl: -en) closing time: *na ~* after hours

de **sluitpost** /sl̥œytpɔst/ (pl: -en): *als ~ op de begroting dienen* be considered unimportant, come at the bottom of the list

de **sluitspier** /sl̥œytspir/ (pl: -en) sphincter

het **sluitstuk** /sl̥œytstʏk/ (pl: -ken) final piece

sluizen /sl̥œyzə(n)/ (sluisde, heeft gesluisd) channel, transfer

de **slungel** /slʏŋəl/ (pl: -s) beanpole

slungelig /ˈslʏŋələɣ/ (adj, adv) lanky

de **slurf** /slʏrf/ (pl: slurven) trunk

slurpen /ˈslʏrpə(n)/ (slurpte, heeft geslurpt) slurp

sluw /slyw/ (adj, adv) sly, crafty, cunning: *de ~e vos* the sly (*or:* cunning) old fox

de **sluwheid** /ˈslywhɛit/ (pl: -heden) slyness, cunning

sm (abbrev) SM, S and M

de **smaad** /smat/ defamation (of character), libel

de **smaak** /smak/ (pl: smaken) taste; flavour: *een goede ~ hebben* have good taste; *van goede* (or: *slechte*) *~ getuigen* be in good (*or:* bad) taste; *de ~ van iets te pakken hebben* have acquired a taste for; *in de ~ vallen bij ...* appeal to ..., find favour with ...; *over ~ valt niet te twisten* there is no accounting for taste(s); *smaken verschillen* tastes differ

het **smaakje** /ˈsmakjə/ (pl: -s) taste: *er zit een ~ aan dat vlees* that meat has a funny taste

de **smaakmaker** /ˈsmakmakər/ (pl: -s) **1** seasoning **2** trendsetter

de **smaakpapil** /ˈsmakpapɪl/ (pl: -len) taste bud

de **smaakstof** /ˈsmakstɔf/ (pl: -fen) flavour(ing), seasoning

smaakvol /ˈsmakfɔl/ (adj, adv) tasteful; in good taste: *~ gekleed zijn* be tastefully dressed

smachten /ˈsmɑxtə(n)/ (smachtte, heeft gesmacht) **1** languish: *iem. ~de blikken toewerpen* look longingly at s.o. **2** (+ naar) long (for), yearn (for)

smadelijk /ˈsmadələk/ (adj, adv) humiliating; scornful

de **smak** /smɑk/ (pl: -ken) **1** fall: *een ~ maken* fall with a bang **2** crash, smack: *met een ~ neerzetten* slam (*or:* slap) down **3** heap, pile: *dat kost een ~ geld* that costs a load of money

smakelijk /ˈsmakələk/ (adj, adv) tasty, appetizing: *eet ~!* enjoy your meal

smakeloos /ˈsmakəlos/ (adj, adv) tasteless; lacking in taste

smaken /ˈsmakə(n)/ (smaakte, heeft gesmaakt) taste: *hoe smaakt het?* how does it taste?; *heeft het gesmaakt, meneer?* (or: *mevrouw?*) did you enjoy your meal, sir? (*or:* madam?); *naar iets ~* taste of sth.; [hum] *dat smaakt naar meer* that's very moreish

¹**smakken** /ˈsmɑkə(n)/ (smakte, heeft gesmakt) smack one's lips: *smak niet zo!* don't make so much noise (when you're eating)

²**smakken** /ˈsmɑkə(n)/ (smakte, is gesmakt) crash: *tegen de grond ~* crash to the ground

smal /smɑl/ (adj) narrow: *~le opening* small opening; *een ~ gezichtje* a pinched face; *de ~le weg* [fig] the straight and narrow (path)

het **smaldeel** /ˈsmɑldel/ (pl: -delen) squadron; [fig] contingent

smalend /ˈsmalənt/ (adj, adv) scornful

het **smalspoor** /ˈsmɑlspor/ narrow-gauge railway

de ¹**smaragd** /smaˈrɑxt/ (pl: -en) [gem] emerald

het ²**smaragd** /smaˈrɑxt/ [mineral] emerald

de **smart** /smɑrt/ (pl: -en) **1** sorrow, grief, pain: *gedeelde ~ is halve ~* a sorrow shared is a sorrow halved **2** yearning, longing: *met ~ op iets (iem.) wachten* wait anxiously for sth. (s.o.)

het **smartboard** /ˈsmɑːrdbɔːrt/ (pl: -s) SMART board

smartelijk /ˈsmɑrtələk/ (adj, adv) grievous, painful

het **smartengeld** /ˈsmɑrtəɣɛlt/ (pl: -en) damages; (financial, monetary) compensation

de **smartlap** /ˈsmɑrtlɑp/ (pl: -pen) tear-jerker

de **smart-tv** /ˈsmɑːrteve/ (pl: -'s) smart TV

de **smash** /smɛʃ/ (pl: -es) (overhead) smash

smashen /ˈsmɛʃə(n)/ (smashte, heeft gesmasht) smash

smeden /ˈsmedə(n)/ (smeedde, heeft gesmeed) forge: *twee stukken ijzer aan elkaar ~* weld two pieces of iron (together); *uit één stuk gesmeed* forged in one piece || *plannen ~* make (or: lay) plans

de **smederij** /smedəˈrɛi/ (pl: -en) forge

het **smeedijzer** /ˈsmetɛizər/ (pl: -s) wrought iron

de **smeekbede** /ˈsmeɣbedə/ (pl: -s, -n) plea (for), cry (for)

het/de **smeer** /smer/ grease, oil; polish

smeerbaar /ˈsmerbar/ (adj) spreadable

de **smeerboel** /ˈsmerbul/ mess

het **smeergeld** /ˈsmerɣɛlt/ (pl: -en) bribe(s)

de **smeerkaas** /ˈsmerkas/ (pl: -kazen) cheese spread

de **smeerlap** /ˈsmerlɑp/ (pl: -pen) **1** skunk, bastard **2** pervert; dirty old man

het **smeermiddel** /ˈsmermɪdəl/ lubricant

de **smeerolie** /ˈsmeroli/ lubricant

smeken /ˈsmekə(n)/ (smeekte, heeft gesmeekt) implore, beg: *iem. om hulp ~* beg (for) s.o.'s help

smelten /ˈsmɛltə(n)/ (smolt, heeft/is gesmolten) melt; melt down: *de sneeuw smelt* the snow is melting (*or:* thawing); *deze reep chocolade smelt op de tong* this bar of chocolate melts in the mouth

de **smeltkroes** /ˈsmɛltkrus/ (pl: -kroezen) meltingpot [also fig]

het **smeltpunt** /ˈsmɛltpʏnt/ (pl: -en) melting point, point of fusion

smeren /ˈsmerə(n)/ (smeerde, heeft gesmeerd) **1** grease, oil; lubricate: *de keel smeren* wet one's whistle **2** smear: *crème op zijn huid ~* rub cream on one's skin **3** butter: *brood ~* butter bread, make sandwiches || *'m ~* clear off; make tracks

smerig /ˈsmerəɣ/ (adj, adv) dirty; [stronger] filthy: *een ~e streek (truc)* a dirty (*or:* shabby) trick

de **smering** /ˈsmerɪŋ/ (pl: -en) lubrication

de **smeris** /ˈsmerɪs/ (pl: -sen) cop

de **smet** /smɛt/ (pl: -ten) blemish, taint, stain:

*een ~ op iemands **blazoen*** a blot on one's escutcheon

smetteloos /smˈɛtəlos/ (adj, adv) [also fig] spotless, immaculate: ~ **wit** immaculate(ly) white

smeuïg /smˈøjəх/ (adj, adv) **1** smooth, creamy **2** vivid

smeulen /smˈølə(n)/ (smeulde, heeft gesmeuld) smoulder

de **smid** /smɪt/ (pl: smeden) smith

de **smiezen** /smˈizə(n)/ (pl) [inform]: *iets in de ~ hebben* be on to sth., see the way the land lies; *iem. in de ~ hebben* have s.o. taped; [Am] be wise to s.o.

smijten /smˈɛitə(n)/ (smeet, heeft gesmeten) throw, fling: *met de deuren ~* slam the doors; [fig] *iem. iets naar het hoofd ~* throw sth. in s.o.'s teeth

smikkelen /smˈɪkələ(n)/ (smikkelde, heeft gesmikkeld) tuck in

smiley /smˈɑjli/ (adj) smiley

de **smoel** /smul/ [inform] **1** trap: *houd je ~!* shut your trap!; *iem. op zijn ~ slaan* conk s.o. **2** face: *~en **trekken*** pull faces

het **smoelenboek** /smˈulə(n)buk/ almanac, year book, web page with photos, staff pages

de **smoes** /smus/ (pl: smoezen) excuse: *een ~je **bedenken*** think up a story (or: an excuse)

smoezelig /smˈuzələх/ (adj) grubby, dingy

smoezen /smˈuzə(n)/ (smoesde, heeft gesmoesd) **1** invent (or: cook up) excuses **2** whisper

de **smog** /smɔɡ/ smog

de **smoking** /smˈɔkɪŋ/ (pl: -s) dinner jacket

de **smokkel** /smˈɔkəl/ smuggling

de **smokkelaar** /smˈɔkəlar/ (pl: -s) smuggler

de **smokkelarij** /smokkəlarˈɛi/ (pl: -en) smuggling

smokkelen /smˈɔkələ(n)/ (smokkelde, heeft gesmokkeld) smuggle

de **smokkelwaar** /smˈɔkəlwar/ contraband

de **¹smoor** /smor/: *(er) de ~ **inhebben*** be peeved, be pissed off at sth.

²smoor /smor/ (adj): *~ **op** iem. zijn* have a crush on s.o.

smoorheet /smorhˈet/ (adj) stifling

smoorverliefd /smorvərlˈift/ (adj) smitten (with s.o.)

de **smoothie** /smuˈːθi/ (pl: -s) smoothie

smoren /smˈorə(n)/ (smoorde, heeft gesmoord) **1** smother, choke **2** braise

de **smos** /smɔs/ [Belg]: *een broodje ~* a salad roll

het **smout** /smɑut/ [Belg] lard

de **sms** /ɛsɛmɛs/ **1** short message service **2** text message

de **sms-alert** /ɛsɛmɛsəlyːrt/ (pl: -s) text-message alert

sms'en /ɛsɛmɛsə(n)/ (sms'te, heeft ge-sms't) text: *ik heb haar ge-sms't* I texted her, I sent her a text (message)

smullen /smˈylə(n)/ (smulde, heeft gesmuld) feast (on): *dat wordt ~!* yum-yum!; *om van te ~* finger-lickin' good

de **smulpaap** /smˈylpap/ (pl: -papen) [inform] gourmet

de **smurf** /smyrf/ (pl: -en) smurf

de **smurrie** /smˈyri/ gunge; sludge

snaaien /snˈajə(n)/ (snaaide, heeft gesnaaid) snitch, snatch

de **snaar** /snar/ (pl: snaren) string, chord; snare: *een gevoelige ~ raken* touch a tender spot; *de snaren **spannen*** string; snare

het **snaarinstrument** /snˈarɪnstrymɛnt/ (pl: -en) stringed instrument

de **snack** /snɛk/ (pl: -s) snack

de **snackbar** /snˈɛɡbar/ (pl: -s) snack bar

snakken /snˈɔkə(n)/ (snakte, heeft gesnakt) **1** gasp, pant: *naar adem ~* gasp for breath **2** crave: *~ naar aandacht* be craving (for) attention; *~ naar een sigaret* be gagging (or: dying) for a cigarette

snappen /snˈɔpə(n)/ (snapte, heeft gesnapt) get: *snap je?* (you) see?; *ik snap 'm* I get it; *ik snap niet waar het om gaat* I don't see it; *ik snap er niets van* I don't get it, it beats me

de **snars** /snɑrs/: *geen ~* not a bit; *hij weet er geen ~ van* he doesn't know a thing about it; *ik begrijp er geen ~ van* I haven't got a clue

de **snater** /snˈatər/ [inform] trap: *hou je ~!* shut your trap (or: face)!

snateren /snˈatərə(n)/ (snaterde, heeft gesnaterd) honk

de **snauw** /snɑu/ (pl: -en) growl, snarl

snauwen /snˈɑuwə(n)/ (snauwde, heeft gesnauwd) snarl, growl, snap

snauwerig /snˈɑuwərəх/ (adj, adv) snappish; gruff

de **snavel** /snˈavəl/ (pl: -s) bill; beak: *hou je ~!* shut up!

snedig /snˈedəх/ (adj, adv) witty

de **snee** /sne/ (pl: -ën) **1** slice: *een dun ~tje koek* a thin slice of cake **2** cut; gash **3** [med] incision

de **sneer** /sner/ (pl: sneren) gibe, taunt

de **sneeuw** /snew/ snow: *een dik pak ~* (a) thick (layer of) snow; *natte ~* sleet; [Belg] *zwarte ~ zien* be destitute, live in poverty; *smeltende ~* slush; *het verdwijnt als ~ voor de zon* it vanishes into thin air; *vastzitten in de ~* be snowbound

de **sneeuwbal** /snˈewbɑl/ (pl: -len) snowball

het **sneeuwbaleffect** /snˈewbɑlɛfɛkt/ (pl: -en) domino theory, snowball

sneeuwblind /snˈewblɪnt/ (adj) snow-blind

de **sneeuwbril** /snˈewbrɪl/ (pl: -len) (pair of) snow goggles

de **sneeuwbui** /snˈewbœy/ (pl: -en) snow (shower)

sneeuwen /snˈewə(n)/ (sneeuwde, heeft gesneeuwd) snow: *het sneeuwt hard* (or: *licht*) it is snowing heavily (or: lightly) de **sneeuwgrens** /sne̱wyrɛns/ snowline

de **sneeuwjacht** /sne̱wjɑχt/ blizzard

de **sneeuwketting** /sne̱wkɛtɪŋ/ (pl: -en) (snow) chain

het **sneeuwklokje** /sne̱wklɔkjə/ (pl: -s) snowdrop

de **sneeuwman** /sne̱wmɑn/ (pl: -nen) snowman

de **sneeuwpop** /sne̱wpɔp/ (pl: -pen) snowman

sneeuwruimen /sne̱wrœymə(n)/ (ruimde sneeuw, heeft sneeuwgeruimd) clear snow, shovel (away) snow

de **sneeuwschoen** /sne̱wsχun/ (pl: -en) snowshoe

de **sneeuwschuiver** /sne̱wsχœyvər/ (pl: -s) **1** snow shovel **2** snowplough

de **sneeuwstorm** /sne̱wstɔrm/ (pl: -en) snowstorm

de **sneeuwval** /sne̱wvɑl/ (pl: -len) snowfall

de **sneeuwvlok** /sne̱wvlɔk/ (pl: -ken) snowflake

sneeuwvrij /sne̱wvrɛi̱/ (adj) clear of snow: *de wegen ~ maken* clear the roads of snow

sneeuwwit /sne̱wwɪt/ (adj) snowy; niveous

Sneeuwwitje /sne̱wɪ̱cə/ Snow White

snel /snɛl/ (adj) **1** fast, rapid **2** quick, swift; fast; speedy: *een ~ besluit* a quick decision; *~ achteruitgaan* decline rapidly; *~ van begrip zijn* be quick (on the uptake) ‖ *iem. te ~ af zijn* steal a march on s.o., beat s.o. to the punch

de **snelbinder** /sne̱lbɪndər/ (pl: -s) carrier straps

de **snelheid** /sne̱lhɛit/ (pl: -heden) speed, pace, tempo; velocity: *bij hoge snelheden* at high speeds; *de maximum ~* the speed limit; *op volle ~* (at) full speed; *~ minderen* reduce speed, slow down

de **snelheidsbegrenzer** /sne̱lhɛitsbəχrɛnzər/ (pl: -s) governor, speed limiting device

de **snelheidscontrole** /sne̱lhɛitskɔntro:lə/ (pl: -s) speed(ing) check

de **snelheidsmaniak** /sne̱lhɛrtsmanijɑk/ (pl: -ken) speeder, speed merchant

de **snelheidsovertreding** /sne̱lhɛrtsovərtredɪŋ/ (pl: -en) speeding offence: *een ~ begaan* speed, go over the speed limit, commit a speeding offence

de **snelkoker** /sne̱lkokər/ (pl: -s) pressure cooker

de **snelkookpan** /sne̱lkokpɑn/ (pl: -nen) pressure cooker

de **snelkoppeling** /sne̱lkɔpəlɪŋ/ (pl: -en) [comp] link

snelladen /sne̱ladə(n)/ fast-charge, quickcharge

de **snellader** /sne̱ladər/ (pl: -s) fast-charger, quick-charger

het **snelrecht** /sne̱lrɛχt/ summary justice (or: proceedings): *~ toepassen* carry out accelerated (criminal) proceedings

de **sneltoets** /sne̱ltuts/ (pl: -en) hotkey

de **sneltrein** /sne̱ltrɛin/ (pl: -en) express (train), intercity (train)

de **sneltreinvaart** /sne̱ltrɛinvart/ tearing rush (or: hurry): *hij kwam in een ~ de hoek om* he came tearing round the corner

het **snelverkeer** /sne̱lvərker/ fast (or: through) traffic

snelwandelen /sne̱lwɑndələ(n)/ race walking

de **snelweg** /sne̱lwɛχ/ (pl: -en) motorway; [Am] freeway ‖ *elektronische* (or: *digitale*) *~* electronic (or: digital) highway

snerpen /snɛrpə(n)/ **1** bite, cut: *een ~de kou* cutting (or: piercing) cold **2** squeal, shriek

de **snert** /snɛrt/ pea soup

sneu /snø/ (adj, adv) unfortunate: *wat ~!* how sad!; *een ~ type* a sad little man

sneuvelen /snøvələ(n)/ (sneuvelde, is gesneuveld) **1** fall (in battle), be killed (in action): *~ in de strijd* be killed in action **2** break, get smashed

snibbig /snɪbəχ/ (adj) snappy, snappish

de **snijbloem** /snɛiblum/ (pl: -en) cut flower

de **snijboon** /snɛibon/ (pl: -bonen) French bean; [Am] string bean

de **snijbrander** /snɛibrɑndər/ (pl: -s) oxyacetylene burner, cutting torch

¹**snijden** /snɛi̱də(n)/ (sneed, heeft gesneden) **1** cut, carve; slice **2** [traf] cut in (on s.o.)

²**snijden** /snɛi̱də(n)/ (sneed, heeft gesneden) **1** cut: *uit hout een figuur ~* carve a figure out of wood **2** cross, intersect

snijdend /snɛi̱dənt/ (adj) cutting: *een ~e wind* a piercing (or: biting) wind

de **snijmachine** /snɛi̱mɑʃinə/ (pl: -s) cutter, cutting machine; slicer; shredder

de **snijmais** /snɛi̱mɑjs/ green maize (fodder)

de **snijplank** /snɛi̱plɑŋk/ (pl: -en) breadboard; chopping board; carving board

het **snijpunt** /snɛi̱pynt/ (pl: -en) crossing; intersection

de **snijtand** /snɛi̱tɑnt/ (pl: -en) incisor

het **snijvlak** /snɛi̱vlɑk/ (pl: -ken) [fig] borderline, cusp: *op het ~ van kunst en wetenschap* where art and science intersect, on the borderline between art and science

de **snijwond** /snɛi̱wont/ (pl: -en) cut

de **snik** /snɪk/ (pl: -ken) gasp: *de laatste ~ geven* breathe one's last; *tot aan zijn laatste ~* to his dying day ‖ *niet goed ~* cracked, off one's rocker

snikheet /snɪkhe̱t/ (adj) sizzling (hot), scorching (hot)

snikken /snɪkə(n)/ (snikte, heeft gesnikt) sob

de **snip** /snɪp/ (pl: -pen) snipe

de **snipper** /snɪpər/ (pl: -s) snip, shred; clipping: *in ~s scheuren* tear (in)to shreds

de **snipperdag** /snɪpərdɑχ/ (pl: -en) day off

snipperen /snɪpərə(n)/ (snipperde, heeft gesnipperd) shred, cut up (fine)

snipverkouden /snɪpfərkɑ̯u̯də(n)/ (adj) (all) stuffed up: ~ *zijn* have a streaming cold

de **snit** /snɪt/ (pl: -ten): *het is naar de* **laatste** ~ it's the latest thing (in fashion)

de **snob** /snɔp/ (pl: -s) snob

snoeien /snu̯jə(n)/ (snoeide, heeft gesnoeid) **1** trim; prune **2** cut back, prune: *in een begroting* ~ prune a budget

de **snoeischaar** /snu̯jsxar/ (pl: -scharen) pruning shears

de **snoek** /snuk/ (pl: -en) pike

de **snoekbaars** /snu̯gbars/ (pl: -baarzen) pikeperch

de **snoep** /snup/ sweets; [Am] candy

snoepen /snu̯pə(n)/ (snoepte, heeft gesnoept) eat sweets; [Am] eat candy

de **snoeper** /snu̯pər/ (pl: -s) s.o. with a sweet tooth ‖ *een* **ouwe** ~ an old goat, a dirty old man

het **snoepgoed** /snu̯pxut/ confectionery, sweets; [Am also] candy

het **snoepje** /snu̯pjə/ (pl: -s) sweet; [Am] candy

het **snoepreisje** /snu̯prɛɪ̯ʃə/ (pl: -s) facility trip; [Am] junket

de **snoepwinkel** /snu̯pwɪŋkəl/ (pl: -s) sweetshop; [Am] candy store: *als een kind* **in** *een* ~ like a kid in a sweetshop (*or:* candy store)

het **snoer** /snur/ (pl: -en) **1** string, rope: *kralen* **aan** *een* ~ *rijgen* string beads **2** flex, lead; [Am] cord

de **snoes** /snus/ (pl: snoezen) sweetie, pet, poppet

de **snoeshaan** /snu̯shan/ (pl: -hanen) queer customer (*or:* fellow)

de **snoet** /snut/ (pl: -en) **1** snout **2** face, mug: *een* **aardig** *~je* a pretty little face

snoeven /snu̯və(n)/ (snoefde, heeft gesnoefd) swagger, brag

snoezig /snu̯zəx/ (adj, adv) cute, sweet

de **snol** /snɔl/ (pl: -len) [inform] tart

snood /snot/ (adj, adv): *snode* **plannen** *hebben* be scheming

de **snor** /snɔr/ (pl: -ren) **1** moustache: *zijn* ~ *laten staan* grow a moustache **2** whiskers ‖ *dat* **zit** *wel* ~ that's fine, all right, okay, Bob's your uncle!

de **snorfiets** /snɔrfits/ (pl: -en) moped

het **snorhaar** /snɔrhar/ (pl: -haren) **1** (hair of a) moustache **2** whisker

de **snorkel** /snɔrkəl/ (pl: -s) snorkel

snorkelen /snɔrkələ(n)/ (snorkelde, heeft/is gesnorkeld) snorkel

snorren /snɔrə(n)/ (snorde, heeft gesnord) whirr, buzz, hum: *een ~de* **kat** a purring cat

de **snorscooter** /snɔrskutər/ (pl: -s) (motor)scooter

het/de **snot** /snɔt/ (nasal) mucus (*or:* discharge); snot

de **snotaap** /snɔtap/ (pl: -apen) brat, whippersnapper

de **snotneus** /snɔtnøs/ (pl: -neuzen) **1** runny

nose **2** (tiny) tot, (little) kid **3** brat

snotteren /snɔtərə(n)/ (snotterde, heeft gesnotterd) **1** sniff(le) **2** blubber

snowboarden /snobo:rdə(n)/ (snowboardde, heeft/is gesnowboard) go snowboarding

snuffelen /snʏfələ(n)/ (snuffelde, heeft gesnuffeld) **1** sniff (at) **2** nose (about), pry (into): *in laden* ~ rummage in drawers

de **snufferd** /snʏfərt/ (pl: -s) [inform] hooter ‖ *ik gaf hem een klap* **op** *zijn* ~ I gave him one on the kisser

het **snufje** /snʏfjə/ (pl: -s) **1** novelty; newest device (*or:* gadget): *het* **nieuwste** ~ the latest thing **2** dash: *een* ~ *zout* a pinch of salt

snugger /snʏɣər/ (adj, adv) [inform] bright, clever

de **snuisterij** /snœystərɛɪ̯/ (pl: -en) bauble, trinket

de **snuit** /snœyt/ (pl: -en) snout: *de* ~ *van een* **varken** a pig's snout

snuiten /snœytə(n)/ (snoot, heeft gesnoten) blow (one's nose)

de **snuiter** /snœytər/ (pl: -s): *een* **rare** ~ a strange guy, a weirdo

snuiven /snœyvə(n)/ (snoof, heeft gesnoven) **1** sniff(le), snort: *cocaïne* ~ sniff cocaine; ~ *als een paard* snort like a horse **2** sniff (at)

snurken /snʏrkə(n)/ (snurkte, heeft gesnurkt) snore

so 1 *schriftelijke overhoring* [Dutch] quiz, written test **2** *secundair onderwijs* [Belg] secondary education

de **soa** /so̯wa/ *seksueel overdraagbare aandoening* VD, venereal disease

de **soap** /sop/ (pl: -s) soap

de **soapie** /sopi/ [Dutch] soap star

de **soapster** /sopstɛr/ soap star

sober /so̯bər/ (adj, adv) austere, frugal: *in ~e* **bewoordingen** in plain words (*or:* language); *hij* **leeft** *zeer* ~ he lives very austerely (*or:* frugally)

de **soberheid** /so̯bərhɛit/ austerity, frugality

¹**sociaal** /so̯ʃal/ (adj) social: *hoog op de sociale* **ladder** high up on the social scale; *iemands sociale* **positie** s.o.'s social position

²**sociaal** /so̯ʃal/ (adv) **1** socially **2** socially-minded: ~ *denkend* humanitarian, socially aware

de **sociaaldemocraat** /so̯ʃaldemokrat/ (pl: -democraten) social democrat

sociaaldemocratisch /so̯ʃaldemokratis/ (adj) social democratic

het **socialisme** /so̯ʃalɪsmə/ socialism

de **socialist** /so̯ʃalɪst/ (pl: -en) socialist

socialistisch /so̯ʃalɪstis/ (adj, adv) socialist(ic)

de **social media** /so̯ʃəlmiːdijə/ (pl) social media

de **sociëteit** /so̯ʃetɛit/ (pl: -en) **1** association, club: *lid van een* ~ *worden* become a member of (*or:* join) an association **2** association (building), club(house) **3** society

de **sociologie** /soʃoloɣi/ sociology
sociologisch /soʃoloɣis/ (adj, adv) sociological
de **socioloog** /soʃolox/ (pl: -logen) sociologist
de **soda** /soda/ **1** (washing) soda **2** soda (water): *een whisky-soda* a whisky and soda
de **sodemieter** /sodəmitər/ [Dutch]: *als de ~!* like crazy; *iem. op z'n ~ geven* beat the hell out of s.o.; *dat gaat je geen ~ aan* that's none of your bloody business
¹**sodemieteren** /sodəmitərə(n)/ (sodemieterde, is gesodemieterd) [Dutch; inform] tumble
²**sodemieteren** /sodəmitərə(n)/ (sodemieterde, heeft gesodemieterd) [Dutch; inform] chuck
soebatten /subɑtə(n)/ (soebatte, heeft gesoebat): [Dutch; inform] *eindeloos ~ over iets* have endless discussions about sth.
het **soelaas** /sulas/: *dat biedt ~* that is a consolation
de **soenniet** /sunit/ (pl: -en) Sunni
de **soep** /sup/ (pl: -en) soup; consommé: *een ~ laten trekken* make a stock (*or:* broth) || *het is niet veel ~s* it's not up to much; *in de ~ lopen* come badly unstuck; *dat is linke ~* that's a risky business
het **soepballetje** /subɑləcə/ (pl: -s) meatball
het **soepbord** /subɔrt/ (pl: -en) soup bowl
soepel /supəl/ (adj, adv) **1** supple, pliable **2** supple; flexible; (com)pliant: *een ~e regeling* a flexible arrangement **3** supple: *~e bewegingen* supple (*or:* lithe) movements
de **soepelheid** /supəlhɛit/ suppleness, flexibility
de **soepgroente** /supxruntə/ (pl: -n) vegetables for soup
de **soepkop** /supkɔp/ (pl: -pen) soup cup
de **soeplepel** /suplepəl/ (pl: -s) **1** soup spoon **2** [Dutch] soup ladle
de **soepstengel** /supstɛŋəl/ (pl: -s) breadstick
het **soepzootje** /supsocə/ mess, shambles
de **soesa** /suza/ fuss, to-do, bother
soeverein /suvərɛin/ (adj, adv) sovereign
de **soevereiniteit** /suvərɛinitɛit/ sovereignty
soezen /suzə(n)/ (soesde, heeft gesoesd) doze, drowse
soezerig /suzərəx/ (adj) drowsy, dozy
de **sof** /sɔf/ flop, washout
de **sofa** /sofa/ (pl: -'s) sofa, couch
het **sofinummer** /sofinʏmər/ (pl: -s) [roughly] National Insurance Number; [Am] [roughly] Social Security Number
het **softbal** /sɔftbɑl/ softball
softballen /sɔf(t)bɑlə(n)/ (softbalde, heeft gesoftbald) play softball
het **softijs** /sɔftɛis/ soft ice-cream, Mr. Softy
de **softporno** /sɔftpɔrno/ soft porn(ography)
de **software** /sɔftwɛːr/ software: *kwaadaardige ~* malware
de **soigneur** /swɑŋør/ (pl: -s) helper; [boxing]

[roughly] second
de **soja** /soja/ (sweet) soy (sauce)
de **sojaboon** /sojabon/ (pl: -bonen) soya bean
de **sojamelk** /sojamɛlk/ soya milk
de **sojaolie** /sojaoli/ soya bean oil
de **sojasaus** /sojasɑus/ soy sauce
het **sojavlees** /sojavles/ soya meat
de **sok** /sɔk/ sock: *hij haalde het op zijn ~ken* he did it effortlessly || *iem. van de ~ken rijden* bowl s.o. over, knock s.o. down
de **sokkel** /sɔkəl/ (pl: -s) pedestal
de **sol** /sɔl/ (pl: -len) [mus] so(h), sol, G
het **solarium** /solarijʏm/ (pl: solaria) solarium
de **soldaat** /sɔldat/ (pl: soldaten) **1** (common) soldier, private: *de gewone soldaten* the ranks **2** soldier; troops: *de Onbekende Soldaat* the Unknown Soldier
het **soldaatje** /sɔldacə/ (pl: -s) toy soldier, tin soldier: *~ spelen* play (at) soldiers
het/de **soldeer** /sɔlder/ solder
de **soldeerbout** /sɔldərbɑut/ (pl: -en) soldering iron
het **soldeersel** /sɔldərsəl/ (pl: -s) solder
de **solden** /sɔldə(n)/ [Belg] sale
solderen /sɔldərə(n)/ (soldeerde, heeft gesoldeerd) solder
de **soldij** /sɔldɛi/ pay(ment)
solidair /solidɛːr/ (adj, adv) sympathetic: *~ zijn* show solidarity (with)
de **solidariteit** /solidaritɛit/ solidarity: *uit ~ met* in sympathy with
solide /solidə/ (adj, adv) **1** solid; hard-wearing **2** steady
de **solist** /solɪst/ (pl: -en) soloist
solitair /solitɛːr/ (adj, adv) solitary
sollen /sɔlə(n)/ (solde, heeft gesold) (+ met) trifle with: *hij laat niet met zich ~* he won't be trifled with
de **sollicitant** /sɔlisitɑnt/ (pl: -en) applicant
de **sollicitatie** /sɔlisita(t)si/ (pl: -s) application
de **sollicitatiebrief** /sɔlisita(t)sibrif/ (pl: -brieven) (letter of) application
het **sollicitatiegesprek** /sɔlisita(t)siɣəsprɛk/ (pl: -ken) interview (for a position, job)
solliciteren /sɔlisitərə(n)/ (solliciteerde, heeft gesolliciteerd) apply (for)
het/de **solo** /solo/ (pl: -'s, soli) solo
de **solocarrière** /solokarijɛrə/ (pl: -s) solo career
het **soloconcert** /solokɔnsɛrt/ solo concert
de **solutie** /soly(t)si/ (pl: -s) (rubber) solution
de **som** /sɔm/ (pl: -men) sum: *een ~ geld* a sum of money; *~men maken* do sums
Somalië /somalijə/ Somalia
de **Somaliër** /somalijər/ (pl: -s) Somali
Somalisch /somalis/ (adj) Somali
somber /sɔmbər/ (adj, adv) **1** dejected, gloomy: *het ~ inzien* take a sombre (*or:* gloomy) view (of things) **2** gloomy; dark: *~ weer* gloomy weather
de **somma** /sɔma/ sum

de **sommelier** /sɔməljeː/ (pl: -s) sommelier, wine waiter

sommeren /sɔmeːrə(n)/ (sommeerde, heeft gesommeerd) summon(s), call (up)on

sommige /sɔməɣə/ (ind pron) some, certain: ~*n* some (people)

soms /sɔms/ (adv) **1** sometimes **2** perhaps, by any chance: *heb je Jan ~ gezien?* have you seen John by any chance?; *dat is toch mijn zaak, of niet ~?* that's my business, or am I mistaken?

de **sonar** /soːnar/ (pl: -s) sonar

de **sonate** /soːnaːtə/ (pl: -s) sonata

de **sonde** /sɔndə/ (pl: -s) **1** probe **2** [med] catheter

de **sondevoeding** /sɔndəvudɪŋ/ (pl: -en) dripfeed

het **songfestival** /sɔŋfɛstival/ (pl: -s) song contest: *het Eurovisie ~* the Eurovision Song Contest

de **songtekst** /sɔŋtɛkst/ lyric(s)

het **sonnet** /sɔnɛt/ (pl: -ten) sonnet

de **¹soort** /sort/ (pl: -en) species: *de menselijke ~* the human species

het/de **²soort** /sort/ (pl: -en) **1** sort, kind, type: *ik ken dat ~* I know the type; *in zijn ~* in its way, of its kind; *in alle ~en en maten* in all shapes and sizes **2** sort (of), kind (of): *als een ~ vis* (rather) like some kind of a fish ‖ *~ zoekt ~* like will to like; birds of a feather flock together; [inform] *een ~ van tevreden* kind (*or:* sort) of satisfied

soortelijk /sortələk/ (adj, adv) specific

het **soortement** /sortəmɛnt/ [inform] a sort of, a kind of

soortgelijk /sortχəlɛik/ (adj) similar; of the same kind

de **soos** /sos/ [Dutch] club

het **sop** /sɔp/ (pl: -pen) (soap)suds: *het ruime ~ kiezen* stand out to sea; *het ~ is de kool niet waard* it's more trouble than it's worth

het **sopje** /sɔpjə/ (soap)suds: *zal ik de keuken nog een ~ geven?* shall I give the kitchen a(nother) wash?

soppen /sɔpə(n)/ (sopte, heeft gesopt) dunk

de **¹sopraan** /sopran/ [singer] soprano

de **²sopraan** /sopran/ [voice] soprano

de **sorbet** /sɔrbɛt/ (pl: -s) sorbet

sorry /sɔri/ (int) sorry: *~ dat ik het zeg* I'm sorry to have to say so, but …

sorteren /sɔrteːrə(n)/ (sorteerde, heeft gesorteerd) sort (out): *op maat ~* sort according to size ‖ *effect sorteren* have (*or:* produce) an effect, be effective

de **sortering** /sɔrteːrɪŋ/ (pl: -en) selection, range, assortment

SOS /ɛsoɛs/ *Save our Souls* SOS: *een SOS(-signaal) uitzenden* broadcast an SOS (message)

de **soufflé** /sufleː/ (pl: -s) soufflé

souffleren /sufleːrə(n)/ (souffleerde, heeft gesouffleerd) prompt

de **souffleur** /suflør/ (pl: -s) prompter

de **soul** /sol/ soul (music)

de **sound** /saunt/ (pl: -s) sound

de **soundbite** /saundbɑjt/ (pl: -s) sound bite

de **soundcheck** /sauntʃɛk/ (pl: -s) soundcheck

de **soundtrack** /sauntrɛk/ (pl: -s) soundtrack

het **souper** /supeː/ (pl: -s) supper, dinner

de **souteneur** /sutənør/ (pl: -s) pimp

het **souterrain** /sutərɛ̃/ (pl: -s) basement

het **souvenir** /suvənir/ (pl: -s) souvenir

de **sovjet** /sɔvjɛt/ (pl: -s) soviet: *de Opperste Sovjet* the Supreme Soviet

de **Sovjet-Unie** /sɔvjɛtyni/ Soviet Union

sowieso /zowizoː/ (adv) in any case, anyhow, definitely: *dat is ~ geen optie* that's not an option anyway; *het wordt ~ laat op dat feest* that party will definitely go on until late

de **¹spa** /spa/ **1** spade **2** spa

de **²spa®** /spa/ mineral water

de **spaak** /spak/ (pl: spaken) spoke: [Dutch] *iem. een ~ in het wiel steken* put a spoke in s.o.'s wheel ‖ *~ lopen* go wrong

de **spaan** /span/ (pl: spanen) **1** chip (of wood): *er bleef geen ~ van heel* there was nothing left of it **2** skimmer

de **spaander** /spandər/ (pl: -s) chip, splinter

de **spaanplaat** /spamplat/ (pl: -platen) chipboard

Spaans /spans/ (adj) Spanish: *Spaanse peper* chilli, hot pepper ‖ *zeg het eens op z'n ~* say it in Spanish

de **spaarbank** /sparbaŋk/ (pl: -en) savings bank: *geld op de ~ hebben* have money in a savings bank (*or:* savings account)

het **spaarbankboekje** /sparbaŋbukjə/ (pl: -s) deposit book

de **spaarcenten** /sparsɛntə(n)/ (pl) savings

de **spaarder** /spardər/ (pl: -s) saver

het **spaargeld** /sparɣɛlt/ (pl: -en) savings

de **spaarlamp** /sparlamp/ (pl: -en) low-energy light bulb

de **spaarpot** /sparpɔt/ (pl: -ten) **1** money box, piggy bank **2** savings, nest egg: *een ~ aanleggen* start saving for a rainy day; *zijn ~ aanspreken* draw on one's savings

het **spaarpunt** /sparpʏnt/ (pl: -en) loyalty point

de **spaarrekening** /sparekənɪŋ/ (pl: -en) savings account

de **spaarstand** /sparstant/ energy saving mode, power save mode

het **spaartegoed** /spartəɣut/ (pl: -en) savings balance

het **spaarvarken** /sparvarkə(n)/ (pl: -s) piggy bank

spaarzaam /sparzam/ (adj, adv) **1** thrifty, economical: *hij is erg ~ met zijn lof* he's very sparing in (*or:* with) his praise; *~ zijn met zijn woorden* not waste words **2** scanty, sparse: *de doodstraf wordt ~ toegepast* the death penalty is seldom imposed

de **spaarzegel** /sparzeɣəl/ (pl: -s) trading

stamp

de **spade** /spɑdə/ (pl: spaden) spade

de **spagaat** /spaɣat/ (pl: spagaten) splits: *een ~ maken* do the splits ‖ *zich in een ~ bevinden* be in two minds, be in a dilemma

de **spaghetti** /spaɣɛti/ spaghetti: *een sliert ~* a strand of spaghetti; [pol] *bestuurlijke ~* administrative shambles; *een ~ van kabels* cable spaghetti

de **spalk** /spɑlk/ (pl: -en) splint

spalken /spɑlkə(n)/ (spalkte, heeft gespalkt) put in splints

de **spam** /spɛm/ spam

de **spambox** /spɛmbɔks/ (pl: -en) spam folder

het **spamfilter** /spɛmfɪltər/ spam filter

spammen /spɛmə(n)/ (spamde, heeft gespamd) spam

het **span** /spɑn/ (pl: -nen) team; [of pers] couple: *een ~ paarden* a team of horses

het **spandoek** /spɑnduk/ (pl: -en) banner: *een ~ met zich meedragen* carry a banner

de **spaniël** /spɛnəl/ (pl: -s) spaniel

de **Spanjaard** /spɑnart/ (pl: -en) Spaniard

Spanje /spɑnjə/ Spain

de **spankracht** /spɑnkrɑxt/ tension; muscle tone; resilience

spannen /spɑnə(n)/ (spande, heeft gespannen) **1** stretch, tighten **2** harness ‖ *het zal erom ~ wie er wint* it will be a close match (*or*: race); *dat spant de kroon* that takes the cake

spannend /spɑnənt/ (adj) exciting, thrilling: *een ~ moment* a tense moment; *een ~ verhaal* an exciting story

de **spanning** /spɑnɪŋ/ (pl: -en) **1** tension; [fig also] suspense: *~ en sensatie* excitement and suspense; *de ~ stijgt* the tension mounts; *de ~ viel van haar af* that was a load off her shoulders; *ze zaten vol ~ te wachten* they were waiting anxiously; *in ~ zitten* be in suspense **2** tension: *onder ~ staan* be live; *een ~ van 10.000 volt* a charge of 10,000 volts

de **spanningsboog** /spɑnɪŋzboɣ/ (pl: -bogen) voltage curve: [fig] *een korte ~ hebben* have a short attention span

het **spanningsveld** /spɑnɪŋsfɛlt/ (pl: -en) [csp fig] area of tension

het **spant** /spɑnt/ (pl: -en) rafter, truss

de **spanwijdte** /spɑnwɛitə/ (pl: -n, -s) wingspan; wingspread

de **spar** /spɑr/ (pl: -ren) spruce

de **sparappel** /spɑrɑpəl/ (pl: -s, -en) fir cone

¹**sparen** /spɑrə(n)/ (spaarde, heeft gespaard) save (up): *voor een nieuwe auto ~* save up for a new car; *zijn krachten sparen* conserve one's energy

²**sparen** /spɑrə(n)/ (spaarde, heeft gespaard) **1** save, spare **2** collect ‖ *spaar me de details* spare me the details, all right?

de **spareribs** /spɛːrɪps/ (pl) spareribs

sparren /spɛrə(n)/ (sparde, heeft gespard) work out; spar

de **sparringpartner** /spɛrɪŋpɑːrtnər/ (pl: -s) sparring-partner

spartelen /spɑrtələ(n)/ (spartelde, heeft gesparteld) flounder, thrash about: *het kleine kind spartelde in het water* the little child splashed about in the water

spastisch /spɑstis/ (adj, adv) spastic

de **spat** /spɑt/ (pl: -ten) **1** splash **2** speck, spot

de **spatader** /spɑtadər/ (pl: -en) varicose vein

het **spatbord** /spɑdbɔrt/ (pl: -en) mudguard; [Am] fender

de **spatel** /spɑtəl/ (pl: -s) spatula

de **spatie** /spa(t)si/ (pl: -s) space, spacing, interspace: *iets typen met een ~* type sth. with interspacing

de **spatiebalk** /spa(t)sibɑlk/ (pl: -en) space bar

de **spatlap** /spɑtlɑp/ (pl: -pen) mud flap

spatten /spɑtə(n)/ (spatte, heeft gespat) splash, sp(l)atter: *vonken ~ in het rond* sparks flew all around; *er is verf op mijn kleren gespat* some paint has splashed on my clothes; *zij spatte (mij) met water in mijn gezicht* she spattered water in my face; *uit elkaar ~ burst*; [fig] *het enthousiasme spatte ervanaf* the enthusiasm was obvious, people were wildly enthusiastic

de **speaker** /spikər/ (pl: -s) speaker

de **specerij** /spesərɛi/ (pl: -en) spice, seasoning

de **specht** /spɛxt/ (pl: -en) woodpecker

¹**speciaal** /speʃal/ (adj) special: *in dit speciale geval* in this particular case

²**speciaal** /speʃal/ (adv) especially, particularly, specially: *ik doel ~ op hem* I mean him in particular; *~ gemaakt* specially made

de **speciaalzaak** /speʃalzak/ (pl: -zaken) specialist shop

de **special** /spɛʃəl/ (pl: -s) special (issue): *een ~ over de Kinks* a special on the Kinks

de **specialisatie** /speʃaliza(t)si/ (pl: -s) specialization

zich **specialiseren** /speʃalizerə(n)/ (specialiseerde zich, heeft zich gespecialiseerd) (+ in) specialize (in)

het **specialisme** /speʃalɪsmə/ (pl: -n) specialism

de **speclalist** /speʃalɪst/ (pl: -en) specialist

specialistisch /speʃalɪstis/ (adj, adv) specialist(ic)

de **specialiteit** /speʃalitɛit/ (pl: -en) speciality

de **specie** /spesi/ (pl: -s) cement, mortar

de **specificatie** /spesifika(t)si/ (pl: -s) specification: *~ van een nota vragen* request an itemized bill

specificeren /spesifiserə(n)/ (specificeerde, heeft gespecificeerd) specify, itemize

specifiek /spesifik/ (adj, adv) specific

het **specimen** /spesimɛn/ (pl: -s) specimen, exemplar

spectaculair /spɛktakylɛːr/ (adj) spectacular

het **spectrum** /spɛktrəm/ (pl: spectra) spectrum

het/de **speculaas** /spekylas/: *gevulde ~* [roughly]

spiced cake filled with almond paste
de **speculaaspop** /spekylɑspɔp/ (pl: -pen) [roughly] gingerbread man
de **speculant** /spekylɑnt/ (pl: -en) speculator
de **speculatie** /spekyla(t)si/ (pl: -s) speculation
speculeren /spekylɤrə(n)/ (speculeerde, heeft gespeculeerd) **1** (+ op) speculate (on) **2** speculate
de **speech** /spiːtʃ/ (pl: -es) speech: *een ~ afsteken* deliver a speech
speechen /spiːtʃə(n)/ (speechte, heeft gespeecht) give (*or:* make) a speech
de **speed** /spiːd/ speed
de **speedboot** /spiːdbot/ (pl: -boten) speedboat
de **speeddate** /spiːtdet/ (pl: -s) speed date
speeddaten /spiːtdetə(n)/ (speeddatete, heeft gespeeddatet) go to a speed dating event
het **speeksel** /speksəl/ saliva
de **speelautomaat** /spelɑutomat/ (pl: -automaten) slot machine
de **speelbal** /spelbɑl/ (pl: -len): *het schip was een ~ van de golven* the ship was the waves' plaything
de **speeldoos** /speldos/ (pl: -dozen) **1** music box **2** toybox
de **speelfilm** /spelfɪlm/ (pl: -s) (feature) film
het **speelgoed** /spelɣut/ toy(s): *een stuk ~* a toy
de **speelhal** /spelhɑl/ (pl: -len) amusement arcade
de **speelhelft** /spelhɛlft/ (pl: -en) half
de **speelkaart** /spelkart/ (pl: -en) playing card
de **speelkameraad** /spelkamərat/ (pl: -kameraden) playfellow, playmate
het **speelkwartier** /spelkwɑrtir/ (pl: -en) [Dutch] playtime; break
de **speelplaats** /spelplats/ (pl: -en) playground, play area: *op de ~* in the playground
de **speelruimte** /spelrœymtə/ (pl: -n, -s) **1** play, latitude: *~ hebben* have some play; *iem. ~ geven* leave s.o. a bit of elbow room **2** play area, room to play
speels /spels/ (adj) **1** playful; [esp animal] frisky **2** playful; light
de **speelsheid** /spelshɛrt/ playfulness
de **speeltafel** /speltafəl/ (pl: -s) gaming table
het **speeltje** /spelcə/ (pl: -s) (little) toy
het **speeltoestel** /speltustɛl/ (pl: -len) playground (*or:* outdoor) equipment
de **speeltuin** /speltœyn/ (pl: -en) playground
het **speelveld** /spelvɛlt/ (pl: -en) (sports, playing) field: [econ] *een gelijk ~* a level playing field
de **speen** /spen/ (pl: spenen) **1** (rubber) teat; [Am] nipple **2** teat
de **speer** /sper/ (pl: speren) spear; javelin ‖ *als een ~* like a rocket
de **speerpunt** /sperpʏnt/ (pl: -en) spearhead: *de ~en van een beleid* the spearheads of a policy

speerwerpen /sperwɛrpə(n)/ throw(ing) the javelin: *het ~ winnen* win the javelin (event)
het **spek** /spɛk/ bacon; fat
spekglad /spɛkxlɑt/ (adj) (very) slippery
spekken /spɛkə(n)/ (spekte, heeft gespekt) lard: *zijn portemonnee ~* line his own pockets; *zijn verhaal met anekdotes ~* spice one's story with anecdotes
het **spekkie** /spɛki/ (pl: -s) [roughly] marshmallow
de **speklap** /spɛklɑp/ (pl: -pen) [Dutch] thick slice of fatty bacon
het **spektakel** /spɛktakəl/ (pl: -s) **1** spectacle, show: *het ~ is afgelopen* the show is over **2** uproar, fuss: *het was me een ~* it was a tremendous fuss
het **spel** /spɛl/ (pl: -en, -len) **1** game; gambling **2** game, match: [cards] *een goed* (*or: sterk*) *~ in handen hebben* have a good hand; *doe je ook een ~letje mee?* do you want to join in? (*or:* play); *het ~ meespelen* play the game, play along (with s.o.); *zijn ~ slim spelen* play one's cards well **3** play: *hoog ~ spelen* play for high stakes, play high; *vals ~* cheating; *vuil* (*or: onsportief*) *~* foul play **4** acting, performance ‖ *een ~ kaarten* a pack (*or:* deck) of cards; *buiten ~ blijven* stay (*or:* keep) out of it; *in het ~ zijn* be involved; be in question, be at stake; *er is een vergissing in het ~* there is an error somewhere; *zijn leven* (*or: alles*) *op het ~ zetten* risk/stake one's life (*or:* everything); *vrij ~ hebben* have free play, have an open field
de **spelbreker** /spɛlbrekər/ (pl: -s) spoilsport
de **spelcomputer** /spɛlkɔmpjutər/ (pl: -s) games computer
de **speld** /spɛlt/ (pl: -en) pin: *je kon er een ~ horen vallen* you could have heard a pin drop; *daar is geen ~ tussen te krijgen* there's no flaw in that argument
spelden /spɛldə(n)/ (speldde, heeft gespeld) pin
het **speldenkussen** /spɛldə(n)kʏsə(n)/ (pl: -s) pincushion
de **speldenprik** /spɛldə(n)prɪk/ (pl: -ken) pinprick: *~ken uitdelen* needle (s.o.), hit out
het **speldje** /spɛlcə/ (pl: -s) **1** pin **2** pin, badge
¹**spelen** /spelə(n)/ (speelde, heeft gespeeld) **1** be set (in), take place (in): *de film speelt in New York* the film is set in New York **2** play: *de wind speelde met haar haren* the wind played (*or:* was playing) with her hair
²**spelen** /spelə(n)/ (speelde, heeft gespeeld) **1** play: *al ~d leren* learn through play; *vals ~* a) cheat; b) [mus] play out of tune; [sport] *voor ~* play up front **2** act, play **3** play: *piano ~* play the piano **4** play, perform **5** be of importance, count: *dat speelt geen rol* that is of no account; *die kwestie speelt nog steeds* that is still an (important) issue

spelenderwijs /speləndərwɛis/ (adv) without effort, with (the greatest of) ease

de **speleoloog** /spelejolo̱x/ (pl: -logen) speleologist

de **speler** /spe̱lər/ (pl: -s) player; gambler

de **spelfout** /spe̱lfaut/ (pl: -en) spelling mistake (or: error)

de **speling** /spe̱lɪŋ/ (pl: -en) **1** play: *een ~ van de natuur* a freak of nature **2** play; slack; margin

de **spelleider** /spe̱lɛidər/ (pl: -s) instructor; emcee

spellen /spe̱lə(n)/ (spelde, heeft gespeld) spell: *correct ~* spell correctly; *een woord verkeerd ~* misspell a word || *de krant ~* read the newspaper word by word

het **spelletje** /spe̱ləcə/ (pl: -s) game: *ergens een ~ van maken* take (or: treat) sth. lightly; [fig] *een ~ spelen met iem.* give s.o. the runaround, have a little game with s.o.

de **spelling** /spe̱lɪŋ/ (pl: -en) spelling

het **spelonk** /spelo̱ŋk/ (pl: -en) cave, cavern

de **spelregel** /spe̱lreɣəl/ (pl: -s) rule of play (or: the game): *je moet je aan de ~s houden* you must stick to the rules; *de ~s overtreden* break the rules

de **spelshow** /spe̱lʃo/ game show

de **spelt** /spelt/ spelt

het **speltbrood** /spe̱ltbrot/ (pl: -broden) spelt bread

de **spelverdeler** /spe̱lvərdelər/ (pl: -s) playmaker

de **spencer** /spe̱nsər/ (pl: -s) spencer

spenderen /spende̱rə(n)/ (spendeerde, heeft gespendeerd) spend

het **sperma** /spe̱rma/ sperm; cum

de **spermabank** /spe̱rmabɑŋk/ (pl: -en) sperm bank

de **spertijd** /spe̱rtɛit/ (pl: -en) curfew

het **spervuur** /spe̱rvyr/ barrage, curtain fire: *een ~ van vragen* a barrage of questions

de **sperwer** /spe̱rwər/ (pl: -s) sparrowhawk

de **sperzieboon** /spe̱rzibon/ (pl: -bonen) green bean

de **spetter** /spe̱tər/ (pl: -s) **1** spatter **2** hunk

spetteren /spe̱tərə(n)/ (spetterde, heeft gespetterd) sp(l)atter; crackle

spetterend /spe̱tərənt/ (adj) splendid, smashing: *een ~ optreden* a splendid performance

de **spetterplaat** /spe̱tərplat/ (pl: -platen) splash plate (to prevent public urination)

de **speurder** /spø̱rdər/ (pl: -s) detective, sleuth

speuren /spø̱rə(n)/ (speurde, heeft gespeurd) investigate, hunt: *naar iets ~* hunt (or: search) for sth.

de **speurhond** /spø̱rhɔnt/ (pl: -en) tracker (dog), bloodhound

de **speurtocht** /spø̱rtɔxt/ (pl: -en) search

het **speurwerk** /spø̱rwɛrk/ investigation, detective work

spichtig /spɪ̱xtəx/ (adj, adv) lanky, spindly: *een ~ meisje* a skinny girl

de **spie** /spi/ (pl: -ën) pin; wedge

spieden /spi̱də(n)/ (spiedde, heeft gespied): *~d om zich heen kijken* look furtively around

de **spiegel** /spi̱ɣəl/ (pl: -s) mirror: *vlakke* (or: *holle, bolle*) *~s* flat (or: concave, convex) mirrors; *in de ~ kijken* look at o.s. (in the mirror)

het **spiegelbeeld** /spi̱ɣəlbelt/ (pl: -en) **1** reflection **2** mirror image

het **spiegelei** /spi̱ɣəlɛi/ (pl: -eren) fried egg

spiegelen /spi̱ɣələ(n)/ (spiegelde, heeft gespiegeld) reflect, mirror

spiegelglad /spi̱ɣəlɣlɑt/ (adj) as smooth as glass; icy; slippery

de **spiegeling** /spi̱ɣəlɪŋ/ (pl: -en) reflection

de **spiegelruit** /spi̱ɣəlrœyt/ (pl: -en) plate-glass window

het **spiegelschrift** /spi̱ɣəlsxrɪft/ mirror writing

het **spiekbriefje** /spi̱gbrifjə/ (pl: -s) crib (sheet)

spieken /spi̱kə(n)/ (spiekte, heeft gespiekt) copy, use a crib: *bij iem. ~* copy from s.o.

de **spier** /spir/ (pl: -en) muscle: *de ~en losmaken* loosen up the muscles, limber up, warm up; *hij vertrok geen ~ (van zijn gezicht)* he didn't bat an eyelid

de **spierbal** /spi̱rbɑl/ (pl: -len): *zijn ~len gebruiken* flex one's muscle(s)

de **spierkracht** /spi̱rkrɑxt/ muscle (power), muscular strength

de **spiermassa** /spi̱rmɑsa/ muscle mass

spiernaakt /spirna̱kt/ (adj) stark naked

de **spierpijn** /spi̱rpɛin/ (pl: -en) sore muscles, aching muscles, muscular pain

het **spierweefsel** /spi̱rwefsəl/ (pl: -s) muscular tissue

spierwit /spirwɪ̱t/ (adj) (as) white as a sheet

de **spies** /spis/ (pl: spiezen) **1** spear **2** skewer

de **spijbelaar** /spɛi̱bəlar/ (pl: -s) truant

spijbelen /spɛi̱bələ(n)/ (spijbelde, heeft gespijbeld) play truant

de **spijker** /spɛi̱kər/ (pl: -s) nail: *de ~ op de kop slaan* hit the nail on the head; *~s met koppen slaan* get down to business; *~s op laag water zoeken* split hairs

de **spijkerbroek** /spɛi̱kərbruk/ (pl: -en) (pair of) jeans: *ik heb een nieuwe ~* I've got a new pair of jeans; *waar is mijn ~?* where are my jeans?

¹**spijkeren** /spɛi̱kərə(n)/ (spijkerde, heeft gespijkerd) drive in nails

²**spijkeren** /spɛi̱kərə(n)/ (spijkerde, heeft gespijkerd) nail

spijkerhard /spɛikərhɑ̱rt/ (adj) (as) hard as a rock; [fig] (as) hard as nails: *~e journalisten* hard-boiled journalists

het **spijkerjasje** /spɛi̱kərjɑʃə/ denim jacket, jeans jacket

het **spijkerschrift** /spɛi̱kərsxrɪft/ cuneiform script

de **spijkerstof** /spɛi̱kərstɔf/ (pl: -fen) [Dutch]

denim

de **spijl** /spɛil/ (pl: -en) bar; rail(ing)

de **spijs** /spɛis/ (pl: spijzen) foods, victuals

de **spijskaart** /spɛiskart/ (pl: -en) menu

de **spijsvertering** /spɛisfərterɪŋ/ digestion: *een slechte ~ hebben* suffer from indigestion

de **spijt** /spɛit/ regret: *daar zul je geen ~ van hebben* you won't regret that; *geen ~ hebben* have no regrets; *daar zul je ~ van krijgen* you'll regret that; *tot mijn (grote) ~* (much) to my regret

spijten /spɛitə(n)/ (speet, heeft gespeten) regret, be sorry: *het spijt me dat ik u stoor* I'm sorry to disturb you; *het spijt me u te moeten zeggen ...* I'm sorry (to have) to tell you ...

spijtig /spɛitəx/ (adj, adv) regrettable

de **spijtoptant** /spɛitɔptant/ (pl: -en) **1** s.o. who (bitterly) regrets a decision or choice **2** criminal suspect who collaborates with police

de **spike** /spɑjk/ (pl: -s) spikes

de **spikkel** /spɪkəl/ (pl: -s) fleck, speck

spiksplinternieuw /spɪksplɪntərniw/ (adj) spanking new, brand new

de **spil** /spɪl/ (pl: -len) **1** pivot **2** pivot, key figure: *zij was de ~ van de organisatie* she was the key figure of the organization

de **spillebeen** /spɪləben/ spindleshanks

de **spin** /spɪn/ (pl: -nen, -s) **1** spider: *nijdig als een ~* furious, absolutely wild **2** [on bike] spider **3** spin: *een bal veel ~ geven* give a ball a lot of spin

de **spinazie** /spinazi/ spinach: *~ à la crème* creamed spinach

het **spinet** /spinɛt/ (pl: -ten) spinet

spinnen /spɪnə(n)/ (spinde/spon, heeft gespind) **1** spin: *garen ~* spin thread (or: yarn) **2** purr **3** [pol] spinmongering **4** [sport] do spinning

het **spinnenweb** /spɪnə(n)wɛp/ (pl: -ben) cobweb, spider('s) web

het **spinnewiel** /spɪnəwil/ (pl: -en) spinning wheel

het **spinrag** /spɪnrɑx/ cobweb, spider('s) web: *zo fijn (or: zo dun, zo teer) als ~* as fine (or: thin, delicate) as gossamer

de **spion** /spijɔn/ (pl: -nen) spy

de **spionage** /spijɔnaʒə/ espionage, spying

spioneren /spijɔnerə(n)/ (spioneerde, heeft gespioneerd) spy

de **spiraal** /spiral/ (pl: spiralen) spiral

het/de **spiraalmatras** /spiralmatrɑs/ (pl: -sen) spring mattress

het **spiraaltje** /spiralcə/ (pl: -s) IUD, coil

de **spirit** /spɪrɪt/ spirit, guts

het **spiritisme** /spiritɪsmə/ spiritualism

spiritueel /spiritywel/ (adj, adv) spiritual

de **spiritus** /spiritys/ methylated spirits, alcohol

het **¹spit** /spɪt/ (pl: -ten) spit: *aan het ~ gebraden* broiled on the spit; *kip van 't ~* barbecued chicken

het/de **²spit** /spɪt/ (pl: -ten) lumbago

het/de **¹spits** /spɪts/ **1** peak, point: *de ~ van een toren* the spire **2** rush hour **3** [sport] forward line: *in de ~ spelen* play forward **4** striker || *het (or: de) ~ afbijten* open the batting; *iets op de ~ drijven* bring sth. to a head

²spits /spɪts/ (adj, adv) pointed, sharp: *~ toelopen* taper (off), end in a point

de **spitsboog** /spɪtsboːx/ (pl: -bogen) pointed arch

spitsen /spɪtsə(n)/ (spitste, heeft gespitst) prick

de **spitskool** /spɪtskol/ (pl: -kolen) pointed cabbage, hearted cabbage

de **spitsstrook** /spɪtstrok/ hard shoulder used as running lane during rush hour, hard shoulder running

de **spitstechnologie** /spɪtstɛxnoloɣi/ (pl: -ën) [Belg] state-of-the-art technology

het **spitsuur** /spɪtsyr/ (pl: -uren) rush hour: *buiten de spitsuren* outside the rush hour; *in het ~* during the rush hour

spitsvondig /spɪtsfɔndəx/ (adj, adv) clever

spitten /spɪtə(n)/ (spitte, heeft gespit) dig: *land ~* turn the soil over

de **spitzen** /ʃpɪtsən/ (pl) point shoes, ballet shoes

de **spleet** /splet/ (pl: spleten) crack: *zijn ogen tot ~jes knijpen* screw up one's eyes

het **spleetoog** /spletox/ (pl: -ogen) slit-eye, slant-eye

splijten /splɛitə(n)/ (spleet, heeft/is gespleten) split || *zijn optreden splijt de partij* his performance/speech has divided the party

de **splijtstof** /splɛitstɔf/ (pl: -fen) nuclear fuel, fissionable material

de **splijtzwam** /splɛitswɑm/ (pl: -men) divisive element

de **splinter** /splɪntər/ (pl: -s) splinter

splinternieuw /splɪntərniw/ (adj) brand-new

de **splinterpartij** /splɪntərpartɛi/ (pl: -en) splinter group

het **split** /splɪt/ slit; placket

de **spliterwt** /splɪtɛrt/ (pl: -en) split pea

de **splitpen** /splɪtpɛn/ (pl: -nen) split pin

¹splitsen /splɪtsə(n)/ (splitste, heeft gesplitst) **1** divide, split **2** separate, split up

zich **²splitsen** /splɪtsə(n)/ (splitste zich, heeft zich gesplitst) split (up), divide: *daar splitst de weg zich* the road forks there

de **splitsing** /splɪtsɪŋ/ (pl: -en) **1** splitting (up), division **2** fork, branch(ing): *bij de ~ links afslaan* turn left at the fork

de **spoed** /sput/ speed/ speed: *op ~ aandringen* stress the urgency of the matter; *met ~* with haste, urgently; *~!* [on letters] urgent

de **spoedbehandeling** /spudbəhandəlɪŋ/ (pl: -en) emergency treatment

de **spoedcursus** /sputkʏrzʏs/ (pl: -sen) intensive course, crash course het **spoeddebat** /spu̱debɑt/ (pl: -ten) emergency debate

spoedeisend /sput̲ɛɪ̲sənt/ (adj) [Dutch] urgent: *de afdeling ~e **hulp*** the accident and emergency department; [Am] the emergency room

spoeden /spu̱də(n)/ (spoedde zich, heeft zich gespoed) [form] speed

het **spoedgeval** /spu̱tχəval/ (pl: -len) emergency (case), urgent matter

¹**spoedig** /spu̱dəχ/ (adj) **1** near: ~*e **levering*** prompt (*or:* swift) delivery **2** speedy, quick: *een ~ **antwoord*** a quick answer

²**spoedig** /spu̱dəχ/ (adv) shortly, soon: *zo ~ mogelijk* as soon as possible

de **spoel** /spul/ (pl: -en) **1** reel; [Am] spool; bobbin **2** shuttle

de **spoelbak** /spu̱lbɑk/ (pl: -ken) washbasin

¹**spoelen** /spu̱lə(n)/ (spoelde, is gespoeld) wash: *naar zee* (*or: aan land*) ~ wash out to sea (*or:* ashore)

²**spoelen** /spu̱lə(n)/ (spoelde, heeft gespoeld) rinse (out): *de **mond** ~* rinse one's mouth (out)

de **spoeling** /spu̱lɪŋ/ (pl: -en) rinse; rinsing: *een ~ **geven*** rinse (out)

de **spoiler** /spɔ̱jlər/ (pl: -s) spoiler

spoken /spo̱kə(n)/ (spookte, heeft gespookt) **1** prowl (round, about): *nog laat **door** het huis ~* prowl about in the house late at night **2** be haunted: *in dat bos spookt het* that forest is haunted

de **sponning** /spɔ̱nɪŋ/ (pl: -en) groove, rebate

de **spons** /spɔns/ (pl: sponzen) sponge

de **sponsor** /spɔ̱nsɔr/ (pl: -s) sponsor

sponsoren /spɔnsɔ̱rə(n)/ (sponsorde, heeft gesponsord) sponsor

de **sponsoring** /spɔ̱nsərɪŋ/ sponsoring

spontaan /spɔntaːn/ (adj, adv) spontaneous

de **spontaniteit** /spɔntanit̲ɛɪ̲t/ (pl: -en) spontaneity

het **spook** /spok/ (pl: spoken) ghost; phantom: *overal spoken **zien*** see ghosts everywhere

spookachtig /spo̱kɑχtəχ/ (adj, adv) ghostly

het **spookbeeld** /spo̱gbelt/ (pl: -en) nightmare, spectre

het **spookhuis** /spo̱khœys/ (pl: -huizen) haunted house

de **spookrijder** /spo̱krɛɪdər/ (pl: -s) ghostrider

de **spookverschijning** /spo̱kfərsχɛɪnɪŋ/ (pl: -en) spectre, ghost

de ¹**spoor** /spor/ spur: *een paard de sporen **geven*** spur a horse; *zijn sporen **verdiend** hebben* have won one's spurs

het ²**spoor** /spor/ **1** track, trail: *ik ben het ~ **bijster** (kwijt)* I've lost track of things; *op het **goede** ~ zijn* be on the right track (*or:* trail); *de politie **heeft** een ~ **gevonden*** the police have found a clue; *iem. **op** het ~ komen* track s.o. down, trace s.o.; *iem. **op** het ~ zijn* be on s.o.'s track **2** track **3** trace: *sporen van **geweld(pleging)***

marks of violence **4** track, trail: *op een **dood** ~ komen (raken)* get into a blind alley; *uit het ~ raken* run off the rails

de **spoorbaan** /spo̱rban/ (pl: -banen) railway

het **spoorboekje** /spo̱rbukjə/ (pl: -s) (train, railway) timetable

de **spoorboom** /spo̱rbom/ (pl: -bomen) [Dutch] level-crossing barrier

de **spoorbreedte** /spo̱rbretə/ (pl: -s) (railway) gauge

de **spoorbrug** /spo̱rbrʏχ/ (pl: -gen) railway bridge

de **spoorlijn** /spo̱rlɛin/ (pl: -en) railway

spoorloos /spo̱rlos/ (adj) without a trace: *mijn **bril** is ~* my glasses have vanished

spoorslags /spo̱rslɑχs/ (adv) at full speed

de **spoorverbinding** /spo̱rvərbɪndɪŋ/ (pl: -en) (railway) connection

de **spoorvorming** /spo̱rvɔrmɪŋ/ **1** (road) rutting **2** ruts

de **spoorweg** /spo̱rwɛχ/ (pl: -en) railway (line)

de **spoorwegmaatschappij** /spo̱rwɛχmatsχɑpɛɪ/ (pl: -en) railway (company)

het **spoorwegnet** /spo̱rwɛχnɛt/ (pl: -ten) railway (network)

de **spoorwegovergang** /spo̱rwɛχovərɣɑŋ/ (pl: -en) level crossing: *bewaakte ~* guarded level crossing

spoorzoeken /spo̱rzukə(n)/ tracking

sporadisch /sporaːdis/ (adj, adv) sporadic: *maar ~ **voorkomen*** be few and far between

de **spore** /spo̱rə/ [bot] spore, sporule

¹**sporen** /spo̱rə(n)/ (spoorde, heeft/is gespoord) travel by rail (*or:* train)

²**sporen** /spo̱rə(n)/ (spoorde, heeft gespoord) (+ met) be consistent with, be in line with || *hij spoort **niet*** he's not all there

het **sporenonderzoek** /spo̱rə(n)ɔndərzuk/ (pl: -en) forensic investigation

de **sporenplant** /spo̱rə(n)plɑnt/ cryptogam

de **sport** /spɔrt/ (pl: -en) **1** sport(s): *een ~ **beoefenen*** practise (*or:* play) a sport; *veel* (*or: weinig*) *aan ~ **doen*** go in for (*or:* not go in for) sports **2** rung: *de **hoogste** ~ bereiken* reach the highest rung (of the ladder)

de **sportartikelen** /spɔ̱rtɑrtikələ(n)/ (pl) sports equipment

de **sportarts** /spɔ̱rtɑrts/ (pl: -en) sports doctor (*or:* physician)

de **sportclub** /spɔ̱rtklʏp/ (pl: -s) sports club

de **sportdag** /spɔ̱rtdɑχ/ (pl: -en) sports day

de **sportdrank** /spɔ̱rtdrɑŋk/ (pl: -en) sports drink, energy drink

sporten /spɔ̱rtə(n)/ (sportte, heeft gesport): *Jaap sport **veel*** Jaap does a lot of sport

de **sporter** /spɔ̱rtər/ (pl: -s) sportsman

de **sportfiets** /spɔ̱rtfits/ (pl: -en) sports bicycle, racing bicycle

de **sporthal** /spɔ̱rtɦɑl/ (pl: -len) sports hall (*or:* centre)

sportief /spɔrtif/ (adj, adv) **1** sports, sporty:

een ~ evenement a sports event; *een ~ jasje* a casual (*or:* sporty) jacket **2** sport(s)-loving, sporty **3** sportsmanlike: *~ zijn* be sporting (*or:* a good sport) (about sth.); *iets ~ opvatten* take sth. well

de **sportiviteit** /spɔrtivitɛit/ sportsmanship

de **sportkleding** /spɔrtkledɪŋ/ sportswear

de **sportliefhebber** /spɔrtlifhɛbər/ (pl: -s) sports enthusiast

de **sportman** /spɔrtmɑn/ (pl: -nen) sportsman

het **sportpark** /spɔrtpɑrk/ (pl: -en) sports park

de **sportschoen** /spɔrtsχun/ (pl: -en) sport(s) shoe

de **sportschool** /spɔrtsχol/ (pl: -scholen) **1** fitness centre; [inform] gym **2** [Dutch] school for martial arts

de **sporttas** /spɔrtɑs/ (pl: -sen) sports bag, kitbag

het **sportterrein** /spɔrtɛrɛin/ (pl: -en) sports field, playing field

de **sportuitslagen** /spɔrtœytslaɣə(n)/ (pl) sports results

het **sportveld** /spɔrtfɛlt/ (pl: -en) sports field, playing field

de **sportvereniging** /spɔrtfərenəɣɪŋ/ (pl: -en) sports club

het **sportvliegtuig** /spɔrtflixtœyχ/ (pl: -en) private pleasure aircraft

de **sportvrouw** /spɔrtfrɑu/ (pl: -en) sportswoman

de **sportwagen** /spɔrtwaɣə(n)/ (pl: -s) sport(s) car

de **sportzaal** /spɔrtsal/ (pl: -zalen) fitness centre, gym

de **spot** /spɔt/ (pl: -s) **1** mockery: *de ~ drijven met* poke fun at, mock **2** (advertising) spot **3** spot(light)

spotgoedkoop /spɔtχutkop/ (adj, adv) dirt cheap

het **spotlight** /spɔtlɑjt/ (pl: -s) spotlight: *in de ~s staan* be in the limelight (*or:* spotlight)

de **spotprent** /spɔtprɛnt/ (pl: -en) cartoon

de **spotprijs** /spɔtprɛis/ (pl: -prijzen) bargain price, giveaway price

spotten /spɔtə(n)/ (spotte, heeft gespot) **1** joke, jest **2** mock: *hij laat niet met zich ~* he is not to be trifled with ‖ *daar moet je niet mee ~* that is no laughing matter

de **spotter** /spɔtər/ (pl: -s) **1** mocker, scoffer **2** spotter, observer

de **spouwmuur** /spɑumyr/ (pl: -muren) cavity wall

de **spraak** /sprak/ speech

het **spraakgebrek** /sprakχəbrɛk/ (pl: -en) speech defect

de **spraakherkenning** /sprakhɛrkɛnɪŋ/ speech recognition

de **spraakles** /spraklɛs/ (pl: -sen) speech training; speech therapy

spraakmakend /sprakmakənt/ (adj) talked-about, discussed

de **spraakverwarring** /sprakvərwɑrɪŋ/ (pl: -en) babel, confusion of tongues

spraakzaam /spraksam/ (adj) talkative

de **sprake** /sprakə/: *er is geen ~ van* that is (absolutely) out of the question; *er is hier ~ van ... it* is a matter (*or:* question) of ...; *iets ter brengen* bring sth. up; *ter ~ komen* come up; *geen ~ van!* certainly not!

sprakeloos /sprakəlos/ (adj, adv) speechless: *iem. ~ doen staan* leave s.o. speechless

sprankelen /sprɑŋkələ(n)/ (sprankelde, heeft gesprankeld) sparkle

het **sprankje** /sprɑŋkjə/ (pl: -s) spark: *er is nog een ~ hoop* there is still a glimmer of hope

de **spray** /sprej/ (pl: -s) spray

sprayen /sprejə(n)/ (sprayde, heeft gesprayd) spray

de **spreadsheet** /sprɛtʃiːt/ (pl: -s) spreadsheet

de **spreekbeurt** /spregbørt/ (pl: -en) talk

de **spreekbuis** /spregbœys/ (pl: -buizen) spokesman, spokesperson

de **spreekkamer** /sprekamər/ (pl: -s) consulting room, surgery

het **spreekkoor** /sprekor/ (pl: -koren) chant(ing): *spreekkoren aanheffen* break into chants

de **spreektaal** /sprektal/ spoken language

het **spreekuur** /sprekyr/ (pl: -uren) office hours; [med] surgery (hours): *~ houden* have office hours, have surgery; *op het ~ komen* come during office hours

de **spreekvaardigheid** /sprekfardəχhɛit/ fluency, speaking ability

het **spreekverbod** /sprekfərbɔt/ (pl: -en) ban on public speaking: *iem. een ~ opleggen* ban s.o. from speaking in public

het **spreekwoord** /sprekwort/ (pl: -en) proverb, saying: *zoals het ~ zegt* as the saying goes

spreekwoordelijk /sprekwordələk/ (adj, adv) proverbial

de **spreeuw** /sprew/ (pl: -en) starling

de **sprei** /sprɛi/ (pl: -en) (bed)spread

spreiden /sprɛidə(n)/ (spreidde, heeft gespreid) **1** spread (out): *het risico ~* spread the risk; *de vakanties ~* stagger holidays **2** spread (out), space

de **spreiding** /sprɛidɪŋ/ **1** spread(ing), dispersal **2** spacing; spread: *de ~ van de macht* the distribution of power

¹**spreken** /sprekə(n)/ (sprak, heeft gesproken) speak, talk: *de feiten ~ voor zich* the facts speak for themselves; *het spreekt vanzelf* it goes without saying; *daar spreekt u mee!* speaking; *spreek ik met Jan?* is that Jan?; *bij wijze van ~* so to speak, in a manner of speaking

²**spreken** /sprekə(n)/ (sprak, heeft gesproken) **1** speak, tell: *een vreemde taal ~* speak a foreign language **2** speak, talk to (*or:* with): *iem. niet te ~ krijgen* not be able to get in

touch with s.o. ‖ *niet te ~ zijn over iets* be unhappy (*or:* be not too pleased) about sth.

¹sprekend /sprɛkənt/ (adj) **1** speaking, talking: *een ~e film* a talking film; *een ~e papegaai* a talking parrot **2** strong, striking: *een ~e gelijkenis* a striking resemblance **3** expressive

²sprekend /sprɛkənt/ (adv) exactly: *zij lijkt ~ op haar moeder* she looks exactly (*or:* just) like her mother; *dat portret lijkt ~ op Karin* that picture captures Karin perfectly

de **spreker** /sprɛkər/ (pl: -s) speaker

sprenkelen /sprɛŋkələ(n)/ (sprenkelde, heeft gesprenkeld) sprinkle

de **spreuk** /sprøk/ (pl: -en) maxim, saying: *oude ~* old saying

de **spriet** /sprit/ (pl: -en) blade

het/de **springconcours** /sprɪŋkɔŋkur/ (pl: -en) jumping competition

springen /sprɪŋə(n)/ (sprong, heeft/is gesprongen) **1** jump, leap, spring; vault: *hoog* (*or: ver, omlaag*) ~ jump high (*or:* far, down); *over een sloot ~* leap a ditch; *staan te ~ om weg te komen* be dying to leave; *zitten te ~ om iets* be bursting (*or:* dying) for sth. **2** burst; explode; blast; pop: *mijn band is gesprongen* my tyre has burst; *een snaar is gesprongen* a string has snapped; *op ~ staan* a) be about to explode; b) be bursting ‖ *op groen ~* change to green

het **springkasteel** /sprɪŋkɑstel/ bouncy castle

de **springlading** /sprɪŋladɪŋ/ (pl: -en) explosive charge

springlevend /sprɪŋlevənt/ (adj) alive (and kicking)

de **springplank** /sprɪŋplɑŋk/ (pl: -en) springboard

de **springstof** /sprɪŋstɔf/ (pl: -fen) explosive

het **springtij** /sprɪŋtɛi/ (pl: -en) spring tide

het **springtouw** /sprɪŋtɑu/ (pl: -en) skipping rope

het **springuur** /sprɪŋyr/ (pl: -uren) [Belg; educ] free period

de **springveer** /sprɪŋver/ (pl: -veren) box spring

de **springvloed** /sprɪŋvlut/ (pl: -en) spring tide

de **sprinkhaan** /sprɪŋkhan/ (pl: -hanen) grasshopper; [Africa and Asia] locust

de **sprinklerinstallatie** /sprɪŋklərɪnstɑla(t)si/ (pl: -s) sprinkler system

de **sprint** /sprɪnt/ (pl: -s) sprint

sprinten /sprɪntə(n)/ (sprintte, heeft/is gesprint) sprint

de **sprinter** /sprɪntər/ (pl: -s) sprinter

de **sprits** /sprɪts/ (pl: -en) (Dutch) short biscuit

sproeien /sprujə(n)/ (sproeide, heeft gesproeid) spray, water; sprinkle; irrigate

de **sproeier** /sprujər/ (pl: -s) sprinkler; jet; spray nozzle; irrigator

de **sproet** /sprut/ (pl: -en) freckle: *~en in het gezicht hebben* have a freckled face

sprokkelen /sprɔkələ(n)/ (sprokkelde, heeft gesprokkeld) gather wood (*or:* kindling): *hout ~* gather wood

de **sprong** /sprɔŋ/ (pl: -en) leap, jump; vault: *hij gaat met ~en vooruit* he's coming along by leaps and bounds; [fig] *de ~ wagen* take the plunge

het **sprookje** /sprɔkjə/ (pl: -s) fairy tale ‖ *iem. ~s vertellen* lead s.o. up the garden path

sprookjesachtig /sprɔkjəsɑxtəx/ (adj, adv) fairy-tale; [fig] fairy-like: *de grachten waren ~ verlicht* the canals were romantically illuminated

de **sprot** /sprɔt/ (pl: -ten) sprat

de **spruit** /sprœyt/ **1** shoot **2** sprig, sprout

spruiten /sprœytə(n)/ (sproot, is gesproten) **1** sprout **2** result from

de **spruitjes** /sprœycəs/ (pl) (Brussels) sprouts

de **spruw** /spryw/ thrush

spugen /spyɣə(n)/ (spuugde, heeft gespogen/gespuugd) **1** spit **2** throw up, be sick

spuien /spœyə(n)/ (spuide, heeft gespuid) spout, unload: *kritiek ~* pour forth criticism

het **spuigat** /spœyɣɑt/ (pl: -en) scupper: *dat loopt de ~en uit* that's going too far, that's past bearing

de **spuit** /spœyt/ (pl: -en) **1** syringe, squirt **2** needle; shot

de **spuitbus** /spœydbʏs/ (pl: -sen) spray (can)

¹spuiten /spœytə(n)/ (spoot, is gespoten) squirt, spurt; gush

²spuiten /spœytə(n)/ (spoot, heeft gespoten) **1** squirt, spurt; erupt: *lak op iets ~* spray lacquer on sth. **2** spray(-paint) **3** inject: *hij spuit* he's a junkie; *iem. plat ~* knock s.o. out (with an injection)

de **spuiter** /spœytər/ (pl: -s) junkie

de **spuitgast** /spœytxɑst/ (pl: -en) hoseman

het **spuitje** /spœycə/ (pl: -s) **1** needle **2** shot

het **spuitwater** /spœytwatər/ seltzer, soda water

het **spul** /spʏl/ (pl: -len) **1** gear, things; togs; belongings **2** stuff, things

de **spurt** /spʏrt/ (pl: -s) spurt: *er de ~ in zetten* step on it

spurten /spʏrtə(n)/ (spurtte, heeft/is gespurt) spurt, sprint

sputteren /spʏtərə(n)/ (sputterde, heeft gesputterd) sputter, cough

het **spuug** /spyx/ spittle, spit

spuugzat /spyxsɑt/ (adj): *iets ~ zijn* be sick and tired of sth.

spuwen /spywə(n)/ (spuwde, heeft gespuwd) **1** spit, spew **2** spew (up), throw up

de **spyware** /spɑjwɛːr/ spyware

het **squadron** /skwɑdrən/ (pl: -s) squadron

het **squash** /skwɔʃ/ squash

de **squashbaan** /skwɔʒban/ (pl: -banen) squash court

squashen /skwɔʒə(n)/ (squashte, heeft gesquasht) play squash

sr. *senior* Sr.

Sri Lanka /srilɑŋka/ Sri Lanka

de **Sri Lankaan** /srilɑŋkan/ (pl: Sri Lankanen) Sri Lankan

Sri Lankaans /srilɑŋkans/ (adj) Sri Lankan

sst /st/ (int) (s)sh, hush

de **staaf** /staf/ (pl: staven) bar

de **staafmixer** /stafmɪksər/ (pl: -s) hand blender

de **staak** /stak/ (pl: staken) stake, pole, post

het **staakt-het-vuren** /staktətfyrə(n)/ ceasefire

het **staal** /stal/ **1** steel: *zo hard* **als** ~ as hard as iron **2** sample: *een (mooi)* ~*tje van zijn soort humor* a fine example of his sense of humour

de **staalborstel** /stalbɔrstəl/ (pl: -s) wire brush

de **staalindustrie** /stalɪndystri/ (pl: -ën) steel industry

de **staalkaart** /stalkart/ (pl: -en) sampling

de **staalwol** /stalwɔl/ steel wool

staan /stan/ (stond, heeft gestaan) **1** stand: *gaan* ~ stand up; *achter* (or: *naast*) *elkaar* **gaan** ~ queue (or: line) up; *die gebeurtenis staat geheel* **op** *zichzelf* that is an isolated incident; *zich* ~*de* **houden** a) stay (or: remain) standing; b) [fig] not succumb, hold firm; [iron] *hij stond erbij en* **keek** *ernaar* he just stood there and watched, he stood idly by **2** stand, be: *hoe* ~ *de* **zaken?** how are things?; *er* **goed** **voor** ~ look good; *zij* ~ **sterk** they are in a strong position; *buiten iets* ~ not be involved in sth.; *de snelheidsmeter stond* **op** *80 km/uur* the speedometer showed 80 km/h; *zij staat* **derde** *in het algemeen klassement* she is third in the overall ranking **3** look **4** say, be written: *er staat niet* **bij** *wanneer* it doesn't say when; *in de tekst staat daar niets over* the text doesn't say anything about it; *wat staat er* **op** *het programma?* what's on the programme? **5** stand still: *blijven* ~ stand still **6** leave, stand: *hij kon nauwelijks spreken, laat* ~ *zingen* he could barely speak, let alone sing; *laat* ~ *dat ...* not to mention (that) ..., let alone (that) ...; *zijn baard* **laten** ~ grow a beard **7** insist (on) ‖ *ergens van* ~ *(te)* **kijken** be flabbergasted; *iem. zeggen waar het* **op** *staat* tell s.o. the way it is; *er staat hem wat te* **wachten** there is sth. in store for him; *ze staat al een uur te* **wachten** she has been waiting (for) an hour

staand /stant/ (adj) standing: ~*e* **passagier** standing passenger; ~*e* *lamp* floor (or: standing) lamp ‖ *iem.* ~*e* **houden** stop s.o.; *zich* ~*e* **houden** keep going, carry on; ~*e* **houden** *(dat)* maintain (that)

de **staanplaats** /stamplats/ (pl: -en) standing room; terrace

de **staar** /star/ cataract, stare; film

de **staart** /start/ (pl: -en) **1** tail: *met de* ~ *kwispelen* wag its tail **2** pigtail; ponytail

het **staartbeen** /stardben/ (pl: -deren, -benen) tail-bone, coccyx

de **staartdeling** /stardelɪŋ/ (pl: -en) long division

de **staartster** /startstɛr/ (pl: -ren) comet

de **staartvin** /startfɪn/ (pl: -nen) tail fin

de **staat** /stat/ (pl: staten) **1** state, condition, status: *burgerlijke* ~ marital status; *in* **goede** ~ *verkeren* be in good condition; *in* *prima* ~ *van onderhoud* in an excellent state of repair **2** condition: *in* ~ *zijn ...* be able (to); *tot alles in* ~ *zijn* be capable of anything **3** state, country, nation, power; the body politic: *de* ~ *der* **Nederlanden** the kingdom of the Netherlands **4** council, board: [Dutch] *de* **Provinciale** *Staten* the Provincial Council **5** statement, record, report, survey ‖ *in alle staten zijn* be frenzied (or: agitated), be beside o.s.

de **staatkunde** /statkyndə/ politics, political science

staatkundig /statkyndəχ/ (adj, adv) political

het **staatsbedrijf** /statsbədrɛɪf/ (pl: -bedrijven) state enterprise

het **staatsbelang** /statsbəlɑŋ/ state (or: national) interest

het **staatsbestel** /statsbəstɛl/ system of government, polity

het **staatsbezoek** /statsbəzuk/ (pl: -en) state visit

het **Staatsblad** /statsblɑt/ (pl: -en) [Dutch] law gazette

Staatsbosbeheer /statsbɔzbəher/ Forestry Commission

de **staatsburger** /statsbyrɣər/ (pl: -s) citizen; subject

het **staatsburgerschap** /statsbyrɣərsχɑp/ citizenship, nationality

de **Staatscourant** /statskurɑnt/ [Dutch] Government Gazette

het **staatsexamen** /statsɛksamə(n)/ (pl: -s) state exam(ination), university entrance examination

het **staatsgeheim** /statsχəhɛim/ (pl: -en) official secret, state secret

de **staatsgreep** /statsχrep/ (pl: -grepen) coup (d'état)

het **staatshoofd** /statshoft/ (pl: -en) head of state

het **staatsieportret** /statsipɔrtrɛt/ (pl: -ten) official portrait

de **staatsinrichting** /statsɪnrɪχtɪŋ/ (pl: -en) civics

de **staatslening** /statslenɪŋ/ (pl: -en) national loan

de **staatsloterij** /statslotərɛi/ (pl: -en) state lottery, national lottery

de **staatsman** /statsmɑn/ (pl: -lieden) statesman

het **staatsrecht** /statsrɛχt/ constitutional law

de **staatsschuld** /statsχylt/ (pl: -en) government debt

de **staatssecretaris** /stˈatsɪkrətɑrɪs/ (pl: -sen) [Dutch and Belg] State Secretary

stabiel /stabˈil/ (adj) stable; firm

de **stabilisatie** /stabilizˌa(t)si/ stabilization

stabiliseren /stabilizˌerə(n)/ (stabiliseerde, heeft gestabiliseerd) stabilize, steady; firm (up)

de **stabiliteit** /stabilitˌɛit/ stability; balance; steadiness

het **stabiliteitspact** /stabilitˌɛitspɑkt/ stability pact

het **stabureau** /stˈabyro/ (pl: -s) standing desk

de **stacaravan** /stˈakɛrəvɛn/ (pl: -s) caravan

staccato /stɑkˈato/ (adv) staccato

de **stad** /stɑt/ (pl: steden) town; city; borough: ~ en *land aflopen* search high and low, look everywhere (for); *de ~ uit zijn* be out of town

het **stadhuis** /stɑthˈœys/ (pl: -huizen) town hall, city hall

het **stadion** /stˈadijɔn/ (pl: -s) stadium

het **stadionverbod** /stˈadijɔnvərbɔt/ (pl: -en) football banning order

het **stadium** /stˈadijʏm/ (pl: stadia) stage, phase

het **stadsbestuur** /stˈɑtsbəstyr/ (pl: -besturen) town council, city council, municipality

de **stadsbus** /stˈɑtsbʏs/ (pl: -sen) local bus

het **stadsdeel** /stˈɑtsdel/ (pl: -delen) quarter, area, part of town; district; [roughly] borough

het **stadslicht** /stˈɑtslɪxt/ (pl: -en) parking light

de **stadsmens** /stˈɑtsmɛns/ (pl: -en) city dweller, townsman

de **stadsmuur** /stˈɑtsmyr/ (pl: -muren) town wall, city wall

de **stadstaat** /stˈɑtstat/ (pl: -staten) city-state

de **stadsvernieuwing** /stˈɑtsfərniwɪŋ/ (pl: -en) urban renewal

de **stadswijk** /stˈɑtswɛik/ (pl: -en) ward, district, area

de **staf** /stɑf/ (pl: staven) **1** staff, (walking) stick; wand **2** management; administration; [Am] faculty **3** [mil] staff, corps

de **stafchef** /stˈɑfʃɛf/ (pl: -s) chief of staff

de **staffel** /stˈɑfəl/ (pl: -s) **1** graduated calculation of interest **2** incremental discount

de **staffelkorting** /stˈɑfəlkɔrtɪŋ/ staggered discount

de **stafhouder** /stˈɑfhaudər/ (pl: -s) [Belg] president of the Bar Council

de **stafkaart** /stˈɑfkart/ (pl: -en) topographic map, ordnance survey map

het **staflid** /stˈɑflɪt/ (pl: -leden) staff member

de **stage** /stˈaʒə/ (pl: -s) work placement; teaching practice; [med] housemanship; [Am] intern(e)ship: ~ *lopen* do a work placement practice

de **stageplaats** /stˈaʒəplats/ (pl: -en) trainee post

de **stagiair** /staʒˈɛːrə/ (pl: -s) student on work placement; student teacher

de **stagnatie** /stɑɣnˈa(t)si/ (pl: -s) stagnation

stagneren /stɑɣnˌerə(n)/ (stagneerde, is gestagneerd) stagnate, come to a standstill

de **sta-in-de-weg** /stˈaɪndəwɛx/ (pl: -s) obstacle

¹**staken** /stˈakə(n)/ (staakte, heeft gestaakt) **1** strike, go on strike: *gaan* ~ go (or: come out) on strike **2** tie

²**staken** /stˈakə(n)/ (staakte, heeft gestaakt) cease, stop, discontinue; suspend: *zijn pogingen* ~ cease one's efforts; *het verzet* ~ cease resistance

de **staker** /stˈakər/ (pl: -s) striker

de **staking** /stˈakɪŋ/ (pl: -en) strike (action), walkout: *in* ~ *zijn* (or: *gaan*) be (or: come out) on strike

de **stakingsbreker** /stˈakɪŋzbrekər/ (pl: -s) strike-breaker; [depr] scab

de **stakker** /stˈɑkər/ (pl: -s) wretch, poor soul (or: creature, thing): *een arme* ~ a poor beggar

de **stal** /stɑl/ (pl: -len) stable; cowshed; sty; fold: *iets van* ~ *halen* dig sth. out (or: up) (again)

de **stalactiet** /stalɑktˈit/ (pl: -en) stalactite

de **stalagmiet** /stalɑɣmˌit/ (pl: -en) stalagmite

stalen /stˈalə(n)/ (adj) steel, steely: *met een ~ gezicht* stony-faced

stalken /stˈɑlkə(n)/ (stalkte, heeft gestalkt) stalk

de **stalker** /stˈɑlkər/ stalker

de **stalking** /stˈɑlkɪŋ/ stalking

de **stalknecht** /stˈɑlknɛxt/ (pl: -en, -s) stableman, stable hand, groom

stallen /stˈɑlə(n)/ (stalde, heeft gestald) store, put up (or: away); garage

het **stalletje** /stˈɑləcə/ (pl: -s) stall, stand, booth

de **stalling** /stˈɑlɪŋ/ (pl: -en) garage; shelter

de **stam** /stɑm/ (pl: -men) **1** trunk, stem, stock **2** stock, clan **3** tribe, race

het **stamboek** /stˈɑmbuk/ (pl: -en) pedigree; studbook; herdbook

het **stamboekvee** /stˈɑmbukfe/ pedigree(d) cattle

de **stamboom** /stˈɑmbom/ (pl: -bomen) family tree, genealogical tree; genealogy; pedigree

het **stamcafé** /stˈɑmkafe/ (pl: -s) favourite pub; [Am] favorite bar; [British] local; [Am] hangout

de **stamcel** /stˈɑmsɛl/ (pl: -len) stem cell

stamelen /stˈamələ(n)/ (stamelde, heeft gestameld) stammer, stutter, sp(l)utter

de **stamgast** /stˈɑmɣɑst/ (pl: -en) regular (customer)

het **stamhoofd** /stˈɑmhoft/ (pl: -en) chieftain, tribal chief, headman

de **stamhouder** /stˈɑmhaudər/ (pl: -s) son and heir, family heir

de **staminee** /staminˈe/ (pl: -s) [Belg] pub

stammen /stˈɑmə(n)/ (stamde, is gestamd) descend (from), stem (from); date (back to, from)

de **stammenstrijd** /stˈɑmə(n)strɛit/ (inter)tribal dispute, tribal war

¹stampen /stɑmpə(n)/ (stampte, heeft gestampt) stamp: *met* zijn voet ~ stamp one's foot

²stampen /stɑmpə(n)/ (stampte, heeft gestampt) pound, crush, pulverize: *gestampte aardappelen* mashed potatoes

de **stamper** /stɑmpər/ (pl: -s) **1** stamp(er), pounder; masher **2** [bot] pistil

de **stampij** /stɑmpɛɪ/ hullabal(l)oo, hubbub, uproar: ~ *maken* raise hell, kick up a row (*or:* fuss)

de **stamppot** /stɑmpɔt/ (pl: -ten) [roughly] stew, hotchpotch; mashed potatoes and cabbage

stampvoeten /stɑmpfutə(n)/ (stampvoette, heeft gestampvoet) stamp one's feet

stampvol /stɑmpfɔl/ (adj) packed; full to the brim; full up

de **stamtafel** /stɑmtafəl/ (pl: -s) table (reserved) for regulars

de **stamvader** /stɑmvadər/ (pl: -s) ancestor, forefather

de **stand** /stɑnt/ (pl: -en) **1** posture, bearing: *een ~ aannemen* assume a position **2** position: *de ~ van de dollar* the dollar rate; *de ~ van de zon* the position of the sun **3** state, condition: *de burgerlijke ~* the registry office **4** score: *de ~ is* 2-1 the score is 2-1 **5** estate, class, station, order: *mensen van alle rangen en ~en* people from all walks of life **6** existence, being: *iets in ~ houden* preserve sth., maintain sth.; *tot ~ brengen* bring about, achieve; *tot ~ komen* come about, be established **7** stand

de **¹standaard** /stɑndart/ (pl: -s) **1** stand, standard **2** standard, prototype

²standaard /stɑndart/ (adj, adv) standard

de **standaardisatie** /stɑndardiza(t)si/ standardization

standaardiseren /stɑndardizerə(n)/ (standaardiseerde, heeft gestandaardiseerd) standardize: *het gestandaardiseerde type* the standard model

de **standaarduitvoering** /stɑndartœytfurɪŋ/ (pl: -en) standard type (*or:* model, design)

het **standaardwerk** /stɑndartwɛrk/ (pl: -en) standard work (*or:* book)

het **standbeeld** /stɑndbelt/ (pl: -en) statue: *een levend ~* a living statue

stand-by /stɛndbɑj/ (adj) standby

standhouden /stɑnthɑudə(n)/ (hield stand, heeft standgehouden) hold out, stand up

de **stand-in** /stɛntɪn/ (pl: -s) stand-in

het **standje** /stɑncə/ (pl: -s) **1** position, posture **2** rebuke

het **standlicht** /stɑntlɪxt/ (pl: -en) [Belg] sidelight, parking light

de **standplaats** /stɑntplats/ (pl: -en) stand: ~ *voor* taxi's taxi rank; [Am] taxi stand

het **standpunt** /stɑntpʏnt/ (pl: -en) standpoint, point of view: *zijn ~ bepalen* define one's position; *bij zijn ~ blijven* hold one's ground

standrechtelijk /stɑntrɛxtələk/ (adj, adv) summary: *een ~e executie* a summary execution

het **standsverschil** /stɑn(t)sfərsxɪl/ (pl: -len) class difference, social difference

de **stand-upcomedian** /stɛndʏpkɔmidijən/ stand-up comedian

standvastig /stɑntfɑstəx/ (adj, adv) firm, perseverant, persistent

de **standwerker** /stɑntwɛrkər/ (pl: -s) hawker, (market, street) vendor

de **stang** /stɑŋ/ (pl: -en) stave, bar, rod; crossbar ‖ *iem. op ~ jagen* needle s.o.

de **stank** /stɑŋk/ (pl: -en) stench, bad (*or:* foul, nasty) smell

het **stanleymes** /stɛnlimɛs/ (pl: -sen) Stanley knife

stansen /stɑnsə(n)/ (stanste, heeft gestanst) punch

stante pede /stɑntəpedə/ (adv) on the spot, this minute

de **stap** /stɑp/ (pl: -pen) **1** step, footstep, pace, stride: *een ~ in de goede richting doen* take a step in the right direction; ~*(je) voor ~(je)* inch by inch, little by little; *een ~(je) terug doen* take a step down (in pay); *een ~ vooruit* a step forward **2** [fig] step, move; grade: *~pen ondernemen tegen* take steps against **3** step, tread ‖ *op ~ gaan* set out (*or:* off)

de **stapel** /stapəl/ (pl: -s) **1** pile, heap, stack **2** stock ‖ *te hard van ~ lopen* go too fast

het **stapelbed** /stapəlbɛt/ (pl: -den) bunk beds

stapelen /stapələ(n)/ (stapelde, heeft gestapeld) pile up, heap up, stack

stapelgek /stapəlɣɛk/ (adj, adv) **1** crazy, (as) mad as a hatter, (raving) mad **2** mad, crazy

het **stapelhuis** /stapəlhœys/ (pl: -huizen) [Belg] warehouse

de **stapelwolk** /stapəlwɔlk/ (pl: -en) cumulus, woolpack

stappen /stɑpə(n)/ (stapte, heeft/is gestapt) **1** step, walk: *eruit ~* quit, get/step out; do o.s. in, catch the bus **2** go out, go for a drink

het **stappenplan** /stɑpə(n)plɑn/ (pl: -nen) step-by-step plan

stapvoets /stɑpfuts/ (adv) at walking pace: ~ *rijden* drive slowly, crawl along

de **star** /stɑr/ (adj, adv) **1** frozen, stiff; glassy **2** rigid, inflexible, uncompromising

staren /starə(n)/ (staarde, heeft gestaard) **1** stare, gaze **2** peer: *zich blind ~ op iets* be fixated on sth.

de **start** /stɑrt/ (pl: -s) start: [car] *een koude ~* a cold start; *een vliegende ~ maken* get off to (*or:* make) a flying start; *een valse ~* a false start; *van ~ gaan* **a)** start; **b)** proceed

de **startbaan** /stɑrdban/ (pl: -banen) runway;

airstrip

het **startblok** /stɑrdblɔk/ (pl: -ken) starting block: [fig] *in de ~ken staan* be ready to go

starten /stɑrtə(n)/ (startte, heeft/is gestart) start, begin; take off; [sport] be off

de **starter** /stɑrtər/ (pl: -s) starter: *~s op de **woningmarkt*** first-time (home)buyers

het **startgeld** /stɑrtxɛlt/ (pl: -en) entry fee

de **startkabel** /stɑrtkabəl/ (pl: -s) jump lead; [Am] jumper cable

startklaar /stɑrtklar/ (adj) ready to start (*or:* go); ready for take-off

de **startmotor** /stɑrtmotər/ (pl: -en) starter, starting motor

de **startpagina**® /stɑrtpaɣina/ start page

het **startpunt** /stɑrtpʏnt/ (pl: -en) starting point

het **startschot** /stɑrtsxɔt/ (pl: -en) starting shot

het **startsein** /stɑrtsɛɪn/ starting signal: *iem. het ~ geven* give s.o. the green light

stateloos /statəlos/ (adj) stateless

het **statement** /stetmənt/ (pl: -s) statement: *een ~ maken* make a statement

de **Staten** /statə(n)/ (pl) [Dutch] (Dutch) Provincial Council

de **Statenbijbel** /statə(n)bɛibəl/ (Dutch) Authorized Version (of the Bible)

de **Staten-Generaal** /statə(n)ɣenəral/ (pl) States General, Dutch parliament

het **statief** /statif/ (pl: statieven) tripod, stand

het **statiegeld** /sta(t)siɣɛlt/ deposit: *geen ~* non-returnable

statig /statəɣ/ (adj, adv) 1 stately, grand: *een ~e dame* a queenly woman, a woman of regal bearing 2 solemn

het **station** /sta(t)ʃɔn/ (pl: -s) (railway) station: *centraal ~* central station; *~ Oldenzaal* Oldenzaal station; [fig] *dat is een gepasseerd ~* it's too late for that, that ship has sailed

stationair /staʃonɛ:r/ (adj) stationary: *een motor ~ laten draaien* let an engine idle

de **stationcar** /steʃənka:r/ (pl: -s) estate (car); [Am] station wagon

stationeren /sta(t)ʃɔnərə(n)/ (stationeerde, heeft gestationeerd) station, post

de **stationschef** /sta(t)ʃɔnʃɛf/ (pl: s) stationmaster

de **stationshal** /sta(t)ʃɔnshɑl/ (pl: -len) station concourse

de **stationsrestauratie** /sta(t)ʃɔnsrɛstora(t)si/ (pl: -s) station buffet

statisch /statis/ (adj) static

de **statistiek** /statɪstik/ (pl: -en) statistics

statistisch /statɪstis/ (adj, adv) statistical

de **status** /statʏs/ 1 (social) status, standing 2 (legal) status

de **statusregel** /statʏsreɣəl/ (pl: -s) status line

het **statussymbool** /statʏsɪmbol/ (pl: -symbolen) status symbol

statutair /statytɛ:r/ (adj, adv) statutory

de **statuur** /statyr/ stature: *hij heeft **onvoldoende** ~ voor die functie* he has insufficient stature for this position; *iem. **van** zijn ~* s.o. of his stature

het **statuut** /statyt/ (pl: statuten) statute, regulation

staven /stavə(n)/ (staafde, heeft gestaafd) substantiate, prove

de **steak** /stek/ (pl: -s) (beef)steak

het/de **steaming** /sti:mɪŋ/ [Belg] [roughly] racketeering

stedelijk /stedələk/ (adj) municipal, urban: *de ~e bevolking* the urban population

de **stedeling** /stedəlɪŋ/ (pl: -en) town-dweller; townspeople

de **stedenbouwkunde** /stedə(n)bɑukʏndə/ urban development

steeds /stets/ (adv) 1 always, constantly: *iem. ~ aankijken* keep looking at s.o.; *~ weer* time after time, repeatedly 2 increasingly, more and more: *~ groter* bigger and bigger; *~ slechter worden* go from bad to worse; *het regent nog ~* it is still raining

de **steeg** /steɣ/ (pl: stegen) alley(way)

de **steek** /stek/ (pl: steken) 1 stab; thrust; prick; stab wound: [fig] *iem. een ~ onder water geven* have a dig at s.o. 2 sting; bite 3 shooting pain, stabbing pain; twinge: *een ~ in de borst* a twinge in the chest 4 stitch: *een ~ laten vallen* a) drop a stitch; b) [fig] make a gaffe, make a mistake || *iem. in de ~ laten* let s.o. down; *ik zie geen ~* I can't see a (blind) thing; *zij heeft geen ~ uitgevoerd* she hasn't done a stroke of work

steekhoudend /stekhɑudənt/ (adj) convincing, valid

de **steekpartij** /stekpartɛi/ (pl: -en) knifing

de **steekpenningen** /stekpɛnɪŋə(n)/ (pl) bribe(s); kickback(s)

de **steekproef** /stekpruf/ (pl: -proeven) random check, spot check, (random) sample survey

de **steeksleutel** /steksløtəl/ (pl: -s) (open-end, fork) spanner (*or:* wrench)

de **steekvlam** /stekflɑm/ (pl: -men) (jet, burst of) flame, flash

de **steekwagen** /stekwaɣə(n)/ (pl: -s) handtruck

het **steekwapen** /stekwapə(n)/ (pl: -s) stabbing weapon

de **steekwond** /stekwɔnt/ (pl: -en) stab wound

de **steel** /stel/ (pl: stelen) 1 stalk, stem 2 handle; stem

de **steelpan** /stelpɑn/ (pl: -nen) saucepan

steels /stels/ (adj) stealthy

de **¹steen** /sten/ 1 stone; [Am] rock; [large] rock; pebble 2 stone; brick; cobble(stone): *ergens een ~tje toe bijdragen* do one's bit towards sth.; chip in with 3 [sport] man; piece || *de onderste ~ moet boven komen* we must get to the bottom of this

het/de **²steen** /sten/ stone || *~ en been klagen* complain bitterly de **steenarend** /stenarənt/ (pl: -en) golden eagle

de **steenbok** /stembɔk/ (pl: -ken) ibex, wild goat

de **Steenbok** /stembɔk/ (pl: -ken) [astrology] Capricorn

de **Steenbokskeerkring** /stembɔkskerkrɪŋ/ tropic of Capricorn

steengrillen /stenɣrɪlə(n)/ (steengrilde, heeft gesteengrild) stone grill

de **steengroeve** /stenɣruvə/ (pl: -n) (stone) quarry

het **steenkolenengels** /stenkolə(n)ɛŋəls/ broken English

de **steenkool** /stenkol/ coal

steenkoud /stenkɑut/ (adj) freezing (cold), ice-cold: *ik heb het* ~ I am freezing

de **steenpuist** /stempœyst/ (pl: -en) boil

steenrijk /stenrɛɪk/ (adj) immensely rich

het **steenslag** /stenslɑx/ road-metal; chippings

de **steentijd** /stentɛit/ Stone Age

het **steentje** /stentʃə/ (pl: -s) small stone; pebble: *een ~ **bijdragen*** do one's bit

de **steenweg** /stenwɛx/ (pl: -en) [Belg] (paved) road

de **steenworp** /stenwɔrp/ (pl: -en): *hij woont **op** een ~ afstand* he lives within a stone's throw

steevast /stevɑst/ (adj, adv) invariable, regular

steggelen /stɛɣələ(n)/ (steggelde, heeft gesteggeld) bicker, squabble; haggle

de **steiger** /stɛiɣər/ (pl: -s) 1 landing (stage, place) 2 scaffold(ing): *in de ~s staan* a) be in scaffolding; b) [fig] be under way (*or*: construction)

steigeren /stɛiɣərə(n)/ (steigerde, heeft gesteigerd) rear (up)

steil /stɛil/ (adj, adv) steep; precipitous: *een ~e **afgrond*** a sharp drop; ~ **haar** straight hair; *ergens ~ van achterover slaan* be flabbergasted by sth.

steilen /stɛilə(n)/ (steilde, heeft gesteild) straighten, flat-iron

de **steiltang** /stɛiltɑŋ/ (pl: -en) flat-iron

de **stek** /stɛk/ (pl: -ken) 1 cutting, slip 2 niche, den: *dat is zijn **liefste** ~* that is his favourite spot

stekeblind /stekəblɪnt/ (adj) (as) blind as a bat

de **stekel** /stekəl/ (pl: -s) prickle, thorn; spine

de **stekelbaars** /stekəlbars/ (pl: -baarzen) stickleback

stekelig /stekələx/ (adj) 1 prickly, spiny, bristly 2 [fig] sharp, cutting

het **stekelvarken** /stekəlvɑrkə(n)/ (pl: -s) porcupine; hedgehog

¹**steken** /stekə(n)/ (stak, heeft gestoken) 1 stick: *ergens in **blijven** ~* get stuck (*or*: bogged) (down) in sth. 2 sting: *de **zon** steekt* there is a burning sun 3 thrust, stab || *daar steekt iets **achter*** there is sth. behind it; *dat steekt hem* that sticks in his throat

²**steken** /stekə(n)/ (stak, heeft gestoken) 1 stab: *alle banden waren **lek** gestoken* all the tyres had been punctured 2 sting, cut 3 sting, prick 4 stick 5 put, place: *veel **tijd** in iets ~* spend a lot of time on sth.; *zijn geld **in** een zaak ~* put one's money in(to) an undertaking || *asperges ~* harvest asparagus

stekend /stekənt/ (adj, adv) stinging, sharp

stekken /stɛkə(n)/ (stekte, heeft gestekt) slip, strike: *planten ~* take (*or*: strike) cuttings of plants

de **stekker** /stɛkər/ (pl: -s) plug

de **stekkerauto** /stɛkərɑuto/ (pl: -'s) plug-in car

de **stekkerdoos** /stɛkərdos/ (pl: -dozen) multiple socket

het **stel** /stɛl/ (pl: -len) 1 set: *ik neem **drie** ~ kleren mee* I'll take three sets of clothes with me 2 couple: *een **pasgetrouwd** ~* newly-weds 3 couple, lot || *het hoeft niet op ~ en **sprong*** there's no rush

stelen /stelə(n)/ (steelde, heeft gesteeld) steal: *uit ~ gaan* go thieving; *dat **kan** me gestolen **worden*** I'd be well shot of it, I'd be better off without that

de **stellage** /stɛlaʒə/ (pl: -s) stand, stage, platform

stellen /stɛlə(n)/ (stelde, heeft gesteld) 1 put, set: *iem. iets **beschikbaar** ~* put sth. at s.o.'s disposal 2 set, adjust: *een **machine** ~* adjust (*or*: regulate) a machine 3 suppose: *stel het **geval** van een leraar die … *take the case of a teacher who … 4 manage, (make) do: *we zullen **het** met minder moeten ~* we'll have to make do with less

het **stelletje** /stɛlɛcə/ (pl: -s) 1 bunch: *een ~ ongeregeld* a disorderly bunch 2 couple, pair

stellig /stɛləx/ (adj, adv) definite, certain

de **stelling** /stɛlɪŋ/ (pl: -en) 1 scaffold(ing) 2 rack 3 proposition 4 theorem, proposition: *de ~ van **Pythagoras*** the Pythagorean theorem || ~ **nemen** tegen make a stand against, set one's face against

de **stellingname** /stɛlɪŋnamə/ (pl: -s, -n) position, stand

stelpen /stɛlpə(n)/ (stelpte, heeft gestelpt) staunch, stem

de **stelplaats** /stɛlplats/ (pl: -en) [Belg] depot

de **stelregel** /stɛlreɣəl/ (pl: -s) principle: *een **goede** ~* a good rule to go by

de **stelschroef** /stɛlsxruf/ (pl: -schroeven) setscrew

het **stelsel** /stɛlsəl/ (pl: -s) system

¹**stelselmatig** /stɛlsəlmatəx/ (adj) systematic

²**stelselmatig** /stɛlsəlmatəx/ (adv) always, invariably: *systematisch te **laat** komen* always (*or*: invariably) arrive late

de **stelt** /stɛlt/ (pl: -en) stilt || *de boel **op** ~en zet-*

ten raise hell

de **steltloper** /stɛltlopər/ (pl: -s) grallatorial bird

de **stem** /stɛm/ (pl: -men) **1** voice: *zijn ~ verliezen* lose one's voice; *met luide ~* out loud; *een ~ van binnen* an inner voice; *zijn ~ verheffen* raise one's voice **2** part, voice **3** vote: *beiden behaalden een gelijk aantal ~men* it was a tie between the two; *met algemene ~men aangenomen* adopted unanimously; *de meeste ~men gelden* the majority decides; *de ~men staken* there is a tie; *de ~men tellen* count the votes; *zijn ~ uitbrengen* cast one's vote, vote

de **stemband** /stɛmbɑnt/ (pl: -en) vocal cord

het **stembiljet** /stɛmbɪljɛt/ (pl: -ten) ballot (paper)

het **stembureau** /stɛmbyro/ (pl: -s) **1** polling station; [Am] polling place **2** polling committee

de **stembus** /stɛmbʏs/ (pl: -sen) ballot box: *naar de ~ gaan* go to the polls

de **stemcomputer** /stɛmkɔmpjutər/ (pl: -s) voting computer

het **stemdistrict** /stɛmdɪstrɪkt/ (pl: -en) constituency; borough; ward

het **stemgeluid** /stɛmɣəlœyt/ (pl: -en) voice

stemgerechtigd /stɛmɣərɛxtəxt/ (adj) entitled to vote

stemhebbend /stɛmhɛbənt/ (adj) voiced

het **stemhokje** /stɛmhɔkjə/ (pl: -s) (voting) booth

stemloos /stɛmlos/ (adj) voiceless, unvoiced

stemmen /stɛmə(n)/ (stemde, heeft gestemd) **1** vote: *ik stem voor (or: tegen)* I vote in favour (or: against) **2** [mus] tune; tune up || *iem. gunstig ~* put s.o. in the right mood, get in s.o.'s good books

de **stemmer** /stɛmər/ (pl: -s) tuner

stemmig /stɛməx/ (adj, adv) sober, subdued

de **stemming** /stɛmɪŋ/ (pl: -en) **1** mood: *in een slechte (or: goede) ~ zijn* be in a bad (or: good) mood; *de ~ zit erin* there's a general mood of cheerfulness **2** feeling: *er heerst een vijandige ~* feelings are hostile **3** vote: *een geheime ~* a secret ballot; *een ~ houden* take a vote; *een voorstel in ~ brengen* put a proposal to the vote **4** [mus] tuning

de **stemmingswisseling** /stɛmɪŋswɪsəlɪŋ/ (pl: -en) mood swings

de **stempel** /stɛmpəl/ **1** seal **2** stamp; postmark

de **stempelautomaat** /stɛmpəlɑutomat/ (pl: -automaten) stamping machine

¹**stempelen** /stɛmpələ(n)/ (stempelde, heeft gestempeld) [Belg] be unemployed (or: on the dole)

²**stempelen** /stɛmpələ(n)/ (stempelde, heeft gestempeld) stamp; postmark

het **stempelgeld** /stɛmpəlɣɛlt/ [Belg] unem-

ployment benefit, the dole

het **stempelkussen** /stɛmpəlkʏsə(n)/ (pl: -s) inkpad

de **stemplicht** /stɛmplɪxt/ compulsory voting

het **stemrecht** /stɛmrɛxt/ (right to) vote, voting right; franchise; suffrage

de **stemverheffing** /stɛmvərhɛfɪŋ/ (pl: -en) raising of one's voice: *zij sprak met ~* she raised her voice as she spoke

de **stemvork** /stɛmvork/ (pl: -en) tuning fork

de **stemwijzer**® /stɛmwɛizər/ voting aid

het/de **stencil** /stɛnsəl/ (pl: -s) stencil, handout

stencilen /stɛnsələ(n)/ (stencilde, heeft gestencild) duplicate, stencil

stenen /stenə(n)/ (adj) stone; brick: *het stenen tijdperk* the Stone Age

de **stengel** /stɛŋəl/ (pl: -s) **1** stalk, stem **2** stick

de **stengun** /stɛŋɣʏn/ (pl: -s) sten gun

stenigen /stenəɣə(n)/ (stenigde, heeft gestenigd) stone

de **stennis** /stɛnɪs/ [inform] commotion: *~ maken* kick up a row

het/de **steno** /steno/ stenography, shorthand

de **stenograaf** /stenoɣraf/ (pl: -grafen) shorthand writer; [Am] stenographer

de **stenografie** /stenoɣrafi/ stenography

de **step** /stɛp/ (pl: -pen) scooter

de **steppe** /stɛpə/ (pl: -n) steppe

de **ster** /stɛr/ (pl: -ren) star: *een vallende ~* a shooting star; [fig] *hij speelt de ~ren van de hemel* his playing is out of this world

de **stereo** /sterejo/ stereo(phony)

stereotiep /sterejotip/ (adj, adv) stock, stereotypic(al): *een ~e uitdrukking* a cliché

de **stereotoren** /sterejotorə(n)/ (pl: -s) music centre

het **stereotype** /sterejotipə/ stereotype

het **sterfbed** /stɛrvbɛt/ (pl: -den) deathbed: *op zijn ~ zal hij er nog berouw over hebben* he'll regret it to his dying day

sterfelijk /stɛrfələk/ (adj) mortal

het **sterfgeval** /stɛrfxəval/ (pl: -len) death

de **sterfte** /stɛrftə/ (pl: -n, -s) **1** death **2** mortality

het **sterftecijfer** /stɛrftəsɛifər/ (pl: -s) mortality rate

steriel /steril/ (adj) **1** sterile **2** sterile, infertile

de **sterilisatie** /steriliza(t)si/ (pl: -s) sterilization

steriliseren /sterilizerə(n)/ (steriliseerde, heeft gesteriliseerd) sterilize; fix

de **steriliteit** /sterilitɛit/ sterility

¹**sterk** /stɛrk/ (adj) **1** strong, powerful, tough: *~e thee* strong tea **2** strong, sharp: *een ~e stijging* a sharp rise; *een ~e wind* a strong wind || *~er nog* indeed, more than that

²**sterk** /stɛrk/ (adv) **1** strongly, greatly, highly: *een ~ vergrote foto* a much enlarged photograph; *iets ~ overdrijven* greatly exaggerate sth. **2** well || *zij staat (nogal) ~* she has a

strong case; *dat lijkt me* ~ I doubt it, I wouldn't count on it

de **sterkedrank** /stɛrkədrɑŋk/ strong drink, liquor

sterken /stɛrkə(n)/ (sterkte, heeft gesterkt) strengthen: *in zijn mening gesterkt worden* be confirmed in one's views

de **sterkte** /stɛrktə/ (pl: -n, -s) **1** strength, power, intensity; volume; loudness: *de* ~ *van een* **geluid** (or: *van het* **licht**) the intensity of a noise (or: the light); *op* **volle** (or: **halve**) ~ at full (or: half) strength; *een zonnebril* **op** ~ prescription sunglasses **2** fortitude, courage: ~ *(gewenst)!* all the best!, good luck! **3** strength, potency

de **stern** /stɛrn/ (pl: -en) tern

het **sterrenbeeld** /stɛrə(n)belt/ (pl: -en) sign of the zodiac

de **sterrenhemel** /stɛrə(n)heməl/ starry sky

het **sterrenhotel** /stɛrə(n)hotɛl/ (pl: -s) luxury hotel

de **sterrenkijker** /stɛrə(n)kɛikər/ (pl: -s) telescope

de **sterrenkunde** /stɛrə(n)kʏndə/ astronomy

de **sterrenkundige** /stɛrə(n)kʏndəɣə/ (pl: -n) astronomer

de **sterrenmix** /stɛrəmɪks/ (pl: -en) tea blended with liquorice and star anise

het **sterrenstelsel** /stɛrə(n)stɛlsəl/ (pl: -s) stellar system

de **sterrenwacht** /stɛrə(n)wɑxt/ (pl: -en) observatory

het **sterretje** /stɛrəcə/ (pl: -s) **1** sparkler: ~*s zien* see stars **2** star, asterisk

de **sterveling** /stɛrvəlɪŋ/ (pl: -en) mortal: *er was* **geen** ~ *te bekennen* there wasn't a (living) soul in sight

sterven /stɛrvə(n)/ (stierf, is gestorven) die: ~ *aan een ziekte* die of an illness; ~ *aan zijn verwondingen* die from one's injuries; *op* ~ *na* **dood zijn** be as good as dead

de **stethoscoop** /stetoskop/ (pl: stethoscopen) stethoscope

de **steun** /støn/ (pl: -en) **1** support, prop: *een* ~*tje in de rug* a bit of encouragement (or: support), a helping hand **2** support, assistance: *dat zal een* **grote** ~ *voor ons zijn* that will be a great help to us **3** support, aid, assistance

de **steunbeer** /stømber/ (pl: -beren) buttress

¹**steunen** /stønə(n)/ (steunde, heeft gesteund) lean (on), rest (on)

²**steunen** /stønə(n)/ (steunde, heeft gesteund) **1** support, prop (up): *een* **muur** ~ support (or: prop up) a wall **2** [fig] support, back up: *iem. ergens* **in** ~ back up s.o. in sth.

de **steunfraude** /stønfrɑudə/ (pl: -s) social security fraud

de **steunkous** /støŋkɑus/ (pl: -en) support stocking

de **steunpilaar** /stømpilar/ (pl: -pilaren) pillar

[also fig]

het **steunpunt** /stømpʏnt/ (pl: -en) (point of) support

de **steuntrekker** /støntrɛkər/ (pl: -s) person on the dole; [Am] person on welfare (benefit)

de **steunzool** /stønzol/ (pl: -zolen) arch support

de **steur** /stør/ (pl: -en) sturgeon

de **steven** /stevə(n)/ (pl: -s) [shipp] stem; stern

¹**stevig** /stevəx/ (adj) **1** substantial, hearty **2** robust, hefty; [fig] stiff; [fig] heavy: *een* ~*e* **hoofdpijn** a splitting headache **3** solid, strong, sturdy **4** tight, firm: *een* ~ **pak** *slaag* a good hiding **5** substantial, considerable

²**stevig** /stevəx/ (adv) **1** solidly, strongly: *die ladder staat niet* ~ that ladder is a bit wobbly **2** tightly, firmly: *we moeten er* ~ *tegenaan gaan* we really need to get (or: buckle) down to it

de **stevigheid** /stevəxhɛit/ sturdiness, strength, solidity

de **steward** /scuwərt/ (pl: -s) steward; flight attendant

de **stewardess** /scuwɑrdɛs/ (pl: -en) stewardess, (air) hostess

stichtelijk /stɪxtələk/ (adj, adv) devotional, pious

stichten /stɪxtə(n)/ (stichtte, heeft gesticht) found, establish: *een* **gezin** ~ start a family

de **stichter** /stɪxtər/ (pl: -s) founder

de **stichting** /stɪxtɪŋ/ (pl: -en) foundation, establishment

de **stick** /stɪk/ (pl: -s) stick

de **sticker** /stɪkɛr/ (pl: -s) sticker

het **stickie** /stɪki/ (pl: -s) joint, stick

de **stiefbroer** /stivbrur/ (pl: -s) stepbrother

de **stiefdochter** /stivdɔxtər/ (pl: -s) stepdaughter

het **stiefkind** /stifkɪnt/ (pl: -eren) stepchild

de **stiefmoeder** /stifmudər/ (pl: -s) stepmother

de **stiefvader** /stifadər/ (pl: -s) stepfather

de **stiefzoon** /stifson/ (pl: -s, -zonen) stepson

de **stiefzuster** /stifsʏstər/ (pl: -s) stepsister

¹**stiekem** /stikəm/ (adj) **1** sneaky **2** secret

²**stiekem** /stikəm/ (adv) **1** in an underhand way, on the sly **2** in secret: *iets* ~ **doen** do sth. on the sly; ~ **weggaan** steal (or: sneak) away

de **stiekemerd** /stikəmərt/ (pl: -s) [Dutch] sneak, sly dog

de **stielman** /stilmɑn/ (pl: -nen) [Belg] craftsman, skilled worker

de **stier** /stir/ (pl: -en) bull

de **Stier** /stir/ (pl: -en) [astrology] Taurus

het **stierengevecht** /stirə(n)ɣəvɛxt/ (pl: -en) bullfight

de **stierenvechter** /stirə(n)vɛxtər/ (pl: -s) bullfighter

stierlijk /stirlək/ (adv): [inform] *ik* **verveel** *me* ~ I'm bored stiff (or: to tears)

de **stift** /stɪft/ (pl: -en) **1** cartridge **2** felt-tip

(pen)

de **stifttand** /stɪftɑnt/ (pl: -en) crowned tooth

het **stigma** /stɪxma/ (pl: -'s, -ta) stigma

stigmatiseren /stɪxmatizerə(n)/ (stigmatiseerde, heeft gestigmatiseerd) stigmatize

¹**stijf** /stɛif/ (adj) **1** stiff, rigid: ~ *van de kou* numb with cold **2** stiff, wooden

²**stijf** /stɛif/ (adv) **1** stiffly, rigidly: *zij hield het pak ~ vast* she held on to the package with all her might **2** stiffly, formally

de **stijfheid** /stɛifhɛit/ (pl: -heden) stiffness

stijfjes /stɛifjəs/ (adj, adv) stiff, formal

de **stijfkop** /stɛifkɔp/ (pl: -pen) stubborn person, pigheaded person

het/de **stijfsel** /stɛifsəl/ paste

de **stijgbeugel** /stɛixbøɣəl/ (pl: -s) stirrup

stijgen /stɛiɣə(n)/ (steeg, is gestegen) **1** rise; climb: *een ~de lijn* an upward trend **2** increase, rise: *de prijzen* (or: *lonen*) ~ prices (or: wages) are rising

de **stijging** /stɛiɣɪŋ/ (pl: -en) rise, increase

de **stijl** /stɛil/ (pl: -en) **1** style; register: *ambtelijke* ~ officialese; *journalistieke* ~ journalese; *het onderwijs nieuwe* ~ the new style of education; *in de* ~ *van* after the fashion of **2** post || *dat is geen* ~ that's no way to behave

het **stijldansen** /stɛildɑnsə(n)/ ballroom dancing

de **stijlfiguur** /stɛilfiɣyr/ (pl: -figuren) figure of speech, trope

stijlloos /stɛilos/ (adj, adv) **1** tasteless, lacking in style **2** ill-mannered

de **stijltang** /stɛiltɑŋ/ (pl: -en) styler

stijlvol /stɛilvɔl/ (adj, adv) stylish, fashionable

stik /stɪk/ (int) [inform] oh heck, oh damn; nuts (to you); get lost

stikdonker /stɪɡdɔŋkər/ (adj) [inform] pitch-dark, pitch-black

stikken /stɪkə(n)/ (stikte, is gestikt) **1** suffocate, choke; be stifled: *in iets* ~ choke on sth.; ~ *van het lachen* be in stitches **2** (+ in) be bursting (with); be up to one's ears (in) **3** drop dead: *iem. laten* ~ leave s.o. in the lurch; stand s.o. up **4** stitch **5** be full (of), swarm (with): *dit opstel stikt van de fouten* this essay is riddled with errors

de **stikstof** /stɪkstɔf/ nitrogen

¹**stil** /stɪl/ (adj) **1** quiet, silent **2** still, motionless **3** quiet, calm: *de ~le tijd* the slack season, the off season || *Stille Nacht* Silent Night

²**stil** /stɪl/ (adv) **1** quietly **2** still **3** quietly, calmly

de **stiletto** /stɪlɛto/ (pl: -'s) flick knife; [Am] switchblade

¹**stilhouden** /stɪlhɑudə(n)/ (hield stil, heeft stilgehouden) stop, pull up

²**stilhouden** /stɪlhɑudə(n)/ (hield stil, heeft stilgehouden) **1** keep quiet, hold still **2** keep quiet, hush up: *zij hielden hun huwelijk stil* they got married in secret

de **stille** /stɪlə/ (pl: -n) plain-clothes policeman

stilleggen /stɪlɛɣə(n)/ (legde stil, heeft stilgelegd) stop, shut down, close down: *het verkeer* ~ stop the traffic

stillen /stɪlə(n)/ (stilde, heeft gestild) satisfy

stilletjes /stɪlɛcəs/ (adv) **1** quietly **2** secretly, on the sly

het **stilleven** /stɪlevə(n)/ (pl: -s) still life

stilliggen /stɪlɪɣə(n)/ (lag stil, heeft stilgelegen) **1** lie still (or: quiet) **2** lie idle, be idle: *het werk ligt stil* work is at a standstill

stilstaan /stɪlstan/ (stond stil, heeft stilgestaan) **1** stand still, pause, come to a standstill: *heb je er ooit bij stilgestaan dat ... has it ever occurred to you that ...* **2** stand still, stop, be at a standstill

de **stilstand** /stɪlstɑnt/ **1** standstill, stagnation: *tot ~ brengen* bring to a standstill (or: halt) **2** [Belg] stop: *deze trein heeft ~en te Lokeren en te Gent* this train stops at Lokeren and Ghent

de **stilte** /stɪltə/ **1** silence, quiet: *een minuut ~* a minute's silence; *de ~ verbreken* break the silence **2** quiet, privacy, secrecy

stilzetten /stɪlzɛtə(n)/ (zette stil, heeft stilgezet) (bring to a) stop

stilzitten /stɪlzɪtə(n)/ (zat stil, heeft stilgezeten) sit still, stand still

het **stilzwijgen** /stɪlzwɛiɣə(n)/ silence

stilzwijgend /stɪlzwɛiɣənt/ (adj, adv) tacit, understood: ~ *aannemen* (or: *veronderstellen*) *dat ...* take (it) for granted that ...; *een contract ~ verlengen* automatically renew a contract

de **stimulans** /stimylɑns/ (pl: -en) stimulus

stimuleren /stimylerə(n)/ (stimuleerde, heeft gestimuleerd) stimulate, encourage; boost [com]

de **stimulus** /stimylʏs/ (pl: stimuli) stimulus, incentive

de **stinkbom** /stɪŋbɔm/ (pl: -men) stink bomb

het **stinkdier** /stɪŋdir/ (pl: -en) skunk

stinken /stɪŋkə(n)/ (stonk, heeft gestonken) stink, smell: *uit de mond* ~ have bad breath; [fig] *die zaak stinkt* there's sth. fishy about that, that business stinks || [inform] *erin* ~ **a)** walk right into it (or: the trap); **b)** fall for sth., rise to the bait, be fooled

stinkend /stɪŋkənt/ (adj) stinking, smelly: [fig] *zijn ~e best doen* do one's absolute best

de **stip** /stɪp/ (pl: -pen) **1** dot; speck **2** [sport] (penalty) spot (or: mark)

stippelen /stɪpələ(n)/ (stippelde, heeft gestippeld) dot, speckle

de **stippellijn** /stɪpəlɛin/ (pl: -en) dotted line

stipt /stɪpt/ (adj, adv) exact, punctual; prompt; strict: ~ *om drie uur* at three o'clock sharp; ~ *op tijd* right on time

de **stiptheid** /stɪptɛit/ accuracy; punctuality; promptness; strictness

de **stiptheidsactie** /stɪptɛitsɑksi/ (pl: -s)

work-to-rule, go-slow; [Am] slow-down (strike)

stockeren /stɔkᵊrə(n)/ (stockeerde, heeft gestockeerd) [Belg] stock

stoeien /stuɪə(n)/ (stoeide, heeft gestoeid) play around: *met het idee* ~ toy with the idea (of)

de **stoel** /stul/ (pl: -en) chair; seat: *een luie (gemakkelijke)* ~ an easy chair; *pak een* ~ take a seat; *de poten onder iemands* ~ *wegzagen* cut the ground from under s.o.'s feet; pull the rug from under s.o.

stoelen /stulə(n)/ (stoelde, heeft gestoeld) be based (on)

de **stoelendans** /stulə(n)dɑns/ (pl: -en) musical chairs

de **stoelgang** /stulɣɑŋ/ (bowel) movement, stool(s)

de **stoeltjeslift** /stulcəslɪft/ (pl: -en) chairlift

de **stoemp** /stump/ [Belg] [roughly] stew, hotchpotch

de **stoep** /stup/ (pl: -en) **1** pavement; [Am] sidewalk **2** (door)step: *onverwachts op de* ~ *staan bij iem.* turn up on s.o.'s doorstep

de **stoeprand** /stuprɑnt/ (pl: -en) kerb; [Am] curb

de **stoeptegel** /stupteɣəl/ paving stone

stoer /stur/ (adj, adv) tough: ~ *doen* act tough; ~*e taal* tough language; *een* ~*e jongen* a tough guy || *een* ~*e jas* a cool jacket

de **stoet** /stut/ (pl: -en) procession, parade

de **stoethaspel** /stuthɑspəl/ (pl: -s) clumsy person, bungler

de **¹stof** /stɔf/ (pl: -fen) **1** substance; matter **2** material, cloth, fabric **3** (subject) matter, material: ~ *tot nadenken hebben* have food for thought

het **²stof** /stɔf/ (pl: -fen) dust: ~ *afnemen* dust; *in het* ~ *bijten* bite the dust; *iem. in het* ~ *doen bijten* make s.o. grovel, make s.o. eat dirt; *veel* ~ *doen opwaaien* kick up (*or:* raise) a dust, cause a great deal of controversy

de **stofdoek** /stɔvduk/ (pl: -en) duster, (dust)-cloth

stoffelijk /stɔfələk/ (adj) material

¹stoffen /stɔfə(n)/ (adj) cloth, fabric

²stoffen /stɔfə(n)/ (stofte, heeft gestoft) dust

de **stoffer** /stɔfər/ (pl: -s) [Dutch] brush: ~ *en blik* dustpan and brush

stofferen /stɔfeːrə(n)/ (stoffeerde, heeft gestoffeerd) **1** upholster **2** [roughly] decorate; furnish with carpets and curtains

de **stoffering** /stɔfeːrɪŋ/ (pl: -en) soft furnishings; [Am] fabrics; cloth; upholstery

stoffig /stɔfəɣ/ (adj) dusty; [fig also] mouldy

de **stofjas** /stɔfjɑs/ (pl: -sen) dustcoat, duster

de **stofwisseling** /stɔfwɪsəlɪŋ/ metabolism

stofzuigen /stɔfsœyɣə(n)/ (stofzuigde, heeft gestofzuigd) vacuum, hoover

de **stofzuiger** /stɔfsœyɣər/ (pl: -s) vacuum (cleaner), hoover

de **stok** /stɔk/ (pl: -ken) stick; cane: *zij kregen het aan de* ~ *over de prijs* they fell out over the price; [fig] *een* ~ *achter de deur* the big stick

het **stokbrood** /stɔgbroːt/ (pl: -broden) baguette, French bread

stokdoof /stɔgdoːf/ (adj) [Dutch] stone-deaf, (as) deaf as a post

¹stoken /stoːkə(n)/ (stookte, heeft gestookt) **1** heat **2** make trouble

²stoken /stoːkə(n)/ (stookte, heeft gestookt) **1** stoke (up); feed; light, kindle: *op olie gestookt* oil-fired; *een vuurtje* ~ light a fire **2** burn: *kolen* ~ burn coal **3** stir up: *ruzie* ~ stir up strife **4** distil || *de tanden* ~ use a toothpick, clean between one's teeth with a toothpick

de **stoker** /stoːkər/ (pl: -s) **1** fireman, stoker; [fig] firebrand; troublemaker **2** distiller

het **stokje** /stɔkjə/ (pl: -s) stick; perch: *het* ~ *doorgeven aan iem.* hand over to s.o.; *het* ~ *overnemen* take up the baton; *ergens een* ~ *voor steken* put a stop to sth.; *van zijn* ~ *gaan* pass out, faint

stokken /stɔkə(n)/ (stokte, is gestokt) catch, halt: *de aanvoer van voedsel stokt* food supplies have broken down; *zijn adem stokte* his breath caught in his throat, his breath stopped short

stokoud /stɔkɔut/ (adj) ancient

het **stokpaardje** /stɔkparcə/ (pl: -s) hobby-horse: *iedereen heeft wel zijn* ~ everyone has his fads and fancies

stokstijf /stɔkstɛif/ (adj, adv) (as) stiff as a rod; stock-still

de **stokvis** /stɔkfɪs/ (pl: -sen) stockfish

de **stol** /stɔl/ (pl: -len) stollen

de **stola** /stoːla/ (pl: -'s) stole

stollen /stɔlə(n)/ (stolde, is gestold) solidify; coagulate; congeal; set; clot

de **stolp** /stɔlp/ (pl: -en) (bell-)glass

het **stolsel** /stɔlsəl/ (pl: -s) coagulum; clot

stom /stɔm/ (adj) **1** dumb, mute **2** stupid, dumb: *ik voelde me zo* ~ I felt such a fool; *iets* ~*s doen* do sth. stupid

de **stoma** /stoːma/ (pl: -'s) fistula; colostomy

stomdronken /stɔmdrɔŋkə(n)/ (adj) dead drunk

¹stomen /stoːmə(n)/ (stoomde, heeft/is gestoomd) steam

²stomen /stoːmə(n)/ (stoomde, heeft gestoomd) dry-clean: *een pak laten* ~ have a suit cleaned

de **stomerij** /stoːmərɛi/ (pl: -en) dry cleaner's

de **stomheid** /stɔmhɛit/ dumbness, muteness; speechlessness: [Dutch] *met* ~ *geslagen zijn* be dumbfounded

stommelen /stɔmələ(n)/ (stommelde, heeft/is gestommeld) stumble

de **stommeling** /stɔməlɪŋ/ (pl: -en) fool, idiot

het **stommetje** /stɔməcə/: ~ *spelen* keep one's

mouth shut

de **stommiteit** /stɔmitεit/ (pl: -en) stupidity: ~*en begaan* make stupid mistakes

de **¹stomp** /stɔmp/ (pl: -en) **1** stump, stub **2** thump; punch

²stomp /stɔmp/ (adj) blunt: *een ~e neus* a snub nose

stompen /stɔmpə(n)/ (stompte, heeft gestompt) thump; punch

stompzinnig /stɔmpsɪnəx/ (adj, adv) obtuse, dense, stupid: ~ *werk* monotonous (*or:* stupid) work

stomtoevallig /stɔmtuvɑlεx/ (adv) accidentally, by a (mere) fluke

stomverbaasd /stɔmvərbast/ (adj, adv) astonished, amazed, flabbergasted

stomvervelend /stɔmvərvεlənt/ (adj) deadly dull, boring; really annoying: ~ *werk moeten doen* have to do deadly boring work

stomweg /stɔmwεx/ (adv) simply, just

stoned /stont/ (adj) high, stoned: *zo ~ als een garnaal* stoned to the gills (*or:* eyeballs), (as) high as a kite

de **stoof** /stof/ (pl: stoven) footwarmer

de **stoofpeer** /stofper/ (pl: -peren) cooking pear

de **stoofschotel** /stofsxotəl/ (pl: -s) stew, casserole

het **stoofvlees** /stofles/ **1** braising meat **2** stew, potroast, braised meat

de **stookolie** /stokoli/ fuel oil

de **stoom** /stom/ steam: ~ *afblazen* let off steam; *op ~ komen* gather steam

het **stoombad** /stombɑt/ (pl: -en) steam bath, Turkish bath

de **stoomboot** /stombot/ (pl: -boten) steamboat, steamer

de **stoomcursus** /stomkʏrzʏs/ (pl: -sen) crash course, intensive course

de **stoommachine** /stomɑʃinə/ (pl: -s) steam engine

het **stoomstrijkijzer** /stomstrεikεizər/ (pl: -s) steam iron

de **stoomtrein** /stomtrεin/ (pl: -en) steam train

de **stoomwals** /stomwɑls/ (pl: -en) steamroller: [fig] *als een ~ over iets heen gaan* crush sth.

de **stoornis** /stornɪs/ (pl: -sen) disturbance, disorder

de **stoorzender** /storzεndər/ (pl: -s) jammer, jamming station

de **stoot** /stot/ thrust; punch; stab; gust: *een ~ onder de gordel* a blow below the belt

het **stootblok** /stodblɔk/ (pl: -ken) buffer (stop)

het **stootje** /stocə/ (pl: -s) thrust; push; nudge: *wel tegen een ~ kunnen* stand rough handling (*or:* hard wear); be thick-skinned

het **stootkussen** /stotkʏsə(n)/ (pl: -s) **1** buffer, pad **2** buffer, fender

de **¹stop** /stɔp/ (pl: -pen) **1** fuse: *alle ~pen sloegen bij hem door* he blew a fuse **2** stop, break: *een sanitaire ~ maken* stop to go to the bathroom

²stop /stɔp/ (int) **1** stop! **2** stop (it)

het **stopbord** /stɔbɔrt/ (pl: -en) stop sign

het **stopcontact** /stɔpkɔntɑkt/ (pl: -en) (plug-)-socket, power point, electric point, outlet

het **stoplicht** /stɔplɪxt/ (pl: -en) traffic light(s)

de **stopnaald** /stɔpnalt/ (pl: -en) darning needle

de **stoppel** /stɔpəl/ (pl: -s) stubble, bristle

de **stoppelbaard** /stɔpəlbart/ (pl: -en) stubbly beard, stubble; five o'clock shadow

¹stoppen /stɔpə(n)/ (stopte, is gestopt) stop: *stop!* stop!

²stoppen /stɔpə(n)/ (stopte, heeft gestopt) **1** fill (up); stuff: *een gat ~* fill a hole **2** put (in(to)): *iets in zijn mond ~* put sth. in(to) one's mouth **3** stop: *de keeper kon de bal niet ~* the goalkeeper couldn't save the ball **4** darn, mend

de **stopplaats** /stɔplats/ (pl: -en) stop, stopping place

het **stopsein** /stɔpsεin/ (pl: -en) stop sign, halt sign

de **stopstreep** /stɔpstrep/ (pl: -strepen) halt line

de **stoptrein** /stɔptrεin/ (pl: -en) slow train

het **stopverbod** /stɔpfərbɔt/ (pl: -en) stopping prohibition; no stopping, clearway

de **stopverf** /stɔpfεrf/ putty

de **stopwatch** /stɔpwɔtʃ/ (pl: -es) stopwatch

het **stopwoord** /stɔpwort/ (pl: -en) stopgap

stopzetten /stɔpsεtə(n)/ (zette stop, heeft stopgezet) stop, bring to a standstill (*or:* halt); discontinue; suspend

¹storen /storə(n)/ (stoorde, heeft gestoord) have poor reception; crackle

²storen /storə(n)/ (stoorde, heeft gestoord) **1** disturb; interrupt; interfere: *dat lawaai stoort me* that noise is disturbing (me); *niet ~!* do not disturb!; *iem. in zijn werk ~* disturb s.o. at his work; *stoor ik?* a) am I interrupting (you)?; b) is this a convenient time? **2** take notice (of), mind: *zij stoorde er zich niet aan* she took no notice of it

storend /storənt/ (adj, adv) interfering; annoying: *~e bijgeluiden* irritating background noise; *~e fouten* annoying errors; *ik vind het niet ~* it doesn't bother me

de **storing** /storɪŋ/ (pl: -en) **1** disturbance; interruption; trouble; failure; breakdown **2** interference, static **3** [meteorology] disturbance; depression

de **storm** /stɔrm/ (pl: -en) gale, storm: *een ~ in een glas water* a storm in a teacup; *het loopt ~* there is a real run on it

stormachtig /stɔrmɑxtəx/ (adj, adv) **1** stormy, blustery **2** stormy; tumultuous

stormen /stɔrmə(n)/ (stormde, is gestormd) storm, rush: *naar voren ~* rush forward (*or:* ahead) de **stormloop** /stɔrmlop/ rush, run

stormlopen /stɔrmlopə(n)/ (liep storm, heeft stormgelopen): *het loopt storm* there's quite a rush, there's a run on it

de **stormram** /stɔrmram/ (pl: -men) battering-ram

de **stormvloed** /stɔrmvlut/ (pl: -en) storm tide, storm flood (*or:* surge)

de **stormvloedkering** /stɔrmvlutkerɪŋ/ (pl: -en) storm surge barrier, flood barrier

het **stort** /stɔrt/ (pl: -en) dump, tip

de **stortbak** /stɔrdbɑk/ (pl: -ken) cistern, tank

de **stortbui** /stɔrdbœy/ (pl: -en) downpour, cloudburst

¹**storten** /stɔrtə(n)/ (stortte, is gestort) fall, crash: *in elkaar* ~ **a)** collapse, cave in [bldg]; **b)** collapse, crack up

²**storten** /stɔrtə(n)/ (stortte, heeft gestort) **1** throw, dump **2** pay, deposit: *het gestorte* ***bedrag*** *is …* the sum paid is …

zich ³**storten** /stɔrtə(n)/ (stortte zich, heeft zich gestort) **1** throw o.s.: *zich* ***in de politiek*** ~ dive into politics **2** (+ op) throw o.s. (into), dive (into), plunge (into)

de **storting** /stɔrtɪŋ/ (pl: -en) payment, deposit

de **stortkoker** /stɔrtkokər/ (pl: -s) (garbage) chute (*or:* shoot)

de **stortplaats** /stɔrtplats/ (pl: -en) dump, dumping ground (*or:* site)

de **stortregen** /stɔrtreɣə(n)/ (pl: -s) downpour

stortregenen /stɔrtreɣənə(n)/ (stortregende, heeft gestortregend) pour (with rain, down)

de **stortvloed** /stɔrtflut/ (pl: -en) torrent, deluge, flood

¹**stoten** /stotə(n)/ (stootte, heeft/is gestoten) bump, knock, hit: *pas op, stoot je* ***hoofd*** *niet* mind your head; *op moeilijkheden* ~ run into difficulties; *iem.* ***van zijn voetstuk*** ~ knock s.o. off his pedestal

²**stoten** /stotə(n)/ (stootte, heeft gestoten) **1** thrust, push: *niet* ~*!* handle with care!; *een vaas* ***van de kast*** ~ knock a vase off the sideboard **2** play (*or:* shoot) (a ball)

zich ³**stoten** /stotə(n)/ (stootte zich, heeft zich gestoten) bump (o.s.): *we stootten ons* ***aan de*** *tafel* we bumped into the table

de **stotteraar** /stotərar/ (pl: -s) stutterer, stammerer

stotteren /stotərə(n)/ (stotterde, heeft gestotterd) stutter, stammer

stout /stɑut/ (adj, adv) naughty: ~ *zijn* misbehave

stoutmoedig /stɑutmudəx/ (adj, adv) bold, audacious

stouwen /stɑuwə(n)/ (stouwde, heeft gestouwd) stow, cram

stoven /stovə(n)/ (stoofde, heeft gestoofd) stew, simmer

de **stoverij** /stovərɛi/ (pl: -en) [Belg] stew

de **straal** /stral/ (pl: stralen) **1** beam, ray **2** jet;

trickle **3** radius: *binnen een* ~ *van 10 kilometer* within a radius of 10 km || *iem.* ~ ***voorbijlopen*** walk right past s.o.

de **straaljager** /straljaɣər/ (pl: -s) fighter jet

de **straalkachel** /stralkɑχəl/ (pl: -s) electric heater

het **straalvliegtuig** /stralvliχtœyχ/ (pl: -en) jet

de **straat** /strat/ (pl: straten) street: *een* ***doodlopende*** ~ dead end street; *de* ***volgende*** ~ *rechts* the next turning to the right; *de* ~ ***opbreken*** dig up the street; *op* ~ *staan* be (out) on the street(s); *de* ~ *op gaan* take to (*or:* hit) the streets; *drie straten verderop* three streets away

straatarm /stratɑrm/ (adj) penniless

de **straatbende** /stradbɛndə/ street gang

het **straatgevecht** /stratχəvɛχt/ (pl: -en) street fight, riot

de **straathond** /strathont/ (pl: -en) cur, mutt

het **straatje** /stratɕə/ (pl: -s) alley, lane: *een* ~ *omlopen* walk around the block, take an airing

de **straatjongen** /stratjoŋə(n)/ (pl: -s) street urchin

de **straatlantaarn** /stratlɑntarn/ (pl: -s) street lamp

de **straatlengte** /stratlɛŋtə/ (pl: -n, -s): *met een* ~ *winnen* win by a mile

het **straatmeubilair** /stratməbilɛ:r/ street furniture

de **straatmuzikant** /stratmyzikɑnt/ busker

Straatsburg /stratsbʏrχ/ Strasbourg

de **straatsteen** /stratsten/ (pl: -stenen) paving brick

de **straattaal** /stratal/ bad language

de **straatventer** /stratfɛntər/ (pl: -s) vendor

de **straatverlichting** /stratfərlɪχtɪŋ/ street lighting

het **straatvoedsel** /stratfutsəl/ street food

het **straatvuil** /stratfœyl/ street refuse; [Am] street garbage

de **straatwaarde** /stratwardə/ street value

de ¹**straf** /strɑf/ (pl: -fen) punishment; penalty: *een zware* (or: *lichte*) ~ a heavy (*or:* light) punishment; *een* ~ ***ondergaan*** pay the penalty; *zijn* ~ *ontlopen* get off scot-free; *voor* ~ for punishment

²**straf** /strɑf/ (adj, adv) stiff, severe: ~*fe* ***taal*** hard words

strafbaar /strɑvbar/ (adj) punishable: *een* ~ *feit* an offence, a punishable (*or:* penal) act; *dat* ***is*** ~ that's an offence; *iets* ~ ***stellen*** attach a penalty to sth., make sth. punishable

de **strafbal** /strɑvbɑl/ (pl: -len) [sport] penalty (shot)

de **strafbank** /strɑvbɑŋk/ **1** dock: *op het* ~*je zitten* be in the dock **2** [sport] penalty box (*or:* bench)

het **strafblad** /strɑvblɑt/ police record, record of convictions (*or:* offences)

de **strafcorner** /strɑfkɔ:rnər/ (pl: -s) penalty

corner

de **strafexpeditie** /strɑfɛkspedi(t)si/ (pl: -s) punitive expedition

straffeloos /strɑfəlos/ (adj, adv) unpunished

straffen /strɑfə(n)/ (strafte, heeft gestraft) punish, penalize

het **strafhof** /strɑfhɔf/ (pl: -hoven) criminal court

het **strafkamp** /strɑfkɑmp/ (pl: -en) prison camp, penal colony

de **strafmaat** /strɑfmat/ (pl: -maten) sentence, penalty

de **strafpleiter** /strɑfplɛɪtər/ (pl: -s) criminal lawyer, advocate, counsellor

het/de **strafport** /strɑfpɔrt/ surcharge

het **strafproces** /strɑfprosɛs/ (pl: -sen) criminal action, criminal proceedings

het **strafpunt** /strɑfpʏnt/ (pl: -en) penalty point: *een ~ geven* award a penalty point

het **strafrecht** /strɑfrɛχt/ criminal law, criminal justice

strafrechtelijk /strɑfrɛχtələk/ (adj, adv) criminal: *iem. ~ vervolgen* prosecute s.o.

de **strafschop** /strɑfsχɔp/ (pl: -pen) penalty (kick), spot kick: *scoren uit een ~* score from a penalty; *een ~ nemen* take a penalty; *een serie ~pen* a penalty shoot-out

het **strafschopgebied** /strɑfsχɔpχəbit/ (pl: -en) penalty area, penalty box

de **strafvermindering** /strɑfərmɪndərɪŋ/ reduction of (one's) sentence, remission

de **strafvervolging** /strɑfərvɔlɣɪŋ/ (criminal) prosecution, criminal proceedings: *tot ~ overgaan* prosecute, institute criminal proceedings

de **strafvordering** /strɑfɔrdərɪŋ/ criminal proceedings: *wetboek van ~* Code of Criminal Procedure

het **strafwerk** /strɑfwɛrk/ lines, (school) punishment: *~ maken* do (or: write) lines; do impositions (or: an imposition)

de **strafworp** /strɑfwɔrp/ (pl: -en) penalty throw; foul shot

de **strafzaak** /strɑfsak/ (pl: -zaken) criminal case, criminal trial

strak /strɑk/ (adj, adv) **1** tight; taut: *iem. ~ houden* keep s.o. on a tight rein; *een ~ lijf* a sleek (or: strong) body; *~ trekken* stretch, pull tight **2** fixed, set, intent: *~ voor zich uit kijken* sit staring (fixedly) **3** fixed, set; stern; tense

strakblauw /strɑkblɑu/ (adj) clear blue, sheer blue, cloudless

straks /strɑks/ (adv) **1** later, soon, next: *~ meer hierover* I'll return to this later; *tot ~* so long, see you later (or: soon) **2** before you know it, if you don't watch out, next thing: *~ val je nog* if you don't watch out, you'll fall (down/over)

stralen /stralə(n)/ (straalde, heeft gestraald)

1 radiate, beam **2** shine, beam, radiate

stralend /stralənt/ (adj, adv) **1** radiant, brilliant; [stronger] dazzling **2** radiant, beaming **3** glorious, splendid

de **straling** /stralɪŋ/ (pl: -en) radiation

stram /strɑm/ (adj, adv) stiff, rigid

het **stramien** /stramin/ pattern

het **strand** /strɑnt/ (pl: -en) beach, seaside: *naar het ~ gaan* go to the beach

stranden /strɑndə(n)/ (strandde, is gestrand) **1** be cast (or: washed) ashore; run aground (or: ashore); be stranded **2** fail: *een plan laten ~* wreck a project **3** be stranded

het **strandhuisje** /strɑnthœyʃə/ (pl: -s) beach cabin

de **strandjutter** /strɑntjʏtər/ (pl: -s) beachcomber; wrecker

de **strandstoel** /strɑntstul/ (pl: -en) deck chair

de **strateeg** /stratex/ (pl: strategen) strategist

de **strategie** /strateɣi/ (pl: -ën) strategy

strategisch /strateɣis/ (adj, adv) strategic

de **stratenmaker** /stratə(n)makər/ (pl: -s) paviour, road worker; road mender

de **stratosfeer** /stratosfer/ stratosphere

de **stream** /stri:m/ (pl: -s) [comp] stream

streamen /stri:mə(n)/ (streamde, heeft gestreamd) stream

de **streber** /strebər/ (pl: -s) careerist, (social) climber

de **streefdatum** /strevdatʏm/ (pl: -data) target date

de **streek** /strek/ (pl: streken) **1** trick; prank; antic; caper: *een stomme ~ uithalen* do sth. silly **2** region, area: *in deze ~* in these parts (or: this part) of the country **3** stroke ‖ *op ~ zijn* get on; *van ~ zijn* a) be out of sorts; b) be upset, be in a dither; c) be upset, be out of order

de **streekbus** /strebʏs/ (pl: -sen) regional (or: county, country) bus

de **streekroman** /strekromɑn/ (pl: -s) regional novel

het **streekvervoer** /strekfərvur/ regional transport

de **streep** /strep/ (pl: strepen) **1** line, score; mark(ing): [fig] *daar hebben we een ~ onder gezet* that's a closed book (or: issue) now **2** stripe, line; band; bar; streak: *iem. over de ~ trekken* win s.o. over **3** stripe, chevron

het **streepje** /strepjə/ (pl: -s) thin line, narrow line; hyphen; dash; slash ‖ *een ~ voor hebben* be privileged, be in s.o.'s favour (or: good books)

de **streepjescode** /strepjəskodə/ (pl: -s) bar code

¹**strekken** /strɛkə(n)/ (strekte, heeft gestrekt) **1** extend, stretch, go **2** last, go: *zolang de voorraad strekt* while stocks lasts

²**strekken** /strɛkə(n)/ (strekte, heeft gestrekt) stretch, unbend, extend, straighten

de **strekking** /strɛkɪŋ/ (pl: -en) import; tenor;

purport; purpose; intent; effect: *de ~ van het*
verhaal the drift of the story

strelen /streːlə(n)/ (streelde, heeft gestreeld)
caress, stroke, fondle

de **streling** /streːlɪŋ/ (pl: -en) caress

stremmen /strɛmə(n)/ (stremde, heeft ge-
stremd) block, obstruct

de **stremming** /strɛmɪŋ/ (pl: -en) **1** blocking: ~
van het ***verkeer*** traffic jam, blocking of the
traffic **2** coagulation

het **stremsel** /strɛmsəl/ (pl: -s) coagulant

de **¹streng** /strɛŋ/ (pl: -en) **1** twist, twine, skein,
hank **2** strand

²streng /strɛŋ/ (adj, adv) **1** severe, hard: *het*
vriest ~ there's a sharp frost; *een ~e* ***winter*** a
severe winter **2** severe, strict; stringent; rigid; harsh: *~e* ***eisen*** stern demands; *een ~e* ***on-***
derwijzer a stern (*or:* strict) teacher; *~* ***straf-***
fen punish severely

strepen /streːpə(n)/ (streepte, heeft gestreept) line, streak, stripe

de **stress** /strɛs/ stress, strain

stressbestendig /strɛzbəstɛndəx/ (adj) immune to stress; stress resistant; robust

stressen /strɛsə(n)/ (streste, heeft gestrest)
work under stress

het **stretch** /strɛtʃ/ stretchy material (*or:* fabric),
elastic

de **stretcher** /strɛtʃər/ (pl: -s) stretcher

het **¹streven** /streːvə(n)/ **1** striving (for), pursuit
(of); endeavour: *het ~* ***naar*** *onafhankelijkheid*
the pursuit of independence **2** ambition, aspiration, aim: *een* ***nobel*** *~* a noble ambition

²streven /streːvə(n)/ (streefde, heeft ge-
streefd) strive (for, after), aspire (after, to),
aim (at): *je doel* ***voorbij*** *~* defeat your object

de **striem** /strim/ (pl: -en) slash, score; weal;
welt

striemen /strimə(n)/ (striemde, heeft ge-
striemd) slash, score

de **strijd** /strɛit/ **1** fight, struggle; combat; battle: *de ~* ***aanbinden*** *tegen iets* fight against
sth.; *hevige* (*or:* *zware*) *~* fierce battle (*or:*
struggle, fighting), battle royal; *~* ***leveren***
wage a fight, put up a fight (*or:* struggle); *de*
~ ***om*** *het bestaan* the struggle for life; *ten ~e*
trekken go to battle (*or:* war) (against)
2 strife, dispute, controversy, conflict: *inner-*
lijke ~ inner struggle (*or:* conflict); *in ~* ***met***
de wet against the law

strijdbaar /strɛidbar/ (adj) militant, warlike: *we moeten ons ~* ***tonen*** we must fight
hard

de **strijdbijl** /strɛidbɛil/ (pl: -en) battle-axe;
tomahawk: *de ~* ***begraven*** bury the hatchet

strijden /strɛidə(n)/ (streed, heeft gestre-
den) **1** struggle, fight, wage war (against,
on); battle **2** compete, contend

de **strijder** /strɛidər/ (pl: -s) fighter; warrior;
combatant

strijdig /strɛidəx/ (adj) **1** contrary (to), ad-

verse (to), inconsistent (with) **2** conflicting;
incompatible (with)

de **strijdkrachten** /strɛitkrɑxtə(n)/ (pl) (armed) forces (*or:* services)

de **strijdkreet** /strɛitkret/ (pl: -kreten) battle
cry, war cry

strijdlustig /strɛitlʏstəx/ (adj) pugnacious,
combative; militant

het **strijdperk** /strɛitpɛrk/ (pl: -en) arena

het **strijdtoneel** /strɛitonel/ scene of battle (*or:*
action): [fig] *van het ~* ***verdwijnen*** leave the
fray, give up the fight

de **strijkbout** /strɛigbaut/ (pl: -en) iron

¹strijken /strɛikə(n)/ (streek, heeft gestre-
ken) brush, sweep || *met de eer gaan ~* carry
off the palm (for), take the credit (for)

²strijken /strɛikə(n)/ (streek, heeft gestre-
ken) **1** smooth, spread, brush **2** stroke, brush
3 iron || *de* ***zeilen*** *~* lower (*or:* strike) the sails

het **strijkgoed** /strɛikxut/ clothes that need to
be ironed; ironed clothes

het **strijkijzer** /strɛikɛizər/ (pl: -s) iron, flat-iron

het **strijkinstrument** /strɛikɪnstrymɛnt/ (pl:
-en) stringed instrument: *de ~en* the strings

het **strijkorkest** /strɛikorkɛst/ (pl: -en) string
orchestra

de **strijkplank** /strɛikplɑŋk/ (pl: -en) ironing
board

de **strijkstok** /strɛikstɔk/ (pl: -ken) bow || *er*
blijft veel ***aan*** *de ~ hangen* the rake-off is considerable

de **strik** /strɪk/ (pl: -ken) **1** bow **2** snare, trap

het **strikje** /strɪkjə/ (pl: -s) bow tie

strikken /strɪkə(n)/ (strikte, heeft gestrikt)
1 tie in a bow: *zijn* ***das*** *~* knot a tie **2** snare
3 trap (into)

strikt /strɪkt/ (adj, adv) strict; stringent; rigorous: *~* ***vertrouwelijk*** strictly confidential

de **strikvraag** /strɪkfrax/ (pl: -vragen) catch
(*or:* trick) question

de **string** /strɪŋ/ **1** thong **2** (character) string

stringent /strɪŋɣɛnt/ (adj) stringent

de **strip** /strɪp/ (pl: -s, -pen) **1** strip; slip; band
2 comic strip, (strip) cartoon

het **stripboek** /strɪbuk/ (pl: -en) comic (book)

de **stripfiguur** /strɪpfiɣyr/ (pl: -figuren) comic(-
strip) character

strippen /strɪpə(n)/ (stripte, heeft gestript)
strip

de **strippenkaart** /strɪpə(n)kart/ (pl: -en)
[Dutch] [roughly] bus and tram card

de **stripper** /strɪpər/ (pl: -s) (male/female)
stripper

de **striproman** /strɪproman/ (pl: -s) graphic
novel

de **striptease** /strɪpti:s/ striptease

de **striptekenaar** /strɪptekənar/ (pl: -s) strip
cartoonist

het **stripverhaal** /strɪpfərhal/ (pl: -verhalen)
comic (strip)

het **stro** /stro/ straw

de **strobloem** /stroblum/ (pl: -bloemen) straw-flower, everlasting (flower)

het **strobreed** /strobret/: iem. **geen** ~ in de weg leggen not put the slightest obstacle in s.o.'s way

stroef /struf/ (adj, adv) **1** rough, uneven **2** stiff, difficult, awkward; jerky; brusque; tight **3** stiff, staid; awkward; stern; difficult (to get on with); remote; reserved; stand-offish

de **strofe** /strofə/ (pl: -n) stanza, strophe

de **strohalm** /strohalm/ (pl: -en) (stalk of) straw: zich **aan** een (laatste) ~ vastklampen clutch at a straw (or: at straws)

de **strohoed** /strohut/ (pl: -en) straw (hat)

stroken /strokə(n)/ (strookte, heeft ge-strookt) tally, agree, square: dat strookt niet **met** elkaar these things do not match; dat strookt niet **met** mijn plannen that does not fit my plans

de **stroman** /stroman/ (pl: -nen) straw man, man of straw, puppet, figurehead

stromen /stromə(n)/ (stroomde, heeft/is gestroomd) **1** stream, pour, flow: een **snel** ~de rivier a fast-flowing river; het **water** stroomde de dijk over the water flooded over the dike **2** pour, flock || ~de **regen** pouring rain

de **stroming** /stromɪŋ/ (pl: -en) **1** current, flow **2** movement, trend, tendency

strompelen /strompələ(n)/ (strompelde, is gestrompeld) stumble, totter, limp

de **stronk** /stroŋk/ (pl: -en) **1** stump, stub **2** stalk

de **stront** /stront/ [inform] shit, dung, filth: er is ~ **aan** de knikker the shit has hit the fan, we're in the shit; [vulg] iem. **in** de ~ laten zakken let s.o. down

het **strontje** /stroncə/ (pl: -s) sty(e)

het **strooibiljet** /strojbɪljɛt/ (pl: -ten) handbill, pamphlet, leaflet

¹**strooien** /strojə(n)/ (adj) straw: een ~ **dak** a thatched roof, a thatch

²**strooien** /strojə(n)/ (strooide, heeft ge-strooid) scatter; strew; sow; sprinkle; dredge: **zand (pekel)** ~ bij gladheid grit icy roads

het **strooizout** /strojzaut/ road salt

de **strook** /strok/ (pl: stroken) **1** strip; band **2** strip, slip; label; tag; stub; counterfoil

de **stroom** /strom/ (pl: stromen) **1** stream, flow; current; flood: de zwemmer **werd** door de ~ **meegesleurd** the swimmer was swept away by the current (or: tide) **2** stream, flood: een ~ **goederen** a flow of goods; er kwam een ~ **van klachten** binnen complaints came pouring in **3** (electric) power, (electric) current: er **staat** ~ op die draad that is a live wire; **onder** ~ staan be live (or: charged)

stroomafwaarts /stromafwarts/ (adj, adv) downstream, downriver

de **stroomdraad** /stromdrat/ live wire, contact wire, electric wire

stroomlijnen /stromlɛinə(n)/ (stroomlijn-de, heeft gestroomlijnd) streamline

stroomopwaarts /stromopwarts/ (adj, adv) upstream, upriver

het **stroomschema** /stromsxema/ flow chart (or: sheet, diagram)

de **stroomsterkte** /stromstɛrktə/ **1** current intensity **2** force of the current

de **stroomstoot** /stromstot/ (pl: -stoten) (current) surge; pulse; transient

de **stroomstoring** /stromstorɪŋ/ (pl: -en) electricity failure, power failure

het **stroomverbruik** /stromvərbrœyk/ electricity consumption, power consumption

de **stroomversnelling** /stromvərsnɛlɪŋ/ (pl: -en) rapid: **in** een ~ geraken gain momentum, develop (or: move) rapidly; be accelerated

de **stroomvoorziening** /stromvorzinɪŋ/ electricity (or: power) supply

de **stroop** /strop/ (pl: stropen) syrup; treacle: ~ (om iemands mond) **smeren** butter s.o. up, softsoap s.o.

de **strooptocht** /stroptoxt/ (pl: -en) (predatory) raid: **op** ~ gaan naar ... ransack the house (or: city, ...) for ...

de **stroopwafel** /stropwafəl/ (pl: -s) syrup waffle

de **strop** /strop/ (pl: -pen) **1** halter, (hangman's) rope; noose; snare; trap **2** bad luck, tough luck; raw deal; financial blow (or: setback); loss

de **stropdas** /stropdas/ (pl: -sen) tie

stropen /stropə(n)/ (stroopte, heeft ge-stroopt) **1** skin **2** poach

de **stroper** /stropər/ (pl: -s) poacher

stroperig /stropərəx/ (adj) **1** syrupy **2** [fig] smooth(-talking)

de **stroperij** /stropərɛi/ (pl: -en) poaching

de **strot** /strot/ (pl: -ten) throat; gullet: het **komt** me de ~ **uit** I'm sick of it; ik krijg het niet **door** mijn ~ I couldn't eat it to save my life; the words stick in my throat

het **strottenhoofd** /strotə(n)hoft/ (pl: -en) larynx

de **strubbelingen** /strʏbəlɪŋə(n)/ (pl) difficulties; trouble; frictions

structureel /strʏktyrel/ (adj, adv) structural; constructional

structureren /strʏktyrerə(n)/ (structureer-de, heeft gestructureerd) structure, structuralize

de **structuur** /strʏktyr/ (pl: structuren) structure, texture, fabric

de **structuurverf** /strʏktyrvɛrf/ (pl: -verven) cement paint

de **struif** /strœyf/ (pl: struiven) (contents of an) egg

de **struik** /strœyk/ (pl: -en) **1** bush, shrub **2** bunch; head

het **struikelblok** /strœykəlblok/ (pl: -ken)

stumbling block, obstacle

struikelen /strœykələ(n)/ (struikelde, is gestruikeld) stumble (over), trip (over)

het **struikgewas** /strœykxəwɑs/ (pl: -sen) bushes, shrubs, brushwood

de **struikrover** /strœykrovər/ (pl: -s) highwayman, footpad

struinen /strœynə(n)/ (struinde, heeft gestruind) forage (about/around)

struis /strœys/ (adj) robust

de **struisvogel** /strœysfoɣəl/ (pl: -s) ostrich

de **struisvogelpolitiek** /strœysfoɣəlpolitik/ ostrich policy: *een ~ volgen* refuse to face facts, bury one's head in the sand

het **stucwerk** /stʏkwɛrk/ stucco(work)

de **stud** /stʏt/ (pl: -s) egghead

de **studeerkamer** /stydɛrkamər/ study

de **student** /stydɛnt/ (pl: -en) student; undergraduate; (post)graduate: *~ Turks* student of Turkish

de **studentenbeweging** /stydɛntə(n)bəweɣɪŋ/ student movement

het **studentencorps** /stydɛntə(n)kɔːr/ (pl: -corpora) [Dutch] [roughly] student(s') union

de **studentenflat** /stydɛntə(n)flɛt/ (pl: -s) **1** [roughly] hall of residence, student apartments **2** student flat, student dorm

het **studentenhuis** /stydɛntə(n)hœys/ (pl: -huizen) student(s') house

de **studentenstop** /stydɛntə(n)stɔp/ (pl: -s) (student) quota

de **studententijd** /stydɛntə(n)tɛit/ (pl: -en) college days, student days

de **studentenvereniging** /stydɛntə(n)vərenəɣɪŋ/ (pl: -en) [roughly] student union

studentikoos /stydɛntikos/ (adj) typical of a student, student-like

studeren /stydɛrə(n)/ (studeerde, heeft gestudeerd) **1** study; go to (*or:* be at) university/college: *Marijke studeert* Marijke is at university (*or:* college); *oude talen ~* read classics; *hij studeert nog* he is still studying (*or:* at college); *verder ~* continue one's studies; *~ voor een examen* study (*or:* revise) for an exam **2** practise (music): *piano ~* practise the piano

de **studie** /stydi/ (pl: -s) study: *met een ~ beginnen* take up a (course of) study

het **studieadvies** /stydiɑtfis/ (pl: -adviezen) recommendation for further education: *bindend ~* decision regarding the continuation of the course

de **studieadviseur** /stydiɑtfizør/ (pl: -s) supervisor; [Am] adviser

de **studiebegeleiding** /stydibəɣəlɛidɪŋ/ (pl: -en) tutoring, coaching

de **studiebeurs** /stydibørs/ (pl: -beurzen) grant

het **studieboek** /stydibuk/ (pl: -en) textbook, manual

de **studiebol** /stydibɔl/ (pl: -len) bookworm, scholar

de **studiefinanciering** /stydifinɑnsirɪŋ/ student grant(s)

de **studiegenoot** /stydiɣənot/ (pl: -genoten) fellow student

de **studiegids** /stydiɣɪts/ (pl: -en) prospectus; [Am] catalog

het **studiehuis** /stydihœys/ (pl: -huizen) [Dutch] educational reform stimulating private study

het **studiejaar** /stydijar/ (pl: -jaren) (school) year; university year, academic year

de **studiemeester** /stydimestər/ (pl: -s) [Belg] [roughly] supervisor

het **studieprogramma** /stydiproɣrama/ (pl: -'s) course programme, study programme, syllabus

het/de **studiepunt** /stydipʏnt/ (pl: -en) credit

de **studiereis** /stydirɛis/ (pl: -reizen) study tour (*or:* trip)

de **studierichting** /stydirɪxtɪŋ/ (pl: -en) subject, course(s), discipline, branch of study (*or:* studies)

de **studieschuld** /stydisxʏlt/ (pl: -en) student loan

de **studietoelage** /styditulaɣə/ (pl: -n) scholarship, (study) grant

de **studiewijzer** /stydiwɛizər/ (pl: -s) course directory, study guide

de **studiezaal** /stydizal/ (pl: -zalen) reading room

de **studio** /stydijo/ (pl: -'s) studio

het **stuf** /stʏf/ eraser

de **stuff** /stʏf/ dope, stuff; pot; grass; weed

stug /stʏx/ (adj, adv) **1** stiff, tough **2** surly, dour, stiff ‖ *~ doorwerken* work (*or:* slog) away; *dat lijkt me ~* that seems pretty stiff (*or:* tall, steep) to me

het **stuifmeel** /stœyfmel/ pollen

de **stuifsneeuw** /stœyfsnew/ powder (*or:* drifting) snow

de **stuip** /stœyp/ (pl: -en) convulsion; [small] twitch; fit; spasm: *iem. de ~en op het lijf jagen* scare s.o. stiff, scare the (living) daylights out of s.o.

stuiptrekken /stœyptrɛkə(n)/ (stuiptrekte, heeft gestuiptrekt) convulse, be convulsed, become convulsed

de **stuiptrekking** /stœyptrɛkɪŋ/ (pl: -en) convulsion, spasm; [small] twitch

het **stuitbeen** /stœydben/ (pl: -deren) tailbone, coccyx

stuiten /stœytə(n)/ (stuitte, heeft/is gestuit) **1** encounter, happen upon, chance upon, stumble across **2** meet with, run up against **3** bounce, bound

stuitend /stœytənt/ (adj, adv) revolting, shocking

de **stuiter** /stœytər/ (pl: -s) big marble, taw, bonce

stuiteren /stœytərə(n)/ (stuiterde, heeft/is gestuiterd) play at marbles

het **stuitje** /stœycə/ tail bone

stuiven /stœyvə(n)/ (stoof, heeft/is gestoven) **1** blow, fly about, fly up **2** dash, rush, whiz ‖ [Belg] *het zal er ~* there'll be a proper dust-up

de **stuiver** /stœyvər/ (pl: -s) [Dutch] five-cent piece

stuivertje-wisselen /stœyvərcəwɪsələ(n)/ change (*or:* trade) places

het ¹**stuk** /stʏk/ (pl: -ken) **1** piece, part, fragment; lot; length: *iets in ~ken snijden* cut sth. up (into pieces); *uit één ~ vervaardigd* made in (*or:* of) one piece **2** piece, item: *een ~ gereedschap* a piece of equipment, a tool; *per ~ verkopen* sell by the piece, sell singly; *twintig ~s vee* twenty head of cattle; *een ~ of tien appels* about ten apples, ten or so apples **3** (postal) article, (postal) item **4** piece, article **5** document, paper **6** piece, picture **7** piece, play **8** piece ‖ *op geen ~ken na* not nearly; *klein van ~* small, of small stature, short; *iem. van zijn ~ brengen* unsettle (*or:* unnerve, disconcert) s.o.

²**stuk** /stʏk/ (adj) **1** apart, to pieces **2** out of order, broken down, bust: *iets ~ maken* break (*or:* ruin) sth.

de **stukadoor** /stykadoːr/ (pl: -s) plasterer

stuken /stykə(n)/ (stuukte, heeft gestuukt) [Dutch] plaster

stukgaan /stʏkxan/ (ging stuk, is stukgegaan) **1** break down, fail; break to pieces **2** break; [inform] exhaust oneself, knacker oneself: *in de laatste beklimming ging ik helemaal stuk* the last climb finished me off ‖ [inform] *we gingen helemaal stuk van dat filmpje* the video made us totally crack up

het **stukgoed** /stʏkxut/ (pl: -eren) general cargo; (load of) packed goods

het **stukje** /stʏkjə/ (pl: -s) **1** small piece, little bit: *~ bij beetje* bit by bit, inch by inch **2** short piece

het **stukloon** /stʏkloːn/: *tegen ~ werken* work at piece rate, be paid by the piece

¹**stuklopen** /stʏkloːpə(n)/ (liep stuk, is stukgelopen) go wrong, break down: *een stukgelopen huwelijk* a broken marriage

²**stuklopen** /stʏkloːpə(n)/ (liep stuk, heeft stukgelopen) wear out

stukmaken /stʏkmakə(n)/ (maakte stuk, heeft stukgemaakt) break (to pieces)

de **stukprijs** /stʏkprɛis/ (pl: -prijzen) unit price

de **stulp** /stʏlp/ (pl: -en) **1** hovel, hut **2** bellglass

de **stumper** /stʏmpər/ (pl: -s) wretch

de **stunt** /stʏnt/ (pl: -s) stunt, tour de force, feat

stuntelen /stʏntələ(n)/ (stuntelde, heeft gestunteld) bungle, flounder

stuntelig /stʏntələx/ (adj, adv) clumsy

stunten /stʏntə(n)/ (stuntte, heeft gestunt) stunt: *met de prijzen ~* sell at record low prices; *Rode Duivels ~ op WK* Red Devils amaze at World Cup

de **stuntman** /stʏntman/ (pl: -nen) stunt man

de **stuntprijs** /stʏntprɛis/ (pl: -prijzen) incredibly (*or:* record) low price; price breakers

stuntvliegen /stʏntfliyə(n)/ stunt flying, aerobatics

het **stuntwerk** /stʏntwɛrk/ stuntwork

sturen /styrə(n)/ (stuurde, heeft gestuurd) **1** steer; drive; guide **2** send; forward [goods]; dispatch; address: *van school ~* expel (from school)

de **stut** /stʏt/ (pl: -ten) prop, stay, support

stutten /stʏtə(n)/ (stutte, heeft gestut) prop (up), support

het **stuur** /styr/ (pl: sturen) steering wheel; [car] wheel; [shipp] helm; rudder; controls; handlebars: *aan het ~ zitten* be at (*or:* behind) the wheel; *de macht over het ~ verliezen* lose control (of one's car, bike)

de **stuurbekrachtiging** /styrbəkraxtəyɪŋ/ power steering

het **stuurboord** /styrboːrt/ starboard

de **stuurboordzijde** /styrboːrtsɛɪdə/: *aan ~* on the starboard side

de **stuurgroep** /styrɣrup/ (pl: -en) steering committee

de **stuurhut** /styrhʏt/ (pl: -ten) pilothouse, wheel house

de **stuurinrichting** /styrɪnrɪxtɪŋ/ steerage, steering-gear

de **stuurknuppel** /styrknʏpəl/ (pl: -s) control stick (*or:* lever), (joy) stick

stuurloos /styrloːs/ (adj, adv) out of control, rudderless, adrift

de **stuurman** /styrman/ (pl: stuurlui) **1** mate: *de beste stuurlui staan aan wal* the best coaches are in the sands **2** [sport] helmsman; cox(swain)

stuurs /styrs/ (adj, adv) surly, sullen

het **stuurslot** /styrslɔt/ (pl: -en) steering wheel lock

het **stuurwiel** /styrwil/ (pl: -en) (steering) wheel; control wheel; [shipp] helm

de **stuw** /styw/ (pl: -en) dam, barrage, floodcontrol dam

de **stuwdam** /stywdam/ (pl: -men) dam, barrage, flood-control dam

stuwen /stywə(n)/ (stuwde, heeft gestuwd) **1** drive, push, force, propel, impel **2** stow, pack, load

de **stuwkracht** /stywkraxt/ (pl: -en) force, drive; thrust

het **stuwmeer** /stywmeːr/ (pl: -meren) (storage) reservoir

de **stylist** /stilɪst/ (pl: -en) stylist

de **subcultuur** /sʏpkʏltyr/ (pl: subculturen) subculture; (the) underground

subiet /sybiːt/ (adv) immediately, at once

het **subject** /sʏpjɛkt/ (pl: -en) subject

subjectief /sʏpjɛktif/ (adj, adv) subjective, personal

de **subjectiviteit** /sʏpjɛktivitɛit/ subjectivity

subliem /syblịm/ (adj, adv) sublime, fantastic, super

het **submenu** /sỵpmǝny/ (pl: -'s) [comp] submenu; cascading menu

de **subsidie** /sypsịdi/ (pl: -s) subsidy; (financial) aid; grant; allowance: *een ~ geven voor* grant a subsidy for

subsidiëren /sypsidijẹrǝ(n)/ (subsidieerde, heeft gesubsidieerd) subsidize, grant (an amount)

de **substantie** /sypstạnsi/ (pl: -s) substance, matter

substantieel /sypstɑn(t)fẹl/ (adj, adv) substantial

het **substantief** /sypstɑntịf/ (pl: substantieven) noun

substitueren /sypstitywẹrǝ(n)/ (substitueerde, heeft gesubstitueerd) substitute

de **substitutie** /sypstity(t)si/ (pl: -s) substitution

de ¹**substituut** /sypstitỵt/ (pl: substituten) substitute

het ²**substituut** /sypstitỵt/ (pl: substituten) substitute

subtiel /syptịl/ (adj, adv) subtle, sophisticated; delicate

de **subtop** /sỵptɔp/ second rank

het **subtotaal** /sỵptotal/ (pl: subtotalen) subtotal

subtropisch /syptrọpis/ (adj) subtropical

subversief /sypfɛrsịf/ (adj) subversive

het **succes** /syksɛs/ (pl: -sen) success, luck: *een goedkoop ~je boeken* score a cheap success; *veel ~ toegewenst!* good luck!; *~ met je rijexamen!* good luck with your driving test!; *een groot ~ zijn* be a big success, be a hit

de **succesformule** /syksɛsfɔrmylǝ/ (pl: -s) formula for success

het **succesnummer** /syksɛsnʏmǝr/ (pl: -s) hit

de **successie** /syksɛsi/ (pl: -s) succession: *voor de vierde maal in ~* for the fourth time in succession (*or:* a row)

het **successierecht** /syksɛsirɛxt/ (pl: -en) inheritance tax

successievelijk /syksɛsịvǝlǝk/ (adv) successively, one by one

succesvol /syksɛsfɔl/ (adj, adv) successful

Sudan /sudạn/ (the) Sudan

de ¹**Sudanees** /sudanẹs/ (pl: Sudanezen) Sudanese

²**Sudanees** /sudanẹs/ (adj) Sudanese

sudderen /sỵdǝrǝ(n)/ (sudderde, heeft gesudderd) simmer

de **sudoku** /sudọku/ sudoku

het/de ¹**suède** /sywɛːdǝ/ suede

²**suède** /sywɛːdǝ/ (adj) suede

het **Suezkanaal** /sywɛskanal/ Suez Canal

suf /syf/ (adj, adv) drowsy, dozy; dopey; groggy

suffen /sỵfǝ(n)/ (sufte, heeft gesuft) nod, (day)dream

de **sufferd** /sỵfǝrt/ (pl: -s) dope, fathead

suggereren /syɣǝrẹrǝ(n)/ (suggereerde, heeft gesuggereerd) suggest, imply

de **suggestie** /syɣɛsti/ (pl: -s) suggestion; proposal: *een ~ doen* make a suggestion (*or:* proposal)

suggestief /syɣɛstịf/ (adj, adv) suggestive, insinuating

suïcidaal /sywisidạl/ (adj) suicidal

de **suïcide** /sywisịdǝ/ (pl: -s, -n) suicide: *~ plegen* commit suicide

de **suiker** /sœykǝr/ (pl: -s) sugar: *~ doen in* put sugar in

de **suikerbiet** /sœykǝrbit/ (pl: -en) sugar beet

de **suikerfabriek** /sœykǝrfabrik/ (pl: -en) sugar refinery

het **Suikerfeest** /sœykǝrfest/ Sugar feast, Eid al-Fitr

het **suikerklontje** /sœykǝrklɔncǝ/ (pl: -s) lump of sugar, sugar cube

de **suikeroom** /sœykǝrom/ (pl: -s) **1** rich uncle **2** rich benefactor; sugar daddy

de **suikerpatiënt** /sœykǝrpaʃɛnt/ (pl: -en) diabetic

de **suikerpot** /sœykǝrpɔt/ (pl: -ten) sugar bowl

het **suikerriet** /sœykǝrit/ sugar cane

de **suikerspin** /sœykǝrspɪn/ (pl: -nen) candy floss; [Am] cotton candy

de **suikertante** /sœykǝrtɑntǝ/ (pl: -s) rich aunt

suikervrij /sœykǝrvrɛi/ (adj) sugar-free; diabetic

het **suikerzakje** /sœykǝrzɑkjǝ/ (pl: -s) sugar bag

de **suikerziekte** /sœykǝrziktǝ/ diabetes

de **suite** /swịtǝ/ (pl: -s) suite (of rooms)

suizen /sœyzǝ(n)/ (suisde, heeft gesuisd) rustle; sing; whisper

de **sukade** /sykạdǝ/ candied peel

de **sukkel** /sỵkǝl/ (pl: -s) dope, idiot, twerp

de **sukkelaar** /sỵkǝlar/ (pl: -s) wretch, poor soul (*or:* beggar)

sukkelen /sỵkǝlǝ(n)/ (sukkelde, heeft/is gesukkeld) be ailing, be sickly, suffer (from sth.): *hij sukkelt met zijn gezondheid* he is in bad health || *in slaap ~* doze off, drop off

het **sukkelgangetje** /sỵkǝlɣɑŋǝcǝ/ jog(trot), shambling gait

de **sul** /syl/ (pl: -len) softy, sucker

het **sulfaat** /sylfạt/ (pl: sulfaten) sulphat; [Am] sulfate

het **sulfiet** /sylfịt/ sulphite; [Am] sulfite

de **sulky** /sỵlki/ (pl: -'s) sulky

sullig /sỵlǝx/ (adj, adv) **1** soft **2** dopey, silly

de **sultan** /sỵltɑn/ (pl: -s) sultan

summier /symịr/ (adj, adv) summary, brief

het **summum** /sỵmʏm/ the height (of)

de **super** /sypǝr/ (adj, adv) super, great, first class

de **superbenzine** /sypǝrbɛnzinǝ/ 4 star petrol; [Am] high octane gas(oline)

de **superette** /sypǝrɛtǝ/ (pl: -s) [Belg] small self-service shop de **supergeleiding** /sypərɣəlɛidɪŋ/ (pl: -en) superconductivity

de **superieur** /syperijør/ (pl: -en) superior

de **superioriteit** /syperijoritɛrt/ superiority

de **superlatief** /sypərlatif/ (pl: superlatieven) superlative (degree)

de **supermaan** /sypərman/ (pl: -manen) super-moon

de **supermacht** /sypərmɑχt/ (pl: -en) super-power

de **supermarkt** /sypərmɑrkt/ (pl: -en) super-market

de **supermens** /sypərmɛns/ superman, super-woman

supersonisch /sypərsonis/ (adj) supersonic

de **supertanker** /sypərtɛŋkər/ (pl: -s) super-tanker

de **supervisie** /sypərvizi/ supervision

de **supervisor** /sypərvizor/ (pl: -s) supervisor

het **supplement** /sypləmɛnt/ (pl: -en) supplement

de **suppoost** /sypost/ (pl: -en) attendant

de **supporter** /sypɔrtər/ (pl: -s) supporter

de **suprematie** /syprema(t)si/ supremacy

surfen /sy:rfə(n)/ (surfte/surfde, heeft/is gesurft/gesurfd) **1** be surfing (or: surf-boarding); windsurfing **2** [comp] surf

de **surfer** /sy:rfər/ (pl: -s) surfer; windsurfer

het **surfgedrag** /syrfχədrɑχ/ browsing behaviour, internet use

de **surfgeschiedenis** /syrfχəsχidənɪs/ browsing history

het **surfpak** /syrfpɑk/ (pl: -ken) surfer's wetsuit

de **surfplank** /sy:rfplɑŋk/ (pl: -en) surfboard; sailboard

Surinaams /syrinɑms/ (adj) Surinamese; Surinam

Suriname /syrinamə/ Surinam

de **Surinamer** /syrinamər/ (pl: -s) Surinamese

de **surprise** /syrprizə/ (pl: -s) surprise (gift)

het **surrealisme** /syrejalɪsmə/ surrealism

surrealistisch /syrejalɪstis/ (adj, adv) surrealist(ic)

het **surrogaat** /syroɣat/ (pl: surrogaten) surro-gate

de **surseance** /syrsejãsə/ (pl: -s): ~ *van betaling* moratorium, suspension of payment

de **surveillance** /syrvɛiãsə/ surveillance; supervision; duty

de **surveillancewagen** /syrvɛiãsəwaɣə(n)/ (pl: -s) patrol car

de **surveillant** /syrvɛiɑnt/ (pl: -en) [Dutch] supervisor, observer; invigilator

surveilleren /syrvɛiɛrə(n)/ (surveilleerde, heeft gesurveilleerd) supervise; invigilate; (be on) patrol

de **survivaltocht** /syrvɑjvɑltɔχt/ (pl: -en) survival trip

de **sushi** /suʃi/ (pl: -'s) sushi

sussen /sysə(n)/ (suste, heeft gesust) **1** soothe, lull: *op ~de toon* in a soothing voice; *je geweten* ~ soothe (or: salve, ease) your conscience **2** quiet down, settle: *een ruzie* ~ settle an argument

de **SUV** /ɛsjuvi:/ *sports utility vehicle* SUV

s.v.p. /ɛsfepe/ *s'il vous plaît* please

de **swastika** /swɔstika/ (pl: -'s) swastika

de **Swaziër** /swazijər/ (pl: -s) Swazi

Swaziland /swazilɑnt/ Swaziland

Swazisch /swazis/ (adj) Swazi

de **sweater** /swɛtər/ (pl: -s) sweater, jersey

het **sweatshirt** /swɛtʃy:rt/ (pl: -s) sweatshirt

swingen /swɪŋə(n)/ (swingde, heeft geswingd) swing

swipen /swɑjpə(n)/ (swipete, heeft geswipet) swipe

switchen /swɪtʃə(n)/ (switchte, heeft/is geswitcht) switch; change (or: swop) over

de **syfilis** /sifilɪs/ syphilis

de **syllabe** /sɪlabə/ (pl: -n) syllable

de **syllabus** /sɪlabys/ (pl: -sen, syllabi) syllabus

de **symbiose** /sɪmbijozə/ symbiosis

de **symboliek** /sɪmbolik/ (pl: -en) symbolism

symbolisch /sɪmbolis/ (adj, adv) symbolic(al): *een ~ bedrag* a nominal amount

symboliseren /sɪmbolizerə(n)/ (symboliseerde, heeft gesymboliseerd) symbolize, represent

het **symbool** /sɪmbol/ (pl: symbolen) symbol

de **symfonie** /sɪmfoni/ (pl: -ën) symphony

het **symfonieorkest** /sɪmfoniɔrkɛst/ (pl: -en) symphony orchestra

de **symmetrie** /sɪmetri/ symmetry

symmetrisch /sɪmetris/ (adj, adv) symmetrical

de **sympathie** /sɪmpati/ (pl: -ën) sympathy, feeling: *zijn ~ betuigen* express one's sympathy

sympathiek /sɪmpatik/ (adj, adv) sympathetic, likable, congenial: *ik vind hem erg ~* I like him very much; *~ staan tegenover iem. (iets)* be sympathetic to(wards) s.o. (sth.)

sympathiseren /sɪmpatizerə(n)/ (sympathiseerde, heeft gesympathiseerd) sympathize (with)

het **symposium** /sɪmpozijym/ (pl: symposia, -s) symposium, conference

symptomatisch /sɪmtomatis/ (adj, adv) symptomatic

het **symptoom** /sɪmtom/ (pl: symptomen) symptom, sign: *een ~ zijn van* be symptomatic (or: a symptom) of

de **symptoombestrijding** /sɪmtombəstrɛidɪŋ/ treatment of (the) symptoms

de **synagoge** /sinaɣoɣə/ (pl: -n) synagogue

de **synchronisatie** /sɪŋχroniza(t)si/ (pl: -s) synchronization

synchroon /sɪŋχron/ (adj, adv) synchronous, synchronic

syndicaal /sɪndikal/ (adj, adv) [Belg] (trade) union

het **syndicaat** /sɪndikat/ (pl: syndicaten) syndicate

het **syndroom** /sɪndrǫm/ (pl: syndromen) syndrome

de **synode** /sinǫdə/ (pl: -n, -s) synod

het **¹synoniem** /sinonim/ (pl: -en) synonym
²synoniem /sinonim/ (adj) synonymous (with)

syntactisch /sɪntǫktis/ (adj, adv) syntactic(al)

de **syntaxis** /sɪntǫksɪs/ syntax

de **synthese** /sɪntęzə/ (pl: -n, -s) synthesis

de **synthesizer** /sɪntəsɑjzər/ (pl: -s) synthesizer

synthetisch /sɪntętis/ (adj, adv) synthetic, man-made

Syrië /sįrijə/ Syria

de **Syriër** /sįrijər/ (pl: -s) Syrian

het **¹Syrisch** /sįris/ Syrian
²Syrisch /sįris/ (adj) Syrian

het **systeem** /sistęm/ (pl: systemen) system; method: *daar **zit** geen ~ in* there is no system (*or:* method) in it; [socc] *spelen volgens het **4-3-3-systeem*** play in the 4-3-3 line-up

de **systeembeheerder** /sistęmbəherdər/ (pl: -s) system manager

de **systematiek** /sɪstematįk/ system

systematisch /sistemątis/ (adj, adv) **1** methodical, systematic: *een ~ **overzicht*** a systematic survey; *~ te **werk** gaan* proceed systematically (*or:* methodically) **2** always, invariably: *~ te **laat** komen* always/invariably be late

t

de **t** /te/ (pl: t's) t, T

taai /taj/ (adj, adv) tough, hardy: ~ *vlees* tough meat; *houd je* ~ **a)** take care (of yourself); **b)** [Am] hang in there; **c)** chin up

het/de **taaitaai** /tajtaj/ [Dutch] gingerbread

de **taak** /tak/ (pl: taken) **1** task, job, duty; responsibility; assignment: *een zware* ~ *op zich nemen* undertake an arduous task; *het is niet mijn* ~ *dat te doen* it is not my place to do that; *iem. een* ~ *opgeven (opleggen)* set s.o. a task; *tot* ~ *hebben* have as one's duty; *niet voor zijn* ~ *berekend zijn* be unequal to one's task **2** [educ] assignment

de **taakbalk** /tagbalk/ (pl: -en) taskbar

de **taakleerkracht** /taklerkraxt/ (pl: -en) remedial teacher

de **taakleraar** /taklerar/ (pl: -leraren) [Belg] remedial teacher

de **taakomschrijving** /takomsxreivin/ (pl: -en) job description

de **taakstraf** /takstraf/ (pl: -fen) community service

het **taakuur** /takyr/ (pl: -uren) non-teaching period, free period

de **taakverdeling** /takfərdelin/ division of tasks (or: labour)

de **taal** /tal/ (pl: talen) language; speech; language skills: *vreemde talen* foreign languages; *zich een* ~ *eigen maken* master a language; *de* ~ *van het lichaam* body language || ~ *noch teken geven* not give a sign of life; *gore* ~ *uitslaan* use foul language

de **taalbarrière** /talbar(i)jɛːrə/ (pl: -s) language barrier

de **taalbeheersing** /talbəhersin/ **1** mastery of a language **2** applied linguistics

de **taalcursus** /talkyrsys/ (pl: -sen) language course

de **taalfout** /talfaut/ (pl: -en) language error

het **taalgebied** /talɣəbit/ (pl: -en): *het Franse* ~ French-speaking regions

het **taalgebruik** /talɣəbrœyk/ (linguistic) usage, language

het **taalgevoel** /talɣəvul/ linguistic feeling

de **taalgrens** /talɣrɛns/ (pl: -grenzen) language boundary

de **taalkunde** /talkyndə/ linguistics

taalkundig /talkyndəx/ (adj, adv) linguistic: ~ *ontleden* parse

het **taallab** /talap/ (pl: -s) [Belg] language laboratory

de **taalstrijd** /talstreit/ linguistic conflict

de **taalvaardigheid** /talvardəxhɛit/ language proficiency; [as school subject] (Dutch) language skills

de **taalwetenschap** /talwetə(n)sxɑp/ linguistics

de **taart** /tart/ (pl: -en) cake; pie; tart

het **taartje** /tarcə/ (pl: -s) a (piece of) cake; a tart (or: pie)

de **taartpunt** /tartpʏnt/ (pl: -en) slice/piece of cake

de **taartschep** /tartsxɛp/ (pl: -pen) cake-slice, cake-server

het **taartvorkje** /tartforkjə/ (pl: -s) cake-fork

de **tab** /tɑp/ (pl: -s) tab: *een* ~ *geven* insert a tab, press tab

de **tabak** /tabɑk/ tobacco

de **tabaksaccijns** /tabɑksɑksɛɪns/ (pl: -accijnzen) tobacco duty (excise, tax)

de **tabaksplant** /tabɑksplɑnt/ (pl: -en) tobacco plant

het **tabblad** /tɑblɑt/ (pl: -en) **1** file tab **2** [comp] tab

de **tabel** /tabɛl/ (pl: -len) table

het/de **tabernakel** /tabərnakəl/ (pl: -s) tabernacle

het **tableau** /tablo/ (pl: -s) **1** tray, platter **2** scene, picture

het/de **¹tablet** /tablɛt/ (pl: -ten) tablet; bar: *een ~je innemen tegen de hoofdpijn* take a pill for one's headache

de **²tablet** (pl: -s) tablet (computer)

de **tabloid** /tɛblɔjt/ tabloid

het **tabloidformaat** /tɛblɔjtformat/ tabloid size

het **¹taboe** /tabu/ (pl: -s) taboo: *een* ~ *doorbreken* break a taboo

²taboe /tabu/ (adj) taboo: *iets* ~ *verklaren* pronounce sth. taboo

het **taboeret** /taburɛt/ (pl: -ten) tabouret

de **taboesfeer** /tabusfer/ taboo: *iets uit de* ~ *halen* stop sth. being taboo, legitimate sth.

de **tachograaf** /taxoɣraf/ (pl: -grafen) **1** tachometer **2** tachograph

tachtig /tɑxtəx/ (num) eighty: *mijn oma is* ~ *(jaar oud)* my grandmother is eighty (years old); *de jaren* ~ the eighties; *in de* ~ *zijn* be in one's eighties

tachtigjarig /tɑxtəxjarəx/ (adj) **1** eighty-year-old: *een ~e* an eighty-year-old **2** eighty years'

tachtigste /tɑxtəxstə/ (num) eightieth

tackelen /tɛkələ(n)/ (tackelde, heeft getackeld) [sport] tackle

de **tackle** /tɛkəl/ (pl: -s) tackle

de **tact** /tɑkt/ tact: *iets met* ~ *regelen* use tact in dealing with sth.

de **tacticus** /tɑktikys/ (pl: tactici) tactician

de **tactiek** /tɑktik/ tactics; strategy: *dat is niet de juiste* ~ *om zoiets te regelen* that is not the way to go about such a thing; *van* ~ *veranderen* change (or: alter) one's tactics

tactisch /tɑktis/ (adj, adv) tactical; tactful: *iets* ~ *aanpakken* set about sth. tactically (or:

shrewdly)
tactloos /tɑktlos/ (adj, adv) tactless: ~ *op-treden* show no tact
tactvol /tɑktfɔl/ (adj, adv) tactful
de **Tadzjiek** /tadʒik/ (pl: -en) Tajik
het ¹**Tadzjieks** /tadʒiks/ Tajiki
²**Tadzjieks** /tadʒiks/ (adj) Tajiki
Tadzjikistan /tɑdʒikistɑn/ Tadzhikistan
het **taekwondo** /tajkwɔndo/ taekwondo
de **tafel** /tafəl/ (pl: -s) table: *de* ~ *afruimen* (or: *dekken*) clear (or: lay) the table; *aan* ~ *gaan* sit down to dinner; *om de* ~ *gaan zitten* sit down at the table (and start talking); *iem. onder* ~ *drinken* drink s.o. under the table; *het ontbijt staat op* ~ breakfast is on the table (or: ready); *ter* ~ *komen* come up (for discussion); *van* ~ *gaan* leave the table ‖ *de* ~ *van zeven* the seven-times table
het **tafelkleed** /tafəlklet/ (pl: -kleden) table-cloth
het **tafellaken** /tafəlakə(n)/ (pl: -s) table-cloth
de **tafelpoot** /tafəlpot/ (pl: -poten) table-leg
het **tafeltennis** /tafəltɛnɪs/ table tennis
tafeltennissen /tafəltɛnɪsə(n)/ (tafeltenniste, heeft getafeltennist) play table tennis
de **tafeltennisser** /tafəltɛnɪsər/ (pl: -s) table-tennis player
het **tafelvoetbal** /tafəlvudbɑl/ table football
de **tafelwijn** /tafəlwɛin/ (pl: -en) table wine
het **tafelzilver** /tafəlzɪlvər/ silver cutlery, silverware
het **tafereel** /tafərel/ (pl: taferelen) tableau, scene
de **tag** /tɛ:k/ (pl: -s) tag
taggen /tɛɡə(n)/ (tagde, heeft getagd) tag
de **tahoe** /tahu/ [Dutch] tofu
het **tai chi** /tajtʃi/ tai chi, t'ai chi (ch'uan)
de **taiga** /tɑjɡa/ (pl: -'s) taiga
de **taille** /tɑjə/ (pl: -s) waist: *een dunne* ~ *hebben* have a slender waist
Taiwan /tɑjwɑn/ Taiwan
de ¹**Taiwanees** /tɑjwanes/ (pl: Taiwanezen) Taiwanese
²**Taiwanees** /tɑjwanes/ (adj) Taiwanese
de **tak** /tɑk/ (pl: -ken) branch; fork; section: *een* ~ *van sport* a branch of sports; *de wandelende* ~ the stick insect; [Am] the walking stick
het/de **takel** /takəl/ (pl: -s) tackle: *in de* ~*s hangen* be in the sling
takelen /takələ(n)/ (takelde, heeft getakeld) hoist: *een auto uit de sloot* ~ hoist a car (up) out of the ditch
de **takelwagen** /takəlwaɣə(n)/ (pl: -s) breakdown lorry; [Am] tow truck
het **takenpakket** /takə(n)pɑkɛt/ job responsibilities (in a job)
het **takkewijf** /tɑkəwɛrf/ (pl: -wijven) [vulg] bitch
de **taks** /tɑks/ (pl: -en) **1** regular (or: usual) amount, share: *ik zit aan mijn* ~ I've had enough **2** tax

het **tal** /tɑl/ number: ~ *van voorbeelden* numbers of (or: numerous) examples
talen /talə(n)/ (taalde, heeft getaald) care (about/for)
de **talenknobbel** /talə(n)knɔbəl/ linguistic talent, gift (or: feel) for languages
het **talenpracticum** /talə(n)prɑktikʏm/ (pl: -practica) language lab(oratory)
het **talent** /talɛnt/ (pl: -en) **1** talent; gift; ability: *ze heeft* ~ she is talented; *verborgen* ~*en* hidden talents **2** talent(ed person): *aanstormend* ~ raging talent, up-and-coming talent
de **talentenjacht** /talɛntə(n)jɑxt/ (pl: -en) talent scouting
¹**talentvol** /talɛntfɔl/ (adj) talented, gifted
²**talentvol** /talɛntfɔl/ (adv) ably, with great talent
het **talenwonder** /talə(n)wɔndər/ (pl: -en) linguistic genius
de **talg** /tɑlx/ **1** sebum **2** tallow
de **talisman** /talɪsmɑn/ (pl: -s) talisman
de **talk** /tɑlk/ **1** talc **2** tallow
het/de **talkpoeder** /tɑlkpudər/ talcum powder
de **talkshow** /tɔːkʃo/ (pl: -s) talk show
talloos /tɑlos/ (adj, adv) innumerable, countless
talmen /tɑlmə(n)/ (talmde, heeft getalmd) tarry, put off
talrijk /tɑlrɛik/ (adj) numerous, many
het **talud** /talʏt/ incline, slope; bank
tam /tɑm/ (adj) **1** tame, tamed; domestic: *een* ~*me vos* a tame fox; ~ *maken* domesticate; tame **2** tame, gentle: *een* ~ *paard* a gentle (or: tame) horse
de **tamboer** /tɑmbuːr/ (pl: -s) drummer
de **tamboerijn** /tɑmburɛin/ (pl: -en) tambourine
tamelijk /tamələk/ (adv) fairly, rather: ~ *veel bezoekers* quite a lot of visitors
de **Tamil** /tamil/ Tamil
de **tampon** /tɑmpɔn/ (pl: -s) tampon
de **tamtam** /tɑmtɑm/ (pl: -s) **1** tom-tom **2** fanfare: ~ *maken over iets* make a fuss about (or: a big thing) of sth.; *met veel* ~ with great fanfare
de **tand** /tɑnt/ (pl: -en) **1** tooth: *er breekt een* ~ *door* he/she is cutting a tooth (or: teething); *met lange* ~*en eten* dawdle over one's food; *een* ~ *laten vullen* (or: *trekken*) have a tooth filled (or: extracted); *zijn* ~*en laten zien* show (or: bare) one's teeth; *zijn* ~*en poetsen* brush one's teeth; *iem. aan de* ~ *voelen* grill s.o.; *tot de* ~*en gewapend zijn* be armed to the teeth; [fig] *de* ~ *des tijds* the ravages of time **2** tooth; prong; cog: *de* ~*en van een kam* (or: *hark, zaag*) the teeth of a comb (or: rake, saw)
de **tandarts** /tɑndɑrts/ (pl: -en) dentist
de **tandartsassistente** /tɑndɑrtsɑsɪstɛntə/ (pl: -s) dentist's assistant
het **tandbederf** /tɑndbədɛrf/ caries, tooth de-

cay, dental decay

tandeloos /tɑndəlos/ (adj) toothless

de **tandem** /tɛndəm/ (pl: -s) tandem

de **tandenborstel** /tɑndə(n)bɔrstəl/ (pl: -s) toothbrush

tandenknarsen /tɑndə(n)knɑrsə(n)/ (tandenknarste, heeft getandenknarst) gnash (*or:* grind) one's teeth

de **tandenstoker** /tɑndə(n)stokər/ (pl: -s) toothpick

de **tandglazuur** /tɑntxlazyr/ (dental) enamel

de **tandheelkunde** /tɑnthelkʏndə/ dentistry

tandheelkundig /tɑnthelkʏndəχ/ (adj) dental

de **tandpasta** /tɑntpɑsta/ (pl: -'s) toothpaste

de **tandplak** /tɑntplɑk/ (dental) plaque

het **tandrad** /tɑntrɑt/ (pl: -raderen) gear (wheel)

de **tandradbaan** /tɑntrɑdban/ (pl: -banen) rack railway, cog railway

het/de **tandsteen** /tɑntsten/ tartar

de **tandtechnicus** /tɑntɛχnikʏs/ (pl: -technici) dental technician

het **tandvlees** /tɑntfles/ gums: *gevoelig* ~ sensitive gums; [fig] *op zijn* ~ *haalde hij de finish* he reached the finish on his last legs

het **tandwiel** /tɑntwil/ (pl: -en) gearwheel, cogwheel; chainwheel; sprocket wheel

de **tandzijde** /tɑntsɛɪdə/ dental floss

tanen /tanə(n)/ (taande, is getaand) wane, fade

de **tang** /tɑŋ/ (pl: -en) **1** tongs; (pair of) pliers; (pair of) pincers **2** shrew, bitch

de **tangens** /tɑŋəns/ (pl: -en, tangenten) tangent

de **tango** /tɑŋgo/ (pl: -'s) tango

tanig /tanəχ/ (adj) **1** tawny **2** *een* ~*e grijsaard* a wiry old man

de **tank** /tɛŋk/ (pl: -s) tank: *een volle* ~ *benzine* a full (*or:* whole) tank of petrol; [Am] a full (*or:* whole) tank of gas; *de* ~ *volgooien* fill up (the tank)

de **tankauto** /tɛŋkɑuto/ (pl: -'s) tank lorry; [Am] tank truck

tanken /tɛŋkə(n)/ (tankte, heeft getankt) fill up (with): *ik heb 25 liter getankt* I put 25 litres in (the tank); *ik tank meestal super* I usually take four star; [Am] I usually take super

de **tanker** /tɛŋkər/ (pl: -s) tanker

het **tankstation** /tɛŋksta(t)ʃɔn/ (pl: -s) filling station

de **tankwagen** /tɛŋkwaɣə(n)/ (pl: -s) tank lorry; [Am] tank truck

het/de **tannine** /taninə/ (pl: -s, -n) tannin

de **tantaluskwelling** /tɑntalʏskwɛlɪŋ/ (pl: -en) (sheer) torment

de **tante** /tɑntə/ (pl: -s) **1** aunt, auntie **2** [hum] woman, female: *een lastige* ~, *geen gemakkelijke* ~ a fussy (*or:* difficult) lady/woman

Tanzania /tɑnzanija/ Tanzania

de **Tanzaniaan** /tɑnzanijan/ (pl: Tanzanianen) Tanzanian

Tanzaniaans /tɑnzanijans/ (adj) Tanzanian

de **tap** /tɑp/ (pl: -pen) **1** plug; bung; stopper; tap **2** tap; spigot: *bier van de* ~ beer on tap (*or:* draught) **3** bar: *achter de* ~ *staan* serve at the bar

de **tapas** /tɑpɑs/ (pl) tapas

de **tapasbar** /tɑpɑsbɑr/ (pl: -s) tapas bar

het **tapbier** /tɑbir/ draught beer; [Am] draft beer

tapdansen /tɛbdɑnsə(n)/ (tapdanste, heeft getapdanst) tap-dance

de **tapdanser** /tɛbdɑnsər/ (pl: -s) tap-dancer

de **tape** /tep/ (pl: -s) tape

de **tapenade** /tapənadə/ tapenade

het **tapijt** /tapɛit/ (pl: -en) carpet; [small] rug: *een vliegend* ~ a magic carpet

de **tapijttegel** /tapɛiteɣəl/ (pl: -s) carpet tile (*or:* square)

de **tapir** /tapir/ (pl: -s) tapir

de **tapkast** /tɑpkɑst/ (pl: -en) bar

de **tapkraan** /tɑpkran/ (pl: tapkranen) tap

tappen /tɑpə(n)/ (tapte, heeft getapt) **1** tap, draw (off); serve: *hier wordt bier getapt* they sell beer here; *bier* ~ tap beer **2** crack: *moppen* ~ crack (*or:* tell) jokes

taps /tɑps/ (adj, adv) tapering, conical; conically

de **taptoe** /tɑptu/ (pl: -s) tattoo

de **tapvergunning** /tɑpfərɣʏnɪŋ/ (pl: -en) licence to sell spirits; [Am] liquor license

de **tarbot** /tɑrbɔt/ (pl: -ten) turbot

het **tarief** /tarif/ (pl: tarieven) tariff, rate; fare: *het gewone* ~ *betalen* pay the standard charge (*or:* rate); *vast* ~ fixed (*or:* flat) rate; *tegen verlaagd* ~ at a reduced tariff (*or:* rate); *het volle* ~ *berekenen* charge the full rate

de **tarra** /tɑra/ tare (weight)

de **tartaar** /tɑrtar/ steak tartare

de **Tartaar** /tɑrtar/ Tartar

tarten /tɑrtə(n)/ (tartte, heeft getart) defy, flout: *de dood* ~ brave death; *het noodlot* ~ tempt fate

de **tarwe** /tɑrwə/ wheat

de **tarwebloem** /tɑrwəblum/ wheat flour

het **tarwebrood** /tɑrwəbrot/ (pl: -broden) wheat bread

het **tarwegras** /tɑrwəɣrɑs/ wheatgrass

de **tas** /tɑs/ (pl: -sen) **1** bag; satchel; (brief)case; (hand)bag: *een plastic* ~ a plastic bag **2** [Belg] cup

de **tasjesdief** /tɑʃəzdif/ (pl: -dieven) bag snatcher, purse snatcher

Tasmanië /tɑsmanijə/ Tasmania

de **tast** /tɑst/ **1** touch **2** groping, feeling: *hij greep op de* ~ *naar de lamp* he groped (*or:* felt) for the lamp; *iets op de* ~ *vinden* find sth. by touch

tastbaar /tɑstbar/ (adj, adv) tangible

tasten /tɑstə(n)/ (tastte, heeft getast)

1 grope **2** dip: *in zijn beurs* ~ dip into one's purse; [fig] *in het duister* ~ be in the dark

de **tastzin** /tɑ(st)sɪn/ touch; feeling

de **tatoeage** /tatuwaʒə/ (pl: -s) tattoo

tatoeëren /tatuwerə(n)/ (tatoeëerde, heeft getatoeëerd) tattoo: *zich laten* ~ have o.s. tattooed

de **taugé** /tɑuge/ bean sprouts

de **tautologie** /tɑutoloɣi/ (pl: -ën) tautology, tautologism

t.a.v. 1 *ten aanzien van* with regard to **2** *ter attentie van* attn., (for the) attention (of)

de **taxateur** /tɑksatør/ (pl: -s) appraiser; assessor

de **taxatie** /tɑksa(t)si/ (pl: -s) **1** assessment, appraisal: *een* ~ *verrichten* make an assessment **2** estimation **3** valuation

taxeren /tɑkserə(n)/ (taxeerde, heeft getaxeerd) evaluate, value (at): *de schade* ~ assess the damage

de **taxfreeshop** /tɛksfri:ʃɔp/ (pl: -s) duty free (shop)

de **taxi** /tɑksi/ (pl: -'s) taxi, cab: *een* ~ *bestellen* call a cab

de **taxichauffeur** /tɑksiʃofør/ (pl: -s) taxi driver

taxiën /tɑksijə(n)/ (taxiede, heeft/is getaxied) taxi

de **taxistandplaats** /tɑksistɑntplats/ (pl: -en) taxi rank; [Am] taxi stand

de **taxus** /tɑksʏs/ (pl: -sen) yew (tree)

de **tbc** /tebese/ TB

de **T-bonesteak** /tibonstek/ (pl: -s) T-bonesteak

de **tbs** /tebeɛs/ [Dutch] *terbeschikkingstelling* detention during Her/His Majesty's pleasure; detention in a hospital || ~ *krijgen* be detained under a hospital order

t.b.v. 1 *ten behoeve van* on behalf of **2** *ten bate van* in favour of

¹**te** /tə/ (adv) too: *te laat* too late; late, overdue; *dat is een beetje te* that's a bit much; *te veel om op te noemen* too much (*or:* many) to mention

²**te** /tə/ (prep) **1** to: *dreigen te vertrekken* threaten to leave; *zij ligt te slapen* she is sleeping (*or:* asleep); *een dag om nooit te vergeten* a day never to be forgotten **2** in: *te Parijs aankomen* arrive in Paris **3** to, for: *te koop* for sale || *te voet* on foot

het **teakhout** /tikhɑut/ teak

het **team** /tim/ (pl: -s) team: *een* ~ *samenstellen* put together a team; *samen een* ~ *vormen* team up together

de **teamgeest** /timɣest/ team spirit

de **teamgenoot** /ti:mɣənot/ (pl: -genoten) teammate

het **teamverband** /timvɛrbɑnt/ team: *in* ~ *werken* work in (*or:* as) a team

de **techneut** /tɛxnøt/ (pl: -en) boffin

de **technicus** /tɛxnikʏs/ (pl: technici) engineer, technician

de **techniek** /tɛxnik/ (pl: -en) **1** technique, skill: *over onvoldoende* ~ *beschikken* possess insufficient skills **2** engineering, technology

technisch /tɛxnis/ (adj) technical, technological, engineering: *de ~e dienst* the technical department; *een ~e storing* a technical hitch; *een ~e term* a technical term; *hij is niet erg* ~ he is not very technical(ly-minded); *een Lagere* (*or: Middelbare*) *Technische School* a junior (*or:* senior) secondary technical school; *een Hogere Technische School* (*or: Technische Universiteit*) a college (*or:* university) of technology

de **technologie** /tɛxnoloɣi/ technology

technologisch /tɛxnoloɣis/ (adj, adv) technological

de **teckel** /tɛkkəl/ (pl: -s) dachshund

de **teddybeer** /tɛdiber/ (pl: -beren) teddy bear

teder /tedər/ (adj, adv) tender

de **tederheid** /tedərhɛit/ tenderness

de **teef** /tef/ (pl: teven) bitch: *een loopse* ~ a bitch on (*or:* in) heat

de **teek** /tek/ (pl: teken) tick

de **teelaarde** /telardə/ humus, leaf mould

de **teelbal** /telbɑl/ (pl: -len) testicle

de **teelt** /telt/ (pl: -en) **1** culture, cultivation, production: *de* ~ *van druiven* the cultivation of grapes **2** culture; crop; harvest: *eigen* ~ home-grown

de **teen** /ten/ (pl: tenen) toe; [garlic] clove: *de grote* (*or: kleine*) ~ the big (*or:* little) toe; *op zijn tenen lopen* [fig] push o.s. to the limit; *van top tot* ~ from head to foot; *gauw op zijn ~tjes getrapt zijn* be quick to take offence, be touchy

de **teenslipper** /tenslɪpər/ (pl: -s) flip-flop

het ¹**teer** /ter/ tar

²**teer** /ter/ (adj, adv) delicate: *een tere huid* a delicate skin

de **teerling** /terlɪŋ/ (pl: -en): [fig] *de* ~ *is geworpen* the die is cast

de **tegel** /teɣəl/ (pl: -s) **1** tile; paving stone: *~s zetten* tile **2** [comp] tile

tegelijk /təɣəlɛik/ (adv) at the same time (*or:* moment), also, as well: ~ *met* at the same time as; *hij is dokter en* ~ *apotheker* he is a doctor as well as a pharmacist

tegelijkertijd /təɣələik ərtɛit/ (adv) at the same time (*or:* moment), simultaneously

het **tegelpad** /teɣəlpɑt/ tile, path; flagstone path

de **tegelvloer** /teɣəlvlur/ (pl: -en) tiled floor

de **tegelwand** /teɣəlwɑnt/ (pl: -en) tiled wall

de **tegelzetter** /teɣəlzɛtər/ (pl: -s) tiler

tegemoet /təɣəmut/ (adv): *iem.* ~ *gaan* (*or: komen, lopen*) go to meet s.o.; go (*or:* come, walk) towards s.o.; *aan iemands wensen* ~ *komen* meet s.o.'s wishes; *iem. een heel eind* ~ *komen* meet s.o. (more than) half way; *iets* ~ *zien* await (*or:* face) sth., look forward to sth.

tegemoetkomen /təɣəmutkomən/ (kwam

tegemoet, heeft/is tegemoetgekomen)
meet, come towards: *aan bezwaren* ~ meet
(*or:* give in to) objections

tegemoetkomend /təɣəmutkomənt/
(adj) oncoming, approaching: ~ *verkeer* oncoming traffic

de **tegemoetkoming** /təɣəmutkomɪŋ/ (pl:
-en) subsidy, contribution: *een* ~ *in* a contribution towards, a grant for

het **¹tegen** /teɣə(n)/ (pl: -s) con(tra), disadvantage: *alles heeft zijn **voor** en* ~ everything has its advantages and disadvantages; *de **voors** en ~s op een rij zetten* weigh the pros and cons; *de argumenten **voor** en* ~ the arguments for and against

²tegen /teɣə(n)/ (adv) against: *zijn **stem** ~ uitbrengen* vote against (*or:* no); *ergens iets (op)* ~ *hebben* mind sth., have sth. against sth.; be opposed to sth., object to sth.; *iedereen **was** ~* everybody was against it; *hij was **fel** ~* he was dead set against it

³tegen /teɣə(n)/ (prep) **1** against: ~ *de **stroom** in* against the current **2** (up) to, against: *iets ~ iem. **zeggen*** say sth. to s.o. **3** against, to, with: *vriendelijk* (*or: lomp*) ~ *iem. zijn* be friendly towards (*or:* rude to) s.o.; *daar kun je niets op ~ **hebben*** you cannot object to that; *zij **heeft** iets ~ hem* she has a grudge against him; *daar **is** toch niets op ~?* nothing wrong with that, is there?; *hij **kan** niet ~ vliegen* flying doesn't agree with him; *ergens niet ~ **kunnen*** not be able to stand (*or:* take) sth.; *er is niets ~ **te doen*** it can't be helped; *zich ~ brand **verzekeren*** take out fire insurance **4** against, counter to; in contravention of: *dat is ~ de **wet*** that is illegal (*or:* against the law) **5** towards, by, come: ~ *elf **uur*** towards eleven (o'clock), just before eleven o'clock; *by eleven; een man van ~ de **zestig*** a man getting (*or:* going) on for sixty **6** (up) against **7** against, for, at: ~ *elke **prijs*** whatever the cost; *een lening ~ 7,5 % **rente*** a loan at 7.5 % interest **8** to, (as) against: *tien ~ **één*** ten to one

tegenaan /teɣə(n)an/ (adv) (up) against: *er flink ~ **gaan*** go hard at it; *ergens (toevallig)* ~ *lopen* hit (*or:* chance) upon sth., run into sth.; [fig] *ergens voortdurend ~ **lopen*** keep running into the same problem(s)

de **tegenaanval** /teɣə(n)anval/ (pl: -len) counter-attack: *in de ~ **gaan*** counter-attack, strike (*or:* hit) back

het **tegenargument** /teɣə(n)arɣymɛnt/ (pl: -en) counter-argument

het **tegenbericht** /teɣə(n)bərɪxt/ (pl: -en) notice (*or:* message) to the contrary: *zonder ~ reken ik op uw komst* if I don't hear otherwise, I'll be expecting you

het **tegenbod** /teɣə(n)bɔt/ counter-offer

het **tegendeel** /teɣə(n)del/ opposite: *het **bewijs** van het ~ leveren* provide proof (*or:* evidence)

to the contrary

het **tegendoelpunt** /teɣə(n)dulpʏnt/ (pl: -en) goal against one('s team): *twee ~en **krijgen*** concede two goals; *een ~ **maken*** score in reply

tegendraads /teɣə(n)drats/ (adj, adv) contrary, awkward

het **tegeneffect** /teɣə(n)ɛfɛkt/ **1** counter-effect **2** backspin

tegengaan /teɣə(n)ɣan/ (ging tegen, is tegengegaan) combat, fight

het **tegengas** /teɣə(n)ɣas/: ~ *geven* resist, put up a fight

tegengesteld /teɣə(n)ɣəstɛlt/ (adj, adv) opposite: *in ~e **richting*** in the opposite direction

het **tegengestelde** /teɣə(n)ɣəstɛldə/ opposite

het **tegengif** /teɣə(n)ɣɪf/ antidote

de **tegenhanger** /teɣə(n)haŋər/ (pl: -s) counterpart

tegenhouden /teɣə(n)hɑudə(n)/ (hield tegen, heeft tegengehouden) **1** stop: *ik **laat** me door niemand ~* I won't be stopped by anyone **2** prevent, stop

tegenin /teɣə(n)ɪn/ (adv) opposed to, against: *ergens ~ **gaan*** oppose sth.

de **tegenkandidaat** /teɣə(n)kandidat/ (pl: -kandidaten) opponent, rival (candidate)

tegenkomen /teɣə(n)komə(n)/ (kwam tegen, is tegengekomen) **1** meet: *iem. op straat* ~ run (*or:* bump) into s.o. on the street; [fig] *zichzelf ~* discover sth. about o.s. **2** stumble across (*or:* upon); run across

het **tegenlicht** /teɣə(n)lɪxt/ backlight(ing)

de **tegenligger** /teɣə(n)lɪɣər/ (pl: -s) oncoming vehicle, approaching vehicle

de **tegenmaatregel** /teɣəmatreɣəl/ (pl: -en) countermeasure

tegennatuurlijk /teɣənatyrlək/ (adj, adv) unnatural, abnormal

het **tegenoffensief** /teɣə(n)ɔfɛnsif/ (pl: -offensieven) counter-offensive

tegenop /teɣə(n)ɔp/ (adv) up: *er ~ **zien** om …* not look forward to …, || *daar **kan** ik niet ~* that's too much for me; *niemand **kon** tegen hem op* nobody could match (*or:* beat) him

tegenover /teɣə(n)ɔvər/ (prep) **1** across, facing, opposite: ~ *elkaar **zitten*** sit opposite (*or:* facing) each other; *de huizen **hier** ~* the houses across from here (*or:* opposite) **2** against, as opposed to: *daar **staat** ~ dat je …* on the other hand you … **3** towards; before: *hoe **sta** je ~ die kwestie?* how do you feel about that matter? || *staat er nog iets ~?* what's in it (for me)?

tegenovergesteld /teɣə(n)ovərɣəstɛlt/ (adj) opposite; reverse

tegenoverstellen /teɣə(n)ovərstɛlə(n)/ (stelde tegenover, heeft tegenovergesteld) provide (*or:* offer) (sth.) in exchange; set (sth.) against: *ergens een financiële **vergoe-***

ding ~ offer compensation for sth.

de **tegenpartij** /te̯ɣə(n)pɑrtɛi̯/ (pl: -en) opposition; (the) other side: *een **speler** van de* ~ a player from the opposing team

de **tegenpool** /te̯ɣə(n)pol/ (pl: -polen) opposite

de **tegenprestatie** /te̯ɣə(n)prɛsta(t)si/ (pl: -s) sth. done in return (*or:* exchange): *een* ~ *leveren* do sth. in return

de **tegenslag** /te̯ɣə(n)slɑx/ (pl: -en) setback, reverse: ~ *hebben* (or: *ondervinden*) meet with (*or:* experience) adversity

tegenspartelen /te̯ɣə(n)spɑrtələ(n)/ (spartelde tegen, heeft tegengesparteld) **1** struggle **2** grumble (at, over, about), protest

het **tegenspel** /te̯ɣə(n)spɛl/ (pl: -en) defence; response: ~ *bieden* offer resistance

de **tegenspeler** /te̯ɣə(n)spelər/ (pl: -s) co-star

de **tegenspoed** /te̯ɣə(n)sput/ adversity, misfortune

de **tegenspraak** /te̯ɣə(n)sprak/ **1** objection, protest, argument: *geen* ~ *duldend* peremptory, pontifical **2** contradiction: *dat is in **flagrante** ~ met* that is in flagrant contradiction to (*or:* with)

tegenspreken /te̯ɣə(n)sprekə(n)/ (sprak tegen, heeft tegengesproken) **1** object, protest, argue (with); answer back, talk back **2** deny, contradict: *dat **gerucht** is door niemand tegengesproken* nobody disputed (*or:* refuted) the rumour; *zichzelf* ~ contradict o.s.

tegensputteren /te̯ɣə(n)spʏtərə(n)/ (sputterde tegen, heeft tegengesputterd) protest, grumble

tegenstaan /te̯ɣə(n)stan/ (stond tegen, heeft tegengestaan): *dat **eten** staat hem tegen* he can't stomach that food; *zijn **manieren** staan me tegen* I can't stand his manners

de **tegenstand** /te̯ɣə(n)stɑnt/ opposition; resistance: ~ *bieden (aan)* offer resistance (to)

de **tegenstander** /te̯ɣə(n)stɑndər/ (pl: -s) opponent: ~ *van iets zijn* be opposed to sth.

de **tegenstelling** /te̯ɣə(n)stɛlɪŋ/ (pl: -en) contrast: *in* ~ *met* (or: *tot*) in contrast with (*or:* to), contrary to

tegenstemmen /te̯ɣə(n)stɛmə(n)/ (stemde tegen, heeft tegengestemd) vote against

de **tegenstrever** /te̯ɣə(n)strevər/ (pl: -s) opponent

tegenstribbelen /te̯ɣə(n)strɪbələ(n)/ (stribbelde tegen, heeft tegengestribbeld) struggle (against), resist

tegenstrijdig /te̯ɣə(n)strɛi̯dəx/ (adj, adv) contradictory, conflicting

de **tegenstrijdigheid** /te̯ɣə(n)strɛi̯dəxhɛit/ (pl: -heden) contradiction, inconsistency

tegenvallen /te̯ɣə(n)vɑlə(n)/ (viel tegen, is tegengevallen) disappoint: *dat valt mij **van** je tegen* you disappoint me

de **tegenvaller** /te̯ɣə(n)vɑlər/ (pl: -s) disap-

pointment: *een **financiële** ~* a financial setback

de **tegenvoeter** /te̯ɣə(n)vutər/ (pl: -s) antipode

het **tegenvoorstel** /te̯ɣə(n)vorstɛl/ (pl: -len) counter-proposal

tegenwerken /te̯ɣə(n)wɛrkə(n)/ (werkte tegen, heeft tegengewerkt) work against (one, s.o.), cross, oppose

de **tegenwerking** /te̯ɣə(n)wɛrkɪŋ/ (pl: -en) opposition

tegenwerpen /te̯ɣə(n)wɛrpə(n)/ (wierp tegen, heeft tegengeworpen) object, argue

de **tegenwerping** /te̯ɣə(n)wɛrpɪŋ/ (pl: -en) objection

het **tegenwicht** /te̯ɣə(n)wɪxt/ (pl: -en) counterbalance

de **tegenwind** /te̯ɣə(n)wɪnt/ (pl: -en) headwind; [fig] opposition: *wij **hadden** ~* we had the wind against us

[1]**tegenwoordig** /teɣə(n)wo̯rdəx/ (adj) present, current: *de ~e **tijd*** the present (tense)

[2]**tegenwoordig** /teɣə(n)wo̯rdəx/ (adv) now(adays), these days: *de jeugd **van** ~* today's youth

de **tegenwoordigheid** /teɣə(n)wo̯rdəxhɛit/ presence: *in* ~ *van* in the presence of; ~ *van geest* presence of mind

de **tegenzet** /te̯ɣə(n)zɛt/ (pl: -ten) countermove, response

de **tegenzin** /te̯ɣə(n)zɪn/ dislike; [stronger] aversion: *hij doet alles **met** ~* he does everything reluctantly

tegenzitten /te̯ɣə(n)zɪtə(n)/ (zat tegen, heeft tegengezeten) be against, go against

het [1]**tegoed** /təɣu̯t/ (pl: -en) balance

[2]**tegoed** /təɣu̯t/ (adv): *zich ~ **doen** aan* feast on, tuck into, indulge in; *iets ~ **hebben*** have sth. owing (to) one; *hij **heeft** nog € 100 van mij* ~ I still owe him € 100; *dat **hebben** we nog* ~ that's still in store for us; *dat **heb** je nog van me* ~ **a)** I (still) owe you one; **b)** I'll pay you back

de **tegoedbon** /təɣu̯dbɔn/ (pl: -nen) credit note

het **tehuis** /təhœy̯s/ (pl: tehuizen) home; hostel; shelter: ~ *voor ouden van dagen* old people's home

de **teil** /tɛil/ (pl: -en) (wash)tub; washing-up bowl

het/de **teint** /tɛːnt/ complexion

teisteren /tɛi̯stərə(n)/ (teisterde, heeft geteisterd) ravage; sweep: *door de **oorlog** geteisterd* war-stricken

tekeergaan /təke̯rɣan/ (ging tekeer, is tekeergegaan) rant (and rave), storm, carry on (about sth.): *tegen iem.* ~ rant and rave at s.o.

het **teken** /te̯kə(n)/ (pl: -s) **1** sign; indication: *het is een **veeg** ~* it promises no good; *een ~ van leven* a sign of life **2** sign; symbol; signal: *een*

~ **geven** om te beginnen (or: vertrekken) give a signal to start (or: leave); het is een ~ **aan** de wand the writing is on the wall **3** mark ‖ het congres staat **in** het ~ van ... the theme of the conference will be ...

de **tekenaar** /tẹkənɑr/ (pl: -s) artist; draughtsman

de **tekendoos** /tẹkə(n)dos/ (pl: -dozen) set (or: box) of drawing instruments

tekenen /tẹkənə(n)/ (tekende, heeft getekend) **1** draw; [fig] portray; depict: **figuurtjes** ~ doodle; met potlood (or: houtskool, krijt) ~ draw in pencil (or: charcoal, crayon) **2** sign: hij tekende **voor** vier jaar he signed on for four years; **was** getekend ... signed

tekenend /tẹkənənt/ (adj) characteristic (of), typical (of)

de **tekenfilm** /tẹkə(n)fɪlm/ (pl: -s) (animated) cartoon

de **tekening** /tẹkənɪŋ/ (pl: -en) **1** drawing; design; plan: een ~ op **schaal** a scale drawing **2** pattern; marking

de **tekenles** /tẹkənlɛs/ (pl: -sen) drawing lesson

het **tekenpapier** /tẹkəmpɑpir/ drawing-paper

het **tekenpotlood** /tẹkəmpɔtlot/ (pl: -potloden) drawing pencil

de **tekentafel** /tẹkə(n)tɑfəl/ (pl: -s) drawing table (or: stand): [fig] iets **terugsturen** naar de ~ send sth. back to the drawing board

het **tekort** /təkɔrt/ (pl: -en) **1** deficit, shortfall **2** shortage, deficiency: een ~ **aan** vitamines a vitamin deficiency

tekortdoen /təkɔrtdun/ (deed tekort, heeft tekortgedaan): **iem.** ~ wrong s.o.; de **waarheid** ~ not be quite truthful, squeeze the truth

tekortkomen /təkɔrtkomə(n)/ (kwam tekort, is tekortgekomen) run short (of): hij komt drie **euro** tekort he's three euros short; we komen **handen** tekort we're short-handed (or: short of staff, short-staffed); we komen drie **man** tekort we're three men short; **niets** ~ lack for nothing, not go short; zij kwam **ogen en oren tekort** [roughly] her eyes were popping out of her head, [roughly] she didn't know where to start

de **tekortkoming** /təkɔrtkomɪŋ/ (pl: -en) shortcoming, failing

tekortschieten /təkɔrtsχitə(n)/ (schoot tekort, heeft tekortgeschoten) not come up to the mark, not be up to scratch: **woorden** schieten tekort om ... there are no words to (describe, express, say ...)

de **tekst** /tɛkst/ (pl: -en) **1** text; lines: **lopende** ~ running text **2** words, lyrics

de **tekstballon** /tɛkstbɑlɔn/ (pl: -nen) balloon

het **tekstbericht** /tɛkstbərɪχt/ (pl: -en) text message: iem. een ~je **sturen** text s.o.

het **tekstbestand** /tɛkstbəstɑnt/ (pl: -en) [comp] text file

de **tekstschrijver** /tɛkstsχreivər/ (pl: -s) script-

writer; copywriter; songwriter

de **tekstverklaring** /tɛkstfərklɑrɪŋ/ (pl: -en) close reading

de **tekstverwerker** /tɛkstfərwɛrkər/ (pl: -s) word processor

de **tekstverwerking** /tɛkstfərwɛrkɪŋ/ word processing

de **tel** /tɛl/ **1** count: ik ben de ~ **kwijt** I've lost count **2** moment, second: in twee ~len ben ik klaar I'll be ready in two ticks (or: a jiffy) **3** account: weinig **in** ~ zijn not count for much ‖ op zijn ~len **passen** watch one's step, mind one's p's and q's; [Belg] van geen ~ zijn be of little (or: no) account

telbaar /tɛlbɑr/ (adj) countable: ~ **naamwoord** count(able) noun

telebankieren /tẹləbɑŋkirə(n)/ (telebankierde, heeft getelebankierd) computerized banking

de **telecommunicatie** /tẹləkɔmynika(t)si/ telecommunication

de **telefax** /tẹləfɑks/ (pl: -en) **1** (tele)fax **2** (tele)fax (machine)

telefoneren /tẹləfonẹrə(n)/ (telefoneerde, heeft getelefoneerd) telephone, phone, call: hij **zit te** ~ he's on the phone; met iem. ~ telephone s.o.

de **telefonie** /tẹləfoni/ **1** telephony **2** telephone system

telefonisch /tẹləfonis/ (adj, adv) by telephone: ben je ~ **bereikbaar?** can you be reached by phone?; we hebben ~ **contact** met elkaar gehad we have talked to each other on the phone

de **telefonist** /tẹləfonɪst/ (pl: -en) telephonist, (switchboard) operator

de **telefoon** /tẹləfon/ (pl: -s) **1** telephone, phone: **draagbare (draadloze)** ~ cellular (tele)phone, cellphone, mobile phone; de ~ **gaat** the phone is ringing; blijft u even **aan** de ~? would you hold on for a moment please?; **per** ~ by telephone; zijn ~ **op stil** zetten mute his phone; zijn ~ **uitschakelen** turn off his phone **2** receiver: de ~ **neerleggen** put down the receiver (or: phone); de ~ **opnemen** answer the phone **3** (telephone) call: er is ~ **voor** u there's a (phone) call for you

de **telefoonaansluiting** /tẹləfonanslœytɪŋ/ (pl: -en) (telephone) connection

de **telefoonbeantwoorder** /tẹləfombəɑntwordər/ (pl: -s) answering machine

het **telefoonboek** /tẹləfombuk/ (pl: -en) (telephone) directory, phone book

de **telefooncel** /tẹləfɔnsɛl/ (pl: -len) telephone box (or: booth)

de **telefooncentrale** /tẹləfɔnsɛntralə/ (pl: -s) (telephone) exchange; switchboard

het **telefoongesprek** /tẹləfɔnɣəsprɛk/ (pl: -ken) **1** telephone conversation **2** phone call

de **telefoongids** /tẹləfɔnɣɪts/ (pl: -en) (telephone) directory, phone book de **telefoonkaart** /teləfo̯nkart/ (pl: -en) phonecard

de **telefoonlijn** /teləfo̯nlɛin/ telephone line

het **telefoonnummer** /teləfo̯nʏmər/ (pl: -s) (phone) number: *geheim* ~ ex-directory number

de **telefoonrekening** /teləfo̯nrekənɪŋ/ (pl: -en) telephone bill

de **telefoonseks** /teləfo̯nsɛks/ telephone sex

de **telefoontik** /teləfo̯ntɪk/ (telephone) unit

het **telefoontje** /teləfo̯ncə/ (pl: -s) (phone) call: *een ~ plegen* make a call

het **telefoontoestel** /teləfo̯ntustɛl/ (pl: -len) telephone

de **telegraaf** /teləɣra̯f/ (pl: -grafen) telegraph

telegraferen /teləɣrafe̯rə(n)/ (telegrafeerde, heeft getelegrafeerd) telegraph: *hij telegrafeerde naar Parijs* he telegraphed (*or:* cabled) Paris

de **telegrafie** /teləɣrafi̯/ telegraphy

het **telegram** /teləɣra̯m/ (pl: -men) telegram: *iem. een ~ sturen* telegraph (*or:* cable) s.o.; *per* ~ by telegram (*or:* cable)

de **telegramstijl** /teləɣra̯mstɛil/ telegram style

de **telelens** /te̯lelɛns/ (pl: -lenzen) telephoto lens

de **telemarketeer** /te̯ləma:rkəti:r/ (pl: -s) telemarketer

de **telemarketing** /te̯ləma:rkətɪŋ/ telemarketing

telen /te̯lə(n)/ (teelde, heeft geteeld) grow, cultivate

het **teleonthaal** /te̯leɔnthal/ [Belg] helpline

de **telepathie** /teləpati̯/ telepathy

telepathisch /teləpa̯tis/ (adj, adv) telepathic

de **teler** /te̯lər/ (pl: -s) grower

de **telescoop** /teləsko̯p/ (pl: -scopen) telescope

teleshoppen /te̯ləʃɔpə(n)/ (teleshopte, heeft geteleshopt) teleshopping

de **teletekst** /te̯lətɛkst/ teletext

teleurstellen /təlø̯rstɛlə(n)/ (stelde teleur, heeft teleurgesteld) disappoint, let down, be disappointing: *zich teleurgesteld voelen* feel disappointed; *stel mij niet teleur* don't let me down; *teleurgesteld zijn over iets (iem.)* be disappointed with sth. (in s.o.)

teleurstellend /təlø̯rstɛlənt/ (adj) disappointing

de **teleurstelling** /təlø̯rstɛlɪŋ/ (pl: -en) disappointment

televergaderen /te̯ləvərɣadərə(n)/ teleconferencing

de **televisie** /teləvi̯zi/ (pl: -s) television; television set: *(naar de) ~ kijken* watch television

het **televisiecircuit** /teləvi̯zisɪrkwi/ (pl: -s) television circuit; CCTV

de **televisiefilm** /teləvi̯zifɪlm/ (pl: -s) TV film

de **televisiekijker** /teləvi̯zikɛikər/ (pl: -s) (television) viewer

de **televisieomroep** /teləvi̯ziɔmrup/ (pl: -en) television company

het **televisieprogramma** /teləvi̯ziprɔɣrama/ television programme

de **televisieserie** /teləvi̯ziseri/ (pl: -s) television series

het **televisietoestel** /teləvi̯zitustɛl/ (pl: -len) television set, TV set

de **televisie-uitzending** /teləvi̯ziœytsɛndɪŋ/ (pl: -en) television broadcast (*or:* programme)

de **televisiezender** /teləvi̯zizɛndər/ (pl: -s) **1** television channel; [Am] television station **2** television transmitter (*or:* mast)

het **telewerken** /te̯ləwɛrkə(n)/ teleworking

de **telex** /te̯lɛks/ telex: *per* ~ by telex

de **telg** /tɛlx/ (pl: -en) descendant

de **telganger** /tɛ̯lɣaŋər/ (pl: -s) ambler

telkens /tɛ̯lkəns/ (adv) **1** every time, in each case: ~ *en* ~ *weer*, ~ *maar weer* again and again, time and (time) again **2** repeatedly

[1]**tellen** /tɛ̯lə(n)/ (telde, heeft geteld) **1** count: *tot tien* ~ count (up) to ten **2** count, matter: *het enige dat telt bij hem* the only thing that matters to him

[2]**tellen** /tɛ̯lə(n)/ (telde, heeft geteld) **1** count: *wel (goed)* geteld zijn er dertig there are thirty all told **2** number, have; consist of: *het huis telde 20 kamers* the house had 20 rooms

de **teller** /tɛ̯lər/ (pl: -s) **1** [maths] numerator: *de* ~ *en de noemer* the numerator and the denominator **2** counter, meter

de **telling** /tɛ̯lɪŋ/ (pl: -en) count(ing): *de ~ bijhouden* keep count (*or:* score)

het **telraam** /tɛ̯lram/ (pl: telramen) abacus

het **telwoord** /tɛ̯lwort/ (pl: -en) numeral

temeer /təme̯r/ (adv) all the more

temmen /tɛ̯mə(n)/ (temde, heeft getemd) **1** tame, domesticate: *zijn driften* (*or:* *hartstochten*) ~ control one's urges (*or:* passions) **2** tame; break

de **temmer** /tɛ̯mər/ (pl: -s) tamer

de **tempel** /tɛ̯mpəl/ (pl: -s) temple

het **temperament** /tɛmpəramɛ̯nt/ (pl: -en) **1** temperament, disposition **2** spirit

de **temperatuur** /tɛmpəraty̯r/ (pl: temperaturen) temperature: *iemands ~ opnemen* take s.o.'s temperature; *op* ~ *moeten komen* have to warm up

de **temperatuurstijging** /tɛmpəraty̯rstɛiɣɪŋ/ rise (*or:* increase) in temperature

temperen /tɛ̯mpərə(n)/ (temperde, heeft getemperd) temper, mitigate

het **tempo** /tɛ̯mpo/ (pl: -'s) **1** tempo, pace: *het jachtige* ~ *van het moderne leven* the feverish pace of modern life; *het ~ aangeven* set the pace; *het ~ opvoeren* increase the pace **2** [mus] tempo, time **3** speed: ~ *maken* make good time

temporiseren /tɛmporize̯rə(n)/ (temporiseerde, heeft getemporiseerd) stall, play for time

ten /tɛn/ (prep) at, in, to, on: ~ *huize van* at the house/home of, at …'s place; ~ *westen van* (to the) west of; ~ *tweede* secondly, in the second place

de **tendens** /tɛndɛns/ (pl: -en) tendency, trend

tendentieus /tɛndɛnʃøs/ (adj, adv) tendentious, biased

tenderen /tɛndɛrə(n)/ (tenderde, heeft getenderd) tend (towards/to)

teneinde /tɛnɛində/ (conj) so that, in order to

tenenkrommend /tenə(n)krɔmənt/ (adj) cringe-making

de **teneur** /tənør/ tenor

de **tengel** /tɛŋəl/ (pl: -s) paw

tenger /tɛŋər/ (adj) slight, delicate: ~ *gebouwd* slightly built

tenietdoen /tənidun/ (deed teniet, heeft tenietgedaan) annul, nullify, undo

tenietgaan /tənitxan/ (ging teniet, is tenietgegaan) perish

de **tenlastelegging** /tɛnlɒstələɣɪŋ/ (pl: -en) [law] charge, indictment

tenminste /tɛmɪnstə/ (adv) at least: *ik doe het liever niet*, ~ *niet meteen* I'd rather not, at least not right away; *dat is* ~ *iets* that is at least sth.

ten minste /tɛmɪnstə/ (adv) see *minst*

het **tennis** /tɛnɪs/ tennis

de **tennisarm** /tɛnɪsɑrm/ tennis elbow

de **tennisbaan** /tɛnɪzban/ (pl: -banen) tennis court: *verharde* ~ hard court

de **tennisbal** /tɛnɪzbɑl/ (pl: -len) tennis ball

de **tennishal** /tɛnɪshɑl/ (pl: -len) indoor tennis court(s)

het/de **tennisracket** /tɛnɪsrɛkət/ (pl: -s) tennis racket

tennissen /tɛnɪsə(n)/ (tenniste, heeft getennist) play tennis

de **tennisser** /tɛnɪsər/ (pl: -s) tennis player

de **tenor** /tənɔr/ (pl: -en) tenor

tenslotte /tɛnslɔtə/ (adv) after all: ~ *is zij nog maar een kind* after all she's only a child

ten slotte /tɛnslɔtə/ (adv) see *slot*

de **tent** /tɛnt/ (pl: -en) 1 tent; stand: *een* ~ *opslaan* (or: *opzetten, afbreken*) pitch (or: put up, take down) a tent; *iem. uit zijn* ~ *lokken* draw s.o. out 2 place, joint || *ze braken de* ~ *bijna af* you could hardly keep them in their seats

de **tentakel** /tɛntakəl/ (pl: -s) tentacle

het **tentamen** /tɛntamə(n)/ (pl: -s) exam: ~ *doen* take an exam

het **tentenkamp** /tɛntə(n)kɑmp/ (pl: -en) (en)-camp(ment), campsite

de **tentharing** /tɛntharɪŋ/ (pl: -en) tent peg

de **tentluifel** /tɛntlœyfəl/ (pl: -s) tent awning

tentoonspreiden /tɛntonsprɛidə(n)/ (spreidde tentoon, heeft tentoongespreid) display; show (off)

tentoonstellen /tɛntonstɛlə(n)/ (stelde tentoon, heeft tentoongesteld) exhibit, display: *tentoongestelde voorwerpen* exhibits, articles on display

de **tentoonstelling** /tɛntonstɛlɪŋ/ (pl: -en) exhibition, show, display

de **tentstok** /tɛntstɔk/ (pl: -ken) tent pole

het **tentzeil** /tɛntsɛil/ (pl: -en) canvas

het/de **tenue** /təny/ (pl: -s) dress, uniform

de **tenuitvoerlegging** /tɛnœytfurlɛɣɪŋ/ (pl: -en) execution

tenzij /tɛnzɛi/ (conj) unless, except(ing)

de **tepel** /tepəl/ (pl: -s) nipple; teat

ter /tɛr/ (prep) at, to, in, on: ~ *plaatse* on the spot, locally

de **teraardebestelling** /tɛrardəbəstɛlɪŋ/ (pl: -en) [form] burial, funeral

terdege /tɛrdeɣə/ (adv) thoroughly, properly

de **terdoodveroordeelde** /tɛrdotfərordeldə/ (pl: -n) condemned man/woman

[1] **terecht** /tərɛxt/ (adj) correct, appropriate: *een* ~*e opmerking* an appropriate remark

[2] **terecht** /tərɛxt/ (adv) 1 found (again): *haar horloge is* ~ her watch has been found 2 rightly: *hij is voor zijn examen gezakt, en* ~ he failed his examination and rightly so

terechtbrengen /tərɛxtbrɛŋə(n)/ (bracht terecht, heeft terechtgebracht): *niet veel* ~ *van iets* not make much of sth., not have much success with sth.

terechtkomen /tərɛxtkomə(n)/ (kwam terecht, is terechtgekomen) 1 fall, land, end up (in, on, at): *lelijk* ~ have (or: take) a nasty fall 2 turn out all right: *wat is er van hem terechtgekomen?* what has happened to him?

terechtkunnen /tərɛxtkynə(n)/ (kon terecht, heeft terechtgekund) 1 go into, enter 2 (get) help (from): *voor al uw vragen kunt u terecht bij* … if you have any questions, please contact …; *daarmee kun je overal terecht* that will do (or: be acceptable) everywhere

terechtstaan /tərɛxtstan/ (stond terecht, heeft terechtgestaan) stand trial, be tried: ~ *wegens diefstal* be tried for theft

terechtstellen /tərɛxtstɛlə(n)/ (stelde terecht, heeft terechtgesteld) execute, put to death

de **terechtstelling** /tərɛxtstɛlɪŋ/ (pl: -en) execution

terechtwijzen /tərɛxtwɛizə(n)/ (wees terecht, heeft terechtgewezen) reprimand, reprove, put s.o. in one's place

de **terechtwijzing** /tərɛxtwɛizɪŋ/ (pl: -en) reprimand

teren /terə(n)/ (teerde, heeft geteerd) live (on, off)

tergen /tɛrɣə(n)/ (tergde, heeft getergd) provoke (deliberately), badger, bait: *iem. zo* ~ *dat hij iets doet* provoke s.o. into (doing) sth.

tergend /tɛrɣənt/ (adj, adv) provocative: ~ *langzaam* exasperatingly slow

de **¹tering** /terɪŋ/ (pl: -en) consumption, tuberculosis || *krijg toch de ~!* bugger off!

²tering /terɪŋ/ (int) bugger

terloops /tɛrlops/ (adj, adv) casual, passing

de **term** /tɛrm/ (pl: -en) term, expression: *in bedekte ~en iets meedelen* speak about sth. in guarded terms

de **termiet** /tɛrmit/ (pl: -en) termite, white ant

de **termijn** /tɛrmɛin/ (pl: -en) **1** term, period: *op korte* (or: *op lange*) ~ in the short (or: long) term; *op kortst mogelijke* ~ as soon as possible **2** deadline: *een ~ vaststellen* set a deadline **3** instalment **4** [pol] term of office: *gekozen voor een tweede* ~ elected for a second term (of office)

de **termijnmarkt** /tɛrmɛinmɑrkt/ (pl: -en) forward market, futures market: *de ~ voor goud* the forward market in gold, gold futures

terminaal /tɛrminal/ (adj) terminal, final: *terminale zorg* terminal care

de **terminal** /tʏrmɪnəl/ (pl: -s) terminal

de **terminologie** /tɛrminoloɣi/ (pl: -ën) terminology, jargon

de **terminus** /tɛrminʏs/ (pl: termini) [Belg] terminus

ternauwernood /tɛrnɑuwərnot/ (adv) hardly, scarcely, barely

terneergeslagen /tɛrneːrɣəslaɣə(n)/ (adj) depressed, downcast: *een ~ indruk maken* seem down

de **terp** /tɛrp/ (pl: -en) mound, terp

de **terpentijn** /tɛrpəntɛin/ turpentine

het **¹terracotta** /tɛrakɔta/ terra cotta

²terracotta /tɛrakɔta/ (adj) terracotta

het **terrarium** /tɛrarijʏm/ (pl: -s, terraria) terrarium

het **terras** /tɛrɑs/ (pl: -sen) **1** pavement café; [Am] sidewalk café; outdoor café: *op een ~je zitten* sit in an outdoor café **2** terrace, patio **3** terrace, sunroof

de **terrashaard** /tɛrɑshart/ (pl: -en) outdoor fireplace

het **terrein** /tɛrɛin/ (pl: -en) **1** ground(s), territory; terrain: *de voetbalclub speelde op eigen* ~ the football team played on home turf; *eigen* ~ (or: *privéterrein*) private property; *het* ~ *verkennen* a) [literally] explore the area; b) [fig] scout (out) the territory; ~ *winnen* gain ground **2** [fig] field, ground: *zich op bekend* ~ *bevinden* be on familiar ground; *zich op gevaarlijk* ~ *begeven* be on slippery ground, be on thin ice; *onderzoek doen op een bepaald* ~ do research in a particular area (or: field)

de **terreinwagen** /tɛrɛinwaɣə(n)/ (pl: -s) all-terrain vehicle

de **terreinwinst** /tɛrɛinwɪnst/ territorial gain: ~ *boeken* gain ground

de **terreur** /tɛrør/ terror

het **terreuralarm** /tɛrøralɑrm/ terror alert, terror alarm

de **terreurcel** /tɛrørsɛl/ (pl: -len) terrorist cell

de **terreurdreiging** /tɛrørdrɛiɣɪŋ/ terror threat

de **terriër** /tɛrijər/ (pl: -s) terrier

de **terrine** /tɛrinə/ (pl: -s) tureen

territoriaal /tɛritor(i)jal/ (adj) territorial

het **territorium** /tɛritor(i)jʏm/ (pl: territoria) territory

terroriseren /tɛrorizɛrə(n)/ (terroriseerde, heeft geterroriseerd) terrorize

het **terrorisme** /tɛrorɪsmə/ terrorism

de **terrorist** /tɛrorɪst/ (pl: -en) terrorist

terroristisch /tɛrorɪstis/ (adj, adv) terrorist(ic): *een ~ aanslag* a terrorist attack

terstond /tɛrstɔnt/ (adv) **1** at once, immediately **2** presently, shortly

tertiair /tɛr(t)sjɛːr/ (adj) tertiary: ~ *onderwijs* higher education

de **terts** /tɛrts/ (pl: -en) [mus] tierce, third: *grote* ~ major third; *kleine* ~ minor third

terug /tərʏx/ (adv) **1** back: *hij wil zijn fiets* ~ he wants his bike back; *ik ben zo* ~ I'll be back in a minute; *heb je* ~ *van 20 euro?* do you have change for 20 euros?; *wij moeten* ~ we have to go back; *heen en* ~ back and forth; ~ *naar af* back to square one; ~ *uit het buitenland* back from abroad; ~ *van weg geweest* a) be back again; b) [fig] have made a comeback **2** [Belg] again || *daar heeft hij niet van* ~ that's too much for him

terugbellen /tərʏxbɛlə(n)/ (belde terug, heeft teruggebeld) call back

terugbetalen /tərʏɣbətalə(n)/ (betaalde terug, heeft terugbetaald) pay back, refund

de **terugbetaling** /tərʏɣbətalɪŋ/ (pl: -en) repayment, reimbursement

de **terugblik** /tərʏɣblɪk/ review, retrospect(ive)

terugblikken /tərʏɣblɪkə(n)/ (blikte terug, heeft teruggeblikt) look back

terugbrengen /tərʏɣbrɛŋə(n)/ (bracht terug, heeft teruggebracht) **1** bring back, take back, return: *een geleend boek* ~ return a borrowed book **2** restore: *iets in de oorspronkelijke staat* ~ restore sth. to its original state **3** reduce, cut back: *de werkloosheid* (or: *inflatie*) ~ reduce unemployment (or: inflation)

terugdeinzen /tərʏɣdɛinzə(n)/ (deinsde terug, is teruggedeinsd) shrink, recoil: *voor niets* ~ stop at nothing

terugdenken /tərʏɣdɛŋkə(n)/ (dacht terug, heeft teruggedacht) think back to: *met plezier aan iets* ~ remember sth. with pleasure

terugdoen /tərʏɣdun/ (deed terug, heeft teruggedaan) **1** put back **2** return, do in return: *doe hem de groeten terug* return the compliments to him

terugdraaien /tərʏɣdrajə(n)/ (draaide terug, heeft teruggedraaid) reverse, change,

undo: *een* **maatregel** ~ reverse a measure
terugfluiten /tərʏxflœytə(n)/ (floot terug, heeft teruggefloten) call back
teruggaan /tərʏxan/ (ging terug, is teruggegaan) go back, return: ~ *in de geschiedenis* (or: *tijd*) go back in history (or: time); *naar huis* ~ go back home
de **teruggang** /tərʏxaŋ/ decline, decrease: *economische* ~ economic recession
de **teruggave** /tərʏxavə/ restoration, return, restitution: ~ *van de* **belasting** income tax refund
teruggetrokken /tərʏxətrɔkə(n)/ (adj) retired, withdrawn: *een* ~ *leven leiden* lead a retired (or: secluded) life
teruggeven /tərʏxevə(n)/ (gaf terug, heeft teruggegeven) **1** give back, return: *ik zal je het boek morgen* ~ I'll return the book (to you) tomorrow **2** give (back), refund: *hij kon niet* ~ *van vijftig euro* he couldn't change a fifty-euro note
terughalen /tərʏxhalə(n)/ (haalde terug, heeft teruggehaald) **1** call back **2** [comp] recover: *gewiste* **bestanden** ~ recover deleted files **3** pull back, withdraw: *producten* ~ *uit de* **winkels** recall products from shops
terughoudend /tərʏxhaudənt/ (adj) reserved, reticent
de **terugkeer** /tərʏxker/ return, comeback, recurrence
terugkeren /tərʏxkerə(n)/ (keerde terug, is teruggekeerd) return, come back, go back; recur: *naar huis* ~ return home; *een* **jaarlijks** ~d *festival* a recurring yearly festival
¹**terugkijken** /tərʏxkɛikə(n)/ (keek terug, heeft teruggekeken) look back (on, upon)
²**terugkijken** /tərʏxkɛikə(n)/ (keek terug, heeft teruggekeken) watch again
terugkomen /tərʏxkomə(n)/ (kwam terug, is teruggekomen) **1** return, come back; recur: *ze kan elk moment* ~ she may be back (at) any moment; *weer* ~ *bij het begin* come full circle; *daar kom ik nog* **op** *terug* I'll come back to that; *op een beslissing* ~ reconsider a decision; *hij is er* **van** *teruggekomen* he changed his mind **2** bounce (back): *mijn* **mailtje** *kwam weer terug* my email bounced
de **terugkomst** /tərʏxkɔmst/ return: *bij zijn* ~ on his return
terugkoppelen /tərʏxkɔpələ(n)/ (koppelde terug, heeft teruggekoppeld) give feedback (information) (to); submit (to)
terugkrabbelen /tərʏxkrɑbələ(n)/ (krabbelde terug, is teruggekrabbeld) back out; go back on; cop out, opt out
terugkrijgen /tərʏxkrɛiɣə(n)/ (kreeg terug, heeft teruggekregen) **1** get back, recover, regain: *zijn* **goederen** ~ get one's goods (or: things) back **2** get in return: *te weinig* **(wissel)geld** ~ be short-changed
terugleggen /tərʏxlɛɣə(n)/ (legde terug,

heeft teruggelegd) put back
de **terugloop** /tərʏxlop/ fall(ing-off), decrease
teruglopen /tərʏxlopə(n)/ (liep terug, is teruggelopen) **1** walk back; flow back **2** drop, fall, decline: *de* **dollar** *liep nog verder terug* the dollar suffered a further setback
terugnemen /tərʏxnemə(n)/ (nam terug, heeft teruggenomen) take back; retract: [fig] *gas* ~ ease up (or: off), take things easy; *zijn* **woorden** ~ retract (or: take back) one's words
de **terugreis** /tərʏxrɛis/ (pl: -reizen) return trip
terugrijden /tərʏxrɛidə(n)/ (reed terug, heeft/is teruggereden) drive back; ride back
terugroepen /tərʏxrupə(n)/ (riep terug, heeft teruggeroepen) call back, recall; call off: *de* **acteurs** *werden tot driemaal toe teruggeroepen* the actors had three curtain calls
terugschakelen /tərʏxsxakələ(n)/ (schakelde terug, heeft/is teruggeschakeld) change down, shift down
terugschrijven /tərʏxsxrɛivə(n)/ (schreef terug, heeft teruggeschreven) write back
terugschrikken /tərʏxsxrɪkə(n)/ (schrok terug, is teruggeschrikt) **1** recoil; shy **2** [fig] recoil, baulk: ~ *van de hoge bouwkosten* baulk at the high construction costs; *nergens* **voor** ~ be afraid of nothing
terugslaan /tərʏxslan/ (sloeg terug, heeft teruggeslagen) **1** hit back, strike back **2** [fig] strike back **3** backfire: *de* **motor** *slaat terug* the engine backfires **4** blow back, move back
de **terugslag** /tərʏxslɑx/ **1** recoil(ing); backfire: *het geweer* **had** *een ontzettende* ~ the gun had a terrible kick (or: recoil) **2** reaction, backlash: *een* ~ **krijgen** be set back, experience a backlash
terugspelen /tərʏxspelə(n)/ (speelde terug, heeft teruggespeeld) play back
terugspoelen /tərʏxspulə(n)/ (spoelde terug, heeft teruggespoeld) rewind
terugsturen /tərʏxstyrə(n)/ (stuurde terug, heeft teruggestuurd) send back, return
de **terugtocht** /tərʏxtɔxt/ (pl: -en) journey back, journey home
de **terugtraprem** /tərʏxtrɑprɛm/ (pl: -men) hub brake, back-pedalling brake
terugtreden /tərʏxtredə(n)/ (trad terug, is teruggetreden) withdraw (from)
¹**terugtrekken** /tərʏxtrɛkə(n)/ (trok terug, heeft teruggetrokken) **1** withdraw: **troepen** ~ withdraw (or: pull back) troops **2** draw back, pull back
zich ²**terugtrekken** /tərʏxtrɛkə(n)/ (trok zich terug, heeft zich teruggetrokken) **1** retire, retreat: *zich* ~ **op** *het platteland* retreat to the country **2** withdraw (from): *zich* **voor** *een examen* ~ withdraw from an exam
de **terugval** /tərʏxfal/ reversion, relapse; [com] spin
terugvallen /tərʏxfalə(n)/ (viel terug, is te-

ruggevallen) (+ op) fall back on

terugverlangen /təryꭓfərlɑŋə(n)/ (verlangde terug, heeft terugverlangd) recall longingly: *naar huis ~* long to go back home

terugvinden /təryꭓfɪndə(n)/ (vond terug, heeft teruggevonden) find again, recover

terugvragen /təryꭓfraꭖə(n)/ (vroeg terug, heeft teruggevraagd) ask back

de **terugwedstrijd** /təryꭓwɛtstrɛit/ (pl: -en) [Belg] return match

de **terugweg** /təryꭓwɛꭏ/ (pl: -en) way back: *op de ~ gaan we bij oma langs* on the way back we shall drop in on grandma

terugwerken /təryꭓwɛrkə(n)/ (werkte terug, heeft teruggewerkt) be retrospective, be retroactive: *met ~de kracht* retrospectively

terugzetten /təryꭓsɛtə(n)/ (zette terug, heeft teruggezet) put back, set back, replace: *de wijzers ~* put (or: move) back the hands; *de teller ~ op nul* reset the counter (to zero)

terugzien /təryꭓsin/ (zag terug, heeft teruggezien) see again

terwijl /tɛrwɛil/ (conj) **1** while: *~ hij omkeek, ontsnapte de dief* while he looked round, the thief escaped **2** whereas, while: *hij werkt over, ~ zijn vrouw vandaag jarig is* he is working overtime even though his wife has her birthday today

terzijde /tɛrzɛidə/ (adv) aside: *~ leggen* put aside; *iem. ~ staan* assist s.o., stand by s.o.

de **test** /tɛst/ (pl: -s) test: *een schriftelijke ~* a written test

het **testament** /tɛstamɛnt/ (pl: -en) **1** will: *een ~ maken* (or: *herroepen*) make (or: revoke) a will **2** Testament

testamentair /tɛstamɛntɛːr/ (adj, adv) testamentary

het **testbeeld** /tɛstbelt/ (pl: -en) test card

de **testcase** /tɛstkes/ (pl: -s) test (case), experiment

testen /tɛstə(n)/ (testte, heeft getest) test: [sport] *hij is positief getest op doping* he tested positive for doping

de **testikel** /tɛstikəl/ (pl: -s) testicle

het **testosteron** /tɛstosterɔn/ testosterone

de **testpiloot** /tɛstpilot/ (pl: -piloten) test pilot

de **tetanus** /tetanʏs/ tetanus

de **teug** /tøꭓ/ (pl: -en) draught; [Am] draft; pull: *met volle ~en van iets genieten* enjoy sth. thoroughly (or: to the full); *hij dronk het glas in één ~ leeg* he emptied the glass at a draught, he tossed off his drink

de **teugel** /tøꭖəl/ (pl: -s) rein: *de ~s in handen nemen* take (up) the reins, assume control

teut /tøt/ (adj) [inform] **1** dawdler **2** bore

teuten /tøtə(n)/ (teutte, heeft geteut) [inform] **1** dilly-dally, dawdle **2** drivel, chatter

het **teveel** /təvel/ surplus

tevens /tevəns/ (adv) also, besides, as well

as; at the same time: *hij was voorzitter en ~ penningmeester* he was chairman and treasurer at the same time; *de zesde en ~ laatste aflevering* the sixth and final episode; *de kantine wordt ~ gebruikt als bingohal* the canteen is also used as a bingo hall

tevergeefs /təvərꭖefs/ (adj, adv) in vain, vainly

tevoorschijn /təvorsꭓɛin/ (adv): *tevoorschijn komen* appear; come out; *tevoorschijn brengen* produce; *zijn zakdoek tevoorschijn halen* take out one's handkerchief

tevoren /təvorə(n)/ (adv) before, previously: *van ~* before(hand), in advance; *we waren er ruim van ~* we were there in plenty of time

tevreden /təvredə(n)/ (adj) satisfied, contented

de **tevredenheid** /təvredənhɛit/ satisfaction: *werk naar ~ verrichten* work satisfactorily; *tot volle ~ van* to the complete satisfaction of

tevredenstellen /təvredə(n)stɛlə(n)/ (stelde tevreden, heeft tevredengesteld) satisfy

tevree /təvre/ (adj) satisfied, happy

de **tewaterlating** /təwatərlatɪŋ/ (pl: -en) launching

teweegbrengen /təweꭖbrɛŋə(n)/ (bracht teweeg, heeft teweeggebracht) bring about; bring on; produce

tewerkstellen /təwɛrkstɛlə(n)/ (stelde tewerk, heeft tewerkgesteld) employ; hire

het/de **textiel** /tɛkstil/ textile

de **textielindustrie** /tɛkstilɪndʏstri/ textile industry

tezamen /təzamə(n)/ (adv) together

de **tgv** /teꭖeve/ High Speed Train

t.g.v. 1 *ten gevolge van* as a result of, resulting from **2** *ter gelegenheid van* on the occasion of

het **Thai** /tɑj/ Thai

Thailand /tɑjlɑnt/ Thailand

de **Thailander** /tɑjlɑndər/ (pl: -s) Thai

Thais /tɑjs/ (adj) Thai

thans /tɑns/ (adv) at present, now

het **theater** /tejatər/ (pl: -s) **1** theatre; cinema; [Am] movie theater **2** dramatic arts, performing arts, (the) stage

de **theatervoorstelling** /tejatərvorstɛlɪŋ/ (pl: -en) theatre performance

theatraal /tejatral/ (adj, adv) theatrical

de **thee** /te/ tea: *~ met citroen* tea with lemon, lemon tea; *~ drinken* drink (or: have) tea; *~ inschenken* pour out tea; *een kopje ~* a cup of tea; *~ laten trekken* brew tea; *op de ~ komen* come to tea; *slappe ~* weak tea; *~ met een smaakje* flavoured tea; *sterke ~* strong tea; *~ zetten* make tea; *zwarte ~* black tea

de **theedoek** /teduk/ (pl: -en) tea towel

theedrinken /tedrɪŋkə(n)/ (dronk thee, heeft theegedronken) have tea

het **theelepeltje** /telepəlcə/ (pl: -s) teaspoon; teaspoonful het **theelichtje** /tˈɛlɪxjə/ (pl: -s) hot plate (for tea); tea-warmer

de **Theems** /tems/ Thames

de **theemuts** /tˈemʏts/ (pl: -en) (tea-)cosy

de **theepauze** /tˈepɑuzə/ (pl: -s) tea break

de **theepot** /tˈepɔt/ (pl: -ten) teapot

het **theeservies** /tˈesɛrvis/ (pl: -serviezen) tea service

het **theewater** /tˈewatər/ tea-water: ~ *opzetten* put the kettle on (for tea) || *boven zijn* ~ *zijn* have had a drop too much

het **theezakje** /tˈezɑkjə/ (pl: -s) tea bag

het **theezeefje** /tˈezefjə/ (pl: -s) tea strainer

het **thema** /tˈema/ (pl: -'s) theme, subject (matter): *een* ~ *aansnijden* broach a subject

het **themakanaal** /tˈemakanal/ (pl: -kanalen) specialty channel

het **themapark** /tˈemapɑrk/ (pl: -en) theme park

de **thematiek** /tematˈik/ theme(s)

thematisch /tematˈis/ (adj, adv) thematic

de **theologie** /tejoloɣˈi/ theology, divinity

theologisch /tejoloɣˈis/ (adj, adv) theological

de **theoloog** /tejolˈox/ (pl: -logen) theologian

de **theoreticus** /tejorˈetikʏs/ (pl: theoretici) theoretician, theorist

[1]**theoretisch** /tejorˈetis/ (adj) theoretic(al)

[2]**theoretisch** /tejorˈetis/ (adv) theoretically, in theory

de **theorie** /tejorˈi/ (pl: -ën) theory, hypothesis: ~ *en praktijk* theory and practice; *in* ~ *is dat mogelijk* theoretically (speaking) that's possible

de **therapeut** /terapˈœyt/ (pl: -en) therapist

therapeutisch /terapˈœytis/ (adj, adv) therapeutic(al)

de **therapie** /terapˈi/ (pl: -ën) **1** therapy **2** (psycho)therapy: *in* ~ *zijn* be having (*or*: undergoing) therapy

de **thermiek** /tɛrmˈik/ thermals, up-currents

de **thermometer** /tɛrmometər/ (pl: -s) thermometer: *de* ~ *daalt* (*or*: *stijgt*) the thermometer is falling (*or*: rising); *de* ~ *stond op twintig graden Celsius* the thermometer read (*or*: stood at) twenty degrees centigrade

de **thermosfles**® /tɛrmosflɛs/ (pl: -sen) thermos (flask)

de **thermoskan**® /tɛrmoskɑn/ (pl: -nen) thermos (jug)

de **thermostaat** /tɛrmostˈat/ (pl: -staten) thermostat

de **these** /tˈezə/ (pl: -n, -s) thesis

de **thesis** /tˈezɪs/ (pl: theses) [educ] thesis, dissertation; master's thesis

thomas /tˈomɑs/: *een ongelovige* ~ a doubting Thomas

de **Thora** /tˈora/ Torah

de **thriller** /θrˈɪlər/ (pl: -s) thriller

het [1]**thuis** /tœys/ home, hearth: *hij heeft geen* ~ he has no home; *mijn* ~ my home; *bericht van* ~ *krijgen* receive news from home

[2]**thuis** /tœys/ (adv) **1** home: *de artikelen worden kosteloos* ~ *bezorgd* the articles are delivered free; *wel* ~! safe journey! **2** at home: *verzorging* ~ home nursing; *doe maar of je* ~ *bent* make yourself at home; *zich ergens* ~ *gaan voelen* settle down (*or*: in); [sport] *spelen we zondag* ~? are we playing at home this Sunday?; *iem. (bij zich)* ~ *uitnodigen* ask s.o. round (*or*: to one's house); *zich ergens* ~ *voelen* feel at home (*or*: ease) somewhere; *hij was niet* ~ he wasn't in (*or*: at home), he was out; *bij ons* ~ at our place, at home, back home; *bij jou* ~ (over) at your place || *samen uit, samen* ~ we stick together, we're in this together

thuisbankieren /tœyzbɑŋkirə(n)/ (thuisbankierde, heeft thuisgebankierd) home banking

thuisbezorgen /tœyzbəzɔrɣə(n)/ (bezorgde thuis, heeft thuisbezorgd) deliver (to the house, door)

de **thuisbioscoop** /tœyzbijoskop/ home cinema

thuisblijven /tœyzblɛivə(n)/ (bleef thuis, is thuisgebleven) stay at home, stay in

thuisbrengen /tœyzbrɛŋə(n)/ (bracht thuis, heeft thuisgebracht) **1** bring home, see home; take home: *de man werd ziek thuisgebracht* the man was brought home sick **2** place: *iets (iem.) niet thuis kunnen brengen* not be able to place sth. (s.o.)

de **thuisclub** /tœysklʏp/ (pl: -s) home team

het **thuisfront** /tœysfrɔnt/ home front

de **thuishaven** /tœyshavə(n)/ (pl: -s) home port, port of register (*or*: registry); home base, haven

thuishoren /tœyshorə(n)/ (hoorde thuis, heeft thuisgehoord) **1** belong, go: *dat speelgoed hoort hier niet thuis* those toys don't belong here; *waar hoort dat thuis?* where does that go? **2** be from, come from: *waar* (*or*: *in welke haven*) *hoort dat schip thuis?* what is that ship's home port? (*or*: port of registry?)

thuishouden /tœyshɑudə(n)/ (hield thuis, heeft thuisgehouden) keep at home || *hou je handen thuis!* keep (*or*: lay) off me!, (keep your) hands off (me)!

de **thuishulp** /tœyshʏlp/ home help

thuiskomen /tœyskomə(n)/ (kwam thuis, is thuisgekomen) come home, come back, get back: *je moet* ~ you're wanted at home; *ik kom vanavond niet thuis* I won't be in tonight

de **thuiskomst** /tœyskomst/ homecoming, return: *behouden* ~ safe return

het **thuisland** /tœyslɑnt/ (pl: -en) **1** homeland **2** home country

thuisloos /tœyslos/ (adj) homeless

de **thuismarkt** /tœysmɑrkt/ (pl: -en) domestic market

de **thuisreis** /tœysrɛis/ (pl: -reizen) homeward

journey: *hij is **op** de ~* he is bound for home

de **thuisvakantie** /tœy̯sfakɑnsi/ (pl: -s) staycation

de **thuisverpleging** /tœy̯sfərplexɪŋ/ home nursing, home care

de **thuiswedstrijd** /tœy̯swɛtstrɛit/ (pl: -en) home game (*or:* match)

het **thuiswerk** /tœy̯swɛrk/ outwork; cottage industry: ~ *doen* take in outwork

de **thuiswerker** /tœy̯swɛrkər/ (pl: -s) outworker

thuiswonend /tœy̯swonənt/ (adj) living at home: *~e **kinderen*** children who (still) live with their parents

de **thuiszorg** /tœy̯sɔrx/ home care

de **ti** /ti/ (pl: ti's) [mus] te, ti

de **TIA** /tija/ *transient ischaemic attack* TIA

Tibet /tibɛt/ Tibet

de **Tibetaan** /tibɛtan/ (pl: Tibetanen) Tibetan

Tibetaans /tibɛtans/ (adj) Tibetan

de **tic** /tɪk/ (pl: -s) **1** trick, quirk: *zij heeft een ~ om alles te bewaren* she's got a quirk of hoarding things **2** tic, jerk **3** [roughly] shot: *een **tonic** met een ~* a tonic with a shot (of gin), a gin and tonic

het **ticket** /tɪkət/ (pl: -s) ticket

de **tiebreak** /tɑjbrek/ (pl: -s) tie break(er)

tien /tin/ (num) ten; [in dates] tenth: *zij is ~ jaar* she is ten years old (*or:* of age); *een **man** of ~* about ten people; *~ **tegen** één dat …* ten to one that … ‖ *een ~ **voor** Engels* top marks for English; an A+ for English

tiende /tində/ (adj) tenth, tithe: *een ~ gedeelte*, *een ~* a tenth (part), a tithe

tienduizend /tindœy̯zənt/ (num) ten thousand ‖ *enige ~en* some tens of thousands

de **tiener** /tinər/ (pl: -s) teenager

tienjarig /tinjarəx/ (adj) decennial, ten-year

de **tienkamp** /tinkɑmp/ (pl: -en) decathlon

tiens /cɛ̃/ (int) [Belg] well, well

het **tiental** /tintɑl/ (pl: -len) ten: *na enkele ~len jaren* after a few decades

tientallig /tintɑləx/ (adj) decimal, denary

het **tientje** /tincə/ (pl: -s) ten euros; ten-euro note

het **tienvoud** /tinvɑut/ (pl: -en) tenfold

tieren /tirə(n)/ (tierde, heeft getierd) rage ‖ *welig ~* flourish; *welig ~d onkruid* rampant weeds

de **tiet** /tit/ (pl: -en) [inform] boob, knocker

tig /tɪx/ (num) umpteen; zillions: *ik heb het al ~ keer gezegd* I've already said it umpteen times

het **tij** /tɛi/ (pl: -en) tide: *het is **hoog** (or: **laag**) ~* it's high (*or:* low) tide, the tide is in (*or:* out); [fig] *het ~ proberen te **keren*** try to stem (*or:* turn) the tide

de **tijd** /tɛit/ (pl: -en) **1** time: *in de **helft** van de ~* in half the time; *in een **jaar** ~* (with)in a year; *dat waren **andere** ~en* those were the days, times have changed; *na **bepaalde** ~* after

some (*or:* a) time, eventually; *een **hele** ~ geleden* a long time ago; *een ~ **lang*** for a while (*or:* time); *vrije ~* spare (*or:* free) time, time off, leisure (time); *het **duurde** een ~je voor ze eraan gewend was* it took a while before (*or:* until) she got used to it; *ik **geef** je vijf seconden de ~* I'm giving you five seconds; *de ~ **hebben*** have time; *heb je even ~?* have you got a moment? (*or:* a sec?); *~ **genoeg** hebben* have plenty of time; have time enough; *~ **kosten*** take time; *de ~ **nemen** voor iets* take one's time over sth.; *~ **opnemen*** record the time; *dat **was** me nog eens een ~!* those were the days!; *~ **winnen*** gain time; play for time; *uw ~ is **om*** your time is up; *binnen de kortst mogelijke ~* in (next to) no time; *het heeft **in** ~en niet zo geregend* it hasn't rained like this for ages; *sinds **enige** ~* for some time (past); *de ~ zal het **leren*** time will tell; *de ~ van **aankomst*** the time of arrival; *vorig jaar om **dezelfde** ~* (at) the same time last year; *het **is** ~* it's time; time's up; *~ **tekortkomen*** run out (*or:* run short) of time; *zijn ~ **uitzitten*** serve (*or:* do) one's time; *eindelijk! het **werd** ~* at last! it was about time (too)!; *het **wordt** ~ dat …* it is (high) time that …; *morgen **om** deze ~* (about, around) this time tomorrow; *op **vaste** ~en* at set (*or:* fixed) times; *de brandweer kwam net **op** ~* the fire brigade arrived just in time; *stipt **op** ~* punctual; on the dot; *op ~ naar bed gaan* go to bed in good time; *te **allen** ~e* at all times; *te **zijner** ~* in due course, when appropriate; *tegen die ~* by that time, by then; *van ~ **tot** ~* from time to time; *van die ~ **af*** from that time (on, onwards), ever since, since then; *veel ~ in beslag nemen* take up a lot of time **2** time(s), period, age: *de **laatste** ~* lately, recently; *hij heeft een **moeilijke** ~ gehad* he has been through (*or:* had) a hard time; *de goede **oude** ~* the good old days; *zijn (beste) ~ **gehad** hebben* be past one's best (*or:* prime); *de ~en **zijn veranderd*** times have changed; *in deze ~ van het jaar* at this time of (the) year; *met zijn ~ **meegaan*** keep up with (*or:* move with) the times; *dat was **voor** mijn ~* that was before my time (*or:* day); *dat was **voor** die ~ heel ongebruikelijk* in (*or:* for) those days it was most unusual; *je moet te **eerste** ~ nog rustig aandoen* to begin with (*or:* at first) you must take it easy; *een ~je* a while **3** season, time **4** tense: *de **tegenwoordige** (or: **verleden**) ~* the present (*or:* past) tense; *toekomende ~* future tense

de **tijdbom** /tɛidbɔm/ (pl: -men) time bomb: [fig] *een **tikkende** ~* a ticking time bomb

[1] **tijdelijk** /tɛidələk/ (adj) temporary, provisional, interim: *~ **personeel*** temporary staff

[2] **tijdelijk** /tɛidələk/ (adv) temporarily

tijdens /tɛidəns/ (prep) during

het **tijdgebrek** /tɛitxəbrɛk/ lack of time

de **tijdgeest** /tɛitxest/ spirit of the age (*or:*

times)

de **tijdgenoot** /tɛitχənot/ (pl: -genoten) contemporary

de **tijdgrens** /tɛitχrɛns/ time limit

¹**tijdig** /tɛidəχ/ (adj) timely: ~e *hulp is veel waard* timely help is of great value

²**tijdig** /tɛidəχ/ (adv) in time; on time

de **tijding** /tɛidɪŋ/ (pl: -en) news

tijdlang /tɛitlɑŋ/ (adv) while; for a while

de **tijdlijn** /tɛitlɛin/ (pl: -en) timeline

tijdloos /tɛitlos/ (adj, adv) timeless, ageless

de **tijdnood** /tɛitnot/ lack (*or:* shortage) of time: *in ~ zitten* be pressed for time

het **tijdpad** /tɛitpɑt/ (pl: -en) time schedule

het **tijdperk** /tɛitpɛrk/ (pl: -en) period, age, era: *het ~ van de **computer*** the age of the computer; *het **stenen** ~* the Stone Age

tijdrekken /tɛitrɛkə(n)/ time wasting; playing for time

de **tijdrit** /tɛitrɪt/ (pl: -ten) time trial

tijdrovend /tɛitrovənt/ (adj) time-consuming: *dit **is** zeer ~* this takes up a lot of time

het **tijdsbesef** /tɛitsbəsɛf/ notion of time

het **tijdsbestek** /tɛitsbəstɛk/ (period of) time: *binnen een ~ van* within (the period of)

het **tijdschema** /tɛitsχema/ (pl: -'s) schedule, timetable: *we lopen achter **op** het ~* we're (running) behind schedule

het **tijdschrift** /tɛitsχrɪft/ (pl: -en) periodical, journal, magazine

de **tijdsdruk** /tɛitsdrʏk/ pressure of time

de **tijdslimiet** /tɛitslimit/ (pl: -en) time limit, deadline: *de ~ **overschrijden*** exceed (*or:* go over) the time limit

het **tijdstip** /tɛitstɪp/ (pl: -pen) (point of, in) time; moment

de **tijdstraf** /tɛitstrɑf/ (pl: -fen) time penalty

het **tijdsverschil** /tɛitsfərsχɪl/ (pl: -len) time difference

het **tijdvak** /tɛitfɑk/ (pl: -ken) period

het **tijdverdrijf** /tɛitfərdrɛif/ pastime

de **tijdverspilling** /tɛitfərspɪlɪŋ/ waste of time

de **tijdwinst** /tɛitwɪnst/ gain in time: *enige ~ boeken* gain some time

de **tijdzone** /tɛitso:nə/ (pl: -s) time-zone

de **tijger** /tɛiɣər/ (pl: -s) tiger

de **tijgerprint** /tɛiɣərprɪnt/ (pl: -s) tiger print

de **tijm** /tɛim/ thyme

de **tik** /tɪk/ (pl: -ken) tap; slap; tick: *iem. een ~ **om** de oren* (or: **op** de vingers) *geven* give s.o. a cuff on the ear (*or:* a rap on the knuckles)

de **tikfout** /tɪkfɑut/ (pl: -en) typing error (*or:* mistake)

het **tikje** /tɪkjə/ (pl: -s) **1** touch, clip: *de bal een ~ geven* clip the ball **2** touch, shade: *zich een ~ **beter** voelen* feel slightly better

het **tikkeltje** /tɪkəlcə/ touch, shade

¹**tikken** /tɪkə(n)/ (tikte, heeft getikt) tap; tick: *de **wekker** tikte niet meer* the alarmclock had stopped ticking; *tegen het raam ~* tap at (*or:* on) the window

²**tikken** /tɪkə(n)/ (tikte, heeft getikt) **1** tap: *de maat ~* tap (out) the beat; *iem. **op** de schouder ~* tap s.o. on the shoulder **2** type: *een **brief** ~* type a letter

het **tikkertje** /tɪkərcə/ tag: ~ *spelen* play tag

til /tɪl/: *er zijn grote veranderingen **op** ~* there are big changes on the way

de **tilapia** /tilɑpija/ tilapia

¹**tillen** /tɪlə(n)/ (tilde, heeft getild) lift (a weight): *ergens niet (zo) **zwaar** aan ~* not feel strongly about

²**tillen** /tɪlə(n)/ (tilde, heeft getild) **1** lift, raise: *iem. **in** de hoogte ~* lift s.o. up (in the air); *niet te ~* as heavy as lead **2** cheat, swindle: *iem. **voor** 50 euro ~* take s.o. for 50 euros, cheat (*or:* swindle) s.o. out of 50 euros

de **tillift** /tɪlɪft/ hoist, lift

de **tilt** /tɪlt/: *op ~ **slaan*** hit the roof

het **timbre** /tɛ̃brə/ (pl: -s) [mus] timbre

timen /tɑjmə(n)/ (timede, heeft getimed) time

de **time-out** /tɑjmɑut/ (pl: -s) time-out: *een ~ **nemen*** take a time-out, take a breather

timide /timidə/ (adj) timid, shy

de **timing** /tɑjmɪŋ/ timing

¹**timmeren** /tɪmərə(n)/ (timmerde, heeft getimmerd) hammer: *goed kunnen ~* be good at carpentry; *de hele boel in elkaar ~* smash the whole place up

²**timmeren** /tɪmərə(n)/ (timmerde, heeft getimmerd) build, put together: *een **boekenkast** ~* build a bookcase

de **timmerman** /tɪmərmɑn/ (pl: timmerlieden, timmerlui) carpenter

het **timmermansoog** /tɪmərmɑnsoχ/: *een ~ **hebben*** have an accurate eye

het **timmerwerk** /tɪmərwɛrk/ carpentry, woodwork

het **tin** /tɪn/ tin

tingelen /tɪŋələ(n)/ (tingelde, heeft getingeld) tinkle, jingle: *op de piano ~* tinkle away at the piano

tinnen /tɪnə(n)/ (adj) tin, pewter: ~ *soldaatjes* tin soldiers

de **tint** /tɪnt/ (pl: -en) tint, hue: *iets een **feestelijk** ~je geven* give sth. a festive touch; *Mary had een **frisse** (or: **gelige**) ~* Mary had a fresh (*or:* sallow) complexion; *warme ~en* warm tones

tintelen /tɪntələ(n)/ (tintelde, heeft getinteld) tingle

de **tinteling** /tɪntəlɪŋ/ (pl: -en) tingle, tingling

tinten /tɪntə(n)/ (tintte, heeft getint) tint, tinge

de **tip** /tɪp/ (pl: -s) **1** tip; corner: *een ~je van de **sluier** oplichten* lift (*or:* raise) (a corner of) the veil **2** tip, lead, clue; tip-off: *iem. een ~ **geven*** tip s.o. off, give s.o. a tip-off

het **tipgeld** /tɪpχɛlt/ tip-off money

de **tipgever** /tɪpχevər/ (pl: -s) (police) informer; tipster

de **tippel** /tɪpəl/ (pl: -s) toddle, walk: *een **hele** ~*

quite a walk

de **tippelaarster** /tɪpəlarstər/ (pl: -s) street-walker

tippelen /tɪpələ(n)/ (tippelde, heeft getippeld) be on (or: walk) the streets, solicit

de **tippelzone** /tɪpəlzɔːnə/ (pl: -s) streetwalkers' district

tippen /tɪpə(n)/ (tipte, heeft getipt) **1** tip (s.o.) off; [Am; to police also] finger **2** tip (as) **3** tip, touch lightly, finger lightly: *aan iets (iem.) niet kunnen ~* have nothing on sth. (s.o.)

tipsy /tɪpsi/ (adj) tipsy

tiptop /tɪptɔp/ (adj, adv) tip-top, A 1: *~ in orde* in apple-pie order, in tip-top (or: A 1) condition

de **tirade** /tiradə/ (pl: -s) tirade

de **tiran** /tirɑn/ (pl: -nen) tyrant

de **tirannie** /tiraniy/ (pl: -ën) tyranny

tiranniek /tirɑnik/ (adj, adv) tyrannical

tiranniseren /tirɑnizerə(n)/ (tiranniseerde, heeft getiranniseerd) tyrannize (over)

de **Tiroler** /tirolər/ (pl: -s) Tyrolean

het **tissue** /tɪʃu/ (pl: -s) paper handkerchief

de **titel** /titəl/ (pl: -s) **1** title; heading **2** title; (university) degree: *een ~ behalen* get a degree; win a title; *de ~ veroveren* (or: *verdedigen*) win (or: defend) the title || *op persoonlijke ~* **a)** personally; **b)** speaking as a private person

de **titelhouder** /titəlhaudər/ (pl: -s) title-holder

de **titelpagina** /titəlpayina/ (pl: -'s) title-page, title

de **titelrol** /titəlrɔl/ (pl: -len) title role

de **titelsong** /titəlsɔŋ/ (pl: -s) title track

de **titelverdediger** /titəlvərdedəɣər/ (pl: -s) titleholder, defender

de **titularis** /titylɑrɪs/ (pl: -sen) [Belg] class teacher

tja /ca/ (int) well

de **tjalk** /cɑlk/ (pl: -en) Dutch sailing vessel

de **tjaptjoi** /cɑpcɔj/ chop suey

tjilpen /cɪlpə(n)/ (tjilpte, heeft getjilpt) chirp; peep; tweet

tjirpen /cɪrpə(n)/ (tjirpte, heeft getjirpt) chirp, chirrup; chirr

tjokvol /cɔkfɔl/ (adj) chock-a-block, chock-full: *de zaal was ~* the hall was jam-packed (or: chock-a-block)

tjonge /cɔŋə/ (int) dear me

de **tl-buis** /teɛlbœys/ (pl: tl-buizen) strip light, neon light (or: tube, lamp)

t.n.v. *ten name van* in the name of

de **toa** /towa/ [Dutch] *technisch onderwijsassistent* school laboratory assistant

de **toast** /tost/ (pl: -s) (piece, slice of) toast

de **tobbe** /tɔbə/ (pl: -s) (wash)tub

tobben /tɔbə(n)/ (tobde, heeft getobd) **1** worry, fret **2** struggle: *opa tobt met zijn been* grandpa is troubled by his leg

toch /tɔx/ (adv) **1** nevertheless, still, yet, all

the same: *ik doe het (lekker) ~* I'll do it anyway; *maar ~* (but) still, even so **2** rather, actually **3** indeed **4** anyway, anyhow: *het wordt ~ niks* it won't work anyway; *nu je hier ~ bent* since you're here || *dat kunnen ze ~ niet menen?* surely they can't be serious?; *we hebben het ~ al zo moeilijk* it's difficult enough for us as it is

de **tocht** /tɔxt/ (pl: -en) **1** draught; breeze: *op de ~ zitten* sit in a draught; *~ voelen* feel a draught **2** journey, trip: *een ~ maken met de auto* go for a drive in the car

tochtdicht /tɔxdɪxt/ (adj) draughtproof

tochten /tɔxtə(n)/ (tochtte, heeft getocht) be draughty: *het tocht hier* there's a draught here

tochtig /tɔxtəx/ (adj) draughty; breezy

het **tochtje** /tɔxjə/ (pl: -s) trip, ride, drive

de **tochtstrip** /tɔxtstrɪp/ (pl: -s) draught excluder, weather strip(ping)

¹**toe** /tu/ (adv) **1** to(wards) **2** too, as well: *dat doet er niet ~* that doesn't matter **3** to, for: *aan iets ~ komen* get round to sth. **4** shut, closed || *aan vakantie ~ zijn* be ready for (or: in need of) a holiday; *er slecht aan ~ zijn* be in a bad way; *tot nu ~* so far, up to now; *dat was nog tot daaraan ~* there's no great harm in that, that doesn't matter so much

²**toe** /tu/ (int) **1** come on **2** please, do **3** come on, go on **4** there now

het ¹**toebehoren** /tubəhorə(n)/ accessories; attachments

²**toebehoren** /tubəhorə(n)/ (behoorde toe, heeft toebehoord) belong to

toebereiden /tubərɛɪdə(n)/ (bereidde toe, heeft toebereid) prepare

toebrengen /tubrɛŋə(n)/ (bracht toe, heeft toegebracht) deal, inflict, give: *iem. een wond ~* inflict a wound on s.o.

toedekken /tudɛkə(n)/ (dekte toe, heeft toegedekt) cover up; tuck in, tuck up: *iem. warm ~* tuck s.o. in nice and warm

toedichten /tudɪxtə(n)/ (dichtte toe, heeft toegedicht) attribute (to)

toedienen /tudinə(n)/ (diende toe, heeft toegediend) administer, apply: *medicijnen ~* administer medicine

het ¹**toedoen** /tudun/ agency, doing: *dit is allemaal door jouw ~ gebeurd* this is all your doing

²**toedoen** /tudun/ (deed toe, heeft toegedaan) add: *wat doet het er toe?* what does it matter?, what difference does it make?; *wat jij vindt, doet er niet toe* your opinion is of no consequence

de **toedracht** /tudrɑxt/ facts, circumstances: *de ware ~ van de zaak* what actually happened

toedragen /tudraɣə(n)/ (droeg toe, heeft toegedragen) bear: *iets een warm hart ~* be well disposed towards sth.; fully support sth.

zich **toe-eigenen** /tuɛiɣənə(n)/ (eigende zich

toe, heeft zich toegeëigend) appropriate

de **toef** /tuf/ (pl: -en) tuft: *een ~ slagroom* a blob of cream

toegaan /tuɣan/ (ging toe, is toegegaan) happen, go on: *het gaat er daar ruig aan toe* there are wild goings-on there

de **toegang** /tuɣaŋ/ (pl: -en) **1** entrance, entry, access: *iem. de ~ ontzeggen* refuse s.o. admittance (or: access), bar s.o.; *verboden ~* no admittance **2** access; admittance; admission: *bewijs van ~* ticket (of admission); *~ hebben tot een vergadering* be admitted to a meeting; *zich ~ verschaffen* gain access (to)

het **toegangsbewijs** /tuɣaŋzbəwɛɪs/ (pl: -bewijzen) (admission) ticket, pass

de **toegangscode** /tuɣaŋskodə/ (pl: -s) access code

het **toegangspoortje** /tuɣaŋsporcə/ (pl: -s) gate; turnstile

de **toegangsprijs** /tuɣaŋsprɛis/ (pl: -prijzen) entrance fee, price of admission

de **toegangsweg** /tuɣɑŋswɛх/ (pl: -en) access (road), approach

toegankelijk /tuɣɑŋkələk/ (adj) accessible, approachable: *moeilijk* (or: *gemakkelijk*) *~* difficult (or: easy) of access; *~ voor het publiek* open to the public

de **toegankelijkheid** /tuɣɑŋkələkhɛit/ accessibility, approachability

toegedaan /tuɣədan/ (adj) dedicated

toegeeflijk /tuɣeflək/ (adj) indulgent, lenient: *~ zijn tegenover een kind* indulge a child

de **toegeeflijkheid** /tuɣefləkhɛit/ indulgence, lenience

toegepast /tuɣəpɑst/ (adj) applied

¹**toegeven** /tuɣevə(n)/ (gaf toe, heeft toegegeven) **1** yield, give in; give way: *onder druk ~* submit under pressure **2** admit, own: *hij wou maar niet ~* he wouldn't own up

²**toegeven** /tuɣevə(n)/ (gaf toe, heeft toegegeven) **1** indulge, humour; pamper; spoil, allow (for), take into account: *over en weer wat ~* give and take **2** admit, grant: *zijn nederlaag ~* admit defeat **3** throw in, add: *op de koop ~* include in the bargain

toegewijd /tuɣəwɛit/ (adj) devoted, dedicated: *een ~e verpleegster* a dedicated nurse

de **toegift** /tuɣɪft/ (pl: -en) encore: *een ~ geven* do an encore

de **toehoorder** /tuhordər/ (pl: -s) listener

toejuichen /tujœyxə(n)/ (juichte toe, heeft toegejuicht) **1** cheer; clap; applaud **2** applaud: *een besluit ~* welcome a decision

de **toejuiching** /tujœyxɪŋ/ (pl: -en) **1** applause **2** acclaim

toekennen /tukɛnə(n)/ (kende toe, heeft toegekend) **1** ascribe to, attribute to **2** award, grant: *macht ~ aan* assign authority to

de **toekenning** /tukɛnɪŋ/ award, grant

toekeren /tukerə(n)/ (keerde toe, heeft

toegekeerd) turn to

toekijken /tukɛikə(n)/ (keek toe, heeft toegekeken) **1** look on, watch **2** sit by (and watch)

toekomen /tukomə(n)/ (kwam toe, is toegekomen) **1** belong to, be due: *iem. de eer geven die hem toekomt* do s.o. justice **2** approach: *daar ben ik nog niet aan toegekomen* I haven't got round to that yet

toekomend /tukomənt/ (adj) future

de **toekomst** /tukɔmst/ future: *in de nabije* (or: *verre*) *~* in the near (or: distant) future; *de ~ voorspellen* tell fortunes; *de ~ lacht hem toe* the future looks rosy for him

toekomstig /tukɔmstəх/ (adj) future, coming || *zijn ~e echtgenote* his bride-to-be; *de ~e eigenaar* the prospective owner

de **toekomstmuziek** /tukɔmstmyzik/: *dat is nog ~* that's still in the future

de **toekomstvisie** /tukɔmstfizi/ (pl: -s) vision for the future

toelaatbaar /tuladbar/ (adj) permissible, permitted

toelachen /tulaхə(n)/ (lachte toe, heeft toegelachen) smile at || *het geluk lacht ons toe* fortune smiles on us

de **toelage** /tulaɣə/ (pl: -n) allowance; grant

toelaten /tulatə(n)/ (liet toe, heeft toegelaten) **1** permit, allow: *als het weer het toelaat* weather permitting **2** admit, receive: *zij werd niet in Nederland toegelaten* she was refused entry to the Netherlands

het **toelatingsexamen** /tulatɪŋsɛksamə(n)/ (pl: -s) entrance exam(ination)

toeleggen /tulɛɣə(n)/ (legde toe, heeft toegelegd) add (to)

het **toeleveringsbedrijf** /tuleverɪŋzbədrɛif/ (pl: -bedrijven) supplier, supply company

toelichten /tulɪхtə(n)/ (lichtte toe, heeft toegelicht) explain, throw light on, clarify: *zijn standpunt ~* explain one's point of view; *als ik dat even mag ~* if I may go into that briefly

de **toelichting** /tulɪхtɪŋ/ (pl: -en) explanation, clarification: *dat vereist enige ~* that requires some explanation

de **toeloop** /tulop/ onrush, rush; flood

toelopen /tulopə(n)/ (liep toe, is toegelopen) taper (off), come (or: run) to a point

toeluisteren /tulœystərə(n)/ (luisterde toe, heeft toegeluisterd) listen (to): *aandachtig ~* listen carefully

het **toemaatje** /tumacə/ (pl: -s) [Belg] extra, bonus

¹**toen** /tun/ (adv) **1** then, in those days, at the (or: that) time: *er stond hier ~ een kerk* there used to be a church here **2** then, next: *en ~?* (and) then what?, what happened next?

²**toen** /tun/ (conj) when, as: *~ hij binnenkwam* when he came in

de **toenaam** /tunam/ surname: *iem. met naam*

en ~ *noemen* mention s.o. by name

de **toenadering** /tu̯naːdərɪŋ/ (pl: -en) advance; approach

de **toename** /tu̯naːmə/ (pl: -n) increase, growth: *een ~ van het verbruik* an increase in consumption

de **toendra** /tu̯ndraː/ (pl: -'s) tundra

toenemen /tu̯neːmə(n)/ (nam toe, is toegenomen) increase, grow; expand: *in ~de mate* increasingly, to an increasing extent; *in kracht ~* grow (or: increase) in strength

toenmalig /tu̯mɑːləx/ (adj) then: *de ~e koning* the king at the (or: that) time

toentertijd /tu̯ntərtɛɪt/ (adv) then, at the time

toepasselijk /tupɑsələk/ (adj) appropriate, suitable

toepassen /tu̯pɑsə(n)/ (paste toe, heeft toegepast) **1** use, employ **2** apply, adopt; enforce: *een methode ~* use a method; *in de praktijk ~* use in (actual) practice

de **toepassing** /tu̯pɑsɪŋ/ (pl: -en) **1** use, employment: *niet van ~ (n.v.t.)* not applicable (n/a); *van ~ zijn op* apply to **2** application: *in ~ brengen* put into practice

de **toer** /tur/ (pl: -en) **1** trip, tour; ride; drive **2** revolution: *op volle ~en draaien* go at full speed, be in top gear; *hij is een beetje over zijn ~en* he's in a bit of a state **3** job, business ‖ *op de lollige ~ gaan* act the clown

de **toerbeurt** /turbørt/ (pl: -en) turn: *bij ~* in rotation, by turns; *we doen dat bij ~* we take turns at it

toereikend /turɛɪkənt/ (adj) sufficient; adequate

toerekeningsvatbaar /turekənɪŋsfɑdbaːr/ (adj) accountable, responsible

toeren /tu̯rə(n)/ (toerde, heeft/is getoerd) go for a ride; go for a drive

het **toerental** /tu̯rə(n)tɑl/ (pl: -len) rpm *(revolutions per minute)*

de **toerenteller** /tu̯rə(n)tɛlər/ (pl: -s) revolution counter

de **toerfiets** /turfits/ (pl: -en) touring bicycle, sports bicycle

het **toerisme** /turɪsmə/ tourism

de **toerist** /turɪst/ (pl: -en) tourist

de **toeristenbelasting** /turɪstə(n)bəlɑstɪŋ/ tourist tax

het **toeristenseizoen** /turɪstə(n)sɛizun/ (pl: -en) tourist season

toeristisch /turɪstis/ (adj) tourist: *een ~e trekpleister* a tourist attraction

het **toernooi** /turnoːj/ (pl: -en) tournament

toerusten /tu̯rvstə(n)/ (rustte toe, heeft toegerust) equip; furnish: *een leger ~* equip an army; *toegerust met* equipped (or: fitted) (out) with

toeschietelijk /tusxitələk/ (adj) accommodating, obliging

toeschieten /tu̯sxitə(n)/ (schoot toe, is toe-

geschoten) rush forward

de **toeschouwer** /tu̯sxɑuwər/ (pl: -s) **1** spectator; viewer; audience: *veel ~s trekken* draw a large audience **2** onlooker, bystander

toeschrijven /tu̯sxrɛivə(n)/ (schreef toe, heeft toegeschreven) **1** blame, attribute: *een ongeluk ~ aan het slechte weer* blame an accident on the weather **2** attribute, ascribe: *dit schilderij wordt toegeschreven aan Vermeer* this painting is attributed to Vermeer

¹**toeslaan** /tu̯slan/ (sloeg toe, heeft toegeslagen) **1** hit home, strike home **2** strike: *de inbreker slaat opnieuw toe* the burglar strikes again ‖ *de paniek slaat toe* panic kicks in, he/she starts panicking

²**toeslaan** /tu̯slan/ (sloeg toe, heeft toegeslagen) slam (shut)

de **toeslag** /tu̯slɑx/ (pl: -en) **1** surcharge **2** bonus: *een ~ voor vuil werk* a bonus for dirty work

toespelen /tu̯speːlə(n)/ (speelde toe, heeft toegespeeld) pass (to); slip (to)

de **toespeling** /tu̯speːlɪŋ/ (pl: -en) allusion, reference: *~en maken* drop hints, make insinuations

de **toespijs** /tu̯spɛis/ (pl: toespijzen) **1** dessert, sweet, pudding **2** side dish

toespitsen /tu̯spɪtsə(n)/ (spitste toe, heeft toegespitst) intensify

de **toespraak** /tu̯sprak/ (pl: toespraken) speech; address: *een ~ houden* make a speech

toespreken /tu̯spreːkə(n)/ (sprak toe, heeft toegesproken) speak to, address

toestaan /tu̯stan/ (stond toe, heeft toegestaan) allow, permit: *uitstel* (or: *een verzoek*) *~* grant a respite (or: a request)

de **toestand** /tu̯stɑnt/ (pl: -en) state, condition, situation: *de ~ van de patiënt is kritiek* the patient is in a critical condition; *de ~ in de wereld* the state of world affairs ‖ *~en maken* make a fuss (about)

toesteken /tu̯steːkə(n)/ (stak toe, heeft toegestoken) extend, put out, hold out: *de helpende hand ~* extend (or: lend) a helping hand

het **toestel** /tu̯stɛl/ (pl: -len) **1** apparatus, appliance; set: *vraag om ~ 212* ask for extension 212 **2** plane

het **toestelnummer** /tu̯stɛlnʏmər/ (pl: -s) extension (number)

toestemmen /tu̯stɛmə(n)/ (stemde toe, heeft toegestemd) agree (to), consent (to): *erin ~ dat ...* agree that ..., agree to (...ing)

de **toestemming** /tu̯stɛmɪŋ/ (pl: -en) agreement, consent, approval (of); permission: *zijn ~ geven* (or: *verlenen, weigeren*) *aan iem.* give (or: grant, refuse) permission to s.o.

toestoppen /tu̯stɔpə(n)/ (stopte toe, heeft toegestopt) slip

toestromen /tu̯stroːmə(n)/ (stroomde toe,

is toegestroomd) stream to(wards), flow (*or:* flock, crowd) towards

toesturen /t<u>u</u>styrə(n)/ (stuurde toe, heeft toegestuurd) send; remit

de **toet** /tut/ (pl: -en) face

toetakelen /t<u>u</u>takələ(n)/ (takelde toe, heeft toegetakeld) **1** beat (up), knock about: *hij is lelijk toegetakeld* he has been badly beaten (up) **2** rig out

toetasten /t<u>u</u>tastə(n)/ (tastte toe, heeft toegetast) take, seize; help o.s.

de **toeter** /t<u>u</u>tər/ (pl: -s) **1** tooter **2** horn

¹toeteren /t<u>u</u>tərə(n)/ (toeterde, heeft getoeterd) hoot, honk

²toeteren /t<u>u</u>tərə(n)/ (toeterde, heeft getoeterd) bellow

het **toetje** /t<u>u</u>cə/ (pl: -s) dessert: *als ~ is er fruit* there is fruit for dessert

toetreden /t<u>u</u>tredə(n)/ (trad toe, is toegetreden) join

de **toetreding** /t<u>u</u>tredɪŋ/ (pl: -en) joining, entry (into)

de **toets** /tuts/ (pl: -en) **1** test, check: *een schriftelijke ~* a written test, a test paper **2** key: *een ~ aanslaan* strike a key

toetsen /t<u>u</u>tsə(n)/ (toetste, heeft getoetst) test, check: *iets aan de praktijk ~* test sth. out in practice

het **toetsenbord** /t<u>u</u>tsə(n)bɔrt/ (pl: -en) keyboard; console

het **toeval** /t<u>u</u>val/ coincidence, accident, chance: *bij ~* by accident (*or:* chance); *door een ongelukkig ~* by mischance; *stom ~* by sheer accident; *(by) a (mere) fluke; *niets aan het ~ overlaten* leave nothing to chance

toevallen /t<u>u</u>valə(n)/ (viel toe, is toegevallen) fall to; accrue to

¹toevallig /tuv<u>a</u>ləx/ (adj) accidental: *een ~e ontmoeting* a chance meeting; *een ~e voorbijganger* a passer-by

²toevallig /tuv<u>a</u>ləx/ (adv) by (any) chance: *elkaar ~ treffen* meet by chance

de **toevalligheid** /tuv<u>a</u>ləxɦɛit/ (pl: -heden) coincidence

de **toevalstreffer** /t<u>u</u>valstrɛfər/ (pl: -s) chance hit, stroke of luck

toeven /t<u>u</u>və(n)/ (toefde, heeft getoefd) [form] stay: *het is daar goed ~* it is a nice place to stay

de **toeverlaat** /t<u>u</u>vərlat/ support: *hij was hun steun en ~* he was their help and stay

toevertrouwen /t<u>u</u>vərtrɑuwə(n)/ (vertrouwde toe, heeft toevertrouwd) **1** entrust: *dat is hem wel toevertrouwd* leave that to him, trust him for that **2** confide (to): *iets aan het papier ~* commit sth. to paper

de **toevloed** /t<u>u</u>vlut/ flow

de **toevlucht** /t<u>u</u>vlʏxt/ refuge, shelter: *dit middel was zijn laatste ~* this (expedient) was his last resort; *~ zoeken bij* take refuge with

het **toevluchtsoord** /t<u>u</u>vlʏxtsort/ (pl: -en)

(port, house, haven of) refuge

toevoegen /t<u>u</u>vuɣə(n)/ (voegde toe, heeft toegevoegd) add: *suiker naar smaak ~* add sugar to taste

de **toevoeging** /t<u>u</u>vuɣɪŋ/ (pl: -en) addition; additive

de **toevoer** /t<u>u</u>vur/ supply

toewensen /t<u>u</u>wɛnsə(n)/ (wenste toe, heeft toegewenst) wish: *iem. veel geluk ~* wish s.o. all the best (*or:* every happiness)

de **toewijding** /t<u>u</u>wɛidɪŋ/ devotion

toewijzen /t<u>u</u>wɛizə(n)/ (wees toe, heeft toegewezen) assign, grant: *het kind werd aan de vader toegewezen* the father was awarded (*or:* granted, given) custody of the child; *een prijs ~* award a prize

toezeggen /t<u>u</u>zɛɣə(n)/ (zegde toe/zei toe, heeft toegezegd) promise

de **toezegging** /t<u>u</u>zɛɣɪŋ/ (pl: -en) promise: *~en doen* make promises

toezenden /t<u>u</u>zɛndə(n)/ (zond toe, heeft toegezonden) send (to)

het **toezicht** /t<u>u</u>zɪxt/ supervision: *~ houden op* supervise, oversee; look after; *onder ~ staan van* be supervised by; *onder verscherpt ~* under close surveillance

de **toezichthouder** /t<u>u</u>zɪxtɦɑudər/ (pl: -s) supervisor

toezien /t<u>u</u>zin/ (zag toe, heeft toegezien) **1** look on, watch: *machteloos ~* stand by helplessly **2** see, take care: *hij moest er op ~ dat alles goed ging* he had to see to it that everything went all right

toezwaaien /t<u>u</u>zwajə(n)/ (zwaaide toe, heeft toegezwaaid) wave to: *iem. lof toezwaaien* give praise to s.o.

tof /tɔf/ (adj, adv) **1** decent, O.K.: *een ~fe meid* a decent girl, an O.K. girl **2** great

de **toffee** /t<u>ɔ</u>fe/ (pl: -s) toffee

de **tofoe** /t<u>ɔ</u>fu/ tofu

de **toga** /t<u>ɔ</u>ɣa/ (pl: -'s) gown, robe: *een advocaat in ~* a robed lawyer

Togo /t<u>ɔ</u>ɣo/ Togo

de **¹Togolees** /toɣol<u>e</u>s/ (pl: Togolezen) Togolese

²Togolees /toɣol<u>e</u>s/ (adj) Togolese

het **toilet** /twal<u>ɛ</u>t/ (pl: -ten) toilet, lavatory: *een openbaar ~* a public convenience; [Am] a rest room; *naar het ~ gaan* go to the toilet

het **toiletartikel** /twal<u>ɛ</u>tartikəl/ (pl: -en) toiletry; toilet requisites (*or:* things)

de **toiletjuffrouw** /twal<u>ɛ</u>tjʏfrɑu/ (pl: -en) lavatory attendant

het **toiletpapier** /twal<u>ɛ</u>tpapir/ toilet paper (*or:* tissue)

de **toiletrol** /twal<u>ɛ</u>trɔl/ (pl: -len) toilet paper

de **toilettafel** /twal<u>ɛ</u>tafəl/ (pl: -s) dressing table

de **toilettas** /twal<u>ɛ</u>tɑs/ (pl: -sen) toilet bag

de **toiletverfrisser** /twal<u>ɛ</u>tfərfrɪsər/ (pl: -s) toilet freshener, lavatory freshener

tokkelen /t<u>ɔ</u>kələ(n)/ (tokkelde, heeft/is getokkeld) strum

het **tokkelinstrument** /tɔkəlɪnstrymɛnt/ (pl:
-en) plucked instrument

de **toko** /tɔko/ (pl: -'s) general shop; Indonesian
shop: [fig] *alleen oog hebben voor je eigen ~*
only be interested in one's own patch

de **tol** /tɔl/ (pl: -len) **1** top: *mijn hoofd draait als
een ~* my head is spinning **2** toll: *ergens ~ voor
moeten* **betalen** [fig] have to pay the price for
sth.; *~ heffen (or:* take) (a) toll (on)
tolerant /tolerɑnt/ (adj, adv) tolerant

de **tolerantie** /tolerɑn(t)si/ tolerance
tolereren /tolererə(n)/ (tolereerde, heeft
getolereerd) tolerate, put up with

de **tolheffing** /tɔlhɛfɪŋ/ (pl: -en) toll collection

de **tolk** /tɔlk/ (pl: -en) interpreter
tolken /tɔlkə(n)/ (tolkte, heeft getolkt) interpret
tollen /tɔlə(n)/ (tolde, heeft getold) **1** play
with (*or:* spin) a top **2** spin, whirl: *zij stond te
~ van de slaap* she was reeling with sleep

de **tolweg** /tɔlwɛx/ (pl: -en) toll road; turnpike

de **tomaat** /tomat/ (pl: tomaten) tomato

de **tomatenketchup** /tomatə(n)kɛtʃʏp/ (pl: -s)
(tomato) ketchup

de **tomatenpuree** /tomatə(n)pyre/ tomato
purée

het **tomatensap** /tomatə(n)sɑp/ tomato juice

de **tomatensoep** /tomatə(n)sup/ tomato soup

de **tombe** /tɔmbə/ (pl: -s, -n) tomb
tomeloos /toməlos/ (adj, adv) unbridled,
uncontrolled: *tomeloze* **energie** boundless
(*or:* unbridled) energy

de **tompoes** /tɔmpus/ (pl: tompoezen) vanilla
slice

de **tompouce** /tɔmpus/ (pl: -s) vanilla slice

de **tomtom** /tɔmtɔm/ (pl: -s) sat nav, GPS

de **ton** /tɔn/ (pl: -nen) **1** cask, barrel **2** [Dutch] a
hundred thousand euros **3** (metric) ton

de **tondeuse** /tɔndøzə/ (pl: -s) (pair of) clip-
pers, trimmers; shears

het **toneel** /tonel/ (pl: tonelen) **1** stage: *op het ~
verschijnen* enter the stage, appear on the
stage; *iets ten tonele voeren* stage sth., put
sth. on the scene; [fig] *van het ~ verdwijnen*
quit the scene, make one's exit **2** scene,
spectacle **3** theatre

het **toneelgezelschap** /tonelɣəzɛlsxɑp/ (pl:
-pen) theatrical company, theatre company

de **toneelkijker** /tonelkɛikər/ (pl: -s) (pair of)
(opera) glasses

de **toneelschool** /tonelsxol/ (pl: -scholen) drama school

de **toneelschrijver** /tonelsxrɛivər/ (pl: -s)
playwright

het **toneelspel** /tonelspɛl/ (pl: -en) **1** play
2 play-acting
toneelspelen /tonelspelə(n)/ (speelde toneel, heeft toneelgespeeld) **1** act, play
2 play-act, dramatize: *wat kun jij ~!* what a
play-actor you are!

de **toneelspeler** /tonelspelər/ (pl: -s) **1** actor,
player **2** play-actor

het **toneelstuk** /tonelstʏk/ (pl: -ken) play: *een ~
opvoeren* perform a play

de **toneelvereniging** /tonelvərenəxɪŋ/ (pl:
-en) drama club

de **toneelvoorstelling** /tonelvorstɛlɪŋ/ (pl:
-en) theatrical performance
tonen /tonə(n)/ (toonde, heeft getoond)
show; display

de **toner** /tonər/ (pl: -s) toner

de **tong** /tɔŋ/ (pl: -en) **1** tongue: *met dubbele ~
spreken* speak thickly, speak with a thick
tongue; *de ~en kwamen los* the tongues
were loosened, tongues were wagging; *zijn ~
uitsteken tegen iem.* put out one's tongue at
s.o.; *op zijn ~ bijten* bite one's tongue; *het ligt
vóór op mijn ~* it's on the tip of my tongue;
[fig] *over de ~ gaan* be on many lips, be
talked about; [fig] *een scherpe ~ hebben* have
a sharp tongue, be sharp-tongued **2** sole

de **tongval** /tɔŋval/ (pl: -len) accent

de **tongzoen** /tɔŋzun/ (pl: -en) French kiss
tongzoenen /tɔŋzunə(n)/ (tongzoende,
heeft getongzoend) French kiss

de **tonic** /tɔnɪk/ (pl: -s) tonic

de **tonijn** /tonɛin/ (pl: -en) tunny(fish), tuna
(fish)

de **tonnage** /tɔnaʒə/ tonnage: *bruto ~* gross
tonnage

de **tonsil** /tɔnsɪl/ (pl: -len) tonsil

de **toog** /tox/ (pl: togen) **1** cassock, soutane
2 bar **3** counter

de **tooi** /toj/ (pl: -en) decoration(s), orna-
ment(s); plumage
tooien /tojə(n)/ (tooide, heeft getooid)
adorn

de **toom** /tom/ (pl: tomen) bridle, reins: *in ~
houden* (keep in) check, keep under control

de **toon** /ton/ (pl: tonen) **1** tone; note: *een halve ~* a semitone, a half step; *de ~ aangeven*
a) give the key; **b)** [fig] lead (*or:* set) the tone;
c) set the fashion; *een ~tje lager zingen*
change one's tune; *uit de ~ vallen* not be in
keeping, not be incongruous; be the odd
man out; [fig] *de juiste ~ aanslaan* strike the
right note **2** tone (colour), timbre
toonaangevend /tonanɣevənt/ (adj) authoritative, leading

de **toonaard** /tonart/ (pl: -en): *in alle ~en* in
every possible way
toonbaar /tombar/ (adj) presentable

de **toonbank** /tombɑŋk/ (pl: -en) counter: *illegale cd's onder de ~ verkopen* sell bootleg CDs
under the counter; [fig] *over de ~ vliegen* sell
like hot cakes

het **toonbeeld** /tombelt/ (pl: -en) model, paragon, example

de **toonder** /tondər/ (pl: -s) bearer: *een cheque
aan ~* a cheque (payable) to bearer

de **toonhoogte** /tonhoxtə/ (pl: -n, -s) pitch: *de*

juiste ~ *hebben* be at the right pitch

de **toonladder** /tonlɑdər/ (pl: -s) scale: ~*s spelen* play (*or:* practise) scales

toonloos /tonlos/ (adj) toneless, flat

de **toonsoort** /tonsort/ (pl: -en) [mus] key

de **toonzaal** /tonzal/ (pl: -zalen) showroom

de **toorn** /torn/ wrath, anger

de **toorts** /torts/ (pl: -en) torch

de **toost** /tost/ toast: *een* ~ (*op iem.*) *uitbrengen* propose a toast (to s.o.)

toosten /tostə(n)/ (toostte, heeft getoost) toast: ~ *op* drink (a toast) to

de **¹top** /tɔp/ (pl: -pen) **1** top, tip; peak: *aan (op) de* ~ *staan* be at the top; *van* ~ *tot teen* from head to foot **2** top, peak, height ǁ ~ *tien* top ten; [Belg] *hoge* ~*pen scheren* be successful; *een Europese* ~ a European summit (conference)

²top /tɔp/ (int) **1** it's a deal (*or:* bargain), you're on!, done! **2** cool!, great!

de **topaas** /topas/ topaz

de **topambtenaar** /tɔpɑmtənar/ (pl: -ambtenaren) key official

de **topconditie** /tɔpkɔndi(t)si/ (tip-)top condition (*or:* form)

de **topconferentie** /tɔpkɔnfɛrɛnsi/ (pl: -s) summit (conference, meeting); summit talks, top-level talks

de **topdrukte** /tɔbdrʏktə/ rush hour

de **topfunctie** /tɔpfʏŋksi/ (pl: -s) top position, leading position

de **topfunctionaris** /tɔpfʏŋkʃɔnarɪs/ (pl: -sen) key official

de **tophit** /tɔphɪt/ (pl: -s) smash hit

het **topje** /tɔpjə/ (pl: -s) **1** tip: *het* ~ *van de ijsberg* the tip of the iceberg **2** top

de **topklasse** /tɔpklɑsə/ (pl: -n) top class; [sport] premier league

topless /tɔpləs/ (adj) topless

de **topman** /tɔpmɑn/ (pl: -nen) senior man (*or:* executive), top-ranking official, senior official: ~ *in het bedrijfsleven* captain of industry

de **topografie** /topoɣrafi/ (pl: -ën) topography

het **topoverleg** /tɔpovərlɛx/ top-level talks, summit talks

toppen /tɔpə(n)/ (topte, heeft getopt) top, head

de **topper** /tɔpər/ (pl: -s) **1** top **2** (smash) hit **3** top match **4** ace **5** leading figure

de **topprestatie** /tɔprɛsta(t)si/ (pl: -s) top performance, record performance: *een* ~ *leveren* turn in a top performance

het **toppunt** /tɔpʏnt/ (pl: -en) **1** height, top: *dat is het* ~! that's the limit!, that beats everything!; *het* ~ *van waanzin* sheer (*or:* utter) madness **2** top, highest point; summit

de **topscorer** /tɔpskorər/ (pl: -s) top scorer

de **topsnelheid** /tɔpsnɛlhɛit/ (pl: -heden) top speed: *op* ~ *rijden* drive at top speed

de **topspin** /tɔpspɪn/ topspin

de **topsport** /tɔpsport/ top-class sport

de **topvorm** /tɔpfɔrm/ top(-notch) form

topzwaar /tɔpswar/ (adj) top-heavy

de **tor** /tɔr/ (pl: -ren) beetle

de **toreador** /torejadɔr/ (pl: -s) toreador

de **toren** /torə(n)/ (pl: -s) **1** tower; steeple; spire: *in een ivoren* ~ *zitten* live in an ivory tower; [fig] *hoog van de* ~ *blazen* **a)** beat the drum; **b)** be demanding **2** rook

de **torenflat** /torə(n)flɛt/ (pl: -s) high-rise flat(s); [Am] high-rise apartment(s)

torenhoog /torə(n)hox/ (adj) towering; sky-high

de **torenspits** /torə(n)spɪts/ (pl: -en) steeple, spire

de **torenvalk** /torə(n)vɑlk/ (pl: -en) kestrel, windhover

de **tornado** /tɔrnado/ (pl: -'s) tornado

tornen /tɔrnə(n)/ (tornde, heeft getornd) unsew, unstitch: *er valt aan deze beslissing niet te* ~ there's no going back on this decision

torpederen /tɔrpəderə(n)/ (torpedeerde, heeft getorpedeerd) torpedo

de **torpedo** /tɔrpedo/ (pl: -'s) torpedo

torsen /tɔrsə(n)/ (torste, heeft getorst) bear, suffer

de **torsie** /tɔrsi/ torsion

de **torso** /tɔrso/ (pl: -'s) torso

de **tortelduif** /tɔrtəldœyf/ (pl: -duiven) turtledove

tossen /tɔsə(n)/ (toste, heeft getost) toss (up, for)

de **tosti** /tɔsti/ (pl: -'s) [Dutch] toasted ham and cheese sandwich

het **tostiapparaat** /tɔstiɑparat/ (pl: -apparaten) (sandwich) toaster

tot /tɔt/ (prep) **1** (up) to, as far as: *de trein rijdt* ~ *Amsterdam* the train goes as far as Amsterdam; ~ *hoever*, ~ *waar?* how far?; ~ *bladzijde drie* up to page three **2** to, until: *van dag* ~ *dag* from day to day; ~ *zaterdag!* see you on Saturday!; ~ *de volgende keer* until (the) next time; ~ *nog (nu) toe* so far; ~ *en met 31 december* up to and including 31 December; *van 3* ~ *12 uur* from 3 to (*or:* till) 12 o'clock; *van maandag* ~ *en met zaterdag* from Monday to Saturday; [Am also] Monday through Saturday **3** at: ~ *elke prijs* at any price ǁ *iem.* ~ *president kiezen* elect s.o. president

totaal /total/ (adj, adv) total, complete: *een totale ommekeer (ommezwaai)* an about-turn, an about-face; *totale uitverkoop* clearance sale; *iets* ~ *anders* sth. completely different; *het is* € *33,-* ~ it's 33 euros in all; *in* ~ in all (*or:* total); ~ *niet* absolutely not

het **totaalbedrag** /totalbədrɑx/ (pl: -en) total (sum, amount)

totalitair /totalitɛːr/ (adj, adv) totalitarian

de **totaliteit** /totalitɛit/ (pl: -en) totality

total loss /totəllɔs/ (adj): *een auto* ~ *rijden* smash (up) a car, wreck a car

totdat /todɑt/ (conj) until

de **totempaal** /totəmpal/ (pl: -palen) totem pole

de **toto** /toto/ tote; [socc] (football) pools: *in de ~ geld winnen* win money on the pools

de **totstandkoming** /totstɑntkomɪŋ/ coming about, realization

toucheren /tuʃerə(n)/ (toucheerde, heeft getoucheerd) **1** receive **2** hit

het/de **touchscreen** /tɑtʃskriːn/ touch screen

de **toupet** /tupɛt/ (pl: -ten) toupee

de **tour** /tur/ (pl: -s) **1** outing, trip **2** tour

de **touringcar** /turɪŋkaːr/ (pl: -s) (motor) coach; [Am] bus

de **tournee** /turne/ (pl: -s) tour: *op ~ zijn* be on tour

het/de **tourniquet** /turnikɛt/ (pl: -s) turnstile; revolving door(s)

de **touroperator** /turopəretər/ (pl: -s) tour operator

het **touw** /tɑu/ (pl: -en) rope, (piece of) string: *ik kan er geen ~ aan vastknopen* I can't make head or tail of it; *iets met een ~ vastbinden (dichtbinden)* tie sth. (up) ‖ *in ~ zijn* be busy, be hard at it; *iets op ~ zetten* set sth. on foot, start sth.

de **touwladder** /tɑuladər/ (pl: -s) rope ladder

het **touwtje** /tɑucə/ (pl: -s) (piece of) string: *de ~s in handen hebben* be pulling the strings, be running the show

touwtjespringen /tɑucəsprɪŋə(n)/ (sprong touwtje, heeft touwtjegesprongen) skipping

touwtrekken /tɑutrɛkə(n)/ tug-of-war

t.o.v. *ten opzichte van* with respect to, with regard to

de **tovenaar** /tovənar/ (pl: -s) magician, sorcerer, wizard

de **toverdrank** /tovərdrɑŋk/ (pl: -en) magic potion

¹**toveren** /tovərə(n)/ (toverde, heeft getoverd) work magic; do conjuring tricks

²**toveren** /tovərə(n)/ (toverde, heeft getoverd) conjure (up): *iets tevoorschijn ~* conjure up sth.

de **toverheks** /tovərhɛks/ (pl: -en) sorceress, magician

de **toverij** /tovərɛi/ (pl: -en) magic, sorcery

de **toverslag** /tovərslɑx/: *als bij ~* like magic

de **toverspreuk** /tovərsprøk/ (pl: -en) (magic) spell, (magic) charm

de **toverstaf** /tovərstaf/ (pl: -staven) magic wand

toxisch /tɔksis/ (adj) toxic, poisonous

traag /trax/ (adj, adv) slow: *hij is nogal ~ van begrip* he isn't very quick in the uptake; *~ op gang komen* get off to a slow start

de **traagheid** /traxhɛit/ slowness: *de ~ van geest* slowness (of mind)

de **traan** /tran/ (pl: tranen) tear; teardrop: *in tranen uitbarsten* burst into tears, burst out crying; *tranen met tuiten huilen* cry buckets,

cry one's eyes out; *geen ~ om iets laten* not shed tears over sth.

het **traangas** /tranɣɑs/ tear-gas

de **traanklier** /tranklir/ (pl: -en) tear gland

het **tracé** /trase/ (pl: -s) (planned) route

traceren /traserə(n)/ (traceerde, heeft getraceerd) trace

trachten /trɑxtə(n)/ (trachtte, heeft getracht) attempt, try

de **tractor** /trɑktor/ (pl: -s) tractor

de **traditie** /tradi(t)si/ (pl: -s) tradition: *een ~ in ere houden* uphold a tradition

traditiegetrouw /tradi(t)siɣətrɑu/ (adj, adv) traditional; true to tradition

traditioneel /tradi(t)ʃonel/ (adj, adv) traditional

de **tragedie** /traɣedi/ (pl: -s) tragedy

de **tragiek** /traɣik/ tragedy

tragikomisch /traɣikomis/ (adj) tragicomic

tragisch /traɣis/ (adj, adv) tragic: *het ~e is de tragedy of it is …*

de **trailer** /trelər/ (pl: -s) trailer

¹**trainen** /trenə(n)/ (trainde, heeft getraind) train; work out: *(weer) gaan ~* go into training (again)

²**trainen** /trenə(n)/ (trainde, heeft getraind) train: *een elftal ~* train (or: coach) a team; *zijn geheugen ~* train one's memory; *zich ~ in iets* train for sth.

de **trainer** /trenər/ (pl: -s) trainer, coach

traineren /trɛnerə(n)/ (traineerde, heeft getraineerd) delay: *hij probeert de zaak alleen maar te ~* he's just dragging his feet

de **training** /trenɪŋ/ (pl: -en) training, practice; workout: *een zware ~* a heavy workout

de **trainingsbroek** /trenɪŋzbruk/ (pl: -en) tracksuit bottoms, jogging bottoms; [Am] sweat pants

het **trainingshesje** /trenɪŋshɛʃə/ (pl: -s) training bib (or: vest)

het **trainingspak** /trenɪŋspɑk/ (pl: -ken) tracksuit, jogging suit

het **traject** /trajɛkt/ (pl: -en) route, stretch; section

het **traktaat** /trɑktat/ (pl: traktaten) **1** treaty **2** tract

de **traktatie** /trɑktat͜si/ (pl: -s) treat

trakteren /trɑkterə(n)/ (trakteerde, heeft getrakteerd) treat: *~ op gebakjes* treat s.o. to cake; *ik trakteer* this is my treat

de **tralie** /trali/ (pl: -s) bar: *achter de ~s zitten* be behind bars

de **tram** /trɛm/ (pl: -s) tram: *met de ~ gaan* take the (or: go by) tram

de **tramhalte** /trɛmhɑltə/ (pl: -s) tramstop

het **trammelant** /trɑmələnt/ [inform] trouble: *daar krijg je ~ mee* that will get you into trouble

de **trampoline** /trɑmpolinə/ (pl: -s) trampoline

trampolinespringen /trɑmpolinəsprɪŋə(n)/ trampolining

de **trance** /trãs/ (pl: -s) trance: *iem. in ~ brengen* send s.o. into a trance

tranen /trɑnə(n)/ (traande, heeft getraand) run, water: *~de ogen* running (*or:* watering) eyes

de **transactie** /trɑnsɑksi/ (pl: -s) transaction, deal

trans-Atlantisch /trɑnsɑtlɑntis/ (adj) transatlantic

het/de **transfer** /trɑnsfyːr/ (pl: -s) transfer

het **transferium** /trɑnsfɛrijʏm/ [roughly] Park and Ride

de **transfermarkt** /trɑnsfyːrmɑrkt/ transfer market

de **transfersom** /trɑnsfyːrsɔm/ (pl: -men) transfer fee

de **transformatie** /trɑnsfɔrmɑ(t)si/ (pl: -s) transformation

de **transformator** /trɑnsfɔrmɑtɔr/ (pl: -en, -s) transformer

transformeren /trɑnsfɔrmɛrə(n)/ (transformeerde, heeft getransformeerd) transform in(to)

de **transfusie** /trɑnsfyzi/ (pl: -s) transfusion

de **transistor** /trɑnzɪstɔr/ (pl: -s) transistor

de **transistorradio** /trɑnzɪstɔradijo/ (pl: -'s) transistor (radio)

de **transit** /trɑnzit/ transit

transitief /trɑnzitif/ (adj) transitive

het/de **transito** /trɑnzito/ transit

de **transitzone** /trɑnzɪtsɔːnə/ (pl: -s) **1** transit area **2** transit zone

de **transmissie** /trɑnsmɪsi/ (pl: -s) transmission

het ¹**transparant** /trɑnspɑrɑnt/ (pl: -en) transparency, overhead sheet

²**transparant** /trɑnspɑrɑnt/ (adj) transparent

de **transpiratie** /trɑnspirɑ(t)si/ (pl: -s) perspiration

transpireren /trɑnspirɛrə(n)/ (transpireerde, heeft getranspireerd) perspire

de **transplantatie** /trɑnsplɑntɑ(t)si/ (pl: -s) transplant(ation)

transplanteren /trɑnsplɑntɛrə(n)/ (transplanteerde, heeft getransplanteerd) transplant

het **transport** /trɑnspɔrt/ (pl: -en) transport; [esp Am] transportation: *tijdens het ~ in* (*or:* during) transit

de **transportband** /trɑnspɔrdbɑnt/ (pl: -en) conveyer (belt)

het **transportbedrijf** /trɑnspɔrdbədrɛif/ (pl: -bedrijven) transport company, haulier

¹**transporteren** /trɑnspɔrtɛrə(n)/ (transporteerde, heeft getransporteerd) transport

²**transporteren** /trɑnspɔrtɛrə(n)/ (transporteerde, heeft getransporteerd) wind (the film) (on)

de **transporteur** /trɑnspɔrtØr/ (pl: -s) carrier

de **transportkosten** /trɑnspɔrtkɔstə(n)/ (pl) transport costs (*or:* charges)

de **transportonderneming** /trɑnspɔrtɔndərnemɪŋ/ (pl: -en) *see transportbedrijf*

de **transseksualiteit** /trɑnsɛksywalitɛit/ transsexualism

de ¹**transseksueel** /trɑnsɛksywel/ (pl: -seksuelen) transsexual

²**transseksueel** /trɑnsɛksywel/ (adj) transsexual

de **trant** /trɑnt/ **1** style, manner: *in dezelfde ~* (all) in the same key **2** kind: *iets in die ~* sth. of the kind (*or:* sort)

de **trap** /trɑp/ (pl: -pen) **1** (flight of) stairs; (flight of) steps: *een steile ~* steep stairs; *de ~ afgaan* go down(stairs); *de ~ opgaan* go upstairs; *boven* (*or:* onder, beneden) *aan de ~ at* the head (*or:* at the foot, at the bottom) of the stairs **2** kick: *vrije ~* free kick; *iem. een ~ nageven* [fig] hit s.o. when he is down **3** step **4** [linguistics] degree: *de ~pen van vergelijking* the degrees of comparison; *overtreffende ~* superlative; *vergrotende ~* comparative

de **trapeze** /trapɛzə/ (pl: -s) trapeze

het **trapezium** /trapɛzijʏm/ (pl: -s) trapezium; [Am] trapezoid

de **trapgevel** /trɑpxevəl/ (pl: -s) (crow-)stepped gable

de **trapleuning** /trɑplønɪŋ/ (pl: -en) (stair) handrail; banister

de **traplift** /trɑplɪft/ (pl: -en) stairlift

traploos /trɑplos/ (adj) stepless

de **traploper** /trɑplopər/ (pl: -s) stair carpet

trappelen /trɑpələ(n)/ (trappelde, heeft getrappeld) stamp: *~de paarden* stamping (and pawing) horses; *~ van ongeduld* strain at the leash; be dying (to do sth., go somewhere)

de **trappelzak** /trɑpəlzɑk/ (pl: -ken) infant's sleeping bag

¹**trappen** /trɑpə(n)/ (trapte, heeft/is getrapt) step, stamp: *ergens in ~* fall for sth., rise to the bait, buy sth.

²**trappen** /trɑpə(n)/ (trapte, heeft getrapt) kick, boot: *tegen een bal ~* kick a ball; *eruit getrapt zijn* have got the boot (*or:* sack); have been kicked out || *lol ~* horse about (*or:* around), lark about (*or:* around)

het **trappenhuis** /trɑpə(n)hœys/ (pl: -huizen) (stair)well

de **trapper** /trɑpər/ (pl: -s) pedal: *op de ~s gaan staan* throw one's weight on the pedals

de **trappist** /trɑpɪst/ (pl: -en) Trappist

het **trappistenbier** /trɑpɪstə(n)bir/ Trappist beer

het **trapportaal** /trɑpɔrtal/ (pl: -portalen) landing

trapsgewijs /trɑpsxəwɛis/ (adj, adv) gradual, step-by-step

het **trapveldje** /trɑpfɛlcə/ (pl: -s) grassplot

het/de **trauma** /trɑuma/ (pl: -'s) trauma

de **traumahelikopter** /trɑumahelikɔptər/

trauma helicopter

het **traumateam** /trɑumati:m/ (pl: -s) medical emergency team

traumatisch /trɑumɑtis/ (adj) traumatic

de **travestie** /travɛsti/ (pl: -ën) transvestism

de **travestiet** /travɛstit/ (pl: -en) transvestite

de **trawler** /trɔːlər/ (pl: -s) trawler

de **trechter** /trɛxtər/ (pl: -s) funnel

de **tred** /trɛt/ (pl: -en) step, pace: *gelijke ~ houden met* keep pace with

de **trede** /tredə/ (pl: -n) step; rung

treden /tredə(n)/ (trad, is getreden) step: *in details ~* go into detail(s); *in contact ~ met iem.* contact s.o.; *in het huwelijk ~ (met)* get married (to s.o.); *naar buiten ~ met iets* come out, make sth. public; *naar voren ~* **a)** come forward; **b)** [fig] stand out

de **tredmolen** /trɛtmolə(n)/ (pl: -s) treadmill

de **tree** /tre/ (pl: -ën, -s) *see* trede

de **treeplank** /treplɑŋk/ (pl: -en) footboard

treffen /trɛfə(n)/ (trof, heeft getroffen) **1** hit: *getroffen door de bliksem* struck by lightning **2** meet: *niemand thuis ~* find nobody (at) home **3** hit, strike: *getroffen worden door* meet with; be stricken by **4** make: *voorbereidingen ~* make preparations || *je treft het (goed)* you're lucky (*or:* in luck); *zij hebben het met elkaar getroffen* they are happy with one another, they get on like a house on fire

treffend /trɛfənt/ (adj, adv) striking; apt: *een ~e gelijkenis* a striking similarity

de **treffer** /trɛfər/ (pl: -s) hit; goal

het **trefpunt** /trɛfpʏnt/ (pl: -en) meeting place; crossroads

het **trefwoord** /trɛfwort/ (pl: -en) headword; reference

trefzeker /trɛfsekər/ (adj, adv) accurate

de **trein** /trɛin/ (pl: -en) train: *met de ~ reizen* go by train; *iem. van de ~ halen* meet s.o. at the station || *dat loopt als een ~* it's going like a bomb, there's no stopping it

de **treinbestuurder** /trɛimbəstyrdər/ (pl: -s) train driver

de **treinconducteur** /trɛinkɔndʏktør/ (pl: -s) guard; [Am] conductor

het **treinkaartje** /trɛinkarcə/ (pl: -s) train ticket

het **treinongeluk** /trɛinɔŋɣəlʏk/ train accident

de **treinramp** /trɛinrɑmp/ (pl: -en) train disaster

de **treinreis** /trɛinrɛis/ (pl: -reizen) train journey

de **treinreiziger** /trɛinrɛizəɣər/ (pl: -s) rail(way) passenger

het **treinstel** /trɛinstɛl/ (pl: -len) train unit

het **treinverkeer** /trɛinvərker/ train traffic, rail traffic

de **treiteraar** /trɛitərar/ (pl: -s) tormentor

treiteren /trɛitərə(n)/ (treiterde, heeft getreiterd) torment

de **trek** /trɛk/ (pl: -ken) **1** pull **2** stroke **3** fea-

ture, line **4** (characteristic) feature, trait: *dat is een naar ~je van haar* that is a nasty trait of hers **5** appetite: *~ hebben* feel (*or:* be) hungry; *heeft u ~ in een kopje koffie?* do you feel like a cup of coffee, would you care for a cup of coffee? **6** popularity: *in ~ zijn* be popular, be in demand **7** migration || *geen ~ aan een sigaar doen* take a puff at a cigar; *niet aan zijn ~ken komen* come into one's own

de **trekhaak** /trɛkhak/ (pl: -haken) drawbar; tow bar

de **trekharmonica** /trɛkhɑrmonika/ (pl: -'s) accordion; concertina

¹**trekken** /trɛkə(n)/ (trok, heeft/is getrokken) **1** pull: *iem. aan zijn haar ~* pull s.o.'s hair; *aan een sigaar ~* puff at (*or:* draw) a cigar **2** go, move; travel; migrate: *de verkiezingskaravaan trekt het hele land door* the election caravan is touring the whole country; *in een huis ~* move into a house **3** stretch: *met zijn been ~* walk with a stiff leg || *deze planken zijn krom getrokken* these planks are warped; *thee laten ~* brew tea

²**trekken** /trɛkə(n)/ (trok, heeft getrokken) **1** draw; extract; pull (out) **2** lead: *een project ~* lead a project **3** draw, attract: *de aandacht ~* attract attention; *publiek* (*or:* *kopers*) *~* draw an audience (*or:* customers); *volle zalen ~* play to (*or:* draw) full houses **4** pull, draw, tow **5** draw; [maths] extract: *een conclusie ~* draw a conclusion || *gezichten ~* make (*or:* pull) (silly) faces; *ik trek het niet langer* I can't hold out any longer

de **trekker** /trɛkər/ (pl: -s) **1** hiker **2** trigger: *de ~ overhalen* pull the trigger **3** truck, lorry: *~ met oplegger* truck and trailer **4** tractor

de **trekking** /trɛkɪŋ/ (pl: -en) draw

de **trekkracht** /trɛkrɑxt/ (pl: -en) tractive power, pulling power

de **trekpleister** /trɛkplɛistər/ (pl: -s) draw, attraction: *een toeristische ~* a tourist attraction

de **trekschuit** /trɛksxœyt/ (pl: -en) tow barge

de **trektocht** /trɛktɔxt/ (pl: -en) hike, hiking tour

de **trekvogel** /trɛkfoɣəl/ (pl: -s) migratory bird, bird of passage

het **trema** /trema/ (pl: -'s) diaeresis

de **trend** /trɛnt/ (pl: -s) trend: *tegen de ~ in gaan* buck the trend

de **trendbreuk** /trɛndbrøk/ (pl: -en) deviation from a trend

trendgevoelig /trɛntxəvuləx/ (adj, adv) subject to trends

de **trendsetter** /trɛntsɛtər/ (pl: -s) trendsetter

trendy /trɛndi/ (adj) trendy: *~ zijn* be (really) in, be the in-thing

treuren /trørə(n)/ (treurde, heeft getreurd) **1** sorrow, mourn, grieve: *~ om een verlies* mourn a loss **2** be sorrowful, be mournful

treurig /trørəx/ (adj, adv) sad, tragic, unhappy: *een ~ gezicht* a sorry (*or:* gloomy) sight; *a sad* (*or:* dejected) face

de **treurigheid** /trø̱rəχhɛit/ sorrow, sadness

de **treurmars** /trø̱rmɑrs/ (pl: -en) funeral march

het **treurspel** /trø̱rspɛl/ (pl: -en) tragedy

de **treurwilg** /trø̱rwɪlχ/ (pl: -en) weeping willow

treuzelen /trø̱zələ(n)/ (treuzelde, heeft getreuzeld) dawdle: *~ met zijn werk* dawdle over one's work

de **triangel** /trija̱ŋəl/ (pl: -s) triangle

de **triatlon** /trija̱tlɔn/ (pl: -s) triathlon

het **tribunaal** /tribyna̱l/ (pl: tribunalen) tribunal

de **tribune** /triby̱nə/ (pl: -s) stand; gallery

het **tricot** /tri̱ko/ (pl: -s) tricot

triest /trist/ (adj, adv) **1** sad **2** melancholy, depressing, dreary

het **triktrak** /trɪ̱ktrɑk/ backgammon

het **triljard** /trɪljɑ̱rt/ (pl: -en) a thousand quadrillions; [Am] octillion

het **triljoen** /trɪljṵn/ (pl: -en) quintillion

trillen /trɪ̱lə(n)/ (trilde, heeft getrild) vibrate; tremble; shake: *met ~de stem* in a trembling voice

de **trilling** /trɪ̱lɪŋ/ (pl: -en) **1** vibration; tremor **2** trembling, shaking

de **trilogie** /triloχi̱/ (pl: -ën) trilogy

de **trilplaat** /trɪ̱lplat/ (pl: -platen) vibration plate

de **trimbaan** /trɪ̱mban/ (pl: -banen) [Dutch] keep-fit trail

het **trimester** /trimɛ̱stər/ (pl: -s) trimester; term: *midden in het ~* (in) mid-term

¹**trimmen** /trɪ̱mə(n)/ (trimde, heeft/is getrimd) do keep-fit (exercises); jog; work out

²**trimmen** /trɪ̱mə(n)/ (trimde, heeft getrimd) trim

de **trimmer** /trɪ̱mər/ (pl: -s) jogger

het **trimpak** /trɪ̱mpɑk/ tracksuit

de **trimschoen** /trɪ̱msχun/ (pl: -en) training shoe, jogging shoe

het **trio** /tri̱jo/ (pl: -'s) trio

de **triomf** /trijɔ̱mf/ (pl: -en) triumph

triomfantelijk /trijɔmfɑ̱ntələk/ (adj, adv) triumphant

triomferen /trijɔmfe̱rə(n)/ (triomfeerde, heeft getriomfeerd) triumph

de **triomftocht** /trijɔ̱mftɔχt/ (pl: -en) triumphal procession

de **trip** /trɪp/ (pl: -s) **1** trip **2** (acid) trip

het **triplex** /tri̱plɛks/ plywood

triplo /tri̱plo/: *in ~* in triplicate

trippelen /trɪ̱pələ(n)/ (trippelde, heeft/is getrippeld) trip, patter

trippen /trɪ̱pə(n)/ (tripte, heeft getript) trip (out): *hij tript op hardrockmuziek* he gets off on hard rock (music)

de **trits** /trɪts/ (pl: -en): *een hele ~* a battery (of); [Am] a bunch (of)

triviaal /trivija̱l/ (adj) trivial

troebel /tru̱bəl/ (adj) turbid, cloudy: *in ~ water vissen* fish in troubled waters

de **troef** /truf/ (pl: troeven) trumps, trump (card): *welke kleur is ~?* what suit is trumps?; *zijn laatste ~ uitspelen* play one's trump card

de **troep** /trup/ (pl: -en) **1** troop; pack **2** mess: *gooi de hele ~ maar weg* just get rid of the whole lot; *~ maken* make a mess **3** [mil] troop: [fig] *voor de ~en uit lopen* jump the gun, chafe at the bit **4** company

de **troepenmacht** /tru̱pə(n)mɑχt/ (pl: -en) (military) force

het **troeteldier** /tru̱təldir/ (pl: -en) cuddly toy, soft toy

het **troetelkind** /tru̱təlkɪnt/ (pl: -kinderen) darling, pet; spoiled child

de **troetelnaam** /tru̱təlnam/ (pl: -namen) pet name

troeven /tru̱və(n)/ (troefde, heeft getroefd) [cards] trump, play trumps

de **trofee** /trofe̱/ (pl: -ën) trophy

de **troffel** /trɔ̱fəl/ (pl: -s) trowel

de **trog** /trɔχ/ (pl: -gen) trough

Trojaans /troja̱ns/ (adj) Trojan

Troje /tro̱jə/ Troy

de **trojka** /trɔ̱jka/ (pl: -'s) troika, triumvirate

de **trol** /trɔl/ (pl: -len) troll

de **trolleybus** /trɔ̱libʏs/ (pl: -sen) trolleybus

de **trom** /trɔm/ (pl: -men) drum: [fig] *met stille ~ vertrekken* slip away

de **trombone** /trɔmbo̱ːnə/ (pl: -s) trombone

de **trombonist** /trɔmboni̱st/ (pl: -en) trombonist

de **trombose** /trɔmbo̱zə/ thrombosis

de **trommel** /trɔ̱məl/ (pl: -s) **1** drum: *de ~ slaan* beat the drum **2** box

trommelen /trɔ̱mələ(n)/ (trommelde, heeft getrommeld) drum: *op de tafel ~* drum (on) the table ‖ *een groep mensen bij elkaar ~* drum up a group of people

de **trommelrem** /trɔ̱məlrɛm/ (pl: -men) drum brake

het **trommelvlies** /trɔ̱məlvlis/ (pl: -vliezen) eardrum, tympanum

de **trompet** /trɔmpɛ̱t/ (pl: -ten) trumpet

trompetten /trɔmpɛ̱tə(n)/ (trompette, heeft getrompet) trumpet

trompetteren /trɔmpɛ̱tərə(n)/ (trompetterde, heeft getrompetterd) trumpet

de **trompettist** /trɔmpɛtɪ̱st/ (pl: -en) trumpet player

de **tronie** /tro̱ni/ (pl: -s) mug

de **troon** /tron/ (pl: tronen) throne: *de ~ beklimmen (bestijgen)* come to (*or:* ascend) the throne; *afstand doen van de ~* abdicate (*or:* renounce) the throne; *iem. van de ~ stoten* dethrone s.o.

de **troonopvolger** /tro̱nɔpfɔlχər/ (pl: -s) heir (to the throne)

de **troonpretendent** /trɔ̱mpretɛndɛnt/ (pl: -en) **1** pretender to a/the throne **2** candidate

(for)

de **troonrede** /trɔ̯nredə/ (pl: -s) Queen's speech, King's speech

de **troonsafstand** /trɔnsɑfstɑnt/ abdication (of the throne): ~ **doen** abdicate

de **troonsbestijging** /trɔnzbəstɛɪɣɪŋ/ accession (to the throne)

de **troost** /trost/ comfort, consolation: *een bakje* ~ a) [Dutch] a cup of coffee; b) [British] a cuppa; *een* **schrale** ~ cold (*or:* scant) comfort/consolation; ~ **putten** *uit de gedachte* find comfort in the idea

troosteloos /trostəlos/ (adj, adv) disconsolate; cheerless: *een* ~ **landschap** a dreary (*or:* desolate) landscape/scene

troosten /trostə(n)/ (troostte, heeft getroost) comfort, console: *zij was* **niet** *te* ~ she was beyond (all) consolation

de **troostprijs** /trostprɛis/ (pl: -prijzen) consolation prize

het **troostvoedsel** /trostfutsəl/ comfort food

de **tropen** /trɔpə(n)/ (pl) tropics

de **tropenjaren** /trɔpə(n)jarə(n)/ (pl) [fig] hard and difficult years

het **tropenrooster** /trɔpə(n)rostər/ (pl: -s) work schedule suited to a tropical climate

tropisch /tropis/ (adj, adv) tropical: *het is hier* ~ *(warm)* it is sweltering here

de **tros** /trɔs/ (pl: -sen) 1 cluster; bunch 2 hawser: *de* ~*sen* **losgooien** cast off, unmoor

de **trostomaat** /trɔstomat/ (pl: -tomaten) vine tomato

de ¹**trots** /trɔts/ pride, glory: *ze is de* ~ *van haar* **ouders** she is her parents' pride and joy; *met* **gepaste** ~ with justifiable pride

²**trots** /trɔts/ (adj, adv) proud

trotseren /trɔtserə(n)/ (trotseerde, heeft getrotseerd) 1 defy; brave: *de* **blik(ken)** ~ *(van)* outface, outstare 2 stand up (to)

het **trottoir** /trɔtwar/ (pl: -s) pavement; [Am] sidewalk

de **troubadour** /trubadur/ (pl: -s) troubadour

de ¹**trouw** /trɑu/ fidelity, loyalty, faith(fulness); allegiance: *te* **goeder** ~ *zijn* be bona fide, in good faith; *te* **kwader** ~ mala fide, in bad faith

²**trouw** /trɑu/ (adj, adv) faithful: ~*e* **onderdanen** loyal subjects; *elkaar* ~ **blijven** be (*or:* remain) faithful/true to each other

het **trouwboekje** /trɑubukjə/ (pl: -s) [roughly] marriage certificate

de **trouwdag** /trɑudɑx/ (pl: -en) wedding day

trouweloos /trɑuwəlos/ (adj, adv) perfidious, disloyal

¹**trouwen** /trɑuwə(n)/ (trouwde, is getrouwd) get married: *ik ben* **er** *niet* **mee** *getrouwd* I'm not wedded (*or:* tied) to it; *ze trouwde* **met** *een arts* she married a doctor; **voor** *de wet* ~ get married in a registry office

²**trouwen** /trɑuwə(n)/ (trouwde, heeft getrouwd) marry

trouwens /trɑuwəns/ (adv) 1 mind you: *ik vind haar* ~ *wel heel aardig* mind you, I do think she's very nice; *hij komt niet; ik* ~ *ook niet* he isn't coming; neither am I for that matter 2 by the way: ~, *was Jan er ook?* by the way, was Jan there as well?

de **trouwerij** /trɑuwerɛi/ (pl: -en) wedding

de **trouwjurk** /trɑujʏrk/ (pl: -en) wedding dress

de **trouwpartij** /trɑupɑrtɛi/ (pl: -en) 1 wedding (party) 2 wedding ceremony, marriage ceremony

de **trouwplannen** /trɑuplɑnə(n)/ (pl): ~ **hebben** be going (*or:* planning) to get married

de **trouwring** /trɑurɪŋ/ (pl: -en) wedding ring

de **truc** /trʏk/ (pl: -s) trick: *een* ~ *met* **kaarten** a card trick; *dat* **is** *de* ~ that's the secret

de **trucage** /trʏkaʒə/ (pl: -s) trickery

de **truck** /trʏk/ (pl: -s) articulated lorry; [Am] trailer truck; truck

de **trucker** /trʏkər/ (pl: -s) lorry-driver; [Am] trucker

de **truffel** /trʏfəl/ (pl: -s) truffle

de **trui** /trœy/ (pl: -en) 1 jumper; sweater 2 jersey, shirt: *de* **gele** ~ the yellow jersey

de **trukendoos** /trʏkə(n)dos/ box of tricks

de **trust** /trʏst/ (pl: -s) trust, cartel

de **trut** /trʏt/ (pl: -ten) [inform] cow: *stomme* ~*!* silly cow!

trutten /trʏtə(n)/ (trutte, heeft getrut) fiddle around

truttig /trʏtəx/ (adj, adv) [inform] frumpy

de **try-out** /trɑjɑut/ (pl: -s) tryout; public rehearsal

de **tsaar** /tsar/ (pl: tsaren) tsar, czar

het **T-shirt** /tiʃʏːrt/ (pl: -s) T-shirt, tee shirt

Tsjaad /tʃat/ Chad

de **Tsjadiër** /tʃadijər/ (pl: -s) Chadian

Tsjadisch /tʃadis/ (adj) Chadian

de **Tsjech** /tʃɛx/ (pl: -en) Czech

Tsjechië /tʃɛxijə/ Czech Republic

het ¹**Tsjechisch** /tʃɛxis/ Czech

²**Tsjechisch** /tʃɛxis/ (adj) Czech

Tsjecho-Slowakije /tʃɛxoslowakɛijə/ Czechoslovakia

de **Tsjetsjeen** /tʃetʃen/ (pl: Tsjetsjenen) Chechen

het ¹**Tsjetsjeens** /tʃetʃens/ Chechen

²**Tsjetsjeens** /tʃetʃens/ (adj) Chechen

Tsjetsjenië /tʃetʃenijə/ Chech(e)nia

het **tso** /teɛso/ [Belg] secondary technical education

de **tsunami** /tsunami/ tsunami

de **tuba** /tyba/ (pl: -'s) tuba

de **tube** /tybə/ (pl: -s) tube

de **tuberculose** /tybɛrkylozə/ tuberculosis

de **tucht** /tʏxt/ discipline: *de* ~ **handhaven** maintain (*or:* keep) discipline

het **tuchtcollege** /tʏxtkɔleʒə/ (pl: -s) disciplinary tribunal

het **tuchtrecht** /tʏxtrɛxt/ disciplinary rules

de **tuchtschool** /tʏxtsχol/ (pl: -scholen) youth custody centre

tuffen /tʏfə(n)/ (tufte, heeft/is getuft) chug; drive

de **tuibrug** /tœybrʏχ/ (pl: -gen) rope bridge, cable bridge

het **tuig** /tœyχ/ (pl: -en) **1** harness **2** riff-raff: *langharig **werkschuw** ~* long-haired workshy layabouts **3** tackle

tuigen /tœyɣə(n)/ (tuigde, heeft getuigd) harness; tackle (up); bridle

het **tuigje** /tœyχjə/ (pl: -s) safety harness

de **tuimelaar** /tœymələr/ (pl: -s) tumbler, wobbly clown, wobbly man

tuimelen /tœymələ(n)/ (tuimelde, is getuimeld) tumble, topple

de **tuimeling** /tœyməlɪŋ/ (pl: -en) tumble, fall: *een ~ **maken*** tumble, fall

het **tuimelraam** /tœyməlram/ (pl: -ramen) pivot(al) window

de **tuin** /tœyn/ (pl: -en) garden || *iem. **om de ~** leiden* lead s.o. up the garden path

de **tuinbank** /tœymbaŋk/ (pl: -en) garden bench

de **tuinboon** /tœymbon/ (pl: -bonen) broad bean

de **tuinbouw** /tœymbau/ horticulture, market gardening

het **tuinbouwbedrijf** /tœymbaubədrɛif/ (pl: -bedrijven) market garden

de **tuinbouwschool** /tœymbausχol/ (pl: -scholen) horticultural school (*or:* college)

de **tuinbroek** /tœymbruk/ (pl: -en) dungarees, overalls

het **tuincentrum** /tœynsɛntrʏm/ (pl: -centra) garden centre

de **tuinder** /tœyndər/ (pl: -s) market gardener

tuinen /tœynə(n)/ (tuinde, is getuind): *erin ~* fall for it

het **tuinfeest** /tœynfest/ (pl: -en) garden party

het **tuingereedschap** /tœynɣəretsχap/ garden(ing) tools

het **tuinhuisje** /tœynhœyʃə/ (pl: -s) garden house

de **tuinier** /tœynir/ (pl: -s) gardener

tuinieren /tœynirə(n)/ (tuinierde, heeft getuinierd) garden

de **tuinkabouter** /tœyŋkabautər/ (pl: -s) garden gnome

de **tuinkers** /tœyŋkɛrs/ (garden) cress

de **tuinman** /tœyman/ (pl: tuinlieden) gardener

de **tuinslak** /tœynslak/ (pl: -ken) garden snail; garden slug

de **tuinslang** /tœynslaŋ/ (pl: -en) (garden) hose

de **tuinstoel** /tœynstul/ (pl: -en) garden chair

de **tuit** /tœyt/ (pl: -en) **1** spout **2** nozzle

¹**tuiten** /tœytə(n)/ (tuitte, heeft getuit) tingle, ring: *mijn **oren** ~* my ears are ringing

²**tuiten** /tœytə(n)/ (tuitte, heeft getuit) purse: *de **lippen** ~* purse one's lips

tuk /tʏk/ (adj) keen (on): *daar ben ik ~ op* I'm keen on (*or:* mad about) that || *ik **had** je lekker ~ gisteren, hè?* I really had you fooled yesterday, didn't I?; *iem. ~ **hebben*** pull s.o.'s leg

het **tukje** /tʏkjə/ (pl: -s) nap: *een ~ **doen*** take a nap

tukken /tʏkə(n)/ (tukte, heeft getukt) nap, doze

de **tulband** /tʏlbant/ (pl: -en) turban

de **tulp** /tʏlp/ (pl: -en) tulip

de **tulpenbol** /tʏlpə(n)bol/ (pl: -len) tulip bulb

de **tulpvakantie** /tʏlpfakan(t)si/ (pl: -s) [Dutch] half-term holiday, spring holiday

de **tumor** /tymor/ (pl: -en) tumour: *kwaadaardige* (or: *goedaardige*) *~* malignant (*or:* benign) tumour

het **tumult** /tymʏlt/ (pl: -en) tumult, uproar

tumultueus /tymʏltywøs/ (adj) tumultuous

de **tune** /cu:n/ (pl: -s) tune

de **tuner** /cu:nər/ (pl: -s) tuner

Tunesië /tynezijə/ Tunisia

de **Tunesiër** /tynezijər/ (pl: -s) Tunisian

Tunesisch /tynezis/ (adj) Tunisian

de **tunnel** /tʏnəl/ (pl: -s) tunnel: *er gloort licht aan het **eind** van de ~* there's light at the end of the tunnel

de **tunnelvisie** /tʏnəlvizi/ tunnel vision

de **turbine** /tʏrbinə/ (pl: -s) turbine

de **turbo** /tʏrbo/ (pl: -'s) **1** turbo((super)charger) **2** turbo(-car) || *turbostofzuiger* high-powered vacuum cleaner

turbulent /tʏrbylɛnt/ (adj) turbulent; tempestuous

de **turbulentie** /tʏrbylɛn(t)si/ (pl: -s) turbulence

tureluurs /tyrəlyrs/ (adj) mad, whacky, crazy: *het is om ~ (van) te **worden*** it's enough to drive anybody mad (*or:* up the wall)

turen /tyrə(n)/ (tuurde, heeft getuurd) peer, gaze, stare: *in de verte ~* gaze into the distance

de **turf** /tʏrf/ (pl: turven) **1** peat **2** tally **3** tome

het/de **turfmolm** /tʏrfmolm/ peat dust

Turijn /tyrɛin/ Turin

de **Turk** /tʏrk/ (pl: -en) Turk

Turkije /tʏrkɛiə/ Turkey

de **Turkmeen** /tʏrkmen/ (pl: Turkmenen) Turkmen

Turkmeens /tʏrkmens/ (adj) Turkoman, Turkman

Turkmenistan /tʏrkmɛnistan/ Turkmenistan

de ¹**turkoois** /tʏrkɔis/ [gem] turquoise

het ²**turkoois** /tʏrkɔis/ [mineral] turquoise

Turks /tʏrks/ (adj) Turkish

turnen /tʏrnə(n)/ (turnde, heeft geturnd) practise gymnastics, perform gymnastics

de **turner** /tʏrnər/ (pl: -s) gymnast

de **turnmat** /tʏrmat/ (pl: -ten) gym mat

turquoise /tʏrkwazə/ (adj) turquoise

turven /tʏrvə(n)/ (turfde, heeft geturfd) tally

tussen /tʏsə(n)/ (prep) **1** between: ~ *de middag* at lunchtime; *dat blijft ~ ons (tweeën)* that's between you and me **2** among: *het huis stond ~ de bomen* in the house stood among(st) the trees; ~ *vier muren* within four walls ‖ *iem. er (mooi) ~ nemen* have s.o. on, take s.o. in; *als er niets ~ komt, dan …* unless sth. unforeseen should occur

tussenbeide /tʏsə(n)bɛidə/ (adv) between, in: ~ *komen* interrupt, butt in; step in, intervene; intercede

de **tussendeur** /tʏsə(n)dør/ (pl: -en) communicating door, dividing door

tussendoor /tʏsə(n)dor/ (adv) **1** through; between them **2** between times: *proberen ~ wat te slapen* try to snatch some sleep

het **tussendoortje** /tʏsə(n)dortʃə/ (pl: -s) snack

de **tussenhandel** /tʏsə(n)handəl/ distributive trade(s)

de **tussenhandelaar** /tʏsə(n)handəlar/ (pl: -s, -handelaren) middleman

tussenin /tʏsə(n)ɪn/ (adv) in between, between the two, in the middle

het **tussenjaar** /tʏsə(n)jar/ (pl: -jaren) gap year: *een ~ nemen* take a gap year

de **tussenjas** /tʏsə(n)jɑs/ (pl: -sen) between-seasons coat

de **tussenkomst** /tʏsə(n)kɔmst/ **1** intervention **2** mediation

de **tussenlanding** /tʏsə(n)lɑndɪŋ/ (pl: -en) stop(over)

tussenliggend /tʏsə(n)lɪɣənt/ (adj) intervening

de **tussenmuur** /tʏsə(n)myr/ (pl: -muren) partition; dividing wall

de **tussenpaus** /tʏsə(n)pɑus/ (pl: -en) [fig] transitory figure

de **tussenpersoon** /tʏsə(n)pɛrson/ (pl: -personen) go-between, intermediary: *als ~ fungeren* act as an intermediary

de **tussenpoos** /tʏsə(n)pos/ (pl: -pozen): *met korte tussenpozen* at short intervals; *met tussenpozen* every so often

de **tussenruimte** /tʏsə(n)rœymtə/ (pl: -n, -s) space: *met gelijke ~n plaatsen* space evenly

de **tussenstand** /tʏsə(n)stɑnt/ (pl: -en) [roughly] score (so far); half-time score

de **tussenstop** /tʏsə(n)stɔp/ (pl: -s) stop(over)

de **tussentijd** /tʏsə(n)tɛit/ (pl: -en) **1** interim: *in de ~* in the meantime, meanwhile **2** [sport] split time: *de snelste ~* fastest split time

tussentijds /tʏsə(n)tɛits/ (adj) interim: *~e verkiezingen* by-elections

tussenuit /tʏsə(n)œyt/ (adv) out (from between two things) ‖ *er ~ knijpen* do a bunk, cut and run

het **tussenuur** /tʏsə(n)yr/ (pl: -uren) **1** free hour **2** free period

tussenvoegen /tʏsə(n)vuɣə(n)/ (voegde tussen, heeft tussengevoegd) insert

de **tussenwand** /tʏsə(n)wɑnt/ (pl: -en) partition

de **tussenweg** /tʏsə(n)wɛɣ/ (pl: -en) middle course

de **tussenwoning** /tʏsə(n)wonɪŋ/ (pl: -en) terraced house, town house

de **tut** /tʏt/ (pl: -ten) [inform] frump

tutoyeren /tytwɑjerə(n)/ (tutoyeerde, heeft getutoyeerd) be on first-name terms

tuttig /tʏtəɣ/ (adj) [inform] frumpy, prissy

de **tutu** /tyty/ (pl: -'s) tutu

de **tv** /teve/ (pl: tv's) TV, television: *tv kijken* watch TV; *wat komt er vanavond op (de) tv?* what's on (TV) tonight?

tv-kijken /tevekɛikə(n)/ (keek tv, heeft tv-gekeken) watch TV

de **tv-serie** /teveseri/ (pl: -s) TV series

t.w. *te weten* namely; viz

twaalf /twalf/ (num) twelve; [in dates] twelfth: *~ dozijn* gross; *om ~ uur 's nachts* at midnight; *om ~ uur 's middags* at (twelve) noon ‖ *de grote wijzer staat al bijna op de ~* the big hand is nearly on the twelve

twaalfde /twalvdə/ (num) twelfth

het **twaalftal** /twalftɑl/ (pl: -len) dozen, twelve

het **twaalfuurtje** /twalfyrtʃə/ (pl: -s) midday snack, lunch

twee /twe/ (num) two; [in dates] second: *~ keer per week* twice a week; *een stuk of ~ a couple of; ~ weken* a fortnight, two weeks; *in ~ën delen* divide in two; halve; *zij waren met hun ~ën* there were two of them ‖ *hij eet en drinkt voor ~* he eats and drinks (enough) for two; *~ aan ~* in twos

de **tweebaansweg** /twebɑnswɛɣ/ (pl: -en) **1** two-lane road **2** dual carriageway; [Am] divided highway

het **tweed** /twi:d/ (pl: -s) tweed

tweedaags /twedaxs/ (adj) two-day

de **¹tweede** /twedə/ (pl: -n) half: *anderhalf is gelijk aan drie ~n* one and a half is the same as three halves

²tweede /twedə/ (num) second: [Dutch] *de Tweede Kamer* the Lower House (*or:* Chamber); *~ keus* second rate, seconds; *als ~ eindigen* **a)** finish second; **b)** be runner-up; **c)** [fig] come off second best; *ten ~* in the second place

het **tweedegeneratieslachtoffer** /twedəɣenəra(t)sislɑxtɔfər/ (pl: -s) second generation victim

tweedegraads /twedəɣrats/ (adj) second-degree: *tweedegraads verbranding* second-degree burn; [Dutch] *tweedegraadsbevoegdheid* lower secondary school teaching qualification

tweedehands /twedəhɑnts/ (adj, adv) second-hand

het **tweedehandsje** /twedəhɑn(t)ʃə/ (pl: -s) [inform] second-hand item

tweedejaars /twedəjars/ (adj) second-year

het **Tweede Kamerlid** /twedəkamərlɪt/ (pl: -leden) [Dutch] member of the Lower House

het **tweedekansonderwijs** /twedəkɑnsɔndərwɛis/ secondary education for adults

tweedelig /twedeləχ/ (adj) two-piece: *een ~ badpak* a two-piece (bathing-suit)

de **tweedelijnszorg** /twedəlɛɪnsɔrχ/ secondary health care

de **tweedeling** /twedelɪŋ/ (pl: -en) split: *sociale ~* social divide

tweederangs /twedərɑŋs/ (adj) second-class

de **tweedracht** /twedrɑχt/ discord

tweeduizend /twedœyzənt/ (num) two thousand

twee-eiig /tweɛiəχ/ (adj) fraternal

het **tweegevecht** /tweɣəvɛχt/ (pl: -en) man-to-man fight, duel

tweehandig /twehɑndəχ/ (adj, adv) ambidext(e)rous

tweehonderd /twehɔndərt/ (num) two hundred

tweehoog /twehoχ/ (adv) on the second floor; [Am] on the third floor

tweejarig /twejarəχ/ (adj) **1** two-year(-old) **2** biennial

de **tweekamerwoning** /twekamərwonɪŋ/ (pl: -en) two-room flat

de **tweekamp** /twekɑmp/ (pl: -en) twosome

de **tweekwartsmaat** /twekwɑrtsmat/ (pl: -maten) two-four time

tweeledig /twreledəχ/ (adj, adv) double, twofold

de **tweeling** /twelɪŋ/ (pl: -en) **1** twins: *zij zijn een ~* they are twins; *eeneiige (or: twee-eiige) ~en* identical (*or:* fraternal) twins **2** twin

de **tweelingbroer** /twelɪŋbrur/ (pl: -s) twin brother

de **Tweelingen** /twelɪŋə(n)/ (pl) [astrology] Gemini, Twins

de **tweelingzus** /twelɪŋzʏs/ (pl: -sen) twin sister

tweemaal /twemal/ (adv) twice: *zich wel ~ bedenken* think twice

tweemaandelijks /twemandələks/ (adj) **1** bimonthly: *een ~ tijdschrift* a bimonthly **2** two-month

tweemotorig /twemotorəχ/ (adj) twin-engined

de **twee-onder-een-kapwoning** /tweɔndərənkɑpwonɪŋ/ (pl: -en) [Dutch] semi-detached house; [Am] (one side of a) duplex

het **tweepersoonsbed** /twepɛrsonzbɛt/ (pl: -den) double bed

de **tweepersoonskamer** /twepɛrsonskamər/ (pl: -s) double(-bedded) room; twin-bedded room

tweeslachtig /tweslɑχtəχ/ (adj) bisexual

de **tweespalt** /twespɑlt/ discord

de **tweesprong** /twesprɔŋ/ (pl: -en) fork, crossroads

tweestemmig /twestɛmɘχ/ (adj, adv) in two voices; two part

de **tweestrijd** /twestrɛit/ internal conflict: *in ~ staan* be torn between (two things)

de **tweet** /twi:t/ (pl: -s) tweet

het **tweetal** /twetal/ (pl: -len) pair, couple

tweetalig /twetaləχ/ (adj) bilingual

tweetallig /twetɑləχ/ (adj) binary

tweeten /twi:tə(n)/ (tweette, heeft getweet) tweet

tweetjes /twecəs/ (num): *wij ~* we two; *zij waren met hun ~* there were two of them

de **tweeverdiener** /tweʋərdinər/ (pl: -s) two-earner; two-earner family, double-income family

het **tweevoud** /twevɑut/ (pl: -en) **1** double, duplicate: *in ~* in duplicate **2** binary, double (of a number)

tweevoudig /twevɑudəχ/ (adj, adv) double, twofold

de **tweewieler** /twewilər/ (pl: -s) two-wheeler

tweezijdig /twezɛidəχ/ (adj) two-sided

de **tweezitsbank** /twezɪtsbɑŋk/ (pl: -en) two-person settee, two-seater settee

de **twijfel** /twɛifəl/ (pl: -s) doubt: *het voordeel van de ~* the benefit of the doubt; *boven (alle) ~ verheven zijn* be beyond all doubt; *iets in ~ trekken* cast doubt on sth., question sth.; *zonder ~* no doubt, doubtless, undoubtedly

de **twijfelaar** /twɛifəlar/ (pl: -s) doubter; sceptic

twijfelachtig /twɛifəlɑχtəχ/ (adj, adv) **1** doubtful **2** dubious: *de ~e eer hebben om …* have the dubious honour of (doing sth.)

twijfelen /twɛifələ(n)/ (twijfelde, heeft getwijfeld) doubt: *daar valt niet aan te ~* that is beyond (all) doubt

het **twijfelgeval** /twɛifəlɣəval/ (pl: -len) dubious case, doubtful case

de **twijg** /twɛiχ/ (pl: -en) twig

twinkelen /twɪŋkələ(n)/ (twinkelde, heeft getwinkeld) twinkle

de **twinkeling** /twɪŋkəlɪŋ/ (pl: -en) twinkling

twintig /twɪntəχ/ (num) twenty; [in dates] twentieth: *de jaren ~* the Twenties, the 1920s; *zij was in de ~* she was in her twenties; *er waren er in de ~* there were twenty odd

de **twintiger** /twɪntəɣər/ (pl: -s) person in his (*or:* her) twenties

twintigste /twɪntəχstə/ (num) twentieth: *een shilling was een ~ pond* a shilling was a twentieth of a pound

de **twist** /twɪst/ (pl: -en) quarrel: *een ~ bijleggen* settle a quarrel (*or:* dispute)

de **twistappel** /twɪstɑpəl/ (pl: -s) apple of discord

twisten /twɪstə(n)/ (twistte, heeft getwist) **1** dispute: *daarover wordt nog getwist* that is still a moot point (*or:* in dispute); *over deze vraag valt te ~* this is a debatable (*or:* an arguable) question **2** quarrel: *de ~de partijen* the contending parties

de **twitteraar** /twɪtərar/ (pl: -s) tweeter

het **Twitterbericht** /twɪtərbərɪxt/ (pl: -en) tweet

twitteren /twɪtərə(n)/ (twitterde, heeft ge-twitterd) twitter

de **tycoon** /tɑjkuːn/ (pl: -s) tycoon

de **tyfoon** /tɑjfuːn/ (pl: -s) typhoon

de **tyfus** /tifʏs/ typhoid

het/de **type** /tipə/ (pl: -s) type, character: *een on-guur ~* a shady customer; *hij is mijn ~ niet* he's not my type

de **typefout** /tipfɑut/ (pl: -en) typing error, typo

de **typemachine** /tipmaʃinə/ (pl: -s) typewriter

typen /tipə(n)/ (typte, heeft getypt) type: *een getypte brief* a typed (*or:* typewritten) letter; *blind ~* touch-type

typeren /tiperə(n)/ (typeerde, heeft gety-peerd) typify, characterize: *dat typeert haar* that is typical of her

typerend /tiperənt/ (adj) typical (of)

typisch /tipis/ (adj, adv) **1** typical: *dat is ~ mijn vader* that's typical of my father; *~ Amerikaans* typically American; *het ~e van de zaak* the curious part of the matter **2** pecu-liar

de **typist** /tipɪst/ (pl: -en) typist

typografisch /tipoɣrafis/ (adj) typograph-ic(al)

t.z.t. *te zijner tijd* in due time, in due course

u

u /y/ (pers pron) you: *als ik u was* if I were you || *een machine waar je u tegen zegt* an impressive (*or:* awesome) machine

de **ufo** /ˈyfo/ (pl: -'s) *unidentified flying object* UFO

Uganda /uˈɣɑnda/ Uganda

de **Ugandees** /uˈɣɑndes/ (pl: Ugandezen) Ugandan

de **ui** /œy/ (pl: uien) onion

de **uiensoep** /ˈœyə(n)sup/ onion soup

de **uier** /ˈœyər/ (pl: -s) udder

de **uil** /œyl/ (pl: -en) owl

de **uilenbal** /ˈœylə(n)bɑl/ (pl: -len) **1** (owl's) pellet **2** dimwit, nincompoop

het **uilskuiken** /ˈœylskœykə(n)/ (pl: -s) [fig, inform] ninny, nitwit

¹**uit** /œyt/ (adj) **1** out, away: *de bal is* ~ the ball is out; *die vlek gaat er niet* ~ that stain won't come out **2** over: *de school gaat* ~ school is over; school is out; *het is* ~ *tussen hen* it is finished between them; *het is* ~ *met de pret* the game (*or:* party) is over now **3** (gone) out: *de lamp is* ~ the light is out (*or:* off) **4** out, after: *op iets* ~ *zijn* be out for (*or:* after) sth. || *dit boek is pas* ~ this book has just been published

²**uit** /œyt/ (adv) out: *hij liep de kamer* ~ he walked out of the room; *Ajax speelt volgende week* ~ Ajax are playing away next week || *moet je ook die kant* ~? are you going that way, too?; *voor zich* ~ *zitten kijken* sit staring into space; *ik zou er graag eens* ~ *willen* I would like to get away sometime; *de aankoop heb je er na een jaar* ~ the purchase will save its cost in a year

³**uit** /œyt/ (prep) **1** out (of), from: ~ *het raam kijken* look out of the window; *een speler* ~ *het veld sturen* order a player off (the field) **2** off: *2 km* ~ *de kust* 2 kilometres off the coast **3** (out) of: *iets* ~ *ervaring kennen* know sth. from experience; ~ *zichzelf* of itself; of one's own accord [pers] **4** out of, from: ~ *bewondering* out of (*or:* in) admiration; *zij trouwden* ~ *liefde* they married for love

uitademen /ˈœytadəmə(n)/ (ademde uit, heeft uitgeademd) breathe out, exhale

uitbaggeren /ˈœydbɑɣərə(n)/ (baggerde uit, heeft uitgebaggerd) dredge

uitbalanceren /ˈœydbɑlɑnserə(n)/ (balanceerde uit, heeft uitgebalanceerd) balance

uitbannen /ˈœydbɑnə(n)/ (bande uit, heeft uitgebannen) banish; ban

uitbarsten /ˈœydbɑrstə(n)/ (barstte uit, is uitgebarsten) **1** burst out: *in lachen* ~ burst out laughing; *in tranen* ~ burst into tears **2** erupt

de **uitbarsting** /ˈœydbɑrstɪŋ/ (pl: -en) **1** outburst; eruption **2** bursting out: *tot een* ~ *komen* come to a head

uitbaten /ˈœydbatə(n)/ (baatte uit, heeft uitgebaat) [Belg] run

de **uitbater** /ˈœydbatər/ (pl: -s) manager

uitbeelden /ˈœydbeldə(n)/ (beeldde uit, heeft uitgebeeld) portray, represent: *een verhaal* ~ act out a story

de **uitbeelding** /ˈœydbeldɪŋ/ (pl: -en) portrayal, representation

uitbesteden /ˈœydbəstedə(n)/ (besteedde uit, heeft uitbesteed) **1** board out: *de kinderen een week* ~ board the children out for a week **2** farm out, contract (out)

uitbetalen /ˈœydbətalə(n)/ (betaalde uit, heeft uitbetaald) pay (out); cash

de **uitbetaling** /ˈœydbətalɪŋ/ (pl: -en) payment

uitbijten /ˈœydbɛitə(n)/ (beet uit, heeft uitgebeten) **1** bite (out) **2** eat away: *dat zuur bijt uit* that acid is corrosive

¹**uitblazen** /ˈœydblazə(n)/ (blies uit, heeft uitgeblazen) take a breather, catch one's breath

²**uitblazen** /ˈœydblazə(n)/ (blies uit, heeft uitgeblazen) **1** blow (out); breathe out: *de laatste adem* ~ breathe one's last **2** blow out

uitblijven /ˈœydblɛivə(n)/ (bleef uit, is uitgebleven) **1** stay away; stay out **2** fail to occur (*or:* appear, materialize): *de gevolgen bleven niet uit* the consequences (soon) became apparent

uitblinken /ˈœydblɪŋkə(n)/ (blonk uit, heeft uitgeblonken) excel: ~ *in* excel in

de **uitblinker** /ˈœydblɪŋkər/ (pl: -s) brilliant person (*or:* student): *in sport was hij geen* ~ he did not shine in sports

uitbloeien /ˈœydblujə(n)/ (bloeide uit, is uitgebloeid) leave off flowering: *de rozen zijn uitgebloeid* the roses have finished flowering

de **uitbouw** /ˈœydbɑu/ (pl: -en) extension, addition

uitbouwen /ˈœydbɑuwə(n)/ (bouwde uit, heeft uitgebouwd) **1** build out; add on to **2** develop, expand

de **uitbraak** /ˈœydbrak/ break, jailbreak

uitbraken /ˈœydbrakə(n)/ (braakte uit, heeft uitgebraakt) vomit

uitbrakken /ˈœydbrɑkə(n)/ (brakte uit, heeft/is uitgebrakt) get over a hangover

¹**uitbranden** /ˈœydbrɑndə(n)/ (brandde uit, is uitgebrand) **1** burn up **2** be burnt down (*or:* out)

²**uitbranden** /ˈœydbrɑndə(n)/ (brandde uit, heeft uitgebrand) burn down, burn out

de **uitbrander** /ˈœydbrɑndər/ (pl: -s) dressing down, telling-off

¹**uitbreiden** /œydbrɛidə(n)/ (breidde uit, heeft uitgebreid) extend, expand: *zijn **kennis** ~* extend one's knowledge

zich ²**uitbreiden** /œydbrɛidə(n)/ (breidde zich uit, heeft zich uitgebreid) extend, expand; spread

de **uitbreiding** /œydbrɛidɪŋ/ (pl: -en) **1** extension, expansion **2** extension, addition; development

uitbreken /œydbrekə(n)/ (brak uit, heeft/is uitgebroken) break out: *er is **brand** (or: een **epidemie**) uitgebroken* a fire (*or:* an epidemic) has broken out; *een **muur** ~* knock down (a part of) a wall

uitbrengen /œydbrɛŋə(n)/ (bracht uit, heeft uitgebracht) **1** bring out, say: *een **toost** ~* propose a toast to s.o.; *hij kon geen **woord** ~* he couldn't bring out (*or:* utter) a word, the words stuck in his throat **2** make, give: *verslag ~ van een vergadering* give an account of a meeting **3** bring out; release; publish: *een nieuw **merk** auto ~* put a new make of car on the market

uitbroeden /œydbrudə(n)/ (broedde uit, heeft uitgebroed) hatch (out): *eieren ~* hatch (out) eggs; *hij zit een **idee** uit te broeden* he is brooding over an idea

uitbuiten /œydbœytə(n)/ (buitte uit, heeft uitgebuit) exploit, use: *een **gelegenheid** ~* make the most of an opportunity

de **uitbuiter** /œydbœytər/ (pl: -s) exploiter

de **uitbuiting** /œydbœytɪŋ/ (pl: -en) exploitation

uitbundig /œydbʏndəx/ (adj, adv) exuberant

uitchecken /œytʃɛkə(n)/ (checkte uit, heeft uitgecheckt) [airport] check out; [Dutch; public transport] touch out

uitdagen /œydaɣə(n)/ (daagde uit, heeft uitgedaagd) challenge: *tot een duel ~* challenge s.o. to a duel

uitdagend /œydaɣənt/ (adj, adv) defiant: *~ gekleed gaan* dress provocatively

de **uitdager** /œydaɣər/ (pl: -s) challenger

de **uitdaging** /œydaɣɪŋ/ (pl: -en) challenge, provocation: *de ~ aangaan* accept the challenge

uitdelen /œydelə(n)/ (deelde uit, heeft uitgedeeld) distribute, hand out

uitdenken /œydɛŋkə(n)/ (dacht uit, heeft uitgedacht) invent, devise, think up

uitdeuken /œydøkə(n)/ (deukte uit, heeft uitgedeukt) beat out (a dent, dents)

uitdiepen /œydipə(n)/ (diepte uit, heeft uitgediept) **1** deepen **2** explore (*or:* study) in depth

uitdijen /œydɛiə(n)/ (dijde uit, is uitgedijd) **1** expand, swell, grow: *de **stad** dijt naar alle kanten uit* the town is spreading in all directions **2** put on weight

uitdoen /œydun/ (deed uit, heeft uitge-

daan) **1** take off, remove: *zijn **kleren** ~* take off one's clothes **2** turn off, switch off

uitdokteren /œydɔktərə(n)/ (dokterde uit, heeft uitgedokterd) work out, figure out

uitdossen /œydɔsə(n)/ (doste uit, heeft uitgedost) dress up, deck out

uitdoven /œydovə(n)/ (doofde uit, heeft uitgedoofd) extinguish; stub out

de **uitdraai** /œydraj/ (pl: -en) print-out

uitdraaien /œydrajə(n)/ (draaide uit, heeft uitgedraaid) **1** turn off, switch off; turn out, put out **2** unscrew **3** print out

uitdragen /œydraɣə(n)/ (droeg uit, heeft uitgedragen) propagate, spread

uitdrijven /œydrɛivə(n)/ (dreef uit, heeft uitgedreven) drive out, expel; exorcize

uitdrogen /œydroɣə(n)/ (droogde uit, is uitgedroogd) dry out; dry up

uitdrukkelijk /œydrʏkələk/ (adj, adv) express, distinct: *iets ~ **verbieden*** expressly forbid sth.

uitdrukken /œydrʏkə(n)/ (drukte uit, heeft uitgedrukt) **1** express, put: *zijn **gedachten** ~* express (*or:* convey, voice) one's thoughts; *om het **eenvoudig** uit te drukken* in plain terms, to put it plainly (*or:* simply) **2** stub out, put out ǁ *de waarde van iets **in** geld ~* express the value of sth. in terms of money

de **uitdrukking** /œydrʏkɪŋ/ (pl: -en) **1** expression, idiom; term: *een **vaste** ~* a fixed expression **2** expression, look: *een **verwilderde** ~ in zijn ogen* a wild (*or:* haggard) look in his eyes ǁ *~ **geven** aan* express, voice

uitdunnen /œydʏnə(n)/ (dunde uit, heeft/is uitgedund) thin (out), deplete: *het **deelnemersveld** is flink uitgedund* the number of participants has thinned out

uiteendrijven /œytəndrɛivə(n)/ (dreef uiteen, heeft uiteengedreven) scatter, disperse

uiteenlopen /œytənlopə(n)/ (liep uiteen, is uiteengelopen) vary, differ, diverge: *de **meningen** liepen zeer uiteen* opinions were sharply (*or:* much) divided; *sterk ~* vary (*or:* differ) widely

uiteenlopend /œytənlopənt/ (adj) various, varied

uiteenvallen /œytənvɑlə(n)/ (viel uiteen, is uiteengevallen) fall apart, collapse; break up

uiteenzetten /œytənzɛtə(n)/ (zette uiteen, heeft uiteengezet) explain, set out

de **uiteenzetting** /œytənzɛtɪŋ/ (pl: -en) explanation, account: *een ~ **houden** over een kwestie* give an account of sth.

het **uiteinde** /œytɛində/ (pl: -n) **1** extremity, tip, (far) end **2** end, close; end of the year: *iem. een **zalig** ~ wensen* wish s.o. a happy New Year

¹**uiteindelijk** /œytɛindələk/ (adj, adv) final, ultimate, last: *de ~e **beslissing*** the final decision

²**uiteindelijk** /œytɛindələk/ (adv) finally,

eventually, in the end: ~ **belandde** ik in Rome eventually I ended (or: landed) up in Rome
uiten /œytə(n)/ (uitte, heeft geuit) utter, express, speak
uit-en-ter-na /œytɛntɛrnɑ/ (adv) **1** endlessly **2** down to the finest detail, thoroughly
uitentreuren /œytəntrœrə(n)/ (adv) over and over again, continually
uiteraard /œytərɑrt/ (adv) of course; naturally
het **¹uiterlijk** /œytərlək/ **1** appearance, looks: hij **heeft** zijn ~ niet **mee** his looks are against him; mensen **op** hun ~ beoordelen judge people by their looks **2** (outward) appearance, show: dat is alleen maar **voor** het ~ that's just for appearance's sake (or: for show)
²uiterlijk /œytərlək/ (adj) outward, external: op de ~e **schijn** afgaan judge by appearances
³uiterlijk /œytərlək/ (adv) **1** outwardly, from the outside, externally: ~ scheen hij **kalm** outwardly he seemed calm enough **2** at the (very) latest, not later than: ~ **(op)** 1 november not later than November 1; **tot** ~ 10 juli until July 10 at the latest
uitermate /œytərmɑtə/ (adv) extremely
¹uiterst /œytərst/ (adj) **1** far(thest), extreme, utmost: het ~e **puntje** the (extreme) tip, the far end; ~ **rechts** (the) far right **2** greatest, utmost: zijn ~e **best** doen om te helpen do one's level best to help, bend over backwards to help **3** final, last: een ~e **poging** a last-ditch effort; ~e **verkoopdatum** sell-by date; sell before/by
het **²uiterst** /œytərst/ (adv) extremely, most
het **uiterste** /œytərstə/ (pl: -n) **1** extreme, utmost, limit: **tot** ~n vervallen go to extremes; **van** het ene ~ in het andere (vervallen) go from one extreme to the other **2** utmost, extreme, last: bereid zijn **tot** het ~ te gaan be prepared to go to any length **3** extremity, end
de **uiterwaard** /œytərwart/ (pl: -en) (river) foreland, water meadow
uitfluiten /œytflœytə(n)/ (floot uit, heeft uitgefloten) hiss (at), give (s.o.) the bird: uitgefloten **worden** receive catcalls; get the bird
uitfoeteren /œytfutərə(n)/ (foeterde uit, heeft uitgefoeterd) [inform] storm at; [Am] bawl out
uitgaan /œytxan/ (ging uit, is uitgegaan) **1** go out, leave: het **huis** (de **deur**) ~ leave the house; een **avondje** ~ have a night out; **met** een meisje ~ go out with a girl, take a girl out, date a girl **2** be over, be out; break up; go out: de **school** (or: de **bioscoop**) gaat uit school (or: the film) is over **3** (+ van) start (from), depart (from), take for granted, assume: ze zijn **ervan** uitgegaan dat ... it has been assumed that ... ‖ die **vlekken** gaan er niet **uit** these spots won't come out
uitgaand /œytxant/ (adj) outgoing, outward; outbound; outward bound: ~e **brieven**

(or: **post**) outgoing letters (or: post)
de **uitgaansavond** /œytxansavɔnt/ (pl: -en) (regular) night out
de **uitgaansgelegenheid** /œytxansxəleɣə(n)hɛit/ (pl: -heden) place of entertainment
het **uitgaansleven** /œytxanslevə(n)/ nightlife: een **bruisend** ~ a bustling nightlife
het **uitgaansverbod** /œytxansfərbɔt/ (pl: -verboden) curfew
de **uitgang** /œytxɑŋ/ (pl: -en) exit, way out
de **uitgangspositie** /œytxɑŋspozi(t)si/ (pl: -s) point of departure: zich in een **goede** (or: **slechte**) ~ bevinden om ... be in a good (or: bad) position for sth.
het **uitgangspunt** /œytxɑŋspʏnt/ (pl: -en) point of departure, starting point
de **uitgave** /œytxavə/ (pl: -n) **1** outlay; spending; expenditure, costs: de ~n voor **defensie** defence expenditure **2** edition; issue **3** publication, production
het **uitgavenpatroon** /œytxavəpatron/ pattern of spending
uitgeblust /œytxəblʏst/ (adj) washed out: een ~e **indruk** maken look washed out
uitgebreid /œytxəbrɛit/ (adj, adv) extensive, comprehensive; detailed: iets ~ **behandelen** discuss sth. at length
uitgehongerd /œytxəhɔŋərt/ (adj) famished, starving
uitgekiend /œytxəkint/ (adj) sophisticated, cunning
uitgekookt /œytxəkokt/ (adj) sly, shrewd
uitgelaten /œytxəlatə(n)/ (adj, adv) elated, exuberant
het **uitgeleide** /œytxəlɛidə/ send-off, escort: iem. ~ **doen** see s.o. off
uitgelezen /œytxələzə(n)/ (adj) exquisite; superior; select
uitgemaakt /œytxəmakt/ (adj) established, settled
uitgemergeld /œytxəmɛrɣəlt/ (adj) emaciated, gaunt
uitgeprocedeerd /œytxəprosədert/ (adj) exhausted of all legal procedures
uitgeput /œytxəpʏt/ (adj) **1** exhausted, worn out: ~ **van** pijn exhausted with pain **2** empty; flat **3** exhausted, at an end: onze **voorraden** zijn ~ our supplies have run out (or: are exhausted)
uitgerekend /œytxərekənt/ (adv) precisely, of all (people, things), very: ~ **jij!** you of all people!; ~ **vandaag** today of all days
uitgeslapen /œytxəslapə(n)/ (adj) wide awake, rested
uitgesloten /œytxəslotə(n)/ (adj) out of the question, impossible
uitgesproken /œytxəsprokə(n)/ (adj, adv) marked, clear(-cut): een ~ **voorkeur** a marked preference; met de ~ **bedoeling** (om) te ... with the explicit aim to ...; ~ **lelijk** undenia-

bly ugly

uitgestorven /œytχəstɔrvə(n)/ (adj) **1** deserted, desolate **2** extinct

uitgestrekt /œytχəstrɛkt/ (adj) vast, extensive

uitgeteld /œytχətɛlt/ (adj) exhausted, deadbeat; [sport] (counted) out: ~ *op de bank liggen* lie on the couch, dead to the world; *ze is in september* ~ she is due in September

uitgeven /œytχevə(n)/ (gaf uit, heeft uitgegeven) **1** spend, pay: *geld aan boeken* (or: *als water*) ~ spend money on books (or: like water) **2** issue, emit: *vals geld* ~ pass counterfeit money **3** publish **4** pass off (as): *zich voor iem. anders* ~ impersonate s.o., pose as s.o. else

de **uitgever** /œytχevər/ (pl: -s) publisher

de **uitgeverij** /œytχevərɛi/ (pl: -en) publishing house (or: company), publisher('s)

uitgewerkt /œytχəwɛrkt/ (adj) elaborate, detailed

uitgewoond /œytχəwont/ (adj) run-down, dilapidated

[1]**uitgezonderd** /œytχəzɔndərt/ (prep) except for, apart from: *niemand* ~ with no exceptions, bar none

[2]**uitgezonderd** /œytχəzɔndərt/ (conj) except(ing), apart from, but, except for the fact that: *iedereen ging mee,* ~ *hij* everyone came (along), except for him, everybody but him came (along)

de **uitgifte** /œytχɪftə/ (pl: -n) issue, distribution

uitgillen /œytχɪlə(n)/ (gilde uit, heeft uitgegild) scream (out), shriek (out): *hij gilde het uit van de pijn* he screamed with pain

uitglijden /œytχlɛidə(n)/ (gleed uit, is uitgegleden) **1** slip, slide **2** slip (and fall): ~ *over een bananenschil* slip on a banana peel

de **uitglijder** /œytχlɛidər/ (pl: -s) [Dutch] blunder, slip(-up)

uitgraven /œytχravə(n)/ (groef uit, heeft uitgegraven) **1** dig up, excavate **2** dig out: *een sloot* ~ deepen (or: dig out) a ditch

uitgroeien /œytχrujə(n)/ (groeide uit, is uitgegroeid) **1** grow (into), develop (into) **2** grow out, expose your roots

de **uithaal** /œythal/ (pl: uithalen) hard shot, sizzler

uithakken /œythɑkə(n)/ (hakte uit, heeft uitgehakt) **1** chop (or: cut, hack) away **2** cut out

[1]**uithalen** /œythalə(n)/ (haalde uit, heeft uitgehaald) (take a) swing: ~ *in de richting van de bal* take a swing (or: swipe) at the ball

[2]**uithalen** /œythalə(n)/ (haalde uit, heeft uitgehaald) **1** take out, pull out, remove; unpick, undo; extract **2** empty, clear out, clean out; draw: *een vogelnest* ~ take the eggs from a bird's nest **3** play, do: *een grap met iem.* ~ play a joke on s.o.; *wat heb je nu weer uitgehaald!* what have you been up to

now! **4** be of use, help: *het haalt niets uit* it is no use (or: all in vain)

het **uithangbord** /œythɑŋbɔrt/ (pl: -en) sign(board): *mijn arm is geen* ~ I can't hold this forever

[1]**uithangen** /œythɑŋə(n)/ (hing uit, heeft uitgehangen) **1** hang out **2** be, hang out

[2]**uithangen** /œythɑŋə(n)/ (hing uit, heeft uitgehangen) **1** hang out, put out: [fig] *de vlag* ~ hang out the flags **2** play, act

uitheems /œythems/ (adj) exotic, foreign

de **uithoek** /œythuk/ (pl: -en) remote corner, outpost: *tot in de verste ~en van het land* to the farthest corners of the country; *in een ~ wonen* live in the back of beyond

uithollen /œythɔlə(n)/ (holde uit, heeft uitgehold) **1** scoop out, hollow out **2** erode: *de democratie* ~ undermine (or: erode) democracy

uithongeren /œythɔŋərə(n)/ (hongerde uit, heeft uitgehongerd) starve (out): *de vijand* ~ starve the enemy out (or: into submission)

uithoren /œythorə(n)/ (hoorde uit, heeft uitgehoord) interrogate, question

uithouden /œythɑudə(n)/ (hield uit, heeft uitgehouden) **1** stand, endure: *hij kon het niet langer* ~ he could not take (or: stand) it any longer **2** stick (it) out: *het ergens lang* ~ stay (or: stick it out) somewhere for a long time

het **uithoudingsvermogen** /œythɑudɪŋsfərmoɣə(n)/ staying power, endurance: *geen* ~ *hebben* lack stamina

uithuilen /œythœylə(n)/ (huilde uit, heeft uitgehuild) cry to one's heart's content

uithuwelijken /œythywələkə(n)/ (huwelijkte uit, heeft uitgehuwelijkt) marry off, give in marriage

de **uiting** /œytɪŋ/ (pl: -en) utterance, expression, word(s): ~ *geven aan zijn gevoelens* express (or: vent, air) one's feelings; *tot* ~ *komen* in manifest (or: reveal) itself in

het **uitje** /œycə/ (pl: -s) **1** outing, (pleasure) trip, excursion **2** cocktail onion

uitjoelen /œytjulə(n)/ (joelde uit, heeft uitgejoeld) *see uitjouwen*

uitjouwen /œytjɑuwə(n)/ (jouwde uit, heeft uitgejouwd) boo, hoot at, jeer at

uitkafferen /œytkɑfərə(n)/ (kafferde uit, heeft uitgekafferd) [inform] give (s.o.) a bawling, bite (s.o.'s) head off

uitkammen /œytkɑmə(n)/ (kamde uit, heeft uitgekamd) comb (out), search

uitkauwen /œytkɑuwə(n)/ (kauwde uit, heeft uitgekauwd) chew (up)

uitkeren /œytkerə(n)/ (keerde uit, heeft uitgekeerd) pay (out), remit

de **uitkering** /œytkerɪŋ/ (pl: -en) payment, remittance; benefit; allowance, pension: *recht hebben op een* ~ be entitled to benefit; *een* *maandelijkse* ~ a monthly allowance; *van een* ~ *leven* live on social security; be on the dole

de **uitkeringstrekker** /œytkerɪŋstrɛkər/ (pl: -s) social security recipient, benefit claimant

uitkienen /œytkinə(n)/ (kiende uit, heeft uitgekiend) [inform] figure out

uitkiezen /œytkizə(n)/ (koos uit, heeft uitgekozen) choose, select: *je hebt het maar voor het* ~ (you can) take your pick

de **uitkijk** /œytkɛik/ (pl: -en) lookout, watch: *op de* ~ *staan* be on the watch (*or:* lookout) (for), keep watch (for)

¹**uitkijken** /œytkɛikə(n)/ (keek uit, heeft uitgekeken) **1** watch out, look out, be careful: *kijk uit!* watch it!, watch out!; ~ *met oversteken* take care crossing the street **2** overlook, look out on: *dit raam kijkt uit op de zee* this window overlooks the sea **3** look out (for), watch (for): *naar een andere baan* ~ watch (*or:* look) out for a new job **4** look forward (to): *naar de vakantie* ~ look forward to the holidays

²**uitkijken** /œytkɛikə(n)/ (keek uit, is uitgekeken) tire (of sth.): *gauw uitgekeken zijn op iets* quickly tire of sth.

de **uitkijkpost** /œytkɛikpɔst/ (pl: -en) lookout; observation post

de **uitkijktoren** /œytkɛiktorə(n)/ (pl: -s) watchtower

uitklapbaar /œytklɑbar/ (adj) folding, collapsible: *deze stoel is* ~ *tot een bed* this chair converts into a bed

uitklappen /œytklɑpə(n)/ (klapte uit, heeft/is uitgeklapt) fold (out)

uitklaren /œytklarə(n)/ (klaarde uit, heeft uitgeklaard) clear (through customs)

uitkleden /œytkledə(n)/ (kleedde uit, heeft uitgekleed) undress, strip (off): *zich* ~ undress, strip (off)

uitkloppen /œytklɔpə(n)/ (klopte uit, heeft uitgeklopt) beat (out), shake (out): *een kleed* ~ beat a carpet

uitknijpen /œytknɛipə(n)/ (kneep uit, heeft uitgeknepen) squeeze (out, dry): *een puistje* ~ squeeze out a pimple

uitknippen /œytknɪpə(n)/ (knipte uit, heeft uitgeknipt) cut, clip: *prentjes* ~ cut out pictures

de **uitknop** /œytknɔp/ (pl: -pen) off-switch

uitkomen /œytkomə(n)/ (kwam uit, is uitgekomen) **1** end up, arrive at: *op de hoofdweg* ~ join (onto) the main road **2** lead (to), give out (into, on to): *die deur komt uit op de straat* ~ this door opens (out) on to the street **3** come out, sprout **4** hatch (out) **5** be revealed (*or:* disclosed): *het kwam uit* it was revealed, it transpired **6** (+ voor) admit: *voor zijn mening durven* ~ stand up for one's opinion; *eerlijk* ~ *voor* admit openly, be honest about **7** prove to be true (*or:* correct), come

true; come out, work out; be right: *die som komt niet uit* that sum doesn't add up; *mijn voorspelling kwam uit* my prediction proved correct (*or:* came true) **8** [sport] play; [cards] lead: *met klaveren* (*or: troef*) ~ lead clubs (*or:* trumps) **9** appear, be published: *een nieuw tijdschrift laten* ~ publish a new magazine **10** turn out, work out: *bedrogen* ~ be deceived; *dat komt (me) goed uit* that suits me fine, that's very timely (*or:* convenient) **11** show up, stand out, come out, be apparent: *iets goed laten* ~ show sth. to advantage; *tegen de lichte achtergrond komen de kleuren goed uit* the colours show up (*or:* stand out) well against the light background

de **uitkomst** /œytkɔmst/ (pl: -en) (final, net) result, outcome

uitkopen /œytkopə(n)/ (kocht uit, heeft uitgekocht) buy out

uitkotsen /œytkɔtsə(n)/ (kotste uit, heeft uitgekotst) [inform] throw up, spew up

uitkramen /œytkramə(n)/ (kraamde uit, heeft uitgekraamd): *onzin* ~ talk nonsense

uitkrijgen /œytkrɛiyə(n)/ (kreeg uit, heeft uitgekregen) **1** get off, get out of: *zijn laarzen niet* ~ not be able to get one's boots off **2** finish, get to the end of

de **uitlaat** /œytlat/ (pl: uitlaten) exhaust (pipe); [Am] muffler; funnel

de **uitlaatgassen** /œytlatχɑsə(n)/ (pl) exhaust fumes

de **uitlaatklep** /œytlatklɛp/ (pl: -pen) **1** outlet valve; exhaust valve, escape valve **2** [fig] outlet

de **uitlaatpijp** /œytlatpɛip/ (pl: -en) [car] exhaust pipe

de **uitlaatservice** /œytlatsɤrvɪs/ (pl: -s) dog-walking service

uitlachen /œytlɑχə(n)/ (lachte uit, heeft uitgelachen) laugh at, deride, scoff (at), ridicule: *iem. in zijn gezicht* ~ laugh in s.o.'s face

uitladen /œytladə(n)/ (laadde uit, heeft uitgeladen) unload; discharge [ship]

uitlaten /œytlatə(n)/ (liet uit, heeft uitgelaten) show out (*or:* to the door), see out (*or:* to the door), let out; discharge: *een bezoeker* ~ show a visitor out (*or:* to the door); *de hond* ~ take the dog out (for a walk)

de **uitlating** /œytlatɪŋ/ (pl: -en) utterance, statement, comment

de **uitleg** /œytlɛχ/ explanation, account: *haar* ~ *van wat er gebeurd was* her account of what had happened

uitleggen /œytlɛɣə(n)/ (legde uit, heeft uitgelegd) explain, interpret: *dromen* ~ interpret dreams; *verkeerd* ~ misinterpret, misconstrue

uitlekken /œytlɛkə(n)/ (lekte uit, is uitgelekt) **1** drain; drip dry: *groente laten* ~ drain vegetables **2** get out, leak out: *het plan is uitgelekt* the plan has got (*or:* leaked) out

uitlenen /œytlenə(n)/ (leende uit, heeft uitgeleend) lend (out), loan

zich **uitleven** /œytlevə(n)/ (leefde zich uit, heeft zich uitgeleefd) live it up, let o.s. go

uitleveren /œytleverə(n)/ (leverde uit, heeft uitgeleverd) extradite; hand over: *iem. aan de politie* ~ hand s.o. over (or: turn s.o. in) to the police

de **uitlevering** /œytleverɪŋ/ (pl: -en) extradition

uitlezen /œytlezə(n)/ (las uit, heeft uitgelezen) **1** read to the end, read through, finish (reading) **2** [comp] read

uitlijnen /œytlɛinə(n)/ (lijnde uit, heeft uitgelijnd) **1** align **2** align, line up

uitloggen /œytlɔɣə(n)/ (logde uit, heeft uitgelogd) log off, log out

uitlokken /œytlɔkə(n)/ (lokte uit, heeft uitgelokt) provoke, elicit, stimulate: *een discussie* ~ provoke a discussion; *hij lokt het zelf uit* he is asking for it (or: trouble)

de **uitloop** /œytlop/ extension: *een* ~ *tot vier jaar* an extension to four years

uitlopen /œytlopə(n)/ (liep uit, is uitgelopen) **1** run out (of), walk out (of), leave: *de straat* ~ walk down the street **2** sprout, shoot, come out **3** result in, end in: *dat loopt op niets* (or: *een mislukking*) *uit* that will come to nothing (or: end in failure); *die ruzie liep uit op een gevecht* the quarrel ended in a fight **4** draw ahead (of): *hij is al 20 seconden uitgelopen* he's already in the lead by 20 seconds **5** overrun its (or: one's) time: *de receptie liep uit* the reception went on longer than expected **6** run: *uitgelopen oogschaduw* smeared (or: smudged) eyeshadow; *de verf is uitgelopen* the paint has run ‖ *het hele dorp is uitgelopen* the whole village has turned out

de **uitloper** /œytlopər/ (pl: -s) runner, stolon; foothill; tail end

uitloten /œytlotə(n)/ (lootte uit, heeft uitgeloot) **1** eliminate by lottery **2** draw, select

uitloven /œytlovə(n)/ (loofde uit, heeft uitgeloofd) offer, put up: *een beloning* ~ offer (or: put up) a reward

uitmaken /œytmakə(n)/ (maakte uit, heeft uitgemaakt) **1** break off; finish; terminate: *het* ~ break (or: split) up **2** constitute, make up: *deel* ~ *van* be (a) part of; *een belangrijk deel van de kosten* ~ form (or: represent) a large part of the cost **3** matter, be of importance: *het maakt mij niet(s) uit* it is all the same to me, I don't care; *wat maakt dat uit?* what does that matter?; *weinig* ~ make little difference **4** determine, establish; make out: *dat maakt hij toch niet uit* that's not for him to decide; *dat maak ik zelf nog wel uit* I'll be the judge of that **5** (+ voor) call, brand: *iem. voor dief* ~ call s.o. a thief

uitmelken /œytmɛlkə(n)/ (molk uit, heeft uitgemolken) bleed dry (or: white), strip

bare: *een onderwerp* ~ flog a subject to death

uitmesten /œytmɛstə(n)/ (mestte uit, heeft uitgemest) **1** clean out, muck out: *een stal* ~ muck out a stable **2** clean up, tidy up: *een kast* ~ tidy up (or: clear out) a cupboard

uitmeten /œytmetə(n)/ (mat uit/meette uit, heeft uitgemeten) **1** measure (out) **2** [fig] make much of, enlarge

uitmonden /œytmɔndə(n)/ (mondde uit, heeft/is uitgemond) **1** flow (out), discharge, run into **2** lead to, end in: *het gesprek mondde uit in een enorme ruzie* the conversation ended in a fierce quarrel

uitmoorden /œytmordə(n)/ (moordde uit, heeft uitgemoord) massacre, butcher

uitmunten /œytmʏntə(n)/ (muntte uit, heeft uitgemunt) stand out, excel

uitmuntend /œytmʏntənt/ (adj, adv) excellent, first-rate

uitnodigen /œytnodəɣə(n)/ (nodigde uit, heeft uitgenodigd) invite, ask: *iem. op een feestje* ~ invite (or: ask) s.o. to a party

de **uitnodiging** /œytnodəɣɪŋ/ (pl: -en) invitation: *een* ~ *voor de lunch* an invitation to lunch

uitoefenen /œytufenə(n)/ (oefende uit, heeft uitgeoefend) **1** practise, pursue, be engaged in **2** exert; exercise; wield: *kritiek* ~ *op* criticize, censure

de **uitoefening** /œytufenɪŋ/ exercise; exertion; practice: *in de* ~ *van zijn ambt* in the performance (or: discharge, exercise) of his duties

uitpakken /œytpakə(n)/ (pakte uit, heeft uitgepakt) unwrap, unpack: [fig] *flink* ~ pull out all the stops, spare no expense

uitpersen /œytpɛrsə(n)/ (perste uit, heeft uitgeperst) squeeze; crush

de **uitploeg** /œytpluχ/ (pl: -en) [sport] away team

uitpluizen /œytplœyzə(n)/ (ploos uit, heeft uitgeplozen) unravel; sift (out, through): *iets helemaal* ~ get to the bottom of sth.

¹**uitpraten** /œytpratə(n)/ (praatte uit, is uitgepraat) finish (talking), have one's say: *iem. laten* ~ let s.o. finish, hear s.o. out

²**uitpraten** /œytpratə(n)/ (praatte uit, heeft uitgepraat) talk out (or: over), have out: *we moeten het* ~ we'll have to talk this out (or: over); *een ruzie* ~ clear up an argument

uitprinten /œytprɪntə(n)/ (printte uit, heeft uitgeprint) print (out)

uitproberen /œytproberə(n)/ (probeerde uit, heeft uitgeprobeerd) try (out), test

uitpuilen /œytpœylə(n)/ (puilde uit, heeft/is uitgepuild) bulge (out), protrude: *~de ogen* bulging (or: protruding) eyes

uitputten /œytpʏtə(n)/ (putte uit, heeft uitgeput) **1** exhaust, finish (up): *de voorraad raakt uitgeput* the supply is running out **2** exhaust, wear out

de **uitputting** /œytpʏtɪŋ/ (pl: -en) exhaustion, fatigue: *de ~ van de olievoorraden* the exhaustion of oil supplies

uitrangeren /œytrɑnʒerə(n)/ (rangeerde uit, heeft uitgerangeerd) sidetrack, shunt

uitrazen /œytrazə(n)/ (raasde uit, heeft/is uitgeraasd) let (*or:* blow) off steam; blow out: *de kinderen laten ~* let the children have their fling

uitreiken /œytrɛikə(n)/ (reikte uit, heeft uitgereikt) distribute, give out; present: *diploma's ~* present diplomas; *iem. een onderscheiding ~* confer a distinction on s.o.

de **uitreiking** /œytrɛikɪŋ/ (pl: -en) distribution; presentation

het **uitreisvisum** /œytrɛisfizʏm/ (pl: -visa) exit visa

uitrekenen /œytrekənə(n)/ (rekende uit, heeft uitgerekend) calculate, compute ‖ *zij is begin maart uitgerekend* the baby is due at the beginning of March

[1]**uitrekken** /œytrɛkə(n)/ (rekte uit, is uitgerekt) stretch: *de trui is in de was uitgerekt* the sweater has stretched in the wash

[2]**uitrekken** /œytrɛkə(n)/ (rekte uit, heeft uitgerekt) stretch (out); elongate: *een elastiek ~* stretch out a rubber band; *zich ~* stretch o.s. (out)

uitrichten /œytrɪχtə(n)/ (richtte uit, heeft uitgericht) do, accomplish: *dat zal niet veel ~* that won't help much

uitrijden /œytrɛidə(n)/ (reed uit, is uitgereden) drive to the end (of); ride to the end (of) ‖ *mest ~* spread manure (*or:* fertilizer)

de **uitrijkaart** /œytrɛikart/ (pl: -en) exit ticket

de **uitrit** /œytrɪt/ (pl: -ten) exit: *~ vrijhouden s.v.p.* please keep (the) exit clear

uitroeien /œytrujə(n)/ (roeide uit, heeft uitgeroeid) exterminate, wipe out

de **uitroeiing** /œytrujɪŋ/ (pl: -en) extermination

de **uitroep** /œytrup/ (pl: -en) exclamation, cry

uitroepen /œytrupə(n)/ (riep uit, heeft uitgeroepen) **1** exclaim, shout, cry (out), call (out) **2** call, declare: *een staking ~* call a strike; *hij werd tot winnaar uitgeroepen* he was declared (*or:* voted) the winner

het **uitroepteken** /œytruptekə(n)/ (pl: -s) exclamation mark

uitroken /œytrokə(n)/ (rookte uit, heeft uitgerookt) smoke out: *vossen ~* smoke out foxes

uitrollen /œytrolə(n)/ (rolde uit, heeft uitgerold) unroll: *de tuinslang ~* unreel the garden hose

[1]**uitrukken** /œytrʏkə(n)/ (rukte uit, is uitgerukt) turn out: *de brandweer rukte uit* the fire brigade turned out

[2]**uitrukken** /œytrʏkə(n)/ (rukte uit, heeft uitgerukt) tear out, pull out: *planten ~* root

up (*or:* uproot) plants

[1]**uitrusten** /œytrʏstə(n)/ (rustte uit, heeft/is uitgerust) rest

[2]**uitrusten** /œytrʏstə(n)/ (rustte uit, heeft uitgerust) equip, fit out: *uitgerust met 16 kleppen* fitted out with 16 valves

de **uitrusting** /œytrʏstɪŋ/ (pl: -en) equipment, kit, outfit, gear: *zijn intellectuele ~* his intellectual baggage; *ze waren voorzien van de modernste ~* they were fitted out with the latest equipment

uitschakelen /œytsχakələ(n)/ (schakelde uit, heeft uitgeschakeld) **1** switch off: *de motor ~* cut (*or:* stop) the engine **2** [fig] eliminate; knock out: *door ziekte uitgeschakeld zijn* be out of circulation through ill health

uitscheiden /œytsχɛidə(n)/ (scheidde uit/ schee uit, is uitgescheiden/uitgescheden) [inform] (+ met) stop (-ing), cease (to, -ing): *ik schei uit met werken als ik zestig word* I'll stop working when I turn sixty; *schei uit!* cut it out!; knock it off!

uitschelden /œytsχɛldə(n)/ (schold uit, heeft uitgescholden) abuse, call names: *iem. ~ voor dief* call s.o. a thief

[1]**uitscheuren** /œytsχørə(n)/ (scheurde uit, is uitgescheurd) tear: *het knoopsgat is uitgescheurd* the buttonhole is torn

[2]**uitscheuren** /œytsχørə(n)/ (scheurde uit, heeft uitgescheurd) tear out

uitschieten /œytsχitə(n)/ (schoot uit, is uitgeschoten) shoot out, dart out: *het mes schoot uit* the knife slipped

de **uitschieter** /œytsχitər/ (pl: -s) peak, highlight

uitschijnen /œytsχɛinə(n)/: [Belg] *iets laten ~* let it be understood, hint at sth.

het **uitschot** /œytsχɔt/ **1** refuse **2** scum, dregs

uitschreeuwen /œytsχrewə(n)/ (schreeuwde uit, heeft uitgeschreeuwd) cry out: *het ~ van pijn* cry out (*or:* yell, bellow) with pain

uitschrijven /œytsχrɛivə(n)/ (schreef uit, heeft uitgeschreven) **1** write out, copy out: *aantekeningen ~* write out notes **2** call; hold; organize **3** write out: *een recept ~* write out a prescription; *rekeningen ~* make out accounts ‖ *iem. als lid ~* strike s.o.'s name off the membership list

uitschudden /œytsχʏdə(n)/ (schudde uit, heeft uitgeschud) shake (out)

uitschuifbaar /œytsχœyvbar/ (adj) extending

uitschuiven /œytsχœyvə(n)/ (schoof uit, heeft uitgeschoven) **1** slide out, pull out **2** extend: *een tafel ~* extend (*or:* pull out) a table

[1]**uitslaan** /œytslan/ (sloeg uit, is uitgeslagen) grow mouldy, become mouldy; sweat ‖ *een ~de brand* a blaze

uitstel

²uitslaan /œytslan/ (sloeg uit, heeft uitgeslagen) **1** beat out, strike out: *het stof* ~ beat
(*or:* shake) out the dust **2** shake out, beat
out: *een stofdoek* ~ shake out a duster **3** utter, talk: *onzin* ~ talk rot

de **uitslag** /œytslɑχ/ (pl: -en) **1** rash; damp: *daar
krijg ik* ~ *van* that brings out (*or:* gives me) a
rash **2** result, outcome: *de* ~ *van de verkiezingen* (or: *van het examen*) the results of the
elections (*or:* examination)

uitslapen /œytslapə(n)/ (sliep uit, heeft/is
uitgeslapen) have a good lie-in, sleep late:
goed uitgeslapen zijn [fig] be pretty astute (*or:*
shrewd); *tot* 10 *uur* ~ stay in bed until 10
o'clock

uitsloven /œytslovə(n)/ (sloofde zich uit,
heeft zich uitgesloofd) slave away, work o.s.
to death

de **uitslover** /œytslovər/ (pl: -s) eager beaver,
show-off

de **uitsloverij** /œytslovərɛi/ (pl: -en) showing-
off

uitsluiten /œytslœytə(n)/ (sloot uit, heeft
uitgesloten) **1** shut out, lock out: *zij wordt
van verdere deelname uitgesloten* she has been
disqualified **2** exclude, rule out: *die mogelijkheid kunnen we niet* ~ that is a possibility
we can't rule out (*or:* ignore); *dat is uitgesloten* that is out of the question

uitsluitend /œytslœytənt/ (adj, adv) only;
exclusively: ~ *volwassenen* adults only

de **uitsluiting** /œytslœytɪŋ/ (pl: -en) **1** exclusion; [sport] disqualification **2** exception:
met ~ *van* exclusive of, to the exclusion of

het **uitsluitsel** /œytslœytsəl/ (pl: -s) definite answer

de **uitsmijter** /œytsmɛitər/ (pl: -s) **1** [Dutch]
bouncer **2** fried bacon and eggs served on
slices of bread **3** final number of a show

uitsnijden /œytsnɛidə(n)/ (sneed uit, heeft
uitgesneden) cut (out); carve (out): *een laag
uitgesneden japon* a low-cut (*or:* low-necked)
dress

de **uitspanning** /œytspɑnɪŋ/ (pl: -en) café,
pub

het **uitspansel** /œytspɑnsəl/ firmament, welkin

uitsparen /œytsparə(n)/ (spaarde uit, heeft
uitgespaard) **1** save (on), economize (on):
dertig euro ~ save thirty euros **2** leave blank
(*or:* open): *openingen* ~ leave spaces

de **uitsparing** /œytsparɪŋ/ (pl: -en) cutaway;
notch

de **uitspatting** /œytspɑtɪŋ/ (pl: -en) splurge;
extravagance: *zich overgeven aan ~en* indulge in excesses

uitspelen /œytspelə(n)/ (speelde uit, heeft
uitgespeeld) **1** finish, play out **2** play, lead:
mensen tegen elkaar ~ play people off
against one another

uitsplitsen /œytsplɪtsə(n)/ (splitste uit,
heeft uitgesplitst) itemize, break down

uitspoelen /œytspulə(n)/ (spoelde uit,
heeft uitgespoeld) rinse (out), wash (out)

uitspoken /œytspokə(n)/ (spookte uit,
heeft uitgespookt) [inform] be (*or:* get) up to

de **uitspraak** /œytsprak/ (pl: uitspraken)
1 pronunciation, accent: *de* ~ *van het Chinees*
the pronunciation of Chinese **2** pronounce-
ment, judgement **3** [law] judgement, sentence; verdict: ~ *doen* pass judgement, pass
(*or:* pronounce) sentence

uitspreiden /œytsprɛidə(n)/ (spreidde uit,
heeft uitgespreid) spread (out), stretch (out)

uitspreken /œytsprekə(n)/ (sprak uit,
heeft/is uitgesproken) **1** pronounce; articulate: *hoe moet je dit woord ~?* how do you
pronounce this word? **2** say, express: *iem. laten* ~ let s.o. have his say, hear s.o. out **3** declare, pronounce: *een vonnis* ~ pronounce
judgement

uitspringen /œytsprɪŋə(n)/ (sprong uit, is
uitgesprongen) stand out

uitspugen /œytspyɣə(n)/ (spoog uit/spuug-
de, heeft uitgespogen/uitgespuugd) spit
out

¹uitstaan /œytstan/ (stond uit, heeft uitge-
staan) stand (*or:* stick, jut) out, protrude

²uitstaan /œytstan/ (stond uit, heeft uitge-
staan) stand, endure, bear: *hitte* (or: *lawaai*)
niet kunnen ~ not be able to endure the heat
(*or:* noise); *iem. niet kunnen* ~ hate s.o.'s guts
|| *ik heb nog veel geld* ~ I have a lot of money
out (at interest)

uitstallen /œytstɑlə(n)/ (stalde uit, heeft
uitgestald) display, expose (for sale); [fig]
show off

het **uitstalraam** /œytstɑlram/ (pl: -ramen)
[Belg] shop window, display window

het **uitstapje** /œytstɑpjə/ (pl: -s) trip, outing,
excursion: *een* ~ *maken* take (*or:* make) a
trip, go on an outing

uitstappen /œytstɑpə(n)/ (stapte uit, is uit-
gestapt) get off (*or:* down), step out, get out:
allemaal ~! all change (here!)

het **uitsteeksel** /œytsteksəl/ (pl: -s) projection,
protuberance

het **uitstek** /œytstɛk/: *bij* ~ pre-eminently

¹uitsteken /œytstekə(n)/ (stak uit, heeft uit-
gestoken) **1** stick out, jut out, project, protrude **2** stand out: *de toren steekt boven de
huizen uit* the tower rises (high) above the
houses; *boven alle anderen* ~ tower above all
the others

²uitsteken /œytstekə(n)/ (stak uit, heeft uit-
gestoken) **1** hold out, put out **2** reach out,
stretch out: *zijn hand naar iem.* ~ extend one's
hand to s.o.

uitstekend /œytstekənt/ (adj, adv) excellent, first-rate: *van ~e kwaliteit* of high quality

het **uitstel** /œytstɛl/ delay, postponement, de-
ferment: ~ *van betaling* postponement (*or:*

extension) of payment; *zonder* ~ without delay || [Belg; law] *met* ~ suspended; *van* ~ komt *afstel* tomorrow never comes; one of these days is none of these days

uitstellen /ˈœytstɛlə(n)/ (stelde uit, heeft uitgesteld) put off, postpone, defer: *voor onbepaalde tijd* ~ postpone indefinitely

uitsterven /ˈœytstɛrvə(n)/ (stierf uit, is uitgestorven) die (out); become extinct: *het dorp* was uitgestorven the village was deserted

uitstijgen /ˈœytstɛiɣə(n)/ (steeg uit, is uitgestegen) surpass

uitstippelen /ˈœytstɪpələ(n)/ (stippelde uit, heeft uitgestippeld) outline, map out, trace out; work out: *een route* ~ map out a route

de **uitstoot** /ˈœytstot/ (pl: uitstoten) discharge, emissions

uitstorten /ˈœytstɔrtə(n)/ (stortte uit, heeft uitgestort) **1** pour out (*or:* forth), empty (out): *zijn hart* ~ bij iem. pour out (*or:* unburden, open) one's heart (to s.o.) **2** pour out: *zijn woede* ~ over iem. vent one's rage upon s.o.

uitstoten /ˈœytstotə(n)/ (stootte uit, heeft uitgestoten) **1** expel, cast out: iem. ~ *uit de groep* expel (*or:* banish) s.o. from the group **2** emit, utter: *onverstaanbare klanken* ~ emit (*or:* utter) unintelligible sounds **3** eject; emit

¹**uitstralen** /ˈœytstralə(n)/ (straalde uit, heeft/is uitgestraald) radiate, emanate

²**uitstralen** /ˈœytstralə(n)/ (straalde uit, heeft uitgestraald) [also fig] radiate, give off, exude: *zelfvertrouwen* ~ radiate (*or:* exude, ooze) self-confidence

de **uitstraling** /ˈœytstralɪŋ/ (pl: -en) radiation, emission; [fig] aura: *een enorme* ~ *hebben* [roughly] possess charisma, have a certain magic

¹**uitstrekken** /ˈœytstrɛkə(n)/ (strekte uit, heeft uitgestrekt) **1** stretch (out), reach (out), extend: *met uitgestrekte armen* with outstretched arms **2** extend

zich ²**uitstrekken** /ˈœytstrɛkə(n)/ (strekte zich uit, heeft zich uitgestrekt) extend, stretch (out): *zich* ~ *over* extend over

uitstrijken /ˈœytstrɛikə(n)/ (streek uit, heeft uitgestreken) spread, smear

het **uitstrijkje** /ˈœytstrɛikjə/ (pl: -s) (cervical) smear, swab

uitstrooien /ˈœytstrojə(n)/ (strooide uit, heeft uitgestrooid) scatter, spread

de **uitstroom** /ˈœytstrom/ (out)flow

de **uitstulping** /ˈœytstʏlpɪŋ/ (pl: -en) bulge

uitsturen /ˈœytstyrə(n)/ (stuurde uit, heeft uitgestuurd) send out; [sport] send off (the field): *iem. op iets* ~ send s.o. for sth.

uittekenen /ˈœytekənə(n)/ (tekende uit, heeft uitgetekend) draw, trace out: *ik kan die plaats wel* ~ I know every detail of that place

uittesten /ˈœytɛstə(n)/ (testte uit, heeft uit-

getest) test (out), try (out), put to the test

uittikken /ˈœytɪkə(n)/ (tikte uit, heeft uitgetikt) type out

de **uittocht** /ˈœytɔxt/ (pl: -en) exodus, trek

de **uittrap** /ˈœytrɑp/ (pl: -pen) goal kick

uittrappen /ˈœytrɑpə(n)/ (trapte uit, heeft uitgetrapt) **1** kick (the ball) into play, take a goal kick **2** put out of play (*or:* into touch, over the line) **3** kick off

uittreden /ˈœytredə(n)/ (trad uit, is uitgetreden) resign (from): *vervroegd* ~ retire early, take early retirement

de **uittreding** /ˈœytredɪŋ/ (pl: -en) **1** resignation, retirement **2** leaving

¹**uittrekken** /ˈœytrɛkə(n)/ (trok uit, zijn uitgetrokken) go out, march out: *erop* ~ *om* set out to

²**uittrekken** /ˈœytrɛkə(n)/ (trok uit, heeft uitgetrokken) **1** take off; pull off: *zijn kleren* ~ take off one's clothes; undress **2** put aside, set aside, reserve: *een bedrag voor iets* ~ put (*or:* set) aside a sum (of money) for sth.

het **uittreksel** /ˈœytrɛksəl/ (pl: -s) excerpt, extract

uittypen /ˈœytipə(n)/ (typte uit, heeft uitgetypt) type out

uitvaardigen /ˈœytfardəɣə(n)/ (vaardigde uit, heeft uitgevaardigd) issue, put out; [law also] make

de **uitvaart** /ˈœytfart/ (pl: -en) funeral (service), burial (service)

het **uitvaartcentrum** /ˈœytfartsɛntrʏm/ (pl: -centra) funeral parlour, mortuary

de **uitvaartdienst** /ˈœytfardinst/ (pl: -en) funeral service, burial service

de **uitval** /ˈœytfɑl/ (pl: -len) **1** outburst, explosion **2** (hair) loss **3** absence (from work)

uitvallen /ˈœytfɑlə(n)/ (viel uit, is uitgevallen) **1** burst out, explode, blow up: ~ *tegen iem.* lash out at s.o. **2** fall (*or:* drop, come) out: *zijn haren vallen uit* he is losing his hair **3** drop out, fall out; break down; be cancelled: *de lessen vallen uit* the classes have been cancelled; *de stroom is uitgevallen* there's a power failure **4** turn out, work out: *we weten niet hoe de stemming zal* ~ we don't know how (*or:* which way) the vote will go **5** be absent through illness

de **uitvaller** /ˈœytfɑlər/ (pl: -s) person who drops out, casualty

de **uitvalsbasis** /ˈœytfɑlzbazɪs/ operating base

de **uitvalsweg** /ˈœytfɑlswɛx/ (pl: -en) main traffic road (out of a town)

uitvaren /ˈœytfarə(n)/ (voer uit, is uitgevaren) sail, put (out) to sea, leave port

uitvechten /ˈœytfɛxtə(n)/ (vocht uit, heeft uitgevochten) fight out: *iets met iem.* ~ fight (*or:* have) sth. out with s.o.

uitvegen /ˈœytfeɣə(n)/ (veegde uit, heeft uitgeveegd) **1** sweep out, clean out **2** wipe out; erase: *een woord* op het schoolbord ~

wipe (*or:* rub) out a word on the blackboard

uitvergroten /ˈœytfərɣrotə(n)/ (vergrootte uit, heeft uitvergroot) **1** enlarge, magnify, blow up **2** [fig] exaggerate, magnify, zoom in on

de **uitvergroting** /ˈœytfərɣrotɪŋ/ (pl: -en) enlargement, blow-up

uitverkocht /ˈœytfərkɔxt/ (adj) **1** sold out: *onze* **kousen** *zijn* ~ we have run out of stockings **2** sold out, booked out, fully booked: *voor een* ~*e* **zaal** *spelen* play to a full house

de **uitverkoop** /ˈœytfərkop/ (clearance, bargain) sale

uitverkoren /ˈœytfərkorə(n)/ (adj) chosen; elect

uitvinden /ˈœytfɪndə(n)/ (vond uit, heeft uitgevonden) **1** invent **2** find out, discover

de **uitvinder** /ˈœytfɪndər/ (pl: -s) inventor

de **uitvinding** /ˈœytfɪndɪŋ/ (pl: -en) invention; gadget: *een* ~ **doen** invent sth.

uitvissen /ˈœytfɪsə(n)/ (viste uit, heeft uitgevist) dig (*or:* fish, ferret) out

uitvlakken /ˈœytflɑkə(n)/ (vlakte uit, heeft uitgevlakt) wipe out: [fig] *dat moet je* **niet** ~ that's not to be sneezed at

het **uitvloeisel** /ˈœytflujsəl/ (pl: -s, -en) consequence

de **uitvlucht** /ˈœytflʏxt/ (pl: -en) excuse, pretext: ~*en* **zoeken** make excuses; dodge (*or:* evade) the question

uitvoegen /ˈœytfuɣə(n)/ (voegde uit, heeft uitgevoegd) exit

de **uitvoegstrook** /ˈœytfuxstrok/ (pl: -stroken) deceleration lane

de **uitvoer** /ˈœytfur/ (pl: -en) **1** export: *de* **in-** *en* ~ *van goederen* the import and export of goods **2** exports **3** execution: *een opdracht* **ten** ~ *brengen* carry out an instruction (*or:* order)

uitvoerbaar /ˈœytfurbar/ (adj) feasible, workable, practicable

de **uitvoerder** /ˈœytfurdər/ (pl: -s) [Dutch] works foreman

uitvoeren /ˈœytfurə(n)/ (voerde uit, heeft uitgevoerd) **1** export **2** do: *hij voert* **niets** *uit* he doesn't do a stroke (of work) **3** perform, carry out: *plannen* ~ carry out (*or:* execute) plans

uitvoerend /ˈœytfurənt/ (adj) executive: ~ **personeel** staff carrying out the work

uitvoerig /ˈœytfurəx/ (adj, adv) comprehensive, full; elaborate; detailed: *iets* ~ **beschrijven** (or: **bespreken**) describe (*or:* discuss) sth. at great/some length

de **uitvoering** /ˈœytfurɪŋ/ (pl: -en) **1** carrying out, performance: *werk* **in** ~ road works (ahead), men at work; work in progress **2** performance; execution **3** design, construction; workmanship: *wij hebben dit model* **in** *twee* ~*en* we have two versions of this model

de **uitvoerrechten** /ˈœytfurɛxtə(n)/ (pl) export duty

uitvouwen /ˈœytfɑuwə(n)/ (vouwde uit, heeft uitgevouwen) unfold, fold out, spread out

uitvreten /ˈœytfretə(n)/ (vrat uit, heeft uitgevreten) be up to: *wat heeft hij nou weer uitgevreten?* what has he been up to now?

de **uitvreter** /ˈœytfretər/ (pl: -s) sponger, parasite

uitvullen /ˈœytvʏlə(n)/ (vulde uit, heeft uitgevuld) justify: *links uitgevuld* left-justified

uitwaaien /ˈœytwajə(n)/ (waaide uit/woei uit, is uitgewaaid) **1** blow out, be blown out **2** get a breath of (fresh) air

het/de **uitwas** /ˈœytwɑs/ (pl: -sen) excrescence, morbid growth; excesses

uitwasemen /ˈœytwasəmə(n)/ (wasemde uit, heeft uitgewasemd) **1** evaporate **2** steam; perspire

uitwassen /ˈœytwɑsə(n)/ (waste uit, heeft uitgewassen) **1** wash (out); swab (out) **2** wash out (*or:* away)

de **uitwedstrijd** /ˈœytwɛtstrɛit/ (pl: -en) away match (*or:* game)

de **uitweg** /ˈœytwɛx/ (pl: -en) way out; answer: *hij* **zag** *geen andere* ~ *meer dan onder te duiken* he had no choice but to go into hiding

uitweiden /ˈœytwɛidə(n)/ (weidde uit, heeft uitgeweid) expatiate (on), hold forth

uitwendig /ˈœytwɛndəx/ (adj, adv) external, outward, exterior: *een geneesmiddel voor* ~ **gebruik** a medicine for external use

¹**uitwerken** /ˈœytwɛrkə(n)/ (werkte uit, is uitgewerkt) wear off; have spent one's force: *de* **verdoving** *is uitgewerkt* (the effect of) the anaesthetic has worn off

²**uitwerken** /ˈœytwɛrkə(n)/ (werkte uit, heeft uitgewerkt) **1** work out, elaborate: *zijn* **aantekeningen** ~ work up one's notes; *een* **idee** ~ develop an idea; *uitgewerkte* **plannen** detailed plans **2** work out, compute: **sommen** ~ work out sums

de **uitwerking** /ˈœytwɛrkɪŋ/ (pl: -en) **1** effect, result: *de* **beoogde** ~ *hebben* have the desired (*or:* intended) effect, be effective; *de medicijnen hadden* **geen** ~ the medicines had no effect (*or:* didn't work) **2** working out, elaboration **3** working out, computation

de **uitwerpselen** /ˈœytwɛrpsələ(n)/ (pl) excrement; droppings

uitwijken /ˈœytwɛikə(n)/ (week uit, is uitgeweken) get out of the way (of); make way (for): *rechts* ~ swerve to the right; *vliegverkeer moest* **naar** *Oostende* ~ air traffic was diverted to Ostend

uitwijzen /ˈœytwɛizə(n)/ (wees uit, heeft uitgewezen) **1** show, reveal: *de* **tijd** *zal het* ~ time will tell **2** deport; expel

de **uitwijzing** /ˈœytwɛizɪŋ/ (pl: -en) deportation; expulsion

uitwisselbaar /œytwɪsəlbar/ (adj) interchangeable, exchangeable

uitwisselen /œytwɪsələ(n)/ (wisselde uit, heeft uitgewisseld) exchange; swap: *ervaringen ~* compare notes

de **uitwisseling** /œytwɪsəlɪŋ/ (pl: -en) exchange, swap

het **uitwisselingsprogramma** /œytwɪsəlɪŋsproɣrama/ (pl: -'s) exchange programme

uitwissen /œytwɪsə(n)/ (wiste uit, heeft uitgewist) wipe out, erase; efface: *een opname ~* wipe (*or:* erase) a recording; *sporen ~* cover up one's tracks

uitwonend /œytwonənt/ (adj) (living) away from home: *een ~e dochter* one daughter living away from home

de **uitworp** /œytwɔrp/ (pl: -en) throw(-out)

uitwrijven /œytfrɛivə(n)/ (wreef uit, heeft uitgewreven) **1** rub; polish (up): *zijn ogen ~* rub one's eyes **2** spread, rub over

uitwringen /œytfrɪŋə(n)/ (wrong uit, heeft uitgewrongen) wring out

¹**uitzaaien** /œytsajə(n)/ (zaaide uit, heeft uitgezaaid) sow, disseminate

zich ²**uitzaaien** /œytsajə(n)/ (zaaide zich uit, heeft zich uitgezaaid) [med] metastasize; spread: *de kanker had zich uitgezaaid* the cancer had spread (*or:* formed secondaries)

de **uitzaaiing** /œytsajɪŋ/ (pl: -en) [med] spread, dissemination

uitzakken /œytsɑkə(n)/ (zakte uit, is uitgezakt) sag, give way: *een uitgezakt lichaam* a sagging body

het **uitzendbureau** /œytsɛndbyro/ (pl: -s) (temporary) employment agency, temp(ing) agency: *voor een ~ werken* temp, do temping

uitzenden /œytsɛndə(n)/ (zond uit, heeft uitgezonden) broadcast, transmit: *de tv zendt de wedstrijd uit* the match will be televised (*or:* be broadcast)

de **uitzending** /œytsɛndɪŋ/ (pl: -en) broadcast, transmission: *een rechtstreekse ~* a direct (*or:* live) broadcast; *u bent nu in de ~* you're on the air now

de **uitzendkracht** /œytsɛntkrɑxt/ (pl: -en) temporary worker (*or:* employee), temp

het **uitzendwerk** /œytsɛntwɛrk/ work as a temp(orary)

het/de **uitzet** /œytsɛt/ (pl: -ten) outfit; trousseau

uitzetten /œytsɛtə(n)/ (zette uit, heeft uitgezet) **1** throw out, put out, expel; deport: *ongewenste vreemdelingen ~* deport (*or:* expel) undesirable aliens **2** switch off, turn off: *het gas ~* turn the gas off **3** expand, enlarge; extend

de **uitzetting** /œytsɛtɪŋ/ (pl: -en) ejection, expulsion; deportation; eviction

het **uitzicht** /œytsɪxt/ (pl: -en) **1** view, prospect, panorama: *vrij ~* unobstructed view; *met ~ op* with a view of, overlooking, looking (out) onto **2** prospect, outlook: *~ geven* op promo-

tie hold out prospects (*or:* the prospect) of promotion

uitzichtloos /œytsɪxtlos/ (adj) hopeless, dead-end

uitzieken /œytsikə(n)/ (ziekte uit, heeft/is uitgeziekt) fully recover

uitzien /œytsin/ (zag uit, heeft uitgezien) face, front, look out on: *een kamer die op zee uitziet* a room with a view of the sea, a room facing the sea

uitzingen /œytsɪŋə(n)/ (zong uit, heeft uitgezongen) hold out, manage

uitzinnig /œytsɪnəx/ (adj, adv) delirious, wild: *een ~e menigte* a frenzied (*or:* hysterical) crowd

uitzitten /œytsɪtə(n)/ (zat uit, heeft uitgezeten) sit out, stay until the end of: *zijn tijd ~* sit out (*or:* wait out) one's time

uitzoeken /œytsukə(n)/ (zocht uit, heeft uitgezocht) **1** select, choose, pick out **2** sort (out) **3** sort out, figure out

uitzonderen /œytsɔndərə(n)/ (zonderde uit, heeft uitgezonderd) except, exclude

de **uitzondering** /œytsɔndərɪŋ/ (pl: -en) exception: *een ~ maken voor* make an exception for; *een ~ op de regel* an exception to the rule; *met ~ van* with the exception of, excepting, save; *bij hoge ~* very exceptionally

uitzonderlijk /œytsɔndərlək/ (adj, adv) exceptional, unique

uitzoomen /œytsumə(n)/ zoom out

uitzuigen /œytsœyɣə(n)/ (zoog uit, heeft uitgezogen) **1** squeeze dry, bleed dry, exploit **2** vacuum (out)

de **uitzuiger** /œytsœyɣər/ (pl: -s) bloodsucker, extortionist

uitzwaaien /œytswajə(n)/ (zwaaide uit, heeft uitgezwaaid) send off, wave goodbye to

uitzwermen /œytswɛrmə(n)/ (zwermde uit, is uitgezwermd) swarm out, swarm off

uitzweten /œytswetə(n)/ (zweette uit, heeft uitgezweet) sweat out

de **uk** /ʏk/ (pl: ukken) toddler, kiddy

ultiem /ʏltim/ (adj) ultimate, last-minute

het **ultimatum** /ʏltimatʏm/ (pl: -s) ultimatum: *een ~ stellen* give (s.o.) an ultimatum

de **ultrafijnstof** /ʏltrafɛinstɔf/ ultrafine particulate matter; ultrafine particles

ultralinks /ʏltralɪŋks/ (adj, adv) extreme left

ultramodern /ʏltramodɛrn/ (adj) ultramodern

ultrarechts /ʏltrarɛx(t)s/ (adj, adv) extreme right

ultraviolet /ʏltravijolɛt/ (adj) ultraviolet

het **umc** /yɛmse/ (pl: -'s) [Dutch] *universitair medisch centrum* university medical centre

de **umlaut** /ʏmlaut/ (pl: -en) umlaut (mark)

unaniem /ynanim/ (adj, adv) unanimous: *~ aangenomen* adopted unanimously

undercover /ʌndərkǫvər/ (adv) undercover

de **underdog** /ʌndərdɔːk/ (pl: -s) underdog

het **understatement** /ʌndərstɛtmənt/ (pl: -s) understatement

de **¹uni** /yni/ (pl: -'s) uni

²uni /yni/ (adj) unicolour(ed)

het **unicum** /ynikʏm/ (pl: -s): *dit is een ~ this is unique, this is a unique event*

de **unie** /yni/ (pl: -s) union, association: *Europese Unie* European Union

de **unief** /ynif/ (pl: -s) [Belg] university

uniek /ynik/ (adj, adv) unique

het **uniform** /ynifǫrm/ (pl: -en) uniform: *een ~ dragen* wear a uniform

uniformeren /ynifǫrmerə(n)/ (uniformeerde, heeft geüniformeerd) make uniform

uniseks /yniseks/ (adj) unisex

de **unit** /junɪt/ (pl: -s) unit

universeel /ynivɛrzel/ (adj, adv) universal: *de universele **rechten** van de mens* the universal rights of man

universitair /ynivɛrzitɛːr/ (adj) university: *iem. met een ~e **opleiding*** s.o. with a university education

de **universiteit** /ynivɛrzitɛit/ (pl: -en) university: *hoogleraar **aan** de ~ van Oxford* professor at Oxford University; *naar de ~ gaan* go to the university; [Am also] go to college

het **universum** /ynivɛrzʏm/ universe

unzippen /ʌnzɪpə(n)/ (unzipte, heeft geünzipt) unzip, decompress, unpack

de **update** /ʏbdet/ (pl: -s) update

updaten /ʏbdetə(n)/ (updatete, heeft geüpdatet) update

de **upgrade** /ʏpgret/ (pl: -s) upgrade

upgraden /ʏpgredə(n)/ (upgradede, heeft geüpgraded) upgrade

uploaden /ʏplodə(n)/ (uploadde, heeft geüpload) upload

het **uppie** /ʏpi/ [inform]: *in z'n ~* on (*or:* by) one's lonesome

up-to-date /ʏptudet/ (adj) up-to-date

het **uranium** /yranijʏm/ uranium: *verrijkt ~* enriched uranium

het/de **urban** /ʏːrbən/ urban music

urenlang /yrə(n)lɑŋ/ (adj, adv) interminable, endless: *er werd ~ **vergaderd*** the meeting went on for hours

urgent /ʏrɣɛnt/ (adj) urgent

de **urgentie** /ʏrɣɛnsi/ urgency

de **urgentieverklaring** /ʏrɣɛnsivərklɑrɪŋ/ (pl: -en) certificate of urgency (*or:* need)

de **urine** /yrinə/ urine

urineren /yrinerə(n)/ (urineerde, heeft geürineerd) urinate

het **urineverlies** /yrinəvərlis/ loss of urine

het **urinoir** /yrinwar/ (pl: -s) urinal

de **URL** /yɛrɛl/ *uniform resource locator* URL

de **urn** /ʏrn/ (pl: -en) urn

de **urologie** /yroloɣi/ urology

de **uroloog** /yrolọx/ (pl: urologen) urologist

Uruguay /urugwɑj/ Uruguay

de **Uruguayaan** /urugwajan/ (pl: Uruguayanen) Uruguayan

Uruguayaans /urugwajans/ (adj) Uruguayan

de **USA** /juɛse/ (pl) *United States of America* USA

de **usance** /yzɑ̃sə/ (pl: -s) custom, common practice

de **USB-poort** /yɛzbeport/ (pl: -en) USB port

de **USB-stick** /yɛzbɛstɪk/ (pl: -s) USB flash drive, USB stick

de **user** /juːzər/ (pl: -s) [comp] user

de **utiliteitsbouw** /ytilitɛrtsbɑu/ commercial and industrial building

de **utopie** /ytopi/ (pl: -ën) utopia, utopian dream

utopisch /ytopis/ (adj) utopian

het **uur** /yr/ (pl: uren) **1** hour: *lange uren maken* put in (*or:* work) long hours; *verloren ~(tje)* spare time (*or:* hour); *het **duurde** uren* it went on for hours, it took hours; *een ~ **in** de wind stinken* stink to high heaven; *over een ~* in an hour; *25 euro **per** ~ verdienen* earn 25 euros an hour; *100 kilometer **per** ~* 100 kilometres per (*or:* an) hour; *per ~ betaald worden* be paid by the hour; *kun je hier binnen **twee** ~ zijn?* can you be here within two hours?; *het is een ~ **rijden*** it is an hour's drive; *uren schrijven* invoice for hours worked **2** hour, period, lesson: *we hebben het **derde** ~ wiskunde* we have mathematics for the third lesson **3** o'clock: *op het **hele** ~* on the hour; *op het **halve** ~* on the half hour; *hij kwam **tegen** drie ~* he came around three o'clock; *om ongeveer **acht** ~* round about eight (o'clock); *om **negen** ~ precies* at nine o'clock sharp **4** hour, moment: *het ~ van de **waarheid** is aangebroken* the moment of truth is upon us; *zijn **laatste** ~ heeft geslagen* his final hour has come; his number is up

het **uurloon** /yrlon/ (pl: uurlonen) hourly wage, hourly pay: *zij werkt **op** ~* she is paid by the hour

het **uurtarief** /yrtarif/ (pl: -tarieven) hourly rate

het **uurtje** /yrcə/ (pl: -s) hour: *in de **kleine** ~s thuiskomen* come home in the small hours

het **uurwerk** /yrwɛrk/ (pl: -en) clock, timepiece

de **uurwijzer** /yrwɛizər/ (pl: -s) hour hand

de **uv-index** /yveɪndɛks/ UV index

de **uv-straling** /yvestralɪŋ/ ultraviolet radiation

uw /yw/ (poss pron) your: *het uwe* yours

uwerzijds /ywərzɛrts/ (adv) on your part

uzelf /yzɛlf/ (ref pron) yourself, yourselves

V

de **v** /ve/ (pl: v's) v, V
vaag /vax/ (adj, adv) vague, faint, dim: *ik heb zo'n ~ vermoeden dat ...* I have a hunch (*or:* a sneaking suspicion) that ...
de **vaagheid** /vaxhɛit/ (pl: -heden) vagueness
vaak /vak/ (adv) often, frequently: *dat gebeurt niet ~* that doesn't happen very often; *steeds vaker* more and more (frequently)
vaal /val/ (adj) faded
de **vaan** /van/ (pl: vaans) flag, standard
het **vaandel** /vandəl/ (pl: -s) banner, flag
de **vaandrig** /vandrɪx/ (pl: -s) [Dutch] reserve officer candidate
het **vaantje** /vancə/ (pl: -s) (small) flag, pennant
het **vaarbewijs** /varbəwɛis/ (pl: -bewijzen) navigation licence
vaardig /vardəx/ (adj) skilful, proficient
de **vaardigheid** /vardəxhɛit/ (pl: -heden) skill, skilfulness; proficiency: *sociale vaardigheden* social skills; *~ in het schrijven* writing skill
de **vaargeul** /varxøl/ (pl: -en) channel, waterway
de **vaarroute** /varutə/ (pl: -s) sea lane
de **vaars** /vars/ (pl: vaarzen) heifer
de **vaart** /vart/ (pl: -en) **1** speed; [also fig] pace: *in volle ~* at full speed (*or:* tilt); *de ~ erin houden* keep up the pace; *het zal zo'n ~ niet lopen* it won't come to that (*or:* get that bad); *~ minderen* reduce speed, slow down; *ergens ~ achter zetten* hurry (*or:* speed) things up, get a move on **2** navigation, (sea) trade: *de wilde ~* tramp shipping
de **vaartijd** /vartɛit/ sailing time
het **vaartuig** /vartœyx/ (pl: -en) vessel, craft
het **vaarwater** /varwatər/ (pl: -s, -en) water(s): *in rustig ~* in smooth water(s)
de **vaarweg** /varwɛx/ (pl: -en) waterway
het **vaarwel** /varwɛl/ farewell: *iem. ~ zeggen* bid s.o. farewell
de **vaas** /vas/ (pl: vazen) vase
de **vaat** /vat/ washing-up, dishes
de **vaatdoek** /vaduk/ (pl: -en) dishcloth
de **vaatwasmachine** /vatwasmaʃinə/ (pl: -s) dishwasher
de **vaatwasser** /vatwasər/ (pl: -s) dishwasher: *kan in de ~* dishwasher proof
vacant /vakɑnt/ (adj) vacant, free, open: *een ~e betrekking* a vacancy, an opening
de **vacature** /vakatyrə/ (pl: -s) vacancy, opening: *voorzien in een ~* fill a vacancy
de **vacaturebank** /vakatyrəbɑŋk/ (pl: -en) job vacancy department
het **vaccin** /vaksɛ̃/ (pl: -s) vaccine

de **vaccinatie** /vaksina(t)si/ (pl: -s) vaccination
vaccineren /vaksinɛrə(n)/ (vaccineerde, heeft gevaccineerd) vaccinate
de **vacht** /vaxt/ (pl: -en) **1** fleece; fur; coat **2** sheepskin **3** fur, pelt: *de ~ van een beer* a bearskin
het **vacuüm** /vakywym/ (pl: -s) vacuum: *~ verpakken* vacuum-pack
vacuümverpakt /vakywymvərpɑkt/ (adj) vacuum-packed, vacuum-sealed
de **vader** /vadər/ (pl: -s) father: *~tje en moedertje spelen* play house; *natuurlijke* (*or:* *wettelijke*) *~* natural (*or:* legal) father; *het Onze Vader* the Lord's Prayer; *hij zou haar ~ wel kunnen zijn* he is old enough to be her father; *van ~ op zoon* from father to son; *zo ~, zo zoon* like father, like son
Vaderdag /vadərdɑx/ Father's Day
het **vaderland** /vadərlɑnt/ (pl: -en) (native) country: *voor het ~ sterven* die for one's country; *een tweede ~* a second home
vaderlands /vadərlɑnts/ (adj) national, native: *de ~e geschiedenis* national history
de **vaderlandsliefde** /vadərlɑntslivdə/ patriotism, love of (one's) country
[1]**vaderlijk** /vadərlək/ (adj) **1** paternal **2** fatherly
[2]**vaderlijk** /vadərlək/ (adv) in a fatherly way, like a father
het **vaderschap** /vadərsxɑp/ paternity, fatherhood
de **vaderskant** /vadərskɑnt/ father's side, paternal side: *familie van ~* paternal relatives, relatives on one's father's side
vadsig /vɑtsəx/ (adj, adv) (fat and) lazy
de **vagebond** /vaɣəbɔnt/ (pl: -en) vagabond, tramp
vagelijk /vaɣələk/ (adv) vaguely, faintly
het **vagevuur** /vaɣəvyr/ purgatory
de **vagina** /vaɣina/ (pl: -'s) vagina
vaginaal /vaɣinal/ (adj) vaginal
het **vak** /vak/ (pl: -ken) **1** section, square, space; box **2** compartment; pigeon-hole; shelf: *de ~ken bijvullen* fill the shelves **3** trade; profession: *een ~ leren* learn a trade; *een ~ uitoefenen* practise a trade, be in a trade (*or:* business); *zijn ~ verstaan* understand one's business, know what one is about; *overdrijven is ook een ~* I think you're overreacting a bit **4** subject; course: *exacte ~ken* (exact) sciences; science and maths
de **vakantie** /vakɑnsi/ (pl: -s) holiday(s); [esp Am] vacation: *een week ~* a week's holiday; *de grote ~* the summer holidays; *prettige ~!* have a nice holiday!; *een geheel verzorgde ~* a package tour; *~ hebben* have a holiday; *~ nemen* take a holiday; *met ~ gaan* go on holiday; *aan ~ toe zijn* be ready for (*or:* in need of) a holiday
het **vakantieadres** /vakɑn(t)siadrɛs/ (pl: -sen) holiday address

de **vakantiebaan** /vakɑ̄n(t)siban/ (pl: -banen) holiday job

de **vakantiedag** /vakɑ̄nsidɑχ/ (pl: -en) (day of one's) holiday

de **vakantieganger** /vakɑ̄nsiɣɑŋər/ (pl: -s) holidaymaker

het **vakantiegeld** /vakɑ̄nsiɣɛlt/ (pl: -en) holiday pay

het **vakantiehuis** /vakɑ̄nsihœys/ (pl: -huizen) holiday cottage

de **vakantiespreiding** /vakɑ̄n(t)sisprɛɪdɪŋ/ staggering of holidays; [Am] staggering of vacation

de **vakantietijd** /vakɑ̄nsitɛit/ (pl: -en) holiday period (or: season)

de **vakantietoeslag** /vakɑ̄n(t)situslɑχ/ (pl: -toeslagen) holiday pay

het **vakantiewerk** /vakɑ̄nsiwɛrk/ holiday job, summer job

vakbekwaam /vɑgbəkwɑ̄m/ (adj) skilled

de **vakbekwaamheid** /vɑgbəkwɑ̄mhɛit/ (professional) skill

de **vakbeurs** /vɑgbørs/ (pl: vakbeurzen) trade fair

de **vakbeweging** /vɑgbəweɣɪŋ/ trade unions

het **vakblad** /vɑgblɑt/ (pl: -en) trade journal

de **vakbond** /vɑgbɔnt/ (pl: -en) (trade) union

de **vakbondsleider** /vɑgbɔntslɛidər/ (pl: -s) (trade) union leader

de **vakcentrale** /vɑksɛntralə/ (pl: -s) trade union federation

het **vakdiploma** /vɑgdiploma/ (pl: -'s) (professional) diploma

het **vakgebied** /vɑkχəbit/ (pl: -en) field (of study)

de **vakgroep** /vɑkχrup/ (pl: -en) [roughly] department

de **vakidioot** /vɑkidijot/ (pl: -idioten) narrow-minded specialist, … freak

het **vakjargon** /vɑkjɑrɣɔn/ (pl: -s) (technical) jargon

het **vakje** /vɑkjə/ **1** compartment **2** box **3** pigeon-hole

de **vakkennis** /vɑkɛnɪs/ professional knowledge, expert knowledge; know-how

het **vakkenpakket** /vɑkə(n)pɑkɛt/ (pl: -ten) examination subjects

vakkenvullen /vɑkə(n)vvlə(n)/ supermarket stocking

de **vakkenvuller** /vɑkə(n)vvlər/ (pl: -s) stock clerk, grocery clerk

¹**vakkundig** /vɑkʏndəχ/ (adj) skilled, competent

²**vakkundig** /vɑkʏndəχ/ (adv) competently, with great skill: *het is ~ gerepareerd* it has been expertly done

de **vakliteratuur** /vɑklitəratyr/ professional literature

de **vakman** /vɑkmɑn/ (pl: vaklui, vaklieden, -nen, vakmensen) expert, professional; skilled worker

het **vakmanschap** /vɑkmɑnsχɑp/ skill; craftsmanship: *het ontbreekt hem aan ~* he lacks skill

de **vaktaal** /vɑktal/ jargon

de **vakterm** /vɑktɛrm/ (pl: -en) technical term

de **vakvereniging** /vɑkfərenəɣɪŋ/ (pl: -en) (trade) union

het **vakwerk** /vɑkwɛrk/ craftmanship, workmanship: *~ afleveren* produce excellent work

de **val** /vɑl/ (pl: -len, -len) **1** fall (off, from); trip: *een vrije ~ maken* skydive; *hij maakte een lelijke ~* he had a nasty fall; *ten ~ komen* fall (down), have a fall; *iem. ten ~ brengen* bring s.o. down **2** (down)fall, collapse: *de regering ten ~ brengen* overthrow (or: bring down) the government **3** trap; snare: *een ~ opzetten* set (or: lay) a trap **4** trap, frame-up: *in de ~ lopen* walk (or: fall) into a trap; rise to (or: swallow) the bait

de **valavond** /vɑlavɔnt/ [Belg] dusk, twilight

Valentijnsdag /valəntɛinzdɑχ/ St Valentine's Day

de **valhelm** /vɑlhɛlm/ (pl: -en) (crash) helmet

valide /validə/ (adj) **1** able-bodied **2** valid

het **valies** /valis/ (pl: -en) (suit)case

het **valium**® /valijʏm/ Valium

de **valk** /vɑlk/ (pl: -en) falcon

de **valkuil** /vɑlkœyl/ (pl: -en) pitfall, trap

de **vallei** /vɑlɛi/ (pl: -en) valley

vallen /vɑlə(n)/ (viel, is gevallen) **1** fall, drop: *er valt sneeuw* (or: *hagel*) it is snowing (or: hailing); *uit elkaar ~* fall apart, drop to bits; *zijn blik laten ~ op* let one's eye fall on **2** fall (over); trip (up): *iem. doen ~* make s.o. fall; trip s.o. up; *zij kwam lelijk te ~* she had a bad fall; *met ~ en opstaan* by trial and error; *van de trap ~* fall (or: tumble) down the stairs **3** come, fall: *dat valt buiten zijn bevoegdheid* that falls outside his jurisdiction **4** drop: *iem. laten ~* drop (or: ditch) s.o.; *hij liet de aanklacht ~* he dropped the charge **5** go (for), take (to): *zij valt op donkere mannen* she goes for dark men || *Kerstmis valt op een woensdag* Christmas (Day) is on a Wednesday; *het ~ van de avond* nightfall; *er vielen doden* (or: *gewonden*) there were fatalities (or: casualties); *er viel een stilte* there was a hush, silence fell; *met haar valt niet te praten* there is no talking to her; *er valt wel iets voor te zeggen om …* there is sth. to be said for …

het **valluik** /vɑlœyk/ (pl: -en) trapdoor

de **valpartij** /vɑlpɑrtɛi/ (pl: -en) spill, fall: *de gladheid leidde tot veel ~en* the icy conditions caused a lot of accidents

de **valreep** /vɑlrep/ (pl: valrepen) gangway, gangplank || *op de ~* right at the end, at the final (or: last) moment

¹**vals** /vɑls/ (adj) **1** false, fake, phoney; pseudo- **2** wrong, false: *een spoor* a false trail **3** [mus] flat; sharp; false **4** mean, vicious: *een*

~ *beest* a vicious animal **5** forged, fake, false, counterfeit: *een ~e Vermeer* a forged (*or:* fake) Vermeer **6** false, artificial; mock; imitation: ~ *haar* false hair

²**vals** /vɑls/ (adv) falsely: ~ *spelen* play out of tune; cheat (at cards); ~ *zingen* sing out of tune, sing off key

het **valscherm** /vɑlsxɛrm/ (pl: -en) parachute

valselijk /vɑlsələk/ (adv) falsely, wrongly

de **valsemunter** /vɑlsəmʏntər/ (pl: -s) [Dutch] counterfeiter, forger

de **valsheid** /vɑlshɛit/ **1** spuriousness: *overtuigd van de ~ van het schilderij* convinced that the painting is a fake **2** forgery, fraud, counterfeiting: ~ *in geschrifte* forgery

de **valstrik** /vɑlstrɪk/ (pl: -ken) snare, trap: *iem. in een ~ lokken* lead (*or:* lure) s.o. into a trap

de **valuta** /vɑlyta/ (pl: -'s) currency

de **valutahandel** /vɑlytahɑndəl/ (foreign) exchange dealings

de **vampier** /vɑmpir/ (pl: -s) vampire

¹**van** /vɑn/ (adv) of, from: *je kunt er wel een paar ~ nemen* you can have some (of those)

²**van** /vɑn/ (prep) **1** from: *hij is ~ Amsterdam* he's from Amsterdam; ~ *dorp tot dorp* from one village to another; ~ *een bord eten* eat from (*or:* off) a plate **2** from: ~ *de vroege morgen tot de late avond* from (the) early morning till late at night; ~ *tevoren* beforehand, in advance; ~ *toen af* from then on, from that day (*or:* time) (on) **3** of: *het hoofd ~ de school* the head(master) of the school; *de trein ~ 9.30 uur* the 9.30 train; *een foto ~ mijn vader* a) a picture of my father's; **b)** a picture of my father; ~ *wie is dit boek?* het is ~ *mij* whose book is this? it's mine **4** (made, out) of: *een tafel ~ hout* a wooden table **5** by, of: *dat was niet slim ~ Jan* that was not such a clever move of Jan's; *het volgende nummer is ~ Van Morrison* the next number is by Van Morrison; *een plaat ~ de Stones* a Stones record, a record by the Stones ‖ *drie ~ de vier* three out of four; *een jas met ~ die koperen knopen* a coat with those brass buttons; ~ *dat geld kon hij een auto kopen* he was able to buy a car with that money; *daar niet ~ niet* that's not the point; *ik geloof ~ niet* I don't think so; *ik verzeker u ~ wel* I assure you I do; *het lijkt ~ wel* it seems (*or:* looks) like it; *het goedkoopste ~ het goedkoopste* the cheapest of the cheap

vanaf /vɑnɑf/ (prep) **1** from, as from; [Am] as of; beginning; since: ~ *de 16e eeuw* from the 16th century onward(s); ~ *vandaag* as from today; [Am] as of today **2** from, over: *prijzen ~ ...* prices (range) from ...

vanavond /vɑnavɔnt/ (adv) tonight, this evening

vanbinnen /vɑmbɪnə(n)/ (adv) (on the) inside

vanboven /vɑmbovə(n)/ (adv) **1** on the top,

on the upper surface, above **2** from above

vanbuiten /vɑmbœytə(n)/ (adv) **1** from the outside **2** on the outside **3** by heart: *iets ~ kennen* (or: *leren*) know (*or:* learn) sth. by heart

vandaag /vɑndax/ (adv) today: ~ *de dag* nowadays, these days, currently; *tot op de dag van* ~ to this very day, to date; ~ *is het maandag* today is Monday; ~ *over een week* a week from today, in a week's time, a week from now; *de krant van* ~ today's paper; *liever* ~ *dan morgen* the sooner the better ‖ ~ *of morgen* one of these days, soon

de **vandaal** /vɑndal/ (pl: vandalen) vandal

vandaan /vɑndan/ (adv) **1** away, from: *we moeten hier ~!* let's go away! **2** out of, from: *waar heb je die oude klok ~?* where did you pick up (*or:* get) that old clock?; *waar kom (ben) jij ~?* where are you from?, where do you come from? ‖ *hij woont overal ver ~* he lives miles from anywhere

vandaar /vɑndar/ (adv) therefore, that's why

het **vandalisme** /vɑndalɪsmə/ vandalism

vandoor /vɑndor/ (adv) off, away: *ik moet er weer ~* I have to be off; *hij is er met het geld ~* he has run off with the money

vaneen /vɑnen/ (adv) separated, split up

vangen /vɑŋə(n)/ (ving, heeft gevangen) **1** catch; capture; (en)trap: *een dief ~* catch a thief **2** catch **3** make: *twintig piek per uur ~* make five quid an hour; [Am] make ten bucks an hour

het **vangnet** /vɑŋnɛt/ (pl: -ten) **1** (trap-)net **2** safety net

de **vangrail** /vɑŋrel/ (pl: -s) crash barrier

de **vangst** /vɑŋst/ (pl: -en) catch, capture; haul: *de politie deed een goede ~* the police made a good catch (*or:* haul)

de **vanille** /vɑnijə/ vanilla

het **vanille-ijs** /vɑnijɛis/ vanilla ice cream

vanjewelste /vɑnjəwɛlstə/ (adj): *een succes* ~ a howling success; *een klap* ~ a huge (*or:* tremendous) blow

vanmiddag /vɑmɪdax/ (adv) this afternoon

vanmorgen /vɑmɔrɣə(n)/ (adv) this morning; in the morning: ~ *vroeg* early this morning

vannacht /vɑnɑxt/ (adv) tonight; last night: *je kunt ~ blijven slapen, als je wil* you can stay the night, if you like; *hij kwam ~ om twee uur thuis* he came home at two o'clock in the morning

vanouds /vɑnʌuts/ (adv): *het was weer als ~* it was just like old times again

vanuit /vɑnœyt/ (prep) **1** from; out of: *ik keek ~ mijn raam naar beneden* I looked down from (*or:* out of) my window **2** starting from

vanwaar /vɑnwar/ (adv) **1** from where **2** why: ~ *die haast?* what's the hurry?

vanwaaraf /vɑnwarɑf/ (adv) from where/

which: *het dak ~ geschoten werd* the roof from which the shots were fired

vanwege /vɑnweɣə/ (prep) because of, owing to, due to, on account of

vanzelf /vɑnzɛlf/ (adv) **1** by o.s., of o.s., of one's own accord **2** as a matter of course, automatically: *alles ging (liep) als ~* everything went smoothly; *dat spreekt ~* that goes without saying

¹vanzelfsprekend /vɑnzɛlfsprekənt/ (adj) obvious, natural, self-evident

²vanzelfsprekend /vɑnzɛlfsprekənt/ (adv) obviously, naturally, of course: *als ~ aannemen* take sth. for granted

de **¹varen** /varə/n/ (pl: -s) fern

²varen /varə(n)/ (voer, heeft/is gevaren) sail: *het schip vaart 10 knopen* the ship sails at 10 knots; *hij wil gaan ~* he wants to go to sea (*or:* be a sailor); *alle voorzichtigheid laten ~* throw (*or:* fling) all caution to the wind(s)

de **varia** /varija/ (pl) miscellany

variabel /varijabəl/ (adj) variable, flexible: *~e werktijden* flexible working hours

de **variabele** /varijabələ/ (pl: -n) variable

de **variant** /varijɑnt/ (pl: -en) variant, variation: *een ~ op* a variant of, a variation on

de **variatie** /varija(t)si/ (pl: -s) variation, change: *voor de ~* for a change

variëren /varijerə(n)/ (varieerde, heeft gevarieerd) vary, differ: *sterk ~de prijzen* widely differing prices

het **variété** /varijete/ (pl: -s) variety, music hall

de **variëteit** /varijetɛit/ (pl: -en) variety, diversity

het **varken** /vɑrkə(n)/ (pl: -s) pig; hog; [offensive] swine: *zo lui als een ~* bone idle (*or:* lazy)

de **varkensfokkerij** /vɑrkənsfokərɛi/ (pl: -en) pig farm

de **varkenshaas** /vɑrkənshas/ (pl: -hazen) pork tenderloin (*or:* steak)

de **varkenspest** /vɑrkə(n)spɛst/ swine fever

de **varkensstal** /vɑrkə(n)stal/ (pl: -len) pigsty; pig house

het **varkensvlees** /vɑrkənsfles/ pork

het **varkensvoer** /vɑrkə(n)sfur/ pigfeed, pigfood; (pig)swill

de **vaseline** /vazəlinə/ vaseline

¹vast /vɑst/ (adj) **1** fixed, immovable: *~e vloerbedekking* wall-to-wall carpet(ing) **2** fixed, stationary: *~ raken* get stuck (*or:* caught, jammed); *~e datum* fixed date; *~e inkomsten* a fixed (*or:* regular) income; *~e kosten* fixed (*or:* standing) charges; *een ~e prijs* a fixed (*or:* set) price; *een ~e telefoon* a landline (telephone), a fixed line telephone **3** firm, steady: *met ~e hand* with a steady (*or:* sure) hand; *~e overtuiging* firm conviction **4** permanent; regular; steady: *~ adres* fixed address; *een ~e betrekking* a permanent position; *~e klanten* regular costumers; [inform] regulars **5** solid: *~ voedsel* solid food

6 firm: *~e vorm geven* shape **7** tight, firm **8** established, standing: *een ~ gebruik* a (set) custom; *een ~e regel* a fixed (*or:* set) rule

²vast /vɑst/ (adv) **1** fixedly, firmly **2** certainly, for certain (*or:* sure): *hij is het ~ vergeten* he must have forgotten (it); [Dutch] *~ en zeker,* [Belg] *zeker en ~* definitely, certainly **3** for the time being, for the present: *begin maar ~ met eten* go ahead and eat (*or:* start eating)

vastberaden /vɑstbəradə(n)/ (adj) resolute, firm, determined

vastbesloten /vɑstbəslotə(n)/ (adj) determined

zich **vastbijten** /vɑstbɛitə(n)/ (beet zich vast, heeft zich vastgebeten) [fig] cling to: *zich in een onderwerp ~* get (*or:* sink) one's teeth into a subject

vastbinden /vɑstbɪndə(n)/ (bond vast, heeft vastgebonden) tie (up, down), bind (up), fasten: *zijn armen werden vastgebonden* his arms were tied (*or:* bound) (up)

het **vasteland** /vɑstəlɑnt/ **1** continent **2** mainland; Continent

de **¹vasten** /vɑstə(n)/ fast(ing)

²vasten /vɑstə(n)/ (vastte, heeft gevast) fast

Vastenavond /vɑstə(n)avɔnt/ Shrove Tuesday

de **vastentijd** /vɑstə(n)tɛit/ **1** Lent **2** fast, time of fasting

het **vastgoed** /vɑstχut/ real estate (*or:* property)

vastgrijpen /vɑstχrɛipə(n)/ (greep vast, heeft vastgegrepen) grasp, clasp

de **vastheid** /vɑsthɛit/ **1** firmness **2** fixity **3** invariability **4** solidity **5** consistency

vasthouden /vɑsthaudə(n)/ (hield vast, heeft vastgehouden) hold (fast); grip; detain: *iemands hand ~* hold s.o.'s hand; *hou je vast!* brace yourself (for the shock)!

vasthoudend /vɑsthaudənt/ (adj) tenacious; persistent; persevering

zich **vastklampen** /vɑstklɑmpə(n)/ (klampte zich vast, heeft zich vastgeklampt) cling, clutch, hang on

vastklemmen /vɑstklɛmə(n)/ (klemde vast, heeft vastgeklemd) clip (on), tighten: *de deur zat vastgeklemd* the door was jammed

vastleggen /vɑstlɛɣə(n)/ (legde vast, heeft vastgelegd) **1** tie up: *zich niet ~ op iets, zich nergens op ~* refuse to commit o.s., leave one's options open; be non-committal **2** set down, record: *iets schriftelijk ~* put sth. down in writing

vastliggen /vɑstlɪɣə(n)/ (lag vast, heeft vastgelegen) be tied up, be fixed: *die voorwaarden liggen vast in het contract* those conditions have been laid down in the contract

vastlijmen /vɑstlɛimə(n)/ (lijmde vast, heeft vastgelijmd) glue (together), stick (together)

vastlopen /vɑstlopə(n)/ (liep vast, is vastgelopen) **1** jam, get jammed: *het schip is vast-gelopen* the ship has run aground **2** [fig] get stuck, be bogged down: *de onderhandelingen zijn vastgelopen* negotiations have reached a deadlock

vastmaken /vɑstmakə(n)/ (maakte vast, heeft vastgemaakt) fasten; tie up; do up, button up; secure

vastpakken /vɑstpɑkə(n)/ (pakte vast, heeft vastgepakt) grip, grasp; grab

vastpinnen /vɑstpɪnə(n)/ (pinde vast, heeft vastgepind) pin down, peg down: *iem. op iets ~* pin (*or:* peg) s.o. down to sth.

vastplakken /vɑstplɑkə(n)/ (plakte vast, heeft vastgeplakt) stick together, glue together

vastroesten /vɑstrustə(n)/ (roestte vast, is vastgeroest) rust

vastspijkeren /vɑ(st)spɛikərə(n)/ (spijkerde vast, heeft vastgespijkerd) nail (down); tack

vaststaan /vɑstan/ (stond vast, heeft vast-gestaan) **1** be certain: *het staat nu vast, dat* it is now definite (*or:* certain) that; *de datum stond nog niet vast* the date was still uncertain (yet) **2** be fixed: *zijn besluit staat vast* his mind is made up

vaststaand /vɑ(st)stant/ (adj) certain; final: *een ~ feit* an established (*or:* a recognized) fact

vaststellen /vɑstɛlə(n)/ (stelde vast, heeft vastgesteld) **1** fix, determine, settle, arrange: *een datum ~* settle on (*or:* fix) a date; *een prijs ~* fix a price **2** decide (on), specify; lay down: *op vastgestelde tijden* at stated times (*or:* intervals) **3** find, conclude **4** determine, establish: *de doodsoorzaak ~* establish (*or:* determine) the cause of death; *de schade ~* assess the damage

de **vaststelling** /vɑ(st)stɛlɪŋ/ (pl: -en) **1** arrangement **2** conclusion **3** decree, assessment

vastvriezen /vɑstfrizə(n)/ (vroor vast, is vastgevroren) freeze (in)

vastzetten /vɑstsɛtə(n)/ (zette vast, heeft vastgezet) **1** fix, fasten; secure **2** tie up, lock up, settle (on): *zijn spaargeld voor vijf jaar ~* tie up one's savings for five years

vastzitten /vɑstsɪtə(n)/ (zat vast, heeft vastgezeten) **1** be stuck; be jammed: *~ in de file* be stuck in a tailback, traffic-jam **2** be stuck (*or:* fixed): *daar zit heel wat aan vast* there is (a lot) more to it (than meets the eye) **3** be locked up, be behind bars: *hij heeft een jaar vastgezeten* he has been inside for a year **4** be in a fix **5** be tied (down) (to), be committed (to): *hij heeft het beloofd; nu zit hij eraan vast* he made that promise, he can't get out of it now

de **¹vat** /vɑt/ hold, grip; handle: *geen ~ op iem. hebben* have no hold over s.o.

het **²vat** /vɑt/ barrel; cask; drum: *een ~ petroleum*

an oil drum; *bier van het ~* draught beer

vatbaar /vɑdbar/ (adj) **1** susceptible to, liable to: *hij is zeer ~ voor kou* he is very prone to catching colds **2** amenable (to), open to: *hij is niet voor rede ~* he's impervious (*or:* not open) to reason

het **Vaticaan** /vatikan/ Vatican

Vaticaanstad /vatikanstɑt/ Vatican City

vatten /vɑtə(n)/ (vatte, heeft gevat) catch

de **vazal** /vazɑl/ (pl: -len) vassal

v.Chr. *voor Christus* BC

vechten /vɛxtə(n)/ (vocht, heeft gevochten) **1** fight; combat: *wij moesten ~ om in de trein te komen* we had to fight our way into the train **2** fight (for, against): *tegen de slaap ~* fight off sleep; *hij vecht voor zijn leven* he's fighting for his life

de **vechter** /vɛxtər/ (pl: -s) fighter, combatant

de **vechtersbaas** /vɛxtərzbas/ (pl: -bazen) hooligan, hoodlum

de **vechtlust** /vɛxtlʏst/ fight, fighting spirit

de **vechtpartij** /vɛxtpɑrtɛi/ (pl: -en) fight, brawl

de **vechtsport** /vɛxtsport/ (pl: -en) combat sport

de **vector** /vɛktɔr/ (pl: -en) vector

de **¹vedergewicht** /vedərɣəwɪxt/ [boxer] featherweight

het **²vedergewicht** /vedərɣəwɪxt/ featherweight

vederlicht /vedərlɪxt/ (adj, adv) feathery

de **vedette** /vədɛtə/ (pl: -s, -n) star, celebrity

het **vee** /ve/ cattle: *een stuk ~* a head of cattle

de **veearts** /veɑrts/ (pl: -en) veterinary (surgeon); [Am] veterinarian; vet

de **¹veeg** /vex/ (pl: vegen) **1** wipe; lick **2** streak; smudge: *er zit een zwarte ~ op je gezicht* there's a black smudge on your face

²veeg /vex/ (adj) **1** fatal **2** ominous, fateful: *een ~ teken* a bad sign (*or:* omen)

de **veehandel** /vehɑndəl/ cattle trade

de **veehouder** /vehɑudər/ (pl: -s) cattle breeder, cattle farmer; [Am] rancher

de **veehouderij** /vehɑudərɛi/ (pl: -en) cattle farm; [Am] cattle ranch

de **veejay** /vidʒe/ veejay, VJ

¹veel /vel/ (ind pron) much, many, a lot, lots: *~ geluk!* good luck!; *weet ik ~* how should I know?; *~ te* far too much (*or:* many); *één keer te ~* (just) once too often

²veel /vel/ (adv) much, a lot: *hij was kwaad, maar zij was nog ~ kwader* he was angry, but she was even more so; *ze lijken ~ op elkaar* they are very much alike

³veel /vel/ (num) many, a lot ‖ *het zijn er ~* there's a lot of them

veelal /velɑl/ (adv) **1** usually **2** mostly

veelbelovend /velbəlovənt/ (adj, adv) promising: *~ zijn* show great promise

veelbetekenend /velbətekənənt/ (adj, adv) meaning(ful): *iem. ~ aankijken* give s.o.

a meaning look

veelbewogen /velbəwoɣə(n)/ (adj) eventful; hectic, turbulent; chequered

veeleer /veler/ (adv) [form] rather

veeleisend /velɛisənt/ (adj) demanding, particular (about)

veelgesteld /velɣəstɛlt/ (adj): ~e vragen frequently asked questions *(FAQ)*

de **veelheid** /velhɛɪt/ multitude

de **veelhoek** /velhuk/ (pl: -en) polygon

veelomvattend /velomvɑtənt/ (adj) comprehensive, extensive

de **veelpleger** /velpleɣər/ multiple offender

veelsoortig /velsortəχ/ (adj) multifarious, varied

veelstemmig /velstɛməχ/ (adj) polyphonic

het **veelvoud** /velvɑut/ (pl: -en) **1** multiple: *30 is een ~ van 5* 30 is a multiple of 5; *zijn salaris bedraagt een ~ van het hare* his salary is many times larger than hers **2** range/wealth of: *een ~ aan mogelijkheden* a range of possibilities

de **veelvraat** /velvrat/ (pl: -vraten) glutton

veelvuldig /velvʏldəχ/ (adj) frequently, often

veelzeggend /velzɛɣənt/ (adj) telling, revealing: *dat is ~* that is saying a lot

veelzijdig /velzɛidəχ/ (adj) many-sided, versatile: *haar ~e belangstelling* her varied interests; *een ~e geest* a versatile mind

de **veemarkt** /vemɑrkt/ (pl: -en) cattle market

het **veen** /ven/ (pl: venen) peat

de **veenbes** /vembɛs/ (pl: -sen) cranberry

de **¹veer** /ver/ **1** feather **2** spring

het **²veer** /ver/ ferry

de **veerboot** /verbot/ (pl: -boten) ferry(boat)

de **veerdienst** /verdinst/ (pl: -en) ferry (service, line)

de **veerkracht** /verkrɑχt/ elasticity, resilience

veerkrachtig /verkrɑχtəχ/ (adj) elastic, springy, resilient

de **veerman** /vermɑn/ (pl: veerlieden, veerlui) ferryman

de **veerpont** /verpont/ (pl: -en) ferry(boat)

veertien /vertin/ (num) fourteen: *vandaag over ~ dagen* in a fortnight('s time), two weeks from today; *~ dagen* fourteen days; a fortnight; *het zijn er ~* there are fourteen (of them)

veertiende /vertində/ (num) fourteenth

veertig /fertəχ/ (num) forty: *in de jaren ~* in the forties; *hij loopt tegen de ~* he is pushing forty; *~ plus* more than 40 % fat

de **veertiger** /fertəɣər/ (pl: -s) man of forty: *hij is een goede ~* he is somewhere in his forties

veertigjarig /fertəχjarəχ/ (adj) **1** forty years', fortieth: *~e bruiloft* fortieth wedding anniversary **2** forty-year-old

veertigste /fertəχstə/ (num) fortieth

veertigurig /fertəχyrəχ/ (adj) forty-hour: *de ~e werkweek* the forty-hour week

de **veestal** /vestɑl/ (pl: -len) cowshed

de **veestapel** /vestapəl/ (pl: -s) (live)stock

de **veeteelt** /vetelt/ stock breeding, cattle breeding

het **veevervoer** /veːvərvur/ transport of livestock (*or:* cattle)

het **veevoer** /vevur/ feed

de **veewagen** /vewaɣə(n)/ (pl: -s) cattle truck; cattle lorry

de **vegaburger** /veɣabʏrɣər/ (pl: -s) veggie burger

de **veganist** /veɣanɪst/ (pl: -en) vegan

veganistisch /veɣanɪstis/ (adj) vegan

vegen /veɣə(n)/ (veegde, heeft geveegd) **1** sweep, brush: *de schoorsteen ~* sweep the chimney **2** wipe: *voeten ~ a.u.b.* wipe your feet please || [comp] *veeg met je vinger over het scherm* swipe your finger over the screen; [sport] *geveegd worden* get crushed

de **veger** /veɣər/ (pl: -s) (sweeping) brush: *~ en blik* dustpan and brush

de **vegetariër** /veɣetarijər/ (pl: -s) vegetarian

vegetarisch /veɣetaris/ (adj) vegetarian: *ik eet altijd ~* I'm a vegetarian

de **vegetatie** /veɣeta(t)si/ (pl: -s) vegetation

vegeteren /veɣetərə(n)/ (vegeteerde, heeft gevegeteerd) vegetate

het **vehikel** /vehikəl/ (pl: -s) vehicle

veilen /vɛilə(n)/ (veilde, heeft geveild) sell by auction: *antiek* (or: *huizen*) *~* auction antiques (*or:* houses)

veilig /vɛiləχ/ (adj, adv) safe, secure; (all-)clear: *~ verkeer* [roughly] road safety; *iets ~ opbergen* put sth. in a safe place; *~ thuiskomen* return home safe(ly); *~ en wel* safe and sound

de **veiligheid** /vɛiləχhɛit/ safety, security: *de openbare ~* public security; *iets in ~ brengen* bring sth. to (a place of) safety

de **veiligheidsagent** /vɛiləχhɛitsaɣɛnt/ (pl: -en) security officer

de **veiligheidsbril** /vɛiləχhɛitsbrɪl/ (pl: -len) safety goggles, protective goggles

de **veiligheidsdienst** /vɛiləχhɛitsdinst/ (pl: -en) security forces: *binnenlandse ~* (counter)intelligence

het **veiligheidsglas** /vɛiləχhɛitsχlɑs/ safety (*or:* shatterproof) glass

de **veiligheidsgordel** /vɛiləχhɛitsχordəl/ (pl: -s) safety belt; seat belt

veiligheidshalve /vɛiləχhɛitshɑlvə/ (adv) for reasons of safety (*or:* security)

de **veiligheidsmaatregel** /vɛiləχhɛitsmatreɣəl/ (pl: -en, -s) security measure

de **Veiligheidsraad** /vɛiləχhɛitsrat/ Security Council

het **veiligheidsslot** /vɛiləχhɛitslot/ (pl: -en) safety lock

de **veiligheidsspeld** /vɛiləχhɛitspɛlt/ (pl: -en) safety pin

veiligstellen /vɛiləχstɛlə(n)/ (stelde veilig,

heeft veiliggesteld) safeguard, secure: *zijn* **toekomst** ~ provide for the future

de **veiling** /vɛilɪŋ/ (pl: -en) auction

het **veilinghuis** /vɛilɪŋhœys/ (pl: -huizen) auctioneering firm

de **veilingmeester** /vɛilɪŋmestər/ (pl: -s) auctioneer

de **veilingsite** /vɛilɪŋsɑjt/ auction site

veinzen /vɛinzə(n)/ (veinsde, heeft geveinsd) pretend, feign

het **vel** /vɛl/ (pl: -len) **1** skin: *het is om uit je ~ te springen* it is enough to drive you up the wall; *~ over been zijn* be all skin and bone; *lekker in zijn ~ zitten* feel good **2** sheet

het **veld** /vɛlt/ (pl: -en) field; open country (*or:* fields); pitch; square: *in geen ~en of wegen was er iem. te zien* there was no sign of anyone anywhere; *een speler uit het ~ sturen* send a player off (the field) ‖ *uit het ~ geslagen zijn* be confused, be taken aback; *het ~ ruimen* step down

het **veldbed** /vɛldbɛt/ (pl: -den) camp bed

het **veldboeket** /vɛldbukɛt/ (pl: -ten) bouquet of wild flowers

de **veldfles** /vɛltflɛs/ (pl: -sen) water bottle

de **veldheer** /vɛltheːr/ (pl: -heren) general

het **veldhospitaal** /vɛlthɔspital/ (pl: -hospitalen) field hospital

de **veldloop** /vɛltlop/ (pl: -lopen) cross-country (race)

de **veldmaarschalk** /vɛltmarsχalk/ (pl: -en) Field Marshal; [Am] General of the Army

de **veldmuis** /vɛltmœys/ (pl: -muizen) field vole, field mouse

veldrijden /vɛltrɛidə(n)/ cyclo-cross (racing)

de **veldsla** /vɛltsla/ lamb's lettuce

de **veldslag** /vɛltslɑχ/ (pl: -en) (pitched) battle

de **veldspeler** /vɛltspeːlər/ (pl: -s) fielder

de **veldtocht** /vɛltɔχt/ (pl: -en) campaign

het **veldwerk** /vɛltwɛrk/ fieldwork: *het ~ verrichten* do the donkey work, do the spadework

de **veldwerker** /vɛltwɛrkər/ (pl: -s) field worker

velen /veːlə(n)/ stand, bear

velerlei /veːlərlɛi/ (adj) many, multifarious: *op ~ gebied* in many fields; *~ oorzaken* a variety of causes

de **velg** /vɛlχ/ (pl: -en) rim

vellen /vɛlə(n)/ (velde, heeft geveld) cut down, fell: *bomen ~* cut down trees; *een oordeel over iets ~* pass judgement on sth.

de **velo** /veːlo/ [Belg] bike

het/de **velours** /vəluːr/ velour(s)

het **ven** /vɛn/ (pl: -nen) pool; hollow

de **vendetta** /vɛndɛta/ (pl: -'s) vendetta, blood feud

Venetië /veːneː(t)sijə/ Venice

de **Venezolaan** /veːnezolan/ (pl: Venezolanen) Venezuelan

Venezolaans /veːnezolans/ (adj) Venezuelan

Venezuela /veːnezywela/ Venezuela

het **venijn** /vənɛin/ poison, venom: *het ~ zit in de staart* the sting is in the tail

venijnig /vənɛinəχ/ (adj, adv) vicious; venomous: *~e blikken* malicious looks

de **venkel** /vɛŋkəl/ fennel

de **vennoot** /vɛnot/ (pl: vennoten) partner

de **vennootschap** /vɛnotsχɑp/ (pl: -pen) **1** partnership, firm; [Am also] company **2** trading partnership: *besloten ~* private limited company; *naamloze ~* public limited company

de **vennootschapsbelasting** /vɛnotsχɑpsbəlɑstɪŋ/ corporation tax

het **venster** /vɛnstər/ (pl: -s) window

de **vensterbank** /vɛnstərbɑŋk/ (pl: -en) windowsill

de **vensterenveloppe** /vɛnstərɛnvəlɔp/ (pl: -n) window envelope

het **vensterglas** /vɛnstərɣlas/ (pl: -glazen) window glass; window-pane

de **vent** /vɛnt/ (pl: -en) **1** fellow, guy, bloke: *een leuke ~* a dishy bloke (*or:* guy) **2** son(ny), lad(die)

venten /vɛntə(n)/ (ventte, heeft gevent) hawk, peddle

de **venter** /vɛntər/ (pl: -s) street trader, hawker, pedlar

het **ventiel** /vɛntil/ (pl: -en) valve

de **ventilatie** /vɛntila(t)si/ ventilation

de **ventilator** /vɛntilatɔr/ (pl: -s, -en) fan, ventilator

¹**ventileren** /vɛntilerə(n)/ (ventileerde, heeft geventileerd) air

²**ventileren** /vɛntilerə(n)/ (ventileerde, heeft geventileerd) ventilate, air: *zijn mening ~* ventilate (*or:* air) one's opinion

de **ventweg** /vɛntwɛχ/ (pl: -en) [Dutch] service road

¹**ver** /vɛr/ (adj) distant, far; far-off; far off; a long way: *~re landen* distant (*or:* far-off) countries; *de ~re toekomst* the distant future; *in een ~ verleden* in some distant (*or:* remote) past; *een ~re reis* a long journey

²**ver** /vɛr/ (adv) **1** far; a long way: *hij sprong zeven meter ~* he jumped a distance of seven metres; *~ gevorderd zijn* be well advanced; *het zou te ~ voeren om ...* it would be going too far to ...; *~ vooruitzien* look well (*or:* way) ahead; *hoe ~ is het nog?* how much further is it?; *hoe ~ ben je met je huiswerk?* how far have you got with your homework?; *dat gaat te ~!* that is the limit!; *nu ga je te ~!* now you're going too far!; *~ weg* a long way off, far away; *het is zo ~!* here we go, this is it; *ben je zo ~?* (are you) ready?; *van ~ komen* come a long way, come from distant parts; *~ te zoeken zijn* be miles away; [fig] not be about (*or:* around) **2** (by) far, way: *~ heen zijn* be far gone; *zijn tijd ~ vooruit zijn* be way ahead of

one's time
veraangenamen /vərȧŋənamə(n)/ (veraangenaamde, heeft veraangenaamd) sweeten, make more pleasant
verachtelijk /vərȧχtələk/ (adj, adv) despicable
verachten /vərȧχtə(n)/ (verachtte, heeft veracht) despise, scorn
de **verachting** /vərȧχtɪŋ/ contempt
de **verademing** /vərȧdəmɪŋ/ relief
veraf /vɛrȧf/ (adv) far away, far off, a long way away (*or:* off)
verafgelegen /vɛrȧfχələχə(n)/ (adj) faraway; far away; remote
verafgoden /vərȧfχodə(n)/ (verafgoodde, heeft verafgood) idolize
verafschuwen /vərȧfsχywə(n)/ (verafschuwde, heeft verafschuwd) loathe, detest
de **veranda** /vərȧndȧ/ (pl: -'s) veranda
¹**veranderen** /vərȧndərə(n)/ (veranderde, is veranderd) **1** change: *de tijden* ~ times are changing **2** change, switch: *van huisarts* ~ change one's doctor; *van onderwerp* ~ change the subject
²**veranderen** /vərȧndərə(n)/ (veranderde, heeft veranderd) **1** alter, change: *een jurkje* ~ alter a dress; *dat verandert de zaak* that changes things; *daar is niets meer aan te* ~ nothing can be done about that **2** change, turn (into): *Jezus veranderde water in wijn* Jesus turned water into wine
de **verandering** /vərȧndərɪŋ/ (pl: -en) **1** change; variation: ~ *van omgeving* change of scene(ry); *voor de* ~ for a change **2** alteration: *een* ~ *aanbrengen in* make an alteration (*or:* a change) to
veranderlijk /vərȧndərlək/ (adj) changeable, variable; unsettled; fickle
verankeren /vərȧŋkərə(n)/ (verankerde, heeft verankerd) anchor; [fig] embed
verantwoord /vərȧntwort/ (adj) **1** safe; sensible **2** well-considered, sound: *-e voeding* a well-balanced (*or:* sensible) diet
verantwoordelijk /vərȧntwordələk/ (adj) responsible: *de -e minister* the minister responsible; *iem. voor iets* ~ *stellen* hold s.o. responsible for sth.
de **verantwoordelijkheid** /vərȧntwordələkhɛit/ (pl: -heden) responsibility: *de* ~ *voor iets op zich nemen* take (*or:* assume) responsibility for sth.; *de* ~ *voor een aanslag opeisen* claim responsibility for an attack
¹**verantwoorden** /vərȧntwordə(n)/ (verantwoordde, heeft verantwoord) justify, account for: *ik kan dit niet tegenover mijzelf* ~ I cannot square this with my conscience
zich ²**verantwoorden** /vərȧntwordə(n)/ (verantwoordde zich, heeft zich verantwoord) justify, answer (to s.o. for sth.)
de **verantwoording** /vərȧntwordɪŋ/ (pl: -en) **1** account: ~ *afleggen* render account; *aan*

iem. ~ *verschuldigd zijn* be accountable (*or:* answerable) to s.o.; *iem. ter* ~ *roepen* call s.o. to account **2** responsibility: *op jouw* ~ you take the responsibility
¹**verarmen** /vərȧrmə(n)/ (verarmde, is verarmd) become impoverished, be reduced to poverty
²**verarmen** /vərȧrmə(n)/ (verarmde, heeft verarmd) impoverish || *verarmd uranium* depleted uranium
verassen /vərȧsə(n)/ (veraste, heeft verast) incinerate, cremate
het ¹**verbaal** /vɛrbȧl/ (pl: verbalen) booking, ticket
²**verbaal** /vɛrbȧl/ (adj) verbal
verbaasd /vərbȧst/ (adj) surprised, astonished, amazed: ~ *zijn over iets* be surprised (*or:* amazed) at sth.
verbaliseren /vɛrbȧlizȩrə(n)/ (verbaliseerde, heeft geverbaliseerd) book
het **verband** /vərbȧnt/ (pl: -en) **1** bandage: *een* ~ *aanleggen* put on a bandage **2** connection; context; relation(ship): *in* ~ *met* a) in connection with, with reference to; b) due to; *in dit* ~ ... in this respect; *in landelijk* (*or:* *Europees*) ~ at a national (*or:* European) level; *in ruimer* ~ in a wider context; ~ *houden met iets* be connected with sth.; *dit houdt* ~ *met het feit dat* this has to do with the fact that; *de woorden uit hun* ~ *rukken* take words out of context
de **verbanddoos** /vərbȧndos/ (pl: -dozen) first-aid kit, first-aid box
verbannen /vərbȧnə(n)/ (verbande, heeft verbannen) banish, exile: ~ *zijn* be banished, be under a ban
de **verbanning** /vərbȧnɪŋ/ (pl: -en) banishment, exile
verbasteren /vərbȧstərə(n)/ (verbasterde, heeft verbasterd) corrupt
¹**verbazen** /vərbȧzə(n)/ (verbaasde, heeft verbaasd) amaze, surprise, astonish: *dat verbaast me niets* that doesn't surprise me in the least
zich ²**verbazen** /vərbȧzə(n)/ (verbaasde zich, heeft zich verbaasd) be surprised (*or:* amazed) (at)
de **verbazing** /vərbȧzɪŋ/ surprise, amazement, astonishment: *wie schetst mijn* ~ imagine my surprise; *dat wekte* ~ that came as a surprise; *tot mijn* ~ *hoorde ik* ... I was surprised to hear ...; *van de ene* ~ *in de andere vallen* go from one surprise to the next
verbazingwekkend /vərbȧzɪŋwɛkənt/ (adj, adv) astonishing, surprising; amazing
¹**verbeelden** /vərbȩldə(n)/ (verbeeldde, heeft verbeeld) represent, be meant (*or:* supposed) to be: *dat moet een badkamer* ~! that is supposed to be a bathroom!
zich ²**verbeelden** /vərbȩldə(n)/ (verbeeldde zich, heeft zich verbeeld) imagine, fancy: *dat ver-*

beeld je je maar you are just imagining it (*or:* things); *hij verbeeldt zich heel wat* he has a high opinion of himself; *verbeeld je maar niet!* don't go getting ideas (into your head)!

de **verbeelding** /vərbɛldɪŋ/ **1** imagination: *dat spreekt tot de ~* that appeals to one's imagination **2** conceit(edness), vanity: *~ hebben* be conceited, think a lot of o.s.

verbergen /vərbɛrɣə(n)/ (verborg, heeft verborgen) hide, conceal: *zij hield iets voor hem verborgen* she was holding sth. back from him

verbeten /vərbɛtə(n)/ (adj) grim, dogged

¹**verbeteren** /vərbɛtərə(n)/ (verbeterde, is verbeterd) improve, get better: *verbeterde werkomstandigheden* improved working conditions

²**verbeteren** /vərbɛtərə(n)/ (verbeterde, heeft verbeterd) **1** improve: *zijn Engels ~* improve (*or:* brush up) one's English **2** correct **3** beat, improve on: *een record ~* break a record

de **verbetering** /vərbɛtərɪŋ/ (pl: -en) **1** improvement: *het is een hele ~ vergeleken met …* it's a great improvement on … **2** correction; rectification; marking

verbeurdverklaren /vərbɔrtfərklarə(n)/ (verklaarde verbeurd, heeft verbeurdverklaard) seize, confiscate

verbieden /vərbidə(n)/ (verbood, heeft verboden) forbid; ban; suppress: *verboden toegang* no admittance; *verboden in te rijden* no entry (*or:* access); *verboden te roken* no smoking; *verboden voor onbevoegden* no unauthorized entry; no trespassing

verbijsterd /vərbɛistərt/ (adj) bewildered, amazed, baffled

verbijsteren /vərbɛistərə(n)/ (verbijsterde, heeft verbijsterd) bewilder, amaze

de **verbijstering** /vərbɛistərɪŋ/ bewilderment, amazement

zich **verbijten** /vərbɛitə(n)/ (verbeet zich, heeft zich verbeten) be (almost) bursting; bite one's lips

verbinden /vərbɪndə(n)/ (verbond, heeft verbonden) **1** join (together), connect (to, with): *~ met* join to, link up to (*or:* with) **2** connect, link **3** bandage **4** connect, attach, join (up): *er zijn geen kosten aan verbonden* there are no expenses involved **5** connect (with), put through (to): *ik ben verkeerd verbonden* I have got a wrong number; *kunt u mij met de heer Jefferson ~?* could you put me through to Mr Jefferson?

de **verbinding** /vərbɪndɪŋ/ (pl: -en) **1** connection, link: *een ~ tot stand brengen* establish (*or:* make) a connection **2** connection: *een directe ~* a direct connection; a through train; *de ~en met de stad zijn uitstekend* connections with the city are excellent **3** con-

nection: *geen ~ kunnen krijgen* not be able to get through; *de ~ werd verbroken* the connection was broken, we (*or:* they) were cut off **4** compound: *een chemische ~* a chemical compound

de **verbintenis** /vərbɪntənɪs/ (pl: -sen) **1** obligation, commitment **2** agreement, contract: *een ~ aangaan* enter into (*or:* make) an agreement **3** association; relationship

verbitterd /vərbɪtərt/ (adj, adv) bitter (at, by), embittered (at, by)

de **verbittering** /vərbɪtərɪŋ/ bitterness

verbleken /vərblekə(n)/ (verbleekte, is verbleekt) **1** (turn, go) pale, turn white, go white **2** fade

verblijden /vərblɛɪdə(n)/ (verblijdde, heeft verblijd): *iem. met iets ~* make s.o. happy with sth.

het **verblijf** /vərblɛif/ (pl: verblijven) **1** stay **2** residence; accommodation: *de verblijven voor de bemanning* (*or:* *het personeel*) the crew's (*or:* servants') quarters

de **verblijfkosten** /vərblɛifkɔstə(n)/ (pl) accommodation expenses, living expenses

de **verblijfplaats** /vərblɛifplats/ (pl: -en) (place of) residence, address: *iem. zonder vaste woon- of ~* s.o. with no permanent home or address

de **verblijfsstatus** /vərblɛifstatʏs/ asylum status

de **verblijfsvergunning** /vərblɛifsfərɣʏnɪŋ/ (pl: -en) residence permit

verblijven /vərblɛivə(n)/ (verbleef, heeft/is verbleven) **1** stay: *hij verbleef enkele maanden in Japan* he stayed in Japan for several months **2** live

verblinden /vərblɪndə(n)/ (verblindde, heeft verblind) dazzle, blind: *een ~de schoonheid* a dazzling (*or:* stunning) beauty

verbloemen /vərblumə(n)/ (verbloemde, heeft verbloemd) disguise, gloss over, cover up

verbluffend /vərblʏfənt/ (adj, adv) staggering, astounding: *~ snel handelen* act amazingly (*or:* incredibly) quickly

verbluft /vərblʏft/ (adj) staggered, stunned: *~ staan kijken* be dumbfounded

het **verbod** /vərbɔt/ (pl: -en) ban, prohibition; embargo: *een ~ uitvaardigen* impose (*or:* declare) a ban

verboden /vərbodə(n)/ (adj) forbidden, banned, prohibited: *tot ~ gebied verklaren* declare (*or:* put) out of bounds; *~ wapenbezit* illegal possession of arms; *~ te roken* no smoking

het **verbodsbord** /vərbɔtsbort/ (pl: -en) prohibition sign

verbolgen /vərbɔlɣə(n)/ (adj) enraged (by, at)

het **verbond** /vərbɔnt/ (pl: -en) **1** treaty, pact: *een ~ sluiten* (*or:* *aangaan*) *met* make (*or:* enter) into a treaty with **2** union

verbonden /vərbɔndə(n)/ (adj) **1** committed, bound **2** allied, joined (together) **3** bandaged, dressed **4** joined (to), united (with); bound (to), wedded (to): *aan een instelling ~ zijn* be attached to an institution; *zich met iem. ~ voelen* feel a bond with s.o. || *verkeerd ~* wrong number

verborgen /vərbɔryə(n)/ (adj) hidden, concealed

verbouwen /vərbɑuwə(n)/ (verbouwde, heeft verbouwd) **1** cultivate, grow **2** carry out alterations, renovate

verbouwereerd /vərbɑuwərɛrt/ (adj) dumbfounded, flabbergasted

de **verbouwing** /vərbɑuwɪŋ/ (pl: -en) alteration, renovation: *gesloten wegens ~* closed for repairs (*or:* alterations)

¹**verbranden** /vərbrɑndə(n)/ (verbrandde, is verbrand) **1** burn down, burn up: *hij is bij dat ongeluk levend verbrand* he was burnt alive in that accident **2** burn; scorch: *het vlees staat te ~* the meat is burning

²**verbranden** /vərbrɑndə(n)/ (verbrandde, heeft verbrand) **1** burn (down), incinerate **2** burn; scald: *zijn gezicht is door de zon verbrand* his face is sunburnt

de **verbranding** /vərbrɑndɪŋ/ (pl: -en) **1** burning, incineration **2** burn; scald

de **verbrandingsmotor** /vərbrɑndɪŋsmotər/ (pl: -en) (internal-)combustion engine

verbrassen /vərbrɑsə(n)/ (verbraste, heeft verbrast) squander, dissipate

¹**verbreden** /vərbrɛdə(n)/ (verbreedde, heeft verbreed) broaden, widen

zich ²**verbreden** /vərbrɛdə(n)/ (verbreedde zich, heeft zich verbreed) broaden (out): *de weg verbreedt zich daar* the road broadens (out) there

verbreiden /vərbrɛidə(n)/ (verbreidde, heeft verbreid) spread

verbreken /vərbrɛkə(n)/ (verbrak, heeft verbroken) **1** break (up): *een zegel ~* break a seal **2** break (off), sever: *een relatie ~* break off a relationship

verbrijzelen /vərbrɛizələ(n)/ (verbrijzelde, heeft verbrijzeld) shatter, crush

verbroederen /vərbrudərə(n)/ (verbroederde, heeft verbroederd) fraternize (with)

verbrokkelen /vərbrɔkələ(n)/ (verbrokkelde, heeft/is verbrokkeld) crumble

verbruien /vərbrœyjə(n)/ (verbruide, heeft verbruid): *hij heeft het bij mij verbruid* I wash my hands of him now

het **verbruik** /vərbrœyk/ consumption

verbruiken /vərbrœykə(n)/ (verbruikte, heeft verbruikt) consume, use up

de **verbruiker** /vərbrœykər/ (pl: -s) consumer, user

de **verbruikzaal** /vərbrœyksal/ (pl: -zalen) dining area

verbuigen /vərbœyɣə(n)/ (verboog, heeft verbogen) bend, twist

de **verbuiging** /vərbœyɣɪŋ/ (pl: -en) declension

¹**verdacht** /vərdɑxt/ (adj) **1** suspected: *iem. ~ maken* cast a slur on s.o., smear s.o. **2** suspicious, questionable: *een ~ zaakje* a questionable (*or:* shady) business

²**verdacht** /vərdɑxt/ (adv) suspiciously: *dat lijkt ~ veel op ...* that looks suspiciously like ...; *de kinderen zijn ~ stil* the children are strongly quiet

de **verdachte** /vərdɑxtə/ (pl: -n) suspect

de **verdachtenbank** /vərdɑxtə(n)bɑŋk/ dock, witness box; [Am] witness stand: *in het ~je zitten* be under suspicion

de **verdachtmaking** /vərdɑxtmakɪŋ/ (pl: -en) imputation; insinuation; slur

verdagen /vərdaɣə(n)/ (verdaagde, heeft verdaagd) adjourn: *een zitting ~* adjourn a session

de **verdaging** /vərdaɣɪŋ/ (pl: -en) postponement; adjournment

verdampen /vərdɑmpə(n)/ (verdampte, heeft/is verdampt) evaporate, vaporize

de **verdamping** /vərdɑmpɪŋ/ evaporation, vaporization

verdedigbaar /vərdedəɣbar/ (adj) **1** defensible **2** defensible, justifiable

verdedigen /vərdedəɣə(n)/ (verdedigde, heeft verdedigd) **1** defend: *een ~de houding aannemen* be on the defensive **2** defend, support: *zijn belangen ~* stand up for (*or:* defend) one's interests; *zich ~* defend (*or:* justify) o.s.

de **verdediger** /vərdedəɣər/ (pl: -s) **1** defender, advocate **2** counsel (for the defence) **3** [sport] defender, back: *centrale ~* central defender; *vrije ~* libero

de **verdediging** /vərdedəɣɪŋ/ (pl: -en) **1** defence: [sport] *in de ~ gaan* go on the defensive; [fig] *in de ~ schieten* be on the defensive **2** counsel (for the defence), defence

verdeeld /vərdelt/ (adj) divided: *hierover zijn de meningen ~* opinions are divided on this (problem, issue, question)

de **verdeeldheid** /vərdeltɦɛit/ discord, dissension: *er heerst ~ binnen de partij* the party is divided (*or:* split); *~ zaaien* spread discord

de **verdeelsleutel** /vərdelsløtəl/ (pl: -s) key, ratio, formula

de **verdeelstekker** /vərdelstɛkər/ (pl: -s) adapter

verdekt /vərdɛkt/ (adj) concealed, hidden: *zich ~ opstellen* conceal o.s., take cover

¹**verdelen** /vərdelə(n)/ (verdeelde, heeft verdeeld) **1** divide, split (up): *die kwestie verdeelt hen tot op het bot* opinions are completely divided over the issue; *verdeel en heers* divide and rule **2** divide (up), distribute: *de buit ~* divide the loot **3** spread: *de taken ~*

allocate (*or:* share) (out) the tasks

zich **²verdelen** /vərde̯lə(n)/ (verdeelde zich, heeft zich verdeeld) divide, split (up): *de rivier verdeelt zich hier in twee takken* the river divides (*or:* forks) here

verdelgen /vərde̯lɣə(n)/ (verdelgde, heeft verdelgd) eradicate

het **verdelgingsmiddel** /vərde̯lɣɪŋsmɪdəl/ pesticide; insecticide; weedkiller

de **verdeling** /vərde̯lɪŋ/ (pl: -en) **1** division **2** distribution

verdenken /vərde̯ŋkə(n)/ (verdacht, heeft verdacht) suspect (of): *zij wordt ervan verdacht, dat ... she is under the suspicion of ...; iem. van diefstal* ~ suspect s.o. of theft

de **verdenking** /vərde̯ŋkɪŋ/ (pl: -en) suspicion: **onder** ~ *staan* be suspected (*or:* under suspicion); *iem. in hechtenis nemen* **op** ~ **van** *moord* arrest s.o. on suspicion of murder

¹verder /vɛrdər/ (adj) **1** (the) rest of **2** further, subsequent

²verder /vɛrdər/ (adv) **1** farther, further: *twee* **regels** ~ two lines (further) down; *hoe* **ging** *het* ~? how did it go on?; ~ **lezen** go on (*or:* continue) reading, read on **2** further, furthermore, in addition, moreover: ~ **verklaarde** *zij ...* she went on (*or:* proceeded) to say ... **3** for the rest, apart from that: *is er* ~ *nog iets?* anything else?

het **verderf** /vərdɛrf/ ruin, destruction: *iem. in het* ~ *storten* ruin s.o., bring ruin upon s.o.

verderfelijk /vərdɛrfələk/ (adj) pernicious: *~e* **invloeden** baneful influences

verderop /vɛrdərɔp/ (adv) further on, farther on: *zij woont vier* **huizen** ~ she lives four houses (further) down; ~ *in de straat* down (*or:* up) the street

verderven /vərdɛrvə(n)/ deprave, corrupt

verdichten /vərdɪxtə(n)/ (verdichtte, heeft verdicht) condense

de **verdichting** /vərdɪxtɪŋ/ **1** condensation **2** [fig] condensing

het **verdichtsel** /vərdɪxtsəl/ (pl: -s) fabrication, invention

¹verdiend /vərdint/ (adj) deserved: *volkomen* ~ richly deserved; *dat is zijn ~e* **loon** it serves him right, he had it coming to him

²verdiend /vərdint/ (adv) deservedly: *de thuisclub* **won** ~ *met 3-1* the home team won deservedly by 3 to 1

¹verdienen /vərdinə(n)/ (verdiende, heeft verdiend) **1** earn, make money: *zij verdient* **uitstekend** she is very well paid **2** pay: *dat baantje verdient* **slecht** that job does not pay well

²verdienen /vərdinə(n)/ (verdiende, heeft verdiend) **1** earn, make, be paid: *een goed* **salaris** ~ earn a good salary; *zuur* *verdiend* hard-earned, hard-won **2** deserve, merit: *dat voorbeeld verdient geen* **navolging** that example ought not to be followed

de **verdienste** /vərdinstə/ (pl: -n) **1** wages, pay, earnings; profit: *zonder ~n zijn* be out of a job, earn no money **2** merit: *een man van* ~ a man of (great) merit

verdienstelijk /vərdinstələk/ (adj, adv) deserving, (praise)worthy: *zich* ~ **maken** make o.s. useful

¹verdiepen /vərdipə(n)/ (verdiepte, heeft verdiept) deepen, broaden: *zijn* **kennis** ~ gain more in-depth knowledge

zich **²verdiepen** /vərdipə(n)/ (verdiepte zich, heeft zich verdiept) (+ in) go (deeply) into, be absorbed in: *verdiept zijn* **in** be engrossed (*or:* absorbed) in

de **verdieping** /vərdipɪŋ/ (pl: -en) floor, storey: *een huis* **met** *zes ~en* a six-storeyed house; **op** *de tweede* ~ on the second floor; [Am] on the third floor

de **verdikking** /vərdɪkɪŋ/ (pl: -en) thickening, bulge

verdisconteren /vərdɪskɔnte̯rə(n)/ (verdisconteerde, heeft verdisconteerd) discount

verdoen /vərdu̯n/ (verdeed, heeft verdaan) waste (away), fritter (away), squander: *ik zit hier mijn* **tijd** *te* ~ I am wasting my time here

verdoezelen /vərdu̯zələ(n)/ (verdoezelde, heeft verdoezeld) blur, disguise: *de ware* **toedracht** ~ fudge (*or:* disguise) the real facts

verdonkeremanen /vərdɔŋkərəma̯nə(n)/ (verdonkeremaande, heeft verdonkeremaand) embezzle; suppress

verdoofd /vərdo̯ft/ (adj) stunned, stupefied, numb

verdord /vərdɔrt/ (adj) shrivelled; withered; parched: *~e* **bladeren** withered leaves

verdorie /vərdo̯ri/ (int) [inform] darned

verdorren /vərdɔrə(n)/ (verdorde, is verdord) shrivel (up), parch; wither (up); wilt

verdorven /vərdɔrvə(n)/ (adj) depraved, perverted: *een* ~ **mens** a wicked person, a pervert

verdoven /vərdo̯və(n)/ (verdoofde, heeft verdoofd) stun, stupefy; benumb: *~de* **middelen** drugs, narcotic(s); *de patiënt wordt* **plaatselijk** *verdoofd* the patient receives a local anaesthetic

de **verdoving** /vərdo̯vɪŋ/ (pl: -en) **1** anaesthesia, anaesthetic **2** stupor

verdraagzaam /vərdra̯xsam/ (adj) tolerant: ~ **jegens** *elkaar zijn* be tolerant of each other

de **verdraagzaamheid** /vərdra̯xsamhɛit/ tolerance

verdraaid /vərdra̯it/ (adj) **1** darn(ed) **2** distorted, twisted

verdraaien /vərdra̯jə(n)/ (verdraaide, heeft verdraaid) **1** turn **2** distort; twist: *de* **waarheid** ~ distort the truth; *iemands* **woorden** ~ twist s.o.'s words, misquote s.o. **3** disguise: *zijn* **stem** ~ disguise (*or:* mask) one's voice

de **verdraaiing** /vərdra̯jɪŋ/ (pl: -en) distortion,

twist

het **verdrag** /vərdrɔx/ (pl: -en) treaty, agreement: *een ~ sluiten* enter into (*or:* make) a treaty

verdragen /vərdraɣə(n)/ (verdroeg, heeft verdragen) **1** bear, endure, stand: *hij kan de gedachte niet ~, dat ...* he cannot bear (*or:* stand) the idea that ... **2** bear, stand, put up with, take: *ik kan veel ~, maar nu is 't genoeg* I can stand (*or:* take) a lot, but enough is enough

het **verdriet** /vərdrit/ grief (*or:* distress) (at, over), sorrow (at): *iem. ~ doen (aandoen)* distress s.o., give s.o. pain (*or:* sorrow); *~ hebben* be in distress; grieve

verdrietig /vərdritəx/ (adj) sad, grieved: *~ maken* sadden

verdrievoudigen /vərdrivɑudəɣə(n)/ (verdrievoudigde, heeft/is verdrievoudigd) triple, treble: *de winst is verdrievoudigd* profit has tripled

verdrijven /vərdrɛivə(n)/ (verdreef, heeft verdreven) drive away, chase away, dispel: *de pijn ~* dispel the pain

¹**verdringen** /vərdrɪŋə(n)/ (verdrong, heeft verdrongen) **1** push away (*or:* aside) **2** shut out; repress; suppress

zich ²**verdringen** /vərdrɪŋə(n)/ (verdrong zich, heeft zich verdrongen) crowd (round): *de menigte verdrong zich voor de etalage* people crowded round the shop window

¹**verdrinken** /vərdrɪŋkə(n)/ (verdronk, is verdronken) drown: *~ in het huiswerk* be swamped by homework; *hij verdrinkt in die jas* that coat is miles too big for him

²**verdrinken** /vərdrɪŋkə(n)/ (verdronk, heeft verdronken) drink away; drown

de **verdrinkingsdood** /vərdrɪŋkɪŋzdot/ death by drowning

verdrogen /vərdroɣə(n)/ (verdroogde, is verdroogd) **1** dry out, dry up, dehydrate: *dat brood is helemaal verdroogd* that loaf (of bread) has completely dried out **2** shrivel (up), wither (away, up)

verdrukken /vərdrʏkə(n)/ (verdrukte, heeft verdrukt) oppress, repress

de **verdrukking** /vərdrʏkɪŋ/ (pl: -en): *in de ~ raken (komen)* get into hot water (*or:* a scrape); *tegen de ~ in* despite the obstacles

verdubbelen /vərdʏbələ(n)/ (verdubbelde, heeft/is verdubbeld) double: *met verdubbelde energie* with redoubled energy

verduidelijken /vərdœydələkə(n)/ (verduidelijkte, heeft verduidelijkt) explain, make (more) clear, clarify

de **verduidelijking** /vərdœydələkɪŋ/ (pl: -en) explanation: *ter ~* by way of illustration

verduisteren /vərdœystərə(n)/ (verduisterde, heeft verduisterd) **1** darken, dim: *de zon ~* blot out the sun **2** embezzle

de **verduistering** /vərdœystərɪŋ/ (pl: -en)

1 darkening **2** eclipse **3** embezzlement

verdunnen /vərdʏnə(n)/ (verdunde, heeft verdund) **1** thin; dilute: *melk met water ~* dilute milk with water **2** thin (out)

de **verdunning** /vərdʏnɪŋ/ (pl: -en) thinning, dilution

verduren /vərdyrə(n)/ (verduurde, heeft verduurd) bear, endure, suffer: *heel wat moeten ~* have to put up with a great deal; *het zwaar te ~ hebben* a) have a hard (*or:* rough) time of it; b) suffer great hardship(s)

verduurzamen /vərdyrzamə(n)/ (verduurzaamde, heeft verduurzaamd) **1** preserve, cure **2** make (more) sustainable: *de bananenproductie ~* make banana production more sustainable; *de economische groei ~* ensure that economic growth persists

verdwaald /vərdwalt/ (adj) lost; stray: *een ~e kogel* a stray bullet; *~ raken* lose one's way

verdwaasd /vərdwast/ (adj) foolish; groggy: *~ voor zich uit staren* stare vacantly into space

verdwalen /vərdwalə(n)/ (verdwaalde, is verdwaald) lose one's way, get lost, go astray

verdwijnen /vərdwɛinə(n)/ (verdween, is verdwenen) disappear; vanish: *een verdwenen boek* a missing (*or:* lost) book; *mijn kiespijn is verdwenen* my toothache has worn off (*or:* disappeared); *geleidelijk ~* fade out (*or:* away), melt away; *spoorloos ~* vanish without (leaving) a trace

de **verdwijning** /vərdwɛinɪŋ/ (pl: -en) disappearance

de **verdwijntruc** /vərdwɛintryk/ (pl: -s) disappearing act, vanishing trick

veredelen /vəredələ(n)/ (veredelde, heeft veredeld) ennoble, elevate, refine

de **veredeling** /vəredəlɪŋ/ refinement; improvement; upgrading

vereenvoudigen /vərenvɑudəɣə(n)/ (vereenvoudigde, heeft vereenvoudigd) simplify: *de vereenvoudigde spelling* simplified spelling

de **vereenvoudiging** /vərenvɑudəɣɪŋ/ (pl: -en) simplification; reduction [fraction]

vereenzamen /vərenzamə(n)/ (vereenzaamde, is vereenzaamd) grow lonely, become lonely

vereenzelvigen /vərenzɛlvəɣə(n)/ (vereenzelvigde, heeft vereenzelvigd) identify: *zij vereenzelvigde zich met Julia Roberts* she identified (herself) with Julia Roberts

de **vereerder** /vərerdər/ (pl: -s) worshipper, admirer

vereeuwigen /vərewəɣə(n)/ (vereeuwigde, heeft vereeuwigd) immortalize

vereffenen /vərɛfənə(n)/ (vereffende, heeft vereffend) settle, square; smooth out: *iets* (*or:* *een rekening*) *met iem. te ~ hebben* have to settle an account

de **vereffening** /vərɛfənɪŋ/ (pl: -en) settlement, payment

vereisen /vərɛisə(n)/ (vereiste, heeft vereist) require, demand: *ervaring vereist* experience required; *de vereiste zorg aan iets besteden* give the necessary care (*or:* attention) to sth.

het/de **vereiste** /vərɛistə/ (pl: -n) requirement: *aan de ~n voldoen* meet (*or:* fulfil) the requirements; *dat is een eerste ~* that is a prerequisite (*or:* a must)

¹**veren** /vɛrə(n)/ (adj) feather: *een ~ pen* a quill (pen)

²**veren** /vɛrə(n)/ (veerde, heeft geveerd) **1** be springy: *het veert niet meer* it has lost its spring (*or:* bounce) **2** spring: *overeind ~* spring to one's feet

verend /vɛrənt/ (adj) springy, elastic: *een ~ matras* a springy (*or:* bouncy) mattress

verenigbaar /vərɛnəχbar/ (adj) compatible (with), consistent (with)

verenigd /vərɛnəχt/ (adj) united, allied

de **Verenigde Arabische Emiraten** /vərɛnəχdəarabisəemiratə(n)/ (pl) United Arab Emirates

de **Verenigde Staten** /vərɛnəχdəstatə(n)/ (pl) United States (of America)

het **Verenigd Koninkrijk** /vərɛnəχtkonɪŋkrɛik/ United Kingdom

verenigen /vərɛnəχə(n)/ (verenigde, heeft verenigd) unite (with), combine, join (to, with): *zich ~ in een organisatie* form an organisation; *het nuttige met het aangename ~* mix (*or:* combine) business with pleasure

de **vereniging** /vərɛnəχɪŋ/ (pl: -en) club, association, society: *~ van eigenaren* owners' association; *een ~ oprichten* found an association

vereren /vərɛrə(n)/ (vereerde, heeft vereerd) worship, adore

¹**verergeren** /vərɛrɣərə(n)/ (verergerde, is verergerd) worsen, become worse, grow worse, deteriorate: *de toestand verergert* the situation is deteriorating (*or:* growing worse)

²**verergeren** /vərɛrɣərə(n)/ (verergerde, heeft verergerd) worsen, make worse, aggravate

de **verering** /vərɛrɪŋ/ (pl: -en) **1** worship, veneration **2** [rel] devotion, cult: *de ~ van Maria* the devotion to Maria, the Maria cult

de **verf** /vɛrf/ (pl: verven) paint; dye: *pas op voor de ~!* (watch out,) fresh (*or:* wet) paint!; *het huis zit nog goed in de ~* the paintwork (on the house) is still good ‖ *niet uit de ~ komen* not live up to its promise, not come into its own

de **verfbom** /vɛrvbom/ (pl: -men) paint bomb

de **verfdoos** /vɛrvdos/ (pl: -dozen) paint box, (box of) paints

verfijnen /vərfɛinə(n)/ (verfijnde, heeft

verfijnd) refine: *zijn techniek ~* refine (*or:* polish (up)) one's technique

de **verfijning** /vərfɛinɪŋ/ (pl: -en) refinement, sophistication

verfilmen /vərfɪlmə(n)/ (verfilmde, heeft verfilmd) film, turn (*or:* make) into a film: *een roman ~* film a novel, adapt a novel for the screen

de **verfilming** /vərfɪlmɪŋ/ (pl: -en) film version, screen version

de **verfkwast** /vɛrfkwɑst/ (pl: -en) paintbrush

de **verflaag** /vɛrflaχ/ (pl: -lagen) coat (*or:* layer) of paint: *bovenste ~* topcoat

verflauwen /vərflɑuwə(n)/ (verflauwde, is verflauwd) fade

verfoeien /vərfujə(n)/ (verfoeide, heeft verfoeid) detest, loathe

verfomfaaid /vərfɔmfajt/ (adj) dishevelled, tousled

verfraaien /vərfrajə(n)/ (verfraaide, heeft verfraaid) embellish (with)

de **verfraaiing** /vərfrajɪŋ/ (pl: -en) embellishment

verfrissen /vərfrɪsə(n)/ (verfriste, heeft verfrist) refresh, freshen up: *zich ~* freshen up, refresh (o.s.)

verfrissend /vərfrɪsənt/ (adj) refreshing, invigorating

de **verfrissing** /vərfrɪsɪŋ/ (pl: -en) refreshment: *enige ~en gebruiken* take (*or:* have) some refreshments

het **verfrissingsdoekje** /vərfrɪsɪŋzdukjə/ (pl: -s) wet wipe, refreshing wipe

de **verfroller** /vɛrfrolər/ (pl: -s) paint roller

verfrommelen /vərfrɔmələ(n)/ (verfrommelde, heeft verfrommeld) crumple (up), rumple (up)

de **verfspuit** /vɛrfspœyt/ (pl: -en) paint sprayer), spray gun

de **verfstof** /vɛrfstɔf/ (pl: -fen) paint; dye (base); pigment

de **verfverdunner** /vɛrfərdʏnər/ (pl: -s) thinner

vergaan /vərɣan/ (verging, is vergaan) **1** fare: *vergane glorie* lost (*or:* faded) glory **2** perish, pass away: *horen en zien vergaat je erbij* the noise is enough to waken the dead **3** perish, decay, rot **4** perish; [fig] be consumed with; be wrecked (*or:* lost); founder: *ik verga van de kou* I am freezing to death; *~ van de honger* be starving to death; *~ van de dorst* be dying of thirst ‖ *ik weet niet hoe het hem is ~* I don't know what has become of him

vergaand /vərɣant/ (adj) far-reaching, drastic

de **vergaarbak** /vərɣarbɑk/ (pl: -ken) reservoir

vergaderen /vərɣadərə(n)/ (vergaderde, is vergaderd) meet, assemble: *hij heeft al de hele ochtend vergaderd* he has been in conference all morning; *de raad vergaderde twee uur lang* the council sat for two hours

de **vergadering** /vərɣadərɪŋ/ (pl: -en) meeting, assembly: *het verslag van een* ~ the minutes of a meeting; *gewone (algemene)* ~ general meeting (*or:* assembly); *een* ~ *bijwonen* (or: *houden*) attend (*or:* hold) a meeting; *de* ~ *sluiten* close (*or:* conclude) the meeting; *een* ~ *leiden* chair a meeting

de **vergaderzaal** /vərɣadərzal/ (pl: -zalen) meeting hall, assembly room, conference room

vergallen /vərɣɑlə(n)/ (vergalde, heeft vergald) embitter, spoil

vergankelijk /vərɣɑŋkələk/ (adj) transitory, transient; fleeting

zich **vergapen** /vərɣapə(n)/ (vergaapte zich, heeft zich vergaapt) gaze at, gape at: *zich* ~ *aan een motor* gape (in admiration) at a motorbike

vergaren /vərɣarə(n)/ (vergaarde, heeft vergaard) gather

vergassen /vərɣɑsə(n)/ (vergaste, heeft vergast) **1** gas **2** gasify

de **vergassing** /vərɣɑsɪŋ/ **1** gasification **2** gassing

¹**vergeefs** /vərɣefs/ (adj) vain, futile; in vain: *een* ~*e reis* a futile (*or:* useless) journey; ~*e pogingen* vain (*or:* futile, useless) attempts

²**vergeefs** /vərɣefs/ (adv) in vain: ~ *zoeken* look in vain

vergeetachtig /vərɣetɑxtəx/ (adj) forgetful

het **vergeetboek** /vərɣedbuk/: *in het* ~ *raken* be(come) forgotten, sink into oblivion

het **vergeet-mij-nietje** /vərxetmɛinicə/ (pl: -s) forget-me-not

vergelden /vərɣɛldə(n)/ (vergold, heeft vergolden) repay; reward; take revenge on: *kwaad met kwaad* ~ pay back (*or:* repay) evil with evil

de **vergelding** /vərɣɛldɪŋ/ (pl: -en) repayment; reward; revenge; retaliation: *ter* ~ *werden krijgsgevangenen doodgeschoten* prisoners of war were shot in retaliation (*or:* reprisal)

de **vergeldingsmaatregel** /vərɣɛldɪŋsmatreɣəl/ (pl: -en) reprisal

vergelen /vərɣelə(n)/ (vergeelde, is vergeeld) yellow, go yellow, turn yellow

het **vergelijk** /vərɣəlɛik/ (pl: -en) agreement; settlement

vergelijkbaar /vərɣəlɛigbar/ (adj) comparable: *meel en vergelijkbare producten* flour and similar products; ~ *zijn met* be comparable to

vergelijken /vərɣəlɛikə(n)/ (vergeleek, heeft vergeleken) compare; compare with sth.; compare to sth.: *vergelijk artikel 12, tweede lid* see (*or:* cf.) article 12, subsection two; *niet te* ~ *zijn met* be (*or:* bear) no comparison with, not be comparable to; *vergeleken met vroeger is er veel veranderd* compared

with (*or:* by contrast with) the past a lot has changed

de **vergelijking** /vərɣəlɛikɪŋ/ (pl: -en) **1** comparison; analogy: *de trappen van* ~ the degrees of comparison; *in* ~ *met* in (*or:* by) comparison with; *ter* ~ by way of comparison, for comparison **2** [maths] equation

de **vergelijkingssite** /vərɣəlɛikɪŋsɑjt/ (pl: -s) comparison site

vergemakkelijken /vərɣəmɑkələkə(n)/ (vergemakkelijkte, heeft vergemakkelijkt) simplify, facilitate: *dat dient om het leven te* ~ that serves to make life easier

vergen /vɛrɣə(n)/ (vergde, heeft gevergd) demand, require; tax: *het uiterste* ~ *van iem.* strain (*or:* try) s.o. to the limit

de **vergetelheid** /vərɣetəlhɛit/ oblivion: *in de* ~ *raken* be(come) forgotten, fall into oblivion

¹**vergeten** /vərɣetə(n)/ (adj) forgotten; neglected: ~ *schrijvers* forgotten (*or:* obscure) writers

²**vergeten** /vərɣetə(n)/ (vergat, is vergeten) **1** forget, slip one's mind: *alles is* ~ *en vergeven* everything is forgiven and forgotten, (there are) no hard feelings; *dat ben ik glad* ~ clean forgot(ten); *dat kun je wel* ~ you can kiss that goodbye! **2** forget, overlook; leave behind: *ze waren* ~ *zijn naam op de lijst te zetten* they had forgotten to put his name on the list; *niet te* ~ not forgetting (*or:* omitting) **3** forget, put out of one's mind: *zijn zorgen* ~ forget one's worries; *vergeet het maar!* forget it!, no way!

vergeven /vərɣevə(n)/ (vergaf, heeft vergeven) **1** forgive: *ik kan mezelf nooit* ~, *dat ik ...* I can never forgive myself for (...ing) **2** poison: *het huis is* ~ *van de stank* the house is pervaded by the stench; ~ *van de luizen* lice-ridden, crawling with lice **3** give (away): *zij heeft zes vrijkaartjes te* ~ she has six free tickets to give away

vergevensgezind /vərɣevə(n)sxəzɪnt/ (adj) forgiving

de **vergeving** /vərɣevɪŋ/ forgiveness; pardon; absolution: *iem. om* ~ *vragen voor iets* ask s.o.'s forgiveness for sth.

vergevorderd /vɛrɣəvɔrdərt/ (adj) (far) advanced

zich **vergewissen** /vɛrɣəwɪsə(n)/ (vergewiste zich, heeft zich vergewist) ascertain, make certain, make sure

vergezellen /vɛrɣəzɛlə(n)/ (vergezelde, heeft vergezeld) accompany; attend (on): *iem. op (de) reis* ~ accompany s.o. on a journey

het **vergezicht** /vɛrɣəzɪxt/ (pl: -en) (panoramic, wide) view, vista

vergezocht /vɛrɣəzɔxt/ (adj) far-fetched

het/de **vergiet** /vərɣit/ (pl: -en) colander; strainer: *zo lek als een* ~ leak like a sieve

vergieten /vərɣitə(n)/ (vergoot, heeft vergoten) shed

het **vergif** /vərɣɪf/ (pl: -fen) poison; venom: *dodelijk* ~ lethal (*or:* deadly) poison

de **vergiffenis** /vərɣɪfənɪs/ forgiveness; pardon; absolution

vergiftig /vərɣɪftəɣ/ (adj) poisonous; venomous

vergiftigen /vərɣɪftəɣə(n)/ (vergiftigde, heeft vergiftigd) poison

de **vergiftiging** /vərɣɪftəɣɪŋ/ (pl: -en) poisoning: *hij stierf door* ~ he died of poisoning

zich **vergissen** /vərɣɪsə(n)/ (vergiste zich, heeft zich vergist) be mistaken (*or:* wrong), make a mistake: *zich lelijk* ~ be greatly mistaken; *vergis je niet* make no mistake; *als ik mij niet vergis* if I'm not wrong (*or:* mistaken); *zich in de persoon* ~ mistake s.o.; *zich in iem.* ~ be mistaken (*or:* wrong) about s.o.; *als hij dat denkt, vergist hij zich* if he thinks that he'll have to think again; ~ *is menselijk* to err is human

de **vergissing** /vərɣɪsɪŋ/ (pl: -en) mistake, error: *iets per* ~ *doen* do sth. by mistake (*or:* inadvertently); *een* ~ *maken* (or: *begaan*) make (*or:* commit) a mistake (*or:* an error)

vergoeden /vərɣudə(n)/ (vergoedde, heeft vergoed) **1** make good, compensate for, refund: *onkosten* ~ pay expenses; *iem. de schade* ~ compensate (*or:* pay) s.o. for the damage **2** compensate, make up (for): *dat vergoedt veel* that makes up for a lot

de **vergoeding** /vərɣudɪŋ/ (pl: -en) **1** compensation, reimbursement: ~ *eisen* claim damages; *een* ~ *vragen voor* charge for **2** allowance, fee; expenses: *tegen een geringe* ~ for a small fee

vergoelijken /vərɣuləkə(n)/ (vergoelijkte, heeft vergoelijkt) smooth over

vergokken /vərɣɔkə(n)/ (vergokte, heeft vergokt) gamble away

vergooien /vərɣojə(n)/ (vergooide, heeft vergooid) throw away, waste: *zijn leven* ~ throw (*or:* fritter) away one's life

vergrendelen /vərɣrɛndələ(n)/ (vergrendelde, heeft vergrendeld) bolt, (double) lock: *een toetsenbord* ~ lock a keyboard

het **vergrijp** /vərɣrɛip/ (pl: -en) offence: *een licht* ~ a minor offence

zich **vergrijpen** /vərɣrɛipə(n)/ (vergreep zich, heeft zich vergrepen) assault; violate: *zich aan iem.* ~ assault s.o.

vergrijzen /vərɣrɛizə(n)/ (vergrijsde, is vergrijsd) age, get old: *Nederland vergrijst* the population of the Netherlands is ageing

de **vergrijzing** /vərɣrɛizɪŋ/ ageing

vergroeien /vərɣrujə(n)/ (vergroeide, is vergroeid) grow crooked; grow deformed, become deformed

het **vergrootglas** /vərɣrotχlɑs/ (pl: -glazen) magnifying glass

vergroten /vərɣrotə(n)/ (vergrootte, heeft vergroot) **1** increase: *de kansen* (or: *risico's*) ~ increase the chances (*or:* risks) **2** enlarge: *de kamer* ~ extend (*or:* enlarge) the room **3** magnify, enlarge; blow up

de **vergroting** /vərɣrotɪŋ/ (pl: -en) **1** increase: ~ *van de omzet* increase in the turnover **2** enlargement

vergruizen /vərɣrœyzə(n)/ (vergruisde, heeft vergruisd) pulverize, crush

verguizen /vərɣœyzə(n)/ (verguisde, heeft verguisd) abuse

verguld /vərɣʏlt/ (adj) **1** gilded, gilt, gold-plated **2** pleased, flattered: *Laurette was er vreselijk mee* ~ Laurette was absolutely delighted with it

vergulden /vərɣʏldə(n)/ (verguldde, heeft verguld) gild, gold-plate

de **vergunning** /vərɣʏnɪŋ/ (pl: -en) **1** permission **2** permit; licence: *een restaurant met volledige* ~ a fully licensed restaurant; *een* ~ *verlenen* (or: *intrekken*) grant (*or:* suspend) a licence

het **verhaal** /vərhal/ (pl: verhalen) story: *de kern van het* ~ the point of the story; *om een lang* ~ *kort te maken* to cut a long story short; *sterke verhalen* tall stories; *zijn* ~ *doen* tell (*or:* relate) one's story; ~*tjes vertellen* tell tales ‖ *het is weer het bekende* ~ it's the same old story; *iem. op* ~ *laten komen* let s.o. get one's breath back

verhalen /vərhalə(n)/ (verhaalde, heeft verhaald) recover, recoup: *de schade op iem.* ~ recover the damage from s.o.

verhandelen /vərhɑndələ(n)/ (verhandelde, heeft verhandeld) trade (in), sell

de **verhandeling** /vərhɑndəlɪŋ/ (pl: -en) [Belg] (mini-)dissertation

zich **verhangen** /vərhɑŋə(n)/ (verhing zich, heeft zich verhangen) hang o.s.

verhapstukken /vərhɑpstʏkə(n)/ [inform] settle; do, finish (off)

verhard /vərhɑrt/ (adj) **1** hard; paved: ~*e wegen* metalled roads; [Am] paved roads **2** [fig] hardened, callous

¹**verharden** /vərhɑrdə(n)/ (verhardde, is verhard) harden: *in het kwaad* ~ become set in evil ways

²**verharden** /vərhɑrdə(n)/ (verhardde, heeft verhard) harden; metal; pave: *een tuinpad* ~ pave a garden path

de **verharding** /vərhɑrdɪŋ/ (pl: -en) hardening; metalling; paving: *een* ~ *van standpunten* a hardening of points of view

verharen /vərharə(n)/ (verhaarde, is verhaard) moult; shed (hair): *de kat is aan het* ~ the cat is moulting

verheerlijken /vərherləkə(n)/ (verheerlijkte, heeft verheerlijkt) idolize, glamourize: *de zanger werd als een afgod verheerlijkt* the singer was worshipped like an idol; *geweld* ~ glorify violence

¹**verheffen** /vərhɛfə(n)/ (verhief, heeft ver-

heven) **1** raise, lift **2** [fig] raise, elevate; up-lift; lift up: *iets tot regel ~* make sth. the rule

zich ²**verheffen** /vərhɛfə(n)/ (verhief zich, heeft zich verheven) rise: *zich hoog ~ boven de stad* rise (*or:* tower) above the city

verheffend /vərhɛfənt/ (adj) elevating: *een weinig ~ schouwspel* an unedifying spectacle

¹**verhelderen** /vərhɛldərə(n)/ (verhelderde, is verhelderd) clear (up)

²**verhelderen** /vərhɛldərə(n)/ (verhelderde, heeft verhelderd) clarify: *een ~d antwoord* an illuminating answer

verhelen /vərhɛlə(n)/ (verheelde, heeft verheeld) conceal, hide

verhelpen /vərhɛlpə(n)/ (verhielp, heeft verholpen) put right, remedy

het **verhemelte** /vərhɛməltə/ (pl: -n, -s) palate, roof of the mouth: *een gespleten ~* a cleft palate

verheugd /vərhøxt/ (adj) glad, pleased: *zich bijzonder ~ tonen (over iets)* take great pleasure in sth.

zich **verheugen** /vərhøɣə(n)/ (verheugde zich, heeft zich verheugd) be glad, be pleased (*or:* happy): *zich ~ op* look forward to

verheugend /vərhøɣənt/ (adj) joyful: *~ nieuws* good news

verheven /vərhɛvə(n)/ (adj) elevated; [fig] above (to), superior (to): *boven iedere verdenking ~* above (*or:* beyond) all suspicion

verhevigen /vərhɛvəɣə(n)/ (verhevigde, heeft/is verhevigd) intensify

verhinderen /vərhɪndərə(n)/ (verhinderde, heeft verhinderd) prevent: *iemands plannen ~* obstruct (*or:* foil) s.o.'s plans; *dat zal mij niet ~ om tegen dit voorstel te stemmen* that won't prevent me from voting against this proposal; *verhinderd zijn* be unable to come (*or:* attend)

de **verhindering** /vərhɪndərɪŋ/ (pl: -en) absence, inability to come: *bij ~* in case of absence

verhit /vərhɪt/ (adj) **1** hot; flushed **2** heated: *~te discussies* heated discussions

verhitten /vərhɪtə(n)/ (verhitte, heeft verhit) **1** heat **2** inflame, stir up: *dat verhitte de gemoederen* that made feelings run high

de **verhitting** /vərhɪtɪŋ/ heating(-up)

verhoeden /vərhudə(n)/ (verhoedde, heeft verhoed) prevent, forbid: *God verhoede dat je ziek wordt* God forbid that you should be ill

verhogen /vərhoɣə(n)/ (verhoogde, heeft verhoogd) **1** raise: *een dijk ~* raise a dike **2** increase: *de prijzen ~* raise (*or:* increase) prices

de **verhoging** /vərhoɣɪŋ/ (pl: -en) **1** raising **2** elevation, platform; rise: *de spreker stond op een ~* the speaker stood on a (raised) platform **3** increase, rise **4** temperature, fever: *ik had wat ~* I had a slight temperature

verhongeren /vərhɔŋərə(n)/ (verhonger-de, is verhongerd) **1** starve (to death), die of starvation: *de kinderen waren half verhongerd* the children were famished (*or:* half starved) **2** starve, go hungry

het **verhoor** /vərhor/ (pl: verhoren) interrogation, examination

verhoren /vərhorə(n)/ (verhoorde, heeft verhoord) **1** interrogate, question; cross-examine: *getuigen ~* hear witnesses **2** hear, answer; grant: *een gebed ~* answer (*or:* hear) a prayer

zich **verhouden** /vərhaudə(n)/ (verhield zich, heeft zich verhouden) be as, be in the proportion of: *60 verhoudt zich tot 12 als 5 tot 1* 60 is to 12 as 5 to 1

de **verhouding** /vərhaudɪŋ/ (pl: -en) **1** relation(ship), proportion: *in ~ tot* in proportion to; *naar ~ is dat duur* that is comparatively expensive **2** affair, relationship **3** proportion: *gevoel voor ~en bezitten* have a sense of proportion

verhoudingsgewijs /vərhaudɪŋsxəwɛis/ (adv) comparatively, relatively

het **verhuisbericht** /vərhœyzbərɪxt/ (pl: -en) change of address card

de **verhuiswagen** /vərhœyswaɣə(n)/ (pl: -s) removal van

verhuizen /vərhœyzə(n)/ (verhuisde, is verhuisd) move (house), relocate ‖ *iem. ~* move s.o.

de **verhuizer** /vərhœyzər/ (pl: -s) remover

de **verhuizing** /vərhœyzɪŋ/ (pl: -en) move, moving

verhullen /vərhʏlə(n)/ (verhulde, heeft verhuld) veil, conceal (from): *niets ~de foto's* revealing photos

verhuren /vərhyrə(n)/ (verhuurde, heeft verhuurd) let; [Am] rent; lease out

het **verhuur** /vərhyr/ letting; [Am] rental

het **verhuurbedrijf** /vərhyrbədrɛif/ leasing company, hire company (*or:* firm); [esp Am also] rental company (*or:* agency)

de **verhuurder** /vərhyrdər/ (pl: -s) letter; [Am] renter; landlord; landlady

verifiëren /verifijɛrə(n)/ (verifieerde, heeft geverifieerd) verify, examine, audit, prove

verijdelen /vərɛidələ(n)/ (verijdelde, heeft verijdeld) frustrate, defeat: *een aanslag ~* foil an attempt on s.o.'s life

de **vering** /vɛrɪŋ/ (pl: -en) springs; [car] suspension

verjaard /vərjart/ (adj) time-barred, super-annuated

de **verjaardag** /vərjardɑx/ (pl: -en) birthday: *vandaag is het mijn ~* today is my birthday

het **verjaardagscadeau** /vərjardɑxskado/ birthday present

het **verjaardagsfeest** /vərjardɑxsfest/ (pl: -en) birthday party

de **verjaardagskalender** /vərjardɑxs-kalɛndər/ (pl: -s) birthday calendar

verjagen /vərjaɣə(n)/ (verjaagde/verjoeg, heeft verjaagd) drive away, chase away

verjaren /vərjarə(n)/ (verjaarde, is verjaard) become prescribed, become (statute-)-barred, become out-of-date

de **verjaring** /vərjarɪŋ/ (pl: -en) prescription; limitation

de **verjaringstermijn** /vərjarɪŋstɛrmɛɪn/ period of limitation

verjongen /vərjɔŋə(n)/ (verjongde, heeft verjongd) rejuvenate, make young

de **verjonging** /vərjɔŋɪŋ/ (pl: -en) rejuvenation

de **verjongingskuur** /vərjɔŋɪŋskyr/ (pl: -kuren) rejuvenation cure: *een ~ ondergaan hebben* [fig] have undergone rejuvenation, be revitalized

verkapt /vərkɑpt/ (adj) veiled, disguised; in disguise

verkassen /vərkɑsə(n)/ (verkaste, is verkast) [inform] move (house)

verkavelen /vərkavələ(n)/ (verkavelde, heeft verkaveld) parcel out, (sub)divide

de **verkaveling** /vərkavəlɪŋ/ (pl: -en) allotment, subdivision

het **verkeer** /vərker/ **1** traffic: *doorgaand ~* through traffic; *druk ~* heavy traffic; *handel en ~ trade* (*or:* traffic) and commerce; *langzaam ~* slow vehicles; *langzaam rijdend en stilstaand ~* slow moving and stationary traffic; *veilig ~* road safety; *het overige ~ in gevaar brengen* be a danger to other road-users **2** association: *in het maatschappelijk ~* in society; *in het dagelijks ~* in everyday life **3** movement: *er bestaat vrij ~ tussen die twee landen* there is freedom of movement between the two countries

verkeerd /vərkert/ (adj, adv) **1** wrong: *een verdediger op het ~e been zetten* wrong-foot a defender; *een ~e diagnose* a faulty diagnosis; *de ~e dingen zeggen* say the wrong things; *het eten kwam in mijn ~e keelgat* the food went down the wrong way; *op een ~ spoor zitten* be on the wrong track; *iets ~ aanpakken* go about sth. the wrong way; *hij doet alles ~* he can't do a thing right; *pardon, u loopt ~* pardon me, but you're going the wrong way (*or:* in the wrong direction); *het liep ~ met hem af* he came to grief (*or:* to a bad end); *iets ~ spellen* (or: *uitspreken, vertalen*) misspell (*or:* mispronounce, mistranslate) sth.; *~ verbonden zijn* have dialled a wrong number; *we zitten ~* we must be wrong; *hij had iets ~s gegeten* sth. he had eaten had upset him; *je hebt de ~e voor* you've mistaken your man **2** wrong; inside out: *zijn handen staan ~* he's all thumbs; *~ om* the other way round; upside down

de **verkeersagent** /vərkersaɣɛnt/ traffic policeman (*or:* policewoman)

het **verkeersbord** /vərkerzbɔrt/ (pl: -en) road sign, traffic sign

de **verkeersbrigadier** /vərkerzbriɣadir/ (pl: -s) lollipop man (*or:* lady)

de **verkeerschaos** /vərkersxaɔs/ traffic chaos

de **verkeersdrempel** /vərkerzdrɛmpəl/ (pl: -s) speed ramp

de **verkeershinder** /vərkershɪndər/ traffic disruption

de **verkeersleider** /vərkerslɛidər/ (pl: -s) air-traffic controller

de **verkeersleiding** /vərkerslɛidɪŋ/ (pl: -en) traffic department; [aviation] air-traffic control, ground control

het **verkeerslicht** /vərkerslɪxt/ (pl: -en) traffic lights: *het ~ sprong op groen* the traffic lights changed to green

het **verkeersongeval** /vərkersɔŋɣəvɑl/ (pl: -len) road accident, traffic accident

de **verkeersopstopping** /vərkersopstopɪŋ/ (pl: -en) traffic jam

de **verkeersovertreding** /vərkersovərtredɪŋ/ (pl: -en) traffic offence

het **verkeersplein** /vərkersplɛin/ (pl: -en) roundabout; [Am] rotary (intersection)

de **verkeerspolitie** /vərkerspoli(t)si/ traffic police

de **verkeersregel** /vərkersreɣəl/ (pl: -s) traffic rule

het **verkeersslachtoffer** /vərkerslɔxtɔfər/ (pl: -s) road casualty, road victim: *het aantal ~s* the toll on the road(s)

de **verkeerstoren** /vərkerstorə(n)/ (pl: -s) control tower

de **verkeersveiligheid** /vərkersfɛiləxhɛit/ road safety, traffic safety

de **verkeersvlieger** /vərkersfliɣər/ (pl: -s) airline pilot

de **verkeerswisselaar** /vərkerswɪsəlar/ (pl: -s) [Belg] cloverleaf junction

verkennen /vərkɛnə(n)/ (verkende, heeft verkend) explore, scout (out); [mil] reconnoitre: *de boel ~* explore the place; *de markt ~* feel out the market

de **verkenner** /vərkɛnər/ (pl: -s) **1** scout **2** (Boy) Scout, Girl Scout

de **verkenning** /vərkɛnɪŋ/ (pl: -en) exploration, scout(ing)

verkeren /vərkerə(n)/ (verkeerde, heeft verkeerd) be (in): *in de hoogste kringen ~* move in the best circles

de **verkering** /vərkerɪŋ/ (pl: -en) courtship: *vaste ~ hebben* go steady; *~ krijgen met iem.* start going out with s.o.

verketteren /vərkɛtərə(n)/ (verketterde, heeft verketterd) execrate, decry, denounce

verkiesbaar /vərkizbar/ (adj) eligible (for election): *zich ~ stellen als president* run for president; *zich ~ stellen* stand for office

verkieslijk /vərkislək/ (adj) preferable

verkiezen /vərkizə(n)/ (verkoos, heeft verkozen) prefer (to): *lopen boven fietsen ~* prefer walking to cycling de **verkiezing** /vərkizɪŋ/ (pl: -en) election: *algemene ~en* general elections; *tussentijdse ~en* [roughly] by-elections; *~en uitschrijven* call (for) an election

de **verkiezingscampagne** /vərkizɪŋskampaɲə/ (pl: -s) election campaign

het **verkiezingsdebat** /vərkizɪnzdəbɑt/ (pl: -ten) election debate

het **verkiezingsprogramma** /vərkizɪŋsproɣrama/ (pl: -'s) (electoral) platform: *iets als punt in het ~ opnemen* make sth. a plank in one's platform

de **verkiezingsstrijd** /vərkizɪŋstrɛit/ electoral struggle

de **verkiezingsuitslag** /vərkizɪŋsœytslɑχ/ (pl: -en) election result: *de ~ bekendmaken* declare the poll

¹**verkijken** /vərkɛikə(n)/ give away, let go by: *die kans is verkeken* that chance has gone by

zich ²**verkijken** /vərkɛikə(n)/ (verkeek zich, heeft zich verkeken) make a mistake, be mistaken: *ik heb me op hem verkeken* I have been mistaken in him

verkikkerd /vərkɪkərt/ (adj) [inform] nuts (on, about), gone (on)

verklaarbaar /vərklarbar/ (adj) explicable, explainable; understandable: *om verklaarbare redenen* for obvious reasons

verklappen /vərklɑpə(n)/ (verklapte, heeft verklapt) give away, let out: *een geheim ~* tell a secret

¹**verklaren** /vərklarə(n)/ (verklaarde, heeft verklaard) **1** explain, elucidate: *iemands gedrag ~* account for s.o.'s conduct **2** declare; certify: *iem. krankzinnig ~* certify s.o. insane; *iets ongeldig ~* declare sth. invalid; *een huis onbewoonbaar ~* condemn a house

zich ²**verklaren** /vərklarə(n)/ (verklaarde zich, heeft zich verklaard) explain o.s.: *verklaar je nader* explain yourself

de **verklaring** /vərklarɪŋ/ (pl: -en) **1** explanation: *dat behoeft geen nadere ~* that needs no further explanation **2** statement; testimony: *een beëdigde ~* a sworn statement; *een ~ afleggen* make a statement

zich **verkleden** /vərkledə(n)/ (verkleedde zich, heeft zich verkleed) **1** change (one's clothes): *ik ga me ~* I'm going to change (my clothes); *zich ~ voor het eten* dress for dinner **2** dress up

verkleinen /vərklɛinə(n)/ (verkleinde, heeft verkleind) **1** reduce, make smaller: *op verkleinde schaal* on a reduced scale **2** reduce, diminish, lessen

de **verkleining** /vərklɛinɪŋ/ (pl: -en) reduction

het **verkleinwoord** /vərklɛinwort/ (pl: -en) diminutive

verkleumd /vərklømt/ (adj) numb (with cold)

verkleumen /vərklømə(n)/ (verkleumde, is verkleumd) grow numb: *we staan hier te ~* we are freezing in (or: out) here

verkleuren /vərklørə(n)/ (verkleurde, is verkleurd) discolour, lose colour; fade: *deze trui verkleurt niet* this sweater will keep its colour; *de grote steden ~ snel* the big cities are rapidly becoming more ethnically diverse

de **verkleuring** /vərklørɪŋ/ (pl: -en) fading; discoloration

verklikken /vərklɪkə(n)/ (verklikte, heeft verklikt) give away; squeal on: *iets ~* blab sth., spill the beans

de **verklikker** /vərklɪkər/ (pl: -s) telltale, tattler; informer; grass

verklooien /vərkloːjə(n)/ (verklooide, heeft verklooid) botch up

verknallen /vərknɑlə(n)/ (verknalde, heeft verknald) blow, spoil: *je hebt het mooi verknald* you've made a hash of it

zich **verkneukelen** /vərknøkələ(n)/ (verkneukelde zich, heeft zich verkneukeld) exult (over), gloat (over)

verknippen /vərknɪpə(n)/ (verknipte, heeft verknipt) **1** cut up **2** spoil in cutting

verknipt /vərknɪpt/ (adj) hung-up, kooky, nutty: *een ~e figuur* a weirdo, a nut(case)

verknocht /vərknɔχt/ (adj) devoted (to), attached (to)

verknoeien /vərknujə(n)/ (verknoeide, heeft verknoeid) botch (up), spoil, mess up: *de boel lelijk ~* make a fine mess of things

verkoelend /vərkulənt/ (adj) cooling, refreshing

de **verkoeling** /vərkulɪŋ/ (pl: -en) cooling

de **verkoeverkamer** /vərkuvərkamər/ recovery room

de **verkokering** /vərkokərɪŋ/ compartmentalization

verkommeren /vərkɔmərə(n)/ (verkommerde, is verkommerd) sink into poverty, pine away

verkondigen /vərkɔndəɣə(n)/ (verkondigde, heeft verkondigd) proclaim, put forward

de **verkondiging** /vərkɔndəɣɪŋ/ (pl: -en) proclamation; preaching

de **verkoop** /vərkop/ (pl: verkopen) sale(s): *~ bij opbod* (sale by) auction; *iets in de ~ brengen* put sth. up for sale (or: on the market)

verkoopbaar /vərkobar/ (adj) saleable, marketable

de **verkoopcijfers** /vərkopsɛifərs/ (pl) sales figures

de **verkoopleider** /vərkoplɛidər/ (pl: -s) sales manager

de **verkoopmakelaar** /vərkopmakəlar/ (pl: -s) sales agent (or: broker)

het **verkooppraatje** /vərkopracə/ (pl: -s) sales pitch

de **verkoopprijs** /vərkoprɛis/ (pl: -prijzen) selling price

het **verkooppunt** /vərkopʏnt/ (pl: -en) (sales)

outlet, point of sale

de **verkoopster** /vɛrko̱ːpstər/ (pl: -s) saleswoman; shop assistant

de **verkoopvoorwaarden** /vɛrko̱ːpfoːrwaːrdə(n)/ (pl) terms and conditions of sale

verkopen /vərko̱ːpə(n)/ (verkocht, heeft verkocht) **1** sell: *nee* ~ give (s.o.) no for an answer; *met winst* (or: *verlies*) ~ sell at a profit (or: loss); *éénmaal! andermaal! verkocht!* going! going! gone! **2** give: *iem. een dreun* ~ clobber s.o.

de **verkoper** /vərko̱ːpər/ (pl: -s) salesman; shop assistant

de **verkoping** /vərko̱ːpɪŋ/ (pl: -en) (public) sale, auction: *bij openbare* ~ by auction

verkorten /vərko̱rtə(n)/ (verkortte, heeft verkort) shorten, abridge, condense; reduce

verkouden /vərko̱udə(n)/ (adj): ~ *worden* catch (a) cold; ~ *zijn* have a cold

de **verkoudheid** /vərko̱uthɛit/ (common) cold: *een* ~ *opdoen* catch (a) cold

verkrachten /vərkra̱xtə(n)/ (verkrachtte, heeft verkracht) rape, (sexually) assault

de **verkrachter** /vərkra̱xtər/ (pl: -s) rapist

de **verkrachting** /vərkra̱xtɪŋ/ (pl: -en) rape

verkrampen /vərkra̱mpə(n)/ (verkrampte, is verkrampt) go tense, tense up

verkrampt /vərkra̱mt/ (adj) contorted; [fig] constrained

¹**verkreukelen** /vərkrø̱ːkələ(n)/ (verkreukelde, is verkreukeld) crumple: *een verkreukeld pak* a creased suit

²**verkreukelen** /vərkrø̱ːkələ(n)/ (verkreukelde, heeft verkreukeld) rumple (up), crumple (up): *papier* ~ crumple up paper

verkrijgbaar /vərkrɛi̱ybaːr/ (adj) available: *het formulier is* ~ *bij de administratie* the form can be obtained from the administration; *zonder recept* ~ over-the-counter

verkrijgen /vərkrɛi̱yə(n)/ (verkreeg, heeft verkregen) **1** receive, get **2** obtain, come by, secure: *een betere positie* ~ secure a better position; *moeilijk te* ~ hard to come by

verkroppen /vərkro̱pə(n)/: *iets niet kunnen* ~ be unable to take sth.

verkrotten /vərkro̱tə(n)/ (verkrotte, is verkrot) decay, become run-down: *verkrotte huizen* slummy (or: dilapidated) houses

verkruimelen /vərkrœy̱mələ(n)/ (verkruimelde, heeft verkruimeld) crumble

verkwanselen /vərkwa̱nsələ(n)/ (verkwanselde, heeft verkwanseld) bargain away, fritter away, squander

verkwikken /vərkwɪ̱kə(n)/ (verkwikte, heeft verkwikt) refresh

verkwikkend /vərkwɪ̱kənt/ (adj) refreshing, invigorating, stimulating

verkwisten /vərkwɪ̱stə(n)/ (verkwistte, heeft verkwist) waste; squander

verkwistend /vərkwɪ̱stənt/ (adj) prodigal; wasteful

de **verkwister** /vərkwɪ̱stər/ (pl: -s) squanderer, waster

de **verkwisting** /vərkwɪ̱stɪŋ/ (pl: -en) waste(fulness), squandering: *het is pure* ~ it's an utter waste

verlagen /vərla̱yə(n)/ (verlaagde, heeft verlaagd) lower; reduce: *(met) 30 %* ~ lower (or: reduce) by 30 % ‖ *zich* ~ *tot* stoop to, lower o.s. to

de **verlaging** /vərla̱yɪŋ/ (pl: -en) lowering; reduction

¹**verlammen** /vərla̱mə(n)/ (verlamde, is verlamd) become paralysed (or: numb)

²**verlammen** /vərla̱mə(n)/ (verlamde, heeft verlamd) paralyse: *de schrik verlamde mij* I was paralysed with fear

verlammend /vərla̱mənt/ (adj, adv) paralysing

de **verlamming** /vərla̱mɪŋ/ (pl: -en) paralysis

het ¹**verlangen** /vərla̱ŋə(n)/ (pl: -s) longing, desire; craving: *aan iemands* ~ *voldoen* comply with s.o.'s wish

²**verlangen** /vərla̱ŋə(n)/ (verlangde, heeft verlangd) (+ naar) long (for), crave: *ik verlang ernaar je te zien* I long to see you; [stronger] I'm dying to see you

³**verlangen** /vərla̱ŋə(n)/ (verlangde, heeft verlangd) want, wish for; demand: *wat kun je nog meer* ~ what more can you ask for?; *dat kunt u niet van mij* ~ you can't expect me to do that

het **verlanglijstje** /vərla̱ŋlɛiscə/ (pl: -s) list of gifts wanted

¹**verlaten** /vərla̱tə(n)/ (adj) **1** deserted: *een* ~ *huis* an abandoned house **2** desolate, lonely **3** abandoned

²**verlaten** /vərla̱tə(n)/ (verliet, heeft verlaten) **1** leave: *het land* ~ leave the country; *de school* ~ leave school **2** abandon, leave: *vrouw en kinderen* ~ leave (or: abandon) one's wife and children

de **verlatenheid** /vərla̱tənhɛit/ desolation, abandonment: *een gevoel van* ~ a feeling of desolation

het ¹**verleden** /vərle̱də(n)/ past: *het* ~ *laten rusten* let bygones be bygones; *teruggaan in het* ~ go back in time

²**verleden** /vərle̱də(n)/ (adj) past: *het* ~ *deelwoord* the past (or: perfect) participle; ~ *tijd* past tense; *voltooid* ~ *tijd* past perfect (or: pluperfect) (tense); ~ *week* last week

verlegen /vərle̱yə(n)/ (adj, adv) **1** shy: ~ *zijn tegenover meisjes* be shy with girls **2** (+ om) in need of, at a loss for, pressed for: *ik zit niet om werk* ~ I have my work cut out as it is

de **verlegenheid** /vərle̱yə(n)hɛit/ **1** shyness **2** embarrassment, trouble: *iem. in* ~ *brengen* embarrass s.o.

verleggen /vərlɛ̱yə(n)/ (verlegde, heeft verlegd) move, shift; push back

verleidelijk /vərlɛi̱dələk/ (adj, adv) tempting, inviting, seductive: *een ~ aanbod* a tempting offer

verleiden /vərlɛidə(n)/ (verleidde, heeft verleid) **1** tempt, invite, entice: *iem. ertoe ~ om iets te doen* tempt s.o. into doing sth. **2** seduce

de **verleider** /vərlɛidər/ (pl: -s) seducer, tempter

de **verleiding** /vərlɛidɪŋ/ (pl: -en) temptation; seduction: *de ~ kunnen weerstaan* be unable to resist (the) temptation; *in de ~ komen om* feel (or: be) tempted to

de **verleidster** /vərlɛitstər/ seducer, temptress

verlenen /vərlɛnə(n)/ (verleende, heeft verleend) grant, confer: *iem. onderdak ~* take s.o. in; harbour s.o.; *voorrang ~* give way (or: priority); [traf] give right of way; [Am] yield

het **verlengde** /vərlɛŋdə/ extension: *in elkaars ~ liggen* be in line

verlengen /vərlɛŋə(n)/ (verlengde, heeft verlengd) **1** extend, lengthen **2** extend, prolong: *een (huur)contract ~* renew a lease; *zijn verblijf ~* prolong one's stay; *verlengd worden* go into extra (or: injury) time; [Am] go (into) overtime

de **verlenging** /vərlɛŋɪŋ/ (pl: -en) **1** extension; [sport] extra time, injury time; [Am] overtime **2** lengthening, extension

het **verlengsnoer** /vərlɛŋsnur/ (pl: -en) extension lead

het **verlengstuk** /vərlɛŋstʏk/ (pl: -ken) extension (piece): [fig] *het ~ zijn van* be a continuation of

verlept /vərlɛpt/ (adj) withered, wilted

verleren /vərlɛrə(n)/ (verleerde, heeft verleerd) forget (how to); unlearn: *je bent het schaken blijkbaar een beetje verleerd* your chess seems a bit rusty; *om het niet (helemaal) te ~* just to keep one's hand in

verlevendigen /vərlɛvəndəɣə(n)/ (verlevendigde, heeft verlevendigd) revive; enliven

verlicht /vərlɪxt/ (adj) **1** lit (up), lighted, illuminated: *helder ~* well-lit, brightly lit **2** relieved, lightened: *met ~ gemoed* with (a) light heart

verlichten /vərlɪxtə(n)/ (verlichtte, heeft verlicht) **1** light, illuminate **2** relieve, lighten: *dat verlicht de pijn* that relieves (or: eases) the pain

de **verlichting** /vərlɪxtɪŋ/ (pl: -en) **1** light(ing), illumination **2** lightening: *~ van straf* mitigation of punishment

verliefd /vərlift/ (adj) in love (with), amorous, loving: *~ worden op iem.* fall in love with s.o.; *zwaar ~ zijn* be madly (or: deeply) in love || *hij keek haar ~ aan* he gave her a fond (or: loving) look

de **verliefdheid** /vərliftheit/ (pl: -heden) being in love, love

het **verlies** /vərlis/ (pl: verliezen) loss: *~ lijden* suffer a loss; make a loss; *met ~ verkopen* sell at a loss; *met ~ draaien* make a loss (or: losses); *niet tegen zijn ~ kunnen* be a bad loser

verliesgevend /vərlisxevənt/ (adj) loss-making

de **verliespost** /vərlispɔst/ (pl: -en) loss-making activity

verliezen /vərlizə(n)/ (verloor, heeft/is verloren) **1** lose: *zijn bladeren ~* defoliate; *de macht ~* fall from power; *terrein ~* lose ground **2** lose, miss: *er is geen tijd te ~* there is no time to lose (or: to be lost)

de **verliezer** /vərlizər/ (pl: -s) loser: *een slechte ~* a bad loser

verlinken /vərlɪŋkə(n)/ (verlinkte, heeft verlinkt) [inform] tell on, grass on

verloederen /vərludərə(n)/ (verloederde, is verloederd) degenerate

de **verloedering** /vərludərɪŋ/ corruption

het **verlof** /vərlɔf/ (pl: verloven) **1** leave, permission: *~ krijgen om …* obtain permission to … **2** leave (of absence); furlough: *buitengewoon ~* special leave; *met ~ zijn* be on leave

verlokkelijk /vərlɔkələk/ (adj, adv) tempting

de **verlokking** /vərlɔkɪŋ/ (pl: -en) temptation

verloochenen /vərloxənə(n)/ (verloochende, heeft verloochend) renounce

verloofd /vərloft/ (adj) engaged (to)

de **verloofde** /vərlofdə/ (pl: -n, -s) fiancé; fiancée

het **verloop** /vərlop/ **1** course, passage: *na ~ van tijd* in time, after some time **2** course, progress, development: *voor een vlot ~ van de besprekingen* for smooth progress in the talks **3** turnover, wastage: *natuurlijk ~* natural wastage

de **verloopstekker** /vərlopstɛkər/ (pl: -s) adapter

verlopen /vərlopə(n)/ (verliep, is verlopen) **1** (e)lapse, go by, pass **2** expire: *mijn rijbewijs is ~* my driving licence has expired **3** go (off): *vlot ~* go smoothly **4** drop off, fall off, go down(hill)

verloren /vərlorə(n)/ (adj) lost: *~ moeite* wasted effort; *een ~ ogenblik* an odd moment; *voor een ~ zaak vechten* fight a losing battle

de **verloskamer** /vərlɔskamər/ (pl: -s) delivery room

de **verloskunde** /vərlɔskʏndə/ obstetrics

verloskundig /vərlɔskʏndəx/ (adj) obstetric

de **verloskundige** /vərlɔskʏndəɣə/ (pl: -n) midwife; obstetrician

verlossen /vərlɔsə(n)/ (verloste, heeft verlost) **1** deliver (from), release (from), save (from): *een dier uit zijn lijden ~* put an animal out of its misery **2** deliver (of)

de **verlosser** /vərlɔsər/ (pl: -s) saviour, rescuer:

verlossing

de Verlosser our Saviour, the Redeemer

de **verlossing** /vərlɔsɪn/ (pl: -en) deliverance, release

verloten /vərlotə(n)/ (verlootte, heeft verloot) raffle (off)

zich **verloven** /vərlovə(n)/ (verloofde zich, heeft zich verloofd) get engaged (to)

de **verloving** /vərlovɪn/ (pl: -en) engagement: *zijn ~ verbreken* break off one's (*or:* the) engagement

verluiden /vərlœydə(n)/ (verluidde, heeft verluid): *naar verluidt* it is reported that, it is understood that, allegedly

verlummelen /vərlʏmələ(n)/ (verlummelde, heeft verlummeld) fritter away

het **vermaak** /vərmak/ (pl: vermaken) amusement, enjoyment, pleasure: *onschuldig ~* good clean fun

vermaard /vərmart/ (adj) renowned (for), celebrated (for), famous (for)

vermageren /vərmaɣərə(n)/ (vermagerde, is vermagerd) lose weight, become thin(ner), get thin(ner); slim: *sterk vermagerd* emaciated, wasted

de **vermageringskuur** /vərmaɣərɪnskyr/ (pl: -kuren) slimming diet: *een ~ ondergaan* be (*or:* go) on a (slimming, reducing) diet

vermakelijk /vərmakələk/ (adj, adv) amusing

vermaken /vərmakə(n)/ (vermaakte, heeft vermaakt) **1** amuse, entertain: *zich ~* enjoy (*or:* amuse) o.s., have fun **2** bequeath, make over

vermalen /vərmalə(n)/ (vermaalde, heeft vermalen) grind

vermanen /vərmanə(n)/ (vermaande, heeft vermaand) admonish, warn

de **vermaning** /vərmanɪn/ (pl: -en) admonition

zich **vermannen** /vərmɑnə(n)/ (vermande zich, heeft zich vermand) screw up one's courage, take heart

vermeend /vərment/ (adj) supposed, alleged

vermeerderen /vərmerdərə(n)/ (vermeerderde, heeft/is vermeerderd) increase, enlarge, grow: *~ met 25 %* increase by 25 per cent

vermelden /vərmɛldə(n)/ (vermeldde, heeft vermeld) **1** mention **2** state, give

vermeldenswaard /vərmɛldə(n)swart/ (adj) worth mentioning, worthy of mention

de **vermelding** /vərmɛldɪn/ (pl: -en) mention, statement: *eervolle ~* honourable mention; *onder ~ van ...* giving (*or:* stating, mentioning) ...

vermengen /vərmɛnə(n)/ (vermengde, heeft vermengd) mix; blend

de **vermenging** /vərmɛnɪn/ (pl: -en) mix(ture), mixing, blend(ing)

¹**vermenigvuldigen** /vərmenəxfʏldəɣə(n)/ (vermenigvuldigde, heeft vermenigvuldigd) **1** duplicate **2** [maths] multiply: *vermenigvuldig dat getal met 8* multiply that number by 8

zich ²**vermenigvuldigen** /vərmenəxfʏldəɣə(n)/ (vermenigvuldigde zich, heeft zich vermenigvuldigd) multiply, increase; reproduce

de **vermenigvuldiging** /vərmenəxfʏldəɣɪn/ (pl: -en) multiplication: *tafel van ~* multiplication table

de **vermicelli** /vɛrmisɛli/ vermicelli

vermijden /vərmɛidə(n)/ (vermeed, heeft vermeden) avoid: *angstvallig ~* shun, fight shy of

verminderd /vərmɪndərt/ (adj, adv) diminished, reduced: *~ toerekeningsvatbaar* not fully accountable for one's actions

verminderen /vərmɪndərə(n)/ (verminderde, heeft verminderd) decrease, reduce: *de uitgaven ~* cut (back on) expenses

de **vermindering** /vərmɪndərɪn/ (pl: -en) decrease, reduction: *~ van straf* reduction of (a) sentence

verminken /vərmɪnkə(n)/ (verminkte, heeft verminkt) mutilate

de **verminking** /vərmɪnkɪn/ (pl: -en) mutilation

de **vermissing** /vərmɪsɪn/ (pl: -en) loss; absence

vermist /vərmɪst/ (adj): *iem. (iets) als ~ opgeven* report s.o. missing, report sth. lost

de **vermiste** /vərmɪstə/ (pl: -n) missing person

vermits /vərmɪts/ (adv) [Belg] since, as, because

vermoedelijk /vərmudələk/ (adj, adv) supposed: *de ~e dader* the suspect; *de ~e oorzaak* the probable cause

het ¹**vermoeden** /vərmudə(n)/ (pl: -s) **1** conjecture, surmise **2** suspicion: *ik had er geen flauw ~ van* I didn't have the slightest suspicion (*or:* the faintest idea); *ik had al zo'n ~, ik had er al een ~ van* I had my suspicions (all along)

²**vermoeden** /vərmudə(n)/ (vermoedde, heeft vermoed) suspect, suppose: *dit heb ik nooit kunnen ~* this is the last thing I expected

vermoeid /vərmujt/ (adj) tired (with), weary (of): *dodelijk ~* dead tired, completely worn-out; *er ~ uitzien* look tired

de **vermoeidheid** /vərmujthɛit/ tiredness; weariness; fatigue: *~ van de ogen* eye strain

vermoeien /vərmujə(n)/ (vermoeide, heeft vermoeid) tire (out), weary, fatigue; exhaust

vermoeiend /vərmujənt/ (adj) tiring; wearisome; tiresome

het **vermogen** /vərmoɣə(n)/ (pl: -s) **1** fortune; property; capital **2** power, capacity **3** power, ability: *naar mijn beste ~* to the best of my ability

vermogend /vərmoɣənt/ (adj) rich, wealthy: *~e mensen* people of substance de **vermogensaanwas** /vərmoɣə(n)sanwɑs/ capital gain

de **vermogensbelasting** /vərmoɣə(n)zbəlɑstɪŋ/ wealth tax

vermolmd /vərmɔlmt/ (adj) mouldered, decayed, rotten

vermommen /vərmɔmə(n)/ (vermomde, heeft vermomd) disguise, dress up: *vermomd als* disguised as

de **vermomming** /vərmɔmɪŋ/ (pl: -en) disguise

vermoorden /vərmordə(n)/ (vermoordde, heeft vermoord) murder; assassinate: [Belg] *zwijgen als vermoord* be silent as the grave

vermorzelen /vərmɔrzələ(n)/ (vermorzelde, heeft vermorzeld) crush, smash up

de **vermout** /vɛrmut/ vermouth

vermurwen /vərmʏrwə(n)/ (vermurwde, heeft vermurwd) mollify

vernauwen /vərnɑuwə(n)/ (vernauwde, heeft vernauwd) narrow (down), constrict, contract ‖ *zich* ~ narrow

de **vernauwing** /vərnɑuwɪŋ/ (pl: -en) narrowing, constriction: ~ *van de* **bloedvaten** stricture (*or:* stenosis) of the blood vessels

vernederen /vərnedərə(n)/ (vernederde, heeft vernederd) humble; humiliate

vernederend /vərnedərənt/ (adj) humiliating; degrading

de **vernedering** /vərnedərɪŋ/ (pl: -en) humiliation: *een* ~ **ondergaan** suffer a humiliation (*or:* an indignity)

vernederlandsen /vərnedərlɑntsə(n)/ (vernederlandste, is vernederlandst) become Dutch, turn Dutch

vernemen /vərnemə(n)/ (vernam, heeft vernomen) learn, be told (*or:* informed) (of)

verneuken /vərnøkə(n)/ (verneukte, heeft verneukt) [vulg] **1** shaft, screw (around), con: *laat je niet* ~ don't let them screw you around; *je wordt verneukt waar je bij staat* it's a rip-off (*or:* con) **2** [vulg] fuck up: *hij heeft het verneukt* he fucked it up

vernielen /vərnilə(n)/ (vernielde, heeft vernield) destroy, wreck

de **vernieling** /vərnilɪŋ/ (pl: -en) destruction, devastation: ~*en* **aanrichten** go on the rampage; *zij ligt helemaal in de* ~ she's a complete wreck

de **vernielzucht** /vərnilzʏxt/ destructiveness, vandalism

vernietigen /vərnitəɣə(n)/ (vernietigde, heeft vernietigd) destroy, ruin; annihilate: *iemands* **verwachtingen** ~ dash s.o.'s expectations

vernietigend /vərnitəɣənt/ (adj, adv) destructive, devastating: *een* ~ **oordeel** a scathing judgment

de **vernietiging** /vərnitəɣɪŋ/ (pl: -en) destruction; annihilation

vernieuwen /vərniwə(n)/ (vernieuwde,

heeft vernieuwd) **1** renew, modernize; renovate **2** renew, restore

de **vernieuwer** /vərniwər/ (pl: -s) **1** renewer; renovator **2** innovator

de **vernieuwing** /vərniwɪŋ/ (pl: -en) **1** renewal, modernization; renovation; rebuilding **2** modernization, renovation; reform: *allerlei* ~*en* **aanbrengen** carry out all sorts of renovations

het/de **vernis** /vərnɪs/ (pl: -sen) varnish

vernissen /vərnɪsə(n)/ (verniste, heeft gevernist) varnish

vernoemen /vərnumə(n)/ (vernoemde, heeft vernoemd) name after, call after

het **vernuft** /vərnʏft/ ingenuity, genius

vernuftig /vərnʏftəx/ (adj) ingenious, witty

veronachtzamen /vərɔnɑxtsamə(n)/ (veronachtzaamde, heeft veronachtzaamd) neglect

veronderstellen /vərɔndərstɛlə(n)/ (veronderstelde, heeft verondersteld) suppose, assume: *ik veronderstel van* **wel** I suppose so

de **veronderstelling** /vərɔndərstɛlɪŋ/ (pl: -en) assumption, supposition: *in* de ~ *verkeren dat* … be under the impression that …

verongelijkt /vərɔŋɣəlɛɪkt/ (adj, adv) aggrieved, wronged

verongelukken /vərɔŋɣəlʏkə(n)/ (verongelukte, is verongelukt) **1** have an accident; be lost, be killed **2** (have a) crash; be wrecked, be lost [ship]: *het vliegtuig verongelukte* the plane crashed

verontreinigen /vərɔntrɛɪnəɣə(n)/ (verontreinigde, heeft verontreinigd) pollute, contaminate

de **verontreiniging** /vərɔntrɛɪnəɣɪŋ/ (pl: -en) pollution, contamination: *de* ~ *van het* **milieu** environmental pollution

verontrust /vərɔntrʏst/ (adj) alarmed, worried, concerned

verontrusten /vərɔntrʏstə(n)/ (verontrustte, heeft verontrust) alarm, worry: *zich* ~ *over iets* be disturbed (*or:* worried) about sth., to worry about sth.

verontrustend /vərɔntrʏstənt/ (adj) alarming, worrying, disturbing

¹**verontschuldigen** /vərɔntsxʏldəɣə(n)/ (verontschuldigde, heeft verontschuldigd) excuse, pardon: *iem.* ~ excuse s.o.

zich ²**verontschuldigen** /vərɔntsxʏldəɣə(n)/ (verontschuldigde zich, heeft zich verontschuldigd) apologize, excuse: *zich laten* ~ beg to be excused; *zich vanwege ziekte* ~ excuse o.s. on account of illness

de **verontschuldiging** /vərɔntsxʏldəɣɪŋ/ (pl: -en) **1** excuse, apology: ~*en* **aanbieden** apologize, offer one's apologies **2** excuse, defence: *hij* **voerde** *als* ~ *aan dat* he offered the excuse that

verontwaardigd /vərɔntwardəxt/ (adj, adv) indignant (about, at) de **verontwaardiging** /vərɔntwardəɣɪŋ/ indignation, outrage: *tot grote ~ van* to the great indignation of

de **veroordeelde** /vərordeldə/ (pl: -n) condemned man (*or:* woman), convict
veroordelen /vərordelə(n)/ (veroordeelde, heeft veroordeeld) **1** condemn; [law] sentence; find guilty: *~ tot de betaling van de kosten* order (s.o.) to pay costs **2** condemn; denounce

de **veroordeling** /vərordelɪŋ/ (pl: -en) **1** [law] conviction; sentence: *voorwaardelijke ~* suspended sentence **2** condemnation; denunciation
veroorloven /vərorlovə(n)/ (veroorloofde, heeft veroorloofd) permit, allow; afford: *zo'n dure auto kunnen wij ons niet ~* we can't afford such an expensive car
veroorzaken /vərorzakə(n)/ (veroorzaakte, heeft veroorzaakt) cause, bring about: *schade ~* cause damage
verorberen /vərɔrbərə(n)/ (verorberde, heeft verorberd) consume
verordenen /vərɔrdənə(n)/ (verordende, heeft verordend) **1** decree **2** order

de **verordening** /vərɔrdənɪŋ/ (pl: -en) regulation(s), ordinance, statute
verouderd /vərɑudərt/ (adj) old-fashioned, (out)dated
verouderen /vərɑudərə(n)/ (verouderde, is verouderd) become obsolete (*or:* antiquated), date, go out of date

de **veroudering** /vərɑudərɪŋ/ obsolescence, getting (*or:* becoming) out of date

de **veroveraar** /vərovərar/ (pl: -s) conqueror: *Willem de Veroveraar* William the Conqueror
veroveren /vərovərə(n)/ (veroverde, heeft veroverd) conquer, capture, win: *de eerste plaats ~ in de wedstrijd* take the lead

de **verovering** /vərovərɪŋ/ (pl: -en) conquest, capture
verpachten /vərpɑxtə(n)/ (verpachtte, heeft verpacht) lease (out): *verpachte grond* land on lease
verpakken /vərpɑkə(n)/ (verpakte, heeft verpakt) pack (up), package: *een cadeau in papier ~* wrap a present in paper

de **verpakking** /vərpɑkɪŋ/ (pl: -en) packing, wrapping, paper

het **verpakkingsmateriaal** /vərpɑkɪŋsmateriˌjal/ (pl: -materialen) packing material
verpatsen /vərpɑtsə(n)/ (verpatste, heeft verpatst) [inform] flog
verpauperen /vərpɑupərə(n)/ (verpauperde, is verpauperd) impoverish, go down (in the world), be reduced to poverty: *een verpauperde stad* a run-down town

de **verpaupering** /vərpɑupərɪŋ/ deterioration, impoverishment
verpesten /vərpɛstə(n)/ (verpestte, heeft verpest) [inform] poison, contaminate, spoil:

de sfeer ~ spoil the atmosphere

het **verpinken** /vərpɪŋkə(n)/: [Belg] *zonder (te) ~* without batting an eyelid
¹verplaatsen /vərplɑtsə(n)/ (verplaatste, heeft verplaatst) move; shift: *zijn activiteiten ~* shift one's activities

zich **²verplaatsen** /vərplɑtsə(n)/ (verplaatste zich, heeft zich verplaatst) **1** move, shift, change places **2** project o.s., put o.s. in s.o. else's shoes: *zich in iemands positie ~* imagine o.s. in s.o. else's position

de **verplaatsingskosten** /vərplɑtsɪŋsˌkostə(n)/ (pl) [Belg] call out charge
verplanten /vərplɑntə(n)/ (verplantte, heeft verplant) transplant

het **verpleeghuis** /vərpleɣhœys/ (pl: -huizen) nursing home, convalescent home

de **verpleeghulp** /vərpleɣhʏlp/ (pl: -en) nurse's aide, nursing auxiliary, medical orderly

de **verpleegkundige** /vərpleɣkʏndəɣə/ (pl: -n) nurse: *gediplomeerd ~* trained (*or:* qualified) nurse

de **verpleegster** /vərpleɣstər/ (pl: -s) nurse
verplegen /vərpleɣə(n)/ (verpleegde, heeft verpleegd) nurse, care for: *~d personeel* nursing staff

de **verpleger** /vərpleɣər/ (pl: -s) (male) nurse

de **verpleging** /vərpleɣɪŋ/ nursing, care: *zij gaat in de ~* she is going into nursing
verpletteren /vərplɛtərə(n)/ (verpletterde, heeft verpletterd) **1** crush, smash **2** [fig] shatter: *dit bericht verpletterde haar* the news shattered her
verpletterend /vərplɛtərənt/ (adj, adv) crushing: *een ~e nederlaag* a crushing defeat
verplicht /vərplɪxt/ (adj, adv) **1** compelled, obliged: *zich ~ voelen om* feel compelled to **2** compulsory, obligatory: *~e lectuur* required reading (matter); *~ verzekerd zijn* be compulsorily insured; *iets ~ stellen* make sth. compulsory
verplichten /vərplɪxtə(n)/ (verplichtte, heeft verplicht) oblige, compel: *de wet verplicht ons daartoe* the law obliges us to do that

de **verplichting** /vərplɪxtɪŋ/ (pl: -en) obligation, commitment; liability: *financiële ~en* financial liabilities (*or:* obligations); *sociale ~en* social duties; *~en aangaan* enter into obligations (*or:* a contract); *zijn ~en nakomen* fulfil one's obligations
verpoten /vərpotə(n)/ (verpootte, heeft verpoot) transplant
verprutsen /vərprʏtsə(n)/ (verprutste, heeft verprutst) bungle, botch
verpulveren /vərpʏlvərə(n)/ (verpulverde, heeft verpulverd) pulverize; [+ direct object also] crush

het **verraad** /vərat/ treason, treachery, betrayal: *~ plegen* commit treason

verraden /vər_a_də(n)/ (verraadde, heeft verraden) **1** betray, commit treason: *iem.* **aan** *de politie* ~ squeak (*or:* rat) on s.o. **2** betray: *een* **geheim** ~ betray (*or:* let out) a secret; *niets* ~, *hoor!* don't breathe a word!

de **verrader** /vər_a_dər/ (pl: -s) traitor, betrayer; squealer

verraderlijk /vər_a_dərlək/ (adj, adv) treacherous

verrassen /vər_a_sə(n)/ (verraste, heeft verrast) (take by) surprise: *door noodweer verrast* caught in a thunderstorm; *onaangenaam verrast zijn* be startled, be taken aback

de **verrassing** /vər_a_sɪŋ/ (pl: -en) **1** surprise; shock: *voor iem. een* ~ *in petto* **hebben** have a surprise in store for s.o.; *het* **was** *voor ons geen* ~ *meer* it didn't come as a surprise to us **2** surprise, amazement: *tot mijn* ~ *bemerkte ik … I* was surprised to see that …

verrast /vər_a_st/ (adj, adv) surprised; amazed: ~ **keek** *hij* **op** he looked up in surprise

verre /vɛrə/ (adv): ~ **van** *dat!* far from it!; *het is* ~ **van** *eenvoudig* it's anything but easy

verregaand /vɛrəɣant/ (adj, adv) far-reaching, outrageous; radical: *in* ~*e* **staat** *van ontbinding* in an advanced state of decomposition

verregenen /vərəɣenə(n)/ (verregende, is verregend) spoil by rain; rain off; drench

verrek /vərɛk/ (int) [inform] gosh, (good) gracious

verrekenen /vərɛkenə(n)/ (verrekende, heeft verrekend) settle, deduct, adjust; pay out: *iets* **met** *iets* ~ balance sth. with sth.

de **verrekening** /vərɛkenɪŋ/ (pl: -en) settlement

de **verrekijker** /vərɛkɛikər/ (pl: -s) binoculars; telescope

¹**verrekken** /vərɛkə(n)/ (verrekte, is verrekt) [inform] die, kick the bucket: ~ **van** *de honger* starve; ~ **van** *de pijn* be groaning with pain; ~ **van** *de kou* perish with cold

²**verrekken** /vərɛkə(n)/ (verrekte, heeft verrekt) strain; pull; twist, wrench; sprain: *een* **pees** ~ stretch a tendon; **zich** ~ strain o.s.

verrekt /vərɛkt/ (adj, adv) [inform] strained

verreweg /vɛrəwɛx/ (adv) (by) far, much; easily: *dat* **is** ~ *het beste* that's easily (*or:* much) the best; *hij* **is** ~ *de sterkste* he's far and away the strongest

verrichten /vərɪxtə(n)/ (verrichtte, heeft verricht) perform; conduct; carry out: **wonderen** ~ work wonders, perform miracles

de **verrichting** /vərɪxtɪŋ/ (pl: -en) **1** performance **2** action; operation

verrijden /vərɛidə(n)/ (verreed, heeft verreden) **1** move; wheel; drive **2** compete in, compete for: *een* **kampioenschap** ~ organize (*or:* hold) a championship; *een wedstrijd* **laten** ~ run off a race

verrijken /vərɛikə(n)/ (verrijkte, heeft verrijkt) enrich: *zijn* **kennis** ~ improve one's knowledge; **zich** ~ *ten koste van een ander* get rich at the expense of s.o. else; *verrijkt* **voedsel** fortified food

de **verrijking** /vərɛikɪŋ/ enrichment

verrijzen /vərɛizə(n)/ (verrees, is verrezen) (a)rise; spring up [bldg]; shoot up

de **verrijzenis** /vərɛizənɪs/ resurrection

zich **verroeren** /vərurə(n)/ (verroerde zich, heeft zich verroerd) move: *je* **kunt** *je hier nauwelijks* ~ you can hardly move in here; *verroer* **je** *niet* don't move

verroest /vərust/ (adj) rusty

verroesten /vərustə(n)/ (verroestte, is verroest) rust, get rusty: *verroest* **ijzer** rusty iron

verrot /vərɔt/ (adj) rotten; bad; putrid, wretched: *door en door* ~ rotten to the core; *iem.* ~ **schelden** tear into s.o., call s.o. all sorts of names; *iem.* ~ **slaan** knock the living daylights out of s.o.

verrotten /vərɔtə(n)/ (verrotte, is verrot) rot, decay: **doen** ~ rot (down); decay

de **verrotting** /vərɔtɪŋ/ rot(ting), decay: *dit hout is* **tegen** ~ *bestand* this wood is treated for rot

verruilen /vərœylə(n)/ (verruilde, heeft verruild) (ex)change, swap

verruimen /vərœymə(n)/ (verruimde, heeft/is verruimd) widen, broaden; liberalize: *zijn* **blik** ~ widen (*or:* broaden) one's outlook; **mogelijkheden** ~ create more possibilities

de **verruiming** /vərœymɪŋ/ widening, broadening; liberalization

verrukkelijk /vərʏkələk/ (adj, adv) delightful, gorgeous; delicious

de **verrukking** /vərʏkɪŋ/ (pl: -en) delight

verrukt /vərʏkt/ (adj) delighted, overjoyed

verruwen /vərywə(n)/ (verruwde, is verruwd) coarsen; become vulgar; become brutalized

de **verruwing** /vərywɪŋ/ coarsening, vulgarization

het ¹**vers** /vɛrs/ (pl: verzen) **1** verse: *Lucas 6,* ~ **10** St Luke, chapter 6, verse 10 **2** verse, stanza; couplet: *dat is* ~ **twee** that's another story **3** verse, poem; rhyme

²**vers** /vɛrs/ (adj, adv) fresh, new: ~ **bloed** fresh (*or:* young, new) blood; ~*e* **eieren** new-laid eggs; ~*e* **sneeuw** fresh (*or:* new-fallen) snow; ~ **blijven** keep fresh (*or:* good); ~ **van** *de pers* hot from the press

verschaald /vərsxa_lt/ (adj): ~ **bier** stale (*or:* flat) beer

verschaffen /vərsxafə(n)/ (verschafte, heeft verschaft) provide (with), supply (with): *het leger verschafte hem een complete* **uitrusting** the army issued him with a complete kit

verschalken /vərsxalkə(n)/ (verschalkte,

verschansen

heeft verschalkt) outwit, (out)fox: *de keeper* ~ outmanoeuvre the keeper

zich **verschansen** /vərsxɑnsə(n)/ (verschanste zich, heeft zich verschanst) entrench o.s., barricade o.s., take cover: *zich in zijn kamer ~* barricade o.s. in one's room

het **verscheiden** /vərsxɛɪdə(n)/ [form] departure

verscheidene /vərsxɛɪdənə/ (num) several, various

de **verscheidenheid** /vərsxɛɪdənhɛit/ variety, diversity; assortment; range: *een grote ~ aan gerechten* a wide variety of dishes

verschepen /vərsxepə(n)/ (verscheepte, heeft verscheept) ship (off, out)

de **verscheping** /vərsxepɪŋ/ (pl: -en) shipping

verscherpen /vərsxɛrpə(n)/ (verscherpte, heeft verscherpt) tighten (up): *het toezicht ~* tighten up control

verscheuren /vərsxørə(n)/ (verscheurde, heeft verscheurd) 1 tear (up); shred; rip (up): *een door oorlog verscheurd land* a war-torn country 2 maul, tear to pieces (*or:* apart)

het **verschiet** /vərsxit/: *dat ligt nog in het ~* that's is still in store

verschieten /vərsxitə(n)/ (verschoot, is verschoten) fade: *de gordijnen zijn verschoten* the curtains are (*or:* have) faded ‖ *van kleur ~* a) blush, go red; b) rapidly become multicultural

verschijnen /vərsxɛɪnə(n)/ (verscheen, is verschenen) 1 appear, surface; emerge 2 appear, turn up 3 appear, come out, be published

de **verschijning** /vərsxɛɪnɪŋ/ (pl: -en) 1 appearance; publication 2 figure, presence: *een indrukwekkende ~* an imposing presence

het **verschijnsel** /vərsxɛɪnsəl/ (pl: -en) phenomenon; symptom; sign: *een eigenaardig ~* a strange phenomenon

het **verschil** /vərsxɪl/ (pl: -len) 1 difference, dissimilarity, distinction: *~ van mening* a difference of opinion; *een groot ~ maken* make all the difference; *~ maken tussen* draw a distinction between, differentiate between; *~ maken* make a difference; *met dit ~, dat ...* with one difference, namely that ...; *een ~ van dag en nacht* a world of difference 2 difference, remainder: *het ~ delen* split the difference

verschillen /vərsxɪlə(n)/ (verschilde, heeft verschild) differ (from), be different (from); vary: *van mening ~ met iem.* disagree with s.o., differ with s.o.; *smaken ~* tastes differ; everyone to his taste

verschillend /vərsxɪlənt/ (adj, adv) 1 different (from), various: *wij denken daar ~ over* we don't see eye to eye on that 2 several, various, different: *bij ~e gelegenheden* on various occasions

verscholen /vərsxolə(n)/ (adj) hidden; secluded: *het huis lag ~ achter de bomen* the house was tucked away behind the trees

verschonen /vərsxonə(n)/ (verschoonde, heeft verschoond) change: *de baby ~* change the baby's nappy; *de bedden ~* put clean sheets on the beds; *zich ~* put on clean clothes

de **verschoning** /vərsxonɪŋ/ (pl: -en) change of underwear

de **verschoppeling** /vərsxopəlɪŋ/ (pl: -en) outcast

verschralen /vərsxralə(n)/ (verschraalde, is verschraald) decrease

¹**verschrikkelijk** /vərsxrɪkələk/ (adj) terrible; devastating; excruciating: *een ~e hongersnood* a devastating famine; *~e sneeuwman* Abominable Snowman, yeti; *een ~ kabaal* an infernal racket

²**verschrikkelijk** /vərsxrɪkələk/ (adv) terribly, awfully; terrifically: *Sander maakte een ~ mooi doelpunt* Sander scored a terrific goal

de **verschrikking** /vərsxrɪkɪŋ/ (pl: -en) terror, horror: *de ~en van de oorlog* the horrors of war

verschroeien /vərsxrujə(n)/ (verschroeide, heeft verschroeid) scorch; singe; sear: *de tactiek van de verschroeide aarde* scorched earth policy

verschrompelen /vərsxrompələ(n)/ (verschrompelde, heeft/is verschrompeld) shrivel (up); atrophy: *een verschrompeld gezicht* a wizened face

zich **verschuilen** /vərsxœylə(n)/ (verschool zich/ verschuilde zich, heeft zich verscholen) hide (o.s.), lurk: *zich in een hoek ~* hide (o.s.) in a corner

verschuiven /vərsxœyvə(n)/ (verschoof, heeft verschoven) 1 move, shift; shove aside 2 postpone

de **verschuiving** /vərsxœyvɪŋ/ (pl: -en) 1 shift 2 postponement

verschuldigd /vərsxYldəxt/ (adj) due; indebted: *iem. veel dank ~ zijn* be greatly indebted to s.o.; *het ~e geld* the money due; *iem. iets ~ zijn* be indebted to s.o., owe s.o. sth.

de **versheid** /vɛrshɛit/ freshness

het/de **vershoudfolie** /vɛrshɑutfoli/ cling film

de **versie** /vɛrzi/ (pl: -s) version

de **versierder** /vərsirdər/ (pl: -s) womanizer, ladykiller

versieren /vərsirə(n)/ (versierde, heeft versierd) 1 decorate: *de kerstboom ~* trim the Christmas tree; *straten ~* decorate the streets 2 pick up, get off with

de **versiering** /vərsirɪŋ/ (pl: -en) decoration

de **versiertoer** /vərsirtur/: *op de ~ gaan* try to pick up s.o., try to make s.o.

versimpelen /vərsɪmpələ(n)/ (versimpelde, heeft versimpeld) (over)simplify

versjacheren /vərʃ_oxərə(n)/ (versjacherde, heeft versjacherd) squander

versjouwen /vərʃ_ouwə(n)/ (versjouwde, heeft versjouwd) drag away

verslaafd /vərsl_aft/ (adj) addicted (to), hooked (on): ~ **raken** *aan drugs* contract the drug habit; **aan** *de drank* (*or: het spel*) ~ *zijn* be addicted to drink (*or:* gambling)

de **verslaafde** /vərsl_avdə/ (pl: -n) alcoholic; (drug) addict; junkie

verslaan /vərsl_an/ (versloeg, heeft verslagen) defeat; beat [sport]: *iem.* ~ **met** *schaken* defeat s.o. at chess

het **verslag** /vərsl_ax/ (pl: -en) report; commentary: *een* **direct** ~ *van de wedstrijd* a live commentary on the match; ~ **uitbrengen** report on, give an account of

verslagen /vərsl_axə(n)/ (adj) **1** defeated, beaten **2** dismayed

de **verslagenheid** /vərsl_axənhɛit/ dismay (at), consternation (at)

de **verslaggever** /vərsl_axevər/ (pl: -s) reporter; commentator

de **verslaggeving** /vərsl_axevɪŋ/ (pl: -en) (press) coverage

zich **verslapen** /vərsl_apə(n)/ (versliep zich, heeft zich verslapen) oversleep: *hij had zich drie* **uur** ~ he overslept and was three hours late

verslappen /vərsl_opə(n)/ (verslapte, is verslapt) slacken; flag; wane: *de* **pols** *verslapt* the pulse is getting weaker

verslavend /vərsl_avənt/ (adj, adv) addictive

de **verslaving** /vərsl_avɪŋ/ addiction, (drug-)dependence

verslechteren /vərsl_ɛxtərə(n)/ (verslechterde, is verslechterd) get worse, worsen, deteriorate

verslepen /vərsl_epə(n)/ (versleepte, heeft versleept) drag (off, away); tow (away)

versleten /vərsl_etə(n)/ (adj) **1** worn(-out), shabby: *tot* **op** *de draad* ~ threadbare **2** worn-out; burnt-out: *een* ~ **paard** an old nag

de **versleuteling** /vərsl_øtəlɪŋ/ [comp] encryption

verslijten /vərsl_ɛitə(n)/ (versleet, heeft versleten) wear out: *hij had al drie* **echtgenotes** *versleten* he had already got through three wives

zich **verslikken** /vərsl_ɪkə(n)/ (verslikte zich, heeft zich verslikt) **1** choke: *pas op, hij verslikt* **zich** watch out, it has gone down the wrong way; *zich* **in** *een graat* ~ choke on a bone **2** underrate, underestimate

verslinden /vərsl_ɪndə(n)/ (verslond, heeft verslonden) devour; eat up; eat: *die auto verslindt* **benzine** that car drinks petrol; *een* **boek** ~ devour a book

verslingerd /vərsl_ɪŋərt/ (adj): *zij is* ~ **aan** *slagroomgebakjes* she is mad about cream cakes

versloffen /vərsl_ɔfə(n)/ (verslofte, is ver-

sloft) [Dutch]: *de boel* **laten** ~ let things go

verslonzen /vərsl_ɔnzə(n)/ (verslonsde, is verslonsd) degrade

versmaden /vərsm_adə(n)/ (versmaadde, heeft versmaad): *dat is* **niet** *te* ~ that's not to be sneezed at (*or:* despised)

¹**versmallen** /vərsm_alə(n)/ (versmalde, heeft/is versmald) narrow

zich ²**versmallen** /vərsm_alə(n)/ (versmalde zich, heeft zich versmald) narrow, become narrow(er): *ginds versmalt de* **weg** *zich* the road gets narrow(er) there

versmelten /vərsm_ɛltə(n)/ (versmolt, is versmolten) blend, merge

de **versnapering** /vərsn_apərɪŋ/ (pl: -en) snack, titbit

versnellen /vərsn_ɛlə(n)/ (versnelde, heeft/is versneld) quicken, accelerate, speed up

de **versnelling** /vərsn_ɛlɪŋ/ (pl: -en) **1** acceleration; increase (in) **2** gear: *in* **de eerste** ~ *zetten* put into first gear; *in* **een hogere** ~ *schakelen* change up; move into gear; *een auto met* **automatische** ~ a car with automatic transmission; *een fiets* **met** *tien* ~*en* a ten-speed bike

de **versnellingsbak** /vərsn_ɛlɪŋzbɑk/ (pl: -ken) gearbox

versnijden /vərsn_ɛidə(n)/ (versneed, heeft versneden) **1** cut up **2** adulterate

versnipperen /vərsn_ɪpərə(n)/ (versnipperde, heeft versnipperd) **1** cut up (into pieces) **2** fragment; fritter away

versoberen /vərs_obərə(n)/ (versoberde, heeft versoberd) economize, cut down (on expenses)

versoepelen /vərs_upələ(n)/ (versoepelde, heeft/is versoepeld) relax; liberalize

verspelen /vərsp_elə(n)/ (verspeelde, heeft verspeeld) forfeit, lose: *een* **kans** ~ throw away a chance; *zijn* **rechten** ~ forfeit one's rights

versperren /vərsp_ɛrə(n)/ (versperde, heeft versperd) block; barricade: *iem. de* **weg** ~ bar s.o.'s way; *de* **weg** ~ block the road

de **versperring** /vərsp_ɛrɪŋ/ (pl: -en) barrier, barricade

verspillen /vərsp_ɪlə(n)/ (verspilde, heeft verspild) waste; fritter away

de **verspilling** /vərsp_ɪlɪŋ/ (pl: -en) **1** wasting: ~ *van* **energie** wasting energy **2** waste: *wat een* ~*!* what a waste!

versplinteren /vərspl_ɪntərə(n)/ (versplinterde, heeft/is versplinterd) smash; splinter: *die* **plank** *is versplinterd* that plank has splintered

verspreid /vərspr_ɛit/ (adj, adv) scattered: *een* *over het hele land* ~*e* **organisatie** a nationwide organization; *haar speelgoed* **lag** ~ *over de vloer* the floor was strewn with her toys; **wijd** ~ widespread; widely (*or:* commonly) held

¹**verspreiden** /vərspr_ɛidə(n)/ (verspreidde,

heeft verspreid) **1** spread, disperse, distribute; circulate: *een kwalijke* **geur** ~ give off a ghastly smell; *licht* ~ shed light; *warmte* ~ give off heat **2** disperse

zich ²**verspreiden** /vərsprɛidə(n)/ (verspreidde zich, heeft zich verspreid) spread (out): *de menigte verspreidde* **zich** the crowd dispersed

de **verspreiding** /vərsprɛidɪŋ/ spread, distribution

zich **verspreken** /vərsprekə(n)/ (versprak zich, heeft zich versproken) make a slip (*or:* mistake)

de **verspreking** /vərsprekɪŋ/ (pl: -en) slip of the tongue, mistake

¹**verspringen** /vɛrsprɪŋə(n)/ (sprong ver, heeft vergesprongen) do the long jump: *zij sprong zes* **meter** *ver* she jumped six metres

²**verspringen** /vərsprɪŋə(n)/ (versprong, is versprongen) **1** jump **2** stagger: *~de naden* staggered seams

de **verspringer** /vɛrsprɪŋər/ long jumper; [Am] broad-jumper

de **versregel** /vɛrsreɣəl/ (pl: -s) line (of poetry)

verst /vɛrst/ (adj, adv) furthest, farthest: *het ~e* **punt** the farthest point; *dat is in de ~e* **verte** *niet mijn bedoeling* that's the last thing I intended

verstaan /vərstan/ (verstond, heeft verstaan) **1** (be able to) hear: *helaas verstond ik zijn* **naam** *niet* unfortunately I didn't catch his name; *ik versta geen* **woord!** I can't hear a word that is being said; *hij kon* **zichzelf** *nauwelijks* ~ he could hardly hear himself speak **2** understand: *heb ik* **goed** ~ *dat …* did I hear you right …; *te* ~ *geven* give (s.o.) to understand (that) **3** understand, mean: *wat versta jij* **daaronder?** what do you understand by that? **4** know: *zijn* **vak** ~ know one's trade

verstaanbaar /vərstambar/ (adj, adv) **1** audible **2** understandable: *zich ~* **maken** make o.s. understood

het **verstand** /vərstɑnt/ **1** (power of) reason, (powers of) comprehension; brain(s): **gebruik** *toch je ~!* use your brains!; **gezond** ~ common sense; *met zijn* **volle** ~ *iets doen* do sth. in full possession of one's faculties, do sth. in full consciousness; *een goed ~* **hebben** have a good head on one's shoulders; *iem. iets* **aan** *het ~* **brengen** drive sth. home to s.o.; *dat gaat mijn ~ te boven* that's beyond me **2** knowledge, understanding: ~ **hebben** *van* know about, understand, be a good judge of; *daar heb ik* **geen** ~ *van* I don't know the first thing about that

¹**verstandelijk** /vərstɑndələk/ (adj) intellectual: *~e* **vermogens** intellect, intellectual powers

²**verstandelijk** /vərstɑndələk/ (adv) rationally

de **verstandhouding** /vərstɑnthɑudɪŋ/ (pl: -en) understanding; relations: *een blik van* ~

an understanding look; *een* **goede** ~ *hebben met* be on good terms with

verstandig /vərstɑndəx/ (adj, adv) sensible: *iets* ~ **aanpakken** go about sth. in a sensible way

het **verstandshuwelijk** /vərstɑn(t)shywələk/ (pl: -en) **1** marriage of convenience **2** alliance of convenience

de **verstandskies** /vərstɑntskis/ (pl: -kiezen) [Dutch] wisdom tooth

de **verstandsverbijstering** /vərstɑntsfərbɛistərɪŋ/ madness: *handelen in een* **vlaag** *van* ~ act in a fit of madness (*or:* insanity)

verstarren /vərstɑrə(n)/ (verstarde, is verstard) become rigid, freeze: *verstarde* **tradities** fossilized traditions

verstedelijken /vərstedələkə(n)/ (verstedelijkte, is verstedelijkt) urbanize

de **verstedelijking** /vərstedələkɪŋ/ urbanization

versteend /vərstent/ (adj) petrified; [also fig] fossilized

het **verstek** /vərstɛk/ (pl: -ken) default (of appearance): ~ **laten gaan** be absent, fail to appear

de **verstekeling** /vərstekəlɪŋ/ (pl: -en) stowaway

verstelbaar /vərstɛlbar/ (adj) adjustable

versteld /vərstɛlt/ (adj) stunned: *iem.* ~ **doen staan** astonish s.o.; ~ **staan** *(van iets)* be dumbfounded

verstellen /vərstɛlə(n)/ (verstelde, heeft versteld) **1** adjust **2** mend, repair

versterken /vərstɛrkə(n)/ (versterkte, heeft versterkt) **1** strengthen; intensify: **geluid** ~ amplify sound **2** fortify

de **versterker** /vərstɛrkər/ (pl: -s) amplifier

de **versterking** /vərstɛrkɪŋ/ (pl: -en) strengthening, reinforcement; amplification: *het leger* **kreeg** ~ the army was reinforced

versterven /vərstɛrvə(n)/ (verstierf, is verstorven) starve

verstevigen /vərsteveɣə(n)/ (verstevigde, heeft verstevigd) strengthen, consolidate; prop up: *zijn* **positie** ~ consolidate one's position

verstijven /vərstɛivə(n)/ (verstijfde, is verstijfd) stiffen: ~ *van* **kou** grow numb with cold; ~ *van schrik* be petrified with fear

verstikken /vərstɪkə(n)/ (verstikte, heeft verstikt) smother, choke

verstikkend /vərstɪkənt/ (adj) suffocating: *~e* **hitte** stifling heat

de **verstikking** /vərstɪkɪŋ/ (pl: -en) suffocation

¹**verstoken** /vərstokə(n)/ (adj) deprived (of)

²**verstoken** /vərstokə(n)/ (verstookte, heeft verstookt) spend on heating

verstokt /vərstokt/ (adj) hardened, confirmed: *een ~e* **vrijgezel** a confirmed bachelor

verstomd /vərstomt/ (adj): ~ **doen staan**

strike dumb, astound; ~ *staan* be dumb-founded (*or:* flabbergasted)

verstommen /vərst*ɔ*mə(n)/ (verstomde, is verstomd) become silent: *het lawaai verstom-de* the noise died down

verstoord /vərst*ort*/ (adj) annoyed, upset

verstoppen /vərst*ɔ*pə(n)/ (verstopte, heeft verstopt) hide: *verstopt raken* a) clog/foul up, become choked (up); b) [nose] stuff up; *zijn geld* ~ hide (*or:* stash) away one's money

het **verstoppertje** /vərst*ɔ*pərcə/ hide-and-seek: ~ *spelen* play (at) hide-and-seek

de **verstopping** /vərst*ɔ*pɪŋ/ (pl: -en) **1** block-age **2** constipation

verstopt /vərst*ɔ*pt/ (adj) blocked (up): *mijn neus is* ~ my nose is all stuffed up; *het riool is* ~ the sewer is clogged

verstoren /vərst*o*rə(n)/ (verstoorde, heeft verstoord) disturb: *het evenwicht* ~ upset the balance; *de stilte* ~ break the silence

de **verstoring** /vərst*o*rɪŋ/ (pl: -en) disruption: ~ *van de openbare orde* disorderly conduct

verstoten /vərst*o*tə(n)/ (verstootte, heeft verstoten) cast off, cast out: *een kind* ~ dis-own a child

verstrekken /vərstr*ɛ*kə(n)/ (verstrekte, heeft verstrekt) supply with, provide with; distribute: *de bank zal hem een lening* ~ the bank will grant him a loan

verstrekkend /v*ɛ*rstrɛkənt/ (adj) far-reach-ing

de **verstrekking** /vərstr*ɛ*kɪŋ/ (pl: -en) supply, provision

verstrijken /vərstr*ɛi*kə(n)/ (verstreek, is verstreken) go by; elapse; expire: *de termijn verstrijkt op 1 juli* the term expires on the 1st of July

verstrikken /vərstr*ɪ*kə(n)/ (verstrikte, heeft verstrikt) entangle: *in iets verstrikt raken* get entangled in sth.

verstrooid /vərstr*o*jt/ (adj) absent-minded

de **verstrooidheid** /vərstr*o*jthɛit/ absent-mindedness: *uit* ~ *iets doen* do sth. from ab-sent-mindedness

verstrooien /vərstr*o*jə(n)/ (verstrooide, heeft verstrooid) scatter, spread: *de as van een overledene* ~ scatter a deceased person's ashes

de **verstrooiing** /vərstr*o*jɪŋ/ (pl: -en) **1** enter-tainment, diversion **2** scattering, dispersion

verstuiken /vərst*œy*kə(n)/ (verstuikte, heeft verstuikt) sprain

de **verstuiver** /vərst*œy*vər/ (pl: -s) spray, atom-izer

versturen /vərst*y*rə(n)/ (verstuurde, heeft verstuurd) send (off): *iets naar iem.* ~ send sth. to s.o.; *per post* ~ mail

versuft /vərs*y*ft/ (adj) dizzy, dazed; stunned

de **versukkeling** /vərs*y*kəlɪŋ/: *in de* ~ *raken* be ailing, fall into a decline

versus /v*ɛ*rsʏs/ (prep) versus

het **vertaalbureau** /vərt*a*lbyro/ (pl: -s) transla-tion agency

de **vertaalslag** /vərt*a*lslɔx/ (pl: -en) applying an idea, rule, etc. from one situation to an-other

zich **vertakken** /vərt*ɑ*kə(n)/ (vertakte zich, heeft zich vertakt) branch (off)

de **vertakking** /vərt*ɑ*kɪŋ/ (pl: -en) **1** branching (off) **2** ramification, branch

vertalen /vərt*a*lə(n)/ (vertaalde, heeft ver-taald) translate; interpret: *vrij* ~ give a free translation; *uit het Engels in het Frans* ~ trans-late from English into French

de **vertaler** /vərt*a*lər/ (pl: -s) translator: *be-ëdigd* ~ sworn translator

de **vertaling** /vərt*a*lɪŋ/ (pl: -en) translation: *een* ~ *maken* do a translation

de **verte** /v*ɛ*rtə/ (pl: -n, -s) distance: *in de* ~ in the distance, far away; *het lijkt er in de* ~ *op* there is a slight resemblance; *in de verste* ~ *niet* not remotely; *uit de* ~ from a distance

vertederen /vərt*e*dərə(n)/ (vertederde, heeft vertederd) soften, move: *zij keek het kind vertederd aan* she gave the child a tender look

de **vertedering** /vərt*e*dərɪŋ/ **1** endearment, softening **2** tenderness

verteerbaar /vərt*e*rbar/ (adj) digestible; [fig also] palatable; acceptable: *licht* ~ *voed-sel* light food

vertegenwoordigen /vərt*e*ɣə(n)-wordəɣə(n)/ (vertegenwoordigde, heeft ver-tegenwoordigd) represent

de **vertegenwoordiger** /vərt*e*ɣə(n)-wordəɣər/ (pl: -s) **1** representative **2** (sales) representative

de **vertegenwoordiging** /vərt*e*ɣə(n)-wordəɣɪŋ/ (pl: -en) **1** representation **2** dele-gation

vertekend /vərt*e*kənt/ (adj) distorted

vertekenen /vərt*e*kənə(n)/ (vertekende, heeft vertekend) distort

vertellen /vərt*ɛ*lə(n)/ (vertelde, heeft ver-teld) tell: *een mop* ~ crack a joke; *moet je mij ~!* you're telling me!; *dat wordt verteld* so they say; *zal ik je eens wat ~?* you know what?; *let me tell you sth.; *wat vertel je me nou?* I can't believe it!; *je kunt me nog meer* ~ tell me another (one); *iets verder* ~ *aan ande-ren* pass sth. on to others; *vertel het maar niet verder* this is just between us

de **verteller** /vərt*ɛ*lər/ (pl: -s) narrator

de **vertelling** /vərt*ɛ*lɪŋ/ (pl: -en) story, tale

¹**verteren** /vərt*e*rə(n)/ (verteerde, heeft ver-teerd) be consumed (*or:* eaten away): *dat la-ken verteert door het vocht* that sheet is mouldering away with the damp; *door ver-driet verteerd worden* be eaten up (*or:* eat one's heart out) with grief

²**verteren** /vərt*e*rə(n)/ (verteerde, heeft ver-teerd) digest: *niet te* ~ indigestible

verticaal /vɛrtik<u>a</u>l/ (adj, adv) vertical: *in verticale stand* in (an) upright position

het **vertier** /vərt<u>i</u>r/ entertainment, diversion

vertikken /vərt<u>ɪ</u>kə(n)/ (vertikte, heeft vertikt) refuse (flatly)

zich **vertillen** /vərt<u>ɪ</u>lə(n)/ (vertilde zich, heeft zich vertild) strain o.s. (in) lifting: [fig] *zich aan iets ~* bite off more than one can chew

vertimmeren /vərt<u>ɪ</u>mərə(n)/ (vertimmerde, heeft vertimmerd) alter, renovate

vertoeven /vərt<u>u</u>və(n)/ (vertoefde, heeft vertoefd) sojourn, stay

vertolken /vərt<u>ɔ</u>lkə(n)/ (vertolkte, heeft vertolkt) **1** express, voice **2** play, interpret

de **vertolker** /vərt<u>ɔ</u>lkər/ (pl: -s) interpreter, performer; exponent, mouthpiece: *een ~ van het levenslied* a performer of the popular ballad

de **vertolking** /vərt<u>ɔ</u>lkɪŋ/ (pl: -en) interpretation

¹**vertonen** /vərt<u>o</u>nə(n)/ (vertoonde, heeft vertoond) **1** show: *geen gelijkenis ~ met* bear no resemblance to; *tekenen ~ van* show signs of **2** show, present: *kunsten ~* do tricks

zich ²**vertonen** /vərt<u>o</u>nə(n)/ (vertoonde zich, heeft zich vertoond) show one's face, turn up: *je kunt je zo niet ~ in het openbaar* you're not fit to be seen in public (like this); *ik durf me daar niet meer te ~* I'm afraid to show my face there now

de **vertoning** /vərt<u>o</u>nɪŋ/ (pl: -en) **1** show(ing), presentation **2** show, production: *het was een grappige ~* it was a curious spectacle

het **vertoon** /vərt<u>o</u>n/ showing, producing: *met veel ~* with great ostentation, with a lot of showing off; *op ~ van een identiteitsbewijs* on presentation of an ID

vertragen /vərtr<u>a</u>yə(n)/ (vertraagde, heeft/is vertraagd) slow down; be delayed: *een vertraagde filmopname* a slow-motion film scene

de **vertraging** /vərtr<u>a</u>yɪŋ/ (pl: -en) delay: *~ ondervinden* be delayed

vertrappen /vərtr<u>ɑ</u>pə(n)/ (vertrapte, heeft vertrapt) tread on, trample underfoot

het **vertrek** /vərtr<u>ɛ</u>k/ (pl: -ken) **1** departure; sailing: *bij zijn ~* on his departure; *op het punt van ~ staan* be about to leave **2** room

de **vertrekhal** /vərtr<u>ɛ</u>khɑl/ (pl: -len) departure hall

¹**vertrekken** /vərtr<u>ɛ</u>kə(n)/ (vertrok, is vertrokken) leave: *wij ~ morgen naar Glasgow* we are off to (or: leave for) Glasgow tomorrow

²**vertrekken** /vərtr<u>ɛ</u>kə(n)/ (vertrok, heeft vertrokken) pull, distort: *zonder een spier te ~* without batting an eyelid; *een van angst vertrokken gezicht* a face contorted (or: distorted, twisted) with fear

het **vertrekpunt** /vərtr<u>ɛ</u>kpʏnt/ (pl: -en) start(ing) point); point of departure

het **vertreksein** /vərtr<u>ɛ</u>ksɛin/ departure signal, green light

de **vertrektijd** /vərtr<u>ɛ</u>ktɛit/ (pl: -en) time of departure

¹**vertroebelen** /vərtr<u>u</u>bələ(n)/ (vertroebelde, is vertroebeld) become clouded

²**vertroebelen** /vərtr<u>u</u>bələ(n)/ (vertroebelde, heeft vertroebeld) cloud; obscure: *dat vertroebelt de zaak* that confuses (or: obscures) the issue

vertroetelen /vərtr<u>u</u>tələ(n)/ (vertroetelde, heeft vertroeteld) pamper

vertrouwd /vərtr<u>au</u>t/ (adj) **1** reliable, trustworthy: *een ~ persoon* a trusted person **2** familiar (with): *zich ~ maken met die technieken* familiarize o.s. with those techniques

de **vertrouwdheid** /vərtr<u>au</u>thɛit/ familiarity

vertrouwelijk /vərtr<u>au</u>wələk/ (adj, adv) intimate, confidential: *~ met iem. omgaan* be close to s.o.; *~ met elkaar praten* have a heart-to-heart talk; *een ~e mededeling* a confidential communication

de **vertrouwelijkheid** /vərtr<u>au</u>wələkhɛit/ confidentiality

de **vertrouweling** /vərtr<u>au</u>wəlɪŋ/ (pl: -en) confidant(e)

het ¹**vertrouwen** /vərtr<u>au</u>wə(n)/ confidence, trust: *op goed ~* on trust; *ik heb er weinig ~ in* I'm not very optimistic; *~ hebben in de toekomst* have faith in the future; *~ wekken* inspire confidence; *vol ~ zijn* be confident; *iem. in ~ nemen* take s.o. into one's confidence; *goed van ~ zijn* be (too) trusting

²**vertrouwen** /vərtr<u>au</u>wə(n)/ (vertrouwde, heeft vertrouwd) trust: *hij is niet te ~* he is not to be trusted; *ik vertrouw erop dat …* I trust that …; *op God ~* trust in God; *iem. voor geen cent ~* not trust s.o. an inch

de **vertrouwensarts** /vərtr<u>au</u>wə(n)sɑrts/ (pl: -en) doctor at an advice centre

de **vertrouwenskwestie** /vərtr<u>au</u>wə(n)skwɛsti/ (pl: -s) matter of confidence ‖ *de ~ stellen* ask for a vote of confidence

de **vertrouwenspersoon** /vərtr<u>au</u>wə(n)spɛrson/ (pl: -personen) confidential advisor

vertrouwenwekkend /vərtr<u>au</u>wə(n)wɛkənt/ (adj) inspiring confidence

vertwijfeld /vərtw<u>ɛi</u>fəlt/ (adj, adv) despairing: *~ raken* (be driven to) despair

de **vertwijfeling** /vərtw<u>ɛi</u>fəlɪŋ/ (pl: -en) despair, desperation

veruit /vɛr<u>œy</u>t/ (adv) by far: *~ de beste zijn* by far and away the best

vervaardigen /vərv<u>a</u>rdəyə(n)/ (vervaardigde, heeft vervaardigd) make: *met de hand vervaardigd* made by hand; *deze tafel is van hout vervaardigd* this table is made of wood

de **vervaardiging** /vərv<u>a</u>rdəxɪŋ/ manufacture, construction

vervaarlijk /vərv<u>a</u>rlək/ (adj, adv) tremendous

¹**vervagen** /vərv<u>a</u>yə(n)/ (vervaagde, is ver-

vaagd) become faint (*or:* blurred); dim; fade (away)

²**vervagen** /vərvaɣə(n)/ (vervaagde, heeft vervaagd) blur, dim: *de tijd heeft die herinneringen vervaagd* time has dimmed those memories

het **verval** /vərvɑl/ **1** decline: *het ~ van de goede zeden* the deterioration of morals; *dit gebouw is flink in ~ geraakt* this building has fallen into disrepair **2** fall

de **vervaldatum** /vərvɑldatʏm/ (pl: -data) expiry date

¹**vervallen** /vərvɑlə(n)/ (adj) **1** dilapidated **2** bedraggled

²**vervallen** /vərvɑlə(n)/ (verviel, is vervallen) **1** fall into disrepair **2** lapse: *in oude fouten ~* relapse into old errors; *tot armoede ~* be reduced to poverty **3** expire: *400 arbeidsplaatsen komen te ~* 400 jobs are to go (*or:* disappear); *die mogelijkheid vervalt* that possibility is no longer open; *de vergadering vervalt* the meeting has been cancelled

vervalsen /vərvɑlsə(n)/ (vervalste, heeft vervalst) **1** forge, counterfeit **2** tamper (with): *een cheque ~* forge a cheque

de **vervalser** /vərvɑlsər/ (pl: -s) forger, counterfeiter

de **vervalsing** /vərvɑlsɪŋ/ (pl: -en) forgery, counterfeit

vervangen /vərvɑŋə(n)/ (verving, heeft vervangen) replace, take the place of, substitute: *niet te ~* irreplaceable

de **vervanger** /vərvɑŋər/ (pl: -s) replacement, substitute: *de ~ van de minister* the substitute minister

de **vervanging** /vərvɑŋɪŋ/ (pl: -en) replacement, substitution

het **vervangingsinkomen** /vərvɑŋɪŋsɪŋkomə(n)/ (pl: -s) [Belg] payment, remittance

de **verve** /vɛrvə/ verve: *met veel ~* with a great deal of verve, with animation

verveeld /vərvelt/ (adj) bored, weary: [Belg] *~ zitten met iets* not know what to do about sth.; *~ toekijken* watch indifferently

verveelvoudigen /vərvelvɑudəɣə(n)/ (verveelvoudigde, heeft verveelvoudigd) multiply

¹**vervelen** /vərvelə(n)/ (verveelde, heeft verveeld) bore, annoy: *tot ~s toe* ad nauseam, over and over again

zich ²**vervelen** /vərvelə(n)/ (verveelde zich, heeft zich verveeld) be(come) bored: *ik verveel me dood* I am bored stiff

vervelend /vərvelənt/ (adj, adv) **1** boring **2** annoying: *een ~ karwei* a chore; *wat een ~e vent* what a tiresome fellow; *doe nu niet zo ~* don't be such a nuisance; *wat ~!* what a nuisance!

de **verveling** /vərvelɪŋ/ boredom: *louter uit ~* out of pure boredom

vervellen /vərvɛlə(n)/ (vervelde, is verveld) peel

verven /vɛrvə(n)/ (verfde, heeft geverfd) **1** paint **2** dye

verversen /vərvɛrsə(n)/ (ververste, heeft ververst) **1** refresh **2** change, freshen

de **verversing** /vərvɛrsɪŋ/ (pl: -en) replacement

¹**vervlaamsen** /vərvlamsə(n)/ (vervlaamste, is vervlaamst) become Flemish

²**vervlaamsen** /vərvlamsə(n)/ (vervlaamste, heeft vervlaamst) make Flemish

vervliegen /vərvliɣə(n)/ (vervloog, is vervlogen) **1** fly **2** evaporate

vervloeken /vərvlukə(n)/ (vervloekte, heeft vervloekt) curse: *hij zal die dag ~!* he will rue the day!

vervoegen /vərvuɣə(n)/ (vervoegde, heeft vervoegd) inflect ‖ *zich ~ bij* apply at

de **vervoeging** /vərvuɣɪŋ/ (pl: -en) conjugation

het **vervoer** /vərvur/ transport, transportation: *ik kon geen ~ krijgen* I couldn't get (*or:* find) any transport; *met het openbaar ~* by public transport; *tijdens het ~ beschadigde goederen* goods damaged in transit

het **vervoerbedrijf** /vərvurbədrɛif/ (pl: -bedrijven) [goods] haulier; haulage firm; passenger transport company: *gemeentelijk ~* municipal (*or:* city) transport company

de **vervoerder** /vərvurdər/ (pl: -s) transporter, carry

vervoeren /vərvurə(n)/ (vervoerde, heeft vervoerd) transport

de **vervoering** /vərvurɪŋ/ (pl: -en): *in ~ raken* be transported, be carried away (by)

het **vervoermiddel** /vərvurmɪdəl/ (pl: -en) (means of) transport: *openbare ~en* public service vehicles

het **vervoersbewijs** /vərvurzbəwɛis/ (pl: -bewijzen) ticket; card

het **vervolg** /vərvɔlx/ (pl: -en) **1** future: *in het ~* in the future **2** continuation (of), sequel (to) **3** continuation: *~ op blz. 10* continued on page 10

vervolgen /vərvɔlɣə(n)/ (vervolgde, heeft vervolgd) **1** continue: *wordt vervolgd* to be continued **2** pursue; persecute **3** [law] sue; prosecute: *iem. gerechtelijk ~* take legal action against s.o.

vervolgens /vərvɔlɣəns/ (adv) then: *~ zei hij … he* went on to say …

de **vervolging** /vərvɔlɣɪŋ/ (pl: -en) **1** persecution **2** [law] legal action (*or:* proceedings), prosecution: *tot ~ overgaan* (decide to) prosecute

het **vervolgonderwijs** /vərvɔlxɔndərwɛis/ secondary education

de **vervolgopleiding** /vərvɔlxɔplɛidɪŋ/ (pl: -en) continuation course; [Am] continuing education (course); advanced training

het **vervolgverhaal** /vərvɔlxfərhal/ (pl: -verhalen) serial (story)

vervolmaken /vərvɔlmakə(n)/ (vervolmaakte, heeft vervolmaakt) (make) perfect

vervormen /vərvɔrmə(n)/ (vervormde, heeft vervormd) **1** transform; deform; disfigure **2** distort: *geluid vervormd* **weergeven** distort a sound

de **vervorming** /vərvɔrmɪŋ/ (pl: -en) transformation; disfiguring; deforming

¹**vervreemden** /vərvremdə(n)/ (vervreemdde, is vervreemd) become estranged (or: alienated): *van zijn werk vervreemd* **raken** lose touch with one's work; *van elkaar* ~ drift apart

²**vervreemden** /vərvremdə(n)/ (vervreemdde, heeft vervreemd) alienate, estrange: *zich* ~ *van* alienate o.s. from

de **vervreemding** /vərvremdɪŋ/ (pl: -en) alienation, estrangement

vervroegen /vərvruɣə(n)/ (vervroegde, heeft vervroegd) advance, (move) forward: *vervroegde* **uittreding** early retirement

vervuilen /vərvœylə(n)/ (vervuilde, heeft vervuild) pollute, make filthy, contaminate

de **vervuiler** /vərvœylər/ (pl: -s) polluter, contaminator: *de* ~ **betaalt** the polluter pays

de **vervuiling** /vərvœylɪŋ/ pollution, contamination: *de* ~ *van het* **milieu** environmental pollution

vervullen /vərvylə(n)/ (vervulde, heeft vervuld) **1** fill: *dat vervult ons* **met** *zorg* that fills us with concern; *van iets vervuld zijn* be full of sth. **2** fulfil; perform: *tijdens het* ~ *van zijn plicht* in the discharge of his duty **3** fulfil, realize: *iemands* **wensen** ~ comply with s.o.'s wishes

de **vervulling** /vərvylɪŋ/ fulfilment; discharge; realization: *een droom ging* **in** ~ a dream came true

verwaaid /vərwajt/ (adj) windblown

verwaand /vərwant/ (adj, adv) conceited, stuck-up

de **verwaandheid** /vərwanthɛit/ conceit(edness), arrogance: *naast zijn schoenen lopen van* ~ be too big for one's boots

verwaardigen /vərwardəɣə(n)/ (verwaardigde zich, heeft zich verwaardigd) condescend

verwaarloosbaar /vərwarlozbar/ (adj) negligible

verwaarloosd /vərwarlost/ (adj) neglected

verwaarlozen /vərwarlozə(n)/ (verwaarloosde, heeft verwaarloosd) neglect

de **verwaarlozing** /vərwarlozɪŋ/ neglect; negligence

verwachten /vərwɑxtə(n)/ (verwachtte, heeft verwacht) **1** expect: *daar moet je ook niet* **alles** *van* ~ don't set your hopes too high; *lang verwacht* long-awaited; *dat had ik* **wel** *verwacht* that was just what I had expected **2** expect, be expecting: *ze verwacht een* **baby** she is expecting (a baby), she is in the family way

de **verwachting** /vərwɑxtɪŋ/ (pl: -en) **1** anticipation: *in* ~ *zijn* be expecting, be an expectant mother **2** expectation; outlook: *de* ~*en waren* **hoog gespannen** expectations ran high; *het overtrof haar* **stoutste** ~*en* it surpassed her wildest expectations; ~*en* **wekken** arouse (one's) hopes; **beneden** *de* ~*en blijven* fall short of expectations, disappoint; *aan de* ~ *beantwoorden* come up to one's expectations; **naar** ~ *zal het bedrijf morgen worden heropend* expectations are that the business will reopen tomorrow

de ¹**verwant** /vərwɑnt/ (pl: -en) relative, relation

²**verwant** /vərwɑnt/ (adj) **1** related (to) **2** kindred: *daar* **voel** *ik* **me** *niet mee* ~ I feel no affinity for (or: with) that

de **verwantschap** /vərwɑntsxɑp/ (pl: -pen) relationship, affinity, connection

het **verwantschapsonderzoek** /vərwɑntsxɑpsɔndərzuk/ (pl: -en) kinship analysis

verward /vərwɑrt/ (adj, adv) **1** confused; (en)tangled: *een* ~ **persoon** a deranged person **2** confused, muddled, incoherent

verwarmen /vərwɑrmə(n)/ (verwarmde, heeft verwarmd) warm, heat: *de* **kamer** *was niet verwarmd* the room was unheated; *een glas hete* **melk** *zal je wat* ~ a glass of hot milk will warm you up

de **verwarming** /vərwɑrmɪŋ/ (pl: -en) heating (system): *centrale* ~ *aanleggen* put in central heating; *de* ~ *hoger* (or: *lager*) *zetten* turn the heat up (or: down)

de **verwarmingsinstallatie** /vərwɑrmɪŋsɪnstala(t)si/ (pl: -s) heating system

de **verwarmingsketel** /vərwɑrmɪŋsketəl/ (pl: -s) (central heating) boiler

verwarren /vərwɑrə(n)/ (verwarde, heeft verward) **1** tangle (up), confuse: ~*d* **werken** lead to confusion **2** (+ met) confuse, mistake: *u verwart hem* **met** *zijn broer* you mistake him for his brother; *niet* **te** ~ **met** not to be confused with

de **verwarring** /vərwɑrɪŋ/ (pl: -en) entanglement, confusion; muddle: *er* **ontstond** *enige* ~ *over zijn identiteit* some confusion arose concerning (or: as to) his identity; ~ **stichten** cause confusion; *in* ~ *raken* become confused

verwateren /vərwatərə(n)/ (verwaterde, is verwaterd) become diluted (or: watered down), peter out: *de* **vriendschap** *tussen hen is verwaterd* their friendship has cooled off

verwedden /vərwɛdə(n)/ (verwedde, heeft verwed) bet: *ik wil er* **alles** *om* ~ *dat ...* I'll bet you anything that ...

het **verweer** /vərwer/ (pl: verweren) defence

verweerd /vərwert/ (adj) weather-beaten

het **verweerschrift** /vərwersxrɪft/ (pl: -en) (written) defence; pleading

verwekken /vərwɛkə(n)/ (verwekte, heeft verwekt) beget, father: *kinderen* ~ beget (*or:* father) children

de **verwekker** /vərwɛkər/ (pl: -s) begetter, father: *de ~ van het kind* the child's natural father

verwelken /vərwɛlkə(n)/ (verwelkte, is verwelkt) **1** wilt, wither **2** [fig] fade: *~de schoonheid* fading beauty

verwelkomen /vərwɛlkomə(n)/ (verwelkomde, heeft verwelkomd) welcome, greet; salute: *iem. hartelijk* ~ give s.o. a hearty welcome

verwend /vərwɛnt/ (adj) **1** spoilt, pampered: *zij is een ~ kreng* she is a spoilt brat **2** discriminating: *een ~ publiek* a discriminating public (*or:* audience)

verwennen /vərwɛnə(n)/ (verwende, heeft verwend) spoil, indulge: *zichzelf* ~ indulge (*or:* pamper) o.s.

verwensen /vərwɛnsə(n)/ (verwenste, heeft verwenst) curse

de **verwensing** /vərwɛnsɪŋ/ (pl: -en) curse

¹**verweren** /vərwerə(n)/ (verweerde, is verweerd) weather; erode; become weather-beaten

zich ²**verweren** /vərwerə(n)/ (verweerde zich, heeft zich verweerd) defend o.s.; put up a fight: *voor hij zich kon* ~ before he could defend himself

verwerkelijken /vərwɛrkələkə(n)/ (verwerkelijkte, heeft verwerkelijkt) realize: *een droom* (or: *wens*) ~ make a dream (*or:* wish) come true

verwerken /vərwɛrkə(n)/ (verwerkte, heeft verwerkt) **1** process, handle, convert: *zijn maag kon het niet* ~ his stomach couldn't digest it; *huisvuil tot compost* ~ convert household waste into compost **2** incorporate: *de nieuwste gegevens zijn erin verwerkt* the latest data are incorporated (in it) **3** cope with: *ze heeft haar verdriet nooit echt goed verwerkt* she has never really come to terms with her sorrow **4** absorb, cope with: *stadscentra kunnen zoveel verkeer niet* ~ city centres cannot absorb so much traffic

de **verwerking** /vərwɛrkɪŋ/ processing, handling, assimilation, incorporation: *bij de ~ van deze gegevens* in processing (*or:* handling) these data

verwerpelijk /vərwɛrpələk/ (adj) reprehensible, objectionable

verwerpen /vərwɛrpə(n)/ (verwierp, heeft verworpen) reject, vote down, turn down

verwerven /vərwɛrvə(n)/ (verwierf, heeft verworven) obtain, acquire; achieve

de **verwerving** /vərwɛrvɪŋ/ acquisition, obtaining

verweven /vərwevə(n)/ (inter)weave: *hun belangen zijn nauw* ~ their interests are closely knit; *met elkaar* ~ *zijn* be interwoven

verwezenlijken /vərwezə(n)ləkə(n)/ (verwezenlijkte, heeft verwezenlijkt) realize; fulfil; achieve: *plannen* (or: *voornemens*) ~ realize one's plans (*or:* intentions)

de **verwezenlijking** /vərwezə(n)ləkɪŋ/ realization, fulfilment

verwijderd /vərwɛidərt/ (adj) remote, distant: *(steeds verder) van elkaar* ~ *raken* drift (further and further) apart; *een kilometer van het dorp* ~ a kilometre out of the village

verwijderen /vərwɛidərə(n)/ (verwijderde, heeft verwijderd) remove: *iem. uit zijn huis* ~ evict s.o.; *iem. van het veld* ~ send s.o. off (the field)

de **verwijdering** /vərwɛidərɪŋ/ (pl: -en) **1** removal: ~ *van school* expulsion from school **2** estrangement: *er ontstond een ~ tussen hen* they drifted apart

verwijfd /vərwɛift/ (adj) effeminate, sissy

het **verwijsbriefje** /vərwɛizbrifjə/ (pl: -s) (doctor's) referral (letter)

het **verwijt** /vərwɛit/ (pl: -en) reproach, blame: *elkaar ~en maken* blame one another; *iem. ~en maken* reproach s.o.

verwijten /vərwɛitə(n)/ (verweet, heeft verweten) reproach, blame: *iem. iets* ~ reproach s.o. with sth., blame s.o. for sth.

verwijtend /vərwɛitənt/ (adj, adv) reproachful: *iem.* ~ *aankijken* look at s.o. reproachfully

verwijzen /vərwɛizə(n)/ (verwees, heeft verwezen) refer: *een patiënt naar een specialist* ~ refer a patient to a specialist

de **verwijzing** /vərwɛizɪŋ/ (pl: -en) reference; referral: *onder* ~ *naar* with reference to, referring to

verwikkelen /vərwɪkələ(n)/ (verwikkelde, heeft verwikkeld) involve, implicate, mix up

de **verwikkeling** /vərwɪkəlɪŋ/ (pl: -en) complication

verwilderd /vərwɪldərt/ (adj) **1** wild, neglected: *een ~e boomgaard* a neglected (*or:* an overgrown) orchard **2** wild, unkempt, dishevelled **3** wild, mad: *er* ~ *uitzien* look wild (*or:* haggard)

verwisselbaar /vərwɪsəlbar/ (adj) exchangeable, convertible: *onderling* ~ interchangeable

verwisselen /vərwɪsələ(n)/ (verwisselde, heeft verwisseld) **1** (ex)change, swap **2** mistake, confuse: *ik had u met uw broer verwisseld* I had mistaken you for your brother

de **verwisseling** /vərwɪsəlɪŋ/ (pl: -en) (ex)change, interchange, swap

verwittigen /vərwɪtəɣə(n)/ (verwittigde, heeft verwittigd) inform, advise, notify

verwoed /vərwut/ (adj, adv) passionate, ardent, impassioned: *~e pogingen doen* make frantic efforts

verwoest /vərwust/ (adj) destroyed, devastated, ravaged

verwoesten /vərwu̱stə(n)/ (verwoestte, heeft verwoest) destroy, devastate, lay waste

verwoestend /vərwu̱stənt/ (adj, adv) devastating, destructive

de **verwoestijning** /vərwustɛɪnɪŋ/ desertification

de **verwoesting** /vərwu̱stɪŋ/ (pl: -en) devastation; ravages; destruction

verwonden /vərwo̱ndə(n)/ (verwondde, heeft verwond) wound; injure

verwonderd /vərwo̱ndərt/ (adj) surprised; [stronger] amazed; astonished

verwonderen /vərwo̱ndərə(n)/ (verwonderde, heeft verwonderd) amaze, astonish

de **verwondering** /vərwo̱ndərɪŋ/ surprise; [stronger] amazement; astonishment: *het hoeft geen ~ te **wekken** dat ...* it comes as no surprise that ...

verwonderlijk /vərwo̱ndərlək/ (adj) surprising

de **verwonding** /vərwo̱ndɪŋ/ (pl: -en) injury; wounding; wound: *~en **oplopen*** sustain injuries, be injured

verwoorden /vərwo̱rdə(n)/ (verwoordde, heeft verwoord) put (in(to) words), express

verworden /vərwo̱rdə(n)/ (verwerd, is verworden) degenerate, deteriorate

de **verworvenheid** /vərwo̱rvənhɛɪt/ (pl: -heden) attainment, achievement

verwringen /vərwrɪ̱ŋə(n)/ twist; distort; contort: *een **van** pijn verwrongen gezicht* a face contorted with pain

de **veryupping** /vərjy̱pɪŋ/ yuppification, gentrification

verzachten /vərzɑ̱xtə(n)/ (verzachtte, heeft verzacht) soften; ease: *pijn ~* relieve (or: alleviate) pain

verzachtend /vərzɑ̱xtənt/ (adj) mitigating, extenuating

verzadigd /vərza̱dəxt/ (adj) **1** satisfied, full (up) **2** saturated: *een ~e **arbeidsmarkt*** a saturated labour market

verzadigen /vərza̱dəɣə(n)/ (verzadigde, heeft verzadigd) saturate

de **verzadiging** /vərza̱dəɣɪŋ/ satisfaction, saturation

het **verzadigingspunt** /vərza̱dəɣɪŋspʏnt/ saturation point

verzaken /vərza̱kə(n)/ (verzaakte, heeft verzaakt) **1** fail: *zijn **plicht** ~* neglect one's duty, fail in one's duty **2** revoke: *ze heeft verzaakt!* she revoked!

verzakken /vərzɑ̱kə(n)/ (verzakte, is verzakt) subside; settle; sink; sag: *de **grond** verzakt* the ground has subsided (or: is subsiding)

de **verzakking** /vərzɑ̱kɪŋ/ (pl: -en) subsidence, collapse

de **verzamelaar** /vərza̱məlar/ (pl: -s) collector

de **verzamel-cd** /vərza̱məlsede/ compilation CD

¹**verzamelen** /vərza̱mələ(n)/ (verzamelde, heeft verzameld) gather (together), assemble; meet: *zich ~* gather, assemble; congregate; *we verzamelen (ons) **op** het plein* we assembled (or: met) in the square

²**verzamelen** /vərza̱mələ(n)/ (verzamelde, heeft verzameld) **1** collect; gather; compile: *krachten ~* summon up (one's) strength; *de verzamelde **werken** van ...* the collected works of ... **2** collect, save

de **verzameling** /vərza̱məlɪŋ/ (pl: -en) **1** collection; gathering; assembly; compilation: *een **bonte** ~ aanhangers* a motley collection of followers; *een ~ **aanleggen*** build up (or: put together) a collection **2** [maths] set

de **verzamelnaam** /vərza̱məlnam/ (pl: -namen) collective term, generic term, umbrella term

de **verzamelplaats** /vərza̱məlplats/ (pl: -en) meeting place (or: point); assembly point

de **verzamelstaat** /vərza̱məlstat/ (pl: -staten) summary (list, table)

de **verzamelwoede** /vərza̱məlwudə/ mania for collecting things

verzanden /vərza̱ndə(n)/ (verzandde, is verzand) get bogged down

verzegelen /vərze̱ɣələ(n)/ (verzegelde, heeft verzegeld) seal, put (or: set) a seal on: *een **woning** ~* put a house under seal

de **verzegeling** /vərze̱ɣəlɪŋ/ (pl: -en) sealing, seal: *een ~ **aanbrengen** (or: **verbreken**)* affix (or: break) a seal

verzeild /vərzɛ̱ɪlt/ (adj): *hoe **kom** jij hier ~?* what brings you here?; *in moeilijkheden ~ **raken*** run into (or: hit) trouble, run into difficulties

de **verzekeraar** /vərze̱kərar/ (pl: -s) insurer; assurer

verzekerd /vərze̱kərt/ (adj) **1** assured (of), confident (of): *succes ~!* success guaranteed!; *u kunt ervan ~ **zijn** dat* you may rest assured that **2** insured: *het ~e **bedrag*** the sum insured

de **verzekerde** /vərze̱kərdə/ (pl: -n) policyholder; insured party, assured party

verzekeren /vərze̱kərə(n)/ (verzekerde, heeft verzekerd) **1** ensure; assure: *iem. **van** iets ~* assure s.o. of sth. **2** guarantee, assure **3** insure; assure: *zich ~ (tegen)* insure o.s. (against)

de **verzekering** /vərze̱kərɪŋ/ (pl: -en) **1** assurance, guarantee: *ik kan u de ~ **geven**, dat ...* I can give you an assurance that ... **2** insurance; assurance: *sociale ~* national insurance, social security; *een ~ **aangaan** (afsluiten)* take out insurance (or: an insurance policy) **3** insurance company, assurance company

de **verzekeringsagent** /vərze̱kərɪŋsaɣɛnt/ (pl: -en) insurance agent

de **verzekeringsmaatschappij** /vərze̱-

kərɪŋsmatsχɑrɛi/ (pl: -en) insurance company, assurance company

de **verzekeringspolis** /vərzɛkərɪŋspolɪs/ (pl: -sen) insurance policy

de **verzekeringspremie** /vərzɛkərɪŋspremi/ (pl: -s) insurance premium

de **verzekeringsvoorwaarden** (pl) policy conditions

verzelfstandigen /vərzɛlfstɑndəyə(n)/ (verzelfstandigde, heeft verzelfstandigd) make independent; privatize

verzenden /vərzɛndə(n)/ (verzond, heeft verzonden) send, mail, dispatch; [goods] ship: *per schip* ~ ship

de **verzender** /vərzɛndər/ (pl: -s) sender, shipper, consignor

de **verzending** /vərzɛndɪŋ/ (pl: -en) dispatch, mailing, shipping, forwarding

de **verzendkosten** /vərzɛntkostə(n)/ (pl) shipping (or: mailing, postage) costs

verzengen /vərzɛŋə(n)/ (verzengde, heeft/is verzengd) scorch: *een ~de hitte* a blistering heat

het **verzet** /vərzɛt/ resistance: *in* ~ *komen (tegen)* offer resistance (to); *in het* ~ *gaan* enter the resistance

het **verzetje** /vərzɛcə/ (pl: -s) diversion, distraction: *hij heeft een* ~ *nodig* he needs a bit of variety (or: a break)

de **verzetsbeweging** /vərzɛtsbəweyɪŋ/ (pl: -en) resistance (movement), underground

de **verzetsstrijder** /vərzɛtstrɛidər/ (pl: -s) resistance fighter, member of the resistance (or: underground)

¹**verzetten** /vərzɛtə(n)/ (verzette, heeft verzet) move (around), shift: *een vergadering* ~ put off (or: reschedule) a meeting; *heel wat werk* ~ be able to take on (or: do, shift) a lot of work

zich ²**verzetten** /vərzɛtə(n)/ (verzette zich, heeft zich verzet) resist, offer resistance (or: opposition): *bij zijn arrestatie verzette hij zich* he resisted when they tried to arrest him

verzieken /vərzikə(n)/ (verziekte, heeft verziekt) spoil, ruin: *de sfeer* ~ spoil the atmosphere

verziend /vɛrzint/ (adj) long-sighted

de **verziendheid** /vɛrzinthɛit/ long-sightedness

de **verzilting** /vərzɪltɪŋ/ salinization, salinity

verzilveren /vərzɪlvərə(n)/ (verzilverde, heeft verzilverd) **1** (plate with) silver, silverplate: *verzilverde lepels* plate(d) spoons **2** cash, convert into (or: redeem for) cash

verzinken /vərzɪŋkə(n)/ (verzonk, is verzonken) sink (down, away), submerge: *in gedachten verzonken zijn* be lost (or: deep) in thought

verzinnen /vərzɪnə(n)/ (verzon, heeft verzonnen) invent, think/make (or: dream, cook) up, devise: *een smoesje* ~ think up (or:

cook up) an excuse

het **verzinsel** /vərzɪnsəl/ (pl: -s) fabrication, invention, figment of one's imagination

verzitten /vərzɪtə(n)/: *gaan* ~ change seats

het **verzoek** /vərzuk/ (pl: -en) **1** request, appeal, petition: *dringend* ~ urgent request, entreaty; *aan een* ~ *voldoen* comply with a request; *op* ~ *van mijn broer* at my brother's request; *vriendelijk* ~ *om ...* you are kindly requested to ..., we kindly request you to ... **2** petition, appeal: *een* ~ *indienen* petition, appeal, make a petition (or: an appeal)

verzoeken /vərzukə(n)/ (verzocht, heeft verzocht) request; petition; ask, beg: *mag ik om stilte* ~ silence please, may I have a moment's silence

de **verzoeking** /vərzukɪŋ/ (pl: -en) temptation

het **verzoeknummer** /vərzuknʏmər/ (pl: -s) request

het **verzoekschrift** /vərzuksχrɪft/ (pl: -en) petition, appeal

verzoenen /vərzunə(n)/ (verzoende, heeft verzoend) reconcile, appease: *zich met iem.* ~ become reconciled with s.o.

verzoenend /vərzunənt/ (adj, adv) conciliatory, expiatory

de **verzoening** /vərzunɪŋ/ (pl: -en) reconciliation

verzorgd /vərzɔrχt/ (adj) well cared-for, carefully kept (or: tended): *een goed* ~ *gazon* a well-tended lawn; *er* ~ *uitzien* be well dressed (or: groomed)

verzorgen /vərzɔryə(n)/ (verzorgde, heeft verzorgd) look after, (at)tend to, care for: *tot in de puntjes verzorgd* taken care of down to the last detail

de **verzorgende** /vərzɔryəndə/ care giver, carer

de **verzorger** /vərzɔryər/ (pl: -s) attendant, caretaker: *ouders, voogden of ~s* parents or guardians

de **verzorging** /vərzɔryɪŋ/ care, maintenance, nursing: *medische* ~ medical care

de **verzorgingsflat** /vərzɔryɪŋsflɛt/ (pl: -s) warden-assisted flat; [Am] retirement home with nursing care

de **verzorgingsstaat** /vərzɔryɪŋstat/ welfare state

het **verzorgingstehuis** /vərzɔryɪŋstəhœys/ (pl: -tehuizen) home; home for the elderly; old people's home, rest home

verzot /vərzɔt/ (adj) crazy (about), mad (about, for): *ik ben* ~ *op kersen* I love cherries, I adore cherries

verzuchten /vərzʏχtə(n)/ (verzuchtte, heeft verzucht) sigh

het **verzuim** /vərzœym/ (pl: -en) omission; nonattendance; absence: ~ *wegens ziekte* absence due to illness

verzuimen /vərzœymə(n)/ (verzuimde, heeft verzuimd) **1** omit; neglect; fail: *zijn* *plicht* ~ neglect one's duty; ~ *te betalen* not pay **2** be absent, fail to attend: *een les* ~ cut (*or:* skip) (a) class

verzuipen /vərz<u>œy</u>pə(n)/ (verzoop, is verzopen) [inform] **1** drown, be drowned **2** be flooded

verzuren /vərz<u>y</u>rə(n)/ (verzuurde, is verzuurd) sour, turn sour, go sour; go off; acidify: *verzuurde* **grond** acid soil

verzwakken /vərzw<u>a</u>kə(n)/ (verzwakte, heeft/is verzwakt) weaken, grow weak; enfeeble; impair

verzwaren /vərzw<u>a</u>rə(n)/ (verzwaarde, heeft verzwaard) make heavier; [fig also] increase; strengthen: *de dijken* ~ strengthen the dykes; *exameneisen* ~ make an examination stiffer

verzwarend /vərzw<u>a</u>rənt/ (adj) aggravating: *diefstal met* ~*e* **omstandigheden** aggravated theft

verzwelgen /vərzw<u>ɛ</u>lɣə(n)/ (verzwolg/verzwelgde, heeft verzwolgen) devour; engulf

verzwijgen /vərzw<u>ɛi</u>ɣə(n)/ (verzweeg, heeft verzwegen) keep silent about; withhold; suppress; conceal: *iets voor iem.* ~ keep (*or:* conceal) sth. from s.o.; *een schandaal* ~ hush up a scandal

verzwikken /vərzw<u>ɪ</u>kə(n)/ (verzwikte, heeft verzwikt) sprain, twist: *zijn* **enkel** ~ sprain one's ankle

het **vest** /vɛst/ (pl: -en) waistcoat, vest; cardigan: *een pak met* ~ a three-piece suit

de **vestiaire** /vɛstij<u>ɛ:</u>rə/ (pl: -s) cloakroom

de **vestibule** /vɛstib<u>y</u>lə/ (pl: -s) hall(way), entrance hall, vestibule

¹**vestigen** /vɛst<u>ə</u>ɣə(n)/ (vestigde, heeft gevestigd) direct, focus: *ik heb mijn hoop* **op** *jou gevestigd* I'm putting (all) my hopes in you; *zijn* **naam** ~ make one's name

zich ²**vestigen** /vɛst<u>ə</u>ɣə(n)/ (vestigde zich, heeft zich gevestigd) settle: *zich ergens* ~ establish o.s., settle somewhere

de **vestiging** /vɛst<u>ə</u>ɣɪŋ/ (pl: -en) branch, office; outlet

de **vestigingsplaats** /vɛst<u>ə</u>ɣɪŋsplats/ (pl: -en) place of business, registered office, seat; [pers] place of residence

de **vesting** /vɛstɪŋ/ (pl: -en) fortress, fort, stronghold

het **vestingwerk** /vɛstɪŋwɛrk/ (pl: -en) fortification

de **vestzak** /vɛ(st)sak/ (pl: -ken) waistcoat pocket, watch pocket: [fig] *dat is* **vestzakbroekzak** that's just a shifting of funds

het ¹**vet** /vɛt/ (pl: -ten) fat; oil; grease; dripping; lard: *iets in het* ~ *zetten* grease sth.

²**vet** /vɛt/ (adj, adv) **1** fat; rich; creamy **2** fatty, greasy, rich **3** fat; plum(my): *een* ~*te* **buit** rich spoils **4** greasy, oily: *een* ~*te* **huid** a greasy (*or:* an oily) skin **5** bold: ~*te* **letters** bold (*or:* heavy) type, boldface; ~ *gedrukt* in bold (*or:*

heavy) type ‖ ~*te* **pech** tough luck; ~ *saai* really boring, mega boring

vetarm /vɛt<u>a</u>rm/ (adj) low-fat

de **vete** /v<u>e</u>tə/ (pl: -s) feud, vendetta

de **veter** /v<u>e</u>tər/ (pl: -s) lace: *zijn* ~*s* **vastmaken** (*strikken*) do up (*or:* tie) one's shoelaces; *je* ~ *zit los!* your shoelace is undone!

de **veteraan** /vetər<u>a</u>n/ (pl: veteranen) veteran

de **veteranenziekte** /vetər<u>a</u>nə(n)zɪktə/ Legionnaire's disease

de ¹**veterinair** /vetərin<u>ɛ:</u>r/ (pl: -s) veterinary surgeon

²**veterinair** /vetərin<u>ɛ:</u>r/ (adj) veterinary

het **vetgehalte** /v<u>ɛ</u>tχəhaltə/ (pl: -s, -n) fat content, percentage of fat

de **vetkuif** /v<u>ɛ</u>tkœyf/ (pl: vetkuiven) greased quiff

vetmesten /v<u>ɛ</u>tmɛstə(n)/ (mestte vet, heeft vetgemest) fatten (up), feed up

het **veto** /v<u>e</u>to/ (pl: -'s) veto: *het recht van* ~ *hebben* have the right (*or:* power) of veto; *zijn* ~ *over iets* **uitspreken** veto sth., exercise one's veto against sth.

het **vetoogje** /v<u>ɛ</u>toxjə/ (pl: -s) drop of fat, fat globule

het **vetorecht** /v<u>e</u>torɛχt/ veto

de **vetplant** /v<u>ɛ</u>tplant/ (pl: -en) succulent

de **vetpot** /v<u>ɛ</u>tpɔt/: *dat is geen* ~ you won't exactly make a fortune

de **vetrol** /v<u>ɛ</u>trɔl/ (pl: -len) roll of fat; [hum] spare tyre

vettig /v<u>ɛ</u>təχ/ (adj, adv) **1** fatty; greasy: *een* ~*e* **glans** an oily sheen **2** greasy; oily

de **vetvlek** /v<u>ɛ</u>tflɛk/ (pl: -ken) grease stain, greasy spot (*or:* mark): *vol* ~*ken* greasestained

vetvrij /vɛtfr<u>ɛi</u>/ (adj) **1** greaseproof: ~ *papier* greaseproof paper **2** fat-free, non-fat

de **vetzak** /v<u>ɛ</u>tsak/ (pl: -ken) fatso, fatty

de **vetzucht** /v<u>ɛ</u>tsʏχt/ fatty degeneration, (morbid) obesity

het **vetzuur** /v<u>ɛ</u>tsyr/ (pl: -zuren) fatty acid

het **veulen** /v<u>ø</u>lə(n)/ (pl: -s) foal; colt; filly

de **vezel** /v<u>e</u>zəl/ (pl: -s) fibre; thread; filament: [fig] *tot in zijn (diepste)* ~*s* through and through, to the core

vezelrijk /v<u>e</u>zəlrɛik/ (adj) high-fibre

vgl. *vergelijk* cf., cp.

de **V-hals** /v<u>e</u>hals/ (pl: V-halzen) V-neck

via /v<u>i</u>ja/ (prep) via, by way of, by, through; by means of: ~ *de* **snelweg** *komen* take the motorway; [Am] take the expressway; *ik hoorde* ~ *mijn* **zuster***, dat …* I heard from (*or:* through) my sister that …; *iets* ~ ~ *horen* learn (*or:* hear) of sth. in a roundabout way, hear sth. on the grapevine

het **viaduct** /vijad<u>ʏ</u>kt/ (pl: -en) viaduct, flyover, crossover; [Am] overpass

de **viagra** /vij<u>a</u>ɡra/ viagra

de **vibrafoon** /vibraf<u>o</u>n/ (pl: -s) vibraphone, vibes

de **vibratie** /vibra̱(t)si/ (pl: -s) vibration
de **vibrator** /vibra̱tor/ (pl: -s) vibrator
vibreren /vibre̱rə(n)/ (vibreerde, heeft gevibreerd) vibrate
de **vicaris** /vika̱rəs/ (pl: -sen) vicar
de **vicepremier** /vi̱səprəmje/ vice-premier
de **vicepresident** /vi̱səprezidɛnt/ vice-president; vice-chairman
vice versa /visəvɛ̱rza/ (adv) vice versa
de **vicevoorzitter** /vi̱səvorzɪtər/ vice-chairman, deputy chairman
vicieus /visijø̱s/ (adj) vicious
victoriaans /vɪktorija̱ns/ (adj) Victorian
de **victorie** /vɪkto̱ri/ (pl: -s) victory: ~ *kraaien* shout victory
de **video** /vi̱dejo/ (pl: -'s) video (tape, recorder): *iets op* ~ *zetten* record sth. on video
de **videoband** /vi̱dejobɑnt/ (pl: -en) videotape
de **videobewaking** /vi̱dejobəwakɪŋ/ closed circuit TV
de **videocamera** /vi̱dejokaməra/ (pl: -'s) video camera
de **videocassette** /vi̱dejokɑsɛtə/ (pl: -s) video cassette
videochatten /vi̱dejotʃɛtə(n)/ videochatting
de **videoclip** /vi̱dejoklɪp/ (pl: -s) videoclip
de **videofilm** /vi̱dejofɪlm/ (pl: -s) video (film, recording)
de **videojockey** /vi̱dejodʒɔki/ (pl: -s) videojockey
de **videorecorder** /vi̱dejorikɔːrdər/ (pl: -s) video (recorder), VCR, video cassette recorder
de **videoscheidsrechter** /vi̱dejosχɛɪtsrɛχtər/ (pl: -s) [socc] video assistant referee *(VAR)*; [tennis] video umpire
het **videospel** /vi̱dejospɛl/ (pl: -en) video game
de **videotheek** /videjote̱k/ (pl: videotheken) video shop
vief /vif/ (adj, adv) lively, energetic
vier /vir/ (num) four; [in dates] fourth: ~ *mei* the fourth of May; *een gesprek onder* ~ *ogen* a private conversation, a tête-à-tête; *zo zeker als tweemaal twee* ~ *is* as sure as I'm standing here; *half* ~ half past three; *ze waren met z'n* ~*en* there were four of them; *hij kreeg een* ~ *voor wiskunde* he got four out of ten for maths
de **vierbaansweg** /vi̱rbɑnswɛχ/ (pl: -en) four-lane motorway; dual carriageway; [Am] divided highway
vierde /vi̱rdə/ (num) fourth: *de* ~ *klas* the fourth form; [Am] the fourth grade; *ten* ~ fourthly, in the fourth place; *het is vandaag de* ~ today is the fourth; *drie* ~ three fourths, three-quarters; *als* ~ *eindigen* come in fourth
vierdelig /vi̱rdeləχ/ (adj) four-part; four-piece
vieren /vi̱rə(n)/ (vierde, heeft gevierd) **1** celebrate; observe; commemorate: *dat gaan we* ~ this calls for a celebration **2** pay

out, slacken: *een touw (laten)* ~ pay out a rope
de **vierhoek** /vi̱rhuk/ (pl: -en) quadrangle, rectangle, square
de **viering** /vi̱rɪŋ/ (pl: -en) celebration; observance; commemoration; [rel] service: *ter* ~ *van* in celebration of
vierjarig /vi̱rjarəχ/ (adj) four-year-old; four-year('s); four-yearly
het **¹vierkant** /vi̱rkɑnt/ (pl: -en) square; quadrangle
²vierkant /vi̱rkɑnt/ (adj) square: *de kamer meet drie meter in het* ~ the room is three metres square, the room is three by three (metres) ‖ *iem.* ~ *uitlachen* laugh at s.o. outright
de **vierkwartsmaat** /vi̱rkwɑrtsmat/ (pl: -maten) four-four time, quadruple time, common time (*or:* measure)
de **vierling** /vi̱rlɪŋ/ (pl: -en) quadruplets, quads
viermaal /vi̱rmal/ (adv) four times
het **vierspan** /vi̱rspɑn/ (pl: -nen) four-in-hand
de **viersprong** /vi̱rsprɔŋ/ (pl: -en) crossroads
het **viertal** /vi̱rtal/ (pl: -len) (set of) four; foursome
het **vieruurtje** /vi̱ryrcə/ (pl: -s) [Belg] tea break, mid-afternoon snack
de **viervoeter** /vi̱rvutər/ (pl: -s) quadruped, four-footed animal
het **viervoud** /vi̱rvɑut/ (pl: -en) quadruple
de **vierwielaandrijving** /vi̱rwilandrɛivɪŋ/ four-wheel drive
vies /vis/ (adj, adv) **1** dirty, filthy **2** nasty, foul: *een* ~ *drankje* a nasty (*or:* vile) mixture ‖ *bij een* ~ *zaakje betrokken zijn* be involved in dirty (*or:* funny) business; *ergens niet* ~ *van zijn* not be averse to sth.; *die film viel* ~ *tegen* that film was a real let-down
de **viespeuk** /vi̱spøk/ (pl: -en) pig: *een oude* ~ a dirty old man
Vietnam /vjɛtnɑm/ Vietnam
de **Vietnamees** /vjɛtname̱s/ (pl: Vietnamezen) Vietnamese
de **viewer** /vju̱wər/ (pl: -s) viewer
de **viezerik** /vi̱zərɪk/ (pl: -en) pig, slob, dirty sod
de **viezigheid** /vi̱zəχhɛit/ dirt, grime
het **vignet** /vɪɲɛ̱t/ (pl: -ten) **1** device, logo, emblem **2** sticker
de **vijand** /vɛi̱ɑnt/ (pl: -en) enemy: *dat zou je je ergste* ~ *nog niet toewensen* you wouldn't wish that on your worst enemy; *gezworen* ~*en* sworn (*or:* mortal) enemies
vijandelijk /vɛiɑ̱ndələk/ (adj, adv) enemy, hostile
de **vijandelijkheid** /vɛiɑ̱ndələkhɛit/ (pl: -heden) hostility, act of war
vijandig /vɛiɑ̱ndəχ/ (adj, adv) hostile, inimical: *een* ~*e daad* a hostile act; *iem.* ~ *gezind zijn* be hostile towards s.o.
de **vijandigheid** /vɛiɑ̱ndəχhɛit/ hostility, animosity, enmity
de **vijandschap** /vɛi̱ɑntsχɑp/ (pl: -pen) enmity,

hostility, animosity: *in ~ leven* be at odds (with)

vijf /vɛif/ (num) five; [in dates] fifth: *~ juni* the fifth of June; *om de ~ minuten* every five minutes; *het is over vijven* it is past (*or:* gone) five; *een stuk of ~* about five, five or so, five-odd; *een briefje van ~* a five-pound note || *na veel vijven en zessen* after a great deal of shilly-shallying

vijfde /vɛivdə/ (num) fifth: *auto met ~ deur* hatchback; *ten ~* fifthly, in the fifth place; *als ~ eindigen* come in fifth

de **vijfenzestigpluskaart** /vɛifə(n)sɛstəxplʏskɑrt/ (pl: -en) senior citizen's ticket (*or:* pass)

de **vijfenzestigplusser** /vɛifə(n)sɛstəxplʏsər/ (pl: -s) senior citizen, pensioner

de **vijfhoek** /vɛifhuk/ (pl: -en) pentagon

het **vijfjarenplan** /vɛifjarə(n)plɑn/ (pl: -nen) five-year plan

vijfjarig /vɛifjarəx/ (adj) five-year-old; five-year('s'); five-yearly

de **vijfling** /vɛiflɪŋ/ (pl: -en) quintuplets, quins: *zij kreeg een ~* she had quintuplets (*or:* quins)

het **vijftal** /vɛiftɑl/ (pl: -len) (set of) five: *een ~ jaren* (about) five years, five (or so) years; *een vrolijk ~* a merry fivesome

vijftien /vɛiftin/ (num) fifteen; [in dates] fifteenth: *~ maart* the fifteenth of March; *rugnummer ~* number fifteen; *een man of ~* about fifteen people, fifteen or so people

vijftig /fɛiftəx/ (num) fifty: *de jaren ~* the fifties; *hij is in de ~* he is in his fifties; *tegen de ~ lopen* be getting on for (*or:* be pushing) fifty

de **vijftiger** /fɛiftəɣər/ (pl: -s) s.o. in his fifties

de **vijg** /vɛix/ fig (tree) || [Belg] *dat zijn ~en na Pasen* that is (*or:* comes) too late to be of use

het **vijgenblad** /vɛiɣə(n)blɑt/ (pl: -eren, -en) fig leaf

de **vijgenboom** /vɛiɣə(n)bom/ (pl: -bomen) fig (tree)

de **vijl** /vɛil/ (pl: -en) file

vijlen /vɛilə(n)/ (vijlde, heeft gevijld) file

de **vijs** /vɛis/ (pl: vijzen) [Belg] screw

de **vijver** /vɛivər/ (pl: -s) pond

de **vijzel** /vɛizəl/ **1** jack **2** Archimedean screw

de **Viking** /vikɪŋ/ (pl: -en) Viking

het **Vikingschip** /vikɪŋsxɪp/ (pl: -schepen) Viking ship

de **villa** /vila/ (pl: -'s) villa: *halve ~* semi-detached house

de **villawijk** /vilawɛik/ (pl: -en) (exclusive) residential area

villen /vɪlə(n)/ (vilde, heeft gevild) skin, flay

het **vilt** /vɪlt/ felt

vilten /vɪltə(n)/ (adj) felt

het **viltje** /vɪlcə/ (pl: -s) beer mat

de **viltstift** /vɪltstɪft/ (pl: -en) felt-tip (pen)

de **vin** /vɪn/ (pl: -nen) **1** fin; flipper: *geen ~ verroeren* not raise (*or:* lift) a finger, not move a

muscle **2** fin; vane

vinden /vɪndə(n)/ (vond, heeft gevonden) **1** find, discover, come across; strike: *dat boek is nergens te ~* that book is nowhere to be found; *ergens voor te ~ zijn* be (very) ready to do sth., be game for sth.; *iem. (iets) toevallig ~* happen (*or:* chance) upon s.o. (sth.) **2** find, think of **3** think, find: *ik vind het vandaag koud* I think it's (*or:* I find it) cold today; *ik zou het prettig ~ als …* I'd appreciate it if …; *hoe vind je dat?* what do you think of that?; *zou je het erg ~ als …?* would you mind if …?; *ik vind het goed* that's fine by me, it suits me fine; *vind je ook niet?* don't you agree?; *daar vind ik niets aan* it doesn't do a thing for me || *het met iem. kunnen ~* get on (*or:* along) with s.o.; *zich ergens in kunnen ~* agree with sth.; *zij hebben elkaar gevonden* **a)** they have come to terms (over it); **b)** they have found each other

de **vinder** /vɪndər/ (pl: -s) finder, discoverer

de **vind-ik-leuk** /vɪntɪkløk/ (pl: -s) [media] like

de **vind-ik-niet-leuk** /vɪntɪknitløk/ (pl: -s) [media] dislike

de **vinding** /vɪndɪŋ/ (pl: -en) idea, invention

vindingrijk /vɪndɪŋrɛik/ (adj) ingenious, inventive: *een ~e geest* a fertile (*or:* creative) mind

de **vindingrijkheid** /vɪndɪŋrɛikhɛit/ ingenuity, inventiveness, resourcefulness

de **vindplaats** /vɪntplats/ (pl: -en) place where sth. is found, site, location

de **vinger** /vɪŋər/ (pl: -s) finger: *groene ~s hebben* have green fingers; [Am] have a green thumb; *lange ~s hebben* have sticky fingers; *met een natte ~* roughly, approximately; *als je hem een ~ geeft,* neemt hij de hele hand give him an inch and he'll take a mile; *hij heeft zich in de ~s gesneden* [fig] he got (his fingers) burned; *de ~ opsteken* put up (*or:* raise) one's hand; *iets door de ~s zien* turn a blind eye to sth., overlook sth.; *iets in de ~s hebben* be a natural at sth.; *een ~ in de pap hebben* have a finger in the pie; *met de ~s knippen* snap one's fingers; *hij had haar nog met geen ~ aangeraakt* he hadn't put (*or:* laid) a finger on her; *op de ~s van één hand te tellen zijn* be few and far between; *iem. op de ~s tikken* rap s.o. over the knuckles; *iem. op zijn ~s kijken* breathe down s.o.'s neck; *dat had je op je ~s kunnen natellen* that was to be expected

de **vingerafdruk** /vɪŋərɑvdrʏk/ (pl: -ken) fingerprint: *~ken nemen (van)* fingerprint s.o., take s.o.'s fingerprints

de **vingerhoed** /vɪŋərhut/ (pl: -en) thimble

de **vingertop** /vɪŋərtɔp/ (pl: -pen) fingertip

de **vingerverf** /vɪŋərvɛrf/ finger paint

vingervlug /vɪŋərvlʏx/ (adj) sticky-fingered

de **vingerwijzing** /vɪŋərwɛizɪŋ/ (pl: -en) hint, clue

de **vingerzetting** /vɪŋərzɛtɪŋ/ (pl: -en) fingering

de **vink** /vɪŋk/ (pl: -en) **1** finch; chaffinch
2 check (mark), tick

vinnig /vɪnəχ/ (adj, adv) sharp, caustic

vintage /vɪntɪtʃ/ (adj) vintage, antique: ~ *kleding* vintage clothing, antique fashion

het **vinyl** /vinil/ vinyl

violet /vijolɛt/ (adj) violet

de **violist** /vijolɪst/ (pl: -en) violinist

de **viool** /vijol/ (pl: violen) violin, fiddle: *(op de)* ~ *spelen* play the violin (*or:* fiddle); *eerste* ~ first violin; *hij speelt de eerste* ~ he is (*or:* plays) first fiddle

het **vioolconcert** /vijolkɔnsɛrt/ (pl: -en) violin concerto

de **vioolsleutel** /vijolsløtəl/ G clef, violin clef

het **viooltje** /vijolcə/ (pl: -s) violet: *Kaaps* ~ African violet

de **vip** /vɪp/ (pl: -s) VIP

viraal /viral/ (adj) viral: *een virale infectie* a viral infection, a virusinfection; ~ *gaan* go viral, break the Internet

viral /vɑjrəl/ (adj): ~ *gaan* go viral, break the Internet

viriel /viril/ (adj) virile

de **viroloog** /viroloχ/ (pl: -logen) virologist

virtueel /vɪrtywel/ (adj, adv) virtual, potential: *een* ~ *winkelcentrum* a virtual shopping centre

virtuoos /vɪrtywos/ (adj, adv) virtuoso

de **virtuositeit** /vɪrtywozitɛit/ virtuosity

virulent /virylɛnt/ (adj) virulent

het **virus** /virʏs/ (pl: -sen) virus

de **virusinfectie** /virʏsɪnfɛksi/ (pl: -s) virus infection, viral infection

de **virusscan** /virʏskɛn/ (pl: -s) virus scan

de **virusscanner** /virʏskɛnər/ (pl: -s) virus scanner

de **virusziekte** /virʏsiktə/ (pl: -n, -s) viral disease

de **vis** /vɪs/ (pl: -sen) fish: *een mand* ~ a basket of fish; *er zit hier veel* ~ the fishing's good here; *zo gezond als een* ~ fit as a fiddle; *zich voelen als een* ~ *in het water* feel like a fish in water; *zich voelen als een* ~ *op het droge* feel like a fish out of water; *vette* ~ oily fish

de **Vis** /vɪs/ (pl: -sen) Pisces, Piscean

de **visagist** /vizaʒɪst/ (pl: -en) cosmetician, beauty specialist, beautician

de **visakte** /vɪsɑktə/ (pl: -n, -s) [Dutch] fishing licence

de **visboer** /vɪzbur/ (pl: -en) fishmonger

viseren /vizerə(n)/ (viseerde, heeft geviseerd) **1** aim at, have in view **2** [Belg] criticise

de **visgraat** /vɪsχrat/ (pl: visgraten) fish bone

de **vishandel** /vɪshɑndəl/ fish trade; fish shop; [Am] fish dealer

de **visie** /vizi/ (pl: -s) view, outlook, point of view: *een man met* ~ a man of vision

het **visioen** /vizjun/ (pl: -en) vision: *een* ~ *hebben* see (*or:* have) a vision

de ¹**visionair** /viʒonɛːr/ (pl: -s) visionary

²**visionair** /viʒonɛːr/ (adj) visionary

de **visitatie** /vizita(t)si/ (pl: -s) **1** search **2** visitation

de **visite** /vizitə/ (pl: -s) **1** visit; call: *bij iem. op* ~ *gaan* pay s.o. a visit, call on s.o., visit **2** visitors, guests, company

het **visitekaartje** /vizitəkarcə/ (pl: -s) visiting card; (business) card: *zijn* ~ *achterlaten* make one's mark, establish one's presence

visiteren /viziterə(n)/ (visiteerde, heeft gevisiteerd) examine, inspect; search

de **viskom** /vɪskɔm/ (pl: -men) fishbowl

de **vismarkt** /vɪsmɑrkt/ (pl: -en) fish market

het **visnet** /vɪsnɛt/ (pl: -ten) fish net, fishing net

de **visschotel** /vɪsχotəl/ (pl: -s) fish dish

vissen /vɪsə(n)/ (viste, heeft gevist) **1** fish; angle: *op haring* ~ fish for herring; *parels* ~ dive (*or:* fish) for pearls **2** drag, dredge ‖ *naar* een complimentje ~ fish (*or:* angle) for a compliment

de **Vissen** /vɪsə(n)/ (pl) [astrology] Pisces

de **visser** /vɪsər/ (pl: -s) fisherman; angler

de **visserij** /vɪsərɛi/ (pl: -en) fishing, fisheries, fishery

de **vissersboot** /vɪsərzbot/ (pl: -boten) fishing boat

de **vissersvloot** /vɪsərsflot/ fishing fleet

de **vissoep** /vɪsup/ fish soup

de **visstand** /vɪstɑnt/ fish stock

de **visstick** /vɪstɪk/ (pl: -s) fish finger

visualiseren /vizywalizerə(n)/ (visualiseerde, heeft gevisualiseerd) visualize

visueel /vizywel/ (adj, adv) visual: ~ *gehandicapt* visually handicapped

het **visum** /vizʏm/ (pl: visa) visa: *een* ~ *aanvragen* apply for a visa

de **visumplicht** /vizʏmplɪχt/ visa requirement

de **visvangst** /vɪsfɑŋst/ fishing, catching of fish: *van de* ~ *leven* fish for one's living

de **visvergunning** /vɪsfərɣʏnɪŋ/ (pl: -en) fishing licence (*or:* permit)

de **visvijver** /vɪsfɛivər/ (pl: -s) fishpond

het **viswater** /vɪswatər/ (pl: -s, -en) fishing ground(s)

het **viswijf** /vɪswɛif/ (pl: -wijven) [offensive] fishwife

de **viswinkel** /vɪswɪŋkəl/ (pl: -s) fish shop, fishmonger's (shop); [Am] fish dealer

vitaal /vital/ (adj) vital: *hij is nog erg* ~ *voor zijn leeftijd* he's still very active for his age

de **vitaliteit** /vitalitɛit/ vitality, vigour

de **vitamine** /vitaminə/ (pl: -s) vitamin: *rijk aan* ~ rich in vitamins, vitamin-rich

het **vitaminegebrek** /vitaminəɣəbrɛk/ lack (*or:* deficiency) of vitamins, vitamin deficiency

het/de **vitrage** /vitraʒə/ (pl: -s) net curtain

de **vitrine** /vitrinə/ (pl: -s) **1** (glass, display) case, showcase **2** shop window, show window

vitten /vɪtə(n)/ (vitte, heeft gevist) find fault,

carp

de **vivisectie** /vivisɛksi/ (pl: -s) vivisection

het **vizier** /vizi̯r/ (pl: -s) **1** sight: *iem. in het ~ krijgen* spot s.o., catch sight of s.o. **2** visor

de **vj** /vi̯dʒe/ (pl: vj's) VJ, veejay

de **vla** /vla/ (pl: -'s) **1** [roughly] custard **2** flan; [Am] (open-faced) pie

de **vlaag** /vlax/ (pl: vlagen) **1** gust, squall **2** fit, flurry: *in een ~ van verstandsverbijstering* in a frenzy, in a fit of insanity; *bij vlagen* in fits and starts, in spurts (*or:* bursts)

de **vlaai** /vlaj/ (pl: -en) flan; [Am] (open-faced) pie

het **¹Vlaams** /vlams/ Flemish

   ²Vlaams /vlams/ (adj) Flemish ‖ *~e gaai* jay

de **Vlaamse** /vlamsə/ Flemish woman

   Vlaanderen /vlandərə(n)/ Flanders

de **vlag** /vlax/ (pl: -gen) flag; colours; ensign: *met ~ en wimpel slagen* pass with (*or:* come through with) flying colours; *de Britse ~* the Union Jack

   vlaggen /vlaɣə(n)/ (vlagde, heeft gevlagd) put out the flag

de **vlaggenmast** /vlaɣə(n)mɑst/ (pl: -en) flagpole, flagstaff

het **vlaggenschip** /vlaɣə(n)sxɪp/ (pl: -schepen) flagship

de **vlaggenstok** /vlaɣə(n)stɔk/ (pl: -ken) flagpole, flagstaff

het **¹vlak** /vlɑk/ (pl: -ken) **1** surface, face; facet: *het voorste* (*or: achterste*) *~* the front (*or:* rear) face **2** sphere, area, field: *op het menselijke ~* in the human sphere

   ²vlak /vlɑk/ (adj) **1** flat, level, even: *iets ~ strijken* level off sth., level sth. out **2** flat, shallow

   ³vlak /vlɑk/ (adv) **1** flat **2** right, immediately, directly: *~ tegenover elkaar* right (*or:* straight) opposite each other **3** close: *~ achter je* right (*or:* just) behind you; *~ bij de school* close to the school, right by the school; *het is ~ bij* it's no distance at all; *het is hier ~ in de buurt* it's just round the corner; [Am] it's just around the corner; *het ligt ~ voor je neus* it is staring you in the face, it's right under your nose

   vlakaf /vlɑkɑf/ (adv) [Belg] plainly, bluntly

   vlakbij /vlɑgbɛi̯/ (adv) nearby: *ik woon hier ~* I live nearby (*or:* close by)

de **vlakgom** /vlɑkxɔm/ rubber, eraser

de **vlakte** /vlɑktə/ (pl: -n, -s) plain: *een golvende ~* a rolling plain; *zich op de ~ houden* not commit o.s., leave (*or:* keep) one's options open; *na twee klappen ging hij tegen de ~* a couple of blows laid him flat

de **vlaktemaat** /vlɑktəmat/ (pl: -maten) surface measurement

de **vlam** /vlɑm/ (pl: -men) **1** flame: *~ vatten* catch fire; burst into flames; *in ~men opgaan* go up in flames; *de ~ sloeg in de pan* **a)** the pan caught fire; **b)** [fig] the fat was in the fire **2** flame: *een oude ~* an old flame

de **Vlaming** /vlamɪŋ/ (pl: -en) Fleming

   vlammen /vlɑmə(n)/ (vlamde, heeft gevlamd) **1** flame **2** [sport] shine, kick ass: *morgen wil ik ~ op de 1500 meter* I plan to kick ass at the 1500m race tomorrow

   vlammend /vlɑmənt/ (adj) fiery, burning: *een ~ protest* a burning protest

de **vlammenwerper** /vlɑmə(n)wɛrpər/ (pl: -s) flame-thrower

de **vlammenzee** /vlɑmə(n)ze/ sea of flame(s)

de **vlamverdeler** /vlɑmvərdelər/ (pl: -s) stove mat

het **vlas** /vlɑs/ flax

   vlassen /vlɑsə(n)/ (vlaste, heeft gevlast) (+ op) be eager for

de **vlecht** /vlɛxt/ (pl: -en) braid, plait, tress: *een valse ~* a tress of false hair

   vlechten /vlɛxtə(n)/ (vlocht, heeft gevlochten) braid, plait, twine

het **vlechtwerk** /vlɛxtwɛrk/ plaiting

de **vleermuis** /vlermœys/ (pl: -muizen) bat

het **vlees** /vles/ **1** flesh; meat: *dat is ~ noch vis* that is neither fish, flesh, nor good red herring; *in eigen ~ snijden* queer one's own pitch; *mijn eigen ~ en bloed* my own flesh and blood; *gebraden ~* roast meat **2** flesh, pulp

de **vleesboom** /vlezbom/ (pl: -bomen) myoma, fibroid

   vleesetend /vlesetənt/ (adj) carnivorous

de **vleeseter** /vlesetər/ (pl: -s) meat-eater; carnivore

   vleesgeworden /vlesxəwordə(n)/ (adj) the incarnation of

het **vleesmes** /vlesmɛs/ (pl: -sen) carving knife

de **vleesschotel** /vlesxotəl/ (pl: -s) meat course (*or:* dish)

de **vleestomaat** /vlestomat/ (pl: -tomaten) beefsteak tomato

de **vleesvork** /vlesfɔrk/ (pl: -en) carving fork

de **vleeswaren** /vleswarə(n)/ (pl) meat products, meats: *fijne ~* (assorted) sliced cold meat; cold cuts

de **vleeswond** /vleswɔnt/ (pl: -en) flesh wound

de **vleet** /vlet/: *hij heeft boeken bij de ~* he has (got) lots of books

de **vlegel** /vleɣəl/ (pl: -s) brat, lout

   vleien /vlɛiə(n)/ (vleide, heeft gevleid) flatter, butter up: *ik voelde me gevleid door haar antwoord* I was (*or:* felt) flattered by her answer

   vleiend /vlɛiənt/ (adj, adv) flattering, coaxing

de **vleierij** /vlɛiərɛi̯/ (pl: -en) flattery: *met ~ kom je nergens* flattery will get you nowhere

de **vlek** /vlɛk/ (pl: -ken) **1** spot, mark, stain; blemish; blotch: *die ~ gaat er in de was wel uit* that spot will come out in the wash **2** [fig] blot, blemish ‖ *blinde ~ (in het oog)* blind spot (in the eye); [fig] *een blinde ~ voor iets hebben* have a blind spot for sth.

vlekkeloos /vlɛ̱kəlos/ (adj) spotless, immaculate

vlekken /vlɛ̱kə(n)/ (vlekte, heeft gevlekt) spot, stain

de **vlerk** /vlɛrk/ boor, lout

de **vleugel** /vlø̱ɣəl/ (pl: -s) **1** wing: *zijn ~s uitslaan* [also fig] spread (*or:* stretch) one's wings; [sport] *over de ~s spelen* play up and down the wings **2** grand piano

vleugellam /vlø̱ɣəlɑm/ (adj) broken-winged: *iem. ~ maken* paralyze s.o., render s.o. powerless

de **vleugelmoer** /vlø̱ɣəlmur/ (pl: -en) wing nut, butterfly nut

de **vleugelspeler** /vlø̱ɣəlspelər/ (pl: -s) [sport] (left, right) winger

het **vleugje** /vlø̱xjə/ (pl: -s) breath, touch: *een ~ ironie* a tinge of irony; *een ~ romantiek* a romantic touch

vlezig /vle̱zəx/ (adj) **1** fleshy **2** plump

de **vlieg** /vlix/ (pl: -en) fly: *twee ~en in één klap (slaan)* kill two birds with one stone; *hij doet geen ~ kwaad* he wouldn't harm (*or:* hurt) a fly

de **vliegangst** /vli̱xɑŋst/ fear of flying

de **vliegbasis** /vli̱ɣbazɪs/ (pl: -bases) airbase

het **vliegbrevet** /vli̱xbrəvɛt/ (pl: -ten) pilot's licence, flying licence: *zijn ~ halen* qualify as a pilot, get one's wings

het **vliegdekschip** /vli̱ɣdɛksxɪp/ (pl: -schepen) (aircraft) carrier

vliegen /vli̱ɣə(n)/ (vloog, heeft/is gevlogen) fly; race: *de dagen ~ (om)* the days are simply flying; *hij ziet ze ~* he has got bats in the belfry; *eruit ~* get sacked; *met KLM ~* fly KLM ‖ *erin ~* fall for sth.

de **vliegenier** /vliɣəni̱r/ (pl: -s) airman, aviator

de **vliegenmepper** /vli̱ɣə(n)mɛpər/ (pl: -s) (fly) swatter

¹**vliegensvlug** /vli̱ɣənsfly̱x/ (adj) lightning

²**vliegensvlug** /vli̱ɣənsfly̱x/ (adv) as quick as lightning, like lightning (*or:* a shot)

de **vliegenzwam** /vli̱ɣə(n)zwɑm/ (pl: -men) fly agaric

de **vlieger** /vli̱ɣər/ (pl: -s) kite: *een ~ oplaten* fly a kite

vliegeren /vli̱ɣərə(n)/ (vliegerde, heeft gevliegerd) fly kites (*or:* a kite)

het **vlieggewicht** /vli̱xəwɪxt/ flyweight

de **vlieghoogte** /vli̱xhoxtə/ (pl: -n) altitude

de **vlieginstructeur** /vli̱xɪnstryktør/ (pl: -s) flying instructor

de **vliegmaatschappij** /vli̱xmatsxɑpɛi/ (pl: -en) airline

de **vliegramp** /vli̱xrɑmp/ (pl: -en) plane crash

de **vliegschaamte** /vli̱xsxamtə/ flygskam, flight shame

het/de **vliegticket** /vli̱xtɪkət/ airline ticket

het **vliegtuig** /vli̱xtœyx/ (pl: -en) aeroplane; [Am] airplane; aircraft, plane: *~jes vouwen* make paper aeroplanes (*or:* airplanes); *met*

het ~ reizen fly, travel by air (*or:* plane)

de **vliegtuigkaper** /vli̱xtœyxkapər/ (pl: -s) (aircraft) hijacker

de **vliegtuigkaping** /vli̱xtœyxkapɪŋ/ (pl: -en) (aircraft) hijack(ing)

de **vliegtuigstand** /vli̱xtœyxstɑnt/ [media] flight mode

het **vliegveld** /vli̱xfɛlt/ (pl: -en) airport

het **vliegverbod** /vli̱xfərbɔt/ grounding; flight restriction

het **vliegwiel** /vli̱xwil/ (pl: -en) fly(wheel), driving wheel

de **vlier** /vlir/ (pl: -en) elder(berry)

de **vliering** /vli̱rɪŋ/ (pl: -en) attic, loft

het **vlies** /vlis/ (pl: vliezen) film; skin

vlijen /vlɛ̱iə(n)/ (vlijde, heeft gevlijd) lay down, nestle

vlijmscherp /vlɛimsxɛ̱rp/ (adj) razor-sharp

de **vlijt** /vlɛit/ diligence, application

vlijtig /vlɛ̱itəx/ (adj, adv) diligent, industrious

de **vlinder** /vlɪ̱ndər/ (pl: -s) butterfly: *~s in mijn buik* butterflies in my stomach

de **vlinderdas** /vlɪ̱ndərdɑs/ (pl: -sen) bow tie

de **vlinderslag** /vlɪ̱ndərslɑx/ butterfly stroke

de **vlo** /vlo/ (pl: vlooien) flea: *onder de ~oien zitten* be flea-ridden

de **vloed** /vlut/ (pl: -en) (high) tide, flood (tide), rising tide: *het is nu ~* the tide is in; *bij ~* at high tide; *een ~ van klachten* a flood (*or:* deluge) of complaints

de **vloedgolf** /vlu̱txɔlf/ (pl: -golven) **1** groundswell **2** tidal wave

de **vloedlijn** /vlu̱tlɛin/ (pl: -en) high-water line

het **vloei** /vluj/ tissue paper: *een pakje shag met ~* (a packet of) rolling tobacco and cigarette papers

vloeibaar /vlu̱jbar/ (adj) liquid, fluid: *~ voedsel* liquid food; *~ maken* liquefy

vloeien /vlu̱jə(n)/ (vloeide, heeft/is gevloeid) **1** flow, stream: *in de kas ~* flow in **2** blot, smudge

vloeiend /vlu̱jənt/ (adj, adv) flowing, liquid: *~e kleuren* blending colours; *een ~e lijn* a flowing line; *hij spreekt ~ Engels* he speaks English fluently

het **vloeipapier** /vlu̱jpapir/ **1** blotting paper **2** tissue paper; cigarette paper

de **vloeistof** /vlu̱jstɔf/ (pl: -fen) liquid, fluid

het **vloeitje** /vlu̱jcə/ (pl: -s) [Dutch] cigarette paper

de **vloek** /vluk/ (pl: -en) curse: *er ligt een ~ op dat huis* a curse rests on that house; *een ~ uitspreken (over iem., iets)* curse s.o. (sth.); [fig] *in een ~ en een zucht* in no time, in the twinkling of an eye

vloeken /vlu̱kə(n)/ (vloekte, heeft gevloekt) curse, swear (at): *op iets ~* curse (*or:* swear) at sth.

de **vloer** /vlur/ (pl: -en) floor: *planken ~* planking; strip flooring; *met iem. de ~ aanvegen* mop (*or*: wipe) the floor with s.o.; *ik dacht dat ik door de ~ ging* I didn't know where to put myself; *veel mensen **over** de ~ hebben* have a lot of visitors; *hij komt daar **over** de ~ he is a regular visitor there

de **vloerbedekking** /vlurbədɛkɪŋ/ (pl: -en) floor covering: *vaste* ~ wall-to-wall carpet(ting)
vloeren /vlurə(n)/ (vloerde, heeft gevloerd) floor

het **vloerkleed** /vlurklet/ (pl: -kleden) carpet; [small] rug

de **vloermat** /vlurmɑt/ (pl: -ten) floor mat

de **vloertegel** /vlurteɣəl/ (pl: -s) (paving) tile (*or*: stone): *~s **leggen*** pave, lay (paving) tiles

de **vloerverwarming** /vlurvərwɑrmɪŋ/ (pl: -en) underfloor heating

het/de **vlog** /vlɔɣ/ (pl: -s) vlog
vloggen /vlɔɣə(n)/ (vlogde, heeft gevlogd) vlog

de **vlogger** /vlɔɣər/ (pl: -s) vlogger

de **vlok** /vlɔk/ (pl: -ken) **1** flock; tuft: *~ken **stof*** whirls of dust **2** flake: *~ken **op** brood* bread with chocolate flakes

de **vlonder** /vlɔndər/ (pl: -s) **1** (wooden) platform, planking **2** pallet
vlooien /vloːjə(n)/ (vlooide, heeft gevlooid) groom

de **vlooienband** /vloːjə(n)bɑnt/ (pl: -en) flea collar

de **vlooienmarkt** /vloːjə(n)mɑrkt/ (pl: -en) flea market

de **vloot** /vloːt/ (pl: vloten) fleet

het **vlos** /vlɔs/ floss (silk)

het **¹vlot** /vlɔt/ (pl: -ten) raft: *op een ~ de rivier oversteken* raft across the river

²vlot /vlɔt/ (adj, adv) **1** facile; fluent; smooth: *een ~te **pen*** a ready pen; *~ **spreken*** speak fluently **2** smooth; ready; prompt: *een zaak ~ **afwikkelen*** settle a matter promptly; *het ging heel ~* it went off without a hitch; *~ van begrip **zijn*** be quick-witted **3** sociable, easy to talk to: *hij **is** wat ~ter **geworden*** he has loosened up a little **4** easy, comfortable: *hij **kleedt** zich heel ~* he is a sharp dresser **5** afloat

vlotjes /vlɔcəs/ (adv) smoothly, easily; promptly: *alles ~ **laten** verlopen* have things run smoothly

vlotten /vlɔtə(n)/ (vlotte, heeft/is gevlot) go smoothly: *het werk **wil** niet ~* we are not making any progress (*or*: headway)

de **vlucht** /vlʏɣt/ (pl: -en) **1** flight, escape: *op de ~ slaan* flee, run (for it); *voor de politie **op** de ~ zijn* be on the run from the police; *iem. **op** de ~ jagen* put s.o. to flight **2** flight: *wij wensen u een **aangename** ~* we wish you a pleasant flight; *binnenlandse ~* domestic flight **3** [cycling] breakaway, escape (from the peloton) || *een **hoge** ~ nemen* boom, expand enormously

de **vluchteling** /vlʏɣtəlɪŋ/ (pl: -en) fugitive; [pol] refugee: *een **economische** ~* an economic refugee; *een **politieke** ~* a political refugee

het **vluchtelingenkamp** /vlʏɣtəlɪŋə(n)kɑmp/ (pl: -en) refugee camp
vluchten /vlʏɣtə(n)/ (vluchtte, is gevlucht) flee, escape, run away: *uit het land ~* flee (from) the country; *een bos **in** ~* take refuge in the woods

het **vluchtgedrag** /vlʏɣtɣədrɑɣ/ flight

de **vluchtheuvel** /vlʏɣthøvəl/ (pl: -s) traffic island

het **vluchthuis** /vlʏɣthœys/ (pl: -huizen) [Belg] refuge (*or*: shelter) for battered women
vluchtig /vlʏɣtəɣ/ (adj, adv) **1** brief; [depr] cursory; quick: *~e **kennismaking*** casual acquaintance; *iets ~ **doorlezen*** glance over (*or*: through) sth., skim through sth. **2** volatile

de **vluchtleider** /vlʏɣtlɛidər/ (pl: -s) flight controller

de **vluchtleiding** /vlʏɣtlɛidɪŋ/ (pl: -en) flight (*or*: mission) control (team), ground control

het **vluchtmisdrijf** /vlʏɣtmɪzdrɛif/ [Belg] hit-and-run: *pleger van een ~* hit-and-run driver

de **vluchtpoging** /vlʏɣtpoɣɪŋ/ (pl: -en) attempted escape

de **vluchtrecorder** /vlʏɣtrikɔːrdər/ (pl: -s) flight recorder, black box

de **vluchtstrook** /vlʏɣtstrok/ (pl: -stroken) [Dutch] hard shoulder; [Am] shoulder

de **vluchtweg** /vlʏɣtwɛɣ/ (pl: -en) escape route
vlug /vlʏɣ/ (adj, adv) **1** fast, quick: *~ **lopen*** run fast; *~ ter been **zijn*** be quick on one's feet; *iem. te ~ af zijn* be too quick for s.o. **2** quick; nimble; agile **3** quick, fast, prompt: *hij was ~ **klaar*** he was soon ready; *iets ~ **doornemen*** (or: **bekijken**) glance over (*or*: through) sth.; *~ iets **eten*** have a quick snack **4** quick, sharp: *hij **behoort** niet tot de ~sten* he's none too quick; *hij **was** er al ~ **bij*** he was quick at everything; *~ **in** rekenen* quick at sums

het **vmbo** /veɛmbeo/ [Dutch] *voorbereidend middelbaar beroepsonderwijs* lower vocational professional education

het **vmbo-b** [Dutch; educ] pre-vocational secondary education (block or day release)

het **vmbo-g** [Dutch; educ] pre-vocational secondary education (combined programme)

het **vmbo-k** [Dutch; educ] pre-vocational secondary education (middle management vocational programme)

het **vmbo-t** [Dutch; educ] pre-vocational secondary education (theoretical programme)

de **VN** /veɛn/ (pl) *Verenigde Naties* UN

de **VN-vredesmacht** /veɛnvredəsmɑɣt/ UN peace-keeping force

het **vo** /veo/ [Dutch] *voortgezet onderwijs* secondary education
vocaal /vokal/ (adj) vocal

het **vocabulaire** /vokabylɛːr(ə)/ vocabulary

het **vocht** /vɔxt/ **1** liquid; fluid: ~ *afscheiden* discharge fluid; secrete fluid **2** moisture, damp-(ness): *de hoeveelheid* ~ *in de lucht* the humidity in the air

vochtig /vɔxtəx/ (adj) damp, moist: *een* ~ *klimaat* a damp climate; *de lucht* is ~ the air is damp; *zijn ogen werden* ~ his eyes became moist

de **vochtigheid** /vɔxtəxhɛit/ **1** moistness, dampness **2** moisture; humidity

het/de **vod** /vɔt/ (pl: -den) **1** rag: *een ~je papier* a scrap of paper **2** trash, rubbish: *dit is een* ~ this is trash ‖ *iem. achter de ~den zitten* keep s.o. (hard) at it

¹**voeden** /vudə(n)/ (voedde, heeft gevoed) be nourishing (*or:* nutritious)

²**voeden** /vudə(n)/ (voedde, heeft gevoed) feed: *die vogels ~ zich met insecten* (*or:* met zaden) these birds feed on insects (*or:* seeds); *zij voedt haar kind zelf* she breast-feeds her baby

het **voeder** /vudər/ (pl: -s) fodder, feed

voederen /vudərə(n)/ (voederde, heeft gevoederd) feed

de **voeding** /vudɪŋ/ (pl: -en) **1** feeding, nutrition: *kunstmatige* ~ artificial (*or:* forced) feeding **2** food; feed: *eenzijdige* ~ an unbalanced diet; *gezonde* (*or:* natuurlijke) ~ health (*or:* natural) food **3** power supply

de **voedingsbodem** /vudɪŋzbodəm/ (pl: -s) breeding ground

de **voedingsindustrie** /vudɪŋsɪndystri/ (pl: -ën) food industry

het **voedingsmiddel** /vudɪŋsmɪdəl/ (pl: -en) food; foodstuff: *gezonde ~en* healthy (*or:* wholesome) foods

de **voedingsstof** /vudɪŋstɔf/ (pl: -fen) nutrient

de **voedingsvezels** /vudɪŋsfezəls/ (pl) nutritional fibre

de **voedingswaarde** /vudɪŋswardə/ nutritional value

het **voedsel** /vutsəl/ food: *plantaardig* ~ vegetable food; ~ *tot zich nemen* take food (*or:* nourishment)

de **voedselbank** /vutsəlbɑŋk/ (pl: -en) food bank

de **voedselhulp** /vutsəlhʏlp/ food aid

de **voedselketen** /vutsəlketə(n)/ food chain

het **voedselpakket** /vutsəlpɑkɛt/ (pl: -ten) food parcel

de **voedselveiligheid** /vutsəlvɛiləxhɛit/ food safety

de **voedselvergiftiging** /vutsəlvərɣɪftəɣɪŋ/ food poisoning

voedzaam /vutsam/ (adj) nutritious, nourishing

de **voeg** /vux/ (pl: -en) joint; seam: *de ~en van een muur* dichtmaken (aanstrijken) point (the brickwork of) a wall; *uit zijn ~en barsten* come apart at the seams

de **voege** /vuɣə/: [Belg] *in* ~ *treden* take effect, come into force

voegen /vuɣə(n)/ (voegde, heeft gevoegd) **1** join (up): *hierbij voeg ik een biljet van € 100,-* I enclose a 100-euro note; *zich bij iem.* ~ join s.o.; *stukken bij een dossier* ~ add documents to a file **2** point

het **voegwoord** /vuxwort/ (pl: -en) conjunction

voelbaar /vulbar/ (adj, adv) tangible, perceptible: *het ijzer wordt* ~ *warmer* the iron is getting perceptibly hotter

¹**voelen** /vulə(n)/ (voelde, heeft gevoeld) **1** feel: *het voelt hard* (or: *ruw, zacht*) it feels hard (*or:* rough, soft) **2** be fond (of), like: *iets gaan* ~ *voor iem.* grow fond of s.o. **3** feel (like), like the idea (of): *veel voor de verpleging* ~ like the idea of nursing; *ik voel wel iets voor dat plan* I rather like that plan; *ik voel er niet veel voor (om) te komen* I don't feel like coming

²**voelen** /vulə(n)/ (voelde, heeft gevoeld) **1** feel: *leven* ~ feel the baby move; *dat voel ik!* that hurts!; *zijn invloed doen* ~ make one's influence felt; *als je niet wil luisteren, moet je maar* ~ (you'd better) do it or else!; *voel je (hem)?* get it? **2** feel (for, after): *laat mij eens* ~ let me (have a) feel

zich ³**voelen** /vulə(n)/ (voelde zich, heeft zich gevoeld) feel: *zich lekker* ~ feel fine, feel on top of the world

de **voeling** /vulɪŋ/ touch, contact: ~ *houden met* maintain contact with, keep in touch with

de **voelspriet** /vulsprit/ (pl: -en) feeler, antenna

het **voer** /vur/ feed; [also fig] food: ~ *geven* feed; ~ *voor psychologen* a fit subject for a psychologist

de **voerbak** /vurbɑk/ (pl: -ken) (feeding) trough, manger

¹**voeren** /vurə(n)/ (voerde, heeft gevoerd) lead, guide: *dat zou (mij, ons) te ver* ~ that would be getting too far off the subject; *de reis voert naar Rome* the trip goes to Rome

²**voeren** /vurə(n)/ (voerde, heeft gevoerd) **1** line **2** feed ‖ *een harde politiek* ~ pursue a tough policy; *een proces* ~ go to court (over); *iem. dronken* ~ get (*or:* make) s.o. drunk

de **voering** /vurɪŋ/ (pl: -en) lining

de **voertaal** /vurtal/ (pl: -talen) language of instruction [educ]; [at conferences etc] official language

het **voertuig** /vurtœyx/ (pl: -en) vehicle

de **voet** /vut/ (pl: -en) **1** foot: *op blote ~en* barefoot; *op grote* ~ *leven* live in (great) style; *iem. op staande* ~ *ontslaan* dismiss s.o. on the spot; *iem. op vrije ~en stellen* set s.o. free; [Belg] *met iemands ~en spelen* make a fool of s.o.; [Belg] *ergens zijn ~en aan vegen* drag one's feet; *de ~en vegen* wipe one's feet; *dat heeft heel wat ~en in de aarde* that'll take some doing; *onder de ~ gelopen worden* be overrun; *iem. op de ~ volgen* follow in s.o.'s footsteps; *de gebeurtenissen* (or: *de ontwikkelingen*) *op de ~ volgen* keep a close track of events (or: developments); *te ~ gaan* walk, go on foot; *zich uit de ~en maken* take to one's heels; *met iets uit de ~en kunnen* be able to manage with (or: handle) sth.; *iem. voor de ~en lopen* hamper s.o., get in s.o.'s way (or: under s.o.'s feet); *geen ~ aan de grond krijgen* have no success; *~ bij stuk houden* stick to one's guns **2** foot, base: *de ~ van een glas* the stem (or: base) of a glass **3** footing; terms: *zij staan op goede* (or: *vertrouwelijke*) *~ met elkaar* they are on good (or: familiar) terms (with each other); *op ~ van oorlog leven* be on a war footing ‖ *dat is hem ten ~en uit* that's (so) typical of him, that's him all over

de **voetafdruk** /vу̲tavdrʏk/ (pl: -ken) footmark, footprint: *ecologische ~* ecological footprint

het **voetbad** /vу̲tbɑt/ (pl: -en) footbath

de [1]**voetbal** /vу̲tbɑl/ (pl: -len) [ball] football

het [2]**voetbal** /vу̲tbɑl/ [sport] football: *Amerikaans ~* American football; *betaald ~* professional football

de **voetbalbond** /vу̲tbɑlbɔnt/ football association

de **voetbalclub** /vу̲tbɑlklʏp/ football club

de **voetbalcompetitie** /vу̲tbɑlkɔmpəti(t)si/ (pl: -s) football competition

het **voetbalelftal** /vу̲tbɑlɛlftɑl/ football team: *het ~ van Ajax* the Ajax team

de **voetbalfan** /vу̲tbɑlfɛn/ (pl: -s) football fan

de **voetbalknie** /vу̲tbɑlkni/ (pl: -ën) cartilage trouble

voetballen /vу̲tbɑlə(n)/ (voetbalde, heeft gevoetbald) play football

de **voetballer** /vу̲tbɑlər/ (pl: -s) football player

het **voetbalpasje** /vу̲tbɑlpɑʃə/ (pl: -s) football identity card

de **voetbalschoen** /vу̲tbɑlsxun/ football boot

het **voetbalstadion** /vу̲tbɑlstadijɔn/ football stadium, soccer stadium

de **voetbalsupporter** /vу̲tbɑlsʏpɔrtər/ (pl: -s) football supporter

de **voetbaluitslagen** /vу̲tbɑlœytslaɣə(n)/ (pl) football results

het **voetbalvandalisme** /vу̲tbɑlvɑndɑlɪsmə/ football hooliganism

het **voetbalveld** /vу̲tbɑlvɛlt/ football pitch

de **voetbalwedstrijd** /vу̲tbɑlwɛtstrɛit/ football match

het **voeteneind** /vу̲tə(n)ɛint/ (pl: -en) foot

de **voetfout** /vу̲tfɑut/ (pl: -en) foot-fault

de **voetganger** /vу̲txɑŋər/ (pl: -s) pedestrian

de **voetgangersbrug** /vу̲txɑŋərzbrʏx/ (pl: -gen) footbridge, pedestrian bridge

het **voetgangersgebied** /vу̲txɑŋərsxəbit/ (pl: -en) pedestrian precinct (or: area)

de **voetgangersoversteekplaats** /vу̲t-χɑŋərsovərstekplɑts/ (pl: -en) pedestrian crossing, zebra crossing

het **voetje** /vу̲cə/ (pl: -s) (little, small) foot: *~ voor ~* inch by inch

het **voetlicht** /vу̲tlɪxt/ (pl: -en) footlights: *iets voor het ~ brengen* bring sth. out into the open

de **voetnoot** /vу̲tnot/ (pl: -noten) **1** footnote **2** note in the margin, critical remark (or: comment)

het **voetpad** /vу̲tpɑt/ (pl: -en) footpath

de **voetreis** /vу̲trɛis/ (pl: -reizen) walking-trip, walking-tour, hike

het **voetspoor** /vу̲tspor/ (pl: -sporen) footprint; track; trail

de **voetstap** /vу̲tstɑp/ (pl: -pen) (foot)step

voetstoots /vу̲tstots/ (adv) without further ado, just like that

het **voetstuk** /vу̲tstʏk/ (pl: -ken) base; pedestal: *iem. op een ~ plaatsen* put (or: place) s.o. on a pedestal; [fig] *iem. van zijn ~ stoten* knock s.o. off his pedestal

de **voettocht** /vу̲toxt/ (pl: -en) walking tour, hiking tour

het **voetvolk** /vу̲tfɔlk/ foot soldiers; infantry

de **voetzoeker** /vу̲tsukər/ (pl: -s) jumping jack; [roughly] firecracker

de **voetzool** /vу̲tsol/ (pl: -zolen) sole (of the, one's foot)

de **vogel** /vо̲ɣəl/ (pl: -s) **1** bird: [Belg] *een ~ voor de kat zijn* be irretrievably lost; *de ~ is gevlogen* the bird has flown **2** customer, character: *het is een rare ~* he's an odd character; *Joe is een vroege ~* Joe's an early bird

de **vogelgriep** /vо̲ɣəlɣrip/ bird flu, avian influenza

het **vogelhuis** /vо̲ɣəlhœys/ (pl: -huizen) aviary; nesting box

de **vogelkooi** /vо̲ɣəlkoj/ (pl: -en) birdcage

het **vogelnest** /vо̲ɣəlnɛst/ (pl: -en) bird's nest: *~en uithalen* go (bird-)nesting

de **vogelpest** /vо̲ɣəlpɛst/ bird flu, avian influenza, fowl pest

de **vogelpik** /vо̲ɣəlpɪk/ [Belg] darts

de **vogelspin** /vо̲ɣəlspɪn/ (pl: -nen) bird spider

de **vogeltrek** /vо̲ɣəltrɛk/ bird migration

de **vogelverschrikker** /vо̲ɣəlvərsxrɪkər/ (pl: -s) scarecrow

de **vogelvlucht** /vо̲ɣəlvlʏxt/ (pl: -en) bird's-eye view: *iets in ~ behandelen* sketch sth. briefly; *iets in ~ tekenen* draw a bird's-eye view of sth.

vogelvrij /voɣəlvrɛi/ (adj) outlawed

de **voicemail** /vɔjsmel/ [telecom] voice mail

vol /vɔl/ (adj, adv) **1** full (of), filled (with): *~ nieuwe ideeën* full of new ideas; *een huis ~ mensen* a house full of people; *met ~le mond praten* talk with one's mouth full; *iets ~ maken (gieten, stoppen)* fill sth. up; *helemaal ~* full up, packed; *~ van iets zijn* be full of sth.; *een ~ gezicht* a full (or: chubby) face; *zij is een ~le nicht van me* she's my first cousin **2** full (of), covered (with, in): *de tafel ligt* ~ *boeken* the table is covered with books; *de kranten staan er* ~ *van* the papers are full of it **3** complete, whole: *een ~le dagtaak* a full day's work; [fig also] *het kostte hem acht ~le maanden* it took him a good (*or:* all of) eight months; *in het ~ste vertrouwen* in complete confidence; *een ~le week de tijd hebben* have a full (*or:* whole) week || *ten ~le* fully, entirely; *iem. voor* ~ *aanzien* take s.o. seriously

volautomatisch /vɔlɑutomɑtis/ (adj) fully automatic

de ¹**volbloed** /vɔlblut/ (pl: -s, -en) thoroughbred: *Arabische* ~ Arab (thoroughbred)

²**volbloed** /vɔlblut/ (adj) **1** full-blood(ed); pedigree: ~ *rundvee* pedigree cattle **2** thoroughbred

volbrengen /vɔlbrɛŋə(n)/ (volbracht, heeft volbracht) complete, accomplish

voldaan /vɔldan/ (adj) **1** satisfied, content(ed): *een* ~ *gevoel* a sense of satisfaction; ~ *zijn over iets* be satisfied (*or:* content) with sth. **2** paid: *voor* ~ *tekenen* receipt, sign for receipt

¹**voldoen** /vɔldun/ (voldeed, heeft voldaan) (+ aan) satisfy; meet; carry out; comply with: *aan de behoeften van de markt* ~ meet the needs of the market; *niet* ~ *aan* fall short of

²**voldoen** /vɔldun/ (voldeed, heeft voldaan) pay, settle: *een rekening* (*or: de kosten*) ~ pay a bill (*or:* the costs)

de ¹**voldoende** /vɔldundə/ (pl: -s, -n) pass (mark); a bare pass: *een* ~ *halen voor wiskunde* pass (one's) maths

²**voldoende** /vɔldundə/ (adj) sufficient, satisfactory: *één blik op hem is* ~ *om ...* one look at him is enough to ...; *jouw examen was net* ~ you only just scraped through your exam; *het is niet* ~ *om van te leven* it is not enough to live on; *ruimschoots* ~ ample, more than enough

³**voldoende** /vɔldundə/ (adv) sufficiently, enough: *heb je je* ~ *voorbereid?* have you done enough preparation?

de **voldoening** /vɔldunɪŋ/ satisfaction

voldongen /vɔldɔŋə(n)/ (adj): *voor een* ~ *feit geplaatst worden* be presented with a fait accompli

voldragen /vɔldraɣə(n)/ (adj) full-term

volgeboekt /vɔlɣəbukt/ (adj) fully booked, booked up

de **volgeling** /vɔlɣəlɪŋ/ (pl: -en) follower; [rel also] disciple

¹**volgen** /vɔlɣə(n)/ (volgde, heeft/is gevolgd) **1** follow; be next: *nadere instructies* ~ further instructions will follow; *hier* ~ *de namen van de winnaars* the names of the winners are as follows; *op elkaar* ~ follow one another; *als volgt* as follows; *wie volgt?* who's next? **2** follow (on): *daaruit volgt dat ...* it follows

that ...

²**volgen** /vɔlɣə(n)/ (volgde, heeft gevolgd) **1** follow: *een spoor* (*or: de weg*) ~ follow a trail (*or:* the road) **2** follow, attend **3** follow; pursue: *zijn hart* ~ follow the dictates of one's heart; *iem. op Twitter* ~ follow s.o. on Twitter || *ik kan je niet* ~ I don't follow you

volgend /vɔlɣənt/ (adj) following, next: *de* ~*e keer* next time (round); *wie is de* ~*e?* who's next?; *het gaat om het* ~*e* the problem is (*or:* the facts are) as follows

volgens /vɔlɣəns/ (prep) according to; in accordance with: ~ *mijn horloge is het drie uur* it's three o'clock by my watch; ~ *mij ...* I think ..., in my opinion ...

het **volgnummer** /vɔlɣnʏmər/ (pl: -s) serial number

volgooien /vɔlɣojə(n)/ (gooide vol, heeft volgegooid) fill (up): *de tank* ~ fill (up) the tank, fill her up

de **volgorde** /vɔlɣɔrdə/ (pl: -n, -s) order; sequence: *in de juiste* ~ *leggen* put in the right order; *in willekeurige* ~ at random; *niet op* ~ out of order, not in order

volgroeid /vɔlɣrujt/ (adj) full(y)-grown

de **volgwagen** /vɔlɣwaɣə(n)/ (pl: -s) **1** car in a (funeral, wedding) procession **2** (official) following car

volgzaam /vɔlɣsam/ (adj) docile, obedient

volharden /vɔlhɑrdə(n)/ (volhardde, heeft volhard) persevere, persist

de **volharding** /vɔlhɑrdɪŋ/ perseverance, persistence

¹**volhouden** /vɔlhɑudə(n)/ (hield vol, heeft volgehouden) persevere, keep on: *we zijn ermee begonnen, nu moeten we* ~ now we've started we must see it through; ~*!* keep it up!, keep going!

²**volhouden** /vɔlhɑudə(n)/ (hield vol, heeft volgehouden) **1** carry on, keep up: *dit tempo is niet vol te houden* we can't keep up this pace **2** maintain, insist: *zijn onschuld* ~ insist on one's innocence; *iets hardnekkig* ~ stubbornly maintain sth.

de **volhouder** /vɔlhɑudər/ (pl: -s) stayer

de **volière** /vɔljɛːrə/ (pl: -s) aviary; birdhouse

het **volk** /vɔlk/ (pl: -en, -eren) **1** people, nation, race **2** people, populace, folk: *een man uit het* ~ a working(-class) man; *het gewone* ~ the common people **3** people: *het circus trekt altijd veel* ~ the circus always draws a crowd

de **Volkenbond** /vɔlkə(n)bɔnt/ League of Nations

de **volkenkunde** /vɔlkə(n)kʏndə/ cultural anthropology

het **volkenrecht** /vɔlkə(n)rɛxt/ international law

de **volkerenmoord** /vɔlkəmort/ (pl: -en) genocide

¹**volkomen** /vɔlkomə(n)/ (adj) complete, total

²**volkomen** /vɔlkoːmə(n)/ (adv) completely: *dat is ~ juist* that's perfectly true

het **volkorenbrood** /vɔlkoːrə(n)broːt/ wholemeal bread; [Am] whole-wheat bread

de **volksbuurt** /vɔlksbyrt/ (pl: -en) working-class area (*or:* district)

de **volksdans** /vɔlksdɑns/ (pl: -en) folk dance

het **volksdansen** /vɔlksdɑnsə(n)/ folk dancing

de **volksgezondheid** /vɔlksxəzɔnthɛit/ public health, national health

de **volksheld** /vɔlkshɛlt/ (pl: -en) popular hero, national hero

de **volkshuisvesting** /vɔlkshœysfɛstɪŋ/ **1** public housing **2** (public) housing department

het **volkslied** /vɔlksliːt/ (pl: -eren) **1** national anthem **2** folk song

de **volksmenner** /vɔlksmɛnər/ (pl: -s) [depr] demagogue, agitator

de **volksmond** /vɔlksmɔnt/: *in de ~* in popular speech (*or:* parlance); *in de ~ heet dit* this is popularly called

de **volksmuziek** /vɔlksmyzik/ folk music

de **volkspartij** /vɔlkspɑrtɛi/ (pl: -en) people's party

de **volksraadpleging** /vɔlksraːtpleɣɪŋ/ (pl: -en) referendum, plebiscite

de **volksrepubliek** /vɔlksrepybliːk/ (pl: -en) people's republic: *de ~ China* the People's Republic of China

de **volksstam** /vɔlkstɑm/ (pl: -men) crowd, horde

de **volkstaal** /vɔlkstaːl/ (pl: -talen) vernacular, everyday language

de **volkstelling** /vɔlkstɛlɪŋ/ (pl: -en) census: *er werd een ~ gehouden* a census was taken

de **volkstuin** /vɔlkstœyn/ (pl: -en) allotment (garden)

de **volksuniversiteit** /vɔlksynivɛrzitɛit/ (pl: -en) [roughly] adult education centre

de **volksverhuizing** /vɔlksfərhœyzɪŋ/ (pl: -en) **1** migrations of a nation **2** (mass) migration

de **volksverlakkerij** /vɔlksfərlɑkərɛi/ deception (of the public)

het **volksvermaak** /vɔlksfərmaːk/ (pl: -vermaken) popular amusement (*or:* entertainment)

de **volksvertegenwoordiger** /vɔlksfərteɣə(n)woːrdəɣər/ (pl: -s) representative (of the people), member of parliament, MP; [Am] Congressman

de **volksvertegenwoordiging** /vɔlksfərteɣə(n)woːrdəɣɪŋ/ (pl: -en) house (*or:* chamber) of representatives, parliament

de **volksverzekering** /vɔlksfərzekərɪŋ/ (pl: -en) [Dutch] national insurance, social insurance

de **volksvijand** /vɔlksfɛiɑnt/ (pl: -en) public enemy, enemy of the people: *roken is ~ nummer één* smoking is public enemy number one

de **volkswoede** /vɔlkswudə/ popular fury (*or:* anger)

volledig /vɔledəx/ (adj, adv) **1** full, complete: *~e betaling* payment in full; *het schip is ~ uitgebrand* the ship was completely burnt out; *ik lees u de titel ~ voor* I'll read you the title in full **2** full, full-time: *~e (dienst)betrekking* full-time job

de **volledigheid** /vɔledəxhɛit/ completeness: *voor de ~* for the sake of completeness

volledigheidshalve /vɔledəxhɛitshɑlvə/ (adv) for the sake of completeness

volleerd /vɔleːrt/ (adj) fully-qualified

de **vollemaan** /vɔleˌmaːn/ full moon: *het is ~* there is a full moon; *bij ~* when the moon is full, at full moon

volleren /vɔlerə(n)/ (volleerde, heeft gevolleerd) [sport] volley

de ¹**volleybal** /vɔlibɑl/ (pl: -len) [ball] volleyball

het ²**volleybal** /vɔlibɑl/ [sport] volleyball

volleyballen /vɔlibɑlə(n)/ (volleyballde, heeft gevolleybald) play volleyball

vollopen /vɔlopə(n)/ (liep vol, is volgelopen) fill up, be filled: *de zaal begon vol te lopen* the hall was getting crowded; *het bad laten ~* run the bath

¹**volmaakt** /vɔlmaːkt/ (adj) perfect, consummate

²**volmaakt** /vɔlmaːkt/ (adv) perfectly: *ik ben ~ gezond* I am in perfect health

de **volmacht** /vɔlmɑxt/ (pl: -en) **1** power (of attorney), mandate, authority: *bij ~* by proxy **2** warrant, authorization

volmondig /vɔlmɔndəx/ (adj, adv) wholehearted, frank: *~ iets bekennen* (*or:* *toegeven*) confess (*or:* admit) sth. frankly; *een ~ ja* a straightforward (*or:* heartfelt) 'yes'

volop /vɔlɔp/ (adv) in abundance, plenty, a lot of: *~ ruimte* ample room; *het is ~ zomer* it is the height of summer; *er was ~ te eten* there was food in abundance

het **volpension** /vɔlpɛnʃɔn/ full board

volproppen /vɔlprɔpə(n)/ (propte vol, heeft volgepropt) cram; stuff: *volgepropte trams* overcrowded (*or:* jam-packed) trams; *zich ~* stuff o.s.

volslagen /vɔlslaːɣə(n)/ (adj, adv) complete, utter: *een ~ onbekende* a total stranger; *~ belachelijk* utterly ridiculous

volslank /vɔlslɑŋk/ (adj) plump; well-rounded

volstaan /vɔlstaːn/ (volstond, heeft volstaan) **1** be enough, be sufficient, do: *dat volstaat* that will do **2** limit o.s. (to)

volstoppen /vɔlstɔpə(n)/ (stopte vol, heeft volgestopt) stuff (full), fill to the brim (*or:* top)

volstrekt /vɔlstrɛkt/ (adj, adv) total, complete: *ik ben het ~ niet met hem eens* I disagree entirely with him

de **volt** /vɔlt/ (pl: -s) volt

het/de **voltage** /vɔltaʒə/ (pl: -s) voltage

voltallig /vɔltɑlləx/ (adj) complete, full, entire: *het ~e bestuur* the entire committee; *de ~e vergadering* the plenary assembly (or: meeting)

voltijds /vɔltɛits/ (adj) full-time

voltooid /vɔltoːjt/ (adj) complete, finished: *een ~ deelwoord* a past (or: perfect) participle; *de ~ tegenwoordige* (or: *verleden*) *tijd* the perfect (or: pluperfect)

voltooien /vɔltoːjə(n)/ (voltooide, heeft voltooid) complete, finish

de **voltooiing** /vɔltoːjɪŋ/ (pl: -en) completion

de **voltreffer** /vɔltrɛfər/ (pl: -s) direct hit

voltrekken /vɔltrɛkə(n)/ (voltrok, heeft voltrokken) execute; celebrate; perform

de **voltrekking** /vɔltrɛkɪŋ/ (pl: -en) celebration; performing

voluit /vɔlœyt/ (adv) in full

het **volume** /vɔlymə/ (pl: -n, -s) volume, loudness

de **volumeknop** /vɔlyməknɔp/ (pl: -pen) volume control (or: knob)

volumineus /vɔlyminøs/ (adj) voluminous

volvet /vɔlvɛt/ (adj) full-cream

volwaardig /vɔlwaːrdəx/ (adj) full; able(-bodied): *een ~ lid* a full member

¹**volwassen** /vɔlwɑsə(n)/ (adj) adult, grown-up; mature; full-grown; ripe: *~ gedrag* mature (or: adult) behaviour; *ik ben een ~ vrouw!* I'm a grown woman!; *toen zij ~ werd* on reaching womanhood; *~ worden* grow to maturity, grow up

²**volwassen** /vɔlwɑsə(n)/ (adv) in an adult (or: a mature) way: *zich ~ gedragen* behave like an adult

de **volwassene** /vɔlwɑsənə/ (pl: -n) adult, grown-up

het **volwassenenonderwijs** /vɔlwɑsənə(n)ɔndərwɛis/ adult education

de **volwassenheid** /vɔlwɑsənhɛit/ adulthood, maturity

de **volzin** /vɔlzɪn/ (pl: -nen) sentence

de **vondeling** /vɔndəlɪŋ/ (pl: -en) abandoned child: *een kind te ~ leggen* abandon a child

de **vondst** /vɔnst/ (pl: -en) invention, discovery: *een ~ doen* make a (real) find; *een gelukkige ~* a lucky strike

de **vonk** /vɔŋk/ (pl: -en) spark || *de ~ sloeg over* a) the audience caught on; b) they fell in love; *de ~en vliegen eraf* a) they're attacking it with zeal; b) sparks are flying

vonken /vɔŋkə(n)/ (vonkte, heeft gevonkt) spark(le), shoot sparks

het **vonnis** /vɔnɪs/ (pl: -sen) judgement; sentence; verdict: *een ~ vellen (uitspreken) over* pass (or: pronounce, give) judgement on

vonnissen /vɔnɪsə(n)/ (vonniste, heeft gevonnist) sentence, convict; pass judgement (or: sentence) (on)

de **voodoo** /vuːduː/ voodoo

de **voogd** /voːxt/ (pl: -en) guardian: *toeziend ~* co-guardian, joint guardian; *~ zijn over iem.* be s.o.'s guardian

de **voogdij** /voːxdɛi/ (pl: -en) guardianship: *onder ~ staan* (or: *plaatsen*) be (or: place) under guardianship

de **voogdijminister** /voːxdɛiminɪstər/ (pl: -s) [Belg] minister in charge

de **voogdijraad** /voːxdɛiraːt/ (pl: -raden) [Dutch] guardianship board

de ¹**voor** /voːr/ (pl: voren) 1 furrow 2 wrinkle, furrow

het ²**voor** /voːr/ (pl: -s) pro, advantage: *~ en tegen van een voorstel* the pros and cons of a proposition

³**voor** /voːr/ (adv) 1 in (the) front: *een kind met een slab ~* a child wearing a bib; *de auto staat ~* the car is at the door; *hij is ~ in de dertig* he is in his early thirties; *~ in het boek* near the beginning of the book 2 ahead, in the lead: *vier punten ~* four points ahead; *zij zijn ons ~ geweest* they got (t)here before (or: ahead of) us 3 for, in favour: *ik ben er niet ~* I'm not in favour of that

⁴**voor** /voːr/ (prep) 1 for: *zij is een goede moeder ~ haar kinderen* she is a good mother to her children; *dat is net iets ~ hem* a) that is just the thing for him; b) that is just like him; *dat is niets ~ mij* that is not my kind of thing (or: my cup of tea) 2 ahead, in front of: *de dagen die ~ ons liggen* the days (that lie) ahead of us 3 before, for 4 before, ahead of: *~ zondag* before Sunday; *tien ~ zeven* ten to seven 5 for, instead of: *ik zal ~ mijn zoon betalen* I'll pay for my son 6 for, in favour of: *ik ben ~ FC Utrecht* I'm a supporter of FC Utrecht || *wat zijn het ~ mensen?* what sort of people are they?

⁵**voor** /voːr/ (conj) before: *~ hij vertrok, was ik al weg* I was already gone before he left

vooraan /voːraːn/ (adv) in (the) front: *~ lopen* walk at the front; *iets ~ zetten* put sth. (up) in front

vooraanstaand /voːraːnstaːnt/ (adj) prominent, leading

vooraf /voːrɑf/ (adv) beforehand, in advance: *een ~ verklaring* an explanation in advance; *je moet ~ goed bedenken wat je gaat doen* you need to think ahead about what you're going to do

voorafgaan /voːrɑfxaːn/ (ging vooraf, is voorafgegaan) precede, go before, go in front (of): *de weken ~de aan het feest* the weeks preceding the celebration

voorafgaand /voːrɑfxaːnt/ (adj) preceding, foregoing: *~e toestemming* prior permission

het **voorafje** /voːrɑfjə/ (pl: -s) appetizer, hors d'oeuvre

vooral /voːrɑl/ (adv) especially, particularly: *dat moet je ~ doen* do that (or: go ahead) by all means; *ga ~ vroeg naar bed* be sure to go to bed early; **maak** *haar ~ niet **wakker*** don't wake her up whatever you do; *vergeet het ~ niet* whatever you do, don't forget it; *~ omdat* especially because

vooraleer /voral̯er/ (conj) [form] afore, before

vooralsnog /voralsnɔx/ (adv) as yet, for the time being

het **voorarrest** /vorarɛst/ remand, custody, detention: *in ~ zitten* be on remand, be in custody; *in ~ gehouden worden* be taken into custody

de **vooravond** /voravɔnt/ (pl: -en) eve

de **voorbaat** /vorbat/: *bij ~ dank* thank (or: thanking) you in advance; *bij ~ kansloos zijn* not stand a chance from the very start

de **voorbank** /vorbaŋk/ (pl: -en) front seats

voorbarig /vorbarəx/ (adj, adv) premature: *~ spreken* (or: *antwoorden*) speak (or: answer) too soon

voorbedacht /vorbədaxt/ (adj) [law]: *met ~en rade* intentionally, with premeditation

het **voorbeeld** /vorbelt/ (pl: -en) example, model; instance: *een afschrikwekkend ~* a warning; *het goede voorbeeld geven* set a good example; *een ~ stellen* make an example of s.o.; *iemands ~ volgen* follow s.o.'s lead (or: example); *tot ~ dienen* serve as an example (or: a model) for

de **voorbeeldfunctie** /vorbeltfʏŋksi/ exemplary function: *een ~ vervullen* serve as an example to others

voorbeeldig /vorbeldəx/ (adj, adv) exemplary, model: *een ~ gedrag* exemplary conduct

het **voorbehoedmiddel** /vorbəhutmɪdəl/ (pl: -en) contraceptive

het **voorbehoud** /vorbəhaut/ restriction, reservation; condition: *iets onder ~ beloven* make a conditional promise; *zonder ~* without reservations

voorbehouden /vorbəhaudə(n)/ reserve: *alle rechten ~* all rights reserved; *wijzigingen ~* subject to modification(s)

voorbereiden /vorbərɛidə(n)/ (bereidde voor, heeft voorbereid) prepare, get ready: *zich ~ op een examen* prepare for an exam; *op alles voorbereid zijn* be ready for anything

voorbereidend /vorbərɛidənt/ (adj) preparatory: *~ wetenschappelijk onderwijs* pre-university education; *~e werkzaamheden* groundwork

de **voorbereiding** /vorbərɛidɪŋ/ (pl: -en) preparation: *~en treffen* make preparations

de **voorbeschouwing** /vorbəsxauwɪŋ/ (pl: -en) preview

de **voorbespreking** /vorbəsprekɪŋ/ (pl: -en) preliminary talk

voorbestemmen /vorbəstɛmə(n)/ (bestemde voor, heeft voorbestemd) predestine, predetermine: *voorbestemd zijn om te ...*

predestined (or: fated) to ...

[1] **voorbij** /vorbɛi/ (adj) past; over: *die tijd is ~* those days are gone; *~e tijden* bygone times

[2] **voorbij** /vorbɛi/ (adv) **1** past, by: *wacht tot de trein ~ is* wait until the train has passed **2** beyond, past: *hij is die leeftijd allang ~* he is way past that age; *je bent er al ~* you have already passed it

[3] **voorbij** /vorbɛi/ (prep) beyond, past: *we zijn al ~ Amsterdam* we've already passed Amsterdam; *hij ging ~ het huis* he went past the house

voorbijgaan /vorbɛiɣan/ (ging voorbij, is voorbijgegaan) pass by, go by: *de jaren gingen voorbij* the years passed by; *een kans voorbij laten gaan* pass up a chance; *er gaat praktisch geen week voorbij of ...* hardly a week goes by when (or: that) ... || *in het ~* incidentally, by the way, in passing

voorbijgaand /vorbɛiɣant/ (adj) transitory, passing: *van ~e aard* of a temporary nature

de **voorbijganger** /vorbɛiɣaŋər/ (pl: -s) passerby

voorbijkomen /vorbɛikomə(n)/ (kwam voorbij, is voorbijgekomen) come past, come by, pass (by)

voorbijrijden /vorbɛirɛidə(n)/ (reed voorbij, is voorbijgereden) drive past; ride past

voorbijschieten /vorbɛisxitə(n)/ (schoot voorbij, is voorbijgeschoten) whizz by || *zijn doel ~* overshoot the mark

voorbijtrekken /vorbɛitrɛkə(n)/ (trok voorbij, is voorbijgetrokken) pass: *hij zag zijn leven aan zijn oog ~* he saw his life pass before his eyes

voorbijvliegen /vorbɛivliɣə(n)/ (vloog voorbij, is voorbijgevlogen) fly (by): *de weken vlogen voorbij* the weeks just flew (by)

de **voorbode** /vorbodə/ (pl: -s) forerunner, herald; [fig] omen: *de zwaluwen zijn de ~n van de lente* the swallows are the heralds of spring

voordat /vordɑt/ (conj) **1** before; until: *alles was gemakkelijker ~ hij kwam* things were easier before he came; *~ ik je brief kreeg, wist ik er niets van* I knew nothing about it until I got your letter **2** before (that): *maar niet ~ ...* but not before ...

het **voordeel** /vordel/ (pl: -delen) **1** advantage, benefit: *Federer staat op ~* advantage Federer; *zijn ~ met iets doen* take advantage of sth.; *~ hebben bij* profit (or: benefit) from; *hij is in zijn ~ veranderd* he has changed for the better; *3-0 in het ~ van Nederland* 3-0 for the Dutch side (or: team); *iem. het ~ van de twijfel gunnen* give s.o. the benefit of the doubt **2** advantage, plus point: *de voor- en nadelen* the advantages and disadvantages; *een ~ behalen* gain an advantage

de **voordeelregel** /vordelreɣəl/ advantage rule: *de ~ toepassen* apply the advantage

voorkeurstem

rule

voordelig /vordeləɤ/ (adj, adv) **1** profitable, lucrative: ~ *kopen* get a bargain **2** economical, inexpensive: ~*er zijn* be cheaper; ~ *in* het gebruik be economical in use, go a long way

de **voordeur** /vordør/ (pl: -en) front door

¹**voordoen** /vordun/ (deed voor, heeft voorgedaan) show, demonstrate

zich ²**voordoen** /vordun/ (deed zich voor, heeft zich voorgedaan) act, appear, pose: zich *flink* ~ put on a bold front; zich ~ *als* politieagent pose as a policeman

de **voordracht** /vordraxt/ (pl: -en) lecture: een ~ *houden* over read a paper on, give a lecture on

voordragen /vordrayə(n)/ (droeg voor, heeft voorgedragen) **1** recite **2** nominate, recommend

voordringen /vordrɪŋə(n)/ (drong voor, is voorgedrongen) push forward (or: past, ahead), jump the queue

de **voordringer** /vordrɪŋər/ (pl: -s) queuejumper

de **voorfilm** /vorfɪlm/ (pl: -s) short

voorgaan /voryan/ (ging voor, is voorgegaan) **1** go ahead (or: before), lead (the way): *dames* gaan voor ladies first; iem. *laten* ~ let s.o. go first; gaat u voor! after you!, lead the way **2** take precedence, come first: het belangrijkste *moet* ~ the most important has to come first

voorgaand /voryant/ (adj) preceding, former, last, previous: op de ~e *bladzijde* on the preceding page

de **voorganger** /voryaŋər/ (pl: -s) predecessor

het **voorgebergte** /voryəbɛrxtə/ promontory, headland

voorgekookt /voryəkokt/ (adj) precooked, parboiled: ~e *aardappelen* precooked potatoes; ~e *rijst* parboiled rice || het *was* allemaal ~ it was all pre-arranged

voorgeleiden /voryəlɛidə(n)/ (geleidde voor, heeft voorgeleid) bring in

voorgenomen /voryənomə(n)/ (adj) intended, proposed: de ~ *maatregelen* the proposed measures

het **voorgerecht** /voryərɛxt/ (pl: -en) first course, starter

de **voorgeschiedenis** /voryəsxidənɪs/ previous history; [of pers] ancestry; past history

voorgeschreven /voryəsxrevə(n)/ (adj) prescribed, required

de **voorgevel** /voryevəl/ (pl: -s) face

voorgeven /voryevə(n)/ (gaf voor, heeft voorgegeven) pretend

het **voorgevoel** /voryəvul/ (pl: -ens) premonition; foreboding: een *angstig* ~ an anxious foreboding; ergens een ~ van *hebben* have a premonition about sth.

voorgoed /voryut/ (adv) for good, once

and for all: dat *is* nu ~ voorbij that is over and done with now

de **voorgrond** /voryront/ (pl: -en) foreground: op de ~ *treden*, zich *op* de ~ *plaatsen* come into prominence; iets *op* de ~ *plaatsen* place sth. in the forefront; hij dringt zich altijd *op* de ~ he always pushes himself forward

de **voorhamer** /vorhamər/ (pl: -s) sledge(hammer)

de **voorhand** /vorhant/: *op* ~ beforehand, in advance

voorhanden /vorhandə(n)/ (adj) on hand, in stock: *niet* meer ~ unavailable

voorhebben /vorhɛbə(n)/ (had voor, heeft voorgehad) **1** have on, wear: een *schort* ~ have on (or: wear) an apron **2** have in front of: de *verkeerde* ~ have got the wrong one (in mind) || het *goed* met iem. ~ mean well by a person, wish a person well

voorheen /vorhen/ (adv) formerly, in the past

de **voorheffing** /vorhɛfɪŋ/ (pl: -en) advance tax payment

de **voorhoede** /vorhudə/ (pl: -s) forward line, forwards

de **voorhoedespeler** /vorhudəspelər/ (pl: -s) forward

het **voorhoofd** /vorhoft/ (pl: -en) forehead

de **voorhoofdsholteontsteking** /vorhoftsholtəontstekɪŋ/ (pl: -en) sinusitis

voorhouden /vorhaudə(n)/ (hield voor, heeft voorgehouden) represent, confront: iem. zijn slechte *gedrag* ~ confront s.o. with his bad conduct

de **voorhuid** /vorhœyt/ (pl: -en) foreskin

voorin /vorɪn/ (adv) in (the) front; at the beginning

vooringenomen /vorɪŋɣənomə(n)/ (adj) biased, prejudiced

het **voorjaar** /vorjar/ (pl: -jaren) spring, springtime

de **voorjaarsmoeheid** /vorjarsmuhɛit/ springtime fatigue

de **voorjaarsvakantie** /vorjarsfakan(t)si/ (pl: -s) spring holidays; [Am] spring vacation

de **voorkamer** /vorkamər/ (pl: -s) front room

de **voorkant** /vorkant/ (pl: -en) front: de ~ *van* een *auto* the front of a car

voorkauwen /vorkauwə(n)/ (kauwde voor, heeft voorgekauwd) repeat over and over

de **voorkennis** /vorkɛnɪs/ foreknowledge; inside knowledge: ~ *hebben* van have prior knowledge of; handel *met* ~ insider trading (or: dealing)

de **voorkeur** /vorkør/ preference: mijn ~ *gaat uit naar* I (would) prefer; de ~ *geven* aan give preference to; *bij* ~ preferably

de **voorkeursbehandeling** /vorkørzbəhandəlɪŋ/ (pl: -en) preferential treatment

de **voorkeurstem** /vorkørstɛm/ (pl: -men) preference vote

het **¹voorkomen** /vo̯rkomə(n)/ **1** appearance, bearing: *nu krijgt de zaak een geheel ander ~* things are now looking a lot different **2** occurrence, incidence: *het regelmatig ~ van ongeregeldheden* the recurrence of disturbances

²voorkomen /vo̯rkomə(n)/ (kwam voor, is voorgekomen) **1** occur, happen **2** occur, be found: *die planten komen overal voor* those plants grow everywhere **3** appear: *hij moet ~* he has to appear in court **4** seem, appear: *dat komt mij bekend voor* that rings a bell, that sounds familiar

³voorkomen /vo̯rko̯mə(n)/ (voorkwam, heeft voorkomen) prevent: *om misverstanden te ~* to prevent (any) misunderstandings; *we moeten ~ dat hij hier weggaat* we must prevent him from leaving; *~ is beter dan genezen* prevention is better than cure

voorkomend /vo̯rkomənt/ (adj) occurring: *dagelijks ~e zaken* everyday events, recurrent matters; *een veel ~ probleem* a common problem; *zelden ~* unusual, rare

de **voorkoming** /vo̯rkomɪŋ/ prevention: *ter ~ van ongelukken* to prevent accidents

voorlaatst /vo̯rla̯tst/ (adj) last but one

het **voorland** /vo̯rlant/ (pl: -en) future: *dat is ook haar ~* that's also in store for her

voorlangs /vo̯rlaŋs/ (adv) along the front (of sth.): [sport] *de bal ~ schieten* shoot across the goal

voorlaten /vo̯rlatə(n)/ (liet voor, heeft voorgelaten) allow to go first, give precedence to

voorleggen /vo̯rlɛɣə(n)/ (legde voor, heeft voorgelegd) present: *iem. een plan ~* present s.o. with a plan; *een zaak aan de rechter ~* bring a case before the court

de **voorletter** /vo̯rlɛtər/ (pl: -s) initial (letter): *wat zijn uw ~s?* what are your initials?

voorlezen /vo̯rlezə(n)/ (las voor, heeft voorgelezen) read aloud, read out loud: *iem. een brief* (or: *de krant*) *~* read aloud a letter (or: the newspaper) to s.o.; *kinderen houden van ~* children like to be read to; *~ uit een boek* read aloud from a book

voorlichten /vo̯rlɪxtə(n)/ (lichtte voor, heeft voorgelicht) **1** inform: *zich goed laten ~* seek good advice; *we zijn verkeerd voorgelicht* we were misinformed **2** tell (s.o.) the facts of life

de **voorlichter** /vo̯rlɪxtər/ (pl: -s) press officer, information officer

de **voorlichting** /vo̯rlɪxtɪŋ/ (pl: -en) information: *de afdeling ~* public relations department; *seksuele ~* sex education; *goede ~ geven* give good advice

de **voorlichtingsdienst** /vo̯rlɪxtɪŋzdinst/ (pl: -en) (public) information service

de **voorliefde** /vo̯rlivdə/ predilection, preference, fondness

voorliegen /vo̯rliɣə(n)/ (loog voor, heeft voorgelogen) lie to

voorlopen /vo̯rlopə(n)/ (liep voor, heeft voorgelopen) **1** walk (or: go) in front **2** be fast: *de klok loopt vijf minuten voor* the clock is five minutes fast

de **voorloper** /vo̯rlopər/ (pl: -s) precursor, forerunner

¹voorlopig /vo̯rlopəχ/ (adj) temporary, provisional: *een ~e aanstelling* a temporary appointment; *~ verslag* interim report

²voorlopig /vo̯rlopəχ/ (adv) for the time being: *hij zal het ~ accepteren* he will accept it provisionally; *~ niet* not for the time being; *~ voor een maand* for a month to begin with

voormalig /vo̯rmaləχ/ (adj) former

de **voorman** /vo̯rman/ (pl: -nen) foreman

de **voormiddag** /vo̯rmɪdaχ/ (pl: -en) **1** morning **2** [Dutch] early afternoon

de **voorn** /vo̯rn/ (pl: -s) roach

de **¹voornaam** /vo̯rnam/ first name: *iem. bij zijn ~ noemen* call s.o. by his first name

²voornaam /vo̯rnam/ (adj, adv) **1** distinguished, prominent: *een ~ voorkomen* a dignified (or: distinguished) appearance **2** main, important: *de ~ste dagbladen* the leading dailies; *de ~ste feiten* the main facts

het **voornaamwoord** /vo̯rnamvort/ (pl: -en) pronoun: *aanwijzend ~* demonstrative pronoun; *bezittelijk ~* possessive pronoun; *betrekkelijk ~* relative pronoun; *persoonlijk ~* personal pronoun

voornamelijk /vo̯rnaməlik/ (adv) mainly, chiefly

het **¹voornemen** /vo̯rnemə(n)/ (pl: -s) intention; resolution: *goede ~s voor het nieuwe jaar* New Year's resolutions; *zij is vol goede ~s* she is full of good intentions; *het vaste ~ iets te bereiken* the determination to achieve sth.

zich **²voornemen** /vo̯rnemə(n)/ (nam zich voor, heeft zich voorgenomen) resolve: *hij had het zich heilig voorgenomen* he had firmly resolved to do so; *zij bereikte wat ze zich voorgenomen had* she achieved what she had set out (or: planned) to do

voornoemd /vo̯rnumt/ (adj) above-mentioned

de **vooronderstelling** /vo̯rɔndərstɛlɪŋ/ (pl: -en) presupposition

het **vooronderzoek** /vo̯rɔndərzuk/ (pl: -en) preliminary investigation: *gerechtelijk ~* hearing

het **vooroordeel** /vo̯rordel/ (pl: -oordelen) prejudice: *een ~ hebben over* be prejudiced against; *zonder vooroordelen* unbiased, unprejudiced

vooroorlogs /vo̯rorloχs/ (adj) pre-war

voorop /vo̯rɔp/ (adv) in front, in the lead, first: *het nummer staat ~ het bankbiljet* the number is on the front of the banknote; *~ staat, dat …* the main thing is that …

vooropgaan /vo̯rɔpχan/ (ging voorop, is

vooropgegaan) lead (the way)

de **vooropleiding** /vorɔplɛidɪŋ/ (pl: -en) (preliminary, preparatory) training

vooroplopen /vorɔplopə(n)/ (liep voorop, heeft vooropgelopen) **1** walk (or: run) in front **2** lead (the way): ~ *in de modewereld* be a trendsetter in the fashion world

vooropstaan /vorɔpstan/ (stond voorop, heeft vooropgestaan): *wat vooropstaat, is …* the main thing is that …

vooropstellen /vorɔpstɛlə(n)/ (stelde voorop, heeft vooropgesteld) **1** assume: *laten we dit ~: …* let's get one thing straight right away: …; *ik stel voorop dat hij altijd eerlijk is geweest* to begin with, I maintain that he has always been honest **2** put first (and foremost): *de volksgezondheid ~* put public health first (and foremost)

de **voorouders** /voraudərs/ (pl) ancestors, forefathers

voorover /vorovər/ (adv) headfirst, face down: *met het gezicht ~ liggen* lie face down(ward); *~ tuimelen* tumble headfirst (or: forward)

de **voorpagina** /vorpaɣina/ (pl: -'s) front page: *de ~'s halen* make the front pages

de **voorpoot** /vorpot/ (pl: -poten) foreleg, forepaw

de **voorpret** /vorprɛt/ pleasurable anticipation

het **voorproefje** /vorprufjə/ (pl: -s) (fore)taste

het **voorprogramma** /vorproɣrama/ (pl: -'s) curtain-raiser; supporting programme; shorts: *een concert van … met … in het ~* a … concert with … as supporting act

de **voorraad** /vorat/ (pl: voorraden) **1** stock, supply: *de ~ goud* the gold reserve(s); *de ~ opnemen* take stock; *zolang de ~ strekt* as long as (or: while) supplies/stocks last; *niet meer in ~ zijn* not be in stock anymore; *uit ~ leverbaar* available from stock **2** supplies, stock(s): *~ inslaan voor de winter* lay in supplies for the winter; *we zijn door onze ~ heen* we have gone through our supplies

de **voorraadkast** /voratkɑst/ (pl: -en) store cupboard; [Am] supply closet

voorradig /voradəx/ (adj) in stock (or: store), on hand: *in alle kleuren ~* available in all colours

de **voorrang** /voraŋ/ right of way, priority: *~ hebben op* have (the) right of way over; *verkeer van rechts heeft ~* traffic from the right has (the) right of way; *geen ~ verlenen* fail to yield, fail to give (right of) way; *~ verlenen aan verkeer van rechts* give way (or: yield) to the right; *(de) ~ hebben (boven)* have (or: take) priority (over); *met ~ behandelen* give preferential treatment; [feelings] *om ~ strijden* fight to gain the upper hand

de **voorrangsweg** /voraŋswɛx/ (pl: -en) major road

het **voorrecht** /vorɛxt/ (pl: -en) privilege: *ik had*

het ~ hem te verwelkomen I had the honour (or: privilege) of welcoming him

voorrekenen /vorekənə(n)/ (rekende voor, heeft voorgerekend) figure out, work out

voorrijden /vorɛidə(n)/ (reed voor, heeft/is voorgereden) drive up to the front (or: entrance, door)

de **voorrijkosten** /vorɛikɔstə(n)/ (pl) call-out charge

de **voorronde** /vorɔndə/ (pl: -n, -s) qualifying round, preliminary round

de **voorruit** /vorœyt/ (pl: -en) windscreen; [Am] windshield

voorschieten /vorsxitə(n)/ (schoot voor, heeft voorgeschoten) advance, lend: *ik zal het even ~* I'll lend you the money

de **voorschoot** /vorsxot/ (pl: -schoten) apron, pinafore

het **voorschot** /vorsxɔt/ (pl: -ten) advance, loan

voorschotelen /vorsxotələ(n)/ (schotelde voor, heeft voorgeschoteld) dish up, serve up

het **voorschrift** /vorsxrɪft/ (pl: -en) **1** prescription, order: *op ~ van de dokter* on doctor's orders **2** regulation, rule: *aan de ~en voldoen* satisfy (or: meet) the requirements; *volgens ~* as prescribed (or: directed)

voorschrijven /vorsxrɛivə(n)/ (schreef voor, heeft voorgeschreven) prescribe: *rust ~* prescribe rest; *op de voorgeschreven tijd* at the appointed time

het **voorseizoen** /vorsɛizun/ (pl: -en) pre-season

de **voorselectie** /vorsəlɛksi/ (pl: -s) pre-selection

voorsorteren /vorsɔrterə(n)/ (sorteerde voor, heeft voorgesorteerd) get in lane: *rechts ~* get in the right-hand lane

het **voorspel** /vorspɛl/ (pl: -en) **1** prelude, prologue: *het ~ van de oorlog* the prelude to the war **2** foreplay

voorspelbaar /vorspɛlbar/ (adj) predictable

voorspelen /vorspelə(n)/ (speelde voor, heeft voorgespeeld) play

voorspellen /vorspɛlə(n)/ (voorspelde, heeft voorspeld) **1** predict, forecast: *iem. een gouden toekomst ~* predict a rosy future for s.o.; *ik heb het u wel voorspeld* I told you so **2** promise: *dat voorspelt niet veel goeds* that doesn't bode well

de **voorspelling** /vorspɛlɪŋ/ (pl: -en) **1** prophecy **2** prediction: *de ~en voor morgen* the (weather) forecast for tomorrow

voorspiegelen /vorspiɣələ(n)/ (spiegelde voor, heeft voorgespiegeld) delude (with images of …)

de **voorspoed** /vorsput/ prosperity: *in voor- en tegenspoed* for better or for worse; *voor- en tegenspoed* ups and downs

voorspoedig /vorspudəx/ (adj, adv) successful, prosperous: *alles verliep ~* it all went off well

de **voorspraak** /vorsprak/ intercession

de **voorsprong** /vorspron/ (pl: -en) (head) start, lead: *hij won met grote ~* he won by a large margin; *iem. een ~ geven* give s.o. a head start; *een ~ hebben op iem.* have the jump (*or:* lead) on s.o.

voorst /vorst/ (adj) first, front: *op de ~e bank zitten* be (*or:* sit) in the front row

voorstaan /vorstan/ (stond voor, heeft voorgestaan) stand (*or:* be) in front: *de auto staat voor* the car is (out) at the front

de **voorstad** /vorstat/ (pl: -steden) suburb

de **voorstander** /vorstandər/ (pl: -s) supporter, advocate: *ik ben er een groot ~ van* I'm all for it

het **voorstel** /vorstɛl/ (pl: -len) proposal, suggestion: *iem. een ~ doen* make s.o. a proposal (*or:* proposition)

voorstelbaar /vorstɛlbar/ (adj) imaginable, conceivable

¹**voorstellen** /vorstɛlə(n)/ (stelde voor, heeft voorgesteld) **1** introduce: *zich ~ aan* introduce o.s. to **2** suggest, propose **3** represent, play **4** represent, depict: *het schilderij stelt een huis voor* the painting depicts a house ‖ *dat stelt niets voor* that doesn't amount to anything

zich ²**voorstellen** /vorstɛlə(n)/ (stelde zich voor, heeft zich voorgesteld) imagine, conceive: *dat kan ik me best ~* I can imagine (that); *ik kan mij zijn gezicht niet meer ~* I can't recall his face; *daar kan ik me niets bij ~* **a)** I'm not getting the point; **b)** I can't see that happening; *wat moet ik me daarbij ~?* what exactly do you mean?; *stel je voor!* just imagine!

de **voorstelling** /vorstɛlɪŋ/ (pl: -en) **1** show-(ing), performance: *doorlopende ~* non-stop (*or:* continuous) performance **2** representation, depiction **3** impression, idea: *dat is een verkeerde ~ van zaken* that is a misrepresentation; *zich een ~ van iets maken* picture sth., form an idea of sth.

het **voorstellingsvermogen** /vorstɛlɪŋsfərmoɣə(n)/ (power(s) of) imagination

voorstemmen /vorstɛmə(n)/ (stemde voor, heeft voorgestemd) vote for

de **voorsteven** /vorstevə(n)/ (pl: -s) stem, prow

de **voorstopper** /vorstopər/ (pl: -s) centre back

voort /vort/ (adv) on(wards), forward

voortaan /vortan/ (adv) from now on

de **voortand** /vortant/ (pl: -en) front tooth

het ¹**voortbestaan** /vordbəstan/ continued existence (*or:* life), survival: *in zijn ~ bedreigd worden* be threatened

²**voortbestaan** /vordbəstan/ (bestond voort, heeft voortbestaan) continue to exist

¹**voortbewegen** /vordbəweɣə(n)/ (bewoog voort, heeft voortbewogen) drive, move on (*or:* forward): *het karretje werd door stroom voortbewogen* the buggy was driven by electricity

zich ²**voortbewegen** /vordbəweɣə(n)/ (bewoog zich voort, heeft zich voortbewogen) move on (*or:* forward)

voortborduren /vordbordyrə(n)/ (borduurde voort, heeft voortgeborduurd) embroider, elaborate: *op een thema ~* elaborate (*or:* embroider) on a theme

voortbrengen /vordbrɛŋə(n)/ (bracht voort, heeft voortgebracht) produce, create, bring forth: *kinderen ~* produce children

het **voortbrengsel** /vordbrɛŋsəl/ (pl: -en) product

voortduren /vordyrə(n)/ (duurde voort, heeft voortgeduurd) continue, go on, wear on

voortdurend /vordyrənt/ (adj, adv) constant, continual; continuous: *een ~e dreiging* a constant threat (*or:* menace); *haar naam duikt ~ op in de krant* her name keeps cropping up in the (news)papers

het **voorteken** /vortekə(n)/ (pl: -s, -en) omen, sign

de **voortent** /vortɛnt/ (pl: -en) front bell (end), (front) extension; awning

voortgaan /vortxan/ (ging voort, is voortgegaan) continue

de **voortgang** /vortxaŋ/ progress

voortgezet /vortxəzɛt/ (adj) continued, further: *~ onderwijs* secondary education

voortijdig /vortɛidəx/ (adj, adv) premature, untimely: *de les werd ~ afgebroken* the lesson was cut short; *~ klaar zijn* be finished ahead of time

voortkomen /vortkomə(n)/ (kwam voort, is voortgekomen) (+ uit) stem (from), flow (from): *de daaruit ~de misstanden* the resulting (*or:* consequent) abuses

voortleven /vortlevə(n)/ (leefde voort, heeft voortgeleefd) live on: *zij leeft voort in onze herinnering* she lives on in our memory

voortmaken /vortmakə(n)/ (maakte voort, heeft voortgemaakt) hurry up, make haste

het **voortouw** /vortau/: *het ~ nemen* take the lead

zich **voortplanten** /vortplantə(n)/ (plantte zich voort, heeft zich voortgeplant) **1** reproduce, multiply **2** propagate, be transmitted: *geluid plant zich voort in golven* sound is transmitted (*or:* travels) in waves

de **voortplanting** /vortplantɪŋ/ reproduction, multiplication, breeding: *geslachtelijke ~* sexual reproduction

het **voortplantingsorgaan** /vortplantɪŋsorɣan/ (pl: -organen) reproductive organ

voortreffelijk /vortrɛfələk/ (adj, adv) excellent, superb: *hij danst ~* he dances superbly (*or:* exquisitely)

voortrekken /vortrɛkə(n)/ (trok voor, heeft voorgetrokken) favour, give preference to: *de een boven de ander ~* favour one person above another

de **voortrekker** /vo̱rtrɛkər/ (pl: -s) **1** pioneer **2** Venture Scout; [Am] Explorer

voorts /vorts/ (adv) furthermore, moreover, besides

zich **voortslepen** /vo̱rtslepə(n)/ (sleepte zich voort, heeft zich voortgesleept) drag on, linger: *een zich al jarenlang ~de kwestie* a lingering question

de **voortuin** /vo̱rtœyn/ (pl: -en) front garden; [Am] front yard

voortvarend /vortfa̱rənt/ (adj, adv) energetic, dynamic

voortvloeien /vo̱rtflujə(n)/ (vloeide voort, is voortgevloeid) result (from), arise (from)

voortvluchtig /vortfly̱xtəx/ (adj) fugitive: *hij is ~* he is on the run

voortzetten /vo̱rtsɛtə(n)/ (zette voort, heeft voortgezet) continue, carry on (or: forward): *de kennismaking ~* pursue the acquaintance; *iemands werk ~* carry on s.o.'s work

¹**vooruit** /vorœy̱t/ (adv) **1** ahead, further: *hiermee kan ik weer een tijdje ~* this will keep me going for a while **2** before(hand), in advance: *zijn tijd ~ zijn* be ahead of one's time; *ver ~* well in advance

²**vooruit** /vorœy̱t/ (int) get going, let's go, come on, go on: *~! aan je werk* come on, time for work; *nou, ~ dan maar* **a)** all right then let's do it; **b)** all right then I'll do it; **c)** go ahead

vooruitbetalen /vorœy̱dbətalə(n)/ (betaalde vooruit, heeft vooruitbetaald) prepay, pay in advance

de **vooruitblik** /vorœy̱dblɪk/ (pl: -ken) preview, look ahead: *een ~ op het volgende seizoen* a preview of (or: look ahead at) the coming season

vooruitdenken /vorœy̱dɛŋkə(n)/ (dacht vooruit, heeft vooruitgedacht) think ahead

vooruitgaan /vorœy̱txan/ (ging vooruit, is vooruitgegaan) progress, improve: *zijn gezondheid gaat vooruit* his health is improving; *er financieel op ~* be better off (financially); profit (financially)

de **vooruitgang** /vorœy̱txaŋ/ (pl: -en) progress; improvement

vooruitkijken /vorœy̱tkɛikə(n)/ (keek vooruit, heeft vooruitgekeken) look ahead

vooruitkomen /vorœy̱tkomə(n)/ (kwam vooruit, is vooruitgekomen) get on (or: ahead), get somewhere, make headway: *moeizaam ~* progress with difficulty

vooruitlopen /vorœy̱tlopə(n)/ (liep vooruit, is vooruitgelopen) anticipate, be ahead (of): *~d op* in advance of; *op de gebeurtenissen ~* anticipate events

vooruitstrevend /vorœytstre̱vənt/ (adj) progressive

het **vooruitzicht** /vorœy̱tsɪxt/ (pl: -en) prospect, outlook: *goede ~en hebben* have good prospects; *iem. iets in het ~ stellen* hold out the prospect of sth. to s.o.

vooruitzien /vorœy̱tsin/ (zag vooruit, heeft vooruitgezien) look ahead (or: forward): *regeren is ~* foresight is the essence of government

vooruitziend /vorœy̱tsint/ (adj) far-sighted; visionary

de **voorvader** /vo̱rvadər/ (pl: -en) ancestor, forefather

het **voorval** /vo̱rval/ (pl: -len) incident, event

voorvallen /vo̱rvalə(n)/ (viel voor, is voorgevallen) occur, happen

de **voorvechter** /vo̱rvɛxtər/ (pl: -s) champion, advocate

de **voorverkiezing** /vo̱rvərkizɪŋ/ (pl: -en) preliminary election; [Am] primary (election)

de **voorverkoop** /vo̱rvərkop/ advance booking (or: sale(s)): *de kaarten in de ~ zijn goedkoper* the tickets are cheaper if you buy them in advance

voorverpakt /vo̱rvərpɑkt/ (adj) pre-packed

voorverwarmen /vo̱rvərwarmə(n)/ (verwarmde voor, heeft voorverwarmd) preheat

het **voorvoegsel** /vo̱rvuxsəl/ (pl: -s) prefix

voorwaar /vorwa̱r/ (adv) indeed, truly

de **voorwaarde** /vo̱rwardə/ (pl: -n) **1** condition, provision: *onder ~ dat ...* provided that ..., on condition that ...; *onder geen enkele ~* on no account, under no circumstances; *iets als ~ stellen* state (or: stipulate) sth. as a condition **2** [com] condition; terms: *wat zijn uw ~n?* what are your terms?

voorwaardelijk /vorwa̱rdələk/ (adj, adv) conditional, provisional: *~e invrijheidstelling* (release on) parole; *hij is ~ overgegaan* he has been put in the next class on probation; [Am] he has been put in the next grade on probation; *~ veroordelen* give a suspended sentence; put on probation

¹**voorwaarts** /vo̱rwarts/ (adj, adv) forward(s), onward(s): *een stap ~* a step forward(s)

²**voorwaarts** /vo̱rwarts/ (int) forward: *~ mars!* forward march!

de **voorwas** /vo̱rwas/ pre-wash

de **voorwedstrijd** /vo̱rwɛtstrɛit/ (pl: -en) preliminary competition (or: game)

voorwenden /vo̱rwɛndə(n)/ (wendde voor, heeft voorgewend) pretend, feign

het **voorwendsel** /vo̱rwɛntsəl/ (pl: -s) pretext, pretence: *onder valse ~s* under false pretences; *onder ~ van* under the pretext of

het **voorwerk** /vo̱rwɛrk/ (pl: -en) preliminary work

het **voorwerp** /vo̱rwɛrp/ (pl: -en) object: *het lijdend ~* the direct object; *meewerkend ~* indirect object; *gevonden ~en* lost property

het **voorwiel** /vo̱rwil/ (pl: -en) front wheel

de **voorwielaandrijving** /vo̱rwilandrɛivɪŋ/

front-wheel drive

het **voorwoord** /v<u>o</u>rwort/ (pl: -en) foreword, preface

voorzeggen /v<u>o</u>rzεɣə(n)/ (zei/zegde voor, heeft voorgezegd) prompt: *het antwoord ~* whisper the answer; *niet ~!* no prompting!

de **voorzet** /v<u>o</u>rzεt/ (pl: -ten) cross, centre; ball into the area: *een goede ~ geven* cross the ball well, send in a good cross

het **voorzetsel** /v<u>o</u>rzεtsəl/ (pl: -s) preposition

voorzetten /v<u>o</u>rzεtə(n)/ (zette voor, heeft voorgezet) **1** put (*or:* place) in front (of) **2** put forward, set forward; put ahead **3** cross; hit the ball into the area

voorzichtig /vorz<u>ɪ</u>xtəx/ (adj, adv) **1** careful, cautious: *~! breekbaar! fragile! handle with care!; wees ~! be careful!; iem. het nieuws ~ vertellen* break the news gently to s.o.; *~ te werk gaan* proceed cautiously (*or:* with caution) **2** cautious; discreet: *~ naar iets informeren* make discreet inquiries (about sth.)

de **voorzichtigheid** /vorz<u>ɪ</u>xtəxhεit/ caution, care

voorzichtigheidshalve /vorzɪxtəxhεits-h<u>a</u>lvə/ (adv) as a precaution

¹**voorzien** /vorz<u>i</u>n/ (adj) provided: *wij zijn al ~* we have been taken care of (*or:* seen to); *het gebouw is ~ van videobewaking* the building is equipped with CCTV; *de deur is ~ van een slot* the door is fitted with a lock

²**voorzien** /vorz<u>i</u>n/ (voorzag, heeft voorzien) **1** foresee, anticipate: *dat was te ~* that was to be expected **2** (+ in) provide (for), see to: *in een behoefte ~* fill a need; *in zijn onderhoud kunnen ~* be able to support o.s. (*or:* to provide for o.s.) **3** (+ van) provide (with), equip (with): *het huis is ~ van centrale verwarming* the house has central heating

de **voorzienigheid** /vorz<u>i</u>nəxhεit/ providence: *Gods ~* divine providence

de **voorziening** /vorz<u>i</u>nɪŋ/ (pl: -en) **1** provision, service: *sociale ~en* social services; *sanitaire ~en* sanitary facilities; *~en treffen* make arrangements **2** provision: *een voorlopige ~* an interim provision

de **voorzijde** /v<u>o</u>rzεidə/ (pl: -n) front (side)

voorzitten /v<u>o</u>rzɪtə(n)/ (zat voor, heeft voorgezeten) chair

de **voorzitter** /v<u>o</u>rzɪtər/ (pl: -s) chairman: *mijnheer* (*or:* *mevrouw*) *de ~* Mr Chairman, Madam Chairman (*or:* Chairwoman); *~ zijn* chair a (*or:* the) meeting

het **voorzitterschap** /v<u>o</u>rzɪtərsxap/ chairmanship

de **voorzorg** /v<u>o</u>rzɔrx/ (pl: -en) precaution: *uit ~ iets doen* do sth. as a precaution(ary measure)

de **voorzorgsmaatregel** /v<u>o</u>rzɔrxsmatreɣəl/ (pl: -en) precaution, precautionary measure: *~en nemen (treffen) tegen* take precautions against

voos /vos/ (adj) **1** dried-out **2** hollow **3** rotten

¹**vorderen** /v<u>o</u>rdərə(n)/ (vorderde, is gevorderd) (make) progress, move forward, make headway: *naarmate de dag vorderde* as the day progressed (*or:* wore on)

²**vorderen** /v<u>o</u>rdərə(n)/ (vorderde, heeft gevorderd) **1** demand, claim: *het te ~ bedrag is … the amount due is …; geld ~ van iem.* demand money from s.o. **2** requisition

de **vordering** /v<u>o</u>rdərɪŋ/ (pl: -en) **1** progress, headway: *~en maken* (make) progress, make headway **2** demand, claim: *een ~ instellen tegen iem.* put in (*or:* submit) a claim against s.o.; *~ op iem.* claim against s.o.

voren /v<u>o</u>rə(n)/ (adv): *kom wat naar ~* come closer (*or:* up here) a bit; *naar ~ komen* **a)** come forward; **b)** [fig] come up, come to the fore; *van ~* from (*or:* on) the front (side); *van ~ af aan* from the beginning

vorig /v<u>o</u>rəx/ (adj) **1** last, previous: *de ~e avond* the night before, the previous night; *in het ~e hoofdstuk* in the preceding (*or:* last) chapter; *de ~e keer* (the) last time **2** earlier, former: *haar ~e man* her former husband

de **vork** /vɔrk/ (pl: -en) fork

de **vorkheftruck** /v<u>o</u>rkhεftryk/ (pl: -s) forklift (truck)

de **vorm** /vɔrm/ (pl: -en) **1** form, shape, outline: *naar ~ en inhoud* in form and content; *de lijdende ~ van een werkwoord* the passive voice (*or:* form) of a verb **2** mould, form **3** (proper) form; shape; build: *in goede ~ zijn* be in good shape (*or:* condition)

vormelijk /v<u>o</u>rmələk/ (adj, adv) **1** formal **2** formalistic

vormen /v<u>o</u>rmə(n)/ (vormde, heeft gevormd) **1** shape, form, mould **2** form, make (up), build (up): *die delen ~ een geheel* those parts make up a whole; *zich een oordeel ~* form an opinion

vormend /v<u>o</u>rmənt/ (adj) formative: *algemeen ~ onderwijs* general (*or:* non-vocational) education

de **vormfout** /v<u>o</u>rmfaut/ (pl: -en) technicality

vormgeven /v<u>o</u>rmɣevə(n)/ (gaf vorm, heeft vormgegeven) design

de **vormgever** /v<u>o</u>rmɣevər/ (pl: -s) designer, stylist

de **vormgeving** /v<u>o</u>rmɣevɪŋ/ design, style, styling: *een heel eigen ~* a very personal (*or:* individual) style

de **vorming** /v<u>o</u>rmɪŋ/ (pl: -en) **1** formation **2** education, training

het **vormsel** /v<u>o</u>rmsəl/ confirmation

de ¹**vorst** /vɔrst/ (pl: -en) sovereign, monarch: *iem. als een ~ onthalen* entertain s.o. like a prince

de ²**vorst** /vɔrst/ frost, freeze: *vier graden ~* four degrees below freezing; *lichte ~* slight frost; *matige ~* moderate frost; *strenge ~* hard (*or:*

severe, sharp) frost; *bij* ~ in frosty weather, in case of frost; *we krijgen* ~ there's (a) frost coming

vorstbestendig /vɔrstbəstɛndəx/ (adj) frost-resistant

vorstelijk /vɔrstələk/ (adj, adv) princely, royal, regal, lordly: *een* ~ *salaris* a princely salary; *iem.* ~ *belonen* reward s.o. generously

het **vorstendom** /vɔrstə(n)dɔm/ (pl: -men) principality, princedom

het **vorstenhuis** /vɔrstə(n)hœys/ (pl: -huizen) dynasty, royal house

de **vorstin** /vɔrstɪn/ (pl: -nen) queen, princess, sovereign's wife, ruler's wife

de **vorstschade** /vɔr(st)sxadə/ frost damage

het **vorstverlet** /vɔrstfərlɛt/ hold-ups due to frost

vorstvrij /vɔrstfrɛɪ/ (adj) frost-free

de **vos** /vɔs/ (pl: -sen) fox: *een troep* ~*sen* a pack of foxes; *een sluwe* ~ a sly old fox; *een* ~ *verliest wel zijn haren, maar niet zijn streken* the leopard cannot change his spots

de **vossenjacht** /vɔsə(n)jɑxt/ (pl: -en) **1** treasure hunt **2** fox hunt: *op* ~ *gaan (zijn)* go fox-hunting, ride to (*or:* follow) the hounds

de **vouw** /vɑu/ (pl: -en) crease, fold: *een scherpe* ~ a sharp crease; *zo gaat je broek uit de* ~ that will take the crease out of your trousers

vouwbaar /vɑubar/ (adj) foldable

de **vouwcaravan** /vɑukɛrəvɛn/ (pl: -s) folding caravan; [Am] folding trailer

de **vouwdeur** /vɑudər/ (pl: -en) folding door

vouwen /vɑuwə(n)/ (vouwde, heeft gevouwen) fold: *de handen* ~ fold one's hands (in prayer); *naar binnen* ~ fold in(wards); turn in

de **vouwfiets** /vɑufits/ (pl: -en) folding (*or:* collapsible) bike

de **voyeur** /vwɑjœr/ (pl: -s) voyeur, peeping Tom

de **vraag** /vrax/ (pl: vragen) **1** question; request: *een pijnlijke* ~ *stellen* ask an embarrassing (*or:* a delicate) question; *de* ~ *brandde mij op de lippen* the question was on the tip of my tongue; *vragen stellen* (or: *beantwoorden*) ask (*or:* answer) questions; *veelgestelde vragen* FAQ *(frequently asked questions)* **2** demand, call: ~ *en aanbod* supply and demand; *niet aan de* ~ *kunnen voldoen* be unable to meet the demand; *er is veel* ~ *naar tulpen* there's great demand (*or:* call) for tulips **3** question, problem, assignment **4** question, issue, problem, topic: *dat is zeer de* ~ that is highly debatable (*or:* questionable); *het is nog de* ~, *of* ... it remains to be seen whether ...

de **vraagbaak** /vraxbak/ (pl: vraagbaken) **1** oracle **2** handbook, encyclopedia **3** FAQ *(frequently asked questions)*

het **vraaggesprek** /vraxəsprɛk/ (pl: -ken) interview

de **vraagprijs** /vraxprɛis/ (pl: -prijzen) asking price

het **vraagstuk** /vraxstʏk/ (pl: -ken) problem, question

het **vraagteken** /vraxtekə(n)/ (pl: -s) question mark; [fig also] mystery: *de toekomst is een groot* ~ the future is one big question mark

de **vraatzucht** /vratsʏxt/ gluttony

vraatzuchtig /vratsʏxtəx/ (adj, adv) gluttonous, greedy

de **vracht** /vrɑxt/ (pl: -en) **1** freight(age), cargo; load: ~ *innemen* take in cargo (*or:* freight(age)) **2** load, burden, weight: *onder de* ~ *bezwijken* succumb under the burden **3** load, shipment **4** (cart)load, ton(s)

de **vrachtbrief** /vrɑxtbrif/ (pl: -brieven) waybill; consignment note; delivery note, forwarding note

het **vrachtschip** /vrɑxtsxɪp/ (pl: -schepen) freighter, cargo ship

het **vrachtverkeer** /vrɑxtfərker/ cargo trade, goods transport(ation); lorry traffic; [Am] truck traffic

het **vrachtvervoer** /vrɑxtfərvur/ goods carriage, cargo transport(ation)

het **vrachtvliegtuig** /vrɑxtflixtœyx/ (pl: -en) cargo plane (*or:* aircraft)

de **vrachtwagen** /vrɑxtwaɣə(n)/ (pl: -s) lorry; [Am] truck; van

de **vrachtwagenchauffeur** /vrɑxtwaɣə(n)ʃofør/ lorry driver; [Am] truck driver; [Am] trucker

¹**vragen** /vraɣə(n)/ (vroeg, heeft gevraagd) **1** ask (for): ~ *staat vrij* ask away, asking doesn't cost anything; *zou ik u iets mogen* ~? would you mind if I asked you a question?, can I ask you sth.?; ~ *hoe laat het is* ask (for) the time; *een politieagent de weg* ~ ask a policeman for (*or:* to show one) the way **2** ask (after, about), inquire (after, about): *daar wordt niet naar gevraagd* that's beside the point; *naar de bekende weg* ~ ask what one already knows (*or:* for the sake of asking) **3** ask, demand, request: *de rekening* ~ (*or:* call) for the bill **4** ask (for), call (for): *erom* ~ ask for it; *dat is om moeilijkheden* ~ that's asking for trouble

²**vragen** /vraɣə(n)/ (vroeg, heeft gevraagd) **1** ask, invite **2** ask, request: *hoeveel vraagt hij voor zijn huis?* how much does he want for his house?; *gevraagd: typiste* wanted: typist; *je vraagt te veel van jezelf* you're asking (*or:* demanding) too much of yourself; *veel aandacht* ~ demand a great deal of attention

¹**vragend** /vraɣənt/ (adj) interrogative: *een* ~ *voornaamwoord* an interrogative (pronoun)

²**vragend** /vraɣənt/ (adj, adv) questioning

de **vragenlijst** /vraɣə(n)lɛist/ (pl: -en) list of questions; questionnaire; inquiry form

de **vragensteller** /vraɣə(n)stɛlər/ questioner, inquirer, interviewer

de **VR-bril** /viːrbrɪl/ (pl: -len) VR headset

de **vrede** /vrе̲də/ **1** peace: ~ *sluiten* met conclude the peace with; ~ *stichten* make peace **2** peace, quiet(ude): ~ met iets *hebben* be resigned (or: reconciled) to sth.; accept sth.

vredelievend /vredəli̲vənt/ (adj, adv) peaceful, peace-loving

de **vrederechter** /vrе̲dərɛχtər/ (pl: -s) [Belg] justice of the peace

de **vredesactivist** /vrе̲dəsɑktivɪst/ (pl: -en) peace activist

het **vredesakkoord** /vrе̲dəsɑkort/ (pl: -en) peace agreement (or: treaty)

de **vredesbeweging** /vrе̲dəzbəweγɪŋ/ (pl: -en) peace movement

de **vredesconferentie** /vrе̲dəskonferɛnsi/ (pl: -s) peace conference

de **vredesduif** /vrе̲dəzdœyf/ (pl: -duiven) dove of peace

de **vredesmacht** /vrе̲dəsmɑχt/ peacekeeping force

vredesnaam /vrе̲dəsnam/: hoe is het *in* ~ mogelijk? how on earth is that possible?, for crying out loud, how is that possible?

de **vredesonderhandelingen** /vrе̲dəsɔndərhɑndəlɪŋə(n)/ (pl) peace negotiations (or: talks)

de **vredesoperatie** /vrе̲dəsopəra(t)si/ (pl: -s) peace operation

het **Vredespaleis** /vrе̲dəspalɛis/ Peace Palace

de **vredespijp** /vrе̲dəspɛip/ (pl: -en) pipe of peace: de ~ *roken* smoke the pipe of peace, keep the (or: make) peace

het **vredesproces** /vrе̲dəsprosɛs/ peace process

de **vredestichter** /vrе̲dəstɪχtər/ (pl: -s) peacemaker

de **vredestijd** /vrе̲dəstɛit/ peacetime

het **vredesverdrag** /vrе̲dəsfərdrɑχ/ (pl: -en) peace treaty

vredig /vrе̲dəχ/ (adj) peaceful, quiet

vreedzaam /vrе̲tsam/ (adj, adv) peaceful, non-violent

¹**vreemd** /vremt/ (adj) **1** strange, odd, unfamiliar, unusual: een ~e *gewoonte* an odd (or: a strange) habit; *het* ~e is, dat ... the odd (or: strange, funny) thing is that ... **2** foreign, strange, imported: zij *is* hier ~ she is a stranger here **3** foreign, exotic: ~ *geld* foreign currency; ~e *talen* foreign languages **4** strange, outside: ~ *gaan* have an (extramarital) affair

²**vreemd** /vremt/ (adv) strangely, oddly, unusually: ~ *doen* behave in an unusual way; ~ *genoeg* strangely enough, strange to say

de **vreemde** /vrе̲mdə/ **1** foreigner, stranger **2** stranger, outsider: dat hebben ze *van* geen ~ it's obvious who they got that from (or: where they learnt that)

de **vreemdeling** /vrе̲mdəlɪŋ/ (pl: -en) **1** stranger: hij is een ~ *in* zijn eigen land he is a stranger in his own country **2** immigrant, alien: *ongewenste* ~en unwanted immigrants

het **vreemdelingenbeleid** /vrе̲mdəlɪŋə(n)bəlɛit/ immigration policy

de **vreemdelingendienst** /vrе̲mdəlɪŋə(n)dinst/ immigration and naturalisation service

de **vreemdelingenhaat** /vrе̲mdəlɪŋə(n)hat/ xenophobia

het **vreemdelingenlegioen** /vrе̲mdəlɪŋə(n)leγijun/ foreign legion

vreemdgaan /vrе̲mtχan/ (ging vreemd, heeft/is vreemdgegaan) cheat, sleep around, have extramarital relations

vreemdsoortig /vremtso̲rtəχ/ (adj) peculiar, strange, odd

de **vrees** /vres/ (pl: vrezen) fear, fright: hij greep haar vast *uit* ~ dat hij zou vallen he grabbed hold of her for fear he should fall

de **vreetpartij** /vrе̲tpɑrtɛi/ (pl: -en) blow-out

de **vreetzak** /vrе̲tsɑk/ (pl: -ken) glutton, pig

de **vrek** /vrɛk/ (pl: -ken) miser, skinflint, Scrooge

vrekkig /vrɛ̲kəχ/ (adj, adv) miserly, stingy

¹**vreselijk** /vrе̲sələk/ (adj, adv) **1** terrible, awful: ~e *honger hebben* have a ravenous appetite; we *hebben* ~ *gelachen* we nearly died (of) laughing **2** terrifying, horrible: een ~e *moord* a shocking (or: horrible) murder

²**vreselijk** /vrе̲sələk/ (adv) terribly, awfully, frightfully: ~ *gezellig* awfully nice

het ¹**vreten** /vrе̲tə(n)/ **1** fodder; food; forage; slops **2** grub, nosh

²**vreten** /vrе̲tə(n)/ (vrat, heeft gevreten) eat (away), gnaw (at), prey (on): het schuldbesef vrat *aan* haar the sense of guilt gnawed at her (heart)

³**vreten** /vrе̲tə(n)/ (vrat, heeft gevreten) **1** feed: dat *is* niet te ~! that's not fit for pigs! **2** stuff (or: cram, gorge) (o.s.): zich te barsten ~ stuff o.s. to the gullet (or: sick) **3** feed, eat **4** eat (up), devour: *kilometers* ~ burn up the road; dat toestel vrе̲ét *stroom* this apparatus simply eats up electricity

de **vreugde** /vrø̲γdə/ (pl: -n) joy, delight, pleasure: *tot* mijn ~ hoor ik I am delighted to hear

de **vreugdekreet** /vrø̲γdəkret/ cry (or: shout) of joy

vreugdeloos /vrø̲γdəlos/ (adj, adv) joyless, cheerless

vreugdevol /vrø̲γdəvol/ (adj, adv) joyful

het **vreugdevuur** /vrø̲γdəvyr/ (pl: -vuren) bonfire

vrezen /vrе̲zə(n)/ (vreesde, heeft gevreesd) fear, dread, be afraid (of, that): ik vrees het *ergste* I fear the worst; *God* ~ fear God; ik vrees *van* niet (or: wel) I'm afraid not (or: so); ik vrees *dat* hij niet komt I'm afraid he won't come (or: show up)

de **vriend** /vrint/ (pl: -en) **1** friend: ~en en *vriendinnen!* friends!; iemands *beste* ~ s.o.'s best (or: closest) friend; *dikke* ~en zijn be (very) close friends; even *goede* ~en no hard feelings, no offence; van je ~en moet je het maar hebben with friends like that who needs enemies; *hij verraste ~ en **vijand*** he surprised friend and foe **2** (boy)friend: *ze **heeft** een ~(je)* she has a boyfriend ‖ *iem. **te** ~ houden* remain on good terms with s.o.

vriendelijk /vrịndələk/ (adj, adv) **1** friendly, kind, amiable: *~ lachen* give a friendly smile; ***zou** u zo ~ **willen zijn** om …* would you be kind enough (*or:* so kind) as to …; *dat **is** erg ~ van u* that's very (*or:* most) kind of you **2** pleasant

de **vriendelijkheid** /vrịndələkhɛit/ (pl: -heden) friendliness, kindness, amiability

de **vriendenclub** /vrịndə(n)klʏp/ (pl: -s) circle of friends

de **vriendendienst** /vrịndə(n)dinst/ (pl: -en) friendly turn, kind turn, act of friendship

de **vriendenkring** /vrịndə(n)krɪŋ/ (pl: -en) circle of friends

het **vriendenprijsje** /vrịndə(n)prɛiʃə/ (pl: -s) give-away: *voor* een ~ for next to nothing

de **vriendin** /vrindị̣n/ (pl: -nen) **1** (girl)friend, (lady) friend: *zij zijn **dikke** ~nen* they're the best of friends **2** girl(friend): *een **vaste** ~ hebben* have a steady girl(friend), go steady

de **vriendjespolitiek** /vrịncəspolitik/ favouritism, nepotism

de **vriendschap** /vrịntsxɑp/ (pl: -pen) friendship: *~ **sluiten*** make (*or:* become) friends, strike up a friendship; *uit ~ iets doen* do sth. out of friendship

vriendschappelijk /vrintsxɑ̣pələk/ (adj, adv) friendly, amicable; in a friendly way: *~e **wedstrijd*** friendly match; *~ met elkaar **omgaan*** be on friendly terms

vriesdrogen /vrịzdroɣə(n)/ (vriesdroogde, heeft gevriesdroogd) freeze-dry, lyophilize

de **vrieskist** /vrị̣skɪst/ (pl: -en) (chest-type) freezer, deep-freeze

de **vrieskou** /vrị̣skɑu/ frost

het **vriespunt** /vrị̣spʏnt/ freezing (point): *temperaturen **boven** (or: **onder, rond**) het ~* temperatures above (*or:* below, about) freezing (point)

het **vriesvak** /vrị̣sfɑk/ (pl: -ken) freezing compartment, freezer

het **vriesweer** /vrị̣swer/ freezing weather, frosty weather

vriezen /vrị̣zə(n)/ (vroor, heeft gevroren) freeze: *het vriest vijf **graden*** it's five (degrees) below freezing; *het vriest **dat** het kraakt* there's a sharp frost in the air

de **vriezer** /vrị̣zər/ (pl: -s) freezer, deep-freeze

¹**vrij** /vrɛi/ (adj) **1** free, open, unrestricted: *~e **handel*** free trade; *de ~e **slag*** freestyle; *een ~ **uitzicht*** hebben have a clear (*or:* an open) view; *de **weg** is ~* the road is clear; *weer op ~e **voeten** zijn* be outside again **2** free, complimentary **3** free, vacant: *die **wc** is ~* that lavatory is free (*or:* vacant, unoccupied); *de handen* — *hebben* have a free hand, have one's hands free; *een stoel ~ **houden*** reserve a seat

²**vrij** /vrɛi/ (adv) quite, fairly, rather, pretty: *het komt ~ **vaak** voor* it occurs quite (*or:* fairly) often

vrijaf /vrɛiɑ̣f/ (adj) off: *een halve **dag** ~* a half-holiday, half a day off; *~ **nemen*** take a holiday (*or:* some time off)

vrijblijvend /vrɛiblị̣jvənt/ (adj, adv) **1** without (*or:* free of) obligations: *een ~e **offerte*** doen make an offer free of engagement **2** [depr] (too) easy, loose, informal

de **vrijbrief** /vrɛ̣ibrif/ (pl: -brieven) [fig] licence

de **vrijbuiter** /vrɛ̣ibœytər/ (pl: -s) freebooter

de **vrijdag** /vrɛ̣idɑx/ (pl: -en) Friday: ***Goede** Vrijdag* Good Friday

¹**vrijdags** /vrɛ̣idɑxs/ (adj) Friday

²**vrijdags** /vrɛ̣idɑxs/ (adv) on Fridays

de **vrijdenker** /vrɛ̣idɛŋkər/ (pl: -s) freethinker

vrijelijk /vrɛ̣ijələk/ (adv) freely, without restraint

de **vrijemarkteconomie** /vrɛijəmɑ̣rktekonomi/ free marker economy

vrijen /vrɛ̣iə(n)/ (vrijde/vree, heeft gevrijd/gevreeën) **1** neck, pet: *die twee **zitten** lekker te ~* those two are having a nice cuddle **2** make love, go to bed: *veilig ~* have safe sex

de **vrijer** /vrɛ̣iər/ (pl: -s) boyfriend, lover, sweetheart, (young) man

de **vrijetijdsbesteding** /vrɛiətɛ̣itsbestedɪŋ/ leisure activities, recreation

de **vrijetijdskleding** /vrɛiətɛ̣itskledɪŋ/ casual clothes (*or:* wear)

het **vrije-uitloopei** /vrɛijəœ̣ytlopɛi/ (pl: -eren) free-range egg

het **vrijgeleide** /vrɛiɣəlɛ̣idə/ (pl: -n, -s) (letter of) safe-conduct, safeguard, pass(port), permit

¹**vrijgeven** /vrɛ̣iɣevə(n)/ (gaf vrij, heeft vrijgegeven) give time off, give a holiday

²**vrijgeven** /vrɛ̣iɣevə(n)/ (gaf vrij, heeft vrijgegeven) release: *de **handel** ~* decontrol the trade; *iets **voor** publicatie ~* release sth. for publication

vrijgevig /vrɛiɣẹvəx/ (adj, adv) generous, free with, liberal with

de **vrijgevigheid** /vrɛiɣẹvəxhɛit/ generosity, liberality

de **vrijgezel** /vrɛiɣəzɛ̣l/ (pl: -len) bachelor, single: *een **verstokte** ~* a confirmed bachelor

de **vrijgezellenavond** /vrɛiɣəzɛ̣lə(n)avɔnt/ (pl: -en) **1** stag-night; hen-party **2** singles night

de **vrijhandel** /vrɛ̣ihɑndəl/ free trade

de **vrijhaven** /vrɛ̣ihavə(n)/ (pl: -s) free port

de **vrijheid** /vrɛ̣ihɛit/ freedom, liberty: *het is hier ~, **blijheid*** it's Liberty Hall here; *~ van **godsdienst** (or: **meningsuiting**)* freedom of religion (*or:* speech); ***persoonlijke** ~* personal freedom (*or:* liberty); *kinderen veel ~ **geven*** give (*or:* allow) children a lot of freedom; *iem. **in** ~ stellen* set s.o. free (*or:* at liberty), free/release s.o.

het **vrijheidsbeeld** /vrɛ̱iɦɛitsbelt/: *het Vrij-heidsbeeld* the Statue of Liberty

de **vrijheidsberoving** /vrɛ̱iɦɛitsbərovɪŋ/ deprivation of liberty (*or:* freedom)

de **vrijheidsstraf** /vrɛ̱iɦɛitstraf/ (pl: -fen) imprisonment, detention

de **vrijheidsstrijder** /vrɛ̱iɦɛitstrɛidər/ (pl: -s) freedom fighter

vrijhouden /vrɛ̱iɦɑudə(n)/ (hield vrij, heeft vrijgehouden) **1** keep (free), reserve; set aside: *een* **plaats** ~ keep a place (*or:* seat) free; *de* **weg** ~ keep the road open (*or:* clear) **2** pay (for), stand (s.o. sth.)

het **vrijkaartje** /vrɛ̱ikarcə/ (pl: -s) free ticket

vrijkomen /vrɛ̱ikomə(n)/ (kwam vrij, is vrijgekomen) **1** come out; be set free, be released **2** be released; be set free **3** become free (*or:* available): *zodra er een* **plaats** *vrijkomt* as soon as there is a vacancy (*or:* place)

vrijlaten /vrɛ̱ilatə(n)/ (liet vrij, heeft vrijgelaten) **1** release, set free (*or:* at liberty); liberate; emancipate **2** leave free (*or:* vacant); leave clear: *deze* **ruimte** ~ *s.v.p.* please leave this space clear

de **vrijlating** /vrɛ̱ilatɪŋ/ release

vrijmaken /vrɛ̱imakə(n)/ (maakte vrij, heeft vrijgemaakt) reserve, keep (free): *tijd* ~ make time (for)

de **vrijmarkt** /vrɛ̱imɑrkt/ (pl: -en) unregulated street market

de **vrijmetselaar** /vrɛimɛ̱tsəlar/ (pl: -s) freemason, Mason

de **vrijmetselarij** /vrɛimɛtsəlarɛ̱i/ Freemasonry, Masonry

vrijmoedig /vrɛimu̱dəx/ (adj) frank, outspoken

de **vrijplaats** /vrɛ̱iplats/ (pl: -en) refuge: *een* ~ *voor* **talent** a paradise (*or:* mecca) for talented people

vrijpleiten /vrɛ̱iplɛitə(n)/ (pleitte vrij, heeft vrijgepleit) clear (of), exonerate (from)

vrijpostig /vrɛipo̱stəx/ (adj) impertinent, impudent, saucy

de **vrijspraak** /vrɛ̱isprak/ acquittal

vrijspreken /vrɛ̱isprekə(n)/ (sprak vrij, heeft vrijgesproken) acquit (from), clear: *vrijgesproken worden van een beschuldiging* be cleared of (*or:* be acquitted on) a charge

vrijstaan /vrɛ̱istan/ (stond vrij, heeft vrijgestaan) be free (to), be allowed (to), be permitted (to), be at liberty (to)

vrijstaand /vrɛ̱istant/ (adj) apart, free; detached: *een* ~ *huis* a detached house

vrijstellen /vrɛ̱istɛlə(n)/ (stelde vrij, heeft vrijgesteld) exempt; excuse; release: *vrijgesteld van militaire dienst* exempt from military service

de **vrijstelling** /vrɛ̱istɛlɪŋ/ (pl: -en) exemption, release, freedom: ~ *verlenen van* exempt from; *een* ~ *hebben* **voor** *wiskunde* be exempted from the maths exam

de **vrijster** /vrɛ̱istər/ (pl: -s) spinster: *een* **oude** ~ an old maid

vrijuit /vrɛio̱ɛyt/ (adv) freely: *u kunt* ~ **spreken** you can speak freely ‖ ~ **gaan a)** not be to blame; **b)** get off (*or:* go) scot-free, go clear/free

vrijwaren /vrɛ̱iwarə(n)/ (vrijwaarde, heeft gevrijwaard) (safe)guard (against): *gevrijwaard* **tegen** protected from; *gevrijwaard* **blijven** *van blessures* remain free from injury

vrijwel /vrɛ̱iwɛl/ (adv) nearly, almost, practically: *dat is* ~ **hetzelfde** that's nearly (*or:* almost) the same; ~ **niets** hardly anything, next to nothing; ~ **tegelijk** aankomen arrive almost simultaneously (*or:* at the same time); *het komt* ~ *op hetzelfde neer* it boils down to pretty well the same thing

vrijwillig /vrɛiwɪ̱ləx/ (adj, adv) voluntary; volunteer; of one's own free will, of one's own volition: ~ *iets op zich* **nemen** volunteer to do sth., take on sth. voluntarily

de **vrijwilliger** /vrɛiwɪ̱ləɣər/ (pl: -s) volunteer: *er* **hebben** *zich nog geen* ~*s* **gemeld** so far nobody has volunteered

het **vrijwilligerswerk** /vrɛiwɪ̱ləɣərswɛrk/ voluntary work, volunteer work

vrijzinnig /vrɛɪzɪ̱nəx/ (adj, adv) **1** [Dutch] liberal **2** [Belg] unbelieving

de **vroedvrouw** /vru̱tfrɑu/ (pl: -en) midwife

vroeg /vruх/ (adj, adv) **1** early: *van* ~ *tot* **laat** from dawn till dusk (*or:* dark); ~ *of* **laat** sooner or later, eventually; *je moet er* ~ **bij zijn** you've got to get in quickly; *hij* **toonde** *al* ~ *tekentalent* he showed artistic talent at an early age; *volgende week is* ~ **genoeg** next week is soon enough; *niet* ~*er dan* ... not before ..., ... at the earliest; *het is* **nog** ~ **a)** the day is still young; **b)** the night is still young; *'s morgens* ~ early in the morning **2** early; young; premature: *een te* ~ **geboren** *kind* a premature baby

de **vroegboekkorting** /vru̱ybukɔrtɪŋ/ early-bird discount

[1]**vroeger** /vru̱ɣər/ (adj) previous, former: *zijn* ~*e* **verloofde** his former (*or:* ex-fiancée)

[2]**vroeger** /vru̱ɣər/ (adv) formerly, before, previously: ~ **heb** ik ook wel gerookt I used to smoke; ~ **stond** hier een kerk there used to be a church here; *het Londen van* ~ London as it used to be (*or:* once was)

het **vroegpensioen** /vru̱xpɛnʃun/ early retirement

vroegrijp /vru̱xrɛip/ (adj) precocious; forward; early-ripening: ~*e* **kinderen** precocious (*or:* forward) children

de **vroegte** /vru̱xtə/: *in alle* ~ at (the) crack of dawn, bright and early

vroegtijdig /vruxtɛ̱idəx/ (adj, adv) early, premature

vrolijk /vro̱lək/ (adj, adv) cheerful, merry: ~ **behang** cheerful (*or:* bright) wallpaper; *het* *was er een ~e boel* they were a merry crowd; *een ~e frans* quite a lad, a happy-go-lucky fellow; ~ *worden* get (a bit, rather) merry; *een ~ leventje leiden* lead a merry life

vroom /vrom/ (adj, adv) pious, devout

de **vrouw** /vrɑu/ (pl: -en) **1** woman: *een alleenstaande ~* a single (*or:* an unattached) woman; *achter de ~en aanzitten* chase (after) women, womanize; *de werkende ~* working women; career woman; *een ~ achter het stuur* a woman driver; *Vrouw Holle* Mother Carey **2** wife: *man en ~* husband (*or:* man) and wife; *hoe gaat het met je ~?* how's your wife?; *een dochter van zijn eerste ~* a daughter by his first wife **3** queen **4** mistress, lady: *de ~ des huizes* lady (*or:* mistress) of the house

vrouwelijk /vrɑuwələk/ (adj) **1** female; woman: *een ~e arts* a woman doctor; *de ~e hoofdrol* the leading lady role (*or:* part) **2** feminine, womanly: *~e charme* feminine charm; *de ~e intuïtie* woman's intuition

de **vrouwenarts** /vrɑuwə(n)ɑrts/ (pl: -en) gynaecologist

de **vrouwenbesnijdenis** /vrɑuwə(n)bəsnɛɪdənɪs/ female genital mutilation *(FGM)*

de **vrouwenbeweging** /vrɑuwə(n)bəweɣɪŋ/ feminist movement, women's (rights) movement

het **vrouwenblad** /vrɑuwə(n)blɑt/ (pl: -en) women's magazine

de **vrouwengek** /vrɑuwə(n)ɣɛk/ (pl: -ken) ladies' man, womanizer

de **vrouwenhandel** /vrɑuwə(n)hɑndəl/ trade (*or:* traffic) in women; white slave trade

de **vrouwenjager** /vrɑuwə(n)jaɣər/ (pl: -s) womanizer, ladykiller

de **vrouwenstem** /vrɑuwə(n)stɛm/ (pl: -men) female voice, woman's voice

vrouwonvriendelijk /vrɑuɔnvrɪndələk/ (adj) disadvantageous to women

het **vrouwtje** /vrɑucə/ (pl: -s) **1** woman; wife(y): *een oud ~* a little old woman, a granny; *hij kijkt te veel naar de ~s* he's too keen on women (*or:* the ladies) **2** mistress **3** female

vrouwvriendelijk /vrɑuvrɪndələk/ (adj, adv) women-friendly

de **vrucht** /vrʏxt/ (pl: -en) **1** fruit: *~en op sap* fruit in syrup; *verboden ~en* forbidden fruit **2** foetus, embryo: *een onvoldragen ~* a foetus that has not been carried to term **3** [fig] fruit(s), reward(s): *zijn werk heeft weinig ~en afgeworpen* he has little to show for his work; *~en afwerpen* bear fruit; *de ~en van iets plukken* reap the fruit(s) (*or:* rewards) of sth.

vruchtbaar /vrʏxtbar/ (adj) **1** fruitful, productive **2** fertile; fruitful: *de vruchtbare periode van de vrouw* a woman's fertile period; *een vruchtbare bodem vinden* find fertile soil

de **vruchtbaarheid** /vrʏxtbarhɛit/ fertility, fruitfulness

het **vruchtbeginsel** /vrʏxtbəɣɪnsəl/ (pl: -s) ova-

ry

vruchteloos /vrʏxtəlos/ (adj, adv) fruitless, futile

de **vruchtenpers** /vrʏxtə(n)pɛrs/ (pl: -en) fruit press

het **vruchtensap** /vrʏxtə(n)sɑp/ (pl: -pen) fruit juice

de **vruchtentaart** /vrʏxtə(n)tart/ (pl: -en) fruit tart

het **vruchtgebruik** /vrʏ(ɣt)xəbrœyk/ [law] usufruct

het **vruchtvlees** /vrʏxtfles/ flesh (of a, the fruit), (fruit) pulp

het **vruchtwater** /vrʏxtwatər/ amniotic fluid, water(s)

de **vruchtwateronderzoek** /vrʏxtwatərɔndərzuk/ (pl: -en) amniocentesis

de **VS** /vɛs/ (pl) *Verenigde Staten* US, USA

de **V-snaar** /vesnar/ (pl: V-snaren) V-belt

het **vso** /vɛso/ [Dutch; educ] *voortgezet speciaal onderwijs* special secondary education

het **V-teken** /veteka(n)/ V-sign

vuig /vœyx/ (adj, adv) foul; mean, low: *~e laster* foul slander

het **¹vuil** /vœyl/ **1** refuse, rubbish; [Am esp] garbage: *iem. behandelen als een stuk ~* treat s.o. like dirt; *~ storten* tip (*or:* dump, shoot) rubbish; *verboden ~ te storten* dumping prohibited, no tipping (*or:* dumping) **2** dirt, filth

²vuil /vœyl/ (adj, adv) **1** dirty, filthy; polluted: *de ~e kopjes* the dirty (*or:* used) cups; *een ~e rivier* a dirty (*or:* polluted) river **2** dirty, foul: *iem. een ~e streek leveren* play a dirty (*or:* nasty trick) on s.o.; *~e viezerik* (or: *leugenaar*) dirty (*or:* filthy) swine/liar **3** dirty, nasty: *iem. ~ aankijken* give s.o. a dirty (*or:* filthy, nasty) look

de **vuilak** /vœylɑk/ (pl: -ken) [inform] pig, rotter, nasty piece of work, skunk

de **vuiligheid** /vœyləχhɛit/ dirt, filth

vuilmaken /vœylmakə(n)/ (maakte vuil, heeft vuilgemaakt) make dirty, dirty, soil

het **vuilnis** /vœylnɪs/ refuse, rubbish; [Am esp] garbage

de **vuilnisauto** /vœylnɪsauto/ (pl: -'s) dustcart; [Am] garbage truck, trash truck

de **vuilnisbak** /vœylnɪzbɑk/ (pl: -ken) dustbin, rubbish bin; [Am] garbage can, trash can

het **vuilnisbakkenras** /vœylnɪzbɑkə(n)rɑs/ (pl: -sen) mongrel

de **vuilnisbelt** /vœylnɪzbɛlt/ (pl: -en) rubbish dump

de **vuilnishoop** /vœylnɪshop/ (pl: -hopen) rubbish dump; [Am] garbage heap

de **vuilniskoker** /vœylnɪskokər/ (pl: -s) rubbish chute

de **vuilnisman** /vœylnɪsmɑn/ (pl: -nen) binman; [Am esp] garbage collector

de **vuilniszak** /vœylnɪsɑk/ (pl: -ken) rubbish bag, refuse bag

de **vuilophaaldienst** /vœylɔphaldinst/ (pl:

-en) refuse collection

de **vuilstortplaats** /vœ͜ylstɔrtplɑts/ (pl: -en) rubbish dump

het **vuiltje** /vœ͜ylcə/ (pl: -s) smut, speck of dirt (or: dust, grit): *een ~ in het oog hebben* have sth. (or: a smut) in one's eye || *er is geen ~ aan de lucht* everything is absolutely fine; [Am] everything is peachy keen

de **vuilverbranding** /vœ͜ylvərbrɑndɪŋ/ (pl: -en) (waste, refuse, garbage) incinerator

de **vuilverwerking** /vœ͜ylvərwɛrkɪŋ/ waste processing

de **vuist** /vœ͜yst/ (pl: -en) fist: *met gebalde ~en* with clenched fists; *een ~ maken* take a stand (or: hard line); *met de ~ op tafel slaan* bang one's fist on the table; take a hard line; *op de ~ gaan* come to blows; *uit het ~je eten* eat with one's fingers || *voor de ~ (weg)* off the cuff, ad lib

de **vuistregel** /vœ͜ystreɣəl/ (pl: -s) rule of thumb

de **vuistslag** /vœ͜ystslɑx/ (pl: -en) punch

vulgair /vʏlɣɛːr/ (adj, adv) vulgar, common; rude

de **vulkaan** /vʏlkan/ (pl: vulkanen) volcano

de **vulkaanuitbarsting** /vʏlkanœydbɑrstɪŋ/ volcanic eruption

vulkanisch /vʏlkanis/ (adj) volcanic: *~e stenen* volcanic rocks

vullen /vʏlə(n)/ (vulde, heeft gevuld) **1** fill (up); inflate: *het eten vult ontzettend* the meal is very filling **2** fill (up); stuff; pad: *een gat ~* fill (up) a hole; *een kip met gehakt ~* stuff a chicken with mince

de **vulling** /vʏlɪŋ/ (pl: -en) **1** filling; stuffing **2** cartridge, refill

de **vulpen** /vʏlpɛn/ (pl: -nen) fountain pen

het **vulpotlood** /vʏlpɔtlot/ (pl: vulpotloden) propelling pencil; [Am] refillable lead pencil

vunzig /vʏnzəx/ (adj) dirty, filthy

¹**vuren** /vʏrə(n)/ (adj) pine, deal

²**vuren** /vʏrə(n)/ (vuurde, heeft gevuurd) fire: *staakt het ~* cease fire

het **vurenhout** /vʏrə(n)hɑut/ pine(wood), deal

vurenhouten /vʏrə(n)hɑutə(n)/ (adj) pine, deal

vurig /vʏrəx/ (adj, adv) **1** fiery, (red-)hot: *~e kolen* coals of fire **2** fiery, ardent, fervent; devout; burning: *~e paarden* fiery (or: high-spirited) horses; *een ~ voorstander van iets* a strong (or: fervent) supporter of sth.; *daarmee was zijn ~ste wens vervuld* it fulfilled his most ardent wish

de **VUT** /vʏt/ [Dutch] *vervroegde uittreding* early retirement: *in de ~ gaan* retire early, take early retirement

de **VUT-regeling** /vʏtreɣəlɪŋ/ (pl: -en) [Dutch] [roughly] early-retirement scheme

het **vuur** /vyr/ (pl: vuren) **1** fire: *voor iem. door het ~ gaan* go through fire (and water) for s.o.; *het huis staat in ~ en vlam* the house is in

flames; *ik zou er mijn hand voor in het ~ durven steken* I'd stake my life on it; *in ~ en vlam zetten* set ablaze (or: on fire); *met ~ spelen* play with fire; *iem. zwaar onder ~ nemen* let fly at s.o.; *een pan op het ~ zetten* put a pan on the stove; *tussen twee vuren zitten* get caught in the middle (or: in the firing line); *een ~ aansteken* light a fire; *iem. het ~ na aan de schenen leggen* make it (or: things) hot for s.o.; *een ~ uitdoven* put out (or: extinguish) a fire; *open ~* open flames (or: fire) **2** fire, ardour, fervour: *in het ~ van zijn betoog* in the heat of his argument || *eigen ~* friendly fire

de **vuurbal** /vyrbɑl/ (pl: -len) fireball, ball of fire

de **vuurdoop** /vyrdop/ baptism of fire

het **vuurgevecht** /vyrɣəvɛxt/ (pl: -en) gunfight

de **vuurhaard** /vyrhart/ (pl: -en) seat of the fire

Vuurland /vyrlɑnt/ Tierra del Fuego

de **vuurlinie** /vyrlini/ (pl: -s) firing line, line of fire

het **vuurpeloton** /vyrpelətɔn/ (pl: -s) firing squad

de **vuurpijl** /vyrpɛil/ (pl: -en) rocket

de **vuurproef** /vyrpruf/ (pl: -proeven) trial by fire; [fig] ordeal; acid test: *de ~ doorstaan* stand the test; *de ~ ondergaan* undergo a severe ordeal

vuurrood /vyrot/ (adj) crimson, scarlet: *~ aanlopen* turn crimson (or: scarlet)

vuurspuwend /vyrspywənt/ (adj) erupting; fire-breathing; fire-spitting

de **vuurspuwer** /vyrspywər/ (pl: -s) [roughly] fire-eater

de **vuursteen** /vyrsten/ flint

het **vuurtje** /vyrcə/ (pl: -s) **1** (small) fire: *het nieuws ging als een lopend ~ door de stad* the news spread through the town like wildfire **2** light: *iem. een ~ geven* give s.o. a light

de **vuurtoren** /vyrtorə(n)/ (pl: -s) lighthouse

vuurvast /vyrvɑst/ (adj) fireproof, flame-resistant, heat-resistant: *een ~ schaaltje* an ovenproof (or: a heat-resistant) dish

het **vuurvliegje** /vyrvlixjə/ (pl: -s) firefly

het **vuurwapen** /vyrwapə(n)/ (pl: -s) firearm, gun; arm

het **vuurwerk** /vyrwɛrk/ **1** firework **2** (display of) fireworks

de **vuurzee** /vyrze/ (pl: -ën) blaze, sea of fire (or: flame(s))

de **VVV®** /veveve/ [Dutch] *Vereniging voor Vreemdelingenverkeer* Tourist Information Office

v.w.b. *voor wat betreft* as far as … is concerned

het **vwo** /veweo/ [Dutch] *voorbereidend wetenschappelijk onderwijs* pre-university education

W

de **w** /we/ (pl: w's) w, W

de **WA** /wea/ [Dutch] *wettelijke aansprakelijkheid* third-party liability

de **waadvogel** /wa̱tfoɣəl/ wader

de **waaghals** /wa̱xhɑls/ (pl: -halzen) daredevil

de **waagschaal** /wa̱xsxɑl/: *zijn leven in de ~
stellen* take one's life in one's (own) hands

het **waagstuk** /wa̱xstʏk/ (pl: -ken) risky enterprise

waaien /wa̱jə(n)/ (waaide/woei, heeft ge-
waaid) **1** blow; be blown: *het waait hard* it's
very windy, there's a strong wind blowing; *er
woei een harde storm* a storm was blowing
2 wave, fly || *laat maar ~* let it rip

de **waaier** /wa̱jər/ (pl: -s) fan

waaiervormig /wajərvɔ̱rməx/ (adj, adv)
fan-shaped

de **waakhond** /wa̱khɔnt/ (pl: -en) watchdog

waaks /waks/ (adj) watchful

de **waakvlam** /wa̱kflɑm/ (pl: -men) pilot light
(or: flame)

waakzaam /wa̱ksam/ (adj, adv) watchful

de **waakzaamheid** /wa̱ksamhɛit/ watchful-
ness

de **Waal** /wal/ (pl: Walen) [pers] Walloon

het **¹Waals** /wals/ Walloon

²Waals /wals/ (adj) Walloon

de **waan** /wan/ delusion: *iem. in de ~ laten* not
spoil s.o.'s illusions

de **waanzin** /wa̱nzɪn/ madness: *dat is je reinste
~* that is pure nonsense (or: sheer madness)

waanzinnig /wanzɪ̱nəx/ (adj, adv) mad: *~
populair zijn* be wildly popular

de **waanzinnige** /wanzɪ̱nəɣə/ (pl: -n) madman, maniac; madwoman

de **¹waar** /war/ (pl: waren) goods, ware(s): *iem. ~
voor zijn geld geven* give value for money

²waar /war/ (adj) **1** true, real, actual: *de ware
oorzaak* the real (or: actual) cause; *'t is toch
niet ~!* you don't say!, not really!; *het is te
mooi om ~ te zijn* it's too good to be true;
echt ~? is that really true?, really?; *eerlijk ~!*
honest! **2** true; actual; real: *een ~ genot* a
regular (or: real) treat; *hij is de ware (jakob)*
he's Mr Right **3** true, correct || *dat is ~ ook …*
that reminds me …, by the way …

³waar /war/ (adv) **1** where; that; which: *de boodschap ~ hij niet
aan gedacht had* the message (that, which) he
hadn't remembered; *het dorp ~ hij geboren is*
the village where (or: in which) he was born
3 wherever; everywhere; anywhere: *meer*

welvaart dan ~ ook more prosperity than anywhere else **4** really, actually: *dat is ~ gebeurd*
it really (or: actually) happened

waaraan /waran/ (adv) **1** what … to: *~ ligt
dit?* what is the reason for it?; *~ heb ik dit te
danken?* what do I owe this to?, to what do I
owe this? **2** what (or: which) … to/of: *het huis
~ ik dacht* the house (which) I was thinking of
3 whatever … to (or: of): *~ je ook denkt*
whatever you're thinking of (or: about)

waarachter /warɔ̱xtər/ (adv) **1** behind
which **2** behind what (or: which)

waarachtig /warɔ̱xtəx/ (adj, adv) truly,
really

waarbij /warbɛ̱i/ (adv) at (or: by, near) …
which: *een ongeluk ~ veel gewonden vielen* an
accident in which many people were injured

de **waarborg** /wa̱rbɔrx/ (pl: -en) guarantee;
security

waarborgen /wa̱rbɔrɣə(n)/ (waarborgde,
heeft gewaarborgd) guarantee

de **waarborgsom** /wa̱rbɔrxsɔm/ (pl: -men)
deposit; [law] bail

de **¹waard** /wart/ (pl: -en) landlord

²waard /wart/ (adj) worth, worthy (of sth.,
s.o.): *laten zien wat je ~ bent* show s.o. what
you're made of; *hij is haar niet ~* he's not
worthy of her; *na een dag werken ben ik 's
avonds niets (meer) ~* after a day's work I'm
no good for anything; *veel ~ zijn* be worth a
lot

de **waarde** /wa̱rdə/ (pl: -n) **1** value: *(zeer) veel ~
aan iets hechten* value sth. highly; *weinig ~
aan iets hechten* attach little value to sth.;
iem. in zijn ~ laten accept s.o. as he is; *in ~ dalen* depreciate, decrease (or: diminish) in value; *iem. niet op zijn juiste ~ schatten* underestimate s.o.; *ter ~ van …* at (the value of),
worth …; *voorwerpen van ~* objects of value,
valuables; *van ~ zijn, ~ hebben* be valuable,
be of value **2** value, reading: *de gemiddelde
~n van de zomertemperaturen* the average
summer temperature || *een vaste ~* a stalwart
friend/supporter

de **waardebon** /wa̱rdəbɔn/ (pl: -nen) voucher,
coupon; gift voucher (or: coupon)

waardeloos /wa̱rdəlos/ (adj) worthless: *dat
is ~* that's useless (or: hopeless)

het **waardeoordeel** /wa̱rdəordel/ (pl: -oorde-
len) value judgement

waarderen /warde̱rə(n)/ (waardeerde,
heeft gewaardeerd) appreciate, value: *hij
weet een goed glas wijn wel te ~* he likes (or:
appreciates) a good glass of wine

waarderend /wa̱rdərənt/ (adj, adv) appre-
ciative: *zich (zeer) ~ over iem. uitlaten* speak
(very) highly of s.o.

de **waardering** /warde̱rɪŋ/ (pl: -en) appreciation, esteem: *~ ondervinden (van)* win the
esteem (or: regard) (of); *als blijk van ~* as a
tribute of one's appreciation (or: esteem)

waardevast /wardəvɑst/ (adj) stable (in value); index-linked; inflation-proof

waardevol /wardəvɔl/ (adj) valuable, useful: ~le **voorwerpen** valuables, objects of value

waardig /wardəχ/ (adj, adv) dignified, worthy

de **waardigheid** /wardəχhɛit/ (pl: -heden) dignity, worth: iets **beneden** zijn ~ achten think sth. beneath one's dignity (or: beneath one)

de **waardin** /wardɪn/ (pl: -nen) landlady

waardoor /wardor/ (adv) **1** (as a result of) what, how: ~ **ben** je van gedachten **veranderd?** what made you change your mind?; ik weet ~ het **komt** I know how it happened, I know what caused it **2** through which, by which, (which, that) … through (or: by); (as a result of) which: de buis ~ het gas **stroomt** the tube through which the gas flows; het begon te regenen, ~ de weg nog gladder **werd** it started to rain, which made the road even more slippery

¹**waargebeurd** /warɣəbørt/ (adj) true

²**waargebeurd** /warɣəbørt/ (adj): een **waargebeurd** verhaal a true story

waarheen /warhen/ (adv) **1** where, where … to: ~ **zullen** wij vandaag **gaan?** where shall we go today? **2** where, to which, (which, that) … to: de plaats ~ ze me **stuurden** the place to which they directed me **3** wherever: ~ u ook **gaat** wherever you (may) go

de **waarheid** /warhɛit/ (pl: -heden) truth, fact: de ~ **achterhalen** get at (or: find out) the truth; om (u) de ~ te **zeggen** to be honest (with you), to tell (you) the truth; de ~ ligt in het midden the truth lies (somewhere) in between; een ~ **als** een koe a truism; ver **bezijden** de ~ zijn be far removed from the truth; de **naakte** ~ the naked truth

waarheidsgetrouw /warhɛitsχətrɑu/ (adj, adv) truthful, true

waarin /warɪn/ (adv) **1** where, in what: ~ **schuilt** de fout? where's the mistake? **2** in which, where, (which, that) … in: de tijd ~ wij leven the age (that, which) we live in **3** wherever, in whatever: ~ de fout ook gemaakt is wherever the mistake was made

waarlangs /warlɑŋs/ (adv) **1** what … past (or: along) **2** past which, along which, (which, that) … past (or: along): de **weg** ~ hij gaat the way he is going, the road along which he is going **3** past whatever, along whatever: ~ zij ook **kwamen** whatever way they came along

waarlijk /warlək/ (adv) truly, really

¹**waarmaken** /warmakə(n)/ (maakte waar, heeft waargemaakt) **1** prove **2** fulfil: de gewekte **verwachtingen** (niet) ~ (fail to) live up to expectations

zich ²**waarmaken** /warmakə(n)/ (maakte zich

waar, heeft zich waargemaakt) prove o.s.

waarmee /warme/ (adv) **1** what … with (or: by): ~ **sloeg** hij je? what did he hit you with? **2** with which, by which; which; (which) … with (or: by): de **boot** ~ ik vertrek the boat on which I leave **3** (with, by) whatever: ~ hij ook **dreigde,** zij werd niet bang whatever he threatened her with she didn't get scared

het **waarmerk** /warmɛrk/ (pl: -en) stamp

waarmerken /warmɛrkə(n)/ (waarmerkte, heeft gewaarmerkt) stamp: een gewaarmerkt **afschrift** a certified (or: an authenticated) copy

waarna /warna/ (adv) after which: ~ Paul als spreker **optrad** after which Paul spoke (or: took the floor)

waarnaar /warnar/ (adv) **1** what … at (or: of, for): ~ **smaakt** dat? what does it taste of? **2** to which; after (or: for, according to) which, (which, that) … to (or: after, for): het **hoofdstuk** ~ ze verwees the chapter (that, which) she referred to **3** whatever … to (or: at, for), wherever: ~ ik hier ook zoek, ik vind nooit wat whatever I look for here, I never find anything

waarnaast /warnast/ (adv) **1** what … next to (or: beside) **2** (which, that) … next to (or: beside) **3** whatever … next to (or: beside): ~ je dit schilderij ook **hangt** whatever you hang this picture next to

waarneembaar /warnembar/ (adj, adv) perceptible: **niet** ~ imperceptible

¹**waarnemen** /warnemə(n)/ (nam waar, heeft waargenomen) replace (temporarily), fill in, take over (temporarily), act: de **zaken** voor iem. ~ fill in for (or: replace) s.o.

²**waarnemen** /warnemə(n)/ (nam waar, heeft waargenomen) observe, perceive

waarnemend /warnemənt/ (adj) temporary, acting

de **waarnemer** /warnemər/ (pl: -s) **1** observer **2** representative, deputy, substitute

de **waarneming** /warnemɪŋ/ (pl: -en) **1** observation, perception **2** substitution

waarom /warɔm/ (adv) **1** why, what … for: ~ **denk** je dat? why do you (or: what makes you) think so?; ~ in vredesnaam? why on earth?, why for goodness' sake? **2** why, (which, that) … for: de **reden** ~ hij het deed the reason (why, that) he did it **3** for whatever, whatever … for: ~ hij het ook doet, hij moet ermee ophouden! whatever he does it for, he has to stop it!

waaromheen /warɔmhen/ (adv) **1** what … (a)round **2** (a)round which: het **huis** ~ een tuin lag the house which was surrounded by a garden

waaronder /warɔndər/ (adv) **1** what … under (or: among), among what **2** under which; among which [inform]: de **boom** ~ wij zaten the tree under which we were sitting;

hij had een **schat** *aan boeken,* ~ *heel zeldzame* he had a wealth of books, including some very rare ones **3** under whatever, whatever … under: ~ *hij ook* **keek,** *hij vond het niet* whatever he looked under, he couldn't find it

waarop /warɔp/ (adv) **1** what … on (*or:* for), where **2** (which, that) … on/in (*or:* by, to): *de* **dag** ~ *hij aankwam* the day (on which) he arrived; *de* **manier** ~ *beviel me niet* I didn't like the way (in which) it was done; *op het* **tijdstip** ~ at the time that **3** whatever … on: ~ *je nu ook staat, ik wil dat je naar beneden komt* whatever you are standing on now, I want you to get down

waarover /warovər/ (adv) **1** what … over (*or:* about, across): ~ *gaat het?* what is it about? **2** (which, that) … over (*or:* about, across): *de* **auto** ~ *ik met je vader gesproken heb* the car of (*or:* about) which I've spoken with your dad **3** whatever … about: ~ *de discussie dan ook* **gaat,** … whatever the discussion is about, …

waarschijnlijk /warsχεinlək/ (adj, adv) probable, likely: *dat* **lijkt** *mij heel* ~ that seems quite likely to me; ~ *niet* I suppose not; *meer dan* ~ more than likely

de **waarschijnlijkheid** /warsχεinləkhεit/ probability, likelihood, odds: *naar alle* ~ in all probability (*or:* likelihood)

waarschuwen /warsχywə(n)/ (waarschuw-de, heeft gewaarschuwd) **1** warn, alert: *ik heb* **je** *gewaarschuwd* I gave you fair warning, I told you so **2** warn, notify: *een* **dokter** *laten* ~ call a doctor; *de* **politie** ~ call the police **3** warn, caution: *ik waarschuw* **je** *voor de laatste maal* I'm telling you for the last time; *wees gewaarschuwd* you've been warned

de **waarschuwing** /warsχywɪŋ/ (pl: -en) warning; caution; reminder; notice: [sport] *een* **officiële** ~ *krijgen* be booked (*or:* cautioned); *Waarschuwing! Zeer brandbaar!* Caution! Highly flammable!

het **waarschuwingsbord** /warsχywɪŋzbɔrt/ (pl: -en) warning sign

waartegen /wartexə(n)/ (adv) **1** what … against (*or:* to): ~ *helpt dit middel?* what is this medicine for? **2** against which, to which, (which, that) … against (*or:* to): *de* **muur** ~ *een ladder staat* the wall against which a ladder is standing; *een* **raad** ~ *niets in te brengen valt* a piece of advice to which no objections can be made **3** whatever … against (*or:* to)

waartoe /wartu/ (adv) **1** what … for (*or:* to), why **2** (which, that) … for (*or:* to) **3** whatever … for (*or:* to): ~ *dit ook moge leiden* whatever this may lead to

waartussen /wartʏsə(n)/ (adv) **1** what … between (*or:* among, from): ~ *moeten wij* **kiezen?** a) what are we (supposed) to choose between; b) what are the alternatives? **2** be-

tween (*or:* among, from) which, (which, that) … between (*or:* among, from) **3** whatever … between (*or:* among, from)

waaruit /warœyt/ (adv) **1** from what: ~ *be-***staat** *de opdracht?* what does the assignment consist of? **2** from which: *het boek* ~ *u ons net voorlas* the book from which you read to us just now

waarvan /warvɑn/ (adv) **1** what … from (*or:* of): ~ *maakt hij dat?* what does he make that of? (*or:* from?); of (*or:* from) what does he make that? **2** (which, that) … from; of whom [of pers]; whose: *100* **studenten,** ~ *on-geveer de helft chemici* 100 students, of whom about half are chemists; *op* **grond** ~ on the basis of which; *dat is een* **onderwerp** ~ *hij veel verstand heeft* that is a subject he knows a lot about **3** whatever … from

waarvandaan /warvɑndan/ (adv) **1** where … from **2** (which, that) … from **3** wherever … from: ~ *je ook belt, draai altijd eerst een 0* wherever you call from, always dial an 0 first

waarvoor /warvor/ (adv) **1** what … for (*or:* about): ~ *dient dat?* what's that for? **2** what … for: ~ *doe je dat?* what are you doing that for? **3** (which, that) … for: *een gevaar* ~ *ik u* **gewaarschuwd heb** a danger I warned you about **4** whatever … for: ~ *hij het ook doet, het is in elk geval niet het geld* whatever he does it for, it's not the money, that's for sure

waarzeggen /warzɛɣə(n)/ (waarzegde, heeft waargezegd) tell fortunes, divine the future

de **waarzegger** /warzɛɣər/ (pl: -s) fortune-tell-er; crystal-gazer

de **waarzegster** /warzɛɣstər/ fortune-teller

het **waas** /was/ haze; [fig] air; aura, film: *een* ~ *van* **geheimzinnigheid** a shroud of secrecy; *een* ~ **voor** *de ogen krijgen* get a mist (*or:* haze) before one's eyes

de **wacht** /wɑχt/ (pl: -en) **1** watchman **2** watch; lookout: *(de)* ~ **houden** be on (*or:* stand) guard; [Belg] *van* ~ *zijn* be on night (*or:* weekend) duty, be on call **3** watch, guard || *iets* **in** *de* ~ *slepen* carry off sth., pocket (*or:* bag) sth.

wachten /wɑχtə(n)/ (wachtte, heeft ge-wacht) **1** wait, stay: *op de bus* ~ wait for the bus; ~ *tot iem. terugkomt* wait till s.o. returns **2** wait, await: *je moet* **er** *niet te lang* **mee** ~ don't put it off too long; *iem.* **laten** ~ keep s.o. waiting; *waar wacht je nog* **op?** what are you waiting for?; *op zijn beurt* ~ await one's turn; [fig] *daar kun je* **op** ~ you can count on it, that's to be expected; *er zijn nog drie* ~*den voor u* hold the line, there are three callers before you **3** wait, await (s.o.), be in store for (s.o.): *er* **staan** *ons moeilijke tijden te* ~ difficult times lie ahead of us; *er wachtte hem een onaangename* **verrassing** there was an unpleasant surprise in store for him de **wachter** /wɑxtər/ (pl: -s) guard(sman), watchman

het **wachtgeld** /wɑxtxɛlt/ (pl: -en) reduced pay

de **wachtkamer** /wɑxtkamər/ (pl: -s) waiting room

de **wachtlijst** /wɑxtlɛist/ (pl: -en) waiting list

wachtlopen /wɑxtlopə(n)/ (liep wacht, heeft wachtgelopen) be on patrol, be on (guard) duty

de **wachtpost** /wɑxtpɔst/ (pl: -en) watch (or: sentry, guard) post

de **wachtstand** /wɑx(t)stɑnt/ (pl: -en) suspension mode, suspended mode

de **wachttijd** /wɑxtɛit/ (pl: -en) wait, waiting period

het **wachtwoord** /wɑxtwort/ (pl: -en) password

het **wad** /wɑt/ (pl: -den) (mud) flat(s), shallow(s) || *de* Wadden the (Dutch) Wadden

waden /wadə(n)/ (waadde, heeft/is gewaad) wade

waf /wɑf/ (int) woof

de **wafel** /wafəl/ (pl: -s) waffle; wafer

het **wafelijzer** /wafɛlɛizər/ (pl: -s) waffle iron

de **waffel** /wɑfəl/ (pl: -s) [inform] trap, gob

de ¹**wagen** /waɣə(n)/ (pl: -s) 1 wagon; cart; van; pram 2 car: *met de ~ komen* come by car

²**wagen** /waɣə(n)/ (waagde, heeft gewaagd) 1 risk: *het erop ~* chance (or: risk) it; *wie niet waagt, die niet wint* nothing ventured, nothing gained 2 venture, dare: *zijn kans ~* try one's luck; *waag het eens!* just you dare! || *aan elkaar gewaagd zijn* be well (or: evenly) matched

het **wagenpark** /waɣə(n)pɑrk/ (pl: -en) fleet (of cars, vans, taxis, buses)

wagenwijd /waɣə(n)wɛit/ (adv) wide open: *wagenwijd openstaan* be open wide

wagenziek /waɣə(n)zik/ (adj) carsick

waggelen /wɑɣələ(n)/ (waggelde, heeft/is gewaggeld) totter, stagger; waddle; toddle

de **wagon** /waɣɔn/ (pl: -s) (railway) carriage; coach; wagon; van

de **wagonlading** /waɣɔnladɪŋ/ (pl: -en) wagonload

het **wak** /wɑk/ (pl: -ken) hole: *hij zakte in een ~ en verdronk* he fell through the thin ice and (was) drowned

de **wake** /wakə/ (pl: -n) watch; wake

waken /wakə(n)/ (waakte, heeft gewaakt) 1 watch, keep watch, stay awake: *bij een zieke ~* sit up with a sick person 2 watch, guard: *over iemands eigendommen ~* watch over (or: guard) s.o.'s property; [Dutch] *ervoor ~ dat iets gebeurt* make sure sth. does not happen

wakker /wɑkər/ (adj, adv) awake: *daar lig ik niet van ~* I'm not going to lose any sleep over it; *~ schrikken* wake up with a start; *iem. ~ schudden* shake s.o. awake; *~ worden* wake up

de **wal** /wɑl/ (pl: -len) 1 bank, embankment; wall 2 quay(side), waterside: *aan de ~ on shore*; *van ~ steken* push off, go ahead, proceed; *iem. van de ~ in de sloot helpen* bring s.o. from bad to worse 3 shore: *aan ~ brengen* land, bring (sth., s.o.) ashore 4 bag || *van twee ~letjes eten* butter one's bread on both sides, play a double game

walgelijk /wɑlɣələk/ (adj, adv) disgusting, revolting: *een ~e stank* a nauseating stench

walgen /wɑlɣə(n)/ (walgde, heeft gewalgd) be nauseated, be disgusted, be revolted: *ik walg ervan* it turns my stomach

de **walging** /wɑlɣɪŋ/ disgust, revulsion, nausea

het **Walhalla** /wɑlhɑla/ Valhalla

de **walkietalkie** /wɔːkitɔːki/ (pl: -s) walkie-talkie

de **walkman**® /wɔːkmɛːn/ (pl: -s) walkman

Wallonië /wɑlonijə/ the Walloon provinces in Belgium

de **walm** /wɑlm/ (pl: -en) (thick, dense) smoke

walmen /wɑlmə(n)/ (walmde, heeft gewalmd) smoke

de **walnoot** /wɑlnot/ walnut

de **walrus** /wɑlrʏs/ (pl: -sen) walrus

de **wals** /wɑls/ (pl: -en) 1 roller 2 steamroller, roadroller; (rolling) mill 3 waltz

¹**walsen** /wɑlsə(n)/ (walste, heeft gewalst) waltz

²**walsen** /wɑlsə(n)/ (walste, heeft gewalst) roll, steamroller; roll

de **walvis** /wɑlvɪs/ (pl: -sen) whale

het **wanbedrijf** /wɑmbədrɛif/ (pl: -bedrijven) [Belg] criminal offence

het **wanbegrip** /wɑmbəɣrɪp/ (pl: -pen) fallacy, misconception, wrong idea, false idea

het **wanbeheer** /wɑmbəheːr/ mismanagement

het **wanbeleid** /wɑmbəlɛit/ mismanagement

de **wanbetaler** /wɑmbətalər/ (pl: -s) defaulter

de **wanbetaling** /wɑmbətalɪŋ/ (pl: -en) default, non-payment

de **wand** /wɑnt/ (pl: -en) wall; face; side; skin: *een buis met dikke ~en* a thick-walled tube

de **wandaad** /wɑndat/ (pl: -daden) outrage, misdeed

de **wandel** /wɑndəl/ walk

de **wandelaar** /wɑndəlar/ (pl: -s) walker; hiker

wandelen /wɑndələ(n)/ (wandelde, heeft/is gewandeld) walk; ramble; hike: *met de kinderen gaan ~* take the children for a walk

wandelend /wɑndələnt/ (adj) walking

de **wandelgang** /wɑndəlɣɑŋ/ (pl: -en): *ik hoorde het in de ~en* I just picked up some gossip

de **wandeling** /wɑndəlɪŋ/ (pl: -en) walk; ramble; [sport] hike: *een ~ maken* have (or: go for) a walk

het **wandelpad** /wɑndəlpɑt/ (pl: -en) footpath

de **wandelstok** /wɑndəlstɔk/ (pl: -ken) walking stick

de **wandeltocht** /wɑndəltɔxt/ (pl: -en) walking tour

de **wandelwagen** /wɑndəlwaɣə(n)/ (pl: -s)

warm

buggy, pushchair; [Am] stroller

het **wandkleed** /wɒntkleːt/ (pl: -kleden) tapestry, wall hanging(s)

de **wandluis** /wɒntlœys/ (pl: -luizen) bedbug

het **wandmeubel** /wɒntmøbəl/ (pl: -s) wall unit

het **wandrek** /wɒntrɛk/ (pl: -ken) wall bars

de **wang** /wɑŋ/ (pl: -en) cheek: *bolle ~en* round (*or:* chubby) cheeks

het **wangedrag** /wɑŋɣədrɑx/ misbehaviour, bad conduct

de **wanhoop** /wɑnhoːp/ despair, desperation: *de ~ nabij zijn* be on the verge of despair

de **wanhoopsdaad** /wɑnhoːpsdaːt/ (pl: -daden) act of despair, desperate act

wanhopen /wɑnhoːpə(n)/ (wanhoopte, heeft gewanhoopt) despair

wanhopig /wɑnhoːpəx/ (adj, adv) desperate, despondent, despairing: *iem. ~ **maken*** drive s.o. to despair; *zich ergens ~ aan **vastklampen*** hang on to sth. like grim death; *~ **zijn*** be in despair, be desperate

wankel /wɑŋkəl/ (adj, adv) shaky, unstable: *~ **evenwicht*** shaky balance; *~e **stoelen*** rickety chairs

wankelen /wɑŋkələ(n)/ (wankelde, heeft gewankeld) stagger, wobble

wankelmoedig /wɑŋkəlmudəx/ (adj, adv) unstable, irresolute, wavering

de **wanklank** /wɑŋklɑŋk/ (pl: -en) dissonance

¹**wanneer** /wɑneːr/ (adv) when: *~ dan **ook*** whenever

²**wanneer** /wɑneːr/ (conj) **1** when: *~ de zon ondergaat, wordt het koeler* when the sun sets it gets cooler **2** if: *hij zou beter opschieten, ~ hij meer zijn best deed* he would make more progress if he worked harder **3** whenever, if: *(altijd) ~ ik oesters eet, word ik ziek* whenever I eat oysters I get ill

de **wanorde** /wɑnɔrdə/ disorder, disarray: *de keuken was in de **grootste** ~* the kitchen was in a colossal mess

wanordelijk /wɑnɔrdələk/ (adj, adv) disorderly

de **wanprestatie** /wɑmprɛsta(t)si/ (pl: -s) **1** failure **2** poor performance: *een ~ **leveren*** put up a poor performance, perform poorly

de **wansmaak** /wɑnsmaːk/ bad taste

wanstaltig /wɑnstɑltəx/ (adj) misshapen, deformed

de ¹**want** /wɑnt/ (pl: -en) mitt(en)

²**want** /wɑnt/ (conj) because, as, for

wanten /wɑntə(n)/: *hij weet **van** ~* he knows the ropes (*or:* what's what)

de **wantoestand** /wɑntustɑnt/ (pl: -en) disgraceful state of affairs

het ¹**wantrouwen** /wɑntrɑuwə(n)/ distrust, suspicion

²**wantrouwen** /wɑntrɑuwə(n)/ (wantrouwde, heeft gewantrouwd) distrust, mistrust

wantrouwend /wɑntrɑuwənt/ (adj, adv)

suspicious (of), distrustful

wantrouwig /wɑntrɑuwəx/ (adj, adv) suspicious: *~ van aard* have a suspicious nature

de **wanverhouding** /wɑnvərhɑudɪŋ/ (pl: -en) disproportion, imbalance

de **WAO** /weaoː/ [Dutch] *Wet op de Arbeidsongeschiktheidsverzekering* disability insurance act

de **WAO'er** /weaoːər/ [Dutch] recipient of disablement insurance benefits

het **wapen** /waːpə(n)/ (pl: -s) **1** weapon; arms: *de ~s neerleggen* lay down arms **2** (coat of) arms: *een leeuw in zijn ~ voeren* bear a lion in one's coat of arms

het **wapenbezit** /waːpə(n)bəzɪt/ possession of firearms (*or:* weapons)

wapenen /waːpənə(n)/ (wapende, heeft gewapend) arm; armour; reinforce

het **wapenfeit** /waːpə(n)fɛɪt/ (pl: -en) **1** feat of arms **2** feat, exploit

de **wapenkunde** /waːpə(n)kʏndə/ heraldry

de **wapenstilstand** /waːpə(n)stɪlstɑnt/ (pl: -en) **1** armistice; suspension of arms (*or:* hostilities); ceasefire **2** [fig] truce

de **wapenstok** /waːpə(n)stɔk/ (pl: -ken) [roughly] baton

het **wapentuig** /waːpə(n)tœyx/ armaments

de **wapenvergunning** /waːpə(n)vərɣʏnɪŋ/ (pl: -en) firearms licence, gun licence

de **wapenwedloop** /waːpə(n)wɛtloːp/ arms race

wapperen /wɑpərə(n)/ (wapperde, heeft gewapperd) blow, fly, stream; flap; flutter: *laten ~* fly, blow, stream, wave ‖ *de handjes laten ~* get busy, buckle down

de **war** /wɑr/ tangle, muddle, confusion: *in de ~ zijn* be confused; *iem. in de ~ brengen* confuse s.o.; *de boel in de ~ sturen* make a (proper) mess of things; *plannen in de ~ sturen* upset s.o.'s plans

de **warboel** /wɑrbul/ muddle, mess; tangle

ware /waːrə/: *als het ~* as it were, so to speak; *~ het niet, dat ...* were it not for ...

warempel /waːrɛmpəl/ (int) [inform] truly, really

de **waren** /waːrə(n)/ (pl) goods, commodities

het **warenhuis** /waːrə(n)hœys/ (pl: -huizen) (department) store

het **warhoofd** /wɑrhoːft/ (pl: -en) scatterbrain

¹**warm** /wɑrm/ (adj) **1** warm, hot: *het ~ **hebben*** be warm (*or:* hot); *het begon (lekker) ~ te **worden*** in de kamer the room was warming up; *iets ~s* sth. warm (*or:* hot) (to eat, drink) **2** enthusiastically: *~ **lopen** voor iets* feel enthusiasm for sth. **3** warmly, pleasantly **4** warm, warm-hearted, ardent: *een ~ **voorstander** van iets zijn* be an ardent (*or:* a fervent) supporter of sth. **5** warmed up, enthusiastic **6** warm, pleasant ‖ *je **bent** ~!* you are (getting) warm! (*or:* hot!); *niet ~ of koud van iets **worden*** blow neither hot nor cold, be

quite indifferent to sth.

²**warm** /wɑrm/ (adv) warmly: *iem. iets ~ aan-bevelen* recommend sth. warmly to s.o.

warmbloedig /wɑrmblu̱dəχ/ (adj) warm-blooded

warmdraaien /wɑrmdrajə(n)/ (draaide warm, heeft/is warmgedraaid) warm up

warmen /wɑrmə(n)/ (warmde, heeft gewarmd) warm (up), heat (up)

de **warming-up** /wɔrmɪŋʏp/ (pl: -s) warm-up (exercise)

warmlopen /wɑrmlopə(n)/ (liep warm, is warmgelopen) **1** have warmed to, feel (great) enthusiasm for (s.o., sth.): *hij loopt niet erg warm voor het plan* he has not really warmed to the plan **2** [sport] warm up, limber up

warmpjes /wɑrmpjəs/ (adv) warmly ‖ [fig] *er ~ bij zitten* be comfortably off, be well off

de **warmte** /wɑrmtə/ warmth, heat: *~ (af)ge-ven* give off (or: emit) heat

de **warmtebron** /wɑrmtəbrɔn/ (pl: -nen) source of heat

het **warmtefront** /wɑrmtəfrɔnt/ (pl: -en) warm front

de **warmwaterkraan** /wɑrmwa̱tərkran/ (pl: -kranen) hot(-water) tap

warrig /wɑrəχ/ (adj) knotty, tangled; [fig] confused; muddled

wars /wɑrs/ (adj) averse (to)

Warschau /wɑrʃɑu/ Warsaw

de **wartaal** /wɑrtal/ gibberish, nonsense: *~ uit-slaan* talk double Dutch (or: gibberish)

de **warwinkel** /wɑrwɪŋkəl/ mess, muddle

de ¹**was** /wɑs/ (pl: -sen) wash, washing; laundry; linen: *de fijne ~* the fine (or: delicate) fabrics; *de vuile ~ buiten hangen* wash one's dirty linen in public; *iets in de ~ doen* put sth. in the wash; *de ~ doen* do the wash (or: laundry)

het/de ²**was** /wɑs/ (pl: -sen) wax: *meubels in de ~ zet-ten* wax furniture ‖ *goed in de slappe ~ zitten* have plenty of dough

de **wasautomaat** /wɑsautomat/ (pl: wasauto-maten) (automatic) washing machine

wasbaar /wɑzbar/ (adj) washable

de **wasbak** /wɑzbɑk/ (pl: -ken) washbasin, sink

de **wasbeer** /wɑzber/ (pl: wasberen) racoon

de **wasbenzine** /wɑzbɛnzinə/ benzine

de **wasdroger** /wɑzdroɣər/ (pl: -s) (tumble-)-dryer

de **wasem** /wɑsəm/ (pl: -s) steam, vapour

wasemen /wɑsəmə(n)/ (wasemde, heeft gewasemd) steam

het **wasgoed** /wɑsχut/ wash, laundry, linen

het **washandje** /wɑshɑncə/ face cloth; [Am] wash rag

de **wasknijper** /wɑsknɛipər/ (pl: -s) clothes-peg

het **waskrijt** /wɑskrɛit/ grease pencil

de **waslijn** /wɑslɛin/ (pl: -en) clothes line

de **waslijst** /wɑslɛist/ (pl: -en) shopping list,

catalogue

de **wasmachine** /wɑsmaʃinə/ (pl: -s) (automat-ic) washing machine

de **wasmand** /wɑsmɑnt/ (pl: -en) (dirty) clothes basket

het **wasmiddel** /wɑsmɪdəl/ detergent

het/de **waspoeder** /wɑspudər/ (pl: -s) washing-powder, soap powder

het **wasrek** /wɑsrɛk/ (pl: -ken) drying rack

¹**wassen** /wɑsə(n)/ (adj) wax: *een ~ beeld* a wax figure

²**wassen** /wɑsə(n)/ (wies, is gewassen) **1** grow **2** rise ‖ *bij ~de maan* while the moon is waxing

³**wassen** /wɑsə(n)/ (waste, heeft gewassen) **1** wash; launder; clean: *waar kan ik hier mijn handen ~?* where can I wash my hands?; *zich ~* **a)** wash, have a wash; **b)** have (or: take) a bath; **c)** wash o.s.; *iets op de hand ~* wash sth. by hand **2** wash, do the wash(ing)

het **wassenbeeldenmuseum** /wɑsə(n)be̱l-də(n)myzejʏm/ waxworks

de **wasserette** /wɑsərɛtə/ (pl: -s) launderette

de **wasserij** /wɑsərɛi̯/ (pl: -en) laundry

de **wasstraat** /wɑstrat/ (pl: -straten) (automat-ic) car wash

de **wastafel** /wɑstafəl/ (pl: -s) washbasin

de **wasverzachter** /wɑsfərzɑχtər/ (pl: -s) fab-ric softener

¹**wat** /wɑt/ (ind pron) **1** sth.; anything; what-ever: *ze heeft wel ~* she has got a certain sth.; *wil je ~ drinken?* would you like sth. to drink?; *zie jij ~?* do (or: can) you see any-thing?; *het is altijd ~ met hem* there is always sth. up with him **2** some, a bit (of); a little; a few: *geef me ~ suiker* (or: *geld*) give me some sugar (or: money); *geef mij ook ~* let me have some too; *~ meer* a bit (or: little) more; *~ minder* a bit (or: little) less ‖ *heel ~ boeken* quite a few books; a whole lot of books; *dat scheelt nogal ~* that makes quite a (bit of a) difference; *~ kun jij mooi tekenen* how well you draw!; *~ een onzin* what (absolute) non-sense; *~! komt hij niet?* what! isn't he coming?

²**wat** /wɑt/ (pron) what; which; whatever: *~ bedoel je daar nou mee?* just what do you mean by that?; [stronger] just what is that supposed to mean?; *wát ga je doen?* you are going to do what?; *~ heb je 't liefste, koffie of thee?* which do you prefer, coffee or tea?; *~ zeg je?* what did you say?; sorry?, come again?; (I beg your) pardon?; *~ is het voor iem.?* what's he (or: she) like?

³**wat** /wɑt/ (pron) that; which: *geef hem ~ hij nodig heeft* give him what he needs; *alles ~ je zegt, klopt* everything you say is true; *en ~ nog belangrijker is* and what's (even) more (im-portant); *doe nou maar ~ ik zeg* just do as I say; *je kunt doen en laten ~ je wilt* you can do what (or: as you) please ‖ *ze zag eruit als een verpleegster, ~ ze ook was* she looked like a

nurse, which in fact she was (too)

⁴wat /wɑt/ (adv) **1** somewhat, rather; a little, a bit: *hij is ~ traag* he is a little slow, he is on the slow side **2** very, extremely: *hij is er ~ blij mee* (or: *trots op*) he is extremely pleased with it (or: proud of it) **3** isn't it (or: that, he) …, …, aren't they (or: those) …: *~ mooi hè, die bloemen* aren't they beautiful, those flowers; *~ lief van je!* how nice of you!; [iron] *~ ben je weer vriendelijk* I see you're your usual friendly self again; *~ ze niet verzinnen tegenwoordig* the things they come up with these days; *~ wil je nog meer?* what more do (or: can) you want?; *~ zal hij blij zijn!* how happy (or: pleased) he will be!

het **water** /wɑtər/ (pl: -en) **1** water: [fig] *~ bij de wijn doen* compromise; *de bloemen ~ geven* water the flowers; *hard ~* hard water; *in het ~ vallen* **a)** fall into the water; **b)** fall through; **c)** be a washout; *bij laag ~* at low water (or: tide); *stromend ~* running water; *een schip te ~ laten* launch a ship; *iets boven ~ halen* [fig] unearth (or: dig up) sth. **2** water; waterway: *stilstaand water* stagnant water

waterafstotend /wɑtərɑfstotənt/ (adj) water-repellent; waterproof

de **waterafvoer** /wɑtərɑfur/ drainage (of water); sewage disposal

het **waterballet** /wɑtərbɑlɛt/ (pl: -ten) [hum] wet affair

het **waterbed** /wɑtərbɛt/ (pl: -den) waterbed

de **waterbouwkunde** /wɑtərbɑukʏndə/ hydraulic engineering: *weg- en ~* civil engineering

waterbouwkundig /wɑtərbɑukʏndəx/ (adj) hydraulic

de **waterbron** /wɑtərbrɔn/ (pl: -nen) spring

de **waterdamp** /wɑtərdɑmp/ (water) vapour

waterdicht /wɑtərdɪxt/ (adj) waterproof; watertight: *een ~ alibi* a watertight alibi

waterdoorlatend /wɑtərdɔrlɑtənt/ (adj) porous

de **waterdruppel** /wɑtərdrʏpəl/ (pl: -s) drop of water

wateren /wɑtərə(n)/ (waterde, heeft gewaterd) urinate

de **waterfiets** /wɑtərfits/ (pl: -en) [Dutch] pedalo, pedal boat

de **watergolf** /wɑtərɣɔlf/ (pl: -golven) **1** wave **2** set

watergolven /wɑtərɣɔlvə(n)/ (watergolfde, heeft gewatergolfd) set: *zijn haar laten ~* have one's hair set

het **waterhoen** /wɑtərhun/ moorhen

het **waterhoofd** /wɑtərhoft/ (pl: -en) hydrocephalus

de **waterhoogte** /wɑtərhoxtə/ water level

de **waterhuishouding** /wɑtərhœyshɑudɪŋ/ **1** soil hydrology **2** water management

waterig /wɑtərəx/ (adj) **1** watery; slushy: *~e soep* thin soup **2** watery; [fig] wishy-washy:

een ~ zonnetje a watery sun

het **waterijsje** /wɑtərɛiʃə/ ice lolly; [Am] popsicle

het **waterkanon** /wɑtərkanɔn/ (pl: -nen) water cannon

de **waterkans** /wɑtərkɑns/ (pl: -en) [Belg] remote chance

de **waterkant** /wɑtərkɑnt/ (pl: -en) waterside, waterfront: *aan de ~* on the waterfront

de **waterkering** /wɑtərkerɪŋ/ (pl: -en) dam, dike

de **waterkers** /wɑtərkɛrs/ (water)cress

de **waterkoker** /wɑtərkokər/ (pl: -s) electric kettle

waterkoud /wɑtərkɑut/ (adj) clammy

de **waterkracht** /wɑtərkrɑxt/ hydropower

de **waterlanders** /wɑtərlɑndərs/ (pl) waterworks

de **waterleiding** /wɑtərlɛidɪŋ/ (pl: -en) **1** water pipe (or: supply): *een huis op de ~ aansluiten* to connect a house to the water main(s) **2** waterworks, water pipes: *een bevroren ~* a frozen water pipe

het **waterleidingbedrijf** /wɑtərlɛidɪŋbədrɛif/ (pl: -bedrijven) waterworks

de **waterlelie** /wɑtərleli/ (pl: -s) water lily

de **waterloop** /wɑtərlop/ (pl: -lopen) watercourse

de **Waterman** /wɑtərmɑn/ (pl: -nen) [astrology] Aquarius

de **watermeloen** /wɑtərməlun/ (pl: -en) watermelon

het **watermerk** /wɑtərmɛrk/ (pl: -en) watermark

de **watermeter** /wɑtərmetər/ (pl: -s) water meter

de **watermolen** /wɑtərmolə(n)/ (pl: -s) watermill

de **waterontharder** /wɑtərɔnthɑrdər/ (pl: -s) water softener

de **wateroverlast** /wɑtərovərlɑst/ flooding

de **¹waterpas** /wɑtərpɑs/ (pl: -sen) spirit level; [Am] level

²waterpas /wɑtərpɑs/ (adj) level: *~ maken* level

het **waterpeil** /wɑtərpɛil/ water level

de **waterpijp** /wɑtərpɛip/ (pl: -en) water pipe, hookah

het **waterpistool** /wɑtərpistol/ (pl: -pistolen) water pistol

de **waterplant** /wɑtərplɑnt/ (pl: -en) water plant

de **waterpokken** /wɑtərpokə(n)/ (pl) chickenpox

de **waterpolitie** /wɑtərpoli(t)si/ river police; harbour police

het **waterpolo** /wɑtərpolo/ water polo

de **waterpomp** /wɑtərpɔmp/ (pl: -en) water pump

de **waterpomptang** /wɑtərpɔmptɑŋ/ (pl: -en) adjustable-joint pliers; [large] (adjustable) pipe wrench

de **waterput** /wⱥtərpyt/ (pl: -ten) well

het **waterrad** /wⱥtərɑt/ (pl: -eren) water wheel
waterrijk /wⱥtərɛik/ (adj) watery, full of water

de **waterschade** /wⱥtərsχadə/ water damage

het **waterschap** /wⱥtərsχɑp/ (pl: -pen) [Dutch] **1** district water board **2** water board district

de **waterscheiding** /wⱥtərsχɛidɪŋ/ (pl: -en) watershed [also fig]

de **waterscooter** /wⱥtərskutər/ (pl: -s) aquascooter

de **waterski** /wⱥtərski/ (pl: -'s) water-ski
waterskiën /wⱥtərskijə(n)/ water-skiing

de **waterslang** /wⱥtərslɑŋ/ (pl: -en) hose(pipe)

de **watersnood** /wⱥtərsnot/ flood(ing)

de **watersnoodramp** /wⱥtərsnotrɑmp/ (pl: -en) flood (disaster)

de **waterspiegel** /wⱥtərspiɣəl/ water surface; water level

de **watersport** /wⱥtərspɔrt/ (pl: - en) water sport, aquatic sport

de **waterstaat** /wⱥtərstat/ see minister

de **waterstand** /wⱥtərstɑnt/ (pl: -en) water level: bij hoge (or: lage) ~ at high (or: low) water

de **waterstof** /wⱥtərstɔf/ hydrogen

de **waterstofbom** /wⱥtərstɔvbɔm/ (pl: -men) hydrogen bomb, fusion bomb, H-bomb

het **waterstofperoxide** /wⱥtərstɔfpɛrɔksidə/ hydrogen peroxide

de **waterstraal** /wⱥtərstral/ (pl: -stralen) jet of water
watertanden /wⱥtərtɑndə(n)/ (watertand-de, heeft gewatertand): deze chocolaatjes **doen** mij ~ these chocolates make my mouth water

de **watertoren** /wⱥtərtorə(n)/ (pl: -s) water tower
watertrappelen /wⱥtərtrɑpələ(n)/ tread water

de **waterval** /wⱥtərvɑl/ (pl: -len) waterfall; fall: de **Niagara** ~len Niagara Falls

de **waterverf** /wⱥtərvɛrf/ watercolour

het **watervliegtuig** /wⱥtərvlixtœyx/ (pl: -en) seaplane, water plane

de **watervogel** /wⱥtərvoɣəl/ (pl: -s) waterbird

de **watervrees** /wⱥtərvres/ hydrophobia: ~ **hebben** be hydrophobic

de **waterweg** /wⱥtərwɛχ/ (pl: -en) waterway

het **waterwingebied** /wⱥtərwɪŋɣəbit/ (pl: -en) water-collection area

de **waterzuivering** /wⱥtərzœyvərɪŋ/ **1** water treatment **2** water treatment plant

het **watje** /wɑcə/ (pl: -s) **1** wad of cotton wool; [Am] wad of absorbent cotton **2** wally

de **watt** /wɑt/ (pl: -s) watt

de **watten** /wⱥtə(n)/ (pl) cotton wadding, cotton wool; [Am] absorbent cotton: een **prop (dot)** ~ a plug (or: wad) of cottonwool; iem. **in** de ~ leggen pamper (or: mollycoddle) s.o.

het **wattenstaafje** /wⱥtə(n)stafjə/ (pl: -s) cotton bud; [Am] cotton swab
wauwelen /wⱥuwələ(n)/ (wauwelde, heeft gewauweld) [inform] chatter; jabber; drone (on)

de **WA-verzekering** /weɑvərzekərɪŋ/ third-party insurance

de **wax** /wɑks/ wax
waxen /wɑksə(n)/ (waxte, heeft gewaxt) wax

het **waxinelichtje** /wɑksinəlɪχjə/ (pl: -s) tea-light
wazig /wⱥzəχ/ (adj, adv) **1** hazy; blurred: alles ~ **zien** see everything (as if) through a haze (or: in a blur) **2** muzzy, drowsy: met een ~e **blik** in de ogen with a dazed look in the eyes

de **wc** /wese/ (pl: wc's) **1** watercloset toilet, lavatory; bathroom; [Am] rest room: ik moet **naar** de wc I have to go to the bathroom (or: toilet) **2** toilet(bowl)

de **wc-bril** /wesebrɪl/ (pl: -len) toilet seat

het **wc-papier** /wesepapir/ toilet paper

de **wc-rol** /weserɔl/ (pl: wc-rollen) toilet roll
we /wə/ (pers pron) we, us: laten we **gaan** (or: **ophouden**) let's go (or: stop)

het **web** /wɛp/ (pl: -ben) **1** web **2** [comp] Web

de **webapp** /wɛpɛp/ (pl: -s) web app

de **webbrowser** /wɛbrauzər/ (pl: -s) web browser

de **webcam** /wɛpkɛm/ webcam

de **webhosting** /wɛphostɪŋ/ web hosting

de **weblink** /wɛplɪŋk/ (pl: -s) weblink

het/de **weblog** /wɛploχ/ weblog

de **webmaster** /wɛpma:stər/ web master

de **webpagina** /wɛpaɣina/ (pl: -'s) web page

de **webserver** /wɛpsʏrvər/ (pl: -s) web server

de **website** /wɛpsɑjt/ (pl: -s) website

de **webwinkel** /wɛpwɪŋkəl/ (pl: -s) web shop, web store
wecken /wɛkə(n)/ (weckte, heeft geweckt) [Dutch] can, preserve

de **weckfles** /wɛkflɛs/ (pl: -sen) [Dutch] preserving jar

de **wedde** /wɛdə/ (pl: -n) pay, salary
wedden /wɛdə(n)/ (wedde, heeft gewed) bet (on): met iem. ~ **om** een tientje dat het s.o. ten euros that; denk jij dat Ron vandaag komt? - ik wed **van** wel you think Ron will come today? - I bet he will

de **weddenschap** /wɛdə(n)sχɑp/ (pl: -pen) bet: een ~ **verliezen** lose a bet

de **weddeschaal** /wɛdəsχal/ (pl: -schalen) [Belg] salary scale

de **wederdienst** /wedərdinst/ (pl: -en) favour in return

de **wedergeboorte** /wedərɣəbortə/ (pl: -n) rebirth

de **wederhelft** /wedərhɛlft/ (pl: -en) consort; [inform] other half

de **wederhoor** /wedərhor/ [law]: **hoor** en ~

toepassen listen to both sides, listen to the other side

wederkerend /wedərkɛrənt/ (adj) reflexive: *een ~ voornaamwoord* a reflexive pronoun

wederkerig /wedərkɛrəx/ (adj, adv) mutual, reciprocal

wederom /wedərǫm/ (adv) (once) again, once more

de **wederopbouw** /wedərǫbau/ reconstruction, rebuilding

de **wederopstanding** /wedərǫpstandɪŋ/ resurrection

wederrechtelijk /wedərɛxtələk/ (adj, adv) unlawful, illegal

¹**wederzijds** /wedərzɛits/ (adj) mutual, reciprocal: *de liefde* was ~ their love was mutual

²**wederzijds** /wedərzɛits/ (adv) mutually

de **wedijver** /wɛtɛivər/ competition, rivalry

wedijveren /wɛtɛivərə(n)/ (wedijverde, heeft gewedijverd) strive (for)

de **wedloop** /wɛtlop/ (pl: wedlopen) race

de **wedren** /wɛtrɛn/ (pl: -nen) race

de **wedstrijd** /wɛtstrɛit/ (pl: -en) match, competition, game: *een ~ bijwonen* attend a match; *een ~ fluiten* referee a match; *met nog drie ~en te spelen* with three games (still) to go

de **weduwe** /wedywə/ (pl: -n) widow: *groene ~* housebound wife

het **weduwepensioen** /wedywə(n)pɛnʃun/ (pl: -en) widows' benefit (*or*: pension)

de **weduwnaar** /wedywnar/ (pl: -s, weduwnaren) widower

de ¹**wee** /we/ labour pain, contraction: *de ~ën zijn begonnen* labour has started

²**wee** /we/ (adj) sickly: *een ~ë lucht* a sickly smell

³**wee** /we/ (int) woe: *o ~ als je het nog eens doet* woe betide you if you do it again

de **weeffout** /wefaut/ (pl: -en) flaw, weaving fault

het **weefgetouw** /wefxətau/ (pl: -en) loom

het **weefsel** /wefsəl/ (pl: -s) **1** fabric, textile; weave **2** tissue, web

de **weegbree** /wexbre/ plantain

de **weegbrug** /wexbrʏx/ (pl: -gen) weighbridge

de **weegschaal** /wexsxal/ (pl: -schalen) (pair of) scales, balance: *twee weegschalen* two pairs of scales, two balances

de **Weegschaal** /wexsxal/ (pl: -schalen) [astrology] Libra

de ¹**week** /wek/ (pl: weken) week: *een ~ rust* a week's rest; *volgende ~ dinsdag* next Tuesday; *een ~ weggaan* go away for a week; *door de ~* on weekdays; *over een ~ in* a week from now; *dinsdag over een ~* Tuesday week, a week from Tuesday; *morgen over twee weken* two weeks from tomorrow; *vandaag een*

~ geleden a week ago today

de ²**week** /wek/ (pl: weken) soak: *de was in de ~ zetten* put the laundry in (to) soak

³**week** /wek/ (adj) **1** soft: *~ worden* soften; *een ~ gestel* a weak constitution **2** weak, soft-hearted

het **weekblad** /wegblɑt/ (pl: -en) weekly, (news) magazine

het **weekdier** /wegdir/ (pl: -en) mollusc

het **weekeinde** /wekɛində/ (pl: -n) weekend: *in het ~* at the weekend; [Am] on the weekend

de **weekenddienst** /wikɛndinst/ (pl: -en) weekend duty

de **weekendtas** /wikɛntɑs/ holdall; [Am] carryall

weekhartig /wekhɑrtəx/ (adj) tenderhearted, softhearted

weeklagen /weklayə(n)/ (weeklaagde, heeft geweeklaagd) lament

het **weekoverzicht** /wekovərzɪxt/ (pl: -en) review of the week

de **weelde** /weldə/ luxury, over-abundance, wealth

weelderig /weldərəx/ (adj, adv) luxuriant; lush; sumptuous

de **weemoed** /wemut/ melancholy, sadness

weemoedig /wemudəx/ (adj, adv) melancholic, sad

Weens /wens/ (adj) Viennese

het ¹**weer** /wer/ **1** weather: *mooi ~ spelen (tegen iem.)* put on a show of friendliness; *~ of geen ~* come rain or shine **2** weathering: *het ~ zit in het tentdoek* the tent is weather-stained || *hij is altijd in de ~* he is always on the go; *vroeg in de ~ zijn* be up and at it early

²**weer** /wer/ (adv) **1** again: *morgen komt er ~ een dag* tomorrow is another day; *het komt wel ~ goed* it will all turn out all right; *nu ik ~* now it's my turn; *wat moest hij nu ~?* what did he want now?; *wat nu ~?* now what? **2** back: *heen en ~ gaan* (or: *reizen*) go (*or*: travel) back and forth; *heen en ~ lopen* pace up and down || *zo moeilijk is het nou ook ~ niet* it's not all that hard

weerbaar /werbar/ (adj) able-bodied: *~ zijn* have spirit

weerbarstig /werbɑrstəx/ (adj, adv) stubborn, unruly

het **weerbericht** /werbərɪxt/ (pl: -en) weather forecast (*or*: report)

de **weerga** /werya/ (adj): *zonder ~* unparalleled

weergalmen /weryɑlmə(n)/ (weergalmde, heeft weergalmd) echo, resound: *de straten weergalmden van het gejuich* the streets resounded with the cheers

weergaloos /weryalos/ (adj, adv) unequalled, unparalleled

de **weergave** /weryavə/ (pl: -n) reproduction; account

weergeven /weryevə(n)/ (gaf weer, heeft weergegeven) **1** reproduce, render, represent; recite; convey **2** reproduce, repeat, report: *dit onderzoek geeft de **feiten** juist weer* this study presents the facts accurately **3** reflect

de **weergod** /wẹryɔt/ (pl: -en) weather god

de **weerhaak** /wẹrhak/ (pl: -haken) barb, beard

de **weerhaan** /wẹrhan/ (pl: -hanen) weathercock, weathervane

weerhouden /werhɑudə(n)/ (weerhield, heeft weerhouden) **1** hold back, restrain: *iem. ervan ~ **om** iets te doen* stop (*or:* keep) s.o. from doing sth. **2** [Belg] retain, keep: *de beslissing is ~* the decision is upheld

de **weerkaart** /wẹrkart/ (pl: -en) weather chart, weather map

weerkaatsen /werkạtsə(n)/ (weerkaatste, heeft/is weerkaatst) reflect; reverberate; (re-)echo: *de muur weerkaatst het **geluid*** the wall echoes the sound; *het geluid weerkaatst **tegen** de muur* the sound reflects off (*or:* from) the wall

de **weerklank** /wẹrklɑŋk/ echo: *geen ~ **vinden*** meet with/find no response

weerklinken /werklɪŋkə(n)/ (weerklonk, heeft weerklonken) **1** resound, ring out: *een **schot** weerklonk* a shot rang out **2** resound, reverberate

de **weerkunde** /wẹrkʏndə/ meteorology

weerkundig /werkʏ̣ndəχ/ (adj) meteorological

de **weerkundige** /werkʏ̣ndəɣə/ (pl: -n) meteorologist, weather expert

weerlegbaar /werlɛ̣ɣbar/ (adj) refutable

weerleggen /werlɛ̣ɣə(n)/ (weerlegde, heeft weerlegd) refute

de **weerlegging** /werlɛ̣ɣɪŋ/ refutation

het/de **weerlicht** /wẹrlɪχt/ (heat, sheet) lightning

weerlichten /wẹrlɪχtə(n)/ (weerlichtte, heeft geweerlicht) lighten

weerloos /wẹrlos/ (adj) defenceless

de **weerman** /wẹrmɑn/ (pl: -nen) weatherman

de **weeromstuit** /werɔ̣mstœyt/: *van de ~* on the rebound; *ik moest **van de** ~ ook lachen* I had to laugh too

het **weeroverzicht** /wẹrovərzɪχt/ (pl: -en) weather survey: *en nu het ~* and now for a look at the weather

het **weerpraatje** /wẹrpracə/ (pl: -s) (the) weather in brief, weather report

de **weerschijn** /wẹrsχɛɪn/ reflection

de **weersgesteldheid** /wẹrsχəstɛlthɛɪt/ weather situation: *bij elke ~* in all weathers

de **weerskanten** /wẹrskɑntə(n)/ (pl): *aan ~ van de tafel* (*or:* het raam) on both sides of the table (*or:* window); *van* (*or:* **aan**) *~* from (*or:* on) both sides

de **weerslag** /wẹrslɑχ/ repercussion: *zijn ~ **hebben** op* have repercussions on; *zijn ~ **krijgen** in ...* be reflected in ..., become apparent in ...

de **weersomstandigheden** /wẹrsɔmstɑndəχhedə(n)/ (pl) weather conditions

weerspannig /werspɑ̣nəχ/ (adj, adv) recalcitrant, rebellious, refractory

weerspiegelen /werspịɣələ(n)/ (weerspiegelde, heeft weerspiegeld) reflect

de **weerspiegeling** /werspịɣəlɪŋ/ (pl: -en) reflection: *een **getrouwe** ~ van iets* a true reflection (*or:* mirror) of sth.

weerstaan /werstạn/ (weerstond, heeft weerstaan) resist, stand up to

de **weerstand** /wẹrstɑnt/ (pl: -en) **1** resistance, opposition: *~ **bieden*** offer resistance; *~ **ontmoeten*** meet with opposition **2** aversion

het **weerstandsvermogen** /wẹrstɑn(t)sfərmoɣə(n)/ resistance

het **weerstation** /wẹrsta(t)ʃɔn/ (pl: -s) weather station

de **weersverwachting** /wẹrsfərwɑχtɪŋ/ (pl: -en) weather forecast

de **weerwil** /wẹrwɪl/: *in ~ van* despite, in spite of, notwithstanding

de **weerwolf** /wẹrwɔlf/ (pl: -wolven) werewolf

het **weerwoord** /wẹrwort/ (pl: -en) answer, reply

het ¹**weerzien** /wẹrzin/ reunion; meeting: *tot ~s* goodbye, until the next time

²**weerzien** /wẹrzin/ (zag weer, heeft weergezien) meet again, see again

de **weerzin** /wẹrzɪn/ disgust, reluctance, aversion, distaste: *iets **met** ~ doen* do sth. with great reluctance

weerzinwekkend /werzɪnwɛ̣kənt/ (adj, adv) disgusting, revolting

de **wees** /wes/ (pl: wezen) orphan

het **weesgegroetje** /wesχəχrụcə/ (pl: -s) Hail Mary: *tien ~s **bidden*** say ten Hail Marys

het **weeshuis** /wẹshœys/ (pl: -huizen) orphanage

het **weeskind** /wẹskɪnt/ (pl: -eren) orphan (child)

de **weet** /wet/: *iets **aan** de ~ komen* find out sth.; *ergens geen ~ **van** hebben* have no knowledge of sth., be unaware of sth.

de **weetal** /wẹtɑl/ (pl: -len) know(-it)-all; [Am also] wise guy

weetgierig /wetχịrəχ/ (adj, adv) inquisitive

het **weetje** /wẹcə/ (pl: -s): *allerlei ~s* all kinds of trivia

de ¹**weg** /wɛχ/ (pl: -en) **1** road, way, track: *zich een ~ **banen*** work (*or:* edge) one's way through; *de ~ **kwijt** zijn* a) have lost one's way; b) [fig] lose it, lose one's marbles; *(iem.) **in** de ~ staan* stand in s.o.'s (*or:* the) way; *op ~ **gaan*** set off (on a trip), set out (for), go; *iem. **op** ~ **helpen*** set s.o. up; *iem. **uit** de ~ gaan* keep (*or:* get) out of s.o.'s way, avoid s.o.; *een misverstand **uit** de ~ helpen* clear up a misunderstanding; *op de **goede*** (*or:* **verkeerde**) *~ zijn* be on the right (*or:* wrong) track; *een **kortere** ~ nemen* take a short cut **2** way, channel, means: *de ~ van de minste **weerstand*** the line (*or:* road) of least resistance **3** way, journey: *nog een **lange** ~ voor zich hebben* have a long way to go ‖ *zijns weegs **gaan*** go one's way

²**weg** /wɛχ/ (adv) **1** gone: *een mooie pen **is** nooit ~* a nice pen always comes in useful; *~ **wezen!*** (let's) get away from here!; (let's) get out of here!; *~ **met** …* away (*or:* down) with … **2** crazy **3** away ‖ *ze **heeft** veel ~ van haar zus* she takes after her sister, she is very like her sister

de **wegbereider** /wɛχbərɛɪdər/ (pl: -s) pioneer

wegblazen /wɛχblazə(n)/ (blies weg, heeft weggeblazen) blow away, blow off

wegblijven /wɛχblɛɪvə(n)/ (bleef weg, is weggebleven) stay away

wegbranden /wɛχbrɑndə(n)/ (brandde weg, heeft weggebrand): *die man is niet weg te bránden* there's no getting rid of that man

wegbrengen /wɛχbrɛŋə(n)/ (bracht weg, heeft weggebracht) **1** take (away), deliver **2** see (off)

wegcijferen /wɛχsɛɪfərə(n)/ ignore: *zichzelf ~* efface o.s.

de **wegcode** /wɛχkodə/ (pl: -s) [Belg] traffic regulations; [roughly] Highway Code

het **wegdek** /wɛχdɛk/ (pl: -ken) road (surface)

wegdenken /wɛχdɛŋkə(n)/ (dacht weg, heeft weggedacht) think away: *internet is niet meer **uit** onze maatschappij weg te denken* it's impossible to imagine life today without the Internet

wegdoen /wɛχdun/ (deed weg, heeft weggedaan) **1** dispose of, part with, get rid of **2** put away

wegdragen /wɛχdraɣə(n)/ (droeg weg, heeft weggedragen) carry away, carry off

wegdrijven /wɛχdrɛɪvə(n)/ (dreef weg, is weggedreven) float away, drift away

wegdrukken /wɛχdrʏkə(n)/ (drukte weg, heeft weggedrukt) **1** shove away, push away **2** *iem. ~* dismiss (*or:* reject) s.o.'s call

wegduiken /wɛχdœykə(n)/ (dook weg, is weggedoken) duck (away); dive away

wegduwen /wɛχdywə(n)/ (duwde weg, heeft weggeduwd) push away, push aside

wegen /weɣə(n)/ (woog, heeft gewogen) weigh: *zwaarder ~ dan* outweigh; *zich laten ~* have o.s. weighed, be weighed

de **wegenbelasting** /weɣə(n)bəlɑstɪŋ/ road tax

de **wegenbouw** /weɣə(n)bɑu/ road building (*or:* construction)

de **wegenkaart** /weɣə(n)kart/ (pl: -en) road map

het **wegennet** /weɣənɛt/ (pl: -ten) road network (*or:* system)

wegens /weɣəns/ (prep) because of, on account of, due to: *terechtstaan ~ …* be tried on a charge of …

de **wegenwacht**® /weɣə(n)wɑχt/ (pl: -en)

[Netherlands] (AA) patrolman; AAA attendant

de **Wegenwacht**® /weɣə(n)wɑχt/ [Dutch] road-service; [roughly] AA-patrol, RAC-patrol; [Am] AAA road service

weggaan /wɛχan/ (ging weg, is weggegaan) **1** go away, leave: *Joe is bij zijn vrouw weggegaan* Joe has left his wife; *~ **zonder** te betalen* leave without paying; *ga weg!* go away!, get lost!; get away!, you're kidding! **2** go away: *de pijn gaat al weg* the pain is already getting less

de **weggebruiker** /wɛχəbrœykər/ (pl: -s) road user

weggeven /wɛχevə(n)/ (gaf weg, heeft weggegeven) give away

het **weggevertje** /wɛχevərcə/ (pl: -s) giveaway; dead giveaway

wegglijden /wɛχlɛɪdə(n)/ (gleed weg, is weggegleden) slip (away): *de auto gleed weg in de modder* the car slipped in the mud

weggooien /wɛχojə(n)/ (gooide weg, heeft weggegooid) throw away, throw out, discard: *dat is weggegooid **geld*** that is money down the drain

de **weggooiverpakking** /wɛχojvərpɑkɪŋ/ disposable container (*or:* packaging, package)

weghalen /wɛχhalə(n)/ (haalde weg, heeft weggehaald) remove; take away: *alle huisraad werd **uit** het huis weggehaald* the house was stripped (bare)

de **weghelft** /wɛχhɛlft/ (pl: -en) side of the road

wegjagen /wɛχjaɣə(n)/ (jaagde weg/joeg weg, heeft weggejaagd) chase away: *klanten ~ door de hoge prijzen* frighten customers off by high prices

wegkijken /wɛχkɛikə(n)/ (keek weg, heeft weggekeken) frown away: *hij werd weggekeken* they stared at him coldly until he left

wegkomen /wɛχkomə(n)/ (kwam weg, is weggekomen) get away: *de meeste favorieten zijn **goed** weggekomen bij de start* the favourites got (off to) a good start; ***slecht*** (or: ***goed***) *~ bij iets* come off badly (*or:* well) with sth.; *ik maakte dat ik wegkwam* I got out of there

wegkruipen /wɛχkrœypə(n)/ (kroop weg, is weggekropen) crawl away, creep away

wegkwijnen /wɛχkwɛinə(n)/ (kwijnde weg, is weggekwijnd) pine away, waste away

weglaten /wɛχlatə(n)/ (liet weg, heeft weggelaten) leave out, omit

wegleggen /wɛχlɛɣə(n)/ (legde weg, heeft weggelegd) **1** put aside, put away **2** lay aside, set aside, save

de **wegligging** /wɛχlɪɣɪŋ/ road-holding

weglopen /wɛχlopə(n)/ (liep weg, is weggelopen) **1** walk away, walk off: *dat loopt niet weg* that can wait; *~ **voor** een hond* run away from a dog **2** run away, walk out; run off: *een weggelopen* **kind** a runaway (child) **3** run off, run out

wegmaken /wɛxmakə(n)/ (maakte weg, heeft weggemaakt) lose

de **wegmarkering** /wɛxmɑrkerɪŋ/ (pl: -en) road marking

wegmoffelen /wɛxmɔfələ(n)/ (moffelde weg, heeft weggemoffeld) quickly hide; cover up

wegnemen /wɛxnemə(n)/ (nam weg, heeft weggenomen) remove, take away; dispel || *dat neemt* **niet** *weg, dat ik hem aardig vind* all the same I like him; *dat neemt* **niet** *weg, dat het geld verdwenen is* that doesn't alter the fact that the money has disappeared

de **wegomlegging** /wɛxɔmlɛɣɪŋ/ (pl: -en) diversion; [Am] detour

wegpesten /wɛxpɛstə(n)/ (pestte weg, heeft weggepest) harass (*or:* pester) (s.o.) until he leaves

wegpinken /wɛxpɪŋkə(n)/ (pinkte weg, heeft weggepinkt): *een* **traantje** ~ wipe away a tear

de **wegpiraat** /wɛxpirat/ (pl: wegpiraten) road hog

wegpoetsen /wɛxputsə(n)/ (poetste weg, heeft weggepoetst) gloss over

wegpromoveren /wɛxpromoverə(n)/ (promoveerde weg, heeft weggepromoveerd) kick upstairs

wegraken /wɛxrakə(n)/ (raakte weg, is weggeraakt) **1** faint **2** get lost

wegrennen /wɛxrɛnə(n)/ (rende weg, is weggerend) run off (*or:* away)

het **wegrestaurant** /wɛxrɛstorɑnt/ (pl: -s) transport cafe, wayside restaurant

wegrijden /wɛxrɛidə(n)/ (reed weg, is weggereden) drive off (*or:* away); ride off (*or:* away): *de* **auto** *reed met grote vaart weg* the car drove off at high speed

wegroepen /wɛxrupə(n)/ (riep weg, heeft weggeroepen) call off (*or:* away)

wegschoppen /wɛxsxɔpə(n)/ (schopte weg, heeft weggeschopt) kick away

wegslaan /wɛxslan/ (sloeg weg, heeft weggeslagen) knock off (*or:* away): *de golven hebben een* **stuk** *van de duinen weggeslagen* the waves have washed away part of the dunes; [fig] *zij is er niet* **(van)** *weg te slaan* she can hardly be dragged away (from it)

wegslepen /wɛxslepə(n)/ (sleepte weg, heeft weggesleept) tow away; drag away

wegslikken /wɛxslɪkə(n)/ (slikte weg, heeft weggeslikt) swallow (down): *ik moest even* **iets** ~ I had to swallow hard

wegsluipen /wɛxslœypə(n)/ (sloop weg, is weggeslopen) sneak away, sneak off

wegsmelten /wɛxsmɛltə(n)/ (smolt weg, is weggesmolten) melt away

¹**wegspoelen** /wɛxspulə(n)/ (spoelde weg, is

weggespoeld) be washed (*or:* carried, swept) away

²**wegspoelen** /wɛxspulə(n)/ (spoelde weg, heeft weggespoeld) **1** wash away, carry away; flush down **2** wash down

wegstemmen /wɛxstɛmə(n)/ (stemde weg, heeft weggestemd) vote out (of office), vote down

wegsterven /wɛxstɛrvə(n)/ (stierf weg, is weggestorven) die away (*or:* down), fade away

wegstoppen /wɛxstɔpə(n)/ (stopte weg, heeft weggestopt) hide away, stash away: *weggestopt* **zitten** be hidden (*or:* tucked) away

wegstrepen /wɛxstrepə(n)/ (streepte weg, heeft weggestreept) cross off, cross out, delete: *twee zaken* **tegen** *elkaar* ~ have two things cancel each other out

wegsturen /wɛxstyrə(n)/ (stuurde weg, heeft weggestuurd) send away

wegtrappen /wɛxtrɑpə(n)/ (trapte weg, heeft weggetrapt) kick away: *de* **bal** ~ kick the ball away

wegtrekken /wɛxtrɛkə(n)/ (trok weg, is weggetrokken) draw off, move away, withdraw: *mijn* **hoofdpijn** *trekt weg* my headache is going (*or:* disappearing) || *met een wit weggetrokken* **gezicht** white-faced

wegvagen /wɛxfaɣə(n)/ (vaagde weg, heeft weggevaagd) wipe out, sweep away

wegvallen /wɛxfɑlə(n)/ (viel weg, is weggevallen) **1** be omitted (*or:* dropped): *er is een* **regel** (or: **letter**) *weggevallen* a line (*or:* letter) has been left out **2** fall away

wegvegen /wɛxfeɣə(n)/ (veegde weg, heeft weggeveegd) wipe (*or:* sweep, brush) away

het **wegverkeer** /wɛxfərker/ road traffic

de **wegversmalling** /wɛxfərsmɑlɪŋ/ (pl: -en) narrowing of the road; road narrows

de **wegversperring** /wɛxfərspɛrɪŋ/ (pl: -en) roadblock

het **wegvervoer** /wɛxfərvur/ road transport

wegvliegen /wɛxfliɣə(n)/ (vloog weg, is weggevlogen) **1** fly away (*or:* off, out) **2** sell like hot cakes

wegvoeren /wɛxfurə(n)/ (voerde weg, heeft weggevoerd) carry away, carry off

wegwaaien /wɛxwajə(n)/ (waaide weg/ woei weg, is weggewaaid) be blown away, fly away, fly off

wegwerken /wɛxwɛrkə(n)/ (werkte weg, heeft weggewerkt) get rid of; polish off; put away; smoothe away: *iets* **op** *een foto* ~ block out sth. on a photo; *de bedrading is weggewerkt* **in** *de plint* the wiring is tucked away behind the skirting board

de **wegwerker** /wɛxwɛrkər/ (pl: -s) [Dutch] roadmender; [Am] road worker

de **wegwerkzaamheden**

/wɛxwɛrksamhedə(n)/ (pl) road works

het **wegwerpartikel** /wɛxwɛrpɑrtikəl/ disposable article; disposables

de **wegwerpbeker** /wɛxwɛrbekər/ disposable cup

wegwerpen /wɛxwɛrpə(n)/ (wierp weg, heeft weggeworpen) throw away, throw out

de **wegwerpmaatschappij** /wɛxwɛrpmatsxɑpɛi/ consumer society

de **wegwerpverpakking** /wɛxwɛrpfərpɑkɪŋ/ (pl: -en) disposable container

wegwezen /wɛxwezə(n)/ clear off, clear out, push off, buzz off, scram: *jongens, ~!* let's get out of here!; *hé, jij daar, ~!* buzz off!, scram!

wegwijs /wɛxwɛis/ (adj) familiar, informed

de **wegwijzer** /wɛxwɛizər/ (pl: -s) signpost

wegzakken /wɛxsɑkə(n)/ (zakte weg, is weggezakt) sink

wegzetten /wɛxsɛtə(n)/ (zette weg, heeft weggezet) set aside, put aside, put away (*or:* aside): *ik kon mijn auto nergens ~* I couldn't find anywhere to park ‖ *iem. ~ als leugenaar* brand s.o. as a liar

wegzinken /wɛxsɪŋkə(n)/ (zonk weg, is weggezonken) sink, go under, subside

de **wei** /wɛi/ (pl: -den) *see* weide

de **weide** /wɛidə/ (pl: -n) **1** meadow; pasture; grasslands **2** playground, playing field

weiden /wɛidə(n)/ (weidde, heeft geweid) graze, pasture

weids /wɛits/ (adj) grand

de **weifelaar** /wɛifəlar/ (pl: -s) waverer

weifelen /wɛifələ(n)/ (weifelde, heeft geweifeld) waver, hesitate, be undecided: *na enig ~ koos ik het groene jasje* after some hesitation I opted for the green jacket

de **weigeraar** /wɛiɣərar/ (pl: -s) refuser

weigerachtig /wɛiɣərɑxtəx/ (adj) unwilling, reluctant; uncooperative

¹**weigeren** /wɛiɣərə(n)/ (weigerde, heeft geweigerd) fail; jam; be jammed: *de motor weigert* the engine won't start

²**weigeren** /wɛiɣərə(n)/ (weigerde, heeft geweigerd) refuse, reject; turn down: *een visum ~* withhold a visa; *iem. iets ~* deny s.o. sth.

de **weigering** /wɛiɣərɪŋ/ (pl: -en) refusal; denial

het **weiland** /wɛilɑnt/ (pl: -en) pasture (land), grazing (land), meadow

¹**weinig** /wɛinəx/ (ind pron) little, not much, not a lot: *~ Engels kennen* not know much English; *~ of (tot) geen geld* little or no money; *er ~ van weten* not know a lot about it; *dat is veel te ~* that's insufficient (*or:* quite inadequate); *twintig pond te ~ hebben* be twenty pounds short

²**weinig** /wɛinəx/ (adv) **1** little: *~ bekende feiten* little-known facts; *er ~ om geven* care little about it; *dat scheelt maar ~* it's a close

thing **2** hardly ever: *~ thuis zijn* not be in often

³**weinig** /wɛinəx/ (num) few, not many: *slechts ~ huizen staan leeg* there are only a few unoccupied houses; *~ of (tot) geen mensen* few if any people

¹**wekelijks** /wekələks/ (adj) weekly: *onze ~e vergadering* our weekly meeting

²**wekelijks** /wekələks/ (adv) **1** weekly, once a week, every week: *~ samenkomen* meet once a week **2** a week, per week: *hij verdient ~ 500 euro* he earns 500 euros a week

weken /wekə(n)/ (weekte, heeft/is geweekt) soak

¹**wekenlang** /wekə(n)lɑŋ/ (adj, adv) lasting several weeks

²**wekenlang** /wekə(n)lɑŋ/ (adv) for weeks (on end)

wekken /wɛkə(n)/ (wekte, heeft gewekt) **1** wake (up); call: *tot leven ~* bring into being **2** awaken, arouse, stir, excite; create: *iemands belangstelling ~* arouse (*or:* excite) s.o.'s interest; *vertrouwen ~* inspire confidence

de **wekker** /wɛkər/ (pl: -s) alarm (clock): *de ~ op zes uur zetten* set the alarm for six (o'clock)

de **wekkerradio** /wɛkəradijo/ (pl: -'s) radio alarm (clock), clock radio

het ¹**wel** /wɛl/ (pl: -len) welfare, well-being: *zijn ~ en wee* his fortunes

²**wel** /wɛl/ (adv) **1** well: *en (dat) nog ~ op zondag* and on a Sunday, too! **2** rather, quite: *het was ~ aardig* it was all right; *'hoe is het ermee?' 'het gaat ~'* 'how are you?' 'all right'; *ik mag dat ~* I quite like that; *het kan er ~ mee door* it'll do **3** probably: *het zal ~ lukken* it'll work out (all right); *dat zal ~ niet* I suppose not; *je zult ~ denken* what will you think?; *hij zal het ~ niet geweest zijn* I don't think it was him; *dat kan ~ (zijn)* that may be (so); *hij zal nu ~ in bed liggen* he'll be in bed by now **4** as much as; as many as; as often as: *dat kost ~ 100 euro* it'll cost as much as 100 euros; *wat moet dat ~ niet kosten* I hate to think (of) what that costs **5** at least, just as: *dat is ~ zo makkelijk* it would be a lot easier that way; *het lijkt me ~ zo verstandig* it seems sensible to me **6** completely, all: *we zijn gezond en ~ aangekomen* we arrived safe and sound ‖ *och, ik mag hem ~* oh, I think he's all right; *dat dacht ik ~* I thought as much; *wat zullen de mensen er ~ van zeggen?* what'll people say?; *heeft hij het ~ gedaan?* did he really do it?; *hij komt ~* he will come (all right); *kom jij? misschien ~!* will you come?, I might!; *het is wél waar* but it ís true; *'ik doe het niet', 'je doet het ~!'* 'I won't do it', 'oh yes you will!'; *jij wil niet? ik ~!* you don't want to? well I do!; *liever ~ dan niet* as soon as not; *nietes! wélles!* **a)** 'tisn't! 'tis!; **b)** [Am] it isn't, it is so! (*or:* too!); **c)** [depending on verb in previous sentence] didn't!

did!; ~ **eens** once in a while; ever; *dat komt ~ eens voor* it happens at times; *heb je ~ eens Japans gegeten?* have you ever eaten Japanese food?; *dát ~* granted, agreed; *hij wou ~* he was all for it

³**wel** /wɛl/ (int) well, why: *~? wat zeg je daarvan?* well? what do you say to that? ‖ *~ allemachtig!* well I'll be damned!; *~ nee!* of course not!

het **welbehagen** /wɛlbəhaɣə(n)/ pleasure: *een gevoel van ~* a sense of well-being
welbekend /wɛlbəkɛnt/ (adj) well-known, famous; familiar
welbeschouwd /wɛlbəsxɑut/ (adj, adv) all things considered, all in all
welbespraakt /wɛlbəsprakt/ (adj) eloquent
welbesteed /wɛlbəstet/ (adj) well-spent

het **welbevinden** /wɛlbəvɪndə(n)/ well-being
welbewust /wɛlbəwʏst/ (adj, adv) deliberate, well-considered

de **weldaad** /wɛldat/ (pl: weldaden) benefaction, charity
weldadig /wɛldadəx/ (adj) benevolent
weldenkend /wɛldɛnkənt/ (adj) rightminded, right-thinking

de **weldoener** /wɛldunər/ (pl: -s) benefactor
weldra /wɛldra/ (adv) presently
weleens /wɛlens/ (adv) once in a while, sometimes: *wil je ~ luisteren!* will you just listen (to me)!

het **weleer** /wɛler/ olden days (or: times)
welgemanierd /wɛlɣəmanirt/ (adj, adv) well-mannered
welgemeend /wɛlɣəment/ (adj) well-meaning, well-meant
welgesteld /wɛlɣəstɛlt/ (adj) well-to-do, well-off
welgeteld /wɛlɣətɛlt/ (adv) all-in-all, all told
welgevallen /wɛlɣəvalə(n)/: *zich iets laten ~* put up with sth., submit to
welgezind /wɛlɣəzɪnt/ (adj) well-disposed (towards)
welig /weləx/ (adj) luxuriant, abundant
welingelicht /wɛlɪnɣəlɪxt/ (adj) well-informed
weliswaar /wɛlɪswar/ (adv) it's true, to be sure: *ik heb het ~ beloofd, maar ik kan het nu niet doen* I did promise (, it's true), but I cannot do it now
welja /wɛlja/ (int) yes of course: *~, lach er maar om* go on, laugh; *~, spot er maar mee* that's right, make fun of it

¹**welk** /wɛlk/ (ind pron) whatever, any (… what(so)ever); whichever; any: *~e kleur je ook (maar) wilt, om het even ~e kleur je wilt* take any colour whatsoever; *om ~e reden ook* for any reason whatsoever; *~e van de twee je ook kiest* whichever of the two you choose; *(geef me er maar een,) het geeft niet ~e*

any (of them) will do; either (of them) will do
²**welk** /wɛlk/ (pron) which, what; which one: *om ~e reden?, met ~e bedoeling?* what for?; *~e van die twee is van jou?* which of those two is yours?
³**welk** /wɛlk/ (pron) **1** who; whom; which: *de man ~e u gezien hebt, is hier* the man (whom) you saw is here **2** which: *wij verkopen koffie en thee, ~e artikelen veel aftrek vinden* we sell coffee and tea, (articles) which are much in demand; *… vanuit ~e overtuiging hij ertoe overging om … …* from which conviction he proceeded to …
welkom /wɛlkɔm/ (adj) welcome: *je bent altijd ~* you're always welcome; *iem. hartelijk ~ heten* give s.o. a hearty (or: cordial) welcome ‖ *~ thuis* welcome home
¹**wellen** /wɛlə(n)/ (welde, is geweld) well (up)
²**wellen** /wɛlə(n)/ (welde, heeft geweld) **1** simmer **2** steep
welles /wɛlɛs/ (int) [inform] yes, it is (or: does): *nietes! ~!* it isn't! it is!

het **welles-nietesspelletje** /wɛləsnitəspɛləcə/ intellectual tug-of-war
welletjes /wɛlɛcəs/ (adj) [inform] quite enough: *'t is zo ~* that will do
wellicht /wɛlɪxt/ (adv) perhaps, possibly
welluidend /wɛlœydənt/ (adj, adv) melodious

de **wellust** /wɛlʏst/ voluptuousness, sensuality
wellustig /wɛlʏstəx/ (adj, adv) sensual, voluptuous
welnee /wɛlne/ (int) of course not, certainly not

het **welnemen** /wɛlnemə(n)/: *met uw ~* by your leave
welnu /wɛlnʏ/ (int) well then: *~, laat eens horen* well then, tell me (your story)
welopgevoed /wɛlɔpxəvut/ (adj) well-bred: *~e kinderen* well brought up children
weloverwogen /wɛlovərwoɣə(n)/ (adj, adv) **1** (well-)considered: *in ~ woorden* in measured words **2** deliberate: *iets ~ doen* do sth. deliberately

de **welp** /wɛlp/ **1** cub **2** Cub Scout
het **welslagen** /wɛlslaɣə(n)/ success
welsprekend /wɛlsprekənt/ (adj) eloquent
de **welsprekendheid** /wɛlsprekənthɛɪt/ eloquence
de **welstand** /wɛlstant/ **1** good health **2** wellbeing
de ¹**weltergewicht** /wɛltərɣəwɪxt/ welterweight
het ²**weltergewicht** /wɛltərɣəwɪxt/ welterweight
welterusten /wɛltərʏstə(n)/ (int) goodnight, sleep well
welteverstaan /wɛltəvərstan/ (adv) that is, if you get my meaning

de **welvaart** /wɛlvart/ prosperity

de **welvaartsmaatschappij** /wɛlvarts-matsχɑpɛi/ affluent society

de **welvaartsstaat** /wɛlvartstat/ welfare state

welvarend /wɛlvarənt/ (adj) thriving; well-to-do

welverdiend /wɛlvərdint/ (adj) well-deserved; well-earned; just

de **welving** /wɛlvɪŋ/ (pl: -en) curve, curvature

welwillend /wɛlwɪlənt/ (adj, adv) kind, sympathetic; favourable: *~ staan tegenover iets* be favourably disposed towards sth.

de **welwillendheid** /wɛlwɪlənthɛit/ benevolence, kindness: *dankzij de ~ van* by (or: through) the courtesy of

het **welzijn** /wɛlzɛin/ welfare, well-being

het **welzijnswerk** /wɛlzɛinswɛrk/ welfare work, social work

de **welzijnswerker** /wɛlzɛinswɛrkər/ (pl: -s) social worker

wemelen /wemələ(n)/ (wemelde, heeft gewemeld) teem (with), swarm (with): *zijn opstel wemelt van de fouten* his essay is full of mistakes

wendbaar /wɛndbar/ (adj) manoeuvrable

¹**wenden** /wɛndə(n)/ (wendde, heeft gewend) turn (about): *hoe je het ook wendt of keert* whichever way you look at it

zich ²**wenden** /wɛndə(n)/ (wendde zich, heeft zich gewend) (+ tot) turn (to), apply (to)

de **wending** /wɛndɪŋ/ (pl: -en) turn: *het verhaal een andere ~ geven* give the story a twist; *een verrassende ~ nemen* take an unexpected turn

wenen /wenə(n)/ (weende, heeft geweend) weep

Wenen /wenə(n)/ Vienna

de **wenk** /wɛŋk/ (pl: -en) sign, wink, nod

de **wenkbrauw** /wɛŋgbrɑu/ (pl: -en) (eye)brow: *de ~en fronsen* frown; *de ~en optrekken* raise one's eyebrows

het **wenkbrauwpotlood** /wɛŋgbrɑupotlot/ eyebrow pencil

wenken /wɛŋkə(n)/ (wenkte, heeft gewenkt) beckon, signal, motion

wennen /wɛnə(n)/ (wende, is gewend) **1** get (or: become) used (to), get (or: become) accustomed (to): *dat zal wel ~* you'll get used to it **2** adjust, settle in (or: down)

de **wens** /wɛns/ (pl: -en) **1** wish, desire: *zijn laatste ~* his dying wish; *mijn ~ is vervuld* my wish has come true; *het gaat naar ~* it is going as we hoped it would; *is alles naar ~?* is everything to your liking? **2** wish, greeting: *de beste ~en voor het nieuwe jaar* best wishes for the new year ‖ *de ~ is de vader van de gedachte* the wish is father to the thought

de **wensdroom** /wɛnzdrom/ (pl: -dromen) fantasy, pipe dream

wenselijk /wɛnsələk/ (adj, adv) desirable; advisable: *ik vind het ~ dat ...* I find it advisable to ...

wensen /wɛnsə(n)/ (wenste, heeft gewenst) wish, desire: *dat laat aan duidelijkheid niets te ~ over* that is perfectly clear; *nog veel te ~ overlaten* leave a lot to be desired; *ik wens met rust gelaten te worden* I want to be left alone; *iem. goede morgen* (or: *een prettige vakantie*) *~ wish* s.o. good morning (or: a nice holiday)

de **wenskaart** /wɛnskart/ (pl: -en) greetings card

wentelen /wɛntələ(n)/ (wentelde, heeft/is gewenteld) roll, turn (round), revolve

de **wenteltrap** /wɛntəltrɑp/ (pl: -pen) spiral staircase, winding stairs (or: staircase)

de **wereld** /werəlt/ (pl: -en) world, earth: *zij komen uit alle delen van de ~* they come from the four corners (or: from every corner) of the world; *aan het andere eind van de ~* on the other side of the world; *wat is de ~ toch klein!* isn't it a small world!; *de ~ staat op zijn kop* it's a mad (or: topsy-turvy) world; *een kind ter ~ brengen* (*helpen*) bring a child into the world; *de rijkste man ter ~* the richest man in the world; *er ging een ~ voor hem open* a new world opened up for him; *de derde ~* the Third World; *dat is de omgekeerde ~* that's putting things on their heads

de **Wereldbank** /werəldbɑŋk/ World Bank

het **wereldbeeld** /werəldbelt/ world-view

de **wereldbeker** /werəldbekər/ (pl: -s) World Cup

wereldberoemd /werəldbərumt/ (adj) world-famous

de **wereldbol** /werəldbɔl/ (pl: -len) (terrestrial) globe

de **wereldburger** /werəldbʏrɣər/ (pl: -s) cosmopolitan, world citizen

het **werelddeel** /werəldel/ (pl: -delen) continent

Werelddierendag /werəldirə(n)dɑχ/ World Animal Day

het **werelderfgoed** /werəltɛrfχut/ world heritage

de **wereldhaven** /werəlthavə(n)/ (pl: -s) international (sea)port

de **wereldkaart** /werəltkart/ (pl: -en) map of the world

de **wereldkampioen** /werəltkɑmpijun/ (pl: -en) world champion

het **wereldkampioenschap** /werəltkɑmpijunsχɑp/ (pl: -pen) world championship; [Am] world's championship

wereldkundig /werəltkʏndəχ/ (adj) public: *iets ~ maken* make sth. public

de **wereldleider** /werəltlɛidər/ world leader

wereldlijk /werəltlək/ (adj) worldly, secular

de **wereldmacht** /werəltmɑχt/ (pl: -en) world power

de **wereldmarktleider** /werəltmɑrktlɛidər/ (pl: -s) world market leader

het **Wereldnatuurfonds** /werəltnatʏrfɔn(t)s/ World Wildlife Fund

de **wereldomroep** /wɛrəltɔmrup/ (pl: -en)
world service

de **wereldoorlog** /wɛrəltorlɔx/ (pl: -en) world
war: *de Tweede Wereldoorlog* the second
World War, World War II

de **wereldpremière** /wɛrəltprəmjɛːrə/ (pl: -s)
world première

het **wereldrecord** /wɛrəltrəkɔːr/ (pl: -s) world
record

de **wereldreis** /wɛrəltrɛis/ (pl: -reizen) journey
around the world, world tour

de **wereldreiziger** /wɛrəltrɛizəyər/ (pl: -s)
globe-trotter

het **wereldrestaurant** /wɛrəltrɛstorɑnt/ (pl:
-s) world cuisine restaurant

werelds /wɛrəlts/ (adj) worldly, secular

wereldschokkend /wɛrəltsxɔkənt/ (adj)
earth-shaking

de **wereldstad** /wɛrəltstɑt/ (pl: -steden) metropolis

de **wereldtentoonstelling** /wɛrəltɛnton-
stɛlɪŋ/ (pl: -en) world fair

de **wereldtitel** /wɛrəltitəl/ (pl: -s) world title

de **wereldvrede** /wɛrəltfredə/ world peace

wereldvreemd /wɛrəltfremt/ (adj) un-
worldly; other-worldly

wereldwijd /wɛrəltwɛit/ (adj) worldwide

de **wereldwinkel** /wɛrəltwɪnkəl/ (pl: -s) third-
world (aid) shop

het **wereldwonder** /wɛrəltwɔndər/ (pl: -en):
de zeven ~en the Seven Wonders of the
World

de **wereldzee** /wɛrəltse/ (pl: -ën) ocean

¹**weren** /wɛrə(n)/ (weerde, heeft geweerd)
avert, prevent, keep out: *vervuilende auto's
worden geweerd uit het centrum* high-polluting cars are banned from the city centre

zich ²**weren** /wɛrə(n)/ (weerde zich, heeft zich
geweerd) **1** resist, combat **2** exert oneself:
zich flink ~ make energetic efforts

de **werf** /wɛrf/ (pl: werven) **1** shipyard; dockyard: *een schip van de ~ laten lopen* launch a
ship **2** yard **3** [Belg] (building) site

het **werk** /wɛrk/ (pl: -en) work, job, task: *het verzamelde ~ van W.F. Hermans* W.F. Hermans'
(collected) works; *ze houden hier niet van half
~* they don't do things by halves here; *dat is
een heel ~* it's quite a job; *het is onbegonnen
~* it's a hopeless task; *aangenomen ~* contract work; *ongeschoold ~* unskilled work;
(vast) ~ hebben have a regular job; *aan het ~
gaan* set to work; *aan het ~ houden* keep going; *iedereen aan het ~!* everybody to their
work!; *iem. aan het ~ zetten* put (*or:* set) s.o.
to work; *er is ~ aan de winkel* there is work to
be done; *~ in uitvoering* roadworks; *ieder ging
op zijn eigen manier te ~* everyone set about it
in their own way; *het vuile ~ opknappen* do
the dirty work || *ze wilden er geen ~ van ma-
ken* they didn't want to take the matter in
hand; *alles in het ~ stellen* make every effort

to; *een goed begin is het halve ~* well begun is
half done; the first blow is half the battle;
vele handen maken licht ~ many hands make
light work

werkbaar /wɛrgbar/ (adj) workable, feasible

de **werkbalk** /wɛrgbɑlk/ tool bar

de **werkbank** /wɛrgbɑŋk/ (pl: -en) bench;
(work)bench

de **werkbespreking** /wɛrgbəsprekɪŋ/ (pl: -en)
[roughly] discussion of progress

het **werkbezoek** /wɛrgbəzuk/ (pl: -en) working
visit

het **werkcollege** /wɛrkɔleʒə/ (pl: -s) seminar,
tutorial

de **werkdag** /wɛrgdɑx/ (pl: -en) working day,
workday, weekday

de **werkdruk** /wɛrgdrɪk/ pressure of work

werkelijk /wɛrkələk/ (adj) real; true

de **werkelijkheid** /wɛrkələkhɛit/ reality: *de
alledaagse ~* everyday reality; *~ worden*
come true; *in ~* actually; *dat is in strijd met de ~*
that conflicts with the facts

werkeloos /wɛrkəlos/ (adj) idle: *~ toezien*
stand by and do nothing, stand by and
watch; *see werkloos*

werken /wɛrkə(n)/ (werkte, heeft gewerkt)
1 work; operate: *de tijd werkt in ons voordeel*
time is on our side; *iem. hard laten ~* work s.o.
hard; *hard ~* work hard; *aan iets ~* work at
(*or:* on) sth.; *~ op het land* work the soil (*or:*
land); [Dutch] *werk ze* have a good (*or:* nice)
day (at work) **2** work, function: *dit apparaat
werkt heel eenvoudig* this apparatus is simple
to operate; *zo werkt dat niet* that's not the
way it works **3** work, take effect: *de pillen
begonnen te ~* the pills began to take effect
|| *zich kapot ~* work one's fingers to the bone;
een ongewenst persoon eruit ~ get rid of an
unwanted person; *zich omhoog ~* work one's
way up (*or:* to the top); *zich in de nesten ~* get
into trouble (*or:* a scrape), tie o.s. up

werkend /wɛrkənt/ (adj) working; employed: *snel ~e medicijnen* fast-acting medicines

de **werker** /wɛrkər/ (pl: -s) worker

de **werkervaring** /wɛrkɛrvarɪŋ/ work experience

het **werkgeheugen** /wɛrkxəhøyə(n)/ (pl: -s)
main memory

de **werkgelegenheid** /wɛrkxəleyənhɛit/ employment

de **werkgever** /wɛrkxevər/ (pl: -s) employer

de **werkgeversorganisatie** /wɛrkxevərs-
ɔryaniza(t)si/ (pl: -s) employers' organization
(*or:* federation)

de **werkgroep** /wɛrkxrup/ (pl: -en) study
group, working party

de **werking** /wɛrkɪŋ/ (pl: -en) **1** working, action, functioning: *buiten ~* out of order; *in ~
stellen* put into action; activate; *de wet treedt*

1 januari in ~ the law will come into force (*or:* effect) on January 1st **2** effect(s)

het **werkje** /wɛrkjə/ (pl: -s) pattern

de **werkkamer** /wɛrkamər/ (pl: -s) study

het **werkkamp** /wɛrkɑmp/ (pl: -en) **1** project week **2** (hard) labour camp

de **werkkleding** /wɛrkledɪŋ/ workclothes, working clothes

het **werkklimaat** /wɛrklimat/ (pl: -klimaten) work climate, work atmosphere

de **werkkracht** /wɛrkrɑχt/ (pl: -en) worker, employee

de **werkkring** /wɛrkrɪŋ/ (pl: -en) post, job; working environment

werkloos /wɛrklos/ (adj) unemployed, out of work (*or:* a job)

de **werkloosheid** /wɛrklosheit/ unemployment

het **werkloosheidscijfer** /wɛrklosheitsɛifər/ (pl: -s) unemployment figure

de **werkloosheidsuitkering** /wɛrklosheitsœytkerɪŋ/ (pl: -en) unemployment benefit; [Am] unemployment compensation

de **werkloze** /wɛrklozə/ (pl: -n) unemployed person

de **werklust** /wɛrklʏst/ zest for work, willingness to work

de **werkmaatschappij** /wɛrkmatsχɑpɛi/ (pl: -en) subsidiary (company)

de **werknemer** /wɛrknemər/ (pl: -s) employee

de **werknemersorganisatie** /wɛrknemərsɔrɣaniza(t)si/ (pl: -s) (trade) union

de **werkonderbreking** /wɛrkɔndərbrekɪŋ/ (pl: -en) (work) stoppage, walkout

het **werkpaard** /wɛrkpart/ (pl: -en) workhorse

de **werkplaats** /wɛrkplats/ (pl: -en) workshop, workplace: [Dutch] *sociale* ~ sheltered workshop

de **werkplek** /wɛrkplɛk/ (pl: -ken) workplace; workstation

het **werkstation** /wɛrksta(t)ʃɔn/ (pl: -s) workstation

de **werkster** /wɛrkstər/ (pl: -s) **1** (woman, female) worker **2** cleaning lady

de **werkstraf** /wɛrkstrɑf/ (pl: -fen) community service

de **werkstudent** /wɛrkstydɛnt/ (pl: -en) student working his way through college with a (part-time) job

het **werkstuk** /wɛrkstʏk/ (pl: -ken) **1** piece of work **2** [educ] paper, project

de **werktafel** /wɛrktafəl/ (pl: -s) work table, desk

het **werkterrein** /wɛrktɛrɛin/ (pl: -en) working space, work area

de **werktijd** /wɛrktɛit/ (pl: -en) working hours; office hours: *na* ~ after hours; *onder* ~ during working hours

het **werktuig** /wɛrktœyχ/ (pl: -en) tool; piece of equipment, machine

de **werktuigbouwkunde** /wɛrktœyχbaukʏndə/ mechanical engineering

werktuiglijk /wɛrktœyχlək/ (adj, adv) mechanical, automatic

het **werkuur** /wɛrkyr/ (pl: -uren) working hour, hour of work

de **werkvergunning** /wɛrkfərɣʏnɪŋ/ (pl: -en) work permit

de **werkverschaffing** /wɛrkfərsχɑfɪŋ/ (unemployment) relief work(s); [fig] work for the sake of it

de **werkvloer** /wɛrkflur/ shop floor

de **werkweek** /wɛrkwek/ (pl: -weken) **1** (working) week **2** study week, project week: *op* ~ *zijn* have a study week (*or:* project week)

de **werkweigering** /wɛrkwɛiɣərɪŋ/ refusal to work

de **werkwijze** /wɛrkwɛizə/ (pl: -n) method (of working); procedure; (manufacturing) process; routine: *dit is de normale* ~ this is (the) standard (operating) procedure

de **werkwillige** /wɛrkwɪləɣə/ (pl: -n) nonstriker

het **werkwoord** /wɛrkwort/ (pl: -en) verb: *onregelmatig* ~ irregular verb; *sterke* (or: *zwakke*) ~*en* strong (*or:* weak) verbs

werkzaam /wɛrksam/ (adj, adv) **1** working, active; employed; engaged **2** active, industrious: *hij blijft als adviseur* ~ he will continue to act as (an) adviser

de **werkzaamheden** /wɛrksamhedə(n)/ (pl) activities; duties; operations; proceedings, business: ~ *aan de metro* work on the underground

de **werkzoekende** /wɛrksukəndə/ (pl: -n) jobseeker, person in search of employment

werpen /wɛrpə(n)/ (wierp, heeft geworpen) have puppies (*or:* kittens): *onze hond heeft (drie jongen) geworpen* our dog has had (three) pups

de **werper** /wɛrpər/ (pl: -s) pitcher

de **werphengel** /wɛrphɛŋəl/ (pl: -s) casting rod

de **wervel** /wɛrvəl/ (pl: -s) vertebra

wervelend /wɛrvələnt/ (adj) sparkling: *een* ~*e show* a spectacular show

de **wervelkolom** /wɛrvəlkolɔm/ (pl: -men) vertebral column, spinal column, spine, backbone

de **wervelstorm** /wɛrvəlstɔrm/ (pl: -en) cyclone, tornado, hurricane

de **wervelwind** /wɛrvəlwɪnt/ (pl: -en) whirlwind, tornado: *als een* ~ like a whirlwind

werven /wɛrvə(n)/ (wierf, heeft geworven) **1** recruit **2** [Belg] appoint

wervend /wɛrvə(n)t/ (adj) attractive, compelling: *een* ~*e tekst* an attractive text

de **werving** /wɛrvɪŋ/ (pl: -en) recruitment; enlistment; enrolment: ~ *en selectie* recruitment and selection

de **wesp** /wɛsp/ (pl: -en) wasp

het **wespennest** /wɛspənɛst/ (pl: -en) wasps'

nest

de **wespentaille** /wɛspə(n)tɑjə/ (pl: -s) wasp waist

west /wɛst/ (adj, adv) **1** west(erly), westward; to the west **2** west(erly); from the west

de **West-Duitser** /wɛsdœytsər/ (pl: -s) West German

West-Duitsland /wɛsdœytslɑnt/ West Germany

westelijk /wɛstələk/ (adj, adv) west, westerly, western, westward: ~ *van* (to the) west of; *de* ~*e Jordaanoever* the West Bank

het **westen** /wɛstə(n)/ west: *het* ~ *van Nederland* the west(ern part) of the Netherlands; *het wilde* ~ the (Wild) West, the Frontier ‖ *buiten* ~ *raken* pass out; *iem. buiten* ~ *slaan* knock s.o. out (cold); *buiten* ~ *zijn* be out (cold)

de **westenwind** /wɛstə(n)wɪnt/ (pl: -en) west-(erly) wind

de **westerlengte** /wɛstərlɛŋtə/ longitude west: *op 15°* ~ at 15° longitude west

de **westerling** /wɛstərlɪŋ/ (pl: -en) Westerner; westerner

de **western** /wɛstərn/ (pl: -s) western

¹**westers** /wɛstərs/ (adj) western

²**westers** /wɛstərs/ (adv) in a western fashion (*or:* manner)

West-Europa /wɛstøropɑ/ Western Europe

West-Europees /wɛstøropes/ (adj) West-(ern) European

West-Indië /wɛstɪndijə/ (the) West Indies

de **westkust** /wɛstkyst/ (pl: -en) west coast

de **wet** /wɛt/ (pl: -ten) **1** law, statute: *een ongeschreven* ~ an unwritten rule; *de* ~ *naleven* (*or: overtreden*) abide by (*or:* break) the law; *de* ~ *schrijft voor dat ...* the law prescribes that ...; *de* ~ *toepassen* enforce the law; *volgens de* ~ *is het een misdaad* it's a crime before the law; *volgens de Engelse* ~ under English law; *bij de* ~ *bepaald* regulated by law; *in strijd met de* ~ unlawful; against the law; *voor de* ~ *trouwen* marry at a registry office; *de* ~ *van Archimedes* Archimedes' principle **2** law, rule: *iem. de* ~ *voorschrijven* lay down the law to s.o.

het **wetboek** /wɛdbuk/ (pl: -en) code, lawbook: *burgerlijk* ~ civil code; ~ *van strafrecht* penal code

het ¹**weten** /wetə(n)/ knowledge: *buiten mijn* ~ without my knowledge; *naar mijn beste* ~ to the best of my knowledge; *te* ~ namely, that is to say; *zeker* ~*!* no buts about it!, absolutely!

²**weten** /wetə(n)/ (wist, heeft geweten) know, manage: *dat weet zelfs een kind!* even a fool knows that!; *ik had het kunnen* ~ I might have known; *laat maar* ~ (please) let me know; *ik zal het u laten* ~ I'll let you know; ~ *te ontkomen* manage to escape; *ik zou weleens willen* ~ *waarom hij dat zei* I'd like to know why he said that; *daar weet ik alles van* I know all about it; *ik weet het!* I've got it!; *voor je het weet, ben je er* you're there before you know it; *ze hebben het geweten* they found out (to their cost); *hij wou er niets van* ~ he wouldn't hear of it; *nu weet ik nóg niets!* I'm no wiser than I was (before)!; *je weet wie het zegt* look who is talking; *je moet het zelf (maar)* ~ it's your decision; *je zou beter moeten* ~ you should know better (than that); *hij wist niet hoe gauw hij weg moest komen* he couldn't get away fast enough; *als dat geen zwendel is dan weet ik het niet (meer)* if that isn't a fraud I don't know what is; *ik zou niet* ~ *waarom (niet)* I don't see why (not); *weet je wel, je weet wel* you know; *iets zeker* ~ be sure about sth.; *voor zover ik weet* as far as I know; *iets te* ~ *komen* find out sth.; *als je dat maar weet!* keep it in mind!; *niet dat ik weet* not that I know; *weet je nog?* (do you) remember?; *weet ik veel!* search me! ‖ *ik wist niet wat ik zag!* I couldn't believe my eyes!; *je weet (het) maar nooit* you never know

de **wetenschap** /wetə(n)sχɑp/ (pl: -pen) **1** knowledge **2** learning; science; scholarship; learning

wetenschappelijk /wetə(n)sχɑpələk/ (adj, adv) scholarly; scientific: [Dutch] *voorbereidend* ~ *onderwijs* pre-university education; ~ *personeel* academic staff; [Am] faculty

de **wetenschapper** /wetənsχɑpər/ (pl: -s) scholar; scientist; academic

wetenswaardig /wetə(n)swɑrdəχ/ (adj) interesting; informative

de **wetenswaardigheid** /wetə(n)swɑrdəχhɛɪt/ (pl: -heden) piece of information

wetgevend /wɛtχevənt/ (adj) legislative: *de* ~*e macht* the legislature

de **wetgever** /wɛtχevər/ (pl: -s) legislator

de **wetgeving** /wɛtχevɪŋ/ (pl: -en) legislation

de **wethouder** /wɛthɑudər/ (pl: -s) [Dutch] alderman, (city, town) councillor: *de* ~ *van volkshuisvesting* the alderman for housing

wetmatig /wɛtmɑtəχ/ (adj, adv) systematic

het **wetsartikel** /wɛtsɑrtikəl/ (pl: -en, -s) section of a (*or:* the) law

de **wetsbepaling** /wɛtsbəpalɪŋ/ (pl: -en) statutory provision, legal provision

de **wetsdokter** /wɛtsdɔktər/ (pl: -s, wetsdoktoren) [Belg] police physician

het **wetsontwerp** /wɛtsɔntwɛrp/ (pl: -en) bill: *een* ~ *aannemen* pass (*or:* adopt) a bill

de **wetsovertreding** /wɛtsovərtredɪŋ/ (pl: -en) violation of a (*or:* the) law

het **wetsvoorstel** /wɛtsforstɛl/ (pl: -len) [Dutch] bill

de **wetswijziging** /wɛtswɛɪzəχɪŋ/ (pl: -en) amendment: *een* ~ *invoeren* amend the law, make a statutory change

de **wetswinkel** /wɛtswɪŋkəl/ (pl: -s) law centre

wettelijk /wɛtələk/ (adj, adv) legal, statutory: ~e *aansprakelijkheid* legal liability; *be-neden de ~e leeftijd* underage; **wettelijke-aansprakelijkheidsverzekering** third-party insurance

wetteloos /wɛtəlos/ (adj, adv) lawless

wetten /wɛtə(n)/ (wette, heeft gewet) whet

wettig /wɛtəχ/ (adj, adv) legal; legitimate; valid: *de ~e eigenaar* the rightful owner

wettigen /wɛtəγə(n)/ (wettigde, heeft gewettigd) legalize

weven /weːvə(n)/ (weefde, heeft geweven) weave

de **wever** /weːvər/ (pl: -s) weaver

de **wezel** /weːzəl/ (pl: -s) weasel: *zo bang als een ~* as timid as a hare

het **¹wezen** /weːzə(n)/ (pl: -s) **1** being, creature: *geen levend ~ te bespeuren* not a living soul in sight **2** being, nature; essence; substance: *haar hele ~ kwam ertegen in opstand* her whole soul rose against it

²wezen /weːzə(n)/ be: *dat zal wel waar ~!* I bet!; *kan ~, maar ik mag hem niet* be that as it may, I don't like him; *wij zijn daar ~ kijken* we've been there to have a look; *laten we wel ~* (let's) be fair (*or:* honest) (now); *een studie die er ~ mag* a substantial study; *weg ~!* off with you!

wezenlijk /weːzənlək/ (adj, adv) essential: *van ~ belang* essential, of vital importance; *een ~ verschil* a substantial difference

wezenloos /weːzə(n)los/ (adj, adv) vacant: *zich ~ schrijven* write o.s. silly; *zich ~ schrikken* be scared out of one's wits

whatsappen® /ʋotsɛpə(n)/ (whatsappte, heeft gewhatsappt) whatsapp

de **whatsappgroep®** /ʋotsɛpχrup/ (pl: -en) Whatsapp group

de **whiplash** /ʋɪpleʃ/ (pl: -es) whiplash (injury)

de **whirlpool** /ʋyːlpuːl/ (pl: -s) whirlpool, jacuzzi

de **whisky** /ʋɪski/ whisky: *Amerikaanse whiskey* bourbon; *Ierse whiskey* Irish whiskey; *Schotse ~* Scotch (whisky); *~ puur* a straight (*or:* neat) whisky

de **whisky-soda** /ʋɪskisoda/ (pl: -'s) whisky and soda

de **whizzkid** /ʋɪskɪt/ (pl: -s) whizzkid

de **wichelroede** /ʋɪχəlrudə/ (pl: -n) divining rod, dowsing rod

het **wicht** /ʋɪχt/ (pl: -en) child

wie /ʋi/ (pron) **1** who; whose; which: *van ~ is dit boek?* whose book is this?; *~ heb je gezien?* who have you seen?; *met ~ (spreek ik)?* who is this? (*or:* that?); *~ van jullie?* which of you?; *~ er ook komt, zeg maar dat ik niet thuis ben* whoever comes, tell them I'm out **2** who; whose: *de man ~ns dood door ieder betreurd wordt* the man whose death is generally mourned; *het meisje (aan) ~ ik het boek gaf* the girl to whom I gave the book **3** whoever:

~ anders dan Jan? who (else) but John?; *~ dan ook* anybody, anyone, whoever || *~ niet akkoord gaat …* anyone who disagrees …

wiebelen /ʋibələ(n)/ (wiebelde, heeft gewiebeld) **1** wobble **2** rock: *ze zat te ~ op haar stoel* she was wiggling about on her chair

wieden /ʋidə(n)/ (wiedde, heeft gewied) weed

wiedes /ʋidəs/ (adj) [inform] *dat is nogal ~* don't I know it, I should think so

de **wiedeweerga** /ʋidəweːrγa/: *als de ~* like greased lightning; on the double

de **wieg** /ʋiχ/ (pl: -en) cradle: *van de ~ tot het graf verzorgd* looked after from the cradle to the grave || *in de ~ gelegd zijn voor …* be cut out (*or:* shaped) for, be fitted (*or:* born) by nature to

wiegen /ʋiγə(n)/ (wiegde, heeft gewiegd) rock

de **wiegendood** /ʋiγə(n)dot/ cot death; [Am] crib death; SIDS *(sudden infant death syndrome)*

de **wiek** /ʋik/ (pl: -en) **1** sail, vane **2** wing

het **wiel** /ʋil/ (pl: -en) wheel: *het ~ weer uitvinden* re-invent the wheel; *iem. in de ~en rijden* put a spoke in s.o.'s wheel || [fig] *het vijfde ~ aan de wagen zijn* be the odd man out

de **wielbasis** /ʋilbazɪs/ wheelbase

de **wieldop** /ʋildop/ (pl: -pen) hubcap

de **wielerbaan** /ʋilərban/ (pl: -banen) bicycle track, cycling track

de **wielerploeg** /ʋilərpluχ/ (pl: -en) (bi)cycling team

de **wielersport** /ʋilərsport/ (bi)cycling

de **wielklem** /ʋilklɛm/ (pl: -men) wheel clamp

het **wielrennen** /ʋilrɛnə(n)/ (bi)cycle racing

de **wielrenner** /ʋilrɛnər/ (pl: -s) (racing) cyclist, bicyclist, cycler

het **wieltje** /ʋilcə/ (pl: -s) (little) wheel; castor: *dat loopt op ~s* that's running smoothly

de **wienerschnitzel** /winərʃnɪtsəl/ (pl: -s) Wiener schnitzel

wiens /ʋins/ (pron) whose

het **wier** /ʋir/ **1** alga **2** seaweed

de **wierook** /ʋirok/ incense: *~ branden* burn incense

de **wiet** /ʋit/ weed, grass

de **wietplantage** /ʋitplantaʒə/ (pl: -s) grow house

de **wifi** /ʋifi/ [comp] Wi-Fi

de **wig** /ʋɪχ/ (pl: -gen) wedge

de **wigwam** /ʋɪχwam/ (pl: -s) wigwam

wij /ʋɛi/ (pers pron) we: *(beter) dan ~* (better) than we are; *~ allemaal* all of us, we all

wijd /ʋɛit/ (adj, adv) **1** wide: *een ~e blik* a broad view; *met ~ open ogen* wide-eyed **2** wide, loose: *~er maken* let out, enlarge **3** wide, broad: *de ~e zee* the open sea || *~ en zijd* far and wide, in all directions

wijdbeens /ʋɛidbens/ (adv) with legs wide apart

wijden /wɛidə(n)/ (wijdde, heeft gewijd) **1** devote: *zijn aandacht* **aan** *iets ~* devote o.s. to sth. **2** [rel] consecrate; ordain: *gewijde* **muziek** sacred music

de **wijding** /wɛidɪŋ/ (pl: -en) consecration

wijdlopig /wɛitlopəx/ (adj, adv) verbose; windy, long-winded: *een ~* **verhaal** a long-winded story

de **wijdte** /wɛitə/ (pl: -n, -s) breadth, distance: *de ~* **tussen** *de banken* the space between the benches

wijdverbreid /wɛitfərbrɛit/ (adj) widespread

wijdverspreid /wɛitfərsprɛit/ (adj) widespread; rife; rampant

wijdvertakt /wɛitfərtɑkt/ (adj) many-branched, ramified

het **wijf** /wɛif/ [inform] bitch: *een* **oud** *~ an* old bag; *stom ~!* stupid bitch (*or:* cow)!; *een* **lekker** *~ a bit of all right, a looker, a cracker

het **wijfje** /wɛifjə/ female

het **wij-gevoel** /wɛiɣəvul/ (feeling of) solidarity, team spirit

de **wijk** /wɛik/ (pl: -en) district, area: *de* **deftige** *~en* the fashionable areas || *de ~* **nemen** *naar Engeland* take refuge in England

de **wijkagent** /wɛikaɣɛnt/ (pl: -en) policeman on the beat, local bobby

het **wijkcentrum** /wɛiksɛntrʏm/ (pl: wijkcentra) community centre

wijken /wɛikə(n)/ (week, is geweken) give in (to), give way (to), yield (to): *hij weet van* **geen** *~* he sticks to his guns; *het* **gevaar** *is geweken* the danger is over

het **wijkgebouw** /wɛikxəbau/ (pl: -en) **1** community centre **2** local branch

de **wijkverpleegkundige** /wɛikfərplexkʏndəxə/ (pl: -n) district nurse

wijlen /wɛilə(n)/ (adj) late, deceased: *~ de* **heer** *Smit* the late Mr Smit

de **wijn** /wɛin/ (pl: -en) wine: *oude ~ in nieuwe zakken* old wine in new bottles

de **wijnazijn** /wɛinazɛin/ wine vinegar

de **wijnboer** /wɛimbur/ (pl: -en) winegrower

de **wijnbouw** /wɛimbau/ winegrowing, viniculture

de **wijnfles** /wɛinflɛs/ (pl: -sen) wine bottle

de **wijngaard** /wɛinɣart/ (pl: -en) vineyard

het **wijnglas** /wɛinɣlɑs/ (pl: -glazen) wineglass; rummer

de **wijnhandelaar** /wɛinhɑndəlar/ (pl: -s, wijnhandelaren) wine merchant

het **wijnjaar** /wɛinjar/ (pl: -jaren) wine-year

de **wijnkaart** /wɛinkart/ (pl: -en) wine list

de **wijnkelder** /wɛinkɛldər/ (pl: -s) (wine) cellar

de **wijnkenner** /wɛinkɛnər/ (pl: -s) connoisseur of wine

de **wijnkoeler** /wɛinkulər/ (pl: -s) wine cooler

de **wijnoogst** /wɛinoxst/ (pl: -en) vintage, grape harvest

de **wijnrank** /wɛinrɑnk/ (pl: -en) (branch of a) vine

de **wijnstok** /wɛinstɔk/ (pl: -ken) (grape)vine

de **wijnstreek** /wɛinstrek/ (pl: -streken) wine(growing) region

de **wijnvlek** /wɛinvlɛk/ (pl: -ken) birthmark

de **¹wijs** /wɛis/ (pl: wijzen) **1** way, manner: *bij wijze van spreken* so to speak, as it were; *bij wijze van uitzondering* as an exception **2** tune: *hij kan geen ~* **houden** he sings (*or:* plays) out of tune; *van de ~ raken* get in a muddle; *iem. van de ~ brengen* put s.o. out (*or:* off) his stroke; *hij liet zich niet* **van** *de ~ brengen* he kept a level head (*or:* his cool) || **onbepaalde** *~ infinitive

²wijs /wɛis/ (adj, adv) wise: **ben** *je niet (goed) ~?* are you mad? (*or:* crazy?); *ik* **werd** *er niet wijzer van* I was none the wiser for it; *ik kan er niet ~ uit* **worden** I can't make head or tail of it

de **wijsbegeerte** /wɛizbəɣertə/ (pl: -n) philosophy

wijselijk /wɛisələk/ (adv) wisely, sensibly: *hij* **hield** *~ zijn mond* wisely, he kept silent

de **wijsgeer** /wɛisxer/ (pl: -geren) philosopher

wijsgerig /wɛisxərəx/ (adj, adv) philosophic(al)

de **wijsheid** /wɛishɛit/ (pl: -heden) wisdom; piece of wisdom: *hij meent de ~ in pacht te* **hebben** he thinks he knows it all; *waar* **heb** *je die ~ vandaan?* my, aren't you (*or:* we) clever?; *~ komt met de jaren* the longer we live the more we learn

de **wijsheidstand** /wɛishɛitstɑnt/ (pl: -en) [Belg] wisdom tooth

het **wijsje** /wɛiʃə/ (pl: -s) tune

wijsmaken /wɛismakə(n)/ (maakte wijs, heeft wijsgemaakt) fool, kid: *laat je niks ~!* don't buy that nonsense!; *maak dat je* **grootje** (*or: de* **kat***) wijs* tell that to the marines!, tell me another one!

de **wijsneus** /wɛisnøs/ (pl: -neuzen) know(-it)-all

de **wijsvinger** /wɛisfɪŋər/ (pl: -s) forefinger

wijten /wɛitə(n)/ (weet, heeft geweten) blame (s.o. for sth.)

de **wijting** /wɛitɪŋ/ (pl: -en) whiting

het **wijwater** /wɛiwatər/ holy water

de **wijze** /wɛizə/ (pl: -n) **1** manner, way **2** wise man (*or:* woman); learned man (*or:* woman)

¹wijzen /wɛizə(n)/ (wees, heeft gewezen) **1** point: *naar een punt ~* point to a spot; [fig] *met de vinger* **naar** *iem. ~* point the finger at s.o.; *er moet* **op** *worden gewezen dat ...* it should be pointed out that ... **2** indicate: *alles wijst* **erop** *dat ...* everything seems to indicate that ...

²wijzen /wɛizə(n)/ (wees, heeft gewezen) show, point out: *de* **weg** *~ lead (*or:* show) the way

zich **³wijzen** /wɛizə(n)/ (wees zich, heeft zich gewezen) show: *dat wijst zich* **vanzelf** that is self-evident

de **wijzer** /wɛizər/ (pl: -s) indicator; hand; pointer: *met de ~s van de* **klok** *mee* clockwise; *de* **grote** (or: *de* **kleine**) ~ the minute (*or:* hour) hand

de **wijzerplaat** /wɛizərplat/ (pl: -platen) dial
wijzigen /wɛizəɣə(n)/ (wijzigde, heeft gewijzigd) alter, change

de **wijziging** /wɛizəɣɪŋ/ (pl: -en) alteration, change: *~en* **aanbrengen** *in* make changes in

de **wikkel** /wɪkəl/ (pl: -s) wrapper
wikkelen /wɪkələ(n)/ (wikkelde, heeft gewikkeld) wind; wrap (up); enfold
wikken /wɪkə(n)/ weigh (up): *na lang ~ en* **wegen** after much deliberation, after mature consideration

de **wil** /wɪl/ will; wish: *geen* **eigen** *~ hebben* have no mind of one's own; *met een beetje* **goeie** *~ gaat het best* with a little good will it'll all work out; *een* **sterke** *~ hebben* be strongwilled; *zijn ~* **is** *wet* his word is law; *tegen ~ en* **dank** willy-nilly, reluctantly; *iem.* **ter** *~le zijn* oblige s.o., do s.o. a favour

het ¹**wild** /wɪlt/ **1** game: ~, *vis en* **gevogelte** fish, flesh and fowl **2** wild: *in het ~ leven* (or: *groeien*) live (*or:* grow) (in the) wild
²**wild** /wɪlt/ (adj, adv) wild: *~e* **dieren** wild animals; *~* **enthousiast** *zijn over iets* go overboard about sth.; *in het ~e (weg)* at random; *zich ~* **schrikken** have the fright of one's life, be scared out of one's wits

de **wilde** /wɪldə/ (pl: -n) savage

de **wildebras** /wɪldəbrɑs/ (pl: -sen) (young) tearaway

de **wildernis** /wɪldərnɪs/ (pl: -sen) wilderness

de **wildgroei** /wɪltɣruj/ proliferation
wildkamperen /wɪltkɑmpərə(n)/ (kampeerde wild, heeft wildgekampeerd) camp wild

het **wildpark** /wɪltpɑrk/ (pl: -en) wildlife park; game park (*or:* reserve)
wildplassen /wɪltplɑsə(n)/ (plaste wild, heeft wildgeplast) urinate in public

de **wildstand** /wɪltstɑnt/ wildlife population

het **wildviaduct** /wɪltfijadykt/ (pl: -en) wildlife viaduct
wildvreemd /wɪltfremt/ (adj) completely strange, utterly strange: *een ~ iem.* a perfect stranger
wildwatervaren /wɪltwɑtərvarə(n)/ white-water rafting

de **wildwestfilm** /wɪltwɛstfɪlm/ (pl: -s) western

het **wildwesttafereel** /wɪltwɛstafərel/ (pl: -taferelen): *het* **was** *een ~* it was bedlam, it was like sth. out of a Western

de **wilg** /wɪlx/ (pl: -en) willow (tree)
wilgen /wɪlɣə(n)/ (adj) willow

het **wilgenhout** /wɪlɣə(n)hɑut/ willow (wood)

de **willekeur** /wɪləkør/ **1** will; discretion: *naar ~ at will*, at one's (own) discretion **2** arbitrariness, unfairness; capriciousness

willekeurig /wɪləkørəx/ (adj, adv) **1** arbitrary; random; indiscriminate: *neem een ~e* **steen** take any stone (you like) **2** arbitrary, high-handed; capricious

¹**willen** /wɪlə(n)/ (wilde/wou, heeft gewild) want, wish, desire: *het is (maar) een* **kwestie** *van ~* it's (only) a matter of will; *ik wil wel een* **pilsje** I wouldn't mind a beer; *wil je wat* **pinda's?** would you like some peanuts?; *ik wil het niet* **hebben** I won't have (*or:* allow) it; *niet ~* **luisteren** refuse to listen; *ik wil niets meer met hem* **te maken hebben** I've done with him; *ik wil wel* **toegeven** *dat ...* I'm willing to admit that ...; *ik wou net* **vertrekken** *toen ...* I was just about (*or:* going) to leave when ...; *dat had ik best eens ~* **zien!** I would have liked to have seen it!; *ja,* **wat** *wil je?* what else can you expect?; *wat wil je nog meer?* what more do you want?; *wilt u* **dat** *ik het raam openzet?* shall I open the window (for you)?; *ik wou* **dat** *ik een fiets had* I wish I had a bike; *of je wilt of niet* whether you want to or not; *we moesten wel glimlachen, of we wilden of niet* we could not help but smile (*or:* help smiling); *dat* **ding** *wil niet* the thing won't (*or:* refuses to) go; *de motor wil niet* **starten** the engine won't start ‖ *men wil* **er** *niet aan* people are not buying (it), nobody is interested

²**willen** /wɪlə(n)/ (aux vb, wilde/wou, heeft gewild) will, would: *wil je me de melk even* **(aan)geven?** could (*or:* would) you pass me the milk, please?; *wil je me even* **helpen?** would you mind helping me?

willens /wɪlə(n)s/ (adv): [Dutch] *~ en* **wetens**, [Belg] **wetens** *en ~* knowingly

willoos /wɪlos/ (adj, adv) unresisting: *~* **liet** *de jongen zich* **meevoeren** the boy went along without a struggle

de **wilsbeschikking** /wɪlzbəsχɪkɪŋ/ (pl: -en) will, testament

de **wilskracht** /wɪlskrɑxt/ will-power, will, backbone

de **wilsverklaring** /wɪlsfərklarɪŋ/ (pl: -en) **1** living will **2** declaration of intent

de **wimpel** /wɪmpəl/ (pl: -s) pennon, pennant

de **wimper** /wɪmpər/ (pl: -s) (eye)lash

de **wind** /wɪnt/ (pl: -en) wind; breeze; gale: *bestand zijn tegen* **weer** *en ~* be wind and weatherproof; *geen* **zuchtje** *~* not a breath of wind, dead calm; *een* **harde** (or: **krachtige**) *~* a high (*or:* strong) wind; *de ~* **gaat liggen** the wind is dropping; *de ~ van voren* **krijgen** get lectured at; *kijken uit welke hoek de ~* **waait** see which way the wind blows; *de ~* **mee** *hebben* **a)** have the wind behind one; **b)** [fig] have everything going for one; [fig] *een* *waarschuwing* **in** *de ~ slaan* disregard a warning; *tegen de ~ in* against the wind, into the teeth of the wind; *het gaat hem voor de ~* he is doing well, he is flying high ‖ *~en laten* break wind

de **windbuil** /wɪndbœyl/ (pl: -en) windbag, gasbag

de **windbuks** /wɪndbʏks/ (pl: -en) air rifle, air-gun

het **windei** /wɪntɛi/ (pl: -eren): *dat zal hem geen ~eren leggen* he'll do well out of it

winden /wɪndə(n)/ (wond, heeft gewonden) wind, twist, entwine; wrap

de **windenergie** /wɪntenɛrʒi/ wind energy

winderig /wɪndərəx/ (adj) **1** windy, blowy; breezy; stormy; windswept **2** windy, flatulent

de **windhaan** /wɪnthan/ (pl: -hanen) weathercock

de **windhond** /wɪnthɔnt/ (pl: -en) greyhound; whippet

de **windhoos** /wɪnthos/ (pl: -hozen) whirlwind

het **windjack** /wɪntjɛk/ (pl: -s) windcheater; [Am] windbreaker

het **windjak** /wɪntjɑk/ (pl: -ken, -s) windcheater

de **windkracht** /wɪntkrɑxt/ **1** wind-force: *wind met ~* **7** force 7 wind(s) **2** wind power, wind energy

de **windmolen** /wɪntmolə(n)/ (pl: -s) windmill: *tegen ~s vechten* tilt at windmills, fight windmills

het **windmolenpark** /wɪntmolə(n)pɑrk/ (pl: -en) wind park (or: farm)

de **windowdressing** /wɪndodrɛsɪŋ/ window dressing

de **windrichting** /wɪntrɪxtɪŋ/ (pl: -en) wind direction; points of the compass

de **windroos** /wɪntros/ (pl: -rozen) compass card

het **windscherm** /wɪntsxɛrm/ (pl: -en) windbreak

de **windsnelheid** /wɪntsnɛlhɛit/ (pl: -heden) wind speed

de **windsterkte** /wɪntstɛrktə/ wind-force

windstil /wɪntstɪl/ (adj) calm, windless, still

de **windstoot** /wɪntstot/ (pl: -stoten) gust (of wind); squall

de **windstreek** /wɪntstrek/ (pl: -streken) quarter, point of the compass

windsurfen /wɪntsʏːrfə(n)/ (windsurfte/windsurfde, heeft/is gewindsurft/gewindsurfd) go windsurfing

de **windsurfer** /wɪntsʏːrfər/ (pl: -s) windsurfer

de **windtunnel** /wɪntʏnəl/ (pl: -s) wind tunnel

de **windvaan** /wɪntfan/ (pl: -vanen) **1** (wind)vane **2** [fig] person who jumps on the bandwagon, weathercock

de **windvlaag** /wɪntflax/ (pl: -vlagen) gust (of wind); blast; squall

de **windwijzer** /wɪntwɛizər/ (pl: -s) weathercock, weathervane

de **windzak** /wɪntsɑk/ windsock, air sock

de **wingerd** /wɪŋərt/ (pl: -s, -en) (grape)vine

het **wingewest** /wɪŋɡəwɛst/ (pl: -en) conquered land, colony

de **winkel** /wɪŋkəl/ (pl: -s) shop, store: *een ~ in modeartikelen* a boutique, a fashion store; *~s kijken* go window-shopping

de **winkelbediende** /wɪŋkəlbədində/ shop-assistant, counter-assistant, salesman, saleswoman

het **winkelcentrum** /wɪŋkəlsɛntrʏm/ (pl: -centra) shopping centre (or: precinct)

de **winkeldief** /wɪŋkəldif/ (pl: -dieven) shoplifter

de **winkeldiefstal** /wɪŋkəldifstɑl/ (pl: -len) shoplifting

winkelen /wɪŋkələ(n)/ (winkelde, heeft gewinkeld) shop, go shopping, do some (or: the) shopping

de **winkelgalerij** /wɪŋkəlxɑlərɛi/ (pl: -en) (shopping-)arcade

de **winkelhaak** /wɪŋkəlhak/ (pl: -haken) **1** three-cornered tear, right-angled tear **2** (carpenter's) square

de **winkelier** /wɪŋkəlir/ (pl: -s) shopkeeper, retailer, tradesman

de **winkelketen** /wɪŋkəlketə(n)/ (pl: -s) chain of shops (or: stores), store chain

het **winkelmandje** /wɪŋkəlmɑncə/ (pl: -s) **1** [in shop] shopping basket **2** [Internet] basket: *toevoegen aan ~* add to basket

het **winkelpersoneel** /wɪŋkəlpɛrsonel/ shop-workers, shop staff (or: personnel)

de **winkelprijs** /wɪŋkəlprɛis/ (pl: -prijzen) retail price, shop price; [Am] store price

de **winkelstraat** /wɪŋkəlstrat/ (pl: -straten) shopping street

de **winkelwagen** /wɪŋkəlwaxə(n)/ (pl: -s) (shopping) trolley; [Am] pushcart: [online shopping] *in ~* add to cart

de **winnaar** /wɪnar/ (pl: -s) winner, victor; winning team

¹**winnen** /wɪnə(n)/ (won, heeft gewonnen) win: *het ~de doelpunt* the winning goal; *je kan niet altijd ~* you can't win them all; *~ bij het kaarten* win at cards; *~ met 7-2* win 7-2, win by 7 goals (or: points) to 2; *(het) ~ van iem.* beat s.o., have the better of s.o.

²**winnen** /wɪnə(n)/ (won, heeft gewonnen) **1** win, gain; mine; extract: *zout uit zeewater ~* obtain salt from sea water **2** win, gain; enlist; secure: *iem. voor zich ~* win s.o. over

de **winning** /wɪnɪŋ/ winning, extraction; reclamation

de **winst** /wɪnst/ (pl: -en) **1** profit; return; earning(s); winning: *netto ~* net returns (or: gain, profit); *~ behalen* (or: *opleveren*) gain (or: make, yield) a profit; *tel uit je ~* it can't go wrong; *op ~ spelen* play to win **2** gain, benefit, advantage: *een ~ van drie zetels in de Kamer behalen* gain three seats in Parliament

het **winstbejag** /wɪnstbəjɑx/ pursuit of profit: *iets uit ~ doen* do sth. for money (or: profit) de **winstdeling** /wɪnzdelɪŋ/ (pl: -en) profit-sharing, participation

de **winst-en-verliesrekening** /wɪnstɛnvərlɪsrekənɪŋ/ (pl: -en) profit-and-loss account

winstgevend /wɪnstxevənt/ (adj) profitable, lucrative; remunerative; [fig] fruitful; economic

de **winstmarge** /wɪnstmɑːrʒə/ (pl: -s) profit margin, margin of profit

het **winstoogmerk** /wɪnstoxmɛrk/ (pl: -en) profit motive: *instelling* **zonder** ~ non-profit institution

het **winstpunt** /wɪnstpʏnt/ (pl: -en) point (scored)

de **winstuitkering** /wɪnstœytkerɪŋ/ (pl: -en) (payment of a) dividend

de **winter** /wɪntər/ (pl: -s) winter: *hartje* ~ the dead (*or*: depths) of winter; *we* **hebben** *nog niet veel* ~ **gehad** we haven't had much wintry weather (*or*: much of a winter) yet; *'s* ~*s* in (the) winter, in (the) wintertime

de **winteravond** /wɪntərɑvɔnt/ (pl: -en) winter evening

de **winterband** /wɪntərbɑnt/ (pl: -en) winter (*or*: snow) tyre

de **winterdag** /wɪntərdɑx/ (pl: -en) winter('s) day

de **winterdepressie** /wɪntərdeprɛsi/ seasonal affective disorder, SAD

de **winterhanden** /wɪntərhɑndə(n)/ (pl) chilblained hands

de **winterjas** /wɪntərjɑs/ (pl: -sen) winter coat

het **winterkoninkje** /wɪntərkonɪŋkjə/ (pl: -s) wren

de **wintermaanden** /wɪntərmɑndə(n)/ (pl) winter months

de **winterpeen** /wɪntərpen/ (pl: -penen) winter carrot

winters /wɪntərs/ (adj, adv) wintery: *zich* ~ **aankleden** dress for winter

de **winterslaap** /wɪntərslap/ hibernation, winter sleep: *een* ~ **houden** hibernate

de **winterspelen** /wɪntərspelə(n)/ (pl) winter games: *de* **Olympische** *Winterspelen* the Winter Olympics

de **wintersport** /wɪntərspɔrt/ (pl: -en) winter sports: *met* ~ *gaan* go skiing, go on a winter sports holiday

de **wintertijd** /wɪntərtɛit/ wintertime, winter season

het **winterweer** /wɪntərwer/ winter weather, wintry weather

de **win-winsituatie** /wɪnwɪnsitywa(t)si/ (pl: -s) win-win situation

de **wip** /wɪp/ (pl: -pen) **1** seesaw: *op* *de* ~ *zitten* have one's job on the line **2** skip, hop: *in een* ~ in a flash (*or*: jiffy, tick), in no time; *met een* ~ *was hij bij de deur* he was at the door in one bound **3** [vulg] lay, screw

de **wipneus** /wɪpnøs/ (pl: wipneuzen) turned-up nose, snub nose

[1]**wippen** /wɪpə(n)/ (wipte, heeft gewipt) **1** hop, bound; skip **2** whip, pop: *er even* **tussenuit** ~ nip (*or*: pop) out for a while; *zij zat* **met** *haar stoel te* ~ *van ongeduld* she sat tilting her chair with impatience **3** play on a seesaw

[2]**wippen** /wɪpə(n)/ (wipte, heeft gewipt) **1** topple, overthrow, unseat **2** [sport] knock out

de **wirwar** /wɪrwɑr/ criss-cross, jumble, tangle; snarl; maze: *een* ~ *van* **steegjes** a rabbit warren

wis /wɪs/ (adj, adv) certain, sure: *iem. van een* ~*se* **dood** *redden* save s.o. from certain death; ~ *en* **waarachtig** upon my word

de **wisent** /wiz̧ɛnt/ (pl: -en) wisent, European bison

de **wiskunde** /wɪskʏndə/ mathematics; maths; [Am] math

de **wiskundeknobbel** /wɪskʏndəknɔbəl/ gift (*or*: head) for mathematics

de **wiskundeleraar** /wɪskʏndəlerar/ (pl: -leraren) mathematics teacher

wiskundig /wɪskʏndəx/ (adj, adv) mathematic(al)

wispelturig /wɪspəltyrəx/ (adj, adv) inconstant, fickle, capricious

de [1]**wissel** /wɪsəl/ (pl: -s) **1** substitute, sub: *een* ~ *inzetten* put in a substitute **2** change, switch **3** [sport] lane change: *een foute* ~ a lane change error

het/de [2]**wissel** /wɪsəl/ (pl: -s) points, switch: *een* ~ *overhalen* (*or*: **verzetten**) change (*or*: shift) the points

de **wisselautomaat** /wɪsəlɑutomat/ (pl: -automaten) (automatic) money changer, change machine

de **wisselbeker** /wɪsəlbekər/ (pl: -s) challenge cup

de **wisselbouw** /wɪsəlbɑu/ rotation of crops

[1]**wisselen** /wɪsələ(n)/ (wisselde, heeft gewisseld) change, vary

[2]**wisselen** /wɪsələ(n)/ (wisselde, heeft gewisseld) **1** change, exchange: *van plaats* ~ change places **2** change, give change: *kunt u* ~? can you change this? **3** exchange; bandy: *van gedachten* ~ *over* exchange views (*or*: ideas) about

het **wisselgeld** /wɪsəlɣɛlt/ change, (small, loose) change: *te weinig* ~ **terugkrijgen** be short-changed

het **wisselgesprek** /wɪsəlɣəsprɛk/ (pl: -ken) call waiting

de **wisseling** /wɪsəlɪŋ/ (pl: -en) change: *een* ~ *in het bestuur* a change of management; *de* ~ *van de* **wacht** the changing of the guard; *de* ~ *van de* **seizoenen** the change of seasons

het **wisselkantoor** /wɪsəlkantor/ (pl: -kantoren) exchange office

de **wisselkoers** /wɪsəlkurs/ (pl: -en) exchange-rate, rate of exchange

de **wisseloplossing** /wɪsələplɔsɪŋ/ (pl: -en)

[Belg] alternative solution

de **wisselslag** /wɪsəlslɑx/ (individual) medley

de **wisselspeler** /wɪsəlspelər/ (pl: -s) substitute, reserve; sub

de **wisselstroom** /wɪsəlstrom/ alternating current, AC

het **wisselstuk** /wɪsəlstʏk/ (pl: -ken) [Belg] (spare) part

de **wisseltruc** /wɪsəltryk/ (pl: -s) fast-change trick

wisselvallig /wɪsəlvɑləx/ (adj) changeable, unstable; uncertain; precarious

de **wisselwerking** /wɪsəlwɛrkɪŋ/ (pl: -en) interaction, interplay

wissen /wɪsə(n)/ (wiste, heeft gewist) **1** wipe **2** erase; [comp] delete

de **wisser** /wɪsər/ (pl: -s) wiper

het **wissewasje** /wɪsəwɑʃə/ (pl: -s) trifle

het **wit** /wɪt/ **1** white **2** cut-price

het **witbrood** /wɪtbrot/ (pl: -broden) white bread

het **witgoed** /wɪtxut/ [roughly] white goods

witheet /wɪthet/ (adj): ~ *van woede* boiling (over) with anger, fuming with anger

witjes /wɪcəs/ (adj) pale, white: ~ *om de neus zien* look white about the gills

de **witkalk** /wɪtkɑlk/ whitewash, whit(en)ing

het **witlof** /wɪtlof/ [Dutch] chicory

het **witloof** /wɪtlof/ [Belg] chicory

de **witregel** /wɪtreɣəl/ (pl: -s) extra space (between the lines)

de **Wit-Rus** /wɪtrʏs/ (pl: -sen) White Russian, Belorussian

Wit-Rusland /wɪtrʏslɑnt/ White Russia, Belorussia

het **¹Wit-Russisch** /wɪtrʏsis/ Belarusian

²Wit-Russisch /wɪtrʏsis/ (adj) Belarusian

het **witsel** /wɪtsəl/ whitewash, whit(en)ing

de **witteboordencriminaliteit** /wɪtəbordə(n)kriminalitɛit/ white-collar crime

de **wittebroodsweken** /wɪtəbrotswekə(n)/ (pl) honeymoon

de **wittekool** /wɪtəkol/ (pl: -kolen) white cabbage

witten /wɪtə(n)/ (witte, heeft gewit) whitewash

de **witvis** /wɪtfɪs/ (pl: -sen) catfish

witwassen /wɪtwɑsə(n)/ (waste wit, heeft witgewassen) launder

het **WK** /weka/ *wereldkampioenschap* World Championship

de **wodka** /wɔtka/ vodka

de **woede** /wudə/ **1** rage, fury, anger: *buiten zichzelf van* ~ *zijn* be beside o.s. with rage (or: anger) **2** mania

de **woedeaanval** /wudəanvɑl/ (pl: -len) tantrum, fit (of anger)

woeden /wudə(n)/ (woedde, heeft gewoed) rage, rave

woedend /wudənt/ (adj, adv) furious, infuriated

de **woede-uitbarsting** /wudəœydbɑrstɪŋ/ (pl: -en) outburst of anger

woef /wuf/ (int) bow-wow, woof

de **woeker** /wukər/ usury

de **woekeraar** /wukərar/ (pl: -s) usurer; profiteer

woekeren /wukərə(n)/ (woekerde, heeft gewoekerd) **1** practise usury; profiteer **2** make the most (of): *met* de ruimte ~ use (or: utilize) every inch of space **3** grow rank (or: rampant)

de **woekering** /wukərɪŋ/ (pl: -en) uncontrolled growth; rampant growth

de **woekerpolis** /wukərpolɪs/ (pl: -sen) profiteering insurance policy

de **woekerprijs** /wukərprɛis/ (pl: -prijzen) usurious price, exorbitant price

woela /wula/ (int) [inform] no joke, no shit

¹woelen /wulə(n)/ (woelde, heeft gewoeld) **1** toss about: *zij lag maar te* ~ she was tossing and turning **2** churn (about, around)

²woelen /wulə(n)/ (woelde, heeft gewoeld) **1** turn up (the soil) **2** grub (up), root (out): *de varkens* ~ *de wortels bloot* the pigs are grubbing up the roots

woelig /wuləx/ (adj, adv) restless: ~*e tijden* turbulent times

de **woensdag** /wunzdɑx/ (pl: -en) Wednesday: *'s* ~*s* Wednesday; on Wednesdays

¹woensdags /wunzdɑxs/ (adj) Wednesday

²woensdags /wunzdɑxs/ (adv) on Wednesdays

de **woerd** /wurt/ (pl: -en) drake

woest /wust/ (adj, adv) **1** savage, wild: *een* ~ *voorkomen hebben* have a fierce countenance **2** rude, rough **3** furious, infuriated: *in een* ~*e bui* in a fit of rage **4** waste; desolate

de **woesteling** /wustəlɪŋ/ (pl: -en) brute

de **woestenij** /wustənɛi/ (pl: -en) wilderness, waste(land)

de **woestijn** /wustɛin/ (pl: -en) desert

de **wok** /wɔk/ (pl: -ken) wok

wokken /wɔkə(n)/ (wokte, heeft gewokt) stir fry

de **wol** /wɔl/ wool: *zuiver* ~ 100 % (or: pure) wool; [fig] *onder* de ~ *kruipen* turn in

de **wolf** /wɔlf/ (pl: wolven) wolf

het **wolfraam** /wɔlfram/ tungsten

de **wolk** /wɔlk/ (pl: -en) cloud || *een* ~ *van een baby* a bouncing baby; [fig] *in* de ~*en zijn* (over iets) be over the moon about sth., tread (or: walk) on air

de **wolkbreuk** /wɔlgbrøk/ (pl: -en) cloudburst

wolkeloos /wɔlkəlos/ (adj) cloudless, unclouded: *een wolkeloze hemel* a clear sky

het **wolkendek** /wɔlkə(n)dɛk/ blanket (or: layer) of clouds

de **wolkenkrabber** /wɔlkə(n)krɑbər/ (pl: -s) skyscraper

het **wolkenveld** /wɔlkə(n)vɛlt/ (pl: -en) mass of cloud(s) het **wolkje** /wɔlkjə/ cloudlet, little cloud, small cloud: *er is geen ~ aan de lucht* there isn't a cloud in the sky

wollen /wɔlə(n)/ (adj) woollen, wool

wollig /wɔləx/ (adj, adv) woolly: *~ taalgebruik* woolly language

de **wolvin** /wɔlvɪn/ (pl: -nen) she-wolf

de **wond** /wɔnt/ (pl: -en) wound; injury: *een gapende ~* a gaping wound, a gash; *Joris had een ~je aan zijn vinger* Joris had a cut (*or:* scratch) on his finger

het **wonder** /wɔndər/ (pl: -en) **1** wonder, miracle: *het is een ~ dat …* it is a miracle that …; *geen ~* no (*or:* small) wonder, not surprising **2** wonder, marvel: *de ~en van de natuur* the wonders (*or:* marvels) of nature || *~ boven ~* by amazing good fortune

wonderbaarlijk /wɔndərbarlək/ (adj, adv) miraculous; strange; curious

het **wonderkind** /wɔndərkɪnt/ (pl: -eren) (child) prodigy

wonderlijk /wɔndərlək/ (adj) strange, surprising

het **wondermiddel** /wɔndərmɪdəl/ (pl: -en) panacea; miracle drug

de **wonderolie** /wɔndəroli/ castor oil

wonderschoon /wɔndərsxon/ (adj, adv) wonderful, exceptionally beautiful

wonderwel /wɔndərwɛl/ (adv) wonderfully well: *hij voelde zich er ~ thuis* he felt wonderfully at home

wonen /wonə(n)/ (woonde, heeft gewoond) live: *op zichzelf gaan ~* set up house, go and live on one's own

de **woning** /wonɪŋ/ (pl: -en) house; home: *iem. uit zijn ~ zetten* evict s.o.

de **woningbouw** /wonɪŋbɑu/ house-building, house-construction: *sociale ~* council housing; [Am] public housing

de **woningbouwvereniging** /wonɪŋbɑuvərenəɣɪŋ/ (pl: -en) housing association (*or:* corporation)

de **woninginrichting** /wonɪŋɪnrɪxtɪŋ/ home furnishing(s)

de **woningmarkt** /wonɪŋmɑrkt/ (pl: -en) housing market

de **woningnood** /wonɪŋnot/ housing shortage

woonachtig /wonɑxtəx/ (adj): *hij is ~ in Leiden* he is a resident of Leiden

het **woonblok** /womblɔk/ (pl: -ken) block

de **woonboot** /wombot/ (pl: -boten) houseboat

het **woonerf** /wonɛrf/ (pl: -erven) residential area (with restrictions to slow down traffic)

de **woongroep** /wonɣrup/ (pl: -en) commune

het **woonhuis** /wonhœys/ (pl: -huizen) (private) house; home

de **woonkamer** /wonkamər/ (pl: -s) living room

de **woonkeuken** /wonkøkə(n)/ (pl: -s) open kitchen, kitchen-dining room

de **woonomgeving** /wonɔmɣevɪŋ/ environment

de **woonplaats** /womplats/ (pl: -en) (place of) residence, address; city; town

de **woonruimte** /wonrœymtə/ (pl: -n, -s) (housing, living) accommodation

de **woonst** /wonst/ (pl: -en) [Belg] **1** house **2** (place of) residence

de **woonwagen** /wonwaɣə(n)/ (pl: -s) caravan; [Am] (house) trailer

de **woonwagenbewoner** /wonwaɣə(n)bəwonər/ (pl: -s) caravan dweller; [Am] trailer park resident

het **woonwagenkamp** /wonwaɣə(n)kɑmp/ caravan camp; [Am] trailer camp

het **woon-werkverkeer** /wonwɛrkførker/ commuter traffic

de **woonwijk** /wonwɛik/ (pl: -en) residential area; housing estate; district; quarter

het **woon-zorgcomplex** /wonzɔrxkɔmplɛks/ sheltered accommodation

het **woord** /wort/ (pl: -en) word: *in ~ en beeld* in pictures and text; *met andere ~en* in other words; *daar heb ik geen ~en voor* I've no words for that; *geen goed ~ voor iets over hebben* not have a good word to say about sth.; *het hoogste ~ voeren* do most of the talking; *hij moet altijd het laatste ~ hebben* he always has to have the last word; *iem. aan zijn ~ houden* keep (*or:* hold) s.o. to his promise; *het ~ geven aan* give the floor to; *zijn ~ geven* give one's word; *het ~ nemen* get up to speak; *het ~ tot iem. richten* address (*or:* speak to) s.o.; *iem. aan het ~ laten* allow s.o. to finish (speaking); *in één ~* in a word, in sum (*or:* short); *op zijn ~en letten* be careful about what one says; *iem. te ~ staan* speak to (*or:* see) s.o.; *niet uit zijn ~en kunnen komen* not be able to express o.s., fumble for words; *met twee ~en spreken* [roughly] be polite; *te gek voor ~en* too crazy (*or:* ridiculous, absurd) for words

woordblind /wordblɪnt/ (adj) dyslexic

de **woordblindheid** /wordblɪntheit/ dyslexia

de **woordbreuk** /wordbrøk/ breaking of one's word (*or:* promise)

woordelijk /wordələk/ (adj, adv) word for word; literal(ly)

het **woordenboek** /wordə(n)buk/ (pl: -en) dictionary: *een ~ raadplegen* consult a dictionary; refer to a dictionary

de **woordenlijst** /wordə(n)lɛist/ (pl: -en) list of words; vocabulary

de **woordenschat** /wordə(n)sxɑt/ **1** lexicon **2** vocabulary

de **woordenstrijd** /wordə(n)strɛit/ (verbal) dispute

de **woordenwisseling** /wordə(n)wɪsəlɪŋ/ (pl: -en) **1** exchange of words, discussion **2** argument het **woordgebruik** /wo̱rtχəbrœyk/ use of words

het **woordje** /wo̱rcə/ (pl: -s) word: *een goed ~ doen voor iem.* put in (*or:* say) a (good) word for s.o.; *een hartig ~ met iem. spreken* give s.o. a (good) talking-to; *ook een ~ meespreken* say one's piece

de **woordkeus** /wo̱rtkøs/ choice of words, wording

de **woordsoort** /wo̱rtsort/ (pl: -en) part of speech

de **woordspeling** /wo̱rtspelɪŋ/ (pl: -en) pun, play on words

de **woordvoerder** /wo̱rtfurdər/ (pl: -s) **1** speaker **2** spokesman

¹**worden** /wo̱rdə(n)/ (werd, is geworden) will be, come to, amount to: *dat wordt dan € 2,00 per vel* that will be 2.00 euros per sheet

²**worden** /wo̱rdə(n)/ (aux vb, werd, is geworden) be: *er werd gedanst* there was dancing; *de bus wordt om zes uur gelicht* the post will be collected at six o'clock

³**worden** /wo̱rdə(n)/ (werd, is geworden) **1** be, get: *het wordt laat* (or: *kouder*) it is getting late (*or:* colder); *hij wordt morgen vijftig* he'll be fifty tomorrow **2** become: *hij wilde altijd al schrijver ~* he has always wanted to be (*or:* become) a writer; *dat wordt niets* it won't work, it'll come to nothing; [inform] *dat gaat hem niet ~* that's not on the cards, that's not going to happen; *wat is er van hem geworden?* whatever became of him?

de **wording** /wo̱rdɪŋ/ genesis, origin: *een stad in ~* a town in the making

de **workaholic** /wy:rkəho̱lɪk/ (pl: -s) workaholic

de **work-out** /wy:rkɑut/ work-out

de **workshop** /wy:rkʃɔp/ (pl: -s) workshop

de **worm** /wɔrm/ (pl: -en) worm

de **worp** /wɔrp/ (pl: -en) throw(ing); shot

de **worst** /wɔrst/ (pl: -en) sausage: *dat zal mij ~ wezen* I couldn't care less

de **worstelaar** /wo̱rstəlar/ (pl: -s) wrestler

worstelen /wo̱rstələ(n)/ (worstelde, heeft geworsteld) struggle; wrestle [sport]: *zich door een lijvig rapport heen ~* struggle (*or:* plough) (one's way) through a bulky report

de **worsteling** /wo̱rstəlɪŋ/ (pl: -en) struggle, wrestle

het **worstenbroodje** /wo̱rstə(n)brocə/ (pl: -s) [roughly] sausage roll

de **wortel** /wo̱rtəl/ (pl: -s) root; carrot: *3 is de ~ van 9* 3 is the square root of 9; *~ schieten* take root

wortelen /wo̱rtələ(n)/ (wortelde, heeft/is geworteld) be rooted, root: [fig] *een diepgeworteld wantrouwen* a deep distrust, an instinctive distrust

het **wortelkanaal** /wo̱rtəlkanal/ (pl: -kanalen) root canal

het **wortelteken** /wo̱rtəltekə(n)/ (pl: -s) radical sign

het **worteltje** /wo̱rtəlcə/ carrot

het **worteltrekken** /wo̱rtəltrɛkə(n)/ extraction of the root(s)

het **woud** /wɑut/ (pl: -en) forest

de **woudloper** /wɑutlopər/ (pl: -s) trapper

would-be /wudbi/ (adj) would-be

de **wraak** /vrak/ revenge, vengeance: *~ nemen op iem.* take revenge on s.o.

de **wraakactie** /vra̱kɑksi/ (pl: -s) act of revenge (*or:* vengeance, retaliation)

wraakzuchtig /vraksʏχtəχ/ (adj) (re)vengeful, vindictive

het **wrak** /vrak/ (pl: -ken) wreck: *zich een ~ voelen* feel a wreck

wraken /vra̱kə(n)/ (wraakte, heeft gewraakt) **1** object to: *de gewraakte passage* the passage objected to **2** challenge

het **wrakhout** /vra̱khɑut/ (pieces of) wreckage; driftwood

het **wrakstuk** /vra̱kstʏk/ (pl: -ken) piece of wreckage; wreckage

wrang /vrɑŋ/ (adj, adv) **1** sour, acid, tart: *een ~e appel* a sour (*or:* tart) apple **2** unpleasant, nasty, ironic; wry: *het is ~ dat juist hij werd gekozen* it is ironic (*or:* painful) that he of all people was elected

de **wrap** /rɛp/ wrap

de **wrat** /vrɑt/ (pl: -ten) wart

wreed /vret/ (adj, adv) cruel

de **wreedheid** /vre̱thɛit/ (pl: -heden) cruelty

de **wreef** /vref/ (pl: wreven) instep

wreken /vre̱kə(n)/ (wreekte, heeft gewroken) revenge; avenge: *zich voor iets op iem. ~* revenge o.s. on s.o. for sth.

de **wreker** /vre̱kər/ (pl: -s) avenger, revenger

de **wrevel** /vre̱vəl/ resentment; [stronger] rancour

wrevelig /vre̱vələχ/ (adj) **1** peevish, tetchy, grumpy **2** resentful

wriemelen /vri̱mələ(n)/ (wriemelde, heeft gewriemeld) fiddle (with)

wrijven /vrɛi̱və(n)/ (wreef, heeft gewreven) **1** rub: *zijn in de handen ~* rub one's hands; *neuzen tegen elkaar ~* rub noses; *wrijf het er maar in* go on, rub it in **2** polish: *de meubels ~* polish the furniture

de **wrijving** /vrɛi̱vɪŋ/ (pl: -en) friction

wrikken /vrɪ̱kə(n)/ (wrikte, heeft gewrikt) lever, prize

¹**wringen** /vrɪ̱ŋə(n)/ (wrong, heeft gewrongen) pinch

²**wringen** /vrɪ̱ŋə(n)/ (wrong, heeft gewrongen) **1** wring: *zich in allerlei bochten ~* wriggle; squirm **2** wring; press

de **wringer** /vrɪ̱ŋər/ (pl: -s) wringer, mangle

de **wroeging** /vru̱χɪŋ/ (pl: -en) remorse

¹**wroeten** /vru̱tə(n)/ (wroette, heeft gewroet) root, rout: *in iemands verleden ~* pry into s.o.'s past

²**wroeten** /vru̱tə(n)/ (wroette, heeft ge-

wroet) burrow, root (up): *de grond **onderste-**
boven ~* root up the earth

de **wrok** /vrɔk/ resentment, grudge; [stronger]
rancour

de **wrong** /vrɔŋ/ (pl: -en) roll, wreath; chignon;
bun

wuft /wʏft/ (adj, adv) frivolous

wuiven /wœyvə(n)/ (wuifde, heeft ge-
wuifd) wave

wulps /wʏlps/ (adj, adv) voluptuous

wurgen /wʏrɣə(n)/ (wurgde, heeft ge-
wurgd) strangle

de **wurgslang** /wʏrxslɑŋ/ (pl: -en) constrictor
(snake)

de **¹wurm** /wʏrm/ worm

het **²wurm** /wʏrm/ mite: *het ~ **kan** nog niet **pra-**
ten* the poor mite can't talk yet

wurmen /wʏrmə(n)/ (wurmde, heeft ge-
wurmd) squeeze, worm

de **WW** /wewe/ [Dutch] *Werkloosheidswet* Unemployment Insurance Act: *in de WW lopen
(zitten)* be on unemployment (benefit), be on
the dole

de **WW-uitkering** /weweœytkerɪŋ/ (pl: -en)
[Dutch] unemployment benefit(s)

X

de **x** /ɪks/ (pl: x'en) x, X

het **x-aantal** /ɪksantɑl/ (pl: -len) n: *een ~ kamers* n rooms

de **xantippe** /ksɑntɪpə/ (pl: -s) Xanthippe

de **x-as** /ɪksɑs/ (pl: -sen) x-axis

de **X-benen** /ɪkzbenə(n)/ knock knees: *~ heb-ben* be knock-kneed, have knock knees

het **X-chromosoom** /ɪksχromozom/ (pl: X-chromosomen) X chromosome

de **xenofobie** /ksenofobi/ xenophobia

de **xtc** /ɛkstəsi/ xtc

de **xylofoon** /ksilofon/ (pl: -s) xylophone

y

de **y** /iɡrɛk/ (pl: y's) y, Y
het **yang** /jɑŋ/ yang
de **y-as** /ɛiɑs/ (pl: -sen) y-axis
het **Y-chromosoom** /ɛixromozom/ (pl: Y-chromosomen) Y chromosome
de **yen** /jɛn/ (pl: -s) yen
    yes /jɛs/ (int): *reken maar van* ~! you bet!
de **yeti** /jeti/ (pl: -'s) yeti
het **yin** /jɪn/ yin
de **yoga** /joɣa/ yoga
de **yoghurt** /joɣʏrt/ yogurt
de **ypsilon** /ɪpsilɔn/ (pl: -s) upsilon

Z

de **z** /zɛt/ (pl: z's) z, Z

het **zaad** /zat/ (pl: zaden) **1** seed **2** sperm, semen; [vulg] cum ‖ *op zwart ~ zitten* be broke

de **zaadbal** /zadbɑl/ (pl: -len) testicle

de **zaadcel** /zatsɛl/ (pl: -len) germ cell; sperm cell

zaaddodend /zadodənt/ (adj) spermicidal

de **zaadlozing** /zatlozɪŋ/ (pl: -en) seminal discharge, ejaculation

de **zaag** /zaɣ/ (pl: zagen) saw

het **zaagblad** /zaɣblɑt/ **1** saw (blade) **2** sawwort

de **zaagmachine** /zaɣmaʃinə/ (pl: -s) saw

het **zaagsel** /zaɣsəl/ sawdust

zaaien /zajə(n)/ (zaaide, heeft gezaaid) sow: *onrust ~* create unrest; *interessante banen zijn dun gezaaid* interesting jobs are few and far between

de **zaaier** /zajər/ (pl: -s) sower

het **zaaigoed** /zajɣut/ sowing seed

de **zaak** /zak/ (pl: zaken) **1** thing; object **2** matter, affair, business: *de normale gang van zaken* the normal course of events; *zich met zijn eigen zaken bemoeien* mind one's own business; *dat is jouw ~* that is your concern; *de ~ in kwestie* the matter in hand **3** business, deal: *goede zaken doen (met iem.)* do good business (with s.o.); *er worden goede zaken gedaan in …* trade is good in …; *zaken zijn zaken* business is business; *hij is hier voor zaken* he is here on business **4** business; shop: *op kosten van de ~* on the house; *een ~ hebben* run a business; *een auto van de ~* a company car **5** case, things: *weten hoe de zaken ervoor staan* know how things stand, know what the score is **6** point, issue: *dat doet hier niet ter zake* that is irrelevant, that is beside the point; *kennis van zaken hebben* know one's facts; be well-informed (on the matter) **7** case, lawsuit: *Maria's ~ komt vanmiddag voor* Maria's case comes up this afternoon **8** affair: *Binnenlandse Zaken* Home (*or:* Internal) Affairs; *Buitenlandse Zaken* Foreign Affairs **9** cause

de **zaakgelastigde** /zakɣəlɑstəɣdə/ (pl: -n) agent

het **zaakje** /zakjə/ (pl: -s) little matter/business (*or:* affair, thing); small deal; job: *ik vertrouw het ~ niet* I don't trust the set-up

de **zaakvoerder** /zakfurdər/ (pl: -s) [Belg] manager

de **zaakwaarnemer** /zakwarnemər/ (pl: -s) (business) minder

de **zaal** /zal/ (pl: zalen) **1** room; hall **2** hall; ward; auditorium **3** hall, house: *een stampvolle ~* a crowded (*or:* packed) hall, a full house; *de ~ lag plat* it brought the house down

de **zaalhuur** /zalhyr/ hall rent

de **zaalsport** /zalsport/ (pl: -en) indoor sport

het **zaalvoetbal** /zalvudbɑl/ indoor football

zacht /zɑxt/ (adj, adv) **1** soft; smooth: *een ~e landing* a smooth landing; *~e sector* social sector **2** mild **3** kind, gentle: *op zijn ~st gezegd* to put it mildly **4** quiet, soft: *met ~e stem* in a quiet voice

zachtaardig /zɑxtardəx/ (adj, adv) good-natured, gentle

zachtgekookt /zɑxtɣəkokt/ (adj) soft-boiled

de **zachtheid** /zɑxthɛit/ softness

zachtjes /zɑxjəs/ (adv) softly; quietly; gently: *~ doen* be quiet; *~ rijden* drive slowly; *~ aan!* easy does it!, take it easy!; *~!* hush!, quiet!

zachtjesaan /zɑxjəsan/ (adv): *we moeten zo ~ vertrekken* we must be going soon

zachtmoedig /zɑxtmudəx/ (adj, adv) mild(-mannered)

zachtzinnig /zɑxtsɪnəx/ (adj, adv) **1** good-natured, mild(-mannered) **2** gentle, kind(ly); tender

het **zadel** /zadəl/ (pl: -s) saddle

zadelen /zadələ(n)/ (zadelde, heeft gezadeld) saddle (up)

de **zadelpijn** /zadəlpɛin/ saddle-soreness: *~ hebben* be saddlesore

zagen /zaɣə(n)/ (zaagde, heeft gezaagd) **1** saw (up) **2** saw, cut: *planken* (*or:* *figuren*) *~* saw into planks (*or:* shapes)

de **zagerij** /zaɣərɛi/ (pl: -en) sawmill

de **zak** /zɑk/ (pl: -ken) **1** bag; [large] sack: *een ~ patat* a bag (*or:* packet) of chips; *een plastic ~* a plastic bag; [fig] *iem. de ~ geven* give s.o. the sack, sack s.o.; [fig] *in ~ en as zitten* be in sackcloth and ashes **2** pocket: *geld op ~ hebben* have some money in one's pockets (*or:* on one) **3** purse: *uit eigen ~ betalen* pay out of one's own purse; *een duit in het ~je doen* put in one's pennyworth; [Am] put in one's two cents **4** [inform] bore, jerk; [stronger] bastard: *een slappe ~* a wimp, an idiot

de **zakagenda** /zɑkaɣɛnda/ pocket diary; [Am] (small) agenda

het **zakboekje** /zɑgbukjə/ (pl: -s) (pocket) notebook

het **zakcentje** /zɑksɛncə/ (pl: -s) pocket money

de **zakdoek** /zɑgduk/ (pl: -en) handkerchief

zakelijk /zakələk/ (adj, adv) **1** business-(like), commercial **2** business(like), objective **3** compact, concise: *een ~e stijl van schrijven* a terse style of writing **4** practical, real(istic); down-to-earth

de **zakelijkheid** /zakələkhɛit/ professionalism

het **zakencentrum** /zₐkə(n)sɛntrʏm/ (pl: -centra) business centre

het **zakendoen** /zₐkə(n)dun/ business

het **zakenkabinet** /zₐkə(n)kabinɛt/ (pl: -ten) government which is not supported by a parliamentary majority

het **zakenleven** /zₐkə(n)levə(n)/ business (life), commerce

de **zakenman** /zₐkə(n)mɑn/ (pl: zakenlui, zakenlieden) businessman: *een gewiekst ~* a shrewd (*or:* an astute) businessman

de **zakenreis** /zₐkə(n)rɛis/ (pl: -reizen) business trip

de **zakenrelatie** /zₐkə(n)rela(t)si/ (pl: -s) business relation

de **zakenvriend** /zₐkə(n)vrint/ (pl: -en) business associate

de **zakenvrouw** /zₐkə(n)vrɑu/ (pl: -en) businesswoman

de **zakenwereld** /zₐkə(n)werəlt/ business world

het **zakformaat** /zₐkfɔrmat/ (pl: zakformaten) pocket size

het **zakgeld** /zₐkχɛlt/ pocket money, spending money, allowance

zakken /zₐkə(n)/ (zakte, is gezakt) **1** fall, drop; sink: *in elkaar ~* collapse **2** fall (off), drop, come down, go down; sink: *de hoofdpijn is gezakt* the headache has eased; *het water is gezakt* the water has gone down (*or:* subsided) **3** fail, go down

zakkenrollen /zₐkə(n)rɔlə(n)/ pick pockets

de **zakkenroller** /zₐkə(n)rɔlər/ (pl: -s) pickpocket: *pas op voor ~s!* beware of pickpockets!

de **zakkenvuller** /zₐkə(n)vʏlər/ (pl: -s) [inform] profiteer

zakkerig /zₐkərəχ/ (adj, adv) baggy

de **zaklamp** /zₐklɑmp/ (pl: -en) (pocket) torch; [Am] flashlight

de **zaklantaarn** /zₐklɑntarn/ (pl: -s) (pocket) torch, flashlight

zaklopen /zₐklopə(n)/ (run a) sack race

het **zakmes** /zₐkmɛs/ (pl: -sen) pocket knife

het **zakwoordenboek** /zₐkwordə(n)buk/ (pl: -en) pocket dictionary

het **zalencentrum** /zₐlə(n)sɛntrʏm/ function rooms

de **zalf** /zɑlf/ (pl: zalven) ointment, salve: *met ~ insmeren* rub ointment (*or:* salve) on

zalig /zaləχ/ (adj, adv) gorgeous, glorious, divine: *~ weer* gorgeous weather; *hij kookt ~* he cooks divinely ‖ *~ kerstfeest* Merry Christmas; *iem. ~ verklaren* beatify s.o.

zaligmakend /zaləχmakənt/ (adj): *dat is ook niet ~* that won't bring universal happiness either

de **zaligverklaring** /zaləχfərklarɪŋ/ (pl: -en) [rel] beatification

de **zalm** /zɑlm/ (pl: -en) salmon

de **zalmforel** /zɑlmforɛl/ (pl: -len) salmon trout

zalmkleurig /zɑlmklørəχ/ (adj) salmon, salmon-coloured

zalven /zɑlvə(n)/ (zalfde, heeft gezalfd) put (*or:* rub) ointment on

zalvend /zɑlvənt/ (adj, adv) unctuous, suave

de **zalving** /zɑlvɪŋ/ (pl: -en) anointment (with)

Zambia /zɑmbija/ Zambia

de **Zambiaan** /zɑmbijan/ (pl: Zambianen) Zambian

Zambiaans /zɑmbijans/ (adj) Zambian

het **zand** /zɑnt/ sand: *~ erover* let's forget it, let bygones be bygones; [fig] *iem. ~ in de ogen strooien* throw dust in s.o.'s eyes

de **zandafgraving** /zɑntɑfχravɪŋ/ (pl: -en) sandpit

de **zandbak** /zɑndbɑk/ (pl: -ken) sandbox

de **zandbank** /zɑndbɑŋk/ (pl: -en) sandbank

zanderig /zɑndərəχ/ (adj) sandy

de **zandgrond** /zɑntχront/ (pl: -en) sandy soil

het **zandkasteel** /zɑntkɑstel/ (pl: -kastelen) sandcastle

de **zandkorrel** /zɑntkɔrəl/ (pl: -s) grain of sand

de **zandloper** /zɑntlopər/ (pl: -s) hourglass; egg-timer

het **zandpad** /zɑntpɑt/ (pl: -en) sandy path

het/de **zandsteen** /zɑntsten/ sandstone

de **zandstorm** /zɑntstɔrm/ (pl: -en) sandstorm

zandstralen /zɑntstralə(n)/ (zandstraalde, heeft gezandstraald) sandblast

het **zandstrand** /zɑntstrɑnt/ (pl: -en) sandy beach

de **zandverstuiving** /zɑntfərstœyvɪŋ/ (pl: -en) sand drift, drifting sand

de **zandvlakte** /zɑntflɑktə/ (pl: -n, -s) sand flat, sand(y) plain

de **zandweg** /zɑntwɛχ/ (pl: -en) sand track (*or:* road), dirt track

de **zandzak** /zɑntsɑk/ (pl: -ken) sandbag

de **zang** /zɑŋ/ (pl: -en) song, singing; warbling

de **zanger** /zɑŋər/ (pl: -s) singer; vocalist

zangerig /zɑŋərəχ/ (adj) melodious; singsong

het **zangkoor** /zɑŋkor/ (pl: -koren) choir

de **zangleraar** /zɑŋlerar/ (pl: -leraren, -s) singing teacher

de **zangvereniging** /zɑŋvərenəχɪŋ/ (pl: -en) choir, choral society

de **zangvogel** /zɑŋvoɣəl/ (pl: -s) songbird

zaniken /zanəkə(n)/ (zanikte, heeft gezanikt) nag; moan; whine

zappen /zɛpə(n)/ (zapte, heeft/is gezapt) zap

¹**zat** /zɑt/ (adj) **1** drunken; drunk **2** fed up: *ik ben het zat* I'm fed up (with it)

²**zat** /zɑt/ (adv) plenty; to spare: *zij hebben geld ~* they have plenty (*or:* oodles) of money; *tijd ~* time to spare, plenty of time

de **zaterdag** /zatərdɑχ/ (pl: -en) Saturday

¹**zaterdags** /zatərdɑχs/ (adj) Saturday

²**zaterdags** /zatərdɑχs/ (adv) on Saturdays

de **zatlap** /zɑtlɑp/ (pl: -pen) boozer
ze /zə/ (pers pron) **1** she, her: *ze* **komt** *zo* she is just coming **2** they, them: *roep ze eens* just call them; *daar* **moesten** *ze eens iets aan* **doen** they ought to do sth. about that
de **zebra** /zebra/ (pl: -'s) zebra
het **zebrapad** /zebrapɑt/ (pl: -en) pedestrian crossing, zebra crossing
de **zede** /zedə/ (pl: -n) **1** custom; usage: *~n en* **gewoonten** customs and traditions **2** morals, manners || *een meisje van* **lichte** *~n* a girl of easy virtue
zedelijk /zedələk/ (adj, adv) moral
zedeloos /zedəlos/ (adj, adv) immoral, corrupt
het **zedendelict** /zedə(n)delɪkt/ (pl: -en) sexual offence
de **zedenleer** /zedə(n)ler/ [Belg; educ] ethics
het **zedenmisdrijf** /zedəmɪzdrɛɪf/ (pl: -misdrijven) sexual offence
de **zedenpolitie** /zedə(n)poli(t)si/ vice squad
de **zedenpreek** /zedə(n)prek/ (pl: -preken) sermon
de **zedenzaak** /zedə(n)zak/ vice case
zedig /zedəχ/ (adj, adv) modest
de **zee** /ze/ (pl: -ën) sea: *een ~ van* **tijd** oceans (*or:* heaps) of time; *aan ~* by the sea, on the coast; *met iem.* **in** *~ gaan* join in with s.o., throw in one's lot with s.o.
de **zeearend** /zearənt/ (pl: -en) white-tailed eagle
de **zeearm** /zeɑrm/ (pl: -en) arm of the sea, inlet
het **zeebanket** /zebɑnkɛt/ seafood
de **zeebenen** /zebenə(n)/ (pl): *~* **hebben** have got one's sea legs, be a good sailor
de **zeebeving** /zebevɪŋ/ (pl: -en) seaquake
de **zeebodem** /zebodəm/ (pl: -s) ocean floor, seabed, bottom of the sea
de **zeebonk** /zebɔŋk/ (pl: -en) sea dog
de **zeeduivel** /zedœyvəl/ (pl: -s) angler, anglerfish
de **zee-egel** /zeeɣəl/ (pl: -s) sea urchin
de **zee-engte** /zeɛŋtə/ (pl: -n, -s) strait
de **zeef** /zef/ (pl: zeven) sieve; strainer: *zo lek* **als** *een ~ zijn* leak like a sieve
de **zeefdruk** /zevdrʏk/ (pl: -ken) silk-screen (print)
het **zeegat** /zeɣɑt/ (pl: -en) tidal inlet (*or:* outlet)
het **zeegezicht** /zeɣəzɪχt/ (pl: -en) seascape
de **zeehaven** /zehavə(n)/ (pl: -s) harbour, seaport
de **zeeheld** /zehɛlt/ (pl: -en) sea hero
de **zeehond** /zehɔnt/ (pl: -en) seal
het **zeeklimaat** /zeklimat/ maritime climate, oceanic climate
de **zeekoe** /zeku/ (pl: zeekoeien) sea cow
de **zeekreeft** /zekreft/ (pl: -en) lobster
Zeeland /zelɑnt/ Zeeland
de **zeeleeuw** /zelew/ (pl: -en) sea lion
de **zeelieden** /zelidə(n)/ (pl) seamen, sailors

de **zeelucht** /zelʏχt/ sea air
het **¹zeem** /zem/ shammy, chamois
het/de **²zeem** /zem/ shammy, chamois
de **zeemacht** /zemɑχt/ navy; naval forces
de **zeeman** /zemɑn/ (pl: zeelieden, zeelui) sailor
de **zeemeermin** /zemermɪn/ (pl: -nen) mermaid
de **zeemeeuw** /zemew/ (pl: -en) (sea)gull
de **zeemijl** /zemɛil/ (pl: -en) nautical mile
de **zeemist** /zemɪst/ (pl: -en) sea mist
het **zeemleer** /zemler/ chamois (*or:* shammy) leather, washleather
zeemleren /zemlerə(n)/ (adj) chamois, shammy
de **zeemogendheid** /zemoɣənthɛit/ (pl: -heden) maritime power, naval power
het **zeeniveau** /zenivo/ (pl: -s) sea level
de **zeeolifant** /zeolifɑnt/ (pl: -en) elephant seal, sea elephant
de **zeep** /zep/ (pl: zepen) **1** soap **2** (soap)suds || *iem. om ~ brengen* kill s.o.; do s.o. in
het **zeepaardje** /zeparcə/ (pl: -s) sea horse
het **zeepbakje** /zebɑkjə/ (pl: -s) soap dish
de **zeepbel** /zebɛl/ (pl: -len) (soap) bubble
de **zeepkist** /zepkɪst/ (pl: -en) soapbox
het/de **zeeppoeder** /zepudər/ washing powder, detergent
het **zeepsop** /zepsɔp/ (soap)suds
het **¹zeer** /zer/ pain, ache; sore: *dat* **doet** *~* that hurts
²zeer /zer/ (adj) sore, painful, aching: *een ~* **hoofd** an aching head
³zeer /zer/ (adv) very, extremely, greatly: *~ tot mijn verbazing* (very) much to my amazement
de **zeereis** /zerɛis/ (pl: zeereizen) (sea) voyage; passage
de **zeerob** /zerɔp/ (pl: -ben) seal
de **zeerover** /zerovər/ (pl: -s) pirate
het **zeeschip** /zesχɪp/ (pl: zeeschepen) seagoing vessel, ocean-going vessel
de **zeeslag** /zeslɑχ/ (pl: -en) sea battle, naval battle; [game] battleships
de **zeespiegel** /zespiɣəl/ (pl: -s) sea level
de **zeestraat** /zestrat/ (pl: -straten) strait
Zeeuws /zews/ (adj) Zeeland
Zeeuws-Vlaanderen /zewsflɑndərə(n)/ Zeeland Flanders
de **zeevaart** /zevart/ seagoing; shipping
de **zeevaartschool** /zevartsχol/ (pl: -scholen) nautical college
zeevarend /zevarənt/ (adj) maritime, seagoing
de **zeevis** /zevɪs/ (pl: -sen) saltwater fish, sea fish
zeevissen /zevɪsə(n)/ (deep-)sea fishing
zeewaardig /zewardəχ/ (adj) seaworthy
het **zeewater** /zewatər/ seawater, salt water
de **zeewering** /zewerɪŋ/ (pl: -en) seawall
het **zeewier** /zewir/ seaweed

de **zeewind** /zéwɪnt/ (pl: -en) sea breeze, sea wind

zeeziek /zézik/ (adj) seasick

het **zeezout** /zézɑut/ sea salt

de **zege** /zéɣə/ (pl: -s) victory, triumph; win

de ¹**zegel** /zéɣəl/ stamp

het ²**zegel** /zéɣəl/ seal: *zijn ~ ergens op* **drukken,** *zijn ~* **hechten** *aan iets* set one's seal on sth.; give one's blessing to sth.

de **zegelring** /zéɣəlrɪŋ/ (pl: -en) signet ring

de **zegen** /zéɣə(n)/ **1** blessing; benediction: [iron] *mijn ~* **heb** *je (voor wat het waard is)* you've got my blessing(, for what it's worth) **2** blessing, boon: *dat is een ~* **voor** *de mensheid* that is a blessing (*or:* boon) to mankind

zegenen /zéɣənə(n)/ (zegende, heeft gezegend) bless

zegerijk /zéɣərɛɪk/ (adj) victorious, triumphant

de **zegetocht** /zéɣətɔχt/ (pl: -en) triumphal march, victory march

zegevieren /zéɣəvirə(n)/ (zegevierde, heeft gezegevierd) triumph

zeggen /zɛɣə(n)/ (zei, heeft gezegd) **1** say, tell: *dat gezegd* **hebbende** *... having said that ...; wat* **wil** *je daarmee ~?* what are you trying to say?, what are you driving at?; *wat ik ~* **wou** by the way; *wat zeg je?* what did you say?; [inform] sorry?, come again?; *wat zegt u?* (I beg your) pardon?, sorry?; *wie zal het ~?* who can say? (*or:* tell?); *zegt u het* **maar** yes, please?; *zeg dat* **wel** you can say that again; *ze ~ dat hij heel rijk is* he is said (*or:* reputed) to be very rich; *wat zeg je me daarvan!* how about that!, well I never!; *dat is toch zo, zeg* **nou zelf** it is true, admit it; *hoe zal ik het ~?* how shall I put it?; *nou je* **het** *zegt* now (that) you mention it; *zo gezegd, zo gedaan* no sooner said than done; **zonder** *iets te ~* without (saying) a word; *zeg* **maar** *'Tom'* call me 'Tom'; *niets te ~ hebben* have no authority; have no say **2** say, mean: *dat* **wil** *~ that means, i.e.; that is (to say)* **3** say, prove: *dat zegt* **niets** that says (*or:* proves) nothing **4** say, state || *laten we ~ dat ...* let's say that ...

de **zeggenschap** /zɛɣənsχɑp/ say, voice: *~* **over** *iets krijgen* get control (*or:* authority) over sth.

de **zeggingskracht** /zɛɣɪŋskrɑχt/ power of expression, eloquence

het **zegje** /zɛχjə/: *ieder wil zijn ~* **doen** everyone wants to have their say

de **zegsman** /zɛχsmɑn/ (pl: zegslieden, zegslui) informant, authority

de **zegswijze** /zɛχswɛɪzə/ (pl: -n) phrase, saying

de **zeik** /zɛik/ [inform] piss

zeiken /zɛikə(n)/ (zeikte, heeft gezeikt/gezeken) [inform] **1** piss **2** go on, harp (*or:* carry) on

de **zeikerd** /zɛikərt/ (pl: -s) [Dutch; inform] bugger

zeikerig /zɛikərəχ/ (adj, adv) [inform] fretful, whiny

zeiknat /zɛiknɑt/ (adj) [inform] sopping (wet)

het **zeil** /zɛil/ (pl: -en) **1** sail: *alle ~en* **bijzetten** employ full sail; pull out all the stops; *onder ~ gaan* **a)** set sail; **b)** [fig] doze off **2** floor covering **3** canvas, sailcloth; tarpaulin

de **zeilboot** /zɛilbot/ (pl: -boten) sailing boat

het/de **zeildoek** /zɛilduk/ canvas

zeilen /zɛilə(n)/ (zeilde, heeft/is gezeild) sail

de **zeiler** /zɛilər/ (pl: -s) yachtsman, yachtswoman, sailor

het **zeiljacht** /zɛiljɑχt/ (pl: -en) yacht

de **zeilplank** /zɛilplɑŋk/ (pl: -en) sailboard

het **zeilschip** /zɛilsχɪp/ (pl: -schepen) sailing ship

de **zeilsport** /zɛilsport/ sailing

de **zeiltocht** /zɛiltɔχt/ (pl: -en) sailing trip, sailing voyage

de **zeilwedstrijd** /zɛilwɛtstrɛit/ (pl: -en) sailing match; regatta

de **zeis** /zɛis/ (pl: -en) scythe

zeker /zékər/ (adj, adv) **1** safe: *(op) ~* **spelen** play safe; *hij heeft het ~e* **voor** *het onzekere genomen* he did it to be on the safe side **2** sure, certain: *iets ~* **weten** know sth. for sure; *om ~ te* **zijn** to be sure; [Dutch] *vast en ~!,* [Belg] *~ en* **vast!** definitely; *~* **weten!** to be sure!, sure is (*or:* are)...! **3** probably: *je* **wou** *haar ~* **verrassen** I suppose you wanted to surprise her; *je hebt het ~ al* *af* you must have finished it by now **4** at least: *~* **dertig** *gewonden* at least thirty (people) injured || *~* **niet** certainly not; *op ~e* **dag** one day; *in ~e* **zin** in a way; *een ~e* **meneer** *Pietersen* a (certain) Mr Pietersen

de **zekerheid** /zékərhɛit/ (pl: zekerheden) **1** safety; safe keeping: *iem. een* **gevoel** *van ~ geven* give s.o. a sense of security; *voor alle ~* for safety's sake, to make quite sure **2** certainty; confidence || **sociale** *~* social security

de **zekering** /zékərɪŋ/ (pl: -en) (safety) fuse: *de ~en* **zijn doorgeslagen** the fuses have blown

zelden /zɛldə(n)/ (adv) rarely, seldom: *~ of* **nooit** rarely if ever

zeldzaam /zɛltsam/ (adj, adv) rare

de **zeldzaamheid** /zɛltsamhɛit/ (pl: -heden) rarity

zelf /zɛlf/ (dem pron) self, myself, yourself, himself, herself, itself, ourselves, yourselves, themselves, oneself: *~ een zaak* **beginnen** start one's own business; *~* **gebakken** *brood* home-made bread; *ik kook ~* I do my own cooking; *al* **zeg** *ik het ~* although I say it myself; *het* **huis** *~ is onbeschadigd* the house itself is undamaged

de **zelfbediening** /zɛlvbədinɪŋ/ self-service

het **zelfbedieningsrestaurant** /zɛlvbədinɪŋsrɛstorɑnt/ (pl: -s) self-service restaurant

het **zelfbedrog** /zɛlvbədrɔx/ self-deception

het **zelfbeeld** /zɛlvbelt/ self-image: *een laag ~ hebben* suffer from low self-esteem, suffer from poor self-image

de **zelfbeheersing** /zɛlvbəhersɪŋ/ self-control: *zijn ~ verliezen* lose control of o.s.

het **zelfbeklag** /zɛlvbəklɑx/ self-pity

de **zelfbeschikking** /zɛlvbəsxɪkɪŋ/ self-determination

het **zelfbestuur** /zɛlvbəstyr/ self-government

de **zelfbevrediging** /zɛlvbəvredəyɪŋ/ masturbation

zelfbewust /zɛlvbəwy̆st/ (adj, adv) self-confident, self-assured

het **zelfbewustzijn** /zɛlvbəwy̆(st)sɛɪn/ self-awareness

zelfde /zɛlvdə/ (adj) similar, very (same): *in deze ~ kamer* in this very room

de **zelfdiscipline** /zɛlvdisiplinə/ self-discipline

de **zelfdoding** /zɛlvdodɪŋ/ (pl: -en) suicide: *hulp bij ~* assisted suicide

zelfgenoegzaam /zɛlfxənŭxsam/ (adj) conceited

zelfingenomen /zɛlfɪŋənomə(n)/ (adj) conceited

de **zelfkant** /zɛlfkɑnt/ (pl: -en): *aan de ~ van de maatschappij leven* live on the fringe(s) (*or:* border(s)) of society

de **zelfkennis** /zɛlfkɛnɪs/ self-knowledge

de **zelfkritiek** /zɛlfkritik/ self-criticism

het **zelfmedelijden** /zɛlfmedəlɛɪdə(n)/ self-pity

de **zelfmoord** /zɛlfmort/ (pl: -en) suicide: *~ plegen* commit suicide

de **zelfmoordaanslag** /zɛlfmortɑnslɑx/ (pl: -en) suicide attack

de **zelfmoordterrorist** /zɛlfmortɛrorɪst/ suicide bomber (*or:* terrorist)

de **zelfontplooiing** /zɛlfontplojɪŋ/ self-development; self-realization

de **zelfontspanner** /zɛlfontspɑnər/ (pl: -s) self-timer

de **zelfoverschatting** /zɛlfovərsxɑtɪŋ/ overestimation of o.s.: *aan ~ lijden* overestimate o.s.

het **zelfportret** /zɛlfportrɛt/ (pl: -ten) self-portrait

het **zelfrespect** /zɛlfrɛspɛkt/ self-respect

zelfrijdend /zɛlfrɛɪdənt/ (adj) driverless, autonomous: *een ~e auto* an autonomous car

zelfrijzend /zɛlfrɛɪzənt/ (adj) self-raising

zelfs /zɛlfs/ (adv) even: *~ zijn vrienden vertrouwde hij niet* he did not even trust his friends; *~ in dat geval* even then so

de **zelfscankassa** /zɛlfskɛŋkɑsa/ (pl: -'s) self-checkout

de **zelfspot** /zɛlfspot/ self-mockery

zelfstandig /zɛlfstɑndəx/ (adj, adv) independent; self-employed: *~ gaan wonen* go and live on one's own

de **zelfstandige** /zɛlfstɑndəyə/ (pl: -n): *een kleine ~* a self-employed person, a small businessman (*or:* trader)

de **zelfstandigheid** /zɛlfstɑndəxhɛit/ independence

de **zelfstudie** /zɛlfstydi/ (pl: -s) private study, home study

de **zelfverdediging** /zɛlfərdedəyɪŋ/ self-defence: *uit ~ handelen* act in self-defence

zelfverklaard /zɛlfərklɑrt/ (adj) self-proclaimed, self-declared

de **zelfverloochening** /zɛlfərloxənɪŋ/ self-denial

het **zelfvertrouwen** /zɛlfərtrɑuwə(n)/ (self-)confidence

het **zelfverwijt** /zɛlfərwɛit/ self-reproach

zelfverzekerd /zɛlfərzɛkərt/ (adj, adv) (self-)assured

zelfvoldaan /zɛlfoldan/ (adj) self-satisfied

de **zelfwerkzaamheid** /zɛlfwɛrksamhɛit/ self-activation; self-motivation; independence

zelfzuchtig /zɛlfsy̆xtəx/ (adj, adv) selfish

de **¹zemel** /zemᵊl/ (pl: -en, -s) bran

de **²zemel** /zemᵊl/ (pl: -s) twaddler

de **zemelen** /zemᵊlə(n)/ (pl) bran

zemen /zemə(n)/ (zeemde, heeft gezeemd) leather

het **zenboeddhisme** /zɛmbudɪsmə/ Zen (Buddhism)

de **zendamateur** /zɛntamatør/ (pl: -s) (radio) ham, amateur radio operator; CB-er

de **zendeling** /zɛndəlɪŋ/ (pl: -en) missionary

¹zenden /zɛndə(n)/ (zond, heeft gezonden) broadcast, transmit

²zenden /zɛndə(n)/ (zond, heeft gezonden) send: *iem. om de dokter ~* send for the doctor

de **zender** /zɛndər/ (pl: -s) **1** broadcasting station, transmitting station **2** sender **3** emitter, transmitter

de **zendgemachtigde** /zɛntxəmɑxtəydə/ (pl: -n) broadcasting licence-holder

de **zending** /zɛndɪŋ/ (pl: -en) supply; parcel; package

het **zendingswerk** /zɛndɪŋswɛrk/ missionary work

de **zendinstallatie** /zɛntɪnstɑla(t)si/ (pl: -s) transmitting station (*or:* equipment)

de **zendmast** /zɛntmɑst/ (pl: -en) (radio, TV) mast; radio tower, TV tower

de **zendpiraat** /zɛntpirat/ (pl: -piraten) radio pirate

het **zendstation** /zɛntsta(t)ʃon/ (pl: -s) broadcasting station, transmitting station

de **zendtijd** /zɛntɛit/ (pl: -en) broadcast(ing) time

de **zenuw** /zenyw/ (pl: -en) nerve; nerves: *stalen ~en* nerves of steel; *de ~en hebben* have the jitters; *ze was óp van de ~en* she was a nervous wreck; *op iemands ~en werken* get (or: grate) on s.o.'s nerves

de **zenuwaandoening** /zenywandunɪŋ/ (pl: -en) nervous disorder

zenuwachtig /zenywaχtəχ/ (adj, adv) nervous: ~ zijn **voor** het examen be jittery before the exam

de **zenuwachtigheid** /zenywaχtəχhɛit/ nervousness

de **zenuwbehandeling** /zenywbəhandəlɪŋ/ (pl: -en) root treatment, root-canal therapy

de **zenuwcel** /zenywsɛl/ (pl: -len) neuron

het **zenuwgas** /zenywγas/ (pl: -sen) nerve gas

het **zenuwgestel** /zenywγəstɛl/ nervous system

de **zenuwinzinking** /zenywɪnzɪŋkɪŋ/ (pl: -en) nervous breakdown

de **zenuwlijder** /zenywlɛidər/ (pl: -s) [inform] neurotic

de **zenuwontsteking** /zenywontstekɪŋ/ (pl: -en) neuritis

zenuwslopend /zenywslopənt/ (adj) nerve-racking; [Am] nerve-wracking

het **zenuwstelsel** /zenywstɛlsəl/ (pl: -s) nervous system

het **zenuwtrekje** /zenywtrɛkjə/ (pl: -s) (nervous) tic

de **zenuwziekte** /zenywziktə/ (pl: -n, -s) nervous disease

de **zeperd** /zepərt/ (pl: -s) [Dutch; inform] fizzle, flop: een ~ **halen** fall flat (on one's face)

de **zeppelin** /zɛpəlɪn/ (pl: -s) Zeppelin

de **zerk** /zɛrk/ (pl: -en) tombstone

de **zero tolerance** /zirotolərəns/ zero tolerance

zes /zɛs/ (num) six; [in dates] sixth: **hoofdstuk** ~ chapter six; iets **in** ~sen delen divide sth. into six (parts); wij zijn **met** z'n ~sen there are six of us; **met** ~ tegelijk in sixes; ~ **min** barely a six; voor dat proefwerk **kreeg** hij een ~ he got six for that test; **een** ~je six (out of ten), a mere pass mark

zesde /zɛzdə/ (num) sixth

de **zeshoek** /zɛshuk/ (pl: -en) hexagon

de **zesjescultuur** /zɛʃəskyltyr/ culture of mediocrity

de **zesjesklant** /zɛʃəsklɑnt/ (pl: -en) a mediocre student

het **zestal** /zɛstɑl/ (pl: -len) six

zestien /zɛstin/ (num) sixteen; [in dates] sixteenth

zestiende /zɛstində/ (num) sixteenth

zestig /sɛstəχ/ (num) sixty: in de **jaren** ~ in the sixties; voor **in** de ~ zijn be just over sixty; hij loopt **tegen** de ~ he is close on sixty; he is pushing sixty

de **zestiger** /sɛstəɣər/ (pl: -s) sixty-year-old, sexagenarian

de **zet** /zɛt/ (pl: -ten) **1** move: een ~ **doen** make a move; jij bent **aan** ~ (it's) your move **2** push: iem. een ~ **geven** push s.o., give s.o. a push; **geef** me eens een ~je give me a boost, will

you; [fig] het **laatste** ~je geven give (s.o.) the last (or: final) push

de **zetbaas** /zɛdbas/ (pl: zetbazen) manager

de **zetel** /zetəl/ (pl: -s) seat; [Belg] armchair

zetelen /zetələ(n)/ (zetelde, heeft/is gezeteld) be established, have one's seat; reside

de **zetfout** /zɛtfɑut/ (pl: -en) misprint

het **zetmeel** /zɛtmel/ starch

de **zetpil** /zɛtpɪl/ (pl: -len) suppository

zetten /zɛtə(n)/ (zette, heeft gezet) **1** set, put; move: enkele **stappen** ~ take a few steps; iem. **eruit** ~ eject, evict s.o.; throw s.o. out; een apparaat in elkaar ~ fit together, assemble a machine; contrive, think up **2** make || zet de muziek **harder** (or: **zachter**) turn up (or: down) the music; zich ergens **toe** ~ put one's mind to sth.

de **zetter** /zɛtər/ (pl: -s) compositor

de **zeug** /zøχ/ (pl: -en) sow

zeulen /zølə(n)/ (zeulde, heeft gezeuld) [inform] lug, drag

de **zeur** /zør/ (pl: -en) bore, nag

zeuren /zørə(n)/ (zeurde, heeft gezeurd) nag, harp; whine: wil je niet zo **aan** mijn kop ~ stop badgering me; iem. aan het hoofd ~ (om, over) nag s.o. (into, about)

¹**zeven** /zevə(n)/ (zeefde, heeft gezeefd) sieve, sift; strain

²**zeven** /zevə(n)/ (num) seven; [in dates] seventh: morgen **wordt** ze ~ tomorrow she'll be seven || een ~ **voor** Nederlands (a) seven for Dutch

zevende /zevəndə/ (num) seventh

zeventien /zevə(n)tin/ (num) seventeen; [in dates] seventeenth

zeventiende /zevəntində/ (num) seventeenth

zeventig /sevəntəχ/ (num) seventy

de **zever** /zevər/ (pl: -s) drivel

zeveren /zevərə(n)/ (zeverde, heeft gezeverd) **1** slobber, slaver **2** drivel

z.g.a.n. zo goed als nieuw as good as new, virtually new

zgn. zogenaamd so-called

zich /zɪχ/ (ref pron) **1** himself, herself, itself, oneself, themselves; him(self); her(self), it(self), one(self), them(selves): geld **bij** ~ hebben have money on one; iem. **bij** ~ hebben have s.o. with one **2** yourself, yourselves: **vergist** u ~ niet? aren't you mistaken?

het **zicht** /zɪχt/ **1** sight, view: iem. het ~ **belemmeren** block s.o.'s view; het einde is **in** ~ the end is in sight (or: view); **uit** het ~ **verdwijnen** disappear from view **2** insight

zichtbaar /zɪχtbar/ (adj, adv) visible: ~ **opgelucht** visibly relieved; niet ~ **met** het blote oog not visible to the naked eye

de **zichtrekening** /zɪχtrekənɪŋ/ (pl: -en) [Belg] current account

zichzelf /zɪχsɛlf/ (ref pron) himself, herself, itself, oneself, themselves, self: niet ~ **zijn** not be oneself; *in* ~ *praten* talk to oneself; *op* ~ *wonen* live on one's own; *tot* ~ *komen* come to oneself; *uit* ~ of one's own accord; *voor* ~ *beginnen* start a business of one's own

ziedend /zi̯dənt/ (adj) seething, furious, livid

ziek /zik/ (adj) ill, sick: ~ *van iemands gezeur worden* get sick of s.o.'s moaning; ~ *worden* fall ill (*or:* sick); *zich* ~ *melden* report sick

het **ziekbed** /zi̯gbɛt/ (pl: -den) **1** sickbed: *aan het* ~ *gekluisterd zijn* be confined to one's (sick)bed **2** illness: *na een kort* ~ after a short illness

de **zieke** /zi̯kə/ (pl: -n) patient, sick person
ziekelijk /zi̯kələk/ (adj) **1** sickly **2** morbid, sick

de **ziekenauto** /zi̯kə(n)ɑuto/ (pl: -'s) ambulance

het **ziekenbezoek** /zi̯kə(n)bəzuk/ (pl: -en) visit to a (*or:* the) patient

de **ziekenboeg** /zi̯kə(n)buɣ/ (pl: -en) sickbay

de **ziekenbroeder** /zi̯kə(n)brudər/ (pl: -s) [Dutch] male nurse

het **ziekenfonds** /zi̯kə(n)fɔnts/ (pl: -en) [roughly] (Dutch) National Health Service: *ik zit in het* ~ I'm covered by the National Health Service

het **ziekenhuis** /zi̯kə(n)hœys/ (pl: -huizen) hospital

de **ziekenhuisopname** /zi̯kə(n)hœysɔpnamə/ (pl: -n, -s) hospitalization

de **ziekenverpleger** /zi̯kə(n)vərpleɣər/ (pl: -s) nurse

de **ziekenwagen** /zi̯kə(n)waɣə(n)/ (pl: -s) ambulance

de **ziekte** /zi̯ktə/ (pl: -n, -s) **1** illness, sickness **2** disease, illness: *de* ~ *van Weil* Weil's disease; *een ernstige* ~ a serious disease (*or:* illness); *een* ~ *oplopen* develop a disease (*or:* an illness)

het **ziektebeeld** /zi̯ktəbelt/ (pl: -en) syndrome

de **ziektekiem** /zi̯ktəkim/ (pl: -en) germ (of a, the disease)

de **ziektekosten** /zi̯ktəkɔstə(n)/ (pl) medical expenses

de **ziektekostenverzekering** /zi̯ktəkɔstə(n)vərzekərɪŋ/ (pl: -en) medical insurance, health insurance

het **ziekteverlof** /zi̯ktəvərlɔf/ sick leave

het **ziekteverloop** /zi̯ktəvərlop/ course of a disease

de **ziekteverwekker** /zi̯ktəvərwɛkər/ (pl: -s) pathogen

het **ziekteverzuim** /zi̯ktəvərzœym/ absence through illness; absenteeism

de **ziektewet** /zi̯ktəwɛt/ [Dutch] (Dutch) Health Law: *in de* ~ *lopen* be on sickness benefit (*or:* sick pay); [Am] be (out) on sick leave

de **ziel** /zil/ (pl: -en) soul: *zijn* ~ *en zaligheid voor iets over hebben* sell one's soul for sth.; *zijn* ~ *ergens in leggen* put one's heart and soul into

sth.; *hoe meer* ~*en, hoe meer vreugd* the more the merrier

het **zielenheil** /zi̯lə(n)hɛɪl/ salvation (of one's soul)

de **zielenpiet** /zi̯ləpit/ (pl: -en) [inform] poor soul

zielig /zi̯ləɣ/ (adj, adv) **1** pitiful, pathetic: *ik vind hem echt* ~ I think he's really pathetic; *wat* ~! how sad! **2** petty

zielloos /zi̯los/ (adj) **1** lifeless, inanimate **2** soulless

zielsbedroefd /zilzbədru̯ft/ (adj) brokenhearted, heart-broken

zielsgelukkig /zi̯lsɣəlʏkəɣ/ (adj) ecstatic, blissfully happy

zielsveel /zi̯lsfel/ (adv) deeply, dearly: ~ *van iem. houden* love s.o. (with) heart and soul

zieltogend /zi̯ltoɣənt/ (adj) moribund

¹**zien** /zin/ (zag, heeft gezien) **1** see **2** look: *Bernard zag zo bleek als een doek* Bernard was (*or:* looked) as white as a sheet

²**zien** /zin/ (zag, heeft gezien) **1** see: *ik zie hem dat nog niet doen* I can't see him doing it; *zich ergens laten* ~ show one's face somewhere; *waar zie je dat aan?* how can you tell?; *ik zie aan je gezicht dat je liegt* I can tell by the look on your face that you are lying; *tot* ~s goodbye; *ik zie het al voor* me I can just see it; *het niet meer* ~ *zitten* have had enough (of it); not be able to see one's way out (of a situation); *zie je, ziet u?* you see?; see? **2** see (to it): *je moet maar* ~ *hoe je het doet* you'll just have to manage || *dat* ~ *we dán wel weer* we'll cross that bridge when we come to it; *mij niet ge~* count me out!, not for me!

zienderogen /zindəroɣə(n)/ (adv) visibly

de **ziener** /zi̯nər/ (pl: -s) seer

de **zienswijze** /zi̯nswɛɪzə/ (pl: -n) view

de **zier** /zir/ [inform] the least bit: *het kan mij geen* ~ *schelen* I couldn't care less

ziezo /zizo̯/ (int) there (we, you are)

de **zigeuner** /siɣønər/ (pl: -s) Gypsy
zigzag /zɪxsɑx/ (adv) zigzag
zigzaggen /zɪxsɑɣə(n)/ (zigzagde, heeft/is gezigzagd) zigzag

de ¹**zij** /zɛi/ (pl: zijden) side: ~ *aan* ~ side by side

het ²**zij** /zɛi/ silk

³**zij** /zɛi/ (pers pron) **1** she **2** they [pl]

het **zijaanzicht** /zɛɪɑnzɪxt/ (pl: -en) side-view

de **zijde** /zɛɪdə/ (pl: zijden) **1** side: *op zijn andere* ~ *gaan liggen* turn over; *van vaders* ~ from one's father's side **2** silk
zijdeachtig /zɛɪdəɑxtəɣ/ (adj) silky
zijdelings /zɛɪdəlɪŋs/ (adj, adv) indirect
zijden /zɛɪdə(n)/ (adj) silk

de **zijderups** /zɛɪdərʏps/ (pl: -en) silkworm

de **zijdeur** /zɛɪdør/ (pl: -en) side door
zijig /zɛɪjəx/ (adj) silky

de **zijinstromer** /zɛɪɪnstromər/ (pl: -s) **1** [Dutch] lateral entry teacher **2** [Belg] s.o. receiving further education de **zijkamer** /zɛɪkamər/ (pl: -s) room at (or: to) the side

de **zijkant** /zɛɪkɑnt/ (pl: -en) side

de **zijlijn** /zɛɪlɛin/ (pl: -en) **1** branch (line) **2** sideline; touchline

het **¹zijn** /zɛin/ being, existence

²zijn /zɛin/ (was, is geweest) be: *als ik jou was, zou ik ...* if I were you, I would ...; *we ~ er* here we are; *er was eens een koning ...* once (upon a time) there was a king ...; *dát is nog eens lopen* (now) that's what I call walking; *er ~ mensen die ...* there are people who ...; *dat ~ mijn ouders* those are my parents; *die beker is van tin* that cup is made of pewter; *er voor iem. ~* be there for s.o.; *wat is er?* what's the matter?; what is it?; *het is zoals het is* it is what it is || *hij is voetballen* he is (out) playing football; *als het ware* as it were, so to speak; *ware het niet, dat ...* were it not for ...

³zijn /zɛin/ (aux vb, was, is geweest) **1** have: *er waren gunstige berichten binnengekomen* favourable reports had come in **2** be: *hij is ontslagen* he has been fired

⁴zijn /zɛin/ (poss pron) his, its, one's: *vader ~ hoed* father's hat; *dit is ~ huis* this is his house; *ieder het ~e geven* give every man his due

het **zijpad** /zɛipɑt/ (pl: -en) side path

de **zijrivier** /zɛirivir/ (pl: -en) tributary

het/de **zijspan** /zɛispɑn/ (pl: -nen) sidecar

de **zijspiegel** /zɛispiɣəl/ (pl: -s) wing mirror

het **zijspoor** /zɛispor/ (pl: zijsporen) siding: *iem. op een ~ brengen (zetten)* put s.o. on the sidelines; sideline s.o.

de **zijstraat** /zɛistrat/ (pl: -straten) side street: *ik noem maar een ~* just to give an example

de **zijtak** /zɛitɑk/ (pl: -ken) **1** side branch **2** branch

zijwaarts /zɛiwarts/ (adj, adv) sideward, sideways

de **zijweg** /zɛiwɛɣ/ (pl: -en) side road

de **zijwind** /zɛiwɪnt/ (pl: -en) side wind, crosswind

het **zikavirus** /zikavirʏs/ Zika virus

zilt /zɪlt/ (adj) [form] salt(y); briny

het **zilver** /zɪlvər/ silver

het/de **zilverdraad** /zɪlvərdrat/ **1** silver wire **2** silver thread

zilveren /zɪlvərə(n)/ (adj) **1** silver **2** silver(y)

zilverkleurig /zɪlvərklørəɣ/ (adj) silver(y)(-coloured)

de **zilvermeeuw** /zɪlvərmew/ (pl: -en) herring gull

het **zilverpapier** /zɪlvərpapir/ silver paper, silver foil

de **zilversmid** /zɪlvərsmɪt/ (pl: -smeden) silversmith

de **zilverspar** /zɪlvərspɑr/ (pl: -ren) silver fir

het **zilveruitje** /zɪlvərœycə/ (pl: -s) pearl onion, cocktail onion

de **zilvervliesrijst** /zɪlvərvlisrɛɪst/ brown rice

de **Zimbabwaan** /zɪmbɑpwaːn/ (pl: Zimbabwanen) Zimbabwean

Zimbabwaans /zɪmbɑpwaːns/ (adj) Zimbabwean

Zimbabwe /zɪmbɑpwə/ Zimbabwe

de **zin** /zɪn/ (pl: -nen) **1** sentence **2** senses: *bij ~nen komen* come to; come to one's senses **3** mind: *zijn eigen ~ doen* do as one pleases; *zijn ~nen op iets zetten* set one's heart on sth. **4** liking: *ergens (geen) ~ in hebben* (not) feel like sth.; *het naar de ~ hebben* find sth. to one's liking; *~ of geen ~* whether you like it or not **5** sense, meaning: *in de letterlijke ~ van het woord* in the literal sense of the word **6** sense, point || *kwaad in de ~ hebben* be up to no good

zindelijk /zɪndələk/ (adj) toilet-trained; clean; house-trained

zingen /zɪŋə(n)/ (zong, heeft gezongen) sing: *zuiver* (or: *vals*) *~* sing in (or: out) of tune

de **zingeving** /zɪŋɣevɪŋ/ giving meaning (to)

het **zink** /zɪŋk/ zinc

¹zinken /zɪŋkə(n)/ (adj) zinc

²zinken /zɪŋkə(n)/ (zonk, is gezonken) sink: *diep gezonken zijn* have fallen low

de **zinkput** /zɪŋkpʏt/ (pl: -ten) cesspit, cesspool

zinloos /zɪnlos/ (adj, adv) **1** meaningless: *zinloos geweld* random violence **2** useless, futile: *het is ~ om ...* there's no sense (or: point) (in) ...(-ing)

de **zinloosheid** /zɪnloshɛit/ **1** meaninglessness **2** uselessness

het **zinnebeeld** /zɪnəbelt/ (pl: -en) symbol

zinnelijk /zɪnələk/ (adj, adv) sensual

zinnen /zɪnə(n)/ (zinde, heeft gezind): *dat zinde haar helemaal niet* she did not like that at all; *op wraak ~* be intent (or: bent) on revenge

zinnenprikkelend /zɪnə(n)prɪkələnt/ (adj) titillating

zinnig /zɪnəɣ/ (adj) sensible: *het is moeilijk daar iets ~s over te zeggen* it's hard to say anything meaningful about that

de **zinsbegoocheling** /zɪnzbəɣoxəlɪŋ/ (pl: -en) illusion

de **zinsbouw** /zɪnzbau/ sentence structure

het **zinsdeel** /zɪnzdel/ (pl: -delen) part (of a, the sentence); tag

de **zinsnede** /zɪnsnedə/ (pl: -n) phrase

de **zinsontleding** /zɪnsɔntledɪŋ/ (pl: -en) parsing (down to the level of the clause)

zinspelen /zɪnspelə(n)/ (zinspeelde, heeft gezinspeeld) allude (to), hint (at)

de **zinspeling** /zɪnspelɪŋ/ (pl: -en) allusion (to), hint

het **zinsverband** /zɪnsfərbɑnt/ context

het **zintuig** /zɪntœyx/ (pl: -en) sense

zintuiglijk /zɪntœyxlək/ (adj, adv) sensual, sensory

zinvol /zɪnvɔl/ (adj) significant; advisable; a

good idea

het **zionisme** /zijonɪsmə/ Zionism

het **zipbestand** /zɪbəstɑnt/ (pl: -en) zip file

zippen /zɪpə(n)/ (zipte, heeft gezipt) zip, pack, compress

de **zit** /zɪt/ sit

het **zitbad** /zɪdbɑt/ (pl: -en) hip bath

de **zitbank** /zɪdbɑŋk/ (pl: -en) sofa, settee

de **zithoek** /zɪthuk/ (pl: -en) sitting area

het **zitje** /zɪcə/ (pl: -s) **1** sit(-down); seat **2** table and chairs

de **zitkamer** /zɪtkamər/ (pl: -s) living room

de **zitplaats** /zɪtplats/ (pl: -en) seat

de **zit-slaapkamer** /zɪtslapkamər/ (pl: -s) bed-sitting-room; [Am] one-room apartment, studio apartment

zitten /zɪtə(n)/ (zat, heeft gezeten) **1** sit: *blijf* ~ **a)** stay sitting (down); **b)** remain seated; *~ blijven* repeat a year; *gaan* ~ **a)** sit down; **b)** take a seat; *zit je goed? (lekker?)* are you comfortable?; *aan de koffie* ~ be having coffee; *waar zit hij toch?* where can he be?; *ernaast* ~ be wrong, be out; be off (target); *wij ~ nog midden in de examens* we are still in the middle of the exams; *zonder benzine* ~ be out of petrol; *(bijna) zonder geld* ~ have run short of money **2** be: *op een kantoor* ~ be (or: work) in an office **3** fit: *goed* ~ be a good fit **4** be (... -ing), sit (... -ing): *we ~ te eten* we are having dinner (or: lunch); *in zijn eentje ~ zingen* sit singing to o.s. ‖ *met iets blijven* ~ be left (or: stuck) with sth.; *laat maar* ~ that's all right; (let's) forget it; *hij heeft zijn vrouw laten* ~ he has left his wife (in the lurch); *met iets* ~ be at a loss (what to do) about sth.; *hoe zit het (dan) met ...?* what about ... (then)?; [sport] *de bal zit* it's a goal!, it has (gone) in!, it's in the back of the net!; *het blijft niet* ~ it won't stay put; *hoe zit dat in elkaar?* how does it (all) fit together?; how does that work?; *daar zit wat in* you (may) have sth. there; there's sth. in that; *onder de modder* ~ be covered with mud; *het zit er (dik) in* there's a good chance of (that (happening)); *eruit halen wat erin zit* make the most (out) of sth.; *dat zit wel goed (snor)* that will be all right; *alles zit hem mee* (or: *tegen*) everything is going his way (or: against him); *hij zit overal aan* he cannot leave anything alone; *achter de meisjes aan* ~ chase ((around) after) girls; *mijn taak zit er weer op* that's my job out of the way; *er al heel wat kilometers op hebben* ~ have many kilometres on the clock

de **zittenblijver** /zɪtə(n)blɛivər/ (pl: -s) repeater, pupil who stays down a class

zittend /zɪtənt/ (adj) **1** sitting, seated **2** sedentary **3** incumbent

de **zitting** /zɪtɪŋ/ (pl: -en) **1** seat **2** session, meeting

het **zitvlak** /zɪtflɑk/ (pl: -ken) seat, bottom

het **zitvlees** /zɪtfles/: *geen ~ hebben* not be able

to sit still

¹**zo** /zo/ (adv) **1** so, like this (or: that), this way, that way: *zó doe je dat!* that's the way you do it!; *zó is het!* that's the way it is!; *als dat zo is* ... if that's the case ...; *zo zijn er niet veel* there aren't many like that; *zo iets geks heb ik nog nooit gezien* I've never seen anything so crazy; *zij heeft er toch zo een hekel aan* she really hates it; *een jaar of zo* a year or so **2** as, so: *het is allemaal niet zo eenvoudig* it's not as simple as it seems (or: as all that); *half zo lang* (or: *groot*) half as long (or: big); *hij is niet zo oud als ik* he is not as old as I am; *zo goed als ik kon* as well as he could; *zo maar* just like that; without so much as a by-your-leave; *zo nu en dan* every now and then **3** right away: *ik ben zo terug* I'll be back right away; *zo juist* just now ‖ *het was maar zo zo* it was just so-so

²**zo** /zo/ (conj) if: *zo ja, waarom; zo nee, waarom niet* if so, why; if not, why not; *een van de grootste, zo niet de grootste* one of the greatest, if not the greatest; *je moet je huiswerk maken, zo niet, dan krijg je een aantekening* you must do your homework, otherwise you'll get a bad mark

³**zo** /zo/ (int) well, so: *goed zo, Jan!* well done, John!; *o zo!* so there; *zo, dat is dat* well (then), that's that; *mijn vrouw heeft een nieuwe computer aangeschaft! zo!* my wife has bought herself a new computer. Really?

het **zoab** /zowɑp/ porous asphalt

zoal /zoɑl/ (adv): *wat heeft hij ~ meegebracht?* what (kind of things) did he bring with him?

zoals /zoɑls/ (conj) like; as: *een meisje ~ jij* a girl like you; *~ gewoonlijk* as usual; *~ dat heet* as they call that; as they say; *~ je wilt* as (or: whatever) you like

¹**zodanig** /zodanəx/ (dem pron) such: *als ~* as such

²**zodanig** /zodanəx/ (adv) so (much)

zodat /zodɑt/ (conj) so (that), (so as) to: *ik zal het eens tekenen, ~ je kunt zien wat ik bedoel* I'll draw it so (that) you can see what I mean

de **zode** /zodə/ (pl: -n) turf: *dat zet geen ~n aan de dijk* that's no use, that won't get us anywhere

zodoende /zodundə/ (adv) (in) this, (in) that way; that's why, that's the reason

zodra /zodra/ (conj) as soon as: *~ ik geld heb, betaal ik u* I'll pay you as soon as I have the money; *~ hij opdaagt* the moment he shows up

zoek /zuk/ (adj) missing, gone: *~ raken* get lost ‖ *op* ~ *gaan (zijn) naar iets* look for sth.; *op* ~ *naar het geluk* in pursuit of happiness; *het eind is* ~ then there is no way out, then it's hopeless

de **zoekactie** /zukɑksi/ (pl: -s) search (operation)

zoeken /zu̱kə(n)/ (zocht, heeft gezocht) **1** look for, search for: *we moeten een **uitweg** ~* we've got to find a way out; *zoek je **iets**?* have you lost sth.?; *hij wordt gezocht (wegens diefstal)* he is wanted (for theft) **2** look for, search for, be after: *jij hebt hier **niets** te ~* you have no business (being) here; *zoiets had ik **achter** haar niet gezocht* I hadn't expected that of her

het **zoeklicht** /zu̱klɪxt/ (pl: -en) searchlight, spotlight

de **zoekmachine** /zu̱kmaʃinə/ (pl: -s) search engine

de **zoekmachineoptimalisatie** /zu̱kmaʃinəɔptimaliza(t)si/ search engine optimization

zoekmaken /zu̱kmakə(n)/ (maakte zoek, heeft zoekgemaakt) **1** mislay, lose **2** waste (on)

het **zoekplaatje** /zu̱kplacə/ (pl: -s) [roughly] (picture) puzzle

zoekraken /zu̱krakə(n)/ (raakte zoek, is zoekgeraakt) get mislaid, be misplaced

de **zoektocht** /zu̱ktoxt/ (pl: -en) search (for), quest (for)

de **Zoeloe** /zu̱lu/ (pl: -s) Zulu

zoemen /zu̱mə(n)/ (zoemde, heeft gezoemd) buzz

de **zoemer** /zu̱mər/ (pl: -s) buzzer

de **zoemtoon** /zu̱mton/ (pl: -tonen) buzz; hum; tone; signal

de **zoen** /zun/ (pl: -en) kiss

zoenen /zu̱nə(n)/ (zoende, heeft gezoend) kiss

zoet /zut/ (adj) **1** sweet: *lekker ~* nice and sweet **2** sweet, good: *iem. ~ **houden*** keep s.o. happy (*or:* quiet); *daar ben je nog wel even ~ **mee*** that will keep you busy for a while

de **zoetekauw** /zu̱təkau/ (pl: -en) sugar lover, s.o. with a sweet tooth

zoeten /zu̱tə(n)/ (zoette, heeft gezoet) sweeten

het **zoethoudertje** /zu̱thaudərcə/ (pl: -s) sop

het **zoethout** /zu̱thaut/ liquorice

zoetig /zu̱təx/ (adj) sweetish

de **zoetigheid** /zu̱təxhɛit/ (pl: -heden) sweet(s)

het **zoetje** /zu̱cə/ (pl: -s) sweetener

zoetsappig /zutsɑ̱pəx/ (adj, adv) namby-pamby, sugary

de **zoetstof** /zu̱tstɔf/ (pl: -fen) sweetener

het **¹zoetzuur** /zutsy̱r/ (sweet) pickles

²zoetzuur /zutsy̱r/ (adj) **1** slightly sour (*or:* sharp) **2** pickled; sweet-and-sour

zoeven /zu̱və(n)/ (zoefde, heeft/is gezoefd) whizz (past)

zo-even /zoe̱və(n)/ (adv) see *zojuist*

zogeheten /zoɣəhe̱tə(n)/ (adj, adv) so-called

zogen /zo̱ɣə(n)/ (zoogde, heeft gezoogd) breastfeed

zogenaamd /zoɣəna̱mt/ (adj, adv) so-called, would-be: *ze **was** ~ **verhinderd*** sth.

supposedly came up (to prevent her from coming)

zogezegd /zoɣəzɛ̱xt/ (adv) as it were, so to speak: *het **is** ~ een kwajongen* he's what you'd call a young brat

zo goed /zoɣu̱t/ (adv): *~ **als** ie kon* as well as he could; *~ **als** nieuw* as good as new; *~ **als** onmogelijk* virtually impossible; *~ **als** niemand* hardly anybody

zoiets /zo̱its/ (adv): *~ heb ik nog nooit gezien* I have never seen anything like it; *er is ook nog ~ als* there is such a thing as

zojuist /zojœ̱yst/ (adv) just (now)

¹zolang /zolɑŋ/ (adv) meanwhile, meantime

²zolang /zolɑ̱ŋ/ (conj) as long as: *(voor) ~ het **duurt*** [iron] as long as it lasts

de **zolder** /zɔ̱ldər/ (pl: -s) attic, loft

de **zoldering** /zɔ̱ldərɪŋ/ (pl: -en) see *zolder*

de **zolderkamer** /zɔ̱ldərkamər/ (pl: -s) attic room, room in the loft

de **zoldertrap** /zɔ̱ldərtrɑp/ (pl: -pen) attic stairs (*or:* ladder)

zomaar /zo̱mar/ (adv) just (like that), without (any) warning: *~ **ineens** suddenly; **waarom** doe je dat? ~* why do you do that? just for the fun of it

de **zombie** /zɔ̱mbi/ (pl: -s) zombie

de **zomer** /zo̱mər/ (pl: -s) summer: *van (in) de ~* in the summer

de **zomeravond** /zo̱məravɔnt/ (pl: -en) summer('s) evening

de **zomerdag** /zo̱mərdɑx/ (pl: -en) summer('s) day

zomers /zo̱mərs/ (adj) summery

de **zomerspelen** /zo̱mərspelə(n)/ (pl) summer games: *de **Olympische** Zomerspelen* the Summer Olympics

de **zomertijd** /zo̱mərtɛit/ summer(time); summer time

de **zomervakantie** /zo̱mərvakɑnsi/ (pl: -s) summer holiday

zomin /zomɪ̱n/ (adv): *net ~ **als*** no more than; *ik weet het net ~ **als** jij* your guess is as good as mine

de **zon** /zɔn/ (pl: -nen) sun: *de ~ **gaat op** (or: **gaat onder**)* the sun is rising (*or:* setting); *er is niets nieuws **onder** de ~* there is nothing new under the sun; *in de **volle** ~* right in the sun; *af en toe ~* sunny periods

zo'n /zɔn/ (dem pron) **1** such (a): *in ~ **geval** zou ik niet gaan* I wouldn't go if that were the case **2** such (a): *ik heb ~ **slaap*** I am so sleepy **3** just like **4** about **5** one of those || *~ **beetje*** more or less; *ik vind haar ~ **meid*** I think she's a terrific girl

de **zonaanbidder** /zɔ̱nambɪdər/ (pl: -s) sun-worshipper

de **zondaar** /zɔ̱ndar/ (pl: -s) sinner

de **zondag** /zɔ̱ndax/ (pl: -en) Sunday

¹zondags /zɔ̱ndɑxs/ (adj) Sunday

²zondags /zɔ̱ndɑxs/ (adv) on Sundays

het **zondagskind** /zɔndɑxskɪnt/ (pl: -eren) Sunday's child

de **zondagsrust** /zɔndɑxsrʏst/ Sunday('s) rest

de **zondagsschool** /zɔndɑxsxol/ (pl: -scholen) Sunday school

de **zonde** /zɔndə/ (pl: -n) **1** sin **2** shame: *het zou ~ van je tijd zijn* it would be a waste of time

de **zondebok** /zɔndəbɔk/ (pl: -ken) scapegoat, whipping boy
zonder /zɔndər/ (prep) without || *~ meer* just like that; of course; without delay

de **zonderling** /zɔndərlɪŋ/ (pl: -en) strange character, odd character

de **zondeval** /zɔndəval/ fall
zondig /zɔndəx/ (adj, adv) sinful
zondigen /zɔndəɣə(n)/ (zondigde, heeft gezondigd) sin

de **zondvloed** /zɔntflut/ Flood

de **zone** /zoːnə/ (pl: -s) zone; belt

het **zonenummer** /zoːnənʏmər/ (pl: -s) [Belg] area code
zonet /zɔnɛt/ (adv) [inform] just (now): *hij is ~ thuisgekomen* he('s) just got home (now)

de **zonkracht** /zɔnkrɑxt/ UV index

het **zonlicht** /zɔnlɪxt/ sunlight
zonnebaden /zɔnəbadə(n)/ (zonnebaadde, heeft gezonnebaad) sunbathe

de **zonnebank** /zɔnəbɑŋk/ (pl: -en) sunbed, solarium

de **zonnebloem** /zɔnəblum/ (pl: -en) sunflower

de **zonnebrand** /zɔnəbrɑnt/ **1** sunburn **2** sun(tan) lotion (*or:* cream); sunscreen

de **zonnebrandcrème** /zɔnəbrɑntoli/ sun(tan) lotion (*or:* cream); sunscreen

de **zonnebril** /zɔnəbrɪl/ (pl: -len) (pair of) sunglasses

de **zonnecel** /zɔnəsɛl/ (pl: -len) solar cell

de **zonnecollector** /zɔnəkɔlɛktor/ (pl: -s, -en) solar collector

de **zonne-energie** /zɔnəenɛrʒi/ solar energy

de **zonnehemel** /zɔnəheməl/ (pl: -s) sunbed
zonneklaar /zɔnəklaːr/ (adj) obvious

de **zonneklep** /zɔnəklɛp/ (pl: -pen) (sun) visor
zonnen /zɔnə(n)/ (zonde, heeft gezond) sunbathe

het **zonnepaneel** /zɔnəpanel/ (pl: -panelen) solar panel

het **zonnescherm** /zɔnəsxɛrm/ (pl: -en) (sun)blind; parasol

de **zonneschijn** /zɔnəsxɛin/ sunshine

de **zonneslag** /zɔnəslɑx/ (pl: -en) sunstroke

de **zonnesteek** /zɔnəstek/ (pl: -steken) sunstroke: *een ~ krijgen* get sunstroke

het **zonnestelsel** /zɔnəstɛlsəl/ (pl: -s) solar system

de **zonnestraal** /zɔnəstral/ (pl: -stralen) ray of sun(shine)

het **zonnetje** /zɔnəcə/ (pl: -s) **1** little sun; [fig] little sunshine: [fig] *ze is het ~ in huis* she is our little sunshine **2** sun(shine): *in het ~ zitten* sit in the sun; *iem. in het ~ zetten* make s.o. the centre of attention || *lopen als een ~* run like a dream

de **zonnewijzer** /zɔnəwɛizər/ (pl: -s) sundial
zonnig /zɔnəx/ (adj) sunny: *een ~e toekomst* a bright future

de **zonsondergang** /zɔnsɔndərɣɑŋ/ (pl: -en) sunset

de **zonsopgang** /zɔnsɔpxɑŋ/ (pl: -en) sunrise

de **zonsverduistering** /zɔnsfərdœystərɪŋ/ (pl: -en) eclipse of the sun

de **zonwering** /zɔnwerɪŋ/ awning, sunblind; (venetian) blind

de **zoo** /zo/ (pl: -s) zoo

het **zoogdier** /zoɣdir/ (pl: -en) mammal

de **zooi** /zoj/ (pl: -en) [inform] **1** mess **2** heap, load

het **zooitje** /zojcə/ *see zootje*

de **zool** /zol/ (pl: zolen) **1** sole **2** insole

de **zoölogie** /zooloɣi/ zoology
zoölogisch /zooloɣis/ (adj) zoological

de **zoom** /zom/ (pl: zomen) **1** hem **2** edge

de **zoomlens** /zumlɛns/ (pl: -lenzen) zoom lens

de **zoon** /zon/ (pl: zonen, -s) son: *Angelo is de jongste ~* Angelo is the youngest (*or:* younger) son; *de oudste ~* **a)** the oldest son; **b)** the elder son; **c)** the eldest son; *de verloren ~* the Prodigal Son

het **zootje** /zocə/ (pl: -s) [inform] **1** heap, load: *het hele ~* the whole lot; *een ~ ongeregeld* a mixed bag; a motley crew **2** mess

de **zorg** /zɔrx/ (pl: -en) **1** care, concern: *iets met ~ behandelen* handle sth. carefully **2** concern, worry: *geen ~en hebben* have no worries; *dat is een (hele) ~ minder* that's (quite) a relief; *zich ~en maken over* worry about; *'t zal mij een ~ wezen, mij een ~* I couldn't care less; *dat is van later ~* we'll worry about that later
zorgelijk /zɔrɣələk/ (adj) worrisome, alarming
zorgeloos /zɔrɣəlos/ (adj, adv) carefree

de **zorgeloosheid** /zɔrɣəlosheit/ freedom from care (*or:* worry)
zorgen /zɔrɣə(n)/ (zorgde, heeft gezorgd) **1** see to, take care of; provide; supply: *voor het eten ~* see to the food; *daar moet jij voor ~* that's your job **2** care for, look after, take care of **3** see (to), take care (to)

het **zorgenkind** /zɔrɣə(n)kɪnt/ (pl: -eren) problem child; source of concern

de **zorgplicht** /zɔrxplɪxt/ duty to provide for

de **zorgsector** /zɔrxsɛktor/ (pl: -s, -en) social service sector

de **zorgtoeslag** /zɔrxtuslɑx/ [Dutch] health care allowance

het **zorgverlof** /zɔrxfərlɔf/ care leave

de **zorgverzekeraar** /zɔrxfərzekəraːr/ (pl: -s) health insurer, health insurance company

de **zorgverzekering** /zɔrxfərzekərɪŋ/ (pl: -en) health insurance, medical insurance
zorgvuldig /zɔrxfʏldəx/ (adj, adv) careful,

meticulous, painstaking: *een ~ onderzoek* a careful (*or:* thorough) examination

de **zorgvuldigheid** /zɔrχfɤldəχhɛit/ care, carefulness, precision

zorgwekkend /zɔrχwɛkənt/ (adj) worrisome, alarming: *zijn toestand is ~* his condition is worrying

zorgzaam /zɔrχsam/ (adj, adv) careful, considerate: *een ~ huisvader* a caring father

de **¹zot** /zɔt/ fool, idiot

²zot /zɔt/ (adj, adv) crazy, idiotic; silly

het **¹zout** /zɑut/ (pl: -en) (common) salt

²zout /zɑut/ (adj) **1** salty **2** salted

zoutarm /zɑutɑrm/ (adj) low-salt

zouteloos /zɑutəlos/ (adj) insipid, flat, dull

zouten /zɑutə(n)/ (zoutte, heeft gezouten) salt

het **zoutje** /zɑucə/ (pl: -s) salt(y) biscuit, cocktail biscuit: *Japanse ~s* Japanese rice crackers, senbei

zoutloos /zɑutlos/ (adj) salt-free

de **zoutzak** /zɑutsɑk/ (pl: -ken) salt-bag: *hij zakte als een ~ in elkaar* he collapsed (like a burst balloon)

het **zoutzuur** /zɑutsyr/ hydrochloric acid

zoveel /zovel/ (num) **1** as much, as many: *net ~* just as much (*or:* many); *dat is tweemaal ~* that's twice as much (*or:* many) **2** so, that much (*or:* many): *om de ~ dagen* every so many days; *niet zóveel* not (as much as) that

zoveelste /zovelstə/ (num) such-and-such; umpteenth

¹zover /zovɛr/ (adv) so far, this far, that far: *ben je ~?* (are you) ready?; *het is ~* the time has come, here we go!; *~ zijn we nog niet* we haven't reached that stage yet, that is still a long way off

²zover /zovɛr/ (conj) as far: *voor ~ ik weet niet* not to my knowledge, not that I know of; *in ~re* insofar, insomuch

zowaar /zowar/ (adv) actually

zowat /zowɑt/ (adv) [inform] almost: *ze zijn ~ even groot* they're about the same height

zowel /zowɛl/ (adv) both, as well as: *~ de mannen als de vrouwen* both the men and the women; the men as well as the women

z.o.z. /zɛtozɛt/ *zie ommezijde* p.t.o., please turn over

zozeer /zozer/ (adv) so much (so): *dat niet ~* not that so much, not so much that; *~ dat ...* so much so that ...

zozo /zozo/ (adv) so-so

z.s.m. *zo spoedig mogelijk* asap, as soon as possible

de **zucht** /zyχt/ (pl: -en) **1** desire, longing, craving **2** sigh: *een diepe ~ slaken* heave a deep sigh; *een ~ van verlichting slaken* breathe (*or:* heave) a sigh of relief

zuchten /zyχtə(n)/ (zuchtte, heeft gezucht) sigh

zuid /zœyt/ (adj, adv) south, south(ern); southerly

Zuid-Afrika /zœytafrika/ South Africa

de **Zuid-Afrikaan** /zœytafrikan/ (pl: Zuid-Afrikanen) South African

het **¹Zuid-Afrikaans** /zœytafrikans/ Afrikaans

²Zuid-Afrikaans /zœytafrikans/ (adj) **1** South African **2** Afrikaans

Zuid-Amerika /zœytamerika/ South America

de **Zuid-Amerikaan** /zœytamerikan/ (pl: Zuid-Amerikanen) South American

Zuid-Amerikaans /zœytamerikans/ (adj) South American

¹zuidelijk /zœydələk/ (adj) **1** southern **2** south(ern); southerly

²zuidelijk /zœydələk/ (adv) (to the) south, southerly, southwards

het **zuiden** /zœydə(n)/ south: *ten ~ (van)* (to the) south (of)

de **zuidenwind** /zœydə(n)wɪnt/ (pl: -en) south (*or:* southern, southerly) wind

de **zuiderbreedte** /zœydərbretə/ southern latitude: *op 4° ~* at a latitude of 4° South

de **zuiderburen** /zœydərbyrə(n)/ (pl) neighbours to the south

de **zuiderkeerkring** /zœydərkerkrɪŋ/ tropic of Capricorn

Zuid-Europa /zœytøropa/ Southern Europe

Zuid-Europees /zœytøropes/ (adj) Southern European

Zuid-Holland /zœythɔlɑnt/ South Holland

Zuid-Hollands /zœythɔlɑnts/ (adj) South Holland

Zuid-Korea /zœytkoreja/ South Korea

de **Zuid-Koreaan** /zœytkorejan/ (pl: Zuid-Koreanen) South Korean

Zuid-Koreaans /zœytkorejans/ (adj) South Korean

de **zuidkust** /zœytkʏst/ (pl: -en) south(ern) coast

¹zuidoost /zœytost/ (adj) south-east(ern); south-easterly

²zuidoost /zœytost/ (adv) south-east(wards), to the south-east

Zuidoost-Azië /zœytostazijə/ South-East Asia

¹zuidoostelijk /zœytostələk/ (adj) south-east(ern); south-easterly

²zuidoostelijk /zœytostələk/ (adv) (to the) south-east, south-easterly

het **zuidoosten** /zœytostə(n)/ south-east; South-East

de **zuidpool** /zœytpol/ South Pole

de **Zuidpool** /zœytpol/ Antarctic

de **zuidpoolcirkel** /zœytpolsɪrkəl/ Antarctic Circle

het **zuidpoolgebied** /zœytpolɣəbit/ Antarctic, South Pole

Zuid-Sudan /zœytsudan/ South Sudan

de **¹Zuid-Sudanees** /zœytsudan<u>ε</u>s/ (pl: Zuid-Sudanezen) South Sudanese

²Zuid-Sudanees (adj) South Sudanese

de **zuidvrucht** /z<u>œ</u>ytfrʏχt/ (pl: -en) subtropical fruit

¹zuidwaarts /z<u>œ</u>ytwarts/ (adj) southward, southerly

²zuidwaarts /z<u>œ</u>ytwarts/ (adv) south-(wards)

¹zuidwest /zœytw<u>ε</u>st/ (adj) south-west(ern); south-westerly

²zuidwest /zœytw<u>ε</u>st/ (adv) south-west-(wards), to the south-west

¹zuidwestelijk /zœytw<u>ε</u>stələk/ (adj) south-west(ern); south-westerly

²zuidwestelijk /zœytw<u>ε</u>stələk/ (adv) (to the) south-west, south-westerly, south-west-wards

het **zuidwesten** /zœytw<u>ε</u>stə(n)/ south-west; South-West

de **zuidwester** /zœytw<u>ε</u>stər/ (pl: -s) **1** south-wester **2** sou'wester

de **Zuidzee** /z<u>œ</u>ytse/: de **Stille** ~ the Pacific (Ocean)

de **zuigeling** /z<u>œ</u>yɣəlɪŋ/ (pl: -en) infant, baby

¹zuigen /z<u>œ</u>yɣə(n)/ (zoog, heeft gezogen) suck (on, away at)

²zuigen /z<u>œ</u>yɣə(n)/ (zoog, heeft gezogen) **1** suck; nurse **2** vacuum, hoover

de **zuiger** /z<u>œ</u>yɣər/ (pl: -s) piston

de **zuigfles** /z<u>œ</u>yχflεs/ (pl: -sen) feeding bottle

de **zuiging** /z<u>œ</u>yɣɪŋ/ (pl: -en) suction

de **zuigkracht** /z<u>œ</u>yχkrɑχt/ **1** suction (power, force) **2** attraction

de **zuignap** /z<u>œ</u>yχnɑp/ (pl: -pen) sucker

het/de **zuigtablet** /z<u>œ</u>yχtablεt/ (pl: -ten) lozenge

de **zuil** /zœyl/ (pl: -en) pillar, column, pile

zuinig /z<u>œ</u>ynəχ/ (adj, adv) **1** economical, frugal, thrifty; sparing: ~ **op** iets zijn be careful about sth. **2** economical; efficient: een motor ~ **afstellen** tune (up) an engine to run efficiently; een ~e **auto** a fuel-efficient car

de **zuinigheid** /z<u>œ</u>ynəχhεit/ economy, frugality, thrift(iness)

¹zuipen /z<u>œ</u>ypə(n)/ (zoop, heeft gezopen) [inform] booze ǁ zich **zat** ~ get sloshed (or: plastered)

²zuipen /z<u>œ</u>ypə(n)/ (zoop, heeft gezopen) [inform] drink: die auto zuipt **benzine** that car just eats up petrol

de **zuiplap** /z<u>œ</u>yplɑp/ (pl: -pen) [inform] boozer, drunk(ard)

de **zuippartij** /z<u>œ</u>ypɑrtεi/ (pl: -en) [inform] drinking bout (or: spree)

het/de **zuivel** /z<u>œ</u>yvəl/ dairy produce/products

de **zuivelfabriek** /z<u>œ</u>yvəlfabrik/ (pl: -en) dairy factory, creamery

het **zuivelproduct** /z<u>œ</u>yvəlprodʏkt/ (pl: -en) dairy product

¹zuiver /z<u>œ</u>yvər/ (adj) **1** pure: van ~ **leer** genuine leather **2** clear, clean, pure **3** correct,

true, accurate: een ~ **schot** an accurate shot

²zuiver /z<u>œ</u>yvər/ (adv) **1** purely **2** [mus] in tune

zuiveren /z<u>œ</u>yvərə(n)/ (zuiverde, heeft gezuiverd) clean, purify; clear; cleanse: de **lucht** ~ clear the air; zich ~ van een verdenking clear o.s. of a suspicion

de **zuiverheid** /z<u>œ</u>yvərhεit/ purity; soundness; accuracy

de **zuivering** /z<u>œ</u>yvərɪŋ/ (pl: -en) **1** purification **2** [pol] purge, purging: etnische ~ ethnic cleansing

de **zuiveringsinstallatie** /z<u>œ</u>yvərɪŋsɪnstala(t)si/ (pl: -s) purification plant; sewage-treatment plant

¹zulk /zʏlk/ (dem pron) such: ~e **mensen** people like that; ~e **zijn** er ook that kind also exists

²zulk /zʏlk/ (adv) such: het zijn ~e **lieve** mensen they're such nice people

zullen /zʏlə(n)/ (aux vb, zou) **1** shall; will; should; would: maar het zou nog erger **worden** but worse was yet to come; dat zul je nu altijd **zien!** isn't that (just) typical!; **wat** zou dat? so what?, what's that to you? **2** will, would, be going (or: about) to: zou je **denken?** do you think (so)?; als ik het kon, zou ik het **doen** I would (do it) if I could; hij zou fraude **gepleegd hebben** he is said to have committed fraud; dat zal vorig jaar **geweest zijn** that would be (or: must have been) last year; wie zal het **zeggen?** who's to say?, who can say?; zou hij ziek **zijn?** can he be ill? (or: sick?); dat zal **wel** I bet it is; I suppose it will; I dare say

de **zult** /zʏlt/ [Dutch] brawn; [Am] headcheese

de **zuring** /zyrɪŋ/ sorrel

de **¹zus** /zʏs/ (pl: -sen) sister; sis

²zus /zʏs/ (adv) so: mijnheer ~ of **zo** Mr so-and-so, Mr something-or-other

het **zusje** /zʏʃə/ (pl: -s) sister, sis; little sister

de **zuster** /zʏstər/ (pl: -s) **1** sister **2** [Dutch] nurse

de **zusterstad** /zʏstərstɑt/ (pl: -steden) twin town

het **¹zuur** /zyr/ (pl: zuren) **1** acid **2** [roughly] pickles; pickled vegetables (or: onions) **3** heartburn, acidity (of the stomach)

²zuur /zyr/ (adj, adv) **1** sour: de **melk** is ~ the milk has turned sour **2** acid

de **zuurkool** /zyrkol/ sauerkraut

de **zuurpruim** /zyrprœym/ (pl: -en) sourpuss, crab (apple)

de **zuurstof** /zyrstɔf/ oxygen

het **zuurstofmasker** /zyrstɔfmɑskər/ (pl: -s) oxygen mask

de **zuurstok** /zyrstɔk/ (pl: -ken) stick of rock

de **zuurtegraad** /zyrtəɣrat/ (degree of) acidity

het **zuurtje** /zyrcə/ (pl: -s) acid drop

zuurverdiend /zyrvərdint/ (adj) hard-earned

de **zwaai** /zwaj/ (pl: -en) swing, sweep; sway; wave

de **zwaaideur** /zwajdør/ (pl: -en) swing-door

zwaaien /zwajə(n)/ (zwaaide, heeft/is gezwaaid) swing, sway; wave; flourish; brandish; wield: **met** zijn armen ~ wave one's arms || er zal **wat** ~ there'll be the devil to pay

het **zwaailicht** /zwajlɪχt/ (pl: -en) flashing light

de **zwaan** /zwan/ (pl: zwanen) swan

het **zwaantje** /zwancə/ [Belg] motorcycle policeman

¹**zwaar** /zwar/ (adj, adv) **1** heavy, rough; full-bodied, strong: dat is tien **kilo** ~ that weighs ten kilos; ~der **worden** put on (or: gain) weight; twee pond **te** ~ two pounds overweight (or: too heavy) **2** difficult, hard: zware **ademhaling** hard breathing, wheezing; een zware **bevalling** a difficult delivery; een ~ **examen** a stiff (or: difficult) exam; hij **heeft** het ~ he is having a hard time of it **3** heavy, serious: ~ **verlies** a heavy loss **4** heavy; deep

²**zwaar** /zwar/ (adv) heavily, heavy, hard, seriously, badly: ~ **gewond** badly (or: seriously, severely) wounded || ergens te ~ aan **tillen** attach too much importance to sth., make heavy weather of sth.; het ~ te pakken hebben **a)** have it bad(ly); **b)** have a bad case

zwaarbeladen /zwarbəladə(n)/ (adj) heavy laden, heavily laden

zwaarbewolkt /zwarbəwɔlkt/ (adj) overcast

het **zwaard** /zwart/ (pl: -en) sword

de **zwaardvis** /zwartfɪs/ (pl: -sen) swordfish

zwaargebouwd /zwarɣəbaut/ (adj) heavily built; heavy-set; large-boned, thickset

zwaargewapend /zwarɣəwapənt/ (adj) heavily armed

de ¹**zwaargewicht** /zwarɣəwɪχt/ [boxer] heavyweight

het ²**zwaargewicht** /zwarɣəwɪχt/ heavyweight

zwaargewond /zwarɣəwɔnt/ (adj) badly, seriously wounded (or: injured)

zwaarmoedig /zwarmudəχ/ (adj) melancholy, depressed: ~ **kijken** look melancholy (or: depressed)

de **zwaarmoedigheid** /zwarmudəχhɛit/ **1** depressiveness, melancholy **2** melancholia; depression **3** melancholy, gloom, dejection

de **zwaarte** /zwartə/ **1** heaviness, weight **2** weight, size, strength

de **zwaartekracht** /zwartəkrɑχt/ gravity, gravitation

het **zwaartepunt** /zwartəpʏnt/ centre, central point, main point

zwaarwegend /zwarweɣənt/ (adj) weighty, important

zwaarwichtig /zwarwɪχtəχ/ (adj, adv) weighty, ponderous

de **zwabber** /zwɑbər/ (pl: -s) mop

zwabberen /zwɑbərə(n)/ (zwabberde, heeft gezwabberd) **1** mop **2** deviate: [fig]

een ~d **beleid** an erratic policy

de **zwachtel** /zwɔχtəl/ (pl: -s) bandage

de **zwager** /zwaɣər/ (pl: -s) [Dutch] brother-in-law

zwak /zwɑk/ (adj, adv) **1** weak, feeble: de zieke is nog ~ **op** zijn benen the patient is still shaky on his legs **2** weak; delicate: een ~ke **gezondheid** hebben be in poor health **3** weak, poor, bad: ~ zijn **in** iets be bad (or: poor) at sth., be weak in sth. **4** weak, vulnerable **5** weak, insubstantial; poor **6** weak, faint || een ~ **voor** iem. hebben have a soft (or: tender) spot for s.o.

zwakalcoholisch /zwɑkɑlkohoʊlis/ (adj) undistilled: ~e **dranken** undistilled alcoholic beverages, beers and wines

zwakbegaafd /zwɑɡbəɣaft/ (adj) retarded

de **zwakheid** /zwɑkhɛit/ (pl: -heden) weakness, failing

de **zwakkeling** /zwɑkəlɪŋ/ (pl: -en) weakling

de **zwakstroom** /zwɑkstrom/ low-voltage current, weak current

de **zwakte** /zwɑktə/ (pl: -s, -n) see zwakheid

zwakzinnig /zwɑksɪnəχ/ (adj) mentally handicapped

de **zwakzinnigheid** /zwɑksɪnəχhɛit/ mental defectiveness (or: deficiency)

zwalken /zwɑlkə(n)/ (zwalkte, heeft gezwalkt) **1** drift about, wander **2** waver, keep changing one's mind: een ~d **beleid** an incoherent (or: inconsistent) policy

de **zwaluw** /zwalyw/ (pl: -en) swallow: één ~ maakt nog geen zomer one swallow does not make a summer

de **zwam** /zwɑm/ (pl: -men) fungus

zwammen /zwɑmə(n)/ (zwamde, heeft gezwamd) [inform] drivel, jabber

de **zwamneus** /zwɑmnøs/ (pl: -neuzen) [inform] gasbag, windbag

de **zwanenhals** /zwanə(n)hɑls/ (pl: -halzen) U-trap, gooseneck

de **zwanenzang** /zwanə(n)zɑŋ/ swan song

de **zwang** /zwɑŋ/: **in** ~ zijn be in vogue, be fashionable, be in fashion

zwanger /zwɑŋər/ (adj) pregnant, expecting

de **zwangerschap** /zwɑŋərsχɑp/ (pl: -pen) pregnancy

de **zwangerschapsgymnastiek** /zwɑŋərsχɑpsχɪmnɑstik/ antenatal exercises

de **zwangerschapsonderbreking** /zwɑŋərsχɑpsondərbrekɪŋ/ (pl: -en) termination of pregnancy, abortion

de **zwangerschapstest** /zwɑŋərsχɑpstɛst/ (pl: -s) pregnancy test

het **zwangerschapsverlof** /zwɑŋərsχɑpsfərlof/ maternity leave

zwart /zwɑrt/ (adj, adv) **1** black, dark: een ~ **bladzijde** in de geschiedenis a black page in history; ~e **goederen** black-market goods **2** black, dirty || ~ **op** wit in writing, in black and white

het **zwartboek** /zwɑrdbuk/ (pl: -en) black book

de **zwartepiet** /zwɑrtəpit/ (pl: -en): *elkaar de ~ toespelen* (try to) blame each other; *iem. de ~ toespelen* pass the buck to s.o.

zwartgallig /zwɑrtχɑləχ/ (adj) melancholic, morbid

de **zwarthandelaar** /zwɑrthɑndəlɑr/ (pl: -s, -handelaren) black marketeer, profiteer

zwartkijken /zwɑrtkɛɪkə(n)/ (keek zwart, heeft zwartgekeken) **1** [historical] evade paying the TV licence **2** be pessimistic, see everything black

de **zwartkijker** /zwɑrtkɛikər/ (pl: -s) pessimist, worrywart

zwartmaken /zwɑrtmakə(n)/ (maakte zwart, heeft zwartgemaakt): *iem. ~* blacken s.o.'s good name (*or:* s.o.'s character)

zwart-op-wit /zwɑrtɔpwɪt/ (adv) in black and white, in writing

zwartrijden /zwɑrtrɛidə(n)/ (reed zwart, heeft zwartgereden) **1** evade paying road tax; [Am] evade paying highway tax **2** dodge paying the fare

de **zwartrijder** /zwɑrtrɛidər/ (pl: -s) **1** road-tax dodger **2** fare-dodger

het **zwartwerk** /zwɑrtwɛrk/ moonlighting

zwartwerken /zwɑrtwɛrkə(n)/ (werkte zwart, heeft zwartgewerkt) moonlight, work on the side

zwart-wit /zwɑrtwɪt/ (adv) black-and-white

de **zwavel** /zwavəl/ sulphur

het **zwaveldioxide** /zwavəldijɔksidə/ sulphur dioxide

het **¹zwavelzuur** /zwavəlzyr/ sulphuric acid

²zwavelzuur /zwavəlzyr/ (adj) sulphuric acid

Zweden /zwedə(n)/ Sweden

de **Zweed** /zwet/ (pl: Zweden) Swede, Swedish woman

het **¹Zweeds** /zwets/ Swedish

²Zweeds /zwets/ (adj) Swedish

de **zweefduik** /zwevdœyk/ (pl: -en) [sport] swallow dive; [Am] swan dive

de **zweefmolen** /zwefmolə(n)/ (pl: -s) whirligig

de **zweeftrein** /zweftrɛɪn/ levitation train, maglev train

zweefvliegen /zwefliyə(n)/ (zweefvliegde, heeft gezweefvliegd) glide

de **zweefvlieger** /zwefliyər/ (pl: -s) glider pilot

het **zweefvliegtuig** /zwefliχtœyχ/ (pl: -en) glider

de **zweefvlucht** /zweflyχt/ (pl: -en) glide

de **zweem** /zwem/ trace, hint: *zonder een ~ van twijfel* without a shadow of a doubt

de **zweep** /zwep/ (pl: zwepen) whip, lash; crop

de **zweepslag** /zwepslɑχ/ (pl: -en) **1** lash, whip(lash) **2** whiplash (injury)

de **zweer** /zwer/ (pl: zweren) ulcer; abscess; boil

het **zweet** /zwet/ sweat: *het ~ breekt hem uit* he's in a (cold) sweat; *baden in het ~* swelter

de **zweetband** /zwedbɑnt/ (pl: -en) sweatband

de **zweetdruppel** /zwedrʏpəl/ (pl: -s) drop (*or:* bead) of sweat

de **zweethanden** /zwethɑndə(n)/ (pl) sweaty hands

de **zweetlucht** /zwetlʏχt/ body odour

de **zweetvoeten** /zwetfutə(n)/ (pl) sweaty feet

zwelgen /zwɛlyə(n)/ (zwolg/zwelgde, heeft gezwolgen) wallow

zwellen /zwɛlə(n)/ (zwol, is gezwollen) swell: *doen ~* **a)** swell; **b)** belly, billow; **c)** bulge

de **zwelling** /zwɛlɪŋ/ (pl: -en) swell(ing)

het **zwembad** /zwɛmbɑt/ (pl: -en) (swimming) pool

de **zwemband** /zwɛmbɑnt/ (pl: -en) water ring

het **zwembandje** /zwɛmbɑncə/ (pl: -s) [hum] spare tyre, love handles

de **zwembroek** /zwɛmbruk/ (pl: -en) bathing trunks, swimming trunks

het **zwemdiploma** /zwɛmdiploma/ (pl: -'s) swimming certificate

zwemen /zwemə(n)/ (zweemde, heeft gezweemd) incline to, tend to

de **zwemles** /zwɛmlɛs/ (pl: -sen) swimming lesson: *op ~ zitten* take swimming lessons

zwemmen /zwɛmə(n)/ (zwom, heeft/is gezwommen) swim: *verboden te ~* no swimming allowed; *gaan ~* go for a swim

de **zwemmer** /zwɛmər/ (pl: -s) swimmer

het **zwempak** /zwɛmpak/ (pl: -ken) swimming suit, swimsuit

de **zwemshort** /zwɛmʃɔːrt/ (pl: -s) swimming shorts

het **zwemvest** /zwɛmvɛst/ (pl: -en) life jacket (*or:* vest)

het **zwemvlies** /zwɛmvlis/ (pl: -vliezen) **1** web **2** flipper

de **zwemvogel** /zwɛmvoyəl/ (pl: -s) web-footed bird

de **zwemwedstrijd** /zwɛmwɛtstrɛit/ (pl: -en) swimming competition (*or:* contest)

de **zwendel** /zwɛndəl/ swindle, fraud

de **zwendelaar** /zwɛndəlar/ (pl: -s) swindler, fraud

zwendelen /zwɛndələ(n)/ (zwendelde, heeft gezwendeld) swindle

de **zwengel** /zwɛŋəl/ (pl: -s) handle; crank

zwenken /zwɛŋkə(n)/ (zwenkte, is gezwenkt) swerve; [shipp] sheer: *naar rechts ~* swerve to the right

¹zweren /zwerə(n)/ (zwoor/zweerde, heeft gezworen) ulcerate; fester

²zweren /zwerə(n)/ (zwoer, heeft gezworen) swear; vow: *ik zou er niet op durven ~* I wouldn't take an oath on it; *ik zweer het (je)* I swear (to you)

de **zwerfkat** /zwɛrfkɑt/ (pl: -ten) stray cat

het **zwerfkind** /zwɛrfkɪnt/ (pl: -eren) young vagrant, vagrant child, runaway

de **zwerftocht** /zwɛrftoxt/ (pl: -en) ramble; wandering

het **zwerfvuil** /zwɛrfœyl/ (street) litter

de **zwerm** /zwɛrm/ (pl: -en) swarm; flock

zwermen /zwɛrmə(n)/ (zwermde, heeft gezwermd) swarm

zwerven /zwɛrvə(n)/ (zwierf, heeft gezworven) **1** wander, roam, rove **2** tramp (about), knock about **3** lie about

de **zwerver** /zwɛrvər/ (pl: -s) **1** wanderer, drifter **2** tramp, vagabond

¹**zweten** /zwetə(n)/ (zweette, heeft gezweet) sweat

²**zweten** /zwetə(n)/ (zweette, heeft gezweet) sweat

zweterig /zwetərəx/ (adj) sweaty

zwetsen /zwɛtsə(n)/ (zwetste, heeft gezwetst) blather; boast; brag: *hij kan enorm ~* he talks a lot of hot air

de **zwetser** /zwɛtsər/ (pl: -s) boaster, bragger

zweven /zwevə(n)/ (zweefde, heeft gezweefd) **1** be suspended: *boven een afgrond ~* hang over an abyss **2** float; glide **3** hover: *tussen hoop en vrees ~* hover between hope(s) and fear(s)

zwevend /zwevənt/ (adj) **1** floating: *een ~ plafond* a false ceiling **2** floating: *~e kiezer* floating voter

zweverig /zwevərəx/ (adj) **1** woolly, free-floating **2** dizzy

zwichten /zwɪxtə(n)/ (zwichtte, is gezwicht) yield, submit; give in: *voor de verleiding ~* yield to the temptation

zwiepen /zwipə(n)/ (zwiepte, heeft gezwiept) bend: *de takken zwiepten in de wind* the branches swayed in the wind

de **zwier** /zwir/: *aan de ~ gaan* go on a spree

zwieren /zwirə(n)/ (zwierde, heeft/is gezwierd) sway, reel; whirl

zwierig /zwirəx/ (adj, adv) elegant, graceful; dashing; flamboyant

het ¹**zwijgen** /zwɛiyə(n)/ silence: *het ~ verbreken* break the silence; *er het ~ toe doen* let sth. pass

²**zwijgen** /zwɛiyə(n)/ (zweeg, heeft gezwegen) be silent: *~ als het graf* be silent as the grave; *zwijg!* hold your tongue!, be quiet!

het **zwijggeld** /zwɛixɛlt/ (pl: -en) hush money

de **zwijgplicht** /zwɛixplɪxt/ oath of secrecy

zwijgzaam /zwɛixsam/ (adj) silent, incommunicative, reticent

de **zwijm** /zwɛim/: *in ~ liggen* be in a dead faint; *in ~ vallen* go off in a swoon

zwijmelen /zwɛimələ(n)/ (zwijmelde, heeft gezwijmeld) swoon

het **zwijn** /zwɛin/ (pl: -en) swine: *een wild ~* a wild boar

zwijnen /zwɛinə(n)/ (zwijnde, heeft ge-

zwijnd) [inform] be lucky

de **zwijnenstal** /zwɛinə(n)stɑl/ (pl: -len) pigsty

de **zwik** /zwɪk/: *de hele ~* the whole lot

zwikken /zwɪkə(n)/ (zwikte, is gezwikt) sprain, wrench

de **Zwitser** /zwɪtsər/ (pl: -s) Swiss

Zwitserland /zwɪtsərlɑnt/ Switzerland

Zwitsers /zwɪtsərs/ (adj) Swiss

zwoegen /zwuyə(n)/ (zwoegde, heeft gezwoegd) **1** plod; drudge, slave (away); toil; labour **2** heave, pant

zwoel /zwul/ (adj) sultry; muggy

het **zwoerd** /zwurt/ (pl: -en) rind

de **zzp'er** /zɛtsɛtpejər/ (pl: -s) self-employed person

English–Dutch

a

180 draai van 180°: *do a ~* een draai van 180° maken

24/7 [inform] vierentwintig uur per dag, zeven dagen per week: *the baby cried ~* de baby huilde de hele dag door

411 (the) [Am; inform] info, gegevens: *the ~ on s.o.* (or: *sth.*) de gegevens van, over iem. (*or*: iets)

¹a (n) **1** a, A **2** de eerste, de hoogste (rang/graad), eersteklas ‖ *A-1* prima, eersteklas

²a (art) **1** een **2** per: *five times a day* vijf keer per dag **3** dezelfde, hetzelfde: *all of an age* allemaal even oud

AA 1 *Automobile Association* [roughly] ANWB **2** [Am] *Alcoholics Anonymous* AA

AA-patrol wegenwacht

ab [inform] *abdominal muscle* buikspier

¹abandon (n) ongedwongenheid, vrijheid: *with ~* uitbundig

²abandon (vb) **1** in de steek laten, aan zijn lot overlaten: *~ a baby* een baby te vondeling leggen; *the order to ~ ship* het bevel het schip te verlaten **2** opgeven, afstand doen van: *~ all hope* alle hoop laten varen **3** [sport] afgelasten

abandoned 1 verlaten, opgegeven **2** verdorven, losbandig, schaamteloos **3** ongedwongen, ongeremd, uitbundig

abandonment 1 achterlating; het in de steek laten **2** het prijsgeven

abate verminderen, afnemen: *the wind ~d* de wind ging liggen

abattoir slachthuis^h, abattoir^h

abbey 1 abdij **2** abdijkerk

abbot abt

abbreviate 1 inkorten, verkorten **2** afkorten

abbreviation 1 inkorting, verkorting **2** afkorting

ABC 1 abc^h; alfabet^h **2** eerste beginselen

abdicate aftreden: *~ from the throne* troonsafstand doen

abdomen buik

abdominal buik-, onderbuik-

abduct ontvoeren, wegvoeren

abduction ontvoering, kidnapping

aberrant afwijkend, abnormaal

aberration 1 afwijking **2** afdwaling; misstap ‖ *in a moment of ~* in een vlaag van verstandsverbijstering

abhor verafschuwen, walgen van

abhorrent weerzinwekkend: *that's ~ to him* zoiets verafschuwt hij

abide blijven ‖ *~ by* a) zich neerleggen bij, zich houden aan; **b)** trouw blijven aan

ability bekwaamheid, vermogen^h, bevoegdheid

abject 1 rampzalig, ellendig, miserabel: *~ poverty* troosteloze armoede **2** verachtelijk, laag

ablaze 1 in lichterlaaie: *set ~* in vuur en vlam zetten **2** schitterend, stralend

able 1 bekwaam, competent **2** in staat, de macht/mogelijkheid hebbend: *be ~ to* kunnen

able-bodied gezond van lijf en leden

ably *see* **able**

abnormal 1 abnormaal, afwijkend **2** uitzonderlijk

abnormality abnormaliteit; afwijking

¹aboard (adv) aan boord: *all ~!* instappen!

²aboard (prep) aan boord van

abolish afschaffen, een eind maken aan: *~ the death penalty* de doodstraf afschaffen

abolition afschaffing

abominable afschuwelijk, walgelijk: *Abominable Snowman* verschrikkelijke sneeuwman

abominate verfoeien, verafschuwen

abomination walgelijk iets, gruwel

aboriginal inheems, autochtoon, oorspronkelijk

abort [comp] afbreken

abortion 1 abortus **2** miskraam^+h

abortive vruchteloos, mislukt

abound overvloedig aanwezig zijn, in overvloed voorkomen, wemelen (van)

¹about (adv) **1** ongeveer, bijna: *that's ~ it* dat moet het zo ongeveer zijn; *~ twenty pence* ongeveer twintig pence **2** [indicating place and direction] rond, rondom, in het rond, in de buurt: *there's a lot of flu ~* er heerst griep **3** om(gekeerd) [also fig]: *the wrong way ~* omgekeerd; *~ turn!* rechtsomkeert!; [Am] *~ face!* rechtsomkeert!

²about (prep) **1** rond, om … heen **2** rondom; in (de buurt van) [also fig]: *there was an air of mystery ~ the boy* de jongen had iets geheimzinnigs over zich **3** door … heen, over: *travel ~ the country* in het land rondreizen **4** over, met betrekking tot: *be quick ~ it* schiet eens wat op **5** omstreeks, omtrent, ongeveer: *~ midnight* rond middernacht ‖ *while you are ~ it* als je toch bezig bent; *what ~ it?* nou, zo what?, wat wil je nu zeggen?; *what* (or: *how*) *~ a cup of coffee?* zin in een kop koffie?

about-face [Am] [also fig] totale ommekeer; draai van 180°: [mil] *~!* rechtsom(keert)!

about-turn [also fig] totale ommekeer; draai van 180°: [mil] *~!* rechtsom(keert)!

¹above (adv) **1** boven, hoger: *from ~* a) van boven; **b)** [fig] uit de hemel; *the ~* a) het bovengenoemde; **b)** de bovengenoemde personen **2** hoger, meer: *twenty and* ~ twintig en meer; *imposed **from*** ~ van hogerhand opgelegd

²**above** (prep) **1** boven **2** hoger dan, meer dan: ~ *fifty* meer dan vijftig || ~ *all* vooral

aboveboard eerlijk, openlijk, rechtuit

abrasion schaafwond

¹**abrasive** (n) schuurmiddel[h]

²**abrasive** (adj) **1** schurend, krassend **2** ruw, kwetsend: ~ *character* irritant karakter

abreast 1 zij aan zij, naast elkaar, op een rij: *two* ~ twee aan twee **2** in gelijke tred, gelijk, op dezelfde hoogte: *keep wages* ~ *of* de lonen gelijke tred doen houden met

abridge verkorten, inkorten

abroad in/naar het buitenland: *(back) from* ~ (terug) uit het buitenland

abrupt 1 abrupt, plotseling **2** kortaf

¹**abs** *abdominal muscles* buikspieren: *exercise* one's ~ buikspieroefeningen doen

²**abs** (adv) [inform] absoluut, echt: ~ *gorgeous* echt geweldig

ABS *Anti-lock Braking System* ABS *(antiblokkeersysteem)*

abscess abces[h], ettergezwel[h]

absence 1 afwezigheid, absentie: *he was condemned **in** his* ~ hij werd bij verstek veroordeeld **2** gebrek[h]: *in the* ~ *of* proof bij gebrek aan bewijs

absent afwezig, absent: [mil] ~ *without* **leave** weggebleven zonder verlof

absentee afwezige; [educ] absent

absent-minded verstrooid, afwezig

absolute 1 absoluut, geheel, totaal: ~ *proof* onweerlegbaar bewijs **2** onvoorwaardelijk: ~ *promise* onvoorwaardelijke belofte

absolution absolutie, vergiffenis

absolve 1 vergeven, de absolutie geven **2** ontheffen, kwijtschelden: ~ *s.o. from a promise* iem. ontslaan van een belofte

absorb absorberen, (in zich) opnemen, opzuigen

absorbed geabsorbeerd: ~ *in* a book verdiept in een boek; ~ *in thought* in gedachten verzonken

absorption absorptie: *complete* ~ *in sport* volledig opgaan in sport

abstain (+ from) zich onthouden (van)

abstinence onthouding

¹**abstract** (n) **1** samenvatting, uittreksel[h] **2** abstract kunstwerk[h]

²**abstract** (adj) abstract, theoretisch, algemeen

³**abstract** (vb) **1** onttrekken, ontvreemden **2** afleiden **3** samenvatten

absurd absurd, dwaas, belachelijk

absurdity absurditeit; dwaasheid

abundance overvloed, weelde, menigte

abundant 1 overvloedig **2** rijk: *a river* ~ *in fish* een rivier rijk aan vis

¹**abuse** (n) **1** misbruik[h], verkeerd gebruik[h]

2 scheldwoorden **3** mishandeling: *child* ~ kindermishandeling

²**abuse** (vb) **1** misbruiken **2** mishandelen **3** schelden, uitschelden

abusive beledigend: *become* ~ beginnen te schelden

ABV *alcohol by volume* alcoholpercentage[h]

abyss afgrond, peilloze diepte

AC *alternating current* wisselstroom

¹**academic** (n) academicus, wetenschapper

²**academic** (adj) academisch; [fig] abstract; theoretisch

academy academie, genootschap[h], school voor speciale opleiding

accede [form] **1** toestemmen: ~ *to his request* zijn verzoek inwilligen **2** aanvaarden: ~ *to the throne* de troon bestijgen **3** toetreden

¹**accelerate** (vb) sneller gaan, het tempo opvoeren, optrekken

²**accelerate** (vb) versnellen

acceleration 1 versnelling; acceleratie [car] **2** bespoediging

accelerator gaspedaal[h]

¹**accent** (n) accent[h] [also fig]; klemtoon, uitspraak: *the* ~ *is on exotic flowers* de nadruk ligt op exotische bloemen

²**accent** (vb) accentueren [also fig]; de klemtoon leggen op, (sterk) doen uitkomen

accept 1 aannemen, aanvaarden, accepteren: *an* ~*ed fact* een (algemeen) aanvaard feit; *be* ~*ed practice* algemeen gebruikelijk zijn **2** aanvaarden, tolereren, verdragen **3** goedvinden, goedkeuren, erkennen: *all members* ~*ed the proposal* alle leden namen het voorstel aan

acceptable 1 aanvaardbaar, aannemelijk **2** redelijk

acceptance 1 aanvaarding, overneming **2** gunstige ontvangst, bijval **3** instemming, goedkeuring **4** [com] accept[h], acceptatie

access 1 (+ to) toegang (tot), toegangsrecht[h], toelating: *no (public)* ~ verboden toegang **2** omgangsrecht[h], bezoekrecht[h]: *he has been denied* ~ *to his children* hij mag zijn kinderen niet zien

accessibility toegankelijkheid

accessible (+ to) toegankelijk (voor), bereikbaar (voor); [fig] begrijpelijk (voor)

accessory 1 medeplichtige **2** accessoire[h]

access provider internetaanbieder; internetprovider

accident 1 toeval[h], toevalligheid, toevallige omstandigheid: *by* ~ bij toeval, toevallig **2** ongeluk[h], ongeval[h]: *by* ~ per ongeluk

accidental toevallig, onvoorzien, niet bedoeld: ~*(ly) on purpose* per ongeluk expres

accident-prone gemakkelijk ongelukken krijgend

acclaim toejuiching, bijval, gejuich[h]: *receive (critical)* ~ (door de critici) toegejuicht

worden
acclamation toejuiching; gejuich^h || *by* ~
bij acclamatie
acclimatize acclimatiseren
accommodate 1 huisvesten, onderbrengen **2** plaats hebben voor **3** aanpassen; (met elkaar) in overeenstemming brengen [plans, ideas]: ~ *o.s.* *(to)* zich aanpassen (aan)
accommodating inschikkelijk, meegaand, plooibaar
accommodation 1 logies^h; onderdak^h, woonruimte **2** schikking: *come* to an ~ tot een vergelijk komen
accommodations [Am] **1** onderdak^h, verblijfplaats, logies^h **2** plaats, ruimte
accompaniment begeleiding: *white wine makes a* **good** ~ *to fish dishes* witte wijn past goed bij visgerechten; *to the* ~ *of trumpets* begeleid door trompetten
accompany 1 begeleiden, vergezellen: ~*ing* **letter** bijgaande brief **2** [mus] begeleiden
accomplice medeplichtige
accomplish 1 volbrengen, voltooien **2** tot stand brengen, bereiken
accomplished 1 volleerd; talentvol **2** volbracht; voltooid: ~ *fact* voldongen feit
accomplishment 1 prestatie **2** bekwaamheid, vaardigheid **3** voltooiing, vervulling
accord akkoord^h, schikking, overeenkomst, verdrag^h: *of* one's own ~ uit eigen beweging
accordance: *in* ~ *with* overeenkomstig, in overeenstemming met
accordingly 1 dienovereenkomstig **2** dus
according *to* volgens, naar … beweert
accost aanklampen; lastigvallen
account 1 verslag^h, beschrijving, verklaring; uitleg [of behaviour]: *by all* ~*s* naar alles wat men hoort; *annual* ~ jaarverslag^h; *give* (or: *render*) *an* ~ *of* verslag uitbrengen over **2** rekening; factuur [also fig]: *settle* an ~ *with* s.o. de rekening vereffenen met iem. **3** rekenschap, verantwoording: *bring* (or: *call*) *s.o. to* ~ *for sth.* iem. ter verantwoording roepen voor iets; *give* (or: *render*) ~ *of* rekenschap afleggen over **4** beschouwing, aandacht: *take* sth. *into* ~, *take* ~ *of sth.* rekening houden met iets **5** belang^h, waarde, gewicht^h: *of no* ~ van geen belang **6** voordeel^h: *put* (or: *turn*) sth. *to* (good) ~ zijn voordeel met iets doen || *do* (or: *keep*) (the) ~*s* boekhouden^h; *on* ~ *of* wegens; *on no* ~ in geen geval
accountability verantwoordelijkheid, aansprakelijkheid
accountable 1 verantwoordelijk **2** verklaarbaar
accountancy accountancy, boekhouding
accountant accountant, (hoofd)boekhouder
account for 1 rekenschap geven van, ver-

slag uitbrengen over **2** verklaren, uitleggen, veroorzaken: *his disease accounts for his strange* **behaviour** zijn ziekte verklaart zijn vreemde gedrag **3** vormen, uitmaken: *computer games accounted* **for** *two-thirds of his spending* computerspelletjes vormden twee derde van zijn uitgaven **4** bekend zijn: *the* **rest** *of the passengers still have to be accounted for* de overige passagiers worden nog steeds vermist
accounting period boekhoudkundige periode
accredit 1 toeschrijven; toekennen **2** accrediteren
accumulate (zich) opstapelen, (zich) ophopen: ~ *a* **fortune** een fortuin vergaren
accumulation 1 opeenstapeling, opeenhoping, accumulatie **2** aangroei
accumulative 1 opeenstapelend; ophopend **2** aangroeiend; vermeerderend
accuracy nauwkeurigheid, correctheid, exactheid
accurate nauwkeurig, correct
accusation beschuldiging, aanklacht
accuse beschuldigen, aanklagen
accused beschuldigd, aangeklaagd
accuser aanklager
accustom (ge)wennen, gewoon maken: ~*ed* *to* gewend aan
ace 1 [cards] aas^{+h}, één^h; [fig] troef **2** [sport, esp tennis] ace **3** [inform] uitblinker: *an* ~ *at arithmetic* een hele piet in het rekenen
acerbity wrangheid, zuurheid, bitterheid
acetate acetaat^h
¹**ache** (n) (voortdurende) pijn: ~*s and* **pains** pijntjes
²**ache** (vb) **1** (pijn) lijden [also fig] **2** pijn doen, zeer doen **3** [inform] (hevig) verlangen, hunkeren: *be aching to do sth.* staan te popelen om iets te doen; ~ *for* hunkeren naar
achieve 1 volbrengen, voltooien, tot stand brengen **2** bereiken [goal etc]; presteren: ~ *success* succes behalen
achievement 1 prestatie **2** voltooiing **3** het bereiken
achiever iem. die goed presteert: *low* ~ iem. die minder presteert
Achilles heel achilleshiel; zwak punt
¹**acid** (n) **1** zuur^h, zure vloeistof/drank **2** [inform] acid, lsd^h
²**acid** (adj) **1** zuur, zuurhoudend: ~ *rain* zure regen **2** bits, bijtend
acid test vuurproef [fig]
acknowledge 1 erkennen, accepteren **2** toegeven: ~ *sth.* **to** *s.o.* ten opzichte van iem. iets toegeven **3** ontvangst bevestigen van: *I herewith* ~ *(receipt of) your* **letter** hierbij bevestig ik de ontvangst van uw brief **4** een teken van herkenning geven aan [by means of a nod, greeting]

acknowledgement 1 erkenning, acceptatie **2** dank, bewijs^h van dank: *in ~ of* als dank voor **3** ontvangstbevestiging, kwitantie

acne acne, jeugdpuistjes

acorn eikel

acoustic akoestisch

acoustics 1 geluidsleer **2** akoestiek [in concert hall etc]

acquaint op de hoogte brengen, in kennis stellen, vertrouwd maken: *~ s.o. of* (or: *with*) *the facts* iem. op de hoogte stellen van de feiten

acquaintance 1 kennis, bekende **2** kennissenkring **3** bekendheid, vertrouwdheid, kennis: *have a nodding ~ with s.o.* iem. oppervlakkig kennen **4** kennismaking: *make s.o.'s ~* kennismaken met iem.

acquainted bekend; op de hoogte: *be ~ with sth.* iets kennen

acquiesce [form] (zwijgend) instemmen; zich schikken

acquiescence instemming, berusting

acquire 1 verwerven, verkrijgen, aanleren: *~d characteristics* aangeleerde eigenschappen; *it's an ~d taste* je moet het leren waarderen [food, drink, etc] **2** aanschaffen, (aan)kopen

acquisition aanwinst, verworven bezit^h, aankoop

acquisitive hebzuchtig, hebberig

acquit vrijspreken: *be ~ed (on a charge) of murder* vrijgesproken worden van moord || [form] *~ o.s. well* **a)** zich goed van zijn taak kwijten; **b)** zich goed gedragen

acquittal vrijspraak

acre 1 acre [4,047 square metres] **2** (-s) landerijen, grondgebied^h, groot gebied^h

acrid bijtend [also fig]; scherp, bitter

acrimonious bitter, scherp, venijnig

acrobat acrobaat

acrobatic 1 acrobatisch **2** soepel, lenig

acronym acroniem^h; letterwoord^h

¹across (adv) **1** [place] overdwars, gekruist: *it measured fifty yards ~* het had een doorsnede van vijftig yards **2** [place] aan de overkant **3** [direction; also fig] over, naar de overkant: *the actor came ~ well* de acteur kwam goed over (bij het publiek); *put a message ~* een boodschap overbrengen **4** [in crossword] horizontaal

²across (prep) (tegen)over [also fig]; dwars, gekruist, aan (naar) de overkant van: *look ~ the hedge* kijk over de haag; *from ~ the sea* van overzee; *the people ~ the street* **a)** de overburen; **b)** de mensen aan de overkant (van de straat)

across-the-board algemeen (geldend) [taxes etc]; voor iedereen

acrylic acryl

¹act (n) **1** handeling, daad, werk^h **2** besluit^h,

bepaling, wet: *~ of Parliament* wet van het Parlement; [Am] *~ of Congress* wet van het Congres **3** akte, (proces)stuk^h **4** [theatre] bedrijf^h, akte **5** [circus] nummer^h, act **6** [inform; depr] komedie: *put on an ~* komedie spelen || [rel] *Acts* (or: *Acts of the Apostles*) Handelingen (van de Apostelen); *~ of God* overmacht, force majeure [force of nature]; *catch* (or: *take*) *s.o. in the (very) ~* iem. op heterdaad betrappen; [inform] *get in on the ~, get into the ~* meedoen (om zijn deel van de koek te hebben); [inform] *get one's ~ together* orde op zaken stellen, zijn zaakjes voor elkaar krijgen

²act (vb) **1** zich voordoen, zich gedragen: *he ~s like a madman* hij gedraagt zich als een krankzinnige **2** handelen, optreden, iets doen **3** fungeren, optreden: *~ as chairman* het voorzitterschap waarnemen **4** werken, functioneren **5** acteren, spelen **6** komedie spelen, zich aanstellen

³act (vb) **1** uitbeelden, spelen, uitspelen: *~ out one's emotions* zijn gevoelens naar buiten brengen **2** [theatre] spelen, opvoeren, acteren **3** spelen, zich voordoen als: *~ the fool* de idioot uithangen || *she doesn't ~ her age* zij gedraagt zich niet naar haar leeftijd

acting waarnemend, plaatsvervangend, tijdelijk

action 1 actie, daad, handeling, activiteit: *a man of ~* een man van de daad; *take ~* maatregelen nemen, tot handelen overgaan; *~s speak louder than words* geen woorden maar daden **2** gevechtsactie, strijd: *be killed in ~* in de strijd sneuvelen **3** proces^h, klacht, eis || *the ~ of the novel takes place in London* de roman speelt zich af in Londen

action figure actiefiguur

activate activeren, actief maken, in werking brengen

active 1 actief, werkend, in werking: *an ~ remedy* een werkzaam middel; *an ~ volcano* een werkende vulkaan **2** actief, bedrijvig: *lead an ~ life* een actief leven leiden **3** [econ] actief, productief || *be under ~ consideration* (ernstig) overwogen worden; [com] *~ securities* (or: *stocks*) actieve fondsen, druk verhandelde fondsen; [mil] *on ~ service* aan het front; [Am] in actieve (or: feitelijke) dienst

activity 1 activiteit, bedrijvigheid, drukte: *economic ~* conjunctuur, economische bedrijvigheid **2** werking, functie

act on 1 inwerken op, beïnvloeden **2** opvolgen, zich laten leiden door: *she acted on his advice* zij volgde zijn raad op

actor acteur [also fig]; toneelspeler

actress actrice [also fig]; toneelspeelster

actual werkelijk, feitelijk, eigenlijk: *~ figures* reële cijfers; *~ size* ware grootte; *what were his ~ words?* wat zei hij nou precies?

actuality werkelijkheid; feit^h, realiteit || *in ~*

eigenlijk; in werkelijkheid
actually 1 eigenlijk, feitelijk, werkelijk
2 zowaar, werkelijk, echt: *they've ~ paid me!*
ze hebben me zowaar betaald! || *You've met
John, haven't you? - Actually, I haven't* Je kent
John, hè? - Nee, ik ken hem niet
act up [inform] last bezorgen; haperen [of
machine]; zich slecht gedragen [of children]
acumen [form] scherpzinnigheid
acupuncture acupunctuur
acute 1 acuut, ernstig, hevig **2** scherp(zin-
nig), fijn; gevoelig [wit, senses] || *an ~ angle*
een scherpe hoek; *~ accent* accent aigu [on
letter: é]
ad [inform] *advertisement* advertentie
AD *Anno Domini* n.Chr., na Christus || *AD 79*
79 n.Chr.
adage adagiumʰ; spreuk
adamant vastbesloten, onbuigzaam
adamantly resoluut: *be ~ opposed to sth.*
fel tegen iets gekant zijn
¹adapt (vb) (+ to) zich aanpassen (aan)
²adapt (vb) aanpassen, bewerken, geschikt
maken: *~ a novel for TV* een roman voor de tv
bewerken
adaptability aanpassingsvermogenʰ
adaptable buigzaam, soepel, flexibel
adaptation 1 aanpassing(sprocesʰ) **2** bewerking: *an ~ of a novel by Minette Walters*
een bewerking van een roman van Minette
Walters
adapter 1 adapter; verloopstekker **2** verdeelstekker
¹add (vb) **1** bijdragen **2** (op)tellen, (een) optelling maken
²add (vb) **1** toevoegen, erbij doen: *value ~ed
tax* belasting op de toegevoegde waarde,
btw **2** optellen: *~ five to three* tel vijf bij drie
op
ADD *attention deficit disorder* ADD, aan-
dachtstekortstoornis
addendum addendumʰ; aanvulling
adder adder
addict verslaafde; [fig] fanaat; enthousiasteling
addicted verslaafd: *~ to alcohol* alcoholver-
slaafd; *~ to gambling* gokverslaafd
addiction verslaving, verslaafdheid
addictive verslavend
addition 1 toevoeging, aanwinst, bijvoeg-
selʰ **2** optelling: *in ~* bovendien, daarbij; *in ~
to* behalve, naast
additional bijkomend, aanvullend, extra
additive additiefʰ; toevoeging
add-on 1 uitbreidingspakketʰ; aanvulling
2 randapparaatʰ
¹address (n) **1** adresʰ [also comp] **2** toespraak **3** aanspreekvorm, aanspreektitel
²address (vb) **1** richten, sturen: *~ complaints
to our office* richt u met klachten tot ons bureau; *o.s. to* a) zich richten tot; b) zich be-

zighouden met, zich toeleggen op **2** adresseren **3** toespreken, een rede houden voor:
the teacher ~ed the pupils de onderwijzer
sprak tegen de leerlingen **4** aanspreken: *you
have to ~ the judge as 'Your Honour'* je moet
de rechter met 'Edelachtbare' aanspreken
address bar adresbalk
address book adresboekʰ
addressee geadresseerde
¹add up (vb) [inform] **1** steek houden, kloppen: *the evidence does not ~* het bewijsmateriaal deugt niet **2** (+ to) als uitkomst geven;
[fig] neerkomen (op); inhouden: *these numbers ~ to 499* deze getallen zijn samen 499;
this so-called invention does not ~ to much deze
zogenaamde uitvinding stelt weinig voor
²add up (vb) optellen
¹adept (n) expert
²adept (adj) (+ at, in) bedreven (in), deskundig, ingewijd
adequacy geschiktheid, bekwaamheid
adequate 1 voldoende, net (goed) genoeg
2 geschikt, bekwaam
adhere 1 kleven, aankleven, vastkleven,
hechten **2** (+ to) zich houden (aan), vasthouden (aan), blijven bij
adherence het vasthouden
adherent aanhanger, voorstander, volgeling
¹adhesive (n) kleefstof, plakmiddelʰ, lijm
²adhesive (adj) klevend, plakkend: *~ plaster*
hechtpleister; *~ tape* plakbandʰ
adjacent 1 aangrenzend **2** nabijgelegen
adjective bijvoeglijk naamwoordʰ
¹adjoin (vb) aan elkaar grenzen
²adjoin (vb) grenzen aan
adjourn 1 verdagen, uitstellen **2** schorsen,
onderbreken: *the court ~ed at six* het hof
ging om zes uur uiteen
adjudicate oordelen, arbitreren, jureren: *~
(up)on a matter* over een zaak oordelen
adjunct 1 toevoegselʰ, aanhangselʰ **2** adjunct [employee, civil servant]
adjust 1 regelen, in orde brengen, rechtzetten **2** afstellen, instellen, bijstellen: *use
button A to ~ the volume* gebruik knop A om
de geluidssterkte in te stellen **3** taxeren;
vaststellen [damage] **4** (zich) aanpassen, in
overeenstemming brengen, harmoniseren: *~
(o.s.) to new circumstances* (zich) aan nieuwe
omstandigheden aanpassen
adjustable regelbaar, verstelbaar
adjustment 1 aanpassing **2** regeling;
schikking
¹ad lib (adj) onvoorbereid, geïmproviseerd
²ad lib (vb) improviseren
³ad lib (adv) **1** ad libitum, naar believen
2 onvoorbereid, geïmproviseerd
administer 1 beheren, besturen **2** toepassen, uitvoeren: *~ justice* rechtspreken **3** toe-
dienen, verschaffen || *~ to s.o.'s needs* in ie-

mands behoeften voorzien
administrate beheren, besturen
administration beheer[h], administratie,
bestuur[h] || ~ *of an* ***oath*** afneming van een eed
Administration [Am] regering, bestuur[h],
ambtsperiode
administrative administratief, beheers-,
bestuurs-
administrator 1 bestuurder, beheerder
2 [comp] systeembeheerder
admirable 1 bewonderenswaard(ig)
2 voortreffelijk, uitstekend
admiral admiraal: *Admiral of the* ***Fleet*** op-
peradmiraal [British Navy]
Admiralty mile zeemijl
admiration bewondering, eerbied
admire bewonderen
admirer bewonderaar, aanbidder
admissible 1 aannemelijk, aanvaardbaar,
acceptabel **2** geoorloofd [also law]; toelaatbaar
admission 1 erkenning, bekentenis, toegeving: *an ~ of* ***guilt*** een schuldbekentenis
2 toegang, toegangsprijs, entree **3** opname
¹admit (vb) **1** toelaten, ruimte laten: *these
facts ~ of one interpretation only* deze feiten
zijn maar voor één interpretatie vatbaar
2 toegang geven **3** erkennen, toegeven, bekennen
²admit (vb) **1** binnenlaten, toelaten: *he was
~ted to hospital* hij werd in het ziekenhuis
opgenomen **2** toelaten, mogelijk maken: *his
statement ~s more than one interpretation* zijn
verklaring is voor meer dan één interpretatie
vatbaar **3** erkennen, toegeven, bekennen:
he ~ted having ***lied*** hij gaf toe dat hij gelogen
had
admittance toegang: *no ~* geen toegang
admittedly 1 toegegeven **2** weliswaar
admonish waarschuwen, berispen
admonition waarschuwing, berisping
ad nauseam tot vervelens toe
adolescence puberteit, adolescentie
¹adolescent (n) puber, tiener, adolescent
²adolescent (adj) **1** opgroeiend **2** puber-
achtig, puberaal, jeugd-
adopt 1 adopteren, aannemen, (uit)kiezen
2 overnemen, aannemen: *~ an* ***idea*** een idee
overnemen **3** aannemen, gebruiken, toepassen: *~ modern* ***techniques*** nieuwe technieken in gebruik nemen **4** aannemen, aanvaarden, goedkeuren: *~ a* ***proposal*** een
voorstel aanvaarden
adoption 1 adoptie, aanneming **2** aanneming, het aannemen **3** gebruik[h], toepassing
4 aanvaarding, goedkeuring, aanneming
adoptive adoptief, aangenomen, pleeg-:
an ~ ***child*** een geadopteerd kind; *~* ***parents***
pleegouders, adoptiefouders
adorable schattig, lief
adoration aanbidding, verering

adorbs [inform] schattig
adore 1 aanbidden, bewonderen **2** [rel]
aanbidden, vereren **3** [inform] dol zijn op
adorn versieren, mooi maken
adrenaline adrenaline
adrenalized vol adrenaline
adrift 1 op drift **2** stuurloos; losgeslagen
[also lit]; hulpeloos, doelloos
adroit handig: *be ~ at* (or: *in*) *carpentering*
goed kunnen timmeren
adulation ophemeling; bewieroking
¹adult (n) volwassene [also animal]
²adult (adj) **1** volwassen, volgroeid, rijp
2 voor volwassenen: *~* ***education*** volwassenenonderwijs[h]; [euph] *~* ***movie*** pornofilm
adulterate vervalsen, versnijden
adulterer overspelige man
adulteress overspelige vrouw
adulterous overspelig
adultery overspel[h]
adulthood volwassenheid; meerderjarigheid
¹advance (n) **1** voorschot[h], vooruitbetaling
2 avance, eerste stappen, toenadering
3 vooruitgang [also fig]; vordering, ontwikkeling, verbetering: *in ~* **a)** vooraf[h], van tevoren [time]; **b)** vooruit, voorop [space]; *to be
paid in ~* vooraf te voldoen
²advance (adj) vooraf, van tevoren, bij
voorbaat: *~* ***booking*** reservering (vooraf); *~*
notice vooraankondiging
³advance (vb) vooruitgaan, voortbewegen,
vorderen, vooruitgang boeken: *the troops ~d
against* (or: *on*) *the enemy* de troepen nader-
den de vijand
⁴advance (vb) **1** vooruitbewegen, vooruit-
brengen, vooruitschuiven, vooruitzetten
2 promoveren, bevorderen (in rang): *~ s.o.
to a higher position* iem. bevorderen **3** bevorderen; steunen [plan] **4** naar voren brengen,
ter sprake brengen: *~ one's opinion* zijn mening naar voren brengen **5** voorschieten,
vooruitbetalen
advanced 1 (ver)gevorderd **2** geavanceerd, modern, vooruitstrevend: *~* ***ideas*** pro-
gressieve ideeën
advancement 1 vordering **2** bevordering,
verbetering, vooruitgang
advantage 1 voordeel[h], gunstige omstandigheid: *have the ~ of* (or: *over*) *s.o.* iets
voorhebben op iem. **2** voordeel[h], nut[h], profijt[h]: *take (full) ~ of sth.* (gretig) gebruik (or:
misbruik) maken van iets **3** overwicht[h]: *get
the ~* de bovenhand krijgen **4** [tennis] voordeel[h]
advantageous 1 voordelig, nuttig, gunstig **2** winstgevend
advent aankomst, komst; nadering [of sth.
or s.o. important]
Advent [rel] advent
adventure avontuur[h], riskante onderne-

ming
adventurer avonturier, gelukzoeker, huurling, speculant
adventurous 1 avontuurlijk, onderne-mend **2** avontuurlijk, gewaagd, gedurfd
adverb bijwoord^h
adverbial bijwoordelijke bepaling
advergame gamecommercial, advergame
adversary tegenstander, vijand
adverse 1 vijandig: ~ *criticism* afbrekende kritiek **2** ongunstig, nadelig
adversity tegenslag, tegenspoed: *in (time of)* ~ in (tijden van) tegenspoed
advert [inform] *advertisement* advertentie
advertise 1 adverteren, reclame maken (voor), bekendmaken, aankondigen **2** (+ for) een advertentie plaatsen (voor)
advertisement advertentie: *classified* ~*s* rubrieksadvertenties
advertising reclame
advice 1 raad, advies^h: *give s.o. a piece* (or: *bit*) *of* ~ iem. een advies geven; *act on* (or: *follow, take*) *s.o.'s* ~ iemands advies opvol-gen; *on* the doctor's ~ op doktersadvies **2** [com] verzendadvies^h, verzendbericht^h
advisability raadzaamheid, wenselijkheid
advisable raadzaam, wenselijk
¹**advise** (vb) informeren, inlichten: ~ *s.o. of sth.* iem. van iets op de hoogte brengen
²**advise** (vb) adviseren, (aan)raden: ~ *(s.o.) against sth.* (iem.) iets afraden; ~ *(s.o.) on sth.* (iem.) advies geven omtrent iets || *be well* ~*d to …* er verstandig aan doen om …
adviser adviseur, raadsman
advocacy 1 verdediging; voorspraak **2** ad-vocatuur
¹**advocate** (n) verdediger, voorstander
²**advocate** (vb) bepleiten, verdedigen, voor-staan: *he* ~*s strong measures against truants* hij bepleit maatregelen tegen spijbelaars
adware [comp] adware [reclamesoftware]
¹**aerial** (n) antenne
²**aerial** (adj) lucht-, in de lucht, bovengronds
aerobatics stuntvliegen^h
aerobic 1 aerobic: ~ *dancing* aerobic(dan-sen) **2** [biology] aeroob
aerodrome vliegveld^h, (kleine) luchthaven
aeronautics luchtvaart(kunde)
aeroplane vliegtuig^h
aerosol can spuitbus
aerospace 1 ruimte; kosmos, heelal^h **2** ruimtevaartindustrie
aesthetics esthetica, schoonheidsleer, es-thetiek
afar (van) ver(re), veraf, ver weg: *from* ~ van verre
affable vriendelijk; innemend
affair 1 zaak, aangelegenheid: *current* ~*s* lopende zaken, actualiteiten; *foreign* ~*s* bui-tenlandse zaken; *that is my* ~ dat zijn mijn zaken, dat gaat je niets aan **2** [inform] affai-

re, kwestie, ding^h, zaak(je^h) **3** verhouding
affect 1 voorwenden, doen alsof **2** zich voordoen als, spelen: ~ *the grieving widow* de diepbedroefde weduwe uithangen **3** (ont)-roeren, aangrijpen: *his death* ~*ed me deeply* ik was diep getroffen door zijn dood **4** beïn-vloeden, treffen: *how will the new law* ~ *us?* welke invloed zal de nieuwe wet op ons hebben? **5** aantasten, aanvallen: *smoking* ~*s your health* roken is slecht voor de gezond-heid
affected 1 voorgewend, hypocriet: ~ *po-liteness* niet gemeende beleefdheid **2** ge-maakt **3** ontroerd, aangedaan **4** getroffen, betrokken: *the* ~ *area* het getroffen gebied **5** aangetast: ~ *by pollution* aangetast door vervuiling
affection genegenheid: ~ *for* (or: *to-ward(s)*) genegenheid tot, liefde tot (*or:* voor)
affectionate hartelijk, warm, lief(heb-bend): ~*ly (yours)* veel liefs [in letters]
affiliate (zich) aansluiten, opnemen, aan-nemen
affiliation connectie; band, verwantschap || *what is your religious* ~? tot welke kerk be-hoor je?
affinity 1 (aan)verwantschap^h **2** affiniteit, overeenkomst, sympathie: *feel* ~ *with* (or: *for*) sympathie voelen voor
affinity group belangengroep
affirm bevestigen, beamen, verzekeren
affirmation 1 bevestiging, verzekering **2** [law] belofte
¹**affirmative** (n) bevestiging: *answer in the* ~ bevestigend (*or:* met ja) antwoorden
²**affirmative** (adj) bevestigend; positief || [Am] ~ *action* voorkeursbehandeling, posi-tieve discriminatie
¹**affix** (n) toevoegsel^h, aanhangsel^h
²**affix** (vb) toevoegen, (aan)hechten, kleven; vastmaken [also fig]: ~ *one's name to a letter* een brief ondertekenen
afflict kwellen, treffen, teisteren: *be* ~*ed with leprosy* lijden aan lepra
affliction 1 aandoening: ~*s of old age* ou-derdomskwalen **2** nood; onheil^h, ramp
affluence overvloed; rijkdom, welvaart
affluent rijk, overvloedig, welvarend: *the* ~ *society* de welvaartsstaat
afford zich veroorloven, zich permitteren, riskeren: *I cannot* ~ *a holiday* ik kan me geen vakantie veroorloven
¹**affront** (n) belediging
²**affront** (vb) (openlijk) beledigen
Afghan Afghaan(se)
Afghanistan Afghanistan
afield ver (van huis); ver weg [also fig]
aflame in brand; in vuur en vlam; gloeiend [also fig]: ~ *with autumn colours* met vlam-mende herfstkleuren

afloat 1 vlot(tend), drijvend, varend **2** aan boord, op zee ‖ nasty **rumours** are ~ er zijn gemene roddels in omloop

afoot [oft depr] op gang, in voorbereiding, in aantocht: there is **trouble** ~ er zijn moeilijkheden op til

aforesaid bovengenoemd

afraid bang, angstig, bezorgd: she was ~ to wake her grandfather ze durfde haar grootvader niet wakker te maken; ~ **of** sth. bang voor iets; don't be ~ **of** asking for help vraag gerust om hulp; I'm ~ I'm late het spijt me, maar ik ben te laat; I'm ~ **not** helaas niet, ik ben bang van niet; I'm ~ I can't help you ik kan u helaas niet helpen

afresh opnieuw, andermaal: **start** ~ van voren af aan beginnen

Africa Afrika

¹African (n) Afrikaan(se) ‖ ~ **violet** Kaaps viooltje

²African (adj) Afrikaans

¹African American (n) Afro-Amerikaan(se)

²African American (adj) Afro-Amerikaans

Afro afrokapsel[h]; afrolook

¹after (adj) later, volgend

²after (adv) na, nadien, erachter: five **years** ~ vijf jaar later; **shortly** ~ spoedig daarna; they lived happily **ever** ~ zij leefden nog lang en gelukkig

³after (prep) **1** achter, na: **cloud** ~ cloud de ene wolk na de andere; Jack ran ~ **Jill** Jack liep Jill achterna; ~ **you** na u, ga je gang **2** [time] na: **day** ~ day dag in dag uit; it's ~ two o'clock het is over tweeën; **time** ~ time keer op keer **3** na, met uitzondering van: the greatest (composer) ~ Beethoven op Beethoven na de grootste (componist) **4** naar, volgens, in navolging van: Jack **takes** ~ his father Jack lijkt op zijn vader ‖ ~ **all** toch, per slot (van rekening); **be** ~ sth. uit zijn op iets, iets najagen

⁴after (conj) nadat, als, toen, wanneer: come back ~ finishing that job kom terug als je met die klus klaar bent

aftercare nazorg

afterlife leven na de dood; hiernamaals[h]

aftermath nasleep, naspel[h]

afternoon middag; [Belg] namiddag [also fig]: **in** (or: during) the ~ 's middags

afters toetje[h]

after-sales service klantenservice

afterthought 1 latere overweging **2** latere toevoeging, postscriptum[h]

afterwards later, naderhand

again 1 opnieuw, weer, nog eens: **time** and (time) ~ telkens opnieuw; (the) **same** ~! schenk nog eens in!, hetzelfde nog eens!; be **o.s.** ~ hersteld zijn, er weer bovenop zijn; **back** (or: **home**) ~ weer terug (or: thuis); **never** ~ nooit meer; **once** ~ nog een keer, voor de zoveelste keer; **now** and ~ nu en dan; ~ and **again** telkens opnieuw **2** nogmaals ‖

what is his name ~? hoe heet hij ook (al) weer?

against 1 [place or direction; also fig] tegen, tegen … aan, in strijd met: a race ~ the **clock** een race tegen de klok; ~ the **current** tegen de stroom in; evidence ~ John bewijs(materiaal) tegen John; vaccination ~ the measles inenting tegen de mazelen **2** tegenover, in tegenstelling met: 18, as ~ the 30 sold last year 18, tegenover de 30 die vorig jaar zijn verkocht

¹age (n) **1** leeftijd, ouderdom: **be** your ~! doe niet zo kinderachtig!; **be** (or: **come**) **of** ~ meerderjarig zijn (or: worden); **look** one's ~ er zo oud uitzien als men is; **what** is your ~? hoe oud ben je?; **at** the ~ **of** ten op tienjarige leeftijd; **in** his (old) ~ op zijn oude dag; ten years **of** ~ tien jaar oud; **under** ~ minderjarig, te jong **2** mensenleven[h], levensduur **3** eeuw, tijdperk[h]: the Stone Age het stenen tijdperk, de steentijd **4** (-s) [inform] eeuwigheid: wait for ~s een eeuwigheid wachten; you've been ~s je bent vreselijk lang weggebleven

²age (vb) verouderen, ouder worden: he **has** ~d a lot hij is erg oud geworden

age bracket leeftijdsgroep

¹aged (adj) oud: ~ **ten** tien jaar oud

²aged (adj) oud, (hoog)bejaard ‖ **the** ~ de bejaarden

ageing veroudering(sproces[h])

ageism leeftijdsdiscriminatie

ageless leeftijdloos, nooit verouderend, eeuwig (jong)

agency 1 bureau[h], instantie, instelling: **travel** ~ reisbureau[h] **2** agentuur, agentschap[h], vertegenwoordiging **3** bemiddeling, tussenkomst, toedoen[h]: **through** (or: **by**) the ~ of friends door toedoen van vrienden

agenda agenda: the main point on the ~ het belangrijkste punt op de agenda

agent 1 agent, tussenpersoon, bemiddelaar, vertegenwoordiger: **secret** ~ geheim agent **2** middel[h]: **cleansing** ~ reinigingsmiddel[h]

age-old eeuwenoud

agglomeration opeenhoping, (chaotische) verzameling

aggravate 1 verergeren: ~ an **illness** een ziekte verergeren **2** [inform] ergeren, irriteren

aggravation 1 verergering **2** ergernis

aggregate totaal[h]: **in** (the) ~ alles bij elkaar genomen, alles bij elkaar opgeteld

aggregation samenvoeging; verzameling, aggregatie: **state** of ~ aggregatietoestand

aggression agressie

aggressive 1 agressief, aanvallend: ~ salesmen opdringerige verkopers **2** ondernemend, ambitieus

aggressor aanvaller

aggrieved gekrenkt, gekwetst: feel (o.s.) ~

at (or: *by, over*) *sth.* zich gekrenkt voelen door iets

aghast (+ at) ontzet (door), verbijsterd, verslagen

agile lenig, beweeglijk, soepel

agility 1 behendigheid, vlugheid **2** alertheid

agitate optreden, strijden (voor/tegen): ~ *for* (or: *against*) actie voeren voor (or: tegen)

agitated geërgerd; geagiteerd

agitation 1 actie, strijd **2** opschudding, opgewondenheid, spanning

agitator oproerkraaier

aglow gloeiend; stralend [also fig]

agnostic agnost, agnosticus

ago geleden: *ten years* ~ tien jaar geleden; *not long* ~ kort geleden

agog opgewonden; vol verwachting

agonize vreselijk lijden; worstelen [fig]: ~ *over* zich het hoofd breken over

agonizing kwellend, hartverscheurend: *an* ~ *decision* een moeilijke beslissing

agony (ondraaglijke) pijn, kwelling, foltering

agony aunt [inform] Lieve Lita

agony column rubriek voor persoonlijke problemen

agrarian agrarisch; landbouw-

¹agree (vb) **1** akkoord gaan, het eens zijn, het eens worden, afspreken: ~ *to do sth.* afspreken iets te zullen doen; ~ *on sth.* het ergens over eens zijn; ~ *to sth.* met iets instemmen, in iets toestemmen; ~ *with s.o. about sth.* het met iem. over iets eens zijn; ~*d!* akkoord! **2** overeenstemmen, goed opschieten, passen: ~ *with* kloppen met

²agree (vb) **1** bepalen, overeenkomen, afspreken: ~ *a price* een prijs afspreken **2** goedkeuren, aanvaarden: ~ *a plan* een plan goedkeuren

agreeable prettig, aangenaam: *the terms are not* ~ *to us* de voorwaarden staan ons niet aan

agreement 1 overeenkomst, overeenstemming, afspraak, contract[h]: *be in* ~ *about* (or: *on, with*) 't eens zijn over, akkoord gaan met **2** instemming, goedkeuring

agriculture landbouw

agritourism agrotoerisme[h]

aground aan de grond, vast

ahead 1 voorop: [sport] *be* ~ leiden, voorstaan; *go* ~ voorop gaan **2** vooruit, voorwaarts, van tevoren, op voorhand: *full speed* ~*!* met volle kracht vooruit!; *look* (or: *plan*) ~ vooruitzien; *straight* ~ rechtdoor

ahead of voor: *the days* ~ *us* de komende dagen; ~ *his time* zijn tijd vooruit; *straight* ~ *you* recht voor je

ahoy ahoi

¹aid (n) **1** hulp, bijstand, assistentie: *come* (or: *go*) *to s.o.'s* ~ iem. te hulp komen; *in* ~ *of*

ten dienste van; *first* ~ eerste hulp (bij ongelukken), EHBO **2** hulpmiddel[h], apparaat[h], toestel[h]: *audiovisual* ~*s* audiovisuele hulpmiddelen **3** helper, assistent

²aid (vb) helpen, steunen, bijstaan

aide 1 aide de camp, adjudant **2** assistent, naaste medewerker, helper

AIDS *Acquired Immune Deficiency Syndrome* aids

AIDS inhibitor aidsremmer

¹ail (vb) ziek(elijk) zijn, sukkelen; iets mankeren [also fig]

²ail (vb) schelen, mankeren

ailment kwaal, ziekte, aandoening

¹aim (n) **1** (streef)doel[h], bedoeling, plan[h] **2** aanleg: *take* ~ *(at)* aanleggen (op), richten (op)

²aim (vb) proberen, willen: ~ *to be an artist* kunstenaar willen worden; ~ *at doing sth.* iets willen doen, van plan zijn iets te doen; *what are you* ~*ing at?* wat wil je nu eigenlijk?

³aim (vb) richten, mikken, aanleggen: ~ *high* hoog mikken; [fig] ambitieus zijn; ~ *(a gun) at* (een vuurwapen) richten op

aimless doelloos, zinloos

¹air (n) **1** lucht, atmosfeer, dampkring, luchtruim[h], hemel: *in the open* ~ in de openlucht; *get some (fresh)* ~ een frisse neus halen; *by* ~ met het vliegtuig, per luchtpost **2** [radio, TV] ether: *be on the* ~ in de ether zijn, uitzenden, uitgezonden worden **3** bries(je[h]), lichte wind **4** voorkomen[h], sfeer, aanzicht[h]: *have an* ~ *of superiority* (or: *loneliness*) een superieure (or: eenzame) indruk maken **5** houding, manier van doen, aanstellerij: *give o.s.* ~*s*, *put on* ~*s* zich aanstellen, indruk proberen te maken ‖ *rumours are in the* ~ het gerucht doet de ronde; *my plans are still (up) in the* ~ mijn plannen staan nog niet vast

²air (vb) **1** drogen, te drogen hangen **2** luchten, ventileren **3** bekendmaken, luchten, ventileren: ~ *one's grievances* (or: *ideas*) uiting geven aan zijn klachten (or: ideeën)

airbag airbag

air base luchtmachtbasis

airboat moerasboot

airborne 1 in de lucht, door de lucht vervoerd **2** per vliegtuig getransporteerd: ~ *troops* luchtlandingstroepen

airbrush 1 spuitlakken **2** retoucheren [photo]

air con airco, airconditioning

air corridor luchtweg; luchtcorridor

aircraft vliegtuig[h]

aircraft carrier vliegdekschip[h]

aircrew vliegtuigbemanning

airfield vliegveld[h], luchthaven

air force luchtmacht, luchtstrijdkrachten

air gun 1 luchtbuks; windbuks **2** verfspuit

air hostess stewardess

air kiss kus in de lucht

airlift luchtbrug
airline luchtvaartmaatschappij
airliner passagiersvliegtuig[h]
airmail luchtpost: *by* ~ per luchtpost
airplane [Am] vliegtuig[h]
air pollution luchtvervuiling
airport luchthaven, vliegveld[h]
air punch je vuisten in de lucht steken
air quotes luchthaakjes
air rage agressie in het vliegtuig
air raid luchtaanval
airship luchtschip[h], zeppelin
airsick luchtziek
airside afgeschermd gedeelte[h] van een luchthaven
airspace luchtruim[h] [of country]
airstrip landingsstrook
airtight luchtdicht; [fig] sluitend; onweerlegbaar: *his alibi is* ~ hij heeft een waterdicht alibi
air time 1 zendtijd **2** beltijd
airy 1 luchtig; fris **2** luchthartig, zorgeloos **3** vluchtig: ~ *promises* loze beloften
aisle 1 zijbeuk [church] **2** gang(pad[h]); middenpad[h] [church, train, theatre, etc]: *lead s.o. up the* ~ iem. naar het altaar leiden/brengen; [in shop] *he walked up and down the ~s looking for peanut butter* hij liep langs de schappen op zoek naar pindakaas || *we had them rolling in the ~s* het publiek lag in een deuk
aitch h: *drop one's ~es* de h's inslikken
ajar op een kier
akimbo (met de handen) in de zij
akin (+ to) verwant (aan), gelijk(soortig)
alabaster albast[h]: ~ *skin* albasten huid
alacrity monterheid, bereidwilligheid, enthousiasme[h]
[1]**alarm** (n) **1** alarm[h], schrik, paniek: *take* ~ *at* opschrikken van, in paniek raken bij **2** alarm[h], waarschuwing, alarmsignaal[h]: *raise* (or: *sound*) *the* ~ alarm geven **3** wekker **4** alarmsysteem[h], alarminstallatie
[2]**alarm** (vb) alarm slaan
[3]**alarm** (vb) alarmeren, opschrikken, verontrusten: *look ~ed* verschrikt kijken
alarm clock wekker: *he set the* ~ *for 6 o'clock* hij zette de wekker op zes uur
alarming alarmerend, onrustbarend, verontrustend
alas helaas
Albania Albanië
[1]**Albanian** (n) Albanees, Albanese
[2]**Albanian** (adj) Albanees
albatross albatros || *an* ~ *around one's neck* een blok aan zijn been
albeit zij het: *a small difference, ~ an important one* een klein verschil, zij het een belangrijk verschil
album 1 album[h], fotoalbum[h], poëziealbum[h] **2** grammofoonplaat, cd
albumen eiwit[h]

alchemy alchemie
alcohol alcohol
[1]**alcoholic** (n) alcoholicus
[2]**alcoholic** (adj) alcoholisch, alcoholhoudend
alcolock alcoholslot[h]
alcopop alcopop [mixdrankje]
alder els, elzenboom
alderman [roughly] wethouder, [roughly] gedeputeerde; [Belg] [roughly] schepen
ale ale, (licht, sterk gehopt) bier[h]
[1]**alert** (n) alarm(signaal)[h], luchtalarm[h]: *on the* ~ *(for)* op zijn hoede (voor)
[2]**alert** (adj) **1** alert, waakzaam, op zijn hoede: ~ *to danger* op gevaar bedacht **2** levendig, vlug
[3]**alert** (vb) alarmeren, waarschuwen, attent maken: ~ *s.o. to the danger* iem. wijzen op het gevaar
A level *advanced level* Brits (examenvak[h] op) eindexamenniveau[h]: *pass one's ~s* zijn eindexamen halen, [roughly] slagen voor vwo
alga alg; zeewier[h]
algal 1 algenachtig **2** algen-: ~ *growth* algengroei
algebra algebra
algebraic algebraïsch
Algeria Algerije
[1]**Algerian** (n) Algerijn(se)
[2]**Algerian** (adj) Algerijns
algorithm algoritme[h], handelingsvoorschrift[h]
[1]**alias** (n) **1** alias, bijnaam, schuilnaam **2** [comp] alias, gebruikersnaam
[2]**alias** (adv) alias, anders genoemd
alibi 1 alibi[h] **2** [inform] excuus[h], uitvlucht
Alice band haarband; diadeem[+h]
[1]**alien** (n) vreemdeling, buitenlander, buitenaards wezen[h]
[2]**alien** (adj) **1** vreemd, buitenlands **2** afwijkend: ~ *to his nature* strijdig met zijn aard
alienate vervreemden; doen bekoelen [friendship]
alienation vervreemding
[1]**alight** (adj) brandend, in brand: *set* ~ aansteken
[2]**alight** (vb) afstappen, uitstappen, afstijgen: ~ *from a horse* van een paard stijgen
align 1 zich richten, op één lijn liggen **2** (+ with) zich aansluiten (bij)
alignment het op één lijn brengen, het in één lijn liggen: *out of* ~ ontzet, uit zijn verband
[1]**alike** (adj) gelijk(soortig), gelijkend: *they are very much* ~ ze lijken heel erg op elkaar
[2]**alike** (adv) gelijk, op dezelfde manier: *treat all children* ~ alle kinderen gelijk behandelen
alimony alimentatie
alive 1 levend, in leven **2** levendig, actief: ~ *and kicking* springlevend || ~ *to* bewust van,

op de hoogte van [a fact etc]
alkaline alkalisch; basisch
¹all (n) gehele bezit[h]: *her jewels* are her ~ haar juwelen zijn haar gehele bezit
²all (pron) **1** alle(n), allemaal, iedereen: [tennis] *thirty* ~ dertig gelijk; *one and* ~, ~ *and sundry* alles en iedereen, jan en alleman; *they have* ~ *left*, ~ *of them have left* ze zijn allemaal weg **2** alles, al, allemaal: *when* ~ *is (said and) done* uiteindelijk; *it's* ~ *one* (or: *the same*) *to me* het kan me (allemaal) niet schelen; *above* ~ bovenal, voor alles **3** de grootst mogelijke: *with* ~ *speed* zo snel mogelijk; [inform] *of* ~ ...! nota bene!; *today of* ~ *days* uitgerekend vandaag **4** enig(e): *beyond* ~ *doubt* zonder enige twijfel **5** één en al; [Am] puur; zuiver: *he was* ~ *ears* hij was één en al oor; [Am] *it's* ~ *wool* het is zuivere wol **6** al(le), geheel: ~ *(the) angles (taken together) are 180°* alle hoeken van een driehoek (samen) zijn 180°; *with* ~ *my heart* van ganser harte; ~ *(the) morning* de hele morgen **7** al(le), ieder, elk: ~ *(the) angles are 60°* alle hoeken zijn 60° ‖ *once and for* ~ voorgoed, voor eens en altijd; *after* ~ per slot van rekening, toch, tenslotte; *he can't walk at* ~ hij kan helemaal niet lopen; *if I could do it at* ~ als ik het maar enigszins kon doen; [after thank you] *not at* ~ niets te danken, graag gedaan; *for* ~ *I know* voor zover ik weet; *in* ~ in 't geheel, in totaal; ~ *in* ~ al met al
³all (adv) helemaal, geheel, volledig; [inform] heel; erg: ~ *right* in orde, oké; *if it's* ~ *the same to her* als het haar niets uitmaakt; *I've known it* ~ *along* ik heb het altijd al geweten; ~ *at once* plotseling; ~ *over again* van voren af aan; [Am] *books lay scattered* ~ *over (the place)* er lagen overal boeken; ~ *round* overal; [fig] in alle opzichten; ~ *too soon* (maar) al te gauw; *I'm* ~ *for it* ik ben er helemaal voor ‖ ~ *the same* toch, desondanks; [inform] *it's not* ~ *that difficult* zo (vreselijk) moeilijk is het nu ook weer niet; ~ *out* a) uit alle macht; b) op volle snelheid; *that's Jack* ~ *over* a) [inform] dat is nou typisch Jack; b) hij lijkt precies op Jack
allay [form] **1** verminderen, verlichten, verkleinen **2** kalmeren, (tot) bedaren (brengen): ~ *all fears* alle angst wegnemen
all but bijna, vrijwel: *he was* ~ *dead* hij was bijna dood; ~ *impossible* vrijwel onmogelijk
allegation bewering, (onbewezen) beschuldiging
allege [form] beweren, aanvoeren: *the ~d thief* de vermeende dief
allegiance trouw, loyaliteit: *pledge* ~ *to the flag* trouw zweren aan de vlag
allegory symbolische voorstelling
alleluia halleluja[h]
allergic (+ to) allergisch (voor); [inform, fig] afkerig: *be* ~ *to gluten* een glutenallergie

hebben
allergy (+ to) allergie (voor)
alleviate verlichten, verzachten
alleviation verlichting, verzachtend middel[h]
alley 1 steeg(je[h]), (door)gang **2** laan(tje[h]), pad[h] **3** kegelbaan ‖ *blind* ~ doodlopende steeg
alley cat [Am] zwerfkat
alliance 1 verdrag[h], overeenkomst, verbintenis **2** bond, verbond[h], vereniging, (bond)genootschap[h]
allied 1 verbonden [also fig]; verenigd: *the Allied Forces* de geallieerden; *(closely)* ~ *to* (nauw) verwant met
alligator alligator
all-in [inform] *all-inclusive* all-in, alles inbegrepen, inclusief
allocate toewijzen, toekennen
allocation toewijzing
allot toewijzen, toebedelen
allotment 1 toegewezen deel[h], aandeel[h] **2** toewijzing, toekenning **3** perceel[h] [rented from government]; volkstuintje[h]
all-out [inform] volledig, intensief: *go* ~ alles op alles zetten
allow 1 toestaan, (toe)laten, veroorloven: *no dogs ~ed* honden niet toegelaten; ~ *o.s.* zich veroorloven **2** voorzien in, mogelijk maken, zorgen voor: *the plan ~s one hour for lunch* het plan voorziet in één uur voor de lunch **3** toekennen, toestaan, toewijzen: ~ *twenty per cent off (for)* twintig procent korting geven (op) **4** toegeven, erkennen: *we must* ~ *that he is clever* we moeten toegeven dat hij slim is
allowance 1 toelage, uitkering, subsidie **2** deel[h], portie, rantsoen[h] **3** vergoeding, toeslag **4** korting, aftrek ‖ *make (an)* ~ *for, make ~(s) for* rekening houden met
allow for rekening houden met: *allowing for his young age* gezien zijn jeugdige leeftijd
alloy legering, metaalmengsel[h]
all-purpose voor alle doeleinden; universeel
¹all right (adj) **1** gezond, goed, veilig, ongedeerd **2** goed (genoeg), aanvaardbaar, in orde: *his work is* ~ zijn werk is acceptabel; *it's* ~ *by me* van mij mag je; *if that's* ~ *with you* als jij dat goed vindt; *would you like a cup of coffee? I'm* ~, *thanks* wil je een kopje koffie? Nee, dank je
²all right (adv) **1** in orde, voldoende: *he's doing* ~ hij doet het aardig **2** inderdaad, zonder twijfel: *he's crazy* ~ hij is inderdaad écht gek **3** begrepen, in orde, (dat is) afgesproken: *can we go to the movies?* ~ mogen we naar de film? oké
all-round allround, veelzijdig
All Saints' Day Allerheiligen [1 November]
All Souls' Day Allerzielen [2 November]

all-terrain geschikt voor elk terrein: ~ *bike* mountainbike; ~ *vehicle* terreinwagen

all-time van alle tijden: *an ~ record* een (langdurig) ongebroken record; *an ~ high* (or: *low*) een absoluut hoogtepunt (or: dieptepunt)

allude to zinspelen op, toespelingen maken op

allure aantrekkingskracht, charme

allusion (+ to) zinspeling (op), toespeling

¹**ally** (n) bondgenoot, medestander, geallieerde: *the Allies* de geallieerden

²**ally** (vb) (zich) verenigen, (zich) verbinden: ~ *o.s. with* een verbond sluiten met

almanac almanak

almighty 1 almachtig: *the Almighty* de Almachtige **2** [inform] allemachtig, geweldig: *an ~ din* een oorverdovend lawaai

almond amandel [fruit]

almost bijna, praktisch, haast: ~ *all of them* haast iedereen

alms aalmoes

almshouse hofjeʰ, armenhuisʰ

aloft 1 omhoog; opwaarts [also fig]: *smoke kept rising* ~ er bleef maar rook opstijgen **2** [shipp] in de mast, in 't want

¹**alone** (adj) alleen, afzonderlijk, in zijn eentje

²**alone** (adv) **1** slechts, enkel, alleen **2** alleen, in zijn eentje: *go it* ~ het op zijn eentje opknappen; *leave* (or: *let*) ~ met·rust laten, afblijven van; *he cannot walk, let* ~ *run* hij kan niet eens lopen, laat staan rennen

¹**along** (adv) **1** door, verder, voort: *he brought his dog* ~ hij had zijn hond bij zich; *come* ~ kom mee; *go* ~ *(with)* meegaan (met); *I suspected it all* ~ ik heb het altijd wel vermoed; ~ *with* samen met **2** langs: *come ~ anytime* (je bent) altijd welkom

²**along** (prep) langs, door: *flowers* ~ *the path* bloemen langs het pad

alongside naast: ~ *the road* aan de kant van de weg

¹**aloof** (adj) afstandelijk, koel

²**aloof** (adv) op een afstand, ver: *keep* (or: *hold, stand*) ~ *(from)* zich afzijdig houden (van)

aloud hardop, hoorbaar

alp berg; alp

alphabet alfabetʰ; abcʰ [also fig]

alphabetical alfabetisch

alpha geek [inform] topnerd

alpha male alfaman; [fig] leider

alpine alpien; berg-: ~ *skiing* het alpineskiën

Alps (the) Alpen

already reeds, al (eerder)

¹**Alsatian** (n) **1** Elzasser, Elzassische **2** Duitse herder(shond)

²**Alsatian** (adj) Elzassisch

also ook, bovendien, eveneens

altar altaarʰ

altar boy misdienaar

alter 1 (zich) veranderen, (zich) wijzigen **2** [Am; inform; euph] helpen [pet]; castreren, steriliseren

alteration 1 wijziging, verandering **2** [Am; inform; euph] castratie, sterilisatie

altercation onenigheid, twist, ruzie, geruzieʰ

¹**alternate** (adj) afwisselend, beurtelings: *on ~ days* om de (andere) dag

²**alternate** (vb) afwisselen, verwisselen: *alternating current* wisselstroom

alternation (af)wisseling

¹**alternative** (n) alternatiefʰ, keuze, optie

²**alternative** (adj) alternatiefʰ: ~ *facts* alternatieve feiten

although hoewel, ofschoon

altitude hoogte

alto 1 altpartij, altinstrumentʰ, altstem **2** alt, altzanger(es)

altogether 1 totaal, geheel, helemaal: *at 50 he stopped working* ~ met 50 hield hij helemaal op met werken **2** in totaal, alles bij elkaar: *there were 30 people* ~ er waren in totaal 30 mensen

alt-right [Am] *alternative right* alt-right: *the ~ movement* de alt-rightbeweging

altruism altruïsmeʰ

aluminium aluminiumʰ

alumnus oud-student; oud-leerling, alumnus

always 1 altijd, steeds, voorgoed: *he's ~ complaining* hij loopt voortdurend te klagen **2** in elk geval, altijd nog: *we can ~ sell the boat* we kunnen altijd nog de boot verkopen

always-on: ~ *internet access* permanente internetverbinding

a.m. *ante meridiem* vm., voor de middag: *at 5 ~* om vijf uur 's ochtends

Am *America(n)*

amalgamate (doen) samensmelten, (zich) verbinden, annexeren, in zich opnemen

amass vergaren, opstapelen

¹**amateur** (n) amateur, liefhebber

²**amateur** (adj) [oft depr] amateur(s)-, amateuristisch

amaze verbazen, verwonderen, versteld doen staan

amazement verbazing, verwondering

amazing verbazingwekkend, verbazend

ambassador ambassadeur, vertegenwoordiger, (af)gezant

amber 1 amber(steen)ᵗʰ, barnsteenᵗʰ **2** amber(kleur); [traffic light] geelʰ, oranjeʰ

Amber alert [Am] amber alertʰ

ambience sfeer, stemming, ambiance

ambiguity dubbelzinnigheid

ambiguous dubbelzinnig, onduidelijk

ambition ambitie, eerzucht

ambitious ambitieus, eerzuchtig

ambivalence ambivalentie: *feel some ~* gemengde gevoelens hebben

ambivalent ambivalent, tegenstrijdig

¹amble (n) **1** telgang; pasgang [of horse] **2** kuierpas, kalme gang

²amble (vb) **1** in de telgang lopen **2** kuieren, op zijn gemak wandelen

ambulance ziekenwagen, ambulance

ambulant ambulant, in beweging, rondtrekkend

ambush hinderlaag, val(strik): *lie* (or: *wait*) *in ~* in een hinderlaag liggen

amen amen, het zij zo: [fig] *say ~ to sth.* volledig met iets instemmen

amenable 1 handelbaar, plooibaar **2** ontvankelijk (voor): *~ to reason* voor rede vatbaar

amend verbeteren [eg text, bill]; (bij amendement) wijzigen

amendment 1 amendement[h] **2** verbetering, rectificatie

amends genoegdoening, schadeloosstelling, compensatie: *make ~* a) schadevergoeding betalen; b) het weer goedmaken

amenity (sociale) voorziening, gemak[h]: *this house has all the amenities* dit huis is van alle gemakken voorzien

America Amerika

¹American (n) **1** Amerikaan(se): *Latin ~* iem. uit Latijns-Amerika, Latijns-Amerikaan(se) **2** Amerikaans(-Engels)[h]

²American (adj) Amerikaans: *~ Indian* (Amerikaanse) indiaan

amethyst 1 amethist[h] **2** violet[h], violetkleur, purperviolet[h]

amiable beminnelijk, vriendelijk

amicable amicaal, vriend(schapp)elijk: *come to an ~ agreement* een minnelijke schikking treffen

amidst te midden van, tussen, onder

¹amiss (adj) **1** verkeerd, gebrekkig: *there is nothing ~ with her* ze mankeert niets **2** misplaatst, ongelegen: *an apology would not be ~* een verontschuldiging zou niet misstaan

²amiss (adv) verkeerd, gebrekkig, fout, foutief: *take sth. ~* iets kwalijk nemen

ammonia ammoniak

ammunition munitie

amnesia amnesie, geheugenverlies[h]

amnesty amnestie, generaal pardon[h]

amoeba amoebe

amok: *run ~* amok maken, als een bezetene tekeergaan

among(st) onder, te midden van, tussen: *customs among(st) the Indians* gebruiken bij de indianen; *among(st) themselves* onder elkaar; *we have ten copies among(st) us* we hebben samen tien exemplaren

amoral amoreel, immoreel

amorous amoureus, verliefd

amount 1 hoeveelheid, grootte: *any ~ of*

money een berg geld **2** totaal[h], som, waarde: *to the ~ of* ten bedrage van

amount to 1 bedragen, oplopen tot, bereiken: *it does not ~ much* het heeft niet veel te betekenen **2** neerkomen op, gelijk staan met: *his reply amounted to a refusal* zijn antwoord kwam neer op een weigering

amp [inform] **1** ampere ampère **2** amplifier versterker

ampere ampère

ampersand en-teken[h] [the & sign]

ample 1 ruim, groot, uitgestrekt **2** rijk(elijk), overvloedig: *have ~ resources* bemiddeld zijn

amplifier versterker

amplify 1 vergroten, vermeerderen **2** [elec] versterken

amputate amputeren, afzetten

amuse amuseren, vermaken, bezighouden: *be ~d at* (or: *by, with*) *sth.* iets amusant vinden

amusement 1 amusement[h], vermaak[h] **2** plezier[h], pret, genot[h]: *watch in ~* geamuseerd toekijken

amusement arcade automatenhal

amusing vermakelijk, amusant

amygdala [anatomy] amygdala

an *see ²a*

anachronism anachronisme[h]

anachronistic 1 anachronistisch **2** ouderwets

anaemia bloedarmoede

¹anaesthetic (n) verdovingsmiddel[h]

²anaesthetic (adj) verdovend, narcotisch

anaesthetist anesthesist

anaesthetize verdoven, onder narcose brengen

anagram anagram[h]

anal anaal, aars-

analogous (+ to, with) analoog (aan), overeenkomstig (met), parallel

analogue analoog: *~ watch* horloge met wijzerplaat

analogy analogie, overeenkomst: *on the ~ of, by ~ with* naar analogie van

analyse analyseren, ontleden, ontbinden

analysis analyse [also maths]; onderzoek[h], ontleding

analyst analist(e), scheikundige

analytical analytisch

anaphylactic shock anafylactische shock

anarchist anarchist

anarchy anarchie

anatomy 1 (anatomische) bouw **2** anatomie, ontleding, analyse

ancestor 1 voorouder, voorvader **2** oertype[h], voorloper, prototype[h]

ancestral voorouderlijk, voorvaderlijk

ancestry 1 voorgeslacht[h], voorouders, voorvaderen **2** afkomst, afstamming

anchor anker[h]: *~ man* vaste presentator [of news and current affairs programmes]

anchorage 1 verankering **2** ankerplaats
anchovy ansjovis
ancient antiek, klassiek, uit de oudheid: ~ *history* de oude geschiedenis
Ancients (the) de antieken
ancillary 1 ondergeschikt, bijkomstig: ~ *industry* toeleveringsbedrijf[h] **2** helpend, aanvullend
and 1 en, (samen) met, en toen, dan: *children* **come** ~ **go** kinderen lopen in en uit; ~ *so* **forth**, ~ *so* **on** enzovoort(s); ~*/or* en/of **2** [intensifier or repetition] en (nog), (en) maar: *thousands* ~ *thousands of people* duizenden en nog eens duizenden mensen **3** [between two verbs] te, om te: *try* ~ *finish it* probeer het af te maken ‖ *nice* ~ *quiet* lekker rustig
Andorra Andorra
¹Andorran (n) Andorrees, Andorrese
²Andorran (adj) Andorrees
androgynous 1 androgyn, hermafrodiet **2** [bot] tweeslachtig
anecdotal anekdotisch
anecdote anekdote
anemone anemoon, zeeanemoon
anesthet- see anaesthet-
anew 1 opnieuw, nogmaals, weer **2** anders
angel 1 engel, beschermengel, engelbewaarder **2** schat, lieverd
angelic 1 engelachtig; hemels **2** [inform] lief
¹anger (n) woede, boosheid: *be filled with* ~ *at sth.* woedend zijn om iets
²anger (vb) boos maken
anger management agressiebeheersing
¹angle (n) **1** hoek [also maths]; kant, uitstekende punt[h]: *at an* ~ *(with)* schuin (op) **2** gezichtshoek, perspectief[h]; [fig] gezichtspunt[h]; standpunt[h]: *look at sth. from a different* (or: *another*) ~ iets van een andere kant bekijken
²angle (vb) (+ for) vissen (naar) [also fig]; hengelen (naar)
angle bracket punthaak
angler visser, hengelaar
Anglican anglicaans
anglicism anglicisme[h]
angling hengelsport
Anglo-American Engels-Amerikaans; Anglo-Amerikaans
¹Anglo-Saxon (n) **1** Oudengels[h] **2** Angelsakser **3** (typische) Engelsman
²Anglo-Saxon (adj) **1** Angelsaksisch **2** [Am] Engels
³Anglo-Saxon (adv) Oudengels
Angola Angola
¹Angolan (n) Angolees, Angolese
²Angolan (adj) Angolees
angry boos, kwaad: *be* ~ *about* (or: *at*) *sth.* boos zijn over iets; *be* ~ *at* (or: *with*) *s.o.* boos zijn op iem.
anguish leed[h], pijn
anguished gekweld; vol angst; vol smart

angular 1 hoekig, hoekvormig, hoek- **2** kantig, met scherpe kanten
¹animal (n) dier[h], beest[h]
²animal (adj) **1** dierlijk: ~ *husbandry* veeteelt **2** vleselijk, zinnelijk: ~ *desires* vleselijke lusten
animal ambulance dierenambulance
animal kingdom (the) dierenrijk[h]
¹animate (adj) **1** levend, bezield **2** levendig, opgewekt
²animate (vb) **1** leven geven, bezielen **2** verlevendigen, opwekken **3** animeren, aanmoedigen, inspireren
animated levend(ig), bezield, geanimeerd ‖ ~ *cartoon* tekenfilm
animation 1 animatiefilm, tekenfilm, poppenfilm **2** het maken van animatiefilms, animatie **3** levendigheid, opgewektheid, animo[h]
animosity vijandigheid, haat, wrok
aniseed anijszaad(je[h]), anijs
ankle enkel
anklet 1 enkelring **2** [Am] enkelsok, halve sok
annals annalen [also fig]; kronieken, jaarboeken
¹annex (n) **1** aanhangsel[h], addendum[h], bijlage **2** aanbouw, bijgebouw[h], dependance
²annex (vb) **1** aanhechten, (bij)voegen **2** annexeren, inlijven; [inform; iron] zich toe-eigenen
annexation 1 aanhechting **2** annexatie, inlijving
annihilate vernietigen; tenietdoen [also fig]
annihilation vernietiging
anniversary 1 verjaardag, jaardag, gedenkdag **2** verjaarsfeest[h], jaarfeest[h]
¹annotate (vb) (+ up)on) aantekeningen maken (bij), commentaar schrijven (op)
²annotate (vb) annoteren
announce 1 aankondigen, bekendmaken, melden **2** omroepen
announcement aankondiging, bekendmaking, mededeling
announcer 1 omroeper **2** aankondiger
annoy 1 ergeren, kwellen, irriteren: *be* ~*ed at sth.* zich over iets ergeren; *be* ~*ed with s.o.* boos zijn op iem. **2** lastigvallen, hinderen, plagen
annoyance 1 ergernis, kwelling **2** last, hinder, plaag
¹annual (n) **1** eenjarige plant **2** jaarboek[h]
²annual (adj) **1** jaarlijks: [bookkeeping] ~ *accounts* jaarrekening; ~ *income* jaarinkomen[h] **2** eenjarig
annuity jaargeld[h], jaarrente
annul 1 vernietigen, tenietdoen, schrappen **2** ongeldig verklaren, herroepen, annuleren
annunciation aankondiging, afkondiging
Annunciation (the) Maria-Boodschap

anoint 1 [rel] zalven **2** inwrijven, insmeren

anomaly anomalie, onregelmatigheid

anonymity anonimiteit

anonymous anoniem

anorak 1 anorak, parka **2** watje[h], nerd, studiebol, kluns

anorexic 1 anorexiapatiënt **2** eetlustremmer

another 1 een ander(e), nog één **2** andere, verschillende: *that's* ~ *matter* dat is een heel andere zaak; *for* one reason or ~ om een of andere reden; *in* one way or ~ op een of andere wijze **3** nog een, een tweede, een andere: *have* ~ *biscuit* neem nog een koekje

¹answer (n) antwoord[h], reactie, oplossing, resultaat[h]: *he gave* (or: *made*) *no* ~ hij gaf geen antwoord; *no* ~ er wordt niet opgenomen, ik krijg geen gehoor; *my only* ~ *to that* mijn enige reactie daarop

²answer (vb) **1** antwoorden, een antwoord geven: *Mary couldn't* ~ Mary wist er geen antwoord op **2** voldoende zijn, aan het doel beantwoorden: *one word would* ~ één woord zou volstaan

³answer (vb) **1** antwoorden (op), beantwoorden, een antwoord geven op: ~ *your father!* geef je vader antwoord! **2** reageren op: ~ *the telephone* de telefoon opnemen; ~ *the door* de deur opendoen (als er gebeld wordt) **3** beantwoorden aan, voldoen aan: ~ *the description* aan het signalement beantwoorden

answerable 1 verantwoordelijk, aansprakelijk: *be* ~ *to s.o. for sth.* bij iem. voor iets verantwoording moeten afleggen **2** beantwoordbaar

answer back 1 zich verdedigen **2** brutaal antwoorden, (schaamteloos) wat terugzeggen, tegenspreken

answer for verantwoorden, verantwoordelijk zijn voor: *I can't answer for the consequences* ik kan niet voor de gevolgen instaan

answering machine antwoordapparaat[h]

answerphone antwoordapparaat[h]

answer to 1 gehoorzamen: *my dog answers to the name of Dixie* mijn hond luistert naar de naam Dixie **2** zich verantwoorden tegenover: ~ *the headmaster for your behaviour* je bij de directeur voor je gedrag verantwoorden **3** beantwoorden aan

ant mier

antagonist tegenstander; antagonist

antagonistic vijandig

antagonize tegen zich in het harnas jagen

¹Antarctic (n, the) **1** Antarctica, zuidpool, zuidpoolgebied[h] **2** Zuidelijke IJszee

²Antarctic (adj) antarctisch, zuidpool-: ~ *Circle* zuidpoolcirkel

antecedent iets voorafgaands, voorafgaand feit[h]: ~*s* antecedenten

antedate voorafgaan aan

antelope antilope

antenatal prenataal: ~ *care* zwangerschapszorg

antenna 1 [Am] antenne **2** voelhoorn, (voel)spriet, antenne

anterior 1 voorste, eerste, voor- **2** voorafgaand: ~ *to* vroeger dan, voorafgaand aan

anthem 1 themalied[h], lijflied[h]: *national* ~ volkslied[h] **2** populair pop- of rocknummer[h]

anthology anthologie, bloemlezing

anthracite antraciet[h]

anthropology antropologie, studie van de mens

anti tegen, anti, tegenstander van, strijdig met

anti-aircraft luchtdoel-; luchtafweer-

¹antibiotic (n) antibioticum[h]

²antibiotic (adj) antibiotisch

antibody antistof, antilichaam[h]

antic capriool, gekke streek

anticipate 1 vóór zijn, voorkomen, ondervangen, de wind uit de zeilen nemen **2** 'verwachten, tegemoet zien, hopen op: *trouble is* ~*d* men rekent op moeilijkheden **3** een voorgevoel hebben van **4** anticiperen, vooruitlopen (op): *I won't* ~ ik wil niet op mijn verhaal vooruitlopen

anticipation 1 verwachting; afwachting: *thanking you in* ~ bij voorbaat dank **2** voorgevoel[h], voorpret

anticlimax anticlimax

anticlockwise linksomdraaiend, tegen de wijzers van de klok (in)

anticoagulant antistollingsmiddel[h]

antidepressant kalmeringsmiddel[h]

antidote tegengif[h]

antifreeze antivries(middel)[h]

antipathetic antipathiek: ~ *to any new idea* voor geen enkel nieuw idee te vinden

antipathy antipathie, vooringenomenheid, afkeer

¹antiquarian (n) **1** oudheidkundige, oudheidkenner **2** antiquair **3** antiquaar, handelaar in oude boeken, prenten, enz.

²antiquarian (adj) **1** oudheidkundig **2** antiquarisch

antiquated ouderwets, verouderd, achterhaald

antique 1 antiek, oud **2** ouderwets

antiquities antiquiteiten, overblijfselen, oudheden

antiquity 1 ouderdom **2** oudheid

anti-Semite antisemiet

anti-Semitism antisemitisme[h]

antiseptic antiseptisch, ontsmettend

antiskid antislip

antisocial 1 asociaal **2** ongezellig

anti-terrorist antiterreur-

antithesis antithese, tegenstelling, tegenstrijdigheid, tegengestelde[h]

antithetic tegengesteld, tegenstrijdig

antitoxin tegengif^h

antitrade: ~ *wind* antipassaatwind

anti-vaxxer vaccinatieweigeraar

antler geweitak^h: ~*s* gewei^h

antsy ongedurig

anus anus, aars

anvil aambeeld^h

anxiety bezorgdheid, ongerustheid, vrees

anxious 1 bezorgd, ongerust: *you needn't be ~ about me* je hoeft je over mij geen zorgen te maken **2** verontrustend, zorgwekkend, beangstigend **3** [inform] verlangend: *he was ~ to leave* hij stond te popelen om te mogen vertrekken

^1**any** (pron) **1** [number or amount] enig(e), enkele, wat: *I cannot see ~ houses* ik zie geen huizen; *have you got ~ paper?* heb je papier?; *~ child can tell you that* elk kind kan je dat vertellen; *I didn't get ~* ik heb er geen enkele gehad; *few, if ~* weinig of geen, zo goed als geen **2** iem., iets, om het even wie (wat), wie (wat) ook: *~ will do* geef me er maar een, het geeft niet welke

^2**any** (adv) [in negative and interrogative sentences] enigszins, in enig opzicht: *are you ~ happier here?* ben je hier gelukkiger?; *I cannot stand it ~ longer* ik kan er niet meer tegen

anybody om het even wie, wie dan ook, iem., iedereen: *she 's not just ~* ze is niet de eerste de beste

anyhow 1 toch (maar) [at the end of a sentence]: *it's probably not worth it but let me see it ~* het heeft waarschijnlijk geen zin, maar laat me het toch maar zien **2** hoe dan ook [at the beginning of a sentence, after a pause]: *~, I have to go now, sorry* hoe dan ook, ik moet nu gaan, het spijt me **3** ongeordend, slordig, kriskras: *he threw his clothes down just ~* hij gooide zijn kleren zomaar ergens neer

anymore nog, meer, opnieuw, langer: *it's not hurting ~* het doet geen pijn meer

anyone *see* anybody

anyplace [Am; inform] waar dan ook: *sleep ~ you like* slaap waar je wilt

^1**anything** (n) alles: *she guards her jewels, her books, her ~* ze bewaakt haar juwelen, haar boeken, alles wat ze heeft

^2**anything** (pron) om het even wat, wat dan ook, iets, (van) alles: *she didn't eat ~* ze at niets; *~ but safe* allesbehalve veilig; *if ~ this food is even worse* dit eten is zo mogelijk nog slechter

^3**anything** (adv) enigszins, in enige mate; [+ negation] enigszins (niet): *it isn't ~ much* het heeft niet veel om het lijf

anytime [inform] wanneer (dan) ook, om het even wanneer: *he can come ~ now* hij kan nu elk ogenblik komen; *come ~ you like* kom wanneer je maar wilt

anyway 1 toch (maar): *he had no time but*

helped us ~ hij had geen tijd maar toch hielp hij ons **2** hoe dan ook, in ieder geval: *~, I must be off now* in ieder geval, ik moet er nu vandoor **3** eigenlijk: *why did he come ~?* waarom kwam hij eigenlijk?

^1**anywhere** (adv) **1** overal, ergens, om het even waar **2** in enigerlei mate, ergens: *she isn't ~ near as tall as me* ze is lang niet zo groot als ik

^2**anywhere** (conj) waar … maar …: *go ~ you like* ga waar je maar naartoe wilt

aorta aorta

apart 1 los, onafhankelijk, op zichzelf **2** van elkaar (verwijderd), op … afstand, met … verschil: *five miles ~* op vijf mijlen (afstand) van elkaar **3** uit elkaar, aan stukken, kapot: *take ~* uit elkaar halen, demonteren ‖ *~ from* behalve, afgezien van

apartheid apartheid

apartment 1 kamer, vertrek^h **2** [esp pl] appartement^h, appartementen, reeks kamers **3** [Am] flat, etage

apathetic apathisch; lusteloos

apathy apathie, lusteloosheid, onverschilligheid

^1**ape** (n) (mens)aap; [fig] na-aper

^2**ape** (vb) na-apen

aperture 1 opening, spleet **2** lensopening

apex top, tip, hoogste punt^h; [fig] toppunt^h; hoogtepunt^h

apiarist imker, bijenhouder

apiculture bijenteelt

apiece elk, per stuk: *she gave us £10 ~* ze gaf ons elk £10

aplomb aplomb^h, zelfverzekerdheid

apocalyptic apocalyptisch

apogee hoogste punt^h, toppunt^h

apologetic verontschuldigend, schuldbewust

apologize zich verontschuldigen, zijn excuses aanbieden

apology verontschuldiging: *~ for absence* bericht van verhindering; *offer an ~ to s.o. for sth.* zich bij iem. voor iets verontschuldigen

apoplexy beroerte

apostle apostel

apostrophe apostrof, weglatingsteken^h

app *application* app

appal met schrik vervullen: *they were ~led at (or: by) it* ze waren er ontsteld over

appalling verschrikkelijk

apparatus apparaat^h, toestel^h, machine ‖ *the men set up their ~* de mannen stelden hun apparatuur op

apparel [form] kleding; gewaad^h

apparent duidelijk, blijkbaar, kennelijk: *~ly he never got your letter* blijkbaar heeft hij je brief nooit ontvangen

apparition verschijning, spook^h, geest

^1**appeal** (n) **1** verzoek^h, smeekbede **2** [law] appel^h, (recht^h van) beroep^h: *lodge an ~* be-

roep aantekenen **3** aantrekkingskracht
²**appeal** (vb) **1** verzoeken, smeken **2** aantrekkelijk zijn voor, aanspreken, aantrekken **3** in beroep gaan, appelleren: *~ against that decision* tegen die beslissing beroep aantekenen
appealing 1 smekend, meelijwekkend **2** aantrekkelijk, aanlokkelijk
appeal to een beroep doen op; appelleren aan [feelings, common sense]: *may we ~ your generosity?* mogen wij een beroep doen op uw vrijgevigheid?
¹**appear** (vb) **1** verschijnen, voorkomen: *he had to ~ before court* hij moest voorkomen **2** opdagen **3** optreden
²**appear** (vb) **1** schijnen, lijken: *so it ~s* 't schijnt zo te zijn **2** blijken: *he ~ed to be honest* hij bleek eerlijk te zijn
appearance 1 verschijning, optredenʰ: *he put in* (or: *made*) *an ~ at the party* hij liet zich even zien op het feest **2** uiterlijkʰ, voorkomenʰ: *~s schijn; ~s are deceptive* schijn bedriegt; *keep up ~s* de schijn ophouden
appease kalmeren, bedaren, sussen, verzoenen
appendicitis blindedarmontsteking
appendix 1 aanhangselʰ **2** [med] appendixʰ
appetite 1 eetlust, honger, trek: *lack of ~* gebrek aan eetlust **2** begeerte, zin: *whet s.o.'s ~* iem. lekker maken
appetizer 1 aperitiefʰ **2** voorgerecht(je)ʰ, hapjeʰ
appetizing eetlust opwekkend, smakelijk; appetijtelijk
¹**applaud** (vb) applaudisseren
²**applaud** (vb) toejuichen [also fig]; prijzen, loven
applause applausʰ, toejuiching
apple appel ‖ *the ~ of his eye* zijn oogappel; *Big Apple* New York
applecart: *upset the ~* een streep door de rekening halen
apple-pie order: *everything is in ~* alles is volmaakt in orde
appliance 1 middelʰ, hulpmiddelʰ **2** toestelʰ, gereedschapʰ, apparaatʰ
applicable 1 toepasselijk, van toepassing, bruikbaar: *not ~* niet van toepassing **2** geschikt, passend, doelmatig
applicant sollicitant, aanvrager
application 1 sollicitatie: *letter of ~* sollicitatiebrief **2** aanvraag(formulierʰ) **3** [comp] toepassing, programmaʰ, app **4** toepassing, gebruikʰ: *for external ~ only* alleen voor uitwendig gebruik **5** het aanbrengen [eg unction on wound] **6** aanvraag, verzoekʰ: *on ~* op aanvraag **7** ijver, vlijt, toewijding
application software toepassingsprogrammatuur
applied toegepast: *~ physics* toegepaste

natuurkunde
¹**apply** (vb) **1** van toepassing zijn, betrekking hebben (op), gelden: *these rules don't ~ to you* dit reglement geldt niet voor u **2** zich richten, zich wenden: *~ within* (or: *next door*) hier (or: *hiernaast*) te bevragen **3** (+ for) solliciteren (naar), inschrijven (voor), aanvragen: *to whom should I ~ for this job?* bij wie moet ik solliciteren voor deze baan?
²**apply** (vb) **1** aanbrengen, (op)leggen, toedienen: *~ this lotion to the skin* wrijf de huid in met deze lotion **2** toepassen, aanwenden, gebruiken: *~ the brakes* remmen ‖ *~ o.s. (to)* zich inspannen (voor), zich toeleggen (op)
appoint 1 vaststellen, bepalen, vastleggen: *at the ~ed time* op de vastgestelde tijd **2** benoemen, aanstellen
appointment 1 afspraak: *by ~* volgens afspraak **2** aanstelling, benoeming
appraisal schatting, waardering, evaluatie
appraise schatten, waarderen, evalueren
¹**appreciate** (vb) stijgen [in price, value]
²**appreciate** (vb) **1** waarderen, (naar waarde) schatten; dankbaar zijn voor, dankbaarheid tonen voor: *he doesn't feel ~d* hij voelt zich niet gewaardeerd; *I would really ~ it if you would listen to me* ik zou het erg waarderen als je naar me luistert; *we ~ your efforts* we waarderen je inzet **2** zich bewust zijn van, zich realiseren, erkennen: *we ~ how important this is for you* we zijn ons ervan bewust hoe belangrijk dit voor je is
appreciation 1 waardering, beoordeling **2** waardering, erkenning
apprehend aanhouden, in hechtenis nemen
apprehension 1 vrees, bezorgdheid: *she had ~s for her safety and about her future* ze maakte zich zorgen over haar veiligheid en haar toekomst **2** aanhouding, arrestatie
apprehensive ongerust, bezorgd
apprentice leerjongen, leerling
¹**approach** (n) **1** toegang(sweg), oprit; aanvliegroute [of aeroplane] **2** aanpak, (wijze van) benadering **3** contactʰ, toenadering: *make ~es to s.o.* bij iem. avances maken, met iem. contact zoeken **4** benadering: *it's the nearest ~ to ...* het is bijna ..., het lijkt het meeste op ...
²**approach** (vb) naderen, (naderbij) komen
³**approach** (vb) **1** naderen, komen bij **2** contact opnemen met, aanspreken, benaderen **3** aanpakken [of problem]
approbation officiële goedkeuring
¹**appropriate** (adj) geschikt, passend, toepasselijk: *where ~* waar nodig, waar van toepassing, in voorkomende gevallen; *~ for, ~ to* geschikt voor
²**appropriate** (vb) **1** bestemmen, toewijzen **2** (zich) toe-eigenen: *he had ~d large sums to himself* hij had zich grote bedragen toegeëi-

gend
approval goedkeuring, toestemming: *on* ~
op zicht
approve 1 formeel akkoord gaan (met),
goedkeuren: *parliament has ~d the proposed*
budget het parlement is akkoord gegaan
met de begroting; *these medicines have been*
~d for the Dutch market deze medicijnen zijn
goedgekeurd voor de Nederlandse markt
2 goedkeuren, positief staan tegenover: *his*
parents do not ~ of his long hair zijn ouders zijn
het er niet mee eens dat hij lang haar heeft
approximate bij benadering (aangegeven), naar schatting: *~ly three hours* ongeveer
drie uur
apricot abrikoos
April april
April fool 1 aprilgrap
April Fools' Day één april
a priori van tevoren, vooraf
apron 1 schort[h], voorschoot[h] **2** platform[h]
[at airport]
apron string: *he is **tied** to his wife's ~s* hij
loopt aan de leiband van zijn vrouw
apt 1 geschikt, passend **2** geneigd **3** begaafd: ~ *at* goed in
aptitude 1 geschiktheid **2** neiging **3** aanleg, talent[h], begaafdheid
aquafarming aquacultuur
aquaplaning 1 het waterskiën **2** [traf]
aquaplaning[h]
aquarium aquarium[h]
Aquarius [astrology] (de) Waterman
aquascooter waterscooter
aquatic water-
aqueduct aquaduct[h]
¹Arab (n) **1** Arabier, Arabische **2** Arabische
volbloed
²Arab (adj) Arabisch
Arabia Arabië
Arabian Arabisch
Arabic Arabisch: ~ *numerals* Arabische cijfers
¹arable (n) bouwland[h], landbouwgrond, akkerland[h]
²arable (adj) bebouwbaar, akker-
arbiter 1 leidende figuur[+h], toonaangevend iem. **2** scheidsrechter
arbitrary 1 willekeurig, grillig **2** eigenmachtig **3** scheidsrechterlijk
¹arbitrate (vb) arbitreren, als bemiddelaar
optreden: ~ *between* the parties tussen de
partijen bemiddelen
²arbitrate (vb) aan arbitrage onderwerpen,
scheidsrechterlijk (laten) regelen
arbitration arbitrage; scheidsrechterlijke
beslissing: *go to* ~ het geschil aan arbitrage
onderwerpen
arbour prieel[h]
arc 1 (cirkel)boog **2** [elec] lichtboog, vlam-
boog

arcade 1 arcade, zuilengang **2** winkelgalerij
arcade game videospel[h]
¹arch (n) **1** boog, gewelf[h], arcade: *triumphal*
~ triomfboog **2** voetholte
²arch (adj) ondeugend, schalks, guitig: *an* ~
glance (or: *smile*) een schalkse blik (*or:* guitig
lachje)
³arch (vb) (+ across, over) (zich) welven
(over), zich uitspannen
⁴arch (vb) **1** (over)welven, overspannen
2 krommen, buigen: *the cat ~ed its **back*** de
kat zette een hoge rug op
archaeologist archeoloog, oudheidkundige
archaeology archeologie, oudheidkunde
archaic verouderd, ouderwets
archangel aartsengel
archbishop aartsbisschop
archenemy aartsvijand
archer boogschutter
archetype archetype[h]; [fig] schoolvoorbeeld[h]
archipelago archipel, eilandengroep
architect 1 architect **2** ontwerper **3** [fig]
maker, schepper, grondlegger
architecture architectuur, bouwkunst,
bouwstijl
archives 1 archief[h] [storage location] **2** archieven [documents stored]
archivist archivaris
archway overwelfde doorgang; poort
arctic 1 (noord)pool-: *Arctic **Circle*** noordpoolcirkel **2** ijskoud
Arctic (the) noordpoolgebied[h], Arctica[h]
ardent vurig, hevig, hartstochtelijk
ardour vurigheid, hartstocht
arduous moeilijk, zwaar, lastig
area 1 oppervlakte: *a farm of 60 square kilo-*
metres in ~ een boerderij met een oppervlakte van 60 vierkante kilometer **2** gebied[h] [also
fig]; streek, domein[h] **3** ruimte, plaats
area code [Am] netnummer[h]
arena arena; strijdperk[h] [also fig]
Argentina Argentinië
Argentine (the) Argentinië
¹Argentinian (n) Argentijn(se)
²Argentinian (adj) Argentijns
argot jargon[h]
arguable 1 betwistbaar, aanvechtbaar
2 aantoonbaar, aanwijsbaar
arguably misschien wel, vermoedelijk,
waarschijnlijk: *this is* ~ *the most beautiful violin*
concerto ever dit is misschien wel het mooiste
vioolconcert ooit
¹argue (vb) **1** argumenteren, pleiten: *they*
were ~ing against (or: *for*) zij pleitten tegen
(*or:* voor) **2** (+ about, over) redetwisten
(over), debatteren **3** twisten, ruziën, kibbelen: *don't* ~ *with me!* spreek me niet tegen!
²argue (vb) **1** doorpraten, bespreken **2** stel-

len, aanvoeren, bepleiten **3** overreden, overhalen: *I managed to ~ him into coming* ik kon hem overreden om te komen

argument 1 argument[h], bewijs[h], bewijsgrond: *a strong ~ for* (or: *against*) een sterk argument voor (or: tegen) **2** ruzie, onenigheid, woordenwisseling **3** hoofdinhoud; korte inhoud [of book] **4** bewijsvoering, betoog[h], redenering: *let us, for the sake of ~, suppose …* stel nu eens (het hypothetische geval) dat … **5** discussie, gedachtewisseling

argumentation argumentatie, bewijsvoering

arid dor, droog, schraal, onvruchtbaar

Aries [astrology] (de) Ram

arise 1 zich voordoen, gebeuren, optreden: *difficulties have ~n* er zijn moeilijkheden ontstaan **2** voortkomen, ontstaan: *~ from* voortkomen uit, het gevolg zijn van

aristocracy [also fig] **1** aristocratie **2** aristocraten, aristocratie, adel

aristocrat aristocraat

¹arithmetic (n) **1** rekenkunde **2** berekening

²arithmetic (adj) rekenkundig: *~ progression* rekenkundige reeks

ark ark: *Noah's ~* Ark van Noach

¹arm (n) **1** arm [of human being, animal; also fig]: *~ in arm* arm in arm, gearmd; *at ~'s length* op een afstand, op gepaste afstand; *within ~'s reach* binnen handbereik; *a list as long as your ~* een ellenlange lijst; *twist s.o.'s ~* iemands arm omdraaien; [fig] forceren, het mes op de keel zetten **2** mouw **3** armleuning **4** afdeling, tak **5** (-s) wapenen, (oorlogs)wapens, bewapening: *lay down* (one's) *~s* de wapens neerleggen; *present ~s* het geweer presenteren **6** (-s) oorlogvoering, strijd **7** (-s) wapen[h], familiewapen[h] || *be up in ~s about* (or: *over, against*) *sth.* verontwaardigd zijn over iets

²arm (vb) zich (be)wapenen [also fig]

³arm (vb) (be)wapenen [also fig]; uitrusten: *~ed with relevant information* gewapend met (or: voorzien van) alle belangrijke informatie

armada armada, oorlogsvloot: *the (Spanish) Armada* de (Spaanse) Armada [of 1588]

armadillo gordeldier[h]

armament 1 wapentuig[h] [of tank, ship, aeroplane] **2** bewapening

armchair leunstoel: *~ critics* stuurlui aan wal; *~ shopping* thuiswinkelen

armed gewapend: *an ~ conflict* een gewapend conflict; *~ forces* strijdkrachten

armed response unit interventie-eenheid

Armenia Armenië

¹Armenian (n) Armeniër, Armeense

²Armenian (adj) Armeens

armistice wapenstilstand, bestand[h]

armlock armklem

armour 1 wapenrusting, harnas[h] **2** pantser[h], pantsering, pantserbekleding **3** beschutting, dekking, schuilplaats

armoured 1 gepantserd: *~ car* pantserwagen **2** gewapend [glass, concrete etc] **3** geharnast

armoury 1 wapenkamer, wapenmagazijn[h] **2** wapens, wapensysteem[h] **3** arsenaal[h] [also fig]

armpit oksel

armrest (stoel)leuning

arms race bewapeningswedloop

arm-wrestling het armworstelen; het armdrukken

army leger[h] [also fig]; massa, menigte: *join the ~* in dienst gaan; *an ~ of locusts* een grote zwerm sprinkhanen

aroma aroma[h], geur

aromatic aromatisch, geurig

¹around (adv) **1** rond [also fig]; in de vorm van een cirkel: *the other way ~* andersom; *a way ~* een omweg; *bring ~* tot een andere mening brengen, overreden; *people gathered ~ to see* mensen verzamelden zich om te kijken; *pass it ~* geef het rond; *turn ~* (zich) omdraaien **2** in het rond, aan alle kanten, verspreid: *news gets ~ fast* nieuws verspreidt zich snel **3** [proximity] in de buurt: *for miles ~* kilometers in de omtrek; *stay ~* blijf in de buurt **4** [approximation] ongeveer, omstreeks: *he's ~ sixty* hij is rond de zestig; *~ fifty people* om en nabij de vijftig mensen

²around (prep) **1** rond, rondom, om … heen: *~ the corner* om de hoek; *a chain ~ his neck* een ketting om zijn hals **2** [proximity] in het rond, rondom, om … heen: *only those ~ him* alleen zijn naaste medewerkers **3** [in all directions] door, rond, her en der in: *all ~ the country* door het hele land

arousal 1 opwinding, prikkeling, ophitsing **2** het (op)wekken, uitlokking

arouse 1 wekken [also fig]; uitlokken, doen ontstaan: *~ suspicion* wantrouwen wekken **2** opwekken, prikkelen, ophitsen

¹arrange (vb) **1** maatregelen nemen, in orde brengen: *~ for sth.* iets regelen, ergens voor zorgen **2** overeenkomen, het eens zijn: *~ with s.o. about sth.* iets overeenkomen met iem.

²arrange (vb) **1** (rang)schikken, ordenen, opstellen **2** bijleggen, rechtzetten, rechttrekken **3** regelen, organiseren, arrangeren, zorgen voor: *~ a meeting* een vergadering beleggen **4** [mus] arrangeren

arrangement 1 ordening, (rang)schikking, opstelling **2** afspraak, regeling, overeenkomst **3** maatregel, voorzorg **4** [mus] arrangement[h], bewerking **5** plan[h]

¹array (n) **1** serie, collectie, reeks **2** gelid[h], marsorde, slagorde

²array (vb) (in slagorde) opstellen, verzamelen, (in het gelid) schikken

arrears 1 achterstand: *in* ~ *with* one's work (or: *rent*) achter met zijn werk (*or:* huur) **2** (geld)schuld: *be in* ~ achter(op) zijn [payment]

¹arrest (n) **1** stilstand [of growth, movement]: [med] *cardiac* ~ hartstilstand **2** bedwinging; beteugeling [of disease, decay etc] **3** arrestatie, aanhouding, (voorlopige) hechtenis: *place* (or: *put*) *under* ~ in arrest nemen; *under* ~ in arrest

²arrest (vb) **1** tegenhouden, bedwingen **2** arresteren, aanhouden **3** boeien, fascineren

arresting boeiend, fascinerend

arrival 1 (aan)komst: *on* ~ bij aankomst **2** binnengevaren schip", binnengekomen trein (vliegtuig"): [fig] *new* ~ pasgeborene **3** nieuwkomer, nieuweling

arrive 1 aankomen, komen, arriveren [of persons, things]: *he ~d at the station at 2 o'clock sharp* hij kwam stipt om 2 uur aan op het station; *their third child ~d two* **weeks** *early* hun derde kind kwam twee weken te vroeg **2** arriveren, het (waar)maken **3** aanbreken; komen [of time]

arrive at bereiken [also fig]; komen tot: ~ *a* **conclusion** tot een besluit komen, een conclusie trekken

arrogance arrogantie; aanmatiging

arrogant arrogant, verwaand

arrow pijl

arse [vulg] **1** reet **2** klootzak, lul

arsenal [mil] arsenaal", (wapen)arsenaal"

arsenic 1 arsenicum", arseen" **2** rattenkruit"

arsey [vulg] irritant, hufterig

arson brandstichting

arsonist brandstichter, pyromaan

art 1 kunst, bekwaamheid, vaardigheid: *~s and* **crafts** kunst en ambacht; *work of* ~ kunstwerk"; *the* **black** ~ zwarte kunst **2** kunst(greep), truc, list **3** kunst(richting): *the* **fine** *~s* de schone kunsten **4** [educ] tekenen

artefact kunstvoorwerp"

arterial slagaderlijk; arterieel: ~ *road* verkeersader

artery slagader; [fig] verkeersader; handelsader

artful listig, spitsvondig

art gallery kunstgalerie

art-house: ~ *film* cultfilm, filmhuisfilm

arthritis artritis, jicht, gewrichtsontsteking

artichoke artisjok

article 1 artikel", stuk", tekstfragment": *a* **newspaper** ~ een krantenartikel **2** [law] (wets)artikel", bepaling **3** [com] artikel", koopwaar, handelswaar: ~ *of* **clothing** kledingstuk" **4** [linguistics] lidwoord": *definite* (or: *indefinite*) ~ bepaald (*or:* onbepaald)

lidwoord **5** (-s) contract", statuten, akten

¹articulate (adj) **1** zich duidelijk uitdrukkend [pers] **2** duidelijk; helder (uitgedrukt/verwoord) [thought etc]

²articulate (vb) duidelijk spreken, articuleren

³articulate (vb) **1** articuleren, duidelijk uitspreken **2** (helder) verwoorden, onder woorden brengen

articulated geleed: ~ *bus* gelede bus, harmonicabus; ~ *lorry* vrachtwagen met aanhanger

articulation articulatie

artifice 1 truc, kunstgreep, list **2** handigheid **3** listigheid

artificial 1 kunstmatig: ~ *intelligence* kunstmatige intelligentie **2** kunst-, namaak-: ~ *flowers* kunstbloemen **3** gekunsteld, gemaakt: *an* ~ *smile* een gemaakte glimlach

artillery [mil] **1** artillerie, geschut" **2** artillerie [part of army]

artisan handwerksman, vakman, ambachtsman

artist 1 (beeldend) kunstenaar (kunstenares) **2** artiest

artiste (variété)artiest(e)

artistic artistiek

artist's impression 1 robotfoto **2** schetsontwerp"

artless argeloos, onschuldig

Arts (the) letteren

artwork 1 kunst **2** illustraties

arty [oft depr] **1** kitscherig **2** artistiekerig

Aruba Aruba

arugula [Am] rucola

¹as (pron) die, dat: *the same as* **he** *had seen* dezelfde die hij gezien had

²as (adv) even, zo: *as fast as John* zo snel als John ‖ *as* **well** *as* zowel ... als, niet alleen ... maar ook; *as* **from** *now* van nu af

³as (prep) **1** [nature, role, function etc] als, in de rol van, in de hoedanigheid van: *Mary starring as Juliet* Mary in de rol van Julia **2** [comparison] als, gelijk: *as light as a feather* vederlicht ‖ *as* **such** als zodanig

⁴as (conj) **1** [agreement or comparison] (zo)als, naarmate, naargelang: *he lived as a* **hermit** *(would)* hij leefde als een kluizenaar; *cheap as cars* **go** goedkoop voor een wagen; *it's bad enough as it is* het is zo al erg genoeg; *as he later* **realized** zoals hij later besefte; *as it* **were** als het ware, om zo te zeggen; *such as* zoals; *he was so kind as to tell me all about it* hij was zo vriendelijk om mij alles daarover te vertellen **2** terwijl, toen: *Jim sang as he scrubbed* Jim zong onder het schrobben **3** aangezien, daar, omdat: *as he was poor* daar hij arm was ‖ *as* **for**, *as to* wat betreft; *as* **from** *today* vanaf vandaag, met ingang van vandaag

asap *as soon as possible* z.s.m., zo spoedig mogelijk

asbestos asbest[h]

ASBO *anti-social behaviour order* [roughly] rechterlijk doenormaalbevel[h]

[1]**ascend** (vb) **1** (op)stijgen, omhooggaan **2** oplopen [of slope, terrain]

[2]**ascend** (vb) **1** opgaan, naar boven gaan, beklimmen **2** bestijgen [throne]

ascendancy overwicht[h], overhand: *have* (or: *gain*) *(the)* ~ *over* overwicht hebben (or: behalen) op

Ascension Hemelvaart: ~ *Day* Hemelvaartsdag

ascent bestijging, opstijging, (be)klim-(ming), het omhooggaan

ascertain vaststellen, bepalen, te weten komen, ontdekken

[1]**ascetic** (n) asceet, iem. die zich onthoudt van weelde en genoegens

[2]**ascetic** (adj) ascetisch, zich onthoudend van weelde en genoegens

ASCII *American Standard Code for Information Interchange* ASCII

ascribe (+ to) toeschrijven (aan)

ASD *autistic spectrum disorder* ASS *(autismespectrumstoornis)*

ash 1 es, essenhout[h] **2** (-es) as [after burning of corpse etc]

ashamed beschaamd: *feel* ~ zich schamen; *be* ~ *of* zich schamen over

ashen asgrauw; vaal **2** (lijk)bleek

ashore 1 kustwaarts, landwaarts **2** aan land, aan wal, op het strand

ashtray asbak

Ash Wednesday Aswoensdag

Asia Azië: ~ *Minor* Klein-Azië

[1]**Asian** (n) Aziaat, Aziatische

[2]**Asian** (adj) Aziatisch

[1]**aside** (n) terloopse opmerking

[2]**aside** (adv) terzijde, opzij, zijwaarts: [fig] *brush* ~ *protests* protesten naast zich neerleggen; *set* ~ **a)** opzijzetten; **b)** sparen [money] ‖ [Am] ~ *from* afgezien van, behalve

asinine ezelachtig [also fig]; dwaas

[1]**ask** (vb) vragen, informeren, navraag doen: ~ *for advice* om raad vragen; [inform] ~ *for it* erom vragen, het uitlokken

[2]**ask** (vb) **1** vragen, verzoeken: ~ *s.o. a question* iem. een vraag stellen; ~ *a favour of s.o.* iem. om een gunst vragen **2** eisen, verlangen: *that's too much to* ~ dat is te veel gevraagd **3** vragen, uitnodigen ‖ [inform] *if you* ~ *me* volgens mij, als je het mij vraagt

askance achterdochtig, wantrouwend: *look* ~ *at s.o. (sth.)* iem. (iets) wantrouwend aankijken (bekijken)

askew scheef, schuin

aslant schuin; naar één kant

asleep in slaap, slapend: *fall* ~ in slaap vallen; *fast* (or: *sound*) ~ in een diepe slaap

A/S level *Advanced Supplementary level* A/S-(examen)niveau[h]

asparagus asperge

aspect 1 gezichtspunt[h], oogpunt[h] **2** zijde, kant, facet[h]

aspen esp(enboom), ratelpopulier: *tremble like an* ~ *leaf* trillen als een espenblad

asperity ruwheid, scherpheid

[1]**asphalt** (n) asfalt[h]

[2]**asphalt** (vb) asfalteren

asphyxia verstikking(sdood)

asphyxiate doen stikken

aspirant kandidaat

aspirate 1 opzuigen, door zuigen verwijderen **2** [linguistics] aspireren

aspiration 1 aspiratie, streven[h], ambitie **2** inademing **3** aspiratie, opzuiging, wegzuiging, afzuiging **4** [linguistics] aspiratie

aspire sterk verlangen, streven: ~ *after,* ~ *to sth.* naar iets streven

aspirin aspirine, aspirientje[h]

ass 1 ezel [also fig]; domoor: *make an* ~ *of o.s.* zichzelf belachelijk maken **2** [Am; vulg] reet

assail [form] aanvallen [also fig]; overvallen: *be* ~*ed with* (or: *by*) *doubt* overmand zijn door twijfel

assailant aanvaller, belager

assassin moordenaar, sluipmoordenaar, huurmoordenaar

assassinate 1 vermoorden **2** vernietigen [character, reputation]

assassination (sluip)moord

[1]**assault** (n) **1** aanval [also fig] **2** [mil] bestorming **3** daadwerkelijke bedreiging: ~ *and battery* mishandeling, geweldpleging; *physical* ~ lichamelijk geweld; *sexual* ~ aanranding

[2]**assault** (vb) **1** aanvallen [also fig] **2** [mil] bestormen

assay analyseren; keuren [metal, ore]

[1]**assemble** (vb) zich verzamelen, samenkomen

[2]**assemble** (vb) **1** assembleren, samenbrengen, verenigen; [techn] in elkaar zetten; monteren **2** ordenen

assembler assembleerprogramma[h]

assembly 1 samenkomst, vergadering, verzameling **2** assemblage, samenvoeging, montage **3** assemblee

assembly language assembleertaal

assembly line montageband; lopende band

[1]**assent** (n) toestemming, aanvaarding

[2]**assent** (vb) toestemmen, aanvaarden: ~ *to sth.* met iets instemmen

assert 1 beweren, verklaren **2** handhaven, laten gelden; opkomen voor [rights]: ~ *o.s.* op zijn recht staan, zich laten gelden

assertion 1 bewering; verklaring **2** handhaving

assertive 1 stellig, uitdrukkelijk, beslist **2** zelfbewust, zelfverzekerd, assertief

assess 1 bepalen; vaststellen [value, amount, damage] **2** belasten; aanslaan [person, estate] **3** taxeren, schatten, ramen, beoordelen: ~ *the situation* de situatie beoordelen

assessment 1 belasting, aanslag **2** schatting, taxatie, raming **3** vaststelling, bepaling **4** beoordeling

assessor taxateur, schade-expert

asset 1 goedʰ, bezitʰ; [fig also] waardevolle eigenschap; pluspuntʰ, aanwinst: *health is the greatest* ~ gezondheid is het grootste goed **2** [econ] creditpost **3** (-s) activa, baten, bedrijfsmiddelen: *~s and liabilities* activa en passiva, baten en lasten

assiduous volhardend, vlijtig

assign 1 toewijzen, toekennen, aanwijzen: ~ *s.o. a task* iem. een taak toebedelen **2** bepalen; vaststellen [day, date]; opgeven, aanwijzen **3** aanwijzen, aanstellen, benoemen: ~ *s.o. to a post in Berlin* iem. voor een functie in Berlijn aanwijzen

assignment 1 taak, opdracht; [Am; educ] huiswerkʰ **2** toewijzing, toekenning, bestemming

assimilate zich assimileren, opgenomen worden, gelijk worden: ~ *into,* ~ *with sth.* opgenomen worden in iets

assist helpen, bijstaan, assisteren

assistance hulp, bijstand, assistentie

assistance dog hulphond

¹assistant (n) **1** helper, assistent, adjunct **2** bediende, hulp

²assistant (adj) assistent-, hulp-, ondergeschikt

assisted dying hulp bij zelfdoding, euthanasie

assisted-living: ~ *facility* verzorgingshuisʰ; woon-zorgcomplexʰ

¹associate (n) **1** partner, compagnon **2** (met)gezel, kameraad, makker

²associate (adj) toegevoegd, bijgevoegd, mede-: ~ *member* buitengewoon lid

³associate (vb) **1** zich verenigen, zich associëren **2** (+ with) omgaan (met)

⁴associate (vb) verenigen, verbinden; [also fig] associëren; in verband brengen: *closely ~d with* nauw betrokken bij

association 1 vereniging, genootschapʰ, gezelschapʰ, bond **2** associatie, verbandʰ, verbinding **3** samenwerking, connectie: *in ~ with* samen met, in samenwerking met **4** omgang, vriendschap

Association football voetbalʰ

assort sorteren, ordenen, classificeren: ~ *with* indelen bij

assorted 1 gemengd, gevarieerd **2** bij elkaar passend: *ill-~* slecht bij elkaar passend

assortment 1 assortimentʰ, collectie, ruime keuze **2** sortering, ordening

assuage 1 kalmeren, verzachten, verlichten, (tot) bedaren (brengen) **2** bevredigen; stillen [hunger, desire]; lessen [thirst]

assume 1 aannemen, vermoeden, veronderstellen **2** overnemen, nemen, grijpen **3** op zich nemen: *he ~d the role of benefactor* hij speelde de weldoener **4** voorwenden: *~d name* aangenomen naam, schuilnaam

assuming ervan uitgaande dat

assumption vermoedenʰ, veronderstelling

assurance 1 zekerheid, vertrouwenʰ **2** zelfvertrouwenʰ **3** verzekering, levensverzekering **4** verzekering, belofte, garantie: *quality* ~ kwaliteitsbewaking, kwaliteitscontrole

assure verzekeren: ~ *s.o. of one's support* iem. van zijn steun verzekeren

asterisk asterisk, sterretjeʰ

asteroid asteroïde, kleine planeet

asthma astma⁺ʰ

astonish verbazen, versteld doen staan: *be ~ed at sth.* zich over iets verbazen, stomverbaasd zijn over iets

astonishment verbazing

astound ontzetten, verbazen, schokken

astounding verbazingwekkend

astray verdwaald: *go* ~ verdwalen, de verkeerde weg op gaan; *lead s.o.* ~ iem. op een dwaalspoor brengen

astride schrijlings, wijdbeens, dwars ‖ *she sat* ~ *her horse* ze zat schrijlings op haar paard

astrology astrologie

astronaut astronaut, ruimtevaarder

astronomer astronoom, sterrenkundige

astronomical astronomisch [also fig]; sterrenkundig

astronomy astronomie, sterrenkunde

astute scherpzinnig, slim, sluw

asylum 1 asielʰ, toevlucht(soordʰ): *political* ~ politiek asiel **2** (krankzinnigen)inrichting

asylum seeker asielzoeker; vluchteling

asymmetric asymmetrisch: ~ *bars* brug met ongelijke leggers

¹at (n) [comp] at, apenstaartjeʰ

²at (prep) **1** [place, time, point on a scale] aan, te, in, op, bij: *at my aunt's* bij mijn tante; *at Christmas* met Kerstmis; *at the corner* op de hoek; *cheap at 10p* goedkoop voor 10 pence; *at that time* toen, in die tijd; *we'll leave it at that* we zullen het daarbij laten **2** [activity or profession] bezig met: *at work* aan het werk; *they're at it again* ze zijn weer bezig **3** [skill] op het gebied van: *my mother is an expert at wallpapering* mijn moeder kan geweldig goed behangen **4** door, naar aanleiding van, als gevolg van, door middel van, via: *at my command* op mijn bevel; *at a glance* in één oogopslag

atheism atheïsmeʰ, godloochening

atheist atheïst, godloochenaar

athleisure modieuze sport- en fitnesskle-

ding
athlete atleet
athletic 1 atletisch **2** atletiek-
athletics atletiek
¹Atlantic (n, the) Atlantische Oceaan
²Atlantic (adj): the ~ *Ocean* de Atlantische Oceaan
atlas atlas
ATM [Am] *automatic teller machine* geldautomaat, pinautomaat
atmosphere 1 dampkring; atmosfeer [also unit of pressure] **2** (atmo)sfeer, stemming
atmospheric atmosferisch, lucht-, dampkrings-
atoll atolʰ, ringvormig koraaleilandʰ
atom 1 [science] atoomʰ **2** zeer kleine hoeveelheid, greintjeʰ
atomic atoom-, kern-, nucleair: ~ *power* atoomkracht; atoommogendheid; ~ *power station* kerncentrale
atomize verstuiven, vernevelen
atomizer verstuiver
atone for goedmaken
atonement vergoeding, boetedoening: *make ~ for* goedmaken
atop boven op, bovenaan
atrocious 1 wreed, monsterachtig **2** afschuwelijk slecht
atrocity 1 wreedheid **2** afschuwelijkheid
atrophy [also fig] wegkwijnen
at sign [comp] apenstaartjeʰ
attach (aan)hechten, vastmaken, verbinden: ~ *too much importance* **to** *sth.* ergens te zwaar aan tillen
attaché attaché
attaché case diplomatenkoffertjeʰ
attachment 1 hulpstukʰ: ~s toebehorenʰ, accessoires **2** aanhechting, verbinding **3** gehechtheid, genegenheid, trouw **4** [comp] attachmentʰ, bijlage
¹attack (n) **1** aanval, (scherpe) kritiek: *be under* ~ aangevallen worden **2** aanpak
²attack (vb) **1** aantasten, aanvreten **2** aanpakken: ~ *a problem* een probleem aanpakken
³attack (vb) aanvallen [also fig]; overvallen
attain bereiken, verkrijgen: ~ *old age* een hoge leeftijd bereiken
attainment 1 verworvenheid, kundigheid **2** het bereiken, verwerving
¹attempt (n) **1** (+ to) poging (tot): ~ *at conciliation* toenaderingspoging **2** aanval, aanslag: ~ *on s.o.'s life* aanslag op iemands leven
²attempt (vb) proberen, wagen
¹attend (vb) **1** aanwezig zijn: ~ *at church* de dienst bijwonen **2** opletten, (aandachtig) luisteren
²attend (vb) **1** bijwonen, aanwezig zijn bij, zitten op [school]: *will you be ~ing his lecture?* ga je naar zijn lezing? **2** zorgen voor, verplegen **3** letten op, bedienen **4** begeleiden,

vergezellen; [fig] gepaard gaan met
attendance 1 opkomst, aantal aanwezigen **2** aanwezigheid: *compulsory* ~ verschijningsplicht, verplichte aanwezigheid **3** dienst, toezichtʰ: *doctor in* ~ dienstdoende arts
attendant 1 bediende, knecht **2** begeleider, volgeling: ~s gevolgʰ **3** bewaker, suppoost
attendee deelnemer, aanwezige: *conference* ~s congresgangers
attend to 1 aandacht schenken aan, luisteren naar **2** zich inzetten voor, zorgen voor, bedienen: *attend to s.o.'s interests* iemands belangen behartigen; *are you being attended to?* wordt u al geholpen?
attention 1 aandacht, zorg: *this plant needs a lot of* ~ deze plant vraagt veel zorg; *pay* ~ opletten; *have a short ~ span* een korte spanningsboog hebben; *for the ~ of* ter attentie van **2** belangstelling, erkenning **3** attentie, hoffelijkheid || *be* (or: *stand*) *at* ~ in de houding staan
attention span concentratieperiode: *he has a short* ~ hij heeft een korte spanningsboog, hij kan zich niet lang concentreren
attentive 1 aandachtig, oplettend **2** attent, hoffelijk
attenuate 1 verdunnen, dunner worden, versmallen **2** verzwakken, verminderen; dempen [sound]: *with old age memories* ~ met de oude dag vervagen de herinneringen
¹attest (vb) (+ to) getuigen (van), getuigenis afleggen (van)
²attest (vb) **1** plechtig verklaren, officieel bevestigen **2** getuigen van, betuigen
attic vliering, zolder(kamer)
attire gewaadʰ, kledij
attitude 1 houding, stand, attitude **2** houding, gedragʰ: ~ *of mind* instelling **3** standpuntʰ, opvatting
attorney 1 procureur, gevolmachtigde: *power of* ~ volmacht **2** [Am] advocaat
Attorney General 1 procureur-generaal **2** [Am] minister van Justitie
attract aantrekken [also fig]; lokken, boeien
attraction 1 aantrekkelijkheid, aantrekking(skracht) **2** attractie, bezienswaardigheid
attractive aantrekkelijk, attractief
¹attribute (n) **1** eigenschap, (essentieel) kenmerkʰ **2** attribuutʰ, symboolʰ
²attribute (vb) toeschrijven, toekennen
attribution toeschrijving
attune doen overeenstemmen, afstemmen: *my ears are not ~d to modern jazz* mijn oren zijn niet gewend aan moderne jazz
aubergine aubergine
auburn kastanjebruin
¹auction (n) veiling, verkoop bij opbod: *put*

up for ~ veilen, bij opbod verkopen
²**auction** (vb) veilen, verkopen bij opbod
audacious 1 dapper, moedig **2** roekeloos **3** brutaal
audacity 1 dappere daad, waagstukʰ **2** dapperheid **3** roekeloosheid **4** brutaliteit, onbeschoftheid
audible hoorbaar, verstaanbaar
audience 1 publiekʰ, toehoorders, toeschouwers **2** (+ with) audiëntie (bij)
¹**audit** (n) **1** accountantsonderzoekʰ, accountantscontrole **2** accountantsverslagʰ **3** balans, afrekening
²**audit** (vb) (de boeken/rekeningen) controleren
audition auditie, proefoptredenʰ
auditor 1 toehoorder, luisteraar **2** (register)accountant; [Belg] bedrijfsrevisor
auditorium gehoorzaal, auditoriumʰ, aula
auditory auditief; gehoor-: ~ *nerve* gehoorzenuw
augment vergroten, (doen) toenemen, vermeerderen
augur: [form] ~ *well* (or: *ill*) *for* goeds (*or:* kwaads) voorspellen voor
augury voorspelling, voortekenʰ: *a hopeful* ~ een gunstig voorteken
august verheven, groots
August augustus
aunt tante
auntie [inform] tantetjeʰ
aura aura, sfeer, waasʰ: *he has an ~ of respectability* hij heeft iets waardigs over zich
aural oor-; van het oor
auspices auspiciën, bescherming: *under the ~ of Her Majesty* onder de bescherming van Hare Majesteit
auspicious 1 gunstig, voorspoedig **2** veelbelovend
¹**Aussie** (n) [inform] Australiër
²**Aussie** (adj) [inform] Australisch
austere 1 streng, onvriendelijk, ernstig **2** matig, sober, eenvoudig
austerity 1 soberheid, matiging **2** (strenge) eenvoud, soberheid **3** beperking, bezuiniging(smaatregel), inlevering: ~ *drive* bezuinigingscampagne
¹**Australasian** (n) bewoner van Australaz-Azië [Oceania]
²**Australasian** (adj) Austraal-Aziatisch
Australia Australië
¹**Australian** (n) Australiër, Australische
²**Australian** (adj) Australisch
Austria Oostenrijk
¹**Austrian** (n) Oostenrijker, Oostenrijkse
²**Austrian** (adj) Oostenrijks
authentic authentiek, onvervalst, origineel
authenticate (voor) echt verklaren: ~ *a will* een testament bekrachtigen
authenticity 1 authenticiteit; echtheid **2** oprechtheid

author auteur, schrijver, maker, schepper
¹**authoritarian** (n) autoritair iem., eigenmachtig individuʰ
²**authoritarian** (adj) autoritair, eigenmachtig
authoritative 1 gebiedend, autoritair: *he has an ~ manner* hij dwingt respect af **2** gezaghebbend
authority 1 autoriteit, overheidsinstantie, overheidspersoon: *the competent authorities* de bevoegde overheden, het bevoegd gezag **2** rechtʰ, toestemming **3** autoriteit, deskundige: *an ~ on the subject* een autoriteit op dit gebied **4** autoriteit, gezagʰ, wettige macht: *abuse of* ~ machtsmisbruikʰ **5** autoriteit, (moreel) gezagʰ, invloed: *you cannot deny his* ~ je kunt niet ontkennen dat hij iem. van aanzien is **6** volmacht, machtiging
authority figure gezagdrager, gezagdraagster
authorization 1 autorisatie, machtiging, volmacht **2** vergunning, goedkeuring
authorize 1 machtigen, recht geven tot, volmacht verlenen: ~*d agent* gevolmachtigd vertegenwoordiger, gevolmachtigde **2** goedkeuren, inwilligen, toelaten
autism autismeʰ
autistic autistisch
auto [Am; inform] auto
autobiographical autobiografisch
autobiography autobiografie
autocracy autocratie
autogas lpgʰ, autogasʰ
autograph handschriftʰ; handtekening [of celebrity]
autoimmunity auto-immuniteit
automate automatiseren
¹**automatic** (n) automatisch wapenʰ
²**automatic** (adj) automatisch, zelfwerkend, zonder na te denken: *he ~ally thought of her* hij dacht onwillekeurig aan haar
automobile [Am] auto
autonomous autonoom, met zelfbestuur: ~ *state* autonome staat
autonomy autonomie, zelfbestuurʰ, onafhankelijkheid: ~ *of the individual* onafhankelijkheid van het individu
autopilot *automatic pilot* automatische piloot
autopsy [med] autopsie, lijkschouwing, sectie
autoreply autoreply, automatische beantwoording
autumn [also fig] herfst, najaarʰ, nadagen: *in (the)* ~ in het najaar (*or:* de herfst)
¹**auxiliary** (n) **1** helper, hulpkracht, assistent **2** hulpmiddelʰ **3** hulpwerkwoordʰ
²**auxiliary** (adj) **1** hulp-, behulpzaam, helpend: ~ *troops* hulptroepen; ~ *verb* hulpwerkwoordʰ **2** aanvullend, supplementair, reserve-

¹avail (n) nut[h], voordeel[h], baat: *to no* ~ nutteloos, vergeefs

²avail (vb) baten, helpen, van nut zijn ‖ *Joe ~ed himself of the opportunity* Joe maakte van de gelegenheid gebruik

availability beschikbaarheid, verkrijgbaarheid, leverbaarheid, aanwezigheid

available beschikbaar, verkrijgbaar, leverbaar: *Mr Jones was not* ~ *for comment* meneer Jones was niet beschikbaar voor commentaar

avalanche lawine; [fig] vloed(golf); stortvloed

avarice gierigheid, hebzucht

avaricious hebzuchtig, gierig

avatar 1 incarnatie; belichaming **2** [comp] avatar

Ave *avenue* ln, laan

avenge wreken, wraak nemen (voor)

avenger wreker

avenue 1 avenue; (brede) laan **2** oprijlaan [to castle, estate] **3** weg [only fig]; toegang, middel[h]: *explore every* ~ alle middelen proberen

¹average (n) gemiddelde[h], middelmaat; [also fig] doorsnee: *eight is the* ~ *of ten and six* acht is het gemiddelde van tien en zes; *above (the)* ~ boven het gemiddelde; *below (the)* ~ onder het gemiddelde ‖ *on (the)* ~ gemiddeld, door de bank genomen

²average (adj) gemiddeld, midden-, doorsnee-: ~ *man* de gewone man

³average (vb) het gemiddelde berekenen

¹average out (vb) [inform] gemiddeld op hetzelfde neerkomen: *the profits averaged out at fifty pounds a day* de winst kwam gemiddeld neer op vijftig pond per dag

²average out (vb) [inform] een gemiddelde berekenen van

averse (+ to) afkerig (van), tegen, afwijzend

aversion 1 (+ to) afkeer (van): *take an* ~ *to* een afkeer krijgen van **2** persoon (iets) waar men een hekel aan heeft

avert 1 (+ from) afwenden (van) [eyes]; afkeren **2** voorkomen, vermijden, afwenden: ~ *danger* het gevaar keren

avian vogel-, ornithologisch

avian flu vogelgriep

aviary vogelhuis[h], vogelverblijf[h]

aviation 1 luchtvaart, vliegkunst **2** vliegtuigbouw

avid 1 gretig, enthousiast: *an* ~ *reader* een grage lezer **2** verlangend

avocet kluut

avoid (ver)mijden, ontwijken: *they couldn't* ~ *doing it* zij moesten het wel doen

avoidance vermijding, het vermijden

avow 1 toegeven, erkennen **2** (openlijk) bekennen; belijden [belief etc]: *they are ~ed enemies* het zijn gezworen vijanden

avuncular als een (vriendelijke) oom, vaderlijk

await opwachten, verwachten, tegemoet zien ‖ *a warm welcome ~s them* er wacht hen een warm welkom

¹awake (adj) **1** wakker: *wide* ~ klaarwakker [also fig] **2** waakzaam, alert: ~ *to* zich bewust van

²awake (vb) **1** ontwaken [also fig]; wakker worden **2** (+ to) zich bewust worden (van), gaan beseffen

³awake (vb) **1** wekken, wakker maken **2** bewust maken

awakening 1 het ontwaken **2** bewustwording

¹award (n) **1** beloning, prijs **2** toekenning [of reward, prize, damages]

²award (vb) **1** toekennen [prize]; toewijzen **2** belonen

aware zich bewust, gewaar: *politically* ~ politiek bewust; *be* ~ *of* zich bewust zijn van

awareness bewustzijn[h]: *lack of* ~ onwetendheid

¹away (adj) uit-: ~ *match* uitwedstrijd

²away (adv) **1** weg [also fig]; afwezig, op (een) afstand, uit: *give* ~ weggeven **2** voortdurend, onophoudelijk: *she was chatting* ~ ze zat aan één stuk door te kletsen ‖ *I'll do it right* ~ ik zal het meteen doen

awe ontzag[h], eerbied: *hold* (or: *keep*) *s.o.* ~ ontzag hebben voor iem.; *stand in* ~ *of* groot ontzag hebben voor

awe-inspiring ontzagwekkend

awesome 1 ontzagwekkend, ontzag inboezemend **2** [inform] gaaf, geweldig, fantastisch

awesomesauce [inform] briljant, supergoed

awful [inform] afschuwelijk, enorm: *an* ~ *lot* ontzettend veel

awfully [inform] erg, vreselijk, ontzettend: *thanks* ~ reuze bedankt; ~ *nice* vreselijk aardig

awhile korte tijd, een tijdje

awkward 1 onhandig, onbeholpen **2** onpraktisch **3** ongelegen; ongunstig [date, time] **4** gênant: ~ *situation* pijnlijke situatie **5** opgelaten, niet op zijn gemak

awning luifel, kap, markies, zonnescherm[h]

AWOL: *go* ~ verdwijnen, met de noorderzon vertrekken

awry scheef [also fig]; schuin, fout: *go* ~ mislukken

¹axe (n) bijl; [fig] *have an* ~ *to grind* ergens zelf een bijbedoeling mee hebben

²axe (vb) **1** ontslaan, aan de dijk zetten **2** afschaffen, wegbezuinigen

axis as(lijn), spil

axle [techn] (draag)as, spil

Azerbaijan Azerbeidzjan

¹Azerbaijani (n) Azerbeidzjaan(se)

²**Azerbaij<u>a</u>ni** (adj) Azerbeidzjaans
<u>a</u>zure hemelsblauw, azuurblauw; [fig] wolkeloos

b

b *born* geb., geboren

B2B *business to business* b2b; business-to-business

BA *Bachelor of Arts* Bachelor of Arts [university degree]

¹**babble** (n) gebabbel^h, gewauwel^h, gelets^h

²**babble** (vb) babbelen

babe 1 [dated] kindje^h, baby **2** [inform] liefje^h, schatje^h **3** [inform] mooie meid ‖ ~ *in the* **woods** naïeveling

babel 1 spraakverwarring **2** wanorde; chaos

baboon baviaan [also fig; depr]; lomperd

baby 1 baby, zuigeling, kleuter **2** jongste, benjamin **3** [fig] klein kind^h, kinderachtig persoon **4** jong^h [of animal] **5** schatje^h **6** [inform] persoon, zaak: *that's your* ~ dat is jouw zaak ‖ [fig] *be left* **carrying** (or: **holding**) *the* ~ met de gebakken peren blijven zitten

baby boomer babyboomer, geboortegolver

baby grand [mus] kleine vleugel

baby minder babysitter, oppas

baby shower babyshower

baby sit babysitten

babysitter babysitter, oppas

bachelor 1 vrijgezel **2** bachelor [lowest university degree]: *Bachelor of* **Arts** bachelor in de letteren; *Bachelor of* **Science** bachelor in de exacte wetenschappen

¹**back** (n) **1** rug, achterkant: *behind s.o.'s* ~ achter iemands rug [also fig] **2** achter(hoede)speler, verdediger, back **3** achterkant, achterzijde, keerzijde, rug: *back to* **back** a) ruggelings, rug tegen rug; b) achtereenvolgens **4** (rug)leuning **5** achterste deel^h: [fig] *at the* ~ *of one's mind* in zijn achterhoofd; *at the* ~ achterin^h **6** [sport] achter^h ‖ *know like the* ~ *of one's* **hand** als zijn broekzak kennen; [fig] *with one's* ~ *to the* **wall** met zijn rug tegen de muur; [inform] *get* (or: *put*) *s.o.'s* ~ *up* iem. irriteren; [inform] *get off s.o.'s* ~ iem. met rust laten; *pat o.s. on the* ~ tevreden zijn over zichzelf; *put one's* ~ *into sth.* ergens de schouders onder zetten; *glad to* **see** *the* ~ *of s.o.* iem. liever zien gaan dan komen; *stab s.o. in the* ~ iem. een dolk in de rug steken, iem. verraden; *turn one's* ~ *on* de rug toekeren

²**back** (adj) **1** achter(-): ~ *room* a) achterkamer(tje); b) [also fig] ergens achteraf; ~ *seat* a) achterbank [of car]; b) [fig] tweede plaats **2** terug- **3** ver (weg), (achter)afgelegen

4 achterstallig **5** oud [of edition]: ~ *issue* (or: *number*) oud nummer [of magazine]

³**back** (vb) krimpen [of wind]

⁴**back** (vb) **1** (onder)steunen [also fin]; schragen, bijstaan **2** [inform] wedden (op), gokken op: [fig] ~ *the wrong* **horse** op het verkeerde paard wedden

⁵**back** (vb) achteruit bewegen, achteruitrijden, (doen) achteruitgaan: ~ *out* achteruit wegrijden

⁶**back** (adv) **1** achter(op), aan de achterkant: [Am] ~ *of* achter **2** achteruit, terug **3** terug [also fig]; weer thuis **4** [inform] in het verleden, geleden, terug: ~ *in* 1975 al in 1975 **5** op (enige) afstand: *a few miles* ~ een paar mijl terug **6** achterom ‖ ~ *and* **forward** (or: *forth*) heen en weer

backache rugpijn

back away (also + from) achteruit weglopen (van), zich terugtrekken

backbencher gewoon Lagerhuislid^h

backbite kwaadspreken (over), roddelen (over)

backbone ruggengraat [also fig]; wervelkolom, wilskracht, pit

backbreaking slopend, zwaar

back-burner [inform] op een laag pitje zetten

backchat [inform] tegenspraak; brutale opmerking

backcountry 1 afgelegen (berg)streek **2** [Austr] binnenland^h

backdate 1 met terugwerkende kracht in doen gaan **2** antidateren

back door achterdeur

back down terugkrabbelen, toegeven

backdrop 1 [theatre] achterdoek^h **2** achtergrond

backfire 1 terugslaan [of engine]; naontsteking hebben **2** mislopen, verkeerd aflopen

background achtergrond [also fig]: *remain in the* ~ op de achtergrond blijven

backhanded: ~ *compliment* dubieus compliment

backie 1 [traf] ritje^h op de bagagedrager: *give s.o. a* ~ iem. meenemen op de bagagedrager **2** [inform] rugselfie

backing 1 (ruggen)steun, ondersteuning **2** achterban, medestanders **3** [mus] begeleiding

backlash tegenstroom, verzet^h, reactie

backlight 1 [photography] tegenlicht^h **2** [screen] achtergrondverlichting

backlog achterstand

back off terugdeinzen, achteruitwijken

back out (+ of) zich terugtrekken (uit), afzien (van)

backpack rugzak

backpacking [inform] rugzaktoerisme^h

backroom politics achterkamertjespolitiek

back-seat driver passagier die 'meerijdt'; [Am; fig] stuurman aan de wal

backside 1 [inform] achterwerk^h, zitvlak^h **2** achtereinde^h

backslash backslash

backslide 1 terugvallen [in bad behaviour]; vervallen **2** afvallig worden

¹backspace (n) backspacetoets

²backspace (vb) met de cursor een positie teruggaan

back-stabbing achterbaks gedrag^h

backstage achter het podium, achter de schermen, in het geheim

backstair(s) 1 privé-, heimelijk: *backstair gossip* achterklap **2** achterbaks, onderhands

backstop 1 [Am; baseball] achtervanger **2** [fig] vangnet^h; noodoplossing

back street achterbuurt(en)

back-street clandestien: *~ abortion* illegale abortus

backstroke rugslag

back-to-back opeenvolgend ‖ *~ housing* [roughly] rijtjeshuizen

backtrack 1 terugkeren **2** terugkrabbelen

backup 1 vervanging **2** reserve **3** [comp] back-up

¹back up (vb) **1** [Am] een file vormen **2** [Am] achteruitrijden [of car]

²back up (vb) **1** (onder)steunen, staan achter, bijstaan **2** bevestigen [story]

back-up 1 (ruggen)steun, ondersteuning **2** reserve, voorraad **3** reservekopie (van computerbestand^h) **4** [Am] file

backward 1 achter(lijk); achtergebleven [in development]; traag, niet bij **2** achteruit(-), ruggelings: *a ~ glance* een blik achterom

backwards 1 achteruit [also fig]; achterwaarts, ruggelings: *~ and forward(s)* heen en weer **2** naar het verleden, terug

backwater 1 (stil) binnenwater^h; [fig] gat^h; afgelegen stadje^h; [fig] impasse; (geestelijke) stagnatie **2** achterwater^h

backwoods binnenlanden

backyard 1 plaatsje^h, achterplaats; [fig] achtertuin: *in one's own ~* in zijn eigen achtertuin **2** [Am] achtertuin

bacon bacon^h, spek^h ‖ [inform] *bring home the ~* de kost verdienen; [inform] *save one's ~* zijn hachje redden, er zonder kleerscheuren afkomen

bacterial bacterieel; bacterie-

bacterium bacterie

¹bad (n) **1** het slechte, het kwade: *go to the ~* de verkeerde kant opgaan **2** debet^h, schuld: *be £ 300 to the ~* voor 300 pond in het krijt staan

²bad (adj) **1** slecht, minderwaardig, verkeerd: *a ~ conscience* een slecht geweten; [inform] *make the best of a ~ job* het beste er van (zien te) maken; *go ~* bederven; *bad-*

mannered ongemanierd; *not half, not so ~* niet zo gek **2** kwaad, kwaadaardig, stout: *in ~ faith* te kwader trouw; *from ~ to worse* van kwaad tot erger **3** ziek, naar, pijnlijk **4** erg, ernstig, lelijk: *~ debt* oninbare schuld; *be in a ~ way* er slecht aan toe zijn **5** ongunstig: *make the best of a ~ bargain* er het beste van maken; *that looks ~* dat voorspelt niet veel goeds **6** schadelijk: *~ for your liver* slecht voor je lever **7** vol spijt: *I feel ~ about that* dat spijt me

bad ass [Am; inform] rotzak; ruziezoeker

bad-ass [Am; inform] **1** retegoed, steengoed, keigaaf **2** stoer; eigenwijs

baddie slechterik

badge badge^+h, insigne^h, politiepenning

¹badger (n) das [animal]

²badger (vb) lastigvallen: *I ~ed him into working for me* ik drong zolang aan dat hij toch maar besloot voor mij te gaan werken

badly 1 slecht: *do ~* een slecht resultaat behalen, het er slecht van afbrengen **2** erg, zeer, hard: *I need it ~* ik heb het hard nodig; *~ wounded* zwaar gewond

bae [inform] *before anyone else* [roughly] schatje^h

baeless [inform] single

baffle verbijsteren, van zijn stuk brengen: *a problem that has ~d biologists for years* een probleem dat biologen al jaren voor raadsels stelt

bafflement verbijstering

¹bag (n) **1** zak, baal: *~s under the eyes* wallen onder de ogen **2** zak, tas, koffer **3** zak vol; [fig] grote hoeveelheid: *the whole ~ of tricks* de hele santenkraam; [inform] *~s of money* hopen geld **4** vangst [game] ‖ *a mixed ~* een allegaartje; [inform] *it's in the ~* het is in kannen en kruiken

²bag (vb) vangen; schieten [game, fowl]

baggage bagage

baggy zakachtig, flodderig: *~ cheeks* hangwangen

bag lady zwerfster

bagpipes doedelzak

Bahamas (the) Bahama's

Bahrain Bahrein

¹Bahraini (n) Bahreiner, Bahreinse

²Bahraini (adj) Bahreins

¹bail (n) borg(stelling), borgtocht, borgsom: *out on ~* vrijgelaten op borgtocht

²bail (vb) hozen

³bail (vb) **1** vrijlaten tegen borgstelling **2** leeghozen

Bailey bridge baileybrug

bailiff 1 [law] deurwaarder **2** [Am; law] gerechtsdienaar

¹bail out (vb) hozen

²bail out (vb) **1** door borgtocht in vrijheid stellen, vrijkopen **2** [inform] uit de penarie helpen **3** leeghozen

¹bait (n) aas^h, lokaas^h; [fig] verleiding: *swallow* (or: *take*) *the* ~ toebijten, toehappen; [fig also] erin trappen

²bait (vb) **1** van lokaas voorzien **2** ophitsen [animal, esp dogs] **3** treiteren, boos maken

bake bakken (in een oven): *~d beans* witte bonen in tomatensaus

baked beans witte bonen in tomatensaus

bake-off bakwedstrijd

baker bakker: [fig] *~'s dozen* dertien

baker's dozen dertien

bakery 1 bakkerij **2** bakkerswinkel

baking soda 1 zuiveringszout^h **2** [culinary] baksoda

baking tin bakvorm

balaclava bivakmuts

¹balance (n) **1** balans, weegschaal: [fig] *his fate is* (or: *hangs*) *in the* ~ zijn lot is onbeslist **2** [com] balans: ~ *of payments* betalingsbalans; *strike a* ~ [fig] een compromis (*or:* het juiste evenwicht) vinden **3** [fin, com] saldo^h, tegoed^h, overschot^h: ~ *in hand* kasvoorraad; ~ *due* debetsaldo^h **4** evenwicht^h, balans: ~ *of power* machtsevenwicht^h; *redress the* ~ het evenwicht herstellen || *on* ~ alles in aanmerking genomen

²balance (vb) **1** schommelen, balanceren, slingeren **2** [com] sluiten [of balance sheet]; gelijk uitkomen, kloppen: *the books* ~ de boeken kloppen, de administratie klopt

³balance (vb) **1** wegen; [fig] overwegen; tegen elkaar afwegen **2** in evenwicht brengen, balanceren **3** [com] opmaken, laten kloppen; sluitend maken [balance sheet]: ~ *the books* het boekjaar afsluiten

balanced evenwichtig, harmonisch: ~ *diet* uitgebalanceerd dieet

balance sheet balans

balcony balkon^h, galerij

bald 1 kaal; [fig also] sober; saai: ~ *as a coot* kaal als een biljartbal; ~ *tyre* gladde band **2** naakt, bloot

balderdash onzin

baldly gewoonweg, zonder omwegen, regelrecht

bale baal

baleful 1 noodlottig **2** onheilspellend [eg glance]

¹bale out (vb) **1** hozen **2** het vliegtuig uitspringen [with parachute]

²bale out (vb) uithozen, leeghozen

¹balk (n) balk

²balk (vb) **1** weigeren, stokken, blijven steken: *the horse ~ed at the fence* het paard weigerde de hindernis **2** (+ at) terugschrikken (van/voor), bezwaar maken (tegen)

³balk (vb) verhinderen: ~ *s.o.'s plans* iemands plannen in de weg staan

Balkan Balkan-

Balkans Balkan

¹ball (n) **1** bal; [sport only] worp; schop, slag: *the* ~ *is in your court* nu is het jouw beurt [also fig]; *set* (or: *start*) *the* ~ *rolling* de zaak aan het rollen brengen **2** bol, bolvormig voorwerp^h, bal **3** prop, kluwen^h, bol **4** rond lichaamsdeel^h; bal [of foot]; muis [of hand]; oogbol, oogappel **5** kogel **6** bal^h, dansfeest^h **7** [inform] plezier^h, leut, lol

²ball (n) balspel^h; [Am] honkbal^h: *play* ~ met de bal spelen; [Am] honkbal spelen; [fig] meewerken

ballad ballade

ballast ballast; [fig] bagage

ballet 1 ballet^h, balletkunst **2** stuk balletmuziek

ball game balspel^h; [Am esp] honkbalwedstrijd || *we are now in a whole new* ~ de zaak staat er nu heel anders voor; *it's anybody's* ~ het kan nog alle kanten op

ballistic ballistisch || [Am; inform] *go* ~ in woede uitbarsten, ontploffen

¹balloon (n) **1** (lucht)ballon: *the* ~ *goes up* de ballon stijgt op; [fig] de pret begint; de moeilijkheden beginnen **2** ballon(netje^h) [in cartoon]

²balloon (vb) **1** per luchtballon reizen **2** opzwellen, bol gaan staan

ballot 1 stem, stembiljet^h, stembriefje^h: ~ *box* stembus; *cast one's* ~ zijn stem uitbrengen **2** stemming, stemronde: *let's take* (or: *have*) *a* ~ laten we erover stemmen

ballot screen keuzescherm^h

ballpark [Am] honkbalveld^h || *in the* ~ ongeveer juist, raak; *that's at least in the* ~ dat komt in ieder geval in de buurt

ball-park ongeveer juist: *a* ~ *figure* een ruwe schatting

ball pit ballenbak

ballroom balzaal, danszaal

balm balsem [also fig]; troost

balmy zacht; mild

balsam 1 [also fig] balsem **2** balsemboom

Baltic Baltisch: ~ *Sea* Oostzee

balustrade balustrade

bamboo bamboe*^h

bamboozle [inform] **1** bedriegen, beetnemen: ~ *s.o. out of his money* iem. zijn geld afhandig maken **2** in de war brengen

¹ban (n) verbod^h: ~ *on smoking* rookverbod^h; *impose a* ~ een verbod instellen

²ban (vb) **1** verbieden, verbannen, uitsluiten: *he was ~ned from driving* hij mocht geen auto meer rijden; *high-polluting cars are ~ned from the city centre* vervuilende auto's worden geweerd uit het centrum **2** verwerpen, afwijzen: ~ *the bomb* weg met de atoombom

banal [oft depr] banaal, gewoon, alledaags

banana banaan: *a hand of ~s* een kam bananen

bananas [inform] knettergek: *go* ~ stapelgek worden

¹band (n) **1** band [also fig]; riem, ring;

(dwars)streep [on animal]; reep, rand, boordʰ: *a rubber* ~ een elastiekje **2** bende, groep, troep **3** band, orkestʰ, (dans)orkestjeʰ, fanfare, popgroep

²band (vb) zich verenigen: ~ *together against* zich als één man verzetten tegen

¹bandage (n) verbandʰ

²bandage (vb) verbinden

band-aid [Am; inform] **1** pleister **2** lapmiddelʰ, tijdelijke oplossing

b and b *bed and breakfast* logiesʰ met ontbijt

bandit bandiet

bandsman muzikant

bandstand muziektent

bandwagon 1 muziekwagen **2** [fig] iets dat algemene bijval vindt: *climb* (or: *jump*) *on the* ~ **a)** met de massa meedoen; **b)** aan de kant van de winnaar gaan staan

band width bandbreedte

bandy heen en weer doen bewegen ‖ ~ *words with s.o.* ruzie maken met iem.; ~ *about* **a)** te pas en te onpas noemen; **b)** verspreiden, rondbazuinen; *have one's name bandied about* voortdurend genoemd worden

bandy-legged met O-benen

bane 1 last, pest, kruisʰ: *the* ~ *of my existence* (or: *life*) een nagel aan mijn doodskist **2** vloek, verderfʰ

¹bang (n) **1** klap, dreun, slag **2** knal, ontploffing, schotʰ **3** plotselinge inspanning: *start off with a* ~ hard aan het werk gaan, hard van stapel lopen ‖ [inform] *go off with a* ~ een reuzesucces oogsten

²bang (vb) **1** knallen, dreunen **2** (+ on) bonzen (op), kloppen, slaan ‖ ~ *about* lawaai maken

³bang (vb) **1** stoten, bonzen, botsen **2** dichtgooien, dichtsmijten **3** smijten, (neer)smakken

⁴bang (adv) **1** precies, pats, vlak: ~ *in the face* precies in zijn gezicht; [inform] ~ *on* precies goed, raak; ~ *on time* precies op tijd **2** plof, boem, paf: *go* ~ uiteenbarsten, in elkaar klappen

⁵bang (int) boem!, pats!, pang!

bang away 1 [inform] hard werken, ploeteren **2** ratelen; er op los knallen [firearms]

banger 1 worstjeʰ **2** stukʰ (knal)vuurwerk

Bangladesh Bangladesh

¹Bangladeshi (n) Bengalees, Bengalese

²Bangladeshi (adj) Bengalees

bangle armband

banish verbannen, uitwijzen, toegang ontzeggen, verwijderen: ~ *those thoughts from your mind* zet die gedachten maar uit je hoofd

banishment ballingschap, verbanning

banister 1 (trap)spijl **2** (trap)leuning

¹bank (n) **1** bank, mistbank, wolkenbank,

sneeuwbank, zandbank, ophoging, aardwal **2** oever, glooiing **3** bank [money, also in games]: *break the* ~ de bank doen springen

²bank (vb) **1** (also + up) zich opstapelen, een bank vormen; ~ *up* zich ophopen **2** (over)hellen [in a bend] **3** een bankrekening hebben: *who(m) do you* ~ *with?* welke bank heb jij? ‖ [inform] ~ *on* vertrouwen op

³bank (vb) **1** opstapelen, ophopen **2** doen hellen [eg an aeroplane, road]; doen glooien **3** (+ up) opbanken, afdekken; inrekenen [fire]

bank account bankrekening

banker bankier

bank holiday nationale feestdag

banking bankwezenʰ

banknote bankbiljetʰ

bankrupt failliet

bankruptcy bankroetʰ, faillissementʰ

banner banier [also fig]; vaandelʰ: *under the* ~ *of* onder de vlag van

banner ad banner

banner headline krantenkop over hele pagina

banns geboden; (kerkelijke) huwelijksaankondiging: *call the* ~ een huwelijk (kerkelijk) afkondigen, in ondertrouw gaan

banoffee pie banaan-toffeetaart

banquet banketʰ, feestmaalʰ, smulpartij

¹banter (n) geplaagʰ, scherts

²banter (vb) schertsen

³banter (vb) plagen, pesten

baptism doop: ~ *of fire* vuurdoop

Baptist 1 doper: *John the* ~ Johannes de Doper **2** doopsgezinde

baptize dopen

¹bar (n) **1** langwerpig stukʰ [of hard material]; staaf, stang, baar, reep; [sport] latʰ: ~ *of chocolate* reep chocola; ~ *of gold* baar goud; ~ *of soap* stuk zeep **2** afgrendelend iets, tralie, grendel, slagboom, afsluitboom; [fig] obstakelʰ; hindernis: *put behind* ~*s* achter (de) tralies zetten **3** streep; balk [on weapon, as mark of distinction] **4** bar [also as part of pub]; buffetʰ **5** balie [in courthouse]; gerechtʰ, rechtbank: *be tried at (the)* ~ in openbare terechtzitting berecht worden

²bar (vb) **1** vergrendelen, afsluiten, opsluiten, insluiten: ~ *o.s. in* (or: *out*) zichzelf binnensluiten (or: buitensluiten) **2** versperren [also fig]; verhinderen **3** verbieden: ~ *s.o. from participation* iem. verbieden deel te nemen

³bar (prep) behalve, uitgezonderd

Bar (the) advocatuur, balie, advocatenstand; [Am] orde der juristen: *read* (or: *study*) *for the* ~ voor advocaat studeren

barb 1 weerhaak, prikkel **2** steek [fig]; hatelijkheid

¹barbarian (n) **1** barbaar [also hist]; onbeschaafd iem., primitieveling **2** woesteling

²**barbarian** (adj) barbaars

barbaric barbaars, ruw, onbeschaafd, wreed

barbarity barbaarsheid; wreedheid

barbarous barbaars, onbeschaafd, wreed

barbecue barbecue, barbecuefeest[h]

barbed 1 met weerhaken **2** [fig] scherp; bijtend [remarks, words] ‖ ~ **wire** prikkeldraad[+h]

barber herenkapper: *the* ~*'s* de kapper(szaak)

bar-code streepjescode, barcode

bard bard, dichter

¹**bare** (adj) **1** naakt: *in his* ~ *skin* in zijn blootje; *lay* ~ blootleggen **2** kaal, leeg: *the* ~ *facts* de naakte feiten **3** enkel, zonder meer: *the* ~ *necessities (of life)* het strikt noodzakelijke

²**bare** (vb) **1** ontbloten: ~ *one's teeth* zijn tanden laten zien **2** blootleggen, onthullen: ~ *one's soul* zijn gevoelens luchten

barebacked met blote rug; ongezadeld

barefaced onbeschaamd, brutaal

barefoot blootsvoets: *walk* ~ op blote voeten lopen

barely nauwelijks, amper: ~ *enough* to eat nauwelijks genoeg te eten

¹**bargain** (n) **1** afspraak, akkoord[h], transactie: *make* (or: *strike*) *a* ~ tot een akkoord komen **2** koopje[h] ‖ *into* the ~ op de koop toe

²**bargain** (vb) onderhandelen, dingen ‖ *more than he* ~*ed for* meer dan waar hij op rekende

bargaining chip onderhandelingstroef

¹**barge** (n) schuit, aak, sloep

²**barge** (vb) [inform] stommelen: ~ *into* (or: *against*) *sth.* ergens tegenaan botsen ‖ ~ *in* **a)** binnenvallen; **b)** zich bemoeien

barge-pole vaarboom ‖ [inform] *I wouldn't touch* him with a ~ ik wil helemaal niets met hem te maken hebben

baritone bariton

¹**bark** (n) **1** blaffend geluid[h], geblaf[h], ruw stemgeluid[h]: *his* ~ *is worse than his bite* (het is bij hem) veel geschreeuw en weinig wol **2** schors, bast

²**bark** (vb) (+ at) blaffen (tegen): [fig] ~ *at s.o.* iem. afblaffen; *be* ~*ing up the wrong tree* op het verkeerde spoor zijn, aan het verkeerde adres zijn

³**bark** (vb) (uit)brullen, aanblaffen, luid aanprijzen: ~ *(out) an order* een bevel schreeuwen

barking: ~ *mad* knettergek, compleet gestoord

barley gerst

barman barman

barn 1 schuur **2** [Am] stal, loods: *a* ~ *of a house* een kast van een huis

barnacle goose brandgans

barn owl kerkuil

barnstorm op tournee gaan

barnyard boerenerf[h], hof

barometer barometer [also fig]; maatstaf

baron 1 baron **2** [Am] magnaat

baroness barones

baronet baronet

baroque barok

barrack 1 barak, keet **2** (-s) kazerne

barrage 1 stuwdam **2** versperring **3** spervuur[h] [also fig]; barrage

barrel ton, vat[h] ‖ *scrape* the ~ zijn laatste duiten bijeenschrapen, de laatste reserves gebruiken; *over a* ~ hulpeloos

barrel bomb vatbom

barrel organ draaiorgel[h]

barren 1 onvruchtbaar, steriel; [also fig] nutteloos **2** dor, bar, kaal

¹**barricade** (n) barricade, versperring

²**barricade** (vb) barricaderen, versperren, afzetten: ~ *o.s. in one's room* zich opsluiten in zijn kamer

barrier barrière, hek[h], slagboom, hindernis

barring behalve, uitgezonderd: ~ *very bad weather* tenzij het zeer slecht weer is; *he's the greatest singer,* ~ *none* hij is de allerbeste zanger, niemand uitgezonderd

barrister 1 advocaat **2** [Am] jurist

barrow 1 kruiwagen **2** draagbaar **3** handkar

bartender [Am] barman

¹**barter** (n) ruilhandel

²**barter** (vb) **1** ruilhandel drijven **2** loven en bieden

³**barter** (vb) **1** (+ for) ruilen (voor/tegen) **2** opgeven [in exchange for sth.]: ~ *away one's freedom* zijn vrijheid prijsgeven

¹**base** (n) **1** basis, voetstuk[h], grondlijn, grondvlak[h]: *the* ~ *of the mountain* de voet van de berg **2** grondslag, fundament[h]; [fig] uitgangspunt[h] **3** hoofdbestanddeel[h] **4** basiskamp[h], basis, hoofdkwartier[h] **5** [sport] honk[h]: *catch s.o. off* ~ iem. onverwacht treffen **6** [pizza] bodem

²**base** (adj) **1** laag, minderwaardig: *a* ~ *action* een laffe daad **2** onedel [metal]; onecht [coin]

³**base** (vb) **1** (+ (up)on) baseren (op); gronden (op) [also fig]: ~ *oneself on* uitgaan van; ~*d (up)on mere gossip* slechts op roddel berustend **2** vestigen

baseball honkbal[h]

baseless ongegrond, ongefundeerd

basement souterrain[h], kelder

¹**bash** (n) **1** dreun, stoot, mep **2** [inform] fuif ‖ [inform] *have a* ~ *(at sth.)* iets eens proberen

²**bash** (vb) botsen, bonken

³**bash** (vb) slaan, beuken: ~ *the door down* de deur inbeuken

bashful verlegen

-bashing [inform] het afranselen; [fig] het fel bekritiseren: *union-bashing* zwaar uithalen naar de vakbond ‖ *bible-bashing* het fa-

natiek verkondigen van de Bijbel
basic 1 basis-, fundamenteel, minimum-: ~
data hoofdgegevens; ~ *pay* (or: *salary*) basis-
loonʰ **2** [inform] basaal, rudimentair
basically eigenlijk, voornamelijk
basics [oft inform] grondbeginselen, basiskennis
basil basilicumʰ
basin 1 kom, schaal, schotel **2** waterbek-
kenʰ, bak **3** bekkenʰ, stroomgebiedʰ **4** wasbak, waskom, fonteintjeʰ **5** bassinʰ, (haven)-
dokʰ
basis basis, fundamentʰ; [fig] grondslag;
hoofdbestanddeelʰ: *on the* ~ *of* op grond van
bask [also fig] zich koesteren
basket 1 mand, korf; winkelmandjeʰ; [bas-
ketball] basket: [Internet] *add* this item to
your ~ voeg dit product toe aan je winkelmandje; *make* (or: *shoot*) *a* ~ scoren
2 schuitjeʰ, gondel
¹basketball (n) basketbalʰ [sport]
²basketball (n) basketbalʰ [ball]
¹Basque (n) Bask, Baskische
²Basque (adj) Baskisch
¹bass (n) baars, zeebaars
²bass (n) basʰ ‖ ~ *guitar* basgitaar
bass clef bassleutel, f-sleutel
bass drum grote trom; bassdrum
bassoon fagot, basson
bastard 1 bastaard, onecht kindʰ **2** [in-
form; depr] smeerlap, schoft **3** [inform] vent:
you lucky ~! geluksvogel die je bent!
baste bedruipen [with fat]
bastion bastionʰ [also fig]; bolwerkʰ
¹bat (n) **1** vleermuis **2** knuppel; [cricket, table tennis] batʰ; [baseball] slaghoutʰ, knuppel; [tennis] racketʰ ‖ [inform] *have* ~s *in the
belfry* een klap van de molen gehad hebben;
[inform] *off one's own* ~ uit eigen beweging,
op eigen houtje; [Am; inform] *(right) off the* ~
direct
²bat (vb) **1** batten **2** knipp(er)en [eyes]: *without* ~*ting an* **eye(lid)** zonder een spier te vertrekken
batch partij, groep, troep: *a* ~ *of* letters een
stapel brieven
batch processing batchverwerking
¹bath (n) **1** badʰ: *have* (or: *take*) *a* ~ een bad
nemen **2** zwembadʰ **3** (-s) badhuisʰ, kuur-
oordʰ
²bath (vb) een bad nemen
¹bathe (n) badʰ, zwempartij
²bathe (vb) **1** zich baden, zwemmen **2** [Am]
een bad nemen, zich wassen **3** (+ in) baden
(in) [fig]; opgaan
³bathe (vb) **1** baden, onderdompelen: ~*d in
sunshine* met zon overgoten **2** betten [eg
wound]
bathrobe 1 badjas **2** [Am] kamerjas
bathroom 1 badkamer **2** [euph] toiletʰ, wc
bathtub badkuip

baton stok, wapenstok, gummistok, dirigeerstok; [sport] estafettestokjeʰ: *under the*
~ *of* onder leiding van, gedirigeerd door
battalion bataljonʰ
¹batten (n) lat, plank
²batten (vb) **1** (+ (up)on) zich vetmesten
(met) **2** (+ (up)on) parasiteren (op)
¹batter (n) beslagʰ
²batter (vb) beuken, timmeren: ~ *(away) at*
inbeuken op
³batter (vb) slaan, timmeren op, havenen
battery 1 batterij [also mil]; reeks: *a* ~ *of
questions* een spervuur van vragen **2** (elektrische) batterij, accu(mulator) **3** [law] aanranding
battery charger batterijoplader
¹battle (n) **1** (veld)slag, gevechtʰ, competitie: *fight a losing* ~ een hopeloze strijd voeren **2** overwinning: *youth is* **half** *the* ~ als je
maar jong bent
²battle (vb) slag leveren [also fig]; strijden: ~
through the crowd zich een weg banen door
de menigte
battle-axe 1 strijdbijl **2** [inform] dragonder; kenau
battlefield slagveldʰ [also fig]
battleground gevechtsterreinʰ [also fig];
slagveldʰ
battleship slagschipʰ
batty [inform] getikt
bauble snuisterij, prulʰ
bauxite bauxietʰ
Bavaria Beierenʰ
Bavarian Beiers
¹bawdy (n) schuine praat, schuine grap
²bawdy (adj) schuin, vies
bawl schreeuwen: ~ *at s.o.* iem. toebrullen ‖
~ *out* uitfoeteren; ~ *one's eyes* **out** tranen
met tuiten huilen
¹bay (n) **1** baai, zeearm, golf **2** (muur)vakʰ
3 nis, erker **4** afdeling, vleugel; ruimte [in
bldg etc] **5** laurier(boom): ~ *leaf* laurierblad
6 luid geblafʰ ‖ *hold* (or: *keep*) *at* ~ op een
afstand houden
²bay (adj) voskleurig [horse]
³bay (vb) (aan)blaffen, huilen
bayonet bajonet, bajonetsluiting
bay window erker
bay wreath lauwerkrans
bazaar bazaar
bazillion [esp Am; inform] onbepaald
groot getalʰ, massa, tig: *make* ~s *of dollars*
zakken vol dollars verdienen
BBC *British Broadcasting Corporation* BBC
BB cream camouflagecrème met uv-be-
scherming
BBQ *barbecue* BBQ
BC *before Christ* v.Chr., voor Christus
bcc *blind carbon copy* bcc
BCNU [inform] *be seeing you* tot ziens, later
BD *bipolar disorder; see bipolar*

¹be (vb) **1** zijn, bestaan, voorkomen, plaats-hebben **2** geweest (gekomen) zijn: *has the postman been?* is de postbode al geweest?
²be (aux vb) **1** aan het … zijn: *they were read-ing* ze waren aan het lezen, ze lazen **2** worden, zijn: *he has been murdered* hij is vermoord **3** mocht, zou: *if this were to happen, were this to happen* als dit zou gebeuren
³be (vb) **1** zijn: *she is a teacher* zij is lerares; *the bride-to-be* de aanstaande bruid; *be that as it may* hoe het ook zij **2** [+ indication of size or quantity] (waard/groot/oud) zijn, kosten, meten, duren: *it's three pounds* het kost drie pond; *it is three minutes* het duurt drie minuten **3** zijn, zich bevinden; plaatshebben [also fig]: *it was in 1953* het gebeurde in 1953; *what's behind this?* wat steekt hier achter?
4 zijn, betekenen: *what's it to you?* wat gaat jou dat aan? **5** bedoeld zijn, dienen: *an axe is to fell trees with* een bijl dient om bomen om te hakken ‖ [inform] *be nowhere* ver achter-liggen; *as is* zoals hij is
be about 1 rondhangen, rondslingeren **2** er zijn, beschikbaar zijn: *there is a lot of flu about* er is heel wat griep onder de mensen **3** op het punt staan: *he was about to leave* hij ging net vertrekken
beach strandʰ, oever
beachcomber strandjutter
beachhead bruggenhoofdʰ [on beach]
beacon 1 (vuur)bakenʰ, vuurtoren, lichtba-kenʰ **2** bakenzender, radiobakenʰ; bakenʰ **3** grenspaaltjeʰ, grenssteen
bead 1 kraal **2** (-s) kralen halssnoerʰ **3** druppel, kraal: *~s of sweat* zweetdruppels
beadle bode, ceremoniemeester; pedel [at university]
beady kraalvormig: *black ~ eyes* zwarte kraaloogjes ‖ *keep a ~ eye on s.o.* iem. scherp in de gaten houden
beagle brak, kleine jachthond
beak snavel, bek, snuit, mondstukʰ
beaker beker(glasʰ)
be-all (the) essentie: *the ~ and end-all of sth.* de alfa en omega van iets
¹beam (n) **1** balk **2** boom, disselboom, ploegboom **3** straal, stralenbundel **4** geleide straal, bakenstraal: *be off ~* [inform] ernaast zitten, fout zijn **5** stralende blik (glimlach)
²beam (vb) stralen, schijnen
bean 1 boon **2** [Am; inform] knikker, kop, hersens ‖ [inform] *spill the ~s* zijn mond voorbijpraten
bean counter [hum] boekhouder(tje)
bean sprouts taugé
¹bear (n) **1** beer **2** ongelikte beer, bullebak
²bear (vb) **1** houden [of ice] **2** dragen [of wall] **3** vruchten voortbrengen, vruchtbaar zijn **4** (aan)houden [of direction]; (voort)-gaan, lopen: *~ (to the) left* links afslaan **5** druk uitoefenen, duwen, leunen: *~ hard*

(or: *heavily, severely*) *(up)on* zwaar drukken op [fig] **6** (+ (up)on) invloed hebben (op), van invloed zijn (op), betrekking hebben (op)
³bear (vb) **1** dragen: *~ fruit* vruchten voort-brengen; [fig] vruchten afwerpen; *~ away a prize, ~ off a price* een prijs in de wacht slepen **2** (over)brengen **3** vertonen, hebben: *~ signs* (or: *traces*) *of* tekenen (or: sporen) ver-tonen van **4** hebben (voelen) voor, toedra-gen, koesteren **5** verdragen, uitstaan: *his words won't ~ repeating* zijn woorden zijn niet voor herhaling vatbaar **6** voortbrengen, ba-ren: *borne by* geboren uit
bearable draaglijk, te dragen
beard 1 baard **2** weerhaak
bear down persen, druk uitoefenen ‖ *~ (up)on* zwaar drukken op
bearer 1 drager: *the ~ of a passport* de houder van een paspoort **2** bode, bood-schapper: *the ~ of this letter* de brenger dezes **3** toonder [of cheque etc]: *pay to ~* betaal aan toonder
bear-hug [inform] houdgreep, onstuimige omhelzing
bearing 1 verbandʰ, betrekking: *have no ~ on* los staan van **2** betekenis, strekking **3** (-s) positie, ligging, plaats: *get* (or: *take*) *one's ~s* zich oriënteren, poolshoogte nemen **4** het dragen **5** houding, voorkomenʰ, gedragʰ, optredenʰ
be around even aanlopen, bezoeken
bear out (onder)steunen, bekrachtigen, staven: *bear s.o. out* iemands verklaring be-vestigen
bear up zich (goed) houden, zich redden: *~ against sth.* ergens tegen opgewassen zijn
bear with geduld hebben met
beast 1 beestʰ [also fig]: *~ of prey* roofdierʰ **2** rund
beastly beestachtig: *~ stench* walgelijke stank; *~ drunk* stomdronken
¹beat (n) **1** slag **2** (vaste) ronde, (vaste) rou-te: *be on one's ~* zijn ronde doen **3** [mus] rit-meʰ, beat
²beat (vb) **1** slaan, bonzen, beuken, woeden; kloppen [of heart, blood]; fladderen [of wing] **2** een klopjacht houden **3** zich (moei-zaam) een weg banen
³beat (vb) **1** slaan (op), klutsen; kloppen [rug]; fladderen met [wing]: [inform] *~ s.o.'s brains out* iem. de hersens inslaan; *the recipe to ~ all recipes* het recept dat alles slaat; *~ back* terugslaan, terugdrijven **2** (uit)smeden, pletten **3** banen [path] **4** verslaan, eronder krijgen; breken [record]: [inform] *can you ~ that?* heb je ooit zoiets gehoord? **5** uitput-ten: *he was dead ~* hij was (dood)op **6** afzoe-ken **7** [Am; inform] ontlopen [punishment] ‖ [inform] *~ it!* smeer 'm!
¹beat down (vb) branden [of sun]

²**beat down** (vb) **1** neerslaan **2** intrappen [door] **3** naar beneden brengen; drukken [price] **4** afdingen (bij/op)

beaten 1 veel betreden; gebaand [of road, track; also fig]: *be off the ~ track* verafgelegen zijn **2** gesmeed, geplet: *~ gold* bladgoudʰ **3** verslagen

beater 1 klopper [of egg, carpet] **2** [hunting] drijver

beating afstraffing [also fig]: *take some* (or: *a lot of*) *~* moeilijk te overtreffen zijn

beatitude 1 zaligverklaring **2** (geluk)zaligheid

beat off afslaan, terugdrijven, afweren

beat up 1 [inform] in elkaar slaan **2** (op)kloppen, klutsen **3** [inform] optrommelen, werven

beautician schoonheidsspecialist(e)

beautiful 1 mooi, fraai, prachtig **2** heerlijk; verrukkelijk [of weather]

beautify verfraaien, (ver)sieren, mooi maken

beauty 1 schoonheid: *that is the ~ of it* dat is het mooie ervan **2** [inform] pracht(exemplaarʰ), juweeltjeʰ

beauty parlour schoonheidssalon⁺ʰ

beaver bever

beaver away [inform] zwoegen, ploeteren

because 1 omdat, want **2** (het feit) dat

because of wegens, vanwege

beck tekenʰ, knik, gebaarʰ: *be at s.o.'s ~ and call* iem. op zijn wenken bedienen

beckon wenken, gebaren, een teken geven

¹**become** (vb) (+ of) gebeuren (met), worden (van), aflopen (met)

²**become** (vb) **1** passen: *it ill ~s you* het siert je niet **2** eer aandoen **3** (goed) staan [of clothes]

³**become** (vb) worden, (ge)raken: *~ mayor* burgemeester worden

becoming gepast, behoorlijk: *as is ~* zoals het hoort

¹**bed** (n) **1** bedʰ, slaapplaats, huwelijkʰ; legerʰ [of animal]; bloembedʰ, tuinbedʰ: *~ and board* kost en inwoning; *~ and breakfast* logies met ontbijt; *double* (or: *single*) *~* tweepersoonsbedʰ, eenpersoonsbedʰ; *spare ~* logeerbedʰ; *wet one's ~* bedwateren **2** (rivier)bedding **3** bedding, grondslag, onderlaag, (bodem)laag

²**bed** (vb) **1** [inform] naar bed gaan met **2** planten: *~ out* uitplanten

bedbug bedwants

bedding 1 beddengoedʰ **2** onderlaag, grondslag, bedding **3** gelaagdheid

bedevil treiteren, dwarszitten, achtervolgen, (ernstig) bemoeilijken

bedfellow bedgenoot, bedgenote ‖ *adversity makes strange ~s* tegenspoed maakt vijanden tot vrienden

bedlam gekkenhuisʰ [also fig]; gestichtʰ;

[inform] heksenketel

Bedouin bedoeïen

be down 1 beneden zijn; minder, gezakt zijn [lit and fig] **2** uitgeteld zijn; [fig] somber zijn: [inform] *~ with the flu* geveld zijn door griep **3** buiten bedrijf zijn; plat liggen [of computer] ‖ [inform] *~ on s.o.* iem. aanpakken, iem. fel bekritiseren; *he is down to his last pound* hij heeft nog maar één pond over

bedpan (onder)steek

bedraggled 1 doorweekt **2** verfomfaaid, toegetakeld, sjofel

bedridden bedlegerig

bedroom slaapkamer

bedside manner [roughly] optreden van dokter aan het ziekbed

bedspread sprei

bedstead ledikantʰ

bedtime bedtijd

bedtime story verhaaltjeʰ voor het slapen gaan

bee 1 bij **2** [inform] gril ‖ [inform] *have a ~ in one's bonnet (about sth.)* **a)** door iets geobsedeerd worden; **b)** niet helemaal normaal zijn (op een bepaald punt)

beech beuk, beukenhoutʰ

¹**beef** (n) **1** rundvleesʰ: *corned ~* cornedbeefʰ **2** [inform] kracht, spierballen **3** [inform] ruzie

²**beef** (vb) [inform] kankeren, mopperen, zeuren

beefcake [inform] (foto's van) gespierde kerels; krachtpatsers

beefeater 1 koninklijke lijfwacht **2** hellebaardier van de Tower **3** [Am; inform] Engelsman

beef jerky gedroogde reepjes rundvlees

beefsteak biefstuk, runderlap(jeʰ)

beef up [inform] versterken, opvoeren

beehive 1 bijenkorf [also fig] **2** suikerbroodʰ [hairdo]

beekeeper bijenhouder, imker

beeline rechte lijn: [inform] *make a ~ for* (or: *to*) regelrecht afstevenen op

¹**beep** (n) **1** getoeterʰ, toet **2** fluittoon, pieptoon; piep(jeʰ) [indicating time]

²**beep** (vb) **1** toeteren **2** piepen

beeper pieper, portofoon, semafoon

beer bierʰ, glasʰ bier

beer o'clock [inform] biertijd: *it's ~* het is tijd voor een biertje

beeswax (bijen)was

beet 1 biet **2** [Am] rode biet

beetle kever, tor

beetroot 1 (bieten)kroot, rode biet **2** beetwortel, suikerbiet

befall [form] overkomen, gebeuren (met)

befit [form] passen

be for zijn voor, voorstander zijn van ‖ *you're for it!* er zwaait wat voor je!

¹**before** (adv) **1** voorop, vooraan, ervoor

2 vroeger, eerder, vooraf: *three* **weeks** ~ drie weken geleden

²before (prep) **1** [time] vóór, vroeger dan, alvorens: ~ *Christmas* voor Kerstmis; ~ *long* binnenkort **2** [place] voor, voor … uit, tegenover: *put a bill* ~ *parliament* een wetsontwerp bij het parlement indienen ‖ *put friendship* ~ *love* vriendschap hoger achten dan liefde; ~ *all else* bovenal

³before (conj) alvorens, voor

beforehand vooraf, van tevoren, vooruit

befriend een vriend zijn voor, bijstaan

¹beg (vb) **1** opzitten [of dog] **2** de vrijheid nemen, zo vrij zijn: *I* ~ *to differ* ik ben zo vrij daar anders over te denken

²beg (vb) **1** bedelen: ~ *for* bedelen om, smeken **2** (dringend/met klem) verzoeken, smeken, (nederig) vragen

beget 1 [Bible] verwekken **2** [form] voortbrengen; veroorzaken

¹beggar (n) bedelaar(ster), schooier ‖ ~*s can't be choosers* [roughly] lieverkoekjes worden niet gebakken

²beggar (vb) te boven gaan: ~ *(all)* **description** alle beschrijving tarten

begin beginnen, aanvangen, starten: *life* ~*s at sixty* met zestig begint het echte leven ‖ *to* ~ *with* om te beginnen, in de eerste plaats

beginning 1 beginʰ, aanvang: *from* ~ *to end* van begin tot einde; *in the* ~ aanvankelijk **2** (-s) (prille) beginʰ

begrudge misgunnen, benijden, niet gunnen

beguile 1 bedriegen, verleiden: ~ *into* ertoe verleiden (te) **2** korten, verdrijven: *we* ~*d the time by playing cards* we kortten de tijd met kaartspelen **3** charmeren, betoveren

beguiling verleidelijk

behalf: *on* ~ *of my father* namens mijn vader; *in my* ~ voor mij

behave zich gedragen, zich goed gedragen: ~ *(yourself)!* gedraag je!

behaviour gedragʰ, houding, optredenʰ: *be on one's best* ~ zichzelf van zijn beste kant laten zien

behead onthoofden

¹behind (n) [inform; euph] achtersteʰ

²behind (adv) **1** [movement, place or space] erachter, achteraan, achterop, achterin, achterom, voorbij **2** [delay or arrears] achterop, achter, achterstallig: *they* **fell** ~ ze raakten achter [also fig]

³behind (prep) **1** [place, direction or time; also fig] achter, voorbij, verder dan, om: *the house* ~ *the* **church** het huis achter de kerk; *put one's problems* ~ *one* zijn problemen van zich afzetten **2** [delay or arrears] achter op, later dan, onder: *the bus is* ~ *schedule* de bus heeft vertraging **3** achter, aan de oorsprong van: *the real* **reasons** ~ *the quarrel* de echte redenen voor de ruzie **4** achter, ter onder-

steuning van: *we* **are** (or: **stand**) ~ *you* wij staan achter je, steunen je

behindhand 1 achter(stallig) **2** achter, achterop: *be* ~ *with one's work* achter zijn met zijn werk

behold [form] aanschouwen: [hum] *lo* **and** ~*!* welwel!, en ziedaar!

beholder aanschouwer; toeschouwer

beige beigeʰ

be in 1 binnen zijn, er zijn, aanwezig zijn: *the new fabrics aren't in yet* de nieuwe stoffen zijn nog niet binnen **2** geaccepteerd zijn, erbij, aanvaard, opgenomen zijn; in de mode zijn, in zijn [of things]: ~ *on* meedoen aan ‖ [inform] *we're in* **for** *a nasty surprise* er staat ons een onaangename verrassing te wachten

being 1 wezenʰ, schepselʰ, bestaanʰ, zijnʰ, existentie: *bring* (or: *call*) **into** ~ creëren, doen ontstaan; *come into* ~ ontstaan **2** wezenʰ, essentie, aard, het wezenlijke

Belarus Wit-Rusland

belated laat

¹belch (n) boer, oprisping

²belch (vb) **1** boeren **2** (uit)braken, uitbarsten: *the volcano* ~*ed out rocks* de vulkaan spuwde stenen (uit)

beleaguer 1 belegeren **2** zwaar bekritiseren

¹Belgian (n) Belg, Belgische

²Belgian (adj) Belgisch

Belgium België

belie 1 een valse indruk geven van, tegenspreken **2** logenstraffen: *the* **attack** ~*d our hopes for peace* de aanval logenstrafte onze hoop op vrede **3** niet nakomen

belief 1 (geloofs)overtuiging **2** geloofʰ, vertrouwenʰ: *beyond* ~ ongelofelijk, onbegrijpelijk, niet te geloven/begrijpen **3** geloofʰ, mening: *to the* **best** *of my* ~ naar mijn beste weten

believe 1 geloven, gelovig zijn **2** (+ in) geloven (in), vertrouwen hebben (in) **3** geloven, menen, veronderstellen **4** geloven, voor waar aannemen: *I'll* ~ *anything* **of** *James* James acht ik tot alles in staat

believer 1 gelover; iem. die gelooft **2** gelovige

belittle onbelangrijk(er) doen lijken, kleineren

Belize Belize

¹Belizean (n) Belizaan(se)

²Belizean (adj) Belizaans

bell klok, bel, belsignaalʰ ‖ *that* **rings** *a* ~ dat komt me ergens bekend voor

bell-boy piccolo

bellhop [Am] piccolo

bellicose strijdlustig, oorlogszuchtig, agressief

belligerent 1 oorlogvoerend **2** strijdlustig, uitdagend, agressief

¹bellow (n) gebrul^h, geloei^h
²bellow (vb) loeien, brullen
bellows blaasbalg: *a (pair of)* ~ een blaasbalg
bell pepper paprika
belly 1 [inform] buik, maag, schoot **2** ronding [as of a stomach]; uitstulping, onderkant: *the ~ of an aeroplane* de buik van een vliegtuig
bellyache buikpijn
belly button navel
belly-up: [inform] *go* ~ failliet gaan
belong 1 passen, (thuis)horen: *it doesn't ~ here* dat hoort hier niet (thuis) **2** [inform] thuishoren, zich thuis voelen, op z'n plaats zijn: *a sense of ~ing* het gevoel erbij te horen
belongings persoonlijke eigendommen, bagage
belong to 1 toebehoren aan, (eigendom) zijn van **2** horen bij, lid zijn van: *which group do you ~?* bij welke groep zit jij?
Belorussia Wit-Rusland
beloved bemind, geliefd
¹below (adv) beneden, eronder, onderaan: *she lives in the flat* ~ ze woont in de flat hieronder; *see* ~ zie verder
²below (prep) **1** onder, beneden, lager (gelegen) dan; [fig] (verscholen/verborgen) achter: *the flat* ~ *ours* de flat onder de onze **2** ondergeschikt, lager dan, minder dan: ~ *average* minderwaardig, slecht; ~ *the average* onder het gemiddelde
¹belt (n) **1** gordel, (broek)riem, ceintuur **2** drijfriem: *fan* ~ ventilatorriem **3** (transport)band, lopende band **4** [esp as second part of compound] zone, klimaatstreek, klimaatgebied^h: *a* ~ *of low pressure* een lagedrukgebied ‖ *hit below the* ~ onder de gordel slaan; *tighten one's* ~, [Am also] *pull one's* ~ *in* de buikriem aanhalen; *under one's* ~ in zijn bezit, binnen
²belt (vb) **1** omgorden **2** een pak slaag geven (met een riem) ‖ ~ *out* brullen, bulken
belt up zijn veiligheidsgordel aandoen
bemoan [form] beklagen
bemused 1 verbijsterd, verdwaasd **2** verstrooid
bench 1 bank, zitbank **2** (parlements)zetel; bank [in House of Commons] **3** rechterstoel **4** werkbank **5** [sport] reservebank, strafbank(je^h) **6** rechtbank, de rechters **7** [sport] de reservebank, de reservespelers
benchmark standaard, maatstaf
bench-press bankdrukken
¹bend (n) **1** buiging, kromming, knik **2** bocht, draai: *a sharp* ~ *in the road* een scherpe bocht in de weg ‖ *(go) (a)round the* ~ knettergek (worden)
²bend (vb) **1** buigen, zwenken: ~ *down* zich bukken, vooroverbuigen ‖ ~ *over backwards* zich vreselijk uitsloven

³bend (vb) **1** buigen, krommen, verbuigen: [fig] ~ *the rules* de regels naar zijn hand zetten; ~ *down* (or: *up*) naar beneden (*or:* boven) buigen **2** onderwerpen, (doen) buigen, plooien: ~ *s.o.* *to one's will* iem. naar zijn hand zetten
bender 1 [inform] feest^h; zuippartij: *on a* ~ aan het zuipen, aan de drugs **2** [vulg] homo
¹beneath (adv) eronder, daaronder, onderaan
²beneath (prep) **1** onder, beneden, lager dan **2** achter, verborgen achter **3** onder, onder de invloed van: *bent* ~ *his burden* onder zijn last gebukt **4** beneden, onder, beneden de waardigheid van: *he thinks manual labour is* ~ *him* hij vindt zichzelf te goed voor handenarbeid
benediction [rel] zegening
benefactor weldoener
beneficent weldadig
beneficial voordelig, nuttig, heilzaam
beneficiary begunstigde
¹benefit (n) **1** voordeel^h, profijt^h, hulp: *give s.o. the* ~ *of the doubt* iem. het voordeel van de twijfel geven; *friend with ~s* vriend(in) om af en toe seks mee te hebben **2** uitkering, steun, steungeld^h: *be on ~s* in de bijstand zitten **3** benefiet^h, liefdadigheidsvoorstelling, benefiet-
²benefit (vb) voordeel halen, baat vinden
³benefit (vb) ten goede komen aan, goed doen voor
benevolent 1 welwillend, goedgunstig **2** liefdadig, vrijgevig
Bengal Bengaals
¹Bengali (n) Bengaal(se)
²Bengali (adj) Bengaals
benign 1 vriendelijk **2** zacht, gunstig, heilzaam: *a* ~ *climate* een zacht klimaat **3** goedaardig: *a* ~ *tumour* een goedaardig gezwel
benignant 1 beminnelijk, welwillend **2** goedaardig
Benin Benin
¹Beninese (n) Beniner, Beninse
²Beninese (adj) Benins
¹bent (n) neiging, aanleg, voorliefde, zwak^h
²bent (adj) **1** afwijkend, krom, illegaal **2** [inform] omkoopbaar **3** [vulg] homoseksueel **4** vastbesloten: ~ *on* uit op
be off 1 [inform] ervandoor gaan [also fig]; vertrekken, weg zijn, wegwezen; [sport] starten; weg zijn; beginnen [talking]: ~ *to a bad start* slecht van start gaan **2** verwijderd zijn [also fig]: *Easter was two weeks off* het was nog twee weken vóór Pasen **3** afgelast zijn, niet doorgaan **4** [inform] bedorven zijn [of food] **5** afgesloten zijn [of water, gas, electricity] ‖ [inform] *be badly off* er slecht voorstaan
¹be on (vb) [inform] op kosten zijn van; betaald worden door: *the drinks are on John*

John trakteert
²**be on** (vb) **1** aan (de gang) zijn; aan staan [of light, radio etc]: *the **match** is on* de wedstrijd is bezig **2** gevorderd zijn: *it was **well** on into the night* het was al diep in de nacht **3** doorgaan, gehandhaafd worden: *the party is on* het feest gaat door **4** [inform] toegestaan zijn: *that's not on!* dat doe je niet! **5** op het toneel staan; spelen [of actor] **6** op het programma staan [radio, TV, play] || [inform] ~ ***about*** *sth.* het hebben over iets; [depr] altijd maar zeuren over iets; [inform] ~ ***to*** *sth.* iets in de gaten hebben

be out 1 (er)uit zijn, (er)buiten zijn, weg zijn, er niet (meer) zijn **2** [inform] uit zijn, voorbij zijn: *before the **year** is out* voor het jaar voorbij is **3** uit(gedoofd) zijn **4** openbaar (gemaakt) zijn, gepubliceerd zijn: *the **results** are out* de resultaten zijn bekend **5** [inform] onmogelijk zijn, niet mogen: *rough **games** are out!* geen ruwe spelletjes! **6** ernaast zitten: *his **forecast** was well out* zijn voorspelling was er helemaal naast **7** in staking zijn **8** laag zijn [of tide]: *the **tide** is out* het is laagtij **9** [cricket, baseball] uit zijn || [inform] ~ ***to do*** *sth.* van plan zijn iets te doen; ~ ***for*** *o.s.* zijn eigen belangen dienen

be out of 1 uit zijn, buiten zijn: ~ ***it*** er niet bij horen **2** zonder zitten: *he is out of a **job*** hij zit zonder werk; *we're out of **sugar*** we hebben geen suiker meer || [inform] *be well out of **it*** er mooi van af (gekomen) zijn

¹**be over** (vb) [with 'all'; inform] **1** overal bekend zijn in: *it's all over the **office*** het hele kantoor weet ervan **2** niet kunnen afblijven van, (overdreven) enthousiast begroeten

²**be over** (vb) **1** voorbij, over zijn: [inform] *that's over and **done** with* dat is voor eens en altijd voorbij **2** overschieten, overblijven: *there's a bit of fabric over* er schiet een beetje stof over **3** op bezoek zijn [from a distant country]: *Henk is over **from** Australia* Henk is over uit Australië

bequeath [form] vermaken, nalaten
bequest legaatʰ
berate [form] uitschelden; een fikse uitbrander geven
bereave beroven, doen verliezen || *the ~d* de nabestaanden
bereavement 1 sterfgevalʰ, overlijdenʰ **2** verliesʰ: *we **sympathize** with you in your ~* wij betuigen onze oprechte deelneming met uw verlies
beret baret
Bermuda Bermuda
berry bes
berserk woest, razend: *go ~* razend worden
¹**berth** (n) **1** kooi, hut **2** ligplaats, ankerplaats, aanlegplaats
²**berth** (vb) aanleggen, ankeren

beseech smeken, dringend verzoeken
beset 1 [esp passive] belegeren [also fig]; overvallen, omsingelen: *young people, ~ **by** doubts* door twijfel overvallen jongeren **2** insluiten, versperren, bezetten
beside naast, bij, langs, dichtbij, vergeleken bij: *it's ~ the **point*** het doet hier niet ter zake || *be ~ o.s. **with** joy* buiten zichzelf van vreugde zijn
¹**besides** (adv) **1** bovendien, daarenboven: *Tina bought a new suit and a blouse ~* Tina kocht een nieuw pak en ook nog een bloes **2** anders, daarnaast, behalve dat **3** trouwens
²**besides** (prep) behalve, buiten, naast: *I can do nothing ~ wait* ik kan alleen maar wachten
besiege 1 belegeren **2** bestormen: ~ *s.o. **with** questions **about*** iem. bestormen met vragen over
besmirch 1 bevuilen; besmeuren **2** [fig] bekladden; schaden
bespatter 1 bespatten **2** bekladden [also fig]; belasteren, uitschelden
¹**best** (n) (de/het) beste: *with the ~ of **intentions*** met de beste bedoelingen; *to the ~ of my **knowledge** (and belief)* voor zover ik weet; *at ~* op z'n best (genomen), hoogstens; *at the ~ of times* onder de gunstigste omstandigheden || ***get** (or: **have**) the ~ of it* de overhand krijgen (or: hebben); *it is (all) **for** the ~* het komt allemaal wel goed
²**best** (adj) best(e) || ~ ***man*** getuige [of bridegroom]; bruidsjonker; *the ~ **part** of* het merendeel van
³**best** (adv) **1** het best: ~ ***before** 10 February* ten minste houdbaar tot 10 februari **2** meest: *those ~ **able** to pay* zij die het gemakkelijkste kunnen betalen
best-before date houdbaarheidsdatum
bestial [also fig] beestachtig, dierlijk
bestie [inform] beste vriend/vriendin
bestow verlenen, schenken
bestseller 1 bestseller, succesartikelʰ, succesproductʰ **2** successchrijver
¹**bet** (n) **1** weddenschap: *lay (or: **make, place**) a ~ (on sth.)* wedden (op iets) **2** inzet **3** iets waarop men wedt, kans, keuze: *your **best** ~ is* je maakt de meeste kans met; *a **safe** ~* een veilige keus; *it's a **safe** ~ to assume that …* je kunt er zonder meer vanuit gaan dat …
²**bet** (vb) **1** wedden, verwedden: ~ ***on** sth.* op iets wedden **2** [inform] wedden, zeker (kunnen) zijn van
be through 1 klaar zijn, er doorheen zijn: *I'm through **with** my work* ik ben klaar met mijn werk **2** [inform] ermee zitten, er de brui aan geven; afgedaan hebben [of things]: ~ ***with** sth.* ergens zijn buik van vol hebben, iets zat zijn; *I'm through **with** you* ik trek mijn handen van je af **3** verbonden zijn, verbinding hebben
be to 1 moeten: *what am I to **do*** wat moet ik

doen? **2** [+ negation] mogen: *visitors are not to **feed** the animals* bezoekers mogen de dieren niet voeren **3** gaan, zullen: *we are to **be** married next year* we gaan volgend jaar trouwen **4** zijn te: *Molly is nowhere to be **found*** Molly is nergens te vinden

betray 1 verraden, in de steek laten **2** verraden, uitbrengen, verklappen: *his eyes ~ed his thoughts* zijn ogen verraadden zijn gedachten

betrayal (daad van) verraad[h]

betrayer verrader

betrothal verloving

betrothed 1 verloofde, aanstaande (bruid/bruidegom) **2** verloofden, aanstaande bruid en bruidegom

[1]**better** (n) **1** (-s) beteren[h], meerderen, superieuren **2** iets beters **3** verbetering: *change for the ~* ten goede veranderen || *his emotions got the ~ of him* hij werd door zijn emoties overmand

[2]**better** (adj) **1** beter: *~ luck next time!* volgende keer beter!; *he is little ~ than a thief* hij is nauwelijks beter dan een dief **2** groter; grootste [part]: *the ~ part of the day* het grootste gedeelte van de dag **3** hersteld, genezen || *I'm none the ~ for it* ik ben er niet beter van geworden

[3]**better** (adv) **1** beter **2** meer: *I like prunes ~ than figs* ik hou meer van pruimen dan van vijgen

betterment verbetering

[1]**between** (adv) ertussen, tussendoor: *two gardens with a fence ~* twee tuinen met een schutting ertussen

[2]**between** (prep) tussen [two]; onder: *~ school, her music and her friends she led a busy life* met de school, haar muziek en haar vrienden, had ze alles bij elkaar een druk leven; *they wrote the book ~ them* ze schreven het boek samen; *~ you and me, ~ ourselves* onder ons (gezegd); *I was sitting ~ my two sisters* ik zat tussen mijn twee zussen in

betwixt (er)tussen

be up 1 in een hoge(re) positie zijn [also fig]: *petrol's up again* de benzine is weer duurder geworden **2** op zijn, opstaan, wakker zijn **3** op zijn, over zijn: [inform] *it's all up with him* het is met hem gedaan **4** ter discussie staan, in aanmerking komen: *~ for discussion* ter discussie staan **5** zijn, wonen, studeren **6** aan de gang zijn, gaande zijn: *get sth. up and running* iets werkend krijgen, iets aan de praat krijgen; *what's up?* **a)** [inform] hoe gaat het?, alles kits?; **b)** wat is er aan de hand?; *what's up with you?* wat is er met jou aan de hand? || *~ against a problem* op een probleem gestoten zijn; [inform] *~ against it* in de puree zitten; *be well up in sth.* goed op de hoogte zijn van iets

be up to 1 komen tot: *I'm up to my ears in work* ik zit tot over m'n oren in het werk **2** in z'n schild voeren, uit zijn op: *he is up to sth.* hij voert iets in zijn schild, hij is iets van plan; *what are you up to now?* wat voer je nu weer in je schild? **3** [esp with negation] voldoen aan, beantwoorden aan: *it wasn't up to our expectations* het beantwoordde niet aan onze verwachtingen **4** [with negation or interrogative] aankunnen, berekend zijn op, aandurven: *he isn't up to this job* hij kan deze klus niet aan || *it's up to you* dat is aan jou

beverage drank: *alcoholic ~s* alcoholhoudende dranken

bevvy [inform] drankje[h]

bewail betreuren

beware oppassen, op zijn hoede zijn, voorzichtig zijn: *~ of the dog* pas op voor de hond

bewilder verbijsteren, van zijn stuk brengen

bewitch beheksen, betoveren, bekoren

be with [inform] **1** (kunnen) volgen, (nog) snappen: *are you still with me?* volg je me nog? **2** aan de kant staan van, op de hand zijn van, partij kiezen voor **3** horen bij: *we are with the coach party* wij horen bij het busgezelschap

[1]**beyond** (n) het onbekende, het hiernamaals: *the great ~* het grote onbekende

[2]**beyond** (adv) **1** verder, daarachter, aan de overzijde, daarna **2** daarenboven, meer, daarbuiten

[3]**beyond** (prep) **1** voorbij, achter, verder dan: *the hills ~ the city* de heuvels achter de stad **2** naast, buiten, behalve, meer dan || *~ belief* ongelofelijk, onbegrijpelijk, niet te geloven/begrijpen; *~ hope* er is geen hoop meer; *it is ~ me* dat gaat mijn verstand te boven

BF [inform] *boyfriend* vriend, vriendje[h]

BFF [inform] *best friend forever* hartsvriend(in), allerbeste vriend(in)

Bhutan Bhutan

[1]**Bhutanese** (n) Bhutaan(se)

[2]**Bhutanese** (adj) Bhutaans

bi [inform] bi *(biseksueel)*

[1]**bias** (n) **1** neiging, tendens, vooroordeel[h], vooringenomenheid: *without ~* onbevooroordeeld **2** [one-sided weighting] eenzijdige verzwaring [of ball]; afwijking [in shape or movement of ball]; effect[h]

[2]**bias** (vb) bevooroordeeld maken, beïnvloeden: *he was ~ed against foreigners* hij zat vol vooroordelen tegen buitenlanders

biased 1 vooringenomen, bevooroordeeld **2** tendentieus, in een bepaalde richting sturend

bib slab, slabbetje[h]

Bible 1 Bijbel **2** [fig] bijbel

biblical Bijbels

bibliographer bibliograaf

bibliography bibliografie, literatuurlijst

bicameral tweekamer-: *a ~ legislature* een wetgevend lichaam met twee kamers

bicarbonate bicarbonaat^h, zuiveringszout^h: *~ of soda* natriumbicarbonaat^h, zuiveringszout^h

bicentenary tweehonderdjarig jubileum^h

bicentennial [Am] tweehonderdjarig jubileum^h

bicker ruziën

¹**bicycle** (n) fiets

²**bicycle** (vb) fietsen

¹**bid** (n) **1** bod^h **2** prijsopgave, offerte **3** [cards] bod^h, beurt (om te bieden) **4** poging [to obtain sth.]; gooi: *a ~ for the presidency* een gooi naar het presidentschap

²**bid** (vb) **1** bevelen, gelasten **2** heten, zeggen: *~ s.o. farewell* iem. vaarwel zeggen **3** (uit)nodigen

³**bid** (vb) **1** bieden, een bod doen (van): *~ 5 dollars for sth.* 5 dollar voor iets bieden **2** een prijsopgave indienen **3** dingen: *~ for the public's favour* naar de gunst van het publiek dingen

bidder bieder: *the highest ~* de meestbiedende

bidding 1 het bieden **2** gebod^h, bevel^h: *do s.o.'s ~* iemands bevelen uitvoeren; [depr] naar iemands pijpen dansen

bide: *~ one's time* zijn tijd afwachten

biennial tweejarig

bifocals dubbelfocusbril

bifurcate zich splitsen; zich vertakken

¹**big** (adj) **1** groot, omvangrijk, dik, zwaar: *~ game* grof wild; *~ money* grof geld, het grote geld; *~ with child* (hoog)zwanger **2** belangrijk, invloedrijk, voornaam; [inform] langverwacht: *~ business* het groot kapitaal, de grote zakenwereld **3** groot, ouder, volwassen: *my ~ sister* mijn grote zus **4** [inform] groot(s), hoogdravend, ambitieus: [inform] *have ~ ideas* ambitieus zijn, het hoog in de bol hebben ‖ *be too ~ for one's boots* het hoog in de bol hebben; [iron] *~ deal!* **a)** en wat dan nog?, nou en?; **b)** lekker belangrijk!; *what's the ~ hurry?* vanwaar die haast?; *what's the ~ idea?* wat is hier aan de hand?

²**big** (adv) [inform] veel, duur, ruim: *pay ~ for sth.* veel voor iets betalen

bigamy bigamie, met twee personen gelijktijdig gehuwd zijn

big bang theory (the) oerknaltheorie

big data big data [pl]

bigheaded [inform] verwaand

bigot dweper, fanaticus

bigoted onverdraagzaam

bigotry onverdraagzaamheid

¹**big-time** (adj) [inform] top-, eersteklas(-): *~ athlete* topatleet

²**big-time** (adv) [inform] enorm, gigantisch: *you owe me ~* je mag me wel superdankbaar zijn; *I agree ~* daar ben ik het helemaal mee

eens; *you messed up ~* je hebt er een puinhoop van gemaakt

bigwig [inform; oft iron] hoge ome, hoge piet, bobo

¹**bike** (n) [inform] **1** fiets **2** [Am] motorfiets

²**bike** (vb) [inform] **1** fietsen **2** [Am] motorrijden

bilateral 1 tweezijdig, tweevoudig **2** bilateraal, wederzijds (bindend), tussen twee landen (partijen): *a ~ meeting* een bilaterale ontmoeting, een bila

bilberry bosbes

bile 1 gal **2** galstoornis **3** [fig] zwartgalligheid, humeurigheid

bilingual tweetalig

bilious 1 misselijk **2** afschuwelijk **3** [form] zwartgallig, humeurig

¹**bill** (n) **1** rekening, factuur, nota: *foot the ~ (for)* de hele rekening betalen (voor) **2** lijst, aanplakbiljet^h, (strooi)biljet^h, programma^h: *~ of fare* menu^{+h}; *stick no ~s* verboden aan te plakken **3** certificaat^h, bewijs^h, brief, rapport^h **4** bek, snavel, neus **5** [Am] (bank)biljet^h **6** [fin] wissel, schuldbekentenis **7** wetsvoorstel^h, wetsontwerp^h ‖ *fill (or: fit) the ~* geschikt zijn, aan iemands wensen tegemoetkomen

²**bill** (vb) **1** aankondigen, aanplakken **2** op de rekening zetten, de rekening sturen

billboard [Am] aanplakbord^h, reclamebord^h

¹**billet** (n) **1** kwartier^h, bestemming, verblijfplaats **2** inkwartieringsbevel^h

²**billet** (vb) inkwartieren, onderbrengen: *the troops were ~ed at our school* de troepen werden ondergebracht in onze school

billiards (Engels) biljart^h, het biljartspel

billion miljard, duizend miljoen; [fig] talloos

¹**billow** (n) **1** (zware) golf, hoge deining **2** [fig] golf, vloedgolf, zee

²**billow** (vb) deinen, golven, bol staan: *the ~ing sea* de golvende zee

billy goat (geiten)bok

bimonthly tweemaandelijks

bin vergaarbak, bak, mand, trommel, vuilnisbak, broodtrommel

binary binair, tweevoudig, dubbel(-)

¹**bind** (vb) (aaneen)plakken, zich (ver)binden, vast worden

²**bind** (vb) **1** (vast)binden, bijeenbinden, boeien **2** bedwingen, aan banden leggen, hinderen: *be snow-bound* vastzitten in de sneeuw **3** verplichten, verbinden, dwingen: *she is bound to come* ze moet komen, ze zal zeker komen; *~ s.o. to secrecy* iem. tot geheimhouding verplichten **4** (in)binden [book]; van een band voorzien ‖ *~ (up) a wound* een wond verbinden; *I'll be bound* ik ben er absoluut zeker van; *he is bound up in his job* hij gaat helemaal op in zijn werk

binder 1 binder [also agriculture; also machine]; boekbinder **2** band, snoer^h, touw^h, windsel^h **3** map, omslag^{+h}, ringband **4** bindmiddel^h

bindery (boek)binderij

bindi bindi

¹binding (n) band, boekband, verband^h

²binding (adj) bindend

bindweed woekerkruid^h

binge [inform] feest^h, braspartij: ~ *eating* feesten, gaan stappen; *go on the* ~ feesten, gaan stappen

binge-drink bingedrinken, comazuipen

binge drinking comazuipen^h

binge-view bingekijken

binge-watch bingekijken

bin liner vuilniszak

binoculars (verre)kijker, veldkijker, toneelkijker

biochemistry biochemie

biodegradable (biologisch) afbreekbaar

biodiversity biodiversiteit

bioengineering biotechniek

biofuel biobrandstof

biographer biograaf, biografe

biographical biografisch

biography biografie, levensbeschrijving

biohazard risico^h op besmetting met (micro-)organismen

biological biologisch

biologist bioloog

biology biologie

biomeat kweekvlees^h

biometric biometrisch: ~ *data* biometrische gegevens

bionic 1 bionisch **2** [inform] supervlug, supersterk

biopic [inform] *biographic picture* filmbiografie

bioprint [med] bioprinten

biosphere biosfeer

biotech *biotechnology* biotechnologie: *a ~ company* een biotechbedrijf

biowaste bioafval^h

bipartisan tweepartijen-

bipartite tweedelig, tweeledig, tweezijdig: *a ~ contract* een tweezijdig contract

biplane tweedekker

bipolar 1 tweepolig **2** bipolair; manisch-depressief: ~ *disorder* bipolaire stoornis

birch 1 berk(enboom) **2** berkenhout^h

bird 1 vogel: ~ *of passage* trekvogel; [fig] passant, doortrekkend reiziger; ~ *of prey* roofvogel **2** [inform] vogel, kerel **3** [inform] stuk^h, meisje^h ‖ *they are ~s of a feather* ze hebben veel gemeen; *kill two ~s with one stone* twee vliegen in één klap slaan; *the ~ is* (or: *has*) *flown* de vogel is gevlogen; [inform] *give s.o. the ~* iem. uitfluiten; *a ~ in the hand* (*is worth two in the bush*) beter één vogel in de hand dan tien in de lucht; *~s of a feather flock*

together soort zoekt soort

bird-brained [inform] stompzinnig; onnozel

bird flu vogelgriep

bird's-eye panoramisch, in vogelvlucht: *a ~ view of the town* een panoramisch gezicht op de stad

bird watcher vogelaar

biro balpen

birth 1 geboorte; [fig] ontstaan^h; begin^h, oorsprong: *give ~ to* het leven schenken aan **2** afkomst, afstamming: *of noble ~* van adellijke afkomst; *he is French by ~* hij is Fransman van geboorte

birth certificate geboorteakte

birthday verjaardag: *happy ~!* gefeliciteerd!

birthday suit [hum] adamskostuum^h

birthmark moedervlek

birthplace 1 geboorteplaats; geboortehuis^h **2** bakermat

birth rate geboortecijfer^h

birthright 1 geboorterecht^h **2** eerstgeboorterecht^h

biscuit 1 biscuit^h, cracker **2** [Am] zacht rond koekje^h

bisect in tweeën delen, splitsen, halveren

bisexual biseksueel

bishop 1 bisschop **2** [chess] loper

bit 1 beetje^h, stukje^h, kleinigheid: *by ~s and pieces* in stukjes en beetjes; *~s and bobs* ditjes en datjes; [inform] *do one's ~* zijn steen(tje) bijdragen; [inform] *~ by ~* bij beetjes, stukje voor stukje; *not a ~ (of it)* helemaal niet(s), geen zier; *not a ~ better* geen haar beter; *quite a ~* heel wat; *your eye's a ~ red* je oog is een beetje rood **2** ogenblik^h, momentje^h: *wait a ~!* wacht even! **3** (ge)bit^h [mouthpiece for horse]: *take the ~ between its teeth* **a)** op hol slaan [of horse]; **b)** (te) hard van stapel lopen **4** boorijzer^h **5** schaafijzer^h, schaafbeitel, schaafmes^h **6** bit^h [smallest unit of information]

bitch 1 teef; wijfje^h [of dog, fox] **2** [vulg; offensive] teef, kreng^h (van een wijf), trut **3** [vulg; offensive] eikel

bitcoin bitcoin

¹bite (n) **1** beet, hap [of je^h]; beetje^h [food]: *have a ~ to eat* iets eten **3** beet [when fishing] **4** vinnigheid, bits(ig)heid, scherpte: *there was a ~ in the air* er hing een vinnige kou in de lucht

²bite (vb) **1** bijten, toebijten; (toe)happen [also fig]; zich (gemakkelijk) laten beetnemen, steken; prikken [of insects]: [fig] *~ one's lip(s)* zich verbijten **2** bijten; inwerken [of acids; also fig] **3** voelbaar worden; effect hebben [esp with sth. negative] ‖ *~ off more than one can chew* te veel hooi op zijn vork nemen; *once bitten, twice shy* [roughly] door schade en schande wordt men wijs

bitstream [comp] datastroom
¹bitter (n) **1** bitterʰ (bier) **2** bitterheid, het bittere ‖ *take the* ~ *with the sweet* het nemen zoals het valt
²bitter (adj) bitter [also fig]; bijtend, scherp, venijnig, verbitterd
bittern roerdomp
bittersweet bitterzoet [also fig]: [Am] ~ *chocolate* extrapure chocolade
bitumen bitumenʰ
bivouac bivakʰ
biweekly veertiendaags, tweewekelijks, om de veertien dagen
bizarre bizar, zonderling
bizjet [inform] zakenvliegtuigʰ
¹blab (vb) zijn mond voorbij praten, loslippig zijn
²blab (vb) (er)uit flappen
blabbermouth [depr] kletskous
¹black (n) **1** zwartʰ: ~ *and white* zwart-witʰ [film; also fig] **2** (roet)zwartʰ, zwarte kleurstof **3** zwarte, neger(in) **4** zwart schaakstukʰ, zwarte damsteen
²black (adj) **1** zwart, (zeer) donker; [fig also] duister: *be in s.o.'s* ~ *book(s)* bij iem. slecht aangeschreven staan; *Black Death* de Zwarte Dood [plague epidemic]; ~ *eye* donker oog, blauw oog [after blow]; ~ *market* zwarte markt; ~ *sheep* zwart schaap [fig]; ~ *spot* zwarte plek, rampenplek [where many accidents happen]; ~ *tie* a) zwart strikje; b) smoking **2** zwart, vuil, besmeurd **3** zwart, (zeer) slecht, somber, onvriendelijk: *give s.o. a* ~ *look* iem. onvriendelijk aankijken ‖ ~ *ice* ijzel; ~ *and blue* bont en blauw [beaten]
³black (vb) **1** zwart maken; poetsen [(black) shoes] **2** bevuilen **3** besmet verklaren [ship's cargo, by strikers] ‖ ~ *s.o.'s eye* iem. een blauw oog slaan
blackball deballoteren; als lid afwijzen
blackberry 1 braam(struik) **2** braam(bes)
blackbird merel
blackboard (school)bordʰ
blackcurrant zwarte bes
blacken 1 zwart maken, bekladden **2** [fig] zwartmaken: ~ *s.o.'s reputation* iem. zwart maken
blackguard schurk, bandiet
black-hat [comp] [pers] met kwade bedoelingen; [activities] niet toegestaan ‖ ~ *methods* illegale technieken
black-hat hacker criminele hacker, cracker
black-hat hacking cracking
blackhead mee-eter, vetpuistjeʰ
¹blackjack (n) [Am] ploertendoder
²blackjack (n) blackjackʰ
¹blacklist (n) zwarte lijst
²blacklist (vb) op de zwarte lijst plaatsen
¹blackmail (n) afpersing, chantage
²blackmail (vb) chanteren, (geld) afpersen

van, afdwingen (onder dreiging): ~ *s.o. into sth.* iem. iets afdwingen
blackmailer afperser; chanteur
blackout 1 verduistering; stroomuitval **2** black-out, tijdelijke bewusteloosheid, tijdelijk geheugenverliesʰ, tijdelijke blindheid
blacksmith smid, hoefsmid
black spot 1 [traf] gevaarlijk puntʰ **2** probleemgebiedʰ: *unemployment* ~ gebied met veel werklozen
black-tie avondkleding: ~ *dinner* diner in avondkleding
bladder blaas
blade 1 lemmetʰ [of knife]; bladʰ [of axe, saw]; kling [of sword]; (scheer)mesjeʰ, dunne snijplaat; ijzerʰ [of skate] **2** blaadjeʰ [eg of grass]; halm: *a* ~ *of grass* een grassprietje **3** [sport] onderbeenprothese
blader [inform] skater (op rollerblades)
¹blame (n) schuld, blaam; verantwoording [for sth. bad]: *bear* (or: *take*) *the* ~ de schuld op zich nemen; *play the* ~ *game* zwartepieten
²blame (vb) **1** de schuld geven aan, verwijten, iets kwalijk nemen: *I don't* ~ *Jane* ik geef Jane geen ongelijk; *he is to* ~ het is zijn schuld **2** afkeuren, veroordelen
blameless onberispelijk, vlekkeloos, onschuldig
¹blanch (vb) bleek worden, wit wegtrekken: ~ *at that remark* verbleken bij die opmerking
²blanch (vb) [cooking] blancheren
bland 1 (zacht)aardig, vriendelijk **2** mild, niet te gekruid, zacht **3** neutraal, nietszeggend **4** flauw, saai **5** nuchter, koel
¹blank (n) **1** leegte, leemte: *his memory is a* ~ hij weet zich niets meer te herinneren **2** blanco formulierʰ **3** losse patroon [of gun]; losse flodder **4** niet, niet in de prijzen vallend lotʰ: *draw a* ~ niet in de prijzen vallen; [fig] bot vangen
²blank (adj) **1** leeg, blanco, onbeschreven: *a* ~ *cartridge* een losse patroon; *a* ~ *cheque* een blanco cheque **2** uitdrukkingsloos, onbegrijpend, ongeïnteresseerd: *a* ~ *look* een wezenloze blik ‖ *a* ~ *refusal* een botte weigering
¹blanket (n) (wollen) deken, bedekking; [fig] (dikke) laag
²blanket (adj) allesomvattend, algemeen geldig: *a* ~ *insurance* een pakketverzekering; *a* ~ *rule* een algemene regel
blare schallen, lawaai maken, luid klinken
blasphemous godslasterlijk
blasphemy (gods)lastering, blasfemie
¹blast (n) **1** (wind)vlaag, rukwind **2** sterke luchtstroom [eg with explosion] **3** explosie [also fig]; uitbarsting **4** stoot [eg on trumpet]; (claxon)signaalʰ ‖ *he was working at full* ~ hij werkte op volle toeren
²blast (vb) **1** opblazen, doen exploderen, bombarderen **2** vernietigen, verijdelen, ruï-

neren **3** [euph] verwensen, vervloeken: ~
him! laat hem naar de maan lopen!
blasted [inform] **1** getroffen [by lightning
etc] **2** verschrompeld, verdwenen
blast furnace hoogoven
blast-off lancering [of rocket]
blatant 1 schaamteloos, onbeschaamd
2 overduidelijk, opvallend: *a ~ lie* een regelrechte leugen **3** hinderlijk, ergerlijk
¹blather (n) gekletsʰ, onzin, nonsens
²blather (vb) dom kletsen
¹blaze (n) **1** vlammen(zee), (verwoestend)
vuurʰ, brand **2** uitbarsting, plotselinge uitval: *a ~ of anger* een uitbarsting van woede
3 felle gloed [of light, colour]; vol lichtʰ,
schittering
²blaze (vb) **1** (fel) branden, gloeien, in lichterlaaie staan; [also fig] in vuur en vlam
staan [of rage, excitement]: *the quarrel ~d up*
de ruzie laaide op **2** (fel) schijnen, verlicht
zijn, schitteren
³blaze (vb) [also fig] banen [road, trail]; aangeven, merken: *~ a trail* een pad banen, een
nieuwe weg inslaan
blaze away 1 oplaaien [of fire]; oplichten,
opvlammen **2** erop los schieten
¹bleach (n) bleekmiddelʰ
²bleach (vb) bleken, bleek worden (maken),
(doen) verbleken
bleak 1 guur [eg of weather]; troosteloos,
grauw **2** ontmoedigend, deprimerend, somber: *~ prospects* sombere vooruitzichten
3 onbeschut, aan weer en wind blootgesteld, kaal
bleary-eyed met wazige blik
¹bleat (n) blatend geluidʰ, geblaatʰ; [fig] ge-
zanikʰ
²bleat (vb) blaten, blèren, mekkeren; [fig]
zeuren; zaniken
¹bleed (vb) **1** bloeden, bloed verliezen: [fig]
her heart ~s for the poor ze heeft diep medelijden met de armen **2** uitlopen; doorlopen
[of colour] **3** (vloeistof) afgeven, bloeden;
afscheiden [eg of plant] **4** uitgezogen worden, bloeden, afgezet worden
²bleed (vb) **1** doen bloeden, bloed afnemen
van, aderlaten **2** uitzuigen, laten bloeden
3 onttrekken [eg liquid]
bleeding [inform] verdomd
bleeding-edge allermodernst; allernieuwst
¹bleep (n) piep, hoge pieptoon
²bleep (vb) (op)piepen, oproepen met piep-
signaal
bleeper pieper [of paging system]
blemish vlek [also fig]; smet, onvolkomenheid
¹blend (n) mengselʰ [eg of tea, coffee, whis-
ky]; melange⁺ʰ, mengeling
²blend (vb) zich vermengen, bij elkaar passen: *~ in with* harmoniëren met

³blend (vb) mengen, combineren
blender mengbeker, mixer
bless 1 zegenen, (in)wijden: *~ o.s.* een kruis
slaan; [fig] zich gelukkig prijzen **2** Gods zegen vragen voor **3** begunstigen, zegenen
4 vereren [eg God]; aanbidden, loven
blessed 1 heilig, (door God) gezegend
2 gelukkig, (geluk)zalig, gezegend: *the
whole ~ day* de godganse dag; *every ~ thing*
alles, maar dan ook alles
blessing 1 zegen(ing): *a ~ in disguise* een
geluk bij een ongeluk; *count your ~!* wees blij
met wat je hebt! **2** goedkeuring, aanmoediging, zegen
¹blight (n) **1** plantenziekte, meeldauw;
soort bladluis **2** afzichtelijkheid, afschuwelijkheid **3** vloek
²blight (vb) **1** aantasten [with plant disease];
doen verdorren **2** een vernietigende uitwerking hebben op, zwaar schaden, verwoesten: *a life ~ed by worries* een leven dat vergald werd door de zorgen
blimey [vulg] verdikkeme
¹blind (n) **1** schermʰ, jaloezie, zonneschermʰ,
rolgordijnʰ **2** voorwendselʰ, uitvlucht, dekmantel
²blind (adj) **1** blind; [fig] ondoordacht; roekeloos: *~ fury* blinde woede; *as ~ as a bat* zo
blind als een mol, stekeblind; *the ~* de blinden **2** blind, zonder begrip, ongevoelig: *be ~
to s.o.'s faults* geen oog hebben voor de fouten van iem. **3** doodlopend; [fig] zonder
vooruitzichten ‖ *turn a ~ eye to sth.* iets door
de vingers zien, een oogje dichtknijpen voor
iets
³blind (vb) **1** verblinden, blind maken, misleiden **2** verduisteren, overschaduwen
3 blinddoeken
⁴blind (adv) blind(elings), roekeloos ‖ *~
drunk* stomdronken
¹blindfold (adj) geblinddoekt: *~ chess*
blindschaken
²blindfold (vb) blinddoeken; [fig] misleiden
blindman's buff blindemannetjeʰ
blind spot 1 blinde vlek [in eye] **2** blinde
hoek **3** zwakke plek: *I have a ~ where politics
is concerned* van politiek heb ik geen kaas
gegeten
bling bling
blini blini
¹blink (n) **1** knipoog, (oog)wenk **2** glimp,
oogopslag **3** flikkering, schijnselʰ ‖ [inform]
on the ~ niet in orde, defect
²blink (vb) **1** met half toegeknepen ogen
kijken, knipogen **2** knipperen, flikkeren,
schitteren
³blink (vb) knippe(re)n met
blink at een oogje dichtdoen voor: *~ illegal
practices* illegale praktijken door de vingers
zien
blinkered [depr] met oogkleppen; be-

krompen
blinkers oogkleppen; [fig] kortzichtigheid
blip 1 piep, bliep **2** [radar] echo
blipvert flitsreclame
bliss (geluk)zaligheid, het einde, puur genotʰ
bliss out [inform] uit zijn dak gaan
B-list tot de subtop behorend; tweederangs
¹**blister** (n) **1** (brand)blaar **2** bladder, blaas
²**blister** (vb) **1** blaren krijgen **2** (af)bladderen, blazen vormen
³**blister** (vb) doen bladderen, verschroeien, blaren veroorzaken op
blistering 1 verschroeiend, verzengend: *the ~ sun* de gloeiend hete zon **2** vernietigend
blithe [form] **1** vreugdevol, blij **2** zorgeloos, onbezorgd
blithering stom, getikt: *you ~ idiot!* stomme idioot die je bent!
¹**blitz** (n) **1** blitzkrieg; bliksemoorlog **2** Duitse bomaanvallen op Londen in 1940 **3** (intensieve) campagne **4** snelschakenʰ: *a ~ game* een snelschaakpartij **5** [culinary] vermaling: *give* the mixture a quick *~* vermaal het mengsel in de keukenmachine
²**blitz** (vb) **1** bombarderen **2** [culinary] in een keukenmachine mengen
blizzard (hevige) sneeuwstorm
bloated opgezwollen, opgezet, opgeblazen
blob klodder, druppel, spat
bloc [pol] blokʰ, groep, coalitie
¹**block** (n) **1** blokʰ [also pol]; stronk, (hak)blokʰ, kapblokʰ, steenblokʰ, beulsblokʰ **2** blokʰ [of buildings]; huizenblokʰ; (groot) gebouwʰ: *~ of flats* flatgebouwʰ; *walk around* the *~* een straatje omlopen **3** versperring, stremming; [psychology, sport] blokkering; obstructie
²**block** (vb) [sport] blokkeren, blokken, obstructie plegen
³**block** (vb) **1** versperren, blokkeren: *~ off* afsluiten, blokkeren **2** belemmeren, verhinderen, tegenhouden: *he ~ed my plans* hij reed mij in de wielen **3** [sport, psychology] blokkeren, obstructie plegen tegen || *~ in* (or: *out*) ontwerpen, schetsen
¹**blockade** (n) blokkade, afsluiting, versperring
²**blockade** (vb) blokkeren, afsluiten, belemmeren, verhinderen
blockage 1 verstopping, opstopping, obstakelʰ **2** stagnatie, stremming
blockbuster kassuccesʰ
blockhead domkop, stommerik
blog blog⁺ʰ
blogger blogger
blogstream op internet gepubliceerde blogs
bloke kerel, gozer, vent

¹**blond** (n) **1** blond iem.; [woman] blondjeʰ; blondine **2** iem. met een lichte huidkleur **3** blondʰ
²**blond** (adj) **1** blond **2** met een lichte huidkleur
blood 1 bloedʰ: *in cold ~* in koelen bloede; *draw first ~* de eerste klap uitdelen; *it makes your ~ boil* het maakt je razend; *let ~* aderlaten **2** temperamentʰ, aard, hartstocht **3** bloedverwantschapʰ, afstamming, afkomst: *blue ~* blauw bloed; *bring in fresh ~* vers bloed inbrengen; *be* (or: *run*) *in one's ~* in het bloed zitten; *~ is thicker than water* het hemd is nader dan de rok
bloodbath bloedbadʰ; slachtpartij
blood clot bloedstolselʰ
bloodcurdling ijzingwekkend, huiveringwekkend, bloedstollend
bloodhound bloedhond; [fig] speurder; detective
bloodless 1 bloedeloos **2** bleek, kleurloos **3** saai, duf
blood relation bloedverwant(e)
blood revenge eerwraak
bloodshed bloedvergietenʰ
bloodshot bloeddoorlopen
blood sport [depr] jachtʰ; bloedige sport
bloodstream bloedstroom, bloedbaan
bloodthirsty bloeddorstig, moorddadig
blood vessel bloedvatʰ, ader
¹**bloody** (adj) **1** bloed-, bloedrood, bebloed: *~ nose* bloedneus **2** bloed(er)ig **3** bloeddorstig, wreed **4** verdraaid: *he's a ~ fool* hij is een domme idioot
²**bloody** (adv) [inform] erg: *you're ~ well right* je hebt nog gelijk ook
bloody-minded [inform] dwars, koppig
¹**bloom** (n) **1** bloem [esp of cultivated plants]; bloesem **2** bloei(tijd), kracht, hoogste ontwikkeling: *in* the *~ of one's youth* in de kracht van zijn jeugd **3** waasʰ, dauw **4** blos, gloed
²**bloom** (vb) **1** bloeien, in bloei zijn **2** in volle bloei komen [also fig]; tot volle ontplooiing komen **3** floreren, gedijen **4** blozen; stralen [esp of woman] **5** zich ontwikkelen, (op)bloeien, uitgroeien
bloomer [inform] blunder, flater, miskleun
blooming verdraaid
¹**blossom** (n) [also fig] bloesem, bloei: *be in ~* in bloesem staan
²**blossom** (vb) **1** ontbloeien; tot bloei komen [of fruit trees] **2** zich ontwikkelen, opbloeien, zich ontpoppen
¹**blot** (n) vlek [also fig]: *the building was a ~ on the landscape* het gebouw ontsierde het landschap
²**blot** (vb) vlekken maken, knoeien, kliederen, vlekken (krijgen); vloeien (met vloeipapier)
³**blot** (vb) **1** bevlekken, bekladden **2** ontsieren **3** (af)vloeien, drogen met vloeipapier

blotch vlek, puist, smet

blot out 1 (weg)schrappen, doorhalen
2 verbergen, aan het gezicht onttrekken, bedekken: *clouds* ~ *the sun* wolken schuiven voor de zon **3** vernietigen, uitroeien

blotting paper vloei(papier)ʰ

blouse bloes [worn by women]; blauwe (werk)kiel

¹blow (n) **1** wind(vlaag), rukwind, storm, stevige bries **2** slag, klap, mep: *come to* (or: *exchange*) ~*s* slaags raken; ~ *by* ~ *account* gedetailleerd verslag; *without* (striking) a ~ zonder slag of stoot, zonder geweld **3** (tegen)slag, ramp, schok

²blow (vb) **1** (uit)blazen, fluiten, weerklinken, (uit)waaien, wapperen: ~ *down* neergeblazen worden, omwaaien; [inform] ~ *in* **a)** (komen) binnenvallen, (komen) aanwaaien; **b)** inwaaien; *the scandal will* ~ *over* het schandaal zal wel overwaaien **2** hijgen, blazen, puffen **3** stormen, hard waaien **4** [elec] doorsmelten, doorbranden; doorslaan [of fuse] ‖ [inform] ~ *hot and cold* (about) veranderen als het weer

³blow (vb) **1** blazen (op/door), aanblazen, afblazen, opblazen, rondblazen, uitblazen, wegblazen; snuiten [nose]; doen wapperen, doen dwarrelen: *the door* was ~*n* open de deur waaide open; *the wind blew her hair* de wind waaide door haar haar; ~ *away* wegblazen, wegjagen; *the wind blew the trees down* de wind blies de bomen om(ver); ~ *in* **a)** doen binnenwaaien; **b)** doen springen [window-pane]; ~ *off* **a)** wegblazen, doen wegwaaien; **b)** laten ontsnappen [steam]; ~ *over* om(ver)blazen, doen omwaaien; ~ *sky-high* in de lucht laten vliegen; [fig] geen spaan heel laten van **2** doen doorslaan, doen doorbranden **3** bespelen, blazen op, spelen op **4** [inform] verprutsen, verknoeien **5** [vulg] pijpen, afzuigen

blow-dry föhnen

blow-dryer föhn, haardroger

blower 1 aanjager, blower, ventilator **2** [inform] telefoon

blowfly vleesvlieg

blowjob [vulg] pijpbeurt

blowout 1 klapband, lekke band **2** lekʰ **3** uitbarsting [of oil well, gas well]; eruptie **4** [inform] eetfestijnʰ, vreetpartij **5** [Am; sport; inform] makkelijke overwinning

¹blow out (vb) **1** uitwaaien, uitgaan **2** springen, klappen, barsten **3** ophouden te werken [of electrical appliances]; uitvallen, doorbranden

²blow out (vb) **1** uitblazen, uitdoen **2** doen springen, doen klappen **3** buiten bedrijf stellen [electrical appliances] ‖ ~ *one's brains* zich voor de kop schieten

¹blow up (vb) **1** ontploffen, exploderen, springen **2** [inform] in rook opgaan, verij-

deld worden **3** opzwellen, opgeblazen worden **4** (in woede) uitbarsten, ontploffen **5** sterker worden [of wind, storm]; komen opzetten; [fig] uitbreken; losbarsten

²blow up (vb) **1** opblazen, laten ontploffen; vullen [with air] **2** opblazen, overdrijven **3** aanblazen [fire]; aanwakkeren, (op)stoken **4** doen opwaaien, opjagen, opdwarrelen **5** [photo] (uit)vergroten

blow-up 1 explosie, ontploffing **2** uitbarsting, ruzie, herrie **3** [photo] (uit)vergroting

blowy winderig

¹blubber (n) **1** blubber **2** [inform] gejankʰ, gegrienʰ

²blubber (vb) grienen, snotteren, janken

blubbery dik; vet

bludgeon (gummi)knuppel, knots

¹blue (n) **1** blauwʰ **2** blauwselʰ [to dye linen blue] **3** [the] blauwe lucht: *out of the* ~ plotseling, als een donderslag bij heldere hemel **4** blauwtjeʰ [butterfly] **5** lidʰ (kleur) van een conservatieve politieke partij; tory; conservatief

²blue (adj) **1** blauw, azuur: ~ *blooded* van adellijke afkomst; ~ *with cold* blauw van de kou **2** gedeprimeerd, triest, somber **3** conservatief; tory **4** [inform] obsceen, porno-, gewaagd: ~ *film* (or: *movie*) pornofilm, seksfilm ‖ *wait till one is* ~ *in the face* wachten tot je een ons weegt; *once in a* ~ *moon* (hoogst) zelden, zelden of nooit; *cry* (or: *scream, shout*) ~ *murder* moord en brand schreeuwen

blueberry bosbes

bluebottle aasvlieg, bromvlieg

blue-collar hand-; fabrieks- [worker(s)]

blueprint blauwdruk, ontwerpʰ, schets

blue ribbon hoogste onderscheiding, eerste prijs

blue-rinse met een blauwe kleurspoeling

blues 1 blues: *play a* ~ een blues spelen **2** [inform] zwaarmoedigheid, melancholie

bluestocking [oft depr] geleerde vrouw

blue tit pimpelmees

¹bluff (n) **1** hoge, steile oever, steile rotswand, klifʰ **2** bluf: *call one's* ~ **a)** iem. uitdagen; **b)** iemands uitdaging aannemen

²bluff (adj) kortaf maar oprecht, plompverloren maar eerlijk

³bluff (vb) **1** bluffen [also in poker]; brutaal optreden **2** doen alsof, voorwenden

⁴bluff (vb) **1** overbluffen, overdonderen **2** misleiden, bedriegen, doen alsof: ~ *one's way out of a situation* zich uit een situatie redden

¹blunder (n) blunder, miskleun

²blunder (vb) **1** blunderen, een stomme fout maken, een flater slaan **2** strompelen, (voort)sukkelen, zich onhandig voortbewegen: ~ *into a tree* tegen een boom op knallen

blunt 1 bot, stomp **2** afgestompt, ongevoelig, koud **3** (p)lomp, ongezouten, onomwonden: *tell* s.o. sth. ~*ly* iem. iets botweg vertellen

¹blur (n) onduidelijke plek, wazig beeld^h, verflauwde indruk

²blur (vb) **1** vervagen, vaag worden **2** vlekken

³blur (vb) **1** bevlekken, besmeren; [fig] bekladden **2** onscherp maken, troebel maken: ~*red* *photographs* onscherpe foto's

blurb flaptekst

blurry onduidelijk, onscherp, vaag

blurt eruit flappen; eruit gooien: ~ *out* eruit flappen

¹blush (n) (schaamte)blos, (rode) kleur, schaamrood^h

²blush (vb) blozen, een kleur krijgen, rood worden

¹bluster (n) **1** tumult^h, drukte, geloei^h; gebulder^h [of storm]; geraas^h; getier^h [of angry voices] **2** gebral^h, opschepperij

²bluster (vb) **1** razen, bulderen, tieren **2** loeien, loeien; huilen [of wind] **3** brallen, opscheppen

blvd boulevard

boar 1 beer [male pig] **2** wild zwijn^h, everzwijn^h

¹board (n) **1** plank, (vloer)deel^h **2** (aanplak)bord^h, scorebord^h, schild^h, plaat; bord^h [basketball and korfball]; (schaak)bord^h, (speel)bord^h **3** [shipp] boord^h: *go by the* ~ **a)** overboord slaan; **b)** volledig mislukken [of plans etc]; *on* ~ aan boord van **4** kost, kostgeld^h, onderhoud^h, pension^h: ~ *and lodging* kost en inwoning; *full* ~ vol pension **5** raad, bestuur(slichaam)^h: ~ *of directors* raad van bestuur; *editorial* ~ redactie; *be on the* ~ in het bestuur zitten, bestuurslid zijn ‖ *sweep the* ~ grote winst(en) boeken, zegevieren; [inform] *take on* ~ begrijpen, accepteren, aannemen [of new ideas etc]; *above* ~ open, eerlijk; *across the* ~ over de hele linie, iedereen, niemand uitgezonderd

²board (vb) in de kost zijn

³board (vb) **1** beplanken, beschieten, betimmeren, bevloeren **2** in de kost hebben **3** uit huis doen, in de kost doen **4** aan boord gaan van; instappen [aeroplane]; opstappen [motorcycle]: ~ *a ship* zich inschepen **5** [shipp] enteren

boarder pensiongast, kostganger, kostleerling, intern

boarding beplanking, betimmering, schutting

boarding card instapkaart

boarding-house kosthuis^h, pension^h

boarding pass instapkaart

boarding school kostschool, internaat^h

boardroom bestuurskamer, directiekamer

boardsailing [sport] het plankzeilen, het (wind)surfen

¹boast (n) **1** [depr] bluf, grootspraak **2** trots, roem, glorie

²boast (vb) opscheppen, overdrijven, sterke verhalen vertellen: ~ *about,* ~ *of* opscheppen over, zich laten voorstaan op

³boast (vb) **1** in het (trotse) bezit zijn van, (kunnen) bogen op (het bezit van) **2** [depr] opscheppen

boaster opschepper, praatjesmaker

boat 1 (open) boot, vaartuig^h, (dek)schuit, sloep: [fig] *be (all) in the same* ~ (allen) in hetzelfde schuitje zitten **2** [Am] (zeewaardig) schip^h; (stoom)boot [used esp by non-sailors] **3** (jus)kom, sauskom ‖ *burn one's* ~*s* z'n schepen achter zich verbranden; *miss the* ~ de boot missen, zijn kans voorbij laten gaan; [inform] *push the* ~ *out* de bloemetjes buiten zetten; [inform] *rock the* ~ de boel in het honderd sturen, spelbreker zijn

boatswain bootsman, boots

¹bob (n) **1** hangend voorwerp^h, (slinger)gewicht^h; lens [of timepiece]; gewicht^h; strik [of kite]; lood^h [of plumb line]; dobber, waker **2** bob(slee) **3** gecoupeerde staart **4** plotselinge (korte) beweging, sprong, (knie)buiging, knicks **5** bob(bed kapsel^h), kortgeknipte kop, jongenskop ‖ [inform] *Bob's your uncle* klaar is Kees, voor mekaar

²bob (vb) **1** bobben, rodelen, bobsleeën **2** (zich) op en neer (heen en weer) bewegen, (op)springen, dobberen: ~ *up* (plotseling) tevoorschijn komen, komen boven drijven, opduiken **3** buigen, een (knie)buiging maken

³bob (vb) **1** (kort) knippen [hair] **2** couperen, kortstaarten **3** heen en weer (op en neer) bewegen, doen dansen, laten dobberen, knikken

bobbin spoel, klos, bobine

bobby [inform] bobby, oom agent, politieman

bobcat rode lynx

¹bobsleigh (n) bob(slee)

²bobsleigh (vb) bobsleeën, bobben

¹bodily (adj) lichamelijk: ~ *harm* lichamelijk letsel

²bodily (adv) **1** met geweld **2** lichamelijk, in levende lijve **3** in z'n geheel, met huid en haar

body 1 lichaam^h, romp, lijk^h: *just enough to keep* ~ *and soul together* net genoeg om je te redden **2** persoon; [law] rechtspersoon; [inform] mens; ziel **3** grote hoeveelheid, massa **4** voornaamste deel^h, grootste (centrale) deel^h, kern, meerderheid; schip^h [of church]; casco^h; carrosserie [of car]; romp [of aeroplane]; klankkast [of musical instrument]: *the* ~ *of a letter* de kern van een brief **5** lichaam^h, groep, korps^h: *the Governing Body is* (or: *are*) *meeting today* het bestuur vergadert vandaag; *they left in a* ~ ze vertrokken als één man **6** voorwerp^h, object^h, lichaam^h: *heavenly bodies* hemellichamen **7** bodystocking

body bag lijkzak
body count aantal gesneuvelden
bodyguard lijfwacht
body mass index *BMI* BMI, queteletindex
body search fouillering
body-shaming [media] het bekritiseren
van iemands lichaam of gewicht
bodywork carrosserie
boffin [inform] expert
bog 1 (veen)moeras[h] **2** [inform] plee, wc
bog down 1 gehinderd worden, vastlopen
2 vast komen te zitten (in de modder) ‖ *get
bogged down in details* in details verzanden
bogey 1 boeman, (kwel)duivel, kwade
geest **2** spookbeeld[h], schrikbeeld[h] **3** [golf]
bogey, score van 1 slag boven par voor een
hole **4** snotje[h]
boggle 1 terugschrikken, terugdeinzen
2 duizelen: *the mind ~s* het duizelt me
boggy moerassig, drassig
bogus vals, onecht, nep-, vervalst
boho [inform] bohemien
¹boil (n) **1** steenpuist **2** kookpunt[h], kook
²boil (vb) **1** (staan te) koken, het kookpunt
bereiken, gekookt worden: *~ing hot* kokend
heet; *~ down* inkoken; *~ over* a) overkoken;
b) [fig] uitbarsten (in woede), tot uitbarsting
komen **2** (inwendig) koken: *~ing with anger*
ziedend van woede ‖ [inform] *~ down to*
neerkomen op, in het kort, in grote lijnen
³boil (vb) koken, aan de kook brengen ‖ [in-
form] *~ down* kort samenvatten, de hoofd-
lijnen aangeven
boiler boiler, stoomketel
boisterous 1 onstuimig, luid(ruchtig)
2 ruw, heftig; stormachtig [of wind, weather
etc]
bold 1 (stout)moedig, doortastend **2** [oft
depr] brutaal: *as ~ as brass* (honds)brutaal
3 krachtig, goed uitkomend **4** vet (gedrukt)
‖ *put a ~ face on the matter* zich goedhouden
boldface [printing] vette letter
bold-faced 1 brutaal, schaamteloos **2** vet
gedrukt
Bolivia Bolivia
¹Bolivian (n) Boliviaan(se)
²Bolivian (adj) Boliviaans
bollard korte paal, bolder; meerpaal
[shipp]; verkeerszuiltje[h], verkeerspaaltje[h]
bollocks [vulg] **1** gelul[h] **2** kloten
boloney [inform] onzin, (flauwe)kul, gelul[h]
Bolshevism bolsjewisme[h]
bolster 1 (onder)kussen[h], hoofdmatras[+h]
2 steun, ondersteuning, stut
bolster up 1 met kussen(s) (onder)steunen
2 schragen, ondersteunen; opkrikken [also
fig]: *~ s.o.'s morale* iem. moed inspreken
¹bolt (n) **1** bout **2** grendel, schuif **3** bliksemstraal, bliksemflits **4** sprong, duik: *make a ~
for it* er vandoor gaan ‖ *a ~ from the blue* een
complete verrassing

²bolt (vb) **1** [inform] op de loop gaan, de benen nemen; op hol slaan [of horse] **2** (plot-
seling/verschrikt) op(zij)springen, wegspringen **3** doorschieten, (vroegtijdig, te vroeg) in
het zaad schieten **4** met bouten bevestigd
zitten **5** sluiten, een grendel hebben
³bolt (vb) **1** (snel) verorberen: *~ down food*
eten opschrokken **2** vergrendelen, op slot
doen **3** met bout(en) bevestigen
⁴bolt (adv) recht: *~ upright* kaarsrecht
bolt cutter betonschaar
¹bomb (n) **1** bom **2** [inform] bom geld: *cost
a ~* kapitalen kosten **3** [inform] hit, klapper,
daverend succes[h]: *go like a ~* a) als een trein
lopen; b) scheuren [of car]
²bomb (vb) **1** bommen werpen **2** razen, racen
³bomb (vb) bombarderen
bombard bombarderen, met bommen,
granaten bestoken; [fig] bestoken; lastigvallen: *~ s.o. with questions* vragen afvuren op
iem.
bombardment bombardement[h], bomaan-
val
bombastic hoogdravend, gezwollen
bomber 1 bommenwerper **2** bommen-
gooier [pers]
bomb scare bommelding
bombshell granaat[h], bom; [inform, fig]
donderslag; (onaangename) verrassing:
drop a ~ een sensationele mededeling doen
bona fide te goeder trouw, bonafide, betrouwbaar
bonanza 1 rijke (erts)vindplaats [esp of
gold, silver, oil]; rijke oliebron, mijn; [fig]
goudmijn **2** grote (winst)opbrengst
bond 1 band, verbond[h], verbondenheid,
binding **2** verbintenis, contract[h], verplichting
3 obligatie, schuldbekentenis **4** verbinding,
hechting; [chem] verbinding **5** (-s) boeien,
ketenen, gevangenschap
bondage 1 slavernij **2** onderworpenheid,
het gebonden zijn, gebondenheid
bonded 1 in douaneopslag (geplaatst)
2 aan elkaar gelijmd, gelaagd
¹bone (n) **1** bot[h], been[h], graat: *I can feel it* (or:
it is) *in my ~s* ik weet het zeker, ik voel het
aankomen **2** kluif, stuk[h] been, bot[h] ‖ *~ of
contention* twistappel; *make no ~s about* niet
aarzelen om; *have a ~ to pick with s.o.* met
iem. een appeltje te schillen hebben
²bone (adj) benen, van been, ivoren
³bone (vb) uitbenen, ontgraten
⁴bone (adv) extreem, uitermate: *~ dry* kurkdroog; *~ idle* (or: *lazy*) aartslui
boneheaded stom, achterlijk, idioot
bonfire vuur[h] in de openlucht, vreugdevuur[h], vuur[h] om dode bladeren (afval) te verbranden
bonkers gek, maf, getikt
bonnet 1 bonnet, hoed **2** beschermkap,

boot

schoorsteenkap; motorkap

bonus 1 bonus, premie, gratificatie **2** bijslag, toelage **3** [inform] meevaller, extraatje[h]

bony 1 benig, mager **2** met veel botten (graten)

¹boo (n) boe, kreet van afkeuring, gejouw[h], boegeroep[h] || *wouldn't* (or: *couldn't*) *say ~ to a goose* **a)** dodelijk verlegen zijn; **b)** zo bang als een wezel zijn

²boo (vb) boe roepen, (weg)joelen, (uit)jouwen

boob [inform] **1** flater, blunder **2** [inform] tiet

boo-boo [inform] flater; blunder

booby [inform] stommerd, domkop, idioot

booby prize poedelprijs

¹booby trap (n) boobytrap, valstrikbom

²booby trap (vb) een boobytrap plaatsen bij

boodle 1 omkoopgeld[h], smeergeld[h] **2** (smak) geld

boohoo geblèr[h], huiltje[h]

¹book (n) **1** boek[h], boekdeel[h], boekwerk[h]; [inform] telefoonboek[h] **2** boek[h] [chapter of bible, poem etc] **3** tekstboekje[h]; libretto[h] [of opera etc]; manuscript[h]; script [of play] **4** (schrijf)boek[h], schrift[h], blocnote **5** boekje[h] [cards, matches, stamps] **6** register[h], lijst, boek[h]; lijst van aangegane weddenschappen [at races]: *make* (or: *keep*) (a) *~* wedmakelen, bookmaker zijn **7** (-s) boeken, kasboek[h], kantoorboek[h], journaal[h] **8** (-s) boek[h], register[h], (leden)lijst || *bring s.o. to ~ for sth.* iem. voor iets rekenschap laten afleggen, iem. zijn gerechte straf doen ondergaan; *read s.o. like a ~* iem. volkomen door hebben; [inform] *throw the ~ (of rules) at s.o.* **a)** iem. maximum straf toebedelen; **b)** iem. de les lezen; *by the ~* volgens het boekje; *in my ~* volgens mij, mijns inziens

²book (vb) een plaats bespreken, een kaartje nemen, reserveren || *~ in* **a)** zich laten inschrijven [in hotel register]; **b)** inchecken [at airport]

³book (vb) **1** boeken, reserveren, bestellen: *~ a passage* passage boeken; *~ed up* volgeboekt, uitverkocht; [of person] bezet **2** inschrijven, registreren, noteren **3** bekeuren, een proces-verbaal opmaken tegen: *I was ~ed for speeding* ik werd wegens te hard rijden op de bon geslingerd **4** [sport] een gele kaart geven

Book (the) het Boek (der Boeken), de Heilige Schrift, de Bijbel

book debt vordering; uitstaande schuld

book end boekensteun

bookie [inform] bookmaker

booking 1 bespreking, reservering, boeking **2** verbalisering **3** [sport] gele kaart

booking office bespreekbureau[h], plaats-(kaarten)bureau[h], loket[h]

bookish 1 leesgraag, verslaafd aan boeken, geleerd: *~ person* boekenwurm, kamergeleerde **2** stijf

bookkeeper boekhouder

bookkeeping boekhouding, het boekhouden

booklet boekje[h]

bookmaker bookmaker

bookmark boekenlegger

bookshop boekwinkel, boekhandel

bookstore [Am] boekwinkel; boekhandel

book token boekenbon

book up een plaats bespreken, reserveren

bookworm boekenwurm

¹boom (n) **1** (dof/hol) gedreun[h], gebulder[h], gedaver[h] **2** hausse, (periode van) economische vooruitgang **3** (hoge) vlucht, grote stijging, bloei, opkomst **4** [shipp] giek, spriet **5** [shipp] (laad)boom **6** galg; statief[h] [of microphone etc] **7** (haven)boom; versperring [of harbour entrance]

²boom (vb) **1** een dof geluid maken, dreunen, bulderen; rollen [of thunder] **2** een (hoge) vlucht nemen, zich snel ontwikkelen, bloeien; sterk stijgen [of price]: *business is ~ing* het gaat ons voor de wind **3** (snel) in aanzien stijgen

³boom (vb) (also + out) bulderend uiten

¹boomerang (n) boemerang [also fig]

²boomerang (vb) als een boemerang terugkeren, 'n boemerangeffect hebben

boom town explosief gegroeide stad

¹boon (n) **1** zegen, weldaad, gemak[h] **2** gunst, wens

²boon (adj) monter, vrolijk: *~ companion* goede kameraad, boezemvriend(in), hartsvriend(in)

boor [depr] lomperd; vlegel

boorish lomp, boers, onbehouwen

¹boost (n) **1** duw (omhoog), zetje[h], (onder)-steun(ing) **2** verhoging, (prijs)opdrijving **3** stimulans, aanmoediging, versterking: *a ~ to one's spirits* een opkikker(tje)

²boost (vb) **1** (omhoog)duwen, een zetje geven, ondersteunen: *~ s.o. up* iem. een duwtje (omhoog) geven **2** verhogen, opdrijven; opvoeren [price, production etc] **3** [Am] aanprijzen, reclame maken voor **4** stimuleren, aanmoedigen, bevorderen: *~ one's spirits* iem. opvrolijken **5** verhogen [pressure]; versterken [radio signal]

booster 1 hulpkrachtbron, hulpversterker, aanjager, aanjaagpomp, startmotor **2** verbetering, opkikker

¹boot (n) **1** laars; hoge schoen: *~s on the ground* (inzet van) grondtroepen; *put the ~ in* in elkaar trappen, erop inhakken **2** schop, trap **3** ontslag[h]: *give s.o. the ~* iem. ontslaan, iem. eruit schoppen **4** kofferbak, bagageruimte

²boot (vb) **1** schoppen, trappen **2** (also + up)

[comp] opstarten, booten
boot camp [Am] bootcamp[h]
boot<u>ee</u> kort laarsje[h], gebreid babysokje[h]
booth 1 kraam, marktkraam, stalletje[h], (feest)tent **2** hokje[h], stemhokje[h], telefooncel; (luister)cabine [in record shop etc]: *polling* ~ stemhokje[h]
bootlace 1 veter voor laars **2** schoenveter
[1]**bootleg** (n) illegale kopie [of record, CD]
[2]**bootleg** (adj) illegaal (geproduceerd) [liquor, records, CDs]
[3]**bootleg** (vb) smokkelen, clandestien (drank) stoken (verkopen)
bootlegger (drank)smokkelaar, illegale drankstoker (drankverkoper)
bootless [form] vergeefs; vruchteloos
booty 1 buit, roof **2** winst, prijs, beloning **3** [Am; inform] kont
booty call [Am; inform] **1** (uitnodiging voor een) seksdate **2** scharrel
[1]**booze** (n) **1** sterkedrank: *on the* ~ aan de drank **2** zuippartij
[2]**booze** (vb) zuipen
boozer 1 kroeg **2** zuiplap, dronkaard
boozy [inform] **1** drankzuchtig **2** dronken **3** met alcohol: *a* ~ *lunch* een lunch met veel drank
[1]**border** (n) **1** grens, grenslijn, afscheiding **2** rand, band, bies, lijst
[2]**border** (vb) begrenzen, omzomen, omranden
[1]**borderline** (n) grens(lijn), scheidingslijn
[2]**borderline** (adj) **1** grens-, twijfelachtig: ~ *case* grensgeval[h] **2** net (niet) acceptabel, op het kantje
border (up)on grenzen aan, liggen naast, belenden
[1]**bore** (n) **1** vervelend persoon **2** vervelend iets **3** boorgat[h] **4** kaliber[h], diameter; boring [of a cylinder, firearm] **5** boor
[2]**bore** (vb) vervelen
[3]**bore** (vb) **1** (een gat) boren, drillen, een put slaan **2** boren, doorboren, uitboren; kalibreren [weapons]; een gat boren in **3** doordringen, zich (een weg) banen, moeizaam vooruitkomen
bored 1 verveeld: *I'm* ~ ik verveel me; *I'm* ~ *stiff* ik verveel me kapot **2** geïrriteerd: *I'm getting very* ~ *with his behaviour* ik begin me behoorlijk te ergeren aan zijn gedrag
boredom verveling
boring vervelend, saai, langdradig
born 1 geboren, van geboorte: ~ *and bred* geboren en getogen; ~ *again* herboren; *not* ~ *yesterday* niet op z'n achterhoofd gevallen **2** geboren, voorbestemd: ~ *to be a leader* voor het leiderschap in de wieg gelegd **3** geboren, van nature: *he is a* ~ *actor* hij is een rastoneelspeler **4** geboren, ontstaan, voortgekomen
borough 1 stad, (stedelijke) gemeente:

municipal ~ (stedelijke) gemeente **2** kiesdistrict[h]
borrow 1 lenen, ontlenen **2** pikken
Borstal [hist] jeugdgevangenis; opvoedingsgesticht[h]
Bosnia and Herzegovina Bosnië en Herzegovina
[1]**Bosnian** (n) Bosniër, Bosnische
[2]**Bosnian** (adj) Bosnisch
bosom 1 borst, boezem **2** borststuk[h] [of piece of clothing] **3** ruimte tussen borst en kleding, boezem
boson [science] boson: *Higgs* ~ higgsdeeltje[h]
[1]**boss** (n) baas, chef, voorman
[2]**boss** (vb) commanderen, de baas spelen (over): ~ *s.o. around* iem. lopen te commanderen
botanic(al) 1 botanisch, plantkundig **2** plantaardig, uit planten verkregen
botany plantkunde, botanica
[1]**botch** (n) knoeiwerk[h], knoeiboel, puinhoop
[2]**botch** (vb) **1** verknoeien: ~ *it up* het verknallen **2** oplappen, slecht repareren
[1]**both** (num) beide(n), allebei, alle twee: *I saw them* ~ ik heb ze allebei gezien; ~ *of them* alle twee
[2]**both** (conj) [with 'and'] zowel, beide: ~ *Jack and Jill got hurt* Jack en Jill raakten allebei gewond; *he was* ~ *tall and fat* hij was lang én dik
[1]**bother** (n) **1** last, lastpost: *I hope I'm not being a* ~ *to you* ik hoop dat ik u niet tot last ben **2** moeite, probleem[h], moeilijkheid: *we had a lot of* ~ *finding the house* het heeft ons veel moeite gekost om het huis te vinden
[2]**bother** (vb) **1** de moeite nemen, zich de moeite geven: *don't* ~ *about that* maak je daar nu maar niet druk om; *don't* ~ doe maar geen moeite **2** lastigvallen, dwarszitten, irriteren: *his leg* ~*s him a lot* hij heeft veel last van zijn been; *I can't be* ~*ed* dat is me te veel moeite; *that doesn't* ~ *me* daar zit ik niet mee
bothersome vervelend, lastig
botnet botnet[h], zombienetwerk[h]
Botswana Botswana
[1]**Botswanan** (n) Botswaan(se)
[2]**Botswanan** (adj) Botswaans
[1]**bottle** (n) fles; [fig] drank: *a* ~ *of rum* een fles rum; *our baby is brought up on the* ~ onze baby wordt met de fles grootgebracht
[2]**bottle** (vb) **1** bottelen, in flessen doen **2** inmaken
bottle bank glasbak
bottleneck flessenhals [also fig]; knelpunt[h]
bottle up opkroppen: ~ *your anger* je woede opkroppen
[1]**bottom** (n) **1** bodem, grond, het diepst: *from the* ~ *of my heart* uit de grond van mijn hart **2** onderste deel[h], voet, basis: *from the* ~ *up* van bij het begin, helemaal (opnieuw)

3 het laagste punt: *the ~ of the **garden*** achterin de tuin **4** achterste[h], gat[h] **5** kiel; [fig] schip[h]; bodem || *I'll get **to** the ~ of this* ik ga dit goed uitzoeken

²bottom (adj) onderste, laatste, laagste

bottom line 1 saldo[h] **2** einduitkomst; resultaat[h], kern: *the ~ of the **lesson*** de moraal van het verhaal **3** bodemprijs; grens

bough tak

boulder kei, zwerfkei, rotsblok[h]

¹bounce (n) **1** vermogen tot stuit(er)en **2** stuit; terugsprong [of ball] **3** levendigheid, beweeglijkheid **4** opschepperij

²bounce (vb) **1** stuit(er)en, terugkaatsen: *~ **back** after a setback* er na een tegenslag weer bovenop komen **2** [inform] wiebelen, ervandoor gaan **3** (op)springen, wippen **4** ongedekt zijn; geweigerd worden [of cheque] **5** terugkomen [of email]: *my **email** ~d* mijn mailtje kwam weer terug, mijn mailtje kon niet afgeleverd worden

³bounce (vb) **1** laten stuit(er)en, kaatsen, stuit(er)en **2** [inform] eruit gooien, ontslaan

bouncer 1 uitsmijter **2** iem. die (iets dat) stuit

bouncing gezond, levendig, flink

bouncy 1 levendig, levenslustig **2** die kan stuiten: *a ~ **mattress*** een goed verende matras

bouncy castle springkussen[h], springkasteel[h]

¹bound (n) **1** (-s) grens; [maths] limiet: *out of ~s* verboden terrein, taboe [also fig] **2** sprong **3** stuit; terugsprong [of ball] || *keep within the ~s of reason* redelijk blijven

²bound (adj) **1** zeker: *he is ~ **to** pass his exam* hij haalt zijn examen beslist **2** op weg, onderweg: *this train is ~ **for** Poland* deze trein gaat naar Polen **3** gebonden, vast: *she is completely ~ **up in** her research* ze gaat helemaal op in haar onderzoek

³bound (vb) **1** springen **2** stuit(er)en, terugkaatsen

⁴bound (vb) begrenzen, beperken

-bound 1 [roughly] gehinderd door, [roughly] vastzittend aan: *be **snowbound*** vastzitten in de sneeuw **2** gebonden in: *leather~ books* in leer gebonden boeken

boundary grens, grenslijn

boundless grenzeloos

bountiful 1 vrijgevig, gul, royaal **2** overvloedig, rijk

bounty 1 gulheid, vrijgevigheid **2** (gulle) gift, donatie **3** premie, bonus

bounty hunter premiejager

bouquet 1 boeket[h], bos bloemen, ruiker **2** bouquet[h]; geur en smaak [of wine]

bourgeois (klein)burgerlijk; bourgeois

bout 1 vlaag, tijdje[h], periode; aanval [of illness]: *~s of **activity*** vlagen van activiteit; *~s of migraine* migraineaanvallen **2** wedstrijd

[of boxing, wrestling]

boutique boetiek

bovine runderachtig, runder-

¹bow (n) **1** buiging: *take a ~* applaus in ontvangst nemen **2** boeg [foremost part of ship]

²bow (n) **1** boog, kromming **2** boog, handboog **3** strijkstok **4** strik

³bow (vb) **1** buigen, een buiging maken **2** buigen, zich gewonnen geven: *he ~ed **to** the inevitable* hij legde zich bij het onvermijdelijke neer

⁴bow (vb) **1** buigen, krommen **2** strijken [of violinist]

bowel 1 darm: *~s* ingewanden **2** binnenste[h]: *deep in the ~s of the earth* in de diepste diepten van de aarde

bower tuinhuisje[h], prieel(tje)[h]

¹bowl (n) **1** kom, schaal, bekken[h] **2** [Am; geography] kom, komvormig gebied[h], bekken[h] **3** kop [of pipe] **4** [Am] amfitheater[h], stadion[h]

²bowl (n) [sport] bowl

³bowl (vb) **1** [cricket] bowlen **2** voortrollen, rollen || *the batsman was ~ed **(out)*** de slagman werd uitgegooid

bowl along 1 vlot rijden; rollen [of car] **2** vlotten; lekker gaan [of work]

bowlegged met O-benen

bowler hat bolhoed

bowling alley kegelbaan, bowlingbaan, bowlingcentrum[h]

bowl over 1 omverlopen **2** van z'n stuk brengen

bow out officieel afscheid nemen; zich terugtrekken [from a high position]

bow tie strikje[h], vlinderdas

¹box (n) **1** doos, kist, bak, trommel, bus **2** loge, hokje[h]; cel e.d. [in theatre]: *telephone ~*, [Am] *call ~* telefooncel; *witness ~* getuigenbank **3** beschermhoes **4** kader[h], omlijning, omlijnd gebied[h] **5** mep, draai om de oren, oorveeg: *give s.o. a ~ **on** the ears* iem. een draai om de oren geven **6** buis, tv, televisie

²box (vb) **1** boksen (tegen/met) **2** in dozen doen **3** een draai om de oren geven: *~ s.o.'s **ears*** iem. een draai om z'n oren geven

boxer 1 bokser **2** boxer [dog]

box in opsluiten, insluiten: *feel boxed in* zich gekooid voelen

boxing het boksen, bokssport

Boxing Day tweede kerstdag

box junction [roughly] kruispunt[h] dat te allen tijde vrijgelaten moet worden

box number (antwoord)nummer[h]

box office bespreekbureau[h], loket[h]; kassa [of cinema]: *be **bad** ~* geen publiek trekken

boxwood palmhout[h]; bukshout[h]

¹boy (n) **1** jongen, knul, zoon(tje)[h]: *that's my ~* grote jongen, bravo knul; *~s will be **boys*** zo zijn jongens nu eenmaal **2** [Am] man, jon-

gen, vent: *come on, **old*** ~ vooruit, ouwe jongen || *jobs **for** the* ~s vriendjespolitiek
²boy (int) [Am] (t)jonge jonge
¹boycott (n) boycot
²boycott (vb) boycotten
boyf [inform] vriendjeʰ
boyfriend vriend(jeʰ), vrijer
boyhood jongenstijd, jongensjaren
boy scout padvinder
bps *bits per second* bps
bra *brassière* beha
¹brace (n) **1** klamp, (draag)beugel, (muur)-anker **2** steun, stut **3** booromslag+ʰ: ~ *and bit* boor **4** band, riem **5** [dentistry] beugel **6** (-s) bretels **7** koppelʰ, paarʰ, stelʰ: *three* ~ *of partridge* drie koppel patrijzen
²brace (vb) **1** vastbinden, aantrekken, aanhalen **2** versterken, verstevigen, ondersteunen **3** schrap zetten: ~ *o.s. for a shock* zich op een schok voorbereiden
bracelet armband
bracing verkwikkend, opwekkend, versterkend
bracken varenvegetatie; varens
¹bracket (n) **1** steun, plankdrager **2** haakjeʰ, accolade: *in* ~s, ***between*** ~s tussen haakjes **3** klasse, groep: *the lower **income*** ~ de lagere inkomensgroep
²bracket (vb) **1** tussen haakjes zetten **2** (also + *together*) koppelen, in een adem noemen, in dezelfde categorie plaatsen **3** (onder)-steunen [with a brace]
brackish brak; niet zuiver
brag (+ *about*, *of*) opscheppen (over)
braggart opschepper
braid 1 vlecht **2** galon+ʰ, boordselʰ, tres
braille brailleʰ, blindenschriftʰ
¹brain (n) **1** hersenen, hersens; breinʰ [as organ] **2** [inform] knappe kop, breinʰ, genieʰ **3** breinʰ, intelligentie, hoofdʰ: *she **has** (a lot of)* ~s ze heeft (een goed stel) hersens; *pick s.o.'s* ~(s) iem. om advies vragen
²brain (vb) de hersens inslaan
brain drain uittocht van het intellect
brain freeze plotselinge hoofdpijn tijdens het eten of drinken van iets kouds: *eating ice-cream always **gives** me* ~ ik krijg altijd hoofdpijn als ik ijs eet || [fig] *I **had*** ~ *during my oral exam* ik wist even niks meer tijdens mijn mondeling examen
brainiac [esp Am; inform] knappe kop; nerd
brainpower intelligentie, intellectueel vermogenʰ
brainstorm 1 black-out **2** [Am] ingeving **3** brainstorm(sessie)
brainteaser hersenkraker; puzzel, moeilijke vraag
brainwash hersenspoelen
brainwave ingeving, goed ideeʰ: *he suddenly **had** a* ~ hij had opeens een ingeving

brainy slim, knap, intelligent
braise [cooking] smoren
¹brake (n) **1** rem: *apply* (or: *put on*) *the* ~s remmen; [fig] matigen, temperen **2** stationcar, combi
²brake (vb) (af)remmen
brake pad remblokjeʰ
bramble 1 braamstruik **2** doornstruik **3** braam
bran zemelen
¹branch (n) **1** tak, loot **2** vertakking; arm [of river, road etc] **3** tak, filiaalʰ, bijkantoorʰ, plaatselijke afdeling
²branch (vb) zich vertakken, zich splitsen: ~ *off* zich splitsen, afbuigen
branch out zijn zaken uitbreiden, zich ontwikkelen
¹brand (n) **1** merkʰ, merknaam, soort+ʰ, typeʰ **2** brandmerkʰ
²brand (vb) **1** (brand)merken, markeren: ~*ed goods* merkartikelen **2** brandmerken
brandish zwaaien met: ~ *a **sword*** (dreigend) zwaaien met een zwaard
brandy 1 cognac **2** brandewijn
¹brass (n) **1** messingʰ, geelkoperʰ **2** koperʰ, koperen instrumenten **3** [inform] duiten, centen
²brass (adj) koperen || [inform] *get down to* ~ *tacks* spijkers met koppen slaan
brassy 1 (geel)koperen, koperkleurig **2** brutaal **3** blikkerig [sound]; schel
brat snotaap, rotkindʰ
¹brave (adj) dapper, moedig: *put a* ~ *face on* zich sterk houden
²brave (vb) trotseren, weerstaan
bravery moed, dapperheid
¹brawl (n) vechtpartij, knokpartij
²brawl (vb) knokken, op de vuist gaan
brawn spierkracht, spieren
¹bray (n) schreeuw [of donkey]; gebalkʰ
²bray (vb) balken [of donkey]
brazen brutaal
brazen out: [inform] *brazen **it** out* zich er brutaal doorheen slaan
Brazil Brazilië
¹Brazilian (n) Braziliaan(se)
²Brazilian (adj) Braziliaans
BRB [inform] *be right back* ben zo terug
¹breach (n) **1** breuk, bres, gatʰ **2** breuk, schending: ~ *of **contract*** contractbreuk; ~ *of the peace* ordeverstoring
²breach (vb) **1** doorbreken, een gat maken in **2** verbreken, inbreuk maken op
bread 1 broodʰ: ~ *and **butter*** boterham(men); [fig] dagelijkse levensbehoeften, levensonderhoudʰ; *a **loaf** of* ~ een brood; *slice of* ~ boterham **2** broodʰ, kost, levensonderhoudʰ: *daily* ~ dagelijks brood, dagelijkse levensbehoeften
bread-and-butter fundamenteel, basis-
breadline armoedegrens, bestaansmini-

mum^h: *be on the* ~ op de armoedegrens leven
breadth 1 breedte [of dimensions]
2 breedte, strook; baan [of material, wallpaper etc] **3** ruimte, uitgestrektheid
breadwinner broodwinner; kostwinner
¹**break** (n) **1** onderbreking, verandering, breuk, stroomstoring: *a* ~ *for lunch* een lunchpauze; *there was a* ~ *in the* **weather** het weer sloeg om **2** uitbraak, ontsnapping; [cycling] demarrage: *make a* ~ *for it* proberen te ontsnappen **3** [tennis] servicedoorbraak **4** [inform] kans, geluk^h: *lucky* ~ geluk^h, meevaller; *give s.o. a* ~ iem. een kans geven, iem. een plezier doen **5** begin^h; het aanbreken [of day]: ~ *of day* dageraad
²**break** (vb) **1** breken, kapot gaan, het begeven: *his* **voice** *broke* hij kreeg de baard in zijn keel; ~ *with* breken met [eg tradition, family] **2** ontsnappen, uitbreken; [cycling] demarreren: ~ *free* (or: *loose*) ontsnappen, losbreken **3** ophouden, tot een einde komen; omslaan [of weather] **4** plotseling beginnen; aanbreken [of day]; losbreken; losbarsten [of storm] **5** bekendgemaakt worden [of news] **6** plotseling dalen, kelderen; ineenstorten [of prices on stock exchange] ‖ [inform; also com] ~ *even* quitte spelen
³**break** (vb) **1** breken [also fig]; kapot maken, (financieel) ruïneren; laten springen [bank]: ~ *cover* uit de schuilplaats komen; ~ *the law* de wet overtreden; ~ *a record* een record verbeteren **2** onderbreken [eg trip] **3** temmen; dresseren [horse] **4** (voorzichtig) vertellen [(bad) news]; tactvol vertellen **5** schaven; bezeren [skin] **6** ontcijferen; breken [code] **7** [tennis] doorbreken [service]
breakable breekbaar
breakage breuk, het breken, barst ‖ *£10 for* ~ £10 voor breukschade
¹**breakaway** (n) **1** afgescheiden groep **2** uitval, demarrage, aanval^h
²**breakaway** (adj) afgescheiden
break away (+ from) wegrennen (van), ontsnappen (aan); [fig] zich losmaken (van)
breakdown 1 defect^h, mankement^h **2** instorting, zenuwinstorting **3** uitsplitsing, specificatie: ~ *of costs* kostenverdeling, uitsplitsing van de kosten
¹**break down** (vb) **1** kapot gaan; defect raken [of machine]; verbroken raken [of connections] **2** mislukken [of talks, marriage etc] **3** instorten [of human being] **4** zich laten uitsplitsen: *the procedure can be broken down into five easy steps* de werkwijze kan onderverdeeld worden in vijf eenvoudige stappen, de werkwijze valt uiteen in vijf eenvoudige stappen
²**break down** (vb) **1** afbreken [wall; also fig]; vernietigen, slopen; inslaan, intrappen [door] **2** uitsplitsen, analyseren; [chem] afbreken

breaker 1 sloper **2** breker, brandingsgolf
break-even break-even, evenwichts-: ~ *point* (punt van) evenwicht tussen inkomsten en uitgaven
¹**breakfast** (n) ontbijt^h: *continental* ~ ontbijt met koffie en croissants enz.; *have* ~ ontbijten; [fig] *have s.o. for* ~ gehakt van iem. maken, iem. helemaal afmaken
²**breakfast** (vb) ontbijten
¹**break in** (vb) **1** interrumperen: ~ *on* interrumperen, verstoren **2** inbreken
²**break in** (vb) **1** africhten, dresseren **2** inlopen [shoes]
break-in inbraak: *car* ~ auto-inbraak, autokraak
breaking news belangrijk nieuws^h; zojuist binnengekomen bericht^h
breakneck halsbrekend: *at (a)* ~ *speed* in razende vaart
¹**break off** (vb) **1** afbreken [eg of branch] **2** pauzeren **3** ophouden met praten, zijn mond houden
²**break off** (vb) **1** afbreken [eg branch; also fig: negotiations etc] **2** verbreken [relationship with s.o.]; ophouden met
breakout uitbraak, ontsnapping
break out 1 uitbreken **2** (also + of) ontsnappen (uit), uitbreken, ontkomen (aan) ‖ ~ *in* bedekt raken met, onder komen te zitten [eg small stains]
breakthrough doorbraak
¹**break through** (vb) doorbreken; [fig] een doorbraak maken
²**break through** (vb) doorbreken [also fig]
¹**break up** (vb) **1** uit elkaar vallen, in stukken breken; [fig] ten einde komen; ontbonden worden [of meeting]: *their* **marriage** *broke up* hun huwelijk ging kapot **2** uit elkaar gaan [of marriage] partners, group of people etc]
²**break up** (vb) **1** uit elkaar doen vallen, in stukken breken; [fig] onderbreken, doorbreken [routine, part of text] **2** kapot maken [marriage] **3** verspreiden; uiteenjagen [group of people] **4** beëindigen; een eind maken aan [quarrel, fight, meeting]: *break it up!* hou ermee op! **5** doen instorten, in elkaar doen klappen
break-up 1 opheffing; beëindiging [business] **2** scheiding [of lovers]
breakwater golfbreker
bream brasem
breast 1 borst, voorzijde, borststuk^h **2** hart^h, boezem ‖ *beat one's* ~ groot misbaar van verdriet maken
breast stroke schoolslag
breath 1 adem(haling), lucht, het ademen: *get one's* ~ *(back) (again)* weer op adem komen; *out of* ~ buiten adem **2** zuchtje^h (wind), licht briesje^h **3** vleugje^h: *not a* ~ *of suspicion* geen greintje argwaan ‖ *take one's* ~ *away* perplex doen staan

breathalyser blaaspijpje[h]
¹breathe (vb) **1** ademen, ademhalen; [form] leven: *I can't* ~ ik krijg geen lucht; ~ *in* inademen; ~ *out* uitademen **2** op adem komen, uitblazen, bijkomen
²breathe (vb) **1** inademen **2** uitblazen, uitademen **3** inblazen, ingeven: ~ *new life into* nieuw leven inblazen
breather 1 pauze, adempauze **2** beetje beweging, wandeling
breathing space pauze; rustperiode
breathless 1 buiten adem, hijgend, ademloos **2** ademloos, gespannen
breath test blaasproef, blaastest
breech delivery stuitbevalling
breeches kniebroek; [inform] lange broek
¹breed (n) ras[h], aard, soort[+h]
²breed (vb) zich voortplanten, jongen
³breed (vb) **1** kweken, telen, fokken; [fig] voortbrengen **2** kweken, opvoeden, opleiden: *well bred* goed opgevoed, welgemanierd
breeder fokker
breeding 1 het fokken, het kweken, fokkerij, kwekerij **2** voortplanting, het jongen **3** opvoeding, goede manieren
breeding ground 1 broedgebied[h] **2** [fig] broedplaats; kweekplaats: *a* ~ *for new talent* een kweekvijver voor nieuw talent; *a* ~ *for terrorists* een broedplaats voor terroristen
¹breeze (n) bries, wind
²breeze (vb) [inform] (zich) vlot bewegen: ~ *in* (vrolijk) binnen komen waaien
breezy 1 winderig, tochtig **2** opgewekt, levendig, vrolijk
brevity 1 kortheid **2** beknoptheid, bondigheid
¹brew (n) brouwsel[h], bier[h]
²brew (vb) **1** bierbrouwen **2** trekken [of tea] **3** broeien, dreigen, op komst zijn ‖ ~ *up* thee zetten
³brew (vb) **1** brouwen [beer]; zetten [tea] **2** brouwen, uitbroeden
brewer brouwer
brewery brouwerij
brewpub brouwerijcafé[h]
Brexit brexit: *a no-deal* ~ een harde brexit
Brexiteer brexitvoorstander
¹bribe (n) **1** steekpenning, smeergeld[h] **2** lokmiddel[h]
²bribe (vb) (om)kopen, steekpenningen geven, smeergeld betalen
bribery omkoperij
¹brick (n) **1** baksteen **2** blok[h] [toy] ‖ *drop a* ~ iets verkeerds zeggen, een blunder begaan
²brick (vb) metselen: ~ *up,* ~ *in* dichtmetselen, inmetselen
bricklayer metselaar
brickwork metselwerk[h]
bridal bruids-, huwelijks-, bruilofts-
bride bruid

bridegroom bruidegom
bridesmaid bruidsmeisje[h]
¹bridge (n) **1** brug: [fig] *burn one's* ~*s* zijn schepen achter zich verbranden **2** neusrug **3** brug [of glasses frame] **4** kam [of string instrument]
²bridge (n) bridge[h] [cards]
³bridge (vb) overbruggen, een brug slaan over
bridgehead bruggenhoofd[h] [also fig]
¹bridle (n) hoofdstel[h]; [fig] breidel; toom
²bridle (vb) (verontwaardigd) het hoofd in de nek gooien
³bridle (vb) **1** (een paard) het hoofdstel aandoen **2** breidelen, in toom houden
bridle path ruiterpad[h]
¹brief (n) **1** stukken, bescheiden, dossier[h] **2** (-s) (dames)slip, herenslip
²brief (adj) kort, beknopt, vluchtig: *a* ~ *look at the newspaper* een vluchtige blik in de krant; ~ *and to the point* kort en krachtig; *in* ~ om kort te gaan, kortom
³brief (vb) instrueren, aanwijzingen geven
briefcase aktetas, diplomatenkoffertje[h]
briefing (laatste) instructies, briefing, instruering
brigade brigade, korps[h]
brigadier brigadegeneraal [in British army]; brigadecommandant
brigand (struik)rover, bandiet
bright 1 hel(der) [also fig]; licht, stralend: *always look on the* ~ *side* of things de dingen altijd van de zonnige kant bekijken; ~ *red* helderrood **2** opgewekt, vrolijk **3** slim, pienter: *a* ~ *idea* een slim idee
brighten 1 (doen) opklaren; ophelderen [also fig]: *the sky is* ~*ing up* de lucht klaart op **2** oppoetsen, oprvolijken: *she has* ~*ed up his whole life* dankzij haar is hij helemaal opgeleefd
brill [inform] fantastisch
brilliance 1 schittering **2** virtuositeit; genialiteit
brilliant 1 stralend, fonkelend, glinsterend: ~ *stars* fonkelende sterren; ~ *red* hoogrood **2** briljant, geniaal **3** geweldig, fantastisch, gaaf
¹brim (n) **1** (boven)rand, boord[h]: *full to the* ~ tot de rand toe vol, boordevol [of a glass] **2** rand [of a hat]
²brim (vb) boordevol zijn, tot barstens toe gevuld zijn: *her eyes* ~*med with tears* haar ogen schoten vol tranen
brine 1 pekel(nat)[h] **2** het zilte nat
bring 1 (mee)brengen, (mee)nemen, aandragen: *his cries brought his neighbours running* op zijn kreten kwamen zijn buren aangesneld; ~ *a case before the court* een zaak aan de rechter voorleggen **2** opleveren, opbrengen: ~ *a good price* een goede prijs opbrengen **3** teweegbrengen, leiden tot,

broke

voortbrengen: *I can't ~ myself to kill an animal* ik kan me(zelf) er niet toe brengen een dier te doden; *you've brought this problem (up)on yourself* je hebt je dit probleem zelf op de hals gehaald ‖ *~ home to* duidelijk maken, aan het verstand brengen

bring about veroorzaken, teweegbrengen, aanrichten: *~ changes* veranderingen teweegbrengen

bring along 1 meenemen, meebrengen **2** opkweken, in de ontwikkeling stimuleren **3** doen gedijen

bring (a)round overhalen, ompraten, overreden

bring back 1 terugbrengen, retourneren, mee terugbrengen **2** in de herinnering terugbrengen, doen herleven, oproepen: *this song brings back memories* dit liedje brengt (goede) herinneringen boven **3** herinvoeren, herintroduceren: *~ capital punishment* de doodstraf weer invoeren

bring down 1 neerhalen; neerschieten [aeroplane, bird] **2** aan de grond zetten **3** [sport] neerleggen, onderuithalen; ten val brengen [opponent] **4** ten val brengen; omverwerpen [government] **5** drukken, verlagen; terugschroeven [costs]

bring forth [form] voortbrengen; [fig] veroorzaken; oproepen [protest, criticism]

bring in 1 binnenhalen [harvest] **2** opleveren, afwerpen, inbrengen **3** bijhalen, opnemen in, aanwerven: *~ experts to advise* deskundigen in de arm nemen **4** inrekenen [detainee] **5** komen aanzetten met; introduceren [new fashion]; indienen [bill]

bring off 1 in veiligheid brengen, redden uit **2** [inform] voor elkaar krijgen, fiksen: *we've brought it off* we hebben het voor elkaar gekregen

bring on veroorzaken, teweegbrengen

bring out 1 naar buiten brengen, voor de dag komen met; [fig also] uitbrengen **2** op de markt brengen; uitbrengen [product] **3** duidelijk doen uitkomen: *this photo brings out all the details* op deze foto zijn alle details goed te zien

bring round bij bewustzijn brengen, bijbrengen ‖ *~ to* (het gesprek) in de richting sturen van

bring up 1 naar boven brengen **2** grootbrengen, opvoeden **3** ter sprake brengen, naar voren brengen **4** [inform] uitbraken, overgeven, uitkotsen

brink (steile) rand, (steile) oever: *on* (or: *to*) *the ~ of war* op de rand van oorlog

briny deep (the) [form] het zilte nat; het ruime sop

brisk 1 kwiek, vlot: *~ trade* levendige handel **2** verkwikkend; fris [of wind]

brisket borststuk[h] [beef]

¹bristle (n) stoppel(haar[h])

²bristle (vb) recht overeind staan [of hair]: *~ (up)* zijn stekels opzetten, nijdig worden; *~ with anger* opvliegen van woede; *~ with* wemelen van

Brit *Briton* Brit(se)

Britain Groot-Brittannië

Britannia (Vrouwe) Brittannia

Britannic [form] Brits

British Brits, Engels: *the ~ Empire* het Britse Rijk; *the ~* de Britten

Briton Brit(se)

Brittany Bretagne

brittle broos, breekbaar, onbestendig, wankel

bro [inform] **1** *brother* broer **2** maat, gabber: *hey, what's up ~?* hé man, hoe gaat het ermee?

broach 1 aanspreken; openmaken [bottle etc] **2** aansnijden, ter sprake brengen; beginnen over [topic]

¹broad (n) **1** brede (ge)deel(te)[h] **2** [Am; inform] wijf[h], mokkel[h] ‖ *the Norfolk Broads* de Norfolkse plassen

²broad (adj) **1** breed, uitgestrekt, in de breedte: *~ bean* tuinboon; *~ shoulders* brede schouders; *~ly speaking* in zijn algemeenheid **2** ruim(denkend) **3** gedurfd, onbekrompen, royaal **4** duidelijk, direct: *a ~ hint* een overduidelijke wenk **5** grof, plat, lomp: *~ Scots* met een sterk Schots accent **6** ruim, globaal, ruw **7** helder, duidelijk: *in ~ daylight* op klaarlichte dag

broadband breedband

broadband internet access breedband-internet[h]

¹broadcast (n) (radio-)uitzending, tv-uitzending

²broadcast (vb) **1** uitzenden, in de lucht zijn **2** op de radio (*or:* televisie) zijn

³broadcast (vb) **1** breedwerpig zaaien; [fig] rondbazuinen; rondstrooien **2** uitzenden: *a ~ing station* een zendstation

broaden (zich) verbreden, breder worden (maken): *reading ~s the mind* lezen verruimt de blik

broad-minded ruimdenkend, tolerant

broadsheet serieuze krant (op groot formaat)

broccoli broccoli

brochure brochure, folder, prospectus[+h]: *advertising ~s* reclamefolders

brogue 1 gaatjesschoen **2** zwaar accent[h]; [esp] Iers, Schots accent[h]

¹broil (vb) (liggen) bakken

²broil (vb) [esp Am] **1** grillen, roosteren **2** stoven: *~ing hot* smoorheet, bloedheet

broiler 1 grill, braadrooster[h] **2** braadkuiken[h], slachtkuiken[h]

broke [inform] platzak, blut, aan de grond, bankroet: *stony* (or: *flat*) *~* finaal aan de grond, zonder een rooie cent

broken 1 gebroken, kapot, stuk: ~ *colours* gebroken kleuren; ~ *English* gebrekkig Engels; ~ *home* ontwricht gezin; *a* ~ *marriage* een stukgelopen huwelijk **2** oneffen [of terrain]; ruw, geaccidenteerd **3** onderbroken, verbrokkeld: *a* ~ *journey* een reis met veel onderbrekingen

broken-down versleten, vervallen

¹broker (n) (effecten)makelaar

²broker (vb) als makelaar optreden

³broker (vb) (als makelaar) regelen

brokerage 1 makelaardij **2** courtage; makelaarsloon[h]

brolly [inform] paraplu

bronchitis bronchitis

¹bronze (n) **1** bronzen (kunst)voorwerp[h] **2** bronzen medaille, brons[h], derde plaats **3** brons[h], bronskleur

²bronze (vb) bronsachtig worden, bruinen

³bronze (vb) bronzen, bruinen

Bronze Age bronstijd, bronsperiode

brooch broche

¹brood (n) gebroed[h], broed(sel[h]); kroost[h] [also fig]

²brood (vb) **1** broeden **2** tobben, piekeren, peinzen: *she just sits there ~ing* ze zit daar maar te piekeren; ~ *about* (or: *on, over*) tobben over, piekeren over; ~ *over* one's *future* inzitten over zijn toekomst

broody 1 broeds **2** bedrukt, somber

¹brook (n) beek, stroompje[h]

²brook (vb) dulden: *this **matter** ~s no delay* deze kwestie kan geen uitstel lijden

broom 1 bezem, schrobber **2** [bot] brem

broomstick bezemsteel

Bros *Brothers* Gebr. [Gebroeders]: *Jones ~* Gebr. Jones

broth bouillon, vleesnat[h], soep

brothel bordeel[h]

brother 1 broer: *he has been like a ~ to me* hij is als een broer voor me geweest **2** broeder, kloosterbroeder **3** [inform] makker, gast

brotherhood broederschap: *Muslim Brotherhood* moslimbroederschap

brother-in-law zwager

brow 1 wenkbrauw: *knit one's **brows*** (de wenkbrauwen) fronsen **2** voorhoofd[h] **3** bovenrand, (overhangende) rotsrand, top, kruin

browbeat overdonderen, intimideren

brown bruin: ~ *bread* bruinbrood[h], volkorenbrood[h]; ~ *paper* pakpapier[h]

brownie goede fee, nachtelfje[h]

Brownie padvindster; kabouter [from 7 to 11 years of age]

brownie point [inform] schouderklopje[h], wit voetje[h]

¹browse (n) **1** [esp singular] het grasduinen, het neuzen: *have a good ~ through* flink grasduinen in **2** (jonge) scheuten [as food for animals]

²browse (vb) **1** grasduinen, (in boeken) snuffelen, (rond)neuzen **2** weiden, (af)grazen

browser zoekprogramma[h]

bruh [inform] vriend, maat

¹bruise (n) kneuzing [also of fruit]; blauwe plek

²bruise (vb) blauwe plek(ken) vertonen, gekneusd zijn

³bruise (vb) kneuzen, bezeren

bruiser krachtpatser, rouwdouwer

Brunei Brunei

¹Bruneian (n) Bruneier, Bruneise

²Bruneian (adj) Bruneis

brunt eerste stoot, zwaartepunt[h], toppunt[h]: *she bore the (full) ~ of his anger* zij kreeg de volle laag

¹brush (n) **1** borstel, kwast; penseel[h] [of artist, painter]; brushes: [fig] *tarred with the same ~* uit hetzelfde (slechte) hout gesneden **2** (af)borsteling **3** lichte aanraking, beroering **4** schermutseling, kort treffen[h] **5** kreupelhout[h], onderhout[h] **6** kreupelbos[h], met dicht struikgewas begroeid gebied[h]

²brush (vb) **1** afborstelen, opborstelen, uitborstelen, afvegen, wegvegen, uitvegen **2** strijken (langs/over), rakelings gaan (langs): *the cat's whiskers ~ed my cheek* de snorharen van de kat streken langs mijn wang

brush aside 1 opzijschuiven, wegschuiven [resistance, opposition etc]; uit de weg ruimen **2** terzijde schuiven, naast zich neerleggen: *brush **complaints** aside* klachten wegwuiven

¹brush off (vb) zich laten wegborstelen, (door borstelen) loslaten

²brush off (vb) **1** wegborstelen, afborstelen **2** (zich van) iem. afhouden, afschepen: *I won't be brushed off* ik laat me niet afschepen

brush-off [inform] afscheping, afpoeiering, de bons: *give s.o. the ~* **a)** iem. met een kluitje in het riet sturen; **b)** iem. de bons geven

brush up opfrissen, ophalen, bijspijkeren: ~ *(on) your **English*** je Engels ophalen

brushwood onderhout[h], kreupelhout[h], sprokkelhout[h]

brusque bruusk, abrupt, kort aangebonden

Brussels sprouts spruitjes

brutal bruut, beestachtig, meedogenloos: ~ *frankness* genadeloze openhartigheid

brutality bruutheid, wreedheid, onmenselijkheid

¹brute (n) **1** beest[h], dier[h] **2** bruut, woesteling

²brute (adj) bruut, grof: ~ *force* grof geweld

B Sc *Bachelor of Science* [roughly] Bachelor (of Science)

BSE *bovine spongiform encephalopathy*

BSE; gekkekoeienziekte
BSI *British Standards Institution* [roughly]
NNI[h]; Nederlands Normalisatie-instituut[h]
BST *British Summer Time*
BTL *below the line* reactiegedeelte[h] bij een
bericht op een site
btw *by the way* T2H [tussen haakjes]; trouwens
[1]**bubble** (n) **1** (lucht)bel(letje[h]): *blow* ~*s* bellen blazen **2** glaskoepel **3** [fig] zeepbel, bal-
lonnetje[h]
[2]**bubble** (vb) **1** borrelen, bruisen, pruttelen
2 glimmen, stralen: ~ *over* with enthusiasm
overlopen van enthusiasme
bubble gum klapkauwgom[h]
bubble wrap noppenfolie[+h]; bubbeltjes-
plastic[h]
[1]**bubbly** (n) champagne
[2]**bubbly** (adj) **1** bruisend, sprankelend **2** jolig
bubonic: ~ *plague* builenpest
buccaneer boekanier, zeerover, vrijbuiter
[1]**buck** (n) **1** mannetjesdier[h]; bok [of deer];
ram(melaar) [of rabbit, hare] **2** dollar ‖ [in-
form] *pass the* ~ *(to s.o.)* de verantwoordelijkheid afschuiven (op iem.), (iem.) de zwartepiet toespelen
[2]**buck** (vb) bokken [of horse]; bokkenspron-
gen maken
[3]**buck** (vb) **1** afwerpen [horseman, horse-
woman]; afgooien **2** [Am; inform] tegenwerken: *you can't go on ~ing the system* je
kunt je niet blijven verzetten tegen het systeem
[1]**bucket** (n) emmer: [inform, fig] *it came
down in ~s* het regende dat het goot ‖ [in-
form] *kick the* ~ het hoekje omgaan, de pijp
uitgaan
[2]**bucket** (vb) [inform] gieten, plenzen; bij
bakken neervallen [of rain also]
bucket list bucketlist, wensenlijstje[h]
bucket seat kuipstoel [in car or aeroplane]
[1]**buckle** (n) gesp
[2]**buckle** (vb) **1** met een gesp sluiten, aange-
gespt (kunnen) worden **2** kromtrekken, ontzetten, ontwricht raken **3** wankelen, wijken,
bezwijken
[3]**buckle** (vb) (vast)gespen: ~ *up* a belt een
riem omdoen
[1]**buck up** (vb) [inform] opschieten
[2]**buck up** (vb) [inform] opvrolijken: ~, *things
will be all right* kop op, het komt wel weer
goed
buckwheat 1 boekwit **2** boekweitmeel[h]
bucolic landelijk, bucolisch
[1]**bud** (n) knop, kiem: *nip* in the ~ in de kiem
smoren; [fig] *in the* ~ in de dop
[2]**bud** (vb) knoppen, uitlopen
Buddha 1 Boeddha **2** Boeddhabeeld[h],
boeddha
Buddhism boeddhisme[h]

budding ontluikend, aankomend, in de
dop
buddy [inform] **1** maat, vriend, kameraad
2 buddy [of AIDS patient] **3** [as form of address; Am] maatje[h], makker
[1]**budge** (vb) **1** zich (ver)roeren, (zich) bewegen, zich verplaatsen: *the screw won't* ~ ik
krijg geen beweging in die schroef **2** veranderen: *not* ~ *from* one's opinion aan zijn mening vasthouden
[2]**budge** (vb) (een klein stukje) verplaatsen,
verschuiven, verschikken: *not* ~ *one* **inch** geen
duimbreed wijken
budgerigar (gras)parkiet
[1]**budget** (n) **1** begroting, budget[h] **2** rijksbegroting
[2]**budget** (adj) voordelig, goedkoop: ~ *prices*
speciale aanbiedingen
[3]**budget** (vb) **1** budgetteren, de begroting
opstellen **2** huishouden
[4]**budget** (vb) in een begroting opnemen, reserveren, ramen
[1]**buff** (n) **1** [inform] enthousiast, liefhebber,
fanaat **2** rundleer[h], buffelleer[h] **3** vaalgeel[h],
bruingeel[h], buff: ~ *yellow* vaalgeel **4** [in-
form] nakie[h], blootje[h]: *in the* ~ naakt
[2]**buff** (vb) polijsten, opwrijven
buffalo buffel, karbouw, bizon
buffed [Am; inform] (goed) gespierd: *get* ~
(meer) spieren kweken
[1]**buffer** (n) buffer, stootkussen[h], stootblok[h]
[2]**buffer** (vb) als buffer optreden voor, beschermen, behoeden
[1]**buffet** (n) slag [also fig]; klap, dreun
[2]**buffet** (vb) **1** dressoir[h], buffet[h] **2** buffet[h],
schenktafel **3** niet-uitgeserveerde maaltijd:
cold ~ koud buffet
[3]**buffet** (vb) **1** meppen, slaan, beuken **2** teisteren, kwellen, treffen: ~*ed by* **misfortunes**
geteisterd door tegenslag
buffoon hansworst, potsenmaker, clown
[1]**buff up** (vb) trainen
[2]**buff up** (vb) [leather] opwrijven, doen
glanzen
[1]**bug** (n) **1** halfvleugelig insect[h], wants, bedwants **2** [Am] insect[h], beestje[h], ongedierte[h]
3 [inform] virus[h] [also fig]; bacil, bacterie
4 [inform] obsessie **5** [inform] mankement[h],
storing, defect[h] **6** [inform] afluister-
apparaatje[h], verborgen microfoontje[h]
[2]**bug** (vb) [inform] **1** afluisterapparatuur
plaatsen in **2** [Am] irriteren, ergeren, lastigvallen: *what is* ~*ging him?* wat zit hem dwars?
bugger 1 [vulg] lul(hannes), zak(kenwas-
ser) **2** [vulg] sodomiet, homofiel **3** ~ (arme)
drommel, (arme) donder, kerel ‖ ~ *him!* hij
kan de tering krijgen
bugger off ophoepelen
bugger up verpesten, verzieken
buggy 1 licht rijtuigje[h], open autootje[h]
2 [Am] kinderwagen **3** wandelwagen

bugle hoorn [for military signals]

¹build (n) (lichaams)bouw, gestalte, vorm

²build (vb) **1** bouwen **2** (in kracht) toenemen, aanwakkeren, verhevigen, groeien, aanzwellen: *tension built within her* de spanning in haar nam toe

³build (vb) **1** (op)bouwen, maken: *~ a fire* een vuur maken **2** vormen, ontwikkelen, ontplooien **3** samenstellen, vormen, opbouwen **4** (+ on) baseren (op), grondvesten, onderbouwen: *~ one's hopes on* zijn hoop vestigen op **5** inbouwen [also fig]; opnemen: *this clause was not built into my contract* deze clausule was niet in mijn contract opgenomen

builder aannemer, bouwer

building 1 gebouwʰ, bouwwerkʰ, pandʰ **2** bouw, het bouwen, bouwkunst

¹build up (vb) **1** aangroeien, toenemen, zich opstapelen: *tension was building up* de spanning nam toe **2** (geleidelijk) toewerken (naar)

²build up (vb) **1** opbouwen, ontwikkelen, tot bloei brengen: *~ a firm from scratch* een bedrijf van de grond af opbouwen **2** ophemelen, loven, prijzen

build-up 1 opstopping, opeenhoping, opeenstapeling: *a ~ of traffic* een verkeersopstopping **2** ontwikkeling, opbouw, vorming **3** (troepen)concentratie

built-in ingebouwd [also fig]; aangeboren: *~ cupboard* muurkast

built-up 1 samengesteld, geconstrueerd **2** bebouwd, volgebouwd

bulb 1 bol(letjeʰ), bloembol; [by extension] bolgewasʰ: *~ fields* bollenvelden **2** (gloei)-lamp

bulbous bolvormig: *~ nose* stompe neus

Bulgaria Bulgarije

¹Bulgarian (n) Bulgaar(se)

²Bulgarian (adj) Bulgaars

¹bulge (n) bobbel

²bulge (vb) **1** (op)zwellen, uitdijen **2** bol staan, opbollen, uitpuilen: *~ out* uitpuilen

bulk 1 (grote) massa, omvang, volumeʰ: *~ buying* in het groot inkopen; *in ~* **a)** onverpakt, los; **b)** in het groot **2** (scheeps)lading, vracht **3** grootste deelʰ, merendeelʰ, grosʰ: *the ~ of the books have already been sold* het merendeel van de boeken is al verkocht **4** kolos, gevaarteʰ, massa **5** (scheeps)ruimʰ

bulkhead (waterdicht) schotʰ, scheidingswand, afscheiding

bulky lijvig, log, dik, omvangrijk

bull 1 stier, bul; mannetjeʰ [of whale, elephant etc]: *like a ~ in a china shop* als een olifant in een porseleinkast; *take the ~ by the horns* de koe bij de hoorns vatten **2** (pauselijke) bul **3** [vulg] kletspraat, gekletsʰ, gezeikʰ

bulldog buldog

bulldoze 1 met een bulldozer bewerken

2 [inform] (plat)walsen, doordrukken, zijn zin doordrijven

bulldozer bulldozer

bullet (geweer)kogel, patroonʰ ‖ *bite (on) the ~* door de zure appel heen bijten

bulletin (nieuws)bulletinʰ, dienstmededeling

bulletin board [Am] mededelingenbordʰ, prikbordʰ

bullet point opsommingstekenʰ, bolletjeʰ

bullfight stierengevechtʰ

bullfrog brulkikvors

bullish 1 optimistisch **2** [fin] oplopend, stijgend

bull market stijgende markt [at stock exchange]

bullock 1 os **2** jonge stier, stiertjeʰ

bullring arena [for bull fights]

bull's-eye 1 roos [target] **2** schotʰ in de roos [also fig]; rake opmerking **3** [type] toverbal [peppermint]

bull shark stierhaai

¹bullshit (n) [vulg] gekletsʰ, kletspraat, gezeikʰ

²bullshit (vb) [vulg] lullen, zeiken: *don't ~ me* neem me niet in de zeik, lul niet

bull terrier bulterriër

¹bully (n) **1** bullebak, beul, kwelgeest **2** [hockey] afslag

²bully (adj) [also iron] prima: *~ for you* bravo!, wat geweldig van jou!

³bully (vb) koeioneren, intimideren: *~ s.o. into doing sth.* iem. met bedreigingen dwingen tot iets

bullyboy [inform] (gehuurde) zware jongen, vechtersbaas

bully off [hockey] de afslag verrichten

bulrush 1 bies, mattenbies, stoelbies **2** lisdodde **3** [rel] papyrus(plant)

bulwark 1 (verdedigings)muur, wal, schans **2** bolwerkʰ [also fig]; bastionʰ **3** [shipp] verschansing

¹bum (n) [vulg] **1** kont, gatʰ, achtersteʰ **2** [Am, Austr; depr] zwerver, schooier, landloper, bedelaar **3** (kloot)zak, mislukkeling, nietsnut

²bum (adj) [vulg] waardeloos, rottig

bum along [inform] toeren, rustig rijden

bum around [inform] lanterfanten, lummelen, rondhangen

bumble 1 mompelen, brabbelen, bazelen: *to keep bumbling on about sth.* blijven doorzeuren over iets **2** stuntelen, klungelen

bumblebee hommel

bumf [inform] [depr] papierrommel, papiertroep, papierwinkel

¹bump (n) **1** bons, schok, stoot **2** buil, bult; hobbel [in road, terrain]

²bump (vb) **1** bonzen, stoten, botsen **2** hobbelen, schokken: *we ~ed along in our old car* we denderden voort in onze oude auto

burning

³**bump** (vb) stoten tegen, botsen tegen, rammen: *don't ~ your **head*** stoot je hoofd niet

⁴**bump** (adv) pats-boem, pardoes

bumper 1 (auto)bumper, stootkussenʰ, stootrand; [Am] buffer; stootblokʰ **2** iets vols, iets groots, overvloed: ~ *crop* (or: *harvest*) recordoogst

bumph see *bumf*

bump into [inform] tegen het lijf lopen, toevallig tegenkomen

bump off [inform] koud maken, vermoorden

bumptious opdringerig, verwaand

bump up [inform] opkrikken, opschroeven

bumpy hobbelig, bobbelig

bun 1 (krenten)bolletjeʰ, broodjeʰ: [hum] *have a ~ in the **oven*** in verwachting zijn **2** (haar)knot(jeʰ)

¹**bunch** (n) **1** bos(je)ʰ, bundel, tros: *a ~ of **grapes*** een tros(je) druiven; *a ~ of **keys*** een sleutelbos **2** [inform] troep(jeʰ), groep(jeʰ), stel(letje)ʰ: *the **best** of the ~* de beste van het stel

²**bunch** (vb) samendringen, samendrommen

¹**bundle** (n) bundel, bosʰ, pak(ket)ʰ, zenuwbundel, spierbundel, vezelbundel: *he is a ~ of nerves* hij is één bonk zenuwen

²**bundle** (vb) **1** bundelen, samenbinden, samenpakken, samenvouwen: ~ *up old newspapers* een touwtje om oude kranten doen **2** proppen, (weg)stouwen, (weg)stoppen, induwen, inproppen

Bundt cake [culinary] tulband

¹**bung** (n) stop, kurk, afsluiter

²**bung** (vb) keilen, gooien, smijten

bungalow bungalow

bungee jumping bungeejumping

bungle (ver)knoeien, (ver)prutsen

bung up [inform] verstoppen, dichtstoppen: *my **nose** is bunged up* mijn neus zit verstopt

bunion (eelt)knobbel

bunk (stapel)bedʰ, kooi ‖ [inform] *do a ~* ertussenuit knijpen, 'm smeren

bunk-bed stapelbedʰ

bunker [mil, sport] bunker

bunk-up duwtjeʰ

bunny [child language] (ko)nijntjeʰ

bunny chow uitgehold broodʰ, gevuld met curry

bunting 1 gors, vink **2** dundoekʰ, vlaggetjes

¹**buoy** (n) **1** boei, ton(boei) **2** redding(s)boei

²**buoy** (vb) **1** drijvend houden: *~ed (up) **by** the sea* drijvend op de zee **2** schragen, ondersteunen, dragen

buoyant 1 drijvend **2** opgewekt, vrolijk, luchthartig

buoy up opvrolijken, opbeuren

bur klis, klit

burble 1 kabbelen **2** leuteren, ratelen, kwekken

¹**burden** (n) **1** last, vracht, verplichting: *beast of ~* lastdierʰ, pakdierʰ, pakezel, pakpaardʰ; ~ *of **proof*** bewijslast; *be a ~ **to** s.o.* iem. tot last zijn **2** leidmotiefʰ, grondthemaʰ, hoofdthemaʰ, kern

²**burden** (vb) belasten, beladen, overladen, (zwaar) drukken op

burdensome (lood)zwaar, bezwarend, drukkend

bureau 1 schrijftafel **2** [Am] ladekast **3** dienst, bureauʰ, kantoorʰ, departementʰ, ministerieʰ

bureaucracy bureaucratie

bureaucrat [oft depr] bureaucraat

bureaucratic bureaucratisch

bureau de change geldwisselkantoorʰ

burgeon [bot] uitbotten, uitlopen; [fig] snel groeien

burgh 1 stad, (stedelijke) gemeente **2** kiesdistrictʰ

burglar inbreker

burglary inbraak

burgle inbreken (in), inbraak plegen (bij), stelen (bij)

Burgundy 1 Bourgondië **2** bourgogne(wijn), Bourgondische wijn **3** bordeauxroodʰ

burial begrafenis

burka boerka

Burkina Faso Burkina Faso

¹**Burkinese** (n) Burkinees, Burkinese

²**Burkinese** (adj) Burkinees

burkini boerkini

burlap jute

burlesque koddig, kluchtig

burly potig, zwaar, flink

Burma Birma

¹**Burmese** (n) Birmaan(se)

²**Burmese** (adj) Birmaans

¹**burn** (n) brandwond, brandgaatjeʰ

²**burn** (vb) **1** branden, gloeien: ~ *low* uitgaan, uitdoven; *~ing **for** an ideal* in vuur en vlam voor een ideaal; ~ *with* anger koken van woede **2** branden, afbranden, verbranden, ontbranden, in brand staan (steken): *the soup ~t my **mouth*** ik heb mijn mond aan de soep gebrand; ~ *away* opbranden, wegbranden; [fig] verteren; ~ *off* wegbranden, afbranden, schoonbranden, leegbranden; ~ *to death* door verbranding om het leven brengen

³**burn** (vb) **1** verteren **2** werken op, gebruiken als brandstof **3** in brand steken

burn down (tot de grond toe) afbranden, platbranden

burner 1 brander; pit [of cooking apparatus etc] **2** wegwerptelefoon

burner phone wegwerptelefoon

burning brandend, gloeiend, dringend: *a ~ **issue*** een brandend vraagstuk

burnish (op)glanzen, gaan glanzen, polijsten

¹**burn out** (vb) **1** uitbranden; opbranden [also fig] **2** doorbranden [of electrical appliance etc]; doorslaan

²**burn out** (vb) **1** uitbranden: *the shed was completely burnt out* de schuur was volledig uitgebrand **2** door brand verdrijven uit, door brand dakloos maken **3** [inform] overwerken, over de kop werken: *burn o.s. out* zich over de kop werken **4** doen doorbranden

burnt gebrand, geschroeid, gebakken: ~ *offering* (or: *sacrifice*) brandofferʰ

burnt-out 1 opgebrand, uitgeblust, versleten **2** uitgebrand **3** dakloos [because of fire] **4** [inform] doodmoe, uitgeput, afgepeigerd

¹**burn up** (vb) **1** oplaaien, feller gaan branden **2** [inform] scheuren, jakkeren, hard rijden **3** [Am; inform] laaiend (van woede) zijn

²**burn up** (vb) verstoken, opbranden

¹**burp** (n) [inform] boer(tjeʰ), oprisping

²**burp** (vb) [inform] (laten) boeren; een boertje laten doen [baby]

burqa boerka

¹**burrow** (n) legerʰ [of rabbit etc]; hol(letjeʰ), tunnel(tjeʰ)

²**burrow** (vb) **1** een leger graven; [fig] zich nestelen; beschutting zoeken **2** wroeten, graven, zich (een weg) banen: [fig] ~ *into somebody's secrets* in iemands geheimen wroeten

bursar thesaurier, penningmeester

¹**burst** (n) uitbarsting, ontploffing; demarrage: ~ *of anger* woede-uitbarsting; ~ *of laughter* lachsalvoʰ

²**burst** (vb) **1** losbarsten, uitbarsten, doorbreken, uit elkaar springen: ~ *forth*, ~ *out* uitroepen, uitbarsten; ~ *out crying* in huilen uitbarsten; ~ *into* tears in tranen uitbarsten **2** op barsten, springen staan, barstensvol zitten: *be ~ing to come* staan te popelen om te komen

³**burst** (vb) doorbreken, openbreken, verbreken, forceren, inslaan, intrappen: *the river will ~ its banks* de rivier zal buiten haar oevers treden; [fig] ~ *one's sides (with) laughing* schudden van het lachen

burst in komen binnenvallen, binnenstormen, (ruw) onderbreken

Burundi Burundi

¹**Burundian** (n) Burundiër, Burundische

²**Burundian** (adj) Burundisch

bury 1 begraven **2** verbergen, verstoppen: ~ *one's hands* in one's pockets zijn handen (diep) in zijn zakken steken **3** verzinken [also fig]: *buried in thoughts* in gedachten verzonken; ~ *o.s. in one's books* (or: *studies*) zich in zijn boeken (or: studie) verdiepen

¹**bus** (n) **1** (auto)bus: [fig] *miss the* ~ de boot missen; *go by* ~ de bus nemen **2** [inform]

bak, kar **3** [inform] kist, vliegtuigʰ

²**bus** (vb) met de bus gaan (vervoeren), de bus nemen, per bus reizen, op de bus zetten

busby kolbak, berenmuts

bush 1 struik, bosjeʰ **2** struikgewasʰ, kreupelhoutʰ **3** rimboe, woestenij, wildernis ‖ *beat about the* ~ ergens omheen draaien, niet ter zake komen

bushed [inform] bekaf, doodop, uitgeput

Bushman Bosjesman

bush meat bushmeatʰ [vlees van wilde dieren]

business 1 handel, zaken: *get down to* ~ ter zake komen, spijkers met koppen slaan; *mean* ~ het serieus menen; *be in* ~ (bezig met) handel drijven; [fig] startklaar staan; *on* ~ voor zaken **2** iets afdoends, ruwe behandeling, standjeʰ **3** (ver)plicht(ing), taak, verantwoordelijkheid, werkʰ: [inform] *my affairs are no* ~ *of yours* (or: *none of your* ~) mijn zaken gaan jou niets aan; *have no* ~ *to do sth.* ergens niet het recht toe hebben; *I will make it my* ~ *to see that …* ik zal het op me nemen ervoor te zorgen dat …; [inform] *mind your own* ~ bemoei je met je eigen (zaken) **4** agenda, programmaʰ: [inform] *like nobody's* ~ als geen ander; [on agenda of meeting] *any other* ~ rondvraag, wat verder ter tafel komt **5** aangelegenheid, affaire, zaak, kwestie: *I'm sick and tired of this whole* ~ ik ben dit hele gedoe meer dan zat **6** moeilijke taak, hele kluif **7** zaak, winkel, bedrijfʰ

business card adreskaartjeʰ, kaartjeʰ, visitekaartjeʰ

business hours kantooruren; openingstijden

businessman zakenman

busker (bedelend) straatmuzikant

bus shelter bushokjeʰ; abri

bus stop bushalte

¹**bust** (n) **1** buste, borstbeeldʰ **2** boezem, buste, borsten

²**bust** (adj) [inform] kapot, stuk, naar de knoppen: *go* ~ op de fles gaan

³**bust** (vb) [inform] **1** barsten, breken, kapotgaan **2** op de fles gaan, bankroet gaan

⁴**bust** (vb) [inform] **1** breken, mollen, kapotmaken **2** laten springen, doorbreken, verbreken, bankroet laten gaan, platzak maken **3** arresteren, aanhouden **4** een inval doen in; huiszoeking doen bij [by police]

busted [Am; inform] betrapt, gesnapt; er gloeiend bij

¹**bustle** (n) drukte, bedrijvigheid

²**bustle** (vb) druk in de weer zijn, jachten, zich haasten: ~ *with* bruisen van

bust-up [inform] **1** stennis, herrie **2** [Am] mislukking [of marriage]; het stuklopen

¹**busy** (adj) **1** bezig, druk bezet, bedrijvig: *she is* ~ *at* (or: *with*) her work ze is druk aan het werk **2** [Am] bezet; in gesprek [of tele-

phone]

²**busy** (vb) bezighouden, zoet houden: ~ *o.s. with* collecting stamps postzegels verzamelen om iets omhanden te hebben

busybody bemoeial

¹**but** (adv) **1** slechts, enkel, alleen, maar, pas: *I could* ~ *feel sorry for her* ik kon enkel medelijden hebben met haar; *I know* ~ *one* ik ken er maar één **2** (en) toch, echter, anderzijds

²**but** (prep) behalve, buiten, uitgezonderd: *he wanted nothing* ~ ***peace*** hij wilde slechts rust; *the last* ~ ***one*** op één na de laatste

³**but** (conj) **1** [exception] behalve, buiten, uitgezonderd: *what could I do* ~ *surrender?* wat kon ik doen behalve me overgeven? **2** [contrast] maar (toch), niettemin, desondanks: *not a man* ~ *an **animal*** geen mens maar een dier; ~ *then* (again) (maar) anderzijds, maar ja; ~ *yet* niettemin

butane butaanʰ; butagasʰ

butch [inform] **1** manwijfʰ, pot **2** ruwe klant, vechtersbaas

¹**butcher** (n) slager, slachter: *the* ~'s de slager(ij)

²**butcher** (vb) **1** slachten **2** afslachten, uitmoorden

butchery 1 slachting, bloedbadʰ **2** het slachten [for consumption]

but for ware het niet voor, als niet

¹**butt** (n) **1** mikpuntʰ [of mockery] **2** doelwitʰ, roos **3** (dik) uiteindeʰ, kolf, handvatʰ, restantʰ, eindjeʰ, peuk; [inform] achtersteʰ; krent; [Am] romp; tors: [Am; inform] *kiss s.o.'s* ~ iem. in zijn kont kruipen, vreselijk slijmen bij iem. **4** [Am] sigaret, peuk **5** (bier)vatʰ, wijnvatʰ, (regen)ton **6** ram, kopstoot, stoot [with head or horns]

²**butt** (vb) rammen [with head or horns]; stoten, een kopstoot geven

butt-dial [Am; inform] broekzakbellen

butter boter || *(he looks as if)* ~ *wouldn't melt in his mouth* hij lijkt van de prins geen kwaad te weten

buttercup boterbloem

butterfingers [inform] stuntel, stoethaspel; [ball game] slecht vanger

butterfly 1 vlinder **2** vlinderslag

buttermilk karnemelk, botermelk

butternut squash flespompoen

butter up [inform] vleien, stroop om de mond smeren, slijmen

butthurt [Am; inform] op zijn teentjes getrapt

butt in [inform] tussenbeide komen, onderbreken

buttock 1 bil **2** (-s) achtersteʰ, achterwerkʰ

button 1 knoop(jeʰ) **2** (druk)knop, knopjeʰ **3** [Am] button, rond insigneʰ || [Am; inform] *on the* ~ **a)** precies, de spijker op z'n kop; **b)** in de roos

button bar knoppenbalk

¹**buttonhole** (n) knoopsgatʰ

²**buttonhole** (vb) in zijn kraag grijpen, staande houden

¹**button up** (vb) [inform] zijn kop houden

²**button up** (vb) dichtknopen, dichtdoen: [Am; inform] ~ *your lip* hou je kop || *that job is buttoned up* dat is voor elkaar

¹**buttress** (n) steunbeer; [fig] steunpilaar

²**buttress** (vb) (also + up) versterken met steun(beer); [fig] (onder)steunen

buxom weelderig; mollig

¹**buy** (n) **1** aankoop, aanschaf, koop **2** koopjeʰ, voordeeltjeʰ

²**buy** (vb) [inform] geloven, accepteren, (voor waar) aannemen: *don't* ~ *that **nonsense*** laat je niks wijsmaken

³**buy** (vb) aankopen, inkopen, opkopen, aanschaffen: *peace* was dearly bought de vrede werd duur betaald; ~ *time* tijd winnen; ~ *back* terugkopen; ~ *up* opkopen, overnemen || [inform] ~ *it* gedood worden; *rent* to ~ huurkopen

buyer 1 koper, klant **2** inkoper [of department store etc]

¹**buzz** (n) **1** bromgeluidʰ, gonsgeluidʰ, zoemgeluidʰ, geroezemoesʰ **2** [inform] belletjeʰ, telefoontjeʰ: *give* mother a ~ bel moeder even

²**buzz** (vb) **1** zoemen, brommen, gonzen; roezemoezen **2** druk in de weer zijn **3** op een zoemer drukken, (aan)bellen || [Am; inform] ~ *along* opstappen [after visit]

buzzard buizerd

buzz cut [Am] stekeltjes, gemillimeterd haarʰ

buzzer zoemer

buzz in [inform] (iem.) binnenlaten met behulp van een elektronische deurontsluiter: *can you buzz me in?* kun je me binnenlaten?

buzz word modewoordʰ

¹**by** (adv) langs, voorbij: *in years **gone** by* in vervlogen jaren || *by and **by*** straks; *by and **large*** over 't algemeen

²**by** (prep) **1** [nearness] bij, dichtbij, vlakbij, naast; [on compass card] ten: *sit by my side* kom naast mij zitten; *by **o.s.*** alleen **2** [way, medium etc] door, langs, via, voorbij: *travel by **air*** vliegen; *taught by **radio*** via de radio geleerd **3** [time] tegen, vóór, niet later dan; [by extension] op; om [certain time]; in [certain year]: *finished by **Sunday*** klaar tegen zondag; *by **now*** nu (al) **4** [instrument, means etc] door, door middel van, per, als gevolg van: *by **accident*** per ongeluk; *he missed by an **inch*** hij miste op een paar centimeter; *I did it all by **myself*** ik heb het helemaal alleen gedaan **5** ten opzichte van, wat … betreft: *paid by the **hour*** per uur betaald; *play by the **rules*** volgens de regels spelen; *that is fine by me* ik vind het best, wat mij betreft is het goed **6** [time or circumstance] bij, tijdens: *by **day***

overdag **7** [sequence] na, per: *he got worse by the **hour*** hij ging van uur tot uur achteruit ‖ *swear by the **Bible*** (or: ***Koran***) op de Bijbel (*or:* Koran) zweren

bye [inform] tot ziens, dag

by-election tussentijdse verkiezing

bygone voorbij, vroeger

bygones: *let ~ be ~* men moet geen oude koeien uit de sloot halen

by-law 1 (plaatselijke) verordening, gemeenteverordening **2** [Am] (bedrijfs)voorschrift^h, (huis)regel: *~s* huishoudelijk reglement^h

¹bypass (n) **1** [traf] rondweg, ringweg **2** [techn] omloopkanaal^h, omloopleiding, omloopverbinding **3** [med] bypass

²bypass (vb) om … heen gaan, mijden

by-product 1 bijproduct^h **2** bijverschijnsel^h; neveneffect^h

bystander omstander, toeschouwer

byte byte

byway zijweg ‖ [fig] *the ~s of **literature*** de minder bekende paden van de letterkunde

byword 1 spreekwoord^h, gezegde^h, zegswijze **2** belichaming, synoniem^h, prototype^h: *Joe is a ~ **for** laziness* Joe is het prototype van de luilak

C

C 1 *Celsius* **2** *cent* **3** *centigrade* **4** *circa* ca.
cab 1 [Am] taxi **2** [inform; traf] cabine, bok, cockpit
cabaret 1 variétérestaurant[h] **2** show; variété[h]
cabbage 1 kool: *Chinese* ~ Chinese kool; paksoi; *red* ~ rodekool; *white* ~ wittekool **2** [inform] slome duikelaar[h], druiloor
cabby [inform] taxichauffeur
cabdriver [esp Am] taxichauffeur
cabin 1 (houten) optrek, huisje[h], hut, kleedhokje[h], badhokje[h]; [railways] seinhuis[h] **2** cabine; (slaap)hut [on ship]; laadruimte; bagageruim[h] [in aeroplane]
cabin cruiser motorjacht[h]
cabinet 1 kast, porseleinkast, televisiemeubel[h], dossierkast **2** kabinet[h], ministerraad **3** kabinetsberaad[h], kabinetsvergadering
¹cable (n) **1** kabel, sleepkabel, trekkabel **2** (elektriciteits)kabel, televisiekabel **3** kabel, kabelvormig ornament[h]; [knitting] kabelsteek
²cable (vb) telegraferen
cable car kabelwagen, gondel, cabine van een kabelbaan
cable television kabeltelevisie
cable tie kabelbinder, tiewrap
cableway kabelbaan
caboodle [inform] troep, zwik, bups: *the whole* ~ de hele bups
cab rank taxistandplaats
cache 1 (geheime) bergplaats **2** (geheime/verborgen) voorraad **3** [comp] tijdelijk geheugen[h], cache(geheugen[h])
cachet distinctie; cachet[h], allure
¹cackle (n) **1** kakelgeluid[h] **2** giechel(lachje[h]), gekraai[h]: ~*s of excitement* opgewonden gilletjes **3** gekakel[h]; [fig] gekwebbel[h]; geklets[h]: [inform] *cut the* ~ genoeg gekletst
²cackle (vb) **1** kakelen; [fig] kwebbelen; kletsen **2** giechelen, kraaien
cacophonous kakofonisch
cacophony kakofonie
cactus cactus
cad [depr] schoft
CAD *computer-aided design* CAD
cadaverous lijkachtig, lijkkleurig
caddie [golf] caddie
caddish schofterig, ploerterig
caddy theeblikje[h], theebusje[h]
cadence 1 stembuiging, toonval, intonatie **2** [mus] cadens **3** cadans, vloeiend ritme[h]
cadet cadet

¹cadge (vb) [inform; depr] klaplopen, schooien
²cadge (vb) [inform; depr] bietsen, aftroggelen
cadre 1 kader[h] **2** kaderlid[h]
Caesarean section keizersnede
café 1 eethuisje[h], café-restaurant[h], snackbar **2** theesalon+[h], tearoom **3** koffiehuis[h]
cafeteria kantine, zelfbedieningsrestaurant[h]
caff [inform] *see café*
¹cage (n) **1** kooi(constructie) **2** liftkooi, liftbak **3** gevangenis, (krijgs)gevangenkamp[h] **4** [ice hockey] kooi, doel[h]
²cage (vb) kooien, in een kooi opsluiten
cage fighting kooivechten[h]
cagey [inform] **1** gesloten, behoedzaam, teruggetrokken **2** argwanend, achterdochtig
cajole (door vleierij) bepraten, ompraten, overhalen: ~ *s.o.* *into giving money* iem. geld aftroggelen
cake 1 cake, taart, (pannen)koek, gebak[h]: *go* (or: *sell*) *like hot* ~*s* verkopen als warme broodjes, lopen als een trein **2** blok[h] [of compact material]; koek || [inform] *you can't have your* ~ *and eat it* je kunt niet alles willen
Cal 1 *California* **2** *(large) calorie*
calamity onheil[h], calamiteit, ramp(spoed)
calcify verkalken [also fig]
calcium calcium[h]
¹calculate (vb) **1** rekenen, een berekening maken **2** schatten, een schatting maken
²calculate (vb) **1** (wiskundig) berekenen, (vooraf) uitrekenen **2** beramen, bewust plannen: ~*d to attract the attention* bedoeld om de aandacht te trekken **3** incalculeren: ~*d risk* ingecalculeerd risico
calculating berekenend
calculation 1 berekening [also fig] **2** voorspelling, schatting **3** bedachtzaamheid
calculator rekenmachine, calculator
calculus calculus; analyse: ~ *of probabilities* kansrekening
calendar 1 kalender **2** [Am] agenda
calf 1 kalf[h]: *the cow is in* (or: *with*) ~ de koe is drachtig, de koe moet kalven **2** [anatomy] kuit
calibre kaliber[h], gehalte[h], niveau[h], klasse
¹call (n) **1** kreet, roep van dier, roep van vogel: *we heard a* ~ *for help* we hoorden hulpgeroep; *within* ~ binnen gehoorsafstand **2** (kort, formeel, zakelijk) bezoek[h]: *pay a* ~ een visite afleggen; [inform; euph] naar een zekere plaats (or: nummer 100) gaan **3** beroep[h], aanspraak, claim **4** oproep(ing), roep(ing), appel[h], voorlezing van presentielijst; [fin] oproep tot aflossing van een schuld; aanmaning: *the actors received a* ~ *for eight o'clock* de acteurs moesten om acht uur op; *at* ~, *on* ~ (onmiddellijk) beschikbaar, op af-

roep; *the doctor was on* ~ de dokter had bereikbaarheidsdienst **5** reden, aanleiding, noodzaak, behoefte: *there's no ~ for you to worry* je hoeft je niet ongerust te maken **6** telefoontje^h, (telefoon)gesprek^h ‖ *~ to the bar* toelating als advocaat; [euph] *~ of nature* aandrang [to go to the toilet]; natuurlijke behoefte

²**call** (vb) **1** (even) langsgaan (langskomen), (kort) op bezoek gaan; stoppen [at a station]: *the ship ~s at numerous ports* het schip doet talrijke havens aan

³**call** (vb) **1** afroepen, oplezen, opsommen: ~ *out numbers* nummers afroepen **2** (op)roepen, aanroepen; terugroepen [actor]; tot het priesterschap roepen: ~ *a witness* een getuige oproepen **3** afkondigen, bijeenroepen, proclameren: ~ *a meeting* een vergadering bijeenroepen **4** wakker maken, wekken, roepen **5** (be)noemen, aanduiden als: ~ *s.o. a liar* iem. uitmaken voor leugenaar; [inform] *what-d'you-call-it* hoe-heet-het-ook-weer?, dinges; *Peter is ~ed after his grandfather* Peter is vernoemd naar zijn grootvader **6** vinden, beschouwen als: *I ~ it nonsense* ik vind het onzin **7** het houden op, zeggen, (een bedrag) afmaken op: *let's ~ it ten euros* laten we het op tien euro houden **8** [cards] bieden ‖ ~ *into being* in het leven roepen; ~ *away* wegroepen; ~ *forth* oproepen, (naar) boven brengen

⁴**call** (vb) **1** (uit)roepen: ~ *for help* om hulp roepen **2** (op)bellen **3** [cards] bieden

call-back terugroeping

call-box telefooncel

call centre callcenter^h; telefonische helpdesk

call charges voorrijkosten

caller 1 bezoeker **2** beller, iem. die belt

caller display nummerweergave; nummerherkenning

caller ID [techn] nummermelding

call for 1 komen om, (komen) afhalen **2** wensen, verlangen, vragen: ~ *the bill* de rekening vragen **3** vereisen: *this situation calls for immediate action* in deze toestand is onmiddellijk handelen geboden

call-girl callgirl

call in 1 laten komen, de hulp inroepen van, consulteren: ~ *a specialist* er een specialist bij halen **2** terugroepen, terugvorderen, uit de circulatie nemen: *some cars had to be called in* een aantal auto's moest terug naar de fabriek

calling 1 roeping **2** beroep^h

call off afzeggen, afgelasten: ~ *one's engagement* het afmaken

callous 1 vereelt, verhard **2** ongevoelig, gevoelloos

¹**call out** (vb) **1** uitroepen, een gil geven **2** roepen, hardop praten

²**call out** (vb) **1** afroepen, opnoemen **2** te hulp roepen [fire brigade etc]

callow 1 kaal [of birds]; zonder veren **2** groen, jong, onervaren

calltime gesprekstijd

call up 1 opbellen **2** in het geheugen roepen, zich (weer) voor de geest halen **3** [mil] oproepen, te hulp roepen, inschakelen: ~ *reserves* reserves inzetten

call (up)on 1 (even) langsgaan bij, (kort) bezoeken: *we'll call (up)on you tomorrow* we komen morgen bij u langs **2** een beroep doen op, aanspreken

call waiting wisselgesprek^h

¹**calm** (n) **1** (wind)stilte [also fig]; kalmte **2** windstilte [wind-force 0]

²**calm** (adj) kalm, (wind)stil, vredig, rustig

³**calm** (vb) kalmeren: *the gale ~ed (down)* de storm ging liggen

calorie calorie

calumny laster(praat), roddel, geroddel^h

Cambodia Cambodja

¹**Cambodian** (n) Cambodjaan(se)

²**Cambodian** (adj) Cambodjaans

camel kameel, dromedaris

camera fototoestel^h, (film)camera ‖ [law] *in* ~ achter gesloten deuren; *off* ~ buiten beeld

Cameroon Kameroen

¹**Cameroonian** (n) Kameroener, Kameroense

²**Cameroonian** (adj) Kameroens

camisole (mouwloos) hemdje^h

camomile kamille

¹**camouflage** (n) camouflage

²**camouflage** (vb) camoufleren, wegmoffelen

¹**camp** (n) **1** kamp^h, legerplaats; [fig] aanhang van partij: *break* (or: *strike*) ~, *break up* ~ (zijn tenten) opbreken **2** kitsch

²**camp** (adj) **1** verwijfd **2** homoseksueel **3** overdreven, theatraal, bizar **4** kitscherig

³**camp** (vb) kamperen, zijn kamp opslaan

campaign campagne, manoeuvre^h: *advertising* ~ reclamecampagne

campaigner 1 campagnevoerder; activist: [fig] *old* ~ oude rot in het vak **2** [Am] campagnemedewerker [in elections]

campground [Am] kampeerterrein^h; camping

camphor kamfer

campsite kampeerterrein^h, camping

campus campus [university or school grounds]

¹**can** (n) **1** houder [usually of metal]; kroes, kan **2** blik^h, conservenblikje^h, filmblik^h: *in the* ~ gereed **3** [Am; inform] plee **4** [inform] bak, bajes, lik ‖ [Am; inform] ~ *of worms* een moeilijke kwestie; [inform] *carry* (or: *take*) *the* ~ *(back)* ergens voor opdraaien

²**can** (vb) inblikken, conserveren, inmaken ‖ [Am; inform] ~ *it!* hou op!

³can (aux vb) **1** kunnen, in staat zijn te: *I ~ readily understand that* ik kan dat best begrijpen; *could you **help** me please?* zou u mij alstublieft kunnen helpen? **2** kunnen, zou kunnen: *~ this **be** true?* zou dit waar kunnen zijn?; *I could go to the baker's if you like* ik zou naar de bakker kunnen gaan als je wilt **3** mogen, kunnen, bevoegd zijn te: *you ~ **go** now* je mag nu gaan

Canada Canada

¹Canadian (n) Canadees, Canadese

²Canadian (adj) Canadees

canal kanaalʰ, vaart, gracht, (water)leiding

canalization kanalisatie, het in banen leiden

canary kanarie(piet)

¹cancel (vb) tegen elkaar wegvallen, elkaar compenseren, tegen elkaar opwegen: *the **arguments** ~ (each other)* de argumenten wegen tegen elkaar op

²cancel (vb) **1** doorstrepen, doorhalen, (door)schrappen **2** opheffen, ongedaan maken, vernietigen **3** annuleren, afzeggen, opzeggen; intrekken [order]; herroepen, afgelasten **4** ongeldig maken; afstempelen [stamp]

cancellation annulering; ontbinding [of an agreement]; afgelasting [of a game]

¹cancel out (vb) elkaar compenseren, tegen elkaar opwegen

²cancel out (vb) compenseren, goedmaken, neutraliseren: *the pros and cons cancel each other out* de voor- en nadelen heffen elkaar op

cancer kanker, kwaadaardige tumor; [fig] (verderfelijk, woekerend) kwaadʰ

Cancer [astrology] (de) Kreeft: *tropic of ~* Kreeftskeerkring

candelabra armkandelaar

candid open(hartig), rechtuit, eerlijk: *~ **picture*** spontane foto

candidate kandidaat, gegadigde

candidature kandidatuur, kandidaatschapʰ

candle kaars ‖ *burn the ~ at both ends* te veel hooi op zijn vork nemen; *he can't **hold** a ~ to her* hij doet voor haar onder

candlelight kaarslichtʰ

candlestick kandelaar, kaarsenstandaard

candlewick kaarsenpit

can-do [inform] ondernemend: *people with a ~ **attitude*** mensen die van aanpakken weten

candour open(hartig)heid, eerlijkheid, oprechtheid

candy 1 (stukjeʰ) kandijʰ, suikergoedʰ **2** [Am] snoepjeʰ, snoepjes, zuurtjeʰ, zuurtjes, chocola(atjeʰ)

candy bar gevulde (chocolade)reep

candyfloss suikerspin

¹cane (n) **1** dikke stengel, rietstengel, bamboestengel, rotan(stok) **2** rotting, wandelstok, plantensteun **3** [bot] stam, stengel, scheut **4** rietʰ, rotanʰ, bamboe+ʰ, suikerrietʰ: *get the ~* met het rietje krijgen

²cane (vb) **1** met het rietje geven, afranselen **2** matten [of furniture]

canine hondachtig, honds-

canine tooth hoektand

canister bus, trommel, blikʰ

cannabis (Indische) hennep, cannabis, marihuana, wiet

cannabis coffee shop koffieshop

canned ingeblikt, in blik ‖ *~ **music*** ingeblikte muziek, muzak

cannibal kannibaal, menseneter

cannibalism kannibalismeʰ

¹cannon (n) **1** kanonʰ, (stukʰ) geschutʰ, boordkanonʰ: [fig] *a **loose** ~* een ongeleid projectiel **2** [billiards] carambole

²cannon (vb) (op)botsen: *she ~ed **into** me* ze vloog tegen me op

cannonade kanonnade, bombardementʰ

cannonball 1 kanonskogel **2** [swimming] bommetjeʰ: *to **do** a ~* een bommetje doen

cannon fodder kanonnenvoerʰ

canny 1 slim, uitgekookt **2** zuinig, spaarzaam

¹canoe (n) kano

²canoe (vb) kanoën, kanovaren

canola raapzaad(olie), koolzaad(olie)

canon 1 kerkelijke leerstelling; (algemene) regel [also fig]: *the **Shakespeare** ~* (lijst van) aan Shakespeare toegeschreven werken **2** kanunnik

canonize heilig verklaren

canon law canoniek rechtʰ; kerkrechtʰ

canoodle [inform] knuffelen, scharrelen

can opener blikopener

canopy baldakijn+ʰ; [fig] gewelfʰ; kap, dakʰ

cant 1 jargonʰ, boeventaal: *thieves' ~* dieventaal **2** schijnheilige praat

cantankerous ruzieachtig

canteen kantine

¹canter (n) handgalopʰ, rit(jeʰ) in handgalop

²canter (vb) in handgalop gaan (brengen)

¹Cantonese (n) Kantonees, Kantonese

²Cantonese (adj) Kantonees

canvas 1 canvasʰ, zeildoek+ʰ, tentdoekʰ **2** schilderslinnen **3** borduurgaasʰ **4** [shipp] zeilvoering: *under ~* onder vol zeil **5** doekʰ, stukʰ schilderslinnen, (olieverf)schilderijʰ

canvass 1 diepgaand (be)discussiëren, grondig onderzoek doen **2** stemmen werven (in) **3** klanten werven, colporteren: *~ **for** a magazine* colporteren voor een weekblad **4** opiniepeiling houden (over)

canyon cañon, ravijnʰ

¹cap (n) **1** hoofddekselʰ; kapjeʰ [of nurse, domestic servant etc]; muts, pet, baret: *take the ~ round* met de pet rondgaan **2** kapvormig voorwerpʰ; hoed [of mushroom]; kniekap, flessendop, vulpendop, afsluitdop, beschermkapje[h] **3** slaghoedje[h] **4** klappertje[h] **5** [sport] (selectie als) international: *it's his first ~ for England* hij komt voor de eerste keer uit voor Engeland ‖ *~ in hand* onderdanig, nederig; *if the ~ fits, wear it* wie de schoen past, trekke hem aan

²cap (vb) **1** een cap opzetten; [sport; fig] in de nationale ploeg opstellen **2** verbeteren, overtroeven: *to ~ it all* als klap op de vuurpijl, tot overmaat van ramp

capability 1 vermogen[h], capaciteit, bekwaamheid **2** vatbaarheid, ontvankelijkheid **3** (capabilities) talenten, capaciteiten

capable 1 in staat: *he is ~ of anything* hij is tot alles in staat **2** vatbaar: *~ of improvement* voor verbetering vatbaar **3** capabel, bekwaam

capacious ruim: *a ~ memory* een goed geheugen

capacity 1 hoedanigheid: *in my ~ of chairman* als voorzitter **2** vermogen[h], capaciteit, aanleg **3** capaciteit, inhoud, volume[h]: *seating ~* aantal zitplaatsen; *filled to ~* tot de laatste plaats bezet

capacity crowd volle zaal, bak

cape 1 cape **2** kaap, voorgebergte[h]

¹caper (n) **1** [fig] bokkensprong, capriool: *cut ~s* capriolen uithalen, zich idioot gedragen **2** [inform] (ondeugende) streek, kwajongensstreek **3** [inform] karwei[h], klus

²caper (vb) (rond)dartelen, capriolen maken

Cape Verde Islands (the) Kaapverdische Eilanden

¹capital (n) **1** kapitaal[h]: [fig] *make ~ (out) of* munt slaan uit **2** [architecture] kapiteel[h] **3** hoofdletter, kapitaal[h] **4** hoofdstad

²capital (adj) **1** kapitaal, hoofd-: *~ city* (of: *town*) hoofdstad; *~ letters* hoofdletters **2** dood-, dodelijk: *~ punishment* doodstraf

capital gain vermogensaanwas: *~s tax* vermogens(aanwas)belasting

capitalism kapitalisme[h]

¹capitalist (n) kapitalist

²capitalist (adj) kapitalistisch

capitalization 1 kapitalisatie **2** [printing] gebruik van hoofdletters

capitalize kapitaliseren; [fig] *~ (up)on* uitbuiten, munt slaan uit

Capitol Hill 1 Capitol Hill **2** het (Amerikaanse) Congres

capitulate capituleren, zich overgeven

capitulation overgave

caprice gril, kuur, wispelturigheid

Capricorn [astrology] (de) Steenbok: *tropic of ~* Steenbokskeerkring

caps 1 *capital letters* **2** *capsule*

capsize (doen) kapseizen, (doen) omslaan

capsule 1 capsule **2** neuskegel [of rocket]; cabine [of spacecraft]

captain 1 kapitein [also mil]; bevelhebber,

(scheeps)gezagvoerder; [mil] kapitein-terzee: *~ of industry* grootindustrieel **2** [aviation] gezagvoerder **3** [Am] korpscommandant, districtscommandant [of police] **4** voorman, ploegbaas **5** [sport] aanvoerder, captain

captcha captcha

caption 1 titel, kop, hoofd[h] **2** onderschrift[h]; bijschrift[h] [of illustration]; ondertitel(ing) [film, TV]

captivate boeien, fascineren: *he was ~d by Geraldine* hij was helemaal weg van Geraldine

¹captive (n) gevangene [also fig]; krijgsgevangene

²captive (adj) **1** (krijgs)gevangen (genomen); [fig] geketend: *~ audience* een aan hun stoelen gekluisterd publiek; *be taken ~* gevangengenomen worden **2** geboeid, gecharmeerd

captivity gevangenschap [also fig]; krijgsgevangenschap[h]

¹capture (n) **1** gevangene, vangst, buit, prijs **2** vangst, gevangenneming

²capture (vb) **1** vangen, gevangennemen, gevangen houden; [fig] boeien; fascineren: *~ the imagination* tot de verbeelding spreken **2** buitmaken, bemachtigen, veroveren **3** [chess, draughts etc] slaan [piece, man etc]

car 1 auto(mobiel[+h]), motorrijtuig[h], wagen: *by ~* met de auto **2** rijtuig[h]; [Am] (spoorweg)wagon; tram(wagen) **3** gondel [of airship, cableway]

carabiner [climbing] karabijnhaak

carafe karaf

caramel karamel

carat karaat[h]: *pure gold is 24 ~s* zuiver goud is 24 karaat

caravan 1 karavaan **2** woonwagen, kermiswagen **3** caravan, kampeerwagen

carbine karabijn

carbohydrate koolhydraat[h]

carbon 1 koolstof[h] **2** carbon(papier)[h]

carbonated koolzuurhoudend: *~ water* sodawater[h], spuitwater[h]

carbon copy 1 doorslag **2** duplicaat[h], getrouwe kopie

carbon footprint CO_2-voetafdruk

carbon monoxide koolmonoxide[h], kolendamp

carbon trading CO_2-handel

car break-in auto-inbraak

carbs [inform] *carbohydrates* koolhydraten; koolhydraatrijk voedsel[h]

carbuncle 1 karbonkel **2** steenpuist

carburettor carburator

carcass 1 karkas[h]; romp [of slaughtered animal] **2** geraamte[h], skelet[h] ‖ *~ of a car* autowrak[h]

carcinogen carcinogeen[h]; kankerverwekkende stof

carcinogenic kankerverwekkend
card 1 kaart: *house* of ~s kaartenhuis^h; *keep* (or: *play*) *one's ~s close to one's chest* zich niet in de kaart laten kijken, terughoudend zijn **2** programma^h [of sport event] **3** scorestaat, scorekaart [eg of cricket, golf] ‖ *have a ~ up one's sleeve* (nog) iets achter de hand hebben; *he played his ~s right* (or: *well*) hij heeft zijn kansen goed benut; *put (all) one's ~s on the table* open kaart spelen; [inform] *it is on the ~s* het zit er in; *see cards*
¹**cardboard** (n) karton^h, bordpapier^h
²**cardboard** (adj) **1** kartonnen, bordpapieren **2** onecht, clichématig: ~ *characters* stereotiepe figuren
card-carrying 1 officieel **2** actief, geëngageerd
card-embedded met ingebouwde kaart
cardholder bezitter van creditcard; kaarthouder
cardiac hart-: ~ *arrest* hartstilstand
cardigan gebreid vestje^h
¹**cardinal** (n) **1** hoofdtelwoord^h **2** [Roman Catholicism] kardinaal
²**cardinal** (adj) kardinaal, fundamenteel, vitaal: ~ *idea* centrale gedachte; ~ *number* hoofdtelwoord^h
cardiologist cardioloog; hartspecialist
cardiovascular cardiovasculair; hart- en vaat-
cards kaartspel^h: *play* ~ kaarten
¹**care** (n) **1** zorg, ongerustheid: *free from* ~(s) zonder zorgen **2** zorg(vuldigheid), voorzichtigheid: *handle with* ~ (pas op,) breekbaar!; *take* ~ oppletten; *take* ~! a) hou je taai; b) het beste **3** verantwoordelijkheid, zorg, toezicht^h: *take* ~ of zorgen voor, onder zijn hoede nemen; *take* ~ to ervoor zorgen dat; ~ of per adres; *under doctor's* ~ onder doktersbehandeling **4** kinderzorg, kleuterzorg: *take into* ~ opnemen in een kindertehuis
²**care** (vb) **1** erom geven, zich erom bekommeren: *well, who* ~s? nou, en?, wat zou het?; *for all I* ~ wat mij betreft **2** bezwaar hebben: *I don't* ~ *if you do* mij best
³**care** (vb) **1** (graag) willen, zin hebben (in), bereid zijn te: *if only they would* ~ *to listen* als ze maar eens de moeite namen om te luisteren **2** zich bekommeren om, geven om, zich aantrekken van: *I couldn't* ~ *less* het zal me een zorg zijn; *Paul doesn't seem to* ~ *very much* zo te zien kan het Paul weinig schelen
¹**career** (n) **1** carrière, (succesvolle) loopbaan **2** (levens)loop, geschiedenis **3** beroep^h: ~s *master* (or: *mistress*) schooldecaan **4** (grote) vaart, (hoge) snelheid: *at* (or: *in*) *full* ~ in volle vaart
²**career** (vb) voortdaveren: ~ *about* rondrazen
care for 1 verzorgen, letten op, passen op, onderhouden **2** zin hebben in, (graag) wil-

len: *would you care for* a cup of coffee? heb je zin in een kopje koffie? **3** houden van, belangstelling hebben voor: *more* than I ~ meer dan me lief is
carefree 1 onbekommerd, zonder zorgen **2** [depr] onverantwoordelijk, zorgeloos
careful 1 zorgzaam, met veel zorg **2** angstvallig **3** voorzichtig, omzichtig, oplettend: *be* ~ *(about) what you say* let op je woorden **4** zorgvuldig, nauwkeurig: ~ *examination* zorgvuldig onderzoek **5** nauwgezet
careless 1 onverschillig, onvoorzichtig **2** onopplettend **3** onzorgvuldig, slordig, nonchalant
carer thuisverzorger, verzorger, verzorgende
¹**caress** (n) teder gebaar^h, streling
²**caress** (vb) liefkozen, kussen, aanhalen
caretaker 1 conciërge, huismeester **2** huisbewaarder **3** toezichthouder, zaakwaarnemer
careworn afgetobd, (door zorgen) getekend
car ferry autoveer^h, autoveerboot, autoveerdienst, ferry(boot)
cargo lading, vracht, cargo
cargo pants cargobroek
¹**Caribbean** (n, the) Caribisch gebied^h, Caribische zee
²**Caribbean** (adj) Caribisch
caribou kariboe
caricature karikatuur, spotprent
¹**caring** (n) **1** zorg, verzorging **2** hartelijkheid, warmte
²**caring** (adj) **1** zorgzaam, vol zorg, meelevend, attent: *a* ~ *society* een zorgzame maatschappij **2** verzorgend: *a* ~ *job* een verzorgend beroep
car kit carkit
carnage slachting [among people]; bloedbad^h
carnal [oft depr] vleselijk, lichamelijk
carnation anjer, anjelier
carnival 1 carnaval^h, carnavalstijd, carnavalsviering **2** [Am] circus^{+h}, kermis **3** festival^h, beurs, jaarmarkt
carnivore carnivoor; vleeseter
carnivorous vleesetend
carol lofzang, kerstlied^h
carousel 1 [Am] carrousel^{+h} **2** [aviation] bagagecarrousel^{+h}; bagageband
¹**carp** (n) karper(achtige)
²**carp** (vb) [oft depr] zeuren, vitten
car park 1 parkeerterrein^h **2** parkeergarage
carpenter timmerman
carpentry timmerwerk^h, timmerkunst
¹**carpet** (n) (vloer)tapijt^h, (vloer)kleed^h, karpet^h, (trap)loper: ~ *of flowers* bloemenkleed; *fitted* ~ vast tapijt ‖ *sweep under the* ~ in de doofpot stoppen

²**carpet** (vb) **1** tapijt leggen, bekleden: ~ *the stairs* een loper op de trap leggen **2** [inform] een uitbrander geven

carpetbag reistas, valies^h

carpeting 1 tapijt^h **2** [inform] uitbrander

carping 1 muggenzifterig, vitterig: ~ *criticism* kinderachtige kritiek **2** klagerig, zeurderig

carpool carpool, autopool

carport carport

carriage 1 rijtuig^h, koets; [railways] (personen)wagon **2** slee; onderstel^h [of carriage] **3** (lichaams)houding, gang **4** vervoer^h, transport^h, verzending **5** vracht(prijs), vervoerskosten, verzendkosten

carriageway verkeersweg, rijweg, rijbaan

carrier 1 vervoerder van goederen of reizigers, expediteur, transporteur, vrachtvaarder, expeditiebedrijf^h, transportbedrijf^h, vervoerbedrijf^h, luchtvaartmaatschappij, spoorwegmaatschappij, rederij **2** [med, science, chem] drager **3** bagagedrager **4** [mil] vervoermiddel^h voor mensen en materieel, vliegdekschip^h **5** (boodschappen)tas

carrier pigeon postduif

carrion aas^h [putrid flesh]; kadaver^h

carrot 1 peen, wortel(tje^h) **2** [fig, inform] lokmiddel^h: *hold out* (or: *offer*) *a* ~ *to s.o.* iem. een worst voorhouden

¹**carry** (vb) **1** dragen; reiken [eg of voice] **2** in verwachting zijn, drachtig zijn **3** aangenomen worden [eg of bill]; erdoor komen

²**carry** (vb) **1** vervoeren, transporteren, (mee)dragen, steunen, (met zich) (mee)voeren, bij zich hebben, afvoeren; [science] (ge)leiden; (binnen)halen [harvest etc]; drijven: *such a crime carries a severe punishment* op zo'n misdaad staat een strenge straf; *diseases carried by insects* ziekten door insecten overgebracht; ~ *to excess* te ver doordrijven; *the loan carries an interest* de lening is rentedragend; *write 3 and* ~ *2* 3 opschrijven, 2 onthouden; *Joan carries herself like a model* Joan beweegt zich als een mannequin; ~ *into effect* ten uitvoer brengen **2** in verwachting zijn van **3** veroveren, in de wacht slepen: ~ *one's motion* (or: *bill*) zijn motie (or: wetsontwerp) erdoor krijgen **4** met zich meebrengen, impliceren **5** uitzenden, publiceren || ~ *all* (or: *everything*) *before one* in ieder opzicht slagen; ~ *too far* overdrijven

carryall [Am] weekendtas, reistas

carry along stimuleren, aansporen, (voort)drijven

carry away 1 meesleuren, meeslepen, opzwepen **2** wegdragen

carry back doen (terug)denken aan; terugvoeren

carrycot reiswieg

carry forward 1 [bookkeeping] transporteren **2** vorderen met [eg work]; voortzetten **3** in mindering brengen, overbrengen naar volgend boekjaar

carryings-on [inform] **1** (dolle) streken, handel en wandel **2** geflirt^h

carry off 1 winnen, veroveren, in de wacht slepen **2** wegvoeren, ontvoeren, er vandoor gaan met **3** trotseren, tarten || *I managed to carry it off* ik heb me eruit weten te redden

¹**carry on** (vb) **1** doorgaan, zijn gang gaan, doorzetten **2** [inform] tekeergaan, stennis maken, zich aanstellen: *it is a shame how he carried on in there* het is een schande zoals hij daarbinnen tekeer ging **3** [inform; oft depr] scharrelen, het houden met (elkaar)

²**carry on** (vb) **1** voortzetten, volhouden: ~ *the good work!* hou vol!, ga zo door! **2** (uit)voeren, drijven, gaande houden **3** voeren [war, lawsuit]

carry out uitvoeren, vervullen, volbrengen

carry-out [Am] om mee te nemen: ~ *restaurant* afhaalrestaurant^h

¹**carry through** (vb) voortbestaan, voortduren

²**carry through** (vb) erdoor helpen: *his faith carried him through* zijn geloof hield hem op de been

car sharing 1 (het) carpoolen, carpooling **2** (het) autodelen

carsick wagenziek

¹**cart** (n) **1** kar **2** winkelwagentje^h || *put* (or: *set*) *the* ~ *before the horse* het paard achter de wagen spannen

²**cart** (vb) vervoeren in een kar: ~ *off* a prisoner een gevangene (hardhandig) afvoeren^h

cartilage kraakbeen^h

carton kartonnen doos: *a* ~ *of cigarettes* een slof sigaretten; *a* ~ *of milk* een pak melk

cartoon 1 (politieke) spotprent, cartoon **2** strip(verhaal^h): *animated* ~ tekenfilm, animatiefilm **3** tekenfilm, animatiefilm

cartoonist cartoonist

cartridge 1 patroon(huls) **2** (kant-en-klare) vulling, cassette, inktpatroon, gasvulling

cartwheel 1 karrenwiel^h [also fig]; wagenwiel^h **2** radslag: *do* ~s, *turn* ~s radslagen maken

¹**carve** (vb) beeldhouwen

²**carve** (vb) kerven, houwen, beitelen, graveren in: ~ *wood into a figure* uit hout een figuur snijden

³**carve** (vb) voorsnijden [meat, poultry etc]

carve out 1 uitsnijden, afsnijden, (uit)houwen **2** bevechten, zich veroveren: *she has carved out a successful career for herself* zij heeft een succesvolle carrière voor zichzelf opgebouwd

carve up 1 [inform] opdelen, aan stukken snijden **2** [inform] een jaap bezorgen

carving sculptuur, beeld(houwwerk)^h, houtsnede, gravure, reliëf^h

car-wash autowasserette, carwash

¹cascade (n) kleine waterval

²cascade (vb) (doen) vallen (als) in een waterval

¹case (n) **1** geval^h, kwestie, zaak, stand van zaken, voorbeeld^h, patiënt, ziektegeval^h: *former Yugoslavia is a ~ in point* het voormalige Joegoslavië is goed voorbeeld (hiervan); *in ~* voor het geval dat; [Am] indien; *(just) in ~* voor het geval dat; *in ~ of* in geval van, voor het geval dat; *in the ~ of* met betrekking tot; *in any* (or: *no*) *~* in elk (*or:* geen) geval **2** argumenten, bewijs(materiaal)^h, pleidooi^h: *have a strong ~* er sterk voor staan; *make (out) one's ~* aantonen dat men gelijk heeft **3** [law] (rechts)zaak, geding^h, proces^h **4** doos, kist, koffer, zak, tas(je^h), schede, koker, huls, mantel, sloop^{+h}, overtrek^{+h}, cassette, etui^h, omslag^{+h}, band, uitstalkast, vitrine; kast [of watch, piano; for books etc] **5** kozijn^h, raamwerk^h, deurlijst **6** [linguistics] naamval

²case (vb) voorzien van een omhulsel, insluiten, vatten

casebook example schoolvoorbeeld^h; model^h

case history voorgeschiedenis; ziektegeschiedenis

case law jurisprudentie; precedentenrecht^h

case-sensitive hoofdlettergevoelig

¹cash (n) contant geld^h, contanten, cash; [inform] geld^h; centen: *~ on delivery* (onder) rembours, betaling bij levering; *hard ~* munten; [inform] contant geld; *ready ~* baar geld, klinkende munt; *(be) short of ~* krap (bij kas) (zitten); *pay in ~* contant betalen; *~ down* (à) contant

²cash (vb) omwisselen in contanten [cheques etc]; verzilveren, innen

cashcard betaalpas, pinpas

cash cow melkkoe [fig]

cash desk kassa

cash dispenser geldautomaat, flappentap

cashew cashewnoot

cashier 1 kassier **2** caissière, kassabediende

cash in 1 het loodje leggen **2** zijn slag slaan: *~ on* profiteren van

cashless *~ society* plasticgeldmaatschappij

cash machine geldautomaat, pinautomaat

cashmere 1 kasjmieren sjaal **2** kasjmier^h [wool]

cashpoint geldautomaat, flappentap

cash register kasregister^h, kassa

casing 1 omhulsel^h, doos **2** kozijn^h, raamwerk^h, deurlijst

casino casino^h, gokpaleis^h

cask vat^h, fust^h

casket 1 (juwelen)kistje^h, cassette, doosje^h **2** [Am] dood(s)kist

cassava maniok; cassave

casserole braadschotel, ovenschotel,

stoofschotel, eenpansgerecht^h

cassette cassette

¹cast (n) **1** worp, gooi **2** iets wat geworpen wordt; lijn [with a fishing fly for bait] **3** gietvorm, model^h, afdruk **4** gips(verband)^h **5** hoedanigheid, kwaliteit, aard, uitdrukking; uiterlijk^h [of face]: *~ of mind* geestesgesteldheid **6** bezetting [of film, play etc]; cast, rolverdeling

²cast (vb) **1** zijn hengel uitwerpen **2** de doorslag geven, beslissend zijn: *~ing vote* beslissende stem [of chairman, when votes are equally divided]

³cast (vb) **1** werpen, (van zich) afwerpen, uitgooien, laten vallen: [shipp] *~ adrift* losgooien; *~ ashore* op de kust werpen **2** kiezen [actors]; (de) rol(len) toedelen aan, casten **3** gieten [metals; also fig]; een afgietsel maken van

⁴cast (vb) (be)rekenen, uitrekenen, (be)cijferen, calculeren, optellen; trekken [horoscope]: *~ (up) accounts* rekeningen optellen

cast about (koortsachtig) zoeken: *~ for an excuse* koortsachtig naar een excuus zoeken

castanet castagnet

cast aside afdanken, aan de kant schuiven, laten vallen

castaway 1 schipbreukeling **2** aan land gezette schepeling

cast away 1 verwerpen, afwijzen **2** weggooien: *~ one's life* zijn leven vergooien

cast down 1 terneerslaan, droevig stemmen: *~* terneergeslagen **2** neerslaan [eyes] **3** buigen [head]

caste kaste

castellated kasteelachtig

castigate [form] **1** kastijden, tuchtigen **2** hekelen **3** corrigeren; herzien [text]

casting gietstuk^h, gietsel^h

cast iron gietijzer^h

cast-iron 1 gietijzeren **2** ijzersterk: *a ~ will* een ijzeren wil

¹castle (n) **1** kasteel^h, slot^h; burcht [also fig] **2** [chess] toren, kasteel^h || *build ~s in the air* luchtkastelen bouwen, dagdromen

²castle (vb) [chess] rokeren

¹cast off (vb) **1** van zich werpen; weggooien [clothes] **2** afdanken, aan de kant zetten

²cast off (vb) **1** [shipp] (de trossen) losgooien **2** [knitting] minderen, afhechten

cast-off afgedankt, weggegooid: *~ clothes* afdankertjes, oude kleren

castor 1 strooier, strooibus: *a set of ~s* peper-en-zoutstelletje^h, olie-en-azijnstelletje^h **2** zwenkwieltje^h; rolletje^h [of furniture]

castor oil wonderolie

castor sugar poedersuiker

cast out verstoten, verjagen, uitdrijven

castrate 1 castreren **2** ontzielen, beroven van energie **3** kuisen, zuiveren

castration 1 castratie **2** ontzieling **3** kuising, zuivering

cast up 1 doen aanspoelen, aan land werpen **2** optellen, berekenen

¹casual (n) **1** (-s) gemakkelijk zittende kleding **2** tijdelijke (arbeids)kracht

²casual (adj) **1** toevallig **2** ongeregeld, onsystematisch: ~ *labour* tijdelijk werk; ~ *labourer* los werkman **3** terloops, onwillekeurig: *a ~ glance* een vluchtige blik **4** nonchalant, ongeïnteresseerd **5** informeel: ~ *clothes* (or: *wear*) vrijetijdskleding, gemakkelijke kleren **6** oppervlakkig: *a ~ acquaintance* een oppervlakkige kennis

casualty 1 (dodelijk) ongeval[h], ongeluk[h], ramp: ~ *ward* (afdeling) eerste hulp [of hospital] **2** slachtoffer[h], gesneuvelde, gewonde: *suffer heavy casualties* zware verliezen lijden

casuistry drogreden

cat kat: *a lion is a big ~* een leeuw is een grote katachtige || *let the ~ out of the bag* uit de school klappen [esp unintentionally]; *it is raining ~s and dogs* het regent bakstenen; *play ~ and mouse (with s.o.)* kat en muis (met iem.) spelen; *(put) a ~ among the pigeons* een knuppel in het hoenderhok (werpen); *like sth. the ~ brought in* verfomfaaid; *when the ~'s away (the mice will play)* als de kat van huis is, dansen de muizen op tafel

cataclysm catastrofe; grote ramp

catacomb catacombe, (graf)kelder

¹catalogue (n) **1** catalogus **2** (was)lijst, rits, opsomming: *a whole ~ of crimes* een hele rits misdaden

²catalogue (vb) catalogiseren

catalyst katalysator [also fig]

catamaran catamaran

¹catapult (n) katapult

²catapult (vb) met een katapult (be)schieten || *the driver was ~ed through the window* de chauffeur werd door de ruit geslingerd

cataract 1 waterval **2** sterke stroomversnelling [in river] **3** grauwe staar, cataract

catastrophe catastrofe, ramp

¹catcall (n) fluitconcert[h], (afkeurend) gejoel[h]

²catcall (vb) een fluitconcert aanheffen

³catcall (vb) uitfluiten

¹catch (n) **1** het vangen, vangst, buit, aanwinst, visvangst **2** houvast[h], greep **3** hapering [of voice, breath, machine etc]; het stokken **4** [inform] addertje[h] onder het gras, luchtje[h], valstrik **5** vergrendeling, pal, klink

²catch (n) overgooien[h] [ball game]

³catch (vb) **1** vlam vatten, ontbranden **2** pakken, aanslaan: *the engine failed to ~* de motor sloeg niet aan **3** besmettelijk zijn; zich verspreiden [of disease] **4** [baseball] achtervangen, achtervanger zijn **5** klem komen te zitten, blijven haken || *~ at any opportunity* iedere gelegenheid aangrijpen

⁴catch (vb) **1** (op)vangen, pakken, grijpen: *~ fish* (or: *thieves*) vis (or: dieven) vangen; *I*

caught my thumb in the car door ik ben met mijn duim tussen het portier gekomen **2** (plotseling) stuiten op, tegen het lijf lopen **3** betrappen, verrassen: *caught in the act* op heterdaad betrapt; [iron] ~ *me!* ik kijk wel uit! **4** inhalen **5** halen [eg train, bus]; (nog) op tijd zijn voor **6** oplopen, krijgen; opdoen [illness]: ~ *(a) cold* kouvatten **7** trekken [attention etc]; wekken, vangen: ~ *s.o.'s attention* (or: *interest*) iemands aandacht trekken (or: belangstelling wekken) **8** opvangen: ~ *a glimpse of* een glimp opvangen van **9** stuiten, (plotseling) inhouden: *he caught his breath from fear* van angst stokte zijn adem **10** bevangen, overweldigen: [inform] ~ *it* de wind van voren krijgen **11** verstaan, (kunnen) volgen: *I didn't quite ~ what you said* ik verstond je niet goed

catcher vanger; [esp baseball] achtervanger

catching 1 besmettelijk **2** boeiend

catch on [inform] **1** aanslaan, het doen, ingang vinden **2** doorhebben; snappen [idea, joke]

catch out 1 betrappen **2** vangen, erin laten lopen

¹catch up (vb) **1** [inform] een achterstand wegwerken: *John had to ~ on* (or: *in*) *geography* John moest zijn aardrijkskunde ophalen **2** (weer) bij raken, (weer) op de hoogte raken

²catch up (vb) **1** oppakken, opnemen **2** ophouden, opsteken, omhoog houden

³catch up (vb) inhalen, bijkomen, gelijk komen: ~ *to s.o.*, ~ *with s.o.* iem. inhalen || *be caught up in* verwikkeld zijn in

catchword kreet, slogan

catchy 1 pakkend, boeiend **2** gemakkelijk te onthouden; goed in het gehoor liggend [of music etc]

catechism 1 catechismus **2** (godsdienst)onderwijs[h] [in the form of question and answer]; catechese

categorical categorisch, onvoorwaardelijk, absoluut

categorize categoriseren

category categorie, groep

cater maaltijden verzorgen (bij), cateren

caterer 1 cateringbedrijf[h] **2** restaurateur, cateraar, hoteleigenaar, restauranteigenaar

cater for 1 maaltijden verzorgen, cateren: *weddings and parties catered for* wij verzorgen bruiloften en partijen [of dinners etc] **2** in aanmerking nemen, overwegen, rekening houden met **3** zich richten op, bedienen, inspelen op: *a play centre catering for children* een speeltuin die vertier biedt aan kinderen

catering catering, receptieverzorging, dinerverzorging

caterpillar 1 rups **2** rupsband **3** rupsbaan

[fairground attraction]

cater to [depr] zich richten op, bedienen, inspelen op, tegemoetkomen aan: *politicians often ~ the **whims** of the voters* politici volgen vaak de grillen van de kiezers

caterwaul janken (als een krolse kat)

catfight catfight [gevecht of ruzie tussen vrouwen]

catfishing [inform] [media] neppen[h], faken[h]

cat flap kattenluik[h]

cathedral kathedraal

cathode-ray tube kathodestraalbuis, beeldbuis

catholic universeel, algemeen: *a man of ~ tastes* een man met een brede belangstelling

Catholic katholiek

Catholicism katholicisme[h]

catnap hazenslaapje[h]; dutje[h]

cat's-eye kat(ten)oog[h] [reflector]

cat suit jumpsuit, bodystocking

cattery 1 kattenpension[h] **2** kattenfokkerij

cattle (rund)vee[h]: *the ~ **are** grazing* het vee graast

catwalk 1 richel, smal looppad[h]; [shipp] loopbrug **2** lang[+h]; smal podium[h] [for fashion parades etc]; lichtbrug [in theatre]

¹Caucasian (n) **1** Kaukasiër, Kaukasische **2** blanke, lid[h] van het Indo-Europese ras

²Caucasian (adj) **1** Kaukasisch **2** blank, van het Indo-Europese ras

caucus [esp Am] **1** (besloten) partijbijeenkomst **2** (besloten) vergadering van de partijleiding

cauldron ketel, kookpot

cauliflower bloemkool

causal oorzakelijk

causality causaliteit

¹cause (n) **1** oorzaak, reden: *give ~ for* reden geven tot; *there is **no** ~ for alarm* er is geen reden voor ongerustheid **2** zaak, doel[h]: *make common ~ with s.o.* gemene zaak maken met iem. [in politics etc]; *work for a **good** ~* voor een goed doel werken

²cause (vb) veroorzaken, ertoe brengen

'cause [inform] *because*

caustic 1 brandend: *~ **soda** natronloog[+h], caustische soda **2** bijtend [also fig]; sarcastisch

¹caution (n) **1** waarschuwing **2** berisping **3** voorzichtigheid ‖ *throw* (or: *fling*) *~ to the winds* alle voorzichtigheid laten varen; *~!* voorzichtig!; [traf] let op!

²caution (vb) waarschuwen, tot voorzichtigheid manen

cautionary waarschuwend

cautious voorzichtig, op zijn hoede

cavalier 1 nonchalant, onnadenkend **2** hooghartig

cavalry 1 cavalerie; [originally] ruiterij

2 [Am] bereden strijdkrachten, lichte pantsers

¹cave (n) hol[h], grot, spelonk

²cave (vb) een holte vormen, instorten, inzakken

³cave (vb) uithollen, uithakken, indeuken

cave-dweller holbewoner

cave in 1 instorten, invallen, inzakken **2** [inform] zwichten, (onder druk) toegeven

caveman holbewoner

cavern spelonk, diepe grot, hol[h]

caviar kaviaar

cavity 1 holte, gat[h] **2** gaatje[h]: *dental ~* gaatje in tand

cavity wall spouwmuur

caw gekras[h] [of raven]

cayman kaaiman

cc *cubic centimetre(s)* cc, kubieke centimeter

CC cream *colour control cream* camouflagecrème met kleurcorrectie

CCTV *closed circuit television* televisiebewaking, bewaking d.m.v. camera's

CD 1 *Corps Diplomatique* CD[h] **2** *compact disc* cd

CD-ROM *compact disc read-only memory* cd-rom

CE *Common Era* A.D. *(Anno Domini);* na Christus: *1628 CE* 1626 A.D.

¹cease (n): *without ~* onophoudelijk

²cease (vb) ophouden, tot een eind komen, stoppen

³cease (vb) beëindigen, uitscheiden met: *~ fire!* staakt het vuren!; *~ to exist* ophouden te bestaan

cease-fire 1 order om het vuren te staken **2** staakt-het-vuren[h], bestand[h]

ceaseless [form] onafgebroken; aanhoudend

cedar ceder [tree and wood]

Ceefax teletekst

ceiling 1 plafond[h] **2** bovengrens [of wages, prices etc]; plafond[h]: *~ **price** maximum prijs **3** [aviation] hoogtegrens [of aeroplane]; plafond[h]

celebrate 1 vieren **2** opdragen: *~ mass* de mis opdragen

celebration viering, festiviteit

celebrity 1 beroemdheid, beroemd persoon **2** roem, faam

celerity [form] snelheid

celery selderie, bleekselderij

celestial 1 goddelijk, hemels mooi **2** hemels: *~ **body** hemellichaam[h]

celibate ongehuwd

cell cel, batterijcel ‖ *solar ~* zonnecel

cellar 1 kelder **2** wijnkelder

cellist cellist; cellospeler

cellophane cellofaan[h]

cellphone mobiele telefoon, gsm

cellular 1 cellulair, cellig, met cellen: *~ tissue* celweefsel[h] **2** celvormig **3** poreus

celluloid celluloid^h

Celt Kelt [inhabitant of Ireland, Wales, Cornwall, Scotland, Brittany]

¹Celtic (n) Keltisch^h [language]

²Celtic (adj) Keltisch

¹cement (n) cement^h; mortel [also fig]; band, bindende kracht

²cement (vb) cement(er)en, met cement bestrijken || ~ *a union* een verbond versterken

cemetery begraafplaats, kerkhof^h

censer wierookvat^h

¹censor (n) **1** censor **2** zedenmeester

²censor (vb) **1** censureren **2** schrappen

censorship censuur

¹censure (n) afkeuring, terechtwijzing: *a vote of ~* een motie van wantrouwen

²censure (vb) afkeuren, bekritiseren

census 1 volkstelling **2** (officiële) telling

¹cent (n) **1** cent **2** kleine munt || *per ~* percent^h

²cent 1 *centigrade* **2** *century*

centenarian honderdjarig

¹centenary (n) **1** eeuwfeest^h **2** periode van honderd jaar

²centenary (adj) honderdjarig

¹centennial (n) [Am] eeuwfeest^h

²centennial (adj) **1** honderdste, honderdjarig: *~ anniversary* eeuwfeest^h **2** honderd jaar durend

center [Am] *see* ¹centre

centigrade Celsius

centimetre centimeter

centipede duizendpoot

central 1 centraal, midden-: *~ government* centrale regering **2** belangrijkst, voornaamst: *the ~ issue* de hoofdzaak

Central African Republic Centraal-Afrikaanse Republiek

¹centralize (vb) zich concentreren, samenkomen

²centralize (vb) centraliseren, in één punt samenbrengen

¹centre (n) **1** midden^h, centrum^h; middelpunt^h [also fig]; spil, as; [pol] centrumpartij; (zenuw)centrum^h; haard [of storm, rebellion]: *~ of attraction* zwaartepunt^h; [fig] middelpunt van de belangstelling; *~ of gravity* zwaartepunt^h **2** centrum^h, instelling, bureau^h

²centre (adj) middel-, centraal

³centre (vb) zich concentreren, zich richten: *~ (a)round* als middelpunt hebben

⁴centre (vb) **1** in het midden plaatsen **2** concentreren, (in het midden) samenbrengen **3** [techn] centreren

centred 1 geconcentreerd **2** gecentreerd **3** [fig] stabiel, emotioneel in evenwicht

centrefold (meisje^h op) uitklapplaat [in magazine]

centrepiece 1 middenstuk^h [on table] **2** belangrijkste onderdeel^h

centrifugal centrifugaal, middelpuntvliedend

centrifuge centrifuge

century 1 eeuw **2** honderdtal^h

CEO *Chief Executive Officer* algemeen directeur

ceramic keramisch

ceramics keramiek, pottenbakkerskunst

cereal 1 graan(gewas)^h [edible] **2** graanproduct^h [at breakfast]; ontbijtgranen; cornflakes; muesli

cereal bar mueslireep

cerebral hersen-: *~ person* verstandsmens, cerebraal iem.

¹ceremonial (n) **1** plechtigheid **2** ritueel^h **3** ceremonieel^h, het geheel der ceremoniën

²ceremonial (adj) ceremonieel, plechtig

ceremony 1 ceremonie; [rel] rite: *master of ceremonies* ceremoniemeester **2** formaliteit, vorm: *stand (up)on ~* hechten aan de vormen; *without ~* informeel

certain 1 zeker, overtuigd: *are you ~?* weet je het zeker?; *make ~ (that)* zich ervan vergewissen (dat) **2** zeker, vaststaand: *he is ~ to come* hij komt beslist; *for ~* (vast en) zeker **3** zeker, bepaald, een of ander: *a ~ Mr Jones* ene meneer Jones **4** enig, zeker **5** sommige(n): *~ of his friends* enkele van zijn vrienden

certainly zeker, ongetwijfeld, beslist || *~ not!* nee!, onder geen beding!

certainty zekerheid, (vaststaand) feit^h, vaste overtuiging: *I can't say with any ~ if it will work* ik weet (absoluut) niet zeker of het werkt

certificate certificaat^h [law]; getuigschrift^h, legitimatiebewijs^h: *~ of birth* geboorteakte; *Certificate of Secondary Education (CSE)* middelbareschooldiploma; [roughly] mavodiploma^h; *General Certificate of Education (GCE)* middelbareschooldiploma; [roughly] havodiploma^h, [roughly] vwo-diploma^h; [since 1987] *General Certificate of Secondary Education (GCSE)* middelbareschooldiploma [roughly combination of diplomas of higher general secondary education and lower general secondary education]; *~ of marriage* (afschrift van) huwelijksakte; [roughly] trouwboekje^h

certificated gediplomeerd, bevoegd

¹certify (vb) **1** (+ to) getuigen (over/betreffende) **2** [Am] een diploma uitreiken

²certify (vb) **1** (officieel) verklaren: *the bank certified the accounts (as) correct* de bank heeft de rekening gefiatteerd **2** [Am] een certificaat verlenen aan, diplomeren **3** [inform] officieel krankzinnig verklaren: *John should be certified* ze zouden John moeten opbergen

certitude zekerheid, (vaste) overtuiging

cervical 1 hals-, nek- **2** baarmoederhals-: *~ smear* uitstrijkje^h

cervix 1 hals **2** baarmoederhals

cessation beëindiging; het staken

cesspit beerput [also fig]; poel

cf *confer* vgl., vergelijk

ch *chapter* hfst., hoofdstuk

Chad Tsjaad

¹Chadian (n) Tsjadiër, Tsjadische

²Chadian (adj) Tsjadisch

chador gezichtssluier

¹chafe (vb) **1** schuren **2** zich ergeren, ongeduldig zijn: ~ *at*, ~ *under* zich opwinden over
3 tekeergaan

²chafe (vb) **1** warm wrijven **2** schuren,
(open)schaven: *his collar ~d his neck* zijn
boord schuurde om zijn nek **3** ergeren, irriteren

chaff 1 kaf^h [also fig] **2** namaak, nep, prullaria **3** (goedmoedige) plagerij

chaffinch vink

chagrin verdriet^h, boosheid, ergernis

¹chain (n) **1** ketting; keten [also chem]: *a ~ of
office* een ambtsketen **2** reeks, serie: *a ~ of
coincidences* een reeks van toevalligheden
3 groep, maatschappij, keten: *a ~ of hotels*
(or: *shops*) een hotelketen (*or:* winkelketen)
4 bergketen **5** kordon^h **6** (-s) boeien, kete-
nen: *in ~s* geketend [also fig] || [inform] *pull*
(or: *yank*) *s.o.'s ~* iem. op de kast jagen, iem.
in de maling nemen

²chain (vb) ketenen, in de boeien slaan

chain lock kettingslot^h

chain smoker kettingroker

chain store filiaal^h (van een winkelketen)

¹chair (n) **1** stoel, zetel, zitplaats; [fig] positie; functie: *take a ~* ga zitten **2** voorzitters-
stoel, voorzitter(schap^h): *be in* (or: *take*) *the ~*
voorzitten **3** leerstoel **4** [inform] elektrische
stoel

²chair (vb) voorzitten, voorzitter zijn van: ~ *a
meeting* een vergadering voorzitten

chairman voorzitter

chairperson voorzitter, voorzitster

chalice kelk

¹chalk (n) **1** krijt(je)^h, kleurkrijt(je)^h: *a piece
of ~, a stick of ~* een krijtje; [inform] *they are
as different as ~ and cheese* ze verschillen als
dag en nacht **2** krijtstreep **3** krijttekening,
crayon

²chalk (vb) krijten, met krijt schrijven

chalk up opschrijven [on blackboard,
slate] **2** optellen (bij de score), noteren: ~
success (or: *many points*) een overwinning (or:
veel punten) boeken **3** op iemands rekening
schrijven: *chalk it up, please!* wilt u het op
mijn rekening zetten?

¹challenge (n) uitdaging, moeilijke taak,
test: *rise to the ~* de uitdaging aandurven

²challenge (vb) **1** uitdagen, tarten, op de
proef stellen: ~ *s.o. to a duel* iem. uitdagen
tot een duel **2** uitlokken, opwekken: ~ *the
imagination* de verbeelding prikkelen; ~
thought tot nadenken stemmen **3** aanroe-

pen, aanhouden: ~ *a stranger* een vreemde
staande houden **4** betwisten, in twijfel trekken **5** opeisen, vragen: ~ *attention* de aandacht opeisen

challenged [euph] gehandicapt

challenger 1 uitdager **2** betwister, bestrij-
der **3** eiser, vrager **4** mededinger [eg for po-
sition]

chamber 1 [dated] kamer, vertrek^h, slaapkamer: ~ *of horrors* gruwelkamer **2** raad,
college^h, groep: *Chamber of Deputies* huis
van afgevaardigden; *house of commerce* kamer van koophandel **3** afdeling van een
rechtbank, kamer **4** (-s) ambtsvertrekken,
kantoor^h, kabinet^h

chamberlain 1 kamerheer **2** penningmeester

chameleon kameleon^{+h} [also fig]

¹chamois (n) gems

²chamois (n) zeemleren lap

¹champ (n) [inform] *champion* kampioen

²champ (n) aardappelpuree met bosui en
boter

champagne champagne

¹champion (n) **1** kampioen, winnaar
2 voorvechter

²champion (vb) verdedigen, pleiten voor,
voorstander zijn van

championship kampioenschap^h, kampi-
oenswedstrijd

¹chance (n) **1** kans, mogelijkheid, waarschijnlijkheid: *fat ~!* weinig kans!; *give s.o. a
fighting ~ to …* iem. een eerlijke (or: serieuze) kans geven om …; *stand a ~* een redelijke kans maken; *are you Mr Buckett by
(any) ~?* bent u toevallig de heer Buckett?;
(the) ~s are that het is waarschijnlijk dat
2 toevallige gebeurtenis **3** kans, gelegenheid: *a ~ in a million* een kans van één op
duizend **4** risico^h: *take ~s, take a ~* risico's
nemen **5** het lot, de fortuin: *a game of ~* een
kansspel; *leave to ~* aan het toeval overlaten

²chance (adj) toevallig: *a ~ meeting* een toevallige ontmoeting

³chance (vb) (toevallig) gebeuren: *I ~d to be
on the same boat* ik zat toevallig op dezelfde
boot || ~ *(up)on* (toevallig) vinden

chancel koor^h [of church]

chancellery 1 kanselarij **2** kanseliersambt^h

chancellor 1 kanselier, hoofd van een
kanselarij; hoofd van een universiteit [in
England as title of honour] **2** [Am; law] president; voorzitter [of some courts of law]
3 minister van Financiën || *Chancellor of the
Exchequer* minister van Financiën

chancy [inform] gewaagd, riskant, onzeker

chandelier kroonluchter

¹change (n) **1** verandering, afwisseling, variatie: *a ~ for the better* (or: *worse*) een verandering ten goede (or: kwade); *she has had
a ~ of heart* ze is van gedachten veranderd;

for a ~ voor de afwisseling **2** verversing: *a ~ of oil* nieuwe olie **3** [traf] het overstappen **4** wisselgeld[h]: *keep the ~!* laat maar zitten! **5** kleingeld[h]: *give ~ for a banknote* een briefje wisselen ‖ *~ of life* overgang(sjaren); [inform] *get no ~ out of s.o.* geen cent wijzer worden van iem.

[2]**change** (vb) **1** veranderen, anders worden, wisselen **2** zich verkleden, andere kleren aantrekken **3** overstappen: *you have to ~ at Boxtel* u moet in Boxtel overstappen **4** [techn] schakelen: *~ down* terugschakelen; *~ into second gear* in zijn twee zetten

[3]**change** (vb) **1** veranderen, anders maken **2** (ver)ruilen, omruilen, (ver)wisselen: *~ one's clothes* zich omkleden; *~ gear* (over)schakelen; *~ oil* olie verversen **3** [fin] (om)wisselen **4** verschonen: *~ a baby* een baby een schone luier aandoen

changeable veranderlijk; wisselvallig

changeover 1 omschakeling, overschakeling, overgang **2** [sport] het wisselen

change over 1 veranderen, overgaan, omschakelen **2** ruilen (van plaats) **3** omzwaaien: *he changed over from gas to electricity* hij is overgestapt van gas naar elektriciteit

changing room kleedkamer

[1]**channel** (n) **1** kanaal[h], zee-engte: *the Channel* het Kanaal **2** (vaar)geul, bedding **3** kanaal[h], buis, pijp, goot **4** [radio, TV] kanaal[h]; [fig] net[h]; programma[h]

[2]**channel** (vb) **1** kanaliseren, voorzien van kanalen **2** leiden, sturen, in bepaalde banen leiden

channel-hop [inform] **1** [TV] zappen; kanaalzwemmen **2** tripje(s) over het Kanaal maken

Channel Islands (the) Kanaaleilanden

channel-surf [esp Am; inform] zappen; kanaalzwemmen

[1]**chant** (n) **1** lied[h], (eenvoudige) melodie, psalm **2** zangerige intonatie

[2]**chant** (vb) **1** zingen, op één toon zingen **2** roepen, herhalen

Chanukah Chanoeka[h]

chaos chaos, verwarring, wanorde

chaotic chaotisch, verward, ongeordend

[1]**chap** (n) **1** [inform] vent, kerel, knul **2** kloof(je[h]); barst(je[h]) [in lip or skin]; scheur [in soil]

[2]**chap** (vb) splijten, (doen) barsten, kloven

chapel kapel ‖ *are you church or ~?* bent u anglicaans of protestants?

chaplain 1 kapelaan, huisgeestelijke **2** veldprediker, aalmoezenier

chapter 1 hoofdstuk[h]: *give ~ and verse* [inform, fig] alle details geven, tekst en uitleg geven **2** episode, periode: *a whole ~ of accidents* een hele reeks tegenslagen **3** [rel] kapittel[h], kapittelvergadering

chapter house kapittelzaal

[1]**char** (n) **1** charlady, charwoman werkster **2** klus(je[h]), taak, (huishoudelijk) karwei(tje)[h]

[2]**char** (vb) werkster zijn

[3]**char** (vb) verbranden, verkolen, schroeien

character 1 (ken)teken[h], merkteken[h], kenmerk[h], (karakter)trek **2** teken[h], symbool[h], letter, cijfer[h] **3** persoon, type[h]; individu[h] [also depr]: *a suspicious ~* een louche figuur; *he is quite a ~* hij is me d'r eentje **4** personage[h], rol, figuur[h] **5** [inform] excentriek figuur[h] **6** karakter[h], aard, natuur: *out of ~* a) niet typisch; b) ongepast **7** schrift[h], handschrift[h], (druk)letters **8** moed

[1]**characteristic** (n) kenmerk[h], (kenmerkende) eigenschap

[2]**characteristic** (adj) kenmerkend, tekenend

characterize kenmerken, typeren

character set tekenset

charade 1 schertsvertoning **2** (-s) lettergreepraadsel[h]; hints

charcoal 1 houtskool **2** donkergrijs[h], antraciet[h], antracietkleur

[1]**charge** (n) **1** lading [also elec]; belasting **2** lading springstof, bom **3** prijs, kost(en), schuld **4** pupil, beschermeling **5** instructie, opdracht; [mil] (bevel tot de) aanval **6** [law] telastlegging, beschuldiging, aanklacht: *face a ~ of theft* terechtstaan wegens diefstal; *press ~s* een aanklacht indienen **7** zorg, hoede, leiding: *officer in ~* dienstdoend officier; *take ~ of* de leiding nemen over, zich belasten met; *in ~ of* verantwoordelijk voor

[2]**charge** (vb) **1** (aan)rekenen, in rekening brengen: *he ~d me five pounds* hij rekende mij vijf pond **2** beschuldigen, aanklagen: *~ s.o. with theft* iem. van diefstal beschuldigen **3** bevelen, opdragen

[3]**charge** (vb) **1** aanvallen, losstormen op **2** opladen, laden, vullen

charge card klantenkaart; klantenpas

charged 1 emotioneel, sterk voelend **2** geladen, omstreden: *a ~ atmosphere* een geladen atmosfeer

charging cable oplaadkabel

chariot triomfwagen, (strijd)wagen

charisma charisma[h]; uitstraling

charismatic charismatisch, inspirerend

charitable 1 menslievend, welwillend **2** liefdadig, vrijgevig **3** van een liefdadig doel: *~ institutions* liefdadige instellingen **4** mild in zijn oordeel, vergevensgezind

charity liefdadigheidsinstelling, liefdadigheid, (naasten)liefde ‖ *~ begins at home* [roughly] het hemd is nader dan de rok

charlatan charlatan, kwakzalver

[1]**charm** (n) **1** charme, bekoorlijke eigenschap, aantrekkelijkheid **2** tovermiddel[h], toverspreuk: [inform] *it works like a ~* het werkt perfect **3** amulet **4** bedeltje[h] [on bracelet]

[2]**charm** (vb) **1** betoveren, charmeren **2** be-

zweren: ~ *snakes* slangen bezweren
charming charmant, aantrekkelijk
¹chart (n) **1** kaart, zeekaart, weerkaart **2** grafiek, curve, tabel **3** (-s) hitparade
²chart (vb) in kaart brengen, een kaart maken van: ~ *a course* een koers uitzetten
¹charter (n) **1** oorkonde, (voor)recht[h] **2** handvest[h]: *the ~ of the United Nations* het handvest van de Verenigde Naties **3** (firma)-contract[h], statuten **4** het charteren, huur
²charter (vb) **1** een octrooi verlenen aan: ~ed *accountant* (beëdigd) accountant **2** charteren, (af)huren
charwoman werkster
chary 1 voorzichtig **2** verlegen **3** zuinig, karig, spaarzaam **4** kieskeurig
¹chase (n) **1** achtervolging; jacht [also sport]: *give* ~ (to) achternazitten **2** park[h], jachtveld[h] **3** (nagejaagde) prooi **4** steeplechase, wedren met hindernissen
²chase (vb) jagen, zich haasten
³chase (vb) **1** achtervolgen, achternazitten; [fig] najagen: ~ *up* opsporen **2** verjagen, verdrijven: ~ *away* (or: *out, off*) wegjagen
chaser 1 [meteorology] stormjager, tornadojager **2** [roughly] kopstoot [strong alcoholic drink]
chasm kloof, afgrond; [fig also] verschil[h]; tegenstelling
chassis chassis[h], onderstel[h], landingsgestel[h]
chaste kuis
chasten 1 kuisen, zuiveren **2** matigen
chastise kastijden, (streng) straffen
chastity kuisheid
¹chat (n) **1** babbeltje[h], praatje[h] **2** geklets[h], gebabbel[h]
²chat (vb) babbelen, kletsen, praten: ~ *away* erop los kletsen
chatline babbellijn
chat room chatroom, babbelbox
chatshow talkshow, praatprogramma[h]
¹chatter (n) **1** geklets[h] **2** geklapper[h] [of teeth]
²chatter (vb) **1** kwebbelen, (druk) praten: ~ *away* (erop los) praten **2** klapperen [of teeth]
chatterbox kletskous
chat up [inform] proberen te versieren; flirten met
¹chauffeur (n) chauffeur
²chauffeur (vb) vervoeren
chav [inform] aso, asociaal
¹cheap (adj) **1** goedkoop, voordelig: *on the* ~ voor een prikje **2** gemakkelijk **3** ordinair, grof: *a* ~ *kind of humour* flauwe grappen **4** onoprecht, oppervlakkig
²cheap (adv) **1** goedkoop, voordelig **2** vulgair, ordinair
¹cheapen (vb) goedkoop worden, in prijs dalen
²cheapen (vb) **1** goedkoop maken, goedko-

per maken, in waarde doen dalen, verlagen; [fig] afbreuk doen aan **2** afdingen op
¹cheat (n) **1** bedrog[h], afzetterij **2** bedrieger, valsspeler
²cheat (vb) **1** bedrog plegen, vals spelen **2** [inform] ontrouw zijn
³cheat (vb) **1** bedriegen, oplichten, afzetten: ~ *at exams* spieken; ~ *s.o. out of sth.* iem. iets afhandig maken **2** ontglippen (aan), ontsnappen aan
cheater bedrieger, oplichter, afzetter
¹Chechen (n) Tsjetsjeen
²Chechen (adj) Tsjetsjeens
Chechnya Tsjetsjenië
¹check (n) **1** belemmering, oponthoud[h]: *keep a ~ on s.o.*, [Am] *have one's ~s upon s.o.* iem. in de gaten houden **2** proef, test, controle **3** [Am] rekening [in restaurant] **4** kaartje[h], reçu[h], bonnetje[h] **5** ruit(je[h]), ruitpatroon[h], geruite stof **6** controle, bedwang[h]: *without* ~ ongehinderd **7** schaak[h]: ~! schaak!
²check (vb) **1** controleren, testen: ~ *(up) on sth.* iets controleren **2** (doen) stoppen, tegenhouden, afremmen **3** schaak zetten, bedreigen **4** [Am] afgeven [for safekeeping] **5** kloppen, punt voor punt overeenstemmen ‖ ~ *into a hotel* zich inschrijven in een hotel
³check [Am] *see* cheque
checkbox aanvinkvakje[h], checkbox
check card [Am] betaalpas
checked geruit, geblokt
checker 1 [Am] caissière **2** [comp] controle, checker **3** controleur
checkers [Am] damspel[h], dammen
¹check in (vb) zich inschrijven, inchecken
²check in (vb) [Am] **1** registreren, inschrijven **2** terugbrengen
checking account [Am] lopende rekening
checklist checklist, controlelijst
¹checkmate (n) schaakmat[h]
²checkmate (vb) schaakmat zetten
checkout kassa [at supermarket and the like]
check out vertrekken, zich uitschrijven: ~ *of a hotel* vertrekken uit een hotel
checkpoint controlepost
checkroom [Am] **1** bagagedepot[h] **2** garderobe [in hotel, theatre etc]
check-up (algemeen medisch) onderzoek[h]
cheddar kaas
cheek 1 wang: *turn the other* ~ de andere wang toekeren; ~ *by jowl (with)* **a)** dicht bijeen; **b)** (als) twee handen op een buik **2** brutaliteit, lef[h]
cheekbone jukbeen[h]
cheeky brutaal
cheep gefluit[h]; getjilp[h] [of birds]
¹cheer (n) **1** (juich)kreet, schreeuw: ~s hoerageroep[h]; gejuich[h] **2** aanmoediging **3** stemming, humeur[h]: *of* (or: *with*) *good* ~ welge-

moed, vrolijk **4** vrolijkheid

²cheer (vb) juichen, schreeuwen, roepen ‖ ~ *up!* kop op!

³cheer (vb) **1** toejuichen, aanmoedigen: ~ *on* aanmoedigen **2** bemoedigen: ~ *up* opvrolijken

cheerful vrolijk, blij, opgewekt

cheerio [inform] **1** dag!, tot ziens! **2** proost!

cheerleader [Am] cheerleader

cheerless troosteloos; somber

cheers 1 proost! **2** [inform] dag!, tot ziens! **3** [inform] bedankt!

cheery vrolijk; opgewekt

cheese kaas

cheeseburger hamburger met kaas

cheesecake kwarktaart

cheesy 1 kaasachtig **2** [Am; inform] goedkoop; waardeloos

cheetah jachtluipaard^h

chef chef-kok

¹chemical (n) chemisch product^h

²chemical (adj) chemisch, scheikundig

chemist 1 chemicus, scheikundige **2** apotheker **3** drogist

chemistry 1 scheikunde **2** scheikundige eigenschappen; [fig] geheimzinnige werking: *the ~ of love* de mysterieuze werking van de liefde

chemotherapy chemotherapie

cheque cheque

cheque card betaalpas(je^h), bankkaart

chequer schakeren, afwisseling brengen in; [fig] kenmerken door wisselend succes: *a ~ed life* een leven met voor- en tegenspoed

cherish koesteren, liefhebben: ~ *hopes* hoop koesteren

cherry 1 kers **2** kersenboom: *flowering ~* Japanse sierkers **3** kersenhout^h **4** kersrood^h

chess schaak^h, schaakspel^h

chessman schaakstuk^h

chest 1 borst(kas): *get sth. off one's ~* over iets zijn hart luchten **2** kist, kast, bak, doos: ~ *of drawers* ladekast

chest bump chestbump

chestnut 1 kastanje^h, kastanjeboom **2** vos(paard^h) **3** [inform] ouwe mop, bekend verhaal^h **4** kastanjebruin^h: ~ *mare* kastanjebruine merrie

¹chew (n) (tabaks)pruim^h: *a ~ of tobacco* een tabakspruim

²chew (vb) **1** kauwen, pruimen **2** [inform, also fig] herkauwen, (over)denken, bepraten: ~ *sth. over* ergens over nadenken; ~ *over sth.* iets bespreken; ~ *over* (or: *on*) *sth.* nadenken over iets

chewing gum kauwgom^{+h}

chia seed chiazaad^h

¹chic (n) chic, verfijning, stijl

²chic (adj) chic, stijlvol, elegant

chick 1 kuiken^h, (jong) vogeltje^h **2** [inform]

meisje^h, grietje^h, stuk^h **3** kind^h

¹chicken (n) **1** kuiken^h, (jong) vogeltje^h **2** kip **3** kind^h: *Mary is no ~* Mary is niet meer zo piep **4** [inform; depr] lafaard, bangerik **5** [inform] lekker stuk^h, grietje^h ‖ *count one's ~s before they are hatched* de huid verkopen voordat men de beer geschoten heeft

²chicken (adj) [inform] laf, bang

chicken out [inform] ertussenuit knijpen, bang worden

chickenpox waterpokken

chickpea kikkererwt

chicory 1 Brussels lof^h, witlof^h **2** [Am] andijvie

chide [form] berispen; afkeuren

¹chief (n) leider, aanvoerder, opperhoofd^h

²chief (adj) belangrijkst, voornaamst, hoofd-: ~ *accountant* hoofdaccountant; ~ *constable* hoofd van politie in graafschap

chiefly voornamelijk, hoofdzakelijk, vooral

chieftain 1 hoofdman [of tribe etc] **2** bendeleider

chilblain winterhanden, wintervoeten

child 1 kind^h [also fig]: *from a ~* van jongs af (aan); *with ~* zwanger, in verwachting **2** nakomeling **3** volgeling, aanhanger **4** (gees-tes)kind^h, product^h, resultaat^h

child abuse kindermishandeling

childbirth bevalling, kraambed^h

childhood jeugd, kinderjaren: *second ~* kindsheid

childish kinderachtig; kinderlijk

childminding kinderoppas, kinderopvang

child molester kinderlokker

Chile Chili

¹Chilean (n) Chileen(se)

²Chilean (adj) Chileens

¹chill (n) **1** verkoudheid, koude rilling **2** kilte, koelte, frisheid; [fig] onhartelijkheid: *cast a ~ over sth.* een domper zetten op iets

²chill (vb) **1** afkoelen, koud worden **2** chillen ‖ *~ed meat* gekoeld vlees

³chill (adj) [inform] ontspannen, chill, relaxed: *a ~ guy* een toffe gast; *see chilly*

chillax [Am; inform] doe toch eens even rustig

chilli Spaanse peper; chilipeper

chilling angstaanjagend; beangstigend

chill pill [inform] kalmeringstabletje^h [fig]: *take a ~* doe eens even rustig

chill room ontspanningsruimte

chilly 1 koel, kil, koud **2** huiverig **3** onvriendelijk, ongevoelig

chimaera hersenschim; schrikbeeld^h

¹chime (n) **1** klok, klokkenspel^h: *a ~ of bells* een klokkenspel; *ring the ~s* de klokken luiden **2** klokgelui^h **3** harmonie, overeenstemming

²chime (vb) **1** luiden, slaan: ~ *with* in overeenstemming zijn met **2** in harmonie zijn, overeenstemmen

chime in 1 overeenstemmen, instemmen: ~ *with* overeenstemmen met **2** opmerken; invallen [with a remark]; bijvallen: ~ *with* invallen met [remark]

chimney schoorsteen, rookkanaal^h

chimney-piece schoorsteenmantel

chimney sweep(er) schoorsteenveger

chimp [inform] *chimpanzee* chimpansee

chimpanzee chimpansee

chin kin ‖ [inform] *(keep your)* ~ *up!* kop op!

China 1 China: *the People's* **Republic** *of* ~ de volksrepubliek China **2** porselein^h

¹Chinese (n) Chinees, Chinese

²Chinese (adj) Chinees, uit China ‖ ~ *lantern* lampion, papieren lantaarn; ~ *wall* Chinese Muur; [fig] onoverkomelijke hindernis

Chinglish [inform] mengeling van Chinees en Engels

¹chink (n) **1** spleet, opening, gat^h: [fig] *that is the* ~ *in his armour* dat is zijn zwakke plek **2** lichtstraal [as if through a crack]; straaltje^h licht: *a* ~ *of* **light** een lichtstraal **3** kling, het rinkelen

²chink (vb) rinkelen [(as if) of metal, glass]

³chink (vb) **1** doen rinkelen [(like) metal, glass] **2** dichten, (op)vullen

chin-wag [inform] geklets^h; praatje^h

¹chip (n) **1** splintertje^h, scherf **2** fiche^h: [inform] *when the* ~*s are down* als het erop aankomt, als het menens wordt **3** friet, patat **4** (-s) [Am, Austr] chips **5** [techn] chip ‖ *have a* ~ *on one's* **shoulder** prikkelbaar zijn, lichtgeraakt zijn

²chip (vb) afbrokkelen: ~ *away at a piece of wood* hout vorm geven

³chip (vb) **1** (af)kappen, afsnijden, onderbreken, in de rede vallen: ~ *off* afbikken, afbreken **2** beitelen, beeldhouwen

chip and PIN betalen met chipkaart of pinpas, chippen en pinnen

chip in 1 (zijn steentje) bijdragen, lappen **2** opperen, onderbreken

chipmunk aardeekhoorn; wangzakeekhoorn

chipping 1 scherfje^h, stukje^h **2** bik, losse stukjes steen

chirp tjirpen, tjilpen, piepen

chirpy vrolijk; levendig [inform]; spraakzaam

¹chisel (n) beitel

²chisel (vb) beitelen: [fig] ~*led* **features** scherpe gelaatstrekken

chit 1 jong kind^h, hummel **2** [oft depr; for woman] jong ding^h **3** briefje^h, memo^h **4** rekening, bon(netje^h), cheque

chivalrous ridderlijk, galant

chivalry ridderschap^h, ridderlijkheid

chives bieslook^h

chivvy achterna zitten, (op)jagen

chlorine chloor^+h

chlorophyl(l) bladgroen^h

chock-full propvol; tjokvol

¹chocolate (n) **1** chocolaatje^h, bonbon, praline **2** chocolade: *a* **bar** *of* ~ een reep chocolade

²chocolate (adj) **1** chocoladekleurig **2** chocolade, naar chocolade smakend

¹choice (n) **1** keus, keuze, alternatief^h, voorkeur: *the colour of your* ~ de kleur van uw keuze; *a* **wide** ~ *of* een ruim assortiment aan, een ruime keuze aan; *John* **has** *no* ~ *but to come* John moet wel komen; *by* ~ **a)** bij voorkeur; **b)** bewust, uit vrije wil; *for* ~ bij voorkeur; *from* ~ graag, gewillig **2** keuzemogelijkheid, optie

²choice (adj) **1** uitgelezen: ~ *meat* kwaliteitsvlees **2** zorgvuldig gekozen [of words]

choir koor^h

choirboy koorknaap

¹choke (n) choke, gasklep

²choke (vb) (ver)stikken, naar adem snakken, zich verslikken

³choke (vb) **1** verstikken, doen stikken: ~ *a* **fire** een vuur doven **2** verstoppen **3** onderdrukken, inslikken, bedwingen

chokehold 1 [grip] nekklem **2** [fig] wurggreep

choker choker; nauwsluitende halsketting

cholera cholera

choleric zwartgallig

cholesterol cholesterol

choose 1 (uit)kiezen, selecteren: *a lot to* ~ *from* veel om uit te kiezen **2** beslissen, besluiten: *George chose not to* **come** George besloot niet te komen, George kwam liever niet **3** (ver)kiezen, willen, wensen

choos(e)y kieskeurig

¹chop (n) **1** houw, hak, slag **2** karbonade, kotelet **3** (karate)slag **4** (-s) kaken; lippen [of animals] **5** ontslag^h: *get the* ~ ontslagen worden

²chop (vb) **1** hakken, kappen, houwen **2** voortdurend veranderen [also fig]: ~ *and* **change** erg veranderlijk zijn, vaak van mening veranderen

³chop (vb) **1** hakken, kappen, houwen: ~ *down trees* bomen omhakken **2** fijnhakken, fijnsnijden: ~*ped* **liver** (fijn)gehakte lever

chopper 1 hakker, houwer **2** hakmes^h, kapmes^h **3** bijl **4** [inform] helikopter

choppy 1 met korte golfslag: ~ *sea* ruwe zee **2** veranderlijk [of wind] **3** [Am; inform] onsamenhangend [of style]; hortend

chopstick (eet)stokje^h

chop suey tjaptjoi [Chinese dish]

choral 1 koor- **2** gezongen

chord 1 snaar [also fig]: [fig] *that* **strikes** *a* ~ dat herinnert me aan iets **2** [mus] akkoord^h

chore karwei(tje)^h: *do the* ~*s* het huishouden doen

choreography choreografie

chorister koorknaap

chortle luidruchtig gegrinnik^h

chorus 1 koor^h: *answer in* ~ in koor antwoorden **2** refrein^h

chow 1 chowchow [dog] **2** [inform] eten^h, voer^h

chow-chow chowchow [dog]

chowder [esp Am] dikke (vis)soep

^1**chow down** (n) [inform] voer^h, vreten^h

^2**chow down** (vb) [inform] vreten, bikken

Christ Christus

christen 1 dopen **2** als (doop)naam geven, noemen, dopen

Christendom christenheid

christening doop

^1**Christian** (n) christen, christenmens

^2**Christian** (adj) christelijk

Christianity 1 christendom^h **2** christelijkheid

Christian name doopnaam, voornaam

Christmas Kerstmis, kerst(tijd): *the* ~ *season* het kerstseizoen

Christmas cracker knalbonbon

Christmas Eve kerstavond, avond (dag) voor Kerstmis

chrome chroom^h, chromium^h

chromium chromium^h, chroom^h

chromosome chromosoom^h

chronic 1 chronisch, slepend, langdurend; [of disease also] ongeneeslijk **2** [inform] erg, slecht, vreselijk

chronicle kroniek

chronology chronologie

chrysanth(emum) chrysant

chubby [inform] mollig; gevuld [of face]

^1**chuck** (n) **1** aaitje^h [under one's chin]; tikje^h, klopje^h **2** klem [on a lathe]

^2**chuck** (vb) **1** [inform] gooien **2** [inform] de bons geven, laten zitten **3** [inform] ophouden met, laten, opgeven: ~ *it (in)* er de brui aan geven, ermee ophouden

^1**chuckle** (n) lachje^h, gegrinnik^h, binnenpretje^h

^2**chuckle** (vb) **1** grinniken, een binnenpretje hebben **2** leedvermaak hebben

chuffed blij, tevreden

^1**chug** (n) puf, geronk^h

^2**chug** (vb) (also + along) (voort)puffen

chum 1 makker, gabber; maat [esp among boys] **2** [Am] kamergenoot

chump [inform] sukkel ‖ *go off one's* ~ stapelgek worden

chunk brok^h, stuk^h; homp [also fig]: *a* ~ *of cheese* (or: *bread*) een brok kaas, een homp brood

chunky 1 in brokken, met stukjes **2** kort en dik, gedrongen [of animals, persons]

church 1 kerk(gebouw^h): *established* ~ staatskerk **2** kerk(genootschap^h): *the Church of England* de anglicaanse kerk **3** kerk(dienst)

churchgoer kerkgang(st)er

churchyard kerkhof^h, begraafplaats

churlish boers, lomp

^1**churn** (n) **1** karn(ton) **2** melkbus

^2**churn** (vb) **1** roeren [milk or cream] **2** karnen **3** omroeren, laten schuimen ‖ [inform] ~ *out* (in grote hoeveelheden tegelijk) produceren, (in grote hoeveelheden tegelijk) afdraaien [of text]

chute 1 helling, stortkoker **2** stroomversnelling **3** [inform] parachute

chutney chutney

chutzpah gotspe, schaamteloze brutaliteit

CIA [Am] *Central Intelligence Agency* CIA

cider cider, appelwijn

cigar sigaar

cigarette sigaret

C-in-C *Commander-in-chief* opperbevelhebber

cinch [Am] [inform] makkie^h, kinderspel^h ‖ *it's a* ~ dat is een makkie

cinder sintel: ~s as

Cinderella Assepoester

cinema bioscoop, cinema

cinematic film-

cinnamon kaneel^h

cipher 1 nul **2** cijfer^h **3** sleutel [of code] **4** code, geheimschrift^h: *the message was in* ~ de boodschap was in geheimschrift

circa circa, omstreeks

circadian dagelijks terugkomend: ~ *rhythm* dag-en-nachtritme^h, 24 uursritme^h

^1**circle** (n) **1** cirkel **2** kring, ring; [archeology] kring stenen; rotonde, ringlijn, rondweg; balkon^h [in theatre]; [hockey] slagcirkel: *run round in* ~s nodeloos druk in de weer zijn **3** groep, clubje^h, kring ‖ *vicious* ~ vicieuze cirkel

^2**circle** (vb) rondcirkelen, ronddraaien, rondgaan

^3**circle** (vb) omcirkelen

circuit 1 kring, omtrek, ronde **2** (race)baan, circuit^h **3** stroomkring, schakeling **4** [sport] circuit^h ‖ *closed* ~ gesloten circuit

circuit board printplaat

circuitous omslachtig; met een omweg

^1**circular** (n) **1** rondschrijven^h, circulaire **2** rondweg

^2**circular** (adj) **1** rond, cirkelvormig: ~ *saw* cirkelzaag **2** rondlopend, rondgaand, (k)ring-: ~ *road* rondweg **3** ontwijkend, indirect ‖ ~ *letter* circulaire, rondschrijven^h

circulate (laten) circuleren, (zich) verspreiden

circulation 1 oplage **2** omloop, circulatie, distributie: *in* (or: *out of*) ~ in (or: uit) de roulatie **3** bloedsomloop

circumcision besnijdenis

circumference cirkelomtrek

circumflex accent^h circonflexe, dakje^h, kapje^h

circumscribe 1 begrenzen; beperken

2 omcirkelen **3** [geometry] omschrijven
circumspect omzichtig, op zijn hoede, voorzichtig
circumstance 1 omstandigheid, (materiële) positie, (financiële) situatie: *straitened* (or: *reduced*) ~*s* behoeftige omstandigheden; *in* (or: *under*) *the* ~*s* onder de gegeven omstandigheden **2** feit^h, geval^h, gebeurtenis **3** praal, drukte, omhaal: *pomp and* ~ pracht en praal
circumstantial 1 (afhankelijk) van de omstandigheden: ~ *evidence* indirect bewijs **2** bijkomstig, niet essentieel **3** uitvoerig, omstandig
circumvent ontwijken, omzeilen
circus 1 circus^+h **2** (rond) plein^h
CIS *Commonwealth of Independent States* GOS^h, Gemenebest^h van Onafhankelijke Staten
citadel fort^h, citadel, bolwerk^h
citation aanhaling, citaat^h
cite aanhalen, citeren: ~ *examples* voorbeelden aanhalen
citizen 1 burger, stedeling, inwoner **2** staatsburger, onderdaan: *Jeffrey is a British* ~ Jeffrey is Brits onderdaan **3** [Am] niet-militair, burger
citizenship (staats)burgerschap^h
citizenship course inburgeringscursus
citric citroen-: ~ *acid* citroenzuur^h
citrus citrus-
city (grote) stad; [fig] financieel centrum^h: *the City* de oude binnenstad van Londen
city break stedentrip
city council gemeenteraad
city hall [Am] **1** gemeentehuis^h, stadhuis^h **2** stadsbestuur^h
civic 1 burger-, burgerlijk **2** stedelijk, gemeente-: ~ *centre* bestuurscentrum, openbaar centrum
civics leer van burgerrechten en -plichten; [educ] [roughly] maatschappijleer
civil 1 burger-, burgerlijk, civiel: ~ *disobedience* burgerlijke ongehoorzaamheid; ~ *law* Romeins recht; ~ *marriage* burgerlijk huwelijk; ~ *war* burgeroorlog **2** beschaafd, beleefd **3** niet-militair, burger-: ~ *service* civiele dienst, ambtenarij ‖ ~ *engineering* weg- en waterbouwkunde
¹civilian (n) burger, niet-militair
²civilian (adj) burger-, civiel, burgerlijk
civility beleefde opmerking, beleefdheid
civilization 1 beschaving, cultuur, ontwikkeling **2** de beschaafde wereld
civilize 1 beschaven, ontwikkelen, civiliseren **2** opvoeden
civilized 1 beschaafd; ontwikkeld **2** comfortabel **3** beleefd
clad [form] gekleed; bedekt
¹claim (n) **1** aanspraak, recht^h, claim, eis: *lay* ~ *to*, *make a* ~ *to* aanspraak maken op **2** vor-

dering, claim **3** bewering, stelling
²claim (vb) een vordering indienen, een eis instellen, schadevergoeding eisen
³claim (vb) **1** opeisen, aanspraak maken op: ~ *damages* schadevergoeding eisen **2** beweren, verkondigen, stellen
¹clairvoyant (n) helderziende
²clairvoyant (adj) helderziend
¹clam (n) schelpdier^h ‖ *shut up like a* ~ geen mond open doen
²clam (vb): ~ *up* weigeren iets te zeggen
clamber opklimmen tegen, beklimmen
clammy klam, vochtig
clamorous lawaaierig, luidruchtig
¹clamour (n) **1** geschreeuw^h, getier^h **2** herrie, lawaai^h
²clamour (vb) **1** schreeuwen, lawaai maken **2** protesteren, zijn stem verheffen, aandringen: ~ *for* aandringen op
¹clamp (n) **1** klem, klamp, (klem)beugel **2** kram, (muur)anker^h
²clamp (vb) klampen, vastklemmen
clamp down (+ on) een eind maken (aan), de kop indrukken: *we're clamping down on overspending* we willen een eind maken aan de te hoge uitgaven
clam up dichtslaan, dichtklappen, weigeren iets te zeggen
clan geslacht^h, stam, familie, clan
clandestine clandestien, geheim
¹clang (n) metalige klank, galm; luiden [bell]; gekletter^h, gerinkel^h
²clang (vb) (metalig) (doen) klinken, (metalig) (doen) luiden, (metalig) (doen) rinkelen, (doen) galmen
clanger miskleun, blunder, flater: *to drop a* ~ een flater slaan, een blunder begaan
¹clap (n) klap, slag, tik, applaus^h: ~ *of thunder* donderslag
²clap (vb) **1** klappen, slaan, kloppen **2** applaudisseren
³clap (vb) **1** (stevig) plaatsen, zetten, planten, poten: ~ *s.o. in jail* iem. achter de tralies zetten **2** slaan: ~ *s.o. on the back* iem. op de rug slaan **3** klappen in, slaan in: ~ *one's hands* in de handen klappen
clapped-out 1 uitgeteld, afgedraaid **2** gammel, wrakkig
clapper 1 klepel **2** ratel
claptrap 1 holle frasen, goedkope trucs **2** onzin
clarification 1 zuivering; filtrering [liquid, air] **2** opheldering, verklaring, uitleg
¹clarify (vb) helder worden [liquid, fat, air]; [fig] verhelderen; duidelijk worden
²clarify (vb) **1** zuiveren, klaren, doen bezinken **2** ophelderen, duidelijk maken, toelichten
clarinet klarinet
clarion 1 klaroen, signaalhoorn: ~ *call* klaroengeschal^h **2** (klaroen)geschal^h

clarity helderheid, duidelijkheid

¹clash (n) **1** gevecht[h], botsing, conflict[h] **2** (wapen)gekletter[h]

²clash (vb) **1** slaags raken, botsen **2** tegenstrijdig zijn, botsen, in conflict zijn (raken) || *the party ~es with my exam* het feest valt samen met mijn examen

¹clasp (n) gesp, haak, knip

²clasp (vb) **1** vastmaken, dichthaken, vastgespen **2** vastgrijpen, vasthouden: *~ hands* elkaars hand grijpen **3** omvatten, omhelzen

clasp knife zakmes[h], knipmes[h]

¹class (n) **1** stand, (maatschappelijke) klasse **2** rang, klas(se), soort[+h], kwaliteit **3** klas, klasgenoten **4** les, lesuur[h], college[h], cursus **5** categorie, groep, verzameling; [also maths, biology] klasse: *in a ~ of its* (or: *his*) *own* een klasse apart **6** stijl, distinctie

²class (vb) plaatsen, indelen, classificeren: *~ as* beschouwen als

class A drug harddrug uit de zwaarste categorie

¹classic (n) **1** een van de klassieken: *that film is a real ~* die film is een echte klassieker **2** (-s) klassieke talen

²classic (adj) **1** klassiek, tijdloos, traditioneel **2** kenmerkend, typisch, klassiek: *a ~ example* een schoolvoorbeeld

classical 1 klassiek, traditioneel **2** antiek, uit de klassieke oudheid

classification 1 categorie, classificatie, klasse **2** rangschikking, indeling

classified 1 geheim **2** gerubriceerd: *~ ads* rubrieksadvertenties

classify 1 indelen, rubriceren, classificeren **2** geheim verklaren, als geheim aanmerken

classmate klasgenoot, klasgenote

classroom klas(lokaal[h])

classy sjiek, deftig, elegant

¹clatter (n) gekletter[h], gerammel[h], geklepper[h]

²clatter (vb) kletteren, klepperen

clause clausule, bepaling, beding[h] || [linguistics] *main ~* hoofdzin; [linguistics] *subordinate ~* bijzin

claustrophobic claustrofobisch

¹claw (n) **1** klauw **2** poot **3** schaar [of crab etc]

²claw (vb) klauwen, grissen, graaien

clay klei, leem[+h], aarde, modder

¹clean (n) schoonmaakbeurt: *give the room a ~* de kamer een (goede) beurt geven

²clean (adj) **1** schoon, helder; zuiver [air] **2** sierlijk, regelmatig, duidelijk; helder [style] **3** compleet, helemaal: *a ~ break* een radicale breuk **4** oprecht, eerlijk, sportief: *come ~* voor de draad komen (met), eerlijk bekennen **5** onschuldig, netjes, fatsoenlijk, kuis || *make a ~ breast of sth.* iets bekennen, ergens schoon schip mee maken; *wipe the slate ~* met een schone lei beginnen

³clean (vb) schoon(gemaakt) worden, zich laten reinigen

⁴clean (vb) schoonmaken, reinigen, zuiveren: *have a coat ~ed* een jas laten stomen; *~ down* schoonborstelen, schoonwassen

⁵clean (adv) **1** volkomen, helemaal, compleet: *~ forgotten* glad vergeten **2** eerlijk, fair

clean-cut duidelijk, helder: *a ~ decision* een ondubbelzinnige beslissing

cleaner 1 schoonmaker, schoonmaakster, werkster **2** schoonmaakmiddel[h], reinigingsmiddel[h] **3** (-'s) stomerij || [fig] *take s.o. to the ~'s* **a)** iem. uitkleden; **b)** de vloer met iem. aanvegen

cleaning lady schoonmaakster, hulp in de huishouding

cleanly proper, zindelijk, netjes

clean out 1 schoonvegen, uitvegen, uitmesten **2** [inform] kaal plukken, uitschudden; opkopen [stock]; afhandig maken [money]

cleanse reinigen, zuiveren; desinfecteren [wound]

clean-shaven gladgeschoren

¹clean up (vb) de boel opruimen, schoonmaken

²clean up (vb) **1** opruimen **2** (goed) schoonmaken, opknappen: *clean o.s. up* zich opknappen **3** zuiveren; [fig] uitmesten; saneren: *~ the town* de stad (van misdaad) zuiveren

clean-up schoonmaakbeurt [also fig]; sanering

¹clear (n): *be in the ~* buiten gevaar zijn, vrijuit gaan

²clear (adj) **1** helder, schoon, doorzichtig, klaar **2** duidelijk, ondubbelzinnig, uitgesproken: *make o.s. ~* duidelijk maken wat je bedoelt; *do I make myself ~?* is dat begrepen?; *send a ~ message* een duidelijk signaal afgeven **3** netto; schoon [wages, profit etc] **4** compleet, volkomen, absoluut: *a ~ majority* een duidelijke meerderheid **5** vrij, open, op een afstand, veilig, onbelemmerd: *the coast is ~* de kust is veilig || *~ conscience* zuiver geweten

³clear (vb) **1** helder worden; opklaren [of air] **2** weggaan, wegtrekken; optrekken [of fog]: *~ away* optrekken

⁴clear (vb) **1** helder maken, schoonmaken, verhelderen **2** vrijmaken; ontruimen [bldg, street]: *~ the table* de tafel afruimen **3** verwijderen, opruimen **4** zuiveren, onschuldig verklaren: *~ s.o. of suspicion* iem. van verdenking zuiveren **5** (ruim) passeren; springen over [gate]; erlangs kunnen **6** (laten) passeren [Customs]; inklaren, klaren, uitklaren **7** verrekenen; vereffenen [debt]; clearen [cheque]

⁵clear (adv) **1** duidelijk, helder: *his voice came*

through loud and ~ zijn stem kwam luid en helder door **2** op voldoende afstand, een eindje, vrij: *keep* (or: *stay, steer*) ~ *of* uit de weg gaan, (proberen te) vermijden

clearance 1 opheldering, verheldering, verduidelijking **2** ontruiming, opruiming, uitverkoop **3** vergunning, toestemming; (akte van) inklaring [ships]; [aviation] toestemming tot landen (opstijgen) **4** speling, vrije ruimte, tussenruimte: *there was only 2 ft* ~ *between* the two ships er zat maar twee voet speling tussen de twee schepen

clear-cut scherp omlijnd [also fig]; duidelijk, uitgesproken

clear-headed helder denkend, scherpzinnig

clearing 1 open(gekapte) plek [in forest] **2** verrekening, vereffening

clearly 1 duidelijk: *understand* sth. ~ iets goed begrijpen **2** ongetwijfeld

¹**clear off** (vb) [inform] de benen nemen, 'm smeren, afdruipen: ~! opgehoepeld!

²**clear off** (vb) **1** afmaken, een eind maken aan; uit de weg ruimen [arrears] **2** aflossen, afbetalen

¹**clear out** (vb) [inform] de benen nemen, ophoepelen

²**clear out** (vb) **1** uitruimen, leeghalen; uithalen [cupboard, drain]; opruimen [room] **2** [inform] uitputten; leeghalen [stocks]

clear-sighted 1 met scherpe blik [oft fig]; scherpzinnig **2** vooruitziend

¹**clear up** (vb) **1** opklaren [weather] **2** ophouden; bijtrekken [difficulties] **3** (rommel) opruimen

²**clear up** (vb) **1** opruimen; uit de weg ruimen [mess]; afmaken [work] **2** verklaren, uitleggen, ophelderen

clearway autoweg [where there is no stopping]

cleavage 1 scheiding, kloof; breuk [also fig] **2** gleuf; gootjeʰ [between breasts]; decolletéʰ, inkijk

cleave kloven, splijten, hakken, (door)klieven

cleave to [form] hangen aan: ~ *old customs* oude gewoonten trouw blijven

clef [mus] sleutel

¹**cleft** (n) **1** spleet, barst, scheur; kloof [also fig] **2** gleuf; kuiltjeʰ [in chin]

²**cleft** (adj) gespleten; gekloofd [of hoof]: ~ *palate* gespleten gehemelte

clematis clematis, bosrank

clement 1 mild, weldadig, zacht **2** genadig, welwillend

clench 1 dichtklemmen; op elkaar klemmen [jaws, teeth]; dichtknijpen: *with* ~ed *fists* met gebalde vuisten **2** vastklemmen, vastgrijpen

clergy geestelijkheid, geestelijken

clergyman geestelijke, predikant, priester

cleric geestelijke

clerical 1 geestelijk, kerkelijk **2** administratief, schrijf-: *a* ~ *job* een kantoorbaan

clerk 1 (kantoor)beambte, kantoorbediende, klerk **2** secretaris, griffier, (hoofd)administrateur **3** [Am] (winkel)bediende **4** [Am] receptionist

clever 1 knap, slim, intelligent, vernuftig: ~ *at* sth. goed in iets **2** handig

cliché gemeenplaats; clichéʰ

¹**click** (n) klik, tik, klak

²**click** (vb) **1** klikken, tikken, ratelen: [comp] ~ *on* aanklikken; doorklikken **2** [inform] het (samen) kunnen vinden, bij elkaar passen **3** [inform] op z'n plaats vallen; plotseling duidelijk worden [joke, remark]

³**click** (vb) klikken met, laten klikken

click and collect het afhalen van online bestelde goederen bij een fysieke winkel

clickbait klikaasʰ, clickbait

click farm [comp] in het aanklikken en liken van webpagina's gespecialiseerd bedrijf

clicks-and-mortar met winkel en website

click through doorklikken

client 1 cliënt **2** klant, afnemer, opdrachtgever

clientele 1 klantenkring **2** praktijk [of lawyer] **3** vaste bezoekers [of theatre, restaurant etc]

cliff steile rots, klip, klifʰ

cliff-hanger spannende wedstrijd, spannend verhaalʰ

climactic leidend tot een climax

climate 1 klimaatʰ **2** (lucht)streek **3** sfeer, stemming, klimaatʰ: *the* ***present*** *economic* ~ het huidige economische klimaat

climatic klimaat-

climax 1 hoogtepuntʰ, climax, toppuntʰ **2** orgasmeʰ

¹**climb** (n) **1** klim, beklimming **2** helling, klim, weg omhoog

²**climb** (vb) **1** omhoog gaan, klimmen, stijgen, toenemen **2** oplopen; omhooggaan [of road] **3** zich opwerken; opklimmen [rank, position]

³**climb** (vb) klimmen in (op), beklimmen, bestijgen

climber 1 klimmer, klauteraar, bergbeklimmer **2** klimplant

¹**clinch** (n) **1** vaste greep, omklemming **2** [boxing] clinch **3** omarming, omhelzing

²**clinch** (vb) **1** [boxing] (met elkaar) in de clinch gaan, lijf aan lijf staan **2** [inform] elkaar omhelzen

³**clinch** (vb) beklinken, sluiten; afmaken [agreement, transaction]: *that* ~ed *the* ***matter*** dat gaf de doorslag

cling 1 kleven, zich vasthouden, zich vastklemmen **2** dicht blijven bij, hangen, hechten **3** zich vastklampen aan, vasthouden

clinging 1 aanhankelijk, plakkerig

2 nauwsluitend [clothing etc]
clinic 1 kliniek; privékliniek **2** adviesbureau^h, consultatiebureau^h **3** groepspraktijk **4** spreekuur^h
clinical klinisch, onbewogen; zakelijk [attitude]
¹clink (n) gerinkel^h, geklink^h
²clink (vb) klinken, rinkelen, rammelen
³clink (vb) laten rinkelen; klinken met [eg glasses]
¹clip (n) **1** knippende beweging, scheerbeurt, trimbeurt **2** klem, knijper, clip **3** fragment^h, stuk^h; gedeelte^h [from film]; (video)-clip
²clip (vb) knippen, snoeien
³clip (vb) **1** (vast)klemmen, vastzetten: ~ *together* samenklemmen **2** (bij)knippen, afknippen, kort knippen, trimmen; scheren [sheep]; uitknippen [from newspaper, film] **3** afbijten [words]; inslikken [letter(s), syllable]
clip out uitknippen
clipper 1 knipper, scheerder, (be)snoeier **2** klipper(schip^h) **3** (-s) kniptang [of guard] **4** (-s) nagelkniptang **5** (-s) tondeuse
clipping krantenknipsel^h
clique kliek, club(je^h)
clitoris clitoris
¹cloak (n) **1** cape, mantel **2** bedekking, laag **3** dekmantel, verhulling
²cloak (vb) verhullen, verbergen, vermommen
cloakroom 1 garderobe **2** [euph] toilet^h
¹clobber (n) **1** boeltje^h, spullen **2** plunje, kloffie^h
²clobber (vb) **1** aftuigen, een pak rammel geven **2** in de pan hakken
¹clock (n) **1** klok, uurwerk^h **2** [inform] meter, teller, taximeter, prikklok, snelheidsmeter, kilometerteller: *the car had 100,000 miles on the* ~ de auto had 160.000 kilometer op de teller
²clock (vb) klokken [time clock]: ~ *in*, ~ *on* inklokken; *we have to* ~ *at* 8 *o'clock* wij moeten om 8 uur inklokken; ~ *off*, ~ *out* uitklokken
clockwise met de (wijzers van de) klok mee
clockwork uurwerk^h, opwindmechaniek^h: *like* ~ op rolletjes, gesmeerd
clockwork orange gerobotiseerde mens, robot
clod kluit (aarde), klomp (klei), klont
¹clog (n) klomp
²clog (vb) **1** verstopt raken, dicht gaan zitten: ~ *up* a) verstopt raken [drain pipe]; b) vastlopen [machinery] **2** stollen, samenklonteren
³clog (vb) (doen) verstoppen: ~ *up* doen verstoppen, vast laten draaien [machines]; ~*ged with* dirt totaal vervuild
cloister 1 kloostergang; kruisgang **2** kloos-

terleven^h
¹clone (n) kloon, kopie
²clone (vb) klonen: ~*d mobile phone* mobiel met een gekloonde simkaart
¹close (n) **1** einde^h, slot^h, besluit^h: *bring to a* ~ tot een eind brengen, afsluiten **2** binnenplaats, hof(je^h) **3** terrein^h [around church, school etc]
²close (adj) **1** dicht, gesloten, nauw; benauwd [space]; drukkend [weather, air] **2** bedekt, verborgen, geheim, zwijgzaam **3** beperkt, select; besloten [partnership] **4** nabij; naast [relative(s)]; intiem; dik [friend(ship)]; onmiddellijk; direct [vicinity]; getrouw; letterlijk [copy, translation]; gelijk opgaand [contest, struggle]; kort [hair, grass]: ~ *at hand* (vlak) bij de hand, dicht in de buurt; *those two* **are** *very* ~ die twee zijn erg goed bevriend; *at* ~ *range* van dichtbij; [pol, sport] *it's too* ~ *to* **call** het is een nek-aan-nekrace **5** grondig; diepgaand [attention]: *keep a* ~ *watch on s.o.* iem. scherp in de gaten houden || *a* ~ *shave* (or: *thing, call*) op het nippertje
³close (vb) aflopen, eindigen; besluiten [of speaker]
⁴close (vb) **1** dichtmaken, (af)sluiten; hechten [wound]; dichten [hole] **2** besluiten, beëindigen; (af)sluiten [argument, plea] **3** dichter bij elkaar brengen, aaneensluiten **4** afmaken, rond maken; sluiten [agreement, business]
⁵close (adv) **1** dicht, stevig **2** dicht(bij), vlak, tegen: ~ *on* *sixty years* bijna zestig jaar
closed 1 dicht, gesloten **2** besloten, select, exclusief
closed-circuit via een gesloten circuit: ~ *television, CCTV* videobewaking, bewaking d.m.v. camera's
closed-door politics achterkamertjespolitiek
close down 1 sluiten, opheffen; dichtgaan, dichtdoen [of a business] **2** sluiten [of radio and TV programmes]
closefisted gierig; vrekkig
close in 1 korter worden; korten [of days] **2** naderen, dichterbij komen: ~ *(up)on* omsingelen, insluiten [of darkness] **3** (in)vallen [of darkness]
close-knit hecht
¹closet (n) **1** (ingebouwde) kast, bergruimte **2** privévertrek^h
²closet (vb) in een privévertrek opsluiten: [fig] *he was* ~*ed with* *the headmaster* hij had een privéonderhoud met het schoolhoofd
¹close up (vb) dichtgaan [of flowers]
²close up (vb) afsluiten, blokkeren, sluiten
close-up close-up; [fig] indringende beschrijving
closure 1 het sluiten, sluiting **2** slot^h, einde^h, besluit^h
¹clot (n) **1** klonter, klont **2** [inform] stomme-

ling, idioot, ezel

²clot (vb) (doen) klonteren, (doen) stollen: *~ted cream* dikke room

cloth 1 stukʰ stof, doekʰ, lap **2** tafellakenʰ **3** stof, materiaalʰ, geweven stof **4** beroepskledij [of clergymen]; [fig] de geestelijkheid

clothe kleden, aankleden, van kleren voorzien

clothes kleding, kleren, (was)goedʰ

clothes horse droogrekʰ

clothing kleding, kledij

¹cloud (n) **1** wolk; [fig] schaduw; probleemʰ: *under a ~* uit de gratie **2** massa, menigte; zwerm [of insects] || [comp] *the ~* de cloud; *store data in the ~* data (or: gegevens) opslaan in de cloud; *every ~ has a silver lining* achter de wolken schijnt de zon

²cloud (adj) [comp] cloud-, internet-: *~ applications* cloudtoepassingen

³cloud (vb) bewolken, verduisteren; betrekken [also fig]: *the sky ~ed over* (or: *up*) het werd bewolkt

⁴cloud (vb) (zoals) met wolken bedekken, verduisteren; vertroebelen [also fig]: *~ the issue* de zaak vertroebelen

cloudburst wolkbreuk

cloud computing cloudcomputing

cloud storage [comp] het online opslaan van bestanden

cloudy bewolkt, betrokken, duister; troebel [of liquid]; beslagen; dof [of glass]; onduidelijk; verward [of memory]

¹clout (n) **1** [inform] mep, klap **2** (politieke) invloed, (politieke) macht

²clout (vb) een klap geven

clove 1 teen(tjeʰ): *a ~ of garlic* een teentje knoflook **2** kruidnagel

clover klaver || *be* (or: *live*) *in ~* leven als God in Frankrijk

cloverleaf klaverbladʰ; [also fig] verkeersknooppuntʰ

clown clown, grappenmaker, moppentapper

cloy tegenstaan: *cream ~s if you have too much of it* room gaat tegenstaan als je er te veel van eet

¹club (n) **1** knuppel, knots **2** golfstok **3** klaveren [one card] **4** clubgebouwʰ, clubhuisʰ **5** club, sociëteit, vereniging; [inform] *'I've lost my money.' 'Join the ~!'* 'Ik heb mijn geld verloren.' 'Jij ook al!'

²club (vb) een bijdrage leveren || *his friends ~bed together to buy a present* zijn vrienden hebben een potje gemaakt om een cadeautje te kopen

³club (vb) knuppelen

clubbing uitgaanʰ (naar nachtclubs): *she goes ~ every Friday* ze gaat vrijdags altijd uit

clubfoot klompvoet

club sandwich [Am] clubsandwich

clue aanwijzing, spoorʰ, hint: [inform] /

haven't (got) *a ~* ik heb geen idee

clueless stom, dom, idioot

¹clump (n) **1** groep; bosjeʰ [of trees or plants] **2** klont, brokʰ: *a ~ of mud* een modderkluit

²clump (vb) stommelen, zwaar lopen

clumsy 1 onhandig, lomp, log **2** tactloos, lomp

¹cluster (n) bos(je)ʰ, groep(jeʰ)

²cluster (vb) **1** zich groeperen **2** in bosjes groeien, in een groep groeien

³cluster (vb) bundelen, groeperen

¹clutch (n) **1** greep, klauw; [fig also] macht; controle, bezitʰ: *be in the ~es of a blackmailer* in de greep van een chanteur zijn **2** nestʰ (eieren/kuikens); [fig] stelʰ; groep, reeks **3** [techn] koppeling(spedaalʰ): *let the ~ in* koppelen

²clutch (vb) grijpen, beetgrijpen, vastgrijpen, stevig vasthouden

clutch bag enveloptasjeʰ; damestas [without handle]

¹clutter (n) rommel, warboel

²clutter (vb) **1** rommelig maken, onoverzichtelijk maken, in wanorde brengen **2** (op)vullen, volstoppen: *a sink ~ed (up) with dishes* een aanrecht bedolven onder de borden

c/o care of p/a, per adres

Co 1 company **2** county

CO commanding officer bevelvoerend officier

¹coach (n) **1** koets, staatsiekoets **2** diligence **3** spoorrijtuigʰ, spoorwagon **4** bus, reisbus: *go* (or: *travel*) *by ~* met de bus reizen **5** trainer, coach

²coach (vb) **1** in een koets vervoeren **2** trainen, coachen

coachwork koetswerkʰ, carrosserie

coagulate stremmen; stollen

coal 1 steenkool **2** houtskool || *carry* (or: *take*) *~s to Newcastle* water naar de zee dragen; *haul s.o. over the ~s* iem. de les lezen

coalescence samensmelting, samenvoeging

coalition [pol] coalitie, unie, verbondʰ

coalmine kolenmijn

coal pit kolenmijn

coal tit zwarte mees

coarse grof, ruw, ordinair, plat

¹coast (n) kust

²coast (vb) **1** freewheelen, met de motor in de vrijloop rijden **2** [fig] zonder inspanning vooruitkomen, zich (doelloos) laten voortdrijven, zich niet inspannen: *~ to victory* op zijn sloffen winnen

coastal kust-

coaster 1 kustbewoner **2** kustvaarder, coaster **3** onderzetter, bierviltjeʰ

coastguard 1 kustwachter **2** kustwacht

coastline kustlijn

¹coat (n) **1** (over)jas, mantel, jasje^h **2** vacht, beharing, verenkleed^h **3** schil, dop, rok **4** laag, deklaag: ~ *of paint* (or: *dust*) verflaag, stoflaag ‖ ~ *of arms* wapenschild^h, familiewapen^h; ~ *of mail* maliënkolder

²coat (vb) een laag geven, met een laag bedekken

coating laag, deklaag

coat-tails slippen^h ‖ *ride* on the ~ *of* meerijden op het succes van

co-author medeauteur

coax vleien, overreden, overhalen: *the police ~ed the public away from the place of the accident* de politie verwijderde het publiek met zachte hand van de plaats van het ongeluk

coaxial: ~ *cable* coaxiale kabel; coaxkabel

cob 1 mannetjeszwaan **2** maiskolf [without the corn]

cobalt 1 kobalt^h **2** kobaltblauw^h, ultramarijn^h

¹cobble (n) kei, kinderkopje^h, kassei

²cobble (vb) bestraten (met keien), plaveien ‖ ~ *together* in elkaar flansen

cobbler schoenmaker

cobra cobra, brilslang

cobweb 1 spinnenweb^h; web^h [also fig] **2** spinrag^h **3** ragfijn weefsel^h [also fig] ‖ *blow the ~s away* de dufheid verdrijven

cocaine cocaïne

cochineal cochenille [red paint]

¹cock (n) **1** haan; [fig] kemphaan **2** mannetje^h [of birds]; mannetjes- **3** [inform] makker, maat, ouwe jongen **4** kraan, tap **5** [vulg] lul, pik **6** haan [of firearms]: *go off at half ~* a) voortijdig beginnen; b) mislukken (door overijld handelen)

²cock (vb) **1** overeind (doen) staan: ~ *the ears* de oren spitsen **2** spannen [cock of firearm] **3** scheef (op)zetten

cock-a-doodle-doo kukeleku^h

cock-and-bull story sterk verhaal^h, kletsverhaal^h

cockeyed [inform] **1** scheef; schuin **2** onzinnig

cockle kokkel ‖ *it warms the ~s of my heart* dat doet mijn hart goed

Cockney 1 cockney [inhabitant] **2** Cockneydialect^h

cockpit 1 cockpit, stuurhut **2** vechtplaats voor hanen; [fig] slagveld^h **3** [shipp] kuip

cockroach kakkerlak

cocktail cocktail

cock up 1 oprichten, spitsen: ~ *one's ears* de oren spitsen **2** [inform] in de war sturen, in het honderd laten lopen

cock-up [inform] puinhoop, klerezooi

cocky brutaal en verwaand

cocoa 1 warme chocola **2** cacao(poeder^h)

coconut 1 kokosnoot **2** kokos(vlees^h)

¹cocoon (n) **1** cocon, pop **2** overtrek^+h, (beschermend) omhulsel^h

²cocoon (vb) (zich) verpoppen: ~*ed from the outside world* afgeschermd van de buitenwereld; *be ~ed in* een beschermd leven leiden in

cod kabeljauw

COD *cash on delivery, (Am) collect on delivery* betaling bij aflevering, levering onder rembours

coddle 1 zacht koken **2** vertroetelen, verwennen

code 1 code **2** gedragslijn: ~ *of honour* erecode **3** wetboek^h

codify codificeren, schriftelijk vastleggen

co-driver bijrijder

codswallop nonsens, onzin

coed [Am; inform] studente

coeducation gemengd onderwijs^h

coerce 1 dwingen: ~ *s.o. into doing sth.* iem. dwingen iets te doen **2** afdwingen **3** onderdrukken

coercion dwang

coexist co-existeren; (vreedzaam) naast elkaar bestaan

coexistence co-existentie, het (vreedzaam) naast elkaar bestaan

C of E *Church of England* anglicaanse kerk

coffee koffie

coffee shop coffeeshop: *Dutch ~ coffeeshop*

coffer 1 koffer, (geld)kist, brandkast **2** (-s) schatkist; [inform] fondsen

coffin (dood)kist

cog tand(je^h) [of wheel] ‖ [fig, inform] *a ~ in the machine* (or: *wheel*) een klein radertje in een grote onderneming

cogent overtuigend

cognac cognac

cognition 1 kenvermogen^h; het kennen **2** waarneming

cognizance 1 kennis(neming), nota **2** gerechtelijk onderzoek^h

cogwheel tandrad^h

cohabit samenwonen: ~*ing agreement* samenlevingscontract

cohere 1 nauw samenwerken **2** (logisch) samenhangen; coherent zijn

coherence samenhang

coherent samenhangend, begrijpelijk

cohesion (onderlinge) samenhang

¹coil (n) **1** tros [of rope, cable] **2** winding, wikkeling **3** vlecht **4** [elec] spoel **5** [med] spiraaltje^h ‖ *this mortal ~* dit aardse ongerief

²coil (vb) (zich) kronkelen, (op)rollen

¹coin (n) **1** munt(stuk^h), geldstuk^h: *toss* (or: *flip*) *a ~* kruis of munt gooien, tossen **2** gemunt geld^h

²coin (vb) **1** munten; slaan [money] **2** verzinnen, uitvinden: ~ *a word* een woord verzinnen

coinage 1 munt(stelsel^h) **2** munten **3** neologisme^h

coincide 1 (+ with) samenvallen (met) **2** (+

with) overeenstemmen (met), identiek zijn
coïncidence 1 het samenvallen, samenloop (van omstandigheden): *a mere* ~ puur
toeval **2** overeenstemming
coitus [form] coïtus; geslachtsdaad
coke 1 cokes **2** coca-cola **3** [inform] cocaïne
Col *Colonel* kol., kolonel
colander vergiet^h
¹cold (n) **1** verkoudheid: *catch (a)* ~ kouvatten **2** kou ‖ *she was **left** out in the* ~ ze was
aan haar lot overgelaten
²cold (adj) koud, koel; [fig] onvriendelijk: *a* ~
fish een kouwe kikker; [inform] ~ *sweat* het
angstzweet; *it **leaves** me* ~ het laat me koud ‖
~ *comfort* schrale troost; *get* (or: *have*) ~ *feet*
bang worden (or: zijn); [fig] *put sth. in(to)* ~
storage iets in de ijskast zetten; *make s.o.'s
blood **run*** ~ iem. het bloed in de aderen doen
stollen
³cold (adv) **1** in koude toestand **2** [inform]
volledig, compleet: ~ *sober* broodnuchter; *be
turned down* ~ zonder meer afgewezen
worden
cold call verkopen via telefoon; telemarketing bedrijven
cold case onopgelost misdrijf^h, cold case
cold-eyed [look] ijskoud, emotieloos
coldshoulder [inform] de rug toekeren;
negeren
cold sore koortslip
coleslaw koolsalade
colic koliek^{+h}
collaborate 1 samenwerken, medewerken **2** collaboreren; heulen [with enemy]
collaboration 1 samenwerking **2** collaboratie [with the occupier(s)]
collagen collageen^h
¹collapse (n) **1** in(een)storting, in(een)-
zakking **2** val, ondergang **3** inzinking, ver-
val^h van krachten **4** mislukking, fiasco^h
²collapse (vb) **1** in(een)storten, in(een)val-
len, in elkaar zakken **2** opvouwbaar zijn
3 bezwijken **4** mislukken
³collapse (vb) **1** in(een) doen storten, in-
(een) doen vallen, in elkaar doen zakken
2 opvouwen, samenvouwen
collapsible opvouwbaar, inschuifbaar, in-
klapbaar, opklapbaar
¹collar (n) **1** kraag, halskraag **2** boord(je^h),
halsboord^h **3** halsband, halsring **4** halsket-
ting, halssnoer^h **5** gareel^h; haam^h [of horse]
²collar (vb) [inform] in de kraag grijpen, in-
rekenen
collarbone sleutelbeen^h
¹collateral (n) zakelijk onderpand^h
²collateral (adj) **1** bijkomstig; ondergeschikt **2** samengaand; bijkomend: ~ *damage*
nevenschade
colleague collega
¹collect (adj) [Am] te betalen door opgeroepene [telephone]: *a* ~ *call* een telefoonge-

sprek voor rekening van de opgeroepene;
call me ~ bel me maar op mijn kosten
²collect (vb) **1** zich verzamelen **2** [inform]
geld ontvangen
³collect (vb) **1** verzamelen **2** innen, incasseren, collecteren **3** (weer) onder controle krijgen: ~ *one's **thoughts*** (or: *ideas*) zijn gedachten bijeenrapen; ~ *o.s.* zijn zelfbeheersing
terugkrijgen **4** afhalen, ophalen
¹collectable (n) verzamelobject^h
²collectable (adj) gewild
collected kalm, bedaard, beheerst
collection 1 verzameling, collectie **2** collecte, inzameling **3** buslichting **4** het verzamelen, het inzamelen, de incassering **5** in-
casso^h, inning
¹collective (n) **1** groep, gemeenschap, col-
lectief^h **2** gemeenschappelijke onderneming, collectief landbouwbedrijf^h
²collective (adj) gezamenlijk, gemeenschappelijk, collectief
collector 1 verzamelaar **2** collecteur [of
public funds]; ontvanger (der belasting), in-
zamelaar **3** collectant
college 1 hogere beroepsschool, academie;
instituut^h **2** college^h **3** [Am] (kleine) universiteit **4** grote kostschool **5** universiteitsge-
bouw^h, universiteitsgebouwen, schoolge-
bouw^h, schoolgebouwen **6** raad
collegiate 1 behorend tot een college,
universiteit **2** bestaande uit verschillende
autonome afdelingen [of university]
collide botsen, aanrijden, aanvaren; [fig] in
botsing komen
collision botsing, aanrijding, aanvaring;
[fig also] conflict^h
collision course ramkoers [also fig]
colloquial tot de spreektaal behorend, informeel
colloquialism 1 alledaagse uitdrukking
2 informele stijl
collude [form] samenzweren; samenspannen
collywobbles (the) [inform] buikpijn [also
fig]
Cologne Keulen
Colombia Colombia
¹Colombian (n) Colombiaan(se)
²Colombian (adj) Colombiaans
colon 1 dubbelepunt **2** karteldarm
colonel kolonel
¹colonial (n) koloniaal
²colonial (adj) koloniaal, van de koloniën
colonialism kolonialisme^h, koloniaal stel-
sel^h
colonist kolonist
¹colonize (vb) een kolonie vormen
²colonize (vb) koloniseren
colonnade zuilenrij, zuilengalerij
colony kolonie [also biology]
colossal 1 kolossaal, reusachtig, enorm

2 [inform] geweldig, prachtig, groots
colossus kolos [also fig]
¹colour (n) **1** kleur: *loud ~s* opvallende kleuren; [fig] *paint in glowing ~s* zeer enthousiast beschrijven **2** kleurtjeʰ, gelaatskleur: *have little ~* er bleekjes uitzien; *change ~* van kleur verschieten **3** donkere of getinte huidskleur: *people of ~* mensen met een donkere of getinte huidskleur, mensen van kleur **4** soort⁺ʰ, aard, slagʰ **5** (-s) nationale vlag, vaandelʰ **6** clubkleuren, insigneʰ, lintʰ ||
with flying ~s met vlag en wimpel; *give* (or: *lend*) *~ to* geloofwaardiger maken; [inform] *show* one's *(true) ~s* zijn ware gedaante tonen; *feel* (or: *look*) *off ~* zich niet lekker voelen
²colour (vb) **1** kleur krijgen, kleuren **2** blozen, rood worden: *~ up* blozen
³colour (vb) **1** kleuren, verven **2** vermommen **3** verkeerd voorstellen, verdraaien **4** beïnvloeden
colour-blind kleurenblind
coloured 1 gekleurd **2** niet-blank, zwart: *a ~ person* iem. met een donkere huidskleur
colouring 1 verf(stof), kleur(stof) **2** kleuring **3** (gezonde) gelaatskleur
colt 1 veulenʰ, jonge hengst **2** [inform; sport] beginneling, jonge speler
column 1 zuil, pilaar, pijler: *~ of smoke* rookzuil **2** kolom: *the advertising ~s* de advertentiekolommen **3** [mil] colonne
columnist columnist(e)
coma comaʰ
¹comb (n) **1** kam [also of cock etc] **2** honingraat
²comb (vb) **1** kammen **2** [inform] doorzoeken, uitkammen
¹combat (n) strijd, gevechtʰ
²combat (vb) vechten (tegen), (be)strijden
combats combatbroek
combination 1 combinatie, vereniging, verbinding: *in ~ with* samen met, in combinatie met **2** (geheime letter)combinatie **3** samenstelling
¹combine (n) maaidorser, combine
²combine (vb) **1** zich verenigen, zich verbinden **2** samenwerken **3** [chem] zich verbinden
³combine (vb) **1** combineren, verenigen, verbinden, samenvoegen: *~d operations* (or: *exercises*) legeroefeningen waarbij land-, lucht- en zeemacht samenwerken **2** in zich verenigen
comb out [inform] **1** uitkammen, doorzoeken **2** zuiveren, schiften **3** verwijderen; afvoeren [redundant staff]
¹combustible (n) brandstof, brandbare stof
²combustible (adj) **1** (ver)brandbaar, ontvlambaar **2** opvliegend, lichtgeraakt
combustion verbranding: *spontaneous ~* zelfontbranding

come 1 komen, naderen: *in the years to ~* in de komende jaren; *she came running* ze kwam aanrennen; *~ and go* heen en weer lopen; [fig] komen en gaan **2** aankomen, arriveren: *the goods* have *~* de goederen zijn aangekomen; *the train is coming* de trein komt eraan; *I'm coming!* ik kom eraan!; *first ~, first served* die eerst komt, eerst maalt **3** beschikbaar zijn, verkrijgbaar zijn, aangeboden worden: *this suit ~s in two sizes* dit pak is verkrijgbaar in twee maten **4** verschijnen: *that news came as a surprise* dat nieuws kwam als een verrassing **5** meegaan: *are you coming?* kom je mee? **6** gebeuren: *~ what may* wat er ook moge gebeuren; *(now that I) ~ to think of it* nu ik eraan denk; [inform] *how ~?* hoe komt dat?, waarom? **7** staan, komen, gaan: *my job ~s before everything else* mijn baan gaat vóór alles **8** zijn: *it ~s cheaper by the dozen* het is goedkoper per dozijn **9** beginnen, gaan, worden: *the buttons* came *unfastened* de knopen raakten los; *~ to believe* tot de overtuiging komen; *~ to know s.o. better* iem. beter leren kennen **10** (een bepaalde) vorm aannemen || *the life to ~* het leven in het hiernamaals; [inform] *he'll be eighteen ~ September* hij wordt achttien in september; *she doesn't know whether she is coming or going* ze is de kluts kwijt; *~ now!* komkom!, zachtjes aan!
come about gebeuren: *how did the accident ~?* hoe is het ongeluk gebeurd?
¹come across (vb) **1** overkomen [of intention, joke etc]; begrepen worden: *his speech didn't ~ very well* zijn toespraak sloeg niet erg aan **2** [inform] lijken te zijn, overkomen (als): *he comes across to me as quite a nice fellow* hij lijkt me wel een aardige kerel
²come across (vb) aantreffen, vinden, stoten op: *I came across an old friend* ik liep een oude vriend tegen het lijf
come after 1 volgen, komen na, later komen **2** [inform] (achter iem.) aanzitten
come again 1 terugkomen, teruggaan **2** [inform] iets herhalen, iets nog eens zeggen: *~?* zeg 't nog eens
come along 1 meekomen, meegaan **2** opschieten, vooruitkomen: *how is your work coming along?* schiet je op met je werk?; *~!* vooruit! schiet op! **3** zich voordoen, gebeuren: *take every opportunity that comes along* elke kans grijpen die zich voordoet **4** zijn best doen: *~!* komaan!
come apart uit elkaar vallen, losgaan, uit elkaar gaan
come at 1 komen bij, er bij kunnen, te pakken krijgen **2** bereiken, toegang krijgen tot: *the truth is often difficult to ~* het is vaak moeilijk de waarheid te achterhalen **3** er op losgaan, aanvallen: *he came at me with a knife* hij viel me aan met een mes

come aw<u>ay</u> 1 losgaan, loslaten **2** heengaan, weggaan, ervandaan komen
c<u>o</u>meback comeback, terugkeer: *stage* (or: *make, attempt*) *a* ~ een comeback (proberen te) maken
come b<u>a</u>ck 1 terugkomen, terugkeren, een comeback maken **2** weer in de mode komen, weer populair worden **3** weer te binnen schieten: *it'll* ~ *to me in a minute* het schiet me zo wel weer te binnen
c<u>o</u>me between tussenbeide komen, zich bemoeien met
c<u>o</u>me by 1 krijgen, komen aan: *jobs are hard to* ~ werk is moeilijk te vinden **2** oplopen [disease, wound etc]; vinden, tegen het lijf lopen **3** voorbijkomen, passeren
com<u>e</u>dian 1 (blijspel)acteur; komediant [also fig] **2** blijspelauteur **3** komiek
c<u>o</u>medown [inform] **1** val, vernedering, achteruitgang **2** tegenvaller
come d<u>o</u>wn 1 neerkomen, naar beneden komen: [fig] ~ *in the world* aan lagerwal raken **2** overgeleverd worden [of tradition etc] **3** dalen [also of aeroplane]; zakken; lager worden [of price] **4** <u>o</u>verkomen
come d<u>o</u>wn on 1 neerkomen op, toespringen (op), overvallen **2** straffen **3** [inform] krachtig eisen **4** [inform] berispen, uitschelden, uitvaren tegen: *he came down on me like a* **ton** *of bricks* hij verpletterde me onder zijn kritiek
come d<u>o</u>wn to [inform, fig] neerkomen op: *the problem comes down to this* het probleem komt hierop neer
c<u>o</u>medy 1 blijspel[h], komedie **2** humor
c<u>o</u>me from 1 komen uit, afstammen van **2** het resultaat zijn van: *that's what comes from lying to people* dat komt ervan als je liegt tegen mensen
come <u>i</u>n 1 binnenkomen **2** aankomen: *he came in* **second** hij kwam als tweede binnen **3** in de mode komen, de mode worden **4** deelnemen, een plaats vinden: *this is* **where** *you* ~ hier kom jij aan de beurt, hier begint jouw rol **5** voordeel hebben: **where** *do I* ~*?* wat levert het voor mij op? **6** beginnen, aan de beurt komen: *this is* **where** *we* ~ hier begint voor ons het verhaal **7** opkomen; rijzen [of tide] **8** binnenkomen, in ontvangst genomen worden; verkregen worden [of money] **9** dienen, nut hebben: ~ **handy** (or: *useful*) goed van pas komen
come <u>i</u>n for 1 krijgen, ontvangen: ~ *a fortune* een fortuin krijgen **2** het voorwerp zijn van, uitlokken: ~ *a great deal of* **criticism** heel wat kritiek uitlokken
c<u>o</u>me into 1 (ver)krijgen, verwerven, in het bezit komen van: ~ *a fortune* een fortuin erven; ~ *s.o.'s possession* in iemands bezit komen **2** komen in: ~ *blossom* (or: *flower*) beginnen te bloeien; ~ **fashion** in de mode ko-

men **3** binnenkomen
c<u>o</u>mely aantrekkelijk, knap
c<u>o</u>me of 1 komen uit, afstammen van: *he comes of noble* **ancestors** hij stamt uit een nobel geslacht **2** het resultaat zijn van: *that's what comes of being late* dat komt ervan als je te laat bent; *nothing came of* **it** er kwam niets van terecht, het is nooit iets geworden
come <u>o</u>ff 1 loslaten [eg of wallpaper from the wall]; losgaan **2** er afkomen, er afbrengen: ~ **badly** het er slecht van afbrengen **3** lukken, goed aflopen **4** plaatshebben: *Henry's birthday party didn't* ~ Henry's verjaardagsfeestje ging niet door **5** afkomen van, loslaten, verlaten: *has this button* ~ *your coat?* komt deze knoop van jouw jas? **6** afgaan [of price]: *that'll* ~ *your paycheck* dat zal van jouw salaris worden afgetrokken ‖ [inform] *oh,* ~ *it!* schei uit!
come <u>o</u>n 1 naderbij komen, oprukken, (blijven) komen: *I'll* ~ *later* ik kom je wel achterna **2** opschieten, vooruitkomen **3** beginnen; opkomen [of thunderstorm]; vallen [of night]; aangaan [of light]; beginnen (te ontstaan) [of disease etc]: *I've got a cold coming on* ik heb een opkomende verkoudheid **4** op de tv komen **5** opkomen [of actor] **6** beter worden, herstellen; opknappen [of disease] **7** [Am] een grote indruk maken; <u>o</u>verkomen [on TV, radio] **8** aantreffen, stoten op **9** treffen [of sth. undesirable]; overvallen: *the disease came on her suddenly* de ziekte trof haar plotseling ‖ *oh* ~*!* hou toch op!, schei toch uit!
c<u>o</u>me-on [inform] **1** lokmiddel[h], verlokking **2** [Am; inform] uitnodiging, invitatie ‖ [inform] *she* **gave** *me the* ~ *as soon as her husband had left* zodra haar man weg was, begon ze avances te maken
come <u>o</u>ut 1 uitkomen, naar buiten komen: *Lucy came out in the* **top three** Lucy eindigde bij de eerste drie **2** staken, in staking gaan **3** verschijnen, tevoorschijn komen; gepubliceerd worden [of book]; uitlopen, bloeien [of plants, trees]; doorkomen [of sun]: ~ **with** *the truth* met de waarheid voor de dag komen **4** ontdekt worden **5** duidelijk worden, goed uitkomen; er goed op staan [photo] **6** verdwijnen, verschieten; verbleken [of colour]; uitvallen [of hair, teeth] **7** zich voor (tegen) iets verklaren: *the Government came out strong(ly)* **against** *the invasion* de regering protesteerde krachtig tegen de invasie **8** verwijderd worden; er uitgaan [of stain] **9** uitkomen, kloppen; juist zijn [of bill] **10** openlijk uitkomen voor [sexual inclination] ‖ ~ **badly** (or: *well*) het er slecht (*or:* goed) afbrengen; ~ **right** (or: *wrong*) goed (*or:* slecht) aflopen; ~ **for** *s.o.* (*sth.*) iem. (iets) zijn steun toezeggen
come <u>o</u>ver 1 <u>o</u>verkomen, komen over,

oversteken **2** (naar een andere partij) over-lopen **3** langskomen, bezoeken **4** inslaan, <u>o</u>verkomen, aanslaan **5** worden, zich voelen: ~ *dizzy* zich duizelig voelen **6** overk<u>o</u>men, bekruipen: *a strange feeling came over her* een vreemd gevoel bekroop haar; *what has* ~ *you?* wat bezielt je?

come r<u>ou</u>nd [Am] **1** aanlopen, langsko-men, bezoeken **2** bijkomen, weer bij zijn positieven komen **3** overgaan, bijdraaien: *Jim has* ~ Jim heeft het geaccepteerd **4** te-rugkomen, (regelmatig) terugkeren **5** een geschil bijleggen **6** een omweg maken **7** bij-trekken [after angry mood]: *Sue'll soon* ~ Sue komt vast gauw in een beter humeur

com<u>e</u>stible eetbaar

c<u>o</u>met komeet

come thr<u>ou</u>gh 1 doorkomen, overkomen: *the message isn't coming through clearly* het bericht komt niet goed door **2** overleven, te boven komen; doorstaan [disease etc] **3** [Am] slagen, lukken, de bestemming be-reiken **4** [inform] doen als verwacht, over de brug komen

c<u>o</u>me to 1 bijkomen, weer bij zijn positie-ven komen **2** betreffen, aankomen op: *when it comes to speaking clearly* wat duidelijk spre-ken betreft **3** komen tot (aan), komen bij: ~ *an* **agreement** het eens worden; ~ *s.o.'s* **aid** iem. te hulp komen **4** bedragen, (neer)ko-men op: ~ *the same* **thing** op hetzelfde neer-komen **5** te binnen schieten, komen op **6** toekomen, ten deel vallen, gegeven wor-den: *it comes* **naturally** *to him,* [inform] *it comes natural to him* het gaat hem makkelijk af **7** overk<u>o</u>men: *I hope no* **harm** *will* ~ *you* ik hoop dat je niets kwaads overkomt ‖ *he'll never* ~ **anything** er zal nooit iets van hem worden; *he had it coming to* **him** hij kreeg zijn verdiende loon; ~ **nothing** op niets uitdraai-en; *we never thought things would* ~ **this!** we hadden nooit gedacht dat het zo ver zou komen!

come <u>u</u>p 1 uitkomen, kiemen **2** aan de orde komen, ter sprake komen **3** gebeuren, v<u>oo</u>rkomen, zich voordoen **4** vooruitkomen: ~ *in the* **world** vooruitkomen in de wereld **5** [inform] uitkomen, getrokken worden: *I hope my number will* ~ *this time* ik hoop dat mijn lotnummer deze keer wint ‖ ~ **against** in conflict komen met; *our holiday didn't* ~ **to** *our expectations* onze vakantie viel tegen; [inform] *you'll have to* ~ **with** *sth.* better je zult met iets beters moeten komen

come up<u>o</u>n 1 overvallen, overrompelen, komen over **2** aantreffen, stoten op, tegen het lijf lopen

come<u>u</u>ppance [inform] verdiende loon: *get* one's ~ zijn verdiende loon krijgen

¹c<u>o</u>mfort (n) **1** troost, steun, bemoediging: *derive* (or: *take*) ~ *from sth.* troost putten uit

iets **2** comfort<u>h</u>, gemak<u>h</u> **3** welstand, welge-steldheid: *live in* ~ welgesteld zijn

²c<u>o</u>mfort (vb) troosten, bemoedigen

c<u>o</u>mfortable 1 aangenaam, gemakkelijk: *feel* ~ zich goed voelen **2** royaal, vorstelijk **3** rustig, zonder pijn: *have a* ~ **night** een rus-tige nacht hebben **4** welgesteld: *live in* ~ **cir-cumstances** in goeden doen zijn

c<u>o</u>mforter 1 trooster, steun **2** fopspeen

c<u>o</u>mfort food comfortfood<u>h</u>, troosteten<u>h</u>

c<u>o</u>mfortless 1 troosteloos; somber **2** on-gerieflijk

c<u>o</u>mfort stop [inform] plaspauze, sanitaire stop

c<u>o</u>mfort z<u>o</u>ne: *to be* **out of** one's ~ zich on-gemakkelijk voelen

c<u>o</u>mfy [inform] aangenaam; behaaglijk

¹c<u>o</u>mic (n) **1** komiek, grappenmaker **2** (-s) stripboek<u>h</u>, strippagina

²c<u>o</u>mic (adj) **1** grappig, komisch: ~ **relief** vro-lijke noot **2** blijspel-

com<u>i</u>cal [inform] **1** grappig, komisch **2** blijspel-

c<u>o</u>mic strip strip(verhaal<u>h</u>)

¹c<u>o</u>ming (n) komst: *the* ~s *and* **goings** het komen en gaan

²c<u>o</u>ming (adj) **1** toekomstig, komend, aan-staand: *the* ~ **week** volgende week **2** [in-form] veelbelovend, in opkomst

c<u>o</u>ming <u>ou</u>t coming-out, het uit de kast komen

c<u>o</u>mma 1 komma<u>+h</u> **2** cesuur ‖ *inverted* ~s aanhalingstekens

¹comm<u>a</u>nd (n) **1** commando<u>h</u>, leiding, mili-tair gezag<u>h</u>: *be* **in** ~ *of the situation* de zaak onder controle hebben **2** bevel<u>h</u>, order, ge-bod<u>h</u>, opdracht **3** legeronderdeel<u>h</u>, comman-do<u>h</u>, legerdistrict<u>h</u> **4** beheersing, controle, meesterschap<u>h</u>: *have (a) good* ~ *of a language* een taal goed beheersen

²comm<u>a</u>nd (vb) **1** bevelen geven **2** het be-vel voeren

³comm<u>a</u>nd (vb) **1** bevelen, commanderen **2** het bevel voeren over **3** beheersen: ~ *o.s.* zich beheersen **4** bestrijken, overzien: *this hill* ~s *a fine* **view** vanaf deze heuvel heeft men een prachtig uitzicht **5** afdwingen: ~ *respect* eerbied afdwingen

command<u>a</u>nt commandant, bevelvoerend officier

comm<u>a</u>nder 1 bevelhebber, commandant; [shipp] gezagvoerder: ~ *in* **chief** opperbevel-hebber **2** [shipp] kapitein-luitenant-ter-zee **3** commandeur [of knighthood]

comm<u>a</u>nding 1 bevelvoerend, bevelend **2** indrukwekkend, imponerend

comm<u>a</u>ndment 1 bevel<u>h</u>, order, gebod<u>h</u> **2** bevelschrift<u>h</u> **3** [rel] gebod<u>h</u>: *the* **Ten** *Com-mandments* de tien geboden

comm<u>a</u>ndo [mil] commando<u>h</u>, stoottroep, stoottroeper

commemorate herdenken, gedenken, vieren

commence beginnen

commencement beginʰ, aanvang

commend 1 toevertrouwen, opdragen: ~ sth. to s.o.'s care iets aan iemands zorg toevertrouwen **2** prijzen: *highly* ~*ed* met eervolle vermelding **3** aanbevelen

commendation 1 prijs, eerbewijsʰ, eervolle vermelding **2** lof, bijval **3** aanbeveling

¹**comment** (n) **1** (verklarende/kritische) aantekening, commentaarʰ, toelichting: [inform] *no* ~ geen commentaar **2** opmerking **3** [media] reactie: *leave a* ~ een reactie plaatsen **4** gepraatʰ, praatjes

²**comment** (vb) **1** (+ (up)on) commentaar leveren (op) **2** opmerkingen maken, kritiek leveren

commentary 1 commentaarʰ, opmerking **2** uitleg, verklaring **3** reportage: *a running* ~ een doorlopende reportage

commentate verslag geven; commentaar leveren

commentator 1 commentator **2** verslaggever

commerce handel, (handels)verkeerʰ

¹**commercial** (n) reclame, spot

²**commercial** (adj) commercieel [also depr]: ~ *traveller* vertegenwoordiger, handelsreiziger

commiserate (+ with) medelijden hebben (met), medeleven betuigen

¹**commission** (n) **1** opdracht **2** benoeming; aanstelling [of officer]; benoemingsbrief **3** commissie, comitéʰ **4** commissie; verlening [of power, position etc]; machtiging, instructie **5** provisie, commissieloonʰ **6** het begaan [of crime, sin]

²**commission** (vb) **1** opdragen **2** bestellen

commissioner 1 commissaris **2** (hoofd)-commissaris [of police] **3** (hoofd)ambtenaar

commit 1 toevertrouwen: ~ *to memory* uit het hoofd leren **2** in (voorlopige) hechtenis nemen, opsluiten: ~ *s.o. to prison* iemand in hechtenis nemen **3** plegen, begaan, bedrijven: ~ *murder* (or: *an offence*) een moord (or: misdrijf) plegen **4** beschikbaar stellen, toewijzen: ~ *money to a new project* geld uittrekken voor een nieuw project || ~ *o.s.* a) zich verplichten; b) zich uitspreken

commitment 1 verplichting, belofte **2** overtuiging **3** inzet, betrokkenheid **4** (bevelʰ tot) inhechtenisneming, (bevelʰ tot) aanhouding

committal 1 inhechtenisneming, opsluiting, opname **2** toezegging, belofte **3** verwijzing, toewijzing

committed 1 toegewijd, overtuigd **2** betrokken

committee commissie, bestuurʰ, comitéʰ: ~ *of inquiry* onderzoekscommissie

commode 1 ladekast, commode **2** toiletʰ

commodious ruim

commodity 1 (handels)artikelʰ, productʰ, nuttig voorwerpʰ **2** basisproductʰ; [roughly] grondstof

¹**common** (n) **1** gemeenschapsgrond **2** het gewone: *out of the* ~ ongewoon, ongebruikelijk **3** (-s) burgerstand, (gewone) burgerij || *in* ~ gemeenschappelijk, gezamenlijk; *in* ~ *with* evenals, op dezelfde manier als

²**common** (adj) **1** gemeenschappelijk, gemeen: *by* ~ *consent* met algemene instemming; *it is very* ~ het komt heel vaak voor **2** openbaar, publiek: *for the* ~ *good* in het algemeen belang **3** gewoon, algemeen, gebruikelijk, gangbaar: *the* ~ *man* de gewone man, Jan met de pet **4** ordinair: *as* ~ *as muck* (or: *dirt*) vreselijk ordinair || *make* ~ *cause with* onder één hoedje spelen met; ~ *law* gewoonterechtʰ, ongeschreven recht; ~ *sense* gezond verstand

commoner burger, gewone man

common-law (volgens het) gewoonterecht: *they are* ~ *husband and wife* ze zijn zonder boterbriefje getrouwd

commonly gewoonlijk; gebruikelijk, vaak

common-or-garden [inform] huis-tuin-en-keuken-; doodgewoon

¹**commonplace** (n) **1** clichéʰ **2** alledaags iets

²**commonplace** (adj) **1** afgezaagd, clichématig **2** alledaags, gewoon, doorsnee

common-room 1 docentenkamer **2** studentenvertrekʰ, leerlingenkamer

Commons (the) (leden van het) Lagerhuisʰ

Commonwealth Britse Gemenebest

commotion 1 beroering, onrust, opschudding **2** rumoerʰ, lawaaiʰ, herrie

communal gemeenschappelijk: ~ *life* gemeenschapslevenʰ

commune in nauw contact staan, gevoelens uitwisselen, zich één voelen: ~ *with friends* een intiem gesprek met vrienden hebben; ~ *with nature* zich één voelen met de natuur

communicable 1 besmettelijk **2** overdraagbaar [of ideas]

¹**communicate** (vb) **1** communiceren, contact hebben **2** in verbinding staan: *our living room* ~*s with the kitchen* onze woonkamer staat in verbinding met de keuken

²**communicate** (vb) overbrengen, bekendmaken, doorgeven

communication 1 mededeling, boodschap, berichtʰ **2** verbinding, contactʰ, communicatie **3** het overbrengen [of ideas, diseases] **4** (-s) verbindingen, communicatiemiddelen

communion 1 kerkgenootschapʰ, gemeente, gemeenschap **2** gemeenschappelijkheid

Communion [Roman Catholicism] communie; [Protestant] avondmaal[h]
communiqué bekendmaking, bericht[h], communiqué[h]
communism communisme[h]
¹**communist** (n) communist
²**communist** (adj) communistisch
community 1 gemeenschap, bevolkingsgroep **2** overeenkomst(igheid), gemeenschappelijkheid: *a ~ of interests* gemeenschappelijke belangen **3** [Roman Catholicism] congregatie, broederschap **4** bevolking, publiek[h], gemeenschap
community centre buurtcentrum[h], wijkcentrum[h]
community service taakstraf
commutation 1 omzetting [of punishment]; vermindering **2** afkoopsom, het afkopen **3** het pendelen
¹**commute** (vb) pendelen
²**commute** (vb) **1** verlichten, verminderen, omzetten: *~ a sentence from death to life imprisonment* een vonnis van doodstraf in levenslang omzetten **2** veranderen, omzetten, afkopen: *~ an insurance policy into* (or: *for*) *a lump sum* een verzekeringspolis afkopen voor een uitkering ineens
commuter forens, pendelaar
¹**compact** (n) **1** overeenkomst, verbond[h], verdrag[h] **2** poederdoos **3** [Am] middelgrote auto, compact car
²**compact** (adj) **1** compact, samengeperst **2** compact, bondig, beknopt
³**compact** (vb) een overeenkomst aangaan
⁴**compact** (vb) samenpakken, samenpersen
companion 1 metgezel, kameraad **2** vennoot, partner **3** handboek[h], gids, wegwijzer **4** één van twee bij elkaar horende exemplaren
companionship kameraadschap; gezelschap[h]
company 1 gezelschap[h]: *in ~ with* samen met; *request the ~ of* uitnodigen; *keep ~ with* omgaan met, verkering hebben met **2** bezoek[h], gasten: *have* (or: *expect*) *~* bezoek hebben (or: krijgen) **3** compagnonschap[h], compagnon(s) **4** gezelschap[h]: *theatre ~* toneelgezelschap[h] **5** onderneming, firma, bedrijf[h]: [econ] *limited ~* naamloze vennootschap **6** gilde[h], genootschap[h] **7** [mil] compagnie **8** [shipp] bemanning
comparable vergelijkbaar: *my car is not ~ with* (or: *to*) *yours* mijn auto is niet met die van jou te vergelijken
¹**comparative** (n) vergrotende trap
²**comparative** (adj) betrekkelijk, relatief: *they live in ~ comfort now* het gaat ze nu verhoudingsgewijs beter
¹**compare** (n): [form] *beyond* (or: *past, without*) *~* onvergelijkbaar, weergaloos
²**compare** (vb) vergelijkbaar zijn, de verge-

lijking kunnen doorstaan: *our results ~ poorly with theirs* onze resultaten steken mager bij de hunne af
³**compare** (vb) vergelijken: *I'm tall ~d to him* vergeleken bij hem ben ik lang; *~ down* jezelf vergelijken met minder bevoordeelden en daardoor beseffen dat je het zelf zo slecht nog niet hebt
comparison vergelijking: *bear* (or: *stand*) *~ with* de vergelijking kunnen doorstaan met; *by* (or: *in*) *~ with* in vergelijking met
compartment compartiment[h], vakje, (trein)coupé, (gescheiden) ruimte
compass 1 kompas[h]: *the points of the ~* de kompasrichtingen, de windstreken **2** (-es) passer: *a pair of ~es* een passer
compassion medelijden[h]
compassionate medelevend, medelijdend: *~ leave* verlof wegens familieomstandigheden
compatible verenigbaar, bij elkaar passend, aansluitbaar; bruikbaar in combinatie [of technical appliances]: *~ systems* onderling verenigbare systemen; *~ with* aangepast aan; *drinking is not ~ with driving* drinken en autorijden verdragen elkaar niet
compatriot landgenoot, landgenote
compel (af)dwingen, verplichten, noodzaken
compelling 1 fascinerend, onweerstaanbaar, meeslepend **2** onweerlegbaar, overtuigend: *~ evidence* overtuigend bewijs; *make a ~ case for sth.* de noodzaak (or: urgentie) van iets aantonen
¹**compensate** (vb) **1** (+ for) dienen als tegenwicht (voor), opwegen (tegen) **2** compenseren, goedmaken
²**compensate** (vb) vergoeden, vereffenen, goedmaken
compensation compensatie, (onkosten)vergoeding, schadevergoeding, schadeloosstelling
compere conferencier, ceremoniemeester, presentator
compete concurreren, strijden, wedijveren: *competing interests* (tegen)strijdige belangen
competence (vak)bekwaamheid, vaardigheid, (des)kundigheid
competent 1 competent, (vak)bekwaam, (des)kundig **2** voldoende, toereikend, adequaat
competition 1 wedstrijd, toernooi[h], concours[h], competitie **2** rivaliteit, concurrentie
competitive concurrerend: *~ examination* vergelijkend examen
competitor concurrent, (wedstrijd)deelnemer, rivaal
compilation samenstelling, bundel(ing), verzameling
compile samenstellen, bijeenbrengen, bij-

eengaren, verzamelen
complacency [depr] zelfgenoegzaamheid
complacent [oft depr] **1** zelfvoldaan, zelfingenomen **2** passief, laks: *be ~ about sth.* een passieve houding hebben tegenover iets
complain klagen, zich beklagen, een klacht indienen: *~ about sth. to s.o.* bij iem. ergens over klagen
complaint 1 klacht [also law]; grief, kwaal: *lodge a ~ against s.o.* een aanklacht tegen iem. indienen **2** beklag[h], het klagen: *no cause* (or: *ground*) *for ~* geen reden tot klagen
¹complement (n) **1** aanvulling **2** vereiste hoeveelheid, voltallige bemanning
²complement (vb) aanvullen, afronden
complementary aanvullend
¹complete (adj) **1** compleet, volkomen, totaal **2** klaar, voltooid
²complete (vb) vervolledigen, afmaken; invullen [a form]
completion voltooiing, afwerking, afronding
¹complex (n) **1** complex[h] [eg for sports]; samengesteld geheel[h] **2** [psychology] complex[n]; [inform, fig] obsessie
²complex (adj) gecompliceerd, samengesteld, ingewikkeld
complexion 1 huidskleur, uiterlijk[h] **2** aanzien[h], voorkomen[h], aard: *that changed the ~ of the **matter*** dat gaf de kwestie een heel ander aanzien
complexity 1 complicatie, moeilijkheid, probleem[h] **2** gecompliceerdheid, complexiteit
compliance 1 volgzaamheid, meegaandheid: *in ~ with your wish* overeenkomstig uw wens; *~ with the law* naleving van de wet **2** onderdanigheid, onderworpenheid
compliant volgzaam, onderdanig
complicate 1 ingewikkeld(er) worden (maken) **2** verergeren
complicated gecompliceerd; ingewikkeld
complication complicatie, (extra, onvoorziene) moeilijkheid
complicity medeplichtigheid: *~ in* medeplichtigheid aan
¹compliment (n) compliment[h]: *the ~s of the **season*** prettige feestdagen [at Christmas, New Year]; *pay s.o. a ~*, *pay a ~ to s.o. (on sth.)* iem. een complimentje (over iets) maken; *my ~s to your wife* de groeten aan uw vrouw
²compliment (vb) (+ on) complimenteren (met/over), een compliment maken, gelukwensen
complimentary 1 vleiend **2** gratis, bij wijze van geste gegeven: *~ copy* presentexemplaar[h]; *~ tickets* vrijkaartjes
comply zich schikken, gehoorzamen: *refuse to ~* weigeren mee te werken; *~ with* **a)** zich neerleggen bij, gehoor geven aan; **b)** naleven [law]

¹component (n) component, onderdeel[h], element[h]
²component (adj) samenstellend: *~ parts* onderdelen
comport [form] zich gedragen: *he ~ed himself with dignity* hij gedroeg zich waardig
compose 1 schrijven [literary or musical work]; componeren **2** zetten [printed matter] **3** samenstellen, vormen, in elkaar zetten: *~d of* bestaande uit **4** tot bedaren brengen, bedaren, kalmeren: *~ yourself* kalm nou maar **5** bijleggen [difference of opinion]
composed kalm, rustig, beheerst
composer 1 componist **2** auteur; schrijver [of letter, poem]
¹composite (n) samengesteld geheel[h], samenstelling
²composite (adj) samengesteld: *~ photograph* montagefoto, compositiefoto
composition 1 samenstelling, compositie, opbouw: *a piece of his own ~* een stuk van eigen hand **2** het componeren, het (op)stellen **3** kunstwerk[h], muziekstuk[h], compositie, dichtwerk[h], tekst **4** opstel[h], verhandeling **5** mengsel[h], samengesteld materiaal[h], kunststof: *chemical ~s* chemische mengsels **6** het letterzetten
compost compost[+h]
composure (zelf)beheersing
¹compound (n) **1** samenstel[h], mengsel[h], (chemische) verbinding **2** omheinde groep gebouwen, (krijgs)gevangenkamp[h]; omheind gebied[h] [for cattle]
²compound (adj) samengesteld, gemengd, vermengd, gecombineerd: *~ fracture* gecompliceerde breuk; *~ interest* samengestelde interest, rente op rente
³compound (vb) **1** dooreenmengen, vermengen, samenstellen, opbouwen: *~ a recipe* een recept klaarmaken **2** vergroten, verergeren: *the situation was ~ed by his absence* door zijn afwezigheid werd de zaak bemoeilijkt
comprehend 1 (be)vatten, begrijpen, doorgronden **2** omvatten
comprehension 1 begrip[h], bevattingsvermogen[h] **2** [educ] begripstest, leestoets, luistertoets, tekstbegrip[h] **3** (toepassings)bereik[h]
¹comprehensive (n) scholengemeenschap
²comprehensive (adj) allesomvattend, veelomvattend, uitvoerig, uitgebreid: *~ insurance* allriskverzekering; *~ school* middenschool
¹compress (n) kompres[h], drukverband[h]
²compress (vb) samendrukken, samenpersen: *~ed air* perslucht
compression 1 samenpersing **2** dichtheid, compactheid
compressor compressor, perspomp
comprise bestaan uit, bevatten: *the house ~s five rooms* het huis telt vijf kamers

¹compromise (n) compromis^h; tussenoplossing, middenweg, tussenweg
²compromise (vb) een compromis sluiten
³compromise (vb) **1** door een compromis regelen **2** in opspraak brengen, de goede naam aantasten van: *you ~d* ***yourself*** *by accepting that money* door dat geld aan te nemen heb je je gecompromitteerd **3** in gevaar brengen
compulsion dwang, verplichting, druk
compulsive dwingend, gedwongen, verplicht: *a ~* ***smoker*** een verslaafd roker
compulsory 1 verplicht: *~* ***military service*** dienstplicht; [educ] *~* ***subject*** verplicht vak **2** noodzakelijk
compunction schuldgevoel^h, (gewetens)-bezwaar^h, wroeging
compute berekenen, uitrekenen
computer computer: *be ~-savvy* goed met computers overweg kunnen
computerate computervaardig
computer dummy digibeet
computer game computerspel^h: *play a ~* gamen
¹computerize (vb) verwerken met een computer [information]; opslaan in een computer
²computerize (vb) computeriseren, overschakelen op computers
computer-literate vaardig in het gebruik van de computer, goed overweg kunnend met computers
computer moron digibeet
computing computerisering, het werken met computers, computerwerk^h
comrade kameraad, vriend, makker: *~s in* ***arms*** wapenbroeders
comradeship kameraadschap(pelijkheid), vriendschap
¹con (n) **1** *contra* tegenargument^h, nadeel^h, bezwaar^h: *the pros and ~s of this proposal* de voors en tegens van dit voorstel **2** tegenstem(mer) **3** [inform] oplichterij **4** [inform] *convict* veroordeelde, (oud-)gevangene
²con (vb) **1** [inform] oplichten, afzetten, bezwendelen: *~ s.o.* ***out of*** *his money* iem. zijn geld afhandig maken **2** [inform] ompraten, bewerken, overhalen: *he ~ned me* ***into*** *signing* hij heeft me mijn handtekening weten te ontfutselen
con-artist [inform] oplichter
concave hol(rond)
conceal verbergen, verstoppen, achterhouden, geheimhouden: *~ed* ***turning*** let op, bocht [as a traffic sign]
concealment geheimhouding, verzwijging
¹concede (vb) zich gewonnen geven, opgeven
²concede (vb) **1** toegeven: *~* ***defeat*** zijn nederlaag erkennen **2** opgeven, prijsgeven

conceit verwaandheid, ijdelheid, verbeelding
conceited verwaand, ijdel, zelfingenomen
conceivable voorstelbaar, denkbaar, mogelijk
¹conceive (vb) **1** bedenken, ontwerpen: *she ~d a* ***dislike*** *for me* ze kreeg een hekel aan mij **2** opvatten, begrijpen
²conceive (vb) ontvangen [child]; zwanger worden (van)
conceive of zich voorstellen, zich indenken
¹concentrate (vb) (+ (up)on) zich concentreren (op), zich toeleggen
²concentrate (vb) concentreren: *~ one's* ***attention*** *on* zijn aandacht richten op
concentrated 1 geconcentreerd, van sterk gehalte **2** krachtig, intens
concentration concentratie: *power of ~* concentratievermogen^h
concept idee^h, voorstelling, denkbeeld^h
conception 1 ontstaan^h [of idea etc]; ontwerp^h, vinding **2** voorstelling, opvatting, begrip^h: *I have no ~* ***of*** *what he meant* ik heb er geen idee van wat hij bedoelde **3** bevruchting [also fig]
conceptual conceptueel: *~* ***art*** conceptuele kunst; ideeënkunst
¹concern (n) **1** aangelegenheid, belang^h, interesse: *your drinking habits are no ~ of* ***mine*** uw drinkgewoonten zijn mijn zaak niet **2** zorg, bezorgdheid, (gevoel^h van) betrokkenheid: *no cause* ***for*** *~* geen reden tot ongerustheid **3** bedrijf^h, onderneming, firma: *going ~* bloeiende onderneming **4** (aan)deel^h, belang^h
²concern (vb) **1** aangaan, van belang zijn voor: *where* ***money*** *is ~ed* als het om geld gaat; *to whom it* ***may*** *~* aan wie dit leest [salutation of open letter]; *as far as I'm ~ed* wat mij betreft, voor mijn part **2** betreffen, gaan over **3** zich aantrekken, zich interesseren: *~ o.s.* ***about*** (or: *with*) *sth.* zich ergens voor inzetten, zorgen om maken
concerned 1 bezorgd, ongerust **2** geïnteresseerd, betrokken: *all the* ***people*** *~* alle (erbij) betrokkenen, alle geïnteresseerden; *~* ***in*** betrokken bij ‖ *be ~* ***with*** betreffen, gaan over
concerning betreffende, in verband met, over
concert concert^h, muziekuitvoering ‖ *in ~* in onderlinge samenwerking, in harmonie
concerted gecombineerd, gezamenlijk
concession 1 concessie(verlening), vergunning, tegemoetkoming **2** korting; (prijs)reductie [with discount card]
conciliate 1 tot bedaren brengen, kalmeren **2** verzoenen, in overeenstemming brengen
conciliation verzoening
concise beknopt, kort maar krachtig

¹conclude (vb) **1** eindigen, aflopen **2** tot een conclusie (besluit/akkoord) komen

²conclude (vb) **1** beëindigen, (af)sluiten, afronden **2** (af)sluiten, tot stand brengen: *conclude an agreement* een overeenkomst sluiten **3** concluderen, vaststellen

conclusion 1 besluith, beëindiging, sloth: *in ~* samenvattend, tot besluit **2** conclusie, gevolgtrekking: *come to* (or: *draw, reach*) *~s* conclusies trekken; *a foregone ~* een bij voorbaat uitgemaakte zaak; *jump to ~s* (or: *to a ~*) te snel conclusies trekken

conclusive afdoend, overtuigend, beslissend: *~ evidence* overtuigend bewijs

concoct 1 samenstellen, bereiden, brouwen **2** [depr] verzinnen, bedenken, bekokstoven: *~ an excuse* een smoes verzinnen

concord 1 verdragh, overeenkomst, akkoordh **2** harmonie, eendracht, overeenstemming **3** [linguistics] congruentie, overeenkomst

concourse 1 menigte **2** samenkomst, samenloop, bijeenkomst: *a fortunate ~ of circumstances* een gelukkige samenloop van omstandigheden **3** pleinh, promenade, (stations)hal

¹concrete (n) betonh

²concrete (adj) **1** concreet, echt, tastbaar **2** betonnen, beton-: *~ jungle* betonwoestijn

concrete mixer betonmolen

concubine concubine, bijzit

concur samenvallen, overeenstemmen || *~ with s.o.* (or: *in sth.*) het eens zijn met iem. (iets)

concurrent samenvallend; gelijktijdig (optredend, voorkomend)

concussion 1 schok, stoot, klap **2** hersenschudding

condemn 1 veroordelen, schuldig verklaren: *~ed to spend one's life in poverty* gedoemd zijn leven lang armoede te lijden **2** afkeuren, verwerpen

condemnation veroordeling, afkeuring, verwerping

condensation condensatie, condens, condenswaterh

condense condenseren [also fig]; indampen, bekorten, inkorten, verkorten: *~d milk* gecondenseerde melk

condescend 1 zich verlagen, zich verwaardigen **2** neerbuigend doen, neerkijken

condescension neerbuigendheid

condiment 1 kruiderij, specerij **2** bijgerechth, tafelzuurh

¹condition (n) **1** (lichamelijke) toestand, (lichamelijke) staat, (lichamelijke) conditie: *she is in no ~ to work* ze is niet in staat om te werken; *in* (or: *out of*) *~* in (or: niet in) conditie **2** voorwaarde, conditie, bedingh: *on ~ that* op voorwaarde dat **3** omstandigheid: *favourable ~s* gunstige omstandigheden

4 [med] afwijking, aandoening, kwaal: *skin ~* huidaandoening

²condition (vb) bepalen, vaststellen, afhangen (van): *a nation's expenditure is ~ed by its income* de bestedingsmogelijkheden van een land worden bepaald door het nationale inkomen

conditional voorwaardelijk, conditioneel: [linguistics] *~ mood* conditionalis, voorwaardelijke wijs

conditioner crèmespoeling

condolence 1 deelneming, sympathie, medelevenh **2** (-s) condoleantie, rouwbeklagh: *my ~s, sir* gecondoleerd, meneer; *please accept my ~s on …* mijn deelneming met …

condom condoomh, kapotjeh

condominium [Am] **1** flatgebouw met koopflats **2** koopflat

condone vergeven

conducive [form] bevorderlijk; gunstig

¹conduct (n) gedragh, houding, handelwijze

²conduct (vb) **1** leiden, rondleiden, begeleiden: *~ed tour* verzorgde reis, rondleiding **2** [mus] dirigeren, dirigent zijn (van) **3** (zich) gedragen: *~ o.s.* zich gedragen **4** [science, elec] geleiden

conduction [science] geleiding, conductie

conductor 1 conducteur **2** [mus] dirigent, orkestleider **3** [science, elec] geleider

cone 1 kegel **2** (ijs)hoorntjeh **3** dennenappel

confabulation 1 verzinselh **2** praatjeh, babbeltjeh

confectionery 1 banketbakkerij, banketbakkerswinkel **2** gebakh, zoetigheid, suikergoedh

confederation (con)federatie, bond, verbondh

¹confer (vb) confereren, beraadslagen

²confer (vb) verlenen, uitreiken, schenken: *~ a knighthood on s.o.* iem. een ridderorde verlenen

conference conferentie, congresh

confess 1 bekennen, erkennen, toegeven: *I must ~ I like it* ik moet zeggen dat ik het wel prettig vind **2** [rel] (op)biechten, belijden

confession 1 bekentenis, erkenning, toegeving: *on his own ~* naar hij zelf toegeeft **2** [rel] biecht **3** [rel] (geloofs)belijdenis

confessor [rel] **1** biechtvader **2** belijder

confetti confetti

confidant vertrouweling, vertrouwensman

confide toevertrouwen, in vertrouwen mededelen

confide in vertrouwen, in vertrouwen nemen

confidence 1 (zelf)vertrouwenh, geloofh: *in ~* in vertrouwen, vertrouwelijk **2** vertrouwelijke mededeling, geheimh

confidence trick oplichterij

confident (tref)zeker, zelfverzekerd, over-

tuigd
confidential 1 vertrouwelijk **2** vertrouwens-, privé-, vertrouwd
confine 1 beperken **2** opsluiten, insluiten: *be ~d to bed* het bed moeten houden
confined krap; eng, nauw
confinement opsluiting: *solitary ~* eenzame opsluiting
confirm 1 bevestigen, bekrachtigen: *~ by letter* (or: *in writing*) schriftelijk bevestigen **2** bevestigen, goedkeuren: *he hasn't been ~ed in office yet* zijn benoeming moet nog bevestigd worden **3** [Protestantism] confirmeren, (als lidmaat) aannemen **4** [Roman Catholicism] vormen, het vormsel toedienen
confirmation 1 bevestiging, bekrachtiging, goedkeuring: *evidence in ~ of your statement* bewijzen die uw bewering staven **2** [Protestantism] confirmatie, bevestiging als lidmaat **3** [Roman Catholicism] (heilig) vormsel[h]
confiscate in beslag nemen, verbeurd verklaren, afnemen
conflagration grote brand [of forests, buildings]; vuurzee
¹conflict (n) strijd, conflict[h], onenigheid: *armed ~* gewapend conflict[h]
²conflict (vb) **1** onverenigbaar zijn, in tegenspraak zijn, botsen: *~ing interests* (tegen)strijdige belangen **2** strijden, botsen, in conflict komen
conflicted [Am] in tweestrijd: *be* (or: *feel*) *~* a) niet kunnen kiezen; b) het even niet weten
confluence 1 toeloop, menigte **2** samenvloeiing
conform zich conformeren, zich aanpassen
conformity 1 overeenkomst, gelijkvormigheid: *in ~ with* in overeenstemming met, overeenkomstig **2** aanpassing, naleving
confound 1 verbazen, in verwarring brengen, versteld doen staan **2** verwarren, door elkaar halen
confront confronteren, tegenover elkaar plaatsen; [fig] het hoofd bieden aan
confrontation 1 confrontatie **2** het tegenover (elkaar) stellen
confuse in de war brengen, door elkaar halen, verwarren
confused verward, wanordelijk, rommelig
confusion verwarring, wanorde
congeal (doen) stollen
congenial 1 (geest)verwant, gelijkgestemd, sympathiek **2** passend, geschikt, aangenaam
congenital 1 aangeboren **2** [fig] geboren: *a ~ thief* een aartsdief
congestion op(een)hoping, opstopping, verstopping
congestion charging rekeningrijden[h]
conglomeration bundeling, verzameling

Congo Congo
¹Congolese (n) Congolees, Congolese
²Congolese (adj) Congolees
congratulate gelukwensen, feliciteren: *~ o.s. on* zichzelf gelukkig prijzen met
congratulation gelukwens, felicitatie: *~s!* gefeliciteerd!
congregation 1 bijeenkomst, verzameling **2** verzamelde groep mensen, menigte, groep **3** [rel] gemeente, congregatie
congress congres[h], vergadering, bijeenkomst
Congress [Am] het Congres
congruity gepastheid, overeenstemming, overeenkomst
conic(al) m.b.t. een kegel, kegelvormig, conisch
conifer naaldboom, conifeer
conjecture 1 gis(sing), (vage) schatting, vermoeden[h] **2** giswerk[h], speculatie, gokwerk[h]
conjugation 1 [linguistics] vervoeging **2** vereniging, verbinding, koppeling
conjunction 1 verbinding; combinatie, het samengaan: *in ~ with* samen met **2** [linguistics] voegwoord[h]
conjuncture (kritieke) toestand, samenloop van omstandigheden, (crisis)situatie
¹conjure (vb) toveren, goochelen, manipuleren
²conjure (vb) (te voorschijn) toveren, oproepen, voor de geest roepen
conjurer goochelaar, illusionist
conk [inform] een oplawaai geven
conker (wilde) kastanje, paardenkastanje
con man [inform] *confidence man* oplichter; zwendelaar
¹connect (vb) **1** in verbinding komen, in verband staan: *our TV is not yet ~ed* onze tv is nog niet aangesloten; *obesity is ~ed to heart failure* er is een verband tussen zwaarlijvigheid en hartfalen **2** aansluiten, aansluiting hebben: *the five o'clock train ~s to the Thalys* de trein van vijf uur sluit aan op de Thalys; *when they met, Pete and Jane immediately ~ed* toen ze elkaar ontmoetten, hadden Pete en Jane meteen een klik
²connect (vb) **1** verbinden, aaneensluiten, aaneenschakelen; doorverbinden [telephone]: *the islands are ~ed by a bridge* de eilanden staan via een brug met elkaar in verbinding; *could you ~ me to Mr. White, please?* kunt u mij doorverbinden met dhr. White?; *there is no evidence to ~ him to the murder* er is geen bewijs dat hij betrokken is bij de moord; *~ up* verbinden **2** (+ with) in verband brengen (met), een verbinding leggen tussen
connection 1 verbinding, verband[h], aansluiting: *miss one's ~* zijn aansluiting missen [of bus, train]; *in ~ with* in verband met **2** sa-

menhang, coherentie **3** connectie, betrekking, relatie **4** verwant, familielid[h] **5** verbindingsstuk[h] **6** [elec] lichtpunt[h], stopcontact[h], (wand)contactdoos

connive 1 oogluikend toelaten, (even) de andere kant opkijken: ~ *at* oogluikend toelaten, door de vingers zien **2** samenspannen, samenzweren

connotation (bij)betekenis, connotatie

¹conquer (vb) overwinnen, de (over)winnaar zijn

²conquer (vb) **1** veroveren, innemen; bemachtigen [also fig] **2** verslaan, overwinnen, bedwingen: ~ *mountains* bergen bedwingen

conqueror veroveraar, overwinnaar: *William the* Conqueror Willem de Veroveraar

conquest verovering, overwinning; het bedwingen [of a mountain]: *the* Norman Conquest de Normandische verovering

conscience geweten[h]: *in* all ~ met een gerust geweten, waarachtig, werkelijk

conscientious plichtsgetrouw, zorgvuldig: ~ *objector* gewetensbezwaarde, principiële dienstweigeraar

conscious 1 bewust, denkend **2** welbewust, opzettelijk **3** (zich) bewust **4** bewust, bij kennis

consciousness 1 bewustzijn[h]: *lose* ~ het bewustzijn verliezen **2** gevoel[h], besef[h]

¹conscript (n) dienstplichtige

²conscript (vb) oproepen: ~ed *into* the army ingelijfd bij het leger

conscription dienstplicht

consecutive opeenvolgend: *on two* ~ *days* twee dagen achter elkaar

consensus algemene opvatting, overeenstemming

¹consent (n) toestemming, instemming, goedkeuring: *by* **common** (or: **general**) ~ met algemene stemmen; *informed* ~ verklaring van vrijwillige toestemming

²consent (vb) toestemmen, zijn goedkeuring geven, zich bereid verklaren: ~ *to* sth. iets toestaan

consequence 1 consequentie, gevolg[h], gevolgtrekking, resultaat[h] **2** belang[h], gewicht[h]: *of no* ~ van geen belang

consequently dus; derhalve

conservation 1 behoud[h], instandhouding: ~ *of energy* behoud van energie **2** milieubeheer[h], milieubescherming, natuurbescherming, monumentenzorg

conservation area 1 (beschermd) natuurgebied[h] **2** beschermd stads-, dorpsgezicht

conservationist milieubeschermer, natuurbeschermer

conservatism conservatisme[h], behoudzucht

¹conservative (n) conservatief, behoudend persoon; [pol] lid[h] van de Conservatieve Partij

²conservative (adj) **1** conservatief, behoudend, traditioneel (ingesteld) **2** voorzichtig, gematigd, bescheiden: *a ~* **estimate** een voorzichtige schatting

conservatory 1 serre, (planten)kas, broeikas **2** conservatorium[h], muziekacademie, toneelschool

¹conserve (n) jam, ingemaakte vruchten

²conserve (vb) **1** behouden, bewaren, goed houden **2** inmaken

consider 1 overwegen, nadenken over **2** beschouwen, zien: *we ~ him (to be) a* **man** *of genius* we beschouwen hem als een genie **3** in aanmerking nemen, rekening houden met, letten op

considerable aanzienlijk, behoorlijk: *a ~* **time** geruime tijd

considerate attent, voorkomend, vriendelijk

consideration 1 overweging, aandacht: *take* sth. *into* ~ ergens rekening mee houden **2** (punt[h] van) overweging, (beweeg)reden **3** voorkomendheid, attentheid, begrip[h]

¹considering (adv) [at the end of a sentence] alles bij elkaar (genomen): *she has been very successful,* ~ eigenlijk heeft ze het ver gebracht

²considering (prep) gezien, rekening houdend met

consign 1 [com] verzenden, versturen, leveren **2** overdragen, toevertrouwen, in handen stellen: ~ *one's child* **to** *s.o.'s care* zijn kind aan iemands zorg toevertrouwen

consignment (ver)zending

consistency 1 consequentheid, samenhang **2** dikte, stroperigheid

consistent 1 consequent, samenhangend **2** overeenkomend, kloppend, verenigbaar: *be ~* **with** kloppen met

consist in bestaan in, gevormd worden door: *my duties mainly ~ word processing and filing* mijn werkzaamheden bestaan voornamelijk in tekstverwerken en archiveren

consist of bestaan uit, opgebouwd zijn uit: *the convoy consisted of sixteen ships* het konvooi bestond uit zestien schepen

consolation troost, troostrijke gedachte

¹console (n) **1** steunstuk[h], draagsteen **2** toetsenbord[h], (bedienings)paneel[h], controlebord[h], schakelbord[h]; [comp] console **3** radio-, televisie-, grammofoonmeubel[h]

²console (vb) troosten, bemoedigen(d toespreken), opbeuren

¹consolidate (vb) **1** hechter, steviger worden **2** zich aaneensluiten, samengaan, fuseren

²consolidate (vb) **1** verstevigen, stabiliseren **2** (tot een geheel) verenigen

consonant medeklinker

¹consort (n) gade, gemaal[h], gemalin

²consort (vb) omgaan, optrekken: ~ **with**

criminals omgaan met misdadigers

consortium consortium^h; syndicaat^h

conspicuous opvallend, in het oog lopend, opmerkelijk: *be ~ by one's absence* schitteren door afwezigheid

conspiracy samenzwering, complot^h; [law] samenspanning

conspiracy theory complottheorie

conspirator samenzweerder

conspire samenzweren; samenspannen

constable 1 agent, politieman **2** [Am] (ongeüniformeerde) politiefunctionaris onder sheriff; [roughly] vrederechter

constabulary politie(korps^h), politiemacht

constancy 1 standvastigheid, onveranderlijkheid **2** trouw

constant 1 constant, voortdurend, onveranderlijk **2** trouw, loyaal

constellation sterrenbeeld^h; constellatie [also fig]

consternation opschudding

constipation constipatie, verstopping

constituency 1 kiesdistrict^h **2** achterban, kiezers

¹**constituent** (n) **1** kiezer, ingezetene van een kiesdistrict **2** onderdeel^h, bestanddeel^h

²**constituent** (adj): *~ body* kiescollege^h

constitute vormen, (samen) uitmaken, vertegenwoordigen

constitution 1 grondwet **2** conditie, gesteldheid

constitutional grondwettig, grondwettelijk

constrain (af)dwingen, verplichten, noodzaken: *feel ~ed to do sth.* zich ergens toe verplicht voelen

constraint 1 beperking, restrictie **2** dwang, verplichting **3** gedwongenheid, geforceerde stemming, geremdheid

constrict vernauwen, versmallen, beperken

construct construeren, in elkaar zetten, bouwen

construction 1 interpretatie, voorstelling van zaken, uitleg **2** constructie, aanbouw, aanleg, (huizen)bouw, bouwwerk^h: *under ~* in aanbouw

constructive constructief, opbouwend, positief

construe interpreteren, opvatten, verklaren: *giving in now will be ~d as a weakness* nu toegeven zal als zwakheid worden uitgelegd

consul consul

consular consulair

consulate consulaat^h

¹**consult** (vb) overleggen, beraadslagen: *~ about* (or: *upon*) beraadslagen over

²**consult** (vb) raadplegen

consultancy 1 baan als consulterend geneesheer **2** baan als (bedrijfs)adviseur

consultant 1 consulterend geneesheer

2 consulent, (bedrijfs)adviseur, deskundige

consultation 1 vergadering, bespreking **2** overleg^h, raadpleging, consult^h: *in ~ with* in overleg met

consume 1 consumeren, verorberen **2** verbruiken, gebruiken **3** verteren, wegvreten, verwoesten: *~d by* (or: *with*) *hate* verteerd door haat

consumer consument, verbruiker, koper

consumer goods consumptiegoederen

consumerism [Am] consumentisme^h; overdreven consumptiedrang

consumer society consumptiemaatschappij

consummation 1 (eind)doel^h **2** voltooiing, bekroning **3** huwelijksgemeenschap

consumption 1 consumptie, verbruik^h, (ver)tering: *these oranges are unfit for ~* deze sinaasappelen zijn niet geschikt voor consumptie **2** verwoesting, aantasting

¹**contact** (n) **1** contact^h, contactpersoon **2** contactlens **3** contact^h [also elec]; aanraking

²**contact** (vb) **1** in contact brengen, een contact leggen tussen **2** contact opnemen met

contagion 1 besmetting **2** besmettelijke invloed; [fig] virus^h

contagious besmet(telijk); [fig] aanstekelijk

contain 1 bevatten, tellen, inhouden **2** beheersen, onder controle houden, bedwingen: *~ yourself!* beheers je!, hou je in!

container 1 houder, vat^h, bak, doosje^h, bus, verpakking **2** container

contamination vervuiling, besmetting

¹**contemplate** (vb) nadenken, peinzen, in gedachten verzonken zijn

²**contemplate** (vb) **1** beschouwen **2** nadenken over, overdenken, zich verdiepen in **3** overwegen, zich bezinnen op

contemplation overpeinzing, bezinning, overdenking: *lost in ~* in gepeins verzonken

contemplative bedachtzaam, beschouwend

contemporaneous gelijktijdig, in de tijd samenvallend

¹**contemporary** (n) **1** tijdgenoot **2** leeftijdgenoot, jaargenoot

²**contemporary** (adj) **1** gelijktijdig, uit dezelfde tijd **2** even oud **3** eigentijds, hedendaags

contempt minachting, verachting: *beneath ~* beneden alle peil

contemptuous minachtend, verachtend

¹**contend** (vb) wedijveren, strijden: *~ with difficulties* met problemen (te) kampen (hebben)

²**contend** (vb) betogen, (met klem) beweren

contender 1 [sport] uitdager **2** mededinger

¹**content** (n) **1** capaciteit, volume^h, omvang,

inhoud(smaat) **2** inhoud, onderwerp^h **3** ge-
halte^h: *sugar* ~ suikergehalte^h, hoeveelheid
suiker; *nutritional* ~ voedingswaarde **4** (-s)
inhoud [of bottle, bag] **5** (-s) inhoud(sopga-
ve) [of book]: *table of* ~s inhoudsopgave
²**content** (adj) tevreden, blij, content
  content curation [Am] contentbeheer^h
  contented tevreden, blij
  contention 1 standpunt^h, stellingname,
  opvatting **2** geschil^h, conflict^h
  contentious 1 ruzieachtig **2** controversieel; aanvechtbaar
  contentment tevredenheid, voldoening
  content provider informatieleverancier,
  dienstenaanbieder
¹**contest** (n) **1** krachtmeting, strijd, (kracht)-
  proef **2** (wed)strijd, prijsvraag, concours^h
²**contest** (vb) twisten, strijden: ~ *against* (or:
  with) strijden met
³**contest** (vb) betwisten, aanvechten
  contestant 1 kandidaat, deelnemer (aan
  wedstrijd), strijdende partij **2** betwister,
  aanvechter
  context context [also fig]; verband^h, samenhang: *my words were quoted out of* ~
  mijn woorden zijn uit hun verband gerukt
  contiguity 1 aangrenzing, naburigheid
  2 opeenvolging, aan(een)sluiting
  continence zelfbeheersing, matigheid
  continent continent^h, werelddeel^h
  Continent (the) vasteland^h (van Europa)
  [opposite Great Britain]
¹**continental** (n) vastelander, bewoner van
  het Europese vasteland; [Am also] Europeaan
²**continental** (adj) continentaal, het vasteland van Europa betreffende: ~ *breakfast*
  ontbijt met koffie en croissants enz.; ~ *climate* landklimaat^h
  contingency eventualiteit, onvoorziene
  gebeurtenis (uitgave)
  contingency plan rampenplan^h
¹**contingent** (n) **1** afvaardiging, vertegenwoordiging **2** [mil] (troepen)contingent^h
²**contingent** (adj) **1** toevallig, onvoorzien
  2 mogelijk, eventueel **3** bijkomend, incidenteel **4** voorwaardelijk, afhankelijk: *our success is* ~ *(up)on his cooperation* ons slagen
  hangt van zijn medewerking af
  continual [depr] aanhoudend, voortdurend, onophoudelijk
  continuation voortzetting, vervolg^h, con-
  tinuering
¹**continue** (vb) **1** doorgaan, voortgaan, verder gaan, volhouden, zich voortzetten **2** (in
  stand) blijven, voortduren, continueren: *the
  weather* ~s *fine* het mooie weer houdt aan
  3 vervolgen, verder gaan: ~d *on page 106*
  lees verder op bladzijde 106
²**continue** (vb) **1** voortzetten, (weer) doorgaan, voortgaan, verder gaan met, volhou-

den, vervolgen: *to be* ~d wordt vervolgd
  2 handhaven, aanhouden, continueren
  3 verlengen
  continuity 1 tijdsmatig verloop^h, samenhang **2** [film] draaiboek^h **3** [radio, TV] tekst-
  boek^h, draaiboek^h, verbindende teksten
  continuous ononderbroken, continu: ~
  performance doorlopende voorstelling
  contort verwringen
  contortion 1 kronkeling, bocht **2** verwrin-
  ging, ontwrichting
  contour contour [also fig]; omtrek(lijn),
  vorm
  contraband 1 smokkelwaar, smokkel-
  goed^h **2** smokkel(handel)
  contraception anticonceptie
  contraceptive voorbehoed(s)middel^h
¹**contract** (n) contract^h, (bindende) overeenkomst, verdrag^h
²**contract** (vb) een overeenkomst, verdrag
  sluiten, een verbintenis aangaan, contracteren: ~*ing parties* contracterende partijen; ~
  out zich terugtrekken
³**contract** (vb) bij contract regelen, contracteren, aangaan: ~ *out* uitbesteden
⁴**contract** (vb) samentrekken, inkrimpen,
  slinken
  contraction 1 samentrekking, inkorting,
  verkorting **2** [esp pl] wee, barenswee
  contract killer huurmoordenaar
  contract killing huurmoord
  contractor 1 aannemer, aannemersbe-
  drijf^h, handelaar in bouwmaterialen **2** con-
  tractant, iem. die een contract aangaat
  contradict tegenspreken, in tegenspraak
  zijn met, ontkennen
  contradiction 1 tegenspraak, tegenstrijdigheid: ~ *in terms* contradictio in terminis,
  innerlijke tegenspraak **2** weerlegging
  contradictory 1 tegenstrijdig, in tegenspraak: ~ *to* strijdig met **2** ontkennend
  contraflow tweerichtingsverkeer^h op één
  rijbaan
  contrail *condensation trail* condensstreep
  contralto alt
  contraption geval^h, toestand, ding^h, appa-
  raat^h
¹**contrary** (n) tegendeel^h, tegen(over)gestel-
  de^h: *on the* ~ integendeel, juist niet; *if I don't
  hear anything to the* ~ ... zonder tegenbericht
  ...
²**contrary** (adj) **1** tegen(over)gesteld, strijdig: ~ *to* tegen ... in, ondanks **2** ongunstig,
  tegenwerkend, averechts: ~ *winds* tegenwind
³**contrary** (adj) tegendraads, weerbarstig,
  eigenwijs
¹**contrast** (n) contrast^h, contrastwerking;
  [fig also] tegenbeeld^h; verschil^h: *in* ~ *to* (or:
  with) in tegenstelling tot
²**contrast** (vb) contrasteren, (tegen elkaar)

afsteken, (een) verschil(len) vertonen: ~ **with** afsteken bij

³**contrast** (vb) tegenover elkaar stellen, vergelijken

contravene [form] in strijd zijn met; overtreden

contribute een bijdrage leveren, bevorderen: ~ **to** bijdragen tot, medewerken aan

contribution bijdrage, inbreng, contributie

contributor bijdrager

contrite berouwvol, schuldbewust

contrivance 1 apparaatʰ, toestelʰ, (handig) dingʰ 2 (-s) list, truc, slimmigheid(jeʰ) 3 vernuftʰ, vernuftigheid, vindingrijkheid

contrive 1 voor elkaar boksen, kans zien om te: *he had ~d to **meet** her* hij had het zo gepland dat hij haar zou ontmoeten 2 bedenken, uitvinden, ontwerpen 3 beramen, smeden

contrived geforceerd, onnatuurlijk, gemaakt

¹**control** (n) 1 (-s) bedieningspaneelʰ, controlepaneelʰ 2 (-s) controlemiddelʰ, beheersingsmechanismeʰ 3 beheersing, controle, zeggenschapᵃʰ: *passport* ~ paspoortcontrole; *keep under* ~ bedwingen, in toom houden; *get* (or: *go*) *out of* ~ uit de hand lopen 4 bestuurʰ, opzichtʰ, toezichtʰ, leiding: *be **in** ~* de leiding hebben, het voor het zeggen hebben 5 controlekamer, meldkamer

²**control** (vb) 1 controleren, leiden, toezicht uitoefenen op, beheren 2 besturen, aan het roer zitten 3 in toom houden, beheersen, onder controle houden

control freak controlefreak

control key controltoets

controller 1 controleur, controlemechanismeʰ 2 afdelingschef, afdelingshoofdʰ

control tower verkeerstoren

controversial 1 controversieel, aanvechtbaar, omstreden 2 tegendraads

controversy 1 strijdpuntʰ 2 onenigheid, verdeeldheid

conundrum 1 raadselachtige kwestie; vraag 2 strikvraag

convalesce herstellen; herstellende zijn [from a disease]; genezen

convalescence 1 herstelʰ, genezing 2 herstelperiode

convalescent herstellend, genezend, herstellings-: ~ *hospital* (or: *nursing home*) herstellingsoordʰ

convector warmtewisselaar, kachel

¹**convene** (vb) bijeenkomen, samenkomen, (zich) vergaderen

²**convene** (vb) 1 bijeenroepen, samenroepen 2 (voor het gerecht) dagen, dagvaarden

convenience 1 (openbaar) toiletʰ, wc, urinoirʰ: *public ~s* openbare toiletten 2 gemakʰ, comfortʰ: *his house has all the **modern**

~*s* zijn huis is van alle moderne gemakken voorzien; *at* your earliest ~ zodra het u gelegen komt

convenience food gemaksvoedselʰ, kant-en-klaarmaaltijd

convenience goods kant-en-klare consumptiegoederen

convenience store buurtwinkel

convenient 1 geschikt, handig: *they were ~ly **forgotten*** zij werden gemakshalve vergeten 2 gunstig gelegen, gemakkelijk bereikbaar

convent (nonnen)kloosterʰ, kloostergebouwʰ, kloostergemeenschap

convention 1 overeenkomst, verdragʰ 2 bijeenkomst, congresʰ, conferentie 3 gewoonte, gebruikʰ

conventional gebruikelijk, traditioneel: ~ *wisdom* algemene opinie

¹**converge** (vb) samenkomen, samenlopen, samenvallen

²**converge** (vb) naar één punt leiden, doen samenkomen

conversation gesprekʰ, conversatie, praatjeʰ: *make* ~ converseren, een gesprek gaande houden

¹**converse** (n) tegendeelʰ, omgekeerdeʰ

²**converse** (adj) tegenovergesteld, omgekeerd

³**converse** (vb) spreken, converseren

conversion 1 omzetting, overschakeling, omschakeling, omrekening, verbouwing 2 [rel] bekering 3 [rugby, Am football] conversie

¹**convert** (n) bekeerling

²**convert** (vb) (een) verandering(en) ondergaan, veranderen, overgaan

³**convert** (vb) 1 bekeren [also fig]; overhalen 2 omschakelen, overschakelen, omzetten, veranderen, ombouwen, verbouwen, omwisselen, inwisselen, omrekenen: ~ *a **loan*** een lening converteren 3 [comp] converteren

¹**convertible** (n) cabriolet

²**convertible** (adj) 1 inwisselbaar, omwisselbaar 2 met vouwdak, met open dak

convex convex, bol(rond)

convey 1 (ver)voeren, transporteren, (ge)leiden 2 meedelen, duidelijk maken, uitdrukken: *his tone ~ed his real **intention*** uit zijn toon bleek zijn werkelijke bedoeling

conveyor vervoerder, transporteur: ~ *belt* transportband, lopende band

¹**convict** (n) 1 veroordeelde 2 gedetineerde, gevangene

²**convict** (vb) veroordelen, schuldig bevinden: ~*ed of murder* wegens moord veroordeeld

conviction 1 veroordeling 2 (innerlijke) overtuiging, overtuigdheid, (vaste) mening: *carry* ~ overtuigend zijn

convince overtuigen, overreden, overhalen

convivial 1 (levens)lustig, joviaal, uitgelaten **2** vrolijk

convo [inform; Am] *conversation* gesprek[h], praatje[h]

convocation 1 vergadering **2** bijeenroeping

convoluted 1 ingewikkeld; ondoorzichtig **2** [form] (in elkaar) gedraaid; gekronkeld

convoy 1 konvooi[h], geleide[h], escorte **2** escortering

convulsion 1 (-s) stuip(trekking), convulsie **2** uitbarsting, verstoring **3** lachsalvo[h], onbedaarlijk gelach[h]

¹coo (n) roekoe(geluid)[h], gekoer[h]

²coo (vb) koeren, kirren, lispelen

COO *chief operating officer* bedrijfsleider

¹cook (n) kok(kin)

²cook (vb) op het vuur staan, (af)koken, sudderen

³cook (vb) [inform] knoeien met, vervalsen: ~ *the books* knoeien met de boekhouding (*or:* cijfers) ‖ ~ *up* verzinnen

⁴cook (vb) koken, (eten) bereiden

cookbook [Am] kookboek[h]

cooker kooktoestel[h], kookplaat, kookstel[h]

cookery book kookboek[h]

cookie 1 koekje[h]; biscuitje[h], kaakje[h] **2** [comp] cookie[h]

cooky 1 [Am] koekje[h], biscuitje[h] **2** [Am; inform] figuur[+h], type[h], persoon

¹cool (n) **1** koelte, koelheid **2** kalmte, zelfbeheersing, onverstoorbaarheid: *keep your* ~ hou je in

²cool (adj) **1** koel, fris **2** koel, luchtig; licht [of clothing] **3** kalm, rustig, beheerst: *(as)* ~ *as a cucumber* ijskoud, doodbedaard **4** kil, koel, afstandelijk **5** [inform] koel, ongeëmotioneerd: *a* ~ *card* (or: *customer, hand*) een gehaaid figuur, sluwe vos **6** gaaf, cool: *a* ~ *T-shirt* een gaaf T-shirt; *are we* ~? is alles oké tussen ons?

³cool (vb) (af)koelen [also fig]; verkoelen ‖ ~ *it* rustig maar, kalm aan

cooler koeler, koelcel, koeltas; [Am] ijskast

cooling-off period 1 afkoelingsperiode **2** bedenktijd

¹coop (n) kippenren, kippenhok[h]

²coop (vb) opsluiten (in een hok); kooien [of chickens]: ~ *up* (or: *in*) opsluiten, kooien

co-op *co-operative* coöperatieve onderneming

co-operate samenwerken, meewerken

co-operation 1 coöperatie, samenwerkingsverband[h] **2** medewerking, samenwerking, hulp

¹co-operative (n) coöperatie, collectief[h], coöperatief bedrijf[h]

²co-operative (adj) **1** behulpzaam, meewerkend, bereidwillig **2** coöperatief, op

coöperatieve grondslag

¹co-ordinate (n) **1** standgenoot, klassengenoot, soortgenoot, gelijke **2** [maths] coördinaat, waarde, grootheid

²co-ordinate (adj) gelijkwaardig, gelijk in rang

³co-ordinate (vb) (harmonieus) samenwerken

⁴co-ordinate (vb) coördineren, rangschikken (in onderling verband), ordenen

co-ordinator coördinator

coot meerkoet

¹cop (n) **1** [inform] smeris **2** [inform] arrestatie, vangst

²cop (vb) [inform] **1** betrappen, grijpen, vangen **2** raken, treffen ‖ ~ *it* last krijgen

cope het aankunnen, zich weten te redden: ~ *with* het hoofd bieden (aan), bestrijden

copier kopieerapparaat[h]

co-pilot tweede piloot

copious 1 overvloedig **2** productief; vruchtbaar [author etc]

cop out [inform] terugkrabbelen; afhaken

copper 1 (rood) koper[h] **2** koperkleur **3** koperen muntje[h], koper(geld)[h] **4** [inform] smeris

copulation geslachtsgemeenschap

¹copy (n) **1** kopie, reproductie, imitatie, fotokopie **2** exemplaar[h], nummer[h] **3** kopij, (reclame)tekst

²copy (vb) een kopie maken, overschrijven

³copy (vb) **1** kopiëren, een afdruk maken van, overschrijven: ~ *from s.o.* van iem. overschrijven, bij iem. afkijken; ~ *me in on your email* stuur mij een cc'tje; ~ *and paste* **a)** [comp] kopiëren en plakken, copy-pasten; **b)** copy-pasten [plagiarism] **2** navolgen, imiteren, overnemen

¹copybook (n) voorbeeldenboek[h], schrijfboek[h] ‖ [inform] *blot one's* ~ zijn reputatie verspelen, een slechte beurt maken

²copybook (adj) perfect, (helemaal) volgens het boekje

copycat [inform] **1** na-aper, navolger **2** afkijker, spieker[+h]

copyleft copyleft[h]

copy-paste [comp] **1** kopiëren en plakken, copy-pasten **2** [fig] klakkeloos overnemen, knippen en plakken

copyright auteursrecht[h]

coral 1 koraal[h], kraal(tje[h]) **2** koraalrood[h], koraalkleur[h]

cord 1 [anatomy] streng, band: *umbilical* ~ navelstreng **2** koord[h], streng, touw[h], snaar **3** (elektrisch) snoer[h], kabel, draad **4** ribfluweel[h], corduroy[h]

cordial hartelijk

cordiality hartelijkheid, vriendelijkheid

cordon kordon[h], ring

corduroy (fijn) ribfluweel[h]

core binnenste[h], kern, klokhuis[h]; [nuclear

energy] reactorkern; [fig] wezen[h]; essentie, hart[h]: *rotten to the* ~ door en door rot

¹**cork** (n) kurk; drijver [of fishnet, fishing line]; flessenkurk, (rubber) stop

²**cork** (vb) kurken: ~ *up a bottle* een fles kurken

corkscrew kurkentrekker

corm (stengel)knol

cormorant aalscholver

corn 1 likdoorn, eksteroog[h] **2** korrel, graankorrel, maiskorrel, tarwekorrel, zaadje[h], graantje[h] **3** graan[h], koren[h], tarwe; [Am] mais: ~ *on the cob* maiskolf, mais aan de kolf [as cooked food] **4** [inform] sentimenteel gedoe[h]

corned 1 gezouten: ~ *beef* cornedbeef[h] **2** [Am; inform] teut; zat, dronken

¹**corner** (n) **1** hoek, bocht, hoekje[h]: *in a remote* ~ *of the country* in een uithoek van het land; *cut* ~*s* **a)** bochten afsnijden; **b)** het niet zo nauw (meer) nemen **2** [sport] hoekschop || *cut* ~*s* **a)** de uitgaven besnoeien; **b)** formaliteiten omzeilen

²**corner** (vb) een bocht nemen, door de bocht gaan, de hoek omgaan

³**corner** (vb) in het nauw drijven, insluiten, klemzetten

cornerstone hoeksteen [also fig]; steunpilaar

cornet 1 [mus] kornet **2** (ijs)hoorn, cornetto

cornflour maizena, maismeel[h]

corn flower korenbloem

corny [inform] afgezaagd, clichématig, flauw

corollary uitvloeisel[h]; logisch gevolg[h]

¹**coronary** (n) hartinfarct[h], hartaanval

²**coronary** (adj) m.b.t. de krans(slag)ader: ~ *arteries* krans(slag)aderen

coronation kroning

coroner 1 lijkschouwer **2** rechter van instructie

coronet 1 (adellijk) kroontje[h], prinsenkroon, prinsessenkroon **2** diadeem[+h], (haar)kransje[h]

¹**corporal** (n) korporaal

²**corporal** (adj) lichamelijk, lijfelijk, lichaams-: ~ *punishment* lijfstraf

corporate 1 gezamenlijk, collectief, verenigd: ~ *body, body corporate* lichaam[h], rechtspersoon **2** m.b.t. een gemeentebestuur, gemeente-, gemeentelijk **3** m.b.t. een naamloze vennootschap, bedrijfs-, ondernemings-: ~ *identity* bedrijfsidentiteit, huisstijl; ~ *lawyer* bedrijfsjurist

corporation 1 gemeenteraad, gemeentebestuur[h] **2** rechtspersoon, lichaam[h]; [Am] naamloze vennootschap; onderneming: ~ *tax* vennootschapsbelasting

corps 1 [mil] (leger)korps[h], wapen[h], staf **2** korps[h], staf: ~ *de ballet* (corps de) ballet;

diplomatic ~ corps diplomatique

corpse lijk[h]

corpulent dik, zwaarlijvig

corral [Am] (vee)kraal, omheining voor paarden

¹**correct** (adj) **1** correct, juist: *politically* ~ politiek correct **2** onberispelijk, beleefd

²**correct** (vb) **1** verbeteren, corrigeren, nakijken **2** terechtwijzen **3** rechtzetten, rectificeren **4** verhelpen, repareren, tegengaan

correction correctie, verbetering, rectificatie: ~ *fluid* correctievloeistof

corrective verbeterend, correctief

correlation correlatie [also statistics]; wisselwerking, wederzijdse betrekking

correspond 1 (+ to, with) overeenkomen, overeenstemmen (met), kloppen, corresponderen **2** corresponderen, een briefwisseling voeren, schrijven

correspondence 1 overeenkomst, overeenstemming, gelijkenis **2** correspondentie; briefwisseling, mailwisseling: *commercial* ~ handelscorrespondentie

¹**correspondent** (n) correspondent; verslaggever

²**correspondent** (adj) [form] **1** overeenkomend **2** overeenkomstig

corridor 1 gang [also pol]; corridor, galerij **2** luchtweg, corridor, luchtvaartroute, vliegtuigroute

corroboration bevestiging, bekrachtiging

¹**corrode** (vb) vergaan, verteren, verroesten, (weg)roesten

²**corrode** (vb) aantasten, aanvreten, wegvreten

corrosion verroesting, aantasting, roest[+h]

corrugate plooien, golven: ~*d (card)board* golfkarton; *sheets of* ~*d iron* golfplaten

¹**corrupt** (adj) **1** verdorven, immoreel **2** corrupt, omkoopbaar **3** verbasterd, onbetrouwbaar: *a* ~ *form of Latin* verbasterd Latijn

²**corrupt** (vb) slecht worden, (zeden)bederf veroorzaken

³**corrupt** (vb) **1** omkopen, corrupt maken **2** verbasteren, vervalsen, verknoeien

corruption 1 corruptie, omkoperij **2** verbastering **3** bederf[h], verderf[h]

corset korset[h], keurslijfje[h], rijglijfje[h]

cortex cortex

¹**cosh** (n) (gummi)knuppel, ploertendoder

²**cosh** (vb) slaan met een gummiknuppel, aftuigen, neerknuppelen

cosine cosinus

¹**cosmetic** (n) cosmetisch middel[h], schoonheidsmiddel[h]: ~*s* cosmetica

²**cosmetic** (adj) **1** cosmetisch, schoonheids-: ~ *surgery* cosmetische chirurgie **2** [depr] verfraaiend, voor de schone schijn, oppervlakkig

cosmic kosmisch, van het heelal

cosmonaut kosmonaut

cosmopolitan kosmopolitisch

cosset vertroetelen, verwennen

¹cost (n) kost(en), prijs, uitgave: *the ~ of living* de kosten van levensonderhoud; *at all ~s, at any ~* koste wat het kost, tot elke prijs; *at the ~ of* ten koste van; *charged at ~* in rekening gebracht ‖ *count the ~* de nadelen overwegen [before acting]

²cost (vb) kostbaar zijn, in de papieren lopen

³cost (vb) kosten, komen (te staan) op, vergen

¹co-star (n) tegenspeler, tegenspeelster

²co-star (vb) als tegenspeler optreden

Costa Rica Costa Rica

¹Costa Rican (n) Costa Ricaan(se)

²Costa Rican (adj) Costa Ricaans

cost-cutting kostenbesparend: *~ measures* bezuinigingsmaatregelen

cost-effective rendabel

costing kostprijsberekening; raming

costly kostbaar, duur

costume kostuumʰ, pakʰ, (kleder)dracht

costume jewellery namaakbijouterie

¹cosy (n) 1 theemuts 2 eierwarmer

²cosy (adj) knus, behaaglijk, gezellig

cosy up [Am] dicht(er) aankruipen [to s.o.]; [fig] in de gunst proberen te komen [with s.o.]

cot 1 ledikantjeʰ, kinderbed(jeʰ), wieg 2 [Am] veldbedʰ, stretcher

cot death wiegendood

Côte d'Ivoire Ivoorkust

cottage 1 (plattelands)huisjeʰ 2 vakantiehuisjeʰ, zomerhuisjeʰ

cottage cheese [roughly] kwark; [Belg] [roughly] plattekaas

cotton 1 katoenʰ, katoenplant, katoendraadᵗʰ, katoenvezel 2 katoenen stof, katoenweefselʰ

cotton candy [Am] suikerspin

cotton on [inform] het snappen; doorkrijgen

¹couch (n) (rust)bank, sofa, divan

²couch (vb) 1 inkleden, formuleren, verwoorden: *the instructions were ~ed in simple language* de instructies waren in eenvoudige bewoordingen gesteld 2 vellen [spear, lance]

couch surfing het gratis verblijven bij particulieren

couch-surfing 1 (het) couchsurfen 2 (het) bankhangen

cougar 1 poema 2 oudere vrouw met jonge vriend

¹cough (n) 1 hoest: *have a bad ~* erg hoesten 2 kuch(jeʰ), hoestbui, hoestaanval

²cough (vb) 1 hoesten, kuchen 2 sputteren; blaffen [of firearm]: *the engine ~s and misfires* de motor sputtert en hapert

cough up 1 opbiechten, bekennen 2 dokken; ophoesten [money]

council 1 raad, (advies)collegeʰ, bestuurʰ: *municipal ~* gemeenteraad 2 kerkvergadering

council estate woningwetwijk, woningwetbuurt

councillor raadslidʰ

¹counsel (n) 1 raad, (deskundig) adviesʰ 2 overlegʰ 3 raadslieden, advocaat, verdediging ‖ *keep one's own ~* zijn motieven voor zich houden, zich niet blootgeven

²counsel (vb) advies geven, adviseren, aanraden

counselling het adviseren, adviseurschapʰ

counsellor 1 adviseur, consulent(e); [Am] (studenten)decaan; beroepskeuzeadviseur 2 [Am] raadsman, raadsvrouw, advocaat

¹count (n) 1 het uittellen [of a boxer]: *be out for the ~* uitgeteld zijn [also fig] 2 (niet-Engelse) graaf 3 telling, tel, getalʰ: *keep ~* de tel(ling) bijhouden, (mee)tellen; *lose ~* de tel kwijtraken

²count (vb) tellen, meetellen, gelden: *~ for little* (or: *nothing*) weinig (or: niets) voorstellen ‖ *~ against* pleiten tegen

³count (vb) 1 meetellen, meerekenen: *there were 80 victims, not ~ing (in) the crew* er waren 80 slachtoffers, de bemanning niet meegerekend 2 rekenen tot, beschouwen (als), achten: *~ o.s. lucky* zich gelukkig prijzen ‖ *they'll ~ it against you ...* ze zullen het je kwalijk nemen ...

⁴count (vb) tellen, optellen, tellen tot: *~ down* aftellen

countdown het aftellen

¹countenance (n) 1 gelaatʰ, gelaatstrekken, gelaatsuitdrukking 2 aanzichtʰ, aanzienʰ 3 welwillende blik 4 kalmte, gemoedsrust, zelfbeheersing: *lose ~* van zijn stuk raken 5 (morele) steun, instemming, goedkeuring: *we won't give* (or: *lend*) *~ to such plans* we zullen dergelijke plannen niet steunen

²countenance (vb) goedkeuren, (stilzwijgend) toestaan, oogluikend toestaan, dulden

¹counter (n) 1 toonbank, balie, bar, loketʰ, kassa 2 ficheʰ 3 tegenzet, tegenmaatregel, tegenwichtʰ ‖ *over the ~* zonder recept (verkrijgbaar) [of drugs]; *under the ~* onder de toonbank

²counter (adj) 1 tegen(over)gesteld, tegenwerkend, contra- 2 duplicaat-, dubbel

³counter (vb) een tegenzet doen, zich verweren, terugvechten; [boxing] counteren

⁴counter (vb) 1 zich verzetten tegen, tegenwerken, (ver)hinderen 2 beantwoorden, reageren op 3 tenietdoen, weerleggen

⁵counter (adv) 1 in tegenovergestelde richting 2 op tegengestelde wijze: *act* (or: *go*) *~ to* niet opvolgen, ingaan tegen

counteract tegengaan, neutraliseren, tenietdoen

¹**counter-attack** (n) tegenaanval

²**counter-attack** (vb) in de tegenaanval gaan

³**counter-attack** (vb) een tegenaanval uitvoeren op

counterbalance tegenwicht^h

counter-clockwise [Am] linksdraaiend, tegen de wijzers van de klok in (draaiend)

¹**counterfeit** (n) vervalsing, falsificatie

²**counterfeit** (adj) **1** vals, vervalst, onecht **2** voorgewend, niet gemeend

³**counterfeit** (vb) **1** vervalsen, namaken **2** doen alsof

counterfeiter vervalser, valsemunter

counterfoil controlestrookje^h, kwitantiestrook

counterpart tegenhanger

¹**counterpoise** (n) **1** tegenwicht^h, tegendruk **2** evenwicht^h

²**counterpoise** (vb) in evenwicht brengen, opwegen tegen, compenseren

counterproductive averechts; contraproductief

countersign medeondertekenen

counterweight tegen(ge)wicht^h, contragewicht^h

countess gravin, echtgenote van een graaf

countless talloos, ontelbaar

count out [inform] **1** niet meetellen, afschrijven, terzijde schuiven: *if it rains tonight you can count* **me** *out* als het vanavond regent moet je niet op me rekenen **2** [sport] uittellen [boxer] **3** neertellen

country 1 land^h, geboorteland^h, vaderland^h **2** volk^h, natie: *the ~ doesn't support this decision* het land staat niet achter deze beslissing **3** (land)streek, terrein^h **4** platteland^h, provincie: *go for a day* **in** *the ~* een dagje naar buiten gaan

country cousin provinciaal

countryfolk plattelanders, buitenlui

country house landhuis^h, buitenverblijf^h

countryman 1 landgenoot **2** plattelander

countryside platteland^h

count (up)on rekenen (vertrouwen) op

county graafschap^h, provincie

county council graafschapsbestuur^h, provinciaal bestuur^h; [roughly] Provinciale Staten

county court districtsrechtbank; [roughly] kantongerecht^h

county hall provinciehuis^h

coup 1 slimme zet, prestatie, succes^h: *make* (or: *pull off*) *a ~* zijn slag slaan **2** staatsgreep, coup

¹**couple** (n) **1** koppel^h, paar^h, span^h: *a ~ of* **a)** twee; **b)** [inform] een paar, een stuk of twee [not more than three] **2** (echt)paar^h, stel^h: *a married ~* een getrouwd stel, een echtpaar

²**couple** (vb) **1** paren vormen **2** paren, ge-

slachtsgemeenschap hebben

³**couple** (vb) **1** (aaneen)koppelen, verbinden, aanhaken: *~ up* aan elkaar koppelen **2** (met elkaar) in verband brengen, gepaard laten gaan

coupling koppeling, verbinding, koppelstuk^h

coupon 1 bon, kaartje^h, zegel, kortingsbon **2** (toto)formulier^h

courage moed, dapperheid, durf: *muster up* (or: *pluck up, summon up*) *~* moed vatten

courageous moedig, dapper, onverschrokken

courgette courgette

courier 1 koerier, bode **2** reisgids, reisleider

course 1 loop, (voort)gang, duur: *the ~ of events* de loop der gebeurtenissen; *run* (or: *take*) *its ~* zijn beloop hebben, (natuurlijk) verlopen **2** koers, richting, route: *stay the ~* tot het eind toe volhouden; *on ~* op koers **3** manier, weg, (gedrags)lijn **4** cursus, curriculum^h: *an English ~* een cursus Engels **5** cyclus, reeks, serie: *~ of lectures* lezingencyclus **6** [sport] baan **7** [culinary] gang: *a three-~ dinner* een diner van drie gangen; *the main ~* het hoofdgerecht ‖ *of ~* natuurlijk, vanzelfsprekend

courseware educatieve software

coursing hazen- of konijnenjacht met windhonden

¹**court** (n) **1** rechtbank, gerechtsgebouw^h, gerechtszaal, (gerechts)hof^h: *Court of Appeal(s)* hof van beroep; *Court of Claims* bestuursrechtelijk hof [Am]; *~ of inquiry* gerechtelijke commissie van onderzoek; *go to ~* naar de rechter stappen; *settle out of ~* buiten de rechter om schikken **2** hof^h, koninklijk paleis^h, hofhouding **3** [sport] (tennis)baan **4** omsloten ruimte, (licht)hal, binnenhof^h, binnenplaats ‖ *laugh s.o. (sth.)* **out** *of ~* iem. (iets) weghonen; *rule* (or: *put*) **out** *of ~* **a)** uitsluiten [witness, evidence; also fig]; **b)** (iets/iem.) totaal geen kans geven

²**court** (vb) verkering hebben

³**court** (vb) **1** vleien, in de gunst trachten te komen bij **2** flirten met, het hof maken, dingen naar de hand van, vragen om, uitlokken: *~ disaster* om moeilijkheden vragen **3** (trachten te) winnen, streven naar

courteous beleefd, welgemanierd

courtesy beleefdheid, welgemanierdheid, beleefdheidsbetuiging: *(by)* **of** welwillend ter beschikking gesteld door, met toestemming van

court-house gerechtsgebouw^h

courtly 1 hoofs, verfijnd, elegant **2** welgemanierd, beleefd, hoffelijk

¹**court martial** (n) krijgsraad, (hoog) militair gerechtshof^h

²**court martial** (vb) voor een krijgsraad

brengen
courtship 1 verkering(stijd) **2** het hof maken **3** [zoology] balts
courtyard binnenhof^h, binnenplaats, plein^h
cousin neef, nicht, dochter of zoon van tante of oom: *first* ~ volle neef/nicht; [fig] nauwe verwante; *second* ~ achterneef, achternicht, verre neef/nicht
cove 1 inham, kleine baai, kreek **2** beschutte plek, (beschutte) inham
covenant 1 overeenkomst **2** [rel] verbond^h
¹cover (n) **1** bedekking, hoes: ~*s* dekens; dekbed^h **2** deksel^{+h}, klep **3** omslag^{+h}, stofomslag^{+h}, boekband: *read a book from* ~ *to* ~ een boek van begin tot eind lezen **4** enveloppe **5** mes en vork **6** invaller, vervanger **7** dekmantel, voorwendsel^h: *under* ~ *of friendship* onder het mom van vriendschap **8** dekking [also sport]; beschutting, schuilplaats: *take* ~ dekking zoeken, (gaan) schuilen; *under* ~ heimelijk, in het geheim, verborgen **9** dekking [insurance]
²cover (vb) [inform] (+ for) invallen (voor), vervangen
³cover (vb) **1** bedekken, overtrekken: *he was ~ed in* (or: *with*) *blood* hij zat onder het bloed; ~ *over* bedekken **2** beslaan, omvatten, bestrijken **3** afleggen [distance] **4** bewaken [eg access roads] **5** verslaan, verslag uitbrengen over **6** dekken, verzekeren: *we aren't ~ed against* fire we zijn niet tegen brand verzekerd **7** onder schot houden, in bedwang houden **8** beheersen, controleren, bestrijken **9** [sport] dekken, bewaken || *a ~ing letter* (or: *note*) een begeleidend schrijven
coverage 1 dekking [also insurance]; verzekerd bedrag^h (risico^h) **2** berichtgeving, verslag^h, verslaggeving, publiciteit **3** bereik^h
cover charge couvert(kosten)
covering bedekking, dekzeil^h
cover story 1 omslagartikel^h; coverstory **2** dekmantel
¹covert (n) **1** beschutte plaats, schuilplaats **2** kreupelhout^h
²covert (adj) bedekt, heimelijk, illegaal
¹cover up (vb) dekking geven, een alibi verstrekken
²cover up (vb) **1** verdoezelen, wegmoffelen, verhullen: ~ *one's tracks* zijn sporen uitwissen **2** toedekken, inwikkelen
cover-up 1 doofpotaffaire **2** dekmantel, alibi^h
covet begeren
cow koe, wijfje^h: [fig] *sacred* ~ heilige koe || *till the ~s come home* tot je een ons weegt, eindeloos
coward lafaard
cowardice lafheid
cowboy 1 [Am] cowboy, veedrijver **2** beunhaas, knoeier **3** [inform] gewetenloos zakenman: ~ *employers* gewetenloze

werkgevers
cower in elkaar duiken, ineenkrimpen
cowl 1 monnikskap, kap **2** monnikspij **3** schoorsteenkap
co-worker collega, medewerker
cow pat koeienvlaai
cowslip 1 sleutelbloem **2** [Am] dotterbloem
cox stuurman; stuur^h [of rowing boat]
coxcomb ijdeltuit
coy 1 koket **2** ingetogen; terughoudend: *a politician* ~ *about his plans* een politicus die zijn plannen voor zich houdt
cozy see ¹*cosy*
cps characters, cycles per second
CPU Central Processing Unit CVE
¹crab (n) **1** krab **2** [inform] schaamluis
²crab (vb) **1** krabben vangen **2** [inform] kankeren, mopperen
crab apple wilde appel
crabbed 1 chagrijnig, prikkelbaar **2** kriebelig, gekrabbeld; onduidelijk [of handwriting] **3** ingewikkeld
¹crack (n) **1** barst(je^h), breuk, scheur(tje^h) **2** kier, spleet **3** knal(geluid^h), knak, kraak **4** klap, pets **5** [inform] gooi, poging: *have a* ~ *at* een gooi doen naar, proberen **6** grap(je^h), geintje^h **7** [inform] kraan, kei, uitblinker **8** [inform] (zuivere vorm van) cocaïne || *at the* ~ *of dawn* bij het krieken van de dag
²crack (adj) [inform] prima, keur-, uitgelezen: *a* ~ *shot* (or: *marksman*) een eersteklas schutter
³crack (vb) **1** in(een)storten, het begeven, knakken **2** knallen, kraken **3** barsten, splijten, scheuren **4** breken, schor worden; overslaan [of voice]
⁴crack (vb) **1** laten knallen, laten kraken: ~ *a whip* klappen met een zweep **2** doen barsten, splijten, scheuren **3** meppen, slaan **4** de oplossing vinden van: ~ *a code* een code ontcijferen **5** [inform] vertellen: ~ *a joke* een mop vertellen
⁵crack (vb) **1** (open)breken, stukbreken, knappen: ~ *a safe* een kluis openbreken **2** [chem] kraken
crack-brained onzinnig, getikt, dwaas
crackdown (straf)campagne, (politie)optreden^h, actie
crack down on met harde hand optreden tegen
cracker 1 cracker(tje^h), knäckebröd^h **2** knalbonbon **3** [comp] criminele hacker
crackers [inform] gek
cracking [inform] **1** schitterend, uitstekend **2** snel: ~ *pace* stevige vaart || *get* ~ aan de slag gaan
¹crackle (n) geknetter^h, geknap(per)^h, geknisper^h
²crackle (vb) knapp(er)en, knetteren, knisperen; kraken [of telephone]

crack on [inform] (snel) doorgaan

crackpot [inform] zonderling

¹**crack up** (vb) [inform] bezwijken, instorten, eronderdoor gaan

²**crack up** (vb) [inform] **1** ophemelen, roemen, prijzen: *he isn't everything he's cracked up to be* hij is niet zo goed als iedereen zegt **2** in de lach schieten, in een deuk liggen

crack-up [inform] in(een)storting, inzinking

¹**cradle** (n) **1** wieg [also fig]; bakermat: *from the ~ to the grave* van de wieg tot het graf **2** stellage; [shipp] (constructie)bok; haak [of telephone] **3** werkbak, gondel [of working platform]

²**cradle** (vb) **1** wiegen, vasthouden **2** in een wieg leggen **3** op de haak leggen [telephone]

¹**craft** (n) **1** vakʰ, ambachtʰ **2** (kunst)vaardigheid, kunstnijverheid **3** bedrijfstak, branche, (ambachts)gildeʰ

²**craft** (n) **1** boot(jeʰ), vaartuigʰ **2** vliegtuigʰ **3** ruimtevaartuigʰ

craft beer [Am] ambachtelijk bierʰ

craftsman handwerksman; vakman [also fig]

crafty geslepen, doortrapt, geraffineerd

crag steile rots

¹**cram** (vb) **1** zich volproppen, schrokken **2** blokken, stampen

²**cram** (vb) **1** (vol)proppen, aanstampen, (vol)stouwen **2** klaarstomen [pupil] **3** erin stampen [subject matter]

cramp kramp(scheut): *~s* maagkramp; buikkramp

cramped 1 benauwd, krap, kleinbehuisd **2** kriebelig [of handwriting] **3** gewrongen

cranberry veenbes

¹**crane** (n) **1** kraanvogel **2** kraan, hijskraan

²**crane** (vb) de hals uitstrekken, reikhalzen

³**crane** (vb) (reikhalzend) uitstrekken, vooruitsteken

¹**crank** (n) **1** krukas, autoslinger; crank [of bicycle] **2** [inform] zonderling, excentriekeling **3** [Am; inform] mopperkont

²**crank** (vb) aanzwengelen, aanslingeren: *~ up a car* een auto aanslingeren

crankshaft krukas, trapas

cranky 1 [inform] zonderling, bizar **2** [Am; inform] chagrijnig

cranny spleet; scheur

¹**crap** (n) [vulg] **1** stront: *have a ~* een drol leggen **2** kletspraat, gekletsʰ: *a load of ~* een hoop gezever **3** troep, rotzooi

²**crap** (vb) [vulg] schijten, kakken

crap on [fig] doorzagen; tot vervelens toe blijven praten

¹**crash** (n) **1** klap, dreun **2** botsing, neerstorting, ongelukʰ **3** krach, ineenstorting

²**crash** (adj) spoed-: *~ course* stoomcursus, spoedcursus

³**crash** (vb) **1** te pletter slaan, verongelukken, botsen, (neer)storten: *the plates ~ed to the floor* de borden kletterden op de grond **2** stormen **3** dreunen, knallen **4** ineenstorten, failliet gaan; [comp] crashen; down gaan **5** [inform] (blijven) pitten, de nacht doorbrengen

⁴**crash** (vb) te pletter laten vallen

crash barrier vangrail

crash landing buiklanding, noodlanding

crass bot, onbehouwen, lomp: *~ stupidity* peilloze domheid

crate 1 kratʰ, kist **2** [inform] brik, bak **3** [inform] kist, wrakkig vliegtuigʰ

crater krater

crave hunkeren (naar), smachten (naar)

craving hunkering; verlangenʰ

¹**crawl** (n) **1** slakkengang **2** crawl(slag)

²**crawl** (vb) **1** kruipen, sluipen, moeizaam vooruitkomen **2** krioelen, wemelen: *the place was ~ing with vermin* het krioelde er van ongedierte **3** kruipen, kruiperig doen, slijmen: *~ to one's boss* de hielen likken van zijn baas

craze rage, manie, gril

crazy 1 gek, krankzinnig, dol, waanzinnig: *go ~* gek worden; [inform] *~ about fishing* gek van vissen **2** [inform] te gek, fantastisch

creak geknarsʰ, gekraakʰ

¹**cream** (n) **1** (slag)roomʰ **2** crème [for use on skin] **3** crèmeʰ [colour]

²**cream** (vb) **1** room toevoegen aan, in room e.d. bereiden: *~ed potatoes* aardappelpuree **2** inwrijven; insmeren [skin]

³**cream** (vb) romen; afromen [also fig]: *~ off* afromen

cream puff 1 roomsoesjeʰ **2** [inform] slapjanus

cream tea aangeklede thee

¹**crease** (n) vouw, plooi, kreukel: *~ resistant* kreukvrij

²**crease** (vb) persen, een vouw maken in

³**crease** (vb) kreuke(le)n, vouwen, plooien

¹**create** (vb) [inform] tekeergaan, leven maken

²**create** (vb) **1** scheppen, creëren, ontwerpen **2** veroorzaken, teweegbrengen

creation 1 schepping, instelling, oprichting: *the Creation* de schepping **2** creatie, (mode)ontwerpʰ

creative creatief, scheppend, vindingrijk: *~ accounting* creatief boekhouden

creativity creativiteit, scheppingsdrang, scheppingsvermogenʰ

creator schepper

creature 1 schepselʰ, schepping, voortbrengselʰ: *~ of habit* gewoontedierʰ, gewoontemens **2** dierʰ, beestʰ **3** (levend) wezenʰ **4** stakker, mens(jeʰ), creatuurʰ

crèche 1 crèche, kinderdagverblijfʰ **2** [Am] kerststal, krib

credence geloofʰ: *attach* (or: *give*) *no ~ to* geen geloof hechten aan

credentials introductiebrieven, geloofsbrieven, legitimatiebewijsʰ

credibility geloofwaardigheid

credible 1 geloofwaardig, betrouwbaar **2** overtuigend

¹credit (n) **1** kredietʰ: *buy on ~* op krediet kopen; *~ on* a prepaid phone card beltegoedʰ **2** creditʰ, creditzijde, creditpost **3** tegoedʰ, spaarbanktegoedʰ, positief saldoʰ **4** geloofʰ, vertrouwenʰ: *lend ~ to* bevestigen, geloofwaardig maken **5** kredietʰ, kredietwaardigheid, goede naam **6** kredietʰ, krediettermijn **7** eer, lof, verdienste: *it does* you ~, *it is to your ~*, *it reflects ~ on you* het siert je, het strekt je tot eer **8** [Am] studiepuntʰ, examenbriefjeʰ, tentamenbriefjeʰ **9** sieraadʰ: *she's a ~ to our family* ze is een sieraad voor onze familie **10** (-s) titelrol, aftiteling

²credit (vb) **1** geloven, geloof hechten aan **2** crediteren, op iemands tegoed bijschrijven **3** toedenken, toeschrijven: *he is ~ed with the invention* de uitvinding staat op zijn naam

creditable 1 loffelijk, eervol, prijzenswaardig **2** te geloven

credit card creditcard; [roughly] betaalkaart

credit crunch kredietcrisis

creditor crediteur, schuldeiser

credo credoʰ; geloofsbelijdenis

credulity lichtgelovigheid, goedgelovigheid

creed 1 geloofsbelijdenis; credoʰ [also fig] **2** (geloofs)overtuiging, gezindte

creek kreek; inham; bocht, kleine rivier ǁ [inform] *up the ~* in een lastig parket, in de penarie

¹creep (n) **1** [inform] gluiperd, griezel, engerd, slijmerd **2** (the creeps) kriebels, kippenvelʰ, koude rillingen

²creep (vb) kruipen, sluipen: *~ in* binnensluipen; *~ up on* bekruipen, besluipen

creeper 1 kruiper **2** kruipend gewasʰ, klimplant **3** (-s) [Am] kruippakʰ **4** (-s) bordeelsluipers, schoenen met crêpe zolen

creep out [inform] (iem.) schrik aanjagen, de stuipen op het lijf jagen

creepy griezelig, eng, huiveringwekkend

creepy-crawly [inform] beestjeʰ, (kruipend) insectʰ (ongedierteʰ)

cremate cremeren, verassen

cremation crematie

crematorium crematorium(gebouw)ʰ

crescent 1 halvemaan, afnemende maan **2** halvemaanvormig iets, halvemaantjeʰ

cress kers, gewone kers, tuinkers, sterrenkers

¹crest (n) **1** kam, pluim, kuif **2** helmbos, helmpluim, vederbos **3** top, berg-, heuveltop, golfkam: [fig] *he is riding the ~ (of the*

waves) hij is op het hoogtepunt van zijn carrière/succes

²crest (vb) de top bereiken van; bedwingen [mountain]

crestfallen terneergeslagen, teleurgesteld

¹Cretan (n) Kretenzer, Kretenzische

²Cretan (adj) Kretenzisch, Kretenzer

Crete Kreta

crevice spleet; scheur, kloof

crew 1 bemanning: *several ~ are ill* verscheidene bemanningsleden zijn ziek **2** personeelʰ **3** ploeg, roeibootbemanning, roeiploeg

crew cut stekeltjes(haarʰ); crewcut

¹crib (n) **1** [Am] ledikantjeʰ, bedjeʰ, wieg **2** krib, voederbak, ruif **3** kerststal **4** [inform] afgekeken antwoordʰ, spiekwerkʰ, plagiaatʰ **5** [inform] spiekbriefjeʰ

²crib (vb) [inform] **1** spieken, afkijken, overschrijven **2** jatten, pikken

¹crick (n) stijfheid, spitʰ: *a ~ in the neck* een stijve nek

²crick (vb) verrekken, verdraaien, ontwrichten

¹cricket (n) cricketʰ: *that's not ~* dat is onsportief, zoiets doe je niet

²cricket (n) krekel

crier 1 schreeuwer **2** huilebalk **3** [hist] omroeper, stadsomroeper

crime 1 misdaad, misdrijfʰ **2** criminaliteit, (de) misdaad **3** schandaalʰ, schande: *it's a ~ the way he treats us* het is schandalig zoals hij ons behandelt

Crimean Krim-, m.b.t. de Krim

crime scene plaats delict

¹criminal (n) misdadiger

²criminal (adj) **1** misdadig, crimineel: *~ act* misdrijfʰ, strafbare handeling **2** [inform] schandalig **3** strafrechtelijk, crimineel: *~ libel* smaad

crimson karmozijn(rood): *turn ~* (vuur)rood aanlopen, (diep) kleuren/blozen

cringe 1 ineenkrimpen, terugdeinzen, terugschrikken **2** (+ to) kruipen (voor), door het stof gaan (voor), zich vernederen **3** [inform] de kriebel(s) krijgen: *his foolish talk makes me ~* zijn gezwets hangt me mijlenver de keel uit

¹crinkle (n) kreuk, (valse/ongewenste) vouw

²crinkle (vb) (doen) kreuke(le)n, (doen) rimpelen, verfrommelen

crinkly 1 gekreukt; gekreukeld, verfrommeld **2** gekruld; kroezig

¹cripple (n) invalide, (gedeeltelijk) verlamde, kreupele

²cripple (vb) verlammen, invalide maken; [fig] (ernstig) beschadigen: *~d with gout* krom van de jicht

crisis crisis, kritiek stadiumʰ, keerpuntʰ

¹crisp (n) (aardappel)chip

²crisp (adj) **1** knapperig, krokant: *a ~ pound*

note een kraaknieuw biljet van een pond
2 stevig; vers [vegetable etc] **3** fris, helder,
verfrissend: *the ~ autumn **wind*** de frisse
herfstwind **4** helder, ter zake, kernachtig

crispbread knäckebröd^h

crisper groentelade, groentevak^h [in refrig-
erator]

crispy knapperig, krokant

¹criss-cross (adj) kruiselings, kruis-

²criss-cross (vb) **1** (kriskras) (door)kruisen
2 doorsnijden: *train tracks ~ the country*
spoorlijnen doorsnijden het land **3** krassen
maken op, bekrassen

³criss-cross (adv) kriskras, door elkaar

criterion criterium^h

critic criticus, recensent

critical 1 kritisch; streng: *be ~ **of** sth.* ergens
kritisch tegenover staan; *~ **thinker*** kritisch
(*or:* onafhankelijk) denker **2** kritiek; cruciaal:
*the patient's **condition** is ~* de toestand van de
patiënt is kritiek; *of ~ **importance*** van cruci-
aal belang || *~ **writings*** kritieken

criticism 1 kritiek, recensie, bespreking
2 afkeuring, afwijzing

criticize 1 kritiek hebben (op) **2** (be)kritise-
ren, beoordelen, recenseren **3** afkeuren

critique kritiek; recensie; [esp] kunstkritiek

CRM [econ] *customer relationship management* crm^h, klantenrelatiebeheer^h

¹croak (vb) **1** kwaken [of frogs]; krassen [of
ravens and crows]; hees zijn, (ontevreden)
grommen, brommen **2** [inform] het loodje
leggen

²croak (n): *speak **with** a ~* hees zijn, spreken
met schorre stem

Croat Kroaat, Kroatische

Croatia Kroatië

Croatian Kroatisch

crochet haakwerk^h

crock 1 aardewerk(en) pot, kruik **2** pot-
scherf **3** [inform] (oud) wrak^h, kneusje^h,
ouwe knol

crockery aardewerk^h, vaatwerk^h, servies-
goed^h

crock up [inform] in elkaar klappen, instorten

crocodile 1 krokodil: *~ **tears*** krokodillentranen **2** rij (kinderen, 2 aan 2)

crocus krokus

crony makker, maat(je^h), gabber

crook 1 herderstaf **2** bisschopsstaf, krom-
staf **3** bocht, kronkel, buiging: *the ~ of one's
arm* de elleboogholte **4** haak, hoek, luik^h
5 [inform] oplichter, zwendelaar, flessen-
trekker

crooked 1 bochtig, slingerend, kronkelig
2 misvormd; krom(gegroeid) [also with age];
gebocheld **3** oneerlijk, onbetrouwbaar, achterbaks

crooner sentimenteel zanger; crooner

crop 1 krop [of bird] **2** rijzweep(je^h), kar-

wats, rijstokje^h **3** gewas^h, landbouwpro-
duct^h, landbouwproducten **4** oogst [also fig];
graanoogst, lading, lichting: *a whole new ~ of
students* een hele nieuwe lichting studenten
|| *a fine ~ of **hair*** een mooie bos haar

cropper [inform] smak: *come a ~* een
(dood)smak maken; [fig] op z'n bek vallen,
afgaan

crop spraying gewasbespuiting

crop top naveltruitje^h

crop up [inform] opduiken, de kop opsteken, plotseling ter sprake komen: *her name
keeps cropping up in the papers* haar naam
duikt voortdurend op in de krant

¹cross (n) **1** kruis(je^h), crucifix^h, kruisteken^h:
make the sign of the ~ een kruisje slaan (*or:*
maken) **2** kruis^h, beproeving, lijden^h **3** kruising, bastaard **4** [socc] voorzet

²cross (adj) boos, kwaad, uit zijn humeur: *be
~ **with** s.o.* kwaad op iem. zijn

³cross (vb) (elkaar) kruisen

⁴cross (vb) **1** kruisen, over elkaar slaan: *~
one's **arms** (or: **legs**)* zijn armen (*or:* benen)
over elkaar slaan **2** een kruisteken maken
boven: *~ **o.s.*** een kruis slaan **3** (door)strepen,
een streep trekken door: *~ **out** (or: off)* doorstrepen, doorhalen, schrappen [also fig]
4 dwarsbomen; doorkruisen [plan] **5** [biolo-
gy] kruisen

⁵cross (vb) **1** oversteken, overtrekken, doortrekken **2** kruisen, (elkaar) passeren

Cross (the) (Heilige) Kruis^h; kruisiging [of
Christ]; christendom^h

cross-border grensoverschrijdend: *~ **traffic*** grensoverschrijdend verkeer^h

crossbow kruisboog

crossbreed 1 kruising, bastaard **2** gekruist
ras^h, bastaardras^h

¹cross-country (n) cross(country), terrein-
wedstrijd; [athletics] veldloop; [cycling] veld-
rit

²cross-country (adj) **1** terrein- **2** over het
hele land, van kust tot kust: *~ concert **tour***
landelijke concerttournee

cross-dresser travestiet

cross-examine aan een kruisverhoor onderwerpen [also fig]; scherp ondervragen

cross-eyed scheel(ogig): *he is slightly ~* hij
loenst een beetje

crossfire [mil] kruisvuur^h: [fig] *caught **in** the
~* tussen twee vuren zitten

crossfit [sport] crossfit^h

crossing 1 oversteek, overtocht, overvaart
2 kruising, snijpunt^h, kruispunt^h **3** oversteekplaats, zebra **4** overweg: *level ~* gelijkvloer-
se kruising, overweg

cross-legged met gekruiste benen; in
kleermakerszit

crossmatch [med] kruisproef

crossover 1 overstap **2** oversteekplaats
3 [car] cross-over **4** [mus] cross-over

cross-purpose: *talk at ~s* langs elkaar heen praten

cross-reference verwijzing, referentie

crossroads wegkruising, tweesprong, driesprong, viersprong, kruispunt[h]; [fig] tweesprong; beslissend moment[h], keerpunt[h]

cross section dwarsdoorsnede [also fig]; kenmerkende steekproef

cross-stitch kruissteek

crossword kruiswoord(raadsel)[h]

crotch 1 vertakking, vork **2** kruis[h] [of person or article of clothing]

crotchet [mus] kwart[h], kwartnoot

crotchety chagrijnig; knorrig

crouch zich (laag) bukken, ineenduiken, zich buigen: *~ down* ineengehurkt zitten

[1]**crow** (n) **1** kraai, roek **2** gekraai[h] [of cock] **3** kreetje[h], geluidje[h]; gekraai[h] [of baby] ‖ *as the ~ flies* hemelsbreed

[2]**crow** (vb) **1** kraaien [of cock, child]: *the baby ~ed with pleasure* het kindje kraaide van plezier **2** [inform] opscheppen, snoeven ‖ *~ over* (triomfantelijk) juichen over, uitbundig leedvermaak hebben over

crowbar koevoet, breekijzer[h]

[1]**crowd** (n) **1** (mensen)menigte, massa **2** [inform] volkje[h], kliek(je[h]) ‖ *follow* (or: *move with, go with*) *the ~* in de pas lopen, zich conformeren aan de massa

[2]**crowd** (vb) elkaar verdringen: *people ~ed round* mensen dromden samen

[3]**crowd** (vb) **1** (over)bevolken, (meer dan) volledig vullen: *shoppers ~ed the stores* de winkels waren vol winkelende mensen **2** proppen, persen, (dicht) op elkaar drukken ‖ *~ out* buitensluiten, verdringen

crowded vol, druk

crowdfund crowdfunden, financieren via crowdfunding

crowdfunding crowdfunding

crowdsourcing crowdsourcing

crowd-surf crowdsurfen

[1]**crown** (n) **1** krans **2** kroon; [fig] vorstelijke macht; regering; [law] openbare aanklager: *minister of the Crown* zittend minister [in England] **3** hoogste punt[h], bovenste gedeelte[h], (hoofd)kruin, boomkruin; kroon [of tooth, molar] **4** [sport] kampioen(schap)stitel

[2]**crown** (vb) **1** kronen: *~ed heads* gekroonde hoofden, regerende vorsten **2** bekronen, belonen, eren **3** kronen, de top vormen van, sieren **4** voltooien, (met succes) bekronen, de kroon op het werk vormen: *to ~ (it) all* als klap op de vuurpijl; [iron] tot overmaat van ramp

crow's-foot kraaienpootje[h] [wrinkle near corner of the eye]

crucial 1 cruciaal, (alles)beslissend; [inform] zeer belangrijk: *~ point* keerpunt[h] **2** kritiek

cruciate ligament [anatomy] kruisband

crucifix kruisbeeld[h]

crucifixion kruisiging

crucify 1 kruisigen **2** tuchtigen

crude 1 ruw, onbewerkt, ongezuiverd, primitief: *~ oil* ruwe olie, aardolie; *a ~ log cabin* een primitieve blokhut **2** rauw, bot, onbehouwen: *~ behaviour* lomp gedrag

cruel wreed, hard(vochtig), gemeen; [fig] guur; bar

cruelty wreedheid: *~ to animals* dierenmishandeling

cruise 1 een cruise maken **2** kruisen [of aeroplane, car etc]; zich met kruissnelheid voortbewegen, (langzaam) rondrijden, patrouilleren, surveilleren

crumb 1 kruimel, kruim(pje[h]) **2** klein beetje[h], fractie, zweem(pje[h])

crumble ten onder gaan, vergaan, vervallen, afbrokkelen: *crumbling walls* bouwvallige muren ‖ *~ away* a) afbrokkelen; b) verschrompelen

crumpet warm broodje[h] [at breakfast] ‖ [inform] *a nice piece of ~* een lekkere meid

[1]**crumple** (vb) (also + up) verschrompelen, ineenstorten, ineenklappen

[2]**crumple** (vb) (also + up) kreuk(el)en, rimpelen, verfrommelen

[1]**crunch** (n) **1** knerpend geluid[h], geknars[h] **2** beslissend moment[h], beslissende confrontatie: *if* (or: *when*) *it comes to the ~* als puntje bij paaltje komt

[2]**crunch** (vb) **1** (doen) knarsen **2** knauwen (op), (luidruchtig) kluiven, knagen (aan)

crusade kruistocht, felle campagne

[1]**crush** (n) **1** drom, (samengepakte) mensenmenigte **2** [always singular] gedrang[h]: *avoid the ~* de drukte vermijden **3** [inform] overmatig drukke bijeenkomst **4** [inform] (hevige) verliefdheid: *have a ~ on* smoorverliefd zijn op

[2]**crush** (vb) **1** in elkaar drukken, indeuken: *be ~ed to death in a crowd* doodgedrukt worden in een mensenmenigte **2** vernietigen, de kop indrukken: *~ it* a) er helemaal top uitzien; b) iets heel goed doen, iets perfect uitvoeren

[3]**crush** (vb) dringen, (zich) persen

crush barrier dranghek[h]

crushing vernietigend, verpletterend

[1]**crust** (n) **1** korst, broodkorst, kapje[h], korstdeeg[h], bladerdeeg[h]: *the earth's ~* de aardkorst **2** aardkorst **3** (wond)korst **4** [inform] lef[h], brutaliteit ‖ [inform] *off one's ~* getikt

[2]**crust** (vb) met een korst bedekt worden

crusty 1 knapperig **2** chagrijnig, humeurig

crutch kruk [for disabled person]

crux essentie, kern(punt[h])

[1]**cry** (n) **1** kreet, (uit)roep, geschreeuw[h], schreeuw, strijdkreet **2** huilpartij, gehuil[h] **3** diergeluid[h], schreeuw, (vogel)roep **4** roep, smeekbede, appel[h]

²cry (vb) **1** schreeuwen, jammeren: *he cried (out)* **with** *pain* hij schreeuwde het uit van de pijn **2** een geluid geven [of animals, esp birds]; roepen

³cry (vb) **1** huilen, janken: ~ *for sth.* om iets jengelen, om iets huilen; ~ *for joy* huilen van blijdschap **2** roepen, schreeuwen: *the fields are ~ing out for rain* het land schreeuwt om regen ‖ ~ *sth.* **down** iets kleineren, iets afbreken; ~ *off* terugkrabbelen, er(gens) van afzien; [inform] *for ~ing out loud, why did you do it?* waarom heb je dat in vredesnaam gedaan?; [inform] *it's only six o'clock in the morning, for ~ing out loud!* het is verdorie pas zes uur!

crybaby huilebalk

crying hemeltergend, schreeuwend: *a ~ shame* een grof schandaal

cryotherapy cryotherapie, koudetherapie

crypt crypt(e), grafkelder, ondergrondse kapel

cryptic cryptisch, verborgen, geheimzinnig: ~ *crossword* cryptogram^h

¹crystal (n) **1** kristal^h **2** [Am] horlogeglas^h

²crystal (adj) **1** kristal(len): ~ *ball* kristallen bol [of fortune-teller] **2** (kristal)helder

crystal clear glashelder [also fig]

ct *cent* c

cub welp^{+h}, jong^h, vossenjong^h

Cuba Cuba

¹Cuban (n) Cubaan(se)

²Cuban (adj) Cubaans

¹cube (n) **1** kubus, klontje^h, blokje^h: [Am] *a ~ of sugar* een suikerklontje **2** derde macht: ~ *root* derdemachtswortel

²cube (vb) tot de derde macht verheffen: *two ~d is eight* twee tot de derde is acht

cube root derdemachtswortel

cubic 1 kubiek, driedimensionaal: ~ *metre* kubieke meter **2** kubusvormig, rechthoekig **3** kubisch, derdemachts-

cubicle 1 kleedhokje^h **2** toilethokje^h **3** douchecabine, douchecel **4** slaapho(e)kje^h **5** werkplek

¹cuckold (n) bedrogen echtgenoot

²cuckold (vb) bedriegen, ontrouw zijn

¹cuckoo (n) **1** koekoek **2** koekoeksroep **3** [fig] uilskuiken^h, sul ‖ ~ *in the **nest*** ongewenste indringer

²cuckoo (adj) [inform] achterlijk, idioot

cucumber komkommer

cud herkauwmassa [from rumen]: *chew the ~* herkauwen; [fig] prakkeseren, tobben

¹cuddle (vb) dicht tegen elkaar aan (genesteld) liggen: ~ *up* dicht tegen elkaar aankruipen; ~ *up to s.o.* zich bij iem. nestelen

²cuddle (vb) knuffelen, liefkozen

cuddly snoezig, aanhalig: *a ~ toy* een knuffelbeest

¹cudgel (n) knuppel ‖ *take up the ~s for* in de bres springen voor

²cudgel (vb) neerknuppelen

cue 1 aansporing, wenk, hint **2** richtsnoer^h, voorbeeld^h, leidraad: *take one's ~ from* een voorbeeld nemen aan **3** (biljart)keu

¹cuff (n) **1** manchet **2** [Am] (broek)omslag^h **3** klap [with a flat hand]; draai om de oren, pets ‖ [inform] *off the ~* voor de vuist (weg)

²cuff (vb) een draai om de oren geven

cuff link manchetknoop

cul-de-sac 1 doodlopende straat **2** dood punt^h

¹cull (n) selectie

²cull (vb) **1** plukken [flowers etc] **2** verzamelen, vergaren **3** selecteren, uitkammen, uitziften: ~ *from* selecteren uit

culminate culmineren, zijn hoogtepunt bereiken

culpable 1 afkeurenswaardig, verwerpelijk **2** verwijtbaar: ~ *homicide* dood door schuld **3** aansprakelijk, schuldig

culprit 1 beklaagde, verdachte, beschuldigde **2** schuldige, dader, boosdoener

cult 1 rage; [depr] ziekelijke verering **2** sekte, kliek: ~ *book* cultboek^h, exclusief boek **3** cultus, eredienst: ~ *figure* cultfiguur^{+h}

cultivate 1 cultiveren, aanbouwen, bebouwen, ontginnen **2** kweken [eg bacteria] **3** voor zich proberen te winnen, vleien

cultivation 1 [agriculture] cultuur, ontginning, verbouw: *under ~* in cultuur **2** beschaafdheid, welgemanierdheid

cultural cultureel, cultuur-

culture 1 cultuur, beschaving(stoestand), ontwikkeling(sniveau^h) **2** (bacterie)kweek **3** algemene ontwikkeling **4** kweek, cultuur, teelt

¹cum (prep) met, plus, inclusief, annex, zowel als, tevens: *bed-cum-sitting room* zitslaapkamer

²cum (n) [vulg] sperma^h

cumbersome 1 onhandelbaar, log, (p)lomp **2** hinderlijk, lastig, zwaar

cumin komijn

cumulus stapelwolk

cunnilingus het beffen

¹cunning (n) sluwheid, listigheid, slimheid

²cunning (adj) sluw, listig, slim

cunt [vulg] kut

cup 1 kop(je^h), mok, beker **2** [sport] (wissel)beker, cup, bokaal ‖ *between ~ and lip* op de valreep; *my ~ of tea* (echt) iets voor mij

cupboard kast

cupcake 1 cupcake **2** [Am; inform] moppie^h, schatje^h

cup final [sport] bekerfinale

cup-tie [sport] bekerwedstrijd

curable geneesbaar

Curaçao Curaçao

curate hulppredikant; [Roman Catholicism] kapelaan

curative heilzaam; geneeskrachtig

cur<u>a</u>tor beheerder, curator, conservator

¹curb (n) **1** rem, beteugeling **2** [Am] stoeprand

²curb (vb) intomen [also fig]; beteugelen, in bedwang houden ‖ [Am] ~ *your dog!* (hond) in de goot!

curd wrongel; gestremde melk: *~s and whey* wrongel en wei

cu̲rd cheese kwark; [Belg] platte kaas

cu̲rdle stremmen, (doen) stollen: *her blood ~d at the spectacle* het schouwspel deed haar bloed stollen

¹cure (n) **1** (medische) behandeling, kuur **2** (genees)middel^h, medicament^h; remedie^{+h} [also fig] **3** genezing, herstel^h

²cure (vb) **1** kuren, een kuur doen **2** een heilzame werking hebben **3** verduurzaamd worden, roken, drogen

³cure (vb) verduurzamen, conserveren; zouten, roken [fish, meat]; drogen [tobacco]

⁴cure (vb) genezen, beter maken, (doen) herstellen: ~ *o.s. of bad habits* zijn slechte gewoonten afleren

cu̲re-all wondermiddel^h; panacee

cu̲rfew 1 avondklok, uitgaansverbod^h **2** spertijd

curi̲osity 1 curiositeit, rariteit **2** nieuwsgierigheid, benieuwdheid: ~ *killed the cat* [roughly] de duivel heeft het vragen uitgevonden **3** leergierigheid

cu̲rious 1 nieuwsgierig, benieuwd **2** leergierig **3** curieus, merkwaardig: *~ly (enough)* merkwaardigerwijs, vreemd genoeg

¹curl (n) **1** (haar)krul, pijpenkrul **2** krul, spiraal

²curl (vb) **1** spiralen; zich winden [of plant]: *smoke ~ed from the chimney* uit de schoorsteen kringelde rook **2** (om)krullen

³curl (vb) **1** met krullen versieren **2** doen (om)krullen **3** kronkelen om, winden om ‖ *he ~ed his lip* hij keek smalend

⁴curl (vb) krullen [of hair]; in de krul zetten, kroezen

cu̲rler krulspeld, roller, kruller

cu̲rlew wulp

curl u̲p 1 [inform] (doen) ineenkrimpen [in horror, of shame, with joy etc] **2** omkrullen **3** [inform] neergaan, neerhalen, in elkaar (doen) klappen, tegen de vlakte (doen) gaan **4** zich (behaaglijk) oprollen, in elkaar kruipen

cu̲rly krul-: ~ *hair* krullend haar^h, krullen

cu̲rrant 1 krent **2** aalbes: *red* (or: *white*) ~ rode (or: witte) bes

cu̲rrency 1 valuta, munt, (papier)geld^h: *foreign currencies* vreemde valuta's **2** munt-, geldstelsel^h **3** (geld)circulatie, (geld)omloop **4** gangbaarheid: *gain* ~ ingang vinden, zich verspreiden

¹cu̲rrent (n) **1** stroom; stroming [in gas, liquid] **2** loop, gang, tendens **3** (elektrische)

stroom: *alternating* ~ wisselstroom; *direct* ~ gelijkstroom

²cu̲rrent (adj) **1** huidig, actueel **2** gangbaar, geldend, heersend **3** [fin] in omloop

cu̲rrent accou̲nt rekening-courant, (bank)girorekening, lopende rekening

cu̲rrent a̲ffairs actualiteiten, nieuws^h

cu̲rrently momenteel, tegenwoordig

curri̲culum onderwijsprogramma^h, leerplan^h

cu̲rry 1 kerrie(poeder^h) **2** Indiaas gerecht^h, curry: *go for a* ~ uit eten gaan in een Indiaas restaurant; Indiaas halen

¹cu̲rse (n) **1** vloek(woord^h), verwensing, doem: *lay s.o. under a* ~ een vloek op iem. leggen **2** bezoeking, ramp, plaag

²cu̲rse (vb) **1** vervloeken, verwensen, een vloek uitspreken over: [inform] ~ *it!* (or: *you!*) verdraaid! **2** [esp passive] straffen, bezoeken, kwellen: *be ~d with* gebukt gaan onder

³cu̲rse (vb) (uit)vloeken, vloeken (op), (uit)schelden

cu̲rsive aaneengeschreven

cu̲rsory vluchtig, oppervlakkig

curt kortaf, kortaangebonden: *a* ~ *manner* een botte manier van doen

curtai̲l 1 inkorten, bekorten, verkorten **2** verkleinen, verminderen, beperken

¹cu̲rtain (n) **1** gordijn^h, voorhang(sel^h); [fig] barrière: ~ *of smoke* rookgordijn^h **2** [theatre] doek^h, (toneel)gordijn^h, scherm^h

²cu̲rtain (vb) voorzien van gordijnen: ~ *off* afschermen [by means of a curtain]

cu̲rts(e)y reverence, korte buiging

¹curve (n) **1** gebogen lijn, kromme, curve, boog **2** bocht [in road] **3** ronding; welving [of woman] ‖ [Am; inform, fig] *throw s.o. a* ~ iem. op het verkeerde been zetten

²curve (vb) buigen, een bocht (doen) maken, (zich) krommen

¹cu̲shion (n) **1** kussen^h, (lucht)kussen^h **2** stootkussen^h, buffer, schokdemper **3** [billiards] band

²cu̲shion (vb) **1** voorzien van kussen(s) **2** dempen, verzachten; opvangen [bang, shock, effect] **3** in de watten leggen, beschermen: *a ~ed life* een beschermd leventje

cu̲shy [inform] makkelijk, comfortabel: *a ~ job* een luizenbaantje, een makkie

custo̲dian 1 beheerder, conservator, bewaarder **2** voogd **3** [Am] conciërge, beheerder

cu̲stody 1 voogdij, zorg **2** beheer^h, hoede, bewaring **3** hechtenis, voorarrest^h, verzekerde bewaring: *take s.o. into* ~ iem. aanhouden

cu̲stom 1 gewoonte, gebruik^h **2** klandizie **3** (-s) douaneheffing, invoerrechten **4** (-s) douane(dienst)

cu̲stomary 1 gebruikelijk, gewoonlijk, normaal **2** gewoonte-, gebruik(s)-

custom-built op bestelling gebouwd, gebouwd (gemaakt) volgens de wensen van de koper

customer 1 klant, (regelmatige) afnemer **2** [inform] klant, gast: *awkward* ~ rare snijboon, vreemde vogel; *he is a tough* ~ het is een taaie

customer service klantenservice

¹cut (n) **1** slag (snee) met scherp voorwerp, (mes)sne(d)e, snijwond, houw, (zweep)slag **2** afgesneden (*or:* afgehakt, afgeknipt) stukʰ, lap; bout [meat] **3** (haar)knipbeurt **4** vermindering, verlaging **5** coupure, weglating, verkorting **6** snit, coupe **7** doorsnijding, geul, kloof, kanaalʰ, doorgraving, kortere weg: *take a short* ~ een kortere weg nemen **8** [card](aan)deelʰ, provisie, commissie **9** [film] scherpe overgang ‖ ~ *and thrust* (woorden)steekspel, vinnig debat; [inform] *be a* ~ *above* beter zijn dan

²cut (vb) **1** (zich laten) snijden, knippen: *the butter* ~*s easily* de boter snijdt gemakkelijk **2** een inkeping (scheiding) maken, snijden, knippen, hakken, kappen, kerven, maaien ‖ ~ *and run* de benen nemen, 'm smeren; ~ *both ways* a) tweesnijdend zijn; b) voor- en nadelen hebben

³cut (vb) **1** snijden in, verwonden, stuksnijden: ~ *one's finger* zich in zijn vinger snijden **2** afsnijden, doorsnijden, lossnijden, wegsnijden, (af)knippen, (om)hakken, (om)kappen, (om)zagen: ~ *open* openhalen; ~ *away* wegsnijden, weghakken, wegknippen, snoeien; ~ *in half* doormidden snijden, knippen **3** maken met scherp voorwerp, kerven, slijpen, bijsnijden, bijknippen, bijhakken, boren, graveren, opnemen; maken [CD, record]: ~ *one's initials into sth.* zijn initialen ergens in kerven **4** maaien, oogsten; binnenhalen [crop] **5** inkorten; snijden (in) [book, film etc]; afsnijden [route, corner]; besnoeien (op), inkrimpen, bezuinigen: ~ *the travelling time by a third* de reistijd met een derde terugbrengen **6** stopzetten, ophouden met, afsluiten; afsnijden [water, energy]; uitschakelen, afzetten **7** krijgen [tooth]: *I'm* ~*ting my wisdom tooth* mijn verstandskies komt door **8** (diep) raken; pijn doen [of remark etc] **9** negeren, veronachtzamen, links laten liggen: ~ *s.o. dead* (*or: cold*) iem. niet zien staan, iem. straal negeren ‖ [Am; inform] *that doesn't* ~ *it* a) dat voldoet niet; b) daarmee red je het niet

⁴cut (vb) **1** snijden, kruisen **2** [cards] couperen, afnemen **3** [inform] verzuimen, spijbelen, overslaan

cut across 1 afsnijden, doorsteken, een kortere weg nemen **2** strijdig zijn met, ingaan tegen **3** doorbreken, uitstijgen boven: ~ *traditional party loyalties* de aloude partijbindingen doorbreken

¹cut back (vb) snoeien [plants]

²cut back (vb) inkrimpen, besnoeien, bezuinigen

¹cut down (vb) minderen: *you work too much, try to* ~ *a bit* je werkt te veel, probeer wat te minderen

²cut down (vb) **1** kappen, omhakken, omhouwen, vellen **2** inperken, beperken, verminderen: ~ *one's expenses* zijn bestedingen beperken **3** inkorten, korter maken: ~ *an article* een artikel inkorten

cut down on minderen met, het verbruik beperken van: ~ *smoking* minder gaan roken

cute schattig, snoezig, leuk

cuticle 1 opperhuid **2** nagelriem

cutie leuk iem., mooie meid (jongen)

cut in 1 er(gens) tussen komen, in de rede vallen, onderbreken **2** gevaarlijk invoegen [with a vehicle]; snijden: ~ *on* s.o. iem. snijden

cut into 1 aansnijden: ~ *a cake* een taart aansnijden **2** onderbreken, tussenbeide komen, in de rede vallen: ~ *a conversation* zich (plotseling) mengen in een gesprek **3** storend werken op, een aanslag doen op: *this job cuts into my evenings off* deze baan kost me een groot deel van mijn vrije avonden

cutlery bestekʰ, eetgereiʰ, couvertʰ

cutlet [culinary] lapje vleesʰ, (lams)koteletjeʰ, kalfskoteletjeʰ

cut off 1 afsnijden, afhakken, afknippen **2** afsluiten, stopzetten, blokkeren **3** (van de buitenwereld) afsluiten, isoleren: *villages* ~ *by floods* door overstromingen geïsoleerde dorpen **4** onderbreken; verbreken [telephone connection]

cut-off scheiding, grens, afsluiting: ~ *date* sluitingsdatum

¹cut out (vb) **1** uitvallen, defect raken, het begeven: *the engine* ~ de motor sloeg af **2** afslaan: *the boiler cuts out at 90 degrees* de boiler slaat af bij 90 graden

²cut out (vb) **1** uitsnijden, uitknippen, uithakken, modelleren, vormen **2** knippen [dress, pattern]: *cut it out!* hou ermee op! **3** [inform] weglaten, verwijderen, schrappen **4** uitschakelen, elimineren; [inform] het nakijken geven **5** uitschakelen, afzetten ‖ [inform] *be* ~ *for* geknipt zijn voor

cut-out 1 uitgeknipte (*or:* uitgesneden, uitgehakte) figuur⁺ʰ **2** [techn] afslag, (stroom)-onderbreker: *automatic* ~ automatische afslag, thermostaat

cut-price 1 met korting; goedkoop **2** discount-: ~ *shop* discountzaak

cutter 1 iem. die snijdt, gebruiker van scherp voorwerp, knipper, snijder, hakker, houwer, slijper **2** snijwerktuigʰ, snijmachine, schaar, tang, mesʰ; [in butcher's shop] cutter **3** sloep (van oorlogsschipʰ) **4** (motor)barkasʰ [for transport between ship and coast]

5 kotter **6** kustwachter, kustbewakings-
schip[h] **7** [film] filmmonteerder
cut through zich worstelen door, doorbreken, zich heen werken door
¹cutting (n) **1** (afgesneden/afgeknipt/uitge-
knipt) stuk(je)[h] **2** stek [of plant] **3** (kranten)-
knipsel[h]
²cutting (adj) **1** scherp, bijtend: ~ *remark*
grievende opmerking **2** bijtend, snijdend;
guur [of wind]
cutting edge 1 absolute voorhoede;
(spraakmakende) avant-garde **2** voorsprong
cutting-edge allermodernst; allernieuwst,
geavanceerd
cutting room montageruimte
cuttlefish inktvis
¹cut up (vb) zich (in stukken) laten snijden,
zich (in stukken) laten knippen || [inform] ~
rough tekeergaan
²cut up (vb) **1** (in stukken) snijden, knippen
2 in de pan hakken, (vernietigend) verslaan
3 [inform] niets heel laten van, afkraken
4 [inform] (ernstig) aangrijpen: *be ~ about
sth.* zich iets vreselijk aantrekken, ergens ondersteboven van zijn
cyanide cyanide[h]
cyberbullying het cyberpesten, het digi-
pesten
cybercafé internetcafé[h]
cybercop politieagent belast met de be-
strijding van cybercriminaliteit
cybercrime computercriminaliteit
cyclamen cyclaam
¹cycle (n) **1** cyclus **2** kringloop; [fig also] spiraal **3** [elec] trilling, trilling per seconde,
hertz **4** *bicycle* fiets: *go by* ~ met de fiets
gaan **5** *motorbicycle* motorfiets: *go by* ~ met
de motorfiets gaan
²cycle (vb) **1** cirkelen, ronddraaien, kringen
beschrijven **2** fietsen
cyclist fietser, wielrenner
cyclone cycloon, wervelstorm, tyfoon, tornado
cyder *see* cider
cygnet jonge zwaan
cylinder 1 cilinder **2** magazijn[h] [of revolv-
er]; rol, wals, trommel, buis, pijp, (gas)fles
cynical cynisch
cynicism cynisme[h], cynische uitlating
¹Cypriot (n) Cyprioot, Cypriotische
²Cypriot (adj) Cypriotisch
Cyprus Cyprus
czar tsaar; [Am; inform] koning
¹Czech (n) Tsjech(ische)
²Czech (adj) Tsjechisch
Czech Republic Tsjechië

d

d *died* gest., gestorven

¹dab (n) **1** tik(je^h), klopje^h **2** lik(je^h), kwast-(je^h), hoopje^h: *a ~ of paint* (or: *butter*) een likje verf (or: boter) **3** veegje^h: *a ~ with a sponge* (even) een sponsje eroverheen **4** kei, kraan: *he is a ~ (hand) at squash* hij kan ontzettend goed squashen **5** (-s) vingerafdrukken

²dab (vb) opbrengen [paint]: *~ on* (zachtjes) aanbrengen

³dab (vb) **1** (aan)tikken, (be)kloppen **2** betten, deppen

dabble 1 plassen, ploeteren **2** liefhebberen: *~ at* (or: *in*) *arts* (wat) rommelen in de kunst **3** (in water) rondscharrelen [across bottom]

dabbler liefhebber, amateur

dachshund teckel, taks, dashond

dad [inform] pa

daddy papa, pappie

daddy longlegs langpoot(mug); [Am] hooiwagen(achtige); langbeen

Daesh IS *(Islamitische Staat)*

daffodil (gele) narcis

daft 1 halfgaar, niet goed snik **2** idioot, belachelijk, maf

dagger dolk || *at ~s drawn with s.o.* op voet van oorlog met iem.

¹daily (n) **1** dagblad^h, krant **2** werkster, schoonmaakster

²daily (adj) **1** dagelijks: *~ newspaper* dagblad^h **2** geregeld, vaak, constant || *the ~ grind* de dagelijkse sleur

³daily (adv) dagelijks, per dag

dainty 1 sierlijk, verfijnd **2** teer, gevoelig **3** kostelijk, verrukkelijk: *~ food* uitgelezen voedsel **4** kieskeurig, veeleisend

dairy 1 zuivelbedrijf^h, zuivelproducent **2** melkboer, melkman **3** melkvee(stapel)^h

dais podium^h, verhoging

daisy 1 madelief(je^h) **2** margriet, grote madelief || *be pushing up the daisies* onder de groene zoden liggen

dally 1 lanterfanten, (rond)lummelen, klungelen **2** treuzelen || *~ with* a) flirten met; b) spelen (or: stoeien) met [an idea]

¹dam (n) **1** (stuw)dam **2** barrière, belemmering, hinderpaal **3** moederdier^h [quadruped]

²dam (vb) **1** van een dam voorzien, afdammen **2** indammen, beteugelen

¹damage (n) **1** schade, beschadiging, averij **2** (-s) schadevergoeding, schadeloosstelling: *we will claim ~ from them* we zullen schadevergoeding van hen eisen

²damage (vb) beschadigen, schade toebrengen, aantasten

damaged goods 1 beschadigde goederen **2** [inform] beschadigd persoon

¹damn (n) [inform] zak, (malle)moer: *not be worth a (tuppenny) ~* geen ene moer waard zijn; *not give a ~* het geen (ene) moer kunnen schelen

²damn (adj) [inform] godvergeten: *a ~ fool* een stomme idioot

³damn (vb) **1** [inform] vervloeken, verwensen: *I'll be ~ed if I go* ik vertik het (mooi) om te gaan **2** te gronde richten, ruïneren **3** (af)kraken, afbreken: *the play was ~ed by the critics* het stuk werd door de recensenten de grond in geboord **4** vloeken (tegen), uitvloeken

damning belastend, (ernstig) bezwarend, vernietigend

¹damp (n) **1** vocht^h, vochtigheid **2** nevel, damp

²damp (adj) vochtig, nattig, klam || *~ squib* sof, fiasco^h

³damp (vb) **1** bevochtigen **2** smoren, doven, temperen: *~ down* afdekken **3** temperen, doen bekoelen: *~ down s.o.'s enthusiasm* iemands enthousiasme temperen

dampen 1 bevochtigen **2** temperen, ontmoedigen

damper 1 sleutel [of stove]; regelschuif, demper **2** schokdemper, schokbreker **3** (trillings)demper **4** domper, teleurstelling

damsel [dated; hum] jongedame: *a ~ in distress* een jonkvrouw in nood

¹dance (n) **1** dans, dansnummer^h **2** dansfeest^h, bal^h, dansavond **3** dance [EDM]

²dance (vb) (doen/laten) dansen, springen, (staan te) trappelen: *the leaves were dancing in the wind* de blaren dwarrelden in de wind; *her eyes ~d for* (or: *with*) *joy* haar ogen tintelden van vreugde; *~ a baby on one's knee* een kindje op zijn knie laten rijden

dancer danser(es), ballerina

dancing het dansen; danskunst, gedans^h

dandelion paardenbloem

dandle wiege(le)n [child]; laten dansen: *~ a baby on one's knee* een kindje op zijn knie laten rijden

dandruff (hoofd)roos

¹dandy (n) **1** fat, dandy, modegek **2** juweel(tje)^h, prachtstuk^h, prachtfiguur^h

²dandy (adj) **1** fatterig, dandyachtig **2** [Am] tiptop, puik, prima

Dane Deen || *Great ~* Deense dog

danger gevaar^h, risico^h: *be in ~ of* het gevaar lopen te; *out of ~* buiten (levens)gevaar

dangerous gevaarlijk, riskant

¹dangle (vb) bengelen, bungelen, slingeren

²dangle (vb) laten bengelen, slingeren: [fig] *~ sth. before* (or: *in front of*) *s.o.* iem. met iets

trachten te paaien
¹Danish (n) Deen(se)
²Danish (adj) Deens
dank klam
Danube Donau
dapper 1 keurig, netjes, goed verzorgd
2 zwierig
dapple (be)spikkelen, met vlekken bedekken
¹dare (n) **1** uitdaging: *do sth.* **for** *a* ~ iets doen
omdat men wordt uitgedaagd **2** gedurfde
handeling, moedige daad
²dare (vb) uitdagen, tarten: *she* ~d *Bill to hit
her* ze daagde Bill uit haar te slaan
³dare (aux vb) (aan)durven, het wagen, het
lef hebben te: *he does not* ~ *to answer back, he
~ not answer back* hij durft niet tegen te spreken; *how* ~ *(you say such things)?* hoe durf je
zoiets te zeggen? || *I* – *say* ik veronderstel, ik
neem aan, misschien
daredevil waaghals, durfal
¹daring (n) **1** moed, durf, lef[h] **2** gedurfdheid
²daring (adj) **1** brutaal, moedig, gedurfd
2 gewaagd
¹dark (n) **1** donkere kleur **2** donkere plaats
3 duister[h], duisternis: *in the* ~ **a)** in het donker; **b)** [fig] in het geniep; *keep s.o. in the* ~
about sth. iem. ergens niets over laten weten;
be in the ~ *(about sth.)* in het duister tasten
(omtrent iets); *go* ~ **a)** [TV] op zwart gaan;
b) [aviation] van de radar verdwijnen; **c)** in
het niets verdwijnen **4** vallen van de avond:
after (or: *before*) ~ na (or: voor) het donker
²dark (adj) **1** donker, duister, onverlicht: ~
brown donkerbruin **2** somber: *the* ~ *side of
things* de schaduwzijde der dingen **3** verborgen, geheimzinnig **4** donker; laag en vol [of
voice] || ~ *horse* **a)** outsider [in race]; **b)** onbe-
kende mededinger [at elections]
dark chocolate pure chocolade
darkness duisternis, verdorvenheid: *powers of* ~ kwade machten
darknet [comp] darknet[h]
dark Web darkweb[h], diepe web[h]
¹darling (n) schat(je[h]), lieveling
²darling (adj) geliefd, (aller)lief(st)
¹darn (n) stop, gestopt gat[h], stopsel[h]
²darn (vb) stoppen, mazen
³darn (vb) (ver)vloeken, verwensen: ~ *(it)!*
verdorie!, verdraaid!
darned [inform] verdraaid, vervloekt
¹dart (n) **1** pijl(tje[h]) **2** (plotselinge, scherpe)
uitval [also fig]; steek, sprong: *make a* ~ *for
the door* naar de deur springen
²dart (vb) toesnellen, wegsnellen, toeschieten, wegschieten, toestuiven, wegstuiven
dartboard dartbord[h]
darts darts[h], vogelpik
¹dash (n) **1** ietsje[h], tik(kelt)je[h], scheutje[h]: ~ *of
brandy* scheutje cognac **2** (snelle, krachtige)
slag, dreun **3** spurt, sprint, uitval **4** streep [in

Morse code]: *dots and* ~*es* punten en strepen
5 kastlijn, gedachtestreep(je[h])
²dash (vb) **1** (vooruit)stormen, (zich) storten,
denderen: *I'm afraid I must* ~ *now* en nu moet
ik er als de bliksem vandoor; ~ *away* weg-
stormen; ~ *off* er (als de gesmeerde bliksem)
vandoor gaan **2** (rond)banjeren, (met veel
vertoon) rondspringen: ~ *about* rondbanje-
ren
³dash (vb) **1** verbrijzelen, verpletteren; [fig]
verijdelen: *all my **expectations** were* ~*ed* al
mijn verwachtingen werden de bodem inge-
slagen **2** snel doen: ~ *sth. **down*** (of: *off*) iets
nog even gauw opschrijven **3** vervloeken,
verwensen: [inform] ~ *it (all)!* verdraaid!
4 doorspekken, larderen
⁴dash (vb) (met grote kracht) slaan, smijten,
beuken: ~ *down* neersmijten; *the waves* ~*ed
against the rocks* de golven beukten tegen de
rotsen
dashboard dashboard[h]
dash cam dashcamera, dashboardcamera
dashed verdraaid, verduiveld
dashing 1 levendig, wilskrachtig, vlot
2 opzichtig
data 1 feit[h], gegeven[h] **2** gegevens, data, informatie: *insufficient* ~ onvoldoende gegevens; *the* ~ *is* (or: *are*) *being prepared for processing* de informatie wordt gereedgemaakt
voor verwerking
database database
data manager gegevensbeheerder
data stick USB-stick, datastick, geheugenstick
¹date (n) **1** dadel **2** datum, dagtekening
3 afspraak(je[h]) **4** vriend(inne[t])je[h], partner,
'afspraakje[h]', date: *she's my* ~ *for tonight* ik ga
vanavond met haar uit, ze is vanavond mijn
date **5** tijd(perk[h]), periode: *of early* ~, *of an
early* ~ uit een vroege periode || *out of* ~ ver-
ouderd, ouderwets; *to* ~ tot op heden; *up to*
~ **a)** bij (de tijd), modern, geavanceerd;
b) volledig bijgewerkt; *bring up to* ~ bijwerken, moderniseren
²date (vb) **1** verouderen, uit de tijd raken
2 dateren: ~ *back to* stammen uit **3** [Am] af-
spraakjes hebben, uitgaan, daten
³date (vb) **1** dateren, dagtekenen **2** dateren,
de ouderdom vaststellen van: ~ *a **painting***
een schilderij dateren **3** uitgaan met, af-
spraakjes hebben met, vrijen met
dated ouderwets, gedateerd, verouderd
dating agency bemiddelingsbureau[h]
dative derde naamval
datum nulpunt[h] [of scale etc]; (gemiddeld
laag)waterpeil[h]
¹daub (n) **1** lik, klodder, smeer[h] **2** kladschil-
derij[+h], kladderwerk[h] **3** (muur)pleister[h], pleisterkalk
²daub (vb) besmeren, bekladden, besmeuren

daughter dochter
daughter-in-law schoondochter
daunt ontmoedigen, intimideren, afschrikken: *a ~ing prospect* een afschrikwekkend
vooruitzicht
dauntless 1 onbevreesd **2** volhardend,
vasthoudend
dawdle treuzelen, teuten ‖ *~ over one's
food* met lange tanden eten
¹dawn (n) dageraad [also fig]; zonsopgang:
the ~ of civilization de ochtendstond der beschaving; *at ~* bij het krieken van de dag
²dawn (vb) dagen [also fig]; licht worden,
aanbreken, duidelijk worden: *it ~ed on me*
het drong tot me door
day 1 dag, etmaalʰ: *this ~ fortnight* (or:
week) vandaag over veertien dagen (*or:* een
week); *~ and night, night and ~* dag en nacht;
the ~ after tomorrow overmorgen; *the ~ before yesterday* eergisteren; *from ~ one* meteen, vanaf de eerste dag; *~ in, ~ out* dag in,
dag uit; *~ after ~* dag in, dag uit; *~ by ~, from
~ to ~* dagelijks, van dag tot dag **2** werkdag:
an 8-hour ~ een achturige werkdag; *~ off*
vrije dag **3** [in compounds] (hoogtij)dag
4 tijdstipʰ, gelegenheid: *some ~* a) eens,
eenmaal, op een keer; b) bij gelegenheid
5 dag, daglichtʰ: [form] *by ~* overdag **6** tijd,
periode, dag(en): *(in) ~s of old* (or: *yore*) (in)
vroeger tijden; *he has had his ~* hij heeft zijn
tijd gehad; *those were the ~s* dat waren nog
eens tijden; *these ~s* tegenwoordig, vandaag
de dag; *(in) this ~ and age* vandaag de dag
7 slag, strijd: *carry* (or: *save, win*) *the ~* de
slag winnen **8** (-s) levensdagen, levenʰ ‖ *that
will be the ~* dat wil ik zien; *all in a ~'s work* de
normale gang van zaken; *call it a ~* a) het
voor gezien houden; b) sterven; *make s.o.'s ~*
iemands dag goedmaken; *one of those ~s*
zo'n dag waarop alles tegenzit; *to the ~* op
de dag af; *to this ~* tot op de dag van vandaag, tot op heden; *from one ~ to the next*
van vandaag op morgen; [inform] *every other ~* om de haverklap; *the other ~* onlangs,
pas geleden; *she is thirty if she is a ~* ze is op
zijn minst dertig
daybreak dageraad, zonsopgang
day-care dagopvang, kinderopvang: *~ centre* crèche, kinderdagverblijfʰ
¹daydream (n) dagdroom
²daydream (vb) dagdromen; mijmeren
daylight 1 daglichtʰ **2** dageraad ‖ *see ~* iets
in de gaten krijgen
daylight robbery 1 beroving op klaarlichte dag **2** schaamteloze oplichting
day-to-day 1 dagelijks **2** van dag tot dag
daytrip uitjeʰ, uitstapjeʰ, dagjeʰ uit
¹daze (n) verbijstering: *in a ~* verbluft, ontsteld
²daze (vb) verbijsteren, verbluffen
¹dazzle (vb) **1** verblinden **2** verbijsteren

²dazzle (vb) imponeren, indruk maken (op)
DC *direct current* gelijkstroom
D-day *Decision day* D-day, D-dag, kritische
begindag
¹dead (n) hoogte-, dieptepuntʰ: *in the* (or: *at*)
~ of night in het holst van de nacht
²dead (adj) **1** dood, overleden, gestorven:
over my ~ body over mijn lijk; *rise from the ~*
uit de dood opstaan **2** verouderd **3** onwerk-
zaam, leeg, uit, op: *~ battery* lege accu; *cut
out (the) ~ wood* verwijderen van overbodige
franje; *~ and gone* dood (en begraven); [fig]
voorgoed voorbij **4** uitgestorven: *the place is
~* het is er een dooie boel **5** gevoelloos, ongevoelig **6** [sport] uit (het spel) [of ball]
7 volkomen, absoluut: *~ certainty* absolute
zekerheid; *~ loss* a) puur verlies; b) tijdverspilling; c) [inform] miskleun, fiascoʰ **8** abrupt, plotseling: *come to a ~ stop* (plotseling)
stokstijf stil (blijven) staan **9** exact, precies: *~
centre* precieze midden ‖ *~ as a doornail*
morsdood; *~ duck* mislukk(el)ing, verliezer; *~
end* a) doodlopende straat; b) impasse, dood
punt; *come to a ~ end* op niets uitlopen;
[sport] *~ heat* gedeelde eerste (tweede enz.)
plaats; *flog a ~ horse* achter de feiten aanlopen; *~ letter* a) dode letter [of law]; b) onbe-
stelbare brief; *wait for a ~ man's shoes* op iemands bezit azen; *make a ~ set at* a) te lijf
gaan [fig]; b) (vastberaden) avances maken;
~ to the world a) in diepe slaap; b) bewusteloos; *I wouldn't be seen ~ in that dress* voor
geen goud zou ik me in die jurk vertonen
³dead (adv) **1** volkomen, absoluut: *~ straight*
kaarsrecht; *stop ~* stokstijf blijven staan; *~
tired* (or: *exhausted*) doodop, bekaf **2** pal,
onmiddellijk: *~ ahead of you* pal voor je; *~
against* a) pal tegen [of wind]; b) fel tegen
[plan etc]
deadbeat nietsnut
dead beat doodop, bekaf
¹deaden (vb) de kracht verliezen, de helderheid verliezen, verflauwen, verzwakken
²deaden (vb) **1** verzwakken; dempen
[sound]; verzachten, dof maken [colour]
2 ongevoelig maken, verdoven: *drugs to ~
the pain* medicijnen om de pijn te stillen
dead-end 1 doodlopend **2** uitzichtloos: *a ~
job* een baan zonder carrièreperspectief (*or:*
doorgroeimogelijkheden)
deadline (tijds)limiet, uitersteʰ (in)leverda-
tum: *meet the ~* binnen de tijdslimiet blijven;
miss the ~ de tijdslimiet overschrijden
deadlock patstelling
deadly 1 dodelijk [also fig]; fataal **2** [depr]
doods, dodelijk (saai) **3** doods-, aarts- **4** [in-
form] enorm **5** oer-, uiterst: *~ dull* oersaai ‖
the seven ~ sins de zeven hoofdzonden
dead man walking 1 [Am] terdoodveroordeelde die van zijn cel naar de plek van
executie loopt **2** [fig] iem. in een uitzichtloze

situatie

deaf doof [also fig] ‖ as ~ as a *(door)post*
stokdoof; *fall on ~ ears* geen gehoor vinden;
turn a ~ ear to doof zijn voor

deaf-aid (ge)hoorapparaat[h]

deafen verdoven, doof maken, overstemmen

deafening oorverdovend

deaf-mute doofstom

¹**deal** (n) **1** transactie, overeenkomst, handel
2 (grote) hoeveelheid, mate: *a great ~ of
money* heel wat geld **3** [depr] (koe)handeltje[h], deal **4** [cards] gift, het geven, beurt om
te geven: *it's your ~* jij moet geven ‖ *it's a ~!*
afgesproken!, akkoord!; *that's a big ~* dat is
belangrijk, dat betekent veel; *it's no big ~*
a) het is geen probleem; **b)** het stelt niet veel
voor; *what's the big ~?* **a)** wat is het probleem?; **b)** wat maakt het uit?

²**deal** (vb) zaken doen, handelen

³**deal** (vb) geven, (uit)delen: ~ *(out) fairly*
eerlijk verdelen

dealbreaker doorslaggevend punt[h],
breekpunt[h]: *the ~ for me is if he has a job or not*
wat voor mij de doorslag geeft is of hij een
baan heeft

dealer 1 handelaar, koopman, dealer **2** effectenhandelaar

dealing 1 manier van zaken doen, aanpak
2 (-s) transacties, affaires; relaties [business]
3 (-s) betrekkingen, omgang

deal with 1 zaken doen met, handel drijven met, kopen bij **2** behandelen, afhandelen: ~ *complaints* klachten behandelen
3 aanpakken, een oplossing zoeken voor
4 optreden tegen **5** behandelen, omgaan
met: *be impossible to ~* onmogelijk in de
omgang zijn **6** gaan over: *the book deals with
racism* het boek gaat over racisme

dean 1 deken **2** oudste, overste **3** [university] decaan, faculteitsvoorzitter, (studenten)-
decaan

¹**dear** (n) schat, lieverd

²**dear** (adj) **1** dierbaar, lief **2** lief, schattig
3 duur, prijzig **4** beste, lieve; geachte [eg in
salutation]: ~ *Julia* beste Julia; *my ~ lady* mevrouw; ~ *sir* geachte heer; ~ *sirs* mijne heren,
geachte heren **5** dierbaar, lief: *I hold her very
~* ze ligt me na aan het hart ‖ *for ~ life* of zijn
leven ervan afhangt

³**dear** (adv) **1** duur (betaald) [also fig] **2** innig, vurig

dearest liefste

dearly 1 innig, vurig: *wish ~* vurig wensen
2 duur(betaald) [also fig]: *pay ~ for sth.* iets
duur betalen **3** vurig

dearth schaarste, tekort[h]: *a ~ of talent* te
weinig talent

death 1 sterfgeval[h], slachtoffer[h] **2** dood,
overlijden[h]; [fig] einde[h]: *assisted ~* hulp bij
zelfdoding; [fig] *be in at the ~* een onderne-

ming zien stranden; *be the ~ of s.o.* iemands
dood zijn [also fig]; *bore s.o. to ~* iem. stierlijk
vervelen; *war to the ~* oorlog op leven en
dood **3** de Dood, Magere Hein ‖ *at ~'s door*
op sterven, de dood nabij; *dice with ~* met
vuur spelen; *flog to ~* uitentreuren herhalen;
worked to ~ afgezaagd, uitgemolken

death certificate overlijdensakte

death duty successierecht[h]

deathly doods, lijk-: ~ *pale* doodsbleek

death penalty doodstraf

death row [Am] dodencel(len): *be on ~(s)*
ter dood veroordeeld zijn

death warrant 1 executiebevel[h] **2** [fig]
doodvonnis[h], genadeslag

debase 1 degraderen **2** vervalsen **3** verlagen, vernederen

¹**debate** (n) **1** (+ on, about) debat[h] (over),
discussie, dispuut[h]: *that question is open to ~*
dat staat nog ter discussie **2** twist, conflict[h],
strijd **3** overweging, beraad[h]

²**debate** (vb) **1** (+ about, upon) debatteren
(over), discussiëren, een debat houden **2** beraadslagen

³**debate** (vb) bespreken, beraadslagen over,
in debat treden over

debauched liederlijk; verdorven

debauchery losbandigheid

debilitating slopend, uitputtend: ~ *climate* slopend klimaat

¹**debit** (n) **1** schuldpost, debitering, debetboeking **2** debetsaldo[h]

²**debit** (vb) debiteren, als debet boeken

debit card bankpas, pinpas

debris puin[h], brokstukken

debt schuld, (terugbetalings)verplichting:
owe s.o. a ~ of gratitude iem. dank verschuldigd zijn; *get (or: run) into ~* schulden maken

debtor 1 schuldenaar **2** debiteur

debug 1 [roughly] ontluizen, [roughly] van
insecten ontdoen **2** (van mankementen) zuiveren, kinderziekten verhelpen bij **3** (van
fouten) zuiveren, debuggen

debunk [inform] **1** [s.o.] ontmaskeren, onderuithalen, voor joker zetten **2** [sth.] ontkrachten, doorprikken

debut debuut[h]

decade decennium[h], periode van tien jaar

decadence decadentie; verval[h] [in art]

decadent decadent, genotzuchtig

decaf *decaffeinated coffee* cafeïnevrij(e
koffie)

decanter decanteerfles; karaf

decapitate onthoofden

decathlon [athletics] tienkamp

¹**decay** (n) **1** verval[h], (geleidelijke) achteruitgang **2** bederf[h], rotting

²**decay** (vb) **1** vervallen, in verval raken
2 (ver)rotten, bederven, verteren: *sugar may
~ the teeth* suiker kan tot tandbederf leiden

deceased overleden, pas gestorven

deceit bedrog[h], oneerlijkheid
deceive bedriegen, misleiden, om de tuin leiden: *if my ears do not ~ me* als mijn oren me niet bedriegen
decelerate vertragen, afremmen, vaart minderen
December december
decency fatsoen[h], fatsoenlijkheid
decent 1 fatsoenlijk **2** wellevend **3** behoorlijk: *a ~ wage* een redelijk loon **4** geschikt: *a ~ guy* een geschikte kerel
deception 1 misleiding, list, bedrog[h] **2** (valse) kunstgreep, (smerige) truc, kunstje[h]
deceptive bedrieglijk, misleidend: *appearances are often ~* schijn bedriegt
decibel decibel
¹decide (vb) **1** beslissen, een beslissing nemen, een keuze maken **2** besluiten, een besluit nemen: *~ against* afzien van; *we have ~d against it* we hebben besloten het niet te doen
²decide (vb) **1** beslissen, uitmaken: *~ a question* een knoop doorhakken **2** een uitspraak doen in
deciduous loof-: *~ tree* loofboom
¹decimal (n) **1** decimale breuk: *recurring ~* repeterende breuk **2** decimaal getal[h]
²decimal (adj) decimaal: *~ point* decimaalteken[h], komma[+h]
decipher ontcijferen, decoderen
decision beslissing, besluit[h], uitspraak: *arrive at* (or: *take*) *a ~* een beslissing nemen
decision maker beleidsvormer
decisive 1 beslissend, doorslaggevend **2** beslist, gedecideerd, zelfverzekerd
deck 1 (scheeps)dek[h], tussendeke ruimte: *clear the ~s (for action)* [fig] zich opmaken voor de strijd; *below ~(s)*; *on ~* aan dek **2** verdieping van bus **3** [Am] spel[h] (kaarten) **4** (tape)deck[h], cassettedeck[h] || *hit the ~* op je bek vallen; [boxing] neergaan
deck-chair ligstoel, dekstoel
decking [architecture] (vlonder)terras[h]
¹declaim (vb) **1** uitvaren, schelden: *~ against* uitvaren tegen **2** retorisch spreken
²declaim (vb) declameren, voordragen
declaration 1 (openbare/formele) verklaring, afkondiging: *Declaration of Independence* Amerikaanse onafhankelijkheidsverklaring **2** geschreven verklaring: *~ of income* aangifte inkomstenbelasting
¹declare (vb) **1** een verklaring afleggen, een aankondiging doen **2** (+ against, for) stelling nemen (tegen/voor), zich (openlijk) uitspreken (tegen/voor)
²declare (vb) **1** bekendmaken, aankondigen, afkondigen **2** bestempelen als, uitroepen tot: *~ s.o. the winner* iem. tot winnaar uitroepen **3** aangeven [goods at Customs, income etc]: *nothing to ~* niets aan te geven
declination 1 (voorover)helling **2** buiging **3** verval[h], achteruitgang **4** [Am] afwijzing **5** declinatie; [compass] afwijking(shoek)
¹decline (n) **1** verval[h], achteruitgang, aftakeling: *fall* (or: *go*) *into a ~* beginnen af te takelen, in verval raken **2** daling, afname, vermindering: *on the ~* tanend **3** slotfase, ondergang
²decline (vb) **1** (af)hellen, aflopen, dalen **2** ten einde lopen, aftakelen: *declining years* oude dag, laatste jaren **3** afnemen, achteruitgaan
³decline (vb) (beleefd) weigeren, afslaan, van de hand wijzen: *~ an invitation* niet op een uitnodiging ingaan
declutter opruimen, van rommel ontdoen
decode decoderen, ontcijferen
¹decompose (vb) **1** desintegreren, uiteenvallen **2** (ver)rotten, bederven
²decompose (vb) **1** ontleden, ontbinden, afbreken **2** doen rotten
decompress 1 de druk verlagen in, op **2** [comp] uitpakken; decomprimeren
decontaminate ontsmetten, desinfecteren
decorate 1 afwerken, verven, schilderen, behangen **2** versieren, verfraaien: *~ the Christmas tree* de kerstboom optuigen **3** decoreren, onderscheiden, een onderscheiding geven
decoration 1 versiering, decoratie, opsmuk **2** inrichting (en stoffering), aankleding: *interior ~* binnenhuisarchitectuur **3** onderscheiding(steken[h]), decoratie, ordeteken[h], lintje[h]
decorator afwerker (van huis), (huis)schilder, stukadoor, behanger
decorous correct, fatsoenlijk
decoy 1 lokvogel, lokeend **2** lokaas[h], lokmiddel[h]
¹decrease (n) vermindering, afneming, daling
²decrease (vb) (geleidelijk) afnemen, (geleidelijk) teruglopen, (geleidelijk) achteruitgaan
³decrease (vb) verminderen, beperken, verkleinen
¹decree (n) verordening, besluit[h]: *by ~* bij decreet
²decree (vb) verordenen, bevelen
decrepit 1 versleten, afgeleefd, op **2** vervallen, bouwvallig, uitgewoond
decry 1 kleineren, openlijk afkeuren **2** kwaadspreken over, afgeven op
decryption ontcijfering; decodering, decryptie
dedicate 1 wijden, toewijden, in dienst stellen van **2** opdragen, toewijden: *~ a book to s.o.* een boek aan iem. opdragen
dedicated toegewijd, trouw
dedication 1 opdracht **2** (in)wijding, inzegening **3** [singular] toewijding, trouw, toe-

gedaanheid

deduce (logisch) afleiden: *and what do you ~ from that?* en wat maak je daaruit op?

deduct (+ from) aftrekken (van), in mindering brengen (op)

deductible [fin] aftrekbaar

deduction 1 conclusie, gevolgtrekking, slotsom **2** inhouding, korting, (ver)mindering

deed 1 daad, handeling: *in word and in ~* met woord en daad **2** wapenfeit[h], (helden)-daad **3** akte, document[h]

deem [form] achten: *~ sth. an honour* iets als een eer beschouwen

¹deep (n) diepte, afgrond

²deep (adj) **1** diep, diepgelegen, ver(afgelegen): *the ~ end* het diepe [in swimming pool]; *~ in the forest* diep in het bos **2** diep(zinnig), moeilijk, duister, ontoegankelijk **3** diep(gaand); intens [of feelings]; donker [of colours]: *~ in conversation* diep in gesprek **4** dik, achter elkaar: *the people were standing ten ~* de mensen stonden tien rijen dik ‖ *thrown in at the ~ end* in het diepe gegooid, meteen met het moeilijkste (moeten) beginnen; *in ~ water(s)* in grote moeilijkheden

³deep (adv) diep, tot op grote diepte: *~ into the night* tot diep in de nacht

¹deepen (vb) **1** dieper worden **2** toenemen

²deepen (vb) vergroten; versterken

deep-freeze diepvriezen

deep fry frituren

deep-link [comp] dieplinken

deep-seated diepliggend; ingeworteld

deep Web darkweb[h], diepe web[h]

deer hert[h]

def [inform] gaaf, vet, cool

deface 1 beschadigen, verminken **2** onleesbaar maken, bekladden

defamation laster

default 1 afwezigheid: *by ~* bij gebrek aan beter; *in ~ of* bij gebrek aan, bij ontstentenis van **2** verzuim[h]; niet-nakoming [of obligation to pay]; wanbetaling

¹defeat (n) **1** nederlaag **2** mislukking **3** verijdeling, dwarsboming

²defeat (vb) **1** verslaan, overwinnen, winnen van **2** verijdelen, dwarsbomen: *be ~ed in an attempt* een poging zien mislukken **3** verwerpen, afstemmen **4** tenietdoen, vernietigen: *her expectations were ~ed* haar verwachtingen werden de bodem ingeslagen

defeatism moedeloosheid

¹defect (n) mankement[h], gebrek[h]: *a hearing ~* een gehoorstoornis

²defect (vb) **1** overlopen, afvallig worden **2** uitwijken [by seeking asylum]

defective 1 onvolkomen, gebrekkig, onvolmaakt **2** te kort komend, onvolledig

defector overloper, afvallige

defence 1 verdediging, afweer, defensief[h],

bescherming; [law] verweer[h]: *~s* verdedigingswerken; *in ~ of* ter verdediging van **2** verdediging(srede), verweer[h] **3** [sport; also chess] verdediging **4** defensie, (lands)verdediging

defenceless weerloos; machteloos

defend 1 verdedigen, afweren, verweren, als verdediger optreden (voor) **2** beschermen, beveiligen: *~ from* behoeden voor, beschermen tegen

defendant gedaagde, beschuldigde

defender 1 verdediger; [sport] achterspeler **2** titelverdediger

defensive defensief, verdedigend, afwerend: *be on the ~* een defensieve houding aannemen

¹defer (vb) zich onderwerpen, het hoofd buigen: *~ to* eerbiedigen, respecteren, in acht nemen

²defer (vb) opschorten, uitstellen: *~red payment* uitgestelde betaling

deference achting, eerbied, respect[h]

defiance 1 trotsering, uitdagende houding: *in ~ of* in weerwil van, ondanks **2** openlijk verzet[h], opstandigheid: *in ~ of* a) met minachting voor; b) in strijd met

deficiency 1 tekort[h]; gebrek[h]: *~ of food* voedseltekort[h] **2** onvolkomenheid; defect[h]

deficient 1 incompleet, onvolledig **2** ontoereikend, onvoldoende: *~ in iron* ijzerarm **3** onvolwaardig, zwakzinnig

deficit 1 tekort[h], nadelig saldo[h] **2** tekort[h], gebrek[h] **3** [sport] achterstand

defile 1 bevuilen, verontreinigen, vervuilen **2** schenden, ontheiligen

define 1 definiëren, een definitie geven (van) **2** afbakenen, bepalen, begrenzen **3** aftekenen

definite 1 welomlijnd, scherp begrensd **2** ondubbelzinnig, duidelijk **3** uitgesproken, onbetwistbaar **4** beslist, vastberaden **5** [linguistics] bepaald: *~ article* bepaald lidwoord

definitely absoluut, beslist: *~ not* geen sprake van

definition 1 definitie, omschrijving **2** afbakening, bepaling, begrenzing **3** karakteristiek **4** scherpte; beeldscherpte [of TV]: *lack ~* onscherp zijn [eg photo]

definitive 1 definitief, blijvend, onherroepelijk **2** beslissend, afdoend **3** (meest) gezaghebbend, onbetwist **4** ondubbelzinnig

deflate 1 leeg laten lopen; [fig] doorprikken [conceitedness] **2** kleineren, minder belangrijk maken: *feel utterly ~d* zich geheel ontmoedigd voelen **3** [econ] aan deflatie onderwerpen, inkrimpen

deflation deflatie, waardevermeerdering van geld

deflect 1 (doen) afbuigen, (doen) afwijken, uitwijken **2** (+ from) afbrengen (van), afleiden (van)

defoliate ontbladeren
deforest [Am] ontbossen
deformed 1 misvormd, mismaakt **2** verknipt, pervers
deformity misvorming; vergroeiing
defraud bedriegen, bezwendelen: ~ *s.o. of his money* iem. (door bedrog) zijn geld afhandig maken
defray financieren, betalen, voor zijn rekening nemen: ~ *the cost(s)* de kosten dragen
defriend ontvrienden
defrost ontdooien
deft behendig, handig, bedreven
defunct verdwenen, in onbruik
defuse onschadelijk maken [also fig]; demonteren [explosives]: ~ *a crisis* een crisis bezweren
defy 1 tarten, uitdagen: *I ~ anyone to prove I'm wrong* ik daag iedereen uit om te bewijzen dat ik ongelijk heb **2** trotseren, weerstaan: ~ *definition* (or: *description*) elke beschrijving tarten
degenerate 1 degenereren, ontaarden, verloederen **2** verslechteren, achteruitgaan
degradation 1 degradatie; achteruitgang **2** vernedering
degrade 1 degraderen, achteruitzetten, terugzetten: ~ *o.s.* zich verlagen **2** vernederen, onteren
degree 1 graad: *an angle of 45 degrees* een hoek van 45 graden; ~ *of latitude* (or: *longitude*) breedtegraad, lengtegraad **2** (universitaire) graad, academische titel; [also] lesbevoegdheid **3** mate, hoogte, graad, trap: *to a high* (or: *certain*) ~ tot op grote (or: zekere) hoogte; *by ~s* stukje bij beetje, gaandeweg
¹dehydrate (vb) **1** vocht verliezen **2** opdrogen, uitdrogen, verdrogen, verdorren
²dehydrate (vb) vocht onttrekken aan
deice het ijs verwijderen van; ontdooien
deify vergoddelijken
deign zich verwaardigen, zich niet te goed achten: *not ~ to look at* geen blik waardig keuren
deity 1 god(in), godheid **2** (af)god, verafgode figuur[+h]
dejected 1 terneergeslagen, somber **2** bedroefd, verdrietig
dejection 1 neerslachtigheid **2** bedroefdheid, verdriet[h]
¹delay (n) **1** vertraging, oponthoud[h] **2** uitstel[h], verschuiving: *without (any)* ~ zonder uitstel
²delay (vb) treuzelen, tijd rekken (winnen)
³delay (vb) **1** uitstellen, verschuiven **2** ophouden, vertragen, hinderen
¹delegate (n) afgevaardigde, gedelegeerde, ge(vol)machtigde
²delegate (vb) **1** afvaardigen, delegeren **2** machtigen **3** delegeren, overdragen
delegation 1 delegatie, afvaardiging

2 machtiging
delete verwijderen, wissen, doorhalen, wegstrepen: ~ *from* schrappen uit; ~ *as applicable* doorhalen wat niet van toepassing is
deletion 1 (weg)schrapping, doorhaling **2** verwijderde passage
Delhi belly [inform] reizigersdiarree
deli *delicatessen* delicatessenwinkel
¹deliberate (adj) **1** doelbewust, opzettelijk **2** voorzichtig, weloverwogen, bedachtzaam
²deliberate (vb) **1** wikken en wegen, beraadslagen **2** raad inwinnen, te rade gaan
³deliberate (vb) **1** (zorgvuldig) afwegen **2** beraadslagen, zich beraden over
deliberation 1 (zorgvuldige) afweging, overleg[h]: *after much* ~ na lang wikken en wegen **2** omzichtigheid, bedachtzaamheid
delicacy 1 delicatesse, lekkernij **2** (fijn)gevoeligheid, verfijndheid **3** tact
delicate 1 fijn, verfijnd **2** lekker [of foods] **3** teer, zwak, tenger: *a ~ constitution* een teer gestel **4** (fijn)gevoelig **5** tactvol **6** kieskeurig, kritisch **7** netelig
delicious (over)heerlijk, verrukkelijk, kostelijk
¹delight (n) **1** verrukking, groot genoegen[h] **2** genot[h], vreugde: *take ~ in* genot vinden in
²delight (vb) genot vinden
³delight (vb) in verrukking brengen: *she ~ed them with her play* haar spel bracht hen in verrukking
delighted verrukt, opgetogen: *I shall be ~* het zal me een groot genoegen zijn; ~ *at* (or: *with*) opgetogen over
delineate 1 omlijnen, afbakenen **2** schetsen, tekenen, afbeelden
delinquency 1 vergrijp[h], delict[h] **2** criminaliteit, misdadigheid, misdaad
delinquent wetsovertreder, jeugdige misdadiger: *juvenile* ~ jeugddelinquent
delirious 1 ijlend: *become* ~ gaan ijlen **2** dol(zinnig): ~ *with joy* dol(zinnig) van vreugde
delish [inform] heerlijk, verrukkelijk
¹deliver (vb) afkomen, over de brug komen: *he will* ~ *on* his promise hij zal doen wat hij beloofd heeft
²deliver (vb) **1** verlossen, bevrijden: *be ~ed of* verlost worden van, bevallen van **2** ter wereld helpen: ~ *a child* een kind ter wereld helpen **3** bezorgen, (af)leveren **4** voordragen, uitspreken: ~ *a lecture* (or: *paper*) een lezing houden
deliverance verlossing, bevrijding, redding
delivery 1 bevalling, verlossing, geboorte **2** bestelling, levering **3** bevrijding, verlossing, redding **4** bezorging, (post)bestelling **5** voordracht, redevoering || *take ~ of* in ontvangst nemen
delivery room verloskamer

delouse ontluizen

delude misleiden, op een dwaalspoor brengen, bedriegen: ~ *o.s. into* zichzelf wijsmaken dat

deluge 1 zondvloed **2** overstroming, watervloed **3** wolkbreuk, stortbui **4** stortvloed, stroom; waterval [of words etc]

delusion waanideeʰ, waanvoorstelling: ~*s of grandeur* grootheidswaan

demagogue demagoog, oproerstoker

¹demand (n) **1** eis, verzoekʰ, verlangenʰ **2** aanspraak, claim, vordering: *make great* (or: *many*) ~*s on* veel vergen van **3** vraag, behoefte: *supply and* ~ vraag en aanbod; *meet the* ~ aan de vraag voldoen; *be in great* ~ erg in trek zijn

²demand (vb) **1** eisen, verlangen, vorderen: *I* ~ *a written apology* ik eis een schriftelijke verontschuldiging **2** vergen, vragen, (ver)eisen: *this job will* ~ *much of you* deze baan zal veel van u vragen

demanding veeleisend

demarcation afbakening, grens(lijn)

demean verlagen, vernederen: ~ *o.s.* zich verlagen; *such language* ~*s you* dergelijke taal is beneden je waardigheid

demeanour gedragʰ, houding, optredenʰ

demented 1 krankzinnig, gek, gestoord **2** dement, kinds

demerara bruine (riet)suiker

demerge weer uiteengaan

demise 1 het ter ziele gaan **2** [form; euph] overlijdenʰ, dood

demo 1 *demonstration* betoging, demonstratie, protestmars **2** *demonstration* proefopname

demobilize demobiliseren, uit de krijgsdienst ontslaan

democracy 1 democratie **2** medezeggenschap⁺ʰ

democrat democraat

democratic democratisch

demolish 1 slopen, vernielen, afbreken, vernietigen **2** omverwerpen, te gronde richten **3** ontzenuwen, weerleggen

demolition vernieling, afbraak, sloop

demon 1 demon, boze geest, duivel; [fig] duivel(s mens) **2** bezetene, fanaat: *he is a* ~ *chessplayer* hij schaakt als een bezetene

¹demonstrate (vb) demonstreren, betogen

²demonstrate (vb) **1** demonstreren, een demonstratie geven van **2** aantonen, bewijzen **3** uiten, openbaren

demonstration 1 demonstratie, betoging, manifestatie **2** demonstratie, vertoning van de werking **3** bewijsʰ **4** uiting, manifestatie, vertoonʰ

demonstrative 1 (aan)tonend **2** open, extravert **3** [linguistics] aanwijzend: ~ *pronoun* aanwijzend voornaamwoord

demonstrator 1 demonstrateur **2** de-

monstrant, betoger

demoralization 1 demoralisatie, ontmoediging **2** zedelijk bederfʰ

demoralize demoraliseren, ontmoedigen

demote degraderen, in rang verlagen

demotivate demotiveren, ontmoedigen

demure ingetogen; zedig

demystification ontsluiering, opheldering

den 1 holʰ, schuilplaats; legerʰ [of animal] **2** holʰ, (misdadigers)verblijfʰ **3** kamertjeʰ, hokʰ

denial 1 ontzegging, weigering **2** ontkenning **3** verwerping

denier ontkenner

denigrate kleineren, belasten

denim 1 spijkerstof **2** (-s) spijkerbroek

denizen [form or hum] inwoner; bewoner

Denmark Denemarken

denomination 1 (eenheids)klasse, munteenheid, muntsoort, getalsoort, gewichtsklasse: *coin of the lowest* ~ kleinste munteenheid **2** noemer: *reduce fractions to the same* ~ breuken onder een noemer brengen **3** gezindte, kerk(genootschapʰ)

denominational confessioneel; bijzonder

denominator noemer, deler

denote 1 aanduiden, verwijzen naar, omschrijven **2** aangeven, duiden op **3** betekenen, als naam dienen voor

dénouement ontknoping; afloop

denounce 1 hekelen, afkeuren **2** aan de kaak stellen, openlijk beschuldigen

dense 1 dicht, compact, samengepakt: ~*ly populated* dichtbevolkt **2** dom, hersenloos

density 1 dichtheid, compactheid, concentratie **2** bevolkingsdichtheid

¹dent (n) **1** deuk **2** [fig] deuk, knauw || *that made a big* ~ *in our savings* dat kostte ons flink wat van ons spaargeld

²dent (vb) **1** deuken, een deuk maken (krijgen) in **2** [fig] deuken, een knauw geven

dental 1 dentaal, m.b.t. het gebit, tand- **2** tandheelkundig: ~ *floss* tandzijde

dentist tandarts

dentistry tandheelkunde

denture 1 gebitʰ **2** (-s) kunstgebitʰ, vals gebitʰ

denunciation 1 openlijke veroordeling **2** beschuldiging, aangifte, aanklacht **3** opzegging [of pact etc]

deny 1 ontkennen: *there is no* ~*ing that* het valt niet te ontkennen dat **2** ontzeggen, weigeren

deodorant deodorant

¹depart (vb) heengaan, weggaan, vertrekken: ~ *for* vertrekken naar, afreizen naar

²depart (vb) verlaten: ~ *this life* sterven

department 1 afdeling, departementʰ; [education] vakgroep; sectie; instituutʰ [at university] **2** ministerieʰ, departementʰ: *De-*

*partment of **Environment** [roughly] Ministerie van Milieuzaken

department store warenhuis[h]

departure 1 vertrek[h], vertrektijd **2** afwijking: *new* ~ nieuwe koers; *a* ~ *from the agreed policy* een afwijking van het afgesproken beleid

depend afhangen: *it all* ~*s* het hangt er nog maar van af

dependable betrouwbaar

dependence 1 afhankelijkheid: ~ *on luxury* afhankelijkheid van luxe **2** vertrouwen[h] **3** verslaving

¹**dependent** (n) afhankelijke [eg for sustenance]

²**dependent** (adj) afhankelijk: ~ *(up)on* afhankelijk van

depend (up)on 1 afhangen van, afhankelijk zijn van **2** vertrouwen op, bouwen op, zich verlaten op: *can I depend (up)on on that?* kan ik daar op rekenen?

depict (af)schilderen, beschrijven, afbeelden: *in that book his father is* ~*ed as an alcoholic* in dat boek wordt zijn vader afgeschilderd als een alcoholist

depiction afbeelding; afschildering

deplete leeghalen, uitputten

deplorable betreurenswaardig, zeer slecht

deplore betreuren, bedroefd zijn over

deploy 1 inzetten **2** [mil] opstellen

depopulate ontvolken

deport 1 (zich) gedragen, (zich) houden: ~ *o.s.* zich gedragen **2** verbannen, uitzetten

deportation deportatie; verbanning

deportee gedeporteerde, banneling

deportment 1 (lichaams)houding, postuur[h] **2** gedrag[h], manieren, houding

depose 1 afzetten, onttronen **2** getuigen; onder ede verklaren [in writing]

¹**deposit** (n) **1** onderpand[h], waarborgsom, aanbetaling, statiegeld[h] **2** storting **3** deposito[h]; depositogeld[h] [with period of notice] **4** afzetting, ertslaag, bezinksel[h]

²**deposit** (vb) **1** afzetten, bezinken **2** neerleggen, plaatsen **3** deponeren, in bewaring geven, storten

depository opslagruimte, bewaarplaats

depot 1 depot[h], magazijn[h], opslagruimte **2** (leger)depot[h], militair magazijn[h] **3** [Am] spoorwegstation[h], busstation[h]

depravation verdorvenheid, bederf[h]

deprave bederven, doen ontaarden

depravity verdorvenheid

deprecation 1 afkeuring, protest[h] **2** geringschatting

depreciate 1 (doen) devalueren, in waarde (doen) dalen **2** kleineren

depreciation 1 devaluatie, waardevermindering, afschrijving **2** geringschatting

depredation plundering

depressed 1 gedeprimeerd, ontmoedigd

2 noodlijdend, onderdrukt: ~ *area* **a)** noodlijdend gebied; **b)** streek met aanhoudend hoge werkloosheid

depressing deprimerend, ontmoedigend

depression 1 laagte, holte, indruk **2** depressie, lagedrukgebied[h], lage luchtdruk **3** depressie, crisis(tijd) **4** depressiviteit, neerslachtigheid

deprivation 1 ontbering, verlies[h], gemis[h] **2** beroving, ontneming

deprive beroven: *the old man was* ~*d of his wallet* de oude man werd beroofd van zijn portefeuille; *they* ~ *those people of clean water* ze onthouden deze mensen schoon water

deprived misdeeld, achtergesteld, arm: ~ *children* kansarme kinderen

dept 1 department **2** deputy

depth 1 diepte: *he was **beyond*** (or: *out of*) *his* ~ hij verloor de grond onder z'n voeten; *in* ~ diepgaand, grondig **2** diepzinnigheid, scherpzinnigheid **3** het diepst, het holst: *in the* ~*s of Asia* in het hart van Azië; *in the* ~*(s) of winter* midden in de winter

deputation afvaardiging, delegatie

¹**deputy** (n) **1** (plaats)vervanger, waarnemer **2** afgevaardigde, kamerlid[h] **3** hulpsheriff; [roughly] plaatsvervangend commissaris

²**deputy** (adj) onder-, vice-, plaatsvervangend: ~ *director* onderdirecteur

deradicalize deradicaliseren

derail (doen) ontsporen

derange verwarren, krankzinnig maken: *mentally* ~*d* geestelijk gestoord, krankzinnig

derelict verwaarloosd, verlaten

deride uitlachen, bespotten, belachelijk maken: ~ *as* uitmaken voor

derision spot: *be/become an **object** of* ~ bespot worden

derisive spottend; honend

derivation afleiding, afkomst, etymologie

¹**derivative** (n) afleiding

²**derivative** (adj) afgeleid, niet oorspronkelijk

¹**derive** (vb) afstammen: ~ *from* ontleend zijn aan, (voort)komen uit

²**derive** (vb) afleiden, krijgen, halen: ~ *pleasure from* plezier ontlenen aan

dermatologist huidarts; dermatoloog

derogatory geringschattend, minachtend, kleinerend

derp [inform] suf

descale ontkalken

descant [mus] discant, sopraan

¹**descend** (vb) **1** (af)dalen, naar beneden gaan, neerkomen **2** afstammen: *be* ~*ed from* afstammen van

²**descend** (vb) afdalen, naar beneden gaan langs; afzakken [river]

descendant afstammeling, nakomeling

descent 1 afkomst, afstamming: *Charles claims* ~ *from a Scottish king* Charles beweert

af te stammen van een Schotse koning
2 overdracht, overerving **3** afdaling, landing, val **4** helling

describe 1 beschrijven, karakteriseren: *you can hardly ~ his ideas as original* je kunt zijn ideeën toch moeilijk oorspronkelijk noemen **2** beschrijven, trekken: *~ a circle* een cirkel tekenen

description 1 beschrijving, omschrijving: *fit the ~* aan de beschrijving voldoen **2** soort^{+h}, type^h: *weapons of all ~s* (or: *every ~*) allerlei (soorten) wapens

descriptive beschrijvend

desecrate ontheiligen; schenden

¹desert (n) woestijn

²desert (vb) deserteren

³desert (vb) verlaten, in de steek laten: *~ed streets* uitgestorven straten

desertion desertie

deserts: *give s.o. his (just) ~* iem. zijn verdiende loon geven

deserve verdienen, recht hebben op: *one good turn ~s another* de ene dienst is de andere waard

¹design (n) **1** ontwerp^h, tekening, blauwdruk, constructie, vormgeving **2** dessin^h, patroon^h **3** opzet, bedoeling, doel^h: *have ~s against* boze plannen hebben met; *by ~* met opzet

²design (vb) **1** ontwerpen **2** uitdenken, bedenken, beramen: *who ~ed this bank-robbery?* wie beraamde deze bankroof? **3** bedoelen, ontwikkelen, bestemmen: *~ed for children* bedoeld voor kinderen

¹designate (adj) [form] aangesteld: [Am] *~d survivor* reservepresident

²designate (vb) **1** aanduiden; markeren **2** noemen; bestempelen **3** aanstellen, benoemen: [inform] *the ~d driver* de bob

designer designer, ontwerper, tekenaar: *~ clothes* designerkleding

designing listig, berekenend, sluw

desirable 1 wenselijk **2** aantrekkelijk

¹desire (n) **1** (+ for) wens, verlangen^h (naar), wil **2** begeerte, hartstocht

²desire (vb) wensen, verlangen, begeren: *leave much/nothing to be ~d* veel/niets te wensen overlaten

desist (+ from) ophouden (met), uitscheiden (met), afzien (van)

desk 1 werktafel, (schrijf)bureau^h **2** balie, receptie, kas

desk job kantoorbaan

desktop [comp] desktop

desolate 1 verlaten, uitgestorven, troosteloos **2** diepbedroefd, eenzaam: *at 30 he was already ~ and helpless* op zijn dertigste was hij al zo eenzaam en hulpeloos

desolation 1 verwoesting, ontvolking **2** verlatenheid **3** eenzaamheid

¹despair (n) wanhoop, vertwijfeling: *drive s.o. to ~, fill s.o. with ~* iem. tot wanhoop drijven; *be the ~ of s.o.* iem. wanhopig maken

²despair (vb) wanhopen

desperate wanhopig, hopeloos; uitzichtloos [of situation]; vertwijfeld; radeloos [of deeds, people]: *a ~ action* een wanhoopsactie; *she was ~ for a cup of tea* ze verlangde verschrikkelijk naar een kopje thee

despicable verachtelijk

despise verachten, versmaden

despite ondanks: *~ the fact that* ondanks het feit dat

despondent wanhopig; vertwijfeld

despot despoot; tiran

dessert dessert^h

destination (plaats van) bestemming, doel^h, eindpunt^h

destine bestemmen, (voor)beschikken: *be ~d for* bestemd zijn voor

destiny lot^h, bestemming, beschikking

Destiny (nood)lot^h

destitute arm, behoeftig

destroy vernielen, vernietigen, ruïneren: *thousands of houses were ~ed by the earthquakes* door de aardbevingen zijn duizenden huizen vernield

destruction 1 vernietiging, afbraak **2** ondergang

destructive vernietigend; destructief: *~ criticism* afbrekende kritiek

detach (+ from) losmaken (van), scheiden, uit elkaar halen

detached 1 los; vrijstaand [of house]; niet verbonden, geïsoleerd **2** onbevooroordeeld: *~ view of sth.* objectieve kijk op iets **3** afstandelijk, gereserveerd

detachment 1 detachering, detachement^h **2** scheiding **3** afstandelijkheid, gereserveerdheid **4** onpartijdigheid

detail 1 detail^h, bijzonderheid, kleinigheid: *enter* (or: *go*) *into ~(s)* op bijzonderheden ingaan **2** kleine versiering

detailed uitvoerig: *~ information available on request* uitgebreide informatie op aanvraag verkrijgbaar

detain 1 aanhouden, laten nablijven, gevangen houden **2** laten schoolblijven: *Henry was ~ed for half an hour* Henry moest een halfuur nablijven **3** ophouden, vertragen: *I don't want to ~ you any longer* ik wil u niet langer ophouden

detainee (politieke) gevangene, gedetineerde

detect ontdekken, bespeuren

detective detective, speurder, rechercheur

detention 1 opsluiting, (militaire) detentie, hechtenis **2** het schoolblijven: *keep a pupil in ~* een leerling laten nablijven **3** vertraging, oponthoud^h

deter (+ from) afschrikken (van), ontmoedigen, afhouden (van)

detergent wasmiddel^h, afwasmiddel^h, reinigingsmiddel^h

deteriorate verslechteren, achteruitgaan

deterioration achteruitgang; verslechtering

determination 1 vast voornemen^h, bedoeling, plan^h **2** vastberadenheid, vastbeslotenheid

determine 1 besluiten, beslissen: *Sheila ~d to dye her hair green* Sheila besloot haar haar groen te verven **2** doen besluiten, drijven tot

determined beslist, vastberaden, vastbesloten

deterrence afschrikking

deterrent afschrikwekkend middel^h, afschrikmiddel^h, atoombom: *the cameras are a ~ for shoplifters* de camera's hebben een preventieve werking tegen winkeldieven

detest verafschuwen, walgen van

dethrone afzetten, onttronen

¹detonate (vb) ontploffen, exploderen

²detonate (vb) tot ontploffing brengen, laten exploderen

detour 1 omweg, bocht, (rivier)kronkel **2** omleiding

¹detox (n) **1** ontwenning(skuur) **2** ontslakking

²detox (vb) **1** afkicken; ontwennen **2** ontslakken

detoxification centre ontwenningskliniek; afkickcentrum^h

detract: ~ *from* kleineren, afbreuk doen aan, verminderen

detriment (oorzaak van) schade, kwaad^h, nadeel^h: *to the ~ of* ten nadele van

detrimental schadelijk; slecht, nadelig

detritus resten, afval^h: *he waded through the ~ of the party* hij waadde door de resten van het feest

deuce 1 twee [on dice] **2** [tennis] veertig gelijk || *a ~ of a fight* een vreselijke knokpartij

devaluation devaluatie, waardevermindering

devalue devalueren, in waarde (doen) dalen

devastate verwoesten, ruïneren, vernietigen: *he was ~d* hij was er helemaal kapot van

devastation verwoesting

¹develop (vb) **1** ontwikkelen, uitwerken, ontginnen: *~ing country* ontwikkelingsland; *~ a film* een film(pje) ontwikkelen **2** ontvouwen, uiteenzetten

²develop (vb) (zich) ontwikkelen, (doen) ontstaan, (doen) uitbreiden

developer 1 projectontwikkelaar **2** [photo] ontwikkelaar

development 1 ontwikkeling, verloop^h, evolutie, ontplooiing, groei, verdere uitwerking: *await further ~s* afwachten wat er verder komt **2** gebeurtenis **3** (nieuw)bouwproject^h

deviant 1 afwijkend, tegen de norm **2** abnormaal

deviate (+ from) afwijken (van), afdwalen

deviation afwijking [from current norm]; deviatie: ~ *from* afwijking van

device 1 apparaat^h, toestel^h: *a new ~ for squeezing lemons* een nieuw apparaat om citroenen te persen **2** middel^h, kunstgreep, truc **3** devies^h, motto^h, leus **4** embleem^h [on coat of arms] || *left to his own ~s* op zichzelf aangewezen

devil 1 duivel **2** man, jongen, donder, kerel || *give the ~ his due* ere wie ere toekomt, het iem. nageven; ~ *take the hindmost* ieder voor zich en God voor ons allen; *be a ~* kom op, spring eens uit de band; *there'll be the ~ to pay* dan krijgen we de poppen aan het dansen; *the ~ of an undertaking* een helse klus

devil-may-care roekeloos; wie-dan-leeft-die-dan-zorgt

devious 1 kronkelend, slingerend; [fig] omslachtig: ~ *route* omweg **2** onoprecht, onbetrouwbaar, sluw

devise bedenken, beramen

devoid (+ of) verstoken (van), ontbloot (van), gespeend (van)

¹devolve (vb) [form] terechtkomen: *his duties ~d on* (or: *to, upon*) *his secretary* zijn taken werden overgenomen door zijn secretaris || [form] *the property ~d to his son* het land viel toe aan zijn zoon

²devolve (vb) [form] afwentelen; delegeren, overdragen

devote (+ to) wijden (aan), besteden (aan): ~ *o.s. to* zich overgeven aan

devotee 1 (+ of) liefhebber (van), aanbidder, enthousiast **2** aanhanger; volgeling [of religious sect] **3** dweper, fanaticus

devotion 1 toewijding, liefde, overgave: ~ *to duty* plichtsbetrachting **2** het besteden **3** vroomheid

devour 1 verslinden [also fig]; verzwelgen **2** verteren: *(be) ~ed by jealousy* verteerd (worden) door jaloezie

devout 1 vroom **2** vurig, oprecht

dew dauw

dexterity handigheid, behendigheid, (hand)vaardigheid

diabetes diabetes, suikerziekte

¹diabetic (n) diabeticus: *be a ~* diabetes hebben

²diabetic (adj) voor suikerzieken, diabetes-

diabolic(al) afschuwelijk, afgrijselijk, ontzettend

diadem diadeem^(+h)

diagnose een diagnose stellen (van)

diagnosis diagnose

¹diagonal (n) diagonaal

²diagonal (adj) diagonaal

diagram diagram^h, schets, schema^h, grafiek

¹dial (n) **1** wijzerplaat **2** schaal(verdeling);

(afstem)schaal [of radio etc]; zonnewijzer
3 kiesschijf [of telephone] **4** afstemknop [of radio etc]

²**dial** (vb) draaien; bellen [of telephone]

dialect dialect[h]

dialling code 1 netnummer[h] **2** landnummer[h]

dialogue dialoog

dialogue box dialoogvenster[h]

dial-up kies-, geschakeld: *a ~ connection* inbelverbinding

diameter diameter, middellijn, doorsnede

diamond 1 diamant, diamanten sieraad[h] **2** ruit(vormige figuur[+h]) **3** ruiten(kaart) **4** (-s) ruiten [cards]: *Queen of ~s* ruitenvrouw || *it was ~ cut ~* het ging hard tegen hard

diaper [Am] luier

diaphragm diafragma[h], middenrif[h]

diarist dagboekschrijver

diarrhoea diarree [also fig]; buikloop

diary 1 dagboek[h] **2** agenda

diatribe scherpe kritiek; schimprede

dibs [inform]: *call ~ on sth.* iets claimen; *I call ~ die is van mij; ik eerst; *have first ~ on something* de eerste keus hebben bij iets

¹**dice** (n) dobbelsteen; [also fig] kans; geluk[h]: *the ~ are loaded against him* het lot is hem niet gunstig gezind || [Am; inform] *no ~* tevergeefs

²**dice** (vb) in dobbelsteentjes snijden

³**dice** (vb) dobbelen

dices dobbelspel[h]

dicey link, riskant

dick 1 [vulg] lul, pik, piemel **2** [Am; vulg] lul, eikel, zak: *be a total ~ about sth.* verschrikkelijk moeilijk doen over iets **3** [Am; vulg] smeris

dickhead idioot, stommeling

dicky wankel, wiebelig: *a ~ heart* een zwak hart

¹**dictate** (n) ingeving, bevel[h]

²**dictate** (vb) **1** dicteren **2** commanderen, opleggen

dictator dictator

diction 1 voordracht **2** taalgebruik[h], woordkeus

dictionary woordenboek[h]

didactic didactisch

diddle ontfutselen, bedriegen: *he ~d me out of £5* hij heeft me voor £5 afgezet

¹**die** (n) matrijs, stempel[h], gietvorm

²**die** (vb) **1** sterven, overlijden, omkomen: *~ from* (or: *of*) *an illness* sterven aan een ziekte **2** ophouden te bestaan, verloren gaan: *the mystery ~d with him* hij nam het geheim mee in zijn graf **3** uitsterven, wegsterven **4** verzwakken, verminderen, bedaren || *~ away* a) wegsterven [of sound]; b) uitgaan [of fire]; c) gaan liggen [of wind]; *~ down* a) bedaren, afnemen [of wind]; b) uitgaan [of fire]; *~ off* a) een voor een sterven; b) uitsterven; *be dy-*

ing for a cigarette snakken naar een sigaret; *~ of anxiety* doodsangsten uitstaan

die-cast gegoten

diehard 1 taaie[h], volhouder **2** aartsconservatief **3** onverzoenlijke

diesel diesel

¹**diet** (n) **1** dieet[h], leefregel; light, dieet-: *~ soda* frisdrank light; *on a ~* op dieet **2** voedsel[h], voeding, kost: *her ~ consisted of bread and lentils* haar voedsel bestond uit brood en linzen

²**diet** (vb) op dieet zijn; [fig] lijnen

dietary dieet-; eet-: *~ rules* voedselvoorschriften

dietician diëtist(e), voedingsspecialist(e)

differ 1 (van elkaar) verschillen, afwijken: *those twin sisters ~ from one another* die tweelingzusjes verschillen van elkaar **2** van mening verschillen: *~ from s.o.* het met iem. oneens zijn

difference 1 verschil[h], onderscheid[h]: *that makes all the ~* dat maakt veel uit **2** verschil[h], rest: *split the ~* het verschil (samen) delen **3** meningsverschil[h], geschil(punt)[h]

different 1 verschillend, ongelijk, afwijkend: *as ~ as chalk and* (or: *from*) *cheese* verschillend als dag en nacht; [fig] *strike a ~ note* een ander geluid laten horen; *~ from, ~ to* anders dan **2** ongewoon, speciaal || *a horse of a ~ colour* een geheel andere kwestie

¹**differential** (n) **1** verschil in loon[h] **2** koersverschil[h] **3** [techn] differentieel[h]

²**differential** (adj) onderscheidend || [maths] *~ calculus* differentiaalrekening

¹**differentiate** (vb) **1** zich onderscheiden **2** een verschil maken: *~ between* ongelijk behandelen

²**differentiate** (vb) onderscheiden, onderkennen

difficult moeilijk [also of character]; lastig

difficulty 1 moeilijkheid, probleem[h] **2** moeite: *with ~* met moeite

diffident bedeesd, terughoudend

¹**diffuse** (adj) diffuus; wijdlopig [also style]

²**diffuse** (vb) zich verspreiden; verstrooid worden [of light]

diffusion 1 verspreiding **2** [physics] diffusie

¹**dig** (n) **1** por; [fig] steek (onder water): *have a ~ at s.o.* iets hatelijks over iem. zeggen **2** (archeologische) opgraving **3** (-s) kamer(s)

²**dig** (vb) **1** doordringen **2** zwoegen, ploeteren **3** graven, delven, opgraven **4** uitgraven, rooien **5** uitzoeken, voor de dag halen **6** porren **7** vatten, snappen

¹**digest** (n) samenvatting, (periodiek) overzicht[h]

²**digest** (vb) verteren

³**digest** (vb) verteren [also fig]; slikken, verwerken, in zich opnemen

digestion spijsvertering, digestie

¹**digestive** (n) **1** digestief^h **2** volkoren-biscuit^h

²**digestive** (adj) **1** spijsverterings- **2** goed voor de spijsvertering

digger 1 graver, gouddelver **2** graafmachine **3** Australiër

digicam digitale camera

¹**dig in** (vb) **1** zich ingraven **2** aanvallen [food] **3** van geen wijken weten

²**dig in** (vb) **1** ingraven: *dig o.s.* in zich ingraven; [fig] zijn positie verstevigen **2** onderspitten

dig into 1 graven in: *dig sth. into the soil* iets ondergraven, iets onderspitten **2** prikken, slaan, boren in **3** zijn tanden zetten in, diepgaand onderzoeken: *the journalist dug into the scandal* de journalist beet zich vast in het schandaal

digit cijfer^h; getal^h [0 up to and including 9]

digital digitaal

digital money elektronisch geld^h, digitaal geld^h, e-geld^h

dignified waardig, deftig, statig

dignitary (kerkelijk) hoogwaardigheidsbekleder: *the local dignitaries* de dorpsnotabelen

dignity waardigheid: *that is beneath his ~* dat is beneden zijn waardigheid

dig out 1 uitgraven **2** opdiepen, voor de dag halen **3** blootleggen

digress uitweiden: *~ from one's subject* afdwalen van zijn onderwerp

digression (+ on) uitweiding (over)

¹**dig up** (vb) [Am] bijdrage leveren, betalen

²**dig up** (vb) **1** opgraven, uitgraven; omspitten [road] **2** blootleggen, opsporen **3** bij elkaar scharrelen **4** opscharrelen

dike *see* dyke

dilapidated vervallen, bouwvallig

¹**dilate** (vb) uitzetten; zich verwijden

²**dilate** (vb) **1** verwijden; opensperren [eyes] **2** doen uitzetten

dilatory 1 traag, langzaam, laks **2** vertragend

dilemma dilemma^h, netelig vraagstuk^h

diligence ijver, vlijt, toewijding

diligent ijverig, vlijtig

dilly-dally [inform] **1** treuzelen **2** dubben; weifelen

dilute 1 verdunnen, aanlengen: *~ the syrup with water or milk* de siroop met water of melk aanlengen **2** doen verbleken, doen vervallen **3** afzwakken, doen verwateren

¹**dim** (adj) **1** schemerig, (half)duister **2** vaag, flauw: *I have a ~ understanding of botany* ik heb een beetje verstand van plantkunde **3** stom ‖ *take a ~ view* of sth. iets afkeuren, niets ophebben met iets

²**dim** (vb) **1** verduisteren, versomberen **2** temperen, dimmen: *~ the headlights* dimmen men

dime dime; 10 centstuk^h [Am]; cent, stuiver ‖ *a ~ a dozen* dertien in een dozijn

dimension 1 afmeting, grootte, omvang; [fig] kaliber^h; formaat^h **2** dimensie, aspect^h, kwaliteit

diminish verminderen, verkleinen, afnemen, z'n waarde verliezen, aantasten

diminutive 1 verklein- **2** nietig: *a ~ kitten* een piepklein poesje

dimple kuiltje^h

dimwit sufferd, onbenul^h

¹**din** (n) kabaal^h, lawaai^h: *kick up* (or: *make*) *a ~* herrie schoppen

²**din** (vb) **1** verdoven [of noise] **2** inprenten: *~ sth. into s.o.* iets er bij iem. in stampen

dine dineren: *~ out* buitenshuis dineren

diner 1 iem. die dineert, eter, gast **2** restauratiewagen **3** [Am] klein (weg)restaurant^h

ding-dong 1 gebimbam^h; gebeier^h **2** [inform] herrieschopperij; felle discussie

dinghy 1 jol **2** kleine boot, (opblaasbaar) reddingsvlot^h, rubberboot

dingy 1 smerig, smoezelig **2** sjofel, armoedig

dining car restauratiewagen

dining room eetkamer; [in hotel] restaurant^h

dinky 1 snoezig **2** [Am] armzalig

dinner eten^h, avondeten^h, (warm) middagmaal^h: *~ is served* er is opgediend

dinner jacket smoking(jasje)

dinner suit smoking

dinosaur dinosaurus

dint deuk; indruk [also fig]

dioxide dioxide^h

¹**dip** (n) **1** indoping, onderdompeling, wasbeurt; [inform] duik **2** schepje **3** helling, daling; dal^h [landscape] **4** (kleine) daling, vermindering **5** dipsaus

²**dip** (vb) **1** duiken, plonzen, kopje-onder gaan **2** ondergaan, vallen, zinken **3** hellen, dalen **4** tasten, reiken, grijpen: *~ in* toetasten; *~ into one's financial resources* aanspraak doen op zijn geldelijke middelen ‖ *~ into* vluchtig bekijken

³**dip** (vb) **1** (onder)dompelen, (in)dopen; galvaniseren [in bath]; wassen [animals in a bathtub with insecticide] **2** verven, in verfbad dopen **3** dimmen [headlights]

diploma diploma^h

diplomacy diplomatie [also fig]; (politieke) tact, diplomatiek optreden^h

diplomat diplomaat

diplomatic 1 diplomatiek, m.b.t. diplomatieke dienst; [fig] met diplomatie: *~ bag* diplomatieke post(zak) [for embassy etc] **2** subtiel, berekend, sluw

Dipper (the) **1** [Am] Grote Beer: *Big ~* Grote Beer; *Little ~* Kleine Beer **2** waterspreeuw

dipsomaniac (periodiek) alcoholist, kwar-

taaldrinker
dipstick peilstok, meetstok
dire ijselijk, uiterst (dringend): *be in ~ need of water* snakken naar water; *~ poverty* bittere armoede
¹direct (adj) **1** direct, rechtstreeks, onmiddellijk, openhartig: *be a ~ descendant* in een rechte lijn van iem. afstammen; *a ~ hit* een voltreffer **2** absoluut, exact, precies: *~ opposites* absolute tegenpolen ‖ *~ current* gelijkstroom; *~ object* lijdend voorwerp
²direct (vb) **1** richten: *these measures are ~ed against* abuse deze maatregelen zijn gericht tegen misbruik **2** de weg wijzen, leiden: *~ s.o. to the post office* iem. de weg wijzen naar het postkantoor **3** bestemmen, toewijzen **4** leiden, de leiding hebben over, besturen **5** geleiden, als richtlijn dienen voor **6** opdracht geven, bevelen; [law] instrueren
³direct (vb) regisseren, dirigeren
⁴direct (adv) rechtstreeks: *broadcast ~* rechtstreeks uitzenden
direction 1 opzichtʰ, kant, tendens, richting; [fig also] gebiedʰ; terreinʰ: *progress in all ~s* vooruitgang op alle gebieden **2** instructie, bevelʰ, aanwijzing: *at the ~ of, by ~ of* op last van **3** oogmerkʰ, doelʰ **4** leiding, directie, supervisie: *in the ~ of London* in de richting van Londen **5** geleiding, het geleiden **6** directie, regie
directive instructie, bevelʰ
directly 1 rechtstreeks, openhartig **2** dadelijk, zo **3** precies, direct: *~ opposite the door* precies tegenover de deur
director 1 directeur, manager, directielidʰ: *the board of ~s* de raad van bestuur **2** [Am] dirigent **3** regisseur, spelleider
directory 1 adresboekʰ, gids, adressenbestandʰ **2** telefoonboekʰ
dirge lijkzang, treurzang, klaagzang
dirt 1 vuilʰ, modder, drek, viezigheid: *treat s.o. like ~* iem. als oud vuil behandelen **2** lasterpraat, geroddelʰ **3** grond, aarde
dirt bike (cross)motor
dirt road [Am] onverharde weg; zandweg
dirty 1 vies, vuil, smerig **2** laag, gemeen: *give s.o. a ~ look* iem. vuil aankijken; *play a ~ trick on s.o.* iem. een gemene streek leveren **3** [inform] slecht; ruw [of weather] ‖ *wash one's ~ linen in public* de vuile was buiten hangen
disability 1 onbekwaamheid, onvermogenʰ **2** belemmering, nadeelʰ, handicap **3** invaliditeit, lichamelijke ongeschiktheid
disable 1 onmogelijk maken, onbruikbaar, ongeschikt maken **2** invalide maken, arbeidsongeschikt maken: *~d persons* (lichamelijk) gehandicapte mensen; *the ~d* de invaliden
disadvantage nadeelʰ, ongunstige situatie: *at a ~* in het nadeel

disadvantaged minder bevoorrecht
disagree 1 het oneens zijn, verschillen van mening, ruziën **2** verschillen, niet kloppen, niet overeenkomen: *the two statements ~* de twee beweringen stemmen niet overeen
disagreeable 1 onaangenaam **2** slecht gehumeurd, onvriendelijk
disagreement 1 onenigheid, meningsverschilʰ, ruzie **2** verschilʰ, afwijking
disagree with 1 niet liggen; ziek maken: *Italian wine disagrees with me* ik kan niet tegen Italiaanse wijn **2** afkeuren
disallow 1 niet toestaan, verbieden **2** ongeldig verklaren, verwerpen, afkeuren: *~ a goal* een doelpunt afkeuren
disappear verdwijnen
disappoint 1 teleurstellen, niet aan de verwachtingen voldoen, tegenvallen **2** verijdelen [plan]; doen mislukken, tenietdoen
disappointed teleurgesteld: *she was ~ in him* hij viel haar tegen
disappointment teleurstelling
disapproval afkeuring: *the teacher shook her head in ~* de docente schudde afkeurend haar hoofd
disapprove afkeuren, veroordelen: *he wanted to stay on but his parents ~d* hij wilde nog even blijven, maar zijn ouders vonden dat niet goed
¹disarm (vb) de kracht ontnemen, vriendelijk stemmen: *his quiet manners ~ed all opposition* zijn rustige manier van doen nam alle tegenstand weg; *a ~ing smile* een ontwapenende glimlach
²disarm (vb) ontwapenen, onschadelijk maken
disarmament ontwapening
disarrange in de war brengen, verstoren
disarray wanorde, verwarring
disaster ramp, catastrofe; [fig] totale mislukking: *court ~* om moeilijkheden vragen
disastrous rampzalig, noodlottig
disavowal 1 ontkenning, loochening **2** afwijzing
disband uiteengaan, ontbonden worden
disbelief ongeloofʰ: *he stared at us in ~* hij keek ons vol ongeloof aan
disbelieve niet geloven, betwijfelen, verwerpen
disc 1 schijf, parkeerschijf **2** discus **3** (grammofoon)plaat, cd, cd-rom **4** [med] schijf, tussenwervelschijf: *a slipped ~* een hernia **5** [comp] schijf
¹discard (vb) zich ontdoen van, weggooien, afdanken
²discard (vb) [cards] afgooien, ecarteren, niet bekennen
discern 1 waarnemen, onderscheiden, bespeuren: *I could hardly ~ the words on the traffic sign* ik kon de woorden op het verkeersbord nauwelijks onderscheiden **2** onderscheiden,

verschil zien, onderscheid maken
discerning scherpzinnig, opmerkzaam, kritisch
¹discharge (n) **1** bewijsʰ van ontslag **2** lossing, ontlading, het uitladen **3** uitstorting, afvoer, uitstroming; [of gas etc; also fig] uiting **4** schotʰ, het afvuren **5** aflossing, vervulling **6** ontslagʰ van rechtsvervolging, vrijspraak
²discharge (vb) **1** zich ontladen, zich uitstorten; etteren [of wound]: *the river ~s into the sea* de rivier mondt in zee uit **2** [elec] zich ontladen
³discharge (vb) **1** ontladen, uitladen, lossen **2** afvuren, afschieten, lossen **3** ontladen, van elektrische lading ontdoen **4** wegsturen, ontslaan, ontheffen van, vrijspreken, in vrijheid stellen: ~ *the jury* de jury van zijn plichten ontslaan; ~ *a patient* een patiënt ontslaan **5** uitstorten, uitstoten, afgeven **6** vervullen, voldoen, zich kwijten van: ~ *one's duties* zijn taak vervullen
disciple discipel, leerling, volgeling
¹discipline (n) **1** methode, systeemʰ **2** vakʰ, discipline, tak van wetenschap **3** discipline, tucht, orde, controle: *maintain* ~ orde houden
²discipline (vb) **1** disciplineren, onder tucht brengen, drillen **2** straffen, disciplinaire maatregelen nemen tegen
disc jockey diskjockey
disclaim ontkennen, afwijzen, verwerpen, van de hand wijzen
disclaimer 1 ontkenning; afwijzing **2** [law] bewijsʰ van afstand
disclose onthullen [also fig]; bekendmaken, tonen
disco disco, discotheek
discomfit verwarren; in verlegenheid brengen
discomfort 1 ongemakʰ, ontbering, moeilijkheid **2** ongemakkelijkheid, gebrekʰ aan comfort
disconcert 1 verontrusten, in verlegenheid brengen **2** verijdelen [plans]
disconcerting verontrustend
disconnect losmaken, scheiden, loskoppelen; afsluiten [s.o., from gas supply etc]: *we were suddenly ~ed* de (telefoon)verbinding werd plotseling verbroken
disconsolate ontroostbaar; wanhopig
¹discontent (n) **1** grief, bezwaarʰ **2** ontevredenheid
²discontent (adj) (+ with) ontevreden (over/met), teleurgesteld
¹discontinue (vb) tot een einde komen, ophouden
²discontinue (vb) **1** beëindigen, een eind maken aan, ophouden met **2** opzeggen [newspaper etc]
discord 1 onenigheid, twist, ruzie **2** lawaaiʰ
discotheque disco, discotheek
¹discount (n) **1** reductie, korting: *at a ~ of £3* met een korting van drie pond **2** discontoʰ, wisseldiscontoʰ
²discount (vb) **1** disconto geven (nemen); disconteren [Bill of Exchange] **2** korting geven (op) **3** buiten beschouwing laten, niet serieus nemen
discounter discountzaak
discourage 1 ontmoedigen, de moed ontnemen **2** weerhouden, afhouden, afbrengen
discouragement 1 tegenslag **2** ontmoediging **3** moedeloosheid
discourse 1 gesprekʰ, dialoog, conversatie **2** verhandeling, lezing
discourteous onbeleefd, onhoffelijk
discover 1 ontdekken, (uit)vinden: *Tasman ~ed New Zealand* Tasman heeft Nieuw-Zeeland ontdekt **2** onthullen, blootleggen; [fig] aan het licht brengen; bekendmaken **3** aantreffen, bemerken, te weten komen
discovery ontdekking: *a voyage of* ~ een ontdekkingsreis
¹discredit (n) schande, diskredietʰ, opspraak: *bring ~ (up)on o.s., bring o.s. into ~* zich te schande maken
²discredit (vb) **1** te schande maken, in diskrediet brengen **2** wantrouwen, verdenken
discreditable schandelijk, verwerpelijk
discreet 1 discreet **2** bescheiden, onopvallend
discrepancy discrepantie, afwijking, verschilʰ
discrete afzonderlijk
discretion 1 oordeelkundigheid, tact, verstandʰ: *the age* (or: *years*) *of* ~ de jaren des onderscheids **2** discretie, oordeelʰ, vrijheid (van handelen): *at* ~ naar goeddunken; *use one's* ~ naar eigen goeddunken handelen; [film] *viewer* ~ *is advised* niet geschikt voor jeugdige kijkers
¹discriminate (vb) **1** onderscheid maken: ~ *between* verschil maken tussen **2** discrimineren: ~ *against* discrimineren; *she felt ~d against in pay* zij voelde zich qua salaris gediscrimineerd
²discriminate (vb) onderscheiden, herkennen
discriminating 1 opmerkzaam, scherpzinnig **2** onderscheidend, kenmerkend **3** kieskeurig, overkritisch **4** discriminerend
discrimination 1 onderscheidʰ, het maken van onderscheid **2** discriminatie **3** oordeelsvermogenʰ, kritische smaak
discus discus
discuss bespreken, behandelen, praten over: *okay, let's now ~ my pay rise* goed, laten we het nu eens over mijn loonsverhoging hebben

discussion 1 bespreking, discussie, gesprek[h]: *be under* ~ in behandeling zijn **2** uiteenzetting, verhandeling, bespreking

disdain minachting

disease ziekte, aandoening, kwaal: *wasting* ~ kwijnende ziekte

[1]**disembark** (vb) van boord gaan, aan wal gaan, uitstappen

[2]**disembark** (vb) ontschepen, aan land brengen, lossen

disembodied zonder lichaam; onstoffelijk, niet tastbaar

disembowel 1 van de ingewanden ontdoen; ontweien [fish, game] **2** de buik openrijten van

disenchant ontgoochelen, ontnuchteren, uit de droom helpen

disenchantment desillusie

[1]**disengage** (vb) losraken, zich losmaken

[2]**disengage** (vb) losmaken, vrij maken, bevrijden

disengagement 1 bevrijding **2** vrijheid; ongebondenheid, onafhankelijkheid **3** ongedwongenheid **4** verbreking van verloving **5** [mil] terugtrekking

[1]**disentangle** (vb) zich ontwarren

[2]**disentangle** (vb) ontwarren, ontrafelen, oplossen

disfavour 1 afkeuring, lage dunk: *look upon* (or: *regard, view*) *s.o.* **with** ~ iem. niet mogen **2** ongenade, ongunst

disfigurement misvorming, wanstaltigheid

[1]**disgorge** (vb) leegstromen, zich legen, zich uitstorten

[2]**disgorge** (vb) **1** uitbraken, uitstoten **2** uitstorten, uitstromen

[1]**disgrace** (n) schande, ongenade: *be in* ~ uit de gratie zijn

[2]**disgrace** (vb) te schande maken, een slechte naam bezorgen

disgruntled ontevreden: ~ *at sth.* (or: *with s.o.*) ontstemd over iets (iem.)

[1]**disguise** (n) **1** vermomming: *in* ~ vermomd, in het verborgene; *a blessing in* ~ een geluk bij een ongeluk **2** voorwendsel[h], schijn, dekmantel

[2]**disguise** (vb) **1** vermommen **2** een valse voorstelling geven van **3** verbergen, maskeren, verhullen

[1]**disgust** (n) afschuw, afkeer, walging

[2]**disgust** (vb) doen walgen, afkeer opwekken: *she was suddenly ~ed at* (or: *by, with*) *him* plotseling vond ze hem weerzinwekkend

disgusting weerzinwekkend, walgelijk

[1]**dish** (n) **1** schaal, schotel **2** gerecht[h], schotel **3** schotelvormig voorwerp[h], schotelantenne: ~ *aerial* schotelantenne **4** lekker stuk[h], lekkere meid

[2]**dish** (vb) ruïneren, naar de maan helpen, verknallen ‖ ~ *out* **a)** uitdelen [papers, presents etc]; **b)** rondgeven, rondstrooien [advice]

dishcloth vaatdoek

dishearten ontmoedigen

dishevelled slonzig, slordig, onverzorgd

dishonest oneerlijk, bedrieglijk, vals

dishonesty leugenachtigheid; oneerlijkheid

dishonour schande, eerverlies[h], smaad

dish soap afwasmiddel[h]

dish up 1 opdienen, serveren; [fig] presenteren; opdissen [facts etc] **2** het eten opdienen

dishwasher 1 afwasser, bordenwasser **2** afwasmachine, vaatwasmachine

disillusion desillusioneren, uit de droom helpen: *be ~ed at* (or: *about, with*) teleurgesteld zijn over

disinclination tegenzin, onwil, afkeer: *feel a* ~ *to meet s.o.* geen (echte) zin hebben om iem. te ontmoeten

disinfect desinfecteren, ontsmetten

[1]**disinfectant** (n) desinfecterend middel[h], ontsmettingsmiddel[h]

[2]**disinfectant** (adj) desinfecterend, ontsmettend

disinherit onterven

disintegrate 1 uiteenvallen, uit elkaar vallen, vergaan **2** [chem] afbreken

disinterested 1 belangeloos **2** [fig] ongeïnteresseerd, onverschillig

disjointed onsamenhangend; verward [of story, ideas]

disk *see* disc

diskette diskette, floppy(disk)

disk storage schijfgeheugen[h]

[1]**dislike** (n) afkeer, tegenzin: *likes and ~s* sympathieën en antipathieën

[2]**dislike** (vb) niet houden van, een afkeer hebben van, een hekel hebben aan

dislocate 1 verplaatsen **2** onklaar maken, ontregelen; [fig] verstoren; in de war brengen **3** [med] ontwrichten

disloyal ontrouw, trouweloos, niet loyaal

dismal 1 ellendig, troosteloos, somber **2** zwak, armzalig

[1]**dismantle** (vb) uitneembaar zijn [eg of appliance]

[2]**dismantle** (vb) **1** ontmantelen, van de bedekking ontdoen **2** leeghalen, van meubilair (uitrusting) ontdoen, onttakelen **3** slopen, afbreken, uit elkaar halen

[1]**dismay** (n) wanhoop, verbijstering, ontzetting

[2]**dismay** (vb) verbijsteren, ontzetten, met wanhoop vervullen: *be ~ed at* (or: *by*) *the sight* de moed verliezen door de aanblik

dismember 1 uiteenrijten: *the body was ~ed by wolves* het lijk werd door wolven verscheurd **2** in stukken snijden **3** in stukken verdelen

dismiss 1 laten gaan, wegsturen **2** ontslaan, opzeggen **3** van zich afzetten, uit zijn gedachten zetten **4** afdoen, zich (kort) afmaken van, verwerpen: *they ~ed the suggestion* ze verwierpen het voorstel **5** afdanken, laten inrukken **6** [telecom] wegdrukken: *~ s.o.'s call* iem. wegdrukken

dismissal 1 verlof^h om te gaan **2** ontslag^h **3** verdringing, het uit zijn gedachten zetten **4** het terzijde schuiven, verwerping, het afdoen

dismissive minachtend, afwijzend

disobedient ongehoorzaam, opstandig

disobey niet gehoorzamen, ongehoorzaam zijn; negeren [order]; overtreden [rules]

disorder 1 oproer^h, opstootje^h, ordeverstoring **2** stoornis, kwaal, ziekte, aandoening: *Boris suffered from a kidney ~* Boris leed aan een nierkwaal **3** wanorde, verwarring, ordeloosheid

disorientate het gevoel voor richting ontnemen; desoriënteren

disown 1 verwerpen, afwijzen, ontkennen **2** verstoten, niet meer willen kennen

disparage 1 kleineren, geringschatten **2** in diskrediet brengen, verdacht maken, vernederen

disparity ongelijkheid, ongelijksoortigheid, ongelijkwaardigheid: *(a) great ~ of* (or: *in) age between them* een groot leeftijdsverschil tussen hen

¹dispatch (n) **1** bericht^h **2** het wegsturen **3** doeltreffendheid, snelle afhandeling: *with great ~* met grote doeltreffendheid

²dispatch (vb) **1** (ver)zenden, (weg)sturen **2** de genadeslag geven, doden **3** doeltreffend afhandelen **4** wegwerken [food etc]; soldaat maken

dispel verjagen, verdrijven

dispensary 1 apotheek; huisapotheek [in school etc] **2** consultatiebureau^h, medische hulppost

¹dispense (vb) ontheffing geven, vrijstelling verlenen

²dispense (vb) **1** uitreiken, distribueren, geven: *~ justice* het recht toepassen, gerechtigheid doen geschieden **2** klaarmaken en leveren [drugs]: *dispensing chemist* apotheker

dispenser 1 apotheker **2** automaat, houder

dispense with 1 afzien van, het zonder stellen, niet nodig hebben **2** overbodig maken, terzijde zetten

¹disperse (vb) zich verspreiden, uiteengaan

²disperse (vb) **1** uiteen drijven, verspreiden, spreiden, uiteenplaatsen **2** verspreiden, overal bekendmaken **3** verjagen

dispirited moedeloos, somber, mistroostig

displace verplaatsen, verschuiven: *~d people* ontheemden **2** vervangen, verdrin-

gen

displacement 1 verplaatsing **2** vervanging **3** waterverplaatsing [of ship]

¹display (n) **1** tentoonstelling, uitstalling, weergave: *the more expensive models are on ~ in our showroom* de duurdere modellen zijn uitgestald in onze toonzaal **2** vertoning, tentoonspreiding **3** demonstratie, vertoon^h, druktemakerij

²display (vb) **1** tonen, exposeren, uitstallen **2** tentoonspreiden, tonen, aan de dag leggen: *a touching ~ of friendship and affection* een ontroerende blijk van vriendschap en genegenheid **3** te koop lopen met, demonstreren

displease ergeren, irriteren: *be ~d at sth.* (or: *with s.o.*) boos zijn over iets (*or*: op iem.)

displeasure afkeuring; ergernis: *incur s.o.'s ~* zich iemands ongenoegen op de hals halen

disposable 1 beschikbaar: *~ income* besteedbaar inkomen **2** wegwerp-, weggooi-

disposal 1 het wegdoen, verwijdering **2** overdracht, verkoop, schenking **3** beschikking: *I am entirely at your ~* ik sta geheel tot uw beschikking

dispose 1 plaatsen, ordenen, rangschikken, regelen **2** brengen tot, bewegen: *~ s.o. to do sth.* iem. er toe brengen iets te doen

disposed geneigd, bereid: *they seemed favourably ~ to(wards) that idea* zij schenen welwillend tegenover dat idee te staan

dispose of 1 van de hand doen, verkopen, wegdoen **2** afhandelen; uit de weg ruimen [questions, problems etc]

disposition 1 plaatsing, rangschikking, opstelling **2** aard, karakter^h, neiging: *she has a* (or: *is of a) happy ~* zij heeft een opgewekt karakter

dispossess onteigenen, ontnemen: *~ s.o. of sth.* iem. iets ontnemen

disproportionate onevenredig, niet naar verhouding

disprove weerleggen, de onjuistheid aantonen van

¹dispute (n) **1** twistgesprek^h, discussie, woordenstrijd: *the matter in ~* de zaak in kwestie **2** geschil^h, twist: *beyond* (or: *past, without) ~* buiten kijf

²dispute (vb) redetwisten, discussiëren

³dispute (vb) **1** heftig bespreken, heftig discussiëren over **2** aanvechten, in twijfel trekken **3** betwisten, strijd voeren over **4** weerstand bieden aan

disqualification diskwalificatie; uitsluiting

disqualify 1 ongeschikt maken **2** onbevoegd verklaren **3** diskwalificeren, uitsluiten

disquieting onrustbarend; zorgwekkend, verontrustend

disregard 1 geen acht slaan op, negeren: *~*

a warning een waarschuwing in de wind
slaan **2** geringschatten
disrepair verval^h, bouwvalligheid: *the
house had fallen into* ~ (or: *was in* ~) het huis
was vervallen
disrepute slechte naam, diskrediet^h: *bring
into* ~ in diskrediet brengen
disrespect oneerbiedigheid; gebrek aan
respect
disrespectful oneerbiedig; onbeleefd
disrupt 1 uiteen doen vallen, verscheuren
2 ontwrichten, verstoren: *communications
were* ~*ed* de verbindingen waren verbroken
disruption ontwrichting; verstoring; disruptie
diss [Am; inform] beledigen, dissen
dissatisfaction ontevredenheid
dissatisfy niet tevreden stellen: *dissatisfied
with the results* ontevreden over de resultaten
dissect 1 in stukken snijden, verdelen
2 ontleden, grondig analyseren
dissection 1 ontleed deel^h van dier of
plant **2** ontleding, analyse
¹dissemble (vb) huichelen
²dissemble (vb) **1** veinzen; voorwenden
2 verhullen
disseminate uitzaaien, verspreiden
dissemination verspreiding: *the free* ~ *of
information* de vrije verspreiding van informatie
dissension 1 meningsverschil^h **2** tweedracht, verdeeldheid, onenigheid
dissent verschil^h van mening
dissertation 1 verhandeling, dissertatie,
proefschrift^h **2** scriptie
dissident 1 dissident, andersdenkend
2 dissident, andersdenkende
dissimilar ongelijk, verschillend: ~ *in character* verschillend van aard
dissimulation veinzerij
¹dissipate (vb) **1** verdrijven, verjagen, doen
verdwijnen **2** verspillen [eg money, forces];
verkwisten
²dissipate (vb) zich verspreiden: *the mob
rapidly* ~*d* de menigte ging snel uiteen
dissociate scheiden, afscheiden: *it is very
hard to* ~ *the man from what he did* het is erg
moeilijk om de man los te zien van wat hij
heeft gedaan; ~ *o.s. from* zich distantiëren
van
dissolute 1 losbandig **2** verdorven
¹dissolve (vb) oplossen, smelten: [fig] ~
in(to) tears in tranen wegsmelten
²dissolve (vb) **1** oplossen **2** ontbinden [of
parliament]; opheffen
dissonance 1 wanklank **2** onenigheid
dissuade ontraden, afraden
distance 1 afstand, tussenruimte, eind(je)^h;
[fig] afstand(elijkheid); terughoudendheid:
keep one's ~ afstand bewaren; *within walk-*

ing ~ op loopafstand; *in the* ~ in de verte
2 (tijds)afstand, tijdsverloop^h, tijdruimte
distant 1 ver, afgelegen, verwijderd: ~ *relations* verre bloedverwanten **2** afstandelijk:
a ~ *smile* een gereserveerde glimlach
distaste (+ for) afkeer (van), aversie (van),
weerzin: *for once he managed to overcome his*
~ *hard work* eenmaal wist hij zijn afkeer van
hard werken te overwinnen
distasteful onaangenaam; akelig: *such a
way of life is* ~ *to* me zo'n manier van leven
staat mij (vreselijk) tegen
distil 1 distilleren: ~ *water* water distilleren
2 via distillatie vervaardigen, branden, stoken **3** [form] afleiden, de essentie weergeven van
distillery distilleerderij, stokerij
distinct 1 onderscheiden, verschillend,
apart: *four* ~ *meanings* vier afzonderlijke be-
tekenissen **2** duidelijk, goed waarneembaar,
onmiskenbaar: *a* ~ *possibility* een stellige
mogelijkheid
distinction 1 onderscheiding, ereteken^h
2 onderscheid^h, onderscheiding, verschil^h:
draw a sharp ~ *between* een scherp onder-
scheid maken tussen **3** voortreffelijkheid,
aanzien^h, gedistingeerdheid
distinctive onderscheidend, kenmerkend
distinguish 1 indelen, rangschikken **2** onderscheiden, onderkennen: ~ *cause and effect*
oorzaak en gevolg onderscheiden **3** zien,
onderscheiden: *I could* ~ *the tower in the distance* in de verte kon ik de toren onderschei-
den **4** kenmerken, karakteriseren || ~ *be-
tween* onderscheid maken tussen, uit elkaar
houden
distinguished 1 voornaam, aanzienlijk:
distinguished-looking ladies voornaam uit-
ziende dames **2** beroemd, befaamd **3** gedistingeerd
distort 1 vervormen, verwringen: *the frame
of my bike was completely* ~*ed* het frame van
mijn fiets was helemaal vervormd **2** verdraaien, vertekenen: *a* ~*ed version of the
facts* een verdraaide versie van de feiten
distract 1 afleiden **2** verwarren, verbijsteren
distraction 1 vermakelijkheid, ontspanning, vermaak^h **2** afleiding, ontspanning,
vermaak^h **3** gebrek^h aan aandacht **4** verwarring, gekheid: *those children are driving me to*
~ ik word stapelgek van die kinderen
distraught radeloos: ~ *with grief* radeloos
van verdriet
distress 1 leed^h, verdriet^h, zorg **2** nood, armoede **3** gevaar^h, nood: *a ship in* ~ een schip
in nood
distressed 1 (diep) bedroefd **2** bang
3 overstuur, van streek **4** noodlijdend, behoeftig
distress signal noodsein^h; noodsignaal^h

distribute distribueren, verdelen: *the rainfall is evenly ~d throughout the year* de regenval is gelijkmatig over het jaar verdeeld

distribution verdeling, (ver)spreiding, distributie

district 1 district^h, regio **2** streek, gebied^h **3** wijk, buurt: *a residential ~* een woonwijk

district attorney [Am] officier van justitie

¹distrust (n) wantrouwen^h, argwaan, achterdocht

²distrust (vb) wantrouwen, geen vertrouwen stellen in

disturb 1 in beroering brengen [also fig]; verontrusten: *~ing facts* verontrustende feiten **2** storen: *be mentally ~ed* geestelijk gestoord zijn; *please do not ~!* a.u.b. niet storen! **3** verstoren: *~ the peace* de openbare orde verstoren

disturbance 1 opschudding, relletje^h **2** stoornis, verstoring: *a ~ of the peace* een ordeverstoring **3** storing

disunity verdeeldheid, onenigheid

disuse onbruik^h: *fall into ~* in onbruik (ge)-raken

¹ditch (n) sloot, greppel

²ditch (vb) [inform] afdanken, verlaten: *when did she ~ Brian?* wanneer heeft zij Brian de bons gegeven?

¹dither (n) zenuwachtigheid, nerveuze opwinding: *all of a ~* zenuwachtig, opgewonden

²dither (vb) **1** aarzelen **2** zenuwachtig doen

ditto 1 dito^h, idem, hetzelfde **2** duplicaat^h

ditty liedje^h, deuntje^h

divan 1 divan; sofa **2** springbox

¹dive (n) **1** duik, duikvlucht **2** plotselinge snelle beweging, greep, duik: *he made a ~ for the ball* hij dook naar de bal **3** kroeg, tent

²dive (vb) **1** duiken [also fig]; onderduiken, een duikvlucht maken: *~ into one's studies* zich werpen op zijn studie **2** wegduiken **3** tasten, de hand steken (in): *she ~d into her handbag* zij stak haar hand diep in haar tasje

diver duiker

diverge 1 uiteenlopen, uiteenwijken **2** afwijken, verschillen: *his account ~s from the official version* zijn verslag wijkt af van de officiële versie **3** afdwalen

diverse 1 divers, verschillend **2** afwisselend, gevarieerd

diversify 1 diversifiëren; verscheidenheid aanbrengen **2** afwisselen; variëren

diversion 1 afleidingsactie, schijnbeweging **2** afleiding, ontspanning **3** omleiding

diversity 1 ongelijkheid: *their ~ of interests* hun uiteenlopende belangen **2** verscheidenheid, diversiteit

divert 1 een andere richting geven, verleggen, omleiden: *why was their plane ~ed to Vienna?* waarom moest hun toestel uitwijken naar Wenen? **2** afleiden [attention] **3** amu-

seren, vermaken

divest of [form] ontdoen van; beroven van: *~ parental power* uit de ouderlijke macht ontzetten

¹divide (n) **1** waterscheiding **2** scheidslijn

²divide (vb) **1** verdeeld worden **2** onenigheid krijgen **3** zich delen, zich vertakken

³divide (vb) **1** delen, in delen splitsen, indelen **2** scheiden: *~d highway* weg met gescheiden dubbele rijbanen **3** onderling verdelen [also fig]; distribueren, verkavelen: *~d against itself* onderling verdeeld **4** delen: *how much is 18 ~d by 3?* hoeveel is 18 gedeeld door 3?

dividend dividend^h, winstaandeel^h, uitkering (van winst)

divination 1 profetie, voorspelling **2** waarzeggerij

¹divine (adj) **1** goddelijk **2** aan God gewijd: *~ service* godsdienstoefening **3** hemels, verrukkelijk

²divine (vb) **1** waarzeggen **2** (met wichelroede) vaststellen

³divine (vb) gissen, raden, inzien, een voorgevoel hebben van

diviner 1 waarzegger **2** (wichel)roedeloper

divining rod wichelroede

divinity 1 godheid, goddelijkheid, god, goddelijk wezen^h: *the Divinity* de Godheid **2** theologie

divisible deelbaar

division 1 (ver)deling, het delen: *a ~ of labour* een arbeidsverdeling **2** afdeling [organisation, bureau] **3** [mil] divisie **4** scheiding, scheidslijn, afscheiding **5** verschil^h, ongelijkheid, onenigheid: *a ~ of opinion* uiteenlopende meningen

divisive tot ongelijkheid leidend, onenigheid brengend

¹divorce (n) (echt)scheiding

²divorce (vb) scheiden (van), zich laten scheiden van

divorcee gescheiden vrouw of man

divot graszode, divot

divulge onthullen, openbaar maken, bekendmaken

DIY *do-it-yourself* doe-het-zelf

dizzy 1 duizelig, draaierig **2** verward, versuft **3** duizelingwekkend [of height, speed etc]

¹DJ (n) *disc jockey* deejay, dj

²DJ (vb) optreden als dj, draaien

Djibouti Djibouti

¹Djiboutian (n) Djiboutiaan(se)

²Djiboutian (adj) Djiboutiaans

DNA *deoxyribonucleic acid* DNA^h

DNA profiling DNA-onderzoek^h

DNR *do not resuscitate* niet reanimeren

¹do (n) partij, feest^h || *do's and don'ts* wat wel en wat niet mag

dodge

²**do** (vb) **1** doen, handelen, zich gedragen: *he did well to refuse that offer* hij deed er goed aan dat aanbod te weigeren; *she was hard done by* zij was oneerlijk behandeld **2** het stellen, maken, zich voelen: *how do you do* hoe maakt u het?; *he is doing well* het gaat goed met hem **3** aan de hand zijn, gebeuren: *nothing doing* **a)** er gebeurt (hier) niets; **b)** daar komt niets van in **4** klaar zijn, opgehouden zijn (hebben): *be done with s.o.* niets meer te maken (willen) hebben met iem.; *have done with sth.* ergens een punt achter zetten **5** geschikt zijn, voldoen, volstaan: *this copy won't do* deze kopie is niet goed genoeg; *it doesn't do to say such things* zoiets hoor je niet te zeggen; *that will do!* en nou is 't uit! **6** het (moeten) doen, het (moeten) stellen met: *they'll have to do with what they've got* ze zullen het moeten doen met wat ze hebben ‖ *do away with* **a)** wegdoen, weggooien, een eind maken aan; **b)** afschaffen [death penalty, institution etc]; *do for s.o.* het huishouden doen voor iem., werkster zijn bij iem.; *I could do with a few quid* ik zou best een paar pond kunnen gebruiken; *it has got nothing to do with you* jij staat erbuiten

³**do** (vb) **1** doen [sth. abstract]: *do one's best* zijn best doen; *it isn't done* zoiets doet men niet; *what can I do for you?* wat kan ik voor je doen?; [in shop] wat mag het zijn? **2** bezig zijn met [sth. concrete, existing]; doen, opknappen, in orde brengen, herstellen; oplossen [puzzles etc]; studeren: *do one's duty* zijn plicht doen; *do psychology* psychologie studeren; *have one's teeth done* zijn tanden laten nakijken; *do up the kitchen* de keuken opknappen **3** maken, doen ontstaan: *the storm did a lot of damage* de storm richtte heel wat schade aan; *do wonders* wonderen verrichten **4** (aan)doen, geven, veroorzaken: *do s.o. a favour* iem. een dienst bewijzen **5** beëindigen, afhandelen, afmaken; [inform, fig] uitputten; kapotmaken: *I have done cleaning,* [inform] *I am done cleaning* ik ben klaar met de schoonmaak; *done in* bekaf, afgepeigerd; [inform] *do s.o. in* iem. van kant maken **6** [culinary] bereiden, klaarmaken: *well done* goed doorbakken [of meat] **7** rijden, afleggen: *do 50 mph.* 80 km/u rijden **8** [inform] beetnemen, afzetten, neppen: *do s.o. for $100* iem. voor honderd dollar afzetten **9** ontvangen, onthalen: *he does himself well* hij zorgt wel dat hij niets te kort komt **10** [inform] uitzitten [a sentence]: *he has done time in Attica* hij zat vast in Attica ‖ *I've done it again* ik heb het weer verknoeid; *a boiled egg will do me* ik heb genoeg aan een gekookt ei; *over and done with* voltooid verleden tijd; *do up a zip* (or: *a coat*) een rits (or: jas) dichtdoen

⁴**do** (aux vb): [often untranslated] *do you know him?* ken je hem?; [in negative sentence] *I don't know him* ik ken hem niet; [replacing verb] *he laughed and so did she* hij lachte, en zij ook; *I treat my friends as he does his enemies: badly* ik behandel mijn vrienden zoals hij zijn vijanden: slecht; [to ask for consent] *he writes well, doesn't he?* hij schrijft goed, nietwaar?; [with emphasis, in imperative mood] *do come in!* kom toch binnen!; *oh, do be quiet!* o, houd alsjeblieft eens je mond!

doc *doctor* dokter

docile meegaand, volgzaam: *a ~ horse* een mak paard

¹**dock** (n) **1** dokʰ, droogdokʰ, havendokʰ, kade: *floating ~* drijvend dok **2** (-s) haven(s) **3** werf **4** beklaagdenbank: *be in the ~* terechtstaan ‖ *in ~* **a)** in reparatie; **b)** in het ziekenhuis; **c)** op de helling

²**dock** (vb) **1** dokken, de haven binnenlopen, in het dok gaan **2** gekoppeld worden [spacecraft]

³**dock** (vb) **1** couperen [tail etc]; afsnijden, afknippen **2** korten, (gedeeltelijk) inhouden, achterhouden **3** dokken, in het dok brengen **4** koppelen [spacecraft]

docker dokwerker, havenarbeider, stuwadoor

docket 1 bon, kassabon, bewijsstukʰ, reçuʰ **2** korte inhoud [of document, report]

dockland havenbuurt; havenkwartierʰ

dockyard werf

¹**doctor** (n) **1** dokter, arts; [Am] tandarts; veearts: *that is just what the ~ ordered* dat is net wat je nodig hebt **2** doctor [somebody holding the highest university degree]

²**doctor** (vb) **1** [euph] helpen, steriliseren, castreren **2** knoeien met, rommelen met, vervalsen: *~ the accounts* de boeken vervalsen

doctorate doctoraatʰ; doctorstitel

doctrine 1 doctrine, leer **2** dogmaʰ, beginselʰ

¹**document** (n) documentʰ, bewijsstukʰ

²**document** (vb) documenteren, vastleggen

documentary documentaire

documentation 1 documentatie **2** bewijsmateriaalʰ

dodder 1 beven [with old age, weakness] **2** schuifelen, strompelen

doddle eitjeʰ: *it's a ~* het is een eitje, het is heel makkelijk

¹**dodge** (n) **1** (zij)sprong, ontwijkende beweging **2** foefjeʰ, trucjeʰ, slimmigheidjeʰ: *a tax ~* een belastingtruc

²**dodge** (vb) **1** (opzij) springen, snel bewegen, rennen: *the woman ~d behind the chair* de vrouw dook weg achter de stoel **2** uitvluchten zoeken, (eromheen) draaien

³**dodge** (vb) ontwijken, vermijden, ontduiken: *he kept dodging the question* hij bleef de vraag ontwijken

dodgem botsautootje[h]
dodger ontduiker; ontwijker
dodgy 1 slim, gewiekst **2** netelig: ~ *situation* netelige situatie
dodo 1 dodo **2** [Am] sukkel || [inform] *as dead as a* ~ zo dood als een pier
doe wijfje[h] van een konijn
¹dog (n) **1** hond **2** [inform] kerel: *lucky* ~ geluksvogel, mazzelaar || *not a* ~*'s chance* geen schijn van kans; *he is a* ~ *in the* **manger** hij kan de zon niet in het water zien schijnen; *go to the* ~*s* naar de bliksem gaan; *the* ~*s* (wind)hondenrennen
²dog (vb) (achter)volgen, (achter)nazitten
dog collar 1 halsband **2** [hum] boord van een geestelijke
dog-eared met ezelsoren
dogged vasthoudend, volhardend: *it is* ~ *that does it* de aanhouder wint
doggerel 1 rijmelarij **2** kreupelrijm[h]
doggy hondje[h]
dogma dogma[h]
dogmatic 1 dogmatisch **2** autoritair
dogsbody duvelstoejager, sloof: *a general* ~ een manusje-van-alles
doing 1 handeling, het handelen, het (toe)doen: *it is all* *their* ~ het is allemaal hun schuld **2** (-s) daden, handelingen
doldrums 1 neerslachtigheid: *be in the* ~ in de put zitten **2** het stilliggen van een schip **3** [fig] stilstand
dole (the) werkloosheidsuitkering, steun: *be on the* ~ steun trekken
doll 1 pop **2** meisje[h], meid || *Will you do it? You are a* ~*!* Doe je het? Je bent een schat!
dollar dollar
dollop (klein) beetje[h], kwak, scheut
doll up zich optutten: *doll o.s. up* zich uitdossen
dolly [child language] pop(je[h])
dolphin dolfijn
dolt domoor, uilskuiken[h]
domain 1 domein[h], (land)goed[h] **2** gebied[h] [fig]; veld[h], terrein[h]: *the garden is my wife's* ~ de tuin is het domein van mijn vrouw
dome 1 koepel **2** gewelf[h] **3** ronde top: *the* ~ *of a* *hill* de ronde top van een heuvel
¹domestic (n) bediende, dienstbode
²domestic (adj) **1** huishoudelijk, het huishouden betreffend: ~ *economy* (or: *science*) huishoudkunde **2** huiselijk: ~ *violence* huiselijk geweld **3** binnenlands: ~ *trade* binnenlandse handel **4** tam: ~ *animals* huisdieren
domesticate 1 aan het huiselijk leven doen wennen **2** aan zich onderwerpen, temmen, beteugelen, tot huisdier maken
domicile verblijfplaats, woning
dominance overheersing
dominant dominant [also biology]; (over)heersend
dominate domineren, overheersen: ~ *the*

conversation het hoogste woord voeren
domination overheersing, heerschappij
Dominica Dominica
¹Dominican (n) Dominicaan(se)
²Dominican (adj) Dominicaans
Dominican Republic Dominicaanse Republiek
dominion 1 domein[h], (grond)gebied[h], rijk[h] **2** heerschappij, macht
domino dominosteen
dominoes domino(spel)[h]
¹don (n) docent aan een universiteit
²don (vb) [form] aandoen: *she* ~*ned her hat and coat* zij zette haar hoed op en trok haar jas aan
donate schenken, geven: ~ *money* **towards** *sth.* geld schenken voor iets
donation schenking; donatie, bijdrage
done 1 netjes, gepast: *it is not* ~ zoiets doet men niet **2** klaar, gereed, af: *be* ~ *with* klaar zijn met; *have* ~ *with* niets meer te maken (willen) hebben met **3** doodmoe, uitgeput || *hard* ~ *by* oneerlijk behandeld; *she seemed completely* ~ *in* (or: *up*) zij leek volkomen uitgeteld; ~*!* akkoord!, afgesproken!
dongle dongel
donkey ezel [also fig]; domoor, sufferd || [inform] *nodding* ~ jaknikker
donkey's years [inform] eeuwigheid; lange tijd; eeuwigheid: *I haven't heard from her for* ~ het is eeuwen geleden dat ik iets van haar gehoord heb
donor 1 gever, schenker **2** donor
don't verbod[h]: *do's and* ~*s* wat wel en niet mag, geboden en verboden
donut [Am] *see* doughnut
doodah [inform] je-weet-wel; ding(etje)[h]
¹doodle (n) krabbel, figuurtje[h], poppetje[h]
²doodle (vb) krabbelen, figuurtjes tekenen
¹doom (n) **1** noodlot[h], lot[h]: *a sense of* ~ *and foreboding* een gevoel van naderend onheil **2** ondergang, verderf[h]: *meet one's* ~ de ondergang vinden **3** laatste oordeel[h]
²doom (vb) **1** veroordelen, (ver)doemen **2** ten ondergang doemen: *the undertaking was* ~*ed from the* **start** de onderneming was vanaf het begin tot mislukken gedoemd
doomsday dag des oordeels [also fig]; doemdag: *till* ~ eeuwig
door 1 deur, (auto)portier[h]: *answer the* ~ (de deur) opendoen (voor iem. die aangebeld heeft); *show s.o. the* ~ iem. de deur wijzen; *show s.o. to the* ~ iem. uitlaten; *out of* ~*s* buiten(shuis) **2** toegang, mogelijkheid: *leave the* ~ *open* de mogelijkheid openlaten || *lay the blame at s.o.'s* ~ iem. de schuld geven
doorbell (voor)deurbel
do-or-die alles-of-niets-; erop-of-eronder-: ~ *mentality* alles-of-nietshouding
doorknob deurknop
doorstep 1 stoep: *on the* (or: *your*) ~ vlakbij

2 [inform] dikke boterham; pil
doorway deuropening, ingang, deurgat[h]
[1]**dope** (n) **1** sufferd, domoor **2** drugs, verdovende middelen **3** doping, stimulerende middelen **4** info(rmatie), nieuws[h] **5** smeermiddel[h], smeersel[h]
[2]**dope** (vb) verdovende middelen/doping toedienen aan: *they must have ~d his* **drink** zij moeten iets in zijn drankje gedaan hebben
dopehead [inform] drugsgebruiker
dopey [inform] **1** suf **2** dom
do-rag [roughly] bandana
dormant 1 slapend, sluimerend; [biology] in winterslaap **2** latent, verborgen **3** inactief: *a ~* **volcano** een slapende vulkaan
dormitory 1 slaapzaal **2** [Am] studentenhuis[h]
dormouse slaapmuis
dosage dosering, dosis
[1]**dose** (n) dosis [also fig]; hoeveelheid, stralingsdosis ‖ *like a ~ of* **salts** razend vlug
[2]**dose** (vb) doseren, medicijn toedienen aan
[1]**doss** (n) dutje[h]
[2]**doss** (vb) maffen
dosser dakloze
dosshouse logement[h], goedkoop hotelletje[h]
[1]**dot** (n) punt[h] [also music, Morse; on letter]; spikkel, stip ‖ *on the ~* stipt (op tijd)
[2]**dot** (vb) **1** een punt zetten op [also music]: [fig] *~ the i's (and cross the t's)* de puntjes op de i zetten **2** stippelen, (be)spikkelen: *~ted line* stippellijn ‖ *sign on the ~ted* **line** (een contract) ondertekenen
dotage kindsheid, dementie: *be* **in** *his ~* oud en dement zijn
dot-com dotcombedrijf[h], internetbedrijf[h]
dote (up)on dol zijn op, verzot zijn op; [fig] aanbidden; verafgoden
dotty 1 gespikkeld, gestippeld **2** getikt, niet goed snik **3** (+ about) dol (op), gek (op)
[1]**double** (n) **1** dubbel[h], doublet[h]: *~ or* **quits** quitte of dubbel **2** het dubbele, dubbele (hoeveelheid/snelheid e.d.) **3** dubbelganger **4** [film etc] doublure, vervanger, stuntman **5** verdubbeling [of score, board, stake etc in various sports] **6** (-s) [tennis] dubbel(spel)[h]: *mixed ~s* gemengd dubbel ‖ *at* (or: *on) the ~* in looppas; [fig] meteen, onmiddellijk
[2]**double** (adj) **1** dubbel, tweemaal (zo groot/veel): *~ the* **amount** tweemaal zoveel; *~* **bed** tweepersoonsbed[h]; *~* **chin** onderkin, dubbele kin; *~* **cream** dikke room; *~* **entry** (bookkeeping) dubbele boekhouding; *~* **exposure** dubbele belichting; *~* **glazing** (or: **windows**) dubbele beglazing (or: ramen); *~* **standard** het meten met twee maten [fig] **2** oneerlijk, dubbelhartig, vals: *~* **agent** dubbelagent, dubbelspion ‖ *~* **Dutch** koeterwaals[h], onzin
[3]**double** (vb) **1** (zich) verdubbelen, doubleren **2** terugkeren, plotseling omkeren: *~*

(back) **on** *one's tracks* op zijn schreden terugkeren **3** een dubbele rol spelen **4** [film etc] als vervanger optreden: *~* **for** *an actor* een (toneel)speler vervangen
[4]**double** (vb) **1** verdubbelen, doubleren, tweemaal zo groot maken **2** [film etc] als vervanger optreden van **3** [bridge] doubleren
[5]**double** (adv) dubbel, tweemaal (zoveel als), samen
[1]**double back** (vb) terugkeren
[2]**double back** (vb) terugslaan, terugvouwen
double-barrelled 1 dubbelloops **2** tweeledig; met twee oogmerken ‖ *a ~* **name** een dubbele naam
double-bass contrabas
double-breasted met twee rijen knopen, dubbelrijs
[1]**double-dealing** (n) oplichterij, bedrog[h]
[2]**double-dealing** (adj) oneerlijk, vals
double-digit in tientallen: *~* **inflation** inflatie van 10% en meer
double down [Am] **1** de inzet verdubbelen **2** [fig] de inzet verhogen, extra inzetten op: *the president doubled down* **on** *renewable energy* de president zette extra in op duurzame energie
double-edged tweesnijdend [also fig]: *a ~* **argument** een argument dat zowel vóór als tegen kan worden gebruikt
double-quick vliegensvlug, razendsnel, zo snel je kunt
double-talk 1 onzin **2** dubbelzinnigheid, dubbelzinnige opmerking(en)
double-time 1 looppas **2** overwerkgeld[h]; onregelmatigheidstoeslag [of employee]
[1]**double up** (vb) ineenkrimpen [with laughter, in pain]
[2]**double up** (vb) **1** buigen, doen ineenkrimpen: *~ one's legs* zijn benen intrekken **2** opvouwen, omslaan, terugslaan
doubly dubbel (zo), tweemaal (zo): *~* **careful** extra voorzichtig
[1]**doubt** (n) twijfel, onzekerheid, aarzeling: *the* **benefit** *of the ~* het voordeel van de twijfel; *be* **in** *no ~* **about** *sth.* ergens zeker van zijn; *have one's ~s* **about** *sth.* ergens aan twijfelen; *without (a) ~* ongetwijfeld; *no ~* ongetwijfeld, zonder (enige) twijfel
[2]**doubt** (vb) twijfelen (aan), onzeker zijn, betwijfelen: *~* **that** (or: **whether**) (be)twijfelen of
doubtless zeker; ongetwijfeld
douche 1 spoeling [of vagina] **2** [depr] sukkel
douche bag 1 [med] vaginale douche **2** [Am; depr] sukkel, eikel
dough 1 deeg[h] **2** [inform] poen[+h], centen

doughnut donut
dour streng, stug
dove duif [also fig]; aanhanger van vredes-
politiek
dovecot(e) duiventil
dovetail precies passen [also fig]; overeenkomen: *my plans ~ed with his* mijn plannen
sloten aan bij de zijne
dowager douairière
dowdy slonzig, slordig gekleed
¹**down** (n) dons[h], haartjes, veertjes ‖ *have a ~
on s.o.* een hekel hebben aan iem.
²**down** (adj) **1** neergaand, naar onder leidend **2** beneden **3** depressief, verdrietig: *be
~ and out* berooid zijn, aan de grond zitten ‖
cash ~ contante betaling, handje contantje;
~ payment contante betaling; aanbetaling
³**down** (adv) neer, (naar) beneden, omlaag,
onder: *bend ~* bukken, vooroverbuigen; *the
sun goes ~* de zon gaat onder; *up and ~* op en
neer; *~ with the president!* weg met de president! ‖ *come* (or: *go*) *~* de universiteit verlaten [because of holidays or graduation]; *be
sent ~* weggezonden worden van de universiteit; *eight ~ and two to go* acht gespeeld en
nog twee te gaan; *~ under* in Australië en
Nieuw-Zeeland
⁴**down** (prep) **1** vanaf, langs: *~ the coast*
langs de kust; *~ (the) river* de rivier af, verder
stroomafwaarts; *he went ~ the street* hij liep
de straat door **2** neer, af ‖ *~ town* de stad in,
in het centrum
down-and-out [inform] zwerver
down-at-heel [inform] haveloos; sjofel
downbeat [inform] pessimistisch; somber
downcast 1 terneergeslagen, somber,
neerslachtig **2** neergeslagen [eyes]: *~ eyes*
neergeslagen ogen
downer [inform] **1** kalmerend middel[h];
tranquillizer **2** teleurstelling: *be on a ~* depri
zijn
downfall 1 stortbui **2** val; ondergang
downgrade 1 degraderen, in rang verlagen **2** de waarde naar beneden halen van
downhearted terneergeslagen, neerslachtig, ontmoedigd
¹**downhill** (adj) **1** (af)hellend, neerwaarts
2 gemakkelijk: *it's all ~ from here* het is een
makkie vanaf hier
²**downhill** (adv) bergafwaarts, naar beneden: *go ~* verslechteren
download downloaden
downplay afzwakken; bagatelliseren, relativeren
downpour stortbui, plensbui
¹**downright** (adj) **1** uitgesproken, overduidelijk: *a ~ liar* iem. die liegt dat het gedrukt
staat **2** eerlijk, oprecht
²**downright** (adv) volkomen, door en door
¹**downriver** (adj) stroomafwaarts (gelegen)
²**downriver** (adv) stroomafwaarts; met de

stroom mee
down-river racing het wildwatervaren
downshift [Am] **1** [car] terugschakelen
2 [fig] een stapje terug doen
downside 1 nadeel[h]; schaduwzijde, keerzijde **2** [Am] onderkant
downsizing inkrimping, bezuiniging
Down's syndrome syndroom[h] van Down
¹**downstairs** (adj) beneden, op de begane
grond
²**downstairs** (adv) (naar) beneden, de trap
af
downstream stroomafwaarts
down-to-earth nuchter, met beide benen
op de grond
downtown naar de binnenstad, de stad in
downtrodden onderdrukt
downward naar beneden gaand, neerwaarts, aflopend: *~ spiral* neerwaartse spiraal
downwind met de wind mee (gaand)
downy donzig, zacht
dowry bruidsschat
dowse (met een wichelroede) wateraders
(mineralen) opsporen, wichelroede lopen
dowsing-rod wichelroede
dox [media] persoonlijke gegevens
doxing [media] het verzamelen en/of gebruiken van iemands persoonlijke gegevens
¹**doze** (n) sluimering, dutje[h]
²**doze** (vb) sluimeren, dutten, soezen: *~ off*
indutten, in slaap sukkelen
³**doze** (vb) (+ away) verdutten, versuffen
dozen 1 dozijn[h], twaalftal[h] **2** groot aantal[h],
heleboel: *~s (and ~s) of people* een heleboel
mensen; *by the ~* bij tientallen, bij bosjes ‖ *it's
six of one and half a ~ of the other* het is lood
om oud ijzer
dozy slaperig, soezerig
¹**drab** (n) [vulg] slons, slet, hoer
²**drab** (adj) **1** [inform] vaalbruin **2** kleurloos,
saai
draconian draconisch; zeer streng: *~
measures* uiterst harde maatregelen
¹**draft** (n) **1** klad(je[h]), concept[h], schets: *in ~* in
het klad **2** [Am] dienstplicht
²**draft** (vb) **1** ontwerpen, schetsen, een klad-
(je) maken van **2** [Am] indelen, detacheren
3 [Am] oproepen (voor militaire dienst)
draftsman 1 tekenaar, ontwerper **2** opsteller (van documenten)
¹**drag** (n) **1** het slepen, het trekken **2** het
dreggen **3** dreg, dregnet[h], dreganker[h] **4** rem
[fig]; belemmering, vertraging, blok[h] aan het
been: *it was a ~ on the proceedings* het belemmerde de werkzaamheden **5** saai ge-
doe[h], saai figuur[h], vervelend iets (iem.): *it was
such a ~* het was stomvervelend **6** trekje[h] [of
a cigarette]; haaltje[h] **7** door een man gedragen vrouwenkleding: *in ~* in travestie, als
man verkleed

²drag (vb) **1** dreggen: ~ *for* dreggen naar **2** zich voortslepen; kruipen [of time]; lang duren, langdradig zijn: ~ *on* eindeloos duren **3** achterblijven

³drag (vb) afdreggen; afzoeken [river]

⁴drag (vb) (mee)slepen, (voort)trekken, (voort)sleuren, (voort)zeulen: ~ *through* the mire (or: *mud*) door het slijk halen [also fig]; *don't* ~ *my name in* laat mijn naam erbuiten || [comp] ~ *and drop* slepen

drag-and-drop sleep-

drag down 1 slopen, uitputten, ontmoedigen **2** neerhalen [also fig]; verlagen

draggy [inform] duf, saai, vervelend

dragon draak

dragonfly libel, waterjuffer

¹dragoon (n) dragonder [also fig]

²dragoon (vb) (+ into) (met geweld) dwingen tot

drag out 1 eruit trekken [truth etc] **2** rekken [meeting, story etc]; uitspinnen

drag queen [inform] mannelijke travestiet

¹drain (n) **1** afvoerkanaalʰ, afvoerbuis, rioolʰ: *down* the ~ naar de knoppen, verloren; [inform] *circle* the ~ **a)** bijna dood zijn; **b)** [fig] op sterven na dood zijn **2** afvloeiing, onttrekking; [fig] druk; belasting: *it is a great ~ on* his strength het vergt veel van zijn krachten

²drain (vb) **1** weglopen, wegstromen, (uit)-lekken: ~ *away* wegvloeien; [fig] wegebben, afnemen **2** leeglopen, afdruipen **3** afwateren, lozen

³drain (vb) **1** afvoeren, doen afvloeien, afgieten; [fig] doen verdwijnen **2** leegmaken, leegdrinken: ~ *off* afvoeren, leegmaken **3** droogleggen || *a face ~ed of all colour* een doodsbleek gezicht

drainpipe regenpijp, afvoerpijp

drake mannetjeseend, woerd

dram 1 drachme⁺ʰ, dram **2** neutjeʰ

drama toneelstukʰ, dramaʰ

drama queen dramaqueen; aansteller

dramatic 1 dramatisch, toneel-: ~ *irony* tragische ironie **2** indrukwekkend, aangrijpend

dramatist toneelschrijver

¹dramatize (vb) zich aanstellen, dramatisch doen, overdrijven

²dramatize (vb) dramatiseren, als drama bewerken, aanschouwelijk voorstellen

¹drape (n) **1** draperie **2** [Am] gordijnʰ

²drape (vb) **1** bekleden, omhullen, versieren **2** draperen [also fig]

drapery 1 stoffen **2** manufacturenhandel **3** [Am] gordijnʰ

drastic drastisch, ingrijpend

drat verwensen, vervloeken: [inform] *that ~ted animal!* dat vervelende beest!

draught 1 tocht, trek, luchtstroom: [inform] *feel* the ~ op de tocht zitten; [fig] in geldnood verkeren **2** teug; slok [of medicine] **3** drankjeʰ, medicijnʰ, dosis **4** het aftappen: *beer on* ~ bier van het vat **5** schets, conceptʰ, kladʰ **6** damschijf: *(game of)* ~s damspelʰ, het dammen

draughtboard dambordʰ

draught-proof tochtdicht, tochtvrij [of windows etc]

draughtsman 1 tekenaar, ontwerper **2** opsteller [of documents] **3** damschijf

¹draw (n) **1** trek, het trekken: *he is quick on the* ~ hij kan snel zijn revolver trekken; [fig] hij reageert snel **2** aantrekkingskracht, attractie, trekpleister **3** [lottery] trekking, (uit)loting, verloting **4** gelijkspelʰ, remise

²draw (vb) **1** komen, gaan: ~ *to an end* (or: *a close*) ten einde lopen; ~ *level* gelijk komen [in race] **2** aantrekkingskracht uitoefenen, publiek trekken **3** [sport, game] gelijkspelen, in gelijkspel eindigen, remise maken **4** trekken [of tea]

³draw (vb) **1** (aan)trekken, (aan)lokken: ~ *attention to* de aandacht vestigen op **2** (in)-halen: ~ *a deep breath* diep inademen, diep ademhalen **3** ertoe brengen, overhalen **4** (te voorschijn) halen, uittrekken; [fig] ontlokken; naar buiten brengen; (af)tappen [beer etc]: ~ *blood* bloed doen vloeien; [fig] iem. gevoelig raken; *he refused to be ~n* hij liet zich niet uit zijn tent lokken **5** van de ingewanden ontdoen **6** opstellen [text]; opmaken, formuleren; uitschrijven [cheque] **7** trekken [money, wages]; opnemen, ontvangen **8** [sport, game] in gelijkspel doen eindigen || ~ *off* **a)** afleiden [attention]; **b)** weglokken; **c)** aftappen

⁴draw (vb) **1** trekken, slepen; tevoorschijn halen [weapon]; dichtdoen [curtain]: ~ *the blinds* de jaloezieën neerlaten; ~ *back the curtains* de gordijnen opentrekken; ~ *s.o. into a conversation* iem. in een gesprek betrekken **2** tekenen, schetsen: [fig] *one has to ~ the line somewhere* je moet ergens een grens trekken **3** loten, door loting verkrijgen **4** putten [also fig]: ~ *inspiration from* inspiratie opdoen uit; *I'll have to ~ upon my savings* ik zal mijn spaargeld moeten aanspreken || ~ *a conclusion* een conclusie trekken

draw apart uit elkaar gaan, uit elkaar groeien

draw away 1 (+ from) wegtrekken (van), (zich) terugtrekken (van) **2** (+ from) uitlopen (op), een voorsprong nemen (op)

drawback nadeelʰ, bezwaarʰ

draw back (+ from) (zich) terugtrekken (van), terugwijken (van/voor)

drawbridge ophaalbrug

drawer 1 lade: *a chest of* ~s een ladekast **2** (-s) (lange) onderbroek

draw in 1 binnenrijden, komen aanrijden **2** aan de kant gaan rijden **3** ten einde lopen [of day]; schemerig worden; korter worden [of days]

dra**wing 1** tekening **2** het tekenen, tekenkunst: *Yvonne is good at ~* Yvonne is goed in tekenen

dra**wing board** tekentafel: *back to the ~!* terug naar af!; overnieuw!

dra**wing-pin** punaise

dra**wing-room** salon+h, zitkamer

1drawl (n) lijzige manier van praten

2drawl (vb) lijzig praten

drawn 1 vertrokken, strak; afgetobd [face] **2** onbeslist [match]

1draw o**ut** (vb) **1** langer worden [of days] **2** wegrijden [of train etc]

2draw o**ut** (vb) **1** (uit)rekken, uitspinnen **2** aan de praat krijgen, eruit halen, uithoren

1draw u**p** (vb) stoppen, tot stilstand komen: *~ to* naderen, dichter komen bij

2draw u**p** (vb) **1** opstellen; plaatsen [soldiers] **2** opmaken, opstellen, formuleren **3** aanschuiven [chair]; bijtrekken ‖ *draw o.s. up* zich oprichten, zich lang maken

1dread (n) (doods)angst, vrees, schrik

2dread (vb) vrezen, erg opzien tegen, doodsbang zijn (voor): *I ~ to think (of) what will happen to him* ik moet er niet aan denken wat hem allemaal zal overkomen

dreadful vreselijk, ontzettend

dreadlocks rastakapselh, rastavlechten

dreads [inform] *dreadlocks* dreads

1dream (n) droom; [fig] ideaalh: *a ~ of a dress* een beeldige jurk

2dream (vb) dromen, zich verbeelden, zich indenken: *~ up* verzinnen; *she wouldn't ~ of moving* zij piekerde er niet over om te verhuizen

drea**my 1** dromerig **2** [inform] beeldig

drea**ry 1** somber, treurig **2** saai

dredge (op)dreggen, (uit)baggeren: [fig] *~ up old memories* herinneringen ophalen

dregs bezinkselh, droesem: *drink* (or: *drain*) *to the ~* tot op de bodem ledigen **2** [depr] iets waardeloos, uitvaagselh: *~ of society* uitschot van de maatschappij

drench doordrenken, doorweken, kletsnat maken: *sun-drenched beaches* zonovergoten stranden

1dress (n) **1** jurk, japon **2** kleding, dracht

2dress (vb) **1** (aan)kleden, van kleding voorzien, kleren aantrekken: *~ed to kill* opvallend gekleed; *~ up* verkleden, vermommen **2** versieren, opsieren, optuigen: *~ up* a) opdoffen; b) [also fig] mooi doen lijken, aanvaardbaar laten klinken (*or:* maken), leuk brengen **3** [med] verbinden; verzorgen [wound]; verband aanleggen op **4** opmaken, kammen en borstelen, kappen ‖ *~ down* a) roskammen [horse]; b) een pak slaag geven, op z'n donder geven

3dress (vb) **1** zich (aan)kleden, gekleed gaan

2 zich verkleden: *~ for dinner* zich verkleden voor het eten

dre**ssage** dressuur

dress circle balkonh

dre**sser 1** buffetkast, keukenkast **2** [Am] ladekast **3** kleder, kleedster

dre**ssing 1** het (aan)kleden **2** [med] verband(materiaal)h **3** slasaus **4** [Am; culinary] vulling

dre**ssing d**o**wn** schrobbering; uitbrander

dre**ssing-gown 1** badjas **2** ochtendjas

dre**ssmaker** naaister, kleermaker

dress rehearsal generale repetitie

1dri**bble** (n) **1** stroompjeh; [fig] vleugjeh; druppeltjeh, beetjeh **2** [sport] dribbel **3** kwijlh, speekselh

2dri**bble** (vb) **1** (weg)druppelen, langzaam wegstromen; [fig] haast ongemerkt verdwijnen: *the answers ~d in* de antwoorden kwamen binnendruppelen **2** kwijlen **3** [sport] dribbelen

3dri**bble** (vb) (laten) druppelen, langzaam laten vloeien

dried droog, gedroogd: *~ milk* melkpoeder+h

dri**er** droger, haardroger, wasdroger, droogmolen

1dri**ft** (n) **1** afwijking, afdrijving, het zwerven **2** vlaag, sneeuwvlaag, regenvlaag, stofwolk **3** opeenhoping, berg, massa **4** ongeorganiseerde beweging, gang, trek: *the ~ from the country to the city* de trek van het platteland naar de stad **5** strekking, tendens, bedoeling: *the general ~ of the story* de algemene strekking van het verhaal

2dri**ft** (vb) **1** (af)drijven, uiteendrijven [also fig]; (zich laten) meedrijven, (rond)zwalken: *~ away* (or: *off*) geleidelijk verdwijnen **2** opwaaien; (zich) ophopen [of snow]

3dri**ft** (vb) **1** meevoeren, voortdrijven **2** bedekken [with snow, leaves]

dri**ftwood** drijfhouth; wrakhouth

1dri**ll** (n) **1** boor(machine), drilboor **2** het drillen, exercitie, oefening **3** driloefening, het opdreunen, het erin stampen **4** gebruikelijke procedure, normale gang van zaken

2dri**ll** (vb) **1** boren, gaten boren **2** stampen, (mechanisch) leren **3** oefenen, exerceren

3dri**ll** (vb) **1** doorboren **2** aanboren **3** drillen, africhten, trainen **4** erin stampen, erin heien

dri**ly** droog(jes)

1dri**nk** (n) **1** (iets te) drinken, slok, teug: *would you like a ~?* wilt u misschien iets drinken? **2** drank, sterkedrank, alcohol: *food and ~* eten en drinken

2dri**nk** (vb) **1** in zich opnemen, (in)drinken: *~ in s.o.'s words* iemands woorden in zich opnemen **2** drinken op, het glas heffen op: *they drank (to) his health* zij dronken op zijn gezondheid

3dri**nk** (vb) drinken, leegdrinken, opdrinken:

*he ~s like a **fish*** hij zuipt als een ketter; *~ up* opdrinken, (het glas) leegdrinken

drink-driver alcomobilist, automobilist die te veel gedronken heeft

drink to toosten op, een dronk uitbrengen op

¹drip (n) **1** gedruppel[h], druppel, het druppelen **2** infuus[h], infusievloeistof **3** sukkel, slome (duikelaar)

²drip (vb) druipen, druppelen: *~ping **wet*** drijfnat, doornat

³drip (vb) laten druppelen

drip-dry kreukherstellend; strijkvrij

drippy flauw, onnozel

¹drive (n) **1** rit(je[h]), rijtoer: *let's **go** for a ~* laten we een eindje gaan rijden **2** [psychology] drift, drang **3** actie, campagne **4** laan, oprijlaan, oprit **5** (groot) offensief[h], (zware) aanval **6** aandrijving, overbrenging: *front-wheel ~* voorwielaandrijving; *right-hand ~* met het stuur rechts **7** drijfkracht, stuwkracht **8** energie, doorzettingsvermogen[h] **9** diskdrive **10** afslag

²drive (vb) **1** snellen, (voort)stormen, (blijven) doorgaan **2** gooien, schieten, lanceren

³drive (vb) **1** dwingen, brengen tot: *~ s.o. to **despair*** iem. wanhopig maken **2** aandrijven

⁴drive (vb) **1** drijven [also fig]; opjagen, bijeendrijven: *~ **out*** verdrijven, uitdrijven, verdringen **2** rijden, (be)sturen, vervoeren: *~ **in*** binnenrijden; *~ **off*** wegrijden, *~ **up*** voorrijden **3** voortdrijven, duwen; slaan [also sport]: *~ **home*** a) vastslaan, inhameren; b) volkomen duidelijk maken; *~ **in*** a) inslaan [nail etc]; b) inhameren [fig]

drive at doelen op, bedoelen: *what is he driving at?* wat bedoelt hij?

¹drive-in (n) drive-in, bioscoop, cafetaria

²drive-in (adj) drive-in, inrij-

¹drivel (n) gezwam[h], kletskoek

²drivel (vb) zwammen, (onzin) kletsen, zeveren

driver 1 bestuurder, chauffeur, machinist **2** (vee)drijver

driveway oprijlaan, oprit

driving 1 aandrijvend; stuwend [also fig] **2** krachtig, energiek: *~ **rain*** slagregen

driving force 1 drijvende kracht: *the ~ **behind** the reforms* de drijvende kracht achter de hervormingen **2** gangmaker

driving licence rijbewijs[h]

driving mirror achteruitkijkspiegel

¹drizzle (n) motregen

²drizzle (vb) motregenen, miezeren

³drizzle (vb) [culinary] **1** [eg oil] sprenkelen (op) **2** [a dish] besprenkelen

droll komiek, humoristisch

dromedary dromedaris

¹drone (n) **1** hommel, dar **2** gegons[h], gezoem[h], gebrom[h] **3** dreun, eentonige manier van praten **4** drone [aircraft]

²drone (vb) **1** gonzen, zoemen, brommen **2** (op)dreunen [also fig]; monotoon spreken: *~ **on*** (door)zeuren

drool 1 kwijlen: [inform, fig] *~ **about*** (or: *over*) dwepen met, weglopen met **2** [inform] zwammen, leuteren

¹droop (n) hangende houding, het (laten) hangen

²droop (vb) **1** neerhangen, (af)hangen, slap worden, krom staan **2** verflauwen, afnemen, verslappen

¹drop (n) **1** druppel, drupje[h], neutje[h]; [fig] greintje[h]; spoor(tje)[h]: *he has **had** a ~ too much* hij heeft te diep in het glaasje gekeken **2** zuurtje[h] **3** (-s) druppels, medicijn[h]: [inform] *knock-out ~s* bedwelmingsmiddel[h] ‖ *a ~ **in** a **bucket*** (or: *in the **ocean***) een druppel op een gloeiende plaat; *at the ~ of a **hat*** meteen, bij de minste aanleiding, zonder te aarzelen

²drop (vb) **1** druppelen, druipen **2** vallen, omvallen, neervallen, zich laten vallen; [fig] terloops geuit worden: *~ **dead!*** val dood! **3** ophouden, verlopen, uitvallen: *they let the **matter** ~* zij lieten de zaak verder rusten **4** dalen, afnemen, zakken: *the **wind** has ~ped* de wind is gaan liggen ‖ *~ **back*** (or: *behind*) achterblijven, achtergelaten worden; *~ **behind*** achterraken bij

³drop (vb) **1** laten druppelen, laten druipen **2** laten vallen, laten zakken, neerlaten **3** laten varen, laten schieten, opgeven: *~ (the) **charges*** een aanklacht intrekken **4** laten dalen, verminderen, verlagen: *~ one's **voice*** zachter praten **5** terloops zeggen, laten vallen: *~ s.o. a **hint*** iem. een wenk geven; *~ me a **line*** schrijf me maar een paar regeltjes **6** afleveren, afgeven, afzetten: *he ~ped me **at** the corner* hij zette mij bij de hoek af

drop by langskomen; binnenvallen: *drop in on her* even bij haar aanlopen

drop-down menu dropdown, uitklapbaar keuzemenu[h]

drop in langskomen, binnenvallen: *~ **on** s.o.* even aanlopen bij iem.

droplet druppeltje[h]

¹drop off (vb) **1** geleidelijk afnemen, teruglopen **2** [inform] in slaap vallen

²drop off (vb) **1** afzetten, laten uitstappen **2** afgeven

drop out 1 opgeven, zich terugtrekken **2** [Am] vroegtijdig verlaten

drop-out drop-out, voortijdige schoolverlater, verstotene

droppings uitwerpselen [of animals]; keutels

drought (periode van) droogte

drove horde; kudde [cattle]; menigte [people]: *people came **in** ~s* de mensen kwamen in drommen

drown 1 (doen) verdrinken, (doen) verzuipen: *~ one's **sorrows** (in drink)* zijn verdriet

verdrinken **2** (doen) overstromen, onder
water zetten, (rijkelijk) overspoelen; [fig]
overstemmen; overstelpen
¹drowse (vb) slaperig zijn, dommelen, loom
zijn
²drowse (vb) slaperig maken, suf maken,
sloom maken
drowsy 1 slaperig; loom **2** er slaperig uitziend: *a ~ hamlet* een ingeslapen gehuchtje
drubbing 1 pakʰ slaag, aframmeling
2 (zware) nederlaag
¹drudge (n) sloof, zwoeger, werkezel
²drudge (vb) zwoegen, zich afbeulen, eentonig werk doen
drudgery eentonig werkʰ, slaafs werkʰ
¹drug (n) **1** geneesmiddelʰ, medicijnʰ **2** drug,
verdovend middelʰ: [inform] *do ~s* drugs gebruiken, aan de drugs zijn
²drug (vb) medicijn(en) e.d. toedienen, bedwelmen, drogeren, verdoven
drug addict drugsverslaafde
drugstore [Am] klein warenhuisʰ, apotheek, drogisterij
¹drum (n) **1** trom, trommel **2** getrommelʰ,
geroffelʰ, roffel, het trommelen **3** (-s) slag-
werkʰ, drumstelʰ, drums **4** drum, ton, vatʰ
²drum (vb) trommelen, drummen, slagwerker zijn, roffelen, ritmisch tikken ‖ *~ up* optrommelen, bijeenroepen; *~ up trade* een
markt creëren, klanten werven; *~ sth. into
s.o.* (or: *s.o.'s head*) iets bij iem. erin hameren
drum major tamboer-majoor
drummer slagwerker, drummer, tamboer
drumstick 1 trommelstok **2** (gebraden)
kippenpootjeʰ, drumstick
¹drunk (n) dronkaard, zuiplap
²drunk (adj) **1** dronken: *~ and disorderly* in
kennelijke staat; *blind* (or: *dead*) *~* stomdronken **2** door het dolle heen, (brood)-
dronken: *~ with power* tiranniek, machts-
wellustig
drunkard [dated] dronkaard
drunk-driving [Am] het rijden onder invloed
drunken dronken, dronkenmans-
¹dry (adj) **1** droog: *~ land* vaste grond
2 droog, (op)gedroogd; zonder beleg
[bread]; drooggelegd [land; also fig]: *run ~*
opdrogen, droog komen te staan **3** [inform]
dorstig **4** droog, op droge toon (gezegd),
ironisch ‖ *~ cleaner('s)* stomerij; *(as) ~ as dust,
bone-~* gortdroog, kurkdroog; *~ run* repetitie, het proefdraaien
²dry (vb) (op)drogen, droog worden, uitdrogen: *dried milk* melkpoeder ‖ *~ out a)* uitdrogen, grondig droog worden; *b)* afkicken [al-
coholics]; *~ up a)* opdrogen; *b)* [also fig] afnemen tot niets
³dry (vb) (af)drogen, laten drogen ‖ *~ out
a)* grondig droog laten worden; *b)* laten afkicken [alcoholics]

dry-cleaning 1 het chemisch reinigen
2 chemisch gereinigde kleding
dryer *see* drier
drywall 1 gipswand **2** gipsplaat
DTP *desktop publishing* DTP
dual tweevoudig, tweeledig: *~ carriageway*
dubbele rijbaan; *have ~ citizenship* een dubbele nationaliteit hebben; *dual-purpose*
voor twee doeleinden geschikt
dub 1 tot ridder slaan, ridderen **2** noemen,
(om)dopen (tot), de bijnaam geven van
3 (na)synchroniseren, dubben
dubbing het bijmixen [sound]; (na)syn-
chronisatie
dubious 1 twijfelend, aarzelend, onzeker
2 onbetrouwbaar, twijfelachtig
duchess hertogin
duchy hertogdomʰ
¹duck (n) eend, eendvogel ‖ *play ~s and
drakes with*, *make ~s and drakes of* verkwanselen; *take to sth. like a ~ to water* in z'n element zijn
²duck (vb) buigen, (zich) bukken, wegduiken
³duck (vb) **1** plotseling (onder)dompelen,
kopje-onder duwen **2** ontwijken, vermijden
3 snel intrekken [head]
duckboard loopplank [across ditch or mud]
duckling jonge eend, eendjeʰ
duckweed eendenkroosʰ
duct buis [also biology]; kanaalʰ, goot, leiding
duct tape ducttape
dud 1 prulʰ, nepdingʰ **2** blindganger
[bomb, grenade]
dude 1 kerel, vent; [inform] gast **2** [Am]
stadsmens [holidaying on a ranch]
¹due (n) **1** datgene wat iem. toekomt: *give
s.o. his ~* iem. niet tekortdoen, iem. geven
wat hem toekomt **2** (-s) schuld(en), rechten,
contributie
²due (adj) **1** gepast, juist, terecht: *with ~ care*
met gepaste zorgvuldigheid; *in ~ time, in ~
course (of time)* te zijner tijd **2** schuldig, verschuldigd, invorderbaar, verplicht: *postage ~*
ongefrankeerd; *the amount ~* het verschul-
digde bedrag; *fall* (or: *become*) *~* vervallen,
verschijnen [instalment]; *our thanks are ~ to
you* wij zijn u dank verschuldigd **3** verwacht:
the aircraft is ~ at 4.50 p.m. het toestel wordt
om 16 uur 50 verwacht ‖ *~ to* toe te schrijven
aan
³due (adv) precies [only for points of the
compass]: *~ south* pal naar het zuiden
due date 1 [fin] vervaldatum **2** [pregnan-
cy] datum waarop iem. is uitgerekend
duel duelʰ
duet duetʰ
due to wegens, vanwege, door
duff waardeloos, slecht, kapot
duffle bag plunjezak
dugout 1 (boomstam)kano **2** schuilholʰ,

duvet

uitgegraven schuilplaats **3** [sport] dug-out
duh [inform] duh, nogal wiedes
duke hertog
dukedom hertogdom^h
dull 1 saai, vervelend **2** dom, sloom **3** mat
[of colour, sound, pain]; dof **4** bot, stomp
5 bewolkt, betrokken **6** [com] flauw: *the ~
season* de slappe tijd || *as ~ as* **ditchwater** (or:
dishwater) oersaai
duly 1 behoorlijk, naar behoren, terecht
2 stipt, prompt
dumb 1 stom, niet kunnen spreken, zwijgzaam: *to be* **struck** ~ met stomheid geslagen
zijn, sprakeloos zijn **2** dom, stom, suf
¹**dumb-ass** (n) [vulg] dommerik, idioot
²**dumb-ass** (adj) [vulg] extreem dom, idioot
dumbfound verstomd doen staan
dumbo dombo, stomkop
dumb show gebarenspel^h, pantomime
dumbstruck perplex; met stomheid geslagen
¹**dummy** (n) **1** dummy; blinde [cards]; pop;
model^h [of book]; proefpagina, stroman, figurant **2** nepartikel^h **3** fopspeen **4** [inform]
sufferd, uilskuiken^h
²**dummy** (adj) **1** namaak, schijn, nep
2 proef-: *~* **run** het proefdraaien, militaire
oefening
¹**dump** (n) **1** hoop, (vuilnis)belt, (vuil)stort-
plaats **2** dump, tijdelijk depot^h van leger-
goederen **3** [inform] puinhoop, vervallen
woning, desolate stad, desolaat dorp^h || [in-
form] *(down)* **in** *the ~s* in de put, somber
²**dump** (vb) **1** dumpen, storten, lozen, neersmijten **2** dumpen [goods on foreign mar-
ket] **3** achterlaten, in de steek laten
Dumpster [Am] afvalcontainer
dumpy kort en dik
dunce [dated] domkop; langzame leerling
dune duin
dung mest, drek, gier
dungarees overall, jeans, tuinbroek
dungeon kerker
dunghill 1 mesthoop **2** puinhoop
¹**dunk** (vb) **1** onderdompelen [also fig]; (in)-
dopen; soppen [bread in tea etc] **2** [basket-
ball] dunken [scoren]
²**dunk** (n) dunk
duodenum [med] twaalfvingerige darm
¹**dupe** (n) dupe, slachtoffer^h (van bedrog),
bedrogene
²**dupe** (vb) bedriegen, benadelen, duperen
¹**duplex** (n) [Am] halfvrijstaand huis^h; maisonnette
²**duplex** (adj) **1** tweevoudig, dubbel; dubbelzijdig: *~* **printing** dubbelzijdig printen
2 met twee verdiepingen: [Am] *~* **apartment**
maisonnette
¹**duplicate** (n) **1** duplicaat^h, kopie **2** duplo^h:
in ~ in duplo, in tweevoud
²**duplicate** (adj) **1** dubbel, tweevoudig

2 gelijkluidend, identiek
³**duplicate** (vb) **1** verdubbelen, kopiëren,
verveelvuldigen **2** herhalen
duplicity dubbelhartigheid, bedrog^h
durability duurzaamheid
durable duurzaam, bestendig, onverslijtbaar
duration duur: *for* the ~ of zolang … duurt,
tijdens
duress [form] dwang
during tijdens, gedurende, onder: *~* the *afternoon* in de loop van de middag
dusk schemer(ing), duister^h, duisternis
dusky [form] duister; schemerig
¹**dust** (n) **1** stof^h, poeder^{+h} **2** stofwolk: [fig]
when the ~ had **settled** toen de gemoederen
bedaard waren
²**dust** (vb) (af)stoffen, stof afnemen
³**dust** (vb) **1** bestuiven, bestrooien: *~* **crops**
gewas besproeien [from aeroplane] **2** afstoffen
dustbin vuilnisbak
duster 1 stoffer, plumeau **2** stofdoek
dust jacket stofomslag^h
dustman vuilnisman
dust off afstoffen; [fig] opfrissen; ophalen
[old knowledge]
dustpan blik^h [dustpan and brush]
dust-up 1 handgemeen^h **2** rel, oproer^h
dusty 1 stoffig, bestoft, droog **2** als stof ||
not so ~ lang niet gek
¹**Dutch** (n) Nederlands^h, Hollands^h
²**Dutch** (n) Nederlanders, het Nederlandse
volk || [Am; inform] *beat the ~* een bijzondere
prestatie leveren
³**Dutch** (adj) Nederlands, Hollands || *~* **auc-
tion** veiling bij afslag; *~* **bargain** overeenkomst die met een dronk bezegeld wordt; *~*
comfort schrale troost; *~* **courage** jenever-
moed; *~* **door** boerderijdeur, onder- en bo-
vendeur; *~* **treat** feest waarbij ieder voor zich
betaalt; *talk like a ~* **uncle** duidelijk zeggen
waar het op staat; *go ~* ieder voor zich betalen
Dutchman Nederlander, Hollander || *… or I
am a ~* (or: *I am a ~ if …*) ik ben een boon als ik
…
dutiful 1 plicht(s)getrouw **2** gehoorzaam,
eerbiedigend
duty 1 plicht, verplichting, taak, functie,
dienst: *do ~ for* dienstdoen als, vervangen;
off ~ buiten (de) dienst(tijd), in vrije tijd; *on ~*
in functie, in diensttijd **2** belasting, accijns,
invoerrechten, uitvoerrechten, rechten
3 mechanisch arbeidsvermogen^h: *a* **heavy** ~
drilling machine een boormachine voor zwaar
werk **4** (duties) functie, werkzaamheden
5 belasting, accijns, invoerrechten, uitvoerrechten, rechten
duty-free belastingvrij
duvet dekbed^h; donzen dekbed^h

¹dwarf (n) dwerg

²dwarf (adj) dwerg-, dwergachtig

³dwarf (vb) **1** in z'n groei belemmeren, klein(er) maken, klein houden: ~ *plants* miniatuurplanten kweken **2** kleiner doen lijken: *the skyscraper ~ed all the other buildings* bij de wolkenkrabber verzonken alle andere gebouwen in het niet

dwell 1 wonen, verblijven, zich ophouden **2** blijven stilstaan, uitweiden: ~ *(up)on* (lang) blijven stilstaan bij, (lang) doorgaan over

dwelling woning

¹DWI (n) [Am] *driving while intoxicated* (het) rijden onder invloed

²DWI [inform] *deal with it* wen er maar aan

dwindle afnemen, achteruitgaan

¹dye (n) verf(stof), kleurstof

²dye (vb) verven, kleuren

dyed-in-the-wool door de wol geverfd; door en door

dyke 1 dijk, (keer)dam **2** kanaaltjeʰ, sloot, (natuurlijke) waterloop **3** pot, lesbienne

dynamic 1 dynamisch, bewegend **2** voortvarend, actief, energiek

dynamics 1 [mus] dynamiek [also fig] **2** [physics] dynamica; bewegingsleer

dynamite dynamietʰ ‖ *the news was really ~* het nieuws sloeg in als een bom

dynamo dynamo

dynasty dynastie, (vorsten)huisʰ

dysentery bloeddiarree

dysfunctional verstoord; slecht functionerend: *a ~ family* een verstoord gezin(sleven)

dyslexia leesblindheid, dyslexie

dysmorphia [med] dysmorfie, misvorming

dystopia dystopie

e

E 1 [elec] *earth* aarde **2** *east(ern)* O., Oost(e-lijk)

each 1 elk, ieder afzonderlijk: *~ year he grows weaker* ieder jaar wordt hij zwakker **2** elk; ieder [of a group]: *they are a dollar ~* ze kosten een dollar per stuk

each other elkaar, mekaar: *they hate ~'s guts* ze kunnen elkaars bloed wel drinken

eager 1 vurig, onstuimig **2** (+ for) (hevig) verlangend (naar), begerig ‖ [inform] *~ beaver* (overdreven) harde werker

eagle adelaar, arend

eagle-eyed scherpziend; met arendsogen

e-alert e-mailnieuwsbrief

ear 1 oor^h: [fig] *play it by ~* improviseren, op z'n gevoel afgaan; *up to one's ~s* tot over zijn oren **2** gehoor^h, oor^h: *have an ~ for* een gevoel hebben voor **3** (koren)aar **4** oor^h, lus, oog^h, handvat^h ‖ *keep an ~* (or: *one's ~(s)) (close) to the ground* **a)** (goed) op de hoogte blijven [of trends, gossip]; **b)** de boel goed in de gaten houden; *prick up one's ~s* de oren spitsen; *be out on one's ~* ontslagen worden; *be all ~s* een en al oor zijn

earbud oortje^h, oortelefoon

ear canal gehoorgang

eardrum trommelvlies^h

earful: [inform] *give s.o. an ~* iem. onomwonden de waarheid zeggen

earl (Engelse) graaf

¹early (adj) **1** vroeg, vroegtijdig: *~ bird* vroege vogel; vroegboeker; *~ retirement* VUT, vervroegd pensioen; *the ~ bird catches the worm* vroeg begonnen, veel gewonnen; *in the ~ 1960s* in het begin van de jaren zestig **2** spoedig: *an ~ reply* een spoedig antwoord **3** oud, van lang geleden: *the ~ Celts* de oude Kelten

²early (adv) **1** vroeg, (in het) begin, tijdig: *~ on (in)* al vroeg, al in het begin **2** te vroeg: *we were an hour ~* we kwamen een uur te vroeg

early adopter koploper

early-bird vroegboek-: *~ deal* vroegboekactie; *~ discount* vroegboekkorting

earmark reserveren [funds etc]: *~ for* opzijleggen om (… te)

earn 1 verdienen, (ver)krijgen **2** verwerven, (terecht) krijgen: *his behaviour ~ed him his nickname* zijn gedrag bezorgde hem zijn bijnaam

¹earnest (n) ernst: *in (real) ~* menens; *I am in (real) ~* ik meén het

²earnest (adj) ernstig, serieus, gemeend

earnings 1 inkomen^h, inkomsten, verdiensten **2** winst [of business]

earphones koptelefoon

earshot gehoorsafstand: *out of* (or: *within*) *~* buiten (*or:* binnen) gehoorsafstand

¹earth (n) **1** aarde **2** [zoology] hol^h: *go* (or: *run) to ~* **a)** zijn hol invluchten; **b)** onderduiken ‖ *promise the ~* gouden bergen beloven; *down to ~* met beide benen op de grond, nuchter, eerlijk; *why on ~* waarom in vredesnaam

²earth (vb) aarden

earthenware aardewerk^h

earthly 1 aards, werelds: [inform] *no ~ use* absoluut geen zin, geen enkele zin

earthquake aardbeving

earthworm pier, regenworm

earthy 1 vuil (van aarde) **2** materialistisch, aards, grof

earwax oorsmeer^h

earwig oorwurm

¹ease (n) **1** gemak^h, gemakkelijkheid **2** ongedwongenheid, gemak^h, comfort^h: [mil] *stand at ~* op de plaats rust; *at one's ~* op zijn gemak, rustig **3** welbehagen^h: *ill at ~* niet op z'n gemak

²ease (vb) afnemen, minder worden, (vaart) minderen: *~ off* (or: *up) afnemen, verminderen, rustiger aan gaan doen

³ease (vb) **1** verlichten, doen afnemen: *~ back the throttle* gas terugnemen **2** gemakkelijk(er) maken: [fig] *~ s.o.'s mind* iem. geruststellen **3** voorzichtig bewegen: *~ off the lid* voorzichtig het deksel eraf halen

easel (schilders)ezel

easily 1 moeiteloos, rustig, met gemak **2** ongetwijfeld, zonder meer, beslist

¹east (n) het oosten [point of the compass]; oost: *the East* het oostelijk gedeelte, de Oost, de Oriënt

²east (adj) oostelijk: *~ wind* oostenwind

³east (adv) in, uit, naar het oosten: *sail due ~* recht naar het oosten varen

Easter Pasen

Easter Bunny paashaas

¹easterly (n) oostenwind

²easterly (adj) oostelijk

eastern 1 oostelijk, oost(en)-: *Eastern Hemisphere* oostelijk halfrond; *the Eastern bloc* het Oostblok **2** oosters

¹easy (adj) **1** (ge)makkelijk, eenvoudig, moeiteloos: *have ~ access to sth.* makkelijk toegang hebben tot iets **2** ongedwongen: *have an ~ manner* ontspannen manier van doen **3** comfortabel, gemakkelijk: *~ chair* leunstoel, luie stoel **4** welgesteld, bemiddeld: *in ~ circumstances* in goede doen; *have an ~ time (of it)* een gemakkelijk leventje hebben ‖ *by ~ stages* stap voor stap; *on ~ terms* op gemakkelijke condities, op afbetaling

²**easy** (adv) **1** gemakkelijk, eenvoudig: *easier said than done* gemakkelijker gezegd dan gedaan **2** kalm, rustig: *take it ~* het rustig aan doen; *~ does it!* voorzichtig! (dan breekt het lijntje niet)

easygoing 1 laconiek, makkelijk **2** gemakzuchtig, laks

easy-peasy makkelijk, een eitje

¹**eat** (vb) eten: *~ out* buitenshuis eten

²**eat** (vb) **1** (op)eten, vreten **2** verslinden, opvreten: *~en up with curiosity* verteerd door nieuwsgierigheid **3** aantasten, wegvreten || *what's ~ing you?* wat zit je zo dwars?

eavesdrop afluisteren, luistervinkje spelen

e-banking internetbankieren^h

¹**ebb** (n) eb, laag water^h; [fig] *be at a low ~* in de put zitten

²**ebb** (vb) afnemen, wegebben

e-bike *electric bike* elektrische fiets

ebony ebbenhout^h

e-book *electronic book* e-boek^h

ebullient uitbundig, uitgelaten

EC *European Community* EG

e-card 1 e-card [greetings card] **2** smartcard, chipkaart

¹**eccentric** (n) zonderling, excentriekeling

²**eccentric** (adj) zonderling, excentriek

ecclesiastical geestelijk, kerkelijk, kerk-

echelon rang; groep, echelon^h

¹**echo** (n) echo, weerklank

²**echo** (vb) weerklinken, resoneren

³**echo** (vb) **1** echoën, herhalen, nazeggen **2** weerkaatsen

echocardiogram [med] echocardiogram^h

¹**eclipse** (n) eclips, verduistering: *a total ~ of the sun* een volledige zonsverduistering

²**eclipse** (vb) **1** verduisteren **2** overschaduwen, in glans overtreffen

eco-car groene auto; elektrische auto

ecological ecologisch

ecology ecologie

e-commerce internethandel, e-commerce

economic 1 economisch **2** rendabel, lonend, winstgevend

economical 1 zuinig, spaarzaam **2** economisch, voordelig

economics economie (als wetenschap)

economist 1 zuinig iem. **2** econoom

economize (+ on) bezuinigen (op), spaarzaam zijn

economy 1 economie, economisch stelsel^h: *all those strikes are damaging the French ~* al die stakingen brengen de Franse economie veel schade toe **2** besparing, bezuiniging, zuinig gebruik: *we bought a smaller house for reasons of ~* we hebben een kleiner huis gekocht om redenen van bezuiniging

economy class economyclass; toeristenklasse

economy size voordeelverpakking, voordeelpak^h

ecstasy 1 extase, vervoering **2** ecstasy [drug]

Ecuador Ecuador

¹**Ecuadorian** (n) Ecuadoraan(se)

²**Ecuadorian** (adj) Ecuadoraans

ecumenical oecumenisch

eczema eczeem^h

ed *edition* uitg., uitgave

EDC [Am] *explosive detection canine* explosievenhond

¹**eddy** (n) werveling, draaikolk

²**eddy** (vb) (doen) dwarrelen, (doen) kolken

¹**edge** (n) **1** snede, snijkant; scherpte [also fig]; effectiviteit, kracht: *her voice had an ~ to it* haar stem klonk scherp; *take the ~ off* het ergste wegnemen **2** kant, richel **3** rand, boord^h, oever, grens: *on the ~ of* op het punt van || [inform] *have an ~ over* een voorsprong hebben op; *be on ~* gespannen zijn

²**edge** (vb) (langzaam/voorzichtig) bewegen: *~ away* (or: *off*) voorzichtig wegsluipen; *~ up* dichterbij schuiven

³**edge** (vb) omranden: *~d with lace* met een randje kant

edging rand, boord^h, bies

edgy 1 scherp **2** gespannen, prikkelbaar

edible eetbaar, niet giftig

edification stichting, zedelijke en godsdienstige opbouw

edifice gebouw^h, bouwwerk^h, bouwsel^h

edify [form] stichten: *an ~ing homily* een stichtelijke preek

edit bewerken, herschrijven: *an ~ed version* een gekuiste versie; *~ed by* onder redactie van [magazines etc]

edition uitgave, editie, oplage; [fig] versie

editor 1 bewerker, samensteller **2** redacteur **3** uitgever

¹**editorial** (n) hoofdartikel^h, redactioneel artikel^h

²**editorial** (adj) redactioneel, redactie-, redacteurs-

editor-in-chief hoofdredacteur

EDM [mus] *Electronic Dance Music* dance

educate 1 opvoeden, vormen **2** opleiden, onderwijzen: *an ~d person* een gestudeerd iem., intellectueel **3** scholen, trainen

education 1 onderwijs^h, scholing, opleiding **2** opvoeding, vorming **3** pedagogie, opvoedkunde

educational 1 onderwijs- **2** leerzaam; educatief

eel paling || *be as slippery as an ~* zo glad als een aal zijn

eerie angstaanjagend, griezelig

efface 1 uitwissen **2** uit het geheugen bannen || *~ o.s.* zich wegcijferen

¹**effect** (n) **1** resultaat^h, effect^h, gevolg^h, uitwerking: *take ~* resultaat hebben; *to no ~* vruchteloos, tevergeefs **2** uitvoering, voltrekking: *put plans into ~* plannen uitvoeren

3 inhoud, strekking: *words to that* ~ woorden van die strekking **4** werking, (rechts)geldigheid: *come into* ~, *take* ~ van kracht worden **5** (-s) bezittingen, eigendommen || *in* ~ in feite, eigenlijk

²**effect** (vb) bewerkstelligen, teweegbrengen, veroorzaken: ~ *a cure for s.o.* iem. genezen

effective 1 effectief, doeltreffend **2** indrukwekkend, treffend: ~ *speeches* indrukwekkende toespraken **3** van kracht [law etc]

effeminate verwijfd

effervescence 1 levendigheid, uitgelatenheid **2** het bruisen

effete verzwakt, slap, afgeleefd

efficacy werkzaamheid, doeltreffendheid

efficiency 1 efficiëntie, doeltreffendheid, doelmatigheid **2** bekwaamheid **3** productiviteit

efficient 1 efficiënt, doeltreffend, doelmatig **2** bekwaam **3** productief

effigy beeltenis

effluent 1 afvalwater^h, rioolwater^h **2** aftakking, zijrivier, afvoer

effort 1 moeite, inspanning, poging: *make an* ~ *(to do sth.)* zich inspannen iets te doen **2** prestatie: *he has made a jolly good* ~ hij heeft geweldig zijn best gedaan

effrontery brutaliteit

effusion 1 ontboezeming **2** uitstroming

effusive overdadig [of utterances]; uitbundig

e.g. *exempli gratia* bijv.

egalitarian gelijkheids-, gelijkheid voorstaand

egg 1 ei^h: *fried* ~ gebakken ei; *poached* ~ gepocheerd ei; *scrambled* ~*s* roerei^h; ~ *whisk* eierklopper **2** eierstruif **3** eicel || *have* (or: *put*) *all one's* ~*s in one basket* alles op één kaart zetten; [inform] *have* ~ *on one's face* voor schut staan

egg beater [Am] eierklopper

eggcup eierdopje^h

egghead [inform] intellectueel, gestudeerde

eggnog eierdrank

egg on [inform] aanzetten; aansporen

eggplant aubergine

ego 1 ego^h **2** ik-bewustzijn^h **3** eigenwaarde

egocentric 1 egocentrisch **2** egoïstisch, zelfzuchtig

egoism egoïsme^h

egotism eigenwaan

egret (kleine) zilverreiger

Egypt Egypte

¹**Egyptian** (n) Egyptenaar, Egyptische

²**Egyptian** (adj) Egyptisch

EI *Emotional Intelligence* EQ^h *(emotionele-intelligentiequotiënt)*

Eid al-Adha Offerfeest^h

Eid al-Fitr Suikerfeest^h

eiderdown 1 (donzen) dekbed^h **2** eiderdons^h

eight acht

eighteen achttien

eighth achtste: *the* ~ *fastest runner* de op zeven na snelste loper

eightieth tachtigste

eighty tachtig: *in the eighties* in de jaren tachtig

¹**either** (pron) **1** één van beide(n): *use* ~ *hand* gebruik een van je (twee) handen; *choose* ~ *of the colours* kies één van de twee kleuren **2** beide(n), alle twee, allebei: *in* ~ *case*, ~ *way* in beide gevallen, in elk geval; *on* ~ *side* aan beide kanten

²**either** (adv) evenmin, ook niet, bovendien niet: *he can't sing, and I can't* ~ hij kan niet zingen en ik ook niet

³**either** (conj) (+ or) of, ofwel, hetzij: *have* ~ *cheese or a dessert* neem kaas of een toetje

ejaculation 1 zaadlozing, ejaculatie **2** uitroep

eject uitgooien, uitzetten, uitstoten, uitwerpen

ejection 1 verdrijving, (ambts)ontzetting, uitzetting **2** uitwerping

ejector seat schietstoel

e-juice dampvloeistof, rookvloeistof

eke out 1 rekken [also supplies]; aanvullen **2** bijeenscharrelen: ~ *a living* (met moeite) zijn kostje bijeen scharrelen

¹**elaborate** (adj) **1** gedetailleerd, uitgebreid, uitvoerig **2** ingewikkeld

²**elaborate** (vb) (+ (up)on) uitweiden (over)

³**elaborate** (vb) **1** in detail uitwerken, uitvoerig behandelen, uitweiden over **2** (moeizaam) voortbrengen, ontwikkelen

elapse verstrijken, voorbijgaan

¹**elastic** (n) elastiek(je^h)

²**elastic** (adj) **1** elastieken: ~ *band* elastiekje^h **2** elastisch, rekbaar **3** flexibel, soepel

elate verrukken, in vervoering brengen: *be* ~*d at* (or: *by*) *sth.* met iets verguld zijn

¹**elbow** (n) **1** elleboog, (scherpe) bocht **2** [techn] elleboog, knie(stuk^h) || *give s.o. the* ~ iem. de bons geven; *at s.o.'s* ~ naast iem., bij iem. in de buurt

²**elbow** (vb) zich (een weg) banen, met de ellebogen duwen, werken

elbow grease zwaar werk^h, poetswerk^h, schoonmaakwerk^h

elbow-room bewegingsvrijheid, armslag

¹**elder** (n) **1** oudere: *he is my* ~ *by four years* hij is vier jaar ouder dan ik; *the under 60s are more computer-savvy than their* ~*s* mensen onder de 60 kunnen beter met computers overweg dan mensen die ouder zijn **2** oudste [of two] **3** voorganger, ouderling

²**elder** (adj) oudste [of two]; oudere

elderberry vlierbes

eldercare ouderenzorg

elderly op leeftijd, bejaard: *a home for the ~* een bejaardentehuis

eldest oudste [of three or more]

¹**elect** (adj) gekozen [but not yet in office]: *the president ~* de nieuwgekozen president

²**elect** (vb) **1** kiezen, verkiezen (als) **2** besluiten: *~ to become a lawyer* besluiten jurist te worden

election verkiezing, keus: *municipal* (or: *local*) *~(s)* gemeenteraadsverkiezingen

electioneer stemmen werven; op verkiezingscampagne gaan

electoral 1 kies-, kiezers-: *~ register* (or: *roll*) kiesregisterʰ; [Am] *the ~ vote* (stemmen van) kiesmannen; [Am] *win the ~ vote* de meerderheid van de kiesmannen achter zich verzamelen (en daardoor de verkiezingen winnen) **2** electoraal, verkiezings-: *~ campaign* verkiezingscampagne

electorate electoraatʰ, de kiezers

electric 1 elektrisch: *~ chair* elektrische stoel; *~ storm* onweerʰ **2** opwindend, opzwepend **3** gespannen [eg of atmosphere]

electrical elektrisch, elektro-

electrician elektricien, elektromonteur

electricity elektriciteit, elektrische stroom

electrify 1 onder spanning zetten **2** elektrificeren, voorzien van elektrische installaties **3** opwinden, geestdriftig maken

electrocute elektrocuteren, op de elektrische stoel ter dood brengen

electronic elektronisch: *~ banking* elektronisch bankieren, internetbankieren; *~ data processing* elektronische informatieverwerking; *~ scrap* elektronisch afvalʰ, e-schrootʰ

electronics elektronica

elegant elegant, sierlijk

elegy treurdichtʰ, klaagliedʰ

element 1 elementʰ, onderdeelʰ, (hoofd)-bestanddeelʰ: *out of one's ~* als een vis op het droge **2** ietsʰ, watʰ: *there is an ~ of truth in it* er zit wel wat waars in **3** [chem, maths] elementʰ **4** (-s) de elementen [of weather] **5** (-s) (grond)beginselen

elemental 1 essentieel, wezenlijk: *~ needs* basisbehoeften **2** van de elementen [also of weather]: *~ force* natuurkracht; elementaire kracht

elementary 1 eenvoudig, simpel: *~ question* eenvoudige vraag **2** inleidend, elementair: *~ school* lagere school, basisschool **3** [science, chem] elementair

elephant olifant || *white ~* overbodig luxeartikel

elevate 1 opheffen, omhoogbrengen, verhogen **2** verheffen [only fig]; op een hoger plan brengen **3** promoveren, bevorderen: *~d to the presidency* tot president verheven

elevation 1 hoogte, heuvel, ophoging **2** bevordering, promotie **3** verhevenheid

elevator [Am] lift

eleven elf; [sport] elftal; ploeg

elevenses [dated] elfuurtjeʰ; hapje om elf uur

eleventh elfde; [fig] *at the ~ hour* ter elfder ure, op het laatste ogenblik

elf elf, fee

elicit 1 ontlokken, loskrijgen: *~ an answer from s.o.* een antwoord uit iem. krijgen; *elicit a response* een reactie ontlokken **2** teweegbrengen, veroorzaken

eligible in aanmerking komend, geschikt, bevoegd: *~ for (a) pension* pensioengerechtigd

eliminate 1 verwijderen **2** uitsluiten, buiten beschouwing laten: *~ the possibility of murder* de mogelijkheid van moord uitsluiten **3** uitschakelen [in match etc] **4** [inform] van kant maken, uit de weg ruimen

elimination 1 verwijdering, eliminatie **2** uitschakeling [in match etc] **3** uitsluiting; het schrappen [of options]

e-liquid dampvloeistof, rookvloeistof

elite elite

elitist elitair

elk eland

ellipse ellips, ovaalʰ

ellipsis 1 weglatingstekenʰ [three dots] **2** [linguistics] ellips

elm 1 iep, olm **2** iepenhoutʰ, olmenhoutʰ

elocution voordrachtskunst, welbespraaktheid

elongate langer worden (maken), (zich) verlengen, in de lengte (doen) groeien

elope er vandoor gaan [with lover, or to get married in secret]

eloquence welsprekendheid, welbespraaktheid

eloquent welsprekend [of person, argument]

El Salvador El Salvador

else anders, nog meer: *anything ~?* verder nog iets?; *little ~* niet veel meer; *what ~ did you expect?* wat had jij anders verwacht?

elsewhere elders, ergens anders

elucidate (nader) toelichten, licht werpen op, ophelderen

elude 1 ontwijken, ontschieten, ontsnappen aan; [fig] ontduiken; zich onttrekken aan [duties]; uit de weg gaan: *~ capture* weten te ontkomen **2** ontgaan [of fact, name]; ontschieten: *his name ~s me* ik ben zijn naam even kwijt

elusive 1 ontwijkend: *~ answer* ontwijkend antwoord **2** moeilijk te vangen **3** onvatbaar, ongrijpbaar: *an ~ name* een moeilijk te onthouden naam

'em *see* them

emaciate uitgemergeld

e-mail *electronic mail* e-mail, elektronische post

emanate from [form] afkomstig zijn van

emancipate 1 vrijmaken [slaves etc];
emanciperen, zelfstandig maken: *~d women*
geëmancipeerde vrouwen **2** gelijkstellen
voor de wet, emanciperen
emancipation 1 bevrijding [of slaves];
emancipatie **2** emancipatie, gelijkstelling
voor de wet: *the ~ of women* de emancipatie
van de vrouw
embalm balsemen
embankment 1 dijk, dam, wal **2** opge-
hoogde baan, spoordijk **3** kade
embargo embargo[h] [of ships, trade]; blokkade, beslag[h], beslaglegging, verbod[h], belemmering, uitvoerverbod[h]
embark 1 aan boord gaan (nemen), (zich)
inschepen **2** beginnen, van start gaan: *~
(up)on* zich begeven in, beginnen (aan)
embarkation 1 inscheping, inlading, het
aan boord gaan (brengen) **2** het beginnen
embarrass 1 in verlegenheid brengen **2** in
geldverlegenheid brengen, in financiële
moeilijkheden brengen
embarrassed opgelaten, in verlegenheid
gebracht
embarrassing pijnlijk; beschamend; gênant
embarrassment 1 verlegenheid, onbehagen[h] **2** (geld)verlegenheid, (geld)probleem[h]
embassy ambassade, diplomatieke vertegenwoordigers
embattled 1 (voortdurend) in moeilijkheden **2** omsingeld [by enemies]
embed 1 (vast)zetten, vastleggen: *the arrow
~ded itself in his leg* de pijl zette zich vast in
zijn been; *be ~ded in* vastzitten in **2** omsluiten, insluiten, omringen, omgeven **3** inbedden
embellish verfraaien, versieren: *~ a story*
een verhaal opsmukken
ember 1 gloeiend stukje[h] kool **2** (-s) gloeiende as, smeulend vuur[h]; [fig] laatste vonken; resten
embezzle verduisteren, achterhouden
embitter verbitteren, bitter(der) maken
emblem embleem[h], symbool[h]
emblematic symbolisch: *be ~ of* het symbool zijn van
embodiment belichaming
embody 1 vorm geven (aan), uitdrukken: *~
one's principles in actions* zijn principes tot uiting laten komen in daden **2** inlijven: *his
points of view were embodied in the article* zijn
standpunten waren verwerkt in het artikel
¹embrace (n) omhelzing, omarming
²embrace (vb) elkaar omhelzen, elkaar omarmen
³embrace (vb) **1** omhelzen, omarmen, omvatten **2** gebruikmaken van, aangrijpen: *~
an offer* gebruikmaken van een aanbod
embroider 1 borduren **2** opsmukken, verfraaien

embroil verwikkelen; betrekken: *~ o.s. in*
betrokken raken bij
embryo embryo[h]: *in ~* in de kiem (aanwezig), in wording, in de dop
emcee [inform] **1** ceremoniemeester; spelleider **2** [mus] hiphopartiest
em dash kastlijntje[h], lang gedachtestreep-
je[h]
emend corrigeren; verbeteringen aanbrengen [in text]
emendation correctie, verbetering
emerald 1 smaragd(groen) **2** smaragden,
van smaragd
emerge 1 verschijnen, tevoorschijn komen:
~ from (or: *out of*) tevoorschijn komen uit;
[econ] *emerging countries* opkomende landen **2** bovenkomen, opduiken **3** blijken, uitkomen: *after a long investigation it ~d that …*
een langdurig onderzoek heeft uitgewezen
dat …
emergence 1 het bovenkomen **2** het uitkomen **3** het optreden
emergency 1 onverwachte gebeurtenis,
onvoorzien voorval[h] **2** noodsituatie, noodtoestand, noodgeval[h]: *state of ~* noodtoestand; *~ exit* nooduitgang, nooddeur; *in case
of ~* in geval van nood
emergency room [Am] eerstehulp(afdeling)
emergency worker reddingswerker,
hulpverlener
emigrant emigrant(e)
emigrate emigreren, het land verlaten
eminence 1 heuvel, hoogte **2** eminentie
[also as title]; verhevenheid
eminent 1 uitstekend **2** hoog; verheven
[also lit]; aanzienlijk
emission afgifte, uitzending; afscheiding
[of body]; [science] emissie; uitstoot [of (poisonous) gases]
emit 1 uitstralen, uitzenden **2** afscheiden,
afgeven; uitstoten [(poisonous) gases]: *~ a
smell* stank afgeven
emoji [comp] emoji, emoticon[h]
¹emollient (n) verzachtend middel[h]
²emollient (adj) verzachtend, zachtmakend
e-money *electronic money* elektronisch
geld[h]; e-geld[h]
emoticon emoticon[+h]
emotion 1 (gevoels)aandoening, emotie,
gevoelen[h], ontroering: *mixed ~s* gemengde
gevoelens **2** het gevoel, de gevoelswereld
3 bewogenheid
emotional 1 emotioneel, gevoels-, ge-
moeds-: *~ intelligence* emotionele intelligentie **2** ontroerend
emotive roerend; gevoelig
empathy empathie
emperor keizer
emphasis 1 accent[h]; klemtoon [also fig]:
lay (or: *place, put*) *an ~ on sth.* het accent

leggen op iets **2** nadruk, klem, kracht
emphasize benadrukken, de nadruk leggen op
emphatic 1 nadrukkelijk **2** krachtig **3** duidelijk
empire (keizer)rijk^h; imperium^h [also fig]; wereldrijk^h
empirical gebaseerd op ervaring
¹employ (n) (loon)dienst: *in the ~ of* in dienst van
²employ (vb) **1** in dienst nemen, tewerkstellen **2** gebruiken, aanwenden **3** bezighouden: *be ~ed in* bezig zijn, zich bezighouden met
employable bruikbaar, inzetbaar
employee werknemer
employee participation medezeggenschap^{+h}
employer werkgever
employment 1 beroep^h, werk^h, baan **2** bezigheid **3** werkgelegenheid: *full ~* volledige werkgelegenheid **4** gebruik^h, het gebruiken
empower 1 machtigen **2** in staat stellen
empress keizerin
emptiness leegte
¹empty (n): *returned empties* geretourneerde lege flessen/kratten
²empty (adj) **1** leeg, ledig **2** nietszeggend, hol **3** onbewoond, leegstaand: [esp Am] *~ nest* [fig] leeg nest, kinderen het huis uit **4** leeghoofdig, oppervlakkig
³empty (vb) leeg raken, (zich) legen
⁴empty (vb) legen, leegmaken
emu emoe
enable 1 in staat stellen, (de) gelegenheid geven **2** mogelijk maken
enact 1 bepalen, vaststellen **2** tot wet verheffen
enamel 1 (email)lak^{+h}, glazuur^h, vernis^h **2** email^h, (tand)glazuur^h
enamour bekoren, charmeren: *~ed of* (or: *with*) dol, verliefd op
encampment kamp(ement)^h, legerplaats, veldverblijf^h
encapsulate 1 (zich) inkapselen **2** samenvatten
enchant 1 betoveren, beheksen **2** bekoren, verrukken: *be ~ ed by* (or: *with*) verrukt zijn over
encipher coderen
encircle omcirkelen, omsingelen, insluiten
encl *enclosed, enclosure* bijl., bijlage
enclose 1 omheinen, insluiten **2** insluiten; bijsluiten [enclosure etc]
enclosure 1 (om)heining, schutting **2** omheind stuk^h land **3** vak^h, afdeling **4** bijlage
encode coderen
encompass 1 omringen, omgeven **2** bevatten, omvatten
encore toegift, encore^h: *~!* bis!, nog eens!

¹encounter (n) **1** (onverwachte) ontmoeting **2** krachtmeting, confrontatie, treffen^h
²encounter (vb) **1** ontmoeten, (onverwacht) tegenkomen **2** ontmoeten, geconfronteerd worden met: *~ difficulties* moeilijkheden moeten overwinnen
encourage 1 bemoedigen, hoop geven **2** aanmoedigen, stimuleren, in de hand werken
encroach opdringen, oprukken: *the sea ~es further (up)on the land* de zee tast de kust steeds verder aan
encroachment overschrijding; aantasting, inbreuk
encrust 1 met een korst bedekken **2** bedekken, bezetten: *~ed with* precious stones bezet met edelstenen
encrypt coderen, in code weergeven; versleutelen [message, data]
encumber 1 beladen, (over)belasten: *~ed with parcels* met boodschappen beladen **2** hinderen, belemmeren: *~ o.s. with* financial responsibilities zich financiële verplichtingen op de hals halen
encumbrance [form] last; belemmering
encyclop(a)edia encyclopedie
¹end (n) **1** einde^h, afsluiting, besluit^h: *come* (or: *draw*) *to an ~* ten einde lopen, ophouden; *put an ~ to* een eind maken aan, afschaffen; *in the ~* ten slotte, op het laatst, uiteindelijk; *for weeks on ~* weken achtereen **2** einde^h, uiteinde^h: *~ to ~* in de lengte **3** einde^h, verste punt^h, grens; [also fig] uiterste^h **4** kant, onderkant, bovenkant, zijde; [also fig] afdeling; part^h: *place on ~* rechtop zetten **5** einde^h, vernietiging, dood **6** doel^h, bedoeling, (beoogd) resultaat^h: *the ~ justifies the means* het doel heiligt de middelen ‖ *at the ~ of the day* uiteindelijk, als puntje bij paaltje komt; *be at the ~ of one's tether* aan het eind van zijn krachten zijn; *make (both) ~s meet* de eindjes aan elkaar knopen; *that irritates me no ~* dat irriteert me heel erg
²end (vb) **1** eindigen, aflopen: *our efforts ~ed in a total failure* onze pogingen liepen op niets uit **2** ten einde vinden, sterven
³end (vb) **1** beëindigen, een eind maken aan, ophouden met **2** conclusie vormen van **3** vernietigen, een eind maken aan: *~ it (all)* er een eind aan maken, zelfmoord plegen
endanger in gevaar brengen, een gevaar vormen voor, bedreigen: *~ed species* bedreigde diersoorten
en dash half kastlijntje^h, kort gedachtestreepje^h
endear geliefd maken
endearment 1 uiting van genegenheid **2** innemendheid: *terms of ~* lieve woordjes
¹endeavour (n) poging, moeite, inspanning
²endeavour (vb) pogen, trachten, zich inspannen

endemic inheems; plaatsgebonden

ending 1 einde^h, beëindiging, afronding, eindspel^h **2** einde^h, slot^h, afloop: *happy ~* goede afloop

endive andijvie

endless 1 eindeloos **2** [inform] ontelbaar

endorse 1 bevestigen, bekrachtigen, beamen **2** aanprijzen, aanbevelen

endorsement 1 bevestiging; bekrachtiging **2** aantekening [eg on driving licence]

endow 1 begiftigen, subsidiëren, bekostigen **2** schenken, geven aan: *~ed with great musical talent* begiftigd met grote muzikaliteit

endowment 1 gave, begaafdheid, talent^h **2** gift **3** het schenken

endue begiftigen, schenken

endurance 1 uithoudingsvermogen^h, weerstand **2** duurzaamheid || *beyond* (or: *past*) *~* onverdraaglijk, niet uit te houden

endurance training duurtraining

^1**endure** (vb) **1** duren, blijven **2** het uithouden

^2**endure** (vb) **1** doorstaan, uithouden, verdragen **2** ondergaan, lijden

enduring blijvend, (voort)durend

enema klysma^h; lavement^h

enemy vijand, vijandelijke troepen: *the ~ were **thrown** back* de vijand werd teruggeslagen

energetic 1 energiek, vurig, actief **2** krachtig; sterk [protest etc]

energy kracht, energie: *nuclear ~* kernenergie

energy-smart energieslim

enervate ontkrachten, slap maken, verzwakken

enfeeble verzwakken, uitputten

enfold 1 wikkelen; hullen in **2** omsluiten: *~ in one's arms* in de armen sluiten

enforce 1 uitvoeren, op de naleving toezien van; de hand houden aan [rule, law] **2** (af)dwingen **3** versterken, benadrukken

enforcement 1 handhaving, uitvoering **2** dwang

^1**engage** (vb) **1** (+ in) zich bezighouden (met), zich inlaten (met), doen (aan) **2** zich verplichten, beloven, aangaan **3** [techn] in elkaar grijpen, gekoppeld worden **4** (+ with) [mil] de strijd aanbinden (met)

^2**engage** (vb) **1** aannemen, in dienst nemen, contracteren **2** bezetten; in beslag nemen [also fig]: *~ s.o. in conversation* een gesprek met iem. aanknopen **3** beloven, verplichten: *~ o.s. to do sth.* beloven iets te doen **4** [mil] aanvallen **5** [techn] koppelen, inschakelen

engaged 1 verloofd: *~ to* verloofd met **2** bezet, bezig, druk, gereserveerd: *I'm ~* ik heb een afspraak; *the telephone is ~* de telefoon is in gesprek **3** gecontracteerd

engagement 1 verloving **2** afspraak **3** belofte, verplichting: *~s* financiële verplichting **4** gevecht^h **5** contract^h

engaging innemend, aantrekkelijk

engender veroorzaken, voortbrengen

engine motor, machine, locomotief

^1**engineer** (n) **1** ingenieur **2** machinebouwer **3** genieofficier, geniesoldaat: *the (Royal) Engineers* de Genie **4** technicus, mecanicien; [shipp] werktuigkundige **5** [Am] (trein)machinist

^2**engineer** (vb) **1** bouwen, maken, construeren **2** bewerkstelligen, op touw zetten

engineering 1 techniek **2** bouw, constructie

England Engeland

^1**English** (n) Engels^h, de Engelse taal: *the ~* de Engelsen

^2**English** (adj) Engels, in het Engels: *~ **breakfast*** Engels ontbijt, ontbijt met spek en eieren

Englishman Engelsman

English-speaking Engelstalig

Englishwoman Engelse; Engelse vrouw

engrave graveren

engraving 1 gravure **2** graveerkunst

engross geheel in beslag nemen, overheersen: *I was so ~ed in my book that* ik was zo in mijn boek verdiept, dat

engulf overspoelen: *~ed by fear* door angst overmand; *~ed in the waves* door de golven verzwolgen

enhance verhogen, versterken, verbeteren

enhancement verhoging, versterking, verbetering

enhancer prestatieverhogend middel^h, stimulerend middel^h

enigma mysterie^h, raadsel^h

enjoy genieten van, plezier beleven aan: *Dick ~s a good health* Dick geniet een goede gezondheid || *~ o.s.* zich vermaken

enjoyable plezierig, prettig, fijn

enjoyment plezier^h; genot^h; genoegen^h

enkindle aansteken [fig]; doen oplaaien; opwekken [anger, passion]

^1**enlarge** (vb) **1** groeien, groter worden, zich uitbreiden **2** uitgebreid spreken, uitweiden: *~ **(up)on** a subject* uitweiden over een onderwerp **3** uitvergroot worden

^2**enlarge** (vb) vergroten, groter maken

enlighten onderrichten, onderwijzen

enlightened verlicht, rationeel, redelijk: *~ ideas* verlichte opvattingen

enlightenment opheldering, verduidelijking

Enlightenment (the) verlichting

^1**enlist** (vb) dienst nemen, vrijwillig in het leger gaan

^2**enlist** (vb) werven, mobiliseren, in dienst nemen: *~ s.o. in an enterprise* iem. bij een onderneming te hulp roepen

enmity vijandschap, haat(gevoel^h), onmin

enormity 1 gruweldaad, wandaad **2** gruwelijkheid, misdadigheid **3** enorme omvang; immense grootte [of problem etc]
enormous enorm, geweldig groot
¹enough (pron) genoeg, voldoende: *beer* ~ genoeg bier ‖ *be ~ of a man to* wel zo flink zijn om te
²enough (adv) **1** genoeg: ~ *said* genoeg daarover; *oddly* (or: *strangely*) ~ merkwaardig genoeg **2** zeer, heel: *I'm having ~ problems with my own children* ik heb al genoeg problemen met mijn eigen kinderen **3** tamelijk, redelijk: *she paints well* ~ ze schildert vrij behoorlijk
enquire see ¹*inquire*
enquiry see *inquiry*
enrage woedend maken, tot razernij brengen
enrapture verrukken; ~*d at* (or: *by*) in vervoering om, door
enrich 1 verrijken, rijk(er) maken, uitbreiden **2** verrijken, de kwaliteit verhogen: ~*ed uranium* verrijkt uranium
¹enrol (vb) zich inschrijven, zich opgeven
²enrol (vb) **1** inschrijven, opnemen **2** werven, aanwerven, in dienst nemen
ensemble 1 geheelʰ; totaalʰ **2** [theatre, mus] ensembleʰ; gezelschapʰ **3** [fashion] ensembleʰ
ensign 1 insigneʰ, embleemʰ **2** vlag, nationale vlag
enslave knechten, tot slaaf maken, onderwerpen
enslaved tot slaaf gemaakt: *an ~ person* een tot slaaf gemaakte, een slaafgemaakte
ensnare vangen, verstrikken; [also fig] in de val laten lopen
ensue 1 volgen: *the ensuing month* de volgende maand, de maand daarna **2** (+ from) voortvloeien (uit), voortkomen (uit)
ensure 1 veiligstellen, beschermen **2** garanderen, instaan voor: ~ *the safety of our guests* de veiligheid van onze gasten waarborgen **3** verzekeren van
entail met zich meebrengen, noodzakelijk maken, inhouden
entangle verwarren, onontwarbaar maken; [also fig] verstrikken; vast laten lopen
entanglement 1 complicatie, het verstrikt raken **2** gecompliceerde relatie; [esp] affaire **3** hindernis
¹enter (vb) **1** zich laten inschrijven, zich opgeven **2** [theatre] opkomen
²enter (vb) **1** gaan in/op/bij, zich begeven in, zijn intrede doen in: ~ *the Church* priester worden **2** inschrijven, bijschrijven, opschrijven, noteren, boeken, invoeren **3** opgeven, inschrijven **4** toelaten; binnenlaten [as member] **5** deelnemen aan; meedoen aan [competition, fight] **6** inzenden: ~ *sth. in the competition* iets inzenden voor de wedstrijd

³enter (vb) binnengaan; binnenlopen [of ship]; binnendringen
enter into 1 beginnen; aanknopen [conversation] **2** zich verplaatsen in, zich inleven in **3** deel uitmaken van, onderdeel vormen van **4** ingaan op, onder de loep nemen **5** aangaan; sluiten [contract, treaty]
enterprise 1 onderneming **2** firma, zaak **3** ondernemingsgeest, ondernemingszin: *we need a man of* ~ we hebben iem. met initiatief nodig
enterprising ondernemend
¹entertain (vb) **1** een feestje (etentje) geven, gasten hebben **2** vermaak bieden
²entertain (vb) **1** gastvrij ontvangen, aanbieden **2** onderhouden, amuseren **3** koesteren, erop nahouden: ~ *doubts* twijfels hebben **4** overdenken, in overweging nemen: ~ *a proposal* over een voorstel nadenken
entertainer iem. die het publiek vermaakt, zanger, conferencier, cabaretier, goochelaar
entertaining onderhoudend, vermakelijk, amusant
entertainment 1 iets dat amusement biedt, opvoering, uitvoering, show, conference **2** feestʰ, partij, feestmaalʰ **3** gastvrijheid, gastvrij onthaalʰ **4** vermaakʰ, plezierʰ, amusementʰ: *greatly* (or: *much*) *to our* ~ tot onze grote pret **5** amusementswereld(jeʰ), amusementsbedrijfʰ
enthralling betoverend, boeiend
enthrone op de troon zetten, kronen
¹enthuse (vb) (+ about, over) enthousiast spreken/zijn (over)
²enthuse (vb) enthousiast maken
enthusiasm 1 (+ about, for) enthousiasmeʰ (voor), geestdrift (voor/over), verrukking, vervoering **2** vurige interesse, passie
enthusiast 1 (+ about, for) enthousiasteling (in), fan (van), liefhebber (van) **2** dweper
enthusiastic enthousiast
entice (ver)lokken, verleiden
entire 1 compleet, volledig **2** geheel, totaal **3** gaaf, heel, onbeschadigd
entirely 1 helemaal, geheel (en al), volkomen **2** alleen, enkel, slechts
entirety totaliteit: *in its* ~ in zijn geheel
entitle 1 betitelen, noemen: *a novel* ~*d 'Enduring love'* een roman met als titel 'Enduring love' **2** recht geven op: *be* ~*d to compensation* recht hebben op schadevergoeding
entity bestaanʰ, wezenʰ, het zijn; [law] *legal* ~ rechtspersoon
entrails ingewanden, darmen
¹entrance (n) **1** ingang, toegang, entree **2** binnenkomst **3** opkomst [on stage] **4** entree, toelating; [by extension] toegangsgeldʰ: ~ *fee* toegangsgeldʰ; *no* ~ verboden toegang

²**entrance** (vb) in verrukking brengen, meeslepen

entreat smeken (om), bidden (om), dringend verzoeken

¹**entrench** (vb) **1** zich verschansen, zich ingraven **2** (+ on, upon) inbreuk maken (op)

²**entrench** (vb) stevig vastleggen; verankeren [right, habit etc]

entrenchment loopgravenstelselʰ; verschansing

entrepreneur 1 ondernemer **2** impresario [stage]

entrust toevertrouwen: ~ *sth.* **to** *s.o.*, ~ *s.o.* **with** *sth.* iem. iets toevertrouwen

entry 1 intrede, entree, toetreding, intocht, binnenkomst; [theatre] opkomst **2** toegang: *no* ~ verboden in te rijden **3** ingang, toegang, halʰ **4** notitie, inschrijving, boeking

entwine 1 ineenstrengelen **2** (zich) winden (om)

enumerate 1 opsommen **2** (op)tellen

enunciate (goed) articuleren, (duidelijk) uitspreken

envelop inwikkelen, inpakken; [fig] omhullen; omgeven: *a subject ~ed in mystery* een onderwerp omgeven met geheimzinnigheid

envelope 1 omhulling [also fig] **2** envelop: *padded* ~ luchtkussenenvelop

enviable benijdenswaardig, begerenswaardig

envious (+ of) jaloers (op), afgunstig

environment 1 omgeving **2** milieuʰ, omgeving

environmental milieu-; omgevings-: *the ~ effects of using coal* de gevolgen van het gebruik van steenkool voor het milieu

environmentalist 1 milieudeskundige, milieubeheerder **2** milieuactivist, milieubewust iem.

envisage voorzien; zich voorstellen [in future]

envoy (af)gezant, diplomatiek vertegenwoordiger

¹**envy** (n) afgunst: *he was filled with ~ at my new car* hij benijdde me mijn nieuwe wagen

²**envy** (vb) benijden

enzyme enzymʰ

ep [inform; media] *episode* aflevering

ephemeral kortstondig, voorbijgaand

¹**epic** (n) eposʰ, heldendichtʰ

²**epic** (adj) **1** episch, verhalend **2** heldhaftig **3** [inform] episch, enorm, geweldig: ~ *fail* totale mislukking; ~ *fail!* wat een sof **4** [inform] gaaf, vet

epidemic epidemie

epidermis opperhuid

epigraph epigraaf; opschriftʰ, inscriptie [esp on monument]

epilepsy epilepsie, vallende ziekte

¹**epileptic** (n) epilepticus

²**epileptic** (adj) epileptisch

epilogue 1 epiloog, slotrede **2** naschriftʰ, nawoordʰ

episcopal bisschoppelijk

episode episode, (belangrijke) gebeurtenis, voorvalʰ; aflevering [of serial]

epitaph grafschriftʰ

epithet 1 bijnaam **2** [Am] scheldwoordʰ

epitome belichaming; personificatie: *the ~ of* het toppunt van

epoch 1 keerpuntʰ, mijlpaal **2** tijdvakʰ, tijdperkʰ

epoch-making van grote betekenis; baanbrekend

EQ *Emotional Quotient* EQʰ *(emotionele-intelligentiequotiënt)*

equable gelijkmatig, gelijkmoedig

¹**equal** (n) gelijke, weerga

²**equal** (adj) **1** gelijk, overeenkomstig, hetzelfde: *on* ~ *terms* op voet van gelijkheid; ~ *to* gelijk aan **2** onpartijdig, eerlijk, rechtvaardig: ~ *opportunity* gelijke kansen **3** gelijkmatig, effen

³**equal** (vb) evenaren, gelijk zijn aan: *two and four ~s six* twee en vier is zes

equality gelijkheid, overeenkomst

¹**equalize** (vb) **1** gelijk worden **2** [sport] gelijkmaken

²**equalize** (vb) gelijkmaken, gelijkstellen

equally 1 eerlijk, evenzeer, gelijkmatig **2** in dezelfde mate

equanimity 1 gelijkmoedigheid **2** berusting

equate 1 (+ to, with) vergelijken (met) **2** (+ with) gelijkstellen (aan) **3** gelijkmaken, met elkaar in evenwicht brengen

equation vergelijking

equator evenaar, equator

equatorial 1 equatoriaal **2** tropisch

Equatorial Guinea Equatoriaal-Guinea

Equatorial Guinean Equatoriaal-Guineeër

equestrian ruiter

equilibrium evenwichtʰ

equip (+ with) uitrusten (met), toerusten (met)

equipment uitrusting, installatie, benodigdheden

equity 1 billijkheid, rechtvaardigheid **2** (equities) aandelen

¹**equivalent** (n) equivalentʰ

²**equivalent** (adj) (+ to) equivalent (aan), gelijkwaardig (aan)

equivocal 1 dubbelzinnig **2** twijfelachtig

equivocate 1 eromheen draaien, een ontwijkend antwoord geven **2** een slag om de arm houden

er eh [hesitation]

era era, tijdperkʰ, jaartelling, hoofdtijdperkʰ

eradicate met wortel en al uittrekken; [fig] uitroeien; verdelgen

erase uitvegen, uitwissen
eraser 1 stukje vlakgom, gummetje[h] **2** bordenwisser
e-read [comp] e-lezen
e-reader e-reader
¹erect (adj) recht, rechtop (gaand), opgericht
²erect (vb) **1** oprichten, bouwen, neerzetten **2** stichten, vestigen, instellen
erection 1 erectie **2** gebouw[h] **3** het oprichten, het bouwen, het optrekken **4** het instellen
ergonomic ergonomisch
Eritrea Eritrea
¹Eritrean (n) Eritreeër, Eritreese
²Eritrean (adj) Eritrees
ermine hermelijn
¹erode (vb) wegspoelen
²erode (vb) **1** (also + away) uitbijten [of acid] **2** (also + away) uithollen [of water]; afslijpen, eroderen
erogenous erogeen: ~ *zone* erogene zone
erosion erosie [also fig]
erotic erotisch
err 1 zich vergissen **2** afwijken: ~ *on the side of caution* het zekere voor het onzekere nemen **3** zondigen
errand 1 boodschap: *go on* (or: *run*) ~*s for s.o.* boodschappen doen voor iem. **2** doel[h] [of message]
errand-boy loopjongen
erratic 1 onregelmatig, ongeregeld, grillig **2** excentriek, onconventioneel **3** veranderlijk, wispelturig
error vergissing: ~ *of judgement* beoordelingsfout; *human* ~ menselijke fout; *be in* ~ zich vergissen
error message foutmelding
erudition [form] uitgebreide kennis; eruditie
erupt 1 uitbarsten [of volcano, geyser etc]; (vuur) spuwen, spuiten **2** barsten [also fig]; uitbreken
¹escalate (vb) stijgen [of prices, wages]; escaleren
²escalate (vb) verhevigen, doen escaleren
escalator roltrap
escapade 1 escapade **2** dolle streek, wild avontuur[h]
¹escape (n) ontsnapping, vlucht: *make one's* ~ ontsnappen
²escape (vb) **1** (+ from, out of) ontsnappen (uit/aan), ontvluchten: ~ *with* one's life het er levend afbrengen **2** naar buiten komen; ontsnappen [of gas, steam] **3** verdwijnen, vervagen, vergeten raken
³escape (vb) **1** vermijden, ontkomen aan: ~ *death* de dood ontlopen **2** ontschieten; (even) vergeten zijn [of name, etc] **3** ontgaan: ~ *one's attention* aan iemands aandacht ontsnappen **4** ontglippen, ontvallen
escape artist [roughly] boeienkoning

escape hatch 1 noodluik[h], nooddeur [in ship, plane] **2** uitvlucht
e-scooter e-step
¹escort (n) **1** escorte[+h], (gewapende) geleide[h] **2** begeleider, metgezel
²escort (vb) escorteren, begeleiden, uitgeleide doen
e-signature *electronic signature* elektronische (or: digitale) handtekening
esp *especially* i.h.b., in het bijzonder
especial speciaal, bijzonder
especially 1 speciaal: *bought* ~ *for you* speciaal voor jou gekocht **2** vooral, in het bijzonder, voornamelijk
espionage spionage
Esq *esquire* Dhr.
esquire de (Weledelgeboren) Heer
essay essay[h], opstel[h], (korte) verhandeling
essence 1 essentie, kern **2** wezen[h], geest: *he's the* ~ *of kindness* hij is de vriendelijkheid zelf
¹essential (n) **1** het essentiële, essentie, wezen[h] **2** essentieel punt[h], hoofdzaak **3** noodzakelijk iets, onontbeerlijke zaak: *the basic* ~*s* de allernoodzakelijkste dingen
²essential (adj) **1** (+ for, to) essentieel (voor), wezenlijk **2** (+ for, to) onmisbaar (voor), noodzakelijk (voor)
establish 1 vestigen [also fig]; oprichten, stichten: ~*ed custom* ingeburgerd gebruik; ~ *o.s.* zich vestigen **2** (vast) benoemen, aanstellen **3** vaststellen [facts]; bewijzen || ~*ed church* staatskerk
establishment vestiging, oprichting, instelling
Establishment (the) staatskerk
estate 1 landgoed[h], buiten(verblijf)[h] **2** (land)bezit[h], vastgoed[h] **3** woonwijk **4** stand, klasse **5** [law] boedel **6** plantage || *industrial* ~ industrieterrein[h], industriegebied[h], industriewijk
estate agent makelaar in onroerend goed
estate car stationcar
¹esteem (n) achting, respect[h], waardering: *hold s.o. in high* ~ iem. hoogachten
²esteem (vb) **1** (hoog)achten, waarderen, respecteren **2** beschouwen: ~ *sth. a duty* iets als een plicht zien
esthet- *see aesthet-*
estimable 1 achtenswaardig **2** schatbaar, taxeerbaar
¹estimate (n) **1** schatting: *at a rough* ~ ruwweg **2** (kosten)raming, begroting, prijsopgave **3** oordeel[h]
²estimate (vb) **1** schatten, berekenen: ~ *sth. at £100* iets op 100 pond schatten **2** beoordelen [pers]
estimation 1 (hoog)achting: *hold s.o. in* ~ iem. (hoog)achten **2** schatting, taxatie
Estonia Estland
¹Estonian (n) Est(lander); Estlandse

²Estonian (adj) Estlands

estrangement vervreemding, verwijdering

estuary (wijde) riviermond

et al *et alia, et alii* e.a.

etc *et cetera* enz., etc., enzovoort

etch etsen

eternal eeuwig [also inform]

eternity 1 eeuwigheid [also inform] **2** onsterfelijkheid, het eeuwige leven

ethereal 1 etherisch [also fig]; hemels **2** ijl **3** vluchtig: ~ *oil* etherische olie

ethical ethisch

ethics 1 ethiek, zedenleer **2** gedragsnormen, gedragscode

Ethiopia Ethiopië

¹Ethiopian (n) Ethiopiër, Ethiopische

²Ethiopian (adj) Ethiopisch

ethnic etnisch: ~ *minority* etnische minderheid

ethnicity 1 het behoren tot een bepaald ras of volk **2** volkstrots

ethos ethos^h

etiquette etiquette^h

EU *European Union* EU, Europese Unie

eucalyptus eucalyptus; gomboom

eulogy (+ of, on) lofprijzing (over)

euphemism eufemisme^h

euphony welluidendheid

euphoria euforie, gevoel^h van welbevinden, opgewektheid

euro euro

Europe 1 Europa **2** EU: *leave* ~ uit de EU treden

¹European (n) Europeaan

²European (adj) Europees: ~ *Union* Europese Unie, EU

euro symbol euroteken^h

euthanasia euthanasie

euthanize in laten slapen; euthanasie plegen op

EV 1 *electric vehicle* EV **2** *electronic vaporizer* e-sigaret

evacuate evacueren, ontruimen; [mil] terugtrekken uit

evacuation ontruiming, evacuatie

evade vermijden, (proberen te) ontkomen aan, ontwijken: ~ *one's responsibilities* zijn verantwoordelijkheden uit de weg gaan

evaluate 1 de waarde bepalen van, evalueren **2** berekenen

evaluation 1 waardebepaling, beoordeling, evaluatie **2** berekening

evangelical evangelisch

evangelist evangelist: *the four* ~s de vier evangelisten

evaporate verdampen, (doen) vervliegen; [fig] in het niets (doen) verdwijnen: *my hope has* ~d ik heb de hoop verloren

evasion ontwijking, uitvlucht: ~ *of taxes* belastingontduiking

evasive ontwijkend

eve 1 vooravond: *on the* ~ *of* aan de vooravond van; *on the* ~ *of the race* de dag voor de wedstrijd **2** avond

¹even (adj) **1** vlak, gelijk, glad **2** gelijkmatig, kalm, onveranderlijk: *an* ~ *temper* een evenwichtig humeur **3** even: ~ *and odd numbers* even en oneven getallen **4** gelijk, quitte: *get* ~ *with s.o.* 't iem. betaald zetten; *now we're* ~ *again* nu staan we weer quitte **5** eerlijk: *an* ~ *exchange* een eerlijke ruil

²even (vb) gelijk worden, glad worden

³even (vb) gelijk maken

⁴even (adv) **1** zelfs: ~ *now* zelfs nu; ~ *so* maar toch; ~ *if* (or: *though*) zelfs al **2** [before comparative] nog: *that's* ~ *better* dat is zelfs nog beter

even-handed onpartijdig

evening avond; [fig] einde^h: *good* ~! goedenavond!; *in* (or: *during*) *the* ~ 's avonds; *on Tuesday* ~ op dinsdagavond

even out (gelijkmatig) spreiden, gelijk verdelen, uitsmeren

evensong avonddienst

event 1 gebeurtenis, evenement^h, manifestatie: *the normal* (or: *usual*) *course of* ~s de gewone gang van zaken; *happy* ~ blijde gebeurtenis [birth] **2** geval^h: *at all* ~s in elk geval; *in the* ~ *of his death* in het geval dat hij komt te overlijden **3** uitkomst, afloop: *in the* ~, *he decided to withdraw from the race* uiteindelijk besloot hij zich uit de wedstrijd terug te trekken **4** [sport] nummer^h, onderdeel^h

eventful veelbewogen; rijk aan gebeurtenissen

eventual uiteindelijk

eventuality eventualiteit, mogelijke gebeurtenis

eventually ten slotte, uiteindelijk

even up gelijk worden, gelijkmaken, gelijkschakelen, evenwicht herstellen

ever 1 ooit: *faster than* ~ sneller dan ooit **2** toch, in 's hemelsnaam: *how* ~ *could I do that?* hoe zou ik dat in 's hemelsnaam kunnen? **3** echt, erg, verschrikkelijk, zo ... als het maar kan: *it is* ~ *so cold* het is verschrikkelijk koud **4** immer, altijd, voortdurend: *an ever-growing fear* een steeds groeiende angst; *they lived happily* ~ *after* daarna leefden ze nog lang en gelukkig; ~ *since* van toen af, sindsdien

¹evergreen (n) altijd jeugdig iem. (iets); onsterfelijke melodie [etc]; evergreen

²evergreen (adj) altijdgroen, groenblijvend; [fig] onsterfelijk; altijd jeugdig

everlasting 1 eeuwig(durend), eindeloos **2** onsterfelijk; [fig] onverwoestbaar

every 1 elk(e), ieder(e), alle: [inform] ~ *bit as good* in elk opzicht even goed; ~ *which way* in alle richtingen; ~ *(single) one of them is wrong* ze zijn stuk voor stuk verkeerd; *three*

*out of ~ **seven** drie op zeven; ~ **other** week om de andere week, eens in de twee weken* **2** alle, alle mogelijke: *she was given ~ **opportunity*** ze kreeg alle kansen || ~ ***now** and again* (or: *then*), *~ so **often*** (zo) nu en dan, af en toe
everybody iedereen: *~ **despises** her* iedereen kijkt op haar neer
everyday (alle)daags, gewoon, doordeweeks
everyone *see* everybody
everyplace [Am; inform] overal
everything 1 alles, alle dingen: *~ **but** a success* allesbehalve een succes, bepaald geen succes **2** (+ and) van alles, dergelijke, zo, dat (alles), nog van die dingen: *with exams, holidays **and** ~ she had plenty to think of* met examens, vakantie en zo had ze genoeg om over te denken
everywhere 1 overal **2** overal waar, waar ook: *~ he **looked** he saw decay* waar hij ook keek zag hij verval
evict uitzetten, verdrijven
eviction order bevel[h] tot uitzetting
evidence 1 aanduiding, spoor[h], teken[h]: *bear* (or: *show*) *~ of* sporen dragen van, getuigen van **2** bewijs[h], bewijsstuk[h], bewijsmateriaal[h]: *conclusive ~* afdoend bewijs; *on the ~ of* op grond van **3** getuigenis[+h], getuigenverklaring: *call s.o. **in** ~* iem. als getuige oproepen **4** duidelijkheid, zichtbaarheid, opvallendheid: *be **in** ~* zichtbaar zijn, opvallen
evident duidelijk, zichtbaar, klaarblijkelijk
[1]**evil** (n) **1** kwaad[h], onheil[h], ongeluk[h]: *choose the **least*** (or: *lesser*) *of two ~s* van twee kwaden het minste kiezen **2** kwaad[h], zonde: *speak ~ of* kwaadspreken over **3** kwaal
[2]**evil** (adj) **1** kwaad, slecht, boos: *put off the ~ **day*** (or: *hour*) iets onaangenaams op de lange baan schuiven **2** kwaad, zondig
evince tonen, aan de dag leggen
evocative (gevoelens) oproepend: *it is ~ **of** his earlier paintings* het doet denken aan zijn vroegere schilderijen
evoke oproepen, tevoorschijn roepen, (op)wekken
evolution evolutie, ontwikkeling, groei
evolutionary evolutie-
[1]**evolve** (vb) **1** zich ontwikkelen, zich ontvouwen, geleidelijk ontstaan **2** een ontwikkeling doormaken; transformeren
[2]**evolve** (vb) ontwikkelen, afleiden, uitdenken
e-wallet digitale portemonnee; betaalapp
e-waste e-afval[+h], e-schroot[h]
ewe ooi, wijfjesschaap[h]
ex ex, ex-man, ex-vrouw, ex-verloofde
[1]**exact** (adj) **1** nauwkeurig, accuraat **2** exact, precies: *the ~ **time*** de juiste tijd
[2]**exact** (vb) **1** vorderen [money, payment]; afdwingen, afpersen **2** eisen, vereisen
exacting veeleisend

exactly precies, helemaal, juist, nauwkeurig: *not ~* eigenlijk niet; [iron] niet bepaald
exaggerate 1 overdrijven, aandikken **2** versterken
exaggeration overdrijving
exalt 1 verheffen, verhogen, adelen **2** loven, prijzen **3** in vervoering brengen
exam *examination* examen[h]
examination 1 examen[h]: *sit for* (or: *take*) *an ~* examen doen **2** onderzoek[h], inspectie, analyse: *a **medical** ~* een medisch onderzoek; *on closer ~* bij nader onderzoek; *under ~* nog in onderzoek
examine 1 onderzoeken, onder de loep nemen, nagaan **2** examineren: *~ s.o. **in*** (or: *on*) iem. examineren in
examiner 1 examinator **2** inspecteur
example voorbeeld[h]: *give* (or: *set*) *a good ~* een goed voorbeeld geven; *make an ~ of s.o.* een voorbeeld stellen; *for ~* bijvoorbeeld
exasperate 1 erger maken **2** boos maken, ergeren
exasperation ergernis, ergerlijkheid, kwaadheid
excavate 1 uitgraven, blootleggen, delven **2** uithollen
exceed 1 overschrijden **2** overtreffen, te boven gaan: *they ~ed us in number* zij overtroffen ons in aantal
exceedingly buitengewoon, bijzonder
[1]**excel** (vb) uitblinken, knap zijn
[2]**excel** (vb) overtreffen, uitsteken boven
excellence 1 voortreffelijkheid, uitmuntendheid **2** uitmuntende eigenschap
Excellency excellentie: *His* (or: *Her*) *~* Zijne (or: Hare) Excellentie
excellent uitstekend, voortreffelijk
[1]**except** (vb) uitzonderen, uitsluiten, buiten beschouwing laten
[2]**except** (prep) behalve, uitgezonderd, tenzij, op ... na: *~ **for** Sheila* behalve Sheila
[3]**except** (conj) ware het niet dat, maar, echter, alleen: *I'd buy that ring for you, ~ I've got no money* ik zou die ring best voor je willen kopen, alleen heb ik geen geld
exception uitzondering, uitsluiting: *with the ~ of* met uitzondering van; *an ~ to the rule* een uitzondering op de regel || *take ~ to* bezwaar maken tegen, aanstoot nemen aan
exceptionable 1 verwerpelijk **2** aanvechtbaar
exceptional uitzonderlijk, buitengewoon
excerpt 1 uittreksel[h] **2** stukje[h], fragment[h], passage
[1]**excess** (n) **1** overmaat, overdaad: *in* (or: *to*) *~* overmatig **2** exces[h], buitensporigheid, uitspatting **3** overschot[h], surplus[h], rest **4** eigen risico[h] [of insurance] || *in ~ of* meer dan, boven; *drink to ~* (veel te) veel drinken
[2]**excess** (adj) **1** bovenmatig, buitenmatig **2** extra-: *~ **baggage*** (or: *luggage*) over-

vracht, overgewicht[h]; ~ *postage* strafport[+h]
exc<u>e</u>ssive 1 buitensporig **2** overdadig, overmatig
¹exch<u>a</u>nge (n) **1** ruil, (uit)wisseling, woordenwisseling, gedachtewisseling **2** beurs, beursgebouw[h] **3** telefooncentrale **4** het (om)ruilen, het (uit)wisselen: *in* ~ *for* in ruil voor **5** het wisselen [of money]
²exch<u>a</u>nge (vb) **1** ruilen, uitwisselen, verwisselen: ~ *words* with een woordenwisseling hebben met **2** wisselen, inwisselen
exch<u>e</u>quer schatkist, staatskas
Exch<u>e</u>quer (the) ministerie[h] van Financiën
¹exc<u>i</u>se (n) accijns
²exc<u>i</u>se (vb) uitsnijden, wegnemen
exc<u>i</u>te 1 opwekken, uitlokken, oproepen **2** opwinden: *do not get ~d about it!* wind je er niet over op! **3** prikkelen; stimuleren [also sexually]
exc<u>i</u>ted opgewonden, geprikkeld
exc<u>i</u>tement 1 opwindende gebeurtenis, sensatie **2** opwinding, opschudding, drukte
exc<u>i</u>ting 1 opwindend; spannend **2** stimulerend
exclam<u>a</u>tion 1 uitroep, schreeuw, kreet: ~ *mark* uitroepteken[h] **2** geroep[h], geschreeuw[h], luidruchtig commentaar[h]
excl<u>u</u>de uitsluiten, weren, uitzonderen, verwerpen
excl<u>u</u>ding exclusief; niet inbegrepen
excl<u>u</u>sion uitsluiting, uitzetting, verwerping, uitzondering: *to the* ~ *of* met uitsluiting van
excl<u>u</u>sive exclusief: *mutually* ~ *duties* onverenigbare functies; ~ *rights* alleenrecht[h], monopolie[h]; ~ *of* exclusief, niet inbegrepen
excl<u>u</u>sively uitsluitend, enkel, alleen
excomm<u>u</u>nicate excommuniceren; in de ban doen
excrement uitwerpsel[h], uitwerpselen, ontlasting
excr<u>u</u>ciating tenenkrommend, vreselijk: *it was ~ly funny* het was om je ziek te lachen
exc<u>u</u>rsion 1 excursie, uitstapje[h], pleziertochtje[h] **2** uitweiding: *the teacher made a brief* ~ *into politics* de leraar hield een korte uitweiding over politiek
¹exc<u>u</u>se (n) **1** excuus[h], verontschuldiging: *make one's* (or: *s.o.'s*) ~*s* zich excuseren (voor afwezigheid) **2** uitvlucht, voorwendsel[h]
²exc<u>u</u>se (vb) **1** excuseren, verontschuldigen, vergeven: ~ *my being* late neem me niet kwalijk dat ik te laat ben; ~ *me, can you tell me …?* pardon, kunt u me zeggen …?; ~ *me!* sorry!, pardon! excuseer! ha ha ~d laten weggaan, niet langer ophouden || *may I be ~d?* mag ik van tafel af?, mag ik even naar buiten? [to go to the toilet]; ~ *o.s.* zich excuseren [also for absence]
execute 1 uitvoeren [sentence]; afwikkelen [testament] **2** executeren, terechtstellen

exec<u>u</u>tion 1 executie, terechtstelling **2** uitvoering; volbrenging [of sentence]; afwikkeling [of testament] **3** spel[h], (muzikale) voordracht, vertolking
exec<u>u</u>tioner beul
¹ex<u>e</u>cutive (n) **1** leidinggevend persoon, hoofd[h], directeur **2** uitvoerend orgaan[h], administratie, dagelijks bestuur[h]
²ex<u>e</u>cutive (adj) **1** leidinggevend: ~ *director* lid van de raad van bestuur, directeur [who is member of the Board of Directors]; *chief* ~ *officer* algemeen directeur **2** uitvoerend [also pol]
ex<u>e</u>cutor executeur(-testamentair)
ex<u>e</u>mplary voorbeeldig [of behaviour etc]
exemplific<u>a</u>tion 1 voorbeeld[h], illustratie **2** toelichting
ex<u>e</u>mplify toelichten; illustreren [with an example]
¹ex<u>e</u>mpt (adj) vrij(gesteld), ontheven
²ex<u>e</u>mpt (vb) (+ from) vrijstellen (van), ontheffen, excuseren
¹<u>e</u>xercise (n) **1** (uit)oefening, gebruik[h], toepassing **2** lichaamsoefening, training **3** (-s) militaire oefeningen, manoeuvres
²<u>e</u>xercise (vb) **1** (zich) oefenen, lichaamsoefeningen doen, trainen, fitnessen **2** (uit)oefenen, gebruiken, toepassen: ~ *patience* geduld oefenen; ~ *power* macht uitoefenen **3** uitoefenen, waarnemen; bekleden [office, position] **4** [mil] laten exerceren, drillen
<u>e</u>xercise bike hometrainer
<u>e</u>xercise book schoolschrift[h]
ex<u>e</u>rt uitoefenen, aanwenden, doen gelden: ~ *pressure* pressie uitoefenen; ~ *o.s.* zich inspannen
ex<u>e</u>rtion 1 (zware) inspanning **2** uitoefening, aanwending: *the* ~ *of power* de uitoefening van macht
exhal<u>a</u>tion 1 uitblazing, uitademing **2** uitwaseming, verdamping, uitlaatgas[h]
exh<u>a</u>le uitademen
¹exh<u>a</u>ust (n) **1** uitlaat, uitlaatbuis, uitlaatpijp **2** afzuigapparaat[h] **3** uitlaatstoffen, uitlaatgassen
²exh<u>a</u>ust (vb) **1** opgebruiken, opmaken **2** uitputten, afmatten; [fig] uitputtend behandelen: ~ *a subject* een onderwerp uitputten; *feel ~ed* zich uitgeput voelen
exh<u>a</u>ust fume uitlaatgas[h]
exh<u>a</u>ustion 1 het opgebruiken **2** uitputting
¹exh<u>i</u>bit (n) **1** geëxposeerd stuk[h] **2** geëxposeerde collectie **3** [law] officieel bewijsstuk: ~ *A* eerste/belangrijkste bewijsstuk **4** [Am] tentoonstelling
²exh<u>i</u>bit (vb) **1** tentoonstellen, uitstallen **2** vertonen, tonen, blijk geven van
exhib<u>i</u>tion 1 tentoonstelling, expositie **2** vertoning || *make an* ~ *of o.s.* zich belachelijk aanstellen

exhilarate 1 opwekken, opvrolijken **2** versterken, stimuleren

exhilarating 1 opwekkend, opbeurend **2** versterkend, stimulerend

exhort aanmanen, oproepen

exhume opgraven; [fig] aan het licht brengen

exile 1 balling, banneling **2** ballingschap: *send into* ~ in ballingschap zenden

exist 1 bestaan, zijn, voorkomen, gebeuren **2** (over)leven, bestaan, voortbestaan: *how can they* ~ *in these conditions?* hoe kunnen zij in deze omstandigheden overleven?

existence 1 bestaanswijze, levenswijze **2** het bestaan, het zijn: *come into* ~ ontstaan

existent 1 bestaand **2** levend, in leven **3** huidig, actueel

existential existentieel; bestaans-

¹exit (n) **1** uitgang **2** afslag; uitrit [of motorway] **3** vertrek[h]: *make one's* ~ van het toneel verdwijnen, weggaan

²exit (vb) afgaan; van het toneel verdwijnen [also fig]

³exit (vb) **1** verlaten, vertrekken uit **2** [comp] afsluiten, verlaten: ~ *the program* het programma afsluiten

exonerate 1 zuiveren, vrijspreken: ~ *s.o. from* all *blame* iem. van alle blaam zuiveren **2** vrijstellen, ontlasten

exorbitant buitensporig, overdreven

exorcism uitdrijving, (geesten)bezwering

exotic exotisch, uitheems, vreemd

expand 1 opengaan, (zich) ontplooien, spreiden **2** (doen) uitzetten, (op)zwellen, (in omvang) doen toenemen **3** (zich) uitbreiden, (zich) ontwikkelen, uitgroeien: *she owns a rapidly ~ing chain of fast-food restaurants* zij bezit een snelgroeiende keten van fastfoodrestaurants **4** uitwerken, uitschrijven || ~ *on sth.* over iets uitweiden

expansion uitbreiding, uitgezet deel[h], vergroting: *sudden industrial* ~ plotselinge industriële groei

expansion card uitbreidingskaart

expat [inform] *expatriate* expat

expatriate *see expat*

expect 1 verwachten, wachten op, voorzien: *I did not* ~ *this* ik had dit niet verwacht **2** rekenen op, verlangen: ~ *too much of s.o.* te veel van iem. verlangen **3** [inform] aannemen, vermoeden: *I* ~ *you're coming too* jij komt zeker ook? || *be ~ing (a baby)* in (blijde) verwachting zijn

expectancy verwachting, afwachting

expectant 1 verwachtend, (af)wachtend, vol vertrouwen: ~ *crowds* menigte vol verwachting **2** toekomstige: ~ *mother* aanstaande moeder

expectation verwachting, afwachting, (voor)uitzicht[h]; vooruitzichten [of inheritance, money]: ~ *of life* vermoedelijke levensduur; *against* (or: *contrary to*) *(all)* ~*(s)* tegen alle verwachting in

expedient geschikt, passend

expedite 1 bevorderen, bespoedigen **2** (snel) afhandelen, afwerken

expedition expeditie, onderzoekingstocht; [by extension] plezierreis; excursie

expeditious snel, prompt

expel 1 verdrijven, verjagen **2** wegzenden, wegsturen, deporteren: ~ *from school* van school sturen

expend 1 besteden, uitgeven, spenderen **2** (op)gebruiken, verbruiken, uitputten

expenditure uitgave(n), kosten, verbruik[h]

expense 1 uitgave, uitgavenpost **2** kosten, uitgave(n), prijs; [fig] moeite; opoffering: *at the* ~ *of* op kosten van; [fig] ten koste van **3** (-s) onkosten: *travelling ~s* reiskosten **4** onkostenvergoeding || *spare no* ~ geen kosten sparen

expensive duur, kostbaar

¹experience (n) ervaring, belevenis, ondervinding, praktijk: *a humbling* ~ een lesje in nederigheid

²experience (vb) ervaren, beleven, ondervinden: ~ *difficulties* op moeilijkheden stoten

experienced ervaren, geschikt, geroutineerd

¹experiment (n) experiment[h], proef(neming), test

²experiment (vb) experimenteren, proeven nemen

experimental 1 experimenteel: ~ *stage* proefstadium[h] **2** empirisch

experimentation proefneming

¹expert (n) expert, deskundige

²expert (adj) ervaren, deskundig, bekwaam: ~ *job* a) vakkundig uitgevoerde klus; b) werkje voor een expert

expertise bekwaamheid; deskundigheid, (vak)kennis

expiration 1 uitademing **2** vervaltijd, expiratie **3** dood

expire 1 verlopen, verstrijken, aflopen, vervallen: *your ticket* ~*s* je kaart wordt ongeldig **2** [form] sterven

expiry einde[h], verval[h], vervaldag, afloop: ~ *date* vervaldatum

explain (nader) verklaren, uitleggen, uiteenzetten, toelichten, verantwoorden, rechtvaardigen: ~ *one's conduct* zijn gedrag verantwoorden; ~ *away* wegredeneren, goedpraten

explanation verklaring, uitleg, toelichting

explanatory verklarend; verhelderend

expletive krachtterm, vloek, verwensing

explicable verklaarbaar

explicit expliciet, duidelijk, uitvoerig, uitgesproken, uitdrukkelijk

¹explode (vb) **1** exploderen, ontploffen,

(uiteen)barsten **2** uitbarsten, uitvallen: ~ *with laughter* in lachen uitbarsten

²**explode** (vb) **1** tot ontploffing brengen, opblazen **2** ontzenuwen, verwerpen: ~*d ideas* achterhaalde ideeën

¹**exploit** (n) (helden)daad, prestatie, wapenfeitʰ

²**exploit** (vb) **1** benutten, gebruikmaken van **2** uitbuiten: ~ *poor children* arme kinderen uitbuiten

exploitation 1 exploitatie, gebruikʰ, ontginning **2** uitbuiting, misbruikʰ

exploration onderzoekʰ, studie

explore 1 een onderzoek instellen **2** onderzoeken, bestuderen: ~ *all possibilities* alle mogelijkheden onderzoeken **3** verkennen

explorer ontdekkingsreiziger, onderzoeker

explosion 1 explosie, ontploffing, uitbarsting **2** uitbarsting, losbarsting, uitval: ~ *of anger* uitval van woede

¹**explosive** (n) explosiefʰ, ontplofbare stof, springstof

²**explosive** (adj) **1** explosief, (gemakkelijk) ontploffend: ~ *population* **increase** enorme bevolkingsgroei **2** opvliegend, driftig

exponent 1 exponent; vertegenwoordiger, verdediger **2** uitvoerder **3** [maths] exponent

¹**export** (n) **1** export, uitvoer(handel) **2** exportartikelʰ

²**export** (vb) exporteren, uitvoeren

expose 1 blootstellen, blootgeven, introduceren **2** tentoonstellen, uitstallen, (ver)tonen: ~ *the goods* de waren uitstallen **3** onthullen, ontmaskeren, bekendmaken **4** [photo] belichten

exposé onthulling; ontmaskering

exposed blootgesteld, onbeschut, kwetsbaar: ~ *pipes* slecht geïsoleerde leidingen; *be* ~ *to* blootstaan aan

exposure 1 blootstelling [to weather, danger, light]: *he died from* (or: *of*) ~ *to the cold* hij stierf door (blootstelling aan) de kou **2** bekendmaking, uiteenzetting, onthulling: *the* ~ *of his* **crimes** de onthulling van zijn misdaden **3** [photo] belichting

expound uiteenzetten

¹**express** (n) sneltrein, snelbus, exprestrein

²**express** (adj) **1** uitdrukkelijk, duidelijk (kenbaar gemaakt), nadrukkelijk: *it was his* ~ *wish it should be done* het was zijn uitdrukkelijke wens dat het gedaan werd **2** snel(gaand), expres-, ijl-: *an* ~ *train* een sneltrein

³**express** (vb) uitdrukken, laten zien, betuigen: *he* ~*ed his* **concern** hij toonde zijn bezorgdheid

⁴**express** (adv) **1** met grote snelheid, met spoed **2** per expresse, met snelpost **3** speciaal

expression 1 uitdrukking, zegswijze

2 (gelaats)uitdrukking, blik **3** [maths] (hoeveelheids)uitdrukking, symboolʰ, symbolen-(verzameling) **4** het uitdrukken: *that's* **beyond** (or: *past*) ~ daar zijn geen woorden voor **5** expressie, uitdrukkingskracht

expressive expressief, betekenisvol, veelzeggend: *this poem is* ~ *of great sorrow* dit gedicht drukt groot verdriet uit

expressway [Am] snelweg

expulsion verdrijving, verbanning, uitwijzing

exquisite 1 uitstekend, prachtig, voortreffelijk **2** fijn, subtiel

extemporize improviseren

¹**extend** (vb) zich uitstrekken [of land, time]; voortduren ‖ ~*ed* **family** (hele) familie

²**extend** (vb) **1** (uitt)rekken, langer (groter) maken, uitbreiden: *an* ~*ing* **ladder** schuifladder **2** uitstrekken, uitsteken, aanreiken **3** (aan)bieden, verlenen, betuigen, bewijzen: ~ *a warm* **welcome** *to s.o.* iem. hartelijk welkom heten

extension 1 aanvulling, verlenging, toevoeging: [comp] *file* ~ extensie **2** (extra) toestel(nummer)ʰ: *ask for* ~ *212* vraag om toestel 212 **3** extension; haarverlenging **4** uitstelʰ, langer tijdvakʰ **5** uitbreiding, vergroting, verlenging: *the* ~ *of a* **contract** de verlenging van een contract

extensive uitgestrekt, groot, uitgebreid: *an* ~ **library** een veelomvattende bibliotheek

extent 1 omvang, grootte, uitgestrektheid: *the full* ~ *of his* **knowledge** de volle omvang van zijn kennis **2** mate, graad, hoogte: *to a certain* ~ tot op zekere hoogte; *to a great* (or: *large*) ~ in belangrijke mate, grotendeels; *to what* ~ in hoeverre

extenuate verzachten, afzwakken: *extenuating* **circumstances** verzachtende omstandigheden

¹**exterior** (n) buitenkant, oppervlakte, uiterlijkʰ: *do not judge people by their* ~*s* beoordeel mensen niet op hun uiterlijk

²**exterior** (adj) buiten-, aan buitenkant

exterminate uitroeien, verdelgen

external 1 uiterlijk, extern **2** (voor) uitwendig (gebruik) ‖ ~ **examination** (or: **examiner**) examen (or: examinator) van buiten de school

extinct 1 uitgestorven **2** niet meer bestaand, afgeschaft **3** uitgedoofd; (uit)geblust [also fig]; dood: *an* ~ **volcano** een uitgedoofde vulkaan

extinction 1 ondergang, uitroeiing: *be threatened by* (or: *with*) *complete* ~ bedreigd worden door totale uitroeiing **2** het doven

extinguish 1 doven, (uit)blussen **2** vernietigen, beëindigen

extinguisher 1 (brand)blusapparaatʰ, brandblusser **2** domper, kaarsendover

extol hoog prijzen, ophemelen, verheerlijken: ~ *s.o.'s talents to the skies* iemands talent hemelhoog prijzen

extort afpersen: ~ *a confession* **from** *s.o.* iem. een bekentenis afdwingen

extortion afpersing; afzetterij

¹**extra** (n) **1** niet (in de prijs) inbegrepen zaak, bijkomend tarief[h] **2** figurant, dummy

²**extra** (adj) extra, bijkomend ‖ ~ *buses for football-supporters* speciaal ingezette bussen voor voetbalsupporters; [sport] ~ *time* verlenging

³**extra** (adv) **1** extra, buitengewoon, bijzonder (veel): ~ *good quality* speciale kwaliteit **2** buiten het gewone tarief: *pay* ~ *for postage* bijbetalen voor portokosten

¹**extract** (n) **1** passage, fragment[h], uittreksel[h] **2** extract[h], aftreksel[h], afkooksel[h]

²**extract** (vb) **1** (uit)trekken, (uit)halen, verwijderen; [fig] afpersen; weten te ontlokken: ~ *a* **confession** een bekentenis afdwingen **2** (uit)halen [minerals etc]; onttrekken, winnen

extraction 1 het winnen [of minerals etc] **2** afkomst, oorsprong: *Americans of Polish and Irish* ~ Amerikanen van Poolse en Ierse afkomst

extracurricular buitenschools

extradite 1 uitleveren [criminal] **2** uitgeleverd krijgen

extramarital buitenechtelijk

extraneous 1 van buitenaf, buiten-, extern **2** onbelangrijk

extraordinary 1 extra: *an* ~ *session* een extra zitting **2** buitengewoon, bijzonder

extraterrestrial buitenaards

extravagant 1 buitensporig, mateloos **2** verkwistend, verspillend: *she is rather* ~ zij smijt met geld

¹**extreme** (n) uiterste[h], extreme[h]: *go from one* ~ *to the other* van het ene uiterste in het andere (ver)vallen; *in the* ~ uitermate, uiterst

²**extreme** (adj) **1** extreem, buitengewoon **2** uiterst, verst **3** grootst, hoogst: ~ *danger* het grootste gevaar

extremely uitermate, uiterst, buitengewoon

extremism extremisme[h]

extremity 1 uiteinde[h] **2** [always singular] uiterste[h] **3** lidmaat[+h]: *the* **upper** *and* **lower** *extremities* armen en benen **4** (extremities) handen en voeten **5** uiterste nood

extricate halen uit, bevrijden, losmaken: ~ *o.s. from difficulties* zich uit de nesten redden

exuberant 1 uitbundig, vol enthousiasme, geestdriftig **2** overdadig, overvloedig: ~ *growth* weelderige groei

exude 1 (zich) afscheiden, afgeven: ~ *sweat* zweet afscheiden **2** (uit)stralen, duidelijk tonen: ~ *happiness* geluk uitstralen

exultation uitgelatenheid, verrukking

¹**eye** (n) **1** oog[h]: ~*s* gezichtsvermogen[h]; blik; kijk; *as* **far** *as the* ~ *can see* zo ver het oog reikt; *catch s.o.'s* ~ iemands aandacht trekken; *close* (or: *shut*) *one's* ~*s to* oogluikend toestaan; *cry* (or: *weep*) *one's* ~*s out* tranen met tuiten huilen; *have an* ~ *for* kijk hebben op; *keep an* ~ *on* in de gaten houden; *keep your* ~*s open* let goed op!; *there is more to it* (or: *in it*) *than meets the* ~ er zit meer achter (dan je zo zou zeggen); *open s.o.'s* ~*s (to)* iem. de ogen openen (voor); *set* (or: *lay*) ~*s on* onder ogen krijgen; *under* (or: *before*) *his very* ~*s* vlak voor (or: onder) zijn ogen; *with an* ~ **to** met het oog op; *all* ~*s* een en al aandacht **2** oog[h]; opening [of needle]; oog[h]; ringetje[h] [for fastener] **3** centrum[h], oog[h]; middelpunt[h] [of storm] **4** [bot] kiem, oog[h] ‖ *do s.o. in the* ~ iem. een kool stoven; *make* ~*s at s.o.* lonken naar iem.; *see* ~ *to* ~ *(with s.o.)* het eens zijn (met iem.); *with one's* ~*s* **shut** met het grootste gemak; [inform] *that was* **one** *in the* ~ *for him* dat was een hele klap voor hem

²**eye** (vb) bekijken, aankijken, kijken naar

eyeball oogappel, oogbal, oogbol: [inform] ~ **to** ~ (vlak) tegenover elkaar

eyebrow wenkbrauw: *raise an* ~ (or: *one's*) ~*s* de wenkbrauwen optrekken; *(be)* **up to** *one's* ~*s (in work)* tot over de oren (in het werk zitten)

eye-catching opvallend

eyeful 1 goede blik: *get* (or: *have*) *an* ~ *(of)* een goede blik kunnen werpen (op) **2** lust voor het oog: *Deborah is quite an* ~ Deborah ziet er heel erg goed uit

eyelash wimper, ooghaartje[h]

eyelet oogje[h]

eye-opener openbaring, verrassing: *it was an* ~ *to him* daar keek hij van op

eyesight gezicht(svermogen)[h]

eyesore ontsiering: *be a* **real** ~ vreselijk lelijk zijn

eyewash [inform] onzin; larie

eyewitness ooggetuige

eyrie 1 roofvogelnest[h] **2** arendsnest[h] [fig]

f

FA *Football Association*

f<u>a</u>ble 1 fabel, mythe, legende **2** verzinsel^h, verzinsels, fabeltje^h, praatje^h

f<u>a</u>bric 1 stof, materiaal^h, weefsel^h **2** bouw, constructie

f<u>a</u>bricate 1 bouwen, vervaardigen, fabriceren **2** verzinnen, uit de duim zuigen

fabric<u>a</u>tion 1 fabricage **2** verzinsel^h

f<u>a</u>bric softener wasverzachter

f<u>a</u>bulous 1 legendarisch, verzonnen **2** fantastisch

faç<u>a</u>de gevel, front^h, voorzijde: [fig] *a ~ of friendliness* een façade van vriendelijkheid

¹f<u>a</u>ce (n) **1** gezicht^h, gelaat^h: *look s.o. in the ~* iem. recht aankijken [also fig]; *meet s.o. ~ to ~* iem. onder ogen komen; *show one's ~* zijn gezicht laten zien; *in (the) ~ of* ondanks, tegenover **2** (gezichts)uitdrukking: *fall on one's ~* (plat) op zijn gezicht vallen; [also fig] zijn neus stoten **3** aanzien^h, reputatie, goede naam: *lose ~* zijn gezicht verliezen, afgaan; *save (one's) ~* zijn gezicht redden **4** (belangrijkste) zijde, oppervlak^h; bodem [earth]; gevel, voorzijde; wijzerplaat [clock]; kant; wand [mountain] || *fly in the ~ of sth.* tegen iets in gaan; *on the ~ of it* op het eerste gezicht

²f<u>a</u>ce (vb) uitzien, het gezicht (de voorkant) toekeren, uitzicht hebben

³f<u>a</u>ce (vb) **1** onder ogen zien, (moedig) tegemoet treden: *let's ~ it,* ... laten we wel wezen, ... **2** confronteren: *Joe was ~d with many difficulties* Joe werd met vele moeilijkheden geconfronteerd **3** staan tegenover, uitzien op: *the picture facing the title page* de illustratie tegenover het titelblad || *~ s.o. down* iem. overbluffen

f<u>a</u>ce cloth washandje^h

f<u>a</u>celess gezichtsloos, grauw; anoniem [of crowd] || *~ transactions* internettransacties

f<u>a</u>ce-lift facelift [also fig]; opknapbeurt

f<u>a</u>ce-plant [inform] op zijn gezicht vallen

f<u>a</u>cer 1 klap in het gezicht **2** onverwachte moeilijkheid, kink in de kabel, probleem^h

¹f<u>a</u>ce time (n) [Am] persoonlijke ontmoeting: *who does not want ~ with the President?* wie wil de president nou niet persoonlijk ontmoeten?

²f<u>a</u>ce time (vb) [esp Am] [media] videobellen, skypen

fac<u>e</u>tious (ongepast) geestig; schertsend; spottend

face v<u>a</u>lue 1 nominale waarde **2** ogen-schijnlijke betekenis, eerste indruk: *take sth. at (its) ~* **a)** iets kritiekloos accepteren; **b)** iets accepteren zonder er verder op in te gaan

¹f<u>a</u>cial (n) [cosmetics] gezichtsbehandeling

²f<u>a</u>cial (adj) gezichts-

fac<u>i</u>le [oft depr] **1** oppervlakkig, luchtig **2** makkelijk, vlot **3** vlot, vaardig; vloeiend [style (of writing)]

fac<u>i</u>litate vergemakkelijken, verlichten: *to ~ matters* om de zaken te vereenvoudigen; voor het gemak, gemakshalve

fac<u>i</u>lities voorzieningen, faciliteiten

fac<u>i</u>lity 1 voorziening, gelegenheid: *research facilities* onderzoeksfaciliteiten **2** vaardigheid, handigheid, talent^h **3** simpelheid; gemakkelijkheid [of task, piece of music]

f<u>a</u>cing 1 bekleding [eg on wall, metal] **2** [fashion] beleg^h

fact 1 feit^h, waarheid, zekerheid: *the ~s of life* de bloemetjes en de bijtjes; *know for a ~* zeker weten **2** werkelijkheid, realiteit: *in ~* in feite || *in ~* bovendien, zelfs, en niet te vergeten

f<u>a</u>ct-finding: *he's on a ~ mission* hij is op onderzoeksreis om feitenmateriaal te verzamelen; hij is op inspectiereis

f<u>a</u>ct-free feitenvrij: *~ politics* beleid dat niet op feiten is gebaseerd

f<u>a</u>ction 1 (pressie)groep **2** partijruzie, interne onenigheid

f<u>a</u>ctoid weetje^h, feitje^h

f<u>a</u>ctor 1 factor, omstandigheid **2** agent, vertegenwoordiger, zaakgelastigde

f<u>a</u>ctory fabriek, werkplaats

f<u>a</u>ctory farming bio-industrie

f<u>a</u>ctual feitelijk, werkelijk

f<u>a</u>culty 1 (geest)vermogen^h, functie, zin, zintuig^h: *faculties* verstandelijke vermogens; *the ~ of hearing* (or: *speech*) de gehoorzin, het spraakvermogen **2** (leden van) faculteit, wetenschappelijk personeel^h, staf: *the Faculty of Law* de Juridische Faculteit

fad bevlieging, rage, gril

¹fade (vb) langzaam verdwijnen, afnemen; verflauwen [of enthusiasm]; vervagen [of colours, memories]; verbleken; verschieten [of colours]; verwelken [of flowers]: [film] *~ in* (in)faden, invloeien

²fade (vb) doen verdwijnen, laten wegsterven, laten vervagen: *~ in* (or: *up*) **a)** [radio] het volume (geleidelijk) laten opkomen; **b)** [film] (in)faden, invloeien [of image]

fade aw<u>a</u>y (geleidelijk) verdwijnen; afnemen [of forces]; vervagen [of colours]; wegsterven [of sound]

fade <u>ou</u>t 1 [radio] langzaam (doen) wegsterven; wegdraaien [sound] **2** [film] geleidelijk (doen) vervagen; langzaam uitfaden [of image]

f<u>ae</u>ces [form] fecaliën; ontlasting

fag 1 saai werk^h **2** [Am; inform] homo **3** [inform] peuk, sigaret
fagged (out) [inform] afgepeigerd, kapot
faggot 1 takkenbos, bundel (aanmaak)houtjes **2** bal gehakt **3** vervelend mens^h, (oude) zak **4** [Am; offensive] flikker, homo
¹fail (n) onvoldoende ‖ *without* ~ zonder mankeren
²fail (vb) **1** tekortschieten, ontbreken, het begeven: *words ~ed me* ik kon geen woorden vinden **2** afnemen, opraken, verzwakken **3** zakken, een onvoldoende halen **4** mislukken, het niet halen, het laten afweten **5** failliet gaan
³fail (vb) **1** nalaten, niet in staat zijn, er niet in slagen: *I ~ to see* your point ik begrijp niet wat u bedoelt **2** in de steek laten, teleurstellen **3** zakken voor; niet halen [exam] **4** laten zakken, als onvoldoende beoordelen
¹failing (n) tekortkoming; zwakheid [in character]; fout [in construction]
²failing (prep) bij gebrek aan
failure 1 het falen, het zakken, afgang: *power* ~ stroomstoring, stroomuitval **2** mislukking, fiasco^h, mislukkeling **3** nalatigheid, verzuim^h, onvermogen^h **4** het uitblijven; mislukking [of crop] **5** storing, ontregeling
¹faint (n) flauwte, onmacht: *to fall down in a* ~ flauwvallen
²faint (adj) **1** flauw, leeg, wee: ~ *with* hunger flauw van de honger **2** halfgemeend, zwak: *damn with* ~ *praise* het graf in prijzen **3** laf **4** nauwelijks waarneembaar, vaag; onduidelijk [sound] **5** gering, vaag; zwak [idea, hope]: *I haven't the ~est idea* ik heb geen flauw idee
³faint (vb) flauwvallen
faint-hearted laf; angstig
¹fair (n) **1** markt, bazaar **2** beurs, (jaar)markt, tentoonstelling **3** kermis
²fair (adj) **1** eerlijk, redelijk, geoorloofd: *get a* ~ *hearing* een eerlijk proces krijgen; *by* ~ *means or foul* met alle middelen; ~ *play* fair play, eerlijk spel; [inform] ~ *enough!* dat is niet onredelijk!, oké! **2** behoorlijk, bevredigend, redelijk **3** mooi [weather]; helder [sky] **4** gunstig, veelbelovend: [shipp] ~ *wind* gunstige wind **5** blank, licht(gekleurd); blond [hair, skin] ‖ *the* ~ *sex* het schone geslacht
³fair (adv) **1** eerlijk, rechtvaardig: *play* ~ eerlijk spelen, integer zijn; *to win* ~ *and square* overtuigend winnen; *to be* ~, … aan de andere kant, …, het is eigenlijk wel zo dat … **2** precies, pal, net: ~ *and square* a) precies; b) rechtuit, open(hartig)
fairground kermisterrein^h
fairly 1 eerlijk, billijk **2** volkomen, helemaal: *I was* ~ *stunned* ik stond compleet paf **3** tamelijk, redelijk
fair-minded rechtvaardig, eerlijk

fairness 1 eerlijkheid **2** lichte kleur [of hair, skin]
fair-trade eerlijke handel tussen rijke en arme landen: ~ *agreement* prijsbinding(sovereenkomst)
fairy 1 (tover)fee, elf(je^h) **2** [depr] homo, nicht
fairy cake klein rond, vaak versierd cupcakeje^h
fairyland sprookjeswereld, sprookjesland^h
fairy tale 1 sprookje^h **2** verzinsel^h
faith 1 geloof^h, geloofsovertuiging, vertrouwen^h: *in one's* ~ *on, put one's* ~ *in* vertrouwen stellen in **2** (ere)woord^h, gelofte **3** trouw, oprechtheid: *act in good* ~ te goeder trouw handelen
faithful 1 gelovig, godsdienstig **2** trouw, loyaal **3** getrouw [replica] **4** betrouwbaar [worker]
faithfully 1 trouw **2** met de hand op het hart ‖ *yours* ~ hoogachtend
faith healer gebedsgenezer
faithless 1 ontrouw **2** onbetrouwbaar, vals
¹fake (n) **1** vervalsing, kopie **2** oplichter, bedrieger
²fake (adj) namaak-, vals; vervalst [jewel, painting]
³fake (vb) **1** voorwenden; doen alsof [illness, surprise]: *a ~d robbery* een in scène gezette overval **2** namaken; vervalsen [painting, signature]
fake news nepnieuws^h
falcon valk
¹fall (n) **1** val, smak, het vallen; [fig] ondergang; verderf^h: *the Fall (of man)* de zondeval **2** afname, daling; verval^h [of river]; het zakken [of prices, temperature] **3** (-s) waterval **4** [Am] herfst, najaar^h
²fall (vb) **1** vallen, omvallen; invallen [nightfall]; afnemen; dalen [of prices, barometer, voice]; aflopen; afhellen [of land]: ~ *to pieces* in stukken vallen [also fig]; *the wind fell* de wind nam af, de wind ging liggen; ~ *apart* uiteenvallen; [inform] instorten; *sth. to* ~ *back on* iets om op terug te vallen; ~ *over* omvallen; [inform] ~ *over backwards* zich uitsloven, zich in allerlei bochten wringen; ~ *through* mislukken **2** ten onder gaan, vallen, sneuvelen; ingenomen worden [of town, fortress]; zijn (hoge) positie verliezen: ~ *from power* de macht verliezen **3** betrekken [of face] **4** terechtkomen, neerkomen; [fig] ten deel vallen: *it fell to me to put the question* het was aan mij de vraag te stellen **5** raken: ~ *behind with* achteropraken met ‖ *Easter always ~s on a Sunday* Pasen valt altijd op zondag; ~ *asleep* in slaap vallen; ~ *flat* niet inslaan, mislukken; ~ *short (of)* tekortschieten (voor), niet voldoen (aan)
³fall (vb) worden: ~ *ill* ziek worden; ~ *silent*

farm

stil worden

fallacy 1 denkfout, drogreden **2** vergissing

fall down 1 (neer)vallen, instorten, ten val komen **2** [inform] mislukken, tekortschieten: ~ *on* sth. (or: *the job*) er niets van bakken

fallen 1 gevallen **2** zondig: ~ *angel* (or: *woman*) gevallen engel (or: vrouw) **3** gesneuveld

fall guy [Am; inform] **1** slachtoffer[h] **2** zondebok

fall in 1 instorten, invallen **2** [mil] aantreden, zich in het gelid opstellen

falling-out [inform] ruzie

fall out 1 (+ with) ruzie maken (met) **2** gebeuren, terechtkomen, uitkomen

fall-out 1 radioactieve neerslag **2** het uitvallen, het ophouden

fallow braak, onbewerkt: *lie* ~ braak liggen [also fig]

fallow deer damhert[h]

fall to 1 de verantwoordelijkheid zijn van **2** [form] beginnen met

false 1 onjuist, fout, verkeerd: ~ *pride* ongerechtvaardigde trots; *true* or ~? waar of onwaar? **2** onecht, kunstmatig: ~ *teeth* kunstgebit[h]; *a* ~ *beard* een valse baard **3** bedrieglijk, onbetrouwbaar: ~ *alarm* loos alarm; ~ *bottom* dubbele bodem; *under* ~ *pretences* onder valse voorwendsels

falsehood onwaarheid; leugen

falsify 1 vervalsen, falsificeren **2** verkeerd voorstellen [event] **3** weerleggen [prophecy]

falter 1 wankelen, waggelen **2** aarzelen, weifelen **3** stotteren, stamelen: *Vic's voice* ~*ed* Vics stem beefde

fame 1 roem, bekendheid **2** (goede) naam, reputatie: *of ill* ~ berucht

familiar 1 vertrouwd, bekend, gewoon: *doesn't that look* ~ *to* you? komt dat je niet bekend voor? **2** (+ with) op de hoogte (van), bekend (met) **3** informeel, ongedwongen **4** vrijpostig

familiarity 1 vertrouwdheid, bekendheid: ~ *breeds contempt* wat vertrouwd is wordt gemakkelijk doodgewoon **2** ongedwongenheid **3** vrijpostigheid, vrijheid

familiarize bekendmaken; vertrouwd maken: ~ *o.s. with* zich eigen maken

family 1 (huis)gezin[h], kinderen, gezinsleden **2** familie(leden), geslacht[h]: *run in the* ~ in de familie zitten **3** afkomst, afstamming, familie

family doctor huisarts

family name achternaam

family room 1 huiskamer, woonkamer **2** [tourism] familiekamer

famine 1 hongersnood **2** tekort[h], schaarste, gebrek[h]

famish (laten) verhongeren, uitgehongerd zijn: *the men were* ~*ed* de mannen waren uitgehongerd

famous (+ for) beroemd (om), (wel)bekend

[1]fan (n) **1** waaier **2** ventilator, fan **3** bewonderaar(ster), enthousiast, fan

[2]fan (vb) **1** (toe)waaien; blazen [air]; toewuiven [cool] **2** aanblazen; aanwakkeren [also fig]: ~ *the flames* het vuur aanwakkeren, olie op het vuur gooien

fanatic fanatiekeling(e)

fanaticism fanatisme[h]

fanbase fans

fanciful 1 fantasievol; rijk aan fantasie [style, writer] **2** denkbeeldig, verzonnen, ingebeeld

[1]fancy (n) **1** fantasie, verbeelding(skracht), inbeelding **2** voorkeur, voorliefde, zin: *a passing* ~ een bevlieging **3** veronderstelling, idee[h], fantasie

[2]fancy (adj) **1** versierd, decoratief, elegant: ~ *cakes* taartjes; ~ *dress* kostuum[h]; ~ *goods* fantasiegoed[h], snuisterijen **2** grillig; buitensporig [prices] **3** verzonnen, denkbeeldig

[3]fancy (vb) **1** zich voorstellen, zich indenken **2** vermoeden, geloven: ~ *that!* stel je voor!, niet te geloven! **3** leuk vinden, zin hebben in: ~ *a girl* op een meisje vallen; ~ *some peanuts?* wil je wat pinda's?; ~ *o.s.* een hoge dunk van zichzelf hebben

fancy woman [inform] minnares

fang hoektand; snijtand [of dog or wolf]; giftand [of snake]; slagtand

fantasize fantaseren

fantastic 1 grillig, bizar **2** denkbeeldig **3** enorm, fantastisch, geweldig

fantasy 1 verbeelding, fantasie **2** illusie, fantasie

FAQ *frequently asked questions* vraagbaak; veelgestelde vragen

[1]far (adj) ver, (ver)afgelegen: *at the* ~ *end of the room* aan het andere eind van de kamer

[2]far (adv) **1** ver: ~ *and near* overal; *so* ~ (tot) zó ver, in zoverre; ~ *from easy* verre van makkelijk; *in so* ~ *as*, *as* ~ *as* voor zover; *as* ~ *as I can see* volgens mij **2** lang; ver: *so* ~ tot nu toe; *so* ~ *so good* tot nu toe is alles nog goed gegaan **3** veel, verreweg: ~ *too easy* veel te makkelijk

faraway 1 (ver)afgelegen, ver **2** afwezig, dromerig; ver [of look]

farce 1 klucht **2** schijnvertoning, zinloos gedoe[h]

[1]fare (n) **1** vervoerprijs, ritprijs, vervoerkosten, tarief[h]; [roughly] kaartje[h] **2** kost, voedsel[h], voer[h]: *simple* ~ eenvoudige kost

[2]fare (vb) (ver)gaan || *how did you* ~? hoe is het gegaan?; ~ *well* succes hebben, het goed maken

fare dodger [inform] zwartrijder

[1]farewell (n) afscheid[h], vaarwel[h]

[2]farewell (int) vaarwel, adieu, tot ziens

far-fetched vergezocht

[1]farm (n) boerderij, landbouwbedrijf[h]

²**farm** (vb) boer zijn, boeren, een boerderij hebben

³**farm** (vb) bewerken, bebouwen; cultiveren [land] ‖ ~ **out a)** uitbesteden [work, child]; **b)** overdragen, afschuiven [responsibility]

farmer boer, landbouwer, agrariër

farmers' market [roughly] boerderijwinkel, [roughly] markt met producten van de boerderij

farm-hand boerenknecht, landarbeider

farmhouse boerenhoeve; boerderij

farming het boerenbedrijf

farmstead boerenhoeve

far-off ver(afgelegen), ver weg, lang geleden

far-out 1 afgelegen, ver weg **2** [inform] uitzonderlijk, uitheems; bizar [of clothes, ideas] **3** [inform] fantastisch

far-reaching verstrekkend; verreikend

far-sighted 1 vooruitziend **2** verziend

¹**fart** (n) [vulg] **1** scheet, wind **2** lul, klootzak

²**fart** (vb) [vulg] een scheet laten ‖ ~ **about** (or: *around*) klooien, rotzooien

¹**farther** (adj) verder (weg)

²**farther** (adv) verder, door, vooruit

farthest verst (weg)

farthing [hist] een vierde penny; [roughly] duit [also fig]

fascinate boeien, fascineren

fascination 1 aantrekkingskracht, charme, bekoring **2** geboeidheid

Fascism fascisme[h]

fascist fascist

¹**fashion** (n) **1** gebruik[h], mode, gewoonte: *set a* ~ de toon aangeven; *come into* ~ in de mode raken **2** manier, stijl, trant: *did he change the nappies? yes, after a* ~ heeft hij de baby verschoond? ja, op zijn manier

²**fashion** (vb) vormen, modelleren, maken

fashionable modieus, in (de mode), populair

¹**fast** (n) vasten(tijd)

²**fast** (adj) **1** vast, stevig, hecht: ~ **colours** wasechte kleuren **2** snel, vlug; gevoelig [film]: ~ **food** gemaksvoedsel[h]; ~ **lane** linker rijbaan, inhaalstrook **3** vóór [of clock] ‖ [inform] *make a* ~ **buck** snel geld verdienen; [inform] *pull a* ~ **one on s.o.** met iem. een vuile streek uithalen, iem. afzetten

³**fast** (vb) vasten

⁴**fast** (adv) **1** stevig, vast: ~ **asleep** in diepe slaap; *play* ~ **and loose (with)** het niet zo nauw nemen (met), spelen (met) [s.o.'s feelings] **2** snel, vlug, hard

fasten vastmaken, bevestigen, dichtmaken: ~ **up** one's coat zijn jas dichtdoen

fastener (rits)sluiting; haakje[h] [of dress]

fastening sluiting, slot[h]; bevestiging [of window, door]

fastidious veeleisend, pietluttig, kieskeurig

fast-track snel; snel promotie makend

¹**fat** (n) vet[h], bakvet[h], lichaamsvet[h] ‖ *the* ~ *is in the fire* de poppen zijn aan het dansen; *chew the* ~ kletsen

²**fat** (adj) **1** dik, vet(gemest), weldoorvoed **2** vettig, zwaar; vet [of meat, food] **3** rijk; vruchtbaar [of land]; vet [of clay] **4** groot, dik, lijvig: [iron] *a* ~ *lot* of good that'll do you daar schiet je geen moer mee op, nou, daar heb je veel aan ‖ [inform] *a* ~ *cat* **a)** rijke pief; **b)** (stille) financier, geldschieter [pol]

fatal 1 (+ to) noodlottig (voor), dodelijk; fataal [of illness, accident] **2** rampzalig [of decision]

fatality 1 slachtoffer[h], dodelijk ongeluk[h]: *there were no fatalities* er zijn geen slachtoffers gevallen **2** noodlottigheid

fatally: *see fatal*; ~ *injured* dodelijk gewond; *she tried,* ~, *to cross the river* haar poging de rivier over te steken werd haar noodlottig

fate lot[h], noodlot[h], bestemming: *as sure as* ~ daar kun je donder op zeggen

fateful noodlottig, rampzalig, belangrijk

fatfree vetarm, vetvrij

fathead sufferd

¹**father** (n) **1** vader, huisvader **2** grondlegger, stichter

²**father** (vb) **1** vader zijn van, voor **2** produceren; de geestelijke vader zijn van [eg of plan, book]

Father pater, priester: ~ *Christmas* de Kerstman

fatherhood vaderschap[h]

father-in-law schoonvader

fatherly vaderlijk

fathom vadem; vaam

¹**fatigue** (n) **1** vermoeidheid; moeheid [also of metals] **2** [mil] corvee

²**fatigue** (vb) afmatten, vermoeien

fatigues 1 [mil] gevechtstenue[h] **2** strafcorvee[h]

fat-shaming [inform] het bekritiseren of belachelijk maken van een dik iem.

fatten dik(ker) maken: ~ **up** (vet)mesten

¹**fatty** (n) [inform] vetzak, dikke(rd)

²**fatty** (adj) vettig, vet(houdend): *(un)saturated* ~ *acids* (on)verzadigde vetzuren

fatuous dom, dwaas, stompzinnig

faucet [Am] kraan

¹**fault** (n) **1** fout, defect[h], gebrek[h] **2** overtreding, misstap **3** foute service; fout [tennis] **4** schuld, oorzaak: *at* ~ schuldig **5** [geology] breuk, verschuiving

²**fault** (vb) aanmerkingen maken op, bekritiseren

fault-finding muggenzifterij

faulty 1 defect, onklaar **2** onjuist, verkeerd, gebrekkig

fauna fauna; dierenwereld

¹**fave** (n) [inform] favoriet: *those are her ~s*

dat zijn haar favorieten, daar is ze het gekst op

²**fave** (adj) [inform] favoriet, lievelings-: *he is my ~ football player* hij is mijn favoriete voetballer

¹**favour** (n) **1** genegenheid, sympathie, goedkeuring: *be in* (or: *out of*) *~ with* in de gunst (or: uit de gratie) zijn bij **2** partijdigheid, voorkeur, voortrekkerij **3** gunst, attentie, begunstiging: *do s.o. a ~* iem. een plezier doen ‖ *do me a ~!* zeg, doe me een lol!

²**favour** (vb) **1** gunstig gezind zijn, positief staan tegenover, een voorstander zijn van **2** begunstigen, prefereren, bevoorrechten

favourable 1 welwillend, goedgunstig: *the weather is ~ to us* het weer zit ons mee **2** gunstig, veelbelovend, positief

¹**favourite** (n) **1** favoriet(e) **2** lieveling(e)

²**favourite** (adj) favoriet, lievelings-

favouritism voortrekkerij, vriendjespolitiek

fawn kwispelstaarten ‖ [fig] *~ (up)on* vleien, kruipen voor

¹**fax** (n) **1** fax(apparaat ʰ) **2** fax(bericht ʰ)

²**fax** (vb) faxen, per fax verzenden

faze van streek maken, in de war doen geraken

F-bomb: [Am; inform] *drop the ~* het woord 'fuck' gebruiken

¹**fear** (n) **1** vrees, angst(gevoel ʰ): *in ~ and trembling* met angst en beven; *go in ~ of* bang zijn voor; [inform] *no ~* beslist niet, geen sprake van

²**fear** (vb) **1** vrezen, bang zijn voor **2** vermoeden, een voorgevoel hebben van, vrezen: *~ the worst* het ergste vrezen

fearful 1 vreselijk, afschuwelijk, ontzettend **2** bang, angstig

fearsome afschrikwekkend, ontzaglijk

feasible 1 uitvoerbaar, haalbaar, doenlijk **2** aannemelijk, waarschijnlijk, geloofwaardig

¹**feast** (n) **1** feest ʰ **2** feestmaal ʰ, banket ʰ

²**feast** (vb) feesten, feestvieren

³**feast** (vb) onthalen; trakteren [also fig]: *~ one's eyes (on)* zich verlustigen in de aanblik (van)

feat 1 heldendaad **2** prestatie, knap stuk werk ʰ

feather veer; pluim ‖ *a ~ in one's cap* iets om trots op te zijn, een eer

featherbrained onnozel

featherweight vedergewicht ⁺ʰ

¹**feature** (n) **1** (gelaats)trek: *~s* gezicht ʰ **2** (hoofd)kenmerk ʰ, hoofdtrek **3** hoogtepunt ʰ, specialiteit, hoofdnummer ʰ **4** speciaal onderwerp ʰ; [newspaper] hoofdartikel ʰ

²**feature** (vb) een (belangrijke) plaats innemen, opvallen

feature film speelfilm, hoofdfilm

featureless kleurloos; saai, onopvallend

February februari

feckless lamlendig, futloos

fecundity 1 vruchtbaarheid **2** productiviteit

federal 1 federaal; bonds- **2** [esp Am] nationaal; regerings-: *~ government* centrale regering; landsregering

Federal 1 federaal, bonds- **2** [Am] nationaal, lands-, regerings-

federation 1 federatie, statenbond **2** bond, federatie, overkoepelend orgaan ʰ

fed up [inform] zat, beu, ontevreden: *be ~ with sth.* van iets balen, het zat (or: beu) zijn

fee 1 honorarium ʰ [eg of doctor, lawyer] **2** inschrijfgeld ʰ, lidmaatschapsgeld ʰ **3** (-s) schoolgeld ʰ, collegegeld ʰ

feeble 1 zwak, teer; krachteloos [of creatures] **2** flauw, slap; zwak [eg of excuse, joke]: *a ~ effort* een halfhartige poging

feeble-minded 1 zwakzinnig, zwak begaafd **2** dom

¹**feed** (n) **1** voeding [of animal, baby]; voedering **2** (vee)voer ʰ, groenvoer ʰ

²**feed** (vb) eten; zich voeden; grazen, weiden: *~ on* leven van, zich voeden met [also fig]

³**feed** (vb) **1** voeren, (te) eten geven, voederen: *~ up* vetmesten, volstoppen **2** voedsel geven aan; [fig] stimuleren [imagination] **3** [esp technology] aanvoeren [raw materials]; toevoeren: *~ coins into the pay phone* munten in de telefoon stoppen

feedback terugkoppeling, antwoord ʰ, reactie, feedback

feeder 1 eter: *this fish is a night ~* deze vis eet (or: jaagt) 's nachts **2** toevoer **3** zijtak, zijrivier, aanvoerweg **4** zuigfles

¹**feel** (n) **1** het voelen, betasting **2** gevoel ʰ, feeling **3** routine: *get the ~ of sth.* iets in zijn vingers krijgen

²**feel** (vb) **1** (rond)tasten, (rond)zoeken **2** voelen **3** gevoelens hebben, een mening hebben

³**feel** (vb) **1** voelen, gewaarworden **2** voelen (aan), betasten: *~ s.o.'s pulse* iem. de pols voelen [also fig]; *~ one's way* op de tast gaan [also fig] **3** voelen, gewaarworden: *~ the effects of* lijden onder de gevolgen van **4** voelen, aanvoelen, de indruk krijgen: *I ~ it necessary to deny that* ik vind het nodig dat te ontkennen **5** vinden, menen: *it was felt that … men was de mening toegedaan dat …*

⁴**feel** (vb) **1** zich voelen: *I felt such a fool* ik voelde me zo stom; *~ cold* (or: *warm*) het koud (or: warm) hebben; *~ small* zich klein voelen; *I ~ like sleeping* ik heb zin om te slapen; *I ~ like a walk* ik heb zin in een wandelingetje; *I don't ~ like going out tonight* ik heb geen zin om vanavond uit te gaan **2** aanvoelen, een gevoel geven, voelen

feeler tastorgaan ʰ, voelhoorn, voelspriet;

[fig] proefballonnetjes: *put* (or: *throw*) *out ~s* een balletje opgooien

feel-good positief; een goed gevoel gevend

feeling 1 gevoel^h, gewaarwording: *a sinking ~* een benauwd gevoel **2** emotie, gevoel^h: *~s* gevoelens; *hurt* s.o.'s *~s* iem. kwetsen; *mixed ~s* gemengde gevoelens **3** idee^h, gevoel^h, indruk **4** aanleg, gevoel^h: *a ~ for colour* een gevoel voor kleur **5** opinie, mening, geloof^h **6** opwinding, ontstemming, wrok: *~s ran high* de gemoederen raakten verhit **7** gevoel^h: *have lost all ~ in one's fingers* alle gevoel in zijn vingers kwijt zijn

feign veinzen, simuleren: *~ed* **indifference** gespeelde onverschilligheid

felicitous [form] welgekozen; gelukkig

felicity geluk^h, gelukzaligheid || *express* o.s. *with ~* zijn woorden goed weten te kiezen

feline 1 katachtig **2** katten-

fell omhakken, kappen: [fig] *he ~ed his opponent at a blow* hij velde zijn tegenstander met één klap

¹**fellow** (n) **1** kerel, vent **2** maat, kameraad **3** wederhelft; andere helft [of pair]: *a sock and its ~* een sok en de bijbehorende (sok) **4** lid^h van universiteitsbestuur

²**fellow** (adj) mede-, collega, -genoot: *~ inmate* medegevangene

fellowship 1 genootschap^h **2** broederschap, verbond^h **3** omgang, gezelschap^h **4** vriendschap, kameraadschap(pelijkheid): *~ in misfortune* vriendschap in tegenspoed **5** [educ] beurs, toelage

felony (ernstig) misdrijf^h, zware misdaad

felt vilt^h: *~ pen* viltstift

felt-tip pen viltstift

fem *feminine* vrl., vrouwelijk

¹**female** (n) **1** vrouwelijk persoon, vrouw **2** wijfje^h, vrouwtje^h **3** vrouwspersoon^h

²**female** (adj) vrouwelijk, wijfjes-: *the ~ honey badger* het wijfje van de honingdas || *~ suffrage* vrouwenkiesrecht^h

¹**feminine** (n) de vrouwelijke vorm; vrouwelijk^h

²**feminine** (adj) vrouwen-, vrouwelijk

feminism feminisme^h

feminist feministe

fen moeras(land)^h

¹**fence** (n) **1** hek^h, omheining, afscheiding: [fig] *be* (or: *sit*) *on the ~* geen partij kiezen, geen keuze (kunnen) maken; [fig] *get off the ~* partij kiezen, een standpunt innemen **2** heler

²**fence** (vb) [sport] schermen

³**fence** (vb) omheinen: *~ in* a) afrasteren; b) [fig] inperken

fend: *~ off* afweren [blow]; ontwijken [question]; *~ for* o.s. voor zichzelf zorgen

fender 1 stootrand, stootkussen^h; [Am] bumper **2** [Am] spatbord^h **3** haardscherm^h

fennel venkel

feral wild

¹**ferment** (n) **1** gist(middel^h) **2** onrust, opwinding

²**ferment** (vb) **1** (ver)gisten, (doen) fermenteren **2** in beroering zijn (brengen); onrustig zijn (maken)

fern varen

ferocious woest, ruw, wild, meedogenloos

ferocity woestheid, ruwheid, gewelddadigheid

¹**ferret** (n) fret^h

²**ferret** (vb) rommelen, snuffelen: *~ about* (or: *around*) *among* s.o.'s *papers* in iemands papieren rondsnuffelen || *~ out* uitvissen, uitzoeken

Ferris wheel reuzenrad^h

¹**ferry** (n) **1** veer^h, veerboot, pont **2** veerdienst; veer^h

²**ferry** (vb) **1** overzetten, overvaren **2** vervoeren: *~ children to and from a party* kinderen naar een feestje brengen en ophalen

ferryboat veerboot

fertile 1 vruchtbaar **2** rijk (voorzien), overvloedig: *~ imagination* rijke verbeelding

fertility vruchtbaarheid

fertilize 1 bevruchten, insemineren **2** vruchtbaar maken, bemesten

fertilizer (kunst)mest

fervent vurig, hartstochtelijk, fervent

fervour heftigheid, hartstocht, vurigheid

fester 1 zweren, etteren **2** knagen; irriteren [remark etc]

festival 1 feest^h, feestelijkheid **2** muziekfeest^h, festival^h

festive feestelijk: *the ~ season* de feestdagen

festivity feestelijkheid, festiviteit

festoon met slingers versieren

fetch 1 halen, brengen, afhalen **2** tevoorschijn brengen; trekken [audience, tears] **3** opbrengen [money]: *the painting ~ed £100* het schilderij ging voor 100 pond weg

fetching leuk, aantrekkelijk, aardig

fete feest^h, festijn^h

fetish fetisj

fetter keten, boei, ketting

fetus foetus^+h

feud vete, onenigheid, ruzie

feudal feodaal, leen-

feudalism leenstelsel^h

fever 1 opwinding, agitatie, spanning: *in a ~ of anticipation* in opgewonden afwachting **2** koorts, verhoging

fever blister koortslip

few 1 weinige(n), weinig, enkele(n), een paar: *holidays are ~ and far between* feestdagen zijn er maar weinig; *a ~* een paar, enkele(n) **2** weinig, een paar: *a ~ words* een paar woorden; *every ~ days* om de zoveel dagen || [inform] *there were a good ~* er waren er

nogal wat; *quite* a ~ vrij veel; *quite* a ~ *books* nogal wat boeken
ff *following* e.v., en volgende(n)
F-factor [inform] aantrekkingskracht
fiancé verloofde
fiasco mislukking, fiasco^h
fib leugentje^h: *tell* ~s jokken
fibre 1 vezel **2** draad **3** kwaliteit, sterkte, karakter^h: *moral* ~ ruggengraat
fibreglass fiberglas^h, glasvezel
fibromyalgia fibromyalgie, spierreuma^h
fickle wispelturig, grillig
fiction verzinsel^h, verdichtsel^h, fictie
fictional roman-: ~ *character* romanfiguur
fictitious 1 onecht **2** verzonnen; bedacht [story]; gefingeerd [name, address] **3** denkbeeldig; fictief [event]
¹fiddle (n) viool, fiedel || *play second* ~ *(to)* in de schaduw staan (van)
²fiddle (vb) [inform] **1** vioolspelen, fiedelen **2** lummelen: ~ *about* (or: *around*) rondlummelen **3** friemelen, spelen: ~ *with* morrelen aan, spelen met
³fiddle (vb) **1** spelen **2** [inform] foezelen met, vervalsen, bedrog plegen met: ~ *one's taxes* met belastingaangifte knoeien
fiddlesticks lariekoek, kletskoek
fiddling onbeduidend, nietig: ~ *little screws* pietepeuterige schroefjes
fidelity 1 (natuur)getrouwheid, precisie **2** (+ to) trouw (aan/jegens), loyaliteit
¹fidget (n) zenuwlijer, iem. die niet stil kan zitten
²fidget (vb) de kriebels hebben, niet stil kunnen zitten: ~ *with one's pen* met zijn pen friemelen
¹field (n) **1** veld^h, land^h, weide, akker, vlakte, sportveld^h, sportterrein^h, gebied^h **2** arbeidsveld^h, gebied^h, branche: ~ *of study* onderwerp (van studie) **3** [elec, physics] (kracht)veld^h, draagwijdte, invloedssfeer, reikwijdte: *magnetic* ~ magnetisch veld **4** bezetting [match]; veld^h, alle deelnemers, jachtpartij, jachtstoet **5** concurrentie, veld^h; andere deelnemers: *play the* ~ fladderen, van de een naar de ander lopen
²field (vb) [sport] in het veld brengen; uitkomen met
field day schooluitstapje^h, excursie || *have a* ~ volop genieten
field glasses veldkijker, verrekijker
field hockey hockey^h
Field Marshal [mil] veldmaarschalk
field-test in de praktijk testen
field trip uitstapje^h, excursie
fiend 1 duivel, demon, kwade geest **2** [in compounds] fanaat, maniak
fierce 1 woest, wreed **2** hevig: ~ *dislike* intense afkeer
fiery 1 brandend, vurig **2** onstuimig, vurig, opvliegend: ~ *temperament* fel tempera-

ment
fifteen vijftien
fifteenth vijftiende
fifth vijfde; [mus] kwint
fiftieth vijftigste
fifty vijftig: *a man in his fifties* een man van in de vijftig
fifty-fifty half om half, fiftyfifty: *go* ~ *with s.o.* met iem. samsam doen
fig 1 vijg **2** vijgenboom || *not care* (or: *give*) *a* ~ *(for)* geen bal geven (om)
¹fight (n) **1** gevecht^h, strijd, vechtpartij: *a* ~ *to the finish* een gevecht tot het bittere einde **2** vechtlust, strijdlust: *(still) have plenty* of ~ *in one* zijn vechtlust (nog lang) niet kwijt zijn
²fight (vb) **1** vechten, strijden: ~ *to a finish* tot het bittere eind doorvechten **2** ruziën
³fight (vb) bestrijden, strijden tegen: ~ *off sth.* ergens weerstand tegen bieden; ~ *it out* het uitvechten
fighter vechter, strijder, vechtersbaas
¹fighting (n) het vechten, gevechten
²fighting (adj) strijdbaar, uitgerust voor de strijd: ~ *spirit* vechtlust || *he has a* ~ *chance* als hij alles op alles zet lukt het hem misschien
figment verzinsel^h: ~ *of the imagination* hersenspinsel^h
figurative figuurlijk
¹figure (n) **1** vorm, contour, omtrek, gedaante, gestalte, figuur^h **2** afbeelding; [maths] figuur^h; motief^h: [maths] *solid* ~ lichaam^h **3** personage^h: ~ *of fun* mikpunt van plagerij **4** cijfer^h: *double* ~s getal van twee cijfers **5** bedrag^h, waarde, prijs
²figure (vb) **1** voorkomen, een rol spelen, gezien worden: ~ *in a book* in een boek voorkomen **2** [Am; inform] vanzelf spreken, logisch zijn: *that* ~s dat ligt voor de hand, dat zit er wel in
³figure (vb) [Am; inform] denken, menen, geloven
figurehead 1 [shipp] boegbeeld^h **2** [fig] leider in naam, stroman
figure out 1 berekenen, becijferen, uitwerken **2** [Am] uitpuzzelen, doorkrijgen: *be unable to figure a person out* geen hoogte van iem. kunnen krijgen
figure skating kunstrijden^h
Fiji Fiji
¹Fijian (n) Fijiër, Fijische
²Fijian (adj) Fijisch
filament 1 fijne draad **2** [elec] gloeidraad
filch jatten, gappen
¹file (n) **1** vijl **2** dossier^h, register^h, legger **3** (dossier)map, ordner, klapper **4** [comp] bestand^h **5** rij, file: *in single* ~ in ganzenmars
²file (vb) in een rij lopen, achter elkaar lopen
³file (vb) **1** vijlen, bijvijlen; bijschaven [also fig]: ~ *sth. smooth* iets gladvijlen **2** opslaan, archiveren: ~ *sth. away* iets opbergen
filial kinder-: ~ *piety* respect voor de ouders

filibuster vertragingstactiek
¹Filipino (n) Filipino; Filipijn
²Filipino (adj) Filipijns
¹fill (n) vulling, hele portie: *eat one's* ~ zich rond eten
²fill (vb) **1** (op)vullen, vol maken: ~ *a gap* een leemte opvullen [esp fig] **2** vervullen, bezetten, bekleden: ~ *a vacancy* een vacature bezetten
filler vulling, vulsel^h, vulstof, plamuur^h
fillet filet^(+h), lendenstuk^h, haas: ~ *of pork* varkenshaas
fill in 1 invullen [form] **2** passeren: ~ *time* de tijd doden **3** (+ on) [inform] op de hoogte brengen (van), briefen (over) **4** dichtgooien, dempen
¹filling (n) vulling, vulsel^h
²filling (adj) machtig, voedzaam: *that pancake was rather* ~ die pannenkoek lag nogal zwaar op de maag
filling station benzinestation^h, tankstation^h
fill out 1 opvullen, groter (dikker) maken: ~ *a story* een verhaaltje uitbouwen **2** [Am] invullen [form]
¹fill up (vb) **1** zich vullen, vollopen, dichtslibben **2** benzine tanken
²fill up (vb) **1** (op)vullen; vol doen [tank]; bijvullen **2** invullen [form]
filly merrieveulen^h, jonge merrie
¹film (n) **1** dunne laag, vlies^h: *a* ~ *of dust* een dun laagje stof **2** rolfilm, film **3** (speel)film
²film (vb) **1** filmen; opnemen [scene] **2** verfilmen, een film maken van [book]
filmy dun, doorzichtig
¹filter (n) filter^h, filtertoestel^h, filtreertoestel^h
²filter (vb) uitlekken, doorsijpelen, doorschemeren: *the news* ~*ed out* het nieuws lekte uit
³filter (vb) filtreren, zeven, zuiveren
filter bubble [media] filterbubbel
filth 1 vuiligheid, vuil^h, viezigheid **2** vuile taal, smerige taal
filthy 1 vies, vuil, smerig **2** schunnig || ~ *lucre* vuil gewin, poen^(+h)
fin 1 vin **2** vinvormig voorwerp^h, zwemvlies^h, kielvlak^h, stabilisatievlak^h
¹final (n) **1** finale, eindwedstrijd **2** (-s) (laatste) eindexamen^h: *take one's* ~*s* eindexamen doen
²final (adj) **1** definitief, finaal, beslissend **2** laatste, eind-, slot-: *give* (or: *put*) *the* ~ *touch(es) to* de laatste hand leggen aan
finalize tot een einde brengen, de laatste hand leggen aan, afronden
finally 1 ten slotte, uiteindelijk **2** afdoend, definitief, beslissend: *it was* ~ *decided* er werd definitief besloten
¹finance (n) **1** financieel beheer^h, geldwezen^h, financiën **2** (-s) geldmiddelen, fondsen

²finance (vb) financieren, bekostigen
financial financieel: ~ *year* boekjaar^h
finch vink
¹find (n) (goede) vondst
²find (vb) [law] oordelen
³find (vb) **1** vinden, ontdekken, terugvinden: *I can't* ~ *my keys* ik kan mijn sleutels niet vinden; *he was found dead* hij werd dood aangetroffen **2** (be)vinden, (be)oordelen (als), ontdekken; blijken; [law] oordelen; verklaren, uitspreken: *how did you* ~ *Prague?* wat vond je van Praag?; *it was found that all the vases were broken* alle vazen bleken gebroken te zijn; *be found wanting* niet voldoen, tekortschieten, te licht bevonden worden; *the jury found him not guilty* de gezworenen spraken het onschuldig over hem uit
finder vinder: ~*s keepers* wie wat vindt, mag het houden
finding 1 vondst **2** [esp pl] [esp law] bevinding; uitspraak
find out 1 ontdekken, erachter komen **2** betrappen || *be found out* door de mand vallen
¹fine (n) (geld)boete
²fine (adj) **1** fijn, dun, scherp: *the* ~ *print* de kleine lettertjes **2** voortreffelijk, fijn: *that's all very* ~ allemaal goed en wel **3** fijn, goed: ~ *workmanship* goed vakmanschap **4** in orde, gezond: *I'm* ~, *thanks* met mij gaat het goed, dank je || ~ *arts* beeldende kunst(en); *one of these* ~ *days* vandaag of morgen; *not to put too* ~ *a point* (or: *an edge*) *on it* zonder er doekjes om te winden
³fine (vb) beboeten
⁴fine (adv) **1** fijn, in orde: *it suits me* ~ ik vind het prima **2** fijn, dun: *cut up onions* ~ uien fijn snipperen
finery opschik, opsmuk, mooie kleren
fine-tooth comb stofkam; luizenkam: [fig] *go over sth. with a* ~ iets grondig onderzoeken
finger vinger || [inform] *work one's* ~*s to the bone* zich kapot werken; [inform] *have a* ~ *in every pie* overal een vinger in de pap hebben; *be all* ~*s and thumbs* twee linkerhanden hebben, erg onhandig zijn; *burn one's* ~*s* zijn vingers branden; [inform] *cross one's* ~*s, keep one's* ~*s crossed* duimen; [inform] *give s.o. the* ~ zijn middelvinger naar iem. opsteken; *have one's* ~*s in the till* geld stelen uit de kas (van de winkel waar iem. werkt); *not be able to put* (or: *lay*) *one's* ~ *on sth.* iets niet kunnen plaatsen; *not lift* (or: *move, raise, stir*) *a* ~ geen vinger uitsteken; *let slip through one's* ~*s* door de vingers laten glippen; *twist* (or: *wind*) *s.o. round one's (little)* ~ iem. om zijn vinger winden
finger food kleine hapjes, fingerfood^h
fingermark (vuile) vinger(afdruk)
fingerprint vingerafdruk

fingertip vingertop ǁ *have sth.* **at** *one's* ~*s* iets heel goed kennen

finicky 1 pietepeuterig **2** [depr] pietluttig; kieskeurig

¹finish (n) beëindiging, einde^h, voltooiing: *be in* **at** *the* ~ [fig] bij het einde aanwezig zijn; *(fight)* **to** *the* ~ tot het bittere einde (doorvechten)

²finish (vb) **1** eindigen, tot een einde komen, uit zijn: *the film* ~*es* **at** *11 p.m.* de film is om 11 uur afgelopen; ~ *off with* eindigen met; *we used to* ~ **up** *with a glass of port* we namen altijd een glas port om de maaltijd af te ronden **2** uiteindelijk terechtkomen, belanden: *he will* ~ **up** *in jail* hij zal nog in de gevangenis belanden

³finish (vb) **1** (often + off) beëindigen, afmaken, een einde maken aan: ~ *a book* een boek uitlezen **2** (often + off, up) opgebruiken, opeten, opdrinken **3** afwerken, voltooien, de laatste hand leggen aan: ~ *(up) cleaning* ophouden met schoonmaken

finished 1 (goed) afgewerkt, verzorgd, kunstig **2** klaar, af: *those days are* ~ die tijden zijn voorbij **3** geruïneerd, uitgeput: *he is* ~ **as** *a politician* als politicus is hij er geweest

finishing school etiquetteschool

finishing touch laatste hand: *put the* ~*es to* de laatste hand leggen aan

finite eindig, begrensd, beperkt

finite verb [linguistics] persoonsvorm

Finland Finland

Finn Fin(se)

Finnish Fins

fir 1 spar(renboom) **2** sparrenhout^h, vurenhout^h

¹fire (n) **1** vuur^h, haard(vuur^h): *catch* ~ vlam vatten **2** brand: *set on* ~, *set* ~ *to* in brand steken; *on* ~ in brand; [fig] in vuur (en vlam) **3** het vuren, vuur^h; schot^h [of gun]: *be* (or: *come*) **under** ~ onder vuur genomen worden [also fig] **4** kachel ǁ *play with* ~ met vuur spelen; ~*!* brand!

²fire (vb) **1** in brand steken; doen ontvlammen [also fig]: *it* ~*d him* **with** *enthusiasm* het zette hem in vuur en vlam **2** [inform] de laan uitsturen, ontslaan ǁ ~ **up** bezielen, stimuleren

³fire (vb) **1** stoken, brandend houden: *oil-fired furnace* oliekachel, petroleumkachel **2** bakken [pottery] **3** schieten; (af)vuren [also fig]: ~ *questions* vragen afvuren

firearm vuurwapen^h

firebrand brandhout^h

fire brigade brandweer(korps^h)

firecracker voetzoeker

fire drill brandweeroefening

fire engine brandspuit; brandweerauto

fire escape 1 brandtrap **2** brandladder

fire exit nooduitgang, branddeur

firefighter brandbestrijder, brandweer-

man

firefly glimworm

fire hydrant brandkraan

fireman 1 brandweerman **2** stoker

fireplace 1 open haard **2** schoorsteen, schouw

fireproof vuurbestendig, brandveilig

fire-sale dump-: *sell at* ~ *prices* tegen dumpprijzen verkopen

fireside (the) (hoekje bij de) haard ǁ ~ *chat* informeel gesprek

fire starter [Am] aanmaakblokje^h; [pl] aanmaakmateriaal^h

fire station brandweerkazerne

fire wall 1 brandmuur **2** [comp] firewall

fireworks vuurwerk^h

firing line vuurlinie, vuurlijn [also fig]

¹firm (n) firma

²firm (adj) **1** vast, stevig, hard: *be on* ~ *ground* vaste grond onder de voeten hebben [also fig] **2** standvastig, resoluut: ~ *decision* definitieve beslissing; *take a* ~ *line* zich (kei)hard opstellen

³firm (adv) stevig, standvastig: *stand* ~ op zijn stuk blijven

¹first (adv) **1** eerst: *he told her* ~ hij vertelde het eerst aan haar; ~ *and foremost* in de eerste plaats, bovenal; ~ *of all* in de eerste plaats, om te beginnen **2** liever, eerder: *she'd die* ~ *rather than give in* ze zou eerder sterven dan toe te geven

²first (num) eerste deel, begin: *at* ~ aanvankelijk, eerst ǁ *she came out* ~ ze behaalde de eerste plaats; ~ *form*, [roughly] brugklas [school]; *I'll take the* ~ *train* ik neem de eerstvolgende trein

first-aid eerstehulp-, EHBO-: ~ *box* (or: *kit*) EHBO-doos

first-degree eerstegraads: [law] ~ *murder* moord met voorbedachten rade

firsthand uit de eerste hand

first name voornaam: *be on* ~ *terms* elkaar bij de voornaam noemen

first-rate prima, eersterangs

first responder eerstehulpverlener

first school [roughly] onderbouw

First World eerste wereld, westerse wereld

fiscal fiscaal, belasting(s)-: ~ *year* boekjaar^h; belastingjaar^h

¹fish (n) vis, zeedier^h: ~ *and chips* (gebakken) vis met patat ǁ *like a* ~ *out of water* als een vis op het droge; [inform] *drink like a* ~ drinken als een tempelier; *have other* ~ *to fry* wel wat anders te doen hebben

²fish (vb) vissen [also fig]; hengelen, raden

³fish (vb) (be)vissen: ~ *out a piece of paper from a bag* een papiertje uit een tas opdiepen

fisherman visser, sportvisser

fish finger visstick

fishing rod hengel

fishing tackle vistuig^h, visbenodigdheden

fishmonger vishandelaar, visboer

fishwife visvrouw; [depr] viswijfʰ

fishy 1 visachtig **2** [inform] verdacht: *a ~ story* een verhaal met een luchtje eraan

fission splijting, deling; [biology] (cel)deling; [physics] (kern)splitsing

fissure spleet; kloof

fist vuist

fist bump [inform] boks

fist-bump een boks geven

¹fit (n) **1** vlaag, opwelling, inval: *by* (or: *in*) *~s (and starts)* bij vlagen **2** aanval, stuip; toevalʰ [also fig]: *a ~ of coughing* een hoestbui; *give s.o. a ~* iem. de stuipen op het lijf jagen

²fit (adj) **1** geschikt, passend: *a ~ person to do sth.* de juiste persoon om iets te doen **2** gezond, fit, in (goede) conditie: *as ~ as a fiddle* kiplekker, zo gezond als een vis **3** gepast: *think* (or: *see*) *~ to do sth.* het juist achten (om) iets te doen **4** [inform] knap; seksueel aantrekkelijk

³fit (vb) geschikt zijn, passen, goed zitten: *it ~s like a glove* het zit als gegoten

⁴fit (vb) **1** passen, voegen **2** aanbrengen, monteren: *have a new lock ~ted* een nieuw slot laten aanbrengen

¹fit in (vb) (goed) aangepast zijn, zich aanpassen aan: *~ with your ideas* in overeenstemming zijn met jouw ideeën; *~ with our plans* stroken met onze plannen

²fit in (vb) **1** inpassen, plaats (tijd) vinden voor **2** aanpassen: *fit sth. in with sth.* iets ergens bij aanpassen

fitness 1 het passend zijn: *~ for a job* geschiktheid voor een baan **2** fitheid, goede conditie

fitness steps steps

fitted 1 (volledig) uitgerust, compleet: *~ kitchen* volledig uitgeruste keuken; *~ with* (uitgerust) met, voorzien van **2** vast: *~ carpet* vaste vloerbedekking || *~ sheet* hoeslakenʰ

fitter monteur, installateur

fitting 1 [techn] hulpstukʰ, accessoireʰ **2** [fashion] maat

fit up [inform] onderdak verlenen: *fit s.o. up with a bed* iem. onderdak verlenen

five vijf: *give me ~* **a)** geef me er vijf (van); **b)** [fig] geef me de vijf

five-a-day vijf porties groente en fruit

fivefold vijfvoudig

fiver [inform] briefjeʰ van vijf

¹fix (n) **1** moeilijke situatie, knel: *be in* (or: *get o.s. into*) *a ~* in de knel zitten (*or:* raken) **2** doorgestoken kaart, afgesproken werkʰ: *the election was a ~* de verkiezingen waren doorgestoken kaart **3** shot, dosis

²fix (vb) **1** vastmaken, bevestigen, monteren: *~ sth. in the mind* (or: *memory*) iets in de geest (*or:* het geheugen) prenten **2** vasthouden, trekken [attention]; fixeren [eyes]: *~ one's eyes* (or: *attention*) *(up)on sth.* de blik (*or:*

aandacht) vestigen op iets **3** vastleggen, bepalen; afspreken [price, date, place] **4** regelen, schikken: [depr] *the whole thing was ~ed* het was allemaal doorgestoken kaart **5** opknappen, repareren, in orde brengen **6** [Am] bereiden; maken [meal, drink]: *~ sth. up* iets klaarmaken

fixation 1 bevestiging, bepaling **2** [psychology] fixatie

fixed 1 vast: *~ idea* idee-fixe⁺ʰ **2** voorzien van: *how are you ~ for beer?* hoe staat het met je voorraad bier?

fixed-term voor bepaalde duur: *~ contract* tijdelijk contract

fixer tussenpersoon

fixings [Am; inform] **1** uitrusting, toebehorenʰ **2** garnering; versiering [of a dish]

fix up regelen, organiseren, voorzien van: *fix s.o. up with a job* iem. aan een baan(tje) helpen

¹fizz (n) **1** gebruisʰ, gesisʰ, geschuimʰ **2** [inform] mousserende drank, champagne

²fizz (vb) sissen, (op)bruisen, mousseren

fizzle (zachtjes) sissen, (zachtjes) bruisen || [inform] *~ out* met een sisser aflopen

fizzy bruisend, sissend, mousserend: *~ drink* frisdrank

flabbergast [inform] verstomd doen staan, verbijsteren, overdonderen: *be ~ed at* (or: *by*) verstomd staan door

flabby slap; zwak

flaccid slap, zwak, zacht

¹flag (n) **1** vlag, vaandelʰ, vlaggetjeʰ: *~ of convenience* goedkope vlag; *show the ~* [fig] je gezicht laten zien **2** lisbloem || *keep the ~ flying* doorgaan met de strijd, volharden

²flag (vb) verslappen; verflauwen

³flag (vb) **1** met vlaggen versieren (markeren) **2** doen stoppen (met zwaaibewegingen), aanhouden, aanroepen: *~ (down) a taxi* een taxi aanroepen

flag day collectedag, speldjesdag

flagon 1 schenkkan, flacon **2** kan, fles

flagpole vlaggenstok, vlaggenmast

flagrant flagrant, in het oog springend

flagship vlaggenschipʰ; [fig also] paradepaardjeʰ

flagstaff vlaggenstok, vlaggenmast

¹flail (n) (dors)vlegel

²flail (vb) **1** dorsen **2** wild zwaaien (met): *the boy ~ed his arms in the air* de jongen maaide met zijn armen in de lucht

flair flair⁺ʰ, feeling, fijne neus, bijzondere handigheid

flak [mil] (granaten voor) luchtafweergeschut **2** [inform] scherpe kritiek

¹flake (n) vlok, sneeuwvlok, schilfer; [paint] bladder

²flake (vb) (doen) (af)schilferen, (doen) pellen || [inform] *~ out* **a)** omvallen van vermoeidheid; **b)** gaan slapen; **c)** flauwvallen

flaky 1 vlokkig **2** schilferachtig **3** [Am; inform] geschift **4** [inform] onbetrouwbaar, onstabiel

flamboyant 1 bloemrijk **2** schitterend, vlammend **3** opzichtig, zwierig

¹**flame** (n) **1** vlam, gloed: *~s vuur*ʰ; hitte; *burst into ~(s)* in brand vliegen **2** geliefde, liefde, passie

²**flame** (vb) vlammen, ontvlammen; opvlammen [of passion, love] ‖ *~ out* (or: *up*) (razend) opvliegen, (razend) opstuiven [of pers]

flammable brandbaar, explosief

flan [roughly] kleine vla(ai)

Flanders Vlaanderen

¹**flank** (n) zijkant, flank

²**flank** (vb) flankeren: *~ed by* (or: *with*) *trees* met bomen erlangs

flannel 1 flanelʰ **2** (flanellen) doekjeʰ, washandjeʰ **3** [inform] mooi praatjeʰ, vleierij, smoesjes

¹**flap** (n) **1** geflapperʰ, geklapʰ **2** klep, flap, (afhangende) rand; (neerslaand) bladʰ **3** [inform] staat van opwinding, paniek, consternatie

²**flap** (vb) flapp(er)en, klepp(er)en, slaan

³**flap** (vb) op en neer bewegen, slaan met

¹**flare** (n) **1** flakkerend lichtʰ, flikkering **2** signaalvlam, vuursignaalʰ

²**flare** (vb) (op)flakkeren, (op)vlammen; [fig] opstuiven: *~ up* **a)** opflakkeren; **b)** [also fig] woest worden

flare-up opflakkering, uitbarsting, hevige ruzie

¹**flash** (n) **1** (licht)flits, vlam, (op)flikkering: *~es of lightning* bliksemschichten; *quick as a ~* razend snel; *in a ~* in een flits **2** flits(lichtʰ), flitsapparaatʰ **3** lichtseinʰ, vlagseinʰ **4** kort (nieuws)berichtʰ, nieuwsflits **5** opwelling, vlaag: *a ~ of inspiration* een flits van inspiratie

²**flash** (adj) **1** plotseling (opkomend): *~ flood* (or: *fire*) plotselinge overstroming (or: brand) **2** [inform] opzichtig, poenig

³**flash** (vb) **1** opvlammen; (plotseling) ontvlammen [also fig] **2** plotseling opkomen: *~ into view* (or: *sight*) plotseling in het gezichtsveld verschijnen **3** snel voorbijflitsen, (voorbij)schieten: *~ past* (or: *by*) voorbijvliegen, voorbijflitsen

⁴**flash** (vb) **1** (doen) flitsen, (doen) flikkeren: *~ the headlights* (*of a car*) met de koplampen flitsen **2** pronken met [jewels]: *~ money around* te koop lopen met zijn geld

flashback terugblik

flash card 1 (systeem)kaartjeʰ [educ] **2** [comp] flashkaart, geheugenkaart

flash drive [comp] USB-stick, geheugenstick

flasher 1 flitser, knipperlichtʰ **2** potloodventer [exhibitionist]

flashlight 1 flitslichtʰ, lichtflits, signaallichtʰ **2** [Am] zaklantaarn

flashy opzichtig; poenig, opvallend

flask 1 fles, flacon; [chem] kolf **2** veldfles **3** thermosfles

¹**flat** (n) **1** vlakte, vlak terreinʰ **2** flat, etage, appartementʰ: *a block of ~s* een flatgebouw **3** platte kant, vlakʰ, hand(palm) **4** [Am] lekke band **5** [mus] mol(tekenʰ); [Belg] b-moltekenʰ

²**flat** (adj) **1** vlak, plat **2** laag, niet hoog; plat [also of feet] **3** zonder prik; [Belg] plat [water]; verschaald [beer] **4** effen; gelijkmatig [colour, paint] **5** bot, vierkant; absoluut [negation, refusal] **6** leeg; plat [tyre] **7** saai, oninteressant, mat, smaakloos; flauw [food]: *fall ~* mislukken, geen effect hebben **8** [mus] te laag **9** [mus] mol, mineur

³**flat** (adv) **1** [inform] helemaal: *~ broke* helemaal platzak; *~ out* (op) volle kracht, met alle kracht [advance, work] **2** [inform] botweg, ronduit: *tell s.o. sth.* ~ iem. botweg iets zeggen **3** [mus] (een halve toon) lager, te laag **4** rond, op de kop af, exact: *ten seconds* ~ op de kop af tien seconden

flatbed 1 laadvloer [of truck] **2** pick-up met platte bak

flat-bottomed platboomd, met een platte bodem

flatbread platbroodʰ

flatfish platvis

flat-iron strijkijzerʰ, strijkbout

flatly 1 uitdrukkingsloos, mat; dof [say, speak etc] **2** botweg; kortaf [eg refuse]: *Simon ~ refused to say where he had been* Simon vertikte het gewoon om te zeggen waar hij had gezeten **3** helemaal

flat rate uniform tariefʰ; vast bedragʰ

flat-screen: *a ~ TV* een flatscreen-tv, een tv met een plat beeldscherm

flatten 1 afplatten, effenen: *~ out* afvlakken, effenen **2** flauw(er) maken, dof maken

flatter 1 vleien: *~ o.s.* zich vleien, zichzelf te hoog aanslaan; *I ~ myself that I'm a good judge of character* ik vlei mezelf met de hoop dat ik mensenkennis bezit **2** strelen [ears, eyes] **3** flatteren, mooier afschilderen

flattery 1 vleierij; [teasingly] slijm⁺ʰ **2** gevleiʰ, vleiende woorden

flatulence winderigheid

flaunt 1 pronken met, pralen met, tentoonspreiden: [hum] *if you've got it, ~ it!* wie het breed heeft, laat het breed hangen **2** doen opvallen, (zich) zeer opvallend uitdossen (gedragen)

flautist fluitist, fluitspeler

flavour 1 smaak, aromaʰ, geur; [fig] bijsmaak **2** het karakteristieke, het eigene, het typische: *Camden has its own peculiar ~* Camden heeft iets heel eigens

flavouring smaakstof, aromaʰ, kruidʰ, kruiderij

flaw 1 barst, breuk, scheur **2** gebrek^h; fout [in jewel, stone, character]

fla**wless** gaaf; vlekkeloos, onberispelijk

flax vlas^h [plant, fibre]

fla**xen 1** als, van vlas **2** vlaskleurig: ~ *hair* vlashaar^h; vlasblond haar

flay 1 villen, (af)stropen **2** afranselen; [fig] hekelen

flea 1 vlo **2** watervlo ‖ *go off with a* ~ *in his ear* van een koude kermis thuiskomen; ~ *market* vlooienmarkt, rommelmarkt

fle**abite** vlooienbeet; [fig] iets onbelangrijks; kleinigheid

¹**fleck** (n) vlek(je^h), plek(je^h), spikkel(tje^h)

²**fleck** (vb) (be)spikkelen, vlekken, stippen

fle**dgling** (vliegvlugge) jonge vogel; [fig] beginneling

flee (ont)vluchten

¹**fleece** (n) **1** (schaaps)vacht **2** vlies^h **3** fleece^{+h}

²**fleece** (vb) **1** scheren [sheep] **2** [inform] afzetten; het vel over de oren halen [pers]

fleet 1 vloot, marine, luchtvloot **2** schare, verzameling, groep: *a* ~ *of cars* (or: *taxis*) een wagenpark

flee**ting 1** vluchtig, vergankelijk **2** kortstondig: *a* ~ *glance* een vluchtige blik

Fle**ming** Vlaming

Fle**mish** Vlaams

flesh vlees^h: ~ *and blood* het lichaam, een mens(elijk wezen); *one's own* ~ *and blood* je eigen vlees en bloed, je naaste verwanten

fle**shy 1** vlezig **2** dik

¹**flex** (n) (elektrisch) snoer^h

²**flex** (vb) buigen, samentrekken

flexibi**lity** flexibiliteit; buigzaamheid; soepelheid

fle**xible 1** buigzaam [also fig]; soepel, flexibel: ~ *working* hours variabele werktijd **2** meegaand, plooibaar

flexita**rian** flexitariër

fle**xitime** variabele werktijd(en)

fle**xiworker** flexwerker

¹**flick** (n) **1** tik, mep, slag **2** ruk, schok: *a* ~ *of the wrist* een snelle polsbeweging **3** [inform] film **4** (the flicks) bios

²**flick** (vb) even aanraken, aantikken, afschudden; aanknippen [switch]: ~ *crumbs from* (or: *off*) *the table* kruimels van de tafel vegen ‖ ~ *through* a *newspaper* een krant doorbladeren

¹**fl**i**cker** (n) **1** trilling, (op)flikkering, flikkerend licht^h **2** sprankje^h: *a* ~ *of hope* een sprankje hoop

²**fl**i**cker** (vb) **1** trillen, fladderen, wapperen, flikkeren **2** heen en weer bewegen, heen en weer schieten

fli**ck knife** stiletto

flie**r** *see flyer*

flight 1 vlucht, het vliegen; baan [of projectile, ball]; [fig] opwelling; uitbarsting: *put*

to ~ op de vlucht jagen **2** zwerm, vlucht, troep **3** trap: *a* ~ *of stairs* een trap

fli**ght attendant** steward(ess)

fli**ght mode** [media] vliegtuigstand

fli**ght path 1** vliegroute **2** baan [of satellite]

fli**ght recorder** vluchtrecorder, zwarte doos

fli**ghty** grillig, wispelturig

¹**fl**i**msy** (n) doorslag(papier^h), kopie

²**fl**i**msy** (adj) **1** broos, kwetsbaar, dun **2** onbenullig, onnozel

flinch [also fig] terugdeinzen; terugschrikken [with fear, pain]: *without* ~*ing* zonder een spier te vertrekken

¹**fling** (n) **1** worp, gooi **2** uitspatting, korte, hevige affaire ‖ *have one's* ~ uitspatten

²**fling** (vb) **1** gooien, (weg)smijten, (af)werpen **2** wegstormen, (boos) weglopen

flint vuursteen(tje^h)

¹**flip** (n) tik, mep, (vinger)knip

²**flip** (adj) glad, ongepast, brutaal

³**flip** (vb) [inform] **1** flippen, maf worden **2** boos worden, door het lint gaan

⁴**flip** (vb) **1** wegtikken, wegschieten (met de vingers): ~ *a coin* kruis of munt gooien **2** omdraaien: [Am; inform] ~ *burgers* in een fastfoodrestaurant werken

fli**pchart** flip-over

fli**p-flop** teenslipper

fli**ppant** oneerbiedig, spottend

fli**pper 1** vin, zwempoot **2** zwemvlies^h

fli**p side 1** B-kant (van grammofoonplaat) **2** keerzijde [also fig]

flip through doorbladeren, snel doorlezen

¹**flirt** (n) flirt

²**flirt** (vb) flirten, koketteren

fli**rt with 1** flirten met; [fig] spelen met; overwegen: *we* ~ *the idea of* we spelen met de gedachte om **2** uitdagen, flirten met: ~ *danger* een gevaarlijk spel spelen

¹**flit** (n) [inform] **1** snelle beweging **2** verhuizing: *do a (moonlight)* ~ met de noorderzon vertrekken

²**flit** (vb) fladderen; vliegen: *thoughts* ~*ted through* his *mind* gedachten schoten hem door het hoofd

¹**float** (n) **1** drijvend voorwerp^h, vlot^h, boei, dobber **2** drijver **3** kar, (praal)wagen **4** contanten, kleingeld^h

²**float** (vb) **1** drijven, dobberen **2** vlot komen [of ship] **3** zweven

³**float** (vb) **1** doen drijven **2** vlot maken [ship etc] **3** over water vervoeren **4** in omloop brengen, voorstellen, rondvertellen: ~ *an idea* met een idee naar voren komen

flo**ating 1** drijvend: ~ *bridge* a) pontonbrug; b) kettingpont **2** veranderlijk: ~ *kidney* wandelende nier; ~ *voter* zwevende kiezer

¹**flock** (n) **1** bosje^h, vlokje^h **2** troep, zwerm, kudde

²**flock** (vb) bijeenkomen, samenstromen: *people* ~ed to the cities men trok in grote groepen naar de steden

flog slaan, ervan langs geven

¹**flood** (n) **1** vloed **2** uitstorting, stroom, vloed: ~ of **reactions** stortvloed van reacties **3** overstroming

²**flood** (vb) (doen) overstromen, overspoelen, buiten zijn oevers doen treden: *we were ~ed (out)* **with** letters we werden bedolven onder de brieven

floodgate sluisdeur [fig]; sluis: *open* the ~s de sluizen openzetten

flooding overstroming

floodlight 1 schijnwerper **2** strijklichtʰ, spotlichtʰ

flood tide vloed; hoogtijʰ

¹**floor** (n) **1** vloer, grond: *first* ~ eerste verdieping; [Am] begane grond **2** verdieping, etage **3** vergaderzaal [of parliament]: *a motion* **from** the ~ een motie uit de zaal ‖ *wipe the* ~ with s.o. de vloer met iem. aanvegen

²**floor** (vb) **1** vloeren [also fig]; knock-out slaan, verslaan: *his* **arguments** ~ed me tegen zijn argumenten kon ik niet op **2** van de wijs brengen

floorboard 1 vloerplank **2** bodemplank

floor show floorshow, striptease

¹**flop** (n) **1** smak, plof **2** flop, mislukking

²**flop** (vb) **1** zwaaien, klappen, spartelen: ~ *about* in the water rondspartelen in het water **2** smakken, ploffen: ~ *down* in a chair neerploffen in een stoel **3** [inform] mislukken, floppen; zakken [at examination]

¹**floppy** (n) floppy (disk), diskette, flop

²**floppy** (adj) **1** slap(hangend) **2** [inform] zwak

flora flora

floral 1 gebloemd: ~ *tribute* bloemenhulde **2** m.b.t. flora, plant-

floret 1 bloempjeʰ **2** roosjeʰ [of cauliflower or broccoli]

florid 1 bloemrijk, (overdreven) sierlijk **2** in het oog lopend, opzichtig **3** blozend, hoogrood

florin florijn, gulden

florist 1 bloemist **2** bloemkweker

flotilla 1 flottielje, smaldeelʰ **2** vloot [of small ships]

flotsam 1 drijfhoutʰ, wrakhoutʰ: [fig] ~ *and* **jetsam** uitgestotenen **2** rommel, rotzooi

FLOTUS [inform] *First Lady of the United States* de first lady; de presidentsvrouw

¹**flounce** (n) **1** zwaai, ruk, schok **2** (gerimpelde) strook [on article of clothing, curtain]

²**flounce** (vb) **1** zwaaien [of body]; schokken, schudden **2** ongeduldig lopen: ~ *about* the room opgewonden door de kamer ijsberen

flounder 1 ploeteren **2** stuntelen, van zijn stuk gebracht worden **3** de draad kwijtraken, hakkelen

flour meelʰ, (meel)bloem

¹**flourish** (n) **1** krul, krulletter **2** bloemrijke uitdrukking, stijlbloempjeʰ **3** zwierig gebaarʰ **4** fanfare, geschalʰ

²**flourish** (vb) **1** gedijen, bloeien **2** floreren, succes hebben: *his* **family** were ~ing het ging goed met zijn gezin

³**flourish** (vb) tonen, zwaaien met: *he ~ed a* **letter** in my face hij zwaaide een brief onder mijn neus heen en weer

flout 1 beledigen, bespotten **2** afwijzen, in de wind slaan

¹**flow** (n) **1** stroom, stroming, het stromen: *go* with the ~ met de stroom meegaan **2** vloed, overvloed: *ebb* and ~ eb en vloed

²**flow** (vb) **1** (toe)vloeien, (toe)stromen **2** golven; loshangen [of hair, article of clothing] **3** opkomen [of high tide]: *swim* with the ~ing tide met de stroom meegaan

¹**flower** (n) **1** bloem, bloesem **2** bloei: *the orchids are* **in** ~ de orchideeën staan in bloei

²**flower** (vb) bloeien, tot bloei (ge)komen (zijn)

flower arrangement bloemstukʰ

flowing 1 vloeiend **2** loshangend, golvend

fl. oz. *fluid ounce*

flu *influenza* griep

flub [Am] verknoeien

fluctuate fluctueren, schommelen, variëren

flue schoorsteenpijp, rookkanaalʰ

fluency spreekvaardigheid

fluent vloeiend: *be* ~ *in* English vloeiend Engels spreken

¹**fluff** (n) pluis(jes), donsʰ

²**fluff** (vb) **1** verknallen, verprutsen **2** opschudden [pillow]

fluff out 1 opschudden **2** opzetten

fluffy donzig, pluizig

¹**fluid** (n) vloeistof

²**fluid** (adj) **1** vloeibaar, niet vast, vloeiend **2** instabiel, veranderlijk: *our* **plans** are still ~ onze plannen staan nog niet vast ‖ ~ *ounce* ounce

fluke bof, meevaller, mazzel: *by* a ~ door stom geluk

flummox in verwarring brengen, perplex doen staan

flunk [Am; inform] (doen) zakken [examination]; afwijzen [at examination]

flunkey [oft depr] **1** lakei **2** strooplikker

flunk out [Am; inform] weggestuurd worden

fluorescent fluorescerend: ~ *lamp* tl-buis

fluoride fluorideʰ, fluorwaterstofzoutʰ

flurry vlaag [also fig]; windvlaag, windstoot, (korte) bui: *in a* ~ *of* **excitement** in een vlaag van opwinding

¹**flush** (n) **1** vloed, (plotselinge) stroom, vloedgolf **2** (water)spoeling **3** opwinding: *in*

*the **first** ~ of victory* in de overwinningsroes
4 blos **5** flush, serie kaarten van dezelfde kleur

²flush (adj) **1** goed voorzien, goed bij kas: ~ *with money* goed bij kas **2** gelijk, vlak: ~ *with the wall* gelijk met de muur

³flush (vb) **1** doorspoelen; doortrekken [toilet] **2** kleuren, blozen

⁴flush (vb) **1** (schoon)spoelen: ~ *sth. away* (or: *down*) iets wegspoelen **2** opwinden, aanvuren: *~ed with happiness* dolgelukkig **3** doen wegvliegen: ~ *s.o. out of* (or: *from*) *his hiding place* iem. uit zijn schuilplaats verjagen

¹fluster (n) opwinding, verwarring: *be in a ~* opgewonden zijn

²fluster (vb) van de wijs brengen, zenuwachtig maken

flute fluit

flutist [Am] fluitist

¹flutter (n) **1** gefladder^h, geklapper^h **2** opwinding, drukte: *be in a ~* opgewonden zijn **3** [inform] gokje^h, speculatie

²flutter (vb) **1** fladderen, klapwieken **2** dwarrelen [of leaf] **3** wapperen [of flag] **4** zenuwachtig rondlopen, ijsberen **5** snel slaan, (snel) kloppen

flux 1 vloed, het vloeien, stroom **2** voortdurende beweging, veranderlijkheid: *everything was in a **state** of* ~ er waren steeds nieuwe ontwikkelingen

¹fly (n) **1** vlieg: *die **like** flies* in groten getale omkomen; *not **harm** (or: **hurt**) a ~* geen vlieg kwaad doen **2** gulp ‖ *a ~ in the **ointment*** een kleinigheid die het geheel bederft; *a ~ on the **wall*** een spion; [inform] *there **are** no flies on her* ze is niet op haar achterhoofd gevallen

²fly (vb) **1** vliegen [of bird, aeroplane etc]: ~ *away* wegvliegen; [fig] verdwijnen; ~ *in* (or: *out*) aankomen (*or:* vertrekken) per vliegtuig; ~ *past* (in formatie) over vliegen; ~ *at* **a)** aanvallen, zich storten op [of bird]; **b)** [fig] uitvallen tegen; ~ *into* landen op [airport] **2** wapperen [of flag, hair]; fladderen, vliegen **3** zich snel voortbewegen, vliegen, vluchten; omvliegen [of time]; wegvliegen [of money]: *let ~* **a)** (af)schieten, afvuren; ~ *into* a rage (or: passion, temper) in woede ontsteken ‖ ~ *high* hoog vliegen [fig]; ambitieus zijn

³fly (vb) **1** vliegen, besturen: ~ *a plane in* een vliegtuig aan de grond zetten **2** vliegen (met) [airline company] **3** laten vliegen [pigeon]; oplaten [kite]: ~ *a kite* vliegeren; [fig] een balletje opgooien **4** voeren; laten wapperen [flag] **5** ontvluchten, vermijden

flyboard flyboard^h

flyboarding het flyboarden

fly-drive: *a ~ holiday* een vliegreis inclusief huurauto

flyer 1 vlugschrift^h, folder, flyer **2** piloot, vlieger **3** vliegtuigpassagier

flying 1 vliegend: ~ *jump* (or: *leap*) sprong met aanloop; ~ *saucer* vliegende schotel **2** (zeer) snel, zich snel verplaatsend (ontwikkelend), vliegend: ~ *start* vliegende start [also fig] **3** kortstondig, van korte duur, tijdelijk

flying squad vliegende brigade, mobiele eenheid

flyover viaduct^h [across motorway]

flysheet 1 (reclame)blaadje^h, folder, circulaire **2** informatieblad^h; gebruiksaanwijzing [of catalogue, book]

fly swatter vliegenmepper

flyweight [boxing, wrestling] **1** worstelaar (bokser) in de vliegegewichtklasse, vliegegewicht **2** vliegegewicht^h

foal veulen^h

¹foam (n) **1** schuim^h **2** schuimrubber

²foam (vb) **1** schuimen **2** schuimbekken: ~ *at the **mouth*** schuimbekken [also fig]

fob off 1 wegwuiven, geen aandacht besteden aan **2** afschepen, zich afmaken van: *we won't be fobbed off this time* deze keer laten we ons niet met een kluitje in het riet sturen

fob watch zakhorloge^h

focal m.b.t./van het brandpunt: ~ *distance* (or: *length*) brandpuntsafstand

focal point brandpunt^h [also fig]; middelpunt^h

¹focus (n) **1** brandpunt^h, focus^+h; [fig] middelpunt^h; centrum^h **2** scherpte: *out of* ~ onscherp

²focus (vb) **1** in een brandpunt (doen) samenkomen **2** (zich) concentreren: ~ *on* zich concentreren op; *stay ~ed* gefocust blijven, geconcentreerd blijven

fodder (droog) veevoeder^h; voer^h [also fig]

foe [form] vijand, tegenstander

foetus foetus^+h

¹fog (n) mist; nevel [also fig]; onduidelijkheid, verwarring

²fog (vb) beslaan: *my glasses ~ged up* mijn bril besloeg

fogbound 1 door mist opgehouden **2** in mist gehuld

fogey ouderwets figuur^h, ouwe zeur

foggy mistig, (zeer) nevelig; [also fig] onduidelijk; vaag: [inform] *I haven't the foggiest (idea)* (ik heb) geen flauw idee

foible 1 zwak^h, zwakheid, zwak punt^h **2** gril

¹foil (n) **1** (aluminium)folie, zilverpapier^h **2** contrast^h, achtergrond: *be a ~ to* beter doen uitkomen

²foil (vb) verijdelen, verhinderen, voorkomen

foist opdringen

¹fold (n) **1** vouw, plooi, kronkel(ing), kreuk **2** schaapskooi **3** het vouwen **4** kudde; [fig] kerk; gemeente: *return to the ~* in de schoot van zijn familie terugkeren

²fold (vb) [inform] **1** op de fles gaan, over de kop gaan **2** het begeven, bezwijken

³fold (vb) **1** (op)vouwen: ~ *away* opvouwen, opklappen; ~ *back* terugslaan, omslaan **2** (om)wikkelen, (in)pakken **3** (om)sluiten, omhelzen: ~ *s.o. in one's arms* iem. in zijn armen sluiten **4** hullen [in fog] **5** over elkaar leggen; kruisen [arms]; intrekken [wings]

folder 1 folder, (reclame)blaadjeʰ **2** map-(jeʰ) **3** [comp] map

¹fold up (vb) **1** bezwijken, het begeven, het opgeven **2** failliet gaan, over de kop gaan

²fold up (vb) opvouwen, opklappen

foliage gebladerteʰ, bladʰ, loofʰ

folk [inform] **1** familie, gezinʰ, oude lui: *her ~s were from New Jersey* haar familie kwam uit New Jersey **2** luitjes, jongens, mensen **3** mensen, lieden, lui: *some ~ never learn* sommige mensen leren het nooit

folklore 1 folklore **2** volkskunde

folk-tale volksverhaalʰ, sage, sprookjeʰ

follow volgen, achternalopen, aanhouden; gaan langs [road, direction, river]; achternazitten, vergezellen, bijwonen, komen na, opvolgen, aandacht schenken aan, in de gaten houden, begrijpen; bijhouden [news]; zich laten leiden door; uitvoeren [order, advice]; nadoen [example]; voortvloeien uit: ~ *the rules* zich aan de regels houden; ~ *s.o. about* (or: *around*) iem. overal volgen; ~ *on* verder gaan, volgen [after interruption]; ~ *up* a) (op korte afstand) volgen, in de buurt blijven van; b) vervolgen, een vervolg maken op; c) gebruikmaken van; d) nagaan; *the outcome is as ~s* het resultaat is als volgt; *to* ~ als volgend gerecht; *would you like anything to ~?* wilt u nog iets toe?

follower 1 aanhanger, volgeling: *Marx and Engels had many ~s* Marx en Engels hadden veel aanhangers **2** volger: *how many ~s do you have on Instagram?* hoeveel volgers heb jij op Instagram?

¹following (n) aanhang, volgelingen

²following (adj) **1** volgend **2** mee, in de rug; gunstig [wind]

³following (prep) na, volgende op: ~ *the meeting* na de vergadering

follow-up vervolgʰ, voortzetting, vervolgbrief, tweede bezoekʰ

folly 1 (buitensporig) duur en nutteloos iets **2** dwaasheid, dwaas gedragʰ: *where ignorance is bliss, 'tis ~ to be wise* [roughly] wat niet weet, wat niet deert

foment aanstoken, aanmoedigen, stimuleren

FOMO *fear of missing out* angst iets leuks of belangrijks te missen

fond 1 liefhebbend, teder, innig **2** dierbaar, lief: *his ~est wish was fulfilled* zijn liefste wens ging in vervulling **3** al te lief, al te toe-

geeflijk || *be ~ of* gek zijn op; [inform] er een handje van hebben te

fondle liefkozen, strelen, aaien

fondness 1 tederheid, genegenheid, warmte **2** voorliefde, hang: *his ~ for old proverbs is quite irritating at times* zijn voorliefde voor oude spreekwoorden is soms heel irritant

font 1 (doop)vontʰ **2** fontʰ, lettertypeʰ

food 1 voedingsmiddelʰ, voedingsartikelʰ, levensmiddelʰ, eetwaar: *frozen ~s* diepvriesproducten **2** voedselʰ, etenʰ; voeding [also fig]: ~ *for thought* (or: *reflection*) stof tot nadenken

food processor keukenmachine

foodstuff levensmiddelʰ, voedingsmiddelʰ, voedingsartikelʰ

¹fool (n) **1** dwaas, gek, zot(skap), stommeling: *more ~ him* hij had beter kunnen weten; *make a ~ of s.o.* iem. voor de gek houden **2** nar, zot: *act* (or: *play*) *the ~* gek doen **3** dessertʰ van stijf geklopte room, ei, suiker en vruchten || *he's nobody's* (or: *no*) *~* hij is niet van gisteren

²fool (vb) **1** gek doen: ~ *(about, around) with* spelen met, flirten met **2** lummelen, lanterfanten: ~ *about* (or: *around*) rondlummelen, aanrommelen

³fool (vb) voor de gek houden, ertussen nemen: *he ~ed her into believing he's a guitarist* hij maakte haar wijs dat hij gitarist is

foolery dwaasheid

foolhardy onbezonnen, roekeloos

foolish 1 dwaas, dom, zinloos **2** verbouwereerd, beteuterd || *penny wise, pound ~* [roughly] sommige mensen zijn zuinig als het om kleine bedragen gaat, terwijl ze grote bedragen over de balk gooien

foolproof 1 volkomen veilig **2** kinderlijk eenvoudig **3** onfeilbaar; waterdicht **4** bedrijfszeker

fool's errand vruchteloze onderneming: *send s.o. on a ~* iem. voor niks laten gaan

foosball [esp Am] tafelvoetbalʰ

¹foot (n) **1** voet [also of mountain, stocking]: *put one's feet up* (even) gaan liggen; *stand on one's own feet* op eigen benen staan; *on ~* te voet, op handen **2** (vers)voet **3** poot [of table] **4** voeteneindeʰ [of bed] **5** ondersteʰ, laatste deelʰ, (uit)eindeʰ **6** [measure of length] voet [0.3048 metre] || *have a ~ in both camps* geen partij kiezen; [fig] *feet of clay* fundamentele zwakte; *carry* (or: *sweep*) *s.o. off his feet* iem. meeslepen; [inform] *fall* (or: *land*) *on one's feet* mazzel hebben; *find one's feet* a) beginnen te staan [of child]; b) op eigen benen kunnen staan; *get to one's feet* opstaan; *put one's ~ down* streng optreden; [inform] *plankgas rijden*; [inform] *put one's ~ in it* (or: *one's mouth*) een blunder begaan; [inform] *be rushed off one's feet* zich uit de naad werken; *my ~!* kom nou!; *they say it's easy. Easy my ~!* ze zeggen dat het makkelijk is. Nou, vergeet het maar!

²**foot** (vb) betalen, vereffenen, dokken voor

³**foot** (vb): [inform] *~ it* a) dansen; b) de benenwagen nemen, te voet gaan

footage 1 lengte (in voeten) **2** (stuk) film

foot-and-mouth disease mond-en-klauwzeerʰ

¹**football** (n) **1** voetbal [ball] **2** rugbybal **3** speelbal [fig]

²**football** (n) [Am] Amerikaans footballʰ

footbridge voetbrug

footer voettekst

foothill uitloper [of mountains]

foothold 1 steun(puntʰ) voor de voet, plaats om te staan **2** vaste voet, steunpuntʰ, zekere positie

footing 1 steun (voor de voet), steunpuntʰ, houvastʰ; [fig] vaste voet: *lose one's ~* wegglijden **2** voet, niveauʰ, sterkte **3** voet, verstandhouding, omgang: *on the same ~* op gelijke voet

footlights voetlichtʰ; [by extension] (toneel)carrière

footling 1 dwaas, stom **2** onbeduidend, waardeloos

footloose vrij, ongebonden

footman lakei, livreiknecht

footmark voetafdruk; voetstap

footnote voetnoot; [fig] kanttekening

footpath voetpadʰ, wandelpadʰ

footprint voetafdruk, voetspoorʰ, voetstap: [fig] *ecological ~* ecologische voetafdruk

footsie voetsokjeʰ, kousenvoetjeʰ || *play ~* voetjevrijen

footstep 1 voetstap, voetafdruk; voetspoorʰ [also fig]: *follow* (or: *tread*) *in s.o.'s ~s* in iemands voetsporen treden **2** pas, stap

foppish fatterig, dandyachtig

for 1 voor, om, met het oog op, wegens, bedoeld om, ten behoeve van: *act ~ the best* handelen om bestwil; *long ~ home* verlangen naar huis; *write ~ information* schrijven om informatie; *thank you ~ coming* bedankt dat je gekomen bent; *now ~ it* en nu erop los **2** voor, wat betreft, gezien, in verhouding met: *an ear ~ music* een muzikaal gehoor; *it's not ~ me to* het is niet aan mij om te; *so much ~ that* dat is dat; *I ~ one will not do it* ik zal het in elk geval niet doen; *~ all I care* voor mijn part **3** ten voordele van, ten gunste van, vóór: *~ and against* voor en tegen **4** in plaats van, tegenover, in ruil voor **5** als (zijnde): *left ~ dead* dood achtergelaten **6** over, gedurende, sinds, ver, met een omvang: *it was not ~ long* het duurde niet lang **7** dat ... zou ..., dat ... moet ...: *~ her to leave us is impossible* het is onmogelijk dat zij ons zou verlaten **8** opdat: *~ this to work* it is necessary to

wil dit lukken, dan is het nodig te || *anyone ~ coffee?* wil er iem. koffie?; *and now ~ sth. completely different* en nu iets anders

forage 1 naar voedsel zoeken, foerageren **2** doorzoeken: *~ about* in s.o.'s bag iemands tas doorsnuffelen

foray 1 [mil] inval; strooptocht **2** [inform] uitstapjeʰ, intrede: *John's ~ into science failed* Johns poging zich op het gebied van de wetenschap te wagen mislukte

forbear zich onthouden, zich inhouden, afzien: *he should ~ from quarrels* hij moet zich verre houden van ruzies

forbearance verdraagzaamheid; tolerantie

forbid 1 verbieden, ontzeggen **2** voorkomen, verhoeden, buitensluiten: *God ~!* God verhoede!

forbidden verboden, niet toegestaan

forbidding afstotelijk, afschrikwekkend

¹**force** (n) **1** kracht, geweldʰ, macht: *by ~ of circumstances* door omstandigheden gedwongen; *join ~s (with)* de krachten bundelen (met); *by* (or: *from, out of*) *~ of habit* uit gewoonte **2** (rechts)geldigheid, het van kracht zijn: *a new law has come into ~* (or: *has been put into ~*) een nieuwe wet is van kracht geworden **3** macht, krijgsmacht, legerʰ **4** (the Forces) strijdkrachten

²**force** (vb) **1** dwingen, (door)drijven, forceren: *~ back* terugdrijven; *Government will ~ the prices up* de regering zal de prijzen opdrijven **2** forceren, open-, doorbreken: *the burglar ~d an entry* de inbreker verschafte zich met geweld toegang

forced gedwongen, onvrijwillig, geforceerd: *~ labour* dwangarbeid; *~ landing* noodlanding

forcemeat gehaktʰ

forceps (verlos)tang: *two pairs of ~* twee tangen

forceps delivery tangverlossing

forcible 1 gewelddadig, gedwongen, krachtig **2** indrukwekkend, overtuigend

fore het voorste gedeelte: [fig] *come to the ~* op de voorgrond treden

¹**forearm** (n) onderarm, voorarm

²**forearm** (vb): *forewarned is ~ed* een gewaarschuwd mens telt voor twee

forebear voorvader, voorouder

foreboding voortekenʰ, voorspelling **2** (akelig) voorgevoelʰ

¹**forecast** (n) voorspelling; verwachting [of weather]

²**forecast** (vb) voorspellen, verwachten, aankondigen

foreclosure executie

forecourt voorpleinʰ

forefather voorvader, stamvader

forefinger wijsvinger

forefront voorste deelʰ, voorste gelidʰ,

front[h], voorgevel: *in the ~ of the fight* aan het (gevechts)front

foregather samenkomen, (zich) verzamelen

forego voorafgaan

foregoing voorafgaand, voornoemd, vorig

foregone conclusion uitgemaakte zaak

forehead voorhoofd[h]

foreign 1 buitenlands: *~ aid* ontwikkelingshulp; *~ exchange* deviezen; *Foreign Office* Ministerie van Buitenlandse Zaken **2** vreemd, ongewoon

foreigner buitenlander, vreemdeling

foreman 1 voorzitter van jury **2** voorman, ploegbaas

[1]**foremost** (adj) **1** voorst(e), eerst(e), aan het hoofd: *head ~* met het hoofd naar voren **2** opmerkelijkst, belangrijkst

[2]**foremost** (adv) voorop

forename voornaam

forensic gerechtelijk, (ge)rechts-, forensisch

forensics 1 forensische wetenschap **2** forensisch onderzoek[h], sporenonderzoek[h]

foreplay voorspel[h]

forerunner 1 voorteken[h]; [fig] voorbode **2** voorloper

foresee voorzien, verwachten, vooraf zien

foreseeable 1 te verwachten, te voorzien **2** afzienbaar, nabij: *in the ~ future* in de nabije toekomst

foreshadow aankondigen, voorspellen

foresight 1 vooruitziende blik, het vooruitzien **2** toekomstplanning, voorzorg

foreskin voorhuid

forest woud[h] [also fig]; bos[h]

forestall 1 vóór zijn **2** vooruitlopen op **3** (ver)hinderen, dwarsbomen, voorkomen

forester boswachter, houtvester

foretaste voorproef(je[h])

foretell voorspellen, voorzeggen

forethought toekomstplanning, voorzorg, vooruitziende blik

forever 1 (voor) eeuwig, voorgoed, (voor) altijd **2** onophoudelijk, aldoor: *I was ~ dragging David away from the fireplace* ik moest David aldoor bij de open haard wegslepen

forewarn van tevoren waarschuwen ‖ *~ed is forearmed* een gewaarschuwd man telt voor twee

foreword voorwoord[h]; woord[h] vooraf

[1]**forfeit** (n) het verbeurde, boete, straf

[2]**forfeit** (vb) verbeuren, verspelen, verbeurd verklaren

[1]**forge** (n) **1** smidse, smederij **2** smidsvuur[h]

[2]**forge** (vb) **1** vervalsing(en) maken, valsheid in geschrifte plegen **2** vooruitschieten: *~ ahead* gestaag vorderingen maken

[3]**forge** (vb) **1** smeden [also fig]; bedenken, beramen **2** vervalsen: *a ~d passport* een vals paspoort

forger vervalser, valsemunter

forgery 1 vervalsing, namaak **2** het vervalsen, oplichterij

[1]**forget** (vb) vergeten, nalaten, verwaarlozen: *~ to do sth.* iets nalaten te doen

[2]**forget** (vb) vergeten, niet denken aan, niet meer weten: [inform] *~ (about) it* laat maar, denk er maar niet meer aan; [inform] *So you want to borrow my car? ~ it!* Dus jij wil mijn auto lenen? Vergeet het maar!; *not ~ting* en niet te vergeten, en ook

forgetful vergeetachtig; verstrooid

forget-me-not vergeet-mij-nietje[h]

forgive vergeven ‖ *Dick forgave his sister the money he had lent her* Dick schold zijn zus het geld kwijt dat hij haar geleend had

forgo zich onthouden van, afstand doen van, het zonder (iets) doen

[1]**fork** (n) **1** vork, hooivork, mestvork **2** tweesprong, splitsing

[2]**fork** (vb) **1** zich vertakken, zich splitsen, uiteengaan: *~ed tongue* gespleten tong **2** afslaan, een richting opgaan: *~ right* rechts afslaan

forklift truck vorkheftruck

fork out (geld) dokken

forlorn 1 verlaten, eenzaam **2** hopeloos, troosteloos ‖ *~ hope* hopeloze onderneming, laatste hoop

[1]**form** (n) **1** (verschijnings)vorm, gedaante, silhouet[h] **2** vorm, soort[+h], systeem[h] **3** vorm(geving), opzet, presentatiewijze **4** formulier[h], voorgedrukt vel[h] **5** formaliteit, vast gebruik[h], gewoonte: *true to ~* geheel in stijl, zoals gebruikelijk **6** [sport] conditie, vorm: *be on ~, be in great ~* goed op dreef zijn **7** manier, wijze, vorm **8** (school)klas: *first ~* eerste klas

[2]**form** (vb) zich vormen, verschijnen, zich ontwikkelen

[3]**form** (vb) **1** vormen, modelleren, vorm geven **2** maken; opvatten [plan]; construeren, samenstellen: *~ (a) part of* deel uitmaken van

formal formeel, officieel, volgens de regels

formality 1 vormelijkheid, stijfheid **2** formaliteit

[1]**format** (n) **1** (boek)formaat[h], afmeting, grootte, uitvoering **2** manier van samenstellen, opzet **3** (beschrijving van) opmaak; indeling [of data]

[2]**format** (vb) formatteren, opmaken; indelen [data etc]

formation 1 vorming **2** formatie, opstelling, verband[h]: *fly in ~* in formatie vliegen

formative vormend, vormings-: *the ~ years of his career* de beginjaren van zijn loopbaan

formatting het formatteren, opmaak

[1]**former** (n) leerling [of certain form]: *second-~* tweedeklasser

[2]**former** (dem pron) **1** eerste; eerstgenoemde [of two] **2** vroeger, voorafgaand, vorig: *in*

~ *days* in vroeger dagen
formerly vroeger, eertijds, voorheen
form feed paginadoorvoer; formuliertoevoer
formidable 1 ontzagwekkend, gevreesd **2** formidabel, geweldig, indrukwekkend
formula 1 formule, formulering, formulierʰ; [fig] cliché ͪ **2** formule, samenstelling, receptʰ **3** [Am] flesvoeding
formulate 1 formuleren **2** opstellen, ontwerpen, samenstellen
fornicate [form] overspel plegen
forsake verlaten, in de steek laten, opgeven
fort fortʰ, vesting, sterkte || **hold** the ~ de zaken waarnemen, op de winkel letten
forth voort, tevoorschijn: **bring** ~ **a)** voortbrengen, veroorzaken; **b)** baren || **hold** ~ uitweiden; *and so* ~ enzovoort(s)
forthcoming 1 aanstaand, verwacht, aangekondigd: *her* ~ *album* haar binnenkort te verschijnen album **2** tegemoetkomend, behulpzaam **3** [also with negation] beschikbaar, ter beschikking: *an explanation was not* ~ en verklaring bleef uit
forthright rechtuit, openhartig, direct
forthwith onmiddellijk; terstond
fortieth veertigste
fortification versterking, fortificatie
fortify versterken, verstevigen
fortitude standvastigheid, vastberadenheid
fortnight veertien dagen, twee weken: *a* ~ *on* **Monday** **a)** maandag over veertien dagen; **b)** maandag veertien dagen geleden; *Tuesday* ~ dinsdag over veertien dagen
fortress vesting, versterkte stad, fortʰ
fortuitous 1 toevallig, onvoorzien **2** [inform] gelukkig
fortunate gelukkig, fortuinlijk, gunstig
fortune 1 fortuinʰ, voorspoed, gelukʰ **2** lotgevalʰ, (toekomstige) belevenis: *tell* ~s de toekomst voorspellen **3** fortuinʰ, vermogenʰ, rijkdom: *she* **spends** *a* ~ *on clothes* ze geeft een vermogen uit aan kleren
fortune cookie gelukskoekjeʰ
fortune hunter gelukzoeker
fortune-teller waarzegger
forty veertig: *a man* **in** *his forties* een man van in de veertig
¹forward (n) [sport] voorspeler: *centre* ~ middenvoor
²forward (adj) **1** voorwaarts, naar voren (gericht) **2** vroegrijp: *a* ~ *girl* een vroegrijp meisje **3** arrogant, brutaal **4** voorst, vooraan gelegen **5** gevorderd, opgeschoten **6** vooruitstrevend, modern, geavanceerd **7** termijn-, op termijn: ~ *planning* toekomstplanning
³forward (vb) **1** doorsturen; nazenden [mail]: *he* ~*ed the* **email** *to a friend* hij stuurde

de e-mail door naar een vriend **2** zenden, (ver)sturen, verzenden
⁴forward (adv) **1** voorwaarts, vooruit; naar voren [in space; also fig]: *backward(s) and* ~ vooruit en achteruit, heen en weer **2** vooruit, vooraf; op termijn [in time]: *from today* ~ vanaf vandaag
forwarding address doorstuuradresʰ
forwards voorwaarts, vooruit, naar voren
forward slash slash
¹fossil (n) fossielʰ
²fossil (adj) fossiel: ~ *fuel* fossiele brandstof
foster 1 koesteren, aanmoedigen; [fig] voeden **2** opnemen in het gezin; als pleegkind opnemen [without adoption]: ~ *parent* pleegouder
foster parent pleegouder
¹foul (n) [sport] overtreding, fout
²foul (adj) **1** vuil, stinkend, smerig, vies: ~ *weather* smerig weer **2** vuil, vulgair: *a* ~ *temper* een vreselijk humeur; ~ *language* vuile taal **3** [sport] onsportief, gemeen, vals: [oft fig] ~ *play* onsportief spel, boze opzet, misdaad || *fall* ~ *(of)* in aanvaring komen (met)
³foul (vb) [sport] een overtreding begaan, in de fout gaan
⁴foul (vb) **1** bevuilen, bekladden **2** [sport] een overtreding maken op
foul-mouthed ruw in de mond, vulgair
foul-up 1 verwarring, onderbreking **2** blokkering, mechanisch defectʰ, storing
found 1 grondvesten; funderen [also fig] **2** stichten, oprichten, tot stand brengen: *this bakery was* ~*ed in 1793* deze bakkerij is in 1793 opgericht
foundation 1 stichting, fondsʰ, oprichting **2** fundering [also fig]; fundamentʰ, basis: *the story is completely without* ~ het verhaal is totaal ongegrond
foundation course basiscursus
¹founder (n) stichter, oprichter, grondlegger
²founder (vb) **1** invallen, instorten, mislukken: *the project* ~*ed* **on** *the ill will of the government* het project mislukte door de onwil van de regering **2** zinken, vergaan, schipbreuk lijden
founding father grondlegger; stichter, oprichter
foundling vondeling
foundry (metaal)gieterij
fountain 1 fontein: ~ *pen* vulpen **2** bron [also fig]
fountainhead [form] bron; diepe oorsprong
four vier, viertal, vierspan || *be* **on** *all* ~s op handen en knieën lopen, kruipen
four-leaved clover klavertjevierʰ
four-letter word schuttingwoordʰ
four-poster bed hemelbedʰ

foursome viertal^h, kwartet^h
foursquare 1 vierkant, vierhoekig 2 resoluut, open en eerlijk, vastbesloten
fourteen veertien
fourteenth veertiende
fourth vierde, kwart
fowl kip, hoen^h, haan
¹**fox** (n) vos [also fig]
²**fox** (vb) doen alsof
³**fox** (vb) 1 beetnemen, bedriegen, te slim af zijn 2 in de war brengen
foxglove vingerhoedskruid^h
foxhound jachthond
foxy 1 vosachtig 2 [esp Am; inform] sexy 3 sluw
frack fracken
fraction 1 breuk, gebroken getal^h: *decimal* ~ tiendelige breuk; *vulgar* ~ (gewone) breuk 2 fractie, (zeer) klein onderdeel^h
fractious 1 onhandelbaar, dwars, lastig 2 humeurig, prikkelbaar
fracture 1 fractuur, (bot)breuk, beenbreuk 2 scheur, barst, breuk
fractured [Am; inform] stomdronken; teut, lazarus
fragile breekbaar, broos
fragment fragment^h, deel^h, (brok)stuk^h
fragmentation versplintering
fragrance geur, (zoete) geurigheid
fraidy cat [Am; child language] bangerik
frail breekbaar, zwak, tenger, teer
¹**frame** (n) 1 (het dragende) geraamte [of construction]; skelet^h [wood construction]; frame^h [of bicycle]; raamwerk^h, chassis^h 2 omlijsting, kader^h, kozijn^h; montuur^{+h} [of glasses]; raam^h [of window etc] 3 [oft fig] (gestructureerd) geheel^h, structuur, opzet: ~(s) *of reference* referentiekader^h || ~ *of mind* gemoedsgesteldheid
²**frame** (vb) 1 vorm geven aan, ontwerpen, uitdenken, formuleren, uitdrukken, vormen, vervaardigen, verzinnen, zich inbeelden 2 inlijsten, omlijsten, als achtergrond dienen voor 3 [inform] erin luizen, in de val laten lopen, (opzettelijk) vals beschuldigen: *the swindlers were* ~d de zwendelaars werden in de val gelokt
frame-up complot^h, gearrangeerde beschuldiging, valstrik
framework 1 geraamte^h 2 structuur; kader^h
France Frankrijk
franchise 1 stemrecht^h, burgerrecht^h 2 concessie 3 franchise, systeemlicentie
¹**frank** (adj) (+ with) openhartig (tegen), oprecht, eerlijk: *~ly, I don't give a damn* eerlijk gezegd kan het me geen barst schelen
²**frank** (vb) 1 frankeren 2 stempelen, automatisch frankeren
frankly eerlijk gezegd: ~, *I don't like it* eerlijk gezegd vind ik het niet leuk

frantic 1 dol, buiten zichzelf, uitzinnig: *the noise drove me* ~ het lawaai maakte me hoorndol 2 [inform] verwoed, extreem: ~ *efforts* verwoede pogingen
fraternal broederlijk [also fig]; vriendelijk
fraternity 1 broederlijkheid 2 genootschap^h, broederschap, vereniging: *the medical* ~ de medische stand 3 [Am] studentencorps^h; studentenclub [for men]
fraternize zich verbroederen
fratricide broedermoord, zustermoord
fraud 1 bedrog^h, fraude, zwendel 2 bedrieger, oplichter 3 vervalsing, bedriegerij, oplichterij: *the newly-discovered Rembrandt was a* ~ de pas ontdekte Rembrandt was een vervalsing
fraudster fraudeur
fraudulence bedrog^h, bedrieglijkheid
fraudulent [form] frauduleus, vals
fraught vol, beladen: *the journey was* ~ *with danger* het was een reis vol gevaren
¹**fray** (n) strijd, gevecht^h, twist: *eager for the* ~ strijdlustig
²**fray** (vb) verzwakken, uitputten: *~ed nerves* overbelaste zenuwen
³**fray** (vb) (uit)rafelen, verslijten
frazzled [Am; inform] 1 zat, dronken 2 uitgeput, er helemaal doorheen zittend
¹**freak** (n) 1 gril, kuur, nuk 2 uitzonderlijk verschijnsel^h 3 [inform] fanaticus, freak, fanaat
²**freak** (adj) abnormaal, uitzonderlijk, ongewoon: *a* ~ *accident* een bizar ongeval; ~ *weather* typisch weer
³**freak** (vb): ~ *out* door het lint gaan, helemaal gek worden, flippen
¹**freak out** (vb) bang maken: *that song always freaks me out* ik vind dat nummer altijd heel naar klinken
²**freak out** (vb) door het lint gaan, helemaal gek worden: *he is freaking out on drugs* hij is helemaal high
freckle (zomer)sproet
¹**free** (adj) 1 vrij, onafhankelijk, onbelemmerd: *a* ~ *agent* iem. die vrij kan handelen; ~ *fight* algemeen gevecht; *give* (or: *allow*) *s.o. a* ~ *hand* iem. de vrije hand laten; [socc] ~ *kick* vrije schop; ~ *speech* vrijheid van meningsuiting; *set* ~ vrijlaten, in vrijheid stellen; ~ *from care* vrij van zorgen, onbekommerd; ~ *of charge* gratis, kosteloos 2 vrij, gratis, belastingvrij: [inform] *for* ~ gratis, voor niets 3 vrij, zonder staatsinmenging: ~ *enterprise* (de) vrije onderneming; ~ *trade* vrije handel, vrijhandel 4 vrij, niet bezet, niet in gebruik; [science] ongebonden: *is this seat* ~? is deze plaats vrij? 5 vrijmoedig, vrijpostig: ~ *and easy* ongedwongen, zorgeloos || ~ *pardon* gratie(verlening)
²**free** (vb) 1 bevrijden, vrijlaten 2 verlossen, losmaken, vrijstellen

³free (adv) **1** vrij, los, ongehinderd: *the dogs ran* ~ de honden liepen los **2** gratis

freebie [inform] weggevertje[h], iets dat je gratis krijgt

freebooter vrijbuiter [oft fig]; kaper

freedom 1 vrijheid, onafhankelijkheid: ~ *of the press* persvrijheid; ~ *of speech* vrijheid van meningsuiting **2** vrijstelling, ontheffing, vrijwaring: ~ *from sth.* het vrij zijn van iets; het niet gebukt gaan onder iets

free-floating zich vrij bewegend, rondzwervend; [eg e-scooter] geen vaste parkeerplaats hebbend

free-for-all [inform] **1** algemene ruzie; algemeen gevecht[h] **2** vrij spel[h]; wildwestsituatie

freehold 1 volledig eigendomsrecht **2** vrij bezit

free house pub die (or: café[h] dat) niet onder contract staat bij een brouwerij

¹freelance (adj) freelance, onafhankelijk, zelfstandig

²freelance (vb) freelance werken, als freelancer werken

freeload klaplopen, profiteren, bietsen

freeman 1 vrij man **2** ereburger

freemason vrijmetselaar

freephone (het) gratis bellen [eg an 0800 number]

freepost antwoordnummer[h] || ~ *no. 1111* antwoordnummer 1111

free-range scharrel-: ~ *eggs* scharreleieren

freesia fresia

freestyle 1 [swimming] vrije slag, (borst)-crawl **2** [wrestling etc] vrije stijl

freeware [comp] gratis software

freeway [Am] snelweg, autoweg

freewheel rustig aandoen [also fig]

¹freeze (n) **1** vorst, vorstperiode **2** bevriezing, blokkering, opschorting: *a wage* ~ een loonstop

²freeze (vb) vriezen: *it is freezing in here* het is hier ijskoud; *the government froze all contracts* de regering bevroor alle contracten

³freeze (vb) bevriezen [also fig]; verstijven, ijzig behandelen, opschorten: *make one's blood* ~ het bloed in de aderen doen stollen; ~ *out* [inform] uitsluiten || *frozen with fear* verstijfd van angst

freezer 1 diepvries, diepvriezer **2** vriesvak[h]

¹freezing (n) [inform] vriespunt[h]: *six degrees below* ~ zes graden onder het vriespunt (or: nul)

²freezing (adj) ijskoud, kil [also fig]: *my hands are* ~ ik heb ijskoude handen; *it's* ~ *cold* het is ijskoud; *the atmosphere was* ~ er hing een kille sfeer

freezing point vriespunt[h]

freight vracht(goederen)

freight car [Am] goederenwagon

¹French (n) Frans[h], de Franse taal: *the* ~ de

Fransen

²French (adj) Frans: ~ *bread* (or: *loaf*) stokbrood[h] || ~ *bean* sperzieboon; ~ *fries* patat, friet; ~ *kiss* tongzoen; *take* ~ *leave* er tussenuit knijpen; ~ *windows* openslaande (bal-kon)deuren, openslaande (terras)deuren

¹French kiss (n) tongzoen

²French kiss (vb) tongzoenen

Frenchman Fransman

Frenchwoman Française, Franse

frenetic jachtig; woest; verwoed

frenzy (vlaag van) waanzin, razernij, staat van opwinding

frequency 1 frequentie, (herhaald) voorkomen[h] **2** [science] frequentie, trillingsgetal[h], periodetal[h] **3** [radio] frequentie, golflengte

¹frequent (adj) frequent, veelvuldig: *a* ~ *caller* een regelmatig bezoeker

²frequent (vb) regelmatig bezoeken

fresh 1 vers, pas gebakken, vers geplukt: ~ *from the oven* zo uit de oven, ovenvers **2** nieuw, ander, recent: *a* ~ *attempt* een hernieuwde poging **3** zoet [of water]; niet brak **4** zuiver, helder, levendig: ~ *air* frisse lucht **5** fris, koel, nogal koud: *a* ~ *breeze* een frisse bries [wind-force 5] **6** [inform] brutaal, flirterig

freshen in kracht toenemen, aanwakkeren

freshen up 1 opfrissen, verfrissen **2** zich opfrissen, zich verfrissen

fresher [inform] eerstejaars(student)

freshman eerstejaars(student), groene

freshwater zoetwater-

fret zich ergeren, zich opvreten (van ergernis), zich zorgen maken: *the child is* ~*ting for its mother* het kind zit om z'n moeder te zeuren

fretful geïrriteerd, zeurderig

fretsaw figuurzaag

friar monnik, broeder

friction wrijving [also fig]; frictie, onenigheid

Friday vrijdag: *on* ~*(s)* vrijdags, op vrijdag

fridge [inform] *refrigerator* koelkast, ijskast

fried gebakken: ~ *egg* spiegelei[h]

friend 1 vriend(in), kameraad, kennis, collega: *make* ~*s with s.o.* bevriend raken met; *can we still be* ~*s?* kunnen we vrienden blijven?; ~ *with benefits* vriend(in) met wie iem. af en toe seks heeft; *a* ~ *in need (is a* ~ *indeed)* in nood leert men zijn vrienden kennen **2** vriend(in), voorstander, liefhebber

friendly 1 vriendelijk, welwillend, aardig **2** vriendschappelijk, bevriend, gunstig gezind: ~ *nations* bevriende naties

friendship vriendschap

friendzone [inform] als vriend zien i.p.v. als potentiële geliefde

fries [esp Am] patat; [Belg] frieten

Friesian *see* ¹*Frisian*

frieze fries⁺ʰ, sierlijst

frigate fregatʰ

fright angst, vrees, schrik: **give** a ~ de schrik op 't lijf jagen; *he took ~ at the sight of the knife* de schrik sloeg hem om 't hart toen hij het mes zag

frighten bang maken, doen schrikken, afschrikken: *we were ~ed to **death*** we schrokken ons dood; ~ *s.o. to **death*** iem. de stuipen op het lijf jagen; *be ~ed **of** snakes* bang voor slangen zijn

frightful 1 angstaanjagend **2** [inform] afschuwelijk: *I am ~ly **late*** ik ben vreselijk laat

frigid 1 koud [also fig]; koel, onvriendelijk **2** frigide

frill 1 (sier)strook **2** (-s) franje [also fig]; fraaiigheden, kouwe drukte

fringe 1 franje **2** randgroepering, randverschijnselʰ: *the ~s of **society*** de zelfkant van de maatschappij **3** pony(haarʰ)

fringe benefit secundaire arbeidsvoorwaarde

frisbee frisbee

¹Frisian (n) Friesʰ

²Frisian (n) Fries

¹frisk (vb) huppelen, springen

²frisk (vb) fouilleren: *stop and ~ s.o.* iem. preventief aanhouden en fouilleren

frisky vrolijk, speels

fritter away verkwisten, verspillen

frivolous 1 onbelangrijk, pietluttig, onnozel **2** frivool, lichtzinnig

frizz kroeskop, kroeshaarʰ, krul(len)

¹frizzle (vb) **1** krullen, kroezen **2** sissen; knetteren [in pan]

²frizzle (vb) **1** kroezend maken, doen krullen: ~ *up* friseren **2** laten sissen; laten knetteren [in pan]; braden, bakken

fro *see ¹to*

frock jurk, japon

frog kikker, kikvors: *as mad as a **box** of ~s* zo gek als een deur || *have a ~ in one's throat* een kikker in de keel hebben, schor/hees zijn

frogman kikvorsman

¹frolic (n) pret, lol, gekheid: *the little **boys** were having a ~* de jongetjes waren aan het stoeien

²frolic (vb) **1** (rond)dartelen, rondhossen **2** pret maken

from van, vanaf, vanuit: ~ *one **day** to the next* van de ene dag op de andere; *judge ~ the **facts*** oordelen naar de feiten; *I heard ~ **Mary*** ik heb bericht gekregen van Mary; *recite ~ **memory*** uit het geheugen opzeggen; ~ *bad **to** worse* van kwaad tot erger; *(in) a week ~ **now*** over een week

¹front (n) **1** voorkant, voorste gedeelteʰ: *the driver sits **in** (the) ~* de bestuurder zit voorin; *in ~ **of** voor*, in aanwezigheid van **2** [mil] frontʰ [also fig]; gevechtslinie **3** façade [also fig]; schijn, dekmantel: *show (or: put on) a **bold** ~*

zich moedig voordoen **4** (strand)boulevard, promenade langs de rivier **5** [meteorology] frontʰ

²front (adj) **1** voorst, eerst: ~ *garden* voortuin; ~ *runner* koploper **2** façade-, camouflage-: ~ *organisation* mantelorganisatie || *up ~* eerlijk, rechtdoorzee

frontage 1 frontʰ; voorgevel **2** voorterreinʰ

frontal frontaal, voor-: ~ *attack* frontale aanval

front crawl borstcrawl

front door voordeur

frontier grens(gebiedʰ): *the ~s of **knowledge*** de grenzen van het weten

frontline frontlinie [also fig]

front office administratie, administratieve afdeling

front page voorpagina [of newspaper]

front runner [athletics] koploper

fronts grill

¹frost (n) vorst, bevriezing: *there was five **degrees** of ~* het vroor vijf graden

²frost (vb) **1** bevriezen [plant etc] **2** glaceren [cake] **3** matteren [glas, metal]: ~ed *glass* matglas

frostbite bevriezing

frosting [esp Am] eiwitglazuurʰ

frosty vriezend, (vries)koud; [fig] ijzig; afstandelijk: ~ *welcome* koele verwelkoming

¹froth (n) **1** schuimʰ **2** oppervlakkigheid, zeepbel **3** gebazelʰ

²froth (vb) schuimen, schuimbekken

³froth (vb) doen schuimen; [milk] opschuimen

¹frown (n) frons, fronsende blik, afkeuring

²frown (vb) de wenkbrauwen fronsen, streng kijken, turen; [fig] ~ *at* (or: *on*) afkeuren(d staan tegenover)

frozen 1 bevroren, vastgevroren, doodgevroren: ~ *over* dichtgevroren **2** (ijs)koud [also fig]; ijzig, hard **3** diepvries-, ingevroren: ~ *food* diepvriesvoedselʰ **4** [econ] bevroren, geblokkeerd: ~ *assets* bevroren tegoeden

frugal 1 (+ of) zuinig (met), spaarzaam (met) **2** schraal, karig, sober

fruit 1 vrucht, stukʰ fruit **2** fruitʰ, vruchten: [also fig] *bear ~* vrucht dragen **3** (-s) opbrengst, resultaatʰ

fruit cup bowl, punch, vruchtenbowl

fruiterer fruithandelaar, fruitkoopman

fruitful vruchtbaar [also fig]; productief, lonend

fruition vervulling, verwezenlijking, realisatie: *bring (or: come) to ~* in vervulling doen gaan

fruit machine fruitautomaat, gokautomaat

frumpish slonzig; t(r)uttig

frustrate frustreren, verijdelen: ~ *s.o. in his plans*, ~ *s.o.'s **plans*** iemands plannen dwars-

bomen
frustrating vervelend, frustrerend
frustration 1 frustratie, teleurstelling **2** verijdeling, dwarsboming
¹fry (n) jonge vis, broedselʰ; [fig] kleintjeʰ; jonkieʰ
²fry (vb) braden, bakken, frituren: *fried egg* spiegelei
frying pan koekenpan ‖ *from* (or: *out*) *of the* ~ *into the fire* van de wal in de sloot
ft *foot, feet* ft, voet
FTM *female to male* VNM *(vrouw-naar-man)*
¹fuck (vb) [vulg] neuken, naaien, wippen
²fuck (n): [vulg] *what the* ~ *is going on here?* wat is hier verdomme aan de hand?
fucking [vulg] klote-, kut-; fokking: ~ *a* klootzak; *that's none of your* ~ *business* dat gaat je geen moer aan
¹fuck off (vb) [vulg] opsodemieteren
²fuck off (vb) [vulg] pissig maken
fuck up [vulg] verkloten; verpesten
fuddled verward, in de war, beneveld, dronken
¹fudge (n) **1** onzin, larie **2** zachte karamel
²fudge (vb) **1** knoeien (met), vervalsen **2** er omheen draaien, ontwijken **3** in elkaar flansen
¹fuel (n) brandstof; [fig] voedselʰ: ~ *for dissension* stof tot onenigheid
²fuel (vb) **1** van brandstof voorzien, voeden [fire, oven etc] **2** [fig] voeden, veroorzaken: *~led by* versterkt door, aangewakkerd door
fuel oil stookolie
fug bedomptheid, mufheid
fugitive vluchteling, voortvluchtige
fugue fuga
fulfil volbrengen, vervullen, uitvoeren, voltooien: ~ *a condition* aan een voorwaarde voldoen; ~ *a purpose* aan een doel beantwoorden
fulfilment 1 vervulling **2** voldoening
¹full (n) totaalʰ, geheelʰ: *in* ~ volledig, voluit
²full (adj) vol, volledig: ~ *board* vol(ledig) pension; ~ *to the brim* boordevol; *come* ~ *circle* weer terugkomen bij het begin; [fig] *give* ~ *marks for sth.* iets hoog aanslaan, iets erkennen; ~ *moon* vollemaan; *(at)* ~ *speed* (in) volle vaart; ~ *stop* punt [punctuation mark]; *come to a* ~ *stop* (plotseling) tot stilstand komen; *in* ~ *swing* in volle gang; ~ *of o.s.* vol van zichzelf; *he was* ~ *of it* hij was er vol van
³full (adv) **1** volledig, ten volle: ~ *ripe* helemaal rijp **2** zeer, heel: *know sth.* ~ *well* iets zeer goed weten **3** vlak, recht: *hit s.o.* ~ *on the nose* iem. recht op zijn neus slaan
full-blooded 1 volbloed, raszuiver **2** volbloedig, energiek
full-blown 1 in volle bloei **2** goed ontwikkeld, volledig: ~ *war* regelrechte oorlog
full-grown volwassen, volgroeid
full-scale volledig, totaal, levensgroot

full-time fulltime, met volledige dagtaak: *a* ~ *job* een volledige baan
fully 1 volledig, geheel: ~ *automatic* volautomatisch **2** minstens, ten minste: ~ *an hour* minstens een uur
fully-fledged 1 geheel bevederd [of bird] **2** volwassen, ten volle ontwikkeld **3** (ras)echt, volslagen
fulminate foeteren; fulmineren; heftig uitvaren
fulsome overdreven
¹fumble (vb) struikelen, hakkelen, klunzen
²fumble (vb) **1** tasten, morrelen (aan), rommelen (in): ~ *about* rondtasten **2** [ball game] fumbelen
¹fume (n) (onwelriekende/giftige) damp, rook
²fume (vb) **1** roken, dampen **2** opstijgen [of fume] **3** [fig] koken [with rage]; branden: ~ *at* verbolgen zijn over
fumigate uitroken, zuiveren
¹fun (n) pret, vermaakʰ, plezierʰ: *figure of* ~ groteske figuur, schertsfiguur; ~ *and games* pretmakerij, iets leuks; *make* ~ *of, poke* ~ *at* voor de gek houden, de draak steken met; *for* ~, *for the* ~ *of it* (or: *the thing*) voor de aardigheid; *for* ~, *in* ~ voor de grap
²fun (adj) prettig, amusant, gezellig: *a* ~ *guy* een leuke kerel; *a* ~ *game* een leuk spelletje
¹function (n) **1** functie, taak, werking **2** plechtigheid, ceremonie, receptie, feestʰ: *I have a* ~ *tonight* ik ga vanavond naar een feest (receptie)
²function (vb) functioneren, werken: ~ *as* fungeren als
functional functioneel, doelmatig, bruikbaar
functionality functionaliteit [also comp]
functionary functionaris, beambte
function key functietoets
function room zaal, receptiezaal, feestzaal
fund 1 fondsʰ **2** voorraad, bron, schat: *a* ~ *of knowledge* een schat aan kennis **3** (-s) fondsen, geldʰ, kapitaalʰ: *short of* ~s slecht bij kas
¹fundamental (n) (grond)beginselʰ, grondslag, fundamentʰ
²fundamental (adj) fundamenteel, grond-, basis-
fundamentalism fundamentalismeʰ
funding fondsgelden
fund raiser 1 benefietʰ **2** fondsenwerver
funeral 1 begrafenis(plechtigheid); [Am] rouwdienst **2** [Am] begrafenisstoet **3** [inform] zorg, zaak: *it's your* ~ het is jouw zorg
funereal akelig, droevig, triest: *a* ~ *expression* begrafenisgezichtʰ
funfair 1 pretparkʰ, amusementsparkʰ **2** reizende kermis
fungal schimmel-

fungus fungus, paddenstoel, schimmel
funicular kabelbaan; kabeltrein
funk [inform] schrik, angst: *be in* a *(blue)* ~ in de rats zitten
funky 1 [Am; inform] funky, eenvoudig; gevoelsmatig [of music] **2** [inform] extravagant, cool **3** [Am] stinkend
¹**funnel** (n) **1** trechter **2** koker, pijp; schoorsteen(pijp) [of steamship]
²**funnel** (vb) afvoeren (als) door een trechter: ~ *off* doen afvloeien
funny 1 grappig, leuk **2** vreemd, gek **3** niet in orde, niet pluis: *there is sth.* ~ *about* er is iets niet pluis met **4** misselijk, onwel: *feel* ~ zich onwel voelen ‖ ~ *bone* telefoonbotjeʰ [in elbow]
fur 1 vacht **2** bontʰ, pels(werkʰ), bontjas **3** aanslag, beslagʰ
furious 1 woedend, razend **2** fel, verwoed, heftig: *a* ~ *quarrel* een felle twist
furlough verlofʰ, verloftijd: *on* ~ met verlof
furnace oven, verwarmingsketel, hoogoven
furnish 1 verschaffen, leveren, voorzien van **2** uitrusten, meubileren, inrichten: *a* ~*ed house* een gemeubileerd huis
furnishings woninginrichting
furniture meubilairʰ, meubels: *a* *piece* *of* ~ een meubelstuk
furniture van verhuiswagen
furrow 1 voorʰ, gleuf, groef, rimpel **2** zogʰ; spoorʰ [of ship]
¹**further** (adj) verder, nader: *on* ~ *consideration* bij nader inzien; ~ *education* voortgezet onderwijs voor volwassenen
²**further** (vb) bevorderen, stimuleren: ~ *s.o.'s interests* iemands belangen behartigen
³**further** (adv) verder, nader, elders: *inquire* ~ nadere inlichtingen inwinnen
furthermore verder, bovendien
furthermost verst (verwijderd)
furthest verst, laatst, meest
furtive heimelijk
fury woede(aanval), razernij
¹**fuse** (n) **1** lont **2** (schok)buis, ontsteker **3** zekering, stop: *a* ~ *has blown* er is een zekering gesprongen
²**fuse** (vb) **1** (doen) fuseren [of businesses etc] **2** (doen) uitvallen [of electrical appliance]
fusion fusie(procesʰ), (samen)smelting, mengeling, coalitie, kernfusie
fusion bomb waterstofbom
¹**fuss** (n) (nodeloze) drukte, omhaal, ophef: *I don't understand what all the* ~ *is* *about* ik snap niet waar al die heisa om gemaakt wordt; *kick* up (or: *make*) *a* ~ heibel maken, luidruchtig protesteren; *make a* ~ *of* (or: *over*) overdreven aandacht schenken aan
²**fuss** (vb) (+ about) zich druk maken (om), drukte maken, zich opwinden: ~ *about* ze-

nuwachtig rondlopen
fussy 1 (overdreven) druk, zenuwachtig, bemoeiziek **2** pietluttig, moeilijk: [inform] *I'm not* ~ het is mij om het even
futile vergeefs, doelloos
futility nutteloosheid, doelloosheid
futsal futsalʰ, zaalvoetbalʰ
¹**future** (n) toekomst: *in the* *distant* ~ in de verre toekomst; *for the* (or: *in*) ~ voortaan, in 't vervolg
²**future** (adj) toekomstig, aanstaande: ~ *tense* toekomende tijd
fuzz 1 donsʰ, pluisʰ, donzig haarʰ **2** [inform] smeris [policeman]; de smerissen [the police]
fuzzy 1 donzig, pluizig **2** kroes, krullig **3** vaag **4** verward ‖ [maths] ~ *logic* fuzzy logic, vage logica
FWB [inform] *friend with benefits* vriend(in) om af en toe seks mee te hebben
FWIW [inform] *for what it's worth* voor wat het waard is
f-word vloekwoordʰ
FYI *for your information* ter info(rmatie)

g

g *gram(s)* g, gram
gabble kakelen, kwebbelen: ~ *away* erop los kletsen
gable gevelspits, geveltop
gabled met gevelspits
Gabon Gabon
¹Gabonese (n) Gabonees, Gabonese
²Gabonese (adj) Gabonees
gadfly paardenvlieg, horzel
gadget (handig) dingetjeʰ, apparaatjeʰ, snufjeʰ
gadgetry snufjes
Gaelic Gaelischʰ
gaffe blunder; flater
gaffer chef-technicus [at TV or film shootings]
¹gag (n) **1** (mond)prop **2** (zorgvuldig voorbereid) komisch effectʰ **3** grap
²gag (vb) kokhalzen, braken: ~ *on sth.* zich in iets verslikken
³gag (vb) een prop in de mond stoppen
gaga 1 kierewiet: *go* ~ kinds worden **2** stapel: *be* ~ *about* stapel zijn op
gaggle 1 vlucht (ganzen) **2** (snaterend) gezelschap: *a* ~ *of girls* een stel snaterende meisjes
gaiety vrolijkheid, pret, opgewektheid
¹gain (n) **1** aanwinst **2** groei, stijging, verhoging **3** (-s) winst, opbrengst
²gain (vb) **1** winst maken **2** winnen: ~ *(up)on* terrein winnen op, inhalen **3** groeien **4** voorlopen [of timepiece]: *my watch ~s (three minutes a day)* mijn horloge loopt (elke dag drie minuten meer) voor
³gain (vb) winnen, verkrijgen, behalen: ~ *the victory* (or: *the day*) de overwinning behalen; ~ *weight* aankomen
gainful 1 winstgevend **2** bezoldigd; betaald
gait gang, pas, loop
¹gal (n) meid, meisjeʰ
²gal *gallon(s)*
galactic galactisch; van de Melkweg
galaxy Melkweg
gale storm, harde wind
¹gall (n) **1** gal(blaas) **2** bitterheid, rancune **3** galnoot, galappel **4** brutaliteit, lef+ʰ
²gall (vb) (mateloos) irriteren, razend maken
gallant dapper, moedig; indrukwekkend [of ship, horse]
gallantry 1 moedige daad **2** moed, dapperheid **3** hoffelijkheid
gall bladder galblaas

galleon galjoenʰ
gallery 1 galerij, portiek+ʰ, (zuilen)gang **2** galerij, balkonʰ **3** museumʰ, museumzaal **4** (kunst)galerie **5** engelenbak: [fig] *play to the* ~ op het publiek spelen, effect najagen; commercieel zijn
galley 1 galei **2** kombuis
Gallic Gallisch, Frans
gallicize verfransen
gallon gallon+ʰ [measure of capacity]
¹gallop (n) galop: *at a* ~ in galop, op een galop; [fig] op een holletje
²gallop (vb) galopperen; [fig] zich haasten; vliegen
gallows galg
gallows humour galgenhumor
gallstone galsteen
galore in overvloed, genoeg: *examples* ~ voorbeelden te over
galvanic 1 galvanisch **2** opwindend, opzienbarend
galvanize prikkelen, opzwepen: ~ *s.o. into action* (or: *activity*) iem. tot actie aansporen
Gambia (the) Gambia
¹Gambian (n) Gambiaan(se)
²Gambian (adj) Gambiaans
¹gamble (n) gok(jeʰ) [also fig]; riskante zaak, speculatie: *take a* ~ *(on)* een gokje wagen (op); *it is a* ~ het is een gok
²gamble (vb) **1** gokken, spelen, dobbelen: ~ *on* gokken op **2** speculeren
³gamble (vb) op het spel zetten, inzetten: ~ *away* vergokken
gambler gokker
gambling gokkerij
¹game (n) **1** spelʰ [also fig]; wedstrijd, partij: ~ *of chance* kansspelʰ; *play the* ~ eerlijk (spel) spelen, zich aan de regels houden; *it is all in the* ~ het hoort er (allemaal) bij **2** spelletjeʰ, tijdverdrijfʰ **3** [tennis] game: *(one)* ~ *all* gelijk(e stand); ~ *and (set)* game en set **4** plannetjeʰ: *two can play (at) that* ~ dat spelletje kan ik ook spelen; *none of your (little)* ~s*!* geen kunstjes!; *the* ~ *is up* het spel is uit, nu hangen jullie **5** jachtdierʰ; prooi [also fig] **6** (-s) spelenʰ, (atletiek)wedstrijden **7** (-s) gym(nastiek); sport [at school] || *beat* (or: *play*) *s.o. at his own* ~ iem. een koekje van eigen deeg geven
²game (adj) **1** dapper, kranig, flink **2** bereid(willig), enthousiast: *be* ~ *to do sth.* bereid zijn om iets te doen; *I am* ~ ik doe mee **3** lam; kreupel [of arm, leg]
game changer ingrijpende wijziging, radicale verandering: *that's a (total)* ~ dat verandert alles, dat zet de zaak volledig op zijn kop
gamecock vechthaan
gamekeeper jachtopziener
games computer spelcomputer
game show spelshow

gammon 1 (gekookte) achterham **2** gerookte ham

gamut gamma⁺ʰ [also fig]; toonladder, scala⁺ʰ, reeks: *the whole ~ of human **experience*** het hele register van menselijke ervaringen

gander mannetjesgans ‖ *have/take a ~ **at*** een blik werpen op

gang groep mensen, (boeven)bende, troep; ploeg [workers]: *violent **street** ~s* gewelddadige straatbendes; *a ~ of labourers removing graffiti* een ploeg werklui die graffiti verwijderen

gang-banger 1 groepsverkrachter **2** [Am] lidʰ van een straatbende

gangling slungelig

gangplank loopplank

gangrene 1 koudvuurʰ **2** verrotting

¹**gangsta** (n) [Am; inform] gangster, bendelidʰ

²**gangsta** (adj) [Am; inform] heftig

gangsta rap [Am; inform] gangsterrap

gangster gangster, bendelidʰ

gang up een bende vormen, (samen)klieken, zich verenigen: *~ **against** (or: on)* samenspannen tegen, aanvallen; *~ **with*** zich aansluiten bij, samenspannen met

gangway 1 doorgang **2** (gang)padʰ [in theatre etc] **3** loopplank

gaol *see* ¹*jail*

gap (tussen)ruimte, opening, gatʰ, kloof, barst, ravijnʰ, tekortʰ: ***bridge** (or: **close, fill**) a ~* **a)** een kloof overbruggen; **b)** een tekort aanvullen; *some developing countries are quickly **closing** the ~* sommige ontwikkelingslanden lopen snel de achterstand in

gape 1 gapen, geeuwen **2** geopend zijn, gapen: *gaping **wound*** gapende wond **3** staren: *~ **at*** aangapen, aanstaren

gapper [educ] student op een tussenjaar

gap year tussenjaarʰ: *take a ~* een jaartje ertussenuit gaan

garage garage, garagebedrijfʰ, benzinestationʰ

garb dracht, kledij

garbage 1 afvalʰ, huisvuilʰ **2** rommel

garbage can vuilnisbak, vuilnisvatʰ

garbage collector vuilnisman

garble onvolledige voorstelling geven van, verkeerd voorstellen, verdraaien: *~d **account*** verdraaide voorstelling

¹**garden** (n) tuin [also fig]; groenten, bloementuin: *the ~ of **Eden*** de hof van Eden, het Aards Paradijs; ***lead** up the ~ (path)* om de tuin leiden

²**garden** (vb) tuinieren

gardener tuinman, hovenier, tuinier

gardening het tuinieren, tuinbouw

garden party tuinfeestʰ

gargantuan gigantisch

gargle gorgelen

gargoyle waterspuwer

garish 1 fel, schel **2** bont, opzichtig

garland 1 slinger **2** lauwer(krans)

garlic knoflookʰ

garment kledingstukʰ: *~s* kleren

garner [form] opslaan; vergaren: *~ **in** (or: up)* binnenhalen

¹**garnish** (n) garnering, versiering

²**garnish** (vb) garneren, verfraaien, opkloppen

¹**garotte** (n) wurgpaal; garrot

²**garotte** (vb) verwurgen

garret zolderkamertjeʰ

garrison garnizoenʰ, garnizoensplaats

garter kousenband, jarretelle

gas 1 gasʰ, gifgasʰ, lachgasʰ, mijngasʰ: ***natural** ~* aardgasʰ **2** benzine: ***step** on the ~* gas geven, er vaart achter zetten **3** [inform] gezwamʰ, kletspraat, gekletsʰ

gasbag kletsmeier

gas chamber gaskamer

gas fitter gasfitter

gas guzzler [inform] benzineslokop

gash 1 jaap, gapende wond **2** kloof, breuk

gasket pakking

gaslight 1 gaslamp **2** gaslichtʰ

gas lighter gasaansteker, gasontsteker

gas main hoofd(gas)leiding

gasman meteropnemer

gas mark stand

gasoline 1 gasoline **2** benzine

¹**gasp** (n) snik: *at one's last ~* bij de laatste ademtocht

²**gasp** (vb) **1** (naar adem) snakken, naar lucht happen: *~ **for** breath* naar adem snakken **2** hijgen, puffen, snuiven

³**gasp** (vb) haperend uitbrengen, hijgend uitbrengen: *'call an ambulance!' she ~ed* 'bel een ziekenwagen!', hijgde ze

gas ring gaspit

gas station benzinestationʰ, tankstationʰ

gassy 1 met een hoog koolzuurgehalte, met veel prik **2** [Am] winderig

gastric maag-: *~ **band*** maagband

gastronome fijnproever

gastronomy fijnproeverij

gasworks gasfabriek(en)

gate 1 poort(jeʰ), deur, hekʰ, ingang, afsluitboom, slagboom, sluis(deur), schuif; gate [at airport]; perronʰ: ***anti-theft** ~s* anti-diefstalpoortjes **2** [sport] publiekʰ [number of paying spectators]: *a ~ of **2000*** 2000 man publiek **3** entreegelden

gatecrash (onuitgenodigd) binnenvallen [at party etc]

gatecrasher onuitgenodigde gast, indringer

gatekeeper portierʰ

gate money entreegelden; recette

gatepost deurpost ‖ *between **you** and me and the ~* onder ons gezegd en gezwegen

gateway 1 poort: *the ~ to **success*** de poort

tot succes; *the ~ to **Europe*** de toegangspoort tot Europa **2** [drugs] opstapje[h]: *can marijuana be a ~ to* the use of other drugs? kan cannabis een opstapje zijn naar het gebruik van andere drugs?

¹gather (vb) **1** zich verzamelen, samenkomen: *~ round* bijeenkomen; *~ round* s.o. *(sth.)* zich rond iem. (iets) scharen **2** zich op(een)hopen, zich op(een)stapelen

²gather (vb) **1** verzamelen, samenbrengen, bijeenroepen, op(een)hopen, op(een)stapelen, vergaren, inzamelen, plukken, oogsten, oprapen: *~ (one's) **strength*** op krachten komen; *~ **wood*** hout sprokkelen; *~ **speed*** op snelheid komen **2** opmaken, afleiden, concluderen: *your husband is not in I ~* uw echtgenoot is niet thuis, begrijp ik; *~ **from*** afleiden uit

gathering 1 bijeenkomst, vergadering **2** verzameling, op(een)stapeling, op(een)hoping

gauche onhandig, onbeholpen

gaudy opzichtig, schel, bont

¹gauge (n) **1** standaardmaat, ijkmaat, vermogen[h], capaciteit, inhoud; kaliber[h] [also of firearms]: *narrow-~* film smalfilm **2** meetinstrument[h], meter, kaliber[h]

²gauge (vb) meten, uitmeten, afmeten, opmeten, peilen

gaunt 1 uitgemergeld, vel over been **2** somber

gauntlet kaphandschoen, sporthandschoen, werkhandschoen: *fling* (or: *throw*) *down the ~* iem. uitdagen; *pick* (or: *take*) *up the ~* de uitdaging aanvaarden; *run the ~* spitsroeden (moeten) lopen

gauze gaas[h], verbandgaas[h], muggengaas[h]

gavel voorzittershamer

gawk [inform] gapen: *~ at* sth. naar iets staan gapen

gawky klungelig, onhandig

¹gay (n) homo(seksueel), nicht, lesbienne

²gay (adj) **1** homoseksueel: *~ **marriage*** (or: *blessing*) homohuwelijk[h] **2** vrolijk, opgeruimd **3** fleurig, bont: *~ **colours*** bonte kleuren

gaydar [inform] speciale antenne voor (het ontdekken van) homo's

gaze staren, aangapen: *~ at* (or: *on*) aanstaren

gazelle gazel(le), antilope

gazette krant, dagblad[h]

gazillion [esp Am; inform] onbepaald groot getal[h], massa, tig: *make ~s of dollars* zakken vol dollars verdienen

GB *Great Britain* Groot-Brittannië

GBF [inform] *gay best friend* homovriend

GCE *General Certificate of Education* middelbareschooldiploma[h], havodiploma[h], vwo-diploma[h]

GCSE *General Certificate of Secondary Education* eindexamen[h]

GDPR *General Data Protection Regulation* AVG *(Algemene Verordening Gegevensbescherming)*

¹gear (n) **1** toestel[h], mechanisme[h], apparaat[h], inrichting: *landing ~* landingsgestel[h] **2** transmissie, koppeling, versnelling: *bottom ~* eerste versnelling; *reverse ~* achteruit; *top ~* hoogste versnelling; *change ~* (over)schakelen **3** uitrusting, gereedschap[h], kledij, spullen: *hunting ~* jagersuitrusting

²gear (vb) (over)schakelen, in (een) versnelling zetten: *~ **down*** terugschakelen, vertragen; *~ **up*** opschakelen, overschakelen

gearbox versnellingsbak

gearlever (versnellings)pook

gear to afstemmen op, instellen, afstellen op: *be geared to* ingesteld zijn op, berekend zijn op

gearwheel tandwiel[h], tandrad[h]

gee jee(tje)!

geek sukkel, fanaat: *computer~* computerfanaat

geezer (ouwe) vent

¹gel (n) gel[+h]

²gel (vb) **1** gel(ei)achtig worden, stollen **2** vorm krijgen [of ideas etc]; goed kunnen samenwerken [of people]; lukken

gelatin gelatine(achtige stof)

geld castreren

gelding castraat, gecastreerd paard[h], ruin

gem 1 edelsteen, juweel[h] **2** kleinood[h], juweeltje[h]

Gemini [astrology] (de) Tweelingen

gemstone (half)edelsteen

gender 1 [linguistics] grammaticaal geslacht[h] **2** geslacht[h], sekse **3** gender

gender identity genderidentiteit

gender-neutral geslachtsneutraal, genderneutraal: *~ **clothing*** uniseks kleding

gender pronoun aanspreekvorm: *my boss's preferred ~ is 'she'* mijn baas wil als vrouw aangesproken worden

gene gen[h]

genealogy genealogie, familiekunde

¹general (n) **1** algemeenheid, het algemeen: *in ~* in het algemeen **2** generaal, veldheer

²general (adj) algemeen: *~ **anaesthetic*** algehele verdoving; *~ **election*** algemene, landelijke verkiezingen; *in the ~ **interest*** in het algemeen belang; *the ~ **public*** het grote publiek; *as a ~ **rule*** in 't algemeen, doorgaans ‖ *~ **delivery*** poste restante; *~ **practitioner*** huisarts

generality algemeenheid

generalize generaliseren, veralgemenen, (zich) vaag uitdrukken

generally 1 gewoonlijk, meestal **2** algemeen: *~ **known*** algemeen bekend **3** in het algemeen, ruwweg: *~ **speaking*** in 't algemeen

general-purpose voor algemeen gebruik; universeel

generate genereren, doen ontstaan, voortbrengen; ~ *electricity* elektriciteit opwekken; ~ *heat* warmte ontwikkelen

generation 1 generatie, (mensen)geslacht^h, mensenleven^h **2** generatie, voortplanting, ontwikkeling

generation gap generatiekloof

generator generator

generic 1 de soort betreffende, generiek **2** algemeen, verzamel- || ~ *drugs* merkloze geneesmiddelen

generosity vrijgevigheid, gulheid

generous 1 grootmoedig, edel(moedig) **2** vrijgevig, royaal, gul **3** overvloedig, rijk(elijk)

genesis ontstaan^h, wording

Genesis (het bijbelboek) Genesis

genetic genetisch: ~ *engineering* genetische manipulatie; ~ *fingerprint* genenprint; ~*ally modified* genetisch gemodificeerd

geneticist geneticus

genetics genetica, erfelijkheidsleer

Geneva Genève

genial 1 mild, zacht, aangenaam; warm [of weather, climate etc] **2** vriendelijk, sympathiek

geniality hartelijkheid, sympathie, vriendelijkheid

genital genitaal, geslachts-, voortplantings-

genitalia genitaliën, geslachtsorganen

genitive genitief, tweede naamval

¹**genius** (n) **1** genie^h [pers]: *be a ~ at* geniaal zijn in **2** genialiteit, begaafdheid: *a woman of ~* een geniale vrouw **3** geest: *evil ~* kwade genius

²**genius** (adj) [inform] briljant, geniaal

Genoa Genua^h

genocide genocide, volkerenmoord

genre genre^h, soort^{+h}, type^h

gent gentleman, heer || [inform] *the Gents* het herentoilet

genteel 1 [oft iron] chic, elegant: ~ *poverty* fatsoenlijke/stille armoede **2** aanstellerig

¹**gentile** (n) niet-jood, christen, heiden

²**gentile** (adj) niet-joods, christelijk, ongelovig

gentility deftigheid, voornaamheid

gentle 1 voornaam, van goede afkomst **2** zacht, licht, (ge)matigd(d): ~ *pressure* lichte dwang; *hold* it *gently* hou het voorzichtig vast **3** zacht(aardig), teder, vriendelijk: *the ~ sex* het zwakke geslacht **4** kalm, bedaard, rustig

gentleman 1 (echte) heer: *Ladies and Gentlemen!* Dames en Heren! **2** edelman

gentleman's agreement herenakkoord^h

gentrification 1 gentrificatie, yuppificatie

2 fatsoenering, vernetting

gentry lage(re) adel, voorname stand: *landed ~* (groot)grondbezitters, lage landadel

genuflect [form] een kniebuiging maken

genuine 1 echt, zuiver, onvervalst: ~ *parts* oorspronkelijke onderdelen **2** oprecht, eerlijk

genus 1 soort^{+h}, genre^h, klasse **2** genus^h, geslacht^h

geographer aardrijkskundige, geograaf

geographic(al) aardrijkskundig, geografisch

geography aardrijkskunde, geografie: [inform] *the ~ of the house* de indeling van het huis

geological geologisch

geologist geoloog

geology geologie

geometric(al) meetkundig

geometry meetkunde

Georgia Georgië

Georgian 1 Georgisch [of Georgia] **2** Georgian [of or characteristic of the time of King George]

gerbil woestijnrat

geriatric ouderdoms-; [depr] aftands; oud

geriatrics geriatrie, ouderdomszorg

germ 1 [biology] kiem, geslachtscel; [fig] oorsprong; begin^h **2** [med] ziektekiem, bacil

¹**German** (n) Duits^h, de Duitse taal

²**German** (n) Duitse(r)

³**German** (adj) Duits: ~ *shepherd* Duitse herder(shond) || ~ *measles* rodehond

Germanic 1 Germaans **2** Duits

Germany Duitsland

germ carrier bacillendrager, kiemdrager

germinate [also fig] ontkiemen, ontspruiten: *the idea ~d with him* het idee kwam bij hem op

germ warfare biologische oorlogvoering

gerontology ouderdomskunde

gestation dracht(tijd), zwangerschap(speriode)

gesticulate gebaren

¹**gesture** (n) gebaar^h, geste, teken^h: *a ~ of friendship* een vriendschappelijk gebaar

²**gesture** (vb) gebaren, (met gebaren) te kennen geven

¹**get** (vb) **1** (ge)raken, (ertoe) komen, gaan, bereiken: ~ *rid of sth.* zich van iets ontdoen; *he is ~ting to be an old man* hij wordt een oude man aan het worden; *he never ~s to drive the car* hij krijgt nooit de kans om met de auto te rijden; ~ *lost* verdwalen; ~ *lost!* loop naar de maan!; ~ *to see s.o.* iem. te zien krijgen; ~ *ahead* vooruitkomen, succes boeken; ~ *behind* achteropraken; [fig] ~ *nowhere* (or: *somewhere*) niets (or: iets) bereiken; ~ *there* er komen, succes boeken; ~ *above o.s.* heel wat van zichzelf denken; ~ *at* a) bereiken, te

pakken krijgen, komen aan, komen achter; **b)** [inform] bedoelen; **c)** bekritiseren; **d)** knoeien met; **e)** omkopen; **f)** ertussen nemen; ~ *at the truth* de waarheid achterhalen; *what are you ~ting at?* wat bedoel je daarmee?; ~ *in* contact (or: *touch*) *with* contact opnemen met; ~ *into the car* in de auto stappen; *what has got into you?* wat bezielt je?, wat heb je?; ~ *off* **a)** afstappen van [bicycle, pavement, lawn]; **b)** ontheven worden van [obligation]; ~ *onto s.o.* iem. te pakken krijgen; ~ *on(to) one's bike* op zijn fiets stappen; ~ *out of sth.* ergens uitraken, zich ergens uit redden; ~ *out of the way* uit de weg gaan, plaatsmaken; ~ *over* te boven komen, overwinnen; ~ *over an illness* genezen van een ziekte; *I still can't ~ over the fact that …* ik heb nog steeds moeite met het feit dat …, ik kan er niet over uit dat …; ~ *through* heen raken door [time, money, clothing, work]; ~ *through an exam* slagen voor een examen; ~ *to* bereiken, kunnen beginnen aan, toekomen aan; *where has he got to?* waar is hij naartoe?; ~ *to the top of the ladder* (or: *tree*) de top bereiken **2** beginnen, aanvangen: ~ *going!* (or: *moving!*) vooruit!, begin (nu eindelijk)!; ~ *going* **a)** op dreef komen [of person]; **b)** op gang komen [of party, project, machine etc]; ~ *to like sth.* ergens de smaak van te pakken krijgen || ~ *off the **ground*** van de grond raken; [inform] ~ ***stuffed!*** stik!, val dood!

²**get** (vb) **1** (ver)krijgen, verwerven: ~ *a **glimpse** of* vluchtig te zien krijgen; ~ *one's **hands** on* te pakken krijgen; ~ ***leave*** verlof krijgen; ~ *what is coming to one* krijgen wat men verdient; ~ *sth. **out of** s.o.* iets van iem. loskrijgen **2** (zich) aanschaffen, kopen: *my car was stolen, so I had to* ~ *a new one* mijn auto was gestolen, dus moest ik een nieuwe kopen **3** bezorgen, verschaffen, voorzien: ~ *s.o. some **food*** iem. te eten geven; ~ *sth. **for** s.o.* iem. iets bezorgen, iets voor iem. halen **4** doen geraken, doen komen, gaan, brengen, krijgen, doen: ~ *sth. **going*** iets op gang krijgen, iets op dreef helpen; ~ *s.o. **talking*** iem. aan de praat krijgen; [inform, fig] *it ~s you **nowhere*** je bereikt er niets mee; ~ *sth. **into** one's head* zich iets in het hoofd halen; ~ *sth. **into** s.o.'s head* iets aan iem. duidelijk maken; ~ *s.o. **out of** sth.* iem. aan iets helpen ontsnappen **5** maken, doen worden, bereiden, klaarmaken: ~ ***dinner*** *(ready)* het avondmaal bereiden; *let me* ~ *this **clear*** (or: ***straight***) laat me dit even duidelijk stellen; ~ ***ready*** klaarmaken; ~ *sth. **done*** iets gedaan krijgen **6** nemen, vangen, opvangen, ontvangen, grijpen, (binnen)halen: *go and* ~ *your breakfast!* ga maar ontbijten! **7** overhalen, zover krijgen: ~ *s.o. to **talk*** iem. aan de praat krijgen **8** [inform] hebben, krijgen: *he*

got a mobile phone for his birthday hij kreeg een mobieltje voor zijn verjaardag **9** vervelen, ergeren: *it really ~s me when* ik erger me dood wanneer **10** snappen, begrijpen, verstaan: *he has finally got the **message*** (or: *got **it***) hij heeft het eindelijk door; ~ *sth. (s.o.) **wrong*** iets (iem.) verkeerd begrijpen

³**get** (aux vb) worden: ~ ***killed*** *(in an accident)* omkomen (bij een ongeluk); ~ ***married*** trouwen; ~ ***punished*** gestraft worden

⁴**get** (vb) (ge)raken, worden: ~ ***better*** beter worden; ~ ***used*** *to* wennen aan; ~ ***even*** *with s.o.* het iem. betaald zetten

get across 1 oversteken, aan de overkant komen **2** begrepen worden; aanslaan [of idea etc]; succes hebben **3** overkomen [of person]; bereiken, begrepen worden: ~ *to the audience* zijn gehoor weten te boeien

get along 1 vertrekken, voortmaken, weggaan **2** opschieten, vorderen: *is your work getting along?* schiet het al op met je werk? **3** (zich) redden, het stellen, het maken: *we can ~ **without** your help* we kunnen je hulp best missen **4** (+ with) (kunnen) opschieten (met), overweg kunnen (met): *they ~ very **well*** ze kunnen het goed met elkaar vinden

get (a)round 1 op de been zijn; rondlopen [of person, after illness] **2** rondtrekken, rondreizen, overal komen **3** zich verspreiden; de ronde doen [of news]: *get (a)round to s.o.* iem. ter ore komen **4** gelegenheid hebben, toekomen: *get (a)round **to** sth.* **a)** aan iets kunnen beginnen; **b)** ergens de tijd voor vinden

getaway ontsnapping: *make one's* ~ ontsnappen

get away 1 wegkomen, weggaan: *did you manage to* ~ *this summer?* heb je deze zomer wat vakantie kunnen nemen? **2** ontsnappen, ontkomen: ~ *from* ontsnappen aan; *you can't* ~ *from this* hier kun je niet (meer) onderuit || ~ *from it all* even alles achterlaten, er tussenuit gaan; *he'll never* ~ *with it* dat lukt hem nooit; *some students* ~ *with murder* sommige studenten mogen echt alles en niemand die er wat van zegt; *commit a crime and* ~ *with it* ongestraft een misdaad bedrijven

¹**get back** (vb) terugkomen, teruggaan, thuiskomen: ~*!* terug!, naar buiten! || ~ *at* (or: *on*) *s.o.* het iem. betaald zetten

²**get back** (vb) **1** terugkrijgen, terugvinden **2** terugbrengen, terughalen, naar huis brengen || *get one's own back (on s.o.)* het iem. betaald zetten

get by 1 zich er doorheen slaan, zich redden, het stellen: ~ *without* sth. het zonder iets kunnen stellen **2** (net) voldoen, er (net) mee door kunnen

¹**get down** (vb) dalen: ~ *on one's knees* op zijn knieën gaan (zitten) || ~ *to* sth. aan iets kunnen beginnen, aan iets toekomen; ~ *to*

gibberish

business ter zake komen; ~ **to** *work* aan het werk gaan

²**get down** (vb) **1** doen dalen, naar beneden brengen; naar binnen krijgen [food] **2** deprimeren, ontmoedigen: *it is not just the work that gets you down* het is niet alleen het werk waar je depressief van wordt

get-go: [inform] *from* the ~ vanaf het begin

¹**get in** (vb) **1** binnenkomen; toegelaten worden [to school, university]: ~ **on** sth. aan iets meedoen; [inform] ~ **on** the act mogen meedoen **2** instappen [into vehicle]

²**get in** (vb) **1** binnenbrengen; binnenhalen [harvest]; inzamelen [money]: *get the* **doctor** *in* de dokter er bij halen; *I couldn't get a word in (edgeways)* ik kon er geen speld tussen krijgen, ik kreeg geen kans om ook maar iets te zeggen

¹**get off** (vb) **1** ontsnappen, ontkomen **2** afstappen, uitstappen: *you should* ~ *at Denmark Street* je moet bij Denmark Street uitstappen **3** vertrekken, beginnen: ~ **to** *a good start* flink van start gaan, goed beginnen **4** in slaap vallen **5** vrijkomen, er goed afkomen: ~ *lightly* er licht van afkomen ‖ ~ **with** het aanleggen met, aanpappen met

²**get off** (vb) **1** doen vertrekken, doen beginnen **2** doen vrijkomen, er goed doen afkomen, vrijspraak krijgen voor: *he got me off* **with** *a fine* hij zorgde ervoor dat ik er met een bon af kwam **3** (op)sturen [letter]; wegsturen: *get s.o. off* **to** *school* iem. naar school sturen **4** eraf krijgen: *I can't get the lid off* ik krijg het deksel er niet af **5** uittrekken [clothing, shoes]; afnemen **6** leren, instuderen: *get sth. off* **by** *heart* iets uit het hoofd leren

¹**get on** (vb) **1** vooruitkomen, voortmaken, opschieten: ~ **with** *one's work* goed opschieten met zijn werk **2** bloeien, floreren **3** (+ with) (kunnen) opschieten met, overweg kunnen met **4** oud (laat) worden: *he is getting on (in years)* hij wordt oud, hij wordt een dagje ouder **5** opstappen [horse, bicycle]; opstijgen; instappen [bus, aeroplane] ‖ *he is getting on* **for** *fifty* hij loopt tegen de vijftig; ~ **to** sth. **a)** iets door hebben; **b)** iets op het spoor komen

²**get on** (vb) **1** aantrekken, opzetten: ~*e's hat and coat on* zijn hoed opzetten en zijn jas aantrekken **2** erop krijgen: *I can't get the lid on* ik krijg het deksel er niet op

¹**get out** (vb) **1** uitlekken, bekend worden **2** naar buiten gaan, weggaan, eruit komen **3** ontkomen, maken dat je weg komt, ontsnappen: *no-one here gets out alive* niemand komt hier levend vandaan **4** afstappen, uitstappen

²**get out** (vb) eruit halen (krijgen) [splinter, stains; also fig]

¹**get over** (vb) begrepen worden [of joke, comedian]

²**get over** (vb) overbrengen [meaning etc]; duidelijk maken, doen begrijpen

¹**get through** (vb) (er) doorkomen, zijn bestemming bereiken; goedgekeurd worden [of bill]; aansluiting krijgen [by telephone etc]; begrepen worden: ~ **to a)** bereiken, doordringen tot, contact krijgen met; **b)** begrepen worden door

²**get through** (vb) **1** zijn bestemming doen bereiken, laten goedkeuren; erdoor krijgen [also at exams] **2** duidelijk maken, aan zijn verstand brengen

get-together bijeenkomst

¹**get up** (vb) **1** opstaan, recht (gaan) staan **2** opsteken [of wind, storm etc] ‖ ~ **to a)** bereiken; **b)** gaan naar, benaderen; *what is he getting up* **to** *now?* wat voert hij nu weer in zijn schild?

²**get up** (vb) **1** organiseren; op touw zetten [party, play] **2** maken, ontwikkelen, produceren: ~ **speed** versnellen **3** instuderen, bestuderen ‖ *get one up on s.o.* iem. de loef afsteken; ~ **to** doen bereiken

get-up 1 uitrusting, kostuum[h] **2** uitvoering, formaat[h] **3** aankleding, decor[h]

geyser 1 geiser **2** (gas)geiser

GF [inform] *girlfriend* vriendin, vriendinnetje[h]

Ghana Ghana

¹**Ghanaian** (n) Ghanees, Ghanese

²**Ghanaian** (adj) Ghanees

ghastly verschrikkelijk, afgrijselijk

gherkin augurk

ghetto getto[h]

¹**ghost** (n) **1** geest, spook[h], spookverschijning **2** spook(beeld)[h], fata morgana **3** spoor[h], greintje[h]: *not have the* ~ *of a* **chance** geen schijn van kans hebben; *a* ~ *of a* **smile** een zweem van een glimlach ‖ *give up the* ~ de geest geven, sterven

²**ghost** (vb) [dating] steeds minder reageren en ten slotte het contact verbreken

ghosting 1 identiteitsdiefstal van overleden personen **2** [dating] het niet meer reageren op iemands berichten

ghostly spookachtig

ghost town spookstad

ghostwriter spookschrijver

ghoul gruwelijk, morbide mens[h]; monster[h]

ghoulish 1 gruwelijk; morbide **2** satanisch

GHQ *General Headquarters* hoofdkwartier[h]

GI dienstplichtige

giant reus, kolos; [fig] uitblinker: *Shakespeare is one of the* ~*s of English literature* Shakespeare is een van de allergrootsten in de Engelse literatuur

giant killer reuzendoder [person who beats a favourite]

gibber brabbelen

gibberish gebrabbel[h]

gibbon gibbon

¹**gibe** (n) spottende opmerking

²**gibe** (vb) (be)spotten, schimpen: ~ *at* de draak steken met

giddy 1 duizelig, draaierig, misselijk **2** duizelingwekkend **3** frivool, wispelturig, lichtzinnig

gift 1 cadeauʰ, geschenkʰ, gift: *free* ~ gratis geschenk [by way of promotion] **2** gave, talentʰ, aanleg: *have the* ~ *of (the) gab* a) welbespraakt zijn; **b)** praatziek zijn

gifted begaafd, talentvol, intelligent

gift-horse gegeven paardʰ [fig]; geschenkʰ: *don't look a* ~ *in the mouth* je moet een gegeven paard niet in de bek zien

gift shop cadeauwinkel(tjeʰ)

giftwrap als cadeautje inpakken, in cadeaupapier inpakken

giftwrapped ingepakt als een cadeautje, in geschenkverpakking: *the second goal came* ~ het tweede doelpunt was een cadeautje

gift-wrapping geschenkverpakking

gig 1 optredenʰ, concertʰ **2** [inform; esp Am] baantjeʰ

gigantic gigantisch, reusachtig (groot)

¹**giggle** (n) gegiechelʰ: *have the* ~*s* de slappe lach hebben

²**giggle** (vb) giechelen (van)

gigolo gigolo

gild vergulden; [fig] versieren; opsmukken

gilded verguld; [fig] versierd; sierlijk: *today's* ~ *youth* de rijkeluisjeugd van deze tijd

gill kieuw

gilt 1 goudgerande schuldbrief [with government guarantee] **2** verguldselʰ

gilt-edged 1 goudgerand **2** met rijksgarantie: ~ *shares* goudgerande aandelen

gimme *give me* geef mij, toe (nou), kom op nou

gimmick truc(jeʰ), vondst

gimmicky op effect gericht [of products]

gin gin, jenever

ginger 1 gember(plant) **2** roodachtig bruinʰ; [of person] rooie

ginger ale gemberbierʰ

gingerbread gembercake, gemberkoek, peperkoek

gingerly (uiterst) voorzichtig

ginger up stimuleren, opvrolijken, oppeppen

ginseng ginseng(plant)

gipsy zigeuner(in)

giraffe giraf(fe)

gird 1 [form] omgorden **2** zich gereed maken: [form] ~ *o.s. up* zich vermannen; zich voorbereiden

girder steunbalk, draagbalk, dwarsbalk

girdle gordel, (buik)riem, korsetʰ

girl 1 meisjeʰ **2** dienstmeisjeʰ **3** liefjeʰ, vriendinnetjeʰ

girlfriend vriendin(netjeʰ), meisjeʰ

Girl Guide padvindster

Girl Scout padvindster

giro 1 giro(dienst): *National Giro* postgiro **2** girocheque

girth 1 buikriem; singel **2** omtrek; omvang; [hum] dikke buik: *one metre in* ~ met een omtrek van één meter

gist (the) hoofdgedachte, essentie, kern

give 1 geven, schenken, overhandigen: ~ *him my best wishes* doe hem de groeten van mij; ~ *a dinner* een diner aanbieden **2** geven, verlenen, verschaffen, gunnen: ~ *a prize* een prijs toekennen; *we were* ~*n three hours' rest* we kregen drie uur rust; *he has been* ~*n two years* hij heeft twee jaar (gevangenisstraf) gekregen; ~ *s.o. to understand* (or: *know*) iem. te verstaan (*or:* kennen) geven **3** geven, opofferen, wijden: ~ *one's life for one's country* zijn leven geven voor zijn vaderland **4** doen: ~ *a beating* een pak slaag geven; ~ *a cry* een kreet slaken; ~ *s.o. a sly look* iem. een sluwe blik toewerpen **5** (op)geven, meedelen: *the teacher gave us three exercises (to do)* de onderwijzer heeft ons drie oefeningen opgegeven (als huiswerk); ~ *information* informatie verstrekken **6** produceren, voortbrengen: ~ *off* (af)geven, verspreiden, maken ‖ ~ *or take 5 minutes* 5 minuten meer of minder; ~ *as good as one gets* met gelijke munt betalen; *don't* ~ *me that* (hou op met die) onzin; ~ *s.o. what for* iem. flink op zijn donder geven

give-and-take geven en nemen; compromisʰ

give away 1 weggeven, cadeau doen **2** verraden, verklappen

give-away 1 cadeautjeʰ **2** onthulling, (ongewild) verraadʰ

give in (+ to) toegeven (aan), zich gewonnen geven, zwichten (voor)

¹**given** (adj) **1** gegeven, gekregen, verleend **2** gegeven [also maths]; (wel) bepaald, vastgesteld: *under the* ~ *conditions* onder de gegeven omstandigheden; *at any* ~ *time* om het even wanneer, op elk moment **3** geneigd: ~ *to drinking* verslaafd aan de drank

²**given** (prep) gezien: ~ *the present situation* in het licht van de huidige situatie

³**given** (conj) [often with 'that'] aangezien: ~ *(that) you don't like it* aangezien je het niet leuk vindt

given name voornaam, doopnaam

¹**give out** (vb) uitgeput raken, opraken

²**give out** (vb) **1** afgeven, verspreiden, maken **2** verdelen, uitdelen, uitreiken

¹**give over** (vb) ophouden, stoppen

²**give over** (vb) afzien van, stoppen, opgeven: *I asked the students to* ~ *chewing gum in class* ik verzocht de studenten om geen kauwgom meer te kauwen tijdens de les

¹**give up** (vb) opgeven, zich gewonnen ge-

ven: ~ *on* geen hoop meer hebben voor; *I* ~ *on you* je bent hopeloos

²**give up** (vb) **1** opgeven, afstand doen van, niet langer verwachten, alle hoop opgeven voor; [inform] laten zitten: ~ *one's seat* zijn zitplaats afstaan; ~ *for dead* (or: *lost*) als dood (*or:* verloren) beschouwen [also fig]; ~ *smoking* stoppen met roken **2** ophouden **3** overgeven, overleveren, (toe)wijden: *give o.s. up* zich gevangen geven, zich melden

gizmo dingetjeʰ, apparaatjeʰ

glacial ijs- [also fig]; ijzig, ijskoud: ~ *detritus* gletsjerpuinʰ; ~ *era* ijstijd(vak)

glacier gletsjer

glad blij, gelukkig, verheugd: *be ~ to see the back* of *s.o.* iem. gaarne zien vertrekken; *I'd be ~ to!* met plezier!; *I'll be ~ to help* ik wil je graag helpen [also iron]; ~ *about* (or: *at, of*) blij om, verheugd over

gladden blij maken

gladiator gladiator

gladiolus gladiool

gladly graag, met plezier

glam [inform] *glamorous* (zeer) aantrekkelijk; prachtig, glitter-

glamorous (zeer) aantrekkelijk, bekoorlijk, betoverend (mooi), prachtig, glitter-

glamour betovering, schone schijn

glamping *glamour camping* het luxe kamperen

glampsite glamping

¹**glance** (n) (vluchtige) blik, oogopslag, kijkjeʰ: *at a* ~ met één oogopslag, onmiddellijk

²**glance** (vb) (vluchtig) kijken, een (vluchtige) blik werpen: ~ *at* even bekijken, een blik werpen op

gland klier: *sweat* ~*s* zweetklieren

¹**glare** (n) **1** woeste (dreigende) blik **2** verblindend lichtʰ [also fig]; (felle) glans

²**glare** (vb) **1** fel schijnen, blinken, schitteren: *the sun* ~*d down* on *our backs* de zon brandde (fel) op onze rug **2** boos kijken, woest kijken

glaring verblindend, schitterend, fel: ~ *colours* schreeuwende kleuren **2** dreigend, woest: ~ *eyes* vlammende ogen

glass 1 glasʰ, (drink)glasʰ, brillenglasʰ, spiegel **2** lens **3** glasʰ [drink] **4** glas-(werk)ʰ **5** (-es) bril: *two pairs* of ~*es* twee brillen **6** (-es) verrekijker, toneelkijker || *people who live in* ~ *houses should not throw stones* wie in een glazen huisje zit, moet niet met stenen gooien

glass fibre glasvezel, glasdraad⁺ʰ

glasshouse (broei)kas

glassworks glasfabriek, glasblazerij

glassy glasachtig, glazig, (spiegel)glad

glaucoma glaucoomʰ

¹**glaze** (n) glazuurʰ, glazuurlaag

²**glaze** (vb) (also + over) glazig worden; breken [of eyes]

³**glaze** (vb) in glas zetten: *double-glazed*

windows dubbele ramen

glazing 1 glazuurʰ, glazuurlaag **2** beglazing, ruiten, ramenʰ: *double* ~ dubbel glas, dubbele ramen

¹**gleam** (n) (zwak) schijnselʰ, glans, schittering; straal(tjeʰ) [also fig]: *not a* ~ *of hope* geen sprankje hoop

²**gleam** (vb) (zwak) schijnen, glanzen, schitteren

glean 1 verzamelen, oprapen; vergaren [ears] **2** moeizaam vergaren; (bijeen) sprokkelen [information]: ~ *ideas from everywhere* overal ideeën vandaan halen

glee leedvermaakʰ, vreugde, opgewektheid

glib welbespraakt, vlot, rad van tong, glad, handig

glide 1 glijden, sluipen, zweven **2** [aviation] zweven

glider 1 zweefvliegtuigʰ **2** zweefvlieger

glimmer 1 zwak lichtʰ, glinstering, flikkering **2** straaltjeʰ [fig]: ~ *of hope* sprankje hoop

glimpse glimp: *catch* (or: *get*) *a* ~ *of* eventjes zien, een glimp opvangen van

glisten schitteren, glinsteren, glimmen: ~ *with* schitteren van, fonkelen van

glitch out stoppen als gevolg van een storing

¹**glitter** (n) geschitterʰ, glans, glinstering

²**glitter** (vb) schitteren, blinken, glinsteren: ~ *with* blinken van || *all that* ~*s is not gold* het is niet al goud wat er blinkt

glitz glitter

glitzy opzichtig, opvallend

gloat 1 wellustig staren, begerig kijken **2** zich verlustigen, zich vergenoegen: ~ *over* (or: *on*) zich verkneukelen in

glob [inform] klont; klodder, kwak

global 1 wereldomvattend, wereld-: ~ *warming* opwarming van de aarde ten gevolge van het broeikaseffect; ~ *cloud* netwerk van over de hele wereld verspreide computers die rechtstreeks met elkaar verbonden zijn **2** algemeen, allesomvattend, globaal

globalization globalisering

globalize wereldomvattend, wereldwijd maken

globe globe, aarde, wereldbol

globefish kogelvis

globetrotter globetrotter, wereldreiziger

gloom 1 duisternis, halfduisterʰ: *cast a* ~ *over sth.* een schaduw over iets werpen **2** zwaarmoedigheid, somberheid

gloomy 1 duister; donker **2** mistroostig; somber **3** hopeloos; weinig hoopgevend

glorify 1 verheerlijken, vereren **2** ophemelen, loven, prijzen: [inform] *this isn't a country house but a glorified hut* dit is geen landhuis, maar een veredeld soort hut **3** mooier voorstellen, verfraaien

glorious 1 roemrijk, glorierijk, glorieus, luisterrijk **2** prachtig, schitterend

glory 1 glorie, eer, roem: *I wrote that book for my own personal* ~ ik heb dat boek geschreven voor mijn eigen roem **2** lof, dankzegging

glory in erg genieten van, trots zijn op

gloss 1 lippenglans **2** glans **3** glamour, schone schijn

glossary verklarende woordenlijst; glossarium[h]

glossy glanzend, blinkend, glad: ~ *print* glanzende foto ‖ ~ *magazine* duur blad, glossy

glove handschoen: *fit like a* ~ als gegoten zitten ‖ *throw down the* ~ de handschoen toewerpen

glove compartment dashboardkastje[h], handschoenenkastje[h]

[1]glow (n) gloed; [fig] bezieling; enthousiasme[h]

[2]glow (vb) **1** gloeien, glimmen; [fig] bezield zijn; enthousiast zijn **2** blozen ‖ ~ *with pride* zo trots als een pauw zijn

glowworm glimworm

glucose glucose, druivensuiker

[1]glue (n) lijm

[2]glue (vb) lijmen, plakken: [fig] *his eyes were* ~*d to the girl* hij kon zijn ogen niet van het meisje afhouden

glum mistroostig

[1]glut (n) **1** overvloed **2** overschot[h]

[2]glut (vb) **1** volstoppen: ~ *o.s. with* zich volstoppen met **2** (over)verzadigen, overladen, overvoeren

glutton slokop, gulzigaard, (veel)vraat

gluttony gulzigheid; vraatzucht

gm *gram* g(r)

[1]GM (adj) *genetically modified: GM foods* genetisch gemanipuleerd voedsel

[2]GM *general manager*

GMO *genetically modified organism* ggo[h] *(genetisch gemodificeerd organisme)*

GMT *Greenwich Mean Time* GT, Greenwichtijd

gnarled knoestig, ruw, verweerd

gnash knarsetanden, tandenknarsen: ~ *one's teeth* tandenknarsen

gnat mug, muskiet

[1]gnaw (vb) knagen [also fig]; knabbelen, smart veroorzaken, pijn doen

[2]gnaw (vb) **1** knagen aan [also fig]; kwellen **2** (uit)knagen, afknagen: *the mice have* ~*n a small hole* de muizen hebben een holletje uitgeknaagd

gnome gnoom, aardmannetje[h], kabouter

GNP *gross national product* bnp[h], bruto nationaal product[h]

gnu gnoe

[1]go (n) **1** poging: *have a go at sth.* eens iets proberen **2** beurt, keer: *at* (or: *in*) *one go* in

één klap, in één keer **3** aanval ‖ *make a go of it* er een succes van maken; *(it's) no go* het kan niet, het lukt nooit

[2]go (adj) goed functionerend, in orde, klaar: *all systems (are) go* (we zijn) startklaar

[3]go (vb) **1** gaan, starten, vertrekken, beginnen: *(right) from the word go* vanaf het begin; *go to find s.o.* iem. gaan zoeken; *get going* a) aan de slag gaan; b) op gang komen; *let go* laten gaan, loslaten; [fig] *I wouldn't go so far as to say that* dat zou ik niet durven zeggen; *go about sth.* a) iets aanpakken; b) zich bezighouden met; *go by sth.* zich baseren op, zich laten leiden door; *nothing to go by* niets om op af te gaan; *go off* afgaan van, afstappen van; *go on the pill* aan de pil gaan; *go over* a) doornemen, doorlezen [text]; b) herhalen [explanation]; c) repeteren [part, lesson]; *go through* a) nauwkeurig onderzoeken, doorzoeken; b) nagaan, checken [assertion etc]; c) doornemen [text]; *we go through a difficult time* we maken een moeilijke periode door; *ready, steady, go!* klaar voor de start? af! **2** gaan, voortgaan, lopen, reizen: *go by air* (or: *car*) met het vliegtuig (or: de auto) reizen; *go for a walk* een wandeling maken; *go abroad* naar het buitenland gaan; *go along that way* die weg nemen **3** gaan (naar), wijzen (naar/op); voeren (naar) [also fig]; reiken, zich uitstrekken: *go from bad to worse* van kwaad tot erger vervallen; *the difference goes deep* het verschil is erg groot **4** gaan; (voortdurend) zijn [in a particular condition]: *as things go* in het algemeen; *go armed* gewapend zijn; *how are things going?* hoe gaat het ermee? **5** gaan, lopen, draaien; werken [of appliance, system, factory etc]: *the clock won't go* de klok doet het niet; *go slow* een langzaamaanactie houden **6** gaan; afgaan [of gun]; aflopen; luiden [of bell etc] **7** verstrijken, (voorbij)gaan; verlopen [of time]: *ten days to go to* (or: *before*) *Easter* nog tien dagen (te gaan) en dan is het Pasen **8** gaan; afleggen [distance]: *five miles to go* nog vijf mijl af te leggen **9** gaan; luiden [of poem, story]; klinken [of tune]: *the tune goes like this* het wijsje klinkt als volgt **10** aflopen, gaan, uitvallen: *how did the exam go?* hoe ging het examen?; *go well* goed aflopen, goed komen **11** doorgaan, gebeuren, doorgang vinden: *what he says goes* wat hij zegt, gebeurt ook **12** vooruitgaan, opschieten: *how is the work going?* hoe vordert het (met het) werk? **13** gelden; gangbaar zijn [of money]; gezaghebbend zijn; gezag hebben [of judgement, person]: *that goes for all of us* dat geldt voor ons allemaal **14** wegkomen, eronderuit komen, ervanaf komen: *go unpunished* ongestraft wegkomen **15** (weg)gaan; verkocht worden [of merchandise]: *go cheap* goedkoop verkocht worden; *going!,*

going!, gone! eenmaal! andermaal! verkocht! **16** gaan; besteed worden [of money, time] **17** verdwijnen; verloren gaan [also fig]: *my complaints went **unnoticed*** mijn klachten werden niet gehoord **18** verdwijnen, wijken, afgeschaft worden, afgevoerd worden: *my car must go* mijn auto moet weg **19** weggaan, vertrekken; heengaan [also fig]; sterven, doodgaan: *we must **be** going* we moeten ervandoor **20** gaan, passen, thuishoren: *the **forks** go in the top drawer* de vorken horen in de bovenste la; *where do you want this **cupboard** to go?* waar wil je deze kast hebben? **21** dienen, helpen, nuttig zijn, bijdragen: *this goes to **prove** I'm right* dit bewijst dat ik gelijk heb; *it only goes to **show*** zo zie je maar ‖ *go by the **book*** volgens het boekje handelen; *go and **get** sth.* iets gaan halen; *let o.s. go* a) zich laten gaan, zich ontspannen; b) zich verwaarlozen; *anything goes* alles is toegestaan, alles mag; *go **before*** voorafgaan [in time]; *go one **better*** (één) meer bieden; [fig] het beter doen, overtreffen; *go **easy** on* geen druk uitoefenen op, matig (*or:* voorzichtig) zijn met; *go **easy** with* aardig zijn tegen; *here goes!* daar gaat ie (dan)!; *to* go om mee te nemen [eg hot dishes]; *there **you** go* a) alsjeblieft!; b) daar heb je het (al); *go **west*** het hoekje omgaan, de pijp uitgaan; *go **wrong** a)* een fout maken, zich vergissen; b) fout (*or:* mis) gaan, de mist in gaan; *not much evidence to go on* niet veel bewijs om op af te gaan

⁴**go** (vb) **1** maken; gaan maken [trip etc] **2** afleggen, gaan: *go the shortest **way*** de kortste weg nemen ‖ *go it alone* iets helemaal alleen doen

⁵**go** (vb) worden, gaan: *go **bad*** slecht worden, bederven; *go **blind*** blind worden; *go **broke*** al zijn geld kwijtraken; *we'll have to go **hungry*** we moeten het zonder eten stellen; *the milk went **sour*** de melk werd zuur; *going **fifteen*** bijna vijftien (jaar), naar de vijftien toe

go about 1 rondlopen **2** (rond)reizen **3** de ronde doen; rondgaan [of rumour, gossip] **4** omgang hebben, verkering hebben: *~ **with** s.o.* omgaan met iem.

go across oversteken, overgaan, gaan over

goad drijven; [fig] aanzetten; prikkelen; opstoken: *she ~ed him **on** to take revenge* ze stookte hem op wraak te nemen

go against 1 ingaan tegen, zich verzetten tegen **2** indruisen tegen, in strijd zijn met, onverenigbaar zijn met

go ahead 1 voorafgaan, voorgaan, vooruitgaan: *Peter went ahead **of** the procession* Peter liep voor de stoet uit **2** beginnen, aanvangen: *we went ahead **with** our task* we begonnen aan onze taak; *~!* ga je gang!, begin maar! **3** verder gaan, voortgaan, vervolgen: *we went ahead **with** our homework* we gingen

verder met ons huiswerk

¹**go-ahead** (n, the) [inform] toestemming: *give the ~* het startsein geven, zijn fiat geven

²**go-ahead** (adj) [inform] voortvarend; ondernemend

goal 1 doelʰ: *one's ~ in **life*** iemands levensdoel **2** (eind)bestemming **3** doelʰ, goal: *keep ~* het doel verdedigen, keepen **4** doelpuntʰ, goal: *kick* (or: *make*) *a ~* een doelpunt maken

goal area doelgebiedʰ

goalie [inform] keeper, doelman

goalkeeper [sport] keeper, doelman, doelverdediger

goal kick doeltrap, uittrap, doelschop

goal line [sport] **1** doellijn **2** achterlijn

go along 1 meegaan: *she decided to ~ **with** the children* ze besloot om met de kinderen mee te gaan **2** vorderen, vooruitgaan: *the work was going along nicely* het werk schoot lekker op

go along with 1 meegaan met [also fig]; akkoord gaan met, bijvallen **2** samenwerken met, terzijde staan **3** deel uitmaken van, behoren tot, horen bij

goalpost doelpaal: *move the ~s* [fig, inform] de regels naar zijn hand zetten

go around 1 rondgaan (in), rondlopen; de ronde doen [of rumour etc]; zich verspreiden [of disease]: *you can't ~ **complaining** all of the time!* je kan toch niet de hele tijd lopen klagen! **2** voldoende zijn (voor): *there are enough chairs to ~* er zijn genoeg stoelen voor iedereen ‖ [Am] *what goes around **comes** around* dat komt ervan, wie kaatst, moet de bal verwachten

go-around [aviation] doorstart

go-as-you-please: *~ ticket* algemeen abonnement; passe-partoutʰ

goat 1 geit **2** ezel, stomkop ‖ *get s.o.'s ~* iem. ergeren

go at 1 aanvallen, te lijf gaan; [fig] van leer trekken tegen, tekeergaan tegen **2** verkocht worden voor

goatee sik

goatee beard sik(jeʰ)

go away weggaan, vertrekken: *~ **with** s.o. (sth.)* ervandoor gaan met iem. (iets)

gob 1 rochel, fluim **2** smoel, mond, bek: *shut your ~!* houd je waffel!, kop dicht!

go back 1 teruggaan, terugkeren **2** teruggaan, zijn oorsprong vinden, dateren: *Louis and I ~ a long **time*** Louis en ik kennen elkaar al heel lang; *this tradition goes back **to** the Middle Ages* deze traditie gaat terug tot de middeleeuwen **3** teruggrijpen, terugkeren **4** teruggedraaid worden; teruggezet worden [of clock, watch]: *the **clocks** ~ tonight* de klok wordt vannacht achteruitgezet

go back on 1 terugnemen; terugkomen op [word(s) etc] **2** ontrouw worden, verraden

gobble (op)schrokken: *~ **down** (or: up)* naar

binnen schrokken

gobbledygook [inform] ambtelijk jargon; onbegrijpelijke taal

go-between tussenpersoon, bemiddelaar

go beyond gaan boven, overschrijden, overtreffen, te buiten gaan: ~ one's **duty** buiten zijn boekje gaan, zijn bevoegdheid overschrijden; their teasing is going beyond a **joke** hun geplaag is geen grapje meer

goblet kelk, beker

gobsmacked met de mond vol tanden, stomverbaasd

go by 1 voorbijgaan [also fig]; passeren **2** verstrijken, verlopen, aflopen

god (af)god; [fig] invloedrijk persoon; idool[h] **God** God: in ~'s **name!**, for ~'s **sake!** in godsnaam!; ~ **bless** you! God zegene u!; **thank** ~! goddank!

godchild petekind[h]

goddaughter peetdochter

goddess godin

godfather 1 peetvader, peetoom **2** godfather [Mafia] **3** grondlegger: the ~ **of** modern science de grondlegger van de moderne wetenschap

godforsaken 1 (van) godverlaten **2** triest, ellendig, hopeloos

godmother meter, peettante

go down 1 naar beneden gaan: ~ **to** the Mediterranean naar de Middellandse Zee afzakken **2** dalen [of price, temperature] **3** zinken; ondergaan [ship, person] **4** in de smaak vallen, ingang vinden: ~ like a **bomb** enthousiast ontvangen worden; ~ **with** in de smaak vallen bij, gehoor vinden bij **5** te boek gesteld worden: ~ **in** history de geschiedenis ingaan || ~ **on** one's knees op de knieën vallen [also fig]; ~ **with** measles de mazelen krijgen

godsend meevaller; buitenkansje[h]

godson peetzoon

godspeed: [Am; dated] **wish** him ~ hem een goede reis toewensen

godwit grutto

go far 1 het ver schoppen, het ver brengen **2** toereiken(d zijn), veruit volstaan, lang meegaan || far gone ver heen

go for 1 gaan om, (gaan) halen, gaan naar: Rob went for some more coffee Rob ging nog wat koffie halen; ~ a **walk** een wandeling maken **2** gelden voor, van toepassing zijn op **3** verkocht worden voor, gaan voor: ~ a **song** voor een prikje van de hand gaan **4** aanvallen, te lijf gaan; [also fig; with words] van leer trekken tegen

go forward 1 vooruitgaan [also fig]; vorderen, vooruitgang boeken **2** zijn gang gaan, voortgaan, vervolgen

go-getter doorzetter

goggle staren, turen: ~ **at** aangapen

goggle-eyed met uitpuilende ogen

goggles veiligheidsbril, sneeuwbril, stofbril

go in 1 erin gaan, (erin) passen **2** naar binnen gaan

go in for 1 (gaan) deelnemen aan, opgaan voor; zich aanmelden voor [an exam, competition etc] **2** (gaan) doen aan; een gewoonte maken van [hobby, sport etc]

¹going (n) **1** vertrek[h]: **comings** and ~s komen en gaan [also fig] **2** gang, tempo[h]: be **heavy** ~ moeilijk zijn, een hele klus zijn || while the ~ is **good** nu het nog kan

²going (adj) **1** voorhanden, in omloop: there is a good job ~ er is een goede betrekking vacant; I've got some fresh coffee ~ ik heb nog verse koffie staan **2** (goed) werkend **3** gangbaar, geldend: the ~ **rate** het gangbare tarief

going-over [inform] **1** onderzoek[h] **2** pak[h] slaag

goings-on [inform] voorvallen; gebeurtenissen: there was all **sorts** of ~ er gebeurde van alles

go into 1 binnengaan (in), ingaan **2** gaan in, zich aansluiten bij, deelnemen aan: ~ **business** zakenman worden **3** (nader) ingaan op, zich verdiepen in, onderzoeken: ~ (the) **details** in detail treden

go-kart gocart; skelter

gold 1 goud[h] [also fig] **2** goud[h], goudstukken, rijkdom **3** goud[h], goudkleur: ~ **card** creditcard met speciale voordelen voor de houder **4** gouden medaille, goud[h]: ~ **medallist** goudenmedaillewinnaar

goldcrest goudhaantje[h]

golden gouden; goudkleurig [also fig]: the Golden **Age** de gouden eeuw; ~ **handshake** gouden handdruk; ~ **rule** gulden regel; ~ **wedding** (anniversary) gouden bruiloft || ~ **oldie** gouwe ouwe

golden years [inform] periode na iemands pensioen

goldfinch putter, distelvink

goldfish goudvis

gold rush goudkoorts

golf golf[h] [game]

golfer golfspeler

goliath goliath, reus, krachtpatser

golly gossie(mijne)

gondola 1 gondel [Venetian boat] **2** gondola; open (hang)bak [for displaying articles]

gondolier gondelier

¹gone (adj) **1** verloren [also fig] **2** voorbij, vertrokken || be three **months** ~ in de derde maand zijn [of pregnancy]; **far** ~ ver heen

²gone (prep) over: he is ~ **fifty** hij is over de vijftig, hij is de vijftig voorbij; it's ~ **three** het is over drieën

goner [inform] gedoemde[h]; de klos: you **are** a ~ je gaat eraan

gong 1 gong **2** medaille, lintje[h]

goo kleverig goedje[h]

¹good (n) **1** goed[h], welzijn[h], voorspoed: for the **common** ~ voor het algemeen welzijn; he *will* **come** *to no* ~ het zal slecht met hem aflopen; *for* his (own) ~ om zijn eigen bestwil **2** nut^h, voordeel^h: *it's* **no** ~ (my) talking to her het heeft geen zin met haar te praten **3** goed werk^h, dienst: *be* **after** (or: up **to**) no ~ niets goeds in de zin hebben **4** goedheid, verdienste, deugd(zaamheid): ~ and **evil** goed en kwaad **5** (-s) goederen, (koop)waar^h, handelsartikelen: *deliver* the ~s de goederen (af)leveren; [fig] volledig aan de verwachtingen voldoen **6** (-s) bezittingen ‖ *for* ~ (and all) voorgoed, voor eeuwig (en altijd)

²**good** (adj) **1** goed, knap, kundig: ~ **looks** knapheid; ~ *for* (or: **on**) you goed zo, knap (van je) **2** goed, correct, juist: ~ **English** goed Engels; *my watch keeps* ~ **time** mijn horloge loopt gelijk; *all in* ~ **time** alles op zijn tijd **3** goed, fatsoenlijk, betrouwbaar: (in) ~ **faith** (te) goede(r) trouw **4** aardig, lief, gehoorzaam: ~ **humour** opgewektheid; *put in a* ~ **word** for, say a ~ **word** for een goed woordje doen voor, aanbevelen; *be* so ~ *as to* wees zo vriendelijk, gelieve; *it's* ~ **of** you to help him het is aardig van u om hem te helpen **5** goed, aangenaam, voordelig, lekker, smakelijk, gezond: ~ **buy** koopje^h, voordeeltje^h; ~ *afternoon* goedemiddag; *feel* ~ **a)** zich lekker voelen; **b)** lekker aanvoelen; *too* ~ *to be true* te mooi om waar te zijn **6** afdoend, geldig: *this* **rule** *holds* ~ deze regel geldt **7** aanzienlijk, aardig groot, lang: *stand a* ~ **chance** een goede kans maken; *a* ~ **deal**, *a* ~ **many** heel wat; *a* ~ **hour** (or: ten **miles**) ruim een uur (or: tien mijl) ‖ *all* ~ **things** come to an end aan alle goede dingen komt een einde; *one* ~ *turn* deserves another de ene dienst is de andere waard; *be in s.o.'s* ~ **books** bij iem. in een goed blaadje staan; *as* ~ *as* **gold** erg braaf, erg lief [of child]; *stroke of* ~ **luck** buitenkansje^h; *it's a* ~ **thing** *that* het is maar goed dat; *it's a* ~ **thing** to … het is verstandig om …; *a* ~ **thing** too! maar goed ook!; *too much of a* ~ **thing** te veel van het goede; *make* ~ **time** lekker opschieten; *as* ~ *as* zo goed als, nagenoeg; *be* ~ *at* goed zijn in; *be* ~ *for* another couple of years nog wel een paar jaar meekunnen; ~ies *and* **baddies** de goeien en de slechteriken

¹**goodbye** (n) afscheid^h, afscheidsgroet
²**goodbye** (int) tot ziens: [inform, fig] *you can kiss* ~ to that dat kan je wel vergeten, zeg maar dag met je handje
¹**good-for-nothing** (n) nietsnut
²**good-for-nothing** (adj) niet-deugend; waardeloos
goodish 1 tamelijk goed **2** behoorlijk, tamelijk groot, lang, veel: *a* ~ **number** of people een vrij groot aantal mensen
good-looking knap, mooi
goodness 1 goedheid: *have* the ~ to an-

swer, please wees zo vriendelijk te antwoorden, a.u.b.; ~ **(me)!**, **my** ~!, ~ **gracious!** wel, heb je ooit!; goeie genade!; *for* ~' **sake!** in 's hemelsnaam!; *thank* ~! goddank! **2** gezonde stoffen
good-tempered goedgehumeurd, opgewekt
good-time op amusement belust, gezelligheids-
good will 1 welwillendheid **2** goodwill; (goede) reputatie [part of assets] **3** klantenkring [commercial value of a business]; klanten, zakenrelaties
¹**goody** (n) lekkernij, zoetigheid
²**goody** (int) [child language] jippie!, leuk!
goody bag goodiebag
goody-goody schijnheilig
gooey [inform] **1** kleverig; zacht **2** sentimenteel
¹**goof** (n) **1** sufkop, stommeling **2** blunder, flater
²**goof** (vb) miskleunen, een flater slaan
go off 1 weggaan [also fig]; (van het toneel) afgaan: ~ **with** ertussenuit knijpen met, ervandoor gaan met **2** afgaan [of alarm, gun]; ontploffen [of bomb]; aflopen [of alarm-clock]; losbarsten [also fig] **3** slechter worden, achteruit gaan; verwelken [of flowers]; zuur worden; bederven [of food]: *the veal has gone off* het kalfsvlees is niet goed meer
goofy [inform] **1** [Am] mal **2** met vooruitstekende tanden
google googelen, zoeken op internet
¹**go on** (vb) zich baseren op, afgaan op, zich laten leiden door
²**go on** (vb) **1** voortduren [also fig]; doorgaan (met), aanhouden: *he went on to* **say** *that* hij zei vervolgens dat **2** verstrijken, verlopen, voorbijgaan **3** (door)zaniken, (door)zagen: ~ **about** doorzeuren over **4** gebeuren, plaatsvinden, doorgang vinden: *what is going on?* wat is er aan de hand? ‖ *enough to be going* (or: go) on **with** genoeg om mee rond te komen
goose 1 gans **2** onbenul^h ‖ *he cannot* **say** *boo to a* ~ hij brengt nog geen muis aan het schrikken
gooseberry kruisbes(senstruik) ‖ *play* ~ het vijfde wiel aan de wagen zijn
goosebumps kippenvel^h
gooseflesh kippenvel^h
goose pimples kippenvel^h
go out 1 uitgaan, van huis gaan, afreizen: ~ **with** uitgaan met, verkering hebben met **2** uitgaan [of fire, light] **3** uit de mode raken **4** teruglopen; eb worden [of sea]: *the tide is going out* het is eb ‖ *go (all) out* **for** sth. zich volledig inzetten voor iets
go out of 1 verlaten; uitgaan [a room]: ~ **play** 'uit' gaan [of ball] **2** verdwijnen uit: ~

fashion uit de mode raken; ~ *sight* (or: *view*) uit het zicht verdwijnen; ~ *use* in onbruik raken, buiten gebruik raken

go over 1 (+ to) overlopen (naar), overschakelen (op); overgaan (tot) [other party etc]: *we now ~ to our reporter on the spot* we schakelen nu over naar onze verslaggever ter plaatse **2** aanslaan, overkomen

Gordian: *cut the ~ knot* de (gordiaanse) knoop doorhakken

¹gore (n) [form] geronnen bloed^h; gestold bloed^h

²gore (vb) doorboren; spietsen

gorge kloof, bergengte ‖ *my ~ rises at* ik walg van, ik heb tabak van

gorgeous schitterend, grandioos; prachtig [also of person]

gorilla gorilla

gormless stom, dom, onnozel

go round 1 (rond)draaien **2** rondgaan (in), rondlopen; de ronde doen [of rumour etc]; zich verspreiden [of disease]: *his words kept going round in my head* zijn woorden bleven mij door het hoofd spelen **3** voldoende zijn (voor): *there are enough chairs to ~* er zijn genoeg stoelen voor iedereen **4** (+ to) langsgaan (bij) [s.o.]; *see go around*

gorse brem

gory bloederig, bloedig: *a ~ film* een film met veel bloed en geweld

go-see eerste ontmoeting met potentiële opdrachtgever

goshawk havik

gospel evangelie^h: *take sth. for ~* iets zonder meer aannemen

gossamer 1 herfstdraad, spinrag^h **2** gaas^h, fijn en licht weefsel^h

¹gossip (n) **1** roddel, kletspraat, praatjes **2** roddelaar(ster), kletskous

²gossip (vb) roddelen

gotcha hebbes!, nou heb ik je!, gelukt!

¹goth (n) gothic [mus]

²goth (n) goth [fan]

Gothic 1 [linguistics] Gotisch **2** [architecture] gotisch

go through aangenomen worden [of proposal, bill etc]; erdoor komen ‖ ~ *with* doorgaan met

go to 1 gaan naar [also fig] **2** zich getroosten: ~ *great* (or: *considerable*) *expense* er heel wat geld tegenaan gooien; ~ *great lengths* zich de grootste moeite getroosten, alle mogelijke moeite doen

go-to standaard-: *he is my ~ guy* als er iets gedaan moet worden, klop ik als eerste bij hem aan

gouge (uit)gutsen, uitsteken: ~ *out s.o.'s eyes* iem. de ogen uitsteken

goulash goulash

go under 1 ondergaan, zinken; [fig] er onder door gaan; bezwijken **2** failliet gaan,

bankroet gaan

go up 1 opgaan, naar boven gaan: ~ *in the world* in de wereld vooruitkomen **2** stijgen; omhooggaan [of price, temperature] **3** ontploffen, in de lucht vliegen: ~ *in smoke* (or: *flames*) in rook (or: vlammen) opgaan

gourmet lekkerbek

gout jicht

govern 1 regeren, besturen: *~ing body* bestuurslichaam, raad van beheer **2** bepalen, beheersen, beïnvloeden

governance 1 bestuur^h, beheer^h **2** heerschappij, macht

governess gouvernante

government regering(svorm), (staats)bestuur^h, kabinet^h, leiding: *the Government has* (or: *have*) *accepted the proposal* de regering heeft het voorstel aanvaard

governor 1 gouverneur **2** bestuurder; president [of bank]; directeur [of prison]; commandant [of garrison] **3** [inform] ouwe, ouwe heer, baas

go with 1 meegaan met [also fig]; het eens zijn met: ~ *the times* met de tijd meegaan **2** samengaan, gepaard gaan met, passen bij: *your socks don't ~ your shirt* jouw sokken passen niet bij je overhemd

go without het stellen zonder ‖ *it goes without saying* het spreekt vanzelf

gown 1 toga, tabbaard **2** nachthemd^h, ochtendjas **3** lange jurk, avondjapon **4** operatieschort^h: *surgical ~* operatieschort^h, operatiejas

goy niet-Jood; goj

GP *general practitioner* huisarts

GPO *General Post Office* hoofdpostkantoor^h

GPS *Global Positioning System* gps^h

gr 1 *gram* gr. **2** *gross* gros

¹grab (n) greep, graai: *make a ~ at* (or: *for*) *sth.* ergens naar grijpen; *up for ~s* voor het grijpen

²grab (vb) graaien, grijpen, pakken

³grab (vb) **1** grijpen, vastpakken **2** bemachtigen, in de wacht slepen: ~ *s.o.'s seat* iemands plaats inpikken; *try to ~ the attention* proberen de aandacht op zich te vestigen

grace 1 gratie, charme **2** [goodness] vriendelijkheid, fatsoen^h: *with bad ~* onvriendelijk, met tegenzin **3** uitstel^h, genade: *a day's ~* een dag uitstel [of payment] **4** (dank)gebed^h: *say ~* dank zeggen, bidden (bij maaltijd) **5** genade, goedertierenheid; gunst [of God]: *fall from ~* tot zonde vervallen; [fig] uit de gratie raken, in ongenade vallen ‖ *his smile is his saving ~* zijn glimlach maakt al het overige goed

graceful 1 gracieus, bevallig, elegant **2** aangenaam, correct, charmant

gracious hoffelijk ‖ *good ~!* goeie genade!

grad [inform] *graduate* afgestudeerde

gradation 1 (geleidelijke) overgang, verloopʰ, gradatie **2** nuance(ring), stap, trede: *many ~s of red* vele tinten rood

¹grade (n) **1** rang, niveauʰ, kwaliteit **2** klas [at elementary school] **3** cijferʰ [as a mark for work handed in at school]: *make the ~* slagen, aan de eisen voldoen, carrière maken

²grade (vb) **1** kwalificeren, rangschikken; sorteren [size, quality etc]: *~d eggs* gesorteerde eieren **2** een cijfer geven, beoordelen || *~d reader* voor een bepaald niveau bewerkt boek

grader 1 [Am; educ] leerling uit de … klas, … jaars: *fourth ~* leerling uit de vierde klas **2** iem. die cijfers geeft

grade school basisschool

gradient helling, stijging, hellingshoek: *on a ~* op een helling

gradual geleidelijk, trapsgewijs

¹graduate (n) **1** afgestudeerde **2** gediplomeerde

²graduate (vb) een diploma behalen, afstuderen, een getuigschrift behalen: *he has ~d in law from Yale* hij heeft aan Yale een titel in de rechten behaald

graduate programme mastersopleiding

graduate school instituutʰ voor onderwijs aan masterstudenten of promovendi

graduate student 1 masterstudent (*or:* promovendus) **2** bachelor, doctorandus

graduation 1 schaalverdeling, maatstreep **2** uitreiking van diploma, het afstuderen

graffiti graffiti, opschriften, muurtekeningen

¹graft (n) **1** ent, griffel **2** (politiek) geknoeiʰ, omkoperij, smeergeldʰ **3** zwaar werkʰ

²graft (vb) **1** enten, samenbinden, inplanten **2** verenigen, aan elkaar voegen

grain 1 graankorrel **2** graanʰ, korenʰ **3** korrel(tjeʰ); [fig] greintjeʰ; zier: *take his words with a ~ of salt* neem wat hij zegt met een korreltje zout **4** textuur, vleug; draad [of fabric]; vlam; nerf [in wood]; korrel [of film, metal]; structuur [of rock]: *go against the ~* tegen de draad in gaan [also fig]

gram gram⁺ʰ

grammar 1 spraakkunst, grammatica **2** (correct) taalgebruikʰ

grammar school 1 atheneumʰ; gymnasiumʰ [with Latin and Greek] **2** voortgezet lagere school; [roughly] mavoʰ

grammatical grammaticaal

gramme *see* gram

gramophone grammofoon, platenspeler

gran oma

¹grand (n) **1** vleugel(piano) **2** duizend pondʰ (dollar); [roughly] milleʰ: *it cost me two ~* het kostte me twee mille

²grand (adj) **1** voornaam, gewichtig, groots: *live in ~ style* op grote voet leven **2** grootmoedig: *a ~ gesture* een grootmoedig gebaar **3** prachtig, indrukwekkend **4** reusach-

tig, fantastisch **5** hoofd-, belangrijkste; [in titles] groot-: *~ duke* groothertog || *~ piano* vleugel(piano); *~ jury* jury van 12-23 personen die onderzoekt of het bewijsmateriaal voldoende is om arrestaties te verrichten

grandad opa, grootvader

grandchild kleinkindʰ

granddaughter kleindochter

grandeur grootsheid; pracht

grandfather grootvader

grandiose grandioos, groots, prachtig

grandma oma, grootmoeder

grandmaster [chess, draughts, bridge] grootmeester

grandmother grootmoeder

grandpa opa, grootvader

grandparent grootouder

grandson kleinzoon

grandstand tribune, hoofdtribune, eretribune

granite granietʰ

grannex [inform] mantelzorgwoning

granny oma, opoe, grootjeʰ

granny flat mantelzorgwoning; kangoeroewoning

¹grant (n) subsidie, toelage, beurs

²grant (vb) **1** toekennen, inwilligen, verlenen, toestaan: *~ a request* een verzoek inwilligen; *~ a discount* korting verlenen **2** toegeven, erkennen: *I must ~ you that you've are a better driver than I* ik moet toegeven dat je beter rijdt dan ik || *take sth. for ~ed* iets als (te) vanzelfsprekend beschouwen

granular korrelig, gekorreld

grape druif: *a bunch of ~s* een tros druiven

grapefruit grapefruit, pompelmoes

grape sugar druivensuiker

grapevine 1 wijnstok, wingerd **2** geruchtʰ **3** geruchtencircuitʰ: *I heard it on the ~* het is me ter ore gekomen

graph grafiek, diagramʰ, grafische voorstelling

graphic 1 grafisch, m.b.t. tekenen, schrijven, drukken: *the ~ arts* de grafische kunsten **2** treffend, levendig: *a ~ description* een levendige beschrijving; *~ designer* grafisch ontwerper

graphics grafiek, grafische kunst, grafische media

graphics card grafische kaart, videokaart

graphite grafietʰ

graphology handschriftkunde

graph paper millimeterpapierʰ

grapple (+ with) worstelen (met) [also fig]; slaags raken (met): *~ with a problem* met een probleem worstelen

¹grasp (n) **1** greep [also fig]; macht **2** begripʰ, bevatting, beheersing: *that is beyond my ~* dat gaat mijn pet te boven

²grasp (vb) grijpen, graaien

³grasp (vb) **1** grijpen, vastpakken **2** vatten,

begrijpen: *I ~ed half of what he said* de helft van wat hij zei heb ik begrepen

grasping hebberig, inhalig

¹grass (n) **1** gras^h **2** tipgever, verklikker **3** [inform] marihuana, weed || *cut the ~ from under s.o.'s feet* iem. het gras voor de voeten wegmaaien

²grass (vb) klikken [to police]: *~ on s.o.* iem. verraden, iem. aangeven

grasshopper sprinkhaan

grassroots 1 van gewone mensen, aan de basis: *the ~ opinion* de publieke opinie **2** fundamenteel

grass widow onbestorven weduwe, groene weduwe

grassy 1 grazig, grasrijk **2** grasachtig

¹grate (n) **1** rooster^h, haardrooster^h **2** traliewerk^h **3** haard

²grate (vb) **1** knarsen **2** irriterend werken: *the noise ~d on my nerves* het lawaai werkte op mijn zenuwen

³grate (vb) raspen: *~d cheese* geraspte kaas

grateful dankbaar

grater rasp

gratification voldoening, bevrediging

gratify 1 behagen, genoegen doen **2** voldoen, bevredigen

grating 1 rooster^h, traliewerk^h **2** raster^h

gratis gratis, kosteloos

gratitude dankbaarheid, dank

gratuitous 1 ongegrond, nodeloos **2** gratis, kosteloos

¹grave (n) graf^h, grafkuil; [fig] dood; ondergang: *from the cradle to the ~* van de wieg tot het graf; *dig one's own ~* zichzelf te gronde richten; *rise from the ~* uit de dood opstaan

²grave (adj) **1** belangrijk, gewichtig: *~ issue* ernstige zaak **2** ernstig, plechtig: *a ~ look on his face* een ernstige uitdrukking op zijn gezicht

gravedigger doodgraver

gravel 1 grind^h, kiezel^h **2** kiezelzand^h, grof zand^h

graveyard kerkhof^h, begraafplaats

gravitation zwaartekracht: *law of ~* wet van de zwaartekracht

gravity 1 ernst, serieusheid **2** zwaarte, gewicht^h, dichtheid: *centre of ~* zwaartepunt^h [also fig] **3** zwaartekracht

gravy 1 jus, vleessaus **2** gemakkelijk verdiend geld^h, voordeeltje^h

gravy boat juskom [with spout]

gravy train [inform] goudmijntje^h: *get (a ride) on the ~* gemakkelijk geld verdienen

gray *see ²grey*

¹graze (n) **1** schampschot^h **2** schaafwond, schram

²graze (vb) **1** grazen, weiden **2** schampen, schuren

³graze (vb) **1** laten grazen, weiden, hoeden **2** licht(jes) aanraken, schampen, schuren: *he*

~d his arm against the wall hij schaafde zijn arm tegen de muur

¹grease (n) vet^h, smeer^h

²grease (vb) invetten, oliën, smeren

greasy vettig, vet

¹great (n) groten, vooraanstaande figuren: *Hermans is one of the ~ of Dutch literature* Hermans is een van de groten van de Nederlandse literatuur

²great (adj) **1** groot; nobel [persons]: *a ~ man* een groot man **2** geweldig, fantastisch: *a ~ idea* een geweldig idee **3** groot, belangrijk, vooraanstaand: *Great Britain* Groot-Brittannië; *the Great Wall of China* de Chinese Muur **4** buitengewoon, groot; zwaar [emotions, situations etc] **5** groot, aanzienlijk; hoog [number]: *a ~ deal* heel veel wat; *a ~ many* heel wat, een heleboel **6** lang; hoog [age, time]: *live to a ~ age* een hoge leeftijd bereiken **7** groot, ijverig, enthousiast: *a ~ reader* een verwoed lezer **8** [inform] omvangrijk, dik, reuzen-, enorm: *a ~ big tree* een kanjer van een boom **9** goed, bedreven: *he is ~ at golf* hij is een geweldige golfer || *Great Dane* Deense dog; *at ~ length* uitvoerig; *be in ~ spirits* opgewekt zijn; *set ~ store by* (or: on) grote waarde hechten aan; *the ~est thing since sliced bread* iets fantastisch; *the Great War* de Eerste Wereldoorlog

Great Britain Groot-Brittannië

greatly zeer, buitengewoon: *~ moved* zeer ontroerd

grebe fuut

Grecian Grieks [in style etc]

Greece Griekenland

greed 1 hebzucht, hebberigheid, gulzigheid **2** gierigheid

greedy 1 gulzig: *~ eyes* gulzige blikken **2** hebzuchtig; begerig: *~ for* (or: *of*) *money* geldzuchtig

¹Greek (n) Griek(se)

²Greek (adj) Grieks: [fig] *that is ~ to me* daar snap ik niks van

¹green (n) **1** grasveld^h, brink, dorpsplein^h **2** [golf] green **3** groen^h **4** loof^h, groen gewas^h **5** (-s) (blad)groenten **6** (de) Groenen, (de) milieupartij

²green (adj) **1** groen, met gras begroeid **2** groen, plantaardig: *~ vegetables* bladgroenten **3** groen, onrijp; [fig] onervaren; naïef **4** groen, milieu-: *the ~ party* de Groenen **5** jaloers, afgunstig: *~ with envy* scheel van afgunst

greenback [Am; inform] (Amerikaans) bankbiljet

greenery groen^h, bladeren en groene takken

greenfinch groenling

green gas biogas^h

greengrocer groenteboer, groenteman

greenhorn groentje^h, beginneling

greenhouse broeikas: ~ *effect* broeikaseffect[h]

Greenland Groenland

Greenlander Groenlander, Groenlandse

Greenlandic Groenlands

green wall verticale tuin, groengevel

greenway [Am] groengordel; wandel- of fietspad[h]

Greenwich Mean Time Greenwichtijd

greet 1 begroeten, groeten **2** onthalen, begroeten || *a cold air ~ed us* een vlaag koude lucht kwam ons tegemoet

greeting 1 groet, begroeting, wens: *exchange ~s* elkaar begroeten **2** aanhef [of letter]

gregarious 1 in kudde(n) levend: *a ~ animal* een kuddedier **2** van gezelschap houdend, graag met anderen zijnd

Gregorian gregoriaans: ~ *calendar* gregoriaanse kalender

gremlin 1 pechduiveltje[h], zetduivel **2** kwelgeest, lastpak

grenade (hand)granaat

¹grey (n) **1** schimmel [horse] **2** grijs[h]

²grey (adj) **1** grijs(kleurig): ~ *cells* grijze cellen, hersenen; *his face turned* ~ zijn gezicht werd (as)grauw **2** grijs, bewolkt, grauw **3** somber, treurig, triest: ~ *with* age grijs van de ouderdom; [fig] verouderd

greyed out [comp] niet beschikbaar

greyhound 1 hazewind(hond) **2** greyhoundbus [large coach for long-distance travel]

grid 1 rooster[h], traliewerk[h] **2** raster[h]; coördinatenstelsel[h] [of map] **3** netwerk[h], hoogspanningsnet[h]: [Am] *live off the* ~ zelfvoorzienend leven, in afzondering leven; [Am; fig] *be off the* ~ onvindbaar zijn

gridlock verkeersknoop, het muurvast zitten; [fig] impasse

grief leed[h], verdriet[h], smart: *come to* ~ a) verongelukken; b) vallen; c) [also fig] mislukken, falen

grievance 1 grief, klacht **2** bitter gevoel[h]: *nurse a ~ against s.o.* wrok tegen iem. koesteren

¹grieve (vb) treuren, verdriet hebben: ~ *for s.o.*, ~ *over s.o.'s death* treuren om iemands dood

²grieve (vb) bedroeven, verdriet veroorzaken: *it ~s me to hear that* het spijt mij dat te horen

grievous 1 zwaar, ernstig, verschrikkelijk: [law] ~ *bodily harm* zwaar lichamelijk letsel; *a ~ wound* een ernstige wond **2** pijnlijk

griffin griffioen

¹grill (n) **1** grill, rooster[h] **2** geroosterd (vlees)gerecht[h]

²grill (vb) verhoren, aan een kruisverhoor onderwerpen

³grill (vb) roosteren, grilleren; [fig] bakken:

grilling *on the beach* op het strand liggen bakken

grille 1 traliewerk[h], rooster[h], rasterwerk[h] **2** traliehek(je[h]), kijkraampje[h] **3** radiatorscherm[h] [of car]; sierscherm[h], grille

grim 1 onverbiddelijk, meedogenloos: ~ *determination* onwrikbare vastberadenheid **2** akelig, beroerd: ~ *prospects* ongunstige vooruitzichten

grimace grimas, gezicht[h], grijns: *make ~s* smoelen trekken

grime vuil[h], roet[h]

grimy vuil; groezelig, goor

¹grin (n) **1** brede glimlach **2** grijns, grimas: *take that (silly) ~ off your face!* sta niet (zo dom) te grijnzen!

²grin (vb) grijnzen, grinniken, glimlachen: ~ *and bear it* zich flink houden, op zijn tanden bijten

¹grind (n) **1** geknars[h], schurend geluid[h] **2** inspanning, (vervelend) karwei[h]

²grind (vb) **1** blokken, ploeteren: *he is ~ing away at his maths* hij zit op zijn wiskunde te blokken **2** knarsen, schuren, krassen: ~ *one's teeth* tandenknarsen; ~ *to a halt* tot stilstand komen [also fig] **3** verbrijzelen, (ver)malen, verpletteren; [fig] onderdrukken: ~ *coffee* koffie malen; ~*ing poverty* schrijnende armoede **4** (uit)trappen [also fig]: *Joe ~ed his cigarette into the rug* Joe trapte zijn sigaret in het tapijt (uit) **5** (doen) draaien [(coffee) grinder, barrel organ etc]

grinder 1 molen **2** slijper, slijpmachine **3** maalsteen **4** kies

grind out uitbrengen, voortbrengen; opdreunen [continuously and mechanically]: *the pupil first had to ~ ten irregular verbs* de leerling moest eerst tien onregelmatige werkwoorden opdreunen

grindstone slijpsteen: *go back to the* ~ weer aan het werk gaan

gringo vreemdeling

¹grip (n) **1** greep, houvast[h]: *keep a tight ~ on* stevig vasthouden **2** beheersing, macht, meesterschap[h]; [fig] begrip[h]; vat[h]: *come to ~s with a problem* een probleem aanpakken; *keep* (or: *take*) *a ~ on o.s.* zich beheersen, zichzelf in de hand houden **3** greep, handvat[h] **4** toneelknecht

²grip (vb) pakken [of brake etc]; grijpen [of anchor]

³grip (vb) vastpakken, grijpen, vasthouden; [fig] pakken; boeien: *a ~ping story* een boeiend verhaal

gripe klacht, bezwaar[h], kritiek

grip fastening klittenbandsluiting

grippy ruw, stroef

grisly 1 griezelig, akelig **2** weerzinwekkend, verschrikkelijk

gristle kraakbeen[h] [in meat]

¹grit (n) **1** gruis[h], zand[h] **2** lef[h], durf

²grit (vb) **1** knarsen: ~ *one's teeth* knarsetanden [also fig] **2** met zand bestrooien: ~ *the icy roads* de gladde wegen met zand bestrooien

gritty 1 zanderig, korrelig **2** kranig, moedig, flink

grizzled 1 grijs, grauw **2** grijsharig

grizzly grizzly(beer)

¹groan (n) gekreun^h, gekerm^h, gesteun^h

²groan (vb) **1** kreunen, kermen, steunen: ~ *with pain* kreunen van de pijn **2** grommen, brommen

grocer kruidenier

groceries boodschappen

grocery 1 (groceries) kruidenierswinkel **2** kruideniersbedrijf^h, kruideniersvak^h **3** (groceries) kruidenierswaren, levensmiddelen

grocery store [Am] supermarkt, buurtsuper

grog grog

groggy 1 onvast op de benen, wankel **2** suf, versuft, verdoofd: *I feel* ~ ik voel me suf

groin lies

¹groom (n) **1** bruidegom **2** stalknecht

²groom (vb) **1** verzorgen [horses]; roskammen **2** een keurig uiterlijk geven; uiterlijk verzorgen [pers] ‖ ~ *a candidate for* the Presidency een kandidaat voorbereiden op het presidentschap

groove 1 groef, gleuf, sponning **2** routine, sleur: *find one's* ~, *get into the* ~ zijn draai vinden; *be stuck in the* ~ in een sleur zitten

¹grope (vb) tasten, rondtasten; [fig] zoeken: ~ *for* an answer onzeker naar een antwoord zoeken

²grope (vb) **1** al tastend zoeken: ~ *one's way* zijn weg op de tast zoeken **2** betasten [esp with sexual intentions]

¹gross (n) gros^h, 12 dozijn^h, 144: *by the* ~ bij dozijnen, bij het gros

²gross (adj) **1** grof [also fig]; dik, lomp: ~ *injustice* uitgesproken onrechtvaardigheid; ~ *language* ruwe taal **2** bruto, totaal: ~ *national product* bruto nationaal product

³gross (vb) een bruto winst hebben van, in totaal verdienen

grotesque zonderling, belachelijk

grotto grot

grotty [inform] rottig, vies, waardeloos

grouch mopperen, mokken: *he is always ~ing about his students* hij loopt altijd te mopperen over zijn studenten

¹ground (n) **1** terrein^h **2** grond, reden; basis [of action, reasoning]: *on religious ~s* uit godsdienstige overwegingen **3** grond, aarde; bodem [also fig]: *go to* ~ **a)** zich in een hol verschuilen [of animal]; **b)** onderduiken [of person]; *get off the* ~ van de grond komen **4** gebied^h [fig]; grondgebied^h, afstand: *break*

new (or: *fresh*) ~ nieuw terrein betreden, pionierswerk verrichten; *gain* (or: *make*) ~ **a)** veld winnen; **b)** erop vooruit gaan; *give* (or: *lose*) ~ terrein verliezen, wijken; *hold* (or: *keep, stand*) *one's* ~ standhouden, voet bij stuk houden **5** (-s) gronden, domein^h; park^h [around bldg]: *a house standing in its own ~s* een huis, geheel door eigen grond omgeven ‖ *cut the* ~ *from under s.o.'s feet* iem. het gras voor de voeten wegmaaien; *it suits him down to the* ~ dat komt hem uitstekend van pas

²ground (vb) **1** op de grond terecht komen, de grond raken **2** aan de grond lopen, stranden

³ground (vb) **1** aan de grond houden [aeroplane, pilot]: *the planes have been ~ed by the fog* de vliegtuigen moeten door mist aan de grond blijven **2** laten stranden [ship] **3** [Am; elec] aarden

groundbreaking baanbrekend; grensverleggend

ground control vluchtleiding

ground-floor benedenverdieping, parterre^+h

ground frost vorst aan de grond, nachtvorst

grounding scholing, training, basisvorming

groundless ongegrond

groundnut aardnoot; pinda

groundnut oil arachideolie, aardnotenolie

ground plan plattegrond, grondplan^h; [fig] ontwerp^h; blauwdruk

groundsman 1 terreinknecht **2** tuinman

groundswell vloedgolf [also fig]; zware golving; nadeining [of sea, after storm or earthquake]

groundwork (the) grondslag; basis

¹group (n) groep, geheel^h, verzameling, klasse, familie, afdeling, onderdeel^h

²group (vb) zich groeperen

³group (vb) groeperen, in groepen plaatsen: *we ~ed ourselves round the guide* we gingen in een groep rond de gids staan

¹grouse (n) korhoen^h, Schotse sneeuwhoen^h

²grouse (vb) mopperen, klagen

grovel kruipen [fig]; zich vernederen, zich verlagen: ~ *before* s.o. voor iem. kruipen

¹grow (vb) **1** groeien, opgroeien, ontstaan: ~ *wild* in het wild groeien; ~ *up* **a)** opgroeien, volwassen worden; **b)** ontstaan; ~ *up into* opgroeien tot, zich ontwikkelen tot, worden; ~ *out of* **a)** ontstaan uit; **b)** ontgroeien [bad habit, friends]; ~ *out of one's clothes* uit zijn kleren groeien **2** aangroeien, zich ontwikkelen, gedijen: ~ *to become* uitgroeien tot; ~ *into* sth. big tot iets groots uitgroeien ‖ ~ *up!* doe niet zo kinderachtig!

²grow (vb) **1** kweken, verbouwen, telen: ~ *vegetables* groenten kweken **2** laten staan (groeien) [beard] **3** laten begroeien, bedekken

³**grow** (vb) worden, gaan: *she has ~n (into) a woman* ze is een volwassen vrouw geworden

grower kweker, teler, verbouwer

growing operation [Am] hennepkwekerij, wietplantage

growing pains 1 groeistuipen, groeipijnen **2** kinderziekten [fig]

growl 1 grommen, brommen **2** snauwen, grauwen

grown 1 gekweekt, geteeld **2** volgroeid, rijp, volwassen

grown-up volwassen

grow-op [Am] *growing operation*

growth 1 gewasʰ, productʰ **2** gezwelʰ, uitwasᵗʰ, tumor **3** groei, (volle) ontwikkeling: *reach full ~* volgroeid zijn **4** toename, uitbreiding **5** kweek, productie

growth area groeisector, (snel) groeiende bedrijfstak

grub 1 larve, made, rups **2** etenʰ, voerʰ, hap

grubby vuil, vies, smerig

¹**grudge** (n) wrok, grief: *bear s.o. a ~* een wrok tegen iem. koesteren

²**grudge** (vb) misgunnen, niet gunnen, benijden

grudgingly met tegenzin, niet van harte

gruelling afmattend, slopend

gruesome gruwelijk, afschuwelijk

gruff nors, bars

¹**grumble** (vb) rommelen [of thunder]

²**grumble** (vb) morren, mopperen, brommen: *~ at s.o. about sth.* tegen iem. over iets mopperen

grumpy knorrig, humeurig

grunge [Am] vuilʰ, smerigheid

grunt knorren, brommen, grommen

GSM *Global System for Mobile Communications* gsm

G-string g-strings, tangaslipjeʰ

¹**guarantee** (n) waarborg, garantie(bewijsʰ), zekerheid, belofte

²**guarantee** (vb) **1** garanderen, waarborgen, borg staan voor **2** verzekeren

¹**guard** (n) **1** bewaker, cipier, gevangenbewaarder **2** conducteur [on train] **3** beveiliging, bescherming(smiddelʰ), schermʰ, kap **4** wacht, bewaking, waakzaamheid: *be on* (or: *keep, stand*) *~* de wacht houden, op wacht staan; *the changing of the ~* het aflossen van de wacht; *catch s.o. off (his) ~* iem. overrompelen; *be on (one's) ~ against* bedacht zijn op **5** garde, (lijf)wacht, escorteᵗʰ

²**guard** (vb) **1** (zich) verdedigen, zich dekken **2** zich hoeden, zijn voorzorgen nemen: *~ against sth.* zich voor iets hoeden **3** op wacht staan

³**guard** (vb) **1** bewaken, beveiligen; bewaren [secret] **2** beschermen

guard dog waakhond

guarded voorzichtig; bedekt [terms]

guardian 1 bewaker, beschermer, oppasser **2** voogd(es), curator

guardian angel beschermengel, engelbewaarder

guardianship 1 bescherming **2** voogdij(schapʰ)

guard rail 1 leuning, reling **2** vangrail

Guatemala Guatemala

¹**Guatemalan** (n) Guatemalaan(se), Guatemalteek(se)

²**Guatemalan** (adj) Guatemalaans, Guatemalteeks

guava guave

gue(r)rilla guerrilla(strijder)

¹**guess** (n) gis(sing), ruwe schatting: *your ~ is as good as mine* ik weet het net zomin als jij; *make* (or: *have*) *a ~ (at sth.)* (naar iets) raden; *it is anybody's* (or: *anyone's*) *~* dat is niet te zeggen; *at a ~* naar schatting

²**guess** (vb) **1** raden, schatten, gissen: *keep s.o. ~ing* iem. in het ongewisse laten; *~ at sth.* naar iets raden **2** denken, aannemen: *What is that? - That is his new car, I ~* Wat is dat nou? - Dat is zijn nieuwe auto, neem ik aan

guesswork giswerkʰ; het raden

guest 1 gast, logé: *~ of honour* eregast **2** genodigde, introducé || *be my ~!* ga je gang!

guesthouse pensionʰ

¹**guffaw** (n) bulderende lach

²**guffaw** (vb) bulderen van het lachen

guidance 1 leiding **2** raad, adviesʰ, hulp, begeleiding: *vocational ~* beroepsvoorlichting

¹**guide** (n) **1** gids **2** leidraad **3** padvindster, gids

²**guide** (vb) **1** leiden, gidsen, de weg wijzen, (be)geleiden: *a ~d tour of the head office* een rondleiding in het hoofdkantoor **2** als leidraad dienen voor: *he was ~d by his feelings* hij liet zich leiden door zijn gevoelens

guide dog geleidehond

guideline richtlijn; richtsnoerʰ

guild gildeʰ

guilder gulden

guildhall 1 gildehuisʰ **2** raadhuisʰ, stadhuisʰ

guile slinksheid, bedrogʰ, valsheid: *he is full of ~* hij is niet te vertrouwen

guillotine 1 guillotine, valbijl **2** papiersnijmachine

guilt schuld, schuldgevoelʰ

guilt trip [inform] (sterk) schuldgevoelʰ: *send* (or: *put*) *s.o. on a ~* iem. een schuldgevoel aanpraten

guilty schuldig, schuldbewust: *a ~ conscience* een slecht geweten; *plead not ~* schuld ontkennen

guinea gienjeʰ [old gold coin with a value of 21 shillings]

Guinea Guinee
Guinea-Bissau Guinee-Bissau
guinea fowl parelhoen[h]
[1]**Guinean** (n) **1** Guineeër, Guineese **2** Papoea-Nieuw-Guineeër, Papoea-Nieuw-Guineese
[2]**Guinean** (adj) **1** Guinees **2** Papoea-Nieuw-Guinees
· **guinea pig 1** cavia **2** proefkonijn[h]
guitar gitaar
gulf golf, (wijde) baai
Gulf stream (the) Golfstroom
gull meeuw
gullet keel(gat[h]), strot ‖ *stick in s.o.'s ~* onverteerbaar zijn voor iem.
gullible makkelijk beet te nemen, lichtgelovig, onnozel
gully geul, ravijn[h], greppel
[1]**gulp** (n) **1** teug, slok **2** slikbeweging
[2]**gulp** (vb) schrokken, slokken, slikken: *he ~ed down his drink* hij sloeg zijn borrel achterover
gum 1 (-s) tandvlees[h] **2** gom(hars)[+h] **3** kauwgom[+h]
gumdrop gombal
gumption [inform] **1** initiatief[h], ondernemingslust, vindingrijkheid **2** gewiekstheid, pienterheid
[1]**gun** (n) **1** stuk[h] geschut, kanon[h] **2** vuurwapen[h], (jacht)geweer[h], pistool[h] **3** spuitpistool[h] ‖ *beat* (or: *jump*) *the ~* te vroeg van start gaan; [fig] op de zaak vooruitlopen; *stick to one's ~s* voet bij stuk houden
[2]**gun** (vb) jagen, op jacht zijn (gaan)
[3]**gun** (vb) (also + down) neerschieten, neerknallen: *he was ~ned down from an ambush* hij werd vanuit een hinderlaag neergeknald
gunboat diplomacy machtspolitiek
gunfight vuurgevecht[h]
gunfire geweervuur[h]; (geweer)schoten
gunge smurrie
gunman 1 gangster, (beroeps)moordenaar **2** schutter
gunmetal staalgrijs[h]
gunner 1 artillerist, kanonnier **2** boordschutter
gunpoint: *at ~* onder bedreiging van een vuurwapen, onder schot
gunpowder buskruit[h]
gunrunner wapensmokkelaar
gunshot 1 schot[h]; geweerschot[h], pistoolschot[h] **2** schootsafstand
[1]**gurgle** (n) gekir[h] [of baby]; geklok[h], gemurmel[h]
[2]**gurgle** (vb) kirren, klokken, murmelen
[3]**gurgle** (vb) kirrend zeggen
guru goeroe
[1]**gush** (n) **1** stroom [also fig]; vloed, uitbarsting **2** uitbundigheid, overdrevenheid **3** sentimentaliteit
[2]**gush** (vb) **1** stromen, gutsen **2** dwepen (met), overdreven doen (over)

[3]**gush** (vb) spuiten, uitstorten, doen stromen
gust 1 (wind)vlaag, windstoot **2** uitbarsting: *a ~ of laughter* een lachsalvo
gusto animo[h]: *with (great) ~* enthousiast
gusty stormachtig
[1]**gut** (n) **1** darm **2** (-s) ingewanden **3** buikje[h] **4** (-s) lef[h], durf, moed: *you don't have the ~s* dat durf je toch niet; *I cannot believe you had the ~s to tell him* ik kan niet geloven dat je het lef had om het hem te vertellen ‖ *hate s.o.'s ~s* grondig de pest hebben aan iem.; *sweat* (or: *work*) *one's ~s out* zich een ongeluk werken
[2]**gut** (adj) instinctief, onberedeneerd: *a ~ reaction* een (zuiver) gevoelsmatige reactie; *it's just a ~ feeling* **a)** zo voelt het gewoon; **b)** ik vermoed het
[3]**gut** (vb) **1** van binnen volledig vernietigen/leeghalen [of bldg] **2** [inform] kapotmaken [emotionally]: *I feel ~ted* ik ben er helemaal kapot van
gutless laf; zonder durf
[1]**gutter** (n) goot [also fig]; geul, greppel, dakgoot: *he'll end up in the ~* hij belandt nog in de goot
[2]**gutter** (vb) druipen [of candle]
gutter press (the) schandaalpers; roddelpers
guttural keel-; [linguistics] gutturaal
guv 1 baas [employer] **2** ouwe heer [father] **3** meneer
guy kerel, vent, man: *~s* lui; jongens; mensen; *you and the other ~s* jij en de anderen, de rest van de groep; *where are you ~s going?* waar gaan jullie naartoe?
Guyana Guyana
[1]**Guyanese** (n) Guyaan(se)
[2]**Guyanese** (adj) Guyaans
guyfriend mannelijke kennis, vriend
guzzler zwelger, brasser, zuiper
gym 1 gymlokaal[h] **2** fitnesscentrum[h], sportschool: *go to the ~* naar de sportschool gaan **3** gymnastiek(les)
gymnasium gymnastieklokaal[h]
gymnast gymnast, turner
gymnastics gymnastiek, lichamelijke oefening, turnen[h]
gynaecologist gynaecoloog, vrouwenarts
gypsy zigeuner(in)
gyrate (rond)draaien, wentelen; (rond)tollen
gyroscope gyroscoop

h

h h, H
haberdashery 1 fournituren, garen[h], band[h], fourniturenwinkel **2** [Am] herenmode(artikelen), herenmodezaak
habit 1 habijt[h], ordekleed[h] **2** rijkleding: *riding* ~ rijkleding **3** gewoonte, hebbelijkheid, aanwensel[h]: *fall* (or: *get*) *into the* ~ de gewoonte aannemen; *he has a* ~ *of changing the lyrics in mid-song* hij heeft de gewoonte om midden in het lied de tekst te veranderen; *get out of* (or: *kick*) *the* ~ *of doing sth.* (de gewoonte) afleren om iets te doen; *be in the* ~ *of doing sth.* gewoon zijn iets te doen; *old* ~s *die hard* oude gewoontes zijn hardnekkig, veranderen is niet makkelijk
habitable bewoonbaar
habitat natuurlijke omgeving [of plant, animal]; habitat, woongebied[h]
habitation woning, bewoning
habitual 1 gewoon(lijk), gebruikelijk **2** gewoonte-: ~ *criminal* recidivist
¹hack (n) **1** huurpaard[h], knol **2** broodschrijver **3** houw, snee, jaap, trap(wond)
²hack (vb) **1** hakken, houwen, een jaap geven: ~ *off a branch* een tak afkappen; ~ *at sth.* in iets hakken, op iets in houwen **2** fijnhakken; bewerken [soil] **3** kraken, een computerkraak plegen, hacken
hacker 1 (computer)kraker, hacker **2** computermaniak
hackneyed afgezaagd; banaal [of saying]
hacksaw ijzerzaag, metaalzaag
haddock schelvis
haemophilia hemofilie, bloederziekte
haemorrhage bloeding: *massive* ~s zware bloedingen
haemorrhoids aambeien
hag (lelijke oude) heks
haggard verwilderd uitziend; wild [of look]; met holle ogen, afgetobd
haggle 1 kibbelen **2** pingelen, afdingen: ~ *with s.o. about* (or: *over*) *sth.* met iem. over iets marchanderen
Hague: *The* ~ Den Haag[h], 's-Gravenhage[h]
¹hail (n) (welkomst)groet
²hail (n) hagel(steen); [fig] regen; stortvloed: *a* ~ *of bullets* een regen van kogels
³hail (vb) hagelen [also fig]; neerkomen (als hagel)
⁴hail (vb) **1** erkennen, begroeten als: *the people* ~ed *him* (as) *king* het volk haalde hem als koning in **2** aanroepen: ~ *a taxi* een taxi (aan)roepen

hail from afkomstig zijn van; komen uit
Hail Mary Ave Maria[h], weesgegroet(je[h])
hailstone hagelsteen
hailstorm hagelbui
hair haar[h], haren, hoofdhaar[h]: *let one's* ~ *down* het haar los dragen; [fig] zich laten gaan ‖ *hang by a* ~ aan een zijden draadje hangen; *not harm a* ~ *on s.o.'s head* iem. geen haar krenken; [inform] *keep your* ~ *on!* maak je niet dik!; *split* ~s haarkloven; *tear one's* ~ *(out)* zich de haren uit het hoofd trekken; *without turning a* ~ zonder een spier te vertrekken
haircut 1 het knippen: *have a* ~ zijn haar laten knippen **2** kapsel[h]
hairdo kapsel[h]
hairdresser kapper; [Am] dameskapper
hair extension haarverlenging
hairgrip (haar)speld(je[h])
hairline 1 haargrens **2** *hairline crack* haarscheurtje[h]
hairpin haarspeld: ~ *bend* haarspeldbocht
hair's breadth haarbreed(te) ‖ *escape death by a* ~ op het nippertje aan de dood ontsnappen
hair-splitting haarkloverij
hairstyle kapsel[h], coiffure
hairy 1 harig, behaard **2** riskant
Haiti Haïti
¹Haitian (n) Haïtiaan(se)
²Haitian (adj) Haïtiaans
hake heek
halal halal
halcyon kalm, vredig, gelukkig
hale gezond, kras: ~ *and hearty* fris en gezond
¹half (n) helft, half(je[h]), de helft van: ~ *an hour*, *a* ~ *hour* een half uur; *two and a* ~ twee-en-een-half; *one* ~ een helft ‖ [inform] *go halves with s.o. in sth.* de kosten van iets met iem. samsam delen; *he's too clever by* ~ hij is veel te sluw; [inform] *that was a game and a* ~ dat was me een wedstrijd
²half (pron) de helft: ~ *of six is three* de helft van zes is drie
³half (adv) half; [inform] bijna: *only* ~ *cooked* maar half gaar; *I* ~ *wish* ik zou bijna willen; ~ *as much* (or: *many*) *again* anderhalf maal zoveel; [inform] ~ *seven* half acht; *he didn't do* ~ *as badly as we'd thought* hij deed het lang zo slecht niet als we gedacht hadden; ~ *past* after) one half twee; [inform] ~ *one,* ~ *two etc* half twee, half drie enz.; ~ *and* ~ half om half ‖ [inform] *he didn't* ~ *get mad* hij werd me daar toch razend; [inform] *not* ~ *bad* lang niet kwaad, schitterend; *not* ~ *strong enough* lang niet sterk genoeg
half-baked [fig] halfbakken; halfgaar
half-breed halfbloed, bastaard-
half-caste [depr] halfbloed
half-glazed: ~ *door* deur met een ruit,

deur met half glas
half-hearted halfhartig; halfslachtig
half holiday vrije middag [at schools]
half-life [physics] halfwaardetijd, halve-ringstijd
half-mast halfstok
half-term [school] korte vakantie
half-timbered vakwerk-
half-time 1 [sport] rust: *at* ~ tijdens de rust **2** halve werktijd, deeltijdarbeid, halve dagen: *be on* ~ halve dagen werken, een deeltijdbaan (*or:* halve baan) hebben
¹halfway (adj) **1** in het midden: [sport] ~ *line* middenlijn **2** tamelijk; beetje
²halfway (adv) halverwege: *meet s.o.* ~ iem. tegemoet komen; ~ *through* halverwege
halfway house rehabilitatiecentrumʰ, reclasseringscentrumʰ **2** compromisʰ
halfwit [depr] halvegare
halibut heilbot
halitosis slechte adem
hall 1 zaal, ridderzaal **2** openbaar gebouwʰ, paleisʰ **3** groot herenhuisʰ **4** vestibule, halʰ, gang **5** studentenhuisʰ: ~ *of residence* studentenhuisʰ
hallelujah hallelujaʰ
hallmark stempelʰ [also fig]; gehaltemerkʰ, waarmerkʰ, kenmerkʰ
hallo hallo!, hé!
hallowed gewijd, heilig
Hallowe'en avond voor Allerheiligen
hallstand staande kapstok
hallucinate hallucineren
hallucination hallucinatie, zinsbegoocheling
hallway portaalʰ, halʰ, vestibule
halo 1 halo **2** stralenkrans; [fig] glans
halogen halogeenʰ
¹halt (n) **1** [inform] (bus)halte, stopplaats; stationnetjeʰ **2** haltʰ, stilstand, rust: *call a* ~ *to* een halt toeroepen; *come to a* ~ tot stilstand komen
²halt (vb) halt (doen) houden, stoppen, pauzeren
halter 1 halsterʰ **2** strop
halting weifelend, aarzelend, onzeker: *a* ~ *voice* een stokkende stem
halve halveren, in tweeën delen, tot de helft reduceren
¹ham (n) **1** ham **2** dij, bil: ~*s* achtersteʰ **3** [inform] amateur
²ham (vb) overacteren, overdrijven: ~ *up* zich aanstellen
hamburger 1 hamburger **2** [comp] hamburgermenuʰ
hamburger tax vettaks
ham-fisted onhandig
hamlet gehuchtʰ
¹hammer (n) hamer: *go* (or: *come*) *under the* ~ geveild worden ‖ *go at it* ~ *and tongs* er uit alle macht tegenaan gaan

²hammer (vb) **1** hameren: ~ *(away) at* er op losbeuken **2** [inform] zwoegen: ~ *(away) at* sth. op iets zwoegen
³hammer (vb) **1** hameren, smeden **2** [inform] verslaan, inmaken, een zware nederlaag toebrengen **3** [inform] scherp bekritiseren, afkraken ‖ ~ *out* a compromise solution (moeizaam) een compromis uitwerken
hammered [inform] stomdronken, ladderzat
hammerhead hamerhaai
hammock hangmat
¹hamper (n) **1** (grote) sluitmand; pakmand [for foodstuffs]: *Christmas* ~ kerstpakketʰ **2** [Am] wasmand
²hamper (vb) belemmeren, storen; [fig] hinderen
hamster hamster
¹hamstring (n) **1** hamstring **2** hakpees, achillespees
²hamstring (vb) de achillespees doorsnijden bij, kreupel maken; [fig] verlammen; frustreren
Han Han-Chinezen
¹hand (n) **1** hand; voorpoot [of animals]: *bind* (or: *tie*) s.o. ~ *and foot* iem. aan handen en voeten binden [also fig]; *hold* (or: *join*) ~*s* (elkaar) de hand geven; *shake s.o.'s* ~, *shake* ~*s with s.o.* iem. de hand drukken; *wring one's* ~*s* ten einde raad zijn; ~*s off!* bemoei je er niet mee!; *at* ~ dichtbij; [fig] op handen; *close* (or: *near*) *at* ~ heel dichtbij; *by* ~ **a)** met de hand (geschreven); **b)** in handen, per bode [letter]; *make* (or: *earn*) *money* ~ *over fist* geld als water verdienen **2** arbeider, werkman, bemanningslidʰ: ~*s needed* arbeidskrachten gevraagd; *all* ~*s on deck!* alle hens aan dek! **3** vakman, specialist: *be a poor* ~ *at sth.* geen slag van iets hebben **4** wijzer [of clock]; naald [of meter] **5** kaart(en) [assigned to a player]; hand: *overplay one's* ~ te veel wagen, te ver gaan, zijn hand overspelen; *show* (or: *reveal*) *one's* ~ zijn kaarten op tafel leggen **6** handbreed(te) [approximately 10 cm] **7** kant, zijde, richting: *at my left* ~ aan mijn linkerhand; *on the one* (or: *other*) ~ aan de ene (*or:* andere) kant **8** handschriftʰ, handtekening: *set* (or: *put*) *one's* ~ *to a document* zijn hand(tekening) onder een document plaatsen **9** hulp, steun, bijstand: *give* (or: *lend*) *s.o. a (helping)* ~ iem. een handje helpen **10** controle, beheersing, bedwangʰ: *have the situation well in* ~ de toestand goed in handen hebben; *take in* ~ onder handen nemen; *get out of* ~ uit de hand lopen **11** (-s) macht, beschikking, gezagʰ: *change* ~*s* in andere handen overgaan, van eigenaar veranderen; *put* (or: *lay*) *(one's)* ~*s on sth.* de hand leggen op iets; *the children are off my* ~*s* de kinderen zijn de deur uit; *have time on one's* ~*s* tijd zat hebben **12** toestemming, (huwe-

lijks)belofte; (handels)akkoord^h [with hand-shake]: *ask for s.o.'s* ~ iem. ten huwelijk vragen **13** invloed, aandeel^h: *have a* ~ *in sth.* bij iets betrokken zijn **14** applaus^h, bijval: *the actress got a **big*** (or: ***good***) ~ de actrice kreeg een daverend applaus **15** (-s) [sport] hands^h, handsbal ‖ *wait on* (or: *serve*) *s.o.* ~ *and **foot*** iem. op zijn wenken bedienen; *they are* ~ *in **glove*** ze zijn twee handen op één buik; *try one's* ~ *at (doing) sth.* iets proberen; *get one's* ~ *in at sth.* iets onder de knie krijgen; *go* ~ *in* ~ samengaan; *force s.o.'s* ~ iem. tot handelen dwingen; *lay* (or: *put*) *one's* ~ *on* de hand weten te leggen op; *strengthen one's* ~ zijn positie verbeteren; *my* ~*s are **tied*** ik ben machteloos; *turn one's* ~ *to sth.* iets ondernemen; [euph] *where can I **wash** my* ~*s?* waar is het toilet?; *wash one's* ~*s of sth.* zijn handen van iets aftrekken; *win* ~*s **down*** op één been winnen; *at the* ~ *of s.o.*, *at s.o.'s* ~*s* van(wege) iem., door iem.; *live **from*** ~ *to mouth* van de hand in de tand leven; *cash in* ~ contanten in kas; *we have plenty of time in* ~ we hebben nog tijd genoeg; *out of* ~ **a)** voor de vuist weg; **b)** tactloos; *have s.o. eating out of one's* ~ iem. volledig in zijn macht hebben; *to* ~ bij de hand, dichtbij; *a **hand-to-mouth** existence* een leven van dag tot dag; [roughly] te veel om dood te gaan, te weinig om van te leven; *with one* ~ *(tied) behind one's back* zonder enige moeite; *(at) **first*** (or: ***second***) ~ uit de eerste (*or:* tweede) hand

²**hand** (vb) **1** overhandigen, aanreiken, (aan)geven; ~ *back* teruggeven; ~ *round* ronddelen **2** helpen, een handje helpen, leiden ‖ [inform] *you have to* ~ *it to her* dat moet je haar nageven

handbag handtas(je^h)

handball handbal^h

hand blender staafmixer

handbrake handrem

handcuffs handboeien

hand down 1 overleveren [tradition etc]; overgaan [possession]: *this watch has been handed down in our family for 130 years* dit horloge gaat in onze familie al 130 jaar over van generatie op generatie **2** aangeven

handful 1 handvol **2** [inform] lastig kind^h: *that **child** is a* ~ ik heb mijn handen vol aan dat kind

handicap 1 handicap, nadeel^h, functiebeperking **2** [sport] handicap, (wedren met) voorgift

handicapped gehandicapt, invalide

handicraft handvaardigheid, handenarbeid, handwerk^h

hand in 1 inleveren: *please* ~ *your paper **to** your own teacher* lever alsjeblieft je proefwerk in bij je eigen docent **2** voorleggen, aanbieden, indienen: ~ *one's **resignation*** zijn ontslag indienen

handkerchief zakdoek

¹**handle** (n) **1** handvat^h, hendel, steel **2** knop, kruk, klink **3** heft^h, greep **4** oor^h, hengsel^h ‖ [inform] *fly off the* ~ opvliegen, z'n zelfbeheersing verliezen

²**handle** (vb) **1** aanraken, betasten; bevoelen [with one's hands] **2** hanteren, bedienen, manipuleren: ~ *with care!* voorzichtig (behandelen)! **3** behandelen, omgaan met **4** verwerken, afhandelen **5** aanpakken; bespreken [problem]: *can he* ~ *that **situation?*** kan hij die situatie aan? **6** verhandelen, handelen in

handlebar stuur^h [of bicycle]

handling 1 behandeling; hantering, verwerking **2** beheer^h **3** rijgedrag^h [of car] **4** transport^h

hand-me-down [Am] afdankertje^h

handout 1 gift, aalmoes **2** stencil^h, folder

hand out ronddelen, uitdelen

hand over overhandigen [esp money]; overdragen

hand-pick 1 plukken met de hand **2** zorgvuldig uitkiezen, selecteren

handrail leuning

handroll [culinary] handrol

handsfree handsfree: *you must **phone*** ~ *in a car* in een auto moet je handsfree bellen

handshake handdruk

handsome 1 mooi, schoon; knap [man]; elegant, statig [woman] **2** royaal; gul [reward, prize]; overvloedig, ruim ‖ *come down* ~*(ly)* flink over de brug komen

hands-on praktisch, praktijk-: *she **is** very* ~ ze is erg praktisch ingesteld; ~ *training* praktijkgerichte training

handwriting (hand)schrift^h ‖ [Am] *the* ~ *on the **wall*** het teken aan de wand

handwritten met de hand geschreven

handy 1 bij de hand, binnen bereik **2** handig, praktisch: *come in* ~ van pas komen

handyman 1 klusjesman, manusje-van-alles^h **2** klusser, doe-het-zelver: *I'm not **much** of a* ~ ik ben geen klusser

¹**hang** (n) het vallen; val [of material]; het zitten [of clothing] ‖ [inform] *get* (or: *have*) *the* ~ *of sth.* de slag van iets krijgen (*or:* hebben)

²**hang** (vb) **1** hangen: ~ *loose* **a)** loshangen; **b)** kalm blijven **2** hangen, opgehangen worden **3** zweven, blijven hangen **4** aanhangen, zich vastklemmen, vast (blijven) zitten **5** onbeslist zijn: ~ *in the **balance*** (nog) onbeslist zijn ‖ ~ *behind* achterblijven; [Am] ~ *in (there)* volhouden; *she hung **on(to)** his every word* zij was één en al oor; ~ *onto sth.* proberen te (be)houden; ~ *over one's head* iem. boven het hoofd hangen

³**hang** (vb) **1** (op)hangen [also as punishment]: *he* ~*ed **himself*** hij verhing zich **2** laten hangen: ~ *one's **head** in shame* het hoofd

schuldbewust laten hangen **3** tentoonstellen [painting] || [inform] ~ *it (all)!* ze kunnen van mij allemaal in elkaar storten!; ~ *sth. on s.o.* iem. de schuld van iets geven

hangar hangar, vliegtuigloods

hang (a)round 1 rondhangen, rondlummelen **2** wachten, treuzelen

hang back aarzelen; dralen: ~ *from doing sth.* aarzelen iets te doen

hanger-on (slaafse) volgeling, parasiet, handlanger

hang-glider deltavlieger [appliance as well as user]; zeilvlieger, hangglider

¹**hanging** (n) **1** ophanging **2** [esp pl] wandtapijtʰ

²**hanging** (adj) hangend; **hang-hangman** beul

hang on 1 zich (stevig) vasthouden, niet loslaten, blijven (hangen): ~ *tight!* hou (je) stevig vast!; ~ *to* zich vasthouden aan **2** volhouden, het niet opgeven, doorzetten **3** even wachten; aan de lijn blijven [telephone]: ~ *(a minute)!* ogenblikje!

hangout verblijfʰ, stamkroeg, ontmoetingsplaats, hangplek

¹**hang out** (vb) [inform] uithangen, zich ophouden: *where were you hanging out?* waar heb jij uitgehangen?; *I used to ~ with him* vroeger ben ik veel met hem opgetrokken

²**hang out** (vb) uithangen; ophangen [laundry]; uitsteken [flag]

hangover 1 kater, houten kop **2** overblijfselʰ: *his style of driving is a ~ from his racing days* zijn rijstijl heeft hij overgehouden aan zijn tijd als autocoureur **3** ontnuchtering, ontgoocheling

¹**hang up** (vb) **1** ophangen [telephone]: *and then she hung up on me* en toen gooide ze de hoorn op de haak **2** vastlopen

²**hang up** (vb) **1** ophangen **2** uitstellen, ophouden, doen vastlopen || [inform] *be hung up on* (or: *about*) *sth.* complexen hebben over iets

hang-up complexʰ, obsessie, frustratie

hank streng [yarn]

hanker (+ after, for) hunkeren (naar)

hanky zakdoek

hanky-panky 1 hocus pocus⁺ʰ, bedriegerij **2** gescharrelʰ, overspelʰ

Hanukkah Chanoekaʰ

haphazard toevallig, op goed geluk (af), lukraak

hapless ongelukkig, onfortuinlijk

happen 1 (toevallig) gebeuren: *as it ~s* (or: *~ed*) toevallig, zoals het nu eenmaal gaat; *should anything ~ to* him mocht hem iets overkomen **2** toevallig verschijnen, toevallig komen, gaan || *if you ~ to see* him mocht u hem zien; *I ~ed to notice it* ik zag het toevallig; *I ~ed (up)on it* ik trof het toevallig aan

happening gebeurtenis

happiness gelukʰ

happy 1 gelukkig, blij **2** gepast, passend; gelukkig [language, behaviour, suggestion] **3** voorspoedig, gelukkig: *Happy Birthday* hartelijk gefeliciteerd met je verjaardag; *Happy New Year* Gelukkig nieuwjaar **4** blij; verheugd [in polite phrases]: *I'll be ~ to accept your kind invitation* ik neem uw uitnodiging graag aan || *(strike) the ~ medium* de gulden middenweg (inslaan); [euph] ~ *event* blijde gebeurtenis, geboorte; *many ~ returns (of the day)!* nog vele jaren!

happy-go-lucky zorgeloos; onbezorgd

happy hour happy hourʰ

haptic haptisch

haram haram

harass 1 treiteren, pesten, kwellen **2** teisteren, voortdurend bestoken

harassment kwelling; pesterij

¹**harbour** (n) **1** haven **2** schuilplaats

²**harbour** (vb) **1** herbergen; onderdak verlenen [criminal] **2** koesteren [emotions, ideas]

¹**hard** (adj) **1** hard, vast(staand), krachtig, taai, robuust: ~ *cover* (boek)band, gebonden editie; ~ *currency* harde valuta; *a ~ winter* een strenge winter; ~ *and fast rule* (or: *line*) vaste regel, ijzeren wet **2** hard, hardvochtig: *drive a ~ bargain* keihard onderhandelen; *be ~ on s.o.* onvriendelijk zijn tegen iem. **3** moeilijk, hard, lastig: ~ *labour* dwangarbeid; *she gave him a ~ time* hij kreeg het zwaar te verduren van haar; ~ *of hearing* slechthorend, hardhorend **4** hard, ijverig, energiek: *a ~ drinker* een stevige drinker; *a ~ worker* een harde werker || ~ *cash* baar geld, klinkende munt; *they preferred ~ copy to soft copy* zij verkozen uitdraai boven beeldschermtekst; ~ *feelings* wrok(gevoelens), rancune; ~ *luck* pech, tegenslag; *as ~ as nails* ongevoelig, onverzoenlijk; ~ *shoulder* vluchtstrook; *play ~ to get* moeilijk doen, zich ongenaakbaar opstellen; ~ *by* vlakbij

²**hard** (adv) **1** hard, krachtig, inspannend, zwaar: *be ~ hit* zwaar getroffen zijn; *think ~* diep nadenken; *be ~ on s.o.'s heels* (or: *trail*) iem. op de hielen zitten **2** met moeite, moeizaam: *be hard put (to it) to (do sth.)* het moeilijk vinden (om iets te doen); *old habits die ~* vaste gewoonten verdwijnen niet gauw; *take sth. ~* iets zwaar opnemen, zwaar lijden onder iets

hardback (in)gebonden [book]

hardboard (hard)boardʰ, houtvezelplaat

hard-boiled 1 hardgekookt **2** hard, ongevoelig

hard copy (computer)uitdraai, afdruk

¹**hard-core** (adj) hard

²**hard-core** (adj) onbuigzaam

hard disk harde schijf, vaste schijf, harddisk

hard-earned zuurverdiend

harden 1 (ver)harden, ongevoelig worden,

maken: a ~ed **criminal** een gewetenloze misdadiger **2** gewennen: **become** ~ed to sth. aan iets wennen

hard hat 1 helm [helmet] **2** [inform] bouwvakker

hard-headed praktisch, nuchter, zakelijk

hard-hearted hardvochtig

hardline keihard, een politiek van de harde lijn voerend

hardly nauwelijks, amper: we had ~ **arrived** when it began to rain we waren er nog maar net toen het begon te regenen; I could ~ move ik kon me haast niet bewegen; ~ **anything** bijna niets; ~ **anybody** vrijwel niemand; ~ **ever** bijna nooit

hard-pressed in moeilijkheden; sterk onder druk: be ~ **for** time in tijdnood zitten

hardship ontbering, tegenspoed

hard up slecht bij kas || be ~ **for** sth. grote behoefte aan iets hebben

hardware 1 ijzerwaren, (huis)gereedschap[h] **2** apparatuur [also of computer]; hardware, bouwelementen

hardwood hardhout[h]

hardy 1 sterk, robuust **2** winterhard, wintervast: ~ **annual** winterharde plant; [fig; hum] onderwerp dat regelmatig aan de orde komt, oude bekende

hare haas

harebrained onbezonnen; dwaas

harelip hazenlip

harem harem

haricot snijboon

[1]**harm** (n) kwaad[h], schade: be (or: do) no ~ geen kwaad kunnen; she came to no ~ er overkwam haar geen kwaad; out of ~'s way in veiligheid

[2]**harm** (vb) kwaad doen, schade berokkenen

harmful schadelijk, nadelig

harmless 1 onschadelijk, ongevaarlijk **2** onschuldig

[1]**harmonic** (n) harmonische (toon), boventoon

[2]**harmonic** (adj) harmonisch

harmonica harmonica; mondharmonica

harmonious 1 harmonieus **2** eensgezind

harmony harmonie, eensgezindheid, overeenstemming: be **in** ~ **with** in overeenstemming zijn met **2** goede verstandhouding, eendracht: live **in** ~ in goede verstandhouding leven

[1]**harness** (n) gareel[h], (paarden)tuig[h] || get back into ~ weer aan het werk gaan

[2]**harness** (vb) **1** optuigen; inspannen [horse]; in het gareel brengen **2** aanwenden, gebruiken; benutten [(natural) energy sources]

harp harp

harp on zaniken, zeuren: ~ about sth. doorzeuren over iets

harpoon harpoen

harpsichord klavecimbel[h]

harrow eg

harrowing aangrijpend

harsh 1 ruw, wrang; verblindend [light]; krassend [sound] **2** wreed, hardvochtig

[1]**harvest** (n) oogst(tijd)

[2]**harvest** (vb) **1** oogsten, vergaren **2** verkrijgen, behalen (wat men verdient)

harvester oogstmachine

hash 1 hachee[+h] **2** mengelmoes[h] **3** hasj(iesj) || **make** a ~ of it de boel verknoeien

hashish hasjiesj

hash symbol hekje[h] (#)

hashtag hashtag

[1]**hassle** (n) **1** gedoe[h]: a real ~ een zware opgave, een heel gedoe **2** ruzie

[2]**hassle** (vb) moeilijk maken, dwarszitten, lastigvallen

haste haast, spoed: **make** ~ zich haasten **2** overhaasting

[1]**hasten** (vb) zich haasten

[2]**hasten** (vb) versnellen, bespoedigen

hasty 1 haastig; gehaast **2** overhaast; onbezonnen

hat hoed: at the **drop** of a ~ bij de minste aanleiding, plotseling, zonder aarzeling || knock into a **cocked** ~ a) gehakt maken van, helemaal inmaken; b) in duigen doen vallen; I'll **eat** my ~ if … ik mag doodvallen als …; **keep** sth. under one's ~ iets geheim houden, iets onder de pet houden; **pass** (or: **send, take**) the ~ (round) met de pet rondgaan; [fig] **take** off one's ~ (or: **take** one's ~ off) to s.o. zijn pet(je) afnemen voor iem.; [inform] **talk** through one's ~ bluffen, nonsens verkopen; **throw** (or: **toss**) one's ~ in(to) the ring zich in de (verkiezings)strijd werpen; [comp] **black** ~ cracker; criminele hacker; [comp] **white** ~ hacker met goede bedoelingen die inbreekt om een bedrijf te wijzen op veiligheidslekken

[1]**hatch** (n) **1** onderdeur **2** luik[h] **3** sluisdeur || **down** the ~ proost!

[2]**hatch** (vb) (also + out) uit het ei komen [of chick]; openbreken [of egg(shell)]

[3]**hatch** (vb) **1** (also + out) uitbroeden, broeden **2** beramen [plan]

hatchback 1 (opklapbare) vijfde deur **2** vijfdeursauto

hatchet 1 bijltje[h], (hand)bijl **2** tomahawk, strijdbijl || [inform] **bury** the ~ de strijdbijl begraven, vrede sluiten

hatchet man 1 huurmoordenaar, gangster **2** [depr] handlanger, trawant; [by extension] waakhond; ordehandhaver

hatchling pas uitgekomen jong[h]

[1]**hate** (n) **1** gehate persoon, gehaat iets **2** haat

[2]**hate** (vb) **1** haten, grondig verafschuwen, een hekel hebben aan **2** [inform] het jammer vinden: I ~ having to **tell** you … het spijt

me u te moeten zeggen ...; I ~ to **say** this, but
... ik zeg het niet graag, maar ...
hate crime haatmisdaad
hateful 1 gehaat, weerzinwekkend **2** hatelijk [remark] **3** onsympathiek, onaangenaam, onuitstaanbaar
hater hater: are you a **dog**-~ heb je een hekel aan honden?; he's a ~ hij doet altijd negatief
hatred haat, afschuw
hat tip: ~ **to** my colleague for bringing this to my attention met dank aan mijn collega, die mij hierop wees
haughty trots, arrogant
¹haul (n) **1** haal, trek, het trekken **2** vangst, buit **3** afstand, traject^h: **in** (or: over) the long ~ op lange termijn **4** lading, vracht
²haul (vb) **1** halen, ophalen; inhalen [with effort]: ~ **down** one's flag (or: colours) de vlag strijken; [fig] zich overgeven; ~ **in** the net het net binnenhalen **2** vervoeren **3** slepen [take somebody to court]
haulage 1 het slepen, het trekken **2** vervoer^h, transport^h **3** transportkosten, vervoerkosten: all prices **include** ~ bij alle prijzen zijn de vervoerkosten inbegrepen
haulier vrachtrijder, vervoerder, expediteur
haunch lende, heup, bil, dij: **on** one's ~es op zijn hurken
¹haunt (n) **1** trefpunt^h: we went for a drink at one of his favourite ~s we gingen iets drinken in een van de plaatsen waar hij graag kwam **2** hol^h; schuilplaats [of animals]
²haunt (vb) **1** vaak aanwezig zijn in, zich altijd ophouden in, regelmatig bezoeken: he ~s that **place** daar is hij altijd te vinden **2** rondspoken in, rondwaren in: ~ed **castle** spookkasteel **3** achtervolgen, niet loslaten, (steeds) lastigvallen: that tune has been ~ing me all afternoon dat deuntje speelt de hele middag al door mijn kop
have 1 hebben, bezitten, beschikken over, houden: he has (got) an excellent memory hij beschikt over een voortreffelijk geheugen; ~ **mercy** on us heb medelijden met ons; I've **got** it ik heb het, ik weet het (weer); you ~ **sth.** there daar zeg je (me) wat, daar zit wat in; ~ sth. **about** (or: on, with) one iets bij zich hebben; what does she ~ **against** me? wat heeft ze tegen mij? **2** [as part of a whole] bevatten, bestaan uit: the book has six **chapters** het boek telt zes hoofdstukken **3** krijgen, ontvangen: we've had no **news** we hebben geen nieuws (ontvangen); you can ~ it **back** tomorrow je kunt het morgen terugkrijgen **4** nemen, pakken; gebruiken [food, drink etc]: ~ **breakfast** ontbijten; ~ a **drink** iets drinken, een drankje nemen **5** hebben, genieten van, lijden aan: ~ a good **time** het naar zijn zin hebben **6** hebben, laten liggen, leggen, zetten: let's ~ the **rug** in the hall laten we het ta-

pijt in de hal leggen **7** hebben, maken, nemen: ~ a **bath** (or: shower) een bad (or: douche) nemen; ~ a **try** iets proberen **8** toelaten, accepteren: I won't ~ such **conduct** ik accepteer zulk gedrag niet; I'm not having **any** ik pik het niet, ik pieker er niet over **9** hebben te: I still ~ quite a **bit** of work to do ik heb nog heel wat te doen **10** laten, doen, opdracht geven te: ~ one's **hair** cut zijn haar laten knippen **11** krijgen [child]: ~ a child **by** een kind hebben van **12** zorgen voor: can you ~ the **children** tonight? kun jij vanavond voor de kinderen zorgen? **13** [inform] te pakken hebben [lit and fig]; het winnen van: you've got me there a) jij wint; b) geen idee, daar vraag je me wat **14** [inform] bedriegen, bij de neus nemen: **John's** been had ze hebben John beetgenomen **15** hebben, zijn: I ~ **worked** ik heb gewerkt; he has **died** hij is gestorven; I had **better** (or: best) forget it ik moest dat maar vergeten; I'd **just** as soon die ik zou net zo lief doodgaan || he had it **coming** to him hij kreeg zijn verdiende loon; rumour has **it** that ... het gerucht gaat dat ...; ~ **it** (from s.o.) het (van iem.) gehoord hebben; [inform] ~ had **it** a) hangen, de klos zijn; b) niet meer de oude zijn, dood zijn; c) het zat (or: beu) zijn, er de brui aan geven; ~ it **in** for s.o. een hekel hebben aan iem., het op iem. gemunt hebben, de pik hebben op iem.; ~ it (or: the matter) **out** with s.o. het (probleem) uitpraten met iem.; ~ s.o. **up** (for sth.) iem. voor de rechtbank brengen (wegens iets); ~ nothing **on** niet kunnen tippen aan
haven behouden haven, veilige haven [also fig]; toevluchtsoord^h
have-nots armen
have on 1 aanhebben; dragen [clothes]; ophebben [hat] **2** gepland hebben, op zijn agenda hebben: I've got nothing on tonight vanavond ben ik vrij **3** [inform] voor de gek houden, een loopje nemen met: are you having me on? zit je mij nou voor de gek te houden?
have to moeten, verplicht zijn om te, (be)hoeven: we have (got) to go now we moeten nu weg; he didn't ~ do that dat had hij niet hoeven doen
havoc verwoesting, vernieling, ravage; [fig] verwarring: **play** ~ among (or: with), **make** ~ of, **wreak** ~ on a) totaal verwoesten; b) grondig in de war sturen, een puinhoop maken van
hawk havik; [fig] oorlogszuchtig persoon: **watch** like a ~ zeer nauwlettend in de gaten houden
hawker (straat)venter, marskramer
hawthorn haagdoorn, meidoorn
hay hooi^h || **hit** the ~ gaan pitten; **make** ~ while the sun shines men moet het ijzer smeden als het heet is

hay fever hooikoorts
hay-stack hooiberg
haywire in de war, door elkaar: *my plans went* ~ mijn plannen liepen in het honderd
¹**hazard** (n) **1** gevaarʰ, risicoʰ: *smoking and drinking are health* ~s roken en drinken zijn een gevaar voor de gezondheid **2** kans, mogelijkheid, toevalʰ **3** [golf] (terrein)hindernis
²**hazard** (vb) **1** in de waagschaal stellen, wagen, riskeren **2** zich wagen aan, wagen: ~ *a guess* een gok wagen
hazardous gevaarlijk, gewaagd, riskant
¹**haze** (n) nevel, damp, waasʰ; [fig] vaagheid; verwardheid
²**haze** (vb) (+ over) nevelig worden
hazel hazelaar, hazelnotenstruik
hazelnut hazelnoot
hazy nevelig, wazig; [fig] vaag: *a* ~ *idea* een vaag idee
he hij, die, dat, het: *'Who is he?' 'He's John'* 'Wie is dat?' 'Dat is John'
¹**head** (n) **1** hoofdʰ, kop, hoofdlengte: ~ *and shoulders above* met kop en schouders erbovenuit; [fig] verreweg de beste; ~s *or tails?* kruis of munt?; ~ *first* (or: *foremost*) voorover **2** hoofdʰ, verstandʰ: *it never entered* (or: *came into*) *his* ~ het kwam niet bij hem op; *get* (or: *take*) *sth. into one's* ~ zich iets in het hoofd zetten; *the success has gone to* (or: *turned*) *his* ~ het succes is hem naar het hoofd gestegen; *put one's* ~s *together* de koppen bij elkaar steken; *a* ~ *for mathematics* een wiskundeknobbel **3** persoon, hoofdʰ: *£1 a* ~ £1 per persoon **4** uiteindeʰ, kop **5** hoofdjeʰ, korfjeʰ, kruin **6** top, bovenkant **7** breekpuntʰ, crisis: *that brought the matter to a* ~ daarmee werd de zaak op de spits gedreven **8** boveneindeʰ, hoofd(einde)ʰ **9** voorkant, kop, spits; hoofdʰ [also of team] **10** meerdere, leider, hoofdʰ: ~ *of state* staatshoofdʰ **11** stukʰ (vee); kudde; aantalʰ dieren: *50* ~ *of cattle* 50 stuks vee || *have one's* ~ *in the clouds* met het hoofd in de wolken lopen; *from* ~ *to foot* van top tot teen; *bury one's* ~ *in the sand* de kop in het zand steken; *I could not make* ~ *or tail of it* ik kon er geen touw aan vastknopen; *keep one's* ~ *above water* het hoofd boven water houden; *keep one's* ~ zijn kalmte bewaren; *laugh one's* ~ *off* zich een ongeluk lachen; *lose one's* ~ het hoofd verliezen; *scream* (or: *shout*) *one's* ~ *off* vreselijk tekeergaan; *have one's* ~ *screwed on straight* (or: *right*) verstandig zijn, niet gek zijn
²**head** (vb) gaan, gericht zijn, koers zetten: *the plane* ~ed *north* het vliegtuig zette koers naar het noorden
³**head** (vb) **1** aan het hoofd staan van, voorop lopen: *the general* ~ed *the revolt* de generaal leidde de opstand **2** bovenaan plaatsen, bovenaan staan op **3** overtreffen, voorbijstreven **4** [socc] koppen **5** richten, sturen

headache 1 hoofdpijn **2** probleemʰ, vervelende kwestie: *finding reliable staff has become a major* ~ het vinden van betrouwbaar personeel is een groot probleem geworden
head butt kopstoot
headcase [inform] halvegare
headdress hoofdtooi
header 1 [socc] kopbal **2** duik(eling): *take a* ~ een duikeling maken **3** koptekst
head for afgaan op, koers zetten naar: *he was already heading for the bar* hij liep al in de richting de bar; *you are heading for trouble* als jij zo doorgaat krijg je narigheid
headgear hoofddekselʰ
headhunting 1 het koppensnellen **2** headhunting
heading opschriftʰ, titel, kop
headlamp koplamp
headland kaap; landtong
headlight koplamp
headline (kranten)kop, opschriftʰ: *make* (or: *hit*) *the* ~s volop in het nieuws komen || *the* ~s hoofdpunten van het nieuws
headlong 1 voorover, met het hoofd voorover **2** haastig, halsoverkop
headmaster schoolhoofdʰ, rector
headmistress schoolhoofdʰ
head off 1 onderscheppen, van richting doen veranderen **2** voorkomen
head-on frontaal, van voren: *a* ~ *collision* een frontale botsing
headphones koptelefoon
headquarters hoofdbureauʰ, hoofdkantoorʰ, hoofdkwartierʰ
headrest hoofdsteun [eg in car]
headset koptelefoon
headspace geestestoestand, gemoedstoestand
head start (+ on, over) voorsprong (op) [also fig]; goede uitgangspositie
headstone grafsteen
headstrong koppig, eigenzinnig
heads-up [Am; inform] alert
headway voortgang; vaart [of ship]: [fig] *make* ~ vooruitgang boeken
headwind tegenwind
heady 1 opwindend, wild **2** bedwelmend; dronken makend [wine]
heal (also + over) genezen, (doen) herstellen; dichtgaan [of wound]; [fig] bijleggen; vereffenen
healer genezer || *time is the great* ~ de tijd heelt alle wonden
health gezondheid, gezondheidstoestand: *have* (or: *be in, enjoy*) *good* ~ een goede gezondheid genieten || *drink* (to) *s.o.'s* ~ op iemands gezondheid drinken
health food gezonde (natuurlijke) voeding
healthy gezond, heilzaam: *he has a* ~ *respect for my father* hij heeft een groot ontzag

voor mijn vader

¹heap (n) **1** hoop, stapel, berg **2** boel, massa, hoop: *we've got ~s of time* we hebben nog zeeën van tijd

²heap (vb) **1** (+ up) ophopen, (op)stapelen, samenhopen **2** (+ on, with) vol laden (met), opladen (met) **3** overladen, overstelpen: *she ~ed reproaches (up)on her mother* zij overstelpte haar moeder met verwijten

¹hear (vb) **1** luisteren naar, (ver)horen, behandelen; verhoren [prayer]; overhoren, gehoor geven aan: *please ~ me out* laat mij uitspreken **2** vernemen, kennisnemen van, horen: *we are sorry to ~ that* het spijt ons te (moeten) horen dat

²hear (vb) horen: *~ from* bericht krijgen van, horen van; *~ of (or: about)* horen van (*or:* over) ‖ *~! ~!* bravo!

hearing 1 gehoor^h, hearing, hoorzitting: *he would not even give us a ~* hij wilde zelfs niet eens naar ons luisteren **2** behandeling [of a case] **3** [Am; law] verhoor^h **4** gehoor^h: *she is hard of ~* zij is hardhorend **5** gehoorsafstand: *out of (or: within) ~ distance* buiten (*or:* binnen) gehoorsafstand

hearing aid (ge)hoorapparaat^h

hearsay praatjes, geruchten: *I know it from ~* ik weet het van horen zeggen

hearse lijkwagen

heart 1 hart^h, hartspier, binnenste^h, gemoed^h: *from (or: to) the bottom of my ~* uit de grond van mijn hart; *they have their own interests at ~* zij hebben hun eigen belangen voor ogen; *set one's ~ on* zijn zinnen op iets zetten, iets dolgraag willen; *she took it to ~* zij trok het zich aan, zij nam het ter harte; *in one's ~ of hearts* in het diepst van zijn hart; *with all one's ~* van ganser harte **2** boezem, borst **3** geest, gedachten, herinnering: *a change of ~* verandering van gedachten; *(learn) by ~* uit het hoofd (leren) **4** kern, hart^h, essentie **5** moed, durf: *not have the ~* de moed niet hebben; *lose ~* de moed verliezen; *take ~* moed vatten, zich vermannen ‖ *my ~ bleeds* ik ben diepbedroefd; [iron] oh jee, wat heb ik een medelijden; *cry (or: weep) one's ~ out* tranen met tuiten huilen; *eat one's ~ out* wegkwijnen (van verdriet/verlangen); [hum] *eat your ~ out!* doe dat maar eens na!, daar sta je van te kijken, hè!

heart attack hartaanval; hartinfarct^h

heartbeat hartslag

heartbreaking 1 hartbrekend, hartverscheurend **2** frustrerend, zwaar [work]

heart condition hartkwaal

hearten bemoedigen, moed geven

heartfelt hartgrondig, oprecht

hearth haard(stede); [fig] huis^h; woning: *~ and home* huis en haard

heartily 1 van harte, oprecht, vriendelijk **2** flink, hartig: *eat ~* stevig eten **3** hartgron-

dig: *I ~ dislike that fellow* ik heb een hartgrondige hekel aan die vent

heart-rending hartverscheurend

heart-stopping adembenemend

heartstrings diepste gevoelens; [iron] sentimentele gevoelens: *tug at s.o.'s ~* iem. zeer (ont)roeren

heart-to-heart openhartig gesprek^h

hearty 1 hartelijk, vriendelijk **2** gezond, flink, hartig: *a ~ meal* een stevig maal; *hale and ~* kerngezond **3** [inform] (al te) joviaal

¹heat (n) **1** warmte, hitte **2** vuur^h, drift, heftigheid: *in the ~ of the conversation* in het vuur van het gesprek **3** [inform] druk, dwang, moeilijkheden: *turn (or: put) the ~ on s.o.* iem. onder druk zetten **4** loopsheid: *on ~* loops, tochtig **5** voorwedstrijd, serie, voorronde

²heat (vb) warm worden: *~ up* heet worden

³heat (vb) verhitten, verwarmen: *~ up* opwarmen

heater kachel, verwarming(stoestel^h)

heath 1 heideveld^h, open veld^h **2** dopheide, erica

heathen 1 heiden, ongelovige **2** barbaar

heather heide(kruid^h), struikheide

heating verwarming(ssysteem^h)

heat wave hittegolf

¹heave (n) **1** hijs, het op en neer gaan: *the ~ of the sea* de deining van de zee **2** ruk: *he gave a mighty ~* hij gaf een enorme ruk

²heave (vb) **1** (op)zwellen, rijzen, omhooggaan: *his stomach ~d* zijn maag draaide ervan om **2** op en neer gaan **3** trekken, sjorren: *~ at (or: on)* trekken aan

³heave (vb) **1** opheffen, (op)hijsen **2** slaken: *she ~d a sigh* ze zuchtte diep, ze liet een diepe zucht **3** [inform] gooien, smijten **4** [shipp] hijsen, takelen

heaven hemel; [fig] gelukzaligheid; Voorzienigheid: *in Heaven's name, for Heaven's sake* in hemelsnaam; *thank ~(s)!* de hemel zij dank!

heavenly 1 hemels; goddelijk **2** hemel-: *~ bodies* hemellichamen

heavy 1 zwaar: *~ industry* zware industrie; *~ with* zwaar beladen met; *~ with the smell of roses* doortrokken van de geur van rozen **2** zwaar, hevig, aanzienlijk: *~ traffic* druk verkeer, vrachtverkeer^h **3** moeilijk te verteren [also fig]: *I find it ~ going* ik schiet slecht op **4** serieus [newspaper, part in play]; zwaar op de hand **5** streng **6** zwaar, drukkend **7** zwaarmoedig ‖ *play the ~ father* een (donder)preek houden; *make ~ weather of sth.* moeilijk maken wat makkelijk is; [inform] *be ~ on* veel gebruiken [petrol, make-up]; *time hung ~ on her hands* de tijd viel haar lang

heavy-footed 1 log **2** moeizaam; stroef

heavy-handed 1 onhandig; log, onbeholpen: *be ~ with the salt* erg scheutig zijn met zout **2** tactloos

heavyset zwaargebouwd

heavyweight 1 zwaar iem. **2** worstelaar (bokser) in de zwaargewichtklasse **3** kopstuk^h, zwaargewicht^h

Hebrew Hebreeuws, Joods

heckle 1 steeds onderbreken [speaker] **2** uitjouwen, naroepen

heckler 1 iem. die stelselmatig interrumpeert (en daardoor de orde verstoort) **2** uitjouwer, naroeper

hectic koortsachtig [also fig]; jachtig, druk, hectisch

¹hedge (n) heg, haag

²hedge (vb) een slag om de arm houden, ergens omheen draaien

³hedge (vb) **1** omheinen: ~ *about* (or: *around, in*) *with* omringen met **2** dekken [bets, speculations]

hedge fund [fin] hedgefonds^h

hedgehog egel

hedge in omheinen; [fig] omringen; belemmeren: *hedged in by rules and regulations* door regels en voorschriften omringd

hedgerow haag

hedge sparrow heggenmus

heed aandacht, zorg: *give* (or: *pay*) ~ *to* aandacht schenken aan; *take* ~ *of* nota nemen van, letten op

heedless 1 achteloos, onoplettend: *be* ~ *of* niet letten op, in de wind slaan **2** onvoorzichtig

heel 1 hiel [also of stocking]; hak [also of shoe] **2** uiteinde^h, onderkant; korst [of cheese]; kapje^h [of bread] ‖ *bring* to ~ kleinkrijgen, in het gareel brengen; *dig* one's ~s in het been stijf houden; *he* took to his ~s hij koos het hazenpad; *turn on* one's ~ zich plotseling omdraaien; *down* at ~ met scheve hakken, afgetrapt; [fig] haveloos; *at* (or: *on*) the ~s op de hielen, vlak achter

hefty 1 fors, potig **2** zwaar, lijvig

hegemony hegemonie; overwicht^h

heifer vaars(kalf^h)

height 1 hoogte, lengte, peil^h, niveau^h: *it is only 4 feet in* ~ het is maar 4 voet hoog **2** hoogtepunt^h, toppunt^h: *the* ~ *of summer* hartje zomer; *at its* ~ op zijn hoogtepunt **3** top, piek **4** terreinverheffing, hoogte

heighten 1 hoger (doen) worden, verhogen **2** (doen) toenemen, verhevigen

heinous gruwelijk

heir 1 erfgenaam: ~s erven; *sole* ~ enige erfgenaam **2** opvolger: ~ *to* the throne troonopvolger

heiress erfgename [of fortune]

heirloom erfstuk^h, familiestuk^h

heist [Am; inform] roof(overval)

helicopter helikopter

helicopter parent helikopterouder

helium helium^h

hell hel [also fig]: *she drove* ~ *for leather* zij reed in vliegende vaart ‖ *come* ~ *and* (or: *or*) *high water* wat er zich ook voordoet

hell-bent (+ on, for) vastbesloten (om)

hellhole [inform] hel; afschuwelijke plek

hello 1 hallo: *say* ~ *to him for me* doe hem de groeten van mij **2** hé [to express surprise]

helm helmstok; [also fig] stuurrad^h; roer^h: *at the* ~ aan het roer; *take the* ~ het roer in handen nemen

helmet helm

helmsman roerganger, stuurman

¹help (n) **1** hulp, steun, bijstand: *that's a big* ~! nou, daar hebben we wat aan!, daar schieten we mee op, zeg!; *can we be of any* ~? kunnen wij ergens mee helpen? **2** help(st)er, dienstmeisje^h, werkster **3** huishoudelijk personeel^h **4** remedie^{+h}: *there is no* ~ *for it* er is niets aan te doen

²help (vb) **1** helpen, bijstaan, (onder)steunen, baten: ~ *along* (or: *forward*) vooruithelpen, bevorderen; ~ *out* a) bijspringen; b) aanvullen **2** opscheppen, bedienen: ~ *yourself* ga je gang, tast toe **3** verhelpen, helpen tegen: *it can't be ~ed* er is niets aan te doen **4** voorkomen, verhinderen: *if I can* ~ *it* als het aan mij ligt **5** [+ negation] nalaten, zich weerhouden van: *we could not* ~ *but smile* wij moesten wel glimlachen, of we wilden of niet

help desk helpdesk

helpful 1 nuttig **2** behulpzaam

¹helping (n) portie [food]

²helping (adj) steunend: *lend a* ~ *hand* een handje helpen

helpless 1 hulpeloos: ~ *with* laughter slap van de lach **2** onbeholpen

helter-skelter holderdebolder, halsoverkop, kriskras

¹hem (n) boord^h, zoom: *take the* ~ *up (of sth.)* (iets) korter maken

²hem (vb) (om)zomen: ~ *about* (or: *around*) omringen; *feel ~med in* zich ingekapseld voelen

he-man mannetjesputter

hemisphere halve bol; [geography] halfrond^h: *the northern* (or: *southern*) ~ het noordelijk (or: zuidelijk) halfrond

hemp hennep, cannabis

hen 1 hoen^h, hen, kip **2** pop [of bird] **3** [inform] pop [of bird]

hence 1 van nu (af): *five years* ~ over vijf jaar **2** vandaar

henceforth van nu af aan, voortaan

henchman 1 volgeling, aanhanger **2** trawant

henna henna

hen-party vrijgezellenfeest^h (voor vrouwen)

henpecked onder de plak (zittend): *a ~ husband* een pantoffelheld

hepatitis geelzucht; hepatitis
¹her (pers pron) **1** haar, aan haar: *he gave ~ a watch* hij gaf haar een horloge **2** zij: *that's ~* dat is ze
²her (poss pron) haar: *it's ~ day* het is haar grote dag
¹herald (n) **1** heraut, gezant **2** (voor)bode
²herald (vb) aankondigen: *~ in* inluiden
heraldry heraldiek, wapenkunde
herb kruidʰ: *~s and spices* kruiden en specerijen
herbaceous kruidachtig: *~ border* border van overblijvende (bloeiende) planten
herbal kruiden-
herbivore herbivoor, planteneter
Herculean herculisch
¹herd (n) **1** kudde, troep, horde; [depr] massa: *the common* (or: *vulgar*) *~* de massa
²herd (vb) samendrommen, bij elkaar hokken: *~ with* omgaan met
³herd (vb) hoeden: *~ together* samendrijven
here hier, op deze plaats, hierheen: *where do we go from ~* hoe gaan we nu verder?; *near ~* hier in de buurt; [inform] *~ we are* daar zijn we dan, (zie)zo; *~ you are* hier, alsjeblieft; *~ and now* nu meteen; *over ~* hier(heen); *~, there and everywhere* overal; *that's is neither ~ nor there* dat slaat nergens op, dat heeft er niets mee te maken
hereabouts hier in de buurt; hieromtrent
¹hereafter (n) hiernamaalsʰ
²hereafter (adv) **1** hierna; voortaan, verderop **2** [form] na de dood
hereby **1** hierbij **2** hierdoor
hereditary erfelijk, erf-
heredity **1** erfelijkheid **2** overerving
heresy ketterij
heretic ketter
heretical ketters
herewith hierbij, bij deze(n)
heritage **1** erfenis; erfgoedʰ [also fig] **2** erfdeelʰ
hermaphrodite **1** hermafrodiet **2** [bot] tweeslachtige plant
hermit kluizenaar
hermit crab heremietkreeft
hernia hernia, (lies)breuk
hero **1** held **2** hoofdpersoon, hoofdrolspeler
heroic **1** heroïsch, heldhaftig **2** helden-: *~ age* heldentijd **3** groots, gedurfd
heroin heroïne
heroine **1** heldin **2** hoofdrolspeelster
heroism heldenmoed
heron reiger
herring haring
herring gull zilvermeeuw
hers van haar, de (or: het) hare: *my books and ~* mijn boeken en die van haar; *a friend of ~* een vriend van haar
herself zichzelf, zich, zelf: *she cut ~* ze

sneed zich; *she did it ~* ze deed het zelf
hesitate aarzelen, weifelen: *~ about* (or: *over*) aarzelen over
hesitation aarzeling
hessian jute, zaklinnenʰ
heterogeneous heterogeen, ongelijksoortig
heterosexual heteroseksueel
hew houwen, sabelen, (be)kappen: *~ down* a) kappen, omhakken [trees]; b) neermaaien [people]
hexagon regelmatige zeshoek
hexameter hexameter
hex key inbussleutel
hey hé: *~, you!* hé jij daar!
heyday hoogtijdagen, bloei, beste tijd
hi hallo, hoi: *tell her I said hi* doe haar de groeten
hibernate een winterslaap houden [also fig]
hiccup **1** hik **2** [inform] probleempjeʰ
hiccups (the) de hik
hidden verborgen, geheim: *~ agenda* geheime agenda
¹hide (n) (dieren)huid, velʰ
²hide (vb) zich verbergen: *~ away* (or: *out*) zich schuil houden
³hide (vb) verbergen, verschuilen: *~ from view* aan het oog onttrekken
hide-and-seek verstoppertjeʰ: *play ~* verstoppertje spelen
hideaway [inform] (geheime) schuilplaats
hidebound bekrompen
hideous afschuwelijk, afzichtelijk
hideout schuilplaats
hiding **1** het verbergen **2** het verborgen zijn: *come out of ~* tevoorschijn komen; *go into ~* zich verbergen **3** [inform] pakʰ rammel || [inform] *be on a ~ to nothing* voor een onmogelijke taak staan, geen schijn van kans maken
hiding place schuilplaats, geheime bergplaats
hierarchy hiërarchie
hieroglyph hiëroglief
hi-fi *high fidelity* hifi-geluidsinstallatie, stereo
¹high (n) **1** (hoogte)recordʰ, hoogtepuntʰ, toppuntʰ: *hit a ~* een hoogtepunt bereiken; *an all-time ~* een absoluut hoogtepunt, een absolute topper **2** hogedrukgebiedʰ || *from on ~* uit de hemel
²high (adj) **1** hoog, hooggeplaatst, verheven: *~ command* opperbevelʰ; *a ~ opinion of* een hoge dunk van; *have friends in ~ places* een goede kruiwagen hebben; *~ pressure* a) [meteorology] hoge druk; b) [inform] agressiviteit [of salesmanship]; *~ society* de hogere kringen; *~ tide* hoogwaterʰ, vloed; [fig] hoogtepuntʰ; *~ water* hoogwaterʰ **2** intens, sterk, groot: *~ hopes* hoge verwachtin-

gen **3** belangrijk: ~ *treason* hoogverraad[h]
4 vrolijk: *in* ~ *spirits* vrolijk **5** gevorderd,
hoog, op een hoogtepunt: ~ *season* hoogseizoen[h]; *it's* ~ *time we went* het is de hoogste
tijd om te gaan **6** aangeschoten, zat ‖ *get on
one's* ~ *horse* een hoge toon aanslaan; *the* ~
sea(s) de volle zee; ~ *tea* vroeg warm eten,
vaak met thee; ~ *and dry* gestrand; [fig] zonder middelen; ~ *and mighty* uit de hoogte

³**high** (adv) **1** hoog, zeer **2** schel ‖ *hold one's
head* ~ zijn hoofd niet laten hangen; *feelings
ran* ~ de emoties liepen hoog op; *ride* ~ succes hebben; *search* ~ *and low* in alle hoeken
zoeken

¹**highbrow** (n) (semi-)intellectueel
²**highbrow** (adj) geleerd, intellectueel
high-carb [food] koolhydraatrijk
high-class 1 eersteklas, prima, eerlijk
2 hooggeplaatst, voornaam
high-definition met hoge resolutie
highfalutin [inform] hoogdravend
high-five [inform] een high five geven
high-flyer hoogvlieger, ambitieus persoon
high-grade hoogwaardig
high-handed eigenmachtig, aanmatigend, autoritair
high-impact 1 stootvast, breekvast [mate-
rial] **2** [sport] de gewrichten zwaar belastend **3** [inform, fig] met groot effect, vergaand
highland hoogland[h]
Highlands (the) de Schotse Hooglanden
high-level op hoog niveau
¹**highlight** (n) **1** lichtste deel[h]; [fig] opvallend kenmerk[h] **2** hoogtepunt[h] **3** (-s) coupe
soleil
²**highlight** (vb) naar voren halen, doen uitkomen: *use this pen to* ~ *the relevant passages*
gebruik deze pen maar om de relevant passages te markeren
highlining [sport] (het) koordlopen over
een hoog boven de grond gespannen koord
highly 1 hoog: ~ *paid officials* goed betaalde ambtenaren **2** zeer, erg, in hoge mate
3 met lof: *speak* ~ *of* loven, roemen
high-maintenance 1 onderhouds-
intensief [equipment etc] **2** [inform] veel
aandacht nodig hebbend, lastig [pers]
high-minded hoogstaand, verheven
highness 1 hoogheid: *His* (or: *Her*) *Royal
Highness* Zijne (or: Hare) Koninklijke Hoogheid **2** hoogte, verhevenheid
high-pitched 1 hoog, schel **2** steil [roof]
high-powered krachtig; met groot vermogen; *a* ~ *car* een auto met een krachtige
motor; *a* ~ *manager* een dynamische manager; een topmanager
high-profile opvallend; op de voorgrond
tredend
high-res *see* hi-res
high-rise [Am] hoog: ~ *buildings* hoog-

bouw; ~ *flats* torenflats
high-risk met verhoogd risico: ~ *group* risicogroep
high road hoofdweg, grote weg; [fig] (directe) weg
high school [Am] middelbare school
high-sounding hoogdravend; klinkend
high-speed snel: ~ *rail link* hogesnelheidslijn
high street hoofdstraat: *High-Street fashion* mode voor het grote publiek
high-strung nerveus, overgevoelig
high-tech geavanceerd technisch
high-technology geavanceerde technologie
high-top [Am] (hoge) basketbalschoen
highway grote weg, verkeersweg; [fig] (directe) weg
highwayman struikrover
highway patrol [Am] verkeerspolitie
hijab hoofddoek, hidjab
¹**hijack** (n) kaping
²**hijack** (vb) kapen
hijacker kaper
¹**hike** (n) **1** lange wandeling, trektocht ‖ [Am;
inform] *take a* ~*!* hoepel op!, wegwezen!
²**hike** (vb) lopen, wandelen, trekken
³**hike** (vb) **1** (+ up) ophijsen, optrekken
2 [Am] verhogen
hiker wandelaar
hilarious 1 heel grappig, dolkomisch
2 vrolijk, uitgelaten
hilarity hilariteit, vrolijkheid
hill heuvel ‖ *it is up* ~ *and down dale* het gaat
heuvelop, heuvelaf; *over the* ~ over zijn
hoogtepunt heen
hillbilly [Am; depr] boerenkinkel, boeren-
trien
hillock 1 heuveltje[h] **2** bergje[h] [earth]
hillside helling
hilly heuvelachtig
hilt gevest[h], handvat[h] ‖ *(up)to the* ~ volkomen, tot over de oren
him 1 hem, aan hem **2** hij: ~ *and his jokes* hij
met zijn grapjes
himself zichzelf, zich, zelf: *he cut* ~ hij
sneed zich; *he did it* ~ hij deed het zelf
¹**hind** (n) hinde
²**hind** (adj) achterst ‖ *talk the* ~ *leg(s) off a
donkey* iem. de oren van het hoofd kletsen
hinder 1 belemmeren, hinderen **2** (+ from)
beletten (te), verhinderen, tegenhouden
hindmost achterst
hindquarters achterdeel[h]; achterlijf[h] [of
horse]
hindrance belemmering, beletsel[h], hindernis
hindsight kennis, inzicht[h] achteraf: *with* ~
achteraf gezien
¹**Hindu** (n) hindoe
²**Hindu** (adj) Hindoes

hinge scharnier[h]; [fig] spil
¹hint (n) **1** wenk, hint, tip: *drop a ~* een hint geven; *take a ~* een wenk ter harte nemen **2** vleugje[h], tikje[h]
²hint (vb) aanwijzingen geven: *~ at* zinspelen op
³hint (vb) laten doorschemeren
¹hip (n) heup
²hip (adj) hip, modern ‖ *~, ~, hurrah!* hiep, hiep, hoera!
hippie hippie
hippo nijlpaard[h]
hippopotamus nijlpaard[h]
hipsters 1 heupbroek **2** onderbroek met rechte pijpen
¹hire (n) huur, (dienst)loon[h]: *for* (or: *on*) *~* te huur
²hire (vb) **1** huren: *~ out* verhuren **2** inhuren, (tijdelijk) in dienst nemen
hireling huurling
hire purchase huurkoop: *on ~* op afbetaling
his zijn, van hem, het zijne, de zijne: *these boots are ~* deze laarzen zijn van hem; *a hobby of ~* een hobby van hem; *it was ~ day* het was zijn grote dag
hiss 1 sissen **2** uitfluiten: *~ off* (or: *away, down*) van het podium fluiten
hissy fit [inform] driftbui, woede-uitbarsting: *throw* (or: *have*) *a ~* een driftbui krijgen
historian historicus
historic historisch, beroemd
historical historisch, geschiedkundig
history 1 geschiedenis: *ancient* (or: *past*) *~* verleden tijd **2** historisch verhaal[h] **3** [comp] zoekgeschiedenis: *erase one's ~* zijn geschiedenis wissen
¹hit (n) **1** klap, slag **2** treffer **3** hit, succes-(nummer)[h] **4** buitenkansje[h], treffer **5** goede zet: *make a ~ (with)* succes hebben (bij)
²hit (vb) **1** aanvallen **2** hard aankomen ‖ *~ home* doel treffen
³hit (vb) treffen [also fig]; raken: *be hard ~* zwaar getroffen zijn ‖ [inform] *~ it off (with)* het (samen) goed kunnen vinden (met)
⁴hit (vb) **1** slaan; geven [a blow]: [fig] *~ a man when he is down* iem. een trap nageven; *~ and run* doorrijden na aanrijding; *~ back (at)* terugslaan; [fig] van repliek dienen **2** stoten (op), botsen (tegen)
hit-and-run 1 m.b.t. het doorrijden [after collision] **2** [mil] verrassings- [attack]
hit-and-run driver doorrijder; [Belg] iem. die vluchtmisdrijf pleegt: *he was killed by a ~* hij werd doodgereden door iem. die na de aanrijding is doorgereden
¹hitch (n) **1** ruk, zet, duw **2** storing: *go off without a ~* vlot verlopen
²hitch (vb) **1** vastmaken, vasthaken: *~ a horse to a cart* een paard voor een wagen spannen

2 liften: [inform] *~ a ride* liften ‖ *get ~ed* trouwen; *~ up* optrekken
hitcher 1 [inform] lifter **2** haak, bootshaak
hitchhiker lifter
hither herwaarts: *~ and thither* her en der
hitherto tot nu toe, tot dusver
hit list [inform] **1** dodenlijst **2** zwarte lijst
hit man [Am; inform] huurmoordenaar
hit out 1 krachtig slaan **2** aanvallen ‖ *~ at* uithalen naar
hit (up)on bedenken; komen op [an idea]; bij toeval ontdekken
HIV *human immunodeficiency virus* hiv-virus[h]
hive 1 bijenkorf [also fig] **2** zwerm; [fig] menigte **3** (-s) netelroos
HM *Her Majesty* H.M., Hare Majesteit **2** *His Majesty* Z.M., Zijne Majesteit
HMU *hit me up* bel of mail me even
Ho 1 *Honorary* Ere- **2** *Hono(u)rable* Hoog-(wel)geboren [title for noblemen]
¹hoard (n) **1** (geheime) voorraad, schat **2** opeenhoping
²hoard (vb) hamsteren: *~ up* oppotten
hoarding 1 (tijdelijke) schutting **2** reclamebord[h] **3** verzamelwoede
hoarfrost rijp
hoarse 1 hees, schor **2** met een hese stem
hoary 1 grijs **2** grijsharig, witharig **3** (al)oud, eerbiedwaardig: *a ~ joke* een ouwe bak
¹hoax (n) bedrog[h]: *the bomb scare turned out to be a ~* de bommelding bleek vals (alarm)
²hoax (vb) om de tuin leiden: *~ s.o. into believing that* iem. laten geloven dat …
hob kookplaat [of cooker]
hobble (doen) strompelen; [fig] moeizaam (doen) voortgaan
hobby hobby, liefhebberij
hobby horse 1 hobbelpaard[h] **2** stokpaardje[h] [also fig]
hobgoblin 1 kobold **2** boeman
hobnob (also + with) vriendschappelijk omgaan (met): *he is always ~bing with the manager* hij papt altijd met de directeur aan
hobo [Am] zwerver
hockey 1 hockey[h] **2** [Am] ijshockey[h]
hocus-pocus hocus pocus[+h], gegoochel[h], bedriegerij
hoe schoffel
hog 1 varken[h] **2** zwijn[h] [also fig]; veelvraat ‖ [inform] *go the whole ~* iets grondig doen
hog heaven [inform] staat van innig geluk of uiterste ontspanning: *the boys were in ~* de jongens waren volmaakt gelukkig
hogwash lariekoek; flauwekul
hoi polloi (the) het volk; het gepeupel
¹hoist (n) hijstoestel[h], tillift
²hoist (vb) hijsen, takelen: *~ one's flag* zijn vlag in top hijsen
hoity-toity [inform, dated] hooghartig
hokum [Am; inform] onzin; klets

¹hold (n) **1** greep, houvastʰ; [fig] invloed: *catch/get* (or: *grab, take*) ~ *of* (vast)grijpen, (vast)pakken; *get* a ~ *on* vat krijgen op; *have* a ~ *over s.o.* macht over iem. hebben; *keep* (or: *leave*) ~ *of* vasthouden, loslaten; *take* ~ vastgrijpen; [fig] aanslaan **2** (scheeps)ruimʰ ‖ *on* ~ uitgesteld, vertraagd, in afwachting: *put a project on* ~ een project opschorten; *no* ~*s barred* alle middelen zijn toegestaan, alles mag

²hold (vb) **1** houden, het uithouden, standhouden: ~ *by* (or: *to*) zich houden aan **2** van kracht zijn, gelden, waar zijn: ~ *good* (or: *true*) *for* gelden voor, van toepassing zijn op **3** doorgaan, aanhouden; goed blijven [of weather]

³hold (vb) **1** vasthouden (aan), beethouden; [fig] boeien: *will you* ~ *the line?* wilt u even aan het toestel blijven?; ~ *together* bijeenhouden; ~ *s.o. to his promise* iem. aan zijn belofte houden **2** hebben: ~ *a title* een titel dragen **3** bekleden [eg position] **4** doen plaatsvinden, beleggen, houden: ~ *a conversation* een gesprek voeren **5** in bedwang houden, weerhouden: *there is no* ~*ing her* zij is niet te stuiten **6** [inform] ophouden met, stilleggen, stoppen: ~ *everything!* stop! **7** menen, beschouwen als: ~ *sth. cheap* (or: *dear*) weinig (or: veel) waarde aan iets hechten; ~ *sth. against s.o.* iem. iets verwijten **8** in hechtenis houden, vasthouden ‖ ~ *it!* houen zo!, stop!; ~ *one's own* a) het (alleen) aankunnen; b) zich handhaven, niet achteruitgaan [of a sick person]; ~ *one's own with* opgewassen zijn tegen

holdall reistas, weekendtas

¹hold back (vb) aarzelen, schromen, iets verzwijgen: ~ *from* zich weerhouden van

²hold back (vb) **1** tegenhouden, inhouden, in de weg staan **2** achterhouden, voor zich houden

holder 1 houder, bezitter; drager [of a title] **2** bekleder [of an office]

holding 1 pachtgoedʰ: *small* ~*s* kleine boerenbedrijfjes **2** bezitʰ [of shares etc]; eigendomʰ

¹hold off (vb) uitblijven, wegblijven

²hold off (vb) **1** uitstellen **2** weerstaan, tegenstand bieden aan

hold on 1 volhouden **2** zich vasthouden **3** aanhouden **4** [inform] wachten; niet ophangen [telephone] ‖ [inform] ~*!* stop!, wacht eens even!

hold on to 1 vasthouden, niet loslaten: *whatever you do,* ~ *your dreams* wat je ook doet, geef nooit je dromen op **2** [inform] houden

¹hold out (vb) **1** standhouden, volhouden, het uithouden **2** weigeren toe te geven ‖ ~ *for* blijven eisen; ~ *on* a) weigeren toe te geven aan; b) iets geheim houden voor

²hold out (vb) uitsteken [hand]

hold over 1 aanhouden **2** verdagen, uitstellen

¹hold up (vb) standhouden, het uithouden

²hold up (vb) **1** (onder)steunen **2** omhoog houden; opsteken [hand]: ~ *as an example* tot voorbeeld stellen; ~ *to ridicule* (or: *scorn*) bespotten **3** ophouden, tegenhouden, vertragen **4** overvallen

hold-up 1 oponthoudʰ **2** roofoverval; [fig] overval

hole 1 gatʰ, holte, kuil **2** gatʰ, opening, bres: *make a* ~ *in* een gat slaan in; [fig] duchtig aanspreken; [fig] *pick* ~*s in* ondergraven [eg argument] **3** holʰ [of animal]; legerʰ **4** hokʰ, krotʰ; [Am] isoleercel **5** penibele situatie: *in a* ~ in het nauw, in de knel **6** kuiltjeʰ [in ballgames]; knikkerpotjeʰ; [billiards] zak **7** [golf] hole

hole-in-the-wall [inform] **1** flappentap; geldautomaat **2** [Am] duister tentjeʰ

¹holiday (n) **1** feestdag: *public* ~ officiële feestdag **2** vakantiedag: *ook* ~*s* vakantie; vrije tijd; *take a* ~ vrijaf nemen; *on* ~, *on one's* ~*s* op vakantie

²holiday (vb) met vakantie zijn

holiday-maker vakantieganger

holiness heiligheid

holler [inform; Am] schreeuwen; roepen, blèren

¹hollow (n) **1** holte, kuil **2** leegte

²hollow (adj) **1** hol **2** zonder inhoud, leeg, onoprecht **3** hol [of sound] ‖ *beat s.o.* ~ iem. totaal verslaan

holly hulst

holocaust holocaust, vernietiging

holster holster

holy heilig, gewijd, vroom, godsdienstig: *the Holy Ghost* (or: *Spirit*) de Heilige Geest; *Holy Writ* de Heilige Schrift; [Roman Catholicism] *the Holy See* de Heilige Stoel; ~ *water* wijwaterʰ; *Holy Week* de Goede Week

homage hulde: *pay* (or: *do*) ~ *to* eer bewijzen aan

¹home (n) **1** huisʰ, woning, verblijfʰ, woonhuisʰ **2** thuisʰ, geboortegrond: *arrive* (or: *get*) ~ thuiskomen; *leave* ~ het ouderlijk huis verlaten; *at* (or: *back*) ~ bij ons thuis, in mijn geboortestreek, geboorteplaats; *be at* ~ a) thuis zijn; b) ontvangen; *make yourself at* ~ doe alsof je thuis bent; *(away) from* ~ van huis; *it's a* ~ *from* ~ het is er zo goed als thuis **3** bakermat, zetel, haard: *strike* ~ doel treffen **4** (te)huisʰ, inrichting **5** [sport, game] eindstreep, finish, (thuis)honkʰ ‖ *drive a nail* ~ een spijker er helemaal inslaan; ~ *(in) on* a) zich richten op [of aeroplane etc]; b) koersen op [a beacon]

²home (adj) **1** huis-, thuis-: ~ *base* (thuis)basis; [sport, game] doelʰ, honkʰ; ~ *brew* zelf gebrouwen bier; ~ *help* gezinshulp; ~ *movie* zelf opgenomen film; ~ *remedy* huismiddel-(tje) **2** huiselijk: ~ *life* het huiselijk leven **3** lokaal: *the Home Counties* de graafschappen rondom Londen

Home binnenlands, uit eigen land: *the ~ Office* het Ministerie van Binnenlandse Zaken; *the ~ Secretary* de minister van Binnenlandse Zaken

homebirth thuisgeboorte

homegrown zelfgekweekt, van eigen bodem: ~ *talent* eigen kweek

Homeland Security [Am; pol] ministerie^h van Binnenlandse Veiligheid

homeless dakloos

homely 1 eenvoudig **2** alledaags **3** [Am] lelijk [of persons]

homemade zelfgemaakt: ~ *jam* zelfgemaakte jam

homemaker [Am] [roughly] huismoeder, [roughly] huisvrouw

home shopping het thuiswinkelen

homesick: *be* (or: *feel*) ~ heimwee hebben

homespun 1 zelfgesponnen **2** eenvoudig

homestead hofstede, boerderij

home team thuisploeg

homeward(s) (op weg) naar huis, terugkerend, huiswaarts: *homeward bound* op weg naar huis

home watch buurtpreventie, buurtwacht

homework huiswerk^h; [fig] voorbereiding: *do ~* huiswerk maken; *do one's ~* zich (grondig) voorbereiden

homey huiselijk, gezellig, knus

homicidal moorddadig: ~ *tendencies* moordneigingen

homicide doodslag, moord

homoeopathy homeopathie

homogeneity homogeniteit, gelijksoortigheid

homogeneous homogeen, gelijksoortig

homosexual homoseksueel

¹**Honduran** (n) Hondurees, Hondurese

²**Honduran** (adj) Hondurees

Honduras Honduras

hone slijpen, wetten; [fig] verbeteren

honest 1 eerlijk, oprecht: *earn* (or: *turn*) *an ~ penny* een eerlijk stuk brood verdienen **2** braaf

honestly echt: ~, *did you believe him?* eerlijk, geloofde je hem?

honesty eerlijkheid, oprechtheid: ~ *is the best policy* eerlijk duurt het langst

honey 1 honing; [fig] zoetheid; liefelijkheid **2** [Am] schat; liefje^h [as form of address]

honeybee honingbij

¹**honeycomb** (n) **1** honingraat **2** honingraatmotief^h

²**honeycomb** (vb) doorboren, doorzeven: ~*ed with* doorzeefd met, doortrokken van

honeymoon 1 huwelijksreis **2** wittebroodsdagen

honeysuckle kamperfoelie

¹**honk** (vb) schreeuwen [of goose]

²**honk** (vb) (doen) toeteren, (doen) claxonneren: *he ~ed the horn* hij toeterde

honorary honorair, ere-, onbezoldigd

¹**honour** (n) eer(bewijs^h), hulde, aanzien^h, reputatie: *code of* ~ erecode; *it does him* ~, *it is to his* ~ het strekt hem tot eer; *in* ~ *bound, on one's* ~ moreel verplicht; *do the* ~*s* als gastheer optreden || *Your* (or: *His*) *Honour* Edelachtbare [form of address for judges]

²**honour** (vb) **1** eren, in ere houden, eer bewijzen: ~ *with* vereren met **2** honoreren

honourable 1 eerzaam, respectabel **2** eervol: ~ *mention* eervolle vermelding **3** eerbaar **4** hooggeboren, edelachtbaar: *Most* (or: *Right*) *Honourable* edel(hoog)achtbaar [in titles]

honour killing eerwraak

honours degree [educ] universitaire graad

hooch sterkedrank

hood 1 kap, capuchon **2** overkapping, huif; vouwdak^h [of car]; kap [of carriage, pram] **3** beschermkap, wasemkap

hoodlum 1 gangster; bendelid^h, crimineel **2** (jonge) vandaal

hoodwink bedriegen, voor de gek houden

hoody [inform] **1** hoody **2** straat-, hangjongere **3** bonte kraai

hooey onzin, nonsens, kletskoek

hoof hoef

¹**hook** (n) **1** (telefoon)haak: ~ *and eye* haak en oog; *off the* ~ van de haak [telephone] **2** vishoek, vishaak **3** hoek, kaap, landtong || ~, *line and sinker* helemaal, van a tot z; *by* ~ *or by crook* hoe dan ook, op eerlijke of oneerlijke wijze; *get* (or: *let*) *s.o. off the* ~ iem. uit de puree halen

²**hook** (vb) vastgehaakt worden

³**hook** (vb) **1** vasthaken, aanhaken: ~ *on* vasthaken **2** aan de haak slaan [also fig]; strikken, bemachtigen

hooked 1 haakvormig: *a ~ nose* een haakneus, haviksneus **2** met een haak **3** vast(gehaakt), verstrikt: *her skirt got ~ on a nail* ze bleef met haar rok achter een spijker haken **4** (+ on) verslaafd (aan) [drugs]; [fig] *he is completely ~ on that girl* hij is helemaal bezeten van dat meisje

hooker [Am; inform] hoer

hook up 1 (+ with) aansluiten (op), verbinden (met) **2** aanhaken, vasthaken

hooligan (jonge) vandaal, herrieschopper, hooligan

hoop 1 hoepel, ring **2** [sport] hoepel; [croquet] hoop; ijzeren poortje^h || *put s.o. through the ~(s)* iem. het vuur na aan de schenen leggen

¹**hoot** (n) **1** gekras^h [of owl] **2** getoet^h **3** (ge)boe^h, gejouw^h **4** [inform] giller || [inform] *he*

doesn't give (or: *care*) *a* ~ het kan hem geen zier schelen
²hoot (vb) **1** krassen, schreeuwen **2** toeteren (met) **3** schateren, bulderen van het lachen
³hoot (vb) uitjouwen: ~ *at* s.o., ~ s.o. *off the stage* iem. uitjouwen, iem. wegjouwen
hooter sirene, fabrieksfluit, fabriekssirene
hoover stofzuigen[h]
¹hop (n) **1** hink(el)sprong(etje[h]), huppelsprong(etje[h]) **2** dansje[h], dansfeest[h] **3** reisje[h] **4** (-s) hop(plant), hopbel || *catch* s.o. on the ~ iem. verrassen, bij iem. binnenvallen; *on the* ~ druk in de weer
²hop (vb) hinkelen, huppen, wippen: ~ *in* (or: *out*) instappen, uitstappen
³hop (vb) **1** overheen springen **2** springen in [on bus, train] || [inform] ~ *it!* smeer 'em!, donder op!
¹hope (n) hoop(volle verwachting), vertrouwen[h]; [Belg] betrouwen[h]: ~ *against hope* tegen beter weten in blijven hopen; *lay/set* (or: *pin, put*) *one's* ~s *on* zijn hoop vestigen op; *live* in ~(s) (blijven) hopen
²hope (vb) (+ for) hopen (op): ~ *for the best* er het beste (maar) van hopen
¹hopeful (n) veelbelovend persoon, belofte
²hopeful (adj) hoopvol, hoopgevend, veelbelovend, optimistisch: *I'm not very* ~ *of* success ik heb niet veel hoop op een geslaagde afloop
hopefully 1 hoopvol **2** hopelijk: ~, *he will come* het is te hopen dat hij komt
hopeless hopeloos, wanhopig, uitzichtloos: ~ *at* hopeloos slecht in
horizon horizon [also fig]
horizontal horizontaal, vlak
hormone hormoon[h]
horn 1 hoorn, gewei[h], (voel)hoorn **2** toeter, claxon, trompet: *blow* (or: *sound*) *the* ~ toeteren || *draw* (or: *pull*) *in one's* ~s **a)** terugkrabbelen; **b)** de buikriem aanhalen
hornet horzel
hornet's nest wespennest[h] || *stir up a* ~ zich in een wespennest steken
hornrimmed met hoornen montuur
horny 1 [inform] geil **2** [inform] sexy **3** eeltig **4** van hoorn
horoscope horoscoop: *cast a* ~ een horoscoop trekken
horrendous afgrijselijk, afschuwelijk
horrible afschuwelijk, vreselijk, verschrikkelijk
horrid 1 vreselijk, verschrikkelijk **2** akelig
horrific weerzinwekkend, afschuwelijk
horrify met afschuw vervullen, schokken, ontstellen
horror 1 verschrikking, gruwel, ontzetting **2** (-s) kriebels || *you little* ~! klein kreng dat je bent!
horse 1 paard[h]: *eat* (or: *work*) *like a* ~ eten (or: werken) als een paard **2** (droog)rek[h],

schraag, ezel **3** bok [gymnastic apparatus]; paard[h] **4** heroïne || *a* ~ *of another* (or: *a different*) *colour* een geheel andere kwestie; *(straight) from the* ~'s *mouth* uit de eerste hand; *hold your* ~s! rustig aan!, niet te overhaast!
horse about [inform] dollen; stoeien
horseback paardenrug: *three men on* ~ drie mannen te paard
horseman ruiter, paardrijder
horseplay stoeipartij, lolbroekerij
horsepower paardenkracht
horse racing paardenrennen[h]
horseradish 1 mierik(swortel) **2** mierikswortelsaus
horseshoe (hoef)ijzer[h]
horticulture 1 tuinbouw **2** hovenierskunst
¹hose (n) **1** brandslang, tuinslang **2** kousen, panty's, sokken
²hose (vb) (met een slang) bespuiten, schoonspuiten: ~ *down* a car een auto schoonspuiten
hospice 1 verpleeghuis[h] voor terminale patiënten **2** [Am] wijkverpleger, wijkverpleegster **3** gastenverblijf[h] [in monastery]
hospitable gastvrij, hartelijk
hospital ziekenhuis[h]: *in* ~, [Am] *in the* ~ in het ziekenhuis
hospitality gastvrijheid
hospitalize (laten) opnemen in een ziekenhuis
¹host (n) **1** gastheer **2** waard **3** massa, menigte: ~s *of tourists* horden toeristen
²host (vb) ontvangen, optreden als gastheer bij, op: ~ *a television* **programme** een televisieprogramma presenteren
hostage gijzelaar: *take* s.o. ~ iem. gijzelen
hostel 1 tehuis[h], studentenhuis[h], pension[h] **2** jeugdherberg
hostess 1 gastvrouw **2** hostess **3** stewardess
host family gastgezin[h]
hostile 1 vijandelijk **2** vijandig, onvriendelijk
hostilities vijandelijkheden, oorlogshandelingen
hostility 1 vijandschap **2** vijandelijkheid, vijandige daad
hot 1 heet, warm, gloeiend, scherp, pikant, vurig, hartstochtelijk, heetgebakerd; [inform] geil; opgewonden; [inform; techn] radioactief: ~ **flushes** opvlieger, opvlieging; *with two policemen in* ~ **pursuit** met twee agenten op zijn hielen; *am I getting* ~? word ik warm? [while guessing] **2** vers [of track]; recent; heet (van de naald) [of news]: ~ *off the* **press** vers van de pers || ~ *air* blabla, gezwets[h]; *like a cat on* ~ **bricks,** [Am] *like a cat on a* ~ *tin* **roof** benauwd, niet op zijn gemak; *sell like* ~ *cakes* als warme broodjes de winkel

uitvliegen; *strike while the iron is* ~ het ijzer smeden als het heet is; *a* ~ *potato* een heet hangijzer; ~ *stuff* a) bink; **b)** prima spul; **c)** (harde) porno; **d)** buit, gestolen goed; *be* ~ *on s.o.'s track* (or: *trail*) iem. na op het spoor zijn; *be in* (or: *get into*) ~ *water* in de problemen zitten (*or:* raken); *make it* (or: *the place, things*) *(too)* ~ *for s.o.* iem. het vuur na aan de schenen leggen; *not so* ~ niet zo goed; ~ *on astrology* gek op astrologie; *blow* ~ *and cold* nu eens voor dan weer tegen zijn

hotbed 1 broeikas **2** broeinest[h]

hotblooded 1 vurig, hartstochtelijk **2** opvliegend

hotchpotch hutspot, ratjetoe[h]; [fig] mengelmoes[h]; allegaartje[h]

hot-desk werken vanaf een flexplek; flexwerken

hotel hotel[h]

hothouse (broei)kas

hotkey sneltoets

hot mess [inform] **1** [sth.] puinhoop **2** [s.o.] (heerlijke) chaoot

hotplate kookplaat(je[h]), warmhoudplaat-(je[h])

hot-tempered heetgebakerd, heethoofdig

hot tub hottub, jacuzzi

¹hot up (vb) [inform] warm(er) worden, hevig(er) worden

²hot up (vb) [inform] verhevigen, intensiveren

¹hound (n) (jacht)hond, windhond

²hound (vb): [inform] *be* ~*ed out by envious colleagues* door jaloerse collega's weggepest worden

hour 1 uur[h]; *after* ~*s* na sluitingstijd, na kantoortijd; *on the* ~ op het hele uur; *out of* ~*s* buiten de normale uren; *at the eleventh* ~ ter elfder ure, op het allerlaatste ogenblik **2** moment[h], huidige tijd: *the* ~ *has come* de tijd is gekomen, het is zover

hourglass zandloper

¹hourly (adj) **1** ieder uur; uurlijks **2** per uur: ~ *pay* uurloon[h]

²hourly (adv) ieder uur: *three* ~ elke drie uur

¹house (n) **1** huis[h], woning, behuizing, (handels)huis[h]: ~ *of cards* kaartenhuis[h] [also fig]; ~ *of God* godshuis[h], huis des Heren; *eat s.o. out of* ~ *and home* iem. de oren van het hoofd eten; *move* ~ verhuizen; [fig] *put* (or: *set*) *one's* ~ *in order* orde op zaken stellen; *set up* ~ op zichzelf gaan wonen; *on the* ~ van het huis, (rondje) van de zaak **2** (vorstelijk/adellijk) geslacht[h], koningshuis[h], vorstenhuis[h], adellijke familie **3** bioscoopzaal, schouwburgzaal, voorstelling: [fig] *bring the* ~ *down* staande ovaties oogsten ‖ *like a* ~ *on fire* a) krachtig; **b)** (vliegens)vlug; **c)** prima, uitstekend; *keep* ~ het huishouden doen

²house (vb) huisvesten, onderdak bieden

aan

House volksvertegenwoordiging, kamer: *the* ~ *of Commons* het Lagerhuis; *the* ~ *of Lords* het Hogerhuis; *the* ~*s of Parliament* het parlement, de parlementsgebouwen; *the* ~ *of Representatives* het Huis van Afgevaardigden

house agent makelaar (in onroerend goed)

housebreaking inbraak

housebroken [Am] zindelijk

house dust mite huisstofmijt

house fire woningbrand

¹household (n) (de gezamenlijke) huisbewoners, huisgenoten, huisgezin[h]

²household (adj): *a* ~ *name* begrip[h], bekende naam; *a* ~ *word* gangbare uitdrukking

householder gezinshoofd[h]; bewoner

housekeeper huishoudster

housekeeping huishouding, huishouden[h]

houseman 1 (intern) assistent-arts [in hospital] **2** (huis)knecht

house-proud [depr] (overdreven) proper

houseroom onderdak[h], (berg)ruimte: [fig] *I wouldn't give such a chair* ~ ik zou zo'n stoel niet eens gratis willen hebben

house-to-house huis-aan-huis-

housetrained [of animals] zindelijk

housewarming inwijdingsfeest[h] [of house]

housewife huisvrouw

housework huishoudelijk werk[h]

housing 1 huisvesting, woonruimte **2** [techn] huis[h], omhulsel[h]

housing association woningbouwvereniging

housing estate 1 nieuwbouwproject[h] **2** woonwijk

hovel krot[h], bouwval

hover 1 hangen (boven); (blijven) zweven [of birds etc] **2** rondhangen, blijven hangen ‖ [fig] ~ *between life and death* tussen leven en dood zweven

hovercraft hovercraft

¹how (adv) **1** hoe, hoeveel, hoever: ~ *are things?* hoe gaat het ermee?; [inform] ~ *idiotic can you get?* hoe kan het gekker?; *she knows* ~ *to cook* ze kan koken; ~ *do you like my hat?* wat vind je van mijn hoed?; ~ *do you do?* aangenaam, hoe maakt u het?; ~ *is she (off) for clothes?* heeft ze genoeg kleren?; ~ *about John?* wat doe je (dan) met John? **2** hoe, waardoor, waarom: ~ *come she is late?* hoe komt het dat ze te laat is? ‖ ~ *about going home?* zouden we niet naar huis gaan?; ~ *about an ice-cream?* wat vind je van een ijsje?

²how (conj) zoals: *colour it* ~ *you like* kleur het zoals je wilt

¹however (adv) **1** hoe … ook, hoe dan ook, op welke wijze ook: ~ *you travel,* *you will be tired* hoe je ook reist, je zult moe zijn **2** echter, nochtans, desondanks: *this time, ~, he meant what he said* deze keer echter meende hij het **3** hoe in 's hemelsnaam: *~ did you manage to come?* hoe ben je erin geslaagd te komen?

²however (conj) hoe … maar, zoals … maar: *~ he tried, it wouldn't go in* hoe hij het ook probeerde, het wilde er niet in

¹howl (n) gehuilʰ, brul, gil: *~s of derision* spotgelach, hoongelachʰ

²howl (vb) huilen, jammeren, krijsen: *the wind ~ed* de wind gierde; *~ with laughter* gieren van het lachen ‖ *the speaker was ~ed down* de spreker werd weggehoond

howler giller, flater, blunder

howling gigantisch, enorm

howsoever *see ¹however*

hp 1 *horsepower* pk, paardenkracht **2** *hire purchase* huurkoop: *on (the) hp* op huurkoopbasis; [roughly] op afbetaling

HQ *headquarters* hoofdbureauʰ, hoofdkwartierʰ

HRH *Her Royal Highness* H.K.H., Z.K.H., Hare (Zijne) Koninklijke Hoogheid

hr(s) *hour(s)* uur, uren

HST hogesnelheidstrein

hub 1 naaf **2** centrumʰ, middelpuntʰ **3** overstapluchthaven

hubbub 1 gedruisʰ; kabaalʰ **2** straatrumoerʰ; drukte

¹huddle (n) **1** (dicht opeengepakte) groep, kluwenʰ, menigte **2** samenraapselʰ, bosʰ, troep ‖ *go into a ~* de koppen bij elkaar steken

²huddle (vb) bijeenkruipen: *~ together* bij elkaar kruipen; *the singers ~d together around the microphone* de zangeressen stonden dicht bijeen rond de microfoon

hue kleur [also fig]; tint ‖ *raise a ~ and cry against a new measure* luid protesteren tegen een nieuwe maatregel

huff boze bui: *in a ~* nijdig, beledigd

¹hug (n) omhelzing, knuffel

²hug (vb) **1** omarmen, omhelzen, tegen zich aandrukken **2** (zich) vasthouden aan

huge reusachtig, kolossaal, enorm: *~ly overrated* zwaar overschat

hulk 1 (scheeps)cascoʰ, scheepsromp, hulk **2** vleesklomp, kolos

hull 1 (scheeps)romp **2** (peulen)schil; [fig] omhulselʰ

hullabaloo kabaalʰ; herrie

hullo hallo

¹hum (n) zoemgeluidʰ, bromgeluidʰ, brom, gebromʰ, gezoemʰ

²hum (vb) **1** zoemen, brommen **2** bruisen, (op volle toeren) draaien: *things are beginning to ~* er komt schot in; *~ with activity* gonzen van de bedrijvigheid

³hum (vb) neuriën: *he was just ~ming a tune to himself* hij zat in zichzelf een deuntje te

neuriën

¹human (n) mens

²human (adj) menselijk, mensen-: *~ being* mens; *~ interest* het menselijk element, de gevoelsinbreng [in newspaper articles etc]; *~ nature* de menselijke natuur; *the ~ race* de mensheid; *~ rights* mensenrechten; *I'm only ~* ik ben (ook) maar een mens

humane humaan, menselijk

humanistic humanistisch

humanitarian humanitair, menslievend

humanity 1 mensdomʰ **2** menselijkheid, mensheid, mens-zijnʰ, menslievendheid: *crimes against ~* misdaden tegen de menselijkheid **3** (humanities) geesteswetenschappen

humankind [form] mensheid

¹humble (adj) bescheiden, onderdanig, nederig, eenvoudig: *my ~ apologies* mijn nederige excuses ‖ *eat ~ pie* een toontje lager zingen, inbinden

²humble (vb) vernederen

humbug 1 bedrieger, oplichter **2** pepermuntballetjeʰ, kussentjeʰ **3** onzin, nonsens, larie **4** bluf

humdrum saai, vervelend, eentonig

humid vochtig

humidity vochtigheid

humiliate vernederen, krenken

humiliation vernedering

humility nederigheid, bescheidenheid

hummingbird kolibrie

humorous humoristisch, grappig, komisch

¹humour (n) **1** humor, geestigheid: *sense of ~* gevoel voor humor **2** humeurʰ, stemming: *in a bad ~* slechtgeluimd, in een slechte bui

²humour (vb) tegemoetkomen (aan), paaien, toegeven: *~ a child* een kind zijn zin geven

¹hump (n) **1** bult, bochel **2** [inform] landerigheid: *it gives me the ~* ik baal ervan ‖ *be over the ~* het ergste achter de rug hebben

²hump (vb) **1** welven, bol maken, ronden **2** [inform] torsen, (mee)zeulen

¹hunch (n) voorgevoelʰ, vaag ideeʰ

²hunch (vb) krommen; optrekken [shoulders]; (krom)buigen

hunchback gebochelde, bultenaar

hundred honderd; [fig] talloos: *one ~ per cent* honderd percent, helemaal; *I'm not feeling one ~ per cent* ik voel me niet helemaal honderd procent

hundredth honderdste

¹Hungarian (n) Hongaar(se)

²Hungarian (adj) Hongaars

Hungary Hongarije

¹hunger (n) honger, trek; [fig] hunkering; dorst: *a ~ for sth.* een hevig verlangen naar iets

²hunger (vb) hongeren, honger hebben; [fig] hunkeren; dorsten

hungover katterig; met een kater
hungry 1 hongerig, uitgehongerd: *feel ~* honger hebben **2** (+ for) [fig] hunkerend (naar)
hunk 1 homp, brok[h] **2** [fig] stuk[h]
hunky-dory [inform] prima
¹hunt (n) jacht(partij), vossenjacht; [fig] speurtocht, zoektocht
²hunt (vb) **1** jagen (op), jacht maken (op) **2** zoeken, speuren: *~ high and low for sth.* overal zoeken naar iets **3** opjagen: *a ~ed look* een (op)gejaagde blik
hunt down opsporen, najagen
hunter 1 jager [also fig] **2** jachtpaard[h]
hunting jacht, vossenjacht
hunt out opdiepen, opsporen
huntsman 1 jager **2** jachtmeester
hunt up opzoeken, natrekken
hurdle 1 horde, hindernis; obstakel[h] [also fig] **2** schot[h], horde **3** (-s) horde(loop)
hurl smijten, slingeren: *~ reproaches at one another* elkaar verwijten naar het hoofd slingeren; *the dog ~ed itself at* (or: *on) the postman* de hond stortte zich op de postbode
hurray hoera(atje[h]), hoezee[h], hoerageroep[h] || *hip, hip, ~!* hiep, hiep, hoera!
hurricane orkaan, cycloon
hurried haastig, gehaast, gejaagd
¹hurry (n) haast: *I'm rather in a ~* ik heb nogal haast
²hurry (vb) zich haasten, haast maken, opschieten: *he hurried along* hij snelde voort; *~ up!* schiet op! vooruit!
³hurry (vb) **1** tot haast aanzetten, opjagen **2** verhaasten, bespoedigen: *~ up a job* haast maken met een klus **3** haastig vervoeren
¹hurt (n) **1** pijn(lijke zaak) **2** letsel[h], wond
²hurt (vb) pijn doen: *my feet ~* mijn voeten doen pijn; *it won't ~ to cut down on spending* het kan geen kwaad om te bezuinigen
³hurt (vb) **1** bezeren, verwonden, blesseren: *I ~ my knee* ik heb mijn knie bezeerd **2** krenken, kwetsen, beledigen: *feel ~* zich gekrenkt voelen
hurtful 1 schadelijk **2** kwetsend
hurtle kletteren, razen, suizen
husband man, echtgenoot: *~ and wife* man en vrouw
husbandry landbouw en veeteelt, het boerenbedrijf: *animal ~* veehouderij, veeteelt
¹hush (n) stilte
²hush (vb) verstommen, tot rust komen || *~!* stil!, sst!
³hush (vb) tot zwijgen brengen, doen verstommen: *~ up* verzwijgen, doodzwijgen
hush-hush [inform] (diep) geheim
hush money zwijggeld[h]
husk 1 schil(letje[h]), (mais)vlies[h]: *rice in the ~* ongepelde rijst **2** (waardeloos) omhulsel[h], lege dop

husky eskimohond
hussy brutaaltje[h]: *brazen* (or: *shameless) ~* brutaal nest
¹hustle (n) gedrang[h], bedrijvigheid, drukte: *~ and bustle* drukte, bedrijvigheid
²hustle (vb) **1** dringen, duwen **2** zich haasten, hard werken, druk in de weer zijn
³hustle (vb) **1** (op)jagen, duwen: *she ~d him out of the house* ze werkte hem het huis uit **2** [Am; inform] bewerken [eg customers]
hustler [Am; inform] **1** ritselaar **2** hoer
hut 1 hut(je[h]), huisje[h], keet **2** [mil] barak
hyacinth hyacint
¹hybrid (n) kruising
²hybrid (adj) hybride: *~ car* hybride, hybrideauto
hydrant brandkraan
hydraulic hydraulisch: *~ engineering* waterbouw(kunde)
hydroculture hydrocultuur
hydroelectric hydro-elektrisch
hydrofoil draagvleugel, (draag)vleugelboot
hydrogen waterstof[h]
hydroplane 1 glijboot; speedboot **2** watervliegtuig[h]
hyena hyena
hygiene hygiëne, gezondheidsleer, gezondheidszorg
hygienic hygiënisch
hymn hymne, lofzang, kerkgezang[h]
¹hype (n) **1** kunstje[h], truc, list **2** opgeblazen zaak [by media, advertising]; schreeuwerige reclame, aanprijzing
²hype (vb) enthousiasmeren: *~ up an audience* een publiek opzwepen
hyperbola [maths] hyperbool
hyperbole [form] hyperbool, overdrijving
hyperglycaemia [med] hyperglykemie
hypermarket hypermarkt, weidewinkel
hypersensitivity hypergevoeligheid
hypertension verhoogde bloeddruk; hypertensie
hypertext hypertekst
hyperventilate hyperventileren
hyphen verbindingsstreepje[h], afbrekingsteken[h], koppelteken[h]
hyphenate afbreken, door een koppelteken verbinden
hypnosis hypnose
hypnotic 1 hypnotisch; hypnotiserend **2** slaapopwekkend
hypnotism hypnotisme[h]
hypnotize hypnotiseren [also fig]; biologeren, fascineren
¹hypochondriac (n) hypochonder, zwaarmoedig mens[h]
²hypochondriac (adj) hypochondrisch, zwaarmoedig
hypocrisy hypocrisie
hypocrite hypocriet, huichelaar

hypocritical hypocriet; schijnheilig
hypodermic onderhuids: ~ *needle* injectienaald
hypoglycaemia [med] hypoglykemie
hypothesis hypothese, veronderstelling
hypothetical hypothetisch, verondersteld
hysteria hysterie
hysterical hysterisch

I

I ik, zelf, eigen persoon
Iberian Iberisch
IBS [med] *irritable bowel syndrome* prikkelbaredarmsyndroom^h
IC [inform] *I see* oké, ik snap het
¹ice (n) **1** ijs^h: [fig] *put sth. on ~* iets in de ijskast zetten, iets uitstellen **2** vruchtenijs^h, waterijs(je)^h **3** ijs(je)^h || ***break the ~*** het ijs breken; ***cut no*** (or: *not much*) ***~*** (*with s.o.*) geen (*or:* weinig) indruk maken (op iem.)
²ice (vb) bevriezen, dichtvriezen: *~ over* dichtvriezen || *~d drinks* (ijs)gekoelde dranken
ice age ijstijd
iceberg ijsberg: [esp fig] *the tip of the ~* het topje van de ijsberg
icebound ingevroren, door ijs ingesloten
icebreaker ijsbreker
ice cream ijs(je)^h, roomijs(je)^h
ice cube ijsblokje^h
iced 1 bevroren, gekoeld, ijs-: *~ coffee* ijskoffie **2** geglazuurd: *~ cake* taart met een glazuurlaagje
ice fishing ijsvissen, wakvissen
ice floe ijsschots
Iceland IJsland
Icelander IJslander, IJslandse
Icelandic IJslands
ice rink (overdekte) ijsbaan
ice skate schaatsen
ice tea icetea
icicle ijskegel, ijspegel
icing suikerglazuur^h, glaceersel^h || *(the) ~ on the cake* tierelantijntje(s)
icing sugar poedersuiker
icky goor, vies, smerig
icon ico(o)n^h; [comp] pictogram^h; icoon
iconic iconisch, beeldbepalend
iconoclast beeldenstormer
icy 1 ijzig, ijskoud, ijsachtig: *an ~ look* een ijzige blik **2** met ijs bedekt, bevroren, glad
¹ID *identification* ID; legitimatie(bewijs^h): *get a positive ID on* de identiteit achterhalen van
²ID (vb) de identiteit vaststellen van: *positively ID s.o.* iem. herkennen
ID card legitimatie(bewijs^h), identiteitsbewijs^h
idea idee*^h, denkbeeld^h, begrip^h, gedachte: *is this your ~ of a pleasant evening?* noem jij dit een gezellige avond?
¹ideal (n) ideaal^h
²ideal (adj) **1** ideaal **2** ideëel, denkbeeldig **3** idealistisch

idealism idealisme^h
idealist idealist
idealize idealiseren
identical identiek, gelijk(luidend), gelijkwaardig: *~ twins* eeneiige tweeling
identifiable identificeerbaar; herkenbaar
identification 1 identificatie [also psychology]; legitimatie **2** identiteitsbewijs^h
¹identify (vb) (+ with) zich identificeren (met), zich vereenzelvigen (met)
²identify (vb) **1** identificeren, de identiteit vaststellen van, in verband brengen: *I can't ~ your accent* ik kan uw accent niet thuisbrengen; *s.o. who is identified with a fascist party* iem. die in verband gebracht wordt met een fascistische partij **2** erkennen, vaststellen
identity 1 identiteit, persoon(lijkheid): *a case of mistaken ~* een geval van persoonsverwisseling **2** volmaakte gelijkenis
identity card legitimatie(bewijs^h), identiteitsbewijs^h
ideological ideologisch
ideology ideologie
IDGAF [vulg] *I don't give a fuck* boeien
idiocy idiotie, dwaasheid
idiom 1 idiomatische uitdrukking **2** idioom^h, taaleigen^h, taaleigenaardigheid
idiosyncrasy eigenaardigheid, typerend kenmerk^h
idiosyncratic eigenaardig
idiot idioot
¹idle (adj) **1** werkloos, inactief: *he has been ~ all day* hij heeft de hele dag niets uitgevoerd **2** lui, laks **3** doelloos, zinloos, vruchteloos: *an ~ attempt* een vergeefse poging; *~ gossip* loze kletspraat **4** ongebruikt, onbenut: *~ machines only cost money* stilstaande machines kosten alleen maar geld
²idle (vb) **1** nietsdoen, luieren: *~ about* luieren, rondhangen **2** stationair draaien [of engine]
idle away verdoen; verlummelen [time]
idler leegloper; lanterfanter
idly see ¹*idle*
idol 1 afgod(sbeeld^h), idool^h **2** favoriet
idolatry 1 verafgoding, blinde verering **2** afgoderij
idolize verafgoden
idyl(l) idylle
idyllic idyllisch
i.e. *id est* d.w.z., dat wil zeggen
IED *improvised explosive device* geïmproviseerd explosief^h, bermbom
¹if (n) onzekere factor, voorwaarde, mogelijkheid || *ifs and buts* maren, bedenkingen
²if (conj) **1** indien, als, zo, op voorwaarde dat: *if anything* indien dan al iets, dan ...; *if anything this is even worse* dit is zo mogelijk nog slechter; *if not* zo niet; *if so* zo ja **2** telkens als, telkens wanneer **3** of: *I wonder if she is happy* ik vraag mij af of ze gelukkig is **4** zij

het, (al)hoewel, al: *a talented if arrogant young man* een begaafde, zij het arrogante, jongeman; *protest, if **only** to pester them* protesteer, al was het maar om hen te pesten; *if we failed we did all we could* we hebben wel gefaald maar we hebben gedaan wat we konden **5** warempel, zowaar: *if that isn't Mr Smith!* als dat niet meneer Smith is! ‖ *if **only** als …* maar, ik wou dat

iffy onzeker, dubieus

igloo iglo, Eskimohut, sneeuwhut

¹ignite (vb) ontbranden, vlam vatten

²ignite (vb) aansteken

ignition 1 ontsteking(sinrichting) [of car]: *turn the ~, switch the ~ on* het contactsleuteltje omdraaien, starten **2** ontbranding, ontsteking

ignition key contactsleuteltje[h]

ignoble laag(hartig), onwaardig

ignominious schandelijk, oneervol

ignorance onwetendheid, onkunde, onkundigheid: *keep in ~* in het ongewisse laten

ignorant 1 onwetend, onkundig: *~ of* onkundig van; *I'm very ~ of politics* ik heb helemaal geen verstand van politiek **2** dom, onontwikkeld

ignore negeren

¹ill (n) **1** tegenslag **2** kwaad[h], onheil[h], vloek: *speak ~ of* kwaadspreken van

²ill (adj) **1** ziek, beroerd, ongezond: *fall* (or: *be taken*) *~* ziek worden **2** slecht, kwalijk: *~ fame* slechte naam; *~ health* slechte gezondheid **3** schadelijk, nadelig, ongunstig: *~ effects* nadelige gevolgen **4** vijandig, onvriendelijk: *~ feeling* haatdragendheid

³ill (adv) **1** slecht, kwalijk, verkeerd: *~ at ease* slecht op zijn gemak **2** nauwelijks, amper, onvoldoende: *I can ~ afford the money* ik kan het geld eigenlijk niet missen

ill-advised onverstandig

ill-bred onopgevoed, ongemanierd

ill-considered ondoordacht; onbezonnen

ill-disposed 1 kwaadgezind, kwaadwillig **2** afkerig, onwillig: *~ towards a plan* gekant tegen een plan

illegal onwettig, illegaal, onrechtmatig: *~ drugs* verboden drugs; [comp] *an ~ command* een ongeldige opdracht; [chess] *an ~ move* een onreglementaire zet

illegality onwettigheid, onrechtmatigheid

illegible onleesbaar

illegitimate 1 onrechtmatig, illegaal **2** onwettig [of child]; buitenechtelijk **3** ongewettigd, ongeldig

ill-fated 1 gedoemd te mislukken **2** noodlottig

ill-gotten onrechtmatig verkregen: *~ gains* vuil geld; gestolen goed

illicit onwettig, illegaal, ongeoorloofd

illiteracy analfabetisme[h], ongeletterdheid

illiterate ongeletterd, analfabeet

ill-mannered ongemanierd

ill-natured onvriendelijk

illness ziekte, kwaal

illogical onlogisch, ongerijmd, tegenstrijdig

ill-tempered slecht gehumeurd, humeurig

ill-timed misplaatst, op een ongeschikt ogenblik

ill-treat slecht behandelen; mishandelen

illuminate 1 [also fig] verlichten, licht werpen op **2** met feestverlichting versieren

illumination 1 verlichting; [fig] geestelijke verlichting **2** opheldering, verduidelijking **3** (-s) feestverlichting

illusion 1 illusie, waandenkbeeld[h]: *optical ~* gezichtsbedrog[h]; *cherish the ~ that* de illusie koesteren dat; *be under an ~* misleid zijn **2** (zins)begoocheling, zelfbedrog[h]

illusory denkbeeldig, bedrieglijk

illustrate illustreren, verduidelijken, toelichten

illustration illustratie, toelichting, afbeelding

illustrious illuster, vermaard, gerenommeerd

ILU [inform] *I love you* hartje; ik hou van je

ILYSM [inform] *I love you so much* ik hou heel erg van je

image 1 beeld[h], afbeelding, voorstelling **2** imago[h], image[+h], reputatie: *corporate ~* bedrijfsimago

imageboard [techn] elektronisch prikbord[h]

imager beeldapparaat[h], camera: *thermal ~* infraroodcamera

imagery beeldspraak

imaginable voorstelbaar, denkbaar, mogelijk

imaginary denkbeeldig; imaginair

imagination verbeelding(skracht), voorstelling(svermogen[h]), fantasie

imagine 1 zich verbeelden, zich indenken, fantaseren: *just ~ that!* stel je voor! **2** veronderstellen, aannemen

imaging het afbeelden, het scannen

imaginings [form] waandenkbeelden; waanideeën

imam imam

imbalance onevenwichtigheid, wanverhouding

¹imbecile (n) imbeciel, zwakzinnige, stommeling

²imbecile (adj) imbeciel, zwakzinnig, dwaas

imbecility stommiteit, idioterie

imbroglio gecompliceerde situatie; verwikkeling

imbue (door)drenken [also fig]; verzadigen, doordringen: *~d with hatred* van haat vervuld

IMHO [inform] *in my humble opinion* als je het mij vraagt

imitate 1 nadoen, imiteren: *you should ~ your brother* neem een voorbeeld aan je broer **2** lijken op: *it is wood, made to ~ marble* het is hout dat eruitziet als marmer

imitation imitatie, navolging, namaak: *~ leather* kunstleerʰ

immaculate 1 vlekkeloos, onbevlekt, zuiver: [Roman Catholicism] *Immaculate Conception* onbevlekte ontvangenis **2** onberispelijk

immaterial 1 onstoffelijk, immaterieel **2** onbelangrijk, irrelevant: *all that is ~ to me* dat is mij allemaal om het even

immature onvolgroeid, onrijp, onvolwassen

immaturity onvolgroeidheid; onrijpheid, onvolwassenheid

immeasurable onmetelijk, immens, oneindig

immediacy 1 nabijheid **2** dringendheid, urgentie, directheid

immediate 1 direct, onmiddellijk, rechtstreeks: *an ~ reply* een onmiddellijk antwoord **2** nabij, dichtstbijzijnd, naast: *my ~ family* mijn naaste familie

¹**immediately** (adv) meteen, onmiddellijk

²**immediately** (conj) zodra

immemorial onheuglijk, eeuwenoud, oeroud: *from time ~* sinds mensenheugenis

immense immens, onmetelijk, oneindig: *enjoy o.s. ~ly* zich kostelijk amuseren

immerse 1 (onder)dompelen **2** verdiepen, absorberen, verzinken: *he ~s himself completely in his work* hij gaat helemaal op in zijn werk

immigrant immigrant

immigrate immigreren

immigration immigratie

imminence dreiging, nabijheid; nadering [of danger]

imminent dreigend, op handen zijnd: *a storm is ~* er dreigt onweer

immobile onbeweeglijk, roerloos

immobilize onbeweeglijk maken, stilleggen, lamleggen, inactiveren

immoderate onmatig, overmatig, buitensporig

immodest 1 onbescheiden, arrogant **2** onfatsoenlijk, onbeschaamd

immodesty 1 onbescheidenheid **2** onfatsoenlijkheid

immoral immoreel, onzedelijk, verdorven

immortal onsterfelijk

immortality onsterfelijkheid

immortalize vereeuwigen

immune immuun, onvatbaar, bestand: *~ against* (or: *from, to*) immuun voor; *~ from punishment* vrijgesteld van straf

immune response afweerreactie

immune system immuunsysteemʰ, natuurlijk afweersysteemʰ

immunity onschendbaarheid: *~ from taxation* vrijstelling van belasting

immunization immunisatie, immunisering

immutable onveranderbaar, onveranderlijk

IMO *in my opinion* volgens mij

imp 1 duiveltjeʰ **2** deugniet

impact 1 schok, botsing, inslag: *on ~* op het moment van een botsing **2** schokeffectʰ, (krachtige) invloed, impact

impair schaden, benadelen, verslechteren: *~ one's health* zijn gezondheid schaden

impaired beschadigd, verzwakt: *visually ~* visueel gehandicapt

impairment beschadiging, afbreuk, verslechtering, verzwakking

impart 1 verlenen, verschaffen **2** meedelen, onthullen

impartial onpartijdig, neutraal, onbevooroordeeld

impassable onbegaanbaar

impasse impasse; dood spoorʰ: *talks have reached an ~* de onderhandelingen zitten muurvast

impassioned bezield, hartstochtelijk

impassive ongevoelig, gevoelloos, onbewogen; [sometimes depr] hardvochtig; kil

impatient 1 ongeduldig, geërgerd, onlijdzaam **2** begerig: *the child is ~ his mother* het kind popelt van ongeduld om zijn moeder te zien

impeachment beschuldiging, aanklagingsprocedure

impeccable 1 foutloos, feilloos, vlekkeloos **2** onberispelijk, smetteloos

impede belemmeren, (ver)hinderen

impediment 1 beletselʰ, belemmering **2** (spraak)gebrekʰ

impel 1 aanzetten, aanmoedigen **2** voortdrijven, voortstuwen

impending dreigend, aanstaand

impenetrable ondoordringbaar, ontoegankelijk; [fig] ondoorgrondelijk; onpeilbaar

¹**imperative** (n) gebiedende wijs

²**imperative** (adj) **1** noodzakelijk, vereist **2** verplicht, dwingend **3** gebiedend, autoritair

imperceptible onwaarneembaar, onmerkbaar, onzichtbaar

imperfect onvolmaakt, onvolkomen, gebrekkig

imperfection onvolkomenheid, gebrekʰ, gebrekkigheid, onvolmaaktheid

imperial keizerlijk, rijks-, m.b.t. het Britse rijk: *~ eagle* keizerarend

imperialism imperialismeʰ, expansiedrang

¹**imperialist** (n) imperialist [also depr]

²**imperialist** (adj) imperialistisch [also depr]

imperious [form] **1** heerszuchtig **2** dwingend

impermeable ondoordringbaar, waterdicht

impersonal 1 onpersoonlijk, zakelijk **2** niet menselijk || [linguistics] ~ *pronoun* onbepaald voornaamwoord

impersonate 1 vertolken, (de rol) spelen (van), imiteren **2** zich uitgeven voor

impertinent onbeschaamd, brutaal

imperturbable onverstoorbaar, onwankelbaar

impervious 1 ondoordringbaar **2** onontvankelijk, ongevoelig: ~ *to* ongevoelig voor

impetuous onstuimig, impulsief, heetgebakerd

impetus 1 impuls, stimulans **2** drijvende kracht, drijfkracht, stuwkracht, drijfveer

impinge (up)on 1 treffen, raken, inslaan in **2** beroeren, van invloed zijn op **3** inbreuk maken op

impish ondeugend, schelms

implacable onverbiddelijk, onvermurwbaar

implant 1 (in)planten, (in de grond) steken **2** inprenten, inhameren

implausible onaannemelijk, onwaarschijnlijk

¹implement (n) werktuigʰ, gereedschapʰ, instrumentʰ

²implement (vb) ten uitvoer brengen, toepassen, verwezenlijken: ~ *a new computer network* een nieuw computernetwerk in gebruik nemen

implicate betrekken, verwikkelen

implication 1 implicatie, (onuitgesproken) suggestie: *by* ~ bij implicatie **2** verwikkeling, betrokkenheid

implicit 1 impliciet, onuitgesproken, stilzwijgend **2** onvoorwaardelijk: ~ *faith* onvoorwaardelijk geloof

implore smeken, dringend verzoeken

imply 1 impliceren, met zich meebrengen: *his refusal implies that …* uit zijn weigering blijkt dat … **2** suggereren, duiden op: *are you ~ing that you're going to resign?* wil je daarmee zeggen dat je ontslag gaat nemen?

impolite onbeleefd, onhoffelijk

imponderable onvoorspelbaar

¹import (n) **1** invoerartikelʰ **2** invoer, import

²import (vb) invoeren, importeren: ~ *cars from Japan into Europe* auto's uit Japan invoeren in Europa

importance belang(rijkheid); gewichtʰ, betekenis: *place no ~ on sth.* geen belang aan iets hechten

important belangrijk, gewichtig: ~ *to* belangrijk voor

importation invoer(artikelʰ), import(goederen)

impose 1 opleggen, heffen, afdwingen: ~ *a task* een taak opleggen **2** opdringen: ~ *o.s.* (or: *one's company*) *(up)on* zich opdringen aan

impose (up)on gebruik maken van, tot last zijn, een beroep doen op

imposing imponerend, indrukwekkend, ontzagwekkend

imposition 1 heffing, belasting **2** (opgelegde) last, (zware) taak, druk **3** straf(taak), strafwerkʰ

impossibility onmogelijkheid

impossible onmogelijk: *an* ~ *situation* een hopeloze situatie; *that chap is* ~ *to get along with* die gozer is onmogelijk om mee om te gaan

impostor bedrieger, oplichter

impotence 1 onvermogenʰ; machteloosheid **2** impotentie

impotent 1 machteloos, onmachtig **2** impotent

impound 1 beslag leggen op **2** in een asiel opsluiten

impoverish verarmen, verpauperen

impracticable onuitvoerbaar, onrealiseerbaar

impractical onpraktisch, onhandig

imprecise onnauwkeurig

impregnable onneembaar, onaantastbaar

impregnate 1 doordrenken, impregneren **2** zwanger maken **3** bevruchten

impress 1 bedrukken, afdrukken, indrukken, opdrukken **2** (een) indruk maken op, imponeren: *your boyfriend ~es us* **unfavourably** je vriendje maakt geen beste indruk op ons; *~ed* **at** (or: *by, with*) geïmponeerd door, onder de indruk van **3** inprenten

impression 1 afdruk, indruk **2** indruk, impressie: *make an* ~ *(on)* indruk maken (op); **under** *the* ~ *that …* in de veronderstelling dat …

impressive indrukwekkend, ontzagwekkend

imprint (af)drukken, indrukken, stempelen; [fig] griffen; inprenten

imprison in de gevangenis zetten

imprisonment gevangenneming, gevangenschap

improbability onwaarschijnlijkheid

improbable onwaarschijnlijk, onaannemelijk

¹impromptu (adj) onvoorbereid, geïmproviseerd

²impromptu (adv) voor de vuist (weg), spontaan

improper 1 ongepast, misplaatst **2** onfatsoenlijk, oneerbaar

impropriety 1 ongepastheid **2** onfatsoenlijkheid

improve vooruitgaan, beter worden: *his health is improving* zijn gezondheid gaat vooruit

improvement verbetering, vooruitgang: *that is* **quite** *an* ~ dat is een stuk beter; *an* ~ *in*

the weather een weersverbetering
improve (up)on overtreffen: *improve
(up)on a previous performance* een eerdere
prestatie overtreffen
improvident zorgeloos, verkwistend
improvisation improvisatie
improvise improviseren, in elkaar flansen
imprudent onvoorzichtig; ondoordacht
impudent schaamteloos, brutaal
impulse 1 impuls, puls, stroomstoot **2** opwelling, inval, impuls(iviteit): *act on* ~ impulsief handelen
impulsive impulsief
impunity straffeloosheid: *with* ~ straffeloos, ongestraft
impure 1 onzuiver, verontreinigd **2** onze-
dig
impute toeschrijven, wijten, aanwrijven
¹in (adj) **1** intern, inwonend, binnen- **2** populair, modieus, in **3** exclusief: *in-crowd*
kliekje^h, wereldje^h
²in (adv) binnen, naar binnen, erheen: *built-
in* ingebouwd; *fit sth. in* iets (er)in passen; *the
police moved in* de politie kwam tussenbeide
³in (prep) **1** in: *in my opinion* naar mijn mening; *play in the street* op straat spelen **2** [di-
rection; also fig] in, naar, ter: *in aid of* ten
voordele van **3** [time] in, binnen: *in a few
minutes* over enkele minuten; *in all those
years* gedurende al die jaren **4** [activity, pro-
fession] wat betreft, in: *the latest thing in*
computers het laatste snufje op het gebied
van computers **5** [proportion, size, degree]
in, op, uit: *sell in ones* per stuk verkopen; *one
in twenty* één op twintig **6** [in the shape of]
als: *buy in instalments* op afbetaling kopen
7 in zover dat, in, met betrekking tot, doordat, omdat: *he resembles you in being very
practical* hij lijkt op jou in zoverre dat hij heel
praktisch is || *he was in charge of* hij was ver-
antwoordelijk voor; *in honour of* ter ere van
inability onvermogen^h, onmacht
inaccessible ontoegankelijk, onbereikbaar
inaccurate 1 onnauwkeurig **2** foutief
inaction inactiviteit
inactive 1 inactief; passief **2** ongebruikt;
buiten werking
inactivity inactiviteit
inadequacy ontoereikendheid, tekort^h, tekortkoming, gebrek^h
inadequate ontoereikend, onvoldoende,
ongeschikt
inadmissible ontoelaatbaar, ongeoorloofd: ~ *evidence* ontoelaatbaar bewijs
inadvertent 1 onoplettend, nonchalant
2 onopzettelijk: *I dropped it ~ly* ik heb het
per ongeluk laten vallen
inalienable onvervreemdbaar [of right]
inane leeg, inhoudloos, zinloos
inanimate levenloos, dood

in-app [media] in-app
inapplicable ontoepasselijk, ontoepas-
baar, onbruikbaar
inappropriate ongepast, onbehoorlijk,
misplaatst
inapt 1 ontoepasselijk, ongeschikt **2** onbekwaam, on(des)kundig, onhandig
inarticulate 1 onduidelijk (uitgesproken),
onverstaanbaar, onsamenhangend **2** onduidelijk sprekend
inasmuch as aangezien, omdat
inattentive onoplettend, achteloos
inaudible onhoorbaar
inaugurate installeren, inaugureren, (in
een ambt/functie) bevestigen
inauguration installatie(plechtigheid), inauguratie, inhuldiging
inauspicious onheilspellend; ongunstig
in-between tussen-: ~ *state* tussenfase
inborn aangeboren
inbound [Am] binnenkomend, thuisko-
mend, inkomend, binnenlopend
¹inbox (n) [comp] postvak^h in
²inbox (vb) [comp] mailen naar: *can you* ~ *me
the details?* kun je de gegevens naar me
mailen?
inbreeding inteelt
inc incl.
Inc [Am] *Incorporated* nv, naamloze vennootschap
incalculable 1 onberekenbaar **2** onvoorspelbaar
incandescent 1 gloeiend: ~ *lamp* gloeilamp **2** kwaad, woedend
incapable onbekwaam, machteloos: *drunk
and* ~ dronken en onbekwaam; *be* ~ *of* niet
in staat zijn tot, niet kunnen
incapacitate uitschakelen; ongeschikt maken: *his age ~s him for* work door zijn leeftijd
is hij niet in staat te werken
incapacity onvermogen^h, onmacht: ~ *for
work* arbeidsongeschiktheid
incarnate vleesgeworden, lijfelijk: *the devil*
~ de duivel in eigen persoon
incarnation incarnatie; belichaming
incautious onvoorzichtig
¹incendiary (n) **1** brandstichter **2** opruier
²incendiary (adj) **1** brandgevaarlijk, (licht)
ontvlambaar: ~ *bomb* brandbom **2** opruiend
¹incense (n) wierook(geur)
²incense (vb) kwaad, boos maken: *~d at* (or:
by) zeer boos over
incentive 1 stimulans, aansporing, motief^h
2 (prestatie)premie, toeslag, aanmoedi-
gingspremie
incessant onophoudelijk, voortdurend,
aanhoudend
incest incest, bloedschande
¹inch (n) (Engelse) duim [24.5 mm]; inch^{+h}:
not budge (or: *give, yield*) *an* ~ geen duimbreed wijken; *every* ~ *a gentleman* op-en-top

een heer ‖ *give* him an ~ *and he'll take a mile* als je hem een vinger geeft neemt hij de hele hand; ~ *by* ~ beetje bij beetje; *we came **within** an* ~ *of death* het scheelde maar een haar of we waren dood geweest

²**inch** (vb) schuifelen, langzaam voortgaan: ~ *forward through a crowd* zich moeizaam een weg banen door een menigte

incidence (mate van) optreden[h], frequentie: *a **high** ~ of disease* een hoog ziektecijfer

incident incident[h], voorval[h], gebeurtenis

incidental bijkomend, begeleidend, bijkomstig: ~ *expenses* onvoorziene uitgaven; ~ *to* samenhangend met, gepaard gaande met

incidentally 1 terloops **2** overigens, trouwens, tussen twee haakjes

incident room meldkamer

incinerate (tot as) verbranden, verassen

incipient beginnend, begin-

incision insnijding, inkerving, snee; [med] incisie

incisive 1 scherp(zinnig) **2** doortastend

incisor snijtand

incite 1 opwekken, aanzetten, aansporen **2** bezielen, opstoken, ophitsen

inclement guur, stormachtig

inclination 1 neiging, voorkeur: *have an ~ to get fat* aanleg hebben om dik te worden **2** geneigdheid, zin

¹**incline** (n) helling, glooiing

²**incline** (vb) neigen, geneigd zijn, een neiging hebben: *I ~ to **think** so* ik neig tot die gedachte

³**incline** (vb) **1** (neer)buigen, neigen: ~ *one's **head*** het hoofd neigen **2** beïnvloeden, aanleiding geven: *I **am** ~d to **think** so* ik neig tot die gedachte

¹**inclined** (adj) **1** geneigd; bereid: *if you **feel** so* ~ als u daar zin in heeft **2** aangelegd

²**inclined** (adj) hellend: ~ *plane* hellend vlak

inclose *see* enclose

include 1 omvatten, bevatten, insluiten: *the **price** ~s freight* de prijs is inclusief vracht; [hum] ~ *out* uitsluiten, niet meerekenen **2** (mede) opnemen, bijvoegen, toevoegen

including inclusief; waaronder, onder wie, zoals: *10 **days** ~ today* 10 dagen, vandaag meegerekend; *up to and* ~ tot en met; *200 victims, ~ **women** and children* 200 slachtoffers, onder wie (*or:* waaronder) vrouwen en kinderen

inclusive inclusief: *pages 60 to 100* ~ pagina 60 tot en met 100; *an* ~ *society* een inclusieve samenleving

incoherent incoherent, onsamenhangend

income inkomen[h], inkomsten: *live **within** one's* ~ niet te veel uitgeven, rondkomen

income tax inkomstenbelasting

incoming 1 inkomend, aankomend, binnenkomend: ~ *tide* opkomend tij **2** opvol-

gend, komend: *the* ~ *tenants* de nieuwe huurders

incomparable onvergelijkelijk, onvergelijkbaar

incompatible onverenigbaar, (tegen)strijdig, tegengesteld

incompetence incompetentie; onbekwaamheid

incompetent onbevoegd, onbekwaam

incomplete 1 onvolledig, incompleet **2** onvolkomen, onvoltooid

incomprehensible onbegrijpelijk, ondoorgrondelijk

inconceivable onvoorstelbaar, ondenkbaar

inconclusive 1 niet doorslaggevend, onovertuigend **2** onbeslist

incongruity ongerijmdheid

incongruous 1 ongerijmd, strijdig **2** ongelijksoortig

inconsiderable onaanzienlijk, onbetekenend

inconsiderate onattent, onnadenkend

inconsistency 1 inconsistentie **2** onverenigbaarheid

inconsistent 1 inconsistent, onlogisch **2** onverenigbaar, strijdig

inconsolable ontroostbaar

inconspicuous onopvallend

incontinence incontinentie

incontinent incontinent

incontrovertible onweerlegbaar, onomstotelijk

¹**inconvenience** (n) ongemak[h], ongerief[h]

²**inconvenience** (vb) overlast bezorgen, ongelegen komen

inconvenient storend, ongelegen

incorporate 1 opnemen, verenigen, incorporeren **2** omvatten, bevatten: *this **theory** ~s new ideas* deze theorie omvat nieuwe ideeën

incorporated als naamloze vennootschap erkend: *Jones* ~ [roughly] Jones nv

incorrect incorrect, onjuist, verkeerd, ongepast

incorrigible onverbeterlijk

¹**increase** (n) **1** toename, groei, aanwas: *be on the* ~ toenemen **2** verhoging, stijging

²**increase** (vb) toenemen, (aan)groeien, stijgen

³**increase** (vb) vergroten, verhogen

increasingly in toenemende mate; meer en meer: ~ *worse* hoe langer hoe erger

incredible ongelofelijk, ongeloofwaardig; [inform] verbluffend (goed)

incredulity ongelovigheid

incredulous ongelovig: *be* ~ *of* geen geloof hechten aan, sceptisch staan tegenover

increment 1 toename, (waarde)vermeerdering **2** periodiek[h] [of salary]; periodieke verhoging

incriminate 1 beschuldigen, aanklagen

2 bezwaren, als de schuldige aanwijzen: *incriminating statements* bezwarende verklaringen
incubation 1 uitbroeding **2** broedperiode **3** incubatie(tijd)
¹**incumbent** (n) bekleder van een kerkelijk ambt
²**incumbent** (adj) zittend, in functie zijnd: [Am] *the ~ governor* de zittende gouverneur
incur oplopen, zich op de hals halen: ~ *large debts* zich diep in de schulden steken; ~ *expenses* onkosten maken
incurable ongeneeslijk: ~ *pessimism* onuitroeibaar pessimisme
incursion inval, invasie, strooptocht: [fig] *an ~ upon s.o.'s privacy* een inbreuk op iemands privacy
indebted schuldig, verschuldigd: *be ~ to s.o. for …* iem. dank verschuldigd zijn voor …
indecency onfatsoenlijkheid
indecent onfatsoenlijk, onbehoorlijk, indecent: ~ *assault* aanranding; ~ *exposure* openbare schennis der eerbaarheid, (geval van) exhibitionisme
indecipherable niet te ontcijferen; onleesbaar
indecision 1 besluiteloosheid **2** aarzeling
indecisive 1 niet afdoend: *the battle was ~* de slag was niet beslissend **2** besluiteloos, weifelend
indeed 1 inderdaad: *is it blue? ~ it is* is het blauw? inderdaad **2** in feite, sterker nog: *I don't mind. ~, I would be pleased* ik vind het best. Sterker nog, ik zou het leuk vinden **3** [after a word to be emphasized] echt: *that's a surprise ~* dat is echt een verrassing || *very kind ~* werkelijk zeer vriendelijk
indefatigable onvermoeibaar
indefinite 1 onduidelijk, onbestemd, vaag: *postponed ~ly* voor onbepaalde tijd uitgesteld **2** onbepaald [also linguistics]: ~ *article* onbepaald lidwoord; [linguistics] ~ *pronoun* onbepaald voornaamwoord **3** onzeker, onbeslist
indelible onuitwisbaar
indelicate 1 onbehoorlijk **2** smakeloos, grof **3** tactloos
indemnity 1 schadeloosstelling, herstelbetaling(en) **2** garantie, (aansprakelijkheids)verzekering **3** vrijstelling [of punishment]; vrijwaring
¹**indent** (n) **1** inspringing **2** orderbrief
²**indent** (vb) een schriftelijke bestelling doen
³**indent** (vb) kartelen, kerven, inkepen: *an ~ed coastline* een grillige kustlijn
⁴**indent** (vb) (laten) inspringen [line]
indentation 1 keep, snee **2** inspringing **3** inham, fjord **4** karteling, insnijding
independence onafhankelijkheid
independent 1 onafhankelijk, partijloos: *of ~ means* financieel onafhankelijk; ~

school particuliere school **2** vrijstaand
indescribable onbeschrijfelijk, niet te beschrijven
indestructible onverwoestbaar
indeterminate 1 onbepaald, onbeslist **2** onbepaalbaar **3** onduidelijk, vaag
index 1 index [also science]; indexcijferʰ, verhoudingscijferʰ **2** (bibliotheek)catalogus **3** registerʰ, index || ~ *finger* wijsvinger
India 1 India **2** Brits-Indië, Voor-Indië
¹**Indian** (n) **1** Indiër, Indiase **2** indiaan: *American ~* indiaan; *Red ~* indiaan
²**Indian** (adj) **1** Indiaas **2** indiaans || ~ *corn* maïs; *in ~ file* in ganzenmars; ~ *ink* Oost-Indische inkt; ~ *summer* Indian summer
indicate 1 duiden op, een teken zijn van, een teken zijn voor **2** te kennen geven **3** de noodzaak aantonen van: *surgery seemed to be ~d* een operatie leek wenselijk **4** aangeven, aanwijzen: *the cyclist ~d left* de fietser stak zijn linkerhand uit
indication aanwijzing, indicatie, tekenʰ: *there is little ~ of improvement* er is weinig dat op een verbetering duidt
indicator richtingaanwijzer
indict aanklagen
indictment 1 (aan)klacht **2** (staat van) beschuldiging
indie onafhankelijke platen-, filmmaatschappij
indifference onverschilligheid
indifferent 1 onverschillig: ~ *to hardship* ongevoelig voor tegenspoed **2** (middel)matig
indigenous 1 inheems: *plants ~ to this island* op dit eiland thuishorende planten **2** aangeboren, geboren
indigestion indigestie
indignant verontwaardigd
indignation verontwaardiging
indignity vernedering, belediging, hoon
indirect indirect, niet rechtstreeks: [linguistics] ~ *object* meewerkend voorwerp
indiscreet indiscreet
indiscretion indiscretie, onbescheidenheid: *an ~ of his youth* een misstap uit zijn jeugd
indiscriminate 1 kritiekloos, onzorgvuldig **2** lukraak: *deal out ~ blows* in het wilde weg om zich heen slaan
indispensable onmisbaar, essentieel
indisposition 1 ongesteldheid, onpasselijkheid **2** ongenegenheid, onwil(ligheid)
indisputable onbetwistbaar
indistinct onduidelijk, vaag
indistinguishable niet te onderscheiden
¹**individual** (n) individuʰ; [inform] figuurⁿʰ; typeʰ
²**individual** (adj) **1** individueel, persoonlijk, eigen: *I can't thank you all ~ly* ik kan u niet ieder afzonderlijk bedanken **2** afzonderlijk:

give ~ **attention** to persoonlijke aandacht besteden aan
individualism individualisme[h]
individuality individualiteit: she's a girl of **marked** ~ ze is een uitgesproken persoonlijkheid
indivisible ondeelbaar
indocility hardleersheid
indoctrinate indoctrineren
indolence traagheid, sloomheid
indomitable ontembaar, onbedwingbaar
Indonesia Indonesië
[1]**Indonesian** (n) Indonesiër, Indonesische
[2]**Indonesian** (adj) Indonesisch
indoor binnen-: ~ **aerial** kamerantenne; ~ **sports** zaalsporten
indoors binnen: let's go ~ laten we naar binnen gaan
indubitably zonder twijfel
induce 1 bewegen tot, brengen tot: our reduced prices will ~ people **to** buy onze verlaagde prijzen zullen de mensen tot kopen bewegen; nothing will ~ me to **give** in nooit zal ik toegeven 2 teweegbrengen, veroorzaken, leiden tot; opwekken [contractions]
inducement aansporing; stimulans
induction 1 installatie, inhuldiging, bevestiging 2 opwekking [of contractions] 3 opgewekte geboorte 4 introductie(cursus)
inductive 1 aanleiding gevend, veroorzakend 2 inductief
[1]**indulge** (vb) zich laten gaan, zich te goed doen; [inform] zich te buiten gaan aan drank (eten): ~ **in** zich (de luxe) permitteren (van)
[2]**indulge** (vb) 1 toegeven aan 2 (zich) uitleven (in)
indulgence 1 mateloosheid: ~ **in** strong drink overmatig drankgebruik 2 toegeeflijkheid
indulgent toegeeflijk, inschikkelijk
industrial 1 industrieel 2 geïndustrialiseerd: the ~ **nations** de industrielanden 3 de industriearbeid(ers) betreffende: ~ **dispute** arbeidsconflict[h]
industrialization industrialisatie
industrious vlijtig, arbeidzaam
industry 1 industrie 2 bedrijfsleven[h] 3 vlijt, (werk)ijver
inedible oneetbaar
ineffective 1 ineffectief 2 inefficiënt, ondoelmatig, onbekwaam
ineffectual 1 vruchteloos, vergeefs 2 ongeschikt
inefficient inefficiënt, ondoelmatig, onpraktisch
ineligible ongeschikt: ~ to **vote** niet stemgerechtigd
inept 1 absurd, dwaas 2 onbeholpen, onbekwaam
ineptitude onbekwaamheid
inequality ongelijkheid, verschil[h]

inequitable onrechtvaardig
inequity onrechtvaardigheid
ineradicable onuitroeibaar, onuitwisbaar
inert inert, traag, mat: ~ **gas** edel gas
inescapable onontkoombaar; onvermijdelijk
inestimable onschatbaar
inevitability onvermijdelijkheid; onontkoombaarheid
inevitable onvermijdelijk, onontkoombaar, onafwendbaar
inexact onnauwkeurig
inexcusable onvergeeflijk
inexhaustible 1 onuitputtelijk 2 onvermoeibaar
inexorable onverbiddelijk
inexpensive voordelig, goedkoop
inexperienced onervaren
inexplicable onverklaarbaar
infallible 1 onfeilbaar 2 feilloos: infallibly, she makes the wrong choice ze doet steevast de verkeerde keus
infamous 1 berucht 2 schandelijk
infamy 1 beruchtheid 2 schanddaad
infancy 1 kindsheid, eerste jeugd 2 beginstadium[h]: in its ~ in de kinderschoenen
[1]**infant** (n) jong kind[h]
[2]**infant** (adj) kinder-: ~ **prodigy** wonderkind[h]
infanticide kindermoord
infantile 1 infantiel, kinderachtig, onvolwassen 2 kinder-: ~ **paralysis** kinderverlamming
infantry infanterie, voetvolk[h]
infant school kleuterschool
infatuated gek, dol, (smoor)verliefd: be ~ **with** s.o. (sth.) gek zijn op iem. (iets)
infatuation verliefdheid
infect 1 besmetten [also fig]; infecteren: [fig] an ~ed **computer** een besmette computer 2 vervuilen, bederven
infection infectie, infectieziekte
infectious 1 besmettelijk 2 aanstekelijk
infer 1 (+ from) concluderen (uit), afleiden, opmaken 2 impliceren, inhouden
inference gevolgtrekking
[1]**inferior** (n) ondergeschikte
[2]**inferior** (adj) 1 lager, minder, ondergeschikt 2 inferieur, minderwaardig: ~ **goods** goederen van mindere kwaliteit; be ~ **to** onderdoen voor
inferiority minderwaardigheid
infernal 1 hels, duivels 2 afschuwelijk, vervloekt
inferno inferno[h]; vuurzee
infertile onvruchtbaar
infest teisteren, onveilig maken: be ~ed **with** vergeven zijn van
infestation teistering, het onveilig-zijn/onveilig-worden, plaag
infidel ongelovige
infidelity ontrouw

infiltrate (+ into) infiltreren (in), tersluiks binnendringen

¹infinite (n) oneindigheid: *the* ~ het heelal; *the Infinite* God

²infinite (adj) **1** oneindig, onbegrensd **2** buitengemeen groot

infinitesimal oneindig klein || ~ *calculus* infinitesimaalrekening

infinitive infinitief

infinity oneindigheid, grenzeloosheid

infirm zwak: ~ *of purpose* besluiteloos

infirmary ziekenhuis[h], ziekenafdeling, ziekenzaal

infirmity 1 zwakheid **2** gebrek[h], kwaal

¹inflame (vb) opwinden, kwaad maken: ~d *with rage* in woede ontstoken

²inflame (vb) ontsteken, ontstoken raken: *an* ~d *eye* een ontstoken oog

inflammable ontvlambaar, zeer brandbaar; [fig] opvliegend

inflammation ontsteking, ontbranding

inflatable opblaasbaar

inflate 1 opblazen, doen zwellen **2** inflateren; kunstmatig opdrijven [eg prices]

inflation 1 het opblazen **2** [econ] inflatie: *galloping* ~ wilde inflatie

inflect [linguistics] verbuigen, vervoegen

inflexible onbuigbaar [also fig]; onbuigzaam

inflict 1 opleggen, opdringen: ~ *a penalty (up)on* s.o. iem. een straf opleggen **2** toedienen, toebrengen: ~ *a blow (up)on* s.o. iem. een klap geven **3** teisteren

in-flight tijdens de vlucht: ~ *movie* tijdens de vlucht vertoonde film

inflow toevloed; instroom, toestroom

¹influence (n) **1** invloed, inwerking, macht: ~ *on* (or: *upon*) (onbewuste) invloed op **2** protectie; [inform] kruiwagen || [inform] *under the* ~ onder invloed

²influence (vb) beïnvloeden, invloed hebben op

influencer [media] influencer; beïnvloeder

influential invloedrijk

influenza influenza, griep

influx toevloed, instroming

info *information* info, informatie

inform 1 informeren, op de hoogte stellen: ~ *s.o.* *about* (or: *of*) iem. inlichten over **2** berichten, meedelen

informal 1 informeel, niet officieel **2** ongedwongen: ~ *speech* spreektaal

informant informant, zegsman

informatics informatica

information informatie, inlichting(en), voorlichting: *obtain* ~ informatie inwinnen

information overload overvloed aan informatie

informative informatief, leerzaam

informed ingelicht: *ill-*~ slecht op de hoogte; *an* ~ *decision* een weloverwogen besluit;

make an ~ *choice* een weloverwogen keuze maken

informer geheim agent, politiespion

infrastructure infrastructuur

infrequent zeldzaam

¹infringe (vb) (+ (up)on) inbreuk maken (op)

²infringe (vb) schenden; overtreden [agreement etc]

infuriate razend maken

infuse 1 (in)gieten, ingeven **2** bezielen, inprenten, storten: ~ *courage into* s.o., ~ *s.o. with courage* iem. moed inblazen

ingenious ingenieus, vernuftig

ingenuity 1 vindingrijkheid, vernuft[h] **2** ingenieuze uitvinding

ingenuous 1 argeloos, naïef, onschuldig, ongekunsteld **2** eerlijk, openhartig

inglorious eerloos; schandelijk

ingot baar, (goud)staaf, ingot

ingrained 1 ingeworteld **2** verstokt, doortrapt

ingratiate bemind maken: ~ *o.s. with* s.o. bij iem. in de gunst trachten te komen

ingratitude ondankbaarheid

ingredient ingrediënt[h]

ingrown ingegroeid [of nails]: [fig] ~ *habit* vaste gewoonte

inhabit bewonen, wonen in

inhabitant bewoner, inwoner

inhalation inhalatie, inademing

inhale inademen, inhaleren

inhaler inhaleertoestel[h]

inherent inherent, intrinsiek, eigen: *violence is* ~ *in a dictatorship* geweld is inherent aan een dictatuur

inherit erven, erfgenaam zijn; meekrijgen [vices and virtues etc]

inheritance 1 erfenis, nalatenschap **2** (over)erving

inheritance tax successierecht[h]

inhibit 1 verbieden, ontzeggen **2** hinderen, onderdrukken: ~ *s.o. from doing sth.* iem. beletten iets te doen

inhibited geremd

inhibition 1 geremdheid; verlegenheid **2** remming; vertraging

inhospitable ongastvrij

inhuman onmenselijk; wreed

inhumane onmenselijk; inhumaan

inhumanity wreedheid

inimical 1 vijandig **2** (+ to) schadelijk (voor)

inimitable onnavolgbaar, weergaloos

iniquity onrechtvaardigheid, ongerechtigheid, zonde

¹initial (n) initiaal, beginletter, hoofdletter, voorletter: ~s paraaf

²initial (adj) begin-, eerste, initiaal: ~ *capital* grondkapitaal[h]; ~ *stage* beginstadium[h]

initially aanvankelijk, eerst, in het begin

initiate 1 beginnen, in werking stellen **2** (+

into) inwijden (in)

initiative initiatief^h: *on one's own* ~ op eigen initiatief

inject 1 injecteren **2** inbrengen, introduceren: ~ *a little life into a community* een gemeenschap wat leven inblazen

injection injectie [also fig]; stimulans

in-joke grapje voor ingewijden

injudicious [form] onverstandig; onoordeelkundig

injure 1 (ver)wonden, kwetsen, blesseren: *twelve people were ~d* er vielen twaalf gewonden **2** kwaad doen, benadelen, beledigen

injury 1 verwonding, letsel^h, blessure: *suffer minor injuries* lichte verwondingen oplopen **2** mishandeling **3** schade, onrecht^h

injustice onrechtvaardigheid: *do s.o. an* ~ iem. onrecht doen

¹ink (n) inkt [also of octopus]; drukinkt: [inform] *sling* ~ *at s.o.* het met iem. aan de stok hebben, tegen iem. polemiseren

²ink (vb) **1** met inkt overtrekken, inkleuren **2** tatoeëren: *get ~ed* een tatoeage laten zetten

inkling flauw vermoeden^h, vaag idee^h: *he hasn't an* ~ *of what goes on* hij heeft geen idee van wat er gebeurt

¹inland (adj) binnenlands: ~ *navigation* binnen(scheep)vaart

²inland (adv) landinwaarts

Inland Revenue 1 staatsbelastinginkomsten **2** belastingdienst

in-law aangetrouwd familielid^h: *my ~s* mijn schoonouders, mijn schoonfamilie

inlay 1 inlegsel^h, inlegwerk^h, mozaïek^h **2** informatieblad^h, informatieboekje^h bij cd

inlet 1 inham, kreek **2** inlaat [for liquids]; toegang

in-line skate skate

inmate gevangene; opgenomen patiënt

inmost 1 binnenst **2** diepst, geheimst

inn 1 herberg **2** taveerne, kroeg

innards ingewanden

innate aangeboren, ingeboren: *~ly kind* vriendelijk van nature

inner 1 binnenst, innerlijk: ~ *city* a) binnenstad; b) verpauperde stadskern; ~ *tube* binnenband **2** verborgen, intiem: ~ *life* gemoedsleven^h; *the* ~ *meaning* de diepere betekenis

innings slagbeurt, innings || *have a good* ~ een lang en gelukkig leven leiden

innkeeper waard

innocence onschuld

innocent onschuldig, schuldeloos

innocuous onschadelijk

innovate vernieuwen

innovation vernieuwing, innovatie

innuendo (bedekte) toespeling

innumerable ontelbaar, talloos

inoculation inenting [with vaccine]

inoffensive onschuldig, onschadelijk, geen ergernis wekkend

inoperable 1 [med] inoperabel **2** onuitvoerbaar; onbruikbaar

inopportune ongelegen (komend)

inordinate [form] buitensporig

inorganic anorganisch

in-patient (intern verpleegd) patiënt

input 1 toevoer, invoer, inbreng **2** invoer, input

inquest 1 gerechtelijk onderzoek^h, lijkschouwing **2** jury voor lijkschouwing

¹inquire (vb) (+ into) een onderzoek instellen (naar)

²inquire (vb) (na)vragen, onderzoeken: ~ *after* (or: *for*) *s.o.* naar iemands gezondheid informeren; ~ *of s.o.* bij iem. informeren

inquiry (+ into) onderzoek^h (naar), (na)vraag, enquête, informatie: *make inquiries* inlichtingen inwinnen; *on* ~ bij navraag

inquisition (gerechtelijk) onderzoek^h, ondervraging: *the Inquisition* de inquisitie

inquisitive nieuwsgierig, benieuwd

inroad inbreuk; aantasting: *the holidays make ~s (up)on my budget* de vakantie vormt een aanslag op mijn portemonnee

ins: *the* ~ *and outs* de fijne kneepjes (van het vak), de details

insane krankzinnig [also fig]; onzinnig

insanitary 1 ongezond **2** smerig, besmet

insanity krankzinnigheid, waanzin

insatiable onverzadigbaar

inscribe 1 (+ in(to), on) inschrijven (in), graveren; [fig] inprenten **2** opdragen; van een opdracht voorzien [book etc]

inscription 1 inscriptie, opschrift^h **2** opdracht [in book etc]

inscrutable ondoorgrondelijk, raadselachtig

insect 1 insect^h **2** (nietig) beestje^h; [fig] onderkruiper

insecticide insecticide^h, insectenvergif^h

insecure 1 onveilig, instabiel, wankel **2** onzeker, bang

insecurity onzekerheid; onveiligheid

insemination bevruchting, inseminatie: *artificial* ~ kunstmatige inseminatie

insensible 1 onwaarneembaar, onmerkbaar **2** gevoelloos, bewusteloos **3** ongevoelig, onbewust: *be* ~ *of the danger* zich niet van het gevaar bewust zijn

insensitive ongevoelig, gevoelloos: ~ *to the feelings of others* onverschillig voor de gevoelens van anderen

inseparable on(af)scheidbaar, onafscheidelijk

¹insert (n) tussenvoegsel^h, bijlage, inzetstuk^h, bijsluiter

²insert (vb) inzetten, inbrengen; [comp] invoegen: ~ *a coin* een muntstuk inwerpen

insertion 1 insertie, inplanting **2** tussenvoeging; plaatsing [in newspaper] **3** tussenzetsel[h], inzetstuk[h]

in-service training bijscholing

inset 1 bijvoegsel[h], (losse) bijlage, inlegvel[h], inlegvellen **2** inzetsel[h], tussenzetsel[h]

¹inside (n) binnenkant, binnenste[h]; huizenkant [of pavement or road]

²inside (adj) **1** binnen-: *the ~ track* de binnenbaan; [Am] voordelige positie, voordeel[h] **2** van ingewijden, uit de eerste hand: *~ information* inlichtingen van ingewijden || *~ job* inbraak door bekenden

³inside (adv) **1** [place and direction; also fig] (naar) binnen, aan de binnenkant: *turn sth. ~ out* iets binnenstebuiten keren **2** [inform] in de bak

⁴inside (prep) **1** [place] (binnen)in **2** [time] binnen, (in) minder dan: *~ an hour* binnen een uur

insider ingewijde

insidious verraderlijk, geniepig, bedrieglijk

insight (+ into) inzicht (in), begrip[h] (van)

insignia insignes, onderscheidingstekenen

insignificant onbeduidend, onbelangrijk, gering

insincere onoprecht, hypocriet

insinuate insinueren, toespelingen maken, indirect suggereren: *what are you insinuating?* wat wil je daarmee zeggen? || *he was trying to ~ himself into the minister's favour* hij probeerde bij de minister in de gunst te komen

insinuation bedekte toespeling; insinuatie

insipid 1 smakeloos, flauw **2** zouteloos, banaal, nietszeggend

insist (+ (up)on) (erop) aandringen, volhouden, erop staan: *I ~ (up)on an apology* ik eis een verontschuldiging

insistence 1 aandrang, eis **2** volharding, vasthoudendheid

insistent vasthoudend, dringend, hardnekkig

insofar in zoverre: *~ as* voor zover

insofar as voor zover

insolent onbeschaamd, schaamteloos, brutaal

insoluble onoplosbaar

insolvent insolvent, niet in staat om geldelijke verplichtingen na te komen

insomnia slapeloosheid

insomuch as zodanig dat, aangezien, daar

insouciance zorgeloosheid, onverschilligheid

inspect inspecteren, onderzoeken, keuren

inspection inspectie, onderzoek[h], controle: *on ~* **a)** ter inzage; **b)** bij nader onderzoek

inspector inspecteur, opzichter, controleur

inspiration 1 inspiratie **2** [inform] inval, ingeving

inspire 1 inspireren, bezielen **2** opwekken,

doen ontstaan

instability onvastheid, instabiliteit

install 1 installeren; plechtig bevestigen [in office, dignity] **2** installeren, aanbrengen, plaatsen: *~ central heating* centrale verwarming aanleggen || *~ o.s.* zich installeren, zich nestelen

installation 1 toestel[h], installatie, apparaat[h] **2** installatie; plechtige bevestiging [in office, dignity] **3** installering, vestiging **4** aanleg, installering, montage

instalment 1 (afbetalings)termijn **2** aflevering [of story, TV programme etc]

instance geval[h], voorbeeld[h]: *bijvoorbeeld* || *in the first ~* in eerste instantie, in de eerste plaats

¹instant (n) moment[h], ogenblik(je[h]): *the ~ (that) I saw her* zodra ik haar zag

²instant (adj) **1** onmiddellijk, ogenblikkelijk: *an ~ replay* een herhaling [of television recordings] **2** kant-en-klaar, instant

instantaneous onmiddellijk, ogenblikkelijk

instantly onmiddellijk, dadelijk

instead in plaats daarvan: *~ of* in plaats van

instep 1 wreef [of foot] **2** instap [of shoes]

instigate 1 aansporen, aanstichten, teweegbrengen **2** aanzetten, uitlokken, ophitsen: *~ s.o. to steal* iem. aanzetten tot diefstal

instigation aandrang, instigatie: *at Peter's ~* op aandrang van Peter

instil geleidelijk doen doordringen, bijbrengen, langzaamaan inprenten

instinct instinct[h], intuïtie

instinctive instinctief, intuïtief

¹institute (n) instituut[h], instelling

²institute (vb) stichten, invoeren, op gang brengen, instellen || *~ proceedings against s.o.* een rechtszaak tegen iem. aanspannen

institution 1 instelling, stichting, invoering **2** gevestigde gewoonte, (sociale) institutie, regel **3** instituut[h], instelling, genootschap[h] **4** inrichting, gesticht[h]

instruct 1 onderwijzen, onderrichten, instrueren **2** opdragen, bevelen

instruction 1 onderricht[h], instructie, les **2** voorschrift[h], order, opdracht: *~s for use* handleiding

instructive instructief, leerzaam

instructor instructeur, docent

instrument instrument[h], gereedschap[h]; werktuig[h] [also fig]: *~ of fate* speelbal van het lot

instrumental 1 (+ in) behulpzaam (bij), hulpvaardig: *be ~ in* een cruciale rol spelen bij **2** instrumentaal

insubordinate ongehoorzaam, opstandig

insufferable on(ver)draaglijk, onuitstaanbaar

insufficient ontoereikend, onvoldoende,

te weinig

insular 1 eiland-, geïsoleerd **2** bekrompen, kortzichtig

insulate 1 (+ from) isoleren (van), afschermen (van), beschermen (tegen) **2** isoleren [heat, sound]

insulation 1 isolatie, afzondering **2** isolatiemateriaal[h]

[1]**insult** (n) belediging: *add ~ to injury* de zaak nog erger maken

[2]**insult** (vb) beledigen

insuperable onoverkomelijk, onoverwinnelijk

insupportable on(ver)draaglijk, onuitstaanbaar

insurance 1 verzekering, assurantie, verzekeringspolis **2** [Am] zekerheid, bescherming

insure 1 (laten) verzekeren **2** [Am] garanderen, veiligstellen

insurer verzekeraar

insurgence oproer[h], opstand

insurmountable onoverkomelijk, onoverwinnelijk

insurrection oproer[h], opstand

intact intact, ongeschonden, gaaf

intake 1 inlaat, toevoer(opening), opgenomen hoeveelheid **2** opneming, opname, toegelaten aantal[h], voeding: *an ~ of breath* een inademing

intangible 1 immaterieel: *~ assets* immateriële activa **2** ongrijpbaar; ondefinieerbaar

integer [maths] geheel getal[h]

integral 1 wezenlijk **2** geheel, volledig, integraal

[1]**integrate** (vb) geïntegreerd worden, integreren, deel gaan uitmaken (van)

[2]**integrate** (vb) **1** integreren, tot een geheel samenvoegen **2** als gelijkwaardig opnemen [eg minorities]; integreren

integration integratie

integrity 1 integriteit, rechtschapenheid: *a man of ~* een integer man **2** ongeschonden toestand, eenheid

intel [inform] **1** [mil; Am] militaire inlichtingen(dienst) **2** informatie

intellect intellect[h], verstand(elijk vermogen)[h]

[1]**intellectual** (n) intellectueel

[2]**intellectual** (adj) intellectueel; verstandelijk

intelligence 1 intelligentie, verstand(elijk vermogen)[h] **2** informatie, nieuws[h], inlichtingen **3** (geheime) informatie, inlichtingendienst

intelligent intelligent, slim

intelligible begrijpelijk, verstaanbaar

intemperate 1 onmatig, buitensporig, heftig, drankzuchtig **2** guur [of climate, wind]; extreem

intend 1 van plan zijn, bedoelen, in de zin

hebben: *I ~ to cancel the order* ik ben van plan de order te annuleren; *we ~ them to repair it* we willen dat zij het repareren **2** (voor)bestemmen, bedoelen: *their son was ~ed for the Church* hun zoon was voorbestemd om priester te worden

intense intens, sterk, zeer hevig

[1]**intensify** (vb) intens(er) worden, versterken, toenemen

[2]**intensify** (vb) verhevigen, versterken, intensiveren

intensity intensiteit, sterkte, (mate van) hevigheid

intensive intensief, heftig, (in)gespannen: *~ care* intensieve verpleging, intensive care

[1]**intent** (n) bedoeling, intentie, voornemen[h] || *to all ~s and purposes* feitelijk, in (praktisch) alle opzichten

[2]**intent** (adj) **1** (in)gespannen, aandachtig **2** vastbesloten, vastberaden: *be ~ on revenge* zinnen op wraak

intention 1 bedoeling, oogmerk[h], voornemen[h]: *have no ~ of doing so* (or: *to do so*) er niet over peinzen dat te doen **2** (-s) [inform] bedoelingen, (huwelijks)plannen

intentional opzettelijk; expres

inter ter aarde bestellen, begraven

interact op elkaar inwerken, met elkaar reageren

interaction wisselwerking

interactive interactief

interbreed (onderling) kruisen

intercede 1 ten gunste spreken, een goed woordje doen **2** bemiddelen, tussenbeide komen

intercept onderscheppen, afsnijden

intercession tussenkomst, bemiddeling, voorspraak

[1]**interchange** (n) **1** uitwisseling, ruil(ing), verwisseling **2** knooppunt[h] [of motorways]; verkeersplein[h]

[2]**interchange** (vb) **1** uitwisselen, ruilen **2** (onderling) verwisselen, afwisselen

interchangeable 1 uitwisselbaar, ruilbaar **2** (onderling) verwisselbaar

intercom (the) intercom

intercourse 1 omgang, sociaal verkeer[h], betrekking(en) **2** (geslachts)gemeenschap[h]: *sexual ~* geslachtsgemeenschap

interdenominational oecumenisch

interdependent onderling afhankelijk, afhankelijk van elkaar

interest 1 interesse, (voorwerp[h] van) belangstelling: *show an ~ in* belangstelling tonen voor; *take a great ~ in* zich sterk interesseren voor **2** (eigen)belang[h], interesse, voordeel[h]: *it's in the ~ of the community* het is in het belang van de gemeenschap **3** rente [also fig]; interest: *the rate of ~*, *the ~ rate* de rentevoet; *lend money at 7% ~* geld lenen tegen 7% rente

interested 1 belangstellend, geïnteresseerd, vol interesse 2 belanghebbend, betrokken: *the ~ party* de betrokken partij

interesting interessant, belangwekkend

interface 1 raakvlak[h] [also fig]; grensvlak[h], scheidingsvlak[h] 2 [comp] koppeling, aansluiting, interface

interfaith oecumenisch, van meerdere religies: *the commemoration was an ~ service* de herdenkingsdienst werd geleid door vertegenwoordigers van verschillende religies

interfere hinderen, in de weg staan: *don't ~* hou je erbuiten

interference 1 (ver)storing, belemmering 2 inmenging, tussenkomst, bemoeienis

interfere with 1 aankomen, betasten, knoeien met: *don't ~ that bike* blijf met je handen van die fiets af 2 zich bemoeien met 3 [euph] aanranden, zich vergrijpen aan

[1]**interim** (n) tussentijd: *in the ~* intussen, ondertussen

[2]**interim** (adj) tijdelijk, voorlopig: *an ~ report* een tussentijds rapport

interior 1 inwendig, binnen- 2 binnenshuis, interieur- 3 innerlijk: *~ monologue* monologue intérieur, inwendige monoloog 4 binnenlands

interior decorator binnenhuisarchitect(e)

interject (zich) ertussen werpen, tussenbeide komen, opmerken

interjection 1 tussenwerpsel[h], interjectie 2 uitroep, kreet

[1]**interlock** (vb) in elkaar grijpen, nauw met elkaar verbonden zijn: *these problems ~* deze problemen hangen nauw met elkaar samen

[2]**interlock** (vb) met elkaar verbinden, aaneenkoppelen

interloper indringer

interlude 1 onderbreking, pauze 2 tussenstuk[h], tussenspel[h]

intermarry 1 een gemengd huwelijk aangaan 2 onderling trouwen, binnen de eigen familie trouwen

[1]**intermediary** (n) tussenpersoon, bemiddelaar, contactpersoon

[2]**intermediary** (adj) bemiddelend, optredend als tussenpersoon

intermediate tussenliggend, tussengelegen, tussentijds: *~ course* aanvullende cursus

interminable oneindig (lang), eindeloos

intermingle (zich) (ver)mengen, (vrijelijk) met elkaar omgaan

intermission onderbreking [also in play etc]; pauze, rust: *without ~* ononderbroken

intermittent met tussenpozen (verschijnend/werkend), onderbroken, met onderbrekingen

[1]**intern** (n) [Am] 1 intern, inwonend (co)assistent 2 hospitant(e), stagiair(e)

[2]**intern** (vb) interneren, gevangen zetten; vastzetten [during wartime]

internal 1 inwendig, innerlijk, binnen-: *the ~ ear* het inwendige oor 2 binnenlands, inwendig

internalize zich eigen maken

[1]**international** (n) 1 interland(wedstrijd) 2 international, interlandspeler 3 expat, kenniswerker

[2]**international** (adj) internationaal

internee (politieke) gevangene

Internet (the) internet[h]: *break the ~* viraal gaan, een hit worden op internet

internet account internetaansluiting

internet banking internetbankieren[h]

internet café internetcafé[h]

internment internering

interpersonal intermenselijk

interplay interactie, wisselwerking

interpose 1 tussenplaatsen, invoegen 2 interrumperen, onderbreken 3 naar voren brengen, aanvoeren

[1]**interpret** (vb) als tolk optreden, tolken

[2]**interpret** (vb) 1 interpreteren, uitleggen, opvatten 2 vertolken, interpreteren 3 (mondeling) vertalen

interpretation 1 interpretatie, uitleg 2 het tolken 3 vertolking, interpretatie

interpreter tolk

interracial tussen (verschillende) rassen, voor verschillende rassen

interregnum tussenregering

[1]**interrelate** (vb) met elkaar in verband staan, met elkaar verbonden zijn

[2]**interrelate** (vb) met elkaar in verband brengen

interrogation ondervraging, verhoor[h]

[1]**interrogative** (n) vragend (voornaam)-woord[h]

[2]**interrogative** (adj) vragend; vraag- [also linguistics]: *~ pronoun* vragend voornaamwoord

[1]**interrupt** (vb) storen, onderbreken, in de rede vallen

[2]**interrupt** (vb) 1 onderbreken, afbreken, belemmeren 2 interrumperen, in de rede vallen, storen

interruption 1 onderbreking, afbreking 2 interruptie, het storen

intersection 1 (weg)kruising, kruispunt[h], snijpunt[h] 2 doorsnijding, kruising

intersperse 1 verspreid zetten, (hier en daar) strooien: *a speech ~d with posh words* een met deftige woorden doorspekte toespraak 2 afwisselen, variëren, van tijd tot tijd onderbreken

interstate highway autosnelweg

interstice nauwe tussenruimte, spleet, reet

[1]**intertwine** (vb) zich in elkaar strengelen, (met elkaar) verweven zijn

[2]**intertwine** (vb) ineenstrengelen, dooreenvlechten

interval 1 tussenruimte, interval^h, tussen- tijd: *trams go at* 15-minute *~s* er rijdt iedere 15 minuten een tram **2** pauze, rust **3** interval^h, toonsafstand

intervene 1 tussenbeide komen, zich erin mengen, ertussen komen **2** ertussen liggen: *in the intervening months* in de tussenliggen- de maanden

intervention tussenkomst, inmenging; in- greep [also med]

¹**interview** (n) **1** (persoonlijk) onderhoud^h, sollicitatiegesprek^h **2** interview^h, vraagge- sprek^h **3** verhoor^h

²**interview** (vb) **1** interviewen, een vraag- gesprek houden met, een sollicitatiegesprek voeren met **2** ondervragen

interviewer 1 interviewer **2** ondervrager

¹**interweave** (vb) zich in elkaar strengelen

²**interweave** (vb) in elkaar vlechten; verwe- ven

intestine darm(kanaal^h), (buik)ingewan- den: *large ~* dikke darm; *small ~* dunne darm

intimacy 1 intimiteit, vertrouwelijkheid, intieme mededeling **2** innige verbonden- heid, vertrouwdheid: *they were on terms of ~* er bestond een sterke vriendschapsband tus- sen hen **3** intimiteit, intieme omgang, ge- slachtsverkeer^h

¹**intimate** (adj) **1** intiem [also sexually]; in- nig (verbonden) **2** vertrouwelijk, privé: *~ se- crets* hartsgeheimen; *they are on ~ terms* zij zijn goede vrienden

²**intimate** (vb) suggereren, een hint geven, laten doorschemeren

intimation aanduiding, suggestie, hint

intimidate intimideren, bang maken

into 1 in, binnen-: *look ~ the matter* de zaak bestuderen; [inform] *he's ~ Zen these days* te- genwoordig interesseert hij zich voor zen **2** [change of circumstance] tot, in: *translate ~ Japanese* in het Japans vertalen **3** [duration or distance] tot … in: *far ~ the night* tot diep in de nacht ‖ *run ~ an old friend* een oude vriend tegen het lijf lopen; *talk somebody ~ leaving* iem. ompraten om te gaan

intolerable on(ver)draaglijk, onuitstaan- baar

intolerance onverdraagzaamheid; [also med] intolerantie: *lactose ~* lactose-intole- rantie

intolerant (+ of) onverdraagzaam (tegen- over), intolerant

intonation intonatie, stembuiging

¹**intoxicant** (n) bedwelmend middel^h, alco- holische drank, sterkedrank

²**intoxicant** (adj) bedwelmend, alcoholisch

intoxication 1 bedwelming, dronken- schap **2** vervoering

intractable 1 lastig **2** onhandelbaar

intransigent onbuigzaam, onverzoenlijk, onverzettelijk

intransitive onovergankelijk

intravenous in de ader(en); intraveneus

intrepid onverschrokken, dapper

intricate ingewikkeld, complex, moeilijk

¹**intrigue** (n) intrige, gekonkel^h, samenzwe- ring

²**intrigue** (vb) intrigeren, samenzweren

³**intrigue** (vb) intrigeren, nieuwsgierig ma- ken, boeien

intrinsic intrinsiek, innerlijk, wezenlijk

introduce 1 introduceren, voorstellen, in- leiden: *~ to* a) voorstellen aan [s.o.]; b) kennis laten maken met [sth.] **2** invoeren, introdu- ceren, naar voren brengen: *~ a new subject* een nieuw onderwerp aansnijden

introduction 1 inleiding, introductie, voorwoord^h: *an ~ to the Chinese language* een inleiding tot de Chinese taal **2** introductie, voorstelling, inleiding

introductory inleidend: *~ offer* introduc- tieaanbieding; *~ remarks* inleidende opmer- kingen

introspection introspectie; zelfreflectie

¹**intrude** (vb) **1** (zich) binnendringen, zich opdringen: *intruding into conversations* zich ongevraagd in gesprekken mengen **2** zich opdringen, ongelegen komen, storen: *let's not ~ on his time any longer* laten wij niet lan- ger onnodig beslag leggen op zijn tijd

²**intrude** (vb) **1** binnendringen, indringen, opdringen **2** opdringen, lastigvallen, storen

intruder indringer, insluiper

intrusion binnendringing, indringing, in- breuk: *an ~ (up)on my privacy* een inbreuk op mijn privacy

intuition intuïtie, ingeving: *she had an ~ that things were wrong* ze had een plotselinge ingeving dat de zaak fout zat

intuitive intuïtief

Inuit Inuit

Inuk Inuk

inundate onder water zetten, overstelpen, overstromen

inure gewennen, harden

invade 1 binnenvallen, een inval doen in, binnendringen **2** overstromen: *hundreds of people ~d the newly-opened shopping centre* honderden mensen overstroomden het pas geopende winkelcentrum **3** inbreuk maken op; schenden [privacy]

invader indring(st)er

¹**invalid** (n) invalide

²**invalid** (adj) **1** ongerechtvaardigd, onge- grond, zwak **2** ongeldig, onwettig, nietig: *this will is ~* dit testament is ongeldig

³**invalid** (adj) **1** invalide, gebrekkig **2** invali- den-, zieken-: *~ chair* rolstoel

invalidate ongeldig maken (verklaren), nietig maken: *this automatically ~s the guar- antee* hierdoor komt de garantie automa- tisch te vervallen; *his arguments were ~d* zijn

argumenten werden ontzenuwd
invaluable onschatbaar
invariable onveranderlijk, constant, vast
invariably steevast; steeds, altijd
invasion 1 invasie [also fig]; inval, het binnenvallen **2** inbreuk, schending
invasive 1 invasie-; binnendringend **2** zich verspreidend [of illness]
invective scheldwoord[h], scheldwoorden, getier[h]
inveigh krachtig protesteren, uitvaren, tieren
inveigle verleiden, overhalen: ~ *s.o. into stealing* iem. ertoe brengen om te stelen
invent 1 uitvinden, uitdenken **2** bedenken, verzinnen
invention 1 uitvinding, vinding **2** bedenksel[h], verzinsel[h]
inventive inventief, vindingrijk, creatief
inventor uitvinder
inventory 1 inventaris(lijst), inventarisatie, boedelbeschrijving **2** overzicht[h], lijst
inverse omgekeerd, tegenovergesteld, invert: ~ *ratio* omgekeerd evenredigheid
invert omkeren, inverteren: ~ed *commas* aanhalingstekens
[1]**invertebrate** (n) ongewerveld dier[h]
[2]**invertebrate** (adj) ongewerveld
[1]**invest** (vb) geld beleggen, (geld) investeren
[2]**invest** (vb) investeren, beleggen: *they ~ed all their spare time in the car* ze staken al hun vrije tijd in de auto
[1]**investigate** (vb) een onderzoek instellen
[2]**investigate** (vb) onderzoeken, nasporen
investigation onderzoek[h]
investigative onderzoeks-; onderzoekend: ~ *journalism* onderzoeksjournalistiek
investigator onderzoeker, detective
investment investering, (geld)belegging
inveterate 1 ingeworteld, diep verankerd **2** verstokt, aarts-: ~ *liars* onverbeterlijke leugenaars
invidious 1 aanstootgevend, ergerlijk **2** hatelijk, beledigend
invigilate surveilleren [at examination]
invigorate (ver)sterken, kracht geven
invincible onoverwinnelijk, onomstotelijk || ~ *belief* onwankelbaar geloof
inviolable onschendbaar
invisible onzichtbaar [also fig]; verborgen
invitation uitnodiging, invitatie: an ~ *to a party* een uitnodiging voor een feest
invite 1 uitnodigen, inviteren: ~ *s.o. over* (or: *round*) iem. vragen langs te komen **2** uitnodigen, verzoeken **3** vragen om, uitlokken
invoice factuur
invoke 1 aanroepen, inroepen **2** zich beroepen op, een beroep doen op
involuntary onwillekeurig, onopzettelijk, onbewust: *an ~ movement* een reflexbeweging

involve 1 betrekken, verwikkelen: *whose interests are ~d?* om wiens belangen gaat het?; *the persons ~d* de betrokkenen **2** (met zich) meebrengen, betekenen: *large sums of money are ~d* er zijn grote bedragen mee gemoeid; *this job always ~s a lot of paperwork* dit werk brengt altijd veel administratieve rompslomp met zich mee
involvement 1 betrokkenheid **2** deelname **3** inmenging **4** verhouding; relatie
invulnerable onkwetsbaar [also fig]; onaantastbaar
[1]**inward** (adj) **1** innerlijk, inwendig **2** binnenwaarts, naar binnen gericht
[2]**inward** (adv) **1** binnenwaarts, naar binnen **2** innerlijk, in de geest
in-your-face overdonderend, heftig
I/O *input/output*
iodine jodium(tinctuur[h])
iota jota; [fig] greintje[h]: *not an* ~ geen jota
IOU *I owe you* schuldbekentenis
IP *Internet Protocol* IP[h]
IQ *Intelligence Quotient* IQ[h], intelligentiequotiënt[h]
Iran Iran
[1]**Iranian** (n) Iraniër, Iraanse
[2]**Iranian** (adj) Iraans
Iraq Irak
[1]**Iraqi** (n) Irakees, Irakese
[2]**Iraqi** (adj) Irakees
irascible prikkelbaar, opvliegend
irate ziedend, woedend
ire [form] toorn; woede
Ireland Ierland
iris 1 iris; regenboogvlies[h] [of eye] **2** lis[+h], iris
[1]**Irish** (n) Iers[h], de Ierse taal, (Iers-)Gaelisch[h]
[2]**Irish** (adj) Iers, van Ierland
Irishman Ier
Irishwoman Ierse
iris scan irisscan
irk ergeren, hinderen: *it ~s me to do this job* deze klus staat me tegen
irksome ergerlijk; hinderlijk
[1]**iron** (n) ijzer[h], strijkijzer[h], brandijzer[h]: *rule with a rod of* ~ met ijzeren vuist regeren; *cast* ~ gietijzer[h]; *wrought* ~ smeedijzer[h] || *have too many ~s in the fire* te veel hooi op z'n vork genomen hebben
[2]**iron** (adj) **1** ijzeren **2** ijzersterk: ~ *constitution* ijzeren gestel || *the Iron Curtain* het IJzeren Gordijn
[3]**iron** (vb) strijken: [fig] ~ *out problems* problemen gladstrijken
Iron Age (the) ijzertijd
ironic ironisch: ~*ally* ironisch genoeg
ironing het strijken, strijkgoed[h]
ironmonger ijzerhandelaar
[1]**irony** (n) ironie, spot: *life's ironies* de tegenstrijdigheden van het leven
[2]**irony** (adj) ijzerachtig: *this food has an* ~ *taste* er zit een ijzersmaak aan dit eten

irradiate 1 schijnen op, verlichten: *their faces were ~d with happiness* hun gezicht straalde van geluk **2** bestralen [also with X-rays etc] **3** doen stralen, doen schitteren
[1]**irrational** (n) onmeetbaar getal[h]
[2]**irrational** (adj) irrationeel, onredelijk: *~ behaviour* onberekenbaar gedrag
irreconcilable 1 onverzoenlijk **2** onverenigbaar, onoverbrugbaar
irrecoverable 1 onherstelbaar, hopeloos **2** onherroepelijk **3** oninbaar, oninvorderbaar
irrefutable onweerlegbaar, onbetwistbaar
[1]**irregular** (n) lid[h] van ongeregelde troepen, partizaan, guerrillastrijder
[2]**irregular** (adj) **1** onregelmatig, abnormaal, afwijkend: *in spite of his ~ passport* hoewel zijn paspoort niet in orde was **2** ongeregeld, ongeordend: *she studies very ~ly* ze studeert zeer onregelmatig ‖ *~ verbs* onregelmatige werkwoorden
irrelevance irrelevantie, irrelevant(e) opmerking, vraag …
irrelevant irrelevant, niet ter zake (doend)
irremediable onherstelbaar
irreparable onherstelbaar, niet te verhelpen
irreplaceable onvervangbaar
irrepressible onbedwingbaar, ontembaar, onstuitbaar: *~ laughter* onbedaarlijk gelach
irresistible onweerstaanbaar, onbedwingbaar, onweerlegbaar
irresolute besluiteloos, weifelend, aarzelend
irrespective toch, sowieso: *~ of* ongeacht; *~ of whether it was necessary or not* of het nu noodzakelijk was of niet
irresponsible 1 onverantwoord(elijk) **2** ontoerekenbaar, niet aansprakelijk
irretrievable onherstelbaar, niet meer ongedaan te maken, reddeloos (verloren)
irreverent oneerbiedig, zonder respect
irreversible onomkeerbaar, onherroepelijk, onveranderlijk
irrevocable onherroepelijk, onomkeerbaar
irrigate irrigeren, bevloeien, begieten
irrigation irrigatie, bevloeiing, besproeiing
irritable lichtgeraakt, prikkelbaar, opvliegend
irritant 1 irriterend (or: prikkelend) middel[h] **2** ergernis
irritate 1 irriteren, ergeren, boos maken: *be ~d at* (or: by, with) geërgerd zijn door **2** irriteren; prikkelen [skin etc]
irritation 1 irritatie, ergernis **2** irritatie, branderigheid, branderige plek
IRS *Internal Revenue Service* belastingdienst; fiscus
Is *Island(s), Isle(s)* Eiland(en)
Isaiah Jesaja, Isaias

ISDN *integrated services digital network* ISDN
ISIL *Islamic State of Iraq and the Levant* IS (Islamitische Staat)
ISIS *Islamic State of Iraq and Syria* IS (Islamitische Staat)
Islam islam, islamitische wereld
Islamic islamitisch
island 1 eiland[h] [also fig] **2** vluchtheuvel
islander eilander, eilandbewoner
isle [in specific combinations] eiland[h]
islet eilandje[h]
isn't *is not*
isolate isoleren, afzonderen, afsluiten
isolation isolatie, afzondering, isolement[h]: *in ~* in afzondering, op zichzelf
Israel Israël
[1]**Israeli** (n) Israëli, bewoner van Israël
[2]**Israeli** (adj) Israëlisch
[1]**Israelite** (n) Israëliet, nakomeling van Israël
[2]**Israelite** (adj) Israëlitisch
[1]**issue** (n) **1** uitgave, aflevering; nummer[h] [of magazine] **2** kwestie, (belangrijk) punt[h], probleem[h]: *force the ~* een beslissing forceren; *make an ~ of sth.* ergens een punt van maken; *that's not an ~* dat speelt geen rol, dat doet er niet toe **3** publicatie, uitgave, emissie: *the day of ~* de dag van publicatie
[2]**issue** (vb) uitkomen, verschijnen: *~ forth* (or: out) tevoorschijn komen
[3]**issue** (vb) **1** uitbrengen, publiceren, in circulatie brengen, uitvaardigen: *they ~d a new series of stamps* ze gaven een nieuwe serie postzegels uit **2** uitlenen [books] **3** uitstorten, uitspuwen: *a volcano issuing dangerous gases* een vulkaan die gevaarlijke gassen uitspuwt
isthmus istmus, nauwe verbinding, landengte
it 1 het: *I dreamt it* ik heb het gedroomd; *it is getting on* het wordt laat; *it says in this book that …* er staat in dit boek dat …; *it is reported that* volgens de berichten; *I've got it* ik heb een idee; *she let him have it* ze gaf hem ervan langs; *who is it?* wie is het? **2** hét, het neusje van de zalm, het probleem: *that is it, I've finished* dat was het dan, klaar is Kees; *that is it* dat is 't hem nu juist
IT *information technology* IT, informatietechnologie
[1]**Italian** (n) Italiaan(se)
[2]**Italian** (adj) Italiaans
italic 1 cursief, cursieve drukletter: *the words in ~* de schuingedrukte woorden **2** schuinschrift[h], lopend schrift[h]
italicize cursiveren
Italy Italië
[1]**itch** (n) **1** jeuk, kriebel **2** verlangen[h], hang
[2]**itch** (vb) **1** jeuken, kriebelen: *the wound keeps ~ing* de wond blijft maar jeuken **2** jeuk hebben **3** graag willen: *she was ~ing to tell*

her ze zat te popelen om het haar te vertellen

itchy 1 jeukend **2** rusteloos: *get* ~ *feet* de reiskriebels krijgen

item 1 item^h, punt^h, nummer^h **2** onderdeel^h, bestanddeel^h **3** artikel^h, (nieuws)bericht^h

itemize specificeren

itinerant rondreizend, (rond)trekkend: ~ *preacher* rondtrekkend prediker

itinerary 1 routebeschrijving, reisbeschrijving **2** reisroute

its zijn, haar, ervan: *this coat has had* ~ *day* deze mantel heeft zijn tijd gehad; *the government has lost* ~ *majority* de regering is haar meerderheid kwijt; ~ *strength frightens me* de kracht ervan maakt mij bang

itself 1 zich, zichzelf: *the animal* **hurt** ~ het dier bezeerde zich; *by* ~ alleen, op eigen kracht; *in* ~ op zichzelf **2** zelf: *the* **watch** ~ *was not in the box* het horloge zelf zat niet in de doos

IV bag infuuszak

ivory ivoor^h

Ivory Coast (the) Ivoorkust

ivy klimop^+h

j

j j, J
¹jab (n) **1** por, steek **2** [inform] prik, injectie
²jab (vb) porren, stoten, stompen: *he ~bed his elbow into my side* hij gaf me een por in de ribben
jabber brabbelen, kwebbelen: *~ away* erop los kwebbelen
jack 1 toestelʰ, hefboom, vijzel, krik, stut, stellage, (zaag)bok **2** dierʰ, mannetjeʰ **3** [cards] boer: *~ of hearts* hartenboer
jackal jakhals
jackass ezel [also fig]
jackboot 1 kaplaars [boot] **2** totalitarismeʰ
jackdaw kauw, torenkraai
jacket 1 jas(jeʰ), colbert(jeʰ) **2** omhulselʰ, bekleding, mantel, huls **3** stofomslagʰ [of book] ‖ *potatoes cooked in their ~s* aardappelen in de schil bereid
jacket potato aardappel in de schil
¹jackhammer (n) [Am] drilboor; sloophamer
²jackhammer (vb) [Am] **1** (kapot)boren **2** [fig] beuken ‖ *his heart was ~ing* zijn hart klopte in zijn keel
jack-in-the-box duveltje in een doosje
¹jackknife (n) (groot) knipmesʰ
²jackknife (vb) scharen [of articulated vehicles]
jack-of-all-trades manusje-van-allesʰ
jack off [vulg] zich aftrekken
jackpot pot [at games of hazard]; jackpot: *hit the ~* **a)** (de pot) winnen [at poker etc]; **b)** [fig] een klapper maken, het helemaal maken
jack up opkrikken; [inform, fig also] opvijzelen; opdrijven [prices etc]
jade 1 knol [old horse] **2** jade⁺ʰ, bleekgroenʰ
jaded 1 afgemat, uitgeput **2** afgestompt
jagged getand, gekarteld, puntig: *~ edge* scherpe rand
¹jail (n) gevangenis, huisʰ van bewaring
²jail (vb) gevangen zetten
jailbird bajesklant
jailbreak ontsnapping uit de gevangenis; uitbraak
jailer cipier, gevangenbewaarder
¹jam (n) **1** opstopping, blokkering, stremming **2** knel, knoei, moeilijkheden: *be in* (or: *get into*) *a ~* in de nesten zitten (*or:* raken) **3** jam, marmelade **4** jamsessie
²jam (vb) vast (blijven) zitten, klemmen, blokkeren, vastraken: *the door ~med* de deur raakte klem
³jam (vb) **1** vastzetten, klemmen, knellen **2** (met kracht) drijven, dringen, duwen: *~ the brakes on* op de rem gaan staan **3** (vol)proppen: *he ~med all his clothes into a tiny case* hij propte al zijn kleren in een piepklein koffertje **4** blokkeren, verstoppen, versperren: *the crowds ~med the streets* de massa versperde de straten **5** [radio] storen
Jamaica Jamaica
¹Jamaican (n) Jamaicaan(se)
²Jamaican (adj) Jamaicaans
jam-packed propvol, barstensvol
¹jangle (n) **1** metaalklank, gerinkelʰ **2** wanklank
²jangle (vb) **1** kletteren, rinkelen, rammelen **2** vals klinken, wanklank geven: *the music ~d on my ears* de muziek schetterde in mijn oren
³jangle (vb) irriteren, van streek maken: *it ~d his nerves* het vrat aan zijn zenuwen
janitor 1 portierʰ, deurwachter **2** [Am] conciërge, huisbewaarder
January januari
Japan Japan
¹Japanese (n) Japanner, Japanse
²Japanese (adj) Japans
¹jar (n) **1** (zenuw)schok, onaangename verrassing, ontnuchtering: *suffer a nasty ~* flink ontnuchterd worden **2** pot, (stop)fles, kruik; [inform] glasʰ [beer etc]
²jar (vb) **1** knarsen, vals klinken: [also fig] *~ring note* valse noot, dissonant **2** botsen, in strijd zijn: *~ring opinions* botsende meningen
jargon jargonʰ, vaktaal; [depr] koeterwaalsʰ; taaltjeʰ
jasmin(e) jasmijn
¹jaundice (n) geelzucht
²jaundice (vb) afgunstig maken, verbitteren: *take a ~d view of the matter* een scheve kijk op de zaak hebben
jaunt uitstapjeʰ, tochtjeʰ, snoepreisjeʰ
jaunty 1 zwierig, elegant **2** vrolijk, zelfverzekerd: *a ~ step* een kwieke tred
javelin 1 speer, werpspies **2** [athletics] speerwerpenʰ
¹jaw (n) **1** kaak: *lower* (or: *upper*) *~* onderkaak, bovenkaak **2** praat, gekletsʰ, gezwamʰ, geroddelʰ **3** tegenspraak, brutale praat: *don't give me any ~!* hou je gedeisd! **4** (-s) bek; muil [of animal]
²jaw (vb) **1** kletsen, zwammen, roddelen **2** preken: *~ at s.o.* iem. de les lezen
jawbreaker [Am] toverbal
jaw-dropping [inform] ongelofelijk, onvoorstelbaar
jay Vlaamse gaai
jazz 1 jazz **2** gesnoefʰ **3** onzin, larie ‖ *and all that ~* en nog meer van die dingen
jazzed [Am; inform] opgewonden
jazz up opvrolijken, opfleuren, verfraaien:

they jazzed it up ze brachten wat leven in de brouwerij

jealous 1 jaloers, afgunstig: *~ of* jaloers op **2** (overdreven) waakzaam, nauwlettend: *guard ~ly* angstvallig bewaken

jealousy jaloersheid, afgunst, jaloezie

jeans spijkerbroek, jeans

jeep jeep

¹jeer (n) hatelijke opmerking: *~s* gejouwʰ; hoon

²jeer (vb) jouwen: *~ at s.o.* iem. uitlachen

³jeer (vb) uitjouwen

jell 1 (doen) opstijven, geleiachtig (doen) worden **2** vorm krijgen (geven), kristalliseren: *my ideas are beginning to ~* mijn ideeën beginnen vorm te krijgen

jelly gelei, gelatine(pudding), jam: *beat s.o. to ~* iem. tot moes slaan

jellyfish kwal

jemmy koevoet, breekijzerʰ

jeopardize in gevaar brengen, riskeren, op het spel zetten: *~ one's life* zijn leven wagen

jeopardy gevaarʰ: *put one's future in ~* zijn toekomst op het spel zetten

¹jerk (n) **1** ruk, schok, trek **2** [vulg] lul, zak

²jerk (vb) schokken, beven: *~ to a halt* met een ruk stoppen

³jerk (vb) rukken aan, stoten, trekken aan: *he ~ed the fish out of the water* hij haalde de vis met een ruk uit het water

jerk off [Am; vulg] zich aftrekken

jerk-off [Am; vulg] eikel, hufter

jerky schokkerig, spastisch, hortend: *move along jerkily* zich met horten en stoten voortbewegen

jest 1 grap, mop **2** scherts, gekheid: *in ~* voor de grap

jester nar

Jesus Jezus

¹jet (n) **1** straal [of water etc] **2** (gas)vlam, pit **3** [inform] jet, straalvliegtuigʰ, straalmotor

²jet (vb) **1** spuiten, uitspuiten, uitwerpen: *~ (out) flames* vlammen werpen; *~ out* eruit spuiten **2** [inform] per jet reizen ‖ *~ out* vooruitspringen

jet-black gitzwart

jetfoil draagvleugelboot

jet lag jetlag

jetsam strandgoedʰ

jettison werpen [ship's cargo]; [fig] overboord gooien; prijsgeven

jetty pier, havendam, havenhoofdʰ, golfbreker

Jew 1 Jood **2** [rel] joodʰ

jewel 1 juweelʰ [also fig]; edelsteen, sieraadʰ **2** steen [in timepiece]

jeweller juwelier

jewellery juwelen, sieraden

Jewess 1 Jodin **2** [rel] jodin

Jewish 1 Joods **2** [rel] joods

Jewry Jodendomʰ, de Joden

jib 1 weigeren (verder te gaan) [of horse] **2** terugkrabbelen: *~ at* terugdeinzen voor, zich afkerig tonen van

¹jibe (n) spottende opmerking

²jibe (vb) spotten; schimpen: *~ at* de draak steken met

jiffy momentjeʰ: *I won't be a ~* ik kom zo; *in a ~* in een mum van tijd, in een wip

¹jig (n) **1** sprongetjeʰ **2** jig, gigue [dance]

²jig (vb) op en neer (doen) wippen, (doen) huppelen, (doen) hossen

¹jiggle (vb) schommelen, wiegen

²jiggle (vb) doen schommelen, (zacht) rukken aan, wrikken

jigsaw figuurzaag

jigsaw (puzzle) (leg)puzzel

jihad jihad

jilt afwijzen; de bons geven [lover]

¹jingle (n) **1** geklingelʰ, gerinkelʰ, getinkelʰ **2** [depr] rijmelarij, rijmpjeʰ **3** jingle [on radio]

²jingle (vb) (laten) klingelen, (doen) rinkelen

jinks pretmakerij: *high ~* dolle pret

jinx 1 onheilsbrenger **2** doem, vloek: *put a ~ on s.o.* iem. beheksen

jitters kriebels, zenuwen: *give s.o. the ~* iem. nerveus maken

jittery [inform] zenuwachtig; nerveus

JK [inform] *just kidding* geintje!

jnr *junior* jr.

job 1 karweiʰ, klus, job: *have a ~ to get sth. done* aan iets de handen vol hebben; *make a (good) ~ of sth.* iets goed afwerken; *on the ~* aan het werk, bezig **2** baan(tjeʰ), vakʰ, job, taak: *between ~s* zonder werk, werkloos; [euph] op zoek naar een nieuwe uitdaging; *~s for the boys* vriendjespolitiek **3** [inform] gevalʰ, dingʰ: *that new car of yours is a beautiful ~* die nieuwe auto van jou is een prachtslee **4** [inform] toestand: *make the best of a bad ~* ergens het beste van maken; *he has gone, and a good ~ too* hij is weg, en maar goed ook ‖ *that should do the ~* zo moet het lukken

jobbery ambtsmisbruikʰ, (ambtelijke) corruptie

jobbing klusjes-: *a ~ gardener* een klusjesman voor de tuin

job interview sollicitatiegesprekʰ

jobless zonder werk, werkloos

job satisfaction arbeidsvreugde

job-sharing het werken met deeltijdbanen

jock [inform] **1** [Am] atleet, atlete **2** Schot **3** dj

¹jockey (n) jockey

²jockey (vb) manoeuvreren: *~ for position* met de ellebogen werken

jocular schertsend, grappig

jodhpurs rijbroek: *a pair of ~* een rijbroek

Joe [Am; inform] **1** vent, kerel: *an honest ~* een eerlijke kerel **2** leut, koffie: *a cup of joe* een kopje koffie

¹jog (n) **1** duw(tjeʰ), schok, stootjeʰ **2** sukkeldraf(jeʰ) **3** een stukje joggen

²jog (vb) **1** joggen, trimmen **2** op een sukkeldraf(je) lopen, sukkelen: ~ *along* (or: *on*) voortsukkelen

³jog (vb) (aan)stoten, een duw(tje) geven, (aan)porren ‖ ~ *s.o.'s* **memory** iemands geheugen opfrissen

⁴jog (vb) hotsen, op en neer (doen) gaan, schudden

joggle hotsen, heen en weer (op en neer) (doen) gaan, schudden

jogtrot sukkeldraf(jeʰ), lichte draf

john 1 [Am; inform] wc **2** [Am; inform] klant [of whore]; hoerenloper

johnny kerel, man, vent

¹join (n) verbinding(sstukʰ), voeg, las, naad

²join (vb) **1** samenkomen, zich verenigen, verenigd worden, elkaar ontmoeten, uitkomen op: ~ *up (with)* samensmelten (met) **2** zich aansluiten, meedoen, deelnemen: *can I ~ in?* mag ik meedoen?; ~ *up* dienst nemen (bij het leger), lid worden, zich aansluiten (bij)

³join (vb) **1** verenigen, verbinden, vastmaken: ~ *the main road* op de hoofdweg uitkomen; ~ *up (with)* samenvoegen (met) **2** zich aansluiten bij, meedoen met, deelnemen aan: ~ *the army* dienst nemen (bij het leger); *will you ~ us?* doe je mee?, kom je bij ons zitten?

joiner 1 schrijnwerker, meubelmaker **2** nieuw lid

¹joint (n) **1** verbinding(sstukʰ), voeg, las, naad **2** gewrichtʰ, geleding, scharnierʰ: *out of* ~ [also fig] ontwricht, uit het lid, uit de voegen **3** braadstukʰ, gebraadʰ, (groot) stukʰ vlees **4** [inform] tent, kroeg **5** [inform] joint, stickieʰ

²joint (adj) gezamenlijk, gemeenschappelijk: ~ *account* gezamenlijke rekening; ~ *owners* mede-eigenaars; ~ *responsibility* gedeelde verantwoordelijkheid

joist (dwars)balk, bintʰ, (horizontale) steunbalk

¹joke (n) **1** grap(jeʰ), mop: *practical ~* poets, practical joke; *crack* (or: *tell*) ~*s* moppen tappen; *be* (or: *go*) *beyond a ~* te ver gaan, niet leuk zijn; [inform] *no ~* geen grapje **2** mikpuntʰ [of mockery, wittiness]; spot

²joke (vb) grappen maken, schertsen: *you must be joking!* dat meen je niet!; *joking apart* in alle ernst, nee, nou even serieus

joker 1 grapjas, grappenmaker **2** [cards] joker; [fig] (laatste) troef **3** kerel, (rot)vent

jollity uitgelatenheid, joligheid

¹jolly (adj) **1** plezierig, prettig **2** [also iron] vrolijk, jolig: *a ~ fellow* een lollige vent **3** [inform; euph] (lichtelijk) aangeschoten, dronken ‖ [inform] *it's a ~ shame* het is een

grote schande; *Jolly Roger* piratenvlag

²jolly (vb) vleien, bepraten: ~ *along* (or: *up*) zoet houden, bepraten; ~ *s.o. into sth.* iem. tot iets overhalen

³jolly (adv) [inform] heel, zeer: *you ~ well will!* en nou en of je het doet!

¹jolt (n) schok, ruk, stoot; [fig also] verrassing; ontnuchtering

²jolt (vb) (+ along) (voort)schokken, horten, botsen, stoten

³jolt (vb) schokken; [fig] verwarren: ~ *s.o. out of a false belief* iem. plotseling tot een beter inzicht brengen

Jordan 1 Jordaan [river] **2** Jordanië

¹Jordanian (n) Jordaniër, Jordaanse

²Jordanian (adj) Jordaans

josh plagen, voor de gek houden

jostle (ver)dringen, (weg)duwen, (weg)stoten

¹jot (n) jota [only fig]: *I don't care a ~* het kan me geen moer schelen

²jot (vb) (+ down) (vlug) noteren, neerpennen, opkrabbelen

jotter blocnote, notitieboekjeʰ

journal 1 dagboekʰ, journaalʰ, kasboekʰ **2** dagbladʰ, krant **3** tijdschriftʰ

journalese journalistieke stijl, krantentaal, sensatiestijl

journalism journalistiek

journalist journalist(e)

journalistic journalistiek: ~*ally speaking* vanuit journalistiek oogpunt

¹journey (n) (dag)reis; tocht [over land]

²journey (vb) reizen, trekken

journey planner reisplanner

joust aan een steekspel deelnemen; een steekspel houden [also fig]: ~ *with s.o.* met iem. in het krijt treden

Jove Jupiter

jovial joviaal, vrolijk

jowl kaak, kaaksbeenʰ, wang

joy 1 bron van vreugde: *she's a great ~ to her parents* ze is de vreugde van haar ouders **2** vreugde, genotʰ, blijdschap: *be filled with ~* overlopen van vreugde

joyous [form] blij, opgewekt

joypad gamepad

joyride joyride

joystick 1 knuppel; stuurstang [of aeroplane] **2** bedieningspookjeʰ; joystick [of videogames, computer etc]

JP *Justice of the Peace* politierechter

Jr *Junior* jr.

jubilant 1 uitbundig, triomfantelijk: ~ *shout* vreugdekreet; ~ *at* in de wolken over **2** jubelend, juichend

jubilee jubileumʰ: *diamond ~* diamanten jubileum

judder (heftig) vibreren, trillen, schudden

¹judge (n) **1** rechter **2** scheidsrechter, arbiter, jurylidʰ; beoordelaar [at competition etc]

3 kenner, expert: *good ~ of character* mensenkenner, iem. met veel mensenkennis
²judge (vb) **1** rechtspreken, vonnis vellen **2** arbitreren, als scheidsrechter optreden; [at match] punten toekennen **3** oordelen, een oordeel vellen: *judging by* (or: *from*) *his manner* naar zijn houding te oordelen
³judge (vb) **1** rechtspreken over, berechten **2** beoordelen, achten, schatten: *~ s.o. by his actions* iem. naar zijn daden beoordelen
judgement 1 oordeelʰ, uitspraak, vonnisʰ, schatting: *sit in ~ on* rechter spelen over; *in my ~* naar mijn mening **2** *use one's ~* zijn (gezond) verstand gebruiken; *against one's better ~* tegen beter weten in
Judgement Day dag des oordeels; laatste oordeelʰ
judgmental oordelend, overkritisch: *be ~* zijn oordeel klaar hebben
judicial gerechtelijk, rechterlijk, rechter(s)-: *~ branch* rechterlijke macht; *~ system* gerechtelijk apparaat
judiciary 1 rechtswezenʰ **2** rechterlijke macht
judicious verstandig, voorzichtig
judo judoʰ
¹jug (n) **1** kan(netjeʰ) **2** [Am] kruik, grote (plastic) fles **3** [vulg; Am] tiet
²jug (vb) stoven [hare, rabbit]: *~ged hare* gestoofde haas, hazenpeper
juggernaut grote vrachtwagen, bakbeestʰ
juggle 1 (+ with) jongleren (met) **2** goochelen, toveren **3** (+ with) knoeien (met), frauderen
juggler 1 jongleur **2** goochelaar
Jugoslav *see ¹Yugoslav*
jugular vein halsader: [inform] *go for the ~* naar de keel vliegen
juice sapʰ, levenssapʰ ‖ *let s.o. stew in their own ~* iem. in zijn eigen vet gaar laten koken
juice bar juicebar, sapbar
juicer fruitpers, vruchtenpers
July juli
¹jumble (n) **1** warboel, janboel, troep **2** mengelmoesʰ, allegaartjeʰ
²jumble (vb) dooreengooien, dooreenhaspelen, samenflansen
jumble sale liefdadigheidsbazaar, rommelmarkt
¹jumbo (n) **1** kolos, reus **2** jumbo(jet)
²jumbo (adj) kolossaal, jumbo-, reuzen-
jumbotron [Am; inform] [roughly] zeer groot videoschermʰ
¹jump (n) sprong; [fig] (plotselinge/snelle) stijging; schok, ruk: [fig] *stay one ~ ahead* één stap vóór blijven
²jump (vb) **1** springen; [cycling] wegspringen; demarreren: *~ in* naar binnen springen, vlug instappen; [fig] tussenbeide komen; [fig] *he ~ed at the offer* hij greep het aanbod met beide handen aan; *~ on s.o.* iem. te lijf

gaan; [fig] uitvaren tegen iem. **2** opspringen, opschrikken, een schok krijgen: *he ~ed at the noise* hij schrok op van het lawaai; *~ to one's feet* opspringen **3** zich haasten, overhaast komen (tot): *~ to conclusions* overhaaste conclusies trekken
jumper 1 springer **2** pullover, (dames)trui, jumper **3** [Am] overgooier
jumper cable [Am] startkabel
jumping jack hansworst; trekpop [toy]
jump lead startkabel
jump-start 1 starten met startkabels **2** [fig] een duwtje in de rug geven
jump suit overall
jumpy 1 gespannen **2** lichtgeraakt, prikkelbaar
junction verbinding(spuntʰ), kruispuntʰ; knooppuntʰ [of motorways, railways]
juncture tijdsgewrichtʰ, toestand: *at this ~* onder de huidige omstandigheden
June juni
jungle 1 jungle, oerwoudʰ **2** warboel, warwinkel, chaos: *a ~ of tax laws* een doolhof van belastingwetten
¹junior (n) **1** junior **2** jongere, kleinere: *he's my ~ by two years, he's two years my ~* hij is twee jaar jonger dan ik **3** mindere, ondergeschikte
²junior (adj) **1** jonger, klein(er); junior [after names] **2** lager geplaatst, ondergeschikt, jonger: *~ clerk* jongste bediende
junior college [Am] universiteit [with only the first two years of the course]
junior high (school) [Am] middenschool, brugschool
juniper jeneverbes(struik)
junk 1 (oude) rommel, rotzooi, schrootʰ **2** jonk
junk food junkfoodʰ, ongezonde kost, vette hap
junkie junkie, (drugs)verslaafde
junk mail huis-aan-huispost, reclamedrukwerkʰ; spam
jurisdiction 1 rechtspraak **2** (rechts)bevoegdheid, jurisdictie, competentie: *have ~ of* (or: *over*) bevoegd zijn over
juror jurylidʰ
jury jury
¹just (adj) **1** billijk, rechtvaardig, fair **2** (wel)verdiend: *get* (or: *receive*) *one's ~ deserts* zijn verdiende loon krijgen **3** gegrond, gerechtvaardigd
²just (adv) **1** precies, juist, net: *~ about* zowat, wel zo'n beetje, zo ongeveer; *~ now* net op dit moment, daarnet **2** amper, ternauwernood, (maar) net: *~ a little* een tikkeltje (maar) **3** net, zo-even, daarnet: *they've (only) ~ arrived* ze zijn er (nog maar) net **4** gewoon, (alleen) maar, (nu) eens, nu eenmaal: *it ~ doesn't make sense* het slaat gewoon nergens op; *~ wait and see* wacht

maar, dan zul je eens zien **5** gewoonweg, in één woord, (toch) even ‖ ~ *the* **same** toch, niettemin

ju̱stice 1 rechter: *Justice of the* **Peace** kantonrechter, politierechter; [Belg] vrederechter **2** gerechtigheid, rechtmatigheid, recht^h, rechtvaardigheid, Justitia: *do* ~ *(to)* recht laten wedervaren; *do* ~ *to o.s., do o.s.* ~ zich (weer) waarmaken, aan de verwachtingen voldoen; *to* **do** *him* ~ ere wie ere toekomt **3** gerecht^h, rechtspleging, justitie: *bring s.o. to* ~ iem. voor het gerecht brengen

justifiable 1 gerechtvaardigd, verantwoord, rechtmatig **2** te rechtvaardigen, verdedigbaar

justifica̱tion 1 rechtvaardiging; verantwoording: *there are few* ~*s* **for** *a war* er zijn weinig redenen die een oorlog rechtvaardigen **2** [printing] het opvullen, uitvullen

ju̱stify 1 rechtvaardigen, bevestigen: *we were clearly justified* **in** *sacking him* we hebben hem terecht ontslagen **2** [esp in passive voice] in het gelijk stellen, rechtvaardigen, staven: *am I justified in thinking that …* heb ik gelijk als ik denk dat … **3** [printing] uitvullen: *left-justified* links uitgevuld

jut (also + out) uitsteken, (voor)uitspringen **jute** jute

^1**ju̱venile** (n) jongere, jeugdig persoon
^2**ju̱venile** (adj) jeugdig, kinderlijk: ~ **court** kinderrechter; ~ **delinquency** jeugdcriminaliteit

juveni̱lia jeugdwerken
juxtapo̱se naast elkaar plaatsen

k

K 1 *1000* 1000: *he earns £30K a year* hij verdient £30.000 per jaar **2** *1024 bytes* KB **3** [inform] *okay* oké
kale (boeren)kool
kaleidoscope caleidoscoop
kangaroo kangoeroe
kangaroo court onwettige rechtbank
kapok kapok
karaoke karaokeʰ
karting kartingʰ, gocarting
kayak kajak [of Eskimos]; kano
¹Kazakh (n) Kazach(se)
²Kazakh (adj) Kazachs
Kazakhstan Kazachstan
keel [shipp] kiel
keelhaul 1 kielhalen **2** op z'n nummer zetten, op z'n donder geven: *Julian was ~ed by his boss* Julian kreeg flink op z'n donder van zijn baas
keen 1 scherp [also fig]; bijtend, fel; hevig [of wind, frost, etc; also of fight]: *we're facing ~ competition from small businesses* we kampen met felle concurrentie van kleine ondernemingen **2** scherp; helder [of senses, intelligence etc]: *~ sight* scherp gezichtsvermogen **3** vurig, enthousiast: *a ~ golfer* een hartstochtelijk golfer; *~ on* gespitst op, gebrand op **4** spotgoedkoop
¹keep (n) **1** (hoofd)toren **2** bolwerkʰ, bastionʰ **3** (levens)onderhoudʰ, kost, voedselʰ: *earn your ~* de kost verdienen || *for ~s* voor altijd, voorgoed
²keep (vb) **1** blijven, doorgaan met: *~ left* links houden; *will you please ~ still!* blijf nou toch eens stil zitten!; *how is Richard ~ing?* hoe gaat het met Richard?; *~ abreast of* a) bijhouden; b) [fig] op de hoogte blijven van; *~ back* op een afstand blijven; *~ indoors* in huis blijven; *if the rain ~s off* als het droog blijft; *~ off!* (or: *out!*) verboden toegang!; *~ off* uit de buurt blijven van, vermijden; *~ out of* a) zich niet bemoeien met; b) niet betreden; c) zich niet blootstellen aan **2** goed blijven; vers blijven [of food]: [fig] *your news will have to ~ a bit* dat nieuwtje van jou moet maar even wachten
³keep (vb) **1** houden, zich houden aan, bewaren: *~ a promise* een belofte nakomen; *~ a secret* een geheim bewaren **2** houden, onderhouden, eropna houden, (in dienst) hebben: *~ chickens* kippen houden **3** (in bezit) hebben, bewaren, in voorraad hebben, verkopen: *~ the change* laat maar zitten **4** houden, ophouden, vasthouden, tegenhouden: *~ within bounds* binnen de perken houden; *~ it clean* houd het netjes; *~ sth. going* iets aan de gang houden; *~ s.o. waiting* iem. laten wachten; *what kept you (so long)?* wat heeft je zo (lang) opgehouden?, waar bleef je (nou)?; *~ back* a) tegenhouden, op een afstand houden; b) achterhouden, geheimhouden; *~ down* a) binnenhouden [food]; b) omlaaghouden, laag houden; c) onder de duim houden; d) onderdrukken, inhouden [rage]; *~ one's weight down* z'n gewicht binnen de perken houden; *~ your head down!* bukken!; *~ off* op een afstand houden; *~ s.o. out* iem. buitensluiten; *he tried to ~ the bad news from his father* hij probeerde het slechte nieuws voor z'n vader verborgen te houden; *he couldn't ~ his eyes off the girl* hij kon z'n ogen niet van het meisje afhouden; *~ your hands off me!* blijf met je poten van me af!; *~ them out of harm's way* zorg dat ze geen gevaar lopen; *he kept it to himself* hij hield het voor zich **5** bijhouden [book, diary etc]; houden: *Mary used to ~ (the) accounts* Mary hield de boeken bij **6** houden, aanhouden, blijven in: *~ your seat!* blijf (toch) zitten!
keep at door blijven gaan met: *~ it!* ga zo door!
keeper 1 bewaarder **2** keeper, doelverdediger; [cricket] wicketkeeper
¹keep in (vb) binnen blijven
²keep in (vb) na laten blijven
keeping 1 bewaring, hoede: *in safe ~* in veilige bewaring **2** overeenstemming, harmonie: *in ~ with* in overeenstemming met
keep in with (proberen) op goede voet (te) blijven met: *now that she's old she wishes she had kept in with her children* nu ze oud is, wilde ze dat ze op goede voet was gebleven met haar kinderen
¹keep on (vb) **1** volhouden, doorgaan: *he keeps on telling me these awful jokes* hij blijft me maar van die vreselijke grappen vertellen **2** doorgaan, doorrijden, doorlopen, verder gaan **3** blijven praten, doorkletsen
²keep on (vb) **1** aanhouden, ophouden; blijven dragen [clothing, hat]: *please ~ your safety helmet throughout the tour* houd u alstublieft tijdens de rondleiding uw veiligheidshelm op **2** aanlaten [light]
keepsake aandenkenʰ, souvenirʰ: *for a ~* als aandenken
keep to 1 blijven bij, (zich) beperken tot, (zich) houden (aan): *~ the point* bij het onderwerp blijven; *she always keeps (herself) to herself* ze is erg op zichzelf **2** houden, rijden: *~ the left* links houden
¹keep up (vb) **1** overeind blijven, blijven staan **2** hoog blijven [of price, standard; also fig] **3** (in dezelfde/goede staat) blijven, aanhouden: *I do hope that the weather keeps up*

ik hoop wel dat het weer mooi blijft **4** opblijven **5** bijblijven, bijhouden: ~ *with one's neighbours* niet bij de buren achterblijven; ~ *with* the Joneses z'n stand ophouden; ~ *with the times* bij de tijd blijven

²**keep up** (vb) **1** omhooghouden, ophouden **2** hooghouden: ~ *the costs* de kosten hoog houden; keep *morale* up het moreel hooghouden **3** doorgaan met, handhaven, volhouden: ~ *the conversation* de conversatie gaande houden; ~ *the good work!* ga zo door!

keg vaatje^h: ~ *beer* bier van het vat

kelp kelp; zeewier^h

ken kennis, bevattingsvermogen^h, begrip^h: *that is beyond* (or: *outside*) *my* ~ dat gaat boven mijn pet

kennel 1 hondenhok^h **2** kennel, hondenfokkerij

Kenya Kenia

¹**Kenyan** (n) Keniaan(se)

²**Kenyan** (adj) Keniaans

kerb stoeprand, trottoirband

kerchief [dated] hoofddoek^h; halsdoek^h

ker-ching [inform; hum] kassa!

kerfuffle opschudding

kernel 1 pit, korrel **2** kern, essentie

kerosene kerosine, (lampen)petroleum^h, lampolie, paraffineolie

kestrel torenvalk

kettle ketel: *put the* ~ *on* theewater opzetten

kettledrum keteltrom(mel), pauk

¹**key** (n) **1** sleutel; [fig] toegang; oplossing, verklaring: ~ *to the mystery* sleutel van het raadsel **2** toon; [mus] toonaard, toonsoort; tonaliteit, stijl: *out of* ~, *off* ~ vals **3** toets [of piano, typewriter etc]; klep [of wind instrument]

²**key** (adj) sleutel-, hoofd-, voornaamste: ~ *figure* sleutelfiguur; ~ *question* hamvraag; ~ *witness* hoofdgetuige, voornaamste getuige

³**key** (vb) (+ in) invoeren [by means of keyboard]; intikken

keyboard 1 toetsenbord^h **2** klavier^h **3** klavierinstrument^h, toetsinstrument^h; keyboard^h

key card sleutelkaart

keyhole sleutelgat^h || ~ *surgery* kijkoperatie

keyhole surgery kijkoperatie

keynote 1 grondtoon, hoofdtoon **2** hoofdgedachte, grondgedachte

keynote speech keynotespeech, presentatie van het centrale thema van een congres

keypad (druk)toetsenpaneel(tje)^h [of remote control unit, pocket calculator etc]

key signature voortekening

keystone 1 sluitsteen [of arch] **2** hoeksteen, fundament^h

key up opwinden, gespannen maken: *the boy looked keyed up* de jongen zag er gespannen uit

kg *kilogram(s)* kg

khaki kaki(kleur), kakistof

khakis 1 kakiuniform^h **2** kakibroek

kibbutz kibboets

¹**kick** (n) **1** schop, trap **2** terugslag [of gun] **3** kick, stimulans, impuls: *do sth. for* ~s iets voor de lol doen **4** kracht, fut, energie || *a* ~ *in the pants* een schop onder zijn kont [fig]; *a* ~ *in the teeth* een slag in het gezicht [fig]

²**kick** (vb) **1** schoppen, trappen: [socc] ~ *off* aftrappen **2** terugslag hebben [of gun] **3** er tegenaan schoppen, protesteren: ~ *against* (or: *at*) protesteren tegen || ~ *off* sterven

³**kick** (vb) **1** schoppen, trappen, wegtrappen: ~ *o.s.* zich voor zijn kop slaan; ~ *out* eruit schoppen, ontslaan **2** stoppen met [addiction etc] || ~ *a person when he is down* iem. nog verder de grond in trappen; ~ *upstairs* wegpromoveren

¹**kick around** (vb) **1** rondslingeren: *his old bicycle has been kicking around in the garden for weeks now* zijn oude fiets slingert al weken rond in de tuin **2** in leven zijn, bestaan, rondhollen

²**kick around** (vb) **1** sollen met, grof behandelen **2** commanderen, bazen

kickback 1 smeergeld^h **2** [inform] gezellig feestje^h

kick back relaxen, ontspannen

kick in in werking treden, beginnen (te werken); (plotseling) beginnen mee te spelen [eg of fear]: *but when she saw the rhino at close range, fear kicked in* maar toen ze de neushoorn van dichtbij zag, werd ze ineens bang

kick-off 1 [socc] aftrap **2** begin^h

kicks [inform] sportschoenen

kick-start 1 snel op gang brengen, een impuls geven aan **2** aantrappen; starten [engine]

kickstart(er) trapstarter

¹**kid** (n) **1** jong geitje^h, bokje^h **2** kind^h, joch^h **3** geitenleer^h

²**kid** (adj) **1** jonger: ~ *brother* (or: *sister*) jonger broertje (or: zusje) **2** van geitenleer, glacé: *handle* (or: *treat*) (s.o.) *with* ~ *gloves* (iem.) met fluwelen handschoentjes aanpakken

³**kid** (vb) plagen, in de maling nemen: *no* ~*ding?* meen je dat?; *no* ~*ding!* echt waar!

kid around dollen, een lolletje maken: *he's just kidding around* hij is wat aan het dollen; *I'm not kidding around* ik maak geen grapje

kiddie jong^h, joch^h, knul

kiddo [Am; inform] jochie^h

kidnap ontvoeren, kidnappen

kidney nier

kidult kidult

¹**kill** (n) buit, vangst, (gedode) prooi || *be in at*

the ~ erbij zijn als de vos gedood wordt; [fig] er (op het beslissende moment) bij zijn

²**kill** (vb) **1** [also fig] doden, moorden, ombrengen: *my feet are ~ing me* ik verga van de pijn in mijn voeten; *~ o.s. laughing* (or: *with laughter*) zich een ongeluk lachen; *~ off* afmaken, uit de weg ruimen, uitroeien; *be ~ed* om het leven komen **2** [socc] doodmaken, doodleggen, stoppen ‖ *dressed to ~* er piekfijn uitzien

killer moordenaar

killer whale orka

¹**killing** (n) **1** moord, doodslag **2** groot (financieel) succesʰ: *make a ~* zijn slag slaan, groot succes hebben

²**killing** (adj) **1** dodelijk, fataal **2** slopend, uitputtend

killjoy spelbreker

kill switch 1 noodknop **2** [of mobile phone] toestelblokkering, antidiefstalfunctie

kiln (steen)oven

kilo 1 kilo(gram)⁺ʰ **2** kilometer

kilobyte kilobyte

kilogramme kilogram⁺ʰ

kilometre kilometer

kilowatt kilowatt

kilt kilt

kin familie, verwanten: *kith and ~* vrienden en verwanten; *next of ~* naaste verwanten

¹**kind** (n) **1** soort⁺ʰ, typeʰ, aard: *nothing of the ~* niets van dien aard, geen sprake van; *three of a ~* drie gelijke(n), drie dezelfde(n); *a ~ of* een soort; *all ~s of* allerlei; *I haven't got that ~ of money* zulke bedragen heb ik niet **2** wijze, manier van doen **3** wezenʰ, karakterʰ, soort⁺ʰ ‖ *pay in ~* in natura betalen; [fig] met gelijke munt terugbetalen

²**kind** (adj) vriendelijk, aardig: *with ~ regards* met vriendelijke groeten; *would you be ~ enough to* (or: *so ~ as to*) *open the window* zou u zo vriendelijk willen zijn het raam open te doen

kinda [inform] wel; best, nogal: *he's ~ cute* hij is wel leuk; *I was ~ scared* ik was een beetje bang

kindergarten kleuterschool

¹**kindle** (vb) ontbranden, (op)vlammen, vlam vatten: *such dry wood ~s easily* zo'n droog hout vat gemakkelijk vlam

²**kindle** (vb) **1** ontsteken **2** opwekken, doen stralen, gloeien: *I don't know what ~d their hatred of him* ik weet niet waardoor ze hem zijn gaan haten

kindling aanmaakhoutʰ

¹**kindly** (adj) vriendelijk, (goed)aardig: *in a ~ fashion* vriendelijk

²**kindly** (adv) alstublieft: *~ move your car* zet u a.u.b. uw auto ergens anders neer ‖ *he did not take ~ to all those rules* hij kon niet zo goed tegen al die regels

kindness 1 vriendelijke daad, iets aardigs, gunst **2** vriendelijkheid: *out of ~* uit goedheid

¹**kindred** (n) **1** verwantschap **2** verwanten, familie(leden)

²**kindred** (adj) verwant: *a ~ spirit* een verwante geest

king koning; [card game also] heer

kingcup boterbloem

kingdom koninkrijkʰ, rijkʰ, domeinʰ

kingfisher ijsvogel

kingpin 1 [bowling] koning **2** spil [fig]; centrale figuur: [Am] *drug ~* drugsbaron

King's English standaard Engels, BBC-Engelsʰ

king-size(d) extra lang, extra groot

kink 1 kink; knik [in wire etc] **2** kronkel, eigenaardigheid

kinky 1 pervers **2** sexy; opwindend

kinship verwantschap; [also fig] overeenkomst; verbondenheid: *she felt a deep ~ with the other students in her group* ze voelde een diepe verbondenheid met de andere studenten in haar groep

kinsman (bloed)verwant

kiosk 1 kiosk, stalletjeʰ **2** reclamezuil **3** telefooncel

¹**kip** (n) **1** slaapplaats, bedʰ **2** dutjeʰ, slaap-(jeʰ)

²**kip** (vb) (also + down) (gaan) pitten, (gaan) slapen

kipper gerookte haring

¹**Kirghiz** (n) Kirgies, Kirgizische

²**Kirghiz** (adj) Kirgizisch

Kirghizistan Kirgizië

¹**kiss** (n) kus(jeʰ), zoen(tjeʰ): *blow a ~* een kushandje geven, een kus toewerpen ‖ *~ of life* mond-op-mondbeademing

²**kiss** (vb) **1** kussen, elkaar kussen, (elkaar) zoenen: *~ and be friends* het afzoenen, het weer goedmaken **2** (even/licht) raken; [billiards] klotsen (tegen); een klos maken

kisser snoet, waffel: *he smacked the thief in the ~* hij gaf de dief een klap voor zijn kanis

kissing disease (the) knuffelziekte, ziekte van Pfeiffer

kit 1 (gereedschaps)kist, doos, (plunje)zak **2** bouwdoos, bouwpakketʰ **3** uitrusting, spullen: *did you remember to bring your squash ~?* heb je eraan gedacht je squashspullen mee te brengen?

kitbag plunjezak

kitchen keuken

kitchen garden moestuin, groentetuin

kitchen sink aanrechtʰ

kite 1 vlieger: *fly a ~* vliegeren, een vlieger oplaten; [fig] een balletje opgooien **2** wouw ‖ *go fly a ~* maak dat je weg komt

kitten katjeʰ, poesjeʰ ‖ *have ~s* de zenuwen hebben, op tilt slaan

kitty 1 katjeʰ, poesjeʰ **2** (gezamenlijke) pot;

inzet [in card game]; kas
ki**wi 1** kiwi(vrucht) **2** Nieuw-Zeelander
kla**xon** claxon
kleptoma**niac** kleptomaan
km *kilometre(s)* km
knack 1 vaardigheid, handigheid, slag: *get the ~ of sth.* de slag te pakken krijgen van iets **2** truc, handigheidjeʰ: *there's a ~ in it* je moet de truc even doorhebben
¹**kn**a**cker** (n) sloper
²**kn**a**cker** (vb) [inform] **1** uitputten, afmatten [fig] **2** mollen, naar z'n grootje helpen
kna**ckered 1** bekaf, doodop: *I'm ~* ik ben gesloopt **2** kapot, stuk: *the car radio is ~* de autoradio doet het niet meer
kna**psack** knapzak, plunjezak
knave 1 [cards] boer **2** schurk
knead 1 (dooreen)kneden: *make sure you ~ the dough properly* zorg ervoor dat je het deeg goed kneedt **2** kneden; masseren [eg muscle]
knee knie: *bring s.o. to his ~s* iem. op de knieën krijgen **2** kniestukʰ || *his ~s were knocking together* hij stond te trillen op zijn benen
knee**cap 1** knieschijf **2** kniebeschermer
¹**knee-deep** (adj) kniehoog, kniediep
²**knee-deep** (adj) diep [fig]: *be ~ in debt* tot over de oren in de schulden zitten
knee-jerk [inform] automatisch: *a ~ reaction* een voorspelbare reactie
kneel (also + down) knielen, geknield zitten
knees-up knalfuif, feestʰ
knell doodsklok [also fig]
kni**ckers** slipjeʰ; onderbroek [of woman]
kni**ck-knack** prul(letjeʰ), snuisterij
¹**knife** (n) mesʰ || *turn* (or: *twist*) *the ~* nog een trap nageven
²**knife** (vb) (door)steken, aan het mes rijgen
knife crime 1 gewelddelicten waarbij een steekwapen wordt gebruikt **2** (knife crimes) steekpartij
knight 1 ridder: *~ errant* dolende ridder; ridderlijk persoon **2** [chess] paardʰ
kni**ghthood** ridderorde: *confer a ~ on s.o.* iem. tot ridder slaan
¹**knit** (vb) één worden, vergroeien: *the broken bones ~ readily* de gebroken botten groeien weer snel aan elkaar
²**knit** (vb) **1** breien **2** fronsen, samentrekken **3** verweven, verbinden: *(their interests are) closely ~* (hun belangen zijn) nauw verweven
kni**tting** breiwerkʰ
knob 1 knop, hendel, handvatʰ, schakelaar **2** knobbel, bult: *the ~ on her leg was quite visible* de bult op haar been was goed te zien **3** brok(jeʰ), klontjeʰ
kno**bbly** knobbelig
kno**bby** knobbelig
¹**knock** (n) **1** slag, klap, klop, tik **2** oplazer:

take a lot of ~s heel wat te verduren krijgen
²**knock** (vb) **1** (hard) slaan, meppen, stoten (tegen): *~ a hole* (or: *nail*) *in* een gat (or: spijker) slaan in **2** (af)kraken **3** met stomheid slaan, versteld doen staan
³**knock** (vb) kloppen, tikken: *~ at* (or: *on*) *a door* op een deur kloppen || *~ against sth.* tegen iets (op) botsen; *~ into s.o.* iem. tegen het lijf lopen
kno**ckabout 1** gooi-en-smijt- [of films] **2** rouwdouw
knock about 1 rondhangen, lanterfanten **2** (rond)slingeren **3** rondzwerven, rondscharrelen, van de hand in de tand leven: *~ with* optrekken met, scharrelen (or: rotzooien) met
knock back [inform] **1** achteroverslaan [drink] **2** kosten; een rib uit het lijf zijn van **3** teleurstellen **4** versteld doen staan
knockdown 1 verpletterend, vernietigend **2** afbraak-, spotgoedkoop
knock down 1 neerhalen, tegen de grond slaan; [fig] vloeren **2** slopen, tegen de grond gooien **3** aanrijden, omverrijden, overrijden **4** naar beneden krijgen, afdingen, afpingelen: *knock s.o. down a pound* een pond bij iem. afdingen **5** verkopen [at auction]: *the chair was knocked down at three pounds* de stoel ging weg voor drie pond
kno**cker 1** deurklopper **2** [inform] negatieveling **3** (-s) [inform] tiet
knock-kneed met X-benen
knock off 1 (af)nokken (met), kappen; stoppen [work] **2** goedkoper geven, korting geven **3** in elkaar draaien **4** afmaken, nog doen **5** [inform] jatten, beroven
kno**ck-on** domino(-effectʰ)
kno**ckout 1** [boxing] knock-out **2** [sport] eliminatietoernooiʰ; [roughly] voorronde **3** spetter, juweelʰ: *you look a ~* je ziet eruit om te stelen
knock out 1 vloeren, knock-out slaan **2** verdoven; bedwelmen [of drug] **3** [sport] uitschakelen, elimineren **4** in elkaar flansen: *we knocked out a programme for the festivities* we flansten snel een programma voor de festiviteiten in elkaar
knock over 1 omgooien, neervellen, aanrijden, overrijden, omverrijden **2** versteld doen staan **3** overvallen, beroven
knock together in elkaar flansen, (slordig/haastig) in elkaar zetten
¹**knock up** (vb) [tennis] inslaan
²**knock up** (vb) **1** afbeulen, slopen **2** bij elkaar verdienen [money] **3** zwanger maken
¹**knot** (n) **1** knoop; strik [as decoration] **2** knoop [fig]; moeilijkheid **3** kwast, knoest, noest **4** kluitje mensen **5** band, verbinding, huwelijksband **6** knoop, zeemijl per uur, zeemijl || *get tied (up) into ~s (over)* van de kook raken door, de kluts kwijtraken (van/

over)

²**knot** (vb) **1** (vast)knopen, (vast)binden, een knoop leggen in **2** dichtknopen, dichtbinden

knotty 1 vol knopen, in de knoop (geraakt) **2** kwastig; knoestig [of wood] **3** ingewikkeld, lastig

¹**know** (n): *in the* ~ ingewijd, (goed) op de hoogte

²**know** (vb) **1** weten, kennis hebben (van), beseffen: *if you ~ what I mean* als je begrijpt wat ik bedoel; *for **all** I ~ he may be in China* misschien zit hij in China, wie weet; *you ~* weet je (wel), je weet wel; *not that I ~ of* niet dat ik weet **2** kennen, bekend zijn met: ~ *one's **way*** de weg weten **3** herkennen, (kunnen) thuisbrengen: *I knew Jane by her **walk*** ik herkende Jane aan haar manier van lopen ‖ *don't I ~ it* moet je mij vertellen; ~ *backwards (and forwards)* kennen als zijn broekzak, kunnen dromen; ~ *better than to do sth.* (wel) zo verstandig zijn iets te laten

know-how handigheid, praktische vaardigheid, technische kennis

knowing 1 veelbetekenend: ~ *glance* (or: *look*) blik van verstandhouding **2** bewust: ~*ly hurt s.o.* iem. bewust pijn doen

know-it-all wijsneus; betweter

knowledge kennis, wetenschap, informatie, geleerdheid: *to the **best** of one's ~ (and belief)* naar (zijn) beste weten; *without s.o.'s ~* buiten iemands (mede)weten; *be **common** ~* algemeen bekend zijn

knowledgeable goed geïnformeerd, goed op de hoogte: *be ~ **about*** verstand hebben van

known 1 bekend, algemeen beschouwd, erkend **2** gegeven, bekend ‖ *make o.s. ~ to* zich voorstellen aan

knuckle knokkel ‖ *rap on* (or: *over*) *the ~s* op de vingers tikken; *near the ~* op het randje [of joke]

knuckle down (+ to) zich serieus wijden (aan) [job, chore]; aanpakken, aanvatten: *it's high time you knuckled down to some hard study* het wordt hoog tijd dat je eens flink gaat studeren

knuckle under (+ to) buigen (voor), zwichten (voor)

KO [inform] *knockout* ko

koala koala(beer)

kooky verknipt, geschift

Koran (the) Koran

kosher koosjer, jofel, in orde

kowtow (+ to) door het stof gaan (voor), zich vernederen

kph *kilometres per hour* km/u, kilometer per uur

kudos [inform] lof: ~ *for* … kudos voor …, complimenten voor …; ~ *to all of you for an amazing job* allemaal bedankt voor deze geweldige prestatie

Kurd Koerd

Kurdish Koerdisch

Kuwait Koeweit

¹**Kuwaiti** (n) Koeweiter, Koeweitse

²**Kuwaiti** (adj) Koeweits

kW *kilowatt(s)* kW

¹**Kyrgyz** (n) Kirgies, Kirgizische

²**Kyrgyz** (adj) Kirgizisch

Kyrgyzstan Kirgizië

l

l 1 *left* links **2** *litre(s)* l, liter(s)
L *learner driver* leerling-automobilist
LA *Los Angeles*
lab [inform] *laboratory* lab^h; laboratorium^h
¹label (n) **1** etiket^h, label^h **2** label^h [of CD]; platenmaatschappij **3** etiket^h
²label (vb) **1** etiketteren, labelen, merken **2** een etiket opplakken, bestempelen als
laboratory laboratorium^h, proefruimte
laborious 1 afmattend, bewerkelijk **2** moeizaam
¹labour (n) **1** arbeid; werk^h [in employment] **2** (krachts)inspanning, moeite **3** arbeidersklasse, arbeidskrachten **4** (barens)weeën **5** bevalling: *be in* ~ bevallen
²labour (vb) **1** arbeiden, werken **2** zich inspannen, ploeteren: ~ *at* (or: *over*) *sth.* op iets zwoegen **3** moeizaam vooruitkomen, zich voortslepen
laboured 1 moeizaam **2** gekunsteld
labourer (hand)arbeider, ongeschoolde arbeider: *agricultural* ~ landarbeider
labour force beroepsbevolking
labour market arbeidsmarkt
labour under te kampen hebben met, last hebben van: ~ *the delusion* (or: *illusion*) *that* in de waan verkeren dat
labyrinth doolhof; labyrint^h [also fig]
¹lace (n) **1** veter, koord^h **2** kant(werk^h)
²lace (vb) **1** rijgen, dichtmaken met veter **2** (door)vlechten, (door)weven **3** een scheutje sterkedrank toevoegen aan: ~ *tea with rum* een scheutje rum in de thee doen
lacerate (ver)scheuren
¹lack (n) **1** gebrek^h, tekort^h: *die for* (or: *through*) ~ *of food* sterven door voedselgebrek **2** behoefte
²lack (vb) **1** missen, niet hebben: *he simply ~s courage* het ontbreekt hem gewoon aan moed **2** gebrek hebben aan, te kort komen
lackadaisical lusteloos; futloos
lackey 1 lakei, livreiknecht **2** kruiper
lacking afwezig, ontbrekend: *be* ~ *in* gebrek hebben aan
lacklustre dof, glansloos; mat [of eyes]
laconic kort en krachtig, laconiek
lacquer 1 lak^+h **2** (blanke) lak, vernis^h **3** (haar)lak
lactation 1 het zogen, melkvoeding **2** lactatie(periode), zoogperiode
lad jongen, knul, jongeman ‖ *be one of the ~s* erbij horen
ladder 1 ladder [also fig]; trap(leer), touw-

ladder **2** ladder [in stocking] **3** [sport] ladder, ranglijst
laden zwaar beladen; vol: *branches* ~ *with snow* met sneeuw beladen takken; [fig] ~ *with anxieties* onder zorgen gebukt
Ladies(') dames(toilet^h)
¹ladle (n) soeplepel
²ladle (vb) **1** opscheppen, oplepelen: ~ *out soup* soep opscheppen **2** (+ out) rondstrooien, smijten met
lady 1 dame: *ladies and gentlemen* dames en heren; [Am] *First Lady* presidentsvrouw **2** lady ‖ ~ *doctor* vrouwelijke arts
ladybird lieveheersbeestje^h
ladyboy [inform] transseksueel, travestiet
ladybug [Am] lieveheersbeestje^h
lady-in-waiting hofdame
ladykiller vrouwenjager, (ras)versierder
ladylike 1 ladylike, zoals een dame past, beschaafd **2** elegant
Lady Luck Vrouwe Fortuna; het lot
ladyship lady: *her, your* ~ mevrouw de barones, gravin enz.
¹lag (vb) (+ behind) achterblijven, achteraan komen
²lag (vb) bekleden, betimmeren; isoleren [pipes etc]
lager (blond) bier^h; [fig] pils^h
laggard treuzelaar, laatkomer, slome duikelaar^h
lagging bekleding(smateriaal^h), isolatie-(materiaal^h), het bekleden
lagoon lagune
la(h)-di-da(h) bekakt
laid-back relaxed, ontspannen
lair 1 hol^h; leger^h [of wild animal] **2** hol^h [fig]; schuilplaats
laity 1 leken(dom^h), de leken **2** leken(publiek^h), de leken
lake meer^h, vijver
lamb 1 lam(metje)^h, lamsvlees^h **2** lammetje^h, lief kind^h, schatje^h
lame 1 mank, kreupel **2** onbevredigend, nietszeggend: ~ *excuse* zwak excuus ‖ ~ *duck* slappeling, zielige (or: behoeftige) figuur
¹lament (n) **1** jammerklacht **2** klaaglied^h
²lament (vb) **1** (+ over) klagen (over), jammeren (over) **2** treuren: ~ *for a brother* treuren om een broer
³lament (vb) (diep) betreuren, treuren om, bewenen
lamentable 1 betreurenswaardig, beklagenswaard(ig) **2** erbarmelijk (slecht), bedroevend (slecht)
lamentation 1 geweeklaag^h; jammerklacht **2** leed^h
laminate 1 in dunne lagen splijten **2** lamineren, tot dunne platen pletten, bedekken met (metalen) platen: ~d *wood* triplex, multiplex
lamp lamp

¹**lampoon** (n) satire, schotschrift[h]
²**lampoon** (vb) hekelen
lamp-post lantaarnpaal
lampshade lampenkap
lance lans, spies, speer
lancet lancet[h] [surgical knife]
¹**land** (n) **1** (vaste)land[h] **2** landstreek, staat, gebied[h]: *native* ~ vaderland[h] **3** bouwland[h], aarde, grond, grondgebied[h], lap grond, weiland[h] || *the promised* ~ het beloofde land
²**land** (vb) **1** landen, aan land gaan **2** (be)-landen, neerkomen, terechtkomen: ~ *in a mess* in de knoei raken || [inform] *I* ~*ed up in Athens* uiteindelijk belandde ik in Athene
³**land** (vb) **1** aan wal zetten **2** doen landen; aan de grond zetten [aeroplane] **3** doen belanden, brengen: ~ *s.o. in a mess* iem. in de knoei brengen **4** vangen; binnenhalen, binnenbrengen [fish] **5** in de wacht slepen, bemachtigen
land agent 1 rentmeester **2** onroerend-goedhandelaar
landed 1 land-, grond-, uit land bestaand: ~ *property* grondbezit[h] **2** land bezittend: ~ *gentry* (or: *nobility*) landadel
landfall (het) aan land komen, het vasteland bereiken: *the hurricane made* ~ *in Florida* de orkaan kwam in Florida aan land
landfill gestort afval[h], afvalberg
land forces landstrijdkrachten, landmacht
landing 1 landingsplaats, steiger, aanlegplaats **2** landing [of aeroplane]; het aan wal gaan; aankomst [of ship] **3** overloop, (trap)-portaal[h]
landing craft landingsvaartuig[h], landingsschip[h]
landing gear landingsgestel[h], onderstel[h]
landing net schepnet[h]
landing stage (aanleg)steiger, aanlegplaats, losplaats
landlady 1 hospita, pensionhoudster, waardin **2** huisbazin, vrouw van de huisbaas
landline vaste telefoon(lijn)
landlocked geheel door land omgeven: *a ~ country* een binnenstaat
landlord 1 landheer **2** huisbaas, pensionhouder, waard
landmark 1 grenspaal **2** oriëntatiepunt[h] [also fig]; markering, baken[h] **3** mijlpaal, keerpunt[h]
landowner landeigenaar; grondbezitter
landscape landschap[h], panorama[h]
landslide aardverschuiving [also fig]: *win by a* ~ een verpletterende overwinning behalen
lane 1 (land)weggetje[h], laantje[h], paadje[h] **2** (voorgeschreven) vaarweg, vaargeul **3** luchtcorridor, luchtweg, (aan)vliegroute **4** [traf] rijstrook **5** [sport] baan
language 1 taal: *foreign* ~*s* vreemde talen **2** taalgebruik[h], woordgebruik[h], stijl

3 (groeps)taal, vaktaal, jargon[h] **4** communicatiesysteem[h], gebarentaal, (programmeer)-taal, computertaal **5** taalbeheersing, spraak-(vermogen[h])
language acquisition taalverwerving
languid lusteloos, (s)loom, slap
languish (weg)kwijnen, verslappen, verzwakken
languor 1 apathie, lusteloosheid, matheid **2** lome stilte, zwoelheid, drukkendheid
languorous 1 loom; lusteloos **2** zwoel
lank 1 schraal, (brood)mager, dun **2** krachteloos, slap; sluik [of hair] **3** lang en buigzaam [eg of grass]
lanky slungelachtig
lantern lantaarn
Laos Laos
¹**Laotian** (n) Laotiaan(se)
²**Laotian** (adj) Laotiaans
¹**lap** (n) **1** schoot [also of article of clothing] **2** overlap(ping), overlappend deel[h], overslag **3** [sport] baan, ronde **4** etappe [of trip]
²**lap** (vb) (+ against) kabbelen (tegen), klotsen (tegen)
³**lap** (vb) likken, oplikken: ~ *up* oplikken, opslorpen; [fig] verslinden
¹**lapse** (n) **1** kleine vergissing, fout(je[h]) **2** misstap **3** (tijds)verloop[h], verstrijken van tijd **4** periode, tijd(je[h]); poos(je[h]) [in past]
²**lapse** (vb) **1** (gaandeweg) verdwijnen, achteruitgaan, afnemen: *my anger had soon* ~*d* mijn boosheid was weldra weggeëbd **2** vervallen, terugvallen, afglijden: ~ *into silence* in stilzwijgen verzinken **3** verstrijken, verlopen
lapsed 1 afvallig, ontrouw **2** [law] verlopen, vervallen
laptop (computer) schootcomputer, laptop
lapwing kievit
larceny diefstal
¹**lard** (n) varkensvet[h], (varkens)reuzel
²**lard** (vb) larderen [also fig]; doorspekken, doorrijgen met spek
larder provisiekamer, provisiekast
large 1 groot, omvangrijk, ruim **2** veelomvattend, ver(re)gaand **3** onbevangen, gedurfd **4** edelmoedig, vrijgevig || *as* ~ *as life* a) in levenden lijve, hoogstpersoonlijk; b) onmiskenbaar; ~*r than life* overdreven, buiten proporties; *the murderer is still at* ~ de moordenaar is nog steeds op vrije voeten
largely grotendeels, hoofdzakelijk, voornamelijk
lark 1 grap: *for a* ~ voor de gein **2** leeuwerik
larp *live action role playing* larpen
larva larve, larf
larynx strottenhoofd[h]
lascivious wellustig, geil
laser laser: ~ *beams* laserstralen
laser pointer laserpen
¹**lash** (n) **1** zweepkoord[h], zweepeinde[h]

2 zweepslag **3** wimper
²lash (vb) **1** opzwepen, ophitsen: ~ *s.o. into a fury* iem. woedend maken **2** vastsnoeren, (stevig) vastbinden; [shipp] sjorren
³lash (vb) **1** een plotselinge beweging maken (met), slaan; zwiepen [eg of tail] **2** met kracht slaan (tegen), geselen, teisteren; striemen [of rain]; beuken [of waves]
lash out 1 (+ at) (heftig) slaan, schoppen (naar), uithalen (naar), een uitval doen (naar) **2** (+ at, against) uitvallen (tegen) **3** met geld smijten
lass [Scotland] meisje^h
lassie meisje^h
lassitude vermoeidheid, uitputting
¹lasso (n) lasso, werpkoord^h
²lasso (vb) met een lasso vangen
¹last (n) (schoenmakers)leest ‖ *stick to one's* ~ zich bij zijn leest houden
²last (vb) **1** duren, aanhouden **2** meegaan, intact blijven, houdbaar zijn: *his irritation won't* ~ zijn ergernis gaat wel over; ~ *out* a) niet opraken; b) het volhouden **3** toereikend zijn
³last (vb) toereikend zijn voor, voldoende zijn voor
⁴last (adv) **1** als laatste; [in compounds] laatst-: *come in* ~ als laatste binnenkomen; *last-mentioned* laatstgenoemde; ~ *but not least* (als) laatstgenoemde, maar daarom niet minder belangrijk **2** (voor) het laatst, (voor) de laatste keer: *when did you see her* ~? (or: ~ *see her?*) wanneer heb je haar voor het laatst gezien?
⁵last (num) laatste [of a series]; laatstgenoemde: *breathe one's* ~ zijn laatste adem uitblazen; *fight to* (or: *till*) *the* ~ vechten tot het uiterste; *I don't think we have seen the* ~ *of him* ik denk dat we nog wel terugzien ‖ *at (long)* ~ (uit)eindelijk, ten slotte
⁶last (num) laatste [also fig]; vorige, verleden: *at the* ~ *minute* (or: *moment*) op het laatste ogenblik; ~ *night* gister(en)avond, vannacht; ~ *Tuesday* vorige week dinsdag; *the* ~ *but one* de voorlaatste; *the* ~ *few days* de laatste paar dagen ‖ *that's the* ~ *straw* dat doet de deur dicht; *the* ~ *word in cars* het nieuwste snufje op het gebied van auto's; *down to every* ~ *detail* tot in de kleinste details
last-ditch: ~ *effort* (or: *attempt*) laatste wanhopige poging
lasting blijvend, aanhoudend, duurzaam: *a* ~ *solution* een definitieve oplossing
lastly ten slotte, in de laatste plaats, tot slot
last-minute allerlaatst, uiterst
latch klink [of door, gate]: *on the* ~ op de klink [not locked]
latchkey huissleutel
latchkey child sleutelkind^h
latch on to 1 snappen, (kunnen) volgen

2 hangen aan, zich vastklampen aan
¹late (adj) **1** te laat, verlaat, vertraagd: *five minutes* ~ vijf minuten te laat **2** laat, gevorderd: *in the* ~ *afternoon* laat in de middag; *at a* ~ *hour* laat (op de dag), diep in de nacht; *at the* ~st uiterlijk, op zijn laatst **3** recent, van de laatste tijd, nieuw: *her* ~st *album* haar nieuwste album **4** voormalig, vorig **5** (onlangs) overleden, wijlen: *his* ~ *wife* zijn (onlangs) overleden vrouw
²late (adv) **1** te laat, verlaat, vertraagd: *better* ~ *than never* beter laat dan nooit **2** laat, op een laat tijdstip, gevorderd: ~ *in (one's) life* op gevorderde leeftijd ‖ *of* ~ onlangs, kort geleden
lately onlangs, kort geleden: *have you been there* ~? ben jij er/daar de laatste tijd nog geweest?
late-night laat(st), nacht-: ~ *shopping* koopavond
latent latent; verborgen, sluimerend
later later: ~ *on* a) later, naderhand; b) verderop; *not* ~ *than* uiterlijk
lateral zij-, aan, vanaf, naar de zijkant
laters [inform] later, tot ziens
lath 1 tengel(lat), latwerk^h **2** lat
lather (zeep)schuim^h, scheerschuim^h
¹Latin (n) Latijn^h [language]
²Latin (n) Romaan, iem. die een Romaanse taal spreekt
³Latin (adj) Latijns: ~ *America* Latijns-Amerika
Latin-American Latijns-Amerikaans
Latinx [Am] latinx
latitude 1 hemelstreek, luchtstreek, zone **2** (geografische) breedte, poolshoogte **3** speelruimte, (geestelijke) vrijheid
latrine latrine, wc (van kamp/kazerne)
latte koffie verkeerd
latter 1 laatstgenoemde [of two] **2** laatst-(genoemd) [of two]: *the* ~ *part of the year* het tweede halfjaar; *in his* ~ *years* in zijn laatste jaren
lattice raster(werk)^h, vak-, raam-, traliewerk^h, rooster^h: ~ *window* glas-in-loodraam^h
Latvia Letland
¹Latvian (n) Let(lander); Letlandse
²Latvian (adj) Lets, Letlands
laudable prijzenswaardig
¹laugh (n) **1** lach, gelach^h, lachje^h **2** geintje^h, lolletje^h, lachertje^h: *for* ~s voor de lol ‖ *have the last* ~ het laatst lachen
²laugh (vb) **1** lachen: ~ *to o.s.* inwendig lachen **2** in de lach schieten, moeten lachen
³laugh (vb) **1** lachend zeggen **2** belachelijk maken, uitlachen, weglachen: ~ *off* met een grapje afdoen
laughable lachwekkend, belachelijk
laugh at 1 uitlachen, belachelijk maken **2** lachen om **3** maling hebben aan
laughing 1 lachend, vrolijk, opgewekt

2 om te lachen: *no ~ matter* een serieuze zaak, geen gekheid

laughing stock mikpunt^h (van spot) [also of things]

laughter 1 gelach^h: *burst into ~* in lachen uitbarsten, het uitschateren; *roar with ~* bulderen van het lachen **2** plezier^h, pret, lol

¹launch (n) **1** motorsloep **2** rondvaartboot, plezierboot **3** tewaterlating **4** lancering

²launch (vb) (also + out) (energiek) iets (nieuws) beginnen: *~ out into business for o.s.* voor zichzelf beginnen; *~ into* zich storten op

³launch (vb) **1** lanceren, afvuren, (weg)werpen, (weg)smijten **2** te water laten **3** op gang brengen, (doen) beginnen, op touw zetten

launching pad lanceerplatform^h; [fig] springplank

launder 1 wassen (en strijken) **2** witmaken [black money]

launderette wasserette

laundry 1 wasserij, wasinrichting **2** was, wasgoed^h

laundry list waslijst [also fig]; wensenlijst

laurel 1 laurier **2** lauwerkrans, erepalm **3** (-s) lauweren, roem, eer: *rest on one's ~s* op zijn lauweren rusten

lava lava

lavatory 1 toilet^h, wc, openbaar toilet^h **2** toiletpot

lavender lavendel

¹lavish (adj) **1** kwistig, gul, verkwistend **2** overvloedig, overdadig: *~ praise* overdadige lof

²lavish (vb) kwistig schenken

law 1 wet, recht^h, rechtsregel, wetmatigheid, natuurwet: *~ and order* orde en gezag, recht en orde; *be a ~ unto o.s.* zijn eigen wetten stellen, eigenmachtig optreden **2** wet(geving), rechtsstelsel^h **3** rechten(studie), rechtsgeleerdheid **4** recht^h, rechtsgang, justitie, gerecht^h: *go to ~* naar de rechter stappen, een proces aanspannen **5** (gedrags)code, (spel)regel, norm, beroepscode, sportcode, kunstcode **6** [inform] politie, sterke arm ‖ *take the ~ into one's own hands* het recht in eigen hand nemen; *~ of the jungle* recht van de sterkste; *lay down the ~* a) de wet voorschrijven; b) snauwen, blaffen

law-abiding gezagsgetrouw, gehoorzaam aan de wet

law centre wetswinkel

law court rechtscollege^h, rechtbank, gerechtshof^h

lawful 1 wettig, legaal, rechtsgeldig **2** rechtmatig, geoorloofd, legitiem

lawless 1 wetteloos **2** onstuimig, losbandig, wild

lawmaker wetgever

lawn 1 gazon^h, grasveld^h **2** batist^h, linnen^h

lawnmower grasmaaier, grasmaaimachine

lawsuit proces^h, (rechts)geding^h, (rechts)zaak

lawyer 1 advocaat, (juridisch) raadsman **2** jurist, rechtsgeleerde

lax laks, nalatig: *~ about keeping appointments* laks in het nakomen van afspraken

¹laxative (n) laxeermiddel^h

²laxative (adj) laxerend

¹lay (n) ligging, positie: [Am] *the ~ of the land* de natuurlijke ligging van het gebied; [fig also] de stand van zaken

²lay (adj) leken-, niet-priesterlijk, wereldlijk

³lay (vb) wedden ‖ *~ into* ervan langs geven [also fig]

⁴lay (vb) **1** leggen, neerleggen (= neervlijen) **2** installeren, leggen, plaatsen, zetten; dekken [table]: *the scene of the story is laid in Oxford* het verhaal speelt zich af in Oxford **3** (eieren) leggen **4** in een bepaalde toestand brengen/leggen/zetten, brengen: *~ bare* blootleggen; [fig] aan het licht brengen; *~ low* a) tegen de grond werken; b) (vernietigend) verslaan; c) [fig] vellen [eg of disease]; *~ waste* verwoesten **5** riskeren, op het spel zetten, (ver)wedden: *~ a wager* een weddenschap aangaan ‖ *~ in* a) inslaan; b) opslaan

layabout nietsnut

lay about wild (om zich heen) slaan, te lijf gaan; ervan langs geven [also fig]

lay aside 1 opzijleggen, sparen, wegleggen, bewaren **2** laten varen; opgeven [plan, hope]

lay down 1 neerleggen: *~ one's tools* staken **2** vastleggen, voorschrijven, bepalen: *~ a procedure* een procedure uitstippelen **3** opgeven, laten varen; neerleggen [office]

layer 1 laag: *~ of sand* laag zand **2** legger [chicken]; leghen

layman leek, amateur, niet-deskundige

¹lay off (vb) stoppen, ophouden, opgeven: *~, will you?* laat dat, ja?

²lay off (vb) (tijdelijk) ontslaan, op non-actief stellen, laten afvloeien

lay-off 1 (tijdelijk) ontslag **2** (periode van) tijdelijke werkloosheid

lay on zorgen voor, regelen, organiseren: *~ a car* een auto regelen ‖ *lay it on (thick)* a) (sterk/flink) overdrijven, het er dik opleggen; b) slijmen

layout indeling, ontwerp^h, bouwplan^h

lay out 1 uitgeven, investeren **2** uitspreiden, etaleren; klaarleggen [clothing] **3** afleggen; opbaren [corpse]

lay up 1 opslaan, een voorraad aanleggen van, inslaan **2** uit de roulatie halen, het bed doen houden: *he was laid up with the flu* hij moest in bed blijven met de griep

laze luieren, niksen: *~ about (or: around)*

aanklooien, rondlummelen

lazy 1 lui **2** loom, drukkend: *~ day* lome dag

lazybones [inform] luiwammes

lb *libra* lb., Engels pond, 454 gram

LDR *long distance relationship* langeaf-standsrelatie

L-driver *learner-driver* leerling-automobilist

¹**lead** (n) **1** lood^h **2** (diep)lood^h, peillood^h, paslood^h **3** (potlood)stift, grafiet^h ‖ *swing the ~* zich drukken, lijntrekken

²**lead** (n) **1** leiding, het leiden: *take the ~* de leiding nemen, het initiatief nemen **2** aanknopingspunt^h, aanwijzing, suggestie: *give s.o. a ~* iem. op weg helpen, iem. een hint geven **3** leiding, koppositie, eerste plaats **4** voorsprong **5** hoofdrol; [by extension] hoofdrolspeler **6** (honden)lijn, hondenriem

³**lead** (vb) **1** (weg)leiden; (mee)voeren [by the hand, on a rope etc] **2** brengen tot, overhalen, aanzetten tot: *~ s.o. to think that* iem. in de waan brengen dat **3** leiden [existence, life]: *~ a life of luxury* een weelderig leven leiden ‖ *~ away* meeslepen, blind(elings) doen volgen; *~ (s.o.) on* a) (iem.) overhalen (tot); b) iem. iets wijsmaken; *~ up to* a) (uiteindelijk) resulteren in; b) een inleiding (*or:* voorbereiding) zijn tot

⁴**lead** (vb) **1** leiden, voorgaan, de weg wijzen, begeleiden **2** aan de leiding gaan, aanvoeren, op kop liggen; [sport] voorstaan; een voorsprong hebben op; [fig] de toon aangeven: *Liverpool ~s with sixty **points*** Liverpool staat bovenaan met zestig punten **3** voeren; leiden [of road, route]; [fig] resulteren in: *~ to disaster* tot rampspoed leiden **4** leiden, aanvoeren, het bevel hebben (over) ‖ *~ off (with)* beginnen (met)

leaden 1 loden, van lood **2** loodgrijs, loodkleurig

leader 1 leider, aanvoerder, gids **2** eerste man, partijleider, voorman; [mus] concertmeester; eerste violist; [Am; mus] dirigent **3** [journalism] hoofdcommentaar^h

leaderboard [sport] scorebord^h

leadership 1 leiderschap^h **2** leiding: *the ~ are* (or: *is*) *divided* de leiding is verdeeld

lead-in inleiding

leading 1 voornaam(st), hoofd-, toonaangevend: *~ actor* hoofdrolspeler **2** leidend, (be)sturend ‖ *~ question* suggestieve vraag

leading-edge allermodernst; allernieuwst

lead singer leadzanger

lead time 1 [techn] aanlooptijd **2** [com] levertijd **3** [planning] doorlooptijd

¹**leaf** (n) **1** blad^h [of tree, plant]; (bloem)blad^h **2** blad^h, bladzijde [of book]: [fig] *turn over a new ~* met een schone lei beginnen, een nieuwe weg inslaan; [fig] *take a ~ out of s.o.'s book* een voorbeeld nemen aan iem., iem. navolgen **3** uitklapbare klep; insteekblad^h,

uitschuifblad^h [of table] **4** [as second part in compounds] folie^+h; blad- [of metal]: *gold ~* bladgoud^h

²**leaf** (vb) bladeren: *~ through* (snel) doorbladeren

leaflet 1 blaadje^h **2** foldertje^h, brochure

league 1 [sport] bond, competitie, divisie **2** klasse, niveau^h: *she's not in my ~* ik kan niet aan haar tippen ‖ *in ~ with* in samenwerking met, samenspannend met

¹**leak** (n) **1** lek^h, lekkage, ongewenste ontsnapping: *spring a ~* lek raken; [inform] *take a ~* pissen **2** uitlekking; ruchtbaarheid [of secret data]

²**leak** (vb) lekken, lek zijn, (lekkend) doorlaten; [information] onthullen: *~ information (out) to the papers* gegevens aan de kranten doorspelen; [fig] *~ out* (laten) uitlekken, (onbedoeld) bekend worden

leakage lekkage, lek^h

¹**lean** (adj) mager, schraal, karig

²**lean** (vb) **1** leunen **2** steunen, staan (tegen) **3** zich buigen: *~ down* zich bukken; *~ over to s.o.* zich naar iem. overbuigen **4** hellen, scheef staan ‖ *~ over backwards* zich in (de gekste) bochten wringen, alle mogelijke moeite doen; *~ on* onder druk zetten; *~ to* (or: *towards*) a) neigen tot; b) prefereren; *~ (up)on* steunen op, afhankelijk zijn van

³**lean** (vb) **1** laten steunen, zetten (tegen) **2** buigen, doen hellen: *the Leaning **Tower** of Pisa* de scheve toren van Pisa; *~ one's head back* zijn hoofd achteroverbuigen **3** mager, schraal **4** arm(zalig), weinig opleverend: *~ years* magere jaren

lean-to aanbouw, afdak^h

¹**leap** (n) sprong, gesprongen afstand, plotselinge toename, hindernis, obstakel^h ‖ *by ~s and bounds* halsoverkop; [fig] *a ~ in the dark* een sprong in het duister

²**leap** (vb) (op)springen, vooruitspringen: *~ for joy* dansen van vreugde ‖ *her heart ~ed up* haar hart maakte een sprongetje; *~ at* met beide handen aangrijpen [chance etc]

¹**leapfrog** (n) haasje-over^h, bokspringen^h

²**leapfrog** (vb) sprongsgewijs vorderen

³**leapfrog** (vb) haasje-over spelen, bokspringen

leap year schrikkeljaar^h

¹**learn** (vb) **1** leren, studeren: *~ how to play the piano* piano leren spelen; *~ from experience* door ervaring wijzer worden **2** horen, vernemen, te weten komen: *~ about* (or: *of*) *sth. from the papers* iets uit de krant te weten komen

²**learn** (vb) **1** leren, zich eigen maken, besturen **2** vernemen, horen van, ontdekken: *I ~t it from the papers* ik heb het uit de krant

learned 1 onderlegd, ontwikkeld, geleerd **2** belezen **3** wetenschappelijk, academisch: *~ periodical* wetenschappelijk tijdschrift

learner 1 leerling **2** beginner, beginneling **3** leerling-automobilist

learner's permit [Am] voorlopig rijbewijs

learning 1 studie; onderwijsʰ, het leren **2** kennis; geleerdheid

¹lease (n) **1** pacht, pachtcontractʰ **2** (ver)huur, (ver)huurcontractʰ, (ver)huurovereenkomst **3** pachttermijn, huurtermijn, pachtduur ‖ *a (new) ~ of life* een nieuw leven, een tweede kans

²lease (vb) **1** (ver)pachten **2** (ver)huren, leasen

leaseholder 1 pachter **2** huurder

leash (honden)lijn, riem: *always keep Sarah on the ~* houd Sarah altijd aangelijnd ‖ *strain at the ~* trappelen van ongeduld

¹least (adj) kleinste, geringste: *I haven't the ~ idea* ik heb er geen flauw idee van; *the line of ~ resistance* de weg van de minste weerstand

²least (adv) minst(e): *the ~ popular leader* de minst populaire leider; *to say the ~ (of it)* om het zachtjes uit te drukken; *at (the) ~ seven* ten minste zeven; *it didn't bother me in the ~* het stoorde mij helemaal niet

¹leather (n) leerʰ

²leather (adj) leren, van leer

¹leave (n) **1** toestemming, permissie, verlofʰ: *~ of absence* verlofʰ, vakantie; *by* (or: *with) your ~* met uw permissie **2** verlofʰ, vrij, vakantie: *on ~* met verlof ‖ *take one's ~ of s.o.* a) iem. gedag zeggen; b) afscheid nemen van iem.

²leave (vb) **1** laten liggen, laten staan, achterlaten, vergeten: *~ about* (or: *around) laten* (rond)slingeren **2** laten staan, onaangeroerd laten: *~ (sth.) undone* (iets) ongedaan laten; *be left with* (blijven) zitten met, opgescheept worden met **3** overlaten, doen overblijven: *four from six ~s two* zes min vier is twee **4** afgeven, achterlaten: *~ a note for s.o.* een boodschap voor iem. achterlaten **5** toevertrouwen, in bewaring geven **6** nalaten, achterlaten ‖ *~ it at that* het er (maar) bij laten; *~ (people) to themselves* zich niet bemoeien met (mensen)

³leave (vb) weggaan (bij/van), verlaten, vertrekken (bij/van): *it's time for you to ~, it's time you left* het wordt tijd dat je weggaat

leave behind 1 thuis laten, vertrekken zonder, vergeten (mee te nemen) **2** (alleen) achterlaten, in de steek laten: *John was left behind* John werd (alleen) achtergelaten **3** achter zich laten, passeren

¹leave off (vb) ophouden, stoppen

²leave off (vb) **1** uit laten [not wear any longer]; niet meer dragen **2** staken, stoppen met

leave out 1 buiten laten (liggen/staan) **2** weglaten, overslaan, niet opnemen **3** buitensluiten: *feel left out* zich buitengesloten

voelen

leavings overschotʰ, overblijfselen, etensresten

¹Lebanese (n) Libanees, Libanese

²Lebanese (adj) Libanees

Lebanon Libanon

lecherous 1 wellustig, liederlijk **2** geil, hitsig

¹lecture (n) **1** lezing, verhandeling, voordracht **2** (hoor)collegeʰ, (openbare) les **3** preek, berisping: *read s.o. a ~* iem. de les lezen

²lecture (vb) de les lezen

³lecture (vb) **1** spreken (voor), lezing(en) geven (voor) **2** college geven (aan), onderrichten

lecturer 1 spreker, houder van lezing **2** docent [in higher educ]

LED *light-emitting diode* led

ledge richel, (uitstekende) rand

ledger [bookkeeping] grootboekʰ; [Am also] registerʰ

lee 1 luwte, beschutting, beschutte plek **2** [shipp] lij(zijde)

leech bloedzuiger; [fig] uitzuiger; parasiet ‖ *cling* (or: *stick) like a ~ (to)* niet weg te branden zijn (bij)

leek prei

¹leer (n) **1** wellustige blik **2** wrede grijns, vuile blik

²leer (vb) **1** loeren, grijnzen **2** verlekkerd kijken, wellustige blikken werpen

lees droesem; bezinkselʰ

leeway (extra) speelruimte, speling; [Am] veiligheidsmarge

¹left (n) **1** linkerkant, linksʰ, linkerhand: *keep to the ~* links (aan)houden; *turn to the ~* links afslaan **2** [pol] linksʰ, de progressieven

²left (adj) **1** linker, links **2** [pol] links

³left (adv) **1** links, aan de linkerzijde **2** naar links, linksaf, linksom: *turn ~* links afslaan

left-back linksachter

left-hand links, linker: *~ bend* bocht naar links; *~ drive* linkse besturing [of car]

left-handed 1 links(handig) **2** links, onhandig **3** dubbelzinnig, dubieus: *~ compliment* twijfelachtig compliment

left luggage office bagagedepotʰ

leftover over(gebleven); resterend, ongebruikt

leftovers 1 kliekjes, (etens)restjes **2** kliekjesmaaltijd

left-wing links; progressief

lefty [inform] **1** [pol] lidʰ van de linkervleugel **2** [Am] linkshandige

leg 1 beenʰ **2** poot [of animal]; achterpoot **3** beengedeelteʰ van kledingstuk; beenʰ [of stocking]; (broeks)pijp **4** poot [of furniture etc] **5** gedeelteʰ (van groter geheelʰ); etappe [of trip, competition etc]; estafetteonderdeelʰ; manche [of competition] **6** bout [of calf, lam]: ~ of **mutton** schapenbout **7** schenkel: ~ of **veal** kalfsschenkel ‖ **give** s.o. a ~ up iem. een voetje geven; [fig] iem. een handje helpen; **pull** s.o.'s ~ iem. voor de gek houden; **run** s.o. off his ~s **a)** iem. geen seconde met rust laten; **b)** iem. uitputten; **shake** a ~ opschieten; not **have** a ~ to stand on geen poot hebben om op te staan; **stretch** one's ~s de benen strekken [by means of a walk]; **walk** s.o. off his ~s iem. laten lopen tot hij erbij neervalt

legacy erfenis [also fig]; nalatenschap

legal 1 wettig, legaal, rechtsgeldig: ~ **tender** wettig betaalmiddel **2** wettelijk, volgens de wet **3** juridisch: (free) ~ **aid** kosteloze rechtsbijstand

legality rechtsgeldigheid, rechtmatigheid

legalize legaliseren, wettig maken

legend 1 (volks)overlevering, legende(n) **2** onderschrift[h], opschrift[h]

legendary legendarisch [also fig]

legging 1 beenkap, beenbeschermer, scheenbeschermer **2** legging

legible leesbaar

¹legion (n) legioen[h]

²legion (adj) talrijk: **books** on this subject are ~ er zijn veel/legio boeken over dit onderwerp

¹legionary (n) legionair, legioensoldaat

²legionary (adj) legioens-

legislation wetgeving

legislative 1 wetgevend, bevoegd tot wetgeving **2** wets-, m.b.t. wetgeving

legislator wetgever, lid[h] van een wetgevend lichaam

legit legitimate wettig, legaal, oké

legitimacy 1 wettigheid; rechtmatigheid, legitimiteit **2** geldigheid

legitimate 1 wettig, rechtmatig, legitiem **2** geldig: ~ **purpose** gerechtvaardigd doel

legitimize 1 wettig (or: geldig) maken/ verklaren; autoriseren **2** [fig] legitimeren, rechtvaardigen

legless [inform] stomdronken

leg-pull plagerij, beetnemerij

leg-up steuntje[h], duwtje[h]; zetje[h] [in the right direction]

¹leisure (n) (vrije) tijd, gelegenheid: at ~ vrij, zonder verplichtingen, ontspannen; at one's ~ in zijn vrije tijd, als men tijd heeft, als het schikt

²leisure (adj) **1** vrij: ~ **hours** (or: **time**) vrije uren (or: tijd) **2** vrijetijds-

leisure centre [roughly] recreatiecentrum[h], [roughly] sportcentrum[h]

leisurely zonder haast (te maken), ontspannen, op zijn gemak

leisurewear vrijetijdskleding

lemon 1 citroen **2** [inform] idioot **3** miskoop, maandagochtendexemplaar[h]

lemonade (citroen)limonade

lemon squash 1 citroensiroop **2** citroenlimonade

lemur maki

lend 1 (uit)lenen: ~ s.o. a **book** iem. een boek lenen **2** verlenen, schenken, geven: ~ **assistance** to steun verlenen aan ‖ ~ **itself** to **a)** zich (goed) lenen tot; **b)** vatbaar zijn voor

lender geldschieter

length 1 lengte, omvang, (lichaams)lengte, grootte, gestalte: ~ of a **book** omvang van een boek; three centimetres **in** ~ drie centimeter lang **2** lengte, duur: for the ~ of our **stay** voor de duur van ons verblijf **3** eind(je)[h], stuk(je)[h]: ~ of **rope** eindje touw ‖ go to con**siderable** (or: **great**) ~s erg z'n best doen, zich veel moeite getroosten; at ~ **a)** langdurig; **b)** uitvoerig; **c)** ten slotte; go to all ~s (or: **any** ~(s)) er alles voor over hebben; at some ~ uitvoerig

lengthen verlengen, langer maken: ~ a **dress** een jurk langer maken

lengthy 1 langdurig **2** langdradig

lenience toegevendheid, mildheid

lenient 1 tolerant, toegevend **2** mild, genadig: ~ **verdict** mild vonnis

lens lens

lentil linze

Leo [astrology] (de) Leeuw

leopard luipaard, panter

leotard tricot[h], balletpakje[h], gympakje[h]

leper lepralijder, melaatse

leprosy lepra, melaatsheid

leprous melaats

¹lesbian (n) lesbienne

²lesbian (adj) lesbisch

lesion verwonding; letsel[h]

¹less (adj) kleiner: **no** ~ a person than niemand minder dan

²less (adv) minder: ~ **money** minder geld; he couldn't **care** ~ het kon hem geen barst schelen; **more** or ~ min of meer ‖ **none** the ~ niettemin

³less (prep) zonder, verminderd met, op ... na: a **year** ~ one month een jaar min één maand

lessen (ver)minderen, (doen) afnemen

lesser minder, kleiner, onbelangrijker: to a ~ **extent** in mindere mate

lesson 1 les, leerzame ervaring: let this be a ~ **to** you laat dit een les voor je zijn **2** leerstof **3** lesuur[h] **4** Schriftlezing, Bijbellezing ‖ **teach** s.o. a ~ iem. een lesje leren

lest (voor het geval/uit vrees) dat, opdat niet: she was afraid ~ he leave her ze vreesde dat hij haar zou verlaten

¹let (n) **1** [sport, esp tennis] let(bal), overgespeelde bal **2** beletsel[h], belemmering: without ~ or **hindrance** vrijelijk, zonder (enig) beletsel

²let (vb) **1** verhuurd worden **2** uitbesteed worden ‖ [inform] ~ **on** (about, that) verklappen, doorvertellen (dat); [inform] ~ **on** *(that)* net doen (alsof)

³let (vb) **1** laten, toestaan: ~ *sth.* be **known** iets laten weten; *please,* ~ *me buy this round* laat mij nu toch dit rondje aanbieden **2** laten: ~ *me* **hear** (or: **know**) hou me op de hoogte; ~ *me* **see** eens kijken; ~*'s not talk about it* laten we er niet over praten **3** [maths] stellen, geven: ~ *x be y+z* stel x is y+z, gegeven x is y+z **4** verhuren, in huur geven **5** aanbesteden || ~ *s.o.* **be** iem. met rust laten; ~ **fly** *(at)* uithalen (naar); ~ *s.o.* **get on** *with it* iem. zijn gang laten gaan; ~ **go** *(of)* loslaten, uit zijn hoofd zetten, ophouden (over); ~ *o.s.* **go** zich laten gaan; ~ *s.o.* **have it** iem. de volle laag geven, iem. ervan langs geven; ~ **slip** **a)** laten uitlekken; **b)** missen, voorbij laten gaan [chance]; ~ **through** laten passeren, doorlaten; ~ **into** **a)** binnenlaten in, toelaten tot; **b)** in vertrouwen nemen over, vertellen

let down 1 neerlaten, laten zakken, laten vallen **2** teleurstellen, in de steek laten: *don't let me down* laat me niet in de steek **3** leeg laten lopen [tyre]

let-down afknapper, teleurstelling

lethal dodelijk, fataal

lethargy lethargie, (s)loomheid, loomheid, sloomheid

let in binnenlaten, toelaten: *let o.s. in* zich toegang verschaffen || ~ **for** opschepen met, laten opdraaien voor; *let o.s. in* **for** zich op de hals halen; ~ **on a)** in vertrouwen nemen over, inlichten over; **b)** laten meedoen met

let off 1 afvuren, afsteken, af laten gaan: ~ **fireworks** vuurwerk afsteken **2** excuseren, vrijuit laten gaan, vrijstellen van: *the judge let him off* de rechter liet hem vrijuit gaan; *be* ~ **with** er afkomen met

¹let out (vb) **1** uithalen, van leer trekken: ~ **at** *s.o.* naar iem. uithalen, tegen iem. uitvaren **2** dichtgaan, sluiten; uitgaan [of school etc]

²let out (vb) **1** uitnemen, wijder maken [clothing] **2** laten uitlekken, verklappen, openbaar maken, bekendmaken **3** laten ontsnappen, vrijlaten, laten gaan: *let the air out of a balloon* een ballon laten leeglopen **4** geven [scream] **5** de laan uitsturen, ontslaan, (van school) sturen

letter 1 letter: *to the* ~ naar de letter, tot in detail, tot de kleinste bijzonderheden **2** brief: ~ *to the* **editor** ingezonden brief; ~ *of* **introduction** aanbevelingsbrief; **covering** ~ begeleidend schrijven; **by** ~ per brief, schriftelijk **3** (-s) letteren, literatuur

letter bomb bombrief

letterbox brievenbus

letterhead 1 briefhoofd[h] **2** postpapier[h] met briefhoofd

lettuce sla, salade: *a* **head** *of* ~ een krop sla

let up 1 minder worden, afnemen, gaan liggen: *I hope the wind's going to* ~ *a little* ik hoop dat de wind wat gaat liggen **2** het kalm aan doen, gas terugnemen **3** pauzeren, ophouden (met werken)

leukaemia leukemie, bloedkanker

levee [Am] (rivier)dijk, waterkering

¹level (n) **1** peil[h], niveau[h], hoogte, natuurlijke plaats: ~ *of* **achievement** (or: **production**) prestatiepeil, productiepeil[h]; **find** *one's* ~ plaats vinden **2** vlak[h], (vlak) oppervlak[h], vlakte, vlak land[h] **3** horizontaal **4** [Am] waterpas[+h]; uitbreng] **on** *the* ~ rechtdoorzee, goudeerlijk **5** niveau[h]: *at* **ministerial** ~ op ministerieel niveau

²level (adj) **1** waterpas, horizontaal **2** vlak, egaal, zonder oneffenheden: ~ **teaspoon** afgestreken theelepel **3** (op) gelijk(e hoogte), even hoog: ~ **crossing** gelijkvloerse kruising, overweg; **draw** ~ **with** op gelijke hoogte komen met **4** gelijkmatig, evenwichtig, regelmatig: *in a* ~ **voice** zonder stemverheffing **5** bedaard, kalm: *keep a* ~ **head** zijn verstand erbij houden **6** gelijkwaardig, op gelijke voet **7** strak [of look]; doordringend: *give s.o. a* ~ **look** iem. strak aankijken || (do) *one's* ~ **best** zijn uiterste best (doen)

³level (vb) **1** egaliseren, effenen **2** nivelleren, op gelijk niveau brengen; opheffen [distinction]: ~ **down** tot hetzelfde niveau omlaag brengen; ~ **up** tot hetzelfde niveau omhoog brengen

⁴level (vb) (horizontaal) richten, aanleggen, afvuren; uitbrengen [criticism etc]: ~ *a charge* **against** (or: *at*) *s.o.* een beschuldiging tegen iem. uitbrengen

⁵level (adv) vlak, horizontaal, waterpas

level-headed nuchter, afgewogen

¹lever (n) **1** hefboom, koevoet, breekijzer[h] **2** werktuig[h] [only fig]; pressiemiddel[h], instrument[h] **3** hendel, handgreep, handvat[h]

²lever (vb) opheffen d.m.v. hefboom, tillen, (los)wrikken: ~ *s.o.* **out of** *his job* iem. wegmanoeuvreren

leverage 1 hefboomwerking, hefboomkracht **2** macht, invloed, pressie: *even small groups can* **exert** *enormous political* ~ zelfs kleine groeperingen kunnen enorme politieke pressie uitoefenen

levitate zweven; levitatie ondergaan

levity lichtzinnigheid, lichtvaardigheid, oneerbiedigheid

¹levy (n) heffing, vordering, belastingheffing: **make** *a* ~ *on* een heffing instellen op

²levy (vb) **1** heffen, opleggen: ~ *a* **fine** een boete opleggen **2** vorderen, innen **3** (aan)werven, rekruteren

lewd 1 wellustig **2** obsceen, schunnig

lexicography lexicografie, het samenstellen van woordenboeken

lexicology lexicologie [study of words]

life

lexicon woordenboek[h]
LGBT *lesbian, gay, bisexual, transgender* lhbt'er
LGBTQ+ *lesbian, gay, bisexual, trans, queer and other* lgbtq+, lhbtq+ *(lesbienne, homo, biseksueel, transgender, queer en overige)*
liability 1 (wettelijke ver)plicht(ing): ~ *to pay taxes* belastingplichtigheid **2** (liabilities) passiva, lasten, schulden **3** blok[h] aan het been
liability insurance aansprakelijkheidsverzekering
liable 1 (wettelijk) verplicht: ~ *for tax* belastingplichtig **2** (+ for) aansprakelijk (voor), (wettelijk) verantwoordelijk (voor) **3** vatbaar, vaak lijdend: ~ *to colds* vaak verkouden **4** de neiging hebbend, het risico lopend: *it isn't* ~ *to happen* dat zal niet zo gauw gebeuren
liaison 1 liaison [also mil]; verbinding; [by extension] samenwerkingsverband[h] **2** buitenechtelijke verhouding
liana liaan
liar leugenaar
¹libel (n) **1** smaadschrift[h] **2** smaad, laster, belastering
²libel (vb) **1** belasteren, valselijk beschuldigen **2** een smaadschrift publiceren tegen
¹liberal (n) liberaal, ruimdenkend iem.
²liberal (adj) **1** ruimdenkend, onbevooroordeeld, liberaal **2** royaal, vrijgevig **3** overvloedig, welvoorzien ‖ ~ *arts* vrije kunsten
liberalism liberalisme[h]
liberate bevrijden
liberated bevrijd; geëmancipeerd [socially, sexually]
liberation bevrijding, vrijlating
Liberia Liberia
¹Liberian (n) Liberiaan(se)
²Liberian (adj) Liberiaans
libero [socc] vrije verdediger
libertarian vrijheidsgezinde
libertine 1 losbol **2** libertijn
liberty 1 vrijheid, onafhankelijkheid: ~ *of conscience* gewetensvrijheid; *at* ~ **a)** in vrijheid, op vrije voeten; **b)** vrij, onbezet; **c)** ongebruikt, werkloos **2** vrijheid, vrijmoedigheid: *take liberties with s.o.* zich vrijheden veroorloven tegen iem. ‖ *you're at* ~ *to* het staat je vrij (om) te
Libra [astrology] (de) Weegschaal
librarian bibliothecaris
library bibliotheek, (openbare) leeszaal; uitleenverzameling [of films, CDs etc]
Libya Libië
¹Libyan (n) Libiër, Libische
²Libyan (adj) Libisch
licence 1 vergunning, licentie, verlof[h] **2** verlof[h], permissie, toestemming **3** vrijheid **4** losbandigheid, ongebondenheid **5** (artistieke) vrijheid

license 1 (een) vergunning verlenen (aan): ~*d to sell* **tobacco** met tabaksvergunning; ~*d* **victualler** caféhouder met drankvergunning **2** (officieel) toestemming geven voor
licensee vergunninghouder; licentiehouder [of liquor licence, tobacco licence]
license plate [Am] nummerbord[h]
licentious wellustig
lichen korstmos[h], licheen
¹lick (n) **1** lik, veeg; [by extension] ietsje[h]; klein beetje[h]: *a* ~ *of paint* een kwastje (verf) **2** (vliegende) vaart: *(at) full* ~, *at a* **great** ~ met een noodgang **3** [mus] loopje[h]: *guitar* ~ gitaarloopje[h]
²lick (vb) **1** likken **2** [inform] een pak slaag geven [also fig]; ervan langs geven, overwinnen: ~ *a* **problem** een probleem uit de wereld helpen
³lick (vb) lekken; (licht) spelen (langs) [of waves, flames]: *the* **flames** ~*ed (at) the walls* de vlammen lekten (aan) de muren
licking pak[h] rammel: *the team got a* ~ het team werd ingemaakt
lid 1 deksel[+h], klep **2** (oog)lid[h] ‖ *take the* ~ *off* onthullingen doen; *that* **puts** *the* ~ *on* dat doet de deur dicht
¹lie (n) **1** leugen: *tell a* ~ liegen **2** ligging, situering, positie: *the* ~ *of the land* de natuurlijke ligging van het gebied; [fig] de stand van zaken ‖ *give the* ~ *to* weerleggen
²lie (vb) liegen, jokken
³lie (vb) **1** (plat/uitgestrekt/vlak) liggen, rusten **2** (begraven) liggen, rusten: *here* ~*s …* hier ligt … **3** gaan liggen, zich neerleggen **4** zich bevinden [in a place, situation]; liggen, gelegen zijn: ~ **fallow** braak liggen; *my sympathy* ~*s with …* mijn medeleven gaat uit naar … ‖ *I don't know what* ~*s in store* **for** *me* ik weet niet wat me te wachten staat
lie about 1 luieren, niksen **2** (slordig) in het rond liggen; rondslingeren [of objects]
Liechtenstein Liechtenstein
Liechtensteiner Liechtensteiner, Liechtensteinse
lie down (gaan) liggen: [fig] *we won't* **take** *this lying down* we laten dit niet over onze kant gaan
lie-down [inform] dutje[h]
liege 1 leenheer **2** leenman, vazal
lie in [inform] uitslapen, lang in bed blijven liggen
lie over overstaan, blijven liggen, uitgesteld worden: *let sth.* ~ iets uitstellen
lieu: *in* ~ *of* in plaats van
lie up 1 zich schuilhouden, onderduiken **2** het bed houden, platliggen
lieutenant [mil] luitenant
lie with zijn aan, de verantwoordelijkheid zijn van, afhangen van: *the* **choice** *lies with her* de keuze is aan haar
life 1 levend wezen[h], leven[h]: *several lives*

*were **lost** verscheidene mensen kwamen om het leven; **human** lives mensenlevens **2** leven[h], bestaan[h], levendigheid, bedrijvigheid, levensduur, levensbeschrijving: a **matter** of ~ and death een zaak van leven of dood; make ~ **easy** niet moeilijk doen; you (can) **bet** your ~ nou en of!, wat dacht je!; **bring** to ~ (weer) bijbrengen; [fig] tot leven wekken; **come** to ~ **a)** bijkomen, tot leven komen; **b)** [fig] geïnteresseerd raken; **save** s.o.'s ~ iemands leven redden; **take** one's (own) ~ zelfmoord plegen; **for** ~ voor het leven, levenslang; **for** the ~ of me I couldn't remember it al sla je me dood, ik weet het echt niet meer; this is the ~! dit noem ik nog eens leven! **3** levenslang(e gevangenisstraf) || **take** one's ~ in one's (own) hands zijn leven in de waagschaal stellen; the ~ (and soul) of the **party** de gangmaker van het feest; **start** ~ zijn carrière beginnen; not **on** your ~ nooit van zijn leven*

li**febelt** redding(s)gordel

li**febuoy** redding(s)boei

life-course savings scheme levensloopregeling

li**feguard 1** badmeester, strandmeester **2** lijfwacht

li**fe hack** lifehack, slimme vondst

li**fe insurance** levensverzekering

li**fe jacket** redding(s)vest[h]

li**feless** levenloos; dood; [fig] futloos, lusteloos

li**feline 1** redding(s)lijn **2** vitale verbindingslijn; navelstreng [fig]

li**felong** levenslang; voor het leven

li**fe preserver** [Am] reddingsboei, reddingsvest[h]

li**fer** [inform] tot levenslang veroordeelde

li**fe raft** reddingsvlot[h]

li**fesaver 1** levensreddend middel[h] **2** [inform] redder in de nood

li**fespan** (potentiële) levensduur

li**festyle** levensstijl

li**festyle dise**ase welvaartsziekte

li**fetime** levensduur, mensenleven[h]: the **chance** of a ~ een unieke kans

[1]**lift** (n) **1** lift **2** lift, gratis (auto)rit **3** (ver)heffing

[2]**lift** (vb) **1** (op)stijgen, opgaan, opkomen, omhooggaan, omhoogkomen; ~ **off** opstijgen, starten **2** optrekken [of mist etc]

[3]**lift** (vb) **1** optillen, optrekken, ophijsen: not ~ a **hand** (or: **finger**) geen hand (or: vinger) uitsteken **2** opheffen, afschaffen: ~ a **block-ade** een blokkade opheffen **3** verheffen, op een hoger plan brengen: this news will ~ his **spirits** dit nieuws zal hem opbeuren **4** rooien, uit de grond halen **5** verheffen, luider doen klinken: ~ **up** one's voice zijn stem verheffen

li**ft-off** lancering

li**gament** gewrichtsband

[1]**light** (n) **1** licht[h], verlichting, openbaarheid: **bring** (or: **come**) to ~ aan het licht brengen (or: komen); **reversing** ~ achteruitrijlicht; see the ~ het licht zien, tot inzicht komen; **shed** (or: **throw**) ~ (up)on licht werpen op, klaarheid brengen in **2** vuurtje[h], vlammetje[h]: can you **give** me a ~, please? heeft u misschien een vuurtje voor me? || **set** (a) ~ to sth. iets in de fik steken; see the ~ at the **end** of the tunnel licht in de duisternis zien; a **shining** ~ een lichtend voorbeeld; **in** (the) ~ **of** this statement gezien deze verklaring

[2]**light** (adj) **1** licht, niet zwaar: ~ **clothing** lichte kleding; ~ **food** licht (verteerbaar) voedsel; light; dieetproducten; ~ of **heart** licht-, luchthartig; [sport] ~ **heavyweight** halfzwaargewicht[+h]; ~ **opera** operette; make ~ **work** of zijn hand niet omdraaien voor; **make** ~ of niet zwaar tillen aan **2** licht, verlicht, helder

[3]**light** (vb) **1** ontbranden, vlam vatten **2** aan gaan; gaan branden [of lamp etc] **3** opklaren; oplichten [also of face, eyes]

[4]**light** (vb) **1** aansteken: ~ a **fire** (or: **lamp**) een vuur (or: lamp) aansteken **2** verlichten, beschijnen: ~ed (or: **lit**) **by** electricity elektrisch verlicht

[5]**light** (adv) licht: **sleep** ~ licht slapen; **travel** ~ weinig bagage bij zich hebben

light-a**rmed** lichtgewapend

li**ght bulb** (gloei)lamp

[1]**l**i**ghten** (vb) **1** lichter worden, afnemen in gewicht **2** opleven, opfleuren **3** ophelderen, opklaren **4** klaren, dagen **5** bliksemen, (weer)lichten

[2]**l**i**ghten** (vb) **1** verlichten, ontlasten; [fig] opbeuren **2** verlichten, verhelderen

li**ghter** aansteker

light-hea**ded** licht-, warhoofdig

light-hea**rted** luchthartig

li**ghthouse** vuurtoren

li**ghting** verlichting

li**ghtly 1** licht(jes), een ietsje **2** licht(jes), gemakkelijk **3** luchtig, lichtvaardig || ~ **come**, ~ **go** zo gewonnen, zo geronnen

li**ghtness** lichtheid [also fig]

li**ghtning** bliksem, weerlicht[h]: **forked** ~ vertakte bliksem(straal); **like** (greased) ~ als de (gesmeerde) bliksem; ~ **conductor** bliksemafleider

[1]**light** u**p** (vb) **1** (ver)licht(ing) aansteken, de lamp(en) aandoen **2** [inform] (een sigaar/sigaret/pijp) opsteken || his eyes lit up **with** greed zijn ogen begonnen te glimmen van hebzucht

[2]**light** u**p** (vb) **1** aansteken, ontsteken **2** verlichten

li**ghtweight** lichtgewicht[h] [also fig]

[1]**like** (n) **1** (-s) voorkeuren; ~s and **dislikes** sympathieën en antipathieën **2** soortgenoot, (soort)gelijke: [inform] the ~s **of** us

mensen als wij, ons soort (mensen) **3** [media] like, vind-ik-leuk ‖ *I've never seen* (or: *heard*) *the ~ of it* zoiets heb ik nog nooit meegemaakt (*or:* gehoord)
²like (adj) soortgelijk, (soort)verwant: *they are as ~ as two **peas** (in a pod)* ze lijken op elkaar als twee druppels water
³like (vb) willen, wensen: *if **you** ~* zo u wilt, als je wilt
⁴like (vb) **1** houden van, (prettig) vinden, (graag) willen: *would you ~ a **cup** of tea?* wilt u een kopje thee?; *I'd ~ **to** do that* dat zou ik best willen; *how do **you** ~ your egg?* hoe wilt u uw ei? **2** [media] liken
⁵like (adv) **1** [inform] weet je, wel: *he thinks he's **clever** ~* hij vindt zichzelf best wel slim **2** [inform] nou, zoiets als: *her request was … ~ … unusual, you know* haar verzoek was … nou ja … ongebruikelijk, weet je
⁶like (prep) **1** als, zoals, gelijk aan: *cry ~ a **baby*** huilen als een kind; *it is **just** ~ John to forget it* echt iets voor John om het te vergeten; *~ **that*** zo, op die wijze; *just ~ **that*** zo maar (even); *what is **he** ~?* wat voor iem. is hij?; *what is it ~?* hoe voelt dat nou?; *more ~ ten pounds than nine* eerder tien pond dan negen **2** (zo)als: *take a science ~ **chemistry*** neem nou scheikunde ‖ *it hurts ~ **anything*** het doet erg veel pijn; *that's more ~ **it*** dat begint er op te lijken; *there's **nothing** ~ a holiday* er gaat niets boven een vakantie; *sth. ~ five days* om en nabij vijf dagen
⁷like (conj) **1** zoals, op dezelfde wijze als: [inform] *they ran ~ **crazy*** ze liepen zo hard zij konden; *it was ~ in the old days* het was zoals vroeger **2** [inform] alsof: *it **looks** ~ he will win* het ziet ernaar uit dat hij zal winnen
likeable innemend, aardig, sympathiek
likelihood waarschijnlijkheid: *in all ~* naar alle waarschijnlijkheid
¹likely (adj) waarschijnlijk, aannemelijk; [by extension] kansrijk: *he is the most ~ **candidate** for the job* hij komt het meest in aanmerking voor de baan; *he **is** ~ to become suspicious* hij wordt allicht achterdochtig
²likely (adv) waarschijnlijk: *not ~!* kun je net denken!; *as ~ as not* eerder wel dan niet
like-minded gelijkgestemd
likeness gelijkenis, overeenkomst: *it's a **good** ~* het lijkt er goed op [eg of photo]
likewise 1 evenzo, insgelijks **2** evenzeer
liking voorkeur, voorliefde: *have a ~ **for*** houden van, gek zijn op ‖ *is your room **to** your ~?* is uw kamer naar wens?
lilac 1 sering **2** lilaʰ
lily lelie ‖ *gild the ~* iets mooier, beter maken dan nodig
limb 1 lid(maat)ʰ [plural: ledematen]; arm, beenʰ **2** (dikke/grote) tak ‖ *out on a ~* op zichzelf aangewezen
limbo 1 voorportaalʰ (der hel) **2** vergetel-

heid **3** opsluiting **4** onzekerheid, twijfel: *be in ~* in onzekerheid verkeren
lime 1 limoen **2** linde **3** gebrande kalk
limelight kalklichtʰ: *in the ~* in de schijnwerpers
limestone kalksteen⁺ʰ
limey [Am; inform] Brit, Engelsman
¹limit (n) limiet, (uiterste) grens: [Am] *go the ~* tot het uiterste gaan; [Am; esp mil] *off ~s (to)* verboden terrein (voor); *within ~s* binnen bepaalde grenzen; *you're the ~* je bent onmogelijk
²limit (vb) begrenzen, beperken: *~ing **factors*** beperkende factoren; *~ **to*** beperken tot
limitation beperking, begrenzing: *he **has** (or: **knows**) his ~s* hij heeft (or: kent) zijn beperkingen
limited beperkt, gelimiteerd ‖ *~ (liability) **company*** naamloze vennootschap
limitless onbegrensd
¹limp (n) kreupele (slepende) gang, mankheid: *he **walks** with a ~* hij trekt met zijn been
²limp (adj) (ver)slap(t)
³limp (vb) **1** mank lopen, slecht ter been zijn **2** haperen, horten
limpid (glas)helder
linchpin spil [fig]; hoeksteen
¹line (n) **1** lijn, snoerʰ, koordʰ: *the ~ is **bad*** de verbinding is slecht [telephone] **2** smalle streep, lijn: *we must **draw** the ~ somewhere* we moeten ergens een grens trekken; *in ~ **with*** in het verlengde van; [fig] in overeenstemming met **3** rij (naast/achter elkaar); [mil] linie; stelling: *come (or: **fall**) into ~* op één lijn gaan zitten, zich schikken; [Am] *cut in ~* voordringen, voor je beurt gaan; *read between the ~s* tussen de regels door lezen; *all **along** the ~* **a)** over de (ge)hele linie; **b)** [also fig] van begin tot eind **4** kort briefjeʰ, krabbeltjeʰ: *drop s.o. a ~* iem. een briefje schrijven **5** beleidslijn, gedragslijn: *~ of **thought*** zienswijze, denkwijze **6** koers, route; weg [also fig]: *~ of **least** resistance* weg van de minste weerstand **7** lijndienst **8** spoorlijn, spoorʰ **9** terreinʰ [fig]; vlakʰ, branche: *banking is his ~* hij zit in het bankwezen **10** assortimentʰ, soort artikelʰ **11** lintʰ, lont, bandʰ **12** (-s) (straf)regels, strafwerkʰ **13** (-s) trouwakte **14** (-s) methode, aanpak: *do sth. **along** (or: on) the wrong ~s* iets verkeerd aanpakken ‖ *lay (or: **put**) it on the ~* **a)** betalen; **b)** open kaart spelen; *sign on the dotted ~* **a)** (een contract) ondertekenen; **b)** [inform] niet tegenstribbelen; **c)** in het huwelijksbootje stappen; *toe the ~* in het gareel blijven; *on ~* aan het werk, functionerend; *out of ~* uit de pas, over de schreef
²line (vb) **1** liniëren: *~d **paper*** gelinieerd papier **2** flankeren: *a road ~d **with** trees* een weg met (rijen) bomen erlangs **3** voeren, (van binnen) bekleden: *~d **with** fur* met bont

gevoerd ‖ ~ *one's nest* (or: *pocket, purse*) zijn zakken vullen, zijn beurs spekken

lineage 1 geslacht[h], nageslacht[h] **2** afkomst

linear lineair, lengte-, recht(lijnig): ~ *measure* lengtemaat

linen 1 linnen[h], lijnwaad[h] **2** linnengoed[h]

liner 1 lijnboot **2** lijntoestel[h]

linesman 1 [sport] grensrechter, lijnrechter **2** lijnwerker

¹line up (vb) in de rij gaan staan: [fig] ~ *alongside* (or: *with*) zich opstellen naast

²line up (vb) **1** opstellen in (een) rij(en) **2** op een rij zetten, samenbrengen

linger 1 treuzelen, dralen: ~ *over details* lang stilstaan bij details **2** (zwakjes) voortleven: *the memory ~s on* de herinnering leeft voort

lingo taal(tje)[h], (vak)jargon[h]: *at least I master the* **commercial** ~ *they use over there* in elk geval beheers ik het handelstaaltje dat ze daar spreken

linguist 1 talenkenner, talenwonder[h] **2** taalkundige, linguïst

linguistic taalkundig, linguïstisch

linguistics taalkunde, linguïstiek: *applied* ~ toegepaste taalkunde

lining voering(stof), (binnen)bekleding ‖ *every cloud has a silver* ~ achter de wolken schijnt de zon

¹link (n) **1** schakel [also fig]; verbinding, verband[h]: *missing* ~ ontbrekende schakel **2** presentator **3** (-s) [sport] (golf)links, golfbaan

²link (vb) een verbinding vormen, zich verbinden, samenkomen: ~ *up* zich aaneensluiten

³link (vb) verbinden, koppelen: ~ *hands* de handen ineenslaan

linkman 1 presentator **2** middenvelder **3** bemiddelaar, tussenpersoon

link-up verbinding, koppeling

linoleum linoleum[h]

linseed lijnzaad[h]

lion 1 leeuw **2** idool[h]

lioness leeuwin

lionhearted moedig (als een leeuw)

lionize als een beroemdheid behandelen; op een voetstuk plaatsen

lion's share (the) leeuwendeel[h]

lip 1 lip: [fig] *hang on s.o.'s ~s* aan iemands lippen hangen; *my ~s are sealed* ik zwijg als het graf **2** rand **3** praatjes, grote mond: *we don't want any of your* ~ hou jij je praatjes maar voor je

lippy niet op zijn mondje gevallen, brutaal

lip service lippendienst: *give* (or: *pay*) ~ *to* lippendienst bewijzen aan

lipstick lippenstift

liquefy smelten, vloeibaar worden (maken)

liqueur likeur(tje[h])

¹liquid (n) vloeistof, vocht[h]

²liquid (adj) **1** vloeibaar **2** [com] liquide,

vlottend: ~ *assets* liquide middelen

liquidate elimineren, uit de weg ruimen

liquidity 1 vloeibaarheid **2** [com] liquiditeit

liquidizer mengbeker, sapcentrifuge

liquor alcoholische drank, alcohol; [Am] sterkedrank

liquorice 1 zoethout[h], zoethoutwortel **2** drop[+h]

¹lisp (n) slissende uitspraak, geslis[h]: *he speaks with a* ~ hij slist

²lisp (vb) **1** brabbelen; krompraten [of child] **2** lispelen, slissen

¹list (n) **1** lijst, tabel **2** [shipp] slagzij **3** (-s) strijdperk[h], ring: *enter the ~s (against)* in het krijt treden (tegen)

²list (vb) [shipp] slagzij maken

³list (vb) **1** een lijst maken van, rangschikken in een lijst **2** op een lijst zetten: *~ed buildings* op de monumentenlijst geplaatste gebouwen

listen luisteren: ~ *in (to)* (mee)luisteren (naar), afluisteren; ~ *to* luisteren naar

listener luisteraar

listless lusteloos, futloos

lit 1 aan(gestoken), brandend **2** verlicht, beschenen **3** [inform] dronken, bezopen **4** [inform] supergaaf, superchill, tof: *the concert was* ~ het concert was superchill

litany litanie [also fig]

lite light, dieet-: ~ *ice cream* halfvol ijs

literacy alfabetisme[h], het kunnen lezen en schrijven

literal letterlijk, letter-

literally letterlijk [also fig]

literary 1 literair, letterkundig **2** geletterd: ~ *man* geletterd man, letterkundige

literate geletterd: *only half the children in this group are* ~ niet meer dan de helft van de kinderen in deze groep kan lezen en schrijven

literature 1 literatuur, letterkunde: *the ~ of* (or: *on*) *a subject* de literatuur over een onderwerp **2** [inform] voorlichtingsmateriaal[h]

lithe soepel; buigzaam, lenig

Lithuania Litouwen

¹Lithuanian (n) Litouwer, Litouwse

²Lithuanian (adj) Litouws

litigation proces[h], procesvoering, rechtszaak

litmus paper lakmoespapier(tje[h])

litre liter

litter 1 rommel, rotzooi, troep **2** (stal)stro[h]; afdekstro[h] [for plants]; stalmest **3** nest[h] (jongen), worp: *have a* ~ *of kittens* jongen, jongen krijgen

litterbin afvalbak, prullenmand

¹little (adj) **1** klein: *a* ~ *bit* een (klein) beetje; ~ *finger* pink; *his* ~ *sister* zijn jongere zusje; *her* ~ *ones* haar kinderen; *its* ~ *ones* haar jongen **2** klein(zielig), kleintjes: ~ *minds* klein-geestigen; ~ *things please* ~ *minds* kleine mensen, kleine wensen

²**little** (pron) weinig, beetje: *he got* ~ *out of it* het bracht hem maar weinig op; *make* ~ *of sth.* ergens weinig van begrijpen; ~ *or nothing* weinig of niets; ~ *by* ~ beetje bij beetje; *every* ~ *helps* alle beetjes helpen

³**little** (adv) **1** weinig, amper, gering: ~ *more than an hour* iets meer dan een uur **2** volstrekt niet: ~ *did he know that ...* hij had er geen flauw benul van dat ...

liturgy liturgie

¹**live** (adj) **1** levend, in leven (zijnd): ~ *bait* levend aas; *a real* ~ *horse!* een heus paard! **2** direct, rechtstreeks: ~ *broadcast* directe uitzending **3** levendig, actief: *a* ~ *topic* een actueel onderwerp **4** onder spanning staand: ~ *wire* onder spanning staande draad; [fig] energieke figuur || ~ *ammunition* (or: *cartridges*) scherpe munitie (or: patronen)

²**live** (vb) **1** leven, bestaan: ~ *and let* ~ leven en laten leven; *long* ~ *the Queen!* (lang) leve de koningin!; ~ *together* samenleven, samenwonen; ~ *above* (or: *beyond*) *one's means* boven zijn stand leven; ~ *for* a) leven voor; b) toeleven naar: ~ *with a situation* (hebben leren) leven met een situatie **2** wonen: ~ *in* inwonen, intern zijn; ~ *on one's own* op zichzelf wonen **3** voortleven: *you haven't* ~*d yet!* je hebt nog helemaal niet van het leven genoten!

³**live** (vb) **1** leven: ~ *a double life* een dubbelleven leiden **2** beleven, doormaken, meemaken || ~ *it up* het ervan nemen, de bloemetjes buiten zetten

liveable 1 bewoonbaar **2** leefbaar

liveblog liveblog[+h]

lived-in bewoond, gebruikt: *a home with a* ~ *feel* een huis waar echt geleefd wordt, een gezellig huis

live-in 1 samenwonend **2** inwonend

livelihood levensonderhoud[h]: *earn* (or: *gain*) *one's* ~ de kost verdienen

lively levendig: ~ *colours* sprekende kleuren

liven verlevendigen, opfleuren: ~ *up* opfleuren, opvrolijken

liver lever

livery livrei, uniform[h]

live-screen rechtstreeks uitzenden

livestock vee[h], levende have

live-stream livestreamen

live up to naleven, waarmaken: ~ *one's reputation* zijn naam eer aan doen

livid 1 hels, des duivels: ~ *at* razend op **2** lijkbleek, asgrauw **3** loodgrijs, blauwgrijs

¹**living** (n) **1** inkomen[h], kostwinning: *earn/gain* (or: *get, make*) *a* ~ *(as, out of, by)* de kost verdienen (als) **2** leven[h], levensonderhoud[h]

²**living** (adj) **1** levend, bestaand: *(with)in* ~ *memory* bij mensenheugenis **2** levendig || *he's the* ~ *image of his father* hij is het evenbeeld van zijn vader

living room woonkamer; huiskamer

lizard hagedis

llama lama(wol)

LL B *Bachelor of Laws* Bachelor (in de rechten)

LMAO [inform] *laughing my ass/arse off* ik lig in een deuk, ik lach me rot

¹**load** (n) **1** lading; last [also fig]: *that takes a* ~ *off my mind* dat is een pak van mijn hart **2** belasting, massa **3** (elektrisch) vermogen[h], kracht **4** [inform] hoop, massa's: *they have* ~*s of money* ze barsten van het geld

²**load** (vb) laden [firearms, camera]

³**load** (vb) laden, geladen worden, bevrachten: *the table was* ~*ed with presents* de tafel stond vol met cadeaus

loaded 1 geladen, emotioneel geladen **2** [inform] stomdronken **3** [Am; inform] stoned **4** venijnig, geniepig: *a* ~ *question* een strikvraag

loader 1 lader **2** shovel

loaf 1 brood[h]: *a* ~ *of brown bread* een bruin brood **2** brood(suiker)[h] **3** kop, hersens: *use your* ~ *for once* denk nu eens een keer na

loaf about rondhangen, lummelen

loafer 1 leegloper, lanterfanter **2** [Am] lage schoen, loafer

loam leem[+h]

¹**loan** (n) **1** lening: *apply for a* ~ *with a bank* een lening bij een bank aanvragen **2** leen[h], tijdelijk gebruik[h]: *have sth.* **on** ~ *from s.o.* iets van iem. te leen hebben; *thank you for the* ~ *of your car* bedankt voor het lenen van je auto

²**loan** (vb) (uit)lenen: ~ *money* **to** *a friend* geld aan een vriend lenen

loan shark [inform] woekeraar; uitzuiger

loanword leenwoord[h]

loath ongenegen, afkerig: *the elderly couple were* ~ *to leave the house at night* het oudere echtpaar ging 's avonds niet graag de deur uit

loathe verafschuwen

loathing afkeer

loathsome walgelijk, weerzinwekkend

lob 1 [tennis] lobben **2** [inform] gooien, smijten

¹**lobby** (n) **1** hal[h], portaal[h] **2** foyer **3** lobby, pressiegroep

²**lobby** (vb) lobbyen, druk uitoefenen op de politieke besluitvorming

³**lobby** (vb) in de wandelgangen bewerken; onder druk zetten [MPs]

lobbyist lobbyist; lid van pressiegroep

lobe 1 (oor)lel **2** kwab; lob [of brain, lung]

lobster zeekreeft

¹**local** (n) **1** plaatselijke bewoner, inboorling

2 [inform] stamcafé[h], stamkroeg
²local (adj) plaatselijk, lokaal, buurt-, streek-: ~ *authority* plaatselijke overheid; ~ *call* lokaal gesprek; ~ *government* plaatselijk bestuur
locality plaats, district[h], buurt
localize lokaliseren, tot een bepaalde plaats beperken, een plaats toekennen: *they hoped to ~ the outbreak of polio* ze hoopten de uitbarsting van polio tot een klein gebied te beperken
¹locate (vb) [Am] zich vestigen, gaan wonen, een zaak opzetten
²locate (vb) **1** de positie bepalen van, opsporen: *I can't ~ that village anywhere* ik kan dat dorp nergens vinden **2** vestigen, plaatsen, stationeren: *the estate was ~d on the bank of a river* het landgoed was gelegen aan de oever van een rivier
location 1 plaats, ligging, positie **2** terrein[h], afgebakend land[h] **3** locatie: *filmed on ~ in Australia* op locatie gefilmd in Australië
loch 1 meer[h] **2** smalle (ingesloten) zeearm
¹lock (n) **1** (haar)lok **2** slot[h] [also of firearms]; sluiting: *under ~ and key* achter slot en grendel; [fig] in de gevangenis **3** vergrendeling **4** (schut)sluis **5** houdgreep || ~, *stock, and barrel* in zijn geheel, alles inbegrepen
²lock (vb) sluiten, vergrendeld (kunnen) worden: *the doors wouldn't ~* de deuren wilden niet sluiten
³lock (vb) **1** (af)sluiten, op slot doen **2** wegsluiten; opsluiten [also fig]: *don't forget to ~ away your valuables* vergeet niet je kostbaarheden op te bergen
locker kast(je[h]); kluis [eg for clothing, luggage]
locker room kleedkamer
lock gate sluisdeur
locksmith slotenmaker
¹lock up (vb) afsluiten, alles op slot doen
²lock up (vb) **1** op slot doen, afsluiten **2** opbergen, wegsluiten: ~ *one's gold and silver* zijn goud en zilver veilig opbergen **3** opsluiten; wegstoppen [in prison, madhouse]
lock-up 1 arrestantenhok[h], cachot[h], nor, bajes **2** afsluitbare ruimte, kiosk, dagwinkel, opbergbox
locomotion (voort)beweging(svermogen[h])
locomotive locomotief
locust 1 sprinkhaan **2** [Am] cicade
lodestar leidster [also fig]; poolster
¹lodge (n) **1** (schuil)hut **2** personeelswoning, portierswoning **3** afdeling, (vrijmetselaars)loge
²lodge (vb) **1** verblijven, (tijdelijk) wonen, logeren: ~ *at a friend's*, ~ *with* a friend bij een vriend wonen **2** vast komen te zitten, blijven steken: *the bullet ~d in the ceiling* de kogel bleef in het plafond steken
³lodge (vb) **1** onderdak geven, logeren, (tij-

delijk) huisvesten **2** indienen, voorleggen: ~ *a complaint* een aanklacht indienen
lodger kamerbewoner, (kamer)huurder
lodgings (gehuurde) kamer(s)
loft zolder(kamer), vliering, hooizolder
lofty 1 torenhoog **2** verheven, edel: ~ *ideals* hooggestemde idealen **3** hooghartig, arrogant: *behave loftily to s.o.* (erg) uit de hoogte doen tegen iem.
¹log (n) **1** blok(hout)[h], boomstronk, boomstam **2** logboek[h], scheepsjournaal[h] || *sleep like a ~* slapen als een os
²log (vb) in het logboek opschrijven || ~ *off* uitloggen; *the truck driver had ~ged up 700 miles* de vrachtrijder had er 700 mijl op zitten; ~ *into a computer system* inloggen
logarithm logaritme
logbook 1 logboek[h], scheepsjournaal[h], journaal[h] van een vliegtuig, werkverslag[h], dagboek[h], reisjournaal[h] **2** registratiebewijs[h] [of car]
log cabin blokhut
logger [Am] houthakker
loggerhead: *they are always at ~s with each other* ze liggen altijd met elkaar overhoop
logic logica, redeneerkunde
logical logisch, steekhoudend, vanzelfsprekend (volgend uit)
login [comp] **1** het inloggen: *at ~* tijdens het inloggen **2** loginnaam, gebruikersnaam
logistics logistiek
logjam impasse; knelpunt[h]
logo 1 logotype[h], woordmerk[h] **2** logo[h], beeldmerk[h], firma-embleem[h]
logon 1 het inloggen: *at ~* tijdens het inloggen **2** loginnaam, gebruikersnaam
loin lende
loincloth lendendoek[h]
¹loiter (vb) treuzelen: ~ *about* (or: *around*) rondhangen; ~ *with intent* zich verdacht ophouden
²loiter (vb) verdoen, verlummelen: ~ *away one's time* zijn tijd verdoen
LOL *laughing out loud* lol [lach me rot]
loll (rond)hangen, lummelen, leunen
lollipop (ijs)lolly: ~ *man* klaar-over
lolly 1 lolly **2** [inform] poen[+h]
lone alleen, verlaten, eenzaam: *be* (or: *play*) *a ~ hand* [fig] met niemand rekening houden; ~ *wolf* iem. die zijn eigen weg gaat
lonely eenzaam, verlaten, alleen
loner eenzame, eenling
lonesome eenzaam, alleen: *by* (or: *on*) *his ~* in zijn (dooie) eentje
¹long (adj) lang, langgerekt, langdurig, ver, langlopend: *a ~ haul* a) een hele ruk [eg a long trip]; b) een lange tijd (or: termijn); *to cut a ~ story short* om kort te gaan, samengevat; *in the ~ term* op den duur, op de lange duur; ~ *vacation* zomervakantie; *it won't take ~* het zal niet lang duren; *before ~* bin-

nenkort, spoedig; *he won't stay for ~* hij zal niet (voor) lang blijven ‖ *the ~ arm of the law* de lange arm der wet; *not by a ~ chalk* op geen stukken na, bijlange (na) niet; *make* (or: *pull*) *a ~ face* ongelukkig kijken; [roughly] *a ~* een lang gezicht trekken; *in the ~ run* uiteindelijk; *~ shot* a) kansloos deelnemer; b) gok, waagstuk^h; [Am] *by a ~ shot* veruit, met gemak; [Am] *not by a ~ shot* op geen stukken na, bijlange na niet; *~ in the tooth* lang in de mond, aftands; *take a ~ view* dingen op de lange termijn bekijken; *go a ~ way (towards)* voordelig (in het gebruik) zijn, veel helpen, het ver schoppen

²**long** (vb) (also + for) hevig verlangen (naar), hunkeren: *after two weeks we were ~ing for the city again* na twee weken verlangden we alweer naar de stad

³**long** (adv) lang, lange tijd: *all night ~* de hele nacht; *be ~ in doing sth.* lang over iets doen

longboat barkas; (grote) sloep

longbow (grote) handboog

longevity lang leven^h, lange levensduur

longhand (gewoon) handschrift

¹**longing** (n) verlangen^h, hunkering

²**longing** (adj) vol verlangen, smachtend

longitude (geografische) lengte, longitude

long-lasting langdurig

long-life 1 met een lange levensduur **2** langer houdbaar ‖ *~ batteries* batterijen met een lange levensduur

¹**longlist** (n) longlist, voorlopige lijst

²**longlist** (vb) op een longlist plaatsen

long-lived 1 lang levend **2** van lange duur, hardnekkig

longneck [Am] bierflesje^h met een lange hals

long-sighted 1 verziend **2** vooruitziend

long-tailed tit staartmees

long-term langlopend, op lange termijn: *the ~ unemployed* de langdurig werklozen

long-winded langdradig

loo wc, plee

¹**look** (n) **1** blik, kijkje^h: *let's have a ~* laten we even een kijkje nemen **2** (gelaats)uitdrukking, blik **3** uiterlijk^h, (knap) voorkomen^h, aanzien^h: *by the ~ of it* (or: *things*) zo te zien **4** mode **5** uitzicht^h **6** (-s) uiterlijk^h, schoonheid: *lose one's ~s* minder mooi worden

²**look** (vb) **1** kijken, (proberen te) zien, aandachtig kijken: *~ about* (or: *around*) om zich heen kijken, rondkijken; *~ ahead* vooruitzien [also fig]; *~ on* toekijken; *~ at* kijken naar, beschouwen, onderzoeken; *not ~ at* niet in overweging nemen, niets willen weten van; *~ beyond* verder kijken dan; *~ down the road* de weg af kijken; *~ round the town* een kijkje in de stad nemen; *~ before you leap* bezint eer gij begint **2** uitkijken, uitzien, liggen: *~ to the south* op het zuiden liggen **3** wijzen [in

particular direction]; (bepaalde kant) uitgaan ‖ *~ down (up)on* neerkijken op; *~ forward to* tegemoet zien, verlangen naar; *~ here!* kijk eens (even hier)!, luister eens!; *~ in* aanlopen, aanwippen; [inform] tv kijken; *~ in on s.o.* bij iem. langskomen; *~ after* passen op, toezien op; *~ after o.s., ~ after one's own interests* voor zichzelf zorgen; *~ for* zoeken (naar); *~ for trouble* om moeilijkheden vragen; *~ into* a) even bezoeken; b) onderzoeken; *~ (up)on s.o. as* iem. beschouwen als

³**look** (vb) **1** zijn blik richten op, kijken (naar), zien: *~ what you've done* kijk nou (eens) wat je gedaan hebt **2** eruitzien als: *~ one's age* aan iem. zijn leeftijd afzien

⁴**look** (vb) lijken (te zijn), uitzien, de indruk wekken te zijn: [Am] *~ good* goed lijken te gaan, er goed uitzien; *it ~s like snow* er is sneeuw op komst; *he ~s as if he has a hangover* hij ziet eruit alsof hij een kater heeft

lookalike evenbeeld^h, dubbelganger

looker [inform] schoonheid

looker-on toeschouwer, kijker

look-in [inform] **1** kijkje^h; bezoekje^h **2** kans (op succes)

looking-glass spiegel

lookout 1 het uitkijken: *keep a ~* een oogje in het zeil houden; *be on the ~ for* op zoek zijn naar **2** uitkijkpost **3** uitzicht^h

look over doornemen [eg letters]; doorkijken

look through goed bekijken; grondig/helemaal doornemen, een voor een doornemen [eg documents] ‖ *look right* (or: *straight*) *through s.o.* straal langs iem. heen kijken, doen alsof iem. lucht is

look to 1 zorgen voor, bekommeren over: *~ it that …* zorg ervoor, dat … **2** vertrouwen op, rekenen op: *don't ~ her for help* (or: *to help you*) verwacht van haar geen hulp

¹**look up** (vb) **1** opkijken, de ogen opslaan **2** beter worden [eg of business]; vooruitgaan: *prices are looking up* de prijzen stijgen ‖ *~ to* opkijken naar, bewonderen

²**look up** (vb) **1** opzoeken, naslaan **2** raadplegen **3** (kort) bezoeken, opzoeken

¹**loom** (n) weefgetouw^h

²**loom** (vb) opdoemen [also fig]; dreigend verschijnen, zich flauw aftekenen: *~ large* onevenredig belangrijk lijken, nadrukkelijk aanwezig zijn

¹**loony** (n) gek, dwaas

²**loony** (adj) geschift, gek, getikt

loony-bin gekkenhuis^h

¹**loop** (n) **1** lus, strop, bocht **2** beugel, handvat^h **3** spiraaltje^h ‖ [inform] *be in the ~* tot de incrowd/trendsetters behoren

²**loop** (vb) een lus vormen

³**loop** (vb) **1** een lus maken in, met een lus vastmaken **2** door een lus halen

loophole uitvlucht, uitweg: *~s in the law*

mazen in de wet(geving)

¹loose (n) (staat van) vrijheid, losbandigheid: *there's a killer* **on** *the* ~ er loopt een moordenaar vrij rond

²loose (adj) **1** los, slap, open: ~ *ends* losse eindjes; [fig] onvolkomenheden, onafgewerkte zaken **2** vrij, bevrijd, ongehinderd: *break* (or: *get*) ~ uitbreken, ontsnappen; *cut* ~ a) (met moeite) weggaan, zich losmaken; b) op gang komen; *let* ~ vrij laten, de vrije hand laten, ontketenen **3** wijd, ruim, soepel **4** ongedisciplineerd, lichtzinnig: *have a* ~ *tongue* loslippig zijn ‖ *be at a* ~ *end* niets omhanden hebben; *have a screw* ~ ze zien vliegen, een beetje geschift zijn

³loose (vb) losmaken, bevrijden

⁴loose (adv) losjes

loose-leaf losbladig

loosely losjes, vaag, in het wilde weg

¹loosen (vb) losgaan, ontspannen, verslappen: ~ *up* een warming-up doen, de spieren losmaken

²loosen (vb) los(ser) maken, laten verslappen: *drink* ~s *the tongue* drank maakt spraakzaam; ~ *up* doen ontspannen

¹loot (n) **1** (oorlogs)buit, gestolen goedʰ, prooi **2** poet, poen⁺ʰ, geldʰ

²loot (vb) plunderen, roven

lop afsnoeien, afkappen

lop-eared met hangende oren: *a* ~ *rabbit* een hangoor(konijn)

lopsided 1 scheef, overhellend **2** ongebalanceerd, eenzijdig

¹lord (n) **1** heer, vorst, koning **2** lord, edelachtbare, excellentie: *live like a* ~ als een vorst leven; *My Lord* edelachtbare, heer **3** (the Lords) het Hogerhuis, de leden van het Hogerhuis

²lord (vb) de baas spelen: ~ *it* **over** *s.o.* over iem. de baas spelen

Lord (de) Heer, God: *the* ~'s *Prayer* het Onze Vader

Lord Chancellor voorzitter van het Hogerhuis

lordship Lord [form of address for lord and judge]; edele heer, edelachtbare

lore traditionele kennis, overlevering

lorry vrachtauto

¹lose (vb) **1** verliezen, verlies lijden, er op achteruit gaan: *you can't* ~ daar heb je niets bij te verliezen; ~ *out on sth.* er (geld) bij inschieten **2** achterlopen [of watch etc]

²lose (vb) **1** verliezen, kwijtraken, verspelen: [inform] ~ *one's cool* z'n kalmte verliezen; ~ *count* de tel kwijtraken; ~ *sight* of uit het oog verliezen; ~ *one's temper* boos worden; ~ *no time in (doing sth.)* geen tijd verspillen met (iets); ~ *weight* afvallen, vermageren; ~ *o.s. in* geheel opgaan in **2** doen verliezen, kosten: *her stupid mistake lost us a major customer* haar stomme fout kostte ons een gro-

te klant **3** missen, niet winnen **4** afschudden

loser verliezer: *born* ~ geboren verliezer; *a good* (or: *bad*) ~ een goede (or: slechte) verliezer

loss 1 verliesʰ **2** nadeelʰ, schade **3** achteruitgang, teruggang ‖ *be at a* ~ *(what to do)* niet weten wat men doen moet; *be at a* ~ *for words* met de mond vol tanden staan

lost 1 verloren, weg, kwijt: ~ *property (department, office)* (afdeling/bureau) gevonden voorwerpen **2** gemist: ~ *chance* gemiste kans **3** in gedachten verzonken, afwezig, er niet bij: ~ *in* thought in gedachten verzonken **4** verspild: *sarcasm is* ~ *(up)on him* sarcasme raakt hem niet ‖ *get* ~*!* donder op!

lot 1 portie, aandeelʰ **2** kavel, perceelʰ, partij, (veiling)nummerʰ **3** lotʰ, loterijbriefjeʰ: *cast* (or: *draw*) ~s loten **4** (nood)lotʰ, levenslotʰ: *cast* (or: *throw*) *in one's* ~ *with* mee gaan doen met **5** [Am] stukʰ grond, terreinʰ: *parking* ~ parkeerterreinʰ **6** groep, aantalʰ dingen (mensen), een hoop, een heleboel: ~s *and lots* ontzettend veel, hopen; *this* ~ deze mensen, deze dingen; *a* ~ *of books,* ~s *of books* een heleboel boeken; *that's the* ~ dat is alles; *things have changed quite a* ~ er is nogal wat veranderd

lotion lotion, haarwaterʰ, gezichtswaterʰ

lottery loterij

¹loud (adj) **1** luid(ruchtig), hard **2** opzichtig; schreeuwend [of colour]

²loud (adv) luid(ruchtig), hard, schreeuwerig: ~ *and clear* erg duidelijk, overduidelijk; *out* ~ hardop

loudmouth luidruchtig persoon

loudspeaker luidspreker, box

¹lounge (n) **1** lounge, halʰ, foyer **2** zitkamer, conversatiezaal

²lounge (vb) **1** luieren, (rond)hangen: ~ *about* (or: *around*) rondhangen **2** slenteren, kuieren

louse luis

louse up grondig bederven, verpesten

lousy 1 vol luizen **2** [inform] waardeloos, vuil, beroerd **3** [inform] armzalig [of amount, number etc]

lout lummel, hufter

lovable lief; beminnelijk

¹love (n) **1** liefde, verliefdheid: *mother sends her* ~ moeder laat je groeten; *fall in* ~ *with s.o.* verliefd worden op iem. **2** plezierʰ, genoegenʰ: *music is a great* ~ *of his* muziek is een van zijn grote liefdes **3** liefjeʰ **4** [inform] snoes; geliefd persoon [also man] **5** groeten **6** [tennis] love, nul: ~ *all* nul-nul ‖ *not for* ~ *or money* niet voor geld of goeie woorden; *there is no* ~ *lost between them* ze kunnen elkaar niet luchten of zien

²love (vb) liefde voelen, verliefd zijn

³love (vb) **1** houden van, liefhebben, graag mogen: ~ *dearly* innig houden van **2** dol zijn op, heerlijk vinden: *he ~s (to go) swimming* hij is dol op zwemmen

lovebird 1 dwergpapegaai **2** (-s) [inform] tortelduifjes

loved ones dierbaren

lovelorn [form] vol liefdesverdriet

lovely 1 mooi, lieftallig, aantrekkelijk **2** [inform] leuk, prettig, fijn, lekker

love match huwelijk^h uit liefde

love potion liefdesdrank(je^h)

lover 1 (be)minnaar **2** liefhebber, enthousiast **3** (-s) verliefd paar^h **4** (-s) minnaars, stel^h

lover boy loverboy

lovesick smachtend van liefde, smoorverliefd

lovey liefje^h, schatje^h

¹low (n) **1** laag terrein^h, laagte **2** dieptepunt^h, laag punt^h: *an all-time* ~ een absoluut dieptepunt **3** geloei^h, gebulk^h **4** lagedrukgebied^h

²low (adj) **1** laag, niet hoog, niet intensief: *the Low Countries* de lage landen; *~est common denominator* kleinste gemene deler; *~est common multiple* kleinste gemene veelvoud; *~ point* minimum^h, dieptepunt^h; *~ tide* laagwater^h, eb **2** laag(hartig): *~ trick* rotstreek **3** plat, ordinair: *~ expression* ordinaire uitdrukking **4** zacht, stil, niet luid; laag [tone]: *speak in a ~ voice* zacht praten **5** ongelukkig, depressief: *~ spirits* neerslachtigheid **6** verborgen, onopvallend: *lie ~* zich gedeisd houden **7** zwak, slap, futloos ‖ *keep a ~ profile* zich gedeisd houden; *bring ~* **a)** aan lagerwal brengen; **b)** uitputten; **c)** ziek maken

³low (vb) loeien

⁴low (adv) **1** laag, diep: *aim ~* laag mikken **2** zacht, stil **3** diep [of sound]; laag **4** bijna uitgeput: *run ~* opraken, bijna op zijn

¹lowbrow (n) [inform; depr] niet-intellectueel

²lowbrow (adj) [inform; depr] niet intellectueel; ordinair

low-carb [inform] koolhydraatarm

lowcut laag uitgesneden

¹low-down (n, the) fijne^h van de zaak, feiten, inzicht^h: *have the ~ on* het fijne weten over

²low-down (adj) laag, gemeen

¹lower (adj) **1** lager, lager gelegen, onder-, van lage(r) orde: *~ classes* lagere stand(en); *~ deck* benedendek^h **2** neder-, beneden-: *the Lower Rhine* de Neder-Rijn ‖ *Lower Chamber* (or: *House*) Lagerhuis^h

²lower (vb) afnemen, minder worden, dalen, zakken

³lower (vb) **1** verlagen, doen zakken **2** neerlaten, laten zakken: *~ one's eyes* de ogen neerslaan **3** verminderen, doen afnemen: *~ one's voice* zachter praten

lower-case onderkast; in, met kleine letters

low-fat met laag vetgehalte, mager, halva-, halfvol: *~ margarine* halvarine; *~ milk* magere melk

low-key rustig, ingehouden

lowland laagland^h

Lowlands (the) de Schotse Laaglanden

lowlife proleet, schooier, iem. van lage stand

lowly 1 bescheiden; laag [in rank] **2** eenvoudig, nederig

low-minded laag(hartig)

loyal trouw, loyaal

loyalist (regerings)getrouwe, loyalist

loyalty 1 loyaliteit, trouw: *customer ~* klantentrouw; *~ card* klantenpas **2** (loyalties) banden, binding

lozenge 1 ruit, ruitvormig iets^h **2** (hoest)tablet^h

LP *long-playing record* lp, elpee

LP gas *liquefied petroleum gas* lpg^h, autogas^h

Lt *Lieutenant* lt., luitenant

Ltd *limited* [roughly] nv; naamloze vennootschap

LTNS [inform] *long time no see* lang niet gezien

lubricant 1 smeermiddel^h **2** glijmiddel^h

lubricate (door)smeren, oliën

lucid 1 helder; duidelijk [also fig] **2** bij zijn verstand

luck geluk^h, toeval^h, succes^h: *bad* (or: *hard*) ~ pech; *good* ~ succes; *push one's* ~ te veel risico's nemen, overmoedig worden; *try one's* ~ zijn geluk beproeven; *let's do it once more for* ~ laten we het nog een keer doen, misschien brengt dat geluk; *be out of* ~, be down on *one's* ~ pech hebben; *with* ~ als alles goed gaat; *no such* ~ helaas niet; *as* ~ *would have it* (on)gelukkig, toevallig

luckily gelukkig: *~ for* you, *I found your keys* je hebt geluk dat ik je sleutels heb gevonden

luckless onfortuinlijk

lucky 1 gelukkig, fortuinlijk, toevallig juist: *a ~ thing no-one got hurt* gelukkig raakte er niemand gewond **2** gelukbrengend, geluks-: *~ charm* talisman; *~ dip* grabbelton; [fig] loterij; *~ star* geluksster ‖ *strike* ~ boffen

lucrative winstgevend, lucratief

lucre gewin^h: *filthy ~* vuil gewin

ludicrous belachelijk, bespottelijk

¹lug (n) uitsteeksel^h, handvat^h, oor^h

²lug (vb) (voort)trekken, (voort)zeulen: *~ sth. along* iets meesleuren

luggage bagage: *left ~* afgegeven bagage, bagage in depot

lugubrious luguber, naargeestig, treurig

lukewarm 1 lauw **2** niet erg enthousiast

¹lull (n) korte rust: *a ~ in the storm* een korte windstilte tijdens de storm

²lull (vb) **1** sussen, kalmeren: *~ to sleep* in

slaap sussen **2** in slaap brengen
lullaby slaapliedje^h
lumbago spit^+h
¹lumber (n) **1** rommel, afgedankt meubilair^h **2** [Am] half bewerkt hout^h, timmerhout^h, planken
²lumber (vb) sjokken, zich log voortbewegen: ~ *along* voortsjokken
³lumber (vb) [inform] (met iets vervelends/moeilijks) opzadelen: ~ *(up)* *with* opzadelen met
lumberjack [Am] bosbouwer, houthakker
lumber-room rommelkamer
luminous lichtgevend; [fig] helder; duidelijk
¹lump (n) **1** klont, klomp, brok^h: [fig] *with a* ~ *in my* **throat** met een brok in mijn keel **2** bult, knobbel
²lump (vb) klonteren
³lump (vb) **1** tot een geheel samenvoegen, bij elkaar gooien: ~ *together* onder één noemer brengen **2** slikken: *you'll have to* **like** *it or* ~ *it* je hebt het maar te slikken
lump sum bedrag^h ineens, ronde som
lunacy waanzin
lunar van de maan, maan-: ~ *eclipse* maansverduistering
¹lunatic (n) krankzinnige
²lunatic (adj) krankzinnig, gestoord ‖ *the* ~ *fringe* het extremistische deel [of a group]
¹lunch (n) lunch: *have* ~ lunchen; [fig] *there's no such thing as a* **free** ~ voor niets gaat de zon op
²lunch (vb) lunchen
lunch break lunchpauze; middagpauze
luncheon 1 lunch **2** [Am] lichte maaltijd
lung long
¹lunge (n) stoot, uitval
²lunge (vb) (+ at) uitvallen (naar), een uitval doen
³lunge (vb) stoten
¹lurch (n) ruk, plotselinge slingerbeweging ‖ [inform] *leave s.o. in the* ~ iem. in de steek laten
²lurch (vb) slingeren, strompelen
¹lure (n) **1** lokmiddel^h, lokaas^h **2** aantrekking, verleiding, aantrekkelijkheid
²lure (vb) (ver)lokken, meetronen: ~ *away (from)* weglokken (van); ~ *into* verlokken tot
lurid 1 schril, zeer fel (gekleurd), vlammend **2** luguber, choquerend
lurk 1 op de loer liggen, zich schuilhouden **2** latent (aanwezig) zijn, verborgen zijn
luscious 1 heerlijk: *a* ~ *peach* een overheerlijke perzik **2** weelderig
¹lush (n) [Am; inform] zuiplap
²lush (adj) **1** weelderig; overdadig groeiend **2** [inform] luxueus
lust 1 sterk verlangen^h, lust, aandrift: *a* ~ *for power* een verlangen naar macht **2** wellust(igheid), (zinnelijke) lust: *his* **eyes**, *full of* ~

zijn ogen, vol wellust
lust after hevig verlangen naar; begeren
lustre glans, schittering, luister, roem: *add* ~ *to* glans geven aan
lustrous glanzend, schitterend: ~ *eyes* stralende ogen
lusty 1 krachtig, flink, gezond **2** wellustig
lute luit
Luxembourg Luxemburg
Luxembourger Luxemburger, Luxemburgse
luxuriance overvloed, weelderigheid
luxuriant 1 weelderig, overdadig: ~ *flora* weelderige flora **2** vruchtbaar [also fig]: ~ *imagination* rijke verbeelding
luxurious luxueus, weelderig; duur [eg of habits]
luxury 1 weelde, luxe, overvloed: *a* **life** *of* ~ een luxueus leven **2** luxe(artikel^h) **3** weelderigheid
lymph lymfe, weefselvocht^h
lymph gland lymfeklier; lymfeknoop
lynch lynchen
lynx lynx
lyre lier
¹lyric (n) **1** lyrisch gedicht^h **2** (-s) tekst [of song]
²lyric (adj) lyrisch [of poem, poet]
lyrical lyrisch

m

m 1 *married* geh., gehuwd **2** *masculine* m., mannelijk **3** *metre(s)* m, meter(s) **4** *mile(s)* mijl(en) **5** *million(s)* mln., miljoen(en) **6** *minute(s)* min, minuut, minuten

ma ma

MA *Master of Arts* Master of Arts, drs., doctorandus

ma'am *madam* mevrouw

mac *mackintosh* regenjas

macabre macaber, griezelig

macaroon bitterkoekje[h]

mace 1 goedendag, strijdknots, knuppel **2** scepter; staf [of speaker in House of Commons] **3** foelie

Macedonia Macedonië

¹Macedonian (n) Macedoniër, Macedonische

²Macedonian (adj) Macedonisch

machination intrige

machine 1 machine [also fig]; werktuig[h], apparaat[h] **2** aandrijfmechanisme[h]

machine gun machinegeweer[h]

machinery machinerie [also fig]; machinepark[h], systeem[h], apparaat[h]

machinist monteur, werktuigkundige, machinebankwerker, vakman voor werktuigmachines

¹macho (n) macho

²macho (adj) macho

mackerel makreel

mackintosh regenjas

macrobiotic macrobiotisch

mad 1 gek, krankzinnig: *go* ~ gek worden; *drive s.o.* ~ iem. gek maken **2** dwaas, onzinnig: ~ *project* dwaze onderneming **3** wild, razend; hevig [eg of wind]: *make a* ~ *run for* ... als een gek rennen naar ... **4** hondsdol **5** (+ about, after, for, on) verzot (op) **6** (+ at, about sth.) boos (op), woedend (op/om) || ~ *as a* **hatter,** ~ *as a March* **hare** stapelgek

¹Madagascan (n) Malagassiër, Malagassische

²Madagascan (adj) Malagassisch

Madagascar Madagaskar

madam mevrouw, juffrouw: *excuse me,* ~, *can I help you?* pardon, mevrouw, kan ik u van dienst zijn?

madcap dol, roekeloos: ~ *ideas* dwaze ideeën

mad cow disease gekkekoeienziekte

madden gek worden/maken, woedend worden/maken, irriteren

maddening erg vervelend: ~ *waste of time* ergerlijk tijdverlies

madhouse gekkenhuis[h] [also fig]

madly 1 als een bezetene **2** heel (erg): ~ *in love* waanzinnig verliefd

madman gek

madness 1 krankzinnigheid, waanzin(nigheid) **2** dwaasheid, gekte **3** enthousiasme[h]

maelstrom 1 (enorme) draaikolk **2** maalstroom [also fig]

mafia maffia

mag *magazine* tijdschrift[h]

magazine 1 magazine[h], tijdschrift[h]; radiomagazine[h], tv-magazine[h] **2** magazijn[h] [of gun]

maggot made

¹magic (n) magie [also fig]; toverkunst, betovering: *as if by* ~, *like* ~ als bij toverslag

²magic (adj) **1** magisch, tover- **2** betoverend || ~ *carpet* vliegend tapijt

magical wonderbaarlijk, magisch

magician 1 tovenaar **2** goochelaar [also fig]; kunstenaar

magisterial 1 gezaghebbend [also fig] **2** autoritair **3** magistraal

magistrate 1 magistraat, (rechterlijk) ambtenaar **2** politierechter, vrederechter

magnanimity grootmoedigheid

magnanimous edelmoedig, grootmoedig

magnate magnaat

magnet magneet [also fig]

magnetic 1 magnetisch: ~ *compass* kompas[h]; ~ *needle* magneetnaald; ~ *north* magnetische noordpool **2** onweerstaanbaar

magnetism 1 magnetisme[h] **2** aantrekkingskracht

magnetize 1 magnetiseren **2** boeien, fascineren

magnificence 1 pracht, weelde **2** grootsheid

magnificent 1 prachtig, groots **2** weelderig **3** prima

¹magnify (vb) overdrijven, opblazen

²magnify (vb) **1** vergroten [of lens etc]; uitvergroten **2** versterken [sound]

magnifying glass vergrootglas[h]

magnitude 1 belang[h], belangrijkheid **2** omvang, grootte **3** [astronomy] helderheid

magnolia 1 magnolia, tulpenboom **2** crèmewit[h]

magnum anderhalveliterfles

magpie 1 ekster **2** verzamelaar, hamsteraar

mahogany mahonie[h]

maid 1 hulp, dienstmeisje[h] **2** meisje[h], juffrouw **3** maagd || ~ *of* **honour** (ongehuwde) hofdame

¹maiden (n) **1** meisje[h], juffrouw **2** maagd

²maiden (adj) **1** maagdelijk, van een meisje **2** ongetrouwd [of woman]: ~ *name* meisjesnaam **3** eerste [eg of trip, flight]: *the Titanic sank on her ~ voyage* de Titanic zonk tijdens haar eerste reis

m<u>ai</u>denhead 1 maagdenvlies^h **2** maagdelijkheid [also fig]

¹mail (n) **1** post, brieven **2** mail, e-mail: *check one's ~* zijn mail lezen **3** maliënkolder

²mail (vb) **1** posten, per post versturen **2** mailen **3** (be)pantseren

m<u>ai</u>lbox [Am] brievenbus

m<u>ai</u>ling list adressenlijst, verzendlijst

m<u>ai</u>lman [Am] postbode

maim verminken [also fig]; kreupel maken

¹main (n) **1** hoofdleiding, hoofdbuis, hoofdkabel **2** (-s) (elektriciteits)net^h, elektriciteit, lichtnet^h: *connected to the ~s* (op het elektriciteitsnet) aangesloten **3** (open) zee || *in the ~* voor het grootste gedeelte, in het algemeen

²main (adj) hoofd-, belangrijkste, voornaamste: *~ course* hoofdgerecht^h; *~ line* **a)** hoofdlijn [of railways]; **b)** [Am] hoofdstraat; *~ street* hoofdstraat

m<u>ai</u>nframe mainframe^h, hoofdcomputer

m<u>ai</u>nland vasteland^h

m<u>ai</u>nly hoofdzakelijk, voornamelijk, grotendeels

m<u>ai</u>n stage 1 [venue] grote zaal **2** [festival] hoofdpodium^h

m<u>ai</u>nstay steunpilaar, pijler

m<u>ai</u>nstream 1 heersende stroming **2** hoofdstroom [of river] **3** mainstream [jazz]

maint<u>ai</u>n 1 handhaven, in stand houden: *he ~ed his calm attitude* hij bleef rustig; *~ order* de orde bewaren **2** onderhouden [eg house, family]; zorgen voor, een onderhoudsbeurt geven **3** beweren, stellen: *the suspect ~s his innocence* de verdachte zegt dat hij onschuldig is **4** verdedigen, opkomen voor: *~ an opinion* een mening verdedigen

m<u>ai</u>ntenance 1 handhaving [eg of law] **2** onderhoud^h [of house, machine] **3** levensonderhoud^h, levensbehoeften **4** toelage [of woman, child]; alimentatie

m<u>ai</u>son<u>e</u>tte 1 huisje^h, flatje^h **2** maisonnette

m<u>ai</u>ze mais

maj<u>e</u>stic majestueus, verheven

M<u>a</u>jesty Majesteit, Koninklijke Hoogheid || *on Her* (or: *His*) *~'s service* dienst [on envelope]

¹m<u>a</u>jor (n) **1** meerderjarige **2** majoor **3** [Am] hoofdvak^h [of study] **4** [Am] hoofdvakstudent

²m<u>a</u>jor (adj) **1** groot, groter, voornaamste: *a ~ breakthrough* een belangrijke doorbraak; *the ~ part of* de meerderheid van; *~ road* hoofdweg **2** ernstig, zwaar: *~ operation* zware operatie **3** meerderjarig, volwassen **4** [mus] in majeur: *C ~* C grote terts **5** senior, de oudere: *Rowland ~* Rowland senior

m<u>a</u>jor in [Am] als hoofdvak(ken) hebben, (als hoofdvak) studeren

maj<u>o</u>rity 1 meerderheid: *the ~ of people* de meeste mensen; *the ~ world* de derde wereld, de ontwikkelingslanden **2** meeste: *in the ~* in de meerderheid

m<u>a</u>jorly [inform] uiterst, heel erg: *he is ~ insane* hij is compleet gestoord

¹make (n) **1** merk^h **2** fabricage, vervaardiging || *on the ~* **a)** op (eigen) voordeel uit, op winst uit; **b)** op de versiertoer

²make (vb) **1** doen, zich gedragen, handelen: *~ as if* (or: *though*) **a)** doen alsof; **b)** op het punt staan **2** gaan, zich begeven: *we were making toward(s) the woods* wij gingen naar de bossen || *you'll have to ~ do with this old pair of trousers* je zult het met deze oude broek moeten doen; *~ away* (or: *off*) 'm smeren, ervandoor gaan; *~ away with o.s.* zich van kant maken; *~ off with* wegnemen, meenemen, jatten

³make (vb) **1** maken, bouwen, fabriceren, scheppen, veroorzaken, bereiden; opstellen [law, testament]: *~ coffee* (or: *tea*) koffie (or: thee) zetten; *God made man* God schiep de mens; *~ over a dress* een jurk vermaken; *show them what you are made of* toon wat je waard bent **2** maken, vormen, maken tot, benoemen tot: *the workers made him their spokesman* de arbeiders maakten hem tot hun woordvoerder **3** (ver)krijgen, (be)halen; binnenhalen [profit]; hebben [success]; lijden [loss]; verdienen, scoren; maken [point etc]: *~ a lot of money* veel geld verdienen; [cards] *~ a trick* een slag maken; *he made a lot on this deal* hij verdiende een hoop aan deze transactie **4** laten, ertoe brengen, doen, maken dat: *don't ~ me laugh* laat me niet lachen; *she made the food go round* ze zorgde ervoor dat er genoeg eten was voor iedereen; *you can't ~ me* je kunt me niet dwingen **5** schatten (op), komen op: *what time do you ~ it?* hoe laat heeft u het? **6** worden, maken, zijn: *three and four ~ seven* drie en vier is zeven **7** (geschikt) zijn (voor), (op)leveren, worden: *this student will never ~ a good doctor* deze student zal nooit een goede arts worden; *the man is made for this job* de man is perfect voor deze baan **8** bereiken, komen tot; halen [speed]; gaan; pakken [train]; zien; in zicht krijgen [land]; worden, komen in: *~ an appointment* op tijd zijn voor een afspraak; *~ the front pages* de voorpagina's halen; *~ it* op tijd zijn, het halen; [fig] succes hebben, slagen; *have it made* geslaagd zijn, op rozen zitten **9** doen, verrichten; uitvoeren [research]; geven [promise]; nemen [test]; houden [speech]: *~ an effort* een poging doen, pogen; *~ a phone call* opbellen **10** opmaken [bed] **11** tot een succes maken, het hem doen, de finishing touch geven: *~ sth. of o.s.*

succes hebben [in life] || *this fool can ~ or* **break** *the project* deze gek kan het project maken of breken; *~ sth. do* zich met iets behelpen; *let's ~ it next week* (or: *Wednesday*) laten we (voor) volgende week (or: woensdag) afspreken; *~ the most of* a) er het beste van maken; b) zoveel mogelijk profiteren van; *~ much of* a) belangrijk vinden; b) veel hebben aan; c) veel begrijpen van; *~ nothing of* a) gemakkelijk doen (over), geen probleem maken van; b) niets begrijpen van; *they couldn't ~ anything of my notes* ze konden niets met mijn aantekeningen beginnen
make-believe schijn, fantasie, het doen alsof: *this fight is just ~* dit gevecht is maar spel
make for 1 gaan naar, zich begeven naar: *we made for the nearest pub* we gingen naar de dichtstbijzijnde kroeg **2** bevorderen, bijdragen tot, zorgen voor
¹**make out** (vb) klaarspelen, het maken, zich redden: *the European industry is not making out as bad as everybody says* met de Europese industrie gaat het niet zo slecht als iedereen zegt
²**make out** (vb) **1** uitschrijven, invullen: *~ a cheque to* (or: *in favour of*) een cheque uitschrijven op naam van (or: ten gunste van) **2** beweren, verkondigen: *she makes herself out to be very rich* zij beweert dat ze erg rijk is **3** onderscheiden, zien **4** ontcijferen [eg handwriting] **5** begrijpen, snappen, hoogte krijgen van: *I can't ~ this message* ik snap dit bericht niet
makeover opknapbeurt, metamorfose
maker maker, fabrikant || *meet one's ~* sterven, dood gaan
¹**makeshift** (n) tijdelijke vervanging, noodoplossing
²**makeshift** (adj) voorlopig, tijdelijk, nood-
¹**make up** (vb) **1** zich opmaken, zich schminken **2** zich verzoenen, weer goedmaken || *~ for* weer goedmaken, vergoeden; *~ to s.o.* iem. in de gunst zien te komen; *~ to s.o. for sth.* a) iem. iets vergoeden; b) iets goedmaken met (or: bij) iem.
²**make up** (vb) **1** opmaken, schminken **2** bijleggen; goedmaken [quarrel]: *make it up (with s.o.)* het weer goedmaken (met iem.) **3** volledig maken, aanvullen: *father made up the difference of three pounds* vader legde de ontbrekende drie pond bij **4** vergoeden, goedmaken, teruggeven, terugbetalen: *~ lost ground* de schade inhalen **5** verzinnen: *~ an excuse* een excuus verzinnen **6** vormen, samenstellen: *the group was made up of four musicians* de groep bestond uit vier muzikanten **7** maken, opstellen; klaarmaken [medicine]; bereiden, maken tot (pakje), (kleren) maken (van), naaien **8** opmaken [bed]
make-up 1 make-up, schmink **2** aard, ka-

rakterh, natuur **3** samenstelling, opbouw
making 1 (-s) verdiensten **2** (-s) ingrediënten [also fig]; (juiste) kwaliteiten: *have the ~s of a surgeon* het in zich hebben om chirurg te worden || *in the ~* in de maak, in voorbereiding
maladjusted 1 [psychology] onaangepast **2** [econ] onevenwichtig
malady kwaal, ziekte: *a social ~* een sociale plaag
¹**Malagasy** (n) Malagassiër, Malagassische
²**Malagasy** (adj) Malagassisch
malaise 1 malaise **2** wee gevoel
malapropism grappige verspreking
malaria malaria
Malawi Malawi
¹**Malawian** (n) Malawiër, Malawische
²**Malawian** (adj) Malawisch
Malaysia Maleisië
¹**Malaysian** (n) Maleisiër, Maleisische
²**Malaysian** (adj) Maleisisch
malcontent ontevredene, ontevreden mensh
¹**male** (n) **1** mannelijk persoon **2** mannetjeh [animal]
²**male** (adj) **1** mannelijk [also fig]: *~ chauvinism* (mannelijk) seksisme; *~ choir* mannenkoorh **2** mannetjes-
malefactor boosdoener
malevolence kwaadwilligheid, boosaardigheid
malevolent [esp form] kwaadwillig
malformed misvormd
malfunction storing, defecth
Mali Mali
¹**Malian** (n) Malinees, Malinese
²**Malian** (adj) Malinees
malice 1 kwaadwilligheid, boosaardigheid: *bear ~ towards* (or: *to, against*) s.o. (een) wrok tegen iem. koesteren **2** boos opzet
malicious 1 kwaadwillig; kwaadaardig **2** [law] opzettelijk
malign kwaadwillig; maligne
malignant 1 schadelijk, verderfelijk **2** kwaadwillig, boosaardig **3** kwaadaardig [of disease]: *a ~ tumour* een kwaadaardig gezwel
mall 1 wandelgalerij, promenade **2** winkelpromenade, groot winkelcentrumh **3** [Am] middenberm
mallard wilde eend
malleable [fig] kneedbaar
mallrat [inform] rondhangende jongere in winkelcentrum, hangjongere
mall rat [roughly] hangjongere
malnourished ondervoed
malnutrition slechte voeding, ondervoeding
malpractice 1 [med] medische fout, nalatigheid **2** [law] misdrijfh
malt mout+h, malt+h

Malta Malta

¹Maltese (n) Maltees, Maltese

²Maltese (adj) **1** Maltees; Maltezer: ~ *Cross* Maltezer kruis **2** Maltezisch

maltreatment mishandeling

malversation malversatie, verduistering, wanbeheerʰ

malware malware

mam *mammy* mam(s)

mammal zoogdierʰ

mammoth mammoet

¹man (n) **1** man, de man, echtgenoot, minnaar, partner: ~ *of letters* schrijver, geleerde; ~ *of means* (or: *property*) bemiddeld (*or:* vermogend) man; *the* ~ *in the street* de gewone man, jan met de pet; ~ *about town* man van de wereld, playboy; ~ *and wife* man en vrouw; ~ *of the world* iem. met mensenkennis; *the very* ~ de persoon die men nodig heeft, net wie men zocht; *be* ~ *enough to* mans genoeg zijn om **2** mens, het mensdom: *the rights of Man* de mensenrechten; *to the last* ~ tot op de laatste man; *every* ~ *for himself* ieder voor zich; *as a* ~ als één man; *one* ~, *one vote* enkelvoudig stemrecht **3** ondergeschikte, soldaat: *men* manschappen; *officers and men* officieren en manschappen; *I'm your* ~ op mij mag (*or:* kan) je rekenen ‖ *be enough of a* ~ *to* wel zo flink zijn om te; *(all) to a* ~ eensgezind

²man (vb) **1** bemannen, bezetten: *~ned crossing* bewaakte overweg **2** vermannen: ~ *o.s.* zich vermannen

³man (int) [Am] sjonge!

¹manacle (n) **1** handboei **2** belemmering

²manacle (vb) in de boeien slaan, aan elkaar vastketenen

¹manage (vb) **1** rondkomen, zich behelpen **2** slagen, het klaarspelen: *can you ~?* gaat het?, lukt het (zo)?; *I'll* ~ het lukt me wel **3** als beheerder optreden

²manage (vb) **1** slagen in, weten te, kunnen, kans zien te: *the ~d to escape* hij wist te ontsnappen **2** leiden, besturen; beheren [business]; hoeden [cattle] **3** beheersen, weten aan te pakken, manipuleren **4** hanteren **5** aankunnen, aandurven, in staat zijn tot: *I cannot* ~ *another mouthful* ik krijg er geen hap meer in

manageable handelbaar, beheersbaar

management 1 beheerʰ, managementʰ, bestuurʰ, administratie **2** overlegʰ, beleidʰ: *more luck than (good)* ~ meer geluk dan wijsheid **3** werkgevers

manager 1 bestuurder, chef; directeur [of business]; manager [of sports team]; impresario [of singer] **2** manager, bedrijfsleider: *general* ~ algemeen directeur

managerial bestuurs-, directeurs-, leidinggevend

manatee lamantijn

mancave mancave

mandarin 1 mandarijntjeʰ **2** bureaucraat

Mandarin Mandarijnsʰ [language]; Chineesʰ

mandarin orange mandarijntjeʰ

mandate mandaatʰ, machtiging om namens anderen te handelen

mandatory 1 bevel-: ~ *sign* gebodsbordʰ **2** verplicht: ~ *subject* verplicht (school)vak

mandolin mandoline

mane manen

manège 1 manege, (paard)rijschool **2** rijkunst

mange schurft⁺ʰ, scabiës

manger trog, krib

mange-tout peul(tjeʰ)

¹mangle (n) **1** mangel **2** wringer

²mangle (vb) **1** mangelen, door de mangel draaien **2** verscheuren, verminken, havenen; [fig] verknoeien: *~d bodies* verminkte lichamen

mango mango

mangy 1 schurftig **2** sjofel

manhandle 1 toetakelen, afranselen **2** door mankracht verplaatsen

manhood 1 mannelijkheid **2** volwassenheid

mania 1 manie, waanzin, zucht: *Beatle* ~ Beatlemania, Beatlegekte **2** (+ for) rage (om/voor)

maniac maniak, waanzinnige

manic 1 manisch **2** erg opgewonden, bezeten

¹manicure (n) manicure

²manicure (vb) manicuren

¹manifest (adj) zichtbaar, duidelijk, klaarblijkelijk

²manifest (vb) zichtbaar maken, vertonen: ~ *one's interest* blijk geven van belangstelling

manifestation 1 manifestatie **2** verkondiging, openbaring **3** uiting

manifesto manifestʰ

manifold veelvuldig, verscheiden

manipulate 1 hanteren [appliance] **2** manipuleren [also med] **3** knoeien met [text, figures]

manipulation manipulatie

manipulative manipulatief

mankind het mensdom, de mensheid

manly mannelijk, manhaftig

man-made door de mens gemaakt, kunstmatig: ~ *fibre* kunstvezel

man-mountain [inform] beer van een vent

mannequin 1 mannequin **2** etalagepop

manner 1 manier, wijze: *in a* ~ in zekere zin; *in a* ~ *of speaking* bij wijze van spreken **2** houding, gedragʰ **3** stijl, trant **4** soort⁺ʰ, slagʰ: *all* ~ *of* allerlei **5** (-s) manieren, goed gedragʰ: *bad ~s* slechte manieren; *it's bad ~s*

dat is onbeleefd **6** (-s) zeden, sociale gewoonten
mannerism 1 aanwensel[h] **2** gekunsteld-
heid
mannish manachtig; mannelijk [of wom-
en]
¹manoeuvre (n) manoeuvre[+h]
²manoeuvre (vb) manoeuvreren; [fig] slinks
handelen: ~ *s.o. into a good job* een goed
baantje voor iem. versieren
manor manor, groot (heren)huis[h] met om-
liggende gronden
manpower 1 arbeidskrachten **2** beschik-
bare strijdkrachten
mansion herenhuis[h]
man-size flink, kolossaal
manslaughter doodslag
mantelpiece schoorsteenmantel
mantra mantra[+h]
¹manual (n) **1** handboek[h], handleiding
2 [mus] manuaal[h]
²manual (adj) hand-: ~ *labour* handenarbeid; ~ *worker* handarbeider
¹manufacture (n) **1** fabricaat[h], product[h],
goederen **2** vervaardiging, fabricage, pro-
ductie(proces[h]), makelij
²manufacture (vb) **1** vervaardigen, verwerken, produceren: *manufacturing industry* ver-
werkende industrie **2** verzinnen
manufacturer fabrikant
man up [Am] zich vermannen, je verantwoordelijkheid nemen
¹manure (n) mest
²manure (vb) bemesten, gieren
manuscript manuscript[h], handschrift[h]
many veel, een groot aantal: *how* ~ *books
did you read?* hoeveel boeken heb je gelezen?; *a good* (or: *great*) ~ een groot aantal; ~
of the pages were torn veel bladzijden waren
gescheurd; *three times as* ~ drie keer zo veel;
as ~ *as thirty* wel dertig; *ten mistakes in as* ~
lines tien fouten in tien regels; *and as* ~ *again*
(or: *more*) en nog eens zoveel; *he had had one
too* ~ hij had een glaasje te veel op; ~'s the
time vaak
¹map (n) **1** kaart **2** plan[h], grafische voorstelling ‖ *put on the* ~ de aandacht vestigen op
²map (vb) in kaart brengen: ~ *out* in kaart
brengen; [fig] plannen, indelen; *I've got my
future ~ped out for me* mijn toekomst is al
uitgestippeld
maple esdoorn
maple leaf esdoornblad[h]
mapping afbeelding
mar bederven, verstoren: *make* (or: *mend)
or* ~ *a plan* een plan doen slagen of mislukken
¹marathon (n) marathon(loop)
²marathon (adj) marathon, ellenlang
maraud plunderen, roven
¹marble (n) **1** marmer[h] **2** knikker: *play (at)* ~s
knikkeren ‖ *he has lost his* ~s er zit bij hem

een steekje los
²marble (adj) marmeren, gemarmerd
¹march (n) **1** mars **2** opmars: *on the* ~ in opmars ‖ *steal a* ~ *on s.o.* iem. te vlug af zijn
²march (vb) (op)marcheren, aanrukken:
quick ~*!* voorwaarts mars!
³march (vb) **1** doen marcheren **2** leiden;
voeren [on foot]: *be ~ed away* (or: *off*) weg-
geleid worden
March maart
marching order 1 [mil; esp pl] marsorder
2 ontslag[h]; [hum] afwijzing
march past defilé[h], parade
mare merrie
margarine margarine
margin 1 marge; [Stock Exchange] surplus[h]:
~ *of error* foutenmarge **2** kantlijn
marginal 1 in de kantlijn geschreven: ~
notes kanttekeningen **2** miniem, onbeduidend, bijkomstig: *of* ~ *importance* van ondergeschikt belang
marguerite margriet
marigold 1 goudsbloem **2** afrikaantje[h]
marijuana marihuana
marina jachthaven
¹marinade (n) marinade
²marinade (vb) marineren
¹marine (n) **1** marine, vloot **2** marinier
²marine (adj) zee-: ~ *biology* mariene biologie
mariner zeeman, matroos
marionette marionet
marital echtelijk, huwelijks-: ~ *status* burgerlijke staat
maritime maritiem: ~ *law* zeerecht[h]
marjoram marjolein
¹mark (n) **1** teken[h], leesteken[h]; [fig] blijk[h]: *as
a* ~ *of my esteem* als blijk van mijn achting
2 teken[h], spoor[h], vlek; [fig] indruk: *bear the
~s of* de sporen dragen van; *make one's* ~ zich
onderscheiden **3** (rapport)cijfer[h], punt[h]
4 peil[h], niveau[h]: *above* (or: *below*) *the* ~ boven (or: beneden) peil; *I don't feel quite up to
the* ~ ik voel me niet helemaal fit **5** start-
(streep): *not quick off the* ~ niet vlug (van begrip); *on your ~s, get set, go!* op uw plaatsen!
klaar? af! **6** doel[h], doelwit[h]: [fig] *hit the* ~ in
de roos schieten; [fig] *miss* (or: *overshoot*) *the*
~ het doel missen, te ver gaan, de plank misslaan ‖ *keep s.o. up to the* ~ zorgen dat iem.
zijn uiterste best doet; *overstep the* ~ over de
schreef gaan
²mark (vb) **1** vlekken (maken/krijgen) **2** cijfers geven
³mark (vb) **1** merken, tekenen, onderscheiden: ~ *the occasion* de gelegenheid luister
bijzetten **2** beoordelen, nakijken; cijfers geven voor [schoolwork] **3** letten op [words
etc]: ~ *how it is done* let op hoe het gedaan
wordt **4** te kennen geven, vertonen **5** bestemmen, opzijzetten **6** vlekken; tekenen

[animal] **7** [sport] dekken
Mark model[h], type[h], rangnummer[h]
mark down 1 noteren, opschrijven **2** afprijzen **3** een lager cijfer geven
marked 1 duidelijk: *a ~ preference* een uitgesproken voorkeur **2** gemarkeerd; gemerkt [eg money] **3** bestemd, uitgekozen
marker 1 teller **2** teken[h], merk[h], kenteken[h], mijlpaal, kilometerpaal, baken[h], boekenlegger, scorebord[h] **3** markeerstift
¹market (n) **1** markt, handel, afzetgebied[h]: *be in the ~ for* sth. iets willen kopen; *price o.s. out of the ~* zich uit de markt prijzen **2** marktprijs **3** markt, beurs
²market (vb) inkopen doen, winkelen
³market (vb) **1** op de markt brengen **2** verkopen, verhandelen
marketable 1 verkoopbaar **2** markt-: *~ value* marktwaarde
market-driven marktgestuurd
market garden moestuin
marketing 1 markthandel **2** marketing, marktonderzoek[h]
marketplace marktplein[h]
marking 1 tekening [of animal etc] **2** (ken)teken[h] het nakijken van huiswerk
mark out 1 afbakenen, markeren **2** uitkiezen, bestemmen: *marked out as a candidate for promotion* uitgekozen als promotiekandidaat
marksman 1 scherpschutter **2** [sport] goede scorer, doelpuntenmaker
mark up in prijs verhogen
marmalade marmelade
marmot marmot
¹maroon (n) **1** vuurpijl, lichtsein[h] **2** kastanjebruin[h] **3** marron, boslandcreool
²maroon (vb) **1** achterlaten; [fig] aan zijn lot overlaten **2** isoleren, afsnijden: *~ed by the floods* door de overstromingen ingesloten
marquee grote tent, feesttent
marquis markies
marriage huwelijk[h], echt(verbintenis): *~ of convenience* verstandshuwelijk[h]; *her ~ to* haar huwelijk met; *~ settlement* huwelijksvoorwaarden
marriageable huwbaar
marriage vows trouwbeloften
married gehuwd: *a ~ couple* een echtpaar
marrow 1 (eetbare) pompoen: *vegetable ~* eetbare pompoen **2** merg[h] **3** kern, pit
marry trouwen (met), in het huwelijk treden (met): *~ money* (or: *wealth*) een rijk huwelijk sluiten; *get married* trouwen ‖ *married to* verknocht aan; *he is married to his work* hij is met zijn werk getrouwd; *he is married with three children* hij is getrouwd en heeft drie kinderen
marsh moeras[h]
¹marshal (n) **1** (veld)maarschalk **2** hofmaarschalk **3** hoofd[h] van ordedienst **4** [Am]

hoofd[h] van politie; [roughly] sheriff **5** [Am] brandweercommandant
²marshal (vb) **1** (zich) opstellen **2** leiden, (be)geleiden
marshmallow marshmallow
¹marsupial (n) buideldier[h]
²marsupial (adj) buideldragend
mart handelscentrum[h]
marten 1 [animal] marter **2** [fur] marter(bont)[h]
martial 1 krijgs-: *~ arts* (oosterse) vechtkunsten [karate, judo etc] **2** krijgshaftig
¹Martian (n) Marsbewoner
²Martian (adj) Mars-
¹martyr (n) martelaar [also fig]: *make a ~ of o.s.* zich als martelaar opwerpen
²martyr (vb) de marteldood doen sterven; martelen [also fig]; kwellen
martyrdom 1 martelaarschap[h] **2** marteldood **3** marteling, lijdensweg
¹marvel (n) wonder[h]: *do* (or: *work*) *~s* wonderen verrichten
²marvel (vb) (+ at) zich verwonderen (over), zich verbazen (over)
marvellous prachtig, fantastisch
marzipan marsepein(tje)[h]
masc *masculine* mnl., mannelijk
mascot mascotte
masculine 1 mannelijk **2** manachtig
¹mash (n) (warm) mengvoer[h]
²mash (vb) fijnstampen, fijnmaken: *~ed potatoes* (aardappel)puree **2** mengen, hutselen
mash up vermengen
¹mask (n) masker[h] [also fig]; mom[h]
²mask (vb) zich vermommen, een masker opzetten; [fig] zijn (ware) gelaat verbergen
³mask (vb) **1** maskeren, vermommen **2** verbergen, verhullen
masked gemaskerd
masking tape afplakband[h]
masochist masochist
mason 1 metselaar **2** vrijmetselaar
¹masquerade (n) **1** maskerade **2** vermomming
²masquerade (vb) (+ as) zich vermommen (als), zich voordoen (als)
¹mass (n) **1** massa, hoop, menigte: *in the ~* in massa; *a ~ of* één en al; *the ~es* de massa
²mass (adj) massa-, massaal: *weapons of ~ destruction* massavernietigingswapens; *~ resistance* massaal verzet; *~ shooting* schietpartij waarbij veel slachtoffers vallen
³mass (n) [Roman Catholicism] mis
⁴mass (n) (zich) verzamelen: *~ troops* troepen concentreren
¹massacre (n) **1** bloedbad[h] **2** [fig] afslachting
²massacre (vb) **1** uitmoorden **2** in de pan hakken
¹massage (n) massage

²**massage** (vb) **1** masseren **2** manipuleren; knoeien met [data etc]

massive 1 massief, zwaar **2** groots, indrukwekkend **3** massaal **4** aanzienlijk, enorm

mass-produce in massa produceren

mast mast

¹**master** (n) **1** meester, heer, baas, schoolmeester: ~ *of the* **house** heer des huizes **2** origineel^h, matrijs, master(tape) ‖ *Master of* *Arts* [roughly] doctorandus, [roughly] Master of Arts, [roughly] Master of Science; *Master of* *Ceremonies* ceremoniemeester

²**master** (adj) hoofd-, voornaamste

³**master** (vb) overmeesteren; de baas worden [also fig]; te boven komen

master bedroom grootste slaapkamer

master card hoogste kaart; hoge troef

masterful 1 meesterachtig **2** meesterlijk

master key loper, passe-partout^{+h}

mastermind uitdenken: *he* ~*ed the* **project** hij was het brein achter het project

masterpiece meesterstuk^h, meesterwerk^h

masterstroke meesterzet

mastery 1 meesterschap^h: *the* ~ *over* de overhand op **2** beheersing, kennis

masticate kauwen

masturbate masturberen

¹**mat** (n) **1** mat(je^h) [also fig; sport]; deurmat **2** tafelmatje^h, onderzettertje^h **3** klit: *a* ~ *of* *hair* een wirwar van haren

²**mat** (adj) mat, dof

³**mat** (vb) klitten, in de war raken

⁴**mat** (vb) verwarren, doen samenklitten

¹**match** (n) **1** (or: **meet**) *one's* ~ zijns gelijke vinden; *be more than a* ~ *for* s.o. iem. de baas zijn **2** wedstrijd **3** lucifer **4** huwelijk^h

²**match** (vb) (bij elkaar) passen: ~*ing* **clothes** (or: **colours**) bij elkaar passende kleren (or: kleuren)

³**match** (vb) **1** evenaren, niet onderdoen voor: *can you* ~ *that?* kan je dat net zo goed doen?; *they are* **well** ~*ed* zij zijn aan elkaar gewaagd **2** passen bij: *they are* **well** ~*ed* ze passen goed bij elkaar **3** doen passen; aanpassen [colour]: ~ *jobs and applicants* het juiste werk voor de juiste kandidaten uitzoeken

matchbox lucifersdoosje^h

matchless weergaloos, niet te evenaren

matchmaking het koppelen, het tot stand brengen van huwelijken

¹**mate** (n) **1** maat, kameraad **2** (huwelijks)partner, gezel(lin), mannetje^h; wijfje^h [of birds] **3** helper [of craftsman]; gezel **4** stuurman **5** [chess] mat^h

²**mate** (vb) paren, huwen, zich voortplanten

³**mate** (vb) **1** koppelen, doen paren **2** schaken, mat zetten

¹**material** (n) **1** materiaal^h, grondstof; [fig] gegevens; stof **2** soort^{+h}

²**material** (adj) **1** materieel, lichamelijk: ~

damage materiële schade **2** belangrijk, wezenlijk: *a* ~ *witness* een belangrijke getuige

materialism materialisme^h

materialist(ic) materialistisch

¹**materialize** (vb) **1** werkelijkheid worden: *his* *dreams* never ~*d* zijn dromen werden nooit werkelijkheid **2** tevoorschijn komen [of ghost]

²**materialize** (vb) **1** verwezenlijken, realiseren, uitvoeren **2** materialiseren

maternal moeder-: ~ *love* moederliefde ‖ *grandfather* grootvader van moederszijde

maternity moederschap^h: ~ *home* kraamkliniek

maternity blues [inform] babyblues, postnatale depressie

maternity leave zwangerschapsverlof^h

matey vriendschappelijk: *be* ~ *with* s.o. beste maatjes met iem. zijn

math [Am] wiskunde ‖ [inform] *do* the ~ het rekensommetje maken, iets uitrekenen; [inform] *just do the* ~*!* reken maar uit, ga maar na

mathematical 1 wiskundig **2** precies, exact

mathematician wiskundige

mathematics wiskunde

maths *mathematics* wiskunde

mating season paartijd, bronst

matriarchal matriarchaal

matricide moedermoord(enaar)

matriculation inschrijving, toegang tot universiteit

matrimony huwelijk^h, echt(elijke staat)

matrix 1 gietvorm, matrijs **2** matrix

matron 1 matrone **2** directrice, hoofdverpleegster ‖ ~ *of honour* getrouwd bruidsmeisje

matt mat, niet glanzend

¹**matter** (n) **1** materie, stof **2** stof, materiaal^h, inhoud **3** stof [in, of body] **4** belang^h: *no* ~ het maakt niet uit, laat maar **5** kwestie: *just a* ~ *of* **time** slechts een kwestie van tijd; *no* **laughing** ~ niets om te lachen; *for* that ~, *for the* ~ *of* that wat dat betreft ‖ *as a* ~ *of* **course** vanzelfsprekend; *as a* ~ *of* **fact** eigenlijk; *what is the* ~ *with him?* wat scheelt hem?

²**matter** (vb) van belang zijn, betekenen: *it* *doesn't* ~ het geeft niet, het doet er niet toe; *what does it* ~*?* wat zou het?

matter-of-fact zakelijk, nuchter

matting matwerk^h; matten [as floor covering etc]

mattress matras^{+h}

¹**mature** (adj) **1** rijp, volgroeid **2** volwassen: *behave* ~*ly* zich gedragen als een volwassene **3** weloverwogen **4** belegen [cheese, wine]

²**mature** (vb) **1** rijpen, tot rijpheid komen: ~*d cheese* belegen kaas **2** volgroeien, zich volledig ontwikkelen, volwassen worden **3** vervallen [of Bill of Exchange etc]

maturity 1 rijpheid **2** volgroeidheid, volwassenheid

maul 1 verscheuren; aan stukken scheuren
[also fig] **2** ruw behandelen

Maundy Thursday Witte Donderdag

Mauritania Mauritanië

¹Mauritanian (n) Mauritaniër, Mauritaanse

²Mauritanian (adj) Mauritaans

¹Mauritian (n) Mauritiaan(se)

²Mauritian (adj) Mauritiaans

Mauritius Mauritius

maverick [Am] **1** non-conformist **2** onge-
brandmerkt kalfʰ, veulenʰ

maw 1 pens; maag [of animal] **2** krop [of
bird] **3** muil; bek [fig]

mawkish 1 walgelijk; flauw [of taste]
2 overdreven sentimenteel

max *maximum* max.: [inform] *to the* ~ absoluut, compleet, totaal

maxim spreuk

maximally hoogstens, maximaal

maximize maximaliseren: ~ *one's experience* zo veel mogelijk munt slaan uit zijn ervaring

¹maximum (n) maximumʰ: *at its* ~ op het
hoogste punt

²maximum (adj) maximaal, hoogste: ~
speed topsnelheid

max out [Am; inform] leeghalen, (helemaal) opmaken [credit card]

may 1 mogen: ~ *I ask why you think so?* mag
ik vragen waarom je dat denkt?; *you* ~ *not
leave yet* je mag nog niet vertrekken **2** [pos-
sibility] kunnen: *they* ~ *arrive later* ze komen
misschien later; *come what* ~ wat er ook gebeurt; ~ *I help you?* kan ik u helpen?; *I hope
he* ~ *recover, but I fear he* ~ *not* ik hoop dat hij
beter wordt, maar ik vrees van niet **3** [in
wishes] mogen: ~ *you stay forever young* moge
jij altijd jong blijven

May mei

maybe misschien, wellicht: *as soon as* ~ zo
vlug mogelijk

mayday mayday, noodsignaalʰ

May Day 1 mei, dag van de arbeid

mayfly eendagsvlieg

mayhem rotzooi: *cause* (or: *create*) ~ herrie
schoppen

mayonnaise mayonaise

mayor burgemeester

maypole meiboom

maze doolhof [also fig]

MBA *Master of Business Administration*

me mij, voor mij, ik: *he liked her better than
me* hij vond haar aardiger dan mij; *poor me*
arme ik; *it is me* ik ben het

mead mede

meadow wei(de), graslandʰ

meagre schraal [meal, result etc]

meal 1 maalʰ, maaltijd **2** meelʰ

meals-on-wheels [roughly] tafeltje-dek-
jeʰ

mealy 1 melig **2** bleek [complexion]

¹mean (n) **1** (-s) middelʰ: *by* ~*s of* door middel van; *by no* ~, *not by any (manner of)* ~*s* in
geen geval; *a* ~*s to an end* een middel om een
doel te bereiken **2** (-s) middelen (van bestaan): *live beyond one's* ~*s* boven zijn stand
leven **3** middelmaat; [fig] middenweg **4** gemiddeldeʰ (waarde)

²mean (adj) **1** gemeen, laag, ongemanierd:
~ *tricks* ordinaire trucs **2** gierig **3** armzalig,
armoedig **4** [Am] kwaadaardig, vals **5** gemiddeld, doorsnee- **6** gebrekkig, beperkt:
no ~ *cook* een buitengewone kok, geen
doorsneekok **7** laag; gering [origin]

³mean (vb) het bedoelen: ~ *ill* (or: *well*) *(to,
towards, by s.o.)* het slecht (or: goed) menen
(met iem.)

⁴mean (vb) **1** betekenen, willen zeggen: *it* ~*s
nothing to me* het zegt me niets **2** bedoelen:
what do you ~ *by that?* wat bedoel je daarmee? **3** de bedoeling hebben: ~ *business*
vastberaden zijn, zeer serieus zijn; *I* ~ *to
leave tomorrow* ik ben van plan morgen te
vertrekken **4** menen **5** bestemmen **6** betekenen, neerkomen op: *those clouds* ~ *rain* die
wolken voorspellen regen

meander 1 zich (in bochten) slingeren;
kronkelen [of river] **2** (rond)dolen [also fig]

meanderings slingerpadʰ, kronkelpadʰ,
gekronkelʰ

¹meaning (n) **1** betekenis, zin, inhoud: [dis-
approvingly] *what's the* ~ *of this?* wat heeft
dit te betekenen? **2** bedoeling, strekking

²meaning (adj) veelbetekenend, veelzeggend

meaningful 1 van (grote) betekenis, gewichtig **2** zinvol

meaningless 1 zonder betekenis, nietszeggend **2** zinloos

means test inkomensonderzoekʰ

means-tested inkomensafhankelijk

meantime tussentijd: *in the* ~ ondertussen

meanwhile ondertussen

measles 1 mazelen **2** rodehond

measly 1 met mazelen **2** [inform] armzalig: ~ *tip* hondenfooi

measurable 1 meetbaar: *within a* ~ *distance of* dicht in de buurt van **2** van betekenis, belangrijk

¹measure (n) **1** maatregel, stap: *take strong*
~*s* geen halve maatregelen nemen **2** maat
[also music]; maateenheid, maat(beker);
maat(streep) [mus]; mate, gematigdheid: *a* ~
of wheat een maat tarwe; *in (a) great* (or:
large) ~ in hoge (or: ruime) mate; *made to* ~
op maat gemaakt **3** maatstaf **4** maatstok,
maatlat, maatlintʰ **5** ritmeʰ, melodie

²measure (vb) **1** beoordelen, taxeren **2** opnemen, met de ogen afmeten **3** letten op,
overdenken: ~ *one's words* zijn woorden

wegen

³**measure** (vb) meten, afmeten, opmeten, toemeten, uitmeten, de maat nemen: *the room ~s three **metres** by four* de kamer is drie bij vier (meter); *~ **off*** (or: *out*) afmeten [materiaal etc]; *~ **out*** toemeten

measured weloverwogen, zorgvuldig

measurement 1 afmeting, maat **2** meting

measure up voldoen: *~ **to a)*** voldoen aan; **b)** berekend zijn op (or: voor), opgewassen zijn tegen

meat 1 vleesʰ: *white ~* wit vlees [eg poultry] **2** [Am] eetbaar gedeelteʰ [of fruit, crustacean, egg]; (vrucht)vleesʰ **3** essentie: *there is no real ~ in the story* het verhaal heeft weinig om het lijf **4** fortʰ, sterke kant ‖ *one man's ~ is another man's **poison*** de een traag, de ander graag

meatball gehaktbal

meaty 1 lijvig **2** vleesachtig **3** stevig: *a ~ discussion* een pittige discussie

mechanic mecanicien, technicus, monteur

mechanical 1 mechanisch, machinaal; [fig] ongeïnspireerd **2** ambachtelijk, handwerk- **3** werktuig(bouw)kundig: *~ **engineering*** werktuig(bouw)kunde

mechanics 1 mechanica, werktuigkunde **2** mechanismeʰ **3** techniek

mechanism 1 mechanismeʰ, mechaniekʰ **2** werking **3** techniek

mechanization mechanisering

medal medaille

medallion 1 (grote) medaille **2** medaillonʰ

medallist medaillewinnaar

meddle in zich bemoeien met, zich inlaten met: *don't ~ my affairs* bemoei je met je eigen zaken

meddlesome bemoeiziek

media media

median middel-, midden-, middelst: *~ **point*** zwaartepuntʰ

media-savvy mediawijs

¹**mediate** (vb) overbrengen

²**mediate** (vb) bemiddelen, bijleggen: *~ **between*** bemiddelen tussen

mediation bemiddeling

mediator bemiddelaar, tussenpersoon

medic [inform] medisch student; dokter

¹**medical** (n) (medisch) onderzoekʰ, keuring

²**medical** (adj) medisch: *~ **certificate*** doktersverklaring

medical examiner [Am] lijkschouwer, patholoog-anatoom

medicament medicijnʰ

Medicare ziektekostenverzekering

medication 1 medicamentʰ, medicijnʰ, medicijnen **2** medicatie

medicinal 1 geneeskrachtig **2** geneeskundig, medisch

medicine 1 geneesmiddelʰ: *she **takes** too much ~* ze slikt te veel medicijnen **2** tover-

middelʰ **3** geneeskunde, medicijnen

medieval middeleeuws

mediocre middelmatig

mediocrity middelmatigheid

¹**meditate** (vb) **1** diep nadenken, in gedachten verzonken zijn: *~ **(up)on*** overpeinzen **2** mediteren

²**meditate** (vb) van plan zijn: *~ **revenge*** zinnen op wraak

meditation 1 overpeinzing, bespiegeling: *deep in ~* in gepeins verzonken **2** meditatie

Mediterranean m.b.t. de Middellandse Zee, m.b.t. het Middellandse Zeegebied

¹**medium** (n) **1** middenweg, compromisʰ **2** gemiddeldeʰ, middenʰ **3** mediumʰ, middelʰ: *through the ~ of* door middel van **4** tussenpersoon **5** (natuurlijke) omgeving, milieuʰ **6** uitingsvorm, kunstvorm **7** [spiritism] mediumʰ

²**medium** (adj) gemiddeld, doorsnee-: *in the ~ term* op middellange termijn; [radio] *~ **wave*** middengolf

medlar mispel

medley 1 mengelmoes(je)ʰ **2** [mus] potpourri⁺ʰ, medley

meds [inform] medicijnen

meek 1 gedwee **2** bescheiden **3** zachtmoedig

¹**meet** (n) **1** samenkomst; trefpuntʰ [for hunt] **2** jachtgezelschapʰ **3** [Am; athletics] ontmoeting, wedstrijd

²**meet** (vb) **1** elkaar ontmoeten, elkaar tegenkomen: *~ **up*** elkaar (toevallig) treffen; *~ up **with*** tegen het lijf lopen **2** samenkomen, bijeenkomen **3** kennismaken **4** sluiten; dicht gaan [of article of clothing]

³**meet** (vb) **1** ontmoeten, treffen, tegenkomen: *run to ~ s.o.* iem. tegemoet rennen; [fig] *~ s.o. **halfway*** a) iem. tegemoetkomen; **b)** het verschil (samen) delen **2** (aan)raken **3** kennismaken met: *pleased to ~ you* aangenaam **4** afhalen: *I'll ~ your train* ik kom je van de trein afhalen **5** behandelen, het hoofd bieden: *~ **criticism*** kritiek weerleggen **6** tegemoetkomen (aan), voldoen (aan), vervullen: *~ the **bill*** de rekening voldoen **7** beantwoorden, (onvriendelijk) bejegenen **8** ondervinden, ondergaan, dragen: *~ one's **death*** de dood vinden

meet and greet 1 meet-and-greet; korte ontmoeting [with celebrity] **2** ouderavond [at school]

meeting 1 ontmoeting [also sport]; wedstrijd **2** bijeenkomst, vergadering, bespreking: *meeting-house* kerk

meet with 1 ondervinden, ondergaan: *~ **approval*** instemming vinden **2** tegen het lijf lopen **3** [Am] een ontmoeting hebben met

megabyte megabyte [1 million bytes]

megalomania grootheidswaanzin

megaphone megafoon

megawatt megawatt
meh [inform] bleh, waardeloos
melancholic melancholisch, zwaarmoedig
¹**melancholy** (n) melancholie, zwaarmoedigheid
²**melancholy** (adj) 1 melancholisch, zwaarmoedig 2 droevig, triest
mellow 1 rijp; sappig [of fruit] 2 zacht, warm; vol [of sound, colour, taste] 3 gerijpt, zacht(moedig), mild
melodious melodieus, welluidend
melodrama melodrama^h [also fig]
melody melodie
melon meloen
melt smelten: ~ *in the mouth* smelten op de tong; ~ *down* omsmelten
meltdown het afsmelten [at nuclear power plant]
meltingpoint smeltpunt^h
melting pot smeltkroes [also fig]: *in the* ~ onstabiel
member lid^h, lidmaat^{+h}, (onder)deel^h, element^h, zinsdeel^h, lichaamsdeel^h: ~ *of Parliament* parlementslid^h; ~ *state* lidstaat
membership 1 lidmaatschap^h 2 ledental^h, de leden
membrane membraan^h
meme 1 [biology] meme 2 [comp] meme
memento gedenkteken^h
memo *memorandum* memo^h
memoir 1 biografie 2 verhandeling
memoirs memoires, autobiografie
memorable gedenkwaardig
memorandum memorandum^h, informele nota: ~ *of association* akte van oprichting
¹**memorial** (n) gedenkteken^h, monument^h
²**memorial** (adj) herdenkings-: ~ *service* herdenkingsdienst
memorize 1 uit het hoofd leren 2 onthouden
memory 1 geheugen^h, herinnering: *to the best of my* ~ voor zover ik mij kan herinneren; *within living* ~ bij mensenheugenis; *from* ~ van buiten, uit het hoofd 2 herinnering, aandenken^h: *in* ~ *of, to the* ~ *of* ter (na)gedachtenis aan
memory lane: *go down* ~ terug in je herinnering gaan
¹**menace** (n) 1 (be)dreiging: *filled with* ~ vol dreiging 2 lastpost, gevaar^h
²**menace** (vb) (be)dreigen
¹**mend** (n) herstelling, reparatie ‖ *he's on the* ~ hij is aan de beterende hand
²**mend** (vb) er weer bovenop komen, herstellen, zich (ver)beteren
³**mend** (vb) 1 herstellen, repareren: ~ *stockings* kousen stoppen 2 goedmaken 3 verbeteren
mendicant 1 bedelmonnik 2 bedelaar
¹**menial** (n) [oft depr] dienstbode, knecht, meid

²**menial** (adj) [oft depr] ondergeschikt, oninteressant: *a* ~ *job* een min baantje
menopause menopauze
men's room [Am] herentoilet^h
menstrual 1 menstrueel: ~ *cycle* menstruatiecyclus; ~ *period* menstruatie 2 maandelijks
menstruate menstrueren, ongesteld zijn
menstruation menstruatie, ongesteldheid
menswear herenkleding
mental 1 geestelijk, mentaal, psychisch: ~ *illness* zenuwziekte; ~*ly defective* (or: *deficient, handicapped*) geestelijk gehandicapt; ~*ly retarded* achterlijk 2 hoofd-, met het hoofd: ~ *arithmetic* hoofdrekenen^h; ~ *gymnastics* hersengymnastiek; *make a* ~ *note of sth.* iets in zijn oren knopen 3 psychiatrisch: ~ *hospital* psychiatrische inrichting
mentality mentaliteit
¹**mention** (n) vermelding, opgave: *honourable* ~ eervolle vermelding; *make* ~ *of* vermelden
²**mention** (vb) vermelden: *not to* ~ om (nog maar) niet te spreken van ‖ *don't* ~ *it* geen dank
mentor mentor
menu menu^h, (menu)kaart, maaltijd: *set* ~, *fixed price* ~ keuzemenu^h
menu bar menubalk
mercantile handels-, koopmans-
¹**mercenary** (n) huurling
²**mercenary** (adj) 1 op geld belust 2 gehuurd: ~ *troops* huurtroepen
merchandise koopwaar, artikelen, producten
¹**merchant** (n) groothandelaar, koopman
²**merchant** (adj) 1 koopvaardij-: ~ *shipping* koopvaardij 2 handels-, koopmans-
merciful genadig; mild: ~*ly, he came just in time* gelukkig kwam hij net op tijd
merciless genadeloos: *a* ~ *ruler* een meedogenloos heerser
mercury kwik(zilver)^h
mercy 1 genade, barmhartigheid 2 daad van barmhartigheid, weldaad: *be thankful for small mercies* wees maar blij dat het niet erger is 3 vergevensgezindheid: *throw o.s. on a person's* ~ een beroep doen op iemands goedheid; [oft iron] *left to the (tender)* ~ *of* overgeleverd aan de goedheid van ‖ *at the* ~ *of* in de macht van
mercy killing [euph] euthanasie, de zachte dood
mere louter, puur: *by the* ~*st chance* door stom toeval; *at the* ~ *thought of it* alleen al de gedachte eraan
merely slechts, enkel, alleen
merge 1 (+ with) opgaan (in), samengaan (met), fuseren (met) 2 (geleidelijk) overgaan (in elkaar): *the place where the rivers* ~ de plaats waar de rivieren samenvloeien

merger 1 samensmelting **2** [econ] fusie
meridian meridiaan, middaglijn
¹**merit** (n) **1** verdienste, waarde: *the ~s and demerits of sth.* de voors en tegens van iets; *reward each according to his ~s* elk naar eigen verdienste belonen; *judge sth.* **on** *its (own) ~s* iets op zijn eigen waarde beoordelen **2** (-s) intrinsieke waarde
²**merit** (vb) verdienen, waard zijn
meritocracy meritocratie
mermaid (zee)meermin
merriment 1 vrolijkheid **2** pret, plezier^h, hilariteit
merry 1 vrolijk, opgewekt: *Merry* **Christmas** Vrolijk kerstfeest **2** aangeschoten || *lead s.o. a ~ dance* a) iem. het leven zuur maken; b) iem. voor de gek houden; *make ~* pret maken; *make ~ over* zich vrolijk maken over
merry-go-round draaimolen, carrousel^{+h}; [fig] maalstroom; roes
merrymaking 1 pret(makerij), feestvreugde **2** feestelijkheid
¹**mesh** (n) **1** maas, steek; [fig also] strik **2** net(werk)^h: *a ~ of lies* een netwerk van leugens
²**mesh** (vb) **1** (+ with) ineengrijpen, ingeschakeld zijn; [fig] harmoniëren (met) **2** verstrikt raken
mesmerize magnetiseren, (als) verlammen: *~d at his appearance* gebiologeerd door zijn verschijning
¹**mess** (n) **1** puinhoop, troep, (war)boel, knoeiboel: *his life was a ~* zijn leven was een mislukking; *clear up the ~* de rotzooi opruimen **2** vuile boel **3** moeilijkheid: *get o.s.* **into** *a ~* zichzelf in moeilijkheden brengen **4** mess, kantine
²**mess** (vb) zich bemoeien met iets, tussenkomen: *~ in other people's business* z'n neus in andermans zaken steken || *no ~ing* echt waar
¹**mess about** (vb) prutsen, (lui) rondhangen: *don't ~ with people like him* laat je met mensen zoals hij niet in; *he spent the weekend messing about* hij lummelde wat rond tijdens het weekend
²**mess about** (vb) **1** rotzooien met: *stop messing my daughter about* blijf met je poten van mijn dochter af **2** belazeren
¹**message** (n) **1** boodschap: *the ~ of a* **book** de kerngedachte van een boek; *(I) got the ~* begrepen, ik snap het al; *send s.o. on a ~* iem. om een boodschap sturen **2** bericht^h **3** sms
²**message** (vb) sms'en
messaging elektronische berichtgeving
messenger boodschapper, koerier: *~ from Heaven* gezant des hemels
Messiah Messias, Heiland
Messrs 1 (de) Heren **2** Fa., Firma: *~ Smith & Jones* de Firma Smith & Jones
mess up 1 in de war sturen, verknoeien: *mess things up* ergens een potje van maken

2 smerig maken **3** ruw aanpakken, toetakelen **4** in moeilijkheden brengen
mess-up [inform] warboel: *they made a complete ~ of it* ze hebben de boel grondig verknoeid
mess with lastigvallen: *don't ~ me* laat me met rust
messy 1 vuil, vies **2** slordig, verward
metabolism metabolisme^h, stofwisseling
¹**metal** (n) **1** metaal^h **2** steenslag^h [for road]
²**metal** (adj) metalen
metallic 1 metalen: *~ lustre* metaalglans **2** metaalhoudend
metamorphosis metamorfose, gedaanteverwisseling
metaphor metafoor, beeld^h, beeldspraak
metaphorical metaforisch
metaphysical 1 metafysisch, bovennatuurlijk **2** [oft depr] abstract, te subtiel
metastasis [med] uitzaaiing
metastasize 1 [med] uitzaaien **2** [fig] zich verspreiden
meteor meteoor
meteorite meteoriet
meteorologist weerkundige
mete out toedienen: *~ rewards and punishments* beloningen en straffen uitdelen
meter meter, meettoestel^h
methadone methadon^h
method methode, procedure: *~s of* **payment** wijzen van betaling
methodical methodisch, zorgvuldig
methodology methodologie
meticulous uiterst nauwgezet, pietepeuterig
metre 1 meter **2** metrum^h
metric metriek: *~ system* metriek stelsel
metrical metrisch, ritmisch
metro metro, ondergrondse
metropolis metropool
¹**metropolitan** (n) bewoner van een metropool
²**metropolitan** (adj) hoofdstedelijk
mettle 1 moed, kracht: *a man of ~* een man met pit; *show* (or: *prove*) *one's ~* zijn karakter tonen **2** temperament^h, aard
mew 1 miauwen **2** krijsen
¹**Mexican** (n) Mexicaan(se)
²**Mexican** (adj) Mexicaans || [Am; inform] *~ promotion* bevordering zonder salarisverhoging
Mexico Mexico
mg *milligram(s)*
¹**miaow** (n) miauw, kattengejank^h [also fig]
²**miaow** (vb) m(i)auwen
¹**mic drop** (n) het demonstratief laten vallen van de microfoon na een optreden of toespraak
²**mic drop** (int) [inform] einde discussie, zo gaan we het doen
Michaelmas term herfsttrimester^h

microbe microbe
microbead plastickorreltje^h in schoonheidsproducten
microchip microchip
microfilm microfilm
microloan microlening
micrometer micrometer
micron micron^{+h}, micrometer
microphone microfoon
microprocessor microprocessor [central processing unit of computer]
microscope microscoop^{+h}: *put* (or: *examine*) *under the* ~ onder de loep nemen [also fig]
microscopic microscopisch (klein)
microwave 1 magnetron; [Belg] microgolfoven **2** microgolf
microwave oven magnetron
mid- midden, het midden van: *in mid-air* in de lucht; *from mid-June to mid-August* van half juni tot half augustus; *in mid-ocean* in volle zee
midday middag
midden mesthoop, afvalhoop
¹middle (n) **1** midden^h, middelpunt^h, middellijn, middelvlak^h: *in the* ~ *(of)* middenin; *be caught in the* ~ tussen twee vuren zitten **2** middel^h, taille ‖ *keep to the* ~ *of the road* de (gulden) middenweg nemen
²middle (adj) middelst, midden, tussen-: ~ *age* middelbare leeftijd; *Middle Ages* middeleeuwen; ~ *class* a) bourgeoisie; b) kleinburgerlijk; ~ *finger* middelvinger ‖ ~ *distance* [athletics] middenafstand; *the Middle East* het Midden-Oosten
middle-aged van middelbare leeftijd
middle-class kleinburgerlijk
middleman tussenpersoon, bemiddelaar, makelaar
middlename 1 tweede voornaam **2** tweede natuur: *bad luck is our* ~ we zijn voor het ongeluk geboren; *sobriety is his* ~ hij is de soberheid zelve
middle-of-the-road gematigd
middling middelmatig, tamelijk (goed), redelijk; [inform] tamelijk gezond
midge mug
¹midget (n) dwerg, lilliputter
²midget (adj) lilliputachtig, mini-: ~ *golf* midgetgolf^h
midland binnenland^h, centraal gewest^h
Midlands (the) Midden-Engeland: *a* ~ *town* een stad in Midden-Engeland
midlife crisis midlifecrisis
midnight middernacht: *at* ~ om middernacht
midnight oil (the): *burn the* ~ werken tot diep in de nacht
midriff 1 middenrif^h **2** maagstreek
midst midden^h: *in the* ~ *of the fight* in het heetst van de strijd

midterm midden^h van een politieke ambtstermijn
midway halverwege: *stand* ~ *between* het midden houden tussen
midweek het midden van de week
midwife vroedvrouw
mien [form] voorkomen^h, gelaatsuitdrukking
miffed op de tenen getrapt
¹might (n) macht, kracht: *with* ~ *and main* met man en macht
²might (aux vb) **1** mocht(en), zou(den) mogen: ~ *I ask you a question?* zou ik u een vraag mogen stellen? **2** [possibility] kon(den), zou(den) (misschien) kunnen: *he told her he* ~ *arrive later* hij zei dat hij misschien later kwam; *it* ~ *be a good idea to ...* het zou misschien goed zijn te ...; *you* ~ *have warned us* je had ons wel even kunnen waarschuwen
mighty 1 machtig, krachtig **2** indrukwekkend, kolossaal **3** geweldig
migraine migraine(aanval)
¹migrant (n) migrant; seizoenarbeider
²migrant (adj) migrerend, trek-
migrate trekken, verhuizen
migration migratie, volksverhuizing
migratory zwervend: ~ *bird* trekvogel
mike [inform] *microphone* microfoon
mil milliliter: *an alcohol level of .8 per* ~ een alcoholgehalte van 0,8 pro mille
milady 1 milady **2** elegante vrouw
¹mild (n) licht bier^h
²mild (adj) **1** mild, zacht(aardig), welwillend: *only* ~*ly interested* maar matig geïnteresseerd; *to put it* ~*ly* om het zachtjes uit te drukken **2** zwak, licht, flauw: ~ *flavoured tobacco* tabak met een zacht aroma
mildew 1 schimmel(vorming) **2** meeldauw(schimmel)
mile mijl [1,609.34 metres]; [fig] grote afstand: *she is feeling* ~*s better* ze voelt zich stukken beter; *stick out a* ~ in het oog springen; *my thoughts were* ~*s away* ik was met mijn gedachten heel ergens anders; *recognize s.o. a* ~ *off* iem. van een kilometer afstand herkennen ‖ *run a* ~ *from s.o.* met een boog om iem. heenlopen
mileage 1 totaal aantal afgelegde mijlen **2** profijt^h: *he has got a lot of political* ~ *out of his proposal* met dat voorstel heeft hij heel wat politiek voordeel gehaald
milestone mijlpaal
milieu milieu^h, sociale omgeving
¹militant (n) militant
²militant (adj) militant, strijdlustig
militarism militarisme^h
¹military (n) leger^h, soldaten, strijdkrachten
²military (adj) militair, krijgs- ‖ ~ *service* (leger)dienst; ~ *tribunal* krijgsraad
militate pleiten: ~ *against* pleiten tegen; ~ *for* (or: *in favour of*) pleiten voor (or: ten

gunste van)
mil<u>i</u>tia militie(leger[h]), burgerleger[h]
¹milk (n) melk; [bot] melk(sap[h]): *attested* ~ kiemvrije melk; *semi-skimmed* ~ halfvolle melk; *skim(med)* ~ magere, afgeroomde melk ‖ ~ *run* routineklus, makkie[h]; ~ *and honey* melk en honing [abundance]; *(it's no use) cry(ing) over spilt milk* gedane zaken nemen geen keer
²milk (vb) **1** melken **2** (ont)trekken; sap aftappen van [tree, snake etc] **3** exploiteren, uitbuiten **4** ontlokken [information]; (uit)melken
m<u>i</u>lking machine melkmachine
m<u>i</u>lkman melkboer
m<u>i</u>lksop bangerik, huilebalk
m<u>i</u>lk tooth melktand
m<u>i</u>lky **1** melkachtig, troebel **2** melkhoudend ‖ the Milky *Way* de Melkweg
¹mill (n) **1** molen, pers **2** fabriek ‖ *put s.o. through* the ~ iem. flink onder handen nemen; *have been through* the ~ het klappen van de zweep kennen
²mill (vb) **1** malen **2** (metaal) pletten, walsen
mill ab<u>ou</u>t krioelen, wemelen
¹mill<u>e</u>nnial (n) millennial
²mill<u>e</u>nnial (adj) millennial-: *the* ~ *generation* de millennialgeneratie, de millennials
mill<u>e</u>nnium millennium[h], periode van duizend jaar
m<u>i</u>ller molenaar
m<u>i</u>lligram(me) milligram[h]
m<u>i</u>llimetre millimeter
m<u>i</u>llion miljoen; [fig] talloos: [Am] *thanks a* ~ reuze bedankt; *a chance in a* ~ een kans van één op duizend ‖ *feel like a* ~ *(dollars)* zich kiplekker voelen
million<u>ai</u>re miljonair
m<u>i</u>llionth miljoenste
m<u>i</u>llipede duizendpoot
m<u>i</u>llstone molensteen [also fig]
mil<u>o</u>meter mijlenteller, kilometerteller
mil<u>o</u>rd milord
¹mime (n) **1** mime, (panto)mimespeler, mimekunst **2** nabootsing
²mime (vb) mimen, optreden in mimespel
¹m<u>i</u>mic (n) **1** mime, mimespeler **2** na-aper [also animals]
²m<u>i</u>mic (adj) **1** mimisch: ~ *art* mimiek **2** nabootsend, na-apend
³m<u>i</u>mic (vb) nabootsen, na-apen
m<u>i</u>micry **1** nabootsing **2** mimiek
min **1** *minimum* **2** *Ministry* **3** *minute(s)*
minar<u>e</u>t minaret
¹mince (n) **1** gehakt[h], gehakt vlees[h] **2** [Am] gehakt voedsel[h]
²mince (vb) **1** aanstellerig spreken **2** trippelen
³mince (vb) **1** fijnhakken: ~d *meat* gehakt (vlees) **2** aanstellerig uitspreken: *she didn't ~ her words* zij nam geen blad voor de mond,

ze zei waar het op stond **3** vergoelijken: *not* ~ *the matter* er geen doekjes om winden
m<u>i</u>ncemeat pasteivulling ‖ *make* ~ *of* in de pan hakken, geen stukje heel laten van [an argument]
m<u>i</u>ncer gehaktmolen
¹mind (n) **1** geest, gemoed[h]: *set s.o.'s* ~ *at ease* iem. geruststellen; *have sth.* *on* one's ~ iets op zijn hart hebben **2** verstand[h]: *be clear in one's* ~ *about sth.* iets ten volle beseffen **3** mening, opinie: *have a* ~ *of one's own* er zijn eigen ideeën op na houden; *speak* one's ~ zijn mening zeggen, zeggen wat je op je hart hebt; *be in* two ~s *(about)* het met zichzelf oneens zijn over; *to my* ~ volgens mij **4** bedoeling: *nothing is* **further** *from my* ~! a) ik denk er niet aan!, ik pieker er niet over!; b) dat is helemaal niet mijn bedoeling; *have half a* ~ *to* min of meer geneigd zijn om; [iron] veel zin hebben om; *change* one's ~ zich bedenken; *make* up one's ~ tot een besluit komen, een beslissing nemen **5** wil, zin(nen): *have sth. in* ~ a) iets van plan zijn; b) iets in gedachten hebben **6** aandacht, gedachte(n): *bear in* ~ in gedachten houden; *cross* (or: *enter*) one's ~ bij iem. opkomen; *give* (or: *put, turn*) one's ~ *to* zijn aandacht richten op; *set* one's ~ *to sth.* zich ergens op concentreren; *it'll take my* ~ *off things* het zal mij wat afleiden **7** denkwijze **8** herinnering: *bring* (or: *call*) *sth. to* ~ a) zich iets herinneren; b) doen denken aan; *come* (or: *spring*) *to* ~, *come into one's* ~ te binnen schieten; *keep in* ~ niet vergeten; *it slipped my* ~ het is mij ontschoten; *who do you have in* ~? aan wie denk je?
²mind (vb) oppletten, oppassen: ~ *(you),* I *would prefer not to* maar ik zou het liever niet doen
³mind (vb) **1** denken aan, bedenken, letten op: ~ *one's own* **business** zich met zijn eigen zaken bemoeien; *never* ~ maak je geen zorgen, het geeft niet; *never* ~ *the expense* de kosten spelen geen rol; *never* ~ *what your father said* ongeacht wat je vader zei; [when leaving] ~ *how* you go wees voorzichtig **2** zorgen voor, oppassen, bedienen: *he couldn't walk, never* ~ *run* hij kon niet lopen, laat staan rennen ‖ ~ *you* **go** *to the dentist* denk erom dat je nog naar de tandarts moet
⁴mind (vb) **1** bezwaren hebben (tegen), erop tegen zijn, zich storen aan: *he* **doesn't** ~ *the cold weather* het koude weer deert hem niet; *would* you ~? zou je 't erg vinden?, vindt u het erg? **2** gehoorzamen
m<u>i</u>nd-blowing fantastisch, duizelingwekkend
m<u>i</u>nd-boggling verbijsterend: *it was so* ~ *(to me)* ik kon er echt niet bij
m<u>i</u>nded geneigd: *he could do it if he were* **so** ~ hij zou het kunnen doen als hij er (maar)

zin in had
minder 1 kinderoppas **2** bodyguard
mindful 1 met aandacht **2** opmerkzaam
3 denkend aan: ~ *of* one's duties zijn plichten
indachtig
mindfully 1 aandachtig **2** gebruikmakend
van mindfulnesstechnieken: *work out* ~
mindful fitnessen
mindfulness [psychology] mindfulness
mindless 1 dwaas, dom **2** niet lettend op:
~ *of* danger zonder oog voor gevaar ‖ ~ *violence* zinloos geweld
mind out (+ for) oppassen (voor)
mindreader gedachtelezer
mindset 1 denkrichting **2** obsessie
mind's eye 1 geestesoog[h], verbeelding
2 herinnering
¹mine (n) mijn; [fig] goudmijn: *a* ~ *of* information een rijke bron van informatie
²mine (vb) **1** in een mijn werken, een mijn
aanleggen: ~ *for* gold naar goud zoeken
2 mijnen leggen
³mine (vb) uitgraven
⁴mine (poss pron) **1** van mij: *that box is* ~ die
doos is van mij **2** de mijne(n), het mijne: *a*
friend of ~ een vriend van me
minefield mijnenveld[h] [also fig]
miner mijnwerker
¹mineral (n) **1** mineraal[h] **2** (-s) mineraalwater[h]
²mineral (adj) delfstoffen-, mineraal-: ~ *ores*
mineraalertsen
mineralogy mineralogie
minesweeper mijnenveger
mingle 1 zich (ver)mengen **2** zich mengen
onder: *they didn't feel like mingling* ze hadden
geen zin om met de anderen te gaan praten
[at party]
mingy krenterig
miniature miniatuur
minibar minibar
minicab minitaxi
minimal minimaal
minimize minimaliseren, zo klein mogelijk
maken, vergoelijken
minimum minimum[h]: *keep sth. to a* ~ iets
tot het minimum beperkt houden; ~ *wage*
minimumloon[h]
mining mijnbouw
minion gunsteling, slaafs volgeling, hielenlikker
miniscooter scootmobiel
minister 1 minister: *Minister of the* **Crown**
minister (van het Britse kabinet); *Minister of*
State onderminister **2** geestelijke, predikant
3 gezant
ministerial 1 ministerieel **2** geestelijk
minister to [form] bijstaan, verzorgen
ministry 1 ministerie[h] **2** dienst, verzorging
3 geestelijk ambt[h] [priest, vicar]: *enter the* ~
geestelijke worden

mink 1 nerts **2** nertsbont[h] **3** nertsmantel
¹minor (n) **1** minderjarige **2** bijvak[h] [at Am
university]
²minor (adj) **1** minder, kleiner, vrij klein
2 minder belangrijk, lager, ondergeschikt: ~
poet minder belangrijke dichter; ~ *road* secundaire weg **3** minderjarig **4** [mus] mineur:
in a ~ *key* in mineur [also fig]
minority 1 minderheid **2** minderjarigheid
minster kloosterkerk
minstrel minstreel
¹mint (n) **1** munt [bldg]; [inform] bom duiten; smak geld; [fig] bron **2** pepermuntje[h]
3 [bot] munt
²mint (adj) [inform] vet, kapotgoed
³mint (vb) munten, tot geld slaan; [fig] smeden: ~ *a new* **expression** een nieuwe uitdrukking creëren
mint condition perfecte staat: *in* ~ puntgaaf
minuet menuet[h]
¹minus (n) **1** minteken[h] **2** minus[h], tekort[h];
[fig] nadeel[h]
²minus (adj) **1** negatief [maths, science]
2 [educ] -min, iets minder goed dan: *a B-*~
[roughly] een 8 min
³minus (prep) **1** min(us), min, onder nul:
wages ~ **taxes** loon na aftrekking van belastingen; ~ *six (degrees centigrade)* zes graden
onder nul **2** minder dan: ~ *two* **cm** *in diameter*
minder dan twee cm doorsnede **3** [inform]
zonder: *a teapot* ~ *a* **spout** een theepot zonder tuit
¹minute (n) **1** minuut, ogenblik[h]: ~ *hand*
grote wijzer; *wait a* ~ wacht eens even; *I*
won't be a ~ ik ben zo klaar, ik ben zo terug;
just a ~*!* moment!, ogenblik(je)!; *in a* ~ zo
dadelijk; *the* ~ *(that)* I *saw him* zodra ik hem
zag **2** aantekening, notitie **3** nota, memorandum[h] **4** (-s) notulen
²minute (adj) **1** onbeduidend **2** minutieus,
gedetailleerd
minx brutale meid
miracle mirakel[h], wonder[h]
miraculous miraculeus, wonderbaarlijk
mirage 1 luchtspiegeling, fata morgana
2 droombeeld[h], hersenschim
mire [form] **1** moeras[h] **2** slijk[h] ‖ *be in the* ~ in
de knoei (*or:* puree) zitten
¹mirror (n) spiegel; [fig] weerspiegeling
²mirror (vb) (weer)spiegelen, afspiegelen,
weerkaatsen
mirror version spiegelsite, mirrorsite
mirth vrolijkheid, lol
misadventure tegenspoed, ongeluk[h]:
death by ~ dood door ongeluk
misanthrope misantroop, mensenhater
misapply 1 verkeerd toepassen **2** verduisteren [money]
misapprehension misverstand[h], misvatting: *under the* ~ *that* ... in de waan dat ...

misbeha**ve** zich misdragen, zich slecht gedragen

¹misca**lculate** (vb) zich misrekenen

²misca**lculate** (vb) verkeerd schatten, onjuist berekenen: *I had ~d the distance* ik had de afstand fout geschat

misca**rriage 1** mislukking [of plan]: *~ of justice* rechterlijke dwaling **2** miskraam

misca**rry 1** mislukken, falen **2** een miskraam krijgen

miscegena**tion** rassenvermenging

miscella**neous 1** gemengd, gevarieerd: *~ articles* artikelen over uiteenlopende onderwerpen **2** veelzijdig

miscellany mengeling, mengelwerkʰ

mischa**nce** ongelukʰ, tegenslag: *by ~, through a ~* bij ongeluk

mischief 1 kattenkwaadʰ: *her eyes were full of ~* haar ogen straalden ondeugd uit; *get into ~* kattenkwaad uithalen **2** ondeugendheid **3** onheilʰ, schade: *the ~ had been done* het kwaad was al geschied

mischievous 1 schadelijk, nadelig **2** ondeugend, speels

misconce**ption** verkeerde opvatting

misconduct 1 wangedragʰ, onfatsoenlijkheid **2** ambtsmisdrijfʰ, ambtsovertreding

misconstru**e** verkeerd interpreteren

misdeme**anour** misdrijfʰ

mi**ser** vrek

mi**serable 1** beroerd, ellendig **2** armzalig: *live on a ~ pension* van een schamel pensioentje rondkomen **3** waardeloos

mi**serly** vrekkig

mi**sery 1** ellende, nood: *put an animal out of its ~* een dier uit zijn lijden helpen **2** tegenslag, beproeving **3** pijn, ziekte

misfi**re 1** ketsen, niet afgaan **2** weigeren **3** niet aanslaan

mi**sfit 1** onaangepast iem. **2** niet-passend kledingstukʰ

misfo**rtune** ongelukʰ, tegenspoed

misgi**ving** onzekerheid, bang vermoedenʰ: *they had serious ~s about employing him* ze twijfelden er ernstig aan of ze hem in dienst konden nemen

misgui**ded 1** misleid, verblind **2** ondoordacht

misha**ndle** verkeerd behandelen, slecht regelen

mi**shap** ongeluk(je)ʰ, tegenvaller(tjeʰ): *a journey without ~* een reis zonder incidenten

mi**shmash** mengelmoesʰ, rommeltjeʰ

misinfo**rm** verkeerd inlichten (*or:* informeren)

misinte**rpret** verkeerd interpreteren, verkeerd begrijpen

misinterpreta**tion** verkeerde interpretatie: *open to ~* voor verkeerde uitleg vatbaar

misju**dge** verkeerd (be)oordelen: *~ s.o.* zich in iem. vergissen

misla**y** zoekmaken, verliezen: *I've mislaid my glasses* ik kan mijn bril niet vinden

misle**ad** misleiden, bedriegen, op 't verkeerde spoor brengen

misle**ading** misleidend, bedrieglijk

mismanagement wanbeheerʰ, wanbestuurʰ, -beleidʰ

mi**smatch** verkeerde combinatie, verkeerd huwelijkʰ

miso**gynist** vrouwenhater

mispla**ce** misplaatsen: *a ~d remark* een misplaatste opmerking

¹mi**sprint** (n) drukfout, zetfout

²mi**sprint** (vb) verkeerd drukken: *~ a word* een drukfout maken

misquo**te** onjuist citeren: *~ s.o.'s words* iemands woorden verdraaien

misre**ad** verkeerd lezen: *~ s.o.'s feelings* zich in iemands gevoelens vergissen

misreprese**nt 1** verkeerd voorstellen **2** slecht vertegenwoordigen

¹misru**le** (n) **1** wanbestuurʰ **2** wanorde, anarchie

²misru**le** (vb) slecht (*or:* verkeerd) besturen

¹miss (n) misser, misslag: *give sth. a ~* iets laten voorbijgaan; *I think I'll give it a ~ this year* ik denk dat ik het dit jaar maar eens oversla

²miss (vb) **1** missen: *his shots all ~ed* hij schoot er telkens naast **2** [gerund] ontbreken: *the book is ~ing* het boek is zoek **3** mislopen, falen

³miss (vb) **1** missen, niet raken **2** mislopen, te laat komen voor: *~ s.o.* een afspraak mislopen **3** ontsnappen aan: *he narrowly ~ed the accident* hij ontsnapte ternauwernood aan het ongeluk **4** vermissen, afwezigheid opmerken: *they'll never ~ it* ze zullen nooit merken dat het verdwenen is

Miss 1 Mejuffrouw, Juffrouw: *the ~es Brown* de (jonge)dames Brown **2** [also 'miss'] jongedame

mi**ssile 1** raket: *guided ~* geleide raket **2** projectielʰ

mi**ssing 1** ontbrekend: *the ~ link* de ontbrekende schakel **2** vermist: *killed, wounded or ~* gesneuveld, gewond of vermist **3** verloren, weg

mi**ssion 1** afvaardiging, legatie: [Am] *foreign ~* gezantschapʰ **2** roeping, zending: *her ~ in life* haar levenstaak **3** opdracht: *~ accomplished* taak volbracht, opdracht uitgevoerd

¹mi**ssionary** (n) missionaris, zendeling

²mi**ssionary** (adj) **1** zendings-: *~ work* zendingswerkʰ **2** zendelings-: [fig] *with ~ zeal* met toewijding; met hartstocht

mi**ssion control** controlecentrumʰ

mi**ssion statement** doelstellingen, missie

¹miss out (vb) over het hoofd gezien worden: *she always misses out* ze vist altijd achter het net ‖ *~ on the fun* de pret mislopen

²**miss out** (vb) **1** vergeten **2** overslaan

missus (the) [hum] moeder de vrouw

¹**mist** (n) **1** mist [also fig]; nevel: *lost in the ~ of antiquity* verloren in de nevelen der oudheid **2** waas^h: *see things through a ~* alles in een waas zien

²**mist** (vb) **1** misten **2** (+ over, up) beslaan **3** beneveld worden, wazig worden

¹**mistake** (n) fout, dwaling: *and make no ~* **a)** en vergis je niet; **b)** en houd jezelf niet voor de gek; *my ~* ik vergis me, mijn fout; *by ~* per ongeluk; *and no ~, there's no ~ about it* daar kun je van op aan, en dat is zeker

²**mistake** (vb) **1** verkeerd begrijpen **2** verkeerd kiezen **3** niet herkennen: *there's no mistaking him with his orange hat* je kunt hem eenvoudig niet mislopen met zijn oranje hoed **4** (+ for) verwarren (met)

mistaken verkeerd (begrepen), mis: *~ identity* persoonsverwisseling; *be ~ about* zich vergissen omtrent

mister [without surname] meneer: *what's the time, ~?* hoe laat is het, meneer?

mistletoe maretak

mistress **1** meesteres; bazin: *a dog and its ~* een hond en zijn bazin; *she is her own ~* zij is haar eigen baas; *~ of the house* vrouw des huizes **2** lerares **3** maîtresse

¹**mistrust** (n) wantrouwen^h

²**mistrust** (vb) wantrouwig zijn (over), wantrouwen

misty mistig, nevelig

misunderstand **1** niet begrijpen: *a misunderstood artist* een onbegrepen kunstenaar **2** verkeerd begrijpen

misunderstanding **1** misverstand^h **2** geschil^h **3** onbegrip^h

¹**misuse** (n) **1** misbruik^h: *~ of funds* verduistering van gelden **2** verkeerd gebruik^h

²**misuse** (vb) **1** misbruiken **2** verkeerd gebruiken

mitigate **1** lenigen, verlichten **2** matigen, verzachten: [law] *mitigating circumstances* verzachtende omstandigheden

mitt **1** want **2** [baseball] (vang)handschoen

¹**mix** (n) **1** mengeling, mix **2** mengsel^h

²**mix** (vb) zich (laten) (ver)mengen: *~ with* omgaan met

³**mix** (vb) **1** (ver)mengen **2** bereiden, mixen: *he was ~ing a salad* hij was een slaatje aan het klaarmaken **3** mixen [sound] ‖ *~ it (up)* elkaar in de haren zitten, knokken

mixed gemengd, vermengd: *~ bag* allegaartje^h, ratjetoe^{+h}, een bonte verzameling; *technology is a ~ blessing* de technologie heeft voor- en nadelen; [tennis] *~ doubles* gemengd dubbel

mixed up **1** in de war, versuft **2** betrokken, verwikkeld

mixer mengtoestel^h, (keuken)mixer ‖ *a good ~* een gezellig mens

mixture mengsel^h, mengeling

mix up **1** verwarren: *I kept mixing up the names of those twins* ik haalde steeds de namen van die tweeling door elkaar **2** in de war brengen

mm *millimetre(s)* mm

mnemonic ezelsbruggetje^h, geheugensteuntje^h

MO *modus operandi* werkwijze

¹**moan** (n) **1** gekreun^h, gekerm^h **2** geklaag^h, gejammer^h

²**moan** (vb) **1** kermen, kreunen **2** klagen, jammeren: *what's she ~ing about now?* waarover zit ie nu weer te zeuren?

moat slotgracht

¹**mob** (n) **1** gepeupel^h **2** menigte **3** bende

²**mob** (vb) samenscholen

³**mob** (vb) **1** in bende aanvallen, lastigvallen **2** omstuwen, drommen rondom

¹**mobile** (n) **1** mobile^{+h} **2** mobieltje^h ‖ *~ phone* mobieltje^h, gsm

²**mobile** (adj) **1** beweeglijk, mobiel, los, levendig **2** rondtrekkend [of vehicle, shop]: *a ~ home* een stacaravan

mobility beweeglijkheid, mobiliteit

mobility scooter scootmobiel

mobilize mobiliseren: *he ~d all his forces* hij verzamelde al zijn krachten

mobster bendelid^h; gangster

¹**mock** (adj) onecht, nagemaakt: *~ trial* schijnproces^h

²**mock** (vb) spotten, zich vrolijk maken

³**mock** (vb) **1** bespotten **2** (minachtend) trotseren, tarten

mockery **1** namaaksel^h **2** aanfluiting, schijnvertoning **3** bespotting, hoon: *make a ~ of* de spot drijven met

modal modaal: [linguistics] *~ auxiliary* modaal hulpwerkwoord

mod cons *modern conveniences* modern comfort^h: *house with all ~* huis dat van alle gemakken is voorzien

mode **1** wijze, manier, methode **2** gebruik^h, procedure

¹**model** (n) **1** model^h, maquette, evenbeeld^h **2** type^h [eg of car] **3** exclusief model^h [article of clothing] **4** toonbeeld^h, voorbeeld^h

²**model** (adj) model- **2** perfect: *a ~ husband* een modelechtgenoot

³**model** (vb) mannequin zijn

⁴**model** (vb) **1** modelleren, boetseren **2** vormen naar een voorbeeld: *he ~led his main character on one of his teachers* voor de hoofdpersoon gebruikte hij een van zijn leraren als voorbeeld

model home [Am] kijkwoning, modelwoning

modem *modulator-demodulator* modem^h

¹**moderate** (n) gematigde

²**moderate** (adj) gematigd, matig: *~ prices* redelijke prijzen

³**moderate** (vb) **1** (zich) matigen: *the strikers have ~d their demands* de stakers hebben hun eisen bijgesteld **2** afnemen, verminderen
moderation gematigdheid || *~ in all things* alles met mate
modern modern: *~ history* nieuwe geschiedenis; *~ languages* levende talen
modern-day hedendaags, modern
modernism modernismeʰ
modernize moderniseren, (zich) vernieuwen
modest 1 bescheiden **2** niet groot **3** redelijk
modification 1 wijziging **2** verzachting
modify 1 wijzigen **2** verzachten
modular modulair
module 1 module; [architecture] bouwelementʰ: *lunar ~* maanlandingsvoertuig **2** modulus, maat(staf)
moist vochtig, klam
moisten bevochtigen, natmaken
moisture vochtʰ, vochtigheid
molar kies
Moldova Moldavië
¹**Moldovan** (n) Moldaviër, Moldavische
²**Moldovan** (adj) Moldavisch
mole 1 mol **2** (kleine) moedervlek, vlekjeʰ **3** pier, golfbreker **4** spion, mol
molecular moleculair: *~ weight* moleculegewichtʰ
molecule molecule⁺ʰ
molehill molshoop
molest lastigvallen, molesteren
mollify 1 bedaren **2** vertederen, vermurwen: *be mollified by s.o.'s flatteries* zich laten vermurwen door iemands vleierij **3** matigen, verzachten
mollusc weekdierʰ
molten gesmolten
mom mamma
moment 1 (geschikt) ogenblikʰ, momentʰ: *for the ~* voorlopig; *in a ~* ogenblikkelijk; *just a ~, please* een ogenblikje alstublieft **2** tijdstipʰ: *at the ~* op het ogenblik **3** belangʰ, gewichtʰ: *of (great) ~* van (groot) belang
momentarily [Am] zo meteen, spoedig
momentary kortstondig, vluchtig
momentous gewichtig, ernstig
momentum 1 impuls, hoeveelheid van beweging **2** vaart [also fig]; (stuw)kracht: *gain* (or: *gather*) *~* aan stootkracht winnen
¹**Monacan** (n) Monegask(ische)
²**Monacan** (adj) Monegaskisch
Monaco Monaco
monarch monarch: *absolute ~* absoluut vorst
monarchy monarchie
monastery (mannen)kloosterʰ
Monday maandag: *on ~(s)* maandags, op maandag
monetary monetair

money 1 geldʰ: *one's ~'s worth* waar voor je geld; *made of ~* stinkend rijk; *I'm not made of ~* het geld groeit me niet op de rug; *there is ~ in it* er valt geld aan te verdienen **2** welstand, rijkdom: *~ talks* met geld open je (alle) deuren || *for my ~* wat mij betreft
moneyed 1 [form] welgesteld **2** [form] geldelijk: *~ assistance* geldelijke ondersteuning
money-grubber geldwolf
moneylender financier, geldschieter
moneymaking winstgevend
moneyspinning [inform] winstgevend
money-washing witwassenʰ
Mongolia Mongolië
¹**Mongolian** (n) Mongoliër, Mongolische
²**Mongolian** (adj) Mongolisch
mongrel 1 bastaard(hond) **2** mengvorm
¹**monitor** (n) **1** monitor, leraarshulpjeʰ **2** controleapparaatʰ, monitor
²**monitor** (vb) controleren, meekijken (meeluisteren) met, afluisteren, toezicht houden op
monk (klooster)monnik
monkey 1 aap: [inform] *make a ~ (out) of s.o.* iem. voor aap/voor schut zetten **2** deugniet
monkey business [inform] apenstreken, kattenkwaadʰ
monkey nut apennootjeʰ
monkey puzzle apenboom
monobrow doorlopende wenkbrauw
monochrome monochroom; zwart-wit
monogamous monogaam
monogram monogramʰ, naamtekenʰ
monologue monoloog, alleenspraak
mononucleosis (ziekte van) Pfeiffer
monopolize monopoliseren
monopoly monopolieʰ, alleenrechtʰ
monosyllable eenlettergrepig woordʰ: *speak in ~s* kortaf spreken
monotonous monotoon, eentonig, slaapverwekkend
monsoon 1 moesson(wind), passaatwind **2** (natte) moesson, regenseizoenʰ
monster 1 monsterʰ, gedrochtʰ **2** onmens, beestʰ **3** bakbeestʰ, kanjer: *~ potatoes* enorme aardappelen
monstrosity monstruositeit, wanproductʰ
monstrous 1 monsterlijk **2** enorm
Montenegro Montenegro
month maand || *I won't do it in a ~ of Sundays* ik doe het in geen honderd jaar
¹**monthly** (n) maandbladʰ
²**monthly** (adj, adv) maandelijks
monument monumentʰ, gedenktekenʰ
monumental 1 monumentaal **2** kolossaal
¹**moo** (n) boe(geluid)ʰ [of cow]
²**moo** (vb) loeien
moobs [inform] mannentieten, spiertieten
MOOC *massive open online course* mooc

mooch 1 jatten, gappen **2** [Am] bietsen, schooien

mood 1 stemming, bui: *in no ~ for* (or: *to*) niet in de stemming voor (or: om); *~ swing* plotselinge stemmingswisseling **2** wijs: *imperative ~* gebiedende wijs

moody 1 humeurig, wispelturig **2** slechtgehumeurd

moon maan, satelliet (van andere planeten) || *promise s.o. the ~* iem. gouden bergen beloven; *be over the ~* in de wolken zijn, in de zevende hemel zijn

moonbeam manestraal

¹moonlight (n) maanlicht[h]

²moonlight (vb) **1** een bijbaantje hebben, bijverdienen, klussen **2** zwartwerken

moonlighter iem. die een bijbaantje heeft, schnabbelaar

moonlight flit [inform] vertrek met de noorderzon

moonlit maanbeschenen, met maanlicht overgoten

moon over dagdromen over, mijmeren

moonshine 1 maneschijn **2** geklets[h], dromerij **3** [esp Am] illegaal gestookte sterkedrank

moonstruck 1 maanziek **2** warhoofdig, geschift

¹moor (n) **1** hei(de), woeste grond **2** [Am] veenmoeras[h]

²moor (vb) meren, aanmeren, afmeren, vastmeren, vastleggen

moorhen waterhoen[h]

mooring ligplaats, ankerplaats || *lose one's ~s* zijn houvast verliezen

Moorish Moors, Saraceens

moorland heide(landschap[h])

moose eland [North America]

moot onbeslist, onuitgemaakt: *a ~ point* (or: *question*) een onopgeloste kwestie

¹mop (n) **1** zwabber, stokdweil **2** haarbos, ragebol

²mop (vb) **1** (aan)dweilen, zwabberen **2** droogwrijven, (af)vegen: *~ one's brow* zich het zweet van het voorhoofd wissen **3** betten, opnemen

¹mope (n) **1** kniesoor, brompot **2** kniesbui: *have a ~* klagerig zeuren **3** (the mopes) neerslachtigheid

²mope (vb) kniezen, chagrijnen: *~ about, ~ (a)round* lusteloos rondhangen

moped bromfiets, brommertje[h], snorscooter

mop up 1 opdweilen, opnemen **2** opslokken **3** zuiveren, verzetshaarden opruimen: *mopping-up operations* zuiveringsacties

¹moral (n) **1** moraal, (zeden)les: *the ~ of the story* de moraal van het verhaal **2** stelregel, principe[h] **3** (-s) zeden

²moral (adj) **1** moreel, zedelijk, ethisch: *it's a ~ certainty* het is zo goed als zeker **2** deugdzaam, kuis

morale moreel[h], mentale veerkracht: *the ~ of the troops was excellent* het moreel van de soldaten was uitstekend

moralist moralist

moralistic moralistisch, moraliserend

morality zedenleer, moraal

moralize moraliseren

morass moeras[h]; [fig] poel; [fig] uitzichtloze situatie

moratorium 1 moratorium[h], algemeen uitstel[h] van betaling **2** tijdelijk verbod[h] of uitstel[h], opschorting

morbid 1 morbide, ziekelijk: *a ~ imagination* een ziekelijke fantasie **2** zwartgallig, somber

¹more (pron) meer: *$50, ~ or less* ongeveer vijftig dollar; *a few ~* nog een paar; *there was much ~* er was nog veel meer; *there were many ~* er waren er nog veel meer; *one ~ try* nog een poging; *the ~ people there are the happier he feels* hoe meer mensen er zijn, hoe gelukkiger hij zich voelt; *I was just one ~ candidate* ik was niet meer dan de zoveelste kandidaat || *and what's ~* en daarbij komt nog dat

²more (adv) **1** meer, veeleer, eerder: *~ or less* min of meer, zo ongeveer; *once ~* nog eens, nog een keer; *that's ~ like it* dat begint er al op te lijken, dat is al beter; *I will be ~ than happy to help you* ik zal je met alle liefde en plezier helpen **2** -er, meer: *~ difficult* moeilijker; *~ easily* makkelijker **3** bovendien

moreover bovendien, daarnaast

morgue mortuarium[h]

moribund stervend, ten dode opgeschreven

morning ochtend, morgen; [fig] begin[h]: *good ~* goedemorgen; *he works ~s* hij werkt 's morgens; *in the ~* **a)** 's morgens; **b)** morgenochtend; *at two o'clock in the ~* 's nachts om twee uur; *~!* morgen!

morning coat jacquet[h]

morning dress 1 jacquetkostuum[h] **2** colbertkostuum[h]

¹Moroccan (n) Marokkaan(se)

²Moroccan (adj) Marokkaans

Morocco Marokko

moron [offensive] idioot, zakkenwasser

morose 1 chagrijnig **2** somber

morph veranderen: *~ into* veranderen in

morphine morfine

morsel hap, mondvol, stuk(je)[h]: *he hasn't got a ~ of sense* hij heeft geen greintje hersens

mortal 1 sterfelijk: *the ~ remains* het stoffelijk overschot **2** dodelijk, moordend; fataal [also fig] **3** doods-, dodelijk, zeer hevig (groot): *~ enemy* aartsvijand, doodsvijand; *it's a ~ shame* het is een grof schandaal **4** (op aarde) voorstelbaar: *she did every ~ thing to*

please him ze wrong zich in de gekste bochten om het hem naar de zin te maken
mortality 1 sterftecijfer^h **2** sterfelijkheid
mortally 1 dodelijk **2** doods-, enorm: ~ *wounded* dodelijk gewond
¹mortar (n) **1** vijzel **2** mortier^{+h} **3** mortel, (metsel)specie
²mortar (vb) (vast)metselen
mortar bomb mortiergranaat
¹mortgage (n) hypotheek(bedrag^h)
²mortgage (vb) (ver)hypothekeren; [also fig] verpanden
mortgage interest relief hypotheekrenteaftrek
mortician [Am] begrafenisondernemer
mortification 1 zelfkastijding, versterving **2** gekwetstheid: *to his* ~ tot zijn schande
mortify 1 tuchtigen, kastijden: ~ *the flesh* het vlees doden **2** krenken, kwetsen
mortuary lijkenhuis^h, mortuarium^h
mosaic mozaïek^h
Mosel Moezel
Moslem *see* Muslim
mosque moskee
mosquito mug, muskiet: ~ *net* klamboe, muskietennet^h
moss mos^h
¹most (pron) meeste(n), grootste gedeelte van: *twelve at (the)* ~, *twelve at the very* ~ hoogstens twaalf; *this is the* ~ *I can do* meer kan ik niet doen; *for the* ~ *part* grotendeels
²most (adv) **1** meest, hoogst, zeer: ~ *complicated* zeer ingewikkeld; ~ *of all I like music* voor alles houd ik van muziek **2** -st(e), meest: *the* ~ *difficult problem* het moeilijkste probleem **3** [Am] bijna, haast: ~ *every evening* bijna elke avond
mostly grotendeels, voornamelijk, meestal
MOT [inform] *Ministry of Transport* verplichte jaarlijkse autokeuring
motel motel^h
moth 1 mot: *this sweater has got the* ~ *in it* de mot zit in deze trui **2** nachtvlinder
¹mother (n) **1** moeder [also fig]; bron, oorsprong: *expectant* (or: *pregnant*) ~ aanstaande moeder **2** moeder(-overste) ‖ *shall I be* ~? zal ik (even) opscheppen?
²mother (vb) (be)moederen, betuttelen
motherboard moederbord^h
motherhood moederschap^h
mother-in-law schoonmoeder
mother-of-pearl paarlemoer^h
Mother's Day [Am] Moederdag
mother tongue moedertaal
motif (leid)motief^h, (grond)thema^h
¹motion (n) **1** beweging, gebaar^h, wenk **2** beweging(swijze), gang, loop: *the film was shown in slow* ~ de film werd vertraagd afgedraaid; *put* (or: *set*) *sth. in* ~ iets in beweging zetten **3** motie **4** mechaniek^h, bewegend mechanisme^h ‖ *go through the* ~*s* plicht-

matig verrichten, net doen alsof
²motion (vb) wenken, door een gebaar te kennen geven: *the policeman* ~*ed the crowd to keep moving* de agent gebaarde de mensen door te lopen
motion picture speelfilm
motion sensor bewegingssensor, bewegingsmelder
motivate motiveren
motivation 1 motivering **2** motivatie
motive 1 motief^h, beweegreden: *without* ~ ongegrond, zonder reden(en) **2** leidmotief^h
motley 1 samengeraapt **2** bont, (veel)kleurig: *a* ~ *collection* een bonte verzameling
motor 1 motor **2** auto
motorbike 1 motor(fiets) **2** [Am] bromfiets, brommer
motorcycle motor(fiets)
motor home kampeerauto, camper
motorist automobilist
motorman 1 wagenbestuurder **2** chauffeur
motor scooter scooter
motortruck [Am] vrachtwagen
motorway autosnelweg
MOT-test verplichte jaarlijkse keuring [for cars over 3 years old]; apk
mottled gevlekt, gespikkeld
motto lijfspreuk
¹mould (n) **1** vorm, mal, matrijs, pudding(vorm); [fig] aard; karakter^h: *cast in one* (or: *the same*) ~ uit hetzelfde hout gesneden **2** afgietsel^h **3** schimmel **4** teelaarde, bladaarde
²mould (vb) vormen, kneden: ~ *a person's character* iemands karakter vormen
moulder (tot stof) vergaan, vermolmen, verrotten
moulding 1 afgietsel^h, afdruk **2** lijstwerk^h, profiel^h
mouldy 1 beschimmeld, schimmelig **2** muf **3** afgezaagd; oud
¹moult (n) rui
²moult (vb) ruien, verharen, vervellen
mound 1 hoop aarde, (graf)heuvel; [fig] berg; hoop **2** wal, dam, dijk
¹mount (n) **1** berg, heuvel **2** rijdier^h **3** plateautje^h; zetting [of jewels]; opplakkarton^h, opzetkarton^h [of photo, picture]
²mount (vb) **1** (op)stijgen, (op)klimmen: *the expenses kept* ~*ing up* de uitgaven liepen steeds hoger op **2** een paard bestijgen
³mount (vb) **1** bestijgen, beklimmen, opgaan: *he* ~*ed the stairs* hij liep de trap op **2** te paard zetten, laten rijden: ~*ed police* bereden politie **3** zetten op; opplakken [photos] **4** organiseren, in stelling brengen: ~ *an exhibition* een tentoonstelling organiseren
mountain berg, heuvel, hoop: ~ *bike* mountainbike; ~ *range* bergketen ‖ *make a* ~ *out of a molehill* van een mug een olifant

maken

¹mountain bike (n) terreinfiets

²mountain bike (vb) mountainbiken, terreinfietsen

mountaineer 1 bergbeklimmer **2** bergbewoner

mountainous 1 bergachtig, berg- **2** gigantisch, reusachtig

mountainside berghelling

mountebank 1 kwakzalver **2** charlatan

¹mourn (vb) **1** (+ for, over) rouwen (om), in de rouw zijn, treuren **2** rouw dragen

²mourn (vb) betreuren, bedroefd zijn over

mourner 1 rouwdrager, rouwdraagster **2** rouwklager, rouwklaagster

mournful bedroefd, triest

mourning 1 rouw, rouwdracht: *go into ~* de rouw aannemen **2** rouwtijd

mouse muis

mouseover [comp] mouse-over, tooltip

mouse over [comp] met de muis bewegen over

mousepad [comp] **1** muismatjeʰ **2** touchpad [on laptop]

mousetrap muizenval

moustache snor

¹mouth (n) **1** mond, muil, bek: *a big ~* een grote bek; *keep one's ~ shut* niets verklappen; *it makes my ~ water* het is om van te watertanden; *out of s.o.'s own ~* met iemands eigen woorden; *mouth-to-mouth* mond op mond **2** opening, ingang, toegang; (uit)monding [of river]; mond [of port etc] ‖ *shoot one's ~ off* zijn mond voorbijpraten; *down in the ~* terneergeslagen, ontmoedigd

²mouth (vb) **1** declameren, geaffecteerd (uit)spreken **2** (voor zich uit) mompelen

mouthful 1 mondvol, hapjeʰ **2** [inform] hele mond vol, een lang woord: *a large ~ to swallow* moeilijk te geloven

mouth off [inform] brutaal zijn, een grote bek hebben

mouthpiece 1 mondstukʰ **2** spreekbuis, woordvoerder

mouthwash mondspoeling

movable 1 beweegbaar, beweeglijk, los: *~ scene* coulisse **2** verplaatsbaar, verstelbaar ‖ *~ property* roerend goed

¹move (n) **1** beweging: *get a ~ on* a) in beweging komen, aanpakken; b) opschieten; *large forces were on the ~* grote strijdkrachten waren op de been **2** verhuizing, trek: *be on the ~* op reis zijn, aan het zwerven zijn, op trek zijn [of birds] **3** zet, beurt, slag: *make a ~* een zet doen; *it's your ~* jij bent aan zet **4** stap, maatregel, manoeuvre⁺ʰ: *make a ~* a) opstaan [from table]; b) opstappen, het initiatief nemen; c) maatregelen treffen, in actie komen

²move (vb) **1** (zich) bewegen, zich verplaatsen, van positie veranderen: *it's time to be*

moving het is tijd om te vertrekken; *~ along* doorlopen, opschieten; *~ over* inschikken, opschuiven **2** vooruitkomen, opschieten: *suddenly things began to ~* plotseling kwam er leven in de brouwerij; *keep moving!* blijf doorgaan!, doorlopen! **3** [board game] een zet doen, zetten, aan zet zijn **4** verkeren, zich bewegen: *he ~s in the highest circles* hij beweegt zich in de hoogste kringen **5** verhuizen, (weg)trekken, zich verzetten: *they ~d into a flat* ze betrokken een flat **6** een voorstel doen: *~ for adjournment* verdaging voorstellen

³move (vb) **1** bewegen, (ver)roeren, in beweging brengen: *the police ~d them along* de politie dwong hen door te lopen **2** verplaatsen; [board game] zetten; verschuiven **3** opwekken, (ont)roeren, raken, aangrijpen: *he is ~d to tears* hij is tot tranen toe geroerd **4** aanzetten, aansporen: *be ~d to* zich geroepen voelen om te

¹move about (vb) **1** zich (voortdurend) bewegen, rondlopen, ronddrentelen **2** dikwijls verhuizen

²move about (vb) **1** vaak laten verhuizen, vaak verplanten **2** vaak verplaatsen, rondsjouwen

move in 1 intrekken, gaan wonen; betrekken [house, flat etc]: *~ with s.o.* bij iem. intrekken **2** binnenvallen, optrekken, aanvallen, tussenbeide komen: *the police moved in on the crowd* de politie reed op de menigte in

movement 1 beweging, voortgang, ontwikkeling, impuls, trend, tendens; [med] stoelgang; ontlasting **2** beweging, organisatie: *the feminist ~* de vrouwenbeweging **3** mechaniekʰ **4** [mus] beweging; deelʰ [of symphony etc]

¹move on (vb) **1** verder gaan, opschieten, doorgaan **2** vooruitkomen, promotie maken

²move on (vb) iem. gebieden door te gaan

move out verhuizen, vertrekken

mover 1 indiener van een voorstel **2** verhuizer

move up 1 in een hogere klas komen, in rang opklimmen **2** stijgen, toenemen

movie 1 film: *go to the ~s* naar de film gaan **2** bioscoop **3** (the movies) filmindustrie

moving 1 ontroerend **2** bewegend: [Am] *~ picture* film

moving van verhuiswagen

mow maaien: *~ down soldiers* soldaten neermaaien

mower 1 maaier **2** maaimachine, grasmaaier

¹Mozambican (n) Mozambikaan(se)

²Mozambican (adj) Mozambikaans

Mozambique Mozambique

MP 1 *Member of Parliament* **2** *military police(man)*

MPD [med] *multiple-personality disorder*

MPS *(meervoudigepersoonlijkheidsstoornis)*
mpg *miles per gallon* mijlen per gallon
mph *miles per hour* mijlen per uur
MPV *multipurpose vehicle* MPV, spacewagon, ruimtewagen
Mr *mister* dhr., de heer
Mrs Mevr.
Ms Mw. [instead of Miss or Mrs]
Mt *Mount* Berg
MTF *male to female* MNV *(man-naar-vrouw)*
¹much (adv) veel: *how ~ is it?* hoeveel kost het?; *it's not up to ~* het is niet veel soeps; *her contribution didn't amount to ~* haar bijdrage stelde niet veel voor; *that's not ~ use to me now* daar heb ik nu niet veel aan || *there isn't ~ in it* het maakt niet veel uit; *I thought as ~* zoiets dacht ik al; *it was as ~ as I could do to keep from laughing* ik had de grootst mogelijke moeite om niet te lachen; *he's not ~ of a singer* als zanger stelt hij niet veel voor; *well, so ~ for that* dat was dan dat
²much (adv) **1** [degree] veel, zeer, erg: *she was ~ the oldest* zij was verreweg de oudste; *as ~ as $2 million* (maar) liefst 2 miljoen dollar; *~ as he would have liked to go* hoe graag hij ook was gegaan; *~ to my surprise* tot mijn grote verrassing **2** veel, vaak, dikwijls, lang: *she didn't stay ~* ze bleef niet lang **3** ongeveer, bijna: *they were ~ the same size* ze waren ongeveer even groot
muchness hoeveelheid, grootte: *much of a ~* lood om oud ijzer
¹muck (n) **1** troep, rommel, rotzooi: *make a ~ of a job* niets terecht brengen van een klus, er niets van bakken **2** (natte) mest, drek **3** slijk[h]; viezigheid [also fig]
²muck (vb) bemesten || *~ out* uitmesten; *~ up* verknoeien
¹muck about (vb) **1** niksen, lummelen **2** vervelen, klieren: *~ with* knoeien met
²muck about (vb) **1** pesten **2** knoeien met
muckraking vuilspuiterij
mucous slijm-: *~ membrane* slijmvlies[h]
mud modder, slijk[h]; [fig] roddel; laster: *drag s.o.'s name through the ~* iem. door het slijk halen; *fling* (or: *sling, throw*) *~ at s.o.* iem. door de modder sleuren
¹muddle (n) verwarring, warboel: *in a ~* in de war
²muddle (vb) wat aanknoeien, wat aanmodderen: *~ along* (or: *on*) voortmodderen; *~ through* met vallen en opstaan het einde halen
³muddle (vb) **1** (also + up) door elkaar gooien, verwarren **2** in de war brengen: *a bit ~d* een beetje in de war
muddle-headed warrig, dom
muddy 1 modderig **2** troebel, ondoorzichtig **3** vaal, dof
mudguard spatbord[h]
mud-slinging zwartmakerij, vuilspuiterij:

~ campaign moddercampagne
muesli muesli
¹muff (n) **1** mof **2** misser [originally at ball game]; fiasco[h]
²muff (vb) **1** [sport] missen: *~ an easy catch* een makkelijke bal missen **2** verknoeien: *I know I'll ~ it* ik weet zeker dat ik het verpest
muffle 1 warm inpakken, warm toedekken: *~ up* goed inpakken **2** dempen [sound]: *~d curse* gedempte vloek
muffler 1 das, sjaal **2** geluiddemper; [Am] knalpot
¹mug (n) **1** mok, beker **2** kop, smoel **3** sufferd, sul
²mug (vb) aanvallen en beroven
mugger straatrover
mugging straatroof
muggins sul, sufferd
muggle 1 dreuzel [fantasy fiction] **2** [inform] sukkel
muggy benauwd, drukkend
mugshot portretfoto [for police file]
mug up uit je hoofd leren, erin stampen
mulberry moerbeiboom
mule 1 muildier[h], muilezel: *obstinate* (or: *stubborn*) *as a ~* koppig als een ezel **2** stijfkop, dwarskop
mullet 1 zeebarbeel: *red ~* mul **2** matje[h] [hair style]
multicultural multicultureel
multidimensional gecompliceerd; met veel kanten [eg problem]
multifocal multifocaal
multigenerational meergeneratie-: *~ housing* generatiewonen, kangoeroewonen
multilateral 1 veelzijdig **2** multilateraal
multinational multinationaal
¹multiple (n) [maths] veelvoud[h]: *least* (or: *lowest*) *common ~* kleinste gemene veelvoud
²multiple (adj) **1** veelvoudig: *~ choice* meerkeuze-; *~ shop* (or: *store*) grootwinkelbedrijf[h] **2** divers, veelsoortig **3** [bot] samengesteld
multiple birth meerling
multiplex megabioscoop
multiplication vermenigvuldiging
multiplication table tafel van vermenigvuldiging
multiplicity 1 veelheid, massa **2** veelsoortigheid: *a ~ of ideas* een grote verscheidenheid aan ideeën
¹multiply (vb) **1** zich vermeerderen, aangroeien **2** zich vermenigvuldigen **3** een vermenigvuldiging uitvoeren
²multiply (vb) **1** vermenigvuldigen: *~ three by four* drie met vier vermenigvuldigen **2** vergroten: *~ one's chances* zijn kansen doen stijgen
multipurpose veelzijdig, voor meerdere doeleinden geschikt
multiracial multiraciaal

multistorey car park parkeergarage
multitask multitasken, verschillende taken tegelijkertijd uitvoeren
multitude 1 massa: *a ~ of ideas* een grote hoeveelheid ideeën **2** menigte
1mum (n) mamma
2mum (adj) stil: *keep ~ zijn mondje dicht houden*
3mum (int) mondje dicht!, sst!, niets zeggen!: *~'s the word!* mondje dicht!, niks zeggen!
mumble 1 mompelen **2** knauwen op, mummelen op
mummify mummificeren, balsemen
mummy 1 mummie **2** mammie, mam(s)
mumps de bof
munch kauwen (op): *~ (away at) an apple* aan een appel knagen
munchkin 1 [inform; esp Am] kleintje[h] [pers] **2** munchkin [cat]
mundane gewoon: *~ matters* routinezaken
Munich München
municipal gemeentelijk
municipality 1 gemeente **2** gemeentebestuur[h]
munition 1 munitie **2** (-s) wapens; bommen, granaten
muppet stomkop, gekkie[h]
1mural (n) muurschildering, fresco[h]
2mural (adj) muur-, wand-: *~ painting* muurschildering
1murder (n) **1** moord: *get away with ~* **a)** alles kunnen maken; **b)** precies kunnen doen wat men wil **2** beroerde toestand
2murder (vb) **1** vermoorden, ombrengen **2** verknoeien, ruïneren
murderer moordenaar
murky 1 duister, donker **2** vunzig, kwalijk: *~ affairs* weinig verheffende zaken
1murmur (n) **1** gemurmel[h]; geruis[h] [of brook] **2** gemopper[h] **3** gemompel[h]
2murmur (vb) **1** mompelen **2** ruisen, suizen **3** mopperen: *~ against* (or: *at*) mopperen op, klagen over
Murphy's Law de wet van Murphy
muscle 1 spier: *flex one's ~s* de spieren losmaken **2** (spier)kracht, macht
muscular 1 spier-: *~ dystrophy* spierdystrofie **2** gespierd, krachtig
1muse (n) muze; [fig also] inspiratie: *The Muses* de (negen) muzen, kunsten en wetenschappen
2muse (vb) (+ about, over, on) peinzen (over), mijmeren
museum museum[h]
mush 1 moes[h], brij **2** sentimenteel geklets[h], kletspraat **3** [advertising] geruis[h]
1mushroom (n) **1** champignon **2** (eetbare) paddenstoel
2mushroom (vb) **1** zich snel ontwikkelen,

als paddenstoelen uit de grond schieten **2** paddenstoelvormig uitwaaieren [of smoke]
mushrooming snelle groei, explosieve toename
mushy 1 papperig, zacht: *~ peas* erwtenpuree **2** [inform] halfzacht, sentimenteel
music 1 muziek: *~ hall* variété(theater) **2** bladmuziek, partituur || *face the ~* de consequenties aanvaarden; *piped ~* ingeblikte muziek [in restaurant etc]
1musical (n) musical
2musical (adj) **1** muzikaal **2** welluidend **3** muziek-: *~ sound* klank [as opposed to noise] || *~ chairs* stoelendans
musician musicus, muzikant
music stand muziekstandaard
musk 1 muskus **2** muskusdier[h] **3** muskusplant
muskrat muskusrat
1Muslim (n) moslim
2Muslim (adj) moslims-: *~ community* moslimgemeenschap
Muslimah moslima
1muss (n) [Am] wanorde
2muss (vb) [Am] in de war maken; verknoeien [hair, clothing]: *~ up one's suit* zijn pak ruïneren
mussel mossel
1must (n) noodzaak, vereiste[h], must: *the Millennium Dome is a ~* je moet beslist naar de Millennium Dome toe
2must (aux vb) **1** [command, obligation and necessity] moeten; [in indirect speech also] moest/moesten; [condition] zou(den) zeker: *you ~ come and see us* je moet ons beslist eens komen opzoeken; *if you ~ have your way, then do* als je per se je eigen gang wil gaan, doe dat dan; *~ you have your way again?* moet je nu weer met alle geweld je zin krijgen? **2** [prohibition; with negation] mogen: *you ~ not go near the water* je mag niet dicht bij het water komen **3** [supposition] moeten; [Am also; with negation] kunnen: *you ~ be out of your mind to say such things* je moet wel gek zijn om zulke dingen te zeggen; *s.o. ~ have seen sth., surely?* er moet toch iem. iets gezien hebben?
mustard mosterd: [Am; inform] *cut the ~* het 'm flikken, het maken
1muster (n) **1** inspectie: *pass ~* ermee door kunnen **2** verzameling
2muster (vb) zich verzamelen; bijeenkomen [for inspection]
3muster (vb) **1** verzamelen, bijeenroepen **2** bijeenrapen; verzamelen [courage, powers]: *~ up one's courage* al zijn moed bijeenrapen
must-have iets dat iedereen moet (or: wil) hebben: *three ~ books for parents* drie boeken die elke ouder gelezen moet hebben

musty 1 muf: *~ air* bedompte lucht **2** schimmelig

mutation 1 verandering, wijziging **2** mutatie

¹mute (n) (doof)stomme

²mute (adj) **1** stom **2** zwijgend, stil, sprakeloos ‖ *~ swan* knobbelzwaan

mutilate verminken; toetakelen [also fig]

mutilation verminking

mutineer muiter

¹mutiny (n) muiterij, opstand

²mutiny (vb) muiten

mutt halvegare, idioot

¹mutter (n) **1** gemompel^h **2** gemopper^h

²mutter (vb) **1** mompelen: *he ~ed an oath* hij vloekte zachtjes **2** mopperen: *~ against* (or: *at*) mopperen over

mutton schapenvlees^h

muttonhead stomkop

mutual 1 wederzijds, wederkerig: *~ consent* wederzijds goedvinden **2** gemeenschappelijk, onderling: *~ interests* gemeenschappelijke belangen

muzak achtergrondmuziek, muzak

¹muzzle (n) **1** snuit; muil [of animal] **2** mond; tromp [of gun] **3** muilkorf

²muzzle (vb) muilkorven [also fig]; de mond snoeren

muzzy 1 duf, saai, dof **2** wazig, vaag **3** beneveld, verward

¹my (pron) mijn: *my dear boy* beste jongen; *he disapproved of my going out* hij vond het niet goed dat ik uitging

²my (int) **1** o jee **2** wel: *my, my* welwel

myalgia 1 spierpijn **2** spierreumatiek

Myanmar Myanmar

myopic 1 bijziend, kippig **2** kortzichtig

myself 1 mij, me, mezelf: *I am not ~ today* ik voel me niet al te best vandaag **2** zelf: *I'll go ~* ik zal zelf gaan

mysterious geheimzinnig, mysterieus

mystery 1 geheim^h, mysterie^h, raadsel^h **2** geheimzinnigheid

¹mystic (n) mysticus

²mystic (adj) **1** mystiek **2** occult, esoterisch, alleen voor ingewijden **3** raadselachtig

mystical 1 mystiek **2** occult, esoterisch

mystification mystificatie, misleiding

mystify verbijsteren, verwarren, voor een raadsel stellen: *her behaviour mystified me* ik begreep niets van haar gedrag

mystique 1 aura **2** geheime techniek

myth 1 mythe, mythologie **2** fabel, allegorie **3** verzinsel^h, fictie

mythical 1 mythisch **2** fictief, verzonnen

mythological 1 mythologisch **2** mythisch

mythology mythologie

n

N *North* N., Noord(en)

n/a *not applicable* n.v.t., niet van toepassing

nab (op)pakken, inrekenen

naff niks waard, waardeloos

¹nag (n) **1** klein paard(je^h), pony **2** knol, slecht renpaard^h **3** zeurpiet

²nag (vb) **1** zeuren: *a ~ging headache* een zeurende hoofdpijn; *~ (at) s.o.* iem. aan het hoofd zeuren **2** treiteren

¹nail (n) **1** nagel **2** spijker: *hit the ~ on the head* de spijker op de kop slaan ‖ *pay on the ~* contant betalen

²nail (vb) **1** (vast)spijkeren **2** vastnagelen: *he was ~ed to his seat* hij zat als vastgenageld op zijn stoel **3** te pakken krijgen: *he ~ed me as soon as I came in* hij schoot me direct aan toen ik binnenkwam **4** betrappen ‖ *~ it* het voor elkaar krijgen

nail-biter razend spannende film, razend spannend boek^h

nail down 1 vastspijkeren **2** nauwkeurig vaststellen, bepalen: *John had nailed him down* John had hem precies door **3** vastleggen, houden aan: *it's difficult to nail him down on any subject* hij zegt niet gauw wat hij ergens van denkt; *we nailed him down to his promise* we hielden hem aan zijn belofte **4** zich verzekeren van, veiligstellen: *they've already nailed down the championship* ze zijn al zeker kampioen

nail up 1 dichtspijkeren **2** (op)hangen

naive 1 naïef **2** onnozel, dom

naivety naïviteit, onschuld, onnozelheid

naked 1 naakt, bloot **2** onbedekt, kaal ‖ *the ~ eye* het blote oog; *~ truth* naakte waarheid

¹name (n) **1** naam, benaming: *enter* (or: *put down*) *one's ~ for* zich opgeven voor; *what's-his-~?* hoe heet hij ook alweer?, dinges; *I only know him by ~* ik ken hem alleen van naam; *a man by* (or: *of*) *the ~ of Jones* iem. die Jones heet, een zekere Jones; *he hasn't a penny to his ~* hij heeft geen cent; *I can't put a ~ to it* ik weet niet precies hoe ik het moet zeggen; *first ~* voornaam; *second ~* achternaam **2** reputatie, naam: *make* (or: *win*) *a ~ for o.s.*, *win o.s. a ~* naam maken ‖ *the ~ of the game is ...* waar het om gaat is ...; *call s.o. ~s* iem. uitschelden; *lend one's ~ to* zijn naam lenen aan; *in the ~ of* in (de) naam van

²name (vb) **1** noemen, benoemen, een naam geven: *she was ~d after her mother*, [Am also] *she was ~d for her mother* ze was naar haar moeder genoemd **2** dopen [ship] **3** (op)noemen: *~ your price* noem je prijs **4** benoemen, aanstellen **5** vaststellen: *~ the day* de trouwdag vaststellen ‖ *you ~ it* noem maar op

name-calling het schelden, scheldpartij

namedropping opschepperij, indruk willen maken door met namen te strooien

namely namelijk

namesake naamgenoot

Namibia Namibië

¹Namibian (n) Namibiër, Namibische

²Namibian (adj) Namibisch

nan [child language] oma

¹nancy (n) [depr] mietje^h, nicht, flikker

²nancy (adj) [depr] verwijfd

nanny kinderjuffrouw

nanny state (the) [depr] [roughly] betuttelende verzorgingsstaat

¹nap (n) **1** dutje^h, tukje^h **2** vleug [of fabric]

²nap (vb) dutten, dommelen: *catch s.o. ~ping* iem. betrappen

napa cabbage Chinese kool

nape (achterkant van de) nek

napkin 1 servet^h, doekje^h **2** luier

nappy luier

narcissus (witte) narcis

¹narcotic (n) verdovend middel^h, slaapmiddel^h

²narcotic (adj) verdovend, slaapverwekkend

¹nark (n) verklikker, tipgever

²nark (vb) kwaad maken, irriteren: *she felt ~ed at* (or: *by*) *his words* zijn woorden ergerden haar

narrate vertellen, beschrijven

narration verhaal^h, vertelling, verslag^h

¹narrative (n) verhaal^h, vertelling

²narrative (adj) verhalend, verhaal-, narratief: *~ power* vertelkunst

narrator verteller

¹narrow (n) engte, zee-engte, bergengte

²narrow (adj) **1** smal, nauw, eng: *by a ~ margin* nog net, op het nippertje **2** beperkt, krap: *a ~ majority* een kleine meerderheid **3** bekrompen **4** nauwgezet, precies: *a ~ examination* een zorgvuldig onderzoek ‖ *it was a ~ escape* het was op het nippertje; *in the ~est sense* strikt genomen

narrow down beperken, terugbrengen: *it narrowed down to this* het kwam (ten slotte) hierop neer

narrowly 1 net, juist: *the sailor ~ escaped drowning* de zeeman ontkwam maar net aan de verdrinkingsdood **2** zorgvuldig

narrow-minded bekrompen, kleingeestig

nasal neus-, nasaal: *~ spray* neusspray

nasality neusgeluid^h, nasaliteit

nasturtium Oost-Indische kers

nasty 1 smerig, vuil, vies **2** onaangenaam, onprettig: *the bill was a ~ shock* de rekening zorgde voor een onaangename verrassing

3 lastig, hinderlijk, vervelend **4** gemeen, hatelijk: *a ~ look* een boze blik; *he turned ~ when I refused to leave* hij werd giftig toen ik niet wilde weggaan **5** ernstig, hevig: *a ~ accident* een ernstig ongeluk; *a ~ blow* a) een flinke klap; b) een tegenvaller

nation 1 natie, volk[h] **2** land[h], staat

¹national (n) **1** landgenoot **2** staatsburger, onderdaan

²national (adj) **1** nationaal, rijks-, staats-, volks-: *~ anthem* volkslied[h]; *~ debt* staatsschuld; *~ monument* historisch monument; *~ service* militaire dienst; *National Trust* [roughly] monumentenzorg **2** landelijk, nationaal

nationalism nationalisme[h]

nationalist(ic) nationalistisch

nationality nationaliteit

nationalize 1 nationaliseren **2** naturaliseren **3** tot een natie maken

nationwide landelijk, door het hele land

¹native (n) **1** inwoner, bewoner: *a ~ of Dublin* een geboren Dubliner **2** [oft depr] inboorling, inlander **3** inheemse diersoort, plantensoort

²native (adj) **1** geboorte-: *Native American* indiaan; *a ~ speaker of English* iem. met Engels als moedertaal **2** natuurlijk **3** autochtoon, inheems, binnenlands; [oft depr] inlands: *go ~* zich aanpassen aan de plaatselijke bevolking

nativity geboorte

Nativity (the) geboorte(feest[h]) van Christus, Kerstmis

nativity play kerstspel[h]

NATO *North Atlantic Treaty Organization* NAVO, Noord-Atlantische Verdragsorganisatie

natty 1 sjiek, netjes, keurig **2** handig, bedreven

¹natural (n) natuurtalent[h], favoriet, meest geschikte persoon: *John's a ~ for the job* John is geknipt voor die baan

²natural (adj) **1** natuurlijk, natuur-: *~ forces* natuurkrachten; *~ gas* aardgas[h]; *~ history* natuurlijke historie, biologie **2** geboren, van nature: *he's a ~ linguist* hij heeft een talenknobbel **3** aangeboren **4** normaal **5** ongedwongen

naturalist 1 naturalist **2** natuurkenner

naturalization 1 naturalisatie **2** inburgering **3** het inheems maken [plants, animals]

naturalize 1 naturaliseren **2** doen inburgeren, overnemen **3** inheems maken; uitzetten [plants, animals]: *rabbits have become ~d in Australia* konijnen zijn in Australië een inheemse diersoort geworden

naturally 1 natuurlijk, vanzelfsprekend, uiteraard **2** van nature ‖ *it comes ~ to her* het gaat haar gemakkelijk af

nature 1 wezen[h], natuur, karakter[h]: *he is*

stubborn *by ~* hij is koppig van aard; *in the (very) ~ of things* uit de aard der zaak **2** soort[+h], aard: *sth. of that ~* iets van dien aard **3** de natuur: *~ reserve* natuurreservaat[h]; [fig] *let ~ take its course* de zaken op hun beloop laten; *contrary to ~* wonderbaarlijk, onnatuurlijk

nature conservation natuurbeheer[h]

naturism naturisme[h], nudisme[h]

naught nul, niets: *come to ~* op niets uitlopen

naughty 1 ondeugend, stout **2** slecht, onfatsoenlijk

nausea 1 misselijkheid **2** walging, afkeer

nauseate misselijk maken: *he was ~d at the sight of such cruelty* het zien van zoveel wreedheid vervulde hem met afschuw; *a nauseating taste* een walgelijke smaak

nauseous 1 [esp Am] misselijk **2** [form] misselijk makend, walgelijk [also fig]

nautical nautisch, zee(vaart)-: *~ mile* a) (Engelse) zeemijl [1,853.18 metres]; b) internationale zeemijl [1,852 metres]

naval 1 zee-, scheeps-: *~ architect* scheepsbouwkundig ingenieur **2** marine-, vloot-: *~ battle* zeeslag; *~ officer* marineofficier; *~ power* zeemacht

nave 1 schip[h] [of church] **2** naaf [of wheel]

navel 1 navel **2** middelpunt[h]

navigable 1 bevaarbaar **2** zeewaardig **3** bestuurbaar

¹navigate (vb) een schip/vliegtuig besturen; [also comp] navigeren

²navigate (vb) **1** bevaren **2** oversteken, vliegen over **3** besturen **4** loodsen [fig]; (ge)leiden **5** [comp] navigeren op

navigation navigatie, stuurmanskunst, scheepvaart: *inland ~* binnen(scheep)vaart

navigator 1 [aviation] navigator **2** [shipp] navigatieofficier

navvy 1 grondwerker **2** graafmachine

navy 1 marine **2** oorlogsvloot, zeemacht

nay 1 nee(n) **2** tegenstemmer, stem tegen: *the ~s have it* de motie/het (wets)voorstel is verworpen **3** weigering

NBD [inform] *no big deal* geen probleem, maakt niet uit

NBF [inform] *new best friend* nieuwe beste vriend(in)

NCD [med] *non-communicable disease* niet-overdraagbare ziekte

NE *north-east* N.O., noordoost

¹near (adj) **1** dichtbij(gelegen): *Near East* Nabije Oosten **2** kort [road] **3** nauw verwant **4** intiem; persoonlijk [friend] **5** krenterig, gierig ‖ *he had a ~ escape,* [inform] *it was a ~ thing* het was maar op het nippertje; *it was a ~ miss* het was bijna raak [also fig]

²near (vb) naderen

³near (adv) dichtbij, nabij: *from far and ~* van heinde en ver; *nowhere ~ as clever* lang niet zo slim; *she was ~ to tears* het huilen stond

haar nader dan het lachen
⁴near (prep) dichtbij, nabij, naast: *he lived ~ his sister* hij woonde niet ver van zijn zuster; *go* (or: *come*) *~ to doing sth.* iets bijna doen, op het punt staan iets te doen
nearby dichtbij, nabij gelegen
nearly 1 bijna, vrijwel: *is his book ~ finished?* is zijn boek nu al bijna af? **2** nauw, na, van nabij: *~ related* nauw verwant || *not ~* (nog) lang niet, op geen stukken na
nearside linker: *the ~ wheel* het linker wiel
near-sighted bijziend
neat 1 net(jes), keurig, proper **2** puur; zonder ijs [of drink] **3** handig, vaardig, slim **4** sierlijk, smaakvol **5** [Am] schoon, netto **6** [Am] gaaf, prima **7** kernachtig
nebulous nevelig [also fig]; troebel, vaag
necessarily noodzakelijk(erwijs), onvermijdelijk, per definitie
¹necessary (n) **1** behoefte: *the ~* a) het benodigde; b) geld^h **2** (necessaries) benodigdheden, vereisten **3** (necessaries) (levens)behoeften
²necessary (adj) noodzakelijk, nodig, vereist, essentieel: *~ evil* noodzakelijk kwaad
necessitate 1 noodzaken **2** vereisen, dwingen tot
necessity 1 noodzaak, dwang: *in case of ~* in geval van nood **2** noodzakelijkheid **3** behoefte, vereiste^h **4** nood, armoede
¹neck (n) **1** hals, nek: [sport] *~ and ~* nek aan nek **2** hals(vormig voorwerp^h); [eg] flessenhals **3** zee-engte, landengte, bergengte: *a ~ of land* een landengte || [Am] *~ of the woods* buurt, omgeving; *breathe* down s.o.'s *~* a) iem. op de hielen zitten; b) iem. op de vingers kijken; *get it in the ~* het voor zijn kiezen krijgen; *risk one's ~* zijn leven wagen; *stick one's ~ out* zijn nek uitsteken; *up to one's ~ in (debt)* tot zijn nek in (de schuld)
²neck (vb) vrijen (met), kussen
necklace halsband^h, halssnoer^h, (hals)ketting
necktie [esp Am] stropdas
nectar nectar, godendrank
nectarine nectarine
née geboren
¹need (n) **1** noodzaak: *there's no ~ for you to leave yet* je hoeft nog niet weg (te gaan) **2** behoefte, nood: *as* (or: *if, when*) *the ~ arises* als de behoefte zich voordoet; *have ~ of* behoefte hebben aan; *people in ~ of help* hulpbehoevenden **3** armoede: *a friend in ~* een echte vriend || *if ~ be* desnoods, als het moet
²need (vb) nodig hebben, behoefte hebben aan, vereisen: *they ~ more room to play* ze hebben meer speelruimte nodig; *this ~s to be done urgently* dit moet dringend gedaan worden
³need (aux vb) hoeven, moeten; [+ negation] had (niet) hoeven: *all he ~ do is ...* al wat hij

moet doen is ...; *we ~ not have worried* we hadden ons geen zorgen hoeven te maken
needful noodzakelijk
¹needle (n) **1** naald, breinaald, magneetnaald, injectienaald, dennennaald: *look for a ~ in a haystack* een speld in een hooiberg zoeken **2** sterke rivaliteit: *~ match* wedstrijd op het scherp van de snede || [inform] *get the ~* pissig worden
²needle (vb) **1** naaien, een naald halen door, (door)prikken **2** zieken, pesten
needless onnodig: *~ to say ...* overbodig te zeggen ...
needlework naaiwerk^h, handwerk^h
needs noodzakelijkerwijs: *he ~ must* hij kan niet anders; *at a moment like this, he must ~ go* uitgerekend op een moment als dit moet hij zo nodig weg
needy arm, noodlijdend
nefarious misdadig, schandelijk
negate 1 tenietdoen **2** ontkennen
negation ontkenning
¹negative (n) **1** afwijzing, ontkenning: *the answer is in the ~* het antwoord luidt nee **2** weigering **3** [photo] negatief^h
²negative (adj) **1** negatief: *the ~ sign* het minteken **2** ontkennend, afwijzend: *~ criticism* afbrekende kritiek
¹neglect (n) **1** verwaarlozing **2** verzuim^h: *~ of duty* plichtsverzuim^h
²neglect (vb) **1** verwaarlozen **2** verzuimen, nalaten
negligence nalatigheid, slordigheid
negligible verwaarloosbaar, niet noemenswaardig
¹negotiate (vb) onderhandelen
²negotiate (vb) **1** (na onderhandeling) sluiten, (na onderhandeling) afsluiten **2** nemen, passeren, doorkomen, tot een goed einde brengen: *~ a sharp bend* een scherpe bocht nemen
negotiation 1 onderhandeling, bespreking: *enter into* (or: *open, start*) *~s with* in onderhandeling gaan met **2** (af)sluiting
negotiator onderhandelaar
Negress [offensive] negerin
Negro [offensive] neger
¹neigh (n) (ge)hinnik^h
²neigh (vb) hinniken
neighbour 1 buurman, buurvrouw: *my ~ at dinner* mijn tafelgenoot **2** medemens, naaste: *duty to one's ~* (ver)plicht(ing) ten opzichte van zijn naaste
neighbourhood 1 buurt, wijk **2** nabijheid, omgeving || *I paid a sum in the ~ of 150 dollars* ik heb rond de 150 dollar betaald
neighbouring aangrenzend
¹neither (pron) geen van beide(n): *~ of us wanted him to come* we wilden geen van beiden dat hij kwam; *~ candidate* geen van beide kandidaten

²**neither** (adv) evenmin, ook niet: *she cannot play and ~ can I* zij kan niet spelen en ik ook niet

³**neither** (conj) noch: *she could ~ laugh nor cry* ze kon (noch) lachen noch huilen

neocon [inform] neoconservatief

neologism neologisme^h, nieuw woord^h

neon neon^h

Nepal Nepal

¹**Nepalese** (n) Nepalees, Nepalese

²**Nepalese** (adj) Nepalees

nephew neef(je^h), zoon van broer of zus

nepotism nepotisme^h, vriendjespolitiek, begunstiging van familieleden en vrienden

nerd sul, klungel, nerd

nerdy [inform] sullig, wereldvreemd, nerdachtig

nerve 1 zenuw: [fig] *hit* (or: *touch*) *a ~* een zenuw raken **2** moed, durf, lef^h, brutaliteit: *you've got a ~!* jij durft, zeg!; *lose one's ~* de moed verliezen **3** (-s) zenuwen, zelfbeheersing: *get on s.o.'s ~s* op iemands zenuwen werken

nerve-racking zenuwslopend

nerve-wracking zenuwslopend

nervous 1 zenuwachtig, gejaagd **2** nerveus, zenuw-: *~ breakdown* zenuwinstorting, zenuwinzinking; *(central) ~ system* (centraal) zenuwstelsel **3** angstig, bang: *~ of* bang voor

nervy 1 [inform] zenuwachtig, schrikkerig **2** [Am; inform] koel(bloedig), onverschillig

nest 1 nest^h: *a ~ of robbers* een roversnest **2** broeinest^h, haard ‖ *feather one's ~* zijn zakken vullen

nest egg appeltje^h voor de dorst

¹**nestle** (vb) **1** zich nestelen, lekker (gaan) zitten (liggen) **2** (half) verscholen liggen **3** schurken, (dicht) aankruipen: *~ up against* (or: *to*) *s.o.* dicht tegen iem. aankruipen

²**nestle** (vb) **1** neerleggen **2** tegen zich aan drukken, in zijn armen nemen

¹**net** (n) **1** net^h; [fig] web^h; (val)strik **2** netmateriaal^h, mousseline^{+h}, tule ‖ *surf the Net* internetten, surfen op internet

²**net** (n) nettobedrag^h

³**net** (adj) netto, schoon, zuiver: *~ profit* nettowinst

⁴**net** (vb) (in een net) vangen; [also fig] (ver)-strikken

⁵**net** (vb) **1** (als winst) opleveren, (netto) opbrengen **2** winnen, opstrijken, (netto) verdienen

nether [dated or hum] onder-, neder-, beneden-: *~ world* schimmenrijk^h, onderwereld

Netherlands (the) Nederland

netiquette nettiquette

netizen netizen, internetburger

netting net(werk)^h

¹**nettle** (n) (brand)netel ‖ *grasp the ~* de koe bij de hoorns vatten

²**nettle** (vb) irriteren, ergeren

network 1 net(werk)^h **2** radio- en televisiemaatschappij, omroep **3** computernetwerk^h

networking 1 het werken met een netwerk(systeem) **2** [Am] het netwerken

neural neuraal, zenuw-

neuralgia zenuwpijn, neuralgie

neurology neurologie

¹**neurotic** (n) neuroot, zenuwlijder

²**neurotic** (adj) neurotisch

¹**neuter** (adj) onzijdig [of word, plant, animal]

²**neuter** (vb) helpen, castreren; steriliseren [animal]

neutral 1 neutraal [also chem]; onpartijdig **2** onzijdig, geslachtloos ‖ *in ~ gear* in z'n vrij

neutrality neutraliteit

neutralize neutraliseren

never nooit: *never-ending* altijddurend, oneindig (lang); *never-to-be-forgotten* onvergetelijk ‖ *this'll ~ do* dit is niks, hier kun je niks mee; *he ~ so looked!* hij keek niet eens!

nevermore nooit meer

never-never (the) [inform] huurkoop(systeem^h): *on the ~* op afbetaling

nevertheless niettemin, desondanks, toch

new nieuw, ongebruikt, recent: *~ bread* vers brood; *~ moon* (eerste fase van de) wassende maan, nieuwemaan; *~ town* nieuwbouwstad; *the New World* de Nieuwe Wereld, Noord- en Zuid-Amerika; *~ year* a) jaarwisseling; b) nieuw jaar ‖ *~ broom* frisse wind; *turn over a ~ leaf* met een schone lei beginnen; *break ~ ground* [fig] nieuwe wegen banen; *that's ~ to me* dat is nieuw voor me; *I'm ~ to the job* ik werk hier nog maar pas

newbie nieuwkomer, beginneling

newborn 1 pasgeboren **2** herboren

newcomer nieuwkomer, beginner

newly 1 op nieuwe wijze, anders **2** onlangs, pas, recentelijk: *~ wed* pasgetrouwd **3** opnieuw

newlywed jonggehuwde, pasgetrouwde

news 1 nieuws^h: *break the ~ to s.o.* (als eerste) iem. het (slechte) nieuws vertellen; *that is ~ to me* dat is nieuw voor mij **2** nieuws^h, nieuwsberichten, journaal^h, journaaluitzending

newsagent krantenverkoper, tijdschriftenverkoper

newscast nieuwsuitzending, journaal^h

newsflash nieuwsflits

newsletter nieuwsbrief, mededelingenblad^h

newspaper krant, dagblad^h

newsprint krantenpapier^h

newsreader nieuwslezer

newsreel bioscoopjournaal^h

newsroom redactiekamer

newsstand kiosk

newswire persdienst, nieuwskanaal^h

New Year's Day nieuwjaarsdag
New Year's Eve oudejaarsdag, oudejaarsavond
New Year's resolution goed voornemen
New Zealand Nieuw-Zeeland
¹next (adj) **1** volgend [of place]; na, naast,
dichtstbijzijnd: *she lives ~ door* ze woont
hiernaast; *the ~ turn past the traffic lights* de
eerste afslag na de verkeerslichten; *the ~
best* het beste op één na, de tweede keus;
the ~ but one de volgende op één na **2** volgend [of time]; aanstaand: *the ~ day* de volgende dag, de dag daarop; *~ Monday* aanstaande maandag; *the ~ few weeks* de komende weken
²next (dem pron) (eerst)volgende: *~, please*
volgende graag ǁ *~ of kin* (naaste) bloedver-
want(en), nabestaande(n)
³next (adv) **1** daarnaast: *what ~?* a) wat
(krijgen we) nu?; b) [depr] kan het nog gekker? **2** [time; also fig] daarna, daaropvolgend, de volgende keer: *the ~ best thing* op
één na het beste ǁ *~ to impossible* bijna onmogelijk; *for ~ to nothing* bijna voor niks
next-door aangrenzend: *we are ~ neighbours* we wonen naast elkaar
NGL [inform] *not gonna lie* echt waar, serieus
NGO *non-governmental organization* ngo
NHS *National Health Service* nationaal zie-
kenfondsʰ
nib pen, kroontjespen
¹nibble (n) hapjeʰ
²nibble (vb) knabbelen (aan), knagen (aan):
~ away (or: *off*) wegknabbelen, afknabbe-
len, wegknagen, afknagen
Nicaragua Nicaragua
¹Nicaraguan (n) Nicaraguaan(se)
²Nicaraguan (adj) Nicaraguaans
nice 1 aardig, vriendelijk: *you're a ~ friend!*
mooie vriend ben jij! **2** mooi, goed: *~ work!*
goed zo! **3** leuk, prettig: *have a ~ day* nog
een prettige dag, tot ziens **4** genuanceerd,
verfijnd **5** kies(keurig), precies ǁ *~ and warm*
(or: *fast*) lekker warm (or: hard)
nicety 1 detailʰ, subtiliteit, nuance **2** nauwkeurigheid, precisie ǁ *to a ~* precies, tot in de
puntjes
niche 1 nis **2** stek, plek(tje ʰ), hoekjeʰ: *he has
found his ~* hij heeft zijn draai gevonden
¹nick (n) **1** kerf, keep **2** snee(tjeʰ), kras **3** bajes, nor **4** politiebureauʰ **5** staat, vorm: *in
good ~* in prima conditie, in goede staat ǁ *in
the ~ of time* op het nippertje
²nick (vb) **1** inkepen, inkerven, krassen **2** jatten **3** in de kraag grijpen, arresteren
nickel 1 vijfcentstukʰ [in Canada and Am];
stuiver **2** nikkelʰ
¹nickname (n) **1** bijnaam **2** roepnaam
²nickname (vb) een bijnaam geven (aan)
nicotine nicotine

niece nicht(jeʰ), oomzegster, tantezegster,
dochter van broer of zus
niff lucht, stank
nifty 1 jofel, tof **2** handig
Niger Niger
Nigeria Nigeria
¹Nigerian (n) Nigeriaan(se)
²Nigerian (adj) Nigeriaans
¹Nigerien (n) Nigerees, Nigerese
²Nigerien (adj) Nigerees
niggard vrek
nigger [offensive] nikker, neger
¹niggle (vb) muggenziften, vitten
²niggle (vb) **1** knagen aan, irriteren **2** vitten
op
night nacht, avond: *~ and day* dag en nacht;
stay the ~ blijven logeren; *at* (or: *by*) *'s
nachts, 's avonds; *first ~* première(avond);
last ~ gisteravond, vannacht; *~ owl* nachtbraker, nachtmens ǁ *make a ~ of it* nachtbraken, doorhalen
nightcap slaapmuts(jeʰ) [also drink]
nightclub nachtclub
nightclubbing: *go ~* (de) nachtclubs afgaan
nightdress nachthemdʰ, nachtjapon
nightfall vallen van de avond
nightie [inform] nachtpon
nightingale nachtegaal
nightly nachtelijk, elke nacht (avond), 's
nachts, 's avonds
nightmare nachtmerrie
night shift 1 nachtdienst **2** nachtploeg
night-time nacht(elijk uurʰ)
nightwear nachtkleding, nachtgoedʰ
nighty nachthemdʰ, nachtjapon
nil nihil, nietsʰ, nul: *three-~* drie-nul
nimble 1 behendig, vlug **2** alert, gevat,
spits
nimby [inform] *not in my backyard* niet-in-
mijn-achtertuinprotesteerder: *~ syndrome*
blijf-uit-mijn-buurtsyndroom
nine negen ǁ *he was dressed (up) to the ~s* hij
was piekfijn gekleed
ninepins kegelenʰ, kegelspelʰ
nineteen negentien
nineteenth negentiende
ninetieth negentigste
ninety negentig: *he was in his nineties* hij
was in de negentig
ninny imbeciel, sukkel
ninth negende
¹nip (n) **1** stokjeʰ, borreltjeʰ **2** kneep **3** (bijtende) kou: *there was a ~ in the air* het was
nogal fris(jes)
²nip (vb) nippen, in kleine teugjes nemen
³nip (vb) (+ out) eventjes (weg)gaan, vliegen,
rennen: *~ in* a) binnenwippen; b) naar links
(or: rechts) schieten [in traf]
⁴nip (vb) **1** knijpen, beknellen; bijten [also of
animal] **2** in de groei stuiten: *~ in the bud* in

de kiem smoren

nipper 1 peuter **2** (-s) tang, nijptang, buigtang

nipple 1 tepel **2** [Am] speen [of feeding bottle] **3** (smeer)nippel

nippy 1 vlug, rap **2** fris(jes), koud

niqab (gezichts)sluier, nikab

nit 1 neet, luizeneiʰ **2** stommeling

¹nitpicking (n) muggenzifterij

²nitpicking (adj) muggenzifterig

nitrogen stikstofʰ

nitrous salpeterachtig: ~ *acid* salpeterigzuurʰ; ~ *oxide* lachgasʰ

nitty-gritty (the) kern, essentie: *let's get down to the* ~ laten we nu de harde feiten eens bekijken

nitwit idioot, stommeling

¹nix (n) niks, nietsʰ, nop

²nix (vb) een streep halen door, niet toestaan

¹no (n) **1** neenʰ, weigering **2** tegenstemmer: *I won't* **take** *no for an answer* ik sta erop, je kunt niet weigeren, ik wil geen nee horen

²no (pron) **1** geen, geen enkele, helemaal geen: *on no* **account** onder geen enkele voorwaarde; *there's no* **milk** er is geen melk in huis; *I'm no* **expert** ik ben geen deskundige **2** haast geen, bijna geen, heel weinig, een minimum van: *it's no* **distance** het is vlakbij; *in no* **time** in een mum van tijd

³no (adv) **1** nee(n): *oh no!* 't is niet waar!; *did you tell her? no I didn't* heb je het tegen haar gezegd? neen; *no!* neen toch! **2** niet, in geen enkel opzicht: *he told her in no uncertain terms* hij zei het haar in duidelijke bewoordingen; *let me know whether* **or** *no you are coming* laat me even weten of je komt of niet; *the mayor himself, no* **less** niemand minder dan de burgemeester zelf

no. *number* nr. *(nummer)*

nob 1 kop, hoofdʰ **2** hoge ome

nobble 1 [sport] uitschakelen [horse, dog; esp through doping] **2** omkopen; bepraten [pers] **3** (weg)kapen; jatten [money, prize]

nobility 1 adel, adelstand **2** adeldom **3** edelmoedigheid, nobelheid

¹noble (n) edele, edelman, edelvrouw

²noble (adj) **1** adellijk, van adel **2** edel, nobel: ~ *savage* edele wilde ‖ [chem] ~ *gas* edelgasʰ

nobleman edelman, lidʰ van de adel

nobody niemand, onbelangrijk persoon, nul

no-brainer 1 fluitjeʰ van een cent, koud kunstjeʰ, makkieʰ; vanzelfsprekendheid **2** iem. zonder hersens, dombo

nocturnal nachtelijk, nacht-

¹nod (n) knik(jeʰ), wenk(jeʰ): *give (s.o.) a* ~ (iem. toe)knikken ‖ *on the* ~ **a)** op de lat, op krediet; **b)** zonder discussie (*or:* formele) stemming

²nod (vb) **1** knikken [as greeting, order]; ja

knikken [indicating approval]: *have a* ~*ding* **acquaintance** *with s.o. (sth.)* iem. (iets) oppervlakkig kennen **2** (+ off) indutten, in slaap vallen **3** (zitten te) suffen, niet opletten, een fout maken

³nod (vb) **1** knikken met [head] **2** door knikken te kennen geven [approval, greeting, permission]: ~ *approval* goedkeurend knikken

nodding oppervlakkig: *have a* ~ **acquaintance** *with s.o.* iem. oppervlakkig kennen; *have a* ~ **acquaintance** *with sth.* een vage notie hebben van iets

node 1 knoest, knobbel **2** [science, comp] knoop

Noel [form] Kerstmis

no-frills zonder overbodige extra's: *a* ~ **supermarket** goedkope supermarkt met beperkt productaanbod

no-frill(s) zonder franje, eenvoudig

¹no-go (n) [inform]: *that's a* ~ dat gaat niet lukken, vergeet dat maar

²no-go (adj) verboden, niet toegankelijk: ~ *area* verboden wijk/gebied

nohow op geen enkele manier, helemaal niet, van geen kant: *we couldn't find it* ~ we konden het helemaal nergens vinden

noise 1 geluidʰ **2** lawaaiʰ, rumoerʰ **3** [techn] geruisʰ, ruis, storing

noise nuisance geluidshinder, geluidsoverlast

noisy lawaaierig, luidruchtig, gehorig

nomad 1 nomade **2** zwerver [also fig]

nomadic nomadisch, (rond)zwervend

no-man's-land niemandslandʰ

nominal 1 in naam (alléén), theoretisch, niet echt **2** zo goed als geen, niet noemenswaardig; symbolisch [eg amount]: *at (a)* ~ *price* voor een spotprijs

nominate 1 (+ as, for) kandidaat stellen (als/voor), (als kandidaat) voordragen, nomineren **2** benoemen: ~ *s.o. to* **be** (*or:* **as**) iem. benoemen tot

nomination 1 kandidaatstelling, voordracht, nominatie **2** benoeming

nominee 1 kandidaat **2** benoemde

non-aggression non-agressie, (belofte van) het niet aanvallen: ~ *pact* (*or:* *agreement*) niet-aanvalsverdragʰ

non-aligned niet-gebonden; neutraal [country, politics]

non-binary non-binair

nonchalant nonchalant, onverschillig

non-commissioned zonder officiersaanstelling: ~ *officer* onderofficier

non-committal neutraal; vrijblijvend [reply]

nondescript 1 non-descript, moeilijk te beschrijven **2** nietszeggend, onbeduidend

¹none (pron) geen (enkele), niemand, niets: *I'll have* ~ *of your tricks* ik pik die streken van jou niet; *there is ~ left* er is niets meer over; *~ other* than the President niemand anders dan de president; *~ of the students* niemand van de studenten

²**none** (adv) helemaal niet, niet erg, niet veel: *she was ~ the wiser* ze was er niets wijzer op geworden; *she is none too bright* ze is niet al te slim; *he was ~ too pleased about* (or: *with*) *it* hij was er niet erg blij mee, hij was er niet erg van gecharmeerd

nonentity onbelangrijk persoon (ding^h)

nonetheless niettemin, echter, toch

non-event afknapper

non-existent niet-bestaand

non-iron zelfstrijkend

no-nonsense 1 zakelijk, no-nonsense **2** zonder franjes [eg dress]

nonplussed verbijsterd

nonprofit zonder winstoogmerk, non-profit

nonproliferation non-proliferatie

non-returnable zonder statiegeld

nonsense onzin, nonsens, flauwekul: *make (a) ~ of* tenietdoen, het effect bederven van; *stand no ~* geen flauwekul dulden; *what ~* wat een flauwekul

nonsensical onzinnig, absurd

non-smoking rookvrij

non-stick antiaanbak-, met een antiaanbaklaag

non-stop non-stop, zonder te stoppen; doorgaand [train]; zonder tussenlandingen [flight]; direct [connection]; doorlopend [performance]

non-U [inform; hum] niet gebruikelijk bij de upper class

noob [inform] leek, dombo, nitwit

noodles noedels, mie

nook (rustig) hoekje^h, veilige plek: *search every ~ and cranny* in elk hoekje en gaatje zoeken, overal zoeken

noon middag(uur^h), twaalf uur 's middags

no-one niemand

noose lus, strik, strop

nootropic smartdrug

nope [inform] nee

nor 1 evenmin, ook niet: *you don't like melon? ~ do I* je houdt niet van meloen? ik ook niet **2** [often after neither] noch, en ook niet, en evenmin: *neither Jill ~ Sheila* noch Jill noch Sheila; *she neither spoke ~ smiled* ze sprak noch lachte

Nordic noords, Noord-Europees, Scandinavisch

norm norm, standaard

¹**normal** (n) het normale, gemiddelde^h, normale toestand: *above* (or: *below*) *~* boven (or: onder) normaal

²**normal** (adj) normaal, gewoon, standaard

normalization 1 normalisatie **2** het normaal worden

normalize normaal worden (maken), herstellen, normaliseren

normal time [sport] reguliere speeltijd

Norman Normandisch

normative normatief, bindend

Norseman Noorman

¹**north** (n) het noorden [point of the compass]; noord: *face (the) ~* op het noorden liggen; *the North* het Noordelijk gedeelte

²**north** (adj) noordelijk: *the North Pole* de noordpool; *the North Sea* de Noordzee

³**north** (adv) van, naar, in het noorden: *face ~* op het noorden liggen

northbound iem. die naar het noorden gaat, iets dat naar het noorden gaat [traf, road]

north-east noordoostelijk

northeastern uit het noordoosten, noordoostelijk

¹**northerly** (n) noordenwind

²**northerly** (adj) noordelijk

northern noordelijk, noorden-, noord(-): *the ~ lights* het noorderlicht

North Korea Noord-Korea

¹**North Korean** (n) Noord-Koreaan(se)

²**North Korean** (adj) Noord-Koreaans

North Macedonia Noord-Macedonië

¹**North Macedonian** (n) Noord-Macedoniër, Noord-Macedonische

²**North Macedonian** (adj) Noord-Macedonisch

northward noord(waarts), noordelijk

north-west noordwestelijk

northwestern noordwest(elijk)

Norway Noorwegen

¹**Norwegian** (n) Noor(se)

²**Norwegian** (adj) Noors

nos *numbers* nummers

¹**nose** (n) **1** neus, reukorgaan^h; [fig] reukzin; speurzin: *(right) under s.o.'s (very) ~* vlak voor zijn neus **2** punt^h; neus [of aeroplane, car, shoe] || *cut off one's ~ to spite one's face* woedend zijn eigen glazen ingooien; *follow one's ~* zijn instinct volgen; *have a ~ for sth.* ergens een fijne neus voor hebben; *keep one's ~ to the grindstone* zwoegen, voortdurend hard werken; *keep one's ~ out of s.o.'s affairs* zich met zijn eigen zaken bemoeien; *look down one's ~ at s.o.* de neus voor iem. ophalen, neerkijken op iem.; *pay through the ~ (for)* zich laten afzetten (voor); *poke one's ~ into s.o.'s affairs* zijn neus in andermans zaken steken; *put s.o.'s ~ out of joint* **a)** iem. voor het hoofd stoten; **b)** iem. jaloers maken; *rub s.o.'s ~ in it* (or: *the dirt*) iem. iets onder de neus wrijven; *turn up one's ~ at sth. (s.o.)* zijn neus ophalen voor iets (iem.); *(win) by a ~* een neuslengte vóór zijn

²**nose** (vb) zich (voorzichtig) een weg banen [of ship, car]

nose about rondneuzen (in), rondsnuffelen (in)

nosebleed bloedneus

¹nosedive (n) **1** duikvlucht **2** plotselinge (prijs)daling

²nosedive (vb) **1** een duikvlucht maken **2** plotseling dalen, vallen

nosegay ruiker(tjeʰ), boeketjeʰ

nose job [inform] neuscorrectie

nose out ontdekken, erachter komen

¹nosh (n) etenʰ

²nosh (vb) bikken, eten

nosiness bemoeizucht, nieuwsgierigheid

nostalgia nostalgie, verlangenʰ (naar het verleden)

nostril 1 neusgatʰ **2** neusvleugel

nosy nieuwsgierig: *Nosey Parker* bemoeial, nieuwsgierig aagje

not niet, geen, helemaal niet: ~ *a thing* helemaal niets; *I hope* ~ ik hoop van niet; ~ *to say* misschien zelfs, om niet te zeggen; ~ *at all* helemaal niet; ~ *only ... but (also)* niet alleen ..., maar (ook); ~ *a bus but a tram* geen bus maar een tram; ~ *that I care* niet (om)dat het mij iets kan schelen

¹notable (n) belangrijk persoon; notabele

²notable (adj) opmerkelijk, opvallend

notably in het bijzonder, met name: *others, ~ the Americans and the English, didn't want to talk about it* anderen, met name de Amerikanen en Engelsen, wilden er niet over praten

notary notaris: ~ *public* notaris

notation 1 notatie [music, chess etc]; schrijfwijze: *chemical* ~ chemische symbolen **2** [Am] aantekening, noot

¹notch (n) **1** keep [also fig]; kerf, inkeping **2** graad; stukjeʰ

²notch (vb) **1** (in)kepen, (in)kerven, insnijden **2** (also + up) (be)halen [victory, points]; binnenhalen: *we ~ed up nine victories in a row* we behaalden negen overwinningen op rij

¹note (n) **1** aantekening, notitie: *make ~s* aantekeningen maken; *make a ~ of your expenses* houd bij wat voor onkosten je maakt **2** briefjeʰ, berichtjeʰ, (diplomatieke) nota, memorandumʰ **3** (voet)noot, annotatie **4** (bank)biljetʰ, briefjeʰ **5** [mus] toon, noot **6** (onder)toon, klank: *sound* (or: *strike*) *a ~ of warning* een waarschuwend geluid laten horen **7** aanzienʰ, belangʰ, gewichtʰ: *of* ~ van belang, met een reputatie, algemeen bekend **8** aandacht, nota: *take ~ of* notitie nemen van || *compare ~s* ervaringen uitwisselen

²note (vb) **1** nota nemen van, aandacht schenken aan, letten op **2** (op)merken, waarnemen **3** aandacht vestigen op, opmerken **4** (+ down) opschrijven, noteren

notebook 1 notitieboekjeʰ **2** notebook⁺ʰ

noted (+ for) beroemd (om/wegens), bekend

notepaper postpapierʰ

noteworthy vermeldenswaardig, opmerkelijk

¹nothing (pron) niets; [pers] nul; waardeloos iem.; [matter] kleinigheid; niemendalletje: *she did ~ but grumble* ze zat alleen maar te mopperen || *there was ~ for it but to call a doctor* er zat niets anders op dan een dokter te bellen; *for ~* **a)** tevergeefs; **b)** gratis, voor niets; *there's ~ to it* er is niets aan, het is een makkie; [sport] *there's ~ in it* zij zijn gelijk

²nothing (adv) helemaal niet, lang niet: *my painting is ~ like* (or: *near*) *as good as yours* mijn schilderij is bij lange na niet zo goed als het jouwe

¹notice (n) **1** aankondiging, waarschuwing; opzegging [of contract]: *give one's* ~ zijn ontslag indienen; *we received three month's* ~ de huur is ons met drie maanden opgezegd; *at a moment's* ~ direct, zonder bericht vooraf **2** aandacht, belangstelling, attentie: *I'd like to bring this book to your* ~ ik zou dit boek onder uw aandacht willen brengen; *take (no)* ~ *of* (geen) acht slaan op **3** mededeling, berichtʰ

²notice (vb) (op)merken, zien, waarnemen: *she didn't ~ her friend in the crowd* zij zag haar vriendin niet in de menigte

noticeable 1 merkbaar, zichtbaar, waarneembaar **2** opmerkelijk, opvallend, duidelijk

notice board mededelingenbordʰ, prikbordʰ

notification 1 aangifte **2** informatie, mededeling

notify informeren, bekendmaken, op de hoogte stellen

notion 1 begripʰ **2** ideeʰ, mening, veronderstelling: *she had no ~ of what I was talking about* ze had geen benul waar ik het over had; *the ~ that the earth is flat* het denkbeeld dat de aarde plat is

notoriety beruchtheid

notorious algemeen (ongunstig) bekend, berucht

¹notwithstanding (adv) desondanks, ondanks dat, toch

²notwithstanding (prep) ondanks, in weerwil van: *the road was built ~ fierce opposition* de verkeersweg werd gebouwd ondanks de felle tegenstand

nougat noga

nought nul || *~s and crosses* boter, kaas en eieren, kruisje nulletje

noughties (the) de jaren nul

noun zelfstandig naamwoordʰ

nourish 1 voeden [also fig]: *~ing food* voedzaam eten **2** koesteren: ~ *the hope to* de hoop koesteren om te

nourishment 1 voeding [also fig]; het voeden, het gevoed worden **2** voedselʰ,

etenʰ
¹novel (n) roman
²novel (adj) nieuw, onbekend: ~ *ideas* verrassende ideeën
novelist romanschrijver, schrijver
novelty nieuwigheid, nieuwsʰ, iets onbekends, aardigheidjeʰ: *the ~ soon wore off* het nieuwe was er al snel af, de nieuwigheid was er al gauw af
November november
novice 1 novice **2** beginneling, nieuweling
¹now (n) nuʰ, dit momentʰ: *before ~* vroeger, tot nu toe; *by ~* ondertussen, inmiddels; *for ~* voorlopig; *as from ~, from ~ on* van nu af aan; *until ~, up till ~, up to ~* tot nu toe
²now (adv) **1** nu, tegenwoordig, onder deze omstandigheden: *they'll be here any minute ~* ze kunnen nu elk ogenblik aankomen; *~ what do you mean?* maar wat bedoel je nu eigenlijk?; *(every) ~ and again* (or: *then*) zo nu en dan, af en toe, van tijd tot tijd; *just ~* a) zo-even, daarnet; b) nu, op dit ogenblik; *~ then, where do you think you're going?* zo, en waar dacht jij heen te gaan? **2** nu (dat), gezien (dat): *~ you are here I will show you* nu je hier (toch) bent zal ik het je laten zien
nowadays tegenwoordig, vandaag de dag
nowhere nergens [also fig]; nergens heen: *it got him ~* het leverde hem niets op; *she is ~ near as bright as him* ze is lang niet zo intelligent als hij; *he started from ~ but became famous* hij kwam uit het niets maar werd beroemd
noxious [also fig] schadelijk, ongezond
nozzle 1 tuit, pijp **2** (straal)pijp, mondstukʰ, straalbuis
nub 1 brokʰ, klompjeʰ, stomp(je)ʰ) **2** [singular] kern(punt)ʰ, essentie: *the ~ of the matter* de kern van de zaak
nuclear 1 m.b.t. de kern(en), kern- **2** nucleair, kern-, atoom-: *~ disarmament* nucleaire ontwapening; *~ waste* kernafvalʰ
nucleus kern [also fig]
¹nude (n) naakt iem.: *in the ~* naakt, in zijn nakie
²nude (adj) naakt
¹nudge (n) stoot(je)ʰ, por, duwtjeʰ
²nudge (vb) **1** (zachtjes) aanstoten [with elbow] **2** zachtjes duwen, schuiven **3** [fig] een duwtje in de rug geven
nudist nudist, naturist
nudity naaktheid
nugget 1 (goud)klompjeʰ **2** juweel(tje)ʰ [only fig]: *~ of information* informatie die goud waard is
nuisance 1 lastig iem. (iets), lastpost, lastpak: *make a ~ of o.s.* vervelend zijn **2** (over)last, hinder: *what a ~* wat vervelend
¹nuke (n) [esp Am; inform] **1** atoombom **2** kernwapenʰ
²nuke (vb) [esp Am; inform] **1** met kernwa-

pens vernietigen: *~ 'em* gooi er een bom op **2** [culinary] in de magnetron opwarmen (*or:* bereiden)
null: *~ and void* van nul en gener waarde
nullify 1 nietig verklaren, ongeldig verklaren **2** opheffen, tenietdoen
¹numb (adj) (+ with) verstijfd (van), verdoofd, verkleumd
²numb (vb) **1** verlammen [also fig]; doen verstijven **2** verdoven: *medicines ~ed the pain* medicijnen verzachtten de pijn
¹number (n) **1** getalʰ: *~ 10 bus* (bus)lijn 10; *by ~s* a) stap voor stap; b) [inform] mechanisch, fantasieloos **2** aantalʰ: *a ~ of problems* een aantal problemen; *in ~* in aantal, in getal; *any ~ of* ontelbaar veel **3** nummerʰ: *published in ~s* in afleveringen verschenen **4** gezelschapʰ, groep **5** (-s) aantallen, hoeveelheid, grote aantallen: *win by ~s* winnen door getalsterkte || *have s.o.'s ~* iem. doorhebben; *always think of ~ one* altijd alleen maar aan zichzelf denken; *my ~ one problem* mijn grootste probleem
²number (vb) nummeren, nummers geven
³number (vb) **1** tellen **2** vormen [number]; bedragen: *we ~ed eleven* we waren met ons elven **3** tellen, behoren tot: *I ~ him among my best friends* hij behoort tot mijn beste vrienden || *his days are ~ed* zijn dagen zijn geteld
numberless ontelbaar, talloos
number plate nummerplaat, nummerbordʰ
number sign [Am] hekjeʰ
num(b)skull sufferd, stomkop
¹numeral (n) **1** cijferʰ: *Roman ~s* Romeinse cijfers **2** telwoordʰ
²numeral (adj) getal(s)-, van getallen
numerate met een wiskundige basiskennis, gecijferd: *some of my students are hardly ~* enkele van mijn studenten kunnen nauwelijks rekenen
numerical 1 getallen-, rekenkundig **2** numeriek, in aantal, getals-
numerous talrijk(e), groot, vele
nun non
nunnery [form] vrouwenkloosterʰ, nonnenkloosterʰ
nuptial huwelijks-
¹nurse (n) **1** verpleegster, verpleger, verpleegkundige: *male ~* verpleger, ziekenbroeder; *~!* zuster! **2** kindermeisjeʰ **3** voedster
²nurse (vb) zuigen, aan de borst zijn: *be nursing at one's mother's breast* de borst krijgen
³nurse (vb) **1** verplegen, verzorgen **2** zogen, borstvoeding geven: *nursing mother* zogende moeder **3** behandelen, genezen: *~ s.o. back to health* door verpleging iem. weer gezond krijgen **4** bevorderen, koesteren: *~ a*

grievance (or: *grudge*) *against s.o.* een grief
(*or:* wrok) tegen iem. koesteren
nursemaid 1 kindermeisje[h] **2** verzorgster
nurse practitioner verpleegkundige
nursery 1 kinderkamer **2** crèche, kinderdagverblijf[h] **3** kwekerij
nurseryman kweker
nursery rhyme kinderversje[h]
nursery school peuterklas
nursing verpleging, verzorging, verpleeg-
kunde
nursing home 1 verpleegtehuis[h] **2** particulier ziekenhuis[h]
[1]**nurture** (n) [form] opvoeding, vorming
[2]**nurture** (vb) [form] **1** voeden **2** koesteren,
verzorgen **3** opvoeden
nut 1 noot **2** moer **3** fanaat, gek ‖ *~s and*
bolts grondbeginselen, hoofdzaken; *do*
one's ~ woedend zijn; *she can't sing* ***for*** *~s* ze
kan totaal niet zingen; ***off*** *one's ~* niet goed
bij zijn hoofd
nutcase mafkees
nutcracker notenkraker: *(a **pair** of) ~s* een
notenkraker
nutjob [vulg] gestoorde gek
nutmeg 1 muskaatnoot **2** nootmuskaat
[1]**nutrient** (n) voedingsstof, bouwstof
[2]**nutrient** (adj) voedend, voedings-
nutrition 1 voeding **2** voedingsleer
nutritional voedings-
nutritious voedzaam
nuts gek, getikt: *go ~* gek worden
nutshell notendop [also fig]
nutty 1 met (veel) noten, vol noten **2** naar
noten smakend **3** gek, getikt, gestoord: *as ~*
*as a **fruitcake*** stapelgek, mesjokke
nuzzle 1 (be)snuffelen **2** (zich) nestelen
nylon nylon[+h]: *~s* nylonkousen
nymph nimf
[1]**nymphomaniac** (n) nymfomane
[2]**nymphomaniac** (adj) nymfomaan

O

o' *of* van: *five o'clock* vijf uur
oaf klungel, lomperd
¹oak (n) eik
²oak (adj) eiken, eikenhout
oak-apple galappel, galnoot
OAP *old age pension* AOW, Algemene Ouderdomswet
oar roeispaan, (roei)riem ‖ *put* (or: *shove*) *one's ~ in* zich ermee bemoeien, zijn neus erin steken
oarsman roeier
oasis oase [also fig]
oat haver, haverkorrel ‖ *feel one's ~s* bruisen van energie; [Am also] zelfgenoegzaam doen; *off one's ~s* zonder eetlust
oath 1 eed: *make* (or: *take, swear*) *an ~* een eed afleggen; *under ~* onder ede **2** vloek
oatmeal 1 havermeelʰ, havervlokken **2** havermout(pap)
obdurate 1 onverbeterlijk **2** onverzettelijk
obedience 1 gehoorzaamheid: *passive ~* onvoorwaardelijke gehoorzaamheid **2** [rel] obediëntie
obedient 1 gehoorzaam **2** onderworpen
obeisance 1 buiging **2** eerbied, respectʰ
obese zwaarlijvig
obesity obesitas, zwaarlijvigheid
obey gehoorzamen (aan), opvolgen, toegeven aan
obituary overlijdensberichtʰ [with short biography]
¹object (n) **1** voorwerpʰ, objectʰ **2** doelʰ **3** [linguistics] voorwerpʰ: *direct ~ (of a verb)* lijdend voorwerp; *indirect ~ (of a verb)* meewerkend voorwerp ‖ *money is no ~* geld speelt geen rol
²object (vb) bezwaar hebben (maken): *he ~ed to being called a coward* hij wou niet voor lafaard doorgaan
objectify 1 [sth.] concreet maken **2** [s.o.] als object behandelen of zien, tot lustobject maken
objection bezwaarʰ: *raise ~s* bezwaren maken
objectionable 1 bedenkelijk **2** ongewenst, onaangenaam
¹objective (n) **1** doelʰ, doelstelling, doelwitʰ, operatiedoelʰ **2** objectiefʰ
²objective (adj) objectief, onpartijdig
obligation 1 plicht, (zware) taak **2** verplichting, verbintenis: *lay* (or: *place, put*) *s.o. under an ~* iem. aan zich verplichten
obligatory verplicht

¹oblige (vb) het genoegen doen, ten beste geven: *~ with a song* een lied ten beste geven
²oblige (vb) **1** aan zich verplichten: *(I'm) much ~d (to you)* dank u zeer **2** verplichten; (ver)binden [by promise, contract]: *I feel ~d to say that ...* ik voel me verplicht te zeggen dat ...
obliging attent, voorkomend, behulpzaam
oblique 1 schuin, scheef: *~ stroke* schuine streep **2** indirect, ontwijkend
obliterate uitwissen, wegvagen
obliteration 1 uitroeiing, vernietiging **2** uitwissing, verwijdering **3** afstempeling [of stamps]
oblivion vergetelheid: *fall* (or: *sink*) *into ~* in vergetelheid raken
oblivious 1 vergeetachtig **2** onbewust: *~ of* niet lettend op, vergetend; *~ of* (or: *to*) zich niet bewust van
¹oblong (n) rechthoek, langwerpige figuur
²oblong (adj) rechthoekig
obnoxious [form] **1** aanstootgevend **2** uiterst onaangenaam: *an ~ child* een stierlijk vervelend kind
oboe hobo
obscene obsceen, onzedelijk
obscenities obsceniteiten, schunnige taal
obscenity obsceniteit, vies woord
¹obscure (adj) **1** obscuur, onduidelijk, onbekend **2** verborgen, onopgemerkt
²obscure (vb) **1** verduisteren **2** overschaduwen **3** verbergen
obscurity 1 duisterʰ, duisternis **2** onbekendheid: *live in ~* een obscuur leven leiden **3** onduidelijkheid, onbegrijpelijkheid
obsequious kruiperig, onderdanig
observable waarneembaar, merkbaar
observant 1 opmerkzaam, oplettend **2** in acht nemend; nalevend [law, duty, rites]
observation 1 waarneming, observatie: *keep s.o. under ~* iem. in de gaten (blijven) houden **2** opmerking, commentaarʰ
observatory sterrenwacht
observe 1 opmerken, zeggen: *he ~d that* hij merkte op dat **2** naleven, in acht nemen **3** waarnemen, observeren
observer 1 toeschouwer **2** waarnemer [also aviation]; observeerder, observator
obsess obsederen: *~ed by* (or: *with*) geobsedeerd door
obsession 1 obsessie, dwanggedachte: *have an ~ about sth.* bezeten zijn door iets **2** bezetenheid, het bezeten-zijn
obsessive 1 obsederend **2** bezeten
obsolete verouderd, in onbruik (geraakt), achterhaald
obstacle obstakelʰ, belemmering: *form an ~ to sth.* een beletsel vormen voor iets
obstacle course hindernisbaan: *he had to run an ~* hij moest allerlei hindernissen over-

winnen

obstetrician verloskundige

obstetrics obstetrie, verloskunde

obstinate 1 halsstarrig **2** hardnekkig; koppig

obstruct 1 versperren, blokkeren **2** belemmeren, hinderen **3** [sport, esp football] obstructie plegen tegen

obstruction 1 belemmering, hindernis **2** versperring, obstakel[h] **3** obstructie [also sport, med]

obtain (ver)krijgen, behalen

[1]**obtrude** (vb) opdringerig zijn, zich opdringen

[2]**obtrude** (vb) (+ (up)on) opdringen (aan), ongevraagd naar voren brengen

obtuse 1 stomp: *an ~ angle* een stompe hoek **2** traag van begrip

obviate ondervangen, voorkomen: *~ the necessity* (or: *need*) *of sth.* iets overbodig maken

obvious 1 duidelijk, zonneklaar: *an ~ lie* een aperte leugen **2** voor de hand liggend, doorzichtig **3** aangewezen, juist: *the ~ man for the job* de aangewezen man voor het karweitje

obviously duidelijk, kennelijk

[1]**occasion** (n) **1** gebeurtenis, voorval[h] **2** evenement[h], gelegenheid, feest[h]: *he seemed to be equal to the ~* hij leek tegen de situatie opgewassen te zijn; *we'll make an ~ of it* we zullen het vieren; *on the ~ of your birthday* ter gelegenheid van je verjaardag **3** aanleiding, reden: *give ~ to* aanleiding geven tot; *you have no ~ to leave* jij hebt geen reden om weg te gaan

[2]**occasion** (vb) veroorzaken, aanleiding geven tot

occasional 1 incidenteel, nu en dan voorkomend: *~ showers* verspreide buien **2** gelegenheids-

occasionally nu en dan, af en toe

occidental westers

occult occult, geheim, verborgen: *the ~* het occulte

occupant 1 bezitter, landbezitter **2** bewoner **3** inzittende [of car] **4** bekleder [of office]

occupation 1 beroep[h] **2** bezigheid, activiteit **3** bezetting (door vijand)

occupational m.b.t. een beroep, beroeps-: *~ hazard* beroepsrisico[h]

occupy 1 bezetten, bezit nemen van: *~ a building* een gebouw bezetten **2** in beslag nemen: *it will ~ a lot of his time* het zal veel van zijn tijd in beslag nemen **3** bezighouden: *~ o.s. with* zich bezighouden met **4** bewonen, betrekken

occur 1 voorkomen, aangetroffen worden **2** opkomen, invallen: *it simply did not ~ to him* het kwam eenvoudigweg niet bij hem op

3 gebeuren

occurrence 1 voorval[h], gebeurtenis **2** het voorkomen

ocean oceaan: *the Pacific Ocean* de Stille Zuidzee; *~s of time* zeeën van tijd

ochre oker

o'clock uur: *ten ~* tien uur

octagon achthoek

octave octaaf[+h]

October oktober

octogenarian tachtigjarige

octopus inktvis

oculist oogarts

odd 1 oneven: *~ and even numbers* oneven en even getallen **2** vreemd, ongewoon: *an ~ habit* een gekke gewoonte **3** overblijvend: *the ~ man at the table* de man die aan tafel overschiet [after the others have formed pairs] **4** toevallig, onverwacht: *he drops in at ~ times* hij komt zo nu en dan eens langs **5** los, niet behorend tot een reeks: *an ~ glove* een losse handschoen; *~ job* klusje[h] **6** iets meer dan: *five pounds ~* iets meer dan vijf pond; *60-~ persons* ruim 60 personen ‖ *~ man out* vreemde eend; *which is the ~ man out in the following list?* welke hoort in het volgende rijtje niet thuis?

oddball [Am] gekke vent, rare

oddity 1 eigenaardigheid, vreemde eigenschap **2** gekke vent **3** iets vreemds, vreemd voorwerp[h], vreemde gebeurtenis **4** curiositeit

odd-job man manusje-van-alles[h], klusjesman

oddment overschot[h], overblijfsel[h], restant[h]

odds 1 ongelijkheid, verschil[h]: *that makes no ~* dat maakt niets uit; *what's the ~?* wat doet dat ertoe? **2** onenigheid: *be at ~ with* in onenigheid leven met **3** (grote) kans, waarschijnlijkheid: *the ~ are that she will do it* de kans is groot dat ze het doet **4** verhouding tussen de inzetten bij weddenschap: *take ~ of one to ten* een inzet accepteren van één tegen tien ‖ *~ and ends* prullen; *~ and sods* rommel; *against all (the) ~* tegen alle verwachtingen in; *over the ~* meer dan verwacht

odious hatelijk, weerzinwekkend

odour 1 geur, stank, lucht(je[h]): *an ~ of sanctity* een geur van heiligheid **2** reputatie, naam: *be in good ~ with* goed aangeschreven staan bij

oestrogen oestrogeen[h]

oeuvre (kunst)werk[h]; oeuvre[h]

of 1 van, van … vandaan: *go wide of the mark* ver naast het doel schieten **2** (afkomstig) van, (afkomstig) uit, (veroorzaakt, gemaakt) door: *a colour of your own choice* een kleur die u zelf kunt kiezen; *that's too much to ask of Jane* dat is te veel van Jane gevraagd; *of necessity* uit noodzaak **3** [composition, contents, amount] bestaande uit, van: *a **box** of chocolates* een doos chocola **4** over, van, met betrekking tot: *quick of **understanding*** snel van begrip **5** van, te, bij, met: *men of **courage*** mannen met moed; *be of **importance*** (or: *value*) van belang (*or:* waarde) zijn **6** van, behorend tot: *it's that dog of **hers*** *again* het is die hond van haar weer **7** van, tot, naar, voor: *fear of spiders* angst voor spinnen **8** van, onder: *a **pound** of flour* een pond bloem; *five of **us*** vijf mensen van onze groep ‖ *the **month** of May* de maand mei; *an angel of a **husband*** een engel van een man

ofc [inform] *of course* natuurlijk

¹off (adj) **1** vrij: *my husband **is** ~ today* mijn man heeft vandaag vrij **2** minder (goed), slecht(er): *her singing **was** a bit ~ tonight* ze zong niet zo best vanavond **3** verder (gelegen), ver(ste) **4** rechter(-) [of side of horse, vehicle]; rechts **5** rustig, stil: *during the ~ **season*** buiten het (hoog)seizoen **6** (hoogst) onwaarschijnlijk: *~ **chance*** kleine kans **7** bedorven [of food]; zuur: *this **sausage** is ~* dit worstje is bedorven **8** van de baan, afgelast, uitgesteld: *the **meeting** is ~* de bijeenkomst gaat niet door **9** weg, vertrokken, gestart: *get ~ to a good start* goed beginnen **10** uit‐ (geschakeld), buiten werking, niet aan: *the **water** is ~* het water is afgesloten **11** mis, naast: *his **guess** was slightly ~* hij zat er enigszins naast

²off (adv) **1** verwijderd, weg, (er)af, ver, hiervandaan: *three **miles** ~* drie mijl daarvandaan; *send ~ a letter* een brief versturen **2** af, uit, helemaal, ten einde: *a **day** ~* een dagje vrij; *kill ~* uitroeien; *turn ~ the radio* zet de radio af **3** ondergeschikt, minder belangrijk: *5% ~* met 5% korting ‖ *~ **and on*** af en toe, nu en dan; *be **well*** (or: ***badly***) *~* rijk (*or:* arm) zijn

³off (prep) **1** van, van af: *he got ~ the **bus*** hij stapte uit de bus **2** van de baan, van ... af, afgestapt van: *~ **duty*** vrij (van dienst), buiten dienst; *I've **gone** ~ fish* ik lust geen vis meer **3** van ... af, naast, opzij van, uit: *it was ~ the **mark*** het miste zijn doel [also fig]; *an **alley** ~ the square* een steegje dat op het plein uitkomt **4** onder, beneden, achter zijn, minder dan: *a year or two ~ **sixty*** een jaar of wat onder de zestig

offal 1 orgaanvlees^h, slachtafval^h **2** afval^h, vuil^h, vuilnis^h; [fig] uitschot^h

offbeat [inform] ongebruikelijk, onconventioneel

off-colour onwel, niet lekker

off day ongeluksdag

offence 1 overtreding, misdrijf^h, delict^h, misdaad: *commit an ~* een overtreding begaan **2** belediging: *cause* (or: *give*) *~ to s.o.* iem. beledigen; *take ~ at* aanstoot nemen aan, zich ergeren aan; *he is quick to **take** ~* hij is gauw op z'n teentjes getrapt

¹offend (vb) kwaad doen: *the verdict ~s against all principles of justice* het vonnis is een aanfluiting van alle rechtsprincipes

²offend (vb) beledigen [also fig]; boos maken

offender overtreder, zondaar: *first ~* niet eerder veroordeelde

¹offensive (n) aanval, offensief^h; [fig] campagne; beweging: *take* (or: *go into*) *the ~* aanvallen, in het offensief gaan

²offensive (adj) **1** offensief, aanvallend **2** beledigend, aanstootgevend

¹offer (n) aanbod^h, aanbieding, offerte, voorstel^h: *be **on** ~* in de aanbieding zijn, te koop zijn; *this house is **under** ~* op dit huis is een bod gedaan

²offer (vb) voorkomen, gebeuren, optreden: *as **occasion** ~s* wanneer de gelegenheid zich voordoet

³offer (vb) **1** (aan)bieden, geven, schenken: *~ one's **hand*** zijn hand uitsteken; *he ~ed to **drive** me home* hij bood aan me naar huis te brengen **2** te koop aanbieden, tonen, laten zien

offering 1 offergave **2** aanbieding, aanbod^h: *foreign ~s on the market* buitenlandse koopwaar op de markt

offertory-box offerblok^h, collectebus

offhand 1 onvoorbereid, geïmproviseerd: *avoid making ~ **remarks*** maak geen ondoordachte opmerkingen **2** nonchalant

office 1 ambt^h, openbare betrekking, functie: *hold ~* een ambt bekleden **2** dienst, hulp, zorg: *good ~s* goede diensten **3** kantoor^h, bureau^h ‖ *the **Foreign** ~* het ministerie van Buitenlandse Zaken

office manager officemanager

officer 1 ambtenaar, functionaris, medewerker: *policy ~* beleidsmedewerker **2** iem. die een belangrijke functie bekleedt, directeur, voorzitter: *clerical* (or: *executive*) *~* (hoge) regeringsfunctionaris **3** politieagent **4** officier

¹official (n) beambte, functionaris, (staats)-ambtenaar; [sport] official; wedstrijdcommissaris

²official (adj) officieel; ambtelijk

officialese stadhuistaal, ambtenarenlatijn^h

officiate 1 officieel optreden: *~ as **chairman*** (officieel) als voorzitter dienstdoen **2** [sport] arbitreren

officious bemoeiziek, opdringerig

off-key vals; uit de toon [also fig]

off-licence 1 slijtvergunning **2** slijterij, drankzaak

offline offline; niet-verbonden

offload 1 lossen [vehicle, esp aeroplane] **2** dumpen

off-peak buiten het hoogseizoen, de spits [of use, traf]; goedkoop, rustig: *in the ~ **hours*** tijdens de daluren

offprint overdruk
off-putting ontmoedigend
offset compenseren, opwegen tegen, te-nietdoen: ~ *against* zetten tegenover
offshoot uitloper [also fig]; scheut, zijtak
offshore 1 op zee, voor de kust, buiten-gaats: ~ *fishing* zeevisserij; ~ *wind farm* windmolenpark op zee **2** aflandig: ~ *wind* aflandige wind
¹offside (n) **1** [sport] buitenspel[h], buiten-spelpositie **2** rechterkant [of car, horse, road etc] **3** verste kant
²offside (adj) [sport] buitenspel-: *the ~ rule* de buitenspelregel
offspring kroost[h], nakomeling(en)
offstage 1 achter (de schermen) **2** onzicht-baar
off-the-record onofficieel, binnenskamers
off-topic niets met het onderwerp (van de discussie) te maken hebbend; offtopic
often vaak: *as* ~ *as not* de helft van de ke-ren, vaak; *he was late once* ~ hij kwam één keer te veel te laat || *every so* ~ nu en dan
of the moment in de mode, in
ogre menseneter
oh o!, och!, ach!: *oh no!* dat niet!, o nee!; *oh yes!* o ja!, jazeker!; *oh yes?* zo?, o ja?; *oh well* och, och kom
¹oil (n) **1** (aard)olie; [Belg] petroleum **2** pe-troleum, kerosine, stookolie, diesel(brand-stof), smeerolie **3** olieverf || ~ *and vinegar* (or: *water*) water en vuur; *strike* ~ olie aan-boren; [fig] plotseling rijk worden
²oil (vb) smeren, oliën, insmeren, invetten
oilcake lijnkoek(en), oliekoek(en)
oil-change olieverversing: *do an* ~ de olie verversen
oilcloth wasdoek[h]
oil-fired met olie gestookt
oil painting olieverfschilderij[h] || [hum] *he's no* ~ hij is geen adonis
oil rig booreiland[h]
oilskin 1 oliejas **2** (-s) oliepak[h] **3** geolied doek[h], wasdoek[h]
oil slick olievlek [on water]
oily 1 olieachtig, geolied, vettig **2** kruipe-rig, vleiend
ointment zalf, smeersel[h]
¹OK (n) goedkeuring, akkoord[h], fiat[h]
²OK (adj, adv) oké, OK, in orde, voldoende, akkoord, afgesproken: *are you okay?* gaat het?, alles in orde?; *it looks OK now* nu ziet het er goed uit
³OK (vb) goedkeuren, akkoord gaan met **okay** see *²OK*
¹old (n) vroeger tijden, het verleden: *heroes of* ~ helden uit het verleden
²old (adj) **1** oud, bejaard, antiek, verouderd, ouderwets, in onbruik geraakt: ~ *age* ouder-dom, hoge leeftijd; ~ *maid* oude vrijster; *as* ~ *as the hills* zo oud als de weg naar Rome

2 voormalig, ex-: *the good ~ days* (or: *times*) de goede oude tijd; *pay off* ~ *scores* een oude rekening vereffenen **3** lang bekend: *good ~ John* die beste Jan **4** oud, van de leeftijd van: *a 17-year-~ girl* een zeventienjarig meisje **5** ervaren, bekwaam: *an ~ hand at shoplifter* een doorgewinterde winkeldief || *a chip off the ~ block* helemaal haar moeder; *money for ~ rope* iets voor niets, gauw verdiend geld; ~ *country* a) land in de Oude Wereld; **b)** [with the] moederland[h], geboorteland[h]; *the ~ man* a) de ouwe [also ship's captain]; **b)** de baas [also husband]; **c)** mijn ouweheer; *in any ~ place* waar je maar kan denken; *any ~ thing will do* alles is goed; *the Old World* de Oude Wereld; [Am] (continentaal) Europa, de Oude Wereld
old-age pension ouderdomspensioen[h], AOW
olden: [form] *in ~ days* eertijds, voorheen
old-fashioned ouderwets, verouderd, conservatief
oldie 1 oud nummer[h], oude film of tv-serie: *a golden* ~ een gouwe ouwe **2** oudje[h] [pers]
oldish ouwelijk, nogal oud
old-school ouderwets
oldster oudje[h], ouder lid[h]
old-time oud, van vroeger, ouderwets
old-timer [Am] **1** oudgediende, oude rot **2** oude bewoner **3** iets ouds, oude auto
old-world ouderwets, verouderd, van vroeger
Old-World van de Oude Wereld
O level [dated] *ordinary level* Brits (exa-menvak[h] op) eindexamenniveau[h] [compare 'havo']
¹olive (n) olijf(boom), olijfhout[h]
²olive (adj) **1** olijfkleurig **2** olijfgroen; olijf-bruin [complexion]
olive branch olijftak || *hold out an* ~ de hand reiken
¹Olympian (n) olympiër [also fig]
²Olympian (adj) **1** Olympisch [also fig]; goddelijk, verheven **2** olympisch, van de Olympische Spelen
Olympic olympisch: *the ~ Games* de Olym-pische Spelen
Olympics (the) Olympische Spelen
Oman Oman
¹Omani (n) Omaniet, Omanitische
²Omani (adj) Omanitisch
ombudsman ombudsman
omega omega; [fig] slot[h], besluit[h]
omelet(te) omelet
omen voorteken[h]
OMG [inform] *oh my god* mijn hemel, nee hè
ominous 1 veelbetekenend **2** onheilspel-lend, dreigend
omission weglating, verzuim[h]
omit 1 weglaten, overslaan **2** verzuimen,

nalaten, verwaarlozen
omnibus 1 (auto)bus **2** omnibus(uitgave)
omnipotent almachtig
omnipresence alomtegenwoordigheid
omnipresent alomtegenwoordig
omniscient alwetend
omnivorous allesetend: *an ~ reader* iem.
die alles wat los en vast zit leest
¹on (adj) **1** aan(gesloten), ingeschakeld;
open [appliance, tap etc] **2** aan de gang,
gaande: *the match is on* de wedstrijd is aan
de gang **3** op [stage]: *you're on in five minutes*
je moet over vijf minuten op **4** aan de beurt,
dienstdoend || *I'm on!* oké, ik doe mee; *the
wedding is on* het huwelijk gaat door
²on (adv) **1** in werking, aan, in functie: *the
music came on* de muziek begon; *have you
anything on tonight?* heb je plannen voor
vanavond?; *leave the light on* het licht aan laten **2** [of clothes] aan: *put on your new dress*
trek je nieuwe jurk aan **3** verder, later, voort,
door: *five years on* vijf jaar later; *send on*
doorsturen, nazenden; *later on* later; *and so
on* enzovoort; *(talk) on and on* zonder onderbreking (praten); *from that moment on* vanaf
dat ogenblik **4** [indicating place or direction;
also fig] op, tegen, aan, toe: *they collided
head on* ze botsten frontaal
³on (prep) **1** [indicating place or direction;
also fig] op, in, aan, bovenop: *I have it on
good authority* ik heb het uit betrouwbare
bron; *hang on the wall* aan de muur hangen
2 bij, nabij, aan, verbonden aan: *on your
right* aan de rechterkant; *just on sixty people*
amper zestig mensen **3** [time] op, bij: *arrive
on the hour* op het hele uur aankomen; *come
on Tuesday* kom dinsdag; *on opening the
door* bij het openen van de deur **4** [condi-
tion] in, met: *the patient is on antibiotics* de
patiënt krijgt antibiotica; *be on duty* dienst
hebben; *on trial* op proef **5** over: *take pity on
the poor* medelijden hebben met de armen
6 ten koste van, op kosten van: *this round is
on me* dit rondje is voor mij, ik betaal dit
rondje
on-board aan boord: *~ computer* boordcomputer
¹once (adv) **1** eenmaal, eens, één keer: *~
again* (or: *more*) opnieuw, nog eens; *~ too
often* één keer te veel; *~ or twice* zo nu en
dan, van tijd tot tijd; *(all) at ~* tegelijk(ertijd),
samen; *(just) for (this) ~* (voor) deze ene keer;
~ and for all voorgoed, definitief, voor de
laatste keer; *~ in a while* een enkele keer; *he
only said it the ~* hij zei het maar één keer
2 vroeger, (ooit) eens: *the ~ popular singer* de
eens zo populaire zanger; *~ upon a time there
was ...* er was eens ... || *at ~* onmiddellijk,
meteen; *all at ~* plots(eling), ineens, opeens
²once (conj) eens (dat), als eenmaal, zodra: *~
you are ready, we'll leave* zodra je klaar bent,

zullen we gaan
once-over kijkjeʰ, vluchtig overzichtʰ: *give
s.o. the ~* iem. globaal opnemen, iem. vluchtig bekijken
oncoming 1 naderend, aanstaand **2** tegemoetkomend [also fig]: *~ traffic* tegenliggers
¹one (n) éénʰ: *the figure ~* het cijfer één; *by ~s
and twos* alleen of in groepjes van twee; [fig]
heel geleidelijk
²one (pron) **1** (er) een, (er) eentje: *the best ~s*
de beste(n); *you are a fine ~* jij bent me d'r
eentje; *give him ~* geef hem er een van, geef
hem een knal; *let's have (a quick) ~* laten we
er (gauw) eentje gaan drinken; *the ~ that I
like best* degene die ik het leukst vind; *he was
~ up on me* hij was me net de baas; *this ~'s on
me* ik trakteer!; *this ~* deze hier **2** men: *~
must never pride o.s. on one's achievements*
men mag nooit prat gaan op zijn prestaties
3 een zeker(e), één of ander(e), ene: *~ day
he left* op een goeie dag vertrok hij; *~ Mr
Smith* called *for you* een zekere meneer Smith
heeft voor jou gebeld **4** één, enig; [fig] dezelfde, hetzelfde; [as intensifier] hartstikke:
this is ~ good book dit is een hartstikke goed
boek; *from ~ chore to another* van het ene
klusje naar het andere; *they are all ~ colour* ze
hebben allemaal dezelfde kleur; *~ day out of
six* één op de zes dagen, om de zes dagen; *my
~ and only friend* mijn enige echte vriend || *for
~ thing a)* ten eerste; **b)** (al was het) alleen
maar omdat; *neither ~ thing nor the other*
vlees noch vis, halfslachtig
³one (num) éénʰ: *~ after another* een voor
een, de een na de andere; *~ by ~* een voor
een, de een na de ander; *~ to ~* één op één,
één tegen één || *~ and all* iedereen, jan en al-
leman; *I was ~ too many for him* ik was hem te
slim af; *like ~ o'clock* als een gek, energiek; *I,
for ~,* *will refuse* ik zal in ieder geval weigeren
one another elkaar, mekaar: *they loved ~*
ze hielden van elkaar
one-armed eenarmig: *~ bandit* eenarmige
bandiet [gambling machine]
one-horse 1 met één paard [carriage etc]
2 derderangs, slecht (toegerust): *~ town*
gatʰ
oneliner oneliner
one-man eenmans-: *~ show* solovoorstel-
ling
one-night stand [inform] **1** eenmalig optreden **2** affaire, sekspartner voor één nacht
one-off exclusief, uniek, eenmalig
one-on-one 1 [sport] één tegen één
2 [Am] individueel [eg of education]
one-parent family eenoudergezinʰ
onerous lastig, moeilijk
oneself 1 zich(zelf): *be ~* zichzelf zijn; *by ~*
in z'n eentje, alleen **2** zelf: *one should do it ~*
men zou het zelf moeten doen
one-sided 1 eenzijdig **2** bevooroordeeld,

partijdig

onesie 1 onesie, jumpsuit **2** [Am] romper-
tje^h, kruippakje^h

one-time voormalig, vroeger, oud-

one-track beperkt [fig]; eenzijdig: *he has a*
~ mind hij denkt altijd maar aan één ding

one-trick pony [inform; esp Am] iem. die
maar één ding goed kan

one-upmanship slagvaardigheid, kunst
de ander steeds een slag voor te zijn

one-way in één richting: *~ street* straat met
eenrichtingsverkeer

ongoing voortdurend, doorgaand: *~ re-*
search lopend onderzoek

onion ui || *know* one's *~s* zijn vak verstaan,
van wanten weten

online online, via het internet: *~ banking*
internetbankieren; *~ dating* onlinedating

onlooker toeschouwer, (toe)kijker

¹only (adj) **1** enig: *an ~ child* een enig kind;
we were the ~ people wearing hats we waren
de enigen met een hoed (op) **2** best, (meest)
geschikt, juist

²only (adv) **1** slechts, alleen (maar): *she was ~*
too glad ze was maar al te blij; *~ five minutes*
more nog vijf minuten, niet meer; *if ~* als …
maar, ik wou dat …; *if ~ to*, *if ~ because* al
was het alleen maar om **2** [with expressions
of time] pas, (maar) eerst, nog: *the train has ~*
just left de trein is nog maar net weg; *he ar-*
rived ~ yesterday hij is gisteren pas aangekomen; *I like it, ~ I cannot afford it* ik vind het
mooi, maar ik kan het niet betalen

onrush 1 toeloop, toestroming **2** aanval,
bestorming

onset 1 aanval, (plotselinge) bestorming
2 begin^h, aanvang, aanzet: *the ~ of scarlet fe-*
ver de eerste symptomen van roodvonk

¹onshore (adj) **1** aanlandig, zee-: *~ breeze*
zeebries **2** kust-, aan de kust gelegen, op de
kust gelegen, binnenlands: *~ fishing* kustvis-
serij

²onshore (adv) **1** land(in)waarts, langs de
kust **2** aan land

onside [sport] niet buitenspel

on-site plaatselijk, ter plekke

onslaught (hevige) aanval, (scherpe) uitval, aanslag

on-the-job-training opleiding in de praktijk

onus 1 last, plicht: *the ~ of proof rests with*
the plaintiff de bewijslast ligt bij de eiser
2 blaam, schuld: *put* (or: *shift*) *the ~ onto* de
blaam werpen op

onward voorwaarts, voortgaand: *the ~*
course of events het verdere verloop van de
gebeurtenissen

onwards voorwaarts, vooruit: *move ~*
voortgaan, verder gaan

oompah hoempageluid^h, (eentonig) ge-
hoempapa

oomph [inform] **1** charme **2** geestdrift,
animo^{+h}

oops oei, jee(tje), nee maar, pardon

oops-a-daisy hup(sakee), hoepla(la), hop

¹ooze (n) modder, slijk^h, drab^{+h}

²ooze (vb) **1** binnensijpelen, doorsijpelen,
insijpelen, druipen, druppelen: *~ out of* (or:
from) sijpelen uit **2** (uit)zweten, vocht af-
scheiden, lekken, bloed opgeven || *his cour-*
age ~d away de moed zonk hem in de schoenen

³ooze (vb) afscheiden, uitwasemen; [fig]
druipen van; doortrokken zijn van, uitstralen: *her voice ~d sarcasm* er klonk sarcasme in
haar stem

op *operation* operatie

OP *original poster* [on Internet forum]
plaatser van het eerste berichtje

opacity 1 onduidelijkheid, ondoorgrondelijkheid **2** ondoorschijnendheid

opal 1 opaal^{+h}, opaalsteen **2** opaalglas^h,
melkglas^h

opaque 1 ondoorschijnend, ondoorzichtig;
dekkend [of paint, colour] **2** onduidelijk, onbegrijpelijk **3** [fig] stompzinnig, dom, traag
van begrip

¹open (n) (de) open ruimte, openlucht, open
veld, open zee; [fig] openbaarheid: *bring*
into the ~ aan het licht brengen, bekendmaken; *come* (*out*) *into the ~* **a)** open kaart spelen [of someone]; **b)** aan het licht komen,
ruchtbaarheid krijgen [of something]

²open (adj) **1** open, geopend, met openingen, onbedekt, niet (af)gesloten, vrij: *keep*
one's *eyes ~* goed opletten; [fig] *with one's*
eyes ~ bij zijn volle verstand, weloverwogen;
~ prison open gevangenis; *~ to the public*
toegankelijk voor het publiek **2** open-
(staand), beschikbaar, onbeslist, onbepaald:
~ cheque ongekruiste cheque; *it is ~ to you to*
het staat je vrij te; *lay o.s.* (*wide*) *~ to* zich (helemaal) blootstellen aan **3** openbaar, (algemeen) bekend, duidelijk, openlijk: *~ hostili-*
ties openlijke vijandigheden; *~ secret* publiek geheim **4** open(hartig), oprecht, mededeelzaam: *admit ~ly* eerlijk uitkomen
voor; *be ~ with* open kaart spelen met
5 open(baar), vrij toegankelijk || *keep ~*
house erg gastvrij zijn; *have* (or: *keep*) *an ~*
mind on openstaan voor; *lay o.s. ~ to ridicule*
zich belachelijk maken

³open (vb) **1** opengaan, (zich) openen, geopend worden: *~ into* (or: *onto*) *the garden*
uitkomen in (*or:* op) de tuin **2** openen, beginnen; van wal steken [of speaker] **3** opendoen, (een boek) openslaan

⁴open (vb) **1** openen: *~ a tin* een blik opendraaien **2** openen, voor geopend verklaren,
starten: *~ the bidding* het eerste bod doen
[at auction, at card game]; *~ fire at* (or: *on*)
het vuur openen op

open-air openlucht-, buiten-, in de open-lucht

open-and-shut (dood)eenvoudig: *an ~ case* een uitgemaakte zaak

opencast bovengronds, in dagbouw: ~ *mining* dagbouw

open-ended open, met een open einde: ~ *discussion* vrije discussie

opener openingsnummer^h, openingsronde; eerste manche, ronde [etc]: *a standard* ~ een klassiek begin

openhanded gul, vrijgevig

open-hearted 1 openhartig, eerlijk **2** hartelijk, open

opening 1 opening, begin^h, beginfase, inleiding; [chess, draughts] opening(szet); beginspel^h **2** opening, kans, (gunstige) gelegenheid: *new ~s for trade* nieuwe afzetgebieden **3** vacature **4** opening, het opengaan, geopend worden, bres, gat^h, uitweg: *hours of ~ are Tuesdays 1 to 5* openingsuren dinsdag van 1 tot 5

openly open, openhartig: *you can speak* ~ u kunt vrijuit spreken

open-minded onbevooroordeeld, ruimdenkend

open-mouthed met de mond wijd open(gesperd); [also fig] sprakeloos [with surprise]

^1**open out** (vb) **1** verbreden, breder worden, zich uitbreiden: ~ *into* uitmonden in [of river] **2** opengaan, (naar buiten) openslaan

^2**open out** (vb) openvouwen, openleggen

open-plan met weinig tussenmuren: *an ~ office* een kantoortuin

open season open seizoen^h, jachtseizoen^h, hengelseizoen^h

^1**open up** (vb) **1** opengaan, zich openen, zich ontplooien; [fig] loskomen; vrijuit (gaan) spreken: *in the second half the game opened up* in de tweede helft werd er aantrekkelijker gespeeld **2** (de deur) opendoen

^2**open up** (vb) openen, openmaken, toegankelijk maken, opensnijden

opera opera

operable 1 opereerbaar **2** uitvoerbaar, realiseerbaar

opera glasses toneelkijker

opera house opera(gebouw^h)

^1**operate** (vb) **1** in werking zijn, functioneren; lopen [also of train]; draaien [of engine]; te werk gaan **2** (de juiste) uitwerking hebben, werken; (het gewenste) resultaat geven [of tariff, treaty, law]: *the new cutbacks will not ~ till next month* de nieuwe bezuinigingsmaatregelen gaan pas volgende maand in **3** te werk gaan, opereren; [med also] een operatie doen; ingrijpen

^2**operate** (vb) **1** bewerken **2** bedienen [machine, appliance]; besturen [also car, ship]: *be ~d by* werken op, (aan)gedreven worden

door [steam, electricity] **3** [Am; med] opereren

operating system besturingssysteem^h

operating theatre operatiekamer

operation 1 operatie, handeling, onderneming, campagne, militaire actie, chirurgische ingreep **2** werking: *bring* (or: *put*) *sth. into* ~ iets in werking brengen (or: zetten); *come into* ~ in werking treden, ingaan [of law] **3** bediening

operational operationeel, gebruiksklaar, bedrijfsklaar, gevechtsklaar: ~ *costs* bedrijfskosten

operations room controlekamer [at manoeuvres]; commandopost, hoofdkwartier^h

operative 1 werkzaam, in werking, van kracht: *the ~ force* de drijvende kracht; *become* ~ in werking treden, ingaan [of law] **2** meest relevant, voornaamste

operator 1 iem. die een machine bedient, operateur, telefonist(e), telegrafist(e), bestuurder **2** [inform] gladjanus

operetta operette

ophthalmic oogheelkundig

ophthalmologist oogheelkundige, oogarts

ophthalmology oogheelkunde

opiate opiaat^h, slaapmiddel^h, pijnstiller

opinion 1 mening, oordeel^h, opinie, opvatting: *a matter of* ~ een kwestie van opvatting; *in the ~ of most people* naar het oordeel van de meeste mensen; *in my* ~ naar mijn mening; *be of (the) ~ that* van oordeel zijn dat **2** (hoge) dunk, waardering, (gunstig) denkbeeld^h: *have a high ~ of* een hoge dunk hebben van **3** advies^h, oordeel^h; mening [of expert]: *have a second* ~ advies van een tweede deskundige inwinnen

opinionated koppig, eigenwijs

opinion poll opinieonderzoek^h, opiniepeiling

opium opium^h

opponent opponent, tegenstander, tegenspeler

opportune geschikt, gunstig (gekozen)

opportunism opportunisme^h, het steeds handelen naar de omstandigheden

^1**opportunist** (n) opportunist, iem. die steeds van gunstige gelegenheden gebruik probeert te maken

^2**opportunist** (adj) opportunistisch

opportunity (gunstige/geschikte) gelegenheid, kans: *take* (or: *seize*) *the ~ to* van de gelegenheid gebruikmaken om; *she had ample ~ for doing that* ze had ruimschoots de gelegenheid (om) dat te doen

oppose 1 tegen(over)stellen, contrasteren, tegenover elkaar stellen **2** zich verzetten tegen, bestrijden

opposed 1 tegen(over)gesteld: *be ~ to* tegen(over)gesteld zijn aan **2** tegen, afkerig:

be ~ *to* (gekant) zijn tegen, afkeuren ‖ *as* ~ *to* in tegenstelling met

opposing 1 tegenoverliggend **2** tegenwerkend; [sport] vijandig: *the* ~ **team** de tegenpartij

¹**opposite** (n) tegen(over)gestelde^h, tegendeel^h: *be* ~*s* elkaars tegenpolen zijn

²**opposite** (adj) **1** tegen(over)gesteld, tegenover elkaar gelegen, tegen-: ~ *number* ambtgenoot, collega **2** tegenover, aan de overkant: *the* **houses** ~ de huizen hier tegenover

³**opposite** (adv) tegenover (elkaar), aan de overkant: *she* **lives** ~ ze woont hiertegenover; ~ *to* tegenover

⁴**opposite** (prep) tegenover: *she sat* ~ *a fat boy* ze zat tegenover een dikke jongen

opposition 1 oppositie, het tegen(over)stellen: *in* ~ *to* tegen(over), verschillend van, in strijd met **2** oppositie, verzet^h: *meet with strong* ~ op hevig verzet stuiten **3** oppositie(groep), oppositiepartij

oppress 1 onderdrukken **2** benauwen: ~*ed by* anxiety doodsbenauwd

oppression 1 benauwing, neerslachtigheid **2** onderdrukking(smaatregel), verdrukking

oppressive 1 onderdrukkend, tiranniek **2** benauwend, deprimerend

oppressor onderdrukker, tiran

opt (+ for) opteren (voor), kiezen, besluiten

optic gezichts-, oog-, optisch: ~ *nerve* oogzenuw

optical 1 optisch: ~ *illusion* optisch bedrog, gezichtsbedrog^h **2** gezichtkundig ‖ ~ *fibre* glasvezel

optician opticien

optics optica

optimal optimaal, best, gunstigst

optimism optimisme^h

optimist optimist

optimistic optimistisch

optimum optimum^h

option 1 keus, keuze, alternatief^h: *have* **no** ~ *but to go* geen andere keus hebben dan te gaan **2** [fin] optie

optional keuze-, facultatief, vrij: *an* ~ *extra* accessoire, leverbaar tegen meerprijs

opt out niet meer (willen) meedoen, zich terugtrekken: ~ *of* a) niet meer (willen) meedoen aan [idea, plan]; **b)** afschuiven [responsibility]; **c)** opzeggen [contract]

opulence (enorme) rijkdom, overvloed, weelde

opulent overvloedig, (schat)rijk

or 1 of, en, ofwel, anders gezegd, of misschien, nog, ook: *would you like tea or coffee* wil je thee of koffie **2** of (anders): *tell me or I'll kill you!* vertel het mij of ik vermoord je!

oracle orakel^h

¹**oral** (n) mondeling^h, mondeling examen^h

²**oral** (adj) mondeling, oraal, gesproken: ~ *agreement* mondelinge overeenkomst; ~ *tradition* mondelinge overlevering

¹**orange** (n) sinaasappel

²**orange** (adj) oranje(kleurig)

orange juice jus d'orange, sinaasappelsap^h

orang-utan orang-oetan(g)

oration (hoogdravende) rede(voering): *a funeral* ~ een grafrede

orator (begaafd) redenaar

oratorical retorisch; [sometimes depr] hoogdravend

oratory 1 oratorium^h **2** redenaarskunst

orb bolvormig iets, globe, hemellichaam^h

¹**orbit** (n) **1** kring; (invloeds)sfeer, interessesfeer **2** baan [of planet etc]; omloop, kring(loop)

²**orbit** (vb) een (cirkel)baan beschrijven (rond)

orchard boomgaard

orchestra orkest^h

orchestral orkestraal; orkest-

orchestrate orkestreren, voor orkest arrangeren; [fig] (harmonieus/ordelijk) samenbrengen; organiseren

orchestration orkestratie

orchid orchidee

ordain 1 (tot geestelijke of priester) wijden **2** (voor)beschikken [by God, fate] **3** verordenen

ordeal 1 beproeving, bezoeking; [fig] vuurproef; pijnlijke ervaring **2** godsoordeel^h: ~ *by fire* vuurproef

¹**order** (n) **1** orde, stand, rang, (sociale) klasse, soort^+h, aard: ~ *of* **magnitude** orde (van grootte); *in the* ~ *of* in de orde (van grootte) van, ongeveer, om en (na)bij **2** (rang)orde, volgorde, op(een)volging: *in* alphabetical ~ alfabetisch gerangschikt; *in* ~ *of* importance in volgorde van belangrijkheid **3** ordelijke inrichting, orde(lijkheid), ordening, geregeldheid, netheid; [mil] opstelling; stelsel^h, (maatschappij)structuur: *in good* ~ piekfijn in orde; *out of* ~ defect, buiten gebruik **4** (dag)orde, agenda; reglement^h [of meeting etc]: *call* s.o. *to* ~ iem. tot de orde roepen; *be* **out of** ~ a) buiten de orde gaan [of speaker]; **b)** (nog) niet aan de orde zijn **5** orde, tucht, gehoorzaamheid: *keep* ~ de orde bewaren **6** (klooster)orde, ridderorde **7** bevel^h, order, opdracht, instructie: *on* doctor's ~*s* op doktersvoorschrift **8** bedoeling, doel^h: *in* ~ *to* om, teneinde **9** bestelling, order: *be* **on** ~ in bestelling zijn, besteld zijn **10** [fin] (betalings)opdracht, order(briefje^h): *postal* ~ postwissel ‖ ~*s are* **orders** (een) bevel is (een) bevel; *made* to ~ op bestelling gemaakt; [fig] perfect

²**order** (vb) **1** bevelen, het bevel hebben **2** bestellen, een order plaatsen

³**order** (vb) **1** ordenen, in orde brengen,

(rang)schikken **2** (een) opdracht geven (om), het bevel geven (tot), verzoeken om; voorschrijven [of doctor]: *he ~ed the troops to open fire* hij gaf de troepen bevel het vuur te openen **3** bestellen, een order plaatsen voor ‖ *~ s.o.* **about** (or: *around*) iem. (steeds) commanderen, iem. voortdurend de wet voorschrijven

order book orderboek^h, bestel(lingen)-boek^h

ordered geordend, ordelijk

order form bestelformulier^h

^1**orderly** (n) **1** ordonnans **2** (zieken)oppasser, hospitaalsoldaat

^2**orderly** (adj) ordelijk, geordend, geregeld

order out wegsturen, de deur wijzen

^1**ordinal** (n) rangtelwoord^h

^2**ordinal** (adj) rang-: *~ numbers* rangtelwoorden

ordinance verordening, bepaling, voorschrift^h

^1**ordinary** (n) het gewone: *out of the ~* ongewoon, bijzonder

^2**ordinary** (adj) **1** gewoon, gebruikelijk, normaal, vertrouwd **2** ordinair, middelmatig

ordination [rel] wijding

ordnance 1 (zwaar) geschut^h **2** militaire voorraden en materieel, oorlogsmateriaal^h

ordnance survey map topografische kaart, stafkaart

ore erts^h

organ 1 orgel^h **2** orgaan^h: *~s of speech* spraakorganen **3** orgaan^h, instrument^h, instelling

organ grinder orgeldraaier

organic 1 wezenlijk, essentieel **2** (organisch-)biologisch, natuurlijk: *~ food* natuurvoeding; *~ waste* [roughly] gft-afval^h

organism organisme^h

organist organist, orgelspeler

organization organisatie, structuur, vereniging

^1**organize** (vb) zich organiseren, zich verenigen

^2**organize** (vb) **1** organiseren, regelen, tot stand brengen, oprichten **2** lid worden van [trade union]; zich verenigen in

organizer 1 organisator **2** systematische agenda

orgasm orgasme^h

orgy orgie, uitspatting; [fig] overdaad

oriel (window) erker, erkervenster^h

orient 1 richten **2** oriënteren, situeren: *~ o.s.* zich oriënteren

Orient Oriënt^+h, Oosten^h

oriental oosters, oostelijk, oriëntaal: *~ rug* (or: *carpet*) oosters tapijt

orientation 1 oriëntatie **2** oriënteringsvermogen^h

origin oorsprong, origine, ontstaan^h, bron, afkomst, herkomst, oorzaak: *country of ~*

land van herkomst

^1**original** (n) origineel^h, oorspronkelijke versie

^2**original** (adj) origineel, oorspronkelijk, authentiek: *an ~ mind* een creatieve geest; *~ sin* erfzonde

originality originaliteit, oorspronkelijkheid

originate ontstaan, beginnen, voortkomen: *~ from* (or: *in*) *sth.* voortkomen uit iets

^1**ornament** (n) **1** ornament^h, sieraad^h **2** versiering, decoratie

^2**ornament** (vb) (ver)sieren

ornamental sier-, decoratief: *~ painter* decoratieschilder

ornate sierlijk

ornithologist ornitholoog, vogelkenner

ornithology vogelkunde

^1**orphan** (n) wees

^2**orphan** (vb) tot wees maken

orphanage weeshuis^h

orthodontics orthodontie

orthodox 1 orthodox, rechtgelovig **2** conservatief, ouderwets

orthodoxy 1 orthodoxe praktijk, gewoonte **2** orthodoxie, rechtzinnigheid

orthography spellingleer

orthopaedic orthopedisch

oscillate 1 trillen, (heen en weer) slingeren: *oscillating current* wisselstroom **2** weifelen

oscillation 1 schommeling, trilling **2** besluiteloosheid

osprey visarend

^1**Ossete** (n) Osseet

^2**Ossete** (adj) Ossetisch, Osseets

Ossetia Ossetië^h

ossify (doen) verbenen; [fig] verharden; afstompen

ostentation vertoon^h

ostentatious opzichtig

osteopath orthopedist

ostracize verbannen; [fig] uitstoten

ostrich struisvogel [also fig]

other 1 ander(e), nog een, verschillend(e): *every ~ week* om de (andere) week, eens in de twee weken; *on the ~ hand* daarentegen **2** (nog/weer) andere(n), overige(n), nieuwe: *someone or ~* iemand; *one after the ~* na elkaar; *among ~s* onder andere **3** anders, verschillend: *none ~ than John* niemand anders dan John ‖ *the ~ week* een paar weken geleden

other than behalve, buiten: *there was no-one else ~ his sister* er was niemand behalve zijn zuster; *~ that, ...* afgezien daarvan, ...

^1**otherwise** (adj) anders, verschillend, tegengesteld: *mothers, married and* (or: *or*) *~* moeders, al dan niet gehuwd

^2**otherwise** (adv) anders, overigens: *be ~ engaged* andere dingen te doen hebben; *go* *now; ~ it'll be too late* ga nu, anders wordt het te laat

otter (vis)otter

ought to 1 [command, prohibition, obligation] (eigenlijk) moeten, zou (eigenlijk) moeten: *you ~ be grateful* je zou dankbaar moeten zijn **2** [supposition] moeten, zullen, zou moeten: *this ~ do the trick* dit zou het probleem moeten oplossen, hiermee zou het moeten lukken

ounce (Engels, Amerikaans) ons[h]; [fig] klein beetje[h]: *an ~ of common sense* een greintje gezond verstand

our ons, onze, van ons

ours van ons, de (*or:* het) onze: *the decision is ~* de beslissing ligt bij ons; *a friend of ~* een vriend van ons

ourselves 1 ons, onszelf: *we busied ~ with organizing the party* we hielden ons bezig met het organiseren van het feestje **2** zelf, wij zelf, ons zelf: *we went ~* we gingen zelf

oust 1 verdrijven, uitdrijven, ontzetten, afzetten: *~ s.o. from* (*or:* of) iem. ontheffen van **2** verdringen, vervangen

¹out (adj) **1** uit [of equipment] **2** voor uitgaande post: *~ box* (*or:* *tray*) brievenbak voor uitgaande post

²out (adv) **1** [place, direction; also fig; also sport] uit, buiten, weg: *inside ~* binnenste buiten; *~ in Canada* daarginds in Canada **2** buiten bewustzijn, buiten gevecht, in slaap, dronken **3** niet (meer) in werking, uit **4** uit, openbaar, tevoorschijn: *the sun is ~* de zon schijnt; *~ with it!* vertel op!, zeg het maar!, voor de dag ermee! **5** ernaast [of estimates] ‖ *~ and about* (weer) op de been, in de weer; *~ and away* veruit; *she is ~ for trouble* ze zoekt moeilijkheden

³out (prep) uit, naar buiten: *from ~ the window* vanuit het raam

⁴out (vb) **1** [boxing] knock-out slaan **2** [inform] outen [reveal]

out-and-out volledig, door en door: *an ~ supporter of the programme* een verdediger van het programma door dik en dun

outback [Austr] binnenland[h]

outbalance zwaarder wegen dan, belangrijker zijn dan

outbid meer bieden dan, overtroeven

outbound uitgaand, op de uitreis, vertrekkend: *~ traffic* uitgaand verkeer

outbox postvak[h] uit

outbreak uitbarsting, het uitbreken

outburst uitbarsting, uitval

outcast verschoppeling, verworpene

¹outcaste (n) paria, kasteloze

²outcaste (adj) kasteloos, paria-

outclass overtreffen

outcome resultaat[h], gevolg[h], uitslag

outcry 1 schreeuw, kreet **2** (publiek) protest[h], tegenwerping: *public ~ against* (*or:*

over) publiek protest tegen

outdated achterhaald, ouderwets

outdo 1 overtreffen **2** overwinnen, de loef afsteken

outdoor 1 openlucht-, buiten(shuis)-: *~ advertising* buitenreclame **2** buiten een instelling, thuis zittend, zijnd

outdoors buiten(shuis), in de openlucht

outer buitenste: *~ garments* (*or:* *wear*) bovenkleding; *~ space* de ruimte; *the ~ world* de buitenwereld

outermost buitenste, uiterste

outfit 1 uitrusting, toerusting **2** groep, (reis)gezelschap[h], team[h], ploeg

outflow 1 uitloop, afvoer **2** uitstroming, uitvloeiing, afvloeiing

outgoing 1 hartelijk, vlot **2** vertrekkend, uitgaand: *~ tide* aflopend tij **3** uittredend, ontslag nemend

outgoings uitgaven, onkosten

outgrow 1 ontgroeien (aan), afleren, te boven komen: *~ one's strength* uit zijn krachten groeien **2** boven het hoofd groeien, groter worden dan

outhouse bijgebouw[h], aanbouw

outing 1 uitstapje[h], excursie **2** wandeling, ommetje[h]

outlandish vreemd, bizar, excentriek

outlast langer duren (meegaan) dan, overleven

¹outlaw (n) vogelvrijverklaarde, bandiet

²outlaw (vb) verbieden, buiten de wet stellen, vogelvrij verklaren

outlet 1 uitlaat(klep), afvoerkanaal[h] **2** afzetgebied[h], markt **3** vestiging, verkooppunt[h] **4** [Am] (wand)contactdoos, stopcontact[h]

¹outline (n) **1** omtrek(lijn), contour **2** schets, samenvatting, overzicht[h], ontwerp[h]: *in broad ~* in grote trekken **3** (-s) (hoofd)trekken, hoofdpunten

²outline (vb) **1** schetsen, samenvatten **2** omlijnen, de contouren tekenen van

outlive overleven, langer leven dan

outlook 1 uitkijk(post): *be on the ~ for* uitzien, uitkijken naar **2** uitzicht[h], gezicht[h] **3** vooruitzicht[h], verwachting **4** kijk, oordeel[h]: *a narrow ~ on life* een bekrompen levensopvatting

outmatch overtreffen

outmoded 1 uit de mode **2** verouderd

outnumber in aantal overtreffen, talrijker zijn dan: *be ~ed* in de minderheid zijn

out of 1 [place and direction; also fig] buiten, uit (… weg): *turned ~ doors* de straat opgejaagd, op straat gezet; *~ the ordinary* ongewoon; *feel ~ it* zich buitengesloten voelen; *one ~ four* een op vier **2** uit, vanuit, komende uit: *act ~ pity* uit medelijden handelen **3** zonder, -loos: *~ breath* buiten adem

out-of-date achterhaald, ouderwets

out-patient poliklinisch patiënt

out-patient clinic polikliniek
out-patient treatment poliklinische behandeling
outperform overtreffen, beter doen dan
outpost 1 voorpost **2** buitenpost
outpouring 1 uitvloeiing, afvloeiing, stroom **2** [esp pl] ontboezeming
output opbrengst, productie, prestatie, nuttig effect[h], vermogen[h], uitgangsvermogen[h], uitgangsspanning, uitvoer, output
[1]outrage (n) **1** gewelddaad, wandaad, misdaad, misdrijf[h], aanslag, belediging, schandaal[h]: *terrorist ~s* terreuraanslagen **2** [Am] verontwaardiging
[2]outrage (vb) **1** geweld aandoen, zich vergrijpen aan, overtreden, beledigen **2** [Am] verontwaardigd maken: *I felt ~d by what they had done* ik was buiten mezelf over wat ze gedaan hadden
outrageous 1 buitensporig **2** gewelddadig **3** schandelijk, schaamteloos, afschuwelijk
outrank hoger zijn in rang dan, belangrijker zijn dan
[1]outright (adj) **1** totaal, volledig, grondig **2** volstrekt: *~ nonsense* volslagen onzin **3** onverdeeld, onvoorwaardelijk **4** direct
[2]outright (adv) **1** helemaal, voor eens en altijd **2** ineens: *kill ~* ter plaatse afmaken **3** openlijk
outrun 1 harder (verder) lopen dan, inhalen **2** ontlopen, ontsnappen aan
outset begin[h], aanvang: *from the (very) ~* van meet af aan, vanaf het (allereerste) begin
outshine in glans overtreffen; [fig] overschaduwen
[1]outside (n) **1** buitenkant, buitenste[h], uiterlijk[h] **2** buitenwereld **3** uiterste[h], grens: *at the (very) ~* uiterlijk, op zijn laatst
[2]outside (adj) **1** buiten-, van buiten(af), buitenstaand **2** gering, klein: *an ~ chance* een hele kleine kans
[3]outside (adv) buiten, buitenshuis
outsider 1 buitenstaander **2** zonderling **3** [sport] outsider [horse]
outsize extra groot
outskirts buitenwijken, randgebied[h]: *on the ~ of town* aan de rand van de stad
outsmart te slim af zijn
outsourcing uitbesteding, outsourcing
outspoken open(hartig), ronduit
outstanding 1 opmerkelijk, voortreffelijk **2** onbeslist, onbetaald: *~ debts* uitstaande schulden
outstation buitenpost, afgelegen standplaats
outstay langer blijven dan: *~ one's welcome* langer blijven dan men welkom is
outstrip 1 achter zich laten, inhalen **2** overtreffen

outward 1 buitenwaarts, naar buiten (gekeerd), uitgaand: *~ passage* (or: *journey*) heenreis **2** uitwendig, lichamelijk: *to all ~ appearances* ogenschijnlijk
outwardly klaarblijkelijk, ogenschijnlijk
outwards naar buiten, buitenwaarts: *~ bound* uitgaand, op de uitreis
outweigh 1 zwaarder wegen dan **2** belangrijker zijn dan
outwit te slim af zijn, beetnemen
outwork 1 thuiswerk[h] **2** buitenwerk[h]
outworn 1 versleten, uitgeput **2** verouderd, afgezaagd
[1]oval (n) ovaal[h]
[2]oval (adj) ovaal(vormig), eivormig: *the Oval Office* [fig] het presidentschap
ovary eierstok; [bot] vruchtbeginsel[h]
ovation ovatie, hulde(betoon[h])
oven (bak)oven, fornuis[h]: *like an ~* snikheet
oven glove ovenwant
oven mitt ovenwant
[1]over (adv) **1** [direction; also fig] over-, naar de overkant, omver: *he called her ~* hij riep haar bij zich **2** [place] daarover, aan de overkant, voorbij: *~ in France* (daarginds) in Frankrijk; *~ here* hier, in dit land; *~ there* daarginds; *~ against* tegenover; *~ (to you)* [fig] jouw beurt **3** [degree] boven, meer, te: *some apples were left ~* er bleven enkele appelen over **4** [place] boven, bedekt: *he's mud all ~* hij zit onder de modder **5** ten einde, af, over **6** ten einde, helemaal, volledig: *they talked the matter ~* de zaak werd grondig besproken **7** opnieuw: *~ and over again* telkens weer ‖ *that's him all ~* dat is typisch voor hem
[2]over (prep) **1** [place] over, op, boven … uit: *chat ~ a cup of tea* (even) (bij)kletsen bij een kopje thee; *buy nothing ~ fifty francs* koop niets boven de vijftig frank; *~ and above these problems there are others* behalve deze problemen zijn er nog andere **2** [length, surface etc] doorheen, door, over: *speak ~ the phone* over de telefoon spreken; *~ the past five weeks* gedurende de afgelopen vijf weken **3** [direction] naar de overkant van, over **4** [place] aan de overkant van, aan de andere kant van **5** betreffende, met betrekking tot, over, om: *all this fuss ~ a trifle* zo'n drukte om een kleinigheid **6** [maths] gedeeld door: *eight ~ four equals two* acht gedeeld door vier is twee
overact overdrijven, overacteren
[1]overall (n) **1** (-s) overal **2** (werk)kiel
[2]overall (adj) **1** totaal, geheel, alles omvattend: *~ efficiency* totaal rendement **2** globaal, algemeen
[3]overall (adv) **1** in totaal, van kop tot teen **2** globaal: *~ I was happy with the result* al met al was ik tevreden met de uitslag
[1]overbalance (vb) het evenwicht verliezen, kapseizen, omslaan

²**overbalance** (vb) uit het evenwicht brengen

overbearing dominerend, bazig: ~ *manner* arrogante houding

overboard overboord: *throw* ~ overboord gooien [also fig]

overburden [also fig] overbelasten, overladen

¹**overcast** (n) bewolking

²**overcast** (adj) **1** betrokken, bewolkt **2** donker

¹**overcharge** (vb) overvragen, te veel vragen

²**overcharge** (vb) **1** overdrijven: ~*d with emotion* te emotioneel geladen **2** overvragen, te veel in rekening brengen (voor): ~ *a person* iem. te veel laten betalen

overcoat overjas

¹**overcome** (adj) overwonnen, overmand: ~ *by* the heat door de warmte bevangen; ~ *by* (or: with) grief door leed overmand

²**overcome** (vb) overwinnen, zegevieren (over), te boven komen: ~ *a temptation* een verleiding weerstaan

overconnected verslaafd aan internet en sociale media

overcrowded 1 overvol, stampvol **2** overbevolkt

overdo 1 overdrijven, te veel gebruiken: ~ *things* (or: *it*) te hard werken, overdrijven **2** te gaar koken, overbakken: ~*ne meat* overgaar vlees

¹**overdose** (n) overdosis

²**overdose** (vb) een overdosis toedienen, nemen van

¹**overdraw** (vb) een negatief saldo krijgen, rood komen te staan: *I'm* ~*n* ik sta rood

²**overdraw** (vb) overdrijven

overdress (zich) te netjes kleden, (zich) opzichtig kleden

overdrive overversnelling, overdrive

overdue te laat, over (zijn) tijd, achterstallig

overestimate overschatten

overexpose te lang blootstellen; [photo] overbelichten

¹**overflow** (n) **1** overstroming **2** overschot[h], overvloed

²**overflow** (vb) overstromen, (doen) overlopen: *full to* ~*ing* boordevol

overgrow 1 overgroeien **2** overwoekeren **3** te groot worden voor, ontgroeien

¹**overhang** (n) overhang(end gedeelte[h]), uitsteeksel[h]

²**overhang** (vb) overhangen, uitsteken

³**overhang** (vb) boven het hoofd hangen, voor de deur staan, dreigen

¹**overhaul** (n) revisie, controlebeurt

²**overhaul** (vb) **1** grondig nazien, reviseren; [by extension] repareren **2** [shipp] inhalen, voorbijsteken, voorbijvaren

overhead 1 hoog (aangebracht), in de lucht: ~ *railway* luchtspoorweg **2** algemeen, vast: ~ *charges* (or: *expenses*) vaste bedrijfsuitgaven

overheads algemene onkosten

overhear 1 toevallig horen **2** afluisteren

overjoyed (+ at) in de wolken (over)

overkill overkill

¹**overlap** (n) overlap(ping)

²**overlap** (vb) elkaar overlappen, gedeeltelijk samenvallen

³**overlap** (vb) overlappen, gedeeltelijk bedekken

overlay 1 bekleding, bedekking, (bedden)-overtrek[+h] **2** deklaagje[h]

overleaf aan ommezijde

overload te zwaar (be)laden, overbelasten

overlook 1 overzien, uitkijken op **2** over het hoofd zien, voorbijzien **3** door de vingers zien

overly [Am, Scotland] (al) te, overdreven: ~ *protective* overdreven beschermend

¹**overnight** (adj) **1** van de vorige avond **2** nachtelijk: ~ *journey* nachtelijke reis **3** plotseling [eg success]

²**overnight** (adv) **1** de avond tevoren **2** tijdens de nacht: *stay* ~ overnachten **3** in één nacht, zomaar ineens: *become* famous ~ van de ene dag op de andere beroemd worden

overpass viaduct[h]

overpopulation overbevolking

overpower 1 bedwingen, onderwerpen **2** overweldigen **3** bevangen

overrate overschatten, overwaarderen

¹**overreach** (vb) te ver reiken

²**overreach** (vb) verder reiken dan, voorbijschieten, voorbijstreven: ~ *o.s.* te veel hooi op zijn vork nemen

overreaction te sterke reactie

overriding doorslaggevend, allergrootst

overrule 1 verwerpen, afwijzen; terzijde schuiven [eg objection] **2** herroepen, intrekken, nietig verklaren: ~ *a decision* een beslissing herroepen

¹**overrun** (vb) **1** overstromen **2** [fig] uitlopen

²**overrun** (vb) **1** overstromen [also fig] **2** onder de voet lopen, veroveren **3** overschrijden [time limit] **4** overgroeien

¹**overseas** (adj) overzees, buitenlands: ~ *trade* overzeese handel

²**overseas** (adv) overzee, in (de) overzeese gebieden

oversee toezicht houden (op)

overseer opzichter, voorman

overshadow overschaduwen; [fig] domineren

oversharer iem. die te veel vertelt over zichzelf

overshoot voorbijschieten, verder gaan dan: ~ *the runway* doorschieten op de lan-

dingsbaan
oversight 1 onoplettendheid, vergissing
2 supervisie
over-sixties zestigplussers
oversize(d) bovenmaats, te groot
oversleep (zich) verslapen, te lang slapen
overspill 1 overloop, gemorst water[h]
2 surplus[h] **3** overloop; migratie [of surplus of
population]
overstate overdrijven
overstay langer blijven dan: ~ *one's **welcome*** langer blijven dan de gastvrouw of
gastheer lief is
overstep overschrijden: ~ *one's **authority***
zijn boekje te buiten gaan
overt open(lijk): ~ *hostility* openlijke vijandigheid
overtake inhalen
over-the-counter 1 [com] incourant: ~
securities incourante fondsen **2** [med] zonder (dokters)recept verkrijgbaar
overthrow 1 om(ver)werpen, omgooien
2 omverwerpen, ten val brengen
¹overtime (n) **1** (loon[h] voor) overuren,
overwerk(geld)[h] **2** [Am; sport] (extra) verlenging: *go into* ~ verlengd worden
²overtime (adv) over-: *work* ~ overuren maken
overtone 1 [mus] boventoon **2** [fig] ondertoon, suggestie
overture [mus] ouverture, inleiding, voorstel[h]: [fig] *make ~s (to)* toenadering zoeken
(tot)
¹overturn (vb) omslaan, verslagen worden
²overturn (vb) doen omslaan, ten val brengen
overview overzicht[h], samenvatting
¹overweight (n) over(ge)wicht[h]; te zware
last [also fig]
²overweight (adj) te zwaar, te dik
³overweight (vb) **1** overladen **2** te zeer benadrukken
overwhelm bedelven, verpletteren: ~*ed
with* grief door leed overmand
overwhelming overweldigend, verpletter-
rend: ~ *majority* overgrote meerderheid
¹overwork (vb) te hard werken
²overwork (vb) **1** te hard laten werken, uitputten **2** te vaak gebruiken, tot cliché maken: *an ~ed expression* een afgesleten uitdrukking
ovulate ovuleren
¹owe (vb) schuld(en) hebben: ~ *for everything
one has* voor alles wat men heeft nog (ten
dele) moeten betalen
²owe (vb) **1** schuldig zijn, verplicht zijn, verschuldigd zijn **2** (+ to) te danken hebben
(aan), toeschrijven (aan)
owing 1 verschuldigd, schuldig, onbetaald:
how much is ~ to you? hoeveel heeft u nog te
goed? **2** (+ to) te danken (aan), te wijten

(aan)
owing to wegens, ten gevolge van
owl uil [also fig]
¹own (adj) eigen, van ... zelf, eigen bezit (familie): *an ~ goal* een doelpunt in eigen doel;
be one's ~ man (or: *master*) heer en meester
zijn, onafhankelijk zijn; *not have a moment*
(or: *minute, second*) *to call one's* ~ geen moment voor zichzelf hebben; *you'll have a room
of your* ~ je krijgt een eigen kamer || *beat s.o.
at his ~ game* iem. met zijn eigen wapens
verslaan; *in his ~ (good) time* wanneer het
hem zo uitkomt; *hold one's* ~ **a)** standhouden; **b)** niet achteruitgaan [of health]; *on
one's* ~ in zijn eentje, op eigen houtje
²own (vb) bekennen, toegeven: ~ *up (to)* opbiechten
³own (vb) bezitten, eigenaar zijn van
owner eigenaar
ownership 1 eigendom[h], bezit[h] **2** eigen-
dom(srecht)[h]: *land* of uncertain ~ grond met
onbekende eigenaar
ox os, rund[h]
Oxbridge Oxford en Cambridge
oxidation oxidatie
oxide oxide[h]
oxtail soup ossenstaartsoep
oxygen zuurstof[h]
oyster oester
Oyster card [roughly] ov-chipkaart
oystercatcher scholekster
oz *ounce(s)* ons
ozone 1 ozon[+h] **2** frisse lucht
ozone depletion ozonafbraak

p

¹p (n) p, P ǁ *mind* one's p's and q's op zijn woorden passen

²p 1 *page* p., blz., pagina, bladzijde **2** *penny, pence* penny: *the apples are 12p each* de appels kosten 12 pence per stuk

¹pa (n) pa

²pa *per annum* p.j., per jaar

PA *personal assistant* assistent

¹pace (n) **1** pas, stap, schrede, gang **2** tempoʰ, gang, tred: *force the* ~ het tempo opdrijven; *keep* ~ *(with)* gelijke tred houden (met) ǁ *put* s.o. *through his* ~s iem. uittesten, iem. laten tonen wat hij kan

²pace (vb) stappen, kuieren: ~ *up and down* ijsberen

³pace (vb) (also + off, out) afstappen, afpassen, met stappen afmeten

pacemaker 1 [sport] haas **2** [med] pacemaker

pacific vreedzaam, vredelievend ǁ *the Pacific Ocean* de Grote Oceaan

pacifier [Am] fopspeen

pacifist pacifist

pacify kalmeren, de rust herstellen in

¹pack (n) **1** pakʰ, (rug)zak, last, verpakking, pakketʰ **2** pakʰ, hoop, pakʰ kaarten; [Am] pakjeʰ [cigarettes]: ~ *of lies* pak leugens; ~ *of nonsense* hoop onzin **3** (veldʰ van) pakijsʰ **4** kompresʰ **5** troep, bende, horde, meute; [sport] pelotonʰ [rugby]

²pack (vb) **1** (in)pakken, zijn koffer pakken **2** inpakken, zich laten inpakken ǁ ~ *into* zich verdringen in; ~ *up* ermee uitscheiden

³pack (vb) **1** (in)pakken, verpakken; inmaken [fruit etc]: [fig] ~ *one's bags* zijn biezen pakken; ~*ed lunch* lunchpakket **2** samenpakken, samenpersen: *the theatre was* ~*ed with people* het theater was afgeladen **3** wegsturen: ~ s.o. *off* iem. (ver) wegsturen **4** bepakken, volproppen: ~*ed out* propvol **5** [Am] op zak hebben [eg pistol]; bij de hand hebben ǁ ~ *it in* (or: *up*) ermee ophouden

¹package (n) **1** pakketʰ, pak(jeʰ), bundel; [comp] programmapakketʰ; standaardprogrammaʰ **2** verpakking

²package (vb) **1** verpakken, inpakken **2** groeperen, ordenen

package deal 1 speciale aanbieding **2** packagedeal, koppelverkoop

package holiday pakketreis, geheel verzorgde reis

packed 1 opeengepakt: ~ *(in* (or: *together*))

like *sardines* als haringen opeengepakt **2** volgepropt, overvol: *the theatre was* ~ *with people* het theater was afgeladen

packet 1 pak(jeʰ), stapeltjeʰ: *a* ~ *of cigarettes* een pakje sigaretten; ~ *soup* soep uit een pakje **2** bom geld

packing 1 verpakking **2** pakking, dichtingsmiddelʰ

pact verdragʰ

¹pad (n) **1** kussen(tje)ʰ, vulkussenʰ, opvulselʰ, stootkussenʰ, onderlegger, stempelkussenʰ; [sport] beenbeschermer **2** schrijfblokʰ, blocnote **3** (lanceer)platformʰ **4** bedʰ, verblijfʰ, huisʰ

²pad (vb) **1** draven, trippelen **2** lopen, stappen

³pad (vb) (also + out) (op)vullen: ~*ded envelope* luchtkussenenveloppe

padding opvulling, (op)vulselʰ

¹paddle (n) **1** peddel, roeispaan, schoep **2** vin [eg of seal]; zwempoot ǁ *go for a* ~ gaan peddelen

²paddle (vb) **1** pootje baden **2** (voort)peddelen

paddle boat rader(stoom)boot

paddling pool pierenbadʰ, kinder(zwem)badʰ

paddock kraal; omheinde weide [near stable or racecourse]

paddy woedeaanval

Paddy ler

paddy field rijstveldʰ

padlock hangslotʰ

padre aal(moezenier)

¹pagan (n) heiden

²pagan (adj) heidens

¹page (n) **1** pagina, bladzijde **2** page, (schild)knaap

²page (vb) oproepen, oppiepen

pageant 1 vertoning, spektakelstukʰ **2** historisch schouwspelʰ **3** [Am] schoonheidswedstrijd, missverkiezing

page boy 1 page **2** pagekop(jeʰ)

page break harde paginaovergang

pager pieper, semafoon

pageview [comp] pageview, weergave

paid betaald, voldaan ǁ *put* ~ *to* afrekenen met, een eind maken aan

pail emmer

¹pain (n) **1** pijn, leedʰ, lijdenʰ: *be in* ~ pijn hebben **2** lastpost: *he's a real* ~ *(in the neck)* hij is werkelijk onuitstaanbaar **3** (-s) (barens)weeën, pijnen **4** (-s) moeite, last: *be at* ~*s (to do sth.)* zich tot het uiterste inspannen (om iets te doen)

²pain (vb) pijn doen, leed doen

pained pijnlijk, bedroefd

painful 1 pijnlijk **2** moeilijk **3** [inform] verschrikkelijk (slecht)

painkiller pijnstiller

painstaking nauwgezet, ijverig

¹paint (n) kleurstof, verf: *wet* ~*!* pas geverfd!

²paint (vb) **1** verven, (be)schilderen **2** (af)schilderen, beschrijven, portretteren **3** (zich) verven, (zich) opmaken: ~ *a picture of* een beeld schetsen van

painter 1 (kunst)schilder, huisschilder **2** vanglijn, meertouwʰ

painting 1 schilderijʰ **2** schilderkunst, schilderwerkʰ

paintwork lak⁺ʰ, verfwerkʰ; verflaag [of car etc]

¹pair (n) **1** paarʰ, twee(tal)ʰ): *a* ~ *of gloves* een paar handschoenen; *the* ~ *of them* allebei; *in* ~*s* twee aan twee **2** tweespanʰ ‖ ~ *of scissors* schaar; ~ *of spectacles* bril; ~ *of trousers* broek

²pair (vb) paren, een paar (doen) vormen, (zich) verenigen, koppelen, huwen, in paren rangschikken: ~ *off* in paren plaatsen, koppelen; ~ *up* paren (doen) vormen [work, sport etc]

Pakistan Pakistan

¹Pakistani (n) Pakistaan(se)

²Pakistani (adj) Pakistaans

pal makker

palace 1 paleisʰ **2** het hof

palatable 1 smakelijk, eetbaar **2** aangenaam, aanvaardbaar: *a* ~ *solution* een bevredigende oplossing

palate 1 gehemelteʰ, verhemelteʰ **2** smaak, tong

palatial paleisachtig, schitterend

palaver gewauwelʰ

¹pale (n) **1** (schutting)paal, staak **2** (omheind) gebiedʰ, omsloten ruimte; grenzen [also fig]

²pale (adj) **1** (ziekelijk) bleek, licht-, flets: ~ *blue* lichtblauw **2** zwak, minderwaardig

³pale (vb) (doen) bleek worden, (doen) verbleken

¹Palestinian (n) Palestijn(se)

²Palestinian (adj) Palestijns

palette (schilders)paletʰ

palisade 1 palissade, (paal)heiningʰ **2** (-s) (steile) kliffen

¹pall (n) **1** lijkkleedʰ **2** [Am] doodkist **3** mantel; sluier: ~ *of smoke* rooksluier

²pall (vb) vervelend worden, zijn aantrekkelijkheid verliezen: *his stories began to* ~ *on us* zijn verhaaltjes begonnen ons te vervelen

pall-bearer slippendrager

pallet 1 strozak **2** spatel; strijkmesʰ [of potter] **3** pallet, laadbordʰ, stapelbordʰ

¹palliative (n) pijnstiller

²palliative (adj) **1** verzachtend, pijnstillend **2** vergoelijkend

pallid 1 (ziekelijk) bleek, flets **2** mat, flauw

pallor (ziekelijke) bleekheid, bleke gelaatskleur

pally vriendschappelijk, vertrouwelijk: *be* ~ *with* beste maatjes zijn met

¹palm (n) **1** palm(boom), palm(tak); [by extension] overwinning; verdienste **2** (hand)palm ‖ *have* (or: *hold*) *s.o. in the* ~ *of one's hand* iem. geheel in zijn macht hebben; *grease* (or: *oil*) *s.o.'s* ~ iem. omkopen

²palm (vb) (in de hand) verbergen, wegpikken, achteroverdrukken

palmistry handlijnkunde, handleeskunst

palm off 1 aansmeren, aanpraten: *palm sth. off on s.o.* iem. iets aansmeren **2** afschepen, zoet houden: ~ *s.o. with some story* iem. zoet houden met een verhaaltje

palmy 1 palmachtig, vol palmbomen **2** voorspoedig, bloeiend: [fig] ~ *days* bloeitijd

palpable tastbaar, voelbaar; [fig] duidelijk

palpitation hartklopping, klopping; het bonzen [of heart]

paltry 1 waardeloos, onbetekenend: *two* ~ *dollars* twee armzalige dollars **2** verachtelijk, walgelijk: ~ *trick* goedkoop trucje

pal up vriendjes worden: ~ *with s.o.* goede maatjes worden met iem.

pamper (al te veel) toegeven aan, verwennen

pamphlet pamfletʰ, folder, boekjeʰ

¹pan (n) pan, braadpan, koekenpan, vatʰ, ketel; schaal [of scales]; toiletpot

²pan (vb) **1** (goud)erts wassen **2** [film] pannen; laten meedraaien [camera]

³pan (vb) **1** wassen in goudzeef **2** afkammen, (af)kraken **3** [film] pannen; doen meedraaien [camera]

panacea wondermiddelʰ

Panama Panama

¹Panamanian (n) Panamees, Panamese

²Panamanian (adj) Panamees

pancake pannenkoek, flensjeʰ: *as flat as a* ~ zo plat als een dubbeltje

pancreas pancreas⁺ʰ, alvleesklier

pandemonium 1 hel, hels spektakelʰ **2** heksenketel, chaos, tumultʰ

pane (venster)ruit, glasruit

panel 1 paneelʰ, vlakʰ, (muur)vakʰ, (wand)plaat **2** (gekleurd) inzetstukʰ [of carpet] **3** controlebordʰ, controlepaneelʰ **4** naamlijst **5** panelʰ, comitéʰ, jury

panelling lambrisering, paneelwerkʰ

pang plotselinge pijn, steek, scheut: ~*s of remorse* hevige gewetenswroeging

¹panic (n) paniek: *get into a* ~ *(about)* in paniek raken (over)

²panic (vb) in paniek raken (brengen), angstig worden (maken)

panic button noodknop

panic room beveiligde ruimte, saferoom

pannier 1 (draag)mand, (draag)korf **2** fietstas

panorama panoramaʰ, vergezichtʰ

panoramic panoramisch

paraplegic

pansy 1 [bot] (driekleurig) viooltje[h] **2** [in-form] verwijfde man, jongen; nicht
¹pant (n) hijgende beweging, snak
²pant (vb) **1** hijgen **2** snakken, hunkeren **3** snuiven, blazen; puffen [of steam train]
³pant (vb) hijgend uitbrengen, uitstoten: ~ *out a few words* enkele woorden uitbrengen
panther panter, luipaard, poema
panties slipje[h], (dames)broekje[h]: *a pair of* ~ een (dames)slipje
pantomime 1 (panto)mime[h], gebarenspel[h] **2** (humoristische) kindermusical, sprookjesvoorstelling
pantry provisiekast, voorraadkamer
pants 1 [Am] (lange) broek: [fig] *wear the* ~ de broek aanhebben; *wet one's* ~ het in zijn broek doen, doodsbenauwd zijn **2** damesonderbroek, kinderbroek(je[h]), panty's ∥ *scare s.o.'s* ~ *off* iem. de stuipen op het lijf jagen; *with one's* ~ *down* onverhoeds, met de broek op de enkels
pantyhose [Am] panty
pap 1 pap, brij, moes[h] **2** leesvoer[h]
papa papa, vader
papacy 1 pausdom[h] **2** pausschap[h]; pauselijk gezag[h]
papal 1 pauselijk, van de paus: ~ *bull* pauselijke bul **2** rooms-katholiek
¹paper (n) **1** (blad[h]/vel[h]) papier[h], papiertje[h]: *on* ~ op papier, in theorie **2** dagblad[h], krant(je[h]) **3** (schriftelijke) test: *set a* ~ een test opgeven **4** verhandeling, voordracht: *read* (or: *deliver*) *a* ~ een lezing houden **5** document[h]: *your* ~*s, please* uw papieren, alstublieft
²paper (vb) behangen, met papier beplakken: ~ *over* a) (met papier) overplakken; b) verdoezelen
paperback paperback, pocket(boek[h])
paperclip paperclip
paper feed papierdoorvoer
paperhanger behanger
paper money papiergeld[h], bankbiljetten; cheques
paperweight presse-papier
papist pausgezinde
pappy pappie
paprika paprika(poeder[+h])
Pap test paptest
Papua New Guinea Papoea-Nieuw-Guinea
¹Papua New Guinean (n) Papoea-Nieuw-Guinees, -Guineeër
²Papua New Guinean (adj) Papoea-Nieuw-Guinees
par 1 gelijkheid, gelijkwaardigheid: *be on* (or: *to*) *a* ~ *(with)* gelijk zijn (aan), op één lijn staan (met); *put (up)on a* ~ gelijkstellen, op één lijn stellen **2** gemiddelde toestand: *be up to* ~ zich goed voelen, voldoende zijn ∥ ~ *for the course* de gebruikelijke procedure, wat je kunt verwachten

parable parabel, gelijkenis
parabola parabool
¹parachute (n) parachute
²parachute (vb) aan een parachute neerkomen, parachuteren, aan een parachute neerlaten
¹parade (n) **1** parade, (uiterlijk) vertoon[h], show: *make a* ~ *of* paraderen met **2** stoet, optocht, defilé[h], modeshow: [fig] *rain on s.o.'s* ~ iemands feestje bederven, iemands plezier vergallen **3** paradeplaats
²parade (vb) **1** paraderen, een optocht houden **2** [fig] paraderen: *old ideas parading as new ones* verouderde ideeën opgepoetst tot nieuwe **3** aantreden, parade houden
paradigm voorbeeld[h], model[h]
paradise paradijs[h]
paradox paradox, (schijnbare) tegenstrijdigheid
paraffin 1 paraffine **2** kerosine; paraffine-olie
paraffin oil kerosine; paraffineolie
paragliding paragliding[h], schermvliegen[h]
paragon toonbeeld[h], voorbeeld[h], model[h]: ~ *of virtue* toonbeeld van deugd
paragraph 1 paragraaf, alinea; [law] lid[h] **2** krantenbericht(je)[h]
Paraguay Paraguay
¹Paraguayan (n) Paraguayaan(se)
²Paraguayan (adj) Paraguayaans
parakeet parkiet
¹parallel (n) **1** parallel, evenwijdige lijn; [fig] gelijkenis; overeenkomst: *draw a* ~ *(between)* een vergelijking maken (tussen); *without (a)* ~ zonder weerga **2** parallel, breedtecirkel
²parallel (adj) parallel, evenwijdig; [fig] overeenkomend; vergelijkbaar: [gymnastics] ~ *bars* brug met gelijke leggers; ~ *to* (or: *with*) a) parallel met, evenwijdig aan; b) vergelijkbaar met
Paralympics (the) Paralympische Spelen, Paralympics
paralyse verlammen [also fig]; lamleggen
paralysis verlamming; [fig] machteloosheid; onmacht
paramedic paramedicus
paramount opperst, voornaamst: *of* ~ *importance* van het grootste belang
paranoia [med] paranoia, vervolgingswaanzin, (abnormale) achterdochtigheid
paranoid paranoïde
parapet balustrade, (brug)leuning, muurtje[h]
paraphernalia uitrusting, toebehoren[h], accessoires: *photographic* ~ fotospullen
¹paraphrase (n) omschrijving, parafrase
²paraphrase (vb) omschrijven, in eigen woorden weergeven
paraplegia [med] dwarslaesie
¹paraplegic (n) iem. die gedeeltelijk verlamd is

²paraplegic (adj) tweezijdig verlamd in de benen

parasite 1 parasiet, woekerdierʰ, woekerplant, woekerkruidʰ **2** klaploper, profiteur

parasol parasol, zonneschermʰ

paratroops para(chute)troepen, parachutisten

parcel 1 pak(jeʰ), pakketʰ, bundel **2** perceelʰ, lap grond: *a ~ of land* een lap grond

parcel up inpakken

parch verdorren, uitdrogen: *~ed with thirst* uitgedroogd (van de dorst)

parchment perkament(papier)ʰ

¹pardon (n) **1** vergeving, pardonʰ **2** kwijtschelding (van straf), gratie(verlening), amnestie: *free ~* gratie(verlening); *general ~* amnestie || *(I) beg (your) ~* neemt u mij niet kwalijk [also iron]; *~ pardon,* wat zei u?

²pardon (vb) **1** vergeven, genade schenken, een straf kwijtschelden **2** verontschuldigen: *~ me for coming too late* neemt u mij niet kwalijk dat ik te laat kom

pare 1 (af)knippen, schillen, afsnijden **2** reduceren, besnoeien: *~ down the expenses* de uitgaven beperken

parent 1 ouder, vader, moeder **2** moederdierʰ, moederplant

parentage 1 ouderschapʰ: *child of unknown ~* kind van onbekende ouders **2** afkomst, geboorte

parental ouderlijk, ouder-: *~ leave* ouderschapsverlofʰ

parental leave ouderschapsverlofʰ

parenthesis 1 uitweiding, tussenzin **2** ronde haak, haakjeʰ, haakjes: *in ~* tussen (twee) haakjes [also fig]

parenthetic tussen haakjes: *~ remark* verklarende opmerking

parenthood ouderschapʰ

parenting 1 het ouderschap **2** opvoeding

pariah 1 paria [member of the lowest class in India] **2** verschoppeling

parish 1 parochie, kerkelijke gemeente **2** gemeente, dorpʰ, districtʰ

parishioner parochiaan, gemeentelidʰ

¹Parisian (n) Parijzenaar, Parisienne

²Parisian (adj) Parijs, m.b.t. Parijs

parity 1 gelijkheid, gelijkwaardigheid: *~ of pay* gelijke wedde **2** overeenkomst, gelijkenis **3** pariteit, omrekeningskoers, wisselkoers

¹park (n) **1** (natuur)parkʰ, domeinʰ, natuurreservaatʰ: *national ~* nationaal park, natuurreservaatʰ **2** parkeerplaats

²park (vb) **1** parkeren **2** (tijdelijk) plaatsen, deponeren, (achter)laten: *~ o.s.* gaan zitten

parka parka, anorak

parking het parkeren, parkeergelegenheid: *no ~* verboden te parkeren

parking lot parkeerterreinʰ

parking meter parkeermeter

parkland 1 open graslandʰ [full of trees]

2 parkgrond

parkway [Am] snelweg [through beautiful landscape]

parlance zegswijze, uitdrukking: *in legal ~* in rechtstaal

parley onderhandelen

parliament parlementʰ, volksvertegenwoordiging

parliamentarian parlementslidʰ

parliamentary parlementair, parlements-: *~ party* kamerfractie

parlour salon⁺ʰ, woonkamer, zitkamer: *ice cream ~* ijssalon

parlour game gezelschapsspelʰ, woordspelʰ

parlous gevaarlijk, hachelijk

parochial 1 parochiaal, parochie-, gemeentelijk, dorps- **2** bekrompen, provinciaal

¹parody (n) parodie, karikatuur, nabootsing: *this trial is a ~ of justice* dit proces is een karikatuur van rechtvaardigheid

²parody (vb) imiteren, nadoen, navolgen

parole 1 erewoordʰ, paroolʰ, woordʰ **2** voorwaardelijke vrijlating, parooltijd: *on ~* voorwaardelijk vrijgelaten

paroxysm (gevoels)uitbarsting, uitval: *~ of anger* woedeaanval; *~ of laughter* hevige lachbui

parquet parketʰ, parketvloer

parricide 1 vadermoordenaar, moedermoordenaar **2** vadermoord, moedermoord

¹parrot (n) papegaai [also fig]; naprater

²parrot (vb) papegaaien, napraten: *~ the teacher's explanation* als een papegaai de uitleg van de leraar opzeggen

¹parry (vb) een aanval afwenden [also fig]

²parry (vb) **1** afwenden, (af)weren: *~ a blow* een stoot afwenden **2** ontwijken, (ver)mijden: *~ a question* zich van een vraag afmaken

¹parse (vb) (zich laten) ontleden, (zich laten) analyseren: *the sentence did not ~ easily* de zin was niet makkelijk te ontleden

²parse (vb) taalkundig ontleden [word, sentence]

parsimonious spaarzaam, krenterig

parsley peterselie

parsnip pastinaak

parson predikant [in Church of England]; dominee, pastoor

parsonage pastorie

¹part (n) **1** (onder)deelʰ, aflevering, gedeelteʰ, stukʰ, deelʰ, verzameling: *two ~s of flour* twee delen bloem **2** rol: *play a ~* een rol spelen, doen alsof **3** aandeelʰ, partʰ, functie: *have a ~ in* iets te maken hebben met, een rol spelen in **4** houding, gedragslijn **5** zijde, kant: *take the ~ of* de zijde kiezen van **6** (~s) streek, gebiedʰ, gewestʰ **7** (~s) bekwaamheid, talentʰ, talenten || *~ and parcel of* een essentieel onderdeel van; *in ~(s)* gedeeltelijk, ten dele; *for the most* ~ **a)** meestal, in de meeste gevallen; **b)** vooral

²**part** (vb) van elkaar gaan, scheiden: ~ *(as) friends* als vrienden uit elkaar gaan

³**part** (vb) **1** scheiden, (ver)delen, breken **2** scheiden, afzonderen: *he wouldn't be ~ed from his money* hij wilde niet betalen

⁴**part** (adv) deels, gedeeltelijk, voor een deel

partake (+ of) deelnemen (aan), deelhebben (aan): ~ *in the festivities* aan de festiviteiten deelnemen

part-baked voorgebakken, afbak-

partial 1 partijdig, bevooroordeeld **2** gedeeltelijk, deel-, partieel: ~ *solar eclipse* gedeeltelijke zonsverduistering **3** (+ to) verzot (op), gesteld (op)

partiality partijdigheid, bevoorrechting

participant deelnemer

participate (+ in) deelnemen (aan), betrokken zijn (bij)

participation 1 aandeelʰ **2** participatie, deelname, medezeggenschap⁺ʰ **3** [econ] winstdeling

participle deelwoordʰ: *past* ~ voltooid deelwoord; *present* ~ onvoltooid deelwoord

particle 1 deeltjeʰ, partikelʰ: *fine ~s* fijnstof **2** beetjeʰ, greintjeʰ

¹**particular** (n) **1** bijzonderheid, detailʰ: *in* ~ in het bijzonder, vooral **2** (-s) feiten, (volledig) verslagʰ **3** (-s) personalia, persoonlijke gegevens

²**particular** (adj) **1** bijzonder, afzonderlijk, individueel: *this* ~ *case* dit specifieke geval **2** (+ about, over) nauwgezet (in), kieskeurig (in/op): *he's not over* ~ hij neemt het niet zo nauw **3** bijzonder, uitzonderlijk: *of* ~ *importance* van uitzonderlijk belang; *for no* ~ *reason* zomaar, zonder een bepaalde reden **4** intiem, persoonlijk: ~ *friend* intieme vriend

particularly (in het) bijzonder, vooral, voornamelijk: *not* ~ *smart* niet bepaald slim

¹**particulate** (n) deeltjeʰ; fijnstofʰ

²**particulate** (adj) deeltjes-, partikel-: *ultra-fine* ~ *matter* ultrafijnstofʰ

parting scheiding [also: in hair]

partisan 1 partijganger, aanhanger **2** partizaan

¹**partition** (n) **1** (ver)deling, scheiding **2** scheid(ing)smuur, tussenmuur

²**partition** (vb) (ver)delen, indelen: ~ *off* afscheiden [by means of dividing wall]

partly gedeeltelijk: ~ …, ~ … [also] enerzijds …, anderzijds …

partner partner, huwelijkspartner, vennoot, compagnon: *silent* (or: *sleeping*) ~ stille vennoot ‖ ~ *in crime* medeplichtige

partnership 1 partnerschapʰ: *enter into* ~ *with* met iem. in zaken gaan **2** vennootschap

partridge patrijs

part-time in deeltijd

part with 1 afstand doen van, opgeven

2 verlaten

party 1 partij, medeplichtige: *be a* ~ *to* deelnemen aan, medeplichtig zijn aan; *third* ~ derde **2** (politieke) partij **3** gezelschapʰ, groep: *an coach* ~ een busgezelschap **4** feest(je)ʰ, partijtjeʰ: *that was quite a* ~, [Am] *that was some* ~ dat was me het feestje wel

party line 1 gemeenschappelijke (telefoon)lijn **2** partijlijn, partijprogrammaʰ: *follow the* ~ het partijbeleid volgen

party piece vast nummerʰ [at parties etc]

party-pooper [Am; inform] spelbreker

¹**pass** (n) **1** passage, (berg)pas, doorgang, vaargeul **2** geslaagd examenʰ, voldoende⁺ʰ **3** (kritische) toestand: *it (or: things) had come to such a* ~ *that* … het was zo ver gekomen dat … **4** pas, toegangsbewijsʰ **5** [socc] pass **6** [baseball] vrije loop **7** [tennis] passeerslag **8** [cards] pas ‖ *make a* ~ *at a girl* een meisje proberen te versieren

²**pass** (vb) **1** (verder) gaan, (door)lopen, voortgaan: ~ *along* doorlopen; ~ *to other matters* overgaan naar andere zaken **2** voorbijgaan, passeren, voorbijkomen, overgaan, eindigen: ~ *unnoticed* niet opgemerkt worden **3** passeren, er door(heen) raken **4** circuleren; gangbaar zijn [eg of coins]; algemeen bekendstaan (als): ~ *by* (or: *under*) *the name of* bekendstaan als; ~ *as* (or: *for*) doorgaan voor, dienen als **5** aanvaard worden; slagen [(part of) examination]; door de beugel kunnen [eg rude language] **6** gebeuren, plaatsvinden: *come to* ~ gebeuren **7** [cards] passen **8** overgemaakt worden: *the estate ~ed to the son* het landgoed werd aan de zoon vermaakt **9** [sport] passeren, een pass geven; [tennis] een passeerslag geven

³**pass** (vb) **1** passeren, voorbijlopen: ~ *a car* een auto inhalen **2** (door)geven, overhandigen; uitgeven [money]: *could you* ~ *me that book, please?* kun je mij even dat boek aangeven?; ~ *in* inleveren **3** slagen in: ~ *an exam* voor een examen slagen **4** komen door, aanvaard worden door: *the bill ~ed the senate* het wetsvoorstel werd door de senaat bekrachtigd **5** overschrijden, te boven gaan; overtreffen [eg expectations]: *this ~es my comprehension* dit gaat mijn petje te boven **6** laten glijden, (doorheen) laten gaan: ~ *one's hand across* (or: *over*) *one's forehead* met zijn hand over zijn voorhoofd strijken **7** [sport] passeren, toespelen, doorspelen **8** uiten; leveren [criticism]: ~ *judgement (up)on* een oordeel vellen over **9** vermaken, overdragen **10** doorbrengen [eg time]; spenderen

passable 1 passabel, begaanbaar, doorwaadbaar **2** redelijk, tamelijk, vrij goed

passage 1 doortocht, verloopʰ **2** (rechtʰ op) doortocht, vrije doorgang **3** passage, kanaalʰ, doorgang, (zee)reis, overtocht: *work*

one's ~ voor zijn overtocht aan boord werken **4** gang, corridor **5** passage; plaats [eg in book]
passageway gang, corridor
¹pass away (vb) **1** sterven, heengaan **2** voorbijgaan, eindigen: *the storm passed away* het onweer ging voorbij
²pass away (vb) verdrijven [time]
¹pass by (vb) voorbijgaan; voorbijvliegen [time]
²pass by (vb) over het hoofd zien, geen aandacht schenken aan: *life passes her by* het leven gaat aan haar voorbij
pass down overleveren, doorgeven
passenger 1 passagier, reiziger **2** profiteur [in group]; klaploper
passer-by (toevallige) voorbijganger
¹passing (n) **1** het voorbijgaan, het verdwijnen: *in ~* terloops **2** [euph] het heengaan, dood
²passing (adj) **1** voorbijgaand, voorbijtrekkend **2** vluchtig, oppervlakkig, terloops
passion 1 passie, (hartstochtelijke) liefde, enthousiasmeʰ: *he's got a ~ for skiing* hij is een hartstochtelijk skiër **2** (hevige) gevoelsuitbarsting, woedeaanval
Passion (the) passie(verhaalʰ)
passionate 1 hartstochtelijk, vurig: *~ plea* vurig pleidooi **2** begerig **3** opvliegend
passive passief: *~ resistance* lijdelijk verzet; *~ smoker* meeroker, passieve roker **2** [linguistics] passief, lijdend: *the active and ~ voices* de bedrijvende en lijdende vorm
passkey 1 privésleutel, huissleutel **2** loper
¹pass off (vb) (geleidelijk) voorbijgaan, weggaan, verlopen ‖ *~ as* doorgaan voor
²pass off (vb) **1** negeren **2** uitgeven: *pass s.o. off as* (or: *for*) iem. laten doorgaan voor
¹pass on (vb) **1** verder lopen, doorlopen: *~ to* overgaan tot **2** sterven, heengaan
²pass on (vb) doorgeven, (verder)geven: *~ the decreased costs to the consumer* de verlaagde prijzen ten goede laten komen aan de consument; *pass it on* zegt het voort
¹pass out (vb) **1** flauw vallen, van zijn stokje gaan **2** promoveren [at mil academy]; zijn diploma behalen
²pass out (vb) verdelen, uitdelen, verspreiden
¹pass over (vb) sterven, heengaan
²pass over (vb) **1** laten voorbijgaan, overslaan: *~ an opportunity* een kans laten schieten **2** voorbijgaan aan, over het hoofd zien **3** overhandigen, aanreiken
Passover Pascha [Jewish Easter]
passport 1 paspoortʰ **2** vrijgeleideʰ
pass through 1 ervaren, doormaken: *~ police training* de politieopleiding doorlopen **2** passeren, reizen door
pass up 1 laten voorbijgaan, laten schieten **2** (naar boven) aangeven

password wachtwoordʰ
¹past (n) verleden (tijd): *in the ~* in het verleden, vroeger
²past (adj) **1** voorbij(gegaan), over, gepasseerd **2** vroeger, gewezen **3** verleden: *~ participle* voltooid deelwoord; *~ tense* verleden tijd **4** voorbij(gegaan), geleden: *in times ~* in vroegere tijden **5** voorbij, vorig, laatst: *for some time ~* al enige tijd ‖ *that is all ~ history now* dat is nu allemaal voltooid verleden tijd
³past (adv) voorbij, langs: *a man rushed ~* een man kwam voorbijstormen
⁴past (prep) voorbij, verder dan, later dan: *he cycled ~ our house* hij fietste langs ons huis; *it is ~ my understanding* het gaat mijn begrip te boven; *he is ~ it* hij is er te oud voor, hij kan het niet meer; *half ~ three* half vier
¹paste (n) **1** deegʰ [for pastry] **2** pastei, paté, puree **3** stijfselʰ, stijfselpap, plakselʰ **4** pasta*ʰ, brij(achtige massa)
²paste (vb) **1** kleven; plakken [also comp] **2** uitsmeren **3** pasta maken van
pastel pastelʰ, pastelkleur
paste up aanplakken, dichtplakken
pasteurize pasteuriseren
pastille pastille
pastime tijdverdrijfʰ
pastor predikant, dominee, pastoor
pastoral 1 herders- **2** uiterst lieflijk **3** pastoraal, herderlijk: *~ care* zielzorg, geestelijke (gezondheids)zorg
pastry 1 (korst)deegʰ **2** gebakʰ, gebakjes, taart **3** gebakjeʰ
pastry chef patissier, patisseriechef
pastrycook pasteibakker; banketbakker
pasture weilandʰ, graslandʰ
¹pat (n) **1** klopjeʰ **2** stukjeʰ; klontjeʰ [butter] **3** geklopʰ, getikʰ ‖ *~ on the back* (goedkeurend) (schouder)klopje; [fig] aanmoedigend woordje
²pat (adj) **1** passend: *a ~ solution* een pasklare oplossing **2** ingestudeerd, (al te) gemakkelijk
³pat (vb) tikken
⁴pat (vb) **1** tikken op, (zachtjes) kloppen op, aaien **2** (zacht) platslaan
⁵pat (adv) **1** paraat, gereed: *have one's answer ~* zijn antwoord klaar hebben **2** perfect (aangeleerd), exact (juist): *have* (or: *know*) *sth. (off) ~* iets uit het hoofd kennen
patch 1 lap(jeʰ), stukʰ (stof), ooglap, (hecht)pleister, schoonheidspleister(tjeʰ) **2** vlek **3** lapjeʰ grond, veldjeʰ **4** stuk(je)ʰ, flard: *~es of fog* mistbanken, flarden mist ‖ *not a ~ on* helemaal niet te vergelijken met
patch pocket opgenaaide zak
patch up 1 (op)lappen, verstellen **2** (haastig) bijleggen [quarrel etc] **3** in elkaar flansen, aan elkaar lappen
patchwork 1 lapjeswerkʰ, patchworkʰ: *a ~ of fields* een bonte lappendeken van velden

payable

2 lapwerk^h, knoeiwerk^h
patchwork family samengesteld gezin^h
pate kop, hersens: *bald* ~ kale knikker
¹**patent** (n) patent^h, octrooi^h: ~ *law* octrooi-
wet, octrooirecht^h; ~ *medicine* a) patentge-
neesmiddel(en); b) wondermiddel^h
²**patent** (adj) **1** open(baar) **2** duidelijk ‖ ~
leather lakleer^h
patentee patenthouder
paternal 1 vaderlijk [also fig] **2** van vaders-
zijde: ~ *grandmother* grootmoeder van vaders kant
paternalism paternalisme^h
paternity vaderschap^h
paternity leave vaderschapsverlof^h
path 1 pad^h, weg, paadje^h: *beat* (or: *clear*) *a*
~ zich een weg banen [also fig] **2** baan [eg of
bullet, comet]; route; [fig] weg; pad^h
pathetic zielig, erbarmelijk: ~ *sight* treurig
gezicht
pathfinder 1 verkenner, padvinder **2** pionier, baanbreker
pathological pathologisch; ziekelijk [also
fig]: ~ *liar* pathologische/ziekelijke leugenaar
pathos aandoenlijkheid
pathway pad^h
patience geduld^h: ~ *of Job* jobsgeduld^h;
lose one's ~ zijn geduld verliezen
¹**patient** (n) patiënt
²**patient** (adj) geduldig, verdraagzaam
patio patio, terras^h
patriarch patriarch; [fig] grondlegger
¹**patrician** (n) patriciër, aanzienlijk burger
²**patrician** (adj) patricisch, aanzienlijk, voor-
aanstaand
patricide 1 vadermoordenaar **2** vadermoord
patrimony patrimonium^h, erfdeel^h
patriot patriot
patriotic patriottisch
patriotism patriottisme^h, vaderlandsliefde
¹**patrol** (n) **1** (verkennings)patrouille **2** pa-
trouille, (inspectie)ronde: *on* ~ op patrouille
²**patrol** (vb) patrouilleren, de ronde doen
³**patrol** (vb) afpatrouilleren, de ronde doen
van
patrolman 1 wegenwachter **2** [Am] politieagent
patron 1 patroon^h: ~ *of the arts* iem. die
kunst van kunstenaars ondersteunt **2** (vaste)
klant
patronage 1 steun, bescherming **2** klandizie, clientèle
patroness patrones, beschermheilige
patronize 1 beschermen **2** klant zijn van,
vaak bezoeken **3** uit de hoogte behandelen,
kleineren
patronizing neerbuigend
¹**patter** (n) **1** jargon^h, taaltje^h: *salesman's* ~
verkoperspraatjes **2** gekletsh, gekakel^h **3** ge-

kletter^h; getrippel^h [of feet]
²**patter** (vb) **1** kletsen **2** kletteren **3** trippe-
len
¹**pattern** (n) **1** model^h, prototype^h **2** pa-
troon^h, dessin^h, (giet)model^h, mal, plan^h,
schema^h: *geometric(al)* ~*s* geometrische fi-
guren **3** staal^h, monster^h
²**pattern** (vb) een patroon vormen
³**pattern** (vb) vormen, maken, modelleren: ~
after (or: *on*) modelleren naar; ~ *o.s.* **on** *s.o.*
iem. tot voorbeeld nemen
paucity geringheid, schaarste
paunch buik(je^h), maag **2** pens
pauper arme
¹**pause** (n) pauze, onderbreking, rust(punt^h),
weifeling: ~ *to take* a breath adempauze
²**pause** (vb) **1** pauzeren, pauze houden
2 talmen, blijven hangen **3** aarzelen, nadenken over
pave bestraten [also fig]; plaveien: ~ *with*
flowers met bloemen bedekken
paved 1 bestraat, geplaveid **2** vol (van),
vergemakkelijkt (door)
pavement 1 bestrating, wegdek^h, plavei-
sel^h **2** trottoir^h, voetpad^h, stoep **3** [Am] rijweg, straat
pavement café terrasje^h
pavilion paviljoen^h, cricketpaviljoen^h, club-
huis^h
¹**paw** (n) **1** poot, klauw **2** [inform] hand
²**paw** (vb) **1** krabben **2** onhandig rondtasten
³**paw** (vb) **1** ruw aanpakken, betasten **2** be-
krabben
¹**pawn** (n) **1** (onder)pand^h: *at* (or: *in*) ~ ver-
pand **2** [chess] pion; [fig] marionet: *he was*
only a ~ *in their game* hij was niet meer dan
een pion in hun spel
²**pawn** (vb) verpanden, in pand geven; [fig]
op het spel zetten [life]: ~ *one's* **word** (or:
honour) plechtig beloven op zijn woord van
eer
pawnbroker pandjesbaas
pawnshop pandjeshuis^h, bank van lening
¹**pay** (n) **1** betaling **2** loon^h, salaris^h: *on full* ~
met behoud van salaris
²**pay** (vb) **1** betalen; [fig] boeten: *make s.o.* ~
iem. laten boeten; ~ *down* contant betalen
2 lonend zijn: *it* ~*s to be* **honest** eerlijk duurt
het langst
³**pay** (vb) **1** betalen, afbetalen, vergoeden: ~
cash contant betalen; ~ *over* (uit)betalen
2 belonen [fig]; vergoeden, schadeloosstellen, betaald zetten: ~ *s.o. for his* **loyalty** iem.
voor zijn trouw belonen **3** schenken, verlenen: ~ *attention* opletten, aandacht schenken **4** lonend zijn (voor): *it didn't* ~ *him at all*
het bracht hem niets op ‖ ~ *as you* **earn** loonbelasting
payable betaalbaar, verschuldigd: *make* ~
betaalbaar stellen [Bill of Exchange]; ~ *to* ten
gunste van

pay-as-you-go prepaid
pay back terugbetalen, vergoeden; [fig] betaald zetten: *she paid him back his infidelities* ze zette hem zijn avontuurtjes betaald
paycheck [Am] looncheque, salaris[h]
PAYE *pay as you earn* loonbelasting
payee begunstigde; ontvanger [of Bill of Exchange etc]
payer betaler
pay for betalen (voor), de kosten betalen van; [fig] boeten voor
paying lonend, rendabel
payload 1 betalende vracht [in ship, aeroplane] **2** nuttige last; springlading [in bomb, rocket] **3** netto lading
payment 1 (uit)betaling, honorering, loon[h], (af)betaling **2** vergoeding, beloning, (verdiende) loon[h] **3** betaalde som, bedrag[h], storting: *make monthly ~s on the car* de auto maandelijks afbetalen ‖ *deferred ~, ~ on deferred terms* betaling in termijnen, afbetaling
payment-in-kind betaling in natura
[1]**pay off** (vb) renderen, (de moeite) lonen
[2]**pay off** (vb) **1** betalen en ontslaan **2** (af)-betalen, vereffenen, aflossen
pay-off 1 [fig] afrekening, vergelding **2** resultaat[h], inkomsten, winst **3** climax, ontknoping
payola [Am] **1** omkoperij **2** steekpenning(en)
[1]**pay out** (vb) **1** terugbetalen, met gelijke munt betalen **2** vieren [rope, cable]
[2]**pay out** (vb) **1** uitbetalen **2** (+ on) (geld) uitgeven (voor)
pay-per-view betaal-: *~ television* betaaltelevisie
pay phone munttelefoon, telefooncel
payroll 1 loonlijst **2** loonkosten
payslip loonstrookje[h]
pay station [Am] (publieke) telefooncel
pay train trein met kaartverkoop (en onbemande stations)
pay up betalen, (helemaal) afbetalen; volstorten [shares]: *paid-up capital* gestort kapitaal
paywall betaalmuur
PC 1 *Personal Computer* pc **2** *police constable* politieagent
PCB 1 *polychlorinated biphenyl* pcb **2** *Printed Circuit Board* printplaat
PE *physical education* gymnastiek
pea erwt: *green ~s* erwtjes ‖ *as like as two ~s (in a pod)* (op elkaar lijkend) als twee druppels water
peace 1 vrede, periode van vrede **2** openbare orde: *keep the ~* de openbare orde handhaven **3** rust, kalmte, tevredenheid, harmonie: *~ of mind* gemoedsrust; *hold* (or: *keep*) *one's ~* zich koest houden; *make one's ~ with* zich verzoenen met ‖ *be at ~* de eeuwige rust genieten

peaceful 1 vredig **2** vreedzaam
peacekeeping force vredesmacht
peacemaker vredestichter
peace operation vredesoperatie
[1]**peach** (n) **1** perzik [also colour]: *flat ~* wilde perzik **2** perzikboom **3** prachtexemplaar[h], prachtmeid: *a ~ of a dress* een schattig jurkje
[2]**peach** (vb) klikken, een klikspaan zijn: *~ against* (or: *on*) *an accomplice* een medeplichtige verraden
peacock (mannetjes)pauw [also fig]; dikdoener
[1]**peak** (n) **1** piek, spits, punt[h]; [fig] hoogtepunt[h]; toppunt[h] **2** (berg)piek, (hoge) berg, top **3** klep [of hat]
[2]**peak** (vb) een piek (or: hoogtepunt) bereiken: *the traffic ~s at 6* om 6 uur is het spitsuur
peak hour spitsuur[h]
peak load piekbelasting
peak performance topprestatie
peaky ziekelijk
[1]**peal** (n) **1** klokkengelui[h], klokkenspel[h], carillon[h] **2** luide klank: *~s of laughter* lachsalvo's; *a ~ of thunder* een donderslag
[2]**peal** (vb) **1** luiden **2** galmen, (doen) klinken, luid weerklingen: *~ out* weergalmen
peanut 1 pinda; [also] pindaplant **2** (-s) onbeduidend iets, kleinigheid, een schijntje
peanut butter pindakaas
pear peer
pearl 1 parel **2** paarlemoer[h] ‖ *cast ~s before swine* paarlen voor de zwijnen werpen
peasant 1 (kleine) boer **2** plattelander **3** lomperik, (boeren)kinkel
peasantry 1 plattelandsbevolking **2** boerenstand
pea soup erwtensoep
peat turf, (laag)veen[h]
pebble kiezelsteen, grind[h]
pebble-dash grindpleister[h], grindsteen[+h]
[1]**peck** (n) **1** pik (met snavel) **2** vluchtige zoen
[2]**peck** (vb) (+ at) pikken (in/naar): *~ at* a) vitten op; b) met lange tanden eten van
[3]**peck** (vb) **1** oppikken, wegpikken **2** vluchtig zoenen
pecker [Am; vulg] lul, pik ‖ [inform] *keep your ~ up* kop op!
pecking order pikorde, hiërarchie: *be at the bottom of the ~* niets in te brengen hebben
peckish 1 hongerig **2** [Am] vitterig
pecs [inform] *pectorals* borstspieren
pectoral borst-: *~ cross* borstkruis[h]; *~ fin* borstvin
peculiar 1 vreemd, eigenaardig, excentriek, raar: *I feel rather ~* ik voel me niet zo lekker **2** bijzonder: *of ~ interest* van bijzonder belang **3** (+ to) eigen (aan), typisch (voor): *a habit ~ to the Dutch* een gewoonte die Nederlanders eigen is
peculiarity 1 eigenaardigheid, bijzonder-

penalty

heid, merkwaardigheid **2** eigenheid, (typisch) kenmerk^h
pecuniary [form] **1** financieel: ~ *loss* geldverlies^h **2** [law] met geldboete
pedagogic(al) 1 opvoedkundig, pedagogisch **2** schoolmeesterachtig
pedagogy pedagogiek
¹**pedal** (n) pedaal^h, trapper
²**pedal** (vb) **1** peddelen, fietsen **2** trappen, treden
pedant 1 muggenzifter, betweter **2** boekengeleerde **3** geleerddoener
pedantic pedant, schoolmeesterachtig, frikkerig
¹**peddle** (vb) leuren, venten
²**peddle** (vb) **1** (uit)venten, aan de man brengen: ~ *dope* (or: *drugs*) drugs verkopen **2** verspreiden, verkondigen: ~ *gossip* roddel(praatjes) verkopen
pedestal voetstuk^h, sokkel: [fig] *knock s.o. off his* ~ iem. van zijn voetstuk stoten
pedestrian voetganger: ~ *crossing* voetgangersoversteekplaats; ~ *precinct* autovrij gebied
pediatrician kinderarts
pedicure pedicure
pedigree 1 stamboom, afstamming, goede komaf **2** stamboek^h [of animals]: ~ *cattle* stamboekvee^h
pedlar 1 venter, straathandelaar **2** drugsdealer **3** verspreider [of gossip]
¹**pee** (n) plas, urine: *go* for (or: *have*) a ~ een plasje gaan doen
²**pee** (vb) plassen, een plas(je) doen
¹**peek** (n) (vluchtige) blik, kijkje^h: *have a* ~ *at* een (vlugge) blik werpen op
²**peek** (vb) **1** gluren **2** (+ at) vluchtig kijken (naar)
peekaboo kiekeboe
¹**peel** (n) schil
²**peel** (vb) **1** (also + off) afpellen; afbladderen [of paint]; vervellen: *my nose* ~ed mijn neus vervelde; ~ *off* afschilferen van **2** (+ off) zich uitkleden
³**peel** (vb) schillen, pellen: ~ *off* a) lostrekken, losmaken; b) uittrekken [clothes]; ~ *the skin off* a banana de schil van een banaan afhalen
peeling (aardappel)schil
¹**peep** (n) **1** piep, tjilp(geluid^h) **2** [child language] toeter, claxon **3** kik, woord^h, nieuws^h **4** (vluchtige) blik, kijkje^h: *take a* ~ *at* vluchtig bekijken
²**peep** (vb) **1** (+ at) gluren (naar), loeren (naar), (be)spieden **2** (+ at) vluchtig kijken (naar), een kikje nemen (bij) **3** tevoorschijn komen: ~ *out* opduiken; *the flowers are already* ~*ing through* the soil de bloemen steken hun kopjes al boven de grond uit **4** piepen, tjirpen ‖ ~*ing Tom* voyeur, gluurder
peephole kijkgaatje^h
peeps [inform] mensen, luitjes

¹**peer** (n) **1** gelijke, collega **2** edelman ‖ ~ *of the realm* edelman die lid is van het Hogerhuis
²**peer** (vb) turen, staren, spieden
peerage 1 adel, adeldom^h **2** adelstand
peeress 1 vrouwelijke peer, edelvrouw **2** vrouw van een peer
peer group (groep van) gelijken, leeftijdgenoten, collega's
peerless weergaloos, ongeëvenaard
peer pressure groepsdruk
peeve ergeren, irriteren
peevish 1 chagrijnig, slechtgehumeurd **2** weerbarstig, dwars
¹**peg** (n) **1** pin, pen, plug **2** schroef [of string instrument] **3** (tent)haring **4** kapstok [also fig]: *buy clothes off the* ~ confectiekleding kopen **5** wasknijper ‖ *take s.o. down a* ~ (*or: two*) iem. een toontje lager laten zingen
²**peg** (vb) **1** vastpennen, vastpinnen: *he is hard to* ~ *down* je krijgt moeilijk vat op hem **2** stabiliseren, bevriezen
¹**peg out** (vb) zijn laatste adem uitblazen, het hoekje omgaan
²**peg out** (vb) afbakenen: ~ *a claim* (een stuk land) afbakenen
¹**pejorative** (n) pejoratief, woord met ongunstige betekenis
²**pejorative** (adj) pejoratief, ongunstig
pelican pelikaan
pelican crossing oversteekplaats
pellet 1 balletje^h, bolletje^h, prop(je^h) **2** kogeltje^h, hagelkorrel: ~*s hagel*
pellucid doorzichtig; helder [also fig]
¹**pelt** (n) vacht, huid, vel^h
²**pelt** (vb) **1** (neer)kletteren, (neer)plenzen: ~*ing rain* kletterende regen; *it is* ~*ing (down) with rain* het regent dat het giet **2** hollen: ~ *down* a hill een heuvel afrennen
³**pelt** (vb) bekogelen, beschieten; bestoken [also fig]
pelvic bekken-: ~ *floor* bekkenbodem; ~ *fin* buikvin
pelvis bekken^h, pelvis^h
¹**pen** (n) **1** pen, balpen, vulpen **2** hok^h, kooi, cel
²**pen** (vb) **1** op papier zetten, (neer)pennen **2** opsluiten [also fig]; afzonderen: *all the sheep were* ~*ned in* alle schapen zaten in de schaapskooi
penal 1 strafbaar: ~ *offence* strafbaar feit **2** zwaar, (heel) ernstig: ~ *taxes* zware belastingen **3** straf-: ~ *code* wetboek van strafrecht ‖ ~ *servitude* dwangarbeid
penalize 1 straffen **2** een achterstand geven, benadelen **3** een strafschop toekennen **4** strafbaar stellen, verbieden
penalty 1 straf, geldstraf, gevangenisstraf, (geld)boete: *on* (or: *under*) ~ *of* op straffe van **2** (nadelig) gevolg^h, nadeel^h, schade: *pay the* ~ *of* de gevolgen dragen van **3** handicap,

achterstand, strafpunt^h **4** strafschop
5 [hockey] tijdstraf
penalty area [socc] strafschopgebied^h
penalty box [ice hockey] strafbank, straf-
hok(je^h)
penalty kick [socc] strafschop
penance boete(doening), straf
penchant hang, neiging, voorliefde
¹**pencil** (n) **1** potlood^h, vulpotlood^h, stift
2 (maquilleer)stift
²**pencil** (vb) **1** (met potlood) kleuren, met
potlood merken: *~led* **eyebrows** zwartge-
maakte wenkbrauwen **2** schetsen; tekenen
[also fig]
pencil sharpener puntenslijper
pendant hanger(tje^h), oorhanger
pendent 1 (neer)hangend **2** overhangend,
uitstekend
¹**pending** (adj) hangend, onbeslist, in be-
handeling: *patent ~* octrooi aangevraagd
²**pending** (prep) in afwachting van [eg arri-
val]
pendulum slinger, slingerbeweging: *a*
clock with a ~ een slingeruurwerk
¹**penetrate** (vb) doordringen, penetreren,
binnendringen, indringen
²**penetrate** (vb) **1** doordringen, dringen
door, zich boren in, (ver)vullen **2** doorgronden, penetreren **3** dringen door, zien door:
our eyes couldn't ~ the darkness onze ogen
konden niet door de duisternis heendringen
penetrating doordringend, scherp(zinnig); snijdend [of wind]; scherp; luid [of
sound]
pen-friend penvriend(in), corresponden-
tievriend(in)
penguin pinguïn
penicillin penicilline
peninsula schiereiland^h
penis penis
penitence 1 boete(doening) **2** berouw^h
penitent berouwvol ‖ *be ~* boete doen
¹**penitentiary** (n) federale gevangenis
²**penitentiary** (adj) **1** straf-, boet(e)- **2** her-
opvoedings-, verbeterings-
penknife zak(knip)mes^h
penmanship kalligrafie, schoonschrijf-
kunst
pen-name schrijversnaam, pseudoniem^h
penniless 1 zonder geld, blut, platzak
2 arm, behoeftig
penny penny, stuiver, cent, duit: *it costs 30*
pence het kost 30 penny ‖ *not have* (or: *be*
without) *a ~ to one's* **name** geen rooie duit
bezitten; *a ~ for your* **thoughts** waar zit jij
met je gedachten?; *the ~ has* **dropped** het
kwartje is gevallen, ik snap 't; *spend a ~* een
kleine boodschap doen [to the toilet]; *ten a ~*
dertien in een dozijn; *in for a ~, in for a pound*
wie A zegt, moet ook B zeggen
penny-pinching vrekkig

penny-wise op de kleintjes lettend ‖ *~ and*
pound-foolish zuinig met muntjes maar
kwistig met briefjes
pension pensioen^h: *retire on a ~* met pensioen gaan
pensioner gepensioneerde
pension off 1 pensioneren, met pensioen
sturen **2** afdanken, afschaffen
pensive 1 peinzend, (diep) in gedachten
2 droefgeestig, zwaarmoedig
pentagon vijfhoek
Pentagon (the) ministerie^h van defensie
van de USA
pentathlon vijfkamp
Pentecost 1 [Am] pinksterzondag, Pinkste-
ren **2** [Judaism] pinksterfeest^h, Wekenfeest^h
penthouse dakappartement^h, penthouse^h
pent-up 1 opgesloten, ingesloten, vastzit-
tend **2** opgekropt, onderdrukt: *~ emotions*
opgekropte gevoelens
penultimate voorlaatst, op één na laatst
penury grote armoede, (geld)nood
peony pioen
¹**people** (n) **1** volk^h, gemeenschap, ras^h,
stam: *nomadic ~s* nomadische volken
2 staat, natie **3** mensen, personen, volk^h, lui
4 de mensen, ze, men: *~ say ...* men zegt ...
5 (gewone) volk^h, massa **6** huisgenoten, ou-
welui, (naaste) familie
²**people** (vb) bevolken [also fig]; voorzien
van (inwoners), bewonen
people skills sociale vaardigheden
people watching (het) mensen kijken
pep [inform] fut, vuur^h, energie
¹**pepper** (n) **1** peper [powder, plant, fruit]
2 paprika [plant, fruit]
²**pepper** (vb) **1** (in)peperen, flink kruiden: *~*
a speech with witty remarks een toespraak
doorspekken met grappige opmerkingen
2 bezaaien, bespikkelen: *~ed with* bezaaid
met **3** bekogelen; bestoken [also fig]
peppercorn peperkorrel, peperbol
peppermint pepermunt(je^h)
pepper spray pepperspray
pep up oppeppen, opkikkeren, doen opleven; pikanter maken [dish]
per via, per, door **2** per, voor, elk(e): *60 km*
~ hour zestig km per uur
perceivable 1 waarneembaar **2** begrijpelijk
perceive 1 waarnemen, bespeuren, (be)-
merken **2** bemerken, beseffen
per cent procent^h, percent^h ‖ *I'm one hun-*
dred ~ in agreement with you ik ben het volle-
dig met je eens
percentage 1 percentage^h **2** procent^h,
commissie(loon^h)
perceptible waarneembaar, merkbaar: *he*
worsened perceptibly hij ging zienderogen
achteruit
perception 1 waarneming, gewaarwor-

permeate

ding **2** voorstelling **3** (in)zicht^h, besef^h, visie: *a clear ~ of* een duidelijk inzicht in
perceptive 1 opmerkzaam, oplettend **2** scherp(zinnig), verstandig
¹perch (n) **1** stok(je^h), stang; staaf [for bird] **2** baars ‖ *knock s.o. off his ~* iem. op zijn nummer zetten
²perch (vb) **1** neerstrijken; neerkomen [of birds]; plaatsnemen, zich neerzetten **2** (neer)zetten, (neer)plaatsen, (neer)leggen: *the boy was ~ed on the wall* de jongen zat (hoog) bovenop de muur
percolator koffiezetapparaat^h
percussion slagwerk^h, percussie, slaginstrumenten
perdition verdoemenis, hel
¹perennial (n) overblijvende plant
²perennial (adj) **1** het hele jaar durend **2** vele jaren durend, langdurig, eeuwig, blijvend: *~ snow* eeuwige sneeuw **3** [bot] overblijvend
¹perfect (adj) **1** perfect, volmaakt, uitstekend, volledig, (ge)heel, onberispelijk: *have a ~ set of teeth* een volkomen gaaf gebit hebben; *~ly capable of* heel goed in staat om **2** zuiver, puur: *~ blue* zuiver blauw **3** [linguistics] voltooid: *~ participle* voltooid deelwoord; *~ tense* (werkwoord in de) voltooide tijd **4** volslagen, volledig, totaal: *a ~ stranger* een volslagen onbekende ‖ *have a ~ right (to do sth.)* het volste recht hebben (om iets te doen)
²perfect (vb) **1** perfectioneren, vervolmaken **2** voltooien, beëindigen **3** verbeteren: *~ one's English* zijn Engels verbeteren
perfection 1 perfectie, volmaaktheid: *the dish was cooked to ~* het gerecht was voortreffelijk klaargemaakt **2** hoogtepunt^h, toonbeeld^h
perfectionist perfectionist
perfidious trouweloos, verraderlijk
perforate doorprikken: *stamps with ~d edges* postzegels met tandjes
¹perform (vb) **1** optreden, een uitvoering geven, spelen **2** presteren, werken; functioneren [of machines]: *the car ~s well* de auto loopt goed **3** presteren, het goed doen **4** doen, handelen
²perform (vb) **1** uitvoeren, volbrengen, ten uitvoer brengen: *~ miracles* wonderen doen **2** uitvoeren, opvoeren, (ver)tonen, presenteren
performance 1 voorstelling, opvoering, uitvoering, tentoonstelling: *theatrical ~* toneelopvoering **2** prestatie, succes^h: *a peak ~* een topprestatie **3** uitvoering, volbrenging, vervulling **4** prestaties, werking: *a car's ~* de prestaties van een auto
performance enhancer prestatieverhogend middel^h, stimulerend middel^h
performer 1 uitvoerder **2** artiest

performing 1 gedresseerd, afgericht **2** uitvoerend: *~ arts* uitvoerende kunsten
¹perfume (n) parfum^h, (aangename) geur
²perfume (vb) parfumeren
perfunctory plichtmatig (handelend): *a ~ visit* een routinebezoek, een verplicht bezoekje
perhaps misschien, mogelijk(erwijs), wellicht
peril (groot) gevaar^h, risico^h: *you do it at your ~* je doet het op eigen verantwoordelijkheid
perilous (levens)gevaarlijk, riskant
perimeter omtrek: *secure the ~* de omgeving afzetten, het gebied veiligstellen
¹period (n) periode, tijdperk^h, fase: *bright ~s* opklaringen **2** lestijd, les(uur^h) **3** (menstruatie)periode, ongesteldheid: *she is having her ~* ze is ongesteld **4** punt^h [punctuation mark]: *I won't do it, ~!* ik doe het niet, punt uit!
²period (adj) historisch, stijl-: *~ costumes* historische klederdrachten; *~ furniture* stijlmeubelen
periodical tijdschrift^h
periodic(al) periodiek, regelmatig terugkerend, cyclisch, kring-
peripatetic rondreizend, rondzwervend, (rond)trekkend
peripheral 1 ondergeschikt, marginaal **2** perifeer, rand- [also fig]: [comp] *~ equipment* randapparatuur; *~ shops* winkels aan de rand van de stad
periphery (cirkel)omtrek, buitenkant, rand
periscope periscoop
perish 1 omkomen **2** vergaan, verteren
¹perishable (n) beperkt houdbaar (voedsel)product^h: *~s* snel bedervende goederen
²perishable (adj) **1** kortstondig **2** (licht) bederfelijk, beperkt houdbaar
perishing beestachtig, moordend: *~ cold* beestachtige kou
perjury meineed
perk extra verdienste: *~s* extraatjes; (extra) voordeel^h
perk up opleven, herleven, opfleuren
perky 1 levendig, opgewekt, geestdriftig **2** verwaand
perm 1 permanent^{+h} **2** combinatie; selectie [football pools]
permanence 1 duurzaamheid **2** permanent iem. (iets), vast element^h: *is your new address a ~ or merely temporary?* is je nieuwe adres permanent of slechts tijdelijk?
permanent blijvend, duurzaam: *~ address* vast adres; *~ wave* permanent^{+h}
permanent marker permanente markeerstift
permeate (door)dringen, (door)trekken, zich (ver)spreiden (over): *a revolt ~d the country* een opstand verspreidde zich over het land

permissible toelaatbaar
permission toestemming, vergunning, goedkeuring: *without* (or: *with*) *my ~* zonder (or: met) mijn toestemming
permissive verdraagzaam, tolerant: *the ~ society* de tolerante maatschappij
¹**permit** (n) **1** verlofbrief, pasjeʰ, permissiebriefjeʰ; geleidebiljetʰ [of goods] **2** (schriftelijke) vergunning, toestemming, machtiging
²**permit** (vb) toestaan, toelaten, veroorloven: *weather ~ting* als het weer het toelaat
pernicious 1 schadelijk, kwaadaardig **2** dodelijk, fataal
perp [Am; inform] *perpetrator* dader
¹**perpendicular** (n) loodlijn, verticaal, loodrechte lijn: *be out of (the) ~* niet in het lood staan
²**perpendicular** (adj) loodrecht, heel steil: *~ to* loodrecht op
perpetrate plegen, begaan: *~ a crime* een misdaad plegen
perpetration het plegen, het uitvoeren
perpetual eeuwig(durend), blijvend, permanent, langdurig, onafgebroken: *~ check* eeuwig schaak
perplex 1 verwarren, van zijn stuk brengen, van streek brengen **2** ingewikkeld(er) maken, bemoeilijken, compliceren: *a ~ing task* een hoofdbrekend karwei
perplexity 1 verbijsterend iets **2** verbijstering
perquisite 1 faciliteit, (extra/meegenomen) voordeelʰ **2** extra verdienste
persecute vervolgen, achtervolgen; [fig] kwellen; vervelen: *~ s.o. with questions* iem. voortdurend lastigvallen met vragen
persecution vervolging; [fig] kwelling
perseverance volharding, doorzetting(svermogenʰ)
persevere volhouden, doorzetten: *~ at* (or: *in, with*) volharden in; *~ in doing sth.* volharden in iets, iets doorzetten
Persian Perzisch, Iraans: *~ cat* Perzische kat, pers
persist 1 (koppig) volhouden, (hardnekkig) doorzetten: *~ in* (or: *with*) (koppig) volharden in, (hardnekkig) doorgaan met **2** (blijven) duren, voortduren, standhouden: *the rain will ~ all day* de regen zal de hele dag aanhouden
persistence 1 volharding, vasthoudendheid **2** hardnekkigheid
persistent 1 vasthoudend **2** voortdurend, blijvend, aanhoudend: *~ rain* aanhoudende regen
person 1 persoon, individuʰ, mens: *you are the ~ I am looking for* jij bent degene die ik zoek; *in ~* in eigen persoon **2** persoonlijkheid, karakterʰ, persoon
persona 1 persona, imagoʰ **2** (personae) [esp pl] personageʰ, rol, karakterʰ

personable knap, voorkomend
personage 1 personageʰ, belangrijk persoon **2** personageʰ, rol, karakterʰ
personal 1 persoonlijk, individueel: *from ~ experience* uit eigen ervaring; *for ~ use* voor eigen gebruik **2** persoonlijk, vertrouwelijk, beledigend: *~ remarks* persoonlijke opmerkingen
personality 1 persoonlijkheid, karakterʰ, sterk karakterʰ **2** persoonlijkheid, bekende figuur, beroemdheid
personalize 1 verpersoonlijken **2** merken [with a sign]: *~d stationery* postpapier voorzien van de naam van de eigenaar
personally 1 persoonlijk, in (eigen) persoon, zelf **2** voor mijn part, wat mij betreft **3** van persoon tot persoon: *speak ~ to s.o. about sth.* iets onder vier ogen met iem. bespreken
personal organizer agenda, palmtop (computer)
personification verpersoonlijking, personificatie
personify verpersoonlijken, belichamen, symboliseren
personnel 1 personeelʰ, staf, werknemers: *most of the ~ work* (or: *works*) *from 9 to 6* het meeste personeel werkt van 9 tot 6 **2** personele hulpmiddelen, troepen, manschappen
perspective 1 perspectiefʰ [also fig]; verhouding, dimensie **2** vergezichtʰ, uitzichtʰ, perspectiefʰ **3** gezichtspuntʰ [also fig]; standpuntʰ: *see* (or: *look*) *at sth. in its/the right ~* een juiste kijk op iets hebben **4** toekomstperspectiefʰ, vooruitzichtʰ **5** perspectiefʰ, perspectivisch tekenen; dieptezichtʰ [also fig]: *see* (or: *look*) *at sth. in ~* iets relativeren, iets in het juiste perspectief zien
perspex plexiglasʰ
perspicuous doorzichtig, helder, duidelijk
perspiration transpiratie, zweetʰ
perspire transpireren, zweten
persuade overreden, overtuigen, bepraten: *~ s.o. to do sth.* iem. tot iets overhalen; *o.s. of sth.* a) zich met eigen ogen van iets overtuigen; b) zichzelf iets wijsmaken
persuasion 1 overtuiging, mening, geloofʰ: *people of different ~s* mensen met verschillende (geloofs)overtuiging **2** overtuiging(skracht), overreding(skracht)
persuasive overtuigend
pert vrijpostig, brutaal
pertain to 1 behoren tot, deel uitmaken van **2** eigen zijn aan, passend zijn voor **3** betrekking hebben op, verband houden met
pertinence [form] pertinentie, relevantie
pertinent relevant, toepasselijk: *~ to* betrekking hebbend op
perturb in de war brengen [also fig]; van streek brengen
Peru Peru

per<u>u</u>se 1 doorlezen, nalezen, (grondig) doornemen **2** bestuderen, analyseren

¹Per<u>u</u>vian (n) Peruaan(se)

²Per<u>u</u>vian (adj) Peruaans

perv<u>a</u>de doordringen [also fig]; zich verspreiden in, vervullen: *the author ~s the entire book* de auteur is in het hele boek aanwezig

perv<u>a</u>sive 1 doordringend [also fig]; diepgaand **2** alomtegenwoordig

perv<u>e</u>rse 1 pervers, verdorven, tegennatuurlijk **2** eigenzinnig, koppig, dwars

perv<u>e</u>rsion 1 perversiteit, perversie **2** verdraaiing, vervorming: *a ~ of the law* een valse uitlegging van de wet; *a ~ of the truth* een verdraaiing van de waarheid

¹perv<u>e</u>rt (n) pervers persoon [sexually]; viezerik

²perv<u>e</u>rt (vb) **1** verkeerd gebruiken, misbruiken: *~ the course of justice* verhinderen dat het recht zijn loop heeft **2** verdraaien, vervormen: *his ideas had been ~ed* zijn opvattingen waren verkeerd voorgesteld **3** perverteren, corrumperen, bederven

pescat<u>a</u>rian pescotariër

p<u>e</u>sky [Am; inform] verduiveld; hinderlijk, irriterend

p<u>e</u>ssimism pessimisme^h, zwartkijkerij

p<u>e</u>ssimist pessimist, zwartkijker

pessim<u>i</u>stic pessimistisch; zwartgallig

p<u>e</u>st 1 lastpost **2** schadelijk dier^h, schadelijke plant: *~s* ongedierte^h; *~ control* ongediertebestrijding

p<u>e</u>st control ongediertebestrijding

p<u>e</u>ster kwellen, lastigvallen, pesten: *~ s.o. into doing sth.* iem. door te blijven zeuren dwingen tot het doen van iets

p<u>e</u>sticide pesticide^h, verdelgingsmiddel^h, bestrijdingsmiddel^h

pest<u>i</u>ferous 1 schadelijk **2** verderfelijk **3** vervelend, irriterend

p<u>e</u>stilence pest, (pest)epidemie

p<u>e</u>stilent (dood)vervelend, irriterend

p<u>e</u>stle stamper

¹pet (n) **1** huisdier^h, troeteldier^h **2** lieveling, favoriet

²pet (adj) **1** tam, huis-: *~ snake* huisslang **2** favoriet, lievelings-: *politicians are my ~ aversion* (or: *hate*) aan politici heb ik een hartgrondige hekel; *~ topic* stokpaardje^h

³pet (vb) vrijen: *heavy ~ting* stevige vrijpartij

p<u>e</u>tal bloemblad^h, kroonblad^h

peter <u>ou</u>t 1 afnemen, slinken **2** uitgeput raken, opraken, uitgaan, doven

pet<u>i</u>te klein en tenger, fijn; sierlijk [of woman]

¹pet<u>i</u>tion (n) **1** verzoek^h, smeekbede **2** petitie, smeekschrift^h, verzoek(schrift)^h **3** verzoek(schrift)^h, aanvraag: *file a ~ for divorce* een aanvraag tot echtscheiding indienen

²pet<u>i</u>tion (vb) een verzoek richten tot

pet<u>i</u>tioner 1 petitionaris, verzoeker

2 [law] eiser [in divorce]

¹p<u>e</u>trify (vb) verstenen; tot steen worden [also fig]

²p<u>e</u>trify (vb) **1** (doen) verstenen, tot steen maken **2** doen verstijven, verlammen: *be petrified by* (or: *with*) *terror* verstijfd zijn van schrik

p<u>e</u>trol benzine

petr<u>o</u>leum aardolie

petr<u>o</u>leum j<u>e</u>lly vaseline

p<u>e</u>trolhead [inform] autogek; autoverslaafde

p<u>e</u>trol station tankstation^h, benzinestation^h

p<u>e</u>t shop dierenwinkel

p<u>e</u>tticoat onderrok

p<u>e</u>ttifogging 1 muggenzifterig **2** nietig, onbelangrijk

p<u>e</u>ttish humeurig

p<u>e</u>tty 1 onbetekenend, onbelangrijk: *~ details* onbelangrijke details **2** tweederangs, ondergeschikt: *the ~ bourgeoisie* de lagere middenstand; [shipp] *~ officer* onderofficier **3** klein, gering: *~ crime* kleine criminaliteit

p<u>e</u>tulant prikkelbaar, humeurig

pet<u>u</u>nia petunia

pew kerkbank

p<u>e</u>wit kieviet

¹p<u>e</u>wter (n) tin^h, tinnegoed^h

²p<u>e</u>wter (adj) tinnen: *~ mugs* tinnen kroezen

¹ph<u>a</u>ntom (n) spook^h [also fig]; geest(verschijning)

²ph<u>a</u>ntom (adj) **1** spook-, spookachtig, schimmig: *~ ship* spookschip^h **2** schijn-, denkbeeldig: *~ withdrawals* spookopnames

ph<u>a</u>raoh farao

ph<u>a</u>risee 1 een van de farizeeën **2** farizeeër, schijnheilige

ph<u>a</u>rma de farmaceutische industrie

pharmac<u>eu</u>tical farmaceutisch: *~ chemist* apotheker

pharmac<u>eu</u>ticals farmaceutica, geneesmiddelen

pharmac<u>eu</u>tics farmacie

ph<u>a</u>rmacist apotheker

ph<u>a</u>rmacy apotheek

pharyng<u>i</u>tis keelholteontsteking

phase fase, stadium^h, tijdperk^h: *the most productive ~ in the artist's life* de meest productieve periode in het leven van de kunstenaar; *in ~* **a)** in fase; **b)** corresponderend; *out of ~* niet in fase

phase <u>i</u>n geleidelijk introduceren

phase <u>ou</u>t geleidelijk uit de productie nemen, geleidelijk opheffen

phat [Am; inform] tof, gaaf, cool, vet (goed)

PhD *Doctor of Philosophy* dr., doctor in de menswetenschappen

ph<u>ea</u>sant fazant

phenomenal 1 waarneembaar: *the ~ world* de waarneembare wereld **2** fenomenaal, schitterend: *~ strength* uitzonderlijke kracht

phenomenon fenomeen^h, (natuur)verschijnsel^h

philanthropist mensenvriend

philatelist postzegelverzamelaar

philharmonic filharmonisch

Philippine Filipijns

Philippines (the) Filipijnen

¹philistine (n) cultuurbarbaar

²philistine (adj) acultureel

philosopher filosoof, wijsgeer

philosophical 1 filosofisch, wijsgerig **2** kalm, wijs

philosophy filosofie, levensbeschouwing, opvatting

phlegm 1 slijm^h, fluim **2** flegma^h, onverstoorbaarheid **3** onverschilligheid, apathie

phlegmatic flegmatisch, onverstoorbaar

phobia fobie, (ziekelijke) vrees

phoenix feniks

¹phone (n) telefoon: *on the ~* aan de telefoon

²phone (vb) (op)bellen: *~ back* terugbellen; *~ up* opbellen

phone call telefoontje^h

phone-in belprogramma^h

phonetics fonetiek

¹phoney (n) [inform] **1** onecht persoon, bedrieger **2** namaak(sel^h), nep, bedrog^h

²phoney (adj) vals, onecht, nep

phosphorus fosfor^h

photo foto

photo booth pasfotoautomaat

photocopier fotokopieerapparaat^h

photocopy fotokopie

photodegrade afbreken onder invloed van zonlicht

photofit compositiefoto, montagefoto; [Belg] robotfoto

photogenic fotogeniek

¹photograph (n) foto

²photograph (vb) fotograferen, foto's maken, een foto nemen van

photographer fotograaf

photography fotografie

photon foton^h

photosensitize lichtgevoelig maken

photo shoot fotosessie

photovoltaic: *~ cell* zonnecel

¹phrase (n) **1** gezegde^h, uitdrukking, woordgroep, zinsdeel^h **2** uitdrukkingswijze, bewoordingen: *a turn of ~* een uitdrukking; *he has quite a turn of ~* hij kan zich heel goed uitdrukken || *coin a ~* een uitdrukking bedenken

²phrase (vb) uitdrukken, formuleren, onder woorden brengen

phrase book (ver)taalgids

phraseology idioom^h, woordkeus: *scientific ~* wetenschappelijk jargon

phubbing het negeren van je gesprekspartner door bezig te zijn met je smartphone

physical 1 fysiek, natuurlijk, lichamelijk: *~ education* lichamelijke oefening, gymnastiek; *~ exercise* lichaamsbeweging; *get ~* **a)** handtastelijk worden; **b)** intiem worden **2** materieel **3** natuurkundig, fysisch || *a ~ impossibility* absolute onmogelijkheid

physician arts; geneesheer [oft as opposed to surgeon]; internist

physicist natuurkundige

physics natuurkunde

physio 1 fysiotherapeut(e) **2** fysio(therapie)

physiognomy 1 gezicht^h **2** kenmerk^h, kenteken^h

physiology 1 fysiologie, leer van de lichaamsfuncties van mensen en dieren **2** levensfuncties

physiotherapist fysiotherapeut(e)

physique lichaamsbouw

pi pi [also maths]

pianist pianist(e)

piano piano

pic 1 *picture* foto, plaatje^h, illustratie **2** *picture* film

¹pick (n) **1** pikhouweel^h **2** keus: *take your ~* zoek maar uit, kies maar welke je wilt; *the ~* het beste, het puikje; *the ~ of the bunch* het neusje van de zalm

²pick (vb) **1** hakken (in), prikken; opensteken [lock]: *~ a hole in* een gat maken in **2** peuteren in [eg teeth]; wroeten in; pulken in [nose] **3** afkluiven, kluiven op; ontdoen van [meat] || *~ off* één voor één neerschieten

³pick (vb) **1** (zorgvuldig) kiezen, selecteren, uitzoeken: *~ one's words* zijn woorden zorgvuldig kiezen; *~ and choose* kieskeurig zijn **2** plukken, oogsten **3** pikken [of birds] **4** met kleine hapjes eten, peuzelen (aan): *~ at a meal* zitten te kieskauwen || *~ over* **a)** de beste halen uit; **b)** doorzeuren; *~ at* **a)** plukken aan; **b)** vitten (*or:* hakken) op; *~ on* vitten op

pickaxe pikhouweel^h

¹picket (n) **1** paal, staak **2** post(er), een staker die werkwilligen tegenhoudt

²picket (vb) posten, postend bewaken: *~ a factory* (*or:* *people*) een bedrijf (*or:* mensen) posten

picket line groep posters [at strike]

pickings 1 restjes, kliekjes, overschot^h **2** extraatjes: *there are easy ~ to be made* daar valt wel wat te snaaien

pickle 1 pekel [also fig]; moeilijk parket^h, knoei: *be in a sorry* (*or:* *fine*) *~* zich in een moeilijk parket bevinden **2** zuur^h, azijn: *vegetables in ~* groenten in het zuur **3** (-s) tafelzuur^h, zoetzuur^h

pickled 1 ingelegd (in zuur/zout) **2** in de olie, lazarus

pick-me-up [inform] opkikkertje^h

pick out 1 (uit)kiezen, eruit halen, uitpikken **2** onderscheiden, zien, ontdekken **3** doen uitkomen, afsteken

pickpocket zakkenroller

¹pick up (vb) vaart krijgen; aanwakkeren [of wind]

²pick up (vb) **1** oppakken, opnemen, oprapen: ~ *your* **feet** til je voeten op; pick *o.s.* up overeind krabbelen **2** opdoen, oplopen, oppikken: ~ *speed* vaart vermeerderen; *he picked her up in a bar* hij heeft haar in een bar opgepikt; *where did you pick* **that** *up?* waar heb je dat geleerd? **3** ontvangen; opvangen [radio or light signals] **4** ophalen, een lift geven, meenemen: *I'll pick you up at seven* ik kom je om zeven uur ophalen **5** (terug)vinden, terugkrijgen: ~ *the* **trail** het spoor terugvinden **6** (bereid zijn te) betalen [account] **7** weer beginnen, hervatten: ~ *the* **threads** de draad weer opvatten **8** beter worden, opknappen, er bovenop komen; [econ] opleven; aantrekken: *the* **weather** *is picking up* het weer wordt weer beter

pick-up 1 (taxi)passagier, lifter; [inform] scharreltje^h **2** open bestelauto

pick-up artist [inform] rasversierder

pick-up truck open bestelauto

picky kieskeurig

¹picnic (n) picknick || *it is no* ~ het valt niet mee, het is geen pretje

²picnic (vb) picknicken

¹picture (n) **1** afbeelding, schilderij^h, plaat, prent, schets, foto: *the* **big** (or: *bigger*) ~ het grote geheel, het totaalbeeld **2** plaatje^h, iets beeldschoons^h: *he is the (very)* ~ *of health* hij blaakt van gezondheid **4** (speel)film: *go to the ~s* naar de bioscoop gaan **5** beeld^h [on TV] || *come into the* ~ een rol gaan spelen; *put s.o.* **in** *the* ~ iem. op de hoogte brengen; *the* **larger** ~ het grote geheel, het totaalbeeld

²picture (vb) **1** afbeelden, schilderen, beschrijven: ~ *to o.s.* zich voorstellen **2** zich voorstellen, zich inbeelden

picture gallery schilderijenkabinet^h, galerie voor schilderijen

picture postcard prentbriefkaart, ansichtkaart

picturesque schilderachtig

piddle een plasje doen || *stop piddling around* schiet toch eens op

piddling belachelijk (klein), onbenullig, te verwaarlozen

pidgin mengtaal [on basis of English]

pie 1 pastei **2** taart

¹piebald (n) gevlekt dier^h, bont paard^h

²piebald (adj) gevlekt [esp black and white]; bont

¹piece (n) **1** stuk^h, portie, brok^h, onderdeel^h; deel^h [also techn]; stukje^h (land), lapje^h, eindje^h, schaakstuk^h, damschijf, muntstuk^h, geldstuk^h, artikel^h, muziekstuk^h, toneelstuk^h; [mil] kanon^h; geweer^h: *five* **cents** *a* ~ vijf cent per stuk; *a good* ~ *of* **advice** een goede raad; ~ *of (good)* **luck** buitenkansje^h; *that is a fine* ~ *of* **work** dat ziet er prachtig uit; **come** (or: *go*) *(all) to ~s* (helemaal) kapot gaan, instorten, in (or: uit) elkaar vallen; *say* (or: **speak, state**) *one's* ~ zijn zegje doen, zeggen wat men te zeggen heeft; *in ~s* in stukken; *be all of a* ~ **with** ... helemaal van hetzelfde slag zijn als ..., uit hetzelfde hout gesneden zijn als ...; *of a* ~ in één stuk **2** staaltje^h, voorbeeld^h || *(nasty)* ~ *of* **work** (gemene) vent (or: griet); *give s.o. a* ~ *of one's* **mind** iem. flink de waarheid zeggen; *pick up the ~s* de stukken lijmen

²piece (vb) samenvoegen, in elkaar zetten: ~ **together** aaneenhechten, aaneenvoegen, in elkaar zetten [story]

piecemeal stuksgewijs, geleidelijk, bij stukjes en beetjes

piecework stukwerk^h

pie chart cirkeldiagram^h, taartdiagram^h

pied bont, gevlekt || *the Pied* **Piper** *(of Hamelin)* de rattenvanger van Hamelen

pier 1 pier, havenhoofd^h **2** pijler, brugpijler

pierce doordringen, doorboren: *~d* **ears** gaatjes in de oren

¹piercing (n) piercing, gaatje^h

²piercing (adj) **1** doordringend; onderzoekend [also of look] **2** scherp; snijdend [wind, cold]; stekend [pain]; snerpend [sound]

piety vroomheid; trouw [to parents, relatives]

piffle [inform] nonsens, kletskoek, onzin

piffling belachelijk (klein), waardeloos, onbenullig

pig 1 varken^h, (wild) zwijn^h **2** [inform] varken^h [term of abuse]; gulzigaard, hufter **3** [Am] big **4** smeris || *be ~(gy) in the* **middle** tussen twee vuren zitten; **bleed** *like a (stuck)* ~ bloeden als een rund; *buy a* ~ *in a poke* een kat in de zak kopen; *and ~s might* **fly!** ja, je kan me nog meer vertellen!; *make a* ~ *of o.s.* overdadig eten (en drinken), schranzen

pigeon 1 duif **2** kleiduif || *it is not* **my** ~ het zijn mijn zaken niet

¹pigeon-hole (n) loket^h, hokje^h, (post)vakje^h

²pigeon-hole (vb) **1** in een vakje leggen [document]; opbergen **2** in de ijskast stoppen, opzijleggen, op de lange baan schuiven **3** in een hokje stoppen, een etiket opplakken

piggery 1 varkensfokkerij **2** varkensstal, zwijnerij

piggy big, varkentje^h || *be ~ in the* **middle** tussen twee vuren zitten

piggyback ritje^h op de rug

piggy bank spaarvarken^h

pig-headed koppig, eigenwijs
piglet big, biggetjeʰ
pigment pigmentʰ
pigmentation 1 huidkleuring 2 kleuring
pigsty varkensstal [also fig]
pigtail (haar)vlecht, staartjeʰ
pike 1 piek, spies 2 snoek
¹**pile** (n) 1 (hei)paal, staak, pijler 2 stapel, hoop: ~s of **books** stapels boeken 3 hoop geld, fortuinʰ: he has **made** his ~ hij is binnen 4 aambei 5 (kern)reactor 6 pool [on velvet, carpet]; pluisʰ
²**pile** (vb) zich ophopen: ~ **in** binnenstromen, binnendrommen; ~ **up** zich opstapelen
³**pile** (vb) (op)stapelen, beladen || ~ **it on** (thick) overdrijven
pile driver 1 heimachine 2 harde slag [in boxing]; (harde) trap
pile-up 1 opeenstapeling, op(een)hoping 2 kettingbotsing
pilfer stelen, pikken
pilferer kruimeldief
pilgrim pelgrim
pilgrimage bedevaart, pelgrimstocht
pill 1 pil [also fig]; bittere pil: **sweeten** the ~ de pil vergulden 2 (anticonceptie)pil: be **on** the ~ aan de pil zijn 3 bal
¹**pillage** (n) 1 plundering, roof 2 buit
²**pillage** (vb) plunderen, (be)roven
pillar 1 (steun)pilaar; zuil [also fig] 2 zuil; kolom [smoke, water, air] || driven from ~ to **post** van het kastje naar de muur gestuurd
pillar box brievenbus [of Post Office]
pillbox 1 pillendoosjeʰ 2 klein rond (dames)hoedjeʰ 3 [mil] bunker
¹**pillory** (n) blokʰ, schandpaal: **in** the ~ aan de schandpaal
²**pillory** (vb) aan de kaak stellen, hekelen
pillow (hoofd)kussenʰ
pillowcase kussensloop⁺ʰ
¹**pilot** (n) 1 loods 2 piloot, vlieger: on **automatic** ~ op de automatische piloot 3 gids, leider
²**pilot** (vb) loodsen, (be)sturen, vliegen; (ge)leiden [also fig]: ~ a bill **through** Parliament een wetsontwerp door het parlement loodsen
pilot light 1 waakvlam(metjeʰ) 2 controlelamp(jeʰ)
pilot project proefprojectʰ
pilot scheme proefprojectʰ
pimp pooier
pimple puist(jeʰ), pukkel
¹**pin** (n) 1 speld, sierspeld, broche 2 pin, pen, stift; [techn] splitpen; bout, spie, nagel 3 kegel [bowling] 4 vlaggenstok [in a hole at golf] || I have ~s and **needles** in my arm mijn arm slaapt
²**pin** (vb) 1 (vast)spelden; vastmaken [with pin] 2 doorboren, doorsteken 3 vasthouden, knellen, drukken: ~ s.o. **down** iem. neer-

drukken, iem. op de grond houden || ~ **sth. down** a) iets achterhalen, de vinger op iets leggen; b) iets onder woorden brengen; ~ s.o. **down on** sth. iem. ergens op vastpinnen, iem. ergens aan ophangen
PIN personal identification number persoonlijk identificatienummerʰ, pincode
pinafore (kinder)schortʰ
pinball flipper(spelʰ)
pinball machine flipperkast
pincers 1 (nijp)tang: a **pair** of ~ een nijptang 2 schaar [of lobster]
¹**pinch** (n) 1 kneep 2 klem, nood(situatie): **feel** the ~ de nood voelen 3 snuifjeʰ, klein beetjeʰ: take sth. with a ~ of **salt** iets met een korreltje zout nemen || **at** a ~ desnoods, in geval van nood
²**pinch** (vb) 1 knijpen, dichtknijpen, knellen, klemmen: ~ed **with** anxiety door zorgen gekweld 2 verkleumen, verschrompelen: ~ed **with** cold verkleumd van de kou 3 jatten, pikken, achterover drukken 4 inrekenen, in de kraag grijpen 5 knellen, pijn doen: these **shoes** ~ my toes mijn tenen doen pijn in deze schoenen 6 krenterig zijn, gierig zijn: ~ and **save** (or: **scrape**) krom liggen
pin-cushion speldenkussenʰ
¹**pine** (n) 1 pijn(boom) 2 vurenhoutʰ, grenenhoutʰ, dennenhoutʰ
²**pine** (vb) 1 kwijnen, treuren: ~ **away (from** sth.) wegkwijnen (van iets) 2 (+ after) smachten (naar), verlangen, hunkeren: ~ **to do** sth. ernaar hunkeren iets te doen
pineapple ananas
pine cone dennenappel, pijnappel
¹**ping** (n) ping, kort tinkelend geluidʰ
²**ping** (vb) 'ping' doen [make a short jingling sound]
ping-pong pingpongʰ, tafeltennisʰ
pinhead 1 speldenkop 2 kleinigheid 3 sufferd
pin-hole speldenprik; speldengaatjeʰ
¹**pinion** (n) 1 vleugelpuntʰ 2 [techn] rondselʰ, klein(ste) tandwielʰ
²**pinion** (vb) 1 kortwieken 2 binden; vastbinden [arms]; boeien [hands]
¹**pink** (n) 1 anjelier, anjer 2 roze(rood)ʰ 3 puikjeʰ, toppuntʰ, toonbeeldʰ: **in** the ~ (of health) in blakende gezondheid
²**pink** (adj) 1 roze: ~ **elephants** witte muizen, roze olifanten [a drunk's hallucinations] 2 gematigd links 3 homoseksueel: the ~ **pound** koopkracht van homoseksuelen || be **tickled** ~ bijzonder in zijn schik zijn
pinnacle 1 pinakel, siertorentjeʰ 2 (berg)top, spits, piek; [fig] toppuntʰ
pinny schortʰ
¹**pinpoint** (n) 1 speldenpunt 2 stipjeʰ, kleinigheid, puntjeʰ
²**pinpoint** (vb) uiterst nauwkeurig aanduiden

pinstripe(d) met dunne streepjes [on material, suit]; krijtstreep

pin-striped met krijtstrepen

pint 1 pint [for liquid 0.568 litre, (Am) 0.473 litre] **2** pint, grote pils

pint-size(d) nietig, klein, minuscuul

pin-up pin-up; [Belg] prikkelpop

¹pioneer (n) pionier, voortrekker

²pioneer (vb) pionieren, pionierswerk verrichten (voor), de weg bereiden (voor)

pious 1 vroom **2** hypocriet, braaf **3** vroom, onvervulbaar, ijdel: ~ *hope* (or: *wish*) ijdele hoop, vrome wens

¹pip (n) **1** oogʰ [on dice etc] **2** pit [of fruit] **3** b(l)iep, tikjeʰ, toontjeʰ **4** ster [on uniform] **5** aanval van neerslachtigheid, humeurigheid: *she gives* me the ~ ze werkt op mijn zenuwen

²pip (vb) **1** neerknallen, raken **2** verslaan

¹pipe (n) **1** pijp, buis, leiding(buis), orgelpijp, tabakspijp: ~ *of peace* vredespijp **2** (-s) doedelzak(ken) ‖ *put* that in your ~ and smoke it die kun je in je zak steken

²pipe (vb) **1** fluiten, op de doedelzak spelen **2** door buizen leiden **3** door kabelverbinding overbrengen [music, radio programme]: ~d *music* muziek in blik ‖ ~ *down* zijn mond houden; ~ *up* beginnen te zingen

pipe dream droombeeldʰ, luchtkasteelʰ

pipeline 1 pijpleiding, oliepijpleiding **2** toevoerkanaalʰ, informatiebron ‖ *in* the ~ onderweg, op komst

piper fluitspeler, doedelzakspeler ‖ *pay* the ~ het gelag betalen

¹piping (n) **1** pijpleiding, buizennetʰ **2** het fluitspelen, fluitspelʰ

²piping (adj) schril [voice] ‖ ~ *hot* kokend heet

piquant pikant, prikkelend

¹pique (n) gepikeerdheid, wrevel: *in a fit of* ~ in een kwaaie bui

²pique (vb) kwetsen [pride]; irriteren ‖ ~ *o.s. (up)on* sth. op iets prat gaan

piracy zeeroverij; piraterij [also fig]

piranha piranha

¹pirate (n) **1** piraat [also fig]; zeerover **2** zeeroversschipʰ

²pirate (vb) aan zeeroverij doen

³pirate (vb) **1** plunderen **2** plagiëren, nadrukken, illegale kopieën maken van: ~d *edition* roofdruk

pirate copy illegale kopie

Pisces [astrology] (de) Vissen

¹piss (n) [vulg] pis ‖ *take* the ~ *out of* s.o. iem. voor de gek houden; *are you taking* the ~? zit je mij nou in de maling te nemen?

²piss (vb) [vulg] (be)pissen ‖ ~ *about* (or: *around*) rotzooien; *it is* ~*ing (down)* het stortregent; ~ *off* oprotten

pissed 1 bezopen **2** kwaad: *be* ~ *off at* s.o. woest zijn op iem.

piste skipiste

pistil [bot] stamper

pistol pistoolʰ

piston [techn] zuiger

¹pit (n) **1** kuil, put, (kolen)mijn(schacht) **2** dierenkuil **3** kuiltjeʰ, putjeʰ **4** werkkuil; pits [at racetrack] **5** orkestbak; parterre⁺ʰ [theatre] **6** nestʰ [bed] **7** [Am] pit; steen [of fruit] **8** (the pits) (een) ramp, (een) verschrikking: *do you know that town? it's the* ~*s!* ken je die stad? erger kan niet!

²pit (vb) als tegenstander opstellen, uitspelen: ~ *one's strength against* s.o. zijn krachten met iem. meten

PITA [inform] *pain in the arse/ass* eikel, zeikerd

¹pitch (n) **1** worp: [fig] *make a* ~ *for* sth. een gooi naar iets doen **2** hoogte, intensiteit, top(puntʰ); [mus] toon(hoogte): *perfect* ~ absoluut gehoor **3** [sport] (sport)terreinʰ, veldʰ; [cricket] grasmat: *football* ~ voetbalveldʰ **4** (slim) verkoopverhaalʰ, verkooppraat(jeʰ) **5** standplaats, stalletjeʰ, stek **6** schuinte, (dak)helling **7** pek⁺ʰ

²pitch (vb) **1** afhellen; aflopen [of roof] **2** strompelen, slingeren ‖ ~ *in(to)* aan het werk gaan

³pitch (vb) **1** opslaan [tent, camp] **2** doen afhellen [roof]: ~ed *roof* schuin dak **3** op toon stemmen, (toon) aangeven

pitch-dark pikdonker

pitcher 1 grote (aarden) kruik; [Am] kan **2** [baseball] werper

pitchfork hooivork

piteous meelijwekkend, zielig

pitfall valkuil; [fig] valstrik

pith mergʰ; het wit en de velletjes [of citrus fruit] ‖ *the* ~ *(and marrow) of the matter* de kern van de zaak

pitiful 1 zielig **2** armzalig

pitiless meedogenloos

pit lane pitsstraat

pittance hongerloonʰ: *a mere* ~ een bedroevend klein beetje

¹pity (n) **1** medelijdenʰ **2** betreurenswaardig feitʰ: *it is a thousand* pities het is ontzettend jammer; *what a* ~! wat jammer!; *more's the* ~ jammer genoeg

²pity (vb) medelijden hebben met: *she is much to be pitied* zij is zeer te beklagen

¹pivot (n) spil, draaipuntʰ; [fig] centrale figuur

²pivot (vb) om een spil draaien; [fig] draaien: ~ *(up)on* sth. om iets draaien

pivotal 1 spil-, als spil dienend **2** centraal: ~ *question* cruciale vraag

pix 1 foto's **2** film, de filmindustrie

pixelated met zichtbare pixels (or: beeldpuntjes)

pixie fee, elf

pizza pizza

pizza base pizzabodem

pizzazz pit+ʰ, lefʰ

pl 1 *place* plaats **2** *plural* mv., meervoud

placard plakkaatʰ, aanplakbiljetʰ; protestbordʰ [of protester]

placate tot bedaren brengen, gunstig stemmen

¹place (n) **1** plaats, ruimte: *change ~s with s.o.* met iem. van plaats verwisselen; *fall into ~* duidelijk zijn; *lay* (or: *set*) *a ~ for s.o.* voor iem. dekken; *put* (or: *keep*) *s.o. in his ~* iem. op zijn plaats zetten (*or:* houden); *take ~* plaatsvinden; *take s.o.'s ~* iemands plaats innemen; *out of ~* misplaatst, niet passend (*or:* geschikt); *all over the ~* overal (rondslingerend); *in the first ~* in de eerste plaats **2** (woon)plaats, woning, pleinʰ: *come round to my ~ some time* kom eens (bij mij) langs **3** gelegenheid [pub etc]: *~ of worship* kerk, kapel, e.d. **4** passage [in book] **5** stand, rang, positie: *know one's ~* zijn plaats kennen **6** taak, functie

²place (vb) **1** plaatsen, zetten: *~ an order for goods* goederen bestellen **2** aanstellen, een betrekking geven **3** thuisbrengen, identificeren

placebo placeboʰ, nepgeneesmiddelʰ, zoethoudertjeʰ

placement 1 plaatsing: *product ~* productplaatsing **2** stage, stageplek

placid vreedzaam, kalm

plagiarism plagiaatʰ: *copy-and-paste ~* (plagiaat door) knippen en plakken

plagiarist plagiaris, plagiator

¹plagiarize (vb) plagiaat plegen

²plagiarize (vb) plagiëren

¹plague (n) **1** plaag, teistering **2** pest: *avoid s.o. (sth.) like the ~* iem. (iets) schuwen als de pest; *bubonic ~* (builen)pest **3** lastpost

²plague (vb) **1** teisteren, treffen (+ with) lastigvallen (met), pesten

plaice 1 school **2** [Am] platvis

¹plaid (n) plaid

²plaid (adj) plaid-, met Schots patroon

¹plain (n) vlakte, prairie

²plain (adj) **1** duidelijk: *in ~ language* in duidelijke taal **2** simpel, onvermengd; puur [water, whisky etc]: *~ flour* bloem [without baking powder] **3** ronduit, oprecht: *~ dealing* eerlijk(heid) **4** vlak, effen **5** recht [knitting stitch] **6** volslagen; totaal [nonsense]: *it's ~ foolishness* het is je reinste dwaasheid ‖ *it was ~ sailing all the way* het liep allemaal van een leien dakje

³plain (adv) **1** duidelijk **2** ronduit

plain-clothes in burger(kleren)

plainly 1 ronduit: *speak ~* ronduit spreken **2** zonder meer: *it is ~ clear* het is zonder meer duidelijk

plaintiff aanklager, eiser

plaintive 1 klagend **2** treurig, triest

¹plait (n) vlecht

²plait (vb) vlechten

¹plan (n) **1** planʰ: *what are your ~s for tonight?* wat ga je vanavond doen? **2** plattegrond **3** ontwerpʰ, opzet: *~ of action* (or: *campaign, battle*) plan de campagne **4** schemaʰ, ontwerpʰ

²plan (vb) plannen maken: *he hadn't ~ned for* (or: *on*) *so many guests* hij had niet op zoveel gasten gerekend; *~ on doing sth.* er op rekenen iets te (kunnen) doen

³plan (vb) **1** in kaart brengen, schetsen, ontwerpen **2** plannen, van plan zijn: *he had it all ~ned out* hij had alles tot in de details geregeld

¹plane (n) **1** plataanʰ **2** schaaf **3** vlakʰ, draagvlakʰ; vleugel [of aeroplane] **4** niveauʰ; planʰ **5** vliegtuigʰ

²plane (adj) vlak, plat: *~ geometry* vlakke meetkunde

³plane (vb) **1** glijden; zweven [of aeroplane] **2** schaven, effen maken

plane crash vliegtuigongelukʰ

planet planeet

planetarium planetariumʰ

plank (zware) plank: [fig] *walk the ~* gedwongen ontslag nemen, het veld ruimen

plankton planktonʰ

planner ontwerper; [urban development] planoloog

planning planning, ordening

¹plant (n) **1** plant, gewasʰ **2** fabriek, bedrijfʰ; [elec] centrale **3** machinerie, uitrusting, installatie **4** doorgestoken kaart, vals bewijsmateriaalʰ

²plant (vb) **1** planten; poten [also fish]; aanplanten **2** (met kracht) neerzetten [feet]; plaatsen: *with one's feet ~ed (firmly) on the ground* met beide voeten (stevig) op de grond **3** zaaien **4** onderschuiven; verbergen [stolen goods]; laten opdraaien voor: *~ false evidence* vals bewijsmateriaal onderschuiven

plantain weegbree

plantation 1 beplanting, aanplant **2** plantage

planter 1 planter, plantagebezitter **2** bloembak, bloempot

plaque 1 plaat, gedenkplaat **2** vlek [on skin] **3** tandaanslag

plasma plasmaʰ

plasma screen plasmaschermʰ

plasma TV plasma-tv

¹plaster (n) **1** (hecht)pleister **2** pleisterkalk **3** gipsʰ: *so many Paris* (gebrande) gips

²plaster (vb) **1** (be)pleisteren, bedekken: *~ make-up on one's face* zich zwaar opmaken, z'n gezicht plamuren; *~ over* (or: *up*) dichtpleisteren **2** verpletteren, inmaken

plastered [inform] lazarus

plasterer stukadoor

plastering 1 bepleistering **2** [inform; sport] verpletterende nederlaag

¹plastic (n) plastic^h, kunststof

²plastic (adj) **1** plastisch **2** plastic, synthetisch **3** kunstmatig ‖ ~ *money* plastic geld [with cheque card, credit card]; ~ *surgery* plastische chirurgie

¹plate (n) **1** plaat(je^h), naambordje^h, nummerbord^h, nummerplaat; [geology] plaat [large piece of the earth's crust] **2** bord^h; bordvol^h [food] **3** collecteschaal **4** zilveren (gouden) bestek^h, verzilverd bestek^h, pleet^h ‖ *give* s.o. sth. *on a* ~ iets in de schoot werpen; *have enough on one's* ~ genoeg omhanden hebben

²plate (vb) **1** pantseren **2** verzilveren **3** [culinary] opmaken

plateau plateau^h, tafelland^h; [fig also] stilstand [in growth] ‖ *the pink* ~ het roze plafond

plateful bordvol^h

plate up [culinary] opmaken [of plate]

platform 1 platform^h **2** podium^h **3** balkon^h [of bus, tram] **4** perron^h **5** partijprogramma^h, politiek programma^h

platinum platina^h

platitude open deur, afgezaagde waarheid

platoon peloton^h

platter plat bord^h, platte schotel ‖ *on a* ~ op een gouden schotel

plausible 1 plausibel, aannemelijk **2** bedrieglijk overtuigend

¹play (n) **1** spel^h: ~ *(up)on* **words** woordspeling; *allow full* (or: *free*) ~ *to* sth. iets vrij spel laten **2** toneelstuk^h: *the* ~*s of* **Shakespeare** de stukken van Shakespeare **3** beurt, zet; [Am; esp sport] manoeuvre^+h: *make a* ~ *for* sth. iets proberen te krijgen **4** actie, activiteit, beweging: *bring* (or: *call*) *into* ~ erbij betrekken **5** [techn] speling ‖ *make great* ~ *of* erg de nadruk leggen op, sterk benadrukken

²play (vb) **1** spelen: *a* **smile** ~*ed on her lips* een glimlach speelde om haar lippen; ~ *hide-and-seek*, ~ *at* soldiers verstoppertje (or: soldaatje) spelen; ~ *by* ear op het gehoor spelen; [fig] op zijn gevoel afgaan **2** werken; spuiten [fountain] **3** zich vermaken **4** aan zet zijn [chess] **5** glinsteren; flikkeren [light] ‖ ~ *about* (or: *around*) stoeien, aanklooien; *what on earth are you* ~*ing at?* wat heeft dit allemaal te betekenen?; ~ *(up)on* s.o.'s *feelings* op iemands gevoelens werken

³play (vb) **1** spelen, bespelen; opvoeren [play]; draaien [gramophone record, CD]: ~ *back* a tape een band afspelen **2** richten; spuiten [water] **3** uitvoeren; uithalen [joke]: ~ s.o. *a* **trick** iem. een streek leveren **4** verwedden, inzetten **5** [sport] opstellen [player] ‖ ~ s.o. *along* iem. aan het lijntje houden; ~ sth. *down* iets als minder belangrijk voor-

stellen

playability speelbaarheid

play-act doen alsof, toneelspelen

playback 1 opname op tape **2** weergavetoets

playbill affiche^h [for theatre performance]

playboy playboy

playdate speelafspraakje^h

player speler

playful speels, vrolijk

playgoer schouwburgbezoeker

playground speelplaats

playgroup peuterklasje^h

playhouse 1 schouwburg **2** poppenhuis^h

playing field 1 speelveld^h, sportveld^h: [econ] *level* ~ gelijk speelveld **2** speelweide

playmate 1 speelkameraad **2** pin-up

¹play off (vb) de beslissingsmatch spelen

²play off (vb) uitspelen: *he played his parents off (against each other)* hij speelde zijn ouders tegen elkaar uit

play-off beslissingsmatch

play out 1 beëindigen [game; also fig]: ~ *time* op veilig spelen, geen risico's nemen **2** helemaal uitspelen **3** uitbeelden ‖ *played out* afgedaan, uitgeput

playpen box [for small children]

playtime speelkwartier^h

play up 1 last bezorgen: *my leg is playing up again* ik heb weer last van mijn been **2** benadrukken ‖ ~ *to* s.o. iem. vleien, iem. naar de mond praten

playwright toneelschrijver

PLC *Public Limited Company* nv, naamloze vennootschap

plea 1 smeekbede **2** verweer^h, pleidooi^h

plea bargaining [esp Am] het bepleiten van strafvermindering in ruil voor schuldbekentenis

¹plead (vb) **1** pleiten, zich verdedigen: ~ *guilty* (or: *not guilty*) schuld bekennen (or: ontkennen) **2** smeken, dringend verzoeken: ~ *with* s.o. *for* sth. (or: *to do* sth.) iem. dringend verzoeken iets te doen

²plead (vb) **1** bepleiten **2** aanvoeren [as defence, apology]; zich beroepen op: ~ *ignorance* onwetendheid voorwenden

pleading pleidooi^h; betoog^h

pleasant 1 aangenaam: ~ *room* prettige kamer **2** aardig, sympathiek **3** mooi [weather]

pleasantry grapje^h, aardigheidje^h: *exchange pleasantries* beleefdheden uitwisselen

¹please (vb) **1** naar de zin maken, tevredenstellen **2** wensen: *do as you* ~*!* doe zoals je wilt!; ~ *yourself!* ga je gang!

²please (int) **1** alstublieft: *may I come in,* ~? mag ik alstublieft binnenkomen? **2** alstublieft, wees zo goed: *do come in,* ~*!* komt u toch binnen, alstublieft! **3** graag (dank u): '*A*

beer?' 'Yes, ~' 'Een biertje?' 'Ja, graag'
pleased tevreden, blij: *he was pleased as
Punch* hij was de koning te rijk
pleasing 1 aangenaam, innemend **2** bevredigend
pleasure genoegen^h, plezier^h: *take great ~
in sth.* plezier hebben in iets; *with ~* met genoegen, graag
¹**pleat** (n) platte plooi, vouw
²**pleat** (vb) plooien: *~ed skirt* plooirok
¹**plebeian** (n) proleet
²**plebeian** (adj) proleterig, onbeschaafd
¹**pledge** (n) **1** pand^h, onderpand^h **2** plechtige belofte, gelofte
²**pledge** (vb) **1** verpanden, belenen **2** een
toost uitbrengen op, toosten op **3** plechtig
beloven, (ver)binden: *~ allegiance to* trouw
zweren aan; *~ o.s.* zich (op erewoord) verbinden
plenary 1 volkomen, volledig: *with ~ powers* met volmacht(en) **2** plenair, voltallig: *~
assembly* (or: *session*) plenaire vergadering
(*or:* zitting)
plentiful overvloedig
¹**plenty** (n) overvloed ‖ *he has ~ going for him*
alles loopt hem mee
²**plenty** (adj) overvloedig, genoeg
³**plenty** (adv) ruimschoots
pliable buigzaam, plooibaar; [fig] gedwee
pliant buigzaam, soepel; [fig] gedwee
pliers buigtang, combinatietang: *a pair of ~*
een buigtang
plight (benarde) toestand: *a sorry* (or:
hopeless) *~* een hopeloze toestand
plimsoll gymschoen, gympie^h
¹**plod** (vb) ploeteren, zwoegen: *~ away at
one's work all night* de hele nacht door zwoegen
²**plod** (vb) afsjokken: *~ one's way* zich voortslepen
plodding moeizaam
¹**plop** (n) plons, floep; plof [in water]
²**plop** (vb) met een plons (doen) neervallen,
(laten) plonzen
³**plop** (adv) met een plons
¹**plot** (n) **1** stuk^h grond, perceel^h **2** intrige;
plot [of play, novel]; complot^h **3** [Am] plattegrond, kaart, diagram^h
²**plot** (vb) samenzweren, plannen smeden
³**plot** (vb) **1** in kaart brengen, intekenen; uitzetten [graph, diagram] **2** (also + out) in
percelen indelen [land] **3** beramen; smeden
[conspiracy]
¹**plough** (n) ploeg
²**plough** (vb) ploegen; [fig] ploeteren;
zwoegen: *~ through the snow* zich door de
sneeuw heen worstelen
³**plough** (vb) (om)ploegen: *~ one's way
through sth.* zich (moeizaam) een weg banen
door iets ‖ *~ back profits into equipment*
winsten in apparatuur (her)investeren

plow [Am] ploeg
ploy truc(je^h), list
PLS [inform] *please* a.u.b.
¹**pluck** (n) **1** moed, durf, lef^h **2** het plukken
[of chicken etc]
²**pluck** (vb) **1** (+ at) rukken (aan), trekken
(aan) **2** tokkelen
³**pluck** (vb) **1** plukken [chicken etc; also
flowers]; trekken **2** tokkelen op
plucky dapper, moedig
¹**plug** (n) **1** stop, prop, pen **2** stekker
3 pruim, pluk tabak **4** aanbeveling, reclame,
spot; gunstige publiciteit [on radio, TV] ‖ *pull
the ~ on sth.* iets niet laten doorgaan, een
eind maken aan iets
²**plug** (vb) **1** (also + up) (op)vullen, dichtstoppen **2** neerknallen, neerschieten, beschieten
3 pluggen, reclame maken voor; populair
maken [on radio, TV]; voortdurend draaien
[gramophone records] ‖ *~ in* aansluiten, de
stekker insteken
plughole afvoer, gootsteengat^h
plug-in 1 elektrisch toestel^h **2** [comp] plug-
in **3** stekkerauto [car]
plum 1 pruim **2** pruimenboom **3** donker-
rood^h, donkerpaars^h **4** iets heel goeds, iets
begerenswaardigs, het neusje van de zalm
plumage veren(kleed^h) [of bird]
¹**plumb** (n) (loodje^h van) schietlood^h, pas-
lood^h: *off* (or: *out*) *of ~* niet loodrecht, niet in
het lood
²**plumb** (adj) **1** loodrecht **2** [Am] uiterst: *~
nonsense* je reinste onzin
³**plumb** (vb) **1** loden, peilen met dieplood,
meten met schietlood **2** verticaal zetten,
loodrecht maken **3** (trachten te) doorgronden, peilen
⁴**plumb** (adv) **1** loodrecht, precies in het
lood: *~ in the middle* precies in het midden
2 [Am] volkomen
plumber loodgieter, gas- en waterfitter
plumbing loodgieterswerk^h, (het aanleggen van een) systeem van afvoerbuizen
plumb line loodlijn
plumcake rozijnencake, krentencake
plume 1 pluim, (sier)veer, vederbos
2 pluim, sliert, wolkje^h: *a ~ of smoke* een
rookpluim
¹**plummet** (n) (loodje^h van) loodlijn, (ge-
wicht^h van) dieplood^h, schietlood^h
²**plummet** (vb) (also + down) pijlsnel vallen,
scherp dalen, instorten, neerstorten: *prices
~ed* de prijzen kelderden
plummy 1 (zeer) goed, begerenswaardig:
a ~ job een vet baantje **2** vol [of voice]; te
vol, geaffecteerd
plump stevig [oft euph]; rond, mollig
¹**plump down** (vb) neerploffen, neervallen,
neerzakken
²**plump down** (vb) (plotseling) neergooien,
neerploffen, neerkwakken, laten vallen

¹**plunder** (n) **1** plundering, roof, beroving **2** buit

²**plunder** (vb) (be)stelen, (be)roven, plunderen

¹**plunge** (n) duik, sprong ‖ *take the* ~ de knoop doorhakken, de sprong wagen

²**plunge** (vb) **1** zich werpen, duiken, zich storten **2** (plotseling) neergaan, dalen, steil aflopen **3** (+ into) binnenvallen

³**plunge** (vb) werpen, (onder)dompelen, storten: *he was ~d into grief* hij werd door verdriet overmand

¹**plunk** (vb) neerploffen, luidruchtig (laten) vallen: ~ *down* neersmijten, neergooien

²**plunk** (adv) **1** met een plof **2** precies, juist: ~ *in the middle* precies in het midden

¹**plural** (n) meervoudᵑ, meervoudsvorm

²**plural** (adj) meervoudig, meervouds-

¹**plus** (n) **1** plus⁺ᵑ, plustekenᵑ **2** pluspuntᵑ, voordeelᵑ: *that is a big* ~ dat is een groot voordeel; *on the* ~ *side, we did earn some money* aan de andere kant hebben we wel wat geld verdiend

²**plus** (adj) **1** [maths] plus, groter dan nul **2** [elec] plus, positief **3** ten minste, minimaal, meer (ouder) dan: *she has got beauty* ~ ze is meer dan knap; *you have to be twelve* ~ *for this* hier moet je twaalf of ouder voor zijn

³**plus** (prep) plus, (vermeerderd) met, en, boven nul: *he paid back the loan* ~ *interest* hij betaalde de lening terug met de rente; ~ *six (degrees centigrade)* zes graden boven nul

¹**plush** (n) plucheᵑ

²**plush** (adj) **1** pluchen, van pluche **2** sjiek, luxueus

plus-one [inform] gast

plus sign plus⁺ᵑ, plustekenᵑ, het symbool +

plus-size: ~ *dress* jurk in een grote maat; ~ *women* vrouwen met een maatje meer

¹**ply** (n) **1** [often in compounds] laag [of wood or double material]; velᵑ [of thin wood]: *three-~ wood* triplex⁺ᵑ **2** streng, draad [of rope, wool]

²**ply** (vb) (+ between) een bepaalde route regelmatig afleggen [of bus, ship etc]; pendelen (tussen), geregeld heen en weer rijden (varen) (tussen) ‖ ~ *for hire* passagiers opzoeken [of taxi]

³**ply** (vb) geregeld bevaren, pendelen over

ply with (voortdurend) volstoppen met [food, drink]; (doorlopend) voorzien van ‖ *they plied the MP with questions* ze bestookten het kamerlid met vragen

plywood triplex⁺ᵑ, multiplex⁺ᵑ

p.m. *post meridiem* nm., 's middags

PM *Prime Minister* MP, minister-president

pneumatic pneumatisch, lucht(druk)-: ~ *drill* lucht(druk)boor

pneumonia longontsteking

po po

¹**poach** (vb) stropen, illegaal vissen (jagen): ~

on s.o.'s preserve(s) zich op andermans gebied begeven; [fig] aan iemands bezit (*or:* zaken/werk) komen

²**poach** (vb) **1** pocheren [egg, fish] **2** stropen [game, fish] **3** [sport] afpakken [ball]

PO Box *Post Office Box* postbus

¹**pocket** (n) **1** zak **2** (opberg)vakᵑ, voorvakjeᵑ, map **3** financiële middelen, portemonnee, inkomenᵑ **4** ertsader, olieader **5** klein afgesloten gebiedᵑ; [mil] haard **6** zakformaatᵑ ‖ *have s.o. in one's* ~ iem. volledig in zijn macht hebben; *have sth. in one's* ~ ergens (bijna) in geslaagd zijn; *I was twenty dollars out of* ~ ik ben twintig dollar kwijtgeraakt

²**pocket** (vb) **1** in zijn zak steken, in eigen zak steken **2** opstrijken; (op oneerlijke wijze) ontvangen [money]

pocketbook 1 zakboekjeᵑ, notitieboekjeᵑ **2** portefeuille **3** [Am] pocket(boekᵑ), paperback **4** [Am] (dames)handtas

pocket-dial [telecom] broekzakbellen

pocketful zak vol [also fig]

pocket money zakgeldᵑ

pockmark 1 pokput **2** put, gatᵑ, holte

pockmarked 1 pokdalig **2** vol gaten, met kuilen of holen

pod peul(enschil), (peul)dop, huls

podgy rond, klein en dik, propperig

podium podiumᵑ, (voor)toneelᵑ

poem gedichtᵑ, versᵑ

poet dichter

poetess dichteres

poetic(al) dichterlijk, poëtisch: *poetic licence* dichterlijke vrijheid

poetry poëzie, dichtkunst

poignancy 1 scherpheid **2** ontroering, gevoeligheid

poignant 1 scherp [of taste, emotions]; schrijnend **2** aangrijpend, ontroerend, gevoelig

¹**point** (n) **1** puntᵑ, stip, plek, decimaalteken, kommaᵑ: *in English a decimal* ~ *is used to indicate a fraction: 8.5* in het Engels wordt een decimaalpunt gebruikt om een breuk aan te geven: 8.5 **2** (waarderings)puntᵑ, cijferᵑ: *be beaten on ~s* op punten verliezen **3** (puntig) uiteindeᵑ, (land)punt; tak [antlers]; uitsteekselᵑ **4** puntᵑ, kwestie: *the main* ~ de hoofdzaak **5** karakteristiek, eigenschap: *that's his strong* ~ dat is zijn sterke kant **6** zin, bedoeling, effectᵑ: *get (or: see) the* ~ *of sth.* iets snappen **7** (kompas)streek **8** puntᵑ [exact location, time etc]; kern, essentie: *the* ~ *of the joke* de clou van de grap; ~ *of view* gezichtspuntᵑ, standpuntᵑ; *come (or: get) to the* ~ ter zake komen; *you have a* ~ *there* daar heb je gelijk in, daar zit iets in; *I always make a* ~ *of being in time* ik zorg er altijd voor op tijd te zijn; *I take your ~, ~ taken* ik begrijp wat je bedoelt; *that's beside the* ~ dat

heeft er niets mee te maken, dat staat erbuiten; *that's the whole* ~ daar gaat het nou juist om, dat is de makke; *on the* ~ *of* op het punt van; *that's (not) to the* ~ dat is (niet) relevant; *up to a (certain)* ~ tot op zekere hoogte **9** (-s) [railways] wissel+h **10** contactpunth, stopcontacth ‖ *in* ~ *of fact* a) in werkelijkheid; **b)** bovendien, zelfs; *stretch a* ~ niet al te nauw kijken, van de regel afwijken

²**point** (vb) **1** (+ at, towards) gericht zijn (op), aandachtig zijn (op) **2** (+ at, to) wijzen (naar), bewijzen: ~ *to sth.* ergens naar wijzen, iets suggereren, iets bewijzen

³**point** (vb) **1** scherp maken **2** (+ at, towards) richten (op), (aan)wijzen: ~ *out a mistake* een fout aanwijzen, een fout onder de aandacht brengen **3** voegen [brickwork]

point-blank 1 van vlakbij, korte afstands-, regelrecht: *fire* ~ *at s.o.* van dichtbij op iem. schieten **2** rechtstreeks, (te) direct, bot: *a* ~ *refusal* een botte weigering

pointed 1 puntig, puntvormig **2** scherp, venijnig: *a* ~ *answer* een bits antwoord **3** nadrukkelijk, duidelijk, opvallend

pointer 1 wijzer [on scales etc] **2** aanwijsstok **3** aanwijzing, suggestie, adviesh **4** pointer, staande hond

pointless zinloos, onnodig, onbelangrijk

point out 1 wijzen naar: ~ *sth. to s.o.* iem. op iets attenderen **2** naar voren brengen, in het midden ter sprake brengen: ~ *s.o.'s responsibilities* iem. zijn plichten voorhouden

poise evenwichth; [fig] zelfverzekerdheid; zelfvertrouwenh

poised 1 evenwichtig, stabiel, verstandig **2** zwevend; [fig] in onzekerheid; balancerend: *he was* ~ *between life and death* hij zweefde tussen leven en dood **3** stil (in de lucht hangend) **4** klaar, gereed: *be* ~ *for victory* op het punt staan om te winnen

¹**poison** (n) vergifh, gifh; [fig] schadelijke invloed

²**poison** (vb) **1** vergiftigen **2** bederven [atmosphere, mentality]; verzieken: *their good relationship was* ~*ed by jealousy* hun goede verhouding werd door jaloezie verpest

¹**poke** (n) **1** por, prik, duw **2** vuistslag

²**poke** (vb) **1** (+ out, through) tevoorschijn komen, uitsteken **2** (+ about) (rond)lummelen **3** (+ about) zoeken, snuffelen, (rond)neuzen, zich bemoeien met iets

³**poke** (vb) **1** porren, prikken, stoten: ~ *one's nose into sth.* zijn neus ergens insteken **2** (op)poken; (op)porren [fire]

¹**poker** (n) kachelpook, pook

²**poker** (n) pokerh [cards]

poker face pokergezichth, pokerfaceh

poky benauwd, klein

Poland Polen

polar pool-, van de poolstreken: ~ *bear* ijsbeer

polarize 1 [physics] polariseren [also fig]; in tweeën splitsen **2** sturen, richten: *society today is* ~*d towards material prosperity* de maatschappij is tegenwoordig gericht op materiële welvaart

pole 1 pool; [fig] tegenpool **2** paal, mast, stok, vaarboom ‖ *drive s.o. up the* ~ iem. razend maken; *be* ~*s apart* onverzoenlijk zijn

Pole Pool(se), iem. van Poolse afkomst

polecat 1 bunzing [in Europe] **2** stinkdierh; skunk [in America]

polemic woordenstrijd, pennenstrijd, twist

pole star Poolster

pole vault polsstoksprong, het polsstok(hoog)springen

¹**police** (n) politie, politiekorpsh, politieapparaath

²**police** (vb) **1** onder politiebewaking stellen **2** controleren, toezicht uitoefenen op

police constable [form] politieman, politievrouw

police force politie, politiekorpsh

policeman politieagent ‖ *sleeping* ~ verkeersdrempel

police station politiebureauh

policy 1 beleidh, gedragslijn, politiek **2** polis, verzekeringspolis **3** tactiek, verstandh

policy day heidedag, beleidsdag

policymaker beleidsmaker

polio polio, kinderverlamming

¹**polish** (n) **1** poetsmiddelh **2** glans, glimmend oppervlakh **3** beschaving, verfijning

²**polish** (vb) gaan glanzen, glanzend worden

³**polish** (vb) (also + up) (op)poetsen; polijsten [also fig]; bijschaven: ~ *up his French* zijn Frans oppoetsen; *a* ~*ed performance* een perfecte voorstelling

Polish Pools

polish off wegwerken, afraffelen

polite 1 beleefd, goed gemanierd **2** verfijnd, elegant

politic diplomatiek, verstandig: *the body* ~ de staat, het staatslichaam

political 1 politiek, staatkundig: ~ *prisoner* politieke gevangene **2** overheids-, rijks-, staats- **3** politiek geëngageerd: *he is not a very* ~ *person* hij is niet zo erg in politiek geïnteresseerd

politician (partij)politicus

politics 1 politiek **2** politieke wetenschappen, politicologie **3** politieke overtuiging

¹**poll** (n) **1** stemming, het stemmen: *go to the* ~*s* stemmen **2** aantal (uitgebrachte) stemmen, opkomst **3** opiniepeiling **4** (-s) stembureauh

²**poll** (vb) zijn stem uitbrengen

³**poll** (vb) **1** krijgen; behalen [(preference) vote]: *he* ~*ed thirty per cent of the votes* hij kreeg dertig procent van de stemmen **2** ondervragen, een opiniepeiling houden

pollard 1 geknotte boom **2** [cattle breed-

ing] hoornloos dier[h]
pollen stuifmeel[h]
pollination bestuiving
polling booth stemhokje[h]
pollster enquêteur
poll tax personele belasting
pollute 1 vervuilen, verontreinigen **2** verderven [fig]; verpesten [atmosphere]
pollution 1 vervuiling, (milieu)verontreiniging **2** bederf[h], verderf[h]
polo [sport] polo[h]
poltergeist klopgeest
poly *polytechnic* school voor hoger beroepsonderwijs
polyamory polyamorie
poly bag [inform] diepvrieszak, hersluitbare plastic zak
polygamy veelwijverij
polygon veelhoek, polygoon
polysexual polyseksueel
polysyllabic veellettergrepig
polytechnic [dated] hogeschool
polythene polyethyleen[h], plastic[h]: ~ *bag* plastic tasje
pomegranate granaatappel(boom)
pomp prachtvertoon[h], praal: ~ *and circumstance* pracht en praal
pomposity gewichtigdoenerij, hoogdravendheid
pompous gewichtig, hoogdravend
ponce 1 pooier, souteneur **2** verwijfd type[h]
pond vijver
¹ponder (vb) (+ on, over) nadenken (over), piekeren (over)
²ponder (vb) overdenken, overwegen
ponderous 1 zwaar, massief, log **2** zwaar op de hand, moeizaam, langdradig
¹pong (n) stank, ruft
²pong (vb) stinken, ruften
pontiff paus
pontifical 1 pauselijk **2** [fig] autoritair, plechtig
pontoon 1 ponton, brugschip[h] **2** eenentwintigen[h]
pony 1 pony, ponypaardje[h] **2** renpaard[h] **3** [Am] klein model[h]
ponytail paardenstaart
¹poo (n) [inform] poep
²poo (vb) [inform] poepen
poodle poedel
poof(ter) [inform; offensive] **1** nicht, flikker, poot **2** slappeling, zijig ventje[h]
¹pool (n) **1** poel, plas **2** (zwem)bassin[h], zwembad[h] **3** pot [at games of chance]; (gezamenlijke) inzet **4** (the pools) (voetbal)toto, voetbalpool
²pool (n) poolbiljart
³pool (vb) samenvoegen, bij elkaar leggen; verenigen [money, ideas, means]
pool room biljartgelegenheid, biljartlokaal[h], goklokaal[h]

poop achtersteven, achterdek[h]
pooped uitgeput, vermoeid: ~ *out* uitgeteld, uitgeput
poop scoop hondenpoepschepje[h]
poor 1 arm **2** slecht, schraal, matig: ~ *results* slechte resultaten **3** armzalig, bedroevend: *cut a* ~ *figure* een armzalig figuur slaan **4** zielig, ongelukkig: ~ *fellow!* arme kerel!
poorhouse armenhuis[h]
¹poorly (adj) niet lekker, ziek ‖ ~ *off* a) in slechte doen; b) slecht voorzien
²poorly (adv) **1** arm, armoedig **2** slecht, matig, onvoldoende: *think* ~ *of* geen hoge pet ophebben van
¹pop (n) **1** knal, plof **2** pop(muziek): *top of the* ~*s* (tophit) nummer één **3** pap, pa, papa **4** prik(limonade), frisdrank
²pop (vb) **1** knallen, klappen, ploffen **2** plotseling, onverwacht bewegen, snel komen, snel gaan: ~ *in* even langsgaan; ~ *off* a) opstappen; b) het hoekje omgaan [die]; ~ *open* uitpuilen [of eyes]; ~ *out* a) tevoorschijn schieten; b) uitpuilen; ~ *up* opduiken, (weer) boven water komen, omhoog komen [of illustrations, greetings cards etc] **3** (neer)schieten, (af)vuren: ~ *off* a) afschieten; b) afgeschoten worden **4** laten knallen, laten klappen **5** snel zetten, leggen, brengen, steken: *I'll just* ~ *this letter into the post* ik gooi deze brief even op de bus **6** plotseling stellen; afvuren [questions] **7** slikken, spuiten [drugs, pills]
popcorn popcorn[h], gepofte maïs
pope paus
pop-eyed met uitpuilende ogen, met grote ogen, verbaasd
popgun speelgoedpistooltje[h]
poplar populier, populierenhout[h]
popper drukknoop(je[h])
poppet schatje[h]
poppy papaver, klaproos
poppycock klets(praat)
Poppy Day [in Great Britain] herdenkingsdag voor de gevallenen
poppy seed maanzaad[h]
popsy liefje[h], schatje[h]
populace (the) (gewone) volk[h], massa
popular 1 geliefd, populair, gezien: ~ *with* geliefd bij **2** algemeen, veel verbreid **3** volks-, van, voor het volk: ~ *belief* volksgeloof[h]; ~ *front* volksfront[h]; *the* ~ *vote* de volksstemming; de stem van het volk; [Am] het totaal uitgebrachte stemmen; [Am] *win the* ~ *vote* (in absolute zin) de meeste kiezers achter zich krijgen
popularity populariteit, geliefdheid
popularization popularisering
popularly 1 geliefd **2** algemeen, gewoon(lijk): ~ *known as* in de wandeling bekend als
populate bevolken, bewonen: *densely* ~*d* dichtbevolkt

population 1 bevolking, inwoners, bewoners **2** bevolkingsdichtheid

populist populist; opportunist

pop-up pop-upscherm[h]

pop-up book uitklapboek[h]

pop-up menu pop-upmenu[h]

pop-up toaster broodrooster[+h]

porcelain porselein[h]

porch 1 portaal[h], portiek[+h] **2** [Am] veranda

porcupine stekelvarken[h]

pore porie

pore over zich verdiepen in, aandachtig bestuderen

pork varkensvlees[h]

porn *pornography* porno

pornographic pornografisch

pornography porno(grafie)

porous poreus, waterdoorlatend

porpoise 1 bruinvis **2** dolfijn

porridge 1 (havermout)pap **2** bajes: *do ~* in de bak zitten

port 1 haven, havenstad; [fig] veilige haven; toevluchtsoord[h] **2** bakboord[h], links[h] **3** [comp] poort: *serial ~* seriële poort **4** port(wijn) || *any ~ in a storm* nood breekt wet(ten)

portable 1 draagbaar **2** overdraagbaar: *~ pension* meeneempensioen

portal (ingangs)poort, portaal[h], ingang

portent voorteken[h], voorbode || *a matter of great ~* een gewichtige zaak

porter 1 kruier, sjouwer, drager **2** portier[h]

portfolio portefeuille

porthole patrijspoort

portico portiek[+h], zuilengang

portion gedeelte[h], (aan)deel[h], portie

portion out verdelen, uitdelen

portly [hum] gezet, stevig

portmanteau word porte-manteauwoord[h], samentrekking

portrait portret[h], foto; schildering [also in words]

portray portretteren, (af)schilderen, beschrijven

portrayal portrettering, afbeelding, beschrijving

Portugal Portugal

[1]**Portuguese** (n) Portugees, Portugese

[2]**Portuguese** (adj) Portugees

[1]**pose** (n) houding, vertoon[h]

[2]**pose** (vb) poseren, doen alsof, een pose aannemen: *~ as* zich voordoen als, zich uitgeven voor

[3]**pose** (vb) **1** stellen, voorleggen: *~ a question* een vraag stellen **2** vormen: *~ a threat* (or: *problem*) een bedreiging (or: probleem) vormen

poser moeilijke vraag, lastig vraagstuk[h]

[1]**posh** (adj) chic, modieus

[2]**posh** (adv) bekakt, kakkineus: *talk ~* bekakt

position 1 positie, plaats(ing), ligging, situatie: *be in a ~ to do sth.* in staat zijn iets te doen **2** positie, juiste plaats **3** standpunt[h], houding, mening: *define one's ~* zijn standpunt bepalen **4** rang, (maatschappelijke) positie, stand **5** betrekking, baan

[1]**positive** (n) **1** positief[h] [of photo] **2** positief getal[h]

[2]**positive** (adj) **1** positief **2** duidelijk, nadrukkelijk: *a ~ assertion* een uitspraak die niets aan duidelijkheid te wensen overlaat **3** overtuigd, absoluut zeker: *'Are you sure?'* *'Positive'* 'Weet je het zeker?' 'Absoluut' **4** echt, volslagen, compleet: *a ~ nuisance* een ware plaag **5** zelfbewust, (te) zelfverzekerd **6** wezenlijk, (duidelijk) waarneembaar: *a ~ change for the better* een wezenlijke verbetering || *~ sign* plusteken[h]

posse troep, (politie)macht; groep [with common purpose]

possess 1 bezitten, hebben, beschikken (over) **2** beheersen, meester zijn van, zich meester maken van: *what could have ~ed him?* wat kan hem toch bezield hebben?

possessed 1 bezeten, geobsedeerd: *like one ~* als een bezetene; *~ with rage* buiten zichzelf van woede **2** [form] bezittend: *be ~ of* bezitten

possession 1 bezit[h], eigendom[h], bezitting: *take ~ of* in bezit nemen, betrekken **2** (bal)bezit[h] **3** bezetenheid

possessive 1 bezitterig, hebberig **2** dominerend, alle aandacht opeisend || *~ (pronoun)* bezittelijk voornaamwoord

possessor eigenaar, bezitter

possibility mogelijkheid, kans, vooruitzicht[h]: *there is no ~ of his coming* het is uitgesloten dat hij komt

possible 1 mogelijk, denkbaar, eventueel: *do everything ~* al het mogelijke doen; *if ~* zo mogelijk **2** acceptabel, aanvaardbaar, redelijk

possibly 1 mogelijk, denkbaar, eventueel: *I cannot ~ come* ik kan onmogelijk komen **2** misschien, mogelijk(erwijs), wellicht: *'Are you coming too?' 'Possibly'* 'Ga jij ook mee?' 'Misschien'

possum opossum, buideldrat || *play ~* doen alsof je slaapt

[1]**post** (n) **1** paal, stijl, post **2** [equestrian sports] startpaal, finishpaal, vertrekpunt[h], eindpunt[h] **3** (doel)paal **4** post(bestelling), postkantoor[h], brievenbus: *by return of ~* per kerende post, per omgaande **5** post, (stand)plaats, (leger)kamp[h]: *be at one's ~* op zijn post zijn **6** betrekking, baan, ambt[h]

[2]**post** (vb) **1** (also + up) aanplakken, beplakken **2** posteren, plaatsen, uitzetten **3** (over)plaatsen, stationeren, aanstellen tot **4** (also + off) posten, op de post doen, (ver)sturen **5** op de hoogte brengen, inlichten: *keep s.o. ~ed* iem. op de hoogte houden

postage porto[+h]

postage stamp 1 postzegel **2** [inform] iets kleins; vierkante millimeter, postzegel
postcard briefkaart, ansichtkaart
postdate postdateren, een latere datum geven
postdoc postdoc
poster 1 affiche[h], aanplakbiljet[h], poster **2** [on Internet forum] poster
posterboy [fig] schoolvoorbeeld[h], uithangbord[h], model[h]: *he is the ~ for a healthy lifestyle* hij is het schoolvoorbeeld van iem. die gezond leeft
poster colour plakkaatverf, gouache
postergirl [fig] schoolvoorbeeld[h], uithangbord[h], model[h]: *she is the ~ for high-level sports* zij is het schoolvoorbeeld van een topsporter
posterior later, volgend: *~ to* komend na, volgend op, later dan
posterity nageslacht[h]
¹**postgraduate** (n) afgestudeerde [continues studies at university]; masterstudent
²**postgraduate** (adj) postuniversitair, na de universitaire opleiding komend, postdoctoraal
posthumous postuum, (komend/verschijnend) na de dood
posting stationering, (over)plaatsing
post-it (note) memobriefje[h], geeltje[h]
postman postbode
postmark poststempel[h], postmerk[h]
post-mortem 1 lijkschouwing, sectie **2** nabespreking [esp to find out what went wrong]
post office 1 postkantoor[h] **2** post, posterijen
postpaid franco, port betaald
postpone (+ until, to) uitstellen (tot), opschorten (tot)
postscript postscriptum[h]; naschrift[h] [in letter]
post-traumatic posttraumatisch: *~ stress disorder* posttraumatisch stresssyndroom
post-truth [pol] [roughly] feitenvrij
postulate (zonder bewijs) als waar aannemen, vooronderstellen
¹**posture** (n) **1** (lichaams)houding, postuur[h], pose **2** houding, standpunt[h]
²**posture** (vb) **1** poseren, een gemaakte houding aannemen **2** (+ as) zich uitgeven (voor)
postwar naoorlogs
posy boeket(je)[h]
¹**pot** (n) **1** pot, (nacht)po, potvormig voorwerp[h] (van aardewerk), (gemeenschappelijke) pot, gezamenlijk (gespaard) bedrag[h] **2** hoop [money]; bom **3** hasj(iesj), marihuana **4** aardewerk[h] ‖ *keep* the *~ boiling* de kost verdienen, het zaakje draaiende houden; *go (all) to ~* op de fles gaan, in de vernieling zijn
²**pot** (vb) schieten: *~ at* (zonder mikken) schieten op

³**pot** (vb) **1** (+ up) potten, in een bloempot planten **2** in de zak stoten [billiard ball] **3** op het potje zetten [child]
potato aardappel(plant): *mashed ~(es)* aardappelpuree
potato crisp chips
pot-belly dikke buik, buikje[h], dikzak
potency invloed, kracht
potent 1 krachtig, sterk, effectief **2** (seksueel) potent **3** machtig, invloedrijk
potentate absoluut heerser; [fig] iem. die zich zeer laat gelden
¹**potential** (n) mogelijkheid: *he hasn't realized his full ~ yet* hij heeft de grens van zijn kunnen nog niet bereikt
²**potential** (adj) potentieel, mogelijk, in aanleg aanwezig
pot farm hennepkwekerij, wietplantage
pothole 1 gat[h], put; kuil [in road surface] **2** grot
potion drankje[h] [medicine, magic potion, poison]
potluck: [inform] *take ~* eten wat de pot schaft
pot-roast smoren, stoven, braden
potshot schot[h] op goed geluk af, schot[h] in het wilde weg; [fig] schot[h] in het duister
potted 1 pot-: *~ plant* kamerplant, potplant **2** ingemaakt, in een pot bewaard **3** (erg) kort samengevat
¹**potter** (n) pottenbakker
²**potter** (vb) **1** (+ about) rondscharrelen, rondslenteren, aanrommelen, prutsen **2** (+ away) je tijd verdoen, rondlummelen, lanterfanten
pottery 1 pottenbakkerij **2** aardewerk[h], keramiek
¹**potty** (n) (kinder)po, potje[h]
²**potty** (adj) **1** knetter, niet goed snik, dwaas: *~ about* helemaal wég van **2** onbenullig, pietluttig
potty mouth: [inform] *the child has a ~* het kind slaat smerige taal uit
potty trained zindelijk
POTUS [inform] *President of the United States* de president
pouch 1 zak(je[h]) **2** (zakvormige) huidplooi, buidel, wangzak: *she had ~es under her eyes* zij had wallen onder haar ogen
pouf 1 poef, zitkussen[h] **2** [inform] flikker, homo
poulterer poelier
poultry gevogelte[h], pluimvee[h]
¹**pounce** (n) het stoten [of bird of prey]; het zich plotseling (neer)storten; [fig] plotselinge aanval: *make a ~ at* (or: *on*) zich storten op
²**pounce** (vb) **1** zich naar beneden storten; (op)springen [to seize sth.] **2** plotseling aanvallen; [fig] kritiek uitbrengen
pounce (up)on 1 (weg)graaien, inpikken, begerig grijpen **2** plotseling aanvallen; zich

storten op [also fig]

¹pound (n) **1** pond^h [of weight, currency] **2** depot^h; [for seized goods, towed-away cars etc] asiel^h; omheinde ruimte || *have one's ~ of flesh* het volle pond krijgen

²pound (vb) **1** hard (toe)slaan, flinke klappen uitdelen **2** (herhaaldelijk) zwaar bombarderen, een spervuur aanleggen **3** bonzen [of heart]

³pound (vb) **1** (fijn)stampen, verpulveren **2** beuken op, stompen op

pounding 1 gedreun^h, gebons^h **2** [inform] afstraffing, pak^h slaag

pound note bankbiljet^h van één pond

pound sign 1 pondteken^h **2** [Am] hekje^h [hash]

pound sterling [form] pond sterling^h

pound symbol pondteken^h; [also] hekje^h

¹pour (vb) **1** stromen; (rijkelijk) vloeien [also fig]: *the money kept ~ing in* het geld bleef binnenstromen **2** stortregenen, gieten **3** (thee/koffie) inschenken

²pour (vb) (uit)gieten, doen (neer)stromen

pout (de lippen) tuiten, pruilen (over)

poverty armoede, behoeftigheid

poverty-stricken straatarm

powder 1 poeder^{+h}, (kool)stof^h **2** talkpoeder^h, gezichtspoeder^h **3** (bus)kruit^h

powdered 1 gepoederd, met poeder bedekt **2** in poedervorm (gemaakt/gedroogd): *~ milk* melkpoeder^{+h}; *~ sugar* poedersuiker

powder keg kruitvat^h [also fig]; tijdbom, explosieve situatie

powder puff poederdonsje^h, poederkwastje^h

powder room [euph] damestoilet^h

powdery 1 poederachtig, kruimelig, brokkelig **2** (als) met poeder bedekt, gepoederd

power 1 macht, vermogen^h, mogelijkheid **2** kracht, sterkte **3** invloed, macht, controle: *come in* (or: *into*) *~* aan het bewind komen **4** (vol)macht, recht^h, bevoegdheid: *~ of attorney* volmacht **5** invloedrijk iem. (iets), mogendheid, autoriteit: *the Great Powers* de grote mogendheden **6** (-s) (boze) macht(en), (hemelse) kracht(en) **7** (drijf)kracht, (elektrische) energie, stroom: *electric ~* elektrische stroom **8** macht: *to the ~ (of)* tot de ... macht **9** grote hoeveelheid, groot aantal^h, hoop: *it did me a ~ of good* het heeft me ontzettend goed gedaan || *a ~ behind the throne* een man achter de schermen; *more ~ to your elbow* veel geluk, succes

power bank mobiele oplader

powerboat motorboot

power brakes rembekrachtiging

power cut stroomonderbreking, stroomuitval

powerful 1 krachtig, machtig, invloedrijk **2** effectief, met een sterke (uit)werking: *a ~ speech* een indrukwekkende toespraak

powerless machteloos, zwak

power nap hazenslaap

power-nap krachtslaapje^h

power point stopcontact^h

power station elektriciteitscentrale^h

power steering stuurbekrachtiging

powwow 1 indianenbijeenkomst **2** [inform] lange conferentie, rumoerige bespreking, overleg^h

pp 1 *pianissimo* pp **2** *pages* pp., bladzijden **3** *per pro(curationem)* p.p., bij volmacht, namens

PR *public relations* pr

practicable 1 uitvoerbaar, haalbaar **2** bruikbaar; begaanbaar [of road]

¹practical (n) practicum^h, praktijkles, praktijkexamen^h

²practical (adj) **1** praktisch, in de praktijk, handig **2** haalbaar, uitvoerbaar **3** zinnig, verstandig || *for all ~ purposes* feitelijk, alles welbeschouwd

practicality 1 praktisch aspect **2** bruikbaarheid

practically 1 bijna, praktisch, zo goed als **2** in de praktijk, praktisch gesproken

practice 1 praktijk, toepassing: *put sth. in(to) ~* iets in praktijk brengen **2** oefening, training, ervaring: *be out of ~* uit vorm zijn, het verleerd zijn **3** gewoonte, gebruik^h, normale gang van zaken: *make a ~ of sth.* ergens een gewoonte van maken **4** uitoefening, beoefening, het praktiseren; praktijk [of lawyer, doctor etc]

practise 1 praktiseren, uitoefenen, beoefenen: *~ black magic* zwarte magie bedrijven; *he ~s as a lawyer* hij werkt als advocaat **2** in de praktijk toepassen, uitvoeren **3** oefenen, instuderen, repeteren

practitioner beoefenaar, beroeps(kracht): *medical ~s* de artsen

pragmatic zakelijk, praktisch

Prague Praag

prairie prairie, grasvlakte

¹praise (n) **1** lof, het prijzen, aanbeveling **2** glorie, eer, lof || *~ be (to God)!* God zij geloofd!

²praise (vb) prijzen, vereren

praiseworthy loffelijk, prijzenswaardig

pram kinderwagen

prance 1 steigeren **2** (vrolijk) springen, huppelen, dansen: *~ about* (or: *around*) rondspringen, rondlopen

prank streek, grap

prankster [inform] grappenmaker

prat [inform] idioot, zak, eikel

¹prattle (n) kinderpraat, gebabbel^h

²prattle (vb) babbelen, kleppen, keuvelen

prawn (steur)garnaal

pray 1 bidden, (God) aanroepen **2** hopen, wensen: *we're ~ing for a peaceful day* we hopen op een rustige dag || *he is past ~ing for* hij is niet meer te redden

prayer 1 gebed^h, het bidden **2** (smeek)bede, verzoek^h || *he doesn't have a* ~ hij heeft geen schijn van kans

prayer book gebedenboek^h

preach preken; [fig] een zedenpreek houden

preacher predikant

preachy preek-, moraliserend: ~ *in tone* prekerig van toon

preamble inleiding, voorwoord^h

pre-arrange vooraf regelen, vooraf overeenkomen

precarious 1 onzeker, onbestendig: *he made a* ~ *living* hij had een ongewis inkomen **2** onveilig, gevaarlijk **3** twijfelachtig, niet op feiten gebaseerd

precaution voorzorgsmaatregel, voorzorg: *take* ~*s* voorzorgsmaatregelen treffen

precede voorgaan, vooraf (laten) gaan, de voorrang hebben: *the years preceding his marriage* de jaren voor zijn huwelijk

precedence voorrang, prioriteit, het voorgaan: *give* ~ *to* laten voorgaan, voorrang verlenen aan

precedent 1 precedent^h, vroegere beslissing waarom men zich kan beroepen: *create* (or: *establish, set*) *a* ~ een precedent scheppen; *without* ~ zonder precedent, ongekend **2** traditie, gewoonte, gebruik^h

preceding voorafgaand

precept 1 voorschrift^h, principe^h, grondregel **2** het voorschrijven

precinct 1 (-s) omsloten ruimte [around church, university]; (grond)gebied^h, terrein^h **2** stadsgebied^h: *pedestrian* ~ voetgangersgebied^h; *shopping* ~ winkelcentrum^h **3** [Am] district^h

precincts (the) buurt: *the* ~ *of Bond Street* de omgeving van Bond Street

¹precious (adj) **1** kostbaar, waardevol: ~ *metals* edele metalen **2** dierbaar: *her family is very* ~ *to her* haar familie is haar zeer dierbaar **3** gekunsteld, gemaakt **4** kostbaar, waardeloos

²precious (adv) bar: *he had* ~ *little money* hij had nauwelijks een rooie cent

precipice steile rotswand, afgrond

¹precipitate (adj) overhaast, plotseling

²precipitate (vb) **1** (neer)storten [also fig]; (neer)werpen **2** versnellen, bespoedigen

precipitous 1 (vreselijk) steil **2** als een afgrond, duizelingwekkend hoog **3** overijld; plotseling

precise nauwkeurig, precies: *at the* ~ *moment that* juist op het moment dat

precisely 1 precies: *we'll arrive at 10.30* ~ we komen precies om half elf aan **2** inderdaad, juist, precies

¹precision (n) nauwkeurigheid, juistheid

²precision (adj): ~ *bombing* precisiebombardement^h, nauwkeurig gericht bombardement

preclude uitsluiten: ~ *from* voorkomen, verhinderen, beletten

precocious vroeg(rijp), vroeg wijs

preconceived vooraf gevormd, zich vooraf voorgesteld: *a* ~ *opinion* een vooropgezette mening

preconception vooroordeel^h

precondition eerste vereiste^h, allereerste voorwaarde

precook van tevoren bereiden: ~*ed potatoes* voorgekookte aardappelen

precursor voorloper, voorganger

predation 1 plundering; roof **2** [zoology] predatie

predator roofdier^h

predatory 1 roof-: ~ *bird* roofvogel **2** plunderend: ~ *incursions* strooptochten, plundertochten **3** [depr] roofdierachtig: *a* ~ *female* een mannenverslindster

predecessor 1 voorloper, voorganger **2** voorvader

predestination voorbeschikking

predetermine vooraf bepalen, voorbeschikken: *the colour of s.o.'s eyes is* ~*d by that of his parents* de kleur van iemands ogen wordt bepaald door die van zijn ouders

predicament hachelijke situatie, kritieke toestand

predicate [linguistics] gezegde^h

predict voorspellen, als verwachting opgeven

predictable voorspelbaar, zonder verrassing, saai

prediction voorspelling

predilection voorliefde; voorkeur

predisposition neiging, vatbaarheid, aanleg

predominant overheersend, belangrijkst

predominantly hoofdzakelijk

predominate heersen, regeren, overheersen, de overhand hebben, beheersen

pre-eminent uitstekend, superieur

pre-empt 1 beslag leggen op, zich toe-eigenen, de plaats innemen van **2** overbodig maken, ontkrachten

pre-emptive preventief, voorkomend

preen 1 gladstrijken [feathers] **2** (zich) opknappen, (zich) mooi maken || *he* ~*ed himself on his intelligence* hij ging prat op zijn intelligentie

pre-exist eerder bestaan

prefab montagewoning, geprefabriceerd gebouw^h

prefabricate in onderdelen gereedmaken, volgens systeembouw maken

¹preface (n) voorwoord^h, inleiding

²preface (vb) **1** van een voorwoord voorzien, inleiden **2** leiden tot, het begin zijn van

prefect [English educ] oudere leerling als

ordehandhaver

prefer 1 (+ to) verkiezen (boven), de voorkeur geven (aan), prefereren: *she ~s tea to coffee* ze drinkt liever thee dan koffie; *he ~red to leave rather than to wait* hij wilde liever weggaan dan nog wachten **2** promoveren, bevorderen

preferable verkieslijk, te prefereren: *everything is ~ to* alles is beter dan

preference voorkeur, voorliefde: *in ~ to* liever dan

preferment bevordering, promotie

prefix voorvoegselʰ

pregnancy zwangerschap

pregnant 1 zwanger; drachtig [of animals] **2** vindingrijk, vol ideeën **3** vruchtbaar, vol **4** veelbetekenend: *a ~ silence* een veelbetekenende stilte

prehistoric prehistorisch

prehistory 1 prehistorie **2** voorgeschiedenis

prejudge veroordelen [without trail or interrogation]; vooraf beoordelen

¹prejudice (n) **1** vooroordeelʰ, vooringenomenheid: *without ~* onbevooroordeeld **2** nadeelʰ

²prejudice (vb) **1** schaden, benadelen: *~ a good cause* afbreuk doen aan een goede zaak **2** innemen, voorinnemen

prelate kerkvorst, prelaat

prelim *preliminary examination* tentamenʰ

¹preliminary (n) voorbereiding, inleiding: *the preliminaries* de voorronde(s)

²preliminary (adj) inleidend, voorbereidend

prelude 1 voorspelʰ, inleiding **2** prelude; ouverture [of opera]

premarital voorechtelijk, voordat het huwelijk gesloten is: *~ sex* seks voor het huwelijk

premature 1 te vroeg, voortijdig: *a ~ baby* een te vroeg geboren baby; *his ~ death* zijn vroegtijdige dood **2** voorbarig, overhaast

premeditated opzettelijk, beraamd: *~ murder* moord met voorbedachten rade

premeditation opzetʰ

¹premier (n) eerste minister, minister-president, premier

²premier (adj) eerste, voornaamste

premiership eredivisie

premise 1 vooronderstelling **2** (-s) huisʰ (en erf), zaak: *licensed ~s* caféʰ; *the shopkeeper lives on the ~s* de winkelier woont in het pand

premium 1 beloning, prijs **2** (verzekerings)premie **3** toeslag, extraʰ, meerprijs **4** [fig] hoge waarde: *put s.o.'s work at a ~* iemands werk hoog aanslaan

premonition voorgevoelʰ

prenatal prenataal, voor de geboorte

preoccupation 1 hoofdbezigheid, (voornaamste) zorg **2** het volledig in beslag genomen zijn

preoccupied in gedachten verzonken, volledig in beslag genomen

¹prep (n) huiswerkʰ, voorbereiding(stijd)

²prep (adj) voorbereidend: *~ school* voorbereidingsschool

preparation 1 voorbereiding: *make ~s for* voorbereidingen treffen voor **2** preparaatʰ **3** voorbereiding(stijd), huiswerkʰ, studie

¹prepare (vb) voorbereidingen treffen: *~ for the worst* zich op het ergste voorbereiden

²prepare (vb) **1** voorbereiden, gereedmaken, prepareren, bestuderen, instuderen **2** klaarmaken, (toe)bereiden

prepared 1 voorbereid, gereed **2** bereid: *be ~ to do sth.* bereid zijn iets te doen

prepay 1 vooruitbetalen **2** frankeren: *a prepaid envelope* een gefrankeerde enveloppe

preponderant overwegend, overheersend, belangrijkst

preposition voorzetselʰ

prepossess 1 inspireren **2** in beslag nemen, bezighouden **3** bevooroordeeld maken, gunstig stemmen

preposterous onredelijk, absurd

¹preppy (n) [Am; inform] (ex-)leerling van voorbereidingsschool; kakmeisjeʰ

²preppy (adj) bekakt

prerequisite eerste vereisteʰ: *a ~ of* (or: *for, to*) een noodzakelijke voorwaarde voor

¹prerogative (n) voorrechtʰ

²prerogative (adj) bevoorrecht

¹Presbyterian (n) presbyteriaan

²Presbyterian (adj) presbyteriaans

presbytery 1 priesterkoorʰ **2** (gebied bestuurd door) raad van ouderlingen [Presbyterian Church] **3** pastorie

pre-schooler peuter, kleuter, (nog) niet schoolgaand kindʰ

prescience 1 voorkennis **2** vooruitziendheid

¹prescribe (vb) **1** voorschriften geven, richtlijnen geven **2** (+ for) een advies geven (over), een remedie voorschrijven (tegen)

²prescribe (vb) **1** voorschrijven, opleggen, bevelen **2** aanbevelen: *~ a recipe for* (or: *to*) s.o. iem. een recept voorschrijven

prescription 1 voorschriftʰ [also fig] **2** receptʰ, geneesmiddelʰ

presence 1 aanwezigheid, tegenwoordigheid: *~ of mind* tegenwoordigheid van geest **2** nabijheid, omgeving: *in the ~ of* in tegenwoordigheid van **3** presentie, (indrukwekkende) verschijning, bovennatuurlijk iem. (iets) **4** persoonlijkheid

¹present (n) **1** geschenkʰ, cadeauʰ, giftʰ **2** het heden: *at ~* op dit ogenblik, tegenwoordig; *for the ~* voorlopig

²present (adj) **1** onderhavig, in kwestie: *in the ~ case* in dit geval **2** huidig, tegenwoordig **3** [linguistics] tegenwoordig: ~ *participle* onvoltooid deelwoord; ~ *tense* tegenwoordige tijd **4** tegenwoordig, aanwezig

³**present** (vb) **1** voorstellen, introduceren, voordragen **2** opvoeren, vertonen: ~ *a show* een show presenteren **3** (ver)tonen: ~ *no difficulties* geen problemen bieden **4** aanbieden, schenken, uitreiken: ~ *s.o.* **with** *a prize* iem. een prijs uitreiken **5** presenteren: ~ *arms!* presenteer geweer!

presentable toonbaar, fatsoenlijk

presentation 1 voorstelling **2** schenking, gift, geschenkʰ: *make a ~ of* aanbieden

present-day huidig, modern, gangbaar

presenter presentator

presentiment (angstig) voorgevoelʰ

presently 1 dadelijk, binnenkort **2** [Am] nu, op dit ogenblik

preservation 1 behoudʰ, bewaring **2** staat

preservationist milieubeschermer, natuurbeschermer

preservative 1 bewaarmiddelʰ, conserveringsmiddelʰ **2** voorbehoedmiddelʰ

¹**preserve** (n) **1** jam **2** (natuur)reservaatʰ, wildparkʰ ‖ *poach on another's ~* in iemands vaarwater zitten

²**preserve** (vb) **1** bewaren; levend houden [for future generations]: *only two copies have been ~d* slechts twee exemplaren zijn bewaard gebleven **2** behouden, in stand houden: *well ~d* goed geconserveerd **3** inmaken: *~d fruits* gekonfijt fruit **4** in leven houden, redden

preset vooraf instellen, afstellen

preside 1 als voorzitter optreden **2** (+ over) de leiding hebben (van)

presidency presidentschapʰ, presidentstermijn

president 1 voorzitter **2** president **3** [Am] leidinggevende, directeur

president-elect nieuwgekozen president

presidential presidentieel: ~ *year* jaar met presidentsverkiezingen

¹**press** (n) **1** pers, het drukken, journalisten: *freedom* (or: *liberty*) *of the ~* persvrijheid; *get a good ~* een goede pers krijgen **2** drukpers: *at* (or: *in*) *(the) ~* ter perse **3** drukkerij **4** pers(toestelʰ) **5** menigte, gedrangʰ

²**press** (vb) **1** druk uitoefenen: ~ *ahead* **with** onverbiddelijk doorgaan met **2** persen, strijken **3** dringen, haast hebben: *time ~es* de tijd dringt **4** zich verdringen

³**press** (vb) **1** drukken, duwen, klemmen **2** platdrukken **3** bestoken [also fig]; op de hielen zitten: ~ *s.o.* **hard** iem. het vuur na aan de schenen leggen **4** druk uitoefenen op, aanzetten: ~ *for* an answer aandringen op een antwoord; *be ~ed* **for** money (or: time) in geldnood (or: tijdnood) zitten **5** persen, strijken ‖ [law] ~ *charges* een aanklacht indienen; ~ *home* one's point of view zijn ziens-

wijze doordrijven

Press uitgeverij

press agency persbureauʰ

press baron [inform] krantenmagnaat

press cutting krantenknipselʰ

press gallery perstribune

pressie cadeau(tje)ʰ, geschenkʰ

pressing 1 dringend, urgent **2** (aan)dringend, opdringerig

pressman journalist

press release persberichtʰ

press-stud drukknoopjeʰ

¹**pressure** (n) **1** druk, gewichtʰ: *the ~ of taxation* de belastingdruk **2** stress, spanning: *work under ~* werken onder druk **3** dwang: *a promise made under ~* een afgedwongen belofte; *put the ~ on* [fig] de ketel onder druk zetten

²**pressure** (vb) onder druk zetten

pressure cooker snelkookpan

pressure group pressiegroep; lobby

pressurize 1 onder druk zetten [also fig] **2** de (lucht)druk regelen van: *~d cabin* drukcabine

prestige prestigeʰ, aanzienʰ

prestigious gerenommeerd; prestigieus

presto presto, onmiddellijk: *hey ~!* hocus pocus pas!

presumable aannemelijk, vermoedelijk

¹**presume** (vb) zich vrijheden veroorloven

²**presume** (vb) **1** zich veroorloven, de vrijheid nemen **2** veronderstellen, vermoeden, aannemen

presume (up)on misbruik maken van: *presume (up)on s.o.'s kindness* misbruik maken van iemands vriendelijkheid

presumption 1 (redelijke) veronderstelling **2** reden om te veronderstellen **3** arrogantie, verwaandheid

presumptuous aanmatigend, arrogant

presupposition vooronderstelling, voorwaarde, vereisteʰ

pretence 1 aanspraak, pretentie: ~ *to* aanspraak op **2** valse indruk, schijn: *she made a ~ of laughing* ze deed alsof ze lachte **3** uiterlijk vertoonʰ, aanstellerij: *devoid of all ~* zonder enige pretentie **4** huichelarij

¹**pretend** (vb) **1** voorgeven, (ten onrechte) beweren **2** voorwenden

²**pretend** (vb) doen alsof, komedie spelen

pretender 1 (troon)pretendent **2** huichelaar, schijnheilige

pretension 1 aanspraak **2** pretentie, aanmatiging

pretentious 1 pretentieus, aanmatigend **2** opzichtig

pretext voorwendselʰ, excuusʰ: *under the ~ of* onder voorwendsel van

¹**pretty** (adj) **1** aardig [also iron]; mooi, aantrekkelijk: *a ~ mess* een mooie boel **2** groot, aanzienlijk, veel: *it cost him a ~ penny* het

heeft hem een flinke duit gekost || a ~ **kettle of fish** een mooie boel

²**pretty** (adv) **1** nogal, vrij: ~ **nearly** zo goed als; I have ~ **well** finished my essay ik heb mijn opstel bijna af **2** erg, zeer **3** [Am] aardig, behoorlijk

prevail 1 de overhand krijgen, zegevieren: [form] the author was ~ed **upon** to write an occasional poem de auteur werd overgehaald om een gelegenheidsgedicht te schrijven **2** wijd verspreid zijn, heersen, gelden

prevailing gangbaar, heersend

prevalent 1 heersend, gangbaar, wijd verspreid **2** (over)heersend

prevarication draaierij, uitvlucht

¹**prevent** (vb) in de weg staan

²**prevent** (vb) voorkomen, verhinderen

preventable vermijdbaar

prevention preventie || ~ is **better** than cure voorkomen is beter dan genezen

¹**preventive** (n) **1** obstakelʰ, hindernis **2** voorbehoedmiddelʰ

²**preventive** (adj) preventief, voorkomend: ~ **detention** voorlopige hechtenis

preview voorvertoning

previous voorafgaand, vorig, vroeger: ~ **conviction** eerdere veroordeling

pre-war vooroorlogs

¹**prey** (n) prooi [also fig]; slachtofferʰ: **beast** (or: **bird**) of ~ roofdierʰ, roofvogel; **become** (or: **fall**) (a) ~ **to** ten prooi vallen aan

²**prey** (vb): ~ **(up)on** a) uitzuigen; b) aantasten; c) jagen op; it ~s **on** his mind hij wordt erdoor gekweld

¹**price** (n) **1** prijs [also fig]; som: **set** a ~ on een prijs vaststellen voor; at a low ~ voor weinig geld; at any ~ tot elke prijs; it comes **at** a ~ a) er moet wel voor betaald worden; b) het heeft zijn prijs **2** notering **3** waarde || every man **has** his ~ iedereen is te koop

²**price** (vb) prijzen, de prijs vaststellen van: ~ o.s. **out of** the market zich uit de markt prijzen

price cut prijsverlaging

priceless onbetaalbaar, onschatbaar; [fig] kostelijk

price tag prijskaartjeʰ [also fig]

pricey prijzig, duur

¹**prick** (n) **1** prik: [fig] ~s of **conscience** wroeging, berouwʰ **2** [inform] lul, eikel, schoft **3** [inform] pik

²**prick** (vb) prikken, steken

³**prick** (vb) prikken, (door)steken; prikkelen [also fig]

¹**prickle** (n) stekel, doorn, prikkel

²**prickle** (vb) prikkelen, steken, kriebelen

pride 1 trots, verwaandheid, hoogmoed: take (a) ~ in fier zijn op **2** eergevoelʰ: **false** ~ misplaatste trots, ijdelheid **3** troep [lions]

pride (up)on prat gaan op, trots zijn op

priest priester, pastoor

prig verwaande kwast

prim 1 keurig: ~ and **proper** keurig netjes **2** preuts

primacy voorrang, vooraanstaande plaats

primal [form] oer-; oorspronkelijk: ~ **scream** oerschreeuw, oerkreet **2** voornaamst

primarily hoofdzakelijk, voornamelijk

¹**primary** (n) **1** hoofdzaak **2** [Am] voorverkiezing

²**primary** (adj) **1** voornaamste: of ~ **importance** van het allergrootste belang **2** primair, eerst **3** elementair, grond-: ~ **care** eerstelijnsgezondheidszorg; ~ **colour** primaire kleur; ~ **education** (or: **school**) basisonderwijsʰ, basisschool

primate primaatʰ

Primate aartsbisschop

¹**prime** (n) **1** hoogste volmaaktheid, bloei, hoogtepuntʰ, puikjeʰ: in the ~ of **life** in de kracht van zijn leven; she is well **past** her ~ ze is niet meer zo jong, ze heeft haar beste jaren achter de rug **2** priemgetalʰ

²**prime** (adj) **1** eerst, voornaamst: ~ **suspect** hoofdverdachte **2** uitstekend, prima: [radio, TV] ~ **time** primetime; ~ **quality** topkwaliteit **3** oorspronkelijk, fundamenteel || ~ **number** priemgetalʰ

³**prime** (vb) **1** klaarmaken, prepareren **2** laden [firearm] **3** op gang brengen [by pouring water or oil]; injecteren [engine]

¹**primer** (n) **1** eerste leesboekʰ, abcʰ **2** beknopte handleiding, inleiding

²**primer** (n) grondverf

primeval 1 oorspronkelijk, oer-: ~ **forest** ongerept woud **2** oeroud

primitive 1 primitief **2** niet comfortabel, ouderwets: our **accommodation** there will ~ onze huisvesting daar zal gebrekkig zijn

primrose 1 sleutelbloem **2** lichtgeelʰ

primula primula, sleutelbloem

prince 1 prins: ~ **royal** kroonprins **2** vorst [also fig]; heerser || he **is** my Prince Charming hij is mijn droomprins

princedom 1 prinsdomʰ, vorstendomʰ **2** prinselijke waardigheid

princess prinses

princess royal 1 kroonprinses **2** titel van de oudste dochter van de Britse koning(in)

¹**principal** (n) **1** directeur, directrice **2** hoofdʰ, hoofdpersoon: ~s hoofdrolspelers **3** schoolhoofdʰ **4** [fin] kapitaalʰ, hoofdsom, geleende som

²**principal** (adj) voornaamste

principality prinsdomʰ, vorstendomʰ

Principality (the) Walesʰ

principally voornamelijk, hoofdzakelijk

principle 1 (grond)beginselʰ, uitgangspuntʰ: in ~ in principe **2** principeʰ, beginselʰ || live up (or: **stick** to) one's ~s aan zijn principes vasthouden

prink (zich) mooi maken, (zich) optutten: ~

up zich chic kleden
¹print (n) **1** afdruk; [fig] spoorʰ: *a ~ of a* **tyre** een bandenspoor **2** [art] prent **3** (foto)afdruk, druk: *in ~* gedrukt, verkrijgbaar **4** stempel⁺ʰ **5** gedrukt exemplaarʰ, krant, bladʰ **6** patroonʰ
²print (vb) **1** (+ off) een afdruk maken van; afdrukken [also photo] **2** inprenten || *~ed* **circuit** gedrukte bedrading
³print (vb) **1** (af)drukken: *~ed* **papers** drukwerk; *~ out* een uitdraai maken (van) **2** publiceren **3** in blokletters (op)schrijven **4** (be)stempelen
printer 1 (boek)drukker **2** printer
printing oplage, druk
printing press drukpers
printout uitdraai
print preview [comp] afdrukvoorbeeldʰ
prior vroeger, voorafgaand
priority prioriteit, voorrang: *get one's priorities right* de juiste prioriteiten stellen
prior to vóór, voorafgaande aan
prism prismaʰ
prison 1 gevangenis: *he was sent to ~* hij moest de gevangenis in, hij kreeg gevangenisstraf **2** gevangenisstraf
prison camp interneringskampʰ
prisoner gevangene, gedetineerde: *~ of* **war** krijgsgevangene
prissy preuts, stijf
pristine [form] **1** oorspronkelijk **2** ongerept
privacy 1 persoonlijke levenssfeer **2** geheimhouding, stilte, beslotenheid **3** afzondering
¹private (n) soldaat, militair
²private (adj) **1** besloten, afgezonderd: *~* **celebration** viering in familiekring; *~* **hotel** familiehotelʰ **2** vertrouwelijk, geheim: *~* **conversation** gesprek onder vier ogen; *in ~* in het geheim **3** particulier, niet openbaar: *~* **enterprise** particuliere onderneming; [fig] ondernemingslust; *~* **life** privélevenʰ; *~* **property** privé-eigendom, particulier eigendom; *~* **school** particuliere school **4** persoonlijk, eigen: *~* **detective** privédetective || *~* **eye** privédetective; *~* **means** a) inkomsten anders dan uit loon; b) eigen middelen; *~* **practice** particuliere praktijk; *~* **parts** geslachtsdelen
privation ontbering, gebrekʰ
privatize privatiseren
privet liguster(heg)
¹privilege (n) **1** voorrechtʰ, privilegeʰ **2** onschendbaarheid, immuniteit: *breach of ~* inbreuk op de parlementaire gedragsregels **3** bevoorrechting
²privilege (vb) **1** bevoorrechten, een privilege verlenen **2** machtigen, toestaan **3** vrijstellen
¹prize (n) **1** prijs, beloning **2** prijs(schipʰ), (oorlogs)buit

²prize (vb) **1** waarderen, op prijs stellen **2** openen [with instrument]: *~ a crate* **open** een krat openbreken
prize money prijzengeldʰ
prizewinner prijswinnaar
¹pro (n) **1** *professional* prof, beroeps **2** argumentʰ, stem vóór iets: *the ~s and* **cons** de voor- en nadelen
²pro (adj) **1** pro, voor **2** beroeps-
³pro (adv) (er)vóór, pro
⁴pro (prep) vóór, ter verdediging van
probability waarschijnlijkheid; kans: *in all ~* hoogstwaarschijnlijk; [maths] **theory** *of ~* kansberekening
probable waarschijnlijk, aannemelijk
probably 1 waarschijnlijk **2** ongetwijfeld, vast wel: *~ the greatest singer of all* misschien wel de grootste zanger van allemaal
probation proef(tijd), onderzoekʰ, onderzoeksperiode: *on ~* a) op proef; b) voorwaardelijk in vrijheid gesteld
probation officer reclasseringsambtenaar
¹probe (n) **1** sonde **2** ruimtesonde **3** (diepgaand) onderzoekʰ
²probe (vb) **1** (met een sonde) onderzoeken **2** (goed) onderzoeken, diep graven (in): *~ into* graven naar
problem 1 probleemʰ, vraagstukʰ, kwestie **2** opgave, vraag
problematic(al) 1 problematisch **2** twijfelachtig
procedure 1 procedure, methode, werkwijze **2** [med] ingreep, (kleine) operatie
proceed 1 beginnen, van start gaan **2** verder gaan, doorgaan: *work is ~ing steadily* het werk vordert gestaag **3** te werk gaan, handelen: *how shall we ~* welke procedure zullen we volgen? **4** plaatsvinden, aan de gang zijn **5** zich bewegen, gaan, rijden **6** ontstaan: *~ from* voortkomen uit
proceeding 1 handeling, maatregel **2** optredenʰ, handelwijze **3** (-s) gebeurtenissen, voorvallen **4** (-s) notulen; handelingen [of society etc]; verslagʰ **5** (-s) gerechtelijke actie: *take (or: start)* **legal** *~s* gerechtelijke stappen ondernemen
proceeds opbrengst
proceed to overgaan tot, verder gaan met
¹process (n) **1** procesʰ, ontwikkeling **2** methode **3** (serie) verrichting(en), handelwijze, werkwijze **4** (voort)gang, loop, verloopʰ: *in the ~* en passant; *in (the) ~ of* doende met
²process (vb) (als) in processie gaan, een optocht houden
³process (vb) **1** bewerken, verwerken **2** ontwikkelen (en afdrukken)
procession 1 stoet, optocht, processie: *walk in ~* in optocht lopen **2** opeenvolging
processionary 1 processierups **2** processievlinder

processionary caterpillar processierups: *oak* ~ eikenprocessierups; *pine* ~ dennenprocessierups

processor processor; verwerkingseenheid

proclaim 1 afkondigen, verklaren **2** kenmerken: *his behaviour ~ed him a liar* uit zijn gedrag bleek duidelijk dat hij loog

proclamation afkondiging

procrastination uitstel^h, aarzeling

¹**procreate** (vb) zich voortplanten

²**procreate** (vb) **1** voortbrengen **2** scheppen

procurable verkrijgbaar, beschikbaar

¹**procure** (vb) koppelen, tot ontucht overhalen

²**procure** (vb) verkrijgen, verwerven

¹**prod** (n) **1** por, steek **2** zet [also fig]; duwtje^h

²**prod** (vb) **1** porren, prikken, duwen **2** aansporen, opporren

¹**prodigal** (n) verkwister: *the ~ has returned* de verloren zoon is teruggekeerd

²**prodigal** (adj) **1** verkwistend: *the ~ son* de verloren zoon **2** vrijgevig

prodigious wonderbaarlijk

prodigy 1 wonder^h, bovennatuurlijk verschijnsel^h **2** wonderkind^h

¹**produce** (n) opbrengst, productie: *agricultural* ~ landbouwproducten

²**produce** (vb) **1** produceren, voortbrengen, opbrengen **2** produceren, vervaardigen **3** tonen, produceren, tevoorschijn halen, voor de dag komen met: *~ evidence* (or: *reasons*) bewijzen (or: redenen) aanvoeren **4** uitbrengen, het licht doen zien: *~ a play* een toneelstuk op de planken brengen **5** veroorzaken, teweegbrengen

producer 1 producent, fabrikant **2** [film; TV] producer, productieleider **3** regisseur **4** [radio, TV] samensteller

product 1 product^h, voortbrengsel^h: *agricultural ~s* landbouwproducten **2** resultaat^h, gevolg^h **3** product^h, uitkomst van een vermenigvuldiging

production 1 product^h, schepping **2** [theatre, film] productie **3** productie, vervaardiging, opbrengst **4** het tonen: *on ~ of your tickets* op vertoon van uw kaartje

production line productiestraat; lopende band

productive productief, vruchtbaar

productivity 1 productiviteit **2** rendement^h

prof *professor* prof, professor

¹**profane** (adj) niet kerkelijk, werelds || *~ language* godslasterlijke taal, gevloek^h

²**profane** (vb) ontheiligen

profanity 1 godslastering; (ge)vloek **2** blasfemie

profess 1 beweren, voorwenden **2** verklaren, betuigen: *he ~ed his ignorance on the subject* hij verklaarde dat hij niets van het onderwerp afwist **3** aanhangen

professed 1 voorgewend, zogenaamd **2** openlijk, verklaard, naar eigen zeggen

profession 1 verklaring, uiting **2** beroep^h, vak^h, alle beoefenaren van het vak

¹**professional** (n) **1** beroeps, deskundige **2** professional, prof: *turn ~* beroeps worden

²**professional** (adj) **1** professioneel, beroeps-, prof-: *~ jealousy* broodnijd **2** vakkundig, bekwaam **3** met een hogere opleiding **4** professioneel; opzettelijk [of foul]

professor professor, hoogleraar; [Am also] docent: *~ of chemistry* hoogleraar in de scheikunde

proffer aanbieden, aanreiken

proficiency vakkundigheid, bekwaamheid

proficient vakkundig, bekwaam: *be ~ in French* de Franse taal beheersen

¹**profile** (n) **1** profiel^h, zijaanzicht^h: *in ~* en profil, van opzij **2** silhouet^h, doorsnede **3** profiel^h, karakterschets || *keep a low ~* zich op de achtergrond houden

²**profile** (vb) **1** van opzij weergeven, aftekenen, in silhouet weergeven, een dwarsdoorsnede geven van **2** een karakterschets geven van

¹**profit** (n) **1** winst, opbrengst **2** rente **3** nut^h, voordeel^h, profijt^h: *I read the book much to my ~* ik heb veel aan het boek gehad

²**profit** (vb) **1** nuttig zijn **2** (+ by, from) profiteren (van), profijt trekken

profitable 1 nuttig, voordelig **2** winstgevend

¹**profiteer** (n) woekeraar

²**profiteer** (vb) woekerwinst maken

profligacy 1 losbandigheid **2** verkwisting

¹**profligate** (n) **1** losbol **2** verkwister

²**profligate** (adj) **1** losbandig, lichtzinnig **2** verkwistend

profound 1 wijs, wijsgerig, diepzinnig: *a ~ thinker* een groot denker **2** diepgaand, moeilijk te doorgronden **3** diep, grondig: *~ silence* diepe stilte; *~ly deaf* stokdoof, volkomen doof

profundity 1 diepzinnigheid, wijsgerigheid **2** ondoorgrondelijkheid

profuse 1 gul, kwistig: *be ~ in one's apologies* zich uitputten in verontschuldigingen **2** overvloedig, overdadig: *bleed ~ly* hevig bloeden

progenitor voorvader

progeny 1 nageslacht^h, kinderen **2** volgelingen

prognosis prognose, voorspelling

¹**program** (n) (computer)programma^h

²**program** (vb) programmeren

¹**programme** (n) programma^h

²**programme** (vb) programmeren, een schema opstellen voor

programmer programmeur

¹**progress** (n) voortgang, vooruitgang; [fig]

vordering: *the patient is making* ~ de patiënt gaat vooruit; *in* ~ in wording, aan de gang, in uitvoering

²**progress** (vb) vorderen, vooruitgaan, vooruitkomen; [fig also] zich ontwikkelen

progression 1 opeenvolging, aaneenschakeling **2** voortgang, vooruitgang

¹**progressive** (n) vooruitstrevend persoon

²**progressive** (adj) **1** toenemend, voortschrijdend, voorwaarts; progressief [tax] **2** progressief, vooruitstrevend **3** [linguistics] progressief, duratief: *the* ~ *(form)* de duurvorm, de bezigheidsvorm

prohibit verbieden: *smoking* ~*ed* verboden te roken

prohibition verbodʰ, drankverbodʰ

¹**project** (n) **1** planʰ, ontwerpʰ **2** projectʰ, onderneming **3** projectʰ, onderzoekʰ

²**project** (vb) vooruitspringen, uitsteken: ~*ing shoulder blades* uitstekende schouderbladen

³**project** (vb) **1** ontwerpen, uitstippelen **2** werpen, projecteren: ~ *slides* dia's projecteren **3** afbeelden, tonen **4** schatten

projectile projectielʰ, raket

projection 1 uitstekend deelʰ, uitsprong **2** projectie, beeldʰ **3** raming, planʰ, projectie

projector projector, filmprojector, diaprojector

¹**proletarian** (n) proletariër

²**proletarian** (adj) proletarisch

proletariat proletariaatʰ; arbeidersklasse: *dictatorship* of the ~ dictatuur van het proletariaat

pro-life antiabortus(-)

proliferation 1 woekering, snelle groei **2** verspreiding

prolific vruchtbaar; [fig] met overvloedige resultaten; rijk: *a* ~ *writer* een productief schrijver

prologue proloog, voorwoordʰ, inleiding

prolong 1 verlengen, langer maken **2** verlengen, aanhouden: *a* ~*ed silence* langdurige stilte

prom 1 promenadeconcertʰ; [Am] schoolbalʰ, universiteitsbalʰ; dansfeestʰ **2** promenade, boulevard

¹**promenade** (n) **1** wandeling, het flaneren **2** promenade, boulevard

²**promenade** (vb) **1** wandelen (langs), flaneren **2** wandelen met, lopen te pronken met

prominence 1 verhoging, uitsteekselʰ **2** het uitsteken **3** opvallendheid, bekendheid, belangʰ: *bring* sth. *into* ~ iets bekendheid geven **4** [geog] prominentie

prominent 1 uitstekend, uitspringend: ~ *teeth* vooruitstekende tanden **2** opvallend **3** vooraanstaand, prominent: *a* ~ *scholar* een eminent geleerde

promiscuity 1 willekeurige vermenging **2** onzorgvuldigheid **3** vrij seksueel verkeerʰ, promiscuïteit

promiscuous 1 ongeordend **2** willekeurig **3** promiscue; met willekeurige seksuele relaties

¹**promise** (n) belofte, toezegging: *break* one's ~ zich niet aan zijn belofte houden

²**promise** (vb) **1** een belofte doen, (iets) beloven **2** verwachtingen wekken, veelbelovend zijn

³**promise** (vb) **1** beloven, toezeggen; [inform] verzekeren: *the* ~*d land* het Beloofde Land **2** beloven, doen verwachten: *it* ~*d to be a severe winter* het beloofde een strenge winter te worden

promising veelbelovend

promontory kaap, klip, voorgebergteʰ

promote 1 bevorderen, in rang verhogen **2** bevorderen, stimuleren **3** steunen [eg bill] **4** ondernemen, in gang zetten **5** reclame maken voor

promoter 1 begunstiger, bevorderaar **2** organisator, financier van een manifestatie

promotion 1 bevordering, promotie **2** aanbieding, reclame

promotional 1 bevorderings-: ~ *opportunities* promotiekansen **2** reclame-; advertentie-

¹**prompt** (n) geheugensteuntjeʰ, het voorzeggen, hulp van de souffleur

²**prompt** (adj) prompt, onmiddellijk, vlug, alert: ~ *payment* prompte betaling

³**prompt** (vb) **1** bewegen, drijven: *what* ~*ed you to do that?* hoe kwam je erbij dat te doen? **2** opwekken, oproepen **3** herinneren, voorzeggen, souffleren

⁴**prompt** (adv) precies, stipt: *at twelve o' clock* ~ om twaalf uur precies

prompter souffleur

promptly 1 onmiddellijk, meteen: *he was told the address and* ~ *forgot it* hij had het adres nog niet doorgekregen, of hij was het alweer vergeten **2** stipt: ~ *at four o'clock* precies om vier uur

prone 1 voorover, voorovergebogen **2** vooroverliggend, uitgestrekt **3** geneigd, vatbaar: *he is* ~ *to tactlessness* hij is geneigd tot tactloosheid

prong 1 puntʰ, piek, vorktand **2** tak, vertakking

pronoun [linguistics] voornaamwoordʰ

¹**pronounce** (vb) **1** spreken, articuleren **2** oordelen, zijn mening verkondigen: ~ *(up)on* uitspraken doen over, commentaar leveren op

²**pronounce** (vb) **1** uitspreken **2** verklaren, verkondigen: ~ *judgement* (or: *verdict*) uitspraak doen

pronounced 1 uitgesproken **2** uitgesproken, onmiskenbaar

pronto meteen, onmiddellijk
pronunciation uitspraak
[1]**proof** (n) **1** toets, proefneming: *bring* (or: *put*) *to the* ~ op de proef stellen **2** bewijs[h]: *in* ~ *of his claim* om zijn stelling te bewijzen **3** drukproef **4** proefafdruk
[2]**proof** (adj) bestand [also fig]; opgewassen: ~ *against water* waterdicht, waterbestendig **-proof** -bestendig, -vast, -dicht: *bulletproof* kogelvrij; *childproof* onverwoestbaar [of toys]
proofread proeflezen; drukproeven corrigeren
[1]**prop** (n) **1** stut, pijler, steun, steunpilaar **2** rekwisiet[h], benodigd voorwerp[h] bij toneelvoorstelling
[2]**prop** (vb) ondersteunen [also fig]; stutten
propaganda propaganda, propagandamateriaal[h], propagandacampagne
[1]**propagate** (vb) **1** verspreiden, bekendmaken **2** voortzetten; doorgeven [to next generation] **3** fokken, telen
[2]**propagate** (vb) (zich) voortplanten
propel voortbewegen, aandrijven || ~*ling pencil* vulpotlood
[1]**propellant** (n) **1** drijfgas[h] **2** [fuel] aandrijfbrandstof
[2]**propellant** (adj) voortdrijvend [also fig]; stuwend
propeller propeller
propensity neiging
proper 1 gepast, fatsoenlijk **2** juist, passend: *the* ~ *treatment* de juiste behandeling **3** juist, precies: *the* ~ *time* de juiste tijd **4** geweldig, eersteklas: *a* ~ *spanking* een geweldig pak slaag **5** behorend [to]; eigen [to]: ~ *to* behorend tot, eigen aan **6** eigenlijk, strikt: *London* ~ het eigenlijke Londen || ~ *noun* (or: *name*) eigennaam
properly 1 goed, zoals het moet **2** eigenlijk, strikt genomen **3** correct, fatsoenlijk **4** volkomen, volslagen
property 1 eigenschap, kenmerk[h] **2** perceel[h], pand[h], onroerend goed[h] **3** rekwisiet[h], benodigd voorwerp[h] bij een toneelvoorstelling **4** bezit[h], eigendom[h]: *lost* ~ gevonden voorwerpen **5** bezit[h], vermogen[h], onroerend goed[h]
prophecy 1 voorspelling **2** profetie
[1]**prophesy** (vb) **1** voorspellingen doen **2** als een profeet spreken
[2]**prophesy** (vb) **1** voorspellen, voorzeggen **2** aankondigen
prophet profeet
prophetic profetisch; voorspellend
proponent voorstander, verdediger
[1]**proportion** (n) **1** deel[h], gedeelte[h], aandeel[h] **2** verhouding, relatie: *bear no* ~ *to* in geen verhouding staan tot **3** proportie, evenredigheid: *out of all* ~ buiten alle verhoudingen

[2]**proportion** (vb) **1** aanpassen, in de juiste verhouding brengen **2** proportioneren: *well* ~*ed* goed geproportioneerd
proportional verhoudingsgewijs, proportioneel, evenredig
proposal 1 voorstel[h] **2** huwelijksaanzoek[h]
[1]**propose** (vb) **1** een voorstel doen **2** een huwelijksaanzoek doen
[2]**propose** (vb) **1** voorstellen, voorleggen: ~ *a motion* een motie indienen **2** van plan zijn, zich voornemen **3** een dronk uitbrengen (op)
[1]**proposition** (n) **1** bewering **2** voorstel[h], plan[h] **3** probleem[h], moeilijk geval[h]: *he's a tough* ~ hij is moeilijk te hanteren
[2]**proposition** (vb) oneerbare voorstellen doen aan
propound voorstellen
proprietary 1 eigendoms-, van de eigenaar, particulier: ~ *name* (or: *term*) gedeponeerd handelsmerk **2** bezittend, met bezittingen **3** als een eigenaar, bezittend: *he always has this* ~ *air* hij gedraagt zich altijd alsof alles van hem is
proprietor eigenaar
propriety 1 juistheid, geschiktheid **2** correctheid, fatsoen[h], gepastheid
propulsion 1 drijfkracht **2** voortdrijving, voortstuwing
prop up overeind houden, ondersteunen
prosaic 1 zakelijk **2** alledaags
proscribe 1 verbieden, als gevaarlijk verwerpen **2** verbannen [also fig]; verstoten
prose proza[h]
prosecute 1 voortzetten, volhouden **2** (gerechtelijk) vervolgen, procederen tegen: *trespassers will be* ~*d* verboden voor onbevoegden
prosecution 1 gerechtelijke vervolging, proces[h] **2** [law] eiser
prosecutor 1 eiser, eisende partij **2** [Am] openbare aanklager: *public* ~ openbare aanklager
[1]**prospect** (n) **1** vergezicht[h], panorama[h] **2** idee[h], denkbeeld[h] **3** ligging, uitzicht[h] **4** hoop, verwachting, kans, vooruitzicht[h] **5** potentiële klant, prospect[h]
[2]**prospect** (vb) naar bodemschatten zoeken: ~ *for gold* goud zoeken
prospective 1 voor de toekomst, nog niet in werking **2** toekomstig: *a* ~ *buyer* een gegadigde, een mogelijke koper; ~ *student* aspirant-student
prospector goudzoeker
prosper bloeien, slagen, succes hebben
prosperity voorspoed, succes[h]
prosperous 1 bloeiend; voorspoedig **2** welvarend **3** gunstig
[1]**prostitute** (n) prostitué [man]; prostituee
[2]**prostitute** (vb) **1** prostitueren, tot prostitué (prostituee) maken: ~ *o.s.* zich prostitue-

ren **2** vergooien, verlagen, misbruiken: ~ one's *honour* zich verlagen, z'n eer te grabbel gooien

prostitution prostitutie

¹prostrate (adj) **1** ter aarde geworpen **2** liggend, uitgestrekt, languit **3** verslagen, gebroken: ~ *with grief* gebroken van verdriet

²prostrate (vb) neerwerpen, neerslaan: ~ *o.s.* zich ter aarde werpen, in het stof knielen

prosy saai, vervelend

protagonist 1 voorvechter **2** voorstander **3** [theatre] protagonist; hoofdfiguur

protect 1 beschermen **2** beveiligen, beveiligingen aanbrengen

protection 1 bescherming, beschutting, beschermer: *it's for your own* ~ het is voor uw eigen veiligheid **2** vrijgeleideʰ

protection money protectiegeldʰ, beschermgeldʰ

protective beschermend, beschermings-: ~ *colouring* schutkleur; ~ *sheath* condoomʰ

protector 1 beschermer, beschermheer **2** beschermend middelʰ

protectorate protectoraatʰ, landʰ dat onder bescherming van een ander land staat

protein proteïne⁺ʰ, eiwitʰ

¹protest (n) protestʰ, bezwaarʰ: *enter* (or: *lodge, make*) *a* ~ *against sth.* ergens protest tegen aantekenen

²protest (vb) protesteren, bezwaar maken

³protest (vb) **1** bezweren, betuigen: ~ *one's innocence* zijn onschuld betuigen **2** [Am] protesteren tegen: *they are* ~*ing nuclear weapons* ze protesteren tegen kernwapens

Protestant protestant(s)

protocol 1 protocolʰ **2** officieel verslagʰ, akte, verslagʰ van internationale onderhandelingen

proton protonʰ

prototype prototypeʰ, oorspronkelijk modelʰ

protract voortzetten, verlengen, rekken

protractor gradenboog, hoekmeter

protrude uitpuilen, uitsteken: *protruding eyes* uitpuilende ogen

protuberant gezwollen, uitpuilend

proud 1 trots, fier, zelfverzekerd, hoogmoedig, arrogant **2** trots, vereerd: *I'm* ~ *to know her* ik ben er trots op dat ik haar ken **3** imposant [of thing]

provable bewijsbaar; aantoonbaar

¹prove (vb) **1** blijken: *our calculations* ~*d incorrect* onze berekeningen bleken onjuist te zijn **2** [culinary] rijzen

²prove (vb) bewijzen, (aan)tonen: *of* ~*n authenticity* waarvan de echtheid is bewezen

provenance herkomst

proverb gezegdeʰ, spreekwoordʰ, spreuk

proverbial spreekwoordelijk

¹provide (vb) **1** voorzieningen treffen: ~ *against flooding* maatregelen nemen tegen overstromingen **2** in het onderhoud voorzien, verzorgen: ~ *for children* kinderen onderhouden

²provide (vb) **1** bepalen, eisen, vaststellen: ~ *that …* bepalen dat … **2** voorzien, uitrusten, verschaffen: *they* ~*d us with blankets and food* zij voorzagen ons van dekens en voedsel

provided op voorwaarde dat, (alleen) indien, mits: ~ *that* op voorwaarde dat, mits

providence voorzorg, zorg voor de toekomst, spaarzaamheid

Providence de Voorzienigheid, God

provident 1 vooruitziend **2** zuinig, spaarzaam

providential wonderbaarlijk

provider 1 leverancier **2** kostwinner

providing op voorwaarde dat, (alleen) indien, mits: ~ *(that) it is done properly* mits het goed gebeurt

province 1 provincie, gewestʰ **2** vakgebiedʰ, terreinʰ: *outside one's* ~ buiten zijn vakgebied **3** (-s) plattelandʰ, provincie

¹provincial (n) **1** provinciaal, iem. uit de provincie **2** provinciaaltjeʰ, bekrompen mensʰ

²provincial (adj) provinciaal, van de provincie; [depr] bekrompen

provision 1 bepaling, voorwaarde **2** voorraad, hoeveelheid, rantsoenʰ **3** levering, toevoer, voorziening **4** voorzorg, voorbereiding, maatregelen: *make* ~ *for the future* voor zijn toekomst zorgen **5** (-s) levensmiddelen, provisie, proviandʰ

provisional tijdelijk, voorlopig

proviso voorwaarde, beperkende bepaling

provocation provocatie, uitdaging: *he did it under* ~ hij is ertoe gedreven

provocative provocerend, prikkelend: ~ *clothes* uitdagende kleding

provoke 1 tergen, prikkelen: *his behaviour* ~*d me into beating him* door zijn gedrag werd ik zo kwaad dat ik hem een pak slaag gaf **2** uitdagen, provoceren, ophitsen **3** veroorzaken, uitlokken

prow voorsteven

prowess 1 dapperheid **2** bekwaamheid

¹prowl (n) jacht, roof(tocht), het rondsluipen

²prowl (vb) **1** jagen, op roof uit zijn **2** lopen loeren, rondsluipen, rondsnuffelen: *s.o. is* ~*ing about* (or: *around*) *on the staircase* er sluipt iem. rond in het trappenhuis

prowl car [Am] surveillancewagen [of police]

proximity nabijheid: *in the* ~ in de nabijheid, in de nabije toekomst

proxy 1 gevolmachtigde, afgevaardigde: *stand* ~ *for s.o.* als iemands gemachtigde optreden **2** (bewijsʰ van) volmacht, volmachtbrief: *marry by* ~ bij volmacht trouwen

prude preuts mens
prudence 1 voorzichtigheid, omzichtigheid: *fling* (or: *throw*) ~ *to the winds* alle voorzichtigheid overboord gooien **2** beleid^h, wijsheid
prudent voorzichtig, met inzicht, verstandig
prudential verstandig
¹prune (n) pruimedant, gedroogde pruim
²prune (vb) (be)snoeien [also fig]; korten, reduceren
prurient 1 wellustig **2** obsceen, pornografisch
¹pry (vb) **1** gluren: ~ *about* rondneuzen **2** nieuwsgierig zijn: *I wish you wouldn't* ~ *into my affairs* ik wou dat je je niet met mijn zaken bemoeide
²pry (vb) [Am] (open)wrikken: ~ *open* a chest een kist openbreken
pry bar koevoet, breekijzer^h
PS *postscript* PS, post scriptum
psalm psalm, hymne, kerkgezang^h
pseudo- pseudo-; schijn-
pseudonym pseudoniem^h; schuilnaam
psyche psyche, ziel
psychiatric psychiatrisch
psychiatrist psychiater
psychiatry psychiatrie
psychic 1 psychisch, geestelijk **2** paranormaal, bovennatuurlijk **3** paranormaal begaafd
psycho [inform] psychopaat, gek
psychoanalysis 1 psychoanalyse **2** (leer der) psychoanalyse
psychoanalyst psychoanalyticus
psychological psychologisch: ~ *warfare* psychologische oorlogvoering
psychologist psycholoog
¹psychology (n) karakter^h, aard, psyche
²psychology (n) **1** (wetenschap der) psychologie **2** mensenkennis
psychopath psychopaat, geestelijk gestoorde
psychosis psychose
psychosomatic psychosomatisch
psychotic psychotisch
¹psych out (vb) [Am] in de war raken
²psych out (vb) [Am] **1** analyseren, hoogte krijgen van **2** doorkrijgen, begrijpen: *I couldn't psych him out* ik kon er niet achter komen wat voor iem. hij was **3** intimideren [opponent]
PTO *please turn over* z.o.z., zie ommezijde
pub *public house* café^h, bar, pub, kroeg
pube [inform] schaamhaar [one]: *the* ~s het schaamhaar
puberty puberteit
pubescence 1 beharing **2** begin^h van de puberteit
pub food pubgerechten
pubic van de schaamstreek, schaam-: ~ *hair*

schaamhaar^h
¹public (n) publiek^h, mensen, geïnteresseerden: *in* ~ in het openbaar
²public (adj) **1** openbaar, publiek, voor iedereen toegankelijk, algemeen bekend: ~ *bar* zaaltje in Brits café met goedkoop bier; ~ *conveniences* openbare toiletten; ~ *footpath* voetpad^h, wandelpad^h; ~ *house* café^h, bar, pub; ~ *transport* openbaar vervoer; ~ *utility* nutsbedrijf^h **2** algemeen, gemeenschaps-, nationaal, maatschappelijk: ~ *holiday* nationale feestdag; ~ *interest* het algemeen belang; ~ *opinion* publieke opinie; ~ *school* particuliere kostschool; [Scotland, Am] gesubsidieerde lagere school **3** overheids-, regerings-, publiek-, staats-: ~ *assistance* sociale steun, uitkering; ~ *spending* overheidsuitgaven
publication 1 uitgave, publicatie, boek^h, artikel^h **2** publicatie, bekendmaking
publicity 1 publiciteit, bekendheid, openbaarheid **2** publiciteit, reclame
publicize bekendmaken, adverteren
public relations officer perschef, persvoorlichter
publish 1 publiceren, schrijven **2** uitgeven, publiceren **3** bekendmaken, aankondigen, afkondigen
publisher uitgever(ij)
publishing house uitgeverij
puck 1 kweiduivel **2** ondeugend kind^h **3** [ice hockey] puck
¹pucker (n) vouw, plooi, rimpel
²pucker (vb) samentrekken, rimpelen
pudding 1 pudding [also fig] **2** dessert^h, toetje^h
puddle plas, (modder)poel
pudgy kort en dik, mollig
puerile 1 kinder-, kinderlijk **2** kinderachtig
¹Puerto Rican (n) Porto Ricaan(se)
²Puerto Rican (adj) Porto Ricaans
Puerto Rico Porto Rico
¹puff (n) **1** ademstoot, puf **2** rookwolk **3** trek, haal; puf [on cigarette etc] **4** puf, puffend geluid^h **5** (poeder)dons^h
²puff (vb) **1** puffen, hijgen, blazen **2** roken, dampen: ~ *(away) at* (or: *on*) a cigarette een sigaret roken **3** puffen, in wolkjes uitgestoten worden **4** (also + out) opzwellen, zich opblazen
³puff (vb) **1** uitblazen, uitstoten: ~ *smoke into s.o.'s eyes* iem. rook in de ogen blazen **2** roken; trekken [on cigarette etc] **3** (also + out) opblazen, doen opzwellen: ~*ed up with pride* verwaand, opgeblazen
puffy opgezet, gezwollen, opgeblazen
pug 1 mopshond **2** klei(mengsel^h)
pugilist [form] vuistvechter, bokser
pugnacious strijdlustig
puke overgeven, (uit)braken, kotsen: *it makes me* ~ ik word er kotsmisselijk van

¹pull (n) **1** ruk, trek, stoot; [fig] klim; inspanning, moeite: *a long ~ across the hills* een hele klim over de heuvels **2** trekkracht **3** teug; slok [drink]; trek [on cigar] **4** (trek)knop, trekker, handvat^h **5** invloed, macht: *have a ~ on s.o.* invloed over iemand hebben **6** het trekken, het rukken

²pull (vb) **1** trekken, getrokken worden, plukken, rukken: ~ *at* (or: *on*) *a pipe* aan een pijp trekken **2** zich moeizaam voortbewegen: ~ *away from* achter zich laten **3** gaan [of vehicle, rowing boat]; gedreven worden, roeien, rijden: *the car ~ed ahead of us* de auto ging voor ons rijden; *the train ~ed into Bristol* de trein liep Bristol binnen

³pull (vb) **1** trekken (aan), (uit)rukken, naar zich toetrekken, uit de grond trekken, tappen, zich verzekeren van, (eruit) halen: ~ *customers* klandizie trekken; *he ~ed a gun on her* hij richtte een geweer op haar; *the current ~ed him under* de stroming sleurde hem mee **2** doen voortgaan, voortbewegen **3** verrekken [muscle] **4** (be)roven ‖ ~ *the other one* maak dat een ander wijs

pull back 1 (zich) terugtrekken; [fig] terugkrabbelen, geen woord houden: *the battalion pulled back* het bataljon trok zich terug **2** [fin] bezuinigen, minder geld gaan uitgeven

pull-down menu rolmenu^{+h}

pulley 1 katrol **2** riemschijf

¹pull in (vb) **1** aankomen, binnenlopen, binnenvaren **2** naar de kant gaan (en stoppen) [of vehicle]

²pull in (vb) **1** binnenhalen [money]; opstrijken **2** aantrekken, lokken: *Paul Simon always pulls in many people* Paul Simon trekt altijd veel mensen **3** inhouden: ~ *your stomach* houd je buik in **4** in zijn kraag grijpen [eg thief]; inrekenen

pull off 1 uittrekken, uitdoen **2** bereiken, slagen in: ~ *a deal* in een transactie slagen; *he has pulled it off again* het is hem weer gelukt, hij heeft het weer klaargespeeld

¹pull out (vb) **1** (zich) terugtrekken; [fig] terugkrabbelen: ~ *of politics* uit de politiek gaan **2** vertrekken, wegrijden **3** gaan inhalen, uithalen: *the driver who pulled out had not seen the oncoming lorry* de bestuurder die zijn baan verliet had de naderende vrachtauto niet gezien

²pull out (vb) verwijderen, uitdoen, uittrekken: ~ *a tooth* een kies trekken

pullover pullover

¹pull over (vb) **1** opzijgaan, uit de weg gaan **2** [Am] (naar de kant rijden en) stoppen

²pull over (vb) **1** naar de kant rijden **2** stoppen [vehicle]

pull round 1 bij bewustzijn komen **2** zich herstellen

pull tab lipje^h

pull through erdoor getrokken worden, erdoor komen: *the patient pulls through* de patiënt komt er doorheen

pull together 1 samentrekken **2** samenwerken ‖ *pull yourself together* beheers je

¹pull up (vb) stoppen: *the car pulled up* de auto stopte

²pull up (vb) **1** uittrekken **2** (doen) stoppen: ~ *your car at the side* zet je auto aan de kant **3** tot de orde roepen, op zijn plaats zetten

pull-up 1 rustplaats, wegrestaurant^h **2** optrekoefening [on bar]

pulp 1 moes^h, pap **2** vruchtvlees^h **3** pulp, houtpap **4** rommel **5** sensatieblad^h, sensatieboek^h, sensatieverhaal^h ‖ *beat s.o. to a ~* iem. tot moes slaan

pulpit preekstoel, kansel

pulp magazine sensatieblad^h, pulpblad^h

pulsate kloppen, ritmisch bewegen, trillen

pulse 1 hartslag, pols(slag): *feel* (or: *take*) *s.o.'s ~* iemands hartslag opnemen; [fig] iem. polsen **2** (afzonderlijke) slag, stoot, trilling **3** ritme^h [eg in music] **4** peul(vrucht) **5** peulen^h, peulvruchten

¹pulverize (vb) verpulveren, verpulverd worden

²pulverize (vb) verpulveren; [fig] vernietigen; niets heel laten van

puma poema

¹pump (n) **1** pomp **2** dansschoen **3** [Am] galaschoen

²pump (vb) **1** pompen, pompend bewegen **2** bonzen [of heart]

³pump (vb) **1** pompen: ~ *money into an industry* geld investeren in een industrie **2** (krachtig) schudden [hand] **3** met moeite gedaan krijgen, (erin) pompen, (eruit) stampen: ~ *a witness* een getuige uithoren

pumpkin pompoen

¹pun (n) woordspeling

²pun (vb) woordspelingen maken

¹punch (n) **1** werktuig^h om gaten te slaan, ponsmachine, ponstang, perforator, kniptang **2** (vuist)slag: [boxing] *pull one's ~es* zich inhouden [also fig] **3** slagvaardigheid, kracht, pit: *his speech lacks ~* er zit geen pit in zijn toespraak **4** punch, bowl(drank)

²punch (vb) **1** ponsen **2** slaan: ~ *up* op de vuist gaan **3** [Am] klokken, een prikklok gebruiken: ~ *in* (or: *out*) klokken bij binnenkomst (or: vertrek)

³punch (vb) **1** slaan, een vuistslag geven **2** gaten maken in, perforeren; knippen [ticket]; ponsen

Punch Jan Klaassen: ~ *and Judy* Jan Klaassen en Katrijn

punchbag [boxing] stootzak, zandzak, stootkussen^h

punchball boksbal

punch-drunk versuft; [fig] verward

punch line clou

punch-up knokpartij

punchy [inform] versuft, bedwelmd

punctilious zeer precies, plichtsgetrouw, nauwgezet

punctual punctueel, stipt, nauwgezet

¹**punctuate** (vb) onderbreken: *a speech ~d by* (or: *with*) *jokes* een toespraak doorspekt met grappen

²**punctuate** (vb) leestekens aanbrengen

punctuation interpunctie(tekens)

punctuation mark leesteken^h

¹**puncture** (n) gaatje^h [eg in tyre]; lek^h, lekke band

²**puncture** (vb) lek maken, doorboren; [fig] vernietigen

pundit 1 pandit 2 expert

pungent 1 scherp: ~ *remarks* stekelige opmerkingen 2 prikkelend, pikant: *a ~ smell* een doordringende geur

punish 1 (be)straffen 2 zijn voordeel doen met [somebody's weakness]; afstraffen

punishing slopend, erg zwaar: *a ~ climb* een dodelijk vermoeiende beklimming

punishment 1 straf, bestraffing: *corporal ~* lijfstraf 2 ruwe behandeling, afstraffing

punitive 1 straf- 2 zeer hoog [eg of tax]

¹**punk** (n) 1 punk(er) 2 (jonge) boef, relschopper

²**punk** (adj) 1 waardeloos 2 punk-, van (een) punk(s)

punnet (spanen) mand(je^h) [for fruit, vegetables]; (plastic) doosje^h

¹**punt** (n) punter, platte rivierschuit

²**punt** (vb) 1 bomen, varen in een punter 2 gokken [eg at horse races]

puny nietig, miezerig, onbetekenend

¹**pup** (n) 1 pup(py), jong hondje^h 2 jong^h [eg of otter, seal]

²**pup** (vb) jongen; werpen [of dog]

pupil 1 leerling 2 pupil [of eye]

puppet marionet [also fig]; (houten) pop

puppy 1 puppy^{+h}, jong hondje^h 2 snotneus

puppy fat [inform] babyvet^h

¹**purchase** (n) 1 (aan)koop; ~*s* inkoop; aanschaf; *make ~s* inkopen doen 2 vat^h, greep: *get a ~ on a rock* houvast vinden aan een rots

²**purchase** (vb) zich aanschaffen, (in)kopen

purchaser (in)koper

purchasing power koopkracht

pure 1 puur, zuiver, onvervalst: *a ~ Arab horse* een rasechte arabier; *~ and simple* niets dan, eenvoudigweg 2 volkomen, zuiver, puur

purebred rasecht [of animals]; volbloed-

purée moes^h, puree

purely uitsluitend, volledig, zonder meer: *a ~ personal matter* een zuiver persoonlijke aangelegenheid

purgation zuivering, reiniging

purgatory vagevuur^h, (tijdelijke) kwelling

¹**purge** (n) 1 zuivering 2 laxeermiddel^h

²**purge** (vb) zuiveren, louteren, verlossen

purification zuivering, verlossing, bevrijding

¹**purify** (vb) zuiver worden

²**purify** (vb) zuiveren, louteren

purism purisme^h, (taal)zuivering

¹**puritan** (n) puritein, streng godsdienstig persoon

²**puritan** (adj) puriteins, moraliserend, streng van zeden

purity zuiverheid, puurheid, onschuld

purler smak, harde val: *come* (or: *take*) *a ~* een flinke smak maken

purloin [form] stelen; ontvreemden

purple 1 purper, donkerrood, paarsrood: *he became ~ with rage* hij liep rood aan van woede 2 (te) sierlijk, bombastisch: *a ~ passage* (or: *patch*) een briljant gedeelte [in tedious text]

¹**purport** (n) strekking, bedoeling

²**purport** (vb) beweren: *he ~s to be the inventor of the electric blanket* hij beweert de uitvinder van de elektrische deken te zijn 2 kennelijk bedoelen 3 van plan zijn

purpose 1 doel^h, bedoeling, plan^h, voornemen^h: *accidentally ~* per ongeluk expres; *he did it on ~* hij deed het met opzet 2 zin, (beoogd) effect^h, resultaat^h, nut^h: *all your help will be to no ~* al je hulp zal tevergeefs zijn 3 de zaak waarom het gaat: *his remark is (not) to the ~* zijn opmerking is (niet) ter zake 4 vastberadenheid

purposeful 1 vastberaden 2 met een doel, opzettelijk

¹**purr** (n) 1 spinnend geluid^h; gespin^h [of cat] 2 zoemend geluid^h; gesnor^h [of machine]

²**purr** (vb) 1 spinnen [of cat] 2 gonzen; zoemen [of machine]

¹**purse** (n) 1 portemonnee 2 [Am] damestas(je^h)

²**purse** (vb) samentrekken, rimpelen, tuiten: *indignantly, she ~d her lips* ze tuitte verontwaardigd de lippen

purse strings geldbuideltkoordjes; [fig] financiële macht: *loosen the ~* de uitgaven verhogen; *tighten the ~* bezuinigen; de buikriem aanhalen

pursuance uitvoering, voortzetting: *in (the) ~ of his duty* tijdens het vervullen van zijn plicht

pursuant (ver)volgend, uitvoerend || *~ to your instructions* overeenkomstig uw instructies

pursue 1 jacht maken op, achtervolgen 2 volgen; achternalopen [also fig]; lastigvallen: *this memory ~d him* deze herinnering liet hem niet los 3 doorgaan met, vervolgen: *it is wiser not to ~ the matter* het is verstandiger de zaak verder te laten rusten

pursuer achtervolger; doorzetter

pursuit 1 achtervolging; jacht [also fig]: *in*

~ *of* happiness op zoek naar het geluk **2** bezigheid, hobby

purvey bevoorraden met; leveren [food]

pus pus⁺ʰ, etter

¹push (n) **1** duw, stoot, zet, ruk: *give that door* a ~ geef die deur even een zetje **2** grootscheepse aanval [of army]; offensiefʰ; [fig] energieke poging **3** energie, doorzettingsvermogenʰ, fut **4** druk, nood, crisis: *if* (or: *when*) *it comes to the* ~ als het erop aankomt || *give s.o. the* ~ **a)** iem. ontslaan; **b)** iem. de bons geven; *at* a ~ als het echt nodig is, in geval van nood

²push (vb) **1** duwen, stoten, dringen **2** vorderingen maken, vooruitgaan, verder gaan: ~ *ahead* (or: *forward, on*) (rustig) doorgaan; ~ *ahead/along* (or: *forward, on*) *with* vooruitgang boeken met **3** pushen, dealen

³push (vb) **1** (weg)duwen, een zet geven, voortduwen; [fig] beïnvloeden; dwingen: ~ *the button* op de knop drukken; *he* ~*es the matter too far* hij drijft de zaak te ver door; ~ *s.o. about* (or: *around*) iem. ruw behandelen, iem. commanderen, iem. met minachting behandelen; ~ *back the enemy* de vijand terugdringen; ~ *o.s. forward* zich op de voorgrond dringen; *that* ~*ed prices up* dat joeg de prijzen omhoog **2** druk uitoefenen op, lastigvallen, aandringen bij: *don't* ~ *your luck (too far)!* stel je geluk niet te veel op de proef!; *he* ~*ed his luck and fell* hij werd overmoedig en viel **3** pushen [drugs]

pushback 1 negatieve reactie **2** [aviation] pushback **3** [migrants] (het) terugsturen

push button drukknop

pushcart handkar

pushchair wandelwagen, buggy

pusher 1 (te) ambitieus iem., streber **2** (illegale) drugsverkoper, (drugs)dealer

push in 1 een gesprek ruw onderbreken, ertussen komen, iem. in de rede vallen **2** vordringen

pushing 1 opdringerig **2** vol energie, ondernemend

push off 1 ervandoor gaan, weggaan, ophoepelen: *now* ~, *will you* hoepel nu alsjeblieft eens op **2** uitvaren, van wal steken

push through doordrukken, er doorheen slepen: *we'll push this matter through* we zullen deze zaak erdoor krijgen

pushy 1 opdringerig **2** streberig

puss 1 poes [esp used to call animal]: *Puss in boots* de Gelaarsde Kat **2** poesjeʰ, liefjeʰ, schatjeʰ

pussy 1 poes(jeʰ), kat(jeʰ) **2** [Am] watjeʰ; eiʰ **3** [vulg] kutjeʰ

pussycat [inform] **1** poesjeʰ; katjeʰ **2** schatjeʰ; liefjeʰ

pustule puistjeʰ

¹put (vb) varen, koers zetten: *the ship* ~ *into the port* het schip voer de haven binnen || *his*

sickness ~ *paid to his plans* zijn ziekte maakte een eind aan zijn plannen; ~ *(up)on s.o.* iem. last bezorgen

²put (vb) **1** zetten, plaatsen, leggen, steken; stellen [also fig]; brengen [in a situation]: ~ *pressure (up)on* pressie uitoefenen op; ~ *a price on sth.* een prijskaartje hangen aan; ~ *sth. behind o.s.* zich over iets heen zetten, met iets breken; ~ *the children to bed* de kinderen naar bed brengen; ~ *to good use* goed gebruikmaken van **2** onderwerpen; dwingen, drijven: ~ *s.o. through it* iem. een zware test afnemen, iem. zwaar op de proef stellen **3** (in)zetten, verwedden: ~ *money* on geld zetten op; [fig] zeker zijn van **4** voorleggen, ter sprake brengen: ~ *a proposal before* (or: *to*) *a meeting* een vergadering een voorstel voorleggen **5** uitdrukken, zeggen, stellen: *how shall I* ~ *it?* hoe zal ik het zeggen || *you'll be hard* ~ *to think of a second example* het zal je niet meevallen om een tweede voorbeeld te bedenken; ~ *it* (or: *one, sth.*) *across s.o.* het iem. flikken, iem. beetnemen; *not* ~ *it past s.o. to do sth.* iem. ertoe in staat achten iets te doen; *stay* ~ blijven waar je bent, op zijn plaats blijven

¹put about (vb) laveren, van richting veranderen

²put about (vb) **1** van richting doen veranderen [ship] **2** verspreiden [rumour, lies]

put across overbrengen [also fig]; aanvaardbaar maken, aan de man brengen: *know how to put one's ideas across* zijn ideeën weten over te brengen

put aside opzijzetten, wegzetten; opzijleggen [also of money]; sparen

putative vermeend; vermoedelijk

put back 1 terugzetten, terugdraaien: *put the clock back* de klok terugzetten [also fig] **2** vertragen, tegenhouden: *production has been* ~ *by a strike* de productie is door een staking vertraagd

put by opzijzetten; wegzetten [money]

¹put down (vb) landen [of aeroplane]

²put down (vb) **1** neerzetten, neerleggen **2** onderdrukken [rebellion, crime etc] **3** opschrijven, noteren: *put sth. down to ignorance* iets toeschrijven aan onwetendheid **4** een spuitje geven [sick animal]; uit zijn lijden helpen **5** afzetten; uit laten stappen [passengers] **6** aanbetalen **7** kleineren, vernederen; [fig] op zijn plaats zetten

¹put in (vb) **1** een verzoek indienen, solliciteren: ~ *for* zich kandidaat stellen voor; ~ *for leave* verlof (aan)vragen **2** binnenlopen: ~ *at a port* een haven binnenlopen

²put in (vb) **1** (erin) plaatsen, zetten, inlassen, invoegen: ~ *an appearance* zich (eens) laten zien **2** opwerpen: ~ *a (good) word for s.o.* een goed woordje voor iem. doen **3** besteden [time, work, money]; doorbrengen

[time]: *he ~ a lot of hard* **work** *on the project* hij heeft een boel werk in het project gestopt **4** indienen, klacht, document: *~ a claim for damages* een eis tot schadevergoeding indienen

put off 1 uitstellen, afzeggen **2** afzetten; uit laten stappen [passengers] **3** afschrikken, (van zich) afstoten: *the* **smell** *of that food put me off* de reuk van dat eten deed me walgen **4** afschepen, ontmoedigen **5** van de wijs brengen: *the* **speaker** *was ~ by the noise* de spreker werd door het lawaai van zijn stuk gebracht **6** uitdoen, uitdraaien; afzetten [light, gas, radio etc]

put on 1 voorwenden; aannemen [attitude]: *~ a brave* **face** flink zijn **2** toevoegen, verhogen: *~* **weight** aankomen, zwaarder worden; *put it on* a) aankomen [weight]; b) overdrijven **3** opvoeren, op de planken brengen: *~ a* **play** een toneelstuk op de planken brengen; *put it on* doen alsof **4** aantrekken [clothing]; opzetten [glasses, hat] **5** inzetten; inleggen [extra train etc] **6** in werking stellen; aandoen [light]; aanzetten [radio etc]; opzetten [record, kettle]: *~ a* **brake** (or: *the* **brakes**) afremmen [fig] **7** in contact brengen, doorverbinden: *who put the police on to me?* wie heeft de politie op mijn spoor gezet?

¹put out (vb) uitvaren: *~ to sea* zee kiezen

²put out (vb) **1** uitsteken, tonen: *~* **feelers** zijn voelhoorns uitsteken **2** aanwenden, inzetten, gebruiken **3** uitdoen, doven, blussen: *~ the* **fire** (or: **light**) het vuur (or: licht) doven **4** van zijn stuk brengen **5** storen: *put* **o.s.** *out* zich moeite getroosten, moeite doen **6** buiten zetten [garbage]; eruit gooien, de deur wijzen **7** uitvaardigen, uitgeven; uitzenden [message]: *~ an official* **statement** een communiqué uitgeven **8** uitbesteden [work]: *~ a job* **to** *a subcontractor* een werk aan een onderaannemer uitbesteden || [inform] *I'm just putting it out* **there** ik zeg het maar even, het is maar een idee

¹put over (vb) overvaren

²put over (vb) **1** overbrengen [also fig]; aan de man brengen: *put (a fast) one* (or: *sth.*) *over* **on** *s.o.* iem. iets wijsmaken **2** [Am] uitstellen

putrefy (doen) (ver)rotten, (doen) bederven

putrid (ver)rot, vergaan, verpest

putsch staatsgreep; putsch

put through (door)verbinden [telephone call]

put together 1 samenvoegen, samenstellen, combineren: *more than all the* **others** *~* meer dan alle anderen bij elkaar **2** verzamelen, verenigen || *put* **two** *and two together* a) zijn conclusies trekken; b) logisch nadenken

putty 1 stopverf **2** plamuurʰ || *be ~ in s.o.'s*

hands* als was in iemands handen zijn

¹put up (vb) logeren: *~* **at** *an inn* in een herberg logeren || *I wouldn't ~* **with** *it any longer* ik zou het niet langer meer slikken

²put up (vb) **1** opzetten, oprichten; bouwen [tent, statue etc]: *~ a* **smokescreen** een rookgordijn leggen **2** opsteken, hijsen, ophangen: *put one's* **hands** *up* de handen opsteken [indicating surrender] **3** bekendmaken, ophangen: *~ a* **notice** een bericht ophangen **4** verhogen, opslaan: *~ the* **rent** de huurprijs verhogen **5** huisvesten, logeren **6** beschikbaar stellen [funds]; voorschieten: *who will ~* **money** *for new research?* wie stelt geld beschikbaar voor nieuw onderzoek? **7** bieden, tonen: *the rebels ~ strong* **resistance** de rebellen boden hevig weerstand **8** (te koop) aanbieden: *they ~ their house* **for** *sale* zij boden hun huis te koop aan **9** kandidaat stellen, voordragen: *they put him up* **for** *chairman* zij droegen hem als voorzitter voor || *put s.o. up* **to** *sth.* a) iem. opstoken tot iets; b) iem. op de hoogte brengen van iets; *~* **with** *sth.* iets (moeten) slikken; *I can ~* **with** *that* daar kan ik mee leven

put-up afgesproken: *it's a ~* **job** het is een doorgestoken kaart

¹puzzle (n) **1** raadselʰ, probleemʰ **2** puzzel: **crossword** *~* kruiswoordraadselʰ

²puzzle (vb) peinzen, piekeren

³puzzle (vb) **1** voor een raadsel zetten, verbazen, verbijsteren **2** in verwarring brengen **3** overpeinzen: *~ one's* **brains** *(about, over)* zich het hoofd breken (over); *~ sth. out* iets uitpluizen

puzzled in de war, perplex

puzzler 1 puzzelaar(ster) **2** probleemʰ, moeilijke vraag

puzzling onbegrijpelijk; raadselachtig

¹pygmy (n) pygmee, dwerg; [fig] nietig persoon

²pygmy (adj) heel klein, dwerg-

pyjamas pyjama: *four* **pairs** *of ~* vier pyjama's

pyramid piramide

pyre brandstapel

pyromaniac pyromaan

pyrotechnic vuurwerk-: *a ~* **display** een vuurwerk(show)

pyrrhic: *Pyrrhic* **victory** pyrrusoverwinning

python python

q

QA *quality assurance* kwaliteitsborging, kwaliteitscontrole
Qatar Qatar
¹Qatari (n) Qatarees, Qatarese
²Qatari (adj) Qatarees
Q-tip [Am] wattenstaafjeʰ
¹quack (n) **1** kwakzalver, charlatan **2** kwak [of duck]; gekwaakʰ
²quack (vb) **1** kwaken [of duck] **2** zwetsen, kletsen
quad bike quad
quadrangle 1 vierhoek, vierkantʰ, rechthoek **2** (vierhoekige) binnenplaats, vierkant pleinʰ (met de gebouwen eromheen)
¹quadrilateral (n) vierhoek
²quadrilateral (adj) vierzijdig
quadriplegia [med] [roughly] hoge dwarslaesie
quadruped viervoeter, (als) van een viervoeter
¹quadruple (n) viervoudʰ
²quadruple (adj) vierdelig, viervoudig
quadruplet één van een vierling: ~s vierling
quagmire moerasʰ [also fig]; poel
¹quail (n) kwartel
²quail (vb) (terug)schrikken, bang worden
quaint 1 apart, curieus, ongewoon: *a ~ old building* een bijzonder, oud gebouw **2** vreemd, grillig
¹quake (n) **1** schok **2** aardbeving
²quake (vb) schokken, trillen, bibberen
qualification 1 beperking, voorbehoudʰ: *a statement with many ~s* een verklaring met veel kanttekeningen **2** kwaliteit, verdienste, kwalificatie **3** (bewijsʰ van) geschiktheid: *a medical ~* een medische bevoegdheid **4** beschrijving, kenmerking
qualified 1 beperkt, voorwaardelijk, voorlopig: *~ optimism* gematigd optimisme **2** bevoegd, geschikt: *a ~ nurse* een gediplomeerde verpleegster
¹qualify (vb) zich kwalificeren, zich bekwamen, geschikt zijn, worden: *~ for membership* in aanmerking komen voor lidmaatschap
²qualify (vb) **1** beperken, kwalificeren, (verder) bepalen: *a ~ing exam* een akte-examen **2** geschikt maken, het recht geven **3** verzachten, matigen
qualitative kwalitatief
quality 1 kwaliteit, deugd, capaciteit: *~ of life* leefbaarheid, kwaliteit van het bestaan **2** eigenschap, kenmerkʰ, karakteristiek

3 kwaliteit, waarde, gehalteʰ: *~ newspaper* kwaliteitskrant; *~ time* kwaliteitstijd
qualm 1 (gevoel van) onzekerheid, ongemakkelijk gevoelʰ: *she had no ~s about going on her own* ze zag er niet tegenop om alleen te gaan **2** (gewetens)wroeging
quandary moeilijke situatie, dilemmaʰ, onzekerheid: *we were in a ~ about how to react* we wisten niet goed hoe we moesten reageren
quantify kwantificeren, in getallen uitdrukken, meten, bepalen
quantity 1 hoeveelheid, aantalʰ, som, portie **2** grootheid; [fig] persoon; dingʰ: *an unknown ~* een onbekende (grootheid), een nog niet doorgronde (or: berekenbare) persoon **3** kwantiteit, hoeveelheid, omvang
¹quantum (n) kwantumʰ, (benodigde/wenselijke) hoeveelheid
²quantum (adj) spectaculair: *~ leap* spectaculaire stap vooruit, doorbraak, omwenteling
¹quarantine (n) quarantaine, isolatie
²quarantine (vb) in quarantaine plaatsen; [fig also] isoleren
quark quark
¹quarrel (n) **1** ruzie, onenigheid: *start (or: pick) a ~ (with s.o.)* ruzie zoeken (met iem.) **2** kritiek, reden tot ruzie: *I have no ~ with him* ik heb niets tegen hem
²quarrel (vb) **1** ruzie maken, onenigheid hebben **2** kritiek hebben, aanmerkingen hebben
quarrelsome ruziezoekend
quarry 1 (nagejaagde) prooi, wildʰ **2** (steen)groeve
quart quartʰ, kwart gallon; twee pints [measure of capacity] ‖ *put a ~ into a pint pot* het onmogelijke proberen
quarter 1 kwartʰ, vierde deelʰ: *a ~ of an hour* een kwartier; *three ~s of the people voted* driekwart van de mensen stemde **2** kwart dollar, kwartjeʰ **3** kwartaalʰ; [Am] collegeperiode; academisch kwartaalʰ **4** kwartierʰ [of time, moon]: *for an hour and a ~* een uur en een kwartier (lang); *it's a ~ past (or: to) eight* het is kwart over (or: voor) acht **5** quarter; kwartʰ [weight, size, measure] **6** (wind)richting; windstreek [of compass]; hoek, kant: *I expect no help from that ~* ik verwacht geen hulp uit die hoek **7** (stads)deelʰ, wijk, gewestʰ **8** genade, clementie: *ask for (or: cry) ~* om genade smeken **9** (-s) [oft mil] kwartierʰ, verblijfʰ, woonplaats, legerplaats, kamer(s); [fig] kring: *this information comes from the highest ~s* deze inlichtingen komen uit de hoogste kringen
quarterdeck [shipp] **1** (officiers)halfdekʰ **2** (marine)officieren
quarter-final kwartfinale
¹quarterly (n) driemaandelijks tijdschriftʰ,

kwartaalblad[h]

²**quarterly** (adj) driemaandelijks, viermaal per jaar, kwartaalsgewijs

quartermaster intendant; kwartiermaker

quartet kwartet[h], viertal[h]

quarto kwarto[h]

quartz kwarts[h]

quasi quasi, zogenaamd

¹**quaver** (n) **1** trilling **2** [mus] achtste (noot)

²**quaver** (vb) trillen, beven, sidderen: *in a ~ing voice* met bevende stem

quay kade

queasy 1 misselijk, onpasselijk **2** overgevoelig, kieskeurig: *he has a ~ conscience* hij neemt het erg nauw

¹**queen** (n) **1** koningin **2** [chess] koningin, dame **3** [cards] vrouw, dame: *~ of hearts* hartenvrouw **4** nicht, verwijfde flikker

²**queen** (vb): *~ it over s.o.* de mevrouw spelen ten opzichte van iem.

queen consort gemalin van de koning; koningin

Queen's English standaard Engels, BBC-Engels[h]

¹**queer** (n) **1** [offensive] homo, flikker **2** queer

²**queer** (adj) **1** vreemd, raar, zonderling: *a ~ customer* een rare snuiter **2** verdacht, onbetrouwbaar **3** onwel, niet lekker **4** [offensive] homoseksueel **5** queer || *be in Queer Street* **a)** in moeilijkheden zitten; **b)** schulden hebben

quell onderdrukken, een eind maken aan, onderwerpen

quench 1 doven, blussen **2** lessen [thirst]

querulous 1 klagend **2** klagerig

¹**query** (n) vraag, vraagteken[h]

²**query** (vb) **1** vragen (naar), informeren (naar) **2** in twijfel trekken, een vraagteken plaatsen bij [also lit]; betwijfelen

query language zoektaal

quest zoektocht: *the ~ for the Holy Grail* de zoektocht naar de Heilige Graal

¹**question** (n) **1** vraag: *a leading ~* een suggestieve vraag **2** vraagstuk[h], probleem[h], kwestie: *that is out of the ~* er is geen sprake van, daar komt niets van in; *that is not the ~* daar gaat het niet om **3** twijfel, onzekerheid, bezwaar[h]: *call sth. into ~* iets in twijfel trekken; *beyond (all)* (or: *without*) *~* ongetwijfeld, stellig || *beg the ~* het punt in kwestie als bewezen aanvaarden; *pop the ~ (to her)* (haar) ten huwelijk vragen

²**question** (vb) **1** vragen, ondervragen, uithoren: *~ s.o. about* (or: *on*) *his plans* iem. over zijn plannen ondervragen **2** onderzoeken **3** betwijfelen, zich afvragen: *I ~ whether* (or: *if*) … ik betwijfel het of …

questionable 1 twijfelachtig **2** verdacht

question mark vraagteken[h] [also fig]; mysterie[h], onzekerheid

questionnaire vragenlijst

question time vragenuurtje[h]

¹**queue** (n) rij, file || *jump the ~* voordringen, voor je beurt gaan

²**queue** (vb) een rij vormen, in de rij (gaan) staan

queue-jump voordringen, voor zijn beurt gaan

¹**quibble** (n) spitsvondigheid, haarkloverij

²**quibble** (vb) uitvluchten zoeken, bekvechten: *we don't have to ~ about the details* we hoeven niet over de details te harrewarren

quiche quiche, hartige taart

¹**quick** (n) **1** levend vlees[h] [under skin, nail] **2** hart[h], kern, essentie: *cut s.o. to the ~* iemands gevoelens diep kwetsen **3** [Am] kwik[h]

²**quick** (adj) **1** snel, gauw, vlug: *be as ~ as lightning* bliksemsnel zijn; *~ march!* voorwaarts mars!; *in ~ succession* snel achter elkaar; *he is ~ to take offence* hij is gauw beledigd **2** gevoelig, vlug (van begrip), scherp **3** levendig, opgewekt

³**quick** (adv) [inform] vlug, gauw: *please, come ~* kom alsjeblieft snel

quicken 1 levend worden, (weer) tot leven komen: *his pulse ~ed* zijn polsslag werd weer sterker **2** leven beginnen te vertonen; tekenen van leven geven [of child in womb]

quickie vluggertje[h], haastwerk[h], prutswerk[h]

quickly snel: *~ run inside and get your coat* ren snel naar binnen en pak je jas

quicksand drijfzand[h]

quicksilver kwik(zilver)[h]; [fig] levendig temperament[h]

quickstep quickstep, snelle foxtrot

quick-tempered lichtgeraakt; opvliegend

quick-witted vlug van begrip, gevat, scherp

quid 1 pond[h] [sterling] **2** (tabaks)pruim[h]

quid pro quo vergoeding; compensatie

quiescence rust, stilte

¹**quiet** (n) **1** stilte **2** rust, kalmte: *they lived in peace and ~* zij leefden in rust en vrede

²**quiet** (adj) **1** stil, rustig: *~ as a mouse* muisstil **2** heimelijk, geheim: *keep ~ about last night* hou je mond over vannacht **3** zonder drukte, ongedwongen: *a ~ dinner party* een informeel etentje

¹**quieten** (vb) (also + down) tot bedaren brengen, kalmeren, tot rust brengen: *my reassurance didn't ~ her fear* mijn geruststelling verminderde haar angst niet

²**quieten** (vb) (also + down) rustig worden, bedaren, kalmeren

quietude kalmte, (gemoeds)rust, vrede

quietway [roughly] fietsstraat: *~ route* rustige fietsroute

quilt 1 gewatteerde deken, dekbed[h]: *a continental ~* een dekbed **2** sprei

quince kweepeer

quinine kinine

quintessence 1 kern, hoofdzaak **2** het beste, het fijnste

quintet vijftal[h], (groep van) vijf musici, kwintet[h]

quip 1 schimpscheut, steek **2** geestigheid, woordspeling

quirk 1 spitsvondigheid, uitvlucht **2** geestigheid, spotternij **3** gril, nuk: *a ~ of fate* een gril van het lot **4** (rare) kronkel, eigenaardigheid

quirky 1 spitsvondig **2** grillig; eigenzinnig

¹quit (adj) vrij, verlost, bevrijd: *we are well ~ of those difficulties* goed, dat we van die moeilijkheden af zijn

²quit (vb) **1** ophouden, stoppen: *I've had enough, I ~* ik heb er genoeg van, ik kap ermee **2** opgeven **3** vertrekken, ervandoor gaan, zijn baan opgeven: *the neighbours have already had* **notice** *to ~* de buren is de huur al opgezegd

³quit (vb) **1** ophouden met, stoppen met: *~ complaining about the cold!* hou op met klagen over de kou! **2** verlaten, vertrekken van, heengaan van

quite 1 helemaal, geheel, volledig, absoluut: *~* **possible** best mogelijk; *you're ~* **right** je hebt volkomen gelijk; *that's ~ another matter* dat is een heel andere zaak **2** nogal, enigszins, tamelijk: *it's ~* **cold** *today* het is nogal koud vandaag **3** werkelijk, echt, in feite: *they seem ~* **happy** *together* zij lijken echt gelukkig samen **4** erg, veel: *there were ~ a* **few** *people* er waren flink wat mensen; *that was ~ a* **party** dat was me het feestje wel

quits quitte: *now we* **are** *~* nu staan we quitte

¹quiver (n) **1** pijlkoker **2** trilling, siddering, beving

²quiver (vb) (doen) trillen, (doen) beven, sidderen

¹quiz (n) **1** ondervraging, verhoor[h] **2** test, kort examen[h] **3** quiz

²quiz (vb) **1** ondervragen, uithoren **2** mondeling examineren

quizzical 1 komisch, grappig **2** spottend, plagerig **3** vorsend, vragend: *she gave me a ~* **look** ze keek me met een onderzoekende blik aan

quota 1 quota, evenredig deel[h], aandeel[h] **2** (maximum) aantal[h]

quotation 1 citaat[h], aanhaling, het citeren **2** notering [of Stock Exchange, exchange rate, price] **3** prijsopgave

quotation mark aanhalingsteken[h]

¹quote (n) **1** citaat[h], aanhaling **2** notering [of Stock Exchange etc] **3** aanhalingsteken[h]: *in ~s* tussen aanhalingstekens

²quote (vb) **1** citeren, aanhalen **2** opgeven [price]

quotient quotiënt[h]

r

rabbi rabbi, rabbijn

¹**rabbit** (n) konijn*ʰ*, konijnenbont*ʰ*, konijnen-
vlees*ʰ*

²**rabbit** (vb) **1** op konijnen jagen **2** kletsen,
zeuren

rabbit hole konijnenhol*ʰ*

rabbit warren 1 konijnenveld*ʰ* **2** doolhof,
wirwar van straatjes

rabble kluwen*ʰ*, troep, bende: *the* ~ het gepeupel

rabid 1 razend, woest **2** fanatiek **3** dol,
hondsdol

rabies hondsdolheid

raccoon *see* racoon

¹**race** (n) **1** wedren, wedloop, race: ~ *against*
time race tegen de klok; *the* ~s de (honden)-
rennen, de paardenrennen **2** sterke stroom
3 ras*ʰ* **4** volk*ʰ*, natie, stam, slag*ʰ*, klasse

²**race** (vb) **1** wedlopen, aan een wedloop
deelnemen, een wedstrijd houden **2** rennen,
hollen, snellen **3** doorslaan [of screw,
wheel]; doordraaien [of engine]

³**race** (vb) **1** een wedren houden met, om het
hardst lopen met: *I'll* ~ *you* **to** *that tree* laten
we doen wie het eerst bij die boom is
2 (zeer) snel vervoeren: *they* ~*d the child* **to**
hospital ze vlogen met het kind naar het ziekenhuis **3** laten doordraaien [engine]

racecourse renbaan

racehorse renpaard*ʰ*

racer 1 renner, hardloper **2** renpaard*ʰ*
3 racefiets **4** renwagen **5** raceboot **6** wed-
strijdjacht*ʰ* **7** renschaats: ~s noren

racetrack (ovale) renbaan, circuit*ʰ*

racial raciaal: ~ *discrimination* ras(sen)dis-
criminatie

¹**racing** (n) het wedrennen, het deelnemen
aan wedstrijden

²**racing** (n) rensport

racism 1 racisme*ʰ* **2** rassenhaat

¹**racist** (n) racist

²**racist** (adj) racistisch

¹**rack** (n) **1** rek*ʰ*, (bagage)rek*ʰ* **2** ruif **3** pijnbank: [fig] *be* **on** *the* ~ op de pijnbank liggen,
in grote spanning (*or:* onzekerheid) verkeren **4** kwelling, marteling **5** verwoesting, afbraak, ondergang: *go to* ~ *and* **ruin** geheel
vervallen, instorten **6** [Am; vulg] borsten,
tieten

²**rack** (vb) kwellen, pijnigen, teisteren: ~
one's **brains** zijn hersens pijnigen; ~*ed with*
jealousy verteerd door jaloezie

racket 1 [sport] racket*ʰ* **2** sneeuwschoen

3 lawaai*ʰ*, herrie, kabaal*ʰ*: *kick up a* ~ een rel
(*or:* herrie) schoppen **4** bedriegerij, bedrog*ʰ*,
zwendel **5** [inform] gangsterpraktijken, mis-
dadige organisatie, afpersing, intimidatie

racketeer gangster, misdadiger, afperser

racoon 1 wasbeer **2** wasberenbont*ʰ*

racy 1 markant; krachtig [style, person(ali-
ty)] **2** pittig, kruidig, geurig **3** pikant; gewaagd [story]

radar radar

radial radiaal, stervormig, straal-: ~ *tyre* ra-
diaalband

radiance straling, schittering, pracht

radiant 1 stralend, schitterend: *he was* ~
with joy hij straalde van vreugde **2** stervormig **3** stralings-: ~ *heat* stralingswarmte

¹**radiate** (vb) **1** stralen, schijnen **2** een ster
vormen: *streets radiating* **from** *a square* straten
die straalsgewijs vanaf een plein lopen

²**radiate** (vb) **1** uitstralen, (naar alle kanten)
verspreiden: ~ *confidence* vertrouwen uitstralen **2** bestralen

radiation 1 straling **2** bestraling

radiation sickness stralingsziekte

radiator radiator, radiatorkachel, radia-
teur; koeler [of engine]

¹**radical** (n) **1** basis(principe*ʰ*) **2** wortel(te-
ken*ʰ*) **3** radicaal*ʰ*

²**radical** (adj) **1** radicaal, drastisch **2** fundamenteel, wezenlijk, essentieel **3** wortel-: ~
sign wortelteken*ʰ*

radicalize radicaliseren

radio radio(toestel*ʰ*)

radioactive radioactief

radio button checkbox; hokje*ʰ* dat aangevinkt kan worden

radiogram röntgenfoto

radiography radiografie

radiologist radioloog

radiotherapy [med] bestraling

radish radijs

radium radium*ʰ*

radius straal, radius; halve middellijn [of
circle]: *within* a ~ *of four miles* binnen een
straal van vier mijl

RAF *Royal Air Force*

raffish liederlijk, losbandig, wild

¹**raffle** (n) loterij, verloting

²**raffle** (vb) (also + off) verloten

raft 1 vlot*ʰ*, drijvende steiger **2** reddingvlot*ʰ*
3 grote verzameling: *he worked his way*
through a whole ~ *of letters* hij werkte zich
door een hele berg brieven heen

rafter dakspant*ʰ*

¹**rag** (n) **1** versleten kledingstuk*ʰ*, lomp, vod*ʰ*:
from ~s *to* **riches** van armoede naar rijkdom
2 lapje*ʰ*, vodje*ʰ*, stuk*ʰ*, flard: *I haven't a* ~ *to*
put *on* ik heb niets om aan te trekken **3** vlag,
gordijn*ʰ*, krant, blaadje*ʰ*: *the local* ~ het
plaatselijke blaadje **4** herrie, keet, (studenten)lol ‖ *chew the* ~ mopperen, kankeren

²**rag** (vb) **1** pesten, plagen: *they ~ged the teacher* zij schopten keet bij de leraar **2** te grazen nemen, een poets bakken
ragamuffin schooiertjeʰ
ragbag allegaartjeʰ
rag doll lappenpop
¹**rage** (n) **1** manie, passie, bevlieging: *short hair is (all) the ~ now* kort haar is nu een rage **2** woede, woede-uitbarsting, razernij: *be in a ~* woedend zijn
²**rage** (vb) woeden, tieren, razen; [fig] tekeergaan: *a raging fire* een felle brand
rage-cry huilen van woede
ragged 1 haveloos, gescheurd, gerafeld: *~ trousers* een kapotte broek **2** ruig, onverzorgd: *a ~ beard* een ruige baard **3** ongelijk, getand, knoestig: *~ rocks* scherpe rotsen
ragtag gepeupelʰ, grauwʰ ‖ *~ and bobtail* uitschotʰ, schoremʰ
¹**raid** (n) **1** inval, (verrassings)overval **2** rooftocht, roofoverval: *a ~ on a bank* een bankoverval **3** politieoverval, razzia
²**raid** (vb) **1** overvallen, binnenvallen **2** (be)roven, plunderen, leegroven: *they have been ~ing the fridge as usual* ze hebben zoals gewoonlijk de koelkast geplunderd
raider 1 overvaller **2** kaper(schipʰ) **3** rover
¹**rail** (n) **1** lat, balk, stang **2** leuning **3** omheining, hek(werk)ʰ, slagboom **4** rail, spoorstaafʰ; [fig] trein; spoorwegen: *travel by ~* sporen, per trein reizen **5** reling ‖ *run off the ~s* uit de band springen, ontsporen
²**rail** (vb) (+ against, at) schelden (op), uitvaren (tegen), tekeergaan (tegen)
railcard treinabonnementʰ
railing 1 traliewerkʰ; spijlen [of gate] **2** leuning, reling, hekʰ, balustrade **3** gescheldʰ
raillery scherts, grap(pen), gekheid
rail pass treinabonnementʰ
railroad 1 [Am] per trein vervoeren **2** jagen, haasten, drijven: *~ a bill through Congress* een wetsvoorstel erdoor jagen in het Congres
railway 1 spoorweg, spoorlijn **2** spoorwegmaatschappij, de spoorwegen
railway crossing overweg
railway station spoorwegstationʰ
¹**rain** (n) **1** regen, regenbui, regenval: *it looks like ~* het ziet er naar uit dat het gaat regenen **2** (stort)vloed, stroom: *a ~ of blows* een reeks klappen **3** (the rains) regentijd, regenseizoenʰ
²**rain** (vb) **1** regenen **2** neerstromen **3** doen neerdalen, laten neerkomen: *the father ~ed presents upon his only daughter* de vader overstelpte zijn enige dochter met cadeaus ‖ *it ~s invitations* het regent uitnodigingen
rainbow regenboog
rainbow flag regenboogvlag
rain check nieuw toegangsbewijsʰ [for

match, event]: *I don't want a drink now, but I'll take a ~ on it* ik wil nu niets drinken, maar ik hou het van je tegoed
raincoat regenjas
rain down neerkomen, neerdalen (in groten getale): *blows rained down (up)on his head* een regen van klappen kwam neer op zijn hoofd
rainfall regen(val), neerslag
rain forest regenwoudʰ
rainproof regendicht, tegen regen bestand
rainstorm stortbui
rainy regenachtig, regen-: *save (up)/provide (or: put away, keep) sth. for a ~ day* een appeltje voor de dorst bewaren
raise 1 wekken; opwekken [from death]; wakker maken: *~ expectations* verwachtingen wekken **2** opzetten, tot opstand bewegen **3** opwekken, opbeuren: *the news of her arrival ~d his hopes* het nieuws van haar aankomst gaf hem weer hoop **4** bouwen, opzetten, stichten **5** kweken, produceren, verbouwen **6** grootbrengen, opvoeden: *~ a family* kinderen grootbrengen **7** uiten, aanheffen, ter sprake brengen, opperen: *~ objections to sth.* bezwaren tegen iets naar voren brengen **8** doen ontstaan, beginnen, in het leven roepen: *his behaviour ~s doubts* zijn gedrag roept twijfels op **9** (op)heffen, opnemen; opslaan [eyes]; omhoog doen **10** bevorderen, promoveren **11** versterken, vergroten; verheffen [voice]; vermeerderen, verhogen: *~ the temperature* de verwarming hoger zetten; [fig] de spanning laten oplopen **12** heffen; innen [money]; bijeenbrengen, inzamelen: *~ taxes* belastingen heffen **13** op de been brengen; werven [eg army] **14** opheffen, beëindigen: *~ a blockade* een blokkade opheffen **15** [maths] verheffen tot [power]
raisin rozijn
¹**rake** (n) **1** hark, riek: *as lean as a ~* zo mager als een lat **2** losbol **3** schuinte; val [of mast,]; helling **4** hellingshoek
²**rake** (vb) **1** harken **2** zoeken, snuffelen: *the customs officers ~d through my luggage* de douanebeambten doorzochten mijn bagage van onder tot boven **3** oplopen, hellen
³**rake** (vb) **1** (bijeen)harken [also fig]; vergaren, bijeenhalen: *you must be raking it in* je moet wel scheppen geld verdienen **2** rakelen, poken; [fig] oprakelen: *~ over old ashes* oprakelen, oude koeien uit de sloot halen **3** doorzoeken, uitkammen: *~ one's memory* zijn geheugen pijnigen
rake up 1 bijeenharken, aanharken **2** [inform] optrommelen, opscharrelen **3** oprakelen [also fig]: *~ old stories* oude koeien uit de sloot halen
rakish 1 liederlijk, losbandig **2** zwierig, vlot

3 smalgebouwd, snel, snelvarend

¹rally (n) **1** bijeenkomst, vergadering **2** opleving, herstelʰ **3** [tennis] rally **4** rally, sterrit **5** herstelʰ [of share prices]

²rally (vb) **1** bijeenkomen, zich verzamelen **2** zich aansluiten: ~ *round the flag* zich om de vlag scharen **3** (zich) herstellen, opleven, weer bijkomen **4** weer omhooggaan; zich herstellen [of share prices]

³rally (vb) **1** verzamelen, ordenen, herenigen **2** bijeenbrengen, verenigen, op de been brengen **3** doen opleven, nieuw leven inblazen **4** plagen, voor de gek houden

rally (a)round te hulp komen, helpen, bijspringen

¹ram (n) **1** ram [male sheep] **2** stormram

²ram (vb) **1** aanstampen, vaststampen **2** heien **3** doordringen, overduidelijk maken **4** persen, proppen **5** rammen, bonken, beuken, botsen op

RAM *random-access memory* RAMʰ

Ramadan ramadan; vastenmaand

¹ramble (n) zwerftocht, wandeltocht, uitstapjeʰ

²ramble (vb) **1** dwalen, zwerven, trekken **2** afdwalen, bazelen: *once he gets started he ~s on* als hij eenmaal begonnen is, blijft hij maar doorzeuren **3** wild groeien; woekeren [of plants] **4** kronkelen [of path, river]

rambler 1 wandelaar, trekker, zwerver **2** klimroos

rambling 1 rondtrekkend, ronddolend **2** onsamenhangend, verward: *he made a few ~ remarks* hij maakte een paar vage opmerkingen **3** wild groeiend; kruipend [of plants] **4** onregelmatig, grillig: *~ passages* gangetjes die alle kanten op gaan

rambunctious [Am; inform] **1** onstuimig, onbesuisd, luidruchtig **2** (lekker) eigenzinnig

ramification afsplitsing, vertakking, onderverdeling, implicaties: *all ~s of the plot were not yet known* alle vertakkingen van de samenzwering waren nog niet bekend

ramp 1 helling, glooiing **2** oprit; afrit [also of lorries etc]; hellingbaan **3** verkeersdrempel

¹rampage (n) dolheid, uitzinnigheid: *be on the ~* uitzinnig tekeergaan

²rampage (vb) (uitzinnig) tekeergaan, razen

rampant 1 wild, woest, verwoed **2** (te) weelderig, welig tierend || *crime was ~ in that neighbourhood* de misdaad vierde hoogtij in die buurt

rampart 1 borstwering, wal **2** verdediging, bolwerkʰ

ram raid [inform] ramkraak

ramrod laadstok [to tamp down gunpowder]: *as stiff as a ~* kaarsrecht

ramshackle bouwvallig, vervallen

ranch boerderij, ranch

rancher boer; veefokker

rancid ranzig

rancour wrok, haat

¹random (n): *at ~* op goed geluk af; *fill in answers at ~* zomaar wat antwoorden invullen

²random (adj) willekeurig, toevallig, op goed geluk: *~ check* steekproef

random-access [comp] directe toegang [of memory]: *~ file* direct toegankelijk bestand

randy [inform] geil, wellustig

¹range (n) **1** rij, reeks, keten: *a ~ of mountains* een bergketen **2** woeste (weide)grond **3** schietterreinʰ; testgebiedʰ [of rockets, projectiles] **4** gebiedʰ, kring, terreinʰ **5** sortering, collectie, assortimentʰ **6** groot keukenfornuisʰ **7** bereikʰ, draagkracht, draagwijdte: *the man had been shot at close ~* de man was van dichtbij neergeschoten; *(with)in ~* binnen schootsafstand, binnen bereik

²range (vb) **1** zich uitstrekken **2** voorkomen [of plant, animal]; aangetroffen worden **3** verschillen, variëren: *ticket prices ~ from three to eight pound* de prijzen van de kaartjes liggen tussen de drie en acht pond **4** zwerven, zich bewegen, gaan: *his new book ~s over too many subjects* zijn nieuwe boek omvat te veel onderwerpen

³range (vb) **1** rangschikken, ordenen, (op)stellen **2** doorkruisen, zwerven over, aflopen; [fig] afzoeken; gaan over: *his eyes ~d the mountains* zijn ogen zochten de bergen af **3** weiden, hoeden, houden

ranger 1 boswachter **2** gids; padvindster [14-17 years old] **3** [Am] commandoʰ [soldier]

¹rank (n) **1** rij, lijn, reeks **2** gelidʰ, rij: *the ~ and file* de manschappen; [fig] de gewone man; *close (the) ~s* de gelederen sluiten **3** taxistandplaats **4** rang, positie, graad, de hogere stand: *raised to the ~ of major* tot (de rang van) majoor bevorderd; *pull ~* op zijn strepen gaan staan || *pull ~ on s.o.* misbruik maken van zijn macht ten opzichte van iem.

²rank (adj) **1** (te) weelderig, (te) welig: *~ weeds* welig tierend onkruid **2** te vet [of soil] **3** stinkend **4** absoluut: [fig] *~ injustice* schreeuwende onrechtvaardigheid

³rank (vb) **1** zich bevinden [in a certain position]; staan, behoren: *this book ~s among* (or: *with*) *the best* dit boek behoort tot de beste; *~ as* gelden als **2** [Am] de hoogste positie bekleden

⁴rank (vb) **1** opstellen, in het gelid plaatsen **2** plaatsen, neerzetten, rangschikken: *~ s.o. with Stan Laurel* iem. op één lijn stellen met Stan Laurel

ranking classificatie, (positie in een) rangorde

rankle steken, knagen, woekeren

ransack 1 doorzoeken, doorsnuffelen

2 plunderen, leegroven, beroven

¹ransom (n) **1** losgeld^h, losprijs, afkoopsom **2** vrijlating [for ransom money] ‖ *hold* s.o. *to ~* een losgeld voor iem. eisen [under threat of violence]

²ransom (vb) **1** vrijkopen **2** vrijlaten [for ransom money] **3** losgeld voor iem. eisen

ransomware [comp] gijzelsoftware

¹rant (n) bombast, holle frasen

²rant (vb) **1** bombast uitslaan **2** tieren, te-keergaan: *the schoolmaster started to ~ and rave* de meester begon te razen en te tieren

¹rap (n) **1** tik, slag: *get a ~ over the knuckles* een tik op de vingers krijgen; [fig] op de vingers getikt worden **2** geklop^h, klop **3** zier, beetje^h: *he doesn't give a ~ for her* hij geeft helemaal niets om haar **4** schuld, straf: *I don't want to take the ~ for this* ik wil hier niet voor opdraaien **5** [inform; mus] rap [rhythmic lyrics to music]

²rap (vb) **1** kloppen, tikken: *~ at a door* op een deur kloppen **2** praten, erop los kletsen

³rap (vb) **1** slaan, een tik geven **2** bekritise-ren, op de vingers tikken

rapacious hebzuchtig; inhalig

rapacity hebzucht, roofzucht

¹rape (n) **1** verkrachting **2** koolzaad^h, raap-zaad^h

²rape (vb) verkrachten, onteren

¹rapid (n) stroomversnelling

²rapid (adj) snel, vlug: *~ fire* snelvuur^h; *in ~ succession* snel achter elkaar; [Am] *~ transit* snelverkeer^h [train, tram, underground]

rapidity vlugheid

rapist verkrachter

rap out 1 eruit gooien, er uitflappen **2** door kloppen meedelen, door kloppen te kennen geven: *~ an SOS* met klopsignalen een SOS doorgeven

rapport 1 verstandhouding: *be in ~ with* s.o. een goede verstandhouding met iem. hebben **2** contact

rapt 1 verrukt, in vervoering: *they listened to the new record with ~ attention* helemaal ge-grepen luisterden zij naar de nieuwe plaat **2** verdiept, verzonken

rapture 1 vervoering, verrukking, extase **2** (-s) extase, vervoering: *she was in ~s about* (or: *over*) *her meeting with the poet* zij was ly-risch over haar ontmoeting met de dichter

rapturous hartstochtelijk, meeslepend

rare 1 ongewoon, ongebruikelijk, vreemd **2** zeldzaam **3** halfrauw, niet gaar; kort ge-bakken [of meat]

rarefied 1 ijl, dun **2** verheven

rarely 1 zelden: *he ~ comes home before eight* hij komt zelden voor achten thuis **2** zeldzaam, ongewoon, uitzonderlijk: *a ~ beautiful woman* een zeldzaam mooie vrouw

raring dolgraag, enthousiast

rarity zeldzaamheid, rariteit, schaarsheid

rascal 1 schoft, schurk **2** schavuit, deugniet, rakker

¹rash (n) (huid)uitslag

²rash (adj) **1** overhaast, te snel **2** onstuimig **3** ondoordacht: *in a ~ moment* op een onbe-waakt ogenblik

¹rasp (n) **1** rasp **2** raspgeluid^h, gerasp^h

²rasp (vb) schrapen, krassen: *with ~ing voice* met krakende stem

³rasp (vb) raspen, vijlen, schuren

raspberry 1 frambozenstruik **2** framboos **3** [inform] afkeurend pf!

rat 1 rat **2** deserteur, overloper **3** [Am] ver-rader, klikspaan ‖ *smell a ~* lont ruiken, iets in de smiezen hebben

ratchet up verhogen, opvoeren, opdrijven

¹rate (n) **1** snelheid, vaart, tempo^h **2** prijs, ta-rief^h, koers: *~ of exchange* wisselkoers; *~ of interest* rentevoet **3** (sterfte)cijfer^h, geboor-tecijfer^h **4** (kwaliteits)klasse, rang, graad **5** (-s) gemeentebelasting, onroerendgoed-belasting ‖ *at any ~* in ieder geval, ten min-ste; *at this ~* in dit geval, op deze manier

²rate (vb) gerekend worden, behoren, gel-den: *he ~s as one of the best writers* hij geldt als een van de beste schrijvers

³rate (vb) **1** schatten, bepalen; waarderen [also fig]: *~ s.o.'s income at* iemands inkomen schatten op **2** beschouwen, tellen, rekenen: *~ among* (or: *with*) rekenen onder (or: tot)

rateable 1 te schatten, taxeerbaar **2** be-lastbaar, schatbaar

ratepayer 1 belastingbetaler **2** huiseige-naar

rather 1 liever, eerder: *I would ~ not invite your brother* ik nodig je broer liever niet uit **2** juister (uitgedrukt), liever gezegd: *she is my girlfriend, or ~ she was my girlfriend* zij is mijn vriendin, of liever: ze was mijn vriendin **3** enigszins, tamelijk, nogal, wel: *a ~ shock-ing experience, ~ a shocking experience* een nogal schokkende ervaring **4** meer, sterker, in hogere mate: *they depend ~ on Paul's than on their own income* zij zijn meer van Pauls in-komen afhankelijk dan van het hunne **5** [in-form] jazeker, nou en of

ratify bekrachtigen; goedkeuren [treaty]

rating 1 taxering [rated value, assessment] **2** waarderingscijfer^h [of TV programme]; kijkcijfer^h **3** naam, positie, status

ratio (evenredige) verhouding

¹ration (n) **1** rantsoen^h; portie [also fig] **2** (-s) proviand^h, voedsel^h, rantsoenen

²ration (vb) rantsoeneren, op rantsoen stel-len, distribueren, uitdelen: *petrol is ~ed op* benzine is op de bon

rational 1 rationeel, redelijk **2** (wel)door-dacht, logisch **3** verstandig: *man is a ~ being* de mens is een redelijk wezen

rationale grond(reden), grondgedach-te(n), beweegreden(en)

¹rationalist (n) rationalist

²rationalist (adj) rationalistisch

rationality 1 rationaliteit **2** rede; denkvermogen[h] **3** redelijkheid

¹rationalize (vb) rationaliseren; efficiënter inrichten [business etc]

²rationalize (vb) rationaliseren, aannemelijk maken, verklaren, achteraf beredeneren

rat on laten vallen, verraden, in de steek laten

rat race (the) moordende competitie, carrièrejacht

rattan 1 rotan[h], Spaans riet[h] **2** rotting, wandelstok

¹rattle (n) **1** geratel[h], gerammel[h], gerinkel[h] **2** rammelaar, ratel

²rattle (vb) **1** rammelen, ratelen, kletteren **2** (+ away, on) (door)ratelen, (blijven) kletsen || ~ *through* sth. iets afraffelen, iets gauw afmaken

³rattle (vb) **1** heen en weer rammelen, schudden, rinkelen met **2** [inform] op stang jagen, opjagen, van streek maken

rattlesnake ratelslang

¹rattling (adj) levendig, stevig, krachtig: *a ~ trade* een levendige handel

²rattling (adv) uitzonderlijk, uitstekend: *a ~ good match* een zeldzaam mooie wedstrijd

ratty 1 ratachtig, vol ratten, rat(ten)- **2** geïrriteerd

raucous rauw, schor

raunchy [inform] **1** geil, wellustig **2** rauw, ruig, ordinair **3** [Am] vies, smerig, goor

¹ravage (n) **1** verwoesting(en), vernietiging **2** (-s) vernietigende werking: *the ~s of time* de tand des tijds

²ravage (vb) **1** verwoesten, vernietigen, teisteren: *she came from a country ~d by war* zij kwam uit een door oorlog verwoest land **2** leegplunderen, leegroven

¹rave (n) **1** juichende bespreking **2** wild feest[h], dansfeest[h] || *be in a ~ about* helemaal weg zijn van

²rave (vb) **1** (+ against, at) razen (tegen/op), ijlen, (als een gek) tekeergaan (tegen) **2** (+ about) opgetogen zijn, raken (over), lyrisch worden (over), dwepen (met)

³rave (vb) wild uiting geven aan, zich gek maken

raven raaf

ravenous uitgehongerd, begerig, roofzuchtig

raver [inform] **1** snel figuur; swinger **2** raver [of house party]

ravine ravijn[h]

¹raving (adj) malend, raaskallend

²raving (adv) stapel-: *stark ~ mad* stapelgek, knettergek

ravings wartaal, geraaskal[h]

ravish 1 verrukken, in vervoering brengen, betoveren **2** verkrachten, onteren

ravishing verrukkelijk, betoverend

raw 1 rauw; ongekookt [of vegetables, meat] **2** onuitgewerkt [figures etc]; grof, onaf(gewerkt), onrijp: ~ *material* grondstof; ~ *silk* ruwe zijde **3** groen, onervaren, ongetraind **4** ontveld, rauw, open **5** guur, ruw; rauw [of weather] || ~ *deal* oneerlijke behandeling; *touch s.o. on the ~* iem. tegen het zere been schoppen; *in the ~* ongeciviliseerd, primitief, naakt

rawboned broodmager, vel over been

rawhide 1 ongelooide huid **2** zweep

ray 1 straal [of light etc] **2** sprankje[h], glimp, lichtpuntje[h]: *a ~ of hope* een sprankje hoop **3** rog, vleet

raze met de grond gelijk maken, volledig verwoesten

razor (elektrisch) scheerapparaat[h], scheermes[h]

razor-billed auk alk

razor blade (veiligheids)scheermesje[h]

razor-sharp vlijmscherp [also fig]

razzle braspartij, lol, stappen: *go on the ~* aan de rol gaan, de bloemetjes buiten zetten

RC 1 *Red Cross* Rode Kruis **2** *Roman Catholic* r.-k.

Rd *road* str., straat

¹reach (n) **1** bereik[h] [of arm, power etc; also fig]; reikwijdte: *above* (or: *beyond, out of*) ~ buiten bereik, onbereikbaar, onhaalbaar, niet te realiseren; *within easy ~ of* gemakkelijk bereikbaar van(af) **2** recht[h] stuk rivier [between two bends]

²reach (vb) **1** reiken, (zich) (uit)strekken, (een hand) uitsteken, bereiken; dragen [of sound]; halen: *the forests ~ down to the sea* de bossen strekken zich uit tot aan de zee **2** pakken, (ergens) bij kunnen, grijpen: ~ *down* sth. *from a shelf* iets van een plank afpakken **3** aanreiken, geven, overhandigen **4** komen tot [also fig]; bereiken, arriveren: ~ *a decision* tot een beslissing komen

react 1 reageren [also fig]; ingaan (op) **2** (+ (up)on) uitwerking hebben (op), z'n weerslag hebben (op), veranderen

reaction 1 reactie, antwoord[h], reflex **2** terugslag, weerslag, terugkeer

¹reactionary (n) reactionair, behoudend persoon

²reactionary (adj) reactionair, behoudend

reactivate 1 weer actief maken **2** nieuw leven inblazen

reactor 1 atoomreactor, kernreactor **2** reactievat[h], reactor

read 1 lezen, kunnen lezen, begrijpen, weten te gebruiken: ~ *a magazine* een tijdschrift lezen; ~ *over* (or: *through*) doorlezen, overlezen; ~ *up* bestuderen; ~ *up on* sth. **a)** zijn kennis over iets opvijzelen; **b)** zich op de hoogte stellen van iets; *widely* ~ zeer belezen **2** oplezen, voorlezen: ~ *out loud* hardop lezen; ~ **out** *the instructions* de instructies voorlezen; ~ **to** *a child* een kind voorlezen **3** zich laten lezen, lezen, klinken: *your **essay** ~s like a **translation*** je opstel klinkt als een vertaling **4** uitleggen, interpreteren; voorspellen [future]; [fig] doorgronden, doorzien: *my mother can ~ me **like** a book* mijn moeder weet precies wat ik denk; ~ *the **future*** de toekomst voorspellen; *he ~ more **into** her words than she had meant* hij had meer in haar woorden gelegd dan zij had bedoeld **5** aangeven, tonen, laten zien: *the **thermometer** ~s twenty degrees* de thermometer geeft twintig graden aan **6** uitlezen: ~ *the electricity **meter*** de elektriciteitsmeter uitlezen **7** [dated] studeren: ~ ***Economics*** economie studeren

readability leesbaarheid

readable 1 lezenswaard(ig), leesbaar **2** leesbaar, te lezen

reader 1 lezer [also fig] **2** leesboekʰ, bloemlezing **3** lector [at university]; [Belg] [roughly] docent

readership lezerspubliekʰ; aantalʰ lezers [of newspaper etc]: *a newspaper with a ~ of ten **million*** een krant met tien miljoen lezers

readily 1 graag, bereidwillig **2** gemakkelijk, vlug, dadelijk: *his motives will be ~ **understood*** zijn motivatie is zonder meer duidelijk

readiness 1 bereid(willig)heid, gewilligheid **2** vlugheid, vaardigheid, gemakʰ: ~ *of **tongue*** rapheid van tong **3** gereedheid: *all is in* ~ alles staat klaar

reading 1 het (voor)lezen **2** belezenheid **3** (voor)lezing, voordracht **4** stand; waarde [as read on instrument]: *the ~s on the **thermometer*** de afgelezen temperaturen **5** lectuur, leesstof: *these novels are **required** ~* deze romans zijn verplichte lectuur

reading comprehension leesvaardigheid

¹**readjust** (vb) zich weer aanpassen, weer wennen

²**readjust** (vb) weer aanpassen, opnieuw instellen, bijstellen

read-only onuitwisbaar; niet schrijfbaar, alleen-lezen-: ~ ***memory*** ROMʰ

¹**ready** (n): *at the* ~ klaar om te vuren [of firearm]

²**ready** (adj) **1** klaar, gereed, af: ~, ***steady, go!*** klaar? af! **2** bereid(willig), graag: *I **am** ~ to pay for it* ik wil er best voor betalen **3** vlug, gevat ‖ ~ ***cash*** (or: ***money***) baar geld, klinkende munt; *find a ~ **sale*** goed verkocht worden

ready-made kant-en-klaar, confectie-
ready meal kant-en-klaarmaaltijd
ready-to-wear confectie-

¹**real** (n): *for* ~ in werkelijkheid, echt, gemeend

²**real** (adj) echt, werkelijk, onvervalst: *in* ~ *life*

a) in het echt; **b)** in het gewone leven; [inform] *the* ~ *thing* het echte, je ware ‖ *in* ~ *terms* in concrete termen, in de praktijk

real estate 1 onroerend goedʰ **2** [Am] huizen in verkoop

real-estate agent [Am] makelaar in onroerend goed

realism realismeʰ, werkelijkheidszin

realist realist

realistic 1 realistisch, m.b.t. realisme, natuurgetrouw **2** realistisch, praktisch, werkelijkheidsbewust

reality werkelijkheid, realiteit, werkelijk bestaanʰ: *in* ~ in werkelijkheid, in feite

reality check: [inform] *I think you **need** a ~* je moet de feiten onder ogen zien

realization 1 bewustwording, besefʰ, begripʰ **2** realisatie, realisering, verwezenlijking

realize 1 beseffen, zich bewust zijn of worden, zich realiseren: ***don't** you ~ that …?* zie je niet in dat …? **2** realiseren, verwezenlijken, uitvoeren **3** realiseren, verkopen, te gelde maken

¹**really** (adv) **1** werkelijk, echt, eigenlijk: *I **don't** ~ feel like it* ik heb er eigenlijk geen zin in; *(O) ~?* O ja?, Echt waar? **2** werkelijk, echt, zeer: *it is **really** cold today* het is ontzettend koud vandaag

²**really** (int) waarachtig!, nou, zeg!: ~, *Mike! Mind your manners!* Mike toch! Wat zijn dat voor manieren!; *well ~!* nee maar!

realm 1 koninkrijkʰ, rijkʰ **2** rijkʰ, sfeer; gebiedʰ [fig]: *the ~ of **science*** het domein van de wetenschap

reanimation reanimatie

reap maaien, oogsten, verwerven; opstrijken [profit]

reappear weer verschijnen, opnieuw te voorschijn komen, weer komen opdagen

reappraisal heroverweging

¹**rear** (n) achtergedeelteʰ, achterstukʰ; [fig] achtergrond ‖ *at the* ~, [Am] *in the* ~ achteraan, aan de achterkant

²**rear** (adj) achter-, achterste: ~ *door* achterdeur

³**rear** (vb) (also + up) steigeren

⁴**rear** (vb) grootbrengen, fokken, kweken

rear-admiral schout-bij-nacht

rearguard (the) achterhoede

rearmament herbewapening

rearmost achterste, allerlaatste

rearrange herschikken, herordenen, anders rangschikken

rearview mirror achteruitkijkspiegel

¹**reason** (n) **1** reden, beweegreden, oorzaak: *by ~ **of*** wegens; *with (good)* ~ terecht **2** redelijkheid, gezond verstandʰ: *it **stands** to ~ that* het spreekt vanzelf dat; *anything **(with)in** ~* alles wat redelijk is

²**reason** (vb) **1** redeneren, logisch denken

2 (+ with) redeneren (met), argumenteren (met)

³reason (vb) door redenering afleiden, beredeneren, veronderstellen: ~ *sth. out* iets beargumenteren

reasonable 1 redelijk, verstandig: *beyond ~ doubt* zonder gerede twijfel **2** redelijk, schappelijk, billijk

reasonably vrij, tamelijk, nogal: *it is in a ~ good state* het is in vrij behoorlijke staat

reasoning redenering

¹reassemble (vb) opnieuw vergaderen; opnieuw samenkomen

²reassemble (vb) **1** opnieuw samenbrengen **2** opnieuw samenvoegen

reassert 1 bevestigen **2** (opnieuw) handhaven

reassure geruststellen, weer (zelf)vertrouwen geven

reassuring geruststellend

rebate korting: *tax ~* belastingteruggave

¹rebel (n) rebel, opstandeling

²rebel (vb) (+ against) rebelleren (tegen), zich verzetten (tegen), in opstand komen (tegen)

rebellion opstand, opstandigheid, rebellie

rebellious opstandig

rebirth 1 wedergeboorte **2** herleving, wederopleving

¹reboot (n) reboot; herstart

²reboot (vb) rebooten; herstarten

¹rebound (n) **1** terugkaatsing [of ball] **2** terugwerking, reactie: *on the ~* van de weeromstuit, als reactie

²rebound (vb) terugkaatsen, terugspringen, terugstuiten

¹rebuff (n) afwijzing; weigering [of help, proposal etc]: *he met with* (or: *suffered*) *a ~* hij kwam van een koude kermis thuis

²rebuff (vb) afwijzen, weigeren, afschepen

rebuild 1 opnieuw bouwen, verbouwen, opknappen **2** vernieuwen

¹rebuke (n) berisping, standjeʰ

²rebuke (vb) (+ for) berispen (om/voor), een standje geven (voor)

rebut weerleggen

¹recalcitrant (n) weerspannige, tegenstribbelaar, ongehoorzame

²recalcitrant (adj) opstandig, weerspannig

¹recall (n) **1** terugroeping; terugname: *product ~* terugroepactie **2** herinnering, geheugenʰ: *total ~* absoluut geheugen; *beyond* (or: *past*) *~* onmogelijk te herinneren

²recall (vb) **1** terugroepen; rappelleren [envoy]: *~ the ambassador* de ambassadeur terugroepen **2** terugnemen [present, merchandise etc]; terugroepen [product, by manufacturer]: *~ an email* een e-mail intrekken; *millions of cans of soft drink have been ~ed* er zijn miljoenen blikjes frisdrank teruggehaald

³recall (vb) zich herinneren

¹recap (n) recapitulatie, korte opsomming

²recap (vb) recapituleren, kort samenvatten, samenvattend herhalen

recapitulate recapituleren, kort samenvatten

recapture 1 heroveren **2** oproepen; (zich) in herinnering brengen **3** doen herleven

recede achteruitgaan, zich terugtrekken, terugwijken; [also fig] teruglopen [of value etc]: *a receding forehead* een terugwijkend voorhoofd; *a receding hairline* een kalend hoofd

¹receipt (n) **1** reçuʰ, ontvangstbewijsʰ, kwitantie **2** kassabon **3** ontvangst

²receipt (vb) kwiteren; voor ontvangst tekenen [bill etc]

receive 1 ontvangen, verwelkomen, gasten ontvangen **2** ontvangen, krijgen, in ontvangst nemen **3** opvangen, toelaten, opnemen: *be at* (or: *on*) *the receiving end* al de klappen krijgen

received algemeen aanvaard, standaard-: *Received Standard English* Algemeen Beschaafd Engels

receiver 1 ontvanger [person, appliance] **2** hoorn [of telephone] **3** bewindvoerder **4** heler **5** tuner-versterker

recent 1 recent, van de laatste tijd: *in ~ years* de laatste jaren; *a ~ book* een onlangs verschenen boek **2** nieuw, modern: *~ fashion* nieuwe mode

recently 1 onlangs, kort geleden **2** de laatste tijd: *he has been moody, ~* hij is de laatste tijd humeurig (geweest)

receptacle vergaarbak, container, vatʰ, kom

reception 1 ontvangst [also fig]; onthaalʰ, welkomʰ: *the ~ of his book was mixed* zijn boek werd met gemengde gevoelens ontvangen **2** receptie [at party; in hotel etc] **3** opname [in hospital]

reception centre opvangcentrumʰ

reception desk balie [of hotel, library etc]

receptionist 1 receptionist(e) [eg in hotel] **2** assistent(e) [of doctor etc]

reception room 1 ontvangkamer; receptiezaal **2** [in private house] woonvertrekʰ

receptive ontvankelijk, vatbaar, open

recess 1 vakantie; onderbreking [parliament etc] **2** [Am] (school)vakantie **3** [Am] pauze [between classes] **4** nis, uitsparing, holte **5** uithoek

recession 1 recessie, economische teruggang **2** terugtrekking, terugtreding

recharge herladen; weer opladen [battery etc]

recipe receptʰ, keukenreceptʰ

recipient ontvanger

reciprocal wederkerig, wederzijds: *~ action* wisselwerking

reciprocate 1 beantwoorden [feelings]; vergelden, op gelijke manier behandelen **2** uitwisselen

recital 1 relaas^h, verhaal^h **2** recital^h [music] **3** voordracht [poem, text]

recite 1 reciteren, opzeggen: *Simon can already ~ the alphabet* Simon kan het alfabet al opzeggen **2** opsommen

reckless 1 roekeloos **2** zorgeloos: *~ of danger* zonder zich zorgen te maken over gevaar

¹reckon (vb) **1** (+ on) rekenen (op), afgaan (op) **2** (+ with) rekening houden (met): *she is a woman to be ~ed with* dat is een vrouw met wie je rekening moet houden **3** (+ with) afrekenen (met)

²reckon (vb) **1** berekenen, (op)tellen **2** meerekenen, meetellen, rekening houden met **3** beschouwen, aanzien (voor), houden (voor): *I ~ him among my friends* ik beschouw hem als één van mijn vrienden **4** aannemen, vermoeden, gissen: *I ~ that he'll be home soon* ik neem aan dat hij gauw thuiskomt

reckoner rekenaar: *ready ~* rekentabel

reckoning 1 berekening, schatting **2** afrekening: *day of ~* dag van de afrekening; [fig] dag des oordeels

¹reclaim (n): *he is beyond ~* hij is onverbeterlijk

²reclaim (vb) **1** terugwinnen, recupereren, regenereren: *~ed paper* kringlooppapier **2** droogleggen [land]: *land ~ed from the sea* op de zee teruggewonnen land **3** terugvorderen

reclamation 1 terugwinning **2** terugvordering

¹recline (vb) achterover leunen, (uit)rusten, op de rug liggen

²recline (vb) doen leunen, doen rusten

reclining seat stoel met verstelbare rugleuning

recluse kluizenaar

recognition 1 erkenning **2** waardering, erkentelijkheid **3** herkenning: *change beyond* (or: *out of*) *all ~* onherkenbaar worden

recognizable herkenbaar

recognize 1 herkennen **2** erkennen **3** inzien

¹recoil (n) terugslag, terugloop, terugsprong; terugstoot [of firearm]

²recoil (vb) **1** (+ from) terugdeinzen (voor), terugschrikken (voor), zich terugtrekken **2** terugslaan, teruglopen, terugspringen; terugstoten [of firearm]

recollect zich (moeizaam) herinneren, zich voor de geest halen

recollection herinnering: *to the best of my ~* voor zover ik mij herinner

recommend 1 aanbevelen, aanraden, adviseren: *I can ~ the self-service in this hotel* ik kan u de zelfbediening in dit hotel aanbevelen; *~ed price* adviesprijs **2** tot aanbeveling

strekken **3** toevertrouwen, overgeven, (aan)bevelen

recommendation 1 aanbeveling, aanprijzing, advies^h **2** aanbevelingsbrief

¹recompense (n) vergoeding, schadeloosstelling, beloning: *in ~ for* als vergoeding voor

²recompense (vb) vergoeden, schadeloosstellen: *~ s.o. for sth.* iem. iets vergoeden

reconcile verzoenen, in overeenstemming brengen, verenigen: *become ~d to sth.* zich bij iets neerleggen

reconciliation verzoening, vereniging

reconnaissance verkenning

reconnoitre op verkenning uitgaan, verkennen

reconsider 1 opnieuw bekijken, opnieuw in overweging nemen: *may I ask you to ~ the matter?* mag ik u vragen er nog eens over na te denken? **2** herroepen, herzien, terugkomen op

reconstruct 1 opnieuw opbouwen, herbouwen **2** reconstrueren [events]

reconstruction 1 reconstructie [of event] **2** wederopbouw

¹record (n) **1** verslag^h, rapport^h, aantekening: *for the ~* openbaar, officieel; *off the ~* vertrouwelijk, onofficieel; *all this is off the ~* dit alles blijft tussen ons **2** document^h, archiefstuk^h, officieel afschrift^h **3** vastgelegd feit^h, het opgetekend zijn **4** staat van dienst, antecedenten, verleden^h **5** [mus] plaat; opname

²record (adj) record-: *a ~ amount* een recordbedrag

³record (vb) **1** zich laten opnemen, opnamen maken **2** optekenen, noteren, te boek stellen: *~ed delivery* aangetekend [mail] **3** vastleggen; opnemen [on tape, record]

recorder 1 rechter; voorzitter van Crown Court **2** (tape)recorder **3** blokfluit

recording opname, opgenomen programma^h: *a studio ~* een studio-opname

record-player platenspeler, grammofoon

recount (uitvoerig) vertellen, weergeven

recoup 1 vergoeden, compenseren, schadeloosstellen **2** terugwinnen, inhalen: *~ expenses from a company* onkosten verhalen op een maatschappij

recourse toevlucht, hulp: *have ~ to* zijn toevlucht nemen tot

¹recover (vb) herstellen, genezen, er weer bovenop komen

²recover (vb) terugkrijgen, terugvinden: *~ consciousness* weer bijkomen

recovery 1 herstel^h, recuperatie, genezing: *make a quick ~ from an illness* vlug van een ziekte herstellen **2** het terugvinden, het terugwinnen, het terugkrijgen, herwinning

recreation recreatie, ontspanning, hobby

recreational recreatief, recreatie-, ont-

spannings-
recreation ground speelterrein[h], recrea-
tieterrein[h]
recrimination tegenbeschuldiging, recri-
minatie, tegeneis: *mutual ~s* beschuldigingen over en weer
[1]**recruit** (n) 1 rekruut 2 nieuw lid[h]
[2]**recruit** (vb) rekruten (aan)werven
[3]**recruit** (vb) rekruteren, (aan)werven, aantrekken
recruiter recruiter
recruitment 1 rekrutering; werving 2 versterking
rectangle rechthoek
rectangular rechthoekig
rectification rectificatie
rectify rectificeren, rechtzetten, verbeteren
rectitude 1 rechtschapenheid 2 oprechtheid, eerlijkheid
rector 1 [Anglican Church] predikant, dominee 2 rector [head of university]
rectory predikantswoning; pastorie
rectum rectum[h], endeldarm
[1]**recumbent** (n) ligfiets
[2]**recumbent** (adj) 1 liggend; achteroverleu-
nend: ~ *bike* ligfiets 2 nietsdoend
recuperate herstellen, opknappen, er
weer bovenop komen
recur terugkomen, terugkeren, zich herhalen: *a ~ring dream* een steeds terugkerende
droom; *~ring decimal* repeterende breuk
recurrent terugkomend, terugkerend
recycle recyclen, weer bruikbaar maken: *~d
paper* kringlooppapier
[1]**red** (n) 1 rood[h], rode kleur 2 iets roods
3 rode, communist ‖ *be in the* ~ rood staan
[2]**red** (adj) 1 rood: ~ *currant* rode aalbes; *raise
a* ~ *flag* een alarmbel laten afgaan, een belletje doen rinkelen; *like a* ~ *rag to a bull* als
een rode lap op een stier 2 rood, communistisch ‖ ~ *herring* bokking; [fig] vals spoor, afleidingsmanoeuvre[+h]; *Red Indian* indiaan,
roodhuid; ~ *lead* (rode) menie; ~ *tape* bureaucratie, ambtenarij, papierwinkel; *paint
the town* ~ de bloemetjes buiten zetten; *see*
~ buiten zichzelf raken (van woede)
red-blooded levenskrachtig
redbreast roodborst
redcurrant rode aalbes
redden rood worden (maken), (doen) blozen
reddish roodachtig, rossig
redecorate opknappen; opnieuw schilderen, behangen
redeem 1 terugkopen, afkopen, inlossen;
[fig] terugwinnen: ~ *a mortgage* een hypotheek aflossen 2 vrijkopen, loskopen
3 goedmaken, vergoeden: *a ~ing feature*
een verzoenende trek 4 verlossen, bevrijden, redden
Redeemer Verlosser, Heiland

redemption 1 redding, verlossing, bevrijding: *beyond* (or: *past*) ~ reddeloos (verloren) 2 afkoop, aflossing
redevelop renoveren: ~ *a slum district* een
krottenwijk renoveren
redevelopment 1 nieuwe ontwikkeling
2 renovatie
red-eye: *a* ~ *flight* een nachtvlucht
red-handed op heterdaad
redhead roodharige, rooie
red-hot 1 roodgloeiend; [fig] enthousiast
2 heet van de naald, zeer actueel: ~ *news* allerlaatste nieuws
[1]**redirect** (n) [Internet] doorverwijzing
[2]**redirect** (vb) 1 doorsturen, nasturen 2 [In-
ternet] doorlinken, automatisch doorsturen
rediscovery herontdekking
redistribution herdistributie; herverdeling
red-light district rosse buurt
redneck [Am; inform; depr] (blanke) landarbeider; conservatieveling
redo 1 overdoen, opnieuw doen 2 opknappen
redouble verdubbelen
redress herstellen, vergoeden, goedmaken: ~ *the balance* het evenwicht herstellen
redskin roodhuid
reduce 1 verminderen, beperken, verkleinen, verlagen, reduceren 2 herleiden, reduceren, omzetten, omsmelten 3 (+ to) terugbrengen (tot), degraderen (tot): *be ~d to
tears* alleen nog maar kunnen huilen 4 (+ to)
verpulveren (tot), fijnmaken; klein maken
[also fig]: *his accusations were ~d to nothing*
van zijn beschuldigingen bleef niets overeind
reduction reductie, vermindering, korting
redundancy 1 overtolligheid, overbodig-
heid 2 ontslag[h]; [by extension] werkloosheid
redundancy money afvloeiingspremie
redundant 1 overtollig, overbodig
2 werkloos: *all the workers were made* ~ al de
werknemers moesten afvloeien
reduplicate 1 verdubbelen 2 (steeds) herhalen
reduplication 1 verdubbeling 2 herhaling
reed 1 riet[h], rietsoort 2 riet[h]; tong [in wind
instrument or organ pipe]
re-education 1 omscholing, herscholing
2 heropvoeding
[1]**reef** (n) 1 rif[h] 2 klip 3 [sailing] reef[h], rif[h]
[2]**reef** (vb) [sailing] reven, inhalen, inbinden
reefer 1 jekker 2 marihuanasigaret
[1]**reek** (n) stank
[2]**reek** (vb) 1 (slecht) ruiken; [fig] stinken: *his
statement ~s of corruption* zijn verklaring riekt
naar corruptie 2 roken, dampen, wasemen
[1]**reel** (n) 1 haspel, klos, spoel, (garen)klosje[h]
2 (film)rol
[2]**reel** (vb) 1 duizelen, draaien 2 wervelen,

warrelen **3** wankelen, waggelen: ~ **back** terugdeinzen, terugwijken
re-en<u>a</u>ct 1 weer invoeren **2** weer opvoeren
3 re-ensceneren [crime]; naspelen [battle]
re-<u>e</u>ntry terugkeer, terugkomst: *the ~ of a
spacecraft into the* **atmosphere** de terugkeer
van een ruimtevaartuig in de atmosfeer
re-ex<u>a</u>mine 1 opnieuw onderzoeken
2 [law] opnieuw verhoren
¹ref (n) [inform] *referee* scheids; scheidsrechter
²ref *reference* ref.
ref<u>e</u>r 1 (+ to) verwijzen (naar), doorsturen
(naar) **2** (+ to) toeschrijven (aan), terugvoeren (tot)
¹refer<u>ee</u> (n) **1** scheidsrechter; [fig] bemiddelaar **2** (vak)referent, expert **3** referentie
[person giving the reference]
²refer<u>ee</u> (vb) als scheidsrechter optreden
(bij)
r<u>e</u>ference 1 referentie, getuigschrift^h, pers
die referentie geeft **2** verwijzing: *be* **outside
our terms of** ~ buiten onze competentie vallen **3** zinspeling: **make** *no ~ to* geen toespeling maken op **4** raadpleging: **make** *~ to a
dictionary* een woordenboek naslaan **5** betrekking, verband^h: **in** (or: **with**) ~ **to** in verband met
r<u>e</u>ference book naslagwerk^h
r<u>e</u>ference work naslagwerk^h
refer<u>e</u>ndum referendum^h, volksstemming
refer to 1 verwijzen naar, betrekking hebben op, van toepassing zijn op **2** zinspelen
op, refereren aan, vermelden **3** raadplegen,
naslaan: ~ *a* **dictionary** iets opzoeken in een
woordenboek; *she kept referring to her home
town* ze had het steeds weer over haar geboorteplaats
¹ref<u>i</u>ll (n) (nieuwe) vulling, (nieuw) (op)vul-
sel^h, inktpatroon: *would you* **like** *a ~?* zal ik je
nog eens inschenken?
²ref<u>i</u>ll (vb) opnieuw vullen, (opnieuw) aanvullen, (opnieuw) bijvullen, (opnieuw) opvullen
ref<u>i</u>ll pack navulpak^h
ref<u>i</u>ne zuiveren, raffineren; [fig] verfijnen;
verbeteren
ref<u>i</u>ned verfijnd, geraffineerd; [fig] verzorgd; beschaafd: ~ **manners** goede manieren; ~ **sugar** geraffineerde suiker
ref<u>i</u>nement 1 verbetering, uitwerking
2 raffinage **3** verfijning, raffinement^h,
(over)beschaafdheid
ref<u>i</u>nery raffinaderij
¹ref<u>i</u>t (n) herstel^h, nieuwe uitrusting
²ref<u>i</u>t (vb) hersteld worden, opnieuw uitgerust worden
³ref<u>i</u>t (vb) herstellen, opnieuw uitrusten
refl<u>e</u>ct 1 nadenken, overwegen: *he ~ed
that* ... hij bedacht dat ... **2** weerspiegelen,
weerkaatsen, reflecteren; [fig] weergeven;

getuigen van
refl<u>e</u>ction 1 weerspiegeling, weerkaatsing, reflectie **2** overdenking, overweging:
on ~ bij nader inzien
refl<u>e</u>ctive 1 weerspiegelend, reflecterend
2 bedachtzaam
refl<u>e</u>ctor reflector
refl<u>e</u>ct (up)on 1 nadenken over, overdenken **2** zich ongunstig uitlaten over, een ongunstig licht werpen op: *your impudent behaviour reflects only on* **yourself** je brutale gedrag werkt alleen maar in je eigen nadeel
¹r<u>e</u>flex (n) **1** weerspiegeling: *~es* afspiegeling **2** reflex^h, reflexbeweging: *her ~es* haar
reactievermogen^h
²r<u>e</u>flex (adj) weerkaatst, gereflecteerd: ~
camera spiegelreflexcamera ‖ ~ **action** reflexbeweging
refl<u>e</u>xive [linguistics] reflexief, wederkerend: ~ **pronoun** (or: **verb**) wederkerend
voornaamwoord (*or:* werkwoord)
¹refl<u>oa</u>t (vb) weer vlot raken
²refl<u>oa</u>t (vb) vlot krijgen
¹ref<u>o</u>rm (n) hervorming, verbetering
²ref<u>o</u>rm (vb) verbeteren, hervormen: *Reformed Church* hervormde kerk
reform<u>a</u>tion hervorming, verbetering
Reform<u>a</u>tion (the) de Reformatie
ref<u>o</u>rmer hervormer
refr<u>a</u>ct breken [beams, rays]
refr<u>a</u>ction (straal)breking: **angle** *of ~* bre-
kingshoek
refr<u>a</u>ctory (stijf)koppig, halsstarrig: *a ~ fever* een hardnekkige koorts
¹refr<u>ai</u>n (n) refrein^h
²refr<u>ai</u>n (vb) (+ from) zich onthouden (van),
ervan afzien, het nalaten: *kindly ~ from
smoking* gelieve niet te roken
¹refr<u>e</u>sh (vb) zich verfrissen, zich opfrissen
²refr<u>e</u>sh (vb) **1** verfrissen: ~ *s.o.'s* **memory**
iemands geheugen opfrissen **2** aanvullen,
herbevoorraden
refr<u>e</u>sher course herhalingscursus, bij-
scholingscursus
refr<u>e</u>shing 1 verfrissend, verkwikkend: *a ~
breeze* een lekker koel briesje **2** aangenaam,
verrassend
refr<u>e</u>shment 1 verfrissing [also fig]; ver-
kwikking, verademing **2** (-s) iets te drinken
met een hapje daarbij
refr<u>e</u>shment station verzorgingspost
¹refr<u>i</u>gerate (vb) invriezen
²refr<u>i</u>gerate (vb) koelen
refriger<u>a</u>tion 1 invriezing, het diepvriezen **2** afkoeling
refr<u>i</u>gerator 1 koelruimte, koelkast, ijskast
2 koeler
¹ref<u>ue</u>l (vb) (bij)tanken
²ref<u>ue</u>l (vb) opnieuw voltanken
r<u>e</u>fuge 1 toevlucht(soord^h) [also fig]; schuilplaats, toeverlaat: ~ **from** bescherming te-

gen **2** vluchtheuvel
refugee vluchteling
¹refund (n) terugbetaling, geld^h terug
²refund (vb) terugbetalen, restitueren: ~ *the cost of postage* de verzendkosten vergoeden
refurbish opknappen; [fig] opfrissen: ~ *the office* het kantoor opknappen
refusal 1 weigering, afwijzing **2** optie, (recht^h van) voorkeur: *have (the) first ~ of a house* een optie op een huis hebben
¹refuse (n) afval^h, vuil^h, vuilnis^h
²refuse (vb) weigeren, afslaan, afwijzen: ~ *a request* op een verzoek niet ingaan
refuse collector vuilnisophaler, vuilnisman
refuse dump vuilnisbelt
refutation weerlegging
refute weerleggen
regain 1 herwinnen, terugwinnen: ~ *consciousness* weer tot bewustzijn komen **2** opnieuw bereiken: *I helped him* ~ *his footing* ik hielp hem weer op de been [also fig]
regal koninklijk
regale (+ on, with) vergasten (op), onthalen (op), trakteren (op): ~ *o.s. on* (or: *with*) zich te goed doen aan
regalia 1 rijksinsigniën, regalia **2** onderscheidingstekenen: *the mayor in full* ~ de burgemeester in vol ornaat **3** staatsiegewaad^h
¹regard (n) **1** achting, respect^h: *hold s.o. in high* ~ iem. hoogachten **2** betrekking, verband^h, opzicht^h: *in this* ~ op dit punt **3** aandacht, zorg: *give* (or: *pay*) *no* ~ *to* zich niet bekommeren om; *have little* ~ *for* weinig rekening houden met **4** (-s) groeten, wensen^h ‖ *kind ~s to you all* ik wens jullie allemaal het beste
²regard (vb) **1** beschouwen, aanzien: ~ *s.o. as* iem. aanzien voor **2** betreffen, betrekking hebben op, aangaan: *as ~s* met betrekking tot
regarding betreffende, aangaande
regardless hoe dan ook ‖ *they did it* ~ ze hebben het toch gedaan
regardless of ongeacht, zonder rekening te houden met: ~ *expense* zonder op een cent te letten
regency regentschap^h
¹regenerate (adj) **1** herboren, bekeerd **2** geregenereerd, hernieuwd
²regenerate (vb) [biology] opnieuw (aan)groeien
³regenerate (vb) **1** verbeteren, bekeren, vernieuwen **2** nieuw leven inblazen, doen herleven
regeneration regeneratie
regent 1 regent(es) **2** [Am] curator; bestuurslid^h [of university]
reggae reggae
regicide 1 koningsmoord **2** koningsmoor-

denaar
regime regime^h
regimen 1 regime^h, verloop^h **2** regime^h, kuur
regiment regiment^h; [fig] groot aantal^h
region 1 streek, gebied^h: *~s* sfeer; terrein^h; *the Arctic ~s* de Arctica; *in the* ~ *of* in de buurt van [also fig] **2** gewest^h: *~s* provincie; regio
regional van de streek, regionaal
¹register (n) **1** register^h, (naam)lijst, rol, gastenboek^h, kiezerslijst: *the Parliamentary Register* de kiezerslijst **2** (kas)register^h
²register (vb) **1** zich (laten) inschrijven: ~ *at a hotel* inchecken; ~ *with the police* zich aanmelden bij de politie **2** doordringen tot, (in zich) opnemen
³register (vb) **1** (laten) registreren, (laten) inschrijven; [fig] nota nemen van: ~ *a protest against* protest aantekenen tegen **2** registreren; aanwijzen [eg degrees] **3** uitdrukken, tonen: *her face ~ed surprise* viel verwondering af te lezen **4** (laten) aantekenen; aangetekend versturen [mail]
registered 1 geregistreerd, ingeschreven: ~ *trademark* (wettig) gedeponeerd handelsmerk **2** gediplomeerd, erkend, bevoegd: [Am] ~ *nurse* gediplomeerd verpleegkundige; *State Registered nurse* gediplomeerd verpleegkundige **3** aangetekend [of letter]
register office 1 registratiebureau^h **2** (bureau^h van de) burgerlijke stand
registrar 1 registrator, ambtenaar van de burgerlijke stand **2** archivaris **3** administratief hoofd^h [of university] **4** [law] gerechtssecretaris, griffier **5** [med] stagelopend specialist
registration registratie, inschrijving, aangifte
registry 1 archief^h, registratiekantoor^h **2** (bureau van de) burgerlijke stand **3** register^h **4** registratie
registry office (bureau van de) burgerlijke stand: *married at a* ~ getrouwd voor de wet
regress achteruitgaan, teruggaan
regressive regressief, teruglopend
¹regret (n) **1** spijt, leed(wezen)^h, berouw^h: *greatly* (or: *much*) *to my* ~ tot mijn grote spijt **2** (-s) (betuigingen van) spijt, verontschuldigingen: *have no ~s* geen spijt hebben
²regret (vb) betreuren, spijt hebben van, berouw hebben over: ~ *to inform you* tot onze spijt moeten wij u meedelen
regretful bedroefd, vol spijt
regrettable betreurenswaardig, te betreuren
regrettably 1 bedroevend, teleurstellend: ~ *little response* bedroevend weinig respons **2** helaas, jammer genoeg
¹regular (n) **1** beroepsmilitair): *the ~s* de geregelde troepen **2** vaste klant, stamgast
²regular (adj) **1** regelmatig: *a ~ customer*

een vaste klant; *a ~ job* vast werk; **keep ~** *hours* zich aan vaste uren houden **2** [Am] gewoon, standaard-: *the ~ size* het gewone formaat **3** professioneel: *the ~ army* het beroepsleger **4** echt, onvervalst: *a ~ fool* een volslagen idioot
regularity regelmatigheid
regularize regulariseren, regelen
regulate regelen, reglementeren, ordenen ‖ *a regulating effect* een regulerende werking
regulation regeling, reglement[h], reglementering, (wettelijk) voorschrift[h], bepaling: *rules and ~s* regels en voorschriften
regulator regelaar; kompassleutel [of timepiece]
rehab [Am] *rehabilitation* afkicken[h]; ontwenning: *in ~* in een ontwenningskliniek
rehabilitation 1 rehabilitatie, eerherstel[h] **2** herstelling: *economic ~* economisch herstel
rehabilitation centre revalidatiecentrum[h]
¹rehash (n) herbewerking; [fig] opgewarmde kost: *his latest book is a ~ of one of his earlier ones* zijn jongste boek is een herbewerking van een van zijn eerdere boeken
²rehash (vb) herwerken, opnieuw bewerken
rehearsal repetitie: *dress ~* generale repetitie
¹rehearse (vb) herhalen
²rehearse (vb) repeteren, (een) repetitie houden
rehome een nieuw baasje vinden voor, herplaatsen [pet]
¹reign (n) regering: *~ of terror* schrikbewind[h]; *in the ~ of Henry* toen Hendrik koning was
²reign (vb) regeren; heersen [also fig]: *the ~ing champion* de huidige kampioen
reiki reiki[+h]
reimburse terugbetalen, vergoeden
¹rein (n) teugel: [fig] *give free ~ to s.o. (sth.)* iem. (iets) de vrije teugel laten; [fig] *keep a tight ~ on s.o.* bij iem. de teugels stevig aanhalen
²rein (vb) inhouden [also fig]; beteugelen, in bedwang houden: *~ back* (or: *in, up*) halt doen houden
reincarnation reïncarnatie, wedergeboorte
reindeer rendier[h]
reinforce versterken: *~d concrete* gewapend beton
reinforcement versterking
reinstate herstellen
reinsurance herverzekering
reiterate herhalen
reiteration herhaling
reiterative herhalend
¹reject (n) afgekeurd persoon (voorwerp[h]); afgekeurde [for military service]; uitschot[h]:

~s are sold at a discount tweedekeusartikelen worden met korting verkocht
²reject (vb) **1** verwerpen, afwijzen, weigeren **2** uitwerpen
rejection 1 verwerping, afkeuring, afwijzing **2** uitwerping
reject shop winkel met tweedekeusartikelen
rejoice (+ at, over) zich verheugen (over): *I ~ to hear* het verheugt me te vernemen
rejoicing vreugde, feestviering
¹rejoin (vb) **1** (zich) weer verenigen **2** weer lid worden (van) **3** zich weer voegen bij: *I thought he would ~ his friends, but he went to sit by himself* ik dacht dat hij weer bij zijn vrienden zou gaan staan, maar hij ging apart zitten
²rejoin (vb) antwoorden
rejoinder repliek, (vinnig) antwoord[h]
rejuvenate verjongen; vernieuwen
rejuvenation verjonging
rekindle opnieuw ontsteken, opnieuw aanwakkeren
¹relapse (n) instorting; terugval [into evil]: *have a ~* opnieuw achteruitgaan
²relapse (vb) terugvallen; weer vervallen [into evil]; (weer) instorten: *~ into poverty* weer tot armoede vervallen
¹relate (vb) (+ to) in verband staan (met), betrekking hebben (op)
²relate (vb) **1** verhalen, berichten: *strange to ~ …* hoe onwaarschijnlijk het ook moge klinken, maar … [at beginning of incredible story] **2** (met elkaar) in verband brengen, relateren
related verwant, samenhangend, verbonden: *drug-~ crime* misdaad waarbij drugs een rol spelen; *I'm ~ to her by marriage* zij is aangetrouwde familie van me
relation 1 bloedverwant, familielid[h] **2** bloedverwantschap[h], verwantschap **3** betrekking, relatie, verband[h]: *bear no ~ to* geen verband houden met, geen betrekking hebben op; *in* (or: *with*) *~ to* met betrekking tot, in verhouding tot
relationship 1 betrekking, verhouding **2** bloedverwantschap[h], verwantschap
¹relative (n) familielid[h], (bloed)verwant(e)
²relative (adj) **1** betrekkelijk, relatief: *~ pronoun* betrekkelijk voornaamwoord **2** toepasselijk, relevant
relativity betrekkelijkheid, relativiteit
¹relax (vb) **1** verslappen, verminderen; [fig] ontdooien **2** zich ontspannen, relaxen
²relax (vb) ontspannen, verslappen, verminderen: *~ one's efforts* zich minder inspannen
relaxation ontspanning(svorm)
relaxing rustgevend, ontspannend
¹relay (n) **1** aflossing, verse paarden, nieuwe ploeg, verse voorraad **2** estafettewedstrijd
²relay (vb) heruitzenden; doorgeven [infor-

mation]

relay race estafettewedstrijd

¹**release** (n) **1** bevrijding, vrijgeving, verlossing **2** ontslagʰ; ontheffing [of obligation]; vrijspreking **3** nieuwe film/video/cd/release; het uitbrengen [of film, video, CD]: *on general ~* in alle bioscopen (te zien) **4** (artikelʰ voor) publicatie

²**release** (vb) **1** (+ from) bevrijden (uit), vrijlaten, vrijgeven **2** (+ from) ontslaan (van), vrijstellen; ontheffen (van) [obligation] **3** uitbrengen [film, video]; in de handel brengen [CD]

relegate 1 (+ to) verwijzen (naar) **2** overplaatsen **3** [sport] degraderen

relent minder streng worden, toegeven; [fig] afnemen; verbeteren

relentless 1 meedogenloos, zonder medelijden **2** gestaag, aanhoudend

relevance relevantie

relevant (+ to) relevant (voor): *I've marked the ~ passages* ik heb de desbetreffende passages aangegeven

reliability betrouwbaarheid

reliable betrouwbaar, te vertrouwen, geloofwaardig

reliance vertrouwenʰ

reliant vertrouwend: *be ~ on s.o.* vertrouwen stellen in iem.

relic relikwie **2** overblijfselʰ, souvenirʰ

relief 1 reliëfʰ; [fig] levendigheid; contrastʰ: *bring* (or: *throw) into ~* doen contrasteren [also fig] **2** verlichting, opluchting, ontlasting: *it was a great ~* het was een pak van mijn hart **3** afwisseling, onderbreking: *provide a little light ~* voor wat afwisseling zorgen **4** ondersteuning, steun, hulp **5** ontzetʰ; bevrijding [of city under siege]

relief fund ondersteuningsfondsʰ, hulpfondsʰ

relief map reliëfkaart

relief worker hulpverlener, hulpverleenster

relieve 1 verlichten, oplichten, ontlasten: *~ one's feelings* zijn hart luchten; *~ o.s.* zijn behoefte doen; *~ of a)* ontlasten van, afhelpen van; **b)** [inform] afhandig maken; **c)** ontslaan uit, ontheffen van **2** afwisselen, onderbreken: *a dress ~d with lace* een jurk met kant afgezet **3** ondersteunen, helpen, troosten, bemoedigen **4** aflossen, vervangen **5** [mil] ontzetten, bevrijden

relieved opgelucht

religion 1 godsdienst **2** vroomheid **3** gewetenszaak, heilige plicht: *make a ~ of sth.* van iets een erezaak maken

religious godsdienstig, religieus, vroom

religiously 1 godsdienstig **2** gewetensvol, nauwgezet

relinquish 1 opgeven; prijsgeven [eg religion] **2** afstand doen van [claim, right] **3** los-

laten

¹**relish** (n) **1** genoegenʰ, lust, plezierʰ, zin: *read with great ~* met veel plezier lezen **2** smaak [also fig]; trek: *add* (or: *give) (a) ~ to* prikkelen; *eat with (a) ~* met smaak eten **3** saus **4** pikant smaakjeʰ

²**relish** (vb) **1** smakelijk maken, kruiden **2** genieten van, genoegen scheppen in, zich laten smaken **3** tegemoet zien, verlangen naar: *~ the prospect* (or: *idea)* het een prettig vooruitzicht (or: idee) vinden; *I do not exactly ~ the idea of going on my own* ik kijk er niet echt naar uit om alleen te gaan

¹**relocate** (vb) zich opnieuw vestigen

²**relocate** (vb) opnieuw vestigen; verplaatsen

relocation vestiging elders, verhuizing naar elders

reluctance tegenzin, weerzin, onwil: *with great ~* met grote tegenzin

reluctant onwillig, aarzelend

rely (up)on vertrouwen (op), zich verlaten op, steunen op: *can he be relied upon?* kun je op hem rekenen?

remain 1 blijven, overblijven: *it ~s to be seen* het staat te bezien; *~ behind* achterblijven, nablijven **2** verblijven, zich ophouden **3** voortduren, blijven bestaan

¹**remainder** (n) **1** rest, overblijfselʰ, restantʰ **2** ramsj [of books] **3** verschilʰ [of subtraction]

²**remainder** (vb) opruimen; uitverkopen [books at reduced prices]

remaining overgebleven

remains 1 overblijfselen, ruïnes, resten **2** stoffelijk overschotʰ

¹**remake** (n) remake, nieuwe versie

²**remake** (vb) opnieuw maken, omwerken, een nieuwe versie maken

¹**remand** (n) **1** terugzending [in preventive custody] **2** voorarrestʰ: *on ~* in voorarrest

²**remand** (vb) **1** terugzenden **2** terugzenden in voorlopige hechtenis: *~ into custody* terugzenden in voorlopige hechtenis

remand centre observatiehuisʰ; [roughly] huisʰ van bewaring [for preventive custody]

¹**remark** (n) opmerking: *make a ~* een opmerking maken

²**remark** (vb) (+ (up)on) opmerkingen maken (over)

³**remark** (vb) opmerken, bemerken

remarkable 1 merkwaardig, opmerkelijk **2** opvallend

¹**remarry** (vb) hertrouwen

²**remarry** (vb) opnieuw trouwen met

remedial beter makend, genezend, herstellend, verbeterend

¹**remedy** (n) remedie⁺ʰ, (genees)middelʰ, hulpmiddelʰ: *beyond* (or: *past) ~* ongeneeslijk, onherstelbaar, niet te verhelpen

²**remedy** (vb) verhelpen [also fig]; voorzien in, genezen

¹**remember** (vb) **1** bedenken [in testament; by tipping] **2** gedenken [the dead; in prayers] **3** (+ to) de groeten doen (aan)

²**remember** (vb) (zich) herinneren, onthouden, van buiten kennen, denken aan

remembrance 1 herinnering: *in ~ of* ter herinnering aan **2** herinnering, aandenkenʰ, souvenirʰ **3** (-s) groet

Remembrance Day dodenherdenking

remind herinneren, doen denken: *will you ~ me?* help me eraan denken, wil je?

reminder 1 herinnering **2** betalingsherinnering **3** geheugensteuntjeʰ

reminisce herinneringen ophalen

reminiscence herinnering: *~s* memoires

remiss nalatig: *be ~ in* one's duties in zijn plichten tekortschieten

remission 1 vergeving **2** kwijtschelding **3** vermindering [eg of sentence]

¹**remit** (vb) afnemen

²**remit** (vb) **1** vergeven [sins] **2** kwijtschelden; schenken [debt, sentence]; vrijstellen van **3** doen afnemen/verminderen; laten verslappen [attention]; verzachten; verlichten [pain] **4** terugzenden, zenden, sturen **5** overmaken; doen overschrijven [money]

remittance overschrijving [of money]; overmaking, betalingsopdracht, overgemaakt bedragʰ

remnant 1 restantʰ, rest, overblijfselʰ **2** coupon [material]

remonstrate protesteren: *~ with* s.o. *(up)on* sth. iem. iets verwijten

remorse 1 wroeging **2** medelijdenʰ

remorseless meedogenloos

remote 1 ver (weg), ver uiteen: *~ control* afstandsbediening; *the ~ past* het verre verleden **2** afgelegen **3** gereserveerd, terughoudend **4** gering, flauw: *I haven't the ~st idea* ik heb er geen flauw benul van

removal 1 verwijdering **2** verplaatsing **3** afzetting, overplaatsing **4** verhuizing

removal van verhuiswagen

¹**remove** (vb) verhuizen, vertrekken

²**remove** (vb) **1** verwijderen, wegnemen; opheffen [doubt, fear]; afnemen [hat]; uitwissen [traces]; schrappen; afvoeren [from list]; uitnemen, uittrekken **2** afzetten, ontslaan, wegzenden: *~ s.o. from office* iem. uit zijn ambt ontslaan **3** verhuizen, verplaatsen, overplaatsen

removed verwijderd, afgelegen, ver: *far ~ from the truth* ver bezijden de waarheid || *a first cousin once ~* een achterneef

remover verhuizer

remuneration 1 beloning **2** vergoeding

remunerative winstgevend

renaissance renaissance, herleving

rename herdopen, een andere naam geven

rend 1 scheuren, verscheuren: *~ apart* vaneenscheuren **2** doorklieven, kloven, splijten:

[fig] *a cry rent the skies* (or: *air*) een gil doorkliefde de lucht **3** kwellen; verdriet doen [heart]

render 1 (terug)geven, geven, vergelden, verlenen; verschaffen [assistance]; bewijzen [service]; betuigen [thanks]; uitbrengen [report]; uitspreken [verdict]: *~ good for evil* kwaad met goed vergelden; *services ~ed* bewezen diensten **2** overgeven, overleveren **3** vertalen, omzetten, overzetten: *~ into German* in het Duits vertalen **4** maken, veranderen in

rendering 1 vertolking, weergave **2** vertaling

rendition 1 vertolking **2** vertaling **3** teruggave

renegade afvallige, overloper

renege 1 een belofte verbreken: *~ on* one's word zijn woord breken **2** [cards] verzaken

renew 1 vernieuwen, hernieuwen; oplappen [coat]; verversen; bijvullen [water]; vervangen [tyres] **2** doen herleven, verjongen **3** hervatten; weer opnemen [conversation]; herhalen **4** verlengen [contract]

renewable 1 vernieuwbaar, herwinbaar, recycleerbaar: *~ energy* zonne- en windenergie **2** verlengbaar

renewal 1 vernieuwing, vervanging **2** verlenging

renounce afstand doen van, opgeven, laten varen

renovate 1 vernieuwen, opknappen, renoveren, verbouwen **2** doen herleven

renovation vernieuwing, renovatie

renown faam, roem

renowned vermaard; beroemd

¹**rent** (n) **1** huur, pacht: [Am] *for ~* te huur **2** (meer)opbrengst van landbouwgrond **3** scheur(ing), kloof, barst

²**rent** (vb) **1** huren: *~ to buy* huurkopen **2** (also + out) verhuren

rental 1 huuropbrengst **2** huur(penningen), pacht(geldʰ) **3** [Am] het gehuurde; het verhuurde [eg rented house]

rent arrears achterstallige huur

renunciation 1 afstand, verwerping, verstoting **2** zelfverloochening

reopen 1 opnieuw opengaan, opnieuw openen, weer beginnen; heropenen [of shop etc] **2** hervatten [discussion]

reorganize reorganiseren

¹**repair** (n) herstelling, reparatie, herstelʰ: *in (a) good (state of) ~* in goede toestand, goed onderhouden; *under ~* in reparatie

²**repair** (vb) **1** herstellen, repareren **2** vergoeden, (weer) goedmaken

repairer hersteller, reparateur

reparation 1 herstelʰ, herstelling, reparatie **2** vergoeding, schadeloosstelling: *~s* herstelbetaling

repartee 1 gevatte reactie **2** gevatheid

repatriation repatriëring

repay 1 terugbetalen, aflossen **2** beantwoorden: ~ *kindness* **by** (or: *with*) *ingratitude* goedheid met ondankbaarheid beantwoorden **3** vergoeden, goedmaken **4** betaald zetten

repayment 1 terugbetaling, aflossing **2** vergoeding, vergelding, beloning

¹**repeal** (n) herroeping, afschaffing, intrekking

²**repeal** (vb) herroepen, afschaffen, intrekken

¹**repeat** (n) **1** herhaling **2** heruitzending: *in summer there are **endless** ~s of American soaps* in de zomer krijg je eindeloze herhalingen van Amerikaanse soaps

²**repeat** (vb) **1** zich herhalen, terugkeren: *history ~s **itself*** de geschiedenis herhaalt zich **2** repeteren [eg timepiece, firearm]: *~ing **decimal*** repeterende breuk

³**repeat** (vb) **1** herhalen: *~ a **course*** (or: *year*) blijven zitten [at school] **2** nazeggen, navertellen: *his words will not **bear** ~ing* zijn woorden laten zich niet herhalen

repeatedly herhaaldelijk, steeds weer, telkens

repeater zittenblijver

repeat offender 1 recidivist **2** veelpleger, draaideurcrimineel

repeat order nabestelling

¹**repel** (vb) afkeer opwekken

²**repel** (vb) afweren, terugdrijven; afslaan [offer, attack(er)]; afstoten [damp]

¹**repellent** (n) **1** afweermiddelʰ, insectenwerend middelʰ **2** waterafstotend middelʰ

²**repellent** (adj) **1** afwerend, afstotend **2** weerzinwekkend, walgelijk **3** onaantrekkelijk

repent berouw hebben (over), berouwen

repentance berouwʰ

repercussion 1 terugslag, (onaangename) reactie, repercussie **2** weerkaatsing, echo **3** terugstoot

repertory company repertoiregezelschapʰ

repetition herhaling, repetitie

repetitive (zich) herhalend, herhaald, herhalings-: [med] ~ **strain injury** repetitive strain injury, RSI; muisarm

rephrase herformuleren, anders uitdrukken: ~ *the **question*** de vraag anders stellen

repine morren, klagen

replace 1 terugplaatsen, terugleggen, terugzetten **2** vervangen, in de plaats stellen **3** de plaats innemen van, verdringen

replacement 1 vervanging **2** vervanger, plaatsvervanger, opvolger **3** vervangstukʰ, nieuwe aanvoer; versterking [mil]

replacement cost vervangingswaarde; nieuwwaarde

replay 1 opnieuw spelen, overspelen **2** terugspelen, herhalen

replenish weer vullen, aanvullen, bijvullen

replete (+ with) vol (van), gevuld, volgepropt

replica 1 replica, kopie **2** reproductie; [fig] evenbeeldʰ

replicate 1 herhalen **2** een kopie maken van

¹**reply** (n) antwoordʰ, repliek

²**reply** (vb) antwoorden: ~ **to** antwoorden op, beantwoorden

repo man [inform] iem. van een incassobureau voor autobedrijven

¹**report** (n) **1** rapportʰ, verslagʰ, berichtʰ, schoolrapportʰ **2** knal, slag, schotʰ **3** geruchtʰ, praatjeʰ, praatjes: *the ~ **goes** that …, ~ has it that …* het gerucht doet de ronde dat …

²**report** (vb) **1** rapporteren, berichten, melden: ~ **progress** over de stand van zaken berichten **2** opschrijven, noteren; samenvatten [reports, proceedings] **3** rapporteren, doorvertellen: ~ *s.o.* **to** *the police* iem. bij de politie aangeven **4** verslag uitbrengen, verslag doen, rapport opstellen: ~ **back** verslag komen uitbrengen; ~ **(up)on** *sth.* over iets verslag uitbrengen **5** zich aanmelden, verantwoording afleggen: ~ **to** *s.o.* **for** *duty* (or: *work*) zich bij iem. voor de dienst (*or:* het werk) aanmelden

reportedly naar verluidt, naar men zegt

reporter reporter, verslaggever

reporting berichtgeving, verslaggeving

¹**repose** (n) **1** rust, slaap, ontspanning **2** kalmte

²**repose** (vb) **1** rusten, uitrusten **2** (+ on) berusten (op), steunen

³**repose** (vb) stellen; vestigen [faith, hope]: ~ *confidence* (or: *trust*) **in** *sth.* vertrouwen stellen in iets

repository 1 magazijnʰ, pakhuisʰ, opslagplaats **2** schatkamer [fig]; bron; centrumʰ [of information]

repossess weer in bezit nemen, terugnemen; gedwongen verkopen

represent 1 voorstellen, weergeven, afbeelden **2** voorhouden, onder het oog brengen **3** aanvoeren, beweren: ~ *o.s.* **as** zich uitgeven voor **4** verklaren, uitleggen, duidelijk maken **5** symboliseren, staan voor, betekenen **6** vertegenwoordigen

representation 1 voorstelling, afbeelding, uitbeelding, opvoering **2** vertegenwoordiging **3** protestʰ

¹**representative** (n) **1** vertegenwoordiger, agent **2** afgevaardigde, gedelegeerde, gemachtigde **3** volksvertegenwoordiger: [Am] *House* of *Representatives* Huis van Afgevaardigden

²**representative** (adj) **1** representatief, typisch **2** voorstellend, symboliserend ‖ *be ~ of*

typisch zijn voor

repress 1 onderdrukken [also fig]; verdrukken, in bedwang houden, smoren **2** verdringen

repression 1 onderdrukking, verdrukking **2** verdringing

repressive onderdrukkend; hardvochtig en wreed [of regime]

¹**reprieve** (n) **1** (bevelʰ tot) uitstelʰ; opschorting [of death penalty] **2** kwijtschelding, gratie; omzetting [of death penalty] **3** respijtʰ, verlichting, verademing: *temporary* ~ (voorlopig) uitstel van executie

²**reprieve** (vb) **1** uitstel/gratie verlenen [death penalty] **2** respijt geven [fig]; een adempauze geven

¹**reprimand** (n) (officiële) berisping, uitbrander

²**reprimand** (vb) (officieel) berispen

¹**reprint** (n) **1** overdruk(jeʰ) **2** herdruk

²**reprint** (vb) herdrukken

reprisal represaille, vergelding(smaatregel)

¹**reproach** (n) **1** schande, smaad, blaam: *above* (or: *beyond*) ~ onberispelijk, perfect **2** verwijtʰ, uitbrander, berisping: *a look* of ~ een verwijtende blik

²**reproach** (vb) verwijten, berispen, afkeuren: *I have nothing to* ~ *myself* with ik heb mezelf niets te verwijten

reprocess recyclen, terugwinnen; opwerken [nuclear fuel]

¹**reproduce** (vb) zich voortplanten, zich vermenigvuldigen

²**reproduce** (vb) **1** weergeven, reproduceren, vermenigvuldigen **2** voortbrengen **3** opnieuw voortbrengen, herscheppen; [biology] regenereren

reproduction 1 reproductie, weergave, afbeelding **2** voortplanting

reproductive 1 reproductief **2** voortplantings-: ~ *organs* voortplantingsorganen

reprove berispen, terechtwijzen

reptile 1 reptielʰ **2** (lage) kruiper [fig]

republic republiek [also fig]

¹**republican** (n) republikein

²**republican** (adj) republikeins

repudiate 1 verstoten [woman, child] **2** verwerpen; niet erkennen [debt etc]; afwijzen; ontkennen [accusation]

repudiation 1 verstoting **2** verwerping, (ver)loochening

repugnance afkeer; weerzin: *feel* ~ *towards* sth. weerzin voelen tegen iets

repugnant weerzinwekkend

repulse 1 terugdrijven; terugslaan [enemy]; afslaan [attack]; [fig] verijdelen **2** afslaan; afwijzen [assistance, offer]

repulsive afstotend, weerzinwekkend, walgelijk

reputable achtenswaardig, fatsoenlijk

reputation reputatie, (goede) naam, faam:

have the ~ *for* (or: *of*) *being corrupt* de naam hebben corrupt te zijn

¹**repute** (n) reputatie, (goede) naam, faam: *know s.o.* *by* ~ iem. kennen van horen zeggen

²**repute** (vb) beschouwen (als), houden voor: *be highly* ~*d* een zeer goede naam hebben

reputed 1 befaamd **2** vermeend

reputedly naar men zegt, naar het heet

¹**request** (n) verzoekʰ, (aan)vraag, verzoeknummerʰ: *at the* ~ *of* op verzoek van; *on* ~ op verzoek

²**request** (vb) verzoeken, vragen (om)

request programme verzoekprogrammaʰ

require 1 nodig hebben, behoeven **2** vereisen, eisen, vorderen: *two signatures* ~*d* er zijn twee handtekeningen nodig; ~ *sth. from* (or: *of*) *s.o.* iets van iem. vereisen

requirement 1 eis, (eerste) vereiste: *meet* (or: *fulfil*) *the* ~*s* aan de voorwaarden voldoen **2** behoefte, benodigdheid

¹**requisite 1** vereisteʰ **2** rekwisietʰ, benodigdheid

²**requisite** (adj) vereist, essentieel, nodig

requisition (op)vorderen

requite 1 vergelden, betaald zetten, wreken **2** belonen **3** beantwoorden: ~ *s.o.'s love* iemands liefde beantwoorden

reread herlezen

¹**rerun** (n) herhaling [of film, play etc]

²**rerun** (vb) opnieuw (laten) spelen; herhalen [film, TV programme]

reschedule verplaatsen

¹**rescue** (n) **1** redding, verlossing, bevrijding **2** hulp, bijstand, steun

²**rescue** (vb) redden, verlossen, bevrijden

rescue dog 1 reddingshond **2** asielhond

rescuer redder

rescue-team reddingsploeg

¹**research** (n) (wetenschappelijk) onderzoekʰ

²**research** (vb) onderzoekingen doen, wetenschappelijk werk verrichten, wetenschappelijk onderzoeken: *this book has been well* ~*ed* dit boek berust op gedegen onderzoek

researcher onderzoeker

research student postdoctoraal student; promovendus

resemblance gelijkenis, overeenkomst: *show great* ~ *to s.o.* een grote gelijkenis met iem. vertonen

resemble lijken op

resent kwalijk nemen, verontwaardigd zijn over, zich storen aan: *I* ~ *that remark* ik neem je die opmerking wel kwalijk

resentful 1 boos, verontwaardigd, ontstemd **2** wrokkig, haatdragend

resentment 1 verontwaardiging **2** wrok, haat

reservation 1 middenberm; middenstrook

[of motorway]: *central* ~ middenberm
2 [Am] reservaat^h [for Indians] **3** gereserveerde plaats **4** reserve, voorbehoud^h, bedenking: *without* ~*(s)* zonder voorbehoud **5** reservering, plaatsbespreking: *do you have a* ~*?* heeft u gereserveerd?
¹reserve (n) **1** reserve, (nood)voorraad: *have (or: keep) sth. in* ~ iets in reserve hebben (*or:* houden) **2** reservaat^h: *nature* ~ natuurreservaat^h **3** reservespeler, invaller **4** reservist **5** reserve, voorbehoud^h, bedenking: *without* ~ zonder enig voorbehoud **6** gereserveerdheid, reserve, terughoudendheid
²reserve (vb) **1** reserveren, achterhouden, in reserve houden **2** (zich) voorbehouden [right]: *all rights* ~*d* alle rechten voorbehouden **3** bespreken [seat]; openhouden, laten vrijhouden
reserved 1 gereserveerd, terughoudend, gesloten **2** gereserveerd; besproken [of seat]
reservist reservist
reservoir (water)reservoir^h, stuwmeer^h
reset 1 opnieuw zetten [jewel, leg, plant, book] **2** resetten, opnieuw instellen [also comp]; terugzetten op nul [meter]
reshape een nieuwe vorm geven
reside wonen, zetelen
residence 1 residentie, verblijf^h, verblijfplaats, woonplaats: *take up* ~ *in* gaan wonen in **2** (voorname) woning, villa, herenhuis^h **3** ambtswoning [of governor]
residence permit verblijfsvergunning
¹resident (n) ingezetene, (vaste) inwoner, bewoner
²resident (adj) **1** woonachtig, inwonend, intern: [Am] ~ *alien* vreemdeling met een verblijfsvergunning **2** vast [on inhabitant]
residential woon-, van een woonwijk: ~ *area* (or: *district, quarter*) (deftige/betere) woonwijk; ~ *home* bejaardentehuis^h
residents' association buurtcomité^h
¹residual (n) **1** residu^h; rest [also maths, chem] **2** [chem] bijproduct^h
²residual (adj) achterblijvend; rest-
residue residu^h, overblijfsel^h, rest(ant^h)
¹resign (vb) **1** berusten, zich schikken **2** afstand doen van een ambt, aftreden, ontslag nemen; bedanken [for position]; opgeven [chess]
²resign (vb) **1** berusten in, zich schikken in, zich neerleggen bij: ~ *o.s. to sth., be* ~*ed to sth.* zich bij iets neerleggen **2** afstaan; afstand doen van [right, claim, ownership]; overgeven **3** opgeven [hope]
resignation 1 ontslag^h, ontslagbrief, aftreding, ontslagneming: *hand in/offer* (or: *send in, tender*) *one's* ~ zijn ontslag indienen **2** afstand **3** berusting, overgave
resigned gelaten, berustend
resilience veerkracht [also fig]; herstellingsvermogen^h

resilient veerkrachtig [also fig]
resin (kunst)hars^h: *synthetic* ~ kunsthars^{+h}
resist 1 weerstaan, weerstand bieden (aan), tegenhouden; bestand zijn tegen [cold, heat, damp]; resistent zijn tegen [disease, infection]: ~ *temptation* de verleiding weerstaan **2** zich verzetten (tegen), bestrijden: *this novel* ~*s* **interpretation** deze roman laat zich niet interpreteren
resistance 1 weerstand, tegenstand, verzet^h: *make* (or: *offer*) *no* ~ geen weerstand bieden; [fig] *take the line of least* ~ de weg van de minste weerstand kiezen **2** weerstandsvermogen^h
Resistance (the) verzetsbeweging, verzet^h
resistance fighter verzetsstrijder
resistant weerstand biedend, resistent, bestand: *heat-*~ hittebestendig
¹resit (n) herexamen^h
²resit (vb) opnieuw afleggen [examination]
resolute resoluut, vastberaden, beslist
resolution 1 resolutie, motie, voorstel^h, plan^h **2** besluit^h, beslissing, voornemen^h: *good* ~*s* goede voornemens **3** vastberadenheid, beslistheid, vastbeslotenheid **4** [image] resolutie **5** oplossing, ontbinding, ontleding
¹resolve (n) **1** besluit^h, beslissing, voornemen^h: *a firm* ~ *to stay* een vast voornemen om te blijven **2** [Am] resolutie, motie, voorstel^h **3** vastberadenheid, beslistheid
²resolve (vb) **1** een besluit nemen, besluiten, zich voornemen: *they* ~*d (up)on doing sth.* zij besloten iets te doen **2** zich oplossen, zich ontbinden, uiteenvallen
³resolve (vb) **1** beslissen, besluiten: *he* ~*d to leave* hij besloot weg te gaan **2** oplossen, een oplossing vinden voor **3** opheffen; wegnemen [doubt] **4** ontbinden, (doen) oplossen **5** ertoe brengen, doen beslissen: *that* ~*d us to ...* dat deed ons besluiten om ... **6** besluiten, beëindigen; bijleggen [dispute]
resolved vastbesloten, beslist
resonance resonantie, weerklank, weergalm
resonant 1 resonerend, weerklinkend, weergalmend **2** vol; diep [of voice]
resort 1 hulpmiddel^h, redmiddel^h, toevlucht: *in the last* ~, *as a last* ~ in laatste instantie, in geval van nood; *without* ~ *to* zonder zijn toevlucht te nemen tot **2** resort^h, vakantiecomplex^h
resort to zijn toevlucht nemen tot: ~ *violence* zijn toevlucht nemen tot geweld
resound weerklinken [also fig]; weergalmen
resounding 1 (weer)klinkend **2** zeer groot, onmiskenbaar: *a* ~ *success* een daverend succes
resource 1 hulpbron, redmiddel^h: *left to one's own* ~*s* aan zijn lot overgelaten **2** toevlucht, uitweg **3** vindingrijkheid: *he is full of*

~ (or: *a* **man** *of* ~) hij is (zeer) vindingrijk **4** (-s) rijkdommen, (geld)middelen, voorraden: *natural* ~*s* natuurlijke rijkdommen

resourceful vindingrijk

¹**respect** (n) **1** opzicht^h, detail^h, (oog)punt^h: *in all* (or: *many*) ~*s* in alle (*or:* vele) opzichten; *in some* ~ in zeker opzicht, enigermate **2** betrekking, relatie: *with* ~ *to* met betrekking tot, wat betreft **3** aandacht, zorg, inachtneming: *without* ~ *to* zonder te letten op, ongeacht **4** eerbied, achting, ontzag^h: *be held in the greatest* ~ zeer in aanzien zijn; *with (all due)* ~ als u mij toestaat **5** (-s) eerbetuigingen, groeten, complimenten: *give* her my ~*s* doe haar de groeten; *pay one's last* ~*s to s.o.* iem. de laatste eer bewijzen [at someone's death]

²**respect** (vb) **1** respecteren, eerbiedigen, (hoog)achten **2** ontzien, ongemoeid laten

respectability fatsoen^h, fatsoenlijkheid

respectable 1 achtenswaardig, eerbiedwaardig **2** respectabel, (tamelijk) groot, behoorlijk: *a* ~ *income* een behoorlijk inkomen **3** fatsoenlijk [also iron]

respectful eerbiedig: *yours* ~*ly* met (de meeste) hoogachting

respectively respectievelijk

respiration ademhaling

respirator 1 ademhalingstoestel^h **2** gasmasker^h, rookmasker^h, stofmasker^h

respiratory ademhalings-

respite 1 respijt^h, uitstel^h, opschorting: *work without* ~ zonder onderbreking werken **2** verlichting

resplendent schitterend, prachtig

respond 1 antwoorden **2** (+ to) reageren (op), gehoor geven (aan), gevoelig zijn (voor)

respondent 1 gedaagde [in appeal of divorce proceedings] **2** ondervraagde, geënquêteerde

response 1 antwoord^h, repliek, tegenzet **2** reactie, gehoor^h, weerklank, respons^+h: *meet with no* ~ geen weerklank vinden

responsibility verantwoordelijkheid, aansprakelijkheid: *on one's own* ~ op eigen verantwoordelijkheid

responsible 1 betrouwbaar, degelijk, solide **2** verantwoordelijk; belangrijk [of job] **3** (+ for) verantwoordelijk (voor), aansprakelijk (voor): *be* ~ *to* verantwoording verschuldigd zijn aan

responsive 1 (+ to) ontvankelijk (voor), gevoelig (voor) **2** wakker, alert, geïnteresseerd **3** [web design] responsief

¹**rest** (n) **1** rustplaats, verblijf^h, tehuis^h **2** steun, standaard, houder, statief^h; [billiards] bok **3** [mus] rust(teken^h) **4** rust, slaap, pauze: *come to* ~ tot stilstand komen; *set s.o.'s mind at* ~ iem. geruststellen **5** de rest, het overige, de overigen: *and the* ~ *of it, all*

the ~ *of it* en de rest

²**rest** (vb) **1** rusten, stil staan, slapen, pauzeren: *I feel completely* ~*ed* ik voel me helemaal uitgerust **2** blijven [in a certain condition]: ~ *assured* wees gerust, wees ervan verzekerd **3** braak liggen

³**rest** (vb) **1** laten (uit)rusten, rust geven **2** doen rusten, leunen, steunen

¹**restart** (vb) opnieuw beginnen, starten

²**restart** (vb) weer op gang brengen; [sport] hervatten

restaurant restaurant^h

restful 1 rustig, kalm, vredig **2** rustgevend, kalmerend

resting-place rustplaats [also fig]

restitution restitutie, teruggave, schadeloosstelling

restive 1 weerspannig, onhandelbaar, dwars; koppig [of horse] **2** ongedurig, onrustig; rusteloos [of person]

restless rusteloos, onrustig, ongedurig

restoration 1 restauratie(werk^h), reconstructie **2** herstel^h, herinvoering, rehabilitatie **3** teruggave

restore 1 teruggeven, terugbetalen, terugbrengen **2** restaureren **3** reconstrueren **4** in ere herstellen, rehabiliteren **5** herstellen, weer invoeren, vernieuwen

restrain 1 tegenhouden, weerhouden: ~ *from* weerhouden van **2** aan banden leggen, beteugelen, beperken, in toom houden

restrained 1 beheerst, kalm **2** ingetogen, sober; gematigd [of colour]

restraining order [law] contactverbod^h, straatverbod^h: *take out a* ~ *against s.o.* iem. een contact- of straatverbod (laten) opleggen

restraint 1 terughoudendheid, gereserveerdheid, zelfbeheersing: *without* ~ vrijelijk, in onbeperkte mate **2** ingetogenheid, soberheid

restrict beperken, begrenzen, aan banden leggen: ~ *to* beperken tot

restriction beperking, (beperkende) bepaling, restrictie, voorbehoud^h

restrictive beperkend: ~ *trade practices* beperkende handelspraktijken

restring 1 opnieuw bespannen [eg tennis racket] **2** opnieuw besnaren: ~ *a guitar* een gitaar opnieuw besnaren

rest room [Am] toilet^h [in restaurant, office etc]

rest (up)on (be)rusten op, steunen op

rest with berusten bij

¹**result** (n) **1** resultaat^h, uitkomst; uitslag [of sporting events] **2** gevolg^h, effect^h, uitvloeisel^h: *as a* ~ dientengevolge, als gevolg waarvan; *as a* ~ *of* ten gevolge van **3** uitkomst [of sum]; antwoord^h

²**result** (vb) **1** volgen, het gevolg zijn: ~ *from* voortvloeien uit **2** aflopen, uitpakken: ~ *in*

tot gevolg hebben
resultant resulterend, eruit voortvloeiend
resume 1 opnieuw beginnen, hervatten, hernemen **2** terugnemen, terugkrijgen **3** voortzetten, vervolgen, doorgaan
résumé 1 (korte) samenvatting **2** [Am] cv^h, curriculum vitae^h
resumption hervatting, voortzetting
resurgence heropleving, opstanding
resurrect 1 (doen) herleven, (doen) herrijzen **2** opgraven, weer voor de dag halen
resurrection herleving, opleving, opstanding
Resurrection (the) de verrijzenis, de opstanding
resuscitate 1 weer bijbrengen, reanimeren **2** doen herleven
¹**retail** (n) kleinhandel, detailhandel
²**retail** (vb) in een winkel verkocht worden: ~ *at* (or: *for*) *fifty cents* in de winkel voor vijftig cent te koop zijn
³**retail** (vb) in een winkel verkopen
⁴**retail** (vb) omstandig vertellen
retailer 1 winkelier, kleinhandelaar **2** slijter
retain 1 vasthouden, binnenhouden: *a ~ing wall* steunmuur **2** houden, handhaven, bewaren: *we ~ happy memories of those days* wij bewaren goede herinneringen aan die dagen
retainer 1 voorschot^h [of fee] **2** volgeling, bediende: *an old ~* een oude getrouwe
retaliate wraak nemen
retard ophouden, tegenhouden, vertragen
retarded achtergebleven, achterlijk, geestelijk gehandicapt
retch kokhalzen
retention 1 het vasthouden, het binnenhouden **2** handhaving, behoud^h
¹**rethink** (n) heroverweging, het opnieuw doordenken
²**rethink** (vb) heroverwegen, opnieuw bezien
reticence 1 terughoudendheid, gereserveerdheid **2** het verzwijgen, het achterhouden **3** zwijgzaamheid, geslotenheid
reticent 1 terughoudend, gereserveerd **2** zwijgzaam, gesloten
retina netvlies^h, retina
retinue gevolg^h, hofstoet
retire 1 zich terugtrekken, weggaan, heengaan, zich ter ruste begeven: *~ for the night* (or: *to bed*) zich ter ruste (or: te bed) begeven **2** met pensioen gaan
retired 1 teruggetrokken, afgezonderd, afgelegen **2** gepensioneerd, stil levend, rentenierend
retirement 1 pensionering, het gepensioneerd worden, het met pensioen gaan: *to take early ~* met de vut gaan; [Belg] op brugpensioen gaan **2** afzondering, eenzaamheid

retirement pension ouderdomspensioen^h; AOW
retiring 1 teruggetrokken, niet opdringerig **2** pensioen-: *~ age* de pensioengerechtigde leeftijd
¹**retort** (n) **1** weerwoord^h, repliek, antwoord^h: *say (sth.) in ~* (iets) als weerwoord gebruiken **2** distilleerkolf
²**retort** (vb) een weerwoord geven, antwoorden
³**retort** (vb) (vinnig) antwoorden; [fig] de bal terugkaatsen
retrace 1 herleiden, terugvoeren tot **2** weer nagaan [in memory] **3** terugkeren: *~ one's steps* (or: *way*) op zijn schreden terugkeren
retract intrekken [also fig]; herroepen, afstand nemen van
¹**retreat** (n) **1** toevluchtsoord^h, schuilplaats **2** tehuis^h, asiel^h **3** terugtocht, aftocht: *beat a (hasty) ~* zich (snel) terugtrekken; [fig] (snel) de aftocht blazen **4** retraite
²**retreat** (vb) teruggaan, zich terugtrekken
¹**retrench** (vb) bezuinigen
²**retrench** (vb) besnoeien, inkrimpen, bekorten
retrial nieuw onderzoek^h; revisie
retribution vergelding, straf
retrieval 1 herwinning, het terugvinden **2** herstelling, het verhelpen **3** het redden [data from files] || *beyond* (or: *past*) ~ a) voorgoed verloren; b) onherstelbaar
retrieve 1 terugwinnen, terugvinden, terugkrijgen **2** herstellen, weer goedmaken, verhelpen **3** ophalen [data from files]
retrospect terugblik: *in ~* achteraf gezien
retrospection terugblik, retrospectief^h
retrospective 1 retrospectief, terugblikkend **2** met terugwerkende kracht
¹**return** (n) **1** terugkeer, terugkomst, thuiskomst, terugreis: *the point of no ~* punt waarna er geen weg terug is **2** teruggave [also of tax]; teruggezonden artikel^h: *on sale and ~* op commissie **4** opbrengst, winst, rendement^h: *~ on capital* (or: *investment*) kapitaalopbrengst, resultaat van de investering **5** aangifte, officieel rapport^h **6** verkiezing, afvaardiging **7** terugslag, return, terugspeelbal **8** return(wedstrijd), revanche || *by ~ (of post)* per omgaande, per kerende post; *in ~ for* in ruil voor
²**return** (adj) **1** retour-: *~ ticket* retour(tje) **2** tegen-, terug-: *a ~ visit* een tegenbezoek
³**return** (vb) terugkeren, terugkomen, teruggaan: *~ to a)* terugkeren op; *b)* vervallen in
⁴**return** (vb) **1** retourneren, terugbrengen, teruggeven **2** opleveren, opbrengen **3** beantwoorden, terugbetalen: *~ like for like* met gelijke munt terugbetalen **4** [sport] terugslaan, retourneren, terugspelen **5** kiezen,

verkiezen, afvaardigen
⁵return (vb) antwoorden
returnee 1 repatriant **2** herintreder
return key returntoets, entertoets
¹retweet (n) retweet
²retweet (vb) retweeten, doorsturen
reunion reünie, hereniging, samenkomst
reunite (zich) herenigen, weer bij elkaar komen
reusable geschikt voor hergebruik
¹reuse (n) hergebruikʰ
²reuse (vb) opnieuw gebruiken
rev Reverend Eerw., Eerwaarde
revaluation herwaardering; revaluatie [also fin]
revamp opknappen, vernieuwen, pimpen
¹reveal (n) openbaarmaking, onthulling
²reveal (vb) openbaren, onthullen, bekendmaken
revealing onthullend, veelzeggend
revel pret maken, feestvieren: ~ in erg genieten van, zich te buiten gaan aan
revelation bekendmaking, openbaring, onthulling: it was quite a ~ **to** me dat was een hele openbaring voor mij
revelry pret(makerij), uitgelatenheid
¹revenge (n) **1** wraak(neming), vergelding: take ~ on s.o. for sth. wraak nemen (or: zich wreken) op iem. vanwege iets **2** [sport, game] revanche(partij)
²revenge (vb) wreken, vergelden, wraak nemen
revengeful wraakzuchtig
revenue 1 inkomenʰ, opbrengst; inkomsten [from property, investment etc] **2** inkomsten
revenue tariff belastingtariefʰ
reverberate weerkaatsen [sound, light, heat]; terugkaatsen, echoën, weerklinken: ~ **upon** terugwerken op [also fig]
reverberation weerklank, weerkaatsing
revere (ver)eren, respecteren, eerbied hebben voor
reverence verering, respectʰ, (diepe) eerbied, ontzagʰ: hold s.o. (sth.) in ~ eerbied koesteren voor iem. (iets)
reverend eerwaard(ig)
Reverend (the) Eerwaarde: the ~ **Mr** Johnson de Weleerwaarde Heer Johnson
reverent eerbiedig, respectvol
reversal omkering, om(me)keer
¹reverse (n) **1** tegenslag, nederlaag **2** keerzijde [of coins; also fig]; rugzijde, achterkant **3** achteruit [of car]: put a car **into** ~ een auto in zijn achteruit zetten **4** tegendeelʰ, omgekeerdeʰ, tegengesteldeʰ: but the ~ is also **true** maar het omgekeerde is ook waar ‖ **in** ~ omgekeerd, in omgekeerde volgorde
²reverse (adj) tegen(over)gesteld, omgekeerd, achteraan: ~ **gear** achteruit [of car]; in ~ **order** in omgekeerde volgorde

³reverse (vb) achteruitrijden [of car]; achteruitgaan
⁴reverse (vb) **1** (om)keren, omdraaien, omschakelen; achteruitrijden [car]: ~ one's **policy** radicaal van politiek veranderen **2** herroepen [decision]; intrekken; [law] herzien
revert 1 (+ to) terugkeren (tot) [previous condition]; terugvallen (in) [habit] **2** (+ to) terugkomen (op) [earlier topic of conversation] **3** terugkeren [of property to owner]
¹review (n) **1** terugblik, overzichtʰ, bezinning: be **under** ~ opnieuw bekeken worden **2** parade, inspectie **3** recensie, (boek)bespreking **4** tijdschriftʰ
²review (vb) **1** opnieuw bekijken, herzien **2** terugblikken op, overzien **3** parade houden, inspecteren **4** recenseren, bespreken, recensies schrijven
reviewer recensent
revile (uit)schelden
revise 1 herzien, verbeteren, corrigeren: ~d **edition** herziene uitgave [of book]; enclosed you will find our ~d **invoice** bijgesloten vindt u onze gecorrigeerde factuur **2** repeteren [lesson]; herhalen; studeren [for examination]
revision 1 revisie, herziening, wijziging **2** herhaling [of lesson]; het studeren [for examination]
revitalize nieuwe kracht geven, nieuw leven geven
revival 1 reveilʰ **2** (her)opleving, wedergeboorte, hernieuwde belangstelling **3** herstelʰ [of strengths] ‖ the ~ **of** a play de heropvoering van een toneelstuk
¹revive (vb) **1** herleven, bijkomen, weer tot leven (op krachten) komen **2** weer in gebruik komen, opnieuw ingevoerd worden
²revive (vb) **1** doen herleven, vernieuwen, weer tot leven brengen **2** opnieuw invoeren [old custom]
¹revoke (vb) [cards] verzaken
²revoke (vb) herroepen; intrekken [order, promise, licence]
¹revolt (n) opstand, oproerʰ: stir people to ~ mensen opruien
²revolt (vb) **1** (+ against) in opstand komen (tegen), rebelleren, muiten **2** walgen: ~ **at** (or: against, from) walgen van
³revolt (vb) doen walgen, afstoten; afkerig maken van [also fig]: be ~ed **by** sth. van iets walgen
revolting walgelijk, onsmakelijk, weerzinwekkend
revolution 1 (om)wenteling; draaiing [around centre] **2** rotatie; draai(ing) [around axis]; toer, slag **3** revolutie, (staats)omwenteling **4** ommekeer, omkering: a ~ **in** thought algehele verandering in denkbeelden
revolutionary revolutionair
revolve (rond)draaien, (doen) (rond)wentelen: the discussion always ~s **around** (or:

about) *money* de discussie draait altijd om geld

revolver revolver

revolving draaiend, roterend: ~ *door* draaideur

revulsion walging, afkeer, weerzin: *a ~ against* (or: *from*) een afkeer van, een weerzin tegen

¹rev up (vb) **1** draaien, op toeren komen **2** [fig] opstarten, op gang komen

²rev up (vb) **1** op toeren laten komen **2** [fig] opvoeren, uitbreiden: ~ *one's* **computer** zijn computer versnellen

¹reward (n) beloning, compensatie, loonʰ: *the ~s of* **popularity** de voordelen van populariteit

²reward (vb) belonen

rewarding lonend, de moeite waard; dankbaar [of work, task]

rewind opnieuw opwinden, terugspoelen

¹rewrite (n) **1** bewerking **2** bewerkt boekʰ, artikelʰ

²rewrite (vb) bewerken, herschrijven

rhapsody verhalend gedichtʰ

rhetoric 1 redekunst, retoriek, retorica **2** welsprekendheid, bombast, holle frasen

rhetorical retorisch, gekunsteld ‖ ~ *question* retorische vraag

¹rheumatic (n) reumapatiënt

²rheumatic (adj) reumatisch: ~ *fever* acute reuma

rheumatism reuma⁺ʰ, reumatiek

Rhine (the) Rijn

rhino *rhinoceros* neushoorn

rhinoceros neushoorn

rhododendron rododendron

rhubarb rabarber

¹rhyme (n) **1** rijm(woord)ʰ **2** (berijmd) gedichtʰ, versʰ ‖ *without* ~ *or* **reason** zonder enige betekenis, onzinnig

²rhyme (vb) **1** rijmen, rijm hebben: ~*d verses* rijmende verzen **2** dichten, rijmen

³rhyme (vb) **1** laten rijmen **2** berijmen

rhyming rijmend, op rijm: ~ *slang* rijmend slang

rhythm ritmeʰ, maat

rhythmic(al) ritmisch, regelmatig

¹rib (n) **1** rib **2** baleinʰ [of umbrella] **3** bladnerf **4** ribstukʰ **5** ribbelpatroonʰ [in knitting]

²rib (vb) plagen, voor de gek houden

ribaldry schunnige taal

ribbed geribd: ~ *material* geribbelde stof

ribbon 1 lint(je)ʰ, onderscheiding **2** (-s) flard: [fig] *cut to ~s* in de pan hakken **3** (schrijfmachine)lintʰ

rib cage ribbenkast

rice rijst

rich 1 rijk: ~ *in* rijk aan; *the ~* de rijken **2** kostbaar, luxueus **3** rijkelijk, overvloedig **4** vruchtbaar: ~ *soil* vruchtbare aarde **5** machtig [of food] **6** vol [of sounds]; warm

[of colour] **7** [inform; oft iron] kostelijk [of joke]: *that's (pretty) ~!* **a)** dat is een goeie!; **b)** wat een flater! ‖ *strike it* ~ een goudmijn ontdekken, fortuin maken

riches 1 rijkdom, het rijk-zijn **2** kostbaarheden, weelde

richly volledig, dubbel en dwars: ~ *deserve* volkomen verdienen

¹rick (n) hooimijt

²rick (vb) **1** ophopen **2** verdraaien, verstuiken

rickety gammel, wankel

rickshaw riksja

ricochet (doen) ricocheren, (laten) afketsen: *the bullet ~ted* **off** *the wall* de kogel ketste af op de muur

rid bevrijden, ontdoen van: *be well ~ of s.o.* goed van iem. af zijn; *get ~ of* kwijtraken, van de hand doen

riddance bevrijding, verwijdering: *they've just left. Good ~!* ze zijn net weg. Mooi zo, opgeruimd staat netjes!

-ridden 1 gedomineerd door, beheerst door: *conscience-ridden* gewetensbezwaard **2** vergeven van: *this place is* **vermin-ridden** het wemelt hier van het ongedierte

¹riddle (n) **1** raadselʰ, mysterieʰ **2** (grove) zeef

²riddle (vb) **1** zeven [also fig]; schiften, natrekken **2** doorzeven: *the body was ~d* **with** *bullets* het lichaam was met kogels doorzeefd

riddled gevuld, vol, bezaaid: *the translation was ~* **with** *errors* de vertaling stond vol fouten

¹ride (n) **1** rit(jeʰ), tocht(jeʰ): *can you* **give** *me a ~ to the station?* kan je mij een lift geven tot aan het station? **2** [inform; Am] auto ‖ *take s.o. for a ~* iem. voor de gek houden, iem. in de maling nemen

²ride (vb) **1** rijden, paardrijden **2** rijden, voor anker liggen ‖ ~ *roughshod* over *s.o. (sth.)* nergens naar kijken, niet al te zachtzinnig te werk gaan; ~ *up* omhoogkruipen, opkruipen

³ride (vb) **1** berijden, doorrijden **2** (be)rijden, rijden met: ~ *a* **bicycle** (or: *bike*) op de fiets rijden, fietsen **3** beheersen, tiranniseren: *the robber was ridden by* **fears** de dief werd door schrik bevangen **4** [Am] jennen, kwellen

ride out overleven [also fig]; heelhuids doorkomen: *the ship rode out the* **storm** het schip doorstond de storm

rider 1 (be)rijder, ruiter **2** [law] aanvullingsakte; [bill] amendementʰ **3** [theatre] rider, wensenlijstjeʰ

ridge 1 (berg)kam, richel, bergketen **2** nok [of roof] **3** ribbel **4** golftop **5** rug, (uitgerekt) hogedrukgebiedʰ

¹ridicule (n) spot, hoon

²ridicule (vb) ridiculiseren, bespotten

ridiculous ridicuul, belachelijk

r_i_ding boot rijlaars
rife 1 wijdverbreid, vaak voorkomend: *violence is ~ in westerns* er is veel geweld in cowboyfilms **2** (+ with) goed voorzien (van), legio
riffle through vluchtig doorbladeren
r_i_ff-raff uitschot^h, schorem^h
¹**r_i_fle** (n) geweer^h, karabijn
²**r_i_fle** (vb) doorzoeken, leeghalen: *the burglar had ~d every **cupboard*** de dief had iedere kast overhoop gehaald
r_i_fle range 1 schietbaan **2** schootsafstand, draagwijdte: *within ~* binnen schot(bereik)
rift 1 spleet, kloof **2** onenigheid, tweedracht
¹**rig** (n) **1** tuig^h, tuigage, takelage **2** uitrusting, (olie)booruitrusting **3** plunje, uitrusting: *in **full** ~* in vol ornaat
²**rig** (vb) **1** (op)tuigen, optakelen **2** uitrusten, uitdossen **3** knoeien met, sjoemelen met: *the **elections** were ~ged* de verkiezingen waren doorgestoken kaart
rigging (the) tuig^h, tuigage, takelage, het optuigen
¹**right** (n) **1** rechterkant: ***keep** to the ~* rechts houden; ***on** (or: to) your ~* aan je rechterkant **2** rechterhand; rechtse [in boxing]; rechter(hand)schoen **3** rechts^h, de conservatieven **4** recht^h, voorrecht^h, (gerechtvaardigde) eis: *the ~ of free **speech*** het recht op vrije meningsuiting; *~ of **way*** recht van overpad; [traf] voorrang(srecht); *all ~s **reserved*** alle rechten voorbehouden; *he has a ~ **to** the money* hij heeft recht op het geld; ***within** one's ~s* in zijn recht **5** recht^h, gerechtigheid: *he is **in** the ~* hij heeft gelijk, hij heeft het recht aan zijn kant || ***put** (or: **set**) to ~s* in orde brengen, rechtzetten
²**right** (adj) **1** juist, correct, rechtmatig: *you **were** ~ to tell her* je deed er goed aan het haar te vertellen; ***put** (or: **set**) the clock ~* de klok juist zetten **2** juist, gepast, recht: *strike the ~ **note*** de juiste toon aanslaan; *on the ~ **side** of fifty* nog geen vijftig (jaar oud); *keep on the ~ **side** of the law* zich (keurig) aan de wet houden; *do the ~ **thing*** doen wat juist is, doen wat (zo) hoort; [fig] *be on the ~ **track*** op het goede spoor zitten; *~ **angle*** rechte hoek **3** in goede staat, in orde: *let me see if I've **got** this ~* even kijken of ik het goed begrijp **4** rechts, conservatief **5** eerlijk, betrouwbaar: *the ~ **sort*** het goede soort (mensen); ***Mister** Right* de ware Jakob; *(as) ~ as **rain*** perfect in orde, kerngezond; ***put** (or: **set**) s.o. ~* iem. terechtwijzen; ***see** s.o. ~* zorgen dat iem. aan zijn trekken komt; *~ **enough*** bevredigend, ja hoor **6** waar, echt, heus: *it's a ~ **mess*** het is een puinzooi **7** gelijk: *you **are** ~* je hebt gelijk **8** rechtvaardig, gerechtigd: *it **seemed** only ~ to tell you this* ik vond dat je dit moest weten

³**right** (vb) **1** rechtmaken, recht(op) zetten: *the **yacht** ~ed itself* het jacht kwam weer recht te liggen **2** genoegdoening geven, rehabiliteren **3** verbeteren; rechtzetten [mistakes]: *~ a **wrong*** een onrecht herstellen || *~ **o.s.*** zich herstellen
⁴**right** (adv) **1** naar rechts, aan de rechterzijde: *~ **arm** (or: **hand**)* rechterhand, assistent; *keep on the ~ **side*** rechts houden; *~ and **left*** aan alle kanten, overal, links en rechts; *~, **left** and centre, **left**, ~, and centre* aan alle kanten **2** juist, vlak, regelrecht: *~ **ahead*** recht vooruit; *~ **behind** you* vlak achter je **3** onmiddellijk, direct: *I'll be ~ **back*** ik ben zó terug **4** juist, correct: *nothing seems to **go** ~ for her* niets wil haar lukken **5** helemaal, volledig: *she turned ~ **round*** zij maakte volledig rechtsomkeert **6** zeer, heel, recht || *~ **away*** onmiddellijk; *~ **off*** onmiddellijk; *~ **on** zo mogen wij het horen*
Right Zeer [in forms of address]
right-a_bout in tegenovergestelde richting || *(do a) ~ **turn** (or: **face**)* rechtsomkeert (maken) [also fig]
right-a_ngled rechthoekig, met rechte hoek(en)
r_i_ghteous 1 rechtvaardig, deugdzaam **2** gerechtvaardigd, gewettigd: *~ **indignation*** gerechtvaardigde verontwaardiging
r_i_ghtful 1 wettelijk, rechtmatig: *the ~ **owner*** de rechtmatige eigenaar **2** gerechtvaardigd, rechtvaardig
r_i_ght-hand rechts, m.b.t. de rechterhand: *~ **man*** rechterhand, onmisbare helper; *~ **turn*** bocht naar rechts
right-h_a_nded 1 rechtshandig **2** met de rechterhand toegebracht **3** voor rechtshandigen
r_i_ghtly 1 terecht **2** rechtvaardig, oprecht
right-m_i_nded weldenkend
right-to-l_i_fe antiabortus-
right-w_i_ng van de rechterzijde, conservatief
right-w_i_nger 1 lid^h van de rechterzijde, conservatief **2** rechtsbuiten, rechtervleugelspeler
r_i_gid 1 onbuigzaam, stijf, stug, strak **2** star, verstard
rig_i_dity 1 onbuigzaamheid **2** starheid
r_i_gmarole 1 onzin, gewauwel^h **2** rompslomp
r_i_gorous 1 onbuigzaam, streng, ongenadig **2** rigoureus, nauwgezet, zorgvuldig
r_i_gour 1 gestrengheid, strikte toepassing: *with the utmost ~ of the **law*** met strenge toepassing van de wet **2** hardheid, meedogenloosheid **3** accuratesse, uiterste nauwkeurigheid
rig _o_ut 1 uitrusten, van een uitrusting voorzien **2** uitdossen: *he had rigged **himself** out as a general* hij had zich als generaal uit-

gedost
rig-out plunje, (apen)pak^h
rig up [esp inform] **1** monteren, opstellen **2** in elkaar flansen
rile op stang jagen, nijdig maken, irriteren
rim rand, boord^h, velg; montuur^+h [of glasses]
rime rijp, aangevroren mist
rimless montuurloos [of glasses]
rind schil, korst, zwoerd^h
¹ring (n) **1** ring, kring, piste, arena **2** groepering, bende **3** gerinkel^h, klank; [inform] telefoontje^h: *give* s.o. a ~ iem. opbellen **4** bijklank, ondertoon: *her offer has a **suspicious** ~* er zit een luchtje aan haar aanbod **5** het boksen, bokswereld, ring **6** circus^+h, circuswereld, piste ‖ *make* (or: *run*) ~s *round* s.o. iem. de loef afsteken
²ring (vb) **1** rinkelen, klinken; (over)gaan [of bell]; bellen: ~ *true* oprecht klinken **2** bellen, de klok luiden, aanbellen **3** tuiten [of ears]; weerklinken **4** telefoneren, bellen: ~ *off* opleggen, ophangen [telephone] **5** (+ with) weergalmen (van), gonzen
³ring (vb) **1** doen rinkelen, luiden **2** opbellen, telefoneren naar: *I'll* ~ *you **back** in a minute* ik bel je dadelijk terug
⁴ring (vb) **1** omringen, omcirkelen **2** ringelen; ringen [animals]
ring-binder ringband
ring finger ringvinger
ringleader leider [of group of agitators]
ringlet lange krul
ringmaster circusdirecteur
ringtone beltoon
¹ring up (vb) **1** (al luidend) optrekken [bell] **2** registreren; aanslaan [on cash register]
²ring up (vb) opbellen, telefoneren
rink 1 (kunst)ijsbaan **2** rolschaatsbaan
¹rinse (n) (kleur)spoeling
²rinse (vb) **1** spoelen **2** een kleurspoeling geven aan
¹riot (n) **1** ordeverstoring, ongeregeldheid **2** braspartij, uitbundig feest^h **3** overvloed, weelde: *a* ~ *of **colour*** een bonte kleurenpracht **4** oproer^h, tumult^h **5** dolle pret, pretmakerij ‖ *run* ~ a) relletjes trappen, uit de band springen; b) woekeren [of plants]
²riot (vb) **1** relletjes trappen **2** er ongebreideld op los leven, uitspatten
rioter relschopper
riotous 1 oproerig, wanordelijk **2** luidruchtig, uitgelaten: ~ *assembly* het oproerkraaien **3** denderend
riot police ME, mobiele eenheid
¹rip (n) **1** (lange) scheur, snee **2** losbol, snoeper
²rip (vb) **1** scheuren, splijten **2** vooruitsnellen; scheuren [fig]: *let it* (or: *her*) ~ plankgas geven ‖ *let sth.* ~ iets op zijn beloop laten
³rip (vb) **1** openrijten, losscheuren, afscheu-

ren, wegscheuren: *the bag had been* ~*ped open* de zak was opengereten; ~ *up* aan stukken rijten **2** jatten, pikken: ~ *off* a) te veel doen betalen, afzetten; b) stelen
ripe 1 rijp [also fig]; volgroeid; belegen [of cheese, wine] **2** wijs, verstandig: *of* ~ *age* volwassen, ervaren; *a* ~ *judgement* een doordacht oordeel **3** op het kantje af, plat **4** klaar, geschikt: *the time is* ~ *for action* de tijd is rijp voor actie
ripen rijpen, rijp worden, wijs worden, doen rijpen
rip-off 1 afzetterij **2** diefstal, roof
¹ripple (n) **1** rimpeling, golfje^h, deining **2** gekabbel^h, geruis^h: *a* ~ *of **laughter*** een kabbelend gelach
²ripple (vb) kabbelen, ruisen
³ripple (vb) rimpelen, (doen) golven
rip-roaring lawaaierig, totaal uitgelaten
¹rise (n) **1** helling, verhoging, hoogte **2** stijging [also fig]; verhoging; [Stock Exchange] hausse **3** loonsverhoging **4** het rijzen, het omhooggaan **5** het opgaan, opgang; opkomst [of celestial body]: *the* ~ *of **fascism*** de opkomst van het fascisme **6** oorsprong, begin^h: *give* ~ *to* aanleiding geven tot **7** opkomst, groei ‖ *get a* ~ *out of* s.o. iem. op de kast jagen
²rise (vb) **1** opstaan [also from bed]: ~ *to one's feet* **2** (op)stijgen [also fig]; (op)klimmen: [fig] ~ *to the occasion* zich tegen de moeilijkheden opgewassen tonen **3** opkomen, opgaan; rijzen [of celestial body] **4** promotie maken, bevorderd worden: ~ *in the world* vooruitkomen in de wereld **5** opdoemen, verschijnen **6** toenemen [also fig]; stijgen [of prices] **7** in opstand komen, rebelleren: ~ *in arms* de wapens opnemen **8** ontstaan, ontspringen
riser 1 stootbord^h **2** iem. die opstaat: *a late* ~ een langslaper; *an early* ~ een vroege vogel, iem. die vroeg opstaat
risible 1 lacherig, lachziek **2** lachwekkend
¹rising (n) opstand, revolte
²rising (adj) **1** opkomend, aankomend: *a* ~ *politician* een opkomend politicus **2** stijgend, oplopend: ~ *damp* opstijgend grondwater **3** opstaand, rijzend: *the land of the* ~ *sun* het land van de rijzende zon
¹risk (n) **1** verzekerd bedrag^h **2** risico^h, kans, gevaar^h: *at* ~ in gevaar; *I don't want to run the* ~ *of losing my job* ik wil mijn baan niet op het spel zetten
²risk (vb) **1** wagen, op het spel zetten **2** riskeren, gevaar lopen
risky 1 gewaagd, gevaarlijk **2** gedurfd, gewaagd
rite rite [also fig]; ritus, (kerkelijke) ceremonie
ritual ritueel^h [also fig]; ritus, riten, kerkelijke plechtigheid

¹**rival** (n) rivaal
²**rival** (adj) rivaliserend, mededingend
³**rival** (vb) **1** naar de kroon steken, wedijveren met **2** evenaren
rivalry rivaliteit
river rivier [also fig]; stroom: *~s of blood* stromen bloed; *the ~ Thames* de (rivier de) Theems || *sell s.o. down the ~* iem. bedriegen
river bank rivieroever
riverfront rivieroever, waterkant
¹**riverside** (n) rivieroever, waterkant
²**riverside** (adj) aan de oever(s) (van de rivier)
riverwalk wandelpadʰ langs een kade
¹**rivet** (n) klinknagel
²**rivet** (vb) **1** vastnagelen [also fig]: *he stood ~ed to the ground* hij stond als aan de grond genageld **2** vastleggen, fixeren **3** boeien [also fig]; richten; concentreren [attention, eyes]
riveting geweldig, meeslepend, opwindend: *a ~ story* een pakkend verhaal
rivulet riviertjeʰ, beek(jeʰ)
roach voorn, witvis
road 1 weg, straat, baan: *on the ~ to recovery* aan de beterende hand, herstellende; *rule(s) of the ~* verkeersregels, scheepvaartreglement; *the main ~* de hoofdweg; *subsidiary ~s* secundaire wegen; *hit the ~* **a)** gaan reizen; **b)** weer vertrekken; *one for the ~* een afzakkertje, eentje voor onderweg **2** (-s) [shipp] rede
road accident verkeersongevalʰ
roadblock 1 wegversperring **2** [fig] belemmering, hindernis
road hog wegpiraat, snelheidsmaniak
roadhouse pleisterplaats, wegrestaurantʰ
roadkill doodgereden dieren, aangereden wildʰ
road rage agressie in het verkeer; [Belg] verkeersagressie
road safety verkeersveiligheid
roadshow 1 drive-inshow [of radio broadcasting company] **2** (hit)teamʰ [providing the drive-in show] **3** (band/theatergroep op) tournee **4** promotietour
roadside kant van de weg: *~ restaurant* wegrestaurantʰ
roadsign verkeersbordʰ, verkeerstekenʰ
road tax wegenbelasting
road test 1 testrit **2** [Am] rijexamenʰ
road user weggebruik(st)er
roadway rijweg
roadworks wegwerkzaamheden, werkʰ in uitvoering
roam ronddolen, zwerven: *~ about* (or: *around*) ronddwalen
roaming [telecom] roaming
¹**roar** (n) **1** gebrulʰ, gebulderʰ; geronkʰ [of machine]; het rollen [of thunder] **2** schaterlach, gegierʰ

²**roar** (vb) **1** brullen, bulderen, schreeuwen; rollen [of thunder]; ronken [of machine]; weergalmen **2** schateren, gieren: *~ with laughter* brullen van het lachen
¹**roaring** (adj) **1** luidruchtig, stormachtig **2** voorspoedig, gezond: *a ~ success* een denderend succes; *do a ~ trade* gouden zaken doen
²**roaring** (adv) zeer, erg: *~ drunk* straalbezopen
¹**roast** (n) **1** braadstukʰ **2** kritiek, uitbrander **3** [media] roast
²**roast** (adj) geroosterd, gegrild, gebraden: *~ beef* rosbief, roastbeef; *~ potatoes* (in de oven) gebakken aardappels
³**roast** (vb) de mantel uitvegen, een uitbrander geven
⁴**roast** (vb) **1** roosteren, grillen; poffen [potatoes] **2** branden [coffee]
roasting uitbrander: *give s.o. a good* (or: *real*) *~* iem. een flinke uitbrander geven
rob (be)roven [also fig]; (be)stelen [inform] *~ s.o. blind* iem. een poot uitdraaien
robber rover, dief
robbery diefstal, roof, beroving
robe 1 robe, gewaadʰ **2** ambtsgewaadʰ, toga **3** kamerjas, badjas **4** [Am] plaid, reisdeken
robin roodborstjeʰ
robot robot [also fig]
robust 1 krachtig, robuust, fors, gezond **2** onstuimig, ruw
¹**rock** (n) **1** rots, klip, rotsblokʰ, vast gesteenteʰ, mineraal gesteenteʰ: *as firm as a ~* **a)** muurvast; **b)** betrouwbaar; **c)** kerngezond **2** steun, toeverlaat **3** rock(muziek), rock-'n-roll **4** zuurstok, kaneelstok || *be on the ~s* **a)** op de klippen gelopen zijn, gestrand zijn; **b)** naar de knoppen zijn; **c)** (financieel) aan de grond (zitten)
²**rock** (vb) **1** schommelen, wieg(el)en, deinen **2** (hevig) slingeren, schudden **3** rocken, op rock-'n-roll muziek dansen
³**rock** (vb) **1** (doen) heen en weer schommelen/wiegen **2** heen en weer slingeren, doen wankelen **3** schokken, doen opschrikken
rock-bottom (absoluut) dieptepuntʰ: *fall to ~* een dieptepunt bereiken
rocker schommelstoel || *off one's ~* knettergek)
¹**rocket** (n) **1** raket, vuurpijl **2** raket [self-propelling missile] **3** [inform] uitbrander: *give s.o. a ~* iem. een uitbrander geven
²**rocket** (vb) omhoog schieten, flitsen: *prices ~ up* de prijzen vliegen omhoog
rocket launch raketlancering
rocket science [inform] hogere wiskunde: *that's not ~* dat is echt niet zo moeilijk
rocking chair schommelstoel
rocky 1 rotsachtig **2** steenhard, keihard **3** wankel, onvast

rod 1 stok; scepter [also fig]; heerschappij
2 roe(de), gesel **3** stang **4** stok, hengel,
maatstok **5** [Am; inform] blaffer || *rule with a
~ of iron* met ijzeren vuist regeren
rodent knaagdier[h]
rodeo rodeo
roe 1 ree[+h] **2** kuit: *hard ~* kuit; *soft ~* hom
roebuck reebok, mannetjesree
ROFL [inform] *rolling on floor laughing* lig
dubbel van het lachen
rogue 1 schurk, bandiet **2** [hum] snuiter,
deugniet **3** solitair: *a ~ elephant* een solitaire
olifant
roguery schurkenstreek, gemene streek
rogue state schurkenstaat
roguish 1 schurkachtig, gemeen **2** kwajongensachtig
roisterer lawaaimaker, druktemaker
role 1 rol, toneelrol **2** rol, functie, taak
role play rollenspel[h]
¹roll (n) **1** rol, rolletje[h]: *a ~ of paper* een rol
papier **2** (perkament)rol **3** rol, register[h],
(naam)lijst: *the ~ of honour* de lijst der gesneuvelden **4** broodje[h] **5** buiteling, duikeling **6** schommelgang, waggelgang **7** wals,
rol **8** rollende beweging; geslinger[h] [of ship];
deining [of water]; [fig] golving [of land-
scape] **9** geroffel[h], roffel [eg on drum]; gerommel[h]; gedreun[h] [of thunder, guns]
²roll (vb) **1** rollen, rijden, lopen; draaien [of
press, camera etc]: [fig] *the years ~ed by* de
jaren gingen voorbij; *~ on the day this work is
finished!* leve de dag waarop dit werk af is!
2 zich rollend bewegen, buitelen; slingeren
[of ship]; [fig] rondtrekken; zwerven: [in-
form] *be ~ing in it* (or: *money*) bulken van het
geld, zwemmen in het geld **3** dreunen; roffelen [of drum]
³roll (vb) **1** rollen, laten rollen: *~ on one's
stockings* zijn kousen aantrekken **2** een rollende beweging doen maken; rollen [with
eyes]; doen slingeren [ship]; gooien [dice];
laten lopen [camera] **3** een rollend geluid
doen maken; roffelen [drum]; rollen [r
sound]: *~ one's r's* de r rollend uitspreken
4 oprollen, draaien: [inform] *~ one's own*
shag roken **5** rollen, walsen, pletten **6** [Am;
inform] rollen, beroven
rollator rollator
roll back 1 terugrollen, terugdrijven, terugdringen: *~ the hood of a car* de kap van
een wagen achteruitschuiven **2** weer oproepen, weer voor de geest brengen **3** [Am] terugschroeven [prices]
roll-call appel[h], naamafroeping
¹roller 1 rol(letje[h]), wals, cilinder, krulspeld
2 roller; breker [heavy wave]
rollerblade skeeleren
roller coaster roetsjbaan, achtbaan: *an
emotional ~* een emotionele achtbaan, een
rollercoaster

¹roller skate (n) rolschaats
²roller skate (vb) rolschaatsen
rollicking uitgelaten, vrolijk, onstuimig
rolling rollend, golvend
rolling pin deegrol(ler)
roll-neck rolkraag
roll-on 1 licht korset[h] **2** (deodorant)roller
roll-on roll-off rij-op-rij-af-, roll-on-roll-
off-, roro-: *a ~ ferry* een rij-op-rij-afveerboot
[carrying loaded lorries]
¹roll over (vb) zich omdraaien
²roll over (vb) **1** over de grond doen rollen
2 verlengen [loan, debt]
¹roll up (vb) **1** zich oprollen **2** (komen) aan-
rijden; [fig] opdagen || *~! ~! The best show in
London!* Komt binnen, komt dat zien! De
beste show in Londen!
²roll up (vb) oprollen, opstropen: *roll one's
sleeves up* zijn mouwen opstropen; [fig] de
handen uit de mouwen steken
roll-up [inform] sjekkie[h]
¹roly-poly (n) kort en dik persoon, propje[h]
²roly-poly (adj) kort en dik
ROM *read-only memory* ROM[h]
roman romein(s), niet cursief
¹Roman (n) **1** Romein(se) **2** rooms-katholiek
|| *when in Rome do as the ~s do* 's lands wijs, 's
lands eer
²Roman (adj) **1** Romeins: *~ numerals* Romeinse cijfers **2** rooms-katholiek: *~ Catholic*
rooms-katholiek
¹romance (n) **1** middeleeuws ridderver-
haal[h], romantisch verhaal[h], avonturenro-
man, (romantisch) liefdesverhaal[h], geromantiseerd verhaal[h]; [fig] romantische overdrijving **2** romance, liefdesavontuur[h] **3** romantiek
²romance (vb) avonturen vertellen; [fig]
fantaseren: *~ about one's love-affairs* sterke
verhalen vertellen over zijn liefdesavonturen
Romance Romaans
Romania Roemenië
¹Romanian (n) Roemeen(se)
²Romanian (adj) Roemeens
romantic romantisch
romanticism romantiek [as trend in art]
romanticize romantiseren: *a heavily ~d
version of the early years of Hollywood* een
sterk geromantiseerde versie van de beginjaren van Hollywood
Romany zigeuner-, van de zigeuners
¹romp (n) stoeipartij
²romp (vb) **1** stoeien **2** flitsen, (voorbij)-
schieten || *~ through an exam* met gemak
voor een examen slagen
romper kruippakje[h], speelpakje[h]: *a pair of
~s* een kruippakje
roof dak[h]; [fig] dak[h]; hoogste punt[h]: *~ of the
mouth* gehemelte[h], verhemelte[h]; *go through*
(or: *hit*) *the ~* **a)** ontploffen, woedend worden; **b)** de pan uit rijzen, omhoogschieten

[of prices]

roof box dakkoffer[h]

roofing dakwerk[h], dakbedekking

roofless dakloos, zonder onderdak

roof-rack imperiaal[+h]

rooftop 1 top van het dak **2** dak[h] [flat]: *shout sth. from the ~s* iets van de daken schreeuwen

¹**rook** (n) **1** valsspeler, bedrieger **2** roek **3** [chess] toren

²**rook** (vb) **1** bedriegen, afzetten **2** bedriegen door vals spel

rookie [mil] rekruut, nieuweling, groentje[h]; [Am] nieuwe speler [at baseball etc]

rookie error beginnersfout: *make a ~* een beginnersfout maken, blunderen

¹**room** (n) **1** kamer, vertrek[h], zaal: *~s* appartement[h]; flat **2** ruimte, plaats: *make ~* plaatsmaken **3** ruimte, gelegenheid, kans: *there is still ample ~ for improvement* er kan nog een heel wat aan verbeterd worden

²**room** (vb) [Am] een kamer bewonen, inwonen, op kamers wonen: *she ~ed with us for six months* ze heeft een half jaar bij ons (in)gewoond

roomer [Am] kamerbewoner, huurder

room-mate kamergenoot

room service bediening op de kamer [in hotel]; roomservice

roomy ruim, groot, wijd

roost 1 roest[+h], stok, kippenhok[h] **2** nest[h], bed[h]; slaapplaats [of birds] ‖ *it will come home to ~* je zult er zelf de wrange vruchten van plukken, het zal zich wreken; *rule the ~* de baas zijn, de lakens uitdelen

rooster [Am] haan

¹**root** (n) **1** oorsprong, wortel, basis: *money is the ~ of all evil* geld is de wortel van alle kwaad **2** kern, het wezenlijke: *get to the ~ of the problem* tot de kern van het probleem doordringen ‖ *strike ~, take ~* a) wortel schieten; b) [fig] ingeburgerd raken [of ideas]; *~ and branch* met wortel en tak, grondig; *strike at the ~s of* een vernietigende aanval doen op

²**root** (vb) **1** wortelschieten, wortelen; [fig] zich vestigen; zijn oorsprong hebben **2** wroeten, graven, woelen: *the pigs were ~ing about in the earth* de varkens wroetten rond in de aarde ‖ *~ for the team* het team toejuichen

³**root** (vb) vestigen, doen wortelen: *a deeply ~ed love* een diepgewortelde liefde ‖ *she stood ~ed to the ground* (or: *spot*) ze stond als aan de grond genageld

rootless ontworteld, ontheemd

root out 1 uitwroeten, uitgraven; [fig] tevoorschijn brengen **2** vernietigen, uitroeien

root sign wortelteken[h]

¹**rope** (n) **1** (stuk[h]) touw[h], koord[h], kabel: [boxing] *on the ~s* in de touwen; *know* (or:

learn) *the ~s* de kneepjes van het vak kennen (or: leren); *teach* (or: *show*) *s.o. the ~s* iem. wegwijs maken **2** snoer[h], streng

²**rope** (vb) **1** vastbinden **2** met touwen afzetten **3** [Am] vangen [with a lasso] ‖ *~ s.o. in to help* iem. zover krijgen dat hij komt helpen

rope-ladder touwladder

ropy armzalig, miezerig, beroerd

rosary 1 rozentuin **2** rozenkrans

rose 1 roos, rozenstruik **2** roos, rozet **3** sproeidop, sproeier **4** rozerood[h], dieproze[h] ‖ *it is not all ~s* het is niet allemaal rozengeur en maneschijn; *under the ~* onder geheimhouding

rose-bed rozenperk[h]

rose-coloured rooskleurig [also fig]; optimistisch: *~ spectacles* [fig] een optimistische kijk, een roze bril

rose-hip rozenbottel

rosemary rozemarijn

rose-tinted *see rose-coloured*

rosette rozet

rosewater rozenwater[h]

rose-window roosvenster[h]

rosin hars[h]; [mus] snarenhars[h]

¹**roster** (n) rooster[h], werkschema[h], dienstrooster[h]

²**roster** (vb) inroosteren: *~ed day off* roostervrije dag

rostrum podium[h], spreekgestoelte[h]

rosy 1 rooskleurig, rozig, blozend, gezond **2** rooskleurig, optimistisch

¹**rot** (n) **1** verrotting, bederf[h], ontbinding; [fig] verval[h]; de klad: *then the ~ set in* toen ging alles mis, toen kwam er de klad in **2** vuur[h] [in wood] **3** onzin, flauwekul: *talk ~* onzin uitkramen

²**rot** (vb) **1** rotten, ontbinden, bederven **2** vervallen, ten onder gaan **3** wegkwijnen, wegteren

³**rot** (vb) **1** laten rotten, doen wegrotten **2** aantasten, bederven

rota rooster[h], aflossingsschema[h]

rotary roterend: *~ press* rotatiepers

¹**rotate** (vb) **1** roteren, om een as draaien **2** elkaar aflossen **3** rouleren

²**rotate** (vb) **1** ronddraaien, laten rondwentelen **2** afwisselen

rotation 1 omwenteling, rotatie **2** het omwentelen, rotatie **3** het afwisselen, het aflossen: *the ~ of crops* de wisselbouw; *by* (or: *in*) *~* bij toerbeurt

rotatory 1 rotatie-, omwentelings-, ronddraaiend **2** afwisselend, beurtelings

rote het mechanisch leren (herhalen), het opdreunen, stampwerk[h]: *learn sth. by ~* iets uit het hoofd leren

rotten 1 rot, verrot, bedorven **2** vergaan, verteerd **3** verdorven, gedegenereerd **4** waardeloos, slecht **5** ellendig, beroerd: *she felt ~* ze voelde zich ellendig

rotund 1 rond, cirkelvormig **2** diep, vol **3** breedsprakig, pompeus **4** dik, rond, mollig

rouble roebel

¹rough (n) **1** gewelddadige kerel, agressieveling **2** ruw terrein[h] **3** tegenslag, onaangename kanten: [fig] *take* the ~ *with the smooth* tegenslagen voor lief nemen **4** ruwe staat: *write sth. in* ~ iets in het klad schrijven

²rough (adj) **1** ruw, ruig, oneffen **2** wild, woest: ~ *behaviour* wild gedrag; [fig] *give s.o. a* ~ *passage* (or: *ride*) het iem. moeilijk maken **3** ruw, scherp, naar: ~ *luck* pech, tegenslag; *a* ~ *time* een zware tijd; *it is* ~ *on him* het is heel naar voor hem **4** ruw, schetsmatig, niet uitgewerkt: *a* ~ *diamond* een ruwe diamant; [fig] een ruwe bolster; ~ *copy* eerste schets; ~ *justice* min of meer rechtvaardige behandeling || *live* ~ zwerven, in de openlucht leven

³rough (vb): ~ *it* zich behelpen, op een primitieve manier leven

rough-and-tumble 1 knokpartij **2** ruwe ordeloosheid

¹roughen (vb) ruw worden

²roughen (vb) ruw maken

rough-hewn 1 ruw (uit)gehakt, ruw (uit)gesneden **2** onbehouwen, lomp

rough-house 1 een rel schoppen, geweld plegen **2** ruw aanpakken

roughly ruwweg, ongeveer, zo'n beetje: ~ *speaking* ongeveer

roughneck [Am; inform] gewelddadig iem., ruwe klant

rough out een ruwe schets maken van, (in grote lijnen) schetsen

roughshod onmenselijk, wreed || *ride* ~ *over s.o.* over iem. heen lopen

rough up 1 ruw maken [hair etc] **2** aftuigen, afrossen

roulette roulette

¹round (n) **1** bol, ronding **2** ronde, rondgang, toer: *go the* ~*s* de ronde doen, doorverteld worden **3** schot[h], geweerschot[h] **4** kring, groep mensen **5** [mus] driestemmige (vierstemmige) canon[h] **6** rondheid **7** volledigheid **8** rondte: *in the* ~ **a)** losstaand, vrijstaand [of statue]; **b)** alles welbeschouwd || *a* ~ *of applause* een applaus

²round (adj) **1** rond, bol, bolvormig: ~ *cheeks* bolle wangen **2** rond, gebogen, cirkelvormig: ~ *trip* rondreis; [Am] retour[h] **3** rond, compleet; afgerond [of number]: *in* ~ *figures* in afgeronde getallen || ~ *robin* petitie

³round (vb) **1** ronden, rond maken; [also fig] afronden: ~ *down* naar beneden afronden; ~ *off sharp edges* scherpe randen rond afwerken; ~ *off* besluiten, afsluiten [evening etc] **2** ronden, om(heen) gaan: ~ *a corner* een hoek omgaan || ~ *out* afronden [story, study]; ~ *(up)on s.o.* tegen iem. van leer trekken, zich woedend tot iem. keren

⁴round (adv) **1** [direction; also fig] rond, om: *next time* ~ de volgende keer; *he talked her* ~ hij praatte haar om **2** [place; also fig] rond-om, in het rond: *all* ~ **a)** rondom; **b)** voor alles en iedereen; **c)** in alle opzichten **3** bij, bij zich: *they asked us* ~ *for tea* ze nodigden ons bij hen uit voor de thee; *they brought her* ~ ze brachten haar weer bij (bewustzijn) **4** [time] doorheen: *all (the) year* ~ het hele jaar door

⁵round (prep) **1** om, rondom, om … heen: ~ *the corner* om de hoek **2** omstreeks: ~ *8 o'clock* omstreeks acht uur

¹roundabout (n) **1** draaimolen **2** rotonde, verkeersplein[h]

²roundabout (adj) indirect, omslachtig: *we heard of it in a* ~ *way* we hebben het via via gehoord

roundly 1 ronduit, onomwonden **2** volkomen, volslagen

round-the-clock de klok rond, dag en nacht

round-trip [Am] retour-: ~ *ticket* retourtje[h], retourbiljet[h]

round up 1 bijeenjagen, bijeendrijven **2** grijpen; aanhouden [criminals]; oprollen [gang] **3** naar boven toe afronden

¹rouse (vb) **1** ontwaken, wakker worden **2** in actie komen

²rouse (vb) **1** wakker maken, wekken; [fig] opwekken: ~ *o.s. to action* zichzelf tot actie aanzetten **2** prikkelen **3** oproepen, tevoorschijn roepen: *his conduct* ~*d suspicion* zijn gedrag wekte argwaan

rousing 1 opwindend, bezielend **2** levendig, krachtig: *a* ~ *cheer* luid gejuich

¹rout (n) totale nederlaag, aftocht, vlucht: *put to* ~ een verpletterende nederlaag toebrengen

²rout (vb) **1** verslaan, verpletteren **2** (+ out) eruit jagen, wegjagen: ~ *out of bed* jagen **3** (+ out) opduike(le)n, opsnorren

route route, weg: *en* ~ onderweg **2** [Am] ronde, dagelijkse route

route planner routeplanner

router 1 [comp] router **2** iem. die routes uitstippelt; sorteerder

routine 1 routine, gebruikelijke procedure **2** sleur

¹rove (vb) zwerven, dolen, dwalen: *he has a roving eye* hij kijkt steeds naar andere vrouwen

²rove (vb) doorzwerven, dolen, dwalen

rover zwerver

¹row (n) **1** rel, ruzie **2** herrie, kabaal[h]: *kick up* (or: *make*) *a* ~ luidkeels protesteren

²row (n) **1** rij, reeks: *three days in a* ~ drie dagen achtereen **2** huizenrij, straat met (aan weerszijden) huizen; Straat [in street name] **3** roeitochtje[h]

³**row** (vb) roeien, in een roeiboot varen, per roeiboot vervoeren

⁴**row** (vb) **1** ruzie maken **2** vechten, een rel schoppen

rowanberry lijsterbes

¹**rowdy** (n) lawaaischopper

²**rowdy** (adj) ruw, wild, ordeloos

rower roeier

row house [Am] rijtjeshuis^h

rowing-boat roeiboot

rowing-machine roeitrainer

¹**royal** (n) lid^h van de koninklijke familie

²**royal** (adj) **1** koninklijk, van de koning(in): *Royal Highness* Koninklijke Hoogheid **2** koninklijk, vorstelijk || *treat s.o. ~ly* iem. als een vorst behandelen

royalist royalist, monarchist

royalty 1 iem. van koninklijken bloede, koning(in), prins(es) **2** royalty, aandeel^h in de opbrengst **3** koningschap^h **4** leden van het koninklijk huis

RPM *revolutions per minute* omwentelingen per minuut, -toeren

R rating [Am] [roughly] niet geschikt voor jeugdige kijkers

RSI *Repetitive Strain Injury* RSI; muisarm

RSS *really simple syndication* RSS

RT *retweet* retweet

¹**rub** (n) **1** poetsbeurt, wrijfbeurt **2** hindernis, moeilijkheid: *there's the ~* daar zit de moeilijkheid, dat is het hem juist

²**rub** (vb) **1** schuren langs, wrijven **2** slijten, dun/ruw/kaal worden || *~ up against s.o.* tegen iem. aanlopen

³**rub** (vb) **1** wrijven, afwrijven, inwrijven, doorheen wrijven, poetsen, boenen: *~ one's hands* zich in de handen wrijven **2** schuren **3** beschadigen, afslijten: *~ away* wegslijten, afslijten

rub along 1 zich staande houden, het net klaarspelen **2** het goed samen kunnen vinden

rubber 1 rubber^h, synthetisch rubber^h, rubberachtig materiaal^h **2** wrijver, wisser, gum^+h **3** [Am] overschoen **4** [sport, game] robber, reeks van drie partijen **5** condoom^h

rubber band elastiekje^h

rubber bullet rubberkogel

rubber duck badeend: *~ race* badeendenrace

rubberneck [Am] nieuwsgierige, zich vergapende toerist

rubber stamp 1 stempel^+h **2** marionet [fig]

rubber-stamp automatisch goedkeuren, gedachteloos instemmen met

rubbery rubberachtig, taai

¹**rubbish** (n) **1** vuilnis^h, afval^h **2** nonsens, onzin: *talk ~* zwetsen, kletsen

²**rubbish** (vb) afbrekende kritiek leveren op, afkraken

rubbish bin vuilnisbak

rubbishy waardeloos, onzinnig

rubble puin^h, steengruis^h, steenbrokken

rubella rodehond

rub in inwrijven, (in)masseren || *there's no need to rub it in* je hoeft er niet steeds te te-rug te komen

¹**rub off** (vb) **1** weggewreven worden **2** overgaan op, overgenomen worden: *his stinginess has rubbed off on you* je hebt zijn krenterigheid overgenomen **3** afslijten, minder worden: *the novelty has rubbed off a bit* de nieuwigheid is er een beetje af

²**rub off** (vb) **1** wegvegen, afwrijven **2** afslijten, afschuren

rubric 1 rubriek; titel [of (chapter in) code] **2** rubriek, categorie

rub up 1 oppoetsen, opwrijven **2** ophalen, bijvijlen: *~ one's Italian* zijn Italiaans ophalen || *rub s.o. up the wrong way* iem. tegen de haren instrijken, iem. irriteren

ruby 1 robijn^+h **2** robijnrood^h

ruck 1 de massa **2** de gewone dingen, dagelijkse dingen **2** vouw, kreukel, plooi

rucksack rugzak

ruck up in elkaar kreuke(le)n

ruckus tumult^h, ordeverstoring

ruction kabaal^h, luid protest^h

rudder roer^h

rudderless stuurloos [also fig]

ruddy 1 blozend, gezond **2** rossig, rood(achtig) **3** verdraaide

rude 1 primitief [people]; onbeschaafd **2** ruw, primitief, eenvoudig **3** ongemanierd, grof: *be ~ to s.o.* onbeleefd tegen iem. zijn || [fig] *a ~ awakening* een ruwe teleurstelling; *~ health* onverwoestbare gezondheid

rudiment 1 [biology] rudiment^h **2** (-s) beginselen, grondslagen

rudimentary 1 rudimentair, elementair, wat de grondslagen betreft **2** in een beginstadium

rue spijt hebben van, berouw hebben van: *you'll ~ the day you said this* je zal de dag berouwen dat je dit gezegd hebt

rueful berouwvol, treurig, bedroefd

¹**ruff** (n) **1** plooikraag **2** kraag, verenkraag, kraag van haar

²**ruff** (vb) [cards] troeven

ruffian bruut, woesteling, bandiet

¹**ruffle** (n) ruche [along collar, cuff]; geplooide rand

²**ruffle** (vb) **1** verstoren, doen rimpelen, verwarren: *~ s.o.'s hair* iemands haar in de war maken **2** (+ up) opzetten [feathers] **3** ergeren, kwaad maken, opwinden

rug 1 tapijt^h, vloerkleed^h **2** deken, plaid

rugby rugby^h

rugged 1 ruw, ruig, grof **2** onregelmatig van trekken, doorploegd

rugger rugby^h

¹**ruin** (n) **1** ruïne, vervallen bouwwerk^h **2** on-

dergang, verval^h: *this will be* **the** *~ of him* dit zal hem nog kapot maken **3** (-s) ruïne, bouwval, overblijfsel^h: *in ~s vervallen*, tot een ruïne geworden

²**ruin** (vb) **1** verwoesten, vernietigen **2** ruïneren, bederven: *his story has ~ed my **appetite*** zijn verhaal heeft me mijn eetlust ontnomen **3** ruïneren, tot de ondergang brengen

ruinous 1 vervallen, ingestort, bouwvallig **2** rampzalig, ruïneus

¹**rule** (n) **1** regel, voorschrift^h: *~s of the **road*** verkeersregels, verkeerscode; *according to* (or: *by*) *~* volgens de regels, stipt **2** gewoonte, gebruik^h, regel: *as a ~* gewoonlijk, in het algemeen **3** duimstok, meetlat **4** regering, bewind^h, bestuur^h: *under British ~* onder Britse heerschappij || *~ of **thumb*** vuistregel, nattevingerwerk^h

²**rule** (vb) **1** heersen, regeren, de zeggenschap hebben **2** een bevel uitvaardigen, bepalen, verordenen

³**rule** (vb) **1** beheersen [also fig]; heersen over, regeren: *be ~d **by*** zich laten leiden door **2** beslissen, bepalen, bevelen: *~ sth. **out*** iets uitsluiten, iets voor onmogelijk verklaren **3** trekken [line] || *~d **paper*** gelinieerd papier

ruler 1 heerser, vorst **2** liniaal^{+h}

¹**ruling** (n) regel, bepaling: *give a ~* uitspraak doen

²**ruling** (adj) (over)heersend, dominant

¹**rum** (n) rum

²**rum** (adj) vreemd, eigenaardig

¹**rumble** (n) **1** gerommel^h, rommelend geluid^h **2** [Am] tip, informatie **3** [Am] knokpartij, straatgevecht^h

²**rumble** (vb) **1** rommelen, donderen: *my **stomach** is rumbling* mijn maag knort **2** voortdonderen, voortrollen, ratelen

³**rumble** (vb) **1** mompelen, mopperen, grommen **2** doorhebben, doorzien, in de gaten hebben

rumbling 1 gerommel^h **2** [esp pl] praatje^h, geklets^h

rumbustious onstuimig, onbesuisd, uitgelaten

¹**ruminant** (n) herkauwer

²**ruminant** (adj) herkauwend

ruminate 1 herkauwen **2** peinzen, nadenken, piekeren

¹**rummage** (n) **1** onderzoek^h, het doorzoeken: *I'll have a ~ in the **attic*** ik zal eens op zolder gaan zoeken **2** [Am] rommel, oude spullen, troep

²**rummage** (vb) (+ about, through, among) rondrommelen (in), snuffelen (in), (door)-zoeken

rummage sale rommelmarkt

¹**rumour** (n) gerucht^h, geruchten, praatjes, verhalen: *~ **has** it that you'll be fired* er gaan

geruchten dat je ontslagen zult worden

²**rumour** (vb) geruchten verspreiden, praatjes rondstrooien

rump 1 achterdeel^h; bout [of animal]; stuit [of bird] **2** achterste^h **3** rest(ant^h); armzalig overblijfsel^h [of parliament, administration]

rumple kreuken, door de war maken, verfrommelen

rump steak lendenbiefstuk

rumpus tumult^h, ruzie, geschreeuw^h: *cause* (or: *kick up, **make**) a ~* ruzie maken

¹**run** (n) **1** looppas, het rennen: *make a ~ for it* het op een lopen zetten; *on the ~* **a)** op de vlucht; **b)** druk in de weer **2** tocht, afstand, eindje^h hollen, vlucht, rit, traject^h; route; uitstapje^h [of train, boat]; [skiing] baan; helling; [cricket, hockey] run [a score of 1 point] **3** opeenvolging, reeks, serie; [theatre] looptijd; [mus] loopje^h: *a ~ of **success*** een succesvolle periode **4** (+ on) vraag (naar), stormloop (op): [com] *a ~ **on** copper* een plotselinge grote vraag naar koper **5** terrein^h, veld^h; ren [for animals] **6** eind^h, stuk^h; lengte [of material] **7** [Am] ladder [in stocking] || *we'll **give** them a (good) ~ for their money* we zullen ze het niet makkelijk maken; *give s.o. the ~ of* iem. de (vrije) beschikking geven over; *a ~ on the bank* een run op de bank

²**run** (vb) **1** rennen, hollen, hardlopen **2** gaan, (voort)bewegen, lopen, (hard) rijden, pendelen; heen en weer rijden (varen) [of bus, ferry etc]; voorbijgaan; aflopen [of time]; lopen; werken [of machines]; (uit)lopen, (weg)stromen, druipen; [fig] (voort)duren; zich uitstrekken, gelden: *~ **afoul** of* (or: *foul*) *of* [fig] stuiten op, in botsing komen met; [shipp] *~ **aground*** aan de grond lopen; *feelings ran **high*** de gemoederen raakten verhit **3** rennen, vliegen, zich haasten **4** lopen, zich uitstrekken; gaan [also fig]: *prices are ~ning **high*** de prijzen zijn over het algemeen hoog; *~ **to** extremes* in uitersten vervallen **5** wegrennen, vluchten **6** luiden, klinken: *the third **line** ~s as follows* de derde regel luidt als volgt **7** kandidaat zijn **8** [Am] ladderen [of stocking] || *~ **along!*** vooruit!, laat me eens met rust!; *~ **across** s.o. (sth.)* iem. tegen het lijf lopen, ergens tegen aan lopen; *~ **for** it* op de vlucht slaan, het op een lopen zetten; *~ **through** the minutes* de notulen doornemen

³**run** (vb) **1** rijden (lopen) over; volgen [road]; afleggen [distance]: *~ a **race*** een wedstrijd lopen; *~ s.o. **over*** iem. overrijden **2** doen bewegen, laten gaan, varen, rijden, doen stromen, gieten, in werking stellen, laten lopen; [fig] doen voortgaan; leiden, runnen: *~ a **business*** een zaak hebben; *~ s.o. **close*** (or: *hard*) iem. (dicht) op de hielen zitten; [fig] weinig voor iem. onderdoen **3** smokkelen **4** ontvluchten, weglopen van **5** kandidaat

stellen || ~ a *(traffic-)light* door rood rijden
r**u**nabout wagentje[h], (open) autootje[h]
r**u**n-around het iem. afschepen, het iem.
een rad voor ogen draaien: *give s.o. the ~*
een spelletje spelen met iem., iem. bedriegen
r**u**naway vluchteling, ontsnapte || ~ *inflation* galopperende inflatie
run aw**ay** weglopen, vluchten, op de loop
gaan || *don't ~ with the idea* geloof dat nu
maar niet te snel
r**u**ndown 1 vermindering, afname 2 opsomming, zeer gedetailleerd verslag[h]
run d**ow**n 1 reduceren, verminderen in capaciteit 2 aanrijden 3 opsporen, vinden, te
pakken krijgen: *run a **criminal** down* een misdadiger opsporen 4 kritiseren, naar beneden halen, afkraken: *how dare you run **her**
down?* hoe durf je haar te kleineren?
run-d**ow**n 1 vervallen; verwaarloosd [of
things] 2 uitgeput, verzwakt, doodmoe
r**u**ng sport, trede
[1]run **in** (vb) binnen (komen) lopen
[2]run **in** (vb) 1 oppakken, aanhouden, inrekenen 2 inrijden [car]
r**u**n-in 1 aanloop 2 ruzie, twist, woordenwisseling
r**u**n into 1 stoten op, in botsing komen
met, botsen tegen 2 terechtkomen in: ~ *difficulties* (or: *debts*) in de problemen (or:
schulden) raken 3 tegen het lijf lopen, onverwacht ontmoeten 4 bedragen, oplopen:
the costs ~ thousands of pounds de kosten lopen in de duizenden
r**u**nner 1 agent, vertegenwoordiger, loopjongen, bezorger 2 glijijzer[h] [of skate,
sleigh]; glijgoot, glijplank 3 loper, tafelloper, traploper, vloerloper 4 slingerplant
5 uitloper 6 deelnemer [eg runner, racehorse] || [inform] *do a ~* zich uit de voeten
maken, ervandoor gaan
r**u**nner-**up** tweede, wie op de tweede
plaats eindigt: *runners-up* de overige medaillewinnaars
[1]r**u**nning (n) het rennen; [sport] hardlopen[h]:
out of (or: *in) the ~* kansloos (or: met een
goede kans) (om te winnen) || *make the ~* het
tempo bepalen; [fig] de toon aangeven, de
leiding hebben
[2]r**u**nning (adj) 1 hardlopend, rennend, hollend 2 lopend: ~ *water* stromend water
3 (door)lopend, continu, opeenvolgend: ~
commentary direct verslag || [Am; pol] ~
mate kandidaat voor de tweede plaats; *in ~
order* goed werkend
r**u**nning event loopnummer[h]
r**u**nning gag steeds terugkerende grap
r**u**nny vloeibaar, dun, gesmolten: ~ *nose*
loopneus
[1]run **off** (vb) weglopen, wegvluchten: ~
with s.o. er vandoor gaan met iem.

[2]run **off** (vb) 1 laten weglopen, laten wegstromen, aftappen 2 reproduceren, afdraaien, fotokopiëren
r**u**n-of-the-mill doodgewoon, niet bijzonder, alledaags
run **on** doorgaan, doorlopen, voortgaan:
time ran on de tijd ging voorbij
[1]run **out** (vb) 1 opraken, aflopen: *our supplies* have ~ onze voorraden zijn uitgeput
2 niets meer hebben, te weinig hebben: *we
are running out of time* we komen tijd te kort
3 weglopen, wegstromen
[2]run **out** (vb) 1 uitrollen, afwikkelen; laten aflopen [rope]
[1]run **over** (vb) overlopen, overstromen || ~
with energy overlopen van energie
[2]run **over** (vb) 1 overrijden, aanrijden: *Marco ran over an old lady* Marco reed een oude
dame aan 2 doornemen, nakijken, repeteren
run thr**ou**gh 1 doorboren, doorsteken
2 repeteren, doorlopen
[1]run **up** (vb) (+ against) (toevallig) tegenkomen: ~ *against difficulties* op moeilijkheden
stuiten
[2]run **up** (vb) 1 (doen) oplopen, snel (doen)
toenemen, opjagen: *her **debts** ran up, she ran
up **debts*** ze maakte steeds meer schulden
r**u**n-up voorbereiding(stijd), vooravond: ~
to an election verkiezingsperiode
r**u**nway startbaan, landingsbaan
RUOK [inform] *are you OK?* alles goed?
rup**ee** [fin] roepie [Asian coin, esp of India
and Pakistan]
[1]r**u**pture (n) 1 breuk, scheiding, onenigheid
2 breuk, hernia, ingewandsbreuk
[2]r**u**pture (vb) 1 verbreken, verbroken worden 2 scheuren [of muscle etc] 3 een breuk
krijgen: ~ *o.s. lifting sth.* zich een breuk tillen
r**u**ral landelijk, plattelands, dorps
r**u**se list, truc
[1]r**u**sh (n) 1 heftige beweging, snelle beweging, stormloop, grote vraag, toevloed
2 haast, haastige activiteiten 3 (rushes)
[film] eerste afdruk [before editing] 4 rus,
bies 5 (rushes) biezen [for weaving baskets,
mats etc]
[2]r**u**sh (vb) 1 stormen, vliegen, zich haasten
2 ondoordacht handelen, overijld doen: ~
into marriage zich overhaast in een huwelijk
storten
[3]r**u**sh (vb) 1 meeslepen, haastig vervoeren,
meesleuren 2 opjagen, tot haast dwingen
3 haastig behandelen, afraffelen: ~ *out*
massaal produceren
r**u**sh delivery spoedbestelling
r**u**sh hour spitsuur[h]: *evening* ~ avondspits;
morning ~ ochtendspits
r**u**sh-hour spits-: ~ *traffic* spitsverkeer[h]
r**u**sk (harde) beschuit, scheepsbeschuit
[1]r**u**sset (n) 1 roodbruin[h] 2 winterappel

²**russet** (adj) roodbruin
Russia Rusland
¹**Russian** (n) Rus(sin)
²**Russian** (adj) Russisch
¹**rust** (n) **1** roest⁺ʰ, oxidatie **2** roestkleur, roestbruinʰ
²**rust** (vb) roesten, oxideren
¹**rustic** (n) plattelander, buitenman, boer
²**rustic** (adj) **1** boers, simpel, niet beschaafd **2** rustiek, uit grof materiaal gemaakt: ~ *bridge* rustieke brug [of rough wood] **3** landelijk, dorps, provinciaal
¹**rustle** (n) geruisʰ, geritselʰ
²**rustle** (vb) ruisen, ritselen, een ritselend geluid maken
³**rustle** (vb) **1** [Am] roven [cattle, horses] **2** weten te bemachtigen, bij elkaar weten te krijgen: ~ *up a meal* een maaltijd in elkaar draaien
rustler [Am] veedief
¹**rustproof** (adj) roestvrij
²**rustproof** (vb) roestvrij maken
rusty 1 roestig, verroest **2** verwaarloosd; [fig] verstoft; niet meer paraat: *my French is a bit* ~ mijn Frans is niet meer wat het geweest is
rut 1 voorʰ, groef, spoorʰ **2** vaste gang van zaken, sleur: *get into a* ~ vastroesten in de dagelijkse routine **3** bronst, paartijd
ruthless meedogenloos, wreed, hard
rutting bronstig, in de bronsttijd, paartijd
Rwanda Rwanda
¹**Rwandan** (n) Rwandees, Rwandese
²**Rwandan** (adj) Rwandees
rye 1 rogge **2** whisky, roggewhisky

S

s second sec., seconde

S South Z., Zuid(en)

sabbath sabbat, rustdag: *keep* (or: *break*) *the* ~ de sabbat houden (*or:* schenden)

¹sabbatical (n) sabbatsverlof[h]; verlof[h] [at university]

²sabbatical (adj): ~ *year* sabbatsjaar[h], verlofjaar[h]

¹sabotage (n) sabotage

²sabotage (vb) saboteren, sabotage plegen (op)

sabre sabel

sabre-rattling sabelgekletter[h], (het dreigen met) militair geweld[h]

saccharine 1 suikerachtig, sacharine-, mierzoet **2** [fig] suikerzoet, zoet(sappig)

sachet 1 reukzakje[h] **2** (plastic) ampul [for shampoo] ‖ ~ *of sugar* suikerzakje[h]

¹sack (n) **1** zak, baal, jutezak **2** zak, ontslag[h]: *get the* ~ ontslagen worden; *give s.o. the* ~ iem. de laan uitsturen **3** bed[h]: *hit the* ~ gaan pitten, onder de wol kruipen

²sack (vb) **1** plunderen **2** de laan uitsturen, ontslaan

sackcloth jute ‖ *in* ~ *and ashes* in zak en as, in rouw

sack race zakloopwedstrijd

sacrament sacrament[h]

sacramental tot het sacrament behorend, offer-: ~ *wine* miswijn

sacred 1 gewijd, heilig: ~ *cow* heilige koe **2** plechtig, heilig, oprecht: *a* ~ *promise* een plechtige belofte **3** veilig, onschendbaar

¹sacrifice (n) **1** offer[h], het offeren **2** opoffering, offer[h], het opgeven, prijsgeven[h]

²sacrifice (vb) offeren, een offer brengen

³sacrifice (vb) **1** offeren, aanbieden, opdragen **2** opofferen, opgeven, zich ontzeggen: *he sacrificed his life to save her children* hij gaf zijn leven om haar kinderen te redden

sacrilege heiligschennis

sacrilegious heiligschennend, onterend

sacristan koster

sacristy sacristie

sacrosanct heilig, onaantastbaar: *his spare time is* ~ *to him* zijn vrije tijd is hem heilig

sad 1 droevig, verdrietig, ongelukkig, zielig: *to be ~ly mistaken* er totaal naast zitten **2** schandelijk, bedroevend (slecht)

sadden bedroeven, verdrietig maken, somber stemmen

¹saddle (n) **1** zadel[h]: *be in the* ~ te paard zitten; [fig] de baas zijn, het voor het zeggen

hebben **2** lendenstuk[h], rugstuk[h]: ~ *of lamb* lamszadel[h]

²saddle (vb) **1** (+ up) zadelen, opzadelen: ~ *up one's horse* zijn paard zadelen **2** (+ with, (up)on) opzadelen (met), opschepen (met), afschuiven op: *he ~d all responsibility on her* hij schoof alle verantwoordelijkheid op haar af

saddlebag zadeltas(je[h])

saddle-sore doorgereden, met zadelpijn

saddo [inform] stumper, sukkel

sadism sadisme[h]

sadist sadist(e)

sadistic sadistisch

sadly helaas

safari safari, jachtexpeditie, filmexpeditie: *on* ~ op safari

¹safe (n) brandkast, (bewaar)kluis, safe(loket[h])

²safe (adj) **1** veilig, beschermd: ~ *from attack* beveiligd tegen aanvallen **2** veilig, zeker, gevrijwaard: *as* ~ *as houses* zo veilig als een huis; *be on the* ~ *side* het zekere voor het onzekere nemen; *better (to be)* ~ *than sorry* je kunt beter het zekere voor het onzekere nemen; *play it* ~ op veilig spelen, geen risico nemen **3** betrouwbaar, gegarandeerd: *the party has twenty* ~ *seats* de partij kan zeker rekenen op twintig zetels **4** behouden, ongedeerd: *she arrived* ~ *and sound* ze kwam heelhuids aan

safe conduct vrijgeleide[h], vrije doorgang

safe deposit (brand)kluis, bankkluis

¹safeguard (n) waarborg, bescherming, voorzorg(smaatregel)

²safeguard (vb) beveiligen, beschermen, waarborgen

safehouse safehouse[h]; onderduikadres[h] [in war]

safe-keeping (veilige) bewaring

safe room beveiligde ruimte, paniekkamer

safety veiligheid, zekerheid: ~ *first* veiligheid vóór alles; *let's not split up, there's* ~ *in numbers* laten we ons niet opsplitsen, in een groep is het veiliger

safety belt veiligheidsgordel, veiligheidsriem

safety catch veiligheidspal

safety curtain brandscherm[h]

safety glass veiligheidsglas[h]

safety island vluchtheuvel

safety net vangnet[h] [for acrobats]; [fig; econ] buffer

safety pin veiligheidsspeld

saffron saffraan, oranjegeel

¹sag (n) verzakking, doorzakking, doorbuiging

²sag (vb) **1** (also + down) verzakken, doorzakken, doorbuigen **2** dalen, afnemen, teruglopen: *her spirits ~ged* de moed zonk haar in de schoenen

saga 1 familiekroniek **2** (lang) verhaal[h]

sagacious scherpzinnig, verstandig
sagacity scherpzinnigheid, wijsheid, inzicht^h
¹sage (n) **1** wijze (man), wijsgeer **2** salie
²sage (adj) wijs(gerig), verstandig
Sagittarius [astrology] (de) Boogschutter
said (boven)genoemd, voornoemd
¹sail (n) **1** zeil^h, de zeilen: *set* ~ de zeilen hijsen, onder zeil gaan **2** zeiltocht(je^h), boottocht(je^h): *take s.o. for a* ~ met iem. gaan zeilen **3** molenwiek, zeil^h
²sail (vb) **1** varen, zeilen, per schip reizen: ~ *close to* (or: *near*) *the wind* scherp bij de wind zeilen; [fig] bijna zijn boekje te buiten gaan **2** afvaren, vertrekken, uitvaren: *we're* ~*ing for France tomorrow* we vertrekken morgen naar Frankrijk **3** glijden, zweven, zeilen: *she* ~*ed through her finals* ze haalde haar eindexamen op haar sloffen
³sail (vb) **1** bevaren **2** besturen [ship]
sailing 1 bootreis **2** afvaart, vertrek^h, vertrektijd **3** navigatie, het besturen van een schip **4** zeilsport
sailing ship zeilschip^h
sailor zeeman, matroos: *Andy is a good* (or: *bad*) ~ Andy heeft nooit (or: snel) last van zeeziekte
saint 1 heilige, sint: *All Saints' Day* Allerheiligen **2** engel; [fig] iem. met engelengeduld **Saint** sint, heilig
saintly heilig: *lead a* ~ *life* als een heilige leven
saint's day heiligendag, naamdag
sake belang^h, (best)wil: *for the* ~ *of the company* in het belang van het bedrijf; *we're only doing this for your* ~ we doen dit alleen maar ter wille van jou **2** doel^h, oogmerk^h: *I'm not driving around here for the* ~ *of driving* ik rijd hier niet rond voor de lol
salaam oosterse groet [low bow with right hand on forehead]
salacious 1 geil **2** obsceen, schunnig
salad 1 salade, slaatje^h **2** sla
salad cream slasaus
salamander salamander
salami slicing [fig] kaasschaafmethode
salaried per maand betaald, gesalarieerd
salary salaris^h
salary scale salarisschaal
sale 1 verkoop, afzet(markt): *for* ~ te koop **2** verkoping, veiling, bazaar **3** uitverkoop, opruiming
saleroom veilinglokaal^h
salesclerk winkelbediende
sales department verkoopafdeling
salesgirl winkelmeisje^h, verkoopster
saleslady verkoopster
salesman 1 verkoper, winkelbediende **2** vertegenwoordiger, agent, handelsreiziger ‖ *traveling* ~ handelsreiziger
salesmanship verkoopkunde, verkoop-

techniek
sales pitch verkooppraatje^h
sales representative vertegenwoordiger
sales tax omzetbelasting
saleswoman 1 verkoopster, winkelbediende **2** vertegenwoordigster, agente, handelsreizigster
salient opvallend, belangrijkste
saline zout(houdend), zoutachtig, zilt
saliva speeksel^h
salivate kwijlen [also fig]; speeksel produceren
¹sallow (n) wilg
²sallow (adj) vaal(geel)
sally 1 uitval: *the army made a successful sally* het leger deed een succesvolle uitval **2** uitbarsting, opwelling **3** kwinkslag, (geestige) inval
sally forth 1 een uitval doen **2** erop uit gaan, op stap gaan, naar buiten rennen
salmon 1 zalm **2** zalmkleur
salmon trout zalmforel
saloon 1 zaal, salon^{+h} **2** bar, café^h **3** sedan, gesloten vierdeursauto
¹salt (n) (keuken)zout^h ‖ ~ *cellar* zoutvaatje^h; *the* ~ *of the earth* het zout der aarde; *he's not worth his* ~ hij is het zout in de pap niet waard
²salt (adj) **1** zout, zilt **2** gepekeld, gezouten: ~ *fish* gezouten vis
³salt (vb) **1** zouten, pekelen, inmaken **2** pekelen [roads]; met zout bestrooien **3** [fig] kruiden ‖ *he's got quite some money* ~*ed away* (or: *down*) hij heeft aardig wat geld opgepot
saltpetre salpeter^{+h}
saltshaker zoutvaatje^h, zoutstrooier
saltwater zoutwater-
salty 1 zout(achtig) **2** gezouten, gekruid; pikant [of language]
salubrious heilzaam, gezond
salutary weldadig, heilzaam, gunstig, gezond
salutation 1 aanhef [in letter] **2** begroeting, groet, begroetingskus
¹salute (n) **1** saluut^h, militaire groet, saluutschot^h: *take the* ~ de parade afnemen **2** begroeting, groet
²salute (vb) **1** groeten, begroeten, verwelkomen **2** salueren, een saluutschot lossen (voor)
³salute (vb) eer bewijzen aan, huldigen: *there were several festivals to* ~ *the country's 50 years of independence* er waren verschillende festivals om de vijftigjarige onafhankelijkheid van het land eer te bewijzen
¹salvage (n) **1** berging, redding, het in veiligheid brengen **2** geborgen goed^h, het geborgene: *the divers were not entitled to a share in the salvage* de duikers hadden geen recht op een aandeel in de geborgen goederen **3** bruikbaar afval^h, recycling, hergebruik^h

²**salvage** (vb) **1** bergen, redden, in veiligheid brengen **2** terugwinnen, verzamelen voor hergebruik

salvation 1 redding: *that was my ~* dat was mijn redding **2** verlossing

Salvation Army (the) Leger des Heils

¹**salve** (n) zalf [also fig]; smeersel^h, balsem

²**salve** (vb) sussen, kalmeren, tevreden stellen: *~ one's conscience* zijn geweten sussen

salvia salie

salvo salvo^h, plotselinge uitbarsting: *a ~ of applause* een daverend applaus

¹**same** (dem pron) dezelfde, hetzelfde: *the ~ applies to you* hetzelfde geldt voor jou; *~ here* ik ook (niet), met mij precies zo, idem dito; *they are much the ~* ze lijken (vrij) sterk op elkaar; *it's all the ~ to me* het is mij om het even, het maakt me niet uit; *(the) ~ to you* insgelijks, van 't zelfde; *at the ~ time* tegelijkertijd; *much the ~ problem* vrijwel hetzelfde probleem

²**same** (adv) net zo, precies hetzelfde: *he found nothing, (the) ~ as my own dentist* hij vond niets, net als mijn eigen tandarts

sameness 1 gelijkheid, overeenkomst **2** eentonigheid, monotonie

same-sex homo-: *~ marriage* homohuwelijk^h

¹**Sami** (n) Lap, Same

²**Sami** (adj) Laplands, Samisch

¹**sample** (n) **1** (proef)monster^h, staal^h, voorbeeld^h: *take a ~ of blood* een bloedmonster nemen **2** steekproef

²**sample** (vb) **1** een steekproef nemen uit, monsters trekken uit **2** (be)proeven, testen, keuren

sample copy proefexemplaar^h, proefnummer^h

sanatorium sanatorium^h, herstellingsoord^h

sanctify 1 heiligen **2** rechtvaardigen, heiligen **3** heilig maken, verlossen van zonde(schuld)

sanctimonious schijnheilig

¹**sanction** (n) **1** toestemming, goedkeuring **2** sanctie, dwang(middel^h), strafmaatregel: *apply ~s against racist regimes* sancties instellen tegen racistische regimes

²**sanction** (vb) **1** sanctioneren, bekrachtigen, bevestigen **2** goedkeuren, toestaan, instemmen met

sanctity heiligheid, vroomheid

sanctuary 1 omtrek van (hoog)altaar, priesterkoor^h **2** vogelreservaat^h, wildreservaat^h **3** asiel^h, vrijplaats, wijkplaats, toevlucht(soord^h): *he got up and took ~ in his study* hij stond op en zocht zijn toevlucht in zijn studeerkamer

¹**sand** (n) **1** zand^h **2** (-s) zandvlakte, strand^h, woestijn

²**sand** (vb) **1** met zand bestrooien: *~ slippery*

roads gladde wegen met zand bestrooien **2** (+ down) (glad)schuren, polijsten

sandal sandaal

¹**sandbag** (n) zandzak

²**sandbag** (vb) **1** met zandzakken versterken **2** [Am; inform] dwingen: *he was ~ged into leaving* hij werd gedwongen te vertrekken

sandbank zandbank, ondiepte

sandblast zandstralen

sandbox zandbak

sandcastle zandkasteel^h

sander schuurmachine

sanding machine schuurmachine

sandman (the) zandmannetje^h, Klaas Vaak

¹**sandpaper** (n) schuurpapier^h

²**sandpaper** (vb) schuren

sandpit 1 zandgraverij, zandgroeve **2** zandbak

sandstone zandsteen^{+h}

¹**sandwich** (n) sandwich, dubbele boterham

²**sandwich** (vb) klemmen, vastzetten, plaatsen: *I'll ~ her in between two other appointments* ik ontvang haar wel tussen twee andere afspraken door

sandwich board advertentiebord^h; reclamebord^h [carried on chest and back]

sandwich course cursus waarin theorie en praktijk afwisselend aan bod komen

sandwich man sandwichman

sandy 1 zand(er)ig, zandachtig **2** ros(sig) [of hair]; roodachtig

sane 1 (geestelijk) gezond, bij zijn volle verstand **2** verstandig [of ideas etc]; redelijk

sanguine 1 optimistisch, hoopvol, opgewekt **2** blozend, met een gezonde kleur

sanitarium sanatorium^h, herstellingsoord^h

sanitary 1 sanitair, m.b.t. de gezondheid **2** hygiënisch, schoon: *~ fittings* het sanitair || *~ stop* sanitaire stop

sanitary napkin [Am] maandverband^h

sanitary protection maandverband^h

sanitary towel maandverband^h

sanitation 1 bevordering van de volksgezondheid **2** afvalverwerking, rioolzuivering

sanity 1 (geestelijke) gezondheid **2** verstandigheid, gezond verstand^h

San Marino San Marino

Santa Claus kerstman(netje)

¹**sap** (n) **1** (planten)sap^h **2** levenskracht, energie, vitaliteit: *the ~ of youth* jeugdige levenskracht **3** slagwapen^h, knuppel **4** sul, sukkel, oen

²**sap** (vb) aftappen [also fig]; sap onttrekken aan; [fig] levenskracht onttrekken aan; uitputten: *the tension at the office was ~ping my energy* de spanning op kantoor vrat al mijn energie

sapless futloos

sapphire 1 saffier^{+h} **2** saffierblauw^h

sarcasm sarcasme^h, bijtende spot

sarcastic sarcastisch, bijtend
sarcophagus sarcofaag, stenen doodskist
sardine sardine: *(packed) like ~s* als haringen in een ton
sardonic boosaardig spottend, cynisch
sarky sarcastisch
sash 1 sjerp **2** raam^h, schuifraam^h
sashay nonchalant lopen, paraderen: *the models ~ed down the catwalk* de modellen paradeerden over het podium
¹**sass** (n) tegenspraak, brutaliteit: *I'm not accepting such ~ from anybody* ik accepteer zulke brutale opmerkingen van niemand
²**sass** (vb) brutaal zijn tegen, brutaliseren
¹**Sassenach** (n) Engelsman
²**Sassenach** (adj) Engels
satanic 1 van de duivel **2** satanisch, duivels, hels
satchel (school)tas [oft with shoulder strap]; pukkel
satellite 1 satelliet **2** voorstad, randgemeente: *New Malden is one of the many ~s of London* New Malden is een van de vele voorsteden van Londen **3** satellietstaat, vazalstaat
satellite dish schotelantenne
satellite town satellietstad
satiate (over)verzadigen, bevredigen, overvoeden, overladen: *be ~d with* a) verzadigd zijn van; b) zijn buik vol hebben van
¹**satin** (n) satijn^h
²**satin** (adj) satijnachtig, satijnen, satijnzacht: *~ finish* satijnglans
satire 1 satire, hekeldicht^h, hekelroman **2** satire, bespotting
satiric(al) satirisch
satirize 1 hekelen, bespotten **2** een satire schrijven op
satisfaction 1 genoegen^h, plezier^h, tevredenheid **2** voldoening, bevrediging, zekerheid: *prove sth. to s.o.'s ~* iets tot iemands volle tevredenheid bewijzen **3** genoegdoening, eerherstel^h, voldoening: *demand ~* genoegdoening eisen **4** (af)betaling, terugbetaling, voldoening
satisfactory 1 voldoende, (goed) genoeg **2** voldoening schenkend, bevredigend **3** geschikt
¹**satisfy** (vb) **1** voldoen, toereikend zijn, (goed) genoeg zijn **2** voldoen, genoegen schenken, tevreden stemmen
²**satisfy** (vb) **1** tevredenstellen, genoegen schenken, bevredigen: *be satisfied with* tevreden zijn over **2** vervullen, voldoen aan, beantwoorden aan: *~ the conditions* aan de voorwaarden voldoen **3** nakomen [an obligation]; vervullen **4** bevredigen, verzadigen: *~ one's curiosity* zijn nieuwsgierigheid bevredigen **5** overtuigen, verzekeren: *be satisfied that* ervan overtuigd zijn dat, de zekerheid (verkregen) hebben dat

satsuma mandarijntje^h
saturate 1 doordrenken [also fig]; doordringen, onderdompelen **2** (over)verzadigen, volledig vullen: *the computer market will soon be ~d* de afzetmarkt voor computers zal weldra verzadigd zijn **3** [science, chem] verzadigen: *~d fats* verzadigde vetten
Saturday zaterdag
Saturn Saturnus
satyr halfgod
¹**sauce** (n) **1** saus [also fig]; sausje^h **2** brutaliteit, tegenspraak, vrijpostigheid
²**sauce** (vb) brutaal zijn tegen, een brutale mond opzetten tegen: *don't you ~ me, young man* niet zo'n grote mond tegen mij opzetten, jongeman
sauce boat sauskom
saucepan steelpan
saucer 1 (thee)schoteltje^h **2** schotelantenne
saucy 1 brutaal; (lichtjes) uitdagend [also sexually]: *don't be ~ with me* wees niet zo brutaal tegen mij **2** vlot, knap, tof: *a ~ hat* een vlot hoedje
Saudi Arabia Saudi-Arabië
¹**Saudi Arabian** (n) Saudiër, Saudische
²**Saudi Arabian** (adj) Saudisch; Saudi-Arabisch
sauna sauna
¹**saunter** (n) **1** wandeling(etje^h) **2** slentergang
²**saunter** (vb) drentelen, slenteren: *we spent the afternoon ~ing up and down the pier* de hele middag slenterden we heen en weer op de pier
sausage worst, saucijs
sausage roll saucijzenbroodje^h
¹**savage** (n) **1** wilde, primitieve (mens) **2** woesteling, wildeman **3** barbaar
²**savage** (adj) **1** primitief, onbeschaafd **2** wreed(aardig), woest: *a ~ dog* een valse hond **3** heftig, fel: *~ criticism* meedogenloze kritiek **4** lomp, ongemanierd
savagery wreedheid, ruwheid, gewelddadigheid
savanna(h) savanne
¹**save** (n) redding: *the goalkeeper made a brilliant ~* de doelverdediger wist met een prachtige actie de bal uit het doel te houden
²**save** (vb) **1** sparen (voor), geld opzijleggen, zuinig zijn **2** [sport] een doelpunt (weten te) voorkomen **3** verlossing brengen, redden, verlossen
³**save** (vb) **1** redden, bevrijden, verlossen: *~ the situation* de situatie redden, een fiasco voorkomen **2** (be)sparen, bewaren, opslaan: *~ time* tijd (uit)sparen **3** overbodig maken, voorkomen, besparen: *I've been ~d a lot of trouble* er werd me heel wat moeite bespaard **4** [comp] opslaan, bewaren, saven **5** [sport] voorkomen [goal]; stoppen [penal-

ty, kick] || God ~ the **Queen** God behoede de koningin

⁴save (prep) behalve, met uitzondering van: *everyone ~ Gill* allemaal behalve Gill

saving 1 redding, verlossing **2** besparing: *a ~ of ten dollars* een besparing van tien dollar

savings spaargeld^h

savings account 1 spaarrekening **2** [Am] depositorekening

savings bank spaarbank, spaarkas

saviour 1 redder, bevrijder **2** (de) Verlosser; (de) Heiland [Jesus Christ]

¹savour (n) **1** bijsmaak [also fig]; zweem: *I detected a certain ~ of garlic* ik bespeurde een bijsmaak van knoflook **2** smaak [also fig]; aroma^h, geur: *the ~ of local life* de eigenheid van het plaatselijke leven

²savour (vb) met smaak proeven, genieten (van)

savour of geuren naar [also fig]; rieken naar, iets weg hebben van

¹savoury (n) hartig voorgerecht^h (nagerecht^h), hartig hapje^h

²savoury (adj) **1** smakelijk, lekker **2** hartig, pikant **3** eerbaar, respectabel, aanvaardbaar: *I'll spare you the less – details* ik zal je de minder fraaie bijzonderheden besparen

¹savvy (n) (gezond) verstand^h

²savvy (adj) snugger: *Internet-savvy* handig met internet

¹saw (n) zaag(machine): *circular ~* cirkelzaag

²saw (vb) zagen, gezaagd worden, zich laten zagen

³saw (vb) zagen, in stukken zagen: *~ down a tree* een boom omzagen

sawdust zaagsel^h

sawmill houtzagerij

sax *saxophone* sax

Saxon 1 Angelsaksisch, Oudengels **2** Saksisch

saxophone saxofoon

¹say (n) **1** invloed, zeggen^h, zeggenschap^h: *have a ~ in the matter* iets in de melk te brokkelen hebben, een vinger in de pap hebben **2** zegje^h, mening: *have (or: say) one's ~* zijn zegje doen

²say (vb) zeggen, praten, vertellen: *I couldn't ~* ik zou het niet kunnen zeggen; [inform] *just ~ing* ik zeg het maar even, ik bedoel maar; *so to ~* bij wijze van spreken; *I'd rather not ~* dat zeg ik liever niet, dat houd ik liever voor me; *a man, they ~, of bad reputation* een man, (zo) zegt men, met een slechte reputatie

³say (vb) **1** (op)zeggen, uiten, (uit)spreken: *~ grace (or: one's) prayers* dank zeggen, bidden; *I dare ~ that* het zou zelfs heel goed kunnen dat; *~ no more!* geen woord meer!, praat er mij niet van!, dat zegt al genoeg!; *to ~ nothing of* om nog maar te zwijgen over; *~ to o.s.* bij zichzelf denken; *that is to ~* met an-

dere woorden, dat wil zeggen, tenminste **2** zeggen, vermelden, verkondigen: *to ~ the least* op zijn zachtst uitgedrukt; *she is said to be* very rich men zegt dat ze heel rijk is; *it ~s on the bottle* op de fles staat **3** zeggen, aanvoeren, te kennen geven: *what do you ~ to this?* wat zou je hiervan vinden? **4** zeggen, aannemen, veronderstellen: *let's ~, shall we ~* laten we zeggen; *~ seven a.m.* pakweg zeven uur ('s ochtends) **5** aangeven, tonen, zeggen: *what time does your watch ~?* hoe laat is het op jouw horloge? || *when all is said and done* alles bij elkaar genomen, al met al; *no sooner said than done* zo gezegd, zo gedaan; *it goes without ~ing* het spreekt vanzelf; *you can ~ that again,* you said it zeg dat wel, daar zeg je zoiets, en of!; *~ when* zeg het als 't genoeg is, zeg maar ho

saying gezegde^h, spreekwoord^h, spreuk: *as the ~ goes* zoals het spreekwoord zegt

say-so 1 bewering, woord^h: *why should he believe you on your ~?* waarom zou hij je op je woord geloven? **2** toestemming, permissie

scab 1 onderkruiper, werkwillige, stakingsbreker **2** zwartwerker [non-union member] **3** korst(je^h): *a ~ had formed on her knee* er had zich een korstje gevormd op haar knie

scabbard 1 schede [for sword, knife] **2** holster

scabby schurftig

scabies schurft+^h

scads massa's, hopen^h: *~ of people* massa's mensen

scaffold 1 schavot^h **2** (bouw)steiger, stellage

scaffolding steiger(constructie), stelling(en), stellage

¹scald (n) brandwond, brandblaar, brandvlek

²scald (vb) zich branden [by hot water, steam]

³scald (vb) **1** branden, (doen) branden **2** (uit)wassen, (uit)koken, steriliseren **3** bijna tot kookpunt verhitten [milk]

scalding kokend(heet)

¹scale (n) **1** schub, schaal, (huid)schilfer: [fig] *the ~s fell from her eyes* de schellen vielen haar van de ogen **2** (weeg)schaal: *a pair of ~s* een weegschaal **3** aanslag, ketelsteen+^h **4** schaal(verdeling), schaalaanduiding, maatstok, meetlat: *the ~ of the problem* de omvang van het probleem; *at ~* op grote schaal; [fig] *on a large (or: small) ~* op grote (or: kleine) schaal; *draw to ~* op schaal tekenen **5** [mus] toonladder **6** [maths] schaal

²scale (vb) (af)schilferen, (af)bladderen

³scale (vb) (be)klimmen, (op)klauteren; opgaan [ladder] || *~ back (or: down)* verlagen, verkleinen, terugschroeven; *~ up* verhogen, vergroten, opschroeven

scale drawing schaaltekening

scale model schaalmodel[h]
scalene ongelijkzijdig [of triangle]
[1]scale-up (n) scale-up, jong, snel groeiend bedrijf[h]
[2]scale-up (n) opschaling, het opschalen
scallywag deugniet, rakker, schavuit
[1]scalp (n) hoofdhuid
[2]scalp (vb) scalperen
scalpel scalpel[h], ontleedmes[h], operatiemes[h]
scamp boef(je[h]), rakker, deugniet: *you ~!* (jij) boef!
scamper hollen, rennen, draven
[1]scan (n) **1** onderzoekende blik **2** scan, het aftasten, het onderzoeken
[2]scan (vb) zich laten scanderen [of poem]; metrisch juist zijn: *some of the lines of this song don't ~* sommige regels van dat liedje kloppen metrisch niet
[3]scan (vb) **1** scanderen, in versvoeten verdelen: *the audience were ~ning his **name:** 'Johnson, John-son'* het publiek scandeerde zijn naam: 'John-son, John-son' **2** nauwkeurig onderzoeken, afspeuren, afzoeken **3** snel/vluchtig doorlezen **4** aftasten; scannen [with radar]
scandal 1 schandaal[h], schande **2** achterklap, laster(praat)
scandalize choqueren, ergernis geven: *he didn't know whether to laugh or be ~d* hij wist niet of hij nou moest lachen of zich moest ergeren
scandalmonger kwaadspreker, lasteraar(ster)
scandalous schandelijk, schandalig, aanstootgevend
[1]Scandinavian (n) Scandinaviër, Scandinavische
[2]Scandinavian (adj) Scandinavisch
scanner aftaster, scanner, (draaiende) radarantenne
scant weinig, spaarzaam, gering: *do ~ justice to sth.* iets weinig recht doen
scanty karig, krap, gering
scapegoat zondebok
[1]scar (n) litteken[h], schram, kras
[2]scar (vb): *~ over* een litteken vormen; helen
scarab mestkever
scarce schaars [of food, money, etc]; zeldzaam: *make o.s. ~* zich uit de voeten maken
scarcely 1 nauwelijks, met moeite: *~ ever* haast nooit **2** [iron] zeker niet: *that's ~ the point here* dat is nou niet helemaal waar hier om gaat
scarcity schaarste, gebrek[h]
[1]scare (n) schrik, vrees, paniek: *give s.o. a ~* iem. de stuipen op het lijf jagen
[2]scare (vb) **1** doen schrikken, bang maken **2** (+ off, away) wegjagen, afschrikken
scarecrow vogelverschrikker [also fig]
scared bang: *are you ~ of dogs?* ben jij bang voor honden?; *~ out of one's wits* buiten

zichzelf van schrik, doodsbang; *~ stiff* doodsbang
scare up 1 optrommelen, bij elkaar scharrelen **2** klaarmaken, vervaardigen: *~ a meal from leftovers* uit restjes een maaltijd in elkaar flansen
scarf sjaal(tje[h]), sjerp
scarlatina roodvonk
scarlet scharlaken(rood) || *~ fever* roodvonk
scarper 'm smeren
scar tissue littekenweefsel[h]
scary 1 eng, schrikaanjagend **2** (snel) bang, schrikachtig
scat snel vertrekken: *~!* ga weg!
scathing vernietigend; bijtend [eg sarcasm]
[1]scatter (n) (ver)spreiding, verstrooiing: *a ~ of houses* een paar huizen hier en daar
[2]scatter (vb) verstrooid raken, zich verspreiden
[3]scatter (vb) verstrooien [also science]; verspreiden [also fig]: *all his CDs were ~ed through the room* al zijn cd's lagen verspreid door de kamer; *~ about* (or: *around*) rondstrooien
scatterbrain warhoofd[h]
scattered verspreid (liggend), ver uiteen: *~ showers* hier en daar een bui
scattering verspreiding
scatty gek, warrig
scavenge 1 afval doorzoeken **2** aas eten
scenario scenario[h]; draaiboek[h] [also fig]; (film)script[h]
scene 1 plaats van handeling, locatie, toneel[h]: *change of ~* verandering van omgeving **2** scène [also theatre]; ophef, misbaar[h] **3** decor[h], coulisse(n): *behind the ~s* achter de schermen [also fig] **4** landschap[h] || *set the ~ (for sth.)* (iets) voorbereiden; *steal the ~* de show stelen
scene change decorwisseling [also fig]
scenery 1 decors, coulissen **2** landschap[h]: *change of ~* verandering van omgeving
scenic 1 schilderachtig **2** van de natuur, landschaps- || *~ railway* miniatuurspoorbaan
[1]scent (n) **1** geur; lucht [also hunt] **2** spoor[h] [also fig]: *on a false* (or: *wrong*) *~* op een verkeerd spoor **3** parfum[h], luchtje[h], geurtje[h] **4** reuk(zin); neus [also fig]
[2]scent (vb) **1** ruiken [also fig]; geuren, lucht krijgen van **2** parfumeren: *~ soap* geparfumeerde zeep
sceptic twijfelaar
sceptical (+ about, of) sceptisch (over), twijfelend
scepticism kritische houding
sceptre scepter
schedule 1 programma[h]: *be behind ~* achter liggen op het schema, vertraging hebben; *on ~* op tijd **2** (inventaris)lijst **3** dienstregeling, rooster[h]
scheduled 1 gepland, in het rooster opge-

nomen **2** op een lijst gezet **3** lijn- [service, flight]

¹scheme (n) **1** stelsel[h], ordening, systeem[h] **2** programma[h] **3** oogmerk[h], project[h] **4** plan[h], complot[h] **5** ontwerp[h]

²scheme (vb) plannen maken, plannen smeden: *~ for sth.* iets plannen

³scheme (vb) **1** beramen [plans]; smeden **2** intrigeren: *he was always scheming against her* hij was altijd bezig complotten tegen haar te smeden

schemer 1 plannenmaker **2** intrigant, samenzweerder

scheming sluw

schism scheuring [in church]; afscheiding

schizophrenia schizofrenie

¹schizophrenic (n) schizofreen

²schizophrenic (adj) schizofreen

schmalzy sentimenteel

scholar 1 geleerde: *not much of a ~* geen studiehoofd **2** beursstudent

scholarly wetenschappelijk, geleerd

scholarship 1 (studie)beurs **2** wetenschappelijkheid **3** wetenschap, geleerdheid

scholastic 1 school- **2** schools

¹school (n) **1** school [also of fish etc]; [of thoughts] richting: *~ of thought* denkwijze, (filosofische) school **2** school; [fig] leerschool: *lower* (or: *upper*) *~* onderbouw, bovenbouw; *modern ~* [roughly] mavo[h]; *keep in after ~* na laten blijven; *quit ~* van school gaan; *after ~* na school(tijd); *at ~* op school **3** collegeruimte, examengebouw[h], leslokaal[h] **4** studierichting **5** (universitair) instituut[h], faculteit: *medical ~* faculteit (der) geneeskunde **6** scholing, (school)opleiding

²school (vb) scholen, trainen; africhten [horse]: *~ed in* opgeleid tot

schoolboy schooljongen, scholier

school certificate einddiploma[h]

school crossing patrol klaar-overbrigade

schooldays schooltijd

school friend schoolvriend(in)

schoolgirl schoolmeisje[h]

schooling 1 scholing, onderwijs[h] **2** dressuur

school-marm 1 schooljuffrouw **2** schoolfrik

schoolmaster schoolmeester

schoolmate schoolkameraad

schoolmistress schooljuffrouw

school night avond waarop een school- of werkdag volgt

school run: *do the ~* kinderen naar school brengen of van school halen

school shooting schietpartij op een school

school superintendent 1 schooldirecteur **2** onderwijsinspecteur

schoolteacher 1 onderwijzer(es) **2** leraar

school yard schoolplein[h]

schooner 1 schoener **2** groot bierglas[h] **3** groot sherryglas[h] (portglas[h])

science 1 (natuur)wetenschap: *applied ~* toegepaste wetenschap **2** techniek, vaardigheid

science fiction sciencefiction

scientific 1 wetenschappelijk **2** vakkundig: *a ~ boxer* een bokser met een goede techniek

scientist wetenschapper

sci-fi science fiction

scintillate 1 schitteren, fonkelen **2** vonken **3** sprankelen, geestig zijn: *scintillating humour* tintelende humor

scissors schaar: *a pair of ~* een schaar

¹scoff (n) **1** spottende opmerking: *he was used to ~s about his appearance* hij was gewend aan spottende opmerkingen over zijn uiterlijk **2** mikpunt[h] van spotternij **3** vreten[h]

²scoff (vb) (+ at) spotten (met): *they ~ed the idea* ze maakten spottende opmerkingen over het idee

³scoff (vb) schrokken, vreten

¹scold (vb) (+ at) schelden (op)

²scold (vb) uitvaren tegen: *~ s.o. for sth.* iem. om iets berispen

scolding standje[h], uitbrander

scone scone [small, solid cake]

¹scoop (n) **1** schep, lepel, bak: *three ~s of ice cream* drie bolletjes ijs **2** primeur [in newspaper]; sensationeel nieuwtje[h]

²scoop (vb) **1** scheppen, lepelen: *~ out* opscheppen; *~ up* opscheppen [with hands, spoon] **2** uithollen, (uit)graven **3** binnenhalen; grijpen [money]; in de wacht slepen

scoot rennen, vliegen: *is that the time? I'd better ~* is het al zo laat? Ik moet rennen

scooter 1 step, autoped: *electric ~* elektrische step **2** scooter

scope 1 bereik[h], gebied[h], omvang: *that is beyond* (or: *outside*) *the ~ of this book* dat valt buiten het bestek van dit boek **2** ruimte, armslag, gelegenheid: *this job gives you ~ for your abilities* deze baan geeft je de kans je talenten te ontplooien

¹scorch (vb) razendsnel rijden, vliegen, scheuren

²scorch (vb) **1** (ver)schroeien, (ver)zengen, verbranden **2** verdorren

scorcher 1 snikhete dag **2** scherpe kritiek, scherpe uithaal **3** snelheidsduivel

scorching 1 verschroeiend, verzengend: *a ~ summer afternoon* op een snikhete zomermiddag **2** vernietigend, bijtend

¹score (n) **1** stand, puntentotaal[h], score: *level the ~* gelijkmaken **2** (doel)punt[h] [also fig]; rake opmerking, succes[h]: [fig] *~ off one's opponent* een punt scoren tegen zijn tegenstander **3** getrokken lijn, kerf, kras, striem, schram, lijn **4** reden, grond: *on the ~ of* vanwege **5** grief: *pay off* (or: *settle*) *old ~s* een oude rekening vereffenen **6** onderwerp^h, thema^h, punt^h: *on that ~* wat dat betreft **7** [mus] partituur; [by extension] muziek [for musical etc] ‖ *know the ~* weten hoe de zaken er voorstaan

²score (vb) **1** scoren, (doel)punt maken; puntentotaal halen [eg in test] **2** de score noteren **3** succes hebben **4** geluk hebben ‖ ~ *off* s.o. iem. aftroeven

³score (vb) **1** lijn(en) trekken, (in)kerven, schrammen: ~ *out* (or: *through*) doorstrepen **2** scoren; maken [point]; [fig] behalen; boeken [success]; winnen **3** tellen voor; waard zijn [of point, run] **4** toekennen [points]; geven **5** een score halen van [eg in test] **6** fel bekritiseren, hekelen

scoreboard scorebord^h

scorer 1 scoreteller **2** (doel)puntenmaker

¹scorn (n) (voorwerp^h van) minachting, geringschatting: *pour ~ on* verachten

²scorn (vb) **1** minachten, verachten **2** versmaden, beneden zich achten

scornful negatief: ~ *of* sth. met minachting voor iets

Scorpio [astrology] (de) Schorpioen

scorpion schorpioen

Scot Schot

scotch 1 een eind maken aan; ontzenuwen [theory]; de kop indrukken [rumour] **2** verijdelen [plan]

¹Scotch (n) **1** Schotse whisky **2** de Schotten

²Scotch (adj) Schots: ~ *whisky* Schotse whisky ‖ ~ *broth* Schotse maaltijdsoep

Scotch tape sellotape, plakband^+h

scot-free 1 ongedeerd **2** ongestraft

Scotland Schotland

Scotland Yard Scotland Yard; opsporingsdienst

¹Scots (n) Schots^h

²Scots (adj) Schots

Scotsman Schot

Scotswoman Schotse

¹Scottish (n) de Schotten

²Scottish (adj) Schots

scoundrel schoft

¹scour (vb) rennen: ~ *about after* (or: *for*) sth. rondrennen op zoek naar iets

²scour (vb) **1** (door)spoelen, uitspoelen **2** (+ out) uitschuren, uithollen **3** doorkruisen **4** afzoeken, doorzoeken, afstropen: ~ *the shops for a CD* de winkels aflopen voor een cd

³scour (vb) schuren, schrobben

¹scourge (n) gesel

²scourge (vb) **1** geselen **2** teisteren: *for seven years the country was ~d by war* zeven jaar lang werd het land door oorlog geteisterd

scouring powder schuurmiddel^h

¹scout (n) **1** verkenner **2** talentenjager; scout [in the world of football, film] **3** ver-

kenner, padvinder, gids

²scout (vb) **1** zoeken: ~ *(about, around) for* sth. naar iets op zoek zijn **2** terrein verkennen

³scout (vb) **1** verkennen **2** minachtend afwijzen: *every offer of help was ~ed* elk aanbod om te helpen werd met minachting van de hand gewezen

scoutmaster hopman

¹scowl (n) norse blik

²scowl (vb) (+ at) het voorhoofd fronsen (tegen), stuurs kijken (naar)

¹scrabble (n) gegraai^h

²scrabble (vb) graaien, grabbelen, scharrelen: ~ *about for* sth. naar iets graaien

scrag 1 hals **2** halsstuk^h

scraggy broodmager

scram: ~! maak dat je wegkomt!

¹scramble (n) **1** klauterpartij: *it was a bit of a ~ to reach the top* het was een hele toer om de top te bereiken **2** gedrang^h, gevecht^h **3** motorcross

²scramble (vb) **1** klauteren, klimmen **2** (+ for) vechten (om), zich verdringen **3** zich haasten: ~ *to one's feet* overeind krabbelen

³scramble (vb) **1** door elkaar gooien, in de war brengen **2** roeren [egg] **3** afraffelen **4** vervormen [to encode radio or telephone message]; verdraaien

¹scrap (n) **1** stukje^h, beetje^h, fragment^h: *there's not a ~ of truth in what they've told you* er is niets waar van wat ze je verteld hebben **2** knipsel^h **3** vechtpartij(tje^h), ruzie **4** afval^h, schroot^h **5** (-s) restjes

²scrap (vb) ruziën, bakkeleien

³scrap (vb) **1** afdanken, dumpen; laten varen [ideas, plans] **2** slopen, tot schroot verwerken

scrapbook plakboek^h

¹scrape (n) **1** geschraap^h, geschuur^h **2** gekras^h, kras **3** schaafwond **4** netelige situatie: *get into ~s* in moeilijkheden verzeild raken

²scrape (vb) **1** schuren, strijken, krassen: *the sound of chairs scraping on a tiled floor* het geluid van stoelen die over een tegelvloer schrapen **2** schrapen; zagen [eg on violin] **3** met weinig rondkomen, sober leven **4** het op het kantje af halen [also examination]: ~ *through* in maar net een voldoende halen voor ‖ ~ *along on money from friends* het uit weten te zingen met geld van vrienden

³scrape (vb) **1** (af)schrapen, (af)krabben, uitschrapen **2** schaven [eg knee]: ~ *the paintwork* de verf beschadigen ‖ ~ *together* (or: *up*) bij elkaar schrapen [money]

scraper 1 schraper; (verf)krabber **2** flessenlikker

scrap heap vuilnisbelt, schroothoop: [fig] *throw s.o. (sth.) on the ~* iem. (iets) afdanken

scrap iron schroot^h, oud ijzer^h

scrap paper kladpapier^h

scrappy fragmentarisch
scrapyard autokerkhof[h]
[1]**scratch** (n) **1** krasje[h], schram: *without a ~* ongedeerd **2** startstreep: *start from ~* **a)** [fig] bij het begin beginnen; **b)** met niets beginnen || *up to ~* in vorm, op het vereiste niveau; *come up to ~* het halen
[2]**scratch** (adj) samengeraapt: *a ~ meal* een restjesmaaltijd
[3]**scratch** (vb) scharrelen, wroeten || *~ along* het hoofd boven water weten te houden
[4]**scratch** (vb) **1** (zich) schrammen **2** krabbelen [letter] **3** schrappen, doorhalen **4** terugtrekken **5** (+ together, up) bijeenschrapen [money; information]
[5]**scratch** (vb) krassen, (zich) krabben
scratch card kraslot[h]
scratch paper kladpapier[h]
[1]**scrawl** (n) **1** krabbeltje[h] **2** poot, onbeholpen handschrift[h]
[2]**scrawl** (vb) krabbelen, slordig schrijven
scrawny broodmager
[1]**scream** (n) **1** gil, krijs **2** giller, dolkomisch iets (iem.): *do you know Ernest? He's a ~* ken jij Ernest? Je lacht je gek
[2]**scream** (vb) tieren, razen, tekeergaan
[3]**scream** (vb) gillen, schreeuwen: *~ for water* om water schreeuwen; *~ with laughter* gieren van het lachen
[1]**screech** (n) gil, krijs, schreeuw: *a ~ of brakes* gierende remmen
[2]**screech** (vb) knarsen, kraken, piepen
[3]**screech** (vb) gillen, gieren
[1]**screen** (n) **1** scherm[h]; koorhek[h] [in church] **2** beschutting, bescherming; afscherming [of electrical equipment etc]; muur: *under ~ of night* onder dekking van de nacht **3** doek[h], projectiescherm[h], beeldscherm[h] **4** het witte doek, de film **5** hor, venstergaas[h] **6** zeef, rooster[h]; [fig] selectie(procedure)
[2]**screen** (vb) **1** afschermen [also from radiation]; afschutten, beschermen; dekken [soldier]: *~ off one corner of the room* een hoek van de kamer afschermen **2** beschermen, de hand boven het hoofd houden **3** doorlichten, op geschiktheid testen, screenen **4** vertonen, projecteren: *the feature film will be ~ed at 8.25* de hoofdfilm wordt om 8.25 uur vertoond **5** verfilmen
screening 1 filmvertoning **2** doorlichting **3** afscherming
screenplay scenario[h], script
screen print zeefdruk
screen saver schermbeveiliger; screensaver
screen test screentest, proefopname
screenwriter scenarioschrijver
[1]**screw** (n) **1** schroef **2** propeller, scheepsschroef **3** vrek **4** cipier
[2]**screw** (vb) zich spiraalsgewijs bewegen
[3]**screw** (vb) **1** schroeven, aandraaien: *I could* ~ *his neck* ik zou hem zijn nek wel kunnen omdraaien; *~ down* vastschroeven; *~ on* vastschroeven **2** verfrommelen **3** afzetten: *he's so stupid, no wonder he gets ~ed all the time* hij is zo stom, geen wonder dat hij iedere keer wordt afgezet **4** belazeren, verneuken **5** [vulg] neuken || *~ you!* val dood!
screwball 1 idioot **2** [baseball] omgekeerde curve
screwdriver schroevendraaier
screwed-up 1 verpest **2** verknipt, opgefokt
screw out of afpersen, uitzuigen: *screw money out of s.o.* iem. geld afhandig maken; *screw s.o. out of sth.* zorgen dat iem. iets niet krijgt
screw up 1 verwringen, verdraaien, verfrommelen: *she screwed up her eyes* zij kneep haar ogen dicht **2** verzieken, verknoeien **3** bij elkaar rapen; verzamelen [courage] **4** nerveus maken
screwy excentriek, zonderling
[1]**scribble** (n) **1** gekrabbel[h] **2** briefje[h], kladje[h]
[2]**scribble** (vb) krabbelen
scribe 1 schrijver, klerk **2** schriftgeleerde
scrimmage schermutseling
[1]**scrimp** (vb) zich bekrimpen: *~ and save* heel zuinig aan doen
[2]**scrimp** (vb) beknibbelen op
script 1 geschrift[h] **2** script, manuscript[h], draaiboek[h], tekst **3** schrijfletters, handschrift[h]
script girl regieassistente
scripture heilig geschrift[h]: *the (Holy) Scripture* de Heilige Schrift
scriptwriter scenarioschrijver
[1]**scroll** (n) **1** rol, perkamentrol, geschrift[h] **2** krul
[2]**scroll** (vb) schuiven [moving text on computer screen]; scrollen
scroll bar [comp] schuifbalk
scrolling scrollen[h]
[1]**scrounge** (vb) schooien, bietsen
[2]**scrounge** (vb) **1** in de wacht slepen, achteroverdrukken **2** bietsen
scrounger klaploper, bietser, profiteur
[1]**scrub** (n) **1** met struikgewas bedekt gebied[h] **2** struikgewas[h], kreupelhout[h] **3** het boenen
[2]**scrub** (vb) een schrobber gebruiken, schrobben || *the surgeon was ~bing up* de chirurg was zijn handen aan het schrobben
[3]**scrub** (vb) **1** schrobben, boenen **2** (also + out) schrappen, afgelasten, vergeten
scrubby 1 miezerig **2** met struikgewas bedekt
scrub nurse [Am] ok-verpleegkundige
scrubs [med] operatiekleding
scruff nekvel[h]: *take by the ~ of the neck* bij het nekvel grijpen
scruffy smerig, vuil, slordig
[1]**scruple** (n) scrupule, gewetensbezwaar[h]:

make no ~ *about doing sth.* er geen been in zien om iets te doen

²**scruple** (vb) aarzelen

scrupulous nauwgezet: *~ly clean* kraakhelder

scrutinize in detail onderzoeken, nauwkeurig bekijken

scrutiny 1 nauwkeurig toezicht[h] **2** kritische blik

scud voortscheren, ijlen, snellen: *the children were ~ding downhill on their sledges* de kinderen raasden van de heuvel af op hun sleeën

¹**scuff** (n) slijtplek

²**scuff** (vb) **1** sloffen **2** versleten zijn [of shoe, floor]

³**scuff** (vb) schuren, slepen

¹**scuffle** (n) knokpartij, schermutseling

²**scuffle** (vb) bakkeleien, knokken

¹**scull** (n) **1** korte (roei)riem **2** sculler, éénpersoonsroeiboot met twee korte riemen

²**scull** (vb) roeien

scullery bijkeuken

sculptor beeldhouwer

¹**sculpture** (n) beeldhouwwerk[h], plastiek[h], beeldhouwkunst

²**sculpture** (vb) **1** beeldhouwen **2** met sculptuur versieren, bewerken

scum 1 schuim[h] [on water] **2** uitschot[h] [also fig]; afval[h]: *the ~ of humanity* (or: *the earth*) het schorem, uitschot[h]

¹**scupper** (n) spuigat[h]

²**scupper** (vb) **1** tot zinken brengen **2** (overvallen en) in de pan hakken, (overvallen en) afmaken: *be ~ed* eraan gaan

scurf roos [of skin]

scurrility 1 grofheid **2** grove taal

scurrilous grof

scurry dribbelen, zich haasten: *~ for shelter* haastig een onderdak zoeken

¹**scurvy** (n) scheurbuik[+h]

²**scurvy** (adj) gemeen

¹**scuttle** (n) **1** luik(gat)[h], ventilatieopening **2** kolenbak **3** overhaaste vlucht

²**scuttle** (vb) zich wegscheren: *~ off* (or: *away*) zich uit de voeten maken

³**scuttle** (vb) doen zinken [by making holes]

scuzzy [inform] smerig

¹**scythe** (n) zeis

²**scythe** (vb) (af)maaien [also fig]

SE *southeast* Z.O., zuidoost

sea 1 zee, oceaan; [fig] massa; overvloed: *put (out) to ~* uitvaren; *at ~* op zee; *the seven ~s* de zeven (wereld)zeeën **2** zeegolf, sterke golfslag: *heavy ~* zware zee **3** kust, strand[h] || *be (all) at ~* **a)** verbijsterd zijn; **b)** geen notie hebben

sea battle zeeslag

seabed zeebedding, zeebodem

seabird zeevogel

seaborne over zee (vervoerd/aangevoerd):

~ *supplies* bevoorrading overzee

sea breeze 1 zeebries **2** wind op zee

sea change ommekeer

sea dog zeebonk, zeerob

seafaring zeevarend

seafood eetbare zeevis en schaal- en schelpdieren

seafront strandboulevard; zeekant [of town]

seagoing zeevarend

seagull zeemeeuw

¹**seal** (n) **1** zegel[h]; stempel[h] [also fig]; lakzegel[h], (plak)zegel; [fig] kenmerk[h]; [fig] bezegeling: *set the ~ on* **a)** bezegelen; **b)** [also fig] afsluiten; *under ~ of secrecy* onder het zegel van geheimhouding **2** dichting, dichtingsmateriaal[h], (luchtdichte/waterdichte) afsluiting, stankafsluiting **3** (zee)rob, zeehond, zeeleeuw

²**seal** (vb) **1** zegelen; verzegelen [verdict, orders etc]; [fig] opsluiten **2** dichten, verzegelen, (water)dicht maken; dichtschroeien [meat]: *my lips are ~ed* ik zal er niets over zeggen; *~ off an area* een gebied afgrendelen **3** bezegelen, bevestigen: *~ s.o.'s doom* (or: *fate*) iemands (nood)lot bezegelen

sea lane vaarroute

sea legs zeebenen: *get* (or: *find*) *one's ~* zeebenen krijgen

sea level zeeniveau[h], zeespiegel

sealing wax zegelwas[+h]

sea lion zeeleeuw

seal ring zegelring

sealskin robbenvel[h], sealskin[h]

seam 1 naad, voeg **2** scheurtje[h] [in metal] **3** (steenkool)laag || *burst at the ~s* tot barstens toe vol zitten

seaman zeeman, matroos

seamanship zeemanschap[h], zeevaartkunde

sea mile zeemijl [international: 1,852 metres, British: 1,853.18 metres]

seamless naadloos

seamstress naaister

seamy 1 met een naad **2** minder mooi: *the ~ side of life* de zelfkant van het leven

seaplane watervliegtuig[h]

seaport zeehaven

sear 1 schroeien, verschroeien, (dicht)branden **2** (doen) verdorren, opdrogen, uitdrogen; [fig] verharden

¹**search** (n) grondig onderzoek[h], opsporing, speurwerk[h]; [comp] zoekbewerking, zoekfunctie: *in ~ of* op zoek naar

²**search** (vb) (+ for) grondig zoeken (naar), speuren

³**search** (vb) grondig onderzoeken, fouilleren, naspeuren || *~ me!* weet ik veel!

search engine zoekmachine [on the Internet]

searching 1 onderzoekend [glance]

2 grondig
searchlight zoeklicht^h, schijnwerper
search party opsporingsteam^h
search warrant huiszoekingsbevel^h
seascape zeegezicht^h [painting]
seashell zeeschelp
seashore zeekust
seasick zeeziek
seaside (the) kust, zee(kust)
¹season (n) **1** seizoen^h; [fig] jaar^h: *rainy ~* regentijd **2** geschikte tijd, seizoen^h, jachtseizoen^h, vakantieperiode: *cherries are in ~* het is kersentijd; *a word in ~* een woord op het passende moment, een gepast woord; *in and out of ~* te pas en te onpas **3** feesttijd, kerst- en nieuwjaarstijd: *the ~ of good **cheer*** de gezellige kerst- en nieuwjaarstijd
²season (vb) **1** kruiden [also fig] **2** (ge)wennen, harden: *~ed troops* doorgewinterde troepen **3** laten liggen [wood]
seasonable 1 passend bij het seizoen **2** tijdig **3** passend
seasonal volgens het seizoen; seizoengevoelig [com]: *~ employment* seizoenarbeid
seasonal affective disorder winterdepressie
seasoning 1 het kruiden **2** specerij
season's greetings [roughly] Gelukkig Nieuwjaar
season ticket seizoenkaart, abonnement^h
¹seat (n) **1** (zit)plaats, stoel: *the **back** ~ of a car* de achterbank van een auto; *have* (or: *take*) *a ~* neem plaats **2** zitting [of chair]; wc-bril **3** zitvlak^h **4** zetel [fig]; centrum^h; haard [of disease, fire]: *a ~ of **learning*** een zetel van wetenschap **5** landgoed^h **6** zetel, lidmaatschap^h: *have a ~ **on** a board* zitting hebben in een commissie **7** kiesdistrict^h
²seat (vb) zetten, doen zitten, zetelen: *be ~ed* ga zitten; *be **deeply** ~ed* diep ingeworteld zijn [of feeling, illness etc]
seat belt veiligheidsgordel
seating 1 plaatsing, het geven van een plaats **2** plaatsruimte, zitplaatsen
seawall zeedijk
seaward zeewaarts
seawater zeewater^h
seaweed 1 zeewier^h **2** zeegras^h
seaworthy zeewaardig
sec *second* seconde: *just a ~* een ogenblikje
secateurs snoeischaar, tuinschaar
secession afscheiding, het afscheiden
secluded afgezonderd, teruggetrokken, stil: *a ~ **life*** een teruggetrokken leven; *a ~ **house*** een afgelegen huis
seclusion afzondering, eenzaamheid, rust
¹second (n) **1** seconde; [fig] momentje^h; ogenblikje^h: *I'll be back **in** a ~* ik ben zo terug **2** secondant; getuige [at boxing, duel] **3** (-s) tweede kwaliteitsgoederen, tweede keus (klas) **4** (-s) tweede keer [at meal]: *who would*

like ~s? wie wil er nog?
²second (vb) **1** steunen, bijstaan, meewerken **2** ondersteunen, goedkeuren; bijvallen [proposal etc]
³second (vb) tijdelijk overplaatsen, detacheren
⁴second (adv) **1** op één na: *~ **best*** op één na de beste **2** ten tweede
⁵second (num) tweede, ander(e); [fig] tweederangs; minderwaardig: *~ **class*** tweede klas [also of mail]; *~ **nature*** tweede natuur; *in the ~ **place*** ten tweede, bovendien; *he was ~ to none* hij was van niemand de mindere; *every ~ day* om de andere dag
secondary 1 secundair, bijkomend, bijkomstig, ondergeschikt: *~ **to*** ondergeschikt aan **2** secundair, tweederangs: *~ **to*** inferieur aan **3** [school] secundair, middelbaar: *~ **education*** middelbaar onderwijs; *~ **school*** middelbare school; *~ **modern** (school),* [inform] *~ mod* middelbare school; [roughly] mavo^h; *~ **technical school*** middelbare technische school
second-class 1 tweedeklas-: *~ **mail*** tweedeklaspost **2** tweederangs, inferieur, minderwaardig
second-degree tweedegraads-: *~ **burn*** tweedegraadsverbranding
second-guess 1 [esp Am] achteraf bekritiseren: *~ **yourself*** aan jezelf gaan twijfelen **2** voorspellen: *~ the **mood** of the public* de algehele stemming voorspellen
second hand secondewijzer
second-hand 1 tweedehands: *a ~ **car*** een tweedehands auto **2** uit de tweede hand: *a ~ **report*** een verslag uit de tweede hand
secondly ten tweede, op de tweede plaats
secondment detachering: *he's here **on** ~* hij is bij ons gedetacheerd
second-rate tweederangs, inferieur, middelmatig
secrecy geheimhouding, geheimzinnigheid
¹secret (n) geheim^h, mysterie^h, sleutel: *in ~* in het geheim; *let s.o. **into** a ~* iem. in een geheim inwijden
²secret (adj) **1** geheim, verborgen, vertrouwelijk: *a ~ **admirer*** een stille aanbidder; *~ **ballot*** geheime stemming; *~ **service*** geheime dienst; *keep sth. ~ **from** s.o.* iets voor iem. geheim houden **2** gesloten, discreet **3** verborgen, afgezonderd
secretarial van een secretaresse, secretariaats-
secretariat secretariaat^h
secretary 1 secretaresse **2** secretaris; secretaris-generaal [of department]
Secretary minister: *~ of State* minister
secretary-general secretaris-generaal
secrete 1 verbergen, verstoppen, wegstoppen: *~ sth. **about** one's person* iets op zijn li-

chaam verstoppen **2** afscheiden [of organs, glands]
secretion afscheiding(sproduct^h)
secretive geheimzinnig, gesloten, gereserveerd
secretly 1 in het geheim **2** stiekem
sect sekte, geloofsgemeenschap
¹sectarian (n) sektariër, lid^h van een sekte
²sectarian (adj) sekte-: *a ~ killing* een sektemoord
section 1 sectie, (onder)deel^h, afdeling, lid^h, stuk^h, segment^h, partje^h, wijk, district^h, stadsdeel^h, landsdeel^h; baanvak^h [of railway]: *all ~s of the population* alle lagen van de bevolking **2** groep [within society] **3** (onder)afdeling, paragraaf, lid^h, sectie; katern^h [of newspaper, book] **4** (dwars)doorsnede [also in maths]; profiel^h **5** een vierkante mijl [640 acres] **6** (chirurgische) snee, incisie, (in)snijding, sectie: *c(a)esarean ~* keizersnede ∥ *in ~* in profiel
sectional 1 uitneembaar, demonteerbaar: *~ furniture* aanbouwmeubilair^h **2** sectioneel, m.b.t. een bepaalde bevolkingsgroep: *~ interests* (tegenstrijdige) groepsbelangen
section mark paragraafteken^h
sector sector, (bedrijfs)tak, afdeling, terrein^h, branche
secular 1 wereldlijk, niet-kerkelijk: *~ music* wereldlijke muziek **2** vrijzinnig, niet aan vaste leerstellingen gebonden
secularize verwereldlijken
¹secure (adj) **1** veilig, beschut, beveiligd: *~ against* (or: *from*) veilig voor **2** veilig, stevig, zeker: *a ~ method* of payment een veilige manier van betalen **3** vol vertrouwen
²secure (vb) **1** beveiligen, in veiligheid brengen **2** bemachtigen, zorgen voor: *~ the biggest number of orders* het grootste aantal orders in de wacht slepen **3** stevig vastmaken, vastleggen, afsluiten
security 1 veiligheid(sgevoel^h) **2** veiligheidsvoorziening, verzekering **3** beveiliging, (openbare) veiligheid: *tight ~ is in force* er zijn strenge veiligheidsmaatregelen getroffen **4** obligatie(certificaat^h), effect^h, aandeel^h **5** borg [pers]: *be s.o.'s ~* zich voor iem. borg stellen **6** (waar)borg, onderpand^h: *give as (a) ~* in onderpand geven
security check veiligheidscontrole
Security Council Veiligheidsraad [of United Nations]
security forces politietroepen
security prison bewaakte gevangenis: *maximum, minimum ~* zwaar-, lichtbewaakte gevangenis
security reason veiligheidsoverweging: *for ~s* uit veiligheidsoverwegingen
¹sedate (adj) bezadigd, onverstoorbaar, kalm
²sedate (vb) kalmeren, tot rust brengen, een

kalmerend middel toedienen aan
¹sedative (n) kalmerend middel^h
²sedative (adj) kalmerend, pijnstillend
sedentary (stil)zittend: *~ work* zittend werk; *~ bird* standvogel
sediment sediment^h, neerslag, bezinksel^h; afzetting(smateriaal^h) [by water, wind etc]
sedimentation het neerslaan, afzetting, sedimentatie
sedition ongehoorzaamheid, ordeverstoring
seditious opruiend, oproerig, opstandig
seduce verleiden [also fig]; overhalen: *~ s.o. into sth.* iem. tot iets overhalen
seducer verleider
seduction verleiding(spoging)
seductive verleidelijk
¹see (vb) **1** zien, kijken (naar), aankijken tegen: *worth ~ing* de moeite waard, opmerkelijk; *I cannot ~ him doing it* ik zie het hem nog niet doen; *we shall ~* we zullen wel zien, wie weet; *~ through s.o. (sth.)* iem. (iets) doorhebben **2** zien, begrijpen, inzien: *I don't ~ the fun of doing that* ik zie daar de lol niet van in; *as far as I can ~* volgens mij; *as I ~ it* volgens mij **3** toezien (op), opletten, ervoor zorgen, zorgen voor: *~ to it that* ervoor zorgen dat **4** nadenken, bekijken, zien: *let me ~* wacht eens, even denken; *we will ~ about that* dat zullen we nog wel (eens) zien **5** voor zich zien, zich voorstellen **6** lezen [newspaper etc]; zien: *have you ~n today's papers?* heb je de kranten van vandaag gezien? **7** tegenkomen, ontmoeten: *~ you (later)!, (I'll) be ~ing you!* tot ziens!, tot kijk!; *~ a lot of s.o.* iem. vaak zien **8** ontvangen, spreken met: *Mrs Richards can ~ you now* Mevr. Richards kan u nu ontvangen; *can I ~ you for a minute?* kan ik u even spreken? **9** bezoeken, opzoeken, langs gaan bij: *~ the town* de stad bezichtigen; *~ over* (or: *round*) *a house* een huis bezichtigen **10** raadplegen, bezoeken: *~ a doctor* een arts raadplegen; *you should get that leg ~n to* je moet een dokter naar je been laten kijken **11** meemaken, ervaren, getuige zijn van: *have ~n better days* betere tijden gekend hebben **12** begeleiden, (weg)brengen: *~ a girl home* een meisje naar huis brengen; *~ s.o. out* iem. uitlaten; *I'll ~ you through* ik help je er wel doorheen ∥ *~ sth. out* (or: *through*) iets tot het einde volhouden
²see (n) (aarts)bisdom^h
¹seed (n) **1** zaad(je)^h; kiem [fig]; zaad^h, begin^h: *go* (or: *run*) *to ~* uitbloeien, doorschieten; [fig] verlopen, aftakelen **2** korreltje^h, bolletje^h **3** [sport, esp tennis] geplaatste speler
²seed (vb) zaad vormen, uitbloeien, doorschieten
³seed (vb) **1** zaaien, zaad uitstrooien **2** bezaaien [also fig]; bestrooien **3** [sport, esp

tennis] plaatsen

seedbed 1 zaaibedʰ **2** [fig] voedingsbodem

seedless zonder zaad

seedling zaailing

seedsman zaadhandelaar

seedy 1 slonzig, verwaarloosd, vervallen **2** niet lekker, een beetje ziek, slap

seeing aangezien, in aanmerking genomen dat: ~ *(that) there is nothing I can do* aangezien ik niets kan doen

¹seek (vb) (+ after, for) zoeken (naar): ~ *for a solution* een oplossing zoeken

²seek (vb) **1** nastreven, proberen te bereiken, zoeken **2** vragen, wensen, verlangen **3** opzoeken: ~ *s.o.* **out** naar iem. toekomen, iem. opzoeken **4** proberen (te), trachten (te): ~ *to* **escape** proberen te ontsnappen

seem (toe)schijnen, lijken, eruitzien: *he* ~*s (to be) the* **leader** hij schijnt de leider te zijn; *he* ~*s to have* **done** *it* het ziet ernaar uit dat hij het gedaan heeft; *it would* ~ *to* **me** *that* (or: *as if*) het lijkt mij dat (or: alsof); *he is not satisfied, it* **would** ~ hij is niet tevreden, naar het schijnt; *it* ~*s* **to** *me* mij dunkt

seeming schijnbaar, ogenschijnlijk, onoprecht: *in* ~ **friendship** onder schijn van vriendschap

seemly correct, fatsoenlijk

seep (weg)sijpelen, lekken, doorsijpelen; [fig] doordringen: *the water* ~*s into the* **ground** het water sijpelt weg in de grond

seer 1 ziener, profeet **2** helderziende

¹seesaw (n) wip

²seesaw (vb) **1** wippen, op en neer wippen, op de wip spelen **2** schommelen, zigzaggen, veranderlijk zijn: ~*ing* **prices** schommelende prijzen

seethe koken, zieden, kolken: *he was seething* **with** *rage* hij was witheet van woede

see-through [inform] **1** doorzichtig **2** doorkijk-, doorschijnend: ~ **blouse** doorkijkbloes

segment deelʰ, segmentʰ, part(je)ʰ

segregate afzonderen, scheiden, rassenscheiding toepassen op

segregation afzondering, scheiding, rassenscheiding, apartheid

seismic seismisch, aardbevings-

seismograph seismograaf

seize 1 grijpen, pakken, nemen: ~ *the* **occasion** *with both hands* de kans met beide handen aangrijpen; ~*d* **with** *fear* door angst bevangen **2** in beslag nemen, afnemen **3** bevatten, begrijpen, inzien: *she never seemed to* ~ *the* **point** ze scheen helemaal niet te begrijpen waar het om ging

seize up vastlopen [of machine]; blijven hangen; [fig also] blijven steken; niet verder kunnen

seize (up)on aangrijpen [chance, cause]

seizure 1 confiscatie, inbeslagneming, be-

slaglegging **2** aanval: *epileptic* ~ epileptische aanval

seldom zelden, haast nooit: ~ *if ever,* ~ *or* *never* zelden of nooit

¹select (adj) **1** uitgezocht, zorgvuldig gekozen, geselecteerd **2** exclusief

²select (vb) een keuze maken

³select (vb) (uit)kiezen, uitzoeken, selecteren

selection keuze, selectie, verzameling

selection committee sollicitatiecommissie

selective selectief, uitkiezend

selector 1 lidʰ van selectiecommissie/benoemingscommissie **2** kiezer, keuzeschakelaar

self 1 het zelf, het eigen wezen, het ik **2** persoonlijkheid, karakterʰ: *he is still not quite his* **old** ~ hij is nog steeds niet helemaal de oude **3** de eigen persoon, zichzelf, het eigenbelang: *he never thinks of anything* **but** ~ hij denkt altijd alleen maar aan zichzelf

-self 1 -zelf: *oneself* zichzelf **2** [with emphasis] zelf: *I did it* **myself** ik heb het zelf gedaan

self-absorbed in zichzelf verdiept

self-addressed aan zichzelf geadresseerd: ~ **envelope** antwoordenvelop

self-appointed opgedrongen, zichzelf ongevraagd opwerpend (als): *a* ~ **critic** iem. die zich een oordeel aanmatigt

self-assured zelfverzekerd, vol zelfvertrouwen

self-awareness zelfbewustzijnʰ

self-build doe-het-zelfbouw

self-catering zelf voor eten zorgend, maaltijden niet inbegrepen

self-centred egocentrisch, zelfzuchtig

self-confidence zelfvertrouwenʰ, zelfverzekerdheid

self-confident zelfverzekerd

self-conscious 1 bewust, zich van zichzelf bewust **2** verlegen, niet op zijn gemak

self-contained 1 onafhankelijk **2** vrij; met eigen keuken en badkamer [apartment]

self-contradictory tegenstrijdig

self-control zelfbeheersing

self-defeating zichzelf hinderend, zijn doel voorbijstrevend

self-defence zelfverdediging: *in* ~ uit zelfverdediging

self-denial zelfopoffering, zelfverloochening

self-destruct zichzelf vernietigen

self-determination zelfbeschikking(srechtʰ)

self-doubt onzekerheid

self-drive 1 zonder chauffeur **2** [autonomous] zelfrijdend, automatisch bestuurd

self-driven zelfrijdend, automatisch bestuurd

self-educated autodidactisch: *a ~ man* een autodidact

self-effacing bescheiden

self-employed zelfstandig, met een eigen onderneming, eigen baas

self-esteem gevoel^h van eigenwaarde, trots

self-evident vanzelfsprekend

self-explanatory duidelijk, onmiskenbaar, wat voor zichzelf spreekt

self-fulfilling zichzelf vervullend: *a ~ prophecy* een zichzelf vervullende voorspelling

self-governing autonoom

self-harm zichzelf verwonden

self-help zelfhulp

selfie selfie

selfie stick selfiestick

self-importance gewichtigheid, eigendunk

self-imposed (aan) zichzelf opgelegd

self-indulgence genotzucht

self-inflicted zelf veroorzaakt

self-interest eigenbelang^h

selfish zelfzuchtig, egoïstisch

selfless onbaatzuchtig, onzelfzuchtig

self-made 1 zelfgemaakt **2** opgewerkt, opgeklommen: *a ~ man* een man die alles op eigen kracht bereikt heeft

self-pity zelfmedelijden^h

self-preservation zelfbehoud^h

self-raising zelfrijzend

self-reliant onafhankelijk, zelfstandig

self-respecting zichzelf respecterend

self-righteous vol eigendunk, intolerant

self-righting zichzelf oprichtend [after capsizing]

self-sacrifice zelfopoffering

selfsame precies dezelfde (hetzelfde), identiek

self-satisfaction eigendunk

self-satisfied zelfvoldaan

self-service zelfbediening: *~ restaurant* zelfbedieningsrestaurant^h

self-serving uit eigenbelang

self-starter zelfstarter

self-styled zogenaamd, zichzelf noemend: *~ professor* iem. die zich voor professor uitgeeft

self-sufficient onafhankelijk

self-supporting zelfstandig

self-taught 1 zelf geleerd, zichzelf aangeleerd **2** autodidactisch, zichzelf opgeleid

self-willed eigenwijs

¹**sell** (n) bedrog^h, verlakkerij, zwendel

²**sell** (vb) **1** verkocht worden, verkopen, kosten, in de handel zijn **2** handel drijven, verkopen ‖ *~ up* zijn zaak sluiten

³**sell** (vb) **1** verkopen, in voorraad hebben, handelen in, verkwanselen: *~ off* uitverkopen; *~ at* five pounds (or: *at a loss*) voor vijf

pond (*or:* met verlies) verkopen **2** aanprijzen: *~ o.s.* zichzelf goed verkopen **3** overhalen, warm maken voor, aanpraten: *be sold on* sth. ergens helemaal weg van zijn **4** misleiden, bedriegen, bezwendelen ‖ *~ s.o. short* iem. tekortdoen

sell-by date uiterste verkoopdatum

seller 1 verkoper **2** succes^h, artikel^h dat goed verkoopt

selling point [com] verkoopargument^h, voordeel^h, aanbeveling

selling price verkoopprijs

sellotape plakband^h

sell out 1 door de voorraad heen raken **2** verkocht worden, uitverkocht raken **3** zijn aandeel in een zaak verkopen **4** verraad plegen: *~ to* the enemy samenwerken met de vijand

sell-out 1 volle zaal, uitverkochte voorstelling **2** verraad^h

semblance 1 schijn, uiterlijk^h, vorm: *put on a ~ of* enthousiasm geestdriftig doen **2** gelijkenis **3** afbeelding, beeld^h, kopie ‖ *without a ~ of guilt* zonder ook maar een zweem van schuldgevoel

semen sperma^h, zaad^h

semester semester^h [university]

semicircle 1 halve cirkel **2** halve kring

semicircular halfrond

semicolon puntkomma^{+h}

semiconductor halfgeleider

semi-conscious halfbewust

¹**semi-detached** (n) halfvrijstaand huis^h, huis^h van twee onder een kap

²**semi-detached** (adj) halfvrijstaand

semi-final halve finale

seminal 1 sperma-; zaad- **2** embryonaal; [fig also] in wording **3** vruchtbaar [fig]: *a ~ mind* een oorspronkelijke geest

seminar 1 werkgroep, cursus **2** congres^h

seminary seminarie^h, kweekschool voor priesters

semi-skimmed halfvolle melk

Semite Semiet

Semitic Semitisch

senate 1 senaat, Amerikaanse Senaat **2** senaat, universitaire bestuursraad

senator senator, senaatslid^h, lid^h van de Amerikaanse Senaat

¹**send** (vb) bericht sturen, laten weten: *I sent to warn her* ik heb haar laten waarschuwen

²**send** (vb) **1** (ver)sturen, (ver)zenden **2** sturen, zenden; (doen) overbrengen [by extension]; dwingen tot: *~ to bed* naar bed sturen; *she ~s her love* je moet de groeten van haar hebben; *~ ahead* vooruit sturen; *~ in* a) inzenden, insturen [for evaluation]; b) indienen **3** teweegbrengen, veroorzaken: *the news sent us into deep distress* het nieuws bracht diepe droefenis bij ons teweeg **4** maken, doen worden: *this rattle ~s me crazy* ik

word gek van dat geratel **5** opwinden, meeslepen: *this music really ~s me* ik vind die muziek helemaal te gek ‖ ~ *packing* de laan uit sturen, afschepen

³send (vb) (uit)zenden: ~ *s.o. after her* stuur iem. achter haar aan; ~ *s.o. off the field* iem. uit het veld sturen

send down 1 naar beneden sturen; doen dalen [prices, temperature] **2** verwijderen (wegens wangedrag) [from university] **3** opsluiten [in prison]

sender afzender, verzender: *return to ~* retour afzender

send for 1 (schriftelijk) bestellen **2** (laten) waarschuwen, laten komen: ~ *help* hulp laten halen

¹send off (vb) een bestelbon opsturen: ~ *for* schriftelijk bestellen

²send off (vb) **1** versturen, op de post doen **2** op pad sturen, de deur uit laten gaan **3** wegsturen; [sport] uit het veld sturen

send-off uitgeleide^h, afscheid^h, het uitzwaaien: *give s.o. a ~* iem. uitzwaaien

send on 1 vooruitsturen, (alvast) doorsturen **2** doorsturen [mail]

send out 1 weg sturen, eruit sturen **2** uitstralen, afgeven; uitzenden [signal]

send up 1 opdrijven, omhoogstuwen, doen stijgen: ~ *prices* de prijzen opdrijven **2** parodiëren, de draak steken met **3** opsluiten [in prison]

send-up parodie, persiflage

Senegal Senegal

¹Senegalese (n) Senegalees, Senegalese

²Senegalese (adj) Senegalees

senile 1 ouderdoms- **2** seniel, afgetakeld

senility seniliteit

¹senior (n) **1** oudere, iem. met meer dienstjaren: *she is four years my ~, she is my ~ by four years* ze is vier jaar ouder dan ik **2** oudgediende, senior **3** laatstejaars **4** oudere leerling

²senior (adj) **1** oud, op leeftijd, bejaard, oudst(e): *a ~ citizen* een 65-plusser, een bejaarde **2** hooggeplaatst, hoofd-: *a ~ position* een leidinggevende positie **3** hoger geplaatst, ouder in dienstjaren **4** hoogst in rang **5** laatstejaars **6** ouderejaars **7** senior: *Jack Jones Senior* Jack Jones senior ‖ ~ *service* marine

senior high (school) laatste vier jaar van de middelbare school

seniority 1 (hogere) leeftijd **2** anciënniteit, aantal^h dienstjaren, voorrang op grond van dienstjaren (leeftijd): *their names were listed in the order of ~* hun namen waren gerangschikt op volgorde van het aantal dienstjaren

senior school middelbare school [for children of 14-17 years old]

sensation 1 gevoel^h, (zintuiglijke) gewaar-

wording, sensatie **2** sensatie, beroering: *cause* (or: *create*) *a ~* voor grote opschudding zorgen

sensational 1 sensationeel, opzienbarend, te gek, fantastisch **2** sensatie-, sensatiebelust

sensationalist sensatiebelust, sensatiezoekend

¹sense (n) **1** bedoeling, strekking **2** betekenis, zin: *in a ~* in zekere zin **3** (vaag) gevoel^h, begrip^h, (instinctief) besef^h: ~ *of duty* plichtsbesef^h, plichtsgevoel^h; ~ *of humour* gevoel voor humor **4** (zintuiglijk) vermogen^h, zin, zintuig^h: ~ *of smell* reukzin **5** (gezond) verstand^h, benul^h: *there was a lot of ~ in her words* er stak heel wat zinnigs in haar woorden **6** zin, nut^h: *what's the ~?* wat heeft het voor zin? **7** (groeps)mening, (algemene) stemming **8** (-s) positieven, gezond verstand^h: *bring s.o. to his ~s* a) iem. tot bezinning brengen; b) iem. weer bij bewustzijn brengen ‖ *make ~* a) zinnig zijn; b) ergens op slaan, steekhoudend zijn; *it just doesn't make ~* het klopt gewoon niet, het slaat gewoon nergens op; *make ~ of sth.* ergens uit wijs kunnen (worden); *talk ~* verstandig praten

²sense (vb) **1** (zintuiglijk) waarnemen, gewaar worden **2** zich (vaag) bewust zijn, voelen **3** begrijpen, door hebben: *at last he was beginning to ~ what the trouble was* eindelijk begon hij door te krijgen wat het probleem was

senseless 1 bewusteloos **2** gevoelloos: ~ *fingers* gevoelloze vingers **3** onzinnig, idioot: *a ~ waste of human lives* een zinloze verspilling van mensenlevens

sense organ zintuig^h

sensibility 1 (over)gevoeligheid [for impressions, art]: *offend s.o.'s sensibilities* iemands gevoelens kwetsen **2** lichtgeraaktheid **3** gevoel^h, gevoeligheid, waarnemingsvermogen^h, bewustzijn^h; erkenning [of problem]

sensible 1 verstandig, zinnig **2** praktisch; functioneel [of clothes etc] **3** merkbaar, waarneembaar **4** (+ to) gevoelig (voor), ontvankelijk (voor)

sensitive 1 gevoelig, ontvankelijk **2** precies; gevoelig [of instrument] **3** (fijn)gevoelig, smaakvol **4** lichtgeraakt **5** [photo] (licht)gevoelig **6** gevoelig, geheim: ~ *post* vertrouwenspost ‖ ~ *plant* a) gevoelige plant; b) kruidje-roer-mij-niet^h

sensitivity 1 gevoeligheid **2** (fijn)gevoeligheid, smaak

sensor aftaster, sensor, verklikker

sensory zintuiglijk

sensual sensueel, zinnelijk, wellustig

sensualism genotzucht, wellust

sensuous 1 zinnelijk, zintuiglijk **2** aangenaam, behaaglijk: *with ~ pleasure* vol behagen, behaaglijk

¹sentence (n) **1** (vol)zin: *complex* (or: *compound*) ~ samengestelde zin **2** vonnis^h, vonnissing, (rechterlijke) uitspraak, veroordeling, straf: *under* ~ *of death* ter dood veroordeeld

²sentence (vb) veroordelen, vonnissen: *be ~d to **pay** a fine* veroordeeld worden tot een geldboete

sententious moraliserend, prekerig

sentient (+ of) bewust (van)

sentiment 1 gevoel^h, mening, opvatting: *(those are)* **my** ~s exactly zo denk ik er ook over, precies wat ik wou zeggen **2** (geluk)wens **3** gevoel^h, gevoelens; stemming [also on Stock Exchange, market]; emotie, voorkeur: *be **swayed** by* ~ zich laten leiden door zijn gevoel

sentimental sentimenteel, (over)gevoelig: ~ *value* gevoelswaarde

sentimentality sentimentaliteit

sentry schildwacht: *stand* (or: *keep*) ~ op wacht staan

sepal blaadje^h van een bloemkelk

separable (af)scheidbaar, verdeelbaar: *in his poems form is not* ~ *from content* in zijn gedichten is de vorm niet los te zien van de inhoud

¹separate (adj) afzonderlijk, (af)gescheiden, apart, verschillend, alleenstaand: ~ *ownership* particulier eigendom(srecht); *keep* ~ *from* afgezonderd houden van

²separate (vb) **1** zich (van elkaar) afscheiden, zich afzonderen, zich verdelen, uiteenvallen: ~ *from* zich afscheiden van **2** scheiden, uit elkaar gaan

³separate (vb) afzonderen, losmaken, verdelen: *legally* ~d gescheiden van tafel en bed; *widely* ~d ver uit elkaar gelegen

separates afzonderlijk combineerbare kledingstukken

separation (af)scheiding, afzondering, afscheuring, verschil^h, onderscheid^h, het uiteengaan, vertrek^h, (tussen)ruimte, afstand: *judicial* (or: *legal*) ~ scheiding van tafel en bed

separation allowance alimentatie

separatist separatist, iem. die zich afscheidt; [pol] autonomist; nationalist

sepia sepia

September september

septic 1 (ver)rottings-: ~ *matter* etter **2** ontstoken, geïnfecteerd

sepulchral graf-, begrafenis-; [fig] somber; akelig: *in a* ~ *voice* met een grafstem

sepulchre graf^h, graftombe

sequel 1 gevolg^h, resultaat^h, afloop: *as a* ~ *to* als gevolg van **2** vervolg^h [to a book]; voortzetting

sequence 1 reeks [poems, plays]; opeenvolging, rij, volgorde: *the* ~ *of **events*** de loop der gebeurtenissen; *in* ~ op volgorde, de een

na de ander **2** episode, fragment^h, (onder)deel^h, (film)opname, scène

sequester 1 afzonderen, verborgen houden **2** in bewaring stellen, beslag leggen op

seraglio harem

¹Serb (n) Serviër, Servische

²Serb (adj) Servisch

Serbia Servië

¹Serbian (n) Serviër, Servische

²Serbian (adj) Servisch

serenade serenade(muziek)

serene sereen, helder: *a* ~ *summer **night*** een kalme zomeravond

serenity helderheid, kalmte, rust

serf lijfeigene, slaaf

serfdom lijfeigenschap^h, slavernij

sergeant 1 sergeant, wachtmeester **2** brigadier (van politie)

¹serial (n) **1** feuilleton^h, vervolgverhaal^h, (televisie)serie **2** seriepublicatie

²serial (adj) serieel, in serie, opeenvolgend: ~ *number* volgnummer^h, serienummer^h

serialize 1 als feuilleton publiceren **2** rangschikken, ordenen in reeksen

serial killer seriemoordenaar

series 1 reeks, serie, rij, verzameling, groep: *arithmetical* ~ rekenkundige reeks **2** [elec] serie(schakeling): *in* ~ in serie (geschakeld)

serious 1 ernstig, serieus: ~ *damage* aanzienlijke schade; *after* ~ *thought* na rijp beraad **2** oprecht, gemeend

seriously 1 ernstig, serieus, belangrijk, aanzienlijk: ~ *ill* ernstig ziek **2** echt, heus, zonder gekheid: *but* ~, *are you really thinking of moving?* maar serieus, ben je echt van plan te verhuizen?

seriousness ernst: *in all* ~ in alle ernst, zonder gekheid

sermon preek [also fig]; vermaning: *Sermon on the **Mount*** Bergrede

seropositive seropositief

serotonin serotonine^h

serpent 1 slang, serpent^h **2** onderkruiper

serpentine 1 slangachtig, slangen- **2** kronkelig

serrated zaagvormig, getand, gezaagd: *a* ~ *knife* een kartelmes

serum serum^h

servant 1 dienaar, bediende, (huis)knecht, dienstbode **2** (-s) personeel^h

¹serve (vb) **1** dienen, voorzien in, volstaan, vervullen: ~ *a **purpose*** een bepaald doel dienen; ~ *the **purpose** of* dienstdoen als **2** behandelen, bejegenen: *that* ~s *him **right!*** dat is zijn verdiende loon!, net goed! **3** ondergaan, vervullen, (uit)zitten: *he* ~d *ten **years** in prison* hij heeft tien jaar in de gevangenis gezeten **4** dagvaarden, betekenen: ~ *a **writ** on s.o.*, ~ *s.o. **with** a writ* iem. dagvaarden

²serve (vb) **1** dienen (bij), in dienst zijn van:

[fig] ~ two **masters** twee heren dienen **2** serveren, opdienen: ~ **dinner** het eten opdienen; ~ **at** table bedienen, opdienen **3** dienen, dienstdoen, helpen, baten: that **excuse** ~d him well dat smoesje is hem goed van pas gekomen; are you **being** ~d? wordt u al geholpen? **4** [sport] serveren, opslaan
serve out 1 verdelen, ronddelen **2** uitdienen, uitzitten
server 1 ober, kelner, serveerster **2** opscheplepel **3** dienblad[h] **4** [comp] server
servery 1 buffet[h] [in self-service restaurant] **2** doorgeefluik[h] [between kitchen and dining room]
[1]**service** (n) **1** dienst, (overheids)instelling, bedrijf[h]: secret ~ geheime dienst **2** krijgsmachtonderdeel[h] [army, navy or air force]: on (active) ~ in actieve dienst **3** hulp, bijstand, dienst(verlening): do s.o. a ~ iem. een dienst bewijzen **4** (kerk)dienst **5** verbinding; dienst [by bus, train or boat] **6** onderhoudsbeurt, onderhoud[h], service **7** servies[h] & nutsbedrijf[h] **9** [sport] opslag, service(beurt) **10** gasleiding, waterleiding [in house]; huisaansluiting **11** dienstbaarheid, dienst, het dienen, het dienstbaar zijn: in ~ in dienst [eg of bus or train] **12** nut[h], dienst: at your ~ tot uw dienst **13** bediening, service
[2]**service** (vb) **1** onderhouden, een (onderhouds)beurt geven **2** (be)dienen, voorzien van
serviceable 1 nuttig, bruikbaar, handig **2** sterk, stevig, duurzaam
service area wegrestaurant[h] [with filling station]
service charge 1 bedieningsgeld[h] **2** administratiekosten
service dog hulphond
service flat verzorgingsflat
serviceman militair, soldaat
service provider 1 dienstverlener **2** [comp] provider
service road ventweg, parallelweg
services wegrestaurant[h] (met benzinestation)
service station 1 benzinestation[h], pompstation[h] **2** wegrestaurant[h]
serviette servet(je)[h], vingerdoekje[h]
servile slaafs, onderdanig, kruiperig: ~ **imitation** slaafse navolging
servility slaafsheid, kruiperige houding
serving portie: three ~s of ice-cream drie porties ijs
servitude slavernij, onderworpenheid
sesame sesam(kruid[h]), sesamzaad[h] || Open ~! Sesam, open u!
session 1 zitting [court of law, administration, committee]; vergadering, sessie: secret ~ geheime zitting **2** zittingsperiode, zittingstijd **3** academiejaar[h], semester[h], halfjaar[h] **4** schooltijd **5** bijeenkomst, partij, ver-

gadering **6** (opname)sessie: recording ~ opnamesessie (in studio)
[1]**set** (n) **1** stel[h], span[h], servies[h]; set [pots, pans etc]; reeks: ~ of (false) **teeth** een (vals) gebit **2** kring, gezelschap[h], groep, kliek: the ~ de elite; the **smart** ~ de chic, de hogere standen (or: kringen) **3** toestel[h], radiotoestel[h], tv-toestel[h] **4** stek, loot, jonge plant **5** set, spel[h], partij **6** [maths] verzameling **7** vorm; houding [of head]; ligging [of hills]: the ~ of her **head** de houding van haar hoofd **8** toneelopbouw, scène, (film)decor[h]; [by extension] studiohal; set: on (the) ~ op de set, bij de (film)opname
[2]**set** (adj) **1** vast, bepaald, vastgesteld, stereotiep, routine-, onveranderlijk: ~ **phrase** stereotiepe uitdrukking; ~ **purpose** vast vooropgesteld doel **2** voorgeschreven; opgelegd [book, subject] **3** strak, onbeweeglijk; stijf [face]; koppig, hardnekkig: ~ in one's ways met vaste gewoonten; ~ **fair** a) bestendig [weather]; b) prettig, goed [prospect] **4** klaar, gereed: get ~, ready, steady, go op uw plaatsen, klaar voor de start, af; be all ~ **for** sth. (or: **to do** sth.) helemaal klaar zijn voor iets (or: om iets te doen) **5** volledig en tegen vaste prijs [meal in restaurant]: ~ **dinner** dagschotel, dagmenu[u] **6** geplaatst, gevestigd: eyes ~ deep in the head diepliggende ogen **7** vastbesloten: her mind is ~ **on** pleasure ze wil alleen plezier maken || ~ **square** tekendriehoek
[3]**set** (vb) **1** vast worden; stijf worden [of cement, jelly]; verharden, stollen, een vaste vorm aannemen; bestendig worden [of weather] **2** ondergaan [of sun, moon]: the sun **had** nearly ~ de zon was bijna onder **3** aan elkaar groeien [of broken leg]
[4]**set** (vb) **1** zetten, plaatsen, stellen, leggen, doen zitten: ~ a **trap** een val zetten; ~ **free** vrijlaten, bevrijden; ~ **pen to paper** beginnen te schrijven **2** gelijkzetten [clock, timepiece] **3** opleggen, opdragen, opgeven; geven [example]; stellen, opstellen; (samen)stellen [questions etc]: ~ s.o. a good **example** iem. het goede voorbeeld geven; ~ s.o. a **task** iem. een taak opleggen; ~ **to** work zich aan het werk zetten, beginnen te werken **4** bepalen [date]; voorschrijven; aangeven [size, pace, tone]; vaststellen: ~ the **fashion** de mode bepalen; ~ a **price** on sth. de prijs van iets bepalen **5** brengen, aanleiding geven tot, veroorzaken: that ~ me **thinking** dat bracht me aan het denken **6** stijf doen worden [cement, jelly etc] **7** instellen [camera, lens, appliance] **8** dekken [table]: ~ the **table** de tafel dekken **9** zetten [letters, text] **10** uitzetten [watch, nets]; posteren: ~ a **watch** een schildwacht uitzetten **11** zetten [broken leg]; bij elkaar voegen, samenvoegen **12** op muziek zetten [text]: ~ **to** music op muziek zetten **13** situe-

ren [story, play]: *the novel is ~ in the year* 2020 de roman speelt zich af in het jaar 2020 **14** vestigen [record]: *~ a new record* een nieuw record vestigen ‖ *~ (up)on s.o.* iem. aanvallen; *against that fact you must ~ that …* daartegenover moet je stellen dat …; *~ s.o. against s.o.* iem. opzetten tegen iem.; *~ s.o. beside s.o. else* iem. met iem. anders vergelijken

set about 1 beginnen (met/aan), aanpakken: *the next day they ~ cleaning the house* de dag daarop begonnen ze met het schoonmaken van het huis **2** aanvallen

set apart terzijde leggen, reserveren

set aside 1 terzijde zetten, reserveren; sparen [money]: *~ for* reserveren voor **2** buiten beschouwing laten, geen aandacht schenken aan: *setting aside the details* afgezien van de details

setback 1 inzinking **2** tegenslag, nederlaag

set back terugzetten, achteruitzetten: *the accident has set us back by about four weeks* door het ongeluk zijn we ongeveer vier weken achter (op schema) geraakt

set down 1 neerzetten **2** afzetten; laten afstappen [from vehicle] **3** neerschrijven, opschrijven

set in intreden [season, reaction]; invallen [darkness, thaw]; beginnen: *rain has ~* het is gaan regenen

¹set off (vb) zich op weg begeven, vertrekken: *~ in pursuit* de achtervolging inzetten

²set off (vb) **1** versieren **2** doen uitkomen [colours]: *she wore a dress that ~ her complexion quite well* ze droeg een jurk die haar teint goed deed uitkomen **3** doen ontbranden; tot ontploffing brengen [bomb] **4** doen opwegen, goedmaken: *~ against* doen opwegen tegen **5** doen [laugh, talk]; stimuleren: *set s.o. off laughing* iem. aan het lachen brengen **6** afzetten, afpassen: *a small area was ~ for the smokers* er was een kleine ruimte afgezet voor de rokers

set on ertoe brengen, aansporen

¹set out (vb) **1** zich op weg begeven, vertrekken: *~ for Paris* vertrekken met bestemming Parijs **2** zich voornemen, het plan opvatten

²set out (vb) **1** uitzetten, klaarzetten; opzetten [chessman]: *if you ~ the white pieces, I'll do the black ones* als jij de witte stukken opzet, doe ik de zwarte **2** tentoonstellen; uitstallen [goods] **3** verklaren, uiteenzetten

set point setpunt^h

set square tekendriehoek

sett 1 (dassen)burcht **2** vierkante straatkei

setting 1 ondergang [sun, moon] **2** stand; instelling [of instrument, machine] **3** omlijsting, achtergrond: *the story has its ~ in Sydney* het verhaal speelt zich af in Sydney **4** mon-

tering; aankleding [film, play]

settings instellingen; *see setting*

¹settle (vb) **1** gaan zitten, zich neerzetten, neerstrijken: *~ back in a chair* gemakkelijk gaan zitten in een stoel **2** neerslaan, bezinken [of dust, dregs] **3** zich vestigen, gaan wonen ‖ *~ in a)* zich installeren [in house]; *b)* zich inwerken; *~ for sth.* genoegen nemen met iets; *~ (down) to sth.* zich ergens op concentreren, zich ergens toe zetten

²settle (vb) **1** regelen, in orde brengen **2** vestigen [in place of residence, society] **3** koloniseren: *their forefathers ~d the land in 1716* hun voorvaderen koloniseerden het land in 1716 **4** zetten, plaatsen, leggen: *she ~d herself in the chair* zij nestelde zich in haar stoel **5** (voorgoed) beëindigen; beslissen [argument, doubts]; de doorslag geven: *that ~s it!* dat doet de deur dicht!, dat geeft de doorslag!; *let's ~ this once and for all* laten we dit nu eens en altijd regelen **6** schikken, bijleggen, tot een schikking komen ‖ *~ into* zich thuis doen voelen in; *~ on* vastzetten op

³settle (vb) **1** kalmeren, (doen) bedaren **2** opklaren [liquid]; helderder worden (maken) **3** (+ upon) overeenkomen (m.b.t.), een besluit nemen, afspreken: *~ (up)on a date* een datum vaststellen **4** betalen [eg bill]; voldoen, vereffenen: *~ a claim* schade uitbetalen; *~ up* verrekenen [among each other]; *~ (an account, old score) with s.o.* het iem. betaald zetten

settled vast, onwrikbaar; gevestigd [opinion]; bestendig [weather]; onveranderlijk

¹settle down (vb) **1** een vaste betrekking aannemen, zich vestigen **2** wennen, zich thuis gaan voelen, ingewerkt raken **3** (+ to) zich concentreren (op), zich toeleggen (op): *he finally settled down to his studies* eindelijk ging hij zich toeleggen op zijn studie **4** vast worden [of weather]

²settle down (vb) kalmeren, tot rust komen (brengen)

settlement 1 nederzetting, kolonie, groepje kolonisten, plaatsje^h **2** kolonisatie **3** schikking, overeenkomst **4** afrekening: *in ~ of* ter vereffening van

settler kolonist

set-to 1 vechtpartij **2** ruzie: *there was a bit of a ~ outside the pub* er ontstond ruzie buiten de kroeg

¹set up (vb) zich vestigen: *~ as a dentist* zich als tandarts vestigen

²set up (vb) **1** opzetten [eg tent]; opstellen, monteren, stichten; oprichten [school]; beginnen; aanstellen [committee]; opstellen [rules]; organiseren **2** aanheffen; verheffen [voice] **3** veroorzaken **4** er bovenop helpen, op de been helpen **5** vestigen: *set s.o. up in business* iem. in een zaak zetten **6** beramen [hold-up] **7** belazeren, de schuld in de schoenen schuiven

set-up 1 opstelling [at film shooting] **2** opbouw, organisatie

seven zeven

sevenfold 1 zevenvoudig **2** zevendelig

seven-league: ~ *boots* zevenmijlslaarzen

seventeen zeventien

seventeenth zeventiende

seventh zevende

seventieth zeventigste

seventy zeventig: *he is in his seventies* hij is in de zeventig

¹sever (vb) **1** breken, het begeven, losgaan **2** uiteen gaan, scheiden

²sever (vb) **1** afbreken: ~ *the rope* het touw doorsnijden **2** (af)scheiden: ~ *o.s. from* zich afscheiden van **3** verbreken [relationship etc]

several 1 verscheidene, enkele, een aantal (ervan): *she has written* ~ *books* ze heeft verscheidene boeken geschreven; ~ *of my friends* verscheidene van mijn vrienden **2** apart(e), respectievelijk(e), verschillend(e): *after their studies the students went their* ~ *ways* na hun studie gingen de studenten elk hun eigen weg

severally 1 afzonderlijk, hoofdelijk: *the partners are* ~ *liable* de vennoten zijn hoofdelijk aansprakelijk **2** elk voor zich, respectievelijk

severance 1 verbreking; opzegging [of relations] **2** scheiding, (ver)deling **3** ontslagʰ, verbreking van arbeidscontract

severe 1 streng, strikt **2** hevig, bar: ~ *conditions* barre omstandigheden **3** zwaar, moeilijk, ernstig: ~ *requirements* zware eisen ‖ *leave* (or: *let*) *sth. ~ly alone* ergens z'n handen niet aan willen vuilmaken

severity 1 strengheid, hardheid **2** hevigheid, barheid **3** soberheid, strakheid

sew naaien; hechten [wound]

sewage afvalwaterʰ, rioolwaterʰ: *raw* ~ ongezuiverd afvalwater

sewage works rioolzuiveringsinstallatie

¹sewer (n) rioolʰ; rioolbuis

²sewer (n) naaister

sewerage 1 riolering, rioolstelselʰ **2** (afval)waterafvoer

sewing naaiwerkʰ

sewing machine naaimachine

sew up 1 dichtnaaien, hechten **2** succesvol afsluiten, beklinken, regelen

¹sex (n) **1** geslachtʰ, sekse: *the second* ~ de tweede sekse, de vrouw(en) **2** seks, erotiek **3** seksuele omgang, geslachtsgemeenschap: *have* ~ *with s.o.* met iem. naar bed gaan, vrijen

²sex (vb) seksen, het geslacht vaststellen van

¹sexagenarian (n) zestigjarige, zestiger

²sexagenarian (adj) zestigjarig

sexism seksismeʰ, ongelijke behandeling in

verband met sekse

¹sexist (n) seksist

²sexist (adj) seksistisch

sexless 1 onzijdig, geslachtloos **2** niet opwindend

sex life sekslevenʰ

sex object 1 seksobjectʰ, lustobjectʰ **2** sekssymboolʰ

sex offender zedendelinquent

sextant sextant [navigation instrument]

sextortion seksuele afpersing via internet

sexual 1 seksueel, geslachts-: ~ *harassment* ongewenste intimiteiten [at work]; ~ *intercourse* geslachtsgemeenschap **2** geslachtelijk, m.b.t. het geslacht

sexuality seksualiteit

sex up [inform] [sth.] opleuken, oppimpen **2** [s.o.] opgeilen

sexy sexy, opwindend

sf *sciencefiction* sf

Sgt *sergeant*

sh sst

shabby 1 versleten, af(gedragen), kaal **2** sjofel, armoedig **3** min, gemeen: *what a* ~ *way to treat an old friend!* wat een laag-bijde-grondse manier om een oude vriend te behandelen!

shack 1 hut **2** hokʰ, keet, schuurtjeʰ

shacked up [inform] [roughly] samenwonend: *to be* ~ het bed delen

¹shackle (n) **1** (hand)boei, keten, kluister **2** (-s) belemmering **3** schakel, sluiting

²shackle (vb) **1** boeien, ketenen **2** koppelen, vastmaken **3** belemmeren, hinderen ‖ *be ~d with sth.* met iets opgezadeld zitten

shack up hokken, samenwonen, samenleven: ~ *together* (samen)hokken, samenwonen

¹shade (n) **1** schaduw, lommerʰ: *put s.o.* (*sth.*) *in the* ~ iem. (iets) overtreffen **2** schaduwplek(jeʰ) **3** schakering, nuance: ~*s of meaning* (betekenis)nuances **4** (zonne)schermʰ, (lampen)kap, zonneklep **5** schim, geest, spookʰ **6** tikkeltjeʰ, ietsjeʰ, beetjeʰ **7** (rol)gordijnʰ **8** (-s) duisternis, schemerduisterʰ **9** (-s) zonnebril

²shade (vb) **1** beschermen, beschutten; [fig] in de schaduw stellen: ~ *one's eyes* zijn hand boven de ogen houden **2** afschermen [light]; dimmen **3** arceren, schaduw aanbrengen in

³shade (vb) geleidelijk veranderen, (doen) overgaan ‖ ~ *away* (or: *off*) geleidelijk aan (laten) verdwijnen

shading arcering

¹shadow (n) **1** schaduw, duisterʰ, duisternis, schemerduisterʰ **2** schaduw(beeldʰ) [also fig]; silhouetʰ: *afraid of one's own* ~ zo bang als een wezel; *cast a* ~ *on sth.* een schaduw werpen op iets [also fig] **3** schaduwplek, schaduwhoek, arcering; schaduw [in painting] **4** iem. die schaduwt, spion, detective ‖

*he is the ~ of his former **self*** hij is bij lange na
niet meer wat hij geweest is; *without the ~ of
a **doubt*** zonder ook maar de geringste twijfel
²**shadow** (vb) schaduwen; volgen [by detec-
tive]
shadow-boxing het schaduwboksen
shadow cabinet schaduwkabinetʰ
shadowy 1 onduidelijk, vaag, schimmig
2 schaduwrijk, in schaduw gehuld
shady 1 schaduwrijk **2** onbetrouwbaar,
verdacht, louche
¹**shaft** (n) **1** schacht [of arrow, spear] **2** steel,
stok **3** lichtstraal, lichtbundel, bliksemstraal,
lichtflits **4** koker; schacht [lift, mine]
5 (drijf)as ‖ *get the ~* te grazen genomen
worden
²**shaft** (vb) te grazen nemen, belazeren
¹**shag** (n) **1** warboel, kluwenʰ **2** shag **3** [in-
form] wip, seks
²**shag** (vb) [inform] neuken; naaien, wippen
shagged (out) bekaf, uitgeteld
shaggy 1 harig, ruigbehaard **2** ruig, wild,
woest
shah sjah
¹**shake** (n) **1** het schudden, handdruk: *he said
no with a ~ of the **head*** hij schudde (van) nee
2 milkshake **3** ogenblikjeʰ, momentjeʰ: *in
two ~s (of a lamb's tail)* zo, direct, in een seconde
²**shake** (vb) **1** schudden, schokken, beven,
(t)rillen: *~ with laughter* schudden van het lachen **2** wankelen **3** de hand geven: *~ (on it)!*
geef me de vijf!, hand erop!
³**shake** (vb) **1** doen schudden, schokken,
doen beven **2** (uit)schudden, zwaaien, heen
en weer schudden: *~ dice* dobbelstenen
schudden; *~ off* a) (van zich) afschudden;
b) [also fig] ontsnappen aan; *~ before **use*** (or:
using) schudden voor gebruik **3** geven;
schudden [hand] **4** schokken, verontrusten,
overstuur maken: *mother was tremendously
~n by Paul's **death*** moeder was enorm getroffen door de dood van Paul **5** aan het
wankelen brengen [fig]; verzwakken, verminderen: *these stories have ~n the firm's credit*
deze verhalen hebben de firma in diskrediet
gebracht
shakedown afpersing, geld-uit-de-zak-
klopperij
¹**shake down** (vb) **1** gewend raken, ingewerkt raken **2** goed gaan lopen, werken,
goed afgesteld zijn
²**shake down** (vb) **1** (af)schudden, uitschudden **2** (op de grond) uitspreiden **3** afpersen, geld uit de zak kloppen
shake up 1 (door elkaar) schudden; hutselen **2** wakker schudden; opschrikken; overstuur raken **3** reorganiseren, orde op zaken
stellen
shake-up radicale reorganisatie ‖ *they need*

a thorough ~ ze moeten eens flink wakker
geschud worden
shaky 1 beverig, trillerig, zwak(jes) **2** wankel [also fig]; gammel, onbetrouwbaar: *my
Swedish is rather ~* mijn Zweeds is nogal
zwak
shale gas schaliegasʰ
shall 1 zullen: *how ~ I recognize her?* hoe zal
ik haar herkennen? **2** [command; also promise, threat, plan etc] zullen, moeten: *you ~ do
as I tell you* doe wat ik zeg **3** zullen, moeten:
*~ I **open** the window?* zal ik het raam openzetten?
shallot sjalot
shallow 1 ondiep: *~ dish* plat bord **2** licht;
niet diep [of breathing] ‖ *~ **arguments*** oppervlakkige argumenten
shallows ondiepte, ondiepe plaats, wadʰ
¹**sham** (n) **1** komedie, schijn(vertoning), bedrogʰ: *the **promise** was a ~* de belofte was
maar schijn **2** imitatie **3** bedrieger, hypocriet
²**sham** (adj) **1** namaak-, imitatie-, vals
2 schijn-, gesimuleerd, pseudo-: *a ~ **fight*** een
schijngevecht
³**sham** (vb) voorwenden, doen als of: *~ illness* doen alsof je ziek bent
¹**shamble** (n) schuifelgang(etjeʰ)
²**shamble** (vb) schuifelen; sloffen [also fig]: *a
shambling **gait*** een sukkelgangetje
shambles janboel, troep, bende, zooi: *the
house is a **complete** ~* het huis is een echte
varkensstal
¹**shame** (n) **1** schande, schandaalʰ **2** zonde:
what a ~! het is een schande!, wat jammer!
3 schaamte(gevoelʰ): *have no **sense** of ~* zich
nergens voor schamen **4** schande, smaad,
vernedering: *put to ~* a) in de schaduw stellen; b) beschaamd maken (or: doen staan); *to
my ~* tot mijn (grote) schande; *~ **on** you!*
schaam je!, je moest je schamen!; [to speak-
er] *~!* schandalig!, hoe durft u!
²**shame** (vb) **1** beschamen: *it ~s me to say this*
ik schaam me ervoor dit te (moeten) zeggen
2 schande aandoen, te schande maken **3** in
de schaduw stellen, overtreffen: *your translation ~s all the other **attempts*** jouw vertaling
stelt alle andere pogingen in de schaduw
shamefaced 1 beschaamd **2** beschroomd
shameful 1 beschamend **2** schandelijk,
schandalig
shameless schaamteloos, onbeschaamd
shaming [media] iem. fel bekritiseren of
belachelijk maken
¹**shampoo** (n) shampoo
²**shampoo** (vb) shamponeren; met shampoo
reinigen [car, carpet]
shamrock klaver
shandy shandy
shank 1 (onder)beenʰ, scheenbeenʰ, schenkel **2** schacht [of anchor, column, key] **3** steel
shanks'(s) pony: *go on* (or: *ride*) *shanks'(s)*

pony met de benenwagen gaan

shanty 1 barak, hut, keet **2** zeemansliedje[h]

shanty town sloppenwijk, barakkenkamp[h]

¹shape (n) **1** vorm, gestalte, gedaante, verschijning: *take* ~ (vaste/vastere) vorm aannemen; *in the* ~ *of* in de vorm van **2** bakvorm, gietvorm, model[h], sjabloon[+h] **3** (goede) conditie, (goede) toestand, vorm: *in bad* (or: *good*) ~ in slechte (or: goede) conditie ‖ [+ negation] *in any* ~ *or form* in welke vorm dan ook, van welke aard dan ook; *knock* (or: *lick*) *sth. into* ~ iets fatsoeneren

²shape (vb) (also + up) zich ontwikkelen, zich vormen, vorm aannemen: *we'll see how things* ~ *(up)* we zullen zien hoe de dingen zich ontwikkelen

³shape (vb) **1** vormen, maken, ontwerpen: ~*d like a pear* in de vorm van een peer, peervormig **2** bepalen, vormen, vorm (richting) geven aan: *his theories, which* ~*d mathematical thinking in the 1980s* zijn theorieën, die het wiskundig denken in de jaren tachtig richting gaven

shapeless 1 vorm(e)loos, ongevormd **2** misvormd, vervormd

shapely goedgevormd, welgevormd

¹share (n) **1** aandeel[h], effect[h] **2** (onder)deel[h], aandeel[h], part[h], gedeelte[h], portie: *get one's fair* ~ zijn rechtmatig (aan)deel krijgen ‖ *go* ~*s (with s.o. in sth.)* de kosten (van iets met iem.) delen

²share (vb) **1** (ver)delen: ~ *a bedroom* een slaapkamer delen; ~ *(out) among* (or: *between*) verdelen onder (or: over) **2** deelgenoot maken van: ~ *a secret with s.o.* iem. deelgenoot maken van een geheim

³share (vb) delen, deelnemen: ~ *and share alike* eerlijk delen

shareholder aandeelhouder

share-out verdeling

shareware shareware

shark 1 haai **2** afzetter, woekeraar

¹sharp (n) (noot met) kruis[h] ‖ *F* ~ f-kruis, fa kruis, fis

²sharp (adj) **1** scherp, spits, puntig: *a* ~ *angle* een scherpe hoek **2** schril: *a* ~ *contrast* een schril contrast **3** abrupt, plotseling, steil: *a* ~ *fall* (or: *rise*) *in prices* een scherpe daling (or: stijging) van de prijzen **4** bijtend, doordringend, snijdend: ~ *frost* bijtende vrieskou **5** scherp, pikant, sterk: *a* ~ *flavour* een scherpe smaak **6** hevig, krachtig: *a* ~ *blow* een hevige klap **7** streng, vinnig: *a* ~ *reproof* een scherp verwijt **8** scherpzinnig, bijdehand, pienter, vlug: *keep a* ~ *look-out* scherp uitkijken; *be too* ~ *for s.o.* iem. te slim af zijn **9** geslepen, sluw: *a* ~ *salesman* een gehaaid verkoper **10** stevig, flink, vlug: *at a* ~ *pace* in een stevig tempo ‖ ~ *practice* oneerlijke praktijken, een vuil zaakje

³sharp (adv) **1** stipt, precies, klokslag: *three*

o'clock ~ klokslag drie uur **2** opeens, plotseling, scherp: *turn* ~ *right* scherp naar rechts draaien ‖ *look* ~*!* schiet op, haast je!

sharpen scherp(er) worden (maken), (zich) (ver)scherpen, slijpen

sharpener (punten)slijper

sharper afzetter, oplichter

sharp-eyed scherpziend, waakzaam, alert

sharpish snel, (nu) meteen, direct

sharpshooter scherpschutter

¹shatter (vb) uiteenspatten, barsten, in stukken (uiteen)vallen

²shatter (vb) **1** aan gruzelementen slaan, (compleet) vernietigen: *his death* ~*ed our hopes* zijn dood ontnam ons alle hoop **2** schokken, in de war brengen: ~*ed nerves* geschokte zenuwen **3** afmatten, totaal uitputten: *I feel completely* ~*ed* ik ben doodop

¹shave (n) scheerbeurt: *I badly need a* ~ ik moet me nodig weer eens scheren; *a close* ~ op het nippertje

²shave (vb) **1** (zich) scheren **2** (also + off) (af)schaven, afraspen **3** scheren langs, schampen, rakelings gaan langs

shaver scheerapparaat[h]

shaving 1 het scheren, scheerbeurt **2** schijfje[h]: ~*s* spaanders; schaafkrullen

shawl sjaal(tje[h]), omslagdoek, hoofddoek

she zij, ze; [in some constructions] die; dat, het ‖ *is it a he or a* ~? is het een jongen of een meisje?

sheaf 1 schoof **2** bundel: *he produced a* ~ *of papers from a plastic bag* hij haalde uit een plastic tasje een stapel papieren tevoorschijn

shear 1 (af)scheren: ~*ing sheep* schapen scheren **2** ontdoen, plukken, villen: *shorn of* ontdaan van

shears (grote) schaar, heggenschaar: *a pair of* ~ een schaar

sheath 1 schede, (bescherm)huls, koker **2** nauwaansluitende jurk **3** condoom[h], kapotje[h]

sheathe in de schede steken, van een omhulsel voorzien: *he carefully* ~*d the knife* hij stak het mes zorgvuldig in de schede

sheathing 1 (beschermende) bekleding, omhulling, mantel **2** bekleding

sheath knife steekmes[h]

shebang zootje[h], zaak(je[h]), santenkraam: *the whole* ~ het hele zootje

¹shed (n) schuur(tje[h]), keet, loods

²shed (vb) **1** afwerpen, verliezen, afleggen, afschudden: *the tree had* ~ *its leaves* de boom had zijn bladeren laten vallen; *the lorry* ~ *its load* de vrachtwagen verloor zijn lading **2** storten, vergieten: ~ *hot tears* hete tranen schreien

she-devil duivelin [also fig]

sheen glans, schittering, (weer)schijn

sheep schaap[h] [also fig]; onnozel kind[h], gedwee persoon: *the black* ~ het zwarte schaap

|| *separate the ~ and the* **goats** de goeden van de slechten scheiden, het koren van het kaf scheiden

sheepdog (schaap)herdershond [collie]

sheepfold schaapskooi

sheepish verlegen, onnozel, dom

¹**sheer** (adj) **1** dun, doorschijnend, transparant: *~ nylon* dun nylon **2** erg steil, loodrecht **3** volkomen, je reinste: *that's ~ nonsense* dat is klinkklare onzin!

²**sheer** (vb) [shipp] scherp uitwijken, zwenken || *~ off* uit 't roer lopen; [inform] 'm smeren; *~ away from* mijden

sheet 1 (bedden)laken^h: *fitted ~* hoeslaken^h; *between the ~s* in bed, tussen de lakens **2** blad^h; vel^h [paper] **3** plaat: *a ~ of glass* een glasplaat, een stuk glas **4** gordijn^h, muur, vlaag: *a ~ of flame* een vuurzee

sheet feeder papierinvoer

sheet ice 1 ijs^h, ijslaag [on water] **2** ijzel

sheeting 1 lakenstof^h **2** bekleding(smateriaal^h)

sheet iron bladstaal^h, plaatijzer^h

sheet lightning weerlicht^h, bliksem

sheet music bladmuziek

sheik(h) sjeik

shelf 1 (leg)plank, boekenplank **2** (rots)richel || *be (put, left) on the ~* **a)** afgeschreven worden, in onbruik raken, afgedankt worden; **b)** blijven zitten, niet meer aan een man raken [of woman]

shelf life houdbaarheid: *most dairy products have a limited ~* de meeste zuivelproducten zijn beperkt houdbaar

shelfload: *~s of reports* planken vol rapporten

¹**shell** (n) **1** geraamte^h [of bldg]; skelet^h; romp [of ship]; chassis^h **2** deegbakje^h, pasteikorst **3** huls, granaat^h, patroon^h **4** hard omhulsel^h, schelp, slakkenhuis^h, dop, schaal, schulp: *come out of one's ~* loskomen, ontdooien

²**shell** (vb) **1** van zijn schil ontdoen, schillen, doppen, pellen **2** beschieten, onder vuur nemen, bombarderen

shellfish schaaldier^h, schelpdier^h

shell out dokken, neertellen, ophoesten

shellproof bomvrij

¹**shelter** (n) **1** schuilgelegenheid, schuilkelder, bushokje^h, tramhuisje^h **2** schuilplaats, toevluchtsoord^h, tehuis^h, asiel^h: *~ for battered women* opvang(te)huis voor mishandelde vrouwen **3** (+ from) beschutting (tegen), bescherming: *give ~* onderdak verlenen

²**shelter** (vb) (+ from) schuilen (voor/tegen)

³**shelter** (vb) **1** (+ from) beschutten (tegen), beschermen **2** huisvesten, onderdak verlenen

sheltered accommodation woon-zorgcomplex^h

¹**shelve** (vb) geleidelijk aflopen [of bottom]; glooien, (zacht) hellen

²**shelve** (vb) **1** op een plank zetten **2** op de lange baan schuiven, opschorten: *the plan has been ~d* het plan is op de lange baan geschoven, het plan is in de ijskast gezet

shenanigan 1 trucje^h, foefje^h **2** kattenkwaad^h, bedriegerij

¹**shepherd** (n) (schaap)herder

²**shepherd** (vb) hoeden, leiden, in de gaten houden

shepherdess herderin

shepherd's pie gehakt met een korst van aardappelpuree

sherbet [Am] sorbet

sheriff sheriff

sherry sherry

¹**shield** (n) **1** schild^h **2** beveiliging, bescherming

²**shield** (vb) (+ from) beschermen (tegen), in bescherming nemen

¹**shift** (n) **1** verschuiving, verandering **2** ploeg [workmen] **3** werktijd, arbeidsduur **4** redmiddel^h, hulpmiddel^h || *make ~ without* het stellen zonder

²**shift** (vb) **1** van plaats veranderen, zich verplaatsen, schuiven: *~ing sands* drijfzand **2** wisselen, veranderen: *the scene ~s* de achtergrond van het verhaal verandert **3** zich redden, zich behelpen, het klaarspelen: *~ for o.s.* het zelf klaarspelen

³**shift** (vb) **1** verplaatsen, verschuiven, verzetten: *~ the blame onto* de schuld schuiven op **2** verwisselen, verruilen, veranderen; schakelen [acceleration]: *~ one's ground* plotseling een ander standpunt innemen

shift key hoofdlettertoets

shiftless niet vindingrijk, inefficiënt, onbeholpen

shift work ploegendienst

shifty niet rechtdoorzee, stiekem, onbetrouwbaar

Shiite sjiiet

shilling shilling

shilly-shally dubben, weifelen, aarzelen

¹**shimmer** (n) flikkering, flauw schijnsel^h

²**shimmer** (vb) glinsteren, flakkeren

¹**shin** (n) scheen: *Joe got kicked on the ~s during the match* Joe werd tijdens de wedstrijd tegen zijn schenen geschopt

²**shin** (vb) klauteren; klimmen [using hands and feet]: *~ up a tree* in een boom klimmen

shinbone scheenbeen^h

shindy herrie, tumult^h, opschudding: *kick up a ~* herrie schoppen

¹**shine** (n) **1** schijn(sel^h), licht^h, uitstraling **2** glans, schittering: *take the ~ out of* van zijn glans beroven, maken dat de aardigheid af gaat van **3** poetsbeurt; het poetsen [of shoes] || *take a ~ to s.o.* iem. zomaar aardig vinden

²**shine** (vb) **1** glanzen, glimmen, blinken

2 schitteren, uitblinken: ~ *out* duidelijk naar voren komen

³shine (vb) poetsen [shoes]

⁴shine (vb) schijnen, lichten, gloeien: *he shone his **light** in my face* hij scheen met zijn lantaarn in mijn gezicht

shingle 1 dakspaan, panlat **2** [Am] naambordʰ van arts e.d.: *hang out one's ~* zich vestigen als arts e.d. **3** kiezelʰ, grindʰ, kiezelstrandʰ **4** (-s) gordelroos

shiny glanzend, glimmend

¹ship (n) **1** schipʰ, vaartuigʰ: *on **board** ~* aan boord; [fig] *that ~ has **sailed*** dat is een gepasseerd station, die kans is voorbij **2** vliegtuigʰ, kist **3** ruimteschipʰ

²ship (vb) **1** verschepen, (per schip) verzenden (vervoeren): *~ **off*** (or: *out*) verschepen **2** aan boord nemen, laden **3** binnenkrijgen: *~ **water*** water maken ‖ *~ **off*** wegsturen, wegzenden

shipboard scheepsboordʰ: *on ~* aan boord

shipbuilding scheepsbouw

shipload scheepslading, scheepsvracht

shipmate scheepsmaat, medebemanningslidʰ

shipment 1 zending, vracht, scheepslading **2** vervoerʰ [not only by ship]

shipowner reder

shipper expediteur, verzender

shipping 1 verscheping, verzending **2** scheepvaart

shipping company scheepvaartmaatschappij

shipshape netjes, in orde, keurig

¹shipwreck (n) schipbreuk; [fig] ondergang; mislukking

²shipwreck (vb) schipbreuk (doen) lijden, (doen) mislukken

shipyard scheeps(timmer)werf

shire graafschapʰ

¹shirk (vb) zich drukken

²shirk (vb) zich onttrekken aan

shirt overhemdʰ ‖ *keep one's ~ on* zich gedeisd houden; *put one's ~ on sth.* al zijn geld op iets zetten [horses]

shirtsleeve hemdsmouw: *in one's ~s* in hemdsmouwen

shirty nijdig, kwaad, geërgerd

¹shit (n) **1** stront, kak, poep, het poepen: *have a ~* gaan kakken **2** rommel, rotzooi **3** zeurkous **4** gezeikʰ, gekletsʰ, onzin **5** hasj ‖ *~ **happens*** dat soort dingen gebeuren nu eenmaal

²shit (vb) [vulg] schijten, poepen

³shit (vb) schijten op: *~ o.s.* het in zijn broek doen [also fig]

shitload [vulg] enorme hoeveelheid: *a ~ of money* een smak geld

shitstorm [vulg] **1** rotsituatie **2** [media] commotie: *his Twitter message **caused** a ~* zijn Twitterbericht leidde tot enorme commotie

shitty [vulg] **1** lullig **2** rot-

¹shiver (n) rilling [also fig]; siddering, gevoelʰ van angst (afkeer): *give s.o. the ~s* iem. de rillingen geven

²shiver (vb) rillen [with fear, cold]; sidderen

shivery 1 rillerig, beverig **2** kil [of weather]

shoal 1 ondiepte **2** zandbank **3** menigte, troep; school [of fish]

¹shock (n) **1** aardschok **2** dikke bosʰ [of hair] **3** schok, schrik, (onaangename) verrassing: *come **upon** s.o. **with** a ~* een (grote) schok zijn voor iem. **4** (elektrische) schok **5** shock: *in a **state** of ~* in shocktoestand

²shock (vb) een schok veroorzaken

³shock (vb) **1** schokken, choqueren, laten schrikken: *be ~ed **at*** (or: *by*) geschokt zijn door **2** een schok geven [also elec]; een shock veroorzaken bij

shocking 1 stuitend, schokkend, weerzinwekkend **2** vreselijk, erg: *~ **weather*** rotweerʰ

shockproof schokvast

shock therapy shocktherapie

shock wave schokgolf

shoddy prullig, niet degelijk

shoe 1 schoen **2** hoefijzerʰ **3** remschoen, remblokʰ ‖ *know where the ~ **pinches*** weten waar de schoen wringt, weten waar de pijn zit; *put o.s. in s.o.'s ~s* zich in iemands positie verplaatsen

shoehorn schoenlepel

shoelace (schoen)veter

shoemaker schoenmaker

shoe polish schoensmeer⁺ʰ

shoestring 1 (schoen)veter **2** (te) klein budgetʰ: *on a ~* met erg weinig geld

¹shoo (vb) ks(t) roepen, wegjagen: *~ sth. away* (or: *off*) iets wegjagen

²shoo (int) ks(t)

¹shoot (n) **1** (jonge) spruit, loot, scheut **2** jacht(partij)

²shoot (vb) **1** snel bewegen, (weg)schieten, voortschieten: *~ **ahead*** vooruitschieten **2** schieten [with weapon]: *~ **at*** (or: *for*) a) schieten op; b) (zich) richten op **3** afgaan [of weapon] **4** steken [of pain, wound]: *the pain shot **through*** (or: *up*) *his arm* een stekende pijn ging door zijn arm **5** uitlopen, ontspruiten **6** [sport] (op doel) schieten **7** plaatjes schieten, foto's nemen, filmen ‖ *~!* zeg op!, zeg het maar!

³shoot (vb) **1** (af)schieten [bullet, arrow etc]; afvuren [also fig; questions etc]: *~ **down*** neerschieten; [fig] afkeuren; *~ **off*** a) afschieten, afsteken [fireworks]; b) afvuren [gun] **2** jagen (op) **3** doen bewegen; schuiven [bolt]; spuiten [drugs] **4** (naar doel) schieten [ball]; schieten **5** snel passeren: *he shot the traffic **lights*** hij ging met hoge snelheid door de verkeerslichten **6** schieten [pictures]; opnemen [film] **7** spelen [billiards etc]

sho͟oter 1 schutter **2** [inform] vuurwapen^h **3** [sport] schutter

¹sho͟oting (n) **1** jacht **2** schietpartij **3** opname [film, sequence]

²sho͟oting (adj) **1** schietend **2** stekend: ~ *pains* pijnscheuten ‖ ~ *star* vallende ster

sho͟oting gallery schietbaan

sho͟oting match schietwedstrijd: *the whole* ~ het hele zaakje

¹shoot o͟ut (vb) naar buiten schieten: *the branches are beginning to* ~ de takken beginnen al uit te schieten

²shoot o͟ut (vb) een vuurgevecht leveren over: *they're going to shoot it out* ze gaan het uitvechten (met de revolver)

sho͟ot-out gevecht^h [with small arms]

¹shoot u͟p (vb) omhoog schieten [of plants, children]; snel groeien [of temperature, prices]

²shoot u͟p (vb) kapot schieten, overhoop schieten

¹shop (n) **1** winkel, zaak: *mind the* ~ de winkel runnen; [fig] de touwtjes in handen hebben **2** werkplaats, atelier^h **3** werk^h, zaken, beroep^h: *set up* ~ een zaak opzetten; *talk* ~ over zaken praten ‖ *all over the* ~ door elkaar, her en der verspreid

²shop (vb) winkelen: ~ *around* rondkijken, zich oriënteren (alvorens te kopen) [also fig]

³shop (vb) verlinken [to police]

shopaho͟lic koopziek persoon: *he's a* ~ hij is koopziek

shop assi͟stant winkelbediende

sho͟pbot prijsvergelijker

shop flo͟or (the) **1** werkplaats, werkvloer **2** arbeiders

sho͟pkeeper winkelier

sho͟plifter winkeldief

sho͟pper iem. die winkelt: *the* ~s het winkelpubliek

sho͟pping boodschappen, het boodschappen doen: *Mary always does her* ~ *in Leeds* Mary doet haar boodschappen altijd in Leeds

sho͟pping arcade (overdekte) winkelgalerij

sho͟pping bag boodschappentas

sho͟pping cart winkelwagentje^h

sho͟pping street winkelstraat

shop-so͟iled minder geworden [of goods, because they have lain too long; also fig]; smoezelig

shop ste͟ward vakbondsvertegenwoordiger

sho͟ptalk gepraat^h over het werk

sho͟pwalker (afdelings)chef

shop wi͟ndow etalage

¹shore (n) **1** kust; oever [of lake]: *off the* ~ voor de kust; *on* ~ aan (de) wal, op het land **2** steunbalk

²shore (vb) [also fig] steunen, schragen: ~ *up*

(onder)steunen

sho͟reline waterlijn, oever, kustlijn

¹short (n) **1** korte (voor)film **2** borrel **3** (-s) korte broek, onderbroek

²short (adj) **1** kort, klein, beknopt: ~ *and sweet* kort en bondig; *little* ~ *of* weinig minder dan, bijna; ~ *for* een afkorting van; *in* ~ in het kort **2** kort(durend): *(at)* ~ *notice* (op) korte termijn; ~ *order* snelbuffet^h; *in* ~ *order* onmiddellijk; *in the* ~ *run* op korte termijn; *make* ~ *work of* snel een einde maken aan **3** te kort, onvoldoende, karig, krap: ~ *of breath* kortademig; ~ *change* te weinig wisselgeld; ~ *of money* krap bij kas; *in* ~ *supply* schaars, beperkt leverbaar; ~ *weight* ondergewicht^h; *(be)* ~ *of* (or: *on*) tekort (hebben) aan **4** kortaf, bits **5** bros; kruimelig [eg dough] **6** onverdund [hard liquor]: *a* ~ *drink* (or: *one*) een borrel ‖ ~ *circuit* kortsluiting; ~ *temper* drift(igheid)

³short (adv) **1** niet (ver) genoeg: *four inches* ~ vier inches te kort; *come* (or: *fall*) ~ tekortschieten; [fig] *cut s.o.* ~ iem. onderbreken **2** plotseling: *stop* ~ plotseling ophouden; *be taken* (or: *caught*) ~ nodig moeten ‖ *sell s.o.* ~ iem. tekortdoen; *nothing* ~ *of* a) slechts, alleen maar; b) niets minder dan; ~ *of* behalve, zonder

sho͟rtage gebrek^h, tekort^h, schaarste

sho͟rtbread zandkoek

sho͟rtcake 1 theebeschuit^h **2** [Am] zandgebak^h

short-cha͟nge 1 te weinig wisselgeld geven aan: *be* ~*d* te weinig (wisselgeld) terugkrijgen **2** afzetten

¹short-ci͟rcuit (vb) kortsluiting veroorzaken

²short-ci͟rcuit (vb) **1** kortsluiten **2** verkorten [procedure etc]; vereenvoudigen

sho͟rtcoming tekortkoming

short cu͟t korte(re) weg, sluiproute

sho͟rten verkorten: ~*ed form* verkorting

sho͟rtfall tekort^h

sho͟rthand stenografie, steno^{+h}

short-ha͟nded met te weinig personeel

sho͟rtish vrij kort, aan de korte kant

¹sho͟rtlist (n) aanbevelingslijst [of applicants, candidates]; shortlist

²sho͟rtlist (vb) voordragen, op de voordracht plaatsen, nomineren

short-li͟ved kortdurend, kortlevend

sho͟rtly 1 spoedig, binnenkort, kort: ~ *after* … korte tijd na …; ~ *afterwards* korte tijd later **2** kortaf

short-si͟ghted 1 bijziend **2** kortzichtig

short-te͟mpered opvliegend

short-te͟rm op korte termijn, kortetermijn-: ~ *memory* kortetermijngeheugen^h

short-wa͟ve kortegolf-

short-wi͟nded 1 kortademig **2** kortdurend

sho͟rty [inform] kleintje^h

¹shot (n) **1** schot^h [also sport]; worp, stoot

2 (snedige) opmerking **3** gok, poging: *it's a long ~, but certainly worth trying* het is een hele gok, maar zeker de moeite van het proberen waard; *have* (or: *make*) *a ~ (at sth.)* (ergens) een slag (naar) slaan **4** [photo] opname, kiekje[h] **5** injectie, shot **6** [athletics] (stoot)kogel **7** borrel **8** lading [of firearm]; schroot[h] || *~ in the arm* **a)** stimulans, injectie; **b)** borrel(tje); *a ~ across the bows* een schot voor de boeg, waarschuwing; *a ~ in the dark* een slag in de lucht; *call the ~s* de leiding hebben, het voor het zeggen hebben; *(do sth.) like a ~* onmiddellijk (iets doen)

²**shot** (adj) doorweven, vol: *~ (through) with* doorspekt met || *be ~ of* klaar zijn met, af zijn van

¹**shotgun** (n) (jacht)geweer[h]

²**shotgun** (adj) gedwongen: *~ wedding* (or: *marriage*) moetje[h]

should zou(den), zou(den) moeten, moest(en), mochten: *~ you need any help, please ask the staff* mocht u hulp nodig hebben, wendt u zich dan tot het personeel; *why ~ I listen to him?* waarom zou ik naar hem luisteren?; *the teacher told Sheila that she ~ be more careful* de docent zei tegen Sheila dat zij voorzichtiger moest zijn; *he hoped that he ~ be accepted* hij hoopte dat hij aangenomen zou worden; *if Sheila came, I ~ come too* als Sheila kwam, dan kwam ik ook; *it ~ be easy for you* het moet voor jou gemakkelijk zijn; *yes, I ~ love to* ja, dat zou ik echt graag doen; *I suggest that we ~ leave* ik stel voor dat wij naar huis (zouden) gaan; [sometimes untranslated] *it's surprising he ~ be thought so attractive* het is verbazingwekkend dat hij zo aantrekkelijk wordt gevonden

¹**shoulder** (n) **1** schouder: *stand head and ~s above* met kop en schouders uitsteken boven [also fig] **2** (weg)berm: *hard ~* vluchtstrook **3** schoft [of animal] || *put* (or: *set*) *one's ~ to the wheel* zijn schouders ergens onder zetten, ergens hard aan werken; *rub ~s with* omgaan met; *(straight) from the ~* op de man af, recht voor z'n raap

²**shoulder** (vb) **1** op zich nemen, op zijn schouders nemen: *~ a great burden* (or: *responsibility*) een zware last (or: verantwoording) op zich nemen **2** duwen, (met de schouders) dringen: *he ~ed his way through the crowd* hij baande zich een weg door de menigte

shoulder blade schouderblad[h]

shoulder pad schoudervulling

¹**shout** (n) schreeuw, kreet, gil: *~ of joy* vreugdekreet

²**shout** (vb) schreeuwen, (uit)roepen, brullen, gillen: *~ o.s. hoarse* zich schor schreeuwen; *the audience ~ed down the speaker* het publiek joelde de spreker uit; *~ for joy* het uitroepen van vreugde

shout-out groet: *I want to give a ~ to …* ik wil de groeten doen aan …

¹**shove** (n) duw, zet, stoot

²**shove** (vb) (weg)duwen, dringen (tegen), een zet geven, stoppen, leggen: *~ along* heen en weer duwen, vooruitdringen; *~ it in the drawer* stop het in de la || *~ off* **a)** afschuiven; **b)** afduwen [in boat]; *let's ~ off* laten we er vandoor gaan

¹**shovel** (n) **1** schop, spade, schep **2** schoep [of machine] **3** laadschop

²**shovel** (vb) (op)scheppen, schuiven, opruimen (met een schep): *~ food into one's mouth* eten in zijn mond proppen; *~ a path through the snow* een pad graven door de sneeuw

¹**show** (n) **1** vertoning, show, uitzending, (televisie)programma[h], concert[h], opvoering: *a ~ in the theatre* een toneelopvoering **2** spektakel(stuk)[h], grootse vertoning: *a ~ of force* (or: *strength*) een machtsvertoon; *make a ~ of one's learning* te koop lopen met zijn geleerdheid **3** tentoonstelling **4** poging, gooi, beurt: *a bad* (or: *poor*) *~* een slechte beurt; *good ~!* goed geprobeerd!; *put up a good ~* een goede prestatie leveren **5** uiterlijk[h], schijn, opschepperij: *this is all empty ~* dit is allemaal slechts schijn **6** pracht (en praal) **7** vertoning, demonstratie: *objects on ~* de tentoongestelde voorwerpen || *vote by (a) ~ of hands* d.m.v. handopsteking stemmen; *give the (whole) ~ away* de hele zaak verraden; *steal the ~* de show stelen

²**show** (vb) (zich) (ver)tonen [of film]: *your slip is ~ing* je onderjurk komt eruit; *time will ~* de tijd zal het leren || *it just goes to ~!* zo zie je maar!

³**show** (vb) **1** (aan)tonen, laten zien, tentoonstellen, vertonen: *~ one's cards* (or: *hand*) open kaart spelen [also fig]; *~ (s.o.) the way* **a)** iem. de weg wijzen; **b)** [also fig] een voorbeeld stellen; *~ o.s.* je (gezicht) laten zien, je ware aard tonen; *he has nothing to ~ for his work* zijn werk heeft helemaal niets opgeleverd **2** uitleggen, demonstreren, bewijzen: *he ~ed me how to write* hij leerde me schrijven **3** te kennen geven, tentoonspreiden: *~ bad taste* een slechte smaak getuigen **4** (rond)leiden: *~ s.o. about* (or: *(a)round*) iem. rondleiden; *~ her into the waiting room* breng haar naar de wachtkamer; *~ s.o. over the factory* iem. een rondleiding geven door de fabriek **5** aanwijzen: *the clock ~s five minutes past* de klok staat op vijf over

show business amusementsbedrijf[h], show business

¹**showcase** (n) vitrine [in shop, museum]; uitstalkast

²**showcase** (vb) [Am] onder de aandacht brengen, goed laten uitkomen

showdown 1 [poker] het tonen van zijn kaarten [also fig] **2** directe confrontatie, krachtmeting

¹shower (n) **1** bui: *occasional ~s* hier en daar een bui **2** douche: *have a ~* douchen, een douche nemen **3** stroom, toevloed, golf: *a ~ of arrows* (or: *bullets*) een regen van pijlen (or: kogels)

²shower (vb) **1** zich douchen **2** (toe)stromen: *apples ~ed down the tree* het regende appels uit de boom

³shower (vb) **1** (+ with) overgieten (met), uitstorten, doen neerstromen **2** (+ with) overladen (met), overstelpen: *~ questions on s.o.* een heleboel vragen op iem. afvuren

shower cap douchemuts

showery buiig, regenachtig

showgirl revuemeisje^h

show house modelwoning

showing vertoning, voorstelling, voorkomen^h, figuur^+h: *make a good ~* een goed figuur slaan; *a poor ~* een zwakke vertoning [eg of football team] ‖ *on present ~* zoals de zaak er nu voor blijkt te staan

showman 1 impresario [organiser of concerts, shows] **2** aansteller

¹show off (vb) opscheppen, indruk proberen te maken

²show off (vb) **1** pronken met, etaleren: *don't ~ your knowledge* loop niet zo te koop met je kennis **2** goed doen uitkomen: *your white dress shows off your tanned skin* je witte jurk doet je gebruinde huid goed uitkomen

show-off opschepper

showpiece pronkstuk^h, paradepaardje^h

show pony [inform] aandachtstrekker, uitslover

showroom toonzaal

showrooming producten in een winkel bekijken en daarna via internet aanschaffen

showstopper 1 uitsmijter, hoogtepunt^h **2** obstakel^h; probleem^h

show trial schijnproces^h

¹show up (vb) opdagen, verschijnen

²show up (vb) **1** ontmaskeren, aan het licht brengen: *~ an impostor* een bedrieger ontmaskeren **2** zichtbaar maken: *only strong light shows up her wrinkles* slechts sterk licht toont haar rimpeltjes **3** in verlegenheid brengen: *the pupil's remark showed him up* de opmerking van de scholier zette hem voor gek

show window etalage

showy opvallend, opzichtig

shrapnel 1 (soort) granaat **2** granaatscherven

¹shred (n) **1** stukje^h, reepje^h, snipper: *not a ~ of clothing* geen draadje kleding; *tear sth. to ~s* **a)** iets aan flarden scheuren; **b)** [also fig] niets heel laten van **2** greintje^h: *not a ~ of evidence* niet het minste bewijs, geen enkel bewijs

²shred (vb) verscheuren, versnipperen, in

stukjes snijden

shredder 1 (grove keuken)schaaf [for vegetables, cheese]; rasp **2** versnipperaar

shrew 1 spitsmuis **2** feeks

shrewd slim: *~ guess* intelligente gok; *~ observer* scherp waarnemer

¹shriek (n) schreeuw, gil, (schrille) kreet

²shriek (vb) schreeuwen, gillen: *~ out* uitschreeuwen; *~ with laughter* gieren van het lachen

shrift: *make short ~ of* korte metten maken met

shrill schel, schril, doordringend; [fig] fel: *~ contrast* schril contrast

shrimp garnaal; [inform] klein opdondertje^h

shrine 1 (heiligen)tombe **2** heiligdom^h; [fig] gedenkplaats

¹shrink (n) zielenknijper [psychiatrist]

²shrink (vb) **1** krimpen, afnemen, slinken **2** wegkruipen, ineenkrimpen; [fig] huiveren: *~ back* terugdeinzen

³shrink (vb) doen krimpen, kleiner maken, doen slinken

shrivel verschrompelen, uitdrogen, inkrimpen

shrooms paddo's

¹shroud (n) **1** lijkwade, doodskleed^h **2** [fig] sluier: *wrapped in a ~ of mystery* in een sluier van geheimzinnigheid gehuld

²shroud (vb) (om)hullen, verbergen: *mountains ~ed in mist* in mist gehulde bergen

Shrove Tuesday Vastenavond; vette dinsdag [Tuesday before Ash Wednesday]

shrub struik, heester

¹shrug (n) schouderophalen^h

²shrug (vb) (de schouders) ophalen

shrug off van zich afschudden [clothing]; geen belang hechten aan: *she shrugged off all criticism* zij liet alle kritiek langs haar heen gaan

shrunken gekrompen, verschrompeld

shucks! 1 onzin! **2** krijg nou wat!

¹shudder (n) huivering, rilling

²shudder (vb) **1** huiveren, sidderen, beven: *I ~ to think* ik huiver bij de gedachte **2** trillen

¹shuffle (n) **1** schuifelgang **2** [dance] schuifelpas **3** het schudden [of cards, dominoes]

²shuffle (vb) **1** mengen, door elkaar halen; schudden [cards] **2** heen en weer bewegen, herverdelen: *~ one's papers* in zijn papieren rommelen **3** schuiven: *try to ~ off one's responsibility* zijn verantwoordelijkheid proberen af te schuiven

³shuffle (vb) schuifelen, sloffen: *~ one's feet* met de voeten schuifelen

shufti kijkje^h: *have* (or: *take*) *a ~ at* een blik werpen op

shun mijden, schuwen

shunt afleiden, afvoeren, rangeren; op een

dood spoor zetten [pers]: ~ *a train onto a sid-ing* een trein op een zijspoor rangeren
shush sst!, stilte!
¹shut (adj) dicht, gesloten: *slam the door* ~ de deur dichtsmijten
²shut (vb) sluiten, dichtgaan: *the shop ~s on Sundays* de winkel is 's zondags gesloten
³shut (vb) **1** sluiten, dichtdoen, dichtslaan, dichtdraaien; [fig] stopzetten: ~ *one's eyes* (or: *ears*) *to sth.* iets niet willen zien (*or:* horen); ~ *in by mountains* door bergen ingesloten; ~ *down a plant* een fabriek (voorgoed) sluiten; ~ *out of* de toegang ontzeggen tot **2** opsluiten: ~ *sth. away* iets (veilig) opbergen; ~ *o.s. in* zichzelf opsluiten [eg in room]
shutdown 1 sluiting; stopzetting [of business]; stillegging [eg of nuclear plant] **2** uitschakeling, het afsluiten
shut-eye slaap, dutjeʰ: *have a bit of* ~ een dutje doen
¹shutter (n) **1** blindʰ, (rol)luikʰ: *put up the ~s* de zaak sluiten [temporarily or permanently] **2** sluiter [also of camera]
²shutter (vb) met (een) luik(en) sluiten: *~ed windows* (or: *houses*) vensters (*or:* huizen) met gesloten luiken
shutter speed [photography] sluitertijd
¹shuttle (n) **1** schuitjeʰ [of sewing machine] **2** pendeldienst
²shuttle (vb) pendelen
³shuttle (vb) heen en weer vervoeren
shuttlecock pluimbal; shuttle [badminton]
shuttle service pendeldienst
¹shut up (vb) **1** zwijgen: ~! kop dicht! **2** sluiten [shop etc]
²shut up (vb) **1** sluiten, (zorgvuldig) afsluiten: *they* ~ *the house before they left* ze sloten het huis af voordat ze weggingen; ~ *shop* de zaak sluiten **2** opsluiten, achter slot en grendel zetten, opbergen **3** doen zwijgen, de mond snoeren: *turn the television on, that usually shuts them up* zet de tv maar aan, meestal houden ze dan hun mond dicht
¹shy (n) **1** gooi, worp **2** gooi, poging, experimentʰ: *have a ~ at sth.* een gooi doen naar iets, het (ook) eens proberen
²shy (adj) **1** verlegen: *give s.o. a ~ look* iem. verlegen aankijken **2** voorzichtig, behoedzaam: *fight* (or: *be*) ~ *of* uit de weg gaan **3** schuw; schichtig [animals]
³shy (vb) **1** schichtig opspringen: ~ *at sth.* schichtig worden voor iets [of horses] **2** terugschrikken: ~ *away from sth.* iets vermijden, voor iets terugschrikken
⁴shy (vb) gooien, slingeren
shyster gewetenloos mens [esp lawyer or politician]
Siamese Siamees
Siberian Siberisch
sibling [form] broer, zus
¹sick (n) braakselʰ, spuugselʰ

²sick (adj) **1** misselijk; [fig also] met walging vervuld: *be* ~ overgeven, braken; *be worried* ~ doodongerust zijn; *you make me* ~! ik word niet goed van jou! **2** ziek, sukkelend: *fall* ~ ziek worden; *go* (or: *report*) ~ zich ziek melden **3** wee, onpasselijk makend: *a* ~ *feeling* een wee gevoel **4** ziekelijk, ongezond, morbide; wrang [mockery]: *a* ~ *joke* een lugubere grap; *a* ~ *mind* een zieke geest **5** zat, beu, moe: *I am* ~ *(and tired) of it* ik ben het spuugzat **6** [inform] vet, gaaf ‖ ~ *to death of s.o.* (*sth.*) iem. (iets) spuugzat zijn
sickbay ziekenboeg
sickbed ziekbedʰ
sick benefit ziekengeldʰ
sick call ziekenbezoekʰ [by doctor or clergyman]
¹sicken (vb) **1** ziek worden **2** misselijk worden **3** (+ for) smachten (naar) **4** de eerste tekenen (van een ziekte) vertonen, onder de leden hebben: *be ~ing for measles* de mazelen onder de leden hebben
²sicken (vb) ziek maken, doen walgen
sickening 1 ziekmakend, ziekteverwekkend **2** walgelijk, weerzinwekkend
sickle sikkel
sick leave ziekteverlofʰ: *on* ~ met ziekteverlof
sick list ziekenlijst: *on the* ~ afwezig wegens ziekte
sickly 1 ziekelijk, sukkelend **2** bleek [face, complexion]; flauw [smile] **3** walgelijk [smell]; wee [smell, air]
sickness 1 ziekte **2** misselijkheid
sickness benefit ziektegeldʰ, uitkering wegens ziekte
sick pay ziekengeldʰ
¹side (n) **1** zij(de), (zij)kant, flank; helling [of mountain]; oever [of river]; richting, aspectʰ; trek [of character]: *always look on the bright* ~ *of life* bekijk het leven altijd van de zonnige kant; *take ~s with s.o.* partij voor iem. kiezen; *this* ~ *up* deze kant boven [on boxes before shipping]; *at* (or: *by*) *my* ~ naast mij; ~ *by* ~ zij aan zij; *whose* ~ *are you on, anyway?* aan wiens kant sta jij eigenlijk? **2** bladzijde **3** gedeelteʰ, deelʰ: *he went to the far* ~ *of the room* hij liep tot achter in de kamer **4** gezichtspuntʰ **5** ploeg, teamʰ: *let the* ~ *down* niet aan de verwachtingen van de anderen voldoen ‖ *know (on) which* ~ *one's bread is buttered* weten waar men zijn kaarsje moet laten branden; *the other* ~ *of the coin* de keerzijde van de medaille; *laugh* on the other ~ *of one's face* (or: *mouth*) lachen als een boer die kiespijn heeft; *put* on (or: *to*) *one* ~, *set* on one ~ terzijde leggen, sparen, reserveren; *take* on (or: *to*) *one* ~ terzijde nemen [for a talk]; *on the* ~ **a)** als bijverdienste, zwart; **b)** in het geniep
²side (adj) **1** zij-: ~ *entrance* zijingang **2** bij-, neven-

³side (vb) (+ against, with) partij kiezen (tegen, voor)

sideboard 1 buffetʰ **2** dientafel **3** (-s) bakkebaarden

sideburns bakkebaarden

sidecar zijspanʰ

side dish bijgerechtʰ

side effect 1 bijwerking [of medicine or therapy] **2** neveneffectʰ

sidekick 1 handlanger, ondergeschikte partner **2** sidekick, aangever

sidelight 1 zijlichtʰ; stadslichtʰ [of car] **2** [fig] toevallige informatie: *that throws some interesting ~s on the problem* dat werpt een interessant licht op de zaak

¹sideline (n) **1** bijbaan, nevenactiviteit **2** (-s) [sport] zijlijnen ‖ *be* (or: *sit, stand*) *on the ~s* de zaak van een afstand bekijken

²sideline (vb) van het veld sturen; [fig] buiten spel zetten; negeren

sidelong zijdelings

side-saddle dameszadelʰ

sideshow bijkomende voorstelling; extra attractie [at fairground; in circus]

side-slip zijwaartse slip [of car, aeroplane, skier]

¹sidestep (vb) opzijgaan, uitwijken

²sidestep (vb) ontwijken; uit de weg gaan [also fig; responsibility, problems]

sidestroke zijslag [swimming]

¹sideswipe (n) **1** zijslag, zijstoot **2** schimpscheut, hatelijke opmerking

²sideswipe (vb) schampen (langs), zijdelings raken

sidetrack 1 op een zijspoor zetten [also fig]; rangeren, opzijschuiven **2** van zijn onderwerp afbrengen, afleiden

sidewalk [Am] stoep, trottoirʰ

sideward zijwaarts, zijdelings

sideways zijwaarts, zijdelings

siding 1 rangeerspoorʰ, wisselspoorʰ **2** afbouwmateriaalʰ; buitenbekleding [of wall]

sidle zich schuchter bewegen: *~ up to s.o., ~ away from s.o.* schuchter naar iem. toelopen, schuchter van iem. weglopen

siege belegʰ, belegering, blokkade: *lay ~ to* belegeren; *raise the ~* het beleg opbreken

Sierra Leone Sierra Leone

¹Sierra Leonian (n) Sierra Leoner, Sierra Leoonse

²Sierra Leonian (adj) Sierra Leoons

¹sieve (n) zeef: *a memory like a ~* een geheugen als een zeef

²sieve (vb) ziften [also fig]; zeven, schiften

sift 1 ziften [also fig]; strooien [sugar]: *~ out* uitzeven **2** uitpluizen, doorpluizen: *he ~ed through his papers* hij doorzocht zijn papieren

¹sigh (n) zucht

²sigh (vb) zuchten: *~ for* smachten naar

¹sight (n) **1** (aan)blik, (uit)zichtʰ, schouw-

spelʰ, bezienswaardigheid: *I cannot stand* (or: *bear*) *the ~ of him* ik kan hem niet luchten of zien; *catch ~ of, get a ~ of* in het oog krijgen, een glimp opvangen van; *lose ~ of* uit het oog verliezen [also fig]; *see the ~s* de bezienswaardigheden bezoeken **2** vizierʰ: *have one's ~s set on, set one's ~s on* op het oog hebben, graag willen **3** boel: *he is a ~ too clever* for me hij is me veel te vlug af **4** (ge)zichtʰ, gezichtsvermogen: *loss of ~* het blind worden **5** gezichtʰ, het zien: *at first ~* op het eerste gezicht; *know s.o. by ~* iem. van gezicht kennen **6** (uit)zichtʰ, gezicht(sveld)ʰ: *come into* (or: *within*) *~* zichtbaar worden; *keep in ~ of* binnen het gezichtsveld blijven van; *out of ~, out of mind* uit het oog, uit het hart; *we are (with)in ~ of the end* het einde is in zicht; *stay* (or: *keep*) *out of ~* blijf uit het zicht ‖ *raise* (or: *lower*) *one's ~s* meer (or: minder) verwachten; *out of ~!* fantastisch!, te gek!; *second ~* helderziendheid

²sight (vb) **1** in zicht krijgen, in het vizier krijgen **2** waarnemen, zien: *he was last ~ed in London* hij werd voor het laatst gezien in Londen

sighting waarneming: *there have been numerous ~s of UFO's lately* er zijn de laatste tijd veel vliegende schotels gezien

sightread [mus] van blad spelen (or: zingen)

sightseeing het bezoeken van bezienswaardigheden

sightseer toerist

¹sign (n) **1** tekenʰ, symboolʰ **2** aanwijzing, (ken)tekenʰ, blijkʰ, voortekenʰ **3** wenk, tekenʰ, seintjeʰ **4** (uithang)bordʰ **5** (ken)tekenʰ: *~ of the times* teken des tijds **6** sterrenbeeldʰ: *~ of the zodiac* sterrenbeeldʰ

²sign (vb) **1** (onder)tekenen: *~ one's name* tekenen; *~ in* tekenen bij aankomst, intekenen; *~ on at the Job Centre* inschrijven op het arbeidsbureau; *~ up for a course* zich voor een cursus inschrijven **2** signeren, ondertekenen: *~ed copies are available within* gesigneerde exemplaren zijn binnen verkrijgbaar **3** wenken, een teken geven, gebaren **4** (+ on, up) contracteren [player]

¹signal (n) **1** signaalʰ [also fig; also of radio, TV]; tekenʰ, seinʰ: *~ of distress* noodsignaalʰ **2** sein(apparaatʰ), signaalʰ **3** verkeerslichtʰ

²signal (adj) buitengewoon, glansrijk: *a ~ victory* een glansrijke overwinning

³signal (vb) aankondigen, te kennen geven

⁴signal (vb) (over)seinen, een teken geven

signal box seinhuisjeʰ

signalize doen opvallen, de aandacht vestigen op, opluisteren

signalman seiner; [railways also] sein(huis)wachter

signatory ondertekenaar

signature 1 handtekening **2** [art] handtekening, signatuur

signature campaign handtekeningenactie

signature tune herkenningsmelodie; tune [of radio, TV]

signboard 1 uithangbord^h **2** bord^h met opschrift

signet zegel^h

signet ring zegelring

significance betekenis, belang^h: *a meeting of great historical ~* een ontmoeting van grote historische betekenis

significant belangrijk, veelbetekenend: *be ~ of* aanduiden, kenmerkend zijn voor

signify 1 betekenen, beduiden **2** te kennen geven: *the teacher rose, ~ing that the class was over* de docent stond op, daarmee gaf hij te kennen dat de les afgelopen was

sign language gebarentaal

sign-on herkenningsmelodie [of radio or TV programme]; tune

signpost wegwijzer

¹silence (n) stilte, stilzwijgen^h, stilzwijgendheid, zwijgzaamheid: *put* (or: *reduce*) *s.o. to ~* iem. tot zwijgen brengen; *in ~* in stilte, stilzwijgend; *~!* stil!, zwijg!

²silence (vb) tot zwijgen brengen, het stilzwijgen opleggen, stil doen zijn

silencer 1 geluiddemper [on firearm] **2** knalpot

silent stil, (stil)zwijgend, zwijgzaam, onuitgesproken, stom, rustig: *a ~ film* een stomme film; *keep ~* rustig blijven

silhouette silhouet^h, beeltenis, schaduwbeeld^h, omtrek

silicone silicone^h

¹silk (n) **1** zij(de), zijdedraad **2** King's (Queen's) Counsel

²silk (adj) zijden, zijde-

silken 1 zij(de)achtig **2** zacht

silkworm zijderups

sill 1 vensterbank **2** drempel

¹silly (n) domoor: *of course you're coming with us, ~!* natuurlijk mag je met ons mee, dommerdje!

²silly (adj) **1** dwaas, dom, onverstandig **2** verdwaasd, suf, murw: *knock s.o. ~* iem. murw slaan

silly season komkommertijd

silo silo, voederkuil, (betonnen) voedersleuf

silt slib^h, slik^{+h}

silt up dichtslibben, verzanden

¹silver (n) **1** zilver^h **2** zilvergeld^h **3** zilver(werk)^h; [fig] tafelgerei^h

²silver (adj) **1** van zilver, zilveren, zilver-: *~ foil* zilverfolie^{+h} **2** verzilverd: *~ plate* verzilverd vaatwerk **3** zilverachtig || *~ wedding (anniversary)* zilveren bruiloft

silver bullet [Am] wondermiddel^h, kant-en-klare oplossing

silverfish zilvervisje^h, papiermot

silversmith zilversmid

silvery zilverachtig, zilverkleurig

SIM card simkaart

simian (mens)aap

similar (+ to) gelijk (aan), vergelijkbaar, hetzelfde; [maths] gelijkvormig: *in ~ cases* in vergelijkbare gevallen

similarity 1 vergelijkbaarheid, overeenkomst **2** punt^h van overeenkomst, gelijkenis

similarly 1 op dezelfde manier, op een vergelijkbare manier **2** [at beginning of sentence] evenzo

simile vergelijking; gelijkenis [figure of speech]

¹simmer (n) gesudder^h, gepruttel^h

²simmer (vb) **1** sudderen, pruttelen **2** zich inhouden [of rage, laughter]: *~ down* bedaren

³simmer (vb) aan het sudderen brengen/houden

¹simper (n) onnozele glimlach, zelfvoldane grijnslach

²simper (vb) onnozel glimlachen, zelfvoldaan grijnslachen

simple 1 eenvoudig, eerlijk, simpel: *the ~ life* het natuurlijke leven; *the ~ truth* de nuchtere waarheid **2** dwaas, onnozel **3** eenvoudig, gemakkelijk: *~ solution* eenvoudige oplossing **4** enkel(voudig): *~ forms of life* eenvoudige levensvormen

simple-minded 1 argeloos, onnadenkend **2** zwakzinnig

simpleton dwaas, sul

simplicity 1 eenvoud, ongecompliceerdheid: *it is ~ itself* het is een koud kunstje **2** simpelheid

simplification vereenvoudiging

simplify 1 vereenvoudigen **2** (te) eenvoudig voorstellen, simplificeren

simplistic simplistisch

simply 1 eenvoudig, gewoonweg **2** stomweg **3** enkel, maar, slechts: *if you want to call the nurse, ~ push the red button* als u de zuster wilt roepen, hoeft u alleen maar op de rode knop te drukken

simulate 1 simuleren, voorwenden, doen alsof **2** imiteren, nabootsen: *~d gold* namaakgoud

simulation 1 voorwending, veinzerij **2** nabootsing, imitatie

simultaneity gelijktijdigheid

simultaneous gelijktijdig, simultaan: *~ly with* tegelijk met

¹sin (n) zonde; [fig also] misdaad: *live in ~* in zonde leven, in zonde samenwonen; *for my ~s* voor mijn straf

²sin (vb) (+ against) zondigen (tegen)

¹since (adv) **1** sindsdien, van toen af, ondertussen: *I've lived here ever ~* ik heb hier sindsdien de hele tijd gewoond **2** geleden: *he left some years ~* hij is enige jaren geleden weggegaan

²**since** (prep) sinds, sedert, van ... af: *he has never been the same ~ his wife's **death*** hij is nooit meer dezelfde geweest sinds de dood van zijn vrouw

³**since** (conj) **1** sinds, vanaf de tijd dat: *I **haven't** seen you ~ you were a child* ik heb je niet meer gezien sinds je klein was **2** aangezien, daar: *~ you don't want me around I might as well leave* aangezien je me niet in de buurt wilt hebben, kan ik net zo goed weggaan

sincere eerlijk, oprecht, gemeend

sincerely eerlijk, oprecht, gemeend: *yours ~* met vriendelijke groeten [complimentary close in letter to acquaintances]

sincerity eerlijkheid, gemeendheid: *in all ~* in alle oprechtheid

sine sinus

sinew 1 pees **2** (spier)kracht

sinful 1 zondig, schuldig **2** slecht: *a ~ waste of money* een schandalige geldverspilling

¹**sing** (vb) **1** zingen; suizen [of wind]; fluiten [of bullet] **2** gonzen [of ear] || *~ sth. out* iets uitroepen; *~ out (for)* schreeuwen (om)

²**sing** (vb) bezingen

³**sing** singular enk, enkelvoud

Singapore Singapore

¹**Singaporean** (n) Singaporees, Singaporese

²**Singaporean** (adj) Singaporees

¹**singe** (n) **1** schroeiing **2** schroeiplek

²**singe** (vb) **1** (ver)schroeien **2** krullen; golven [hair]

singer zanger(es)

singing 1 (ge)zangʰ, het zingen **2** zangkunst

¹**single** (n) **1** enkeltjeʰ, enkele reis **2** vrijgezel **3** [mus] single **4** (-s) enkel(spel)ʰ [at tennis]

²**single** (adj) **1** enkel(voudig) **2** ongetrouwd, alleenstaand **3** enig **4** afzonderlijk, individueel: *not a ~ **man** helped* niet één man hielp **5** eenpersoons-: *~ **bed*** eenpersoonsbedʰ **6** enkele reis: *a ~ **ticket*** een (kaartje) enkele reis || *in ~ **file*** achter elkaar (in de rij)

single-handed alleen, solo, zonder steun

single-minded 1 doelbewust **2** vastberaden

singleness concentratie || *~ of **purpose*** doelgerichte toewijding

single out uitkiezen, selecteren

single-parent family eenoudergezinʰ

singlet (onder)hemdʰ, sporthemdʰ

single-use wegwerp-: *~ plastic **bag*** plastic wegwerptasjeʰ

¹**sing-song** (n) **1** dreun: *say sth. in a ~* iets opdreunen **2** samenzang

²**sing-song** (adj) eentonig, zangerig

¹**singular** (n) [linguistics] enkelvoudʰ, enkelvoudsvorm

²**singular** (adj) **1** bijzonder, uitzonderlijk **2** ongewoon, vreemd: *~ **event*** eigenaardige

gebeurtenis

singularity bijzonderheid, eigenaardigheid

Sinhalese Singalees, Singalese [inhabitant of Sri Lanka]

sinister 1 boosaardig, onguur **2** onheilspellend, duister, sinister

¹**sink** (n) **1** gootsteen(bak) **2** wasbak **3** poel (van kwaad): *~ **of iniquity*** poel van verderf

²**sink** (vb) **1** (weg)zinken, (weg)zakken, verzakken: *her **spirits** sank* de moed zonk haar in de schoenen; *his voice sank **to** a whisper* zijn stem daalde tot op fluisterniveau **2** (neer)dalen: *~ **in** one's estimation* in iemands achting dalen **3** afnemen, verflauwen, verdwijnen **4** achteruit gaan, zwakker worden: *the sick **man** is ~ing fast* de zieke man gaat snel achteruit **5** doordringen, indringen (in): *his words will ~ **in*** zijn woorden zullen inslaan || *~ or **swim*** pompen of verzuipen

³**sink** (vb) **1** laten zinken, doen zakken: *~ a ship* een schip tot zinken brengen **2** vergeten, laten rusten: *~ the **differences*** de geschillen vergeten **3** graven, boren: *~ a **well*** een put boren **4** bederven [plan etc]; verpesten || *be sunk **in** thought* in gedachten verzonken zijn; *be sunk* reddeloos verloren zijn

sinner zondaar

sinuous 1 kronkelend, bochtig **2** lenig, buigzaam

sinus holte, opening; [anatomy] sinus

sinusitis voorhoofdsholteontsteking

¹**sip** (n) slokjeʰ, teugjeʰ

²**sip** (vb) **1** met kleine teugjes drinken **2** (+ at) nippen (aan)

siphon (also + off, out) (over)hevelen [also fig]; overtappen: *management ~ed **millions** into plans for the building of a new head office* de directie hevelde miljoenen over naar plannen voor de bouw van een nieuw hoofdkantoor

sir meneer; mijnheer [form of address]: *Dear Sir* geachte heer; *Dear Sirs* mijne heren [in letter]; *no ~!* geen sprake van!

sire 1 vader van dier [of horse] **2** Sire; heer [form of address of emperor, king]

siren 1 (alarm)sirene **2** [mythology] sirene **3** verleidster

sirloin (steak) lendenbiefstuk

sis [inform] sister zusjeʰ

sissy mietjeʰ, watjeʰ

sister 1 zus(ter) **2** non, zuster **3** (hoofd)verpleegster

sisterhood 1 zusterschap, nonnenorde **2** vrouwenbeweging

sister-in-law schoonzus(ter)

¹**sit** (vb) **1** zitten: *~ **tight*** rustig blijven zitten, volhouden **2** zijn, zich bevinden, liggen, staan: *~ **heavy** on the stomach* zwaar op de maag liggen **3** poseren, model staan: *~ **for** a portrait* voor een portret poseren **4** (zitten te)

broeden **5** zitting hebben ‖ ~ **pretty** op rozen zitten; ~ **about** (or: *around*) lanterfanten; ~ **back** gemakkelijk gaan zitten; [fig] zijn gemak nemen, zich terugtrekken; ~ **by** rustig toe zitten te kijken; ~ **down** gaan zitten; ~ **in** als vervanger optreden; ~ **in** on als toehoorder bijwonen; ~ **for** an exam een examen afleggen

²**sit** (vb) **1** laten zitten **2** berijden [horse] **3** afleggen [examination]

sitcom *situation comedy* komische tv-serie

sit-down zittend: ~ *meal* zittend genuttigde maaltijd

¹**site** (n) **1** plaats, locatie **2** (bouw)terrein[h]

²**site** (vb) plaatsen, situeren: *the farm is beautifully* ~*d* de boerderij is prachtig gelegen

site map [comp] sitemap

sit on 1 zitting hebben in **2** onderzoeken **3** laten liggen, niets doen aan **4** terechtwijzen, op z'n kop zitten

sit out 1 uitzitten [eg concert] **2** niet meedoen aan [eg dance]

sitter 1 model[h], iem. die poseert **2** broedende vogel, broedhen **3** *babysitter* kinderoppas, babysit

sitter-in (baby)oppas

¹**sitting** (n) **1** zitting, vergadering **2** tafel, gelegenheid om te eten **3** het zitten **4** het poseren ‖ *he read the story* **at** one ~ hij las het verhaal in één ruk uit

²**sitting** (adj) zittend: ~ *duck* (or: *target*) makkelijk doel(wit), weerloos slachtoffer; ~ *tenant* huidige huurder

sitting room zitkamer, woonkamer, huiskamer

situated 1 geplaatst **2** gelegen, gesitueerd

situation 1 toestand, situatie, omstandigheden **2** ligging, plaats **3** betrekking, baan: ~ *vacant* functie aangeboden, vacature

situation comedy komische tv-serie

sit up 1 rechtop (gaan) zitten: *that will make him* ~ *and* **take** *notice!* daar zal hij van opkijken! **2** opblijven; waken [with sick person]

six zes: *arranged* **by** ~*es* per zes geschikt ‖ *everything is at* ~*es and* **sevens** alles is helemaal in de war; *it's* ~ *of one and half a* **dozen** *of the other, it's* ~ *and two* **threes** het is lood om oud ijzer

sixfold zesvoudig

sixshooter revolver

sixteen zestien

sixteenth zestiende

sixth zesde

sixth form bovenbouw vwo

sixthly ten zesde, op de zesde plaats

sixtieth zestigste

sixty zestig: *in the sixties* in de jaren zestig

sixty-four thousand dollar question hamvraag

size 1 afmeting, formaat[h], grootte, omvang: *trees of various* ~*s* bomen van verschillende grootte **2** maat: *she takes* ~ *eight* ze heeft maat acht; *a* **plus** ~ een grote maat ‖ *cut down to* ~ iem. op zijn plaats zetten

sizeable vrij groot, flink

¹**sizzle** (n) gesis[h], geknetter[h]

²**sizzle** (vb) sissen, knetteren

sizzling snik-: *a* ~ *hot day* een snikhete dag

skanking [inform] dansstijl met wilde (arm)bewegingen

¹**skate** (n) **1** schaats: *get* (or: *put*) *one's* ~*s on* opschieten **2** rolschaats

²**skate** (vb) **1** schaatsen(rijden) **2** rolschaatsen ‖ ~ *over* (or: *round*) sth. ergens luchtig overheen lopen

skateboard skateboard[h], rol(schaats)plank

skateboarding skateboarden[h]

skater 1 schaatser **2** rolschaatser

skating rink 1 ijsbaan, schaatsbaan **2** rolschaatsbaan

skedaddle ervandoor gaan, 'm smeren

skeleton 1 skelet[h], geraamte[h]: *the* ~ *of the building* het geraamte van het gebouw **2** uitgemergeld persoon (dier[h]) **3** schema[h], schets ‖ ~ *in the* **cupboard** (or: *closet*) onplezierig (familie)geheim, lijk in de kast

skeleton key loper

¹**sketch** (n) **1** schets, tekening, beknopte beschrijving **2** sketch, kort toneelstukje[h] (verhaal[h])

²**sketch** (vb) schetsen, tekenen

³**sketch** (vb) (also + in, out) schetsen, kort beschrijven

sketchy schetsmatig, ruw; [fig] oppervlakkig

skew schuin, scheef

¹**skewer** (n) vleespen, spies

²**skewer** (vb) doorsteken [(as if) with skewer]

¹**ski** (n) ski

²**ski** (vb) skiën, skilopen

¹**skid** (n) **1** steunblok[h], steunbalk **2** glijbaan, glijplank **3** remschoen, remblok[h] **4** schuiver, slip, slippartij: *the car went* **into** *a* ~ de wagen raakte in een slip ‖ *put the* ~*s under one's plans* **a)** iem. (iets) ruïneren; **b)** iem. achter zijn vodden zitten

²**skid** (vb) slippen [also of wheel]; schuiven

skidmark remspoor[h] [also fig]

skid row achterbuurt

skier skiër

skiff skiff

skiing skisport; skiën[h]

skilful bekwaam, (des)kundig, vakkundig, ervaren

skill bekwaamheid, vakkundigheid, vaardigheid

skilled bekwaam, vakkundig: ~ *worker* geschoolde arbeider, vakman

skim 1 vluchtig inkijken: ~ *over a* **book** een boek vlug doornemen **2** afromen [milk]; afscheppen [milk] **3** scheren

skimmed afgeroomd: ~ *milk* taptemelk

ski mobile [Am] sneeuwscooter

¹**skimp** (vb) (+ on) bezuinigen (op), beknibbelen: *whatever you do, don't ~ on your food* wat je ook doet, ga in ieder geval niet bezuinigen op het eten

²**skimp** (vb) **1** karig (toe)bedelen, zuinig zijn met **2** kort houden

skimpy karig, schaars

¹**skin** (n) huid [also of aeroplane, ship]; vel^h, pels: *have a **thick** ~* een olifantshuid hebben; *have a **thin** ~* erg gevoelig zijn || *~ and **bone(s)*** vel over been; *escape by the ~ of one's **teeth*** op het nippertje ontsnappen; *get under s.o.'s ~* **a)** iem. irriteren; **b)** bezeten zijn van iem.; *save one's ~* er heelhuids afkomen

²**skin** (vb) **1** villen; (af)stropen [also fig] **2** schillen, pellen **3** oplichten, afzetten || *keep one's eye ~ned* alert zijn, wakker blijven

skin-deep oppervlakkig [also fig]: *his politeness **is** only ~* zijn beleefdheid is alleen maar buitenkant

skin diver sportduiker

skinflint vrek

skinful genoeg drank om dronken van te worden: *he has **had** quite a ~ by the look of him* hij heeft zo te zien al het nodige op

skin game 1 oneerlijk gokspel^h **2** afzetterij, zwendel

skinhead skinhead

skinny broodmager: *a ~ **latte*** een koffie verkeerd met magere melk

skin patch huidpleister, slimme pleister

skint platzak, blut

¹**skip** (n) **1** sprongetje^h **2** afvalcontainer

²**skip** (vb) **1** huppelen, (over)springen **2** touwtjespringen || *~ **over*** overslaan, luchtig overheen gaan

³**skip** (vb) overslaan, weglaten, wegblijven van

skipper 1 kapitein, schipper **2** [sport] aanvoerder van een team

¹**skirmish** (n) **1** schermutseling [also fig] **2** woordenwisseling

²**skirmish** (vb) **1** schermutselen **2** (rede)twisten

¹**skirt** (n) **1** rok **2** rand, zoom, uiteinde^h **3** [inform] stuk^h: *what a **piece** of ~!* wat een stuk!

²**skirt** (vb) **1** begrenzen, lopen langs **2** ontwijken, omzeilen

skirting board plint

skittish 1 schichtig [of horse]; nerveus **2** grillig **3** frivool

skittle kegel

skive zich aan het werk onttrekken, zich drukken: *were you skiving or were you really ill?* was je je aan het drukken, of was je echt ziek?

skulk 1 zich verschuilen **2** sluipen

skull schedel, doodshoofd^h: *~ and cross-bones* doodshoofd met gekruiste beenderen; *he couldn't **get** it into his ~* het drong niet tot zijn hersenen door

skullcap petje^h, kalotje^h, keppeltje^h

skunk 1 stinkdier^h **2** schoft, schooier

sky hemel, lucht: *praise s.o. to the skies* iem. de hemel in prijzen || *the ~ is the **limit*** het kan niet op [of money]

sky-blue hemelsblauw

skydive [parachuting] vrije val maken: *skydiving* vrije val

sky-high hemelhoog; [fig] buitensporig hoog [eg prices]: *blow ~* in de lucht laten vliegen, opblazen; [fig] geen spaan heel laten van

skyjacking (vliegtuig)kaping

¹**skylark** (n) veldleeuwerik

²**skylark** (vb) **1** stoeien **2** pret maken

skylight dakraam^h

skyline 1 horizon **2** skyline; silhouet^h [seen against sky]

skyrocket omhoogschieten [of prices]: *fuel **prices** have ~ed again* de brandstofprijzen zijn weer huizenhoog gestegen

skyscraper wolkenkrabber

slab 1 plaat [eg iron] **2** plat rechthoekig stuk^h steen

¹**slack** (n) **1** los (hangend) deel^h van zeil of touw: *take* up (or: *in*) *the ~* **a)** aantrekken [rope etc]; **b)** [fig] de teugel(s) kort houden **2** steenkoolgruis^h **3** (-s) sportpantalon, lange broek **4** slappe tijd

²**slack** (adj) **1** slap, los: *reign with a ~ **hand*** met slappe hand regeren **2** zwak, laks **3** lui, traag || *~ **water*** stil water, dood getijde

³**slack** (vb) **1** verslappen, (zich) ontspannen **2** los(ser) maken, (laten) vieren **3** de kantjes ervan af lopen, traag werken || *~ **off*** verslappen [in one's work]

¹**slacken** (vb) **1** verslappen, (zich) ontspannen **2** langzamer lopen (rijden) **3** verminderen, afnemen

²**slacken** (vb) los(ser) maken, (laten) vieren: *~ **speed*** vaart minderen

slacker luilak

slag-heap heuvel van mijnafval

¹**slam** (n) **1** harde slag; [baseball] rake slag **2** slem^h [bridge]; alle slagen: *grand ~* groot slem

²**slam** (vb) **1** met een klap dichtslaan, (neer)smijten, dichtsmijten: *~ the **door** (in s.o.'s face)* de deur (voor iemands neus) dichtslaan; *~ **down*** neersmijten **2** harde klap met de hand geven **3** scherp bekritiseren

slam dunk 1 slamdunk **2** [Am; fig] (geheid) succes^h, voltreffer

slam-dunk 1 [basketball] slamdunken **2** [Am; inform] verwerpen, (resoluut) van de hand wijzen

¹**slander** (n) laster(praat)

²**slander** (vb) (be)lasteren

slanderous lasterlijk
slang zeer informele taal, jargonʰ/taal van bepaalde sociale klasse of beroep
¹**slant** (n) **1** helling, schuinte **2** gezichtspuntʰ, kijk, optiek ‖ *the top shelf was* **on** *a ~* de bovenste plank hing scheef
²**slant** (vb) hellen, schuin aflopen
³**slant** (vb) **1** laten hellen, scheef houden **2** niet objectief weergeven: *~ed* **news** nieuwsberichten waarin partij wordt gekozen
¹**slap** (n) klap, mep: *~ on the* **back** vriendschappelijke klap op de rug; [fig] schouderklopjeʰ; *~ in the* **face** klap in het gezicht [also fig]; *~ on the* **wrist** vermaning, lichte straf; *~ and* **tickle** geflirtʰ
²**slap** (vb) **1** een klap geven, meppen: *~ s.o. on the* **back** iem. op zijn schouder kloppen, iem. feliciteren **2** smijten, kwakken: *~* **down** **a)** neersmijten; **b)** [inform] hard aanpakken [eg a wrong]
³**slap** (adv) **1** met een klap, regelrecht **2** eensklaps
slapdash nonchalant, lukraak
slap-happy 1 uitgelaten **2** nonchalant
slapstick 1 gooi-en-smijtfilm **2** grove humor
slap-up super-de-luxe, eersteklas
¹**slash** (n) **1** houw, slag **2** snee, jaap **3** schuine streep
²**slash** (vb) **1** houwen **2** snijden **3** striemen **4** drastisch verlagen [prices] **5** scherp bekritiseren **6** een split maken in: *~ed* **sleeve** mouw met split
¹**slate** (n) **1** leiʰ [rock]; lei [writing tablet]; daklei **2** kandidatenlijst
²**slate** (vb) **1** beleggen [eg meeting]; vaststellen **2** scherp bekritiseren **3** (als kandidaat) voordragen, voorstellen
slatternly slonzig
¹**slaughter** (n) slachting, bloedbadʰ
²**slaughter** (vb) **1** slachten, vermoorden **2** totaal verslaan, inmaken
slaughterhouse slachthuisʰ, abattoirʰ
¹**Slav** (n) Slaaf, Slavische
²**Slav** (adj) Slavisch
¹**slave** (n) slaaf, slavin
²**slave** (vb) zich uitsloven, zwoegen: *~* **away** *(at sth.)* zwoegen (op iets), ploeteren [eg for examination]
slaver kwijlen [also fig]: *that dog is ~ing at the mouth* het kwijl loopt die hond zijn bek uit
slavery 1 slavernij **2** slavenarbeid
Slavic Slavisch
slavish slaafs, onderdanig
slay doden, afmaken, slachten
sleaze goorheid, viesheid
sleazy 1 goor, vies **2** armoedig, goedkoop: *~* **excuse** waardeloos excuus
¹**sled** (n) slee

²**sled** (vb) sleeën
sledge slee
sledgehammer voorhamer, moker: *~* **blow** keiharde slag
¹**sleek** (adj) **1** zacht en glanzend [of hair] **2** (te) keurig verzorgd, opgedoft, opgedirkt **3** mooi gestroomlijnd [of car]
²**sleek** (vb) **1** gladmaken **2** glanzend maken
¹**sleep** (n) **1** slaap, nachtrust: *my foot has* **gone** *to ~* mijn voet slaapt; *not* **lose** *~ over sth.* niet wakker liggen van iets; *put to ~* **a)** in slaap brengen; **b)** wegmaken [anaesthetic]; **c)** een spuitje geven [animal] **2** rust(periode), winterslaap **3** slaap, oogvuilʰ
²**sleep** (vb) slapen, rusten: *~ round the* **clock** de klok rond slapen; *~* **late** uitslapen; *~* **in** **a)** in huis slapen [eg as house-sitter]; **b)** uitslapen; *~* **on** (or: over) *sth.* een nachtje over iets slapen ‖ *let ~ing* **dogs** *lie* men moet geen slapende honden wakker maken; *~* **around** met jan en alleman naar bed gaan; *~* **with** *s.o.* met iem. naar bed gaan
³**sleep** (vb) slaapplaats hebben voor: *this hotel ~s eighty (guests)* dit hotel biedt plaats voor tachtig gasten ‖ *~* **off** *one's hangover* zijn roes uitslapen
sleeper 1 slaper, slaapkop **2** dwarsbalk [of railway]; biel(s) **3** slaapwagen, slaaptrein
sleeping bag slaapzak
sleepover logeerpartij
sleepsuit slaappakjeʰ, rompertjeʰ
sleepwalker slaapwandelaar
sleepy 1 slaperig **2** loom
¹**sleet** (n) natte sneeuw(bui), natte hagel(bui)
²**sleet** (vb) sneeuwen en regenen tegelijk
sleeve 1 mouw **2** koker, mof **3** hoes [of gramophone record] ‖ *have sth. up one's ~* iets achter de hand houden; *laugh in* (or: *up*) *one's ~* in zijn vuistje lachen; *roll up one's ~s* de handen uit de mouwen steken
sleeveless mouwloos
sleigh arrenslee
sleight-of-hand 1 goochelarij; gegoochelʰ [also fig] **2** vingervlugheid
slender 1 slank, tenger **2** schaars, karig: *a ~* **income** een karig inkomen **3** zwak, teer
sleuth 1 speurhond **2** [hum] detective, speurneus
¹**slew** (n) [Am] massa, hoop: *there have been a whole ~* **of** *shooting incidents* er is weer een hele reeks schietpartijen geweest
²**slew** (vb) (rond)zwenken, met kracht omdraaien
¹**slice** (n) **1** plak(jeʰ), snee(tjeʰ), schijf(jeʰ): *~ of* **cake** **a)** stuk taart; **b)** plakje cake; *~ of* **pizza** pizzapunt **2** deelʰ **3** schep ‖ *~ of* **luck** meevaller
²**slice** (vb) **1** (also + up) in plakken snijden **2** snijden: *~d* **bread** gesneden brood **3** (+ off) afsnijden

³slice (vb) kappen [hit (ball)] with spin]
¹slick (n) olievlek [on surface of sea]
²slick (adj) [inform] **1** glad, glibberig, glanzend **2** glad, uitgeslapen, gehaaid **3** oppervlakkig, zich mooi voordoend **4** goed (uitgevoerd), kundig, soepel (draaiend/verlopend)
slicker 1 gladjanus **2** waterafstotende regenjas
¹slide (n) **1** glijbaan **2** sleehelling **3** val; achteruitgang [also fig]: *a dangerous ~ in* oil prices een gevaarlijke daling van de olieprijzen **4** (stoom)schuif **5** dia(positief[h]) **6** (aard)verschuiving, lawine **7** haarspeld
²slide (vb) **1** schuiven: *sliding door* schuifdeur; *sliding scale* variabele schaal, glijdende (loon)schaal **2** slippen **3** (uit)glijden **4** (voort) laten glijden ‖ *~ over* sth. luchtig over iets heen praten
slide rule rekenliniaal[+h]
¹slight (adj) **1** tenger, broos **2** gering, klein, onbeduidend: *~ cold* lichte verkoudheid; *not in the ~est* niet in het minst
²slight (vb) geringschatten, kleineren: *~ing remarks about his teacher* geringschattende opmerkingen over zijn docent
slightly een beetje, enigszins: *~ longer* een beetje langer
¹slim (adj) **1** slank, tenger **2** klein, gering: *~ chance* geringe kans
²slim (vb) afslanken, aan de (slanke) lijn doen
slime slijm[h]
slimy 1 slijmerig [also fig]; glibberig **2** kruiperig
¹sling (n) **1** slinger **2** zwaai, slingering **3** katapult **4** draagdoek, mitella **5** draagriem, draagband **6** lus, (hijs)strop
²sling (vb) **1** (weg)slingeren, zwaaien, smijten: *~ s.o. out* iem. eruit smijten **2** ophangen
slink (weg)sluipen: *~ away* (or: off, out) zich stilletjes uit de voeten maken; *~ in* heimelijk binnensluipen
¹slip (n) **1** misstap [also fig]; vergissing, ongelukje[h]: *~ of the pen* verschrijving; *~ of the tongue* verspreking **2** hoesje[h], (kussen)-sloop[+h] **3** onderrok, onderjurk **4** strookje[h] (papier) **5** stek(je[h]), ent ‖ *give s.o. the ~* aan iem. ontsnappen
²slip (vb) **1** (uit)glijden, slippen: *~ped disc* hernia; *time ~s away* (or: by) de tijd gaat ongemerkt voorbij; *~ through* doorschieten **2** glippen, (snel) sluipen: *~ away* wegglippen; *~ in* (or: out) naar binnen (or: buiten) glippen; *~ through* one's fingers door zijn vingers glippen **3** afglijden, vervallen ‖ *let ~* zich verspreken; *~ up* zich vergissen; *~ into* (or: out) of a dress een jurk aanschieten (or: uittrekken)
³slip (vb) schuiven, slippen, laten glijden: *~ in a remark* een opmerking tussendoor plaatsen **2** ontglippen, ontschieten: *~ one's atten-*

tion ontgaan; *~ one's memory* (or: *mind*) vergeten; *let ~* **a)** zich laten ontvallen; **b)** laten ontsnappen **3** (onopvallend) toestoppen
slip-knot 1 schuifknoop **2** slipsteek
slipover 1 slip-over **2** pullover
slipper pantoffel, slipper
slippery 1 glad, glibberig **2** moeilijk te pakken te krijgen, ontwijkend; [fig also] moeilijk te begrijpen **3** glibberig, riskant **4** onbetrouwbaar, vals ‖ *~ slope* glibberig pad, gevaarlijke koers
slip road oprit, afrit; invoegstrook, uitvoegstrook
slipshod onzorgvuldig, slordig
slipstream 1 schroefwind, luchtbeweging door de propeller veroorzaakt **2** zuiging [behind car]
slip-up vergissing, fout(je[h])
¹slit (n) **1** spleet, gleuf, lange snee **2** split[h] [eg in dress]
²slit (vb) **1** snijden **2** scheuren
slither glijden, glibberen
sliver 1 splinter, scherf **2** dun plakje[h]
slob smeerlap, slons, luie stomkop
slobber 1 kwijlen **2** sentimenteel doen, zwijmelen: *~ over* sth. zwijmelig doen over iets
¹slog (n) **1** geploeter[h], gezwoeg[h] **2** [cricket, boxing] harde klap, woeste slag, uithaal
²slog (vb) **1** (+ at) zwoegen (op), noest doorwerken (aan): *~ away* (at) ijverig doorworstelen (met) **2** ploeteren, sjokken
³slog (vb) [cricket, boxing] hard stoten, uithalen naar, een ontzettende mep geven ‖ *~ it out* het uitvechten
slogan 1 strijdkreet **2** motto[h] **3** slagzin [in advertisement]
¹slop (n) **1** waterige soep, slappe kost **2** spoeling, dun varkensvoer[h] **3** (-s) vuil waswater[h]
²slop (vb) **1** (+ over) overstromen: *~ about* (or: *around*) rondklotsen **2** plassen, kliederen **3** sloffen **4** morsen (op), kliederen (op) ‖ *~ about* (or: *around*) rondhannesen
¹slope (n) helling
²slope (vb) hellen, schuin aflopen, schuin oplopen, glooien: *~ down (to)* aflopen (naar) ‖ *~ off* er vandoor gaan
sloppy 1 slordig, slonzig, onzorgvuldig **2** melig, sentimenteel **3** vies en nat
¹slosh (vb) **1** plassen, ploeteren **2** klotsen
²slosh (vb) **1** klotsen met: *~ about* rondklotsen **2** meppen, een dreun verkopen ‖ *~ the paint on the wall* de verf op de muur kwakken
slot 1 groef, geul, gleuf **2** plaatsje[h], ruimte, zendtijd: *find a ~ for* een plaats inruimen voor [in programme]; [aviation] *landing ~* gereserveerde landingstijd
sloth 1 luiaard **2** luiheid
slot machine 1 automaat **2** [game] fruit-

machine
¹slouch (n) **1** slappe houding, ronde rug
2 zoutzak: *be no ~ at* handig zijn in
²slouch (vb) **1** hangen, erbij hangen **2** een
slappe houding hebben
¹slough (n) **1** moeras^h **2** modderpoel
²slough (n) afgeworpen huid [of snake etc]
¹Slovak (n) Slowaak(se)
²Slovak (adj) Slowaaks
Slovakia Slowakije
¹Slovene (n) Sloveen(se)
²Slovene (adj) Sloveens
Slovenia Slovenië
slovenly slonzig, slordig
¹slow (adj) **1** langzaam, traag, geleidelijk: *~
handclap* traag handgeklap [as sign of bore-
dom]; *~ train* boemeltrein **2** saai, flauw
3 laat ‖ *~ on the uptake* traag van begrip
²slow (vb) vertragen, inhouden: *~ (the car)
down* snelheid minderen; *~ down* het kal-
mer aan doen
³slow (adv) langzaam: *be four minutes ~* vier
minuten achterlopen; *go ~* het langzaamaan
doen
slowdown vertraging, vermindering, pro-
ductievermindering
slow food slowfood^h [ambachtelijk bereid
voedsel]
sludge 1 slijk^h, modder **2** olieklont, olie-
korst
slug 1 naaktslak **2** metaalklomp **3** kogel
4 slok
sluggard luiaard
sluggish traag
¹sluice (n) **1** (afwaterings)sluis **2** sluiskolk
3 sluisdeur
²sluice (vb) (also + out) uitstromen
³sluice (vb) **1** laten uitstromen **2** (also + out,
down) overspoelen, water laten stromen
over
sluice-gate sluisdeur
¹slum (n) achterbuurt, slop^h
²slum (vb): *~ it* armoedig leven
slumber slaap, sluimer
slumdog sloppenwijkbewoner
¹slump (n) ineenstorting, snelle daling: *a ~ in
sales of violent videogames* een sterke daling
in de verkoop van gewelddadige videospel-
letjes
²slump (vb) **1** in elkaar zakken: *~ down to
the floor* op de vloer in elkaar zakken **2** instorten, mislukken; [fin] vallen
¹slur (n) smet, blaam
²slur (vb) brabbelen, onduidelijk (uit)spre-
ken ‖ *that fact was ~red over* aan dat feit
werd achteloos voorbij gegaan
slurp slobberen, (op)slurpen
slush 1 sneeuwbrij **2** dunne modder **3** ge-
zwijmel^h, sentimentele onzin
slut [inform] **1** slons **2** slet, slettebak
sluttish [inform] **1** slonzig **2** sletterig

sly 1 sluw, geslepen **2** geniepig **3** pesterig ‖
on the ~ in het geniep
¹smack (n) **1** smaak **2** vleugje^h **3** trek: *he has
a ~ of inflexibility in him* hij heeft iets onver-
zettelijks **4** smakkend geluid^h, smak **5** klap
6 klapzoen ‖ *have a ~ at sth.* een poging wagen (te)
²smack (vb) (+ of) rieken (naar)
³smack (vb) **1** slaan **2** smakken met [lips]
3 met een smak neerzetten
⁴smack (adv) **1** met een klap: *hit s.o. ~ on the
head* iem. een rake klap op zijn kop geven
2 recht, precies: *~ in the middle* precies in het
midden
smacker 1 klap, smak **2** klapzoen **3** pond^h,
dollar
¹smacking (n) pak^h slaag
²smacking (adj) energiek, vlug: *at a ~ pace*
in een stevig tempo
¹small (n) **1** het smalste gedeelte: *the ~ of the
back* lenden(streek) **2** (-s) kleine was
²small (adj) **1** klein, gering, jong, fijn, onbelangrijk: *~ arms* handvuurwapens; *~ busi-
ness* kleinbedrijf^h; *~ change* kleingeld^h; *~
print* kleine druk; [fig] kleine lettertjes; *~
wonder* geen wonder; *feel* (or: *look*) *~* zich
schamen **2** bescheiden: *in a ~ way* op kleine
schaal **3** slap, licht: *~ beer* [fig] onbelangrijke
zaken ‖ *the ~ hours* de kleine uurtjes
small ad rubrieksadvertentie
small fry [inform] onbelangrijke mensen
smallholder [Am] kleine boer
small-minded kleingeestig
smallpox pokken
small-scale kleinschalig
small talk geklets^h, informeel gesprekje^h
small-time gering, onbelangrijk
small-town 1 van een kleine stad **2** [esp
Am] bekrompen
smarmy zalvend, vleierig: *be polite and
helpful, but never be ~* wees beleefd en hulpvaardig, maar doe nooit kruiperig
¹smart (adj) **1** heftig, fel: *at a ~ pace* met
flinke pas **2** bijdehand, slim, gevat **3** sluw
4 keurig, knap: *how ~ you look!* wat zie je er
mooi uit! ‖ *~ aleck* wijsneus
²smart (vb) **1** pijn doen, steken **2** pijn hebben, lijden: *~ over* (or: *under*) *an insult* zich
gekwetst voelen door een belediging
smart-arse [inform] wijsneus
smart-ass [Am; inform] wijsneus
smart bomb precisiebom
smart card chipkaart, chipknip, bankpas
(met pincode en chip)
smart drug smartdrug
smarten (also + up) opknappen, (zichzelf)
opdoffen
smartmouth [inform] brutale aap
smart TV slimme tv, smart-tv
smartwatch slim horloge^h
¹smash (n) **1** slag, gerinkel^h **2** klap, slag,

dreun **3** ineenstorting, krach, bankroet[h]
4 topper, groot succes[h] **5** [tennis] smash
²smash (vb) **1** slaan op, beuken tegen
2 (also + up) vernielen, in de prak rijden: ~ *in*
in elkaar slaan, inslaan **3** uiteenjagen; verpletteren [enemy] **4** [tennis] smashen
³smash (vb) (also + up) breken, kapot vallen
⁴smash (vb) **1** razen, beuken, botsen: *the car
~ed into the garage door* de auto vloog met
een klap tegen de garagedeur **2** geruïneerd
worden, failliet gaan **3** [tennis] een smash
slaan
smash-and-grab raid etalagediefstal
smashed dronken
smasher 1 iets geweldigs, kanjer: *Lisa is a
real* ~ Lisa is echt een wereldmeid **2** dreun,
vernietigend antwoord[h]
smash hit geweldig succes[h]
smashing geweldig
smash-up klap, dreun, botsing
smattering beetje[h]: *have a ~ of French* een
paar woordjes Frans spreken
¹smear (n) **1** smeer[h], vlek **2** verdachtmaking
3 uitstrijkje[h]
²smear (vb) **1** vies worden, uitlopen **2** afgeven
³smear (vb) **1** smeren, uitsmeren, besmeren
2 vlekken maken op **3** verdacht maken
smear test uitstrijkje[h]
¹smell (n) **1** reuk, geur; [fig] sfeer **2** vieze
lucht || *take a ~ at this* ruik hier eens even aan
²smell (vb) **1** (+ of) ruiken (naar), geuren
(naar) **2** snuffelen **3** (+ of) stinken (naar);
ruiken (naar) [also fig] **4** (+ at) ruiken (aan)
smellies [inform] lekkere geurtjes
smelling-salts reukzout[h]
smell out opsporen, op het spoor komen:
they use sniffer dogs to ~ drug traffickers ze
zetten snuffelhonden in om drugshandela-
ren op te sporen
smelly vies, stinkend
¹smelt (n) spiering
²smelt (vb) **1** uitsmelten [ore] **2** uit erts uitsmelten [metal]
smidge [inform] ietsiepietsie[h]
¹smile (n) glimlach: *wipe the ~ off s.o.'s face*
iem. het lachen doen vergaan; *be all ~s* stralen, van oor tot oor glimlachen
²smile (vb) **1** (+ at) glimlachen (naar/tegen)
2 er stralend uitzien [nature]
³smile (vb) glimlachend uiten: *she ~d her approval* ze glimlachte goedkeurend
smiley smiley
¹smirch (n) vlek; [fig] smet
²smirch (vb) **1** bevuilen **2** [fig] een smet
werpen op
¹smirk (n) zelfgenoegzaam lachje[h]
²smirk (vb) zelfgenoegzaam glimlachen
smite **1** slaan, verslaan, vellen **2** straffen
3 raken, treffen: *smitten with s.o.* smoorverliefd op iem.

smith 1 smid **2** maker, smeder
smithereens: *smash into* (or: *to*) ~ aan diggelen gooien; *blow sth. to* ~ iets opblazen
smithy smederij
smock 1 kieltje[h], schortje[h] **2** jak[h], kiel
¹smoke (n) **1** rook **2** rokertje[h], sigaret
3 damp **4** trekje[h] || *go up in* ~ in rook opgaan;
[fig] op niets uitlopen
²smoke (vb) roken: *~d ham* gerookte ham;
no smoking verboden te roken
smoke alarm rookmelder
smoke-free rookvrij
smoke out 1 uitroken [from hole etc] **2** te
weten komen [eg plans]
smoker 1 roker **2** rookcoupé, rookrijtuig[h]
3 mannenbijeenkomst
smokescreen rookgordijn[h]; [also fig] afleidingsmanoeuvre[+h]
¹smoking (n) het roken
²smoking (adj) [inform] spetterend
smoking gun [fig] hard bewijs[h]
smooch vrijen, knuffelen
¹smooth (adj) **1** glad **2** soepel, gelijkmatig
3 gemakkelijk: *go ~ly* gladjes verlopen; *it's ~
sailing* het gaat van een leien dakje, het is
een makkie **4** rustig **5** overmatig vriendelijk,
glad: ~ *operator* gladjanus **6** zacht smakend
7 zacht; strelend [of voice, sound] || *in ~ wa-
ter* in rustig vaarwater
²smooth (vb) **1** gladmaken, effen maken
2 (also + out) gladstrijken; [fig] (onregelma-
tigheden/verschillen) wegnemen: ~ *down
one's clothes* zijn kleren gladstrijken
smoothie 1 gladde/handige prater
2 smoothie
¹smother (vb) (ver)stikken, (ver)smoren
²smother (vb) **1** (uit)doven **2** smoren, onderdrukken: *all opposition was ~ed* elke
vorm van tegenstand werd onderdrukt **3** (+
in) overladen (met); overdekken (met) [fig];
verstikken: *~ed in cream* rijkelijk met room
bedekt
smoulder (na)smeulen, gloeien
¹smudge (n) vlek; [fig] smet
²smudge (vb) vlekken
³smudge (vb) **1** (be)vlekken, vuilmaken
2 [fig] een smet werpen op, bezoedelen
smudgy 1 vlekkerig, besmeurd **2** wazig
smug zelfvoldaan
smuggle smokkelen
smuggler smokkelaar
smut 1 vuiltje[h], stofje[h] **2** roetdeeltje[h]
3 roet[h], kolenstof[h] **4** vuiligheid: *talk* ~ vuile
taal uitslaan
smutty vuil, goor, vies
snack snack, hapje[h], tussendoortje[h]
snackable [media] hapklaar
snack bar snackbar, cafetaria[+h]
¹snag (n) **1** uitsteeksel[h], punt[h], stomp **2** probleem[h], tegenvaller: *there's a ~ in it somewhere* er schuilt ergens een addertje onder 't

gras **3** (winkel)haak, scheur, haal **4** boom-
(stronk)
²snag (vb) **1** blijven haken met **2** scheuren
[clothing] **3** te pakken krijgen
snail (huisjes)slak [also fig]; slome: ~ *mail*
slakkenpost, gewone post
snail mail [hum] gewone post, slakkenpost
snail's pace slakkengangetje^h
snake slang^h || *a ~ in the grass* een addertje
onder het gras
¹snap (n) **1** klap: *shut a book* (or: *lid*) *with a ~*
een boek (*or:* deksel) met een klap dicht-
doen **2** hap, beet **3** knip [with fingers, scis-
sors] **4** foto **5** karweitje^h van niets, kleinigheid **6** pit^{+h}, energie: *put some ~ into it!* een
beetje meer fut!
²snap (adj) **1** impulsief: ~ *decision* beslissing
van 't moment (zelf) **2** onverwacht, onvoorbereid: ~ *check* (onverwachte) controle
³snap (vb) **1** (weg)grissen, grijpen, (weg)ruk-
ken: ~ *up* op de kop tikken **2** knippen met
[fingers]: ~ *one's fingers* met zijn vingers
knippen **3** kieken, een foto maken van || ~ *it
up* vooruit, aan de slag
⁴snap (vb) **1** (also + at) happen (naar), bijten
2 (af)breken, (af)knappen; het begeven
[also fig] **3** (dicht)klappen, dichtslaan: *the
door ~ped to* (or: *shut*) de deur sloeg dicht
4 (also + out) snauwen || ~ *at* a) grijpen naar;
b) aangrijpen [chance etc]; *I was only ~ped at*
ik werd alleen maar afgesnauwd; ~ *out of it*
ermee ophouden; ~ *to* it vooruit, schiet 'ns
op
⁵snap (int) klap, knal
snapchat snapchatten
snapdragon [bot] leeuwenbek
snap election vervroegde verkiezingen
snap fastener [Am] drukknoopje^h
snappy 1 pittig, levendig **2** chic, net
3 snauwerig, prikkelbaar || *look* ~*!, make* it
~*!* schiet op!
snapshot kiekje^h, snapshot^h, momentopname
snare (val)strik, val: *lay a ~ for s.o.* voor iem.
een valstrik leggen
¹snarl (n) **1** grauw^h, snauw **2** knoop [also
fig]; wirwar || *be in a ~* in de war zijn
²snarl (vb) **1** (+ at) grauwen (tegen), grommen, snauwen **2** in de war raken (brengen)
snarl up 1 in de war raken (brengen), in de
knoop raken (brengen): *get snarled up* verstrikt raken **2** vastlopen [of traf]
snarl-up 1 (verkeers)knoop **2** warboel
¹snatch (n) **1** greep, ruk: *make a ~ at* een
greep doen naar **2** brok^h, stuk^h, fragment^h: *a
~ of conversation* een flard van een gesprek
|| *sleep in ~es* met tussenpozen slapen
²snatch (vb) rukken || ~ *at* grijpen naar, (da-
delijk) aangrijpen
³snatch (vb) **1** (weg)rukken, (weg)grijpen,
bemachtigen: ~ *a kiss* een kus stelen; ~ *away*

wegrukken, wegpakken; *she ~ed the letter
out of my hand* ze rukte de brief uit mijn
hand **2** aangrijpen, gebruikmaken van
snazzy 1 chic **2** opzichtig
¹sneak (n) **1** gluiper(d) **2** klikspaan
²sneak (adj) onverwacht, verrassings-: *a ~
preview* een onaangekondigde voorvertoning
³sneak (vb) sluipen: ~ *away* wegsluipen; ~
(up)on s.o. naar iem. toesluipen || ~ *on s.o.*
over iem. klikken, iem. verraden
⁴sneak (vb) heimelijk doen, smokkelen: ~ *a
smoke* stiekem roken
sneaker 1 sluiper **2** gluiperd **3** klikspaan
4 (-s) gympies
sneaking 1 gluiperig **2** heimelijk **3** vaag: *a
~ suspicion* een vaag vermoeden
sneak-thief insluiper
¹sneer (n) **1** grijns(lach) **2** (+ at) spottende
opmerking (over), hatelijkheid
²sneer (vb) **1** (+ at) grijnzen (naar), spottend
lachen **2** spotten (met)
¹sneeze (n) nies(geluid^h): ~*s* genies^h
²sneeze (vb) niezen || *not to be ~d at* de
moeite waard, niet niks
snick knip(je^h), inkeping
¹snicker (n) **1** hinnikgeluid^h **2** giechel
²snicker (vb) **1** (zacht) hinniken **2** giechelen
snide hatelijk
¹sniff (n) **1** snuivend geluid^h **2** luchtje^h,
snuifje^h: *get a ~ of sea air* de zeelucht opsnuiven
²sniff (vb) **1** snuiven, snuffen **2** snuffelen ||
not to be ~ed at niet te versmaden
³sniff (vb) **1** snuiven **2** besnuffelen **3** ruiken,
de geur opsnuiven van
sniffer dog snuffelhond [for explosives,
drugs]
¹sniffle (n) gesnuif^h, gesnotter^h
²sniffle (vb) snuffen, snotteren
sniffy arrogant, hooghartig
¹snigger (n) giechel
²snigger (vb) gniffelen
¹snip (n) **1** knip: *one ~ of the scissors and 99
balloons flew up into the air* een knip met de
schaar en 99 ballonnen gingen de lucht in
2 snipper, stukje^h, fragment^h **3** koopje^h, bui-
tenkans
²snip (vb) snijden, knippen
³snip (vb) (also + off) (af)knippen, doorknippen, versnipperen
¹snipe (n) snip
²snipe (vb) (+ at) uit een hinderlaag schieten
(op) || *he got tired of critics sniping at him* hij
was het zat door critici aangevallen te worden
sniper sluipschutter
snippet stukje^h, fragment^h, knipsel^h
¹snitch (n) verklikker, verrader
²snitch (vb) klikken: *he ~ed on John* hij verklikte John

³**snitch** (vb) gappen
snivel 1 een loopneus hebben, snotteren **2** grienen, janken
snob snob
snobbery snobisme^h
snobbish snobistisch
snog vrijen
¹**snooker** (n) snooker(biljart)^h
²**snooker** (vb) in het nauw drijven, in een moeilijke positie brengen, dwarsbomen
snoop [inform] (+ about, around) rond-snuffelen
snooty verwaand
¹**snooze** (n) dutje^h
²**snooze** (vb) dutten, een uiltje knappen
¹**snore** (n) gesnurk^h, snurk
²**snore** (vb) snurken
¹**snort** (n) gesnuif^h: *he gave a ~ of contempt* hij snoof minachtend
²**snort** (vb) snuiven: *Ian ~ed with rage* Ian snoof van woede
snot snot^h
snot-nosed [inform]: [Am] *a ~ kid* een snotneus, een snotjongen
snotty 1 snotterig, met snot **2** verwaand, snobistisch
snout snuit
¹**snow** (n) **1** sneeuw [also on TV screen] **2** sneeuwbui **3** sneeuw, cocaïne
²**snow** (vb) **1** sneeuwen **2** neerdwarrelen
³**snow** (vb) ondersneeuwen, overdonderen ‖ *be ~ed in* (or: *up*) ingesneeuwd zijn; *be ~ed under* ondergesneeuwd worden, bedolven worden
¹**snowball** (n) sneeuwbal
²**snowball** (vb) een sneeuwbaleffect hebben, escaleren
³**snowball** (vb) **1** (met sneeuwballen) bekogelen **2** doen escaleren
snowbound ingesneeuwd
snowdrift sneeuwbank
snowdrop sneeuwklokje^h
snowflake 1 sneeuwvlok(je^h) **2** [fig; depr] gevoelig tiepje
snowman sneeuwman, sneeuwpop
snowskating (het) snowskaten
snowstorm sneeuwstorm
snow-white sneeuwwit
Snowwhite Sneeuwwitje
snowy 1 besneeuwd, sneeuwachtig **2** sneeuwwit
Snr *Senior* sr.
¹**snub** (n) bitse afwijzing: *her remark was clearly meant as a ~* haar opmerking was duidelijk bedoeld om te katten
²**snub** (vb) afstoten, afkatten, met de nek aanzien
¹**snuff** (n) snuif(tabak): *take ~* snuiven
²**snuff** (vb) snuiven [tobacco, cocaine]
³**snuff** (vb) **1** snuiten **2** opsnuiven **3** besnuffelen ‖ *~ it* 't hoekje omgaan; *~ out* een eind

maken aan [expectation, uprising etc]
snuffle snotteren
¹**snug** (n) gelagkamer
²**snug** (adj) **1** behaaglijk, beschut, knus: *be as ~ as a bug in a rug* een lekker leventje leiden **2** goed ingericht **3** nauwsluitend **4** ruim [income]
snuggle zich nestelen: *~ up to s.o.* lekker tegen iem. aan gaan liggen ‖ *~ down* lekker onder de dekens kruipen
¹**so** (adj) **1** zo, waar: *is that really so?* is dat echt waar?; *if so* als dat zo is **2** dat, het: *she was skinny but not extremely so* ze was wel mager maar niet extreem; *'She's the prettiest' 'Yes, so she is'* 'Ze is de knapste' 'Dat is ze inderdaad'
²**so** (dem pron) **1** dusdanig, dat: *'You were cheating' 'But so were you'* 'Je hebt vals gespeeld' 'Maar jij ook' **2** iets dergelijks, zo-(iets): *six days or so* zes dagen of zo
³**so** (adv) **1** zo, aldus: *(would you) be so kind as to leave* zou u zo goed willen zijn weg te gaan; *but even so* maar toch; *so far it hasn't happened* tot nu toe is het niet gebeurd; *so long as you don't tell anybody* als je 't maar aan niemand vertelt; *if so* als dat zo is **2** zozeer, zo erg: *she is not so stupid* ze is niet zo dom; *so many came* er kwamen er zo veel **3** daarom, zodoende: *so what?* en dan?, wat dan nog?; *so here we are!* hier zijn we dan!; *so there you are* daar ben je dus ‖ *so long!* tot ziens!; *every so often* nu en dan; *so there* nu weet je het
⁴**so** (conj) **1** zodat, opdat, om: *be careful you don't get hurt* pas op dat je je geen pijn doet **2** zodat, (en) dus: *he is late, so (that) we can't start yet* hij is te laat, zodat we nog niet kunnen beginnen
⁵**so** (int) ziezo
¹**soak** (n) **1** het week maken, het nat maken **2** zuipschuit, drankorgel^h
²**soak** (vb) sijpelen, doortrekken: *~ through the paper* het papier doordrenken
³**soak** (vb) **1** doorweken, (door)drenken: *~ed to the skin* doornat; *~ed through* kletsnat **2** (onder)dompelen: *~ o.s. in* zich verdiepen in **3** afzetten: *~ the rich* de rijken plukken
⁴**soak** (vb) weken, in de week zetten: *~ off* losweken
soaking door en door: *~ wet* doorweekt
soak up 1 opnemen, absorberen **2** kunnen incasseren [criticism, blow]
so-and-so 1 die en die, dinges **2** dit en dat **3** je-weet-wel: *a real ~* een rotzak
¹**soap** (n) **1** zeep **2** soap
²**soap** (vb) (in)zepen
soapbox 1 zeepdoos **2** zeepkist, geïmproviseerd platform^h
soap opera soap (opera)
soapsuds zeepsop^h
soar 1 hoog vliegen; [fig] een hoge vlucht

nemen **2** (omhoog) rijzen, stijgen: *prices ~ed* de prijzen vlogen omhoog **3** zweven

¹**sob** (n) snik

²**sob** (vb) snikken

³**sob** (vb) snikkend vertellen: *~ one's **heart** out* hartverscheurend snikken

¹**sober** (adj) **1** nuchter, niet beschonken: *as ~ as a **judge*** volkomen nuchter **2** matig, ingetogen: *~ colours* gedekte kleuren **3** beheerst, kalm **4** verstandig, afgewogen: *in ~ fact* in werkelijkheid **5** ernstig

²**sober** (vb) (+ down, up) nuchter worden (maken), (doen) bedaren

sobriety 1 nuchterheid, gematigdheid **2** kalmte, ernst

sobriety order alcoholverbod^h

sob story zielig verhaal^h, tranentrekker

so-called zogenaamd

soccer voetbal^h

sociability gezelligheid

sociable gezellig, vriendelijk

¹**social** (n) gezellige bijeenkomst, feestje^h

²**social** (adj) **1** sociaal, maatschappelijk: *man is a ~ **animal*** de mens is een sociaal wezen **2** gezellig, vriendelijk **3** gezelligheids-: *a ~ club* een gezelligheidsvereniging

social bookmarking het delen van favoriete links op internet

socialism socialisme^h

¹**socialist** (n) socialist

²**socialist** (adv) socialistisch

socialize gezellig doen, zich aanpassen: *~ with* omgaan met

social media sociale media

social network sociaal netwerk

social science 1 sociale wetenschap(pen) **2** (-s) maatschappijwetenschappen

social service 1 liefdadig werk^h **2** (-s) sociale voorzieningen

social services 1 sociale voorzieningen **2** (gemeentelijke) sociale dienst

social work maatschappelijk werk^h

social worker maatschappelijk werk(st)er

society 1 vereniging, genootschap^h **2** de samenleving, de maatschappij **3** gezelschap^h: *I try to **avoid** his ~* ik probeer zijn gezelschap te ontlopen **4** society, hogere kringen

sociological sociologisch

sociologist socioloog

sociology sociologie

¹**sock** (n) **1** sok **2** inlegzool(tje^h) **3** (vuist)slag, oplawaai **4** windzak || *pull one's ~s up* er tegen aan gaan; *put a ~ in it* kop dicht

²**sock** (vb) meppen, slaan, dreunen || *~ it to s.o.* **a)** iem. op zijn donder geven; **b)** grote indruk op iem. maken

socket 1 holte, (oog)kas, gewrichtsholte **2** kandelaar **3** sok, mof, buis **4** stopcontact^h, contactdoos, fitting, lamphouder

sock puppet 1 sokpoppetje^h **2** [media]

sokpop [nepaccount]

¹**sod** (n) **1** vent **2** rotklus, ellende **3** (gras)zode: *under the ~* onder de (groene) zoden || *I don't **give** a ~* het interesseert me geen barst

²**sod** (vb): *~ it!* verdomme!

soda 1 soda, natriumcarbonaat^h: *baking ~* **a)** zuiveringszout^h; **b)** baksoda **2** soda(water)^h **3** priklimonade, fris^h

soda water spuitwater^h

sodden 1 doorweekt, doordrenkt **2** klef [of bread etc] **3** opgeblazen; opgezwollen [through drink]: *~ features* opgeblazen gezicht

sodium natrium^h

Sod's Law de wet van 'Sod' [if anything can go wrong, it will]

sofa bank, sofa

soft 1 zacht; gedempt [light] **2** slap [also fig]; week, sentimenteel: *(have) a ~ **spot** for s.o.* een zwak voor iem. hebben **3** niet-verslavend; soft [drugs] **4** eenvoudig: *~ option* gemakkelijke weg **5** onnozel: *have gone ~ in the **head*** niet goed wijs zijn geworden **6** niet-alcoholisch; fris [drink]: *~ **drink*** fris(drank) **7** zwak, gek, verliefd: *be ~ **about** (or: on)* gek (or: verliefd) zijn op, een zwak hebben voor || *~ **loan*** lening op gunstige voorwaarden

soft-boiled 1 zachtgekookt [of egg] **2** [fig] weekhartig

soft copy tekst(en) in elektronische vorm [not on paper]

soft drink fris(drank)

¹**soften** (vb) **1** zacht(er) worden **2** vertederd worden

²**soften** (vb) **1** zacht(er) maken; dempen [light]; ontharden [water] **2** verwennen, verslappen **3** vertederen

softener waterontharder; [esp] wasverzachter

soften up 1 mild stemmen **2** verzwakken, murw maken

softie slappeling, goedzak, dwaas

soft-soap stroop smeren bij, vleien

software software, (computer)programmatuur

software package softwarepakket^h

soggy 1 doorweekt **2** drassig **3** klef [of bread etc]

¹**soil** (n) **1** grond, land^h, teelaarde **2** (vader)land^h: *on Dutch ~* op Nederlandse bodem; *native ~* geboortegrond **3** vervuiling **4** vuil^h; afval^h **5** aarde, grond, land^h

²**soil** (vb) vuil worden

³**soil** (vb) vuilmaken

¹**solace** (n) troost, bemoediging

²**solace** (vb) troosten, opbeuren: *~ o.s. (with sth.)* zich troosten (met iets)

solar van de zon, zonne-: *~ eclipse* zonsverduistering

solar farm zonnepark^h

solar system zonnestelsel[h]
soldering iron soldeerbout
soldier 1 militair, soldaat **2** strijder, voorvechter

soldier on volhouden
¹sole (n) **1** zool [of foot and shoe] **2** tong
[fish and dish]

²sole (adj) **1** enig, enkel **2** exclusief, uitsluitend: ~ *agent* alleenvertegenwoordiger
solely 1 alleen **2** enkel, uitsluitend
solemn 1 plechtig **2** ernstig: *look as ~ as a*
judge doodernstig kijken **3** (plecht)statig
4 belangrijk, gewichtig: ~ *warning* dringende waarschuwing

solemnity 1 plechtigheid **2** plechtstatig-
heid, ceremonieel[h] **3** ernst
¹solicit (vb) **1** een verzoek doen **2** tippelen
²solicit (vb) **1** (dringend) verzoeken: ~ *s.o.'s*
attention iemands aandacht vragen **2** aanspreken [by prostitute]

solicitor 1 procureur **2** rechtskundig adviseur; advocaat [at lower court] **3** notaris
solicitous 1 (+ about, for) bezorgd (om),
bekommerd **2** aandachtig, nauwgezet
solicitude 1 zorg, bezorgdheid, angst
2 aandacht, nauwgezetheid
¹solid (n) **1** vast lichaam[h] **2** (driedimensionaal) lichaam[h] **3** (-s) vast voedsel[h]
²solid (adj) **1** vast, stevig, solide: ~ *rock* vast
gesteente **2** ononderbroken [of time]: *Brug-*
man talked ~ly for three hours Brugman sprak
drie uur aan één stuk **3** betrouwbaar [finan-
cially] **4** driedimensionaal: ~ *geometry* ste-
reometrie **5** unaniem: ~ *vote* eenstemmigheid **6** gegrond, degelijk: ~ *reasons* gegron-
de redenen **7** zuiver, massief, puur: ~ *gold*
puur goud

solidarity solidariteit
solidify hard(er) (doen) worden, (doen)
verharden

solidity 1 hardheid **2** dichtheid, compactheid

soliloquy alleenspraak, monoloog: *teach-*
ing involves more than holding a ~ for fifty min-
utes lesgeven houdt meer in dan vijftig minuten lang een monoloog houden
solitary 1 alleen(levend), solitair **2** eenzelvig **3** afgezonderd, eenzaam: ~ *confinement*
eenzame opsluiting **4** enkel: *give me one ~*
example geef mij één enkel voorbeeld
solitude eenzaamheid
¹solo (n) **1** solo-optreden[h], solovlucht
²solo (adv) solo, alleen: *fly* ~ solo vliegen; *go*
~ een solocarrière beginnen, op de solotoer
gaan

soloist solist(e)
so long tot ziens
solstice zonnestilstand, zonnewende
soluble 1 oplosbaar **2** verklaarbaar
solution oplossing, solutie; [fig] uitweg: ~
for (or: *of, to*) *a problem* oplossing van een

probleem
solve 1 oplossen, een uitweg vinden voor
2 verklaren

solvency solvabiliteit, financiële draagkracht

solvent oplosmiddel[h]
¹Somali (n) Somaliër, Somalische
²Somali (adj) Somalisch
Somalia Somalië
sombre somber, duister, zwaarmoedig
¹some (pron) **1** wat, iets, enkele(n), sommi-
ge(n), een aantal, een of ander(e), een: *she*
bought ~ *oranges* ze kocht een paar sinaas-
appels; ~ *day* you'll understand ooit zul je het
begrijpen; *I've made a cake; would you like ~?*
ik heb een cake gebakken, wil je er wat van
(or: een stukje)?; ~ *say* so er zijn er die dat
zeggen **2** geweldig, fantastisch: *that was ~*
holiday tjonge/nou dat was een fijne vakantie

²some (adv) **1** ongeveer, zo wat: *it costs ~ fif-*
ty pounds het kost zo'n vijftig pond **2** [Am;
inform] enigszins, een beetje: *he was an-*
noyed ~ hij was een tikje geïrriteerd
somebody iemand
some day op een dag, ooit: *we all must die*
~ we moeten allemaal eens sterven
somehow 1 op de een of andere manier,
hoe dan ook, ergens: ~ *(or other) you'll have to*
tell him op de een of andere wijze zul je het
hem moeten vertellen **2** om de een of andere reden, waarom dan ook
someone iemand
someplace [Am] ergens, op een of ander
plaats: *do it ~ else* doe het ergens anders
¹somersault (n) salto (mortale), buiteling:
turn (or: *do*) *a* ~ een salto maken
²somersault (vb) een salto maken
something 1 iets, wat: *he dropped ~* hij
liet iets vallen; *seventy ~* zeventig en nog
wat; *there is ~ in* (or: *to*) *it* daar is iets van aan
2 (+ of) iets, enigszins: *it came as ~ of a sur-*
prise het kwam een beetje als een verrassing
sometime ooit, eens: *I'll show it to you* ~ ik
zal het je weleens laten zien
sometimes soms, af en toe, bij gelegenheid

somewhat enigszins, een beetje: *the soil is*
~ *moist* de aarde is een beetje vochtig
somewhere 1 ergens (heen): *we're getting*
~ *at last* dat lijkt er al meer op **2** ongeveer: ~
about sixty zo'n zestig
somnolence slaperigheid
son zoon, jongen
sonata sonate
song 1 lied(je)[h], wijsje[h] **2** gezang[h] ‖ *don't*
make such a ~ and dance about those old re-
cords maak toch niet zo'n drukte om die
oude platen; *go for a ~* bijna voor niets van
de hand gaan; *on ~* op dreef, op volle toeren, in topvorm

songbird zangvogel

song contest songfestival[h]: *the Eurovision ~* het Eurovisie songfestival

songwriter liedjesschrijver, liedjesschrijfster

sonic m.b.t. geluid(sgolven), geluids-: *~ boom* (or: *bang*) supersone knal

son-in-law schoonzoon

sonnet sonnet[h]

sonny jochie[h], mannetje[h]

sonogram [med] echo, echogram[h]

soon 1 spoedig, gauw, snel (daarna): *speak too ~* te voorbarig zijn; *the ~er the **better** hoe eerder hoe beter; *as ~ **as** zodra (als), meteen toen; *no ~er had he arrived **than** she left* nauwelijks was hij aangekomen of zij ging al weg **2** graag, bereidwillig: *I'd ~er **walk** ik loop liever; *I'd (just) as ~ **stay** home* ik blijf net zo lief thuis

soothe kalmeren, geruststellen, troosten

soothsayer waarzegger

sooty 1 roetig, (als) met roet bedekt **2** roetkleurig

sop doorweken, soppen

sophisticated 1 subtiel, ver ontwikkeld: *a ~ **taste** een verfijnde smaak **2** wereldwijs, ontwikkeld **3** ingewikkeld

sophistication 1 subtiliteit, raffinement[h] **2** wereldwijsheid **3** complexiteit

sophomore [Am] tweedejaarsstudent

sopping doorweekt, doornat: *~ **with** rain* kletsnat van de regen

soppy sentimenteel, zoetig

soprano sopraan(zangeres)

sorcerer tovenaar

sorcery tovenarij

sordid 1 vuil [also fig]; vies: *the ~ **details** de smerige details **2** armzalig, beroerd

¹sore (n) **1** pijnlijke plek, zweer, wond **2** (-s) zeer[h], pijnlijk onderwerp[h]: *recall* (or: *reopen*) *old ~s* oude wonden openrijten

²sore (adj) **1** pijnlijk, irriterend: *a ~ **throat** keelpijn **2** onaangenaam, pijnlijk: *a ~ **point** een teer punt **3** beledigd, kwaad, nijdig: *don't **get** ~ about the money you lost* maak je niet zo nijdig over het geld dat je verloren hebt || *a **sight** for ~ eyes* een aangenaam iets (iem.)

sorehead zeur(kous)

sorely ernstig, in belangrijke mate, pijnlijk: *he was ~ **tempted** hij werd in grote verleiding gebracht

sorrel zuring, soort moeskruid[h]

sorrow verdriet[h], leed[h]: *drown one's ~s* zijn verdriet verdrinken

sorrowful 1 treurig **2** bedroefd

¹sorry (adj) **1** droevig, erbarmelijk: *he came home in a ~ **condition** hij kwam thuis in een trieste toestand **2** naar, ellendig: *be in a ~ **plight** in een ellendige situatie verkeren **3** waardeloos [excuse etc] **4** bedroefd **5** me-

delijdend: *be* (or: *feel*) *~ for s.o.* medelijden hebben met iem. **6** berouwvol: *you'll **be** ~* het zal je berouwen, daar krijg je spijt van

²sorry (int) **1** sorry, het spijt me, pardon **2** wat zegt u?

¹sort (n) **1** soort[h], klasse, type[h]: *just buy him an ice cream, that ~ of **thing** koop maar een ijsje voor hem, of zoiets; *a ~ **of** (a)* een soort van, een of andere; *he is a lawyer **of** ~s* hij is een soort advocaat, hij is zo'n beetje advocaat; *'I'm going alone' 'you'll do nothing **of** the ~!'* 'ik ga alleen' 'daar komt niets van in!'; *all ~s of* allerlei **2** persoon, type[h], slag[h]: *he is a **bad** ~* hij deugt niet **3** [comp] sortering || *be out of ~s* zich niet lekker voelen

²sort (vb) sorteren, klasseren: *~ **letters** brieven sorteren; *~ **over** (or: *through*) sorteren, klasseren

¹sorted (adj) [inform] in orde gemaakt; voor elkaar: *that's your **ticket** ~ je ticket is geregeld

²sorted (int) geregeld

sort of min of meer, zo ongeveer, een beetje: *I feel ~ **ill** ik voel me een beetje ziek; *'are you in charge here?' 'well yes, ~'* 'heeft u hier de leiding?' 'nou, min of meer, ja'

sort out 1 sorteren, indelen, rangschikken **2** ordenen, regelen: *things will sort **themselves** out* de zaak komt wel terecht; *sort **o.s.** out* met zichzelf in het reine komen **3** te pakken krijgen, een opdonder geven: *stop that or I'll come and sort you out* hou daarmee op of je krijgt het met mij aan de stok

so-so zozo, middelmatig

sot dronkaard

sought after veelgevraagd

soul 1 ziel, geest: *poor ~!* (arme) stakker!; *with heart and ~* met hart en ziel; *All Souls' Day* Allerzielen; *not a (living) ~* geen levende ziel, geen sterveling **2** soul || *the (life and) ~ of the party* de gangmaker van het feest; *she is the ~ **of** kindness* zij is de vriendelijkheid zelf

soul-destroying geestdodend, afstompend

soul mate boezemvriend(in), minnaar, minnares

soul-searching het geweten onderzoekend

¹sound (n) **1** geluid[h], klank, toon: *I don't like the ~ of it* het bevalt me niet, het zit me niet lekker; *by the ~ of it* (or: *things*) zo te horen **2** gehoorsafstand **3** zee-engte, zeestraat **4** inham, baai, golf

²sound (adj) **1** gezond, krachtig, gaaf, fit: *be (as) ~ as a **bell*** a) (zo) gezond als een vis zijn; b) perfect functioneren [machine]; *a ~ **mind** in a ~ **body** een gezonde geest in een gezond lichaam **2** correct, logisch; gegrond [argument]; wijs [advice] **3** financieel gezond, evenwichtig, betrouwbaar **4** vast [sleep] **5** hard, krachtig: *a ~ **thrashing** een flink pak ransel

³sound (vb) klinken [also fig]; luiden, galmen: *that ~s reasonable* dat klinkt redelijk ‖ *~ off* a) opscheppen; b) zijn mening luid te kennen geven

⁴sound (vb) **1** laten klinken: *~ a warning* een waarschuwing laten horen **2** uiten, uitspreken **3** blazen [alarm, retreat]; blazen op [eg trumpet] **4** testen [lungs] **5** peilen [also fig]; onderzoeken, polsen: *~ s.o. out about* (or: *on*) *sth.* iem. over iets polsen

⁵sound (adv) vast; diep [sleep]: *~ asleep* vast in slaap

sound barrier geluidsbarrière

sound bite soundbite [korte, kernachtige uitspraak]

sound card geluidskaart

sounding peiling [also fig]: *make* (or: *take*) *~s* poolshoogte nemen, opiniepeilingen houden

sounding board 1 klankbord[h] [also fig]; spreekbuis **2** klankbodem

soundly 1 gezond, stevig **2** vast [asleep]

sound-proof geluiddicht

soundtrack 1 geluidsspoor[h] [of film with sound] **2** (cd met) opgenomen filmmuziek

soup soep ‖ *in the ~* in de puree

soup kitchen 1 gaarkeuken [for poor, homeless] **2** veldkeuken

soup up opvoeren [engine, power]

sour 1 zuur, wrang **2** onvriendelijk; scherp [tongue] **3** guur; onaangenaam [weather] ‖ *~ grapes* de druiven zijn zuur; *go* (or: *turn*) *~* slecht aflopen

source bron [also fig]; oorsprong, oorzaak

source language brontaal

sourpuss zuurpruim

souse 1 doornat maken, (een vloeistof) gieten (over iets) **2** pekelen, marineren

soused bezopen, dronken

¹south (n) het zuiden [point of compass]; zuid: *(to the) ~ of* ten zuiden van; *the South* het zuidelijk gedeelte

²south (adj) zuidelijk

³south (adv) in, uit, naar het zuiden: *down ~* in het zuiden

South Africa Zuid-Afrika: *the Republic of ~* de Republiek Zuid-Afrika

¹South African (n) Zuid-Afrikaan(se)

²South African (adj) Zuid-Afrikaans: *~ Dutch* Afrikaans[h] [language]

southbound op weg naar het zuiden

south-east zuidoostelijk

south-eastern zuidoostelijk

¹southerly (n) zuidenwind

²southerly (adj, adv) zuidelijk

southern zuidelijk: *~ lights* zuiderlicht[h], aurora australis

southerner zuiderling, Amerikaan uit de zuidelijke staten

South Korea Zuid-Korea

¹South Korean (n) Zuid-Koreaan(se)

²South Korean (adj) Zuid-Koreaans

South Pole zuidpool

South Sudan Zuid-Sudan

¹South Sudanese (n) Zuid-Sudanees, Zuid-Sudanese

²South Sudanese (adj) Zuid-Sudanees

southward zuid(waarts), zuidelijk

south-west zuidwestelijk

south-western zuidwestelijk

¹sovereign (n) soeverein, vorst

²sovereign (adj) **1** soeverein, onafhankelijk, heersend, oppermachtig **2** doeltreffend, efficiënt; krachtig [remedy]

sovereignty soevereiniteit, zelfbeschikking, heerschappij

Soviet Sovjet-; Russisch

¹sow (n) zeug

²sow (vb) opwekken, de kiem leggen van: *~ the seeds of doubt* twijfel zaaien

³sow (vb) **1** zaaien [also fig]; verspreiden **2** zaaien, (be)planten, poten

soy soja

spa 1 minerale bron **2** badplaats [near spring]; kuuroord[h]

¹space (n) **1** ruimte **2** afstand, interval[h] **3** plaats, ruimte, gebied[h]: *clear a ~ for s.o. (sth.)* ruimte maken voor iem. (iets) **4** tijdsspanne: *during the ~ of three years* binnen het bestek van drie jaar; *vanish into ~* in het niet verdwijnen

²space (vb) uit elkaar plaatsen, over de tijd verdelen: *~ out* over meer ruimte verdelen, spreiden; *~ out payments* betalen in termijnen

space blanket isolatiedeken, reddingsdeken

space centre ruimtevaartcentrum[h]

spacecraft ruimtevaartuig[h]

spaced out 1 zweverig, high, onder invloed **2** wereldvreemd, excentriek

space flight ruimtevlucht

spaceman ruimtevaarder

space probe ruimtesonde

spaceship ruimteschip[h]

spacing spatie: *single* (or: *double*) *~* met enkele (*or*: dubbele) regelafstand

spacious ruim, groot

spade 1 spade, schop **2** [cards] schoppen(s): *the five of ~s* schoppenvijf ‖ *call a ~ a ~* de dingen bij hun naam noemen

Spain Spanje

spam 1 [culinary] vlees[h], smac **2** [comp] spam, reclamemail

¹span (n) **1** breedte, wijdte, vleugelbreedte; spanwijdte [of aeroplane] **2** (tijd)span(ne) **3** overspanning, spanwijdte

²span (vb) overspannen [also fig]; overbruggen

¹spangle (n) lovertje[h], dun blaadje[h] klatergoud

²spangle (vb) met lovertjes versieren: *~d*

with **stars** met sterren bezaaid
Spaniard Spanjaard, Spaanse
Spanish Spaans ‖ ~ *chestnut* tamme kastanje(boom)
spank (een pak) voor de broek geven, een pak slaag geven
¹**spanking** (n) pakʰ voor de broek
²**spanking** (adj) **1** kolossaal, prima: ~ *new* spiksplinternieuw **2** vlug, krachtig
spanner moersleutel: *adjustable* ~ Engelse sleutel ‖ *throw a* ~ *into the* **works** een spaak in het wiel steken
¹**spar** (n) lange paal, rondhoutʰ
²**spar** (vb) **1** boksen **2** redetwisten
¹**spare** (n) reserve, dubbel, reserveonderdeelʰ, reservewielʰ
²**spare** (adj) **1** extra, reserve: ~ *room* logeerkamer; ~ *tyre* reservewielʰ; [hum] zwembandjeʰ **2** vrij [time] **3** mager ‖ *go* ~ razend worden
³**spare** (vb) **1** het stellen zonder, missen, overhebben: *enough and to* ~ meer dan genoeg; *can you* ~ *me a few moments?* heb je een paar minuten voor mij? **2** sparen, ontzien: ~ *s.o.'s* *feelings* iemands gevoelens sparen **3** sparen, bezuinigen op: *no* **expense** ~*d* het mag wat kosten
sparing zuinig; spaarzaam
¹**spark** (n) vonk; [fig] sprank(jeʰ); greintjeʰ: *a* ~ *of* **compassion** een greintje medelijden ‖ *some* **bright** ~ left the tap running één of andere slimmerik heeft de kraan open laten staan
²**spark** (vb) vonken
³**spark** (vb) **1** ontsteken, doen ontbranden **2** aanvuren, aanwakkeren **3** uitlokken: ~ *off a war* een oorlog uitlokken
sparkie [inform] elektricien
¹**sparkle** (n) fonkeling, glinstering, gefonkelʰ
²**sparkle** (vb) **1** fonkelen, glinsteren: *sparkling with wit* sprankelend van geest(igheid) **2** parelen, (op)bruisen: *sparkling water* spuitwater; *sparkling wine* mousserende wijn **3** spraankelen, geestig zijn
spark plug bougie
spark up er eentje opsteken
sparring partner sparringpartner [also fig]; trainingspartner, oefenmaat
sparrow mus
sparrow hawk sperwer
sparse dun, schaars, karig: *a* ~*ly populated area* een dunbevolkt gebied
sparsity schaarsheid
Spartan spartaans; [fig] zeer hard
spasm 1 kramp, huivering, spasmeʰ: ~*s of laughter* lachkrampen **2** aanval, opwelling: ~*s of* **grief** opwellingen van smart
spastic spastisch, krampachtig
spat klappen, ruzietjeʰ
spate 1 hoge waterstand [of river]: *the rivers*

are in ~ de rivieren zijn gezwollen **2** toevloed, overvloed, stroom: *a* ~ *of* **publications** een stroom publicaties
spatial ruimtelijk, ruimte-
¹**spatter** (n) **1** spat(jeʰ), vlekjeʰ **2** gespatʰ
²**spatter** (vb) **1** (be)spatten, (be)sprenkelen, klateren: *the lorry* ~*ed my clothes* **with** *mud* de vrachtauto bespatte mijn kleren met modder **2** bekladden; besmeuren [also fig]
spatula spatel
¹**spawn** (n) **1** kuit [of fish] **2** kikkerdrilʰ
²**spawn** (vb) **1** kuit schieten **2** verschijnen **3** produceren
¹**speak** (vb) spreken, een toespraak houden: *so to* ~ (om) zo te zeggen, bij wijze van spreken; *strictly* ~*ing* strikt genomen; ~*ing of which* **a)** nu je het zegt, nu we het erover hebben; **b)** trouwens, overigens; ~ *out against sth.* zich tegen iets uitspreken; ~ *up for s.o. (sth.)* het voor iem. (iets) opnemen; *nothing to* ~ *of* niets noemenswaardigs; ~ *ill* (or: *well*) *of s.o. (sth.)* kwaad (or: gunstig) spreken over iem. (iets); ~ *to s.o. (about sth.)* iem. (over iets) aanspreken; [telephone] ~*ing!* spreekt u mee! ‖ *that* ~*s for itself* dat spreekt voor zich; *could you* ~ *up please* kunt u wat harder spreken, a.u.b.; ~ *for sth.* **a)** iets bestellen; **b)** van iets getuigen; **c)** een toespraak houden (or: pleiten) voor [also fig]
²**speak** (vb) (uit)spreken, zeggen, uitdrukken: ~ *one's* **mind** zijn mening zeggen
speaker spreker
Speaker voorzitter van het Lagerhuis
speaking sprekend, levensecht, treffend: *a* ~ *likeness* een sprekende gelijkenis
speaking engagement spreekbeurt
speaking terms: *not be on* ~ *with s.o.* niet (meer) spreken tegen iem., onenigheid met iem. hebben
¹**spear** (n) speer, lans
²**spear** (vb) (met een speer) doorboren, spietsen
¹**spearhead** (n) speerpunt; [fig] spits, leider
²**spearhead** (vb) de spits zijn van [also fig]; leiden; aanvoeren [eg action, campaign]
¹**special** (n) iets bijzonders, extra-editie, speciaal gerechtʰ op menu, speciale attractie, (tv-)special, speciaal programmaʰ
²**special** (adj) speciaal, bijzonder, apart, extra ‖ *Special* **Branch** Politieke Veiligheidspolitie; ~ *delivery* expressebestelling
specialism specialismeʰ, specialisatie
specialist specialist
speciality 1 bijzonder kenmerkʰ, bijzonderheid, detailʰ **2** specialiteit [subject, product etc]
specialization specialisatie
¹**specialize** (vb) **1** zich specialiseren, gespecialiseerd zijn **2** in bijzonderheden treden
²**specialize** (vb) **1** specificeren, speciaal vermelden **2** beperken

specially speciaal, op speciale wijze, bijzonder: *he is not ~ interesting* hij is niet bepaald interessant

species soort, type^h: *the (human) ~, our ~* het mensdom, de menselijke soort

specific 1 specifiek, duidelijk: *be ~* de dingen bij hun naam noemen, er niet omheen draaien **2** specifiek, soortelijk: *~ gravity* soortelijk gewicht

specification 1 specificatie, gedetailleerde beschrijving **2** (-s) technische beschrijving

specify specificeren, precies vermelden

specimen 1 monster^h, staaltje^h **2** (mooi) exemplaar^h, (rare) knakker, eigenaardige kerel

speck vlek, stip, plek(je^h); [fig] greintje^h

¹speckle (n) spikkel, stippel, vlekje^h

²speckle (vb) bespikkelen, stippelen

specs *spectacles* bril

spectacle 1 schouwspel^h, vertoning **2** aanblik, gezicht^h **3** (-s) bril: *a pair of ~s* een bril

spectacular spectaculair, sensationeel

spectator toeschouwer, kijker

spectral 1 spookachtig **2** [physics] spectraal

spectre spook^h, geest; schim [also fig]

speculate speculeren, berekenen: *~ about* (or: *on*) overdenken, overpeinzen; *~ in* speculeren in

speculation 1 beschouwing, overpeinzing **2** speculatie

speculative speculatief, theoretisch, op gissingen berustend

speech 1 toespraak, rede(voering), speech: *Queen's* (or: *King's*) *~* troonrede; *maiden ~* eerste redevoering die iem. houdt, redenaarsdebuut **2** opmerking, uitlating **3** rede: *(in)direct ~* (in)directe rede; *reported ~* indirecte rede **4** spraak(vermogen^h), uiting, taal: *freedom of ~* vrijheid van meningsuiting

speech day prijsuitdeling(sdag) [at school]

speech defect spraakgebrek^h

speechless 1 sprakeloos, verstomd **2** onbeschrijfelijk: *~ admiration* woordeloze bewondering

speech recognition spraakherkenning

speech therapist logopedist

¹speed (n) **1** spoed, haast **2** (rij)snelheid, vaart, gang: *(at) full ~* met volle kracht, in volle vaart **3** versnelling [of bicycle] **4** versnelling(sbak) [of car] **5** (sluiter)snelheid **6** speed, amfetamine^+h

²speed (vb) **1** (te) snel rijden, de maximumsnelheid overschrijden: *~ up* sneller gaan rijden, gas geven **2** (voorbij)snellen [also fig]

³speed (vb) **1** opjagen, haast doen maken: *it needs ~ing up* er moet schot in worden gebracht, er moet tempo in komen **2** versnellen, opvoeren: *~ up (production)* (de productie) opvoeren **3** (+ away) (snel) vervoeren

speedboat speedboot

speed bump verkeersdrempel

speed camera flitspaal

speed dial [telecom] snelkeuzetoets

speeding het te hard rijden

speed limit topsnelheid, maximumsnelheid

speedometer snelheidsmeter

speedway 1 (auto)renbaan, speedwaybaan **2** autosnelweg

speedy snel, vlug, prompt

¹spell (n) **1** bezwering(sformule), ban, betovering: *put a ~ on* (or: *over*) betoveren; *fall under the ~ of* in de ban raken van **2** periode, tijd(je^h), (werk)beurt **3** vlaag, aanval, bui: *cold ~* koudegolf

²spell (vb) (voor)spellen, betekenen, inhouden: *these measures ~ the ruin of* deze maatregelen betekenen de ondergang van

³spell (vb) spellen: *~ out* (or: *over*) uitleggen, nauwkeurig omschrijven

spellbound geboeid, gefascineerd: *hold one's audience ~* het publiek in zijn ban houden

spell-checker spellingcontrole

spelling spelling(wijze)

spend 1 uitgeven, spenderen, besteden: *~ money on* geld spenderen aan **2** doorbrengen, wijden: *~ the evening watching TV* de avond doorbrengen met tv kijken **3** uitputten: *the storm had soon spent its force* de storm was spoedig uitgeraasd

spending cut bezuinigingsmaatregel

spending money [esp Am] zakgeld^h

spending power koopkracht

spendthrift verkwister, verspiller

spent 1 (op)gebruikt, af, leeg: *~ cartridge* lege huls **2** uitgeput, afgemat

sperm 1 spermacel, zaadcel **2** sperma^h, zaad^h

sperm bank spermabank

sperm whale potvis

spew (uit)braken, spuwen: *~ out* uitspugen; *~ up* overgeven

sphere 1 bol, bal, kogel **2** hemellichaam^h, globe, wereldbol **3** sfeer, kring, gebied^h, terrein^h: *~ of influence* invloedssfeer

spherical (bol)rond, bol-

sphinx sfinx

spice kruid^h, kruiden, specerij(en): *add ~ to* kruiden, smaak geven aan

spick and span 1 brandschoon, keurig, in de puntjes **2** (spik)splinternieuw

spicy 1 gekruid, heet **2** geurig **3** pikant [fig]; pittig: *~ story* gewaagd verhaal

spider spin, spinnenkop

spidery 1 spinachtig; [fig] krabbelig [handwriting] **2** broodmager: *~ legs* spillebenen **3** ragfijn

spiel 1 woordenstroom, (breedsprakig) verhaal^h: *the saleman's ~* het verkooppraatje

2 reclametekst [radio]

¹spike (n) **1** (scherpe) punt, pin, piek; prikker [for bills, loose notes etc] **2** (koren)aar **3** (-s) spikes [sports shoe]

²spike (vb) **1** (vast)spijkeren **2** van spijkers (punten) voorzien: ~*d shoes* spikes **3** alcohol toevoegen aan: ~ *coffee with cognac* wat cognac in de koffie doen

spike heel naaldhak

¹spill (n) **1** val(partij), duik **2** stukjeʰ papier (hout) [to light lamp or stove] **3** het afwerpen [of horseman] **4** verspilling

²spill (vb) overlopen, overstromen, uitstromen: *the milk* ~*ed* de melk liep over

³spill (vb) **1** doen overlopen, laten overstromen, morsen (met), omgooien, verspillen: ~ *the wine* met wijn morsen **2** vergieten [blood]; doen vloeien

spillage lozing [eg of oil into sea]

spillway 1 overlaat **2** afvoerkanaalʰ

¹spin (n) **1** draaibeweging, rotatie; [sport] spin; effectʰ [on ball] **2** ritjeʰ, tochtjeʰ: *let's go for a* ~ laten we 'n eindje gaan rijden **3** (terug)val; duik [also fig] **4** spin, tolvlucht || *in a (flat)* ~ in paniek, van de kaart

²spin (vb) tollen, snel draaien: *make s.o.'s head* ~ iemands hoofd doen tollen

³spin (vb) **1** spinnen [also fig] **2** in elkaar draaien, verzinnen; produceren [story] **3** spineffect geven [ball] **4** snel laten ronddraaien: ~ *a coin* kruis of munt gooien; ~ *a top* tollen [game] || ~ *out a)* uitspinnen [story]; **b)** rekken [time]; **c)** zuinig zijn met [money]

spinach spinazie

spindle 1 spindel, (spin)klos, spoel **2** as, spil **3** stang, staaf, pijp

spindly spichtig, stakig

spin doctor spindoctor

spin-drier centrifuge

spin-dry centrifugeren

spine 1 ruggengraat **2** stekel, doorn **3** rug [of book]

spine-chiller horrorfilm, horrorroman, horrorverhaalʰ, griezel-, gruwelfilm

spineless 1 zonder ruggengraat [also fig] **2** karakterloos, slap

spin-off (winstgevend) nevenproductʰ (resultaatʰ), bijproductʰ

spinster 1 oude vrijster **2** ongehuwde vrouw

¹spiral (n) spiraal, schroeflijn

²spiral (adj) **1** spiraalvormig, schroefvormig: ~ *staircase* wenteltrap **2** kronkelend

spire (toren)spits, piek, puntʰ

¹spirit (n) **1** geest, ziel, karakterʰ, bovennatuurlijk wezenʰ: *the Holy Spirit* de Heilige Geest; *kindred* ~*s* verwante zielen **2** levenskracht, energie **3** levenslust, opgewektheid **4** moed, durf, lefʰ **5** zin, diepe betekenis: *the* ~ *of the law* de geest van de wet **6** spiritus, alcohol; [sometimes singular] sterke-

drank(en): *methylated* ~ (brand)spiritus **7** (-s) gemoedsgesteldheid, geestesgesteldheid, stemming: *be in great* (or: *high*) ~*s* opgewekt zijn **8** mensʰ met karakter, karakterʰ **9** (-s) spiritus, geest || *public* ~ gemeenschapszin

²spirit (vb) (+ away, off) wegtoveren, ontfutselen; [fig] heimelijk laten verdwijnen

spirited 1 levendig, geanimeerd **2** bezield, vol energie

spiritless 1 lusteloos, moedeloos **2** levenloos, doods, saai

spirit level waterpas⁺ʰ

spiritual 1 geestelijk, spiritueel **2** mentaal, intellectueel **3** godsdienstig, religieus || ~ *healing* geloofsgenezing

spiritualism 1 spiritualismeʰ **2** spiritismeʰ

spirituality 1 spiritualiteit **2** vroomheid

¹spit (n) **1** spuugʰ, speekselʰ **2** spitʰ, braadspitʰ **3** landtong **4** spade, schop: *dig a hole two* ~(*s*) *deep* een gat twee spaden diep graven **5** geblaasʰ; gesisʰ [of cat] || ~ *and polish* (grondig) poetswerk [eg in army]

²spit (vb) **1** spuwen, spugen **2** sputteren; blazen [eg cat] **3** lichtjes neervallen, druppelen [rain] || *he is the* ~*ting image of his father* hij lijkt als twee druppels water op zijn vader

³spit (vb) (also + out) (uit)spuwen, (uit)spugen, opgeven || ~ *it out!* voor de dag ermee!

¹spite (n) wrok, boosaardigheid: *from* (or: *out of*) ~ uit kwaadaardigheid || *in* ~ *of* ondanks; *in* ~ *of o.s.* of men wil of niet

²spite (vb) treiteren, pesten

spiteful hatelijk

spitfire heethoofd, driftkop

spittle speekselʰ, spuugʰ

¹splash (n) **1** plons **2** vlek, spat **3** gespetterʰ, gespatʰ || *make a* ~ opzien baren

²splash (vb) **1** (rond)spatten, uiteenspatten: ~ *about* rondspatten **2** rondspetteren **3** klateren, kletteren

³splash (vb) **1** (be)spatten **2** laten spatten **3** met grote koppen in de krant zetten

⁴splash (adv) met een plons

splatter 1 spetteren, (be)spatten **2** poedelen **3** klateren, kletteren

¹splay (vb) naar buiten staan [of foot]

²splay (vb) **1** (also + out) (zich) verwijden, (zich) verbreden **2** (also + out) (zich) uitspreiden

spleen 1 milt **2** zwaarmoedigheid, neerslachtigheid **3** boze bui || *vent one's* ~ zijn gal spuwen

splendid 1 schitterend, prachtig **2** groots, indrukwekkend **3** voortreffelijk, uitstekend

splendour 1 pracht, praal **2** glorie, grootsheid

¹splice (n) **1** las, verbinding **2** splits [of rope] **3** houtverbinding

²splice (vb) **1** verbinden, aan elkaar verbinden, een verbinding maken **2** lassen; koppe-

len [film, sound tape] || **get** ~*d* trouwen
splint 1 metaalstrook, metaalstrip **2** spalk
¹**splinter** (n) splinter, scherf
²**splinter** (vb) versplinteren, splinteren
¹**split** (n) **1** spleet, kloof; [fig] breuk; scheiding **2** splitsing **3** (-s) spagaat: *do the* ~*s* een spagaat maken
²**split** (adj) **1** gespleten, gebarsten **2** gesplitst, gescheurd: [sport] ~ *decision* nieteenstemmige beslissing; ~ *level* met halve verdiepingen; ~ *pea* spliterwt; ~ *second* onderdeel van een seconde, flits
³**split** (vb) (+ on) verraden
⁴**split** (vb) **1** splijten, splitsen; [fig] afsplitsen; scheuren: *George and I have* ~ *up* George en ik zijn uit elkaar gegaan; ~ *up into groups* (zich) in groepjes verdelen **2** delen, onder elkaar verdelen: *let's* ~ *(the bill)* laten we (de kosten) delen
splitting fel, scherp, hevig: ~ *headache* barstende hoofdpijn
split-up breuk [after quarrel]; echtscheiding, het uit elkaar gaan
splodge vlek, plek, veeg
splurge 1 uitspatting, het zich te buiten gaan **2** spektakelʰ
¹**splutter** (n) gesputterʰ, gespetterʰ
²**splutter** (vb) **1** sputteren, stamelen, hakkelen **2** sputteren, sissen **3** proesten, spetteren
spod 1 sul, sukkel **2** [comp] nerd, computerfreak
¹**spoil** (n) **1** buit, geplunderde goederen **2** (-s) voordelen, winst
²**spoil** (vb) **1** bederven, (doen) rotten, beschadigen, verpesten: ~ *the fun* het plezier vergallen **2** bederven, verwennen, vertroetelen || *be* ~*ing for a fight* staan te trappelen om te vechten
spoils buit
spoilsport spelbreker
spoke 1 spaak **2** sport, trede || *put a* ~ *in s.o.'s wheel* iem. een spaak in het wiel steken
spokesman woordvoerder, afgevaardigde
spokesmodel fotomodelʰ dat wordt ingezet voor de promotie van een product
spokesperson woordvoerder
¹**sponge** (n) **1** klaploper **2** spons: [boxing] *throw in the* ~ de spons opgooien; [fig] de strijd opgeven **3** wondgaasʰ **4** luchtige cake/taart
²**sponge** (vb) klaplopen, parasiteren: ~ *on s.o.* op iem. (parasi)teren
³**sponge** (vb) **1** sponzen, schoon-, afsponzen **2** afspoelen met een spons
sponge bag toilettasjeʰ
sponge cake luchtige cake (*or:* taart)
sponger 1 sponzenduiker **2** klaploper
¹**sponsor** (n) **1** sponsor, geldschieter **2** peter, meter
²**sponsor** (vb) propageren, steunen, bevorderen, sponsoren

sponsorship sponsoring
spontaneity spontaniteit
spontaneous 1 spontaan, natuurlijk, ongedwongen **2** uit zichzelf, vanzelf: ~ *combustion* zelfontbranding
¹**spoof** (n) **1** poets, bedrogʰ **2** parodie
²**spoof** (vb) **1** voor de gek houden, een poets bakken **2** parodiëren **3** [comp] vervalsen
spook geest, spookʰ
spooky spookachtig, griezelig, eng
spool 1 spoel **2** klos, garenklos
¹**spoon** (n) lepel: *slotted* ~ schuimspaan
²**spoon** (vb): ~ *out* opscheppen, uitdelen
spoon-feed 1 voeren, met een lepel voeren **2** iets met de lepel ingieten, iem. iets voorkauwen
spoonful lepel (vol)
¹**sport** (n) **1** pret, spelʰ, plezierʰ: *in* ~ voor de grap **2** spelʰ, tijdverdrijfʰ **3** sport **4** jacht **5** sportieve meid (kerel)
²**sport** (vb) spelen [of animals]; zich vermaken
³**sport** (vb) pronken met, vertonen, te koop lopen met: *he was* ~*ing a bowler hat* hij liep met een hoge hoed
sporting 1 sportief, eerlijk, fair: ~ *chance* redelijke kans **2** sport-
sports 1 sport **2** sportdag, sportevenementʰ **3** atletiek
sports car sportwagen
sports centre sportcomplexʰ
sports event sportmanifestatie
sportsman 1 sportieve man **2** sportman
sportsmanlike sportief
sportsmanship sportiviteit, zich als een goede winnaar (verliezer) gedragen
sportswear sportkleding
sportswoman 1 sportieve vrouw **2** sportvrouw
sporty 1 sportief, sport- **2** zorgeloos, vrolijk **3** opvallend; bijzonder [of clothes]
¹**spot** (n) **1** plaats, plek: *they were on the* ~ ze waren ter plaatse **2** vlekjeʰ, stip **3** puistjeʰ **4** positie, plaats, functie **5** spot(jeʰ) [advertising etc] **6** spot(lightʰ) **7** beetjeʰ, watʰ: *a* ~ *of bother* een probleempje **8** onmiddellijke levering || *now he is in a (tight)* ~ nu zit hij in de penarie; *he had to leave on the* ~ hij moest op staande voet vertrekken; *put s.o. on the* ~ iem. in het nauw brengen, iem. voor het blok zetten
²**spot** (vb) **1** verkleuren, vlekken krijgen **2** vlekken **3** spetteren, licht regenen: *it is* ~*ting with rain* er vallen dikke regendruppels
³**spot** (vb) **1** vlekken maken in, bevlekken **2** herkennen, eruit halen: ~ *a mistake* een fout ontdekken
⁴**spot** (adv) precies: *arrive* ~ *on time* precies op tijd komen
spot check (onverwachte) steekproef
spotless brandschoon, vlekkeloos; [fig

also] onberispelijk

¹spotlight (n) **1** bundellicht^h, spotlight^h **2** bermlicht^h [of car] ‖ *be in the ~, hold the ~* in het middelpunt van de belangstelling staan

²spotlight (vb) **1** beschijnen **2** onder de aandacht brengen

spot-on [inform] precies (goed)

spotty 1 vlekkerig **2** ongelijkmatig, onregelmatig **3** puisterig

spouse echtgenoot, echtgenote

¹spout (n) **1** pijp, buis **2** tuit **3** stortkoker **4** straal, opspuitende vloeistof, opspuitend zand^h ‖ *up the ~* a) naar de knoppen, verknald [eg money, life]; b) totaal verkeerd [eg figures]; c) hopeloos in de knoei, reddeloos verloren [of person]; d) zwanger

²spout (vb) **1** spuiten, met kracht uitstoten: *the water ~ed from the broken pipe* het water spoot uit de gebarsten leiding **2** galmen, spuien: *she was always ~ing German verses* ze liep altijd Duitse verzen te galmen

¹sprain (n) verstuiking

²sprain (vb) verstuiken

sprat sprot

¹sprawl (n) **1** nonchalante houding **2** slordige massa, vormeloos geheel^h: *the ~ of the suburbs* de uitdijende voorsteden

²sprawl (vb) **1** armen en benen uitspreiden, nonchalant liggen, onderuit zakken **2** zich uitspreiden, alle kanten op gaan: *~ing suburbs* naar alle kanten uitgroeiende voorsteden

¹spray (n) **1** takje^h [also as corsage]; twijg **2** verstuiver, spuitbus **3** straal, wolk **4** nevel, wolk van druppels

²spray (vb) (be)sproeien, (be)spuiten, (een vloeistof) verstuiven

spray-gun spuitpistool^h; verfspuit

¹spread (n) **1** wijdte, breedte; [fig also] reikwijdte **2** uitdijing **3** verbreiding, verspreiding **4** stuk^h land, landbezit^h van één boer **5** smeersel^h **6** (feest)maal^h, onthaal^h **7** dubbele pagina, spread

²spread (vb) **1** zich uitstrekken, zich uitspreiden **2** zich verspreiden, overal bekend worden: *the disease ~ quickly to other villages* de ziekte breidde zich snel uit naar andere dorpen **3** uitgespreid worden: *cold butter does not ~ easily* koude boter smeert niet gemakkelijk

³spread (vb) **1** uitspreiden, verbreiden, verspreiden; [fig also] spreiden; verdelen: *~ out one's arms* zijn armen uitspreiden; *~ the word* (iets) verder vertellen, (iets) verspreiden/doorgeven **2** uitsmeren, uitstrijken **3** bedekken, beleggen, besmeren **4** klaarzetten [meal]; dekken [table]

spreadeagle 1 (zich) met armen en benen wijd neerleggen **2** volkomen verslaan, verpletteren

spreadsheet spreadsheet

spree pret(je^h), lol: *spending ~* geldsmijterij

sprig 1 twijgje^h, takje^h **2** telg, spruit

¹spring (n) **1** bron [also fig]; oorsprong, herkomst **2** (metalen) veer, springveer **3** sprong **4** lente, voorjaar^h: *in (the) ~* in het voorjaar (*or:* de lente)

²spring (vb) **1** (op)springen: *the first thing that ~s to one's mind* het eerste wat je te binnen schiet; *~ to one's feet* opspringen **2** (terug)veren **3** (also + up) ontspringen, ontstaan, voortkomen: *~ from* afstammen van; *~ from* (*or:* out of) voortkomen uit

³spring (vb) **1** springen over [of horse, obstacle] **2** plotseling bekendmaken: *~ sth. on s.o.* iem. met iets verrassen

springboard [also fig] springplank; duikplank

spring-clean voorjaarsschoonmaak, grote schoonmaak

spring roll loempia

spring tide springtij^h, springvloed

springtime lente(tijd), voorjaar^h

springy 1 veerkrachtig **2** elastisch

¹sprinkle (n) **1** regenbuitje^h **2** kleine hoeveelheid ‖ *a ~ of houses* enkele (verspreid liggende) huizen

²sprinkle (vb) **1** sprenkelen [also fig]; strooien **2** bestrooien [also fig]; besprenkelen: *~ with* bestrooien met

sprinkler 1 (tuin)sproeier **2** blusinstallatie

sprinkling kleine hoeveelheid, greintje^h

¹sprint (n) sprint, spurt

²sprint (vb) sprinten

sprinter 1 [sport] sprinter **2** sprinter [train]

sprite 1 (boze) geest **2** elf(je^h)

¹sprout (n) **1** spruit, loot, scheut **2** spruitje^h [vegetable]

²sprout (vb) **1** (ont)spruiten, uitlopen **2** de hoogte in schieten, groeien: *~ up* de hoogte in schieten

³sprout (vb) doen ontspruiten

¹spruce (n) spar, sparrenhout^h

²spruce (adj) net(jes), keurig

³spruce (vb) opdoffen, opdirken, verfraaien

spry levendig, actief: *a ~ old man* een vitale oude man

spud pieper, aardappel

spunk pit^+h, lef^h, durf

¹spur (n) **1** spoor^h [of horseman]: *win one's ~s* zijn sporen verdienen; **b)** [also fig] zich onderscheiden **2** aansporing, prikkel, stimulans: *act on the ~ of the moment* spontaan iets doen **3** uitloper [of mountain]

²spur (vb) **1** de sporen geven **2** aansporen, aanmoedigen: *~ on (to)* aanzetten (tot), aansporen (tot)

spurious 1 onecht, vals, vervalst **2** onlogisch: *~ argument* verkeerd argument

spurn 1 (weg)trappen **2** afwijzen, van de hand wijzen

¹spurt (n) **1** uitbarsting, losbarsting, vlaag, opwelling: *a ~ of flames* een plotselinge vlammenzee **2** sprint(je^h), spurt: *put on a ~* een sprintje trekken **3** (krachtige) straal, stroom, vloed

²spurt (vb) **1** spurten, sprinten **2** spuiten, opspatten: *the blood ~ed out* het bloed gutste eruit

¹sputter (n) gesputter^h, gestamel^h

²sputter (vb) sputteren, proesten, stamelen, brabbelen

¹spy (n) spion(ne), geheim agent(e)

²spy (vb) spioneren, spieden, loeren, een spion zijn: *~ (up)on* bespioneren, bespieden; *~ into* bespioneren, zijn neus steken in

³spy (vb) **1** bespioneren, bespieden **2** ontwaren, in het oog krijgen || *I ~ (with my little eye)* ik zie, ik zie, wat jij niet ziet

spyhole kijkgat^h

spy out 1 verkennen, onderzoeken **2** opsporen

spyware spyware

sq *square* kwadraat^h

¹squabble (n) schermutseling, gekibbel^h

²squabble (vb) kibbelen, overhoop liggen

squad 1 [sport] selectie **2** sectie **3** (politie)-brigade: *drugs ~* narcoticabrigade

squad car patrouilleauto

squadron 1 eskadron^h **2** [navy, air force] eskader^h

squadron leader majoor; eskadercommandant [in air force]

squalid 1 smerig, vuil, vies, gemeen, laag **2** ellendig, beroerd

¹squall (n) **1** vlaag, rukwind, windstoot, bui, storm **2** kreet, gil, schreeuw

²squall (vb) gillen, krijsen, (uit)schreeuwen

squally 1 buiig, regenachtig, winderig **2** stormachtig

squalor 1 misère **2** smerigheid

squander (+ on) verspillen (aan): *~ money* met geld smijten

¹square (n) **1** vierkant^h **2** kwadraat^h, tweede macht **3** plein^h **4** veld^h, hokje^h; ruit [on games' board] **5** (huizen)blok^h **6** oefenplein^h, oefenterrein^h **7** ouderwets persoon || *be back to ~ one* van voren af aan moeten beginnen; *on the ~* **a)** rechtdoorzee; **b)** in een rechte hoek

²square (adj) **1** vierkant, kwadraat-, in het vierkant, fors; breed [of figure]: *~ brackets* vierkante haakjes; *one ~ metre* één vierkante meter; *three metres ~* drie meter in het vierkant **2** recht(hoekig) **3** eerlijk, fair; open(hartig) [eg answer]; regelrecht [eg refusal]: *a ~ deal* een rechtvaardige behandeling, een eerlijke transactie **4** ouderwets **5** stevig [of meal] **6** [sport, esp golf] gelijk: *be (all) ~* gelijk staan || *a ~ peg (in a round hole)* de verkeerde persoon (voor iets); *be ~ with* quitte staan met, op gelijke hoogte (*or:* voet) staan met;

all ~ we staan quitte; [sport] gelijke stand

³square (vb) **1** overeenstemmen, kloppen **2** in een rechte hoek staan

⁴square (vb) **1** vierkant maken **2** rechthoekig maken **3** rechten [shoulders]; rechtzetten **4** in orde brengen, regelen; *~ up* vereffenen; *~ up one's debts* zijn schuld(en) voldoen **5** omkopen **6** kwadrateren, tot de tweede macht verheffen: *three ~d equals nine* drie tot de tweede (macht) is negen **7** [sport] op gelijke stand brengen

⁵square (adv) **1** recht(hoekig), rechtop **2** (regel)recht: *look s.o. ~ in the eye* iem. recht in de ogen kijken **3** eerlijk, rechtvaardig: *play ~* eerlijk spelen **4** rechtuit, open(hartig): *come ~ out with an answer* onomwonden antwoorden

square-built vierkant, hoekig, breed

square dance quadrille

squarely 1 recht(hoekig), rechtop **2** (regel)recht **3** eerlijk: *act ~* eerlijk handelen

square up 1 in gevechtshouding gaan staan: *~ to reality* de werkelijkheid onder ogen zien **2** afrekenen, orde op zaken stellen

¹squash (n) **1** kwast, vruchtendrank **2** gedrang^h, oploop **3** pulp

²squash (vb) **1** geplet worden **2** dringen, zich persen: *can I ~ in next to you?* kan ik er nog bij, naast u?

³squash (vb) **1** pletten, platdrukken **2** verpletteren; de mond snoeren **3** de kop indrukken **4** wringen: *~ in* erin persen

squashy 1 zacht, overrijp **2** drassig || *a ~ pillow* een zacht kussen

¹squat (n) **1** hurkende houding, het hurken **2** ineengedoken houding [of animal] **3** kraakpand^h **4** het kraken [of house]

²squat (adj) **1** gedrongen, plomp **2** gehurkt

³squat (vb) **1** (also + down) (neer)hurken **2** zich tegen de grond drukken [of animal] **3** zich illegaal vestigen [on a stretch of land] **4** als kraker een leegstaand pand bewonen

squatter 1 (illegale) kolonist, landbezetter **2** kraker

¹squawk (n) schreeuw, gekrijs^h

²squawk (vb) krijsen, schril schreeuwen

¹squeak (n) **1** gepiep^h, geknars^h **2** klein kansje^h || *that was a narrow ~* dat was op het nippertje, dat ging nog net

²squeak (vb) **1** piepen, knarsen, gilletjes slaken **2** doorslaan || *~ through* (*or:* by) het nog net halen

squeaky piepend, krakend || *~ clean* brandschoon

squeaky-clean 1 brandschoon **2** [fig, inform] brandschoon: *his ~ image was built on lies* zijn brandschone imago was op leugens gebaseerd

¹squeal (n) **1** gil, schreeuw, gepiep^h **2** klacht

²squeal (vb) **1** krijsen, piepen **2** klikken,

doorslaan: ~ **on** s.o. iem. aanbrengen
squeamish 1 (gauw) misselijk **2** teerge-
voelig, overgevoelig **3** (al te) kieskeurig || *this
film is not for* ~ *viewers* deze film is niet geschikt voor al te gevoelige kijkers
squeegee rubber wisser[h], schuiver, trekker
¹squeeze (n) **1** samendrukking, pressie,
druk: *she gave* his hand a little ~ ze kneep
even in zijn hand; *put* the ~ on s.o. iem. onder
druk zetten **2** gedrang[h] **3** (stevige) handdruk, (innige) omarming **4** beperking,
schaarste || *it was a close* (or: *narrow, tight*) ~
we zaten als haringen in een ton
²squeeze (vb) dringen, zich wringen: ~
through zich erdoorheen wurmen [also fig]
³squeeze (vb) **1** drukken (op), knijpen (in),
(uit)persen, uitknijpen: ~ *a lemon* een citroen uitpersen **2** duwen, wurmen: *how can
she* ~ *so many things into one single day?* hoe
krijgt ze zoveel dingen op één dag gedaan?
3 tegen zich aan drukken, stevig omhelzen
squelch een zuigend geluid maken, ploeteren
squib 1 voetzoeker **2** blindganger **3** schotschrift[h]
squid pijlinktvis
squidgy klef
squiggle kronkel(lijn), krabbel
squillion [hum] ziljoen[h], ontelbaar veel
¹squint (n) **1** scheel oog[h], turend oog[h]
2 (vluchtige) blik: *have* (or: *take*) a ~ at sth.
een blik werpen op iets
²squint (vb) **1** scheel kijken **2** gluren, turen:
~ *at sth.* een steelse blik op iets werpen
squire 1 landjonker; landheer [in England]
2 meneer [form of address among men]
squirm 1 kronkelen, zich in bochten wringen **2** wel door de grond kunnen gaan: *be
~ing with embarrassment* zich geen raad weten van verlegenheid
¹squirrel (n) eekhoorn
²squirrel (vb): *he ~ed away more than he
needed* hij hamsterde meer dan hij nodig had
¹squirt (n) **1** straal [of liquid etc] **2** spuit(je[h]),
waterpistool[h]
²squirt (vb) (krachtig) naar buiten spuiten
³squirt (vb) (uit)spuiten, uitspuwen
sr *senior* sr., sen.
Sri Lanka Sri Lanka
¹Sri Lankan (n) Sri Lankaan(se)
²Sri Lankan (adj) Sri Lankaans
srsly [inform] *seriously* serieus, echt waar
St 1 *Saint* St., H., Sint, Heilige **2** *Street* str.,
straat **3** *strait* zee-engte, straat
¹stab (n) **1** steek(wond), stoot, uithaal
2 pijnscheut, plotse opwelling **3** poging,
gooi: *have* (or: *make*) a ~ at eens proberen || a
~ *in the back* dolkstoot in de rug
²stab (vb) (+ at) (toe)stoten (naar), steken,
uithalen (naar): *a ~bing pain* een stekende
pijn

³stab (vb) (door)steken, neersteken, doorboren: *be ~bed to death* doodgestoken worden
stability stabiliteit, duurzaamheid
stabilize (zich) stabiliseren, in evenwicht
blijven (brengen)
¹stable (n) **1** stal; [fig] ploeg; groep **2** (ren)-
stal || *it is no use shutting the ~ door after the
horse has bolted* als het kalf verdronken is,
dempt men de put
²stable (adj) **1** stabiel, vast, duurzaam
2 standvastig
¹stack (n) **1** (hooi)mijt, houtmijt **2** stapel,
hoop: *~s of money* bergen geld **3** schoorsteen
²stack (vb) **1** (op)stapelen, op een hoop leggen, volstapelen **2** arrangeren: ~ *the cards*
de kaarten vals schikken
¹stack up (vb) **1** een file vormen [of cars,
aeroplanes]; aanschuiven **2** ervoor staan
²stack up (vb) **1** opstapelen **2** ophouden:
traffic was stacked up for miles het verkeer
werd kilometers lang opgehouden
stadium stadion[h]
¹staff (n) **1** staf [also fig]; steun **2** vlaggenstok **3** notenbalk **4** staf [also mil]; perso-
neel[h], korps[h] || *the ~ of life* brood[h]
²staff (vb) bemannen, van personeel voorzien
staff manager personeelschef
staff member staflid[h]
¹stag (n) **1** hertenbok **2** man die alleen op
stap is
²stag (adj) mannen-: ~ *party* vrijgezellen-
feest[h], hengstenbal[h]
¹stage (n) **1** toneel[h] [also fig]; podium[h], platform[h]: *put* on the ~ opvoeren; *be on the* ~ aan
het toneel verbonden zijn **2** fase, stadium[h]:
at this ~ op dit punt, in dit stadium **3** stopplaats, halte aan het eind van een tariefzone
4 etappe, traject[h], tariefzone: *by easy ~s* in
korte etappes; *in ~s* gefaseerd **5** postkoets ||
set the ~ for de weg bereiden voor
²stage (vb) **1** opvoeren, ten tonele brengen
2 produceren **3** regisseren **4** organiseren
stagecoach postkoets
stage door artiesteningang
stage fright plankenkoorts
stage-manage in scène zetten, opzetten
stage manager toneelmeester
¹stagger (n) wankeling
²stagger (vb) wankelen: ~ *along* moeizaam
vooruitkomen
³stagger (vb) **1** doen wankelen; [fig] ont-
hutsen **2** zigzagsgewijs aanbrengen: *a ~ed
road crossing* een kruising met verspringende
zijwegen **3** spreiden [holidays]: *~ed office
hours* glijdende werktijden
staggering 1 wankelend **2** onthutsend,
duizelingwekkend
staging 1 steiger; platform[h] **2** opvoering
stagnant 1 stilstaand **2** stagnerend

stagnate stilstaan, stagneren, stremmen
stag party bokkenfuif; hengstenbal^h
staid 1 bezadigd **2** vast, stellig
¹stain (n) **1** vlek, smet, schandvlek **2** kleurstof
²stain (vb) vlekken
³stain (vb) **1** bevlekken **2** kleuren: ~ed **glass** gebrandschilderd glas
stainless roestvrij [steel]
stair 1 [also pl] trap: a **winding** ~ een wenteltrap **2** trede
staircase trap: a **moving** ~ een roltrap
stairlift traplift
stairway trap
stairwell trappenhuis^h
¹stake (n) **1** staak, paal **2** brandstapel: **go to the** ~ op de brandstapel sterven **3** inzet; [fig] belang^h: **have a** ~ **in** sth. zakelijk belang hebben bij iets || **be at** ~ op het spel staan
²stake (vb) **1** (+ off, out) afpalen [eg land]; afbakenen: ~ **out** a **claim** aanspraak maken op **2** spietsen **3** (+ on) verwedden (om), inzetten (op); [fig] op het spel zetten: I'd ~ **my life on** it ik durf er mijn hoofd om te verwedden || ~ **out** posten bij, in de gaten houden
stakeholder 1 beheerder van de inzet **2** [econ] stakeholder; belanghebbende
stalactite stalactiet, druipsteenpegel
stalagmite stalagmiet, druipsteenkegel
stale 1 niet vers, oud(bakken) **2** afgezaagd **3** mat, afgemat, machinaal
stalemate 1 [chess] pat^h **2** patstelling, dood punt^h
¹stalk (n) **1** [bot] stengel, steel **2** stronk
²stalk (vb) (+ out) (uit) schrijden: the chairman ~ed **out** in anger de voorzitter stapte kwaad op
³stalk (vb) **1** besluipen **2** achtervolgen, stalken **3** rondwaren door
stalker 1 iem. die wild besluipt; jager **2** stalker
¹stall (n) **1** box, hok^h, stal **2** stalletje^h, stand, kraam, tent: **coffee** ~ koffietentje **3** stallesplaats **4** [aviation] overtrokken vlucht
²stall (vb) **1** blijven steken, ingesneeuwd zijn **2** afslaan [of engine] **3** overtrokken raken [of aeroplane] **4** uitvluchten zoeken, tijd rekken
³stall (vb) **1** stallen **2** ophouden, blokkeren
stallion (dek)hengst
¹stalwart (n) trouwe aanhanger
²stalwart (adj) **1** stevig, stoer **2** flink **3** standvastig, trouw
stamen meeldraad
stamina uithoudingsvermogen^h
stammer stotteren, stamelen || **speak** with a ~ stotteren
¹stamp (n) **1** stempel^{+h}; [fig] (ken)merk^h **2** zegel^{+h}, postzegel, waarmerk^h **3** kenmerk^h
²stamp (vb) stampen, trappen
³stamp (vb) **1** stempelen, persen, waarmer-

ken: be ~ed **on** one's memory in zijn geheugen gegrift zijn **2** frankeren, een postzegel plakken op: ~ed addressed **envelope** antwoordenvelop **3** fijnstampen: ~ **out** uitroeien; ~ **on** onderdrukken
stamp collector postzegelverzamelaar
¹stampede (n) **1** wilde vlucht; op hol slaan [of animals]; paniek **2** stormloop
²stampede (vb) op de vlucht slaan, op hol slaan
³stampede (vb) op de vlucht jagen; [fig] het hoofd doen verliezen: don't be ~d **into** selling your house ga nou niet halsoverkop je huis verkopen
stance 1 houding, stand **2** pose, gezindheid: an obvious anti-American ~ een duidelijke anti-Amerikaanse gezindheid
¹stand (n) **1** stilstand, halt^h: **bring** to a ~ tot staan brengen **2** stelling [also mil]; [fig] standpunt^h **3** plaats, positie, post **4** statief^h, standaard **5** stand, kraam **6** standplaats [of taxis etc] **7** tribune, podium^h, getuigenbank
²stand (vb) **1** (rechtop) staan, opstaan: ~ **clear** of vrijlaten [door etc] **2** zich bevinden, staan, liggen **3** stilstaan, halt houden; stoppen [of vehicles] **4** blijven staan, stand houden: ~ **and deliver!** je geld of je leven! **5** gelden, opgaan: the **offer** still ~s het aanbod is nog van kracht **6** zijn, (ervoor) staan, zich in een bepaalde situatie bevinden: I want to know **where** I ~ ik wil weten waar ik aan toe ben **7** kandidaat zijn, zich kandidaat stellen: ~ **for** president against … kandidaat zijn voor het presidentschap met … als tegenkandidaat || I ~ **corrected** ik neem mijn woorden terug; ~ **to lose** sth. waarschijnlijk iets zullen verliezen; ~ **aloof** zich op een afstand houden; ~ **apart** zich afzijdig houden; ~ **easy!** op de plaats rust!; ~ **in** (for s.o.) (iem.) vervangen
³stand (vb) **1** plaatsen, rechtop zetten: ~ everything on its **head** alles op zijn kop zetten **2** verdragen, uitstaan, doorstaan, ondergaan **3** weerstaan **4** trakteren (op): ~ s.o. (to) a **drink** iem. op een drankje trakteren
stand-alone standalone; autonoom
¹standard (n) **1** peil^h, niveau^h: ~ of **living** levensstandaard; **below** ~ beneden peil, beneden de norm **2** vaandel^h [also fig]; standaard, vlag **3** maat(staf), norm **4** standaard(maat) **5** houder [eg candlestick] **6** (munt)standaard: the **gold** ~ de gouden standaard **7** staander, steun, paal **8** hoogstammige plant (struik)
²standard (adj) **1** normaal, gebruikelijk: ~ **size** standaardmaat, standaardgrootte **2** staand: ~ **rose** stamroos
standardization standaardisering, normalisering
standardize standaardiseren, normaliseren
stand aside 1 opzijgaan **2** zich afzijdig

houden
stand b<u>a</u>ck 1 achteruit gaan **2** op een afstand liggen **3** afstand nemen **4** zich op de achtergrond houden
¹st<u>a</u>ndby (n) **1** reserve **2** stand-by
²st<u>a</u>ndby (adj) reserve-, nood-
st<u>a</u>nd by 1 erbij staan **2** werkeloos toezien: ~ and **watch** erbij staan en ernaar kijken, niets doen **3** gereed staan **4** bijstaan, steunen **5** zich houden aan [promise]; trouw blijven aan [somebody]
st<u>a</u>nd d<u>o</u>wn zich terugtrekken, aftreden
st<u>a</u>nd for 1 staan voor, betekenen **2** goedvinden, zich laten welgevallen
st<u>a</u>nd-in vervanger
¹st<u>a</u>nding (n) **1** status, rang, positie: s.o. **of** ~ iem. van aanzien **2** reputatie **3** (tijds)duur: friendship of **long** ~ oude vriendschap
²st<u>a</u>nding (adj) **1** blijvend, van kracht, vast: ~ **committee** permanente commissie; ~ **joke** vaste grap; ~ **order** a) doorlopende order; b) automatische overschrijving; ~ **orders** statuten **2** staand, stilstaand: ~ **ovation** staande ovatie **3** zonder aanloop [of jump etc]
st<u>a</u>nding room staanplaatsen
st<u>a</u>nd-<u>o</u>ff 1 impasse, patstelling **2** evenwichtʰ **3** (periode van) nietsdoenʰ
stand<u>o</u>ffish afstandelijk
st<u>a</u>ndout [Am; inform] uitblinker, schoonheid: Helen's translation **was** a ~ Helens vertaling stak met kop en schouder boven de rest uit
stand <u>ou</u>t 1 duidelijk uitkomen, in het oog vallen **2** zich onderscheiden **3** blijven volhouden: ~ **for** verdedigen
st<u>a</u>ndpoint standpuntʰ [also fig]: **from** a commercial ~ commercieel gezien
St <u>A</u>ndrew's cr<u>o</u>ss 1 andreaskruisʰ **2** Schotse vlag
st<u>a</u>ndstill stilstand: **at** a ~ tot stilstand gekomen
¹st<u>a</u>nd <u>u</u>p (vb) **1** overeind staan **2** gaan staan: ~ and be **counted** voor zijn mening uitkomen; ~ **for** opkomen voor **3** standhouden, overeind blijven; [fig] doorstaan: that won't ~ in **court** daar blijft niets van overeind in de rechtszaal || ~ **to** trotseren
²st<u>a</u>nd <u>u</u>p (vb) laten zitten: she stood **me** up zij is niet op komen dagen
st<u>a</u>nd-up 1 rechtop staand **2** lopend [of supper etc] **3** flink [fight]; stevig || ~ **comedian** conferencier
st<u>a</u>nza coupletʰ, strofe
¹st<u>a</u>ple (n) **1** nietjeʰ **2** krammetjeʰ **3** hoofdbestanddeelʰ [also fig]; hoofdschotel
²st<u>a</u>ple (adj) **1** voornaamste: ~ **diet** hoofdvoedselʰ; ~ **products** stapelproducten **2** belangrijk
³st<u>a</u>ple (vb) (vast)nieten, hechten
st<u>a</u>pler nietmachine
¹st<u>a</u>r (n) **1** ster: Star of **David** davidster;

shooting ~ vallende ster; *thank* one's (lucky) ~s zich gelukkig prijzen **2** asterisk, sterretjeʰ **3** uitblink(st)er, beroemdheid, (film)ster, vedette: all-~ **cast** sterbezetting || the Stars and Stripes (or: **Bars**) Amerikaanse vlag
²st<u>a</u>r (vb) (als ster) optreden
³st<u>a</u>r (vb) **1** met een sterretje aanduiden **2** als ster laten optreden: a **film** ~ring Eddy Murphy een film met (in de hoofdrol) Eddy Murphy
st<u>a</u>rboard stuurboordʰ, rechtsʰ
st<u>a</u>rch 1 zetmeelʰ **2** stijfselʰ
st<u>a</u>rchy 1 zetmeelrijk: ~ **food** meelkost **2** gesteven **3** stijfjes
st<u>a</u>rdom sterrendomʰ; roem
¹st<u>a</u>re (n) starende blik
²st<u>a</u>re (vb) (+ at) staren (naar)
³st<u>a</u>re (vb) staren naar: it is staring you in the **face** het ligt voor de hand; ~ s.o. **down** (or: out) iem. aanstaren tot hij de ogen neerslaat
st<u>a</u>redown [Am] confrontatie
st<u>a</u>rfish zeester
st<u>a</u>rgazer 1 [hum] sterrenkijker **2** dromer
¹st<u>a</u>ring (adj) (te) fel [colour]
²st<u>a</u>ring (adv) volledig: stark ~ **mad** knettergek
¹st<u>a</u>rk (adj) **1** grimmig **2** stijf, onbuigzaam **3** [fig] schril: ~ **contrast** schril contrast **4** verlaten [of landscape]; kaal || ~ **poverty** bittere armoede
²st<u>a</u>rk (adv) volledig: ~ **naked** spiernaakt
st<u>a</u>rkers poedelnaakt
st<u>a</u>rlet (film)sterretjeʰ
st<u>a</u>rling spreeuw
st<u>a</u>rry-<u>ey</u>ed [inform] te idealistisch, wereldvreemd
st<u>a</u>r-spangled met sterren bezaaid || the Star-Spangled **Banner** a) het Amerikaanse volkslied; b) de Amerikaanse vlag
¹st<u>a</u>rt (n) **1** schok, ruk: **give** s.o. a ~ iem. laten schrikken, iem. doen opkijken; **wake** up with a ~ wakker schrikken **2** start: **from** ~ to **finish** van begin tot eind; **false** ~ valse start [also fig]; **get** off to a **good** ~ goed beginnen, een goede start maken; **make** a ~ **on** beginnen met; make a **fresh** (or: **new**) ~ opnieuw beginnen; **for** a ~ om te beginnen; **from** the (very) ~ vanaf het (allereerste) begin **3** startseinʰ **4** voorsprong, voordeelʰ: **give** s.o. a ~ (in life) iem. op gang helpen
²st<u>a</u>rt (vb) **1** beginnen, starten, beginnen te lopen: ~ing next **month** vanaf volgende maand; ~ **out** vertrekken; [fig] zijn loopbaan beginnen; ~ (all) **over** again (helemaal) opnieuw beginnen; ~ **from** beginnen bij; [fig] uitgaan van; to ~ (off) **with** om (mee) te beginnen, in het begin, in de eerste plaats **2** vertrekken, opstijgen, afvaren: ~ (out) **for** op weg gaan naar **3** (op)springen, (op)schrikken: ~ **back** (from) terugdeinzen (voor); ~ **at** (op)schrikken van

4 (plotseling) bewegen; losspringen [of wood]; aanslaan [of engine]; tevoorschijn springen; ~ *for* the door richting deur gaan **5** startsein geven **6** uitpuilen [of eyes]

³start (vb) **1** (doen) beginnen, aan de gang brengen, aanzetten; starten [engine]; aansteken [fire]; op touw zetten; opzetten [business etc]; naar voren brengen [subject] **2** brengen tot, laten: *the dust ~ed me coughing* door het stof moest ik hoesten **3** aannemen, laten beginnen

starter 1 beginner: *a slow ~* iem. die langzaam op gang komt **2** startmotor **3** voorafjeʰ, voorgerechtʰ || *for ~s* om te beginnen

starting block startblokʰ

starting pistol startpistoolʰ

starting point uitgangspuntʰ [also fig]

¹startle (vb) (op)schrikken

²startle (vb) **1** doen schrikken, opschrikken **2** schokken

startling verrassend

¹start off (vb) **1** beginnen: *he started off (by) saying that* hij begon met te zeggen dat **2** vertrekken **3** beginnen te zeggen

²start off (vb) (+ on) aan de gang laten gaan (met), laten beginnen (met)

¹start up (vb) **1** opspringen **2** een loopbaan beginnen: *~ in business* in zaken gaan **3** ontstaan, opkomen

²start up (vb) aan de gang brengen; opzetten [business]; starten [engine]

start-up pas opgericht (internet)bedrijfʰ

star turn hoofdnummerʰ, hoofdattractie

starvation 1 hongerdoodʰ **2** verhongering

starvation wages hongerloonʰ

¹starve (vb) **1** verhongeren: *~ to death* verhongeren **2** honger lijden **3** sterven van de honger

²starve (vb) **1** uithongeren **2** doen kwijnen; [also fig] laten hunkeren; onthouden: *be ~d of* behoefte hebben aan **3** door uithongering dwingen: *be ~d into surrender* door uithongering tot overgave gedwongen worden

¹stash (n) **1** (geheime) opslagplaats **2** verborgen buit; stiekeme voorraad [of drugs]

²stash (vb) (also + away) verbergen, opbergen

¹state (n) **1** toestand, staat: *~ of affairs* stand van zaken; *a poor ~ of health* een slechte gezondheidstoestand **2** (gemoeds)toestand, stemming: *be in a ~* in alle staten zijn **3** staat, natie, rijkʰ **4** staatsie, praal: *~ banquet* staatsiebanket || *lie in ~* opgebaard liggen

²state (vb) **1** (formeel) verklaren, uitdrukken **2** aangeven, opgeven: *at ~ intervals* op gezette tijden, met regelmatige tussenpozen **3** vaststellen, specificeren

state benefit uitkering

stateless staatloos

stately 1 statig **2** waardig **3** formeel || *~ home* landhuisʰ

statement 1 verklaring **2** (bank)afschriftʰ

state-of-the-art hypermodern, uiterst geavanceerd

stateroom 1 staatsiezaal **2** passagiershut **3** (privé)coupé

States (the) Verenigde Staten

statesman staatsman

statesmanlike als een staatsman

statesmanship staatsmanschapʰ

statewide over de gehele staat

static 1 statisch, stabiel: *~ electricity* statische elektriciteit **2** in rust **3** atmosferisch

¹station (n) **1** stationʰ [also of railway, radio, TV]; goederenstationʰ **2** standplaats, plaats, post **3** brandweerkazerne **4** politiebureauʰ **5** [mil] basis, post **6** positie, rang, status: *marry above* (or: *beneath*) *one's ~* boven (or: beneden) zijn stand trouwen

²station (vb) plaatsen, stationeren: *~ o.s.* postvatten

stationary stationair, stilstaand, vast

stationer handelaar in kantoorbenodigdheden, kantoorboekhandel

stationery 1 kantoorbenodigdheden **2** kantoorboekhandel **3** briefpapierʰ en enveloppen: *printed ~* voorbedrukt briefpapier

stationmaster stationschef

statistic statistisch gegevenʰ

statistical statistisch

statistics statistiek(en), cijfers, percentages

statue (stand)beeldʰ: *Statue of Liberty* Vrijheidsbeeld

statuesque 1 als een standbeeld **2** plastisch

statuette beeldjeʰ

stature 1 gestalte, (lichaams)lengte **2** [fig] formaatʰ

status status

status seeker statuszoeker

statute statuutʰ, wet

statutory statutair; volgens de wet

¹staunch (adj) **1** betrouwbaar, trouw **2** solide

²staunch (vb) **1** stelpen **2** tot staan brengen **3** waterdicht maken

stave 1 duig **2** stok, knuppel **3** stang, staaf **4** sport [of ladder, chair]

stave in 1 in duigen slaan **2** een gat slaan in, indrukken, kapotslaan

stave off 1 van zich afhouden, op een afstand houden **2** voorkomen

¹stay (n) **1** verblijfʰ, oponthoudʰ **2** steun [also fig] **3** verbindingsstukʰ [eg in aeroplane] **4** baleinʰ

²stay (vb) **1** blijven: *come to ~, be here to ~* blijven; [fig] zich een blijvende plaats verwerven; *~ for s.o.* wachten op iem. **2** verblijven, logeren: *~ the night* de nacht doorbrengen; *where are you ~ing?* waar overnacht je? **3** stilhouden, ophouden **4** verblijven

³stay (vb) **1** (also + up) (onder)steunen **2** uithouden [sport]: ~ *the* **course** tot het einde toe volhouden

⁴stay (vb) blijven; ~ *seated* blijven zitten; ~ *ahead of the others* de anderen voorblijven; ~ *away* wegblijven; ~ *behind* (achter)blijven; ~ *in (after school)* nablijven; ~ *indoors* binnen blijven; ~ *on* a) erop blijven; b) aanblijven [of light etc]; c) (aan)blijven [in office]; ~ *up* late laat opblijven

staycation [inform] thuisvakantie; vakantie in eigen land

stayer 1 blijverʰ **2** volhouder, doorzetter, langeafstandsloper, langeafstandszwemmer

staying power uithoudingsvermogenʰ

steadfast 1 vast, standvastig **2** trouw

¹steady (n) vrijer, vaste vriend/vriendin

²steady (adj) **1** vast, vaststaand, stabiel: *(as)* ~ *as a* **rock** rotsvast **2** gestaag, geregeld; vast [of job, income etc]; regelmatig [of life]; sterk [of nerves] **3** kalm, evenwichtig: ~ *on!* kalm aan!, langzaam! **4** betrouwbaar, oppassend **5** gematigd [of climate]; matig

³steady (vb) **1** vast/bestendig worden **2** kalm worden

⁴steady (vb) **1** vastheid geven, steunen: ~ *o.s.* zich staande houden **2** bestendigen, stabiliseren

⁵steady (adv) vast, gestaag ‖ *go* ~ vaste verkering hebben

⁶steady (int) **1** kalm aan, rustig **2** [shipp] recht zo

steak 1 (lapje) vleesʰ, runderlapjeʰ **2** (vis)moot **3** visfilet⁺ʰ

steak tartare tartaar

¹steal (vb) **1** stelen **2** sluipen: ~ *away* er heimelijk vandoor gaan; ~ *up on* s.o. iem. besluipen; ~ *over* s.o. iem. bekruipen [of feeling, thought]

²steal (vb) (ont)stelen, ontvreemden: ~ *a ride* stiekem meerijden

stealth heimelijkheid, geheimʰ: *by* ~ stiekem, in het geniep

stealthy heimelijk, stiekem

¹steam (n) stoom(kracht), wasem, condensatie; [fig] kracht(ige gevoelens); vaart: *blow* (or: *let, work*) *off* ~ stoom afblazen, zijn agressie kwijtraken; *run out of* ~ zijn energie verliezen, futloos worden

²steam (vb) **1** stomen, dampen: ~*ing hot* **milk** gloeiend hete melk **2** opstomen; [fig] energiek werken: ~ *ahead* (or: *away*) doorstomen, er vaart achter zetten

³steam (vb) (gaar) stomen, klaarstomen: ~*ed* **fish** (or: *rice*) gestoomde vis (or: rijst)

steamboat stoomboot

steam engine stoommachine

steamer 1 stoompan, stoomketel **2** stoomschipʰ, stoomboot

¹steamroller (n) stoomwals [also fig]

²steamroller (vb) **1** met een stoomwals platwalsen **2** verpletteren, vernietigen: ~ *all*

opposition alle verzet de kop indrukken

¹steam up (vb) beslaan, met condensatie bedekt worden: *my glasses* are steaming up mijn bril beslaat

²steam up (vb) **1** doen beslaan, met condensatie bedekken **2** opgewonden maken, opwinden, ergeren: *don't get steamed up about it* maak je er niet druk om

steamy 1 m.b.t. stoom, dampig **2** heet, sensueel

steed (strijd)rosʰ, paardʰ

¹steel (n) **1** staal [also fig] **2** stukʰ staal: *a man of* ~ een man van staal, een sterke man

²steel (vb) stalen; pantseren [also fig]; harden, sterken: ~ *o.s. to* **do** sth. zich dwingen iets te doen

steelworks staalfabriek

steely stalen, (als) van staal; [fig] onbuigzaam: ~ *composure* ijzige kalmte

¹steep (adj) **1** steil, sterk hellend: *a* ~ **slope** een steile helling **2** scherp (oplopend), snel (stijgend): *a* ~ **rise** *in prices* scherpe prijsstijgingen **3** onredelijk [eg of claim]; sterk [story]

²steep (vb) (in)trekken, weken

³steep (vb) onderdompelen [also fig]

steeple (toren)spits, bovenste deelʰ van een toren

steeplechase [equestrian sport, athletics] steeplechase, hindernisren, hindernisloop

¹steer (n) **1** jonge os **2** stierkalfʰ

²steer (vb) sturen, koers (doen) zetten: *he* ~*ed* *for* home hij ging op huis aan ‖ ~ *clear of* sth. uit de buurt blijven van iets

steering committee stuurgroep

steering wheel stuurwielʰ

steersman stuurman, roerganger

stellar 1 van, m.b.t. de sterren **2** [Am; inform] top-: ~ *year* gloriejaarʰ

¹stem (n) **1** stam [of tree, word]; basisvorm **2** (hoofd)stengel [of flower]; steel(tjeʰ) **3** stamvormig deelʰ; steel [of glass, pipe] **4** voorsteven, boeg: *from* ~ *to* **stern** van de voor- tot de achtersteven; [fig] van top tot teen

²stem (vb) **1** doen stoppen, stelpen **2** het hoofd bieden aan, weerstand bieden aan: ~ *the* **tide** *(of public opinion)* tegen het getijde (van de publieke opinie) ingaan

STEM [Am; educ] *science, technology, engineering, and math* natuur en techniek

stem from stammen uit, voortkomen uit: *his* **bitterness** *stems from all his disappointments* zijn verbittering komt door al zijn teleurstellingen

stench stank

stencil 1 stencilʰ, stencilafdruk **2** modelvorm, sjabloon⁺ʰ

stenography [Am; dated] stenografie, steno⁺ʰ

¹step (n) **1** stap, voetstap, (dans)pas: *break* ~

uit de pas gaan; *fall into* ~ *with* zich aansluiten bij, in de pas lopen met; ~ *by* ~ stapje voor stapje, geleidelijk; *out of* ~ **a)** uit de pas; **b)** [also fig] niet ermee eens; **c)** uit de toon
2 stap, daad: *watch* (or: *mind*) *your* ~ wees voorzichtig, pas op **3** (trap)trede, stoepjeʰ **4** (-s) (stenen) trap, stoep(je)ʰ **5** (-s) trap(ladder)

²step (vb) stappen, gaan: ~ *forward* naar voren komen, zich aanbieden als vrijwilliger; ~ *inside* komt u binnen; ~ *on* the gas (or: *it*) flink gas geven; [fig] opschieten; ~ *out of line* uit het gareel raken
step aside 1 opzij stappen, uit de weg gaan **2** zijn plaats afstaan
stepbrother stiefbroer, halfbroer
stepdaughter stiefdochter
step down 1 aftreden **2** zijn plaats afstaan
stepfather stiefvader
step in 1 binnenkomen **2** tussenbeide komen, inspringen
stepladder trapjeʰ, keukentrap
stepmother stiefmoeder
step off beginnen, starten: ~ *on the wrong foot* op de verkeerde manier beginnen
step out 1 snel(ler) gaan lopen, flink doorstappen **2** (even) naar buiten gaan
stepping stone 1 stapsteen [eg to wade through river] **2** springplank, hulp: *a* ~ *to success* een springplank naar het succes
steps steps
stepsister stiefzuster
stepson stiefzoon
¹step up (vb) naar voren komen, opstaan
²step up (vb) doen toenemen, opvoeren: ~ *production* de productie opvoeren
stereo system stereo-installatie
stereotype stereotype, stereotiep beeldʰ
sterile 1 steriel, onvruchtbaar; [fig] weinig creatief: *a* ~ *discussion* een zinloze discussie **2** steriel, kiemvrij
sterility onvruchtbaarheid, steriliteit
sterilize steriliseren, onvruchtbaar maken, kiemvrij maken
¹sterling (n) pondʰ sterling
²sterling (adj) echt, zuiver, onvervalst; [fig] degelijk, betrouwbaar: *a* ~ *friend* een echte vriend; ~ *silver* 92,5% zuiver zilver
¹stern (n) achterschipʰ, achtersteven
²stern (adj) streng, hard, onbuigzaam, strikt
steroid steroïdeʰ: *anabolic* ~s anabole steroïden
stethoscope stethoscoop
stetson (breedgerande) cowboyhoed
¹stew (n) stoofpot, stoofschotel ‖ *be in* (or: *get into*) *a* ~ opgewonden zijn (or: raken)
²stew (vb) stoven, smoren ‖ *let s.o.* ~ *(in one's own juice)* iem. in zijn eigen vet gaar laten koken
steward 1 rentmeester, beheerder **2** steward, hofmeester **3** ceremoniemeester,

zaalwachter **4** wedstrijdcommissaris, official
St George's cross 1 sint-joriskruisʰ **2** Engelse vlag
¹stick (n) **1** stok, tak, stukʰ hout: *have the wrong end* of the ~ het verkeerd begrijpen **2** staf, stok(je)ʰ **3** staaf(je)ʰ, reep(je)ʰ, stukʰ: *a* ~ *of chalk* een krijtje **4** stok, knuppel **5** stick, hockeystick, (polo)hamer: [fig] *wield the big* ~ dreigen **6** stengel; steel [celeriac] **7** figuur⁺ʰ, snuiter, droogstoppel **8** afranseling [also fig]: *give s.o. some* ~ iem. een pak slaag geven
²stick (vb) **1** klem zitten, vastzitten **2** blijven steken, (blijven) vastzitten **3** plakken [also fig]; (vast)kleven; [inform] blijven: *it will always* ~ *in my mind* dat zal me altijd bijblijven; ~ *together* bij elkaar blijven; ~ *around* rondhangen, in de buurt blijven; ~ *to the point* bij het onderwerp blijven; ~ *to one's principles* trouw blijven aan zijn principes
³stick (vb) **1** (vast)steken, (vast)prikken, bevestigen, opprikken **2** doodsteken, neersteken **3** steken, zetten, leggen: ~ *it in your pocket* stop het in je zak **4** (vast)kleven, vastlijmen, vastplakken **5** [only negative] pruimen, uitstaan, verdragen: *I can't* ~ *such people* ik heb de pest aan zulke mensen
stick at 1 opzien tegen, terugdeinzen voor: ~ *nothing* nergens voor terugdeinzen **2** doorgaan (met), volhouden
sticker 1 plakkertjeʰ, zelfklevend etiketʰ, sticker **2** doorzetter, volhouder
sticking plaster kleefpleister
stick-in-the-mud conservatieveling, vastgeroest iem.
stickleback stekelbaars
stickler (+ for) (hardnekkig) voorstander (van), ijveraar: ~ *for accuracy* pietje-preciesʰ
stick out 1 overduidelijk zijn **2** volhouden, doorbijten: ~ *for sth.* zich blijven inzetten voor iets **3** uitsteken, vooruit steken
¹stick up (vb) **1** omhoogstaan, uitsteken **2** opkomen: ~ *for s.o.* het voor iem. opnemen
²stick up (vb) omhoogsteken, uitsteken: *stick 'em up, stick your hands up* handen omhoog
stick-up overval
sticky 1 kleverig, plakkerig **2** pijnlijk, lastig: *he will come to* (or: *meet*) *a* ~ *end* het zal nog slecht met hem aflopen **3** zwoel, broeierig, drukkend ‖ *she has got* ~ *fingers* ze heeft lange vingers, zij jat
¹stiff (n) [inform] lijkʰ, dooie
²stiff (adj) **1** stijf, stug, gereserveerd **2** vastberaden, koppig: *put up (a)* ~ *resistance* hardnekkig weerstand bieden **3** stram, stroef: *a* ~ *neck* een stijve nek **4** zwaar, moeilijk, lastig: *a* ~ *climb* een flinke klim(partij) **5** sterk, stevig, krachtig: *a* ~ *breeze* een stevige bries **6** (te) groot, overdreven, onre-

delijk: ~ *demands* pittige eisen **7** sterk [alcoholic drink]: *a* ~ *drink* een stevige borrel ‖ *keep a* ~ *upper* **lip** zich flink houden, geen emoties tonen

³stiff (adv) door en door, intens: *bore s.o.* ~ iem. gruwelijk vervelen; *scare s.o.* ~ iem. de stuipen op het lijf jagen

¹stiffen (vb) **1** verstijven **2** verstevigen, in kracht toenemen

²stiffen (vb) **1** dikker maken, doen verdikken **2** verstevigen, krachtiger maken; [also fig] versterken; vastberadener maken

stiff-necked 1 koppig, eigenzinnig **2** verwaand

stiffy [vulg] stijve (piemel)

¹stifle (vb) stikken; smoren [also fig]

²stifle (vb) **1** verstikken, doen stikken, smoren; [fig also] in de doofpot stoppen: *a stifling heat* een verstikkende hitte **2** onderdrukken: ~ *one's laughter* zijn lach inhouden

stigma brandmerk[h], (schand)vlek, stigma[h]

stigmatize stigmatiseren, brandmerken

stile 1 overstap **2** draaihekje[h]

stiletto heel naaldhak

¹still (n) **1** filmfoto, stilstaand (film)beeld[h] **2** distilleertoestel[h]

²still (adj) **1** stil, onbeweeglijk, rustig, kalm: ~ *picture* filmfoto, stilstaand (film)beeld **2** stil, geluidloos, gedempt **3** niet mousserend: ~ *water* mineraalwater zonder prik; plat water; ~ *wine* niet-mousserende wijn

³still (adv) **1** stil: *keep* ~ (zich) stilhouden; *my heart stood* ~ mijn hart stond stil [with fright] **2** nog (altijd): *is he* ~ *here?* is hij hier nog? **3** nog (meer): *he is* ~ *taller, he is taller* ~ hij is nog groter **4** toch, niettemin: ... *but he* ~ *agreed* ... maar hij stemde er toch mee in

stillborn doodgeboren

still life stilleven[h]

stilt 1 stelt **2** paal, pijler

stilted 1 (als) op stelten **2** stijf, gekunsteld

stimulant stimulans, opwekkend middel[h]; [fig] prikkel

stimulate stimuleren, opwekken: ~ *s.o. (in)to more efforts* iem. tot meer inspanningen aanmoedigen

stimulation stimulering

stimulus stimulus; prikkel; [fig] aanmoediging

¹sting (n) **1** angel **2** giftand **3** brandhaar[+h] **4** steek, beet, prikkel(ing)

²sting (vb) **1** steken, bijten; [fig] grieven: *a bee* ~*s* een bij steekt; *his conscience stung him* zijn geweten knaagde **2** prikkelen, branden; [fig] aansporen: *that stung him (in)to action* dat zette hem tot actie aan **3** afzetten, oplichten: ~ *s.o. for a few dollars* iem. een paar dollar lichter maken

stinging 1 stekend, bijtend: *a* ~ *reproach* een scherp verwijt **2** prikkelend

stinging nettle brandnetel

stingy vrekkig, gierig

¹stink (n) **1** stank **2** herrie: *create/kick up* (or: *make, raise*) *a* ~ *about sth.* herrie schoppen over iets

²stink (vb) **1** stinken: *it* ~*s to high heaven* het stinkt uren in de wind **2** oerslecht zijn, niet deugen: *this plan* ~*s* dit plan deugt van geen kanten

stink-bomb stinkbom

stinker 1 stinker(d) **2** iets beledigends, iets slechts, moeilijke opdracht, lastig examen[h]

stinkeye [inform] boze (or: vuile, gemene) blik: *give s.o. the* ~ iem. vuil aankijken

stinking 1 stinkend [also fig]: ~ *rich* stinkend rijk **2** oerslecht, gemeen

¹stint (n) portie, karwei(tje)[h], taak: *do one's daily* ~ zijn dagtaak volbrengen ‖ *without* ~ onbeperkt

²stint (vb) zich bekrimpen, zich beperken

³stint (vb) **1** beperken, inperken **2** zuinig toebedelen, krap houden: ~ *o.s. of food* zichzelf karig voedsel toebedelen

stipulate bedingen, bepalen, als voorwaarde stellen: ~ *for the best conditions* de beste voorwaarden bedingen

¹stir (n) **1** het roeren, het poken: *give the fire a* ~ *pook* het vuur even op **2** beroering, opwinding, sensatie: *cause* (or: *make*) *quite a* ~ (veel) opzien baren, (veel) ophef veroorzaken

²stir (vb) **1** (zich) (ver)roeren, (zich) bewegen **2** opstaan, op zijn

³stir (vb) **1** (+ up) (op)poken, opporren; [fig] aanwakkeren; [fig] aanstoken, opstoken: ~ *one's curiosity* iemands nieuwsgierigheid prikkelen **2** (also + up) (om)roeren

stir-fry roerbakken, wokken

stirring opwekkend, stimulerend, bezielend

stirrup (stijg)beugel

¹stitch (n) **1** steek in de zij **2** steek: *drop a* ~ een steek laten vallen **3** lapje[h], stukje[h] (stof); [fig] beetje[h]: *not do a* ~ *of work* geen lor uitvoeren; *not have a* ~ *on* spiernaakt zijn **4** [med] hechting ‖ *in* ~*es* slap van het lachen, in een deuk (van het lachen)

²stitch (vb) **1** stikken, (vast)naaien, dichtnaaien: ~ *up a wound* een wond hechten **2** borduren

stoat 1 hermelijn **2** wezel

¹stock (n) **1** moederstam [from which grafts are taken] **2** steel **3** familie, ras[h], geslacht[h], afkomst: *be* (or: *come*) *of good* ~ van goede komaf zijn **4** aandeel[h], effect[h] **5** voorraad: ~ *in trade* **a)** voorhanden voorraad; **b)** kneep (van het vak), truc; *while* ~*s last* zolang de voorraad strekt; *take* ~ de inventaris opmaken; [fig] *take* ~ *(of the situation)* de toestand bekijken; *out of* ~ niet in voorraad **6** bouillon **7** aandelen(bezit[h]), effecten, fonds[h]: *his* ~ *is falling* zijn ster verbleekt **8** materiaal[h], materieel^h, grondstof: *rolling* ~ rollend materieel [of railways] **9** vee(stapel)^h **10** (-s) [shipp] stapel(blokken), helling: *on the* ~s op stapel; [fig] in voorbereiding

²**stock** (adj) **1** gangbaar: ~ *sizes* gangbare maten **2** stereotiep, vast: *a* ~ *remark* een stereotiepe opmerking

³**stock** (vb) voorraad inslaan, zich bevoorraden, hamsteren: ~ *up* on sugar suiker inslaan

⁴**stock** (vb) **1** van het nodige voorzien: *a well-stocked department store* een goed voorzien warenhuis **2** in voorraad hebben

stockade **1** houten omheining **2** met houten afzetting omheind terrein^h

stockbroker effectenmakelaar

stock exchange effectenbeurs, beurs(gebouw^h): *the Stock Exchange* de (Londense) Beurs

stockholder aandeelhouder

stocking kous

stock-in-trade **1** (goederen)voorraad **2** gereedschap^h || *that joke* is part of his ~ dat is één van zijn standaardgrappen

stockist leverancier (uit voorraad)

stock market (effecten)beurs

¹**stockpile** (n) voorraad, reserve

²**stockpile** (vb) voorraden aanleggen (van)

stockroom 1 magazijn^h **2** showroom [eg in hotel]

stock size vaste maat, confectiemaat

stock-still doodstil

stocky gedrongen, kort en dik, stevig

stodge zware kost, onverteerbaar eten^h; [fig] moeilijke stof

stodgy 1 zwaar; onverteerbaar [food]; [fig] moeilijk; droog **2** saai, vervelend

stoic stoïcijn

stoic(al) stoïcijns, onaangedaan

¹**stoke** (vb) **1** (also + up) het vuur opstoken **2** (+ up) zich met eten volproppen

²**stoke** (vb) (also + up) aanstoken, opstoken [fire]; opvullen [stove]

stole stola

stolid onverstoorbaar, standvastig

¹**stomach** (n) **1** maag: *on an empty* ~ op een nuchtere maag; [inform] *line his* ~ zijn buikje vullen **2** buik: *lie on one's* ~ op zijn buik liggen **3** eetlust, trek **4** zin: *I have no* ~ *for a fight* ik heb geen zin om ruzie te maken

²**stomach** (vb) slikken, pikken, aanvaarden: *you needn't* ~ *such a remark* zo'n opmerking hoef je niet zomaar te slikken

stomach ache 1 maagpijn **2** buikpijn

¹**stomp** (n) stomp [jazz dance, jazz music]

²**stomp** (vb) stampen

stone 1 steen [also as hard mineral]; pit [of fruit]: *(semi-)precious* ~ (half)edelsteen **2** stone, 14 Engelse pond^h: *he weighs 14* ~(s) hij weegt 90 kilo || *leave* no ~ *unturned* geen middel onbeproefd laten, alles proberen; *rolling* ~ zwerver

Stone Age stenen tijdperk^h

stone-cold steenkoud || ~ *sober* broodnuchter; ~ *dead* morsdood

stoned 1 stomdronken **2** stoned, high

stoneless pitloos, zonder pit

stonemason steenhouwer

stone's throw steenworp: *within a* ~ op een steenworp afstand

stony 1 steenachtig, vol stenen **2** keihard, steenhard; [fig] gevoelloos

stony-broke platzak, blut

stooge 1 [theatre] mikpunt^h, aangever **2** knechtje^h, slaafje^h **3** stroman

stool 1 kruk, bankje^h **2** voetenbank(je^h) **3** ontlasting

¹**stoop** (n) **1** gebukte houding **2** ronde rug, kromme rug

²**stoop** (vb) **1** (zich) bukken, voorover buigen **2** zich verwaardigen **3** zich vernederen, zich verlagen: *he wouldn't* ~ *to lying about his past* hij vond het beneden zijn waardigheid om over zijn verleden te liegen **4** gebogen lopen, met ronde rug lopen

³**stoop** (vb) buigen: ~ *one's head* het hoofd buigen

¹**stop** (n) **1** einde^h, beëindiging, pauze, onderbreking: *bring to a* ~ stopzetten, een halt toeroepen; *put a* ~ *to* een eind maken aan **2** halte, stopplaats **3** afsluiting, blokkade, belemmering **4** punt^h **5** diafragma^h, lensopening **6** pal, plug, begrenzer || *pull out all the* ~s alle registers opentrekken, alles uit de kast halen

²**stop** (vb) **1** ophouden, tot een eind komen, stoppen **2** stilhouden, tot stilstand komen: ~ *short* plotseling halt houden; *they* ~ped *short of actually smashing the windows* ze gingen niet zover, dat ze de ramen daadwerkelijk ingooiden; ~ *at nothing* tot alles in staat zijn, nergens voor terugschrikken **3** blijven, verblijven, overblijven: ~ *by* (even) langskomen; ~ *in* binnenblijven; ~ *off* zijn reis onderbreken; ~ *over* de (vlieg)reis onderbreken

³**stop** (vb) **1** (af)sluiten, dichten, dichtstoppen: ~ *up a leak* een lek dichten **2** verhinderen, afhouden, tegenhouden: ~ *thief!* houd de dief! **3** blokkeren, tegenhouden: ~ *a cheque* een cheque blokkeren **4** een eind maken aan, stopzetten, beëindigen, ophouden met, staken: ~ *work* het werk neerleggen; ~ *it!* hou op!

stopgap 1 noodoplossing **2** invaller **3** stoplap

stopoff kort verblijf^h

stopover reisonderbreking, kort verblijf^h

stoppage 1 verstopping, stremming **2** inhouding: ~ *of pay* inhouden van loon **3** staking, (werk)onderbreking, prikactie

stoppage time (extra) bijgetelde tijd [to make up for interruptions of play]

stopper stop, plug, kurk: *put the* ~(s) on sth.

ergens een eind aan maken
stopping distance afstand tot voorligger
storage opslag, bewaring: [comp] ~ *in the cloud* het online opslaan van bestanden
storage chip geheugenchip
storage space opslagruimte
¹**store** (n) **1** voorraad: *in* ~ in voorraad; *there's a surprise in* ~ *for you* je zult voor een verrassing komen te staan **2** opslagplaats, magazijnʰ, pakhuisʰ **3** (-s) [mil] provisie, goederen, proviandʰ **4** [Am] winkel, zaak **5** warenhuisʰ || *set (great)* ~ *by* veel waarde hechten aan
²**store** (vb) bevoorraden, inslaan
store brand huismerkʰ
storehouse pakhuisʰ, opslagplaats: *Steve is a* ~ *of information* Steve is een grote bron van informatie
storekeeper 1 [Am] winkelier **2** hoofdʰ van het magazijn
storeroom opslagkamer, voorraadkamer
storey verdieping, woonlaag: *the second* ~ de eerste verdieping
stork ooievaar
¹**storm** (n) **1** (hevige) bui, noodweerʰ **2** storm(wind), orkaan: ~ *in a teacup* storm in een glas water, veel drukte om niks **3** uitbarsting, vlaag: ~ *of protests* regen van protesten
²**storm** (vb) **1** stormen, waaien, onweren **2** (+ at) tekeergaan (tegen), uitvallen, razen **3** rennen, denderen: ~ *in* binnen komen stormen
³**storm** (vb) [mil] bestormen, stormlopen op
storm chasing tornadojagenʰ, stormjagenʰ
storm cloud regenwolk, onweerswolk; [fig] donkere wolk; tekenʰ van onheil
storm surge stormvloed
storm trooper stoottroeper
storm window voorzetraamʰ
stormy 1 stormachtig, winderig **2** heftig, ruw: *a* ~ *meeting* een veelbewogen bijeenkomst
story 1 verhaalʰ, relaasʰ: *cut a long* ~ *short* om kort te gaan; *end of* ~*!* punt uit!, einde discussie!; *the (same) old* ~ het oude liedje **2** (levens)geschiedenis, historie **3** vertelling, novelle, verhaalʰ **4** [journalism] (materiaal voor) artikelʰ, verhaalʰ **5** smoesjeʰ, praatjeʰ: *tell stories* jokken **6** verdieping
¹**storybook** (n) verhalenboekʰ
²**storybook** (adv) als in een sprookje, sprookjesachtig: *a* ~ *ending* een gelukkige afloop, een happy end
story line intrige; plotʰ
storyteller 1 verteller **2** [inform] praatjesmaker
¹**stout** (n) stout⁺ʰ, donker bierʰ
²**stout** (adj) **1** moedig, vastberaden: ~ *resistance* krachtig verzet **2** solide, stevig **3** gezet, dik

stout-hearted dapper, moedig, kloek
stove 1 (elektrische) kachel, gaskachel, kolenkachel **2** (elektrisch) fornuisʰ, gasoven, gasfornuisʰ
stow opbergen, inpakken || ~ *it!* kap ermee!, hou op!
stowaway verstekeling
¹**stow away** (vb) zich verbergen [on ship, aeroplane]
²**stow away** (vb) opbergen, wegbergen
straddle schrijlings zitten (op), met gespreide benen zitten (op), wijdbeens staan (boven)
straggle 1 (af)dwalen, achterblijven, van de groep af raken **2** (wild) uitgroeien, verspreid groeien: *straggling houses* verspreid liggende huizen
straggly 1 (onregelmatig) verspreid, verstrooid, schots en scheef **2** verwilderd; verward [hair, beard]
¹**straight** (n) recht stukʰ [of racecourse]
²**straight** (adj) **1** recht, steil; sluik [hair]; rechtop: *(as)* ~ *as a die* kaarsrecht; [fig] goudeerlijk **2** puur, onverdund; [fig] zonder franje; serieus: *a* ~ *rendering of the facts* een letterlijke weergave van de feiten; ~ *whisky* whisky puur **3** open(hartig), eerlijk, rechtdoorzee: ~ *answer* eerlijk antwoord **4** strak, in de plooi, correct: *keep a* ~ *face* zijn gezicht in de plooi houden; *keep (s.o.) to the* ~ *and narrow path* (iem.) op het rechte pad houden **5** ordelijk, geordend, netjes: *put* (or: *set*) *the record* ~ een fout herstellen **6** direct, rechtstreeks **7** hetero(seksueel)
³**straight** (adv) **1** rechtstreeks, meteen, zonder omwegen: *come* ~ *to the point* meteen ter zake raken **2** recht, rechtop: ~ *on* rechtdoor || *think* ~ helder denken; *tell s.o.* ~ iem. eerlijk de waarheid zeggen
straightaway onmiddellijk
¹**straighten** (vb) recht worden, rechttrekken; bijtrekken [also fig]: ~ *up* overeind gaan staan
²**straighten** (vb) rechtzetten; rechttrekken [also fig]: ~ *one's legs* de benen strekken; ~ *the room* de kamer aan kant brengen; ~ *o.s. up* zich oprichten
straighten out 1 recht leggen, rechtmaken **2** op orde brengen: *things will soon straighten out* alles zal gauw op zijn pootjes terechtkomen
straightforward 1 oprecht, open, eerlijk **2** duidelijk
straight up eerlijk (waar), serieus
¹**strain** (n) **1** spanning, druk, trek; [fig] belasting; inspanning **2** overbelasting, uitputting **3** verrekking [of muscles]; verstuiking **4** (-s) flard [of music, poem]; melodie **5** stijl; toon [of expression] **6** (karakter)trek, elementʰ **7** stam, rasʰ, soort

²strain (vb) **1** zich inspannen, moeite doen, zwoegen **2** (+ at) rukken (aan), trekken: ~ *at the leash* aan de teugels trekken, zich los willen rukken [fig]

³strain (vb) **1** spannen, (uit)rekken **2** inspannen, maximaal belasten: ~ *one's eyes* turen, ingespannen kijken **3** overbelasten; [fig] geweld aandoen: ~ *one's voice* zijn stem forceren **4** verrekken [muscles]; verdraaien **5** vastklemmen **6** zeven, laten doorsijpelen **7** afgieten

strained gedwongen, geforceerd, onnatuurlijk: ~ *relations* gespannen verhoudingen

strainer 1 zeef^h **2** vergiet^h **3** filter(doek)^h

strait 1 zee-engte, (zee)straat: *the Straits of Dover* het Nauw van Calais **2** lastige omstandigheden, moeilijkheden: *be in dire ~s* ernstig in het nauw zitten

straitened behoeftig

straitjacket dwangbuis^h; keurslijf^h [also fig]

strait-laced puriteins, bekrompen, preuts

strand streng, snoer^h, draad: *a ~ of pearls* een parelsnoer

stranded gestrand, aan de grond; vast(gelopen) [also fig]

strange 1 vreemd, onbekend, nieuw: *he is ~ to the business* hij heeft nog geen ervaring in deze branche **2** eigenaardig, onverklaarbaar: ~ *to say* vreemd genoeg

stranger vreemde(ling), onbekende, buitenlander: *be a ~ to* ergens part noch deel aan hebben

strangle 1 wurgen **2** onderdrukken; smoren [tendency, cry]

stranglehold wurggreep; verstikkende greep [also fig]: *have a ~ on* in zijn greep hebben

¹strap (n) **1** riem, band(je^h) **2** strop, band^h; reep [also of metal]

²strap (vb) **1** vastbinden, vastgespen **2** (also + up) verbinden, met pleisters afdekken

strapless strapless

strapping flink, potig, stoer

stratagem strategie, truc, plan^h

strategic strategisch

strategist strateeg

strategy strategie, plan^h, methode, beleid^h

stratification 1 laagvorming **2** gelaagdheid, verdeling in lagen

straw 1 stro^h **2** strohalm, strootje^h: *draw ~s* strootjes trekken, het lot laten bepalen wie eerst mag of moet; *clutch at ~s* zich aan iedere strohalm vastklampen; *that's the last ~* dat doet de deur dicht; *the ~ that broke the camel's back* de druppel die de emmer deed overlopen **3** rietje^h [for drinking]

strawberry 1 aardbei(plant) **2** donkerrooze^h

straw man [esp Am] stropop; [fig also] marionet

¹stray (n) **1** zwerver; verdwaalde [also fig]; zwerfdier^h **2** dakloos kind^h

²stray (adj) verdwaald, zwervend: ~ *bullet* verdwaalde kogel; ~ *cats* zwerfkatten

³stray (vb) dwalen; rondzwerven [also fig]: ~ *from the subject* van het onderwerp afdwalen

¹streak (n) **1** streep, lijn, strook: *a ~ of light* een streepje licht **2** (karakter)trek, tikje^h: *there's a ~ of madness in Mel* er zit (ergens) een draadje los bij Mel || *like a ~ of lightning* bliksemsnel

²streak (vb) **1** (weg)schieten, flitsen, snellen **2** streaken, naakt rondrennen

³streak (vb) strepen zetten op, strepen maken in: ~ed *with grey* met grijze strepen

streaker [inform] streaker

streaky gestreept, met strepen; doorregen [of bacon]

¹stream (n) **1** stroom, water^h, beek, stroomrichting **2** (stort)vloed, stroom

²stream (vb) **1** stromen [also fig]; vloeien, druipen: *his face was ~ing with sweat* het zweet liep hem langs het gezicht **2** wapperen, waaien, fladderen

³stream (vb) doen stromen, druipen van: *the wound was ~ing blood* het bloed gutste uit de wond

streamer wimpel, lint^h, serpentine

streaming directe weergave; streaming

streamline stroomlijnen; [fig] lijn brengen in; vereenvoudigen: ~ *an organization* een organisatie efficiënter maken

street straat, weg, straatweg: *dead-end ~* doodlopende straat; *be ~s ahead (of)* ver voorliggen op; *hit the ~s* a) de straat op gaan; b) [eg new car model] in het straatbeeld verschijnen; *in the ~,* [Am] *on the ~* op straat; *take to the ~s* de straat op gaan; *that's (right) up my ~* dat is precies in mijn straatje, dat is net iets voor mij

street address woonadres^h, bezoekadres^h

streetcar [Am] tram

street food streetfood^h, straatvoedsel^h

street level gelijkvloers^h

street lighting straatverlichting

street smarts [Am; inform] straatwijsheid

streetwalker tippelaarster

streetwise door het (straat)leven gehard, door de wol geverfd, slim

strength 1 sterkte [also fig]; kracht(en), vermogen^h: *on the ~ of* op grond van, uitgaand van; *that is not his ~* dat is niet zijn sterkste punt **2** (getal)sterkte, macht, bezetting: *(bring) up to (full) ~* op (volle) sterkte (brengen) **3** gehalte^h, concentratie; zwaarte [of tobacco]; sterkte || *go from ~ to ~* het ene succes na het andere behalen

¹strengthen (vb) sterk(er) worden, in kracht toenemen

²**strengthen** (vb) sterk(er) maken, versterken, verstevigen

strenuous 1 zwaar, inspannend, vermoeiend **2** vol energie, onvermoeibaar, ijverig

¹**stress** (n) **1** spanning, druk, stress, belasting: *(be)* **under** *great* ~ onder (grote) druk staan, zwaar belast worden **2** klem(toon), nadruk, accentʰ; [fig] gewichtʰ; belangʰ: *lay* ~ *on* benadrukken **3** [techn] spanning, druk, (be)last(ing)

²**stress** (vb) **1** benadrukken, de nadruk leggen op: *we can't* ~ *enough that* we kunnen er niet voldoende de nadruk op leggen dat **2** de klemtoon leggen op **3** belasten, onder druk zetten

stressful stressvol, veeleisend

stress mark klemtoontekenʰ, accentʰ

¹**stress out** (vb) [inform] zich druk maken, gestrest raken, in de stress schieten

²**stress out** (vb) [inform] gestrest maken, onder druk zetten: *the job* stressed him out hij raakte gestrest van het werk

¹**stretch** (n) **1** (groot) stukʰ [land, road, sea etc]; uitgestrektheid, vlakte, eind(je)ʰ, stukʰ: ~ *of road* stuk weg **2** tijd, periode; [inform] straftijd: *ten hours* **at** *a* ~ tien uur aan een stuk **3** rek(baarheid), elasticiteit ‖ *not by any* ~ *of the imagination* met de beste wil van de wereld niet; *at full* ~ met inspanning van al zijn krachten; *at a* ~ desnoods, als het moet

²**stretch** (vb) **1** (+ out) zich uitstrekken, (languit) gaan liggen **2** zich uitstrekken (tot), reiken (tot), zich uitrekken **3** rekbaar zijn, elastisch zijn **4** (+ over) duren, zich uitspreiden (over) **5** (uit)rekken [also fig]: ~ *s.o.'s patience* iemands geduld op de proef stellen **6** (aan)spannen, opspannen, strak trekken: ~ *a rope* een touw spannen **7** (uit)strekken, reiken: ~ *o.s.* zich uitrekken **8** tot het uiterste inspannen, forceren: *be fully* ~ed zich helemaal geven **9** ruim interpreteren; het niet zo nauw nemen (met) [rules]; geweld aandoen, overdrijven: ~ *the rules* de regels vrij interpreteren **10** verrekken [muscles]

stretcher brancard, draagbaar

stretch limousine verlengde limousine

stretch mark zwangerschapsstriem

stretchy [inform] elastisch

strew 1 (+ on, over) uitstrooien (over): *books were* ~n all **over** *his desk* zijn bureau was bezaaid met boeken **2** (+ with) bestrooien (met) **3** verspreid liggen op

stricken getroffen, geslagen, bedroefd: ~ *look* verslagen blik

strict strikt, nauwkeurig: ~ *parents* strenge ouders; ~*ly speaking* strikt genomen

stricture aanmerking, afkeuring: *pass* ~*s* (up)on kritiek uitoefenen op

¹**stride** (n) **1** pas, stap, schrede: *get into one's* ~ op dreef komen; *take sth. in (one's)* ~ **a)** er-

gens makkelijk overheen stappen; **b)** iets spelenderwijs doen (*or:* klaren) **2** gang ‖ *make great* ~*s* grote vooruitgang boeken

²**stride** (vb) (voort)stappen, grote passen nemen

strident schel, schril, scherp

strife ruzie, conflictʰ: *industrial* ~ industriële onrust

¹**strike** (n) **1** slag, klap **2** (lucht)aanval **3** staking: *(out)* **on** ~ in staking **4** vondst [of oil etc]; ontdekking; [fig] succesʰ; vangst

²**strike** (vb) **1** strijken; neerlaten [flag]; opbreken [camp, tent] **2** bereiken, sluiten, halen: ~ *a bargain with* het op een akkoordje gooien met **3** aannemen [pose]: ~ *a pose* een houding aannemen **4** ontdekken, vinden, stoten op: ~ *oil* olie aanboren; [fig] fortuin maken **5** een indruk maken op, opvallen, lijken: *did it ever* ~ *you that* heb je er weleens aan gedacht dat, is het jou weleens opgevallen dat **6** opkomen bij; invallen [idea] ‖ ~ *terror into s.o.'s heart* iem. de schrik op het lijf jagen

³**strike** (vb) **1** slaan, uithalen, treffen, raken, botsen (met/op), stoten (op/tegen), aanvallen, toeslaan; aanslaan [string, note]; aansteken [match]: ~ *a blow* een klap uitdelen; *the clock* ~*s* de klok slaat; *struck dumb* met stomheid geslagen; ~ *down* **a)** neerslaan; **b)** [also fig] vellen; **c)** branden [of sun]; ~ *(up)on* **a)** treffen, slaan op; **b)** stoten op, ontdekken; **c)** krijgen, komen op [idea]; *struck by lightning* door de bliksem getroffen **2** staken, in staking gaan **3** (op pad/weg) gaan, beginnen (met): ~ *for home* de weg naar huis inslaan ‖ ~ *home* to s.o. grote indruk maken op iem., geheel doordringen tot iem. [of remark]; *struck on* smoor(verliefd) op

strikebreaker stakingsbreker

strike-call stakingsoproep

strike force aanvalsmacht; [esp] (direct inzetbare) aanvalstroepen

strike off 1 schrappen, royeren **2** afdraaien, drukken

¹**strike out** (vb) **1** (fel) uithalen [also fig]; (fel) tekeergaan **2** nieuwe wegen inslaan: ~ *on one's own* zijn eigen weg inslaan

²**strike out** (vb) schrappen, doorhalen

strike pay stakingsuitkering

striker 1 staker **2** slagman **3** [socc] spits

strike up 1 gaan spelen (zingen), inzetten, aanheffen **2** beginnen: ~ *a conversation (with)* een gesprek aanknopen (met)

striking opvallend, treffend, aantrekkelijk

striking distance bereikʰ: *within* ~ binnen het bereik, binnen loopafstand

¹**string** (n) **1** koordʰ, touw(tje)ʰ, garenʰ: *pull* ~*s* invloed uitoefenen **2** draad, bandʰ **3** snaar **4** (-s) strijkinstrumenten, strijkers **5** aaneenschakeling, reeks, sliert, streng: ~ *of cars* rij auto's ‖ *have two* ~*s* (or: *a second* ~) *to*

one's bow op twee paarden wedden, meer pijlen op zijn boog hebben; *with* no ~s *attached* a) zonder kleine lettertjes; b) zonder verplichtingen (achteraf)

²**string** (vb) **1** (vast)binden **2** (aan elkaar) rijgen, ritsen, aaneenschakelen: ~ *words together* woorden aan elkaar rijgen **3** (+ up) opknopen, ophangen **4** bespannen, besnaren: *highly strung* fijnbesnaard, overgevoelig ǁ *strung up* zenuwachtig, gespannen, opgewonden

¹**string along** (vb) (+ with) zich aansluiten (bij)

²**string along** (vb) belazeren, misleiden, aan het lijntje houden

string band strijkje[h]

string bass [Am] contrabas

string bean [Am] snijboon

stringency strengheid, striktheid: *the ~ of the law* de bindende kracht van de wet

stringent stringent, streng, dwingend: ~ *rule* strikte regel

string orchestra strijkorkest[h]

string quartet strijkkwartet[h]

stringy 1 draderig, pezig: ~ *arm* pezige arm **2** mager, lang en dun

¹**strip** (n) **1** strook, strip, reep **2** kleur(en) [of sports team] ǁ *tear s.o. off a* ~, *tear a* ~ (or: ~s) *off s.o.* iem. uitfoeteren

²**strip** (vb) **1** (also + off) zich uitkleden: ~*ped to the waist* met ontbloot bovenlijf **2** een striptease opvoeren

³**strip** (vb) **1** uitkleden **2** (also + off) van iets ontdoen, pellen, (af)schillen, verwijderen, afscheuren; afhalen [bed]; afkrabben [paint]: ~ *down* uit elkaar halen, ontmantelen [machines]

strip cartoon stripverhaal[h], beeldverhaal[h]

strip club striptent

stripe 1 streep, lijn, strook **2** streep [decoration] **3** opvatting, mening: *of all political* ~s van alle politieke kleuren

striped gestreept

strip-lighting tl-verlichting, buisverlichting

stripped-down sober, simpel, zonder toeters en bellen

stripper [inform] stripper

stripy streperig, met strepen

strive 1 (+ after, for) (na)streven, zich inspannen (voor) **2** vechten

¹**stroke** (n) **1** slag, klap, stoot: *at a* ~ in één klap; *on the* ~ *of twelve* klokslag twaalf (uur), op slag van twaalven **2** aanval, beroerte **3** haal, streep **4** schuine streep **5** streling, aai **6** [rowing] slag(roeier) ǁ ~ *of (good) luck* buitenkansje[h], geluk(je); *he has not done a* ~ *of work* hij heeft geen klap uitgevoerd

²**stroke** (vb) **1** aaien, strelen, (glad)strijken **2** [rowing] de slag aangeven in, slag(roeier) zijn

¹**stroll** (n) wandeling(etje[h]), blokje[h] om: *go for a* ~ een blokje om lopen

²**stroll** (vb) wandelen, kuieren, slenteren

stroller 1 wandelaar **2** [Am] wandelwagen(tje[h]), buggy

strong sterk, krachtig, fors, stevig; zwaar [beer, cigar]; geconcentreerd [solution]; scherp [odour, taste]; drastisch [measure]; hoog [fever, price etc]; onregelmatig [verb]; kras [language]: ~ *arm of the law* (sterke) der wet; ~ *language* (or: *stuff*) krasse taal, gevloek[h]; ~ *nerves* stalen zenuwen; *hold* ~ *views* er een uitgesproken mening op nahouden; *(still) going* ~ nog steeds actief; *two hundred* ~ tweehonderd man sterk; *be* ~ *in* uitblinken in

strong-arm hardhandig, ruw, gewelddadig: ~ *methods* grove middelen

strongbox brandkast, geldkist, safe(loket[h])

stronghold [also fig] bolwerk[h], vesting

strongly 1 sterk: *feel* ~ *about sth.* iets uitgesproken belangrijk vinden **2** met klem, nadrukkelijk

strongman sterke man; machthebber

strong-minded vastberaden, stijfkoppig

strongroom (bank)kluis

strong-willed wilskrachtig, vastberaden

structural structureel, bouw-, constructie-: ~ *alterations* verbouwing

structure 1 bouwwerk[h], constructie, (op)bouw **2** structuur, samenstelling, constructie

¹**struggle** (n) **1** worsteling, gevecht[h], strijd: *put up a* ~ zich verzetten **2** (kracht)inspanning: *quite a* ~ een heel karwei

²**struggle** (vb) worstelen, vechten; [also fig] strijden; zich inspannen: ~ *to* one's *feet* overeind krabbelen

strum betokkelen, tingelen

¹**strut** (n) **1** pompeuze gang **2** stut, steun

²**strut** (vb) pompeus schrijden (op/over), paraderen, heen en weer stappen (op)

¹**stub** (n) **1** stomp(je[h]), eindje[h], peuk **2** reçu-strook; controlestrook [of voucher or cheque book]

²**stub** (vb) **1** stoten: ~ *one's toe* zijn teen stoten **2** (+ out) uitdrukken, uitdoven: ~ *out a cigarette* een sigaret uitmaken

stubble 1 stoppel(s) **2** stoppelveld[h] **3** stoppelbaard

stubborn 1 koppig, eigenwijs **2** weerbarstig: ~ *lock* stroef slot

¹**stucco** (n) stuc[h], pleisterkalk, gipspleister[h]

²**stucco** (vb) pleisteren, stukadoren

stuck 1 vast [also fig]; klem, onbeweeglijk, ten einde raad: *be* ~ *for an answer* met zijn mond vol tanden staan; *get* ~ *with s.o.* met iem. opgezadeld zitten **2** vastgekleefd, vastgeplakt

stuck-up bekakt, verwaand

¹**stud** (n) **1** (sier)spijker, sierknopje[h] **2** knoop(je[h]), overhemdsknoopje[h], boorden-

knoopje[h], manchetknoopje[h] **3** (ren)stal, fokbedrijf[h] **4** fokhengst; dekhengst [also fig]
5 nop [under football shoe]; [Belg] stud
²**stud** (vb) **1** (+ with) beslaan (met), voorzien
van spijkers/knopjes **2** bezetten, bedekken:
~ded **with** quotations vol citaten
student 1 student(e): ~ of **law, law** ~ student in de rechten, rechtenstudent **2** kenner: ~ of **bird-life** vogelkenner
student loan studielening
students' union studentenvereniging
student teacher 1 (leraar-)stagiair(e)
2 iem. die studeert voor onderwijzer
stud farm fokbedrijf[h]
studied weloverwogen, (wel)doordacht: ~
insult opzettelijke belediging; ~ **smile** gemaakte glimlach
studio 1 studio, werkplaats; atelier[h] [of art-
ist] **2** (-s) filmstudio
studio flat eenkamerappartement[h], studio
studious 1 leergierig, ijverig **2** nauwgezet
3 bestudeerd, weloverwogen, opzettelijk: ~
politeness bestudeerde beleefdheid
¹**study** (n) **1** studie, onderzoek[h], aandacht,
attentie **2** studeerkamer; [Belg] bureau[h]
3 (studies) studie(vak[h]): **graduate** studies
postkandidaatsstudie; masteropleiding;
[Belg] derde cyclus
²**study** (vb) studeren, les(sen) volgen, college
lopen: ~ to **be** a **doctor** voor dokter studeren
³**study** (vb) **1** (be)studeren, onderzoeken: ~
law rechten studeren **2** instuderen, van buiten leren
¹**stuff** (n) **1** materiaal[h], (grond)stof, elementen: she **has** the ~ of an actress in her er zit een
actrice in haar **2** spul[h], goed(je[h]), waar: a drop
of the **hard** ~ een lekker neutje; do you **call**
this ~ coffee? noem jij deze troep koffie?
3 troep, rommel: **throw** that ~ away! gooi die
rommel weg! ‖ **do** your ~ eens tonen wat je
kan; **know** one's ~ zijn vak verstaan; that's the
~! (dat is) je ware!, zo mag ik 't horen
²**stuff** (vb) **1** (op)vullen, volproppen, volstoppen: ~ **o.s.** zich volproppen, zich over-
eten; ~ **full** volproppen; my mind is ~ed **with**
facts mijn denkraam zit vol (met) feiten
2 (vol)stoppen, dichtstoppen: ~ed **nose** verstopte neus; my nose is completely ~ed **up** mijn
neus is helemaal verstopt **3** proppen, stoppen, steken, duwen: ~ sth. **in(to)** iets proppen
in **4** opzetten: ~ a **bird** een vogel opzetten
5 farceren, vullen: ~ed **pepper** gevulde paprika ‖ (you can) ~ **yourself!** je kan (van mij)
de pot op!; he can ~ his **job!** hij kan de pot op
met zijn baan
stuffing (op)vulsel[h], vulling, farce ‖ **knock**
(or: **take**) the ~ out of s.o. iem. tot moes slaan,
iem. uitschakelen
stuffy 1 bedompt, benauwd, muf **2** saai,
vervelend **3** bekrompen, preuts
¹**stumble** (n) struikeling, misstap; [fig] blun-

der
²**stumble** (vb) **1** struikelen, vallen **2** hakkelen, haperen, stamelen: ~ **in** one's speech
hakkelen
stumble across tegen het lijf lopen, toevallig ontmoeten, stuiten op, toevallig vinden
stumble into door een toeval belanden in;
terechtkomen in: he stumbled into that **job** hij
kreeg die baan in de schoot geworpen
stumbling block 1 struikelblok[h] **2** steen
des aanstoots
¹**stump** (n) **1** stomp(je[h]), (boom)stronk,
eindje[h], peukje[h] **2** [cricket] wicketpaaltje[h]
²**stump** (vb) stampen
³**stump** (vb) voor raadsels stellen, moeilijke
vragen stellen: that ~ed me daar had ik geen
antwoord op
stumper moeilijke vraag
stump up dokken, betalen, neertellen
stumpy gedrongen, kort en dik
stun 1 bewusteloos slaan **2** schokken, verwarren, verdoven **3** versteld doen staan,
verbazen: be ~ned **into** speechlessness met
stomheid geslagen zijn
stunner schoonheid
stunning ongelofelijk mooi, verrukkelijk,
prachtig
¹**stunt** (n) **1** stunt, (acrobatische) toer, kunstje[h] **2** (reclame)stunt, attractie **3** stuntvlucht
²**stunt** (vb) (in zijn groei) belemmeren
stunt man stuntman
stupefaction verbijstering, (stomme) verbazing
stupefy 1 bedwelmen, verdoven: be stupefied by **drink** door de drank versuft zijn
2 verbijsteren, versteld doen staan
stupendous fantastisch, enorm: a ~ **effort**
een ongelofelijke inspanning
¹**stupid** (n) sufferd
²**stupid** (adj) **1** dom, stom, stompzinnig
2 suf, versuft
stupidity domheid, stommiteit, domme
opmerking, traagheid (van begrip)
stupor (toestand van) verdoving: in a
drunken ~ in benevelde toestand
sturdy 1 sterk, flink, stevig (gebouwd)
2 vastberaden, krachtig
sturgeon steur
¹**stutter** (n) gestotter[h]: **have** a ~ stotteren
²**stutter** (vb) stotteren, stamelen: ~ **out** stot-
terend uitbrengen
sty 1 varkensstal, varkenshok[h] **2** strontje[h]
[small sore on eyelid]
style 1 genre[h], type[h], model[h], vorm: in all
sizes and ~s in alle maten en vormen **2** benaming, (volledige) (aanspreek)titel, (firma)-
naam: trade **under** the ~ of Young & Morris
handel drijven onder de firmanaam Young &
Morris **3** (schrijf)stijl, (schrijf)wijze: spaghetti
Italian ~ spaghetti op zijn Italiaans **4** stijl,

stroming, school: *the new ~ of building* de nieuwe bouwstijl **5** manier van doen, levenswijze, stijl: *the balloon sailed into the air in great ~* de ballon ging zonder enig probleem schitterend omhoog **6** mode, stijl: *in ~* in de mode ‖ *cramp s.o.'s style* iem. in zijn doen en laten belemmeren

stylish 1 modieus, naar de mode (gekleed) **2** stijlvol, elegant, deftig, chic

stylist 1 stilist(e), auteur met (goede) stijl **2** ontwerp(st)er

stylistic stilistisch: *a ~ change* een stijlverandering

stylize stileren: *~d representations* gestileerde afbeeldingen

suave hoffelijk, beleefd; [depr] glad

sub 1 voorschotʰ [wages] **2** duikboot **3** wissel(speler)

sub- ondergeschikt, bijkomend, hulp-: *subpost office* hulppostkantoorʰ

subclass subklasse; onderklasse

¹subconscious (n) onderbewustzijnʰ, onderbewusteʰ

²subconscious (adj) onderbewust

¹subcontract (n) onderaannemingscontractʰ, toeleveringscontractʰ

²subcontract (vb) een onderaannemingscontract (*or:* toeleveringscontract) sluiten (voor): *~ed work* uitbesteed werk

subcontractor onderaannemer

subculture subcultuur

subdivide opsplitsen

subdivision (onder)verdeling, onderafdeling

subdue 1 onderwerpen, beheersen: *~ one's passions* zijn hartstochten beteugelen **2** matigen, verzachten

subdued getemperd, gematigd, gedempt, ingehouden, stil: *~ colours* zachte kleuren

¹subject (n) **1** onderdaan, ondergeschikte **2** onderwerpʰ, themaʰ: *on the ~ of* omtrent, aangaande, over **3** (studie)objectʰ, (school)vakʰ **4** aanleiding, omstandigheid, reden **5** [linguistics] onderwerpʰ

²subject (adj) **1** onderworpen: *~ to foreign rule* onder vreemde heerschappij **2** afhankelijk: *~ to your consent* behoudens uw toestemming **3** onderhevig, blootgesteld: *~ to change* vatbaar voor wijziging(en)

³subject (vb) (+ to) onderwerpen (aan), doen ondergaan

subject index 1 klapper, systematisch registerʰ **2** trefwoordenregisterʰ

subjection onderwerping, afhankelijkheid, onderworpenheid

subjective subjectief

subject matter onderwerpʰ; inhoud [of book]

subjugation onderwerping, overheersing

subjunctive [linguistics] aanvoegende wijs

sublet onderverhuren

sublime subliem, verheven: *(from) the ~ to the ridiculous* (van) het sublieme tot het potsierlijke

submachine gun machinepistoolʰ

submarine duikboot, onderzeeër

submerge 1 (doen) duiken [of submarine]; onderduiken **2** (doen) zinken, (doen) ondergaan, overstromen: *~d rocks* blinde klippen

submersion onderdompeling, overstroming

submission 1 onderwerping, onderdanigheid: *starve the enemy into ~* de vijand uithongeren **2** voorstelʰ

submissive onderdanig, onderworpen

¹submit (vb) toegeven, zwichten, zich overgeven: *~ to s.o.'s wishes* iemands wensen inwilligen; *~ to defeat* zich gewonnen geven

²submit (vb) **1** (+ to) voorleggen (aan): *~ s.o.'s name for appointment* iem. ter benoeming voordragen **2** onderwerpen, overgeven: *~ o.s. to* zich onderwerpen aan **3** indienen [request]; [Internet] verzenden

subnormal beneden de norm

¹subordinate (adj) (+ to) ondergeschikt (aan), onderworpen, afhankelijk: *~ clause* bijzin, ondergeschikte zin

²subordinate (vb) (+ to) ondergeschikt maken (aan), achterstellen (bij)

subordination 1 ondergeschiktheid **2** [linguistics] onderschikking

¹subpoena (n) dagvaarding

²subpoena (vb) dagvaarden

¹subscribe (vb) **1** (+ to) intekenen (voor); zich abonneren (op) [magazine]: *~ for* (vooraf) bestellen **2** (+ to) onderschrijven [opinion] **3** (+ to) (geldelijk) steunen

²subscribe (vb) **1** (onder)tekenen, zijn handtekening zetten onder: *~ one's name (to sth.)* (iets) ondertekenen **2** inschrijven (voor)

subscriber 1 ondertekenaar **2** intekenaar, abonnee

subscription 1 ondertekening **2** abonnementʰ, intekening, inschrijving: *take out a ~ to sth.* zich op iets abonneren **3** contributie, bijdrage, steun

subscription rate abonnementsprijs

subsequent (+ to) volgend (op), later, aansluitend

subsequently vervolgens, nadien, daarna

subservient 1 bevorderlijk, nuttig: *~ to* bevorderlijk voor **2** ondergeschikt **3** kruiperig, onderdanig

subside 1 (be)zinken, (in)zakken, verzakken **2** slinken, inkrimpen, afnemen **3** bedaren

subsidence instorting, verzakking, het wegzakken

subsidiary 1 helpend, steunend, aanvullings-: *~ troops* hulptroepen **2** (+ to) ondergeschikt (aan), afhankelijk (van): *~ subject* bijvakʰ

subsidize subsidiëren

subsidy subsidie

subsist (in) leven (blijven): ~ *on welfare* van een uitkering leven

subsistence 1 bestaan[h], leven[h] **2** onderhoud[h], kost, levensonderhoud[h]

subsistence farming landbouw voor eigen gebruik

subsistence level bestaansminimum[h]: *live at* ~ nauwelijks rondkomen

subsoil ondergrond

subspecies ondersoort

substance substantie, wezen[h], essentie, stof, materie, kern, hoofdzaak: *the* ~ *of his remarks* de kern van zijn opmerkingen; *a man of* ~ een rijk man

substantial werkelijk, aanzienlijk, stoffelijk, degelijk: ~ *meal* stevige maaltijd

substantiate van gronden voorzien, bewijzen, verwezenlijken: ~ *a claim* een bewering hard maken

substantive 1 substantief [also linguistics]; zelfstandig **2** wezenlijk **3** belangrijk ‖ ~ *law* materieel recht

¹**substitute** (n) vervanger, plaatsvervanger; [also sport] invaller, wisselspeler

²**substitute** (adj) plaatsvervangend

³**substitute** (vb) in de plaats stellen (voor), invallen (voor), wisselen: ~ *A by* (of: *with*) *B* A door B vervangen; ~ *A for B* B vervangen door A

substitution vervanging, wissel

subtenant onderhuurder

subterfuge 1 uitvlucht, voorwendsel[h] **2** trucje[h], list

subterranean onderaards, ondergronds

subtitle ondertitel

subtle subtiel, fijn, nauwelijks merkbaar, scherp(zinnig): *smile subtly* fijntjes lachen

subtlety subtiliteit, scherpzinnigheid, subtiel onderscheid[h]

subtract (+ from) aftrekken (van), in mindering brengen (op)

subtraction aftrekking, vermindering

subtropical subtropisch

suburb voorstad, buitenwijk

suburban van de voorstad; [fig] bekrompen

suburbia suburbia[h]; (bewoners van de) voorsteden

subversion 1 ontwrichting **2** ondermijning

subversive ontwrichtend, ondermijnend

subway 1 (voetgangers)tunnel, ondergrondse (door)gang **2** [Am] metro

¹**succeed** (vb) (op)volgen: ~ *to the property* de bezittingen overerven

²**succeed** (vb) slagen, gelukken, succes hebben: ~ *in (doing) sth.* slagen in iets, erin slagen iets te doen

success succes[h], goede afloop, bijval: *be a* ~,

meet with ~ succes boeken; *make a* ~ *of it* het er goed afbrengen

successful succesvol, geslaagd

succession 1 reeks, serie, opeenvolging: ~ *of defeats* reeks nederlagen **2** (troon)opvolging: *law of* ~ successiewet ‖ *in quick* ~ vlak na elkaar

successive opeenvolgend

successor opvolger: ~ *to the throne* troonopvolger

succinct beknopt, kort, bondig

succour hulp, steun

¹**succulent** (n) vetplant

²**succulent** (adj) sappig

succumb (+ to) bezwijken (aan/voor): ~ *to one's enemies* zwichten voor zijn vijanden

¹**such** (adj) **1** zulk(e), zodanig, dergelijke, zo'n: ~ *clothes as he would need* de kleren die hij nodig zou hebben; ~ *as* zoals; *a man* ~ *as Paul* een man als Paul; *I have accepted his help,* ~ *as it is* ik heb zijn hulp aangenomen, ook al is die vrijwel niets waard; *there's no* ~ *thing* automatic translation automatisch vertalen is onmogelijk **2** die en die, dat en dat: *at* ~ *(and* ~*) a place and at* ~ *(and* ~*) a time* op die en die plaats en op dat en dat uur

²**such** (dem pron) zulke, zo iem. (iets), dergelijke(n), zulks: ~ *was not my intention* dat was niet mijn bedoeling ‖ ~ *being the case* nu de zaken er zo voorstaan

suchlike zo'n, zulk(e), dergelijke: *worms and* ~ *creatures* wormen en dergelijke beestjes

¹**suck** (n) slokje[h], teugje[h]

²**suck** (vb) **1** zuigen (aan/op): ~ *sweets* op snoepjes zuigen; ~ *in* opzuigen, in zich opnemen; ~ *up* opzuigen; [fig] ~ *it up* slikken of stikken **2** likken, vleien: ~ *up (to) s.o.* iem. likken, iem. vleien

sucker 1 zuiger, uitloper, scheut **2** onnozele hals, sukkel: *I am a* ~ *for red-headed women* ik val nu eenmaal op vrouwen met rood haar

suckle de borst krijgen (geven), zuigen, zogen

suckling 1 zuigeling **2** jong[h]: ~ *pig* speenvarken[h]

suction zuiging, (kiel)zog[h]

Sudan (the) Sudan

¹**Sudanese** (n) Sudanees, Sudanese

²**Sudanese** (adj) Sudanees

sudden plotseling, haastig, snel, scherp: ~ *death (play-off)* beslissende verlenging; *all of a* ~ plotseling, ineens

suddenly plotseling, opeens, ineens

suds (zeep)sop[h], schuim[h]

sue 1 (gerechtelijk) vervolgen, dagvaarden: ~ *for divorce* (echt)scheiding aanvragen **2** verzoeken, smeken: ~ *for mercy* (iem.) om genade smeken

suede suède[+h]

¹**suffer** (vb) **1** lijden, schade lijden, bescha-

digd worden: ~ *from* lijden aan **2** (+ for) boeten (voor)

²suffer (vb) verdragen, dulden: *not* ~ *fools (gladly)* weinig geduld hebben met dwazen

sufferer lijder; patiënt

suffering pijn, lijden[h]: *severe* ~*s* zware pijn(en)

suffice genoeg zijn (voor), volstaan, voldoen: *your word will* ~ *(me)* uw woord is me voldoende; ~ *(it) to say that* het zij voldoende te zeggen dat

sufficiency 1 voldoende voorraad, toereikende hoeveelheid **2** toereikendheid

sufficient voldoende, genoeg

suffocate (doen) stikken, verstikken

suffocation (ver)stikking

suffrage stemrecht[h], kiesrecht[h]

suffuse bedekken: *eyes* ~*d with* tears ogen vol tranen; ~*d with* light overgoten door licht

¹sugar (n) **1** suiker **2** schat(je[h]), liefje[h] **3** zoete woordjes, vleierij

²sugar (vb) **1** zoeten, suiker doen in **2** aangenamer maken, verzoeten: ~ *the pill* de pil vergulden

sugar beet suikerbiet

sugarcane suikerriet[h]

sugar caster suikerstrooier, strooibus

sugar daddy [Am; inform] rijke (oudere) mainteneur

sugary 1 suikerachtig, suiker- **2** suikerzoet [fig]; stroperig

suggest suggereren, doen denken aan, duiden op, influisteren, ingeven, opperen, aanvoeren, voorstellen, aanraden: ~ *doing* sth. voorstellen iets te doen; ~ *sth.* *to* s.o. iem. iets voorstellen

suggestion 1 suggestie, aanduiding, aanwijzing, mededeling, idee[h], overweging, voorstel[h], raad: *at the* ~ *of* op aanraden van **2** zweem, tikje[h]: *a* ~ *of anger* een zweem van woede

suggestion box ideeënbus

suggestive 1 suggestief, suggererend, veelbetekenend **2** gewaagd, van verdacht allooi, schuin

suicidal 1 zelfmoord- **2** met zelfmoordneigingen

suicide 1 zelfmoord, zelfdoding: *commit* ~ zelfmoord plegen; *assisted* ~ hulp bij zelfdoding **2** zelfmoordenaar

suicide attack zelfmoordaanslag

suicide attempt zelfmoordpoging

suicide belt zelfmoordvest[h], bomgordel

suicide mission zelfmoordaanslag

suicide squad zelfmoordcommando[h]

¹suit (n) **1** kostuum[h], pak[h]: *bathing* ~ badpak[h] **2** [cards] kleur, kaarten van één kleur: *follow* ~ kleur bekennen; [fig] iemands voorbeeld volgen **3** stel[h], uitrusting: ~ *of armour* wapenrusting **4** (rechts)geding[h], proces[h], rechtszaak: *criminal* (or: *civil*) ~ straf-

rechtelijke (*or*: civiele) procedure

²suit (vb) **1** aanpassen, geschikt maken: ~ *one's style to* one's audience zijn stijl aan zijn publiek aanpassen **2** goed zijn voor: *I know what* ~*s me best* ik weet wel wat voor mij het beste is **3** voldoen, aanstaan, bevredigen: ~ s.o. *'s needs* aan iemands behoeften voldoen; ~ *yourself!* **a)** ga je gang maar!; **b)** moet je zelf weten!

³suit (vb) **1** passen (bij), geschikt zijn (voor), staan (bij): *this colour* ~*s* her complexion deze kleur past bij haar teint; ~ s.o. *(down) to the ground* **a)** voor iem. geknipt zijn, precies bij iem. passen; **b)** iem. uitstekend van pas komen **2** gelegen komen (voor), uitkomen (voor), schikken: *that date will* ~ *(me)* die datum komt (me) goed uit

suitability geschiktheid, gepastheid

suitable (+ to, for) geschikt (voor), gepast, passend

suitcase koffer; [Belg] valies[h]

suite 1 stel[h], rij, suite, ameublement[h]: ~ *of rooms* suite; *three-piece* ~ driedelige zitcombinatie **2** suite, gevolg[h]

suited 1 geschikt, (bij elkaar) passend: *well* ~ *to* one another voor elkaar gemaakt **2** gericht (op), beantwoordend (aan)

suitor [form] **1** [law] aanklager; eiser **2** [dated] huwelijkskandidaat

¹sulk (n) boze bui: *have a* ~, *have (a fit of) the* ~*s* een chagrijnige bui hebben

²sulk (vb) mokken, chagrijnig zijn

sulky chagrijnig

sullen 1 nors, stuurs **2** somber: ~ *sky* sombere hemel

sulphur zwavel: ~ *dioxide* zwaveldioxide[h]

sulphuric zwavelachtig, zwavelhoudend: ~ *acid* zwavelzuur[h]

sultan sultan

sultry 1 zwoel, drukkend **2** wellustig, sensueel

sum 1 som, totaal[h], geheel[h], bedrag[h] **2** (re-ken)som, berekening, optelling: *good at* ~*s* goed in rekenen **3** samenvatting, kern, strekking: *in* ~ in één woord

summarily 1 summier, in het kort: *deal* ~ *with* summier behandelen **2** terstond, zonder vorm van proces

summarize samenvatten

¹summary (n) samenvatting, korte inhoud, uittreksel[h]

²summary (adj) summier, beknopt, samenvattend: ~ *account* beknopt overzicht; ~ *statement* verzamelstaat, recapitulatie; ~ *jurisdiction* korte procesgang, snelrecht[h]; ~ *execution* standrechtelijke executie

summation 1 optelling **2** som; totaal[h] **3** samenvatting

summer zomer; [fig] bloeitijd: *in (the)* ~ in de zomer

summer house zomerhuis[h]

summer school zomercursus; vakantie-cursus [at university]
summertime zomerseizoen^h, zomer(tijd)
summer time zomertijd
summery zomers
summing-up samenvatting [by judge]
summit 1 top, hoogste punt^h **2** toppunt^h, hoogtepunt^h: *at the ~* op het hoogste niveau **3** topconferentie
summit meeting topconferentie
summit talks topconferentie
summon 1 bijeenroepen, oproepen **2** dagvaarden
¹summons (n) **1** oproep **2** aanmaning **3** dagvaarding: *serve a ~ on s.o.* iem. dagvaarden
²summons (vb) **1** dringend aanmanen **2** dagvaarden
summon up vergaren, verzamelen: *~ one's courage (to do sth.)* zich vermannen, al zijn moed verzamelen (om iets te doen)
sumptuous weelderig, luxueus, rijk
sum total 1 totaal^h **2** resultaat^h
¹sum up (vb) beoordelen, doorzien: *sum s.o. up as a fool* iem. voor gek verslijten
²sum up (vb) samenvatten
sun zon, zonlicht^h, zonneschijn: *a place in the ~* een plaatsje in de zon; [fig] een gunstige positie; *beneath* (or: *under*) *the ~* onder de zon, op aarde
sunbaked 1 zongedroogd **2** zonovergoten
sunbathe zonnebaden
sunbeam zonnestraal
sunblind zonnescherm^h
sunburn zonnebrand, roodverbrande huid
sunburnt 1 gebruind **2** [Am] verbrand
sundae ijscoupe
Sunday zondag, feestdag, rustdag
Sunday best zondagse kleren: *in one's ~* op zijn zondags
Sunday clothes zondagse kleren: *in one's ~* op zijn zondags
sun deck 1 zonnedek^h **2** dakterras^h
sundial zonnewijzer
sundown zonsondergang: *at ~* bij zonsondergang
sundry divers, allerlei, verschillend: *all and ~* iedereen, jan en alleman
sunflower zonnebloem
sunglasses zonnebril: *a pair of ~* een zonnebril
sunken 1 gezonken, onder water, ingevallen: *~ eyes* diepliggende ogen **2** verzonken, ingegraven, verlaagd: *~ road* holle weg
sunlamp hoogtezon
sunlight zonlicht^h
sunlit door de zon verlicht, in het zonlicht, zonovergoten
¹Sunnite (n) soenniet
²Sunnite (adj) soennitisch
sunny zonnig, vrolijk: *on the ~ side of forty* nog geen veertig
sunny-side up [Am] aan één kant gebakken: *two eggs ~* twee spiegeleieren
sunray zonnestraal
sunrise zonsopgang
sun roof 1 plat dak^h [to sunbathe] **2** schuifdak^h [of car]
sunscreen 1 zonnebrandcrème **2** zonnefilter^h [eg in sun lotion]
sunset zonsondergang, avondrood^h: *at ~* bij zonsondergang; [fig] *in his ~ years* op hoge leeftijd, aan het einde van zijn leven
sunshade zonnescherm^h, parasol, zonneklep
sunshine zonneschijn; [fig] zonnetje^h
sunstroke zonnesteek
suntan (bruine) kleur
suntanned gebruind, bruin
sunup zonsopgang
super super, fantastisch
superabundant zeer overvloedig, al te overvloedig, rijkelijk (aanwezig)
superannuated 1 gepensioneerd **2** verouderd, ouderwets
superannuation 1 pensionering, pensioen^h **2** pensioen^h, lijfrente
superb groots, prachtig, voortreffelijk
superbug resistente bacterie
supercilious uit de hoogte, verwaand
superconductivity supergeleiding
superduper [inform] super; je van het
superficial oppervlakkig, niet diepgaand, vluchtig: *~ wound* ondiepe wond
superfluous overbodig
superglue secondelijm
superhuman bovenmenselijk, buitengewoon
superimpose bovenop leggen, opleggen
superintend toezicht houden (op), controleren, toezien (op)
superintendent 1 (hoofd)opzichter, hoofd^h, directeur **2** hoofdinspecteur [of police]
¹superior (n) **1** meerdere, superieur, hogere in rang, chef **2** overste: *Mother Superior* moeder-overste
²superior (adj) **1** superieur, beter, bovenst, opperst; [fig also] hoger; hoofd-: *~ to a)* beter [quality]; *b)* hoger [rank]; *be ~ to* verheven zijn boven, staan boven **2** hoger, voornaam, deftig **3** verwaand, arrogant: *~ smile* hooghartig lachje ‖ *~ court* hogere rechtbank
superiority superioriteit, grotere kracht, hogere kwaliteit
¹superlative (n) superlatief [also linguistics]; overtreffende trap
²superlative (adj) voortreffelijk, prachtig ‖ [linguistics] *~ degree* superlatief, overtreffende trap
superman superman, supermens

supermarket supermarkt
supernatural bovennatuurlijk
supernaturalistic bovennatuurlijk, supernaturalistisch
supernumerary 1 extra[h], reserve **2** figurant
superpower grootmacht, supermacht
superscript superscript[h] (teken)
supersede vervangen, de plaats doen innemen van, afschaffen
superserver krachtige server
supersonic supersonisch, sneller dan het geluid
superstition bijgeloof[h]
superstitious bijgelovig: ~ *beliefs* bijgeloof[h]
supervise 1 aan het hoofd staan (van), leiden **2** toezicht houden (op), controleren
supervision supervisie, leiding, toezicht[h]
supervisor 1 opzichter, controleur, inspecteur, chef **2** coördinator
supine 1 achteroverliggend, op de rug liggend **2** lui, traag
supper (licht) avondmaal[h], avondeten[h], souper[h]
supplant verdringen, vervangen
supple soepel [also fig]; buigzaam, lenig
¹**supplement** (n) aanvulling, bijvoegsel[h], supplement[h]: *pay a ~* bijbetalen
²**supplement** (vb) aanvullen, van een supplement voorzien: ~ *by* (or: *with*) aanvullen met
supplementary aanvullend, toegevoegd, extra
supplication smeekbede
supplier leverancier
¹**supply** (n) **1** voorraad: *supplies* (mond)voorraad; proviand[h]; benodigdheden **2** bevoorrading, aanvoer, toevoer, levering **3** aanbod[h]: ~ *and demand* vraag en aanbod
²**supply** (vb) **1** leveren, verschaffen, bezorgen, voorzien van: ~ *sth. to s.o.*, ~ *s.o. with sth.* iem. iets bezorgen, iem. van iets voorzien **2** voorzien in, verhelpen, vervullen: ~ *a need* voorzien in een behoefte
supply chain productieketen
¹**support** (n) **1** steun, hulp, ondersteuning: *in ~ of* tot steun van **2** steun(stuk[h]), stut, drager, draagbalk **3** onderhoud[h], levensonderhoud[h], middelen van bestaan
²**support** (vb) **1** (onder)steunen, stutten, dragen **2** steunen, helpen, bijstaan, verdedigen, bijvallen, subsidiëren **3** onderhouden, voorzien in de levensbehoeften van: ~ *o.s.* (or: *one's family*) zichzelf (or: zijn familie) onderhouden **4** verdragen, doorstaan, verduren ‖ ~*ing programme* bijfilm, voorfilm(pje); ~*ing part* (or: *role*) bijrol
supporter 1 verdediger, aanhanger, voorvechter **2** supporter
support group praatgroep

supportive steunend, helpend, aanmoedigend
suppose (ver)onderstellen, aannemen, denken: *he is ~d to be* in London hij zou in Londen moeten zijn; *I'm not ~d to tell you this* ik mag je dit (eigenlijk) niet vertellen; *I ~ so* (or: *not*) ik neem aan van wel (or: niet); ~ *it rains* stel dat het regent, en als het nou regent?
supposed vermeend, vermoedelijk, zogenaamd: *his ~ wealth* zijn vermeende rijkdom
supposedly vermoedelijk, naar alle waarschijnlijkheid, naar verluidt
supposing indien, verondersteld dat: ~ *it rains, what then?* maar wat als het regent?
supposition veronderstelling, vermoeden[h], gissing: *in* (or: *on*) *the ~ that* in de veronderstelling dat
suppository zetpil
suppress onderdrukken, bedwingen, achterhouden: ~ *evidence* (or: *facts*) bewijsstukken (or: feiten) achterhouden; ~ *feelings* gevoelens onderdrukken
suppression onderdrukking
suppressor onderdrukker
supranational supranationaal, bovennationaal
supremacy overmacht, superioriteit: *white ~* gedachtegang dat het blanke ras superieur is aan andere rassen
supreme opperst, hoogst: *Supreme Being* Opperwezen[h], God; *Supreme Court* hooggerechtshof[h]
¹**surcharge** (n) **1** toeslag, strafport[+h] **2** extra belasting
²**surcharge** (vb) **1** extra laten betalen **2** overladen, overbelasten
¹**sure** (adj) **1** zeker, waar, onbetwistbaar: *one thing is ~* één ding staat vast **2** zeker, veilig, betrouwbaar: ~ *proof* waterdicht bewijs **3** zeker, verzekerd, overtuigd: ~ *of o.s.* zelfverzekerd, zelfbewust; *you can be ~ of it* daar kan je van op aan ‖ ~ *card* iem. (iets) waar men op kan bouwen; ~ *thing* a) feit[h], zekerheid; b) [exclamation] natuurlijk!; *be ~ to tell her* vergeet vooral niet het haar te vertellen; *it is ~ to be a girl* het wordt vast een meisje; *just to make ~* voor alle zekerheid
²**sure** (adv) zeker, natuurlijk, ongetwijfeld: ~ *enough!* natuurlijk!; *he promised to come and ~ enough he did* hij beloofde te komen en ja hoor, hij kwam ook; *I don't know for ~* ik ben er niet (zo) zeker van
sure-fire onfeilbaar, zeker: ~ *winner* zekere winnaar
surely 1 zeker, ongetwijfeld, toch: *slowly but ~* langzaam maar zeker; ~ *I've met you before?* ik heb je toch al eens eerder ontmoet?; ~ *you are not suggesting it wasn't an accident?* je wilt toch zeker niet beweren dat het geen ongeluk was? **2** natuurlijk; ga je

gang [in reply to request]
surety 1 borgsteller **2** borg(som): *stand* ~
for s.o. zich borg stellen voor iem.
¹**surf** (n) branding
²**surf** (vb) surfen: ~ *the Net* internetten, (op
het net) surfen
¹**surface** (n) oppervlak[h], oppervlakte [also
fig]: *come* to the ~ tevoorschijn komen, bovenkomen
²**surface** (vb) aan de oppervlakte komen
[also fig]; opduiken, verschijnen
³**surface** (vb) bedekken, bestraten, asfalteren
surface mail landpost, zeepost
surfboard surfplank
surfeit overdaad; overlading [of stomach]:
have a ~ *of* zich ziek eten aan
surfer (branding)surfer
surfing (branding)surfen[h]
¹**surge** (n) **1** (hoge) golf **2** opwelling, vlaag,
golf
²**surge** (vb) **1** golven, deinen, stromen: ~ *by*
voorbijstromen **2** dringen, duwen: *surging*
crowd opdringende massa **3** opwellen; op-
bruisen [of feelings]
surgeon 1 chirurg **2** scheepsdokter
surgery 1 behandelkamer; spreekkamer
[of doctor] **2** spreekuur[h] **3** chirurgie, heel-
kunde: *be* in (or: *have, undergo*) ~ geopereerd worden
surgical chirurgisch, operatief: ~ *procedure*
ingreep ‖ ~ *stocking* steunkous
¹**Surinam** (n) Suriname
²**Surinam** (adj) Surinaams
¹**Surinamese** (n) Surinamer, Surinaamse
²**Surinamese** (adj) Surinaams
surly knorrig, nors
surmise gissing, vermoeden[h]
surmount 1 overwinnen, te boven komen
2 bedekken, overdekken: *peaks* ~ed *with*
snow met sneeuw bedekte toppen
surname achternaam
surpass overtreffen, te boven gaan: ~ *all*
expectations alle verwachtingen overtreffen
¹**surplus** (n) overschot[h], teveel[h], rest(ant[h])
²**surplus** (adj) overtollig, extra: ~ *grain*
graanoverschot[h]
¹**surprise** (n) verrassing, verbazing, verwondering: *come* as a ~ *(to s.o.)* totaal onverwacht komen (voor iem.); *to* my great ~ tot
mijn grote verbazing
²**surprise** (vb) verrassen, verbazen, overvallen, betrappen: *you'd* be ~d! daar zou je van
opkijken!
surprised verrast, verbaasd: *be* ~ *at* zich
verbazen over
surprise visit onverwacht bezoek[h]
surprising verrassend, verbazingwekkend
surreal onwerkelijk
surrealism surrealisme[h]
¹**surrender** (n) overgave

²**surrender** (vb) zich overgeven, capituleren: ~ *to fear* toegeven aan de angst; *the battalion* ~ed *to the Red Army* het bataljon gaf
zich over aan het Rode Leger
³**surrender** (vb) **1** afstaan, afstand doen
van: *the intruders were forced to* ~ *their arms*
de indringers werden gedwongen hun wapens af te geven **2** [sport] incasseren; verliezen, toegeven: *in twenty games the team only*
~ed *fifteen goals* in twintig wedstrijden incasseerde de ploeg slechts vijftien doelpunten
surreptitious heimelijk, stiekem: ~ *glance*
steelse blik
¹**surrogate** (n) **1** plaatsvervanger, substituut **2** vervangend middel[h], surrogaat[h]
²**surrogate** (adj) plaatsvervangend, surro-
gaat- ‖ ~ *mother(hood)* draagmoeder(schap)
surround omringen, omsingelen: ~ed *by*
(or: *with*) omringd door
surroundings omgeving, buurt, streek,
omtrek
surveillance toezicht[h], bewaking: *under*
(close) ~ onder (strenge) bewaking
surveillance airplane verkenningsvlieg-
tuig[h]
¹**survey** (n) **1** overzicht[h]: *a* ~ *of major Dutch*
writers een overzicht van belangrijke Nederlandse schrijvers **2** onderzoek[h] **3** taxering;
taxatierapport[h] [of house] **4** opmeting, opname; kartering [of terrain]
²**survey** (vb) **1** overzien, toezien op **2** onderzoeken **3** taxeren [house] **4** opmeten,
karteren
surveyor 1 opzichter, opzichter, inspecteur
2 landmeter **3** taxateur
survival 1 overleving, het overleven: ~ *of*
the fittest natuurlijke selectie, (het verschijnsel dat) de sterkste(n) overleven **2** overblijfsel[h]
survival kit nooduitrusting
survive overleven, voortbestaan, bewaard
blijven, langer leven dan; [fig] zich (weten
te) handhaven: ~ *an earthquake* een aardbeving overleven; ~ *one's children* zijn kinderen
overleven
survivor overlevende
susceptibility 1 gevoeligheid **2** (suscepti-
bilities) zwakke plek: *wound s.o. in his sus-*
ceptibilities iem. op zijn zwakke plek raken
susceptible (+ to) vatbaar (voor), gevoelig
(voor), onderhevig (aan)
¹**suspect** (n) verdachte
²**suspect** (adj) verdacht
³**suspect** (vb) **1** vermoeden, vrezen, geloven, denken **2** (+ of) verdenken (van), wantrouwen
suspend 1 (op)hangen **2** uitstellen: ~ed
sentence voorwaardelijke straf **3** schorsen
suspender 1 (sok)ophouder **2** (-s) [Am]
bretels: *a pair of* ~s bretels

suspense spanning, onzekerheid: *hold* (or: *keep*) *in ~* in onzekerheid laten
suspension 1 opschorting [of verdict, sentence etc]; onderbreking, uitstel[h] [of payment] **2** vering
suspension bridge hangbrug, kettingbrug
suspicion vermoeden[h], veronderstelling: *have a ~ that* vermoeden dat **2** verdenking: *above ~* boven alle verdenking verheven **3** zweempje[h]: *a ~ of **irony*** een zweempje ironie
suspicious 1 verdacht: *feel ~ about* (or: *of*) *s.o.* iem. wantrouwen **2** wantrouwig, achterdochtig
suss out 1 doorkrijgen [sth.]: *I can't ~ how to remove that wheel clamp* ik kan er maar niet achter komen hoe ik die wielklem eraf moet halen **2** doorhebben [somebody]
sustain 1 (onder)steunen, dragen, staven, bevestigen: *~ing **food*** versterkend voedsel **2** volhouden, aanhouden: *~ a **note*** een noot aanhouden **3** doorstaan: *~ an **attack*** een aanval afslaan **4** ondergaan, lijden, oplopen: *~ a **defeat*** (or: *an **injury***) een nederlaag (or: letsel) oplopen
sustainability duurzaamheid, houdbaarheid
sustainable 1 verdedigbaar **2** duurzaam: *~ solutions* duurzame oplossingen
sustained voortdurend, aanhoudend
sustenance voedsel[h] [also fig]
[1]**suture** (n) hechting
[2]**suture** (vb) hechten
SW South-West(ern) Z.W., zuidwest
[1]**swab** (n) **1** zwabber, stokdweil **2** prop (watten), wattenstokje[h] **3** uitstrijkje[h]; monster[h]: *take a ~* een uitstrijkje maken, een monster nemen
[2]**swab** (vb) zwabberen, (op)dweilen, opnemen
swag [inform] buit || [inform] *he's **got** ~* hij heeft swag, hij heeft stijl
[1]**swagger** (n) **1** geparadeer[h], zwier(ige gang) **2** opschepperij
[2]**swagger** (vb) **1** paraderen, lopen als een pauw **2** opscheppen, pochen
[1]**swallow** (n) **1** zwaluw **2** slok || *one ~ doesn't make a **summer*** één zwaluw maakt nog geen zomer
[2]**swallow** (vb) slikken
[3]**swallow** (vb) **1** (door)slikken, inslikken, binnenkrijgen **2** opslokken, verslinden: *~ up* opslokken, inlijven **3** [fig] slikken, geloven: *~ a **story*** een verhaal slikken **4** inslikken [words or sounds] **5** herroepen, terugnemen: *~ one's **words*** zijn woorden terugnemen **6** onderdrukken, verbijten: *~ one's **pride*** zijn trots terzijde schuiven; *~ hard* zich vermannen
swallow-tailed zwaluwstaartvormig, ge-

vorkt: *~ **coat*** rok(jas)
[1]**swamp** (n) moeras(land)[h]
[2]**swamp** (vb) **1** doen vollopen **2** onder water doen lopen, overstromen **3** bedelven, overspoelen: *~ **with** work* (or: *letters*) bedelven onder het werk (or: de brieven)
swan zwaan || *the Swan of **Avon*** Shakespeare
[1]**swank** (n) **1** opschepper **2** opschepperij
[2]**swank** (vb) opscheppen, zich aanstellen: *~ about in a new fur coat* rondparaderen in een nieuwe bontmantel
swanky 1 opschepperig **2** chic, modieus, stijlvol
swan song zwanenzang
[1]**swap** (n) ruil: *do* (or: *make*) *a ~* ruilen
[2]**swap** (vb) ruilen, uitwisselen: *~ **jokes*** moppen tappen onder elkaar; *~ over* (or: *round*) van plaats verwisselen; *~ for* (in)ruilen tegen
[1]**swarm** (n) zwerm, massa: *~ of **bees*** bijenzwerm; *~s of **children*** drommen kinderen
[2]**swarm** (vb) **1** (uit)zwermen, samendrommen: *~ in* (or: *out*) naar binnen (or: buiten) stromen; *~ about* (or: *round*) samendrommen rond **2** (+ with) krioelen (van), wemelen **3** klimmen: *~ up a tree* in een boom klauteren
swarthy donker, bruin, zwart(achtig)
swastika hakenkruis[h]
swat meppen, (dood)slaan: *~ a **fly*** een vlieg doodmeppen
swathe 1 zwad(e)[h], hoeveelheid met één maai afgesneden gras (koren) **2** (gemaaide) strook, baan: *cut a wide ~ through* flinke sporen achterlaten in
SWAT team [Am] interventieteam[h]
[1]**sway** (n) **1** slingering, zwaai; schommeling [of ship etc] **2** invloed, druk, overwicht[h], dwang: *under the ~ of his **arguments*** overgehaald door zijn argumenten
[2]**sway** (vb) beïnvloeden: *be ~ed by* zich laten leiden door
[3]**sway** (vb) slingeren, (doen) zwaaien; [fig also] (doen) aarzelen: *~ to the music* deinen op de maat van de muziek
swear 1 (+ at, about) vloeken (op/over) **2** zweren, een eed afleggen, met kracht beweren, wedden: *~ an **oath*** een eed afleggen; *~ to do sth.* plechtig beloven iets te zullen doen; *~ by s.o.* (sth.) bij iem. (iets) zweren, volkomen op iem. (iets) vertrouwen **3** beëdigen, de eed afnemen: *sworn **translator*** beëdigd vertaler; *sworn **enemies*** gezworen vijanden; *~ in* beëdigen; *~ to secrecy* (or: *silence*) een eed van geheimhouding afnemen van
swearword vloek, krachtterm
[1]**sweat** (n) **1** zweet[h]: *he was in a **cold** ~* het klamme zweet brak hem uit **2** inspanning, karwei[h]: *a **frightful** ~* een vreselijk karwei **3** eng gevoel[h], angst, spanning: *in a ~* benauwd, bang **4** (oude) rot: *old ~* oude rot

²**sweat** (vb) zweten, (doen) (uit)zweten: ~ *blood* water en bloed zweten; ~ *it out* (tot het einde) volhouden, standhouden, zweten
sweated door uitbuiting verkregen, uitgebuit: ~ *labour* slavenarbeid
sweater sweater, sportvestʰ, (wollen) trui
sweatshop 1 slavenhokʰ 2 illegaal naaiatelierʰ
sweat suit trainingspakʰ, joggingpakʰ
sweaty 1 zwetend, bezweet, zweterig 2 broeierig, heet
Swede Zweed(se)
Sweden Zweden
¹**Swedish** (n) Zweedsʰ [language]
²**Swedish** (adj) Zweeds
¹**sweep** (n) 1 (schoonmaak)beurt, opruiming: *make* a *clean* ~ schoon schip maken 2 veger, schoorsteenveger, straatveger 3 veeg, haal (met een borstel), streek 4 zwaai, slag, draai, bocht: *wide* ~ wijde draai ‖ a ~ *of mountain country* een stuk bergland, een berglandschap
²**sweep** (vb) 1 vegen: ~ *the seas* de zeeën schoonvegen; *be swept from sight* aan het gezicht onttrokken worden; ~ *up* aanvegen, uitvegen, bijeenvegen 2 (laten) slepen 3 (toe)zwaaien, slaan: ~ *aside* (met een zwaai) opzijschuiven; [fig] naast zich neerleggen; ~ *off* (met een zwaai) afnemen [hat] 4 meesleuren, wegsleuren, meevoeren, afrukken: ~ *along* meesleuren, meeslepen; *be swept off one's feet* a) omvergelopen worden; b) [fig] overdonderd worden; c) versteld staan, halsoverkop verliefd worden; *be swept out to sea* in zee gesleurd worden 5 doorkruisen, teisteren, razen over: *the storm swept the country* de storm raasde over het land 6 afzoeken 7 bestrijken 8 (volledig) winnen 9 zich (snel) (voort)bewegen, vliegen: ~ *along* voortsnellen; ~ *by* (or: *past*) voorbijschieten; ~ *down on* aanvallen; ~ *on* voortijlen; ~ *round* zich (met een zwaai) omdraaien; ~ *from* (or: *out of*) *the room* de kamer uit stuiven; ~ *into power* aan de macht komen 10 zich uitstrekken: ~ *down* to *the sea* zich uitstrekken tot aan de zee
sweeper 1 veger, straatveger, schoorsteenveger 2 tapijtenroller, (straat)veegmachine 3 [socc] vrije verdediger, laatste man
sweeping 1 veelomvattend, ingrijpend: ~ *changes* ingrijpende veranderingen 2 radicaal, veralgemenend: ~ *condemnation* radicale veroordeling 3 geweldig, kolossaal: ~ *reductions* reusachtige prijsverlagingen
¹**sweet** (n) 1 lieveling, schatjeʰ 2 snoepjeʰ, lekkersʰ 3 dessertʰ, toetjeʰ
²**sweet** (adj) zoet, lekker, heerlijk, geurig, melodieus: ~ *nature* zachte natuur, beminnelijk karakter; *keep* s.o. ~ iem. te vriend houden; *be* ~ *on* s.o. gek zijn op iem.; *how* ~ *of you* wat aardig van je ‖ ~ *nothings* lieve

woordjes; *have* a ~ *tooth* een zoetekauw zijn
sweetbread zwezerik
¹**sweeten** (vb) zoet(er) worden
²**sweeten** (vb) 1 zoeten, zoet(er) maken 2 verzachten, verlichten, veraangenamen 3 sussen, omkopen, zoet houden
sweetener 1 zoetstof 2 smeergeldʰ, fooi, steekpenning
sweetheart 1 schat 2 liefjeʰ, vriend, vriendin
sweetie 1 liefjeʰ, schatjeʰ 2 snoepjeʰ
sweetmeat 1 snoepjeʰ 2 (-s) snoepgoedʰ
sweetness zoetheid: *yesterday Sarah was all* ~ *and light* gisteren was Sarah een en al beminnelijkheid
sweet pepper paprika
sweet-talk vleien
¹**swell** (n) 1 zwelling, het zwellen, volheid 2 deining
²**swell** (adj) voortreffelijk, prima: a ~ *teacher* een prima leraar
³**swell** (vb) (op)zwellen, bol gaan staan: ~ *out* bollen; ~ *up* (op)zwellen; ~ *with pride* zwellen van trots
⁴**swell** (vb) doen zwellen, bol doen staan: ~ *one's funds* wat bijverdienen
swelling zwelling, het zwellen
sweltering smoorheet, drukkend
¹**swerve** (n) zwenking, wending
²**swerve** (vb) 1 zwenken, plotseling uitwijken: ~ *from* the *path* van het pad afdwalen [also fig] 2 afwijken, afdwalen
³**swerve** (vb) 1 doen zwenken, opzij doen gaan 2 doen afwijken
swift vlug, snel, rap
¹**swig** (n) slok
²**swig** (vb) met grote teugen drinken
³**swig** (vb) naar binnen gieten, leegzuipen
¹**swill** (n) 1 spoeling, spoelbeurt: *give* a ~ uitspoelen 2 afvalʰ 3 varkensdraf, varkensvoerʰ
²**swill** (vb) zuipen, gretig drinken
³**swill** (vb) 1 afspoelen, doorspoelen, uitspoelen: ~ *down* afspoelen; ~ *out* uitspoelen 2 opzuipen, gretig opdrinken: ~ *down* opzuipen
¹**swim** (n) zwempartij: *have* (or: *go*) *for* a ~ gaan zwemmen, een duik (gaan) nemen ‖ *be in* (or: *out of*) *the* ~ (niet) op de hoogte zijn, (niet) meedoen
²**swim** (vb) 1 zwemmen [also fig]; baden 2 vlotten, drijven, zweven: ~*ming in butter* drijvend in de boter 3 duizelen, draaierig worden: *my head is* ~*ming* het duizelt mij
³**swim** (vb) (over)zwemmen: ~ a *river* een rivier overzwemmen
swim bladder zwemblaas
swimmer zwemmer
swimming de zwemsport
swimming costume zwempakʰ, badpakʰ
swimmingly vlot, moeiteloos, als van een

leien dakje: *everything goes on* (or: *off*) ~ alles loopt gesmeerd

swimming pool zwembad[h]

swimming trunks zwembroek

¹swindle (n) (geval[h] van) zwendel, bedrog[h], oplichterij

²swindle (vb) oplichten, afzetten, bedriegen: ~ *money out of* s.o., ~ s.o. *out of* money iem. geld afhandig maken

swindler zwendelaar(ster), oplichter

swine zwijn[h], varken[h]

¹swing (n) 1 schommel 2 schommeling, zwaai, slingerbeweging, forse beweging: ~ *in public opinion* kentering in de publieke opinie 3 (fors) ritme[h] 4 swing(muziek) 5 actie, vaart, gang: *in full* ~ in volle actie; *get into the* ~ *of things* op dreef komen 6 inspiratie || *go with a* ~ van een leien dakje gaan

²swing (vb) 1 met veerkrachtige tred gaan, met zwaaiende gang lopen: ~ *along* (or: *by, past*) met veerkrachtige gang voorbijlopen 2 swingen 3 opgehangen worden: ~ *for* it ervoor gestraft worden 4 slingeren, schommelen, zwaaien: [fig] ~ *into* action in actie komen 5 draaien, (doen) zwenken: ~ *round* (zich) omdraaien, (zich) omgooien; ~ *to* dichtslaan [door etc] 6 (op)hangen: ~ *from the ceiling* aan het plafond hangen 7 beïnvloeden, bepalen, manipuleren: *what* swung *it was the money* wat de doorslag gaf, was het geld 8 wijsmaken: *you can't* ~ *that sort of stuff on her* zoiets maak je haar niet wijs

swing bridge draaibrug

swing by [inform] langsgaan, op bezoek gaan

swing door klapdeur, tochtdeur

swingeing geweldig, enorm: ~ *cuts* zeer drastische bezuinigingen

swinger [inform] 1 snelle jongen 2 iem. die aan partnerruil doet 3 biseksueel

swinging 1 schommelend, slingerend, zwaaiend 2 veerkrachtig: ~ *step* veerkrachtige tred 3 ritmisch, swingend

swing state [Am; pol] swingstaat

swing vote: [esp Am; pol] *hold the* ~ de beslissende stem hebben

¹swipe (n) 1 mep, (harde) slag: *have* (or: *take*) *a* ~ *at* uithalen naar 2 verwijt[h], schimpscheut

²swipe (vb) 1 gappen, jatten, stelen 2 [bank card] door de kaartlezer halen 3 [comp] swipen: ~ *your finger over the screen* veeg met je vinger over het scherm

swipe card magneetkaart

¹swirl (n) 1 (draai)kolk, maalstroom 2 werveling

²swirl (vb) 1 (doen) wervelen, (doen) dwarrelen: ~ *about* rondwervelen, ronddwarrelen 2 (doen) draaien

¹swish (n) 1 zwiep, slag 2 zoevend geluid[h], geruis[h]: *the* ~ *of a cane* het zoeven van een rietje

²swish (adj) chic, modieus

³swish (vb) 1 zoeven, suizen, ruisen: ~ *past* voorbijzoeven 2 zwiepen

⁴swish (vb) doen zwiepen, slaan met: ~*ing tail* zwiepende staart

¹Swiss (n) Zwitser(se)

²Swiss (adj) Zwitsers: ~ *cheese* a) emmentaler; b) [fig] gatenkaas || ~ *roll* opgerolde cake met jam

¹switch (n) 1 schakelaar 2 [railways] wissel[+h] 3 ommezwaai, verandering 4 twijgje[h], loot 5 (valse) haarlok, (valse) haarvlecht

²switch (vb) 1 verwisselen: ~ *(a)round* verwisselen 2 ontsteken

³switch (vb) 1 (om)schakelen, veranderen (van), overgaan (op): ~ *places* van plaats veranderen; ~ *off* a) uitschakelen, afzetten; b) versuffen; ~ *over* a) overschakelen; b) [radio, TV] een ander kanaal kiezen; ~ *through (to)* doorverbinden; ~ *to* overgaan naar 2 draaien, (doen) omzwaaien: ~ *round* omdraaien

switchback 1 bochtige, heuvelige weg 2 achtbaan

switchblade [esp Am] stiletto

switchboard schakelbord[h]

switched-on 1 levendig, alert 2 bij (de tijd), vooruitstrevend 3 high

switch on 1 inschakelen, aanzetten, aandoen 2 stimuleren, doen opleven, inspireren

switch-over 1 overschakeling, omschakeling 2 overgang, verandering

Switzerland Zwitserland

¹swivel (n) (ketting)wartel

²swivel (vb) (rond)draaien: ~ *round in one's chair* ronddraaien in zijn stoel

swivel chair draaistoel

swizz 1 bedrog[h] 2 ontgoocheling

swizzle stick [inform] roerstokje[h]

swollen gezwollen [also fig]; opgeblazen

swollen-headed 1 verwaand, arrogant 2 overmoedig

swoon 1 in vervoering geraken 2 bezwijmen, in onmacht vallen

¹swoop (n) 1 duik 2 veeg, haal: *at one (fell)* ~ met één slag, in één klap

²swoop (vb) stoten [of bird of prey]; (op een prooi) neerschieten; zich storten op [also fig]: ~ *down* stoten

¹swop (n) ruil

²swop (vb) ruilen, uitwisselen: ~ *for* (in)ruilen tegen

sword zwaard[h] || *cross* ~s *(with)* in conflict komen (met); *put to the* ~ over de kling jagen, vermoorden

swordfish zwaardvis

swordsman 1 zwaardvechter 2 schermer

sword swallower degenslikker

sworn 1 gezworen: ~ *enemies* gezworen vijanden 2 beëdigd: ~ *statement* verklaring onder ede

¹swot (n) **1** blokker, stuud, studie(bol) **2** geblok[h], gezwoeg[h]

²swot (vb) blokken op: ~ *sth.* **up,** ~ **up** *on sth.* iets erin stampen, iets repeteren; ~ *for an exam* blokken voor een examen

SWOT: *a* ~ *analysis* een sterkte-zwakteanalyse

swotty [inform] ijverig studerend

sycamore 1 esdoorn **2** plataan[h]

syllable lettergreep

syllabus samenvatting, leerplan[h]

sylph 1 luchtgeest **2** tengere/elegante dame

symbol symbool[h], (lees)teken[h]

symbolic(al) symbolisch: *be symbolic of* voorstellen

symbolism 1 symbolisme[h] **2** symboliek, symbolische betekenis

symbolize symboliseren, symbool zijn van: *a white dove ~s peace* een witte duif is het symbool van vrede

symmetry symmetrie

sympathetic 1 sympathiek, welwillend: *be* (or: *feel*) ~ *to/toward(s) s.o.* iem. genegen zijn **2** meevoelend, deelnemend

sympathize 1 sympathiseren: ~ *with* sympathiseren met, meevoelen met **2** meevoelen, deelneming voelen

sympathizer sympathisant

sympathy sympathie, genegenheid, deelneming: *letter of* ~ condoleancebrief; *feel* ~ *for* meeleven met; *be in* ~ *with* gunstig staan tegenover, begrip hebben voor

symphony symfonie

symphony orchestra symfonieorkest[h]

symptom symptoom[h], (ziekte)verschijnsel[h], indicatie

symptomatic symptomatisch: *be* ~ *of* symptomatisch zijn voor, wijzen op

synagogue synagoge

sync synchronisatie: *be out of* ~ *with* niet gelijk lopen met

synchronic synchroon

¹synchronize (vb) **1** gelijktijdig gebeuren, samenvallen **2** gelijk staan [of clock]

²synchronize (vb) **1** synchroniseren [also film]; (doen) samenvallen (in de tijd): ~ *with* synchroniseren met **2** gelijk zetten [clock]

syndicate 1 syndicaat[h], belangengroepering **2** perssyndicaat[h], persbureau[h]

syndrome syndroom[h], complex[h] van kenmerkende (ziekte)verschijnselen

synod synode

synonym synoniem[h]

synonymous synoniem

synopsis korte inhoud(sbeschrijving), samenvatting, overzicht[h]

syntax syntaxis, zinsbouw

synth *synthesizer*

synthesize 1 maken, samenstellen **2** bij-

eenvoegen, tot een geheel maken **3** synthetisch bereiden, langs kunstmatige weg maken

synthetic synthetisch, op synthese berustend, kunstmatig vervaardigd

syphilis syfilis

Syria Syrië

¹Syrian (n) Syriër, Syrische

²Syrian (adj) Syrisch

¹syringe (n) (injectie)spuit

²syringe (vb) **1** inspuiten, een injectie geven **2** uitspuiten, schoonspuiten

syrup siroop, stroop

system 1 stelsel[h], systeem[h] **2** geheel[h], samenstel[h] **3** methode **4** gestel[h], lichaam[h], lichaamsgesteldheid **5** systematiek || *get sth. out of one's* ~ iets verwerken

systematic systematisch, methodisch

systematize systematiseren, tot een systeem maken

systems analyst systeemanalist(e)

t

t t, T ‖ *cross one's t's (and dot one's i's)* de puntjes op de i zetten, op de details letten; *to a T* precies, tot in de puntjes
ta [inform, child language] dank je
tab 1 lus, ophanglusje^h **2** etiketje^h, label^h **3** klepje^h, flapje^h; lipje^h [of tin] **4** [inform] rekening: *pick up the ~* betalen **5** tabtoets **6** tabblad^h ‖ *keep ~s* (or: *a ~) on* in de gaten houden
tabby 1 cyperse kat **2** poes, vrouwtjeskat
tabernacle [rel] tabernakel^h, (veld)hut, tent
tab key tabtoets
table 1 tafel: *lay the ~* de tafel dekken; *at ~* aan tafel **2** tabel, lijst, tafel: *learn one's ~s* de tafels van vermenigvuldiging leren ‖ *turn the ~s (on s.o.)* de rollen omdraaien; *under the ~* dronken; *drink s.o. under the ~* iem. onder de tafel drinken
tablecloth tafelkleed^h
table-manners tafelmanieren
table-mat onderzetter
tablespoon opscheplepel, eetlepel
tablet 1 (gedenk)plaat, plaquette **2** tablet^h, pil
table-talk tafelgesprekken
table tennis tafeltennis^h
tabletop tafelblad^h
tabloid krant(je^h) [half size of regular newspaper]
tabloid press sensatiepers
taboo taboe^h: *put sth. under ~* iets taboe verklaren
tabs [inform] *tabloids* de roddelpers
tacit stilzwijgend: *~ agreement* stilzwijgende overeenkomst
taciturn zwijgzaam, (stil)zwijgend
¹tack (n) **1** kopspijker(tje^h), nageltje^h; [Am] punaise **2** koers; boeg [while navigating] **3** koers(verandering), strategie, aanpak
²tack (vb) van koers veranderen, het anders aanpakken
³tack (vb) **1** vastspijkeren: [fig] *~ on* toevoegen aan **2** rijgen
tacker nietpistool^h, spijkerpistool^h
¹tackle (n) **1** takel^{+h} **2** [sport] tackle **3** [Am football] tackle, stopper **4** uitrusting, benodigdheden **5** [shipp] takelage, takelwerk^h
²tackle (vb) **1** aanpakken, onder de knie proberen te krijgen: *~ a problem* een probleem aanpakken **2** aanpakken, een hartig woordje spreken met **3** tackelen, (de tegenstander) neerleggen

tacky 1 plakkerig, kleverig **2** haveloos, sjofel **3** smakeloos, ordinair
tact tact
tactful tactvol, omzichtig
tactic 1 tactische zet, tactiek, manoeuvre^{+h} **2** (-s) tactiek
tactical tactisch [also mil]; diplomatiek: *~ voting* strategisch stemgedrag
tactician tacticus
tactile 1 tast-: *~ organs* tastorganen **2** tastbaar, voelbaar: *~ paving* ribbelstroken
tactless tactloos
tad klein beetje^h: *just a ~ depressing* een klein beetje deprimerend
Tadzhikistan Tadzjikistan
¹tag (n) **1** etiket^h [also fig]; insigne^h, label^h **2** [comp] tag **3** stiftje^h [at end of shoe-lace etc] **4** afgezaagd gezegde^h, cliché^h **5** flard, rafel, los uiteinde^h **6** klit haar^h **7** elektronische enkelband
²tag (vb) (+ along) dicht volgen, slaafs achternalopen ‖ *the children were ~ging along behind their teacher* de kinderen liepen (verveeld) achter hun onderwijzer aan
³tag (vb) **1** van een etiket voorzien [also fig]; etiketteren, merken **2** vastknopen, toevoegen: *a label had been ~ged on at the top* aan de bovenkant was een kaartje vastgemaakt **3** [comp] taggen
tagline tagline [slagzin]
¹tail (n) **1** staart **2** onderste^h, achterste deel^h, uiteinde^h, pand^h; sleep [of clothing]; staart [of comet, aeroplane] **3** (-s) munt(zijde) **4** (-s) rokkostuum^h ‖ *with one's ~ between one's legs* met hangende pootjes; *turn ~ and run* hard weglopen; *be on s.o.'s ~* iem. op de hielen zitten
²tail (vb) schaduwen, volgen
tailback file, verkeersopstopping
tailboard laadklep, achterklep
tailcoat jacquet^h, rok, rokkostuum^h
tail end uiteinde^h
¹tailgate (n) [Am] achterklep, laadklep; vijfde deur [of car]
²tailgate (vb) geen afstand houden, bumperkleven
tailgater bumperklever
tail light (rood) achterlicht^h
tail off 1 geleidelijk afnemen, verminderen **2** verstommen **3** uiteenvallen
¹tailor (n) kleermaker
²tailor (vb) **1** maken [clothes]; op maat snijden en aan elkaar naaien **2** aanpassen, op maat knippen: *we ~ our insurance to your needs* wij stemmen onze verzekering af op uw behoeften
tailor-made 1 maat-: *~ suit* maatkostuum^h **2** geknipt, precies op maat
tailwind rugwind
¹taint (n) smet(je^h), vlekje^h
²taint (vb) bederven, rotten, ontaarden

³**taint** (vb) besmetten
Taiw<u>a</u>n Taiwan
¹**Taiwan<u>e</u>se** (n) Taiwanees, Taiwanese
²**Taiwan<u>e</u>se** (adj) Taiwanees
¹**Taj<u>i</u>k** (n) Tadzjiek(se)
²**Taj<u>i</u>k** (adj) Tadzjieks
Taj<u>i</u>kistan Tadzjikistan
¹**take** (n) **1** vangst **2** opbrengst, ont-
vangst(en) **3** [film] opname
²**take** (vb) **1** pakken, aanslaan, wortel schieten **2** effect hebben, inslaan, slagen **3** bijten
[of fish] **4** worden: *he was ~n ill* hij werd ziek
5 vlam vatten || *Gerard ~s after his father* Ge-
rard lijkt op zijn vader; *I took against him at
first sight* ik mocht hem meteen al niet
³**take** (vb) **1** nemen, grijpen, (beet)pakken:
[fig] *~ my grandfather, he is still working* neem
nou mijn opa, die werkt nog steeds **2** veroveren, innemen, vangen; [chess, draughts]
slaan: [chess] *he took my bishop* hij sloeg mijn
loper; *he took me unawares* hij verraste mij
3 winnen, (be)halen **4** nemen, zich verschaffen, gebruiken: *~ the bus* de bus nemen; *this
seat is ~n* deze stoel is bezet; *do you ~ sugar
in your tea?* gebruikt u suiker in de thee?
5 vereisen, in beslag nemen: *it won't ~ too
much time* het zal niet al te veel tijd kosten;
have what it ~s aan de eisen voldoen **6** meenemen, brengen: *that bus will ~ you to the
station* met die bus kom je bij het station; *~
s.o. around* iem. rondleiden; *~ s.o. aside* iem.
apart nemen **7** weghalen, wegnemen: *~ five
from twelve* trek vijf van twaalf af **8** krijgen,
vatten, voelen: *she took an immediate dislike
to him* zij kreeg onmiddellijk een hekel aan
hem; *~ fire* vlam vatten; *~ it into one's head*
het in zijn hoofd krijgen **9** opnemen, noteren, meten: *let me ~ your temperature* laat
mij even je temperatuur opnemen **10** begrijpen: *~ for granted* als vanzelfsprekend
aannemen; *I ~ it that he'll be back soon* ik
neem aan dat hij gauw terugkomt; *~ it badly*
het zich erg aantrekken; *what do you ~ me
for?* waar zie je me voor aan? **11** aanvaarden, accepteren: *~ sides* partij kiezen; *you
may ~ it from me* je kunt van mij aannemen
12 maken, doen; nemen [school subject]: *~ a
decision* een besluit nemen; *~ an exam* een
examen afleggen; *~ notes* aantekeningen
maken; *she took a long time over it* zij deed er
lang over **13** raken, treffen **14** behandelen
[problem etc] **15** gebruiken, innemen || *~ it
or leave it* graag of niet; *~ aback* verrassen,
van zijn stuk brengen, overdonderen; *she
was rather ~n by* (or: *with*) *it* zij was er nogal
mee in haar schik; *~ it (up)on o.s.* het op zich
nemen, het wagen
take ap<u>a</u>rt 1 uit elkaar halen, demonteren
2 een vreselijke uitbrander geven
¹**t<u>a</u>keaway** (n) afhaalrestaurantʰ, afhaalmaaltijd

²**t<u>a</u>keaway** (adj) afhaal-, meeneem-
take aw<u>a</u>y 1 aftrekken **2** weghalen **3** verminderen, verkleinen, afbreuk doen aan: *it
takes sth. away from the total effect* het doet
een beetje afbreuk aan het geheel
take b<u>a</u>ck 1 terugbrengen; [fig] doen denken aan: *it took me back to my childhood* het
deed me denken aan mijn jeugd **2** terugnemen, intrekken
t<u>a</u>kedown [inform] **1** vernedering, kleine-
ring **2** [martial arts] worp waarbij iem. op de
mat gelegd wordt **3** arrestatie op straat
4 [media] procedure waarbij onrechtmatige
inhoud van een website verwijderd wordt
take d<u>o</u>wn 1 afhalen, naar beneden halen
2 [martial arts] neerhalen **3** opschrijven, noteren **4** uit elkaar halen, demonteren, slopen
take-home afhaal-, meeneem-: *~ dinners*
afhaalmaaltijden; *~ exam* tentamen dat je
thuis maakt
take-home p<u>a</u>y nettoloonʰ
take <u>i</u>n 1 in huis nemen, kamers verhuren
aan **2** naar binnen halen, meenemen **3** omvatten, betreffen **4** innemen [clothing];
[shipp] oprollen [sailing] **5** begrijpen, doorzien **6** (in zich) opnemen [surroundings etc];
bekijken **7** bedriegen **8** geabonneerd zijn
op
¹**take <u>o</u>ff** (vb) **1** zich afzetten **2** opstijgen;
starten [also fig; of project etc] **3** (snel) populair worden, succes hebben
²**take <u>o</u>ff** (vb) **1** uittrekken, uitdoen **2** meenemen, wegvoeren: *she took the children off
to bed* zij bracht de kinderen naar bed **3** afhalen, weghalen, verwijderen **4** verlagen
[price] **5** nadoen, imiteren **6** vrij nemen ||
take o.s. off ervandoor gaan, zich uit de voeten maken
take-off 1 start, het opstijgen, vertrekʰ
2 parodie, imitatie
¹**take <u>o</u>n** (vb) tekeergaan, zich aanstellen
²**take <u>o</u>n** (vb) **1** op zich nemen, als uitdaging
accepteren **2** krijgen; aannemen [colour];
overnemen, in dienst nemen **3** het opnemen
tegen, vechten tegen **4** aan boord nemen
take <u>o</u>ut 1 mee naar buiten nemen, mee
uit nemen, naar buiten brengen: [Am] *~
food* een afhaalmaaltijd meenemen; *take s.o.
out for a walk* (or: *meal*) iem. mee uit wandelen nemen, iem. mee uit eten nemen **2** verwijderen, uithalen **3** tevoorschijn halen
4 nemen, aanschaffen: *~ an insurance (policy)*
een verzekering afsluiten **5** buiten gevecht
stellen [opponent] || *take it out of s.o.* veel van
iemands krachten vergen; *don't take it out on
him* reageer het niet op hem af
t<u>a</u>keover overname
take <u>o</u>ver 1 overnemen, het heft in handen nemen **2** navolgen, overnemen
take to 1 beginnen te, gaan doen aan, zich

toeleggen op **2** aardig vinden, mogen: *he did not take **kindly** to it* hij moest er niet veel van hebben **3** de wijk nemen naar, vluchten naar: ~ *one's **bed*** het bed houden; [protest] ~ *the **streets*** de straat op gaan

¹take up (vb) verder gaan [of story, chapter] || ~ **with** bevriend raken met

²take up (vb) **1** optillen, oppakken: ~ *the **hatchet*** de strijdbijl opgraven **2** absorberen [also fig]; opnemen, in beslag nemen: *it nearly took up all the **room*** het nam bijna alle ruimte in beslag **3** oppikken [passengers] **4** ter hand nemen, gaan doen aan: ~ *a **cause*** een zaak omhelzen; ~ ***gardening*** gaan tuinieren **5** vervolgen [story]; hervatten **6** aannemen, aanvaarden, ingaan op: *he took me up **on** my offer* hij nam mijn aanbod aan **7** innemen [position]; aannemen [attitude] || *I'll take you up **on** that* daar zal ik je aan houden

taking: *for the* ~ voor het grijpen

takings verdiensten, recette, ontvangsten

talcum powder talkpoeder^h

tale 1 verhaal(tje)^h: *thereby **hangs** a* ~ daar zit een (heel) verhaal aan vast; **tell** ~s kletsen, roddelen **2** sprookje^h, legende **3** leugen, smoes(je^h) **4** gerucht^h, roddel, praatje^h

talent 1 talent^h, (natuurlijke) begaafdheid, gave **2** talent^h, begaafde persoon

talented getalenteerd, talentvol

taleteller 1 kwaadspreker **2** roddelaar(ster)

¹talk (n) **1** praatje^h; lezing [on radio] **2** gesprek^h: *have a* ~ *(to, with s.o.)* (met iem.) spreken **3** (-s) besprekingen, onderhandelingen **4** gepraat^h **5** gerucht^h, praatjes: *there is* ~ *of* er is sprake van (dat), het gerucht gaat dat **6** geklets^h: *be **all*** ~ praats hebben [but achieving nothing]

²talk (vb) **1** spreken, praten: *now **you're** ~ing* zo mag ik het horen, dat klinkt al (een stuk) beter; *you **can** (or: **can't**)* ~ moet je horen wie het zegt; *do the* ~ing het woord voeren; [at beginning of sentence] ~ing *of plants* over planten gesproken **2** roddelen, praten: ***people** will* ~ de mensen roddelen toch (wel) || ~ *to s.o.* eens ernstig praten met iem.

³talk (vb) **1** spreken (over), discussiëren over, bespreken: ~ *s.o.'s **head** off* iem. de oren van het hoofd praten; ~ *one's **way** out of sth.* zich ergens uitpraten **2** zeggen, uiten || ~ *s.o. **round** to sth.* iem. ompraten tot iets; ~ *s.o. **into** (doing) sth.* iem. overhalen iets te doen; ~ *s.o. **out of** (doing) sth.* iem. iets uit het hoofd praten

talk about 1 spreken over, bespreken, het hebben over: ~ ***problems!*** over problemen gesproken!; ***know** what one is talking about* weten waar men het over heeft; *that's what I'm talking about* **a)** dat bedoel ik nou; **b)** zo mag ik het zien/horen **2** roddelen over: *be talked about* over de tong gaan **3** spreken

van, zijn voornemen uiten (om): *they're talking about **emigrating** to Australia* zij overwegen naar Australië te emigreren

talkative praatgraag, praatziek

talk back (brutaal) reageren: ~ *to s.o.* iem. van repliek dienen

talk down neerbuigend praten: ~ *to one's audience* afdalen tot het niveau van zijn gehoor

talking point discussiepunt^h

talking-to uitbrander: *(give s.o.) a **good*** ~ een hartig woordje (met iem. spreken)

talk of 1 spreken over, bespreken: [at beginning of sentence] *talking of **plants*** over planten gesproken **2** spreken van, het hebben over: ~ ***doing** sth.* van plan zijn iets te doen

talk out 1 uitvoerig spreken over: ~ *a **bill*** door lange redevoeringen het aannemen van een wet verhinderen **2** uitpraten

talk over (uitvoerig) spreken over, uitvoerig bespreken: *talk things over **with** s.o.* de zaak (uitvoerig) met iem. bespreken

talk show praatprogramma^h; talkshow [on TV]

tall 1 lang [of person]; groot; hoog [of tree, mast etc]: *Peter is 6 **feet*** ~ Peter is 1,80 m (lang); *the pole is 10 **feet*** ~ de paal is 3 m hoog **2** overdreven, te groot: ~ ***order*** onredelijke eis; ~ ***story*** sterk verhaal || ~ ***talk*** opschepperij

¹tally (n) **1** rekening **2** inkeping **3** label^h, etiket^h, merk^h **4** score(bord^h) **5** aantekening: ***keep** (a)* ~ *(of)* aantekening houden (van)

²tally (vb) (+ with) overeenkomen (met), gelijk zijn, kloppen

talon klauw [of bird of prey]

tambour 1 trom(mel) **2** schuifklep [of desk]

¹tame (adj) **1** tam, mak **2** meegaand **3** oninteressant, saai

²tame (vb) temmen; [fig] bedwingen

tamper with 1 knoeien met, verknoeien: ~ ***documents*** documenten vervalsen **2** zich bemoeien met **3** komen aan, zitten aan **4** omkopen

tampon tampon

¹tan (adj) geelbruin, zongebruind

²tan (vb) bruin worden [sun]

³tan (vb) **1** bruinen [sun] **2** looien, tanen || ~ *s.o.'s **hide**, ~ the **hide** off s.o.* iem. afranselen

tandem tandem || *in* ~ achter elkaar

tang 1 scherpe (karakteristieke) lucht, indringende geur **2** scherpe smaak; smaakje^h [fig]; zweem, tikje^h

tangent raaklijn, tangens || *fly* (or: *go*) *off at a* ~ een gedachtesprong maken, plotseling van koers veranderen

tangerine 1 feloranje^h **2** tangerine [fruit]

tangible tastbaar [also fig]; voelbaar, concreet: [law] ~ ***assets*** activa

¹tangle (n) **1** knoop; klit [in hair, wool etc]: *in a* ~ in de war **2** verwarring, wirwar

²tangle (vb) **1** in de knoop raken, klitten **2** in verwarring raken, in de war raken: ~ *with s.o.* verwikkeld raken in een ruzie met iem.

¹tango (n) tango

²tango (vb) de tango dansen: *it takes two to tango* **a)** waar twee ruziemaken hebben beiden schuld; **b)** het moet van twee kanten komen

tank 1 (voorraad)tank, reservoir^h **2** tank, pantserwagen

tankard bierpul

tanker tanker

tank up 1 tanken, (bij)vullen **2** zich volgieten, zuipen

tannery looierij

tannin looizuur^h, tannine^{+h}

tanning pak^h slaag: *give* him a good ~! geef hem een goed pak slaag!

tantalize 1 doen watertanden, kwellen **2** verwachtingen wekken

tantalizing (heel) verleidelijk, aantrekkelijk

tantamount (+ to) gelijk(waardig) (aan): *be* ~ *to* neerkomen op

tantrum woede-uitbarsting; driftbui [pl, of small child]: *get into a* ~, *throw a* ~ een woedeaanval krijgen

Tanzania Tanzania

¹Tanzanian (n) Tanzaniaan(se)

²Tanzanian (adj) Tanzaniaans

¹tap (n) **1** kraan, tap(kraan); stop [of vat]: *turn the* ~ *on* (or: *off*) doe de kraan open (*or:* dicht); *on* ~ uit het vat, van de tap; [fig] met-een voorradig, zo voorhanden **2** tik(je^h), klopje^h: *a* ~ *on a* **shoulder** een schouderklopje **3** afluisterapparatuur

²tap (vb) tikken, kloppen: ~ *at* (or: *on*) *the door* op de deur tikken

³tap (vb) **1** doen tikken: ~ *s.o. on the* **shoulder** iem. op de schouder kloppen **2** (af)tappen, afnemen: *her* **telephone** *was* ~ped haar telefoon werd afgeluisterd; [fig] ~ *a person* **for** *information* informatie aan iem. ontfutselen **3** openen; aanbreken [also fig]; aanboren, aansnijden; [fig also] gebruiken: ~ *new* **sources** *of energy* nieuwe energiebronnen aanboren

tap dancing het tapdansen

¹tape (n) **1** lint^h, band^h, koord^h: **insulating** ~ isolatieband^h **2** meetlint^h, centimeter **3** (magneet)band, geluidsband, videoband **4** (plak)band^h: **adhesive** ~ plakband^h

²tape (vb) **1** (vast)binden, inpakken, samenbinden **2** [Am] verbinden, met verband omwikkelen: *his knee was* ~d **up** zijn knie zat in het verband || *have s.o.* ~d *in* iem. helemaal doorhebben

³tape (vb) opnemen, een (band)opname maken (van)

tape measure meetlint^h, centimeter

¹taper (n) **1** (dunne) kaars **2** (was)pit, lontje^h **3** (geleidelijke) versmalling [eg of long object]; spits toelopend voorwerp^h

²taper (vb) **1** taps toelopen, geleidelijk smaller worden: *this stick* ~s **off** *to a point* deze stok loopt scherp toe in een punt **2** (+ off) (geleidelijk) kleiner worden, verminderen, afnemen

³taper (vb) smal(ler) maken, taps doen toelopen

tape recorder bandrecorder

tape recording bandopname

tapestreamer tapestreamer

tapestry 1 wandtapijt^h **2** bekledingsstof van muren

tapeworm lintworm

taproom tapperij, gelagkamer

tap-to-pay contactloos betalen^h

tap water kraanwater^h

¹tar (n) teer^h

²tar (vb) teren, met teer insmeren; [fig] zwartmaken: ~ *and* **feather** *s.o.* iem. met teer en veren bedekken [as punishment]

tarantula vogelspin, tarantula

tardy 1 traag, sloom: ~ **progress** langzame vooruitgang; *he is* ~ *in* **paying** hij is slecht van betalen **2** (te) laat **3** weifelend, onwillig

tare 1 tarra(gewicht^h) [difference between gross and net weight] **2** leeg gewicht^h [of lorry etc]

tares onkruid^h

¹target (n) **1** doel^h, roos, schietschijf; [fig] streven^h; doeleinde^h: *on* ~ op de goede weg, in de goede richting **2** doelwit^h [of mockery, criticism]; mikpunt^h

²target (vb) mikken op: *he* ~s *his* **audiences** *carefully* hij neemt zijn publiek zorgvuldig op de korrel

target date streefdatum

tariff (tol)tarief^h, invoerrechten, uitvoerrechten: *postal* ~s posttarieven

¹tarmac (n) asfalt^h

²tarmac (vb) asfalteren

¹tarnish (n) glansverlies^h, dofheid; [fig] smet

²tarnish (vb) dof worden, verkleuren; aanslaan [of metal]; [fig] aangetast worden

³tarnish (vb) dof maken, doen aanslaan; [fig] bezoedelen: *a* ~ed **reputation** een bezoedelde naam

tarragon dragon

tarry 1 treuzelen, op zich laten wachten **2** (ver)blijven, zich ophouden

¹tart (n) [inform] **1** slet, del **2** (vruchten)-taart(je^h)

²tart (adj) **1** scherp(smakend), zuur, wrang **2** scherp, sarcastisch

tartan 1 Schotse ruit **2** doek^h in Schotse ruit **3** tartan^h, (geruite) Schotse wollen stof

tartar 1 woesteling **2** tandsteen^{+h}

Tartar Tataar

tart up opdirken, optutten: ~ *a house* een huis kitscherig inrichten

¹taser (n) taser, stroomstootwapen[h]

²taser (vb) taseren

task taak, karwei[h], opdracht ‖ **take** s.o. to ~ *(for)* iem. onder handen nemen (vanwege)

taskbar [comp] taakbalk

task bar [comp] taakbalk

task force speciale eenheid [of army, police]; gevechtsgroep

task-juggling multitasking

taskmaster opdrachtgever: *a hard* ~ een harde leermeester

¹taste (n) **1** kleine hoeveelheid, hapje[h], slokje[h], beetje[h], tikkeltje[h]: *have a* ~ *of this cake* neem eens een hapje van deze cake **2** ervaring, ondervinding: *give s.o. a* ~ *of the whip* iem. de zweep laten voelen **3** smaak, smaakje[h], voorkeur, genoegen[h]: *leave a unpleasant* ~ *in the mouth* een onaangename nasmaak hebben [also fig]; *everyone to his* ~ ieder zijn meug; *add sugar to* ~ suiker toevoegen naar smaak **4** smaak, smaakzin, schoonheidszin; gevoel[h] [for proper behaviour, fashion, style etc]: *in good* ~ **a)** smaakvol; **b)** behoorlijk; *sweet to the* ~ zoet van smaak

²taste (vb) smaken: *the pudding ~d of garlic* de pudding smaakte naar knoflook

³taste (vb) **1** proeven, keuren **2** ervaren, ondervinden: ~ *defeat* het onderspit delven

taste bud smaakpapil

tasteful smaakvol

tasteless 1 smaakloos (m.b.t. water enz.) **2** smakeloos (van een slechte smaak)

taster 1 proever; [hist] voorproever **2** voorproefje[h], klein stukje[h]

tasty 1 smakelijk **2** hartig

ta-ta dáág

tatt [inform] tattoo

tatter flard, lomp, vod[h]: *in ~s* aan flarden, kapot [also fig]

tattered 1 haveloos; aan flarden [clothes] **2** in lompen gekleed [pers]

¹tattle (n) **1** geklets[h], geroddel[h] **2** geklik[h]

²tattle (vb) kletsen, roddelen

¹tattoo (n) **1** tatoeage **2** taptoe [drumbeat or clarion call]: *beat* (or: *sound) the* ~ taptoe slaan (or: blazen) **3** tromgeroffel[h]

²tattoo (vb) tatoeëren

tatty slordig, slonzig, sjofel

¹taunt (n) hatelijke opmerking, bespotting: *~s* spot, hoon

²taunt (vb) hekelen: *they ~ed him into losing his temper* ze tergden hem tot hij in woede uitbarstte

Taurus [astrology] (de) Stier

taut strak, gespannen

tautology tautologie

tavern taveerne, herberg

tawdry opzichtig, smakeloos, opgedirkt

¹tax (n) **1** last, druk, gewicht[h]: *be a* ~ *on* veel vergen van **2** belasting, rijksbelasting: *value added* ~ belasting op de toegevoegde waarde, btw

²tax (vb) **1** belasten, belastingen opleggen **2** veel vergen van, zwaar op de proef stellen: ~ *your memory* denk eens goed na

taxation 1 belasting(gelden) **2** belastingsysteem[h]

tax bracket belastingschijf

tax collector (belasting)ontvanger

tax cut belastingverlaging

tax-deductible aftrekbaar van de belastingen

tax evasion belastingontduiking

tax exemption belastingvrijstelling

tax-free belastingvrij

tax haven belastingparadijs[h]

¹taxi (n) taxi

²taxi (vb) **1** (doen) taxiën **2** in een taxi rijden (vervoeren)

taxicab taxi

taxi driver taxichauffeur

taxiway taxibaan

taxman 1 belastingontvanger **2** belastingen, fiscus

taxonomic taxonomisch

taxpayer belastingbetaler

tax rebate belastingteruggave

tax return belastingaangifte

tax with 1 beschuldigen van, ten laste leggen **2** rekenschap vragen voor, op het matje roepen wegens

TB *tuberculosis* tb(c)

TBF *to be fair* eerlijk gezegd

tea 1 thee: *make* ~ theezetten; [hum] *not for all the* ~ *in China* voor geen goud, voor niets ter wereld **2** lichte maaltijd om 5 uur 's middags **3** theeplant, theebladeren

teabag theezakje[h], theebuiltje[h]

¹teach (vb) **1** leren, afleren: *I will* ~ *him to betray our plans* ik zal hem leren onze plannen te verraden **2** doen inzien, leren: *experience taught him that ...* bij ondervinding wist hij dat ...

²teach (vb) onderwijzen, leren, lesgeven: ~ *s.o. chess,* ~ *chess to s.o.* iem. leren schaken; *John ~es me (how) to swim* John leert mij zwemmen; ~ *school* onderwijzer zijn

teacher 1 leraar, docent(e) **2** onderwijzer(es)

teacher training (college) lerarenopleiding

teaching 1 het lesgeven **2** onderwijs[h] **3** leer, leerstelling

tea cloth theedoek, droogdoek

tea-cosy theemuts

teacup theekopje[h]

teak teakhout[h]

tea leaf theeblad[h] ‖ *read the tea leaves* de toekomst voorspellen

¹team (n) **1** teamʰ, (sport)ploeg, elftalʰ **2** spanʰ [of draught animals]
²team (vb) (+ up) een team vormen: ~ **up** **with** samenwerken met, samenspelen met
team bench spelersbank
team-mate teamgenoot
team spirit teamgeest
teamster 1 voerman, menner **2** vrachtwagenchauffeur
teamwork groepsarbeid, samenwerking, samenspelʰ
tea-party theekransjeʰ
teapot theepot
¹tear (n) **1** traan: *move s.o. to* ~s iem. aan het huilen brengen; *shed* ~s *over* tranen storten over [sth. not worthy of tears] **2** drup(pel)
²tear (n) **1** scheur **2** flard
³tear (vb) **1** scheuren, stuk gaan: *silk* ~s *easily* zijde scheurt makkelijk **2** rukken, trekken: ~ *at sth.* aan iets rukken **3** rennen; [fig] stormen; vliegen: *the boy tore **across** the street* de jongen stormde de straat over
⁴tear (vb) **1** (ver)scheuren [also fig]: *the girl tore a **hole** in her coat* het meisje scheurde haar jas; ~ *up* verscheuren; [fig] tenietdoen; [fig] *be torn **between** love and hate* tussen liefde en haat in tweestrijd staan; ~ *in half* (or: *two*) in tweeën scheuren **2** (uit)rukken, (uit)trekken || ~ *down a building* een gebouw afbreken
tear apart 1 verscheuren [fig]; zich vernietigend uitlaten over **2** overhoop halen **3** [inform] uitschelden || *the critics tore his latest **novel** apart* de critici schreven zijn laatste roman de grond in
tearaway herrieschopper
tear away aftrekken, wegtrekken, afscheuren; [fig] verwijderen: *I could hardly tear myself away **from** the party* ik kon het feest maar met tegenzin verlaten
teardrop traan
tearful 1 huilend **2** huilerig
tear gas traangasʰ
tear into in alle hevigheid aanvallen, heftig tekeergaan tegen
tear-jerker tranentrekker, smartlap, sentimentele film, sentimenteel liedjeʰ
tear off afrukken, aftrekken, afscheuren; [fig] verwijderen
tearoom tearoom, theesalon⁺ʰ
¹tease (n) **1** plaaggeest, kwelgeest **2** plagerij, geplaagʰ, flirt
²tease (vb) **1** plagen, lastigvallen, pesten: ~ *s.o. for sth.* iem. lastigvallen om **2** opgewonden maken, opwinden **3** ontlokken || ~ *out* ontwarren [also fig]
teaser 1 plaaggeest, plager **2** moeilijke vraag, probleemgevalʰ
teaspoon theelepeltjeʰ
teastrainer theezeefjeʰ
teat 1 tepel **2** speen

tea towel theedoek, droogdoek
tea-trolley theewagen
tech [inform] *technical college, school*
technical technisch
technicality 1 technische term **2** technisch detailʰ, (klein) formeel puntʰ: *he lost the case on a* ~ hij verloor de zaak door een vormfout
technician technicus, specialist: *dental* ~ tandtechnicus
technique techniek, werkwijze, vaardigheid
technological technologisch: ~ *university* technische universiteit
technology technologie, techniek
tech-savvy technisch onderlegd: *even if you're **not** ~* zelfs als je geen techneut bent
teddy bear teddybeer
tedious vervelend, langdradig, saai
tedium 1 verveling **2** saaiheid, eentonigheid, langdradigheid
tee [golf] tee || *to a* ~ precies, tot in de puntjes
teem 1 wemelen, krioelen, tieren: ~*ing* *with* krioelen van; *his head* ~s *with* new ideas zijn hoofd zit vol nieuwe ideeën; *those forests* ~ *with snakes* die bossen krioelen van de slangen **2** stortregenen, gieten: *it was* ~*ing down* (or: *with*) *rain* het goot
teen 1 tiener **2** (-s) tienerjaren: *boy* (or: *girl*) *in his* (or: *her*) ~s tiener
teenage tiener-: ~ *boy* (or: *girl*) tiener
teenager tiener
teeny(-weeny) piepklein
teeter 1 wankelen, waggelen: [fig] ~ *on the edge of collapse* op de rand van de ineenstorting staan **2** wippen, op de wip spelen
teethe tandjes krijgen [esp milk teeth]
teething troubles kinderziekten [fig]
teetotaller geheelonthouder
telebanking het telebankieren
telecare [med] zorg op afstand
¹telecast (n) tv-uitzending
²telecast (vb) op tv uitzenden
telecommunications 1 telecommunicatietechniek **2** (telecommunicatie)verbindingen
teleconference teleconferentie
telefax telefax
telegram telegramʰ: *by* ~ per telegram
telegraph telegraaf, telegrafie: *by* ~ per telegraaf
telemarketing telefonische verkoop, telemarketing
telepathic telepathisch
telepathy telepathie
¹telephone (n) telefoon, (telefoon)toestelʰ: *by* ~ telefonisch; *on* (or: *over*) *the* ~ telefonisch
²telephone (vb) telefoneren, (op)bellen: *he has just* ~*d **through** from Beirut* hij heeft zojuist uit Beiroet opgebeld

telephone booth telefooncel
telephone call telefoongesprek^h
telephone directory telefoongids
telephoto lens telelens
teleprinter telex, telexapparaat^h: **by** ~ per
telex
Teleprompter [Am] autocue
^1**telescope** (n) telescoop, (astronomische)
verrekijker
^2**telescope** (vb) **1** in elkaar schuiven **2** ineengedrukt worden: *two cars ~d together in
the accident* twee auto's werden bij het ongeval ineengedrukt
^3**telescope** (vb) in elkaar schuiven, ineen-
drukken, samendrukken
telescopic telescopisch, ineenschuifbaar: ~
lens telelens
teleselling telefonische verkoop, telemarketing
teleshopping het telewinkelen, het teleshoppen
teletreatment [med] behandeling op afstand
television televisie, tv(-toestel^h): *watch* ~
tv kijken; *on (the)* ~ op de televisie
television audience 1 televisiekijkers
2 publiek^h bij een tv-opname
television broadcast televisie-uitzending
television commercial reclamespot
television programme televisiepro-
gramma^h
television set televisietoestel^h
teleworking telewerken^h, het thuiswer-
ken
^1**telex** (n) **1** telex, telexbericht^h: *by* ~ per telex **2** telexdienst
^2**telex** (vb) telexen
^1**tell** (vb) **1** spreken, zeggen, vertellen: *as far
as* we can ~ voor zover we weten; *you can
never* ~ je weet maar nooit **2** het verklappen,
het verraden: *don't ~!* verklap het niet!; *~ on
s.o.* iem. verklikken **3** (mee)tellen, meespelen, van belang zijn: *his age will ~ against* him
zijn leeftijd zal in zijn nadeel pleiten
^2**tell** (vb) **1** vertellen, zeggen, spreken: *~ a
secret* een geheim verklappen; [inform] ~
s.o. where he gets off, *~ s.o. to get off* iem. op
zijn plaats, iem. op zijn nummer zetten;
you're ~ing me! vertel mij wat! **2** weten,
kennen, uitmaken: *can you ~ the difference?*
weet (*or:* zie) jij het verschil?; *can she ~ the
time yet?* kan ze al klok kijken?; *there is no
~ing what will happen* je weet maar nooit wat
er gebeurt; *how can I ~ if* (*or:* **whether**) *it is
true or not?* hoe kan ik weten of het waar is
of niet? **3** onderscheiden, uit elkaar houden:
~ truth from lies de waarheid van leugens onderscheiden **4** zeggen, bevelen, waarschuwen: *I told you so!* ik had het je nog gezegd! ‖
all told alles bij elkaar (genomen), over het

geheel; *I'll ~ you what:* let's call him now weet
je wat?: laten we hem nu opbellen; [inform]
~ *s.o. off for sth.* iem. om iets berispen
teller 1 verteller **2** (stemmen)teller [eg in
House of Commons] **3** kassier
telling 1 treffend, raak: *a ~ blow* een rake
klap **2** veelbetekenend, veelzeggend
telling-off uitbrander
tell-tale 1 roddelaar(ster) **2** verklikker
3 teken^h, aanduiding: [fig] *a ~ nod* een veelbetekenend knikje
telly teevee, tv, buis
temerity roekeloosheid
^1**temp** (n) *temporary employee* tijdelijk me-
dewerk(st)er, uitzendkracht
^2**temp** (vb) als uitzendkracht werken, werken via een uitzendbureau
^1**temper** (n) **1** humeur^h, stemming: *be in a
bad* ~ in een slecht humeur zijn, de pest in
hebben **2** kwade bui **3** driftbui, woedeaanval: *fly* (*or:* *get*) *into a* ~ een woedeaanval
krijgen **4** opvliegend karakter^h, drift: *have a
~* opvliegend zijn **5** kalmte, beheersing:
keep (*or:* *lose*) *one's* ~ zijn kalmte bewaren
(*or:* verliezen)
^2**temper** (vb) temperen, matigen
temperament 1 temperament^h [also fig];
aard, gestel^h, vurigheid **2** humeurigheid
temperamental 1 natuurlijk, aangeboren
2 grillig, onberekenbaar, vol kuren
temperance 1 gematigdheid, matigheid,
zelfbeheersing **2** geheelonthouding
temperate 1 matig, gematigd: *~ zone* gematigde luchtstreek **2** met zelfbeheersing
temperature temperatuur, verhoging,
koorts: *have* (*or:* *run*) *a* ~ verhoging hebben
tempest (hevige) storm [also fig]
tempestuous stormachtig [also fig]; hartstochtelijk
template 1 mal, sjabloon^+h **2** [comp] sja-
bloon^+h
temple 1 tempel, kerk **2** slaap [on head]
tempo tempo^h
temporary tijdelijk, voorlopig: *~ buildings*
noodgebouwen; *~ employment agency* uit-
zendbureau^h
tempt 1 verleiden, in verleiding brengen: *I
am ~ed to believe that it's true* ik ben geneigd
te geloven dat het waar is **2** tarten, tergen: *~
Providence* het noodlot tarten
temptation 1 verleidelijkheid **2** verleiding, verzoeking: *lead us not into* ~ leid ons
niet in verzoeking
tempter verleider
tempting verleidelijk
temptress verleidster
ten tien: *I bet you ~ to one* she'll come ik wed
tien tegen één dat ze komt
tenable verdedigbaar, houdbaar
tenacious 1 vasthoudend, hardnekkig
2 krachtig; goed [of memory]

tenacity 1 vasthoudendheid, hardnekkigheid **2** kracht [of memory]

tenancy 1 huur(termijn), pacht(termijn) **2** bewoning, gebruik^h, genot^h

tenant 1 huurder, pachter **2** bewoner

¹tend (vb) **1** gaan [in certain direction]; zich richten, zich uitstrekken: *prices are ~ing downwards* de prijzen dalen **2** neigen, geneigd zijn: *John ~s to* **get** *angry* John wordt gauw boos; *it ~s to* **get** *hot in here in summer* het wordt hier vaak erg warm in de zomer || *~ to* zwemen naar; [Am] aandacht besteden aan

²tend (vb) **1** verzorgen, zorgen voor, passen op: *~ sheep* schapen hoeden **2** [Am] bedienen: *who's ~ing* **bar?** wie staat er achter de bar?

tendency 1 neiging, tendens, trend **2** aanleg: *he has a ~ to grow fat* hij heeft een aanleg tot dik worden

tendentious partijdig, vooringenomen

¹tender (n) **1** verzorger, oppasser, tender **2** tender [of locomotive] **3** offerte, inschrijving: *put out to ~* aanbesteden (voor inschrijving)

²tender (adj) **1** mals [of meat] **2** gevoelig: *~ spot* gevoelige plek **3** broos, teer **4** liefhebbend, teder **5** pijnlijk, zeer: *~ place* gevoelige plek **6** jong, onbedorven: *of ~ age* van prille leeftijd; *he started smoking at the ~ age of 16 years* hij begon al op 16-jarige leeftijd met roken

³tender (vb) inschrijven: *~ for the building of a road* inschrijven op de aanleg van een weg

⁴tender (vb) aanbieden: *~ one's* **resignation** zijn ontslag indienen

tenderfoot groentje^h, nieuwkomer

tender-hearted teerhartig

tenderize mals maken [meat]

tendon (spier)pees

tendril 1 (hecht)rank [of plant] **2** streng, sliert

tenement 1 pachtgoed^h **2** (huur)kamer, appartement^h

tenement house huurkazerne, etagewoning, flatgebouw^h

tenfold tienvoudig

tenner tientje^h, (briefje^h van) tien pond (dollar)

tennis tennis(spel)^h

tennis court tennisbaan

tennis racket tennisracket^h

tenor 1 tenor [singer, part, voice, instrument] **2** gang [of one's life]; loop, verloop^h, (algemene) richting **3** teneur [of text, conversation]; strekking: *get the ~ of what is being said* in grote lijnen begrijpen wat er wordt gezegd

tenpin bowling kegelspel^h; bowling^h

¹tense (n) tijd, werkwoordstijd

²tense (adj) gespannen, in spanning: *a face ~*

with anxiety een van angst vertrokken gezicht

³tense (vb) (+ up) zenuwachtig worden

⁴tense (vb) (+ up) gespannen maken: *~ one's* **muscles** zijn spieren spannen

tension 1 spanning, gespannenheid; strakheid [eg of rope]; zenuwachtigheid: *suffer from* **nervous** *~* overspannen zijn **2** gespannen toestand: *racial ~s* rassenonlusten **3** trekspanning [of solid substance] **4** (elektrische) spanning

tent tent: [also fig] *pitch one's ~* zijn tent opslaan

tentacle tentakel, tastorgaan^h, voelspriet, vangarm

tentative 1 voorlopig: *a ~* **conclusion** een voorzichtige conclusie **2** aarzelend

tenterhooks: *on ~* ongerust, in gespannen verwachting

tenth tiende

tenuous 1 dun, (rag)fijn **2** (te) subtiel **3** vaag, zwak: *a ~* **argument** een zwak argument

tenure 1 pachtregeling **2** ambtstermijn **3** beschikkingsrecht^h, eigendomsrecht^h **4** vaste aanstelling

tepid lauw, halfwarm; [fig] koel; mat

terabyte terabyte

term 1 onderwijsperiode, trimester^h, semester^h, kwartaal^h **2** termijn, periode, duur, tijd, ambtstermijn; zittingsperiode [of court of law, parliament]; huurtermijn, aflossingstermijn, (af)betalingstermijn: *in the* **short** *~* op korte termijn **3** [maths] term, lid^h **4** (vak)term, woord^h, uitdrukking: *~s* bewoordingen; manier van uitdrukken; *tell s.o. in no* **uncertain** *~s* in niet mis te verstane bewoordingen te kennen geven **5** (-s) voorwaarden [of agreement, contract]; condities, bepalingen || *~s of* **reference** taakomschrijving [eg of committee]; *on* **equal** *~s* als gelijken; *to be on friendly ~s with s.o.* op vriendschappelijke voet met iem. staan; **come** *to ~s with* zich verzoenen met, zich neerleggen bij; *in ~s of money* financieel gezien, wat geld betreft; *they are not on speaking ~s* ze spreken niet meer met elkaar, ze hebben onenigheid

¹terminal (n) **1** contactklem **2** eindpunt^h, eindhalte, eindstation^h **3** (computer)terminal

²terminal (adj) **1** eind-, slot-, laatste: *~ station* eindstation^h **2** terminaal, ongeneeslijk **3** van (onderwijs)periode, termijn-: *~ examinations* trimesterexamens, semesterexamens

¹terminate (vb) eindigen, aflopen

²terminate (vb) beëindigen, eindigen, een eind maken aan, (af)sluiten: *~ a contract* een contract opzeggen; *~ a pregnancy* een zwangerschap onderbreken

terminology terminologie, (systeem^h van)

vaktermen
terminus eindpunt[h] [of bus route, railway line]; eindstation[h], eindhalte
termite termiet
[1]**terrace** (n) **1** verhoogd vlak oppervlak[h], (dak)terras[h] **2** bordes[h], (open) tribune, staanplaatsen **3** rij huizen, huizenblok[h]
[2]**terrace** (vb) tot terras(sen) vormen, terrasgewijs aanleggen: *~d garden* terrastuin || *~d house* rijtjeshuis
terrain terrein[h]; gebied[h] [also fig]
terrestrial van de aarde, van het land, aards: *the ~ globe* de aardbol
terrible 1 verschrikkelijk, vreselijk **2** ontzagwekkend, enorm: *a ~ responsibility* een zware verantwoordelijkheid
terribly verschrikkelijk
terrier terriër
terrific geweldig, fantastisch: *at a ~ speed* razendsnel
terrify schrik aanjagen: *be terrified of s.o. (sth.)* doodsbang zijn voor iem. (iets)
terrifying angstaanjagend, afschuwelijk
territorial territoriaal: *~ waters* territoriale wateren, driemijlszone
territory 1 territorium[h], (stuk) grondgebied[h] **2** territorium[h], (eigen) woongebied[h], (grond)gebied[h] **3** (stuk[h]) land[h], gebied[h]; terrein[h] [also fig]; district[h], werkterrein[h]; [com] rayon[h]; handelsgebied[h]: *unknown ~* onbekend gebied
terror 1 verschrikking, plaag: *the ~ of the neighbourhood* de schrik van de buurt **2** lastig iem., rotjoch[h], rotmeid **3** (gevoel van) schrik: *run away in ~* in paniek wegvluchten
terrorism terrorisme[h]
[1]**terrorist** (n) terrorist
[2]**terrorist** (adj) terroristisch, terreur-
terrorize terroriseren, schrik aanjagen
terse beknopt, kort
tertiary tertiair: *a ~ burn* derdegraadsverbranding
[1]**test** (n) **1** test, toets(ing), proef, toets, proefwerk[h]; [chem] reactie: *put sth. to the ~* iets op de proef stellen, iets testen **2** toets, criterium[h], maat(staf) **3** [chem] reageermiddel[h]
[2]**test** (vb) **1** toetsen, testen, aan een test onderwerpen, nagaan, nakijken, onderzoeken **2** veel vergen van, hoge eisen stellen aan: *~ s.o.'s patience* iemands geduld zwaar op de proef stellen; *~ing times* zware tijden
[3]**test** (vb) (d.m.v. een test) onderzoeken: *~ for* onderzoeken (op), het gehalte bepalen van
testament testament[h]: *last will and ~* uiterste wil(sbeschikking), testament[h]
Testament (the) Testament[h] [part of bible]
testator testateur, erflater
test ban treaty kernstopverdrag[h]
test card testbeeld[h]

test case proefproces[h]
test-drive een proefrit maken
tester tester [pers]; testapparaat[h]
testicle teelbal, zaadbal, testikel
testify (+ against, for) getuigen (tegen/voor): *~ to a)* bevestigen; *b)* getuigenis afleggen van; *c)* een teken (*or:* bewijs) zijn van
testimonial 1 getuigschrift[h], aanbevelingsbrief **2** huldeblijk[h], eerbewijs[h]
testimony getuigenverklaring, bewijs[h], blijk[h]: *bear ~ to* getuigen; bevestigen; blijk geven van, wijzen op
testosterone testosteron[h]
test tube reageerbuis
test-tube baby reageerbuisbaby
testy 1 prikkelbaar, opvliegend **2** geërgerd, geïrriteerd: *a ~ remark* een knorrige opmerking
tetchy prikkelbaar [pers]; lichtgeraakt
[1]**tether** (n) tuier [rope used to secure grazing animal] || *at the end of one's ~* uitgeteld, aan het eind van zijn Latijn
[2]**tether** (vb) vastmaken, tuien, (aan een paal) vastleggen, (vast)binden; [fig] aan banden leggen
[1]**text** (n) **1** tekst(gedeelte[h]), gedrukte tekst, inhoud **2** tekst, onderwerp[h], Bijbeltekst **3** sms(-bericht[h])
[2]**text** (vb) sms'en: *~ me when you know* stuur mij maar een sms als je het weet
textbook leerboek[h], studieboek[h], schoolboek[h] || *~ example* schoolvoorbeeld[h]
text editing tekstverwerking
text editor teksteditor
text file tekstbestand[h]
textile weefsel[h], textielproduct[h], stof[h] || *~s* textielindustrie
[1]**text message** (n) sms'je[h], tekstbericht[h]
[2]**text message** (vb) sms'en, tekstbericht(en) versturen aan
texture textuur, weefselstructuur; [by extension] structuur; samenstelling: *the smooth ~ of ivory* de gladheid van ivoor
[1]**Thai** (n) Thai(se)
[2]**Thai** (adj) Thais
Thailand Thailand
Thames (the) Theems || *she won't set the ~ on fire* ze heeft het buskruit niet uitgevonden
than 1 dan, als: *she's better ~ I am* (*or:* *~ me*) zij is beter dan ik; *he would sooner die ~ give in* hij zou (nog) liever sterven dan toegeven; *none other ~ Joe* niemand anders dan Joe **2** of, dan, en, toen
thank 1 (be)danken, dankbaar zijn: *~ you* dank u (wel), (ja) graag, alstublieft; *no, ~ you* (nee) dank u **2** danken, (ver)wijten, verantwoordelijk stellen: *she has herself to ~ for that* het is haar eigen schuld, dat heeft ze aan zichzelf te danken
thankful dankbaar, erkentelijk, blij

thankfully gelukkig: ~, *he's not coming* gelukkig komt hij niet

thankless ondankbaar

thanks dankbaarheid, dankbetuiging, (kort) dankgebed: *a letter of* ~ een schriftelijk bedankje; *received with* ~ in dank ontvangen; [inform] ~*!* bedankt!, merci!; *no,* ~ (nee) dank je (wel), laat maar (zitten)

thanksgiving dankbetuiging, dankzegging

Thanksgiving (Day) [Am] Thanksgiving Day [national holiday; fourth Thursday in November]

thanks to dankzij, door (toedoen van)

thank-you bedankje^h, woord^h van dank: *a* ~ *letter* een bedankbriefje

thanx [inform] dank je

¹**that** (dem pron) **1** die, dat: ~*'s Alice* dat is Alice; ~*'s life* zo is het leven; *at* ~ *point* toen; *do you see* ~ *house?* zie je dat huis daar?; *don't yell like* ~ schreeuw niet zo; *he isn't as stupid as all* ~ zo stom is hij ook weer niet; *that's* ~ dat was het dan, zo, dat zit erop **2** diegene, datgene, hij, zij, dat: *those going by train* diegenen die met de trein gaan **3** die, dat, wat, welke: *the chair(s)* ~ *I bought* de stoel(en) die ik gekocht heb **4** dat, waarop, waarin, waarmee: *the house* ~ *he lives in* het huis waarin hij woont ‖ [inform] *that's it* **a)** dat is 't hem nu juist, dat is (nu juist) het probleem; **b)** dat is wat we nodig hebben, dat is de oplossing; **c)** dit (*or:* dat) is het einde; *we left it at* ~ we lieten het daarbij

²**that** (adv) **1** zo(danig): *she's about* ~ *tall* ze is ongeveer zo groot **2** heel, heel erg, zo: *its not all* ~ *expensive* het is niet zo heel erg duur

³**that** (conj) **1** dat, het feit dat: *it was only then* ~ *I found out* ~ ... pas toen ontdekte ik dat ...; *she knew* ~ *he was ill* ze wist dat hij ziek was **2** [purpose] opdat, zodat **3** [reason or cause] omdat: *not* ~ *I care, but ...* niet dat het mij iets kan schelen, maar ... **4** [consequence] dat, zodat: *so high* ~ *you cannot see the top* zo hoog dat je de top niet kan zien

¹**thatch** (n) **1** strodak^h, rieten dak^h **2** dakstro^h, dekriet^h, dakbedekking

²**thatch** (vb) (een dak) (met stro) bedekken: ~*ed roof* strodak

¹**thaw** (n) dooi

²**thaw** (vb) (ont)dooien, smelten; [fig] ontdooien; vriendelijker worden

¹**the** (adv) **1** [with comparative] hoe, des te: *so much* ~ *better* des te beter; ~ *sooner* ~ *better* hoe eerder hoe beter **2** [with superlative] de, het: *he finished* ~ *fastest* hij was het eerste klaar

²**the** (art) **1** de, het: *she looks after* ~ *children* zij zorgt voor de kinderen; ~ *Italians love spaghetti* (de) Italianen zijn dol op spaghetti; *play* ~ *piano* piano spelen; *ah, this is* ~ *life!* ah, dit is pas leven!; *help* ~ *blind* help de blinden **2** mijn, jouw [etc]: *I've got a pain in* ~ *leg* ik heb pijn in mijn been **3** per, voor elk: *paid by* ~ *week* per week betaald

theatre 1 theater^h, schouwburg **2** toneel^h, toneelstukken, drama^h **3** collegezaal, gehoorzaal, auditorium^h **4** operatiekamer **5** toneel^h, (actie)terrein^h, operatieterrein^h: ~ *of war* oorlogstoneel^h

theatrical 1 toneel-, theater- **2** theatraal, overdreven

thee u, gij

theft diefstal

their 1 hun, haar: *they studied* ~ *French* ze leerden hun Frans; ~ *eating biscuits annoyed her* (het feit) dat zij koekjes aten irriteerde haar **2** zijn, haar: *no-one gave* ~ *address* niemand gaf zijn adres

theirs 1 de hunne, het hunne, van hen: *a friend of* ~ een vriend van hen **2** de zijne, het zijne, van hem, de hare, het hare, van haar: *I forgot my book, could somebody lend me* ~*?* ik ben mijn boek vergeten, kan iem. mij het zijne lenen?

them 1 hen, hun, aan hen, ze: *I bought* ~ *a present* (or: *a present for* ~) ik heb een cadeau voor hen gekocht **2** zij (ze): *I hate* ~ *worrying like that* ik vind het vreselijk als ze zich zulke zorgen maken; *it is* ~ zij zijn het

thematic thematisch: ~ *analysis* thematische analyse

theme 1 thema^h, onderwerp^h, gegeven^h **2** [Am] opstel^h, essay^h **3** [mus] thema^h, hoofdmelodie, herkenningsmelodie

theme park themapark^h, pretpark^h

theme song herkenningsmelodie

themselves 1 zich, zichzelf: *the students kept it to* ~ de studenten hielden het voor zich **2** zelf, zij zelf, hen zelf: *they* ~ *started* zij zelf zijn ermee begonnen

¹**then** (adj) toenmalig: *the* ~ *chairman* de toenmalige voorzitter

²**then** (adv) **1** toen, op dat ogenblik, destijds: *before* ~ voor die tijd; *by* ~ dan, toen, ondertussen **2** dan, (onmiddellijk) daarna, verder: ~ *they went home* daarna zijn ze naar huis gegaan **3** dan (toch), in dat geval: *why did you go* ~*?* waarom ben je dan gegaan? ‖ ~ *and there* onmiddellijk, dadelijk; *but* ~*, why did you do it?* maar waarom heb je het dan toch gedaan?

thence 1 vandaar, van daaruit **2** daarom, dus, daaruit

theologian theoloog, godgeleerde

theological theologisch, godgeleerd

theology theologie, godgeleerdheid

theorem (grond)stelling, principe^h, theorie

theoretical 1 theoretisch **2** denkbeeldig, fictief: ~ *amount* fictief bedrag

theoretician theoreticus

theorize theoretiseren

theory theorie, leer, veronderstelling: ~ *of*

evolution evolutietheorie; *in* ~ in theorie, op papier; [maths] ~ *of chances* kansrekening

therapeutic(al) therapeutisch, genezend

therapy therapie, geneeswijze, (psychiatrische) behandeling

¹**there** (adv) **1** daar, er, ginds; [fig] op dat punt; wat dat betreft: *there's no rush* er is geen haast bij; ~ *I don't agree with you* op dat punt ben ik het niet met je eens; ~ *they come* daar komen ze; *he lives over* ~ hij woont daarginds **2** daar(heen), daarnaartoe: ~ *and back* heen en terug ‖ ~ *you are* a) alstublieft, alsjeblieft; b) zie je wel, wat heb ik je gezegd; ~ *and then* onmiddellijk, ter plekke

²**there** (int) daar, zie je, nou: ~, *what did I tell you!* nou, wat heb ik je gezegd!

thereabouts daar ergens, (daar) in de buurt, daaromtrent; [fig] rond die tijd; (zo) ongeveer: *twenty years or* ~ zo ongeveer twintig jaar

thereafter daarna

thereby daardoor ‖ ~ *hangs a tale* daar zit nog een (heel) verhaal aan vast

therefore daarom, om die reden, dus

therein [form] daarin

thereof daarvan, ervan

thereto [form] daaraan

thereupon daarop

thermal 1 thermisch, warmte- **2** thermaal: ~ *springs* warmwaterbronnen

thermals [inform] thermisch ondergoed

thermometer thermometer

thermonuclear thermonucleair

thermos thermosfles, thermoskan

thermostat thermostaat, warmteregulator

thesaurus thesaurus; [esp] synoniemenwoordenboekʰ

thesis thesis, (hypo)these, (academisch) proefschriftʰ

they 1 zij, ze: ~ *chased each other* ze zaten elkaar achterna; *so* ~ *say* dat zeggen ze toch **2** hij (of zij): *everyone is proud of the work* ~ *do themselves* iedereen is trots op het werk dat hij zelf doet

¹**thick** (n) dichtste, drukste gedeelteʰ, drukte: *be in the* ~ *of it* er midden in zitten ‖ *through* ~ *and thin* door dik en dun

²**thick** (adj) **1** dik; breed [line]; vet [letter, font]; zwaar(gebouwd), (op)gezwollen; dubbel [tongue]: *two inches* ~ twee inch dik **2** dik, dicht; dicht bezaaid; druk; vol; overvloedig, weinig vloeibaar, weinig doorzichtig, mistig; betrokken [weather]: ~ *on the ground* zeer talrijk; *the sky was* ~ *with planes* de lucht zag zwart van vliegtuigen **3** zwaar [accent] **4** dom, traag van begrip **5** [inform] intiem, dik bevriend: *be as* ~ *as thieves* de beste maatjes met elkaar zijn ‖ **6** [inform] sterk, sterk overdreven: *a bit* ~ al te kras ‖ *give s.o. a* ~ *ear* iem. een oorveeg geven; *have*

a ~ *skin* een olifantshuid hebben; *lay it on* ~ flink overdrijven

³**thick** (adv) **1** dik, breed, vet **2** dik, dicht, dicht opeengepakt, dicht op elkaar, talrijk: *blows came* ~ *and fast* het regende slagen

¹**thicken** (vb) dik(ker) worden; gebonden worden [of liquid]; toenemen (in dikte/aantal)

²**thicken** (vb) dik(ker) maken, indikken, doen toenemen (in dikte/aantal): ~ *gravy with flour* saus binden met bloem

thicket (kreupel)bosjeʰ, struikgewasʰ

thickheaded dom, bot (van verstand)

thickness 1 dikte, afmeting in de dikte, dik gedeelteʰ, troebelheid, mistigheid: *length, width, and* ~ lengte, breedte en dikte **2** laag

thickset 1 dicht (beplant/bezaaid) **2** zwaar (gebouwd), dik, gedrongen

thick-skinned dikhuidig; [fig] ongevoelig

thick-witted dom, bot (van verstand)

thief dief ‖ *there is honour among thieves* dieven stelen niet van elkaar

thieve stelen

thievish steels, dieven-, heimelijk

thigh dij

thimble vingerhoed

¹**thin** (adj) **1** dun, smal, fijn, schraal, mager, slank: ~ *air* ijle lucht **2** dun (bezet/gezaaid), dunbevolkt: *a* ~ *audience* een klein publiek; [inform] ~ *on top* kalend **3** dun (vloeibaar), slap, waterig: ~ *beer* schraal bier **4** zwak, armzalig: *a* ~ *excuse* een mager excuus ‖ *disappear* (or: *vanish*) *into* ~ *air* spoorloos (or: volledig) verdwijnen; *the* ~ *end of the wedge* het eerste (kleine) begin; *skate on* ~ *ice* zich op glad ijs wagen; *have a* ~ *skin* erg gevoelig zijn; *have a* ~ *time (of it)* a) een moeilijke tijd doormaken; b) weinig succes boeken

²**thin** (vb) (ver)dunnen, uitdunnen, vermageren

thine van u, uw, de uwe, het uwe

thing 1 dingʰ, dingetjeʰ, zaak(je)ʰ, voorwerpʰ, ietsʰ: *a good* ~ *too!* (dat is) maar goed ook!; *it's a good* ~ *that* het is maar goed dat; *it's a good* ~ *to* je doet er goed aan (om); *a lucky* ~ *no-one got caught* gelukkig werd (er) niemand gepakt; *make a* ~ *of* ergens moeilijk over doen; *not a* ~ *to wear* niks om aan te trekken; *it doesn't mean a* ~ *to me* het zegt me totaal niets; *and another* ~ bovendien, meer nog; *for one* ~ a) in de eerste plaats, om te beginnen; b) immers **2** schepselʰ, wezenʰ, dingʰ: *the poor* ~ de (arme) stakker **3** (favoriete) bezigheid: *do one's (own)* ~ doen waar men zin in heeft **4** (dat) wat gepast is: *the very* ~ *for you* echt iets voor jou; *be not (quite) the* ~ niet passen **5** (dat) wat nodig is: *just the* ~ *I need* juist wat ik nodig heb **6** het belangrijkste (punt, kenmerk): *the* ~ *is that* de kwestie is dat, waar het om gaat is dat **7** (-s) spullen: *pack one's* ~s zijn boeltje bijeenpakken **8** (-s) (algemene) toestand: *that would only* **make** *~s worse* dat zou het allemaal alleen maar verergeren; *how are ~s?,* [inform] **how's** *~s?* hoe gaat het (ermee)? || *have a ~ about* **a)** geobsedeerd zijn door; **b)** dol zijn op; **c)** als de dood zijn voor; *not* **know** *the first ~ about* niet het minste verstand hebben van; **know** *a ~ or two about* het een en ander weten over; *let* *~s rip* (or: *slide*) de boel maar laten waaien; *well, of* **all** *~s!* wel heb ik ooit!; *I'll do it* **first** *~ in the morning* ik doe het morgenochtend meteen; *the* **first** *~ I knew she had hit him* voor ik wist wat er gebeurde had ze hem een mep gegeven

thingamajig dingetje[h], hoe-heet-'t-ook-alweer[h]

thingy [inform] dingetje[h], ding[h] [sth.]; [pers] dinges

[1]**think** (n) **1** gedachte **2** bedenking, overweging: *have a* **hard** *~ about* diep nadenken over || **have** *got another ~ coming* het lelijk mis hebben

[2]**think** (vb) **1** denken, (erover) nadenken, zich (goed) bedenken: *~ for* **o.s.** zelfstandig denken; *~ to* **o.s.** bij zichzelf denken; *~* **back** *to* terugdenken aan; *yes, I ~* **so** ja, ik denk van wel; *~* **twice** er (nog eens) goed over nadenken; *~* **about** **a)** denken aan, nadenken over; **b)** overwegen [idea, proposal, plan]; **c)** (terug)denken aan; *~* **about** *moving* er ernstig over denken om te verhuizen **2** het verwachten, het vermoeden, het in de gaten hebben: *I thought* **as** *much* dat was te verwachten, ik vermoedde al zoiets, dat dacht ik al

[3]**think** (vb) **1** denken, vinden, geloven: *~ s.o.* **pretty** iem. mooi vinden; *~* **out for** *o.s.* voor zichzelf beslissen **2** (na)denken over: *~* **out** overdenken, goed (na)denken over; *~* **over** overdenken, in overweging houden; *~* **through** doordenken, (goed) nadenken over; *~* **up** bedenken, verzinnen; *and to ~ (that)* en dan te moeten bedenken dat; *~* **what** *you're doing* bedenk wat je doet **3** overwegen **4** denken aan, zich herinneren: *he* **didn't** *~ to switch off the headlights* hij vergat de koplampen uit te doen **5** (in)zien, zich voorstellen, begrijpen: *she* **couldn't** *~ how he did it* ze begreep niet hoe hij het voor elkaar had gekregen **6** verwachten, vermoeden, bedacht zijn op: *she* **never** *thought to see us here* ze had nooit verwacht ons hier te treffen || *~* **nothing** *of sth.* iets niets bijzonders vinden, zijn hand voor iets niet omdraaien

thinker denker, geleerde, filosoof

thinking 1 het (na)denken: *way of ~* denkwijze, zienswijze **2** mening, oordeel[h]

thinking cap: *put* on one's *~* diep nadenken

think of 1 denken aan, rekening houden

met: *(just, to) think* **of** *it!* stel je (eens) voor! **2** (erover) denken om, van plan zijn: *be thinking of doing sth.* van plan zijn iets te doen; *he would* **never** *~ (doing) such a thing* zoiets zou nooit bij hem opkomen **3** [after cannot, could not, try, want etc] zich herinneren **4** bedenken, voorstellen, verzinnen, (uit)vinden: *~ a* **number** neem een getal in gedachten **5** aanzien, aanslaan: *think* **highly** *of* een hoge dunk hebben van || *think* **better** *of it* zich bedenken, ervan afzien

think tank denktank, groep specialisten

thin-skinned overgevoelig, lichtgeraakt

third derde; [mus] terts: *~ in line* (als) derde op de lijst; *in ~ (gear)* in zijn drie, in zijn derde versnelling

third-degree derdegraads-

thirdly op de derde plaats

third-party tegenover derden: *~* **insurance** aansprakelijkheidsverzekering, WA-verzekering

third-rate derderangs

Third World derde wereld

[1]**thirst** (n) dorst [also fig]; sterk verlangen[h]

[2]**thirst** (vb) sterk verlangen: *~ after* (or: *for*) snakken naar; *~ after revenge* op wraak belust zijn

thirsty 1 dorstig: *be* (or: *feel*) *~* dorst hebben **2** verlangend: *be ~* **for** snakken naar

thirteen dertien

thirteenth dertiende

thirtieth dertigste

thirty dertig: *he's in his early* (or: *late*) *thirties* hij is voor (or: achter) in de dertig

[1]**this** (dem pron) **1** dit, deze, die, dat: *these are my* **daughters** dit zijn mijn dochters; *what's all ~?* wat is hier allemaal aan de hand?, wat heeft dit allemaal te betekenen?; *~ is where I live* hier woon ik; *do it* **like** *~* doe het zo **2** nu, dit: *~* **is** *a good moment to stop* dit is een goed moment om te stoppen; *after ~* hierna; *at ~* op dit ogenblik; *for all ~* ondanks dit alles **3** [what is just over] laatste, voorbije: *she's so grumpy these* **days** ze is tegenwoordig zo humeurig; *~* **morning** vanmorgen **4** [what is coming] komende, aanstaande: *where are you travelling ~* **summer?** waar ga je de komende zomer naartoe? **5** [inform] een (zekere), zo'n: *~* **fellow** *came cycling along* er kwam een kerel aanfietsen

[2]**this** (adv) zo: *I know ~* **much,** *that the idea is crazy* ik weet in elk geval dat het een krankzinnig idee is

thistle distel

thither daarheen, ginds

thong 1 (leren) riempje[h] **2** (-s) [Am] (teen)slipper; sandaal **3** string [underwear]

thorn 1 doorn **2** doornstruik || *a ~ in one's* **flesh** (or: *side*) een doorn in het vlees (or: oog)

thorny 1 doorn(acht)ig, stekelig **2** lastig

3 ergerlijk
thorough 1 grondig, diepgaand: *a ~ change* een ingrijpende verandering **2** echt, volmaakt: *a ~ fool* een volslagen idioot
¹**thoroughbred** (n) rasdierʰ, raspaardʰ
²**thoroughbred** (adj) volbloed, rasecht; ras- [also fig]
thoroughfare 1 (drukke) verkeersweg, verkeersader, belangrijke waterweg **2** doorgang, doortocht, doorreis: *no ~* geen doorgaand verkeer, verboden toegang, doodlopende weg
thoroughgoing 1 zeer grondig, volledig: *~ cooperation* verregaande samenwerking **2** echt, volmaakt
thou gij: *~ shalt not kill* gij zult niet doden
¹**though** (adv) niettemin, desondanks, toch wel: *I really liked the first part, ~* maar het eerste deel vond ik echt heel goed
²**though** (conj) hoewel: *~ he smiles I do not trust him* hoewel hij glimlacht vertrouw ik hem niet; *~ only six, he is a bright lad* hoewel hij nog maar zes jaar is, is hij een slim jongetje || *as ~* alsof
thought 1 gedachte: *perish the ~!* ik moet er niet aan denken! **2** bedoeling, planʰ: *she had no ~ of hurting him* het was niet haar bedoeling om hem pijn te doen **3** ideeʰ, opinie **4** het denken, gedachte: *in ~* in gedachten verzonken **5** denkwijze **6** de rede, het denkvermogen **7** het nadenken, de aandacht: *after serious ~* na rijp beraad **8** hoop, verwachting: *I had given up all ~ of ever getting away from there* ik had alle hoop opgegeven er nog ooit vandaan te komen || *have second ~s* zich bedenken
thoughtful 1 nadenkend **2** diepzinnig **3** attent, zorgzaam
thoughtless 1 gedachteloos **2** onnadenkend **3** roekeloos **4** onattent, zelfzuchtig
thousand duizend; [fig] talloos
thousandth duizendste
thrash 1 geselen, aframmelen **2** verslaan, niets heel laten van || *~ out a solution* tot een oplossing komen
thrashing 1 pakʰ rammel **2** nederlaag
¹**thread** (n) **1** draad; [fig also] lijn: *lose the ~ of one's story* de draad van zijn verhaal kwijtraken; *take up (or: pick up) the ~s* de draad weer opnemen **2** garenʰ **3** schroefdraad **4** draadjeʰ [on Internet forum] || *hang by a (single) ~* aan een zijden draad hangen
²**thread** (vb) **1** een draad steken in [needle] **2** rijgen [beads] **3** inpassen; inleggen [film, sound tape etc] **4** zich een weg banen door; [fig] zich heen worstelen door **5** banen, zoeken, vinden: *~ one's way through the crowd* zich een weg banen door de menigte
threadbare 1 versleten, kaal **2** armoedig: *a ~ joke* een afgezaagde grap
threat 1 dreigementʰ, bedreiging: *under ~*

of onder bedreiging met **2** gevaarʰ, bedreiging: *they are a ~ to society* ze vormen een gevaar voor de maatschappij
¹**threaten** (vb) **1** dreigen (te gebeuren) **2** er dreigend uitzien: *the weather is ~ing* de lucht ziet er dreigend uit
²**threaten** (vb) **1** bedreigen, een dreigement uiten tegen, een gevaar vormen voor: *peace* is *~ed* de vrede is in gevaar **2** dreigen (met): *they ~ed to kill him* ze dreigden hem te doden
three drie, drietal, drietje, maat drie, drie uur: *~ parts* drie vierde, driekwart
three-cornered 1 driehoekig **2** driehoeks-, tussen drie partijen
¹**three-D** (n) driedimensionale vorm
²**three-D** (adj) driedimensionaal
three-dimensional 1 driedimensionaal **2** stereoscopisch
threefold drievoudig
three-peat [Am; inform] derde overwinning op rij: *pull off a ~* drie keer achterelkaar winnen
three-piece driedelig: *~ suit* driedelig pak
three-quarter driekwart
threesome drietalʰ, driemanschapʰ
threshing machine dorsmachine
threshold 1 drempel [also fig]; aanvang, beginʰ: *~ of pain* pijndrempel **2** ingang
thrice drie maal
thrift zuinigheid, spaarzaamheid
thrifter [Am] koopjesjager
thrifty zuinig, spaarzaam
¹**thrill** (n) **1** beving, golf van ontroering **2** huivering (of fear, horror]: *he felt a ~ of horror* hij huiverde van afgrijzen **3** opwindende gebeurtenis: *it was quite a ~* het was heel opwindend
²**thrill** (vb) **1** beven, aangegrepen worden **2** huiveren
³**thrill** (vb) **1** doen beven, opwinden: *be ~ed (to bits) with sth.* onzettend gelukkig met iets zijn **2** doen huiveren, angst aanjagen
thriller iets opwindends, thriller, spannend misdaadverhaalʰ
thrilling spannend, opwindend
thrillseeker waaghals, avontuurlijk persoon
thrive gedijen, floreren, bloeien: *he seems to ~ on hard work* hard werken schijnt hem goed te doen
throat 1 hals **2** keel, strot: *clear one's ~* zijn keel schrapen || *be at each other's ~s* elkaar in de haren vliegen; *force (or: ram, thrust) sth. down s.o.'s ~* iem. iets opdringen
¹**throb** (n) klop, geklopʰ, gebonsʰ
²**throb** (vb) **1** kloppen **2** bonzen; bonken [of heart]
throe heftige pijn || [fig] *in the ~s of* worstelend met
thrombosis trombose

throne troon, zetel; [fig also] macht; heerschappij

¹throng (n) menigte, mensenmassa

²throng (vb) zich verdringen, toestromen

³throng (vb) vullen, overstelpen, overvol maken: *people* ~*ed the streets* de straten zagen zwart van de mensen

¹throttle (n) [techn] smoorklep

²throttle (vb) **1** doen stikken, (ver)smoren; [fig also] onderdrukken **2** wurgen **3** gas minderen [car]

throttle back afremmen [also fig]; (vaart) minderen

¹through (adj) doorgaand, doorlopend: ~ *train* doorgaande trein; *no* ~ *road* geen doorgaand verkeer

²through (adv) **1** door, verder: *go* ~ *with* doorgaan met **2** door(heen): *read sth.* ~ **a)** iets doornemen; **b)** iets uitlezen **3** klaar, erdoorheen **4** helemaal, van begin tot eind: *get* **soaked** (or: *wet*) ~ doornat worden; ~ *and* **through** door en door, in hart en nieren ‖ *are* you ~? **a)** heeft u verbinding? [telephone]; **b)** [Am] bent u klaar?; *I will* **put** *you* ~ ik zal u doorverbinden

³through (prep) **1** (helemaal) door, via, langs, over, gedurende: *seen* ~ *a child's eyes* gezien met de ogen van een kind; *he remained calm* ~ *the whole trial* hij bleef kalm gedurende het hele proces; ~ *and* **through** helemaal door(heen) [also fig] **2** [manner] door middel van: *he spoke* ~ *his* **representative** hij sprak via zijn vertegenwoordiger **3** [cause] door, wegens, uit: *he could not travel* ~ *illness* hij kon wegens ziekte niet reizen **4** [Am] tot en met: *Monday thru Thursday* van maandag tot en met donderdag

¹throughout (adv) helemaal, door en door, steeds: *our aim has* **been** ~ ... ons doel is steeds geweest ...

²throughout (prep) (helemaal) door, door heel: ~ *the* **country** door/in heel het land

throughput 1 verwerkte hoeveelheid; productie **2** [also comp] verwerkingscapaciteit

throughway [Am] snelweg

¹throw (n) worp, gooi

²throw (vb) met iets gooien/werpen

³throw (vb) **1** werpen, gooien; [fig also] terecht doen komen: ~ *dice* dobbelstenen gooien, dobbelen; *the* **horse** *threw him* het paard wierp hem af; ~ *o.s. into sth.* zich ergens op werpen, zich enthousiast ergens in storten; *be* ~*n (back)* **upon** *one's own resources* op zichzelf worden teruggeworpen **2** richten, (toe)werpen, toezenden: *he threw us a sarcastic* **look** hij wierp ons een sarcastische blik toe **3** afschieten [missile] **4** omzetten, veranderen in **5** draaien [wood, earthenware] **6** snel op zijn plaats brengen/leggen, maken: ~ *the switch* **to** *'off'* de schakelaar op

'uit' zetten **7** maken, hebben, organiseren: [inform] ~ *a* **party** een feest geven, een feestje bouwen **8** [inform] verwarren, van de wijs brengen ‖ ~ *open* openstellen; ~ *s.o. into* confusion iem. in verwarring brengen

throw about rondsmijten: *throw one's* **money** *about* met geld smijten

throw away 1 weggooien **2** verspelen, missen: ~ *a* **chance** een kans verspelen **3** vergooien: *throw one's money away* **on** zijn geld weggooien aan

throw-away 1 wegwerp- **2** zonder nadruk: *a* ~ **remark** een quasinonchalante opmerking

throwback 1 terugslag **2** terugkeer

throw back 1 teruggooien **2** openslaan, opzij werpen: ~ *the* **blankets** de dekens terugslaan ‖ *be thrown back* **on** moeten terugrijpen naar, weer aangewezen zijn op

throw down 1 neergooien **2** afbreken

throw in 1 erin gooien, inwerpen **2** gratis toevoegen: *I'll* ~ *an extra* **battery** ik doe er nog een gratis batterij bij **3** terloops opmerken **4** [sport] ingooien

throw-in [sport] inworp

throw off 1 zich bevrijden van, van zich af schudden **2** uitgooien, haastig uittrekken: ~ *one's* **mask** zijn masker afwerpen [also fig] **3** uitstoten; [also fig] produceren

throw out 1 weggooien, wegdoen **2** verwerpen, afwijzen **3** uiten, suggereren **4** geven, uitzenden: ~ **heat** warmte uitstralen **5** in de war brengen: *now all our* **calculations** *are thrown out* nu zijn al onze berekeningen fout **6** wegsturen, eruit gooien

throw over in de steek laten: *he threw her over* hij heeft haar laten zitten

throw together bij elkaar brengen, samenbrengen: *throw* **people** *together* mensen met elkaar in contact brengen

¹throw up (vb) **1** omhoog gooien, optillen: ~ *one's* **eyes** de ogen ten hemel slaan **2** voortbrengen **3** optrekken, opbouwen: ~ **barricades** barricaden opwerpen **4** opgeven, opzeggen: ~ *one's* **job** zijn baan vaarwel zeggen

²throw up (vb) [inform] overgeven, kotsen

thru see ¹**through**

thrum 1 tokkelen (op); pingelen (op) [guitar] **2** ronken, brommen, dreunen

thrush lijster

¹thrust (n) **1** stoot, duw, zet **2** steek [also fig] **3** druk, (drijf)kracht **4** beweging, streven[h], richting **5** [mil] uitval

²thrust (vb) **1** uitvallen, toestoten **2** dringen, worstelen: ~ *in* zich een weg banen naar binnen

³thrust (vb) **1** stoten **2** steken, stoppen: *he* ~ *his hands into his pockets* hij stak zijn handen in zijn zakken **3** duwen, dringen: *she* ~ *her way* **through** *the crowd* ze worstelde zich door de menigte heen ‖ ~ *sth.* **upon** *s.o.* iem. ergens mee opschepen

¹**thud** (n) plof, slag, bons

²**thud** (vb) (neer)ploffen, bonzen

thug misdadiger, moordenaar

thuggery gewelddadigheid

¹**thumb** (n) duim ‖ *give* the ~s up (or: *down*) goedkeuren, afkeuren; *twiddle* one's ~s duimendraaien; ~s *down* afgewezen; ~s *up!* a) prima!; b) kop op!, hou je taai; *be* **under** *s.o.'s* ~ bij iem. onder de plak zitten

²**thumb** (vb) (+ through) (door)bladeren [eg book]

³**thumb** (vb) **1** beduimelen, vuile vingerafdrukken achterlaten in **2** vragen [lift]; liften: ~ *a ride* liften

thumbnail 1 duimnagel **2** [comp] thumbnail, miniatuur

thumb tack [Am] punaise

¹**thump** (n) dreun, klap

²**thump** (vb) dreunen, bonzen

³**thump** (vb) **1** dreunen op, beuken: he was ~ing *out* a well-known song timmerend op de toetsen speelde hij een bekend liedje **2** stompen **3** een pak slaag geven

⁴**thump** (adv) met een dreun: the boy *ran* ~ with his head against the bookcase de jongen liep 'bam' met zijn hoofd tegen de boekenkast

thumping geweldig

¹**thunder** (n) **1** donder, onweerʰ **2** gedonderʰ [also fig] ‖ *steal* s.o.'s ~ met de eer gaan strijken

²**thunder** (vb) **1** donderen, onweren **2** denderen, dreunen **3** donderen, razen, tekeergaan

³**thunder** (vb) uitbulderen, brullen: ~ *out* curses verwensingen uitschreeuwen

thunderbolt 1 bliksemflits **2** donderslag, schok, klap

thunderclap donderslag [also fig]

thunder-cloud onweerswolk

thundering 1 donderend **2** kolossaal

thunderstorm onweersbui

thunderstruck (als) door de bliksem getroffen

thundery 1 onweerachtig **2** dreigend

Thursday donderdag

thus (al)dus, zo ‖ ~ *far* tot hier toe, tot nu toe

thwart 1 verijdelen, dwarsbomen **2** tegenwerken, tegenhouden

THX *thanks* dank je

thy uw

thyme tijm

thyroid gland schildklier

¹**tick** (n) **1** [zoology] teek **2** tik, getikʰ [of clock] **3** momentjeʰ, ogenblikjeʰ: *in* two ~s in een wip **4** vink(jeʰ); (merk)teken(tjeʰ) [used on checklist] **5** kredietʰ, pof: *on* ~ op de pof

²**tick** (vb) tikken: ~ *away* (or: *by*) a) tikken;

b) voorbijgaan [time] ‖ what *makes* s.o. (sth.) ~ wat iem. drijft; ~ *over* a) stationair draaien [of engine]; b) [inform] zijn gangetje gaan

³**tick** (vb) aanstrepen [on list] ‖ ~ *off* een uitbrander geven

tick box aanvinkvakjeʰ, checkbox

ticker 1 horlogeʰ, klok **2** hartʰ, rikketik

ticker-tape serpentine

¹**ticket** (n) **1** kaart(jeʰ), toegangsbewijsʰ, plaatsbewijsʰ: ~ *tout* zwarthandelaar in kaartjes **2** prijskaartje, etiketʰ **3** bon, bekeuring: *parking* ~ bon voor foutparkeren; *speeding* ~ bon voor te hard rijden **4** [Am] kandidatenlijst ‖ that's *just* the ~ dát is het (precies), dát is precies wat we nodig hebben, dát is wat we zoeken

²**ticket** (vb) **1** etiketteren, prijzen **2** bestemmen, aanduiden **3** [Am] een bon geven

ticket collector (kaartjes)controleur; conducteur

ticketing kaartverkoop

ticket office kassa [eg in theatre]; loketʰ [eg in station]

¹**tickle** (n) gekietelʰ, kietelend gevoelʰ

²**tickle** (vb) **1** kietelen, kriebelen; [fig] (aangenaam) prikkelen **2** amuseren, aan het lachen maken: *be* ~d to *death* zich kostelijk amuseren

ticklish 1 kietelig: *be* ~ niet (or: slecht) tegen kietelen kunnen **2** netelig

tidal getijden-: ~ *river* getijdenrivier

tidal wave getijdengolf, vloedgolf; [fig] golf van emotie

tiddler 1 visjeʰ **2** klein kindʰ; [fig] klein broertjeʰ

tiddly 1 aangeschoten **2** klein

tiddlywinks vlooienspelʰ

tide 1 getij(de)ʰ, tijʰ: *high* ~ vloed; *low* ~ eb; [fig] *turn* the ~ het getijde doen keren **2** stroom; stroming [also fig]: [inform, fig] *swim* (or: *go*) with the ~ met de stroom mee gaan

tidemark hoogwaterlijn

¹**tide over** (vb) helpen over: she gave me £15 to tide me over the next two days ze gaf me £15 om me door de volgende twee dagen te helpen

²**tide over** (vb) (iem.) verder helpen, (iem.) voorthelpen [financially]

tideway 1 stroombedʰ **2** eb in stroombed

tidings tijding(en)

¹**tidy** (n) opbergdoosjeʰ voor prulletjes

²**tidy** (adj) **1** netjes, keurig, op orde **2** proper **3** aardig (groot): ~ *income* aardig inkomen

³**tidy** (vb) opruimen, schoonmaken: ~ *away* opruimen; ~ *up* opruimen, in orde brengen

¹**tie** (n) **1** touw(tje)ʰ, koordʰ **2** (strop)das **3** band, verbondenheid **4** [sport, game] gelijk spelʰ **5** [sport] (afval)wedstrijd, voorronde

²**tie** (vb) **1** vastgemaakt worden **2** een knoop

leggen **3** [sport] gelijk eindigen: *they ~d for a second place* ze deelden de tweede plaats ‖ ~ *in (with)* verband houden (met); [fig] kloppen

³tie (vb) **1** (vast)binden, (vast)knopen: *his hands are ~d* zijn handen zijn gebonden [fig]; ~ *a knot* een knoop leggen; ~ *back* opbinden, bijeen binden [eg hair] **2** (ver)binden **3** binden, beperken: ~ *down* de handen binden, bezighouden; ~ *s.o. down to* iem. zich laten houden aan **4** [sport] gelijk spelen, staan met: *~d game* gelijkspel

tiebreaker beslissingswedstrijd; [tennis] tiebreak

tied (vast)gebonden: ~ *house* gebonden café [selling beer from one particular brewery]

tie-dye met de tie-and-dyetechniek verven

tie-on hang-: ~ *label* hangetiket^h

tiepin dasspeld

tier rij, verdieping; rang [eg in theatre]

¹tie up (vb) **1** afgemeerd worden **2** verband houden **3** kloppen ‖ ~ *with* verband houden met, kloppen met

²tie up (vb) **1** vastbinden, verbinden, dichtbinden: ~ *a dog* een hond vastleggen; [fig] *be tied up with* verband houden met **2** afmeren **3** (druk) bezighouden, ophouden, stopzetten: *be tied up* bezet zijn **4** vastzetten, vastleggen [money]

tiff ruzietje^h

tiger tijger

¹tight (adj) **1** strak, nauw(sluitend), krap: ~ *shoes* te nauwe schoenen **2** propvol: *a ~ schedule* een overladen programma **3** potdicht **4** beklemmend: *be in a ~ corner* (or: *place, spot*) in een lastig parket zitten **5** schaars, krap **6** gierig **7** stevig, vast **8** streng: *keep a ~ grip* (of: *hold*) *on s.o.* iem. goed in de hand houden **9** [inform] dronken ‖ *a ~ squeeze* een hele toer

²tight (adv) vast, stevig: *hold me ~* hou me stevig vast; *good night, sleep ~* goedenacht, welterusten

¹tighten (vb) **1** zich spannen, strakker worden **2** krap worden

²tighten (vb) **1** aanhalen, spannen, vastsnoeren: ~ *one's belt* de buikriem aanhalen [fig] **2** vastklemmen, vastdraaien **3** verscherpen [measure]: ~ *up* verscherpen

tight-fisted krenterig

tight-fitting nauwsluitend

tightknit hecht: *a ~ society* een hechte maatschappij

tight-lipped 1 met opeengeklemde lippen **2** gesloten, stil

tightrope walker koorddanser

tights panty: *(a pair of)* ~ een panty

tightwad vrek

tigress tijgerin

tile 1 (vloer)tegel **2** (dak)pan **3** [comp] tegel ‖ *he has a ~ loose* d'r zit een steekje los bij

hem; *be (out) on the ~s* aan de zwier zijn

¹till (n) geldlade, kassa

²till (vb) bewerken [soil]

³till (prep) [time] tot (aan), voor: ~ *tomorrow* tot morgen; *not ~ after dinner* niet vóór het middageten

⁴till (conj) [time] tot(dat), voordat: *he read ~ Harry arrived* hij las tot Harry (aan)kwam; *it was a long time ~ she came home* het duurde lang voor zij thuis kwam

tiller roer^h, roerpen, helmstok

¹tilt (n) **1** schuine stand: *he wore his hat at a ~* hij had zijn hoed schuin op **2** steekspel^h; [fig] woordenwisseling

²tilt (vb) **1** scheef staan, (over)hellen: ~ *over* wippen, kantelen **2** op en neer gaan, wiegelen, schommelen

³tilt (vb) scheef houden/zetten, doen (over)hellen, kantelen

timber 1 balk **2** (timmer)hout^h ‖ ~*!* van onderen!

timbered in vakwerk uitgevoerd: *a ~ house* een huis in vakwerk

timber yard houthandel

¹time (n) **1** tijd, tijdsduur: *gain* ~ tijd winnen; *kill* ~ de tijd doden; *lose no* ~ geen tijd verliezen, direct doen; *take one's* ~ zich niet haasten; ~ *and (~) again* steeds opnieuw; *in next to no* ~ in een mum van tijd; *let's take some* ~ *off* (or: ~ *out*) laten we er even tussenuit gaan; *I'm working against* ~ ik moet me (vreselijk) haasten, het is een race tegen de klok; *for a* ~ een tijdje; *all the* ~ **a)** de hele tijd, voortdurend; **b)** altijd **2** tijdstip^h, tijd: *do you have the* ~*?* weet u hoe laat het is?; *keep (good)* ~ goed lopen [of clock]; *at the* ~ toen, indertijd; *by the* ~ *the police arrived …* tegen de tijd dat de politie arriveerde …; *what* ~ *is it?, what's the* ~*?* hoe laat is het? **3** (-s) tijdperk^h, periode: *move with the* ~*s* met zijn tijd meegaan; *at one* ~ vroeger, eens; *be behind the* ~*s* achterlopen, niet meer van deze tijd zijn; *once upon a* ~ er was eens **4** gelegenheid, moment^h: *have* ~ *on one's hands* genoeg vrije tijd hebben; *any* ~ altijd, om 't even wanneer; *every* ~ elke keer, altijd, steeds (or: telkens) weer; *many* ~*s, many a* ~ vaak, dikwijls **5** keer, maal^+h: *nine* ~*s out of ten* bijna altijd, negen op de tien keer **6** [mus] maat: *keep* ~ in de maat blijven, de maat houden **7** tempo^h: ~ *signature* maataanduiding ‖ *pass the* ~ *of day with s.o.* iem. goedendag zeggen, even met iem. staan praten; *I had the* ~ *of my life* ik heb ontzettend genoten; *since* ~ *out of mind* sinds onheuglijke tijden; *do* ~ zitten [in prison]; *I have no* ~ *for him* ik mag hem niet, ik heb een hekel aan hem; *mark* ~ [mil] pas op de plaats maken; [fig] een afwachtende houding aannemen; *play for* ~ tijd rekken; ~ *will tell* de tijd zal het uitwijzen; ~*'s up!* het is de hoogste tijd!; *(and) about ~ too!* (en) het werd ook tijd; *~ after ~* keer op keer; *at all ~s* altijd, te allen tijde; *one at a ~* één tegelijk; *at the same ~* **a)** tegelijkertijd; **b)** toch; *at ~s* soms; *for the ~* being voorlopig; *from ~ to ~* van tijd tot tijd; *in ~* **a)** op tijd; **b)** na verloop van tijd; *on ~* **a)** op tijd; **b)** op afbetaling

²**time** (vb) **1** vaststellen; berekenen [time, duration]: *the train is ~d to **leave** at four o'clock* de trein moet om vier uur vertrekken **2** het juiste moment kiezen voor (om te): *his visit was **ill** ~d* zijn bezoek kwam ongelegen **3** klokken

time bomb tijdbom [also fig]
time clock prikklok
time-consuming tijdrovend
time exposure tijdopname
time frame 1 tijd, tijdsbestekʰ **2** tijdschemaʰ, termijn
time-honoured traditioneel
timekeeper 1 uurwerkʰ: *my watch is a good ~* mijn horloge loopt altijd op tijd **2** tijdwaarnemer, tijdopnemer
time lag pauze [between two consecutive occurrences]; tijdsverloopʰ, vertraging, tijdsintervalʰ
timeless 1 oneindig, eeuwig **2** tijd(e)loos
time limit tijdslimiet
timeline 1 [hist] tijdbalk; tijdlijn **2** [media] tijdlijn
timely 1 tijdig **2** van pas komend, gelegen
time out time-out, onderbreking
timepiece uurwerkʰ, klok, horlogeʰ
timer 1 timer [eg on video] **2** tijdopnemer **3** tijdwaarnemer
time-serving opportunistisch
timeshare deeltijdeigenaarschapʰ
time-sharing deeltijdeigenaarschapʰ
time switch tijdschakelaar
¹**timetable** (n) **1** dienstregeling **2** (les)roosterʰ
²**timetable** (vb) plannen, inroosteren
³**timetable** (vb) een rooster maken
time trialist tijdrijder
time warp vervorming van de tijd, tijdsvervorming
time-wasting het tijdrekken, het tijdwinnen, spelbederfʰ
time-worn 1 versleten, oud **2** afgezaagd
time zone tijdzone
timid 1 bang, angstig **2** timide, verlegen
timidity 1 angst **2** bedeesdheid
timing timing
timorous 1 bang, angstig **2** timide, bedeesd
timpani pauk(en)
timpanist paukenist
¹**tin** (n) **1** tinʰ **2** blikʰ **3** blik(jeʰ), conservenblikʰ **4** bus
²**tin** (adj) **1** tinnen: *~ soldier* tinnen soldaatje **2** blikken: *~ can* (leeg) blikje; *~ whistle* blik-

ken fluitje **3** prullerig
³**tin** (vb) inblikken
tincture 1 tinctuur **2** [form] vleugjeʰ **3** tint
tinder 1 tondelʳʰ **2** olie op het vuur
tinderbox 1 tondeldoos **2** [fig] kruitvatʰ
tine 1 scherpe puntʰ; tand [of (pitch)fork] **2** geweitakʰ
tinfoil aluminiumfolieʰ
¹**tinge** (n) tint(jeʰ) [also fig]
²**tinge** (vb) **1** doortrekken: *comedy ~d with tragedy* tragikomedie
¹**tingle** (n) tinteling
²**tingle** (vb) **1** opgewonden zijn, popelen **2** (laten) tintelen; (doen) suizen [of ears]
¹**tinker** (n) ketellapper
²**tinker** (vb) **1** ketellappen **2** (+ at, with) prutsen (aan)
¹**tinkle** (n) **1** gerinkelʰ **2** plasjeʰ **3** telefoontjeʰ
²**tinkle** (vb) **1** rinkelen, tingelen **2** plassen
³**tinkle** (vb) laten rinkelen
tinny 1 tin-, blikachtig **2** metaalachtig [of sound] **3** waardeloos
tin-opener blikopener
tinplate blikʰ
tinpot waardeloos
tinsel klatergoudʰ [also fig]
¹**tint** (n) **1** (pastel)tint **2** kleurshampoo
²**tint** (vb) kleuren
tiny heel klein, nietig
¹**tip** (n) **1** tipjeʰ, topjeʰ, puntʰ; filterʰ [of cigarette]; pomerans [on billiard cue]: *the ~ of the iceberg* het topje van de ijsberg **2** stortʰ, stortplaats; [fig] zwijnenstal **3** fooi **4** tip, raad: *give s.o. a ~ on* iem. een tip geven over **5** tik(jeʰ), duwtjeʰ ‖ *have sth. on the ~ of one's tongue* iets voor op de tong hebben liggen
²**tip** (vb) **1** kiep(er)en, kantelen: *these bunks ~ up* deze slaapbanken klappen omhoog **2** omkantelen: *~ over* omvallen **3** fooien uitdelen
³**tip** (vb) **1** doen overhellen: *~ sth. up* iets schuin houden **2** doen omslaan, omvergooien: *~ over* omgooien **3** (weg)kieperen **4** overgieten **5** aantikken, eventjes aanraken **6** tippen, (als fooi) geven **7** tippen, als kanshebber aanwijzen
tip off waarschuwen, een tip geven
tip-off waarschuwing, hint
tipper 1 fooiengever **2** kiepauto
tipping point omslagpuntʰ
¹**tipple** (n) (sterke)drank, drankjeʰ
²**tipple** (vb) aan de drank zijn, pimpelen
tipster tipgever, informant
tipsy aangeschoten
tiptoe op zijn tenen lopen ‖ *on ~* **a)** op zijn tenen, stilletjes; **b)** vol verwachting
tip-top 1 tiptop, piekfijn **2** chic
tip-up: *a ~ seat* een klapstoeltje
tirade tirade; scheldkanonnade
¹**tire** (n) **1** hoepel **2** [Am] *; see* tyre

²**tire** (vb) **1** moe worden **2** (+ of) het zat (*or: beu*) worden: *I never* ~ *of it* het verveelt me nooit

³**tire** (vb) **1** (also + out) afmatten, vermoeien **2** vervelen

tired 1 moe: ~ *out* doodop **2** afgezaagd ‖ *be* ~ *of sth.* iets zat (*or:* beu) zijn

tireless 1 onvermoeibaar **2** onophoudelijk

tiresome 1 vermoeiend **2** vervelend, saai

tiro beginneling, beginner

tissue 1 doekjeʰ, gaasjeʰ **2** papieren (zak)-doekjeʰ, velletje vloeipapierʰ **3** webʰ, net-werkʰ: ~ *of lies* aaneenschakeling van leugens **4** (cel)weefselʰ

tissue paper zijdepapierʰ

tit 1 mees **2** [inform] tiet, tepel **3** sukkel, klier

titan 1 [mythology] titan **2** kolos

titanic reusachtig

titbit 1 lekker hapjeʰ **2** interessant nieuwtjeʰ, roddeltjeʰ

tit-for-tat vergeldings-, uit wraak

tit-for-tat policy lik-op-stukbeleidʰ

tithe tiend⁺ʰ

titillate prikkelen, aangenaam opwinden

titivate mooi maken, opdirken

title titel, titelbladʰ; [sport] kampioen-(schapʰ); [law] eigendomsrechtʰ; ondertitel; aftiteling [of film]

titled met een (adellijke) titel

title deed eigendomsakte

title-holder titelhouder, titelhoudster

title page titelpagina

titmouse mees

¹**titter** (n) gegiechelʰ

²**titter** (vb) (onderdrukt/nerveus) giechelen

tittle tittel [also fig]; puntjeʰ

¹**tittle-tattle** (n) kletspraat, roddelpraat

²**tittle-tattle** (vb) kletsen

T-junction 1 T-kruising **2** T-stukʰ

TMI *too much information* dat willen we niet weten

¹**to** (adv) **1** [direction] (er)heen: *to and fro* heen en weer **2** [place; also fig] tegen, bij, eraan: *bring s.o. to* iem. bijbrengen

²**to** (prep) **1** naar, naar … toe, tot: *pale to clear blue* bleek tot hel blauw; *drink to her health* op haar gezondheid drinken; *they remained loyal to a man* ze bleven stuk voor stuk trouw; *to my mind* volgens mij; *travel to Rome* naar Rome reizen; *from bad to worse* van kwaad tot erger **2** [place; also fig] tegen, op, in: *I've been to my aunt's* ik ben bij mijn tante gaan logeren; *we beat them eleven to seven* we hebben ze met elf (tegen) zeven verslagen **3** [in comparison] met, ten opzichte van, voor: *use 50 lbs. to the acre* gebruik 50 pond per acre; *superior to synthetic fabric* beter dan synthetische stof; *compared to Jack* vergeleken bij Jack; *true to nature* natuurgetrouw; *I'm new to the place* ik ben hier nieuw; *made*

to size op maat gemaakt **4** [time] tot, tot op, op: *three years ago to the day* precies drie jaar geleden; *stay to the end* tot het einde blijven; *five (minutes) to three* vijf (minuten) voor drie **5** bij, aan, van: *the key to the house* de sleutel van het huis; *there's more to it* er zit meer achter

³**to** [often untranslated] **1** te: *I don't want to apologize* ik wil mij niet verontschuldigen **2** dat, het: *I don't want to* dat wil ik niet

toad [zoology] pad

toadstool paddenstoel

¹**toady** (n) vleier

²**toady** (vb) vleien: ~ *to s.o.* iem. vleien

to-and-fro heen en weer (gaand), schommelend

¹**toast** (n) **1** toost, (heil)dronk: *propose a* ~ *to s.o.* een toost uitbrengen op iem. **2** geroosterde boterham, toast ‖ *have s.o. on* ~ iem. helemaal in zijn macht hebben

²**toast** (vb) **1** roosteren, toast maken van: [fig] ~ *o.s. at the fire* zich warmen bij het vuur **2** toosten op

toaster broodroosterʰ

toastmaster ceremoniemeester [at dinner]

tobacco tabak

tobacconist tabakshandelaar

¹**toboggan** (n) slee

²**toboggan** (vb) sleeën, rodelen

tod: *on one's* ~ in z'n uppie

today vandaag, tegenwoordig

toddle 1 waggelen **2** kuieren: ~ *round* (or: *over*) even aanlopen **3** (also + along) opstappen

toddler dreumes, hummel

to-die-for [inform; hum] voortreffelijk; om je vingers bij af te likken

to-do drukte, gedoeʰ, ophef

toe teen, neus, puntʰ ‖ *turn up one's ~s* de pijp uitgaan; *on one's ~s* alert

toecap neus [of shoe]

toehold steunpuntjeʰ; [fig] houvastʰ; opstapjeʰ

toenail teennagel

toff fijne meneer: *the ~s* de rijkelui

toffee toffee

toffee-nosed snobistisch, verwaand

tofu tofoe, tahoe

toga toga

together 1 samen, bijeen: *come* ~ samenkomen **2** tegelijk(ertijd): *all* ~ *now* nu allemaal tegelijk **3** aaneen, bij elkaar, tegen elkaar: *tie* ~ aan elkaar binden **4** [inform] voor elkaar, geregeld: *get things* ~ de boel regelen **5** achtereen, zonder tussenpozen: *for hours* ~ uren aan een stuk, uren achter elkaar ‖ ~ *with* met

togetherness saamhorigheid

toggle 1 knevel, pin **2** houtjeʰ [on duffel coat]

Togo Togo
¹Togolese (n) Togolees, Togolese
²Togolese (adj) Togolees
togs kloffie^h, plunje
¹toil (n) gezwoeg^h
²toil (vb) **1** (+ at, on) hard werken (aan): ~ *away* ploeteren **2** moeizaam vooruitkomen
toilet 1 wc, toilet^h **2** toilet^h, gewaad^h: *make one's* ~ toilet maken **3** toilettafel, kaptafel
toilet bag toilettas
toilet paper wc-papier^h
toilet roll closetrol, wc-rol
toiletry 1 toiletartikel^h **2** toiletgerei^h
¹token (n) **1** teken^h, blijk^h, bewijs^h: *in ~ of* ten teken van **2** herinnering, aandenken^h **3** bon, cadeaubon **4** munt, fiche^h, penning
²token (adj) symbolisch: ~ *resistance* symbolisch verzet
tolerable 1 draaglijk **2** toelaatbaar **3** redelijk
tolerance 1 verdraagzaamheid, tolerantie: ~ *of* (or: *to*) *hardship* het verdragen van ontberingen **2** toegestane afwijking, tolerantie, speling
tolerant verdraagzaam
tolerate 1 tolereren, verdragen **2** (kunnen) verdragen
toleration verdraagzaamheid
¹toll (n) **1** tol; [fig] prijs: *take a heavy ~* een zware tol eisen **2** kosten van een interlokaal telefoongesprek **3** (klok)geluid^h
²toll (vb) **1** luiden [of bell] **2** slaan [the hour]
toll bridge tolbrug
toll call [Am] interlokaal telefoongesprek^h
toll-free [Am] gratis; zonder kosten [of call]: ~ *800 service* gratis telefoonnummer
toll road tolweg
tom kater || (*every*) *Tom, Dick and Harry* Jan, Piet en Klaas; *peeping Tom* gluurder
Tom Tom; Thomas || (*every*) ~, *Dick and Harry* Jan, Piet en Klaas; *peeping ~* voyeur
tomahawk tomahawk; strijdbijl
tomato tomaat
tomb (praal)graf^h, (graf)tombe, grafmonument^h
tombola tombola [lottery game]
tomboy wilde meid, wildebras, robbedoes
tombstone grafsteen
tomcat kater
tome (dik) boekdeel^h
tomfool stom
tomfoolery 1 dwaasheid, flauw gedrag^h **2** onzin
tommy gun [inform] tommygun; pistoolmitrailleur
tommyrot [inform] volslagen onzin
tomorrow morgen: *the day after ~* overmorgen; ~ *week* morgen over een week
tomtom tamtam, trommel
ton 1 (metrieke) ton [weight; approx 1,016 kg]: [fig] *it weighs (half) a ~* het weegt loodzwaar **2** grote hoeveelheid **3** honderd pond^h, honderd mijl per uur: *do the ~* honderd mijl per uur rijden || *come down like a ~ of bricks* flink tekeergaan

¹tone (n) **1** toon, klank, stem(buiging), tint: *speak in an angry ~* op boze toon spreken **2** intonatie, accent^h **3** [photo] toon, tint **4** [mus] (hele) toon, grote seconde **5** geest; stemming [also of market]: *set the ~* de toon aangeven
²tone (vb) overeenstemmen: ~ (*in*) *with* kleuren bij
³tone (vb) **1** tinten **2** doen harmoniëren: ~ (*in*) *with* doen harmoniëren met, laten passen bij
tone-deaf geen (muzikaal) gehoor hebbend
tone down 1 afzwakken [also fig]: ~ *one's language* op zijn woorden passen **2** verzachten
toneless 1 toonloos, monotoon **2** kleurloos
toner inkt [for printers and copiers]
tongs tang: *pair of ~* tang
tongue 1 tong, spraak **2** taal **3** tongvormig iets; lipje^h [of shoe]; landtong; klepel [of bell] || (*speak*) *with ~ in cheek* spottend (spreken); *hold your ~!* houd je mond!; *have lost one's ~* zijn tong verloren hebben; *set ~s wagging* de tongen in beweging brengen
tongue-in-cheek ironisch, spottend
tongue-tied met de mond vol tanden
tongue-twister tongbreker, moeilijk uit te spreken woord^h/zin
tonic versterkend middel^h [also fig]
tonic water tonic
tonight 1 vanavond **2** vannacht
tonsil (keel)amandel: *have one's ~s out* zijn amandelen laten knippen
tonsil(l)itis amandelontsteking
tonsure tonsuur
too 1 te (zeer): ~ *good to be true* te mooi om waar te zijn **2** [inform] erg, al te: *it's ~ bad* (het is) erg jammer **3** ook, eveneens: *he, ~, went to Rome* híj ging ook naar Rome; *he went to Rome, ~* hij ging ook naar Róme **4** bovendien: *they did it; on Sunday ~!* zij hebben het gedaan; en nog wel op zondag!
¹tool (n) **1** handwerktuig^h, (stuk^h) gereedschap^h, instrument^h: *down ~s* het werk neerleggen [in protest] **2** werktuig^h
²tool (vb) toeren, rijden: ~ *along* rondtoeren, voortsnorren
³tool (vb) bewerken
toolbar [comp] werkbalk
toolbox gereedschapskist
toolkit (set) gereedschappen
tool-shed gereedschapsschuurtje^h
¹toot (n) **1** (hoorn)stoot **2** getoeter^h
²toot (vb) toeteren, blazen (op)
tooth 1 tand [also of comb, saw]; kies: *teeth*

gebit[h]; [fig] *(fight)* ~ *and **nail*** met hand en tand (vechten); [fig] ***armed** to the teeth* tot de tanden gewapend; [fig] ***get** one's teeth into sth.* ergens zijn tanden in zetten **2** (teeth) [inform] kracht, effect[h] ‖ [inform] *be **fed up** to the (back) teeth* er schoon genoeg van hebben; ***kick** in the teeth* voor het hoofd stoten; *the sound **set** his teeth on edge* het geluid ging hem door merg en been

toothache tandpijn, kiespijn

toothbrush tandenborstel

toothed 1 getand **2** met tanden

toothless 1 tandeloos **2** krachteloos

toothpaste tandpasta[+h]

toothpick tandenstoker

toothsome lekker

toothy 1 met grote, vooruitstekende tanden **2** getand

¹tootle (n) getoeter[h]

²tootle (vb) (rond)toeren

³tootle (vb) blazen (op); toeteren (op) [instrument]

tootsy [child language] voet(je[h])

¹top (n) **1** top, hoogste punt[h]; *from ~ to **bottom*** van onder tot boven; *from ~ to **toe*** van top tot teen; *(shout) at the ~ of one's **voice*** luidkeels (schreeuwen); *on ~* boven(aan) **2** bovenstuk[h], bovenkant, tafelblad[h]; dop [of bottle, fountain pen]; top(je[h]) [article of clothing]; deksel[+h], kroonkurk; room [on milk]; bovenrand [of page] **3** beste; belangrijkste[h] [of form, organisation]: *be* (or: *come out*) *(at the) ~ of the **form*** de beste van de klas zijn **4** oppervlakte **5** tol [toy] ‖ *off the ~ of one's **head*** onvoorbereid [speaking]; *(feel) on ~ of the **world*** (zich) heel gelukkig (voelen); [inform] ***blow** one's ~* in woede uitbarsten; ***come** out on ~* overwinnen; ***get** on ~ of sth.* iets de baas worden; ***go** over the ~* **a)** te ver gaan; **b)** uit de loopgraven komen; ***on ~ of** that* daar komt nog bij, bovendien

²top (adj) hoogste, top-: ~ ***drawer*** bovenste la; [fig] *out of the ~ **drawer*** van goede komaf; ~ ***prices*** hoogste prijzen; *at ~ **speed*** op topsnelheid

³top (vb) **1** van top voorzien, bedekken: [fig] *~ **off*** (or: *up*) *sth.* iets bekronen **2** de top bereiken van [eg mountain; also fig] **3** aan de top staan [also fig]; aanvoeren [list, team] **4** overtreffen: *to ~ it **all*** tot overmaat van ramp ‖ *~ and **tail*** afhalen, doppen; *~ **up*** **a)** bijvullen; **b)** [phone] opwaarderen

topaz topaas[+h]

top boot kaplaars

top cat [inform] hoogste baas, leider

topcoat 1 overjas **2** bovenste verflaag, deklaag

top copy origineel[h]

topdog [inform] heer en meester: *be ~* het voor het zeggen hebben

top dollar: [inform] *you need to **pay** ~ for an*

apartment in this town je betaalt de hoofdprijs voor een appartement in deze stad

top-down van boven af; van boven naar beneden [of corporate structure]

top-drawer van goede komaf

top-dress bestrooien [of sand, manure etc]

top-end van hoge kwaliteit

top flight 1 eersteklas, uitstekend **2** best mogelijk

top-gear 1 hoogste versnelling **2** topconditie: *he's back **into** ~* hij draait weer op volle toeren

top hat hoge hoed

top-heavy [also fig] topzwaar

topiary 1 vormboom **2** vormsnoei

topic onderwerp[h] (van gesprek): ~ *of **conversation*** gespreksthema[h]; *off ~* niets met het onderwerp (van de discussie) te maken hebbend

topical 1 actueel **2** plaatselijk [also med] **3** naar onderwerp gerangschikt, thematisch

topicality actualiteit

topknot 1 (haar)knotje[h] **2** strik [in hair] **3** kam [of cock]

topless 1 zonder bovenstuk(je) **2** met topless bediening **3** topless

topmost (aller)hoogst

top-notch eersteklas

top-of-the-bill bekendst; belangrijkst

top-of-the-line eersteklas-, uit het hoogste segment, beste in zijn soort

top-of-the-range eersteklas-, uit het hoogste segment, beste in zijn soort

topper 1 hoge hoed **2** dekmatras[+h], oplegmatras[+h]

topping toplaag(je[h]), sierlaagje[h]

¹topple (vb) (bijna) omvallen, kantelen: ~ ***down*** (or: *over*) omtuimelen

²topple (vb) (bijna) doen omvallen, omkieperen

top-ranking van de hoogste rang; hoogstgeplaatst

tops je van het: ***come** out ~* als de beste uit de bus komen

topsail marzeil[h]

top secret uiterst geheim

topside 1 bovenkant **2** [roughly] biefstuk

topsoil bovenste laag losse (teel)aarde, bovengrond

topsy-turvy ondersteboven (gekeerd), op zijn kop: *the world is **going** ~* de wereld wordt op zijn kop gezet

top-up 1 aanvulling **2** opwaardering [of phone]

top-up card prepaidkaart

top whack [inform] [fin] de hoofdprijs; [general] het maximum: ***pay** ~* de hoofdprijs betalen

¹torch (n) **1** toorts; fakkel [also fig] **2** zaklamp **3** soldeerlamp ‖ ***carry** a* (or: *the*) *~ for s.o.* hopeloos verliefd zijn op iem.

²**torch** (vb) in brand steken
torchlight 1 fakkellicht[h] **2** licht[h] van een zaklantaarn
¹**torment** (n) kwelling
²**torment** (vb) kwellen, plagen: *~ed by mosquitoes* bestookt door muggen
tornado tornado
¹**torpedo** (n) torpedo
²**torpedo** (vb) [also fig] torpederen
torpid 1 gevoelloos **2** traag **3** in winterslaap
torrent [also fig] stortvloed: *the rain fell in ~s* het stortregende
torrential [also fig] als een stortvloed: *~ rains* stortregens
torrid 1 zeer heet, tropisch; verzengend [heat]: *the ~ zone* de tropen **2** intens
torsion torsie; wringing
torso [also fig] torso
tort onrechtmatige daad
tortoise landschildpad
tortoiseshell 1 lapjeskat **2** schildpad[h] [as material]
tortuous 1 kronkelend; slingerend [of road] **2** omslachtig, gecompliceerd, misleidend, bedrieglijk
¹**torture** (n) marteling, zware kwelling
²**torture** (vb) martelen: *~d by doubt* (or: *jealousy*) gekweld door twijfel (*or:* jaloezie)
torture chamber martelkamer, folterkamer
torturer folteraar, beul
Tory conservatief, lid[h] van de conservatieve partij in Groot-Brittannië
tosh onzin
¹**toss** (n) **1** worp **2** beweging, knik, slinger, zwaai, val: *take a ~* van het paard geslingerd worden; [fig] vallen **3** opgooi: [inform] *I don't give a ~* het kan me geen bal schelen; *lose* (or: *win*) *the ~* verliezen (*or:* winnen) bij het tossen
²**toss** (vb) tossen, een munt opgooien, loten: *we'll have to ~ for it* we zullen erom moeten tossen
³**toss** (vb) **1** slingeren: *the ship was ~ed about* het schip werd heen en weer geslingerd **2** schudden, (doen) zwaaien, afwerpen **3** gooien, aangooien, opgooien, in de lucht werpen: *~ hay* hooi keren **4** een munt opgooien met: *I'll ~ you for it* we loten erom
toss off 1 achteroverslaan [drink] **2** razendsnel produceren: *~ a speech* voor de vuist weg een toespraak houden
toss up tossen, kruis of munt gooien
toss-up 1 opgooi **2** [inform] twijfelachtige zaak, onbesliste zaak: *it's a ~ whether* het is een gok of, het is nog maar de vraag of
tot 1 dreumes: *a tiny ~* een kleine hummel **2** scheutje[h] [of hard liquor]
¹**total** (n) totaal[h]
²**total** (adj) totaal, volledig: *~ abstainer* ge-

heelonthouder; *in ~ ignorance* in absolute onwetendheid; *sum ~* totaalbedrag[h]
³**total** (vb) (+ (up) to) oplopen (tot)
⁴**total** (vb) **1** bedragen, oplopen tot **2** (also + up) het totaal vaststellen van
totalitarian totalitair
totality 1 totaal[h] **2** totaliteit
tote (bij zich) dragen [eg gun]; meevoeren
tote bag (grote) draagtas
totter 1 wankelen [also fig] **2** wankelend overeind komen: *~ to one's feet* wankelend opstaan
totty [inform] lekkere wijven
¹**tot up** (vb) (+ to) oplopen (tot), bedragen
²**tot up** (vb) optellen
toucan toekan
¹**touch** (n) **1** aanraking, tik(je[h]); contact[h] [also fig]: *I felt a ~ on my shoulder* ik voelde een tikje op mijn schouder; *be* (or: *keep*) *in ~ with* contact hebben (*or:* onderhouden) met; *I'll be in ~* ik neem nog contact met je op; *lose ~ with* uit het oog verliezen **2** gevoel[h] bij aanraking, tastzin **3** vleugje[h]; snufje[h] [eg salt]; lichte aanval [of disease]: *a ~ of the sun* een lichte zonnesteek **4** stijl, manier: *put the finishing ~(es) to sth.* de laatste hand leggen aan iets; *lose one's ~* achteruitgaan, het verleren **5** [mus] aanslag **6** [sport] deel[h] van veld buiten de zijlijnen [football, rugby] || *play a ~* tikkertje spelen
²**touch** (vb) (elkaar) raken, aan elkaar grenzen
³**touch** (vb) **1** raken [also fig]; aanraken: *you haven't ~ed your meal* je hebt nog geen hap gegeten **2** een tikje geven, aantasten; [fig] aankunnen: *he ~ed his cap* hij tikte zijn pet aan **3** raken, ontroeren: *~ed with pity* door medelijden bewogen **4** treffen, betreffen: *he does not want to ~ politics* hij wil zich niet met politiek inlaten **5** benaderen, bereiken; [fig] evenaren: *the thermometer ~ed 50°* de thermometer liep tot 50° op; *~ s.o. for a fiver* iem. vijf pond aftroggelen
¹**touch-and-go** (n) **1** een dubbeltje op zijn kant, kantje boord **2** veranderlijkheid
²**touch-and-go** (adj) riskant: *it's a ~ state of affairs* het is een dubbeltje op zijn kant
touch at aandoen: *the ship touched at Port Said* het schip deed Port Said aan
touchdown 1 landing [aeroplane] **2** [rugby, Am football] touchdown
¹**touch down** (vb) landen
²**touch down** (vb) [rugby, Am football] aan de grond brengen achter de doellijn [ball; by opponent]
touched 1 ontroerd **2** getikt
touch in [public transport] inchecken
touching ontroerend
touchless [techn] contactloos
touchline zijlijn
touch off 1 afvuren, doen ontploffen **2** de

stoot geven tot
touch out [public transport] uitchecken
touchpaper lont [eg of fireworks]
touchscreen aanraakscherm[h]
touchstone maatstaf
touch-tone toets-, drukknop-: ~ *phone* toetstelefoon
touch-type blind typen
touch up 1 retoucheren **2** bijschaven; [fig] opfrissen [memory]
touch (up)on terloops behandelen
touchy 1 overgevoelig, prikkelbaar **2** netelig
touchy-feely [inform] **1** knuffelig; aanhalig **2** soft; klef
¹tough (n) woesteling, zware jongen
²tough (adj) **1** taai, stoer: *as ~ as old boots* a) vreselijk taai; b) keihard; ~ *as nails* spijkerhard **2** moeilijk, lastig: *a ~ job* een lastig karwei **3** onbuigzaam: *a ~ guy* (or: *customer*) een keiharde; *get ~ with* hard optreden tegen **4** ruw **5** tegenvallend, hard: *it's your ~ luck* het is je eigen stomme schuld; *it's ~ on him* het is een grote tegenvaller voor hem; ~ *(luck)!* pech!, jammer!
³tough (adv) hard, onverzettelijk: *talk ~* zich keihard opstellen [during negotiations]
toughen taai, hard (doen) worden: ~ *up* sterker worden
toughie 1 rouwdouw **2** lastig probleem[h]
toupee haarstukje[h]
¹tour (n) **1** reis, rondreis **2** (+ of) (kort) bezoek[h] (aan): *a guided ~ of* (or: *round*) *the castle* een rondleiding door het kasteel **3** tournee: *on ~* op tournee **4** verblijf[h]: *the ambassador did a four-year ~ in Washington* de ambassadeur heeft vier jaar Washington als standplaats gehad
²tour (vb) **1** (be)reizen, rondreizen **2** op tournee gaan door
tourer 1 touringcar, toerauto **2** toerfiets, toermotor
touring car 1 touringcar, toerauto **2** toerwagen [in motor racing]
tourism toerisme[h]
tourist toerist
tourist class toeristenklasse
tourist office VVV-kantoor[h]
tournament toernooi[h], steekspel[h]
tour operator reisorganisator
tousle in de war maken [hair]
¹tout (n) **1** klantenlokker **2** scharrelaar; handelaar [esp in illegal tickets and information about racehorses]
²tout (vb) **1** klanten lokken, werven: ~ *for business* klanten ronselen **2** sjacheren; handelen [in information about racehorses]
³tout (vb) **1** verhandelen [information about racehorses] **2** op de zwarte markt verkopen [tickets]
¹tow (n) **1** sleep: *take a car in* ~ een auto sle-

pen **2** het (mee)slepen
²tow (vb) (weg)slepen, op sleeptouw nemen, (weg)trekken
towards 1 naar, tot, richting: *her window faced* ~ *the sea* haar raam keek uit op de zee; *he walked* ~ *the signpost* hij ging op de wegwijzer af; *we're saving* ~ *buying a house* we sparen om later een huis te kunnen kopen **2** ten opzichte van, met betrekking tot: *her attitude* ~ *her parents* haar houding ten opzichte van haar ouders **3** [to express time] voor, vlak voor, naar … toe: ~ *six* (o'clock) tegen zessen
tow bar 1 trekhaak **2** [skiing] sleepbeugel [of ski lift]; anker[h]
towel handdoek: *throw in the* ~ de handdoek in de ring gooien; [fig] het opgeven
towelling badstof
¹tower (n) **1** toren, (zend)mast **2** torenflat, kantoorflat || ~ *of strength* steun en toeverlaat, rots in de branding
²tower (vb) (+ over, above) uittorenen (boven), (hoog) uitsteken
tower block torengebouw[h], torenflat
towering 1 torenhoog **2** enorm, hevig: *he's in a ~ rage* hij is razend
towing zone wegsleepzone
town 1 stad **2** gemeente || *go to ~ on sth.* zich inzetten, veel werk maken van iets; [inform] uitspatten, zich uitleven; *(out) on the* ~ (aan het) stappen, (een avondje) uit; *he went up to ~ from Nottingham* hij is vanuit Nottingham naar Londen gegaan
town clerk gemeentesecretaris
town council gemeenteraad
town councillor (gemeente)raadslid[h]
town hall stadhuis[h]
town house 1 huis in de stad **2** huis in stadswijk
townscape stadsgezicht[h]
township 1 gemeente **2** kleurlingenwijk, woonstad
townspeople 1 stedelingen, ingezetenen **2** stadsmensen
towpath jaagpad[h]
towrope sleeptouw[h]
toxic toxisch, giftig, vergiftigings-
toxin toxine[+h]; giftige stof
¹toy (n) speeltje[h], (stuk[h]) speelgoed[h]; [fig] speelbal
²toy (vb) (+ with) spelen (met), zich amuseren (met): *he ~ed with the idea of buying a new car* hij speelde met de gedachte een nieuwe auto te kopen
toyshop speelgoedwinkel
TP *toilet paper* wc-papier[h]
¹trace (n) spoor[h], voetspoor[h]; [also fig] overblijfsel[h]; vleugje[h]: *not a ~ of humour* geen greintje humor; *lose ~ of* uit het oog verliezen; *lost without* ~ spoorloos verdwenen || *kick over the ~s* uit de band springen

²**trace** (vb) **1** (+ out) (uit)tekenen, schetsen; trekken [line] **2** overtrekken **3** volgen, nagaan **4** (+ back) nagaan, naspeuren, opsporen, terugvoeren: *the rumour was ~d back to his aunt* men kwam erachter dat het gerucht afkomstig was van zijn tante **5** vinden, ontdekken: *I can't ~ that book* ik heb dat boek niet kunnen vinden

trace element spoorelementʰ

tracer lichtspoorkogel

tracing paper overtrekpapierʰ

¹**track** (n) **1** spoorʰ: *on the right* (or: *wrong*) ~ op het goede (*or:* verkeerde) spoor [also fig]; *go off the beaten* ~ ongebaande wegen bewandelen [fig]; *be on s.o.'s* ~ iem. op het spoor zijn **2** voetspoorʰ, (voet)afdruk; prent [of animals]: [fig] *cover (up) one's ~s* zijn sporen uitwissen **3** padʰ, bosweg, landweg; [fig also] weg; baan **4** renbaan, racebaan, wielerbaan **5** (spoor)rails **6** rupsband **7** nummerʰ [on CD, gramophone record]; (opname)spoorʰ [on (cassette) tape] ‖ *the wrong side of the (railroad) ~s* de achterbuurten; *lose ~ of* uit het oog verliezen, niet meer op de hoogte blijven van; [inform] *make ~s* 'm smeren; *across the ~s* in de achterbuurten; [inform] *in one's ~s* ter plaatse, ter plekke

²**track** (vb) **1** het spoor volgen van, volgen **2** (+ down) (op)sporen, ontdekken, naspeuren

tracker 1 spoorvolger **2** speurhond

track events [athletics] loopnummers

tracksuit trainingspakʰ

tract 1 uitgestrekt gebiedʰ, landstreek **2** traktaatʰ; verhandeling [rel, ethics] **3** [anatomy] kanaalʰ: *digestive ~* spijsverteringskanaalʰ

traction 1 trekking, het (voort)trekken **2** trekkracht, aandrijving

tractor tractor, (landbouw)trekker

¹**trade** (n) **1** handel, zaken: *Department of Trade and Industry* [roughly] Ministerie van Economische Zaken; *do a good ~* goede zaken doen **2** bedrijfstak, branche **3** handel, (mensen uit) het vak, handelaars **4** vakʰ, ambachtʰ, beroepʰ: *a butcher by ~* slager van beroep **5** passaat(wind)

²**trade** (vb) handel drijven, handelen, zaken doen ‖ ~ *(up)on s.o.'s generosity* misbruik maken van iemands vrijgevigheid

³**trade** (vb) verhandelen, uitwisselen, (om)ruilen: ~ *in an old car for a new one* een oude auto voor een nieuwe inruilen

trade agreement handelsverdragʰ, handelsakkoordʰ

trade association beroepsvereniging

trade deficit handelstekortʰ

trade fair handelsbeurs

trade-in 1 inruilobjectʰ **2** inruil

trademark handelsmerkʰ; [fig] typisch kenmerkʰ [of person]

trade-off 1 inruil [as a compromise] **2** wisselwerking

trade price (groot)handelsprijs

trader 1 handelaar **2** koopvaardijschipʰ

trade relations handelsbetrekkingen

tradesman 1 winkelier **2** leverancier

tradespeople winkeliers [as group]

trade(s) union (vak)bond, vakvereniging

trade unionist vakbondslidʰ, aanhanger van een vakbond

trade wind passaatwind

trading estate industriegebiedʰ

trading partner handelspartner

trading post handelsnederzetting

tradition traditie, overlevering

traditional traditioneel, vanouds gebruikelijk

traditionally traditiegetrouw; vanouds

¹**traffic** (n) **1** verkeerʰ, vervoerʰ, transportʰ **2** handel, koophandel: ~ *in drugs* drugshandel

²**traffic** (vb) **1** handel drijven (in), handelen (in), zaken doen (in) **2** zwarte handel drijven (in), sjacheren (met) ‖ ~ *in arms* wapenhandel drijven

traffic calming snelheidsbeperkende maatregelen

traffic circle rotonde, (rond) verkeerspleinʰ

traffic island vluchtheuvel

traffic jam (verkeers)opstopping

trafficker zwarthandelaar, sjacheraar; dealer [in drugs etc]

traffic lane rijstrook

traffic sign verkeerstekenʰ, verkeersbordʰ

traffic warden parkeercontroleur, parkeerwachter

tragedy tragedie, dramaʰ, tragiek, het tragische

tragic tragisch, droevig

¹**trail** (n) **1** sliert, stroom, rij: ~*s of smoke* rookslierten **2** spoorʰ, padʰ: *a ~ of destruction* een spoor van vernieling; *blaze a* ~ [fig] de weg banen, baanbrekend werk verrichten **3** spoorʰ; prent [of animal]; geur(vlag) [as trace]: *be hard* (or: *hot*) *on s.o.'s* ~ iem. op de hielen zitten

²**trail** (vb) **1** slepen, loshangen: *her gown was ~ing along on the ground* haar japon sleepte over de grond **2** zich (voort)slepen, strompelen **3** kruipen [of plants] **4** (+ behind) [sport] achterliggen, achterstaan, achteraankomen ‖ *his voice ~ed off* zijn stem stierf weg

³**trail** (vb) **1** slepen, sleuren **2** volgen, schaduwen **3** [sport] achterliggen op, achterstaan op

trailer 1 aanhangwagen, oplegger **2** caravan **3** [film] trailer

¹**train** (n) **1** trein: *by* ~ per trein **2** sleep [of dress]; [fig] nasleep **3** gevolgʰ, stoet, sleep **4** rij, reeks, opeenvolging; [fig] aaneenscha-

keling: *a* ~ *of thought* een gedachtegang; *preparations are in* ~ de voorbereidingen zijn aan de gang

²**train** (vb) **1** (zich) trainen, (zich) oefenen **2** een opleiding volgen, studeren: *he is ~ing to be a lawyer* hij studeert voor advocaat

³**train** (vb) **1** trainen, oefenen; africhten [animal] **2** opleiden, scholen **3** leiden [plant] **4** richten, mikken

trained getraind; ervaren: ~ *nurse* gediplomeerd verpleegster

trainee stagiair(e)

trainer trainer, africhter, dompteur **2** (-s) trainingsschoenen

training training, oefening, opleiding: *physical* ~ conditietraining

training college pedagogische academie

traipse sjouwen, slepen ‖ ~ *about* rondslenteren

trait trek(je[h]), karaktertrek, karaktereigenschap

traitor (land)verrader, overloper: *turn* ~ een verrader worden

trajectory baan [of missile]

tram tram: *by* ~ met de tram

tramline 1 tramrail **2** (-s) dubbele zijlijnen [in tennis court]

¹**tramp** (n) **1** getrappel[h], gestamp[h] **2** voettocht, trektocht **3** zwerver, landloper **4** tramp(boot), vrachtzoeker, schip[h] van de wilde vaart

²**tramp** (vb) **1** stappen, marcheren, stampen **2** lopen, trekken, een voettocht maken

³**tramp** (vb) **1** aflopen, doorlopen **2** trappen op, stampen op: ~ *down* plattrappen

¹**trample** (vb) stampen, trappelen, stappen: ~ *(up)on* trappen op; [fig] met voeten treden; ~ *on s.o.'s feelings* iemands gevoelens kwetsen

²**trample** (vb) vertrappen, trappen op

trampoline trampoline

trance trance: *be in a* ~ in trance zijn

tranny [inform; depr] travestiet

tranquil kalm, vredig, rustig

tranquillity kalmte, rust(igheid)

tranquillize kalmeren, tot bedaren brengen

tranquillizer tranquillizer, kalmerend middel[h]

transact verrichten, afhandelen, afwikkelen: ~ *business with s.o.* met iem. zaken doen

transaction 1 transactie, zaak, handelsovereenkomst **2** afhandeling, afwikkeling

transatlantic trans-Atlantisch

transceiver [radio] zendontvanger

transcend 1 te boven gaan **2** overtreffen: *he ~s himself* hij overtreft zichzelf

transcendent superieur, alles (allen) overtreffend, buitengewoon

transcendental transcendentaal, bovenzintuiglijk

transcribe transcriberen, overschrijven, (in een andere spelling) overbrengen; [mus] bewerken: ~ *the music for organ* de muziek voor orgel bewerken

transcript afschrift[h]; kopie

transcription transcriptie, het overschrijven; [mus] bewerking; arrangement[h]

¹**transfer** (n) **1** overplaatsing, overdracht; [sport] transfer[+h] **2** overgeplaatste; [sport] transfer(speler) **3** [fin] overdracht, overschrijving, overboeking **4** overdrukplaatje[h] **5** overstapkaartje[h]

²**transfer** (vb) **1** overstappen: ~ *from the train to the bus* van de trein op de bus overstappen **2** overgeplaatst worden; veranderen [of place, work, school]

³**transfer** (vb) **1** overmaken, overhandigen, overdragen: ~ *one's rights to s.o.* zijn rechten aan iem. (anders) overdragen **2** overplaatsen, verplaatsen, overbrengen **3** overdrukken **4** [sport] transfereren [player]

transferable 1 verplaatsbaar **2** overdraagbaar **3** inwisselbaar; verhandelbaar [cheque etc]

transference overplaatsing, overbrenging

transfix 1 doorboren; doorsteken [eg with lance] **2** (vast)spietsen **3** als aan de grond nagelen, verlammen

¹**transform** (vb) (van vorm/gedaante/karakter) veranderen, een gedaanteverwisseling ondergaan

²**transform** (vb) **1** (van vorm/gedaante/karakter doen) veranderen, hervormen, omvormen: *stress ~ed him into an aggressive man* door de stress veranderde hij in een agressief man **2** [also elec] omzetten, transformeren

transformation transformatie

transformer [elec] transformator

transfuse een transfusie geven (van)

transfusion transfusie

transgender transgender-: ~ *people* transgenders

transgenic transgenetisch [of crop etc]: ~ *mice* transgene muizen

¹**transgress** (vb) **1** een overtreding begaan **2** zondigen

²**transgress** (vb) overtreden, inbreuk maken op, schenden

transient 1 voorbijgaand, kortstondig **2** doorreizend, doortrekkend

transistor transistor

transit doorgang, doortocht: *in* ~ tijdens het vervoer, onderweg

transit camp doorgangskamp[h]

¹**transition** (n) **1** overgang: *period of* ~ overgangsperiode **2** geslachtsverandering

²**transition** (vb) **1** overstappen (op), de overgang maken (naar), overgaan (naar) **2** [gender] in transitie zijn

transitional tussenliggend, overgangs-, tussen-

transitive transitief, overgankelijk

transit visa doorreisvisum[h]

translate 1 vertalen: ~ *a sentence* **from** *English* **into** *Dutch* een zin uit het Engels in het Nederlands vertalen **2** interpreteren, uitleggen, vertolken **3** omzetten; omvormen [also biology]: ~ *ideas into actions* ideeën in daden omzetten

translation vertaling

translator 1 vertaler **2** tolk

translucent doorschijnend

transmission 1 uitzending, programma[h] **2** overbrenging; overdracht [also of disease, heredity] **3** transmissie, overbrenging, versnellingsbak **4** het doorgeven, overlevering

transmit 1 overbrengen; overdragen [also of disease, heredity]: ~ *a message* een boodschap overbrengen **2** overleveren; doorgeven [traditions etc]

transmitter 1 overbrenger, overdrager **2** seintoestel[h], seingever **3** microfoon [of telephone] **4** zender [radio, TV]

transparency 1 dia(positief[h]), projectieplaatje[h], overhead(sheet) **2** doorzichtigheid

transparent 1 doorzichtig [also fig]; transparant: *a ~ lie* een doorzichtige leugen **2** eenvoudig/gemakkelijk te begrijpen

transperson transpersoon

[1]**transpire** (vb) **1** transpireren; waterdamp verdampen [of human being, animal] **2** uitlekken, aan het licht komen, bekend worden: *it ~d that the president himself was involved* het lekte uit dat de president er zelf bij betrokken was

[2]**transpire** (vb) uitwasemen, uitzweten

[1]**transplant** (n) **1** getransplanteerd orgaan[h] (weefsel[h]), transplantaat[h] **2** transplantatie

[2]**transplant** (vb) **1** verplanten, overplanten **2** overbrengen, doen verhuizen **3** transplanteren, overplanten

[1]**transport** (n) vervoer(middel)[h], transport[h]: *public ~* openbaar vervoer; *I'd like to come, but I've no ~* ik zou wel mee willen, maar ik heb geen vervoer

[2]**transport** (vb) vervoeren, transporteren, overbrengen

transport aircraft transportvliegtuig[h]

transportation 1 vervoermiddel[h], transportmiddel[h] **2** vervoer[h], transport[h], overbrenging

transport cafe wegcafé[h], chauffeurscafé[h]

transporter 1 transporteur **2** transportmiddel[h]

transpose 1 anders schikken, (onderling) verwisselen, omzetten **2** [mus] transponeren

transvestite travestiet

[1]**trap** (n) **1** val, (val)strik, hinderlaag, strikvraag: *lay* (or: *set*) *a ~* een val (op)zetten, een strik spannen **2** sifon; stankafsluiter [in drainpipe] **3** [inform] smoel, waffel, bek: *shut your ~!* hou je kop!

[2]**trap** (vb) **1** (ver)strikken, (in een val) vangen; [fig] in de val laten lopen: ~ *s.o.* **into** *a confession* iem. door een list tot een bekentenis dwingen **2** opsluiten: *be ~ped* opgesloten zitten, in de val zitten, vastzitten **3** opvangen [eg energy]

trapdoor valdeur, val, (val)luik[h]

trapeze trapeze

trapper vallenzetter, pelsjager

trappings (uiterlijke) sieraden, (uiterlijk) vertoon

[1]**trash** (n) **1** rotzooi, (oude) rommel, troep **2** onzin, gekletsh **3** afvalh, vuilh, vuilnish **4** nietsnut(ten), uitschot[h], tuig[h]

[2]**trash** (vb) kritiseren; afkraken [book, film etc]

trash can vuilnisemmer

trash talking [Am] ophitsende taal; gescheld[h]

trashy waardeloos, kitscherig: ~ *novel* flutroman

trauma 1 wond, verwonding, letsel[h] **2** [psychology] trauma[h]

traumatic traumatisch, beangstigend

[1]**travel** (n) **1** (lange/verre) reis, rondreis, het reizen: *on our ~s* tijdens onze rondreis **2** (-s) reisverhaal[h], reisverhalen, reizen, reisbeschrijving: *Gulliver's Travels* Gullivers Reizen

[2]**travel** (vb) **1** reizen, een reis maken: *~ling circus* rondreizend circus **2** vertegenwoordiger zijn: ~ *in electrical appliances* vertegenwoordiger in huishoudelijke apparaten zijn **3** zich (voort)bewegen, zich voortplanten, gaan: *news ~s fast* nieuws verspreidt zich snel || *flowers ~ badly* bloemen kunnen slecht tegen vervoer

[3]**travel** (vb) **1** doorreizen, doortrekken; afreizen [also as commercial traveller] **2** afleggen: ~ *500 miles a day* 500 mijl per dag afleggen

travel agency reisbureau[h]

travel ban 1 reisverbod[h] **2** [Am] inreisverbod[h]

traveller 1 reiziger, bereisd man **2** handelsreiziger, vertegenwoordiger **3** zigeuner, zwerver

traveller's cheque reischeque

travelog(ue) (geïllustreerd) reisverhaal[h], reisfilm

[1]**traverse** (vb) schuins klimmen

[2]**traverse** (vb) **1** (door)kruisen, oversteken, (dwars) trekken door, doorsnijden **2** dwars beklimmen [slope]

travesty travestie, karikatuur, parodie: ~ *of justice* karikatuur van rechtvaardigheid

[1]**trawl** (n) **1** sleepnet[h], trawl **2** zoektocht, speurtocht [eg for talent]

[2]**trawl** (vb) met een sleepnet vissen (naar); [fig] uitkammen; uitpluizen: [fig] ~ *for* zorgvuldig doorzoeken

trawler treiler, trawler

tray 1 dienblad^h, (presenteer)blad^h **2** bakje^h, brievenbak(je^h)

traybake plaatcake

treacherous verraderlijk, onbetrouwbaar: ~ *ice* verraderlijk ijs; ~ *memory* onbetrouwbaar geheugen

treachery verraad^h, ontrouw, onbetrouwbaarheid

treacle (suiker)stroop [also fig]

treacly stroperig, kleverig; [fig] (honing)zoet; vleiend

¹tread (n) **1** tred, pas, gang: *a heavy* ~ een zware stap **2** trede, opstapje^h **3** loopvlak^h [of tyre] **4** profiel^h [of tyre]

²tread (vb) treden, stappen, lopen, wandelen: ~ *in the mud* in de modder trappen

³tread (vb) **1** betreden, bewandelen, begaan **2** trappen, vertrappen, intrappen, stuktrappen, uittrappen, vasttrappen; [fig] onderdrukken: ~ *grapes* (met de voeten) druiven persen; ~ *water* watertrappelen **3** heen en weer lopen in, lopen door **4** (zich) banen, platlopen

treadle trapper, pedaal^h

treadmill tredmolen [also fig]

treason hoogverraad^h, landverraad^h

¹treasure (n) **1** schat, kostbaarheid; [inform] juweel^h; parel: *my secretary is a* ~ ik heb een juweel van een secretaresse **2** schat(ten), rijkdom: ~ *of ideas* schat aan ideeën

²treasure (vb) **1** (+ up) verzamelen, bewaren **2** waarderen, op prijs stellen

treasure house schatkamer: *the museum is a* ~ *of paintings* dit museum heeft een schat aan schilderijen

treasurer penningmeester

treasure trove (gevonden) schat, (waardevolle) vondst; rijke bron [also fig]

treasury schatkamer, schatkist; [fig] bron

Treasury (the) Ministerie^h van Financiën

¹treat (n) traktatie, (feestelijk) onthaal^h, feest^h, plezier^h: *it's my* ~ ik trakteer

²treat (vb) **1** trakteren **2** (+ with) onderhandelen (met), (vredes)besprekingen voeren (met), zaken doen (met)

³treat (vb) **1** behandelen [also med]: ~ *s.o. kindly* iem. vriendelijk behandelen **2** beschouwen, afdoen: ~ *sth. as a joke* iets als een grapje opvatten **3** aan de orde stellen; behandelen [subject] **4** trakteren, onthalen

treatable behandelbaar

treatise verhandeling, beschouwing

treatment behandeling, verzorging

treaty verdrag^h, overeenkomst

¹treble (n) jongenssopraan

²treble (adj) driemaal, drievoudig, driedubbel ‖ ~ *recorder* altblokfluit

³treble (vb) verdrievoudigen, met drie vermenigvuldigen

treble clef sopraansleutel

tree boom: *family* ~ stamboom

tree-house boomhut

trefoil [bot] klaver(blad^h)

¹trek (n) tocht; lange reis

²trek (vb) (te voet) trekken

trellis latwerk^h, traliewerk^h

¹tremble (n) trilling, huivering, rilling: *be all of a* ~ over zijn hele lichaam beven

²tremble (vb) **1** beven, rillen, bibberen: *in fear and trembling* met angst en beven **2** schudden [bldg, earth]; trillen **3** huiveren, in angst zitten: *I* ~ *to think* ik moet er niet aan denken, ik huiver bij de gedachte

tremendous 1 enorm, geweldig **2** fantastisch

tremor 1 aardschok, lichte aardbeving **2** huivering, siddering

tremulous 1 trillend, sidderend **2** schuchter, nerveus: ~ *voice* onvaste stem

trench 1 geul, greppel **2** loopgraaf **3** [geology] trog

trenchant scherp, krachtig: ~ *remark* spitse opmerking

trench coat trenchcoat; regenjas

¹trend (n) tendens, neiging, trend: *set the* ~ de toon aangeven

²trend (vb) overhellen, geneigd zijn: *prices are ~ing downwards* de prijzen lijken te gaan zakken

trendsetter trendsetter, voorloper

trendy in, modieus, trendy

trepidation ongerustheid, angst

¹trespass (n) **1** overtreding, inbreuk, schending **2** [rel] zonde, schuld

²trespass (vb) **1** op verboden terrein komen **2** [rel] een overtreding begaan, zondigen

trespasser overtreder: ~*s will be prosecuted* verboden toegang voor onbevoegden

trespass (up)on 1 onrechtmatig betreden [grounds] **2** beslag leggen op, inbreuk maken op; misbruik maken van [time, hospitality]

trestle schraag, onderstel^h

trestle table schragentafel

triad 1 [mus] drieklank **2** drietal^h, triade

trial 1 (gerechtelijk) onderzoek^h, proces^h, rechtszaak **2** proef, experiment^h: *give sth. a* ~ iets testen; *by* ~ *and error* met vallen en opstaan **3** poging **4** beproeving [also fig]; probleem^h: ~*s and tribulations* zorgen en problemen

trial balloon proefballon(netje^h)

trial period proeftijd

triangle driehoek, triangel

triangular 1 driehoekig **2** driezijdig: ~ *contest* driehoeksverkiezing

tribal stam-, stammen-, van een stam

tribe 1 stam, volksstam **2** groep; geslacht^h [related things]

tribesman 1 stamlid^h **2** stamgenoot

tribulation 1 bron van ellende **2** beproeving, rampspoed

tribunal 1 rechtbank, gerecht^h, tribunaal^h **2** [roughly] commissie, [roughly] raad, [roughly] raad van onderzoek

tribune 1 volksleider, demagoog **2** podium^h, tribune

tributary 1 schatplichtige; belastingplichtige [state, person] **2** zijrivier

tribute 1 bijdrage, belasting **2** hulde, eerbetoon^h: **pay** (a) ~ to s.o. iem. eer bewijzen

trice ogenblik^h, moment^h: **in** a ~ in een wip

¹trick (n) **1** truc [also fig]; foefje^h, kneep: know the ~s of the **trade** het klappen van de zweep kennen; **magic** ~s goocheltrucs **2** handigheid, slag: **get** (or: **learn**) the ~ of it de slag te pakken krijgen (van iets) **3** streek, kattenkwaad^h: **play** a ~ (up)on s.o., **play** s.o. a ~ iem. een streek leveren **4** aanwensel^h, tic: you have the ~ **of** pulling your hair when you're nervous je hebt de vreemde gewoonte om aan je haren te trekken als je zenuwachtig bent **5** [cards] slag ‖ this poison should **do** the ~ met dit vergif moet het lukken; not (or: never) **miss** a ~ overal van op de hoogte zijn; be up **to** s.o.'s ~s iem. doorhebben; **how's** ~s? hoe staat het ermee?

²trick (vb) **1** bedriegen, misleiden: ~ s.o. **into** sth. iem. iets aanpraten, iem. ergens inluizen **2** oplichten, afzetten: ~ s.o. **out of** his money iem. zijn geld afhandig maken

trickery bedrog^h

¹trickle (n) **1** stroompje^h, straaltje^h **2** het druppelen

²trickle (vb) **1** druppelen **2** druppelsgewijs komen (gaan): the first guests ~d **in** at ten o'clock om tien uur druppelden de eerste gasten binnen

trickle-down [econ] doordruppel-

trick question strikvraag

trickster oplichter, bedrieger

tricky 1 sluw, listig **2** lastig, moeilijk: ~ **question** lastige vraag

tricycle driewieler

trident drietand

tried beproefd, betrouwbaar

triennial 1 driejaarlijks, om de drie jaar terugkomend **2** driejarig, drie jaar durend

trier volhouder; doorzetter

trifle 1 kleinigheid, wissewasje^h **2** habbekrats, prikje^h, schijntje^h **3** beetje^h: he's a ~ **slow** hij is ietwat langzaam

trifle with 1 niet serieus nemen: she is not a **woman** to be trifled with zij is geen vrouw die met zich laat spotten **2** spelen met

trifling 1 onbelangrijk: of ~ **importance** van weinig belang **2** waardeloos

¹trigger (n) trekker; pal [of pistol]: **pull** the ~ de trekker overhalen; [fig] het startschot geven

²trigger (vb) teweegbrengen, veroorzaken: ~ **off** a) op gang brengen; b) ten gevolge hebben

trigger-happy 1 schietgraag, snel schietend **2** strijdlustig

trigger warning [media] waarschuwing voor mogelijk choquerende inhoud

trigonometry trigonometrie, driehoeksmeting

¹trill (n) **1** roller; triller [of birds] **2** met trilling geproduceerde klank; rollende medeklinker [eg rolling r]

²trill (vb) trillen, kwinkeleren, vibreren ‖ ~ the **r** een rollende r maken

trillion biljoen; [fig] talloos

trilogy trilogie

¹trim (n) **1** versiering; sierstrip(pen) [on car] **2** het bijknippen **3** staat (van gereedheid), conditie: the players were **in** (good) ~ de spelers waren in (goede) vorm

²trim (adj) **1** net(jes), goed verzorgd: a ~ **garden** een keurig onderhouden tuin **2** in vorm, in goede conditie

³trim (vb) **1** in orde brengen, net(jes) maken; (bij)knippen [eg of hair] **2** afknippen; [fig] besnoeien: ~ (down) the **expenditure** de uitgaven beperken **3** versieren: a coat ~med **with** fur een jas afgezet met bont **4** naar de wind zetten [of sails]; [fig] aanpassen; schikken: he ~s his opinions **to** the circumstances hij past zijn mening aan de omstandigheden aan

trimmer 1 snoeimes^h, tuinschaar, tondeuse **2** weerhaan [fig]; opportunist

trimmings 1 garnituur^h, toebehoren^h **2** (af)snoeisel^h, afknipsel^h **3** opsmuk, franje: tell us the story without the ~ vertel ons het verhaal zonder opsmuk

Trinity Drie-eenheid

trinket 1 kleinood^h **2** prul^h, snuisterij

trio 1 drietal^h, trio^h **2** [mus] trio^h

¹trip (n) **1** tocht, reis, uitstapje^h **2** misstap [also fig]; val, vergissing **3** trip [on LSD; also fig]; reuze-ervaring

²trip (vb) **1** (also + up) struikelen, uitglijden **2** huppelen, trippelen: the girl ~ped **across** the room het meisje huppelde door de kamer **3** (+ up) een fout begaan: the man ~ped **up** after a few questions de man versprak zich na een paar vragen

³trip (vb) **1** (also + up) laten struikelen, beentje lichten **2** (also + up) op een fout betrappen **3** (also + up) erin laten lopen, strikken, zich laten verspreken

tripe 1 pens **2** [inform] onzin

¹triple (adj) drievoudig, driedubbel

²triple (vb) verdrievoudigen

triple-play tripleplay-, 3-in-1-

triplet 1 één van een drieling: ~s drieling **2** drietal^h, drie, trio^h

triplets drieling

triplicate triplicaat^h, derde exemplaar^h: **in** ~ in drievoud

tripod driepoot, statief^h

truly

tripper dagjesmens
triptych drieluik[h]
tripwire struikeldraad, valstrik
trite afgezaagd, cliché
¹triumph (n) triomf, overwinning, groot
succes[h]
²triumph (vb) zegevieren: ~ *over difficulties*
moeilijkheden overwinnen
triumphal triomf-, zege-: ~ *arch* triomfboog
triumphant 1 zegevierend **2** triomfantelijk
trivet drievoet; [Am] onderzetter [for pots
and pans etc]
trivial 1 onbelangrijk **2** gewoon, alledaags
3 oppervlakkig
triviality 1 iets onbelangrijks **2** onbelang-
rijkheid
¹Trojan (n) **1** Trojaan **2** [comp] Trojaans
paard[h] || *work like a* ~ werken als een paard
²Trojan (adj) Trojaans: ~ *Horse* paard van
Troje [also fig]; [comp] Trojaans paard
troll 1 sleeplijn [fishing gear] **2** trol [in mythology, comp]
troll army [media] trollenleger[h]
trolley 1 tweewielig (vierwielig) karretje[h],
winkelwagentje[h] **2** tram **3** theewagen || *off
one's* ~ (stapel)gek
trolley bus trolleybus
trolley car tram
trollop [inform] **1** slons, sloddervos **2** slet,
sloerie
trombone trombone, schuiftrompet
¹troop (n) **1** troep, menigte **2** [mil] troep,
peloton[h] **3** (-s) troepen(macht), strijdmach-
ten
²troop (vb) **1** als groep gaan: *his children ~ed
in* zijn kinderen marcheerden naar binnen
2 samenscholen
trooper 1 cavalerist **2** gewoon soldaat
3 (staats)politieagent || *swear like a* ~ vloe-
ken als een ketter
trophy 1 prijs, trofee **2** trofee; zegeteken[h]
[also fig]; aandenken[h]
tropic keerkring: ~ *of Cancer* Kreeftskeerkring; ~ *of Capricorn* Steenbokskeerkring;
the ~s de tropen
tropical tropisch; [fig] heet; drukkend
¹trot (n) **1** draf(je[h]), haastige beweging: *be
on the* ~ ronddraven, niet stilzitten **2** (-s) [in-
form] diarree: *have the* ~s aan de dunne zijn
²trot (vb) **1** draven [also of person] **2** [in-
form] lopen, (weg)gaan
³trot (vb): ~ *out* voor de dag komen met
trotter 1 draver [horse] **2** varkenspoot
¹trouble (n) **1** zorg, bezorgdheid: *that is the
least of my* ~*s!* dat is mij een zorg! **2** tegenslag, narigheid, probleem[h]: *get into* ~ in
moeilijkheden raken **3** ongemak[h], overlast: *I
do not want to be any* ~ ik wil (u) niet tot last
zijn **4** moeite, inspanning: *save o.s. the* ~ zich

de moeite besparen **5** kwaal, ongemak[h]: *he
suffers from back* ~ hij heeft rugklachten
6 onlust, onrust **7** pech, mankement[h]: *the car
has got engine* ~ de wagen heeft motorpech
²trouble (vb) moeite doen: *do not* ~ *to explain* doe geen moeite het uit te leggen
³trouble (vb) **1** verontrusten: *what* ~*s me is
... wat me dwars zit is ...* **2** lastigvallen, storen: *I hope I'm not troubling you* ik hoop dat ik
niet stoor **3** kwellen
troublemaker onruststoker, herrieschopper
troubleshooter probleemoplosser, puin-
ruimer
troublesome lastig
trough 1 trog, drinkbak, eetbak **2** goot
3 laagte(punt[h]); diepte(punt[h]) [on meter, in
statistics etc]
trounce afrossen, afstraffen; [sport; fig] inmaken
troupe troep; groep [esp actors, artists]
trouser broek(s)-: ~ *buttons* broeksknopen
trouser-leg broekspijp
trousers (lange) broek: *a pair of* ~ een (lange) broek; *wear the* ~ de broek aan hebben
trousseau uitzet[+h]
trout (zee)forel || *old* ~ oude tang
trowel troffel || *lay it on with a* ~ het er dik
op leggen, aandikken
Troy Troje
truant 1 spijbelaar: *play* ~ spijbelen **2** lijn-
trekker
truce (tijdelijke) wapenstilstand
truck vrachtwagen, truck || *have no* ~ *with*
geen zaken doen met
trucker [Am] vrachtwagenchauffeur
truckle kruiperig doen: ~ *to s.o.* voor iem.
kruipen
truckle bed [roughly] bed[h] op wieltjes dat
onder een ander bed geschoven kan worden
truckload wagenlading, trucklading
truck stop chauffeurscafé[h]
truculence 1 vechtlust, agressiviteit **2** gewelddadigheid
truculent vechtlustig, agressief
¹trudge (n) trektocht, mars
²trudge (vb) sjokken: ~ *along* zich voortslepen
¹true (adj) **1** waar, juist: *come* ~ werkelijkheid worden **2** echt, waar: ~ *to life* levensecht **3** trouw: *a* ~ *friend* een trouwe vriend
²true (adv) **1** waarheidsgetrouw: *ring* ~ echt
klinken **2** juist
true-blue 1 betrouwbaar, eerlijk **2** onwrikbaar; aarts- [of conservative politician]
true-born rasecht, geboren
true-life waargebeurd
truelove lief(ste)
truffle truffel [also bonbon]
truism 1 waarheid als een koe **2** cliché[h]
truly 1 oprecht: *I am* ~ *grateful to you* ik ben

u oprecht dankbaar **2** echt, werkelijk
3 trouw, toegewijd || *yours* ~ a) hoogach-
tend [complimentary close in letters]; b) de
ondergetekende, [roughly] ik

¹trump (n) troef(kaart) [also fig]: *spades are*
~s schoppen is troef || *come* (or: *turn*) *up ~s*
geluk hebben met

²trump (vb) troeven, troef (uit)spelen || *~ up*
verzinnen; *the charge was clearly ~ed up* de
beschuldiging was duidelijk verzonnen

trump card troefkaart [also fig]: *that was*
my ~ dat was mijn laatste redmiddel

¹trumpet (n) **1** trompet: [fig] *blow one's*
own ~ zijn eigen lof zingen **2** getrompetterʰ
[eg of elephant]

²trumpet (vb) **1** trompet spelen **2** trompetteren

truncate beknotten [also fig]; aftoppen: *~*
a story een verhaal inkorten

truncheon wapenstok

trunk 1 (boom)stam **2** romp, torso **3** hutkoffer [oft also piece of furniture] **4** slurf;
snuit [of elephant] **5** kofferbak [of car] **6** (-s)
korte broek; zwembroek [for men]

trunk call interlokaal telefoongesprekʰ

trunk road hoofdweg

¹truss (n) **1** dakkap, dakspantʰ **2** breukband
3 bundel, bosʰ, pakʰ

²truss (vb) (stevig) inbinden: *~ up* a) inbinden, opmaken [chicken]; b) knevelen

¹trust (n) **1** vertrouwenʰ: *a position of ~* een
vertrouwenspositie **2** (goede) hoop, verwachting **3** zorg, hoede: *commit a child to*
s.o.'s ~ een kind aan iemands zorgen toevertrouwen **4** trust, kartelʰ **5** [law] trust, machtiging tot beheer van goederen voor een begunstigde: *hold property in* (or: *under*) *~* eigendom in bewaring hebben

²trust (vb) **1** vertrouwen: *you should not ~ in*
him je mag hem niet vertrouwen **2** vertrouwen hebben, hopen

³trust (vb) **1** vertrouwen op, aannemen, hopen: *I ~ everything is all right with him* ik hoop
maar dat alles met hem in orde is **2** toevertrouwen: *he ~ed his car to a friend* hij gaf zijn
auto bij een vriend in bewaring

trustee beheerder; bewindvoerder [of capital, estate]; bestuurder, commissaris [of institution, school]

trust fund beheerd fondsʰ

trusting vertrouwend, vriendelijk

trustworthy betrouwbaar

truth 1 waarheid: *to tell the ~ ...* om de
waarheid te zeggen ... **2** echtheid **3** oprechtheid

truthful 1 eerlijk, oprecht **2** waar, (waar-
heids)getrouw

¹try (n) **1** poging: *give it a ~* het eens proberen, een poging wagen **2** [rugby] try

²try (vb) **1** proberen, uitproberen, op de
proef stellen; [also fig] vermoeien: *~ s.o.'s*

patience iemands geduld op de proef stellen; *~ to be* on time proberen op tijd te komen; *tried and found wanting* gewogen en te
licht bevonden; *~ on* aanpassen [clothes]; *~*
out testen, de proef nemen met; *~ sth. on s.o.*
iets op iem. uitproberen; *just ~ and stop me!*
probeer me maar eens tegen te houden!
2 berechten, verhoren: *~ s.o. for murder* iem.
voor moord berechten

trying moeilijk, zwaar: *~ person to deal with*
lastige klant

try-out test, proef: *give s.o. a ~* het met iem.
proberen

tsar tsaar

tsarina tsarina

T-shirt T-shirtʰ

tsunami tsunami, vloedgolf

TT 1 *teetotaller* geheelonthouder **2** *Tourist*
Trophy TT [motorcycle race]

tub 1 tobbe, ton: *have a ~* een bad nemen
2 kuipjeʰ

tuba tuba

tubby tonvormig, rond, dik

tube 1 buis(jeʰ), pijp, slang, huls, koker,
tube **2** binnenband **3** metro **4** [Am] televisie, buis

tuberculosis tuberculose

tube station metrostationʰ

tubular buisvormig: *~ bells* buisklokken,
klokkenspelʰ

¹tuck (n) **1** plooi **2** zoetigheid

²tuck (vb) plooien maken || *~ in!* val aan, tast
toe!; *~ into* flink smullen van

³tuck (vb) **1** plooien **2** inkorten, innemen
3 (+ up) opstropen, optrekken **4** intrekken:
with his legs ~ed up under him in kleermakerszit **5** (also + away) (ver)stoppen, wegstoppen, verschuilen: *~ away* (or: *in*) verborgen
6 (+ in) instoppen: *~ s.o. in* (or: *up*) iem. toedekken; *~ one's shirt into one's trousers* zijn
hemd in zijn broek stoppen

tucked gehurkt

tuck-in smulpartij

tuck shop snoepwinkeltjeʰ

Tuesday dinsdag

tuft bosjeʰ, kwastjeʰ, kuifjeʰ

tufted 1 in bosjes groeiend **2** met, vol bosjes **3** [esp zoology] gekuifd

¹tug (n) **1** ruk, haal: *give a ~ at* (heftig) rukken aan **2** (felle) strijd, conflictʰ: [inform] *~ of*
love touwtrekkerij om (de voogdij over) een
kind [between divorced parents] **3** sleepboot

²tug (vb) (+ at) rukken (aan)

³tug (vb) **1** rukken aan **2** slepen [tug boat]

tugboat sleepboot

tuition 1 schoolgeldʰ, lesgeldʰ **2** onderwijsʰ

tulip tulp

¹tumble (n) **1** val(partij): *have* (or: *take*) *a ~*
vallen **2** warboel: *in a ~* overhoop

²tumble (vb) **1** vallen, tuimelen, struikelen:

~ *down* neerploffen; ~ *down* the stairs van de trap rollen **2** rollen, woelen: ~ *about* rondtollen **3** stormen, lopen: ~ *into* (or: out *of*) bed in zijn bed ploffen, uit zijn bed springen **4** (snel) zakken, kelderen: *tumbling prices* dalende prijzen ‖ ~ *to* snappen

³tumble (vb) **1** doen vallen, omgooien **2** in de war brengen **3** drogen [in tumble drier]

tumbledown bouwvallig

tumble-dryer droogtrommel

tumbler 1 duikelaar **2** acrobaat **3** tuimelglasʰ, (groot) bekerglasʰ **4** [techn] tuimelaar [of lock] **5** droogtrommel

tumbleweed [Am; botany] tuimelkruidʰ, stepperoller

tummy buik(jeʰ)

tummy button navel

tumour tumor

tumult tumultʰ: *in a* ~ totaal verward

tumultuous tumultueus, wanordelijk

tun vatʰ

tuna tonijn

tundra toendra

¹tune (n) **1** wijsjeʰ, melodie; [fig] toon **2** juiste toonhoogte: *sing out of* ~ vals zingen **3** overeenstemming: *it is in* ~ *with the spirit of the time* het is in overeenstemming met de tijdgeest ‖ *call the* ~ de lakens uitdelen; *change one's* ~, *sing another* (or: *dance to another*) ~ een andere toon aanslaan, een toontje lager gaan zingen; *to the* ~ *of £1000* voor het bedrag van £1000

²tune (vb) **1** (+ with) harmoniëren (met) **2** zingen

³tune (vb) **1** stemmen **2** afstemmen [also fig]; instellen: ~ *o.s. to* zich aanpassen aan; ~d *to* afgestemd op **3** afstellen [engine]

tune in afstemmen, de radio (televisie) aanzetten: ~ *to* afstemmen op

tuner 1 [mus] stemmer **2** tuner [separate radio]

¹tune up (vb) stemmen [of orchestra]

²tune up (vb) in gereedheid brengen, afstellen

tunic 1 tunica **2** tuniek, (korte) uniformjas

tuning fork stemvork

Tunisia Tunesië

¹Tunisian (n) Tunesiër, Tunesische

²Tunisian (adj) **1** Tunesisch **2** Tunisch

tunnel 1 tunnel **2** onderaardse gang [of mole etc]

tunny tonijn

turban tulband

turbid 1 troebel, drabbig **2** verward: ~ *emotions* verwarde emoties

turbine turbine

turbot tarbot

turbulence 1 wildheid **2** beroering, onrust

turbulent 1 wild **2** woelig, oproerig: ~ *crowd* oproerige menigte

turd 1 drol **2** verachtelijk persoon

¹turf (n) **1** graszode, plag **2** gras(veld)ʰ: *play on home* ~ een thuiswedstrijd spelen **3** renbaan, racebaan, paardenrennenʰ

²turf (vb): [inform] ~ *s.o.* out iem. eruit knikkeren

turf war [inform] **1** bendeoorlog **2** concurrentiestrijd

turgid 1 [med] (op)gezwollen **2** hoogdravend

Turk Turk(se)

turkey 1 kalkoen **2** [Am] flop ‖ *talk* ~ geen blad voor de mond nemen

Turkey Turkije

Turkish Turks ‖ ~ *bath* Turks bad; ~ *delight* Turks fruit; ~ *towel* ruwe badhanddoek

¹Turkmen (n) Turkmeen(se)

²Turkmen (adj) Turkmeens

Turkmenistan Turkmenistan

turmoil beroering: *the whole country was in (a)* ~ het gehele land was in opschudding

¹turn (n) **1** draai, slag, omwenteling; [fig] ommekeer; kentering [of season]; wisseling: *a few* ~s *of the screwdriver will do* een paar slagen met de schroevendraaier is genoeg; ~ *of the tide* getijwisseling, kentering; ~ *of the century* eeuwwisseling **2** bocht, draai, kromming, afslag: *the next right* ~ de volgende afslag rechts **3** wending, draai, (verandering van) richting: *take a* ~ *for the worse* een ongunstige wending nemen **4** beurt: *take* ~s *at sth.* iets om beurten doen, elkaar aflossen met iets; ~ *and* ~ *about* om en om, om de beurt; *by* ~s om en om, om de beurt; *in* ~ om de beurt, achtereenvolgens, op zijn beurt; *take it in* ~(s) *to do sth.* iets om beurten doen; *out of* ~ **a)** vóór zijn beurt, niet op zijn beurt; **b)** op een ongeschikt moment **5** dienst, daad: *do s.o. a bad* (or: *ill*) ~ iem. een slechte dienst bewijzen **6** aanleg, neiging: *be of a musical* ~ *(of mind)* muzikaal aangelegd zijn **7** korte bezigheid, wandelingetjeʰ, ommetjeʰ, ritjeʰ, tochtjeʰ; nummer(tje)ʰ [in circus, show]; artiest [in show] **8** korte tijd [of participation, work]; poos: *take a* ~ *at the wheel* het stuur een tijdje overnemen **9** slag; winding [in rope etc] **10** schok, draai, schrik: *she gave him quite a* ~ zij joeg hem flink de stuipen op het lijf **11** aanval; vlaag [of rage, illness] ‖ ~ *of phrase* formulering; *at every* ~ bij elke stap, overal

²turn (vb) **1** woelen, draaien: *toss and* ~ *all night* de hele nacht (liggen) draaien en woelen **2** zich richten, zich wenden: *his thoughts* ~ed *to his mother* hij dacht aan zijn moeder; ~ *away (from)* zich afwenden (van), weggaan (van); ~ *to drink* aan de drank raken **3** van richting veranderen, afslaan, een draai maken, (zich) omkeren: *the aeroplane* ~ed *sharply* het vliegtuig maakte een scherpe bocht; ~ *about* zich omkeren; *about* ~! rechtsom(keert)! [order to troops]; ~

(a)round a) zich omdraaien; b) een omme-keer maken, van gedachten (*or:* mening) veranderen; ~ *back* terugkeren, omkeren 4 draaien [of head, stomach]; tollen, duize-len: *my head* is ~*ing* het duizelt mij 5 gisten, bederven || ~ *to* aan het werk gaan; ~ *into* veranderen in, worden; ~ *on* a) draaien om, afhangen van; b) gaan over [of conversa-tion]; *water* ~*s to ice* water wordt ijs; ~ *(up)on s.o.* iem. aanvallen, zich tegen iem. keren

³**turn** (vb) 1 (rond)draaien, doen draaien: *the wheels* ~ *fast* de wielen draaien snel 2 om-draaien, (doen) omkeren, omploegen, om-spitten, omslaan; keren [collar]; omvouwen: *the car* ~*ed* de auto keerde; ~ *about* omke-ren, omdraaien; ~ *(a)round* ronddraaien, omkeren; ~ *back* omvouwen, omslaan; ~ *sth. inside out* iets binnenstebuiten keren; [fig] grondig doorzoeken, overhoophalen; ~ *up-side down* ondersteboven keren; ~ *to page seven* sla bladzijde zeven op 3 draaien [on lathe, at pottery etc]; vormen, maken: ~ *a phrase* iets mooi zeggen 4 verzuren, zuur worden (maken): *the warm weather* ~*ed the milk* door het warme weer verzuurde de melk 5 maken, draaien; beschrijven [circle etc] 6 overdenken, overwegen 7 omgaan [corner]; omdraaien; omzeilen [cape]; om-trekken 8 (doen) veranderen (van), omzet-ten, verzetten, (ver)maken; een wending ge-ven aan [conversation]; bocht laten maken, draaien, afwenden, omleiden: ~ *the car into the garage* de auto de garage indraaien; ~ *into* veranderen in, (ver)maken tot, omzet-ten in; ~ *the conversation to sth. different* het gesprek op iets anders brengen 9 richten, wenden: ~ *your attention to the subject* richt je aandacht op het onderwerp 10 doen worden, maken: *the sun* ~*ed the papers yellow* de zon maakte de kranten geel; [Am] ~ *loose* loslaten, vrijlaten 11 verdraaien; verzwikken [ankle etc] 12 misselijk maken: *Chinese food* ~*s my stomach* Chinees eten maakt mijn maag van streek 13 worden [time, age]; passeren, geweest zijn: *it is* (or: *has*) ~*ed six o'clock* het is zes uur geweest 14 (weg)stu-ren, (weg)zenden: ~ *s.o. adrift* iem. aan zijn lot overlaten; ~ *away* wegsturen, wegjagen, ontslaan; [fig] verwerpen, afwijzen; *we were* ~*ed back at the entrance* bij de ingang werden we teruggestuurd 15 zetten, doen, brengen, laten gaan: ~ *s.o. into the street* iem. op straat zetten 16 omzetten, draaien, een om-zet hebben van; maken [profit]

⁴**turn** (vb) worden: ~ *traitor* verrader wor-den; *the milk* ~*ed sour* de melk werd zuur

turnabout ommekeer

turncoat overloper, afvallige, deserteur

¹**turn down** (vb) achteruitgaan, een recessie doormaken: *our economy* is *turning down* onze economie gaat achteruit

²**turn down** (vb) 1 omvouwen, omslaan: ~ *the sheets* de lakens omslaan 2 (om)keren; omdraaien [card] 3 afwijzen [plan, person]; verwerpen: *they turned your suggestion down* ze wezen je voorstel van de hand 4 lager zetten [gas, light]; zachter zetten [radio, vol-ume]

turner 1 draaier [lathe operator] 2 [Am] spatel, (bak)spaan

¹**turn in** (vb) 1 binnengaan, indraaien 2 naar binnen staan: *his feet* ~ zijn voeten staan naar binnen 3 onder de wol kruipen, erin duiken

²**turn in** (vb) 1 naar binnen vouwen, naar binnen omslaan 2 overleveren; uitleveren [to police] 3 inleveren, geven

turning afsplitsing, aftakking, zijstraat, af-slag, bocht: *the next* ~ *on* (or: *to*) *the right* de volgende straat rechts

turning circle draaicirkel

turning point keerpuntʰ [also fig]: ~ *in* (or: *of*) *s.o.'s life* keerpunt in iemands leven

turnip raap; knol [fodder]

¹**turn off** (vb) 1 afslaan 2 [inform] interesse verliezen, afhaken

²**turn off** (vb) 1 afsluiten [gas, water]: ~ *the gas* draai het gas uit 2 uitzetten, afzetten; uitdoen [eg light] 3 weerzin opwekken bij, doen afknappen: *it really turns me off* ik word er niet goed van

turn-off 1 afslag 2 afknapper

¹**turn on** (vb) enthousiast raken

²**turn on** (vb) 1 aanzetten; aandoen [radio etc]; [fig] laten werken 2 opendraaien; openzetten [water, gas] 3 enthousiast ma-ken, opwinden

turn-on [inform] opwindend persoon, dingʰ

turnout 1 opkomst, publiekʰ, menigte 2 kleding 3 opruimbeurt: *your kitchen needs a good* ~ jouw keuken heeft een flinke schoonmaakbeurt nodig 4 productie

¹**turn out** (vb) 1 (op)komen, verschijnen 2 zich ontwikkelen, aflopen: *things will* ~ *all right* het zal goed aflopen 3 naar buiten staan [of feet etc] 4 [mil] aantreden [of watch]

²**turn out** (vb) 1 uitdoen; uitdraaien [light, stove etc] 2 eruit gooien, wegsturen 3 pro-duceren, afleveren 4 leegmaken, opruimen, een beurt geven: ~ *your handbag* je handtas omkeren 5 uitrusten, kleden 6 optrommelen, bijeenroepen

³**turn out** (vb) blijken (te zijn), uiteindelijk zijn: *the man turned out to be my neighbour* de man bleek mijn buurman te zijn

turnover 1 omzetsnelheid [of articles] 2 omzet 3 verloop³ [of staff] 4 (appel)flap

¹**turn over** (vb) 1 zich omkeren 2 kantelen, omvallen 3 aanslaan; starten [of (car) en-gine]

²**turn over** (vb) **1** omkeren, omdraaien, op zijn kop zetten **2** omslaan [page]; doorbladeren: *please* ~ zie ommezijde **3** starten [car etc] **4** overwegen: *turn sth. over in one's mind* iets (goed) overdenken **5** overgeven; uitleveren, overleveren [to police]

turnover rate omzetsnelheid

turnpike 1 [Am] tolweg **2** [hist] tolweg; tolhekʰ

turn signal [Am] richtingaanwijzer

turnstile tourniquetʰ, draaihekʰ

turntable 1 draaischijf [for locomotives] **2** draaischijf [of record player]; platenspeler

¹**turn up** (vb) **1** verschijnen, komen (opdagen), tevoorschijn komen, voor de dag komen: *your **brooch** has turned up* je broche is terecht **2** zich voordoen: *the **opportunity** will* ~ de gelegenheid doet zich wel voor **3** naar boven gedraaid zijn

²**turn up** (vb) **1** vinden **2** blootleggen, aan de oppervlakte brengen **3** naar boven draaien; opzetten [collar]; omslaan [sleeve, pipe]; omhoogslaan, om(hoog)vouwen; opslaan [eyes]: *turn one's **collar** up* zijn kraag opzetten **4** hoger draaien; harder zetten [radio]

turpentine terpentijn(olie)

turquoise turkoois⁺ʰ

turret 1 torentjeʰ **2** geschutkoepel

turtle 1 (zee)schildpad **2** [Am] zoetwaterschildpad

turtledove tortelduif

turtleneck 1 col **2** coltrui

tusk 1 slagtand **2** scherp uitsteeksel

¹**tussle** (n) vechtpartij, worsteling

²**tussle** (vb) (+ with) vechten (met), worstelen (met)

tutelage voogdijschapʰ

¹**tutor** (n) **1** privéleraar **2** studiebegeleider; [roughly] mentor **3** [Am] docent

²**tutor** (vb) **1** als privéleraar werken **2** [Am] college krijgen van een docent

³**tutor** (vb) (+ in) (privé)les geven (in)

tutorial 1 werkgroep **2** [Am; esp technology] handleiding; [online] tutorial, instructievideo; [DIY] instructiefilmpjeʰ

tuxedo [Am] smoking(kostuumʰ)

TV television tv

¹**twang** (n) **1** tjing; ploink [of string] **2** neusgeluidʰ: *speak **with** a* ~ door de neus praten

²**twang** (vb) **1** geplukt worden [of string] **2** snorren, zoeven [of arrow] **3** spelen [on instrument]; rammen; zagen [on violin]: *~ing **on** a guitar* jengelend op een gitaar

³**twang** (vb) **1** scherp laten weerklinken **2** nasaal uitspreken **3** bespelen, jengelen op, krassen op

¹**tweak** (n) **1** ruk [on ear, nose] **2** verbetering, optimalisatie [adjustments]

²**tweak** (vb) **1** beetpakken (en omdraaien), knijpen in; trekken aan [ear, nose] **2** optimaliseren, verbeteren [adjustments]

twee 1 fijntjes, popperig **2** zoetelijk

tweeds tweed kleding

tweener 1 [inform] tussencategorie **2** [tennis] bal die tussen de benen van de tegenstander door wordt gespeeld

tweep volger

tweeps [inform; media] twitteraars

¹**tweet** (n) **1** tjiep, tjilp; getjilpʰ [of bird] **2** [social networking] twitterbericht

²**tweet** (vb) tjilpen, tjirpen

³**tweet** (vb) [social networking] twitteren

tweeter tweeter; hogetonenluidspreker

tweezers pincet⁺ʰ: *a **pair** of* ~ een pincet

twelfth twaalfde

Twelfth Night driekoningenavond

twelve twaalf

twentieth twintigste

twenty twintig: *in the twenties* in de jaren twintig

twerk [inform] twerken

twice tweemaal, twee keer: *~ a **day*** tweemaal per dag; *~ as **good*** (or: *much*) dubbel zo goed (or: veel); *once or* ~ een keer of twee

¹**twiddle** (n) draai, krul, kronkel

²**twiddle** (vb) zitten te draaien (met/aan), spelen (met), friemelen (met): *~ one's **thumbs*** duimendraaien, luilakken, niksen

¹**twig** (n) twijg, takjeʰ

²**twig** (vb) snappen, begrijpen

twilight 1 schemering [also fig]; vage voorstelling **2** schemerlichtʰ

¹**twin** (n) **1** (een van een) tweeling **2** bijbehorende, tegenhanger **3** (-s) tweeling

²**twin** (adj) tweeling-: *~ **beds*** lits-jumeauxʰ; *~ **towers*** twee identieke torens naast elkaar

¹**twine** (n) streng, vlecht

²**twine** (vb) **1** wikkelen, winden, vlechten: *she ~d her arms **(a)round** my neck* zij sloeg haar armen om mijn nek **2** omwikkelen

³**twine** (vb) zich wikkelen, zich winden: *the vines ~d (themselves) **round** the tree* de ranken slingerden zich om de boom

twin-engined tweemotorig

twinge 1 scheut, steek **2** [fig] knaging [of conscience]; kwelling: *~s of **conscience*** gewetenswroeging

¹**twinkle** (n) **1** schittering, fonkeling: *a **mischievous** ~* een ondeugende flikkering **2** knipoog **3** trilling ‖ *in a ~* in een oogwenk

²**twinkle** (vb) **1** schitteren; fonkelen [of star]: *his eyes ~d **with** amusement* zijn ogen schitterden van plezier **2** trillen

³**twinkle** (vb) knipperen met [eyes] **twinkling**: *in the ~ of an **eye*** in een ogenblik (or: mum van tijd)

twins tweeling

¹**twirl** (n) **1** draai, pirouette **2** krul

²**twirl** (vb) snel (doen) draaien, (doen) tollen, (doen) krullen: *~ one's hair **around** one's fingers* zijn haar rond zijn vingers krullen

¹**twist** (n) **1** draai, draaibeweging, bocht,

kromming; [fig] wending: *a road full of ~s and turns* een weg vol draaien en bochten; *give the truth a ~* de waarheid een beetje verdraaien **2** verdraaiing; vertrekking [of face] **3** afwijking; [of character] trek
²twist (vb) **1** draaien, zich wentelen: *the corners of his mouth ~ed down* zijn mondhoeken trokken naar beneden **2** kronkelen, zich winden **3** zich wringen
³twist (vb) **1** samendraaien, samenstrengelen; [tobacco] spinnen: *~ flowers into a garland* bloemen tot een krans samenvlechten **2** vlechten [eg rope] **3** winden, draaien om: *~ the lid off a jar* het deksel van een jampot afdraaien **4** verdraaien, verwringen; vertrekken [face]; verrekken [muscle]; verstuiken [foot]; omdraaien [arm] **5** [fig] verdraaien [story, words etc]: *a ~ed mind* een verwrongen geest **6** wringen, afwringen, uitwringen
twister 1 bedrieger **2** [Am] wervelwind
¹twit (n) sufferd, domkop
²twit (vb) **1** bespotten **2** verwijten: *~ s.o. about* (or: on) *his clumsiness* iem. (een beetje spottend) zijn onhandigheid verwijten
¹twitch (n) **1** trek, kramp **2** ruk
²twitch (vb) **1** trekken, trillen: *a ~ing muscle* een trillende spier **2** (+ at) rukken (aan)
³twitch (vb) **1** vertrekken: [fig] *he didn't ~ an eyelid* hij vertrok geen spier **2** trekken aan
¹twitter (n) getjilp[h], gekwetter[h] ‖ *all of a ~* opgewonden
²twitter (vb) **1** tjilpen, kwetteren **2** [media] twitteren
twitterer twitteraar
two twee, tweetal: *~ years old* twee jaar oud; *~ or three* een paar, een stuk of wat; *~ by ~* twee aan twee; *arranged in ~s* per twee gerangschikt; *cut in ~* in tweeën gesneden; *an apple or ~* een paar appelen ‖ *in ~ twos* in een paar tellen
two-bit [Am] klein, waardeloos
two-dimensional tweedimensionaal
two-earner tweeverdiener(s)-: *~ couple* tweeverdieners
two-edged [also fig] tweesnijdend
two-faced met twee gezichten; [fig] onoprecht
twofold tweevoudig
two-handed 1 voor twee handen: *~ sword* tweehandig zwaard **2** voor twee personen: *~ saw* trekzaag
two-income family tweeverdienersgezin[h]
twopence (Brits muntstuk[h] van) twee pence ‖ *I don't care ~* ik geef er geen zier om
twopenny twee pence kostend (waard)
¹two-piece (n) **1** deux-pièces[+h] **2** bikini
²two-piece (adj) tweedelig
twosome 1 tweetal[h] **2** spel[h] voor twee
two-stroke tweetakt-

¹two-time (vb) dubbel spel spelen
²two-time (vb) bedriegen, ontrouw zijn
two-way 1 tweerichtings-: *~ traffic* tweerichtingsverkeer[h] **2** wederzijds
tycoon magnaat
¹type (n) **1** type[h], soort[+h], model[h] **2** zetsel[h]: *in ~ gezet*; *in italic ~* in cursief (schrift) **3** drukletter, type[h]
²type (vb) typen, tikken: *~ out* uittikken
typecast steeds eenzelfde soort rol geven [actor]: *be ~ as a villain* altijd maar weer de schurk spelen
typecasting 1 [film] typecasting **2** [fig] (het) in een hokje plaatsen
typeface font[h], lettertype[h]
typescript getypte kopij
typewriter schrijfmachine
typhoid tyfus
typhoon tyfoon
typhus vlektyfus
typical typisch, typerend, kenmerkend: *be ~ of* karakteriseren, kenmerkend zijn voor
typify 1 typeren, karakteriseren **2** symboliseren
typography typografie
tyrannical tiranniek
¹tyrannize (vb) (+ over) als een tiran regeren (over); [fig] de tiran spelen
²tyrannize (vb) tiranniseren
tyranny 1 tirannie **2** tirannieke daad
tyrant tiran
tyre band
tyre-gauge bandspanningsmeter

u

u u, U
U [inform; hum] typisch upper class
ubiquitous overal aanwezig, alomtegenwoordig
U-boat U-boot; onderzeeër
udder uier
UFO *unidentified flying object* ufo, vliegende schotel
Uganda Uganda
¹Ugandan (n) Ugandees, Ugandese
²Ugandan (adj) Ugandees
ugh bah
ugly 1 lelijk, afstotend: [fig] ~ *duckling* lelijk eendje; [inform] *(as)* ~ *as sin* (zo) lelijk als
de nacht **2** dreigend: *an* ~ *look* een dreigende blik **3** [inform] vervelend; lastig [of char-
acter]: *an* ~ *customer* een lastig mens
uh eh
UK *United Kingdom* UK, VK[h], Verenigd Koninkrijk[h]
Ukraine Oekraïne
¹Ukrainian (n) Oekraïner, Oekraïense
²Ukrainian (adj) Oekraïens
ulcer (open) zweer, maagzweer
ulterior verborgen: *an* ~ *motive* een bijbedoeling
¹ultimate (n) maximum[h]; [fig] toppunt[h];
einde[h]
²ultimate (adj) **1** ultiem, uiteindelijk, laatst
2 fundamenteel **3** uiterst, maximaal: *the* ~
chic het toppunt van chic
ultimately uiteindelijk
ultimatum ultimatum[h]
ultra extremistisch, radicaal
ultramarine ultramarijn[h], lazuur(blauw)[h]
ultramodern hypermodern
ultrasound scan echoscopie
ultraviolet ultraviolet[h]
Ulysses Odysseus
um hm, ahum
umbilical navel-: ~ *cord* navelstreng
umbrage ergernis: *give* ~ ergeren; *take* ~ *at*
(or: *over*) zich ergeren aan
¹umbrella (n) **1** paraplu; [fig] bescherming;
overkoepelende organisatie: *under the* ~ *of*
the EU onder de bescherming van de EU
2 (tuin)parasol, zonnescherm[h]
²umbrella (adj) algemeen, verzamel-: ~
term overkoepelende term
¹umpire (n) scheidsrechter, umpire
²umpire (vb) als scheidsrechter optreden (in)
umpteen [inform] een hoop, heel wat, tig
umpteenth [inform] zoveelste, tigste: *he*

checked his watch for the ~ *time* hij keek voor
de zoveelste keer op zijn horloge
UN *United Nations* VN, Verenigde Naties
unabated onverminderd
unable niet in staat: *he was* ~ *to come* hij
was verhinderd
unabridged onverkort, niet ingekort
unacceptable onaanvaardbaar
unaccompanied 1 onvergezeld **2** [mus]
zonder begeleiding
unaccountable onverklaarbaar
unaccustomed 1 ongewoon, ongebruike-
lijk **2** niet gewend: *he is* ~ *to writing letters* hij
is niet gewend brieven te schrijven
unaffected 1 ongedwongen, natuurlijk
2 onaangetast; [fig] niet beïnvloed; ongewijzigd
unafraid niet bang
unaided zonder hulp
unalloyed onvermengd [also fig]; zuiver: ~
metal niet gelegeerd metaal
unambiguous ondubbelzinnig
unanimity 1 eenstemmigheid, unanimi-
teit **2** eensgezindheid
unanimous 1 eenstemmig, unaniem
2 eensgezind
unannounced onaangekondigd
unanswerable 1 onweerlegbaar **2** niet te
beantwoorden
unanswered onbeantwoord
unapproachable ontoegankelijk, onbe-
naderbaar
unarmed ongewapend
unashamed 1 zich niet schamend **2** onbeschaamd
unasked ongevraagd
unassuming pretentieloos; bescheiden
unattached 1 los, niet gebonden, onafhankelijk **2** alleenstaand, ongetrouwd
unattended 1 niet begeleid **2** onbeheerd:
leave sth. ~ iets onbeheerd laten (staan)
unauthorized 1 onbevoegd **2** ongeoorloofd **3** niet geautoriseerd, onofficieel: *an* ~
biography een onofficiële biografie
unavailable niet beschikbaar
unavailing vergeefs, nutteloos
unavoidable onvermijdelijk
unaware (+ of) zich niet bewust (van): *be* ~
that niet weten dat
unawares 1 onverwacht(s): *catch* (or: *take*)
s.o. ~ iem. verrassen (*or*: overrompelen)
2 onbewust
unbalance uit zijn evenwicht brengen, in
verwarring brengen
unbalanced 1 niet in evenwicht, onevenwichtig **2** in de war
unbar ontgrendelen; [fig] openstellen; vrij
maken
unbearable 1 ondraaglijk **2** onuitstaanbaar
unbeaten 1 niet verslagen; ongeslagen

[sport] **2** onovertroffen; ongebroken [record]

unbecoming 1 niet (goed) staand **2** ongepast, onbehoorlijk: *your conduct is ~ for* (or: *to*) *a gentleman!* zo gedraagt een heer zich niet!

unbelief ongeloofⁿ, ongelovigheid
unbelievable ongelofelijk
unbeliever ongelovige
unbending onbuigzaam, onverzettelijk
unbias(s)ed 1 onbevooroordeeld **2** zuiver, niet vertekend
unbind 1 losmaken **2** bevrijden
unblushing 1 schaamteloos **2** niet blozend
unborn 1 (nog) ongeboren **2** toekomstig
unbosom uiten: *~ o.s. (to)* zijn hart uitstorten (bij)
unbowed 1 ongebogen **2** ongebroken [fig]; niet onderworpen
unbridled ongebreideld: *~ tongue* losse tong
unbroken 1 ongebroken, heel **2** ongedresseerd **3** onononderbroken **4** onovertroffen; ongebroken [record]
unbuckle losgespen
unburden 1 ontlasten, van een last bevrijden: *~ one's conscience* zijn geweten ontlasten; *~ o.s.* (or: *one's heart*) *to s.o.* zijn hart uitstorten bij iem. **2** zich bevrijden van, opbiechten
uncalled-for 1 ongewenst, ongepast **2** onnodig: *that remark was ~* die opmerking was nergens voor nodig **3** ongegrond
uncanny geheimzinnig, griezelig
uncaring onverschillig, ongevoelig
unceasing onophoudelijk
unceremonious 1 informeel, ongedwongen **2** niet erg beleefd
uncertain 1 onzeker: *in no ~ terms* in niet mis te verstane bewoordingen; *be ~ of* (or: *about*) *s.o.'s intentions* twijfelen aan iemands bedoelingen **2** onbepaald, vaag **3** veranderlijk: *a woman with an ~ temper* een wispelturige vrouw
uncertainty 1 onzekerheid, twijfel(achtigheid) **2** onduidelijkheid, vaagheid **3** veranderlijkheid, onbetrouwbaarheid
unchallenged onbetwist, zonder tegenspraak: *we cannot let this pass ~* we kunnen dit niet zomaar laten passeren
unchanging niet veranderend; standvastig
uncharitable harteloos, liefdeloos: *an ~ judg(e)ment* een hard oordeel
unchecked 1 ongehinderd **2** ongecontroleerd
uncivil onbeleefd
uncivilized onbeschaafd
unclaimed 1 niet opgeëist **2** niet afgehaald [letter, luggage]
unclassified 1 ongeordend, niet inge-

deeld **2** niet geheim (vertrouwelijk)
uncle oom: [inform] *everyone and their ~* jan en alleman, alles en iedereen
unclean 1 vuil; bevuild [fig]; bevlekt **2** onkuis **3** [rel] onrein: *~ meat* onrein vlees
unclear onduidelijk
Uncle Sam [inform] Uncle Sam, de Amerikaanse regering, het Amerikaanse volk
uncoil (zich) ontrollen
uncoloured ongekleurd [also fig]; objectief
uncomfortable 1 ongemakkelijk, oncomfortabel: *~ situation* pijnlijke situatie **2** niet op zijn gemak, verlegen
uncommitted 1 niet-gebonden, neutraal: *he wants to remain ~* hij wil zich niet vastleggen **2** zonder verplichting(en)
uncommon ongewoon, buitengewoon: *~ly rude* hoogst onbeleefd
uncompromising 1 onbuigzaam, niet toegeeflijk **2** vastberaden
unconcerned 1 onbezorgd **2** onverschillig
unconditional onvoorwaardelijk
¹unconscious (n) het onbewuste, het onderbewuste
²unconscious (adj) **1** onbewust, niet wetend: *be ~ of sth.* zich ergens niet bewust van zijn **2** bewusteloos
uncontested onbetwist: *~ election* verkiezing zonder tegenkandidaten
uncontrollable 1 niet te beheersen, onbedwingbaar **2** onbeheerst: *~ laughter* onbedaarlijk gelach
unconventional 1 onconventioneel, ongebruikelijk **2** natuurlijk **3** niet-conventioneel, nucleair, atoom-
unconvincing niet overtuigend
uncool [inform] niet cool; stom
uncork ontkurken
uncouple ontkoppelen, afkoppelen, loskoppelen
uncouth ongemanierd, grof
¹uncover (vb) zijn hoofddeksel afnemen
²uncover (vb) **1** het (hoofd)deksel afnemen van, opgraven **2** aan het licht brengen, ontdekken
uncritical 1 onkritisch **2** kritiekloos
unction zalving
unctuous zalvend, vleierig
uncut 1 ongesneden, ongemaaid **2** onverkort; ongecensureerd [book, film] **3** ongeslepen [diamond]
undaunted onverschrokken: *~ by* niet ontmoedigd door
undecided 1 onbeslist: *the match was left ~* de wedstrijd eindigde onbeslist **2** weifelend, besluiteloos: *be ~ about* in tweestrijd staan over
undeniable onbetwistbaar: *that is undeniably true* dat is ontegenzeglijk waar
¹under (adv) **1** onder, eronder, hieronder,

daaronder, (naar) beneden, omlaag: *groups of **nine** and ~* groepen van negen en minder **2** in bedwang, onder controle **3** bewusteloos: *the drug **put** her ~ for the day* door het verdovingsmiddel raakte zij de hele dag buiten bewustzijn

²**under** (prep) **1** [place] onder; [fig] onder het gezag van; onder toezicht van: *~ the **cliffs*** aan de voet van de klippen; *he wrote ~ another **name*** hij schreef onder een andere naam; *a place ~ the **sun*** een plekje onder de zon **2** [circumstance] onder, in, in een toestand van, krachtens, tijdens: *~ **construction*** in aanbouw; *the issue ~ **discussion*** het probleem dat ter discussie staat; *collapse ~ the **strain*** het onder de spanning begeven **3** minder dan: *~ **age*** minderjarig; *just ~ a **minute*** net iets minder dan een minuut, net binnen de minuut; *children ~ **six*** kinderen beneden de zes jaar

underachiever onderpresteerder [esp at school]

underage minderjarig: *~ **drinking*** het drinken door jongeren onder de wettelijke leeftijd

¹**underarm** (n) [euph] oksel

²**underarm** (adj, adv) onderhands [esp sport]

undercarriage 1 onderstelʰ [of wagon]; chassisʰ **2** landingsgestelʰ

underclothes ondergoedʰ

undercoat grond(verf)laag

undercover geheim: *~ **man*** spion; stille, detective

undercurrent onderstroom [also fig]; verborgen gedachten, gevoelens

undercut 1 ondergraven, ondermijnen: *~ s.o.'s **authority*** iemands gezag ondermijnen **2** voor een lager loon werken dan; onderbieden **3** [sport] tegeneffect geven

underdeveloped onderontwikkeld [also econ, photo]; (nog) onvoldoende ontwikkeld

underdog underdog, (verwachte) verliezer

underdone niet (helemaal) gaar

underestimate onderschatten, te laag schatten

underexpose onderbelichten

underexposure onderbelichting

underfloor onder de vloer: *~ **heating*** vloerverwarming

underfoot 1 onder de voet(en), op de grond; [fig] onderdrukt: *crush* (or: *trample*) *sth. ~* iets vertrappen **2** in de weg, voor de voeten

undergo ondergaan, doorstaan

undergraduate [inform] student(e) [who does not have a degree yet]; bachelorstudent

¹**underground** (n) metro, ondergrondse: *by ~* met de ondergrondse

²**underground** (adj) ondergronds, (zich) onder de grond (bevindend); [fig] clandestien

³**underground** (adv) ondergronds, onder de grond; [fig] clandestien: *go ~* onderduiken, ondergronds gaan werken

undergrowth kreupelhoutʰ

underhand 1 onderhands, clandestien **2** achterbaks

underhanded 1 onderhands **2** achterbaks

underlie 1 liggen onder, zich bevinden onder **2** ten grondslag liggen aan, verklaren: *underlying **principles*** grondprincipes **3** schuil gaan achter: *underlying **meaning*** werkelijke betekenis

underline onderstrepen [also fig]; benadrukken

undermanned onderbezet

undermine ondermijnen; ondergraven [also fig]; verzwakken

¹**underneath** (n) onderkant

²**underneath** (adv) [place; also fig] onderaan, eronder, aan de onderkant: *what's **written** ~?* wat staat er aan de onderkant geschreven?

³**underneath** (prep) [place] beneden, (vlak) onder: *~ his **coat*** he wore a suit onder zijn jas droeg hij een pak

underpants onderbroek

underpass tunnel(tjeʰ): *take the ~!* ga door het tunneltje!

underperform onderpresteren; achterblijven bij de verwachtingen

underpopulated onderbevolkt

underprivileged (kans)arm, sociaal zwak

underrate 1 te laag schatten [costs] **2** onderschatten, onderwaarderen

underscore onderstrepen [also fig]; benadrukken

undersea onderzees, onderzee-, onderwater-

under-secretary 1 ondersecretaris, tweede secretaris **2** staatssecretaris: *permanent ~* [roughly] secretaris-generaal [of ministry]

underside onderkant, onderzijde

undersigned ondertekend (hebbend): *I, the ~* ik, ondergetekende

undersized te klein, onder de normale grootte

understaffed onderbezet

understand 1 begrijpen, inzien, verstand hebben van, (goed) op de hoogte zijn: *give s.o. to ~ that* iem. te verstaan geven dat; *~ each other* (or: *one another*) elkaar begrijpen, op één lijn zitten; *I simply don't ~* ik snap het gewoon niet; *~ about* verstand hebben van **2** begrijpen, (er) begrip hebben voor: *he begged her to ~* hij smeekte haar begrip voor de situatie te hebben **3** begrijpen, (er)uit opmaken, vernemen: *I understood that you knew him* ik had begrepen dat je hem kende

4 verstaan [language] **5** opvatten: *as I ~ it* zoals ik het zie **6** als vanzelfsprekend aannemen: *that is understood!* (dat spreekt) vanzelf!

understandable begrijpelijk

understandably 1 begrijpelijk **2** begrijpelijkerwijs: ~, *we were all annoyed* begrijpelijkerwijs waren we allemaal geïrriteerd

1understanding (n) **1** afspraak, overeenkomst: *come to* (or: *reach*) *an ~* het eens worden; *on the ~ that* met dien verstande dat **2** (onderling) begrip[h], verstandhouding **3** verstand[h], intelligentie, begrip[h] **4** interpretatie, beoordeling, opvatting: *a wrong ~ of the situation* een verkeerde beoordeling van de situatie

2understanding (adj) begripvol, welwillend

understate 1 (te) zwak uitdrukken **2** te laag opgeven [eg age, income]

understatement understatement[h]: *that's an ~* dat is zwak uitgedrukt

understudy understudy, invaller

undertake 1 ondernemen **2** op zich nemen, beloven, zich verplichten tot **3** garanderen, instaan voor

undertaker begrafenisondernemer

1undertaking (n) het verzorgen van begrafenissen

2undertaking (n) **1** onderneming: *translating the Bible is quite an ~* het is een hele onderneming om de Bijbel te vertalen **2** (plechtige) belofte, garantie

under-the-counter onder de toonbank; clandestien

undertone 1 gedempte toon: *speak in ~s* (or: *an ~*) met gedempte stem spreken **2** ondertoon [fig] **3** lichte tint, zweem: *red with a slight ~ of yellow* rood met een klein beetje geel erin

undervalue onderwaarderen

underwater onder water

underwear ondergoed[h]

underworld onderwereld

underwrite 1 ondertekenen [policy]; afsluiten [insurance]; (door ondertekening) op zich nemen [risk, liability] **2** verzekeren [shipp]; zich garant stellen voor **3** onderschrijven, goedvinden

undeserved onverdiend; onterecht

1undesirable (n) ongewenst persoon; persona non grata

2undesirable (adj) ongewenst; onwenselijk: *~ discharge* oneervol ontslag

undeterred niet ontmoedigd

undies [inform] (dames)ondergoed[h]

undisputed onbetwist

undistinguished niet bijzonder, alledaags, gewoon

undisturbed ongestoord

undivided onverdeeld

1undo (vb) losgaan

2undo (vb) **1** losmaken, losknopen **2** uitkleden **3** tenietdoen, ongedaan maken: *this mistake can never be ~ne* deze fout kan nooit goedgemaakt worden

undoing ondergang

undomesticated 1 ongetemd, wild **2** niet huishoudelijk (aangelegd)

undone 1 ongedaan, onafgemaakt **2** los(gegaan): *come ~* losgaan, losraken

undoubted ongetwijfeld

undreamed onvoorstelbaar: *~ of* onvoorstelbaar

undress (zich) uitkleden

undue 1 overmatig: *exercise ~ influence upon s.o.* te grote invloed op iem. uitoefenen **2** onbehoorlijk

unduly 1 uitermate, overmatig **2** onbehoorlijk **3** onrechtmatig

undying onsterfelijk, eeuwig

unearth 1 opgraven; [fig] opdiepen **2** onthullen

unearthly 1 bovenaards **2** bovennatuurlijk, mysterieus **3** angstaanjagend, eng **4** [inform] onmogelijk [time]: *wake s.o. up at an ~ hour* iem. op een belachelijk vroeg uur wakker maken

uneasy 1 onbehaaglijk: *~ conscience* bezwaard geweten; *be ~ with* zich niet op zijn gemak voelen met **2** bezorgd: *be ~ about, grow ~ at* zich zorgen maken over **3** onrustig [eg during sleep] **4** verontrustend

uneconomic(al) 1 oneconomisch, onrendabel **2** verkwistend

uneducated ongeschoold, onontwikkeld

unemployed 1 ongebruikt **2** werkloos, zonder werk

unemployment werkloosheid: *~ benefit* werkloosheidsuitkering

unemployment benefit werkloosheidsuitkering

unending 1 oneindig, eindeloos **2** onophoudelijk

unenviable niet benijdenswaard(ig); onplezierig [task]

unequal ongelijk(waardig): *~ in size* ongelijk in grootte

unequivocal ondubbelzinnig; duidelijk

unerring onfeilbaar: *~ devotion* niet aflatende toewijding

UNESCO *United Nations Educational, Scientific, and Cultural Organization* Unesco

unethical onethisch

uneven 1 ongelijk; oneffen [eg surface]; onregelmatig **2** van ongelijke kwaliteit

uneventful onbewogen, rustig, saai: *~ day* dag zonder belangrijke gebeurtenissen

unexceptional niet ongewoon; gewoon

unexpected onverwacht

unfailing onuitputtelijk, onophoudelijk

unfair oneerlijk, onrechtvaardig: *~ compe-*

tition oneerlijke concurrentie
unfaithful ontrouw, overspelig
unfaltering 1 zonder te aarzelen **2** onwankelbaar; standvastig: ~ *love* onwankelbare liefde
unfamiliar 1 onbekend, niet vertrouwd **2** ongewoon, vreemd
unfashionable niet modieus
¹unfasten (vb) losgaan
²unfasten (vb) losmaken, losknopen
unfavourable ongunstig
unfeeling gevoelloos [also fig]; hardvochtig
unfettered ontketend [also fig]; vrij
unfinished 1 onaf, onvoltooid: ~ *business* onafgedane kwestie(s) **2** onbewerkt [eg of wood]
unfit 1 ongeschikt **2** in slechte conditie
unflinching 1 onbevreesd **2** vastberaden
unfold 1 (zich) openvouwen **2** (zich) uitspreiden **3** (zich) openbaren, (zich) ontvouwen
unforeseeable onvoorspelbaar
unforgettable onvergetelijk
unforgivable onvergeeflijk
unforgiving 1 onverzoenlijk **2** keihard: *business is* ~ het zakenleven is meedogenloos
unfortunate ongelukkig, betreurenswaardig
unfounded ongegrond
unfriend ontvrienden
unfriendly onvriendelijk, vijandig: ~ *area* onherbergzaam gebied; ~ *reception* koele ontvangst
unfulfilled onvervuld
unfurl (zich) ontrollen; (zich) ontvouwen [eg of flag]
ungainly lomp
unget-at-able [inform] onbereikbaar
ungodly 1 goddeloos **2** [inform] afgrijselijk
ungracious 1 onhoffelijk; lomp **2** onaangenaam: ~ *task* ondankbare taak
ungrateful ondankbaar
unguarded 1 onbewaakt: *in an* ~ *moment* op een onbewaakt ogenblik **2** onbedachtzaam **3** achteloos
unguent zalf
unhappy 1 ongelukkig, bedroefd **2** ongepast
unharmed ongedeerd, onbeschadigd
unhealthy ongezond [also fig]; ziekelijk
unheard niet gehoord, ongehoord: *his advice went* ~ naar zijn raad werd niet geluisterd
unheard-of ongekend, buitengewoon
unheeded genegeerd, in de wind geslagen: *his remark went* ~ er werd geen acht geslagen op zijn opmerking
unhinge 1 uit de scharnieren tillen [door]

2 [inform] uit zijn evenwicht brengen: *his mind is* ~d hij is geestelijk uit evenwicht
unholy 1 goddeloos **2** [inform] verschrikkelijk: [inform] *at an* ~ *hour* op een onchristelijk tijdstip; ~ *noise* heidens lawaai
unhook loshaken
unhurt ongedeerd
unibrow doorlopende wenkbrauw
unicorn eenhoorn
unidentified niet geïdentificeerd: ~ *flying object* vliegende schotel
unification eenmaking, unificatie
¹uniform (n) uniformʰ
²uniform (adj) uniform, eensluidend
uniformity 1 uniformiteit **2** gelijkmatigheid
unify (zich) verenigen, tot één maken
unilateral eenzijdig, van één kant
unimaginable onvoorstelbaar
unimpeachable 1 onbetwistbaar **2** onberispelijk
unimportant onbelangrijk
unimpressed niet onder de indruk
unimpressive weinig indrukwekkend; saai
unintentional onbedoeld, onopzettelijk
uninterested 1 ongeïnteresseerd **2** zonder belangen
uninteresting oninteressant
uninterrupted ononderbroken, doorlopend
union 1 verbondʰ, unie **2** (vak)bond, vakvereniging **3** studentenvereniging **4** huwelijkʰ **5** verbinding, koppelstukʰ
unionist vakbondslidʰ
Union Jack Britse vlag
union leader vakbondsleider
unique uniek; [inform] opmerkelijk
unisex uniseks-
unison 1 koorʰ, het tegelijk spreken: *speak in* ~ in koor spreken **2** harmonie: *work in* ~ eendrachtig samenwerken
unit 1 eenheid, onderdeelʰ, afdeling, meetgrootheid; [techn] apparaatʰ; module: ~ *of account* rekeneenheid **2** combineerbaar onderdeelʰ [of furniture]; unit, blokʰ
unitary eenheids-: ~ *state* eenheidsstaat
¹unite (vb) **1** zich verenigen, samenwerken, fuseren: *they* ~d *in fighting the enemy* samen bestreden zij de vijand **2** zich verbinden, aaneengroeien **3** zich mengen
²unite (vb) **1** verbinden, verenigen, tot een geheel maken **2** in de echt verbinden
united 1 verenigd: *the United Kingdom* het Verenigd Koninkrijk; *the United Nations* de Verenigde Naties; *the United States* de Verenigde Staten **2** saamhorig, hecht, harmonieus **3** gezamenlijk: *with their* ~ *powers* met vereende krachten
United Arab Emirates (the) Verenigde Arabische Emiraten

United Kingdom (the) Verenigd Koninkrijk[h]
United States (the) Verenigde Staten
unity 1 geheel[h], eenheid, samenhang **2** samenwerking **3** harmonie: *at* (or: *in*) ~ eendrachtig, eensgezind
universal 1 universeel, algemeen: ~ *rule* algemeen geldende regel **2** algeheel, alomvattend: ~ *agreement* algemene instemming
universally overal: ~ *present* alomtegenwoordig
universe 1 heelal[h] **2** wereld; [also] gebied[h]
university universiteit, hogeschool
unjust onrechtvaardig
unjustifiable niet te verantwoorden
unkempt 1 ongekamd **2** onverzorgd
unkind 1 onaardig, onvriendelijk **2** ruw
unknown onbekend: ~ *quantity* onbekende grootheid; [fig] onzekere factor ‖ ~ *to us* buiten ons medeweten, zonder dat wij het wisten
unlawful onwettig, illegaal
unleaded loodvrij
unleash losmaken van de riem [dog]; [also fig] ontketenen: ~ *one's rage (up)on s.o.* zijn woede op iem. koelen
unless tenzij, behalve, zonder dat: *I won't go ~ you come with me* ik ga niet tenzij jij meekomt
unlicensed 1 zonder vergunning **2** zonder goedkeuring
¹**unlike** (adj, adv) **1** verschillend, niet gelijkend **2** ongelijkwaardig **3** [maths] tegengesteld
²**unlike** (prep) **1** anders dan, in tegenstelling tot **2** niet typisch voor: *that's ~ John* dat is niets voor John
unlikely 1 onwaarschijnlijk **2** weinig belovend, niet hoopgevend: *he is ~ to succeed* hij heeft weinig kans van slagen
unlimited onbeperkt, ongelimiteerd
unlisted 1 niet geregistreerd: ~ *number* geheim telefoonnummer **2** [fin] incourant
unload 1 lossen, uitladen, leegmaken **2** wegdoen, zich ontdoen van: ~ *responsibilities onto s.o.* de verantwoordelijkheid op iem. afschuiven **3** ontladen [firearm; also fig]; afreageren
unlock 1 openmaken, opendoen, van het slot doen: ~ *the truth* de waarheid onthullen **2** losmaken, bevrijden, de vrije loop laten
unlooked-for onverwacht
unloose(n) 1 losmaken, losknopen, vrijlaten: *old memories were unloose(ne)d* oude herinneringen kwamen boven **2** ontspannen
unlucky ongelukkig: *be ~* pech hebben
unmade onopgemaakt: ~ *bed* onopgemaakt bed
unmanageable 1 onhandelbaar **2** onhanteerbaar, niet te besturen

unmannerly ongemanierd, ruw, onbeschaafd
unmarked 1 ongemerkt; zonder merkteken **2** zonder cijfer; onbeoordeeld ‖ *a novel ~ by psychological insight* een roman die niet uitblinkt door psychologisch inzicht
unmarried ongetrouwd
unmask het masker afnemen, ontmaskeren, onthullen
unmentionable 1 taboe **2** niet (nader) te noemen **3** niet te beschrijven
unmindful zorgeloos, vergeetachtig: ~ *of* zonder acht te slaan op
unmistakable onmiskenbaar, ondubbelzinnig
unmitigated 1 onverminderd, onverzacht **2** absoluut, volkomen: ~ *disaster* regelrechte ramp
unnatural onnatuurlijk, abnormaal
unnecessary 1 onnodig, niet noodzakelijk **2** overbodig
unnerve 1 van zijn stuk brengen, ontmoedigen **2** nerveus maken
unnerving zenuwslopend; verontrustend
unnoticed onopgemerkt
UNO *United Nations Organisation* VN, Verenigde Naties
unobtrusive 1 onopvallend **2** discreet, voorzichtig
unoccupied 1 leeg, onbezet, vrij **2** niet bezig, werkeloos
unofficial onofficieel, officieus, niet bevestigd ‖ ~ *strike* wilde staking
unpack uitpakken: ~ *one's suitcase* (or: *clothes*) zijn koffer (or: kleren) uitpakken
unpaid onbetaald
unparalleled zonder weerga, ongeëvenaard
unpick lostornen: ~ *a seam* (or: *stitches*) een naad (or: steken) lostornen
unpleasant onaangenaam, onplezierig
unpleasantness 1 onaangenaam voorval[h] **2** wrijving, woorden, ruzie **3** onaangenaamheid
unplug de stekker uittrekken van: ~ *the phone* de telefoonstekker eruit trekken; [mus] an ~*ged set* een akoestische set
unplugged [mus] akoestisch
unpolished 1 ongepolijst [also style]; ongepeld [rice] **2** ruw; onbeschaafd [manners]
unpopular impopulair
unprecedented ongekend, nooit eerder voorgekomen
unpredictable onvoorspelbaar
unprepared 1 onvoorbereid, geïmproviseerd **2** onverwacht(s)
unprincipled gewetenloos
unprofessional 1 niet professioneel, onprofessioneel, niet beroeps, amateur- **2** amateuristisch
unproved niet bewezen

unprovided onvoorzien: *he left his family ~ for* hij liet zijn gezin onverzorgd achter; *the cabin was ~ with kitchen utensils* in de hut was geen keukengerei aanwezig

unprovoked niet uitgelokt, zonder aanleiding

unqualified 1 niet gekwalificeerd, onbevoegd **2** onvoorwaardelijk: *~ success* onverdeeld succes

unquestionable onbetwistbaar

unquestionably ongetwijfeld, zonder twijfel: *they are ~ the best team of the USA* dat ze het beste team van Amerika zijn, staat buiten kijf

unquestioned 1 niet ondervraagd **2** onbetwistbaar **3** onbetwist, niet tegengesproken

unquestioning onvoorwaardelijk

unquote een citaat beëindigen, aanhalingstekens sluiten: *he said (quote) 'Over my dead body' (unquote)* hij zei (aanhalingstekens openen) 'Over mijn lijk' (aanhalingstekens sluiten)

¹**unravel** (vb) rafelen, rafelig worden

²**unravel** (vb) ontrafelen [also fig]; uithalen; [fig also] uitzoeken; oplossen

unreal 1 onwerkelijk, denkbeeldig **2** onecht, onwaar, vals

unrealistic onrealistisch

unreasonable 1 redeloos, verstandeloos **2** onredelijk **3** buitensporig, overdreven

unreasoning redeloos, irrationeel, onnadenkend

unrecognized 1 niet herkend **2** niet erkend

unrelated 1 niet verwant **2** geen verband houdend met

unrelenting 1 onverminderd, voortdurend **2** meedogenloos, onverbiddelijk

unreliable onbetrouwbaar

unrelieved 1 eentonig, vlak, saai: *~ by* niet afgewisseld met **2** hevig, sterk, intens

unrequited onbeantwoord: *~ love* onbeantwoorde liefde

unreserved 1 onverdeeld, geheel, onvoorwaardelijk **2** openhartig, eerlijk

unresolved 1 onopgelost; onbeantwoord **2** besluiteloos

unrest onrust, beroering

unrewarding niet lonend, niet de moeite waard; [fig] ondankbaar

unrivalled ongeëvenaard

unroll (zich) uitrollen, (zich) ontrollen; [also fig] (zich) tonen; (zich) onthullen

unruffled kalm, onverstoord

unruly onhandelbaar, weerspannig

unsatisfactory onbevredigend

unsavoury 1 onsmakelijk, vies; [also fig] weerzinwekkend **2** smakeloos, flauw

unscathed ongedeerd, onbeschadigd: *return ~* heelhuids terugkeren

unscientific onwetenschappelijk

unscramble 1 ontcijferen, decoderen **2** ontwarren, uit elkaar halen

¹**unscrew** (vb) **1** losraken **2** losgeschroefd worden

²**unscrew** (vb) **1** losschroeven **2** losdraaien, eraf draaien: *can you ~ this bottle?* krijg jij deze fles open?

unscrupulous zonder scrupules, immoreel, gewetenloos

unseasonable abnormaal voor het seizoen: *an ~ summer* een slechte zomer

unseat 1 afwerpen, uit het zadel werpen, doen vallen, ten val brengen **2** zijn positie afnemen; [pol] zijn zetel doen verliezen

unsecured 1 onbeveiligd **2** [fin] ongedekt: *~ loan* ongedekte lening

unsee [inform] uit zijn geheugen wissen, van zijn netvlies halen: *once you've seen it, you can't ~ it* als je het eenmaal hebt gezien, kun je het niet meer uit je geheugen wissen

unseeing niet(s) ziend, wezenloos

unseemly 1 onbehoorlijk **2** onaantrekkelijk, lelijk

unseen 1 onzichtbaar **2** onvoorbereid: *questions on an ~ text* vragen over een niet bestudeerde tekst

¹**unsettle** (vb) **1** onvast worden; (aan het) wankelen (slaan) [fig]; op losse schroeven komen te staan, onzeker worden **2** van streek raken **3** wisselvallig worden [of weather]

²**unsettle** (vb) **1** doen loskomen, los maken **2** doen wankelen [fig]; op losse schroeven zetten: *unsettling changes* veranderingen die alles op losse schroeven zetten **3** van streek maken

unsettled 1 onzeker, verwar(ren)d: *~ times* onzekere tijden **2** wisselvallig; veranderlijk [weather] **3** onbeslist, (nog) niet uitgemaakt: *this issue is still ~* deze kwestie is nog niet afgedaan **4** in de war

unshrinkable krimpvrij

unsightly onooglijk

unskilled 1 ongeschoold **2** onervaren, onbedreven

unsociable 1 terughoudend, teruggetrokken **2** ongezellig

unsocial asociaal, onmaatschappelijk: *~ hours* ongebruikelijke werktijden

unsolicited ongevraagd

unsophisticated 1 onbedorven, echt, eerlijk **2** onervaren, naïef **3** ongedwongen, ongecompliceerd

unsound 1 ongezond, ziek(elijk): *of ~ mind* krankzinnig, ontoerekeningsvatbaar **2** ongaaf **3** onstevig, zwak **4** ondeugdelijk **5** ongegrond, ongeldig **6** onbetrouwbaar, vals

unsparing 1 kwistig, gul, vrijgevig: *~ of* kwistig met **2** meedogenloos, ongenadig

unspeakable 1 onuitsprekelijk, onuit-

spreekbaar, onbeschrijf(e)lijk **2** afschuwelijk
unspecified ongespecificeerd; niet nader
omschreven
unspoilt onaangetast
unspoken stilzwijgend; onuitgesproken
unsprayed onbespoten
unstable 1 veranderlijk, wisselvallig, onevenwichtig, wispelturig **2** onstabiel [also
science, chem]; labiel: ~ *equilibrium* wankel
evenwicht **3** onvast, los
unstamped ongefrankeerd
unsteady 1 onvast, wankel: *her voice was ~*
haar stem was onvast **2** veranderlijk, wisselvallig **3** onregelmatig
unstinted royaal, gul, kwistig
unstoppable onstuitbaar, niet te stoppen
unstuck los || [inform] *come (badly) ~* in het
honderd lopen, mislukken
unstudied 1 ongekunsteld, natuurlijk
2 ongestudeerd, ongeschoold
unsubscribe [comp] afmelden
unsubstantiated onbewezen; ongefundeerd
unsuccessful 1 niet succesvol, zonder succes **2** niet geslaagd, afgewezen: *be ~* niet
slagen, mislukken
unsuited ongepast: ~ *for* ongeschikt voor
unsure 1 onzeker, onvast **2** onbetrouwbaar, twijfelachtig
unsuspected 1 onverdacht **2** onverwacht;
onvermoed
unsuspecting 1 nietsvermoedend **2** niet
achterdochtig, argeloos
unsustainable 1 niet-duurzaam, verspillend **2** onhoudbaar: *that remark is ~* die bewering is onhoudbaar
unswerving 1 recht, rechtdoor, rechtaan
2 onwankelbaar
untangle 1 ontwarren **2** ophelderen, oplossen
untenable onhoudbaar [also fig]; niet te
verdedigen
unthinkable 1 ondenkbaar, onvoorstelbaar **2** onaanvaardbaar: *it's ~!* geen sprake
van!, daar komt niets van in! **3** onwaarschijnlijk
unthinking 1 onnadenkend: ~ *moment*
onbewaakt ogenblik **2** onbewust, onbedoeld
untidy slordig
untie 1 losknopen, losmaken **2** bevrijden
[person who is tied up]; vrijlaten
until tot, totdat, voor; [+ negation] niet
voor: *I cannot leave ~ Sunday* ik kan niet voor
zondag vertrekken, ik kan pas zondag vertrekken; *I did not know about it ~ today* ik wist
er tot vandaag niets van; *I was very lonely ~ I
met Karen* ik was erg eenzaam tot ik Karen
ontmoette
untimely 1 ongelegen, ongeschikt **2** voortijdig, te vroeg: ~ *death* te vroege dood

untold 1 niet verteld **2** onnoemelijk, onmetelijk
1untouchable (n) onaanraakbare[h]; paria
2untouchable (adj) **1** onaanraakbaar, onrein **2** onaantastbaar
untouched onaangeroerd
untoward 1 ongelegen, ongewenst: ~ *circumstances* ongunstige omstandigheden
2 ongepast
untried 1 niet geprobeerd, onbeproefd
2 niet getest
untroubled 1 ongestoord **2** kalm, rustig
untrue 1 onwaar, niet waar **2** ontrouw,
niet loyaal **3** afwijkend [from norm]; onzuiver, scheef: ~ *tone* onzuivere toon
untruthful 1 leugenachtig; oneerlijk **2** onwaar
1unused (adj) ongebruikt, onbenut: ~ *opportunity* onbenutte gelegenheid
2unused (adj) niet gewend: ~ *to hard work* er
niet aan gewend hard te (moeten) werken
unusual 1 ongebruikelijk, ongewoon
2 opmerkelijk, buitengewoon
unusually bijzonder; erg
unutterable onuitsprekelijk [also fig]; onbeschrijfelijk: ~ *idiot* volslagen idioot
unvarnished onverbloemd
1unveil (vb) de sluier afdoen, de sluier laten
vallen
2unveil (vb) onthullen, ontsluieren; [fig]
openbaren; aan het licht brengen
unwanted 1 ongewenst **2** onnodig
unwarranted ongerechtvaardigd, ongewettigd, ongegrond
unwelcome niet welkom; ongewenst
unwell onwel, ziek
unwieldy 1 onhandelbaar, onhandig, onpraktisch, niet gemakkelijk te hanteren
2 onbehouwen, lomp
unwilling onwillig, niet bereid
1unwind (vb) **1** zich afwikkelen [also fig];
zich ontrollen **2** [inform] zich ontspannen
2unwind (vb) **1** afwikkelen, ontrollen **2** ontwarren
unwise onverstandig
unwitting 1 onwetend, onbewust **2** onopzettelijk, ongewild
unworkable (bijna) onuitvoerbaar; onpraktisch
unworthy 1 onwaardig **2** ongepast: *that
attitude is ~ of you* die houding siert je niet
unwrap openmaken, uitpakken
unwritten 1 ongeschreven **2** mondeling
overgeleverd || ~ *law* ongeschreven wet, ge-
woonterecht[h]
unzip 1 openritsen, losmaken **2** [comp] uitpakken, unzippen
1up (n) **1** (opgaande) helling **2** opwaartse
beweging || *ups and downs* wisselvallighe-
den, voor- en tegenspoed; [inform] *on the
up-and-up* gestaag stijgend; [Am] eerlijk,

openhartig
²up (adj) **1** omhoog-, opgaand, hoog, hoger-(geplaatst): *an up stroke* opwaartse uithaal [with pen] **2** op, uit bed, wakker **3** actief, gezond **4** gestegen, omhooggegaan: *the temperature is up eight degrees* de temperatuur ligt acht graden hoger **5** naar een hoger gelegen plaats gaand [of train]: *the up line* de Londenlijn **6** in aanmerking komend (voor), ter studie: *the house is up for sale* het huis staat te koop **7** verkiesbaar gesteld, kandidaat: *Senator Smith is up for re-election* senator Smith stelt zich herkiesbaar **8** om, voorbij: *time is up* de tijd is om **9** met voorsprong, vóór op tegenstrever **10** duurder (geworden), in prijs gestegen: *coffee is up again* de koffie is weer eens duurder geworden **11** naar boven lopend, omhooggericht || *what's up?* **a)** [inform] hoe gaat het?, alles kits?; **b)** wat is er aan de hand?; *what's up with him?* wat heeft hij?; *up and about* (or: *around*) weer op de been, (druk) in de weer; *road up* werk in uitvoering [warning sign]
³up (vb) [inform] onverwacht doen, plotseling beginnen: *she upped and left* zij vertrok plotseling
⁴up (vb) [inform] (plotseling) de hoogte in jagen, verhogen, (abrupt) doen stijgen: *he upped the offer* hij deed een hoger bod
⁵up (adv) **1** [place or direction] omhoog, op-, uit-: *six floors up* zes hoog; *up the republic* leve de republiek; *live up in the hills* boven in de bergen wonen; *turn up the music* zet de muziek harder; *he went up north* hij ging naar het noorden; *up and down* op en neer, heen en weer; *up till* (or: *to*) *now* tot nu toe; *up to and including* tot en met; *from £4 up* vanaf vier pond; *children from six years up* kinderen van zes jaar en ouder **2** tevoorschijn, zichtbaar: *it will turn up* het zal wel aan het licht komen **3** helemaal, op, door-: *full up* (helemaal) vol **4** [place or direction] in, naar: *he went up to Cambridge* hij ging in Cambridge studeren || [sport] *be two (goals) up* twee goals voorstaan; *I don't feel up to it* ik voel er mij niet toe in staat
⁶up (prep) **1** [place or direction] op, boven in, omhoog: *up (the) river* stroomopwaarts; [theatre] *up stage* achter op de scène; *up the stairs* de trap op **2** [direction towards a central point] naar, in: *up the street* verderop in de straat; *up the valley* (verder) het dal in || *up and down the country* door het gehele land
up-and-coming [inform] veelbelovend
upbeat vrolijk, optimistisch
upbraid verwijten, een (fikse) uitbrander geven: ~ *s.o. for doing sth.* (or: *with sth.*) iem. iets verwijten
upbringing opvoeding
upcoming [Am] voor de deur staand, aanstaande

up-country 1 in/naar/uit het binnenland **2** achtergebleven, naïef
¹update (n) herziening, moderne versie
²update (vb) moderniseren, bijwerken, herzien
upend 1 op zijn kop zetten, ondersteboven zetten **2** omverslaan
¹upgrade (n) **1** (oplopende) helling **2** [comp] upgrade, verbeterde, bijgewerkte versie || *on the* ~ **a)** oplopend, toenemend; **b)** vooruitgang boekend
²upgrade (vb) **1** bevorderen, promotie geven **2** verbeteren, opwaarderen; een nieuwe versie uitbrengen van **3** opschalen: *the tropical storm was ~d to a hurricane* de tropische storm werd opgeschaald naar een orkaan
upheaval omwenteling, opschudding: *social* ~ sociale beroering
¹uphill (adj) **1** hellend, oplopend, (berg)opwaarts **2** (uiterst) moeilijk, zwaar
²uphill (adv) **1** bergop, naar boven, omhoog **2** moeizaam, tegen de stroom in
uphold 1 ophouden, rechthouden, hooghouden **2** (moreel) steunen, goedkeuren **3** (her)bevestigen, blijven bij
upholster stofferen [room, seats]; bekleden
upholstery stoffering, bekleding
upkeep onderhoudskosten
upland 1 hoogland^h, plateau^h **2** binnenland^h
upload [comp] uploaden
upmarket voor de betere inkomensklasse, uit de duurdere prijsklasse: *an* ~ *bookshop* een exclusieve boekhandel
upon see ³on
¹upper (n) **1** bovenleer^h [of footwear] **2** [Am; inform] pepmiddel^h; [fig] stimulans; leuke ervaring || [inform] *be (down) on one's* ~*s* berooid zijn, straatarm zijn
²upper (adj) **1** hoger, boven-, opper-: ~ *arm* bovenarm; ~ *atmosphere* hogere atmosfeer [above troposphere]; ~ *lip* bovenlip **2** hoger gelegen: ~ *reaches of the Nile* bovenloop van de Nijl **3** belangrijker, hoger geplaatst, superieur || *the* ~ *class* de hogere stand, de aristocratie; *have the* ~ *hand* de overhand hebben; *the Upper House* het Hogerhuis, de Senaat, de Eerste Kamer; [inform] *he is wrong in the* ~ *storey* hij is niet goed bij zijn hoofd
upper-class uit de hogere stand, aristocratisch
uppermost hoogst, bovenst, belangrijkst
uppish [inform] verwaand, arrogant
¹upright (n) stijl, staander, stut
²upright (adj) **1** recht(opstaand), loodrecht staand, kaarsrecht **2** oprecht, rechtdoorzee || ~ *piano* pianino, gewone piano
³upright (adv) rechtop, verticaal
uprising opstand
¹upriver (adj) stroomopwaarts (gelegen)

²**upriver** (adv) stroomopwaarts; tegen de stroom in

uproar tumult^h, rumoer^h, herrie

uproarious 1 luidruchtig, uitgelaten **2** lachwekkend

uproot 1 ontwortelen [also fig]; uit zijn vertrouwde omgeving wegrukken [persons] **2** uitroeien

¹**upscale** (adj) [Am] voor de hogere inkomensklasse, duurder

²**upscale** (vb) opschalen, opwaarderen

¹**upset** (n) **1** omverwerping, verstoring, totale ommekeer **2** ontsteltenis: *Sheila has had a terrible ~* Sheila heeft een flinke klap gekregen **3** lichte (maag)stoornis **4** [sport] verrassende nederlaag (wending)

²**upset** (adj) van streek, overstuur, geërgerd

³**upset** (vb) **1** omkantelen, omslaan, omvallen **2** overlopen **3** verstoord worden, in de war raken

⁴**upset** (vb) **1** omstoten, omverwerpen, omgooien **2** doen overlopen **3** in de war sturen, verstoren, van zijn stuk brengen: *a very ~ting experience* een heel nare ervaring **4** ziek maken; van streek maken [stomach]

upshot (the) (eind)resultaat^h; uitkomst

upside 1 voordeel^h; pluspunt^h **2** bovenkant

upside down 1 ondersteboven, omgekeerd **2** compleet in de war

upsize groter maken, opschalen

upskill bijscholen

¹**upstage** (adj) [inform] hooghartig, afstandelijk

²**upstage** (vb) [inform] meer aandacht trekken dan, de show stelen van, in de schaduw stellen

¹**upstairs** (n) de leiding, het management: *~ does not agree* het management gaat niet akkoord

²**upstairs** (adj) m.b.t. de bovenverdieping(en), boven-

³**upstairs** (adv) naar de bovenverdieping(en), de trap op, naar boven

upstanding 1 recht overeind (staand) **2** flinkgebouwd **3** eerlijk, oprecht

¹**upstate** (adj) [Am] meer naar het binnenland gelegen, provinciaal, provincie-, afgelegen

²**upstate** (adv) uit/naar/in het binnenland, noordelijk

upstream tegen de stroom in(gaand), stroomopwaarts

upsurge 1 opwelling, vlaag **2** plotselinge toename

uptake opname [of food, liquid] || *slow* (or: *quick*) *on the ~* niet zo vlug van begrip

uptight [inform] **1** zenuwachtig, gespannen **2** kwaad

up-to-date 1 bijgewerkt, op de hoogte **2** modern, bij(detijds), hedendaags

uptown 1 in/naar/van de bovenstad **2** [Am] in/naar/van de betere woonwijk(en)

upturn 1 beroering **2** verbetering, ommekeer

¹**upvote** (n) upvote; like

²**upvote** (vb) upvoten; liken

upward stijgend, opwaarts, toenemend

upwards (naar) omhoog, naar boven, in stijgende lijn: *from* the knees *~* boven de knieën; *~ of* twenty people meer dan twintig mensen

UR [inform] **1** *you are* je bent **2** *your* jouw

Ural Mountains Oeral

uranium uranium^h: *depleted ~* verarmd uranium

urban stedelijk, stads-: [Am] *~ renewal* stadsvernieuwing; *~ sprawl* suburbanisatie

urban climbing het beklimmen van gebouwen

urbanize verstedelijken, urbaniseren

urban myth broodjeaapverhaal^h

urchin rakker, boefje^h, kwajongen

¹**urge** (n) sterke drang, impuls, neiging, behoefte

²**urge** (vb) **1** drijven, aansporen: *~ on* voortdrijven **2** dringend verzoeken, bidden, smeken **3** bepleiten, aandringen op **4** trachten te overtuigen: *she ~d (up)on us the need for secrecy* zij drukte ons de noodzaak van geheimhouding op het hart

urgency 1 (aan)drang, pressie **2** urgentie, dringende noodzaak

urgent 1 urgent, dringend **2** aanhoudend, hardnekkig

urinal 1 urinaal^h, (pis)fles **2** urinoir^h, openbare waterplaats

urinary urine-

urinate urineren, wateren

urine urine, plas

urine sample urinemonster^h

URL *Universal Resource Locator* URL; [roughly] internetadres^h

urn urn

Uruguay Uruguay

¹**Uruguayan** (n) Uruguayaan(se)

²**Uruguayan** (adj) Uruguayaans

us 1 (voor/aan) ons: *all of us enjoyed it* wij genoten er allen van; *he helps them more than us* hij helpt hen meer dan ons **2** wij, ons: *us girls refused to join in* wij meisjes weigerden mee te doen; *they are stronger than us* ze zijn sterker dan wij **3** [referring to 1st person singular] mij: *let us hear it again* laat het nog eens horen

US *United States* VS, Verenigde Staten

USA 1 *United States of America* VS, Verenigde Staten **2** *United States Army* leger^h van de Verenigde Staten

usable bruikbaar

usage gebruik^h, behandeling, gewoonte, taalgebruik^h

USB *Universal Serial Bus* USB: *~ flash drive* geheugenstick, USB-stick

¹use (n) **1** gebruik[h], toepassing: *make a good ~ of* goed gebruikmaken van; *in ~* in gebruik; *out of ~* in onbruik **2** nut[h], bruikbaarheid: *have no ~ for* **a)** niet kunnen gebruiken; **b)** niets moeten hebben van; *this will be* **of** *~* dit zal goed van pas komen; *it is* **no** *~ arguing* tegenspreken heeft geen zin; *what is* **the** *~ of it?* wat heeft het voor zin?

²use (vb) **1** gebruiken: *~ up* opmaken **2** behandelen: *he was* **ill** *~d* hij werd slecht behandeld

use-by date houdbaarheidsdatum

used gebruikt, tweedehands

¹used to (adj) gewend aan, gewoon aan

²used to (vb) had(den) de gewoonte te, deed, deden: *the winters ~* **be** *colder* de winters waren vroeger kouder; *my father ~* **say:** *'Money doesn't buy you happiness.'* mijn vader zei altijd: 'Met geld koop je geen geluk.'

useful bruikbaar, nuttig: *come in ~* goed van pas komen; *make o.s. ~* zich verdienstelijk maken

useless 1 nutteloos, vergeefs **2** onbruikbaar, waardeloos, hopeloos

user gebruiker, verbruiker; verslaafde [alcohol, drugs]

user-friendly gebruikersvriendelijk

user ID gebruikers-ID; gebruikersnaam

user interface gebruikersinterface

username [comp] gebruikersnaam

¹usher (n) **1** portier[h], zaalwachter **2** plaatsaanwijzer **3** ceremoniemeester

²usher (vb) **1** als portier/plaatsaanwijzer optreden voor, voorgaan, brengen naar: *~* **out** uitlaten, naar buiten geleiden; *~* **into** binnenleiden in **2** (+ in) aankondigen; [fig] inluiden; de voorbode zijn van

usual gebruikelijk, gewoon: *business as ~* de zaken gaan gewoon door, alles gaat zijn gangetje; *as ~* zoals gebruikelijk; *it is ~* **to** het is de gewoonte om

usually gewoonlijk

usurer woekeraar

usurp onrechtmatig in bezit nemen, zich toe-eigenen, zich aanmatigen

usury woeker, woekerrente

utensil 1 gebruiksvoorwerp[h]: *cooking ~s* keukengerei[h] **2** (-s) werktuigen [also fig]; gereedschap[h]

uterine 1 uterus-, baarmoeder- **2** met, van dezelfde moeder: *~* **sister** halfzus met dezelfde moeder

uterus baarmoeder

utilitarian 1 utilitair; nuttigheids- **2** utilitaristisch

utility 1 (openbare) voorziening, nutsbedrijf[h], waterleidings-, gas-, elektriciteitsbedrijf[h] **2** nut[h], nuttigheid

utility company openbaar nutsbedrijf[h]

utility program hulpprogramma[h]

utility room [roughly] bijkeuken

utility value gebruikswaarde

utilize gebruiken, gebruikmaken van

¹utmost (n) **1** uiterste[h] (grens) **2** uiterste best, al het mogelijke: *do one's ~* zijn uiterste best doen

²utmost (adj) uiterst, hoogst: *of the ~* **importance** van het (aller)grootste belang

utopia utopie; droombeeld[h]

¹utter (adj) uiterst, absoluut, volslagen

²utter (vb) **1** uiten; slaken [eg sigh, cry] **2** uitspreken, zeggen **3** in omloop brengen [counterfeit money]

utterance uiting [also linguistics]; uitlating, woorden: *give ~ to* uitdrukking geven aan

utterly 1 uiterst, absoluut **2** volkomen, volslagen: *~* **mad** volslagen krankzinnig

U-turn (totale) ommezwaai; [traf] *no ~s* keren verboden

uvula huig

uxorious 1 dol op zijn echtgenote **2** slaafs [towards wife]

Uzbek Oezbeek(se)

Uzbekistan Oezbekistan

V

kracht zijn **2** redelijkheid [of arguments etc]

v *versus* van

V *volt(s)* V

vacancy 1 vacature **2** lege plaats, leegte, ruimte: *no vacancies* vol [in hotel] **3** afwezigheid

vacant 1 leeg; leeg(staand) [of house]; onbewoond; vrij [of toilet]: ~ *possession* leeg te aanvaarden **2** vacant [of position]; open-(staand) **3** afwezig [of mind]

vacate 1 vrij maken; ontruimen [house] **2** opgeven [position]; neerleggen [office]

¹vacation (n) **1** vakantie [esp of court of law and universities]: *long* ~ zomervakantie **2** ontruiming [of house]

²vacation (vb) [Am] vakantie hebben/houden

vaccinate (+ against) vaccineren (tegen), inenten

vaccination (koepok)inenting, vaccinatie

vaccine vaccinʰ, entstof

vacillate (+ between) aarzelen (tussen), onzeker zijn

vacuity 1 leegheid **2** saaiheid **3** dwaasheid

¹vacuum (n) vacuümʰ, leegte: ~ *cleaner* stofzuiger

²vacuum (vb) stofzuigen

vacuum-packed vacuümverpakt

vagabond vagebond, landloper

vagina vagina

vagrancy landloperij

¹vagrant (n) landloper, zwerver

²vagrant (adj) (rond)zwervend, rondtrekkend

vague 1 vaag, onduidelijk, onscherp: *be ~ about sth.* vaag zijn over iets **2** gering: *I haven't the ~st idea* ik heb geen flauw idee

vain 1 ijdel, verwaand **2** zinloos, nutteloos; vals [hope]; vergeefs [effort, attempt]: *in ~ tevergeefs* **3** triviaal, leeg || *take God's name in ~* Gods naam ijdel gebruiken

vale vallei, dalʰ

valedictorian [Am; school] afscheidsredenaar

valentine 1 liefjeʰ [chosen on St Valentine's Day, 14 February] **2** valentijnskaart

valerian valeriaan

valet 1 lijfknecht, (persoonlijke) bediende **2** hotelbediende

valiant moedig, heldhaftig

valid 1 redelijk [of arguments etc]; steekhoudend, gegrond **2** geldig [of ticket]

validate bevestigen, bekrachtigen

validity 1 (rechts)geldigheid, het van

valley dalʰ, vallei

valour (helden)moed, dapperheid

¹valuable (n) kostbaarheid

²valuable (adj) **1** waardevol, nuttig **2** kostbaar

valuation 1 schatting **2** waarde, beoordeling

¹value (n) **1** (gevoels)waarde, betekenis **2** maatstaf, waarde **3** (gelds)waarde, valuta, prijs: *(get)* ~ *for money* waar voor zijn geld (krijgen); *to the* ~ *of* ter waarde van **4** nutʰ, waarde: *of great* ~ erg nuttig

²value (vb) **1** (+ at) taxeren (op), schatten **2** waarderen, op prijs stellen

value added tax belasting op de toegevoegde waarde, btw

valueless waardeloos

value meal voordeelmenuʰ

valve 1 klep; ventielʰ [also music]; schuif **2** klep(vliesʰ) [of heart, blood vessels]

vamp: ~ *up* opkalefateren, opknappen, pimpen

vampire 1 vampier: ~ *bat* vampier [kind of bat] **2** uitzuiger [fig]

van 1 bestelwagen, busjeʰ; [in compounds often] wagen **2** (goederen)wagon || *in the* ~ *of* in de voorhoede van

vandal vandaal

vandalism vandalismeʰ, vernielzucht

vane 1 vin, bladʰ; schoep [of screw]; vleugel **2** windwijzer, weerhaantjeʰ

vanguard voorhoede [also fig]; spits

¹vanilla (n) vanille

²vanilla (adj) [fig] doorsnee: *plain* ~ *model* basismodelʰ

vanish (plotseling) verdwijnen

vanishing act grote verdwijntruc || *do a* ~ *with sth.* iets snel wegmoffelen

vanishing point 1 verdwijnpuntʰ **2** [fig] puntʰ waarop iets ophoudt (te bestaan); eindeʰ

vanity 1 ijdelheid, verbeelding **2** leegheid

vanity bag damestasjeʰ

vanquish overwinnen [also fig]; verslaan, bedwingen

vantage [Am] voordeelʰ [tennis]; voorsprong

vantage point (voordeel)positie, gunstige ligging: *the cliff offered a great* ~ de klip bood een geweldig uitzicht; *from my* ~ vanuit mijn perspectief

vape dampen

vape pen e-sigaret

vaper damper, e-roker

vapid 1 duf, flauw **2** smakeloos; verschaald [beer]

vaping dampen

vaporize (laten) verdampen

vaporizer verstuiver

vapour damp, gasʰ, wasem

VAR [socc] *video assistant referee* VAR, videoscheidsrechter

variability veranderlijkheid, onbestendigheid

¹**variable** (n) variabele (grootheid), variabele waarde

²**variable** (adj) veranderlijk, wisselend, onbestendig

variance verschilʰ, afwijking; [fig] verschilʰ van mening: *be at* ~ het oneens zijn; *at* ~ *with* in strijd met, in tegenspraak met

¹**variant** (n) variant, afwijkende vorm

²**variant** (adj) afwijkend, alternatief

variation variatie [also music]; (af)wisseling, afwijking

varicoloured veelkleurig

varicose vein spatader

varied gevarieerd, afwisselend

variegated (onregelmatig) gekleurd, (bont) geschakeerd

variety 1 verscheidenheid, afwisseling, variatie, verandering, assortimentʰ: *they sell a wide* ~ *of toys* ze verkopen allerlei verschillende soorten speelgoed **2** variëteit [biology]; verscheidenheid, rasʰ, (onder)soort: ~ *is the spice of life* verandering van spijs doet eten **3** variétéʰ

various 1 gevarieerd, uiteenlopend, verschillend (van soort): *their* ~ *social backgrounds* hun verschillende sociale achtergrond **2** verscheiden, divers: *he mentioned* ~ *reasons* hij noemde diverse redenen

¹**varnish** (n) vernis⁺ʰ, vernislaag [also fig]; lak⁺ʰ; glazuurʰ [of earthenware]: *a* ~ *of civilization* een dun laagje beschaving

²**varnish** (vb) vernissen, lakken; [fig] mooier voorstellen: *she tried to* ~ *over his misbehaviour* ze probeerde zijn wangedrag te verbloemen

varsity 1 universiteit [Oxford and Cambridge] **2** [Am] universiteitsteamʰ [eg of sport]

vary variëren, (doen) veranderen: *with* ~*ing success* met wisselend succes; *prices* ~ *from 15 to 95 pounds* de prijzen lopen uiteen van 15 tot 95 pond

vase vaas

vasectomy vasectomie

vast enorm (groot), geweldig: ~ *auditorium* kolossale aula; ~*ly exaggerated* vreselijk overdreven

vat vatʰ, ton, kuip

VAT *value added tax* btw, belasting op de toegevoegde waarde

¹**Vatican** (n, the) Vaticaanʰ

²**Vatican** (adj) Vaticaans: *the* ~ *Council* het Vaticaans concilie; *a* ~ *decree* een pauselijk besluit

¹**vault** (n) **1** gewelfʰ, boog, (gewelfde) grafkelder (wijnkelder) **2** (bank)kluis **3** sprong; [athletics] polsstoksprong

²**vault** (vb) [also fig] springen (op/over), een sprong maken; [athletics] polsstokhoogspringen

vaunt opscheppen (over) ‖ *her much-vaunted secretary* haar veelgeprezen secretaris

VCR videorecorder

VD *venereal disease* soa, seksueel overdraagbare aandoening

VDU *visual display unit* [roughly] beeldschermʰ, [roughly] terminal

veal kalfsvleesʰ

veer van richting (doen) veranderen, omlopen; (met de klok mee)draaien [of wind]; [fig] een andere kant (doen) opgaan: *the car* ~*ed off* (or: *across*) *the road* de auto schoot (plotseling) van de weg af (*or:* dwars over de weg)

vegan veganist

¹**vegetable** (n) **1** groente, eetbaar gewasʰ **2** plant; [fig] vegeterend mens

²**vegetable** (adj) plantaardig, groente- ‖ ~ *marrow* pompoen

vegetable kingdom (the) plantenrijkʰ

¹**vegetarian** (n) vegetariër

²**vegetarian** (adj) vegetarisch

vegetarianism vegetarismeʰ

vegetate 1 groeien; spruiten [(as if) of plant] **2** vegeteren [fig]

vegetation 1 vegetatie, (planten)groei **2** [med] vegetatie, woekering

veggie [inform] vegetariër

veggieburger groenteburger

veggies [Am; inform] groente

vehemence felheid, hevigheid

vehement fel, heftig, krachtig: ~ *protests* hevige protesten

vehicle 1 voertuigʰ [also fig]; middelʰ, mediumʰ: *language is the* ~ *of thought* taal is het voertuig van de gedachte **2** oplosmiddelʰ, bindmiddelʰ **3** drager, overbrenger

¹**veil** (n) sluier: *draw a* ~ *over sth.* een sluier over iets trekken; [also fig] iets in de doofpot stoppen; *take the* ~ non worden

²**veil** (vb) (ver)sluieren [also fig]: ~*ed threat* verholen dreigement

vein 1 ader, bloedvatʰ, ertsader, nerf **2** vleugjeʰ, klein beetjeʰ: *a* ~ *of irony* een vleugje ironie **3** gemoedstoestand, bui ‖ *in the same* ~ in dezelfde geest, van hetzelfde soort

velcro klittenbandʰ

velocity snelheid

¹**velvet** (n) fluweelʰ

²**velvet** (adj) fluwelen

vend 1 verkopen **2** venten, aan de man brengen

vendetta bloedwraak

vendetta killing eerwraak

vending machine automaat [for soft drinks, sweets, cigarettes etc]

vendor verkoper

¹veneer (n) **1** fineer^h **2** [fig] vernisje^h, dun laagje^h (vernis)

²veneer (vb) **1** fineren **2** [fig] een vernisje geven

venerable 1 eerbiedwaardig **2** hoogeerwaarde [title of archdeacon] **3** [Roman Catholicism] eerwaardig

venerate aanbidden

veneration verering, diepe eerbied

Venetian Venetiaans ‖ ~ **blind** jaloezie

Venezuela Venezuela

¹Venezuelan (n) Venezolaan(se)

²Venezuelan (adj) Venezolaans

vengeance wraak: **take** ~ (up)on s.o. zich op iem. wreken ‖ **work with** a ~ werken dat de stukken eraf vliegen

venial vergeeflijk, onbetekenend

Venice Venetië

venom 1 vergif^h **2** venijn^h, boosaardigheid

venomous 1 (ver)giftig **2** venijnig, boosaardig

¹vent·(n) **1** (lucht)opening, (ventilatie)gat^h, luchtgat^h **2** [also fig] uitlaat, uitweg: **give** ~ to one's feelings zijn hart luchten **3** split^h [in coat etc]

²vent (vb) **1** uiten [feelings]; luchten **2** afreageren: ~ sth. **on** s.o. (sth.) iets afreageren op iem. (iets)

ventilate 1 ventileren, luchten **2** (in het openbaar) bespreken; naar buiten brengen [opinion]

ventilation 1 ventilatie, luchtverversing, ventilatie(systeem^h) **2** openbare discussie **3** uiting; het naar buiten brengen [of opinion etc]

ventilator ventilator

ventriloquist buikspreker

¹venture (n) (gevaarlijke) onderneming, gewaagd project^h, speculatie, avontuurlijke reis/stap

²venture (vb) **1** (aan)durven, wagen (iets te doen), durven (te beweren) **2** (zich) wagen, riskeren: ~ one's **life** zijn leven op het spel zetten; **nothing** ~d, nothing gained wie niet waagt, die niet wint; ~ **out of** doors zich op straat wagen

venture capital risicodragend kapitaal^h

venue 1 plaats van samenkomst, ontmoetingsplaats, trefpunt^h **2** plaats van handeling, locatie, terrein^h, toneel^h

veracity 1 oprechtheid, eerlijkheid **2** geloofwaardigheid, nauwkeurigheid

veranda veranda^h

verb werkwoord^h

verbal 1 mondeling, gesproken, verbaal: ~ **agreement** mondelinge overeenkomst **2** van woorden, woord(en)- **3** woordelijk, woord voor woord: ~ **translation** letterlijke vertaling

verbal diarrhoea [inform] voortdurend geklets^h, gezwam^h

verbalize onder woorden brengen; formuleren

verbatim woordelijk, woord voor woord

verbose breedsprakig

verdant 1 grasgroen **2** met gras bedekt

verdict 1 oordeel^h, vonnis^h, beslissing: ~ **on** oordeel over **2** (jury)uitspraak: **bring** in a ~ uitspraak doen

verge rand; kant [fig]; berm: **bring** s.o. **to** the ~ of despair iem. op de rand van de wanhoop brengen

verge on grenzen aan: verging on the **tragic** op het randje van het tragische

verifiable verifieerbaar: his story is **hardly** ~ de waarheid van zijn verhaal kan moeilijk bewezen worden

verification 1 verificatie, onderzoek^h **2** bevestiging

verify 1 verifiëren, de juistheid nagaan van **2** waarmaken, bevestigen

veritable waar, echt, werkelijk

vermilion vermiljoen^h

vermin 1 ongedierte^h **2** gespuis^h

verminous 1 vol (met) ongedierte **2** door ongedierte overgebracht [disease] **3** vies

¹vernacular (n) landstaal, streektaal

²vernacular (adj) in de landstaal

versatile 1 veelzijdig; [also] flexibel [of mind] **2** ruim toepasbaar, veelzijdig bruikbaar

versatility 1 veelzijdigheid **2** ruime toepasbaarheid

verse 1 vers^h, versregel, dichtregel, Bijbelvers^h **2** vers^h, couplet^h, strofe **3** versvorm, verzen, gedichten: **blank** ~ onberijmde verzen

versed bedreven, ervaren

versification 1 verskunst **2** versbouw

¹versify (vb) **1** rijmen, dichten **2** rijmelen

²versify (vb) op rijm zetten

version versie, variant, interpretatie, lezing, vertaling

Version Bijbelvertaling

versus 1 tegen, contra **2** vergeleken met, tegenover

vertebra (ruggen)wervel

vertebral 1 gewerveld **2** wervel-: ~ **column** wervelkolom

¹vertebrate (n) gewerveld dier^h

²vertebrate (adj) gewerveld

¹vertical (n) **1** loodlijn **2** loodrecht vlak^h **3** loodrechte stand: **out of** the ~ niet loodrecht, uit het lood

²vertical (adj) verticaal, loodrecht

vertigo duizeligheid, draaierigheid

verve vuur^h, geestdrift

¹very (adj) **1** absoluut, uiterst: from the ~ **beginning** vanaf het allereerste begin **2** zelf, juist, precies: the ~ **man** he needed precies de man die hij nodig had; he died in this ~ **room** hij stierf in deze zelfde kamer; this is the ~

thing for me dat is net iets voor mij **3** enkel, alleen (al): *the ~ fact that ...* alleen al het feit dat ...
²**very** (adv) **1** heel, erg: *that is ~* **difficult** dat is erg moeilijk; *the ~ last day* de allerlaatste dag **2** helemaal: *keep this for your ~ own* houd dit helemaal voor jezelf **3** precies: *in the ~ same hotel* in precies hetzelfde hotel
vessel 1 vaartuigʰ, schipʰ **2** [anatomy, bot] vatʰ, kanaalʰ; buis [for blood, fluid] **3** vatʰ [for liquid]
¹**vest** (n) **1** (onder)hemdʰ **2** [Am] vestʰ
²**vest** (vb) toekennen, bekleden: *~ed inter- ests* gevestigde belangen
vestibule 1 vestibule, halʰ **2** kerkportaalʰ
vestige spoorʰ: *not a ~ of regret* geen spoor van spijt
vestment 1 (ambts)kleedʰ, ambtsgewaadʰ **2** [rel] liturgisch gewaadʰ, misgewaadʰ
¹**vet** (n) *veterinary surgeon* dierenarts, vee- arts
²**vet** (vb) **1** medisch behandelen [animal] **2** grondig onderzoeken, (medisch) keuren; [fig] doorlichten
¹**veteran** (n) veteraan; oudgediende [also fig]; oud-soldaat
²**veteran** (adj) **1** door en door ervaren **2** ve- teranen- ‖ *~ car* oldtimer [from before 1916]
Veterans Day [Am] 11 november
veterinarian [Am] dierenarts, veearts
veterinary veeartsenij-: *~ surgeon* dieren- arts, veearts
¹**veto** (n) veto(recht)ʰ
²**veto** (vb) zijn veto uitspreken over, zijn toe- stemming weigeren
vex 1 ergeren, plagen, irriteren **2** in de war brengen
vexation 1 ergernis, irritatie **2** kwelling
vexatious vervelend, ergerlijk
vexed 1 geërgerd, geïrriteerd **2** hachelijk, netelig: *~ question* lastige kwestie
VHF *very high frequency* FM
via 1 via, door, langs: *he left ~ the garden* hij vertrok door de tuin **2** [means] door middel van
viability 1 levensvatbaarheid **2** doenlijk- heid, uitvoerbaarheid
viable 1 levensvatbaar [also fig] **2** uitvoer- baar
viaduct viaductʰ
vial medicijnflesjeʰ
vibe [inform] sfeer(tje), vibe: *a 1970s ~* een jaren 70-sfeertje
vibes *vibrations* vibraties, uitstralende ge- voelens: *have bad ~ about sth.* een slecht ge- voel over iets hebben
vibrant 1 trillend **2** helder [of colour] **3** le- vendig; krachtig [of voice]
vibrate (doen) trillen [also fig]
vibration trilling
vibrator vibrator

vicar 1 predikant; dominee [Anglican Church] **2** [Roman Catholicism] plaatsver- vanger, vicaris
vicarage pastorie
vicarious 1 afgevaardigd **2** indirect
vice 1 gebrekʰ, onvolmaaktheid, slechte ge- woonte **2** ondeugd **3** ontucht, prostitutie **4** handschroef, bankschroef
vice-chairman vicepresident, vicevoorzit- ter
vice-chancellor 1 vicekanselier [of court of law] **2** rector magnificus [of university]
vice-president vicepresident; vicevoorzit- ter
viceroy onderkoning
vice squad zedenpolitie
vicinity 1 buurt, wijk **2** nabijheid, buurt, omgeving
vicious 1 wreed, boosaardig, gemeen: *~ blow* gemene mep **2** gevaarlijk, gewelddadig: *~(-looking) knife* gevaarlijk (uitziend) mes **3** vol kuren [of animals] ‖ *~ circle* **a)** vici- euze cirkel; **b)** [also fig] cirkelredenering
vicissitudes wisselvalligheden
victim 1 slachtofferʰ, dupe: *fall ~ to s.o. (sth.)* aan iem. (iets) ten prooi vallen **2** offerʰ [human, animal]
victimize 1 slachtofferen, doen lijden **2** re- presailles nemen tegen [eg a few persons]; (onverdiend) straffen
victor overwinnaar, winnaar
Victorian victoriaans, negentiende-eeuws; [roughly] (overdreven) preuts; schijnheilig
victorious 1 zegevierend: *be ~* overwin- nen, de overwinning behalen **2** overwin- nings-
victory overwinning, zege
victualler leverancier van levensmiddelen ‖ *licensed ~* caféhouder met vergunning
victuals levensmiddelen, proviandᵗʰ
¹**video** (n) video(film), videorecorder: *~ on demand* video (or: tv, film) op aanvraag; *~ cartridge* (or: *cassette*) videocassette
²**video** (vb) op (de) video opnemen
videodisc videoplaat, beeldplaat
videophone beeldtelefoon
video recorder videorecorder
¹**videotape** (n) videoband
²**videotape** (vb) op videoband opnemen
vie rivaliseren
Vienna Wenen
¹**Viennese** (n) Wener, Weense
²**Viennese** (adj) Weens
Vietnam Vietnam
¹**Vietnamese** (n) Vietnamees, Vietnamese
²**Vietnamese** (adj) Vietnamees
¹**view** (n) **1** bezichtiging, inspectie; [fig] overzichtʰ: *a general ~ of the subject* een al- gemeen overzicht van het onderwerp **2** zienswijze, opvatting: *take a dim* (or: *poor*) *~ of s.o.'s conduct* iemands gedrag maar ma-

tig waarderen; *in my* ~ volgens mij, zoals ik het zie **3** uitzicht^h, gezicht^h; [fig] vooruitzicht^h **4** gezicht^h, afbeelding; [fig] beeld^h **5** bedoeling: *with a* ~ *to* doing sth. met de bedoeling iets te doen **6** zicht^h, gezicht(svermogen)^h **7** zicht^h, uitzicht^h, gezichtsveld^h: *come into* ~ in zicht komen || *have in* ~ op het oog hebben; *in* ~ *of* vanwege, gezien

²**view** (vb) tv kijken

³**view** (vb) **1** bekijken; beschouwen [also fig]: ~ *a house* een huis bezichtigen **2** inspecteren

viewer 1 kijker, tv-kijker **2** viewer [for viewing slides]

viewpoint gezichtspunt^h; oogpunt^h [also fig]

vigil waak, (nacht)wake: *keep* ~ waken

vigilance waakzaamheid, oplettendheid

vigilant waakzaam, oplettend, alert

vigorous 1 krachtig, sterk, vol energie **2** krachtig; gespierd [language] **3** groeizaam; gezond [plants]

vigour 1 kracht, sterkte **2** energie, vitaliteit **3** groeikracht; levenskracht [of plants, animals]

Viking Viking, Noorman

vile 1 gemeen **2** walgelijk; afschuwelijk [eg food] **3** gemeen; beroerd [weather]

villa villa, landhuis^h

village dorp^h: ~ *green* a) dorpsplein^h; b) dorpsweide

villager dorpsbewoner

villain 1 boef, schurk, slechterik: *heroes and* ~*s* helden en schurken **2** rakker, deugniet

villainous schurkachtig, gemeen, doortrapt, heel slecht

villainy 1 schurkenstreek **2** schurkachtigheid, doortraptheid

vim fut, pit^+h

vindicate 1 rechtvaardigen **2** van verdenking zuiveren, rehabiliteren

vindication 1 rechtvaardiging **2** rehabilitatie

vindictive straffend, rancuneus, wraakzuchtig

vine 1 wijnstok, wingerd **2** [Am] kruiper, klimplant

vinegar azijn

vineyard wijngaard

¹**vintage** (n) **1** wijnoogst, wijnpluk **2** wijntijd, (goed) wijnjaar^h **3** jaar^h, jaargang, bouwjaar^h, lichting: *they belong to the 1960* ~ zij zijn van de lichting van 1960

²**vintage** (adj) **1** uitstekend, voortreffelijk: *a* ~ *silent film* een klassieke stomme film **2** oud, antiek: ~ *car* auto uit de periode 1916-1930, klassieke auto

vinyl 1 vinyl^h **2** zeil^h [covering material] **3** grammofoonplaat, lp

viola altviool

violate 1 overtreden, inbreuk maken op, breken: ~ *a treaty* een verdrag schenden **2** schenden, ontheiligen **3** verkrachten

violation 1 overtreding [also sport] **2** schending, schennis **3** verkrachting

violence 1 geweld^h: *acts of* ~ gewelddadigheden **2** gewelddadigheid: *crimes of* ~ geweldmisdrijven **3** hevigheid, heftigheid

violent 1 hevig, heftig, wild: ~ *contrast* schril contrast **2** gewelddadig: ~ *death* gewelddadige dood **3** hel; schreeuwend [colour]

¹**violet** (n) viooltje^h

²**violet** (adj) violet, paars(achtig blauw)

violin 1 viool **2** violist(e)

violinist violist(e)

violist altviolist

violoncello (violon)cello

VIP *very important person* vip, hooggeplaatst persoon, beroemdheid

viper adder [also fig]; serpent^h, verrader

viral viraal, virus-

virally viraal, als een virus: *spread* ~ zich razendsnel verspreiden

¹**virgin** (n) maagd [also of man]

²**virgin** (adj) maagdelijk, ongerept: ~ *snow* vers gevallen sneeuw

Virgin Islands (the) Maagdeneilanden: *the British* ~ de Britse Maagdeneilanden

virginity maagdelijkheid, het (nog) maagd zijn; [fig] ongereptheid

Virgo [astrology] (de) Maagd

virile 1 mannelijk **2** potent

virility 1 mannelijkheid, kracht **2** potentie

virtual feitelijk, eigenlijk, praktisch: *to them it was a* ~ *defeat* voor hen kwam het neer op een nederlaag || ~ *reality* virtuele werkelijkheid

virtually praktisch, feitelijk: *my work is* ~ *finished* mijn werk is zo goed als af

virtue 1 deugd: *make a* ~ *of necessity* van de nood een deugd maken **2** verdienste, goede eigenschap || *by* (or: *in*) ~ *of* op grond van

virtuosity virtuositeit, meesterschap^h

virtuous 1 deugdzaam **2** kuis

virulence 1 kwaadaardigheid, virulentie **2** venijnigheid

virulent 1 (zeer) giftig; dodelijk [poison] **2** kwaadaardig [disease] **3** venijnig, kwaadaardig

virus virus^h

virus scanner virusscanner

visa visum^h

visceral 1 [anatomy] m.b.t. de ingewanden, inwendig; visceraal **2** [fig] diepgeworteld

viscosity kleverigheid, taaiheid, stroperigheid

viscount burggraaf [title between baron and earl]

viscountess burggravin

viscous 1 kleverig **2** taai [also fig]
visibility 1 zicht[h] [meteorology] **2** zicht-baarheid
visible zichtbaar, waarneembaar, merk-baar
vision 1 gezicht(svermogen)[h], het zien: *field of* ~ gezichtsveld[h] **2** visie, inzicht[h]: *a man of* ~ een man met visie **3** visioen[h], droom(beeld[h]) **4** (droom)verschijning **5** (vluchtige) blik, glimp
[1]**visionary** (n) **1** ziener, profeet **2** dromer, idealist
[2]**visionary** (adj) **1** visioenen hebbend **2** dro-merig, onrealistisch **3** denkbeeldig
[1]**visit** (n) bezoek[h]; visite [also of doctor]; (tij-delijk) verblijf[h]: *pay s.o. a* ~ iem. een bezoek-(je) brengen
[2]**visit** (vb) **1** een bezoek afleggen, op bezoek gaan **2** [Am] logeren, verblijven || [Am] ~ *with* een praatje (gaan) maken met
[3]**visit** (vb) **1** bezoeken, op visite gaan bij **2** [Am] logeren bij, verblijven bij **3** inspecte-ren, onderzoeken **4** bezoeken, treffen, teis-teren: *the village was ~ed by the plague* het dorp werd getroffen door de pest
visitation 1 (officieel) bezoek[h], huisbe-zoek[h] **2** beproeving
visitation rights [Am] bezoekrecht[h]
visiting bezoekend, gast-: ~ *professor* gasthoogleraar; [sport] *the* ~ *team* de gasten
visiting hours bezoekuur[h], bezoektijd
visitor bezoeker, gast, toerist
visitor's book gastenboek[h]
visor 1 klep [of hat] **2** zonneklep [of car] **3** vizier[h] [of helmet]
vista 1 uitzicht[h], doorkijk(je[h]), (ver)gezicht[h] **2** perspectief[h], vooruitzicht[h]: *open up new ~s* (or: *a new* ~) nieuwe perspectieven openen
visual 1 visueel: ~ *aids* visuele hulpmidde-len; ~ *arts* beeldende kunsten; ~ *display unit* (beeld)scherm, monitor **2** gezichts-, oog- **3** zichtbaar **4** optisch
visualize 1 zich voorstellen **2** visualiseren, zichtbaar maken
vital 1 essentieel, van wezenlijk belang, onmisbaar: *of* ~ *importance* van vitaal be-lang **2** vitaal, levenskrachtig, levens-: ~ *parts* vitale delen || ~ *statistics* a) bevolkingsstatis-tiek; b) belangrijkste feiten
vitality vitaliteit, levenskracht
vital signs vitale functies
vitamin vitamine
vitiate 1 schaden, schenden, verzwakken **2** bederven; vervuilen [also fig]
vitreous glas-, glazen, van glas, glasachtig, glazig: ~ *enamel* email[h]
vitriol [chem] zwavelzuur[h]; [fig] venijn[h]
vitriolic 1 vitrioolachtig, vitriool- **2** bijtend, venijnig
viva mondeling (her)examen[h]
vivacious levendig, opgewekt

vivacity levendigheid, opgewektheid
vivid 1 helder [colour, light]; sterk **2** leven-dig, krachtig: *a* ~ *imagination* een levendige fantasie
vivisection vivisectie
vixen 1 wijfjesvos **2** feeks
viz *videlicet* nl., namelijk, te weten, d.w.z.
vlogger vlogger
vlogging (het) vloggen
V-neck V-hals
vocabulary woordenlijst, woordenschat
[1]**vocal** (n) **1** lied(je[h]), (pop)song **2** (-s) zang: ~*s: Michael Jackson* zang: Michael Jackson
[2]**vocal** (adj) **1** gesproken, mondeling, vocaal, gezongen: ~ *group* zanggroep **2** zich duide-lijk uitend, welbespraakt **3** stem-: ~ *cords* (or: *chords*) stembanden
vocalist vocalist(e), zanger(es)
vocalization 1 het uitspreken; stemge-bruik[h] **2** [linguistics] vocalisatie
vocalize (met de stem) uiten; zingen
vocation 1 beroep[h], betrekking **2** roeping **3** aanleg, talent[h]: *have a* ~ *for* aanleg hebben voor
vocational beroeps-, vak-: ~ *training* be-roepsonderwijs[h]
vociferate schreeuwen, heftig protesteren
vociferous schreeuwend, lawaaierig, luid-ruchtig
vodka wodka
vogue 1 mode: *be in* ~ in de mode zijn, in zijn **2** populariteit
[1]**voice** (n) **1** stem, (stem)geluid[h], uiting, me-ning: *speak in a low* ~ op gedempte toon spreken; *give* ~ *to* uitdrukking geven aan; *raise one's* ~ a) zijn stem verheffen; b) pro-test aantekenen; *in (good)* ~ goed bij stem **2** vorm: *active* (or: *passive*) ~ bedrijvende (or: lijdende) vorm
[2]**voice** (vb) uiten, verwoorden
voice mail voicemail
voice-over commentaarstem [with film, documentary]
[1]**void** (n) leegte, (lege) ruimte, vacuüm[h]
[2]**void** (adj) **1** leeg, verlaten: ~ *of* zonder, vrij van **2** nietig, ongeldig: *null and* ~ ongeldig, van nul en gener waarde
vol *volume* (boek)deel[h]
volatile 1 vluchtig, (snel) vervliegend **2** veranderlijk, wispelturig
volcanic vulkanisch [also fig]; explosief: ~ *eruption* vulkaanuitbarsting
volcano vulkaan [also fig]; explosieve situ-atie: *dormant* ~ sluimerende vulkaan; *ex-tinct* ~ uitgedoofde vulkaan
volition wil, wilskracht: *by* (or: *of*) *one's own* ~ uit eigen wil, vrijwillig
[1]**volley** (n) **1** salvo[h] [also fig]; (stort)vloed, regen: *a* ~ *of oaths* (or: *curses*) een scheldka-nonnade **2** [sport] volley[h]; [socc] omhaal
[2]**volley** (vb) **1** (gelijktijdig) losbranden; een

salvo afvuren [also fig] **2** in een salvo afgeschoten worden, (tegelijk) door de lucht
vliegen **3** [sport] volleren, een volley maken;
[socc] omhalen

³volley (vb) **1** [sport] uit de lucht slaan
(schieten); [socc] direct op de slof nemen
2 [tennis] volleren, met een volley passeren

¹volleyball (n) volleybalʰ [sport]

²volleyball (n) volleybal [ball]

volt volt

voltage voltageʰ

volume 1 (boek)deelʰ, band, bundel: *speak
~s* boekdelen spreken **2** jaargang **3** hoeveelheid, omvang, volumeʰ **4** volumeʰ, inhoud
5 volumeʰ, (geluids)sterkte: *turn* down *the ~*
het geluid zachter zetten

volume control volumeknop

voluminous omvangrijk, lijvig; wijd [eg
clothing, book]

voluntary 1 vrijwillig, uit eigen beweging:
~ worker vrijwilliger **2** vrijwilligers-: *~ organization* [roughly] stichting **3** gefinancierd door vrijwillige giften [church, school]

¹volunteer (n) vrijwilliger

²volunteer (vb) zich (als vrijwilliger) aanmelden, uit eigen beweging meedoen

³volunteer (vb) **1** (vrijwillig) aanbieden, (uit
eigen beweging) aanbieden **2** uit zichzelf
zeggen [remark, information]

voluntourism vrijwilligerstoerismeʰ

voluptuous 1 sensueel, wellustig **2** weelderig, overvloedig

¹vomit (n) braakselʰ, overgeefselʰ

²vomit (vb) (uit)braken [also fig]; overgeven

voodooism voodoocultus

voracious vraatzuchtig [also fig]: *a ~ reader* een alleslezer

vortex werveling [also fig]; maalstroom

¹vote (n) **1** stem, uitspraak: *cast* (or: *record*)
one's ~ zijn stem uitbrengen; *casting ~* beslissende stem [by chairman, when votes are
equally divided] **2** stemming: *~ of censure*
motie van afkeuring; *~ of confidence* (or: *no-
confidence*) motie van vertrouwen (*or:* wantrouwen); *put* sth. *to the ~* iets in stemming
brengen **3** stemmenaantalʰ: [Am] *the electoral ~* (stemmen van) kiesmannen; *the
floating ~* de zwevende kiezers; [Am] *the
popular ~* het totaal uitgebrachte stemmen;
[Am] *win the popular ~* (in absolute zin) de
meeste kiezers achter zich krijgen **4** stem-
rechtʰ **5** stembriefjeʰ

²vote (vb) stemmen, een stemming houden

³vote (vb) **1** bij stemming verkiezen, stemmen op **2** bij stemming bepalen, beslissen: *~
s.o.* out of *office* (or: *power*) iem. wegstemmen **3** (geld) toestaan **4** uitroepen tot, het
ermee eens zijn dat: *the play was ~d a success*
het stuk werd algemeen als een succes beschouwd **5** voorstellen: *I ~ we leave now* ik
stel voor dat we nu weggaan

vote down afstemmen, (bij stemming)
verwerpen: *~ a proposal* een voorstel verwerpen

vote in verkiezen: *the Conservatives were
voted in again* de conservatieven werden opnieuw verkozen

voter 1 kiezer: *floating ~* zwevende kiezer
2 stemgerechtigde

vouch borg staan: *~ for* instaan voor; garanderen

voucher bon, waardebon, cadeaubon, consumptiebon

vouch for instaan voor, waarborgen, borg
staan voor

¹vow (n) gelofte, eed, plechtige belofte:
make (or: *take*) *a ~* plechtig beloven

²vow (vb) (plechtig) beloven, gelofte afleggen van, zweren

vowel [linguistics] klinker

vox pop [inform] [roughly] straatinterviewʰ

¹voyage (n) lange reis, zeereis, bootreis: *~
home* thuisreis, terugreis; *~ out* heenreis

²voyage (vb) reizen

voyager (ontdekkings)reiziger

voyeur voyeur; gluurder

voyeurism voyeurismeʰ

vs *versus* van, vs.

vulcanization vulkanisatie

vulgar 1 vulgair, laag bij de gronds, ordinair **2** alledaags, gewoon **3** algemeen (be-
kend/aangenomen), van het volk: *~ tongue*
volkstaal || *~ fraction* gewone breuk

vulgarity 1 (vulgarities) platte uitdrukking, grove opmerking **2** (vulgarities) sma-
keloze, onbeschaafde daad **3** platheid, vulgair gedragʰ

vulgarize 1 populariseren, gemeengoed
maken **2** verlagen, onbeschaafd maken

vulnerable kwetsbaar [also fig]; gevoelig

vulture 1 gier **2** aasgier

W

W 1 *watt(s)* W **2** *west(ern)* W
¹wacko (n) [esp Am; inform] idioot
²wacko (adj) [esp Am; inform] lijp, gestoord
wacky mesjogge, kierewiet
wad 1 prop [cotton wool, paper etc]; dot, (op)vulsel[h] **2** pak[h] [letters, money etc] **3** pak-(je[h]); rolletje[h] [banknotes]
¹waddle (n) waggelende gang, eendengang
²waddle (vb) waggelen
wade waden: ~ *through* a boring book een vervelend boek doorworstelen || ~ *in* aanpakken; ~ *into* s.o. (sth.) iem. (iets) hard aanpakken
wader 1 wader **2** waadvogel **3** (-s) lieslaarzen
wading bird waadvogel
wafer 1 wafel(tje[h]) **2** hostie, ouwel
¹waffle (n) **1** wafel **2** gezwets[h], onzin **3** [Am] geaarzel[h], getwijfel[h]
²waffle (vb) **1** wauwelen, kletsen **2** [Am] aarzelen, twijfelen
¹waft (vb) zweven, drijven, waaien
²waft (vb) voeren, dragen, doen zweven
¹wag (n) **1** waggeling, kwispeling **2** grappenmaker
²wag (vb) **1** waggelen, wiebelen; schommelen [while walking]: *set* the tongues ~ging de tongen in beweging brengen **2** kwispelen
³wag (vb) **1** schudden [head]; heen en weer bewegen: *wag* one's finger at s.o. iem. met de vinger dreigen **2** kwispelen
¹wage (n) loon[h], arbeidsloon[h]: *minimum* ~ minimumloon[h]
²wage (vb) voeren [war, campaign]: ~ *war against* (or: *on*) oorlog voeren tegen
wage-cut loonsverlaging
wage demand looneis
wage earner 1 loontrekker **2** kostwinner
wage freeze loonstop
¹wager (n) weddenschap: *lay* (or: *make*) a ~ een weddenschap aangaan
²wager (vb) **1** een weddenschap aangaan **2** verwedden, wedden (om/met), op het spel zetten: *I'll* ~ (you £10) that he'll come ik wed (tien pond met u) dat hij komt
wage settlement loonakkoord[h]
wages floor minimumloon[h]
waggish guitig, ondeugend
¹waggle (n) waggeling, schommeling
²waggle (vb) **1** waggelen, wiebelen, schommelen **2** kwispelen
³waggle (vb) **1** schudden [head]; heen en weer bewegen **2** kwispelen (met)

waggoner vrachtrijder, voerman
wagon 1 wagen, boerenwagen; [Am] wagentje[h]; kar [with ice cream, hot dogs etc] **2** dienwagen(tje[h]), theewagen **3** [Am] stationcar [type of car] **4** goederenwagon **5** vrachtwagen || *go on* the (water) ~ geheelonthouder worden
wagtail kwikstaart
¹wail (n) **1** geweeklaag[h], gejammer[h] **2** geloei[h]; gehuil[h] [of siren]
²wail (vb) **1** klagen, jammeren; huilen [also of wind] **2** loeien; huilen [of siren]
waist 1 middel[h]; taille [also of article of clothing]: *stripped* to the ~ met ontbloot bovenlijf **2** smal(ler) gedeelte[h], vernauwing
waistcoat vest[h] [of suit]
waist-deep tot aan het middel (reikend)
waistline middel[h]; taille [also of article of clothing]
¹wait (n) **1** wachttijd, oponthoud[h] **2** hinderlaag: *lie in* ~ *for* s.o. voor iem. op de loer liggen
²wait (vb) **1** wachten: ~ a *minute!* wacht even!; *I'll do it while* you ~ het is zo klaar, u kunt erop wachten **2** bedienen (aan tafel): ~ *on* s.o. iem. bedienen || ~ *and see* (de dingen) afwachten; ~ *for me!* niet zo vlug!
³wait (vb) afwachten, wachten op: ~ *one's turn* zijn beurt afwachten
waiter kelner
waiting 1 wachttijd **2** bediening: *do* the ~ bedienen **3** dienst: *in* ~ dienstdoend || *no* ~ verboden stil te staan
waiting game afwachtende houding: *play* a ~ de kat uit de boom kijken
waiting list wachtlijst
waiting room wachtkamer
waitress serveerster
waitstaff bedienend personeel[h], bediening
waive 1 afzien van; afstand doen van [rights, privileges] **2** uitstellen; opschorten [problem]
¹wake (n) **1** kielwater[h], kielzog[h] **2** [fig] spoor[h], nasleep: *in the* ~ *of* in het spoor van, in de voetstappen van
²wake (vb) ontwaken; wakker worden [also fig]: *in his waking* **hours** wanneer hij wakker is; ~ *up* ontwaken, wakker worden; ~ *up to* sth. iets gaan inzien
³wake (vb) **1** (also + up) wekken; wakker maken [also fig] **2** bewust maken, doordringen: ~ s.o. up *to* sth. iem. van iets doordringen
wakeful 1 wakend, waakzaam **2** slapeloos: ~ *nights* slapeloze nachten
¹waken (vb) ontwaken, wakker worden
²waken (vb) **1** wekken, wakker maken **2** opwekken
wake-up call 1 wektelefoontje[h] **2** serieuze waarschuwing

¹walk (n) **1** gang, manier van gaan **2** stap; stapvoetse gang [of horse] **3** wandeling: *have* (or: *take*) *a ~*, *go for a ~* een wandeling (gaan) maken; [inform, fig] *a ~ in the **park*** een fluitje van een cent, een makkie, een eitje, kinderspel **4** levenswandel: *~ of life* **a)** beroep[h], roeping; **b)** (maatschappelijke) rang (*or:* stand) **5** wandelgang, voetpad[h] **6** wandelafstand: *it is ten **minutes'** ~* het is tien minuten lopen

²walk (vb) **1** lopen: *~ in one's sleep* slaapwandelen **2** stappen; stapvoets gaan [of horse] **3** (rond)waren, verschijnen ‖ *~ away* (or: *off*) *with* **a)** er vandoor gaan met, stelen; **b)** gemakkelijk winnen; *~ off* opstappen, er vandoor gaan; *~ out* **a)** het werk onderbreken, staken; **b)** opstappen, weglopen [eg at consultation]; *~ out on s.o.* iem. in de steek laten; *~ tall* het hoofd hoog dragen, trots zijn; *~ up!* kom erin!, komt dat zien! [eg at circus]; *~ up to s.o.* op iem. afgaan; [inform] *~ over* met gemak achter zich laten; *~ (all) over s.o.* met iem. de vloer (aan)vegen

³walk (vb) **1** lopen, gaan; te voet afleggen [distance] **2** lopen door/langs/op, bewandelen **3** meelopen met: *~ s.o. **home*** iem. naar huis brengen **4** laten lopen; uitlaten [eg dog]; stapvoets laten lopen [horse]: *~ s.o. off his feet* iem. de benen uit zijn lijf laten lopen

walker 1 wandelaar, voetganger **2** [Am] looprek[h], rollator; loopstoel [for child]

walking papers ontslag(brief): *get one's ~* zijn ontslag krijgen

walkout 1 staking, werkonderbreking **2** het weglopen [from a meeting by way of protest]

walkover gemakkelijke overwinning

walkway 1 gang, wandelgang **2** wandelweg, promenade

¹wall (n) muur, wand: [fig] *a **writing** on the ~* een teken aan de wand ‖ *drive* (or: *push*) *s.o. to the ~* iem. in het nauw drijven; *drive s.o. up the ~* iem. stapelgek maken; [sport] *hit the ~* de man met de hamer tegenkomen

²wall (vb) **1** ommuren **2** dichtmetselen

wallet portefeuille

wallflower 1 muurbloem **2** muurbloempje[h]

¹Walloon (n) Waal(se) [inhabitant of the Walloon provinces in Belgium]

²Walloon (adj) Waals

¹wallop (n) **1** dreun, mep **2** bier[h]

²wallop (vb) aframmelen, hard slaan

¹walloping (n) **1** aframmeling **2** zware nederlaag

²walloping (adj) reusachtig, enorm

wallow 1 (zich) wentelen, (zich) rollen: *~ in the **mud*** zich in het slijk wentelen [fig]; [fig] *~ in **self-pity*** zwelgen in zelfmedelijden **2** rollen; slingeren [of ship]

wall painting 1 muurschildering, fresco[h]

2 muurschilderkunst

wallpaper behang[h]

wall-to-wall kamerbreed [eg carpet]

wally sukkel, stommeling

walnut walnoot

walrus walrus

¹waltz (n) wals [dance (music)]

²waltz (vb) walsen, de wals dansen; [fig] (rond)dansen ‖ *~ off with* er vandoor gaan met

wan 1 bleek; flets [complexion] **2** flauw; zwak [light, smile]

wand toverstokje[h], toverstaf

wander 1 (rond)zwerven, (rond)dwalen: *~ about* rondzwerven **2** kronkelen; (zich) slingeren [of river, road] **3** verdwalen; op de verkeerde weg raken [also fig] **4** afdwalen [also fig]: *~ from* (or: *off*) *one's subject* van zijn onderwerp afdwalen **5** kuieren

wanderer zwerver

wanderings zwerftochten

¹wane (n): *on the ~* aan het afnemen [also fig]

²wane (vb) afnemen, verminderen; [fig] vervallen

¹wangle (n) (slinkse) streek, smoesje[h]

²wangle (vb) weten los te krijgen, klaarspelen: *~ a well-paid job out of s.o.* een goed betaalde baan van iem. weten los te krijgen

³wangle (vb) zich eruit draaien, zich redden: *~ (o.s.) out of a situation* zich uit een situatie weten te redden

¹want (n) **1** behoefte: *meet a long-felt ~* in een lang gevoelde behoefte voorzien **2** gebrek[h], gemis[h]: *drink water **for** ~ of anything better* water drinken bij gebrek aan iets beters **3** tekort[h], nood **4** armoede, behoeftigheid: *live in ~* in armoede leven

²want (vb) behoeftig zijn ‖ *he does not ~ for anything, he ~s for nothing* hij komt niets te kort

³want (vb) **1** (graag) willen, wensen: *I ~ it (to be) **done** today* ik wil dat het vandaag gedaan wordt; *~ in* (or: *out*) naar binnen (*or:* buiten) willen **2** moeten, hoeven: *you ~ to see a psychiatrist* je moet naar een psychiater; *in that case you ~ room 12A, it's just around the corner* in dat geval moet u kamer 12A hebben, die is net om de hoek **3** nodig hebben, vergen, vereisen **4** zoeken; vragen [pers]: *~ed, experienced mechanic* gevraagd: ervaren monteur; *~ed **by** the police **(for** a crime)* gezocht door de politie (voor een misdaad)

wanting 1 te kort, niet voorhanden: *a few pages are ~* er ontbreken een paar bladzijden **2** onvoldoende: *be ~ **in** sth.* **a)** in iets tekortschieten; **b)** iets missen

wanton 1 lichtzinnig [of woman] **2** moedwillig **3** buitensporig, onverantwoord

WAP *wireless application protocol* WAP[h]

¹war (n) oorlog: *~ of **nerves*** zenuw(en)oorlog; **wage** ~ *on* (or: *against*) oorlog voeren tegen [also fig] ‖ *have been in the* ~*s* er gehavend uitzien

²**war** (vb) strijd voeren; strijden [oft fig]: ~ *against* strijden tegen

war baby oorlogsbaby

¹**warble** (n) gekweel[h], gezang[h]

²**warble** (vb) **1** kwelen **2** zingen [of bird]

war crime oorlogsmisdaad

ward 1 (ziekenhuis)afdeling **2** (stads)wijk [as part of constituency] **3** pupil [minor under guardianship]; [fig] beschermeling: ~ *of court* onder bescherming van het gerecht staande minderjarige **4** voogdijschap[h], hoede, curatele **5** afdeling van gevangenis

warden 1 hoofd[h], beheerder; bestuurder [of schools, hospitals etc] **2** [Am] gevangenisdirecteur **3** wachter, opzichter, bewaker, suppoost, conciërge, portier[h]

warder cipier, gevangenbewaarder

ward off afweren, afwenden

wardrobe 1 kleerkast, hangkast **2** garderobe [also in theatre]

wardroom officierenkajuit, officiersmess

ware 1 (koop)waar[h], goederen **2** aardewerk[h]

warehouse pakhuis[h], opslagplaats, magazijn[h]

warfare oorlog(voering); strijd [also fig]

war game oorlogsspel[h]

warhead kop een van raket, torpedo; [nuclear] kernkop

warhorse 1 oorlogspaard[h], strijdros[h] **2** ijzervreter **3** oude rot [in politics]

warlike 1 krijgshaftig, strijdlustig **2** militair, oorlogs-

warlord militair leider

¹**warm** (n) warmte: *come in and have a* ~*!* kom binnen en warm je wat!

²**warm** (adj) **1** warm [also fig]; innemend: ~ *greetings* hartelijke groeten; *give a* ~ *welcome to* hartelijk welkom heten; *keep a place* ~ *for s.o.* een plaats voor iem. openhouden **2** warmbloedig, hartstochtelijk, vurig: *a* ~ *supporter* een vurig aanhanger **3** verhit [also fig]; geanimeerd, heftig: *a* ~ *discussion* een geanimeerde discussie ‖ *make things* ~ *for s.o.* **a)** het iem. moeilijk maken; **b)** iem. straffen

³**warm** (vb) warm worden [also fig]; in de stemming (ge)raken: ~ *to* (or: *toward(s)*) *s.o.* iets gaan voelen voor iem.

⁴**warm** (vb) **1** (ver)warmen **2** opwarmen [also fig]; warm maken

warm-hearted warm, hartelijk

warmonger oorlogs(aan)stoker

warmth [also fig] warmte, hartelijkheid, vuur[h]

¹**warm up** (vb) **1** warm(er) worden [also fig]; op temperatuur komen; [fig] in de stemming raken **2** [sport] een warming-up doen, de spieren losmaken

²**warm up** (vb) **1** opwarmen [also fig]; warm maken, in de stemming brengen **2** (ver)warmen

warm-up opwarming(stijd)

warn 1 waarschuwen: ~ *s.o. of sth.* iem. op iets opmerkzaam maken, iem. voor iets waarschuwen **2** waarschuwen: *the doctor* ~*ed him off drink* de dokter waarschuwde hem geen alcohol te drinken ‖ ~ *s.o. off* iem. weren

warning waarschuwing(steken[h]); [fig] afschrikwekkend voorbeeld[h]: *give a* ~ waarschuwen

¹**warp** (n) **1** schering [in weaving] **2** kromtrekking [in wood]

²**warp** (vb) krom trekken [of wood]

³**warp** (vb) **1** krom trekken [wood] **2** scheeftrekken, bevooroordeeld maken: *his past has* ~*ed his judgment* zijn verleden heeft zijn oordeelsvermogen verwrongen

warpath oorlogspad[h]: *go on the* ~ op het oorlogspad gaan

¹**warrant** (n) **1** bevel(schrift)[h], aanhoudingsbevel[h]: ~ *of arrest* arrestatiebevel[h] **2** machtiging, volmacht **3** (waar)borg **4** rechtvaardiging, grond: *no* ~ *for* geen grond tot

²**warrant** (vb) **1** rechtvaardigen **2** machtigen

³**warrant** (vb) **1** garanderen: ~*ed pure* gegarandeerd zuiver **2** verzekeren: *I* (or: *I'll*) ~ *(you)* dat kan ik je verzekeren

warranty (schriftelijke) garantie

warren 1 konijnenpark[h] **2** doolhof [of streets]; wirwar

warrior 1 strijder, krijger **2** soldaat

Warsaw Warschau

warship oorlogsschip[h]

wart wrat: ~*s and all* met alle gebreken

wartime oorlogstijd

war victim oorlogsslachtoffer[h]

wary 1 omzichtig, alert: ~ *of* op zijn hoede voor **2** voorzichtig

warzone oorlogsgebied[h]

¹**wash** (n) **1** wasbeurt, het wassen: *have a* ~ zich wassen **2** vieze, waterige troep, slootwater[h], slappe thee **3** was(goed[h]) **4** golfslag **5** zog[h], kielwater[h] **6** spoelwater[h] ‖ *it'll come out in the* ~ het zal wel loslopen

²**wash** (vb) **1** zich wassen, zich opfrissen **2** gewassen (kunnen) worden **3** geloofwaardig zijn: *that argument won't* ~ dat argument gaat niet op **4** breken [of wave] ‖ *the stain will* ~ *off* de vlek gaat er (in de was) wel uit

³**wash** (vb) **1** wassen; [fig] zuiveren: ~ *clean* schoonwassen; ~ *off* (eraf) wassen **2** wassen, de was doen **3** meesleuren [of water]; wegspoelen: *be* ~*ed overboard* overboord slaan

washable wasbaar

wash away afwassen, wegspoelen, uitwassen; [fig] reinigen; zuiveren: ~ *s.o.'s sins*

iem. reinigen van zijn zonden
wash cloth [Am] washandje^h
wash down 1 wegspoelen [food, with drink] **2** (helemaal) schoonmaken: ~ *with ammonia* schoonmaken met ammonia
washed-out 1 verbleekt [in the wash] **2** uitgeput **3** [sport] afgelast (wegens regen)
washed-up verslagen, geruïneerd
washer 1 wasser **2** (sluit)ring, afdichtingsring **3** leertje^h **4** wasmachine, wasautomaat
washing was(goed^h)
washing-machine wasmachine
washing-up afwas, vaat: *it's your turn to do the* ~ jij bent aan de beurt om af te wassen
washing-up liquid afwasmiddel^h
washing-up machine afwasmachine, vaatwasser
wash-leather zeem^{+h}, zeemleer^h
¹wash out (vb) (in de was) eruit gaan [of stains]
²wash out (vb) **1** uitwassen, uitspoelen **2** wegspoelen **3** onmogelijk maken [of rain, the match]
wash-out flop, mislukking
wash rag [Am] washandje^h
washroom 1 wasruimte, waslokaal^h **2** [Am] toilet^h
washstand wastafel
¹wash up (vb) **1** [Am] zich opfrissen **2** afwassen, de vaat doen
²wash up (vb) doen aanspoelen [of tide]
washy 1 waterig [of liquid]; slap **2** bleek, kleurloos
wasp wesp
waspish [oft depr] **1** wespachtig **2** giftig, nijdig **3** dun; slank [like a wasp]
wassup [inform] hé, hoe is ie
wastage 1 verspilling; verlies^h [through leakage] **2** verloop^h [of staff]
¹waste (n) **1** woestenij; woestijn [also fig] **2** verspilling: *a ~ of money* zonde van het geld, weggegooid geld; *a ~ of time* tijdverspilling, zonde van je tijd **3** afval(product)^h, puin^h, vuilnis^h: *go to ~, run to ~* verloren gaan, verspild worden
²waste (adj) **1** woest, braak(liggend), verlaten: *lay ~* verwoesten **2** afval-, overtollig
³waste (vb) **1** verspild worden **2** (+ away) wegteren, wegkwijnen
⁴waste (vb) **1** verspillen, verkwisten: *you didn't ~ time on sth.* je liet er geen gras over groeien; ~ *time on sth.* tijd verspillen aan iets **2** verwoesten
wastebasket [Am] afvalbak, prullenmand
wasted dronken
wasteful verspillend, spilziek
wasteland woestenij, onbewoonbaar gebied^h: *a cultural* ~ een cultureel onderontwikkeld gebied; *industrial* ~ braakliggend voormalig industrieterrein
wastepaper papierafval^h

wastepaperbasket prullenmand
wastepipe afvoer(buis)
waste product afvalproduct^h
¹watch (n) **1** horloge^h **2** (watches) (nacht)wake **3** bewaker, wachtpost, nachtwaker **4** waaktijd, wachtkwartier^h, wacht(dienst), bewaking, uitkijk: *keep* ~ *over* waken over **5** wacht, waakzaamheid, hoede: *keep (a) close* ~ *on* (nauwlettend) in de gaten houden, de wacht houden over
²watch (vb) **1** (toe)kijken **2** wachten: ~ *for one's chance* zijn kans afwachten **3** uitkijken: ~ *out* uitkijken, oppassen; ~ *(out) for* uitkijken naar, loeren op **4** de wacht houden
³watch (vb) **1** bekijken, kijken naar **2** afwachten [chance, opportunity]: ~ *one's chance* zijn kans afwachten **3** gadeslaan, letten op: ~ *one's weight* op zijn gewicht letten; ~ *it!* pas op!, voorzichtig!; ~ *yourself* pas op! **4** bewaken; hoeden [cattle] **5** verzorgen, zorgen voor
watchdog waakhond [also fig]; (be)waker
watchful waakzaam, oplettend
watchmaker horlogemaker
watchman bewaker, nachtwaker
watchword 1 wachtwoord^h **2** leus, slogan
¹water (n) **1** water^h: *tread* ~ watertrappelen; *spend money like* ~ geld uitgeven als water **2** water^h, waterstand: *at high* (or: *low*) ~ bij hoogwater; *at low* ~ bij laagwater **3** urine: *make* (or: *pass*) ~ wateren **4** water^h **5** (-s) mineraalwater^h; [fig] (water)kuur: *drink* (or: *take*) *the* ~*s* een kuur doen ‖ ~ *on the brain* waterhoofd^h; *run like* ~ *off a duck's back* niet het minste effect hebben; *hold* ~ steek houden; *fish in troubled* ~*s* in troebel water vissen
²water (vb) **1** tranen, lopen, wateren: *my eyes* ~*ed* mijn ogen traanden **2** watertanden: *make the mouth* ~ doen watertanden **3** water drinken [of animals]
³water (vb) **1** water geven, begieten: ~ *the plants* de planten water geven **2** van water voorzien, bespoelen, besproeien: ~ *down* aanlengen; [fig] afzwakken; *a watered-down version* een verwaterde versie
water biscuit (cream)cracker
waterborne 1 drijvend, vlot **2** over water vervoerd, zee-: ~ *trade* zeehandel
water butt regenton
watercolour 1 aquarel, waterverfschilderij^h **2** waterverf
water cooler 1 koeltank **2** waterkoeler, watertappunt^h: [media] *digital* ~ virtuele koffieautomaat
waterfall waterval
waterfowl watervogel
waterfront waterkant [of city district etc]: *on the* ~ aan de waterkant
water heater boiler; [Am] geiser
water hole waterpoel

w<u>a</u>tering can gieter
w<u>a</u>tering place 1 waterplaats **2** kuuroord^h, badplaats
w<u>a</u>ter level (grond)waterpeil^h
w<u>a</u>terline waterlijn [of ship]
w<u>a</u>terlogged 1 vol water (gelopen) [ship]
2 met water doortrokken [soil, wood]
Waterl<u>oo</u> (verpletterende) nederlaag, beslissende slag: *meet* one's ~ verpletterend verslagen worden
w<u>a</u>terman veerman
w<u>a</u>termark 1 watermerk^h [in paper] **2** waterpeil^h
w<u>a</u>ter meadow uiterwaard
w<u>a</u>ter power waterkracht, hydraulische kracht
¹w<u>a</u>terproof (n) (waterdichte) regenjas
²w<u>a</u>terproof (adj) waterdicht
³w<u>a</u>terproof (vb) waterdicht maken
w<u>a</u>tershed 1 waterscheiding **2** [fig] keerpunt^h
w<u>a</u>terside (the) waterkant
¹w<u>a</u>ter-ski (n) waterski
²w<u>a</u>ter-ski (vb) waterskiën
w<u>a</u>ter snake ringslang
w<u>a</u>terspout 1 waterspuwer, spuier **2** waterhoos
w<u>a</u>ter table grondwaterspiegel
w<u>a</u>tertight [also fig] waterdicht
w<u>a</u>terway 1 waterweg **2** vaarwater^h
w<u>a</u>terwheel waterrad^h
w<u>a</u>ter wings (zwem)vleugels
w<u>a</u>terworks 1 waterleiding(bedrijf^h)
2 waterlanders, tranen: *turn* on the ~ in tranen uitbarsten
w<u>a</u>tery 1 waterachtig, water-, vol water
2 nat, vochtig, tranend: ~ *eye* waterig oog, traanoog^h **3** waterig, smakeloos, flauw, slap, bleek
watt watt
w<u>a</u>ttle 1 lel; halskwab [esp of birds] **2** hordewerk^h, gevlochten rijswerk^h: ~ *and daub* met leem opgevuld vlechtwerk
¹wave (n) **1** golf [also fig]; vloed; [fig] opwelling: ~ *of violence* golf van geweld
2 (haar)golf **3** wuivend gebaar^h **4** golf(beweging), verkeersgolf, aanvalsgolf
²wave (vb) **1** golven, fluctueren **2** wapperen [of flag]
³wave (vb) **1** (toe)wuiven, zwaaien: [fig] ~ *sth. aside* iets van tafel vegen; ~ *s.o. on* iem. gebaren verder te gaan; ~ *at* (or: *to*) s.o. naar iem. zwaaien; ~ *and pay* contactloos betalen
2 krullen, golven
w<u>a</u>ve-and-p<u>a</u>y (het) contactloos betalen
w<u>a</u>velength golflengte [λ; also fig]: *be on* the same ~ op dezelfde golflengte zitten [fig]
w<u>a</u>ver 1 onzeker worden, wankelen **2** aarzelen: ~ *between* aarzelen tussen **3** flikkeren [of light]; flakkeren [of candle]
w<u>a</u>vy golvend, deinend

¹wax (n) **1** (bijen)was: [fig] *be* ~ *in s.o.'s hands* als was in iemands handen zijn **2** (boen)was
3 oorsmeer^h
²wax (vb) wassen, opkomen; toenemen [of water, moon]
w<u>a</u>xen 1 glad als was **2** week als was
w<u>a</u>xwork 1 wassen beeld^h **2** (-s) wassenbeeldententoonstelling, wassenbeeldenmuseum^h
w<u>a</u>xy 1 wasachtig, bleek **2** woedend, opvliegend
¹way (n) **1** weg, route: [fig] *things are going his* ~ het zit hem mee; *lose* the (or: one's) ~ verdwalen, de weg kwijtraken; [fig] *pave* the ~ *(for sth., s.o.)* de weg effenen (voor iets/iem.); [fig] *pay* one's ~ geen schulden maken, zonder verlies werken; *work* one's ~ *through college* werkstudent zijn; ~ *in* ingang; ~ *out* uitgang; [fig] uitweg; *better weather is on the* ~ er is beter weer op komst; *on* the ~ *out* op weg naar buiten; [inform, fig] uit (de mode) rakend; *that's the* ~ *(it is, goes)* zo gaat het nu eenmaal **2** manier, wijze, gewoonte, gebruik^h; [depr] hebbelijkheid: ~ *of life* levenswijze; ~ *of thinking* denkwijze; *in a big* ~
a) op grote schaal; **b)** grandioos; **c)** met enthousiasme; *go the right* (or: *wrong*) ~ *about sth.* iets op de juiste (or: verkeerde) wijze aanpakken; [fig] *find a* ~ een manier vinden, er raad op weten; *set in* one's ~s met vast(geroest)e gewoontes; *one* ~ *and another* alles bij elkaar (genomen); *one* ~ *or another* (or: *the other*) op de een of andere manier; *there are no* ~s *about it* er is geen twijfel (over) mogelijk **3** richting: *look the other* ~ de andere kant opkijken [also fig]; [fig] *I don't know which* ~ *to turn* ik weet me geen raad; *the other* ~ *around* (or: *about*) andersom
4 opzicht^h: *in a* ~ in zekere zin; *in more* ~s *than one* in meerdere opzichten **5** afstand, eind^h, stuk^h: *a long* ~ *away* (or: *off*) een heel eind weg, ver weg; *go a long* ~ *to meet s.o.* iem. een heel eind tegemoetkomen [also fig]
6 (voort)gang, snelheid, vaart: *be under* ~ onderweg zijn; *gather* (or: *lose*) ~ vaart krijgen (or: minderen) [of ship]; *negotiations are well under* ~ onderhandelingen zijn in volle gang **7** ruimte [also fig]; plaats, gelegenheid: *clear* the ~ **a)** de weg banen; **b)** [also fig] ruim baan maken; *give* ~ **a)** toegeven, meegeven; **b)** [also fig] wijken, voorrang geven;
c) doorzakken, bezwijken; *make* ~ *for* plaats maken voor; *put* s.o. *in the* ~ *of sth.* iem. op weg helpen (met iets), iem. aan iets helpen; *out of* the ~ (or: one's) ~ uit de weg [also fig]; *get sth. out of* the ~ iets uit de weg ruimen, iets afhandelen ‖ ~s *and means* geldmiddelen; *make* ~ opschieten [also fig]; *make* one's (own) ~ *(in life, in the world)* in de wereld vooruitkomen; [fig] *go* one's own ~ zijn eigen weg gaan; *go out of* one's (or: *the*) ~ *to …* zijn

(uiterste) best doen om ...; *have a ~ with el-derly people* met ouderen om weten te gaan; *you can't have it both ~s* óf het een óf het an-der; *see one's ~ (clear) to doing sth.* zijn kans schoon zien om iets te doen; *by the ~* ter-loops, trouwens, à propos; *they had done nothing out of the ~* zij hadden niets bijzon-ders gedaan; *by ~ of example* als voorbeeld; *any ~* in ieder geval, hoe dan ook; *either ~* hoe dan ook; [inform] *every which ~* overal, in alle hoeken en gaten; [Am; inform] *no ~!* geen sprake van!

²**way** (adv) ver, lang, een eind: *~ back* ver te-rug, (al) lang geleden

wayfarer [form] trekker; (voet)reiziger

waylay 1 belagen, opwachten 2 onder-scheppen

way-out te gek, geavanceerd, excentriek

waypoint [comp] (GPS-)coördinaten

wayside kant van de weg, berm; [fig] *fall by the ~* afvallen, uitvallen

wayward eigenzinnig, koppig

WC *water closet* wc

we wij, we

weak 1 zwak, slap; week [constitution]; broos: *a ~ argument* een zwakke redenering; *go ~ at the knees* a) slappe knieën krijgen [when in love]; b) op zijn benen staan te tril-len [with fear]; *~ at* (or: *in*) *physics* zwak in natuurkunde 2 flauw, zwak; matig [offer, market, Stock Exchange]: *a ~ demand (for)* weinig vraag (naar) || *have a ~ spot for* een speciaal plekje in zijn hart hebben voor

¹**weaken** (vb) toegeven, zwichten

²**weaken** (vb) verzwakken, afzwakken, (doen) verslappen

weak-kneed 1 besluiteloos, slap, niet wils-krachtig 2 bangelijk, timide, laf

weakling zwakkeling, slappeling

weak-minded 1 zwakzinnig; [fig] achter-lijk 2 zwak [of will, character]

weakness 1 zwakte, slapheid, zwakheid 2 zwak punt^h 3 zwakheid, zonde, fout 4 zwak^h, voorliefde: *he has a ~ for blonde women* hij valt op blonde vrouwen

weaksauce [inform] slappe hap, drie keer niks

weal striem, streep || *for the public ~* voor het algemeen welzijn

wealth 1 overvloed, rijkdom 2 rijkdom-(men), bezit^h, bezittingen, vermogen^h

wealthy rijk, vermogend

wean spenen [child, young] || *~ s.o. (away) from sth.* iem. iets afleren

weapon wapen^h

weaponry wapentuig^h

¹**wear** (n) 1 dracht; het aanhebben [cloth-ing] 2 het gedragen worden [of clothing]; gebruik^h 3 slitage: *show (signs of) ~* slijtage-plekken vertonen 4 sterkte, kwaliteit 5 (pas-sende) kleding, tenue^h: *sportswear* sportkle-

ding || *normal ~ and tear* normale slijtage

²**wear** (vb) 1 goed blijven [also fig]: *this sweater ~s well* deze trui ziet er nog goed uit 2 (also + on, away) voortkruipen [of time]; voortduren: *the meeting wore on* (or: *away*) de vergadering ging maar door

³**wear** (vb) 1 dragen [on one's body]; aan hebben 2 vertonen, hebben, tentoonsprei-den; voeren [colour, flag]: *he ~s a beard* hij heeft een baard 3 uitputten 4 [inform; of-ten with negation] aanvaarden, toestaan: *they won't ~ it* zij nemen het niet

⁴**wear** (vb) [also fig] verslijten, (af)slijten, uit-slijten: *worn clothes* afgedragen kleren; *~ thin* dun worden, slijten; *my patience is ~ing thin* mijn geduld is aan het opraken

wearable draagbaar

wearables 1 kleding 2 draagbare techno-logie, wearables [smartwatch etc]

wear down 1 (af)slijten, verslijten 2 ver-zwakken, afmatten: *~ resistance* tegenstand (geleidelijk) overwinnen

wearing vermoeiend, slopend

wearisome 1 vermoeiend 2 vervelend, langdradig

¹**wear off** (vb) (geleidelijk) minder worden: *the novelty will soon ~* het nieuwtje zal er (wel) gauw af gaan

²**wear off** (vb) verslijten, afslijten

¹**wear out** (vb) afgemat raken: *his patience wore out* zijn geduld raakte op

²**wear out** (vb) uitputten: *wear o.s. out* uit-geput raken, zich uitsloven

³**wear out** (vb) verslijten, afdragen

¹**weary** (adj) 1 moe, lusteloos: *~ of* moe van [also fig] 2 vermoeiend

²**weary** (vb) moe worden: *~ of* moe worden, genoeg krijgen van

³**weary** (vb) vermoeien

¹**weasel** (n) wezel

²**weasel** (vb) (also + out) zich drukken, er tussenuit knijpen: *~ out (of one's duty)* zich onttrekken (aan zijn plicht); *~ words* dub-belzinnig spreken

¹**weather** (n) weer^h: *wet ~* nat weer || *(be, feel) under the ~* a) (zich) niet lekker (voelen); b) dronken (zijn)

²**weather** (vb) verweren

³**weather** (vb) 1 doen verweren 2 door-staan [storm; also fig]; te boven komen

weather-beaten 1 (door storm) bescha-digd (geteisterd) 2 verweerd [of face]

weatherboard 1 waterdorpel 2 houten buitenbekleding [of overlapping planks]

weathercock weerhaan, windwijzer; [fig] draaier; opportunist

weather eye: *keep a ~ open (for)* op zijn hoede zijn (voor), oppassen (voor)

weather forecast weersvoorspelling, weerbericht^h

weatherglass barometer

weatherproof weerbestendig, tegen weer en wind bestand

weathers weersomstandigheden: *in all ~* weer of geen weer

weathervane windwijzer

¹weave (n) **1** weefsel[h] **2** (weef)patroon[h]

²weave (vb) zigzaggen, (zich) slingeren; [traf] weven; van rijstrook wisselen

³weave (vb) zich slingerend banen: *they were weaving their way **through** the full hall* zij baanden zich zigzaggend een weg door de volle hal

⁴weave (vb) **1** vlechten, weven **2** verweven, verwerken **3** maken [story]; ophangen

web 1 (spinnen)web[h] **2** web[h], weefsel[h]; net-(werk)[h] [also fig] **3** val, netten **4** weefsel[h] **5** (zwem)vlies[h]

Web (the) het web

web address webadres[h], internetadres[h]

webbing 1 singel(band), geweven band **2** omboordsel[h]

webcam webcamera, webcam

¹webcast (n) (live-)uitzending via internet; webcast

²webcast (vb) (live) uitzenden via internet; webcasten

web designer websiteontwerper

webhead [inform] internetverslaafde; internettalent[h]

web hosting [comp] webhosting

webinar webinar[+h], webseminar[+h]

weblog weblog[+h], blog[+h]

web page internetpagina

website website

web store webwinkel

web traffic webverkeer[h]

¹wed (vb) paren: *~ **to*** paren aan

²wed (vb) trouwen, huwen: *~ded **couple*** getrouwd paar

wedded 1 huwelijks-, van het huwelijk: *~ life* huwelijksleven[h] **2** verslingerd, getrouwd: [fig] *~ **to** his job* getrouwd met zijn werk

wedding 1 huwelijk[h], huwelijksplechtigheid, bruiloft **2** koppeling, het samengaan: *the ~ of two great **minds*** het samengaan van twee grote geesten

wedding anniversary trouwdag: *celebrate one's 25th ~* zijn 25-jarig huwelijk vieren

wedding breakfast bruiloftsmaal[h], maaltijd of lunch na trouwerij

wedding day trouwdag

wedding gift huwelijkscadeau[h]

wedding planner huwelijksplanner, bruiloftsplanner

wedding ring trouwring

¹wedge (n) **1** wig [also fig]: *drive a ~ between the parties* tweedracht zaaien tussen de partijen **2** wigvorm **3** hoek; punt[h] [of cheese, cake]

²wedge (vb) vastzetten, vastklemmen: *we*

*were ~d (in) **between** the police and the rioters* we zaten ingeklemd tussen de politie en de relschoppers

wedlock huwelijk[h], huwelijkse staat || *born out of ~* buiten huwelijk geboren, onecht

Wednesday woensdag

wee klein: *a ~ **bit*** een klein beetje, ietsje, een pietsje [also iron]

¹weed (n) **1** onkruid[h] **2** tabak, marihuana, hasj, sigaret **3** lange slapjanus

²weed (vb) **1** wieden, verwijderen, schoffelen **2** wieden; zuiveren: *the manager ~ed **out** the most troublesome employees* de manager zette de lastigste werknemers aan de kant

weedkiller onkruidverdelger

weedy 1 vol onkruid **2** slungelig

week week, werkweek: *a ~ **(on) Sunday, Sunday** ~* zondag over een week; *yesterday ~* gisteren een week geleden; *most people work a **38-hour** ~* de meeste mensen hebben een 38-urige werkweek || *~ **in**, ~ **out*** week in, week uit, wekenlang

weekday doordeweekse dag, werkdag, weekdag

weekend weekend[h], weekeinde[h]

¹weekly (n) weekblad[h]

²weekly (adj) wekelijks: *she earns £150 ~* zij verdient 150 pond in de week

weeny heel klein, piepklein

¹weep (n) huilbui: *let them have **their** ~* laat ze maar (uit)huilen

²weep (vb) wenen, huilen: *~ **for** (or: **with) joy*** van vreugde schreien; *no-one will ~ **over** his resignation* niemand zal een traan laten om zijn vertrek

³weep (vb) **1** storten; schreien [tears] **2** huilen, schreien: *~ o.s. to sleep* zichzelf in slaap huilen

weeping met hangende takken, treur-: *~ willow* treurwilg

weepy 1 huilerig, snotterig **2** sentimenteel

wee(-wee) plasje[h]: *do (a) wee(-wee), have a wee(-wee)* een plasje plegen

¹weigh (vb) drukken, een last zijn: *his unemployment ~s **(up)on** him* hij gaat gebukt onder zijn werkloosheid || *~ **in with*** aan komen zetten met, te berde brengen

²weigh (vb) **1** wegen: *it ~s four **kilos*** het weegt vier kilo; *the greengrocer ~ed a bag of potatoes* de groenteman woog een zak aardappelen; *~ **in** (laten) wegen, zich laten wegen; *~ **out*** afwegen **2** overwegen, afwegen: *~ one's **words*** zijn woorden wegen; *~ **up** a)* wikken en wegen; **b)** schatten; **c)** zich een mening vormen over; *~ **up** the situation* de situatie opnemen **3** lichten [anchor, ship] || *~ **down** beladen; [fig] deprimeren; *his marriage problems ~ him **down*** hij gaat gebukt onder zijn huwelijksproblemen

weighbridge weegbrug

weigh-in gewichtscontrole [of boxer before fight; of jockey after race]; wegen na de wedren

¹weight (n) **1** gewicht[h] [for scales]; gewichtsklasse, zwaarte: *~s and measures* maten en gewichten; *lose* ~ afvallen, vermageren; *put on* ~ aankomen, zwaarder worden; *over* ~ te zwaar; *under* ~ te licht **2** gewicht[h], zwaar voorwerp[h] **3** (zware) last; [fig] druk; belasting: *his departure is a* ~ *off my mind* zijn vertrek is een pak van mijn hart **4** belang[h], invloed: *worth one's* ~ *in gold* zijn gewicht in goud waard **5** grootste deel[h], hoofddeel[h], grootste nadruk: *the* ~ *of evidence is against them* het grootste gedeelte van het bewijsmateriaal spreekt in hun nadeel || *carry* ~ gewicht in de schaal leggen, van belang zijn; *give* ~ *to* versterken, extra bewijs leveren voor; *pull one's* ~ [fig] (ieder) zijn steentje bijdragen; *throw one's* ~ *about* (or: *around*) zich laten gelden, gewichtig doen

²weight (vb) **1** verzwaren [also of material] **2** beladen [also fig]; gebukt doen gaan: *~ed down with many parcels* beladen met veel pakjes

weightlifter gewichtheffer

weight-watcher lijner, iem. die goed op zijn lichaamsgewicht let

weighty 1 zwaar **2** belangrijk, zwaarwegend **3** invloedrijk, gezaghebbend

weir 1 (stuw)dam **2** (vis)weer[h]

weird raar, gek, vreemd, eng: ~ *and wonderful* nieuwerwets

weirdo rare (snuiter)

¹welcome (n) **1** welkom[h], verwelkoming **2** onthaal[h]: *they gave the speaker a hearty* ~ zij heetten de spreker hartelijk welkom; *bid s.o.* ~ iem. welkom heten || *outstay one's* ~ langer blijven dan men welkom is, blijven plakken

²welcome (adj) **1** welkom, aangenaam: ~ *change* welkome verandering **2** [roughly] vrij: *you're* ~ *to the use of my books* je mag mijn boeken gerust gebruiken || *'thank you' -'you're* ~*' 'dank u' - 'geen dank'; ~ home, ~ back* welkom thuis

³welcome (vb) **1** verwelkomen, welkom heten **2** (gunstig) onthalen: *we'd* ~ *a change* we zouden een verandering toejuichen

¹weld (n) las(naad)

²weld (vb) **1** lassen **2** samenvoegen, aaneensmeden || *this iron* ~*s well* dit ijzer laat zich goed lassen

welfare 1 welzijn[h], welvaart, voorspoed **2** maatschappelijk werk[h], welzijnszorg **3** bijstand: *be on* ~ van de bijstand leven

welfare state verzorgingsstaat, welvaartsstaat

welfare work maatschappelijk werk[h], welzijnszorg

¹well (n) **1** put, diepe ruimte, diepte, kuil **2** boorput, oliebron **3** koker, schacht

²well (adj) **1** gezond, goed, beter, wel: *she's*

feeling ~ *again* zij voelt zich weer goed **2** goed, in orde, naar wens: *all's* ~ *that ends* ~ eind goed, al goed; ~ *enough* goed genoeg **3** raadzaam, wenselijk: *it would be (just) as* ~ *to confess your little accident* je kan het beste je ongelukje maar opbiechten || *all very* ~ *(, but)* alles goed en wel (maar), dat kan wel zijn (maar); *she's* ~ *in with my boss* zij staat in een goed blaadje bij mijn baas

³well (vb) vloeien, (op)wellen

⁴well (adv) **1** op de juiste manier, goed, naar wens: *behave* ~ zich goed gedragen **2** zorgvuldig, grondig, door en door: ~ *cooked* goed gaar **3** ver, ruim, zeer, een eind: ~ *in advance* ruim van tevoren; *the exhibition was* ~ *worth visiting* de tentoonstelling was een bezoek meer dan waard **4** gunstig, vriendelijk, goedkeurend: *treat s.o.* ~ iem. vriendelijk behandelen **5** redelijkerwijze, met recht: *I cannot very* ~ *refuse to help him* ik kan moeilijk weigeren om hem te helpen **6** verstandig || *be* ~ *off* a) warmpjes bijzitten; b) geluk hebben; ~ *and truly* helemaal; *be* ~ *out of it* er goed van af komen [of sth. unpleasant]; *as* ~ ook, evenzeer, net zo lief, net zo goed; *as* ~ *as* zowel ... als, en, niet alleen ... maar ook; *in theory as* ~ *as in practice* zowel in theorie als in de praktijk; *wish s.o.* ~ iem. succes toewensen; *leave* (or: *let*) ~ *alone* laat maar zo, het is wel goed zo

⁵well (int) **1** zo, nou, wel: ~*, what a surprise* zó, wat een verrassing **2** nou ja, goed dan; jawel [but]: ~*, if she loves the boy* nou ja, als ze van de jongen houdt **3** goed, nu || *oh* ~*, you can't win them all* nou ja, je kan niet altijd winnen; ~ *then?* wel?, nu?

well-advised verstandig, raadzaam

well-appointed goed ingericht, goed voorzien

well-being welzijn[h], gezondheid, weldadig gevoel[h]

well-born van goeden huize

well-bred welopgevoed, beschaafd, welgemanierd

well-disposed (+ towards) welwillend (jegens), vriendelijk (tegen), gunstig gezind

well-done goed doorbakken

well-endowed [inform] fors, weelderig geschapen

well-established 1 voldoende bewezen [eg of principle] **2** reeds lang gevestigd [business]

well-fed 1 goed gevoed **2** weldoorvoed, dik, gezet

well-heeled rijk, vermogend

wellie rubberlaars

well-informed 1 goed op de hoogte, onderlegd **2** goed ingelicht, welingelicht

wellington rubberlaars, kaplaars

well-kept 1 goed onderhouden [of building, garden] **2** goed bewaard [of secret]

well-known bekend, overal bekend

well-matched 1 goed bij elkaar passend **2** aan elkaar gewaagd, tegen elkaar opgewassen

well-meaning goedbedoeld, welgemeend

well-nigh bijna, vrijwel: *it's ~ impossible* het is vrijwel onmogelijk

well off rijk, welgesteld: *you don't know when you're ~* je hebt geen idee hoe goed je 't hebt

well-oiled dronken, in de olie

well-preserved goed geconserveerd [of elderly person]: *grandfather looks ~ at 93* grootvader ziet er nog goed uit op zijn 93e

well-read belezen

wellspring (onuitputtelijke) bron

well-timed op het juiste moment (gedaan/gezegd/komend)

well-to-do rijk, bemiddeld

well-tried beproefd

well-turned-out piekfijn gekleed

well-wisher iem. die iem. het beste toewenst

well-worn afgezaagd, cliché(matig), alledaags

welsh zijn woord niet houden, verplichtingen niet nakomen: *~ on debts* schulden niet (af)betalen

¹Welsh (n) bewoners van Wales

²Welsh (adj) Wels, van Wales, in het Wels || *~ rabbit, ~ rarebit* toast met gesmolten kaas

welsher bedrieger; oplichter [of bookmaker]

Welshman bewoner van Wales

¹welter (n) mengelmoes^h, enorm aantal^h, enorme hoeveelheid

²welter (vb) zich rollen; zich wentelen [also fig]

welterweight (bokser uit het) weltergewicht

¹west (n) het westen: *the West* het westelijk gedeelte

²west (adj) westelijk, west(en)-: *~ wind* westenwind

³west (adv) in/uit/naar het westen, ten westen

westbound in westelijke richting (gaand/reizend)

West Country het zuidwesten van Engeland

¹westerly (n) westenwind

²westerly (adj) westelijk

¹western (n) western, wildwestfilm, wildwestroman

²western (adj) westelijk, west(en)-

westerner westerling

westward(s) westwaarts, westelijk

¹wet (n) **1** nat weer^h, regen **2** nattigheid, vocht^h, vochtigheid **3** sukkel, doetje^h

²wet (adj) **1** nat, vochtig: *~ paint* nat, pas ge-

verfd; *~ through,* wringing *~* kletsnat, helemaal doorweekt **2** regenachtig, nat **3** [inform] slap, sullig, sloom || *~ blanket* a) domper, koude douche; b) spelbreker; *~ dream* natte droom; *he is still ~ behind the ears* hij is nog niet droog achter de oren

³wet (vb) **1** nat maken, bevochtigen **2** plassen in [bed etc]: *~ the bed* bedwateren; *he has ~ his pants again* hij heeft weer in zijn broek geplast

wetting het nat (gemaakt) worden: *get a ~* een bui op zijn kop krijgen

¹whack (n) **1** klap, mep, dreun **2** (aan)deel^h, portie **3** poging: *let me have a ~ at it* laat mij het eens proberen

²whack (vb) een mep geven, een dreun verkopen

whacked doodmoe, uitgeteld, kapot

whacking [inform] enorm, kolossaal

whale walvis || *a ~ of a time* een reusachtige tijd; *they had a ~ of a time* ze hebben een geweldige tijd gehad

whalebone balein^h

whaler walvisvaarder

whaling walvisvangst

wham klap, slag, dreun || *~!* knal!, boem!

wharf kade, aanlegsteiger

whassup [inform] hé, hoe is ie

what 1 wat: *~'s the English for 'gezellig'?* wat is 'gezellig' in het Engels?; *no matter ~* hoe dan ook; *~ do you call that?* hoe heet dat?; *books, clothes, records and ~ have you* boeken, kleren, platen en wat nog allemaal; *~ of it?* en wat (zou dat) dan nog?; *~ about an ice-cream?* wat denken van een ijsje?; *~ did he do that for?* waarom deed hij dat?; *~ if I die?* stel dat ik doodga, wat dan?; *~'s up?* a) [inform] hoe gaat het?, alles kits?; b) wat is er aan de hand?, wat gebeurt er (hier)? **2** wat, dat(gene) wat, hetgeen: *~'s more* bovendien, erger nog; *say ~ you will* wat je ook zegt **3** welke, wat voor, welke (ook), die, dat: *~ work we did was worthwhile* het beetje werk dat we deden was de moeite waard; *~ books do you read?* wat voor boeken lees je? **4** [in exclamations] wat (voor), welk (een): *~ a delicious meal!* wat een lekkere maaltijd! || *~ and ~ not* en wat al niet, enzovoorts enzovoorts; *so ~?* nou en?, wat dan nog?

whatchamacallit hoe-heet-het-ook-alweer^h, dingetje^h

whatever 1 alles wat, wat ook: *I'll stay ~ happens* ik blijf, wat er ook gebeurt **2** om het even wat (welke), wat (welke) dan ook: *have you found your scarf or ~* heb je je sjaal of wat je ook kwijt was gevonden; *any colour ~* om het even welke kleur **3** [in questions and negations] helemaal, totaal, überhaupt: *no-one ~* helemaal niemand **4** wat (toch): *~ happened?* wat is er in 's hemelsnaam ge-

beurd?; ~ *for?* waarom toch?
whatnot wat al niet, noem maar op: *she bought books, records and* ~ ze kocht boeken, platen en noem maar op
whatsisname hoe-heet-ie-ook-alweer, dinges
whatsoever helemaal, absoluut: *no doubt* ~ geen enkele twijfel
wheat tarwe ‖ *separate the* ~ *from the chaff* het kaf van het koren scheiden
wheaten tarwe-: ~ *products* tarweproducten
wheatmeal tarwemeel^h, volkoren tarwemeel^h
¹**wheedle** (vb) flikflooien, vleien
²**wheedle** (vb) **1** (+ into) met gevlei overhalen (tot) **2** (+ out of) aftroggelen, afvleien: ~ *a promise out of* s.o. iem. zover krijgen dat hij een belofte doet
¹**wheel** (n) **1** wiel^h, rad^h, draaischijf **2** stuur^h, stuurrad^h, stuurwiel^h, roer^h: *at* (or: *behind) the* ~ aan het roer, achter het stuur; [fig] aan de leiding **3** auto, kar: *on* ~*s* per auto, met de wagen ‖ *there are* ~*s within* ~*s* het zit zeer ingewikkeld in elkaar
²**wheel** (vb) **1** rollen, rijden **2** (also + (a)round, about) zich omkeren, zich omdraaien, van richting veranderen **3** cirkelen; in rondjes vliegen [of birds] ‖ ~*ing* and *dealing* ritselen, gesjacher, gemarchandeer
³**wheel** (vb) duwen, trekken [sth. on wheels]; (ver)rijden, rollen: *they* ~*ed the patient back to his room* ze reden de patiënt terug naar zijn kamer
wheelbarrow kruiwagen
wheelchair rolstoel
wheel clamp wielklem
wheeler-dealer [esp Am; inform] ritselaar, handige jongen
wheelhouse stuurhut, stuurhuis^h
wheel trim [car] (lichtmetalen) velgen
¹**wheeze** (n) **1** gepiep^h [of breathing] **2** grap, geintje^h **3** plannetje^h, idee^h
²**wheeze** (vb) **1** piepen, fluiten, fluitend ademhalen **2** hijgen, puffen
whelp jong^h, puppy^{+h}, welp^{+h}
¹**when** (adv) **1** [interrogative] wanneer: ~ *will I see you?* wanneer zie ik je weer? **2** wanneer, waarop, dat: *the day* ~ *I went to Paris* de dag waarop ik naar Parijs ging ‖ [when pouring] *say* ~ zeg maar ho; *since* ~ *has he been here?* sinds wanneer is hij al hier?
²**when** (conj) **1** toen: *she came* ~ *he called* ze kwam toen hij riep; ~ *I was a little girl* toen ik een klein meisje was **2** als, wanneer: *he laughs* ~ *you tickle him* hij lacht (telkens) als je hem kietelt **3** als (het zo is dat): *why use gas* ~ *it can explode?* waarom gas gebruiken als (je weet dat) het kan ontploffen? **4** hoewel, terwijl, ondanks (het feit) dat: *the part was plastic* ~ *it ought to have been made of leather*

het onderdeel was van plastic hoewel het van leer had moeten zijn
whence [dated] van waar; waar vandaan; waaruit [also fig]: *dreams* ~ *poetry springs* dromen waaruit dichtkunst ontspringt
whenever 1 telkens wanneer, wanneer ook, om het even wanneer: ~ *we meet he turns away* iedere keer als wij elkaar tegenkomen, draait hij zich om **2** wanneer (toch, in 's hemelsnaam): ~ *did I say that?* wanneer in 's hemelsnaam heb ik dat gezegd?
where 1 [interrogative] waar; waarheen, waarin, waarop [also fig]: ~ *are you going?* waar ga je naartoe? **2** waar, alwaar, waarheen: *Rome,* ~ *once Caesar reigned* Rome, alwaar eens Caesar heerste **3** daar waar, in die omstandigheden waar, waarbij: *nothing has changed* ~ *Rita is concerned* er is niets veranderd wat Rita betreft **4** terwijl, daar waar: ~ *she was shy her brother was talkative* terwijl zij verlegen was, was haar broer spraakzaam
whereabouts verblijfplaats, plaats waar iem. (iets) zich bevindt
whereas hoewel, daar waar, terwijl
whereby [form] waardoor
wherefore [form] waarom; om welke reden
whereof waarvan: *the things* ~ *he spoke* de dingen waarover hij sprak
whereupon waarna, waarop: *he emptied his glass,* ~ *he left* hij dronk zijn glas leeg, waarna hij vertrok
wherever 1 waar (toch, in 's hemelsnaam): ~ *can John be?* waar kan John toch zijn? **2** waar ook, overal waar: *I'll think of you* ~ *you go* ik zal aan je denken waar je ook naartoe gaat
wherewithal middelen, (benodigde) geld^h: *I don't have the* ~ ik heb er geen geld voor
whet wetten, slijpen, (aan)scherpen
whether 1 of: *she wondered* ~ *he would be in* ze vroeg zich af of hij thuis zou zijn; *he wasn't sure* ~ *to buy it* hij wist niet of hij het wel zou kopen **2** (+ or) of, ofwel, zij het, hetzij: ~ *he is ill or not I shall tell him* of hij nu ziek is of niet, ik zal het hem zeggen
whetstone wetsteen, slijpsteen
which 1 welk(e): ~ *colour do you prefer?* welke kleur vind je het mooist? **2** welke (ervan), wie, wat: *he could not tell* ~ *was which* hij kon ze niet uit elkaar houden **3** die, dat, welke, wat: *the clothes* ~ *you ordered* de kleren die je besteld hebt **4** wat, hetgeen, (iets) wat: *he said they were spying on him,* ~ *is sheer nonsense* hij zei dat ze hem bespioneerden, wat klinkklare onzin is
whichever om het even welk(e), welk(e) ook, die(gene) die: ~ *way you do it* hoe je het ook doet
¹**whiff** (n) **1** vleug [of smell]; zweem; flard

[of smoke]; zuchtje^h [of air, wind]; spoor^h [also fig] **2** teug, het opsnuiven, het inademen **3** sigaartje^h

²whiff (vb) (onaangenaam) ruiken, rieken

¹while (n) tijd(je^h), poos(je^h): *a good* ~ geruime tijd; *worth* ~ de moeite waard; *they will make it worth your* ~ je zult er geen spijt van hebben; *(every) once in a* ~ af en toe, een enkele keer; *we haven't seen her for a long* ~ wij hebben haar lang niet gezien; *(for) a* ~ een tijdje, een ogenblik

²while (conj) **1** terwijl, zolang als: ~ *I cook the meal you can clear up* terwijl ik het eten maak kun jij opruimen **2** [contrast] terwijl, hoewel, daar waar: ~ *she has the talent she does not have the perseverance* hoewel ze het talent heeft, zet ze niet door

while away verdrijven

whilst *see* ²*while*

whim gril, opwelling, bevlieging

¹whimper (n) zacht gejank^h, gejammer^h: *without a* ~ zonder een kik te geven

²whimper (vb) janken, jammeren

whimsical grillig, eigenaardig, fantastisch

whimsicality 1 gril, kuur **2** grilligheid

whimsy 1 gril, kuur, opwelling **2** eigenaardigheid

¹whine (n) gejammer^h, gejengel^h

²whine (vb) **1** janken, jengelen **2** zeuren, zaniken

whinge mopperen, klagen, zeuren

¹whinny (n) hinnikend geluid^h, gehinnik^h

²whinny (vb) hinniken

¹whip (n) zweep, karwats, gesel

²whip (vb) **1** snel bewegen, snellen, schieten: *she* ~*ped off her coat* zij gooide haar jas uit; ~ *up* **a)** snel oppakken; **b)** snel in elkaar draaien (*or:* flansen); *he* ~*ped round the corner* hij schoot de hoek om **2** overhands naaien **3** zwepen [also fig]; (met de zweep) slaan, ranselen: *the rain* ~*ped the windows* de regen striemde tegen de ramen **4** kloppen [fresh cream etc]; stijf slaan: ~*ped cream* slagroom **5** verslaan, kloppen, in de pan hakken

whip hand: *have (got) the* ~ *of* (or: *over*) de overhand hebben over

whiplash injury zweepslagtrauma^h

whipping pak^h slaag, aframmeling

whipping cream slagroom

whippy veerkrachtig, buigzaam

whip-round inzameling: *have a* ~ de pet laten rondgaan

¹whirl (n) **1** werveling, draaikolk **2** verwarring, roes: *my thoughts are in a* ~ het duizelt mij **3** drukte, gewoel^h, maalstroom: *a* ~ *of activity* koortsachtige bedrijvigheid **4** poging: *give* it *a* ~ probeer het eens een keer

²whirl (vb) **1** tollen, rondtuimelen: *my head* ~*s* het duizelt mij **2** stormen, snellen, stuiven

³whirl (vb) ronddraaien, wervelen, (doen)

dwarrelen: *he* ~*ed round* hij draaide zich vliegensvlug om

whirligig 1 tol [toy]; molentje^h **2** draaimolen, carrousel^{+h} **3** [fig] mallemolen

whirlpool 1 draaikolk **2** wervelbad^h, bubbelbad^h

¹whirlwind (n) wervelwind, windhoos

²whirlwind (adj) bliksem-, zeer snel: *a* ~ *campaign* een bliksemcampagne

¹whirr (n) gegons^h, gezoem^h, gesnor^h

²whirr (vb) gonzen, zoemen, snorren

¹whisk (n) **1** kwast, plumeau, borstel **2** garde, (eier)klopper

²whisk (vb) **1** zwaaien, zwiepen **2** (also + up) (op)kloppen, stijf slaan

whisk away 1 wegvegen, wegslaan **2** snel wegvoeren, snel weghalen: *the children were whisked off to bed* de kinderen werden snel in bed gestopt

whisker 1 snorhaar^h; snorharen [of cat etc] **2** (-s) bakkebaard(en) || *win by a* ~ met een neuslengte winnen

whiskey [Am, Ireland] (glas^h) whisky

whisky (glas^h) whisky

¹whisper (n) **1** gefluister^h; geruis^h [of wind]: *in a* ~, *in* ~*s* fluisterend **2** gerucht^h, insinuatie **3** het fluisteren, fluistering

²whisper (vb) fluisteren, ruisen, roddelen

¹whistle (n) **1** fluit, fluitje^h **2** gefluit^h, fluitend geluid^h || *wet one's* ~ de keel smeren [with drink]; *blow the* ~ *on sth.* **a)** een boekje opendoen over iets; **b)** een eind maken aan

²whistle (vb) fluiten, een fluitsignaal geven || ~ *up* in elkaar flansen, uit het niets tevoorschijn roepen

whistle-blower klokkenluider

whit grein^h, sikkepit: *not a* ~ geen zier, geen steek

¹white (n) **1** wit^h [also chess, draughts]; het witte **2** oogwit^h **3** blanke

²white (adj) **1** wit, bleek, blank: ~ *Christmas* witte kerst; ~ *coffee* koffie met melk; ~ *as a sheet* lijkbleek, wit als een doek; ~ *tie* **a)** wit strikje [of dress suit]; **b)** rokkostuum^h **2** blank [of human being] || ~ *ant* termiet; ~ *elephant* **a)** witte olifant; **b)** kostbaar maar nutteloos bezit (*or:* geschenk); **c)** weggegooid geld; ~ *ensign* Britse marinevlag; *show the* ~ *feather* zich lafhartig gedragen; ~ *hope* iem. van wie men grote verwachtingen heeft; ~ *lie* leugentje om bestwil; *White Paper* witboek^h; ~ *spirit* terpentine; *bleed s.o.* ~ iem. uitkleden, iem. het vel over de oren halen

whiteboard whiteboard^h, schoolbord^h

white-collar witte boorden-, hoofd-: ~ *job* kantoorbaan; ~ *staff* administratief personeel

Whitehall Whitehall; [fig] de (Britse) regering; Londen

white-hat hacker hacker met goede bedoelingen

white-hat hacking [roughly] hacken met goede bedoelingen
white-hot witheet, witgloeiend
White House Witte Huis; [fig] Amerikaanse president
whitelist toestaan
¹**whiten** (vb) wit worden, opbleken
²**whiten** (vb) witten, bleken
¹**whitewash** (n) 1 witkalk, witsel[h] 2 vergoelijking, dekmantel
²**whitewash** (vb) 1 witten 2 vergoelijken 3 witwassen
whitewater rafting [sport] wildwaterraften[h]
whitey [offensive] blanke || **have** a ~ wit wegtrekken
whither 1 [interrogative] waarheen, waarnaartoe 2 naar daar waar, naar ergens waar: *he knew ~ she had gone* hij wist waar zij heengegaan was
Whit Monday pinkstermaandag, tweede pinksterdag
Whitsun Pinksteren
Whit Sunday pinksterzondag
whittle (+ away, down) (af)snijden [wood]; snippers afsnijden van, besnoeien; [fig] reduceren; beknibbelen: ~ **away** kleiner maken
¹**whiz(z)** (n) gefluit[h], het zoeven, gesuis[h]
²**whiz(z)** (vb) zoeven, fluiten, suizen: *they whiz(z)ed* **past** zij zoefden voorbij
whiz(z)kid briljant jongmens[h], genie[h], wonder[h]
who 1 die, wie: *anyone ~* **disagrees** wie niet akkoord gaat 2 om het even wie, wie dan ook 3 wie: *~* **cares** wat maakt het uit; ~ **knows** *what he'll do next* wie weet wat hij nog zal doen
whodun(n)it detective(roman), detectivefilm
whoever 1 wie (toch): *~ can that* **be?** wie kan dat toch zijn? 2 om het even wie, wie (dan) ook, al wie: *~ you meet, don't speak to them* wie je ook tegenkomt, spreek hen niet aan
¹**whole** (n) geheel[h], totaal[h]: *on the ~* alles bij elkaar, in het algemeen; **the** ~ *of Boston* heel Boston
²**whole** (adj) 1 heel, geheel, totaal, volledig: *~* **number** heel getal; **swallow** *sth. ~* iets in zijn geheel doorslikken; [fig] iets voor zoete koek aannemen 2 geheel, gaaf, gezond || *go (the) ~* **hog** tot het einde toe doorgaan, geen half werk doen; *a ~* **lot** *of people* een heleboel mensen; [Am] *the ~* **shebang** het hele zootje
³**whole** (adv) totaal, geheel: *a ~* **new** *life* een totaal nieuw leven
wholegrain volkoren[h]: *~* **bread** volkorenbrood[h]
wholehearted hartgrondig

wholemeal volkoren
¹**wholesale** (n) groothandel
²**wholesale** (adj) 1 in het groot, groothandel-, grossiers-: *sell ~ in het groot verkopen* 2 massaal, op grote schaal: *~* **slaughter** massamoord
wholesaler groothandelaar, grossier
wholesome 1 gezond, heilzaam 2 nuttig [advice]
wholewheat volkoren
wholly geheel, volledig, totaal
whom 1 wie: *tell ~ you like* zeg het aan wie je wil 2 die, wie: *your father is a man for ~ I have immense respect* jouw vader is iem. voor wie ik enorm veel respect heb
whomever [form] wie ook, om het even wie: *tell ~ you* **meet** zeg het aan iedereen die je tegenkomt
¹**whoop** (n) uitroep; kreet [with joy]
²**whoop** (vb) schreeuwen, roepen; een kreet slaken [with joy] || ~ *it* **up** uitbundig feestvieren
whoopee: *make ~* keet maken, aan de zwier gaan
whooping cough kinkhoest
¹**whoosh** (n) gesuis[h], geruis[h], gesis[h]
²**whoosh** (vb) suizen, ruisen, sissen
whop afranselen, slaan; [fig] verslaan
whopper 1 kanjer 2 grove leugen
whopping [inform] kolossaal, geweldig: *a ~ (great)* **lie** een kolossale leugen
whore [inform] hoer
whorehouse bordeel[h]
whorl 1 krans [of leaves around stem] 2 spiraal [of shell, fingerprint]
whose van wie, wat, welke, waarvan, wiens, wier: *~* **cap** *is this?* wiens pet is dit?, wie zijn pet is dit?; *a writer ~* **books** *are all bestsellers* een schrijver wiens boeken allemaal bestsellers zijn; *children ~* **parents** *work at home* kinderen van wie de ouders thuis werken, kinderen wier de ouders thuis werken
¹**why** (adv) waarom, om welke reden: *~ not* **ask** *him?* waarom vraag je het (hem) niet gewoon? || *the ~s and* **wherefores** het hoe en waarom
²**why** (int) [when surprised] wel allemachtig: *~, if it isn't Mr Smith* wie we daar hebben! Meneer Smith! || *~, a child could answer that* nou zeg, een kind zou dat weten
wick wiek, pit; kousje[h] [of lamp]; katoen[h] || *get on s.o.'s ~* iem. op de zenuwen werken
wicked 1 slecht, verdorven, zondig: *~* **prices** schandelijk hoge prijzen 2 kwaadaardig; gemeen [tongue] 3 schadelijk; kwalijk [cough]; gevaarlijk [storm]; streng [winter] 4 [inform] te gek, fantastisch
wicker vlechtwerk[h]
wicker basket rieten mand
wicker chair rieten stoel

wicket deurtje[h], hekje[h] ‖ [fig] *bat* (or: *be) on a sticky* ~ zich in een moeilijk parket bevinden

¹wide (adj) **1** wijd, breed **2** ruim, uitgestrekt, veelomvattend; rijk [experience]; algemeen [knowledge]: *he has ~ interests* hij heeft een brede interesse **3** wijd open [eyes]: *keep your eyes ~* houd je ogen wijd open **4** ernaast, mis; ver naast [shot, guess]: *~ of the mark* compleet ernaast, irrelevant; *the dart went ~ of the target* het pijltje ging ver naast het doel ‖ *~ boy* gladde jongen; *give s.o. (sth.) a ~ berth* iem. (iets) uit de weg blijven

²wide (adv) **1** wijd, breed **2** helemaal, volledig

wide-angle groothoek-

wide-awake klaarwakker; [inform, fig] uitgeslapen

widely 1 wijd (uiteen), ver uit elkaar **2** breed, over een groot gebied; [also fig] op vele gebieden: *~ known* wijd en zijd bekend **3** sterk, heel, erg: *differ ~* sterk verschillen

widen breder worden, breder maken

wide-ranging breed opgezet, van grote omvang

widescreen breedbeeld(formaat)[h]

wide-screen breedbeeld-: *~ TV* breedbeeldtelevisie

widespread wijdverspreid, wijdverbreid

widget 1 [inform] dingetje[h], apparaatje[h] **2** [comp] widget

¹widow (n) weduwe

²widow (vb) tot weduwe (weduwnaar) maken: *her ~ed father* haar vader, die weduwnaar is

widower weduwnaar

width breedte

wield 1 uitoefenen; bezitten [power, influence] **2** hanteren; gebruiken [tools]

wife vrouw, echtgenote: [inform] *the ~* vrouwlief, mijn vrouw

wi-fi *wireless fidelity* wifi

wig pruik

¹wiggle (n) gewiebel[h]

²wiggle (vb) **1** wiebelen **2** wriemelen, kronkelen

³wiggle (vb) doen wiebelen, op en neer bewegen, heen en weer bewegen: *~ one's toes* zijn tenen bewegen

¹wild (n) **1** woestenij, wildernis: *(out) in the ~s* in de wildernis **2** (vrije) natuur, natuurlijke staat: *in the ~* in het wild

²wild (adj) **1** wild, ongetemd: *~ flower* wilde bloem **2** barbaars, onbeschaafd: *the Wild West* het wilde westen; *run ~* verwilderen [eg of garden] **3** onbeheerst, losbandig **4** stormachtig; guur [of weather, sea] **5** woest; onherbergzaam [of region] **6** dol, waanzinnig: *the ~est nonsense* je reinste onzin **7** woest, woedend: *~ with anger* razend van woede **8** wanordelijk; verward [of hair]

9 fantastisch [of idea]; buitensporig: *the ~est dreams* de stoutste dromen **10** roekeloos, gewaagd **11** woest, enthousiast: *she's ~ about him* ze is weg van hem ‖ *a ~ guess* een gok in het wilde weg; *~ horses wouldn't drag it from me!* voor geen geld ter wereld vertel ik het; *~ camping* vrij kamperen

wild card jokerteken[h]

¹wildcat (n) **1** wilde kat, boskat **2** heethoofd; kat [woman]

²wildcat (adj) **1** onsolide [bank, firm]; (financieel) onbetrouwbaar **2** wild; onofficieel [of strike]

wilderness wildernis [also fig]

wildfire bosbrand, natuurbrand ‖ *spread like ~* als een lopend vuurtje (rondgaan)

wildfowl wild gevogelte[h] [waterfowl]

wild-goose chase dwaze onderneming: *be on a ~* met een dwaze onderneming bezig zijn; *send s.o. on a ~* iem. misleiden

wildlife dieren in het wild

wile list, (sluwe) streek

wilful 1 koppig, eigenzinnig **2** opzettelijk, expres: *~ murder* moord met voorbedachten rade

wiliness sluwheid

¹will (n) **1** testament[h]: *his last ~ (and testament)* zijn laatste wilsbeschikking; *she has a ~ of her own* ze heeft een eigen willetje; *he did it of his own free ~* hij deed het uit vrije wil **2** wil, wilskracht, wens, verlangen[h]: *good* (or: *ill) ~* goede (or: slechte) wil ‖ *at ~* naar goeddunken; *with a ~* vastberaden, enthousiast

²will (vb) **1** willen, wensen, verlangen: *God ~ing* als God het wil; *whether she ~ or no* of ze wil of niet **2** willen, zullen: [emphatically] *I said I would do it and I ~* ik heb gezegd dat ik het zou doen en ik zal het ook doen; *~ you hurry up, please?* wil je opschieten, alsjeblieft?; *that ~ be John* dat zal John wel zijn; *I ~ lend you a hand* ik zal je een handje helpen **3** [habit, repetition] plegen, kunnen: *accidents ~ happen* ongelukken zijn niet te vermijden **4** kunnen, in staat zijn te: *this ~ do* is het genoeg **5** zullen, moeten: *you ~ do as I say* je zult doen wat ik zeg

willful *see* wilful

willies kriebels, de zenuwen: *give s.o. the ~* iem. op de zenuwen werken

willing gewillig, bereid(willig): *~ workers* werkwilligen; *I am ~ to admit that …* ik geef grif toe dat …

willow wilg

willowy slank, soepel, elegant

will power wilskracht: *by sheer ~* door louter wilskracht

willy plasser, piemel

willy-nilly goedschiks of kwaadschiks: *~, he was sent to Spain for a year* hij werd voor een jaar naar Spanje gestuurd, of hij nu wilde of niet

wilt 1 (doen) verwelken, (doen) verdorren **2** hangerig worden, lusteloos worden

w__i__ly sluw, listig, slim

wimp sul, doetje[h]

[1]**win** (n) overwinning

[2]**win** (vb) winnen, zegevieren, de overwinning behalen: ~ *hands* down op zijn gemak winnen; ~ *out* (or: *through*) zich erdoorheen slaan, het (uiteindelijk) winnen

[3]**win** (vb) **1** winnen [competition, prize etc]: *you can't* ~ *'em all* je kunt niet altijd winnen **2** verkrijgen, verwerven; behalen [victory, fame, honour]; winnen [friendship, confidence]; ontginnen [mine, vein]; winnen [ore, oil]: ~ *back* terugwinnen **3** overreden, overhalen: ~ s.o. *over* iem. overhalen

[1]**wince** (n) huivering [of pain, fear]

[2]**wince** (vb) huiveren; ineenkrimpen [of pain etc]; terugdeinzen: ~ *at* s.o.'s words van iemands woorden huiveren

[1]**winch** (vb) windas[h], lier

[2]**winch** (vb) opwinden met een windas

[1]**wind** (n) **1** wind, luchtstroom, tocht, rukwind: [fig] take the ~ from (or: out of) s.o.'s *sails* iem. de wind uit de zeilen nemen; *fair* ~ gunstige wind **2** windstreek, windrichting **3** adem(haling), lucht: *get* back (or: *recover*) one's ~ (weer) op adem komen **4** (buik)wind, darmgassen: *break* ~ een wind laten **5** (-s) blazers(sectie) || *get* ~ of sth. ergens lucht van krijgen; (see) how the ~ blows (or: lies) (kijken) uit welke hoek de wind waait; [inform] get (or: have) the ~ *up* hem knijpen, in de rats zitten; [inform] put the ~ *up* de stuipen op het lijf jagen; (sail) *near* the ~ scherp (bij de wind) (zeilen); [fig] de grens van het toelaatbare (raken); there's sth. *in* the ~ er is iets aan de hand; *second* ~ het weer op adem komen, (nieuwe) energie (voor tweede krachtsinspanning)

[2]**wind** (vb) **1** kronkelen, zich slingeren: *the river* ~s through the landscape de rivier kronkelt door het landschap **2** spiralen, zich draaien: ~ing *staircase* (or: *stairs*) wenteltrap

[3]**wind** (vb) buiten adem brengen; naar adem laten snakken [after thump]

[4]**wind** (vb) **1** winden, wikkelen, (op)rollen: ~ *back* terugspoelen; ~ *in* binnenhalen, inhalen [of (fishing) line] **2** omwinden, omwikkelen **3** opwinden: ~ one's *watch* zijn horloge opwinden

[5]**wind** (vb) winden, spoelen, draaien || ~ *on* (a film) (een filmpje) doorspoelen

windbag [inform] kletsmajoor

windbreak beschutting (tegen de wind)

windbreaker [Am] windjack[h]

windchill gevoelstemperatuur, windverkilling

[1]**wind d__o__wn** (vb) zich ontspannen, uitrusten

[2]**wind d__o__wn** (vb) **1** omlaagdraaien: ~ a *car*

window een portierraampje naar beneden draaien **2** terugschroeven, verminderen

windfall 1 afgewaaide vrucht **2** meevaller, mazzeltje[h], erfenisje[h]

wind farm windmolenpark[h]

winding-__up__ liquidatie, opheffing

wind instrument blaasinstrument[h]

windless windstil

windmill 1 windmolen, windturbine **2** (speelgoed)molentje[h] || *fight* (or: *tilt*) at ~s tegen windmolens vechten

window 1 raam[h], venster[h], ruit: ~ on the *world* venster op de wereld **2** etalage **3** [comp] venster[h] || a ~ of *opportunity* for *peace* een kleine kans op vrede, de deur naar vrede staat op een kier; [inform] *out of* the ~ niet meer meetellend, afgeschreven

window dressing 1 het etaleren, etalage **2** etalage, etalage-inrichting, etalagemateriaal[h] **3** gunstige voorstelling, het mooier presenteren dan het is

window-pane (venster)ruit

window-shop etalages kijken: *go* ~ping etalages gaan kijken

windowsill vensterbank, raamkozijn[h]

windpipe luchtpijp

windscreen vooruit [of car]

windshield 1 windscherm[h] [of motorcycle, scooter] **2** [Am] vooruit [of car]

windshield wiper [Am] ruitenwisser

windsock windzak [at airport]

windsurfing windsurfen

windswept 1 winderig, door de wind geteisterd **2** verwaaid, verfomfaaid

[1]**wind up** (vb) **1** eindigen (als), terechtkomen (in), worden (tot): *he'll* ~ in *prison* hij belandt nog eens in de gevangenis **2** sluiten, zich opheffen

[2]**wind __up__** (vb) **1** opwinden; opdraaien [of spring mechanism]: ~ an *alarm* een wekker opwinden **2** omhoogdraaien, ophalen, ophijsen **3** opwinden, opzwepen: *get* wound up opgewonden raken

[3]**wind up** (vb) besluiten, beëindigen, afronden: ~ a *conversation* (or: *project*) een gesprek (or: project) beëindigen; *winding up* tot besluit, samenvattend

[1]**w__i__ndward** (n) loef(zijde)

[2]**w__i__ndward** (adj) **1** loef-, wind-: ~ *side* loefzijde, windzijde **2** windwaarts, tegen de wind (in)

[3]**w__i__ndward** (adv) windwaarts, tegen de wind in

w__i__ndy 1 winderig, open, onbeschut **2** winderig, opgeblazen; gezwollen [of words] **3** bang

[1]**wine** (n) wijn: *sparkling* ~ mousserende wijn, schuimwijn

[2]**wine** (vb): ~ *and dine* uitgebreid dineren

[1]**wing** (n) **1** vleugel: [fig] *spread* (or: *stretch*) one's ~s op eigen benen gaan staan; [fig]

take *under one's* ~s onder zijn vleugels nemen **2** [architecture] vleugel, zijstuk^h **3** [mil] vleugel, flank **4** [pol; fig] (partij)vleugel **5** [football, rugby; fig] vleugel(speler) **6** (-s) coulisse: *in the* ~s achter de schermen ‖ *clip* *s.o.'s* ~*s* iem. kortwieken; *on the* ~ in de vlucht

²wing (vb) **1** van vleugels voorzien; [fig] vleugels geven; voortjagen **2** vleugellam maken, aan de vleugel verwonden

³wing (vb) vliegen, (als) op vleugels gaan **winger** [football, rugby] vleugelspeler, buitenspeler

wing mirror buitenspiegel, zijspiegel

wing nut vleugelmoer

wingspan vleugelspanning; [aviation] spanwijdte

¹wink (n) **1** knipperbeweging [with eyes]; knipoog(je^h): *give s.o. a* ~ iem. een knipoog geven **2** ogenblik^h [of sleep]: *not get a* ~ *(of sleep)*, *not sleep a* ~ geen oog dichtdoen ‖ *tip s.o. the* ~ iem. een hint geven; *forty* ~s dutje^h

²wink (vb) **1** knipperen (met) (de ogen), knipogen: ~ *at s.o.* iem. een knipoog geven **2** twinkelen

winker richtingaanwijzer, knipperlicht^h

winkle out lospeuteren, uitpersen: *winkle information out of s.o.* informatie van iem. lospeuteren

winner 1 winnaar **2** (kas)succes^h: *be onto a* ~ een lot uit de loterij hebben

winning 1 winnend, zegevierend **2** innemend; aantrekkelijk [smile etc]

winnow 1 wannen, van kaf ontdoen: ~ *the chaff (from the grain)* het kaf (uit het koren) wannen **2** (uit)ziften, schiften

wino zuiplap, dronkenlap

winsome aantrekkelijk, charmant

winter winter: *in (the)* ~ 's winters, in de winter; *last* (or: *this*) ~ afgelopen (*or*: komende) winter

winter sports wintersporten

wintertime wintertijd, winterseizoen^h: *in (the)* ~ in de winter

wintry winters, winter-, guur

win-win win-win-, met alleen maar voordelen: *it's a* ~ *situation* het is een win-winsituatie, je zit altijd goed

¹wipe (n) veeg: *give sth. a* ~ iets even afvegen

²wipe (vb) **1** (af)vegen, (weg)wrijven, (uit)wissen: ~ *one's feet* (or: *shoes*) zijn voeten vegen; ~ *away* wegvegen, wrijven; ~ *down,* *give a* ~*-down* afnemen [with damp cloth]; *please* ~ *that grin off your face* haal die grijns van je gezicht **2** (af)drogen, droog wrijven: ~ *one's hands* zijn handen afdrogen

wipe off 1 afvegen, wegvegen, uitwissen **2** tenietdoen [debt etc]

wipe out 1 uitvegen, uitdrogen, (van binnen) schoonmaken **2** vereffenen, uitwissen

3 wegvagen, met de grond gelijk maken, uitroeien, vernietigen **4** uitvegen, wegvegen, uitwissen ‖ *Jane was wiped out* Jane was bekaf

wiper 1 veger **2** ruitenwisser

wipe up 1 afdrogen: *help to* ~ *(the dishes)* helpen met afdrogen **2** opnemen, opdweilen

¹wire (n) **1** metaalkabel, telefoon-, telegraafkabel, telefoonlijn **2** [Am] telegram^h: *by* ~ telegrafisch, per telegram **3** metaaldraad^{+h}: *barbed* ~ prikkeldraad^{+h}

²wire (vb) [Am] telegraferen: ~ *(to) s.o.* iem. een telegram sturen

³wire (vb) **1** met een draad vastmaken **2** bedraden

wire-cutters draadschaar

wired 1 (met draad) verstevigd [of clothing] **2** op het alarmsysteem aangesloten **3** voorzien van afluisterapparatuur

¹wireless (n) **1** radiotelefonie **2** radio: *on* (or: *over*) *the* ~ op (*or*: via) de radio

²wireless (adj) draadloos, radio-

wiretapping het afluisteren

wiring bedrading

wiry 1 draad-, als draad **2** taai, buigzaam als draad; weerbarstig [hair] **3** pezig

wisdom wijsheid

wisdom tooth verstandskies

wise wijs, verstandig ‖ *it is easy to be* ~ *after the event* achteraf is het (altijd) makkelijk praten; *be* ~ *to sth.* iets in de gaten hebben; *without anyone's being the* ~*r* onopgemerkt, zonder dat er een haan kraait; *come away none the* ~*r* (or: *not much* ~*r*) niets (*or*: weinig) wijzer zijn geworden

wiseass [inform] wijsneus

¹wisecrack (n) grappige opmerking

²wisecrack (vb) een grappige opmerking maken

wiseguy 1 wijsneus, betweter **2** [Am] maffialid^h

wisely wijselijk: *he* ~ *kept his mouth shut* hij hield wijselijk zijn mond

¹wise up (vb) [Am] in de gaten krijgen, doorkrijgen: ~ *to what is going on* in de smiezen krijgen wat er gaande is

²wise up (vb) [Am] uit de droom helpen: *get wised up* uit de droom geholpen worden

¹wish (n) **1** verlangen^h, behoefte, zin **2** wens: *best* (or: *good*) ~*es* beste wensen; [email, letter] *best* ~*es* met vriendelijke groet; *express a* ~ *to* de wens te kennen geven te; *make a* ~ een wens doen

²wish (vb) **1** wensen, willen, verlangen: *what more can you* ~ *for?* wat wil je nog meer? **2** (toe)wensen: ~ *s.o. well* iem. het beste wensen ‖ ~ *away* wegwensen, wensen dat iets niet bestond; *I wouldn't* ~ *that on my worst enemy* dat zou ik mijn ergste vijand nog niet toewensen

wishful wensend, verlangend: ~ *thinking* wishful thinking; [roughly] vrome wens, [roughly] ijdele hoop

wish list verlanglijstje^h

wishy-washy 1 waterig, slap, dun **2** krachteloos, slap, armzalig

wisp 1 bosje^h, bundeltje^h: ~ *of hay* bosje hooi **2** pluimpje^h, plukje^h: ~ *of hair* plukje haar, piek **3** sliert, kringel, (rook)pluim(pje^h): ~s *of music* flarden muziek

wistful 1 weemoedig, droefgeestig **2** smachtend

¹wit (n) **1** gevat iemand **2** scherpzinnigheid **3** geestigheid **4** (-s) verstand^h, benul^h, intelligentie: *have enough* ~ (or: *have the* ~(s)) *to say no* zo verstandig zijn nee te zeggen || *at one's* ~s' *end* ten einde raad; *have* (or: *keep*) *one's* ~s *about one* alert zijn, bijdehand (or: pienter) zijn; *live by* (or: *on*) *one's* ~s op ongeregelde manier aan de kost komen

²wit (vb): *to* ~ te weten, namelijk, dat wil zeggen

witch heks

witchcraft tove(na)rij, hekserij

witch doctor medicijnman

witchery 1 betovering, bekoring, charme **2** tovenarij

with 1 met: *a conversation* ~ *Jill* een gesprek met Jill; *compared* ~ *Mary* vergeleken bij Mary; *angry* ~ *Sheila* kwaad op Sheila **2** [direction] mee met, overeenkomstig (met): *it changes* ~ *the seasons* het verandert met de seizoenen; *sail* ~ *the wind* met de wind zeilen; *come* ~ *me* kom met mij mee **3** [accompaniment, cohesion, characteristic] (samen) met, bij, inclusief, hebbende: *she can sing* ~ *the best of them* ze kan zingen als de beste; *I like it* ~ *sauce* ik eet het graag met saus; *what is* ~ *him?* wat is er met hem (aan de hand)?; *spring is* ~ *us* het is lente; *it's all right* ~ *me* ik vind het goed, mij is het om het even **4** [place; also fig] bij, toevertrouwd aan: *she stayed* ~ *her aunt* ze logeerde bij haar tante **5** [contrast] niettegenstaande, ondanks: *a nice girl,* ~ *all her faults* een leuk meisje, ondanks haar gebreken **6** [means or cause] met, met behulp van, door middel van: *they woke us* ~ *their noise* zij maakten haar wakker met hun lawaai; *pleased* ~ *the results* tevreden over de resultaten; *filled* ~ *water* vol water; *sick* ~ *worry* ziek van de zorgen **7** [time] bij, tegelijkertijd met, samen met: ~ *his death all changed* met zijn dood veranderde alles; *he arrived* ~ *Mary* hij kwam tegelijkertijd met Mary aan; *she's not* ~ *it* **a)** ze heeft geen benul; **b)** ze is hopeloos ouderwets || *I'm* ~ *you there* dat ben ik met je eens; *away* (or: *down*) ~ *him!* weg met hem!; *it's all over* ~ *him* het is met hem afgelopen; *what's up* ~ *him?* wat heeft hij?

¹withdraw (vb) **1** uit de weg gaan, opzij-

gaan **2** zich terugtrekken: *the army withdrew* het leger trok terug **3** zich onttrekken aan, niet deelnemen

²withdraw (vb) **1** terugtrekken: ~ *one's hand* zijn hand terugtrekken **2** onttrekken aan, niet laten deelnemen: ~ *a team from a tournament* een ploeg uit een toernooi terugtrekken **3** terugnemen [remark, promise]; herroepen: ~ *an offer* (or: *a promise*) op een aanbod (or: belofte) terugkomen **4** opnemen [from bank account]: ~ *a hundred pounds* honderd pond opnemen

withdrawal 1 terugtrekking, terugtocht, het terugtrekken **2** intrekking [eg of promise] **3** opname [from bank account] **4** ontwenning [from drug]

withdrawal symptom ontwenningsverschijnsel^h

withdrawn 1 teruggetrokken, op zichzelf (levend) **2** (kop)schuw, bescheiden, verlegen

¹wither (vb) **1** verwelken, verdorren: ~ed *leaves* dorre bla(de)ren **2** vergaan: *my hopes* ~ed *(away)* mijn hoop vervloog

²wither (vb) **1** doen verwelken, doen vergaan **2** vernietigen, wegvagen

withhold onthouden, niet geven, toestaan, inhouden: ~ *one's consent* zijn toestemming weigeren

within [place] binnen in, in: ~ *the organization* binnen de organisatie; *he came to* ~ *five feet from the goal* hij kwam tot op anderhalve meter van het doel; *he returned* ~ *an hour* hij kwam binnen het uur terug || *inquire* ~ informeer binnen

without zonder: *she left* ~ *a word* zij vertrok zonder een woord te zeggen; *it goes* ~ *saying* het spreekt vanzelf || *he had to do* ~ hij moest het zonder stellen

withstand weerstaan, het hoofd bieden: ~ *an attack* een aanval weerstaan **2** bestand zijn tegen, opgewassen zijn tegen: ~ *wind and weather* bestand zijn tegen weer en wind

¹witness (n) **1** (oog)getuige, medeondertekenaar **2** getuigenis^{+h}, getuigenverklaring, (ken)teken^h, bewijs^h: *bear* (or: *give*) ~ *(on behalf of s.o.)* getuigen (ten gunste van iem.) || *bear* ~ *of* (or: *to*) staven, bewijzen

²witness (vb) getuigen, als getuige verklaren: ~ *against s.o.* getuigen tegen iem.

³witness (vb) **1** getuige zijn van, bij: ~ *an accident* getuige zijn van een ongeluk; ~ *a signature* (als getuige) medeondertekenen **2** getuigen van, een teken zijn van

witness box getuigenbank

witter on kletsen, wauwelen

witticism geestige opmerking

witty geestig

¹wizard (n) **1** tovenaar: *he's a* ~ *with a microwave oven* hij kan toveren met een magnetron **2** genie^h

²wizard (adj) waanzinnig, te gek, eindeloos

wizened verschrompeld, gerimpeld, verweerd

wk *week*

¹**wobble** (n) **1** schommeling, afwijking **2** beving, trilling

²**wobble** (vb) waggelen, wankelen

³**wobble** (vb) wiebelen (met): *don't ~ your chair* zit niet met je stoel te wiebelen

wobbly wankel, onvast, wiebelig

woe 1 ramp(spoed), narigheid, ellende **2** smart, weeʰ: *tale of ~* smartelijk verhaal

¹**woeful** smartelijk, verdrietig

¹**wolf** (n) **1** wolf **2** versierder ‖ *keep the ~ from the door* (nog) brood op de plank hebben; *~ in sheep's clothing* wolf in schaapskleren; *cry ~ (too often)* (te vaak) (lichtvaardig) loos alarm slaan

²**wolf** (vb) (also + down) (op)schrokken; naar binnen schrokken [food]

wolf cub wolfsjongʰ, wolfjeʰ

wolf whistle lokfluitjeʰ

woman 1 vrouw, vrouwspersoonʰ, de vrouw, het vrouwelijke geslacht **2** werkster, (dienst)meid **3** maîtresse: *kept ~* maîtresse **4** vrouw, echtgenote

womanhood 1 vrouwelijkheid, het vrouw-zijn **2** de vrouwen, het vrouwelijk geslacht

womanish 1 vrouwelijk, vrouw-, vrouwen- **2** [depr] verwijfd

womanizer rokkenjager, versierder

womankind de vrouwen, het vrouwelijke geslacht

womanly vrouwelijk

womb baarmoeder; [also fig] schoot

Women's Lib *Women's Liberation* vrouwenemancipatiebeweging; [roughly] Dolle Mina

women's refuge blijf-van-mijn-lijfhuisʰ; [Belg] vluchthuisʰ

¹**wonder** (n) **1** wonderʰ, volmaakt voorwerpʰ **2** wonderʰ, mirakelʰ: [fig] *do* (or: *work*) ~s wonderen doen; *~s never cease* de wonderen zijn de wereld nog niet uit **3** verwondering, verbazing, bewondering ‖ *it is little* (or: *no*) *~ that* het is geen wonder dat

²**wonder** (vb) **1** (+ at) verbaasd staan (over), verrast zijn, zich verbazen, (vreemd) opkijken: *I don't ~ at her hesitation* haar aarzeling verbaast me niet; *I shouldn't ~ if* het zou me niet verbazen als **2** benieuwd zijn, zich iets afvragen: *I ~ who will win* ik ben benieuwd wie er gaat winnen; *I ~ whether she noticed* ik vraag me af of ze het gemerkt heeft **3** iets betwijfelen, zich iets afvragen: *Is that so? I ~* O ja? Ik betwijfel het (ten zeerste), O ja? Ik moet het nog zien

wonder boy wonderkindʰ

wonderful schitterend, geweldig, fantastisch

wonderland sprookjeslandʰ, wonderschoon gebiedʰ

wondrous wonder(baarlijk): *~ tales* wondere vertellingen

wonky krakkemikkig, wankel; [fig] slap

woo 1 dingen naar (de gunst van), voor zich trachten te winnen: *~ the voters* dingen naar de gunst van de kiezers **2** het hof maken, dingen naar de hand van

¹**wood** (n) **1** houtʰ: *I haven't had the flu this winter yet, touch ~* ik heb deze winter nog geen griep gehad, laat ik het afkloppen **2** bosʰ: *a walk in the ~s* een wandeling in het bos ‖ *he can't see the ~ for the trees* hij ziet door de bomen het bos niet meer; *out of the ~(s)* in veilige haven, buiten gevaar, uit de problemen

²**wood** (adj) houten

woodcarving houtsnijwerkʰ

woodcraft houtsnijkunst, houtbewerking

woodcut 1 houtsnede **2** hout(snede)blokʰ

woodcutter houthakker

wooded bebost, bosrijk

wooden 1 houten: *~ horse* houten paard, paard van Troje; *~ shoe* klomp **2** houterig, stijf, harkerig

wooden-headed dom, stom

woodland bosrijke streek

woodlouse pissebed

woodman 1 houtvester, boswachter **2** houthakker

woodpecker specht

wood pigeon houtduif

woodpile houtstapel; stapel brandhout

woodsman 1 houtvester, boswachter **2** houthakker

woodwinds houtʰ

woodwork 1 houtbewerking, timmermanskunst **2** houtwerkʰ ‖ *crawl* (or: *come*) *out of the ~* plotseling tevoorschijn komen

woof 1 woef(geluidʰ), waf, geblafʰ **2** inslag [of fabric]

woofer woofer, lagetonenluidspreker

¹**wool** (n) wol ‖ *pull the ~ over s.o.'s eyes* iem. zand in de ogen strooien

²**wool** (adj) wollen, van wol

¹**wool-gathering** (n) verstrooidheid, afwezigheid

²**wool-gathering** (adj) verstrooid, afwezig, aan het dagdromen

woollen wollen, van wol

¹**woolly** (n) wolletjeʰ, trui, wollen kledingstukʰ, ondergoedʰ

²**woolly** (adj) **1** wollen, wollig, van wol **2** onduidelijk, vaag, wollig, warrig

woozy wazig, licht in het hoofd

¹**word** (n) **1** woordʰ, (gesproken) uiting: *~s* tekst; woorden [to song]; *have a ~ in s.o.'s ear* iem. iets toefluisteren; *by ~ of mouth* mondeling; *put ~s in(to) s.o.'s mouth* iem. woorden in de mond leggen; *right from the ~ go* vanaf het begin; *~s fail me* woorden schieten

mij tekort; *say* the ~ een seintje geven; *take s.o. at his* ~ iem. aan zijn woord houden; ~ *for* ~ woord voor woord, woordelijk; *in* other ~*s* met andere woorden; *put into* ~*s* onder woorden brengen; *have a* ~ *with s.o.* iem. (even) spreken; *have* ~*s with s.o.* woorden hebben met iem. **2** (ere)woord[h], belofte: *he is as good as his* ~ wat hij belooft doet hij; *I give you my* ~ ik verzeker het je op mijn erewoord; *keep* one's ~ (zijn) woord houden; *take s.o.'s* ~ *for it* iem. op zijn woord geloven **3** (wacht)woord[h], bevel[h]: *his* ~ *is law* zijn wil is wet **4** nieuws[h], bericht[h], boodschap: *the* ~ *got* round that het bericht deed de ronde dat; *send* ~ *of* berichten || *eat* one's ~*s* zijn woorden inslikken, iets terugnemen; *I could not get a* ~ *in edgeways* ik kon er geen speld tussen krijgen; *weigh* one's ~*s* zijn woorden wegen

²**word** (vb) verwoorden, onder woorden brengen: *I received a carefully* ~*ed letter* ik kreeg een brief die in zorgvuldige bewoordingen gesteld was

word blindness woordblindheid
wording formulering, woordkeus
wordless woordloos; onuitgesproken
wordplay woord(en)spel[h], woordspelingen
word processor tekstverwerker
word wrap woordomslag, automatische tekstoverloop naar volgende regel op scherm
wordy omslachtig; langdradig

¹**work** (n) **1** werk(stuk)[h], arbeid: *a* ~ *of art* een kunstwerk; *have* one's ~ *cut out (for one)* ergens de handen aan vol hebben; *set to* ~ aan het werk gaan; *set about* one's ~ *in the wrong way* verkeerd te werk gaan; *at* ~ aan het werk, op het werk; *men at* ~ werk in uitvoering; *out of* ~ werkloos **2** borduurwerk[h], handwerk[h], naaldwerk[h] **3** (-s) oeuvre[h], werken, verzameld werk[h]: *Joyce's collected* ~*s* de verzamelde werken van Joyce **4** (-s) mechanisme[h] [of clock etc] **5** (-s) zooi, bups, mikmak **6** (-s) fabriek, bedrijf[h], werkplaats || *give s.o. the* ~*s* **a)** iem. flink onder handen nemen; **b)** iem. om zeep helpen; [inform] *gum up the* ~*s* de boel in de war sturen; *shoot the* ~*s* alles op alles zetten, alles riskeren

²**work** (vb) **1** werken, functioneren: *the scheme didn't* ~ het plan werkte niet; ~ *away* (druk) aan het werk zijn; ~ *at* werken aan, zijn best doen op; *it* ~*s by electricity* het loopt op elektriciteit; ~ *on* werken aan iets, bezig zijn met iets; ~ *to* werken volgens **2** gisten, werken **3** raken [in a condition]: *the boy's socks* ~*ed down* de sokken van de jongen zakten af; ~ *round to* toewerken naar, aansturen op

³**work** (vb) **1** verrichten, tot stand brengen, bewerkstelligen: ~ *miracles* (or: *wonders*)

wonderen verrichten **2** laten werken, aan het werk hebben: ~ *s.o. hard* iem. hard laten werken **3** in werking zetten, aanzetten, bedienen, bewerken, in bedrijf houden: ~ *a mine* een mijn exploiteren **4** zich banen [a path through sth.]: ~ one's *way to the top* zich naar de top werken **5** bewerken, kneden, werken met: ~ *clay* kleien, boetseren
workable 1 bedrijfsklaar, gebruiksklaar, bruikbaar **2** uitvoerbaar, haalbaar, werkbaar
workaholic werkverslaafde, workaholic
workaround alternatief[h], alternatieve oplossing
workbench werkbank
workbook 1 werkboek(je[h]) **2** handleiding, instructieboekje[h]
workday werkdag
worker werker, arbeider, werknemer
workflow workflow, werkstroom
work force personeelsbestand[h]
workhorse werkpaard[h] [also fig]; werkezel
work in 1 insteken **2** verwerken: *try to* ~ *some more details* probeer nog een paar bijzonderheden op te nemen || ~ *with* (kunnen) samenwerken met
working werkend, werk-: *the* ~ *class* de arbeidersklasse; ~ *man* arbeider; ~ *mother* buitenshuis werkende moeder
working day werkdag
working drawing constructietekening, werktekening
working knowledge praktijkkennis, praktische beheersing: ~ *of* German voldoende beheersing van het Duits
working week werkweek
workload werk[h], werklast, werkbelasting
workman werkman, arbeider
workmanlike ambachtelijk
workmanship 1 vakmanschap[h], vakkundigheid **2** (hand)werk[h], afwerking
work off wegwerken: ~ *steam* stoom afblazen
workout 1 training **2** intensieve conditietraining, work-out
¹**work out** (vb) **1** zich ontwikkelen, verlopen, (gunstig) uitvallen **2** oplosbaar zijn, uitkomen **3** trainen; fitnessen || ~ *at* (or: *to*) uitkomen op, bedragen
²**work out** (vb) **1** uitwerken; opstellen [plan etc] **2** uitrekenen, uitwerken, berekenen, uitzoeken: *work things out* de dingen op een rijtje zetten; *try if you can work it out for yourself* probeer eens of je er zelf achter kunt komen **3** hoogte krijgen van, doorgronden, doorzien
work permit werkvergunning
workplace werk[h], werkplek: *at* (or: *in*) *the* ~ op het werk
work placement stage: *do a* ~ *at a department store* stage lopen bij een warenhuis

worksheet 1 kladje^h, kladblaadje^h
2 [comp] werkblad^h
workshop 1 werkplaats, atelier^h **2** workshop **3** werkgroep
workstation 1 werkplek **2** werkstation^h
work stoppage werkonderbreking; sta-
king
worktop werkblad^h, aanrecht^h
work-to-rule stiptheidsactie
¹**work up** (vb) (+ to) toewerken (naar)
²**work up** (vb) **1** opbouwen, uitbouwen
2 stimuleren: ~ *an appetite* zich inspannen
zodat men honger krijgt **3** woedend (nerveus) maken: *don't get worked up* maak je
niet druk **4** opwerken, omhoogwerken:
work one's way up from zich omhoogwerken
vanuit **5** (om)vormen: *he's working up his
notes into a book* hij is bezig zijn aantekenin-
genmateriaal uit te werken tot een boek ||
work s.o. (or: *o.s.*) *up* iem. (or: zichzelf) opjui-
nen
world wereld; [fig] hoop; boel, menigte:
make a ~ of difference een hoop verschil uitmaken; *it will do you a ~ of good* daar zul je
reuze van opknappen; *come into the ~* geboren worden; *all the ~ knows, the whole ~
knows* de hele wereld weet het; *why in the ~
did you do this?* waarom heb je dat in 's hemelsnaam gedaan?; *out of this* ~ **a)** niet van
deze wereld; **b)** te gek; *the other* ~ het hier-
namaals; *the Third World* de derde wereld ||
I'd give the ~ to … ik zou er alles (ter wereld)
voor over hebben om …; *think the ~ of s.o.*
een zeer hoge dunk van iem. hebben, iem.
op handen dragen; *they are ~s apart* ze verschillen als dag en nacht; *not for (all) the ~*
voor geen goud; *it is for all the ~ like* (or: *as if*)
het lijkt sprekend op
world-beater superkampioen
World Cup wereldbeker, wereldkampi-
oenschap(pen) [socc]
world-famous wereldberoemd
world-leader 1 [pol] wereldleider **2** [econ]
toonaangevend bedrijf^h
worldly werelds, aards, wereldwijs: ~ *wisdom* wereldwijsheid; ~ *goods* wereldse goederen
worldly-wise wereldwijs
world power wereldmacht
world record wereldrecord^h
world war wereldoorlog
world-weary levensmoe
worldwide wereldwijd, over de hele wereld
¹**worm** (n) **1** worm, hazelworm **2** schroef-
draad
²**worm** (vb) **1** ontwormen [dog, cat etc]
2 wurmen: ~ *one's way into* zich weten in te
dringen in **3** ontfutselen, ontlokken: ~ *a secret out of s.o.* iem. een geheim ontfutselen
worn-out 1 afgedragen, (tot op de draad)

versleten **2** uitgeput, doodop, bekaf
worried bezorgd, ongerust: *a ~ look* een
zorgelijk gezicht
worrisome 1 zorgwekkend, onrustbarend
2 zorgelijk, tobberig
¹**worry** (n) **1** (voorwerp^h van) zorg: [inform]
no worries geen probleem, maak je geen
zorgen, niets aan de hand **2** zorgenkind^h,
bron van zorgen **3** zorg, bezorgdheid, ongerustheid
²**worry** (vb) (+ about, over) zich zorgen ma-
ken (over): *I have enough to ~ about* ik heb al
genoeg aan mijn hoofd; *I should* ~ (zal) mij
een zorg (zijn) || *not to ~!* maak je geen zor-
gen!; ~ *at* **a)** zich het hoofd breken over
[problem]; **b)** aandringen bij [somebody]
³**worry** (vb) lastigvallen, hinderen, storen:
the rain doesn't ~ him de regen deert hem
niet; *oh, that doesn't ~ me* o, daar zit ik niet
(zo) mee, o, daar geef ik niks om; *you'll ~
yourself to death* je maakt je veel te druk
worrying zorgwekkend, zorgelijk
¹**worse** (n) iets slechters, slechtere dingen: *a
change for the* ~ een verandering ten kwade,
een verslechtering
²**worse** (adj, adv) **1** slechter, erger, minder
(goed): *to make things* ~ tot overmaat van
ramp; ~ *still* erger nog **2** zieker, zwakker: *today mother was much ~ than yesterday* van-
daag was moeder zieker dan gisteren || *the ~
for drink* (or: *liquor*) aangeschoten; *he is none
the ~ for* hij is niet minder geworden van, hij
heeft niet geleden onder; *I like him none the ~
for it* ik mag hem er niet minder om
worsen verergeren, verslechteren, bemoeilijken
¹**worship** (n) **1** verering, aanbidding **2** ere-
dienst, godsdienst(oefening) || *Your Worship*
Edelachtbare
²**worship** (vb) **1** naar de kerk gaan **2** van
eerbied vervuld zijn, in aanbidding verzon-
ken zijn
³**worship** (vb) [also fig] aanbidden, vereren
worshipper 1 kerkganger, gelovige
2 aanbidder, vereerder
worst 1 slechtst, ergst: *come off* ~ aan het
kortste eind trekken **2** ziekst, zwakst || *if the
~ comes* to the ~ in het ergste geval; *so you
want to fight, OK, we'll fight. Do your ~!* dus jij
wil vechten, goed, dan vechten we. Kom
maar op!; *at (the)* ~ in het ergste geval
¹**worth** (n) **1** waarde, kwaliteit: *of great ~*
van grote waarde **2** markt-, tegenwaarde: *I
want a dollar's ~ of apples* mag ik voor een
dollar appels?
²**worth** (adj) waard: *land ~ 100,000 dollars*
land met een waarde van 100.000 dollar; *it is
~ (one's) while* het is de moeite waard; ~ *seeing* bezienswaardig; *for what it's ~* voor wat
het waard is; *it's ~ it* het is de moeite waard ||
for all one is ~ uit alle macht

worthwhile de moeite waard, waardevol, nuttig

worthy 1 waardig, waardevol **2** waard: *in clothes ~ of the occasion* in bij de gelegenheid passende kleding; *he isn't ~ of her* hij is haar niet waard **3** [oft iron] achtenswaardig, braaf

would 1 willen, zullen, wensen: *he ~ not hear of it* hij wilde er niet van horen; *I wish he ~ leave me alone* ik wilde dat hij me met rust liet; *I ~ like to show you this* ik zou je dit graag laten zien; *he ~ sooner die than surrender* hij zou liever sterven dan zich overgeven **2** gewoonlijk, steeds, altijd: *we ~ walk to school together* we liepen gewoonlijk samen naar school **3** zou(den): *I ~ try it anyway (if I were you)* ik zou het toch maar proberen (als ik jou was); *he was writing the book that ~ bring him fame* hij was het boek aan het schrijven dat hem beroemd zou maken **4** [supposition] moeten, zullen, zou(den), moest(en): *he ~ be in bed by now* hij zal nu wel in bed liggen; *~ you please shut the door?* wil je de deur sluiten alsjeblieft? **5** [doubt or uncertainty] zou kunnen: *we ~ suggest the following* we zouden het volgende willen voorstellen

would-be 1 [depr] zogenaamd **2** toekomstig, potentieel, mogelijk: *a ~ buyer* een mogelijke koper, een gegadigde

¹wound (n) wond, verwonding; [fig] beledigng || *lick one's ~s* zijn wonden likken [after defeat]

²wound (vb) (ver)wonden; [fig] grieven; krenken: *when he suddenly left her, she felt ~ed and betrayed* toen hij plotseling bij haar wegging, voelde ze zich gekwetst en verraden

wow 1 klapper, groot succesʰ, sensatie **2** wow [of stereo equipment]

wrack verwoesting, vervalʰ, ruïne

wraith (geest)verschijning, schim, spookʰ, spookgestalte

¹wrangle (n) ruzie

²wrangle (vb) ruzie maken, ruziën: *~ with s.o. about (or: over) sth.* met iem. om (*or:* over) iets ruziën

¹wrap (n) **1** omslag(doekʰ), omgeslagen kledingstukʰ, sjaal, stola **2** (reis)deken⁺ʰ || *take the ~s off* onthullen; *under ~s* geheim

²wrap (vb) zich wikkelen

³wrap (vb) **1** inpakken, verpakken **2** wikkelen, omslaan, vouwen **3** (om)hullen, bedekken: *~ped in mist* in nevelen gehuld

wrapper 1 (stof)omslagʰ, kaft⁺ʰ **2** adresband(je)ʰ **3** papiertjeʰ, pakpapierʰ, wikkel

wrapping paper inpakpapierʰ; cadeaupapierʰ

¹wrap up (vb) **1** zich (warm) (aan)kleden **2** zijn mond houden: *~!* kop dicht!

²wrap up (vb) **1** verpakken, inpakken **2** warm aankleden, (goed/stevig) inpakken

3 afwikkelen, afronden, sluiten: *~ a deal* een overeenkomst sluiten || *be wrapped up in* opgaan in; *wrap it up!* hou op!

wrath [form] toorn; woede

wrathful woedend

wreak 1 uitstorten: *~ vengeance (up)on* wraak nemen op **2** veroorzaken, aanrichten

wreath (rouw)krans, (ere)krans || *~ of smoke* kringetje rook

¹wreathe (vb) kringelen, kronkelen

²wreathe (vb) **1** omkransen, om(k)ringen, omhullen: *~d in* om(k)ringd door, gehuld in; [fig] *a face ~ in smiles* een in glimlachen gehuld gelaat **2** (om)wikkelen, (om)strengelen **3** (be)kransen, met een krans tooien

¹wreck (n) **1** wrakʰ [also fig]; ruïne **2** schipbreuk [also fig]; ondergang, vernietiging

²wreck (vb) **1** schipbreuk doen lijden, doen stranden, aan de grond doen lopen; [fig] doen mislukken [plan etc]: *the ship was ~ed on the rocks* het schip liep op de rotsen **2** ruïneren, verwoesten, te gronde richten

wreckage wrakgoedʰ, wrakstukken, brokstukken, restanten

wrecked [inform] **1** straalbezopen **2** zeer high

wrecker 1 berger, bergingsmaatschappij **2** [Am] sloper, sloopbedrijfʰ **3** [Am] takelwagen

wren winterkoninkjeʰ

¹wrench (n) **1** ruk, draai **2** verrekking, verstuiking **3** moersleutel

²wrench (vb) **1** (los)wringen, (los)wrikken, een ruk geven aan: *~ open* openwrikken, openrukken; *~ away* (*or:* off) losrukken, wegrukken, loswrikken **2** verzwikken, verstuiken **3** vertekenen; verdraaien [facts etc]

wrest 1 (los)rukken, (los)wringen, (los)wrikken: [fig] *~ a confession from s.o.* een bekentenis uit iem. persen **2** zich meester maken van, zich toe-eigenen **3** verdraaien; geweld aandoen [meaning, facts]

wrestle worstelen (met/tegen) [also fig]: *~ with problems* met problemen kampen

wrestler worstelaar

wrestling worstelenʰ

wretch 1 stakker, zielenpoot **2** ellendeling, klier **3** schurk, boef, schooier

wretched 1 beklagenswaardig, zielig, droevig **2** ellendig, ongelukkig **3** verachtelijk, laag **4** waardeloos, beroerd, rot-

¹wriggle (n) kronkelbeweging, gekronkelʰ, gewriemelʰ

²wriggle (vb) kronkelen, wriemelen; [fig] zich in allerlei bochten wringen: *~ out of sth.* ergens onderuit proberen te komen

³wriggle (vb) **1** wriemelen met, wriemelend heen en weer bewegen **2** kronkelend afleggen

wring 1 omdraaien: *~ a hen's neck* een kip de nek omdraaien **2** (uit)wringen, (uit)persen, samenknijpen: ~ s.o.'s **hand** iem. stevig de hand drukken **3** afpersen, afdwingen: ~ a confession **from** (or: out **of**) s.o. iem. een bekentenis afdwingen

¹**wrinkle** (n) **1** rimpel, plooi, kreuk **2** foefje^h, kunstje^h **3** tip, idee^h

²**wrinkle** (vb) rimpelen, rimpels (doen) krijgen, kreuke(le)n

wrinkly rimpelig, gerimpeld; kreukelig

wrist 1 pols(gewricht^h) **2** pols(stuk^h) [of clothing]; manchet

wristband 1 horlogebandje^h, pols(arm)-band **2** manchet

wristlet 1 horlogeband(je^h) **2** polsband-(je^h) [sport] **3** armband(je^h)

wristwatch polshorloge^h

writ 1 bevelschrift^h, dwangbevel^h, gerechtelijk schrijven^h: **serve** a ~ on een dagvaarding betekenen aan **2** de Schrift [Bible]

write schrijven, (weg)schrijven: ~ a **cheque** een cheque uitschrijven; ~ **back** terugschrijven, antwoorden; ~ **about** (or: on) a subject over een onderwerp schrijven; ~ away **for** over de post bestellen || nothing to ~ **home** about niet(s) om over naar huis te schrijven; that's not written in stone dat is niet in beton gegoten, dat kan nog anders worden; envy was written all **over** his face de jaloezie stond hem op het gezicht te lezen

write down neerschrijven, opschrijven, op papier vastleggen **2** beschrijven, uitmaken voor, beschouwen (als): write s.o. down (as) a **bore** iem. uitmaken voor een vervelende vent

¹**write in** (vb) schrijven, schriftelijk verzoeken: ~ **for** a free catalogue schrijven om een gratis catalogus

²**write in** (vb) bijschrijven, invoegen, toevoegen, inlassen

¹**write off** (vb) schrijven, over de post bestellen: ~ **for** sth., ~ **to** order sth. schrijven om iets te bestellen

²**write off** (vb) **1** afschrijven [also fig]; afvoeren: ~ **losses** (or: a **car**) verliezen (or: een auto) afschrijven **2** (op)schrijven, in elkaar draaien

write-off 1 afschrijving **2** total loss; weggooier [fig]

write out 1 uitschrijven, voluit schrijven **2** schrijven; uitschrijven [cheque etc] **3** schrappen; uitschrijven [part in TV series]: her **part** was written out haar rol werd geschrapt

writer schrijver, schrijfster, auteur: the (present) ~ ondergetekende

writer's block writer's block^h

write up 1 bijwerken [diary] **2** uitwerken, uitschrijven

writhe wringen, kronkelen, (ineen)krimpen: ~ **with** pain kronkelen van de pijn

writing 1 schrijven^h: **in** ~ schriftelijk

2 (hand)schrift^h **3** schrift^h, schrijfstuur^{+h}: **put** sth. down in ~ iets op schrift stellen **4** (-s) werken, geschriften || the ~ **on the wall** het teken aan de wand

writing desk schrijfbureau^h

writing pad schrijfblok^h, blocnote

¹**wrong** (n) **1** kwaad^h, onrecht^h: **right** and ~ juist en onjuist **2** misstand, wantoestand **3** onrechtmatige daad || be **in** the ~ **a)** het mis hebben; **b)** de schuldige zijn, het gedaan hebben

²**wrong** (adj) **1** verkeerd, fout, onjuist: ~ **number** verkeerd verbonden; (the) ~ **way** round achterstevoren, de verkeerde kant op; go down the ~ **way** in het verkeerde keelgat schieten [of food] **2** slecht, verkeerd, niet goed: **you're** ~ to do this, **it's** ~ of you to do this u doet hier verkeerd aan **3** in de verkeerde richting, de verkeerde kant op || get hold of the ~ **end** of the stick het bij het verkeerde eind hebben; come to the ~ **shop** aan het verkeerde adres (gekomen) zijn; get on the ~ **side** of s.o. iemands sympathie verliezen; on the ~ **side** of sixty de zestig gepasseerd; [Am] the ~ **side** of the tracks de achterbuurten, de zelfkant; **you're** ~ je hebt ongelijk, je vergist je

³**wrong** (vb) **1** onrecht doen, onrechtvaardig behandelen, onredelijk zijn tegen: ~ a **person** iem. tekortdoen **2** onbillijk beoordelen

wrongdoer wetsovertreder; misdadiger

wrongdoing 1 wandaad, overtreding **2** wangedrag^h, misdadigheid

wrongful 1 onterecht, onbillijk **2** onrechtmatig, onwettig

wrong-headed 1 dwars(liggerig), eigenwijs **2** foutief, verkeerd

wrought-up gespannen, nerveus, opgewonden

wry 1 (ver)zuur(d), wrang: ~ **mouth** zuinig mondje **2** (licht) ironisch, spottend, droog; laconiek [of humour]: ~ **smile** spottend lachje

wt weight gewicht

WTF [vulg] what the fuck? [surprise] krijg nou wat; [irritation] in vredesnaam

WWW World Wide Web www

WYSIWYG What You See Is What You Get wysiwyg

X

x 1 (de letter) x **2** onbekende persoon
3 [maths] onbekende grootheid
xenophobe xenofoob, vreemdelingenha-
ter
xenophobia xenofobie, vreemdelingenhaat, vreemdelingenangst
¹**xerox** (n) **1** fotokopie **2** kopieerapparaat[h]
²**xerox** (vb) (foto)kopiëren
XL *extra large* XL; extra groot [clothing]
XLNT [inform] *excellent* uitstekend, prima
Xmas Kerstmis, kerst
X-rated [roughly] (voor) boven de achttien
X-rating keuring boven de 18
¹**X-ray** (n) **1** röntgenstraal **2** röntgenfoto
²**X-ray** (vb) **1** doorlichten [also fig] **2** bestralen
xylophone xylofoon

y

y y, Y
yacht jacht^h [ship]
yachting (wedstrijd)zeilen^h
yachtsman zeiler
yackety-yack [inform] geouwehoer^h, ge-lul^h
yada yada yada [Am; inform] blablabla
yahoo varken^h, schoft
yak jak, knorbuffel
yammer 1 jammeren 2 kakelen
¹yank (n) ruk, sjor
²yank (vb) een ruk geven aan, trekken
Yankee [Am] 1 yankee, yank; [hist] noorderling 2 [depr] Amerikaan
¹yap (n) gekef^h
²yap (vb) 1 keffen 2 [inform] kleppen, kakelen
yard 1 Engelse el [91.4 cm]: *by the* ~ per yard; [fig] ellenlang 2 [shipp] ra 3 (omheind) terrein^h, binnenplaats, erf^h 4 [Am] plaatsje^h, (achter)tuin, gazon^h || *the* Yard Scotland Yard
yardage 1 aantal yards 2 lengte
yardstick meetlat; [fig] maatstaf
yarn 1 lang verhaal^h, (langdradig) verhaal^h 2 garen^h, draad || *spin a* ~ een lang verhaal vertellen
¹yawn (n) geeuw, gaap
²yawn (vb) geeuwen; gapen [also fig]; wijd geopend zijn: *~ing hole* gapend gat
yay [inform] joepie, geweldig
yd *yard*
yds *yards*
¹ye (pers pron) gij, u, jullie, jij
²ye (art) de: *ye olde Spanish Inn* de oude Spaanse herberg
yea 1 stem vóór: *~s and nays* stemmen vóór en tegen 2 voorstemmer
year 1 jaar^h: *a ~ from today* vandaag over een jaar; *all the* ~ *round* het hele jaar door; *for many ~s* sinds jaar en dag; *over the ~s* met de jaren 2 lange tijd; [fig] eeuw 3 (-s) jaren, leeftijd 4 (-s) eeuwigheid; eeuwen: *it has been ~s* het is eeuwen geleden
yearling eenjarig dier^h, eenjarig renpaard^h
yearly jaarlijks, elk jaar: *a ~ income* een jaarinkomen
yearn smachten, verlangen: ~ *after* (or: *for*) smachten naar
yeast gist; [fig] desem
¹yell (n) gil, kreet, schreeuw, aanmoedigingskreet
²yell (vb) gillen, schreeuwen: ~ *one's head off* tekeergaan, tieren

¹yellow (n) 1 geel^h 2 eigeel^h, dooier
²yellow (adj) 1 geel(achtig) 2 laf || [socc] *show s.o. a* ~ *card* iem. een gele kaart geven; ~ *pages* gouden gids
¹yelp (n) 1 gekef^h 2 gejank^h 3 gil
²yelp (vb) 1 keffen 2 janken 3 gillen
Yemen Jemen
¹Yemeni (n) Jemeniet, Jemenitische
²Yemeni (adj) Jemenitisch
yen 1 yen [Japanese currency] 2 verlangen^h
yeoman kleine landeigenaar
yep [Am; inform] ja
¹yes (n) ja^h: *say* ~ ja zeggen, het jawoord geven
²yes (adv) ja; jawel [after negative sentence]
yesterday gisteren^h: *the day before* ~ eergisteren; *~'s weather was terrible* het weer van gisteren was afgrijselijk || *I saw him* ~ *week* ik heb hem gisteren een week geleden gezien
¹yet (adv) 1 nog, tot nu toe, nog altijd: *she has* ~ *to ring up* ze heeft nog steeds niet opgebeld; *as* ~ tot nu toe 2 [in interrogative sentences] al 3 opnieuw, nog: ~ *again* nog een keer 4 toch nog, uiteindelijk: *he'll beat you* ~ hij zal jou nog wel verslaan 5 toch: *and* ~ *he refused* en toch weigerde zij
²yet (conj) maar (toch), doch: *strange* ~ *true* raar maar waar
yeti yeti, verschrikkelijke sneeuwman
yew taxus(boom), taxushout^h
¹Yezidi (n) jezidi
²Yezidi (adj) jezidisch
Yid [offensive] Jood^h, jid
Yiddish Jiddisch^h
¹yield (n) opbrengst, productie, oogst, rendement^h
²yield (vb) 1 opbrengst hebben; vrucht dragen [of tree] 2 zich overgeven [to enemy] 3 toegeven, wijken: ~ *to temptation* voor de verleiding bezwijken 4 voorrang verlenen
³yield (vb) 1 voortbrengen [fruit; also fig: profit, results]; opleveren, opbrengen 2 overgeven, opgeven, afstaan: ~ *(up) one's position to the enemy* zijn positie aan de vijand overgeven 3 toegeven
yielding 1 meegevend, buigzaam 2 meegaand 3 productief, winstgevend
yikes [inform] o jee
yippee [inform] jippie
yob [inform] vandaal
yobbish baldadig, vernielzuchtig; onbeschoft, hondsbrutaal
yobbo vandaal
yodel jodelen
yoga yoga
yogurt yoghurt
¹yoke (n) 1 juk^h [also fig]; heerschappij, slavernij: *throw off the* ~ zich van het juk bevrijden 2 koppel^h, span^h, paar^h 3 draagjuk^h 4 verbintenis; juk^h [of marriage]
²yoke (vb) 1 onder het juk brengen, inspan-

nen, voorspannen **2** koppelen, verbinden:
~*d in marriage* in de echt verbonden
yokel boerenkinkel
yolk dooier
YOLO [inform] *you only live once* yolo
yonder ginds, daar ginder
yore: *of* ~ (van) vroeger, uit het verleden
you 1 jij, jou, je; [form] u: *I saw* ~ *chasing her*
ik heb gezien hoe je haar achterna zat; *Mrs*
Walters **to** ~ voor jou ben ik mevr. Walters
2 jullie, u: *what* **are** ~ *two* **up to?** wat voeren
jullie twee uit? **3** je, men: ~ *can't always get*
what ~ *want* je kunt niet altijd krijgen wat je
wilt; *that's fame* **for** ~ dat noem ik nou nog
eens beroemd zijn
¹**young** (n) **1** de jongelui, de jeugd **2** jongen
[of animal]
²**young** (adj) **1** jong, pasgeboren, klein,
nieuw, vers, fris: ~ *child* klein kind, kindjeʰ; *a*
~ *family* een gezin met kleine kinderen
2 vroeg, net begonnen: *the* **day** (or: **night**) *is*
(still) ~ het is nog vroeg **3** junior, jong(er)e:
the ~*er* **Smith, Smith** *the* ~*er* de jongere Smith
4 jeugdig: *one's* ~ **day(s)** iemands jonge jaren ‖ ~ **blood** nieuw bloed, vers bloed, nieuwe ideeën; *Young* **Turk** revolutionair, rebel; ~
turk wildebras
youngster 1 jongmensʰ **2** jochieʰ, kereltjeʰ
your 1 jouw, jullie, uw, van jou, jullie: *this is*
~ **day** dit is jullie grote dag; *I was surprised at* ~
leaving ik was verbaasd dat je zo hastig vertrok **2** zo'n (fameuze), een: *so this*
is ~ **Hyde** *Park!* dit is dus dat (beroemde)
Hyde Park van jullie!
yours van jou, van jullie, de, het jouwe, de,
het uwe: *take* **what** *is* ~ neem wat van jou is;
a friend **of** ~ een vriend van jou ‖ *sincerely* ~
met vriendelijke groeten
yourself 1 je, zich: *you are not* ~ je bent
niet in je gewone doen; *then you came* **to** ~
toen kwam je bij **2** je zelf, zelf: *it's easier to*
do *it* ~ het is gemakkelijker om het zelf te
doen; *you* ~ *told me* je hebt het me zelf gezegd
yourselves 1 zich, jullie: *you ought to be*
ashamed of ~ jullie zouden je moeten schamen **2** zelf: *finish* *it* ~ maak het zelf af
youth 1 jeugd, jonge jaren **2** jongeman,
jongen **3** tiener: ~*s* jongelui
youthful jeugdig, jong, jeugd-
youth hostel jeugdherberg
¹**yowl** (n) gejankʰ [of animals]
²**yowl** (vb) janken [of animals]
yrs 1 *years* **2** *yours*
yuck bah, gadsie
yucky smerig
¹**Yugoslav** (n) Joegoslaaf, Joegoslavische
²**Yugoslav** (adj) Joegoslavisch, van Joegoslavië
Yugoslavia Joegoslavië
yuletide kersttijd

Yuletide Kerstmis, kerst
yummy 1 lekker, heerlijk **2** prachtig [eg of
colours]
yuppie *young urban professional* yup(pie)

Z

z z, Z
¹Zaïrean (n) Zaïrees, Zaïrese
²Zaïrean (adj) Zaïrees
Zambia Zambia
¹Zambian (n) Zambiaan(se)
²Zambian (adj) Zambiaans
¹zany (n) idioot, halvegare
²zany (adj) **1** grappig, zot, leuk **2** idioot, krankzinnig, absurd
¹zap (n) pit^{+h}, pep ‖ ~! zoef!, flits!, wam!
²zap (vb) [inform] **1** snel gaan, zoeven, racen: *he was ~ping off in his car to Bristol* hij scheurde weg in zijn wagen naar Bristol **2** zappen; kanaalzwemmen [TV]
³zap (vb) raken, treffen
zeal ijver, geestdrift: *show ~ for sth.* voor iets enthousiast zijn
zealot fanatiekeling
zealous 1 ijverig, vurig, enthousiast **2** verlangend, gretig
zebra zebra: ~ *crossing* zebra(pad)
Zen zen, zenboeddhisme^h
zenith toppunt^h, top, piek: *at the ~ of his fame* op het toppunt van zijn roem
¹zero (num) nul, nulpunt, laagste punt, beginpunt: *his chances of recovery were ~* hij had geen enkele kans op herstel
²zero (vb) het vizier instellen, scherp stellen: ~ *in on* **a)** het vuur richten op; **b)** zijn aandacht richten op [problem]; **c)** inhaken op [eg on new market]
zero economic growth nulgroei
zero-emission [car] emissievrij
zero hour 1 [mil] uur^h nul [of operation] **2** kritiek moment^h, beslissend tijdstip^h
zero tolerance lik-op-stukbeleid^h
zest 1 iets extra's, jeu, pit^{+h}: *give* (or: *add*) ~ *to* meer smaak geven aan, wat meer pit geven **2** animo^h, enthousiasme^h: ~ *for life* levenslust, levensvreugde
Zeus Zeus ‖ *by ~!* wel verdorie!, drommels!
¹zigzag (n) zigzag
²zigzag (vb) zigzaggen: *the road ~ged down to the valley* de weg zigzagde naar de vallei toe
³zigzag (adv) zigzag, in een zigzaglijn
zillion eindeloos groot getal^h
Zimbabwe Zimbabwe
¹Zimbabwean (n) Zimbabwaan(se)
²Zimbabwean (adj) Zimbabwaans
Zimmer frame looprek(je)^h, rollator
zinc zink^h
zine *magazine* tijdschrift^h, blad^h

¹zip (n) **1** snerpend geluid^h; gescheur^h [of clothing] **2** rits(sluiting) **3** pit^{+h}, fut: *she's still full of ~* zij zit nog vol energie
²zip (vb) **1** zoeven, scheuren: *bullets ~ped over them* kogels floten over hen heen **2** snel gaan: ~ *by* voorbijsnellen **3** vastgeritst worden, losgeritst worden, ingeritst worden
³zip (vb) **1** ritsen: ~ *up* dichtritsen **2** [comp] inpakken, comprimeren
Zip code [Am] postcode
zip file zipbestand^h, gecomprimeerd bestand^h
zip line tokkelbaan
zipper rits(sluiting)
zippered [of clothes] met een rits
zippy energiek, levendig, vitaal
zip up comprimeren, inpakken
zit [inform] puistje^h, pukkel
zodiac dierenriem
zombie levenloos iem., robot, automaat, zoutzak
ZOMG [inform] *oh my god* o mijn god, o nee hè
¹zone (n) **1** streek, gebied^h, terrein^h, zone: *demilitarized ~* gedemilitariseerde zone **2** luchtstreek **3** ring, kring, streep **4** [Am] postdistrict^h, telefoondistrict^h, treindistrict^h
²zone (vb) bestemmen: ~ *a part of the town as residential* een deel van de stad voor bewoning bestemmen
zone out wegdromen
zoning zonering, indeling in zones; [esp] ruimtelijke ordening, bestemmingsplan^h
zoo *zoological garden* dierentuin
zookeeper dierenverzorger
zoological zoölogisch, dierkundig
zoologist zoöloog, dierkundige
zoology 1 dierkunde, zoölogie **2** dierenleven^h, fauna; dierenwereld [in certain region]
¹zoom (n) **1** gezoem^h **2** [photo] zoom
²zoom (vb) **1** zoemen, snorren **2** snel stijgen [also fig]; de hoogte in schieten **3** [inform] zoeven, hard rijden **4** [photo] zoomen: ~ *in (on)* inzoomen (op); ~ *out* uitzoomen
zoom lens zoomlens, zoomobjectief^h
zucchini [Am] courgette